JANE'S
ALL THE WORLD'S AIRCRAFT
1986-87

Jane's Publishing Company Limited, 238 City Road, London EC1V 2PU, England
Jane's Publishing Inc, 4th Floor, 115 5th Avenue, New York, NY 10003, USA

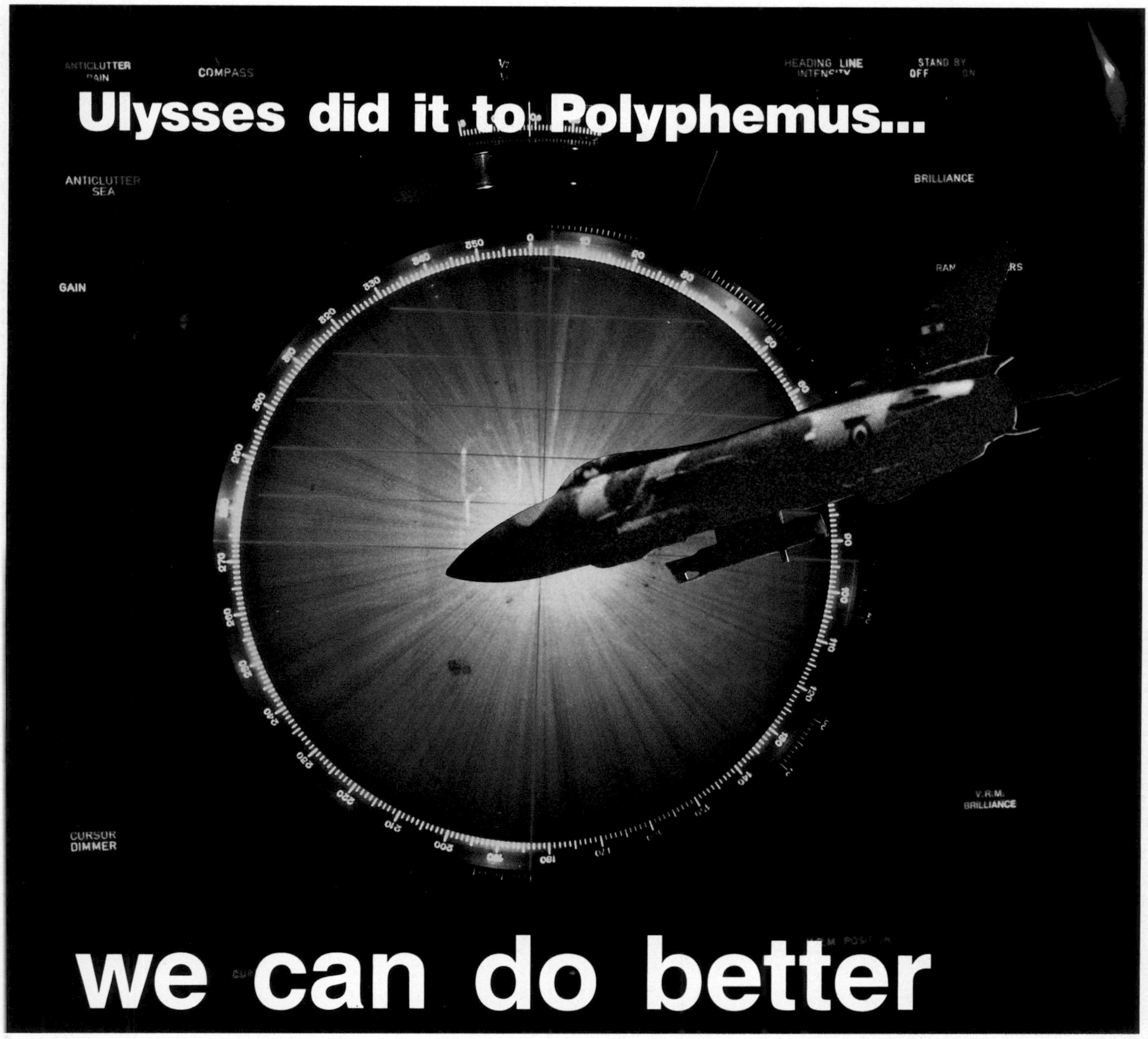

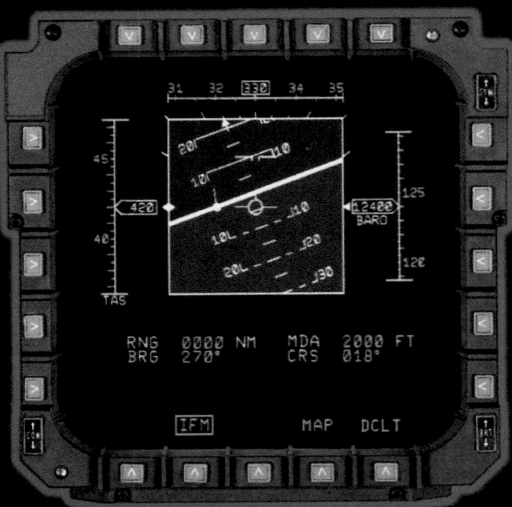

Alphabetical list of advertisers

The AS 30 Laser cuts through 2 meters of concret

Classified list of advertisers

The companies listed advertising in this publication have informed us that they are involved in the fields of manufacture indicated below:-

AC Motors
Aviaexport
Lucas Aerospace

Accelerometers
AGUSTA
Aviaexport
Hughes Aircraft Company

Accessories
Aviaexport
Electronique Serge Dassault
Fokker

Accumulators, cadmium nickel
Aviaexport

Actuators and ultrasonic transducers
EDO Corporation (Western Division/Fullerton Operations)

Actuators, electric
Aviaexport
Grumman Aerospace
Lucas Aerospace

Actuators, hydraulic
AP Precision Hydraulics

Acoustic transducers
EDO Corporation (Western Division)

Aerials aircraft
AGUSTA

Aero-engine test plant
Central Engineering
John Curran
SNECMA

Aero-engines
Aviaexport
FIAT
MTU
SNECMA
Turbomeca

Aeronautical engineers and consultants
AGUSTA
Aviaexport
Fokker
Grumman Aerospace

Aerosystems
Grumman Aerospace

Ailerons
EDO Corporation (Fibre Science Division)

Airborne acoustic & magnetic mine countermeasures systems
EDO Corporation (Government Systems Division)

Airborne surveillance drone systems
Selenia

Airborne video systems
EDO Corporation (Western Division)

Air compressors (cabin) & (engine starting)
Lucas Aerospace

Air compressors for engine starting
Lucas Aerospace

Air-conditioning equipment
Aviaexport
Bronswerk BV

Air control equipment for cabins
Aviaexport
Grumman Aerospace

Air cycle refrigeration packages
Aviaexport

Air dust computer systems
AGUSTA
Aviaexport

Air traffic control equipment
FIAR
Hughes Aircraft Company
Selenia

Aircraft, agricultural
AGUSTA
Omnipol (Foreign Trade Corporation)

Aircraft, agricultural (dusters & sprayers)
Aviaexport
Embraer
Pilatus Aircraft

Aircraft, ambulance
AGUSTA
Aviaexport
Embraer
Pilatus Aircraft

Aircraft, combat
AGUSTA
British Aerospace
Hughes Aircraft Company
Kaman Aerospace Corporation
Selenia

Aircraft, commercial
AGUSTA
British Aerospace
Embraer
Fokker

Aircraft, executive
AGUSTA
Aviaexport
British Aerospace
Embraer
Fokker

Aircraft, integrated data systems
Electronique Serge Dassault
Grumman Aerospace

Aircraft, military
AGUSTA
British Aerospace
CASA
Embraer
Fokker
Grumman Aerospace
Hughes Aircraft Company
Kaman Aerospace Corporation
Pilatus Aircraft
Selenia
Slingsby Aviation
Valmet OY

Aircraft, naval
AGUSTA
British Aerospace
CASA
Fokker
Grumman Aerospace
Hughes Aircraft Company
Kaman Aerospace Corporation

Aircraft, private
AGUSTA
British Aerospace
Embraer
Slingsby Aviation

Aircraft, radio controlled
AGUSTA
Kaman Aerospace Corporation

Aircraft, supersonic
British Aerospace
Grumman Aerospace

Aircraft, training
AGUSTA
British Aerospace
CASA
Embraer
Fokker
Grumman Aerospace
Omnipol (Foreign Trade Corporation)
Pilatus Aircraft
Slingsby Aviation
Valmet OY

Aircraft, transport
AGUSTA
British Aerospace
CASA
Embraer
Grumman Aerospace
Kaman Aerospace Corporation
Omnipol (Foreign Trade Corporation)

Aircraft, v/stol
Aviaexport
British Aerospace
Grumman Aerospace
Hughes Aircraft Company
Pilatus Aircraft

Aircraft canopies
Grumman Aerospace
Lucas Aerospace
Valmet OY

Aircraft construction
DAF Special Products

Aircraft developments
CASA
Embraer
Fokker
Grumman Aerospace
Hughes Aircraft Company
Kaman Aerospace Corporation

Aircraft escape systems
Grumman Aerospace

Aircraft field operations & support
Fokker
Kaman Aerospace Corporation

Aircraft freight handling equipment
Aviaexport

Aircraft integrated data systems
Electronique Serge Dassault

Aircraft mechanical handlers
Aviaexport

Aircraft modifications
Embraer
Fokker
Grumman Aerospace
Hughes Aircraft Company
Kaman Aerospace Corporation
Valmet OY

Aircraft product support
British Aerospace
Embraer
Fokker
Grumman Aerospace
Kaman Aerospace Corporation
Pilatus Aircraft

Aircraft propellers
Aviaexport
Fokker

Aircraft seats
Fokker
Grumman Aerospace

Aircraft supersonic
Selenia

Aircraft wire & cable
Fokker
Grumman Aerospace

Airfield lighting
Aviaexport
Fokker
Grumman Aerospace

Airline technical assistance
Fokker
Grumman Aerospace

Airport ground handling equipment
SNECMA

Airport maintenance equipment
Grumman Aerospace

Airports planning
Fokker

Airspeed indicators
Aviaexport
Thomson CSF/AVS

Air traffic control systems, civilian and military
Hughes Aircraft Company

Alternators
Aviaexport
Lucas Aerospace

Altitude control systems
Aviaexport

Ammunition boosters
SNIA/BPD

Amplifiers
AGUSTA
Electronique Serge Dassault
Fokker

Antennas, aircraft
Elettronica
Fokker
Grumman Aerospace

Antennas
Electronique Serge Dassault
Elettronica
SNECMA

Anti-skid systems
SNECMA

Armaments for aircraft (Asw)
EDO Corporation (Government Systems Division)

Automatic checkout systems
Electronique Serge Dassault

Automatic digital data acquisition systems for engine testing
SNECMA

Automatic pilot
Fokker

Automatic voltage & current regulators
Lucas Aerospace

Auxiliary power plant
FIAT
Fokker
Lucas Aerospace

Avionic systems
Fokker
Hughes Aircraft Company
Selenia
Thomson CSF/AVS

Bars, stainless steel & heat resisting steel
Aviaexport

Batteries
Aviaexport

Batteries, aviation
Aviaexport

Beacon equipment
Thomson CSF/AVS

Belts, safety
Aviaexport

Blades, gas turbine
Aviaexport
SNECMA
Westland Helicopters

Bomb racks
EDO Corporation (Government Systems Division)

Bombsights
Thomson CSF/AVS

Bonding jumpers bus bars
Grumman Aerospace

Brake linings
Goodyear Tyre & Rubber Company

Brakes for aircraft
Aviaexport
Goodyear Tyre & Rubber Company
SNECMA

Cabin cooling (tropical airfield equipment)
Aviaexport

Cabin pressure control systems
Aviaexport
Grumman Aerospace

Cabin pressurising test equipment
Aviaexport
Grumman Aerospace

Cables, electric
Fokker
Grumman Aerospace

Cables, rf
Grumman Aerospace

Canisters
Bronswerk BV

Carbon fibre components
Slingsby Aviation

Coatings, erosion resistant
Fokker
Goodyear Tyre & Rubber Company

Cockpit windows—heated & unheated
Lucas Aerospace

Combat command & control
EDO Corporation (Government Systems Division)

Combustion systems (gas turbine)
Lucas Aerospace

Communications control systems
Grumman Aerospace
Hughes Aircraft

Components
AGUSTA
Aviaexport
Grumman Aerospace
Kaman Aerospace Corporation
Slingsby Aviation

Composite structure
Kaman Aerospace Corporation
Lucas Aerospace
Slingsby Aviation

Computers
AGUSTA
Electronique Serge Dassault
Hughes Aircraft Company
Reflectone
Thomson CSF/AVS

Computers, aerodynamic analogue & digital
Selenia

Connectors/connector accessories
Aviaexport

Constant speed drive test benches
Central Engineering
Lucas Aerospace

Control equipment for aircraft
AP Precision Hydraulics
Aviaexport
Electronique Serge Dassault
Grumman Aerospace

Controls, cockpit
Aviaexport
Fokker
Grumman Aerospace
Thomson CSF/AVS

Controls, main engine fuel
Aviaexport
Grumman Aerospace
Lucas Aerospace
SNECMA

Cooling compressors
Aviaexport

Cooling engines
Lucas Aerospace

Couplings, Self-sealing
AP Precision Hydraulics
Kaman Aerospace Corporation

Cowlings
EDO Corporation (Fibre Science Division)

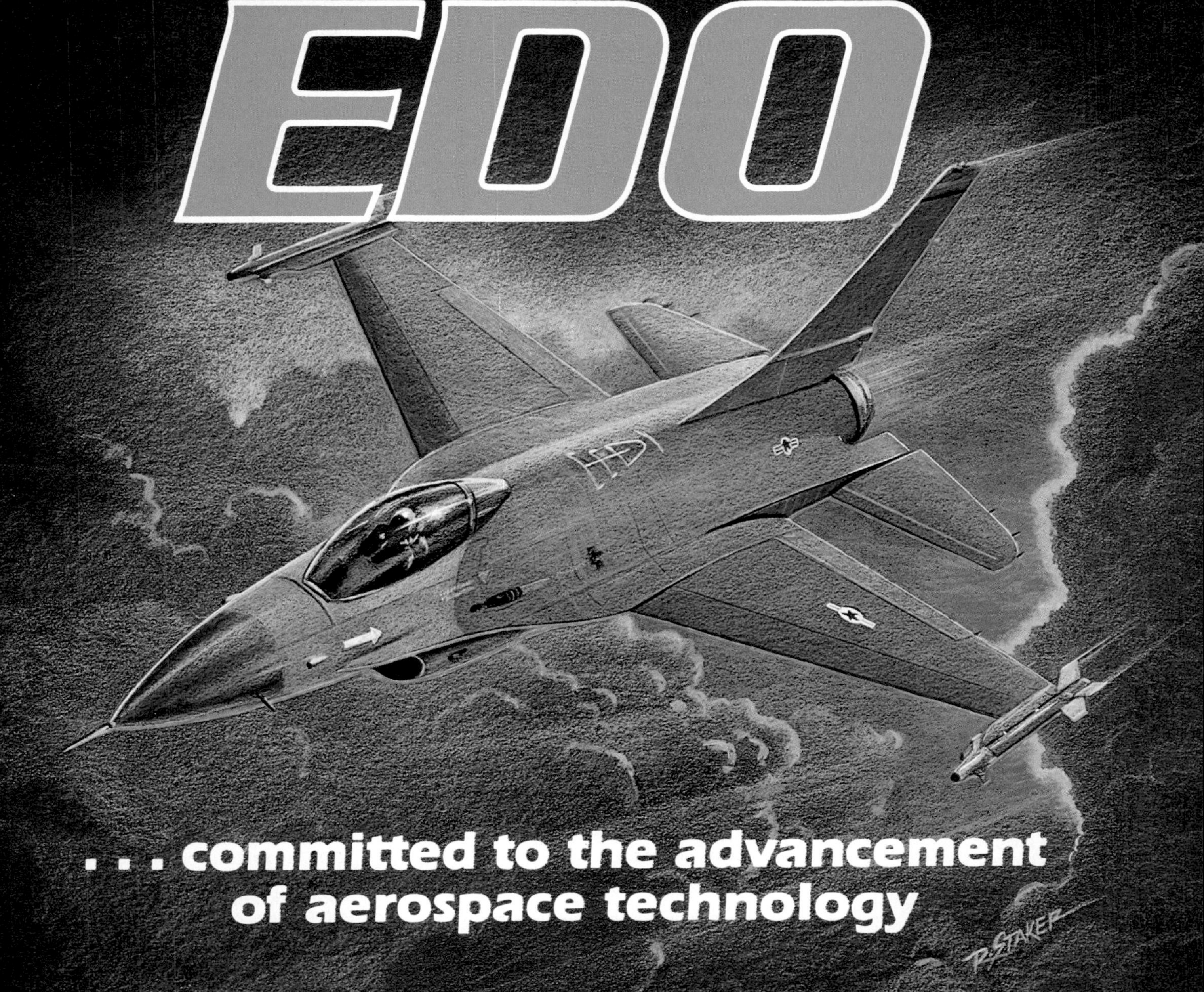

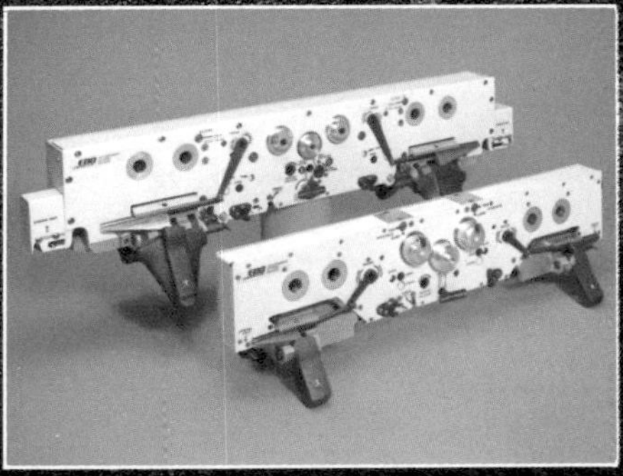

CLASSIFIED LIST OF ADVERTISERS

Data links
Hughes Aircraft Company

Data processing equipment
Central Engineering
Electronique Serge Dassault
Hughes Aircraft Company
SNECMA
Thomson CSF/AVS

Data processing equipment for ATC
Hughes Aircraft Company
Selenia

Data transmission equipment
AGUSTA
Electronique Serge Dassault
Thomson CSF/AVS

Dc generators
Lucas Aerospace

Dc motors
Aviaexport
Lucas Aerospace

Defence & aviation technology
DAF Special Products

Defence contractors
British Aerospace
John Curran
Fokker
Hughes Aircraft Company
Kaman Aerospace Corporation
Slingsby Aviation

Defence data handling & display
Selenia
Thomson CSF/AVS

De-icing equipment
Grumman Aerospace
Lucas Aerospace

Digital data links
Thomson CSF/AVS

Direction finding equipment (triangulation)
AGUSTA
Aviaexport
Hughes Aircraft Company

Display systems
Bendix Flight Systems

Displays, in-cockpit
Fokker
Hughes Aircraft Company
Selenia
Thomson CSF/AVS

Doors
EDO Corporation (Fibre Science Division)

Drive shafts
EDO Corporation (Fibre Science Division)

Drones
Aérospatiale
Flight Refuelling
Kaman Aerospace Corporation
Selenia
Slingsby Aviation

Early warning systems
Canadair
THORN EMI/Pilatus Britten Norman

Ejection seats
Grumman Aerospace
SNECMA

Electric auxiliaries
Aviaexport

Electrical equipment
Aviaexport
Grumman Aerospace
Lucas Aerospace

Electrical wiring assemblies
Aviaexport
Fokker
Grumman Aerospace
Kaman Aerospace Corporation

Electro-hydraulic power packs
AP Precision Hydraulics
Lucas Aerospace

Electro-optical systems
AGUSTA
Barr & Stroud
FIAR
Grumman Aerospace
Hughes Aircraft Company
Thomson CSF/AVS

Electronic countermeasures (ecm)
Electronique Serge Dassault
Elettronica
Hughes Aircraft Company
Selenia
Thomson CSF/AVS

Electronic equipment
AGUSTA
Aviaexport
Electronique Serge Dassault
Grumman Aerospace
Hughes Aircraft Company
Italtel
Lucas Aerospace
Thomson CSF/AVS

Electronic flight controls
AGUSTA
Fokker
Lucas Aerospace
Thomson CSF/AVS

Electronic fuel control systems
Grumman Aerospace
Lucas Aerospace
SNECMA

Electronic map systems
Hughes Aircraft Corporation
Thomson CFS/AVS

Electronic support measures (esm)
Canadair
Elettronica
Selenia
Thomson CSF/AVS

Electronics & guidance
AGUSTA
Electronique Serge Dassault
Grumman Aerospace
Hughes Aircraft Company
Thomson CSF/AVS

Engine compressor cleaning rigs
John Curran

Engine, design and manufacture
SNECMA
Turbomeca

Engine handling equipment
Central Engineering
John Curran

Engine parts fabrication
FIAT

Engine run-up facilities–mobile
John Curran

Engine starting equipment
Central Engineering
FIAT
Lucas Aerospace

Engine testing equipment
Alfa Romeo
Aviaexport
Central Engineering
John Curran

Engines, aircraft
Alfa Romeo
Aviaexport
Omnipol (Foreign Trade Corporation)
SNECMA
Turbomeca

Engines, auxiliary
Aviaexport
Lucas Aerospace
Turbomeca

Engines, v/stol
Aviaexport
Turbomeca

Environmental control systems
Bronswerk BV
Grumman Aerospace

Ew systems
Elettronica
Hughes Aircraft Company
Selenia
Thomson CSF/AVS

Experimental assemblies
Grumman Aerospace
Slingsby Aviation

External crash survivable fuel tanks
EDO Corporation (Fibre Science Division)

Fibre optic recorders
EDO Corporation (Western Division)

Fibre optics
Barr & Stroud
Grumman Aerospace
Hughes Aircraft Company

Filters, air
AP Precision Hydraulics
Aviaexport
Recticel-PRB

Filters, electronic
Aviaexport
Barr & Stroud
Electronique Serge Dassault

Filters—fuel & oil
AP Precision Hydraulics
Aviaexport
Flight Refuelling

Fire suppression systems
Grumman Aerospace
Hughes Aircraft Company

Flight inspection
Canadair

Flight instrument test sets
AGUSTA
Electronique Serge Dassault

Flow gauges
AGUSTA
Aviaexport

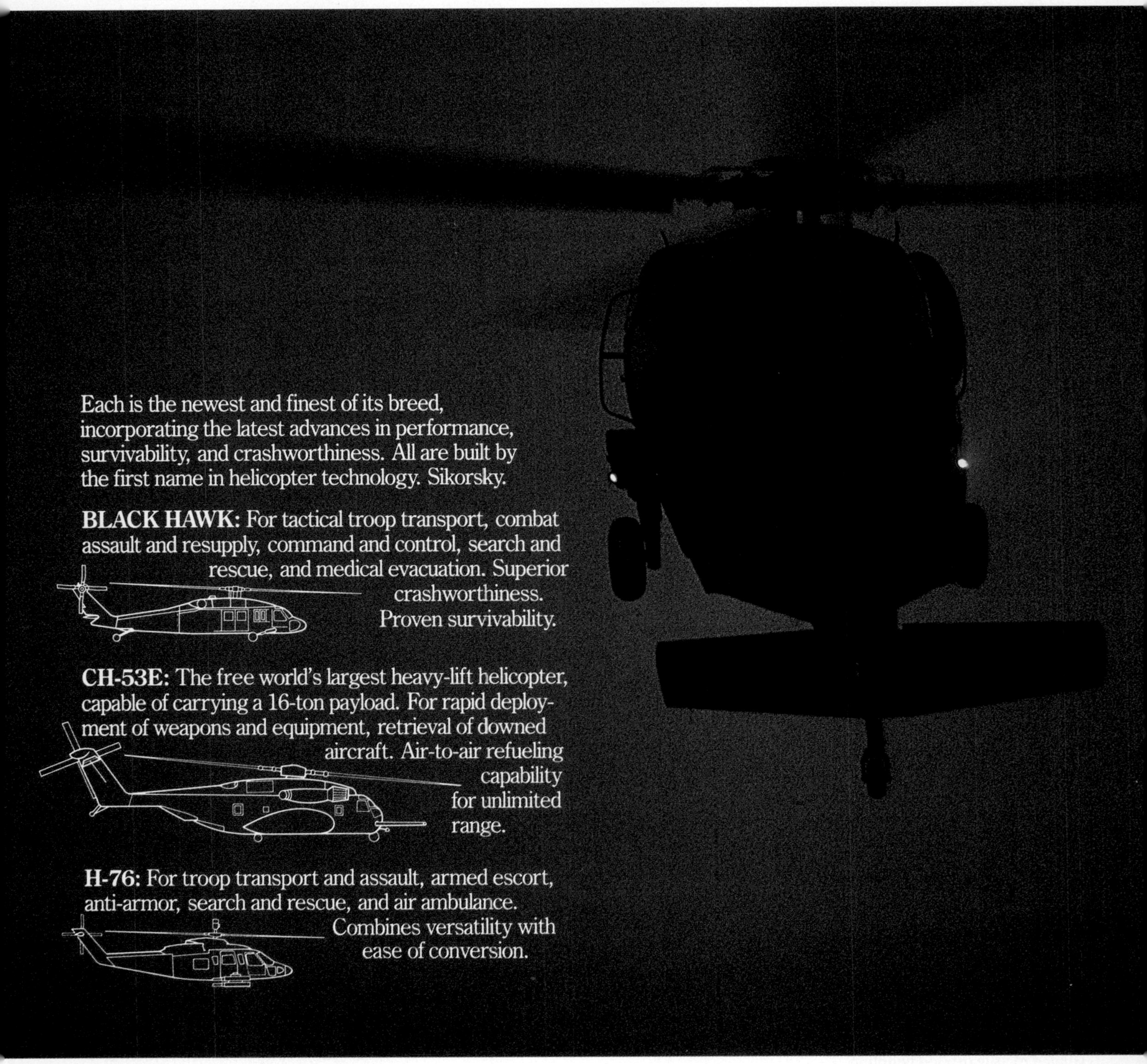

CLASSIFIED LIST OF ADVERTISERS

Flying Controls
AP Precision Hydraulics
Thomson CSF/AVS

Forgings, Steel
SNECMA

Fuel control test benches
AGUSTA
Central Engineering

Fuel flow proportioners
Flight Refuelling
Lucas Aerospace

Fuel pump test benches
Grumman Aerospace

Fuel pumps
Aviaexport
Lucas Aerospace
SNECMA

Fuel sprayers
Lucas Aerospace

Fuel systems protection
Grumman Aerospace
Recticel-PRB

Fuel systems & refuelling equipment
Aviaexport
Flight Refuelling
Grumman Aerospace

Fuel tank pressurisation equipment
Flight Refuelling

Furnishings & aircraft cabins
Aviaexport
Fokker
Grumman Aerospace

Gas turbine starting systems
Lucas Aerospace

Gas turbines
Aviaexport
FIAT
Lucas Aerospace
Turbomeca

Gas turbines, equipment & accessories
Aviaexport
SNECMA

Gauges
Aviaexport

Generator test benches
Central Engineering

Generators
Aviaexport
Lucas Aerospace

Ground support equipment
Bronswerk BV
Electronique Serge Dassault
Grumman Aerospace
Kaman Aerospace Corporation

Guided missile ground handling equipment
Aérospatiale
Hughes Aircraft Company

Guided missiles
AGUSTA
Aérospatiale
Electronique Serge Dassault
Hughes Aircraft Company
Selenia
SNIA/BPD

Hangar test stands
John Curran

Heated windows
Barr & Stroud
Lucas Aerospace

Heated windscreen controllers
Lucas Aerospace

Helicopter gun turrets
Lucas Aerospace

Helicopter parts & components
AGUSTA
AP Precision Hydraulics
Aviaexport
FIAT
Flight Refuelling
Grumman Aerospace
Kaman Aerospace Corporation
Westland Helicopters

Helicopter stabilisation
Kaman Aerospace Corporation

Helicopter surface-to-air refuelling equipment
AGUSTA
Flight Refuelling

Helicopter support
AGUSTA
Kaman Aerospace Corporation
Pilatus Aircraft

Helicopter training & support
AGUSTA
Kaman Aerospace Corporation

Helicopter winches
AGUSTA
Kaman Aerospace Corporation

Helicopters, ambulances
AGUSTA

Helicopters, commercial-executive
AGUSTA
Aviaexport

Helicopters, military-naval
Aérospatiale
AGUSTA
Hughes Aircraft Company
Kaman Aerospace Corporation

High performance aircraft ejection and stores release units.
EDO Corporation (Government Systems Division)

High pressure couplings
AP Precision Hydraulics
Kaman Aerospace Corporation

High-speed research cameras
AGUSTA

Horizon sensors
EDO Corporation (Engineering Division)

Hud
Hughes Aircraft Company
Selenia

Hydraulic actuation systems
AP Precision Hydraulics
Lucas Aerospace
SNECMA

Hydraulic control/systems
AP Precision Hydraulics

Hydraulic equipment
AP Precision Hydraulics
Grumman Aerospace

Hydraulic pressure pumps
AP Precision Hydraulics
Lucas Aerospace
SNECMA

Hydraulic test units, mobile & static
Central Engineering

Hydromechanical engine controls
Lucas Aerospace

Ignition exciters
Lucas Aerospace

Infared detectors
EDO Corporation (Engineering Division)

Inertial navigation & cockpit systems
Hughes Aircraft Company

Infra-red materials
Barr & Stroud
Grumman Aerospace
Hughes Aircraft Company

Infra-red systems
AGUSTA
Barr & Stroud
Electronique Serge Dassault
Elettronica
Grumman Aerospace
Hughes Aircraft Company
Thomson CSF/AVS

Instrument components
AGUSTA

Instruments, aircraft
AGUSTA
Fokker
Thomson CSF/AVS

Instruments, electronic
AGUSTA
Electronique Serge Dassault
Thomson CSF/AVS

Instruments, navigation
AGUSTA
Aviaexport
Electronique Serge Dassault
Thomson CSF/AVS

Instruments—test equipment
AGUSTA
Aviaexport
Central Engineering
Electronique Serge Dassault
Fokker

Integrated marine navigation systems
EDO Corporation (Canada)

Integrated total pneumatic systems
Grumman Aerospace
Lucas Aerospace

Jet engine parts
FIAT
SNECMA

Jet engine test plant
Central Engineering
John Curran
SNECMA

Jet fuel starters
Lucas Aerospace

Jet propulsion engines
SNECMA
Turbomeca

Jet trainer, military
British Aerospace
CASA
Dornier

Joining compound
Goodyear Tyre & Rubber Company

Kevlat components
Slingsby Aviation

Lamps, cockpit
Aviaexport
Lucas Aerospace

Landing Gear
AP Precision Hydraulics

Landing lamps
Aviaexport

Laser countermeasures
EDO Corporation (Engineering Division)

Lasers
Barr & Stroud
Hughes Aircraft Company
Kaman Aerospace Corporation

Laser rangefinders
AGUSTA
Barr & Stroud
FIAR
Hughes Aircraft
Selenia
Thomson CSF/AVS

Lavatories & cabin liners
EDO Corporation (Fibre Science Division)

Lights, aircraft
Aviaexport
Fokker

Lights, landing
Aviaexport

Lights, navigation
Aviaexport
Omnipol (Foreign Trade Corporation)

Linear actuator test benches
Central Engineering

Linear actuators
AP Precision Hydraulics
Lucas Aerospace

Linings—brakes
Goodyear Tyre & Rubber Company

Low altitude airfield attack weapons equipment
Selenia

Low light level tv systems
EDO Corporation (Western Division)

Materials technology
Grumman Aerospace
Hughes Aircraft
Kaman Aerospace Corporation
Slingsby Aviation

Medium lift helicopters
Boeing Helicopters

Metal fittings
Aviaexport

Microphones
Aviaexport

Micro-thermal imaging and remote radiometric analysis instruments
EDO Corporation

Military aircraft training
NAVFCO

Military & commercial electronic
EDO Corporation (Government Systems Division)

Missile launchers
EDO Corporation (Government Systems Division)

Missile optics
AGUSTA
Barr & Stroud
Hughes Aircraft Company
NAVFCO
Thomson CSF/AVS

Missile range control
de Havilland

Missiles for storage
Bronswerk BV

Missiles, guided
Aérospatiale
Electronique Serge Dassault
Hughes Aircraft Company
Selenia
SNIA/BPD

Motor generators
Aviaexport
Lucas Aerospace

Motors, electric
Aviaexport
Lucas Aerospace

Motors, hydraulic
Aviaexport

Night vision equipment
AGUSTA
Barr & Stroud
FIAR
Hughes Aircraft Company

Non-destructive inspect equipment
Fokker
Grumman Aerospace

Oceanographic instrumentation & sonar systems
EDO Corporation (Western Division)

Oil-hydraulic equipment
AP Precision Hydraulics

Optical infared detectors
EDO Corporation

Optical equipment
AGUSTA
Barr & Stroud
Hughes Aircraft Company

Optical gun sights
Barr & Stroud
Hughes Aircraft Company

Overhaul & modification kits
CASA
Fokker
Grumman Aerospace
Kaman Aerospace Corporation

Oxygen apparatus
AGUSTA
Aviaexport

Oxygen breathing apparatus
AGUSTA
Grumman Aerospace

CLASSIFIED LIST OF ADVERTISERS

Parachutes
Aviaexport

Parachutes, special purpose
Aviaexport

Parts for US built aircraft
Grumman Aerospace
Kaman Aerospace Corporation

Passenger cabin windows
Lucas Aerospace

Patrol aircraft, maritime
British Aerospace
CASA
Fokker
Grumman Aerospace
NAVFCO

Periscopes
Barr & Stroud

Piezoelectric ceramics
EDO Corporation (Western Division)
EDO Corporation (Western Division/Fullerton Operations)

Plastic fabrications
Grumman Aerospace
Recticel-PRB
Slingsby Aviation

Plastic fabrications (reinforced with fibreglass)
AGUSTA
Grumman Aerospace
Lucas Aerospace

Plastic mouldings
Grumman Aerospace
Recticel

Pneumatic actuation systems
Lucas Aerospace

Pneumatic component test benches
Central Engineering

Pneumatic controls
Lucas Aerospace

Power—solar cell panels and arrays
Hughes Aircraft Company

Powered flying controls
AP Precision Hydraulics
Lucas Aerospace

Precision gears
Barr & Stroud
Kaman Aerospace Corporation

Precision satellite navigation systems for marine & land geodetic surveys
EDO Corporation (Western Division)

Pressure regulation valves, fluids & gases
Lucas Aerospace

Pressure switches
AP Precision Hydraulics

Private planes, civil & military
Pilatus Aircraft

Propeller test stands
John Curran

Proposals for aircraft ground support operations
John Curran
Grumman Aerospace

Provisioning parts breakdown lists
Grumman Aerospace
Kaman Aerospace Corporation

Pumps, fuel & oil
Lucas Aerospace

Pumps, hydraulic
AP Precision Hydraulics
Lucas Aerospace

Radar for navigation, warning interception, fire control & airfield supervision
Aviaexport
Electronique Serge Dassault
FIAR
Hughes Aircraft Company
Omnipol (Foreign Trade Corporation)
Selenia

Radar processing
Hughes Aircraft Company
Thomson CSF/AVS

Radar reflectors
Electronique Serge Dassault

Radar test set
Electronique Serge Dassault
Grumman Aerospace
Hughes Aircraft Company

Radar towers
John Curran

CLASSIFIED LIST OF ADVERTISERS

Servo actuators
AP Precision Hydraulics
Hughes Aircraft Company
Lucas Aerospace

Sheet metal work
Fokker
Grumman Aerospace
Lucas Aerospace
Valmet OY

Simulators
AGUSTA
Fokker
Grumman Aerospace
Hughes Aircraft Company
NAVFCO
Omnipol (Foreign Trade Corporation)
Reflectone Inc

Simulators, combat
British Aerospace
Hughes Aircraft Company
Reflectone Inc

Sonar
EDO Corporation (Government Systems Division)

Space hardware recovery
Hughes Aircraft Company
SNIA/BPD

Space launchers
Aérospatiale
SNIA/BPD

Space satellites
Aérospatiale
Fokker
Grumman Aerospace
Hughes Aircraft Company
SNIA/BPD

Space systems
AGUSTA
Electronique Serge Dassault
FIAR
Grumman Aerospace
Hughes Aircraft Company
SNIA/BPD

Spacecraft
Grumman Aerospace
Hughes Aircraft Company

Spare parts for US-built aircraft
Grumman Aerospace
Kaman Aerospace Corporation

Starting systems, airborne
Lucas Aerospace

Static inverters
Lucas Aerospace

Steering controls (hydraulic)
AP Precision Hydraulics
Hughes Aircraft Company

Struts & trunnions
EDO Corporation (Government Systems Division)

Surveillance systems
Barr & Stroud
Grumman Aerospace
Hughes Aircraft Company

Switches
Lucas Aerospace

Switchgear
Aviaexport
Lucas Aerospace

Tachometers
Aviaexport

Tactical radios
Hughes Aircraft Company

Targets, aerial
Aérospatiale
Flight Refuelling
Kaman Aerospace Corporation

Target towing winches
Pilatus Aircraft

Technical publications
Hughes Aircraft Company
Kaman Aerospace Corporation

Technical publications, special studies
Hughes Aircraft Company
Kaman Aerospace Corporation

Telemetry equipment
AGUSTA
Hughes Aircraft Company

Temperature control equipment
Lucas Aerospace

Test equipment
Aviaexport
John Curran
Electronique Serge Dassault
Fokker
Grumman Aerospace
Hughes Aircraft Company
Kaman Aerospace Corporation
Valmet OY

Test equipment, radar, air data computer, fire control systems, avionics etc
Aérospatiale
Electronique Serge Dassault
Grumman Aerospace
Hughes Aircraft Company
Thomson CSF/AVS

Test equipment airborne radio
Grumman Aerospace
Hughes Aircraft Company

Test equipment, airfield radio
Hughes Aircraft Company

Test equipment, metal bonding
Aviaexport
Fokker
Hughes Aircraft Company

Test facilities
John Curran
Hughes Aircraft Company

Thermal imaging systems
AGUSTA
Aviaexport
Barr & Stroud
FIAR
Grumman Aerospace
Hughes Aircraft Company
Thomson CSF/AVS

Thrust reversers
Lucas Aerospace
SNECMA

Torsion springs
EDO Corporation (Fibre Science Division)

Training & simulation
Fokker
Hughes Aircraft Company
KHD
Reflectine Inc

Training devices
Aermacchi
Grumman Aerospace
Hughes Aircraft Company
Kaman Aerospace Corporation
KHD
Reflectone Inc
Valmet OY

Transfer of technology
NAVFCO

Transformer rectifier units
de Havilland
Lucas Aerospace

Transport and launching
Bronswerk BV

Troop transport
Sikorsky

Tubes, stainless steel
Aviaexport

Turbofan engines
Alfa Romeo
SNECMA

Turboprop
Pratt & Whitney

Turnkey project management
Hughes Aircraft Company

Tyres for aircraft
Goodyear Tyre & Rubber Company

Unmanned aircraft
Aermacchi
Meteor Construzioni

Undercarriage gear, retractable
AP Precision Hydraulics
SNECMA

Valves
Lucas Aerospace

Valves, control hydraulic
AP Precision Hydraulics

Valves, non-return hydraulic
AP Precision Hydraulics

Valves, relief hydraulic
AP Precision Hydraulics

Voltage & current regulators
Lucas Aerospace

Wheels for aircraft
Goodyear Tyre & Rubber Company
SNECMA

Windscreens—electrically heated
Lucas Aerospace

Wind tunnel testing plant
British Aerospace
John Curran

Wire & cables all types
Grumman Aerospace

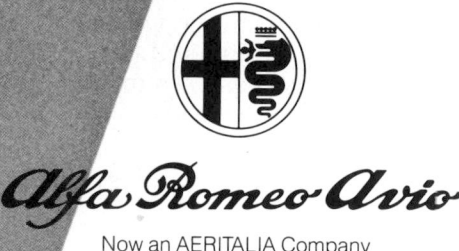

FIAT AVIAZIONE - AN OUTSTANDING, CONTINUING PRESENCE AT THE FOREFRONT OF AIRCRAFT AND MARINE ENGINE TECHNOLOGY:
AEROENGINES
RB 199 FOR THE ALL-WEATHER TORNADO
SPEY M.K. 807 FOR THE AMX LIGHT TACTICAL FIGHTER
T64-P4D FOR THE G 222 TRANSPORT PLANE
V2500 FOR SHORT-HAUL AIRCRAFT
PW 2037 FOR MEDIUM-HAUL AIRCRAFT
PW 4000 AND CF6-80C2 FOR LONG-HAUL AIRCRAFT
ENGINES FOR HELICOPTERS
PT6B-36
T700-CT7
MECHANICAL COMPONENTS FOR HELICOPTERS
SA 321 SUPER FRELON
SA 330 PUMA
SA 360/365 DAUPHIN
MARINE AND INDUSTRIAL TURBINES
LM 2500 IN THE 30,000 HP CLASS
LM 500 IN THE 6,000 HP CLASS
AUXILIARY POWER UNIT
FA 150 - ARGO
FIAT AVIAZIONE

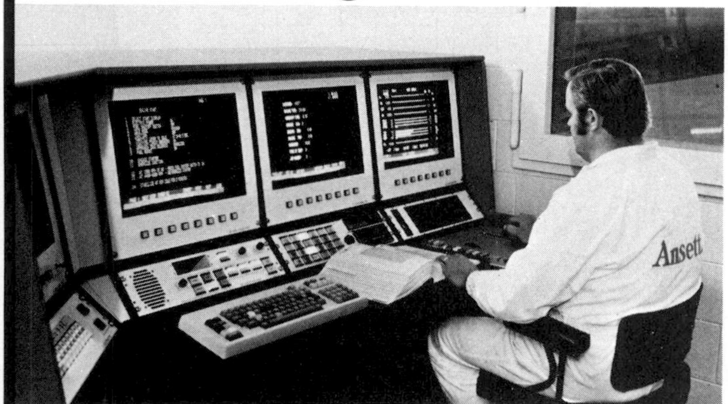

Modern training
and close air support aircraft
such as ALPHA-JET call for
economical, reliable easy-maintenance
engines. These requirements are met by the
double-spool, double-shaft jet turbine
engine LARZAC 04 designed by
GRTS* according to the
modular concept.
Focussed
Power
The manifold
features of the
combat aircraft TORNADO
include independence of
ground equipment and
redundancy – two requirements which
are met by the specially designed
Secondary Power System (SPS).
KHD Luftfahrttechnik GmbH designs, constructs and services gas turbines
and related equipment for air navigation.
KHD
Luftfahrttechnik
KHD-Luftfahrttechnik GmbH
POB 246
6370 Oberursel Germany
Telex 4 10 727 · Phone (0 61 71) 500-1

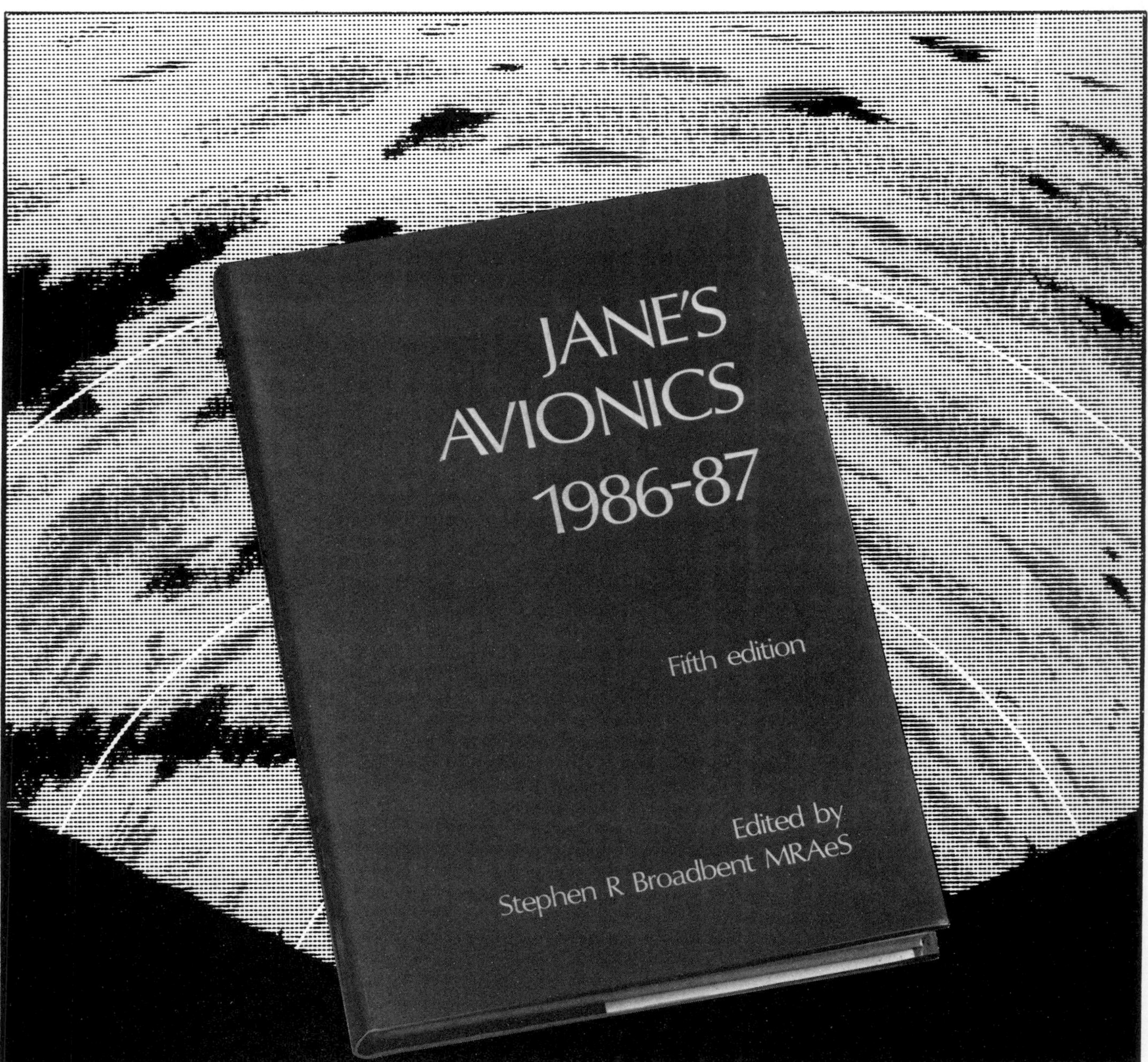

ALL YOU NEED TO KEEP TRACK OF AEROSPACE ELECTRONICS

To navigate successfully the hi-tech world of aviation electronics, you need the expert, up-to-date guidance of Jane's Avionics.

In one volume of detailed technical and commercial information are the latest reports on the development, specifications and operational capabilities of current airborne electronics.

Major sections deal with sensors in terms of anti-submarine warfare, radar, electronic warfare and electro-optics; with data processing, data management and display systems as they affect navigation, flight control and cockpit instruments. Radio communications are examined in detail. The training systems section which includes advanced simulation techniques has been greatly expanded.

For both military and civil use, and complementary to Jane's All the World's Aircraft, Jane's Avionics is the only annual reference work in this highly-specialised and challenging field.

Foreword • Glossary • Sensors • Data processing
Management and displays
Radio Communications • Training systems

Jane's Publishing Co. Ltd.,
238 City Road London EC1V 2PU Tel: 01-251 9281.
Tlx: 894689

Jane's Publishing Inc.,
115 5th Avenue, 4th Floor.
New York, NY10003.
Tel: (212) 254 9097. Tlx: 272562
VNRC UR.

Reach for
JANE'S
AVIONICS 1986-87

For a complete list of all

JANE'S YEARBOOKS

please write to:
The Information Department
Jane's Publishing Company Limited
238 City Road, London EC1V 2PU

At Seca, exceptional service is the rule.

Airplane and helicopter maintenance. All engine O/H and repairs.

Avionics: authorized service center for all major American manufacturers.

Airframe: – maintenance, repairs, and paint jobs.
– A/C modification for special assignments.
– Customized interiors.
– Engine refits.

Engines: Pistons - Turboprops - Turbojets - Turboshafts.
Specialists: LYCOMING - CONTINENTAL - ALLISON - GENERAL ELECTRIC - GARRETT - PRATT & WHITNEY.

FB 01

Aéroport du Bourget - BP 32 - 93350 Le Bourget - France
Tel.: (33/1) 48.35.99.77 - Telex: 220218F SECBG

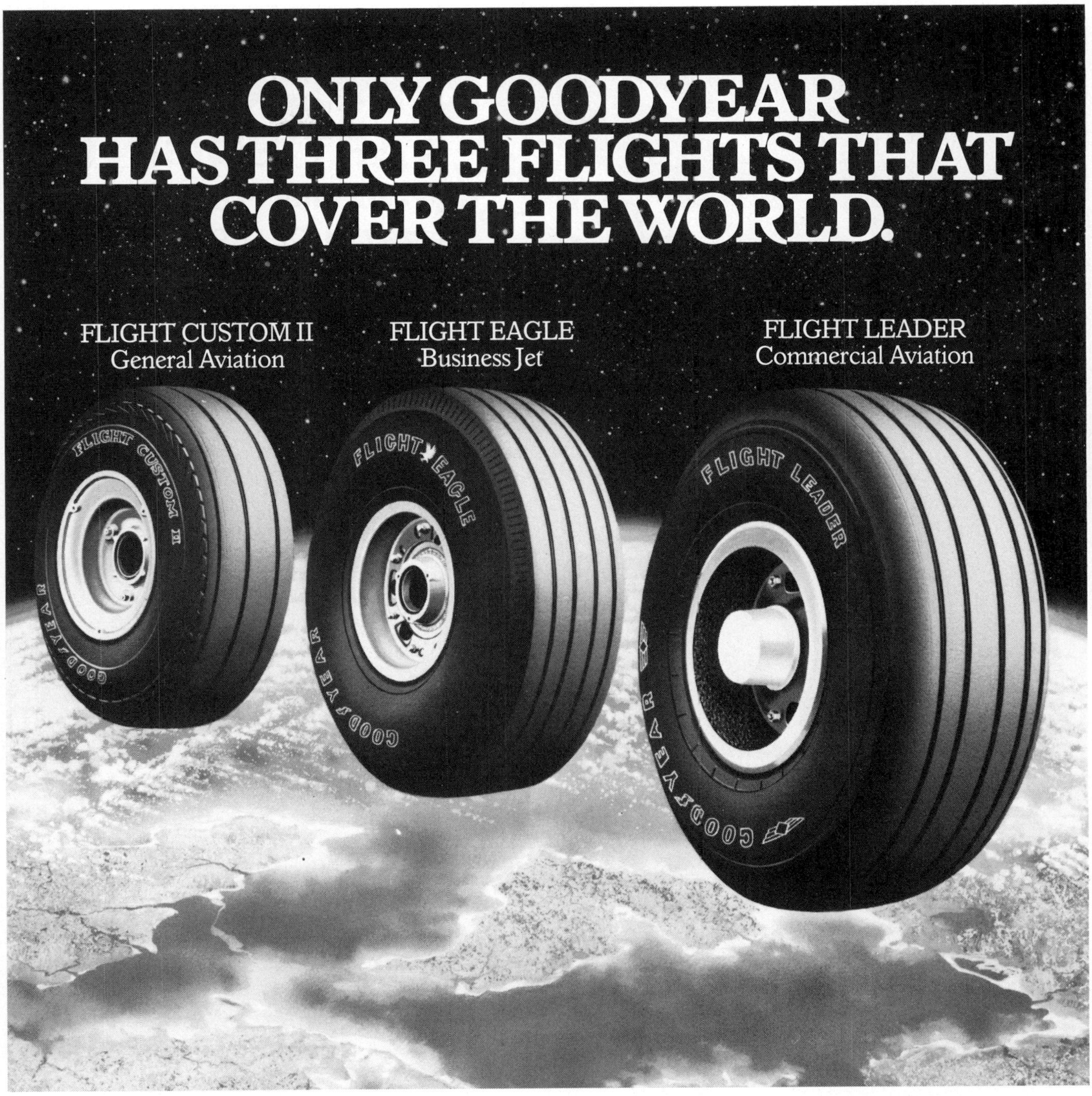

MIRACH 20, MIRACH 70, MIRACH 100, MIRACH 300, MIRACH 600.

OUR PILOT IS LOCATED BOTTOM CENTRE.

Whatever your mission requirement, there is one of our unmanned aircraft that can face the problem without risking a human life. Meteor Costruzioni Aeronautiche ed Elettroniche S.p.A. - Via Nomentana, 146 - 00162 Rome - Italy.

METEOR COSTRUZIONI AERONAUTICHE
ED ELETTRONICHE S.p.A.

Meteor holding spA

A company of **AERITALIA**

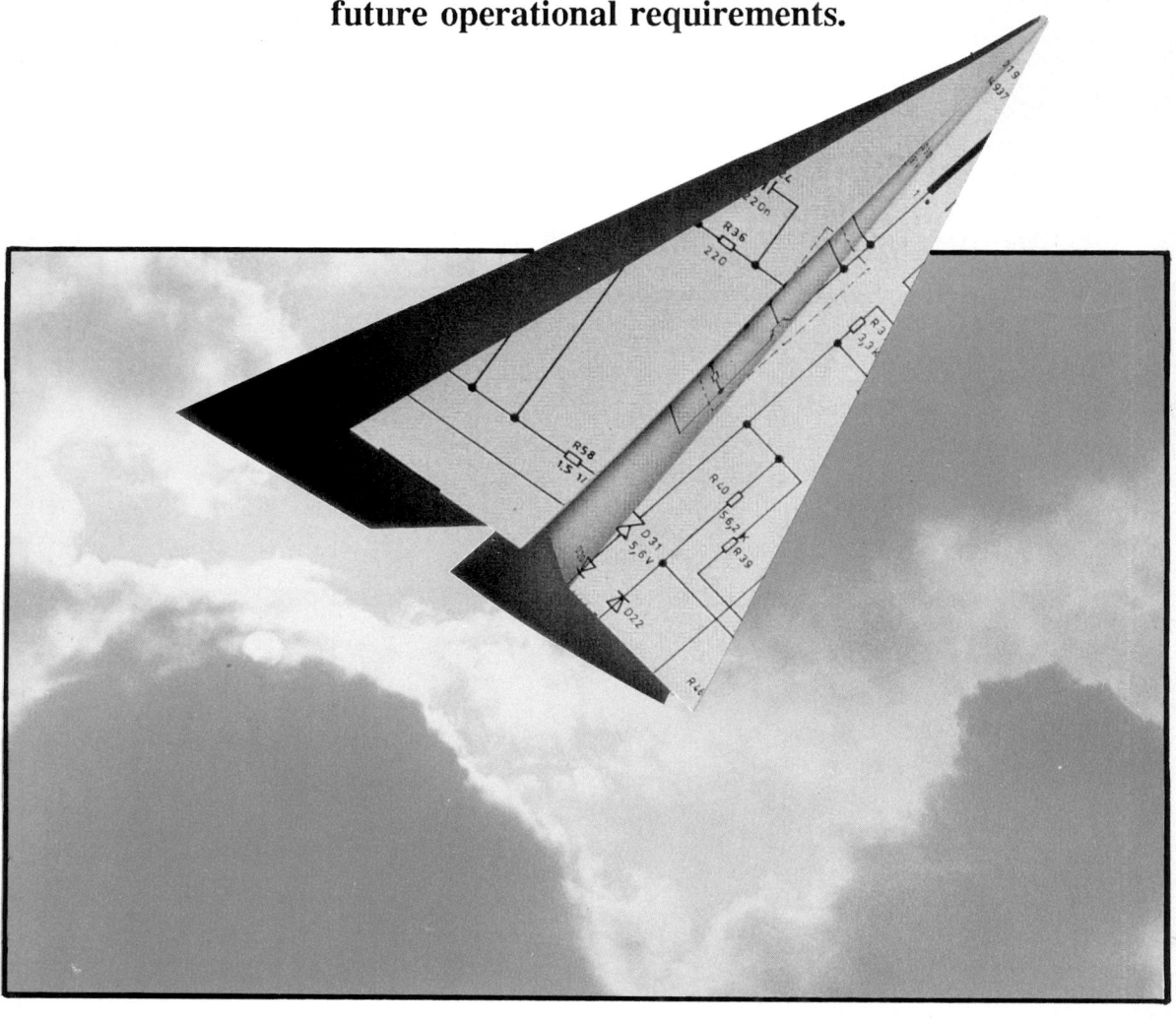

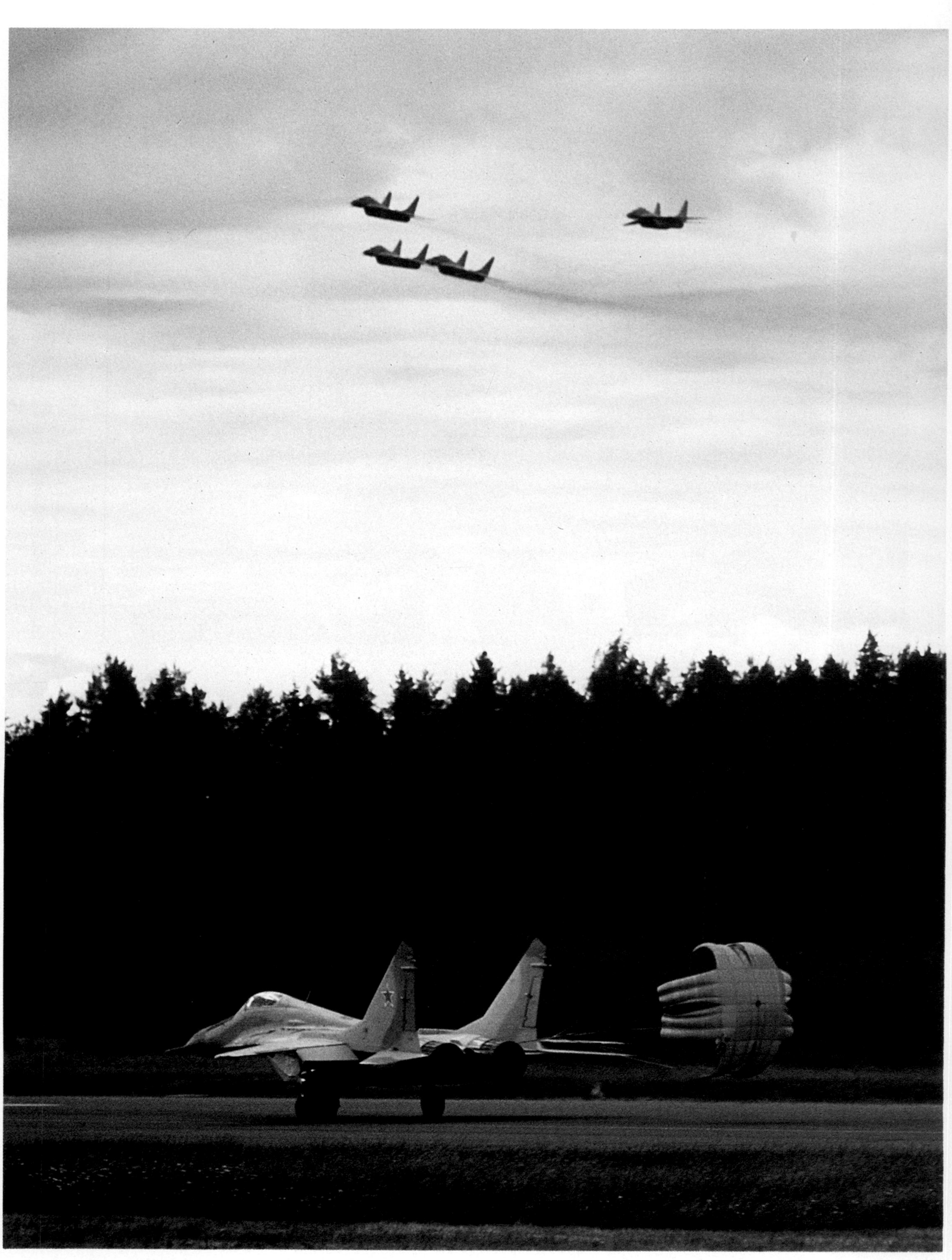

Four MiG-29 counter-air fighters of a Soviet Air Force display team fly over the solo aerobatic aircraft, which is landing at Kuopio-Rissala air base, Finland, with its brake-chute deployed *(Hasse Vallas)*

JANE'S ALL THE WORLD'S AIRCRAFT

FOUNDED IN 1909 BY FRED T. JANE

COMPILED AND EDITED BY
JOHN W R TAYLOR, FRAeS, FRHistS, FSLAET, AFAIAA
ASSISTANT EDITOR
KENNETH MUNSON, AMRAeS, ARHistS

1986-87

ISBN 0 7106-0835-7
JANE'S YEARBOOKS
"Jane's" is a registered trade mark

In the USA and its dependencies
Jane's Publishing Inc, 4th Floor, 115 5th Avenue, New York, NY 10003, USA

CONTENTS

The Editor has been assisted in the compilation of this edition as follows:

Kenneth Munson	AIRCRAFT SECTION: ARGENTINA TO FINLAND, WEST GERMANY TO TURKEY; SAILPLANES; HANG GLIDERS; LIGHTER THAN AIR; RPVS
Maurice Allward	AIRCRAFT SECTION: UNITED KINGDOM; INDEX
Bill Gunston	GLOSSARY; AERO ENGINES
Mike Jerram	AIRCRAFT SECTION: UNITED STATES OF AMERICA
Michael Taylor	SPORT AIRCRAFT; METRIC CONVERSIONS

ADVANCED IMAGE ART

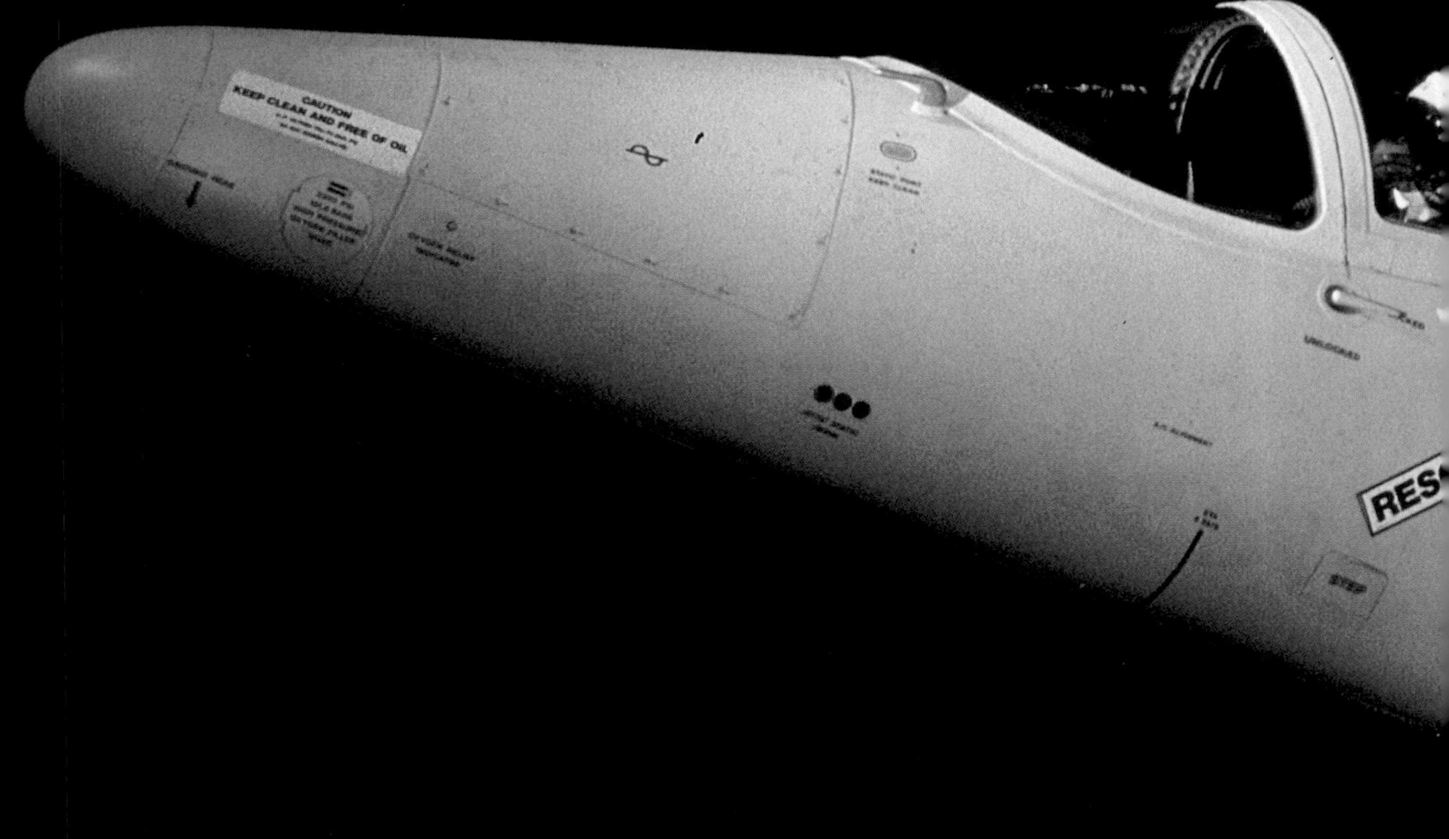

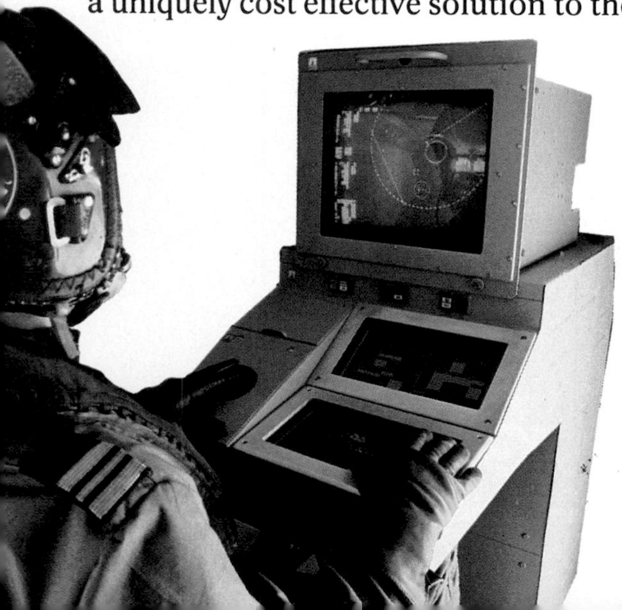

FOREWORD

'Star Wars', President Reagan's Strategic Defense Initiative (SDI) which is intended to provide an impenetrable shield against ballistic missile attack, has dominated military thought during the past year. But while the President has, with the best of intentions, been re-inventing France's 1939 Maginot Line, there have been disturbing reminders that the West will neglect more conventional types of weapon at its peril.

US fighter pilots encounter Soviet 'Bear' strategic bombers over international waters with alarming frequency as the huge missile carriers make simulated attacks on North American targets, probing the defences as they do so. It is easy to dismiss 'Bear' as a lumbering relic of the propeller age. In fact, it has remained in production for more than thirty years because there is still no aircraft that can do better the tasks on which it is deployed. A new supersonic long-range missile carrier, known to NATO as 'Blackjack', was identified on US satellite photographs five years ago; but the Soviet Union never did possess a magic formula to get combat aircraft off the drawing board and into squadron service overnight, as some Western commentators implied in the past.

Satellite reconnaissance appears to have dispelled illusions of this kind. Several years after the Pentagon's *Soviet Military Power* publication warned of the likely production of two new Soviet attack helicopters, there is still no reason to believe that 'Havoc' and 'Hokum' have progressed beyond prototype testing. Fears that 'Hokum' might shoot all NATO helicopters out of the sky in the first ten minutes of any future confrontation were clearly premature. Equally reassuring for those who feared that Soviet designers experience none of the problems encountered by their Western counterparts is the development history of the Sukhoi Su-27 (NATO 'Flanker'), counterpart to the US Air Force's F-15 Eagle. After nine years of flight development, reports suggest that only one modest first-line unit is equipped with Su-27s, while dozens more sit around at Komsomolsk, waiting perhaps for their engines or avionics to be debugged.

Much can be learned from the Soviet sections of this edition of *Jane's*. As always, the facts, figures and photographs were obtained from non-classified sources, without recourse to any private spy system. The book will be credible, and will retain its friends in every country that builds aeroplanes, only so long as it maintains these standards, independent of national or political influence. However, the volume of new and amended information this year is greater than ever before for those who are prepared to read the small print diligently.

* * * * * * *

On 1 July 1986 the Soviet Union provided a rare glimpse of the current state of the art in its combat aircraft design and production centres, when a detachment of six MiG-29s from Kubinka air base, near Moscow, made a goodwill visit to Kuopio-Rissala in Finland.

As the MiGs taxied towards their parking area, spectators were surprised to note that the fighters' engine air intakes appeared to be blanked off. Subsequent inspection of video film showed that the intakes were fitted with doors which closed the ducts when the nosewheel made contact with the runway on landing. Clearly, this was a technique for preventing the low-slung 'mouths' of the big turbofans from hoovering up ice, snow, slush, stones and other foreign objects from the kind of runways that the Warsaw Pact air forces are expected to use year-round. When the doors are closed, the MiG-29 takes in air through louvres above its wingroot leading-edge extensions. The doors open again as the nosewheel lifts off the runway at take-off. All of which is very simple, very practical, very Russian.

Another surprise was to discover that, despite the MiG-29's comparatively small dimensions, in the class of the US Navy's F/A-18 Hornet, it packs a six-barrel 30 mm Gatling type gun in its port wingroot. No underwing weapon pylons were fitted to the aircraft from Kubinka, but the US Department of Defense has referred to six hardpoints for the latest AA-10 and AA-11 air-to-air missiles, or other external stores. These are allied to a large lookdown/shoot-down pulse Doppler radar, said to embody US Hughes Aircraft technology, an infra-red search/track sensor forward of the windscreen, and a pilot's helmet sight linked to the overall weapons system. A voice warning system is said to alert the pilot if he nears the limits of safe flight.

The flying display given by the MiG pilots was impressive, suggesting none of the 'wandering' that MiG-21s exhibit in similar aerobatic manoeuvres, or any need for the wingroot notches and ventral fin of the latest MiG-23s. But no aeroplane is more than a collection of compromises riveted and bonded together.

There was little evidence of the use of weight saving composites in the airframe; ammunition for the gun must be limited by the airflow ducting and other contents of the wingroot; and the MiG does not offer its pilot the superb all-round field of view enjoyed by those who fly F-15s and F-16s. Nor is it likely that the IR sensor is capable of thermal imaging that would pick out an aircraft or cruise missile flying fast and low. And those who suggest that the MiG's pilot might navigate by IR, to avoid radar and radio emissions that would betray his approach to an intended target, should discuss with experts the likely timescale for such techniques.

Whatever their shortcomings, Russia's MiG-29s represent a new level of technology for Soviet design and engineering. Their combat effectiveness depends on other factors such as the competence of their pilots, the TBO of their turbofans and TBMF of their avionics, Soviet Air Force servicing standards, and the extent to which the nation's air defence system has broken free of the ground controlled interception techniques that inhibited pilot initiative in the past.

* * * * * * *

At the beginning of the 1980s, *Jane's* quoted figures showing the depressing standards of combat readiness then achieved by the US air forces. According to Defense Secretary Harold Brown, an average 42 per cent of USAF tactical aircraft were not mission capable at any particular time. The relatively unsophisticated A-10 Thunderbolt II came out best, with only 32·6 per cent of the 243-strong front-line force grounded on average throughout the year. At the other extreme, 65·6 per cent of the 86 F-111Ds were normally not mission capable. Nor was the US Navy in a much healthier state, with an average 47·1 per cent of its 292 F-14A Tomcats unavailable throughout the year, and unimpressive availability of its other five major combat types.

Bearing in mind the 2½ to 1 numerical superiority that has always been enjoyed by the Warsaw Pact air forces in Europe, and the huge efforts made by the Soviet Union to close the technology gap between East and West in recent years, an invitation to study the current state of readiness at Tactical Air Command's Langley Air Force Base in Virginia, in the Spring of 1986, promised to be of outstanding interest. So it proved.

As well as being the Headquarters of TAC, Langley houses the 1st Tactical Fighter Wing. The sight of 72 F-15s lined up wingtip to wingtip on the apron was a little disconcerting to a visitor from terrorist-conscious Europe. In other respects, the whole base displayed an aura of efficient confidence. *Jane's* hosts were the 27th Tactical Fighter Squadron, commanded by Lt Col Bill Rutledge, with 24 F-15s, 30 pilots and 230/260 ground personnel led by Capt Karen Kiever. Each aircraft was logging an average 22 sorties a month, compared with 14 in 1980, with about two minutes per sortie at supersonic speed during attack and disengagement phases. The proportion of aircraft rated non-mission-capable through lack of spares had fallen from 30 per cent to 5·6 per cent in six years;

those non-mission-capable through maintenance backlog had reduced from 40 per cent to 8 per cent. The abort rate was 5 per cent.

Lt Gen Robert E. Kelley, Vice Commander of TAC, admitted that Langley is a little above average; but estimated that the Command would log a total of 738,000 flying hours in 1986, with Holloman, Luke and Nellis AFBs each contributing more flight time than the entire Pacific Air Forces. Nine of the Command's 18 Wings completed 1985 without an accident. The total number of accidents was 15, representing a rate of 2·1 per 100,000 hours. By comparison, the rate in the days of the F-104 was 30 per 100,000 hours.

It would be good to have an opportunity of quoting similar statistics for the Soviet Air Forces, as they represent one vitally important facet of efficient air power. However, the ultimate measure of effectiveness must be in terms of results achieved in action.

In this respect, the Royal Air Force distinguished itself in the USAF's annual Prairie Vortex international bombing competition for the second successive year in 1985. Supported by Victor tanker crews of No. 57 Squadron, aircrew of No. 27 Squadron flew their Tornados to first and second places in the Curtis LeMay Trophy competition, first and second places for the John Meyer Trophy; and second and eighth places for the Mathis Trophy. In doing so, they again outperformed B-52 and F-111 teams of the USAF in both high and low level bombing sorties.

* * * * * * *

Unlike its predecessors, this Foreword is avoiding lengthy comment on political or strategic questions, because weapons like ICBMs, SLBMs and SDI are no longer within its scope. However, one must express some hope now that leaders of East and West are talking of massive reductions in strategic missiles, on the scale discussed for years in *Jane's All the World's Aircraft* and associated writings. Nuclear weapons cannot be disinvented, and a total ban may never be practicable; but international reaction to the civil disaster at Chernobyl power station in the Spring of 1986 helped world leaders to recognise that nuclear weapons must never be used, and that if they were used there would be no victor. Such knowledge focuses attention on the conventional weapons that have to be built in adequate, balanced, numbers to provide an alternative deterrent. Fortunately, they may become more easily affordable through the immense sums saved by cancellation of nuclear weapons, especially as this also makes SDI redundant.

* * * * * * *

One of the major problems within NATO's air forces that remained to be solved in the Autumn of 1986 stems from shortcomings in the Nimrod AEW. Mk 3 early warning aircraft that should have plugged a worrying gap in western air defences long ago. Co-operation between Britain's GEC Avionics and one or other of the American companies with AEW&C experience might have resolved the difficulties; but it seems that commercial interests preclude such partnership, however crucial the problem. So, a straight choice between continued work on Nimrod or an order for Boeing E-3s becomes increasingly urgent.

On the other side of the Atlantic, Congress is trying to limit the worst excesses of those who would lead the United States down an isolationist path. During a debate on one amendment to the FY 1987 defence authorisation bill, Senator John Glenn is reported to have said that he doubted whether there is much expertise abroad that cannot be duplicated in the United States. This prompted a comment in the UK that McDonnell Douglas certainly had no difficulty in duplicating the Harrier, although the speaker suspected they did have some British help. This cast no reflection on McDonnell Douglas, who are splendid partners for anyone; but Europe does seem to have produced a few world-beaters on its own, from the original V/STOL Harrier to the Concorde, which remains the only aircraft in the world able to spend most of its working life at Mach 2.

The United States can, no doubt, duplicate most other types of aircraft, but still finds merit in the European Airbus and Hawk. Do people like Senator John Glenn really believe that the Soviet Union has a better system when it insists on producing virtually all the combat aircraft operated by Warsaw pact air forces, leaving the industries of its allies to jog along on a diet of small helicopters and commuter transports, trainers and sailplanes, and crumbs from the rich man's table in the form of subcontracts for pieces of airliner? Would the Second World War have been won more quickly with only US aircraft, instead of Spitfires, Hurricanes, Lancasters, Mosquitos, Sunderlands and all the rest?

US orders for the modern Airbus family of airliners might deprive Seattle and Long Beach of work and profits, as one US critic of *Jane's* suggested. However, the Airbus programme is providing work to keep considerable numbers of European designers and engineers employed. Even a chief aerodynamicist at NASA Langley had to admit to visitors from the UK last Spring that the supercritical wings used on the Airbus family are probably the best in the world. There could be no higher praise or better reason for maintaining a mutually respectful transatlantic partnership on aerospace programmes.

* * * * * * *

As this edition of *Jane's* closed for press, it was announced that Lockheed and Northrop had been designated prime contractors to build prototypes of the next-generation Advanced Tactical Fighter (ATF) for the USAF, under the designations YF-22A and YF-23A respectively. That these are the manufacturers responsible for America's 'F-19' and ATB stealth aircraft may be coincidental. All that emerged at the time of the announcement was a remark by Lockheed's ATF programme director that his company's fighter will be a single-pilot twin-engined aircraft that will carry all its missiles internally. The YF-22A and YF-23A will each fly with competing Pratt & Whitney YF119 and General Electric YF120 turbofans. The prototypes are intended to be completed and tested within a 50-month demonstration and validation period, at the end of which one will be selected to progress to a five-year full-scale development phase, leading to initial operational capability in the mid-1990s.

Artists' impressions of the ATF published to date are certain to embody modest disinformation. Features to be expected include two-dimensional thrust vectoring jet nozzles of the kind that will be tested on the McDonnell Douglas F-15 STOL demonstrator, to shorten the take-off run. It remains to be seen whether this degree of V/STOL capability will be considered adequate in ten years' time.

Significantly, in October 1986 NASA's Ames Research Center awarded Pratt & Whitney a three-year study contract that could lead to a supersonic research demonstrator capable of true short take-off/vertical landing (STOVL) operation by the early 1990s. The plan is to integrate a derivative of an advanced technology engine such as the PW5000 (forerunner of the ATF's YF119) into four candidate propulsion system concepts. These will comprise ejector augmentor, remote augmented lift, hybrid tandem fan and the Harrier's vectored thrust concept. As the Soviet Union can also be expected to have a new generation of fighters by the mid-1990s, it will be interesting to see if its designers decide to reduce risk by benefiting from Harrier experience, and if this will disadvantage an ATF using a more limited STOL technique.

It has been suggested repeatedly in *Jane's* that intelligent peacetime targeting of a tactical missile force could leave the other side without runways or potential runways within minutes of the start of a conflict. This is no wild surmise. During the Indo-Pakistan War, a squadron of fighters at Dacca was rendered totally unusable when its runway was destroyed. The aircraft themselves remained relatively safe behind concrete enclosures, but could play no part in the fighting.

Except for the US Marine Corps, no air force has yet exhibited a total understanding of what this means. Sweden has come nearest to a next-generation solution with its JAS 39 Gripen fighter. Although in no sense a STOVL aircraft, it shares features of the ATF, embodies canards, and offers potential take-off and landing runs in the 400-500 m (1,300-1,650 ft) bracket. Furthermore, it has been designed from the start for operation from Sweden's numerous, hard-to-spot, road strips. Israel's Lavi and the four-nation Eurofighter must still overcome the peacetime vicissitudes of politics and economics before they come near to confronting an enemy. Normally, this would make the Lavi the better bet; but with both funding and components heavily dependent on the US, the government in Jerusalem is finding it increasingly difficult to resist US proposals for a less costly alternative.

* * * * * * *

Economics have already virtually killed Fairchild Republic's T-46A next generation primary trainer, which seemed set for a 650

HIGH TECHNOLOGY IS OUR BUSINESS

The specialised experience of DAF Trucks in the field of high-quality vehicles was the sound foundation of the independent DAF Special Products division.

In the world of technology DAF Special Products has acquired a special position. Its defence and aviation technology are up to the highest standards. The construction of aircraft landing gears is a striking example.

DAF Special Products accepted the challenge and, together with Menasco Inc., started to build this vital component of the F16 fighter which has already become legendary.

In a relatively short time DAF managed to produce the complete landing gear in keeping with the high-quality standards set.

This has paid dividends because DAF Special Products is now also utilising its know-how and experience in landing gears for other planes (Fokker 50 and Fokker 100), and helicopter components.

At this moment DAF Special Products contributes in the development of the new Nato Helicopters with a revolutionary light-weight crownwheel pignon transmission system.

Not only in the air but also on the ground DAF Special Products gives evidence of its strenght.

Its know-how and experience in the field of defence technology have found a logical sequel in the development and production of infantry vehicles, weapon systems, fuel systems and simulators.

You will meet DAF Special Products in several national and international co-operative ventures: as one of the industrial partners in a consortium, as a project managing organization, as a partner in co-development (Fokker 50), co-production (Leopard) or as a licensee (YPR 765, F16).

To DAF Special Products quality is a matter of course. It was not for nothing that the Dutch Ministry of Defence, acting on behalf of NATO, granted DAF Special Products the AQAP-1 certificate. A guarantee for optimum quality control, from design to final inspection and after-sales service.

DAF Special Products

DAF Special Products The Netherlands Tel.: +3140143056. Telex: 51970.

unit production run a year ago. Work on Boeing's XCH-62 heavy lift research vehicle has been dropped from official funding for the second time. The once-favoured Northrop F-20 export fighter has still found no buyer and seems likely to fade quietly away.

Northrop may not find this too distressing, with huge funding for the ATB continuing and the ATF set to provide further income. The future is altogether gloomier for Fairchild, which may close its Farmingdale, Long Island, factory, former production centre of great US fighters from the P-47 Thunderbolt of the Second World War to the F-84s of Korea and F-105 Thunderchiefs—the mighty 'Thuds'—of Viet-Nam. Yet even this is tolerable by comparison with the disaster which has overtaken the US lightplane industry—supplier of the smaller communications, calibration, forward air control and other support aircraft essential to any air force.

The results are seen clearly in this edition of *Jane's*. Champion Aircraft's range of lightplanes has gone. Piper suspended production of most of its piston-engined models in February 1986, only to resume manufacture of the entire line in July and begin studies for new models. By then, Beech had abandoned its two-seat and four-seat lightplanes, and Cessna had cut its product range from a once-unrivalled total of more than 60 models and variants to just seven, none of them piston engined.

There was one well remembered occasion, in 1932, when this company's listing in *Jane's* occupied only four lines of text under its name and address. In the acerbic style of the Editor of that time, this brief paragraph stated that "The Cessna Aircraft Co. has produced a number of cantilever cabin monoplanes of exceptionally clean design, but has presumably succumbed to the depression and the Company is now believed to be inactive." That belief was to prove misplaced, by a factor of more than 175,000 aircraft built up to 1986.

Few people doubt that Cessna will again fight its way back to leadership in general aviation marketing, on the basis of fine products like its turboprop Caravan I utility transport and turbofan Citation business jets, but this time the problem will be more difficult to overcome. It began with the recession of the early 1980s, although this did not deal general aviation the deadly blow that is sometimes suggested. There have been almost as many transactions involving ownership of light aircraft as in earlier years, but most of the dealings are now in used rather than new aeroplanes.

The more serious explanation for the situation, as explained in last year's *Jane's*, is the product liability 'crisis' that added an average $92,000 to the price of every Cessna sold in 1986, and $80,000 to every Beechcraft. Cessna's Chairman, Russell Meyer, has warned a US Senate subcommittee: "We are on the threshold of seeing an entire industry essentially destroyed because of the uncontrolled impact of the product liability environment, which has lost any reasonable relationship to either negligence, proximate cause or measurable damages."

Beech Aircraft President James S. Walsh told the same subcommittee that a 1978 Beech study had shown that, of the total amount the company spent each year in defence of its products and in settlement of claims, less than 17 per cent ever reached the hands of anyone injured or the survivors of persons killed in Beech aeroplanes. The rest of the money went to courts, lawyers, insurance companies and other parties involved in litigating cases.

Robert J. Wyma of Piper's parent company, Lear Siegler, added that "Today, Piper pays more for product liability insurance than it does for labour to build its aeroplanes—and ours is historically a labour intensive industry".

To the average non-pilot member of the worldwide community, this may seem wrong, but of no personal relevance. However, aviation is by no means the only victim. A letter from a representative of Cessna, in June of this year, stated that "Most of the traditional firework displays scheduled for our 4th of July celebrations have been cancelled, because insurance is either unavailable or unaffordable. And yesterday came the news that one of the most popular ice skating lakes in Wichita will be closed to skating next Winter for the same reason. Where will it end?"

* * * * * * *

At such a time one must admire the courage of small companies like Christen, which has used computer aided design (CAD) techniques to produce an entirely new tandem two-seat lightplane known as the Husky. Intended as a thoroughly modern successor to the Piper Cub, it is expected to capture part of the market left wide open by the big three. If, as hoped, sales build up to 25 a year, supplementing current annual production of 37 or 38 Pitts Specials, Christen's labour force in Afton, Wyoming, could increase from 48 to 60.

In the UK, ARV Aviation and Trago Mills have a similar aim of restoring Britain's long-lost reputation for lightplane manufacture. Promavia of Belgium is another newcomer, possessing even greater ambitions. With financial support from the state, and USAF willingness to provide one of the F109 turbofans developed for the T-46A, it commissioned Dott Ing Stelio Frati of General Avia, Italy, to design for it a side by side two-seat trainer known as the Jet Squalus. This is to be offered to the USAF as a replacement for the T-46A, which may seem a remote possibility. However, the combination of Frati design, an engine developed specially for this application, and extremely low initial and operating costs, must make it attractive when so much emphasis is placed on affordability.

It would be pleasing to see Belgium back among the nations whose industries contribute original designs as well as subcontracting and assembly plants for aircraft developed elsewhere. The quality of the latest original products of nations outside the aviation big league can be appreciated on page after page of this book. Some countries are following the example set postwar by Japan, by beginning with licence assembly, progressing to licence manufacture from locally built components, and then to development and production of their own designs. China's advance in this direction is beginning to generate interesting results—not yet in terms of aircraft to influence world design; but the F-8 II fighter, and the large maritime reconnaissance flying-boat illustrated in the Addenda to this edition, indicate how rapidly the Chinese industry is learning to build on the natural skills and energy of its people.

Brazil has long outgrown the learning phase. By concentrating on unsophisticated commuter transports like the Bandeirante and Brasilia, it has been able to penetrate markets that were once the prerogative of the US manufacturers who invented this class of aircraft. de Havilland of Canada established a world leadership in safe, unhurried STOL transportation. Among countless benefits in every part of the world, this made feasible current plans for a fixed-wing STOLport in the heart of London's old dockland. The reward for DHC was to be put up for sale by its government and acquired by Boeing to fill the bottom end of the latter company's range of airliners for every conceivable stage length and traffic density. This may offer the best hope for continued development of a unique family of aircraft. It is, nevertheless, sad that Canada could not find the money and enthusiasm to keep alive its own highly innovative aviation industry.

Compelled by international disfavour to meet its own military needs, South Africa has made considerable progress towards self sufficiency in combat aircraft during the past year. Parallelling Israel Aircraft Industries' development of the basic Mirage III, via the Nesher, to the Kfir, its Atlas Aircraft Corporation is updating SAAF Mirages to a very superior Cheetah standard, complete with canards, and at the same time developing the Alpha XH-1 attack helicopter from the licence-built Alouette III.

* * * * * * *

Such activities (like the Hughes Aircraft input into the MiG-29's radar) are not strictly what is meant by international collaboration. A few genuine joint ventures, including the former Gates/Piaggio Avanti business aircraft and Saab-Fairchild SF 340A transport, have become single-nation programmes since the last edition went to press. Generally, however, the extent of international teamwork continues to grow.

Most publicised, and in some respects most surprising, international link-up in 1986 was the Sikorsky/Fiat rescue package for Britain's Westland Helicopter company. As most of Westland's successful aircraft since 1947 had been based on Sikorsky designs, it was difficult to see what the US manufacturer had to gain from its offer of capital to prevent an all-European tie-up between Westland, Aérospatiale of France, Agusta of Italy, MBB of Germany, GEC and British Aerospace. This overlooked the UK company's recent advances in helicopter blade design, which led to its BERP (British Experimental Rotor Programme) blades with high performance aerofoil section and paddle shape tips.

On 11 August 1986, a Westland Lynx fitted with BERP III blades set a new world's absolute speed record for helicopters by averaging 216·45 knots (400·87 km/h; 249·09 mph) over a 15/25 km course, subject to FAI homologation. This exceeded by 17·5 knots the former record set by a Soviet Mi-24 (NATO 'Hind'), lending weight to Westland claims that the new blades increase rotor

efficiency by up to 40 per cent. This could provide an incentive for the US Army to decide in favour of the Sikorsky/Boeing team in the competition for the LHX multi-role military helicopter contract. With the Soviet 'Hokum' still a long way from being operational, an LHX fitted with a BERP rotor system by Sikorsky's new UK associate could provide a quick riposte to the US Department of Defense's gloomy comment that: "Hokum will give the Soviets a significant rotary-wing air superiority capability. The system has no current Western counterpart".

The past year has seen other exciting developments in the rotary-wing business. Sikorsky has fitted an X-wing to one of its S-72 rotor systems research aircraft, and flight trials at NASA's Dryden Flight Research Center, Edwards AFB, were due to start in the Autumn of 1986. With a likely speed range from hover, with the X-wing rotor turning, to 300 knots (555 km/h; 345 mph) with it stopped, the S-72 could sire a whole new family of agile and versatile battlefield aircraft.

Meanwhile, the V-22 Osprey series of tilt-rotor aircraft, by Bell and Boeing Vertol, is taking shape under a $1,714 million seven-year development contract approved by US Naval Air Systems Command on 2 May 1986. Total value of the R&D programme, including government furnished equipment and support, is $2,500 million. First flight is scheduled for June 1988 and, if all progresses as planned, the Marine Corps will start to receive its 552 Ospreys, primarily for combat assault and assault support, four years later. The US Air Force is hoping to approve manufacture of 80 for special operations duties by 1993. The US Army wants 231 for multi-mission duties, and the Navy is thinking in terms of 50 for search and rescue, plus 300 more for anti-submarine missions.

There have been unconfirmed reports of similar aircraft under development by the Soviet Mil Bureau, and it would be astonishing if Marat Tishchenko's design team made no attempt to match the V-22. In its basic form, it will combine all the attributes of a helicopter with an ability to haul 6,800 kg (15,000 lb) externally, or carry 24 combat equipped troops at speeds greater than 260 knots (480 km/h; 300 mph). The airframe will be all-composites. Complex mechanisms will permit the wing to be stowed and the rotors folded to create a compact rectangular package for storage on the flight and hangar decks of aircraft carriers.

* * * * * * *

For anyone old enough to remember the time, during the Second World War, when members of the UK public were invited to contribute to Spitfire Funds, to buy aircraft for the Royal Air Force, sums like $2,500 million for the initial development phase of a new aircraft programme are impossible to imagine. How large is a mountain of 2,500,000,000 one-dollar bills? The answer is a lot bigger than one of the Spitfires that could be bought, nominally, for a mere £5,000, or even the V-22 Osprey itself. In fact, one would need three An-124s, the largest aircraft in the world, to carry the bills.

The sums involved in most contracts at government or "big business' level have become meaningless to the public at large. If a person is English, he is pleased to learn that British Airways has placed a contract with Boeing for 16 new-technology 747-400s for delivery in 1989-90. It means that 'his' national airline must be doing well, especially as it expects to need a further 12 similar aircraft in 1991-94. The good folk of Seattle see this same contract as a potential contribution of $4,100 million to Boeing Commercial Airplane Company's income – the largest single order it had received by the Summer of 1986.

They are somewhat resentful that one of their own national operators, Northwest Airlines, should have ordered up to 100 Airbus A320s from Europe, instead of backing Boeing. However, the $3,200,000,000 that the 100 aircraft would inject into European industry would be pleasing to our Englishman if he knew about it. He might even feel that he would benefit personally from Airbus's good fortune if he had been persuaded to buy shares in British Aerospace during Mrs Thatcher's privatisation campaign.

Such is the simple way in which ordinary people view the expediture of vast sums of their money. Unless incited to do so, they usually feel pride, rather than resentment, when their taxes buy something as world-beating, unique, beautiful and thoroughly practical as Concorde. This is why it is preferable to paint models of projects like the US National Aerospace Plane in 'Orient Express' colours rather than refer to it as a potential trans-atmospheric orbital weapon carrier, which is probably a great deal more likely. As one leading member of the US industry commented: "It is still a little early to send grandma to Australia in a ballistic missile".

It is altogether correct that NASA Langley should have in its wind tunnels, in 1986, working models of scramjet engines that might one day propel the National Aerospace Plane. But it makes a great deal more near-term sense that Aérospatiale is studying seriously a second generation Concorde, to carry 200 passengers for 8,000 km (4,320 nm; 4,970 miles) at Mach 2·2. It was a combination of the Royal Aircraft Establishment's wing expertise and French enthusiasm for a 'Super Caravelle' SST that launched the Concorde programme a quarter of a century ago. The 200-seater will cost a great deal of money; but who in the last thousand years would have built a great cathedral or bridge if it had been expected to show a financial profit from day one? Some things *have* to be done, or civilisation grinds to a halt. Continuing to provide supersonic air travel, for a much wider cross-section of the public, after Concorde has reached retirement age, is one of them.

* * * * * * *

During 1985, the Editor travelled to Florida, with his wife, on Concorde. The final stage of what was, to all outward appearances, an afternoon's journey was a 36 minute gentle hop at low altitude, through perfect skies, to West Palm Beach in a piston engined Cessna 402C. The 36 minutes included an unscheduled diversion to Fort Lauderdale to pick up a colleague of the pilot, whose aircraft had been damaged earlier that day. The contrast between the supremely professional Mach 2 Concorde and the relaxing, friendly, Cessna prompted the Editor's wife to tell their children that it had been one of the great days of her life.

This reminds us of the difference between flying and air travel. Flying is sheer enjoyment – the great achievement of our twentieth century. Travel is getting from A to B, where the real pleasure or business is waiting.

For that reason, it is good to discover that flying is not disappearing at the same time as so many of the industry's two- and four-seat light aircraft. This year the aeroplanes that provide such a high proportion of what might be called *real* flying – homebuilts, racing aircraft, microlights, air recreation vehicles, small rotorcraft and suchlike – have been put together in a new section of *Jane's* entitled 'Sport Aircraft'.

A few people will complain because these 'non-professional' types fill 202 pages of a 970-page book intended for a highly professional readership. This overlooks the fact that most professionals find the Sport Aircraft pages of interest and value. In any case, what would one call a *Jane's* denuded of homebuilts and sailplanes, or even RPVs? . . . *Some of the World's Aircraft? Most of the World's Aircraft?* It is a sobering thought that if homebuilts had been omitted from Fred T. Jane's original 1909 edition of *All the World's Air-Ships*, he would have included only the Short-built Wright biplane, the Voisin biplane, and one or two others like the Blériot monoplane – a homebuilt that made the first international aeroplane flight over water, from France to England in 1909, and then went on in production form to carry the pioneer UK Coronation air mail in 1911, become the first real aerobatic display aircraft, and perform the first wartime aerial reconnaissance mission for the Royal Flying Corps in 1914.

Burt Rutan's modern homebuilt canards (themselves casualties of the product liability crisis) have clearly influenced designs like the Starship, on which so much of Beech's future wellbeing may depend. Study of those 202 Sport Aircraft pages will reveal countless other interesting facts to the careful reader, including little-known military applications of certain types – although the best stories may not always be told.

* * * * * * *

So, as always, *Jane's* presents, as far as possible, a comprehensive listing of all the world's aircraft that are in production or under development. This year, the Chinese and Soviet sections give the compilers particular pride. On the debit side, pressures associated with the recession have made it difficult for some smaller companies to provide their usual high standard of co-operation. This explains, no doubt, why one US lightplane manufacturer failed to respond to requests for updated information. As a result, although details of his new models are included, there are no illustrations of them. In general, our friends inside and outside the industries of every nation that builds aeroplanes could not have been more helpful. Our warmest thanks and good wishes are extended to them all.

Whatever is good about this edition of *Jane's* reflects once again the year-round effort and attention to detail of Assistant Editor Kenneth Munson and Compilers Maurice Allward, Bill Gunston, Mike Jerram and Michael Taylor, working closely with our production team and our good friends of Netherwood Dalton in Huddersfield, the printing works from which every edition of this yearbook has come since 1909. Such continuity produces a dedication to accuracy and quality that is all too rare in the mid-eighties. Special thanks are due this year to Michael Taylor, who tackled nobly the task of compiling the Sport Aircraft section, ensuring a consistent style for entries that had differed considerably from section to section in their original form.

Demand for three-view drawings of the highest achievable standard has imposed progressively greater pressure on Dennis Punnett of Pilot Press, whose work has contributed so much to the appearance and reference value of *Jane's* for the past twenty-five years, with the assistance of Michael A. Badrocke. To meet the growing needs of this book and its associated publications, *Jane's* has been fortunate to obtain the services of Mike Keep, an experienced aviation technical artist whose contributions, including some perspective drawings, appear in our book for the first time this year. Hopefully, this strengthening of our team will permit expanded coverage of new designs, to a consistently high standard, in the years ahead.

The list of friends and colleagues who made major contributions to this edition includes many familiar names and a few welcome newcomers, notably Delden Badcock in Australia; Ronaldo S. Olive in Brazil; Neil A. Macdougall in Canada; Wolfgang Wagner in West Germany; Vico Rosaspina in Italy; Eiichiro Sekigawa in Japan; Javier Taibo in Spain; Roland Eichenberger and Dr Ulrich Haller in Switzerland; Tom DeFrank, Jay Miller and Nelson Fuller in the USA; Dipl Ing Andrzej Glass and Dipl Ing Jerzy Grzegorzewski in Poland; William Green and Gordon Swanborough of *Air International*, David Dorrell of *Air Pictorial*, James Gilbert of *Pilot* and Arnold Nayler of *Airship* in the UK; and the editorial staffs of *Flight International* (UK); *Aviation Magazine International* and *Air et Cosmos* (France); *Ultralight Flying* (USA); *FLYGvapenNYTT* (Sweden); *Herkenning* and *de Vliegende Hollander* (Netherlands); *AiReview* (Japan); *Australian Aviation* and *Aircraft* (Australia); *Letectvi + Kosmonautika* (Czechoslovakia); *BIAF* (Israel); *Skrzydlata Polska* (Poland); and *Air Force Magazine* (Washington, DC), with which we continue to enjoy such a valuable special relationship through our bi-monthly *Jane's All the World's Aircraft* Supplements and other contributed features.

As in previous years, our photographic coverage would have been far less complete and informative without the hundreds of prints supplied by Howard Levy, J. M. G. Gradidge, Brian M. Service, Paul R. Duffy, Peter M. Bowers, Austin J. Brown, Don Dwiggins, Katsumi Hinata, Giovanni Masino of Aviodata, Geoffrey P. Jones, Peter Bish, David Davies and Michael Vines of Air Portraits, Stuart MacConnacher, Peter F. Selinger, Ian MacFarlane, Martin Fricke-Kunz and Anton Wettstein. To all of them go our sincere thanks and the hope that we shall be able to count on their continued friendship and help for many more years.

Surbiton, November 1986 JWRT

Glossary

AAM Air-to-air missile.
AATH Automatic approach to hover.
AC Alternating current.
ACLS (1) Automatic carrier landing system; (2) Air cushion landing system.
ADAC Avion de décollage et attérrissage court (STOL).
ADAV Avion de décollage et attérrissage vertical (VTOL).
ADC (1) US Air Force Aerospace Defense Command (no longer active); (2) air data computer.
ADF Automatic direction finding (equipment).
ADG Accessory-drive generator.
ADI Attitude/director indicator.
aeroplane (N America, airplane) Heavier-than-air aircraft with propulsion and a wing that does not rotate in order to generate lift.
AEW Airborne early warning.
AFB Air Force Base (USA).
AFCS Automatic flight control system.
afterburning Temporarily augmenting the thrust of a turbofan or turbojet by burning additional fuel in the jetpipe.
AGREE Advisory Group on Reliability in Electronic Equipment.
Ah Ampère-hours.
AHRS Attitude/heading reference system.
AIDS Airborne integrated data system.
aircraft All man-made vehicles for off-surface navigation within the atmosphere, including helicopters and balloons.
airstair Retractable stairway built into aircraft.
AM Amplitude modulation.
anhedral Downward slope of wing seen from front, in direction from root to tip.
AP Ammonium perchlorate.
APFD Autopilot flight director.
aphelion The point in a solar (Sun-centred) orbit furthest from the Sun.
apogee The point in an Earth-centred orbit furthest from the Earth.
approach noise Measured 1 nm from downwind end of runway with aircraft passing overhead at 112·6 m (370 ft).
APS Aircraft prepared for service; a fully equipped weight.
APU Auxiliary power unit (part of aircraft).
ARINC Aeronautical Radio Inc, US company whose electronic box sizes (racking sizes) are the international standard.
ASE Automatic stabilisation equipment.
ASI Airspeed indicator.
ASIR Airspeed indicator reading.
ASM Air-to-surface missile.
aspect ratio Measure of wing (or other aerofoil) slenderness seen in plan view, usually defined as the square of the span divided by area.
ASPJ Advanced self-protection jammer.
AST Automatic speed trim.
ASV (1) Air-to-surface vessel; (2) Anti surface vessel.
ASW Anti-submarine warfare.
ATC Air traffic control.
ATR Airline transport radio, series of ARINC standard box sizes.
attack, angle of Angle at which airstream meets aerofoil (angle between mean chord and free-stream direction). Not to be confused with angle of incidence (which see).
augmented Boosted by afterburning.
autogyro Rotary-wing aircraft propelled by a propeller (or other thrusting device) and lifted by a freely running autorotating rotor.
AUW All-up weight (term meaning total weight of aircraft under defined conditions, or at specific time during flight). Not to be confused with MTOGW (which see).
avionics Aviation electronics, such as communications radio, radars, navigation systems and computers.
AWACS Airborne warning and control system (aircraft).

bar Non-SI unit of pressure adopted by this yearbook pending wider acceptance of Pa. 1 bar = 10^5 Pa, and ISA pressure at S/L is 1,013·2 mb, or just over 1 bar.
bare weight Undefined term meaning unequipped empty weight.
basic operating weight MTOGW minus payload (thus, including crew, fuel and oil, bar stocks, cutlery etc).
BCAR British Civil Airworthiness Requirements.
Beta mode Propeller or rotor operating regime in which pilot has direct control of pitch.
BFO Beat-frequency oscillator.
BITE Built-in test equipment.
bladder tank Fuel (or other fluid) tank of flexible material.
bleed air Hot high-pressure air extracted from gas-turbine engine compressor or combustor and taken through valves and pipes to perform useful work such as driving machinery or anti-icing by heating surfaces.
blown flap Flap across which bleed air is discharged at high (often supersonic) speed to prevent flow-breakaway.
BOW Basic operating weight.
BPR Bypass ratio.
BTU Non-SI unit of energy (British Thermal Unit) = 0·9478 J.
bus Busbar, main terminal in electrical system to which battery or generator power is supplied.
bypass ratio Airflow through fan duct (not passing through core) divided by airflow through core.

CAA Civil Aviation Authority (UK).
CAB Civil Aeronautics Board (USA).
CAB Pt 298 Sets the commercial standards for non-certificated carriers, mainly commuter airlines.
cabin altitude Height above S/L at which ambient pressure is same as inside cabin.
CAM Cockpit-angle measure (crew field of view).
canards Foreplanes, fixed or controllable aerodynamic surfaces ahead of CG.
CAN 5 Committee on Aircraft Noise (ICAO) rules for new designs of aircraft.
CAR Civil Airworthiness Regulations.
CAS Calibrated airspeed, ASI calibrated to allow for air compressibility according to ISA S/L.
CBR California bearing ratio, measure of ability of airfield surface (paved or not) to support aircraft.
CBU Cluster bomb unit.
CCV Control configured vehicle.
CEAM Centre d'Expériences Aériennes Militaires.
CEAT Centre d'Essais Aéronautiques de Toulouse.
CEP Circular error probability (50/50 chance of hit being inside or outside) in bombing, missile attack or gunnery.
CEV Centre d'Essais en Vol.
CFRP Carbonfibre-reinforced plastics.
CG Centre of gravity.
chaff Thin slivers of radar-reflective material cut to length appropriate to wavelengths of hostile radars and scattered in clouds to protect friendly aircraft.
chord Distance from leading-edge to trailing-edge measured parallel to longitudinal axis.
clean In flight configuration with landing gear, flaps, slats etc retracted.
'clean' Without any optional external stores.
c/n Construction (or constructor's) number.
COINS Computer operated instrument system.
comint communications intelligence.
composite material Made of two constituents, such as filaments or short whiskers plus adhesive.
CONUS Continental USA (ie, excluding Hawaii, etc).
convertible Transport aircraft able to be equipped to carry passengers or cargo.
core Gas generator portion of turbofan comprising compressor(s), combustion chamber and turbine(s).
C/R Counter-rotating (propellers).
CRT Cathode-ray tube.
CSAS Command and stability augmentation system (part of AFCS).
CSD Constant-speed drive (output shaft speed held steady, no matter how input may vary).

daN Decanewtons (Newtons force × 10).
DARPA Defense Advanced Research Projects Agency.
dB Decibel.
DC Direct current.
derated Engine restricted to power less than potential maximum (usually such engine is flat rated).
design weight Different authorities have different definitions; weight chosen as typical of mission but usually much less than MTOGW.
DF Direction finder, or direction finding.
DGAC Direction Générale à l'Aviation Civile.
dibber bomb Designed to cause maximum damage to concrete runways.
dihedral Upward slope of wing seen from front, in direction from root to tip.
DINS Digital inertial navigation system.
disposable load Sum of masses that can be loaded or unloaded, including payload, crew, usable fuel etc; MTOGW minus OWE.
DME Distance-measuring equipment; gives slant distance to a beacon directly ahead.
dog-tooth A step in the leading-edge of a plane resulting from an increase in chord. (See also saw-tooth.)
Doppler Short for Doppler radar—radar using fact that received frequency is a function of relative velocity between transmitter or reflecting surface and receiver.
double-slotted flap One having an auxiliary aerofoil ahead of main surface to increase maximum lift.
dP Maximum design differential pressure between pressurised cabin and ambient (outside atmosphere).
drone Pilotless aircraft, usually winged, following preset programme of manoeuvres.

EAA Experimental Aircraft Association (divided into local branches called Chapters).
EAS Equivalent airspeed, RAS minus correction for compressibility.
ECCM Electronic counter-countermeasures.
ECM Electronic countermeasures.
EFIS Electronic flight instrument(ation) system, in which large multifunction CRT displays replace traditional instruments.
ehp Equivalent horsepower, measure of propulsive power of turboprop made up of shp plus addition due to residual thrust from jet.
EICAS Engine indication (and) crew alerting system.
ekW Equivalent kilowatts, SI measure of propulsive power of turboprop (see ehp).
elevon Wing trailing-edge control surface combining functions of aileron and elevator.
elint electronics intelligence.
ELT Emergency locator transmitter, to help rescuers home on to a disabled or crashed aircraft.
EPA Environmental Protection Agency.
EPNdB Effective perceived noise decibel, SI unit of EPNL.
EPNL Effective perceived noise level, measure of noise effect on humans which takes account of sound intensity, frequency, character and duration, and response of human ear.
EPU Emergency power unit (part of aircraft, not used for propulsion).
ERP Effective radiated power.
ESA European Space Agency.
ESM (1) Electronic surveillance (or support) measures; (2) Electronic signal monitoring.
EVA Extra-vehicular activity, ie outside spacecraft.
EWSM Early-warning support measures.

FAA Federal Aviation Administration.
factored Multiplied by an agreed number to take account of extreme adverse conditions, errors, design deficiencies or other inaccuracies.
FAI Fédération Aéronautique Internationale.
fail-operational System which continues to function after any single fault has occurred.
fail-safe Structure or system which survives failure (in case of system, may no longer function normally).
FAR Federal Aviation Regulations.
FAR Pt 23 Defines the airworthiness of private and air-taxi aeroplanes of 5,670 kg (12,500 lb) MTOGW and below.
FAR Pt 25 Defines the airworthiness of public transport aeroplanes exceeding 5,670 kg (12,500 lb) MTOGW.
FBW Fly by wire (which see).
FDS Flight director system.
feathering Setting propeller or similar blades at pitch aligned with slipstream, to give resultant torque (not tending to turn shaft) and thus minimum drag.
FEBA Forward edge of battle area.
fence A chordwise projection on the surface of a wing, used to modify the distribution of pressure.
fenestron Helicopter tail rotor with many slender blades rotating in short duct.
ferry range Extreme safe range with zero payload.
FFAR Folding-fin (or free-flight) aircraft rocket.
FFVV Fédération Française de Vol à Voile (French gliding authority).
field length Measure of distance needed to land and/or take off; many different measures for particular purposes, each precisely defined.
flaperon Wing trailing-edge surface combining functions of flap and aileron.
flat-four Engine having four horizontally opposed cylinders; thus, flat-twin, flat-six etc.
flat rated Propulsion engine capable of giving full thrust or power for take-off up to high airfield height and/or high ambient temperature (thus, probably derated at S/L).
FLIR Forward-looking infra-red.
fly by wire Flight control system with electrical signalling (ie, without mechanical interconnection between cockpit flying controls and control surfaces).
FM Frequency modulation.
FOL Forward operating location.
footprint A precisely delineated boundary on the surface, inside which the perceived noise of an aircraft exceeds a specified level during take-off and/or landing.
Fowler flap Moves initially aft to increase wing area and then also deflects down to increase drag.
free turbine Turbine mechanically independent of engine upstream, other than being connected by rotating bearings and the gas stream, and thus able to run at its own speed.
Frise aileron Most common manual aileron, with leading-edge that projects below wing to increase drag when aileron is raised.
FSW Forward-swept wing.

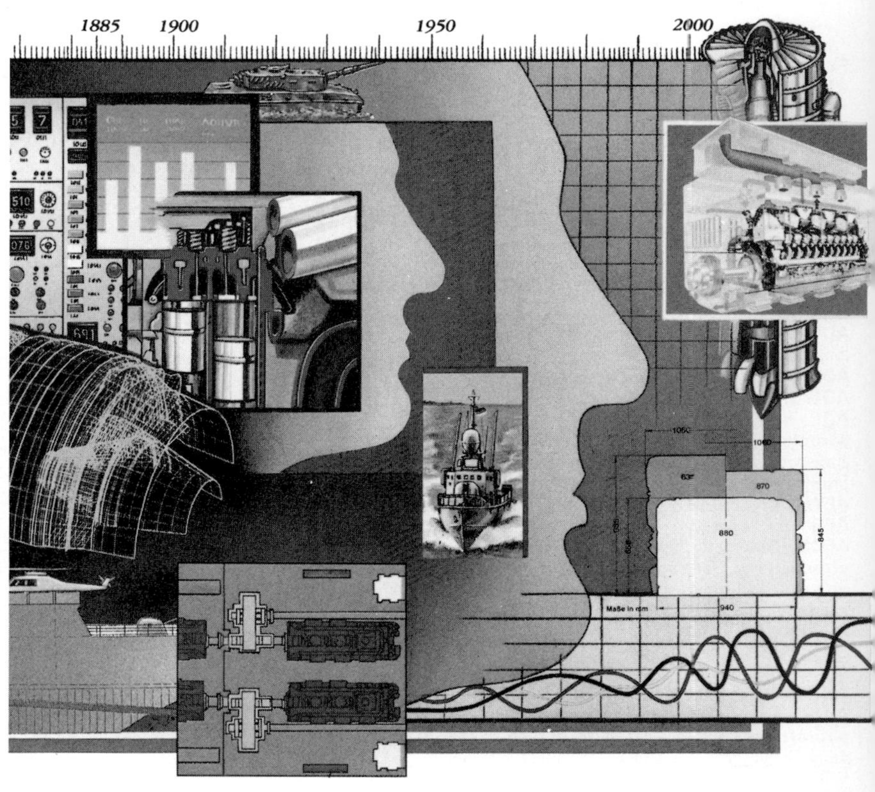

Many great names such as Benz, Daimler, Diesel and Maybach are closely associated with MTU's history. The origins of MTU Motoren- und Turbinen-Union in Munich and Friedrichshafen can be traced back to the beginning of motorization. **Ever since, MTU has been among the world's leaders when it comes to propulsion power on land, sea and in the air.** The MTU Group produces jet and turboshaft engines, industrial gas turbines, diesel engines, power transmissions, and electronic monitoring and control systems. Partnerships in advanced-technology aircraft engine development and production have been established with all internationally renowned manufacturers. MTU products are backed up by a worldwide marketing and service organization.

MTU Group members:

MTU München
MTU Friedrichshafen
MTU Maintenance GmbH
Aktiengesellschaft Kühnle, Kopp & Kausch
L'Orange GmbH
MTU-Turboméca GmbH
Turbo-Union Ltd.
MTU of North America, Inc.
MTU Motores Diesel Ltda.
MTU Argentina S. A.
MTU Asia Pte. Ltd.
MTU Australia Pty. Ltd.

MTU Motoren- und Turbinen-Union Friedrichshafen GmbH
P.O.Box 2040 · D-7990 Friedrichshafen
Telephone (07541) 29-1

8.3/86 Schellenberg, Ogilvy & Mather

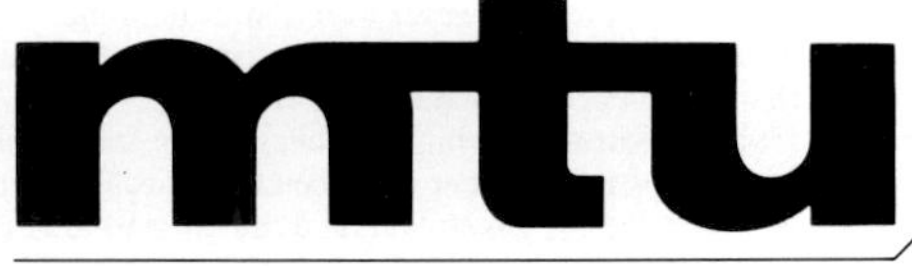

Diesel Propulsion Systems / Gas Turbine Propulsion Systems / Power Generation with Diesel Engines / System Components / Electronic Monitoring and Control Systems / Project Management / Systems Engineering / Product Support

FY Fiscal year (1 July to 30 June in US government affairs).

g Acceleration due to mean Earth gravity, ie of a body in free fall.
gallons Non-SI measure; 1 Imp gal (UK) = 4·546 litres, 1 US gal = 3·785 litres.
GCI Ground-controlled interception.
geostationary Of an Earth satellite, rotating with the Earth and thus always overhead the same point. Corresponds to altitude above Earth's surface of about 35,800 km (22,245 miles).
geostationary orbit An Earth-centred orbit at a height above the Earth's surface of about 35,800 km (22,245 miles) and lying approximately in the plane of the equator. A satellite in such an orbit travelling eastwards will remain over the same point, rotating precisely with the Earth.
geosynchronous See geostationary.
GfK Glassfibre-reinforced plastics (German).
glide ratio Of a sailplane, distance travelled along track divided by height lost in still air.
glove In a swing-wing aeroplane with pivots well out from the centreline it is geometrically impossible to have one-piece pivoted wings because at zero sweep the inner ends would overlap; the answer is fixed inner leading portions called gloves.
GPU Ground power unit (not part of aircraft).
GPWS Ground-proximity warning system.
green aircraft Aircraft flyable but lacking furnishing and customer's choice of avionics.
gross wing area See wing area.
GRP Glassfibre-reinforced plastics.
GS Glideslope, of ILS.
GSE Ground-support equipment (such as special test gear, steps and servicing platforms).
GTS Gas-turbine starter (ie starter is miniature gas turbine).
gunship Helicopter designed for battlefield attack, normally with slim body carrying pilot and weapon operator only.

h Hour(s).
hardened Protected as far as possible against nuclear explosion.
hardpoint Reinforced part of aircraft to which external load can be attached, eg weapon or tank pylon.
helicopter Rotary-wing aircraft both lifted and propelled by one or more power-driven rotors turning about substantially vertical axes.
HF High frequency.
'hot and high' Adverse combination of airfield height and high ambient temperature, which lengthens required TOD.
hovering ceiling Ceiling of helicopter (corresponding to air density at which maximum rate of climb is zero), either IGE or OGE.
HP High pressure.
hp Horsepower.
HSI Horizontal situation indicator.
HUD Head-up display (bright numbers and symbols projected on pilot's windscreen and focussed on infinity so that pilot can simultaneously read display and look ahead).
HVAR High-velocity aircraft rocket.
Hz Hertz, cycles per second.

IAS Indicated airspeed, ASIR corrected for instrument error.
IATA International Air Transport Association.
ICAO International Civil Aviation Organization.
IFF Identification friend or foe.
IFR Instrument flight rules (ie, not VFR).
IGE In ground effect: helicopter performance with theoretical flat horizontal surface just below it.
ILS Instrument landing system.
IMC Instrument meteorological conditions, basically IFR.
IMK Increased manoeuvrability kit.
IMS Integrated multiplex system.
INAS Integrated nav/attack system.
incidence Strictly, the angle at which the wing is set in relation to the fore/aft axis. Wrongly used to mean angle of attack (which see).
inertial navigation Measuring all accelerations imparted to a vehicle and, by integrating these with respect to time, calculating speed at every instant (in all three planes) and by integrating a second time calculating total change of position in relation to starting point.
INS Inertial navigation system.
integral construction Machined from solid instead of assembled from separate parts.
integral tank Fuel or other liquid tank formed by sealing part of structure.
intercom Wired telephone system for communication within aircraft.
inverter Electric or electronic device for inverting (reversing polarity of) alternate waves in AC power to produce DC.
IP Intermediate pressure.
IR Infra-red.
IRAN Inspect and repair as necessary.
IRLS Infra-red linescan (builds TV-type picture showing cool regions as dark and hot regions as light).
IRS Inertial reference system.
ISA International Standard Atmosphere.
ISIS (1 Boeing Vertol) Integral spar inspection system; (2 Ferranti) integrated strike and interception sight.
ITE Involute throat and exit (rocket nozzle).
IVSI Instantaneous VSI.

J Joules, SI unit of energy.
JASDF Japan Air Self-Defence Force.
JATO Jet-assisted take-off (actually means rocket-assisted).
JCAB Japan Civil Airworthiness Board.
JDA Japan Defence Agency.
JGSDF Japan Ground Self-Defence Force.
JMSDF Japan Maritime Self-Defence Force.
JTIDS Joint Tactical Information Distribution System.

Kevlar Aramid fibre used as basis of high-strength composite material.
km/h Kilometres per hour.
kN Kilonewtons (the Newton is the SI unit of force; 1 lbf = 4·448 N).
knot 1 nm per hour.
Krüger flap Hinges down and then forward from below the leading edge.
Küchemann tip Wing tip of curving planform intended to minimise drag at high subsonic speed.
kVA Kilovolt-ampères.
kW Kilowatt, SI measure of all forms of power (not just electrical).

LABS Low-altitude bombing system.
LANTIRN Low-altitude navigation targeting infra-red, night.
LARC Low-altitude ride control.
LBA Luftfahrtbundesamt (Federal German civil aviation authority).
lbf Pounds of thrust.
LCN Load classification number, measure of 'flotation' of aircraft landing gear linking aircraft weight, weight distribution, tyre numbers, pressures and disposition.
LDNS Laser Doppler navigation system.
LED Light-emitting diode.
LGSC Linear glideslope capture.
Lidar Light detection and ranging (laser counterpart of radar).
LITVC Liquid-injection thrust vector control.
LLTV Low-light TV (thus, LLLTV, low-light-level).
Load factor (1) percentage of max payload; (2) stress limit.
LOC Localiser.
localiser Element giving steering guidance in ILS.
loiter Flight for maximum endurance, such as supersonic fighter on patrol.
longerons Principal fore-and-aft structural members (eg, in fuselage).
Loran (Long Range Navigation) Family of hyperbolic navaids based on ground radio emissions.
lox Liquid oxygen.
LP Low pressure.
LRMTS Laser ranger and marked-target seeker.

m Metre(s), SI unit of length.
M or Mach number The ratio of the speed of a body to the speed of sound (1,116 ft; 340 m/sec in air at 15°C) under the same ambient conditions.
MAC US Air Force Military Airlift Command.
MAD Magnetic anomaly detector.
Madar Maintenance analysis, detection and recording.
Madge Microwave aircraft digital guidance equipment.
marker, marker beacon Ground beacon giving position guidance in ILS.
MASTACS Manoeuvrability augmentation system for tactical air combat simulation.
mb Millibars, bar × 10^{-3}.
MBR Marker-beacon receiver.
MEPU Monofuel emergency power unit.
MF Medium frequency.
mg Milligrammes, grammes × 10^{-3}.
MLS Microwave landing system.
MLW Maximum landing weight.
mm Millimetres, metres × 10^{-3}.
MMH Monomethyl hydrazine.
MMO Maximum permitted operating Mach number.
MNPS Minimum navigation performance specification.
monocoque Structure with strength in outer shell, devoid of internal bracing.
MPA Man-powered aircraft.
mph Miles per hour.
MRW Maximum ramp weight.
MTBF Mean time between failures.
MTI Moving-target indication.
MTOGW Maximum take-off gross weight (MRW minus taxi/run-up fuel).
MZFW Maximum zero-fuel weight.
NACA US National Advisory Committee for Aeronautics (now NASA).
Nadge NATO air defence ground environment.
NAS US Naval Air Station.
NASA National Aeronautics and Space Administration.
NASC US Naval Air Systems Command (also several other aerospace meanings).
NATC US Naval Air Training Command or Test Center (also several other aerospace meanings).
NBAA US National Business Aircraft Association.
NDB Non-directional beacon.
NH_4ClO_4 Ammonium perchlorate.
nm nautical mile, 1·8532 km, 1·15152 miles.
NOAA US National Oceanic and Atmospheric Administration.
NOE Nap-of-the-Earth (low flying in military aircraft, using natural cover of hills, trees, etc).
NOGS Night observation gunship.
NOS Night observation surveillance.
Ns Newton-second (1 N thrust applied for 1 second)

OBS Omni-bearing selector.
OCU Operational Conversion Unit.
OEI One engine inoperative.
OGE Out of ground effect; helicopter hovering, far above nearest surface
Omega Long-range hyperbolic navaid.
OMI Omni-bearing magnetic indicator.
omni Generalised word meaning equal in all directions (as in omni-range, omni-flash beacon).
OTPI On-top position indicator (indicates overhead of submarine in ASW).
OUV Osker-Ursinus-Vereinigung (West German chapter of EAA).
OWE Operating weight empty, MTOGW minus payload, usable fuel and oil and other consumables.

PA system Public-address.
pallet (1) for freight, rigid platform for handling by fork-lift or conveyor; (2) for missile, mounting and electronics box outside aircraft.
payload Disposable load generating revenue (passengers, cargo, mail and other paid items), in military aircraft loosely used to mean total load carried of weapons, cargo or other mission equipment.
PD radar Pulse-Doppler.
penaids Penetration aids, such as jammers, chaff or decoys to help aircraft fly safely through hostile airspace.
perigee The point in an Earth-centred orbit nearest to the Earth.
perihelion The point in a solar (Sun-centred) orbit closest to the Sun.
PFA Popular Flying Association (UK).
PHI Position and heading (or homing) indicator.
plane A lifting surface (eg, wing, tailplane).
plume The region of hot air and gas emitted by a helicopter jetpipe.
pneumatic de-icing Covered with flexible surfaces alternately pumped up and deflated to throw off ice.
port Left side, looking forward.
power loading Aircraft weight (usually MTOGW) divided by total propulsive power or thrust at T-O.
pressure fuelling Fuelling via a leakproof connection through which fuel passes at high rate under pressure.
pressure ratio In gas-turbine engine, compressor delivery pressure divided by ambient pressure (in supersonic aircraft, divided by ram pressure downstream of inlet).
primary flight controls Those used to control trajectory of aircraft (thus, not trimmers, tabs, flaps, slats, airbrakes or lift dumpers etc).
propfan A family of new technology propellers characterised by multiple scimitar-shaped blades with thin sharp-edged profile. Single and contra-rotating examples promise to extend propeller efficiency up to about Mach 0·8.
pulse-Doppler Radar sending out pulses and measuring frequency-shift or returns from target(s).
pylon Structure linking aircraft to external load (engine nacelle, drop-tank, bomb etc). Also used in conventional sense in pylon racing.

radius In terms of performance, the distance an aircraft can fly from base and return without intermediate landing
RAE Royal Aircraft Establishment.
RAI Registro Aeronautica Italiano.
ram pressure Increased pressure in forward-facing aircraft inlet, generated by converting (relative) kinetic energy to pressure.
ramp weight Maximum weight at start of flight (MTOGW plus taxi/run-up fuel).
range Too many definitions to list, but essentially the distance an aircraft can fly (or is permitted to fly) with specified load and usually whilst making allowance for specified additional manoeuvres (diversions, stand-off, go-around etc).
RAS Rectified airspeed, IAS corrected for position error.
raster Generation of large-area display, eg TV screen, by close-spaced horizontal lines scanned either alternately or in sequence.

RATT Radio teletype.
redundant Provided with spare capacity or data channels and thus made to survive failures.
refanned Gas-turbine engine fitted with new fan of higher BPR.
rigid rotor Helicopter rotor without articulating hinges (eg, flapping hinge, drag hinge) but with pitch variation.
RLD Rijksluchtvaartdienst. Netherlands civil aviation department.
RMI Radio magnetic indicator (compass).
R/Nav Area navigation, navaid covering whole of local area instead of just crowded airways.
Rotor-kite Rotary-wing aircraft with no internal power, lifted by a freely running autorotating rotor and towed by an external vehicle.
roving Multiple-stands of fibre, as in a rope (but usually not twisted).
RPV Remotely piloted vehicle (pilot in other aircraft or on ground).
RSA Réseau du Sport de l'Air.
RVR Runway visual range.

s Second(s).
SAC US Air Force Strategic Air Command.
safe-life A term denoting that a component has proved by testing that it can be expected to continue to function safely for a precisely defined period before replacement.
salmon (French saumon) Streamlined fairings, usually at wingtip of sailplane, serving same function as endplate and acting also as tip-skid.
SAR (1) Search and rescue; (2) synthetic aperture radar.
SATS (1) Small airfield for tactical support; (2) Small Arms Target System.
saw-tooth Same as dog-tooth.
SCAS Stability and control augmentation system.
second-source Production of identical item by second factory or company.
semi-active Homing on to radiation reflected from target illuminated by radar or laser energy beamed from elsewhere.
service ceiling Usually height equivalent to air density at which maximum attainable rate of climb is 100 ft/min.
servo A device which acts as a relay, usually augmenting the pilot's efforts to move a control surface or the like.
SFAR Special Federal Aviation Regulation(s).
sfc Specific fuel consumption.
SGAC Secrétariat Général à l'Aviation Civile (now DGAC).
shaft Connection between gas turbine and compressor or other driven unit. Two-shaft engine has second shaft, rotating at different speed, surrounding the first (thus, HP surrounds inner LP or fan shaft).
Shoran Short range navigation (radio).
shp Shaft horsepower, measure of power transmitted via rotating shaft.
sideline noise EPNdB measure of aircraft landing and taking off, at point 0·25 nm (2- or 3-engined) or 0·35 nm (4-engined) from runway centreline.
SIF Selective identification facility.
sigint signals intelligence
signature Characteristic 'fingerprint' of all electromagnetic radiation (radar, IR etc).
single-shaft Gas-turbine in which all compressors and turbines are on common shaft rotating together.
S/L Sea level.
SLAR Side-looking airborne radar.
snap-down Air-to-air interception of low-flying aircraft by AAM fired from fighter at a higher altitude.
soft target Not armoured or hardened.
specific fuel consumption Rate at which fuel is consumed divided by power or thrust developed, and thus a measure of engine efficiency. For jet engines (air-breathing, ie not rockets) unit is mg/Ns, milligrams per Newton-second; for shaft engines unit is μg/J, micrograms (millionths of a gram) per Joule (SI unit of work or energy).
specific impulse Measure of rocket engine efficiency; thrust divided by rate of fuel/oxidant consumption per second, the units for mass and force being the same so that the answer is expressed in seconds.
SPILS Stall protection and incidence-limiting system.
spool One complete axial compressor rotor; thus a two-shaft engine may have a fan plus an LP spool.
SSB Single-sideband (radio).
SSR Secondary surveillance radar.
st Static thrust.
stabiliser Fin (thus, horizontal stabiliser = tailplane).
stall strips Sharp-edged strips on wing leading-edge to induce stall at that point.
stalling speed TAS at which aircraft stalls at 1*g*, ie wing lift suddenly collapses.
standard day ISA temperature and pressure.
starboard Right side, looking forward.
static inverter Solid-state inverter of alternating waveform (ie, not rotary machine).
stick-pusher Stall-protection device that forces pilot's control column forward as stalling angle of attack is neared.
stick-shaker Stall-warning device that noisily shakes pilot's control column as stalling angle of attack is neared.
STOL Short take-off and landing. (Several definitions, stipulating allowable horizontal distance to clear screen height of 35 or 50 ft or various SI measures).
store Object carried as part of payload on external attachment (eg bomb, drop-tank).
strobe light High-intensity flashing beacon.
substrate The underlying layer on which something (such as a solar cell or integrated circuit) is made.
supercritical wing Wing of relatively deep, flat-topped profile generating lift right across upper surface instead of concentrated close behind leading edge.
sweepback Backwards inclination of wing or other aerofoil, seen from above, measured relative to fuselage or other reference axis, usually measured at quarter-chord (25%) or at leading-edge.
synchronous See geostationary.
synchronous satellite Geostationary.

t Tonne, 1 Megagram, 1,000 kg.
tabbed flap Fitted with narrow-chord tab along entire trailing-edge which deflects to greater angle than main surface.
tabs Small auxiliary surfaces hinged to trailing-edge of control surfaces for purposes of trimming, reducing hinge moment (force needed to operate main surface) or in other way assisting pilot.
TAC US Air Force Tactical Air Command.
Tacan Tactical air navigation, simple military navaid using ground beacons.
taileron Left and right tailplanes used as primary control surfaces in both pitch and roll.
tailplane Main horizontal tail surface, originally fixed and carrying hinged elevator(s) but today often a single 'slab' serving as control surface.
TANS Tactical air navigation system (Doppler-based computer, control and display unit).
TAS True airspeed, EAS corrected for density (often very large factor) appropriate to aircraft height.
TBO Time between overhauls.
t/c ratio Ratio of the thickness (aerodynamic depth) of a wing or other surface to its chord, both measured at the same place parallel to the fore-and-aft axis.
TFR Terrain-following radar (for low-level attack).
thickness Depth of wing or other aerofoil; maximum perpendicular distance between upper and lower surfaces.
T-O Take-off.
T-O noise EPNdB measure of aircraft taking off, at point directly under flight path 3·5 nm from brakes-release (regardless of altitude).
TOD Take-off distance.
TOGW Take-off gross weight (not necessarily MTOGW).
ton Imperial (long) ton = 1·016 t (Mg), US (short) ton = 0·9072 t.
track Distance between centres of contact areas of main landing wheels measured left/right across aircraft (with bogies, distance between centres of contact areas of each bogie).
transceiver Radio transmitter/receiver.
transfer orbit Orbit, or part of an orbit, linking two others at different heights around the same planetary body.
transponder Radio transmitter triggered automatically by a particular received signal.
TRU Transformer/rectifier unit.
TSO Technical Standard Order (FAA).
turbofan Gas-turbine jet engine generating most thrust by a large-diameter cowled fan, with small part added by jet from core.
turbojet Simplest form of gas turbine comprising compressor, combustion chamber, turbine and propulsive nozzle.
turboprop Gas turbine in which as much energy as possible is taken from gas jet and used to drive reduction gearbox and propeller.
turboshaft Gas turbine in which as much energy as possible is taken from gas jet and used to drive high-speed shaft (which in turn drives external load such as helicopter gearbox).
TVC Thrust vector control (rocket).
TWT Travelling-wave tube.
tyre sizes In simplest form, first figure is rim diameter (in or mm) and second is rim width (in or mm). In more correct three-unit form, first figure is outside diameter, second is max width and third is wheel diameter.

UBE, Ubee Ultra bypass engine, alternative terminology (Boeing) for UDF.
UDF Unducted fan, one form of advanced propulsion system in which gas-turbine blading directly drives large fan (propfan) blades mounted around the outside of the engine pod.
UHF Ultra-high frequency.
unfactored Performance level expected of average pilot, in average aircraft, without additional safety factors.
usable fuel Total mass of fuel consumable in flight, usually 95-98 per cent of system capacity.
US gallon 0·83267 Imperial gallon.

variable-geometry Capable of grossly changing shape in flight, especially by varying sweep of wings.
VD Maximum permitted diving speed
vernier Small thruster, usually a rocket, for final precise adjustment of a vehicle's trajectory and velocity.
VFR Visual flight rules.
VHF Very high frequency.
VLF Very low frequency.
VMO Maximum permitted operating flight speed (IAS, EAS or CAS must be specified).
VNE Never-exceed speed (aerodynamic or structural limit).
VOR VHF omni-directional range, ground navaid usable only when flying along predetermined airways.
VSI Vertical speed (climb/descent) indicator.
VTOL Vertical take-off and landing.

washout Inbuilt wing twist reducing angle of incidence towards the tip.
wheelbase Minimum distance from nosewheel or tailwheel (centre of contact area) to line joining main wheels (centres of contact areas).
wing area Total projected area of clean wing (no flaps, slats etc) including all control surfaces and area of fuselage bounded by leading- and trailing-edges projected to centreline (inapplicable to slender-delta aircraft with extremely large leading-edge sweep angle). Sometimes called gross wing area; net area excludes projected areas of fuselage, nacelles, etc.
wing loading Aircraft weight (usually MTOGW) divided by wing area.
winglet Small auxiliary aerofoil, usually sharply upturned and often swept back, at tip of wing.
wire guidance Guidance of missile or RPV by signals transmitted through fine wire(s) linking it with operator.

zero-fuel weight MTOGW minus usable fuel and other consumables, in most aircraft imposing severest stress on wing.
zero/zero seat Ejection seat designed for use even at zero speed on ground.
ZFW Zero-fuel weight.
μg Microgrammes, grammes × 10^{-6}.

Jane's Aerospace Dictionary (2nd edition) by Bill Gunston (Jane's Publishing Company, £20) provides a listing of over 20,000 current aerospace expressions with definitions.

First Flights

Some first flights made during the period 1 June 1985 to 1 October 1986

JUNE 1985

3 McDonnell Douglas F/A-18B, first Australian manufactured Hornet (A21-104) (USA/Australia)
8 Boudeau MB 10 homebuilt (F-PEMB) (France)
9 Kimbrel Banty microlight (USA)
12 Delemontez-Desjardins D-01 Ibis homebuilt (F-PZIK) (France)
13 Mudry CAP X, second (pre-production) prototype (France)
24 Sikorsky S-76 SHADOW (N765SA) (USA)
26 Partenavia P.68C-TC with De Vore amphibious floats (N68PK), from land (Italy/USA)
26 Bell Model 400 TwinRanger, third prototype (USA)
27 Partenavia P.68C-TC with De Vore amphibious floats (N68PK), from water (Italy/USA)

JULY 1985

3 Sikorsky HH-60A Night Hawk, first flight with full avionics fit (USA)
8 Airbus A310-300 with Pratt & Whitney JT9D-7R4E engines (F-WWCA) (International)
9 Lockheed TriStar K. Mk 1, first Marshall conversion of L-1011-500 for RAF (ZD950) (USA/UK)
9 Smith Bonanza 400 (N1LX) (USA)
9 Prescott Pusher homebuilt (N41PP) (USA)
12 Light Aero Avid Amphibian homebuilt (N47AA) (USA)
25 Politechnika Warszawa PW-2 Gapa sailplane (Poland)
29 Kawasaki XT-4 (56-5601) (Japan)
31 Airbus A300 testbed, first flight with one PW4000 engine (International)

AUGUST 1985

1 WSK-PZL Krosno KR-03 Puchatek sailplane (SP-P336) (Poland)
3 Boeing C-135FR re-engined with CFM56-2B-1 turbofans for French Air Force (USA)
3 Instytut Lotnictwa Z-84 hang glider (Poland)
6 Lockheed TR-1A, first full flight test of PLSS with three aircraft (USA)
7 FMA IA 63 Pampa, second prototype (EX-02) (Argentina)
17 Nanchang Haiyan A (converted CJ-6) agricultural aircraft (China)
17 Melex (PZL Mielec) M-18 Turbine Dromader, first with PT6A-45AG engine (N2856G) (USA/Poland)
20 McDonnell Douglas MD 530F with mast mounted sight (USA)
29 Beechcraft Model 2000 Starship 1 (85% scale prototype), first flight with production standard PT6A-27 engines (USA)
30 Dassault-Breguet Falcon 900, second aircraft (F-WFJC) (France)
30 Bell D292 ACAP (USA)

SEPTEMBER 1985

3 Fokker F28 prototype, first flight as avionics testbed for Fokker 100 (PH-JHG) (Netherlands)
6 Airbus A310-300, second aircraft, first with General Electric CF6-80C2 engines (F-WWCB) (International)
10 Lockheed C-5B Galaxy (USA)
18 PZL Warszawa-Okecie PZL-106BT Turbo-Kruk (SP-PAA) (Poland)
19 Boeing E-3 for Saudi Arabia, with CFM56 engines (USA)
19 Gulfstream Aerospace Gulfstream IV (N404GA) (USA)
19 Centrair 2001 Marianne sailplane (F-WGMA) (France)
24 Airship Industries Skyship 600-02 airship (G-SKSD) (UK)

OCTOBER 1985

3 Rockwell International Shuttle spacecraft *Atlantis* (OV-104) (USA)
6 Ultimate Aircraft Ten Dash One Hundred Albertan homebuilt (C-GIKZ) (Canada)
8 Mudry CAP 230 (F-WZCH) (France)
12 McDonnell Douglas AH-64 Apache, test aircraft for LHX digital flight control system (82-8258) (USA)
15 Fairchild Republic T-46A (84-492) (USA)
16 Aeritalia/Aermacchi/EMBRAER AMX, fourth (first Brazilian assembled) prototype (YA-1/A04/4200) (International)
18 NASA/USAF (General Dynamics) AFTI/F-111, first flight with mission adaptive wing (63-9778) (USA)
28 NAL Asuka QSTOL research aircraft (JQ8501) (Japan)

NOVEMBER 1985

7 Westland Lynx AH. Mk 7 (ZE376) (UK)
7 Sikorsky UH-60A, testbed for US Army/Boeing Vertol ADOCS (USA)
9 Aérospatiale Epsilon, testbed for Turboméca TP 319 engine (01) (France)
12 ARV Super2, second aircraft (G-STWO) (UK)
14 Westland Sea King HC. Mk 4, first production with composites main rotor blades (ZF115) (UK)
17 Wittman O&O Special homebuilt (N41SW) (USA)
20 Panavia Tornado F. Mk 3, first production (ZE154) (International)
20 Classic Waco Classic F-5 (N1935B) (USA)

DECEMBER 1985

5 Panavia IDS Tornado, first flight with HARM missiles (International)
11 Changhe Z-8 (China)
12 Cranfield/BAe Harrier T. Mk 2 VAAC (XW175) (UK)
17 Aermacchi MB-339C (I-AMDA) (Italy)
18 Murphy Sprite homebuilt (EI-BOY) (Ireland)
28 Fokker 50 (PH-OSO) (Netherlands)
30 FMA IA 58C Pucará Charlie (Argentina)

JANUARY 1986

3 Elmwood CH-8 Christavia Mk 4 homebuilt (Canada)
30 Boeing 767-300 (N767S) (USA)
30 Loehle Aviation 5151 Mustang homebuilt (N202XP) (USA)
31 Dornier 228-201, first assembled by HAL (VT-EJN) (Germany/India)

FEBRUARY 1986

5 Westland TT300 (G-17-22; G-HAUL) (UK)
14 EMBRAER EMB-312 Tucano, first flight with Garrett engine (PP-ZTC) (Brazil/UK)
14 ENAER T-35TX Aucán (CC-PZC) (Chile)
15 Beechcraft Model 2000 Starship 1 (N2000S) (USA)
19 Boeing KE-3A for Saudi Arabia (USA)

MARCH 1986

1 Agusta A 129 Mangusta, fifth (final) prototype (Italy)
3 Cessna Model 208B Caravan I (N9767F) (USA)
22 Schleicher ASW 22 BE powered sailplane (D-KKJP) (Germany, Federal Republic)
25 FMA IA 63 Pampa, third prototype (Argentina)
28 Schleicher ASH 25 MB powered sailplane (D-KOWB) (Germany, Federal Republic)

APRIL 1986

11 EMBRAER EMB-312 prototype for Shorts S312 Tucano, first flight in UK (G-14-007; formerly PP-ZTC, see 14 February) (Brazil/UK)
15 Sikorsky S-76 testbed for Turboméca Arriel 1S engines (USA/France)
25 Air Tractor Model AT-503 (USA)
25 CUP F3 microlight (Italy)
25 Cameron D-50P Skystar pressurised hot-air airship (UK)
26 Piasecki Heli-Stat, first free flight (USA)
27 Partenavia P.86 Mosquito (Italy)
30 Fokker 50, second prototype (PH-OSI) (Netherlands)

MAY 1986

2 Schempp-Hirth Nimbus 3D sailplane (D-KCJC) (Germany, Federal Republic)
11 Schleicher ASH 25 sailplane (D-1025) (Germany, Federal Republic)
19 British Aerospace Hawk 200 (ZG200) (UK)
30 GEC Avionics Phoenix RPV (UK)

JUNE 1986

10 Davis Wing DX-1 homebuilt (N5531N *Starship Alpha*) (USA)
11 Gulfstream Aerospace Gulfstream IV, second prototype (N17581) (USA)
14 Beechcraft Starship 1, second prototype (N3042S) (USA)
14 Sikorsky S-70C, testbed for RTM 322 engine (G-RRTM) (USA/International)

JULY 1986

4 Dassault-Breguet Rafale A (France)
4 Kawasaki CH-47J, first assembled from Boeing Vertol CKD kit (Japan/USA)
6 Stemme S 10 sailplane (D-KKST) (Germany, Federal Republic)
18 PZL Mielec M-26 Iskierka (SP-PIA) (Poland)
28 EMBRAER EMB-312 Tucano, second Garrett engined prototype (Brazil)
29 Fairchild Republic T-46A, second FSD aircraft (84-493) (USA)
30 McDonnell Douglas F-4 Phantom II, IAI testbed with PW1120 engine (334) (USA/Israel)
31 Wallis WA-116/X, testbed for Norton engine (G-AVDG) (UK)

AUGUST 1986

1 Schafer (Douglas) DC-3, re-engined with P&WC PT6A-65AR turboprops (USA)
6 BAe ATP (G-MATP) (UK)
8 BAe EAP (ZF534) (UK)
19 Airtech CN-235, first production (ECT-135) (International)
20 Boeing 727-100 testbed; first flight of General Electric GE-36 UDF engine (N32720) (USA)
26 Boeing 707 testbed; first flight of CFM56-5 engine for Airbus A320 (N37681) (USA/International)

SEPTEMBER 1986

5 AAI FanStar (N380AA) (USA)
15 McDonnell Douglas F/A-18C Hornet, first production (USA)
23 Piaggio Avanti (I-PJAV) (Italy)
28 Canadair Challenger 601-3A (Canada)

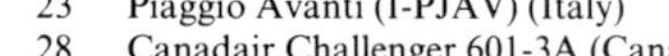

20 August 1986: the historic first-ever flight of a propfan, on the Boeing 727-100 testbed for General Electric's GE-36 unducted fan engine

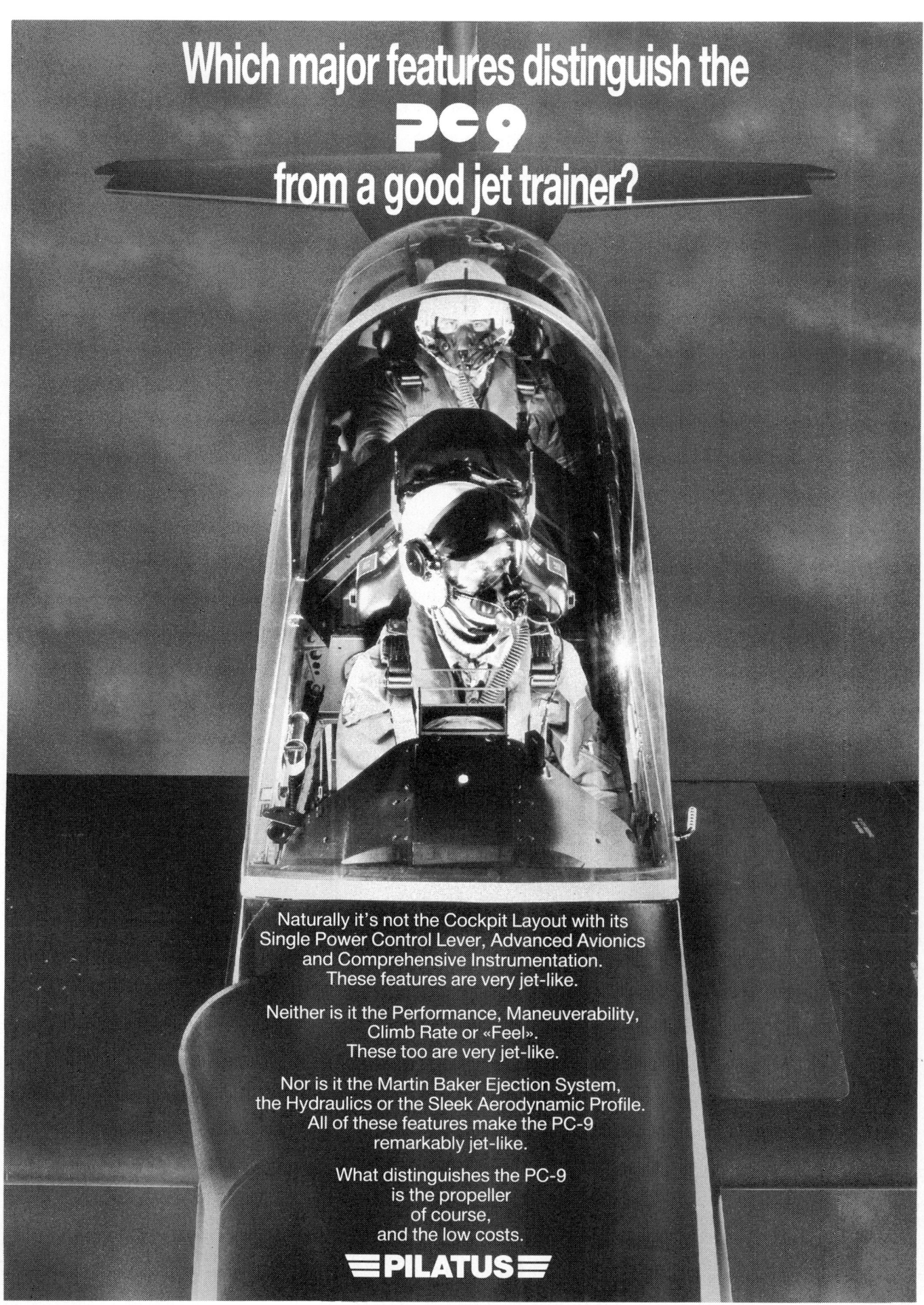

Official Records

Corrected to 1 October 1986

ABSOLUTE WORLD RECORDS

CLASS A

Three records are classed as Absolute World Records for balloons by the Fédération Aéronautique Internationale, as follows:

Duration (USA)
M. L. Anderson, B. L. Abruzzo and L. M. Newman in the gas balloon *Double Eagle II*, on 12-17 August 1978. 137 h 5 min 50 s.

Distance (USA)
B. L. Abruzzo, L. M. Newman, R. Aoki and R. Clark in the gas balloon *Double Eagle V*, from Nagashima, Japan, to Covello, California, USA, on 9-12 November 1981. 4,526·21 nm (8,382·54 km; 5,208·67 miles).

Altitude (USA)
Cdr M. D. Ross and Lt Cdr V. A. Prother in a gas balloon on 4 May 1961. 34,668 m (113,740 ft).

CLASS C

Seven records are classed as Absolute World Records for aeroplanes by the Fédération Aéronautique Internationale, as follows:

Distance in a straight line (USA)
Major Clyde P. Evely, USAF, in a Boeing B-52H Stratofortress, on 10-11 January 1962, from Okinawa to Madrid, Spain. 10,890·27 nm (20,168·78 km; 12,532·3 miles).

Distance in a closed circuit (USA)
Captain William M. Stevenson, USAF, in a Boeing B-52H Stratofortress, on 6-7 June 1962. Seymour Johnson AFB-Bermuda-Sondrestrom (Greenland)-Anchorage (Alaska)-March AFB-Key West-Seymour Johnson AFB. 9,851·54 nm (18,245·05 km; 11,337 miles).

Height (USSR)
Alexander Fedotov in an E-266M (MiG-25) on 31 August 1977. 37,650 m (123,523 ft).

Height in sustained horizontal flight (USA)
Captain Robert C. Helt and Major Larry A. Elliott (USAF) in a Lockheed SR-71A on 28 July 1976 at Beale AFB, California. 25,929·031 m (85,069 ft).

Height, after launch from a 'mother-plane' (USA)
Major R. White, USAF, in the North American X-15A-3 on 17 July 1962, at Edwards AFB, California. 95,935·99 m (314,750 ft).

Speed in a straight line (USA)
Captain Eldon W. Joersz and Major George T. Morgan Jr (USAF) in a Lockheed SR-71A on 28 July 1976 over a 15/25 km course at Beale AFB, California. 1,905·81 knots (3,529·56 km/h; 2,193·17 mph).

Speed in a closed circuit (USA)
Major Adolphus H. Bledsoe Jr and Major John T. Fuller (USAF) in a Lockheed SR-71A on 27 July 1976, over a 1,000 km closed circuit from Beale AFB, California. 1,818·154 knots (3,367·221 km/h; 2,092·294 mph).

CLASS K

Eight records are classed as Absolute World Records for manned spacecraft by the Fédération Aéronautique Internationale, as follows:

Endurance in Earth orbit (USSR)
Leonid Kizim, Vladimir Soloviev and Oleg Atkov on board Soyuz T-10/Salyut-7/Soyuz T-11, from 8 February to 2 October 1984. 236 days 22 h 49 min 4 s.

Altitude (USA)
F. Borman, J. A. Lovell and W. Anders in Apollo 8, on 21-27 December 1968. 203,925 nm (377,668·9 km; 234,673 miles).

Greatest mass lifted to altitude (USA)
F. Borman, J. A. Lovell and W. Anders in Apollo 8, on 21-27 December 1968. 127,980 kg (282,147 lb).

Distance in Earth orbit (USSR)
Anatoli Berezovoi and Valentin Lebedev on board Soyuz T-5/Salyut-7/Soyuz T-7, from 13 May to 10 December 1982, 76,025,908 nm (140,800,000 km; 87,489,056 miles).

Extravehicular duration in space (USSR)
Svetlana Savitskaya from Salyut-7, on 25 July 1984. 3 h 33 min 4 s.

Extravehicular duration on surface of moon or planet (USA)
Eugene A. Cernan, from the Apollo 17 lunar module *Challenger*, on 12, 13 and 14 December 1972, during mission of 7-19 December 1972. 21 h 31 min 44 s.

Number of astronauts remaining simultaneously outside spacecraft (USSR)
A. Eliseiev and E. Khrounov, from Soyuz 4 and 5, for 37 min on 14-18 January 1969. Two astronauts.

Accumulated time in spaceflight (USSR)
Valery Ryumin, on board Soyuz 25, Soyuz 32, Salyut 6, Soyuz 34, Soyuz 35 and Soyuz 37, a total of 361 days 21 h 31 min 55 s.

CLASS P

Four records are classed as Absolute World Records for aerospacecraft by the Fédération Aéronautique Internationale, as follows:

Duration (USA)
John W. Young and crew of five in the Space Shuttle Orbiter OV-102 *Columbia*, on 28 November-8 December 1983. 10 days 7 h 47 min 24 s.

Altitude (USA)
Robert L. Crippen and crew of four in the Space Shuttle Orbiter OV-099 *Challenger*, between 6 and 13 April 1984, 272·047 nm (503·8305 km; 313·066 miles).

Greatest mass lifted to altitude (USA)
V. D. Brand in the Space Shuttle Orbiter OV-102 *Columbia*, on 11 November 1982. 106,882 kg (235,634 lb).

Distance (USA)
J. R. Lousma and C. G. Fullerton in the Space Shuttle Orbiter OV-102 *Columbia*, on 22-30 March 1982. 2,897,953 nm (5,367,009 km; 3,334,904 miles).

WORLD CLASS RECORDS

Following are details of some of the more important world class records confirmed by the FAI:

CLASS C, GROUP I (Aeroplanes with piston engines)

Distance in a straight line (USA)
Cdr Thomas D. Davies, USN, and crew of three in a Lockheed P2V-1 Neptune, on 29 September-1 October 1946, from Perth, Western Australia, to Columbus, Ohio, USA. 9,763·49 nm (18,081·99 km; 11,235·6 miles).

Distance in a closed circuit (USA)
Jerry D. Mullens in the BD-2/Javelin/Mullens Phoenix, on 5-8 December 1981, between Oklahoma City and Jacksonville, USA. 8,695·9 nm (16,104·9 km; 10,007·1 miles).

Height (Italy)
Mario Pezzi, in a Caproni Ca 161*bis*, on 22 October 1938. 17,083 m (56,046 ft).

Speed in a straight line (USA)
Frank Taylor in a modified North American P-51D Mustang, with 2,237 kW (3,000 hp) Rolls-Royce/Packard Merlin V-1650-9 engine, on 30 July 1983, over a 15/25 km course at Mojave, California. 449·31 knots (832·12 km/h; 517·06 mph).

CLASS C, GROUP II (Aeroplanes with turboprop engines)

Distance in a straight line (USA)
Lt Col E. L. Allison and crew in a Lockheed HC-130H Hercules, on 20 February 1972. 7,587·99 nm (14,052·95 km; 8,732·098 miles).

Distance in a closed circuit (USA)
Cdr Philip R. Hite and crew in a Lockheed RP-3D Orion, on 4 November 1972. 5,455·46 nm (10,103·51 km; 6,278·03 miles).

Height (USA)
Donald R. Wilson in an LTV Electrosystems L450F, on 27 March 1972, at Majors Field, Greenville, Texas. 15,549 m (51,014 ft).

Speed in a straight line (USA)
Cdr Donald H. Lilienthal and crew in a Lockheed P-3C Orion, over 15/25 km course on 27 January 1971. 435·26 knots (806·10 km/h; 500·89 mph).

Speed in a closed circuit (USSR)
Ivan Sukhomlin and crew in a Tupolev Tu-114, on 9 April 1960, carrying a 25,000 kg payload over a 5,000 km circuit. 473·66 knots (877·212 km/h; 545·07 mph).

CLASS C, GROUP III (Aeroplanes with jet engines)

Distance in a straight line, distance in a closed circuit, height, speed in straight line and speed in 1,000 km closed circuit
See Absolute World Records.

Speed over a 3 km course at restricted altitude (USA)
Darryl Greenamyer in the modified Red Baron F-104RB Starfighter, on 24 October 1977, at Mud Lake, Tonopah, Nevada. 858·77 knots (1,590·45 km/h; 988·26 mph).

Speed in a 100 km closed circuit (USSR)
Alexander Fedotov in a Mikoyan E-266 (MiG-25), on 8 April 1973. 1,406·641 knots (2,605·1 km/h; 1,618·734 mph).

Speed in a 500 km closed circuit (USSR)
M. Komarov in a Mikoyan E-266 (MiG-25), on 5 October 1967, near Moscow. 1,609·88 knots (2,981·5 km/h; 1,852·62 mph).

Speed around the World (USA)
Walter H. Mullikin and crew of four, in a Boeing 747SP of Pan American, on 1-3 May 1976, from New York City, via Delhi and Tokyo, back to New York, in 1 day 22 h 0 min 50 s. 436·95 knots (809·24 km/h; 502·84 mph).

Greatest payload lifted to a height of 2,000 m (USSR)
Vladimir Terski and crew in an Antonov An-124, near Moscow, on 26 July 1985. 171,219 kg (377,473 lb).

CLASS C.2, ALL GROUPS (Seaplanes)

Distance in a straight line (UK)
Capt D. C. T. Bennett and First Officer I. Harvey, in the Short-Mayo *Mercury*, on 6-8 October 1938, from Dundee, Scotland, to the Orange River, South Africa. 5,211·66 nm (9,652 km; 5,997·5 miles).

Height (USSR)
Georgi Buryanov and crew of two in a Beriev M-10, on 9 September 1961, over the Sea of Azov. 14,962 m (49,088 ft).

Speed in a straight line (USSR)
Nikolai Andrievsky and crew of two in a Beriev M-10, on 7 August 1961, at Joukovski-Petrovskoe, over a 15/25 km course. 492·44 knots (912 km/h; 566·69 mph).

CLASS D, GROUP I (Single-seat sailplanes)

Distance in a straight line (Germany, Federal Republic)
Hans W. Grosse in a Schleicher ASW 12, on 25 April 1972. 788·77 nm (1,460·8 km; 907·70 miles).

Height (USA)
Paul F. Bickle, in a Schweizer SGS 1-23E, on 25 February 1961, at Mojave-Lancaster, California. 14,102 m (46,266 ft).

CLASS D, GROUP II (Two-seat sailplanes)

Distance in a straight line (New Zealand)
S. H. Georgeson and Helen Georgeson in a Schempp-Hirth Janus C, on 31 October 1982, from Alexandra to Gisborne, New Zealand. 536·59 nm (993·76 km; 617·49 miles).

Height (USA)
L. E. Edgar and H. E. Klieforth in a Pratt-Read sailplane, on 19 March 1952, at Bishop, California. 13,489 m (44,256 ft).

CLASS E.1 (Helicopters)

Distance in a straight line (USA).
R. G. Ferry in a Hughes OH-6A, on 6-7 April 1966. 1,923·08 nm (3,561·55 km; 2,213 miles)

Height (France)
Jean Boulet in an Aérospatiale SA 315B Lama on 21 June 1972. 12,442 m (40,820 ft).

Speed in a straight line (USSR)
Gourguen Karapetyan in a Mil A-10 (Mi-24), on 21 September 1978, over a 15/25 km course near Moscow. 198·9 knots (368·4 km/h; 228·9 mph).
Awaiting confirmation is a new record of 216·45 knots (400·87 km/h; 249·09 mph) over a 15/25 km course, set by Trevor Egginton in a Westland Lynx, on 11 August 1986.

Speed in a 100 km closed circuit (USSR)
Boris Galitsky and crew of five in a Mil Mi-6, on 26 August 1964, near Moscow. 183·67 knots (340·15 km/h; 211·36 mph).

Speed in a 500 km closed circuit (USA)
Thomas Doyle in a Sikorsky S-76A, at West Palm Beach, Florida, on 8 February 1982. 186·68 knots (345·74 km/h; 214·83 mph).

CLASS E.2 (Convertiplanes)

Height (USSR)
D. Efremov and crew of two, in the Kamov Ka-22 Vintokryl, on 24 November 1961 at Bykovo. 2,588 m (8,491 ft).

Speed in a straight line (USSR)
D. Efremov and crew of five, in the Kamov Ka-22 Vintokryl, on 7 October 1961, at Joukovski-Petrovskoe, over a 15/25 km course. 192·39 knots (356·3 km/h; 221·4 mph).

Speed in a 100 km closed circuit (New Zealand)
Sqd Ldr W. R. Gellatly and J. G. P. Morton, in the Fairey Rotodyne, on 5 January 1959, White Waltham-Wickham-Radley Bottom-Kintbury-White Waltham. 165·89 knots (307·22 km/h; 190·90 mph).

CLASS E.3 (Autogyros)

Height (UK)
Wing Cdr K. H. Wallis, in a Wallis WA-121/Mc, on 20 July 1982. 5,643·7 m (18,516 ft).

Distance in a straight line (UK)
Wing Cdr K. H. Wallis, in a Wallis WA-116/F, from Lydd Airport, Kent, to Wick, Scotland, on 28 September 1975. 472·092 nm (874·315 km; 543·274 miles).

Distance in a closed circuit (UK)
Wing Cdr K. H. Wallis, in a Wallis WA-116/F on 13 July 1974. 361·91 nm (670·26 km; 416·48 miles).

Speed in a straight line (UK)
Wing Cdr K. H. Wallis, in a Wallis WA-116/F/S, over a 15/25 km course, on 14 October 1984. 102·365 knots (189·58 km/h; 117·80 mph).
Awaiting confirmation is a new record of 104·7 knots (193·9 km/h; 120·48 mph) over a 3 km course, set by Wing Cdr Wallis in the WA-116/F/S on 18 September 1986.

CLASS R (Microlights)

Height (USA)
Richard J. Rowley, in a Mitchell U-2 Superwing, on 17 September 1983. 7,906·5 m (25,940 ft).

Distance in a straight line (France)
Jean-Pierre Mathias, in the ULM *Hotel Ibis*, from Meaux to Biarritz, on 7 July 1984. 375·2 nm (694·8 km; 431·7 miles).

Speed in a straight line (UK)
D. G. Cook, in a CFM Shadow, on 4 August 1983, over a 3 km course at Bungay, Suffolk. 68·18 knots (126·36 km/h; 78·52 mph).

World's fastest helicopter: the Westland Lynx with BERP III rotor which set the first over-400 km/h helicopter speed record on 11 August 1986

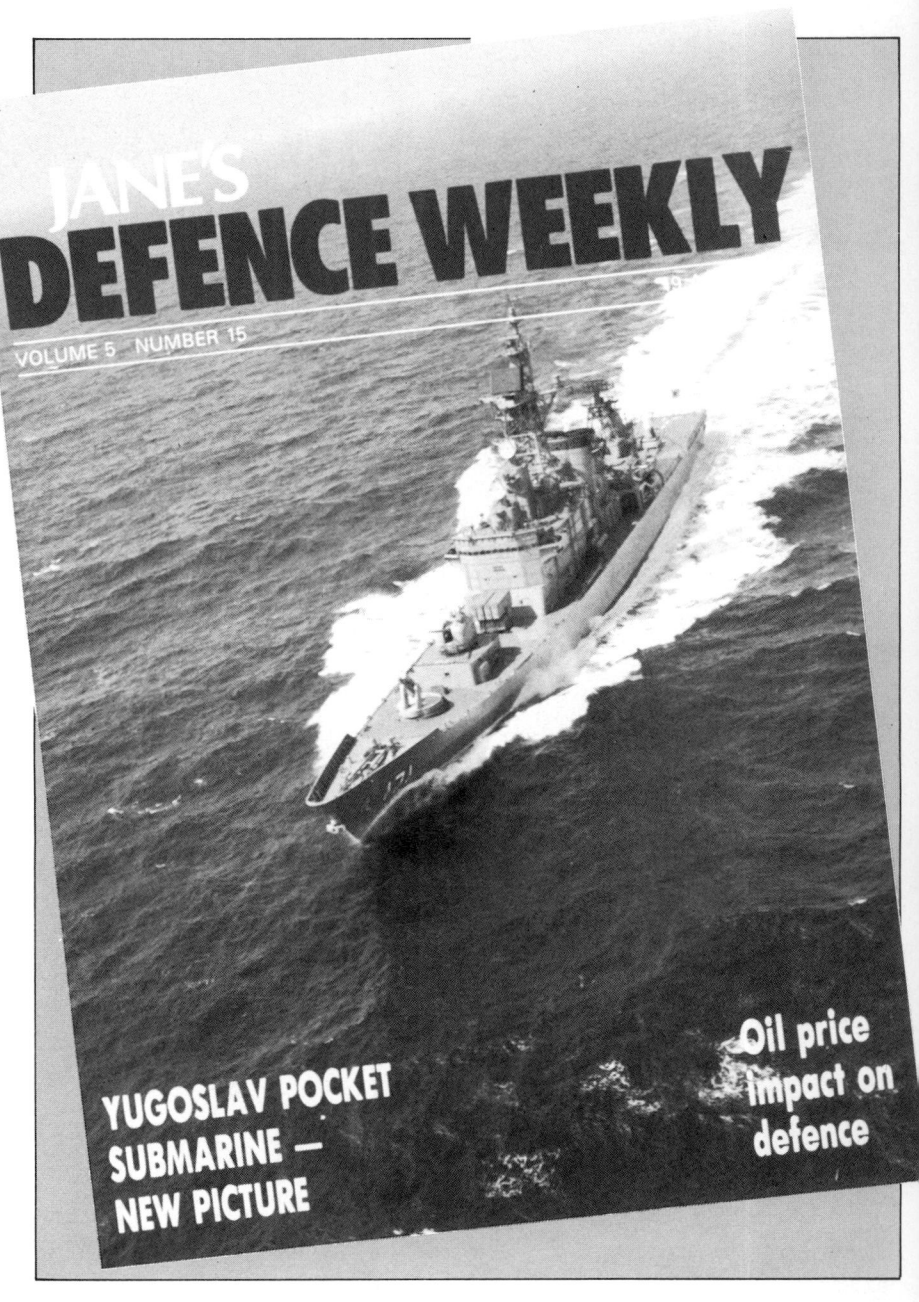

AIRCRAFT

ARGENTINA

AERO BOERO

AERO BOERO SA

Brasil y Alem, 2421 Morteros, Provincia de Córdoba
Telephone: Morteros (0562) 2121 and 2690
PRESIDENT: Hector A. Boero

Aero Boero's activities were seriously affected in 1979 by a tornado and floods, which caused severe damage to a batch of production aircraft, and also to the prototype AB 260 Ag agricultural monoplane.

A new factory came into operation in May 1981. This was being extended in 1986, following sales of the AB 180 RVR to Brazil. The company also reported the possibility of further sales of the AB 115, and is considering setting up a new factory in Brazil.

AERO BOERO 115

The AB 115 three-seat light aircraft was developed from the AB 95 (1969-70 *Jane's*). Thirty had been built by January 1983, including examples of the AB 115 BS ambulance version and 112 kW (150 hp) AB 115/150, descriptions of which can be found in the 1983-84 edition. An order for a trainer version of the standard AB 115 was anticipated in the Summer of 1986, and the following description applies to this version:

TYPE: Two/three-seat light aircraft.

AIRFRAME: As described for AB 180, but with Dacron fabric covering and no tab on rudder.

POWER PLANT: One 86 kW (115 hp) Avco Lycoming O-235-C2A flat-four engine, driving a Sensenich 72-CK-0-50 two-blade fixed-pitch propeller with spinner. Two aluminium fuel tanks in wings, combined capacity 128 litres (28·2 Imp gallons). Refuelling point in top of each tank.

ACCOMMODATION: Pilot and one or two passengers in fully enclosed, heated and ventilated cabin.

SYSTEM: Electrical power provided by one 40A alternator and a 12V battery.

AVIONICS AND EQUIPMENT: Com/nav equipment, blind-flying instrumentation and landing lights optional.

DIMENSIONS, EXTERNAL, AND AREAS: As for AB 180, plus:
Propeller diameter 1·93 m (6 ft 4 in)

WEIGHTS AND LOADINGS:
Weight empty 510 kg (1,124 lb)
Max T-O weight 770 kg (1,698 lb)
Max wing loading 43·9 kg/m² (8·99 lb/sq ft)
Max power loading 8·9 kg/kW (14·77 lb/hp)

PERFORMANCE (at max T-O weight):
Never-exceed speed 118 knots (220 km/h; 136 mph)
Max cruising speed 91 knots (169 km/h; 105 mph)
Stalling speed, power off:
flaps up 41 knots (75 km/h; 47 mph)
flaps down 35 knots (64 km/h; 40 mph)
Max rate of climb at S/L 182 m (597 ft)/min
T-O run 100 m (330 ft)
T-O to, and landing from, 15 m (50 ft) 250 m (820 ft)
Landing run 80 m (265 ft)
Range with max fuel 664 nm (1,230 km; 765 miles)

Aero Boero 115 two/three-seat training and touring aircraft

AERO BOERO 180

The Aero Boero 180 is a higher-powered variant of the AB 150 (see 1983-84 *Jane's*); a total of 60 (all versions) had been manufactured by January 1983, at which time ten more AB 180 RVRs were on order. It has been built in four versions, as follows:

AB 180 RV. Standard version, flown for first time in October 1972. Externally identical to AB 150 RV.

AB 180 RVR. Glider towing version of AB 180 RV, to which it is generally similar except for a cockpit rear window and provision of a towing hook. Production continuing in 1986 for a Brazilian customer.

AB 180 Ag. Agricultural version, certificated in Restricted category.

AB 180 SP. Biplane version of AB 180 Ag, with short span lower wings and enhanced payload/range capability. Prototype only. Details in earlier editions of *Jane's*.

TYPE: Single/three-seat light aircraft.

WINGS: Strut braced high-wing monoplane. Streamline section V bracing strut each side. Wing section NACA 23012 (modified). Dihedral 1° 45′. Incidence 3° at root (3° 30′ on 180 Ag), 1° at tip (2° on 180 Ag). Light alloy structure, including skins. Aluminium alloy flaps and ailerons. No tabs.

FUSELAGE: Welded steel tube structure (SAE 4130), covered with Ceconite.

TAIL UNIT: Wire braced welded steel tube structure, covered with Ceconite. Sweptback fin and rudder, non-swept fixed incidence tailplane with elevators. Ground adjustable tab on rudder; trim tab in port elevator.

LANDING GEAR: Non-retractable tailwheel type, with shock absorption by helicoidal springs inside fuselage. Mainwheels carried on faired-in V struts and half-axles. Mainwheels and tyres size 6·00-6; tailwheel tyre size 2·80-2·50. Hydraulic disc brakes on main units; tailwheel steerable and fully castoring.

POWER PLANT: One 134 kW (180 hp) Avco Lycoming O-360-A1A flat-four engine, driving a Sensenich 76-EM8 fixed-pitch or Hartzell HC-92ZK-8D constant-speed two-blade propeller with spinner. Fuel capacity (two aluminium wing tanks) 200 litres (44 Imp gallons); oil capacity 8 litres (1·75 Imp gallons).

ACCOMMODATION: Pilot and two passengers in 180 RV and RVR; pilot only in 180 Ag. Fully enclosed, heated and ventilated cabin. Cockpit rear window in 180 RVR.

EQUIPMENT: Glider towing hook in AB 180 RVR. Flush fitting underfuselage pod on AB 180 Ag, containing 320 litres (70·4 Imp gallons) of chemical; spraybars fitted along rear bar of V strut and horizontally below wings; electrically operated rotary atomisers (two each side) fitted to rear bar of V strut.

DIMENSIONS, EXTERNAL:
Wing span 10·90 m (35 ft 9 in)
Wing chord, constant 1·61 m (5 ft 3½ in)
Wing aspect ratio 6·98
Length overall 7·27 m (23 ft 10¼ in)
Height overall 2·10 m (6 ft 10½ in)
Wheel track 2·05 m (6 ft 8¾ in)
Wheelbase 5·10 m (16 ft 8¾ in)

AREAS:
Wings, gross 17·55 m² (188·9 sq ft)
Ailerons (total) 1·84 m² (19·81 sq ft)
Trailing-edge flaps (total) 1·94 m² (20·88 sq ft)
Fin 0·93 m² (10·01 sq ft)
Rudder 0·41 m² (4·41 sq ft)
Tailplane 1·40 m² (15·07 sq ft)
Elevators (total, incl tab) 0·97 m² (10·44 sq ft)

WEIGHTS AND LOADINGS (AB 180 RV):
Weight empty 550 kg (1,212 lb)
Max T-O weight 844 kg (1,860 lb)
Max wing loading 51·2 kg/m² (10·5 lb/sq ft)
Max power loading 6·29 kg/kW (10·34 lb/hp)

PERFORMANCE (AB 180 RV/RVR, at max T-O weight except where indicated):
Never-exceed speed 134 knots (249 km/h; 155 mph)
Max level speed at S/L:
180 RV 132 knots (245 km/h; 152 mph)
180 RVR 122 knots (225 km/h; 140 mph)
Max cruising speed at S/L:
180 RVR 108 knots (201 km/h; 125 mph)
Stalling speed, flaps down 40 knots (73 km/h; 45 mph)
Max rate of climb at S/L 360 m (1,180 ft)/min
Rate of climb (180 RVR):
with single-seat sailplane more than 180 m (590 ft)/min
with two-seat sailplane 120 m (394 ft)/min
Time to 600 m (1,970 ft), 75% power, with Blanik two-seat sailplane (180 RVR) 3 min 10 s
Service ceiling more than 7,000 m (22,965 ft)
T-O run 100 m (330 ft)
T-O to 15 m (50 ft), two persons 188 m (615 ft)
Landing from 15 m (50 ft) 160 m (525 ft)
Landing run 60 m (195 ft)
Range with max fuel 636 nm (1,180 km; 733 miles)

Aero Boero 180 RVR glider towing aircraft

AERO BOERO 260 Ag

Aero Boero began the design of this two-seat agricultural aircraft in 1971, and the prototype flew for the first time on 23 December 1972. A number of changes (notably to two-seat configuration instead of the original single-seat layout) were made subsequently, but the prototype was severely damaged by the tornado and floods of 1979. It was fully restored to flying condition, and Argentinian DNA (Dirección Nacional de Aeronavegabilidad) certification was originally hoped for by 1982-83. However, the flight test programme has been more protracted than expected, and work to achieve bilateral DNA/FAA certification under FAR Pt 23 was still in progress in 1986.

TYPE: Two-seat agricultural aircraft.

WINGS: Braced low-wing monoplane, with streamline section overwing struts (two each side) and jury struts. Wing section NACA 23012 (modified). Dihedral 3° from roots. Incidence 3° at root, 0° at tip. Light alloy structure, including skins. Aluminium alloy ailerons and trailing-edge flaps. No tabs. Turned-down wingtips. Large fence on upper surface each side at approx one-third span.

FUSELAGE: Welded steel tube structure (SAE 4130), with skin panels of aluminium at front and plastics at rear.

TAIL UNIT: Wire braced welded steel tube structure with fabric covering. Sweptback fin and rudder; non-swept tailplane and elevators. Trim tab in port elevator.

LANDING GEAR: Non-retractable tailwheel type. Tyre sizes 8·00-6 (main), 2·80-2·50 (tail). Hydraulic disc brakes on main units. Tailwheel steerable and fully castoring.

POWER PLANT: One 194 kW (260 hp) Avco Lycoming O-540-H2B5D flat-six engine, driving either a Sensenich fixed-pitch or a Hartzell or McCauley constant-speed two-blade propeller with spinner. Two aluminium fuel tanks in wings, combined capacity 200 litres (44 Imp gallons). Refuelling point in top of each tank.

ACCOMMODATION: Seats for two persons in heated and ventilated cockpit with framed canopy. Utility compartment on port side, aft of cockpit, with external access.

SYSTEM: Electrical power provided by one 50A alternator and a 12V battery.

AVIONICS AND EQUIPMENT: VHF radio standard. Flush fitting internal tank forward of cockpit for chemical, capacity 600 litres (132 Imp gallons). Spraybars housed inside wings. Chemical is dispersed, by engine driven pump, through two electrically operated rotary atomisers beneath each wing. Twin landing lights in port wing leading-edge.

DIMENSIONS, EXTERNAL:	
Wing span	10·90 m (35 ft 9 in)
Wing chord, constant	1·61 m (5 ft 3½ in)
Wing aspect ratio	6·77
Length overall	7·30 m (23 ft 11½ in)
Height overall	2·04 m (6 ft 8¼ in)
Tailplane span	3·07 m (10 ft 0¾ in)
Wheel track	2·30 m (7 ft 6½ in)
Wheelbase	5·10 m (16 ft 8¾ in)
AREAS: As for AB 180 except:	
Wings, gross	17·55 m^2 (188·9 sq ft)
Fin	1·03 m^2 (11·09 sq ft)
Rudder	0·59 m^2 (6·35 sq ft)

Prototype of the Aero Boero 260 Ag two-seat cropspraying aircraft

WEIGHTS AND LOADINGS:	
Weight empty	690 kg (1,521 lb)
Max T-O weight	1,350 kg (2,976 lb)
Max wing loading	76·92 kg/m^2 (15·76 lb/sq ft)
Max power loading	6·97 kg/kW (11·45 lb/hp)
PERFORMANCE (at max T-O weight):	
Never-exceed speed	135 knots (250 km/h; 155 mph)
Stalling speed, flaps down, engine idling	46 knots (85 km/h; 53 mph)
Max rate of climb at S/L	360 m (1,180 ft)/min
Service ceiling	5,600 m (18,375 ft)
T-O to 15 m (50 ft)	280 m (920 ft)
Landing from 15 m (50 ft)	270 m (886 ft)
Range with max fuel	432 nm (800 km; 497 miles)

CHINCUL

CHINCUL S.A.C.A.I.F.I.

25 de Mayo 489, 4° Piso, Buenos Aires
Telephone: 32 5671/5
Telex: 012 2706 MACUB AR

WORKS: Calle Mendoza entre 6 y 7 (Casilla de Correo 80), San Juan

PRESIDENT: Juan José Beraza

Details of Chincul's licence production of Piper light aircraft were last given in the 1984-85 *Jane's*, although the company itself had not updated its entry since 1981. However, Piper announced in July 1986 that the agreement had "begun to show signs of renewed activity", with two Archer kits recently delivered and two Warrior kits on order.

FMA

FÁBRICA MILITAR DE AVIONES (Area de Material Córdoba) Fuerza Aérea Argentina

Avenida Fuerza Aérea Argentina Km 5½, 5103 Guarnición Aérea Córdoba
Telephone: 45011 to 45015
Telex: 51965 AMCOR AR

GENERAL DIRECTOR:
Brigadeiro Roberto José Engroba

PRODUCTION DIRECTOR:
Comodoro Antonio F. Rizzo Corallo

MAINTENANCE DIRECTOR:
Comodoro Luis H. Pereyra Villán

DIRECTOR OF RESEARCH AND DEVELOPMENT, AND PROGRAMME DIRECTOR, IA 63:
Comodoro Alberto Héctor Lindow

DIRECTOR OF FLIGHT TEST CENTRE:
Mayor D. Horacio A. Orefice Interino

COMMERCIAL MANAGER: H. Francisco Luciano

CHIEF OF PUBLIC RELATIONS:
Vice Comodoro (R) Tidio A. Lazo

The original Fábrica Militar de Aviones (Military Aircraft Factory) came into operation on 10 October 1927 as a central organisation for aeronautical research and production in Argentina. Its name was changed to Instituto Aerotécnico in 1943 and then to Industrias Aeronáuticas y Mecánicas del Estado (IAME) in 1952. In 1957 it became a State enterprise under the title of Dirección Nacional de Fabricaciónes e Investigaciónes Aeronáuticas (DINFIA), but reverted to its original title in 1968. It is now a component of the Area de Material Córdoba (AMC) division of the Argentine Air Force.

FMA comprises two large divisions. The Instituto de Investigaciónes Aeronáuticas y Espacial (IIAE) is responsible for the design of aircraft, and the design, manufacture and testing of rockets, sounding equipment and other equipment. The Fábrica Militar de Aviones itself controls the aircraft manufacturing facilities (Grupo Fabricación) situated in Córdoba, as well as the Centro de Ensayos en Vuelo (Flight Test Centre), to which all aircraft produced in Argentina are sent for certification tests. The laboratories, factories and other aeronautical division buildings occupy a total covered area of approx 253,000 m^2 (2,723,265 sq ft); the Area de Material Córdoba employs more than 3,500 persons, of whom about 2,300 are in the Grupo Fabricación.

In current production is the nationally designed Pucará counter-insurgency aircraft. The IA 63 Pampa basic and advanced jet trainer flew for the first time in October 1984; a go-ahead was still awaited in mid-1986 for the projected ATL twin-turboprop transport, details of which can be found in the 1984-85 *Jane's*. In mid-1986 negotiations were under way with McDonnell Douglas with a view to possible licence production of the A-4 Skyhawk in Argentina.

FMA IA 58 and IA 66 PUCARÁ

This twin-turboprop light attack aircraft, named after a type of stone fortress built by the early South American Indians, flew for the first time on 20 August 1969 with 674 kW (904 ehp) Garrett TPE331-U-303 turboprop engines. It was followed on 6 September 1970 by a second prototype, powered by 761 kW (1,022 ehp) Turboméca Astazou XVI G turboprops, which were adopted as standard for the initial production version.

Four versions of the Pucará have been built, as follows:

IA 58A. Initial (two-seat) production version, of which the first example (A-501) made its first flight on 8 November 1974. Total of 60 ordered originally for the Fuerza Aérea Argentina (FAA), which later ordered 48 more, partly to replace about 24 aircraft lost during the fighting in the South Atlantic in 1982. Deliveries to the FAA began in the Spring of 1976, and the last example was due to be completed in 1986. Currently in service with the FAA's III Brigada Aérea at Reconquista (2° and 3° Escuadrons) and the IX Brigada (4° Escuadron) at Comodoro Rivadavia. Early production IA 58A described in 1983-84 and previous *Jane's*. Some early production aircraft have been converted to single-seat configuration, with extra fuselage fuel tank in place of rear seat; further similar conversions may be planned. Six IA 58As were delivered to the Fuerza Aérea Uruguaya, and a further 40 were being offered for export in early 1986.

IA 58B. As early IA 58A, but with more powerful built-in armament, in a deeper front fuselage, and updated avionics. Prototype only (AX-05), which first flew on 15 May 1979. Forty ordered for FAA in 1980, but cancelled in favour of continued production of IA 58A. Details in 1982-83 *Jane's*.

IA 58C. Improved single-seat version, described separately.

IA 66. Prototype (AX-06), first flown in late 1980 with 746 kW (1,000 shp) Garrett TPE331-11-601W turboprops. Further development unlikely following development of IA 58C. Details in 1984-85 and earlier *Jane's*.

The following description applies to the IA 58A in its final production form:

TYPE: Twin-turboprop close support, reconnaissance and counter-insurgency aircraft; structural design based on MIL-A8860 to 8870 specifications.

WINGS: Cantilever low-wing monoplane. Wing section NACA 64_2A215 at root, NACA 64_1A212 at tip. Dihedral 7° on outer panels. Incidence 2°. No sweepback. Conventional two-spar semi-monocoque fail-safe structure of duralumin, with 075 ST upper and 024 ST lower skins. All-dural electrically controlled hydraulically actuated trailing-edge slotted flaps, inboard and outboard of each engine nacelle. Modified Frise ailerons of duralumin, with magnesium alloy trailing-edges, actuated by push/pull rods. No slats. Balance tab in starboard aileron, electrically operated trim tab in port aileron.

FUSELAGE: Conventional semi-monocoque fail-safe structure of duralumin frames and stringers, built in forward, central and rear main sections. Upper part of nosecone opens upward for access to avionics and equipment.

TAIL UNIT: Cantilever semi-monocoque structure of duralumin; two-spar rudder and elevators have magnesium alloy trailing-edges. Fixed incidence tailplane and elevators mounted near top of fin. Curved dorsal fin. Rudder and elevators actuated by push/pull rods, and each fitted with electrically operated inset trim tab.

LANDING GEAR: Hydraulically retractable tricycle type, with emergency mechanical backup. All units retract forward, steerable nose unit (33° left and right) into fuselage, main units into engine nacelles. Kronprinz

IA 58A Pucará combat aircraft of the Argentine Air Force

Ring-Feder shock absorber in each unit. Single Dunlop wheel on nose unit, twin wheels on main units, all with Dunlop Type III tubeless tyres size 7·50-10. Tyre pressure 3·10 bars (45 lb/sq in) on all units. Dunlop hydraulic disc brakes on mainwheels only. Parking and emergency brake. No anti-skid units. Landing gear suitable for grass strip operation. Provision for 80 m (262 ft) take-off run using three JATO bottles attached to underfuselage pylon.

POWER PLANT: Two 729 kW (978 shp) Turboméca Astazou XVIG turboprop engines, each driving a Ratier-Forest 23LF-379 three-blade variable-pitch fully-feathering metal propeller with spinner. Water injection system, flow rate 2·5 litres (0·55 Imp gallons)/min for 2 min. Electric de-icing of engine air intakes. Fuel in two AMC (Area de Material Córdoba) fuselage tanks (combined capacity 772 litres; 170 Imp gallons) and one AMC self-sealing tank in each wing (combined capacity 508 litres; 111 Imp gallons). Overall usable internal capacity 1,280 litres (281 Imp gallons). Gravity refuelling point for all tanks on top of fuselage aft of cockpit. Fuel system includes two accumulator tanks, permitting up to 30 s of inverted flight. A long-range auxiliary tank, usable capacity 318 or 1,100 litres (70 or 242 Imp gallons) can be attached to the fuselage centreline pylon, and a 318 litre (70 Imp gallon) auxiliary tank on each underwing pylon. Possible external fuel loads are therefore 318, 636, 954, 1,100 or 1,736 litres (70, 140, 210, 242 or 382 Imp gallons); max internal and external usable fuel capacity is 3,016 litres (663 Imp gallons). Oil capacity 11 litres (2·4 Imp gallons).

ACCOMMODATION: Pilot and co-pilot in tandem on Martin-Baker AP06A zero/zero ejection seats beneath single AMC moulded Plexiglas canopy which is hinged at rear and opens upward. Rear (co-pilot) seat elevated 25 cm (10 in) above front seat. Rearview mirror for each crew member. Teleflex heated and bulletproof windscreen, with wiper. Armour plating in cockpit floor, resistant to 7·62 mm ground fire from 150 m (500 ft). Dual controls and blind-flying instrumentation standard. Cockpits heated and ventilated by mixture of engine bleed and external air.

SYSTEMS: Air-conditioning, de-icing and anti-*g* systems optional. Hydraulic system, with air/oil reservoir and two engine driven pumps each delivering 4 litres (0·9 Imp gallons)/min at 175 bars (2,538 lb/sq in), actuates landing gear, flaps, nosewheel steering and mainwheel brakes. Independent pneumatic (compressed air) system on each engine to supply water injection, fuel system, inverted flight accumulators, auxiliary fuel tank transfer, and (port engine only) Dunlop canopy sealing system. Electrical system includes two 28.5V 5kW Turboméca engine driven DC starter/generators; two 250VA Flite-Tronics static inverters (main and standby), fed from DC emergency busbar, for 115/26V single-phase AC power at 400Hz; and a 24V 36Ah SAFT Voltabloc 4006A nickel-cadmium battery. No APU. Main oxygen system uses 5 litre (1·1 Imp gallon) Bendix liquid oxygen bottle and lox converter; separate gaseous oxygen supply for emergency use. L'Hotellier fire detection and extinguishing system, with Graviner extinguisher bottle.

AVIONICS AND EQUIPMENT: Standard avionics include Delta VOR/LOC/ILS, Smiths magnetic compass, Sperry gyro compass and dual artificial horizons, Bendix DFA-73A-1 ADF receiver, Bendix RTA-42A VHF com transceiver, SunAir RE-800 HF com transceiver, Bendix RNA-34 VOR/LOC/glideslope receiver, SunAir ACU-810 HF coupler/amplifier, Delta audio amplifier, and intercom. Optional avionics include ECM, weather radar, IFF, inertial navigation system, Machmeter, and VHF-FM tactical communications system. Standard equipment includes dual Pioneer airspeed and vertical speed indicators, dual Kollsman altimeters, dual Air Precision turn and bank indicators, dual Bendix accelerometers, dual attitude indicators (plus standby), dual bearing/distance/heading indicators, flap position indicator, dual landing gear position indicators, Air Precision chronometer, dual Jaeger engine rpm and AMC torque indicators, dual Brion Leroux propeller pitch indicators, dual Jaeger fuel and oil temperature indicators, dual Faure Herman fuel flow and AMC fuel quantity indicators, heated pitot intake, three pitot static ports, GE landing light in leading-edge of each underwing pylon, AMC taxying light on nosewheel strut, fin-tip anti-collision light, wingtip navigation lights, instrument panel lights and warning lights.

ARMAMENT: Two 20 mm Hispano DCA-804 cannon, each with 270 rds, in underside of forward fuselage; and four 7·62 mm FN-Browning M2-30 machine-guns, each with 900 rds, in sides of fuselage abreast of cockpit. Alkan 115E ejector pylon on centreline beneath fuselage, capacity 1,000 kg (2,205 lb); Alkan 105E pylon, capacity 500 kg (1,102 lb), beneath each wing outboard of engine nacelle. Max external stores load with full internal fuel is 1,500 kg (3,307 lb), including gun and rocket pods, bombs, cluster bombs, incendiaries, mines, torpedoes, air-to-surface missiles, camera pod(s) or auxiliary fuel tank(s). Max external weapons load when carrying drop tanks on the fuselage or wing stations is 1,000 kg (2,205 lb). Typical loads can include twelve 125 kg bombs; seven launchers each with nineteen 2·75 in rockets; a 12·7, 20 or 30 mm gun pod and two 318 litre drop tanks; six 125 kg bombs and sixteen 5 in rockets; six launchers each with forty 74 mm cartridges, plus onboard ECM; twelve 250 lb napalm bombs; three 500 kg delayed action bombs; or two twin-7·62 mm machine-gun pods, plus three launchers each containing nineteen 2·75 in rockets. SFOM 83A3 reflector sight permits weapon release at any desired firing angle; optional Bendix AWE-1 programmer allows release in step or ripple modes of single weapons, pairs or salvos.

Single-seat conversion of standard IA 58A Pucará

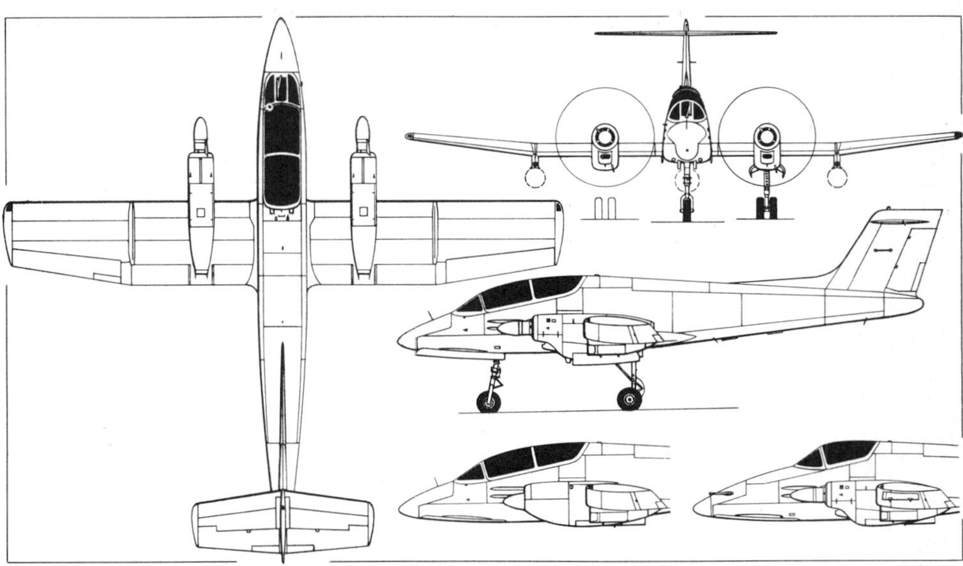

FMA IA 58A Pucará two-seat close support and reconnaissance aircraft, with scrap views of IA 66 (left) and IA 58C *(Pilot Press)*

DIMENSIONS, EXTERNAL:
- Wing span: 14·50 m (47 ft 6⅞ in)
- Wing chord:
  - centre-section (constant): 2·24 m (7 ft 4¼ in)
  - at tip: 1·60 m (5 ft 3 in)
- Wing aspect ratio: 6·94
- Length overall: 14·253 m (46 ft 9⅛ in)
- Length of fuselage: 13·675 m (44 ft 10½ in)
- Fuselage: Max width: 1·32 m (4 ft 4 in)
  - Max depth: 1·95 m (6 ft 4¾ in)
- Height overall: 5·362 m (17 ft 7⅛ in)
- Tailplane span: 4·70 m (15 ft 5 in)
- Wheel track (c/l of shock absorbers): 4·20 m (13 ft 9¼ in)
- Wheelbase: 3·885 m (12 ft 9 in)
- Propeller diameter: 2·59 m (8 ft 6 in)

DIMENSIONS, INTERNAL:
- Cockpit: Length: 2·85 m (9 ft 4¼ in)
  - Max width: 0·81 m (2 ft 8 in)
  - Max height: 1·25 m (4 ft 1¼ in)
  - Floor area: 2·90 m² (31·2 sq ft)
  - Volume: 2·74 m³ (96·8 cu ft)

AREAS:
- Wings, gross: 30·30 m² (326·1 sq ft)
- Ailerons (total): 2·00 m² (21·53 sq ft)
- Trailing-edge flaps (total): 3·54 m² (38·10 sq ft)
- Fin, excl dorsal fin: 3·85 m² (41·76 sq ft)
- Rudder, incl tab: 1·15 m² (12·38 sq ft)
- Tailplane: 4·60 m² (49·51 sq ft)
- Elevators (total, incl tabs): 2·612 m² (28·11 sq ft)

WEIGHTS AND LOADINGS:
- Weight empty, equipped: 4,020 kg (8,862 lb)
- Max fuel load: internal: 1,000 kg (2,205 lb)
  - external: 1,359 kg (2,997 lb)
- Max external stores load: 1,500 kg (3,307 lb)
- Max T-O weight: 6,800 kg (14,991 lb)
- Max zero-fuel weight: 4,546 kg (10,022 lb)
- Max landing weight: 5,600 kg (12,345 lb)
- Max wing loading: 224·4 kg/m² (45·97 lb/sq ft)
- Max power loading: 4·66 kg/kW (7·66 lb/shp)

PERFORMANCE (at AUW of 5,500 kg; 12,125 lb except where indicated):
- Max critical Mach number at max T-O weight: 0·77
- Never-exceed speed at max T-O weight: Mach 0·63 (405 knots; 750 km/h; 466 mph)
- Max level speed at 3,000 m (9,840 ft): 270 knots (500 km/h; 310 mph)
- Max cruising speed at 6,000 m (19,680 ft): 259 knots (480 km/h; 298 mph)
- Econ cruising speed: 232 knots (430 km/h; 267 mph)
- Max speed for landing gear extension (all weights): 150 knots (278 km/h; 172 mph)
- Stalling speed, flaps and landing gear down, AUW of 4,790 kg (10,560 lb): 78 knots (143 km/h; 89 mph)
- Max rate of climb at S/L: 1,080 m (3,543 ft)/min
- Service ceiling: 10,000 m (32,800 ft)
- Service ceiling, one engine out: 6,000 m (19,680 ft)
- Min ground turning radius: 6·50 m (21 ft 4 in)
- T-O run: 300 m (985 ft)
- T-O to 15 m (50 ft): 705 m (2,313 ft)
- Landing from 15 m (50 ft), landing weight of 5,100 kg (11,243 lb): 603 m (1,978 ft)
- Landing run, landing weight as above: 200 m (656 ft)
- Attack radius at T-O weight of 6,500 kg (14,330 lb), 10% reserves of initial fuel:
  - with 1,500 kg (3,307 lb) of external weapons:
    - lo-lo-lo: 121 nm (225 km; 140 miles)
    - lo-lo-hi: 175 nm (325 km; 202 miles)
    - hi-lo-hi: 189 nm (350 km; 217 miles)
  - with 1,200 kg (2,645 lb) of external weapons:
    - lo-lo-lo: 216 nm (400 km; 248 miles)
    - lo-lo-hi: 310 nm (575 km; 357 miles)
    - hi-lo-hi: 350 nm (650 km; 404 miles)
  - with 800 kg (1,764 lb) of ordnance and 450 litres (99 Imp gallons) of external fuel:
    - lo-lo-lo: 310 nm (575 km; 357 miles)
    - lo-lo-hi: 445 nm (825 km; 512 miles)
    - hi-lo-hi: 526 nm (975 km; 606 miles)
- Ferry range at 5,485 m (18,000 ft) with max internal and external fuel: 2,002 nm (3,710 km; 2,305 miles)
- *g* limits: +6/−3

FMA IA 58C PUCARÁ CHARLIE

First details of this single-seat Pucará variant, which was flown for the first time on 30 December 1985, became available in the Autumn of 1984. Its development, based on experience gained during the Falklands/Malvinas campaign of 1982, is intended to extend its attack capability against such targets as helicopters and surface vessels, and to enable it also to carry out a low level air defence role.

Unlike the single-seat IA 58A conversions described in the preceding entry, it is the front cockpit which is deleted in the IA 58C. This enables the existing built-in armament of two 20 mm and four 7·62 mm guns to be supplemented by a 30 mm DEFA 553 cannon in the upper nose with, initially, 270 rounds of ammunition. Externally, provision is made to carry two CITEFA Martin Pescador (Kingfisher) supersonic tactical missiles underwing, or a pair of Matra R.550 Magic air-to-air missiles for self-defence underwing or on two additional Alkan launchers mounted under the tips of strengthened outer wings.

The remaining cockpit has been enlarged, and given added armour protection against hits from light calibre weapons. Improvements and additions to the avionics include an Omega/VLF system with radar altimeter for nap-of-the-earth navigation; a radar warning receiver; new HF and VHF-FM/AM communications; HSI; and ADI with gyro platform. Options include IFF, a Saab RGS-2 or similar lead-computing predictor sight, head-up display, and internal or pod mounted flares, chaff or jamming equipment. Provision is made for wing and tail unit anti-icing.

The IA 58C retains the same power plant as the A version, except that the Astazou XVIG engines now have self-start capability and modified nozzles to reduce their infra-red signature. Maximum take-off and landing weights remain unchanged. Cruising speed at sea level (presumably at max T-O weight) is estimated at 250 knots (463 km/h; 288 mph), and payload/range capability is expected to be increased by up to 20 per cent.

Some Argentine Air Force officials have been quoted as saying that the FAA plans to retrofit its 70 or so IA 58As to IA 58C standard, but whether this will be so, whether a production order will be placed for new-build aircraft, or whether re-equipment will involve a mixture of both will depend on the outcome of flight testing. No official decision had been taken up to March 1986. The FMA's Grupo Fabricación is said to be capable of producing up to three and a half Pucarás per month.

ARMAMENT: Fixed armament as for IA 58A, plus a nose mounted 30 mm DEFA 553 cannon with 270 rds. Two underwing pylon attachments, plus air-to-air missile launchers under each wingtip. Typical weapon combinations can include twelve 125 kg bombs or 250 lb napalm containers; six 125 kg bombs with eight 5 in rockets; three 500 kg retarded bombs; three 220 kg napalm tanks with four launchers each containing forty 74 mm grenades; seven launchers each for nineteen 2·75 in rockets; four such launchers with a 300 litre drop tank, or three launchers with two 300 litre drop tanks; three such rocket launchers with a pair of Matra Magic air-to-air missiles; two Magics and a 1,100 litre drop tank; or two 300 litre drop tanks plus an ECM pod linked automatically with the radar warning receiver.

FMA IA 63 PAMPA

To modernise its military pilot training system, the Fuerza Aérea Argentina decided in the late 1970s to authorise the design of a new jet trainer to replace its ageing Morane-Saulnier MS.760 Paris IIIs, and in 1979 FMA initiated the IA 63 Pampa programme to meet this requirement. An initial concept phase included the study of four possible single-engined and three twin-engined designs before the present configuration, powered by a single Garrett TFE731 turbofan engine, was adopted in early 1980. Detail definition of the design, wind tunnel testing and overall programme planning occupied the remainder of that year, and was followed in early 1981 by the start of the current development phase, which was scheduled to last until 1985. Under contract to the Argentine government, Dornier GmbH of West Germany is providing technical assistance during the development phase, including manufacture of the wings and tailplanes for the prototypes and ground test airframes.

Two IA 63 airframes are being completed for static and fatigue testing. The first flying prototype (EX-01) made a successful first flight on 6 October 1984, and four further test flights were completed before, on 10 October, an 'official' first flight was made to mark the 57th anniversary of the foundation of FMA. First flight of the second prototype took place on 7 August 1985; the third flew during the first half of 1986, and three pre-production aircraft were due to fly before the end of that year.

Plans were to complete flight testing and certification by October 1986, enabling the first 12 production Pampas to be delivered for basic and advanced flying training with the FAA by March 1988. The initial FAA order, confirmed in October 1985, is for 64 aircraft, primarily to replace about 35 Morane-Saulnier Paris III jet trainers. A further 40, for use as combat proficiency trainers, may be ordered later. Production is planned to reach three per month by 1990, when the IA 63 will also become available for export.

For weapons training, the IA 63 can be equipped with a 30 mm DEFA gun pod and underwing practice bombs. Development of an armed version for the light close support role, probably with an uprated engine such as the 19·13 kN (4,300 lb st) TFE731-5, is under consideration.

The single-seat FMA IA 58C Pucará Charlie, with additional nose gun and external ordnance

TYPE: Single-engined basic and advanced jet trainer.

AIRFRAME: Incorporates integrated structures for high-load components such as wing spar box and main frames; numerically controlled, mechanically and chemically milled components; and the use of fibre composites.

WINGS: Cantilever shoulder-wing monoplane. Non-swept tapered wings are of Dornier DoA-7 advanced transonic section, with thickness/chord ratios of 14·5% at root, 12·5% at tip. Two-spar wing box forms integral fuel tank. Hydraulically actuated two-segment single-slotted Fowler trailing-edge flaps inboard of ailerons. Redundant primary controls, actuated hydraulically with assistance by Liebherr servo actuators. Stick forces simulated by artificial feel. Three-axis trim is operated electro-mechanically.

FUSELAGE: Conventional semi-monocoque structure. Hydraulically actuated door type airbrake on each side of upper rear fuselage.

TAIL UNIT: Sweptback fin and rudder; non-swept all-moving anhedral tailplane. Control surface actuation as for ailerons.

LANDING GEAR: Retractable tricycle type, by Servo Hydraulics Lod of Israel, with hydraulic extension/retraction and emergency free-fall extension. Oleo-pneumatic shock absorbers. Single wheel and low-pressure tyre on each unit. Nosewheel retracts rearward, mainwheels inward into underside of engine air intake trunks. Braking system incorporates an anti-skid device; nosewheel steering is optional. Gear is designed for operation from unprepared surfaces.

POWER PLANT: One 15·57 kN (3,500 lb st) Garrett TFE731-2-2N turbofan engine, installed in rear fuselage, with twin lateral air intakes. Standard internal fuel capacity of 980 litres (215·5 Imp gallons) is contained in an integral wing tank of 550 litres (121 Imp gallons) and a 418 litre (92 Imp gallon) flexible fuselage tank with a negative *g* chamber. An additional 415 litres (91 Imp gallons) can be carried in auxiliary tanks installed inside the outer wing panels, to give a max internal capacity of 1,383 litres (304 Imp gallons). Single-point pressure refuelling system. Engine air intakes anti-iced by engine bleed air.

ACCOMMODATION: Instructor and student in tandem (instructor at rear, on elevated seat), on standard ejection seats (Martin-Baker on first prototype) operable also while aircraft is on ground. Ejection procedure can be pre-selected for separate single ejections, or for both seats to be fired from front or rear cockpit. Dual controls standard. One-piece wraparound windscreen. One-piece canopy, with internal screen, is hinged at rear and opens upward. Entire accommodation pressurised and air-conditioned.

SYSTEMS: AiResearch air-conditioning system, supplied by high or low pressure engine bleed air, also provides ram air for negative *g* system and canopy seal. Oxygen system supplied by lox converter. Two independent hydraulic systems, each at pressure of 207 bars (3,000 lb/sq in), supplied by engine driven pumps. Each system incorporates a bootstrap reservoir pressurised at 4 bars (58 lb/sq in). No. 1 system, with flow rate of 16 litres (3·5 Imp gallons)/min, actuates primary flight controls, airbrakes, landing gear and wheel brakes; No. 2 system, with flow rate of 8 litres (1·75 Imp gallons)/min, actuates primary flight controls, wing flaps, emergency and parking brakes, and (if fitted) nosewheel steering. A ram air turbine provides emergency hydraulic power for No. 2 system if pressure in this system drops below minimum. Primary electrical system (28V DC) supplied by an 11·5kW engine driven starter/generator; secondary supply (115/26V AC power at 400Hz) from two static inverters; onboard battery for engine starting.

AVIONICS: Standard avionics package comprises two redundant VHF com transceivers, intercom system, VOR/ILS with marker beacon receiver, DME, and ADF radio compass. Navigation system allows complete navigation/landing training under IFR conditions. Attitude and heading information provided by a three-gyro platform, with magnetic flux valve compass for additional heading reference. Wide range of other avionics available, to customer's requirements.

First two prototypes of the IA 63 Pampa single-engined trainer flying alongside an IA 58A Pucará Pampa. EX-01 nearest camera is fitted with ventral gun pod and underwing stores

ARMAMENT: No built-in weapons. Five attachments for external stores, with max pylon load of 400 kg (882 lb) on each inboard underwing station, 250 kg (551 lb) each on fuselage centreline and outboard underwing pair. With a 30 mm gun pod containing 145 rds on the fuselage station, typical underwing loads can include six Mk 81 bombs, two each Mk 81 and Mk 82 bombs, or one 7·62 mm twin-gun pod and one practice bomb/rocket training container. Gyrostabilised sighting system in each cockpit, with recorder in front sight. Weapon management system adequate for several different tactical configurations.

DIMENSIONS, EXTERNAL:
Wing span 9·686 m (31 ft 9¼ in)
Wing aspect ratio 6·0
Length overall (excl pitot probe) 10·90 m (35 ft 9¼ in)
Height overall 4·29 m (14 ft 1 in)
Tailplane span 4·58 m (15 ft 0⅓ in)
Wheel track 2·66 m (8 ft 8¾ in)
Wheelbase 4·42 m (14 ft 6 in)

AREAS:
Wings, gross reference 15·63 m² (168·2 sq ft)
Vertical tail surfaces (total) 2·52 m² (27·13 sq ft)
Horizontal tail surfaces (total) 4·35 m² (46·82 sq ft)

WEIGHTS AND LOADINGS:
Weight empty 2,627 kg (5,791 lb)
Fuel load:
wings (incl auxiliary tanks) 780 kg (1,719 lb)
fuselage 338 kg (745 lb)
Max underwing load with normal internal fuel 1,160 kg (2,557 lb)
Design gross weight 3,200 kg (7,054 lb)
T-O weight, 'clean' configuration:
968 litres internal fuel 3,700 kg (8,157 lb)
1,383 litres internal fuel 3,800 kg (8,377 lb)
Max T-O weight with external stores 5,000 kg (11,023 lb)
Typical landing weight 3,300 kg (7,275 lb)
Wing loading:
at 'clean' T-O weight:
968 litres internal fuel 236·72 kg/m² (48·51 lb/sq ft)
1,383 litres internal fuel 243·12 kg/m² (49·82 lb/sq ft)
at max T-O weight with external stores 319·90 kg/m² (65·55 lb/sq ft)
Power loading:
at 'clean' T-O weight:
968 litres internal fuel 237·8 kg/kN (2·33 lb/lb st)
1,383 litres internal fuel 244·2 kg/kN (2·39 lb/lb st)
at max T-O weight with external stores 321·4 kg/kN (3·15 lb/lb st)

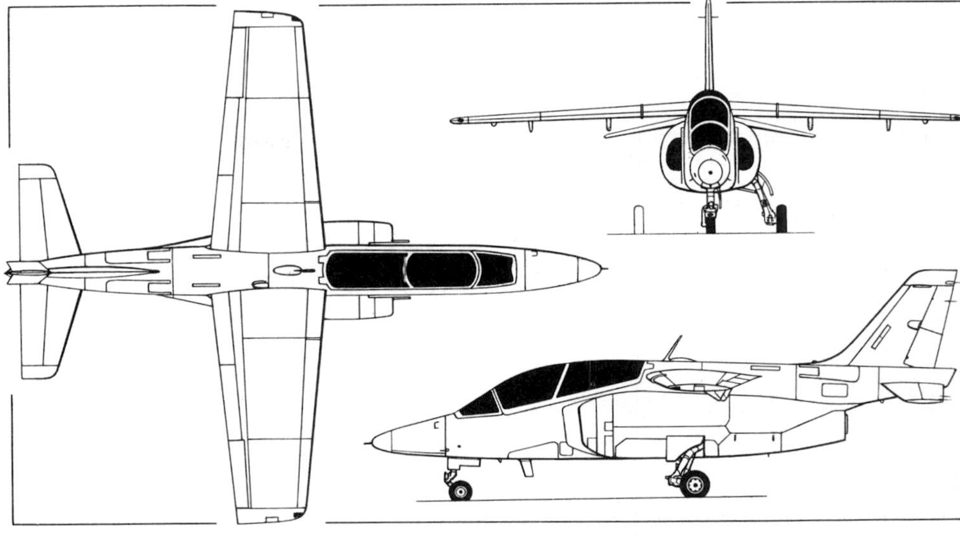

FMA IA 63 Pampa two-seat basic and advanced jet trainer *(Pilot Press)*

PERFORMANCE (initial flight tests, at T-O weight of 3,800 kg; 8,377 lb):
T-O speed 95 knots (176 km/h; 109 mph)
Optimum climbing speed Mach 0·45 (210 knots; 389 km/h; 242 mph)
Approach speed, flaps and landing gear down 120 knots (222 km/h; 138 mph)
Landing speed, flaps and landing gear down 100 knots (185 km/h; 115 mph)
Max rate of climb at S/L 1,600 m (5,250 ft)/min
T-O run 460 m (1,510 ft)
Landing run approx 700 m (2,296 ft)

PERFORMANCE (estimated, ISA, at design gross weight with 50% normal fuel, except where indicated):
Max limiting Mach number at 9,500 m (31,170 ft) 0·81
Max level speed:
at S/L Mach 0·62 (407 knots; 755 km/h; 469 mph)
at 7,000 m (22,965 ft) 442 knots (819 km/h; 509 mph)
Max cruising speed at 4,000 m (13,125 ft) 403 knots (747 km/h; 464 mph)
Max rate of climb at S/L 1,813 m (5,950 ft)/min
Time to 11,000 m (36,000 ft) 10 min 54 s
Turn rate (max sustained) at 4,000 m (13,125 ft) 12·9°/s
Service ceiling 12,900 m (42,325 ft)
T-O run at T-O weight of 3,500 kg (7,716 lb) 400 m (1,312 ft)
T-O to 15 m (50 ft) at S/L, T-O weight of 3,518 kg (7,756 lb) 640 m (2,100 ft)
Landing from 15 m (50 ft), landing weight of 3,300 kg (7,275 lb) 830 m (2,723 ft)
Landing run at landing weight of 3,300 kg (7,275 lb) 515 m (1,690 ft)
Typical mission radius with 30 min reserves:
air-to-air gunnery (hi-hi), T-O weight of 3,950 kg (8,708 lb) with 250 kg (551 lb) external load, 5 min allowance for dogfight 237 nm (440 km; 273 miles)
air-to-ground (hi-lo-hi), T-O weight of 4,860 kg (10,714 lb) with 1,000 kg (2,205 lb) external load, 5 min allowance for weapon delivery 194 nm (360 km; 223 miles)
Range at 300 knots (556 km/h; 345 mph) at 4,000 m (13,125 ft):
968 litres internal fuel 540 nm (1,000 km; 621 miles)
1,383 litres internal fuel 809 nm (1,500 km; 932 miles)
Max endurance at 300 knots (556 km/h; 345 mph) at 4,000 m (13,125 ft), 1,383 litres internal fuel 2 h 48 min
g limit +4·5 max sustained

AUSTRALIA

AAC — *see HDH*

AUSTRALIAN AUTOGYRO
THE AUSTRALIAN AUTOGYRO CO

29 Benning Avenue, Turramurra, Sydney, NSW 2074
Telephone: 4499816
PROPRIETOR: E. R. Minty

AUSTRALIAN AUTOGYRO SKYHOOK

Development history of Mr Ted Minty's Skyhook 'mini-chopper' was recorded in the 1982-83 and earlier editions of *Jane's*. The design has now been perfected, and the Skyhook is in production. A basic 'open frame' model with 1,835 cc Volkswagen engine is known as the **Mk I**; also available are a **Mk II** (unpainted, with enclosed body) and a fully customised **Mk III**. Sales by 1 January 1986 comprised seven Mk Is and two Mk IIIs.

Particular features are the anatomically designed seat/fuel tank (50 sold by beginning of 1986), mounted on rubber blocks at the keel/mast junction, which wraps around the mast to bring pilot and fuel load closer to the CG; an all-new joystick control mechanism to operate the rotor head and blades; and a Stromberg single side draught carburettor with automatically adjustable mixture control. The seat/tank can be fitted also to all versions of the Bensen autogyro (see US part of Sport Aircraft section).

TYPE: Single-seat lightweight autogyro.

ROTOR SYSTEM: Two-blade rotor, with light alloy Rotordyne blades attached directly to a fully adjustable hub bar. Joystick control actuates two nylon encased 6·35 mm (¼ in) stainless steel push/pull cables to operate rotor head and blades.

FUSELAGE: Single keel to which are attached the landing gear, fuselage structure, seat, engine mounting frame, rotor mast and tail unit. Keel and rotor mast are of 5·1 cm (2 in) square section 6061-T6 aluminium alloy with radiused corners. The majority of structural attachments are clamped, rather than bolted or riveted, to reduce to a minimum the number of potential fracture locations in the airframe. Glassfibre fuselage shell on Mks II and III.

Australian Autogyro Co (Minty) Skyhook single-seat autogyro in Mk III production form

TAIL UNIT: Twin rudders, united by a dihedral tailplane attached to the keel. The upper ends of the rudders are braced by double V triangular frames of light alloy and chrome molybdenum steel tube. Rudders manufactured from marine quality aluminium, tailplane from 2024 aluminium sheet. Entire tail assembly operates as a single unit which swivels from side to side to provide directional stability and power-off manoeuvrability.

LANDING GEAR: Non-retractable type with small sprung tailwheel at rear end of keel. Fully sprung steerable nosewheel, linked to rudders. Mainwheels are ultra-light-weight 5 in nylon go-kart rims, each with a 4·00-5 tyre and tube. Disc brakes optional.

Power Plant: One VW engine of 1,835 cc capacity, mounted on chrome molybdenum brackets attached to mast and keel, and driving an HDH two-blade fixed-pitch pusher propeller of Queensland maple which delivers 1·11 kN (250 lb st) at 3,000 rpm and 1·60 kN (360 lb st) at 3,600 rpm. Fuel contained in hollow squab and backrest of pilot's seat, capacity 43 litres (9·5 Imp gallons) plus a reserve of 7 litres (1·5 Imp gallons).

Accommodation: Pilot only, in enclosed cockpit, on rotationally moulded super-strength cross-linked polyethylene seat/fuel tank located just forward of mast/keel junction, close to CG. Aircraft can be flown without fuselage shell and Plexiglas windscreen enclosure if desired. Adjustable vents in fuselage nose provide ventilation when the aircraft is flown with the cockpit enclosed.

Equipment: Standard equipment includes cylinder head high temperature and low fuel warning lights.

Dimensions, external:
- Rotor diameter — 7·01 m (23 ft 0 in)
- Length overall — 3·35 m (11 ft 0 in)
- Height to top of rotor head — 2·06 m (6 ft 9 in)
- Height to top of cockpit canopy — 1·42 m (4 ft 8 in)
- Tailplane span (incl rudders) — 0·86 m (2 ft 10 in)
- Wheel track — 1·68 m (5 ft 6 in)
- Propeller diameter — 1·35 m (4 ft 5 in)

Area:
- Rotor disc — 38·6 m² (415·5 sq ft)

Weights:
- Weight empty: Mk I — 139 kg (306 lb)
- Mks II/III — 161 kg (354 lb)
- Max T-O weight — 271 kg (597 lb)

Performance:
- Max level speed — more than 87 knots (161 km/h; 100 mph)
- Max rate of climb at S/L — 305 m (1,000 ft)/min
- T-O run (depending on headwind) — approx 122 m (400 ft)
- Landing run (with disc brakes) — approx 5 m (15 ft)
- Range with 43 litres (9·5 Imp gallons) fuel at constant 61 knots (113 km/h; 70 mph) — 243 nm (450 km; 280 miles)

CAC — *see HDH*

GAF

GOVERNMENT AIRCRAFT FACTORIES

Fishermen's Bend, Private Bag No. 4, Post Office, Port Melbourne, Victoria 3207
Telephone: (03) 647 3111
Telex: AA 34851 GAFAIR
Works: Avalon Airfield, Beach Road, Lara, Victoria 3212
Telephone: Lara (052) 82 2988
General Manager: J. R. C. Pascoe
Marketing Manager: N. A. Ryan

The Government Aircraft Factories are owned by the Australian government and operated by the Department of Defence. They have a workforce of approximately 2,400 persons. Their functions include the design, development, manufacture, assembly, maintenance and modification of aircraft, target drones and guided weapons. At Avalon airfield, subassembly of components, final assembly, modification, repair and test flying of jet and other aircraft are undertaken.

Current activity includes continuing manufacture of the Ikara anti-submarine missile and (see RPVs and Targets section) the Jindivik target drone. The GAF also produce in-spar wing ribs for the Boeing 757, wing flaps for the Fokker F28 Fellowship, and composite flaps and flap shrouds for the McDonnell Douglas F/A-18. They are responsible for final assembly of all but the first two of the 75 F/A-18 Hornets ordered for the RAAF. The first flight by a GAF assembled Hornet (a TF-18) was made on 26 February 1985, and six had been completed by 1 January 1986.

GOVERNMENT AIRCRAFT FACTORIES NOMAD

The N2 Nomad prototype flew for the first time on 23 July 1971; Australian type certificates for the N22 and N24 initial production versions, described in previous editions of *Jane's*, were issued in May 1975 and October 1977 respectively.

The N22B and N24A were type certificated in August 1975 and May 1978 respectively, and were later awarded US FAR Pt 23 (Normal and Utility category) and FAR Pt 135 Appendix A (Transport category) certification. Type certificates have also been issued in various European, Asian, South American and Pacific countries.

Nomad production was suspended in late 1984 after completion of 170 aircraft; 145 of these had been delivered by early 1986. Main production versions, with totals ordered and/or delivered as at January 1986, were the N22B (35 delivered, including two Floatmasters), N24A (40 delivered), Missionmaster (50 ordered), Searchmaster B (22 ordered) and Searchmaster L (12 delivered). Full details of these models have been given in the 1985-86 and previous editions.

In May 1985, the N22B was recertificated as the **N22C**, with max T-O weight increased to 4,060 kg (8,950 lb). A new force-feed oil filter system downstream of the engines contributes to the increase of less than 23 kg (50 lb) in empty weight.

The following description applies to the N22C:

Type: Twin-turboprop STOL utility aircraft.

Airframe: As described in 1983-84 *Jane's*. No change in tyre pressures.

Power Plant: Two 313 kW (420 shp) Allison 250-B17C turboprop engines, each driving a Hartzell three-blade constant-speed fully-feathering reversible-pitch metal propeller with Beta control. Standard fuel capacity 1,018 litres (224 Imp gallons) plus 20 litres (4·4 Imp gallons) unusable in flexible bag tanks. Provision for internal auxiliary tanks for ferry purposes. An additional fuel capacity of 335 litres (73·7 Imp gallons) is provided by two optional integral tanks, one in each wingtip. Gravity refuelling via overwing point above each pair of tanks. Oil capacity 8·5 litres (1·9 Imp gallons) per engine.

Accommodation: Crew of two on flight deck, but certificated for single-pilot operation in countries where this applies. Access to flight deck by forward opening door on each side or directly from cabin. Main cabin has individual seats for up to 12 passengers at 74 cm (29 in) pitch, with continuous seat tracks and readily removable seats which allow rapid rearrangement of the cabin to suit all-cargo or other alternative loads. Access to main cabin via double doors on port side, with single emergency exit on starboard side. Baggage compartments in nose (with door on each side) and optionally in rear of fuselage (with internal and external access). Whole interior, including flight deck, is heated and ventilated.

N22B short-fuselage version of the GAF Nomad, now available also in an N22C version with higher max T-O weight

Dimensions, external:
- Wing span — 16·46 m (54 ft 0 in)
- Length overall — 12·57 m (41 ft 3 in)
- Height overall — 5·53 m (18 ft 1¾ in)
- Wheel track — 2·90 m (9 ft 6 in)
- Wheelbase — 3·73 m (12 ft 3 in)
- Propeller diameter — 2·29 m (7 ft 6 in)

Dimensions, internal: See 1984-85 *Jane's*

Area:
- Wings, gross — 30·10 m² (324·0 sq ft)

Weights and Loadings (landplane):
- Manufacturer's basic weight empty — 2,092 kg (4,613 lb)
- Operating weight empty — 2,228 kg (4,911 lb)
- Max fuel load (usable): standard — 803 kg (1,770 lb)
- extended range — 1,066 kg (2,350 lb)
- Max T-O weight — 4,060 kg (8,950 lb)
- Max zero-fuel weight — 3,742 kg (8,250 lb)
- Max landing weight — 3,855 kg (8,500 lb)
- Max floor loadings:
  - main cabin — 732 kg/m² (150 lb/sq ft)
  - rear fuselage — 244 kg/m² (50 lb/sq ft)
- Max wing loading — 134·9 kg/m² (27·62 lb/sq ft)
- Max power loading — 6·49 kg/kW (10·65 lb/shp)

Performance (landplane, at max T-O weight, ISA, except where indicated):
- Max cruising speed, AUW of 3,855 kg (8,500 lb):
  - at S/L — 164 knots (304 km/h; 189 mph)
  - at 1,525 m (5,000 ft) — 172 knots (319 km/h; 198 mph)
  - at 3,050 m (10,000 ft) — 176 knots (326 km/h; 203 mph)
- Stalling speed, power off:
  - flaps up — 73 knots (136 km/h; 84 mph) IAS
  - flaps down — 53 knots (99 km/h; 61 mph) IAS
- Max rate of climb at S/L — 424 m (1,390 ft)/min
- En-route rate of climb, one engine out, max continuous power — 52 m (171 ft)/min
- Service ceiling, max cruise rating, 30·5 m (100 ft)/min rate of climb, at AUW of 3,855 kg (8,500 lb) — 7,620 m (25,000 ft)
- Service ceiling, one engine out, max continuous power, conditions as above — 2,010 m (6,600 ft)
- T-O to 15 m (50 ft) at S/L, Normal category — 403 m (1,322 ft)
- Landing from 15 m (50 ft) at S/L, Normal category, at max landing weight — 384 m (1,259 ft)
- Range at 3,050 m (10,000 ft) with max standard fuel, 45 min reserves — 790 nm (1,464 km; 910 miles)

GAF Nomad Searchmaster L, with undernose radome, of Northern Airlines, Australia

HDH

HAWKER DE HAVILLAND LTD (Member company of Hawker Siddeley Group)

PO Box 30, 361 Milperra Road, Bankstown, NSW 2200
Telephone: (02) 772 8111
Telex: AA20719

DIRECTORS:
- B. S. Price (Chairman)
- J. B. Hattersley (Managing)
- J. C. Cross (Finance)
- A. Carolan (Director-General Manager HDH—Melbourne)
- K. E. Odbert (Director-General Manager HDH—Sydney, Perth, Salisbury)
- S. S. Schaetzel (Technical)
- P. A. Smith (Commercial)

Hawker de Havilland is primarily an aerospace and defence company engaged in manufacturing, maintenance and overhaul activities for defence forces, airlines and general aviation operators in Australia and overseas. Its manufacturing activities include a wide range of international subcontracts, current customers including Aérospatiale, Boeing, British Aerospace, General Electric, Lockheed, McDonnell Douglas, Northrop and Pratt & Whitney.

Hawker de Havilland's main activity continues to be the provision of overhaul, modification and repair services to the Australian defence forces, and to a wide variety of other Australian and regional customers in some 25 nations. At Salisbury, South Australia, the emphasis is on research, development and initial production associated with airborne systems. At Perth, HDH is the only defence aircraft facility in Western Australia providing support for military and civil fixed- and rotating-wing airframes, systems, and light piston engines.

Under subcontract to Sikorsky Aircraft (USA), HDH will be responsible for final assembly of seven of the eight S-70B-2 RAWS (role adaptable weapon system) Seahawk helicopters ordered in 1984 for the Royal Australian Navy. Deliveries are due to begin in late 1987 or early 1988.

During 1985 HDH acquired Commonwealth Aircraft Corporation Limited (see page 8). Australian Aircraft Consortium Pty Limited, formerly responsible for the A10 trainer project, also became a wholly owned subsidiary of HDH in 1985.

In December 1985 HDH was nominated as prime contractor for Australian licence production of the Pilatus PC-9 trainer (see Swiss section). First deliveries are due in the second half of 1987.

TRAINER AIRCRAFT DIVISION

DIRECTOR/GENERAL MANAGER: S. S. Schaetzel

Australian Aircraft Consortium Pty Ltd (AAC: see 1985-86 *Jane's*) was formed in 1982 by Commonwealth Aircraft Corporation, Government Aircraft Factories, and Hawker de Havilland Australia to design, develop and produce a new turboprop powered military basic training aircraft, the A10 Wamira, as a potential replacement for the CT4A Airtrainer in RAAF service and for export. In Summer 1985 HDH bought out the GAF share and acquired CAC as a subsidiary, giving it overall control of the programme. AAC then became the Trainer Aircraft Division of HDH. At the same time the competition for the production contract had widened to include two overseas trainers, the EMBRAER/Shorts Tucano and the Pilatus PC-9. On 17 December 1985 the Australian government announced a decision in favour of the PC-9, and HDH was appointed prime contractor for that programme.

The A10B prototype undergoing completion of major assembly in December 1985

HDH A10B

Design of the original A10 was started in June 1982. As a result of a government review of the A10 project, HDH was invited to submit a revised development and production proposal for a more cost-effective version, retaining the essential military standards fundamental to the original A10 design. Definition of this version, known as the A10B, was initiated in May 1985, and assembly of the prototype's major structure was completed in early December 1985. While the December 1985 decision went against the A10B, HDH has been given the rights to the entire A10B programme, and intends to complete development of the aircraft up to the first flight stage. This was expected to occur towards the end of 1986.

TYPE: Two-seat basic trainer.

AIRFRAME: Makes extensive use of corrosion resistant materials, corrosion-proofing and weatherproofing, and is designed to damage-tolerant criteria for long service life with high reliability and ease of maintenance.

WINGS: Cantilever low-wing monoplane. Dihedral from roots. Taper on leading- and trailing-edges. Conventional metal semi-monocoque structure with two spars, ribs and stringer reinforced skins of 2024 Alclad aluminium alloy. Some fairings of GRP. Aluminium alloy trailing-edge flaps (actuated electrically) and mass balanced ailerons (actuated mechanically via pushrods). Balance tab in each aileron; electrically actuated trim tab in port aileron.

FUSELAGE: All-metal non-pressurised semi-monocoque structure with integral fin, stringers, fully machined frames at major load points, and aluminium alloy skins. Some fairings of GRP.

TAIL UNIT: Conventional cantilever all-metal structure, with non-swept surfaces. Integral fin, with dorsal fin; single-spar mass balanced rudder, actuated mechanically via pushrods. Tailplane of similar construction to wings; balanced elevators, attached to tailplane spar and actuated via pushrods. Electrically actuated combined balance/trim tab in rudder. Electrically actuated trim tab in port elevator, balance tab in each elevator.

LANDING GEAR: Retractable tricycle type, with inward retracting single mainwheels and rearward retracting steerable nosewheel. No mainwheel doors. Electro-mechanical actuation, with manual emergency extension. Oleo-pneumatic shock absorber in each unit. All wheels and six-ply tyres by Dunlop Australia, size 7·00-8 (main) and 5·00-5 (nose); tyre pressure 2·9 bars (42 lb/sq in) on all units. Dunlop Australia hydraulic disc brakes on mainwheels; parking brake. Gear suitable for operation from grass or semi-prepared strips.

POWER PLANT: One 559 kW (750 shp) Pratt & Whitney Canada PT6A-25D turboprop engine, flat rated at 455 kW (610 shp) and driving a three-blade Hartzell HC-B3TN-T10173-11R constant-speed fully-feathering reversible-pitch propeller with spinner. Single fuel tank in lower centre fuselage (usable capacity 580 litres; 127·6 Imp gallons), with capability for approx 45 s inverted flight. Single refuelling point on starboard side of fuselage. Oil capacity 16·7 litres (3·7 Imp gallons). Intake lip electrically heated.

ACCOMMODATION: Side by side crashworthy seats for instructor (on right) and pupil, under rearward sliding acrylic canopy. Provision for third seat behind these two. Cockpit equipped with IFR instrumentation and hood, and air-conditioned; engine bleed air provides fresh air, heating and demisting/de-icing for windscreen. Space for baggage in rear of fuselage, with external access.

SYSTEMS: AiResearch 2202200-3 large capacity air-conditioner for 'hot field' operations. Hydraulic system for mainwheel brakes only. No pneumatic system. 28V DC electrical system, incorporating a 28V 200A starter/generator and 22Ah nickel-cadmium battery, with two 125VA static inverters for AC supply. Ground power receptacle in fuselage aft of port wing. Diluter/demand oxygen system for both crew members.

AVIONICS AND EQUIPMENT: Basic flight and navigation equipment standard. Additional nav/com equipment to customer's requirements.

ARMAMENT: Four 'dry' underwing hardpoints, stressed for loads of up to 250 kg (551 lb) each inboard and 150 kg (330 lb) each outboard.

DIMENSIONS, EXTERNAL:

Wing span	11·00 m (36 ft 1 in)
Wing chord: at root	3·03 m (9 ft 11¼ in)
at tip	1·21 m (3 ft 11½ in)
Wing aspect ratio	6·05
Length overall	10·20 m (33 ft 5½ in)
Height overall	3·51 m (11 ft 6¼ in)

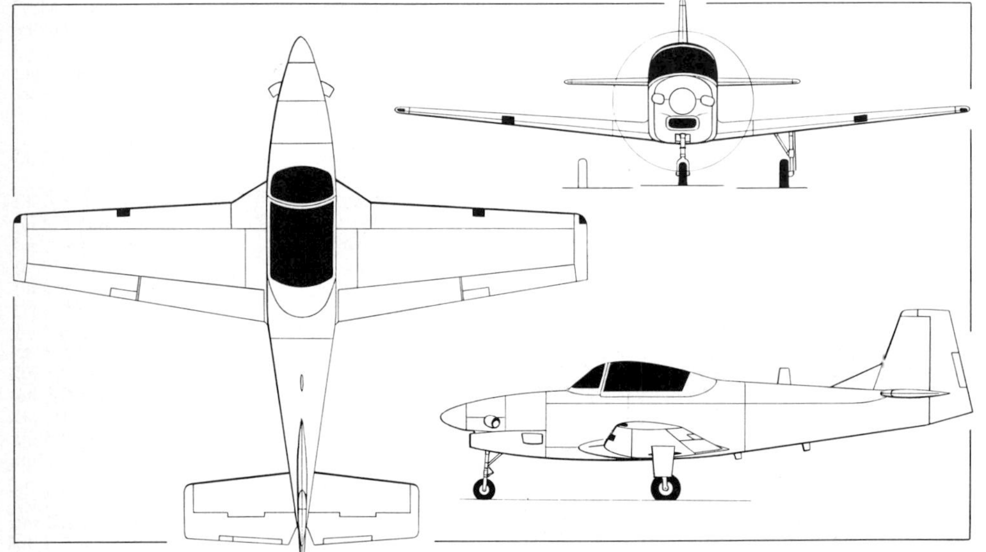

General configuration of the HDH A10B basic trainer *(Pilot Press)*

Elevator span 4·50 m (14 ft 9¼ in)
Wheel track 4·00 m (13 ft 1½ in)
Wheelbase 3·10 m (10 ft 2 in)
Propeller diameter 2·29 m (7 ft 6 in)

AREAS:
Wings, gross reference 20·00 m² (215·3 sq ft)
Vertical tail surfaces (total) 3·43 m² (36·9 sq ft)
Horizontal tail surfaces (total) 5·40 m² (58·1 sq ft)

WEIGHTS AND LOADINGS (Aerobatic category):
Weight empty, equipped 1,580 kg (3,483 lb)
Max T-O weight 2,154 kg (4,749 lb)
Max ramp weight 2,164 kg (4,770 lb)
Max wing loading 107·7 kg/m² (22·06 lb/sq ft)
Max power loading 4·73 kg/kW (7·79 lb/shp)

PERFORMANCE (estimated, at max T-O weight except where indicated):
Never-exceed speed
Mach 0·575 (320 knots; 593 km/h; 368 mph) EAS
Max level speed:
at 4,575 m (15,000 ft)
213 knots (395 km/h; 245 mph)
at S/L 192 knots (356 km/h; 221 mph)
Econ cruising speed:
at 4,575 m (15,000 ft)
156 knots (289 km/h; 180 mph)
at S/L 140 knots (259 km/h; 161 mph)
Stalling speed:
flaps and landing gear up
69 knots (128 km/h; 80 mph) CAS
flaps and landing gear down
58 knots (108 km/h; 67 mph) CAS
Max rate of climb at S/L 640 m (2,100 ft)/min
Time to 3,050 m (10,000 ft) 5 min 18 s
Service ceiling 9,600 m (31,500 ft)
T-O run 284 m (932 ft)
T-O to 15 m (50 ft) 405 m (1,329 ft)
Landing from 15 m (50 ft) 449 m (1,473 ft)
Landing run 243 m (797 ft)
Endurance at 3,050 m (10,000 ft), 50 min reserves 3 h

HAWKER DE HAVILLAND VICTORIA LTD
(Subsidiary of Hawker de Havilland Ltd)

304 Lorimer Street, Port Melbourne, Victoria 3207
POSTAL ADDRESS: Box 779H, GPO Melbourne, Victoria 3001
Telephone: (03) 647 6111
Telex: AA 30721
DIRECTOR/GENERAL MANAGER: A. Carolan
MANAGERS:
D. W. Burton (Aircraft Division)
B. W. Kennedy (Finance and Administration)
J. A. C. Kentwell (Chief Engineer)
D. Osborne (Gas Turbine Division)
D. R. Rees (Market Development)
G. R. Shields (Personnel and Industrial Relations)
D. J. Simmons (Corporate Quality)
I. J. Taylor (Foundries)
PUBLIC AFFAIRS OFFICER: Carmen Rosler

As Commonwealth Aircraft Corporation, HDH Victoria was formed in 1936, and became a wholly owned subsidiary of Hawker de Havilland Ltd on 1 July 1985. The change to its present title took effect on 1 July 1986. HDH Victoria has produced more than 1,750 military aircraft, over 2,500 aero engines, and is a major supplier of equipment and services to the Australian Defence Forces.

The company holds Dept of Aviation approval for civil aviation activities, and maintains a capability for initial design and engineering support of manufacturing and overhaul activities. It employed about 1,750 people in 1986.

Major current programmes include manufacture of airframe components for the McDonnell Douglas F/A-18 Hornet (engine access doors, rear fairings and wing pylons); assembly and testing of the General Electric F404 engine and manufacture of a range of components; life-of-type extension for RAAF Aermacchi MB-326H jet trainers; repair and overhaul, including life-of-type extension of RAAF Mirage major airframe components; repair and overhaul of RAAF Atar 9C and Viper engines; design and manufacture of in-flight catering equipment for Australian airlines; manufacture of escape slides for the McDonnell Douglas DC-10, components for General Electric CF6 engines, and Sikorsky S-70 gearboxes; and design of maintenance trainers for Sikorsky MH-53E helicopters.

An additional programme is the design and installation of the AQS-901 sonics processor into Lockheed P-3 Orions of the RAAF, to counter the threat of faster and quieter nuclear submarines. The AQS-901 can process and present information from a variety of sonobuoys, especially the Barra. The system uses a 920 ATC digital computer and is software controlled, interfacing with an ASQ-114(V) central tactical computer, AN/AQH-4(V)2 recorder/reproducer and AIC-22(V) aircraft intercom system. Other systems added as part of the integration include the Harpoon missile and infra-red detection system cassette recording equipment.

In collaboration with British Aerospace Australia, HDH Victoria has also developed an aircraft fatigue monitoring system known as AFDAS (aircraft fatigue data analysis system), which is currently installed on Mirage III, MB-326H, F/A-18 and F-111 aircraft of the RAAF.

TRANSAVIA
TRANSAVIA DIVISION, TRANSFIELD (NSW) PTY LTD

73 Station Road, Seven Hills, NSW 2147
Telephone: 624 4244
Telex: AA70300 TRANSAC
CHAIRMAN: F. Belgiorno-Nettis, CBE
DIRECTOR: C. Salteri
GENERAL MANAGER: John Corby
SALES MANAGER: Neil McDonald

Transavia, formed in 1964, is a division of Transfield (NSW) Pty Ltd, one of Australia's largest construction companies.

TRANSAVIA PL-12 AIRTRUK/SKYFARMER

The **Airtruk**, designed by Mr Luigi Pellarini, was originally type certificated on 10 February 1966 for spreading dry fertiliser and for seed sowing. Its unusual sesquiplane design gives it a number of significant advantages in agricultural efficiency, manoeuvrability, corrosion resistance and safety. It has exceptional load lifting capacity, and can distribute chemicals over an exceptionally wide swath — up to 32 m (35 yd) — with excellent evenness. Loading is rapid, and risk of damage is minimised, because the loading vehicle approaches the aircraft between the wide-apart twin tails.

A liquid spraying conversion with a capacity of 900 litres (198 Imp gallons), developed in 1968, is capable of covering a 27·5 m (30 yd) spray swath. This version has an engine driven spraypump enclosed in the engine bay so that the pump operates at constant speed in flight without danger of overspeeding and without the need for a brake. The spray system can be operated on the ground for testing and flushing. Spraybooms are attached by quick-clip fasteners.

The prototype flew for the first time on 22 April 1965. Deliveries of production Airtruks began in December 1966, and by early 1986 about 120 (including ten assembled by Flight Engineers Ltd in New Zealand) had been sold for use in Australia, New Zealand, Denmark, Malaysia, South Africa, Taiwan, Thailand and Yugoslavia. Five modified Skyfarmers were provided to China by the Australian government in 1986 to set up an aerial agricultural and training unit in that country during 1986-88.

A general purpose utility version, the **PL-12-U**, developed for passenger/cargo/aerial survey/cropspraying, flew for the first time in December 1970, and received certification in February 1971.

In July 1978 the prototype **Skyfarmer T-300** made its first flight. This differs chiefly in having an Avco Lycoming IO-540 engine, and was followed in 1981 by an improved **Skyfarmer T-300A**. Significant changes in this model include a larger upper-fuselage structure (providing a roomier cockpit and larger hopper throat), and the fitting of new aerodynamically balanced ailerons, horn balanced elevators and electromechanical flaps to reduce pilot workload.

No news of the proposed military **PL-12 MIL** or turboprop **PL-12 550T** (see 1985-86 *Jane's*) has been received for several years. The following description applies to the PL-12, PL-12-U and Skyfarmer, except where a particular version is indicated:

TYPE: Single-engined agricultural (PL-12/Skyfarmer) or multi-purpose (PL-12-U) aircraft.

WINGS: Strut braced sesquiplane. Wing section NACA 23012. Dihedral 1° 30′ on upper wings. Incidence (upper wings) 3° 30′, stub-wings 4°. Conventional all-metal structure, covered with Alclad sheet. All-metal trailing-edge flaps and ailerons, covered with ribbed Alclad sheet, and operated manually. Upper-wing fence on each side of each tailboom to ensure full aileron control, even below stalling speeds. Small stub-wings at base of fuselage, constructed on a 4130 steel leading-edge D box section welded to the integral hopper frame and braced to the upper wings by a V strut on each side.

FUSELAGE: Pod shaped structure comprising 4130 welded steel frame with stainless steel and 2024 Alclad covering. Skyfarmer hopper is integrally structured. Entire one-piece rear cabin is of glassfibre to eliminate corrosion and withstand hard wear and tear.

TAIL UNIT: Twin units, each comprising a fin, rudder and separate T tailplane with elevator, and each carried on a cantilever tapered tubular Alclad boom extending from the upper wings.

LANDING GEAR: Non-retractable tricycle type. Mainwheels carried on pivoted trailing legs supported by Transavia short stroke, heavy duty oleo-pneumatic shock absorbing suspension units. Port and starboard main units are interchangeable. Nosewheel carried on a heavy duty, long stroke straight oleo-suspension unit. All wheels and tyres same size (8·00-6); tyre pressure 1·72 bars (25 lb/sq in) (nose); 2·07 bars (30 lb/sq in) (main). Cleveland disc brakes with parking lock.

POWER PLANT: One 224 kW (300 hp) Continental IO-520-D flat-six engine, driving a McCauley D2A34C58/90AT-2 two-blade constant-speed metal propeller with spinner (300 hp Avco Lycoming IO-540-K1A5 engine and smaller diameter Hartzell three-blade constant-speed propeller in Skyfarmer). Two upper-wing fuel tanks, total capacity 189 litres (41·5 Imp gallons). Optional long range installation of second tank in each upper mainplane, increasing total capacity to 379 litres (83·4 Imp gallons). Refuelling point above upper wings. Oil capacity 11·4 litres (2·5 Imp gallons).

ACCOMMODATION (PL-12/Skyfarmer): Single-seat cockpit, with door on starboard side. Two-seat cabin aft of chemical hopper/tank for carriage of ground crew, with door at rear of lower deck. Accommodation heated and ventilated.

ACCOMMODATION (PL-12-U): Single-seat cockpit as in PL12/Skyfarmer. Large passenger cabin instead of hopper. One passenger on upper deck (back to back with pilot's seat) and four more passengers on lower deck. Doors on upper deck (starboard side) and lower deck (port side).

SYSTEM: 24V electrical system standard, 12V optional.

AVIONICS AND EQUIPMENT: Optional VHF, HF, ADF, artificial horizon and directional gyro. Standard 907 kg (2,000 lb) capacity hopper aft of cockpit. Optional Powermist spray system, Transavia safety take-off weight (STOW) checking system, wire cutter, seed spreader attachment, and cockpit heater.

DIMENSIONS, EXTERNAL:
Upper wing span 11·98 m (39 ft 3½ in)
Upper wing chord:
constant portion 1·76 m (5 ft 9¼ in)
at tip 1·27 m (4 ft 2 in)
Stub-wing span 4·93 m (16 ft 2 in)
Length overall 6·35 m (20 ft 10 in)
Length of fuselage 4·19 m (13 ft 9 in)
Height overall 2·79 m (9 ft 2 in)
Fuselage: Max width 0·97 m (3 ft 2 in)
Tailplane span (each) 2·13 m (7 ft 0 in)
Distance between tailplanes 3·43 m (11 ft 5 in)
Wheel track 2·44 m (8 ft 0 in)
Wheelbase 1·64 m (5 ft 4½ in)
Propeller diameter: PL-12/12-U 2·23 m (7 ft 4 in)
Skyfarmer 2·13 m (7 ft 0 in)
Min propeller ground clearance:
PL-12/12-U 0·30 m (1 ft 0 in)
Skyfarmer 0·36 m (1 ft 2 in)
Passenger door: Height 0·97 m (3 ft 2 in)
Passenger door (PL-12-U, stbd upper):
Height 0·91 m (3 ft 0 in)

Transavia Skyfarmer T-300 agricultural aircraft (Avco Lycoming IO-540 engine)

DIMENSIONS, INTERNAL (PL-12):
- Rear passenger cabin: Length – 1·83 m (6 ft 0 in)
  - Max width – 0·97 m (3 ft 2 in)
  - Max height – 2·03 m (6 ft 8 in)
  - Floor area – 0·37 m² (4 sq ft)
  - Volume: Passenger cabin – 0·85 m³ (30 cu ft)
    - Chemical hopper – 1·02 m³ (36 cu ft)

DIMENSIONS, INTERNAL (PL-12-U):
- Passenger cabin: Length – 2·59 m (8 ft 6 in)
  - Max width – 0·97 m (3 ft 2 in)
  - Max height – 2·08 m (6 ft 10 in)
  - Floor area – 1·50 m² (16·2 sq ft)
  - Volume – 2·15 m³ (76 cu ft)

AREAS:
- Wings, gross – 24·53 m² (264·0 sq ft)
- Ailerons, total – 1·67 m² (18·0 sq ft)
- Trailing-edge flaps, total – 1·67 m² (18·0 sq ft)
- Fins, total – 1·30 m² (14·0 sq ft)
- Rudders, total – 0·56 m² (6·0 sq ft)
- Tailplanes, total – 2·60 m² (28·0 sq ft)
- Elevators, total, incl tabs – 1·30 m² (14·0 sq ft)

WEIGHTS AND LOADINGS:
- Typical weight empty – 1,017 kg (2,242 lb)
- Max T-O weight (agricultural category) – 1,925 kg (4,244 lb)
- Max landing weight – 1,723 kg (3,800 lb)
- Max wing loading – 78·5 kg/m² (16·1 lb/sq ft)
- Max power loading – 8·6 kg/kW (14·15 lb/hp)

PERFORMANCE (at max T-O weight, ISA at S/L, except where indicated):
- Never-exceed speed – 148 knots (274 km/h; 170 mph)
- Max level speed at 915 m (3,000 ft) – 106 knots (196 km/h; 122 mph)
- Max cruising speed (75% power) – 102 knots (188 km/h; 117 mph)
- Stalling speed, power on:
  - flaps up – 47 knots (88 km/h; 55 mph)
  - flaps down – 39 knots (73 km/h; 45 mph)
- Max rate of climb at S/L – 156 m (514 ft)/min
- *Max light-weight rate of climb – 457 m (1,500 ft)/min
- Service ceiling – 3,810 m (12,500 ft)
- *Light-weight service ceiling – 6,890 m (22,600 ft)
- T-O run – 329 m (1,080 ft)
- *Light-weight T-O run – 77 m (252 ft)
- *Light-weight landing run – 82 m (270 ft)

**Weight of empty aircraft plus pilot and 50 per cent standard fuel*

VTOL

VTOL AIRCRAFT PTY LTD

123 Marshall Street, Kotara Heights, NSW 2288
Telephone: (049) 43 5348
CHAIRMAN: Duan A. Phillips

VTOL PHILLICOPTER Mk 1

Design of the Phillicopter, by Mr D. A. Phillips and Mr P. Gerakiteys, began in 1962, and the prototype made its first flight in 1971. The original O-200-C engine was later replaced by a Rolls-Royce Continental O-300 of the same power, as recorded when the aircraft was last described in the 1977-78 edition of *Jane's*.

The Phillicopter was granted Australian type certification in mid-1984, and was exhibited in model form at the 1985 Paris Air Show with the news that Australian production was imminent and foreign licence manufacture was available. Construction of a pre-production Phillicopter began on 10 January 1986, and by February six Mk 1s were on order.

TYPE: Two-seat light helicopter.

ROTOR SYSTEM: Two-blade underslung 'see-saw' main rotor and two-blade tail rotor. Main rotor blades, of NACA 0012 section, are all-metal aluminium alloy units, of untapered planform with no twist, and are bolted to hub. Fixed tab near tip of each blade. Tail rotor blades of similar construction. Main blades do not fold. Main rotor brake optional.

ROTOR DRIVE: Via steel gears in aluminium alloy boxes. Primary gearbox is right angled from engine to drive main rotor via secondary reduction gearbox. Integrated tail rotor gear drive to tail rotor gearbox. Main rotor/engine rpm ratio 1:5·67; tail rotor/engine rpm ratio 1:1.

FUSELAGE: Tubular steel skeletal frame, unclad at rear. Forward portion aluminium clad, with large Perspex 'goldfish bowl' canopy.

TAIL UNIT: Steel tube tail rotor guard, with small triangular underfin. Tailplane incidence ground-adjustable by jack-screws.

LANDING GEAR: Tubular skid type, incorporating ground handling wheels. Elastomeric and torsion leg shock absorption.

POWER PLANT: One 108 kW (145 hp) Continental O-300 flat-four engine in prototype; to be upgraded, probably to 112 kW (150 hp) Avco Lycoming O-320, in production version. Two fuel tanks, total capacity 91 litres (20 Imp gallons), are standard; optional 91 litre (20 Imp gallon) tank available for extended range. Refuelling point in each tank. Oil capacity 5·7 litres (1·25 Imp gallons).

ACCOMMODATION: Side by side seats for pilot and one student/passenger. Door on each side of cabin. Baggage space at base of rotor mast. Cabin ventilated; heating optional.

SYSTEM: 12V battery for engine starting, navigation lights and radio.

AVIONICS AND EQUIPMENT: Radio to customer's requirements. Cargo hook optional.

DIMENSIONS, EXTERNAL:
- Main rotor diameter – 7·77 m (25 ft 6 in)
- Main rotor blade chord – 0·203 m (8 in)
- Tail rotor diameter – 1·22 m (4 ft 0 in)
- Distance between rotor centres – 4·57 m (15 ft 0 in)
- Length overall:
  - both rotors turning – 9·35 m (30 ft 8 in)
  - excluding rotors – 7·01 m (23 ft 0 in)
- Height overall – 2·69 m (8 ft 9 in)
- Height to top of rotor head – 2·59 m (8 ft 6 in)
- Width overall, excluding main rotor – 1·83 m (6 ft 0 in)
- Skid track – 1·83 m (6 ft 0 in)
- Crew/passenger doors (each):
  - Height – 0·76 m (2 ft 6 in)
  - Width – 0·61 m (2 ft 0 in)
  - Height to sill – 0·51 m (1 ft 8 in)

DIMENSIONS, INTERNAL:
- Cabin: Length – 1·22 m (4 ft 0 in)
  - Max width – 1·22 m (4 ft 0 in)
  - Max height – 1·07 m (3 ft 6 in)
  - Floor area – 1·49 m² (16·0 sq ft)
  - Volume – 1·59 m³ (56·0 cu ft)

AREAS:
- Main rotor blades, each – 0·74 m² (8·00 sq ft)
- Tail rotor blades, each – 0·124 m² (1·33 sq ft)
- Main rotor disc – 47·45 m² (510·7 sq ft)
- Tail rotor disc – 1·17 m² (12·57 sq ft)
- Fin – 0·25 m² (2·7 sq ft)
- Tailplane – 0·25 m² (2·7 sq ft)

WEIGHTS:
- Max payload – 217 kg (480 lb)
- Max fuel weight – 64 kg (140 lb)
- Max T-O and landing weight – 703 kg (1,550 lb)

*PERFORMANCE (at max T-O weight):
- Max level speed at S/L – 100 knots (185 km/h; 115 mph)
- Max cruising speed at S/L – 90 knots (167 km/h; 104 mph)
- Econ cruising speed at S/L – 75 knots (139 km/h; 86 mph)
- Max rate of climb at S/L – 366 m (1,200 ft)/min
- Vertical rate of climb at S/L – 122 m (400 ft)/min
- Service ceiling – 4,880 m (16,000 ft)
- Hovering ceiling: IGE – 2,440 m (8,000 ft)
  - OGE – 1,830 m (6,000 ft)
- Range with max fuel – 400 nm (741 km; 460 miles)

**Prototype with 145 hp engine*

Prototype of the VTOL (Phillips) Phillicopter two-seat helicopter

VTOL LIFT ACTIVATOR DISC

VTOL Aircraft has published details of a 'flying saucer' design concept known as the Lift Activator Disc or LAD, able to take off and land vertically. It consists of a revolving disc, spun by a centrally mounted (non-rotating) engine while air drawn in beneath the disc by a blower is expelled at high pressure across the disc's upper surface to generate lift. Centrifugal force created by the spinning motion accelerates the air, increasing the speed of the flow. A separate steerable tail jet gives forward thrust to control direction of movement, serving the same function as the tail rotor on a helicopter, to stabilise the aircraft and keep the central module from turning with the disc.

Crew and passengers are housed in a stationary, circular 'bubble' cabin above the disc, and the entire structure is supported through a bearing on a fixed tripod landing gear. It is claimed that the LAD would be virtually crashproof, since in the event of engine failure it would have the neutral stability of a gyroscope, the flywheel action of the 'coasting' disc continuing to provide sufficient lift for a safe glide back to earth.

The concept is claimed to offer all the advantages of VTOL without the noise and speed limitations of a helicopter, including significantly greater lift per horsepower and forward speed possibly exceeding 400 knots (741 km/h; 460 mph). Radar signature is described as insignificant. Computer calculations, and rudimentary tests with a model of the LAD, have been sufficiently encouraging to proceed to manufacture of a two-seat prototype, which is planned to start in 1988. This will be constructed from composites materials and will probably be powered by a small gas turbine engine. The accompanying diagram illustrates the general principles of the LAD; the prototype is expected to have sprung undercarriage legs, ground handling wheels and added appendages for control. The disc will be 3·05 m (10 ft) in diameter and rotate at 1,000 rpm.

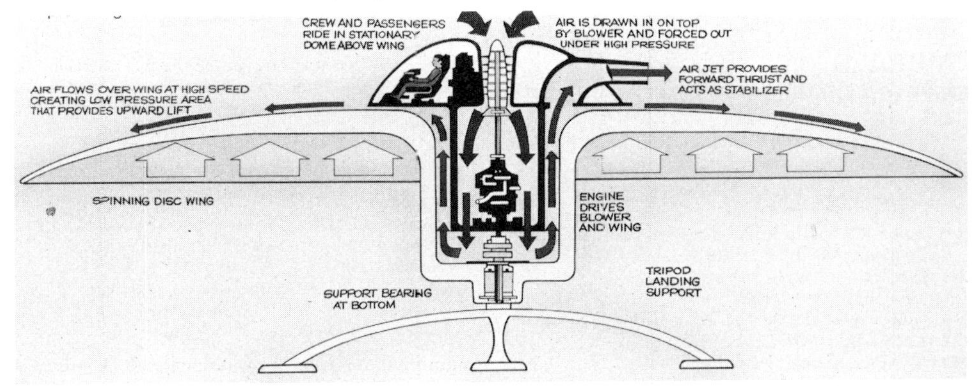

Diagram showing general principles of the VTOL Lift Activator Disc

BELGIUM

PROMAVIA

PROMAVIA SA

Chaussée de Fleurus 181, B-6200 Gosselies-Aéroport
Telephone: (071) 35 08 29
Telex: 51872 SQUAL
President: André L. Delhamende

Promavia SA was formed by a number of industrialists, investment companies and a bank, with offices and facilities near Charleroi Airport. Results of a market survey completed in 1983 confirmed the company's belief that a requirement existed for an 'all-through' jet trainer, built to a specification similar to that which led to the recent US Air Force new generation trainer (NGT). Promavia therefore initiated the Jet Squalus programme, commissioning Dott Ing Stelio Frati of General Avia (see Italian section) to undertake the aircraft's design and prototype construction. Substantial financial backing was obtained from the Belgian government in 1985 to contribute towards prototype research and development.

A description and illustration of the Italian built prototype is given under the General Avia entry in that section. Production, marketing and support of the aircraft, including training programmes, will be undertaken by Promavia, with Sonaca (which see) as major subcontractor. Promavia believes there may be some USAF participation in the flight and static test programmes, and in April 1986 announced an agreement to team with Rockwell International Corporation to submit the Jet Squalus as a possible USAF alternative to the Fairchild T-46A new generation trainer. Under the terms of this agreement, Rockwell would build any examples sold in the USA.

Italian built prototype of the Promavia Jet Squalus new generation trainer *(J. M. G. Gradidge)*

SABCA

SOCIÉTÉ ANONYME BELGE DE CONSTRUCTIONS AÉRONAUTIQUES

Chaussée de Haecht 1470, B-1130 Brussels
Telephone: Brussels (02) 216 80 10
Telex: SABUSH B 21 237
Telefax: (02) 2161570
Chairman of the Board: J. Groothaert
Director/General Manager: P. G. Willekens
Works:
Haren-Brussels: Chaussée de Haecht 1470, B-1130 Brussels
Telephone: Brussels (02) 216 80 10
Telex: SABUSH B 21 237
Gosselies: Aéroport de Gosselies-Charleroi, B-6200 Gosselies
Telephone: Charleroi (071) 35 01 70
Telex: SABGO B 51 251

Founded in 1920, SABCA is the major aerospace company in Belgium. Before the second World War, it produced more than 600 military and civil aircraft of 19 different types, some of its own design and some manufactured under licence. Since the war, SABCA has participated in various European aircraft programmes.

SABCA's current activities are carried out at two manufacturing plants: Haren-Brussels, where 70 per cent of its activities are concentrated, and Gosselies Airport.

At Haren, the company's main effort is directed towards production of aerospace structures and hydraulic systems. In these areas SABCA is manufacturing main frame structures such as wings and nose sections, and other structural components and equipment, for the General Dynamics F-16; Dassault-Breguet/Dornier Alpha Jet; Dassault Mirage F1, Mirage III and Mirage 5; Dassault-Breguet Atlantic 1/Atlantique 2; Airbus A310; Fokker F27 and F28; Aérospatiale SA 330 Puma; Spacelab; and Ariane launchers. Servo controls are produced for the F-16 and the Ariane launchers.

At Gosselies, SABCA is assembling and testing General Dynamics F-16s for Belgium. Deliveries have been made regularly and on schedule since January 1979, and SABCA is now also incorporating modifications to Belgian Air Force and USAFE F-16s. In late 1985 the company was appointed a cruise missile European repair facility.

SABCA's Electronic Division has developed and is producing a laser tank fire control system for the Belgian, Canadian, Australian and other armed forces. More recently, it has designed and developed a universal tank fire control system based on a modular device and adaptable to existing main battle tanks. This division is also manufacturing IFF components and various types of aircraft electronic ground equipment, as well as maintaining existing Doppler equipment.

For many years SABCA has been responsible for the maintenance and overhaul of Belgian and other armed forces' military aircraft, their electronic components and accessories, as well as commercial fixed-wing aircraft and helicopters. It is currently integrating ECM devices in Belgian aircraft.

SABCA is a member of various European industrial consortia; Dassault-Breguet and Fokker have parity holdings in the company.

The company's works occupy a total area of approx 82,000 m² (882,640 sq ft) and in early 1986 employed an average of 1,500 people.

SONACA

SOCIÉTÉ NATIONALE DE CONSTRUCTION AÉROSPATIALE SA

Parc Industriel, Route Nationale Cinq, B-6200 Gosselies

Telephone: Charleroi (071) 34 22 11
Telex: 51241
Telefax: (071) 34 40 35

General Manager: J. Storrer

Directors:
J. Lodewijckx (Finance and Personnel)
P. Wacquez (Manufacturing)
E. Barthelemy (Marketing and Programmes)
J. Maître (Quality Assurance)
G. Krumpmann (Stress and Design)

SONACA SA, formerly Fairey SA (established in 1931), was incorporated on 1 May 1978. Its capital amounts to BF 260 million, of which 50% is held by public institutions and 50% by Belgian industry (FN Herstal 24·4%, SAIT Electronics 12·2%, ACEC 7·3%, SABCA 4·9% and Cartonex 1·2%).

Based at Gosselies Airport, SONACA participates in civil and military aviation manufacturing programmes, co-producing the General Dynamics F-16 combat aircraft (rear fuselage, vertical fin, dorsal fairing and final mating) and components (leading-edge moving surfaces) for the Airbus A310 and A320. It supplies parts for various aircraft, including Aérospatiale and Westland helicopters, the Dassault-Breguet Atlantique 2, Lockheed C-130, Boeing 747SP, Saab SF 340 and Dassault-Breguet/Dornier Alpha Jet. SONACA will be a major subcontractor to Promavia (which see) in the production phase of the Jet Squalus jet trainer (see General Avia entry in the Italian section). The company also designed and sells aircraft galley polycarbonate containers.

SONACA has recently reinforced its R & D capabilities, by increasing the personnel of its engineering office and investing in an IBM Cadam scientific data processing system. Workshops for composite materials and adhesive bonding are equipped with autoclaves, the largest of which has a working length of 10 m (33 ft) and a working diameter of 3 m (10 ft).

In early 1986 the company had a total covered space of 67,500 m² (726,565 sq ft) and a workforce of 1,350.

BRAZIL

EMBRAER

EMPRESA BRASILEIRA DE AERONÁUTICA SA

Av Brig Faria Lima 2170, Caixa Postal 343, 12225 São José dos Campos, SP
Telephone: (123) 25 1711
Telex: (391) 1133589 EBAE BR

Rio Office: Aeroporto Santos-Dumont, Sobreloja, Salão de Embarque No. 2, 20021 Rio de Janeiro, RJ
Telephone: (21) 262 6411
Chairman: Eng Ozires Silva
Chief Executive Officer: Eng Ozilio Carlos da Silva
Commercial Director: Heitor Fernandes Serra
Military Programmes Director: Luiz Thomaz Carrilho Teixeira-Gomes
Technical Director: Eng Guido Fontegalante Pessotti
Industrial Director: Eng Antonio Garcia da Silveira
Production Director: Irajá Buch Ribas
Administration Director: Nelson de Jesus Parada
Financial Director: Adalto Ferreira da Silva
Public Relations: Mário Leme Galvão
Press Relations: Antonio Augusto de Oliveira

US Subsidiary:
Embraer Aircraft Corporation, 276 Southwest 34th Street, PO Box 21623, Fort Lauderdale, Florida 33335
Telephone: (305) 524 5755 and 5744
Telex: (230) 522318 Embraer Fort Lauderdale
Managing Director: Newton Berwig

Paris Office:
Embraer Aviation International, BP 74, Aéroport du Bourget, Zone d'Aviation d'Affaires, 93350 Le Bourget, France
Telephone: (4) 835 9420
Telex: 213498F EBAE PAR
Managing Director: Michel Cury

EMBRAER was created on 19 August 1969, and came into operation on 2 January 1970 to promote the development of the Brazilian aircraft industry. In January 1986 it had an authorised capital of Cr $1,500 billion, of which Cr $227·6 billion had been subscribed by that month. The Brazilian government owns 54·41% of the voting shares, 94·79% of the subscribed capital being held by private shareholders. EMBRAER had a workforce in January 1986 of 7,702 persons and a factory area of 293,000 m² (3,153,825 sq ft). By the end of 1985 EMBRAER had built a total of 3,404 aircraft.

Since August 1974, EMBRAER has had a comprehensive co-operative agreement with Piper Aircraft Corporation involving the manufacture in Brazil of the Seneca and

EMBRAER EMB-110P1A Bandeirante of Air Spirit, showing the current dihedral tailplane

Navajo Chieftain twin-engined aircraft and (currently) three models of four- and six-passenger single-engined types. An agreement for supply of a further 156 Piper aircraft kits, for delivery by the end of 1987, was announced in July 1986. Production of the Piper-licensed Navajo Chieftain has ended. Since 1976, EMBRAER has manufactured components for the Northrop F-5E Tiger II combat aircraft. Under development is the EMB-123 commuter transport.

Agreements concluded in 1983-84 with Sikorsky Aircraft provide for development of EMBRAER's capability to manufacture aircraft components in composite materials, initially for the S-70C helicopter, the EMB-120 Brasilia and the AMX attack aircraft.

EMBRAER has in current production the EMB-110 Bandeirante, the EMB-111 maritime surveillance version of the Bandeirante, the EMB-120 Brasilia commuter transport, the pressurised EMB-121A1 Xingu II twin-turboprop transport aircraft, and the EMB-312 Tucano military trainer. The AMX tactical fighter is under development in partnership with Aeritalia and Aermacchi of Italy. Manufacture of the EMB-201A Ipanema agricultural aircraft, and various EMBRAER built versions of Piper single- and twin-engined light aircraft, is the responsibility of Neiva (which see), which became a subsidiary of EMBRAER in March 1980.

AMX

Details of this military aircraft programme, in which EMBRAER is participating with the Italian companies Aeritalia and Aermacchi, can be found in the International section. The first Brazilian built AMX (prototype A04) made its initial flight on 16 October 1985. The second (A06) was due to join the flight test programme in the fourth quarter of 1986.

EMBRAER EMB-110 BANDEIRANTE (PIONEER)

The Bandeirante twin-turboprop light transport was developed to a Brazilian Ministry of Aeronautics specification calling for a general purpose aircraft capable of carrying out transport, navigation training and aeromedical evacuation missions.

The first of three EMB-100 prototypes (described in the 1970-71 *Jane's*) made its initial flight on 26 October 1968, followed by the first production EMB-110 Bandeirante (C-95/2133) on 9 August 1972. Following Brazilian certification to FAR Pt 23, the first three Bandeirantes were delivered to the Brazilian Air Force on 9 February 1973.

Bandeirantes of various models have been sold to more than 80 operators in 32 countries worldwide. By the end of 1985 the worldwide fleet of Bandeirantes had logged more than 3·7 million flying hours; at that time EMBRAER had delivered 454 Bandeirantes, of which 236 were for export.

Models no longer in regular production include the following (seating capacity in parentheses): EMB-110 (8), EMB-110/C-95 (12), EMB-110A/EC-95 (6), EMB-110B/R-95 (5), EMB-110B1 (14), EMB-110C (15), EMB-110E(J) (7/8), EMB-110K1/C-95A (1,650 kg; 3,637 lb cargo), EMB-110P (18), EMB-110P1 and P1/41 (quick-change versions of P2), EMB-110P1K (as K1), EMB-110P2 (21) and P2/41, and EMB-110S1 (2). Details of these versions, which can still be produced to special order, can be found in the 1984-85 and previous editions of *Jane's*. Principal models in current production are as follows:

EMB-110P1A. Updated version of P1 with the following improvements: 10° tailplane dihedral, to reduce vibration and noise; mass balance relocated to centreline of elevator; mass balance on elevator tab; duplicated control rods to elevator; passenger seats attached to floor only; improved acoustic internal lining; improved emergency exit seals; improved main cabin door seal; new cabin carpet, with foam insulation; and front intake for venting system. First two P1As delivered in December 1983 to Provincetown-Boston Airlines, USA. P1A replaced earlier P1 as standard version from c/n 439 onwards; retrofits available for earlier P1s.

EMB-110P1K. Military utility, cargo and paradropping version of P1 (Brazilian Air Force designation **C-95B**). Thirty delivered by 31 December 1984.

EMB-110P1K SAR. Search and rescue version of P1K (Brazilian Air Force designation **SC-95B**), equipped for inland and overwater search, paradropping, and aeromedical evacuation. Max T-O weight 6,000 kg (13,230 lb). Accommodation for up to six stretchers plus seats for observers and space for inflatable dinghies and other rescue equipment. Two 'bubble' windows in each side of cabin. Independent oxygen system for medevac missions. Five ordered by Brazilian Air Force; operated by 2° Esquadrão of the 10° Grupo de Aviação at Campo Grande.

EMB-110P2A. Replaced former P2 (1984-85 *Jane's*) as third-level commuter transport version, carrying up to 21 passengers. Incorporates same changes as P1A. Detailed description applies mainly to this version.

EMB-110P1A/41 and EMB-110P2A/41. New versions of P1A and P2A, available from 1983, certificated under SFAR Pt 41 for a max T-O weight of 5,900 kg (13,010 lb). These versions replace former P1/41 and P2/41. Power plant and dimensions unchanged. Available also as retrofit to existing P1/41 and P2/41 versions.

EMB-111. Maritime surveillance version, described in 1985-86 and earlier *Jane's*. Supplied to air forces of Brazil (12) and Gabon (1), and Chilean Navy (6). Still available to order.

The following description, except where indicated, applies to the standard production EMB-110P2A:

TYPE: Twin-turboprop general purpose transport.

WINGS: Cantilever low-wing monoplane. Wing section NACA 23016 (modified) at root, NACA 23012 (modified) at tip. Sweepback 0° 19′ 48″ at quarter-chord. Dihedral 7° at 28 per cent chord. Incidence 3°. All-metal two-spar structure, of 2024-T3 and -T4 aluminium alloy, with detachable glassfibre wingtips. Glassfibre wing/fuselage fairing. All-metal statically balanced Frise ailerons and double-slotted flaps. Trim tab in port aileron. De-icing system optional.

FUSELAGE: All-metal semi-monocoque structure of 2024-T3 aluminium alloy. Two upward hinged doors, one on each side of nose, provide access to avionics.

TAIL UNIT: Cantilever all-metal structure, with sweptback vertical surfaces and 10° tailplane dihedral. Glassfibre dorsal fin. Ventral fin. Trim tabs in rudder and port elevator; mass balance on elevator tab and duplicated control rods to elevator. De-icing system optional.

LANDING GEAR: Hydraulically retractable tricycle type, with single wheel and ERAM oleo-pneumatic (nitrogen) shock absorber on each unit. Mainwheel tyre size 670 × 270-12 (10 ply rating), pressure 5·86-6·20 bars (85-90 lb/sq in). Steerable, forward retracting nosewheel unit has tyre size 6·50-8, pressure 4·27-4·69 bars (62-68 lb/sq in).

POWER PLANT: Two 559 kW (750 shp) Pratt & Whitney Canada PT6A-34 turboprop engines, each driving a Hartzell HC-B3TN-3C/T10178H-8R constant-speed three-blade metal propeller with autofeathering and full reverse-pitch capability. Four integral fuel tanks in wings, with total capacity of 1,720 litres (378 Imp gallons). Oil capacity 8·7 litres (1·9 Imp gallons). Gravity refuelling point on top of each wing. Optional de-icing system for engine air inlets and propellers.

ACCOMMODATION: Pilot and co-pilot side by side on flight deck. Seats for up to 21 passengers in main cabin of P2A, at 74 cm (29 in) pitch. P1A has quick-change cabin seating up to 18 persons. Crew/passenger door at front and passenger/baggage door at rear, both on port side; emergency exit over wing on each side, and opposite crew/passenger door on starboard side. Crew/passenger door can also be used as emergency exit. Cabin floor stressed for uniformly distributed loads of up to 488 kg/m² (100 lb/sq ft). Baggage compartment at rear of cabin. Flush type toilet in compartment at rear of cabin. Toilet/lavatory standard. Windscreen de-icing optional.

SYSTEMS: Air cycle air-conditioning system with cooling

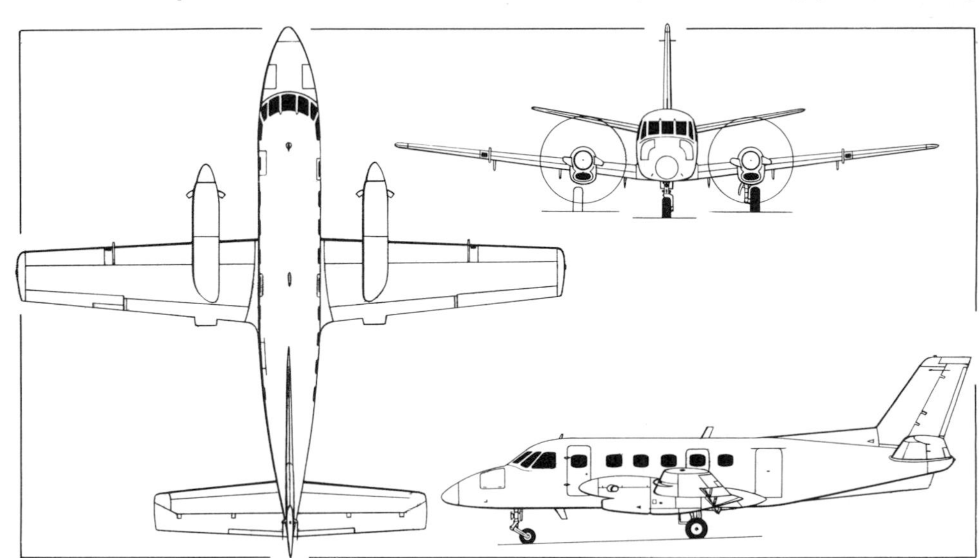

EMBRAER EMB-110P2A Bandeirante, with dihedral tailplane and other changes *(Pilot Press)*

capacity of 25,000 BTU/h and engine bleed heating. Primary hydraulic system for actuation of landing gear, brakes, nosewheel steering and parking/emergency braking. Hydraulic power supply system basically comprises (a) reservoir with electric booster pump and 10 litre (2·2 Imp gallon) capacity; (b) two engine driven, pressure compensated variable delivery pumps, with pump pressure of 207 bars (3,000 lb/sq in) and flow rate of 6·05 litres (1·33 Imp gallons)/min, mounted on engine accessory gearbox; (c) a 0·5 litre (0·11 Imp gallon) capacity pressure accumulator in the pressure line; and (d) hydraulic fluid conforming to MIL-H-5606. Emergency hydraulic system, for landing gear only, consists of handpump in cockpit with 103·5 bars (1,500 lb/sq in) pressure and max flow rate of 15 cc (0·915 cu in) per cycle. Electrical system utilises two starter/generators, giving 200A continuously or 300A for one minute, and one 24V 34Ah nickel-cadmium battery with two 250VA static inverters to supply 115/26V 400Hz AC power. External power receptacle on port side of forward fuselage. Oxygen system for crew and passengers (standard in P2A, optional in P1A), using oxygen cylinder in rear of fuselage with capacity of 3·3 m^3 (115 cu ft) at 128 bars (1,850 lb/sq in) pressure.

Avionics and Equipment: Collins Pro Line, Collins Microline and King Silver Crown II avionics packages available. *Pro Line package* includes two VHF-20 com transceivers; VIR-30A VHF nav VOR/ILS/marker beacon receiver; second VIR-30A; PN-101 pictorial navigation system with 331A-3G pilot's HSI; 331H-3G co-pilot's VOR/ILS indicator; ADF-60 ADF receiver; 332C-10 RMI with NAV 1/ADF 1 on single needle and NAV 2/ADF 2 on double needle; two 387C-4 audio control panels with two 356F-3 speaker amplifiers and eight speakers (flight deck and cabin); PA system; pilot's interphone; and radio master switch. Options to Pro Line package include second ADF-60; second 332C-10 RMI; DME-40 with 339F-12A indicator and NAV 1/HOLD/NAV 2 switching; TDR-90 transponder; second TDR-90; second PN-101 with 331A-3G co-pilot's HSI (instead of co-pilot's AIM-200-DC-FM directional gyro and 331H-3G VOR/ILS indicator); and ALT-50 radar altimeter with 339H-4 indicator. *Microline package* includes two VHF-251 com transceivers; VIR-351 VHF nav receiver with Dorne & Margolin DMH 21-1 nav adapter plus Collins GLS-350 glideslope receiver; second VIR-351 with GLS-350 glideslope receiver only; ADF-650A ADF, including RCR-650A receiver; Aeronetics 7137 RMI with Aeronetics 7100 pilot's dual RMI converter; MKR-350 pilot's marker beacon receiver; PN-101 pilot's pictorial navigation system with 331A-3G HSI; IND-351A co-pilot's VOR/ILS indicator (coupled to NAV 2); two 387C-4 audio control panels with two 356F-3 speaker amplifiers and eight speakers (flight deck and cabin); PA system; pilot's interphone; and radio master switch. Options to Microline package include ANS-351 R/Nav (only if aircraft is equipped also with DME-451); second ADF-650A; one or two DME-451, each with TCR-451 transceiver and IND-451 indicator; one or two TDR-90 transponders; second Aeronetics 7137 RMI for co-pilot, with one or two ADF adapters as appropriate; second PN-101 with 331A-3G co-pilot's HSI (instead of IND-351A and AIM-200-DC-FM directional gyro); second MKR-350; King KI 207 pilot's VOR/ILS indicator repeater, coupled to NAV 2; second KI 207 for co-pilot, coupled to NAV 1; ALT-50A radio altimeter with 339H-4 indicator; AP-106 autopilot with pilot's FD-112V flight director (instead of 331A-3G HSI and RAI-303 artificial horizon on pilot's side); manual electric trim for pitch control, with command for both pilots (Collins 334D-6 trim servo, as used in autopilot); and NAV 1/NAV 2 transfer switch. *Silver Crown II package* includes two KY 196 VHF com transceivers; two KN 53 VHF nav receivers; KR 87 ADF receiver; KNI 582 RMI with NAV 1/ADF 1 on single needle and NAV 2/ADF 2 on double needle; KNR 633 RMI converter; KR 21 pilot's marker beacon receiver; KCS 55A compass system with KI 525A pilot's HSI; KN 72 nav converter; KI 204 co-pilot's VOR/ILS indicator, coupled to NAV 2; two Collins 387C-4 audio control panels with two 356F-3 speaker amplifiers and eight speakers (flight deck and cabin); PA system; pilot's interphone; and radio master switch. Options to Silver Crown II package include one or two KNS 81 R/Nav (only if aircraft is equipped also with KN 63 DME system); second KR 87; one or two KN 63 DME systems, each with KDI 572 indicator; one or two KT 76A transponders; second KNI 582 system; second KCS 55A with KI 525A co-pilot's HSI (instead of directional gyro and KI 204); KN 72 nav converter (required when ordering second KCS 55A without second KNS 81); KI 204 pilot's VOR/ILS indicator, coupled to NAV 2; second KI 204 for co-pilot, coupled to NAV 1; second KR 21 for co-pilot; KRA 405 radio altimeter, with KNI 415 indicator; and two KY 196E wide-bandwidth VHF com transceivers (instead of both KY 196). *In addition to these packages,* other avionics options include Collins HF-200 SSB 20-channel HF transceiver; Bendix M4-D autopilot; King KA 52 autopilot adapter (necessary with King package); Collins AVR-101 cockpit voice recorder (mandatory for French certification); Dorne & Margolin DMELT-6 emergency locator transmitter system (mandatory for US, Canadian and French certification); encoding altimeter (IDC, Smiths or Jaeger); and weather radar (Bendix RDR-1200 or RDR-160).

Search and rescue SC-95B (EMB-110P1K) Bandeirante of the Brazilian Air Force

Dimensions, external:
Wing span 15·33 m (50 ft 3½ in)
Wing chord: at root 2·33 m (7 ft 7¾ in)
at tip 1·37 m (4 ft 6 in)
Wing aspect ratio 8·10
Length overall 15·10 m (49 ft 6½ in)
Length of fuselage 14·59 m (47 ft 10½ in)
Height overall 4·92 m (16 ft 1¾ in)
Fuselage: Max width 1·72 m (5 ft 7¾ in)
Tailplane span 7·54 m (24 ft 9 in)
Wheel track 4·94 m (16 ft 2½ in)
Wheelbase 5·10 m (16 ft 8¾ in)
Propeller diameter 2·36 m (7 ft 9 in)
Distance between propeller centres 4·80 m (15 ft 9 in)
Propeller ground clearance 0·276 m (10¾ in)
Passenger door (rear, port):
Height 1·35 m (4 ft 5¼ in)
Width 0·85 m (2 ft 9½ in)
Crew/passenger door (fwd, port):
Height 1·42 m (4 ft 8 in)
Width 0·63 m (2 ft 1 in)
Passenger and crew emergency exits (three, each):
Height 0·80 m (2 ft 7½ in)
Width 0·63 m (2 ft 1 in)

Dimensions, internal:
Cabin: Max length 9·53 m (31 ft 3¼ in)
Width 1·60 m (5 ft 3 in)
Height 1·60 m (5 ft 3 in)
Floor area 12·00 m^2 (129·2 sq ft)
Volume 20·4 m^3 (720·4 cu ft)
Baggage compartment volume 2·0 m^3 (70·6 cu ft)

Areas:
Wings, gross 29·10 m^2 (313·23 sq ft)
Ailerons (total) 2·16 m^2 (23·25 sq ft)
Flaps (total) 4·90 m^2 (52·74 sq ft)
Fin, excl dorsal fin 3·81 m^2 (41·01 sq ft)
Dorsal fin 0·82 m^2 (8·83 sq ft)
Ventral fin 0·80 m^2 (8·61 sq ft)
Rudder, incl tab 1·69 m^2 (18·19 sq ft)
Tailplane 5·51 m^2 (59·31 sq ft)
Elevators, incl tabs 4·31 m^2 (46·39 sq ft)

Weights and Loadings (A: P2A; B: P1A/41 and P2A/41; C: P1A in passenger configuration):
Weight empty, equipped: A 3,516 kg (7,751 lb)
B, commercial 3,590 kg (7,915 lb)
B, cargo 3,393 kg (7,480 lb)
Fuel weight: A, B, C 1,308 kg (2,883 lb)
Max payload: A 1,681 kg (3,706 lb)
B, commercial 1,561 kg (3,443 lb)
B, cargo 1,712 kg (3,774 lb)
C 1,633 kg (3,600 lb)
Max T-O weight: A 5,670 kg (12,500 lb)
B 5,900 kg (13,010 lb)
Max ramp weight: B 5,930 kg (13,073 lb)
Max landing weight: A 5,670 kg (12,500 lb)
B 5,700 kg (12,566 lb)
Max zero-fuel weight: A, B 5,450 kg (12,015 lb)
Max wing loading: A 195·52 kg/m^2 (40·04 lb/sq ft)
B 202·61 kg/m^2 (41·50 lb/sq ft)
Max power loading: A 5·07 kg/kW (8·33 lb/shp)
B 5·27 kg/kW (8·67 lb/shp)

Performance (at max T-O weight, ISA, except where indicated. A: P2A; B: P1A/41 and P2A/41):
Max level speed at 2,440 m (8,000 ft):
A 248 knots (460 km/h; 286 mph)
Max cruising speed at 2,440 m (8,000 ft):
A 223 knots (413 km/h; 257 mph)
B 222 knots (411 km/h; 256 mph)
Econ cruising speed at 3,050 m (10,000 ft):
A 181 knots (335 km/h; 208 mph)
B 184 knots (341 km/h; 212 mph)
Stalling speed at max landing weight:
A 69 knots (128 km/h; 80 mph) CAS
Max rate of climb at S/L: A 545 m (1,788 ft)/min
B 500 m (1,640 ft)/min
Rate of climb at S/L, one engine out:
A 131 m (430 ft)/min
B 113 m (370 ft)/min
Time to 3,050 m (10,000 ft): A 6 min
Time to 4,575 m (15,000 ft): A 10 min
Service ceiling: A 6,860 m (22,500 ft)
B 6,550 m (21,500 ft)
Service ceiling, one engine out:
A 3,385 m (11,100 ft)
B 3,050 m (10,000 ft)
T-O run:
A, FAR 23.135A 675 m (2,215 ft)
B, FAR 23.135/SFAR 41A 807 m (2,650 ft)
Landing run (non-factored) at max landing weight:
A 850 m (2,790 ft)
B 868 m (2,850 ft)
Range with max fuel (long-range cruising speed, 45 min reserves): A 1,080 nm (2,001 km; 1,244 miles)
B 1,060 nm (1,964 km; 1,220 miles)

EMBRAER EMB-111

Brazilian Air Force designation: P-95

This land based maritime surveillance aircraft, based on the EMB-110 Bandeirante, was designed to meet specifications issued by the Comando Costeiro, the Brazilian Air Force's Coastal Command. The main external differences in this version are the large nose radome, housing search radar, and the addition of wingtip fuel tanks.

The first EMB-111 flew for the first time on 15 August 1977, and 12 were delivered to the Brazilian Air Force. Six were delivered to the Chilean Navy in 1978 and 1979. These aircraft have some mission equipment changes, including full de-icing system, and passive ECM antennae under the nose and at the tail. One EMB-111 was delivered in August 1981 to the Gabonese Air Force.

A description of the EMB-111 can be found in the 1985-86 and earlier editions of *Jane's*.

EMBRAER EMB-111 maritime surveillance aircraft of the Brazilian Air Force

EMBRAER EMB-120 BRASILIA

The EMB-120 Brasilia is a twin-turboprop passenger and cargo transport, design of which was started in September 1979. The first prototype (PT-ZBA) made its initial flight on 27 July 1983, the second (PT-ZBB) on 21 December 1983, and the third (PT-ZBC) on 9 May 1984. These aircraft were used for flight test and certification trials. Nos. 2 and 5 are static and fatigue test aircraft; No. 6 is a pre-series demonstration aircraft.

Certification by the Brazilian CTA was granted on 16 May 1985, and FAA (FAR Pt 25) type approval on 9 July 1985. Bilateral certifications by the British CAA, French DGAC, German LBA and Australian DoT were expected to follow soon afterwards. The first customer, Atlantic Southeast Airlines of the USA, received its first Brasilia at the Paris Air Show in June, and by 1 January 1986 had received six of the ten ordered. By 1 May 1986, total firm orders amounted to 65, with options on a further 99. The first order for the corporate version was received from United Technologies Corporation (USA) in August 1985. Furnished for 18 passengers, it was scheduled for delivery during 1986. Scheduled production rate for that year was three aircraft per month.

TYPE: Twin-turboprop general purpose transport.

WINGS: Cantilever low-wing monoplane. Wing section NACA 23018 (modified) at root, NACA 23012 at tip. Dihedral 6° 30′ from roots at 66 per cent chord. Incidence 2°. Sweepback 0° at 66 per cent chord. Single continuous fail-safe structure, attached to underside of fuselage on three special frames. Main wing box has three spars (at 15, 28 and 66 per cent chord), ribs, stiffeners and skin. Spar caps machined from 2024 or 7050 aluminium alloy extrusions; skin panels are of 2024 or 7475 laminations, chemically milled. Leading-edges of Kevlar reinforced plastics. All-metal hydraulically actuated electrically controlled double-slotted Fowler trailing-edge flap inboard and outboard of each engine nacelle; small plain flap beneath each nacelle. No slats, slots, spoilers or air-brakes. Small fence on each outer wing between outboard flap and aileron. Internally balanced all-metal ailerons. Lateral trimming by tabs (two in starboard aileron, one in port aileron). Ailerons actuated by dual irreversible mechanical actuators operated manually by cable controls. Pneumatic boot de-icing of leading-edges, using engine bleed air.

FUSELAGE: Semi-monocoque pressurised structure, of circular cross-section throughout most of its length. Chemically milled skin, reinforced by extruded stiffeners; C frames attached to skin by shear clips. Entire structure is of 2024, 7050 and 7475 aluminium alloys, and meets the damage tolerance requirements of FAR Pt 25 (Transport category) up to Amendment 25-54. Pressurised area contained within flat bulkhead forward of flight deck and spherical rear bulkhead aft of baggage compartment. Twin ventral strakes under rear fuselage.

TAIL UNIT: Cantilever T tail, of three-spar all-metal construction similar to that of wings. Fixed incidence swept tailplane, with horn balanced elevators. Sweptback fin, with Kevlar reinforced plastics leading-edge; dorsal fin. Serially hinged two-segment rudder actuated hydraulically by Bertea CSD unit. Mechanically actuated trim tab in each half of elevator. Pneumatic boot de-icing of leading-edges, using engine bleed air.

LANDING GEAR: Retractable tricycle type, with Goodrich twin wheels and oleo-pneumatic shock absorber on each unit (main units 12 in, nose unit 8 in). Hydraulic actuation; all units retract forward (main units into engine nacelles). Hydraulically powered nosewheel steering. Goodyear tyres, size 24 × 7·25 in (main), 18 × 5·5 in (nose); pressure 6·90-7·58 bars (100-110 lb/sq in) on main units, 4·14-4·83 bars (60-70 lb/sq in) on nose unit. Goodrich carbon brakes standard (steel optional). Hydro Aire anti-skid system standard; autobrake optional.

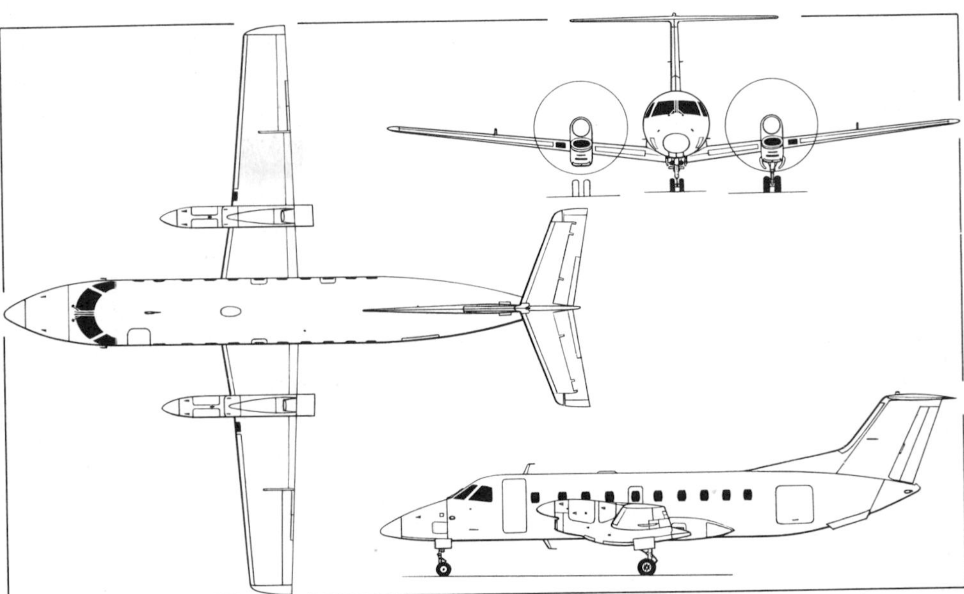

EMBRAER EMB-120 Brasilia twin-turboprop transport *(Pilot Press)*

POWER PLANT: Two Pratt & Whitney Canada PW118 turboprop engines, each rated at 1,342 kW (1,800 shp) for T-O and max continuous power, and driving a Hamilton Standard 14RF-9 four-blade constant-speed reversible-pitch fully-feathering propeller with aluminium spars and glassfibre blades. Fuel in two-cell 1,670 litre (367·4 Imp gallon) integral tank in each wing; total capacity 3,340 litres (734·7 Imp gallons), of which 3,312 litres (728·5 Imp gallons) are usable. Single-point pressure refuelling (beneath outer starboard wing), plus gravity point in upper surface of each wing. Oil capacity 9 litres (2 Imp gallons).

ACCOMMODATION: Pilot and co-pilot on flight deck, with dual controls. Main cabin accommodates cabin attendant and 30 passengers in three-abreast seating at 79 cm (31 in) pitch, with overhead lockable baggage racks, in pressurised and air-conditioned environment. Provisions for wardrobe, galley and toilet. Downward opening main passenger door, with airstairs, forward of wing on port side. Type II emergency exit on starboard side at rear. Overwing Type III emergency exit on each side. Pressurised baggage compartment aft of passenger cabin, with large door on port side. Also available with all-cargo interior; executive or military transport interior; or in mixed-traffic version with 24 or 26 passengers (toilet omitted in latter case), and 900 kg (1,984 lb) of cargo in enlarged rear baggage compartment.

SYSTEMS: AiResearch air-conditioning and pressurisation system (max differential 0·48 bars; 7 lb/sq in), with dual packs of recirculation equipment. Duplicated hydraulic systems (pressure 207 bars; 3,000 lb/sq in), each powered by an engine driven pump, for landing gear, flap, rudder and brake actuation, and nosewheel steering. Emergency standby electric pumps on each system, plus single standby handpump, for landing gear extension. Main electrical power supplied by two 28V 400A DC starter/generators; two 28V 100A DC auxiliary brushless generators for secondary and/or emergency power; one 24V 40Ah nickel-cadmium battery for assisted starting and emergency power. Main and standby 450VA static inverters for 26/115V AC power at 400Hz. Single high-pressure (127·5 bars; 1,850 lb/sq in) oxygen cylinder for crew; individual chemical oxygen generators for passengers. Pneumatic de-icing for wing and tail leading-edges, and engine air intakes; electrically heated windscreens, propellers and pitot tubes; bleed air de-icing of engine air intakes. Optional Garrett GTCP36-150(A) APU in tailcone, for electrical and pneumatic power supply (fitted to second and third prototypes).

AVIONICS: Collins Pro Line II digital avionics package includes as standard dual VHF-22 com transceivers, dual VIR-32 VHF nav receivers, one ADF-60A, one TDR-90 transponder, CLT-22/32/62/92 control heads, one DME-41, one WXR-270 weather radar, dual AHRS-85 digital strapdown AHRS, dual ADI-84, dual EHSI-74, dual RMI-36, one Dorne & Margolin DMELT-81 emergency locator transmitter, dual Avtech audio/interphones, Avtech PA and cabin interphone, Fairchild voice recorder, and IET standby attitude indicator. Optional avionics include third VHF com, second transponder and DME, WXR-300 weather radar, two EFIS-86 electronic flight instrument systems, one MFD-85 multi-function display, one or two J.E.T. RNS-8000 3D or Racal Avionics RN 5000 nav, one APS-65 digital autopilot, one or two FCS-65 digital flight directors, flight entertainment music, one or two Canadian Marconi CMA-771 Alpha VLF/Omega, one or two ALT-55 radio altimeters, altitude alerter/preselect, microwave landing system, ground proximity warning system, flight recorder, and Motorola Selcal. Second (Bendix) and third avionics packages will be available later. Other types of avionics equipment, for special versions of the aircraft, will be as required for the missions concerned.

DIMENSIONS, EXTERNAL:

Wing span	19·78 m (64 ft 10¾ in)
Wing chord: at root	2·81 m (9 ft 2¾ in)
at tip	1·40 m (4 ft 7 in)
Wing aspect ratio	9·92
Length overall	20·00 m (65 ft 7½ in)
Length of fuselage	18·73 m (61 ft 5½ in)
Fuselage: Max diameter	2·28 m (7 ft 5¾ in)
Height overall	6·35 m (20 ft 10 in)
Elevator span	6·94 m (22 ft 9¼ in)
Wheel track (c/l of shock struts)	6·58 m (21 ft 7 in)
Wheelbase	6·97 m (22 ft 10½ in)
Propeller diameter	3·20 m (10 ft 6 in)

EMBRAER EMB-120 Brasilia twin-turboprop passenger transport in the insignia of DLT (Deutsche Luft Transport) of West Germany

Propeller ground clearance (min) 0·48 m (1 ft 7 in)
Passenger door (fwd, port):
Height 1·70 m (5 ft 7 in)
Width 0·774 m (2 ft 6½ in)
Height to sill 1·47 m (4 ft 10 in)
Cargo door (rear, port):
Height 1·36 m (4 ft 5½ in)
Width 1·30 m (4 ft 3¼ in)
Height to sill 1·67 m (5 ft 5¾ in)
Emergency exit (rear, stbd):
Height 1·37 m (4 ft 6 in)
Width 0·51 m (1 ft 8 in)
Height to sill 1·56 m (5 ft 1½ in)
Emergency exits (overwing, each):
Height 0·91 m (3 ft 0 in)
Width 0·51 m (1 ft 8 in)
Emergency exits (flight deck side windows, each):
Min height 0·48 m (1 ft 7 in)
Min width 0·51 m (1 ft 8 in)

DIMENSIONS, INTERNAL:
Cabin, excl flight deck and baggage compartment:
Length 9·35 m (30 ft 8 in)
Max width 2·10 m (6 ft 10¾ in)
Max height 1·76 m (5 ft 9¼ in)
Floor area 14·97 m² (161·14 sq ft)
Rear baggage compartment volume:
30-passenger version 6·40 m³ (226 cu ft)
all-cargo version 2·70 m³ (95 cu ft)
passenger/cargo version 11·00 m³ (388 cu ft)
Cabin, incl flight deck and baggage compartment:
Total volume approx 41·8 m³ (1,476 cu ft)
Max available cabin volume (all-cargo version) 31·10 m³ (1,098 cu ft)

AREAS:
Wings, gross 39·43 m² (424·42 sq ft)
Ailerons (total) 2·88 m² (31·00 sq ft)
Trailing-edge flaps (total) 3·23 m² (34·77 sq ft)
Fin, incl dorsal fin 5·74 m² (61·78 sq ft)
Rudder 2·59 m² (27·88 sq ft)
Tailplane 6·10 m² (65·66 sq ft)
Elevator, incl tabs 3·90 m² (41·98 sq ft)

WEIGHTS AND LOADINGS:
Weight empty, equipped (30 passengers) 6,878 kg (15,163 lb)
Max fuel load 2,682 kg (5,913 lb)
Max payload 3,470 kg (7,650 lb)
Max T-O weight 11,500 kg (25,353 lb)
Max ramp weight 11,580 kg (25,529 lb)
Max landing weight 11,250 kg (24,802 lb)
Max zero-fuel weight 10,500 kg (23,148 lb)
Max wing loading 292 kg/m² (59·8 lb/sq ft)
Max power loading 4·29 kg/kW (7·04 lb/shp)

PERFORMANCE (at max T-O weight, ISA):
Max operating speed 272 knots (504 km/h; 313 mph) EAS
Max level speed at 6,100 m (20,000 ft) 328 knots (608 km/h; 378 mph)
Max cruising speed at 6,100 m (20,000 ft) 298 knots (552 km/h; 343 mph)
Long-range cruising speed at 7,620 m (25,000 ft) 260 knots (482 km/h; 299 mph)
Stalling speed, power off:
flaps up 117 knots (217 km/h; 135 mph) CAS
flaps down 87 knots (162 km/h; 100 mph) CAS
Max rate of climb at S/L 646 m (2,120 ft)/min
Rate of climb at S/L, one engine out 206 m (675 ft)/min
Service ceiling 9,085 m (29,800 ft)
Service ceiling, one engine out 5,240 m (17,200 ft)
FAR Pt 25 T-O field length 1,420 m (4,660 ft)
FAR Pt 135 landing field length, max landing weight at S/L 1,370 m (4,495 ft)
Min ground turning radius 15·76 m (51 ft 8½ in)
Range at 7,620 m (25,000 ft), reserves for 100 nm (185 km; 115 mile) diversion and 45 min hold:
with max (30) passenger payload (2,721 kg; 6,000 lb) 945 nm (1,750 km; 1,088 miles)
with max fuel and 1,920 kg (4,233 lb) payload (21 passengers) 1,610 nm (2,983 km; 1,854 miles)

OPERATIONAL NOISE LEVELS (FAR Pt 36, BCAR-N and ICAO Annex 16):
T-O 78·6 EPNdB
Approach 89·1 EPNdB
Sideline 76·8 EPNdB

EMBRAER EMB-121A1 XINGU II

The Xingu I (see 1983-84 *Jane's*), which first flew on 10 October 1976, was superseded in production by the EMB-121A1 Xingu II. Existing Xingu Is can be retrofitted to this standard, and 47 had been so converted by EMBRAER by the end of 1985.

A first example of the Xingu II (PP-ZCT, the first production Xingu I, re-engined) flew for the first time on 4 September 1981. It retains the same airframe as the Xingu I, but has more powerful Pratt & Whitney Canada PT6A-135 turboprop engines, four-blade propellers, increased fuel capacity, and a small strake added on each side of the tailcone.

Combined production of the Xingu I and II totalled 103 by the beginning of 1986. Production of the Xingu II was due to end that year with the 104th aircraft. An improved standard interior for new-production Xingu IIs (and available as a retrofit on earlier Xingus) was introduced in 1984. This features an improved air-conditioning system, new noise-suppressing materials, redesigned leather seats, new carpeting and toilet installations, foldout tables on each side of the cabin which can be joined in the centre to make a larger surface, and new Collins Pro Line radio communications equipment.

EMBRAER EMB-121A1 Xingu II in French Aéronautique Navale insignia

A detailed description of the Xingu II can be found in the 1985-86 and earlier editions of *Jane's*. The following are the principal details:

TYPE: Twin-turboprop general purpose transport and advanced training aircraft.

AIRFRAME: See 1985-86 *Jane's*.

POWER PLANT: Two 559 kW (750 shp) Pratt & Whitney Canada PT6A-135 turboprop engines, each driving a Hartzell HC-B4TN-3C/T9212B four-blade constant-speed metal propeller with autofeathering and full reverse pitch capability. Two integral fuel tanks in wings, with total capacity of 1,720 litres (378 Imp gallons). Gravity refuelling point on top of each wing. Oil capacity 8·7 litres (1·9 Imp gallons).

ACCOMMODATION: Normal flight crew of two, but certificated for single-pilot operation. Cabin seats up to nine passengers. Downward hinged door on port side, aft of wing, with built-in airstairs. Emergency exit over wing on starboard side. Baggage compartments in nose (unpressurised, with external access via door on each side) and at rear of cabin (pressurised, with internal access). Toilet/lavatory and galley standard. Entire accommodation pressurised and air-conditioned.

SYSTEMS, AVIONICS AND EQUIPMENT: See 1985-86 *Jane's*.

DIMENSIONS, EXTERNAL:
Wing span 14·45 m (47 ft 5 in)
Wing aspect ratio 7·18
Length overall 12·25 m (40 ft 2¼ in)
Height overall 4·74 m (15 ft 6½ in)
Tailplane span 5·58 m (18 ft 3¾ in)
Wheel track 5·24 m (17 ft 2¼ in)
Wheelbase 2·90 m (9 ft 6¼ in)
Propeller diameter 2·36 m (7 ft 9 in)
Passenger door (rear, port):
Height 1·32 m (4 ft 4 in)
Width 0·63 m (2 ft 0¾ in)
Height to sill 1·245 m (4 ft 1 in)

DIMENSIONS, INTERNAL:
Cabin, incl flight deck:
Max length 5·18 m (17 ft 0 in)
Max width 1·74 m (5 ft 8½ in)
Max height 1·52 m (4 ft 11¾ in)
Passenger cabin, incl rear baggage compartment:
Length 3·57 m (11 ft 8½ in)
Floor area 4·24 m² (45·64 sq ft)
Volume 6·9 m³ (243·7 cu ft)
Baggage compartment volume:
nose 0·30 m³ (10·6 cu ft)
rear 0·71 m³ (25·1 cu ft)

AREA:
Wings, gross 27·50 m² (296·0 sq ft)

WEIGHTS AND LOADINGS:
Weight empty, equipped 3,710 kg (8,179 lb)
Max payload (one pilot) 780 kg (1,720 lb)
Max fuel load 1,308 kg (2,884 lb)
Max T-O weight 5,670 kg (12,500 lb)
Max ramp weight 5,700 kg (12,565 lb)
Max zero-fuel weight 4,660 kg (10,273 lb)
Max landing weight 5,340 kg (11,772 lb)
Max cabin floor loading 488 kg/m² (100 lb/sq ft)
Max wing loading 206·2 kg/m² (42·2 lb/sq ft)
Max power loading 5·07 kg/kW (8·33 lb/shp)

PERFORMANCE (at max T-O weight, ISA):
Max operating speed 252 knots (466 km/h; 290 mph) CAS
Max cruising speed at 3,050 m (10,000 ft) 256 knots (474 km/h; 295 mph)
Econ cruising speed at 3,050 m (10,000 ft) 205 knots (380 km/h; 236 mph)
Stalling speed, power off:
flaps up 96 knots (178 km/h; 111 mph) CAS
flaps down 76 knots (141 km/h; 88 mph) CAS
Max rate of climb at S/L 548 m (1,800 ft)/min
Rate of climb at S/L, one engine cut 103 m (340 ft)/min
Service ceiling 8,535 m (28,000 ft)
Service ceiling, one engine out 3,290 m (10,800 ft)
T-O run 580 m (1,903 ft)
T-O to 15 m (50 ft) 767 m (2,516 ft)
Landing from 15 m (50 ft) 850 m (2,789 ft)
Landing run 560 m (1,835 ft)
Min ground turning radius 10·73 m (35 ft 2½ in)
Runway LCN 10
Range at 6,100 m (20,000 ft), 45 min reserves:
with max payload 880 nm (1,630 km; 1,012 miles)
with max fuel 1,268 nm (2,350 km; 1,460 miles)

EMBRAER EMB-121B XINGU III

Development of this 'stretched' version of the Xingu is still in the prototype flying stage.

EMBRAER EMB-123

During the Farnborough Air Show, in September 1986, EMBRAER announced details of its new 19-passenger commuter transport, designated EMB-123. These can be found in the Addenda to this edition of *Jane's*.

EMBRAER EMB-312 TUCANO (TOUCAN)

Brazilian Air Force designation T-27

Design of the EMB-312, by a team under the leadership of Ing Joseph Kovacs, began in January 1978 as part of a programme to develop a new basic trainer for the Brazilian Air Force. On 6 December that year a contract was received from the Departamento de Pesquisas e Desenvolvimento (Department of Research and Development) of the Brazilian Ministry of Aeronautics, for two flying prototypes plus two other airframes for static and fatigue testing.

Characteristics of the EMB-312 include high manoeuvrability, short take-off and landing, the ability to operate from unprepared runways, and a high degree of stability. In addition to meeting the requirements of FAR Pt 23 Appendix A, the aircraft meets MIL and CAA Section K specifications. Its construction embodies such modern techniques as integral numerical control machining, chemical milling, and metal to metal bonding.

The first prototype (Brazilian Air Force serial number 1300) made its initial flight on 16 August 1980, and the second (1301) on 10 December 1980. A third prototype (PP-ZDK), embodying the modifications intended for production Tucanos, flew on 16 August 1982.

The EMB-312 is designated T-27 by the Brazilian Air Force, which has ordered a total of 118 with options for a further 50. Deliveries began on 29 September 1983, with the first six Tucanos going to the Esquadrilha da Fumaça (Smoke Squadron), the aerobatic team of the Brazilian Air Force, and two to the Air Force Academy. By September 1986 EMBRAER had delivered all 118 Tucanos to the FAB as replacements for the Cessna T-37C.

The Egyptian government has ordered 120 Tucanos: 40 for its own air force and 80 for Iraq, with options on 60 more, of which 20 would be for Iraq. EMBRAER built the first ten of these aircraft, which were ferried to Egypt in flyaway condition in 1984. It has since delivered structural components and systems kits for another 70 to AOI in Egypt (which see), which is completing the remainder of the order under licence. Eight Tucanos have been delivered to Honduras, which has four more on option, and deliveries to Venezuela of a total of 30 were under way in Autumn 1986. Production rate was four to five per month in 1986.

EMBRAER teamed with Short Brothers in the UK in 1983-84 to submit the Tucano as a replacement for the Royal Air Force's Jet Provost basic trainers. Its selection for the RAF was announced in early 1985, in a version with British equipment and a more powerful 820 kW (1,100 shp) Garrett TPE331 engine. Details of this version, of which 130 are to be built, can be found in the Shorts entry in the UK section of this edition. The first Garrett engined prototype (PP-ZTC) made its first of six flights in Brazil on 14 February 1986. It was then disassembled and airfreighted to the UK for continued testing.

The following description applies to the standard EMBRAER version:

Type: Tandem two-seat basic trainer.

Wings: Cantilever low-wing monoplane. Wing section NACA 63_2A-415 at root, NACA 63A-212 at tip. Dihedral 5° 30′ at 30% chord. Incidence 1° 25′. Geometric twist 2° 13′. Sweepback 0° 43′ 26″ at quarter-chord. Aluminium alloy two-spar torsion box structure of 2024-T3511 extrusions and 2024-T3 sheet. Single-slotted electrically actuated trailing-edge flaps of 2024-T3, supported on 4130 steel tracks. Frise constant chord balanced ailerons. Electromechanically actuated aileron trim.

Fuselage: Conventional semi-monocoque structure of 2024-T3 aluminium alloy.

Tail Unit: Cantilever all-metal structure, of similar construction to wings. Non-swept fin, with dorsal fin, and horn balanced rudder. Non-swept fixed incidence tailplane and balanced elevators. Small fillet forward of tailplane root on each side. Electromechanically actuated spring trim in rudder and port elevator.

Landing Gear: Hydraulically retractable tricycle type, with single wheel and Piper oleo-pneumatic shock absorber on each unit. Accumulator for emergency extension in the event of hydraulic system failure. Shimmy damper on nose unit. Rearward retracting steerable nose unit; main units retract inward into wings. Parker-Hannifin 40-130 mainwheels, Oldi-DI-1.555-02-OL nosewheel. Tyre sizes 6·50-10 (Type III, 8-ply rating) on mainwheels, 5·00-5 (Type III, 6-ply rating) on nosewheel. Tyre pressures (plus or minus 0·21 bars; 3 lb/sq in in each case) are 5·17 bars (75 lb/sq in) on mainwheels, 4·48 bars (65 lb/sq in) on nosewheel. Parker Hannifin 30-95A hydraulic mainwheel brakes.

Power Plant: One 559 kW (750 shp) Pratt & Whitney Canada PT6A-25C turboprop engine, driving a Hartzell HC-B3TN-3C/T10178-8R three-blade constant-speed fully-feathering reversible-pitch propeller with spinner. Single-lever combined control for engine throttling and propeller pitch adjustment. Two integral fuel tanks in each wing, total capacity 694 litres (152·7 Imp gallons). Fuel tanks lined with anti-detonation plastics foam. Gravity refuelling point in each wing upper surface. Fuel system allows nominally for up to 30 s of inverted flight. (Aircraft was flown inverted for up to 10 min during testing.) Provision for two underwing ferry fuel tanks, total capacity 660 litres (145 Imp gallons).

Accommodation: Instructor and pupil in tandem, on Martin-Baker BR8LC lightweight ejection seats, in air-conditioned cockpit. One-piece fully transparent vacuum formed canopy, opening sideways to starboard, with internal and external jettison provisions. Rear seat elevated. Dual controls standard. Baggage compartment in rear fuselage, with access via door on port side. Cockpit heating and canopy demisting by engine bleed air.

Systems: Freon cycle air-conditioning system, with engine driven compressor. Single hydraulic system, consisting basically of (a) control unit, including reservoir with usable capacity of 1·9 litres (0·42 Imp gallons); (b) an engine driven pump with nominal pressure of 131 bars (1,900 lb/sq in) and nominal flow rate of 4·6 litres (1·01 Imp gallons)/min at 3,800 rpm; (c) landing gear and gear door actuators; (d) filter; (e) shutoff valve; and (f) hydraulic fluid to MIL-H-5606. Under normal operation, hydraulic system actuates landing gear extension/retraction and control of gear doors. Landing gear extension can be performed under emergency operation; emergency retraction may also be possible during landing and T-O with engine running. Reservoir and system are suitable for aerobatics. No pneumatic system. 28V DC electrical power provided by a 6kW starter/generator, 26Ah battery and, for 115V and 26V AC power at 400Hz, a 250VA inverter. Diluter-demand oxygen system conforms to MIL-C-5887 and is supplied individually to each occupant by six MS 21227 D2 type cylinders (total capacity approx 1,200 litres; 264 Imp gallons) at a pressure of 31 bars (450 lb/sq in).

Avionics and Equipment: Standard avionics include two Collins VHF-20A transceivers; two Collins 387C-4 audio systems, one EMBRAER radio transferring system; Telephonics audio control panel; one Collins VIR-31A VOR/ILS/marker beacon receiver; one Collins TDR-90 ATC transponder; one Collins DME-40; one Collins PN-101 gyromagnetic compass; and one Collins ADF-60A. Landing light in each wing leading-edge; taxying lights on nosewheel unit.

Armament: Two hardpoints under each wing, each stressed for a max load of 250 kg (551 lb). Typical loads, on GB100-20-36B pylons, include two 0·30 in C2 machine-gun pods, each with 500 rds; four 25 lb Mk 76 practice bombs; four 250 lb Mk 81 general purpose bombs; or four LM-37/7A or LM-70/7 launchers, each with seven rockets (Avibras SBAT-37 and SBAT-70 respectively). Fixed reflex-type gunsight.

Dimensions, external:

Wing span	11·14 m (36 ft 6½ in)
Wing chord: at root	2·30 m (7 ft 6½ in)
at tip	1·07 m (3 ft 6⅛ in)
Wing aspect ratio	6·4
Length overall	9·86 m (32 ft 4¼ in)
Length of fuselage (excl rudder)	8·53 m (27 ft 11⅞ in)
Fuselage: Max width	1·00 m (3 ft 3¼ in)
Max depth	1·55 m (5 ft 1 in)
Height overall (static)	3·40 m (11 ft 1¾ in)
Tailplane span	4·66 m (15 ft 3½ in)
Wheel track	3·76 m (12 ft 4 in)
Wheelbase	3·16 m (10 ft 4½ in)
Propeller diameter	2·36 m (7 ft 9 in)
Propeller ground clearance (static)	0·33 m (1 ft 1 in)
Baggage compartment door:	
Height	0·60 m (1 ft 11⅝ in)
Width	0·54 m (1 ft 9¼ in)
Height to sill	1·25 m (4 ft 1¼ in)

Dimensions, internal:

Cockpits: Combined length	2·90 m (9 ft 6⅛ in)
Max height	1·55 m (5 ft 1 in)
Max width	0·85 m (2 ft 9½ in)
Baggage compartment volume	0·17 m³ (6·0 cu ft)

Areas:

Wings, gross	19·40 m² (208·82 sq ft)
Ailerons (total)	1·97 m² (21·20 sq ft)
Trailing-edge flaps (total)	2·58 m² (27·77 sq ft)
Fin, incl dorsal fin	2·29 m² (24·65 sq ft)
Rudder, incl tab	1·38 m² (14·85 sq ft)
Tailplane, incl fillets	4·77 m² (51·34 sq ft)
Elevators, incl tab	2·00 m² (21·53 sq ft)

Weights and Loadings:

Basic weight empty	1,810 kg (3,991 lb)
Max internal fuel load (usable)	529 kg (1,166 lb)
Max external stores load	1,000 kg (2,205 lb)
Max T-O weight: 'clean'	2,550 kg (5,622 lb)
with external load	3,175 kg (7,000 lb)
Max ramp weight	3,195 kg (7,044 lb)
Max landing weight: 'clean'	2,800 kg (6,173 lb)
Max zero-fuel weight	2,050 kg (4,519 lb)
Max wing loading:	
'clean'	131·4 kg/m² (26·92 lb/sq ft)
with external stores	163·7 kg/m² (33·52 lb/sq ft)
Max power loading:	
'clean'	4·56 kg/kW (7·50 lb/shp)
with external stores	5·68 kg/kW (9·33 lb/shp)

Performance (at max 'clean' T-O weight except where indicated):

Never-exceed speed	280 knots (519 km/h; 322 mph) EAS
Max level speed at 3,050 m (10,000 ft)	242 knots (448 km/h; 278 mph)
Max cruising speed at 3,050 m (10,000 ft)	222 knots (411 km/h; 255 mph)
Econ cruising speed at 3,050 m (10,000 ft)	172 knots (319 km/h; 198 mph)
Stalling speed, power off:	
flaps and landing gear up	72 knots (133 km/h; 83 mph) EAS
flaps and landing gear down	67 knots (124 km/h; 77 mph) EAS
Max rate of climb at S/L	680 m (2,231 ft)/min
Service ceiling	9,145 m (30,000 ft)
T-O run	380 m (1,250 ft)
T-O to 15 m (50 ft)	710 m (2,330 ft)
Landing from 15 m (50 ft)	605 m (1,985 ft)
Landing run	370 m (1,214 ft)
Range at 6,100 m (20,000 ft) with max fuel, 30 min reserves	995 nm (1,844 km; 1,145 miles)
Ferry range at 6,100 m (20,000 ft) with underwing tanks	1,797 nm (3,330 km; 2,069 miles)

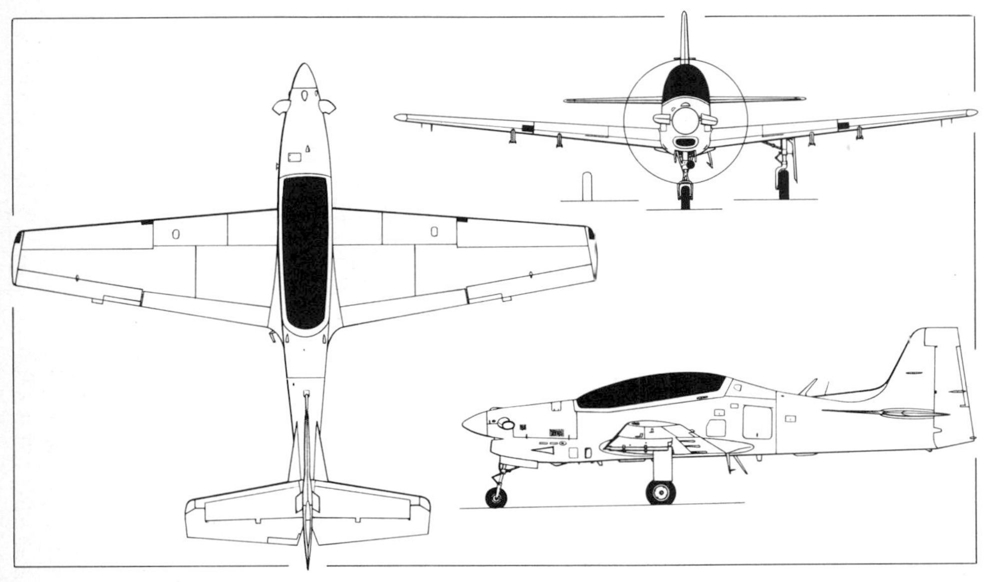

EMBRAER EMB-312 Tucano basic trainer (Pratt & Whitney Canada PT6A-25C turboprop engine)
(Pilot Press)

EMBRAER EMB-312 Tucano tandem two-seat trainer of the Brazilian Air Force

Endurance on internal fuel at econ cruising speed at 6,100 m (20,000 ft), 30 min reserves approx 5 h
g limits: fully Aerobatic category, at max 'clean' T-O weight +6/−3
at max T-O weight with external stores +4·4/−2·2

EMBRAER EMB-201A IPANEMA

The original version of this agricultural aircraft was designed and developed to specifications laid down by the Brazilian Ministry of Agriculture. Design was started in May 1969, and the EMB-200 prototype (PP-ZIP) made its first flight on 30 July 1970. A type certificate was granted on 14 December 1971. Ipanema is the name of a famous beach in Rio, and also of a farm which is the headquarters of the Agricultural Air School of the Ministry of Agriculture, where the EMB-200 was flight tested.

Details of the earlier EMB-200/200A (73 built), EMB-201 (200 built) and EMB-201R (three built) can be found in the 1977-78 and previous editions of *Jane's*. The current production version, first flown on 10 March 1977, is the EMB-201A, of which 253 had been sold by December 1985, bringing total Ipanema sales (all versions) to 529. The EMB-201A incorporates several modifications requested by operators as a result of field experience, including new wing profile, wingtips and other aerodynamic improvements, improved systems, and revised cockpit layout.

Manufacture of the EMB-201A was transferred to EMBRAER's Neiva subsidiary during the second half of 1981.

The 500th EMBRAER Ipanema agricultural aircraft to be delivered

TYPE: Single-seat agricultural aircraft.

WINGS: Cantilever low-wing monoplane. Wing section NACA 23015 (modified), with cambered leading-edges. Dihedral 7° from roots. Incidence 3°. All-metal single-spar structure of 2024 aluminium alloy with all-metal Frise ailerons outboard and all-metal slotted flaps on trailing-edge, and detachable cambered leading-edges. No tabs. Cambered wingtips standard.

FUSELAGE: Rectangular section all-metal safe-life structure, of welded 4130 steel tube with removable skin panels of 2024 aluminium alloy. Structure is specially treated against chemical corrosion.

TAIL UNIT: Cantilever two-spar all-metal structure of 2024 aluminium alloy. Slight sweepback on fin and rudder. Fixed incidence tailplane. Trim tab in starboard elevator.

LANDING GEAR: Non-retractable main- and tailwheels, with oleo shock absorbers in main units. Tailwheel has tapered spring shock absorber. Mainwheels and tyres size 8·50-10. Tailwheel diameter 250 mm (10 in). Tyre pressures: main, 2·07-2·41 bars (30-35 lb/sq in); tailwheel, 3·79 bars (55 lb/sq in). Hydraulic disc brakes on mainwheels.

POWER PLANT: One 224 kW (300 hp) Avco Lycoming IO-540-K1J5D flat-six engine, driving a Hartzell two-blade constant-speed metal propeller with spinner. Integral fuel tanks in each wing leading-edge, with total capacity of 292 litres (64·2 Imp gallons). Refuelling point on top of each tank. Oil capacity 12 litres (2·6 Imp gallons).

ACCOMMODATION: Single horizontally/vertically adjustable seat in fully enclosed cabin with bottom-hinged window/door on each side. Ventilation system in cabin. Inertial shoulder harness standard.

SYSTEM: 28V DC electrical system supplied by a 24Ah BB639/U battery and a Bosch K.1 28V 35A alternator. Power receptacle for external battery (AN-2552-3A type) on port side of forward fuselage.

AVIONICS AND EQUIPMENT: Standard VFR avionics include 720-channel Collins VHF-251S transceiver and Collins RCR-650 ADF transceiver. Hopper for agricultural chemicals has capacity of 680 litres (149·5 Imp gallons) liquid or 750 kg (1,653 lb) dry. Dusting system below centre of fuselage. Spraybooms or Micronair atomisers aft of or above wing trailing-edges respectively.

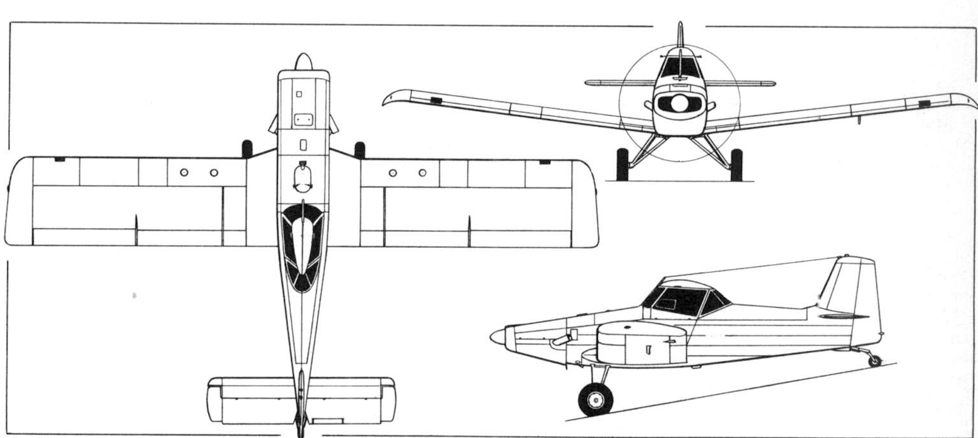

EMBRAER EMB-201A Ipanema single-seat agricultural aircraft *(Pilot Press)*

DIMENSIONS, EXTERNAL:

Wing span	11·20 m (36 ft 9 in)
Wing chord (constant)	1·71 m (5 ft 7½ in)
Wing aspect ratio	6·85
Length overall (tail up)	7·43 m (24 ft 4½ in)
Height overall (tail down)	2·20 m (7 ft 2½ in)
Fuselage: Max width	0·93 m (3 ft 0½ in)
Tailplane span	3·66 m (12 ft 0 in)
Wheel track	2·20 m (7 ft 2½ in)
Wheelbase	5·20 m (17 ft 7¼ in)
Propeller diameter	2·20 m (7 ft 2½ in)

DIMENSIONS, INTERNAL:

Cockpit: Max length	1·20 m (3 ft 11¼ in)
Max width	0·85 m (2 ft 9½ in)
Max height	1·34 m (4 ft 4¾ in)

AREAS:

Wings, gross	19·94 m² (214·63 sq ft)
Ailerons (total)	1·60 m² (17·22 sq ft)
Trailing-edge flaps (total)	2·30 m² (24·76 sq ft)
Fin	0·58 m² (6·24 sq ft)
Rudder	0·63 m² (6·78 sq ft)
Tailplane	3·17 m² (34·12 sq ft)
Elevators (total, incl tab)	1·50 m² (16·15 sq ft)

WEIGHTS AND LOADINGS (N: Normal; R: Restricted category):

Weight empty: N, R	1,011 kg (2,229 lb)
Max payload: N, R	750 kg (1,653 lb)
Max T-O and landing weight: N	1,550 kg (3,417 lb)
R	1,800 kg (3,968 lb)
Max wing loading: N	77·75 kg/m² (15·92 lb/sq ft)
R	90·29 kg/m² (18·49 lb/sq ft)
Max power loading: N	6·92 kg/kW (11·39 lb/hp)
R	8·03 kg/kW (13·23 lb/hp)

PERFORMANCE (at max T-O weight, 'clean' configuration, ISA):

Never-exceed speed:	
N	147 knots (272 km/h; 169 mph)
R	113 knots (209 km/h; 130 mph)
Max level speed at S/L:	
N	124 knots (230 km/h; 143 mph)
R	121 knots (225 km/h; 140 mph)
Max cruising speed (75% power) at 1,830 m (6,000 ft):	
N	115 knots (212 km/h; 132 mph)
R	110 knots (204 km/h; 127 mph)
Stalling speed, power off (N):	
flaps up	56 knots (103 km/h; 64 mph)
8° flap	54 knots (100 km/h; 62 mph)
30° flap	50 knots (92 km/h; 57 mph)
Stalling speed, power off (R):	
flaps up	60 knots (110 km/h; 68 mph)
8° flap	58 knots (107 km/h; 66 mph)
30° flap	53 knots (99 km/h; 61 mph)
Max rate of climb at S/L, 8° flap:	
N	283 m (930 ft)/min
R	201 m (660 ft)/min
Service ceiling, 8° flap: R	3,470 m (11,385 ft)
T-O run at S/L, 8° flap, asphalt runway:	
N	200 m (656 ft)
R	354 m (1,160 ft)
T-O to 15 m (50 ft), conditions as above:	
N	333 m (1,093 ft)
R	564 m (1,850 ft)
Landing from 15 m (50 ft) at S/L, 30° flap, asphalt runway: N	440 m (1,444 ft)
R	500 m (1,640 ft)
Landing run, conditions as above: N	153 m (502 ft)
R	170 m (558 ft)
Range at 1,830 m (6,000 ft), no reserves:	
N	506 nm (938 km; 583 miles)
R	474 nm (878 km; 545 miles)

EMBRAER-PIPER LIGHT AIRCRAFT PROGRAMME

Detailed descriptions of the Piper aircraft built under licence by EMBRAER can be found in the US section of this and earlier editions of *Jane's*. Production of the EMB-710 Carioca (licence PA-28-236 Dakota) and EMB-711T Corisco (PA-28RT-201 Arrow II) has ended. Manufacture of the EMB-711, 712, 720, 721, 810 and 820 is undertaken by EMBRAER's subsidiary, Neiva. The following types were in production in 1986:

EMB-711ST Corisco Turbo. Piper PA-28RT-201T Turbo Arrow IV.

EMB-712 Tupi. Piper PA-28-181 Archer II.

EMB-720D Minuano. Piper PA-32-301 Saratoga.

EMB-810D Seneca III. Piper PA-34-220T Seneca III.

EMB-820C Navajo. Piper PA-31-350 Navajo Chieftain. Production phased out, but available aircraft are being converted to Schafer Comanchero 500 turboprop powered form, as the Neiva **NE-821 Carajá** (which see).

HELIBRAS

HELICÓPTEROS DO BRASIL S/A

Rua Projetada Um 200, Distrito Industrial, Caixa Postal 184, 37500 Itajubá, MG

Telephone: (035) 622 3366 and 622 2455

Telex: 031 2602 HLBR BR

PRESIDENT: José Hugo Castelo Branco

VICE-PRESIDENT DIRECTOR: Alberto Lopes Lavenère-Wanderley

SUPERINTENDENT DIRECTOR: Nivaldo Alves da Silva

COMMERCIAL ASST DIRECTOR: Lionel Paulhiac

PRODUCTION DIRECTOR: Bruno Boulnois

Formed in 1978 and owned jointly by Aérospatiale of France (45%) and the state government of Minas Gerais (55%), Helibras is engaged in a 10 year programme involving the assembly (graduating to local manufacture) of Aérospatiale SA 315B Lama and AS 350B Ecureuil helicopters, known respectively by the Brazilian designations and names **HB 315B Gavião** and **HB 350B Esquilo**. The first assembly hall was officially inaugurated on 28 March 1980. The complete facility will extend over an area of 210,000 m² (2,260,420 sq ft), of which 8,527 m² (91,784 sq ft) is covered at present, with plans to extend this to 18,000 m² (193,750 sq ft) and increase the workforce accordingly. A total of 350 people was employed in 1986.

The first Gaviãos were assembled during the second half of 1979; the first Brazilian assembled Esquilos were also delivered in 1979. By early 1986 Helibras had delivered 68 of these two types of helicopter. Domestic customers then included the Brazilian Navy (nine Esquilos) and various civilian firms and organisations. The Brazilian Navy Esquilos, which serve with the 1° Esquadrão de Helicópteros de Emprego General (squadron of general purpose helicopters), have the service designation **UH-12** and are equipped to carry two Avibrás LM-70/7 pods each containing seven SBAT 70 mm rockets, an FN twin 7·62 mm MAG machine-gun pod, and a door mounted MAG pedestal. Exports had been made to the Bolivian Air Force (nine Gaviãos), Chile (one Gavião), Venezuela (five Esquilos) and Paraguay (two Esquilos).

An aeromedical version of the Esquilo was launched in February 1984. Equipment includes an electrocardiograph, respirator, pacemaker, stretchers, battery operated incubator, oxygen and compressed air cylinders, first aid kit, and a four-way electrical socket for 115V AC (60Hz) and 12V DC power. Apart from the pilot, this version can carry a doctor, nurse and two stretcher patients.

Helibras HB 350B Esquilo (Aérospatiale Ecureuil), one of eight operated by Helijet Aero Taxi of Rio de Janeiro *(Ronaldo S. Olive)*

NEIVA

INDÚSTRIA AERONÁUTICA NEIVA S/A (subsidiary of EMBRAER)

Rua Nossa Senhora de Fátima 360, Vila Antártica, Caixa Postal 10, 18600 Botucatu, SP
Telephone: (0149) 22 1010
Telex: 0142 423 SOAN BR
DIRECTORS:
Eng Antonio Garcia da Silveira (President)
Marcos Baptista dos Santos Jr
MANAGERS:
Luís Carlos Benetti (Engineering)
José Armando Pescatori (Financial and Administrative)
Paulo Urbanavicius (Production)

Neiva became a wholly owned subsidiary of EMBRAER on 10 March 1980. It participates in EMBRAER's general aviation programme, being responsible for all production of the EMB-711ST Corisco Turbo (PA-28RT-201T), EMB-712 (PA-28-181) Tupi, EMB-720D (PA-32-301) Minuano, and EMB-810D (PA-34-220T) Seneca III. In addition, Neiva has for many years built fuselages for the EMBRAER Ipanema agricultural aircraft, and since 1981 has been entirely responsible for Ipanema engineering, manufacture and assembly.

Responsibility for the EMB-820C was transferred to Neiva in mid-1983, when the last five EMBRAER assembled examples were completed by Neiva. Four of these were converted in 1984 to Comanchero 500B configuration (see Schafer entry in US section), in which form they are designated **NE-821 Carajá**. The first Carajá made its initial flight on 9 March 1984, and deliveries began in November of that year. In the Carajá the PT6A-34 engines are derated to 410 kW (550 shp); usable fuel capacity is 1,310 litres (346 US gallons).

NE-821 Carajá, a Schafer Comanchero 500B built under licence by Neiva

WEIGHTS (Carajá):
Weight empty, equipped 2,230 kg (4,916 lb)
Max payload 744 kg (1,640 lb)
Max T-O weight 3,630 kg (8,003 lb)
PERFORMANCE (Carajá):
Max cruising speed at 3,050 m (10,000 ft), max T-O weight, ISA 232 knots (430 km/h; 267 mph)
Max rate of climb at S/L 853 m (2,800 ft)/min
Max operating ceiling 7,315 m (24,000 ft)
T-O to 15 m (50 ft) 540 m (1,772 ft)
Landing from 15 m (50 ft) 563 m (1,847 ft)
Max range, 45 min reserves 971 nm (1,800 km; 1,118 miles)

RIO CLARO

AÉRO CLUBE DE RIO CLARO

Rua Cinco 1152, 13.500 Rio Claro, SP

Under the supervision of Eng Silvio de Oliveira, members of this city flying club are building the prototype of the Super Surubim two-seat aerobatic trainer; two prototypes of a Brazilian version of the Bücker Jungmann aerobatic biplane, named Carcará, made of Brazilian freijó wood and with an engine of US manufacture; and two Araponga gliders (see Sailplanes section).

No news of the Super Surubim has been received since mid-1983, when it was said to be nearing completion. A description and illustration can be found in the 1984-85 *Jane's*.

SÃO CARLOS

ESCOLA DE ENGENHARIA DE SÃO CARLOS São Carlos Engineering School (IPAI Aeronautical Division), University of São Paulo

Universidade de São Paulo, Avenida Dr Carlo Botelho 1465, Caixa Postal 359, 13560 São Paulo, SP
Telephone: (0162) 71 3693
Telex: 166275 USP BR
DIRECTORS OF AERONAUTICAL DIVISION:
Prof Romeu Corsini
Eng Silvio de Oliveira

Between 1945 and 1965 the main aircraft research centre in Brazil was the IPT (Instituto de Pesquisas Tecnologicas: Technical Research Institute) in São Paulo. Created in 1898 to support local industries, it is today one of the ten largest independent research institutes in the world; current activities include metallurgy, and microcircuitry for spacecraft. In about 1938 Dr Frederico Brotero made the discovery that a Brazilian wood known as freijó, stronger and lighter than spruce, was particularly suited to aeroplane construction. Based on this work, an aviation division was created within the IPT to pursue this line of research.

Subsequently, this group began designing aircraft and gliders, which were given an IPT designation followed by a number indicating the sequence of the design. The last aircraft built by the IPT was the IPT-17 laminar-wing sailplane. Its aviation division was transferred to the University of São Paulo where, between 1960 and 1965, four more designs were produced: the SP-18 Onça (Jaguar), SP-19 Galinha (Hen), SP-20 Pinto and SP-21 Ganço (Duck).

An engineering school and research centre known as the IPAI (Industrial Research and Development Institute) was set up at São Paulo University under Prof Romeu Corsini in about 1975. A 2,000 m (6,560 ft) runway, hangars, workshops and other facilities were built at São Carlos, to which the surviving IPT/SP aircraft were brought. These included the SP-18, which was later re-engined and redesignated IPAI-27; other types developed and tested at São Carlos have included the IPAI-26, -29 and -30. Details of these can be found in the 1984-85 or earlier editions of *Jane's*.

Two programmes were current in early 1985: development of metal construction wings for a Paulistinha, and a new version of the IPAI-27 (last described in the 1983-84 *Jane's*).

SUPER ROTOR

M.M. SUPER ROTOR LTDA

Rua Itapeti 541, Tatuapé, 03324 São Paulo (CEP 03324), SP
Telephone: (011) 295 8187
DIRECTOR: Francisco Mattos Jr
MANAGER: José Montalva Perez

SUPER ROTOR AC.4

This all-Brazilian single-seat autogyro was designed in Rio Grande do Sul in the early 1970s, as a private venture, by Eng Altair Coelho. The prototype and production rights were sold subsequently to Sr Francisco Mattos Jr, who introduced a number of modifications before obtaining Brazilian CTA certification. It is produced in both ready to fly and kit forms.

The general appearance of the AC.4 can be seen in the accompanying photograph of the prototype. It has a basic airframe of welded steel tube, a two-blade rotor, and a non-retractable tricycle landing gear with modified go-kart wheels. The rotor blades have one-piece leading-edges of forged aluminium, and trailing-edges of welded aluminium sheet. The prototype was powered by a 63 kW (85 hp) Brazilian modified Volkswagen engine, driving a two-blade wooden pusher propeller, but this is replaced in production aircraft by a 60 kW (80 hp) four-cylinder Retimotor RMV-1, which is a much modified Brazilian redesign of the Volkswagen motorcar engine. Instruments include altimeter, airspeed indicator and compass; equipment includes a battery for engine starting.

By mid-1986 domestic and foreign deliveries of the AC.4, including kits, totalled 160. Modified versions are under development to run on automobile fuel and sugar cane alcohol.

DIMENSIONS: Not known

WEIGHTS:
- Weight empty 166 kg (366 lb)
- Max T-O weight 280 kg (617 lb)

PERFORMANCE:
- Max level speed 86 knots (160 km/h; 99 mph)
- Cruising speed 59 knots (110 km/h; 68 mph)
- Min speed in forward flight 22 knots (40 km/h; 25 mph)
- T-O run, zero wind 150 m (492 ft)
- Landing run, zero wind approx 100 m (328 ft)
- Range with max fuel, 45 min reserves 216 nm (400 km; 248 miles)

Super Rotor AC.4 autogyro

CANADA

AIRTECH

AIRTECH CANADA

Peterborough Municipal Airport, PO Box 415, Peterborough, Ontario K9J 6Z3
Telephone: (705) 743 9483
Telex: 06-962912
PRESIDENT: Bogdan Wolski

Airtech specialises in retrofitting versions of the de Havilland Canada Otter and Beaver with more powerful Polish built engines that offer increased climb rates and considerably greater fuel economy, at lower power settings, than the original engines which they replace.

No 1986 update was received from the company, but at the beginning of the year Airtech was reported to have acquired a former Spanish Air Force C-47/DC-3 with a view to refitting it with ASz-62IR engines and Polish propellers in place of the original Pratt & Whitney R-1830s. The Polish engine was being uprated to 895 kW (1,200 hp) for the purpose, and a first flight in the new form was anticipated in March 1986. In 1986 Airtech also flew a prototype of the PZL-130T Turbo Orlik trainer, further details of which can be found under the WSK-PZL Warszawa-Okecie heading in the Polish section.

Airtech Canada's DHC-3/1000 Otter conversion, powered by a PZL Kalisz ASz-62IR radial engine

AIRTECH CANADA DHC-3/1000 OTTER

Airtech Canada refitted eight de Havilland Canada DHC-3 Otters with Polish PZL-3S radial engines. The first of these made its initial flight in February 1980. Details of this DHC-3/PZL-3S version can be found in the 1983-84 *Jane's*.

Following the first flight of a prototype on 25 August 1983, the Otter conversion is now being offered with a 746 kW (1,000 hp) Polish ASz-62IR engine instead of the 447 kW (600 hp) PZL-3S. Four of these conversions, designated DHC-3/1000, were flying in North and South America by February 1985. An FAA supplemental type certificate had been applied for at that time. Certification is to STA SA83-18 Issue 1.

POWER PLANT: One 746 kW (1,000 hp) PZL Kalisz ASz-62IR nine-cylinder aircooled radial engine, driving a PZL Warszawa AW-2-30 four-blade constant-speed propeller. Fuel capacity as for standard DHC-3; oil capacity 41 litres (9 Imp gallons).

WEIGHTS:
- Weight empty, equipped 2,200 kg (4,850 lb)
- Max T-O weight 3,628 kg (8,000 lb)

PERFORMANCE (at max T-O weight): As for standard DHC-3 except:
- Never-exceed speed 157 knots (291 km/h; 181 mph)
- Max level speed and max cruising speed at S/L 125 knots (232 km/h; 144 mph)
- Econ cruising speed at 1,525 m (5,000 ft) 117 knots (217 km/h; 135 mph)
- Max rate of climb at S/L:
  - at full rated power 552 m (1,810 ft)/min
  - at 602 kW (808 hp) max cruise power 421 m (1,380 ft)/min
- Service ceiling 5,945 m (19,500 ft)
- T-O run 91 m (300 ft)
- T-O to 15 m (50 ft) 182 m (600 ft)
- Max range, allowances for 10 min warm-up, T-O, climb to 1,525 m (5,000 ft), and reserves for 45 min at cruise power 800 nm (1,482 km; 921 miles)

Airtech Canada DHC-2 Beaver floatplane, converted to a Polish PZL-3S radial engine and four-blade propeller

AIRTECH CANADA DHC-2/PZL-3S BEAVER

Although Airtech Canada no longer offers the DHC-3 Otter conversion with PZL-3S engine, it introduced a conversion of the smaller DHC-2 Beaver fitted with this engine, at the request of operators who wanted an increase in power to provide improved performance and safer operation from short airstrips. Four such conversions had been completed by February 1985, three in Canada and one in Peru. The converted Beaver flies under STA SA83-9 Issue 1; application for an FAA STC was to be made during 1985.

POWER PLANT: One 447 kW (600 hp) PZL-3S seven-cylinder aircooled radial engine, driving a PZL US132000A four-blade constant-speed propeller. Fuel capacity 359 litres (79 Imp gallons), or 523 litres (115 Imp gallons) with auxiliary tank in each wingtip.

WEIGHTS:
- Weight empty 1,419 kg (3,129 lb)
- Useful load with full fuel 636 kg (1,402 lb)
- Max T-O weight 2,313 kg (5,100 lb)

PERFORMANCE:
- Normal operating speed and max cruising speed 126 knots (233 km/h; 145 mph) IAS
- Max rate of climb at S/L 488 m (1,600 ft)/min
- T-O to 15 m (50 ft) 305 m (1,000 ft)
- Fuel consumption:
  - at 118 knots (219 km/h; 136 mph) 127 litres (28 Imp gallons)/h
  - at 224 kW (300 hp) 95·5 litres (21 Imp gallons)/h

AVALON

AVALON AVIATION
(a Division of Powell Corporation)

55 Great North Road, Parry Sound, Ontario P2A 2N9
Telephone: (705) 378 2414
Telex: 068-75753
PRESIDENT: Frank D. Powell, QC
GENERAL MANAGER: Bruce D. Powell, BTech
CHIEF PILOT AND OPERATIONS MANAGER: Joe F. Reed
WORKS: Georgian Bay Airport, Parry Sound, Ontario

Powell Corporation was formed, as Georgian Bay Airways Ltd, in 1946, and developed subsequently into a charter and scheduled flying operation specialising in the aerial detection of forest fires and in firefighting support. In 1980 it acquired Avalon Aviation Ltd and its fleet of Canso water bombers, as part of a programme to expand its fire suppression activities.

Avalon currently operates eight Cansos, 13 Piper Aztecs, two Cessna Model 185 amphibians and a DHC-2 Beaver. One of the Cansos has been based at Oslo, Norway, for several years, operating under contract with Haydn Air Charter. The remainder of Avalon's aircraft are maintained at Georgian Bay Airport, in a 2,500 m² (27,000 sq ft) overhaul and maintenance facility opened in 1982.

A description and illustration of Avalon's piston engined Canso water bomber conversion appeared in the 1982-83 *Jane's*. Its proposed **Turbo-Canso**, a heavier duty water bomber with Rolls-Royce Dart turboprop engines, is still in the planning stage. Brief details can be found in the 1984-85 *Jane's*.

Through the Canadian Ministry of Natural Resources, Avalon provides a crewing and maintenance service for the two Canadair CL-215s purchased by the government of Ontario. The aircraft are operated out of Dryden, Ontario, during the fire season, and are refitted by Avalon at Parry Sound during the Winter. Avalon is thus the only non-governmental operator of the CL-215 anywhere in the world.

BELL

BELL HELICOPTER CANADA

Suite 460, 3100 Cote Vertu, St Laurent, Quebec H4R 2J8
Telephone: (514) 333 7040
PRESIDENT: James P. Schwalbe
DIRECTOR, OPERATIONS: Jack Tarpley

The seven-seat Model 400 TwinRanger was announced in February 1983 as the first in a new family of commercial and military single- and twin-engined helicopters on which Bell Helicopter Textron of the USA had been working for the previous three years. On 7 October that year the Canadian government announced the signing of a memorandum of understanding under which Bell had been selected to establish a helicopter industry in Canada, which is the second largest user of helicopters outside the Soviet bloc. A formal contract for this programme, valued at approximately US $210 million in 1982 dollars, was confirmed in January 1984.

Construction began later that year of a new 34,560 m² (372,000 sq ft) facility at Mirabel, Quebec, some 32 km (20 miles) from Montreal. This new plant opened in late 1985, and was expected to have a workforce of about 600 people by the end of 1986. Bell's Canadian facility will begin manufacture with the Model 400A TwinRanger, with Pratt & Whitney Canada PW209T turboshaft engines, followed by the Model 440, which will employ major components manufactured from composite materials. The intention to begin with the Allison 250-C20R powered Model 400 was cancelled in favour of the Model 400A in July 1986.

In due course, Bell expects to transfer US production of the Model 206B JetRanger and 206L LongRanger to the Canadian factory.

BELL MODEL 400A/440 TWINRANGER

Features of the Model 400A include Bell's four-blade 'soft-in-plane' main rotor with composite blades and hub, a Ring Guard tail rotor, an advanced technology transmission and drive system with 'run-dry' capability, and twin PW209T turboshaft engines mated to a combining gearbox. Flight testing of the dynamic components, which are similar to those of the military Model 406 (OH-58D), began in March 1983 using a modified LongRanger (Model 406LM, registered N206N) and were completed later that year. Results achieved with this aerodynamic test prototype, and wind tunnel testing with a one-quarter scale model, enabled Bell to define 95 per cent of the Model 400 series configuration by the time of the January 1984 contract.

Construction of the first Allison engined **Model 400** prototype began on 24 October 1983, and this made its first flight on 30 June 1984. During flight trials it exceeded Canadian government contractual requirements (forward speed of 100 knots; 185 km/h; 115 mph and sideways/rearward speed of 20 knots; 37 km/h; 23 mph), and was subsequently designated as the ground test vehicle. Meanwhile, on 1 June 1984 Bell began building three pre-production Model 400s, the first two of which are being used in the type certification programme; these made their first flights in May and on 26 June 1985. The third pre-production TwinRanger, which flew a few weeks later, is a dedicated demonstration aircraft.

Certification of the standard TwinRanger by the FAA (to FAR Pt 27, Normal category) will be for VFR operation; separate configurations will be available that conform to CAA VFR, and FAA or CAA IFR. Initially the rotor heads, rotor blades, transmission, and other complex components are being manufactured at Fort Worth and shipped to Mirabel, which builds the rest of the airframe and is responsible for final assembly, flight testing and delivery.

Initial production member of the TwinRanger family will now be the **Model 400A**, due to fly in 1987 and become available in 1988. This will be powered by the 699 kW (937 shp) PW209T twin-turbine engine currently being developed by Pratt & Whitney Canada Ltd. From this, in turn, Bell Canada will develop the **Model 440**, which will feature a high level of composite materials in its construction. The 440 is planned to fly in late 1988 and become available to customers in 1989.

Meanwhile, Bell has released preliminary details of a military **Model 400 Combat Twin**. Weighing 1,410 kg (3,110 lb) empty, this would have engine and crew armour, radar warning system, infra-red suppression and low IR reflection paint finish, and a quick-change range of external stores, with a roof mounted sight as a customer option. Max T-O weight remains unchanged.

The following description applies to the standard Model 400A, except where indicated:

TYPE: Seven-seat twin-engined light helicopter.

ROTOR SYSTEM: Four-blade 'soft-in-plane' main rotor and two-blade tail rotor. Each main blade has a high-lift aerofoil section inboard and a high-speed section outboard. Blades are of composite construction, comprising a corrosion resistant Nomex core encased in machine wound glassfibre, strengthened by two upper and two lower filament wound straps, and are interchangeable. Replaceable tip caps are of electroplated nickel. Tail rotor blades are of similar construction. Each main blade has a metal tab at approx 70 per cent radius, and an abrasion protection strip on its leading-edge. Two of the main rotor blades can be folded manually; a rotor brake is optional. Lightweight, advanced composites flex-beam hub has elastomeric bearings and, for each main rotor blade, a one-piece glassfibre yoke to which the blade is attached by two bolts (one quick-release) in a clevis type grip, providing redundant blade retention. Three-degree flapping action is built in, and system requires no lubrication.

ROTOR DRIVE: Transmission is rated at 429 kW (575 shp) for T-O and max continuous operation, and has a 30 min 'run-dry' capability. It is of conventional construction (steel gears in aluminium and magnesium casings), and embodies a liquid inertia vibration eliminator system (LIVE) mounted on the main rotor pylon to absorb rotor vibration. Both engines drive into a combining gearbox that has a rating of 529·5 kW (710 shp) with both engines operating or 343 kW (460 shp) with one engine only, Kaflex greaseless driveshaft for main rotor is driven via main rotor gearbox having one spiral bevel and one single-stage planetary reduction gear. Tail rotor driven via four interchangeable driveshaft sections and a 90° gearbox with a single spiral bevel reduction gear. Four single-system powered actuators (two cyclic, one collective and one directional). Main rotor/engine rpm ratio 0·0639:1, tail rotor/engine rpm ratio 0·4215:1.

FUSELAGE: Fail-safe semi-monocoque cabin structure, comprising roof beam, skin/stringer and honeycomb panels (mainly of conventional aluminium alloys, with some glassfibre and graphite epoxy). Tailboom is an aluminium alloy/honeycomb sandwich monocoque.

TAIL UNIT: Non-moving horizontal stabiliser with small, sweptback (arrowhead) endplate fins. Ring Guard combined fin/tail rotor guard, with small tailskid at its base.

LANDING GEAR: Skid gear, consisting of two longitudinal tubular skids connected by two arched cross-tubes. Each skid is fitted with replaceable wear shoes along bottom, a tow ring on the forward end, and four eyebolts for installation of optional ground handling wheels. Crew boarding step on front cross-tube each side; maintenance steps on rear cross-tube. Emergency flotation kit (optional) includes six skid mounted flotation bags (three each side), an inflation system consisting of a compressed nitrogen filament wound bottle, actuation valve, and associated tubes and flexible lines for gas distribution. Float inflation initiated normally by electrical actuation system energised by water immersion switches, but can also be initiated manually.

POWER PLANT: One Pratt & Whitney Canada PW209T coupled twin-turboshaft engine, rated at 699 kW (937 shp) max for T-O. Fuel in five rupture-resistant aluminium honeycomb tanks (two under cabin floor, two under rearward facing seats, and one main tank at rear of passenger compartment) with a total usable capacity of 719 litres (158 Imp gallons; 190 US gallons). Refuelling point on starboard side at rear of passenger cabin. Oil capacity 5·7 litres (1·25 Imp gallons; 1·5 US gallons) per engine. Engine anti-icing and fire detection systems standard.

ACCOMMODATION: Foam filled seat for pilot, with in-flight adjustable lumbar support. Seating for up to six passengers: one beside pilot, two rearward facing and three forward facing in main cabin. Dual controls optional. Crew door and passenger door on each side; between these, on port side, is an additional door that, when opened with passenger door, provides a wider opening for stretcher or cargo loading. Two stretchers and an intensive care team can be carried in ambulance role; all main cabin seats are removable for cargo operation. Tinted acrylic transparencies, those in doors being openable. Baggage compartment aft of passenger cabin, with external access via door on port side. Entire accommodation heated, ventilated and optionally air-conditioned. Demisting for cockpit and cabin windows.

SYSTEMS: STC approved vapour cycle air-conditioning system optional. Hydraulic system (nominal pressure 69 bars; 1,000 lb/sq in) for cyclic, collective and directional control actuation. Electrical system powered by two 160A engine driven starter/generators and a heavy duty 17Ah nickel-cadmium battery. Nitrogen bottle, pressurised at 207 bars (3,000 lb/sq in), for inflation of emergency flotation bags when fitted.

AVIONICS AND EQUIPMENT: Aircraft is provided with landing lights, position lights, strobe light, instrument lighting, and polyurethane exterior paint finish as standard. Flight instruments are conventional, but engine instruments are mounted in a new, solid state, liquid crystal display offering greater reliability. A priority panel warning system can display, in words, up to six hazards in appropriate order of urgency. To these can be added an electrical system controller developed and produced by VDO of West Germany. Interfaced with the engine starting system, this can monitor electrical power distribution and record, in a diagnostic memory bank, all data required for maintenance following a component failure.

Many FAA approved kits of avionics and equipment, already available for other Bell helicopters, are available

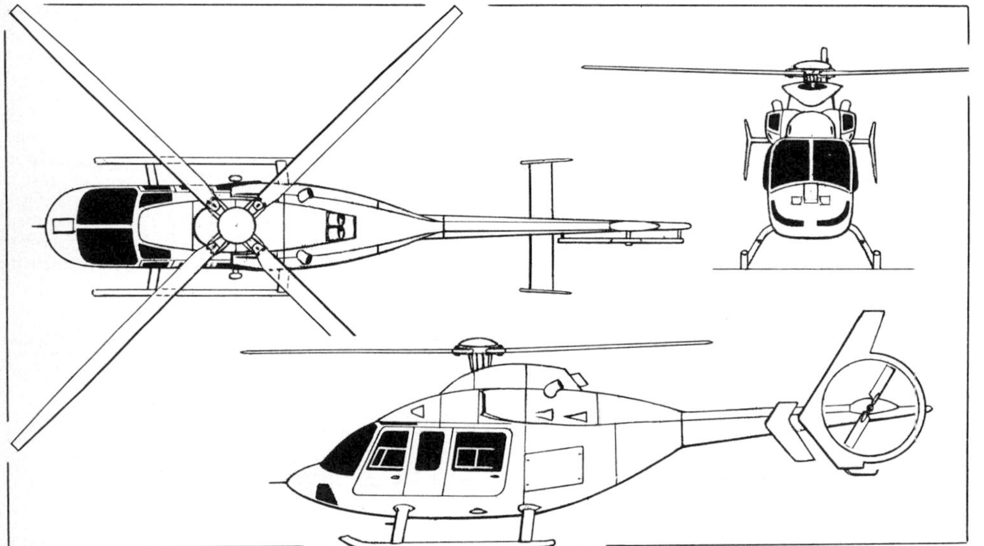

Bell Model 400A TwinRanger light twin-engined helicopter *(Pilot Press)*

as options on the Model 400A. These include King Silver Crown VHF radio (KX 155 transceiver and KMA 24H audio); King navigation equipment (KN 153 VOR/LOC/glideslope receiver, KR 21 marker beacon receiver, KR 87 ADF, KR 10A radio altimeter, KN 63 DME, KI 76A transponder, and KNS 81/KY 196 R/Nav); King IFR package (KMA 24H, KI 229, RMI, and two KX 165); Sperry SPZ-7000 digital AFCS with King KA 52 flight director; stability control augmentation system; dual controls; heater with automatic temperature control; freon type environmental control system; forced-air ventilation; additional soundproofing; de luxe, economy, or mesh seating; shoulder harnesses for all seats; carpet for cabin and crew area; rear cabin audio; engine particle separator, snow deflectors, and fire extinguisher; ground handling wheels; emergency flotation bags; rotor brake; stretchers (two, stowable); electric hoist and 907 kg (2,000 lb) capacity hook for external sling load. Other optional kits, to customer's requirements, can include such items as secure voice communications, full telemetry, loudspeakers, searchlight (up to 30 million candlepower), camera windows, protective armour and wire-cutting cables.

Armament (Combat Twin): Attachment point on each side of fuselage, aft of cabin doors, for two TOW missiles, a seven-round 2·75 in rocket launcher, two Stinger missiles, a twin-7·62 mm machine-gun pod, a 7·62 mm Minigun, or a 20 mm gun pod. Roof mounted sight optional.

Dimensions, external:
- Main rotor diameter: 11·28 m (37 ft 0 in)
- Main rotor blade chord: max: 0·27 m (10¾ in)
  - effective: 0·24 m (9½ in)
- Tail rotor diameter: 1·57 m (5 ft 2 in)
- Tail rotor blade chord (constant): 0·16 m (6·35 in)
- Distance between rotor centres: 6·82 m (22 ft 4⅔ in)
- Length overall, rotors turning: 13·39 m (43 ft 11 in)
- Fuselage: Length: 11·02 m (36 ft 2 in)
  - Max width: 1·31 m (4 ft 3½ in)
- Height: to top of rotor head: 3·20 m (10 ft 6 in)
  - over tail fin: 4·01 m (13 ft 2 in)
- Ground clearance: fuselage (min): 0·51 m (1 ft 8 in)
  - tailskid: 1·12 m (3 ft 8 in)
- Skid track (undeflected): 2·26 m (7 ft 5 in)
- Crew/passenger/stretcher doors:
  - Height (all): 1·04 m (3 ft 5 in)
  - Width: crew: 0·63 m (2 ft 1 in)
    - passenger: 0·91 m (3 ft 0 in)
    - stretcher: 0·37 m (1 ft 2½ in)
  - Height to sill (all): 0·61 m (2 ft 0 in)
- Baggage door: Height: 0·58 m (1 ft 11 in)
  - Width: 0·94 m (3 ft 1 in)
  - Height to sill: 0·69 m (2 ft 3 in)

Dimensions, internal:
- Cabin:
  - Length: fwd: 1·07 m (3 ft 6 in)
    - rear: 1·52 m (5 ft 0 in)
  - Max width: fwd, rear: 1·17 m (3 ft 10 in)
  - Max height: fwd, rear: 1·14 m (3 ft 9 in)
  - Floor area: fwd: 0·53 m² (5·7 sq ft)
    - rear: 0·58 m² (6·2 sq ft)
  - Volume: fwd: 1·13 m³ (40·0 cu ft)
    - rear: 2·26 m³ (80·0 cu ft)
- Baggage compartment:
  - Length: 1·24 m (4 ft 1 in)
  - Max width: 1·07 m (3 ft 6 in)
  - Max height: 0·53 m (1 ft 9 in)
  - Floor area: 0·69 m² (7·4 sq ft)
  - Volume: 0·57 m³ (20·0 cu ft)

Areas:
- Main rotor blades (each): 1·36 m² (14·645 sq ft)
- Tail rotor blades (each): 0·13 m² (1·365 sq ft)
- Main rotor disc: 99·89 m² (1,075·2 sq ft)
- Tail rotor disc: 1·95 m² (20·97 sq ft)
- Ring Guard fin: 1·28 m² (13·78 sq ft)
- Tailplane: 1·04 m² (11·24 sq ft)

Weights and Loadings:
- Manufacturer's weight empty: 1,427 kg (3,146 lb)
- Max usable fuel: 577 kg (1,272 lb)
- Max payload: 717 kg (1,582 lb)
- Max T-O and landing weight: 2,721 kg (6,000 lb)
- Max cabin floor loading: 420 kg/m² (86 lb/sq ft)
- Max disc loading: 27·23 kg/m² (5·58 lb/sq ft)

Performance (preliminary: A at gross weight of 2,041 kg; 4,500 lb, B at 2,268 kg; 5,000 lb, C at T-O weight of 2,495 kg; 5,500 lb):
- Never-exceed speed: 150 knots (278 km/h; 172 mph)
- Max level speed at S/L:
  - A: 133 knots (246 km/h; 153 mph)
  - B: 132 knots (244 km/h; 152 mph)
  - C: 130 knots (241 km/h; 150 mph)
- Operating range cruising speed, S/L to 1,220 m (4,000 ft), ISA: A: 123 knots (228 km/h; 141 mph)
  - B, C: 124 knots (230 km/h; 143 mph)
- Cruising speed for max endurance, S/L, ISA:
  - A: 50 knots (92 km/h; 57 mph)
  - B: 53 knots (98 km/h; 61 mph)
  - C: 57 knots (105 km/h; 65 mph)
- Max rate of climb at S/L, ISA:
  - A: 660 m (2,165 ft)/min
  - B: 556 m (1,825 ft)/min
  - C: 471 m (1,545 ft)/min
- Service ceiling, one engine out, 30 min contingency power, ISA + 20°C: A: 3,445 m (11,300 ft)
  - B: 2,375 m (7,800 ft)
  - C: 1,310 m (4,300 ft)
- Hovering ceiling OGE at T-O power:
  - ISA: A: 5,090 m (16,700 ft)
    - B: 4,145 m (13,600 ft)
    - C: 3,110 m (10,200 ft)
  - ISA + 20°C: A: 4,360 m (14,300 ft)
    - B: 3,260 m (10,700 ft)
    - C: 2,255 m (7,400 ft)
- Operating range, 20 min reserves:
  - S/L, ISA:
    - A, with 537 kg (1,184 lb) of fuel: 327 nm (606 km; 376 miles)
    - B, max fuel: 356 nm (660 km; 410 miles)
    - C, max fuel: 351 nm (650 km; 404 miles)
  - at 1,220 m (4,000 ft), ISA:
    - A, with 537 kg (1,184 lb) of fuel: 368 nm (682 km; 424 miles)
    - B, max fuel: 397 nm (736 km; 457 miles)
    - C, max fuel: 386 nm (715 km; 444 miles)
- Max endurance (S/L, ISA), no reserves:
  - A: 4 h 27 min
  - B: 4 h 41 min
  - C: 4 h 31 min

BLACKHOLE

BLACKHOLE INVESTMENTS LTD

RR4, Kenilworth, Ontario N0G 2E0

President: Charles A. Miller

This company started small-scale production in 1986 of replicas of the 1930s-vintage Bücker Bü 131 Jungmann and Bü 133 Jungmeister, planning to build an initial batch of 14 aircraft. Engine choices include Avco Lycomings of 134-194 kW (180-260 hp), or Warner Super Scarab radials in the same rating bracket. Twelve of the first 14 have been sold to US customers. Although the aircraft are factory built, and plans or kits are not available, they are licensed as homebuilts in Canada in view of the fact that original Bücker drawings are no longer available.

BOEING

BOEING FABRICATION AND SERVICES COMPANY OF CANADA

Arnprior Airport, Arnprior, Ontario K7S 3M1

Telephone: (613) 237 2771 and 623 4267

Details of the SARCUP and VOFUP programmes under which this company (known formerly as Boeing of Canada) upgraded six CH-113 and eight CH-113A helicopters to improved maritime search and rescue standard can be found in the 1985-86 and previous editions of *Jane's*. The latter programme was scheduled for completion in June 1986.

CANADAIR

CANADAIR LIMITED

Cartierville Airport, 1800 Laurentien Boulevard, St Laurent, Quebec H4R 1K2

Postal Address: PO Box 6087, Station 'A', Montreal, Quebec H3C 3G9

Telephone: (514) 744 1511

Telex: 05-826747

Chairman and Chief Executive Officer of Bombardier Inc: Laurent Beaudoin

President and Chief Executive Officer:
Pierre Des Marais II (interim)
Donald C. Lowe (designate)

Executive Vice-President and Chief Operating Officer: Robert D. Richmond

Executive Vice-President: Carl Dean Perry

Corporate Vice-Presidents:
Alan B. Marquis (Finance)
Jacques E. Ouellet (Corporate Resources)
Robert A. Wohl (Administration and Legal)

Vice-Presidents:
Vincent Ambrico (Manufacturing)
Leonard B. Box (Surveillance Systems)
William K. Carr (Government Sales)
Frank M. Francis (Materiel)
Anthony M. Guérin (CL-215 Sales)
Terrance G. Hill (Quality Assurance and Flight Operations)
Robert J. Ross (Engineering)
John F. Smith (Programme Manager, Challenger)
Andreas Throner (Manufacturing, Plants 2 and 3)

Corporate Secretary, and Director, Legal Services:
Robert Lefcort

Canadair Limited's business was carried on between 1976 and 1986 by the Canadian government, which acquired the company from General Dynamics Corporation. In 1982 it came under the control of Canada Development Investment Corporation, giving this Crown corporation the responsibility for managing the government's investment in Canadair's aerospace business. On 18 August 1986 the Canadian government announced the signing of a letter of intent for the sale of Canadair to Bombardier Inc of Montreal. Remaining steps to complete the privatisation process was expected to be taken before the end of the year.

Canadair has been engaged in the manufacture of nearly 4,000 military and commercial aircraft since 1944. It has also been employed in the research, design, development and production of missile components, pilotless surveillance systems and a variety of non-aerospace products. The present Canadair has three plants in the St Laurent complex at Cartierville Airport, and a fourth at Dorval International Airport, Montreal. Total covered floor space is 260,127 m² (2,800,000 sq ft), and total workforce at the beginning of 1986 was 4,700.

The Challenger twin-turbofan executive transport entered production during 1978; manufacture of the fifth series of CL-215 tanker/utility amphibians (c/n 1081 onwards) began in 1984, and go-ahead for a CL-215T turboprop version was announced in 1986; production of the CL-89 and development of the CL-289 and CL-227

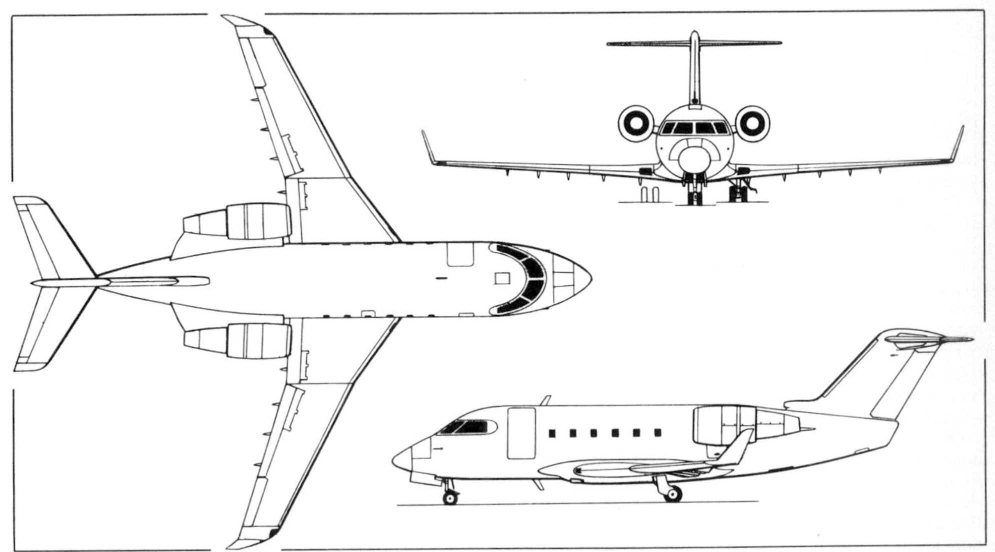

Canadair Challenger 601 (two General Electric CF34-1A turbofan engines) *(Pilot Press)*

surveillance systems (see RPVs and Targets section) continue. Major subcontracts concern outer wing boxes, wing stubs, rear fuselages, forward and aft radomes and main electrical load centres for US Navy and other Lockheed P-3C Orions and the CP-140 Aurora Canadian version of this aircraft; aluminium bulkheads, frames and other machined parts for the McDonnell Douglas F-15; nose barrel assemblies for the McDonnell Douglas F/A-18 Hornet; wing leading-edge components, ailerons and rear cargo doors for the Lockheed C-5B Galaxy transport programme; tailplanes for Northrop F-5 series aircraft; and rear fuselage sections for the Boeing 767. Production of aircraft spares, and the modification, repair and overhaul of aircraft, are also included in the current work programme.

CANADAIR CHALLENGER 600 and 601

Canadian Armed Forces designation: CC-144

In April 1976 worldwide exclusive rights to design, manufacture, market and support the proposed LearStar 600 were acquired from the late William P. Lear Sr; this concept envisaged an aircraft using an advanced technology wing and two high bypass ratio turbofan engines. Canadair's development programme was launched on 29 October 1976. In March 1977, major design changes were announced and the aircraft became known as the Canadair Challenger.

The first of three pre-production Challengers (C-GCGR-X, c/n 1001) made its first flight on 8 November 1978. The second flew on 17 March and the third on 14 July 1979. First flight by a production Challenger was made on 21 September 1979, and this joined the programme in October 1979.

The version with Avco Lycoming engines, originally designated CL-600, is now known as the **Challenger 600**. It received Canadian DoT type approval on 11 August 1980, and FAA certification on 7 November of that year. On 10 April 1982 the prototype of a second version was flown for the first time. Known as the **Challenger 601** (previously CL-601), this has General Electric engines and winglets. The first production 601 (C-GBUU) flew for the first time on 17 September 1982. Canadian DoT and FAA certification were awarded on 25 February and 11 March 1983 respectively, and customer deliveries began shortly afterwards. Twenty-two Challengers were delivered during 1984 and 13 in 1985.

By 1 September 1986, a total of 132 Challengers (82 600s and 50 601s) had been delivered, out of 142 ordered by that date. They include a 600 specially equipped by Dornier of Germany for the Swiss Air-Ambulance service of Zurich. This is fully capable of providing intensive care for four stretcher patients on nonstop flights of more than 3,000 nm (5,550 km; 3,450 miles) and can carry up to eight patients.

By the end of February 1986 a total of 59 Challenger 600s had been retrofitted with winglets, in a continuing programme expected to result in about 80 per cent of the existing 600 fleet being so modified. Winglet retrofit on existing 600s was certificated in 1984.

Thirteen Challenger 601s were ordered during 1985, and production of 14 aircraft was scheduled during 1986. No Model 600s were being produced in early 1986, but this version has not been discontinued, and Canadair is prepared to build more 600s if sufficient orders are received. A new version of the 601, now being offered with a 'glass cockpit' and upgraded engines, is designated **601-3A**, and should begin deliveries in Spring 1987. First flight was scheduled for October 1986.

Canadair has developed specifications for military variants of the Challenger such as flight inspection, maritime surveillance, airborne early warning, electronic warfare training, cargo transport and remote sensing. Several of these variants have been ordered or are under development: the Canadian Dept of Transport has taken delivery of two 601s for use in flight inspection missions, and the Dept of National Defence ordered seven Challenger 600s for service with No. 414 Squadron on electronic support and training, with an eighth for use at the Aeronautical Engineering and Test Establishment at Cold Lake, Alberta, as a testbed for developing such future military applications as maritime reconnaissance. The DND's No. 412 Squadron has four 600s for government transport duties, and four additional 601s were delivered during 1985 as VIP transports. All 16 DND aircraft are fitted with a Litton LTN-91 inertial navigation system. Other military transport versions have been ordered for the Royal Malaysian Air Force (two), West German Luftwaffe (seven 601s for special air missions), and the People's Republic of China (three 601s). The West German Challengers are delivered 'green' to Dornier Reparaturwerft for outfitting. The first was due for delivery to the Luftwaffe in March 1986, with the other six to follow at two-month intervals. Some will be configured as 12/16-passenger transports, one as a passenger/cargo combi, and one as an air ambulance.

On 23/24 August 1983 Challenger 601 c/n 3002 set a new nonstop straight-line distance record in Class C1i by flying from Calgary, Alberta, to Heathrow Airport, London (3,790 nm; 7,023·5 km; 4,364·2 miles), in 9 h 4 min. In all, the FAI has ratified 18 international records by Challengers for time to height, altitude without payload, and altitude in horizontal flight.

Canadair Challenger 600 electronic support and training aircraft of the Department of National Defence. More than 70 per cent of Challenger 600s have now been retrofitted with the 601 winglet modification

TYPE: Twin-turbofan business, cargo and commuter transport.

WINGS: Cantilever low-wing monoplane, built in one piece. Advanced technology section (with winglets on Challenger 601; optional on 600). Thickness/chord ratio 14% at root, 12% at leading-edge sweep break and 10% at tip. Dihedral 2° 20′. Incidence 3°at root. Sweepback at quarter-chord 25°. Two-spar structure, primarily of aluminium alloy; spars covered with skin/stringer panels to form rigid torsion box. Two-section double-slotted trailing-edge flaps. Hydraulically powered aluminium plain ailerons. Inboard spoilers for descent control and ground lift dumping. No tabs. Thermal anti-icing of leading-edges by engine bleed air.

FUSELAGE: Aluminium alloy damage-tolerant semi-monocoque pressurised structure of circular cross-section. Employs chemically milled aluminium alloy skins with riveted frames and stringers, providing optimum strength characteristics while minimising aircraft weight.

TAIL UNIT: Cantilever multi-spar aluminium alloy T tail, with swept vertical and horizontal surfaces. All control surfaces hydraulically powered. Tailplane incidence adjusted by electric trim motor. No tabs.

LANDING GEAR: Hydraulically retractable tricycle type, with twin wheels and Dowty Rotol oleo-pneumatic shock absorbers on each unit. Mainwheels retract inward into wing centre-section, nose unit forward. Nose unit steerable and self-centring. Mainwheels have Goodyear 26 × 6·65 tyres, pressure 11·38 bars (165 lb/sq in); nosewheels have Goodyear 18 × 4·4 tyres, pressure 8·27 bars (120 lb/sq in). Goodyear hydraulically operated multiple-disc carbon brakes with fully modulated anti-skid system.

POWER PLANT: Two 33·36 kN (7,500 lb st) Avco Lycoming ALF 502L-2 or L-3 turbofan engines in Challenger 600; General Electric CF34-1As in Challenger 601, each rated at 40·66 kN; 9,140 lb st with automatic power reserve, or 38·48 kN; 8,650 lb st without APR; or CF34-3A turbofans in 601-3A, ratings of 40·66 kN (9,140 lb st) with/38·48 kN (8,650 lb st) without, APR. One engine is pylon mounted on each side of rear fuselage, fitted with cascade type fan-air thrust reversers. Integral fuel tank in centre-section (capacity 2,839 litres; 624 Imp gallons; 750 US gallons), one in each wing (each 2,725 litres; 600 Imp gallons; 720 US gallons) and auxiliary tank beneath cabin floor; total capacity 9,278 litres (2,041 Imp gallons; 2,451 US gallons). Pressure and gravity fuelling and defuelling. Oil capacity 13·6 litres (3 Imp gallons).

ACCOMMODATION: Pilot and co-pilot side by side on flight deck with dual controls. Blind-flying instrumentation standard. Interiors are installed to customer's specifications. A maximum of 19 passenger seats is approved. Typical installations include toilet, buffet, bar and wardrobe. The baggage compartment, with its own loading door, is accessible in flight. Downward opening door on port side, forward of wing, from c/n 24 onwards. (Upward opening on earlier aircraft.) Door is power assisted on 601-3A. Overwing emergency exit on starboard side. Entire accommodation heated, ventilated and air-conditioned.

SYSTEMS: Sundstrand pressurisation and Garrett air-conditioning systems, max pressure differential 0·64 bars (9·3 lb/sq in) in Challenger 600, 0·62 bars (9·0 lb/sq in) in Challenger 601 and 601-3A. Three independent hydraulic systems, each of 207 bars (3,000 lb/sq in). No. 1 system powers flight controls (via servo-actuators positioned by cables and pushrods); No. 2 system for flight controls and brakes; No. 3 system for flight controls, landing gear extension/retraction, brakes and nosewheel steering. Nos. 1 and 2 systems each powered by an engine driven pump, supplemented by an AC electric pump; No. 3 system by two AC pumps. Two 30kVA engine driven generators supply primary 115/200V three-phase AC electric power at 400Hz. Three transformer-rectifiers to convert AC power to 28V DC; one 43Ah nickel-cadmium battery. Alternative primary power provided by APU and an air driven generator, the latter being deployed automatically if the engine driven generators and APU are inoperative. Stall warning system, with stick shakers and stick pusher. Garrett GTCP-100E gas turbine APU (to be certificated for in-flight operation) for engine start, ground air-conditioning and other services. Electric anti-icing of windscreen, flight deck side windows and pitot heads; Sundstrand bleed air anti-icing of wings, tailplane, engine intake cowls and guide vanes. Gaseous oxygen system, pressure 124 bars (1,800 lb/sq in). Continuous-element fire detectors in each engine nacelle and APU; two-shot extinguishing system for engines, single-shot system for APU.

AVIONICS (except 601-3A): Standard avionics include dual Collins VHF-20A com, dual Collins VIR-30A VOR/ILS/marker beacon receiver, dual Sperry SPZ 600 flight directors, SPZ 600 autopilot with dual servos, dual TDR-90 transponders, dual DME (with HSI display), one ALT-55B radio altimeter, dual C-14 compasses, standby compass, one ADF-60, dual intercom system, comparator warning system, RCA Primus 400 weather radar, HF and other antennae. Provision, at customer's option, for HF com, third VHF com, second ADF, VLF nav, INS, GPWS, ELT, flight data recorder and cockpit voice recorder.

AVIONICS (601-3A): Dual electronic flight instrument systems (EFIS); single multi-function display (MFD); dual laser inertial reference systems (LIRS); dual flight management systems; digital automatic flight control system, with dual channel fail-operational autopilot and flight director; dual digital air data system with V/Nav; four-colour digital weather radar; radar altimeter; dual VHF com; dual VHF nav; dual DME; dual ATC transponders; dual ADF; dual HF com; cockpit voice recorder; standby instruments (artificial horizon, airspeed indicator and altimeter). Systems will be certificated for Cat. II operations. Space provisions for flight data recorder, ELT, VLF/Omega, GPWS, and full provisions for third LIRS.

DIMENSIONS, EXTERNAL:

Wing span: 600	18·85 m (61 ft 10 in)
601, over winglets	19·61 m (64 ft 4 in)
Wing chord: at fuselage c/l	4·89 m (16 ft 0½ in)
at tip	1·27 m (4 ft 1·9 in)
Wing aspect ratio: 600	7·35
601	8·5
Length overall	20·85 m (68 ft 5 in)
Fuselage: Max diameter	2·69 m (8 ft 10 in)
Height overall	6·30 m (20 ft 8 in)
Tailplane span	6·20 m (20 ft 4 in)
Wheel track (c/l of shock struts)	3·18 m (10 ft 5 in)
Wheelbase	7·99 m (26 ft 2½ in)
Passenger door (port, fwd): Height	1·78 m (5 ft 10 in)
Width	0·91 m (3 ft 0 in)
Height to sill	1·61 m (5 ft 3½ in)
Baggage door (port, rear): Height	0·84 m (2 ft 9 in)
Width	0·71 m (2 ft 4 in)
Height to sill	1·61 m (5 ft 3½ in)
Overwing emergency exit (stbd):	
Height	0·91 m (3 ft 0 in)
Width	0·51 m (1 ft 8 in)

DIMENSIONS, INTERNAL:

Cabin: Length, incl galley, toilet and baggage area, excl flight deck	8·61 m (28 ft 3 in)
Max width	2·49 m (8 ft 2 in)
Width at floor level	2·18 m (7 ft 2 in)
Max height	1·85 m (6 ft 1 in)
Floor area	18·77 m² (202 sq ft)
Volume	32·6 m³ (1,150 cu ft)

AREAS:

Wings, gross	48·31 m² (520·0 sq ft)
Ailerons (total)	1·39 m² (15·0 sq ft)
Trailing-edge flaps (total)	7·80 m² (84·0 sq ft)
Fin	9·18 m² (98·8 sq ft)
Rudder	2·03 m² (21·9 sq ft)
Tailplane	6·45 m² (69·4 sq ft)
Elevators (total)	2·15 m² (23·1 sq ft)

WEIGHTS:

Manufacturer's weight empty:	
600	8,464 kg (18,660 lb)
601	9,049 kg (19,950 lb)
601-3A	9,292 kg (20,485 lb)
Typical operating weight empty:	
600	10,562 kg (23,285 lb)
601	11,151 kg (24,585 lb)
601-3A	11,197 kg (24,685 lb)
Max fuel: 600	6,754 kg (14,890 lb)
601, 601-3A	7,559 kg (16,665 lb)
Max payload: 600	2,365 kg (5,215 lb)
601	2,229 kg (4,915 lb)
601-3A	2,184 kg (4,815 lb)
Payload with max fuel: 600	1,395 kg (3,075 lb)
601	907 kg (2,000 lb)
601-3A	862 kg (1,900 lb)
Max T-O weight: 600	18,642 kg (41,100 lb)*
601, 601-3A	19,550 kg (43,100 lb)
Max ramp weight: 600	18,710 kg (41,250 lb)
601, 601-3A	19,618 kg (43,250 lb)
Max landing weight:	
600, 601, 601-3A	16,329 kg (36,000 lb)
Max zero-fuel weight: 600	12,927 kg (28,500 lb)
601	14,061 kg (31,000 lb)
601-3A	13,381 kg (29,500 lb)**
Max wing loading: 600	385·9 kg/m² (79·04 lb/sq ft)
601, 601-3A	404·7 kg/m² (82·88 lb/sq ft)
Max power loading: 600	279·41 kg/kN (2·74 lb/lb st)
601	254·03 kg/kN (2·49 lb/lb st)
601-3A	240·81 kg/kN (2·36 lb/lb st)

**18,710 kg (41,250 lb) with optional winglets*
***14,061 kg (31,000 lb) available optionally*

PERFORMANCE (at max T-O weight except where indicated):

Max cruising speed:	
600, 601, 601-3A	459 knots (851 km/h; 529 mph)
Normal cruising speed:	
600, 601, 601-3A	442 knots (819 km/h; 509 mph)
Long-range cruising speed:	
600	401 knots (743 km/h; 462 mph)
601, 601-3A	424 knots (786 km/h; 488 mph)
Time to initial cruise altitude: 600	25 min
601	21 min
601-3A	20 min
Max operating altitude:	
600, 601, 601-3A	12,500 m (41,000 ft)
Service ceiling, one engine out:	
600, 601, 601-3A	7,315 m (24,000 ft)
Balanced T-O field length (ISA at S/L):	
600 (FAA)	1,737 m (5,700 ft)
601, 601-3A	1,645 m (5,400 ft)
Landing distance at S/L at max landing weight:	
600 (FAA), 601-3A	1,006 m (3,300 ft)
601	1,082 m (3,550 ft)
Min ground turning radius (all)	20·27 m (66 ft 6 in)
Range with max fuel and five passengers, NBAA IFR reserves (200 nm; 370 km; 230 mile alternate) at long range cruising speed:	
600 (basic)	2,800 nm (5,186 km; 3,222 miles)
600 (with fuselage tank)	3,123 nm (5,784 km; 3,594 miles)
601	3,440 nm (6,371 km; 3,959 miles)
601-3A	3,430 nm (6,356 km; 3,950 miles)
Design *g* limit: 600	+2·7
601, 601-3A	+2·6

OPERATIONAL NOISE LEVELS (FAR Pt 36):

T-O: 600	84·7 EPNdB
601, 601-3A	79·9 EPNdB
Sideline: 600	89·5 EPNdB
601, 601-3A	84·8 EPNdB
Approach: 600	91·6 EPNdB
601, 601-3A	89·4 EPNdB

CANADAIR CL-215

The Canadair CL-215 is a twin-engined amphibian, intended primarily for firefighting but adaptable to a wide variety of other duties. It is designed for simplicity of operation and maintenance, and can operate from small airstrips, lakes, ocean bays etc.

The CL-215 made its first flight on 23 October 1967, and its first water take-off on 2 May 1968. Canadian DoT certification in the Utility and Restricted categories was obtained on 7 March 1969, followed by FAA certification in the Restricted category on 15 May of the same year.

By 1 March 1986 sales had been made to the governments of Quebec (15); Manitoba (3); Ontario (2); France (15); Greece (15); Italy (4); Spain (19); Thailand (2); Venezuela (2); and Yugoslavia (5). All aircraft are capable of firefighting and other roles: Spain has eight equipped for SAR and coastal patrol, and Thailand two; the Venezuelan pair are configured as passenger transport aircraft.

Production of the first 80 aircraft was completed in four series. Details of the first and second series can be found in the 1977-78 *Jane's*, and of the third series in the 1979-80 edition.

Continued production of the CL-215 was ensured by new orders for 29 fifth-series water bombers for deployment throughout Canada. Seventeen of these are being funded by the Federal government and 12 by provincial governments. Orders are for Alberta (4), Manitoba (2), Newfoundland (4), Northwest Territories (2), Ontario (7), Quebec (4), Saskatchewan (4) and Yukon (2). Production of the fifth series began in 1985 at a rate of 1½ per month, and by 1 March 1986 three of the 29 had been delivered, two to Ontario and one to the Northwest Territories. Deliveries of all 29 are scheduled for completion in mid-1988.

Canadair CL-215 demonstrating its water bombing capability

The CL-215 firefighting installation consists of two internal tanks, two retractable probes and two drop doors, plus the associated operating systems. It attacks fires in the following ways:

(a) with water or chemical retardants ground loaded at airports; or

(b) with fresh or salt water scooped from a suitable body of water as the aircraft skims across the surface.

The aircraft carries a maximum water or retardant load of 5,346 litres (1,176 Imp gallons). The tanks can be ground filled in 2 min, or scoop filled in 10 s while the aircraft planes at 70 knots (130 km/h; 81 mph). Pickup distance in still air, from 15 m (50 ft) above the surface on approach to 15 m (50 ft) above the surface during climb-out, is 1,200 m (3,935 ft).

On a number of occasions single CL-215s have made over 100 drops totalling more than 534,600 litres (117,600 Imp gallons) in one day. Full loads have been scooped from the Mediterranean in wave heights of up to 2 m (6 ft). In 1983 a Yugoslav CL-215 made 225 drops totalling 1,202,850 litres (264,597 Imp gallons) on fires in one day. Total drops by CL-215s were about half a million by the end of 1985.

A lightweight integrated liquid spray system has been developed and certificated. Four production units have been purchased for the Yugoslav CL-215s. The system, which does not interfere with the primary role of firefighting, is available for retrofit. Uses include the application of oil dispersants and pesticides. Tests conducted at Canadair have shown that the CL-215 can be used to extinguish oil fires by airdropping a suitable foaming agent. Another type of foam agent, mixed on board the aircraft after scooping, has proved particularly effective against forest fires in field trials in France and Spain.

TYPE: Twin-engined multi-purpose amphibian.

WINGS: Cantilever high-wing monoplane. No dihedral. All-metal one-piece fail-safe structure, with front and rear spars at 16 per cent and 49 per cent chord. Spars of conventional construction, with extruded caps and webs stiffened by vertical members. Aluminium alloy skin, with riveted spanwise extruded stringers, is supported at 762 mm (30 in) pitch by interspar ribs. Leading-edge consists of aluminium alloy skin attached to pressed nose-ribs and spanwise stringers. Hydraulically operated all-metal single-slotted flaps, supported by four external hinges on interspar ribs on each wing. Trim tab and geared tab in port aileron, rudder/aileron interconnect tab in starboard aileron. Detachable glassfibre wingtips.

FUSELAGE: All-metal single-step flying-boat hull of conventional fail-safe construction.

TAIL UNIT: Cantilever all-metal fail-safe structure with horizontal surfaces mounted midway up fin. Structure of aluminium alloy sheet, honeycomb panels, extrusions and fittings. Elevators and rudder fitted with dynamic balance, trim tab (port elevator only), spring tabs and geared tabs. Provision for de-icing of leading-edges.

LANDING GEAR: Hydraulically retractable tricycle type. Fully castoring, self-centering twin-wheel nose unit retracts rearward into hull and is fully enclosed by doors. Fifth series aircraft are fitted with nosewheel steering, and a retrofit kit will be made available for earlier aircraft. Main gear support structures retract into wells in sides of hull. A plate mounted on each main gear assembly encloses bottom of wheel well. Mainwheel tyre pressure 5·31 bars (77 lb/sq in); nosewheel tyre pressure 6·55 bars (95 lb/sq in). Hydraulic disc brakes. Non-retractable stabilising floats are each carried on a pylon cantilevered from wing box structure, with breakaway provision.

POWER PLANT: Two 1,566 kW (2,100 hp) Pratt & Whitney R-2800-CA3 eighteen-cylinder radial engines, each driving a Hamilton Standard Hydromatic constant-speed fully-feathering three-blade propeller, with 43E60 hub and type 6903A blades. Two fuel tanks, each of eight flexible cells, in wing spar box, with total usable capacity of 5,910 litres (1,300 Imp gallons). Gravity refuelling through two points above each tank. Oil in two tanks, with total capacity of 272·75 litres (60 Imp gallons), aft of engine firewalls.

ACCOMMODATION (water bomber version): Crew of two side by side on flight deck. Dual controls standard. Two 2,673 litre (588 Imp gallon) water tanks in main fuselage compartment, with retractable pickup probe in each side of hull bottom. Water drop door in each side of hull bottom. Flush doors on port side of fuselage forward and aft of wings. Emergency exit on starboard side aft of wing trailing-edge. Emergency hatch above starboard cockpit. Mooring hatch in upper surface of nose. Side facing canvas folding seats for eight people are located in the forward cabin area.

ACCOMMODATION (other roles): When configured for patrol and search and rescue missions, aircraft has additional stations for a flight engineer, navigator and two observers. Navigator's station, immediately behind flight deck, includes search radar display. Observers' stations in rear fuselage have sliding seats which can be positioned alongside blister windows. Toilet in rear of cabin; galley installed. Additional seats and/or stretchers available. In passenger transport configuration up to 26 forward facing seats can be fitted in a fully furnished interior with toilet and galley. Cargo tiedown fittings for loads of up to 2,268 kg (5,000 lb). Provision for extra cabin windows, to a maximum of 14.

SYSTEMS: Hydraulic system, pressure 207 bars (3,000 lb/sq in), utilises two engine driven pumps (max flow rate 45·5 litres; 10 Imp gallons/min) to actuate landing gear, flaps, water drop doors, pickup probes and wheel brakes. Unpressurised air/oil reservoir. Electric pump in system provides power for emergency actuation of landing gear and brakes and closure of water doors. Electrical system includes two 400VA 115V 400Hz static inverters (800VA in SAR version), two 28V 200A DC generators, one 36Ah lead-acid battery and one aircooled petrol engine driven 28V 200A generator GPU.

AVIONICS AND EQUIPMENT: Standard installation includes dual VHF transceiver, single VHF/FM com, dual VOR/ILS receivers, dual ADF, two marker beacon receivers, ATC transponder and ELT. Optional avionics include HF, DME and radio altimeter. A search radar is optional on the SAR version.

DIMENSIONS, EXTERNAL:

Wing span	28·60 m (93 ft 10 in)
Wing chord (constant)	3·54 m (11 ft 7½ in)
Wing aspect ratio	8·15
Length overall	19·82 m (65 ft 0½ in)
Beam	2·59 m (8 ft 6 in)
Length/beam ratio	7·5
Height overall (on land)	8·98 m (29 ft 5½ in)
Tailplane span	10·97 m (36 ft 0 in)
Wheel track	5·28 m (17 ft 4 in)
Wheelbase	7·23 m (23 ft 8½ in)
Propeller diameter	4·34 m (14 ft 3 in)

Forward door: Height 1·37 m (4 ft 6 in)
Width 1·03 m (3 ft 4 in)
Rear door: Height 1·12 m (3 ft 8 in)
Width 1·03 m (3 ft 4 in)
Water drop door: Length 1·60 m (5 ft 3 in)
Width 0·81 m (2 ft 8 in)
Emergency exit: Height 0·91 m (3 ft 0 in)
Width 0·51 m (1 ft 8 in)

DIMENSIONS, INTERNAL:
Cabin, excl flight deck: Length 9·38 m (30 ft 9½ in)
Max width 2·39 m (7 ft 10 in)
Max height 1·90 m (6 ft 3 in)
Floor area 19·69 m² (212 sq ft)
Volume 35·59 m³ (1,257 cu ft)

AREAS:
Wings, gross 100·33 m² (1,080 sq ft)
Ailerons (total) 8·05 m² (86·6 sq ft)
Flaps (total) 22·39 m² (241 sq ft)
Vertical tail surfaces (total) 17·23 m² (185·5 sq ft)
Rudder, incl tabs 6·02 m² (64·75 sq ft)
Horizontal tail surfaces (total) 28·43 m² (306 sq ft)
Elevators, incl tabs 7·88 m² (84·8 sq ft)

WEIGHTS AND LOADINGS:
Manufacturer's weight empty 12,220 kg (26,941 lb)
Typical operating weight empty 12,738 kg (28,082 lb)
Max fuel weight 4,245 kg (9,360 lb)
Max payload: Water bomber 5,443 kg (12,000 lb)
Utility version 3,864 kg (8,518 lb)
Max T-O weight (land) 19,731 kg (43,500 lb)
Max T-O weight (water) 17,100 kg (37,700 lb)
Max zero-fuel weight 18,143 kg (40,000 lb)
Max landing weight: on land 15,603 kg (34,400 lb)
on water 16,780 kg (37,000 lb)
Cabin floor loading 732 kg/m² (150 lb/sq ft)
Max wing loading 196·66 kg/m² (40·3 lb/sq ft)
Max power loading 6·23 kg/kW (10·36 lb/hp)

PERFORMANCE:
Cruising speed (max recommended power) at AUW of 18,595 kg (41,000 lb) at 3,050 m (10,000 ft) 157 knots (291 km/h; 181 mph)
Stalling speed, 15° flap, AUW of 19,731 kg (43,500 lb) 79 knots (145 km/h; 90 mph)
Stalling speed, 25° flap, AUW of 15,603 kg (34,400 lb), power off 66 knots (123 km/h; 76 mph)

Canadair CL-215T twin-turboprop general purpose amphibian *(Jane's/Mike Keep)*

Max rate of climb at S/L at AUW of 19,731 kg (43,500 lb) at max continuous power 305 m (1,000 ft)/min
Rate of climb at S/L, one engine out, at AUW of 17,100 kg (37,700 lb) at T-O power 75 m (245 ft)/min
T-O to 15 m (50 ft):
from land at AUW of 19,731 kg (43,500 lb) 811 m (2,660 ft)
from water at AUW of 17,100 kg (37,700 lb) 800 m (2,625 ft)
Landing from 15 m (50 ft):
on land at AUW of 15,603 kg (34,400 lb) 732 m (2,400 ft)
on water at AUW of 16,780 kg (37,000 lb) 835 m (2,740 ft)
Range with 1,587 kg (3,500 lb) payload:
at max cruise power 925 nm (1,714 km; 1,065 miles)
at long-range cruise power 1,130 nm (2,094 km; 1,301 miles)

CANADAIR CL-215T

Go-ahead for a turboprop powered version of the CL-215 was confirmed by Canadair in September 1986. Details of this version can be found in the Addenda.

CONAIR

CONAIR AVIATION LTD

Box 220, Abbotsford, British Columbia V2S 4N9
Telephone: (604) 853 1171
Telex: 04-363529

PRESIDENT: L. G. Kerr
VICE-PRESIDENT AND GENERAL MANAGER: K. B. Marsden
DIRECTOR OF OPERATIONS: Barrie Madu
ENGINEERING MANAGER: Bruce D. Emery

Using a mixed fleet of fixed-wing and rotating-wing aircraft, Conair specialises in aerial control services such as forest fire control, oil spill control, insect control, forest fertilisation, and salmonid enhancement. The company also designs and manufactures many speciality aviation systems such as fire retardant delivery systems, dispersal equipment, and various spray systems. Among these are a 1,459 litre (321 Imp gallon) underbelly retardant tank for the Bell 205A helicopter, and an 11,365 litre (2,500 Imp gallon) ventral retardant tank for a firebombing version of the Douglas DC-6B. Sales in 1984-85 included a DC-6 oil spill spraying system to the French Protection Civile, a similar installation to Aeritalia for the G222, and five Bell 205/212 firebombing systems to the National Safety Council of Australia. Since 1978 Conair has also undertaken a number of conversions of Grumman or Canadian built S-2 Tracker aircraft to Conair Firecat air tanker configuration.

In 1986 Conair was awarded a five-year contract to maintain and operate the four Canadair CL-215 water bombers of the Yukon and Northwest Territories.

CONAIR FIRECAT

The Firecat is converted from standard Grumman S-2A (S2F-1) or de Havilland Canada CS2F-1/2/3 Tracker aircraft for specialised fire control operation, and the aircraft so converted are part of the Conair fleet as well as being available for export. Conair is now the Canadian type certificate holder for the S-2F and Firecat (transferred from de Havilland Canada in 1984).

A total of 22 Firecat conversions had been completed by 1 May 1986, comprising 11 for Conair, ten for the French government's Protection Civile and one for the government of Saskatchewan.

The Conair conversion includes raising the cabin floor by 20·3 cm (8 in) and installing a 3,296 litre (725 Imp gallon) retardant tank in the fuselage; modification of the landing gear by fitting larger wheels with low pressure tyres, for soft field operation; inspecting the wing spar caps for corrosion, and repairing or replacing them as necessary; removing 1,361 kg (3,000 lb) of military equipment; completely rewiring the aircraft; and rebuilding/updating the flight deck instrument panels. Options include a choice of hydraulic or pneumatic system for discharge of the retardant, as well as a microcomputer system to control the retardant drop pattern. The retardant tank has four compartments, which can be discharged in a single salvo, two two-door salvos, or four single-door drops.

Special purpose Canadian type approval A-107 was awarded for the Firecat on 1 January 1984.

POWER PLANT: Two 1,100 kW (1,475 hp) Wright 982C9HE2 (R-1820-82) Cyclone nine-cylinder aircooled radial engines, each driving a Hamilton Standard 43D51-355 three-blade constant-speed propeller. Total internal fuel capacity 1,968 litres (433 Imp gallons). Oil capacity 95·5 litres (21 Imp gallons).

ACCOMMODATION: Minimum crew: one pilot.

WEIGHTS:
Operating weight empty 6,895 kg (15,200 lb)
Max payload 4,746 kg (10,464 lb)
Max fuel load 1,418 kg (3,126 lb)
Max T-O weight 11,793 kg (26,000 lb)
Max landing weight 11,113 kg (24,500 lb)

PERFORMANCE (at max T-O weight):
Never-exceed speed 280 knots (519 km/h; 322 mph)
Max level speed at 1,220 m (4,000 ft) 244 knots (452 km/h; 281 mph)
Max cruising speed 220 knots (408 km/h; 253 mph)
Fire-bombing drop speed 120 knots (222 km/h; 138 mph)
Stalling speed, flaps down, power off 82 knots (152 km/h; 95 mph)
Max rate of climb at S/L 366 m (1,200 ft)/min
Rate of climb at S/L, one engine out 170 m (560 ft)/min
Service ceiling 6,860 m (22,500 ft)
Service ceiling, one engine out 4,115 m (13,500 ft)
T-O to 15 m (50 ft) 368 m (1,208 ft)
Landing from 15 m (50 ft) 549 m (1,800 ft)
Minimum field length 915 m (3,000 ft)
Endurance with max payload 4 h 30 min

Conair Firecat conversions of the Grumman S-2 Tracker

CONAIR FIREFIGHTING FOKKER F27

Conair has modified a Fokker F27 Mk 600 commuter transport for firefighting roles, and was preparing to fly the prototype conversion in the Spring of 1986. The company anticipates a world market for at least 30 such conversions, and plans to operate a fleet of six itself.

The extensive modification programme includes installation of a Conair designed and manufactured fire retardant delivery system which will carry 6,364 litres (1,400 Imp gallons) of long-term retardant. The converted aircraft will be readily adaptable to other functions such as transporting cargo and fire crews, infra-red fire detection and mapping, aerial survey and pararescue operations. Unnecessary internal items such as cabin insulation, bulkheads, pressurisation equipment and galleys are deleted, modern avionics installed, and the eight-compartment retardant delivery system fitted in a new underfuselage fairing. The tank can be loaded at a rate of 1,514 litres (333 Imp gallons)/min. Door sequencing and fluid outflow regulators are computer controlled, and the entire vent system can be installed or removed in about 30 min to allow use as a cargo aircraft. The aircraft is crewed by two pilots, and seating for 19 support crew members is retained, together with large cargo volume and large forward (port) freight door.

WEIGHTS:
- Operating weight empty: 10,646 kg (23,471 lb)
- Max payload: 6,731 kg (14,840 lb)
- Max fuel: 4,152 kg (9,153 lb)
- Max T-O weight: 20,411 kg (45,000 lb)
- Max landing weight: 18,143 kg (40,000 lb)

PERFORMANCE (estimated, at max T-O weight except where indicated):
- Never-exceed speed: 259 knots (480 km/h; 298 mph)
- Max cruising speed: 230 knots (426 km/h; 265 mph)
- Firebombing drop speed: 125 knots (232 km/h; 144 mph)
- Min control speed: 80 knots (149 km/h; 92 mph)
- Stalling speed, flaps down, power off: 77 knots (143 km/h; 89 mph)
- Max rate of climb at S/L: 366 m (1,200 ft)/min
- Rate of climb at S/L, one engine out, AUW of 14,060 kg (31,000 lb): 177 m (580 ft)/min
- Service ceiling: 7,620 m (25,000 ft)
- Service ceiling, one engine out, AUW of 14,060 kg (31,000 lb): 5,640 m (18,500 ft)
- T-O to 10·7 m (35 ft): 1,600 m (5,250 ft)
- Landing from 15 m (50 ft) at max landing weight: 987 m (3,240 ft)
- Min field length: 1,525 m (5,000 ft)
- Max endurance: 3 h 24 min

Artist's impression of the Conair firefighting conversion of the Fokker F27

DE HAVILLAND CANADA

THE DE HAVILLAND AIRCRAFT OF CANADA LTD (Division of Boeing of Canada Ltd)

Garratt Boulevard, Downsview, Ontario M3K 1Y5
Telephone: (416) 633 7310
Telex: 06-22128 DE HAV TOR

CHAIRMAN, PRESIDENT AND CHIEF EXECUTIVE OFFICER:
William Brenton Boggs

VICE-PRESIDENTS:
Michael C. W. Davy (Engineering)
Thomas E. Appleton (Marketing and Sales)
William J. Easdale (Personnel)
Joar Gronlund (Customer Support)
Robin W. Butler (Finance)
James Davies (Governmental Affairs)
Robert G. McCall (Operations)
Norman Kingsmore (Manufacturing)

DIRECTOR, PRODUCT ENGINEERING: John Thompson
DIRECTOR, CUSTOMER RELATIONS: Charles Wickes
DIRECTOR, MARKETING: John Giraudy
MANAGER, PUBLIC RELATIONS: Colin S. Fisher

The de Havilland Aircraft of Canada Ltd was established in early 1928 as a subsidiary of The de Havilland Aircraft Co Ltd, and became subsequently a member of the Hawker Siddeley Group. On 26 June 1974 ownership was transferred to the Canadian government until responsible Canadian investors could be found to purchase and operate de Havilland. This was achieved on 31 January 1986 when purchase was completed by The Boeing Company, and de Havilland Canada became a division of Boeing of Canada Ltd.

In mid-1985 facilities covered a total area of 185,806 m² (2 million sq ft), comprising a main plant on the southern border of Downsview airport, leased space on the northern boundary of the airport, and additional leased storage and warehousing space. To handle increased production rates, an expansion at the main plant consisting of an extension for small parts manufacturing, plus a high-bay aircraft assembly and preparation area, was put into service in 1981-82, together with a numerical control profiler building. Two additional assembly bays and a new paint facility were completed in 1984. Approximately 4,500 people were employed by DHC in mid-1986. Repair and overhaul services for the Buffalo, Twin Otter, Dash 7 and Dash 8, by a newly formed Aero Services organisation, were introduced in 1981.

DHC-5D BUFFALO

The turboprop Buffalo, first flown on 9 April 1964, was developed from the piston engined DHC-4 Caribou. Details of its early history have appeared in previous editions of *Jane's*.

Current production version is the DHC-5D, with higher gross weight and improved performance, of which deliveries began in early 1976. A total of 122 Buffalos of all versions had been delivered by June 1985, to customers as listed in the 1985-86 *Jane's*. No further Buffalo sales have been announced since that time, but some unsold aircraft may remain in the DHC inventory. The company did not update this entry in 1986.

The following abbreviated description applies to the DHC-5D:

TYPE: Twin-turboprop STOL utility transport.

AIRFRAME: As described in 1984-85 and earlier *Jane's*.

POWER PLANT: Two General Electric CT64-820-4 turboprop engines, each flat rated at 2,336 kW (3,133 shp) and driving a Hamilton Standard 63E60-25 three-blade constant-speed reversible-pitch fully-feathering metal propeller with Beta control. Fuel in one integral tank in each inner wing, and ten interconnected rubber bag tanks in each outer wing; overall fuel capacity 7,978 litres (1,755 Imp gallons; 2,108 US gallons).

ACCOMMODATION: Crew of three, comprising pilot, co-pilot and crew chief. Main cabin can accommodate roll-up troop seats or folding forward facing seats for 41 combat equipped troops, 35 paratroops, or 24 stretchers and six seats. Provision for toilet in forward part of cabin. Door on each side at rear of cabin. Loading height with rear cargo loading door up and ramp down 2·90 m (9 ft 6 in). Tiedown points in 508 mm (20 in) grid, with additional tiedowns at sides of cabin.

SYSTEMS, AVIONICS AND EQUIPMENT: See 1984-85 *Jane's*.

DIMENSIONS, EXTERNAL:
- Wing span: 29·26 m (96 ft 0 in)
- Length overall: 24·08 m (79 ft 0 in)
- Height overall: 8·73 m (28 ft 8 in)
- Wheel track: 9·29 m (30 ft 6 in)
- Wheelbase: 8·48 m (27 ft 10 in)
- Cabin doors (each side): Height: 1·68 m (5 ft 6 in)
  - Width: 0·84 m (2 ft 9 in)
  - Height to sill: 1·17 m (3 ft 10 in)
- Rear cargo loading door and ramp:
  - Height: 6·33 m (20 ft 9 in)
  - Width: 2·34 m (7 ft 8 in)
  - Height to ramp hinge: 1·17 m (3 ft 10 in)

DIMENSIONS, INTERNAL:
- Cabin, excl flight deck:
  - Length, cargo floor: 9·58 m (31 ft 5 in)
  - Max width: 2·67 m (8 ft 9 in)
  - Max height (aft of wings): 2·08 m (6 ft 10 in)
  - Floor area: 22·48 m² (242 sq ft)
  - Volume (rectangular): 44·74 m³ (1,580 cu ft)

AREA:
- Wings, gross: 87·8 m² (945 sq ft)

WEIGHTS AND LOADINGS (STOL transport mission, firm smooth airfield surface):
- Operational weight empty (incl 3 crew and 680 kg; 1,500 lb allowance for options and avionics): 11,412 kg (25,160 lb)
- Max payload: 8,164 kg (18,000 lb)
- Max normal fuel: 6,212 kg (13,696 lb)
- Max unit load for airdrop: 2,721 kg (6,000 lb)
- Max T-O weight: 22,316 kg (49,200 lb)
- Max landing weight: 21,273 kg (46,900 lb)
- Max zero-fuel weight: 19,731 kg (43,500 lb)
- Max uniform cabin floor loading: 976 kg/m² (200 lb/sq ft)
- Max wing loading: 254·4 kg/m² (52·1 lb/sq ft)
- Max power loading: 4·78 kg/kW (7·85 lb/shp)

PERFORMANCE (at max T-O weight except where indicated, STOL transport mission from firm smooth airfield surface):
- Max cruising speed at 3,050 m (10,000 ft), AUW of 21,200 kg (46,737 lb): 227 knots (420 km/h; 261 mph)
- Stalling speed, 40° flap at 21,273 kg (46,900 lb) AUW: 73 knots (135 km/h; 84 mph)
- Max rate of climb at S/L, normal rated power: 555 m (1,820 ft)/min
- Rate of climb at S/L, one engine out, military power: 116 m (380 ft)/min
- Recommended max operating altitude: 7,620 m (25,000 ft)
- STOL T-O run: 701 m (2,300 ft)
- STOL T-O to 15 m (50 ft), mid-CG: 838 m (2,750 ft)
- STOL landing from 15 m (50 ft): 613 m (2,010 ft)
- STOL landing run: 259 m (850 ft)

de Havilland Canada DHC-5D Buffalo twin-turboprop STOL SAR and transport aircraft of the Canadian Armed Forces

Range at 3,050 m (10,000 ft):
max payload 600 nm (1,112 km; 691 miles)
zero payload 1,770 nm (3,280 km; 2,038 miles)
Max range at 7,620 m (25,000 ft), with ferry tanks
3,300 nm (6,115 km; 3,800 miles)

DHC-6 TWIN OTTER SERIES 300

CAF designation: CC-138
US Army designation: UV-18A
USAF designation: UV-18B

The first of five Twin Otters (CF-DHC-X), powered by two 432 kW (579 ehp) PT6A-6 engines, flew for the first time on 20 May 1965. The fourth and subsequent aircraft of the initial Series 100 version were fitted with PT6A-20 engines; deliveries began in July 1966, shortly after the Twin Otter received FAA Type Approval. All Series are certificated to FAR 23 Pt 135, and the manufacturer's warranty was doubled in 1985 in recognition of the aircraft's 20 years of operation.

Four standard production versions of the Twin Otter have been built, of which the Series 100 (115 built), Series 200 (115 built) and Series 300S (six built) were described in the 1967-68, 1970-71 and 1976-77 *Jane's* respectively. A prototype/demonstrator of a DHC-6-300MR maritime reconnaissance version was flown in 1982, and one aircraft of this type was purchased by the Senegal Department of Fisheries at the end of that year. No sales have yet been announced of the -300M military transport and counter-insurgency versions, introduced at the same time and last described fully in the 1984-85 *Jane's*. There have, however, been (and still are) a large number of military operators of Twin Otters, and a list of these can be found in the 1985-86 edition.

The current standard production version is the Series 300, of which deliveries began in Spring 1969 with the 231st Twin Otter off the line.

By 14 August 1985 a total of 825 Twin Otters had been delivered to over 70 countries, and operating hours totalled more than 9 million.

The Twin Otter is used as a photo survey aircraft in China (People's Republic), Ethiopia, the Sudan and Switzerland. China and Kenya also each have one Twin Otter modified for geophysical survey work. Equipment fitted to these aircraft was detailed in the 1982-83 *Jane's*. Details of a geological survey conversion were given in the 1983-84 edition; a firefighting Twin Otter carrying up to ten smoke jumpers was purchased in late 1983 by the Forest Service of the US Department of Agriculture; and the 1985-86 *Jane's* recorded one Twin Otter modified in 1984 by NFK in Norway for the dispersal of oil spills off the Norwegian coast.

Type: Twin-turboprop STOL transport.

Wings: Strut braced high-wing monoplane. Wing section NACA 6A series mean line; NACA 0016 (modified) thickness distribution. Dihedral 3°. No sweepback. All-metal safe-life structure, each wing being attached to the fuselage by two bolts at the front and rear spar fitting and braced by a single streamline section strut on each side. Light alloy riveted construction is used throughout except for the upper skin panels, which have spanwise corrugated stiffeners bonded to them. All-metal double-slotted full span trailing-edge flaps. All-metal ailerons which also droop for use as flaps. Electrically actuated tab in port aileron; geared trim tabs in port and starboard ailerons. Optional pneumatic-boot de-icing equipment.

Fuselage: Conventional semi-monocoque safe-life structure, built in three sections. Primary structure of frames, stringers and skin of aluminium alloy. Windscreen and cabin windows of acrylic plastics. Cabin floor is of low density aluminium faced sandwich construction and is designed to accommodate distributed loads of up to 976 kg/m² (200 lb/sq ft).

Tail Unit: Cantilever all-metal structure of high strength aluminium alloys. Fin and fixed incidence tailplane are bolted to rear fuselage. Manually operated trim tabs in rudder and elevators. A geared tab is fitted to the rudder to lighten control forces, and a tab fitted to the starboard elevator is linked to the flaps to control longitudinal trim during flap retraction and extension. Optional pneumatic-boot de-icing of tailplane leading-edge.

Landing Gear: Non-retractable tricycle type, with single wheel on each unit. Fully steerable nosewheel. Urethane compression-block shock absorption on main units. Oleo-pneumatic nosewheel shock absorber. Goodyear mainwheel tyres size 11·00-12, pressure 2·62 bars (38 lb/sq in). Goodyear nosewheel tyre size 8·90-12·50, pressure 2·28 bars (33 lb/sq in). Goodrich independent, hydraulically operated disc brakes on mainwheels. Alternatively, high-flotation wheels and tyres, for operation in soft field conditions, are available at customer's option, size 15·0-12·0 for nosewheel and mainwheels. Provision for alternative wheel/ski landing gear. Twin-float gear available optionally; in this configuration aircraft has a shorter nose and is fitted with wing fences and small auxiliary fins.

Power Plant: Two 462 kW (620 shp) Pratt & Whitney Canada PT6A-27 turboprop engines, each driving a Hartzell HC-B3TN-3DY three-blade reversible-pitch fully-feathering metal propeller with Beta control (zero-pitch propeller on floatplane). Two underfloor fuel tanks (eight cells), total capacity of 1,446 litres (318 Imp gallons). Refuelling point for each tank on port side of fuselage. Oil capacity 9·1 litres (2 Imp gallons) per engine. Optional electric de-icing system for propellers and air intakes.

The 800th Twin Otter, a UV-18A (Series 300) for the US Army Alaskan National Guard

Accommodation: Side by side seats for one or two pilots on flight deck, access to which is by a forward opening car type door on each side or via the passenger cabin. Dual controls standard. Windscreen demisting and defrosting standard. Cabin divided by bulkhead into main passenger or freight compartment and baggage compartment. Seats for up to 20 passengers in main cabin. Standard interior is 20-seat commuter layout, with Douglas track, carpets, double windows, individual air vents and reading lights, and airstair door. Optional layouts include 18- or 19-seat commuter versions, and 13/20-passenger utility version with foldaway seats and double cargo doors with ladder. Access to cabin by door on each side of rear fuselage; airstair door on the port side. Optional double door for cargo on port side instead of airstair door. Compartments in nose and aft of main cabin, each with upward hinged door on port side, for 136 kg (300 lb) and 227 kg (500 lb) of baggage respectively; rear baggage hold accessible from cabin in emergency. Emergency exits near front of cabin on each side. Heating of flight deck and passenger cabin by engine bleed air; ventilation via a ram air intake on the port side of the fuselage nose. Oxygen system for crew and passengers optional. Executive, survey or ambulance interiors can be fitted at customer's option. Tiedown cargo rings are installed as standard for the freighter role.

Systems: Hydraulic system, pressure 103·5 bars (1,500 lb/sq in), for flaps, brakes, nosewheel steering and (where fitted) ski retraction mechanism. A handpump in the crew compartment provides emergency pressure for standby or ground operation if the electric pump is inoperative. Accumulators smooth the system pressure pulses and provide pressure for parking and emergency braking. Optional low pressure pneumatic system (1·24 bars; 18 lb/sq in) for operation of autopilot or wing and tail de-icing boots, if fitted. Primary electrical system is 28V DC, with one 200A starter/generator on each engine. One 40Ah 20-cell nickel-cadmium battery (optionally a 36Ah lead-acid battery) for emergency power and engine starting. Separate 3·6Ah battery supplies independent power for engine starting relays and ignition. 250VA main and standby static inverters provide 400Hz AC power for instruments and avionics. External DC receptacle aft of port side cabin door permits operation of complete system on the ground.

Avionics and Equipment: Blind-flying instrumentation standard. Navigation and communications equipment, including weather radar, to customer's specification.

Dimensions, external:
Wing span 19·81 m (65 ft 0 in)
Wing chord (constant) 1·98 m (6 ft 6 in)
Wing aspect ratio 10
Length overall: landplane 15·77 m (51 ft 9 in)
seaplane 15·09 m (49 ft 6 in)
Height overall: landplane 5·94 m (19 ft 6 in)
seaplane (from waterline) 6·04 m (19 ft 10 in)
Tailplane span 6·30 m (20 ft 8 in)
Wheel track (landplane) 3·71 m (12 ft 2 in)
Wheelbase (landplane) 4·53 m (14 ft 10½ in)
Length of floats (seaplane) 9·65 m (31 ft 8 in)
Width over floats (seaplane) 5·18 m (17 ft 0 in)
Seaplane track (c/l of floats) 4·06 m (13 ft 4 in)
Propeller diameter 2·59 m (8 ft 6 in)
Passenger door (port): Height 1·27 m (4 ft 2 in)
Width 0·76 m (2 ft 6 in)
Height to sill 1·32 m (4 ft 4 in)
Passenger door (starboard):
Height 1·15 m (3 ft 9½ in)
Width 0·77 m (2 ft 6¼ in)
Height to sill 1·32 m (4 ft 4 in)
Baggage compartment door (nose):
Mean height 0·69 m (2 ft 3¼ in)
Width 0·76 m (2 ft 5¾ in)
Height to sill 1·32 m (4 ft 4 in)
Baggage compartment door (port, rear):
Max height 0·97 m (3 ft 2 in)
Width 0·65 m (2 ft 1½ in)
Cargo double door (port, rear):
Height 1·27 m (4 ft 2 in)
Width 1·42 m (4 ft 8 in)
Height to sill 1·32 m (4 ft 4 in)

Dimensions, internal:
Cabin, excl flight deck, galley and baggage compartment:
Length 5·64 m (18 ft 6 in)
Max width 1·61 m (5 ft 3¼ in)
Max height 1·50 m (4 ft 11 in)
Floor area 7·45 m² (80·2 sq ft)
Volume 10·87 m³ (384 cu ft)
Baggage compartment (nose):
Volume 1·08 m³ (38 cu ft)
Baggage compartment (rear):
Length 1·88 m (6 ft 2 in)
Volume 2·49 m³ (88 cu ft)

Areas:
Wings, gross 39·02 m² (420 sq ft)
Ailerons (total) 3·08 m² (33·2 sq ft)
Trailing-edge flaps (total) 10·42 m² (112·2 sq ft)
Fin 4·46 m² (48·0 sq ft)
Rudder, incl tabs 3·16 m² (34·0 sq ft)
Tailplane 9·29 m² (100·0 sq ft)
Elevator, incl tabs 3·25 m² (35·0 sq ft)

Weights:
Typical operating weight (20-seat commuter, incl 2 crew and 59 kg; 130 lb of avionics) 3,363 kg (7,415 lb)
Max payload for 100 nm (185 km; 115 miles)
1,941 kg (4,280 lb)
Max fuel weight 1,171 kg (2,583 lb)
Max T-O weight 5,670 kg (12,500 lb)
Max landing weight:
wheels and skis 5,579 kg (12,300 lb)
floats 5,670 kg (12,500 lb)

Performance (at max T-O weight, ISA):
Max cruising speed at 3,050 m (10,000 ft)
182 knots (338 km/h; 210 mph)
Stalling speed:
flaps up 74 knots (138 km/h; 86 mph) EAS
flaps down 58 knots (108 km/h; 67 mph) EAS
Max rate of climb at S/L 488 m (1,600 ft)/min
Rate of climb at S/L, one engine out
104 m (340 ft)/min
Service ceiling 8,140 m (26,700 ft)
Service ceiling, one engine out 3,530 m (11,600 ft)
T-O run: STOL 213 m (700 ft)
CAR Pt 3 262 m (860 ft)
T-O to 15 m (50 ft): STOL 366 m (1,200 ft)
CAR Pt 3 457 m (1,500 ft)
Landing from 15 m (50 ft): STOL 320 m (1,050 ft)
CAR Pt 3 591 m (1,940 ft)
Landing run: STOL 157 m (515 ft)
CAR Pt 3 290 m (950 ft)
Range at long-range cruising speed with 1,134 kg (2,500 lb) payload 700 nm (1,297 km; 806 miles)

DHC-7 DASH 7

CAF designation: CC-132

The Dash 7 quiet STOL airliner project was begun by de Havilland Canada in late 1972, following a worldwide market survey of short-haul transport requirements.

Two pre-production aircraft were built, the first of these (C-GNBX-X) flying on 27 March 1975 and the second (C-GNCA-X) on 26 June 1975. A third airframe was built for structural testing and a fourth for fatigue testing. The first production Dash 7 (C-GQIW, c/n 3), flew on 30 May 1977.

Certification by the Canadian Department of Transport to FAR 25 was received on 2 May 1977; STOL performance is approved under conventional FAR 25 and FAR 121 regulations. In addition, certification has been given for 7°

30′ glideslope and 10·7 m (35 ft) landing reference height adopted by the FAA for STOL aircraft. The first Dash 7 to enter service was c/n 4, with Rocky Mountain Airways (USA), on 3 February 1978. Deliveries of the Dash 7 by mid-1985 had passed the 100 mark, versions including the passenger **Series 100** and the all-cargo **Series 101**.

Certification was planned for 1985 of a version with higher weight and greater fuel capacity, known as the **Series 150**. First customer for this version (one aircraft, for use on ice reconnaissance duties) is the Canadian government, whose aircraft is a specially equipped non-standard example known as the **Dash 7 IR** and is described separately. The standard 150 was intended to replace the Series 100 on the production line in early 1986.

The following description applies to the Series 100 and standard Series 150 except where indicated:

TYPE: Four-engined short/medium-range quiet STOL transport.

WINGS: Cantilever high-wing monoplane, with 4° 30′ dihedral from centre-section. Wing section NACA 63A418 (modified) at root, NACA 63A415 (modified) at tip. Sweepback 3° 12′ at quarter-chord. Incidence 3° at root. Conventional all-metal two-spar bonded skin/stringer structure. Double-slotted flaps, extending over approx 80 per cent of trailing-edge, are actuated mechanically for take-off, by irreversible screwjacks, and hydraulically for landing. Two inboard ground spoilers/lift dumpers and two outboard air spoilers in each upper surface, forward of flaps, also actuated hydraulically. Outboard sections can be operated symmetrically, or differentially in combination with the cable operated ailerons. Trim tab in starboard aileron; servo-tab in each aileron. Pneumatic boot de-icing of leading-edges outboard of the inner nacelles.

FUSELAGE: Conventional all-metal stressed skin pressurised structure, of bonded skin/stringer construction. Basically circular cross-section, with flattened profile under floor level.

TAIL UNIT: Cantilever all-metal T tail, with large dorsal fin. Fixed incidence tailplane, and one-piece cable operated horn balanced elevator with spring tabs. Fore and trailing serially hinged rudders, actuated hydraulically. Pneumatic boot de-icing of tailplane leading-edges and elevator horns.

LANDING GEAR: Menasco retractable tricycle type, with twin wheels on all units. Oleo-pneumatic shock absorbers. Hydraulic retraction, main units forward into inboard engine nacelles, steerable nose unit rearward into fuselage. Goodrich mainwheels and tyres size 30 × 9·00-15, pressure 7·38 bars (107 lb/sq in); nosewheel tyres size 6·50-10, pressure 5·31 bars (77 lb/sq in). Larger, low pressure tyres optional, with pressures of 4·83 bars (70 lb/sq in) on main units, 4·76 bars (69 lb/sq in) on nose unit. Goodrich anti-skid hydraulic braking system for all units. Small retractable tailskid under rear fuselage.

POWER PLANT: Four Pratt & Whitney Canada PT6A-50 turboprop engines, each flat rated at 835 kW (1,120 shp) and driving a Hamilton Standard 24PF-305 constant-speed fully-feathering reversible-pitch four-blade propeller, with Beta control, of slow-turning type (1,320 rpm) to reduce noise level. Propeller blades are of GRP, with forged aluminium spars and foam cores. Fuel in two integral tanks in each wing, total standard capacity 5,602 litres (1,232 Imp gallons), increasable optionally in Srs 150 to 9,747 litres (2,144 Imp gallons). Single pressure refuelling/defuelling point on underside of rear fuselage, aft of pressure dome. Pneumatic de-icing of engine air intakes; electric de-icing for propellers. Oil capacity 23 litres (5 Imp gallons).

ACCOMMODATION: Flight crew of two, plus one or two cabin attendants. Dual controls standard. Seats for 50 passengers at 81 cm (32 in) pitch standard, in pairs on each side of centre aisle, with generous provision for underseat carry-on baggage. Optional high-density seating for 54 passengers at 74 cm (29 in) pitch. Outward opening airstair door at rear on port side. Emergency exits on each side at front of cabin and on starboard side at rear. Baggage compartment in rear fuselage (capacity 998 kg; 2,200 lb), with external access on starboard side and internal access from cabin. Galley, coat rack and toilet at rear of cabin. Optional arrangements include movable bulkhead for mixed freight/passenger loads and (Srs 101/151) large forward freight door on port side. Up to five standard pallets can be accommodated in an all-cargo role. Quick change cargo handling system available optionally. Entire accommodation pressurised and air-conditioned.

SYSTEMS: Cabin pressure differential 0·294 bars (4·26 lb/sq in). Two air cycle systems, driven by engine bleed air, for cabin air-conditioning. Two independent hydraulic systems, each of 207 bars (3,000 lb/sq in). No. 1 system actuates flaps, rudder, wing spoilers and mainwheel brakes; No. 2 system actuates landing gear, nosewheel and backup mainwheel brakes, parking brakes, nosewheel steering, rudder and outboard wing spoilers. Primary DC power provided by four Phoenix 28V 250A 7·5kW starter/generators. 115/200V three-phase AC power at 400Hz from four 10kVA Lucas brushless generators for propeller and windscreen de-icing and standby fuel pumps. Lucas static inverters supply constant frequency 400Hz loads, including engine instrumentation and navigation systems. Nickel-cadmium batteries for engine starting. APU, for cabin air-conditioning and electrics, and engine starting, available optionally.

AVIONICS AND EQUIPMENT: Standard avionics include crew interphone system; cabin PA system; flight data recorder; flight compartment voice recorder; emergency locator transmitter; two independent VHF communications systems; two independent VHF (VOR/ILS) radio navigation systems; one LF (ADF) radio navigation system; one ATC transponder; one DME; one RCA Primus 40 weather radar; one marker beacon receiver; Sperry SPZ-700 autopilot/flight director system, incorporating Z-500 flight computer and ADC-200 central air data computer; Sperry STARS ADI and HSI; Sperry AA-215 radio altimeter; and two Sperry C-14 slaved gyro compasses and VG-14 vertical gyros. Provision for variety of optional avionics to customer's requirements. Standard options include Collins 618M-3 com transceiver, Collins 51RV-4D nav receiver, Collins 51Z-4 glideslope/marker beacon receiver, and Collins 621A-6 transponder.

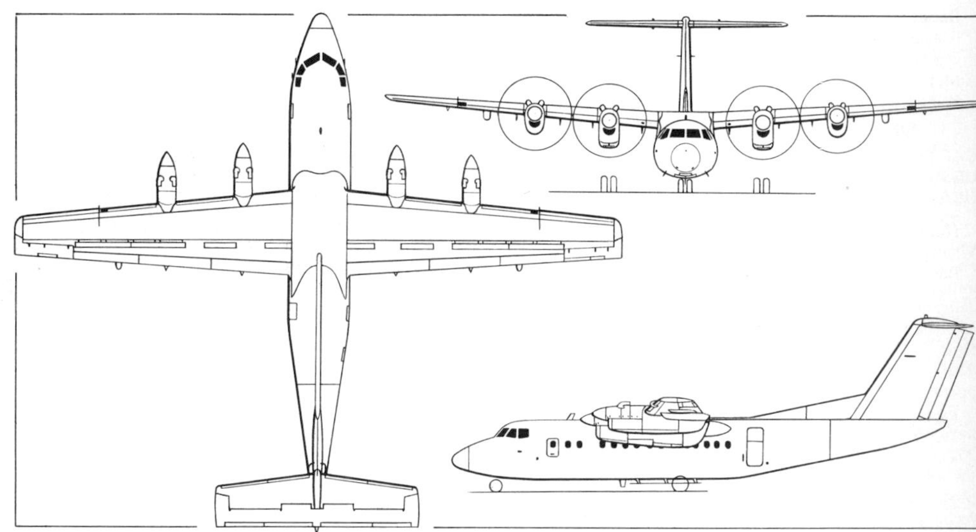

de Havilland Canada DHC-7 Dash 7 four-turboprop STOL transport *(Pilot Press)*

DIMENSIONS, EXTERNAL:

Wing span	28·35 m (93 ft 0 in)
Wing chord: at root	3·81 m (12 ft 6 in)
at tip	1·68 m (5 ft 6 in)
mean aerodynamic	2·99 m (9 ft 9¾ in)
Wing aspect ratio	10
Length overall	24·54 m (80 ft 6 in)
Height overall	7·98 m (26 ft 2 in)
Tailplane span	9·45 m (31 ft 0 in)
Fuselage: Max diameter	2·79 m (9 ft 2 in)
Wheel track	7·16 m (23 ft 6 in)
Wheelbase	8·38 m (27 ft 6 in)
Propeller diameter	3·43 m (11 ft 3 in)
Propeller ground clearance (inboard engines)	1·60 m (5 ft 3 in)
Min propeller/fuselage clearance	0·75 m (2 ft 5·4 in)
Passenger door (rear, port):	
Height	1·75 m (5 ft 9 in)
Width	0·76 m (2 ft 6 in)
Height to sill	1·09 m (3 ft 7 in)
Emergency exit doors (fwd, each):	
Height	0·91 m (3 ft 0 in)
Width	0·51 m (1 ft 8 in)
Height to sill	1·55 m (5 ft 1 in)
Emergency exit door (rear, stbd):	
Height	1·35 m (4 ft 5 in)
Width	0·61 m (2 ft 0 in)
Height to sill	1·09 m (3 ft 7 in)
Baggage hold door (rear, stbd):	
Height	1·02 m (3 ft 4 in)
Width	0·84 m (2 ft 9 in)
Height to sill	1·47 m (4 ft 10 in)
Cargo door (fwd, port, optional):	
Height	1·78 m (5 ft 10 in)
Width	2·31 m (7 ft 7 in)
Height to sill	approx 1·22 m (4 ft 0 in)

DIMENSIONS, INTERNAL:

Cabin, excl flight deck: Length	12·04 m (39 ft 6 in)
Max width	2·60 m (8 ft 6¼ in)
Floor width	2·13 m (7 ft 0 in)
Max height	1·94 m (6 ft 4½ in)
Height under wing	1·85 m (6 ft 1 in)
Volume	54·1 m³ (1,910 cu ft)

de Havilland Canada DHC-7 Dash 7 four-turboprop quiet STOL transport, in the insignia of Grønlandsfly (Greenlandair)

Baggage compartment (rear fuselage):
Max length 2·30 m (7 ft 6½ in)
Volume 6·8 m³ (240 cu ft)

AREAS:
Wings, gross 79·90 m² (860·0 sq ft)
Ailerons (total) 2·16 m² (23·22 sq ft)
Trailing-edge flaps (total) 27·33 m² (294·20 sq ft)
Spoilers (total) 3·63 m² (39·04 sq ft)
Vertical tail surfaces (total, excl dorsal fin) 15·79 m² (170·0 sq ft)
Horizontal tail surfaces (total) 20·16 m² (217·0 sq ft)

WEIGHTS AND LOADINGS:
Basic weight empty (standard 50-passenger layout):
Srs 100 12,247 kg (27,000 lb)
Operating weight empty: Srs 100 12,560 kg (27,690 lb)
Srs 150 12,465 kg (27,480 lb)
Max payload (50 passengers or cargo):
Srs 100 5,130 kg (11,310 lb)
Srs 150 5,225 kg (11,520 lb)
Max fuel: standard 4,563 kg (10,060 lb)
optional 7,938 kg (17,500 lb)
Max T-O weight: Srs 100 19,958 kg (44,000 lb)
Srs 150 21,319 kg (47,000 lb)
Max zero-fuel weight:
Srs 100, 150 17,690 kg (39,000 lb)
Max landing weight: Srs 100 19,050 kg (42,000 lb)
Srs 150 20,411 kg (45,000 lb)
Max cabin floor loading: both 366·2 kg/m² (75 lb/sq ft)
Max wing loading:
Srs 100 249·7 kg/m² (51·16 lb/sq ft)
Srs 150 266·7 kg/m² (54·65 lb/sq ft)
Max power loading:
Srs 100 11·95 kg/kW (19·64 lb/shp)
Srs 150 12·77 kg/kW (20·98 lb/shp)

PERFORMANCE (Srs 100 at max T-O weight, FAR Pt 25, at S/L, ISA, except where indicated):
Max cruising speed at 2,440 m (8,000 ft) at AUW of 18,597 kg (41,000 lb) 231 knots (428 km/h; 266 mph)
Max cruising speed at 4,575 m (15,000 ft) at AUW of 18,597 kg (41,000 lb) 227 knots (420 km/h; 261 mph)
En route rate of climb, flaps and landing gear up:
4 engines, max climb power 372 m (1,220 ft)/min
3 engines, max continuous power 220 m (720 ft)/min
Service ceiling at AUW of 18,597 kg (41,000 lb):
4 engines, max climb power 6,400 m (21,000 ft)
3 engines, max continuous power 3,855 m (12,650 ft)
T-O field length: Srs 100 686 m (2,250 ft)
Srs 150 792 m (2,600 ft)
T-O field length at 3,050 m (10,000 ft), 15° flap 1,829 m (6,000 ft)
Landing field length at max landing weight:
Srs 100, 45° flap 658 m (2,160 ft)
Srs 150, 25° flap 975 m (3,200 ft)
Landing field length at 3,050 m (10,000 ft) at 18,915 kg (41,700 lb) landing weight, 45° flap 823 m (2,700 ft)
Min ground turning radius 8·84 m (29 ft 0 in)
Runway LCN with 32 × 11·50-15 low-pressure tyres, rigid, 30 in relative stiffness 16·2
Range at 4,575 m (15,000 ft) with 50 passengers and baggage, at long-range cruising speed, IFR reserves:
Srs 100 690 nm (1,279 km; 795 miles)
Max range at 4,575 m (15,000 ft) with standard fuel and 2,948 kg (6,500 lb) payload, long-range cruising speed:
Srs 100 1,170 nm (2,168 km; 1,347 miles)
Range at max cruise power, IFR reserves:
Srs 150 (50 passengers) 1,140 nm (2,112 km; 1,313 miles)
Srs 150 (max) 2,525 nm (4,679 km; 2,907 miles)

OPERATIONAL NOISE LEVELS (FAR Pt 36 at S/L, ISA + 10°C, Srs 100 confirmed):
T-O 80·5 EPNdB
Approach on 3° glideslope 91·4 EPNdB
Sideline 82·8 EPNdB

DHC-7 DASH 7 IR

Somewhat later than originally planned, the Dash 7 IR (for ice reconnaissance) entered service with the Department of Environment in Spring 1986. This one-off aircraft, registered C-GCFR, is a specially equipped non-standard example of the Dash 7 Series 150, intended for use in surveying sea ice and icebergs in the shipping and oil drilling regions of the Labrador coast and the Gulf of St Lawrence, where it supplements two Lockheed Electras already used for this purpose by the DoE's Atmospheric Environment Service.

Non-standard features of the Dash 7 IR that are apparent in the accompanying photograph include a special dorsal observation cabin just aft of the flight deck, and a Canadian Astronautics Ltd SLAR 100 side looking radar mounted in a fairing on the port side of the fuselage, to locate ice in shipping lanes and drilling areas. Other mission equipment includes a laser profilometer to measure ice formation contours, photographic mapping equipment, and a data link between the aircraft and ships and drilling rigs in the patrol area.

DHC-8 DASH 8 SERIES 100

The Dash 8 Series 100 is a quiet, fuel-efficient short-haul transport in the 30/40-seat category. The first of four flying prototypes (C-GDNK) made its first flight on 20 June 1983, followed by the second (C-GGMP) on 26 October and the third in November 1983. The fourth aircraft (first with production PW120 engines) was flying by early 1984, followed by the first Dash 8 with production interior in June. Three major subassemblies were completed for structural testing.

C-GCFR, the Canadian government's ice reconnaissance Dash 7 IR

Sized to accommodate 36 to 39 passengers, the Series 100 fits in between the company's 19-passenger Twin Otter and 50-passenger Dash 7. Certification by the Canadian DoT, to FAR Pts 25 and 36 and SFAR No. 27, was awarded on 28 September 1984, and FAA type approval before the end of that year. The first customer Dash 8, one of two Series 100s for NorOntair (c/n 6), was delivered on 23 October 1984, and entered service on 19 December that year.

Two basic versions of the Series 100 are available:

Commuter. Standard local service version, to which the detailed description mainly applies. With full IFR fuel reserves for a 100 nm (185 km; 115 mile) diversion, plus 45 min at long-range cruising speed at 1,525 m (5,000 ft), this version has enough fuel to fly four 100 nm stages without refuelling, carrying a 3,102 kg (6,840 lb) payload of 36 passengers and their baggage.

Corporate. To be marketed in North America exclusively by Innotech Aviation of Montreal, outside North America by DHC, the corporate version will have an extended range capability of up to 2,000 nm (3,706 km; 2,303 miles), plus IFR reserves, with a 544 kg (1,200 lb) payload. In a more typical mission it will be able to carry 17 passengers and their baggage for up to 1,320 nm (2,446 km; 1,520 miles), with reserves, at a max cruising speed of 270 knots (500 km/h; 311 mph). An APU will be standard in this version. Alternative layouts may include a single cabin with first class accommodation for about 24 passengers; the standard commuter interior will also be available for corporate customers.

A 'stretched' Dash 8, the **Series 300**, was announced in 1985 and is described separately.

By 2 September 1986 a total of 109 firm orders had been received for the Series 100, of which 41 had been delivered. A further 36 were on option. Two aircraft ordered by Transport Canada are for use on airways calibration duties; one for a North African oil company is in passenger/cargo configuration with heavy duty floor and an optional medevac conversion package. Six for the Canadian DND are designated **Dash 8M** (for military): four will be equipped for navigation training in Canada, and the other two for passenger/cargo duties in Europe. The Dash 8Ms have long-range fuel tanks, rough-field landing gear, high-strength floors and mission-related avionics.

Sierra Research of Buffalo, New York, a division of LTV Aerospace and Defense Co, was awarded a 1985 contract from the US Air Force to outfit two Dash 8s to serve as airborne platforms for patrols off Florida's Gulf Coast. Scheduled for delivery to Sierra in Spring and Summer 1986, they are equipped as flying data links that will relay telemetry, voice communications and drone tracking data while simultaneously performing radar surveillance functions. Equipment includes a large, electronically steerable phased-array antenna in a starboard-side fuselage fairing, an AN/APS-128D sea surveillance radar in a ventral radome, and extensive internal avionics and electronics. The aircraft are operated by a crew of two. Sierra's work is due to be completed by March 1987, when the aircraft will be delivered to Tyndall AFB, Florida. When in operation, they will enable the USAF to conduct tests and training safely at distances up to 200 nm (370 km; 230 miles) offshore.

The following description applies to the standard Dash 8 Series 100:

TYPE: Twin-turboprop quiet short-range transport.

WINGS: Cantilever high-wing monoplane, with constant chord centre-section and tapered outer panels. Thickness/chord ratio 18% at root, 13% at tip. Sweepback 3° 1′ 48″ at quarter-chord. Dihedral 2° 30′ on outer panels. Drooped inboard leading-edges. Tip to tip torsion box formed by front and rear spars, ribs and skin. Single-slotted Fowler trailing-edge flaps inboard and outboard of engine nacelles. Hydraulically actuated roll control spoilers/lift dumpers forward of each outer flap segment; independent ground spoiler/lift dumper inboard and outboard of each engine nacelle. Mechanically actuated balanced ailerons, with inset tabs. Small stall strip on each wing leading-edge outboard of engine. Pneumatic rubber boot de-icing of leading-edges. Composite materials used for construction of leading-edges, wingtip fairings, flap shrouds, flap trailing-edges and other components.

FUSELAGE: Conventional flush riveted semi-monocoque pressurised structure, of near-circular cross-section. Extensive use of adhesively bonded stringers and cutout reinforcements. Radome, nose bay, wing/fuselage fairings and tailcone of Kevlar and other composites.

TAIL UNIT: Cantilever T tailplane; full span horn balanced elevator, with tabs. Sweptback fin (integral with rear fuselage), large dorsal fin, and two-segment serially hinged hydraulically actuated rudder with yaw damper. Composites used in construction of dorsal fin, fin leading-edge, fin/tailplane fairings, tailplane leading-edges and tips. Pneumatic rubber boot de-icing of tailplane leading-edges.

LANDING GEAR: Retractable tricycle type, by Dowty Equipment of Canada Ltd, with twin wheels on each unit. Steer by wire nose unit retracts forward, main units rearward into engine nacelles. Goodrich mainwheels and brakes; Hydro-Aire Mk 3 anti-skid system. Standard tyre pressures: main 7·93 bars (115 lb/sq in), nose 5·52 bars (80 lb/sq in). Low pressure tyres optional, pressure 4·48 bars (65 lb/sq in) on main units, 3·31 bars (40 lb/sq in) on nose unit. Wheel doors of Kevlar and other composites.

POWER PLANT: Two 1,432 kW (1,800 shp) Pratt & Whitney Canada PW120A turboprop engines, each driving a Hamilton Standard 14SF-7 four-blade constant-speed fully-feathering propeller with reversible pitch. In the event of one engine failing, the other automatically increases power from 1,432 kW (1,800 shp) to 1,491 kW (2,000 shp). Propeller blades have a solid aluminium spar, glassfibre outer shell, nickel erosion sheath outboard,

One of the two Dash 8s being equipped by Sierra Research as airborne data link platforms for the US Air Force

electric de-icing, and Beta control. Engine cowlings, produced by British Hovercraft Corporation, have lower panels, air intakes and rear panels of Kevlar/Nomex sandwich, aluminium side panels, and a titanium firewall. Standard fuel capacity (in-wing tanks) of 3,160 litres (695 Imp gallons); optional auxiliary tank system increases this maximum to 5,655 litres (1,244 Imp gallons). Extended range tanks on corporate version raise maximum capacity to 4,709 litres (1,036 Imp gallons). Pressure refuelling point in rear of starboard engine nacelle; overwing gravity point in each outer wing panel. Oil capacity 19 litres (4·2 Imp gallons) per engine.

ACCOMMODATION: Crew of two on flight deck, plus one attendant in cabin. Dual controls standard, although aircraft will be certificated for single-pilot operation. Standard commuter layout in main cabin provides four-abreast seating, with central aisle, for 36 passengers at 79 cm (31 in) pitch, plus buffet, toilet and large rear baggage compartment. Wardrobe at front of passenger cabin, in addition to overhead lockers and underseat stowage, provides additional carry-on capacity for passengers' baggage. Alternative 40-passenger, mixed passenger/cargo or corporate layouts available at customer's option. Movable bulkhead to facilitate conversion to mixed-traffic or all-cargo configuration. Port side airstair door at front provides access for crew as well as passengers; large inward opening port side door aft of wing for cargo loading. Emergency exit each side, in line with wing leading-edge, and opposite passenger door on starboard side. Entire accommodation pressurised and air-conditioned.

SYSTEMS: Air cycle air-conditioning system provides heating, cooling, ventilation and pressurisation (cabin max differential 0·38 bars; 5·5 lb/sq in). Normal hydraulic installation comprises two independent systems, each having an engine driven variable displacement pump and an electrically driven standby pump; accumulator and handpump for emergency use. Electrical system DC power provided by two starter/generators, two transformer-rectifier units, and two nickel-cadmium batteries. Variable frequency AC power provided by two engine driven AC generators and three static inverters. De-icing system consists of pneumatic system plus electric heating. APU standard in corporate version.

AVIONICS AND EQUIPMENT: Standard factory installed avionics package includes King Gold Crown III com/nav (KTR 908 VHF com, KNR 634 VHF nav, KDF 806 ADF, KDM 706A DME and KXP 756 transponder), Sperry SPZ-800 dual-channel digital AFCS with integrated fail-operational flight director/autopilot system, dual digital air data system, electromechanical flight instruments, and Primus 800 colour weather radar; Sperry electronic flight instrumentation system (EFIS) optional on commuter, standard on corporate version. Avtech audio integrating system. Telephonics PA system. Simmonds fuel monitoring system.

DIMENSIONS, EXTERNAL:

Wing span	25·91 m (85 ft 0 in)
Wing aspect ratio	12·35
Length overall	22·25 m (73 ft 0 in)
Fuselage: Max diameter	2·69 m (8 ft 10 in)
Height overall	7·49 m (24 ft 7 in)
Elevator span	7·92 m (26 ft 0 in)
Wheel track (c/l of shock struts)	7·87 m (25 ft 10 in)
Wheelbase	7·95 m (26 ft 1 in)
Propeller diameter	3·96 m (13 ft 0 in)
Propeller ground clearance	0·94 m (3 ft 1 in)
Propeller/fuselage clearance	0·76 m (2 ft 6 in)
Passenger/crew door (fwd, port):	
Height	1·68 m (5 ft 6 in)
Width	0·76 m (2 ft 6 in)
Height to sill	1·09 m (3 ft 7 in)
Baggage door (rear, port):	
Height	1·52 m (5 ft 0 in)
Width	1·27 m (4 ft 2 in)
Height to sill	1·09 m (3 ft 7 in)

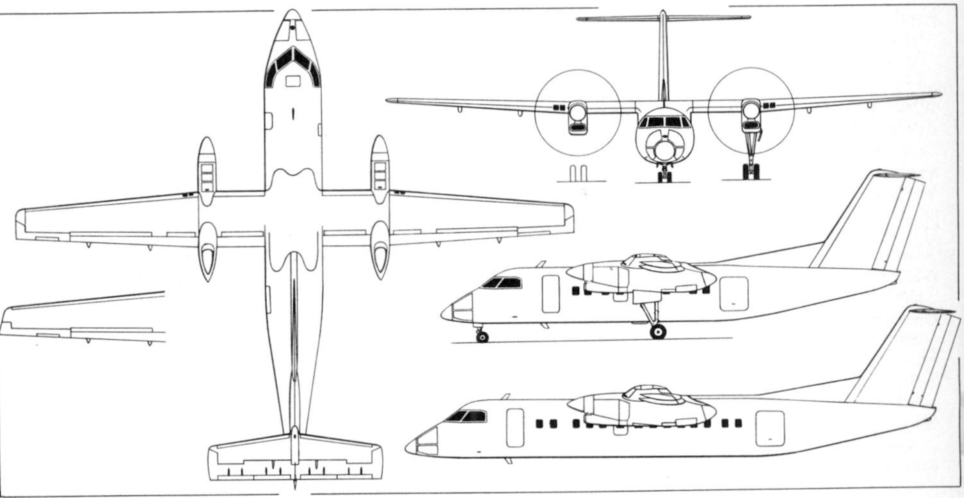

DHC-8 Dash 8 Series 100, with additional side view (bottom) and wingtip of Series 300 *(Pilot Press)*

DIMENSIONS, INTERNAL:

Cabin: Length	9·19 m (30 ft 2 in)
Max width	2·49 m (8 ft 2 in)
Width at floor	2·03 m (6 ft 8 in)
Max height	1·88 m (6 ft 2 in)
Volume	36·8 m³ (1,300 cu ft)
Net volume available for cargo	31·1 m³ (1,100 cu ft)
Baggage compartment volume	8·5 m³ (300 cu ft)

AREAS:

Wings, gross	54·35 m² (585·0 sq ft)
Vertical tail surfaces (total)	14·12 m² (152·0 sq ft)
Horizontal tail surfaces (total)	13·94 m² (150·0 sq ft)

WEIGHTS AND LOADING:

Operating weight empty	9,793 kg (21,590 lb)
Max usable fuel: standard	2,576 kg (5,678 lb)
optional	4,609 kg (10,160 lb)
Max payload: passengers	3,549 kg (7,824 lb)
cargo	4,268 kg (9,410 lb)
Max T-O weight	14,968 kg (33,000 lb)
Max landing weight	14,696 kg (32,400 lb)
Max zero-fuel weight	14,061 kg (31,000 lb)
Max wing loading	275·3 kg/m² (56·4 lb/sq ft)

PERFORMANCE (at max T-O weight except where indicated):

Max cruising speed at 13,834 kg (30,500 lb) AUW:	
at 4,575 m (15,000 ft)	268 knots (497 km/h; 309 mph)
at 6,100 m (20,000 ft)	266 knots (493 km/h; 306 mph)
Stalling speed, flaps down	72 knots (134 km/h; 83 mph)
Max rate of climb at S/L	631 m (2,070 ft)/min
Rate of climb at S/L, one engine out	162 m (530 ft)/min
FAR Pt 25 T-O field length, 15° flap, at max T-O weight:	
ISA at S/L	948 m (3,110 ft)
ISA + 15°C	1,052 m (3,450 ft)
FAR Pt 25 landing field length, 35° flap, at max landing weight	960 m (3,150 ft)
Range:	
full passenger load	890 nm (1,650 km; 1,025 miles)
2,721 kg (6,000 lb) payload	1,150 nm (2,130 km; 1,325 miles)
max cargo payload	150 nm (278 km; 173 miles)

OPERATIONAL NOISE LEVELS (FAR Pt 36 Stage 3 and ICAO Annex 16):

T-O	81 EPNdB
Sideline	86 EPNdB
Approach	95 EPNdB

DHC-8 DASH 8 200M

This designation was quoted in connection with a mockup ASW version of the Dash 8 displayed at the Asian Aerospace exhibition in Singapore in January 1986. Proposed equipment, which would be installed by Boeing Aerospace, included a nose mounted maritime surveillance radar, FLIR, MAD, ESM, inertial navigation system, sonobuoy processing equipment, a universal display and control system, and wing and fuselage weapon attachment points.

DHC-8 DASH 8 SERIES 300

Announced in mid-1985, the Series 300 is a 'stretched' version of the Dash 8 Series 100 in which fore and aft plugs totalling 3·43 m (11 ft 3 in) in length are inserted in the fuselage to increase seating capacity to 50 (standard) or 56 passengers (optional) at a seat pitch of 79 cm (31 in). Other fuselage/cabin changes include a new rear service door on the starboard side, an additional wardrobe, larger lavatory, dual air-conditioning packs, and an optional APU. Wing span is increased by tip extensions, and the Series 300 will be powered by 1,775 kW (2,380 shp) PW137 engines installed in nacelles identical to those of the Series 100. The large rear cargo compartment of the Series 100, and its door, are retained, as are the standard and optional fuel capacities of the Series 100.

First flight, by the converted No. 1 aircraft, is set for Spring 1987, with initial customer deliveries (five for Air Ontario) to be made in the second half of 1988. Orders and options for the Series 300 totalled 23 and 12 respectively by 4 September 1986.

DIMENSIONS, EXTERNAL: As for Series 100 except:

Wing span	27·43 m (90 ft 0 in)
Length overall	25·68 m (84 ft 3 in)
Wheelbase	9·60 m (31 ft 6 in)

de Havilland Canada DHC-8 Dash 8 Series 100 twin-turboprop transport in the insignia of Tyrolean Airways of Austria *(Anton Wettstein)*

WEIGHTS:

Operating weight empty	10,977 kg (24,200 lb)
Max payload (cargo)	5,443 kg (12,000 lb)
Max T-O weight	17,962 kg (39,600 lb)
Max landing weight	17,690 kg (39,000 lb)
Max zero-fuel weight	16,420 kg (36,200 lb)

PERFORMANCE (estimated):

Max cruising speed at 4,575 m (15,000 ft) 284 knots (526 km/h; 327 mph)

Max operating altitude 7,620 m (25,000 ft)

Service ceiling, one engine out (95% MTOW) 3,960 m (13,000 ft)

FAR Pt 25 T-O field length at MTOW, S/L, ISA 1,097 m (3,600 ft)

FAR Pt 25 landing field length at MLW, S/L, ISA 1,052 m (3,450 ft)

Range at max cruising speed, 50 passengers, standard fuel, IFR reserves 800 nm (1,482 km; 921 miles)

HELICOP-JET

HELICOP-JET PROJECT MANAGEMENT

505 West Dorchester Boulevard, Suite 310, Montreal, Quebec H2Z 1A8

Telephone: (514) 879 1671

Telex: 055-61075

PRESIDENT: Pierre Bergeron

VICE-PRESIDENT: Louis Thiffault

Helicop-Jet Project Management was formed in France to progress towards series manufacture of the Helicop-Jet type of 'cold-jet' tip-driven light helicopter which has been under development in France, by M Charles Déchaux, for many years. Its headquarters is in Canada.

HELICOP-JET

A full scale mockup of this 'cold-jet' tip-driven light helicopter, in its original configuration, was first exhibited at the Paris Air Show in June 1969. Construction of a prototype was started by Établissements Charles Déchaux in 1970, and this aircraft made its first flight in December 1976 at Issy-les-Moulineaux. It logged about 60 flying hours, powered by a 186 kW (250 hp) Turboméca Palouste IV air generator, with which it could lift only the pilot.

An improved 002 prototype (F-WZJO), with an Astazou engine, was displayed at the Paris Air Show in June 1979. After preliminary ground testing at Issy, in October 1984, it made its initial flight on 12 December 1984, piloted by M Philippe Fourquaux. This prototype has fulfilled its role as a demonstrator, and is now used for ground development and testing.

Helicop-Jet Project Management next proposes to build a six-seat pre-production prototype with an optimised two-blade rotor of composite materials and driven by either a Turboméca TM 319 turbogenerator or a Pratt & Whitney Canada PW205 or Allison 250-C23 turboshaft engine.

The following description applies to the fully developed 002 prototype, except where indicated:

TYPE: Four-seat tip-driven light helicopter.

ROTOR SYSTEM: One four-blade main rotor; no anti-torque rotor. Blade section NACA 23018. Constant chord blades, each built around a hollow extruded spar and attached to the hub via a laminated torsion strap of high-strength steel. Trailing-edge of each blade consists of a light alloy sheet box structure, bonded over ribs carried by a light spar. The laminated blade attachment straps permit pitch change and flapping without need for the usual blade bearings and stops. Compressed air from engine passes through a large-diameter non-rotating steel rotor mast, via a spherical bearing to the hollow spar of each blade and thence to the blade-tip nozzle. Rotor speed variable from 260-400 rpm, optimised at over 290 rpm.

FUSELAGE: Extensively glazed light alloy cabin made up basically of two roof sections of the Panhard B-24 motor car (lower one inverted), of which M Déchaux has bought the tooling. Twin tailbooms of elliptical section.

TAIL UNIT: Variable incidence horizontal surface between tailbooms, which end in integral endplate fins. Central stainless steel rudder, working in jet efflux, for use particularly during hovering and low-speed flight.

002 prototype of the Helicop-Jet tip-driven light helicopter

LANDING GEAR: Tubular skid type, with attachments for two small ground handling wheels.

POWER PLANT: One Turboméca Astazou IIIA turbo-generator, supplying compressed air for the tip-drive nozzles at an originally planned flow rate of 2·15 kg (4·75 lb)/s and pressure ratio of 3·5:1, and with a residual jet thrust of 20-40 kg (44-88 lb). Single internal fuel tank, capacity 250 litres (55 Imp gallons).

ACCOMMODATION: Seats for four persons in side by side pairs (six in pre-production version). Dual controls. Fully transparent forward hinged door on each side of cabin. Tinted glass optional.

EQUIPMENT: Optional equipment includes radio, intercom, night flying equipment, baggage compartment, winch, rescue and medical equipment and stretcher.

DIMENSIONS, EXTERNAL (A: 002 prototype, B: pre-production version):

Rotor diameter: A	10·00 m (32 ft 10 in)
B	12·00 m (39 ft 4½ in)
Rotor blade chord, constant: A	0·23 m (9 in)
B	0·32 m (1 ft 0¾ in)
Fuselage: Length: A	3·30 m (10 ft 10 in)
Max width: A	1·42 m (4 ft 8 in)
Height overall: A	2·85 m (9 ft 4¼ in)
Skid track: A	2·00 m (6 ft 6¾ in)

AREAS:

Rotor disc: A	78·54 m² (845·4 sq ft)
B	113·10 m² (1,217·4 sq ft)

WEIGHTS AND LOADINGS:

Weight empty: A	650 kg (1,433 lb)
B	552 kg (1,217 lb)
Max T-O weight: A	1,030 kg (2,271 lb)
B, civil (FAR Pt 27)	1,450 kg (3,196 lb)
B, military	1,500 kg (3,307 lb)
Max disc loading: A	13·11 kg/m² (2·69 lb/sq ft)
B, civil (FAR Pt 27)	12·82 kg/m² (2·63 lb/sq ft)
B, military	13·26 kg/m² (2·72 lb/sq ft)

PERFORMANCE (A, demonstrated):

Max cruising speed 84 knots (155 km/h; 96 mph)

PERFORMANCE (B, estimated with TM 319 power plant):

Cruising speed:

at 1,300 kg (2,866 lb) AUW 93 knots (173 km/h; 107 mph)

at 1,500 kg (3,307 lb) AUW 85 knots (157 km/h; 98 mph)

Rate of climb at S/L:

at 900 kg (1,984 lb) AUW	622 m (2,040 ft)/min
at 1,300 kg (2,866 lb) AUW	290 m (950 ft)/min
at 1,500 kg (3,307 lb) AUW	180 m (590 ft)/min

MBB

MBB HELICOPTER CANADA LIMITED (Subsidiary of Messerschmitt-Bölkow-Blohm GmbH)

MARKETING OFFICE: Suite 910, 130 Albert Street, Ottawa, Ontario K1P 5G4

Telephone: (613) 232 1557

Telex: 053-4109

Telefax: (613) 232 5454

VICE-PRESIDENT, MARKETING: E. James Grant

HEAD OFFICE AND WORKS: PO Box 250, Gilmore Road, Fort Erie, Ontario L2A 5M9

Telephone: (416) 871 7772

Telex: 061-5250

Telefax: (416) 871 3320

PRESIDENT: Helge Wittholz

A memorandum of understanding was signed on 13 December 1983 between MBB, of the Federal Republic of Germany, and the government of Canada, for a 20 year project involving the development and manufacture of twin-engined light helicopters in Canada. MBB is developing this engineering capability through a joint venture with Fleet Aerospace Corporation of Fort Erie, Ontario. Of the total investment of $72·6 million, MBB will contribute $37·7 million, the Canadian federal government $20·9 million, and the Ontario government $14 million. A new company, MBB Helicopter Canada Limited, is the focal point for this activity. Fleet Aerospace has a 5% interest in MBB Helicopter Canada Ltd.

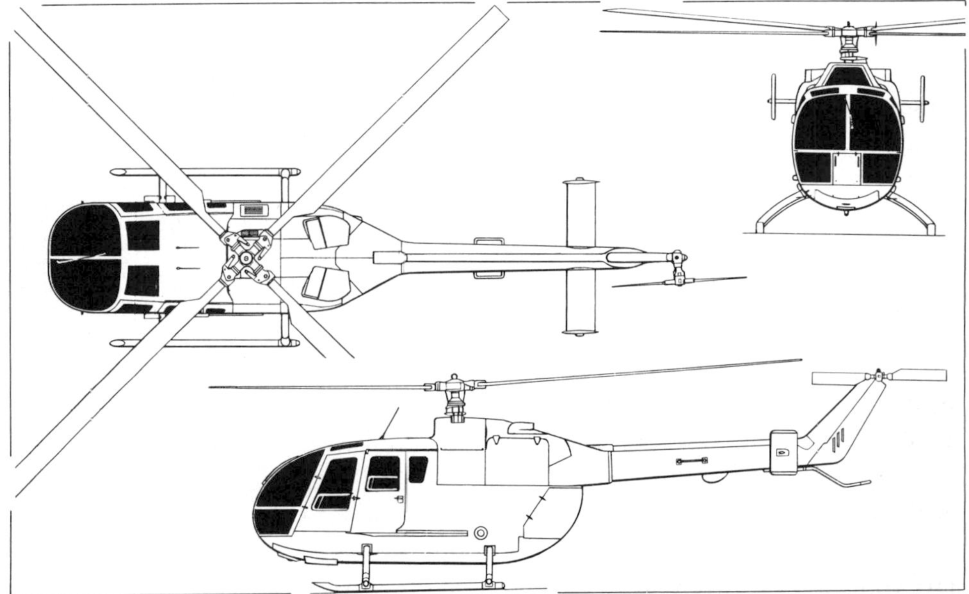

MBB Helicopter Canada Ltd BO 105 LS 'hot and high' helicopter *(Pilot Press)*

Initial production in Canada is of the Allison 250 powered MBB BO 105 LS, the first Canadian examples of which were due to be completed in 1986. At the same time, work is beginning in Canada on major component improvements (eg the dynamic system) to the capabilities of the BO 105 and for incorporation in other MBB helicopters produced in both Germany and Canada. The agreement also includes provision for the development of models powered by the new 298-373 kW (400-500 shp) class Pratt & Whitney Canada STEP turboshaft engine (small turbine engine programme), when this becomes available. These models will be designated BO 205 B. The transfer of technology and design authority from West Germany will enable MBB Helicopter Canada to assume full responsibility for designing and developing derivatives of models offered in Canada, and progressively to increase the Canadian manufacturing content of these later models to 70 per cent.

MBB BO 105 LS

This 'hot and high' version of the BO 105 (L for Lift and S for Stretch) combines the enlarged cabin of the CBS version with more powerful engines and an uprated transmission, permitting operation at a higher gross weight. It was first flown on 23 October 1981. Certification by the LBA was granted in July 1984, and was extended in April 1985 to cover 'hot and high' take-offs and landings at altitudes up to 6,100 m (20,000 ft). It was extended again on 7 July 1986 to cover the A-3 version of the BO 105 LS, with FAA certification expected to follow in Autumn 1986. Canadian production began in early 1986, at which time FAA, British CAA and Canadian DoT certification was being completed.

The description of the BO 105 CBS in the German section applies also to the BO 105 LS, except as follows:

Rotor Drive (BO 105 LS A-3): Main transmission, type ZF-FS 112, is rated for a twin-engine restricted input of 310 kW (416 shp) per engine at T-O power or 294 kW (394 shp) per engine for max continuous operation; or a single-engine restricted input of 368 kW (493 shp) at max continuous power, or 410 kW (550 shp) for 2·5 min at T-O power.

Power Plant: Two Allison 250-C28C turboshaft engines, each rated at 410 kW (550 shp) for 2·5 min, and with 5 min T-O and max continuous power ratings of 373 kW (500 shp) and 368 kW (493 shp) respectively. Fuel capacity as for CB/CBS.

Systems: As for BO 105 CBS, except starter/generators are 200A and stability augmentation system is standard.

Weights:
- Weight empty, basic 1,382 kg (3,047 lb)
- Fuel weight 456 kg (1,005 lb)
- Max T-O weight 2,600 kg (5,732 lb)

Performance (at T-O weight of 2,400 kg; 5,291 lb, ISA, except where indicated):
- Never-exceed speed at S/L 145 knots (270 km/h; 167 mph)
- Max cruising speed at S/L 123 knots (228 km/h; 142 mph)
- Max speed at S/L with external load (AUW of 2,600 kg; 5,732 lb) 100 knots (185 km/h; 115 mph)
- Max rate of climb at S/L 540 m (1,770 ft)/min
- Vertical rate of climb at S/L 252 m (827 ft)/min
- Max operating altitude 6,100 m (20,000 ft)
- Service ceiling, one engine out 2,560 m (8,400 ft)
- Hovering ceiling: IGE 4,265 m (14,000 ft)
- OGE 2,680 m (8,800 ft)
- Range at S/L, standard fuel, max internal payload, no reserves 282 nm (522 km; 324 miles)
- Ferry range at S/L, standard fuel plus two 200 litre (44 Imp gallon) auxiliary tanks, no reserves 482 nm (893 km; 555 miles)
- Endurance at S/L, standard fuel, max internal payload, no reserves 3 h 5 min

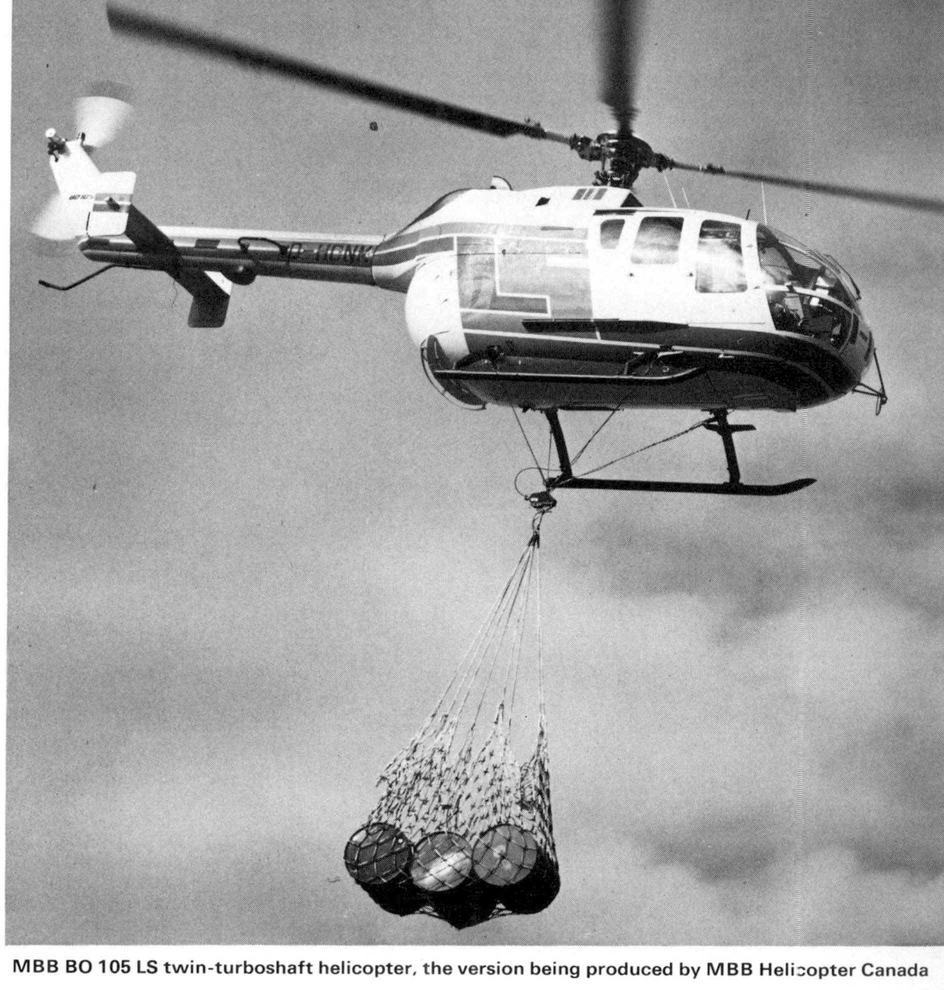

MBB BO 105 LS twin-turboshaft helicopter, the version being produced by MBB Helicopter Canada

MODERN WING

MODERN WING AIRCRAFT LTD

Richmond, British Columbia
President: John Hill

MODERN WING (DE HAVILLAND CANADA) DHC-2 BEAVER

In August 1986 Modern Wing expected to fly the first prototype of a modernised version of the Beaver utility aircraft, and certification was expected by the end of the year. The major change involves replacing the Beaver's original constant chord wings with redesigned, flush riveted wings having tapered outer panels, modified wingtips and higher-lift flaps. Improvements have also been made to the fuselage to reduce drag, and increase payload and speed.

The modifications increase max T-O weight from 2,358 kg (5,200 lb) to 2,721 kg (6,000 lb), but are expected to offer increases of 5-10 per cent in cruising speed and 91·5-122 m (300-400 ft)/min in climb rate, coupled with reductions of 30 per cent in T-O run, 20 per cent in landing run, and 10-15 per cent in fuel consumption.

More than a thousand of the 1,600 Beavers built by de Havilland Canada are still flying, and Modern Wing estimates a sale of 150 sets of new wings in the first five years of production.

NWI

NORTHWEST INDUSTRIES LIMITED (Subsidiary of CAE Industries Ltd)

PO Box 9864, Edmonton International Airport, Edmonton, Alberta T5J 2T2

Telephone: (403) 955 6300
Telex: 037-41574

President: L. H. Prokop

Vice-President and General Manager:
F. A. Maybee

Vice-President, Finance and Administration:
C. H. Fraser

NWI, a wholly owned subsidiary of CAE Industries Ltd, is one of Canada's largest aircraft maintenance, repair, overhaul and modification centres for military and commercial aircraft, including the Lockheed C-130 Hercules, Dassault Falcon, Lockheed T-33 and Canadair CL-41 jet trainers, and the CF-104 Starfighter. In addition to its major in-plant aircraft programmes, mobile repair parties are stationed at CFB Edmonton, CFB Cold Lake and CFB Bagotville in support of the C-130 Hercules, CF-5 and CF-18 aircraft of the Canadian Armed Forces. The company's manufacturing shops produce structural, mechanical and electronic components for its aircraft overhaul and modification programmes and for supply, under subcontract, to North America's principal aerospace manufacturers.

In 1986 NWI was incorporating major structural modifications to the Canadian Armed Forces' fleet of 22 Lockheed C-130E Hercules transport aircraft. In addition to fitting new (Lockheed supplied) C-130H outer wings, the CAF C-130s are receiving structural repairs to the fuselage and a full repaint in new camouflage colours. Depot level inspection, repair and service life extension of 64 CAF T-33A Silver Star jet trainers is providing a comprehensive structural, mechanical and electrical upgrading of these aircraft. Cabin embellishment repairs and tailplane inspections on CAF Dassault-Breguet Falcon 20 aircraft are continuing at NWI's Edmonton International Airport facility.

SPECIALTY

SPECIALTY AIRCRAFT SALES (1984) LTD

Specialty Aircraft Sales developed a Sea Thrush water bomber version of the Ayres Thrush agricultural monoplane, mounted on twin Edo 679-4930 floats and fitted with a 1,514 litre (400 US gallon) water-drop tank instead of the standard hopper. Design began in January 1983, and the prototype (C-GYXL) made its first flight in June of that year. A Canadian Dept of Transport supplementary type certificate (Restricted category) was granted on 19 January 1984, and an FAA STC was awaited in the Spring of 1985. However, a 1986 request for updated information was returned by the Canadian postal authorities indicating that Specialty's former address in Edmonton, Alberta, had been vacated.

All available details of the Sea Thrush were given, with an illustration, in the 1985-86 *Jane's*.

ULTIMATE AEROBATICS — *see Sport Aircraft section*

ZENAIR

ZENAIR LTD

25 King Road, Nobleton, Ontario L0G 1N0
Telephone: (416) 859 4556
PRESIDENT AND DESIGNER: Christophe Heintz

This company was formed by M Christophe Heintz, formerly designer with Avions Pierre Robin of France, to market plans, materials, parts and complete kits of his single-seat, two-seat and three-seat Zénith light aircraft and Zipper microlight (see Sport Aircraft section).

Design began in 1976 of a four/five-seat **CH 400** version of the Zénith which retains the basic configuration of the earlier aircraft but in scaled-up form. Construction of three prototypes began in September 1977, and the first of these was completed and flown in 1984. Production has been postponed pending an improvement in the market. A description and illustration of the Zénith-CH 400 can be found in the 1985-86 and previous editions.

CHILE

CARDOEN

INDUSTRIAS CARDOEN SA

Avenida Providencia 2237, 6° Piso, Santiago
Telephone: 251 1884
Telex: 340997 incar ck
CHIEF ENGINEER: Prof Rene Gonzalez

CARDOEN ATTACK HELICOPTER

Reports that Chile was developing an armed helicopter began to circulate in 1984, and at the FIDA air show at El Bosque in March 1986 Cardoen displayed a mockup of such an aircraft: a twin-turboshaft helicopter apparently based on the MBB BO 105, which is currently being assembled locally by ENAER Chile, though neither MBB nor ENAER is understood to be involved in the Cardoen project. The modifications are generally similar to those by which the French Alouette III has been adapted for a similar role by ICA in Romania and Atlas in South Africa (which see), mainly involving redesign of the forward fuselage and the endplate tail-fins. Initial reports from FIDA suggested that both single- and two-seat versions are proposed, with a first flight likely in late 1986 or early 1987. One or both seats would be provided with armour protection, fuel capacity increased, and the smaller profile would probably permit a higher maximum speed than that of the standard BO 105. An underfuselage Lucas turret mount is provided for a 12·7 mm (0·50 in) ventral gun, aimed by helmet sight, and there are stub-wings in line with the rotor mast, each with two attachments for the carriage of 70 mm rocket pods, bombs, or anti-tank missiles such as Hot or TOW. Other features are believed to include a head-up display, night vision system and digital avionics.

Full size mockup of the proposed Cardoen attack helicopter, based on the BO 105 *(Terry J. Gander)*

ENAER CHILE

EMPRESA NACIONAL DE AERONÁUTICA

Gran Avenida José Miguel Carrera 11087, Par. 36½, El Bosque, Santiago
Telephone: 582707 and 588582
Telex: 645115 ENAER CT
GENERAL MANAGER: Arthur Clark Flores
MANAGER, PRODUCT SUPPORT: Mario Magliocchetti

ENAER is a state owned company formed in 1984, by decision of the Chilean government, from the IndAer industrial organisation which had been set up by the Chilean Air Force in 1980. Aircraft manufacturing started in 1980 with the assembly of 27 Piper PA-28 Dakota light aircraft for Chilean Air Force and flying club use. With a 1986 workforce of about 1,800 people, ENAER's current activities are the design and production of aircraft and electronic warfare equipment.

To replace the Chilean Air Force's Beechcraft T-34s, and to fulfil the eventual need by the air forces of other countries for a basic trainer, ENAER and Piper Aircraft Corporation initiated in October 1980 the design and development of the T-35 Pillán. A turboprop powered version known as the Aucán is now being flight tested.

Meanwhile, in June 1980 Chile embarked upon an industrial transfer programme with CASA of Spain for the manufacture under licence of the CASA C-101BB-02 Aviojet advanced jet trainer, which has the Fuerza Aérea de Chile designation T-36 Halcón. The T-36 has begun to replace the Cessna T-37s being used by the FAC's Escuela de Aviación. An ENAER/CASA programme to develop an attack version of the C-101, with a higher thrust turbofan engine, was initiated during 1982. This version is designated C-101CC-02 by CASA and A-36 by the FAC. It first flew in 1983.

An agreement with MBB of Germany, to assemble BO 105 CBS and LS helicopters in Chile from knocked-down kits, was concluded in 1985, and the first Chilean assembled BO 105 was exhibited at the FIDA air show in El Bosque in March 1986. It was reported at that time that ENAER hoped to secure a Chilean Air Force order for 20-30 of these aircraft, which would have the FAC designation H-61.

ENAER T-35 PILLÁN (DEVIL)

Spanish Air Force designation: E.26 Tamiz

The Pillán is a tandem two-seat, fully aerobatic aircraft, intended for basic, intermediate and instrument flying training. It has been cleared to FAR Pt 23 (Aerobatic category) and military standards. To minimise costs, its design was based on the Piper Cherokee series, utilising in particular many components of the PA-28 Dakota and PA-32 Saratoga.

Two prototypes were developed by Piper, the first of these (designated PA-28R-300 XBT) making its initial flight on 6 March 1981 and the second (PA-28R-300 YBT) at the end of that year. Three further aircraft were delivered by Piper as kits for assembly by ENAER: the first of these (FAC serial number 101) flew on 30 January 1982 and the third in September of that year.

After more than 500 flying hours had been accumulated by the prototypes, a number of modifications were incorporated. These were mostly of a minor nature, the principal ones involving replacement of the original all-moving tailplane and anti-tab by an electrically trimmable tailplane with a conventional elevator, an increase in rudder mass balance, and a deeper canopy.

Series production of the Pillán began in March 1984, initially to fulfil an order for 80 aircraft for the Chilean Air Force. Sixty of these are of the basic **T-35A** primary trainer version, and 20 are **T-35B** instrument trainers with slightly more comprehensive avionics. In July 1984, after prolonged evaluation, the Spanish Air Force ordered 40 **T-35Cs** for use as primary trainers. These have the Spanish designation **E.26 Tamiz**, and are for assembly by CASA from components supplied by ENAER.

The first production T-35 flew for the first time on 28 December 1984 and the first pair were delivered to the Chilean Air Force on 31 July 1985. Six more were due to be delivered to the FAC by December 1985, plus the first two Tamiz kits to CASA. Plans then were to deliver four kits per month to CASA to complete the Spanish order, and to increase overall Pillán output to six per month by late 1986.

ENAER T-35 Pillán trainers of the Chilean Air Force

The following description applies to the T-35B, except where indicated:

TYPE: Two-seat fully aerobatic basic (T-35A/C) and instrument (T-35B) military trainer.

WINGS: Cantilever low-wing monoplane. Wing section NACA 65_2-415 on constant chord inboard panels, NACA 65_2-415 (modified) at tips. Dihedral 7°. Incidence 2° at root, −0° 30′ at tip. Single-spar structure of light alloy, with components mainly from PA-28-236 Dakota (leading-edges) and PA-32R-301 Saratoga (trailing-edges) modified to shorter span. Slotted ailerons and electrically operated single-slotted trailing-edge flaps of light alloy riveted construction, identical to those of Saratoga. Electrically operated trim tab in port aileron.

FUSELAGE: Semi-monocoque structure of aluminium alloy frames and longerons, with riveted skin. Tailcone assembled from Cherokee components, modified to fit narrower fuselage. Two-piece engine cowling of GRP.

TAIL UNIT: Cantilever structure of light alloy with swept-back (38° 43′) vertical surfaces, identical to those of Dakota except for heavier gauge skins, minor reinforcement of fin, and increased rudder mass balance. One-piece non-swept variable incidence tailplane, with electric trim and plastics tips. Full span mass balanced elevator. Tailplane incorporates some standard PA-28 and PA-31 (Navajo/Cheyenne) components; elevator is of all-new design. No elevator or rudder tabs; rudder is trimmed electrically.

LANDING GEAR: Hydraulically retractable tricycle type, with single wheel on each unit. Main gear legs and doors identical to those on PA-32R-301; nose gear assembled from PA-32R-301 and PA-28R-200 components. Main units retract inward, steerable nosewheel rearward. Piper oleo-pneumatic shock absorber in each unit. Emergency free-fall extension. Mainwheels and tyres size 6·00-6 (8 ply), nosewheel and tyre size 5·00-5 (6 ply). Single-disc hydraulic brake on each mainwheel. Parking brake.

POWER PLANT: One 224 kW (300 hp) Avco Lycoming IO-540-K1K5 flat-six engine, driving a Hartzell HC-C3YR-4BF/F7663R-0 three-blade constant-speed metal propeller with spinner. Fuel contained in two integral aluminium tanks in wing leading-edges, total capacity 291·5 litres (64·1 Imp gallons), of which 272·5 litres (60 Imp gallons) are usable. Overwing gravity refuelling point on each wing. Fuel and oil systems permit unlimited inverted flight (up to 40 min flight tested).

ACCOMMODATION: Vertically adjustable seats for two persons, with seat belts and shoulder harnesses, in tandem beneath one-piece transparent jettisonable canopy which opens sideways to starboard. One-piece acrylic windscreen, and one-piece window in glassfibre fairing aft of canopy. Rear (instructor's) seat 22 cm (8⅔ in) higher than front seat. Dual controls standard. Baggage compartment aft of rear cockpit, with external access on port side. Accommodation heated, and canopy demisted, by engine bleed air. Ventilation system as for Piper Dakota.

SYSTEMS: Electrically operated hydraulic system, at 124 bars (1,800 lb/sq in) pressure, for landing gear extension and retraction. Electrical system is 24V DC, powered by a 28V 70A engine driven Prestolite alternator and 24V 17Ah battery, with an inverter for AC power at 400Hz to operate RMIs and attitude indicators. External power socket.

AVIONICS AND EQUIPMENT: (*T-35A*) Optional avionics include dual VHF com, intercom, VOR, marker panel, and ADF. (*T-35B*) Standard package of King avionics includes dual KX 165 VHF-AM com transceivers, dual KMA 24H intercoms, KX 165 VOR/ILS nav, KR 21 marker beacon receiver, KR 87 ADF, KN 63 DME, KT 76A ATC transponder, KCS 55A compass system (dual KI 525 HSIs, dual KNI 582 RMIs, and KA 51A slaving meter); dual AI-904 AA/B attitude director indicators; dual turn and slip indicators; stall warning system; 'landing gear not down' warning system; pitot static system; and vacuum system for gyro instrument operation. Standard instrumentation (*T-35A*) includes airspeed indicator, sensitive altimeter, rate of climb indicator, turn and bank indicator, artificial gyro horizon, directional gyro, vacuum pressure gauge, *g* meter, and magnetic compass (all dual); engine tachometer, manifold pressure gauge, fuel flow indicator, oil temperature and pressure indicators, cylinder head temperature gauge, and exhaust gas temperature gauge (all dual); voltmeter/ammeters (two), fuel quantity indicators (four), fuel pressure indicators (two), digital clocks (two), and outside air temperature gauge (one). Other equipment includes cockpit heating outlets and ventilators (four of each); map compartment (optional); fuel and oil quick-drains; interior instrument panel/map/annunciator/fuel and oil warning lights; exterior navigation/anti-collision strobe lights, landing gear position lights, and a single landing/taxying light in centre of lower engine cowl; external power socket; wing jack pads; tiedown rings; and provision for two underwing hardpoints for external stores.

DIMENSIONS, EXTERNAL:

Wing span	8·81 m (28 ft 11 in)
Wing chord: at root	1·88 m (6 ft 2 in)
at tip	1·26 m (4 ft 1½ in)
inboard (constant)	1·60 m (5 ft 3 in)
mean aerodynamic	1·55 m (5 ft 1 in)
Wing aspect ratio	5·69
Length overall	8·02 m (26 ft 3¾ in)
Height overall	2·34 m (7 ft 8¼ in)
Fuselage: Length	7·66 m (25 ft 1¾ in)
Max width	0·94 m (3 ft 1 in)
Max depth	1·56 m (5 ft 1¼ in)
Tailplane span	3·05 m (10 ft 0 in)
Wheel track	3·02 m (9 ft 11 in)
Wheelbase	2·09 m (6 ft 10¼ in)
Propeller diameter	1·93 m (6 ft 4 in)

DIMENSIONS, INTERNAL:

Cockpit: Length	3·24 m (10 ft 7½ in)
Max width	1·04 m (3 ft 5 in)
Max height	1·48 m (4 ft 10¼ in)

AREAS:

Wings, gross	13·64 m² (146·8 sq ft)
Ailerons (total)	1·10 m² (11·84 sq ft)
Trailing-edge flaps (total)	1·36 m² (14·64 sq ft)
Fin	0·69 m² (7·43 sq ft)
Rudder	0·38 m² (4·09 sq ft)
Tailplane	1·57 m² (16·90 sq ft)
Elevator	0·77 m² (8·29 sq ft)

WEIGHTS AND LOADINGS:

Basic weight empty	833 kg (1,836 lb)
Weight empty, equipped	929 kg (2,048 lb)
Fuel (usable)	196 kg (432 lb)
Max aerobatic T-O weight	1,315 kg (2,900 lb)
Max T-O and landing weight	1,338 kg (2,950 lb)
Max wing loading	98·1 kg/m² (20·1 lb/sq ft)
Max power loading	5·98 kg/kW (9·83 lb/hp)

PERFORMANCE (at max T-O and landing weight, ISA):

Never-exceed speed	241 knots (446 km/h; 277 mph)
Max level speed at S/L	168 knots (311 km/h; 193 mph)
Cruising speed:	
75% power at 2,680 m (8,800 ft)	161 knots (298 km/h; 185 mph)
65% power at 3,900 m (12,800 ft)	150 knots (278 km/h; 173 mph)
55% power at 5,120 m (16,800 ft)	138 knots (255 km/h; 159 mph)
Stalling speed: flaps up	68 knots (125 km/h; 78 mph)
flaps down	63 knots (117 km/h; 73 mph)
Unstick speed	60 knots (111 km/h; 69 mph)
Max speed for flap extension	118 knots (218 km/h; 136 mph)
Max speed for landing gear extension	138 knots (256 km/h; 159 mph)
Approach speed over 15 m (50 ft) obstacle	80 knots (148 km/h; 92 mph)
Landing speed	65 knots (120 km/h; 75 mph)
Max rate of climb at S/L	465 m (1,525 ft)/min
Time to: 1,830 m (6,000 ft)	4 min 42 s
3,050 m (10,000 ft)	8 min 48 s
Service ceiling	5,820 m (19,100 ft)
Absolute ceiling	6,250 m (20,500 ft)
T-O run	293 m (961 ft)
T-O to 15 m (50 ft)	506 m (1,660 ft)
Landing from 15 m (50 ft)	521 m (1,709 ft)
Landing run	243 m (797 ft)
Range with 45 min reserves:	
75% power at 2,440 m (8,000 ft)	590 nm (1,093 km; 679 miles)
65% power at 3,660 m (12,000 ft)	625 nm (1,158 km; 720 miles)
Range, no reserves:	
75% power at 2,440 m (8,000 ft)	685 nm (1,269 km; 789 miles)
65% power at 3,660 m (12,000 ft)	720 nm (1,334 km; 829 miles)
Endurance at S/L: 75% power	4 h 24 min
65% power	4 h 55 min
55% power	5 h 39 min
g limits	+6/−3

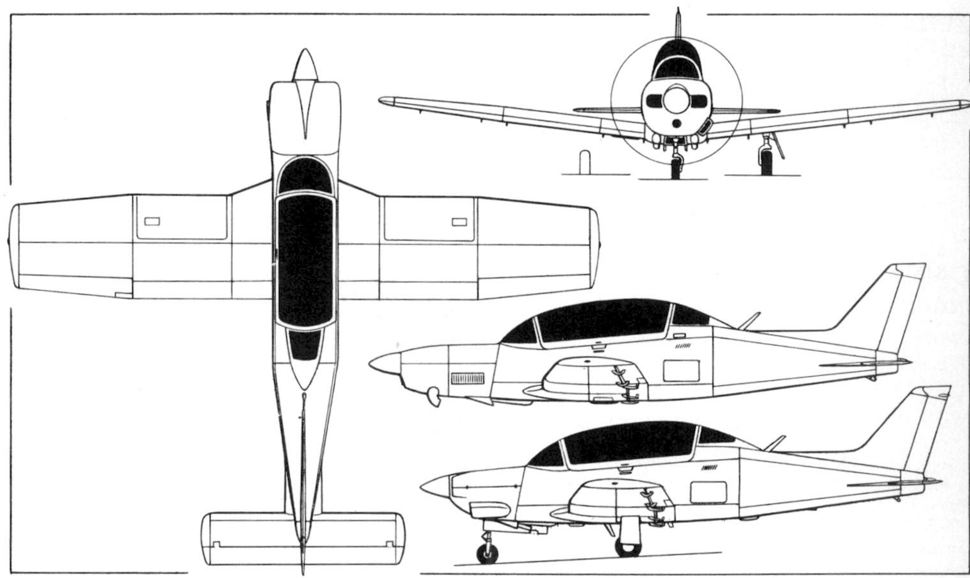

ENAER T-35 Pillán tandem two-seat basic/intermediate trainer, with additional side view (centre) of the T-35TX Aucán *(Pilot Press)*

ENAER T-35TX AUCÁN

Design studies for a turboprop version of the Pillán were completed in 1985. Originally known as the Turbo Pillán, the trainer has now been redesignated T-35TX Aucán and is powered by a 313 kW (420 shp) Allison 250-B17D engine. A prototype (CC-PZC) was shown at the FIDA exhibition in Chile in March 1986, following its first flight on 14 February. Production is planned to start in 1988.

Prototype ENAER Aucán trainer (Allison 250-B17D turboprop engine)

DIMENSIONS, EXTERNAL: As for Pillán except:
Length overall 8·29 m (27 ft 2½ in)
WEIGHTS:
Basic weight empty 1,048 kg (2,310 lb)
Max T-O weight 1,364 kg (3,007 lb)
PERFORMANCE:
Max level speed at S/L 198 knots (367 km/h; 228 mph)
Max cruising speed at 3,050 m (10,000 ft) 186 knots (345 km/h; 214 mph)
Stalling speed at S/L, flaps down 59 knots (109 km/h; 68 mph)
Max rate of climb at S/L 588 m (1,930 ft)/min
Service ceiling 8,535 m (28,000 ft)
T-O run at S/L 178 m (583 ft)
Range 620 nm (1,150 km; 715 miles)

ENAER T-36/A-36 HALCÓN (HAWK)

In 1980 the Chilean Air Force (FAC) ordered an initial batch of 16 C-101BB-02 Aviojet trainers from CASA of Spain, the contract including a licence for local manufacture by ENAER in a progressive programme advancing from assembly of CASA built components to partial manufacture of major components in Chile. The first four aircraft were built and flight tested in Spain, then delivered to the FAC to serve as pattern aircraft in organising the production line. The remaining 12 aircraft on this contract were completed by ENAER. A 17th BB-02 was ordered in July 1984.

Designated **T-36** Halcón by the FAC, the C-101BB-02 differs from the C-101EB for the Spanish Air Force in having a more powerful (16·46 kN; 3,700 lb st) Garrett TFE731-3 turbofan engine instead of the 15·57 kN (3,500 lb st) TFE731-2.

During 1982 ENAER and CASA initiated a programme to develop an attack version of the C-101 with a higher thrust turbofan engine. Designated C-101CC-02 by CASA and **A-36** by the FAC, this flew for the first time in November 1983 and one of the two prototypes was delivered to the FAC later that year. A follow-on order for 21 more C-101s, of which 20 will be A-36s, was placed in July 1984, and the A-36 will replace the Cessna A-37 in FAC service. This version is powered by a TFE731-5 engine of 19·13 kN (4,300 lb st), with a military power reserve (MPR) system which allows the thrust to be increased to 20·91 kN (4,700 lb).

Deliveries of the T-36, to the tactical school of the 1st Air Group of the FAC in northern Chile, began in late 1983. They included the first four (Spanish built) Halcóns, plus the first examples built by ENAER under phase 1A of the multi-stage progression towards partial local manufacture (tail unit and all control surfaces). Aircraft from the follow-on batch of 21 will progress towards phase 3A (Chilean manufacture of electrical and hydraulic systems and small subassemblies) and phase 4 (manufacture of front fuselage). A total of 18 Halcóns had been completed by late 1985. Exhibits at the March 1986 FIDA air show included a T-36 fitted with a ventral 30 mm gun pack and six underwing weapon stations, and an A-36 in naval strike configuration with underwing BAe Sea Eagle missiles.

ENAER MIRAGE 50 UPGRADE

With technical assistance from Israel Aircraft Industries, ENAER has begun to upgrade Dassault-Breguet Mirage 50 fighters by fitting them with non-moving canard surfaces, an inertial navigation system, a computerised head-up display, modified electrical and hydraulic systems, and ENAER Calquen III and Eclipse ECM equipment. The foreplanes are understood to have a different planform from those of the IAI Kfir.

CHINA
(PEOPLE'S REPUBLIC)

The Chinese language is gradually being simplified to a new Latinised or Westernised form of spelling known as Pinyin. Under this system, the transliterated spellings with which Western readers have been familiar for years have, in many cases, undergone some change. For example, Peking is written as Beijing, which conforms more closely with the Chinese pronunciation. Place names in this section are shown first in the current Pinyin spelling, followed where applicable by the 'old' spelling.

STATE AIRCRAFT FACTORIES

Shenyang, Liaoning Province; Xian (Sian), Shaanxi (Shensi) Province; Harbin, Heilongjiang (Heilungkiang) Province; Shanghai Municipality; Beijing (Peking) Municipality; Nanchang, Jiangxi (Kiangsi) Province; Hanzhong (Hanchung), Shaanxi Province; Tianjin (Tientsin) Municipality; Shijiazhuang (Shihchiachuang), Hebei (Hopei) Province; Chengdu, Sichuan Province; and elsewhere

INTERNATIONAL MARKETING:

CATIC (China National Aero-Technology Import and Export Corporation)
67 Jiao Nan Street (PO Box 1671), Beijing
Telephone: 44 2444
Telex: 22318 AEROT CN
PRESIDENT: Sun Zhaoqing
VICE-PRESIDENT: Wang Dawei

ATL (Aircraft Technology Ltd)
1202 Hang Lung Bank Building, 8 Hysan Avenue, Causeway Bay, Hong Kong
Telephone: 5 768227
Telex: 89073 ATEC HX
DIRECTOR: David Y. Chu

Longest established of the Chinese national aircraft factories are those at Shenyang and Harbin. The latter had its origin in the plant of the Manshu Aeroplane Manufacturing Company, one of several aircraft and aero engine manufacturing facilities established in Manchukuo (Manchuria) by the Japanese invaders in 1938. A large flying training school was established by the Japanese at Shenyang (then known as Mukden) in 1940. After the Communist regime came to power in mainland China in 1949 the Manchurian factories were re-established and re-equipped with Soviet assistance. Their early products have been listed in the 1985-86 and earlier editions of *Jane's*. Shenyang and Harbin are still major centres of Chinese aircraft and aero engine production, under the jurisdiction of the Ministry of Aviation Industry. There are design and development centres at Shenyang, Beijing, Harbin and elsewhere. Total workforce of the Chinese aerospace industry was estimated at 350,000 in 1984, although several aircraft factories are engaged also in manufacturing non-aerospace products.

First jet aircraft built in China were the single-seat MiG-15bis and two-seat MiG-15UTI. These were not given Chinese designations. They were followed by the MiG-17F (Chinese designation J-5) and MiG-17PF (J-5 Jia or J-5A). A 'UTI' tandem two-seat conversion of the J-5, known as the JJ-5, was developed by the Chinese, as described in the 1983-84 and earlier editions of *Jane's*. These types were followed by Soviet and Chinese versions of the MiG-19 (J-6), and a more recent fighter designated J-8 is being developed at Shenyang.

Harbin is responsible for the Soviet Ilyushin Il-28 jet bomber (Chinese H-5), and the nationally designed Y-11/Y-12 agricultural/utility light twins. It is also the chief centre for helicopter production, which began with the Mil Mi-4 (Chinese Z-5). Harbin is currently responsible also for the Aérospatiale Dauphin 2 (Z-9) assembly programme, and is sharing production of components for the Mil Mi-8 with the factory at Nanchang.

Aircraft built at Xian (Sian) include the Soviet Tupolev Tu-16 bomber (Chinese designation H-6), and Chinese versions of the MiG-21 (J-7) and Antonov An-24 (Y-7). Xian also produces Wopen-8 (RD-3M) jet engines for the Tu-16/H-6, and since 1980 has manufactured glassfibre header tanks, water float pylons, ailerons and various doors for the Canadair CL-215 water bomber. Xian, Harbin and other Chinese factories also carry out subcontract work on the ATR 42, BAe 146 (cabin doors), Boeing 737-300 (fins and cabin doors), McDonnell Douglas MD-80 (landing gear doors) and Shorts 360 (wing centre-sections and cabin doors).

Nanchang, previously responsible for licence production of the Yak-18A (Chinese designation CJ-5), is currently manufacturing its own development of this aircraft (as the CJ-6), and a Chinese attack aircraft (the Q-5) developed from the J-6/MiG-19. Nanchang has also been suggested as the likely production centre for the Changhe Z-8 helicopter. Other important programmes are those for the Y-8 and Y-10 transport aircraft, at Hanzhong (Shaanxi) and Shanghai respectively. Shanghai is also the centre for co-production of the McDonnell Douglas MD-82 commercial transport aircraft.

Output of older fighters and bombers is now diminishing, with increasing emphasis being placed on the development of new aircraft making use of China's growing technological capability. The reduction of 1 million personnel in China's armed forces manpower is intended to make more funds available during the seventh Five-Year Plan (1986-90) for the purchase of modern weapons and technology, while at the same time shifting emphasis in the aviation industry towards a target of a 60-40 per cent bias in favour of civil aircraft production. As a further step in this direction, increased effort is being made to export Chinese built aircraft (particularly the F-7M, A-5C, Z-9, Y7-100, Y-8 and Y-12) through the newly established, Hong Kong based Aircraft Technology Ltd, in which the Chinese import/export organisation CATIC is a partner with Lucas Aerospace of the UK (40% each) and a Hong Kong businessman (20%).

Priority civil programmes for the period 1986-90 include ongoing development of the Y-7, Y-8 and Y-12; international collaboration programmes to develop other transport aircraft in the 40, 75 and 150 passenger categories; conversion or development of new types of aircraft (including helicopters) for agricultural and forestry work; a 2,000 kg (4,410 lb) light helicopter; and a larger helicopter in the 8,000 kg (17,635 lb) class for multi-role transport use. On the military side, design studies have been initiated at Xian for a 1990s twin-engined supersonic bomber (H-7?), and this factory is also developing another new tandem two-seat military aircraft of which a mockup or prototype was under construction in mid-1985. The latter may be the reported Q-6 attack aircraft, said to be equipped with a 30 mm anti-tank gun system, or (perhaps less likely) a twin-turbofan advanced trainer (CJ-8?). (Designation CJ-7 is believed to apply to a new turboprop trainer programme.) Details of new fighter programmes are much more speculative. Reports continue to persist, without supporting evidence, of a delta-winged J-10 and swept (or swing) winged J-12 under development, with designation 'gaps' explained by a fighter version of 'Fantan-A' (J-9 'Fantan-B'), and possible Chinese production of the MiG-23 (as J-11). While all of these would be logical and credible areas of present/future activity, positive evidence of their factual existence is still awaited. However, China's Aviation Minister did confirm in early 1986 that a new type of fighter would be developed during the seventh Five-Year Plan.

The Air Force of the People's Liberation Army has an operational home defence fighter force of about 4,000 J-5s, J-6s and J-7s, and a tactical air force of more than 1,000 J-5s, H-5s and Q-5s. The PLA Air Force currently deploys a medium bomber force of about 120 Tu-16/H-6s, which are nuclear capable. More than 100 CSS-1 (Dongfeng 2) MRBMs and CSS-2 and CSS-3 (Dongfeng 3 and 4) IRBMs are also deployed in a mobile strategic role, supplemented by a few CSS-4 (Dongfeng 5) KBMs ICBMs able to deliver a 5 mT warhead over a range of 7,000 nm (13,000 km; 8,075 miles).

CHANGHE
CHANGHE AIRCRAFT MANUFACTURING CORPORATION

CHANGHE Z-8

Chinese name: Zhishengji-8 (Vertical take-off aircraft 8) or Zhi-8

Chinese sources have confirmed the existence of this 13,000 kg (28,660 lb) helicopter, which is based on the Aérospatiale SA 321JA Super Frelon and flew for the first time on 11 December 1985. It was developed jointly by the Changhe Aircraft Manufacturing Corporation and the China Helicopter Research and Design Bureau, both located at Jingdezhen in Jiangxi Province. It is planned to complete a batch of ten Zhi-8s by 1990.

First prototype of the Changhe Zhi-8 Chinese version of the Aérospatiale Super Frelon

GUANGZHOU

GUANGZHOU ORLANDO HELICOPTERS LTD

GUANGZHOU (ORLANDO) PANDA

Orlando Helicopter Airways (see US section) initiated a venture in 1985 in which its OHA-S-55 Bearcat will be assembled, and later part-built, in China, by a new company known as Guangzhou Orlando Helicopters Ltd. A 2,323 m^2 (25,000 sq ft) factory is to be built for the purpose at an airfield near the city of Guangzhou.

The 20-year contract, signed on 27 October 1985, provides for the initial assembly in China, from Orlando kits, of ten aircraft. Second and third stage batches of 20 and 30 aircraft respectively will include a proportion of OHA-S-55T Challenger and/or Phoenix turbine powered versions, with 522 kW (700 shp) Avco Lycoming LTS 101-700A-3 engines. Chinese built OHA-S-55s will be marketed, under the name Panda, by Orlando Helicopter Far East Ltd, based in Hong Kong. The contract also contains options for co-production of Orlando modified S-58 and S-61 helicopters.

HARBIN

HARBIN AIRCRAFT MANUFACTURING CORPORATION

General Manager: Li Guangshu

HARBIN (ILYUSHIN) H-5

Chinese name: Hongzhaji-5 (Bomber aircraft 5) or Hong-5

NATO reporting names: Beagle (H-5) and Mascot (HJ-5)

After receiving large numbers of Ilyushin Il-28 three-seat tactical light bombers from the Soviet Union, China began building its own equivalent, as the H-5, in 1966. Production at Harbin, which totalled about 500, ended in about 1982; about 500 H-5s are believed still to equip the air force of the People's Liberation Army, with about 130 more in service with the PLA Navy. Some may be configured for nuclear weapon delivery. Known Chinese versions are:

H-5 (Hongzhaji-5 or Hong-5). Standard three-seat tactical light bomber, similar to basic Il-28. Some early examples were exported to Albania. Production also included torpedo-bomber version similar to Soviet Il-28T.

HJ-5 (Hongzhaji Jiaolianji-5 or Hongjiao-5). Two-seat operational and pilot training version, similar to Soviet Il-28U (NATO reporting name 'Mascot'). Armament and ventral ground mapping radar fairing deleted; 'solid' nose; second, 'stepped' cockpit (with full dual controls) ahead of and below pilot's cockpit. Two or three supplied to each operational H-5 unit.

HZ-5 (Hongzhaji Zhenchaji-5 or Hongzhen-5). Three-seat tactical reconnaissance version, similar to Soviet Il-28R. Wingtip auxiliary fuel tanks standard; weapons bay occupied by alternative packs containing cameras or electronic sensors.

In 1985 China ordered modified Rushton low level towed targets from the FR Group in the UK. These are for use with H-5s of the PLA Navy, to simulate sea-skimming anti-ship missiles.

A full description of the Il-28/H-5 can be found in the 1981-82 *Jane's*, and a shortened version in the 1984-85 edition.

HARBIN Y-11

Chinese name: Yunshuji-11 (Transport aircraft 11) or Yun-11

This twin-engined utility aircraft was designed and developed in China as a potential replacement for the Y-5 (Chinese built Antonov An-2). First flight is believed to have taken place in 1975.

Construction of a pre-production batch of about 15 aircraft began in 1977, and these were used in top-dressing and pest control operations in 1977-78. The Y-11 received Chinese type certification in 1981 and is used primarily in agricultural, forestry and geophysical survey applications. A total of 40 was built, and production has now ended.

The following is a shortened version of the full description which can be found in the 1985-86 and earlier editions of *Jane's*:

Type: Twin-engined agricultural and general purpose aircraft.

Airframe: See 1985-86 *Jane's*.

Power Plant: Two 213 kW (285 hp) Zhuzhou (Chuchow) Huosai-6A (Chinese development of Ivchenko/Vedeneyev AI-14RF) nine-cylinder radial aircooled engines, each driving a two-blade variable-pitch propeller, underslung from wings and fitted with louvred intakes in front of cylinders to control cooling. Two metal fuel tanks between spars of each outer wing, with smaller tank in each engine nacelle. Total fuel capacity 530 litres (116 Imp gallons; 140 US gallons). Normal fuel load carried on agricultural missions is 285 litres (62·5 Imp gallons; 75 US gallons).

Accommodation: Crew of two on flight deck, with separate forward opening door on port side for access. Dual controls. Cabin accommodates seven passengers normally (with removable folding jump seat for an eighth passenger), or equivalent cargo. Cargo/passenger double door on port side of fuselage, in line with wing trailing-edge.

Systems, Avionics and Equipment: See 1985-86 *Jane's*.

Dimensions, external:

Wing span	17·00 m (55 ft 9¼ in)
Length overall	12·017 m (39 ft 5⅛ in)
Height overall	4·64 m (15 ft 2¾ in)
Wheel track (c/l of shock absorbers)	3·45 m (11 ft 3¾ in)
Wheelbase	3·642 m (11 ft 11½ in)
Propeller diameter	2·40 m (7 ft 10½ in)

Area:

Wings, gross	34·00 m^2 (365·97 sq ft)

Harbin Y-11 twin-engined general purpose aircraft

Weights:

Weight empty	2,050 kg (4,519 lb)
Max fuel load	390 kg (860 lb)
Max payload	870 kg (1,918 lb)
Normal T-O and landing weight	3,250 kg (7,165 lb)
Max T-O weight	3,500 kg (7,715 lb)

Performance (at normal T-O weight):

Max level speed	119 knots (220 km/h; 137 mph)
Cruising speed:	
75% power	102 knots (190 km/h; 118 mph)
65% power	94 knots (175 km/h; 109 mph)
57% power	89 knots (165 km/h; 102 mph)
Speed for agricultural operation	86 knots (160 km/h; 99 mph)
Stalling speed, flaps up	57 knots (105 km/h; 65 mph)
Max rate of climb at S/L	246 m (807 ft)/min
Service ceiling	4,000 m (13,125 ft)
STOL T-O and landing run	140 m (459 ft)
Range at 3,000 m (9,845 ft) with max fuel, no reserves	537 nm (995 km; 618 miles)
Range with max payload and 250 kg (551 lb) fuel, 45 min reserves	215 nm (400 km; 248 miles)
Max endurance	7 h 20 min

HARBIN Y-12

Chinese name: Yunshuji-12 (Transport aircraft 12) or Yun-12

This STOL general purpose transport resulted from studies, extending over several years, of possible ways of improving the payload/range capabilities of the piston engined nine/ten-seat Harbin Y-11 general purpose transport. Pratt & Whitney Canada PT6A-11 turboprop engines were adopted for the initial development version, designated **Y-12 I** (originally Y-11T1).

The additional engine power available enabled the basic Y-11 airframe to be scaled up, the principal enlargement being that of the fuselage, which has an increased cross-section and is lengthened to enable up to 17 passengers to be carried in a commuter configuration. The wings, in addition to being 0·235 m (9¼ in) greater in span, have a new aerofoil section intended to afford a 3 per cent increase in maximum speed and 10 per cent increase in rate of climb; they also incorporate additional fuel tanks in the wing spar box. Design and construction of the Y-12 are to FAR Pt 23 and Pt 135 (Annexe A) standards.

Three Y-12 Is were built: one for structure and static testing, the second and third (since fitted out for geophysical

Harbin Y-12 II twin-turboprop utility transport

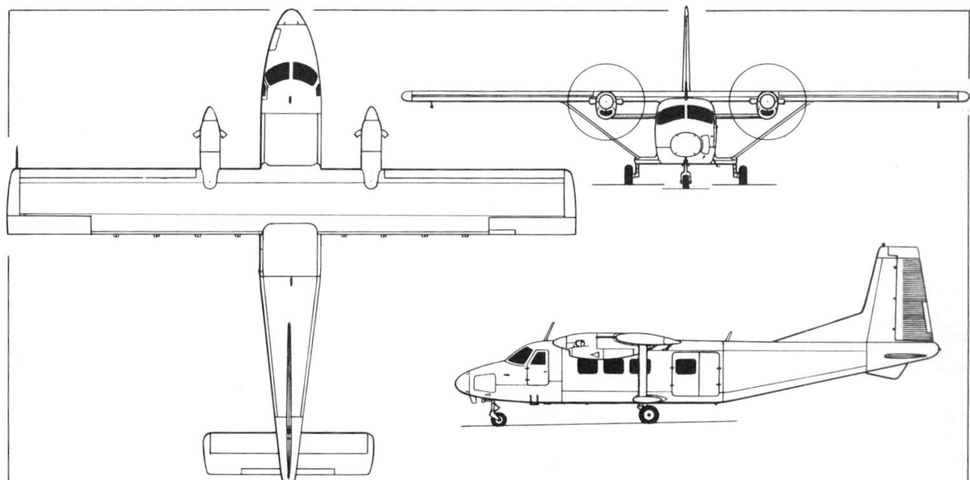

Harbin Y-12 STOL general purpose transport *(Pilot Press)*

survey work and delivered to a Chinese customer) for flight testing. The first flight took place at Harbin on 14 July 1982; the leading-edge slats, which were blanked off for the first flight, were omitted from the second batch of three aircraft (designated **Y-12 II**, originally Y-11T2), which have higher rated PT6A-27 engines. First flight of a Y-12 II took place in 1983.

Domestic certification was received in December 1985, and 18 production Y-12s were due to have been completed by the end of 1986. It is hoped to obtain international certification by the end of 1987, possibly with assistance from the British Civil Aviation Authority.

HAECO (Hong Kong Aircraft Engineering Co) received a 1985 contract similar to that for the Xian Y-7 (which see) to upgrade the avionics and interior of the Y-12. The first Y-12 II for treatment under this programme (c/n 6) was redelivered to China in August 1985, and the details which follow apply to this version except where indicated. A licence agreement for P&WC PT6 engines to be assembled in China was announced in May 1986. China is understood to have a domestic requirement for more than 200 Y-12s, and the aircraft is being offered for export.

TYPE: Twin-turboprop STOL general purpose transport.

WINGS: Braced high-wing monoplane, with constant chord from root to tip. Wing section GA-0417, with thickness/chord ratio of 17%. No dihedral. Two-spar structure, with aluminium alloy skin; Ziqiang-2 resin bonding on 70 per cent of structure and integral fuel tankage in wing spar box. All-metal drooping ailerons and electrically actuated two-section double-slotted flaps along full span of trailing-edges. Trim tab in starboard aileron. Small stub-wings at cabin floor level support the main landing gear units; bracing strut from each stub-wing out to approx one-third span.

FUSELAGE: Conventional semi-monocoque all-metal structure of basically rectangular cross-section, swept upward at rear. Ziqiang-2 resin bonding on 40 per cent of structure.

TAIL UNIT: Cantilever non-swept metal structure, with low-set constant chord tailplane and large dorsal fin. Horn balanced rudder and elevators. Trim tab in rudder and each elevator. Triangular ventral fin under tailcone.

LANDING GEAR: Non-retractable tricycle type, with oleo-pneumatic shock absorber in each unit. Single-wheel main units, attached to underside of stub wings. Single steerable nosewheel. Pneumatic brakes.

POWER PLANT: Two Pratt & Whitney Canada PT6A-11 turboprop engines in Y-12 I, each flat rated at 373 kW (500 shp) and driving a Hartzell HC-B3TN-3B/T10173B-8 three-blade variable- and reversible-pitch propeller with spinner. Y-12 II has 462 kW (620 shp) PT6A-27 turboprops and B-3 propellers. All fuel in tanks in wing spar box, total capacity 1,600 litres (352 Imp gallons; 423 US gallons).

ACCOMMODATION: Crew of two on flight deck, access to which is via a forward opening door on the port side. Four-way adjustable crew seats. Dual controls. Main cabin can accommodate up to 17 passengers in commuter configuration, in three-abreast layout (with aisle), at seat pitch of 79 cm (31 in). Alternative layouts for up to 14 parachutists, or an all-cargo configuration with 11 tie-down rings. Passenger/cargo double door on port side at rear, the rear half of which opens outward and the forward half inward; foldout steps in passenger entrance. Emergency exit opposite passenger door on starboard side. Baggage compartments in nose and at rear of passenger cabin, for 100 kg (220 lb) and 260 kg (573 lb) respectively.

AVIONICS: Standard instrumentation includes BK-450 air-speed indicator, BDP-1 artificial horizon, BG10-1A altimeter, Z3W-3G altitude indicator, ZHZ-4A radio magnetic heading indicator, BC10 rate of climb indicator, ZWH-1 outside air temperature indicator, and ZEY-1 flap position indicator; dual engine torquemeters, interturbine temperature indicators, gas generator tachometers, oil temperature and pressure indicators, and fuel pressure and quantity indicators; HSZ-2 clock; and XDH-10 warning light box.

EQUIPMENT: Hopper for 1,200 litres (264 Imp gallons) of dry or liquid chemical in agricultural version. Appropriate specialised equipment for firefighting, geophysical survey and other missions.

DIMENSIONS, EXTERNAL:

Wing span	17·235 m (56 ft 6½ in)
Wing chord (constant)	2·00 m (6 ft 6¾ in)
Wing aspect ratio	8·67
Length overall	14·86 m (48 ft 9 in)
Height overall	5·575 m (18 ft 3½ in)
Elevator span	5·365 m (17 ft 7¼ in)
Wheel track	3·60 m (11 ft 9¾ in)
Wheelbase	4·698 m (15 ft 5 in)
Propeller diameter: I	2·36 m (7 ft 9 in)
II	2·49 m (8 ft 2 in)
Distance between propeller centres	4·934 m (16 ft 2¼ in)
Fuselage/ground clearance	0·65 m (2 ft 1½ in)
Passenger/cargo door: Height	1·38 m (4 ft 6¼ in)
Width (passenger door only)	0·65 m (2 ft 1½ in)
Width (double door)	1·45 m (4 ft 9 in)
Emergency exit (starboard, rear): Height	0·66 m (2 ft 2 in)
Width	0·68 m (2 ft 2¾ in)
Baggage door (nose, port): Max height	0·56 m (1 ft 10 in)
Width	0·75 m (2 ft 5½ in)

DIMENSIONS, INTERNAL:

Cabin, excl flight deck and rear baggage compartment: Length	4·82 m (15 ft 9¾ in)
Max width	1·46 m (4 ft 9½ in)
Max height	1·70 m (5 ft 7 in)
Volume	12·9 m³ (455·5 cu ft)
Baggage compartment volume: nose	0·77 m³ (27·20 cu ft)
rear	1·89 m³ (66·75 cu ft)

AREAS:

Wings, gross	34·27 m² (368·88 sq ft)
Vertical tail surfaces (total)	5·064 m² (54·51 sq ft)
Horizontal tail surfaces (total)	7·024 m² (75·61 sq ft)

WEIGHTS AND LOADINGS:

Basic weight empty	2,840 kg (6,261 lb)
Operating weight empty	3,000 kg (6,614 lb)
Max fuel load (usable)	1,230 kg (2,711 lb)
Max payload	1,700 kg (3,748 lb)
T-O weight for agricultural operation	4,500 kg (9,921 lb)
Design max T-O and landing weight	5,000 kg (11,023 lb)
Max zero-fuel weight	4,700 kg (10,362 lb)
Max cabin floor loading (cargo)	750 kg/m² (153·7 lb/sq ft)
Max wing loading	145·9 kg/m² (29·90 lb/sq ft)
Max power loading: I	6·71 kg/kW (11·02 lb/shp)
II	5·41 kg/kW (8·89 lb/shp)

PERFORMANCE (at design max T-O weight, ISA):

Max cruising speed at 3,000 m (9,840 ft): I	173 knots (320 km/h; 199 mph)
II	177 knots (328 km/h; 204 mph)
Max rate of climb at S/L: I	390 m (1,280 ft)/min
II	528 m (1,732 ft)/min
Rate of climb at S/L, one engine out: I	36 m (118 ft)/min
II	105 m (344 ft)/min
Service ceiling: I, II	above 7,000 m (22,960 ft)
Service ceiling, one engine out, 15 m (50 ft)/min rate of climb, max continuous power: I	1,750 m (5,740 ft)
II	3,150 m (10,335 ft)
FAR Pt 135 Appendix A landing field length at S/L, paved level runway, zero wind: destination airport (I, II)	733 m (2,405 ft)
alternative airport (I, II)	629 m (2,065 ft)
Range with 800 kg (1,763 lb) payload and max fuel, 45 min reserves: I, II	777 nm (1,440 km; 894 miles)

Harbin Z-9 Haitun twin-turbine light helicopter *(CATIC)*

HARBIN Z-6

Chinese name: Zhishengji-6 (Vertical take-off aircraft 6) or Zhi-6

First indication of the existence of the Z-6 was given in early 1980, when a component was displayed at a trade exhibition in Shanghai. The Z-6 is thought to be a developed version of the Harbin Z-5 (Chinese Mil Mi-4) re-engined with a 1,618 kW (2,170 shp) Shanghai Wozhou-5 (WZ-5) turboshaft engine, developed from the Wojiang-5A (WJ-5A) Chinese version of the Ivchenko AI-24A turboprop. It is believed to be similar in size to the Z-5, but with a redesigned fuselage and a gross weight of about 7,600 kg (16,755 lb). First flight was reportedly in 1968, and a small pre-production batch was completed, but the Z-6 was apparently underpowered and did not go into series production.

HARBIN (AÉROSPATIALE) Z-9 HAITUN (DOLPHIN)

Chinese name: Zhishengji-9 (Vertical take-off aircraft 9) or Zhi-9

A licence agreement was signed on 2 July 1980 between Aérospatiale of France and the Chinese government for the former's SA 365N Dauphin 2 twin-turboshaft helicopter (which see) to be manufactured in China. The first (French built) example for China made its initial acceptance flight in the Beijing area on 6 February 1982. Production is now under way by the Harbin Aircraft Manufacturing Company, and is scheduled to run until 1989.

The agreement is for an initial batch of 50, which are being divided between civil and military duties. About 28 had been completed by the Spring of 1986, including at least nine for the Air Force and one for the Navy. Others are allocated to offshore oil rig support work, and some are configured as air ambulances accommodating four stretchers and two seats or two stretchers and five seats. The aircraft's Arriel IC turboshaft engines are also being produced in China. It is reported that China is seeking a suitable magnetic anomaly detector for installation on naval versions of the Z-9.

The following Chinese published figures for the Z-9 differ from those given for the Dauphin 2 in the French section:

WEIGHTS:

Standard weight empty, excl optional equipment	1,975 kg (4,354 lb)
Max load on cargo sling	1,700 kg (3,748 lb)
Max T-O weight	3,850 kg (8,488 lb)

PERFORMANCE (at max T-O weight):

Max cruising speed at S/L	158 knots (293 km/h; 182 mph)
Max vertical rate of climb at S/L	252 m (827 ft)/min
Service ceiling	4,000 m (13,125 ft)
Hovering ceiling, ISA: IGE	1,950 m (6,400 ft)
OGE	1,020 m (3,350 ft)
Max range at econ cruising speed, no reserves: standard fuel	491 nm (910 km; 565 miles)
with auxiliary tank	572 nm (1,060 km; 658 miles)

HARBIN PS-5

The *Liberation Army Daily* reported on 3 September 1986 that a new flying-boat had entered service with the naval air force of the PLA, following a demonstration to Premier Zhao Zhiyang on 30 August. This is almost certainly the same four-turboprop (WJ-5A) aircraft that was last mentioned in the 1983-84 *Jane's*. Prototypes of that aircraft were said to have flown for the first time in about 1980, in which year members of a US aerospace industry delegation saw two examples of a four-turboprop amphibian under construction.

A photograph of the PS-5, received too late for inclusion on this page, is reproduced in the Addenda. It shows the PS-5 to be a very large aircraft, dimensionally similar to the Shaanxi Y-8 heavy transport, with which it appears to have some features in common.

HUABEI

HUABEI MACHINERY PLANT

HUABEI (ANTONOV) Y-5

Chinese name: Yunshuji-5 (Transport aircraft 5) or Yun-5

NATO reporting name: Colt

The Antonov An-2 general purpose biplane was supplied to, and since 1957 has been built under licence in, China in considerable numbers (nearly 1,000). Its 746 kW (1,000 hp) Shvetsov ASh-62IR engine is built at Zhuzhou (Chuchow) as the Huosai-5 or HS-5. The Y-5 was manufactured initially at Nanchang, and later at Harbin; production was continuing, by the Huabei Machinery Plant at Shijiazhuang, in 1986.

The Y-5 continues to be used extensively both by the PLA Air Force, which has about 300, and in a civil capacity, for agricultural (see 1982-83 *Jane's*) and general transport work. A turboprop version, with an engine believed to be rated at approx 1,380 kW (1,850 shp), was under development in 1986.

A description of the basic An-2 can be found under the WSK-PZL Mielec heading in the Polish section of this edition.

Huabei Y-5 general purpose transport aircraft
(Philip G. Dunnington)

NANCHANG

NANCHANG AIRCRAFT MANUFACTURING COMPANY

NANCHANG CJ-6

Chinese name: Chuji Jiaolianji-6 (Basic training aircraft 6) or Chujiao-6

Developed to replace the Yak-18A/CJ-5 (1980-81 *Jane's*) in the basic training role, the two-seat CJ-6 is reported to have entered production in 1961, with more than 2,000 delivered, including exports to Bangladesh, Korea, Viet-Nam and Zambia. Production, currently by the Hongdu Aircraft Corporation, continued in 1986.

Civil versions known as the **Haiyan** (see following entry) are being developed, and a six-seat utility version has been proposed. The details which follow apply to the standard CJ-6 basic trainer:

AIRFRAME: All-metal cantilever low-wing monoplane. Two-spar wings, with detachable, tapered and dihedralled outer panels. Retractable tricycle landing gear, with low-pressure mainwheel tyres, suitable for operation from grass strips.

POWER PLANT: One 213 kW (285 hp) Zhuzhou Huosai-6A nine-cylinder aircooled radial engine (Chinese version of Ivchenko/Vedeneyev AI-14RF), driving a J9-G1 two-blade variable-pitch propeller. Fuel capacity (two tanks) 100 litres (22 Imp gallons).

DIMENSIONS, EXTERNAL:

Wing span	10·18 m (33 ft 4¾ in)
Length overall	8·46 m (27 ft 9 in)
Height overall	3·25 m (10 ft 8 in)

WEIGHTS:

Weight empty	1,172 kg (2,584 lb)
Max fuel	110 kg (243 lb)
Max T-O weight	1,419 kg (3,128 lb)

PERFORMANCE:

Max level speed	155 knots (286 km/h; 178 mph)
Landing speed	62 knots (115 km/h; 72 mph)
Max rate of climb at S/L	380 m (1,248 ft)/min
Service ceiling	5,080 m (16,665 ft)
T-O run	280 m (920 ft)
Landing run	350 m (1,150 ft)
Endurance	3 h 36 min

NANCHANG HAIYAN (PETREL)

To meet a national requirement for a multi-purpose agricultural and forestry aircraft, the Nanchang Aircraft Manufacturing Company decided to undertake a conversion of its CJ-6 basic trainer (see preceding entry). Work on the conversion started in April 1985, and the **Haiyan A** prototype flew for the first time on 17 August that year.

Little change to the basic, proven airframe of the CJ-6 was necessary. To cater for the higher operating weights involved, the Haiyan A was fitted with a more powerful (257 kW; 345 hp) version of the HS-6A engine and a new-design propeller. Removal of the rear seat allowed a 400 kg (882 lb) insecticide tank to be installed, and another 200 kg (441 lb) of chemical was accommodated in the leading-edge of the wing centre-section. Volumetric capacity in the rear cockpit, without removing the instrument panel, is sufficient to allow 800 kg (1,764 lb) to be carried in this location if desired. The dispersal system consists of four Type 751 underwing sprinkler heads, fed by a modified LB-4 fuel pump, and can be used for both low and ultra-low volume spraying.

Initial flight tests having proved the practicality of the conversion, work was continuing in late 1985/early 1986 mainly to perfect the dispersal system and improve the aircraft's take-off and landing performance. When this is achieved, two production conversions are planned:

Haiyan B. Specialised agricultural and forestry version for cropspraying (dry or liquid pesticide or fertiliser), seed-sowing and forest firefighting.

Haiyan C. Patrol and observation version, with normal CJ-6 rear seat accommodation but having increased fuel capacity to extend endurance to over 6 hours. Suitable for forestry and fishery patrol, cartography, aerial photography, geological survey, coastal and border patrol, with appropriate equipment according to customer requirements.

Nanchang CJ-6 basic trainer, developed from the Yak-18A

The following details apply to the Haiyan A prototype:

DIMENSIONS, EXTERNAL: As for CJ-6

WEIGHTS:

Weight empty	1,214 kg (2,676 lb)
Max T-O weight	2,035 kg (4,486 lb)

PERFORMANCE (at max T-O weight):

Max level speed	160 knots (297 km/h; 185 mph)
Normal operating speed	86 knots (160 km/h; 99 mph)
Operating height: max	6,250 m (20,500 ft)
min	1 m (3 ft)
T-O run	280 m (919 ft)
Landing run	350 m (1,148 ft)
Range	421 nm (780 km; 484 miles)
Endurance	4 h 11 min
Swath width	30 m (98 ft)

NANCHANG Q-5

Chinese name: Qiangjiji-5 (Attack aircraft 5) or Qiang-5

Export designation: A-5

NATO reporting name: Fantan

Design of this twin-jet attack aircraft, derived from the J-6/MiG-19 produced in China, began in 1958, and the first flight was made on 5 June 1965. Misidentified first as F-6bis and then as F-9 by Western reports, its correct designation was first indicated by Chinese officials in 1980. By that time the Q-5 had been in service for some ten years, production having peaked in about 1971 with nearly 100 being manufactured. By 1978 production had almost ended, apart from making good attrition losses, but it was stepped up in about 1981 to meet export orders from North Korea and Pakistan. This important Chinese aircraft continues in production, both for domestic use (**Q-5 III**) and, as the **A-5C**, for export. Current manufacture is said to be by the Hongdu Aircraft Corporation.

The total number in Chinese service in 1986 was thought to be in the region of 600, including up to 100 serving in an air defence role with the air arm of the PLA Navy. The latter version has a small 'teardrop' fairing on the starboard side of the nose, probably housing a gun ranging radar of the 'High Fix' type.

Deliveries of an initial batch of 42 export **A-5Bs** (= **Q-5 II**) to the Pakistan Air Force began in February 1983 and have been completed. Further deliveries of A-5Cs are under way and may eventually provide a total of 140 A-5s to equip eight attack squadrons and an OCU. The first PAF units are No. 16 Squadron at Rafiqui Shorkot, No. 26 at Peshawar and No. 7 at Masroor.

The airframe of the Q-5 is based substantially on that of the J-6 (see 1982-83 *Jane's*), but with a number of significant changes. The main wing structure is basically unchanged and retains the four external attachment points and large boundary layer fences, but the underwing spoilers are omitted and the flaps have undergone some redesign. There are more extensive changes to the centre and front of the fuselage, which is nearly 25 per cent longer than that of the J-6. The purpose of these changes in the original **Q-5 I** was to make room for an internal weapons bay, but this area is no longer used for carrying weapons. Instead, fuselage fuel tank capacity has been increased by approx 70 per cent compared with that carried internally by the J-6. Cockpit canopy opening differs from that on the J-6, and the spine fairing behind it leads to a smaller dorsal fin and larger main fin. The 'solid' ogival nose provides sufficient room for an

Q-5 with additional (ECM?) pods between its underwing rocket launchers and drop tanks

attack radar, although aircraft in service so far have metal skinned noses and clearly do not carry this equipment, which would also require relocation of the nose mounted pitot tube. It is, however, expected to be a feature of the improved **Q-5M/A-5M** now under study (see following entry).

The J-6 power plant is retained, but with twin lateral intakes instead of the single divided nose intake of the Soviet design. Early production Q-5 Is retained also the various louvres and airscoops associated with this installation, but many of these have disappeared from the cleaner looking Q-5 III current production version, referred to in some reports as 'Fantan-C', which also has a relocated tail braking parachute installation similar to that on later production versions of the J-6. Like the J-6, the Q-5 has two wing mounted cannon (23 mm instead of 30 mm); these occupy the revised wing root position outboard of the engine air intake trunks.

A design study has been carried out by the FR Group in the UK to equip the Q-5 as a receiver for in-flight refuelling, with a Xian H-6 bomber adapted to act as the tanker aircraft. Its adoption was under consideration by the Chinese authorities in the Summer of 1986.

TYPE: Single-seat close air support and ground attack aircraft, with capability also for air-to-air combat.

WINGS: Cantilever all-metal mid-wing monoplane, of low aspect ratio, with 4° anhedral from roots. Sweepback at quarter-chord 52° 30'. Multi-spar basic structure with ribs and stressed skin, essentially similar in construction to that of J-6/MiG-19 (see 1982-83 *Jane's*), with three-point attachment to fuselage. Deep, full chord boundary layer fence on each upper surface at mid span. Inboard of each fence is a hydraulically actuated Gouge flap, the inner end of which is angled to give a trailing-edge at right angles to side of fuselage. Hydraulically actuated internally balanced aileron outboard of each fence. Electrically operated inset trim tab at inboard end of each aileron.

FUSELAGE: Conventional all-metal structure of longerons, stringers and stressed skin, built in forward and rear portions which are detachable aft of wing trailing-edge to provide access to engines. Air intake on each side of fuselage, abreast of cockpit; twin jetpipes side by side at rear. Top and bottom 'pen nib' fairings aft of nozzles. Centre-fuselage is 'waisted' in accordance with area rule. Dorsal spine fairing between rear of cockpit and leading-edge of fin. Forward hinged, hydraulically actuated door type airbrake under centre of fuselage, forward of bomb attachment points. Shallow ventral strake under each jetpipe.

TAIL UNIT: Cantilever all-metal stressed skin structure, with sweepback on all surfaces; of generally similar configuration to that of J-6, but with taller main fin and smaller dorsal fin. Mechanically actuated mass balanced rudder, with electrically operated inset trim tab. One-piece hydraulically actuated all-moving tailplane, with anti-flutter weight projecting forward from each tip. Tail warning antenna in tip of fin.

LANDING GEAR: Hydraulically retractable wide-track tricycle type, with single wheel and oleo-pneumatic shock absorber on each unit. Main units retract inward into wings, non-steerable nosewheel forward into fuselage, rotating through 90° to lie flat in gear bay. Mainwheels have size 830 × 205-1 tyres and pneumatic drum brakes. Tail braking parachute, deployable also in flight, in bullet fairing at root of vertical tail trailing-edge beneath rudder (or in tailcone of early production Q-5 I).

POWER PLANT: Two Shenyang Wopen-6 (WP-6) turbojet engines (Chinese version of Tumansky/Mikulin R-9BF-811), each rated at 25·50 kN (5,732 lb st) dry and 31·87 kN (7,165 lb st) with afterburning, mounted side by side in rear of fuselage. Lateral air intake, with small splitter plate, for each engine. Hydraulically actuated nozzles. Internal fuel in three forward and two rear fuselage tanks with combined capacity of 3,720 litres (818·5 Imp gallons). Provision for carrying a 760 litre (167 Imp gallon) drop tank on each inboard underwing pylon, to give max internal/external fuel capacity of 5,240 litres (1,153 Imp gallons). When inboard wing stations are occupied by bombs, a 400 litre (88 Imp gallon) drop tank can be carried instead on each outboard underwing pylon.

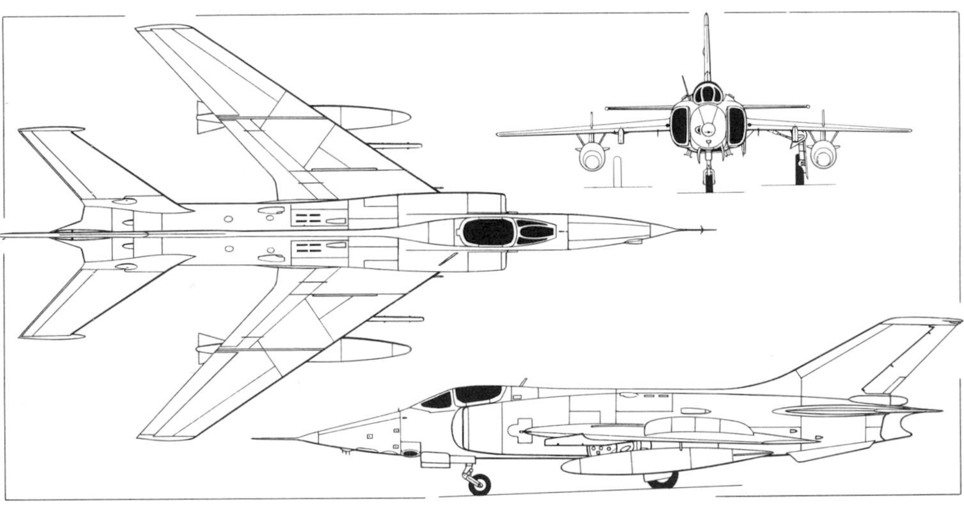

Nanchang Q-5 III 'Fantan' single-seat twin-jet combat aircraft *(Pilot Press)*

ACCOMMODATION: Pilot only, in pressurised cockpit under one-piece jettisonable canopy which is hinged at rear and opens upward. Downward view over nose, in level flight, is 13° 30'. Low-speed seat allows for safe ejection within speed range of 135-458 knots (250-850 km/h; 155-528 mph) at zero height or above. Aircraft in Pakistan service have been refitted with Martin-Baker PKD10 zero/zero seats. Armour plating in some areas of cockpit to protect pilot from anti-aircraft gunfire.

SYSTEMS: Cockpit air-conditioning and pressurisation system. Two independent hydraulic systems, each operating at pressure of 207 bars (3,000 lb/sq in). Primary system actuates landing gear extension and retraction, flaps, airbrake, and afterburner nozzles; auxiliary system supplies power for aileron, rudder and all-moving tailplane boosters, and emergency actuation of main landing gear. Electrical system (28V DC) powered by two 6kW engine driven starter/generators, with two inverters for 115V single-phase and 36V three-phase AC power at 400Hz.

AVIONICS AND EQUIPMENT: Include CT-3 VHF com transceiver, WL-7 radio compass, WG-4 low altitude radio altimeter, LTC-2 horizon gyro, YII-3 IFF, Type 932 radar warning receiver and XS-6 marker beacon receiver. 'High Fix' type gun ranging radar on air defence version. 'Odd Rods' type IFF aerials under nose on Q-5 I/A-5A replaced on Q-5 III/A-5C by a single blade antenna. Space provision in nose and centre-fuselage for additional or updated avionics, including an attack radar. Landing light under fuselage, forward of nosewheel bay and offset to port; taxying light on nosewheel leg.

ARMAMENT AND OPERATIONAL EQUIPMENT: Internal armament consists of one 23 mm cannon (Chinese 23-2), with 100 rds, in each wing root. Eight attachment points normally for external stores: two pairs in tandem under centre of fuselage, and two under each wing (inboard and outboard of mainwheel leg). Fuselage stations can each carry a 250 kg bomb (Chinese 250-2, US Mk 82 or Snakeye, French Durandal, or similar). Inboard wing stations can carry any of these; a 500 or 750 lb bomb; a BL755 600 lb cluster bomb; or 6 kg or 25 lb practice bombs. Normal bomb carrying capacity is 1,000 kg (2,205 lb), max capacity 2,000 kg (4,410 lb). Instead of bombs, the inboard wing stations can each carry a 760 litre drop tank (see 'Power Plant' paragraph) or a launcher for 57 mm (eight Chinese 57-1), 68 mm, or 90 mm (nine Chinese 90-1) rockets. The outboard wing stations can each be occupied by a 400 litre drop tank (when the larger tank is not carried inboard) or, with suitable modification, by air-to-air missiles such as the Chinese PL-2 ('Atoll' derivative), PL-7, AIM-9 Sidewinder and Matra R.550 Magic. Recent photographs have shown the Q-5 with what appear to be two ECM pods, mounted on an additional pylon just outboard of the inner stores station under each wing. Within the overall max T-O weight, all stores mentioned can be carried provided that CG shift remains within the allowable operating range of 31·5 to 38 per cent of mean aerodynamic chord, and more than 22 external stores configurations are possible. The aircraft carries an SH-1J or ABS1A optical sight for level and dive bombing, or for air-to-ground rocket launching. Aircraft in Chinese service can carry a single 5-20 kT nuclear bomb.

DIMENSIONS, EXTERNAL (Q-5 III):

Wing span	9·70 m (31 ft 10 in)
Wing chord (mean aerodynamic)	3·097 m (10 ft 2 in)
Wing aspect ratio	3·37
Length overall:	
incl nose probe	16·255 m (53 ft 4 in)
excl nose probe	15·415 m (50 ft 7 in)
Height overall	4·516 m (14 ft 9¾ in)
Wheel track	approx 4·70 m (15 ft 5 in)
Wheelbase	approx 4·00 m (13 ft 1½ in)

AREAS:

Wings, gross	27·95 m² (300·85 sq ft)
Vertical tail surfaces (total)	4·64 m² (49·94 sq ft)
Horizontal tail surfaces:	
movable	5·00 m² (53·82 sq ft)
total, incl projected fuselage area	8·62 m² (92·78 sq ft)

WEIGHTS AND LOADINGS:

Weight empty	6,494 kg (14,317 lb)
Fuel: max internal	2,883 kg (6,356 lb)
two 400 litre drop tanks	620 kg (1,367 lb)
two 760 litre drop tanks	1,178 kg (2,597 lb)
max internal/external	4,061 kg (8,953 lb)
Max external stores load	2,000 kg (4,410 lb)
Max T-O weight: 'clean'	9,530 kg (21,010 lb)
with max external stores	12,000 kg (26,455 lb)
Max wing loading: 'clean'	341 kg/m² (69·9 lb/sq ft)
with max external stores	429 kg/m² (87·9 lb/sq ft)
Max power loading: 'clean'	149·5 kg/kN (1·47 lb/lb st)
with max external stores	188·3 kg/kN (1·85 lb/lb st)

Nanchang A-5C of the Pakistan Air Force's 'Black Spiders' squadron *(Pakistan Air Force)*

PERFORMANCE (at max 'clean' T-O weight, with afterburning, except where indicated):

Max limiting Mach number (VNE)	Mach 1·5
Max level speed:	
at 11,000 m (36,000 ft)	Mach 1·12 (643 knots; 1,190 km/h; 740 mph)
at S/L	653 knots (1,210 km/h; 752 mph)
T-O speed:	
'clean', 15° flap	162 knots (300 km/h; 186 mph)
with max external stores, 25° flap	178 knots (330 km/h; 205 mph)
*Landing speed:	
25° flap, brake-chute deployed	150-165 knots (278-307 km/h; 172-191 mph)
*Max rate of climb at 5,000 m (16,400 ft)	4,980-6,180 m (16,340-20,275 ft)/min
Service ceiling	15,850 m (52,000 ft)
T-O run:	
*'clean', 15° flap	700-750 m (2,300-2,460 ft)
with max external stores, 25° flap	1,250 m (4,100 ft)
Landing run:	
25° flap, brake-chute deployed	1,060 m (3,480 ft)
Combat radius with max external stores, afterburners off:	
lo-lo-lo (500 m; 1,640 ft)	216 nm (400 km; 248 miles)
hi-lo-hi (8,000/500/8,000 m; 26,250/1,640/26,250 ft)	324 nm (600 km; 373 miles)
Range at 11,000 m (36,000 ft) with max internal and external fuel, afterburners off	nearly 1,080 nm (2,000 km; 1,243 miles)
g limits:	
with full load of bombs and/or drop tanks	5
with drop tanks empty	6·5
'clean'	7·5

* *depending upon airfield altitude and temperature*

NANCHANG Q-5M/A-5M

This improved version of the Q-5/A-5 is the subject of a collaborative study contract signed in July 1986 between CATIC and Aeritalia to upgrade the aircraft's avionics by incorporating a new nav/attack system similar to that used in the AMX aircraft. This would incorporate a ranging radar, inertial navigation system, head-up display, air data computer, central computer and data bus controller. The M (for Modified) version of the Q-5 would also have improved WP-6A turbojets with dry and afterburning ratings of 29·42 kN (6,614 lb st) and 36·77 kN (8,267 lb st) respectively. The changes are expected to increase empty weight to 6,634 kg (14,625 lb); max T-O weight remains unchanged.

PERFORMANCE (estimated):

Max level speed:	
at 11,000 m (36,000 ft)	Mach 1·2 (688 knots; 1,275 km/h; 792 mph)
at S/L	661 knots (1,225 km/h; 761 mph)
Service ceiling	16,000 m (52,500 ft)
T-O run with max external stores, 25° flap	1,200 m (3,937 ft)

SHAANXI

SHAANXI TRANSPORT AIRCRAFT FACTORY

SHAANXI (ANTONOV) Y-8

Chinese name: Yunshuji-8 (Transport aircraft 8) or Yun-8

NATO reporting name: Cub

The Shaanxi Transport Aircraft Factory at Hanzhong (Hanchung), near Xian, is building a Chinese version of the Antonov An-12BP four-turboprop civil/military transport aircraft. Soviet built An-12s have been in service (although not in large numbers) with the country's military services and the civil airline, CAAC, for several years. Redesign of the Chinese version was carried out at Xian, beginning in 1969, and the first Y-8 made its initial flight in 1974.

Outwardly, the Y-8 can be distinguished from the An-12 by its more pointed nose transparencies, which extend the overall length of the aircraft by approx 0·91 m (3 ft). The aircraft's 3,169 kW (4,250 ehp) engines, derived from the Ivchenko AI-20K, are produced at Shanghai under the Chinese designation Wojiang-6 or WJ-6.

The decision to put the Y-8 into production was taken in February 1980, and 26 (including one for static testing) had been completed by the Spring of 1986. At present, Y-8s are in use mainly for specialised long-range cargo flights to such places as Tibet and Hong Kong. The Y-8 has now become a major production priority programme for the 1986-90 period, including the development of a 100-passenger fully pressurised version: the current version has a small pressurised forward cabin for up to 14 passengers in addition to the five-man crew, but the rear cargo hold is unpressurised.

Meanwhile, in an attempt to upgrade the original avionics and equipment, the Canadian firm Litton was requested to provide more modern items such as inertial navigation systems, Doppler and weather radars, radio compasses and transponders. Sully (France) has provided windscreen de-icing installations for two Y-8s. An in-flight refuelling tanker study for the Y-8 has been made by the FR Group of the UK.

On 4 September 1985 Beijing radio reported that the first maritime patrol version of the Y-8 had cleared its technical qualification tests that day. This aircraft (see accompanying photograph) has larger-area nose transparencies, resembling those of the Xian H-6 (Tupolev Tu-16) 'Badger' bomber, and a large 'chin' radome housing the antenna for a Litton Canada APS-504(V)3 search radar. Other equipment includes dual Litton LTN-72R inertial navigation systems, a single LTN-211 Omega navigation system, and Collins radio sets. The maritime surveillance version is expected to be used for both naval patrol and civilian offshore duties such as fishery patrol, pollution monitoring, and support of the oil exploration industry.

A detailed description of the An-12BP can be found in the USSR section of the 1982-83 and earlier editions of *Jane's*. Chinese published details for the Y-8 are as follows:

ACCOMMODATION: Standard seating for crew of six and 96 passengers.

DIMENSIONS, EXTERNAL:

Wing span	38·00 m (124 ft 8 in)
Length overall	34·02 m (111 ft 7½ in)
Fuselage: Max diameter	4·10 m (13 ft 5½ in)
Height overall	11·16 m (36 ft 7½ in)
Rear loading hatch: Length	7·67 m (25 ft 2 in)
Width: min	2·16 m (7 ft 1 in)
max	3·10 m (10 ft 2 in)

DIMENSIONS, INTERNAL:

Cargo hold: Length	13·50 m (44 ft 3½ in)
Width: min	3·00 m (9 ft 10 in)
max	3·50 m (11 ft 5¾ in)
Height: min	2·40 m (7 ft 10½ in)
max	2·60 m (8 ft 6½ in)

AREA:

Wings, gross	121·86 m² (1,311·7 sq ft)

WEIGHTS:

Weight empty, equipped	35,500 kg (78,265 lb)
Max fuel load	22,900 kg (50,485 lb)
Max payload: concentrated	16,000 kg (35,275 lb)
distributed	20,000 kg (44,090 lb)
Max T-O weight	61,000 kg (134,480 lb)
Max landing weight	58,000 kg (127,870 lb)

PERFORMANCE:

Max level speed at 7,000 m (22,965 ft)	357 knots (662 km/h; 411 mph)
Normal cruising speed	297 knots (550 km/h; 342 mph)
Max rate of climb at S/L, AUW of 51,000 kg (112,435 lb)	600 m (1,968 ft)/min
Service ceiling	10,400 m (34,120 ft)
T-O run	1,230 m (4,035 ft)
Landing run	1,100 m (3,609 ft)
Range with max fuel	3,030 nm (5,615 km; 3,490 miles)
Max endurance	10 h 40 min

First photograph to be released of the maritime surveillance version of the Shaanxi Y-8 four-turboprop transport aircraft

SHANGHAI

SHANGHAI AVIATION INDUSTRIAL CORPORATION

VICE-PRESIDENT: Wang Hongnian

SHANGHAI Y-10

Chinese name: Yunshuji-10 (Transport aircraft 10) or Yun-10

The programme to build the first jet airliner of Chinese design and manufacture began in about 1970. Its design was undertaken primarily to demonstrate the Chinese industry's capability to develop an aircraft of this type, utilising JT3D-7 engines available in China in the form of spares for the Boeing 707-320 fleet of CAAC. The Y-10, however, approximates more closely to the seating capacity of the smaller 707-120B, though the fuselage and cabin are shorter and the wing span is greater.

Two prototypes of the Y-10 were built, of which the first was used at Xian in the late 1970s for static load testing. First flight, by the No. 2 aircraft (B-0002), was made on 26 September 1980. Notable long-range flights included one of 1,619 nm (3,000 km; 1,864 miles) from Shanghai to Urumqi in April 1984, and a 1,834 nm (3,400 km; 2,112 mile) flight from Shanghai to Harbin in the following November. Flight testing (200 hours in 120 flights) has been completed, and series production is apparently not intended. A full description of the Y-10 can be found in the 1985-86 *Jane's*.

TYPE: Four-turbofan transport aircraft.

POWER PLANT: Four 84·5 kN (19,000 lb st) Pratt & Whitney JT3D-7 turbofan engines, with thrust reversers, in individual pylon mounted underwing pods.

ACCOMMODATION: Flight crew of five (pilot, co-pilot, flight engineer, navigator and radio operator). Six-abreast seating in air-conditioned and pressurised main cabin for 125 (standard), 149 (all-economy class) or a maximum of 178 passengers. Passenger doors at front and rear of cabin on port side, with service doors opposite them on starboard side. Overwing emergency exit(s) on each side. Provision for upward opening cargo loading door forward of wing on port side. Underfloor baggage compartments forward and aft of wing; overhead baggage lockers above passenger seats.

DIMENSIONS, EXTERNAL:

Wing span	42·242 m (138 ft 7 in)
Length overall (excl probe)	42·933 m (140 ft 10¼ in)
Height overall	13·42 m (44 ft 0⅓ in)
Wheel track	6·60 m (21 ft 7¾ in)
Wheelbase (to c/l of mainwheel bogies)	14·795 m (48 ft 6½ in)

DIMENSIONS, INTERNAL:

Cabin: Length	30·40 m (99 ft 8¾ in)
Max width	3·48 m (11 ft 5 in)
Max height	2·20 m (7 ft 2½ in)
Volume	approx 200 m³ (7,063 cu ft)

AREA:

Wings, gross	244·6 m² (2,632·8 sq ft)

WEIGHTS:

Weight empty, equipped	58,000 kg (127,870 lb)
Max fuel load	51,000 kg (112,435 lb)

Photographs of the Shanghai Y-10 released on 15 September 1984. According to the official caption, it was then configured to carry 149 passengers *(Xinhua)*

Max payload	16,700 kg (36,815 lb)
Max T-O weight	110,000 kg (242,510 lb)
PERFORMANCE:	
Max level speed	525 knots (974 km/h; 605 mph)
Max cruising speed	495 knots (917 km/h; 570 mph)
Normal operating speed	447-458 knots (830-850 km/h; 515-528 mph)
Landing speed	135 knots (250 km/h; 155 mph)
Service ceiling	12,300 m (40,355 ft)
T-O run	2,070 m (6,790 ft)
Landing run	1,925 m (6,315 ft)
Range (approx):	
max payload	3,000 nm (5,560 km; 3,455 miles)
max fuel	3,777 nm (7,000 km; 4,350 miles)

SHANGHAI (MCDONNELL DOUGLAS) MD-82

McDonnell Douglas Corporation announced on 11 January 1984 the signing of a letter of intent with the Shanghai Aviation Industrial Corporation on a co-production programme for 25 MD-82 jet transports.

Shanghai has produced more than 115 sets of landing gear doors for the MD-80 series under subcontract since 1979. Details of this new programme were confirmed in an April 1985 announcement of the sale of 26 MD-82s to China, of which 25 will be finally assembled in Shanghai by 1991. One Douglas built aircraft was delivered in October 1985, followed by the first shipment of major aircraft components in January 1986. Assembly at Shanghai began in April 1986, during which month the second set of subassemblies was despatched from Long Beach. Complete major subassemblies are being supplied by Douglas for the first three MD-82s to be assembled at Shanghai; thereafter, the Chinese industry will take a gradually increasing share in the manufacturing process for the remaining 22. The agreement includes an option for a further 15 aircraft.

Completion of the first Chinese assembled MD-82 is scheduled for the Spring of 1987, with delivery following in July. It would be logical to expect the allocation of a Chinese 'Y' series transport aircraft designation to this programme.

SHENYANG

SHENYANG AIRCRAFT COMPANY

SHENYANG/TIANJIN (MIKOYAN) J-6

Chinese name: Jianjiji-6 (Fighter aircraft 6) or Jian-6

Export designation: F-6

NATO reporting names: Farmer-C (MiG-19SF) and Farmer-D (MiG-19PF)

The J-6 is basically a MiG-19 fighter built in China. Many MiG-19s had been delivered to China in knocked-down form before the deterioration of Moscow-Beijing relations. The designation J-6 was given to the Chinese version of the MiG-19S fighter, which first flew in December 1961 and from mid-1962 became standard equipment in the Air Force of the People's Liberation Army.

Seven versions are known to have been produced at Shenyang, and more recently also at Tianjin (Tientsin):

J-6 (Jianjiji-6 or Jian-6). Chinese equivalent of single-seat MiG-19S/SF day fighter ('Farmer-C'). Superseded by J-6C.

J-6A (Jianjiji-6 Jia or Jian-6A). Chinese version of MiG-19PF limited all-weather fighter ('Farmer-D') with gun and rocket armament.

J-6B (Jianjiji-6 Yi or Jian-6B). Equivalent to limited all-weather MiG-19PM ('Farmer-D'), armed with radar homing missiles (NATO 'Alkali').

J-6C (Jianjiji-6 Bing or Jian-6C). Day fighter development of MiG-19SF/J-6, distinguished externally by relocated brake-chute in bullet fairing at base of rudder.

J-6Xin (Jianjiji-6Xin or Jian-6Xin). Version of Jian-6A/MiG-19PF with Soviet Izumrud (Emerald) intake mounted radar replaced by a Chinese developed airborne interception radar in a needle shaped radome mounted centrally on the intake splitter plate.

JJ-6 (Jianjiji Jiaolianji-6 or Jianjiao-6). Tandem two-seat fighter-trainer version, developed in China.

JZ-6 (Jianjiji Zhenchaji-6 or Jianzhen-6). Single-seat fighter-reconnaissance version, generally similar to Soviet MiG-19R, with cameras mounted in lower forward fuselage instead of the third 30 mm cannon which occupies this position in the fighter-bomber versions.

Production of the J-6 was stepped up from about 1966, and several thousand were built subsequently, including export versions designated **F-6** (fighters) and **FT-6** (two-seat trainers) for Pakistan, Albania, Bangladesh, Egypt, Iran (via North Korea), Iraq (via Egypt and Jordan), Kampuchea, Tanzania (one squadron), and Viet-Nam.

In the PLA Air Force, J-6 variants are still the dominant type, with about 3,000 believed to be in service for air-to-air interception, battlefield interdiction, close support, counter air and tactical reconnaissance. The J-6 also serves in smaller numbers (about 500) with the air force of the PLA Navy.

Chinese sources in 1986 stated that aircraft production at Shenyang had been substantially reduced, and much manufacturing effort diverted to non-aerospace products. This, plus the lack of mention of the F-6 in current export campaigns, suggests that the aircraft is probably no longer in full scale production, though it may continue for a time to meet attrition requirements, any outstanding export orders, and manufacture of components common with the Nanchang Q-5. A detailed structural description of the basic MiG-19SF, modified where possible to apply to Chinese versions of the J-6, can be found in the 1982-83 and earlier editions of *Jane's*, with shortened accounts in subsequent editions up to and including 1985-86.

TYPE: Single-seat day fighter, attack and tactical reconnaissance aircraft.

POWER PLANT: Two Shenyang Wopen-6 turbojet engines, each rated at 25·50 kN (5,732 lb st) dry and 31·87 kN (7,165 lb st) with afterburning. Internal fuel capacity 2,170 litres (477 Imp gallons). Provision for two 760 or 1,140 litre (167 or 251 Imp gallon) underwing drop tanks, raising max total fuel capacity to 3,690 or 4,450 litres (811 or 979 Imp gallons) respectively.

ARMAMENT: See 1985-86 and earlier *Jane's*.

DIMENSIONS, EXTERNAL:	
Wing span	9·20 m (30 ft 2¼ in)
Length overall:	
incl nose probe	14·90 m (48 ft 10½ in)
excl nose probe	12·60 m (41 ft 4 in)
Height overall	3·88 m (12 ft 8¾ in)
Wheel track	4·15 m (13 ft 7½ in)
AREA:	
Wings, gross	25·00 m² (269·1 sq ft)
WEIGHTS:	
Weight empty, nominal	5,760 kg (12,700 lb)
Max external fuel load	approx 907 kg (2,000 lb)
T-O weight 'clean'	7,545 kg (16,634 lb)
Combat T-O weight (two 760 litre drop tanks and two Sidewinders)	8,965 kg (19,764 lb)

Jian-6C (F-6C) single-seat day fighters supplied by China to the Pakistan Air Force *(John Fricker)*

Max T-O weight with external stores
approx 10,000 kg (22,045) lb

PERFORMANCE:
Max level speed, 'clean':
at 11,000 m (36,000 ft)
Mach 1·45 (831 knots; 1,540 km/h; 957 mph)
at low level
Mach 1·09 (723 knots; 1,340 km/h; 832 mph)
Stalling speed, no external stores:
flaps and landing gear up
126 knots (234 km/h; 145 mph)
flaps and landing gear down
120 knots (222 km/h; 138 mph)
Max rate of climb at S/L, with afterburning
more than 9,145 m (30,000 ft)/min
Service ceiling 17,900 m (58,725 ft)
Absolute ceiling 19,870 m (65,190 ft)
T-O run: with afterburning approx 670 m (2,200 ft)
with underwing tanks, no afterburning
900 m (2,953 ft)
Landing run: with brake-chute 600 m (1,970 ft)
without brake-chute 890 m (2,920 ft)
Combat radius with two 760 litre external tanks
370 nm (685 km; 426 miles)
Normal range at 14,000 m (46,000 ft)
750 nm (1,390 km; 863 miles)
Max range with two 760 litre external tanks
1,187 nm (2,200 km; 1,366 miles)
Max endurance at 14,000 m (46,000 ft) 2 h 38 min

SHENYANG J-8

Chinese name: Jianjiji-8 (Fighter aircraft 8) or Jian-8
Export designation: F-8
NATO reporting name: Finback

Development of the J-8 began in the mid-1960s, the first example being completed in about 1969. Initially, it appeared to follow closely the same design philosophy as the Soviet Mikoyan Ye-152A 'Flipper', and a description of it in this form (now called the **J-8 I**) appeared in the 1985-86 *Jane's*.

According to Chinese official sources, only limited production of the J-8 I (about 50 aircraft) was undertaken. An improved version was expected, however, and the possible existence of a J-8 with twin lateral air intakes was reported as long ago as 1979. Confirmation that such a version had been developed came in January 1985, when the Xinhua news agency announced that a J-8 with wing-root intakes had made a successful first flight in early May 1984. Initial flight testing was said to have been very successful, showing a considerable improvement in performance compared with the earlier model. The test programme was continuing in 1986. The new version is designated **J-8 II** in China, or **F-8 II** when offered for export.

The main purpose of the configuration change was twofold, the first being to provide a 'solid' nose with adequate accommodation for a modern AI radar and the second to provide increased airflow for a more powerful engine installation, it being generally conceded that, with its original 59·82 kN (13,448 lb st) WP-7B engines, the J-8 I was underpowered. The power plant problem seems to have been overcome, at least for the time being, by fitting the J-8 II with twin engines designated WP-13A II, almost certainly a Chinese derivative of the Tumansky R-13-300.

In early 1986, US government approval was given for American avionics companies to bid for the avionics upgrade under FMS (foreign military sales) regulations. The requirement was reported to be for 50 shipsets, plus five spare kits, of an avionics suite comprising an AI radar, inertial navigation system, HUD, mission and air data computers, and a data bus. Other details in the Washington report indicated that the improved version of the J-8 was intended for production in the early 1990s, and for service in Manchuria and along China's northern border with the USSR. Most US avionics, however, would be approved only for J-8 IIs for use within China, and other Western alternatives are being sought to enable the aircraft to be exported.

Official details provided during the 1986 Farnborough International air show now make it possible to give the following description of the J-8 II:

TYPE: Single-seat twin-engined air superiority fighter, with secondary ground attack capability.

WINGS: Cantilever mid-wing monoplane. Thin-section delta wings, with slight anhedral and 60° sweepback on leading-edges. Small fence on each upper surface near tip. Two-segment single-slotted trailing-edge flaps on each wing inboard of aileron. Main wing structure is of aluminium alloy and high tensile steel. Control surfaces, which have hydraulically boosted actuation, are of aluminium honeycomb with skins of sheet aluminium.

FUSELAGE: Conventional semi-monocoque structure, 'waisted' between air intakes and tail section in accordance with area rule. Construction is mainly of aluminium alloy, with high tensile steel for main load-bearing members and titanium in high-temperature areas. Dielectric nosecone. Four door-type underfuselage airbrakes, one under each engine air intake trunk and one immediately aft of each mainwheel well. Spine fairing along top of fuselage from cockpit to fin, with small airscoop at foot of fin leading-edge. Additional airscoop at top of rear fuselage on each side, above tailplane.

Shenyang J-8 I fighter in its original form, with single central nose intake

TAIL UNIT: Cantilever sweptback all-metal surfaces, comprising broad chord fin and rudder and low-set all-moving tailplane; 60° sweepback on tailplane leading-edges. (Tailplane anti-flutter weights of J-8 I deleted.) Ventral fin similar to that of MiG-23, main portion of which folds sideways to starboard during take-off and landing, to provide additional directional stability. Rudder and tailplane are of aluminium honeycomb, with sheet aluminium skins; actuation is hydraulically boosted. Dielectric panels at tip of main fin and on non-folding portion of ventral fin leading-edge.

LANDING GEAR: Hydraulically retractable tricycle type, with single wheel and oleo-pneumatic shock absorber on each unit. Nose unit retracts forward, main units inward into centre-fuselage; mainwheels turn to stow vertically inside fuselage, resulting in a slight overwing bulge. Brake-chute in bullet fairing at base of rudder.

POWER PLANT: Two Wopen-13A II turbojet engines (Chinese development of Tumansky R-13-300), each rated at 64·72 kN (14,550 lb st) with afterburning, mounted side by side in rear fuselage with 'pen nib' fairing above and between exhaust nozzles. Lateral, non-swept air intakes, with large splitter plates similar in shape to those of MiG-23. Internal fuel capacity (wing and fuselage tanks) estimated at approx 5,500 litres (1,210 Imp gallons; 1,453 US gallons). Provision for auxiliary fuel tanks on fuselage centreline and each outboard underwing pylon.

ACCOMMODATION: Pilot only, on ejection seat under one-piece canopy hinged at rear and opening upward. Cockpit pressurised, heated and air-conditioned.

SYSTEMS: Two simple air-cycle environmental control systems, one for cockpit heating and air-conditioning and one for radar cooling; cooling air bled from engine compressor. Two independent hydraulic systems (main utility system plus one for flight control surfaces boost), powered by engine driven pumps. DC primary electrical system, with alternators for AC power.

AVIONICS AND OPERATIONAL EQUIPMENT: VHF/UHF and HF/SSB com radio, Tacan, radio compass, radar altimeter, marker beacon receiver, 'Odd Rods' type IFF, radar warning receiver and ECM. Autopilot for attitude and heading hold, altitude hold and stability augmentation. Existing fire control system comprises a monopulse radar, optical gyro gunsight and gun camera. Enlarged avionics bays in nose and fuselage provide room for modernised fire control system.

ARMAMENT: One 23 mm Type 23-3 twin-barrel cannon, with 200 rds, in underfuselage pack immediately aft of nosewheel doors. Seven external stations (one under fuselage and three under each wing) for a variety of stores which can include PL-2B infra-red air-to-air missiles, PL-7 medium-range semi-active radar homing air-to-air missiles, 18-round pods of 57 mm Type 57-2 unguided air-to-air rockets, launchers for 90 mm air-to-surface rockets, bombs, or (centreline and outboard underwing stations only) auxiliary fuel tanks.

DIMENSIONS, EXTERNAL:
Wing span 9·344 m (30 ft 7⅞ in)
Wing aspect ratio 2·07
Length overall, incl nose probe 21·59 m (70 ft 10 in)
Height overall 5·41 m (17 ft 9 in)

Prototype J-8 II landing after a test flight *(CATIC)*

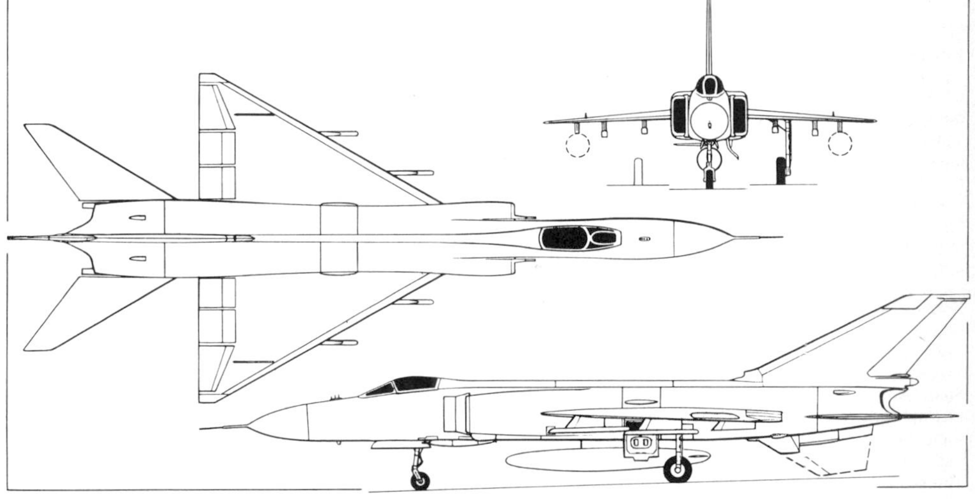
Latest J-8 II version of the 'Finback' twin-jet air superiority fighter *(Pilot Press)*

Wheel track approx 3·80 m (12 ft 7 in)
Wheelbase approx 7·25 m (23 ft 9½ in)
AREA:
Wings, gross 42·2 m² (454·2 sq ft)
WEIGHTS AND LOADINGS:
Weight empty 9,820 kg (21,649 lb)
Normal T-O weight 14,300 kg (31,526 lb)
Max T-O weight 17,800 kg (39,242 lb)
Wing loading:
at normal T-O weight 338·9 kg/m² (69·4 lb/sq ft)
at max T-O weight 421·8 kg/m² (86·4 lb/sq ft)
Power loading:
at normal T-O weight 110·5 kg/kN (1·08 lb/lb st)
at max T-O weight 137·5 kg/kN (1·35 lb/lb st)
PERFORMANCE:
Design max operating Mach number 2·2
Design max level speed
701 knots (1,300 km/h; 808 mph) IAS
Unstick speed 175 knots (325 km/h; 202 mph)
Landing speed 156 knots (290 km/h; 180 mph)
Max rate of climb at S/L 12,000 m (39,370 ft)/min
Acceleration from Mach 0·6 to 1·25 at 5,000 m (16,400 ft) 54 s
Service ceiling 20,000 m (65,620 ft)
T-O run, with afterburning 670 m (2,198 ft)
Landing run, brake-chute deployed 1,000 m (3,280 ft)
Combat radius 432 nm (800 km; 497 miles)
Max range 1,187 nm (2,200 km; 1,367 miles)
g limit in sustained turn at Mach 0·9 at 5,000 m (16,400 ft) +4·83

XIAN

XIAN AIRCRAFT COMPANY

VICE-PRESIDENT AND CHIEF ENGINEER: Yi Zhibin

XIAN (TUPOLEV) H-6

Chinese name: Hongzhaji-6 (Bomber aircraft 6) or Hong-6

NATO reporting name: Badger

First steps to assemble the Tupolev Tu-16 bomber (see USSR section) under licence in China were taken in 1958, but work was suspended in 1960 after the political break with the USSR. A production programme was reinstated some two years later, and the formidable task was undertaken of copying the design without Soviet assistance. Deliveries of the Chinese built H-6 version began in about 1968, and seven of the 26 nuclear devices tested at Lop Nur (Lop Nor) up to 1980 were airdropped from Tu-16/H-6s. Other weapons that can be carried by the H-6 include the C-ASM cruise missile and the C601 air-launched derivative of the Soviet 'Styx'.

Production of this aircraft has been relatively slow, but it is continuing at a low rate, and the number in service is now believed to be about 120, the current version being designated **H-6 IV** or **B-6D**. Mikulin RD-3M engines for the H-6 are built at Xian as the Wopen-8 or WP-8. China is supplying spares for the Tu-16 bombers of the Egyptian Air Force, and the possibility remains that ECM, reconnaissance or other variants may be developed in the future. An aerial tanker design study for the H-6 has been carried out by the FR Group of the UK. This version would serve primarily as a refuelling tanker for the Q-5/A-5 attack aircraft; there are no plans at present for a receiver version of the H-6.

As with other Chinese developments of original Soviet designs, some local modifications have been noted: aircraft carrying C601 missiles, for example, have a bigger and cylindrical 'chin' fairing, presumably housing a Chinese variation of the original radar antenna. One Tu-16/H-6 has been seen with fully circular air intakes, made possible by greater engine/fuselage clearance apparently to overcome intake boundary layer airflow problems. There have also been unconfirmed reports of a four-engined version.

Xian H-6 strategic bomber, based on the Tupolev Tu-16, showing the modified 'chin' radome associated with C601 missile carriage

XIAN (MIKOYAN) J-7

Chinese name: Jianjiji-7 (Fighter aircraft 7) or Jian-7

Export designations: F-7 and F-7M

NATO reporting name: Fishbed

The Chinese version of the Mikoyan MiG-21 day fighter was based originally on a number of Soviet built MiG-21Fs ('Fishbed-Cs') delivered to China before the political break with the USSR in 1960. The task of copying the airframe, the Tumansky R-11 afterburning turbojet engine (built at Chengdu as the Wopen-7 or WP-7) and equipment was accomplished quickly, and the first J-7 made its initial flight in December 1964. The type began to enter service with the air force of the People's Liberation Army in 1965.

Between 60 and 80 J-7s had been completed before production was halted in 1966 by the onset of the Cultural Revolution, but it was resumed subsequently with a number of modifications. An early priority was to extend the very short TBO life (said to be only about 100 hours) of the original power plant, and this was at least doubled in the improved Wopen-7A, which develops 43·1 kN (4,400 kg; 9,700 lb st) dry and 50·0 kN (5,100 kg; 11,243 lb st) with afterburning. Exports of early production J-7/F-7s were made to Albania and Tanzania.

The early model J-7 suffered from the same operational shortcomings as the MiG-21F, namely short endurance and a lack of adequate air-to-air firepower. At the beginning of the 1980s Chinese engineers undertook a further series of modifications aimed at upgrading both handling qualities and combat performance of the aircraft. Major improvements in this version, designated **J-7 II** in China, include use of a Wopen-7B engine, in which the afterburning thrust is increased by 9·8 kN (1,000 kg; 2,205 lb), the addition on the port side of a second 30 mm gun, and the ability to carry an 800 litre (176 Imp gallon) drop tank under the fuselage. The three-position, mechanically movable shock cone in the MiG-21F's nose intake, housing the range-only radar, has been replaced by a more efficient no-step system permitting continuously variable positioning of the centrebody, similar to that introduced on the Soviet built 'Fishbed-E' in the mid-1960s. Introduction of a new zero-height/low-speed ejection seat is accompanied by a new cockpit canopy, hinged at the rear and opening upward, in place of the early pattern MiG-21 canopy which was hinged at the base of the windscreen. The tail braking parachute has been transferred from under the rear fuselage to a 'bullet' fairing beneath the rudder, as on late-production Chinese J-6s and Q-5s. Current export examples of this version, designated **F-7B**, are to this standard.

Components and engines for the F-7 have been exported in some numbers to Egypt, which also ordered up to 160 complete aircraft for its own use (as advanced trainers) and for supply to Iraq. Some of these aircraft, and Egypt's Soviet supplied MiG-21MFs, are being retrofitted with an advanced head-up display and launchers for AIM-9P3/4 Sidewinder air-to-air missiles.

In 1984 China released details of an improved version now known as the **F-7M Airguard**, differing mainly in having more modern Western avionics which include a HUDWACS (head-up display and weapon aiming computer system) instead of the optical sighting system, a more effective ranging radar, new air data computer and radar altimeter, new IFF, and more secure com radio. Other changes include a more efficient electrical power system to cater for the new avionics; two additional underwing stores points; ability to carry the newer and longer-range PL-7 air-to-air missile, which outwardly resembles the Matra Magic; a slightly different version of the Wopen-7B engine; and a relocated nose probe. The F-7M, which is already in service with the PLA Air Force, is being marketed for export by Aircraft Technology Ltd of Hong Kong. According to ATL, one export order for the F-7M had been fulfilled by CATIC before becoming a partner in ATL, and total exports of the F-7 (all models) have exceeded 500. Customer nations have included Egypt, Pakistan, Somalia and Sudan.

Current Soviet versions of the MiG-21 are fully described and illustrated in the USSR section of this edition. China has also developed its own two-seat training version, known as the **JJ-7** or **FT-7**; this is described separately. The following description applies to the current standard F-7B and F-7M Chinese models:

TYPE: Single-seat day fighter and close support aircraft.

WINGS: As for standard MiG-21, with 57° sweepback on leading-edges, 2° anhedral, slotted flaps and balanced ailerons.

FUSELAGE: Generally as MiG-21F except for automatically operated, continuously adjustable shock cone in centre of nose intake, instead of three-step mechanically adjustable centrebody of earlier J-7s. Brake-chute relocated from under rear fuselage to 'bullet' fairing at base of vertical tail. In F-7M, nose probe is relocated above intake, offset to starboard, as on Soviet built MiG-21PFM 'Fishbed-J'.

TAIL UNIT: All-swept surfaces, with all-moving tailplane, as for MiG-21.

LANDING GEAR: Inward retracting mainwheels, with 660 × 220 tyres and LS-16 disc brakes; forward retracting nosewheel, with 500 × 180 tyre and LS-15 double-acting brake. Tail braking parachute at base of vertical tail.

POWER PLANT: One Chengdu Wopen-7B turbojet engine in F-7B (43·1 kN/4,400 kg; 9,700 lb st dry, 59·8 kN/6,100 kg; 13,448 lb st with afterburning). Wopen-7B(BM) in F-7M has same ratings, but kerosene (instead of gasoline) starting. Total internal fuel capacity of 2,385 litres (524·5 Imp gallons), contained in six flexible tanks in fuselage and two integral tanks in each wing. Provision for carrying a 500 or 800 litre (110 or 176 Imp gallon) centreline drop tank, and/or a 500 litre drop tank on each outboard underwing pylon. Max possible internal/external fuel capacity 4,185 litres (920·5 Imp gallons).

Xian F-7B with centreline drop tank and underwing rocket pods *(CATIC)*

ACCOMMODATION: Pilot only, on Chengdu Aircraft Corporation zero-height/low-speed ejection seat operable between 70 and 459 knots (130-850 km/h; 81-528 mph) IAS. One-piece canopy, hinged at rear to open upward.

SYSTEMS: Improved electrical system in F-7M, using three static (instead of four rotary) inverters, to cater for additional avionics. Jianghuai YX-3 oxygen system.

AVIONICS: *(F-7B)* Include CT-3 VHF com radio, WL-7 radio compass, Type 262 radio altimeter, XS-5A marker beacon receiver, Type 222 ranging radar, and Type 602 (Soviet 'Odd Rods' type) IFF transponder. *(F-7M)* GEC Avionics suite includes Type 956 HUDWAC, AD 3400 two-band UHF/VHF multi-function com system, Type 226 Skyranger ranging radar with ECCM, and an air data computer. Other avionics include Type 602 IFF transponder, Type 0101 HR A/2 radar altimeter, WL-7 radio compass, and XS-6A marker beacon receiver. The HUDWAC (head-up display and weapon aiming computer) provides the pilot with displays for instrument flying, with air-to-air and air-to-ground weapon delivery superimposed on the same area of view as the target. It can store 32 weapon parameter functions, allowing both current and future weapon variants to be accommodated. In air-to-air combat its four modes (missiles, conventional gunnery, snapshoot gunnery, or dogfight status) allow for all eventualities. There are also two navigation functions: approach mode, and a standby aiming reticle provided by the HUD.

ARMAMENT: *(F-7B)* Two 30 mm Type 30-1 belt-fed cannon, with 60 rds/gun, in fairings under front fuselage just forward of wing-root leading-edges. One hardpoint under each wing, each capable of carrying a PL-2 ('Atoll' type), PL-2A or similar infra-red homing air-to-air missile, a pod of eighteen 57 mm unguided rockets, or a bomb of up to 250 kg size (500 kg in max overload condition). SM-3A optical or AFS3A computing gunsight interfaced with ranging radar and angle of attack sideslip transmitter, with gun camera mounted on sighting head. *(F-7M)* Gunsight replaced by a GEC Avionics Type 956 head-up display (also showing navigational data) and weapon aiming computer. Contrary to 1985-86 description, weapons carriage remains the function of the *inboard* underwing pylons; it is the outboard ones which are 'wet' for the carriage of drop tanks. The centreline pylon is used for a drop tank only. Each inboard pylon is capable of carrying a PL-2, -2A, -5B or -7 air-to-air missile or, at customer's option, a Matra R.550 Magic; one pod of eighteen Type 57-2 (57 mm) air-to-air and air-to-ground rockets; one pod of seven Type 90-1 (90 mm) air-to-ground rockets; or a 50, 150, 250, or 500 kg bomb. Each outboard pylon can carry one of the above rocket pods, a 50 or 150 kg bomb, or a 500 litre drop tank.

DIMENSIONS, EXTERNAL:
Wing span 7·154 m (23 ft 5⅝ in)
Wing aspect ratio 2·225
Length overall:
excl nose probe 13·945 m (45 ft 9 in)
incl nose probe 14·885 m (48 ft 10 in)
Height overall 4·103 m (13 ft 5½ in)
Tailplane span 3·74 m (12 ft 3¼ in)
Wheel track 2·692 m (8 ft 10 in)
Wheelbase 4·807 m (15 ft 9¼ in)

AREA:
Wings, gross 23·00 m² (247·6 sq ft)

WEIGHTS AND LOADINGS:
Weight empty: F-7B 5,145 kg (11,343 lb)
F-7M 5,275 kg (11,629 lb)
Normal max T-O weight with two PL-2 or PL-7 air-to-air missiles:
F-7B 7,372 kg (16,252 lb)
F-7M 7,531 kg (16,603 lb)
Wing loading at normal max T-O weight:
F-7B 320·52 kg/m² (65·68 lb/sq ft)
F-7M 327·43 kg/m² (67·10 lb/sq ft)
Power loading at normal max T-O weight:
F-7B 123·3 kg/kN (1·21 lb/lb st)
F-7M 125·5 kg/kN (1·23 lb/lb st)

PERFORMANCE (at normal max T-O weight with two PL-2 or PL-7 air-to-air missiles, except where indicated):
Max level speed between 12,500 and 18,500 m (41,010-60,700 ft): F-7B, F-7M Mach 2·05 (1,175 knots; 2,175 km/h; 1,350 mph)
Unstick speed: F-7B, F-7M 167-178 knots (310-330 km/h; 193-205 mph)
Touchdown speed: F-7B, F-7M 162-173 knots (300-320 km/h; 186-199 mph)
Max rate of climb at S/L:
F-7B 9,000 m (29,527 ft)/min
F-7M 10,800 m (35,435 ft)/min
Acceleration from Mach 0·9 to 1·2 at 5,000 m (16,400 ft):
F-7M 35 s
Max sustained turn rate:
F-7M (Mach 0·7 at S/L) 14·7°/s
F-7M (Mach 0·8 at 5,000 m; 16,400 ft) 9·5°/s
Service ceiling: F-7B 18,800 m (61,680 ft)
F-7M 18,200 m (59,710 ft)
Absolute ceiling: F-7B 19,200 m (62,990 ft)
F-7M 18,700 m (61,350 ft)
T-O run: F-7B 800-1,000 m (2,625-3,280 ft)
F-7M 700-950 m (2,297-3,117 ft)

Xian F-7M Airguard Chinese built export version of the MiG-21 ('Fishbed') *(ATL)*

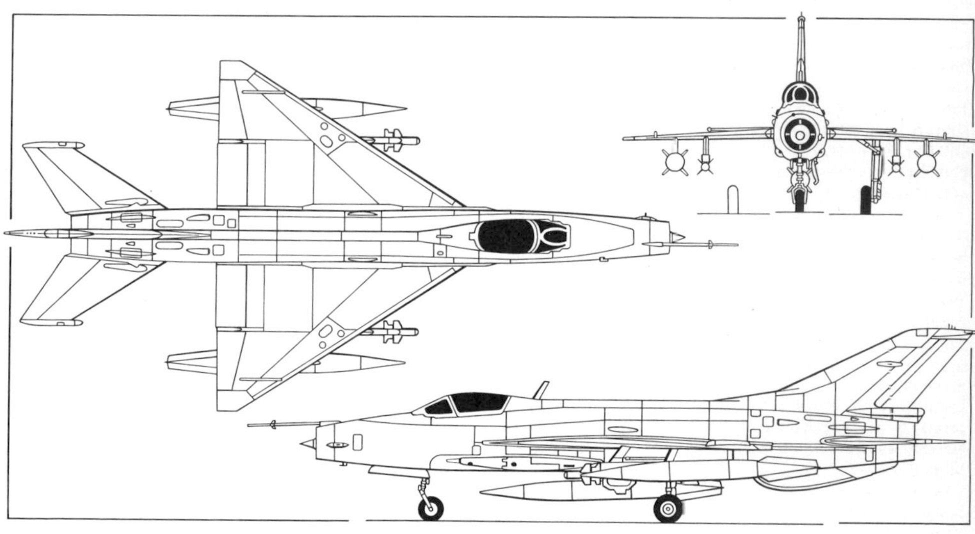

Xian F-7M Airguard single-seat fighter and close support aircraft *(Jane's/Mike Keep)*

Landing run with brake-chute:
F-7B 800-1,000 m (2,625-3,280 ft)
F-7M 600-900 m (1,969-2,953 ft)
Typical mission profiles (F-7M):
Combat air patrol at 11,000 m (36,000 ft) with two air-to-air missiles and three 500 litre drop tanks, incl 5 min combat 45 min
Long range interception at 11,000 m (36,000 ft) at 351 nm (650 km; 404 miles) from base, incl Mach 1·5 dash and 5 min combat, stores as above
Hi-lo-hi interdiction radius, out and back at 11,000 m (36,000 ft), with three 500 litre drop tanks and two 150 kg bombs 324 nm (600 km; 373 miles)
Lo-lo-lo close air support radius with four rocket pods, no external tanks 200 nm (370 km; 230 miles)
Range:
F-7B, two PL-2 missiles only 647 nm (1,200 km; 745 miles)
F-7B, two PL-2s and one 800 litre drop tank 804 nm (1,490 km; 926 miles)
F-7M, two PL-7 missiles and three 500 litre drop tanks 939 nm (1,740 km; 1,081 miles)
F-7M, self-ferry with one 800 litre and two 500 litre drop tanks, no missiles 1,203 nm (2,230 km; 1,385 miles)
g limits: F-7B +7
F-7M +8

XIAN JJ-7

Chinese name: Jianjiji Jiaolianji-7 or Jianjiao-7 (Fighter training aircraft 7)

Export designation: FT-7

The JJ-7 or FT-7 is a tandem two-seat trainer version of the J-7/F-7, generally similar outwardly to its Soviet counterpart, the MiG-21U (NATO 'Mongol-A'), and is said to be capable of providing most of the training necessary for the Shenyang J-8/F-8 fighter as well as the full syllabus for all versions of the J-7/F-7. Avionics are generally as described for the single-seat F-7M.

Differences from the single-seat J-7 include sideways opening (to starboard) twin canopies, the rear one fitted with a retractable periscope, and a removable saddleback fuel tank aft of the second cockpit. A 720 litre (158 Imp gallon) drop tank can be carried under the centre-fuselage, and there is a single underwing pylon each side for such stores as PL-2B air-to-air missiles, 18-round pods of 57 mm rockets, or bombs of up to 250 kg size. If required, the JJ-7 can also be fitted with a Type 23-3 twin-barrel 23 mm gun in an underbelly pack.

DIMENSIONS, EXTERNAL: As J-7 except:
Length overall, incl probe 14·874 m (48 ft 9½ in)

WEIGHTS:
Not known

PERFORMANCE:
Unstick speed 170-181 knots (315-335 km/h; 196-208 mph)
Touchdown speed 165-175 knots (305-325 km/h; 190-202 mph)
Service ceiling 17,300 m (56,760 ft)
Absolute ceiling 17,700 m (58,070 ft)
T-O run 900-1,100 m (2,953-3,609 ft)
Landing run with brake-chute and wheel braking 850-1,100 m (2,789-3,609 ft)
Range at 11,000 m (36,000 ft):
internal fuel only 545 nm (1,010 km; 627 miles)
with 720 litre drop tank 787 nm (1,459 km; 906 miles)
g limit with two PL-2B missiles +7

XIAN (ANTONOV) Y-7 and Y7-100

Chinese name: Yunshuji-7 (Transport aircraft 7) or Yun-7

NATO reporting name: Coke

Civil and military examples of the Antonov An-24 twin-turboprop transport aircraft (40 of which were purchased from the USSR) have been in service with CAAC and the PLA Air Force since about 1970. A 'considerably improved' version of this 48/52-passenger aircraft, known as the **Y-7**, received its Chinese certificate of airworthiness in 1980, following the completion of three prototypes plus two additional airframes for static and fatigue testing. The Y-7 is now in full production at the Xian Aircraft Company factory; its WJ-5A-1 engines (derived from the Ivchenko AI-24A) are manufactured at Shanghai.

Public debut by a pre-production Y-7 took place on 17 April 1982 at Nanyuan Airport, Beijing, and production is believed to have started in 1983, initially to replace Soviet built Il-14s and Il-18s in service with CAAC. First flight of a production Y-7 was announced by the New China news agency (Xinhua) on 1 February 1984, and the initial delivery to CAAC was made shortly afterwards. At first, the CAAC Y-7s were restricted to cargo and charter operations, but in April 1986 the first of the 14 then in service inaugurated scheduled passenger services, and all 14 were due to be reassigned to passenger use by the following July.

Under the first of two similar contracts (the other being for the Harbin Y-12), the Hong Kong Aircraft Engineering Company (HAECO) undertook 'prototype' refurbishment of a 48-passenger production Y-7 in 1985. This programme called for a new three-person flight deck layout, all-new cabin interior with 52 reclining seats, windscreen de-icing, new HF/VHF communications, new navigation equipment, and installation of oxygen, air data and environmental control systems. The aircraft was also fitted with winglets which, by reducing induced drag by 4 per cent, are claimed to offer a 5 per cent reduction in fuel consumption. In this new form the aircraft meets BCAR standards, and is known as the **Y7-100**.

North American, British, French and German firms supplying equipment include Becker, Collins, Hamilton Standard, IDC, Lermer, Litton, Nordam, PTC, Puritan-Bennett, Sfena, Smiths, Sperry and Sundstrand. The Y-7 (registration B-3499) was delivered to HAECO on 27 December 1984 and was returned to China in Y7-100 configuration on 16 August 1985. Information on the programme as it progressed was fed back to China, where two other Y-7s were being similarly upgraded at Xian using kits supplied by HAECO. These were nearing completion in the Spring of 1986.

This initial phase was to be followed by a seven-aircraft second phase, and then by a third involving the surviving examples of China's 40 Soviet built An-24s. The contract with Nordam, which was responsible for the cabin interior redesign, included an option for 50 shipsets of floors, seats, lights and toilets. In the longer term, China estimates a requirement for at least 100 Y-7s by the year 1990, and plans an ongoing development programme intended to lead to a more fuel-efficient **Y7-200** in 1988, with a reduced-weight **Y7-300** and a rear-ramp cargo version appearing about a year later. Boeing Commercial Airplane Company is assisting in the weight reduction programme.

The following description is based on that of the An-24RV, modified where possible to refer to the Y-7 and Y7-100:

Type: Twin-turboprop short/medium-range transport.

Wings: Cantilever high-wing monoplane, with 2° 12′ 2″ anhedral on outer panels. Incidence 3°. Sweepback at quarter-chord on outer panels 6° 50′. All-metal two-spar structure, built in five sections: constant chord centre-section, two tapered inner wings and two tapered outer panels. Mass balanced servo-compensated ailerons, with large glassfibre trim tabs. Hydraulically operated Fowler flaps along entire wing trailing-edges inboard of unpowered ailerons; single-slotted flaps on centre-section, double-slotted outboard of nacelles. Servo tab and trim tab in each aileron. Winglet at each tip on Y7-100.

Fuselage: All-metal semi-monocoque structure in front, centre and rear portions, of bonded/welded construction.

Tail Unit: Cantilever all-metal structure, with single ventral fin. Tailplane dihedral 9°. All controls operated manually. Balance tab in each elevator, trim tab and spring tab in rudder.

Landing Gear (An-24RV): Retractable tricycle type with twin wheels on all units. Hydraulic actuation, with emergency gravity extension. All units retract forward. Mainwheels are size 900 × 300-370, tyre pressure 3·45-4·90 bars (50-71 lb/sq in); nosewheels size 700 × 250, tyre pressure 2·45-3·45 bars (35·5-50 lb/sq in). (Tyre pressures variable to cater for different types of runway.) Disc brakes on mainwheels; steerable and castoring nosewheel unit.

Power Plant: Two Shanghai WJ-5A-1 turboprop engines, each rated at 2,080 kW (2,790 shp) for T-O and 1,976 kW (2,650 shp) at ISA + 23°C; four-blade constant-speed fully-feathering propellers with elongated spinners. Fuel in integral wing tanks immediately outboard of nacelles, and four bag-type tanks in centre-section, total capacity 5,550 litres (1,220 Imp gallons). Provision for four additional tanks in centre-section. Pressure refuelling point in starboard engine nacelle; gravity fuelling point above each tank. One 8·83 kN (1,985 lb st) Type RU 19-300 auxiliary turbojet (or Chinese equivalent ?) in starboard engine nacelle for engine starting, to improve take-off and in-flight performance, and to reduce stability and handling problems if one turboprop engine fails in flight.

Accommodation: Crew of three (Y7-100) or five (Y-7) on flight deck, plus cabin attendant. Standard layout has four-abreast seating, with centre aisle, for 48 (Y-7) or 52 passengers (Y7-100) in air-conditioned, soundproofed (by Tracor) and pressurised cabin. Galley (by Lermer) and toilet at rear on starboard side. Baggage compartments forward and aft of passenger cabin, plus overhead stowage bins in cabin. Passenger door on port side, at rear of cabin, is of airstair type. Doors to forward and rear baggage compartments on starboard side. All doors open inward. Electric windscreen de-icing in Y7-100.

Systems: Hamilton Standard environmental control system in Y7-100 (cabin pressure differential in An-24RV is 0·29 bars; 4·27 lb/sq in). Main and emergency hydraulic systems, pressure 152 bars (2,200 lb/sq in), for landing gear actuation, nosewheel steering, flaps, brakes, windscreen wipers and propeller feathering. Electrical system in An-24RV includes two 27V DC starter/generators, two alternators to provide 115V 400Hz AC supply, and two inverters for 36V 400Hz three-phase AC. Puritan-Bennett passenger oxygen system optional in Y7-100.

Avionics and Equipment (Y7-100): Standard communications equipment comprises Collins 618M-3 dual VHF, Collins 628T-3 single HF, Becker audio selection and intercom, and Sundstrand AV-557C cockpit voice recorder. Standard navigation equipment comprises dual ADI-84A, dual EHSI-74 electronic HSI, dual RMI-36, FGS-65 flight guidance system, dual 51RV-4B VOR/ILS, dual DME-42, dual DF-206 ADF, 860F-4 radio altimeter, 621A-6A ATC transponder, 51Z-4 marker beacon receiver and CWC-80 instrument warning system, all by Collins; Litton LTN-211 VLF/Omega navigation system; Sperry MHRS dual compass system, dual attitude reference and Primus 90 colour weather radar; IDC air data system; Sundstrand UFDR flight data recorder; and KJ-6A autopilot. Gables control units. Other instrumentation by Gould, IDC, Sfena and Smiths.

Dimensions, external:	
Wing span: Y-7	29·20 m (95 ft 9½ in)
Y7-100 (over winglets)	29·637 m (97 ft 2¾ in)
Wing chord: at root	3·50 m (11 ft 5¾ in)
at tip	1·095 m (3 ft 7 in)
Wing aspect ratio	11·7
Length overall	23·708 m (77 ft 9½ in)
Height overall	8·553 m (28 ft 0¾ in)
Fuselage: Max width	2·90 m (9 ft 6¼ in)
Max depth	2·50 m (8 ft 2½ in)
Tailplane span	9·08 m (29 ft 9½ in)
Wheel track (c/l of shock struts)	7·90 m (25 ft 11 in)
Wheelbase	7·90 m (25 ft 11 in)
Passenger door (port, rear):	
Height	1·40 m (4 ft 7 in)
Width	0·75 m (2 ft 5½ in)
Height to sill	1·40 m (4 ft 7 in)
Baggage compartment door (starboard, fwd):	
Height	1·10 m (3 ft 7¼ in)
Width	1·20 m (3 ft 11¼ in)
Height to sill	1·30 m (4 ft 3 in)
Baggage compartment door (starboard, rear):	
Height	1·41 m (4 ft 7½ in)
Width	0·75 m (2 ft 5½ in)
Dimensions, internal:	
Cabin:	
Length, incl flight deck: Y-7	9·90 m (32 ft 5¾ in)

Taken in 1983, this photograph shows An-26s in service with the PLA Air Force. Some of the improvements of the Y7-100 could be applied also to these aircraft in due course *(Xinhua)*

Xian Y-7 (Chinese development of the Antonov An-24) after modification by HAECO of Hong Kong as the prototype Y7-100 *(HAECO)*

Y7-100	10·50 m (34 ft 5½ in)
Max width	2·80 m (9 ft 2¼ in)
Max height	1·90 m (6 ft 2¾ in)
Volume: Y7-100	56·0 m³ (1,978 cu ft)
Baggage compartment volume (Y7-100):	
fwd	4·50 m³ (159 cu ft)
rear	6·70 m³ (237 cu ft)
AREAS:	
Wings, gross	74·98 m² (807·1 sq ft)
Vertical tail surfaces (total)	13·38 m² (144·0 sq ft)
Horizontal tail surfaces (total)	17·23 m² (185·5 sq ft)
WEIGHTS AND LOADINGS:	
Operating weight empty: Y-7	14,235 kg (31,383 lb)
Y7-100	14,900 kg (32,849 lb)
Max fuel (both)	4,790 kg (10,560 lb)
Max payload: Y-7	4,700 kg (10,362 lb)
Y7-100	5,500 kg (12,125 lb)
Max T-O and landing weight (both)	21,800 kg (48,060 lb)
Max wing loading (both)	290·7 kg/m² (59·6 lb/sq ft)
Max power loading (both)	5·24 kg/kW (8·61 lb/shp)
PERFORMANCE (Y7-100 except where indicated):	
Max level speed	279 knots (518 km/h; 322 mph)
Max cruising speed at 4,000 m (13,125 ft):	
Y-7	258 knots (478 km/h; 297 mph)
Y7-100	261 knots (484 km/h; 301 mph)
Econ cruising speed at 6,000 m (19,685 ft)	228 knots (423 km/h; 263 mph)
Max rate of climb at S/L	458 m (1,504 ft)/min
Service ceiling	8,750 m (28,700 ft)
Service ceiling, one engine out	3,900 m (12,800 ft)
T-O run at S/L, FAR Pt 25: ISA	1,248 m (4,095 ft)
ISA + 20°C	1,398 m (4,590 ft)
Landing run	620 m (2,035 ft)
Range:	
max (52-passenger) payload	491 nm (910 km; 565 miles)
max standard fuel	1,025 nm (1,900 km; 1,180 miles)
standard and auxiliary fuel	1,306 nm (2,420 km; 1,504 miles)

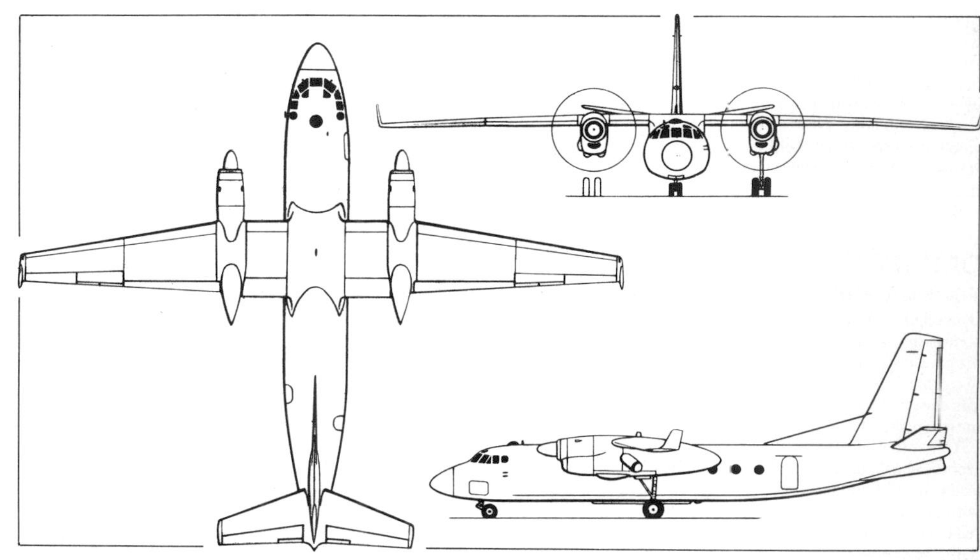

Xian Y7-100 current production version of this twin-turboprop transport aircraft *(Pilot Press)*

FUTURE PROGRAMMES

An outline of China's future plans for civil aircraft development was given in the early part of 1986 by the director of the Ministry of Aviation Industry's civil aircraft bureau, Mr Zhu Yu Li. In addition to continuing with production and new versions of the Y-7, Y-8 and Y-12, an international partner is being sought for a 30/40-passenger commuter airliner programme (existing type or new design), with discussions taking place with Shorts in the UK, a Japanese consortium and de Havilland Canada, among others. A two-year feasibility study (1985-87) for a 75-seat transport, tentatively designated MPC-75, is being undertaken by CATIC and the German company MBB. To follow the Y-8 a new, and possibly propfan/UDF powered, 150-passenger type is being explored with McDonnell Douglas.

Increasing attention is also to be given to helicopter development, hitherto a rather neglected area. With the Z-5 out of production since 1979, the Z-6 programme shelved (and the Z-7 never identified), China's modern helicopter design and manufacturing expertise is restricted to development of the Z-8, a Chinese derivative of the Aérospatiale Super Frelon, and licence production of the same company's Dauphin as the Z-9. To extend this range, discussions are taking place with possible international collaborators concerning development of an 8,000 kg (17,635 lb) class multi-purpose transport helicopter and a small, 2,000 kg (4,410 lb) type for agricultural and forestry work. The latter could also fulfil a current requirement for a small military helicopter. The PLA is said to need about 50 for anti-tank duties, and in 1986 was analysing demonstrations given late the previous year by the Aérospatiale Gazelle, MBB BO 105 and McDonnell Douglas 530MG.

A model of an agricultural aircraft called the **Shennong-1** was displayed at an exhibition in Beijing in the Spring of 1986. Similar in appearance to the Air Tractor AT-400 (see US section), it was said to be proposed with either a piston or a turboprop engine. No other details were given.

COLOMBIA

AVIONES DE COLOMBIA

AVIONES DE COLOMBIA SA

Calle 26 No. 4A-45 Piso 8, Bogotá
Telephone: (282) 9648, 9668 and 9728
Telex: 45 220
WORKS: Aeropuerto Guaymaral, Apartado Aéreo 6876, Bogotá
Telephone: (671) 8211, 8488 and 8502
COMMERCIAL MANAGER: Rafael Urdaneta

This company, established in the 1950s and known formerly as Urdaneta y Galvez Ltda, has been a South American distributor for Cessna aircraft since 1961. In 1969 it began assembling and partly building selected Cessna types under licence (see 1981-82 and earlier editions of *Jane's*), and is now qualified to manufacture complete airframes. Facilities include 464·5 m² (5,000 sq ft) of office space in Bogotá, and 13,935 m² (150,000 sq ft) at Guaymaral, the general aviation airport for Bogotá. Service facilities include complete engine, propeller and avionics workshops. A new office and maintenance facility are shortly to be built at the Eldorado International Airport in Bogotá.

On 31 January 1986 the company had a workforce of 150 persons, and had assembled a total of 1,017 Cessna aircraft. These included 84 Models 150/152, 54 Model 172, 56 Model 172XP, four Model 172RG, six Model 177RG, 70 Model 182, 14 Model 182RG, 36 Model 185, 266 Model 188, 274 Model 206, 70 Model 210, two Model P210, 35 Model 303, 14 Model 310, eight Model 337, nine Model 340, 14 Model 402 and one Model 414.

AVIONES DE COLOMBIA/CESSNA AGTRAINER

Illustrated in an accompanying photograph, the AgTrainer is modified by Aviones de Colombia from the Cessna Model 188 Ag Truck (1984-85 *Jane's*). The cabin is widened to accommodate two persons side by side, increasing the empty weight by approx 91 kg (200 lb). Flight characteristics remain unchanged. Two prototypes have flown (the first of them on 16 September 1976), and by 1 January 1979 these two aircraft had accumulated nearly 2,000 flying hours. The first prototype has been operated by Aeroandes, a local cropspraying flying school.

Seven AgTrainers had been produced by early 1986, of which three were operating in Colombia, three in Central America and one in Ecuador.

POWER PLANT: One 224 kW (300 hp) Continental IO-520-D flat-six engine, driving a McCauley three-blade constant-speed propeller. Fuel capacity 204 litres (45 Imp gallons). Oil capacity 11·4 litres (2·5 Imp gallons).

DIMENSIONS, EXTERNAL:	
Wing span	12·70 m (41 ft 8 in)
Length overall	8·00 m (26 ft 3 in)
Height overall	2·44 m (8 ft 0 in)
Propeller diameter	2·03 m (6 ft 8 in)
DIMENSIONS, INTERNAL:	
Cabin: Max width	1·09 m (3 ft 7 in)
Hopper volume	0·85 m³ (30·0 cu ft)
AREA:	
Wings, gross	19·05 m² (205·0 sq ft)
WEIGHTS:	
Weight empty:	
without dispersal equipment	1,017 kg (2,242 lb)
with dispersal equipment	1,099 kg (2,424 lb)
Max T-O weight:	
Normal category	1,497 kg (3,300 lb)
Restricted category	1,905 kg (4,200 lb)
Max landing weight	1,497 kg (3,300 lb)
PERFORMANCE (at max T-O weight):	
Max level speed at S/L	105 knots (195 km/h; 121 mph)
Max cruising speed (75% power) at 1,980 m (6,500 ft)	98 knots (182 km/h; 113 mph)
Stalling speed, power off:	
flaps up	53 knots (98 km/h; 61 mph) IAS
flaps down	50 knots (92 km/h; 57 mph) IAS
Max rate of climb at S/L	210 m (690 ft)/min
Service ceiling	3,385 m (11,100 ft)
T-O run	207 m (680 ft)
T-O to 15 m (50 ft)	332 m (1,090 ft)
Landing from 15 m (50 ft)	386 m (1,265 ft)
Landing run	128 m (420 ft)
Range, reserves for start, taxi, T-O and 45 min at 45% power	256 nm (474 km; 295 miles)
Endurance, conditions as above	2 h 36 min

Aviones de Colombia/Cessna AgTrainer, a modified Cessna 188 Ag Truck

CZECHOSLOVAKIA

Central direction of the Czechoslovak aircraft industry is by a body known as the Generální Reditelstvi Aero—Ceskoslovenské Letecke Podniky (Trust Aero—Czechoslovak Aeronautical Works), Prague-Letnany, whose General Manager is Josef Skarohlid.

About 29,000 people are employed by the Czechoslovak aircraft industry. Principal factories concerned with aircraft manufacture are the Aero Vodochody National Corporation, Let National Corporation and Zlin Aircraft-Moravan National Corporation, whose current products appear under the appropriate headings in this section. Other Czechoslovak factories engaged in the production of aero-engines and sailplanes are listed in the relevant sections of this edition.

Sales of all aircraft products outside Czechoslovakia are handled by the Omnipol Foreign Trade Corporation.

OMNIPOL
FOREIGN TRADE CORPORATION

Nekázanka 11, 112 21 Prague 1
Telephone: (02) 2140111
Telex: 121297 and 121299
General Manager: Ing Stanislav Fritzl
Sales Manager: Ing František Háva
Publicity Manager: Jan Boček

This concern handles the sales of products of the Czechoslovak aircraft industry outside Czechoslovakia and furnishes all information requested by customers with regard to export goods.

AERO
AERO VODOCHODY NÁRODNÍ PODNIK (Aero Vodochody National Corporation)

Vodochody, p. Odelená Voda, near Prague
Managing Director: Ing Václav Klouda
Vice-Directors:
Ing Josef Sedlácek (Technical)
Josef Spára (Production)
Ing Jaroslav Kucera (Sales)
Ing Jirí Kraus (Works Economy)
Chief Designer: Ing Vlastimil Havelka
Chief Pilot: Antonin Saller

This factory perpetuates the name of one of the three founder companies of the Czechoslovak aircraft industry, which began activities in 1919 with the manufacture of Austrian Phönix fighters. Subsequent well known products included the A 11 military general purpose biplane and its derivatives, and licence manufacture of the French Bloch 200 twin-engined bomber. The present works was established on 1 July 1953.

Aero's major product from 1963-74 was the L-29 Delfin jet basic and advanced trainer, of which approx 3,600 were built. A full description of the L-29, many hundreds of which remain in service, can be found in the 1974-75 *Jane's*. It was superseded in production from 1972 by the L-39.

AERO L-39 ALBATROS

The L-39 basic and advanced jet trainer was developed by a team led by Dipl Ing Jan Vlcek, working in close co-operation with the USSR. Two prototype airframes were built initially, of which the first (X-01) was used for structural testing. The first flight, on 4 November 1968, was made by the X-02 second aircraft (OK-32). By the end of 1970, five flying prototypes (X-02/-03/-05/-06/-07) and one other (X-04) for fatigue testing had been completed. Slightly larger and longer air intake trunks were fitted after preliminary flight tests.

A pre-production batch of ten aircraft began to join the flight test programme in 1971, and series production started in late 1972, following official selection of the L-39 to succeed the L-29 Delfin (1974-75 *Jane's*) as the standard jet trainer for the air forces of the Soviet Union, Czechoslovakia and the German Democratic Republic. Service trials took place in 1973 in Czechoslovakia and the USSR, and by the Spring of 1974 the L-39 had begun to enter service with the Czechoslovak Air Force. Other recipients include Afghanistan (approx 18), Cuba (approx 20), Ethiopia (approx 12), Iraq (60), Libya (approx 160), Romania, Syria (approx 60) and Viet-Nam.

By May 1977, when the L-39 made its first appearance in the West, at the Paris Air Show, some 400-500 were in service with several air forces. Production had totalled more than 1,500 by late 1984, and is expected to continue for at least five more years, at the rate of 200 a year. The Albatros is used in Czechoslovakia for all pilot training, including that of helicopter pilots. On average, pupils solo after approx 14 hours' dual instruction on the L-39 C.

Official Czechoslovak designations for the L-39 are as follows:

L-39 C. Basic version, for basic and advanced flying training, to which the detailed description chiefly applies. Two underwing stations only. In service with the air forces of Afghanistan, Cuba, Czechoslovakia, Germany (Democratic Republic) and USSR. In production.

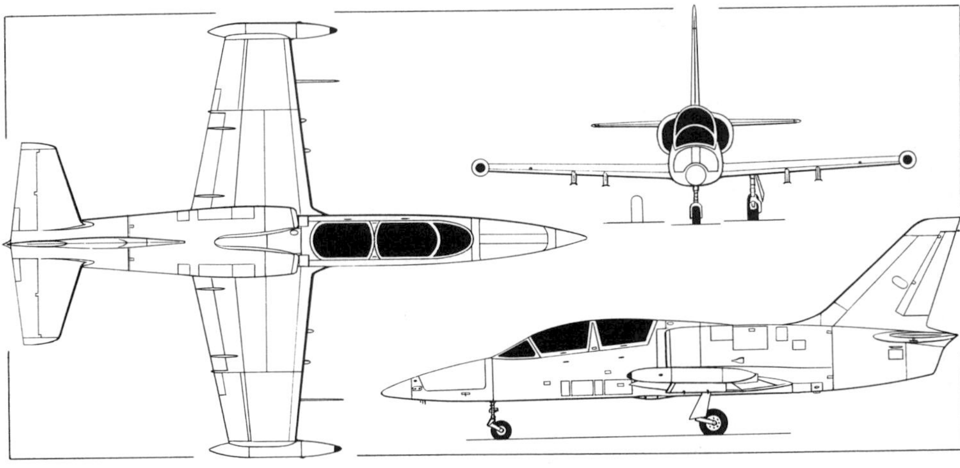

Aero L-39 Z0 Albatros two-seat basic and advanced jet trainer *(Pilot Press)*

L-39 V. As basic L-39 C, but modified as single-seater and equipped with winch and 1,700 m (5,575 ft) cable in rear cockpit for towing KT-04 targets for anti-aircraft artillery training. Prototype (X-08) first flown late 1972.

L-39 ZO. Jet trainer with four underwing weapon stations (Z = Zbrojní: armed) and reinforced wings. Prototype (X-09) first flown 25 August 1975. Export customers include the air forces of Iraq, Libya and Syria. In production.

L-39 ZA. Ground attack and reconnaissance version of L-39 Z0, with underfuselage gun pod and four underwing weapon stations; reinforced wings and landing gear. Prototypes (X-10 and X-11) first flown 1975-76. In service with the air forces of Czechoslovakia and Romania. In production.

L-39 MS. New version with improved airframe, more powerful engine (approx 23·5 kN; 5,300 lb st) and upgraded avionics and equipment, including electronic displays. Prototype flying in 1985, initially with standard AI-25 TL engine. New power plant, available in 1987, will be used to enhance performance rather than payload. In particular, rate of climb will be improved by about 20 per cent. No other details received for publication.

The following description applies to the current production L-39 C basic version, except where indicated:

Type: Two-seat basic and advanced jet trainer; L-39 ZA also has ground attack and reconnaissance capability.

Wings: Cantilever low-wing monoplane, with 2° 30′ dihedral from roots. Wing section NACA 64A012 mod. 5. Incidence 2°. Sweepback 6° 26′ on leading-edges, 1° 45′ at quarter-chord. One-piece all-metal stressed skin structure, with main spar and auxiliary spar; four-point attachment to fuselage. All-metal double-slotted trailing-edge flaps, operated by push/pull rods actuated by a single hydraulic jack. Flaps retract automatically when airspeed reaches 167 knots (310 km/h; 193 mph). Small fence above and below each trailing-edge between flap and aileron. Mass balanced ailerons, each with electrically operated servo tab; port tab, used also for trim, is operated by electromechanical actuator. Flaps deflect 25° for take-off, 44° for landing; ailerons deflect 16° up or down; airbrakes deflect 55° downward. Non-jettisonable wingtip fuel tanks, incorporating landing/taxying lights.

Fuselage: Metal semi-monocoque structure, built in two portions. Front portion consists of three sections, the first of which is a laminated glassfibre nosecone housing avionics, antennae, battery, compressed air and oxygen bottles and the nose landing gear. Next comes the pressurised compartment for the crew. The third section incorporates the fuel tanks, air intakes and the engine bay. The rear fuselage, carrying the tail unit, is attached by five bolts and can be removed quickly to provide access for engine installation and removal. Two airbrakes side by side under fuselage, just forward of wing leading-edge, actuated by single hydraulic jack; these are lowered automatically as airspeed nears a maximum of Mach 0·8.

Close-up of underfuselage gun installation on Aero L-39 ZA

Aero L-39 ZA version of the Albatros, in Czechoslovak Air Force insignia

Tail Unit: Conventional all-metal cantilever structure, with sweepback on vertical surfaces. Variable incidence tailplane. Control surfaces actuated by pushrods. Electrically operated trim tab in each elevator; servo tab in rudder. Elevators deflect 30° up, 20° down; rudder 30° to right and left.

Landing Gear: Retractable tricycle type, with single wheel and oleo-pneumatic shock absorber on each unit. Gear is designed for a touchdown sink rate of 3·4 m (11·15 ft)/s at AUW of 4,600 kg (10,141 lb). Retraction/extension is operated hydraulically, with electrical control. All wheel well doors close automatically after wheels are lowered, to prevent ingress of dirt and debris. Mainwheels retract inward into wings (with automatic braking during retraction), nosewheel forward into fuselage. K24 mainwheels, fitted with Barum tubeless tyres size 610 × 215 mm (610 × 185 mm on early production aircraft), pressure 5·88 bars (85·34 lb/sq in). K25 castoring and self-centering nosewheel, fitted with Barum tubeless tyre size 450 × 165 mm (430 × 150 mm on early production aircraft), pressure 3·92 bars (56·89 lb/sq in). Hydraulic disc brakes and anti-skid units on mainwheels; shimmy damper on nosewheel leg. The L-39 is capable of operation from grass strips (with a bearing strength of 6 kg/cm²; 85 lb/sq in) at up to 4,600 kg (10,141 lb) T-O weight, or from unprepared runways. Landing gear of L-39 ZA reinforced to cater for higher operating weights.

Power Plant: One 16·87 kN (3,792 lb st) Ivchenko AI-25 TL turbofan engine mounted in rear fuselage, with semicircular lateral air intake, fitted with splitter plate, on each side of fuselage above wing centre-section. Fuel in five rubber main bag tanks aft of cockpit, with combined capacity of 1,055 litres (232 Imp gallons), and two 100 litre (22 Imp gallon) non-jettisonable wingtip tanks. Total internal fuel capacity 1,255 litres (276 Imp gallons). Gravity refuelling points on top of fuselage and on each tip tank. Provision for two 350 litre (77 Imp gallon) drop tanks on inboard underwing pylons, increasing total overall fuel capacity to a maximum of 1,955 litres (430 Imp gallons). Fuel system permits up to 20 s of inverted flight.

Accommodation: Crew of two in tandem, on Czechoslovak VS-1-BRI rocket assisted ejection seats, operable at zero height and at speeds down to 81 knots (150 km/h; 94 mph), beneath individual transparent canopies which hinge sideways to starboard and are jettisonable. Rear seat elevated. One-piece windscreen hinges forward to provide access to front instrument panel. Internal transparency between front and rear cockpits. Dual controls standard.

Systems: Cabin pressurised (standard pressure differential 0·227 bars; 3·29 lb/sq in, max overpressure 0·29 bars; 4·20 lb/sq in) and air-conditioned, using engine bleed air and cooling unit. Air-conditioning system provides automatic temperature control from 10° to 25°C at ambient air temperatures from −55°C to +45°C. Main and standby interconnected hydraulic systems, the main system having a variable flow pump with an operating pressure of 147 bars (2,133 lb/sq in) for actuation of landing gear, flaps, airbrakes, ram air turbine and (at 34·3 bars; 500 lb/sq in pressure) wheel brakes. Emergency system, for all of above except airbrakes, incorporates three accumulators. Pneumatic canopy seals supplied by a 2 litre compressed air bottle in nose (pressure 147 bars; 2,133 lb/sq in). Electrical system (27V DC) is powered by a 7·5kVA engine driven generator. If primary generator fails, a V 910 ram air turbine is extended automatically into the airstream and generates up to 3kVA of emergency power for essential services. 12V 28Ah SAM 28 lead-acid battery for standby power and for APU starting. Two 800VA static inverters (the first for radio equipment, ice warning lights, engine vibration measurement and air-conditioning, the second for navigation and landing systems, IFF and air-to-air missiles) provide 115V single-phase AC power at 400Hz. A second circuit incorporates a 500VA rotary inverter and 40VA static inverter to provide 36V three-phase AC power, also at 400Hz. Saphir 5 APU and SV-25 turbine for engine starting. Air intakes and windscreen anti-iced by engine bleed air; normally, anti-icing is sensor-activated automatically, but a manual standby system is also provided. Six-bottle oxygen system for crew, pressure 147 bars (2,133 lb/sq in).

Avionics and Equipment: Standard avionics include R-832 M two-band com radio (VHF 118-140MHz, UHF 220-389MHz); SPU-9 crew intercom; RKL-41 ADF (150-1,800kHz); RV-5 radar altimeter; MRP-56 P/S marker beacon receiver; SRO-2 IFF; and RSBN-5S navigation and landing system. VOR/ILS system available at customer's option. Landing and taxying light in forward end of each tip tank.

Armament (L-39 Z0 and ZA): Underfuselage pod on ZA only, below front cockpit, housing a single 23 mm Soviet GSh-23 two-barrelled cannon; ammunition for this gun (max 150 rds) is housed in fuselage, above gun pod. Gun/rocket firing and weapon release controls, including electrically controlled ASP-3 NMU-39 Z gyroscopic gunsight and FKP-2-2 gun camera, in front cockpit only (no FKP-2-2 in L-39 V). Z0 and ZA have four underwing hardpoints, the inboard pair each stressed for loads of up to 500 kg (1,102 lb) and the outer pair for loads of up to 250 kg (551 lb) each; max underwing stores load 1,100 kg (2,425 lb). Non-jettisonable pylons, each comprising a D3-57D stores rack. Typical underwing stores can include various combinations of bombs (two 500 kg, four 250 kg or six 100 kg); four UB-16-57 M pods each containing sixteen S-5 57 mm air-to-surface rockets; infra-red air-to-air missiles (outer pylons only); a five-camera day reconnaissance pod (port inboard pylon only); or (on inboard stations only) two 350 litre (77 Imp gallon) drop tanks.

Dimensions, external:

Wing span	9·46 m (31 ft 0½ in)
Wing chord (mean)	2·15 m (7 ft 0½ in)
Wing aspect ratio: geometric	4·4
incl tip tanks	5·2
Length overall	12·13 m (39 ft 9½ in)
Height overall	4·77 m (15 ft 7¾ in)
Tailplane span	4·40 m (14 ft 5 in)
Wheel track	2·44 m (8 ft 0 in)
Wheelbase	4·39 m (14 ft 4¾ in)

Areas:

Wings, gross	18·80 m² (202·36 sq ft)
Ailerons (total)	1·23 m² (13·26 sq ft)
Trailing-edge flaps (total)	2·68 m² (28·89 sq ft)
Airbrakes (total)	0·50 m² (5·38 sq ft)
Vertical tail surfaces (total)	3·51 m² (37·78 sq ft)
Tailplane	3·93 m² (42·30 sq ft)
Elevators, incl tabs	1·14 m² (12·27 sq ft)

*Weights and Loadings:

Weight empty, equipped: C	3,459 kg (7,625 lb)
Z0	3,488 kg (7,690 lb)
ZA	3,656 kg (8,060 lb)
Fuel load: fuselage tanks	824 kg (1,816 lb)
wingtip tanks	156 kg (344 lb)
Max external stores load: C	500 kg (1,102 lb)
Z0 and ZA	1,100 kg (2,425 lb)
T-O weight 'clean': ZA	4,549 kg (10,029 lb)
Max T-O weight: C	4,700 kg (10,362 lb)
Z0 and ZA	5,600 kg (12,346 lb)
Max wing loading: C	250·0 kg/m² (51·23 lb/sq ft)
Z0 and ZA	297·9 kg/m² (61·01 lb/sq ft)
Max power loading: C	278·6 kg/kN (2·73 lb/lb st)
Z0 and ZA	332·0 kg/kN (3·25 lb/lb st)

*Performance (at max T-O weight except where indicated):

Max limiting Mach number	Mach 0·80
Max level speed at S/L:	
C	378 knots (700 km/h; 435 mph)
Z0	329 knots (610 km/h; 379 mph)
Max level speed at 5,000 m (16,400 ft):	
C	405 knots (750 km/h; 466 mph)
Z0	340 knots (630 km/h; 391 mph)
ZA	407 knots (755 km/h; 469 mph)
Stalling speed: C	90 knots (165 km/h; 103 mph)
Z0	98 knots (180 km/h; 112 mph)
Max rate of climb at S/L: C	1,320 m (4,330 ft)/min
Z0	810 m (2,657 ft)/min
ZA	1,260 m (4,130 ft)/min
Time to 5,000 m (16,400 ft): C	5 min
Z0	10 min
Service ceiling: ZA	11,000 m (36,100 ft)
C	11,500 m (37,730 ft)
Z0	7,500 m (24,600 ft)
T-O run (concrete): C, ZA	480 m (1,575 ft)
Z0	970 m (3,182 ft)
Landing run (concrete): C	600 m (1,968 ft)
Z0	800 m (2,625 ft)
Range at 5,000 m (16,400 ft), max internal fuel:	
C	540 nm (1,000 km; 621 miles)
Z0	680 nm (1,260 km; 783 miles)
Ferry range: C	944 nm (1,750 km; 1,087 miles)
Endurance at 5,000 m (16,400 ft): C	2 h 30 min
Z0	3 h 20 min
g limits:	
operational, at 4,200 kg (9,259 lb) AUW	+8/−4
ultimate, at 4,200 kg (9,259 lb) AUW	+12
operational, at 5,500 kg (12,125 lb) AUW	+5·2/−2·6

* *A more detailed listing of weight and performance data for earlier versions can be found in the 1982-83 and previous editions*

LET

LET NÁRODNÍ PODNIK (Let National Corporation)

Uherské Hradiste-Kunovice
Telephone: Kunovice 5121/5
Telex: 060387 and 060388
Managing Director: Ing Stanislav Boura
Technical Director: Ing Zdeněk Karásek
Chief Designer: Ing Vlastimil Mertl
Chief Pilot: Frantisek Srnec

The Let plant at Kunovice was established in 1950, its early activities including licence production of the Soviet Yak-11 piston engined trainer under the Czechoslovak designation C-11. It contributed to the production of the Aero 45, was responsible for the L 200 Morava twin-engined air taxi and Z-37 Cmelák agricultural aircraft, and the L 13 Blanik sailplane; it is currently responsible for production of the L-410UVP-E twin-turboprop light transport aircraft and development of the larger L-610.

The factory also produces equipment for radar and computer technology.

LET L-410UVP-E TURBOLET

Design of the L-410 was started in 1966, by a team led by Ing Ladislav Smrcek. The XL-410 prototype (OK-YKE), powered by Pratt & Whitney Canada PT6A-27 turboprop engines, flew for the first time on 16 April 1969. Three additional PT6A-engined prototypes were completed subsequently; the second of these (designated L-410AB) was later test flown with Hartzell HC-B4TN-3 four-blade propellers in a successful demonstration of reduced vibration and cabin noise levels.

Details of the initial L-410A, L-410AF and L-410M production versions can be found in the 1980-81 and earlier editions of *Jane's*. Variants of these included the L-410AS (L-410A with Soviet avionics), the L-410MA (L-410M with M 601 B instead of M 601 A engines), and L-410MU (L-410MA with changes required by Aeroflot).

Standard production version from the beginning of 1979 until late 1985 was the L-410UVP, of which the first of three prototypes made its initial flight on 1 November 1977. Changes included increased wing span and area; fuselage lengthened by 0·47 m (1 ft 6½ in) compared with the L-410M; enlarged vertical tail surfaces; dihedral tailplane; improved cockpit systems and additions to standard instrumentation; introduction of spoilers, automatic bank control flaps, automatic propeller feathering, and anti-skid system for the main landing gear units; fabric covered elevators and rudder; and M 601 B engines with VJ8 508 B propellers. The L-410UVP was developed to comply with Soviet NLGS-2 airworthiness regulations, and in 1980 became the first non-USSR aircraft to receive a type certificate under these regulations. Stringent Aeroflot requirements included the ability to operate in temperatures ranging from −50°C to +45°C; systems were required to be survivable in temperatures as low as −60°C.

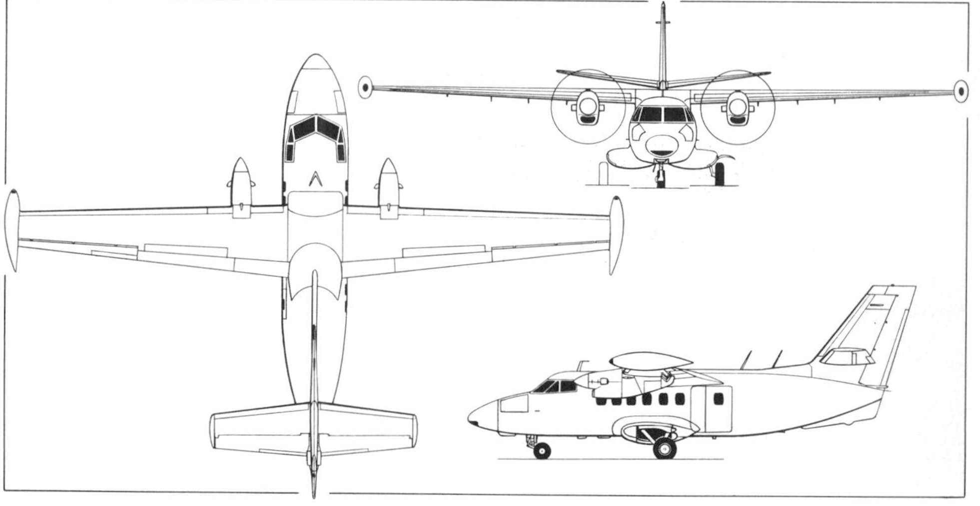

Let L-410UVP-E Turbolet twin-turboprop 19-passenger light transport *(Pilot Press)*

More than 600 L-410s of all versions have been produced for civil and military use, the 500th aircraft for the USSR being delivered to Aeroflot in March 1985. Several hundred more are believed to be required by the Soviet Union.

A prototype (OK-120) was flown in late 1984 of the improved L-410UVP-E, and this entered production in 1985, replacing the UVP. In the UVP-E the rear fuselage has been modified by moving the baggage and toilet compartments further aft, so creating space for four additional passenger seats without increasing overall length. The wings have been reinforced to support two streamlined wingtip tanks, enabling range to be increased by more than 40 per cent. Maximum flap deflection has been increased (to 41°) compared with the UVP, and the spoilers have two fixed deflection angles: 25° (for use in flight) and 72°. Power plant associated changes include a vacuum sintered oil cooler of new design, an oil-to-fuel heat exchanger on each engine firewall to avoid the need for fuel additives at low ambient temperatures, relocation of the engine fire extinguishing bottles under the port rear wing/fuselage fairing and, on the instrument panel, separate speed indicators for each engine and propeller. Cabin improvements include installation of portable oxygen equipment and an improved PA system; a fire extinguishing system is installed in the nose baggage compartment.

The following description applies to the L-410UVP-E:

Type: Twin-turboprop general purpose light transport.

Wings: Cantilever high-wing monoplane. Wing section NACA 63A418 at root, NACA 63A412 at tip. Dihedral 1° 45′. Incidence 2° at root, −0° 30′ at tip. No sweepback at front spar. Conventional all-metal two-spar torsion box structure, attached to fuselage by four-point mountings. Chemically machined skin with longitudinal reinforcement. Hydraulically actuated double-slotted metal flaps, with both slots variable. Spoiler forward of each flap. All-metal ailerons, forward of which are 'pop-up' bank control surfaces that come into operation automatically during single-engine operation and decrease the lift on the side of the running engine. Kléber-Colombes pneumatic de-icing of leading-edges.

Fuselage: Conventional all-metal semi-monocoque spot welded and riveted structure, built in three main portions.

Tail Unit: Conventional cantilever structure, of all-metal construction except for elevators and rudder, which are fabric covered. Vertical tail surfaces swept back 35°; shallow dorsal fin and deeper ventral fin. One-piece tailplane, with 7° dihedral from roots, mounted part-way up fin. Balance tab in rudder and each elevator. Kléber-Colombes pneumatic de-icing of leading-edges.

Landing Gear: Retractable tricycle type, with single wheel on each unit. Hydraulic retraction, nosewheel forward, mainwheels inward to lie flat in fairing on each side of fuselage. Technometra Radotin oleo-pneumatic shock absorbers. Non-braking nosewheel, with servo-assisted steering, fitted with 548 × 221 mm (9·00-6) tubeless tyre, pressure 2·74 bars (39·8 lb/sq in). Nosewheel is also steerable by rudder pedals. Mainwheels fitted with 718 × 306 mm (12·50-10) tubeless tyres, pressure 4·5 bars (65 lb/sq in). All wheels manufactured by Moravan Otrokovice, tyres by Rudy Rijen, Gottwaldow. Moravan Otrokovice hydraulic disc brakes, parking brake and anti-skid units on mainwheels. Metal ski landing gear, with plastics undersurface, optional.

Power Plant: Two 559 kW (750 shp) Motorlet M 601 E turboprop engines, each driving an Avia V 510 five-blade constant-speed reversible-pitch metal propeller with manual and automatic feathering and Beta control. At higher ambient temperatures, engine power can be increased to 590 kW (790 ehp) for short periods by water injection into compressor. De-icing for propeller blades (electrical) and lower intakes; anti-icing flaps inside each nacelle. Eight bag fuel tanks in wings, total capacity 1,290 litres (284 Imp gallons), plus additional 100 kg (220 lb) of fuel in each wingtip tank. Fuel system operable after failure of electrical system. Total oil capacity (incl oil in cooler) 22 litres (4·8 Imp gallons). Water tank capacity (for injection into compressor) 11 litres (2·4 Imp gallons).

Accommodation: Crew of one or two on flight deck, with dual controls. Electric de-icing for windscreen. Standard accommodation in main cabin for 19 passengers, with pairs of adjustable seats on starboard side of aisle and single seats opposite, all at 76 cm (30 in) pitch. Baggage compartment (at rear, accessible from cabin), toilet and wardrobe standard. Cabin heated by engine bleed air. Alternative layouts include all-cargo; ambulance, accommodating six stretchers, five sitting patients and a medical attendant; accommodation for 18 parachutists and a dispatcher/instructor; firefighting configuration, carrying 16 firefighters and a pilot/observer. All-cargo version has protective floor covering, crash nets on each side of cabin, and tiedown provisions; floor is at truckbed height. Aircraft can also be equipped for aerial photography or for calibration of ground navigation aids. Double upward opening doors aft on port side, with stowable steps; right hand door serves as passenger entrance and exit. Both doors open for cargo loading, and can be removed for paratroop training missions. Rearward opening door, forward on starboard side, serves as emergency exit.

Systems: No APU, air-conditioning or pressurisation systems. Duplicated hydraulic systems, No. 1 system actuating landing gear, flaps, spoilers, automatic pitch trim surfaces, mainwheel brakes, nosewheel steering and windscreen wipers. No. 2 system for emergency landing gear extension, flap actuation and parking brake. Electrical system includes AC power from two three-phase 36V 400Hz rotary inverters and two single-phase 115V 400Hz static inverters, guaranteeing against a loss of power for essential instruments; DC power from two 5·6kW generators and two 25Ah batteries. Portable oxygen equipment. Fire extinguisher in nose baggage compartment.

Avionics and Equipment: Standard instrumentation provides for flight in IMC conditions, with all basic instruments duplicated and three artificial horizons. Communications include two VHF with a range of 65 nm (120 km; 75 miles) at 1,000 m (3,280 ft) altitude, and crew intercom. Standard instruments include LUN 1205 horizon gyros, rate of climb indicators, LUN 1215 turn and bank indicator, RMIs, gyro compasses, ILS/SP-50A instrument landing system with marker beacon receiver, ARK-22 ADF, A-037 radio altimeter, SO-69 SSR transponder with encoding altimeter, ASI with stall warning, magnetic compass, GMK-1GE VOR, and analog flight data recorder. Cockpit, instrument and passenger cabin lights, navigation lights, three landing lights in nose (each with two levels of light intensity), crew and cabin fire extinguishers, windscreen wipers, and alcohol spray for windscreen and wiper de-icing, are also standard. Weather radar and VZLU autopilot optional.

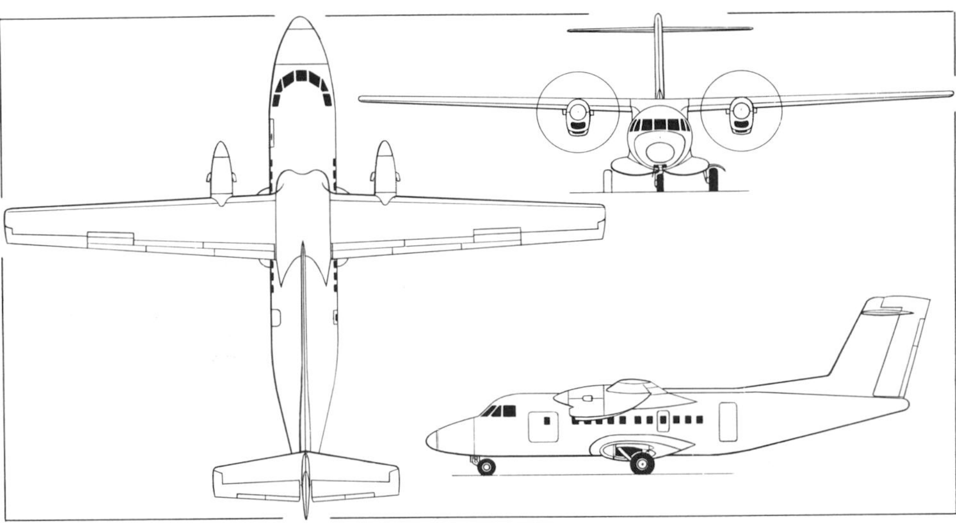

Let L-610 twin-turboprop 40-seat commuter transport *(Pilot Press)*

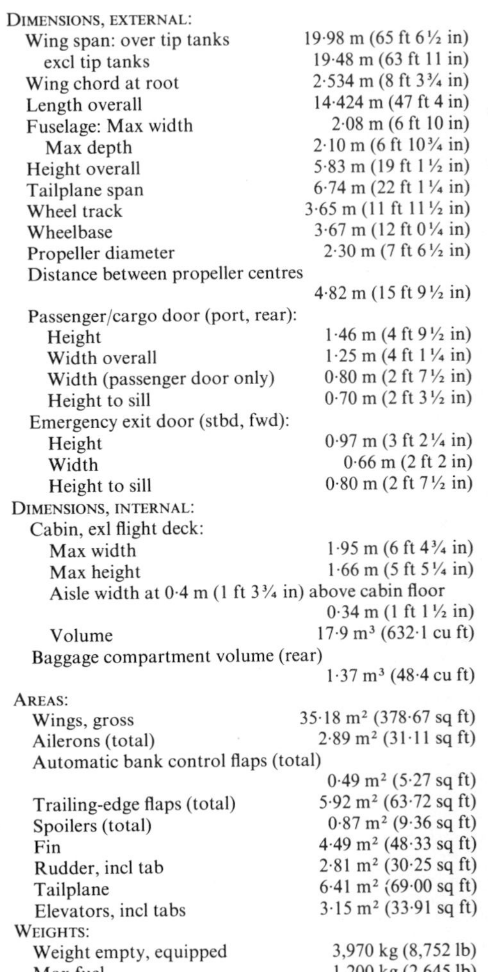

Dimensions, external:

Wing span: over tip tanks	19·98 m (65 ft 6½ in)
excl tip tanks	19·48 m (63 ft 11 in)
Wing chord at root	2·534 m (8 ft 3¾ in)
Length overall	14·424 m (47 ft 4 in)
Fuselage: Max width	2·08 m (6 ft 10 in)
Max depth	2·10 m (6 ft 10¾ in)
Height overall	5·83 m (19 ft 1½ in)
Tailplane span	6·74 m (22 ft 1¼ in)
Wheel track	3·65 m (11 ft 11½ in)
Wheelbase	3·67 m (12 ft 0¼ in)
Propeller diameter	2·30 m (7 ft 6½ in)
Distance between propeller centres	4·82 m (15 ft 9½ in)
Passenger/cargo door (port, rear):	
Height	1·46 m (4 ft 9½ in)
Width overall	1·25 m (4 ft 1¼ in)
Width (passenger door only)	0·80 m (2 ft 7½ in)
Height to sill	0·70 m (2 ft 3½ in)
Emergency exit door (stbd, fwd):	
Height	0·97 m (3 ft 2¼ in)
Width	0·66 m (2 ft 2 in)
Height to sill	0·80 m (2 ft 7½ in)

Dimensions, internal:

Cabin, exl flight deck:	
Max width	1·95 m (6 ft 4¾ in)
Max height	1·66 m (5 ft 5¼ in)
Aisle width at 0·4 m (1 ft 3¾ in) above cabin floor	0·34 m (1 ft 1½ in)
Volume	17·9 m³ (632·1 cu ft)
Baggage compartment volume (rear)	1·37 m³ (48·4 cu ft)

Areas:

Wings, gross	35·18 m² (378·67 sq ft)
Ailerons (total)	2·89 m² (31·11 sq ft)
Automatic bank control flaps (total)	0·49 m² (5·27 sq ft)
Trailing-edge flaps (total)	5·92 m² (63·72 sq ft)
Spoilers (total)	0·87 m² (9·36 sq ft)
Fin	4·49 m² (48·33 sq ft)
Rudder, incl tab	2·81 m² (30·25 sq ft)
Tailplane	6·41 m² (69·00 sq ft)
Elevators, incl tabs	3·15 m² (33·91 sq ft)

Weights:

Weight empty, equipped	3,970 kg (8,752 lb)
Max fuel	1,200 kg (2,645 lb)
Max payload	1,615 kg (3,560 lb)
Max T-O weight	6,400 kg (14,110 lb)
Max landing weight	6,200 kg (13,668 lb)

Performance (at max T-O weight):

Normal cruising speed at 4,200 m (13,780 ft)	202 knots (375 km/h; 233 mph)
Econ cruising speed at 4,200 m (13,780 ft)	197 knots (365 km/h; 227 mph)
Max rate of climb at S/L, ISA	432 m (1,415 ft)/min
Rate of climb at S/L, one engine out, ISA	108 m (355 ft)/min
Absolute ceiling	6,000 m (19,685 ft)
Service ceiling	4,200 m (13,780 ft)
Service ceiling, one engine out	3,650 m (11,975 ft)
Range with max payload, tip tanks empty, 45 min reserves	272 nm (505 km; 313 miles)
Theoretical range with 900 kg (1,984 lb) payload and max fuel, 20 min reserves	744 nm (1,380 km; 857 miles)

L-410UVP-E Turbolet twin-turboprop general purpose transport, with wingtip tanks and five-blade propellers

LET L-610

Intended for certification in 1990 under Soviet ENLG-S civil airworthiness requirements, the L-610 is designed for short-haul operations over stage lengths of 216-324 nm (400-600 km; 248-373 miles). It is scheduled to fly for the first time in late 1987 or early 1988.

Type: Twin-turboprop transport aircraft.

Wings: Cantilever high-wing monoplane. Wing sections MS(1)-0318D at root, MS(1)-0312 at tip, with respective thickness/chord ratios of 18·29% and 12%. Dihedral 2°.

Incidence 3° 8′ 38·4″ at root, 0° at tip. Sweepback 1° at quarter-chord. All-metal fail-safe stressed skin structure, built of high grade aluminium alloys and high strength steel and incorporating sandwich panels. All-metal horn balanced ailerons and single-slotted trailing-edge flaps. Spoiler, of sandwich construction, forward of each outer flap segment. Electro-mechanically actuated trim tab in port aileron. Pneumatic de-icing of leading-edges.

FUSELAGE: Pressurised all-metal semi-monocoque structure, incorporating fail-safe principles. Central portion has a constant circular cross-section.

TAIL UNIT: All-metal structure, with sweptback fin and rudder and long dorsal fin. Non-swept tailplane and elevators mounted near top of fin. Trim tab and balance tab in rudder and each elevator. Pneumatic de-icing of leading-edges.

LANDING GEAR: Retractable tricycle type, with single wheel on each unit. Hydraulic actuation, mainwheels retracting inward to lie flat in fairing each side of fuselage, nosewheel retracting forward. Oleo-pneumatic shock absorber in each unit. Mainwheels are type XK 34-3000.00, with 1,050 × 390 × 480 mm tyres; type XR 25-1000.00 nosewheel has a 720 × 310 × 254 mm tyre. Hydraulic disc brakes and electronically controlled anti-skid units.

POWER PLANT: Two 1,358 kW (1,822 shp) Motorlet M 602 turboprop engines, each driving an Avia V-518 five-blade fully-feathering metal propeller with reversible pitch. Fuel in two integral wing tanks, combined capacity 3,500 litres (770 Imp gallons). Pressure refuelling point in fuselage, gravity points in wings. Oil capacity 30 litres (6·6 Imp gallons).

ACCOMMODATION: Crew of two on flight deck, plus one cabin attendant. Standard accommodation for 40 passengers, four-abreast at seat pitch of 75 cm (29·5 in). Galley, two wardrobes, toilet, freight and baggage compartment, all located at rear of cabin. Passenger door at rear of fuselage, freight door at front, both opening outward on port side. Outward opening service door on starboard side, opposite passenger door, serving also as emergency exit; outward opening emergency exit beneath wing on each side. Entire accommodation pressurised and air-conditioned.

SYSTEMS: Bootstrap type air-conditioning system. Max operating cabin pressure differential 0·3 bars (4·35 lb/sq in). Duplicated hydraulic systems, operating at pressure of 210 bars (3,045 lb/sq in). APU for engine starting and auxiliary on-ground and in-flight power. Electrical system powered by two 115/200V 25kVA variable frequency AC generators, plus a third 8kVA 115/200V three-phase AC generator driven by APU. System also includes two 115V 400Hz inverters (each 1·5kVA), two 27V DC transformer-rectifiers (each 4·5kW), and a 25Ah nickel-cadmium battery for APU starting and auxiliary power supply. Portable oxygen equipment for crew and 10 per cent of passengers. Pneumatic de-icing of wing and tail unit leading-edges, engine inlets and oil cooler; electric de-icing of propeller blades, windscreen, pitot static system and horn balances.

AVIONICS AND EQUIPMENT: Equipped as standard with dual 760-channel VHF com, single HF com, intercom, cabin address system, weather radar, blind-flying instrumentation, dual ILS with two LOC/glideslope receivers and two marker beacon receivers, dual ADF, Doppler velocity sensor, navigation computer, dual compasses, radio altimeter, transponder, GPWS, AFCS, voice recorder, flight recorder, and Category II approach aids.

DIMENSIONS, EXTERNAL:

Wing span	25·60 m (84 ft 0 in)
Wing chord: at root	2·917 m (9 ft 6⅞ in)
at tip	1·458 m (4 ft 9½ in)
Wing aspect ratio	11·703
Length overall	21·419 m (70 ft 3¼ in)
Fuselage: Length	20·533 m (67 ft 4⅜ in)
Max diameter	2·70 m (8 ft 10¼ in)
Distance between propeller centres	7·00 m (22 ft 11½ in)
Height overall	7·608 m (24 ft 11½ in)
Tailplane span	7·908 m (25 ft 11⅓ in)
Wheel track	4·59 m (15 ft 0¾ in)
Wheelbase	6·596 m (21 ft 7¾ in)
Propeller diameter	3·50 m (11 ft 5¾ in)
Propeller ground clearance	1·59 m (5 ft 2½ in)
Passenger door: Height	1·625 m (5 ft 4 in)
Width	0·76 m (2 ft 6 in)
Height to sill	1·448 m (4 ft 9 in)
Freight door: Height	1·30 m (4 ft 3¼ in)
Width	1·25 m (4 ft 1¼ in)
Height to sill	1·448 m (4 ft 9 in)
Service door: Height	1·286 m (4 ft 2⅔ in)
Width	0·61 m (2 ft 0 in)
Emergency exits (underwing, each):	
Height	0·915 m (3 ft 0 in)
Width	0·515 m (1 ft 8¼ in)

DIMENSIONS, INTERNAL:

Cabin: Length	11·10 m (36 ft 5 in)
Max width	2·54 m (8 ft 4 in)
Width at floor	2·02 m (6 ft 7½ in)
Max height	1·825 m (5 ft 11⅞ in)
Floor area	22·4 m² (241·1 sq ft)
Volume	44·1 m³ (1,557·4 cu ft)
Wardrobe volume (total)	1·0 m³ (35·3 cu ft)
Baggage/freight hold volume (total)	4·3 m³ (151·8 cu ft)

AREAS:

Wings, gross	56·0 m² (602·8 sq ft)
Ailerons (total)	3·27 m² (35·20 sq ft)
Trailing-edge flaps (total)	11·29 m² (121·52 sq ft)
Spoilers (total)	3·54 m² (38·10 sq ft)
Fin	8·30 m² (89·34 sq ft)
Rudder, incl tabs	5·54 m² (59·63 sq ft)
Tailplane	7·68 m² (82·67 sq ft)
Elevators (total, incl tabs)	5·82 m² (62·65 sq ft)

WEIGHTS AND LOADINGS:

Operating weight empty	9,000 kg (19,841 lb)
Max fuel	2,650 kg (5,842 lb)
Max payload	3,800 kg (8,377 lb)
Max T-O weight	14,000 kg (30,865 lb)
Max ramp weight	14,040 kg (30,953 lb)
Max landing weight	13,500 kg (29,762 lb)
Max zero-fuel weight	12,800 kg (28,219 lb)
Max wing loading	250 kg/m² (51·2 lb/sq ft)
Max power loading	5·147 kg/kW (8·47 lb/shp)

PERFORMANCE (estimated at max T-O weight):

Never-exceed speed	216 knots (400 km/h; 248 mph) EAS
Max level and max cruising speed at 7,200 m (23,620 ft)	264 knots (490 km/h; 304 mph)
Long range cruising speed at 7,200 m (23,620 ft)	220 knots (408 km/h; 253 mph)
Stalling speed:	
flaps up	93 knots (172 km/h; 107 mph) EAS
flaps down	75 knots (139 km/h; 87 mph) EAS
Max rate of climb at S/L	570 m (1,870 ft)/min
Rate of climb at S/L, one engine out	150 m (492 ft)/min
Service ceiling:	
theoretical	10,750 m (35,270 ft)
practical	10,250 m (33,630 ft)
Service ceiling, one engine out (30·5 m; 100 ft/min rate of climb):	
theoretical	4,750 m (15,585 ft)
practical	3,980 m (13,060 ft)
Min ground turning radius	18·33 m (60 ft 1¾ in)
T-O run	370 m (1,214 ft)
T-O to 10·7 m (35 ft)	613 m (2,011 ft)
Balanced T-O distance	752 m (2,467 ft)
Balanced T-O field length	873 m (2,864 ft)
Landing from 9 m (30 ft)	545 m (1,788 ft)
Landing run	340 m (1,115 ft)
Range, reserves for 45 min hold:	
with max payload	410 nm (760 km; 472 miles)
with max fuel	1,160 nm (2,150 km; 1,336 miles)

ZLIN

MORAVAN NÁRODNÍ PODNIK (Zlin Aircraft Moravan National Corporation)

76581 Otrokovice
Telephone: Gottwaldov 92 2041-44
Telex: Gottwaldov 067 334
MANAGING DIRECTOR: Frantisek Klapil
VICE-DIRECTORS:
Ing Jan Bartoň (Technical)
Ing Vladimír Otřísal (Production)
František Mužný (Sales)
Ing Miroslav Žůrek (Works Economy)
CHIEF DESIGNER: Ing Jirí Navrátil
CHIEF PILOT: Zdenek Polásek
SALES MANAGER: František Mužný

The Moravan works, responsible for production of the famous range of Zlin aerobatic and light touring aircraft, was formed originally on 18 September 1934 as Zlinská Letecká Akciová Spolecnost (Zlin Aviation Joint Stock Co) in Zlin, although manufacture of Zlin aircraft was actually started in 1933 by the Masarykova Letecká Liga (Masaryk League of Aviation). The factory was renamed Moravan after the second World War. Moravan also manufactures items of aircraft equipment.

ZLIN 142

The Zlin 142 is intended for basic and advanced flying training, aerobatic flying and the training of aerobatic pilots, glider towing, and (when equipped with appropriate instrumentation) for night and IFR flying training. It is a progressive development of the Zlin 42 M (see 1980-81 *Jane's*). Design began in the Winter of 1977-78, and the prototype (OK-078) flew for the first time on 29 December 1978. In 1980 it received FAR Pt 23 certification in the Aerobatic, Utility and Normal categories, and production began in 1981. This was continuing in 1985, and 200 had been delivered by 1 January 1986. Exports have been made to Cuba, Germany (Democratic and Federal Republics), Hungary, Poland and Romania.

TYPE: Two-seat fully aerobatic (A), light training (U) and touring (N) aircraft.

WINGS: Cantilever low-wing monoplane. Wing section NACA $63_2$416·5. Dihedral 6° from roots. Sweepforward 4° 20′ at quarter-chord. All-metal structure with single main spar and auxiliary spar; skins (fluted on control

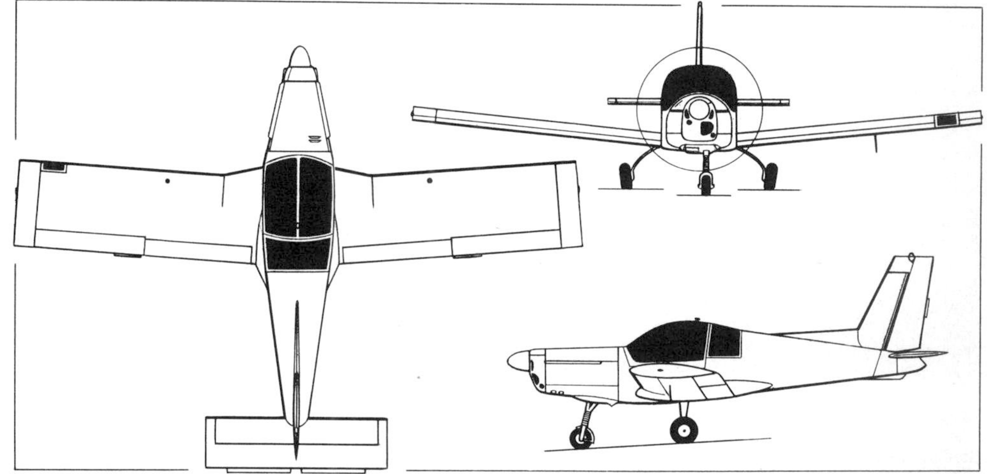

Photograph and three-view drawing *(Pilot Press)* **of the Zlin 142 two-seat aerobatic, training and touring aircraft**

surfaces) of aluminium plated duralumin sheet. All-metal slotted ailerons and flaps all have same dimensions. Mass balanced flaps and ailerons, operated mechanically by control rods. Ground adjustable tab on each aileron.

FUSELAGE: Engine cowlings of sheet metal. Centre-fuselage of welded steel tube truss construction, covered with laminated glassfibre panels. Rear fuselage is all-metal semi-monocoque structure.

TAIL UNIT: Cantilever all-metal structure with skins (fluted on control surfaces) of duralumin sheet. Control surfaces have partial mass and aerodynamic balance. Trim tabs on elevator and rudder. Rudder actuated by control cables, elevator by control rods.

LANDING GEAR: Non-retractable tricycle type, with nosewheel offset to port. Oleo-pneumatic nosewheel shock absorber. Mainwheels carried on flat spring steel legs. Nosewheel steered by rudder pedals. Mainwheels and Barum tyres size 420 × 150, pressure 1·90 bars (27·6 lb/sq in); nosewheel and Barum tyre size 350 × 135, pressure 2·50 bars (36·3 lb/sq in). Hydraulic disc brakes on mainwheels can be operated from either seat. Parking brake standard.

POWER PLANT: One 156·5 kW (210 hp) Avia M 337 AK inverted six-cylinder aircooled inline engine, with supercharger and low-pressure injection pump, driving a two-blade Avia V 500 A constant-speed metal propeller. Fuel tanks in each wing leading-edge, with combined capacity of 125 litres (27·5 Imp gallons). Normal category version has auxiliary 50 litre (11 Imp gallon) tank at each wingtip, increasing total fuel capacity to 225 litres (49·5 Imp gallons). Fuel and oil systems permit inverted flying for up to 3 min. Oil capacity 12 litres (2·6 Imp gallons).

ACCOMMODATION: Individual side by side seats for two persons, the main pilot's seat being to port. Both seats are adjustable and permit the use of back type parachutes. Baggage space aft of seats. Cabin and windscreen heating and ventilation standard. Forward sliding cockpit canopy. Dual controls standard.

SYSTEMS: Electrical system includes a 600W 27V engine driven generator and 24V 25Ah Teledyne battery. External power source can be used for starting the engine.

AVIONICS AND EQUIPMENT: VHF radio with IC (Mesit LUN 3524.20) and IFR instrumentation optional. Standard equipment includes cockpit, instrument and cabin lights; navigation lights; landing and taxying lights; and anti-collision light. Towing gear, for gliders of up to 500 kg (1,102 lb) weight, optional.

DIMENSIONS, EXTERNAL:

Wing span	9·16 m (30 ft 0½ in)
Wing chord (constant portion)	1·42 m (4 ft 8 in)
Length overall	7·33 m (24 ft 0½ in)
Height overall	2·75 m (9 ft 0¼ in)
Elevator span	2·904 m (9 ft 6⅓ in)
Wheel track	2·33 m (7 ft 7¾ in)
Wheelbase	1·66 m (5 ft 5¼ in)
Propeller diameter	2·00 m (6 ft 6¾ in)
Propeller ground clearance	0·40 m (1 ft 3¾ in)

DIMENSIONS, INTERNAL:

Cabin: Length	1·80 m (5 ft 10¾ in)
Max width	1·12 m (3 ft 8 in)
Max height	1·20 m (3 ft 11¼ in)
Baggage space	0·2 m³ (7·1 cu ft)

AREAS:

Wings, gross	13·15 m² (141·5 sq ft)
Ailerons (total)	1·408 m² (15·16 sq ft)
Trailing-edge flaps (total)	1·408 m² (15·16 sq ft)
Fin	0·54 m² (5·81 sq ft)
Rudder, incl tab	0·81 m² (8·72 sq ft)
Tailplane	1·23 m² (13·24 sq ft)
Elevator, incl tabs	1·36 m² (14·64 sq ft)

WEIGHTS AND LOADINGS (A: Aerobatic; U: Utility; N: Normal category):

Basic weight empty (all versions)	730 kg (1,609 lb)
Max T-O weight: A	970 kg (2,138 lb)
U	1,020 kg (2,248 lb)
N	1,090 kg (2,403 lb)
Max landing weight: A	970 kg (2,138 lb)
U	1,020 kg (2,248 lb)
N	1,050 kg (2,315 lb)
Max wing loading: A	73·76 kg/m² (15·11 lb/sq ft)
U	77·57 kg/m² (15·89 lb/sq ft)
N	82·89 kg/m² (16·98 lb/sq ft)
Max power loading: A	6·19 kg/kW (10·17 lb/hp)
U	6·51 kg/kW (10·69 lb/hp)
N	6·96 kg/kW (11·43 lb/hp)

PERFORMANCE (at max T-O weight):

Never-exceed speed (all versions)	179 knots (333 km/h; 206 mph) IAS
Max level speed at 500 m (1,640 ft):	
A, U	125 knots (231 km/h; 143 mph)
N	122 knots (227 km/h; 141 mph)
Max cruising speed at 500 m (1,640 ft):	
A, U	106 knots (197 km/h; 122 mph)
N	102 knots (190 km/h; 118 mph)
Econ cruising speed at 500 m (1,640 ft):	
A	97 knots (180 km/h; 112 mph)
Stalling speed, flaps up:	
A	56 knots (103 km/h; 64 mph) IAS
U	58 knots (107 km/h; 67 mph) IAS
N	60 knots (110 km/h; 69 mph) IAS
Stalling speed, T-O flap setting:	
A	54 knots (99 km/h; 62 mph) IAS
U	56 knots (102 km/h; 64 mph) IAS
N	57 knots (105 km/h; 66 mph) IAS
Stalling speed, flaps down:	
A	48 knots (88 km/h; 55 mph) IAS
U	50 knots (91 km/h; 57 mph) IAS
N	52 knots (95 km/h; 60 mph) IAS
Max rate of climb at S/L, ISA:	
A	330 m (1,082 ft)/min
U	306 m (1,004 ft)/min
N	264 m (866 ft)/min
Service ceiling: A	5,000 m (16,400 ft)
U	4,700 m (15,425 ft)
N	4,300 m (14,100 ft)
T-O run: A	220 m (722 ft)
T-O to 15 m (50 ft): A	440 m (1,444 ft)
U	475 m (1,560 ft)
N	540 m (1,772 ft)
Landing from 15 m (50 ft): A	400 m (1,313 ft)
U	425 m (1,395 ft)
N	460 m (1,510 ft)
Landing run: A	190 m (624 ft)
Range at max cruising speed:	
A, U	283 nm (525 km; 326 miles)
N	513 nm (950 km; 590 miles)
Max range: N	566 nm (1,050 km; 652 miles)
g limits: A	+6/−3·5
U	+5/−3
N	+3·8/−1·5

Zlin Z 50 LS single-seat aerobatic light aircraft

ZLIN Z 50 LS

Production of the Z 50 for export ended in 1981; manufacture of about 50 for the Czechoslovak Federal Aeroclub was undertaken in 1983. Full details of the original Z 50 L version, with 194 kW (260 hp) Avco Lycoming AEIO-540-D4B5 engine, can be found in the 1982-83 *Jane's*. Series production was continuing in 1986 of the more powerful Z 50 LS, to which the following details apply. This version was flown for the first time on 29 June 1981, and in the following year received FAR Pt 23 certification in the Aerobatic and Normal categories. It won the European Aerobatic Championships in 1983 and the World Championships in 1984 and 1986; in 1985 it came 1st and 2nd in the European Championships, and won nine of the first 22 places. A total of 40 Z 50 L/LS had been delivered by mid-1985.

TYPE: Single-seat aerobatic aircraft.

WINGS: Cantilever low-wing monoplane. Wing section NACA 0018 at root, NACA 0012 at tip. Dihedral 1° 7′ 24″. All-metal structure, with single continuous main spar, rear auxiliary spar, and aluminium-clad duralumin skin. All-metal mass balanced ailerons, actuated by pushrods, occupy most of each trailing-edge. Ground adjustable tab on port outer aileron; automatic trim tab on each inboard aileron. No flaps. Provision for fitting wingtip fuel tanks for cross-country flights.

FUSELAGE: All-metal semi-monocoque structure with stressed duralumin skin.

TAIL UNIT: Conventional metal structure. Braced tailplane and fin duralumin covered, elevators and rudder fabric covered. One mechanically adjustable balance tab and one automatic trim tab on elevators; automatic balance tab on rudder. Elevators actuated by pushrods, rudder by cables.

LANDING GEAR: Non-retractable tailwheel type. Mainwheels carried on flat-spring titanium cantilever legs. Mechanical mainwheel brakes actuated by rudder pedals. Fully castoring tailwheel, with flat-spring shock absorption, has automatic locking device to maintain aircraft on a straight track during taxying, take-off and landing. Mainwheel tyres size 350 × 135 mm, pressure 2·5 bars (36 lb/sq in); tailwheel tyre size 200 × 80 mm, pressure 1·0 bar (14·5 lb/sq in). Mainwheel fairings optional.

POWER PLANT: One 224 kW (300 hp) Avco Lycoming AEIO-540-L1B5D flat-six engine, driving a Hoffmann HO-V123K-V/200AH three-blade constant-speed wooden propeller with spinner. Single main fuel tank in fuselage, aft of firewall, capacity 60 litres (13·2 Imp gallons). Auxiliary 50 litre (11 Imp gallon) tank can be attached to each wingtip for cross-country flights only. Fuel and oil systems designed for full aerobatic manoeuvres, including inverted flight. Oil capacity 12 litres (2·64 Imp gallons).

ACCOMMODATION: Single seat under fully transparent sideways opening (to starboard) bubble canopy, which can be jettisoned in an emergency. Seat and backrest are adjustable, and permit the use of a back type parachute. Cockpit ventilated by sliding panel in canopy.

SYSTEM: Electrical system includes an alternator as main power source and a Varley battery. External power socket in fuselage side for engine starting.

AVIONICS: VHF radio optional.

DIMENSIONS, EXTERNAL:

Wing span	8·58 m (28 ft 1¾ in)
Wing span over tip tanks	9·03 m (29 ft 7½ in)
Wing chord: at root	1·73 m (5 ft 8¼ in)
at tip	1·21 m (3 ft 11¾ in)
Wing aspect ratio	5·88
Length overall (tail up)	6·62 m (21 ft 8¾ in)
Height over tail (static)	2·075 m (6 ft 9¾ in)
Elevator span	3·44 m (11 ft 3½ in)
Wheel track	1·90 m (6 ft 2¾ in)
Wheelbase	5·05 m (16 ft 7 in)
Propeller diameter	2·00 m (6 ft 6¾ in)
Propeller ground clearance (tail up)	0·31 m (1 ft 0¼ in)

AREAS:

Wings, gross	12·50 m² (134·55 sq ft)
Ailerons (total)	2·80 m² (30·14 sq ft)
Fin	0·59 m² (6·35 sq ft)
Rudder, incl tab	0·81 m² (8·72 sq ft)
Tailplane	1·66 m² (17·87 sq ft)
Elevators (total, incl tabs)	1·20 m² (12·92 sq ft)

WEIGHTS AND LOADINGS (A: Aerobatic, N: Normal category):

Weight empty: A	600 kg (1,322 lb)
N	610 kg (1,345 lb)
Max T-O weight: A	760 kg (1,675 lb)
N	840 kg (1,852 lb)
Max wing loading: A	60·8 kg/m² (12·45 lb/sq ft)
N	67·2 kg/m² (13·76 lb/sq ft)
Max power loading: A	3·40 kg/kW (5·58 lb/hp)
N	3·75 kg/kW (6·17 lb/hp)

PERFORMANCE (at max Aerobatic T-O weight):

Never-exceed speed	181 knots (337 km/h; 209 mph) CAS
Max level speed at 500 m (1,640 ft), ISA	166 knots (308 km/h; 191 mph)
Max cruising speed at 500 m (1,640 ft), ISA	148 knots (275 km/h; 171 mph)
Stalling speed, engine idling	56 knots (103 km/h; 81 mph) CAS
Max rate of climb at S/L, ISA	840 m (2,755 ft)/min
Service ceiling, ISA	8,175 m (26,820 ft)
T-O run	150 m (492 ft)
T-O to 15 m (50 ft)	300 m (985 ft)
Landing from 15 m (50 ft)	530 m (1,740 ft)
Landing run	300 m (985 ft)
g limits: A	+8/−6
N	+3·8/−1·5

ZLIN Z 37T AGRO TURBO

The piston engined Z-37A Cmelák (Bumble-bee) agricultural aircraft, of which more than 700 were built by Let (651 plus 26 two-seaters) and Moravan, was last described in the 1976-77 *Jane's*. Let then built an XZ-37T prototype (OK-146) of a turboprop version, powered by a 515 kW (691 shp) Walter M 601 B engine, which flew for the first time on 6 September 1981. Brief details of this prototype appeared in the 1982-83 *Jane's*.

In 1982 Moravan began the design and construction of a lower powered turbine engined version known as the Z 37T. Two prototypes of this version were completed initially (OK-072 and OK-074), making their first flights on 12 July and 29 December 1983 respectively; a third was completed in 1985. Certification under BCAR Section K was received in 1984, followed by the start of series production in 1985. First delivery of a production aircraft, to Slov-Air for operational trials, was made in 1985.

Moravan plans to build the Z 37T at an initial rate of 60 a year, and expects that at least 500 will be manufactured eventually. Exports to other Comecon countries were expected to begin during the first half of 1986.

TYPE: Single/two-seat agricultural aircraft.

WINGS: Cantilever low-wing monoplane. Wing section NACA 33015 at root, NACA 44012A at tip. Dihedral 7° on outer panels only. Incidence 3° at root, 0° at tip. All-metal single-spar structure, with auxiliary rear spar, comprising centre-section, built integrally with fuselage, and two outer panels. Linen covered duralumin ailerons, each with ground adjustable tab. All-metal duralumin skinned double-slotted trailing-edge flaps. Leading-edge fixed slats. Outward canted winglet at each tip.

FUSELAGE: Welded steel tube structure, with part-metal, part-linen covering.

TAIL UNIT: Cantilever all-metal two-spar structure. Elevator aerodynamically and mass balanced. Trim tabs in rudder and centre of elevator, latter controlled from cockpit.

LANDING GEAR: Non-retractable tailwheel type, with Technometra oleo-pneumatic mainwheel shock absorbers, Moravan light alloy wheels and Barum tyres. Mainwheel tyres size 556 × 163 × 254 mm, tailwheel tyre size 290 × 110 mm; pressure 3·45 bars (50 lb/sq in) on all units. Moravan hydraulic brakes on mainwheels.

POWER PLANT: One 365 kW (490 shp) Motorlet M 601 Z turboprop engine, driving an Avia VJ7-508Z three-blade constant-speed propeller. Two metal fuel tanks in wing centre-section, combined capacity 350 litres (77 Imp gallons). Fuel can be transported to distant airstrips in four auxiliary tanks with a combined capacity of 500 litres (110 Imp gallons). Gravity refuelling point in top of each wing. Oil capacity 7 litres (1·5 Imp gallons). Air intake filter.

ACCOMMODATION: Pilot in enclosed cockpit, with forward opening window/door on starboard side. Auxiliary seat to rear for one passenger (mechanic or loader). Cockpit heated, and provided with filtered fresh air intake, contoured seat with headrest, rearview mirror and windscreen wiper. Door can be jettisoned in an emergency. Two-seat training version under development.

SYSTEMS: Pneumatic system of 50 bars (725 lb/sq in) pressure, reduced to 30 bars (435 lb/sq in) for agricultural equipment and flaps. Electrical power supplied by 28V 5·6kW DC starter/generator.

AVIONICS AND EQUIPMENT: LUN 3524 VHF radio standard. Hopper/tank capacity (max) 1,000 litres (220 Imp gallons) of liquid or 900 kg (1,984 lb) of dry chemical. Distribution system for both liquid and dry chemicals is operated pneumatically. Chemicals can be jettisoned in 5 s in emergency. Steel cable cutter on windscreen and each mainwheel leg; steel deflector cable runs from tip of windscreen cable cutter to tip of fin. Windscreen washer and wiper standard. Other equipment includes gyro compass, clock, rearview mirror, second (mechanic's) seat, cockpit air-conditioning, ventilation and heating, and anti-collision light. Can be modified for firefighting role.

DIMENSIONS, EXTERNAL:
- Wing span — 13·63 m (44 ft 8½ in)
- Wing chord: at root — 2·39 m (7 ft 10 in)

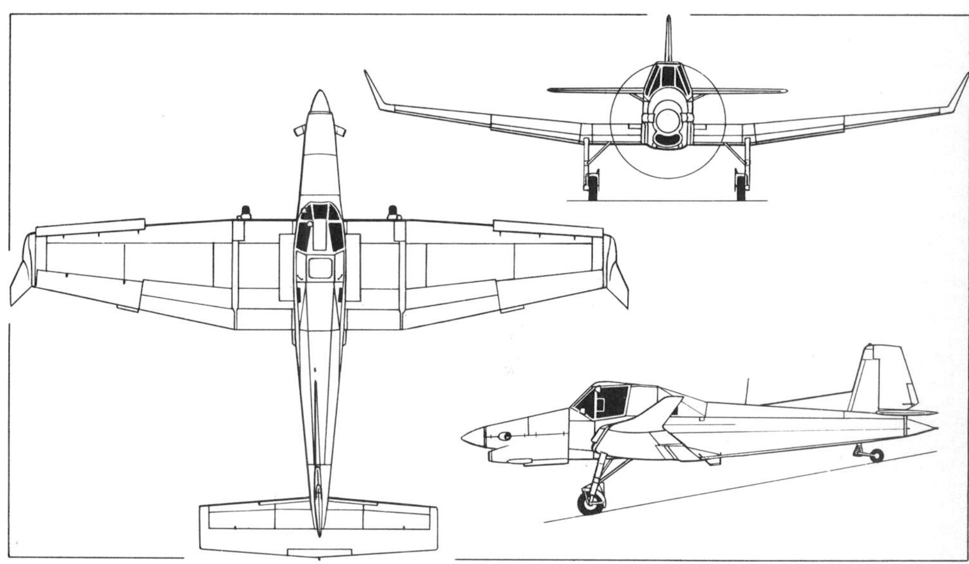

Zlin Z 37T Agro Turbo agricultural aircraft, which entered production in 1985 *(Pilot Press)*

Zlin Z 37T Agro Turbo fitted with agricultural spraygear

- at tip — 1·224 m (4 ft 0¼ in)
- Wing aspect ratio — 6·96
- Length overall (flying attitude) — 10·46 m (34 ft 4 in)
- Fuselage: Max width — 1·70 m (5 ft 7 in)
- Height overall — 3·505 m (11 ft 6 in)
- Elevator span — 5·294 m (17 ft 4½ in)
- Wheel track — 3·30 m (10 ft 10 in)
- Wheelbase — 6·375 m (20 ft 11 in)
- Propeller diameter — 2·50 m (8 ft 2½ in)
- Propeller ground clearance (min) — 0·45 m (1 ft 5¾ in)

AREAS:
- Wings, gross — 26·69 m² (287·3 sq ft)
- Ailerons (total) — 2·428 m² (26·13 sq ft)
- Trailing-edge flaps (total) — 4·37 m² (47·04 sq ft)
- Fin — 1·185 m² (12·76 sq ft)
- Rudder, incl tab — 1·054 m² (11·35 sq ft)
- Tailplane — 2·776 m² (29·88 sq ft)
- Elevator, incl tab — 3·008 m² (32·38 sq ft)

WEIGHTS AND LOADINGS:
- Weight empty with basic agricultural equipment — 1,250 kg (2,756 lb)
- Max payload — 900 kg (1,984 lb)
- Max fuel — 280 kg (617 lb)
- Max T-O weight: ferry flights — 2,260 kg (4,982 lb)
- agricultural, forestry and waterways work — 2,525 kg (5,566 lb)
- Max zero-fuel weight — 2,250 kg (4,960 lb)
- Max wing loading — 89·9 kg/m² (18·41 lb/sq ft)
- Max power loading — 6·67 kg/kW (10·95 lb/shp)

PERFORMANCE (at 2,525 kg; 5,566 lb max T-O weight):
- Never-exceed speed — 153 knots (285 km/h; 177 mph)
- Max level speed at 500 m (1,640 ft) — 118 knots (218 km/h; 135 mph)
- Max cruising speed at 500 m (1,640 ft) — 103 knots (190 km/h; 118 mph)
- Working speed — 78-89 knots (145-165 km/h; 90-103 mph)
- Stalling speed:
  - flaps up — 48 knots (88 km/h; 55 mph)
  - flaps down — 42 knots (77 km/h; 48 mph)
- Max rate of climb at S/L — 252 m (827 ft)/min
- T-O run — 265 m (870 ft)
- T-O to 15 m (50 ft) — 580 m (1,905 ft)
- Landing from 15 m (50 ft) — 720 m (2,365 ft)
- Landing run — 300 m (985 ft)
- Range with max fuel — 188 nm (350 km; 217 miles)
- Swath width: granules — 30 m (98 ft)
  - liquid — 40 m (131 ft)
- *g* limits — +3·2/−1·28

EGYPT

AOI

ARAB ORGANISATION FOR INDUSTRIALISATION

PO Box 70, Cairo
CHAIRMAN: Ahmed Zendou

Aircraft Factory (36), Helwan
CHAIRMAN: Ahmed Heiba

Engine Factory (135), Helwan
CHAIRMAN: Hassen El Gebali

Kader Factory (72), PO Box 287, Orouba Street, Heliopolis
CHAIRMAN: Karim El Leithy

SAKR Factory (333), PO Box 33, Heliopolis
CHAIRMAN: Ahmed F. Ismail

Avionics Factory
CHAIRMAN: Mohamed Nour Youssef

SUBSIDIARIES:
Arab American Vehicle Co (AAVCo)
Arab British Dynamics Co (ABDCo)
Arab British Engine Co (ABECo), Helwan
Arab British Helicopter Co (ABHCo), PO Box 73, Helwan

The AOI was set up in November 1975 by Egypt, Saudi Arabia, Qatar and the United Arab Emirates, with a capital of more than $1,000 million, to provide the basis for an Arab military industry. The main centres of production were to be in the Cairo area, using and building upon the extensive facilities already existing. Initial plans to manufacture the Westland Lynx and its Rolls-Royce Gem engine under licence were terminated in 1979 when Saudi Arabia, Qatar and the UAE withdrew from the partnership following the Camp David agreement between Egypt and Israel.

Since then, however, the AOI has gained strength as a purely Egyptian based organisation, and is now engaged in several important aircraft, aero engine and other military programmes. It is organised into five divisions, which between them have a workforce of about 20,000 people, including approximately 3,000 employed in its four subsidiaries. Rockets, missiles and other weapons are produced by the SAKR Factory near Cairo (except for the Swingfire programme, which is managed by ABDCo); armoured and other military vehicles are manufactured by the Kader Factory, at Heliopolis, and the AAVCo.

Egypt's long term intention is to become completely self-sufficient in the manufacture of arms and other military equipment. It is absorbing a gradual transfer of technology from Western manufacturers, beginning with licence production of aircraft main components, subassemblies and complete systems.

The main centre for this resurgence is Helwan, south of Cairo. Helwan air base is the Egyptian Air Force centre for all major aircraft overhaul and maintenance, as well as its headquarters for maintenance and repair training. Nearby is a large industrial complex, the chief elements of which are an aircraft factory (No. 36) and an aero-engine factory (No. 135), with 3,000 and 3,500 employees respectively. Helwan also accommodates the Arab British Helicopter Company and Arab British Engine Company. By 'reverse engineering', ABECo has also manufactured components for, and overhauled, Soviet TV2-117A turboshaft engines for Egypt's Mil Mi-8 helicopter fleet.

The principal aircraft and engine programmes currently or recently undertaken by the AOI are as follows:

Aérospatiale Gazelle. Fifty-four French built Gazelles supplied earlier now retrofitted to SA 342L standard. December 1981 follow-on contract for 36 aircraft (also SA 342Ls), of which all except six assembled under licence at ABHCo factory at Helwan. Egyptian programme began in June 1983, with first Helwan assembled Gazelle making initial flight at end of September and being handed over to Egyptian Air Force on 1 December 1983. Production completed, including 18 spare Astazou XIVH engines.

Aérospatiale Super Puma. Protocol signed on 10 November 1983, providing for component manufacture (now in progress) and possible ultimate assembly.

Dassault-Breguet Falcon 50. Component manufacture.

Dassault-Breguet Mirage 2000. Egyptian Air Force has ordered 20 (French built), with further 20 on option. Some components for first batch are of Egyptian manufacture; first deliveries scheduled for second half of 1986. Egyptian assembly (possibly from 27th aircraft onward) may be undertaken in second batch.

Dassault-Breguet/Dornier Alpha Jet. Total of 45 ordered by Egypt, comprising 30 (designated **MS1**) to replace Czech L-29 Delfin and MiG-15UTI in the training role and 15 **MS2** ground attack versions to replace the MiG-17. First four in each batch delivered in flyaway condition by France (1982 and 1983 respectively); remaining 26 MS1s and 11 MS2s assembled from French kits by AOI Aircraft Factory. First flight of Egyptian assembled MS1 made on 1 September 1982, first delivery to Egyptian Air Force 4 November 1982. Production completed in 1985. Programme also included manufacture of components (flaps, ailerons, rudders, rear fuselages, exhaust shrouds and 310 litre; 68 Imp gallon drop tanks), as well as licence assembly of 80 Larzac engines by Factory 135.

EMBRAER EMB-312 Tucano. October 1983 contract for 120 Tucanos (80 for Iraq, 40 for Egypt), of which first ten were delivered complete by EMBRAER. Remainder being assembled from Brazilian built kits by Kader Factory at Heliopolis; PT6A-25 engines for these aircraft also being assembled in Egypt. Deliveries of Egyptian assembled Tucanos to the Egyptian Air Force began in November 1985, when three of the 12 aircraft completed by that time were officially accepted. Production rate was then two per month, scheduled to rise to four per month to complete the programme in 1987. Contract includes option for further 60 aircraft (Egypt 40, Iraq 20).

MS2 ground attack version of the Alpha Jet, assembled at the AOI Aircraft Factory in Helwan, with protective ground cover over laser rangefinder in nose

FINLAND

VALMET

VALMET CORPORATION KUOREVESI WORKS

35600 Halli
Telephone: (358) 42 8291
Telex: 28269 VALKU SF

General Manager: Juhani Mäkinen
Marketing: Per Falenius
Research and Development: Jaakko Harjumäki
Production: Arto Tonteri
Accountant: Esko Kurki

Valmet Corporation Kuorevesi Works is affiliated to Valmet Oy, a State owned company consisting of several metal-working factories. It continues the traditions of Ilmailuvoimien Lentokonetehdas, established in 1921, and was formerly a part of the Valmet Oy Tampere factory group, from which it was separated in 1974. It is now an independent factory directly responsible to Valmet's Head Office in Helsinki, and is currently the largest aircraft industry establishment in Finland. Since 1922, the Kuorevesi Works and its predecessors have built 30 different types of aircraft, of which 18 have been of Finnish design. Valmet was responsible for assembly of the 12 Saab 35XS Drakens ordered by Finland in 1970.

Current activities of the Kuorevesi Works include the overhaul and repair of military and civil aircraft, piston engines and instruments. The factory has a covered production area of approximately 17,000 m² (183,000 sq ft) and a February 1986 workforce of 558 people. Linnavuori Works, at Siuro, is concerned primarily with the overhaul and repair of aircraft jet engines.

The Kuorevesi and Linnavuori Works took part in the manufacture and assembly of 46 of the 50 BAe Hawk Mk 51 jet trainers and their Adour Mk 851 jet engines, purchased by the Finnish Air Force from the UK in December 1977. For these aircraft, Valmet manufactured the wing flaps, airbrake, tailplane and fin. The four UK built Hawks were delivered in 1980-81. The first Valmet assembled Hawk was handed over on 20 February 1981. Deliveries were completed on 8 October 1985. The Hawks serve with Finnish Air Force fighter squadrons 11 (at Rovaniemi), 21 (Satakunta) and 31 (Kuopio), and have replaced Fouga Magisters of the Ilmasotakoulu (Central Flying School) at Kauhava; some are also used in a reconnaissance role with the Special Development Unit at Jyvaskyla.

The latest aircraft of Finnish design to be built by Valmet is the L-90 TP turboprop primary and basic trainer.

An agreement to participate in licence production of derivatives of the Avtek 400 (see US section) was signed on 20 March 1985. These would include versions for such duties as surveillance, coastal patrol, geophysical research and liaison.

Valmet L-70 Vinka two-seat trainers of the Finnish Air Force

VALMET L-70 MILTRAINER

Finnish Air Force name: Vinka

A development contract for the L-70 was placed with Valmet by the Finnish Air Force on 23 March 1973. The aircraft, which was originally designated Leko-70, an abbreviation of 'Lentokone', the Finnish word for 'aeroplane', first flew on 1 July 1975. It is named Vinka (a cold Arctic wind) by the Finnish Air Force, to whom 30 Vinkas were delivered during 1980-82, as recorded in earlier editions of *Jane's*. As the L-70 Miltrainer, the aircraft continues to be available for export, and negotiations with a number of air forces were continuing in the Spring of 1986.

The Miltrainer is designed for Aerobatic or Utility use as a two-seater. In civil use, in the Normal category, it is capable of seating up to four persons, depending upon the amount of baggage carried, and fulfils the requirements of FAR Pt 23 in all three categories. In addition to these requirements, the Finnish Air Force specified some special military strength and other requirements for the aircraft. For instance, the Vinka has a fatigue life of more than 8,000 flying hours in heavy military use.

Normal roles include primary flying training, aerobatic training, night and instrument flying training, observation and liaison, tactical training, and ambulance duties. Secondary roles can include search and rescue, supply dropping, weapon training, photo reconnaissance, television monitoring/transmission, glider or target towing, and agricultural operations. The design permits the use of a ski landing gear.

Type: Two-seat training or two/four-seat touring aircraft.

Wings: Cantilever low-wing monoplane. Wing section NACA 63²A615 (modified). Dihedral 6° from roots. Incidence 2°. Fail-safe structure comprising main spar, auxiliary spar, ribs and stringers, of constant chord except for forward-swept wing root leading-edges, and attached to fuselage by steel fittings. Riveted aluminium alloy skin (fluted on flaps and ailerons). Electrically operated slotted flaps, and mass balanced ailerons, on trailing-edges, all of aluminium alloy riveted construction. Ailerons actuated by stainless steel control cables. Flaps and ailerons have fluted skins. Spring tab in each aileron.

Fuselage: Conventional aluminium alloy semi-monocoque fail-safe structure of frames and longerons, with riveted skin. Welded steel tube engine mount and wing carry-through structure; stainless steel firewall. Cockpit floor panels of bonded sandwich.

Tail Unit: Cantilever aluminium alloy structure, with riveted skin (fluted on fin, rudder and elevators). Slight sweepback on vertical surfaces; shallow dorsal fin. Elevators and rudder aerodynamically and mass balanced, and actuated by stainless steel control cables. Geared trim tabs in rudder and each elevator.

Landing Gear: Non-retractable tricycle type. Cantilever

main legs. Automotive Products oleo-pneumatic shock absorber in each unit. Cleveland 40-75S mainwheels, with Goodyear 6·00-6 six-ply tyres, pressure 1·86 bars (27 lb/sq in); Goodyear 395-32926 castoring and self-centering nosewheel, with Goodyear 5·00-5 four-ply tyre, pressure 2·07 bars (30 lb/sq in). Nosewheel steering optional. Cleveland 30-52K hydraulic disc brakes and parking brake. Provision for fitting Finncraft skis.

Power Plant: One 149 kW (200 hp) Avco Lycoming AEIO-360-A1B6 flat-four engine, driving a Hartzell HC-C2YK-4F/FC 7666A-2 two-blade constant-speed propeller with spinner. Christen-801 fuel and oil systems permit up to 1½ min of continuous inverted flight in Aerobatic category. Semi-integral bonded sandwich fuel tank in each wing root ahead of main spar; total capacity 170 litres (37·4 Imp gallons). Gravity fuelling point in top of each tank. Safom reticulated polyurethane foam filling for fuel tanks is optional. Oil capacity 7·5 litres (1·65 Imp gallons).

Accommodation: Side by side seats for instructor and pupil in trainer version, with integral longitudinal central console which serves also to reinforce fuselage floor. Dual controls standard, but instructor's or pupil's control column can be removed if desired. Windscreen and one-piece rearward-sliding fully transparent jettisonable canopy, with steel tube turnover frame. Canopy can be locked in partially open position if required. Provision for two more seats at rear, which can be removed to make room for additional baggage. Up to 280 kg (617 lb) of baggage or freight can be carried internally if aircraft is flown as a single-seater. As ambulance, can accommodate one stretcher patient and medical attendant in addition to pilot. Cockpit heated and ventilated.

System: 28V DC electrical system, with Prestolite 24V 70A alternator and 25Ah nickel-cadmium battery. Ground power receptacle. No hydraulic or pneumatic systems.

Avionics and Equipment: Standard avionics include two VHF transceivers, one ADF, one VOR/ILS with indicator, two RMI, one gyrosyn compass system, and intercom. Standard equipment includes accelerometer, dual airspeed indicators, dual artificial horizons, clock, magnetic compass, dual rate of climb indicators, dual turn and slip indicators, outside air temperature gauge, and tachometer; electrically heated pitot static head; inertia reel shoulder harnesses for front seats; first aid kit; internal and external corrosion proofing; instrument lighting; cockpit utility lights for map reading and as standby instrument lighting; warning lights for alternator, battery temperature and directional gyro; anti-collision beacon; landing and taxying lights in starboard wing leading-edge; navigation lights; and fire extinguisher. Equipment for secondary roles may include reflex gunsight and external load control panel; glider or target towing hook; one long-focus or four short-focus vertical cameras (provision for 35 × 40 cm; 13·8 × 15·75 in aperture, with quick-release panel, in floor of rear cockpit); four underwing pylons (total capacity 300 kg: see following paragraph) for stores; and dispersal equipment for agricultural missions.

Armament and Operational Equipment: Four underwing attachments, the inner pair each stressed for 150 kg (330·5 lb) and the outer pair for 100 kg (220 lb) each; max external load 300 kg (661 lb). As single-seater, can carry four 50 kg bombs; two 100 kg bombs plus two flare pods; four pods each with eighteen 37 mm or six 68 mm rockets; two pods each with twin 7·62 or 5·56 mm machine-guns and 1,000 rds/pod; two such gun pods and two flare pods; two pods each with single 12·7 mm machine-gun and 150 rds/pod; or two reconnaissance or photographic pods. As two-seater, typical loads can include four or eight anti-tank missiles, depending upon type and size; one TV pod (with transmitter) and one searchlight pod; three 10-person life rafts and a searchlight pod; or three 6-person emergency rescue packs and a searchlight pod.

Dimensions, external:

Wing span	9·63 m (31 ft 7¼ in)
Wing chord (constant over most of span)	1·53 m (5 ft 0¼ in)
Wing aspect ratio	6·93
Length overall	7·50 m (24 ft 7¼ in)
Height overall	3·31 m (10 ft 10¼ in)
Tailplane span	3·60 m (11 ft 9¾ in)
Wheel track	2·30 m (7 ft 6½ in)
Wheelbase	1·61 m (5 ft 3½ in)
Propeller diameter	1·88 m (6 ft 2 in)
Propeller ground clearance	0·25 m (9¾ in)

Areas:

Wings, gross	14·00 m² (150·70 sq ft)
Ailerons (total)	1·412 m² (15·20 sq ft)
Trailing-edge flaps (total)	1·90 m² (20·45 sq ft)
Fin	0·87 m² (9·36 sq ft)
Rudder, incl tab	0·79 m² (8·50 sq ft)
Tailplane	2·01 m² (21·64 sq ft)
Elevators, incl tabs	1·01 m² (10·87 sq ft)

Weights and Loadings:

Operating weight empty, equipped	767 kg (1,691 lb)
Max payload with full fuel	380 kg (838 lb)
Max T-O weight: Aerobatic	1,040 kg (2,293 lb)
Utility	1,050 kg (2,315 lb)
Normal	1,250 kg (2,756 lb)
Max wing loading:	
Aerobatic	74·3 kg/m² (15·22 lb/sq ft)
Utility	75·0 kg/m² (15·36 lb/sq ft)
Normal	89·3 kg/m² (18·53 lb/sq ft)
Max power loading:	
Aerobatic	6·97 kg/kW (11·47 lb/hp)
Utility	7·04 kg/kW (11·58 lb/hp)
Normal	8·38 kg/kW (13·78 lb/hp)

HW-350, the last of 46 Valmet assembled BAe Hawks, handed over to the Finnish Air Force on 8 October 1985

Performance (at AUW of 1,000 kg; 2,205 lb):

Never-exceed speed	193 knots (360 km/h; 223 mph)
Max level speed at S/L	127 knots (235 km/h; 146 mph)
Cruising speed (75% power) at 1,525 m (5,000 ft)	120 knots (222 km/h; 138 mph)
Stalling speed, power off:	
flaps up	53 knots (98 km/h; 61 mph)
flaps down	46 knots (85 km/h; 53 mph)
Max rate of climb at S/L	342 m (1,120 ft)/min
Service ceiling	5,000 m (16,400 ft)
T-O run	230 m (755 ft)
Landing run	175 m (575 ft)
Min ground turning radius	8·00 m (26 ft 3 in)
Range with max fuel, no reserves	513 nm (950 km; 590 miles)
Endurance at S/L (65% power)	4 h 48 min
Max endurance, no reserves	6 h 12 min
g limits	+6/−3 (Aerobatic)
	+4·4/−2·02 (Utility)
	+3·3/−1·8 (Normal)

VALMET L-90 TP REDIGO

The L-90 TP is developed from, and is slightly larger than, the L-70, from which it differs primarily in having a turboprop power plant, new wings and retractable landing gear. The prototype (OH-VTP, generally similar to the earlier L-80 TP: see 1985-86 *Jane's*) flew for the first time in June 1986.

Suitable for primary and basic flying training, aerobatic training, night and instrument flight training, tactical training, observation and liaison missions, the L-90 TP is designed to fit a training system that can produce combat-ready pilots within minimum time and cost levels, students proceeding directly from the Redigo to a demanding advanced trainer. Additional roles can include search and rescue, weapons training, photographic reconnaissance and target towing. An alternative all-composites wing (mainly carbonfibre and with the same aerofoil section) has been built for ground fatigue testing and may be flight tested on one of two additional prototypes that are being built.

The following description applies to the first prototype:

Type: Two/four-seat multi-purpose military primary and basic training aircraft. Minimum fatigue life of 10,000 flight hours (fatigue spectrum MIL-A-008866B).

Wings: Cantilever low-wing monoplane. Tapered planform, with extended chord on inboard leading-edges. Generally similar construction to L-70, but with NACA 63-218 (mod) and 63-412 (mod) root and tip sections, 3° root incidence with 3° washout, and slotted Frise ailerons. Geared and/or spring tab in each aileron, trim tab in starboard aileron.

Fuselage and Tail Unit: Generally similar to those described for L-70. Combined trim/geared tab in rudder and each elevator.

Landing Gear: AP Precision Hydraulics electro-hydraulically retractable tricycle type, with single wheel on each unit. Nosewheel retracts rearward, mainwheels inward into wings. Mainwheel tyres size 17·5 × 6·3-6·0 in, pressure 3·79 bars (55 lb/sq in); nosewheel tyre size 14·2 × 4·95-5·0 in, pressure 3·45 bars (50 lb/sq in).

Power Plant: One Allison 250-B17D turboprop engine, max power 313 kW (420 shp), flat rated at 268 kW (360 shp). Hartzell three-blade constant-speed reversible-pitch propeller with spinner. Fuel in four wing tanks, total capacity 360 litres (79 Imp gallons). Refuelling point in each upper wing surface. Fuel system permits inverted flight. Oil capacity 5·7 litres (1·25 Imp gallons).

Accommodation: One or two pilots, side by side, beneath one-piece rearward sliding jettisonable bubble canopy with steel tube turnover frame. Canopy can be locked in partially open position if required. Dual controls standard, but instructor's or pupil's control column can be removed if desired. Provision for two more seats at rear, which can be removed to make room for additional baggage. As ambulance, can accommodate one stretcher patient in addition to pilot. Accommodation heated and ventilated.

Systems: No hydraulic, pneumatic or air-conditioning systems. Electrical system is 24/28V DC, based on alternator/generator and 23Ah battery. Oxygen system for two pilots, capacity 13·3 litres (812 cu in).

Avionics: Standard avionics include VHF, VOR/ILS, ADF, DME and transponder (Collins Pro Line 2). Blind-flying instrumentation standard

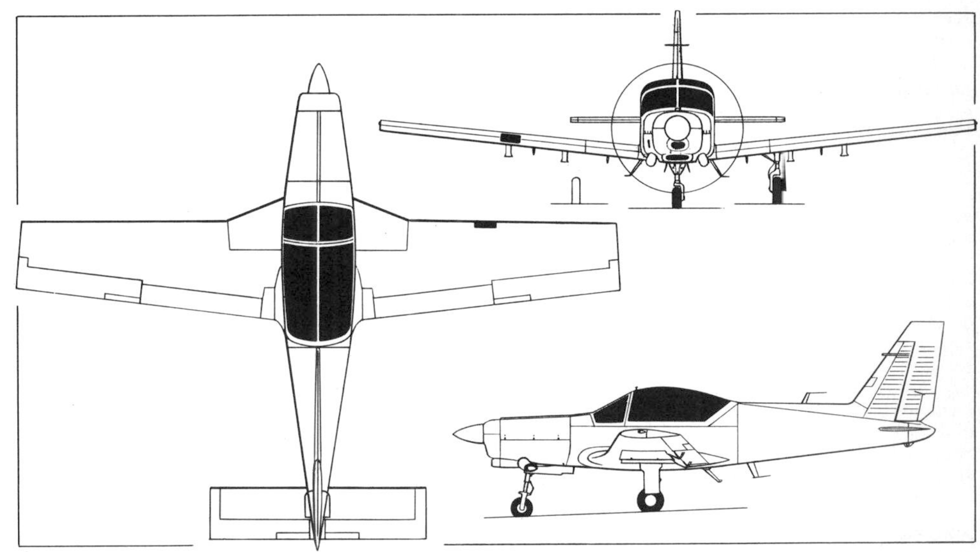

Valmet L-90 TP Redigo turboprop powered development of the L-70 Miltrainer *(Pilot Press)*

ARMAMENT AND OPERATIONAL EQUIPMENT: Six underwing attachments, the inner pair each stressed for 250 kg (551 lb) and the others for 150 kg (331 lb) each; max external load 800 kg (1,764 lb). As single-seater, can carry six 100 kg bombs; two 250 kg bombs plus two 50 kg bombs and two flares; six pods each with eighteen 37 mm or six 68 mm rockets; two rocket pods, two gun pods (each with either two 7·62 mm and 2,000 rds or one 12·7 mm and 300 rds) and two flares; photographic, TV, radar or reconnaissance pods plus flares. As two-seater, typical loads can include six to twelve anti-tank missiles; five liferafts or emergency packs and one searchlight pod; photo and TV pods. Provision for reflector sight, internally mounted cameras (one long-focus or four short-focus), or for target towing with winch and hit counters.

DIMENSIONS, EXTERNAL:

Wing span	10·34 m (33 ft 11 in)
Wing chord: at root	1·83 m (6 ft 0 in)
at tip	1·098 m (3 ft 7¼ in)
Wing aspect ratio	6·98
Length overall	7·90 m (25 ft 11 in)
Length of fuselage	7·38 m (24 ft 2½ in)
Fuselage: Max width	1·22 m (4 ft 0 in)
Height overall	2·85 m (9 ft 4¼ in)
Tailplane span	3·68 m (12 ft 1 in)
Wheel track	3·36 m (11 ft 0¼ in)
Wheelbase	2·13 m (7 ft 0 in)
Propeller diameter	2·19 m (7 ft 2¼ in)
Propeller ground clearance	0·29 m (11½ in)

DIMENSIONS, INTERNAL:

Cockpit: Length	1·81 m (5 ft 11¼ in)
Max width	1·14 m (3 ft 9 in)
Max height	1·02 m (3 ft 4¼ in)

AREAS:

Wings, gross	14·75 m² (158·8 sq ft)
Ailerons (total)	2·00 m² (21·53 sq ft)
Trailing-edge flaps (total)	1·80 m² (19·38 sq ft)
Fin	0·91 m² (9·80 sq ft)
Rudder (aft of hinge)	0·86 m² (9·26 sq ft)
Tailplane	2·09 m² (22·50 sq ft)
Elevators (aft of hinge)	1·20 m² (12·92 sq ft)

WEIGHTS AND LOADINGS:

Weight empty, equipped (Aerobatic)	890 kg (1,962 lb)
Max fuel	280 kg (617 lb)
External stores: max	800 kg (1,764 lb)
with max fuel	600 kg (1,323 lb)
Max T-O weight	1,900 kg (4,189 lb)
Max landing weight	1,700 kg (3,748 lb)
Max wing loading	128·8 kg/m² (26·40 lb/sq ft)
Max power loading	7·08 kg/kW (11·63 lb/shp)

Prototype of the Valmet L-90 TP Redigo two/four-seat multi-stage military trainer

PERFORMANCE (at AUW of 1,350 kg; 2,976 lb):

Max permissible speed in dive	280 knots (520 km/h; 323 mph)
Never-exceed speed	251 knots (465 km/h; 289 mph)
Max level speed at 3,000 m (9,840 ft)	181 knots (335 km/h; 208 mph)
Max speed for flap extension	129 knots (240 km/h; 149 mph)
Stalling speed, engine idling: flaps up	60 knots (110 km/h; 69 mph)
flaps down	54 knots (99 km/h; 62 mph)
Max rate of climb at S/L	612 m (2,008 ft)/min
Rate of climb at 3,000 m (9,840 ft)	612 m (2,008 ft)/min
Time to 3,000 m (9,840 ft)	5 min 30 s
Service ceiling	at least 7,500 m (24,600 ft)
T-O run	195 m (640 ft)
T-O to 15 m (50 ft)	310 m (1,017 ft)
Landing from 15 m (50 ft)	360 m (1,181 ft)
Min ground turning radius	10·80 m (35 ft 5 in)
Range at 6,000 m (19,685 ft) with max fuel, 30 min reserves	more than 755 nm (1,400 km; 870 miles)
Endurance, conditions as above	more than 5 h
g limits:	+7/−3·5 aerobatic
	+2·7 max sustained

FRANCE

AÉROSPATIALE

AÉROSPATIALE SNI

37 boulevard de Montmorency, 75781 Paris Cédex 16
Telephone: 524 43 21
Telex: AISPA 620059 F

HONORARY PRESIDENT: Jacques Mitterrand, Général d'Armée Aérienne (CPN)

BOARD OF DIRECTORS

PRESIDENT: Henri Martre
REPRESENTATIVE OF THE SHAREHOLDERS:
Crédit Lyonnais, represented by Alain Bizot (Asst Managing Director)
REPRESENTATIVES OF THE STATE:
Maurice Bailly (Director of Industrial Programmes and Affairs)
Henri Baquiast (Director of Foreign Economic Affairs)
Guy Boileau (Controller General of Armed Services)
Daniel Tenenbaum (Director General of Civil Aviation)
Jean-Claude Trichet (Asst Director of Treasury Department)
REPRESENTATIVES OF THE EMPLOYEES:
Maurice Adda, Bernard Devert, Georges Marin, Jean Massé, André Sappa, Vincent Valente

GENERAL MANAGEMENT

PRESIDENT AND CHIEF EXECUTIVE OFFICER:
Henri Martre
VICE-PRESIDENT AND DEPUTY CHIEF EXECUTIVE OFFICER:
Roger Chevalier
EXECUTIVE VICE-PRESIDENT: Yves Barbé
SENIOR VICE-PRESIDENTS:
Roger Courot (Inspector General)
Gérard Hibon (International Affairs)
Jean Claude Roqueplo (Labour Relations)
Joseph Millara (Industrial and Technical Matters)
VICE-PRESIDENT:
Jean Picq (Administration and Finance)
DIRECTOR OF THE PRESIDENT'S OFFICE: Bernard Darrieus
DIRECTOR (INFORMATION AND COMMUNICATION):
René Bourone
INDUSTRIAL DIRECTOR: Roger Berthier
CENTRAL TECHNICAL DIRECTOR: Jacques Balazard
DEPUTY DIRECTOR OF INDUSTRIAL RELATIONS (DIRECTOR, HEADQUARTERS ESTABLISHMENT): Marc-André Loiseau

AIRCRAFT DIVISION

DIVISION MANAGER: Jacques Plenier
ASSISTANT DIVISION MANAGER: René Dor
AIRBUS PROGRAMME DIRECTOR: Alain Bruneau
ATR 42 and EPSILON PROGRAMME DIRECTOR:
Jean-Paul Perrais
TRANSALL PROGRAMME DIRECTOR: Jacques Hablot
MILITARY ADVISER: Gen (Retd) C. R. Huguet
FINANCIAL DIRECTOR: Joseph Carpentier
COMMERCIAL DIRECTOR: Henri Paul Puel
FLIGHT TEST DIRECTOR: Henri Perrier
DIRECTOR, SUPPORT SERVICES: Pierre Schaffner
DIRECTOR (QUALITY ASSURANCE): Pierre Lagarde
WORKS AND FACILITIES:
Toulouse. PLANT MANAGER: Jean-Louis Fache
Nantes-Bouguenais. PLANT MANAGER: Daniel Huet
Saint-Nazaire. PLANT MANAGER: Jean-Paul Chandez
Méaulte. PLANT MANAGER: Jean Mousson

HELICOPTER DIVISION

DIVISION MANAGER: Michel Thomas
TECHNICAL MANAGER: Georges Petit
DIRECTOR OF ENGINEERING: René Mouille
ECONOMIC AND COMMERCIAL MANAGER:
Jean-Claude Rebuffel
INDUSTRIAL MANAGER: Fernand Carayon
PRODUCT SUPPORT MANAGER: Yves Birotteau
FLIGHT TEST MANAGER: Jean-Marie Besse
COMMERCIAL MANAGER: Lucien Lordereau
WORKS AND FACILITIES:
Marignane. PLANT MANAGER: Etienne Lefort
La Courneuve. PLANT MANAGER: Lucien Fournier

TACTICAL MISSILES DIVISION

DIVISION MANAGER: Michel Allier
ASSISTANT DIVISION MANAGER: Philippe Girard
SALES DIRECTOR: Pierre Froget
TECHNICAL DIRECTOR: Jean Guillot
DIRECTOR OF DESIGN: Yves de Rougemont
DIRECTOR OF ECONOMIC AFFAIRS: Jacques Pottier
WORKS AND FACILITIES:
Châtillon. PLANT MANAGER: Jean-Claude Renaut
Bourges. PLANT MANAGER: Georges Barroy

SPACE AND BALLISTIC SYSTEMS DIVISION

DIVISION MANAGER: Jean-Charles Poggi
DEPUTY DIVISION MANAGER—DIRECTOR OF MILITARY PROGRAMMES: Gérard Payelle
DIRECTOR OF CIVIL PROGRAMMES: Pierre Madon
INDUSTRIAL AFFAIRS: Jacques Utter
WORKS AND FACILITIES:
Aquitaine. PLANT MANAGER: Jean-Rémy Hugues
Les Mureaux. PLANT MANAGER: Jean Schittenhelm
Cannes. PLANT MANAGER: Lucien Trousse

SUBSIDIARIES

Société Girondine d'Entretien et de Réparation de Matériel Aéronautique (SOGERMA)
Société de Construction d'Avions de Tourisme et d'Affaires (SOCATA)
Société d'Exploitation et de Constructions Aéronautiques (SECA)
Electronique Aérospatiale (EAS)
Société Charentaise d'Equipements Aéronautiques (SOCEA)
Aérospatiale Helicopter Corporation (USA)

Aérospatiale was formed on 1 January 1970, by decision of the French government, as a result of the merger of the former Sud-Aviation, Nord-Aviation and SEREB companies. It had a registered capital of 1,016,500,000 francs, facilities extending over a total area of 8,498,465 m² (91,477,475 sq ft), of which 2,015,345 m² (21,693,175 sq ft) are covered, and a staff (including subsidiary companies) of 39,820 persons on 1 January 1985.

In addition to the programmes of which details follow, Aérospatiale is a partner in the European Airbus programmes (see International section), and participates financially in Helibras (Brazil), Samaero (Singapore) and Maroc Aviation (Morocco). Its activities are devoted 32% to fixed-wing aircraft, 19·3% to helicopters, 32% to tactical missiles, 16·4% to ballistic missiles and space, and 0·3% to other work.

AÉROSPATIALE EPSILON

First details of this tandem two-seat primary/basic trainer were released at the Farnborough Air Show in September 1978. Purpose of the project was to meet a French Air Force requirement for a propeller driven aircraft for use in the initial stages of a more cost effective pilot training scheme than that then operated.

A development contract from the Air Force, for two prototypes and two ground test airframes, was announced by Aérospatiale at the Paris Air Show in June 1979. The first prototype flew for the first time on 22 December that year, followed by the second prototype on 12 July 1980. The flight test development programme was completed in mid-1982. Earlier, on 6 January 1982, a manufacturing programme had been approved, covering delivery of 150 Epsilons at the rate of 30 a year. Contracts for the first two production increments, each of 30 aircraft, were received on 5 March and 30 December 1982 respectively. The first production Epsilon came off the assembly line on 14 June 1983, and flew for the first time on 29 June; deliveries to the Centre d'Expériences Aériennes Militaires (CEAM) at Mont-de-Marsan began on 29 July 1983, and 25 were delivered subsequently to the air base at Cognac, enabling student training on the Epsilon to begin in February 1985. It was planned to have 55 Epsilons at Cognac by the end of 1985. Subsequent aircraft will be assigned to Salon-de-Provence, Aulnat and other training bases. Pupils transition from the Epsilon directly to the Alpha Jet.

The Epsilon programme is handled by the Aircraft Division of Aérospatiale, as prime contractor responsible for the entire programme. Design and manufacture are subcontracted to Socata, the company's light aircraft subsidiary at Tarbes.

An armed version is available to export customers, with four underwing hardpoints for a total 300 kg (661 lb) of external stores with pilot only, or 200 kg (441 lb) with crew of two. Empty weight of this version is 944 kg (2,081 lb), max T-O weight 1,400 kg (3,086 lb), and *g* limits +6/−3. An Epsilon armed with two twin 7·62 mm machine-gun pods could loiter for 30 min at low altitude over a combat area 170 nm (315 km; 195 miles) from its base. First export order, for three armed Epsilons, was placed by the Togolese Air Force in the Autumn of 1984.

The first prototype Epsilon is being used as testbed for the 335 kW (450 shp) TP 319 turboprop developed by Turboméca from the TM 319 turboshaft. The engine is derated to 261 kW (350 shp) for this installation and drives a Ratier-Figeac propeller with three composites blades. First flight was made on 9 November 1985.

The following description applies to the basic version of the Epsilon, as ordered by the French Air Force:

TYPE: Two-seat military primary/basic trainer.

WINGS: Cantilever low-wing monoplane. Wing section RA 1643 at root, RA 1243 at tip. Thickness/chord ratio 16% at root, 12% at tip. Dihedral 5°. Incidence 2°. All-metal light alloy structure, with single main spar and rear auxiliary spar, built in two panels attached directly to sides of fuselage. Press-formed ribs and heavy gauge skin without stringers. Electrically actuated single-slotted flaps. Light alloy ailerons, with spring tabs.

FUSELAGE: Light alloy semi-monocoque structure of four longerons, frames and heavy gauge skin, without stringers.

TAIL UNIT: Cantilever single-spar light alloy structure. Fixed surfaces metal covered; elevators and rudder covered with polyester fabric. Fixed incidence tailplane, with dihedral. Balanced elevators and rudder, with controllable trim tabs. Shallow ventral fin.

LANDING GEAR: Electro-hydraulically retractable tricycle type, with single wheel on each unit. Inward retracting main units and rearward retracting castoring nosewheel. Mainwheel tyres size 380 × 150; nosewheel tyre size 330 × 130. Independent hydraulic single-disc brake on each mainwheel. Parking brake.

POWER PLANT: One 224 kW (300 hp) Avco Lycoming AEIO-540-L1B5D flat-six engine, driving a Hartzell HC-C2YR-4()F/FC 8475-6R two-blade constant-speed metal propeller, with spinner. Fuel in two wing leading-edge tanks, with total capacity of 210 litres (46 Imp gallons; 55·5 US gallons). Refuelling points on wing upper surface. Christen system to permit up to 2 min inverted flight.

ACCOMMODATION: Two seats in tandem, with rear seat raised by 70 mm (2·7 in). Rudder pedals are mechanically adjustable fore and aft. Two-component sliding Plexiglas canopy, with emergency jettison system, plus sideways hinged windscreen. Baggage compartment aft of cabin.

SYSTEMS: Hydraulic systems for actuating landing gear and brakes. 28V electrical system includes engine driven alternator; battery for engine starting and emergency use. Cabin heated and ventilated. Windscreen demister.

AVIONICS AND EQUIPMENT: Standard installation includes blind-flying instrumentation, VHF, UHF, automatic and manual VOR, transponder, ILS capability and Tacan.

ARMAMENT AND OPERATIONAL EQUIPMENT (not on French Air Force Epsilons): Four underwing hardpoints; outboard points each able to carry 80 kg (176 lb), inboard points 160 kg (352 lb). Alternative loads include two Matra pods each containing two 7·62 mm machine-guns, four Matra F2 launchers for Thomson-Brandt 68 mm rockets, six Bavard F4B practice bombs, two 125 kg bombs, two Alkan 500 cartridge launchers, and four land or sea survival kit containers. Associated equipment includes Alkan 663 stores racks, SFOM 83A3 sight and Alkan E105C firing control box.

DIMENSIONS, EXTERNAL:

Wing span	7·92 m (25 ft 11¾ in)
Wing chord: at root	1·46 m (4 ft 9½ in)
at tip	0·92 m (3 ft 0¼ in)
Wing aspect ratio	6·97
Length overall	7·59 m (24 ft 10¾ in)
Height overall	2·66 m (8 ft 8¾ in)
Tailplane span	3·20 m (10 ft 6 in)
Wheel track	2·30 m (7 ft 6½ in)
Wheelbase	1·80 m (5 ft 10¾ in)
Propeller diameter	1·98 m (6 ft 6 in)
Propeller ground clearance	0·25 m (10 in)

AREAS:

Wings, gross	9·00 m² (96·9 sq ft)
Fin	1·02 m² (10·98 sq ft)
Tailplane	2·00 m² (21·53 sq ft)

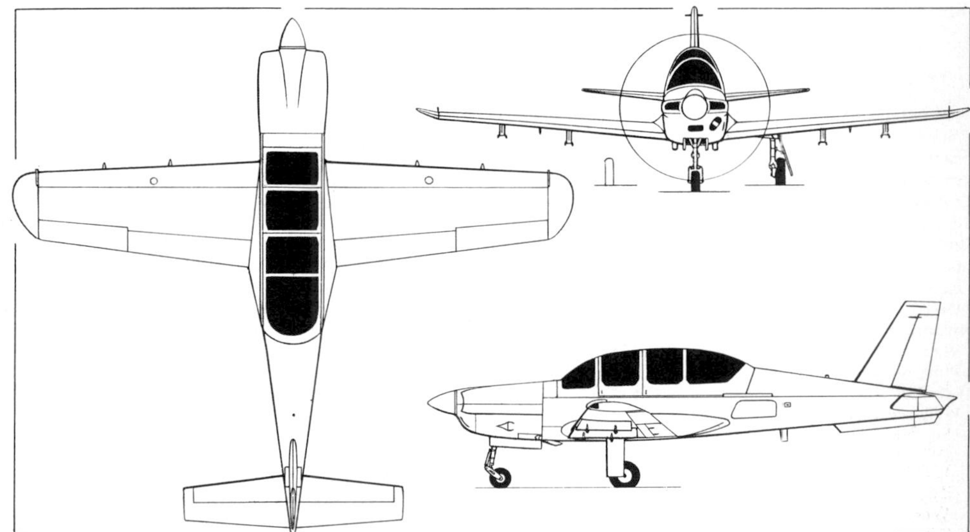

Aérospatiale Epsilon tandem two-seat primary/basic trainer *(Pilot Press)*

Aérospatiale Epsilon (Avco Lycoming AEIO-540-L1B5D engine)

Armed version of Aérospatiale Epsilon carrying two twin-gun packs underwing

Prototype Aérospatiale Epsilon modified as testbed for Turboméca TP 319 turboprop engine

WEIGHTS AND LOADINGS:

Weight empty, equipped	932 kg (2,055 lb)
Fuel weight	150 kg (330 lb)
Max T-O and landing weight	1,250 kg (2,755 lb)
Max wing loading	139 kg/m² (28·4 lb/sq ft)
Max power loading	5·58 kg/kW (9·18 lb/hp)

PERFORMANCE (at max T-O weight):

Never-exceed speed	281 knots (520 km/h; 323 mph)
Max level speed at S/L	205 knots (380 km/h; 236 mph)
Max cruising speed (75% power) at 1,830 m (6,000 ft)	193 knots (358 km/h; 222 mph)
Approach speed	80 knots (148 km/h; 92 mph)
Stalling speed, flaps and landing gear down, power off	62 knots (115 km/h; 72 mph)
Max rate of climb at S/L	564 m (1,850 ft)/min
Service ceiling	7,010 m (23,000 ft)
T-O run	410 m (1,345 ft)
T-O to 15 m (50 ft)	640 m (2,100 ft)
Landing from 15 m (50 ft)	440 m (1,444 ft)
Landing run	250 m (820 ft)
Endurance (75% power)	3 h 45 min
g limits	+6·7/−3·35

AÉROSPATIALE/MBB TRANSALL

Details of the Transall programme can be found in the International section of this edition.

AÉROSPATIALE/MBB HAP/PAH-2/HAC-3G

Details of this Franco-German anti-tank helicopter programme can be found under the Eurocopter heading in the International section.

AÉROSPATIALE/AERITALIA ATR 42/72

Details of the ATR 42/72 programme can be found in the International section.

AÉROSPATIALE SA 315B LAMA

Indian Army name: Cheetah

Design of the SA 315B Lama began in late 1968, initially to meet a requirement of the Indian armed forces, and a prototype was flown for the first time on 17 March 1969. French certification was granted on 30 September 1970 and FAA Type Approval on 25 February 1972.

The Lama combines features of the Alouette II and III, having the airframe (with some reinforcement) of the former and the dynamic components, including the Artouste power plant and rotor system, of the SA 316 Alouette III.

During demonstration flights in the Himalayas in 1969 a Lama, carrying a crew of two and 140 kg (308 lb) of fuel, made the highest landings and take-offs ever recorded, at a height of 7,500 m (24,600 ft).

On 21 June 1972, a Lama set a helicopter absolute height record of 12,442 m (40,820 ft). The pilot was Jean Boulet, holder of the previous record in an SE 3150 Alouette.

The production Lama is capable of transporting an external load of 1,135 kg (2,500 lb) at an altitude of more than 2,500 m (8,200 ft). In an agricultural role, it can be fitted with spraybars and an underbelly tank of 1,135 litres (250 Imp gallons; 300 US gallons) capacity, developed jointly by Aérospatiale Helicopter Corporation and Simplex Manufacturing Company. The tank is equipped with an electrical emergency dump system.

A total of 390 Lamas had been sold for operation in 30 countries by 1 January 1986, of which 383 had been delivered. In addition to manufacture by Aérospatiale, the SA 315B is still produced under licence by HAL for the Indian Army, under the name Cheetah; and is assembled by Helibras in Brazil under the name Gavião.

Type: Turbine-driven general purpose helicopter.

Rotor System: Three-blade main and anti-torque rotors. All-metal main rotor blades, of constant chord, on articulated hinges, with hydraulic drag hinge dampers. Rotor brake standard.

Rotor Drive: Main rotor driven through planetary gearbox, with freewheel for autorotation. Take-off drive for tail rotor at lower end of main gearbox, from where a torque shaft runs to a small gearbox which supports the tail rotor and houses the pitch change mechanism. Cyclic and collective pitch controls are powered.

Fuselage: Glazed cabin has light metal frame. Centre and rear fuselage have triangulated steel tube framework.

Landing Gear: Skid type, with removable wheels for ground manoeuvring. Pneumatic floats for normal operation from water, and emergency flotation gear, inflatable in the air, are available.

Power Plant: One 649 kW (870 shp) Turboméca Artouste IIIB turboshaft engine, derated to 410 kW (550 shp). Fuel tank in fuselage centre-section, with capacity of 575 litres (126·5 Imp gallons; 152 US gallons), of which 573 litres (126 Imp gallons; 151·5 US gallons) are usable.

Accommodation: Glazed cabin seats pilot and passenger side by side in front and three passengers behind. Provision for external sling for loads of up to 1,135 kg (2,500 lb). Can be equipped for rescue (hoist capacity 160 kg; 352 lb), liaison, observation, training, agricultural, photographic and other duties. As an ambulance, can accommodate two stretchers and a medical attendant.

Dimensions, external:
- Main rotor diameter 11·02 m (36 ft 1¾ in)
- Tail rotor diameter 1·91 m (6 ft 3¼ in)
- Main rotor blade chord (constant) 0·35 m (13·8 in)
- Length overall, both rotors turning 12·91 m (42 ft 4¼ in)
- Length of fuselage 10·23 m (33 ft 6¾ in)
- Height overall 3·09 m (10 ft 1¾ in)
- Skid track 2·38 m (7 ft 9¾ in)

Areas:
- Main rotor disc 95·38 m² (1,026·7 sq ft)
- Tail rotor disc 2·87 m² (30·84 sq ft)

Weights:
- Weight empty 1,021 kg (2,251 lb)
- Max T-O weight: normal 1,950 kg (4,300 lb)
- with externally slung cargo 2,300 kg (5,070 lb)

Performance (A, at AUW of 1,950 kg; 4,300 lb. B, at AUW of 2,300 kg; 5,070 lb with slung load):
- Never-exceed speed at S/L:
  - A 113 knots (210 km/h; 130 mph)
- Max cruising speed:
  - A 103 knots (192 km/h; 119 mph)
  - B 65 knots (120 km/h; 75 mph)
- Max rate of climb at S/L: A 330 m (1,080 ft)/min
  - B 234 m (768 ft)/min
- Service ceiling: A 5,400 m (17,715 ft)
  - B 3,000 m (9,840 ft)
- Hovering ceiling IGE: A 5,050 m (16,565 ft)
  - B 2,950 m (9,675 ft)
- Hovering ceiling OGE: A 4,600 m (15,090 ft)
  - B 1,550 m (5,085 ft)
- Range with max fuel: A 278 nm (515 km; 320 miles)

Aérospatiale SA 315B Lama equipped for mountain rescue missions in Switzerland

AÉROSPATIALE ALOUETTE III

The seven-seat Alouette III helicopter was produced by Aérospatiale in two major versions, details of which can be found in the 1981-82 and previous editions of *Jane's*:

SA 316B. Powered by 649 kW (870 shp) Turboméca Artouste IIIB turboshaft engine, derated to 425 kW (570 shp). Prototype flew for first time on 28 February 1959.

SA 319B. Powered by 649 kW (870 shp) Turboméca Astazou XIV turboshaft engine, derated to 447 kW (600 shp). Prototype completed in 1967.

A total of 1,455 Alouette IIIs had been delivered for civil and military operation in 74 countries by 1 May 1985. Production in France has ended, but manufacture of the SA 316B by ICA of Brasov, Romania, continued in 1985, under the designation IAR-316B. ICA has also developed a military gunship version of the Alouette III, known as the IAR-317 Airfox, which is described in the Romanian section of this edition. A further gunship development, the Atlas Alpha, is described in the South African section. SA 316B production by HAL in India, as the Chetak, also continues.

AÉROSPATIALE SA 330 PUMA

The twin-engined SA 330 Puma was developed initially to meet a French Army requirement for a medium sized *hélicoptère de manoeuvre*, able to operate by day or night in all weathers and all climates. In 1967, the SA 330 was selected for the RAF Tactical Transport Programme, and was included in a three-type joint production agreement between Aérospatiale and Westland in the UK.

The first of two SA 330 prototypes flew on 15 April 1965, and the last of six pre-production models on 30 July 1968, followed in September 1968 by the first production aircraft.

Details of six early versions of the Puma can be found in the 1976-77 *Jane's*. The final French production versions were as follows:

SA 330J/L. Civil (J) and military (L) versions introduced in 1976 with main rotor blades of composite materials. Increased max T-O weight, including certification at 7,500 kg (16,535 lb) for cargo-sling mission. Last described fully in 1982-83 *Jane's*.

A total of 692 SA 330 Pumas had been sold by 1 January 1985, in 46 countries. ICA of Brasov, Romania (which see), began manufacture of 100 SA 330H Pumas under licence in 1977, as IAR-330s, and is now the sole producer of this helicopter. Nurtanio of Indonesia (see IPTN) completed the assembly of 11 from knocked-down components in the second quarter of 1983 but, like the parent company, is now concentrating on manufacture of the Super Puma.

AÉROSPATIALE AS 332 SUPER PUMA

The early history of the Super Puma, a list of its improved features compared with the original SA 330 Puma, and details of 1985 versions can be found in the 1985-86 edition of *Jane's*. The first prototype AS 332 Super Puma (F-WZJA) flew for the first time on 13 September 1978. The four versions of the Super Puma introduced in 1986, with uprated Turboméca Makila IA1 engines and 40kVA instead of 20kVA alternators, are as follows:

AS 332B₁. Military version. Standard fuselage, seating up to 23 troops and two crew. Cabin floor reinforced for loads of 1,500 kg/m² (307 lb/sq ft).

AS 332F₁. Naval version, with folding tail rotor pylon, deck landing assist device and anti-corrosion treatment. Suitable for search and rescue, ASW and anti-ship roles.

AS 332L₁. Civil version, with cabin lengthened by 0·76 m (2 ft 6 in) to seat crew of two and up to 24 passengers. Airline

Aérospatiale AS 332F₁ Super Puma equipped with an AM39 Exocet missile

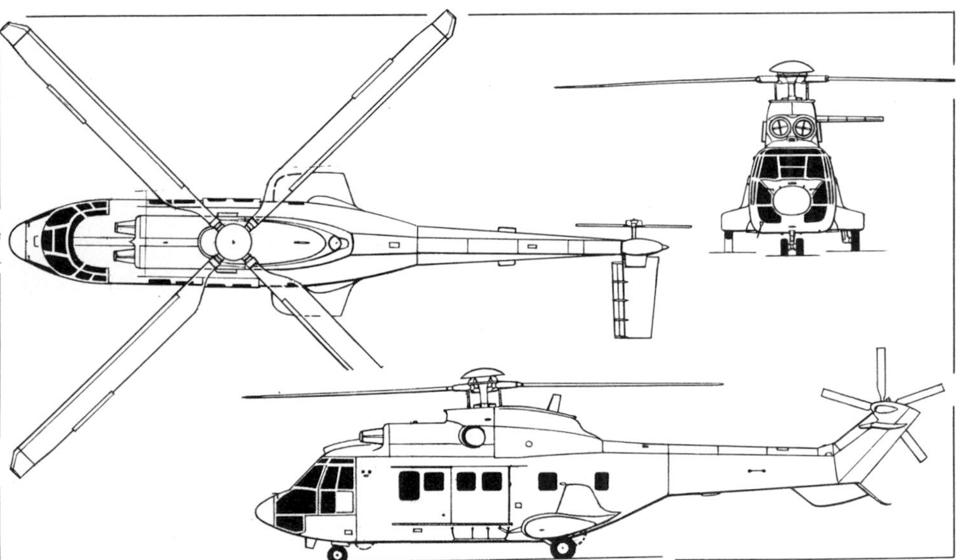

Aérospatiale AS 332L$_1$ Super Puma, with lengthened cabin *(Pilot Press)*

Orchidée battlefield surveillance radar in retracted position under tailboom of Super Puma demonstrator

type ergonomic seat for pilot. Cabin has two additional windows. Fuel capacity increased.

AS 332M$_1$. As 332B$_1$, but with cabin lengthened by 0·76 m (2 ft 6 in) to provide two more seats and two additional windows. Fuel capacity increased.

In early 1986, a Super Puma began flight evaluation of the Orchidée (Observatoire Radar Cohérent Héliporté d' Investigation Des Eléments Ennemis) battlefield surveillance system, intended as a key system for co-ordinating the actions of all French ground forces by the mid-1990s. As can be seen in an accompanying illustration, the Orchidée scanner is carried on a rotating mount under the rear of the helicopter's cabin. When not in use it is retracted upward to stow transversely under the junction of the rear fuselage and tailboom. It is a high-performance Doppler radar, capable of detecting and pinpointing troops and vehicles up to 54 nm (100 km; 62 miles) behind enemy lines while the Super Puma is 27 nm (50 km; 31 miles) inside friendly territory at an altitude of around 3,000 m (9,850 ft). Aérospatiale is industrial prime contractor for Orchidée, in conjunction with Laboratoire Central des Télécommunications, which supplies the radar and is responsible for the surveillance system. This is able to transmit data in real time to mobile ground stations built by Electronique Serge Dassault. Thomson-CSF and Matra are responsible for associated countermeasures.

All Super Puma variants are certificated for IFR category A and B operation, to FAR Pt 29 standards. The first Super Puma (an AS 332L) equipped for operation to IFR Cat II standards was certificated by the DGAC on 7 July 1983 and delivered to Lufttransport of Norway in September 1983. Certification of this version for flight into known icing conditions was granted on 29 June 1983. Corresponding FAA certifications cover Cat II automatic approach, using a SFIM CDV 85 P44 four-axis flight director coupler, and flight into known icing conditions under FAR Pt 25 Appendix C.

Orders for 250 Super Pumas, including six prototypes, for service in 26 countries, had been received by 1 April 1986. They include three for operation by the French Air Force on support duties at nuclear firing ranges in the Pacific; 22 military models for transport duties with the Singapore Air Force; 30 for maritime search and rescue (10), VIP transportation (2) and tactical transport duties (18) with the Spanish armed forces; six naval models, each armed with two Exocet missiles, for Kuwait; other military models for Abu Dhabi (8, incl 2 VIP), Argentina (up to 24), Brazil (8), Chile (3) and Oman (2 for Royal Flight); and 35 AS 332Ls for Bristow Helicopters, whose 19-passenger aircraft, serving offshore oil platforms, are known as **Tigers**. Special equipment on the Tigers includes foldable seats, enlarged windows, large rear baggage compartment, in-flight music, public address system, automatic emergency door jettison, and large capacity liferafts.

Deliveries of the Super Puma from French production began in mid-1981. IPTN of Indonesia (which see) is manufacturing several versions under licence, and 12 of the Spanish tactical transports will be assembled in Spain by CASA.

TYPE: Twin-turbine multi-role helicopter.

ROTOR SYSTEM: Four-blade main rotor, with a fully articulated hub and integral rotor brake. Each drag hinge is fitted with an elastomeric frequency adaptor. The blade cuffs, equipped with horns, are connected by link rods to the swashplate, which is actuated by three hydraulic twin-cylinder servo control units. Each of the moulded blades is made up of a glassfibre roving spar and a composite glassfibre and carbonfibre fabric skin, with Moltoprene filler. The leading-edge is covered with a titanium protective section. The tips are swept. Attachment of each blade to its sleeve by means of two quick-disconnect pins enables the blades to be folded back quickly by manual methods. The five-blade tail rotor has flapping hinges only, and is located on the starboard side of the tailboom. Optional de-icing system, with heating mat on leading-edge of each main and tail rotor blade.

ROTOR DRIVE: Mechanical shaft and gear drive. Modular main gearbox is fitted with two torquemeters and has two separate lubrication circuits. It is mounted on top of the cabin behind the engines, has two separate inputs from the engines and five reduction stages. The first stage drives, from each engine, an intermediate shaft directly driving the alternator and indirectly driving the two hydraulic pumps, with a further shaft drive to the ventilation fan. At the second stage the action of the two units becomes synchronised on a single main driveshaft by means of freewheeling spur gears. If one or both engines are stopped, this enables the drive gears to be rotated by the remaining turbine or the autorotating rotor, thus maintaining drive to the ancillary systems when the engines are stopped. Drive to the tail rotor is via shafting and an intermediate angle gearbox, terminating at a right-angle tail rotor gearbox. Turbine output 23,840 rpm; main rotor shaft 265 rpm, tail rotor shaft 1,278 rpm. The hydraulically controlled rotor brake, installed on the main gearbox, permits stopping of the rotor 15 s after engine shutdown.

FUSELAGE: Conventional all-metal semi-monocoque structure, embodying anti-crash features. Local use of titanium alloy under engine installation, which is outside the main fuselage shell. Monocoque tailboom supports the tail rotor on the starboard side and a horizontal stabiliser with fixed leading-edge slat (and optional pneumatic de-icing) on the port side. Large ventral fin. Optional folding tailboom for aircraft that serve on ships such as frigates.

LANDING GEAR: Retractable tricycle type, of Messier-Hispano-Bugatti high energy absorbing design. All units retract rearward hydraulically, mainwheels into fairings on sides of fuselage. Dual-chamber oleo-pneumatic shock absorbers. Optional 'kneeling' capability for main units. Twin-wheel self-centering nose unit, tyre size 466 × 176, pressure 6.0 bars (85 lb/sq in). Single wheel on each main unit with tyre size 615 × 225-10, pressure 6.0 bars (85 lb/sq in). Hydraulic differential disc brakes, controlled by foot pedals. Lever operated parking brake. Emergency pop-out flotation units can be mounted on main landing gear fairings and forward fuselage.

POWER PLANT: Two Turboméca Makila IA1 turboshaft engines, each with max contingency rating of 1,400 kW (1,877 shp) and max continuous rating of 1,184 kW (1,588 shp). Air intakes protected by a grille against ingestion of ice, snow and foreign objects; but multi-purpose intake is necessary for flight into sandy areas. AS 332B$_1$ has five flexible fuel tanks under cabin floor, with total capacity of 1,560 litres (343 Imp gallons; 412 US gallons). AS 332L$_1$/M$_1$ have a basic fuel system of six flexible tanks with total capacity of 2,060 litres (453 Imp gallons; 544 US gallons). Provision for additional 1,900 litres (418 Imp gallons; 502 US gallons) in four auxiliary ferry tanks installed in cabin. Two external auxiliary tanks are available, with total capacity of 700 litres (154 Imp gallons; 185 US gallons). For long range missions (mainly offshore), special internal auxiliary and external tanks can be fitted to raise the total fuel capacity to 3,090 litres (680 Imp gallons; 816 US gallons) in AS 332L$_1$. This auxiliary tank fits in cargo sling well beneath cabin floor and is quickly removable to permit use of sling. Refuelling point on starboard side of cabin. Fuel system is designed to avoid fuel leakage following a crash, with flexible fuel lines and interconnections between tanks, self-sealing valves and automatic fuel pump shutdown in a crash. Options include a fuel dumping system, pressure refuelling, and crash resistant or self-sealing tanks.

ACCOMMODATION: One pilot (VFR) or two pilots side by side (IFR) on flight deck, with jump seat for third crew member or paratroop dispatcher. Ergonomic seat for pilot on AS 332L$_1$. Provision for composite light alloy/Kevlar armour for crew protection on military models. Door on each side of flight deck and internal doorway connecting flight deck to cabin. Dual controls, co-pilot instrumentation and anti-crash flight deck floor. Max accommodation for 23 passengers in AS 332B$_1$/F$_1$, 24 in AS 332L$_1$ and 25 in AS 332M$_1$. Variety of interiors available for VIP use, or for air ambulance duty carrying six stretchers and eleven seated casualties/attendants, or nine stretchers and three seated. Strengthened floor for cargo carrying, with lashing points. Jettisonable sliding door on each side of main cabin, or port side door with built-in steps and starboard side double door in VIP or airline configurations. Removable panel on underside of fuselage, at rear of main cabin, permits longer loads to be accommodated, and also serves as emergency exit. Removable door with integral steps for access to baggage racks optional. A hatch in the floor below the centreline of the main rotor is provided for carrying loads of up to 4,500 kg (9,920 lb) on an internally mounted cargo sling. A fixed or retractable rescue hoist (capacity 275 kg; 606 lb) can be mounted externally on the starboard side of the fuselage. Cabin and flight deck are heated, ventilated and soundproofed. Demisting, de-icing, washers and wipers for pilots' windscreens.

SYSTEMS: Two independent hydraulic systems, supplied by self-regulating pumps driven by the main gearbox. Each system supplies one set of servo unit chambers, the left-hand system supplying in addition the autopilot, landing gear, rotor brake and wheel brakes. Freewheels in main gearbox ensure that both systems remain in operation, for supplying the servo controls, if the engines are stopped in flight. Other hydraulically actuated systems can be operated on the ground from the main gearbox (when a special disconnect system is installed to permit running of port engine with rotors stationary), or by external power through the ground power receptacle. There is also an independent auxiliary system, fed through a handpump, which can be used in an emergency to lower the landing gear. Three phase 200V AC electrical power supplied by two 40kVA 400Hz alternators, driven by the port side intermediate shaft from the main gearbox and available on the ground under the same conditions as the hydraulic ancillary systems. 28·5V DC power provided from the AC system by two transformer-rectifiers. Main aircraft battery used for self starting and emergency power in flight.

AVIONICS AND EQUIPMENT: Optional communications equipment includes VHF, UHF, tactical HF and HF/SSB radio installations and intercom system. Navigational equipment includes radio compass, radio altimeter, VLF Omega, Decca navigator and flight log, Doppler, and VOR/ILS with glidepath. SFIM 155 autopilot, with provision for coupling to self contained navigation and microwave landing systems. Full IFR instrumentation available optionally. Offshore models have nose mounted radar. The search and rescue version has nose mounted Bendix RDR 1400 or RCA Primus 40 or 50 search radar, Doppler, and Crouzet Nadir or Decca self contained navigation system, including navigation computer, polar indicator, roller map display, hover indicator, route mileage indicator and ground speed and drift indicator. For naval ASW and ASV missions, aircraft can be fitted with nose mounted OMERA type ORB 3214 360° radar, linked to a tactical table in the cabin, and an Alcatel HS 12 sonar station at the rear of the cabin.

ARMAMENT AND OPERATIONAL EQUIPMENT (optional): Typical alternatives for army/air force missions are one 20 mm gun, two 7·62 mm machine-guns, or two pods each containing thirty-six 68 mm rockets or nineteen 2·75 in rockets. Armament and equipment for naval missions includes two AM39 Exocet, six AS.15TT, or one Exocet and 3 AS.15TT missiles, or two torpedoes and sonar, or MAD and sonobuoys.

DIMENSIONS, EXTERNAL:
Main rotor diameter — 15·60 m (51 ft 2¼ in)
Tail rotor diameter — 3·05 m (10 ft 0 in)
Main rotor blade chord — 0·60 m (1 ft 11½ in)
Length overall, rotors turning — 18·70 m (61 ft 4¼ in)
Length of fuselage, incl tail rotor:
AS 332B$_1$/F$_1$ — 15·53 m (50 ft 11½ in)
AS 332L$_1$/M$_1$ — 16·29 m (53 ft 5½ in)
Width, blades folded:
AS 332B$_1$/L$_1$/M$_1$ — 3·79 m (12 ft 5¼ in)
AS 332F$_1$ — 4·04 m (13 ft 3 in)
Height overall — 4·92 m (16 ft 1¾ in)
Height, blades and tail pylon folded:
AS 332F$_1$ — 4·80 m (15 ft 9 in)
Height to top of rotor head — 4·60 m (15 ft 1¼ in)
Width overall, excl rotors — 3·79 m (12 ft 5¼ in)
Wheel track — 3·00 m (9 ft 10 in)
Wheelbase — 4·49 m (14 ft 8¾ in)
Passenger cabin doors, each:
Height — 1·35 m (4 ft 5 in)
Width — 1·35 m (4 ft 5 in)
Floor hatch, rear of cabin:
Length — 0·98 m (3 ft 2¾ in)
Width — 0·70 m (2 ft 3½ in)

DIMENSIONS, INTERNAL:
Cabin: Length: AS 332B$_1$ — 6·05 m (19 ft 10½ in)
AS 332L$_1$/M$_1$ — 6·81 m (22 ft 4 in)
Max width — 1·80 m (5 ft 11 in)
Max height — 1·55 m (5 ft 1 in)
Floor area: AS 332B$_1$ — 7·80 m² (84 sq ft)
Usable volume: AS 332B$_1$ — 11·40 m³ (403 cu ft)
AS 332L$_1$/M$_1$ — 13·30 m³ (469·5 cu ft)

AREAS:
Main rotor disc — 191·1 m² (2,057·4 sq ft)
Tail rotor disc — 7·31 m² (78·64 sq ft)

WEIGHTS:
Weight empty: AS 332B$_1$ — 4,290 kg (9,458 lb)
AS 332F$_1$ — 4,475 kg (9,866 lb)
AS 332L$_1$/M$_1$ — 4,420 kg (9,744 lb)
Max T-O weight:
AS 332B$_1$/F$_1$/M$_1$, internal load — 9,000 kg (19,841 lb)
AS 332L$_1$, internal load — 8,600 kg (18,960 lb)
all versions, with slung load — 9,350 kg (20,615 lb)

PERFORMANCE (at max T-O weight):
Never-exceed speed — 150 knots (278 km/h; 172 mph)
Econ cruising speed at S/L:
AS 332B$_1$/M$_1$ — 141 knots (262 km/h; 163 mph)
AS 332F$_1$ — 130 knots (240 km/h; 149 mph)
AS 332L$_1$ — 144 knots (266 km/h; 165 mph)
Max rate of climb at S/L:
AS 332B$_1$/M$_1$ — 426 m (1,397 ft)/min
AS 332F$_1$ — 372 m (1,220 ft)/min
AS 332L$_1$ — 486 m (1,594 ft)/min
Service ceiling: AS 332L$_1$ — 4,600 m (15,090 ft)
AS 332B$_1$/F$_1$/M$_1$ — 4,100 m (13,450 ft)
Hovering ceiling IGE:
AS 332B$_1$/F$_1$/M$_1$ — 2,700 m (8,850 ft)
AS 332L$_1$ — 3,100 m (10,170 ft)
Hovering ceiling OGE:
AS 332B$_1$/F$_1$/M$_1$ — 1,600 m (5,250 ft)
AS 332L$_1$ — 2,300 m (7,545 ft)

Aérospatiale AS 332M$_1$ Super Puma with lengthened cabin for 25 passengers

Range at S/L, standard tanks, no reserves:
AS 332B$_1$ — 334 nm (618 km; 384 miles)
AS 332F$_1$ — 400 nm (740 km; 460 miles)
AS 332L$_1$ — 470 nm (870 km; 540 miles)
AS 332M$_1$ — 455 nm (842 km; 523 miles)
Range at S/L with external (2 × 350 litre) and auxiliary (330 litre) tanks, no reserves:
AS 332M$_1$ — 596 nm (1,105 km; 686 miles)

AÉROSPATIALE SA 342 GAZELLE

The first prototype of the Gazelle (designated SA 340) made its first flight on 7 April 1967, powered by an Astazou III engine. Details of early versions of the helicopter can be found in the 1979-80 and 1984-85 *Jane's*. Versions currently available are as follows:

SA 342L$_1$. Current basic military version, with higher max T-O weight than earlier models. Powered by Astazou XIVM turboshaft with max rating of 640 kW (858 shp) and max continuous rating of 441 kW (592 shp).

SA 342M. For ALAT (French Army Light Aviation Corps). Differs from SA 342L$_1$ in having an ALAT instrument panel. Optional equipment specified as standard by ALAT includes SFIM PA 85G autopilot, Crouzet Nadir self-contained navigation system, Decca 80 Doppler and night flying equipment. An exhaust deflector remains optional. Order for first increment of planned total of 158 announced in December 1978, each armed with four Hot missiles and gyro stabilised sight for anti-tank warfare. Deliveries to the ALAT trials unit (GALSTA) began on 1 February 1980, and to an operational unit on 9 June 1980.

A two-stretcher ambulance configuration has received FAA supplemental type certification. No major modification is necessary to convert the aircraft to carry two patients longitudinally on the port side of the cabin, one above the other, leaving room for the pilot and a medical attendant in tandem on the starboard side. The dual spineboard arrangement weighs 27 kg (60 lb) and stows into the baggage compartment when not in use.

Under an Anglo-French agreement signed in 1967, Gazelles are produced jointly with Westland Helicopters Ltd; they have also been built under licence in Egypt and Yugoslavia. A total of 1,295 had been sold for civil and military operation in 38 countries by 1 January 1986, of which 1,139 had been delivered. Latest orders include six SA 342Ms for the air force of Angola.

Three Class E1c records were set by the SA 341-01 at Istres on 13 and 14 May 1971 and were unbeaten by mid-1986. These were: 167·28 knots (310·00 km/h; 192·62 mph) in a straight line over a 3 km course; 168·36 knots (312·00 km/h; 193·87 mph) in a straight line over a 15/25 km course; and 159·72 knots (296·00 km/h; 183·93 mph) over a 100 km closed circuit.

The following details apply to the SA 342, except where indicated:

TYPE: Five-seat light utility helicopter.

ROTOR SYSTEM: Three-blade semi-articulated main rotor and 13-blade shrouded fan anti-torque tail rotor (known as a 'fenestron' or 'fan-in-fin'). Rotor head and rotor mast form a single unit. The main rotor blades are of NACA 0012 section, attached to NAT hub by flapping hinges. There are no drag hinges. Each blade has a single leading-edge spar of plastics material reinforced with glassfibre, a laminated glass-fabric skin and honeycomb filler. Tail rotor blades are of die-forged light alloy, with articulation for pitch change only. Main rotor blades can be folded manually for stowage. Rotor brake standard.

ROTOR DRIVE: Main reduction gearbox forward of engine, which is mounted above the rear part of the cabin. Intermediate gearbox beneath engine, rear gearbox supporting the tail rotor. Main rotor/engine rpm ratio 387 : 6,334. Tail rotor/engine rpm ratio 5,918 : 6,334.

FUSELAGE: Cockpit structure is based on a welded light alloy frame which carries the windows and doors. This is mounted on a conventional semi-monocoque lower structure consisting of two longitudinal box sections connected by frames and bulkheads. Central section, which encloses the baggage hold and main fuel tank and supports the main reduction gearbox, is constructed of light alloy honeycomb sandwich panels. Rear section, which supports the engine and tailboom, is of similar construction. Honeycomb sandwich panels are also used for the cabin floors and transmission platform. Tailboom is of conventional sheet metal construction, as are the horizontal tail surfaces and the tail fin.

TAIL UNIT: Small horizontal stabiliser on tailboom, ahead of tail rotor fin.

LANDING GEAR: Steel tube skid type. Wheel can be fitted at rear of each skid for ground handling. Provision for alternative float or ski landing gear.

POWER PLANT: One Turboméca Astazou XIVM turboshaft engine, installed above fuselage aft of cabin and rated at 640 kW (858 shp). Two standard fuel tanks in fuselage (one beneath baggage compartment) with total usable capacity of 545 litres (120 Imp gallons; 144 US gallons). Provision for 200 litre (44 Imp gallon; 53 US gallon) ferry tank inside rear cabin. Total possible usable fuel capacity 745 litres (164 Imp gallons; 197 US gallons). Refuelling point on starboard side of cabin. Oil capacity 14·6 litres (3·2 Imp gallons; 4 US gallons) for engine, 3·5 litres (0·77 Imp gallons; 0·9 US gallons) for gearbox.

ACCOMMODATION: Crew of one or two side by side in front of cabin, with bench seat to the rear for a further three persons. The bench seat can be folded into floor wells to leave a completely flat cargo floor. Access to baggage compartment via rear cabin bulkhead, or via optional door on starboard side. Cargo tiedown points in cabin floor. Forward opening car type door on each side of cabin, immediately behind which are rearward opening

Aérospatiale SA 342L$_1$ Gazelle, armed with four Hot missile launchers

auxiliary cargo loading doors. Baggage compartment at rear of cabin. Ventilation standard. Dual controls optional.

SYSTEMS: Hydraulic system, pressure 40 bars (570 lb/sq in), serves three pitch change jacks for main rotor head and one for tail rotor. 28V DC electrical system supplied by 4kW engine driven generator and 40Ah battery. Optional 26V AC system, supplied by 0·5kVA alternator at 115/200V 400Hz.

AVIONICS AND EQUIPMENT: Optional communications equipment includes UHF, VHF, HF, intercom systems and homing aids. Optional navigation equipment includes radio compass, radio altimeter and VOR. Blind-flying instrumentation and autopilot optional. A variety of operational equipment can be fitted, according to role, including a 700 kg (1,540 lb) cargo sling, 135 kg (300 lb) rescue hoist, one or two stretchers (internally), or photographic and survey equipment.

ARMAMENT: Military loads can include two pods of Brandt 68 mm or FZ 2·75 in rockets, two AS.12 wire guided missiles with APX-Bézu 334 gyro stabilised sight, four or six Hot wire guided missiles with APX 397 gyro stabilised sight, two forward firing 7·62 mm machine-guns, or one GIAT axial 20 mm gun.

DIMENSIONS, EXTERNAL:
Main rotor diameter 10·50 m (34 ft 5½ in)
Tail rotor diameter 0·695 m (2 ft 3⅜ in)
Distance between rotor centres 5·85 m (19 ft 2¼ in)
Main rotor blade chord (constant) 0·30 m (11·8 in)
Length overall 11·97 m (39 ft 3⁵⁄₁₆ in)
Length of fuselage, incl tail rotor 9·53 m (31 ft 3³⁄₁₆ in)
Width, rotors folded 2·04 m (6 ft 8½ in)
Height to top of rotor head 2·72 m (8 ft 11⅛ in)
Height overall 3·19 m (10 ft 5½ in)
Skid track 2·015 m (6 ft 7⁵⁄₁₆ in)
Main cabin doors, each:
Height 1·05 m (3 ft 4⁹⁄₁₆ in)
Width 1·00 m (3 ft 3¼ in)
Height to sill 0·63 m (2 ft 0¾ in)
Auxiliary cabin doors, each:
Height 1·05 m (3 ft 4⁹⁄₁₆ in)
Width 0·48 m (1 ft 6¾ in)
Height to sill 0·63 m (2 ft 0¾ in)

DIMENSIONS, INTERNAL:
Cabin: Length 2·20 m (7 ft 2⁹⁄₁₆ in)
Max width 1·32 m (4 ft 4 in)
Max height 1·21 m (3 ft 11⅝ in)
Floor area 1·50 m^2 (16·1 sq ft)
Volume 1·80 m^3 (63·7 cu ft)
Baggage hold volume 0·45 m^3 (15·9 cu ft)

AREAS:
Main rotor blades, each 1·57 m^2 (16·9 sq ft)
Tail rotor blades, each 0·007 m^2 (0·075 sq ft)
Main rotor disc 86·59 m^2 (932·05 sq ft)
Tail rotor disc 0·37 m^2 (3·98 sq ft)
Fin 0·45 m^2 (4·84 sq ft)
Tailplane 1·80 m^2 (19·4 sq ft)

WEIGHTS AND LOADINGS:
Weight empty: 342L$_1$ 991 kg (2,184 lb)
Max T-O and landing weight:
342L$_1$ 2,000 kg (4,410 lb)
342M 1,900 kg (4,188 lb)
Max disc loading: 342L$_1$ 23·1 kg/m^2 (4·73 lb/sq ft)
342M 21·94 kg/m^2 (4·49 lb/sq ft)

PERFORMANCE (SA 342L$_1$ at max T-O weight):
Never-exceed speed at S/L 151 knots (280 km/h; 174 mph)
Max cruising speed at S/L 140 knots (260 km/h; 161 mph)
Max rate of climb at S/L 468 m (1,535 ft)/min
Service ceiling 4,100 m (13,450 ft)
Hovering ceiling: IGE 3,040 m (9,975 ft)
OGE 2,370 m (7,775 ft)
Range at S/L with standard fuel 383 nm (710 km; 440 miles)

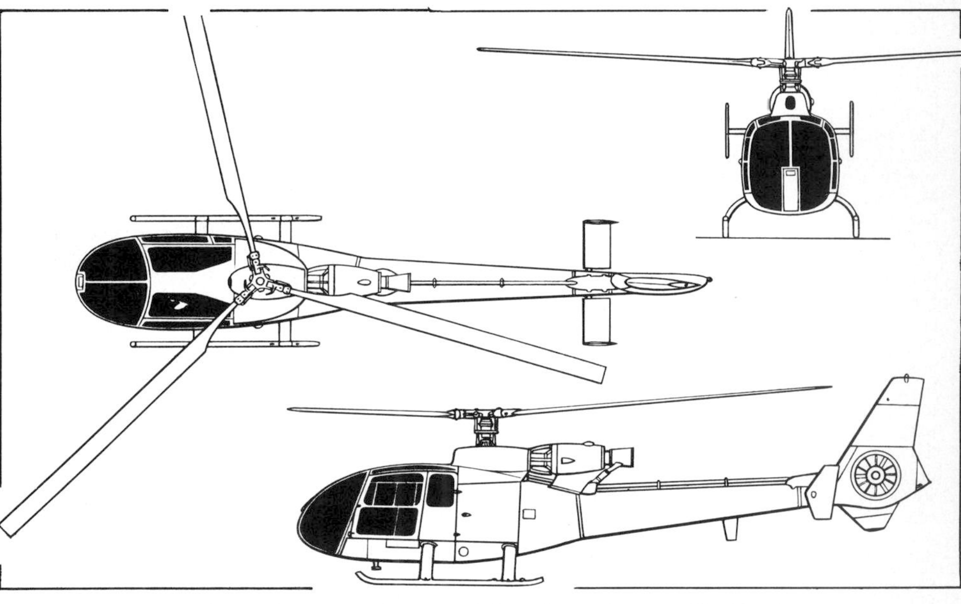

Aérospatiale Gazelle five-seat light utility helicopter *(Pilot Press)*

AÉROSPATIALE AS 350 ECUREUIL/ASTAR

Developed as a successor to the Alouette, the AS 350 Ecureuil (Squirrel) embodies Aérospatiale's Starflex type of main rotor hub, made of glassfibre, with elastomeric spherical stops and oleo-elastic frequency matchers. The first prototype (F-WVKH) flew on 27 June 1974, powered by an Avco Lycoming LTS 101 turboshaft engine. It was followed on 14 February 1975 by a second prototype (F-WVKI) with a Turboméca Arriel turboshaft.

The Avco Lycoming powered version is marketed only in North America, as the **Astar**; and the Arriel powered **Ecureuil** is marketed throughout the rest of the world. Current production versions are as follows:

AS 350B Ecureuil. Basic version with 478 kW (641 shp) Turboméca Arriel 1 turboshaft engine. French certification received on 27 October 1977.

AS 350B$_1$ Ecureuil. 'Hot and high' variant, with 510 kW (684 shp) Arriel 1D turboshaft; uprated transmission, with gearbox able to absorb max input of 440 kW (590 shp); and wide-chord, new section main and tail rotor blades developed originally for the Ecureuil 2/Twinstar. Certificated by DGAC on 9 January 1986.

On 14 May 1985 an AS 350B$_1$, at an AUW of 1,270 kg (2,800 lb) with a crew of two, set three official class E1c records by climbing to 3,000 m in 2 min 59·3 s, 6,000 m in 6 min 54·9 s, and 9,000 m in 13 min 51·5 s.

AS 350D Astar. Current Astar Mk III has 459 kW (615 shp) Avco Lycoming LTS 101-600A-3 turboshaft engine. Otherwise as AS 350B.

AS 350L$_1$ Ecureuil. Military version of AS 350B$_1$, with Arriel 1D turboshaft. Standard features include a taller landing gear, sliding doors, extended instrument panel and airframe reinforcement for axial armament. Provision for armoured seats. First flown in March 1985. Firing trials began in October 1985 and deliveries were in progress in Spring 1986.

Deliveries of the basic AS 350B began in March 1978. FAA certification of the original AS 350C Astar was obtained on 21 December 1977 and the first production delivery was made in April 1978. The AS 350C was superseded in 1978 by the AS 350D. By 1 January 1986 a total of 847 AS 350 Ecureuils and Astars had been delivered. Customers include the Singapore armed forces, which have six, and the Australian government, which has taken delivery of 18 AS 350Bs for RAAF pilot training, liaison, search and rescue, and six more for survey and utility duties with the Royal Australian Navy. Ecureuils are also produced under licence by Helibras of Brazil, with the name Esquilo.

Details of a specially equipped air ambulance version of the Astar were announced in Autumn 1980. Designed to meet American Hospital Association specifications, this accommodates two stretchers, one above the other, across the rear of the cabin, with a bubble door on the starboard side. Stretchers are staggered to facilitate access by the attendant, whose rearward facing seat is on the port side, next to the pilot. Options include a quick-disconnect oxygen system, dual intravenous system, lower stretcher lighting and attendant's swivelling seat.

During 1986, an AS 350B$_1$ Ecureuil with taller landing gear was fitted with a firefighting kit purchased from Conair of Canada, to test its effectiveness in dealing with forest fires in Southern France. The kit consists of a 700 litre (154 Imp gallon; 185 US gallon) streamlined tank which can be refilled in 30 s through a snout while the helicopter hovers over a stretch of water. The experiment proved highly successful and will be repeated in 1987.

Under a French government contract, Aérospatiale expected to fly in 1986 an AS 350 fitted with a 'fenestron' shrouded tail rotor, but this is not expected to become a feature of production Ecureuils of the current series.

TYPE: Five/six-seat light general purpose helicopter.

ROTOR SYSTEM: Three-blade main rotor, with Starflex glassfibre hub in which the three conventional hinges for each blade are replaced by a single balljoint of rubber/steel sandwich construction, requiring no maintenance. Glassfibre blades, with stainless steel leading-edge sheath, produced by an entirely mechanised process. Symmetrical blade section on AS 350B; OA 209 section on wider-chord blades of AS 350B$_1$ and L$_1$. Two-blade tail rotor; each blade comprises a sheet metal skin around a glassfibre spar, the flexibility of which obviates the need for hinges.

ROTOR DRIVE: Simplified transmission, with single epicyclic main gear train. By comparison with Alouette II, number of gear wheels is reduced from 22 to 9 and number of bearings from 23 to 9. Tail rotor driveshaft coupling on engine.

FUSELAGE: Basic structure of light alloy pressings, with skin mainly of thermoformed plastics, including baggage compartment doors.

TAIL UNIT: Horizontal stabiliser, of inverted aerofoil section, mid mounted on tailboom. Sweptback fin, in two sections above and below tailboom.

LANDING GEAR: Steel tube skid type. Taller version standard on military aircraft. Emergency flotation gear optional.

POWER PLANT: One turboshaft engine (for type see individual model listings) mounted above fuselage to rear of cabin. Plastics fuel tanks (self sealing on AS 350L$_1$) with total capacity of 530 litres (116·5 Imp gallons; 140 US gallons).

ACCOMMODATION: Two individual bucket seats at front of cabin and two two-place bench seats are standard. In the alternative layout the two benches are replaced by three armchair seats. Optional ambulance layout described in detail in introductory notes. Large forward hinged door on each side of versions for civil use. Optional sliding door at rear of cabin on port side. (Sliding doors standard on military version.) Baggage compartment aft of cabin, with full-width upward hinged door on starboard side. Top of baggage compartment reinforced to provide platform on each side for inspecting and servicing rotor head.

SYSTEMS: Hydraulic system includes four single-body servo units, operating at 40 bars (570 lb/sq in) pressure, and accumulators to protect against a hydraulic power supply failure. Electrical system includes a 4·5kW engine driven starter/generator, a 16Ah 24V nickel-cadmium battery and a ground power receptacle connected to the busbar which distributes power to the electrical equipment. Cabin air-conditioning system optional.

AS 350B$_1$ 'hot and high' variant of the Aérospatiale Ecureuil five/six-seat light helicopter

AVIONICS AND EQUIPMENT: Optional com/nav radio equipment includes VHF/AM, ICS, VOR/LOC/glideslope, marker beacon indicator, radio compass, HF/SSB, transponder and DME. IFR instrumentation optional. Available equipment includes a SFIM PA 85E, Sperry HelCis or Collins APS-841H autopilot, a 900 kg (1,984 lb) cargo sling, a 135 kg (297 lb) electric hoist, a TV camera for aerial filming, and a 735 litre (161 Imp gallon) Simplex agricultural spraytank and boom system.

ARMAMENT (AS $350L_1$): Provision for wide range of weapons, including 20 mm GIAT M621 gun, 7·62 mm machine-gun pods, Thomson Brandt launchers for twelve 68 mm rockets or Forges de Zeebrugge launchers for seven 2·75 in rockets.

DIMENSIONS, EXTERNAL:
- Main rotor diameter: 10·69 m (35 ft 0¾ in)
- Main rotor blade chord: AS 350B/D: 300 mm (11·8 in)
  - AS $350B_1/L_1$: 350 mm (13·8 in)
- Tail rotor diameter: 1·86 m (6 ft 1¼ in)
- Tail rotor blade chord: AS 350B/D: 185 mm (7·28 in)
  - AS $350B_1/L_1$: 205 mm (8·07 in)
- Length overall: 12·94 m (42 ft 5½ in)
- Length of fuselage, incl tail rotor: 10·93 m (35 ft 10½ in)
- Width of fuselage: 1·80 m (5 ft 10¾ in)
- Height overall: AS $350B/B_1/D$: 3·14 m (10 ft 3½ in)
  - AS $350L_1$: 3·34 m (10 ft 11½ in)
- Skid track: 2·10 m (6 ft 10¾ in)
- Cabin doors (civil versions, standard, each):
  - Height: 1·15 m (3 ft 9¼ in)
  - Width: 1·10 m (3 ft 7¼ in)

DIMENSIONS, INTERNAL:
- Cabin: Length: 2·42 m (7 ft 11¼ in)
  - Width at rear: 1·65 m (5 ft 5 in)
  - Height: 1·35 m (4 ft 5 in)
- Baggage compartment volume: 1·00 m³ (35·31 cu ft)

AREAS:
- Main rotor disc: 89·75 m² (966·1 sq ft)
- Tail rotor disc: 2·72 m² (29·25 sq ft)

WEIGHTS:
- Weight empty: 350B: 1,065 kg (2,348 lb)
  - $350B_1$: 1,108 kg (2,443 lb)
  - 350D: 1,070 kg (2,359 lb)
  - $350L_1$: 1,162 kg (2,562 lb)
- Max T-O weight: normal:
  - 350B/D: 1,950 kg (4,300 lb)
  - $350B_1/L_1$: 2,200 kg (4,850 lb)
  - with max slung load: 350B/D: 2,100 kg (4,630 lb)
  - $350B_1/L_1$: 2,450 kg (5,400 lb)

PERFORMANCE (at normal max T-O weight):
- Never-exceed speed below 500 m (1,640 ft):
  - All versions: 147 knots (272 km/h; 169 mph)
- Max cruising speed at S/L:
  - 350B: 125 knots (232 km/h; 144 mph)
  - $350B_1/D/L_1$: 124 knots (230 km/h; 143 mph)
- Max rate of climb at S/L:
  - 350B, 350D: 480 m (1,575 ft)/min
  - $350B_1/L_1$: 450 m (1,475 ft)/min
- Service ceiling: 350B/D: 4,575 m (15,000 ft)
  - $350B_1/L_1$: 4,500 m (14,760 ft)
- Hovering ceiling IGE: 350B: 2,950 m (9,675 ft)
  - $350B_1/L_1$: 2,870 m (9,415 ft)
  - 350D: 2,500 m (8,200 ft)
- Hovering ceiling OGE: 350B: 2,250 m (7,380 ft)
  - $350B_1/L_1$: 1,920 m (6,300 ft)
  - 350D: 1,800 m (5,900 ft)
- Range with max fuel at S/L, no reserves:
  - 350B: 378 nm (700 km; 435 miles)
  - $350B_1/L_1$: 354 nm (655 km; 407 miles)
  - 350D: 410 nm (760 km; 472 miles)

AÉROSPATIALE AS 355 ECUREUIL 2/TWINSTAR

The AS 355 is a twin-engined version of the AS 350 Ecureuil/Astar family. Many components, such as the main rotor mast and head, tail rotor hub, servo units, cabin and landing gear, are identical to those of the AS 350. The main and tail rotor blades are also identical to those of the current AS $350B_1/L_1$ versions. Major changes apply to the power plant, transmission, fuel system and fuselage structure.

The first of two prototypes (F-WZLA) flew for the first time on 28 September 1979. Details of the AS 355E/F initial production versions can be found in the 1984/85 and earlier editions of *Jane's*.

From January 1984, the AS 355F was superseded by the **AS $355F_1$**, incorporating three significant modifications. Addition of a laminated tab increased the tail rotor blade chord. The max power transmitted to the main gearbox was increased, by setting the torque limiter to 2 × 78% instead of 2 × 73%. Addition of a rotor overspeed alarm set to 410 rpm represented a complementary function of the normal alarm system. These changes permitted increased max T-O weight and payload.

A further increase in max T-O weight is offered by the **AS $355F_2$**, which received DGAC certification on 10 December 1985. This version introduced a load compensator in the yaw channel and an extension of the CG limits.

The AS $355F_2$ is intended primarily for the civil market, in particular for use by companies working in the oil industry. The Armée de l'Air is receiving 50 **AS 355M** military models for surveillance of strategic military bases and other support duties of which the last annual increment of six is

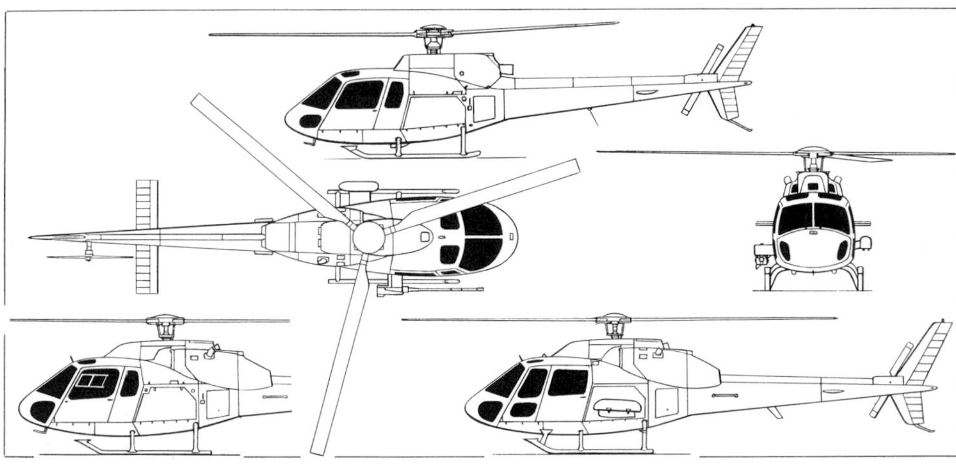

Aérospatiale AS 355M Ecureuil 2, with additional side elevation (top) of single-engined AS 350 and scrap view of AS $355F_1$ *(Pilot Press)*

Aérospatiale AS $355F_1$ Ecureuil 2 twin-turbine five/six-seat light helicopter

scheduled for procurement in 1989. A military version known as the **AS $355M_2$** (embodying the improvements developed for the latest civil variants) is available to other customers. Provision for carrying Matra Mistral infra-red missiles was expected to be introduced on the Armée de l'Air aircraft as deliveries built up. An accompanying illustration shows an alternative weapon load of rockets and a gun. Also available is a TOW anti-tank missile installation.

It is expected that the Allison turboshafts fitted in the AS 355 series will be superseded by Turboméca TM 319s in future versions of this helicopter, including those delivered to the Armée de l'Air from 1987.

By 1 January 1986, a total of 307 AS 355s had been delivered. The version for the North American market is known as the **Twinstar**; aircraft marketed elsewhere are named **Ecureuil 2**.

The following details apply to the AS $355F_2$ and M_2 versions:

TYPE: Twin-turbine light general purpose helicopter.

ROTOR SYSTEM: As for AS $350B_1/L_1$.

ROTOR DRIVE: Single main gearbox, made up of three modules (coupling gearbox with freewheel, angle gearing with spiral bevel gears, and epicyclic gear train including five oscillating planetary gears). Power take-offs for the accessories and tail rotor.

FUSELAGE: Light alloy centre fuselage structure, with deep drawn sheet metal forms of simple geometric design. Cabin skin of thermoformed plastics. Tapered tailboom of light alloy sheet wrapped and riveted around deep drawn sheet metal cylindrical frames.

TAIL UNIT AND LANDING GEAR: As for AS $350B_1/L_1$.

POWER PLANT: Two Allison 250-C20F turboshaft engines, each rated at 313 kW (420 shp) for take-off, mounted above fuselage to rear of cabin. Two structural fuel tanks, with total usable capacity of 730 litres (160 Imp gallons; 193 US gallons), in body structure.

ACCOMMODATION: As for AS $350B_1$, except sliding doors are optional on both sides (standard on military aircraft), and there are three baggage holds with external doors.

SYSTEMS, AVIONICS AND EQUIPMENT: As for AS $350B_1/L_1$, except that twin-body servo command units and a second electrical generator are standard. Options include a second VHF/AM, radio altimeter and casualty installations. Provisions for IFR instrumentation, and SFIM 85 T31 three-axis autopilot and CDV 85 T3 nav coupler.

ARMAMENT (AS $355M_2$): Optional alternative weapons include Brandt or Forges de Zeebrugge rocket packs, Matra or FN machine-gun pods, a GIAT M-621 20 mm gun, and Hot or TOW anti-tank missiles.

DIMENSIONS, EXTERNAL AND INTERNAL:
- As for AS $350B_1/L_1$

WEIGHTS:
- Weight empty: $355F_2$: 1,305 kg (2,877 lb)
  - $355M_2$: 1,360 kg (2,998 lb)

AS $355M_2$ military version of the Ecureuil 2 fitted with Brandt rocket packs

- Max sling load: $355F_2/M_2$: 1,134 kg (2,500 lb)
- Max T-O weight:
  - $355F_2/M_2$, internal load: 2,540 kg (5,600 lb)
  - $355F_2/M_2$, max slung load: 2,600 kg (5,732 lb)

PERFORMANCE (AS $355F_2/M_2$ at max T-O weight, ISA):
- Never-exceed speed (structural limitation): 150 knots (278 km/h; 172 mph)
- Max cruising speed at S/L: 121 knots (224 km/h; 139 mph)
- Max rate of climb at S/L: 390 m (1,280 ft)/min
- Service ceiling: 3,400 m (11,150 ft)
- Hovering ceiling: IGE: 1,800 m (5,900 ft)
  - OGE: 1,350 m (4,425 ft)
- Range with max fuel at S/L, no reserves: 380 nm (703 km; 437 miles)

AÉROSPATIALE SA 365F/AS.15TT DAUPHIN 2

On 13 October 1980, the government of Saudi Arabia placed in France orders for military equipment valued at 14,400 million francs. Known as the Sawari contract, it included the supply of 24 SA 365F Dauphin 2 helicopters, based on the SA 365N (which see). The first four of these are equipped with an Omera ORB 32 radar for search and rescue duties. The remaining 20 are anti-ship helicopters, equipped with Thomson-CSF Agrion 15 radar, Aérospatiale AS.15TT all-weather air-to-surface missiles and Crouzet MAD, for operation from both shore bases and frigates. Subsequent orders include five for Ireland, equipped with Bendix RDR L500 search radar, SFIM L55 autopilot, CDV L55 four-axis flight director/coupler, Crouzet Nadir Mk II nav computer, ESD Cina B Doppler, Crouzet ONS 200A long-distance nav system and five-screen EFIS instrumentation, for fishery surveillance and SAR from ship and shore bases.

An SA 365N (c/n 5100) was modified to flight test the equipment and weapon systems of the SA 365F, and made its first flight in the new configuration on 22 February 1982. It was followed by the first production SA 365F (c/n 6014) on 2 July 1982, equipped as a search and rescue helicopter with arrester hook, search radar, searchlight, self-contained navigation system, automatic hover/transition coupler and rescue winch. This aircraft completed deck landing trials on the French Navy missile frigate *De Grasse* and destroyer *Duperré* in the Summer of 1983, landing in headwinds of up to 90 km/h (56 mph), crosswinds up to 56 km/h (35 mph), tailwinds of 10 km/h (6 mph) and with the ships rolling up to 12°.

The anti-ship version carries the Agrion 15 radar on a roll-stabilised pivot mounting under its nose, to ensure a 360° field of sweep, a total of four AS.15TT missiles, in pairs on an outrigger on each side of the fuselage, and the MAD 'bird' on the port side of the rear fuselage. Agrion 15 is derived from the Iguane radar fitted to the Atlantique ATL2 maritime patrol aircraft, and possesses a track-while-scan capability that enables it to detect threats over long ranges while tracking ten targets simultaneously. Range of the AS.15TT missile is greater than 8 nm (15 km; 9·3 miles). In addition to locating and attacking hostile warships, the SA 365F/AS.15TT can be utilised for coastal surveillance and ship escort duties, and to provide over-the-horizon target designation for long range anti-ship missiles launched from ship or shore. An anti-submarine version is available, initially with MAD, sonobuoys and homing torpedoes, but with provision for Alcatel HS 12 sonar.

The SA 365F carries a normal crew of two, has provision for 10 passengers and is powered by two Turboméca Arriel IM turboshaft engines, each rated at 522 kW (700 shp) for take-off and with a max continuous rating of 465 kW (624 shp). Compared with the SA 365N, it has a larger, carbonfibre 11-blade 'fenestron' to improve hovering performance, particularly in the most severe condition of hovering with the wind from three-quarters aft.

DIMENSIONS, EXTERNAL:
As for SA 365N, except:

Diameter of 'fenestron'	1·10 m (3 ft 7 5/16 in)
Length overall, rotor turning	13·74 m (45 ft 1 in)
Length of fuselage	12·11 m (39 ft 8 3/4 in)
Width over missiles	4·20 m (13 ft 9 1/2 in)
Height to top of tail fin	3·99 m (13 ft 1 in)

WEIGHTS:

Weight empty	2,172 kg (4,788 lb)
Max slung load	1,600 kg (3,527 lb)
Max T-O weight, internal or external load	4,100 kg (9,039 lb)

PERFORMANCE (at max T-O weight):

Never-exceed speed	160 knots (296 km/h; 184 mph)
Max cruising speed at S/L	154 knots (285 km/h; 177 mph)
Max rate of climb at S/L	390 m (1,280 ft)/min
Hovering ceiling: IGE	2,150 m (7,050 ft)
OGE	1,200 m (3,935 ft)
Range with max standard fuel at S/L	467 nm (865 km; 537 miles)

AÉROSPATIALE SA 365N DAUPHIN 2

Chinese designation: Harbin Z-9

The prototype SA 365N (F-WZJD) flew for the first time on 31 March 1979 and was exhibited at the Paris Air Show in June of that year. A second prototype followed a few months later. The first production model (F-WZJJ) introduced changes to the rotor mast fairings, engine cowlings, crew doors, transmission and main rotor blades, as well as larger tail surfaces. French civil certification for VFR operation by day and night was received on 9 April 1981, followed by single-pilot IFR certification on 7 August 1981. FAA certification for VFR category A and B operation was received on 20 November 1981, followed by IFR certification in January 1983. Japanese JCAB certification for single-pilot IFR flight was received on 24 March 1982. Deliveries began early that year.

Production is under way in China (as **Harbin Z-9**), as well as France, following signature on 2 July 1980 of a licence agreement covering a first batch of 50 aircraft. The first SA 365N delivered to China under the terms of the agreement made its initial acceptance flight in the Beijing area on 6 February 1982. Orders for the SA 365N and variants received by Aérospatiale totalled 362 for civil and military use in 34 countries by 1 January 1986, of which 266 had been delivered. The totals include SA 366Gs for the US Coast Guard and SA 365F/AS.15TTs with special equipment for search and rescue, and for attacking surface ships. These variants are described separately.

Aérospatiale SA 365F/AS.15TT Dauphin 2 anti-ship helicopter

A special aeromedical version of the SA 365N, with a flight crew of two, is available in two forms. An 'intensive care' layout is arranged to carry two patients, one on each side of the cabin on a standard NATO stretcher, with space between for the doctor's seat and medical equipment. One of the stretchers can be replaced by seats for two patients, if required. The alternative 'ambulance' configuration provides space for four stretchers, one above the other on each side of the cabin, plus room for the doctor; or a single pair of stretchers, with room for four seated persons on the other side, and a doctor. Stretchers are loaded through nose doors, with 180° opening, on both models. Those in the ambulance layout are fixed to the sides of the cabin, and the patients are carried to them on special mattresses. Six of the 'intensive care' models have been delivered to the Medical Services Flight Department of the Saudi Army.

The following structural description refers to the standard SA 365N, but is generally applicable to all versions:

TYPE: Twin-turbine commercial general purpose helicopter.

ROTOR SYSTEM: Four-blade main rotor. Blades attached by quick disconnect pins to Starflex glassfibre/carbonfibre hub, in which the three conventional hinges for each blade are replaced by a single balljoint of rubber/steel sandwich construction, requiring no maintenance. Blades of new OA 2 section, developed in collaboration with Onera: varying from OA 212 (thickness/chord ratio 12%) at root to OA 207 (7%) at tip, with 10° negative twist from root to tip. Each blade comprises two Z section carbonfibre spars and carbonfibre skin, a solid glassfibre-resin leading-edge covered with a stainless steel sheath, and Nomex honeycomb filling. Leading-edge of carbonfibre tip is swept back at 45°. Ground adjustable tab on trailing-edge of each blade towards tip. Blade chord extended outboard of tab to align with tab trailing-edge. Rotor brake standard. Thirteen-blade 'fenestron' type of metal ducted fan anti-torque tail rotor.

ROTOR DRIVE: Mechanical shaft and gear drive. Transmission shaft from each engine extends forward, through freewheel, to helical and epicyclic reduction stages of main gearbox. Shaft to 'fenestron' driven off bottom of main rotor shaft. Main rotor rpm 349. 'Fenestron' rpm 4,706.

FUSELAGE: Semi-monocoque structure. Bottom structure and framework of front fuselage, primary machined frames fore and aft of the main gearbox platform and at the rear of the centre fuselage, floors under main gearbox and engines, cabin doors, 'fenestron' and fin are all of light alloy (AU4G). Nose and power plant fairings and fin tip of glassfibre/Nomex sandwich. Centre and rear fuselage assemblies, flight deck floor, roof, walls and bottom skins of fuel tanks of light alloy/Nomex sandwich.

TAIL UNIT: Horizontal stabiliser mid-set on rear fuselage, forward of 'fenestron'; swept endplate fins offset 10° to port. Construction of carbonfibre and Nomex/Rohacell sandwich.

LANDING GEAR: Hydraulically retractable tricycle type. Twin-wheel steerable and self-centering nose unit retracts rearward. Single wheel on each rearward retracting main unit, fully enclosed by doors of Kevlar/Nomex sandwich when retracted. All three units embody oleo-pneumatic shock absorber. Mainwheel tyres size 15 × 6·00, pressure 7 bars (101 lb/sq in); nosewheel tyres size 5·00-4, pressure 4 bars (58 lb/sq in). Hydraulic disc brakes.

POWER PLANT: Two Turboméca Arriel IC free turbine turboshaft engines, each rated at 530 kW (710 shp), mounted side by side aft of main rotor driveshaft, with stainless steel firewall between them. Standard fuel in four tanks under cabin floor and a fifth tank in the bottom of the centre-fuselage; total capacity 1,140 litres (250 Imp gallons; 301 US gallons). Provision for auxiliary tank in baggage compartment, with capacity of 180 litres (39·5 Imp gallons; 47·5 US gallons); or ferry tank in place of rear seats in cabin, capacity 475 litres (104·5 Imp gallons; 125·5 US gallons). Refuelling point above landing gear door on port side. Oil capacity 14 litres (3 Imp gallons; 3·7 US gallons).

ACCOMMODATION: Standard accommodation for pilot and co-pilot or passenger in front, and two rows of four seats to rear. High density seating for one pilot and 13 passengers. VIP configurations for four to six persons in addition to pilot. Three forward opening doors on each side. Freight hold aft of cabin rear bulkhead, with door on starboard side. Cabin heated and ventilated.

SYSTEMS: Air-conditioning system optional. Duplicated hydraulic system. Electrical system includes two 4·5kW starter/generators, one 17Ah 24V battery and two 250VA 115V 400Hz inverters.

AVIONICS AND EQUIPMENT: Optional avionics include VHF and HF com/nav, VOR, ILS, ADF, transponder, DME, radar and self contained nav system. Optional equipment includes a SFIM 155 duplex autopilot with SFIM CDV 85 nav coupler, a 1,600 kg (3,525 lb) capacity cargo sling,

Aérospatiale SA 365N Dauphin 2 operated in Gabon by Héli-Union

and 275 kg (606 lb) capacity hoist with 90 m (295 ft) cable length.

DIMENSIONS, EXTERNAL:
- Main rotor diameter 11·93 m (39 ft 1¾ in)
- Diameter of 'fenestron' 0·90 m (2 ft 11 7/16 in)
- Main rotor blade chord: basic 0·385 m (1 ft 3¼ in)
  - outboard of tab 0·405 m (1 ft 4 in)
- Length overall, rotor turning 13·46 m (44 ft 2 in)
- Length of fuselage 11·44 m (37 ft 6½ in)
- Width, rotor blades folded 3·21 m (10 ft 6½ in)
- Height to top of rotor head 3·51 m (11 ft 6¼ in)
- Height overall (tip of fin) 4·01 m (13 ft 2 in)
- Wheel track 1·90 m (6 ft 2¾ in)
- Wheelbase 3·61 m (11 ft 10¼ in)
- Main cabin door (fwd, each side):
  - Height 1·16 m (3 ft 9½ in)
  - Width 1·14 m (3 ft 9 in)
- Main cabin door (rear, each side):
  - Height 1·16 m (3 ft 9½ in)
  - Width 0·87 m (2 ft 10¼ in)
- Baggage compartment door (stbd):
  - Height 0·51 m (1 ft 8 in)
  - Width 0·73 m (2 ft 4¾ in)

DIMENSIONS, INTERNAL:
- Cabin: Length 2·30 m (7 ft 6½ in)
  - Max width 2·03 m (6 ft 8 in)
  - Max height 1·40 m (4 ft 7 in)
  - Floor area 4·20 m² (45·20 sq ft)
  - Volume 5·00 m³ (176 cu ft)
- Baggage compartment volume 1·60 m³ (56·5 cu ft)

AREAS:
- Main rotor disc 111·8 m² (1,203·2 sq ft)
- 'Fenestron' disc 0·636 m² (6·85 sq ft)

WEIGHTS:
- Weight empty, equipped 2,017 kg (4,447 lb)
- Max T-O weight:
  - internal or external load 4,000 kg (8,818 lb)

PERFORMANCE (at T-O weight of 3,850 kg; 8,488 lb):
- Never-exceed speed at S/L 164 knots (305 km/h; 189 mph)
- Max cruising speed at S/L 151 knots (280 km/h; 174 mph)
- Econ cruising speed at S/L 140 knots (260 km/h; 161 mph)
- Max rate of climb at S/L 462 m (1,515 ft)/min
- Service ceiling 4,575 m (15,000 ft)
- Hovering ceiling IGE and OGE 1,050 m (3,445 ft)
- Max range with standard fuel at S/L 475 nm (880 km; 546 miles)
- Endurance with standard fuel 4 h 40 min

AÉROSPATIALE SA 366 DAUPHIN 2

US Coast Guard designation: HH-65A Dolphin

At the 1979 Paris Air Show, Aérospatiale announced that it had won with this aircraft the competition for a helicopter to perform SRR (Short Range Recovery) duties from 18 shore bases, and from icebreakers and cutters, of the US Coast Guard. Current orders are for a total of 99 SA 366Gs, basically similar to the SA 365N but with engines and equipment of US manufacture accounting for about 60 per cent of the total cost of each aircraft.

The SA 366G (known to the Coast Guard as the HH-65A Dolphin) is powered by two Avco Lycoming LTS 101-750A-1 turboshafts, each rated at 507 kW (680 shp) and fitted with a Lucas SDS 300 full authority digital electronic control system. It normally carries a crew of three (pilot, co-pilot and aircrewman/hoist operator). Rockwell Collins is prime contractor for the advanced communications, navigation and all-weather search equipment. The communications package includes dual UHF/VHF transceivers and single UHF/FM and HF systems, plus a data link for automatic transmission of data, such as aircraft position, flight path, ground speed, wind and fuel state, to ship or shore base. Under development is a nose mounted Northrop See Hawk forward looking infra-red sensor to aid rescue operations in bad weather, darkness or high seas. Important design features include the passive failure characteristics of the Dolphin's automatic flight control system, and an omnidirectional airspeed system able to provide information while the aircraft is hovering. Inflatable flotation bags would enable occupants to evacuate the aircraft safely after a forced landing in sea state 5, and would keep the helicopter afloat for subsequent salvage.

The first SA 366G flew for the first time at Marignane on 23 July 1980. It was later shipped to Aérospatiale Helicopter Corporation in Texas for installation of avionics, and flight testing for FAA certification. DGAC certification was received on 20 July 1982. As on the SA 365F/M, the size of the tail fin and carbonfibre 'fenestron' is increased on the operational Coast Guard aircraft, designated **SA 366G-1**. The first was delivered on 19 November 1984, and 22 had been accepted by February 1986. The first life-saving medevac mission was completed on 20 September 1985, when a crewmember of a fishing vessel, his foot almost severed, was hoisted into an HH-65A from New Orleans air station and flown to hospital. Aircraft covered by current contracts will all be in service by 1988.

Two HH-65As, procured with US foreign military sales funding, have been delivered to Israel for evaluation to meet a requirement for up to 20 short range recovery helicopters for the Israeli Defence Force.

Aérospatiale HH-65A Dolphin (SA 366G-1) for the US Coast Guard

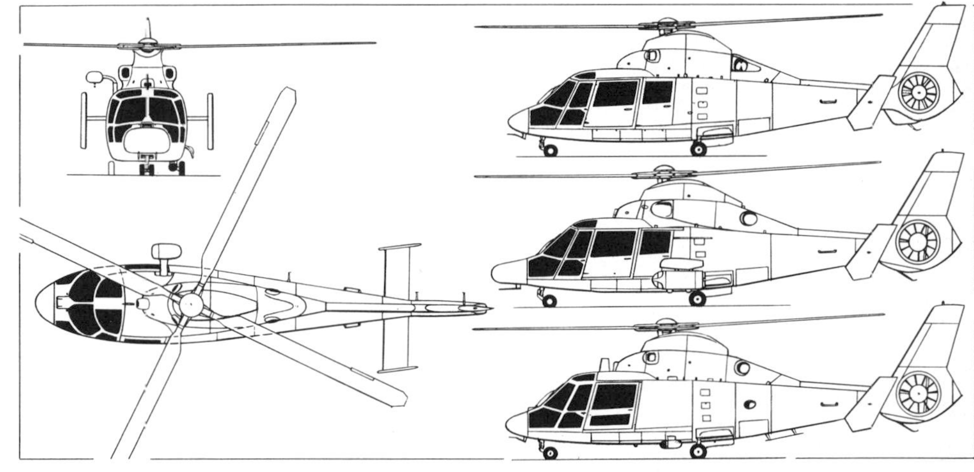

Aérospatiale SA 365M Panther, with added side views of HH-65A Dolphin (SA 366G-1) for US Coast Guard (centre) and SA 365N Dauphin 2 (top) *(Pilot Press)*

WEIGHTS:
- Weight empty, incl mission equipment 2,718 kg (5,992 lb)
- Max T-O weight 4,050 kg (8,928 lb)

PERFORMANCE (at max T-O weight):
- Never-exceed speed 175 knots (324 km/h; 201 mph)
- Max cruising speed 139 knots (257 km/h; 160 mph)
- Hovering ceiling: IGE 2,290 m (7,510 ft)
  - OGE 1,627 m (5,340 ft)
- SRR range 166 nm (307 km; 191 miles)
- Range with max passenger load 216 nm (400 km; 248 miles)
- Range with max fuel 410 nm (760 km; 471 miles)
- Endurance with max fuel 4 h

AÉROSPATIALE SA 365M PANTHER

This multi-role military development of the Dauphin 2 was first flown in prototype form (F-WZJV) on 29 February 1984. It has since undergone considerable refinement, and was first shown in production form, as the Panther, on 30 April 1986. Armament integration and firing trials were scheduled for completion in October 1986. The Panther will be available for delivery in 1988.

The airframe of the Panther is basically similar to that of the SA 365N, but with greater emphasis on survivability in combat areas. Composite materials are used exclusively for the dynamic components and for an increased (15 per cent) proportion of the fuselage structure. The crew seats are armoured, and similar protection will be extended to the flying control servos and engine controls of production Panthers. Other features include a cable cutter, self-sealing fuel tanks and redundant hydraulic circuits. Further development is expected to permit continued operation of the main transmission after total loss of lubricating oil.

Similar attention has been paid to crashworthiness. The crew seats will tolerate 15*g*. The entire basic airframe is designed to withstand an impact at a vertical speed of 7 m (23 ft)/s at max T-O weight; the fuel system is capable of withstanding a 14 m (46 ft)/s crash.

The Panther is powered by two Turboméca TM 333-1M turboshaft engines, each rated at 680 kW (912 shp), and utilises the larger carbonfibre 'fenestron' of the SA 365F. To

Prototype SA 365M Panther fitted with engine IR suppressor and carrying two 20 mm gun pods

reduce IR signature, the airframe is finished in low IR reflecting paint, and the engine efflux is first mixed with cool ambient air and then ejected upward. Noise level is low, and radar signature is minimised by the aircraft's composite structure and special paints. Night operations are made practicable by adaptation of the cockpit to nap-of-the-earth flight using night vision goggles. Equipment can include a Sherloc radar warning receiver, IR jammer and chaff dispenser.

As a high speed assault transport, the Panther will carry a crew of two and eight to ten troops over a radius of action of 215 nm (400 km; 248 miles), or 60 troops per hour over 11 nm (20 km; 12 miles). For close support missions of three-hour duration, the fuselage-side outriggers can each carry a pack of 22 Brandt 68 mm rockets, a launcher for 19 Forges de Zeebrugge 2·75 in rockets or a 20 mm GIAT gun pod with 180 rounds. Three-hour day or night anti-tank missions are possible, carrying four two-round packs of Hot anti-tank missiles with an associated Viviane roof mounted stabilised sight. Operations against fixed-wing aircraft or other helicopters are envisaged, using either 20 mm guns or four two-round packs of Matra Mistral infra-red homing air-to-air missiles. Secondary roles could include armed or unarmed reconnaissance, electronic warfare, target designation, aerial command post, search and rescue, casualty evacuation (four stretchers) and transport of up to 1,600 kg (3,525 lb) of external freight.

Dimensions, external: As for SA 365F, except:
- Length of fuselage — 12·07 m (39 ft 7¼ in)
- Height to top of tail fin — 4·07 m (13 ft 4¼ in)

Weights:
- Basic operating weight, incl 2 crew — 2,690 kg (5,930 lb)
- Max slung load — 1,600 kg (3,527 lb)
- Max T-O weight, internal or external load — 4,100 kg (9,039 lb)

Performance (at max T-O weight):
- Never-exceed speed — 160 knots (296 km/h; 184 mph)
- Max cruising speed at S/L — 150 knots (278 km/h; 172 mph)
- Max rate of climb at S/L — 480 m (1,575 ft)/min
- Hovering ceiling: IGE — 3,200 m (10,500 ft)
- OGE — 2,500 m (8,200 ft)
- Range with max standard fuel at S/L — 400 nm (740 km; 460 miles)

Model of projected design for Hermes aerospacecraft, with doors of cargo bay open

HERMES AEROSPACECRAFT

On 18 October 1985 it was announced that the French Centre National d'Études Spatiales (CNES) had appointed Aérospatiale as industrial prime contractor for the Hermes aerospacecraft programme. Aérospatiale will build the vehicle. Dassault-Breguet will be responsible for the work required to achieve successful flight in the atmosphere.

The Hermes vehicle is envisaged as a delta-wing aircraft with winglets, able to carry two to six persons and up to five tonnes of payload. Placed in low Earth orbit by an Ariane 5 launcher, its primary mission will be to service space stations.

CAGNY

RAYMOND DE CAGNY

5 Square des Bégonias, 91370 Verrières le Buisson
Telephone: 33 (1) 60 11 98 02

M de Cagny is developing a unique side by side three-seat light aircraft, which was first displayed in the form of a full scale mockup at the 1985 Paris Air Show.

CAGNY PERFORMANCE 2000

The design of this all-composites light aircraft was based on the results of a survey carried out among flying clubs in France and overseas. Answers to two of the questions showed a general preference for an Avco Lycoming engine and a three-seat cabin. M Cagny decided to place the three seats of his Performance 2000 side by side, so that the third occupant would share the excellent field of view of the pilots and, being aware of their actions during flying training, might be encouraged to become a pupil pilot.

Current high costs of flying training are expected to be reduced in the Performance 2000 by use of sturdy but lightweight composites, which offer a smooth surface finish, minimal maintenance requirements, easy replacement, and long service life. Positioning of the engine on the fin leading-edge reduces cabin noise, while the shrouded propeller eliminates danger for those around the aircraft on the ground.

First flight of the prototype Performance 2000 will take place no earlier than December 1986. Its construction is being financed by the Nord Pas-de-Calais regional council.

Type: Three-seat light training aircraft.

Wings: Cantilever mid-wing monoplane. Dihedral and sweepback constant from roots, except for inboard trailing-edges which are unswept. All-composites structure with slightly upswept tips. Inset aileron in each outer wing panel; trailing-edge flap in each inboard panel. Wings easily removable.

Fuselage: All-composites semi-monocoque structure of pod and boom form. Retractable steps.

Tail Unit: Cantilever all-composites structure, with sweepback on all surfaces. Tailplane mid-mounted on fin. Elevators and two-section rudder. Shallow ventral fin/bumper on each bottom edge of tailboom.

Landing Gear: Non-retractable tricycle type, with single wheel on each unit. Cantilever main units with composite spring legs. Disc brakes on mainwheels.

Power Plant: One 80 kW (108 hp) Avco Lycoming O-235 flat-four engine, mounted on leading-edge of fin and driving a shrouded three-blade tractor propeller. Shroud braced from fin-tip leading-edge. Provision for alternative engines. One fuel tank, capacity 75 litres (16·5 Imp gallons; 19·8 US gallons).

Accommodation: Three seats side by side in fully enclosed and soundproofed cabin. Seats of semi-reclining type. Baggage hold aft of seats. Access to cabin by means of a downward hinged door. Large wraparound windscreen and canopy, each in one piece. Cabin heated and ventilated.

Mockup of Cagny Performance 2000 three-seat trainer *(Brian M. Service)*

Dimensions, external:
- Wing span — 8·60 m (28 ft 2½ in)
- Length overall — 6·80 m (22 ft 3¾ in)
- Height overall — 2·80 m (9 ft 2¼ in)
- Wheel track — 1·80 m (5 ft 11 in)
- Wheelbase — 2·80 m (9 ft 2¼ in)

Dimensions, internal:
- Cabin: Length — 1·80 m (5 ft 11 in)
- Max width — 1·54 m (5 ft 0½ in)
- Max height — 1·04 m (3 ft 5 in)

Area:
- Wings, gross — 10·80 m² (116·3 sq ft)

Weights and Loadings (estimated):
- Weight empty — 375 kg (827 lb)
- Max baggage — 20 kg (44 lb)
- Max T-O weight — 665 kg (1,466 lb)
- Max wing loading — 61·6 kg/m² (12·6 lb/sq ft)
- Max power loading — 8·31 kg/kW (13·6 lb/hp)

Performance (estimated):
- Max level speed — 118 knots (220 km/h; 136 mph)
- Cruising speed (75% power) — 110 knots (205 km/h; 127 mph)
- Stalling speed: flaps up — 46 knots (85 km/h; 53 mph)
- flaps down — 38 knots (70 km/h; 44 mph)
- Max rate of climb at S/L — 210 m (690 ft)/min
- Service ceiling — 4,000 m (13,125 ft)
- T-O run — 350 m (1,150 ft)
- Landing run — 160 m (525 ft)
- Range with max fuel — 432 nm (800 km; 497 miles)

CENTRAIR

SA CENTRAIR

BP 44, Aérodrome, 36300 Le Blanc
Telephone: (54) 37 07 96 and 37 06 91
Telex: 750272 F

President/Director General: Marc Ranjon

In addition to manufacturing sailplanes and sport aircraft, as described in the appropriate sections of this edition, Centrair is building the prototype of a small business aircraft of advanced concept in collaboration with the École Nationale Supérieure de l'Aéronautique et de l'Espace of Toulouse (ENSAE).

CENTRAIR/ENSAE SUP'AIR

At the 1985 Paris Air Show, ENSAE displayed the full scale mockup of a small single-seat canard known as the Sup'aero, powered by two Microturbo TRS 18 turbojets. The six-seat all-composites Sup'Air, powered by a single rear-mounted piston engine, is a parallel project started by

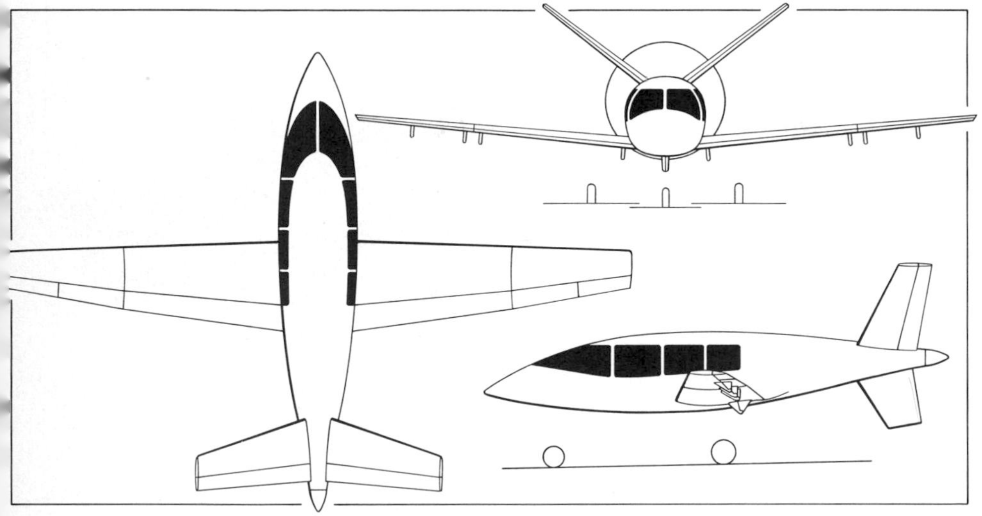

Centrair/ENSAE Sup'Air six-seat business transport *(Jane's/Mike Keep)*

Centrair in 1980, in collaboration with ENSAE, ENSICA, ENSMA and Dassault-Breguet St-Cloud. A prototype of the Sup'Air was under construction by Centrair in Summer 1986, and was expected to be completed in time for demonstration at the 1987 Paris Air Show. The following details should be regarded as provisional:

TYPE: Six-seat business aircraft, conforming to FAR Pt 23.

WINGS: Cantilever low-wing monoplane. Thickness/chord ratio 12%. Dihedral 5° from roots. Incidence 0° 30′. No sweep at quarter-chord. Constructed of carbonfibre and glassfibre, with two spars. Glassfibre ailerons and trailing-edge flaps.

FUSELAGE: Highly streamlined semi-monocoque structure of glassfibre composites, with max cross-section of 1·57 m² (16·9 sq ft).

TAIL UNIT: Cantilever Y type structure of glassfibre composites. V type fixed surfaces and elevators with included angle of 107°.

LANDING GEAR: Retractable tricycle type, with single wheel on each unit. Mainwheels retract inward, nosewheel forward. Oleo-pneumatic shock absorbers. Tyre size: Mainwheels 6·00-5 6PR, nosewheel 5·00-5 6PR.

POWER PLANT: One 179 kW (240 hp) Porsche PFM 3200 turbocharged flat-six engine, mounted in rear fuselage and driving a tail-mounted Hoffmann HOV 123 three-blade variable-pitch propeller with spinner through CIBA Geigy composites extension shaft. Fuel tanks in wings, total capacity 282 litres (62 Imp gallons; 74 US gallons).

ACCOMMODATION: Pilot and five passengers in pairs in enclosed cabin. Upward hinged door.

DIMENSIONS, EXTERNAL:

Wing span	10·80 m (35 ft 5¼ in)
Wing chord: at root	1·56 m (5 ft 1½ in)
at tip	0·66 m (2 ft 2 in)
Wing aspect ratio	9·04
Length overall	8·11 m (26 ft 7¼ in)
Fuselage diameter (max)	1·36 m (4 ft 5½ in)
Height overall	3·31 m (10 ft 10½ in)
Tail unit span	4·67 m (15 ft 4 in)
Wheel track	2·50 m (8 ft 2½ in)
Wheelbase	3·01 m (9 ft 10½ in)
Propeller diameter	2·00 m (6 ft 6¾ in)
Propeller ground clearance	0·85 m (2 ft 9½ in)

DIMENSIONS, INTERNAL:

Cabin: Length	2·93 m (9 ft 7¼ in)
Max width	1·30 m (4 ft 3¼ in)
Height	1·11-1·16 m (3 ft 7¾ in to 3 ft 9½ in)

AREA:

Wings, gross	12·9 m² (138·8 sq ft)

WEIGHTS AND LOADINGS:

Weight empty	826 kg (1,821 lb)
Max fuel	188 kg (415 lb)
Max T-O weight	1,423 kg (3,137 lb)
Max wing loading	110·3 kg/m² (22·6 lb/sq ft)
Max power loading	7·95 kg/kW (13·07 lb/hp)

PERFORMANCE (estimated):

Econ cruising speed at 2,600 m (8,500 ft)	205 knots (380 km/h; 236 mph)
Stalling speed, flaps down	56 knots (103 km/h; 64 mph)
Max rate of climb at S/L	420 m (1,378 ft)/min
Service ceiling	6,700 m (22,000 ft)
Range with max fuel	1,080 nm (2,000 km; 1,242 miles)

DASSAULT-BREGUET

AVIONS MARCEL DASSAULT—BREGUET AVIATION

33 rue du Professeur Victor Pauchet, 92420 Vaucresson

POSTAL ADDRESS: BP 32, 92420 Vaucresson

Telephone: (1) 47 41 79 21

Telex: AMADAS 203944 F

PRESS INFORMATION OFFICE: 27 rue du Professeur Victor Pauchet, BP 32, 92420 Vaucresson

Telephone: (1) 47 41 79 21

WORKS: 92214 Saint-Cloud, 77000 Melun-Villaroche, 95100 Argenteuil, 92100 Boulogne/Seine, 78140 Vélizy-Villacoublay, 33610 Martignas, 33700 Bordeaux-Mérignac, 91120 Brétigny, 33630 Cazaux, 31770 Toulouse-Colomiers, 64600 Biarritz-Anglet, 64200 Biarritz-Parme, 13800 Istres, 74370 Argonay, 93350 Le Bourget, 59113 Lille-Seclin, 86000 Poitiers

PRESIDENT AND CHIEF EXECUTIVE: B. C. Vallières

EXECUTIVE VICE-PRESIDENTS: X. D'Iribarne, J. Estèbe

SECRETARY GENERAL: C. Edelstenne

GENERAL TECHNICAL MANAGER: B. Revellin-Falcoz

GENERAL MANAGER, INTERNATIONAL AFFAIRS: H. de l'Estoile

EXPORT TECHNICAL MANAGER: Y. Thiriet

MILITARY AIRCRAFT SALES MANAGERS: F. Serralta, P. E. Jaillard

CIVIL AIRCRAFT SALES MANAGER: B. Latreille

BUSINESS JET SALES MANAGER: P. Delorme

PRODUCTION MANAGER: J. C. Veber

FLIGHT TEST MANAGER: J. F. Cazaubiel

PRESS INFORMATION MANAGER: Henri Suisse

Avions Marcel Dassault—Breguet Aviation resulted from the merger in December 1971 of Avions Marcel Dassault with Breguet Aviation. In January 1979, 20 per cent of its stock was assigned to the French State, and in November 1981 the State shareholding was raised to 46 per cent. Due to a double voting right of some of its shares, the French State holds a majority control of the company.

Dassault-Breguet is engaged in the development and production of military and civil aircraft, and servo control equipment. Series production of its aircraft is undertaken under a widespread subcontracting programme, with final assembly and flight testing handled by the company. Its 18 separate works and facilities covered 653,335 m² (7,032,500 sq ft), with a total of 15,790 employees, in May 1985.

Dassault-Breguet has established close links with the industries of other countries. The programme for the Atlantique maritime patrol aircraft associates manufacturers in Belgium, France, West Germany, Italy and the Netherlands under the overall responsibility of their respective governments. In the same way the British and French governments are associated in the SEPECAT concern, formed to control the Dassault-Breguet/BAe Jaguar programme; and the West German and French governments are associated in the Dassault-Breguet/Dornier Alpha Jet programme. Purchase of Mirage fighters by Belgium and Spain led to Belgian and Spanish participation in Mirage III/5 and Mirage F1 production. Similarly, purchase of Mirage 2000 fighters by Greece has led to co-production of components for this aircraft by the Hellenic Aerospace Industry. Dassault-Breguet's Biarritz-Parme factory manufactures fuselages for Fokker.

DASSAULT-BREGUET MIRAGE III

The Mirage III was designed initially as a Mach 2 high altitude all-weather interceptor, capable also of performing ground support missions. Developed versions included a two-seat trainer, long range fighter-bomber and reconnaissance aircraft. A total of 1,412 Mirage III/5/50s of all types (incl 870 Mirage IIIs) were ordered and delivered for service in 20 countries, including licence production abroad. They were described fully in the 1985-86 and previous editions of *Jane's*.

DASSAULT-BREGUET MIRAGE 5

The Mirage 5 is a ground attack aircraft using the same airframe and engine as the Mirage III-E. A total of 525 was ordered and built for eleven air forces, including Mirage 5-R reconnaissance variants and two-seat Mirage 5-Ds. Details can be found in the 1985-86 and previous editions of *Jane's*.

DASSAULT-BREGUET MIRAGE 50

The Mirage 50 multi-mission fighter retains the basic airframe of the Mirage III/5 series, but is powered by the SNECMA Atar 9K-50 turbojet, as fitted in the Mirage F1s of the French Air Force and ten other air forces. This gives 70·6 kN (15,873 lb st) with afterburning, representing a thrust increase of between 17 and 23 per cent compared with standard Mirage III/5s.

The prototype Mirage 50 flew for the first time on 15 April 1979. First and only announced customer was the air force of Chile, which ordered a total of sixteen. Further details can be found in the 1985-86 *Jane's*.

MIRAGE ADVANCED TECHNOLOGY UPDATE PROGRAMME

Since 1977, Dassault has been involved in programmes to update the navigation and attack systems, flight aids, radio com/nav, power plant and other features of in-service Mirage III/5/50 aircraft. In particular, several air forces

Demonstration of flight refuelling system now available for Mirage III/5/50 aircraft. The 'buddy' tanker is a Mirage 2000

have awarded Dassault contracts to install an inertial platform, digital computer, CRT head-up display, air-to-ground laser rangefinder and other equipment for improved navigational accuracy, easier target acquisition, and high bombing precision in the various CCIP (continuous computation of the impact point) or CCRP (continuous computation of the release point) modes, including standoff capability through the introduction of CCRP with initial point. Combat efficiency in the air-to-air gunnery mode is improved considerably by display of a highly accurate hotline on the HUD.

All of these improvements are designed to decrease the pilot's task, so enhancing efficiency and survivability, in parallel with improved reliability. Current modernisation programmes, involving the Peruvian Mirage 5 inventory and part of the Egyptian inventory, are in progress in the respective home countries. They are intended, primarily, to add an inertial platform, digital computer and CRT head-up display.

Another major improvement available for the Mirage III/5/50 series is a flight refuelling kit able to offer an increase of 30 to more than 100 per cent in radius of action. Already ordered by one air force for its Mirage 5s, this system was demonstrated in flight before becoming generally available to Mirage operators in 1986. It involves lengthening the nose of the aircraft by 90 mm (3½ in) to accommodate system changes associated with a non-retractable probe on the starboard side, forward of the windscreen, and a single-point pressure refuelling port for both internal and external tanks. Overall refuelling can be accomplished at a rate of 1,000 litres (220 Imp gallons; 264 US gallons)/min. Turnround time between missions can be greatly reduced, at no cost in Mach 2 performance.

DASSAULT-BREGUET MIRAGE 3 NG

This new-generation (Nouvelle Génération) development of the Mirage III/5/50 series is based on the same well-proven airframe, but introduces features which give it much improved air combat performance and survivability in air-to-ground operations. It is powered, like the Mirage 50 and F1, by a SNECMA Atar 9K-50 turbojet engine, rated at 70·6 kN (15,873 lb st) with afterburning. New aerodynamic advances are evident in the added non-retractable swept-back foreplanes and highly-swept wing root leading-edge extensions. It also features a fully fly by wire control system derived from that of the Mirage 2000, and can be equipped for in-flight refuelling.

The navigation/attack system of the Mirage 3 NG is an up to date and highly reliable system composed basically of an inertial platform, CRT head-up display, and optional forward looking sensors such as modernised Cyrano IV radar, a laser rangefinder or Agave air-to-air/air-to-surface radar.

Maximum take-off weight is increased significantly by comparison with the Mirage III. This enables the external load carrying capability to be increased, notably by the addition of four lateral stores stations on the fuselage. Provision is made for adapting the Mirage 3 NG to advanced weapons, and for its use as either a specialised reconnaissance aircraft or a vehicle for mission adapted reconnaissance packs.

The prototype Mirage 3 NG flew for the first time on 21 December 1982. No orders had been announced by Summer 1986.

DIMENSIONS, EXTERNAL:

Wing span	8·22 m (26 ft 11½ in)
Wing aspect ratio	1·94
Length overall	15·65 m (51 ft 4¼ in)
Height overall	4·50 m (14 ft 9 in)
Wheel track	3·15 m (10 ft 4 in)
Wheelbase	4·87 m (15 ft 11¾ in)

AREAS:

Wings, gross	35·00 m² (376·7 sq ft)
Foreplanes	1·00 m² (10·8 sq ft)

WEIGHTS:

T-O weight 'clean'	10,000 kg (22,050 lb)
Max T-O weight	14,700 kg (32,400 lb)

PERFORMANCE:

Max authorised Mach number in level flight	2·2
Max authorised speed in level flight	750 knots (1,390 km/h; 863 mph) IAS
Service ceiling at Mach 2	16,460 m (54,000 ft)

DASSAULT MIRAGE IV-P

Eighteen of the Mirage IV strategic bombers operated by the Commandement des Forces Aériennes Stratégiques (CFAS) of the French Air Force are being modified to carry the ASMP medium-range air-to-surface nuclear missile. Navigation and targeting capabilities are improved by installation of a Thomson-CSF Arcana pulse-Doppler radar and dual inertial systems. Uprated EW equipment includes, typically, a Thomson-CSF jamming pod and a Matra Phimat chaff dispensing pod on the two outboard underwing hardpoints, with external fuel tanks (each 2,000 litres; 440 Imp gallons; 528 US gallons) on the inboard hardpoints. Radar warning receivers are also fitted.

The Mirage IV was last described in the 1969-70 *Jane's*. Modified aircraft, redesignated Mirage IV-P (for pénétration), attained initial operational capability with Gascogne squadron of the 91e Escadre de Bombardement at Mont-de-Marsan on 1 May 1986.

Prototype of the new generation Dassault-Breguet Mirage 3 NG

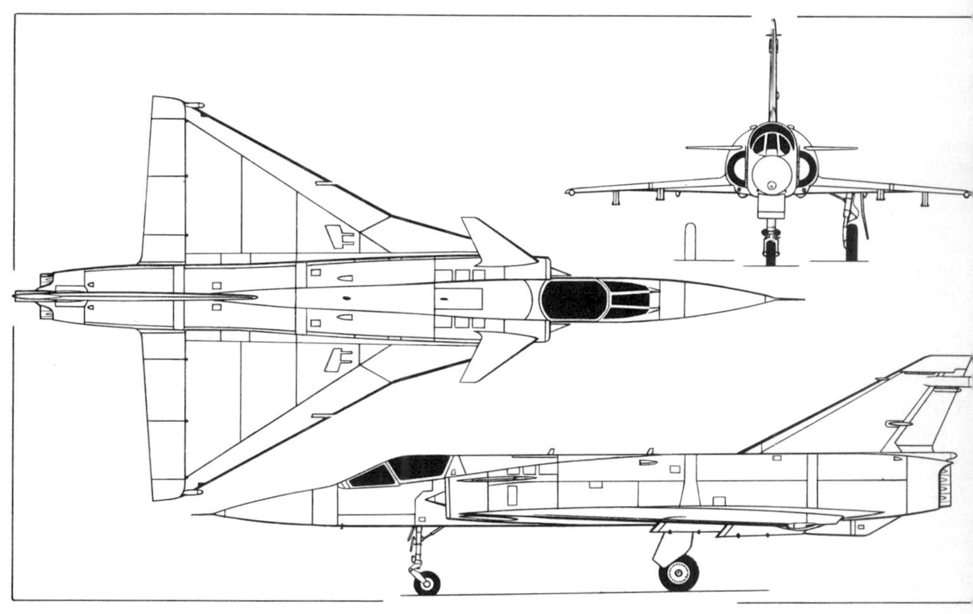

Dassault-Breguet Mirage 3 NG (SNECMA Atar 9K-50 turbojet engine) *(Pilot Press)*

Rocket assisted take-off of a Dassault Mirage IV-P strategic bomber carrying an ASMP test vehicle

DASSAULT-BREGUET MIRAGE F1

Details of the early history of the Mirage F1 can be found in the 1977-78 *Jane's*. The prototype flew for the first time on 23 December 1966 and was followed by three pre-series aircraft.

The primary role of the single-seat Mirage **F1-C** production version, to which the detailed description applies, is that of all-weather interception at any altitude. It is equally suitable for visual ground attack missions, carrying a variety of external loads beneath the wings and fuselage. Other versions include the **F1-B** two-seat version of F1-C, the first of which made its first flight on 26 May 1976; the **F1-D** two-seat version of F1-E; the single-seat **F1-E** multi-role air superiority/ground attack/reconnaissance version for export customers, with an inertial navigation system, nav/attack central computer, CRT head-up display, and a large inventory of external stores; and the single-seat **F1-R** (French Air Force **F1-CR**) day and night reconnaissance variant. Production of the F1-A ground attack version, with reduced equipment and increased fuel, has been completed.

Many F1-Cs of the French Air Force were delivered or modified to **F1-C-200** standard by installation of a removable flight refuelling probe for long range reinforcement capability. Export customers who have F1s equipped with refuelling probes include Iraq, Libya, Morocco, South Africa and Spain.

By 1 April 1986, a total of 715 Mirage F1s had been ordered, comprising 252 (incl 6 prototypes) for the French Air Force and 463 for service with the air forces of Ecuador (F1-B and E), Greece (F1-C), Iraq (F1-B and E), Jordan (F1-B, C and E), Kuwait (F1-B and C), Libya (F1-A, B and E), Morocco (F1-C and E), Qatar (F1-B and E), South

Africa (F1-A and C) and Spain (F1-B, C and E). A total of 672 had been delivered by 1 January. The first production F1 flew on 15 February 1973 and was delivered officially to the French Air Force on 14 March 1973. The first unit to receive the F1 was the 30e Escadre at Reims, which became operational in early 1974. This now has three squadrons of F1-Cs; the 5e Escadre at Orange has two squadrons of F1-Cs and one of F1-Bs; the 12e Escadre at Cambrai has three squadrons of F1-Cs.

Deliveries of the F1-C series to the French Air Force totalled 166, made up of four prototypes, 81 F1-Cs and 81 F1-C-200s. Twenty two-seat F1-Bs began to equip the third squadron at Orange, as the F1 OCU, in June 1980; each aircraft is equipped with the same radar, weapon system and air-to-air missiles as the F1-C, but has no internal guns, and fuel capacity is reduced by 450 litres (99 Imp gallons; 119 US gallons).

The French Air Force has also purchased F1-CRs to replace Mirage III-R/RD aircraft equipping the three squadrons of the 33e Escadre de Reconnaissance, at Strasbourg. These aircraft are intended to carry internally an Omera 33 camera and either an Omera 40 panoramic camera or a SAT Super Cyclope SCM 2400 infra-red sensor, together with a Thomson-CSF Raphaël SLAR and an Omera 400 sight recorder. Further electromagnetic or optical sensors are intended to be carried in an underbelly pack, such as the Thomson-CSF Syrel elint pod. Other equipment includes a Sagem Uliss 47 inertial navigation system and ESD navigation computer. An in-flight refuelling probe is standard (hence -200 added to designation). The first of two F1-CR-200 prototypes, converted from F1-C-200s, flew on 20 November 1981. Sixty-four (incl the two prototypes) were ordered for the French Air Force. The first production F1-CR-200 flew on 10 November 1982, and the first squadron (2/33) became operational in July 1983.

Mirage F1-Cs and F1-C-200s of the French Air Force have Thomson-CSF Cyrano IVM radar of modular construction and optimised for air-to-air missions. The F1-CR-200 has a Cyrano IVMR with added air-to-ground functions for blind let-down, ground mapping, contour mapping and terrain avoidance, plus air-to-ground ranging. Export F1-Cs have a radar similar to Cyrano IV or IVM. Export F1-Es have radar similar to Cyrano IVMR but repackaged to save space.

Mirage F1-EQ5s and EQ6s of the Iraqi Air Force are equipped to carry Exocet anti-ship missiles and laser guided weapons such as the AS.30L missile and Matra 400 kg laser guided bomb.

The Mirage F1 is produced by Dassault-Breguet in co-operation with the Belgian company SABCA, in which Dassault-Breguet has a parity interest, and CASA of Spain, which is building fuselage sections for all Mirage F1s ordered. Dassault-Breguet also has a technical and industrial co-operation agreement with the Armaments Development and Production Corporation of South Africa Ltd, whereby the latter company has rights to build the Mirage F1 under licence.

The following description applies to the F1-C production version for the French Air Force, except where indicated:

TYPE: Single-seat multi-mission fighter and attack aircraft.

WINGS: Cantilever shoulder-wing monoplane. Anhedral from roots. Sweepback 47° 30′ on leading-edges, with extended chord on approximately the outer two-thirds of each wing. All-metal two-spar torsion box structure, making extensive use of mechanically or chemically milled components. Trailing-edge control surfaces of honeycomb sandwich construction, with carbonfibre aileron skin on current production aircraft. Entire leading-edge can be drooped hydraulically (manually for T-O and landing, automatic in combat). Two differentially operating double-slotted flaps and one aileron on each trailing-edge, actuated hydraulically by servo controls. Ailerons are compensated by trim devices incorporated in linkage. Two spoilers on each wing, ahead of flaps.

FUSELAGE: Conventional all-metal semi-monocoque structure. Primary frames are milled mechanically, secondary frames and fuel tank panels chemically. Electric spot welding for secondary stringers and sealed panels, remainder titanium flush riveted or bolted and sealed. Titanium alloy also used for landing gear trunnions, engine firewall and certain other major structures. High tensile steel wing attachment points. Nosecone over radar, and antennae fairings on fin, are of plastics. Large hydraulically actuated door type airbrake in forward underside of each intake trunk.

TAIL UNIT: Cantilever all-metal structure, with sweepback on all surfaces. Single-spar fin. All-moving tailplane mid-set on fuselage, and actuated hydraulically by electric or manual control. Tailplane trailing-edge panels are of honeycomb sandwich construction. Auxiliary fin beneath each side of rear fuselage.

LANDING GEAR: Retractable tricycle type, by Messier-Hispano-Bugatti. Hydraulic retraction, nose unit rearward, main units upward into rear of intake trunk fairings. Twin wheels on each unit. Nose unit steerable and self centering. Oleo-pneumatic shock absorbers. Mainwheel tyres size 605 × 155, pressure 9-11 bars (130-160 lb/sq in). Nosewheel tyres size 360 × 135. Messier-Hispano-Bugatti brakes and anti-skid units. Brake parachute in bullet fairing at base of rudder.

Dassault-Breguet Mirage F1-B two-seat combat trainer of the French Air Force

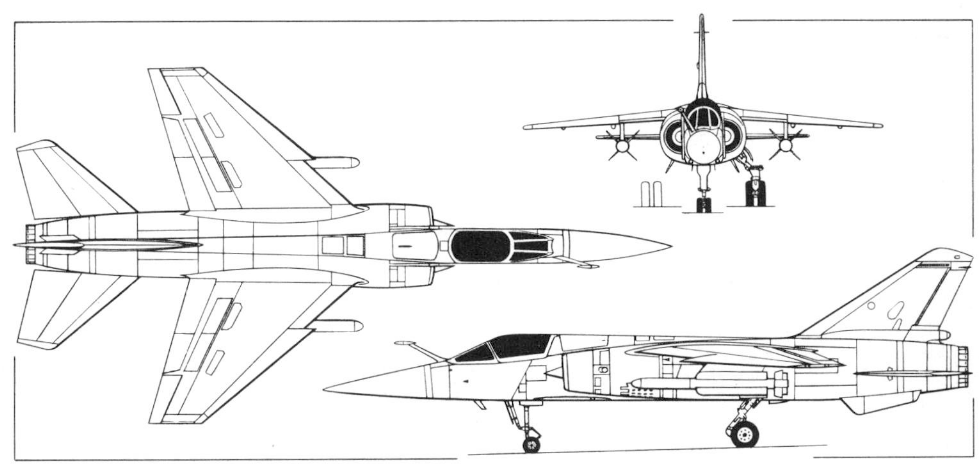

Dassault-Breguet Mirage F1-C-200 single-seat multi-mission fighter and attack aircraft *(Pilot Press)*

Dassault-Breguet Mirage F1-C armed with two Matra Super 530 and two Matra 550 Magic air-to-air missiles

Dassault-Breguet Mirage F1-CR-200 reconnaissance fighter

POWER PLANT: One SNECMA Atar 9K-50 turbojet engine, rated at 70·6 kN (15,873 lb st) with afterburning. Movable semi-conical centrebody in each intake. Fuel in integral tanks in wings (combined capacity 375 litres; 82·5 Imp gallons; 99 US gallons), and three main tanks and one inverted-flight supply tank (combined capacity 3,925 litres; 863·5 Imp gallons; 1,037 US gallons) in fuselage. Total internal fuel capacity 4,300 litres (946 Imp gallons; 1,136 US gallons). Internal tanks able to be pressure refuelled completely in about 6 min. Provision for two jettisonable auxiliary fuel tanks (each 1,130 litres; 248 Imp gallons; 298 US gallons) to be carried on inboard wing pylons, plus a single tank of 2,200 litres (484 Imp gallons; 581 US gallons) capacity on the underfuselage station. Non-retractable, but removable, flight refuelling probe on starboard side of nose optional.

ACCOMMODATION: Single SEM Martin-Baker F1RM4 ejection seat for pilot, under rearward hinged canopy (SEM Martin-Baker F10M rocket seat in latest F1-Cs and in F1-E and F1-CR. Two Mk 10 seats with inter-seat sequence system in F1-B). Cockpit is air-conditioned, and is heated by warm air bled from engine which also heats the radar compartment and certain equipment compartments. Intertechnique liquid oxygen converter, miniature regulator and anti-*g* valve for pilot. No-delay through-the-canopy escape system, with pyrotechnic pre-fragmentation of canopy, on all versions.

SYSTEMS: Two independent hydraulic systems, for landing gear retraction, flaps and flying controls, supplied by pumps similar to those fitted in Mirage III. Electrical system includes two Auxilec 15kVA variable speed alternators, either of which can supply all functional and operational requirements. Emergency and standby power provided by SAFT Voltabloc 40Ah nickel-cadmium battery and ESD static converter. DC power provided by two transformer-rectifiers operating in conjunction with battery.

AVIONICS AND EQUIPMENT: Thomson-CSF Cyrano IV fire control radar in nose. Two UHF transceivers (one UHF/VHF), Socrat 6200 VOR/ILS with Socrat 5600 marker beacon receiver, LMT Tacan, LMT NR-AI-4-A IFF, remote setting interception system, three-axis generator, central air data computer, SFIM spherical indicator with ILS pointers, Crouzet Type 63 navigation indicator, SFENA 505 autopilot and CSF head-up display, with wide field of view double-converter. (Standard equipment on F-1E includes SAGEM Uliss 47 INS, EMD 182 central digital computer for nav/attack computations, TH C8F VE-120C CRT head-up display, Crouzet air data computer and digital armament/nav control panels.)

ARMAMENT AND OPERATIONAL EQUIPMENT: Standard installed armament of two 30 mm DEFA 553 cannon, with 135 rds/gun, mounted in lower central fuselage. Two Alkan universal stores attachment pylons under each wing and one under centre-fuselage, plus provision for carrying one air-to-air missile at each wingtip. Max external combat load 6,300 kg (13,900 lb). Externally mounted weapons for interception role include Matra Super 530 air-to-air missiles under inboard wing pylons and/or Matra 550 Magic (or AIM-9J Sidewinder) air-to-air missiles at each wingtip station. For ground attack, typical loads may include one ARMAT anti-radar missile, or one AM39 Exocet anti-ship missile, or up to fourteen 250 kg bombs, thirty anti-runway bombs or 144 Thomson-Brandt rockets. Other possible external loads include auxiliary fuel tanks, laser designator pod with AS.30L missiles or 400 kg laser guided bombs, air-to-surface missiles, side looking airborne radar pod, active countermeasures pods such as the Thomson-CSF Remora, active ECM jamming pods such as the Thomson-CSF Caiman, a high altitude/long distance reconnaissance pod, and a four-camera reconnaissance pod with an SAT Super Cyclope infra-red scanner/recorder. Typical underwing ECM container for export aircraft is Matra Sycomor, which ejects heat-emitting infra-red cartridges and/or chaff.

DIMENSIONS, EXTERNAL (F1-C):
- Wing span: without missiles — 8·40 m (27 ft 6¾ in)
  - over Magic missiles — approx 9·32 m (30 ft 6¾ in)
- Length overall — 15·30 m (50 ft 2½ in)
- Height overall — 4·50 m (14 ft 9 in)
- Wheel track — 2·50 m (8 ft 2½ in)
- Wheelbase — 5·00 m (16 ft 4¾ in)

AREA:
- Wings, gross — 25·00 m² (269·1 sq ft)

WEIGHTS AND LOADING (F1-C):
- Weight empty — 7,400 kg (16,314 lb)
- T-O weight, 'clean' — 10,900 kg (24,030 lb)
- Max T-O weight — 16,200 kg (35,715 lb)
- Max wing loading — 648 kg/m² (132·7 lb/sq ft)

PERFORMANCE (F1-C):
- Max level speed: high altitude — Mach 2·2
  - low altitude — Mach 1·2 (800 knots; 1,480 km/h; 920 mph EAS)
- Approach speed — 141 knots (260 km/h; 162 mph)
- Landing speed — 124 knots (230 km/h; 143 mph)
- Max rate of climb at S/L (with afterburning) — 12,780 m (41,930 ft)/min
- Max rate of climb at high altitude (with afterburning) — 14,580 m (47,835 ft)/min
- Service ceiling — 20,000 m (65,600 ft)
- Stabilised supersonic ceiling — 16,000 m (52,500 ft)
- T-O run (AUW of 11,500 kg; 25,355 lb) — 600 m (1,970 ft)
- Landing run (AUW of 8,500 kg; 18,740 lb) — 670 m (2,200 ft)
- Combat radius:
  - hi-lo-hi at Mach 0·75/0·88, with fourteen 250 kg bombs and max internal fuel, with reserves — 230 nm (425 km; 265 miles)
  - lo-lo-lo at 400-550 knots (740-1,020 km/h; 460-633 mph), with six 250 kg bombs and two external tanks, with reserves — 325 nm (600 km; 374 miles)
  - hi-lo-hi at Mach 0·8/0·9, with two 250 kg bombs and three external tanks, with reserves — 750 nm (1,390 km; 863 miles)
- Combat air patrol endurance, with two Super 530 missiles and underbelly tank, with reserves, incl one attack at ceiling — 2 h 15 min

DASSAULT-BREGUET MIRAGE 2000

Indian Air Force name: Vajra

The Mirage 2000 was selected on 18 December 1975 as the primary combat aircraft of the French Air Force from the mid-1980s. Under French government contract, it was developed initially as an interceptor and air superiority fighter, powered by a single SNECMA M53 turbofan engine and with Thomson-CSF RDM multi-mode Doppler radar. The Mirage 2000 is equally suitable for reconnaissance, close support, and low altitude attack missions in areas to the rear of a battlefield.

Five prototypes were built, of which four single-seat multi-role models were funded by the French Air Force and one two-seater by the manufacturers. The first single-seater made its first flight, at Istres, on 10 March 1978, only 27 months after programme launch in December 1975. The second flew on 18 September 1978, the third on 26 April 1979 and the fourth on 12 May 1980. The **Mirage 2000B** two-seat trainer version flew on 11 October 1980 and, like its four predecessors, achieved supersonic speed (between Mach 1·3 and 1·5) during its first flight. On the basis of structural testing, the Mirage 2000 airframe was approved for a load factor of +9*g* and rate of roll of 270°/s in subsonic and supersonic flight, clean or with four air-to-air missiles.

A SNECMA M53-2 engine, rated at 83·4 kN (18,740 lb st), was fitted for early prototype testing, and was replaced in 1980 by the uprated M53-5 which also powers initial production aircraft. The first prototype was re-engined subsequently with a more powerful M53-P2, as intended for later production aircraft, and made its first flight in this revised form on 1 July 1983. Meanwhile, the manufacturers' prototype is being used to develop equipment and other changes proposed for future variants and for export models of the Mirage 2000. Further airframes were built for static and fatigue testing.

The first production **Mirage 2000C** made its first flight on 20 November 1982 and deliveries began in 1983. The first production Mirage 2000B flew on 7 October 1983. Escadron de Chasse (EC) 1/2 'Cigognes' was the first French Air Force unit to become operational, at Dijon on 2 July 1984, and now has twelve Mirage 2000Cs and three 2000Bs. EC 3/2 'Alsace' was due to follow in 1986 and Escadron de Chasse et de Transformation (ECT) 2/2 'Côte d'Or' in early 1987. Eventually, these aircraft will equip four wings (escadres), each with three interceptor squadrons. More than 100 of Thomson-CSF's new RDI pulse-Doppler radars are being delivered from late 1986, to replace the RDM in Mirage 2000Cs of the French Air Force.

Following a mid-1979 go-ahead, the first of two prototypes of the **Mirage 2000N** two-seat low-altitude penetration version made its first flight on 2 February 1983; the second flew on 21 September 1983. Strengthened for flight at a typical 600 knots (1,110 km/h; 690 mph) at 60 m (200 ft) above the terrain, this version is intended as a vehicle for the ASMP medium-range air-to-surface nuclear missile, and has ESD Antilope V terrain following radar, two Sagem inertial platforms, improved TRT AHV-12 radio altimeter, Thomson-CSF colour CRT, an Omera vertical camera, and special ECM. Production deliveries were scheduled to start in 1986, and 36 of the planned total of 112 will be in service by 1988, when the 2000N will become operational as a replacement for Mirage III-E and Jaguar nuclear attack aircraft. Two wings with a total of five tactical squadrons will receive this version, beginning with the 4th Escadre at Luxeuil, followed by the 7th at Toul.

Funding approved under the 1985 defence budget brought the total number of aircraft ordered to 134 (66 Cs, 21 Bs and 47 Ns, of which more than 38 Cs and Bs had been completed by the beginning of 1986), excluding the seven prototypes. By the end of the current 1984-88 defence programme, the totals are planned to increase to 139 Cs, 19 Bs and 85 Ns, out of an eventual requirement of 300 to 400 Mirage 2000s of various versions for the French Air Force. Production is being increased progressively to ten aircraft a month in 1988, to satisfy the present level of domestic and export orders. Wings are manufactured at Martignas, fuselages at Argenteuil; final assembly and flight testing take place at Mérignac.

Export customers for the Mirage 2000 include Abu Dhabi, Egypt, India, Peru and Greece. The Egyptians placed an initial firm contract for 20 (16 2000EM and 4 BM, all with M53-P2 engines) in January 1982. India placed an initial order for 40 in October 1982 (36 2000H and 4 TH), all of which were expected to be delivered by mid-1986. The

Dassault-Breguet Mirage 2000, armed with Super 530 and Magic air-to-air missiles, refuelling in flight

four THs and 26 of the Hs have M53-5 engines temporarily; the final 10 Hs will be powered from the start by the M53-P2. First flight by a 2000H (KF-101) was made on 21 September 1984, followed in early 1985 by the first TH (KT-201). The first of two Indian squadrons (No. 7 *Battle Axe*) was formed at Gwalior AB on 29 June 1985, when the Mirage 2000 received the Indian name Vajra (Divine Thunder). A follow-on order for nine aircraft was signed in March 1986. Peru ordered 26 aircraft in December 1982 (24 2000P and 2 DP), but has since reduced the total to 14. Abu Dhabi has ordered 36 (22 2000EAD, 8 RAD and 6 DAD); deliveries were due to begin in 1986. The RAD reconnaissance versions for this customer will be able to carry a COR 2 or Harold surveillance equipment pod; the second 18 for Abu Dhabi will be fitted with Elettronica (Italy) ECM, comprising threat warning receivers and self-protection jammers. Most recent customer is Greece, which in July 1985 signed a contract for 40 (36 2000EGM and 4 BGM).

The following description applies to the single-seat Mirage 2000C, except where indicated:

TYPE: Single-seat interceptor, air superiority and multi-role fighter.

WINGS: Cantilever multi-spar low-wing monoplane of delta planform, with cambered profile. Leading-edge sweepback 58°. Large radius root fairings. Full span two-segment automatic leading-edge flaps provide variable camber in combat, but are retracted during all phases of acceleration and low altitude cruise, to reduce drag. Two-section elevons, forming entire trailing-edge of each wing, have carbonfibre skin, with AG5 light alloy honeycomb core. Fly by wire control system for elevons and flaps, with surfaces actuated by hydraulic servo units. No tabs. Retractable airbrake above and below each wing.

FUSELAGE: Conventional semi-monocoque structure, 'waisted' in accordance with area rule; of conventional all-metal construction except for glassfibre radome and carbonfibre/light alloy honeycomb panel over avionics compartment, immediately aft of canopy. Small fixed strake, with marked dihedral, near leading-edge of each air intake trunk.

TAIL UNIT: Cantilever fin and inset rudder only; latter actuated by fly by wire control system via hydraulic servo units. Much of fin skin and all rudder skin of boron/epoxy/carbon composites with honeycomb core of Nomex (fin) or light alloy (rudder). Sweepback on fin leading-edge 45°. No tab.

LANDING GEAR: Retractable tricycle type by Messier-Hispano-Bugatti, with twin nosewheels, and single wheel on each main unit. Hydraulic retraction, nosewheels rearward, main units inward. Oleo-pneumatic shock absorbers. Electro-hydraulic nosewheel steering, through 45° to each side. Manual disconnect permits nosewheel unit to castor through 360° for ground towing. Light alloy wheels and tubeless tyres, size 360 × 135-6, pressure 8·0 bars (116 lb/sq in) on nosewheels, 750 × 230-15, pressure 15·0 bars (217 lb/sq in) on mainwheels. Messier-Hispano-Bugatti hydraulically actuated carbon composite disc brakes on mainwheels, with anti-skid units. Runway arrester gear standard. Brake-chute in canister above jet nozzle.

POWER PLANT: One SNECMA M53-P2 turbofan engine, rated at 64·3 kN (14,462 lb st) dry and 95·1 kN (21,385 lb st) with afterburning. Movable half-cone centrebody in each air intake. Internal fuel capacity 3,980 litres (875 Imp gallons; 1,051 US gallons) in 2000C, 3,870 litres (851 Imp gallons; 1,022 US gallons) in 2000B. Provision for one jettisonable 1,300 litre (286 Imp gallon; 343 US gallon) fuel tank under centre of fuselage, and a 1,700 litre (374 Imp gallon; 449 US gallon) drop tank under each wing. Total internal/external fuel capacity 8,680 litres (1,909 Imp gallons; 2,292 US gallons) in 2000C, 8,570 litres (1,885 Imp gallons; 2,263 US gallons) in 2000B. Detachable flight refuelling probe forward of cockpit on starboard side.

ACCOMMODATION: Pilot only in 2000C, on Martin-Baker F10Q zero/zero ejection seat, under transparent canopy, in air-conditioned and pressurised cockpit. Canopy hinged at rear to open upward.

SYSTEMS: ABG-Semca air-conditioning and pressurisation system. Two independent hydraulic systems, pressure 280 bars (4,000 lb/sq in), to actuate flying control servo units, landing gear and brakes. Electrical system includes two Auxilec 20110 aircooled 20kVA 400Hz constant frequency alternators, two Bronzavia DC transformers, a SAFT 40Ah battery and ATEI static inverter. Fly by wire flight control system. Eros oxygen system.

AVIONICS AND EQUIPMENT: Thomson-CSF RDM multi-mode radar or RDI pulse-Doppler radar, each with operating range of 54 nm (100 km; 62 miles). (Mirage 2000N will have ESD/Thomson-CSF Antilope V ground-scan radar.) Sagem Uliss 52 inertial platform, ESD Type 2084 central digital computer and Digibus digital data bus, Thomson-CSF TMV-980 data display system (VE-130 head-up and VMC-180 head-down) (two head-down in 2000N), Sfena 605 autopilot, Thomson-CSF/ESD ECM with VCM-65 display, Matra Spirale passive countermeasures, LMT Deltac Tacan, LMT NRAI-7A IFF transponder, Socrat 8900 solid state VOR/ILS and IO-300-A marker beacon receiver, TRT radio altimeter (AHV-6 in 2000B and C, AHV-9 in export aircraft, AHV-12 in 2000N), TRT ERA 7000 V/UHF com transceiver, TRT ERA 7200 UHF or EAS secure voice com, Thomson-CSF Serval radar warning receiver, Crouzet type 90 air data computer, and Thomson-CSF Atlis laser designator and marked target seeker (in pod on forward starboard underfuselage station). Omera vertical camera in 2000N.

ARMAMENT: Two 30 mm DEFA 554 cannon in 2000C (not fitted in B or N), with 125 rds/gun. Nine attachments for external stores, five under fuselage and two under each wing. Fuselage centreline and inboard wing stations each stressed for 1,800 kg (3,968 lb) loads; other four fuselage points for 400 kg (882 lb) each, and outboard wing points for 300 kg (661 lb) each. Typical interception weapons comprise two Matra Super 530 or 530D missiles (inboard) and two Matra 550 Magic or Magic 2 missiles (outboard) under wings. Alternatively, each of the four underwing hardpoints can carry a Magic. Primary weapon for 2000N is ASMP tactical nuclear missile. In an air-to-surface role, the Mirage 2000 can carry up to 6,300 kg (13,890 lb) of external stores, including eighteen Matra 250 kg retarded bombs or Thomson-Brandt BAP 100 anti-runway bombs; sixteen Durandal penetration bombs; one or two Matra BGL 1,000 kg laser guided bombs; five or six Matra Belouga cluster bombs or Thomson-Brandt BM 400 400 kg modular bombs; one Rafaut F2 practice bomb launcher; two Aérospatiale AS 30L, Matra Armat anti-radar, or Aérospatiale AM39 Exocet anti-ship, air-to-surface missiles; four Matra LR F4 rocket launchers, each with eighteen 68 mm rockets; two packs of 100 mm rockets; a Dassault-Breguet CC 630 gun pod, containing two 30 mm cannon and ammunition; a Dassault-Breguet COR 2 multi-camera pod or Dassault-Breguet AA-3-38 Harold long-range oblique photographic (Lorop) pod; a Thomson-CSF Atlis laser designator/marked target seeker pod; two Thomson-CSF DB 3141/3163 self-defence ECM pods; one Thomson-CSF Caiman offensive or intelligence ECM pod; or an Intertechnique 231-300 'buddy' type in-flight refuelling pod. Fuselage centreline and inboard underwing stations are 'wet' for carriage of jettisonable fuel tanks (see 'Power Plant' paragraph for details). For air defence weapon training, a Cubic Corpn AIS (airborne instrumentation subsystem) pod, externally resembling a Magic missile, can replace the Magic on its launch rail, enabling pilot to simulate a firing without carrying the actual missile.

DIMENSIONS, EXTERNAL:

Wing span	9·13 m (29 ft 11½ in)
Wing aspect ratio	2·03
Length overall: 2000C	14·36 m (47 ft 1¼ in)
2000B	14·55 m (47 ft 9 in)
Height overall: 2000C	5·20 m (17 ft 0¾ in)
2000B	5·15 m (16 ft 10¾ in)
Wheel track	3·40 m (11 ft 1¾ in)
Wheelbase	5·00 m (16 ft 4¾ in)

AREA:

Wings, gross	41·0 m² (441·3 sq ft)

WEIGHTS AND LOADINGS:

Weight empty: 2000C	7,500 kg (16,534 lb)
2000B	7,600 kg (16,755 lb)
Max internal fuel: 2000C	3,145 kg (6,933 lb)
2000B	3,055 kg (6,735 lb)

Two-seat Dassault-Breguet Vajra (Mirage 2000TH) for the Indian Air Force

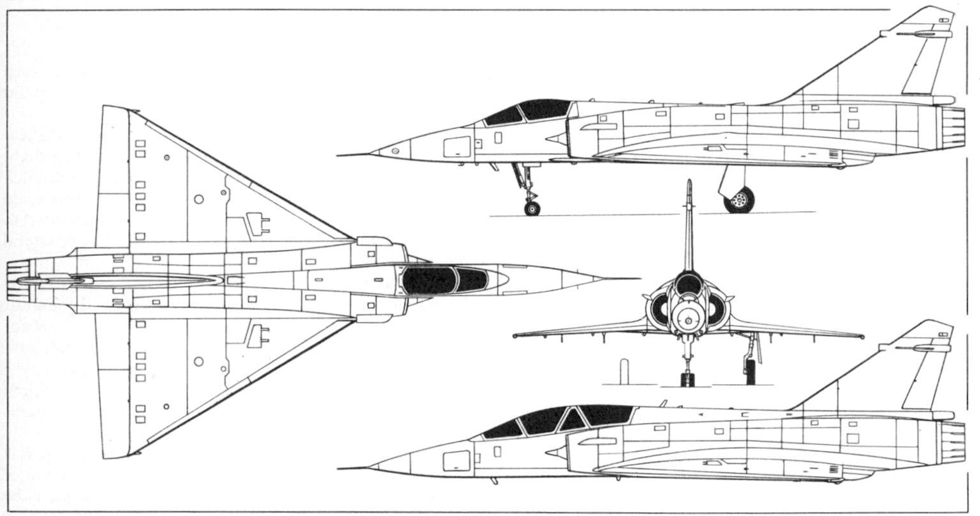
Dassault-Breguet Mirage 2000C, with added side view (lower) of Mirage 2000N *(Pilot Press)*

Dassault-Breguet Mirage 2000N, carrier of the ASMP nuclear missile *(Brian M. Service)*

Max external fuel: 2000C 3,720 kg (8,201 lb)
2000B 3,715 kg (8,190 lb)
Max external stores load 6,300 kg (13,890 lb)
T-O weight 'clean': 2000C 10,860 kg (23,940 lb)
2000B 10,960 kg (24,165 lb)
Max T-O weight: 2000C and B 17,000 kg (37,480 lb)
Max wing loading:
2000C and B 414·63 kg/m² (84·97 lb/sq ft)

PERFORMANCE (Mirage 2000C):
Max level speed over Mach 2·2
Max continuous speed Mach 2·2 (800 knots; 1,482 km/h; 921 mph IAS)
Max speed at low altitude without afterburning, carrying eight 250 kg bombs and two Magic missiles over 600 knots (1,110 km/h; 690 mph)
Min speed in stable flight 100 knots (185 km/h; 115 mph)
Max rate of climb at S/L 17,060 m (56,000 ft)/min
Time to 15,000 m (49,200 ft) and Mach 2 4 min
Time from brake release to intercept target flying at Mach 3 at 24,400 m (80,000 ft) less than 5 min
Service ceiling 18,000 m (59,000 ft)
Range: with four 250 kg bombs more than 800 nm (1,480 km; 920 miles)
with two 1,700 litre drop tanks more than 1,000 nm (1,850 km; 1,150 miles)
with one 1,300 litre and two 1,700 litre drop tanks 1,800 nm (3,335 km; 2,073 miles)
g limits: +9 normal
+13·5 ultimate

DASSAULT-BREGUET SUPER MIRAGE 4000

The Super Mirage 4000 prototype is a twin-turbofan scale-up of the Mirage 2000 that was designed to be suitable for interception as well as low altitude penetration attack at a considerable distance from its base. It flew for the first time on 9 March 1979 and was described fully in the 1984-85 *Jane's*.

In 1986 the Super Mirage 4000 resumed flying in support of the Rafale programme, with particular emphasis on evaluating the behaviour of a delta-canard aircraft in turbulent conditions.

DASSAULT-BREGUET SUPER ETENDARD

At the 1985 Paris Air Show, Dassault-Breguet announced its readiness to relaunch production of the Super Etendard against initial orders for about 40 aircraft. Changes by comparison with the original version would be limited to removal of equipment needed only for deck operations from aircraft carriers, and installation of new fire control and nav/attack systems.

Production of the original, carrier-based, version of this single-seat transonic strike fighter for the navies of France (71 aircraft) and Argentina (14 aircraft) ended in 1983. However, the French Navy is reviewing the possibility of extending and updating the weapon system of aircraft in service, and Super Etendards will be modified to carry the ASMP medium-range air-to-surface nuclear missile under the 1984-88 defence programme. So, while readers are referred to the 1982-83 and previous editions of *Jane's* for a full description of the Super Etendard in its carrier-based form, the following expanded entry on its current armament may be of continuing interest:

ARMAMENT: Two DEFA 30 mm guns, each with 125 rds, in bottom of engine air intake trunks. Underfuselage attachment for two 250 kg bombs, one 600 litre (132 Imp gallon) drop fuel tank, a flight refuelling 'buddy' pack or a reconnaissance pod. Four underwing hardpoints for four 250 kg or 400 kg bombs, two Matra Magic air-to-air missiles, or four rocket pods (each eighteen 68 mm rockets). The inner wing hardpoints can carry two 625 litre or 1,100 litre (137 or 242 Imp gallon; 165 or 290·5 US gallon) fuel tanks, or one AM39 Exocet anti-ship missile and one fuel tank. Standard weapons include AN52 nuclear bomb. Modification to carry ASMP nuclear missile planned. Provision for carrying flare/chaff pods.

DASSAULT-BREGUET RAFALE A (SQUALL)

Known initially as the ACX (advanced combat experimental), the **Rafale A** is an experimental prototype that was built to demonstrate technologies applicable to the tactical combat aircraft (ACT) needed to replace French Air Force Jaguars in the 1990s, and to the ship-based combat aircraft (ACM: avion de combat marine) proposed for deployment on the French Navy's nuclear powered aircraft carrier. The production version will be known as **Rafale B** and is described separately.

Dassault-Breguet Rafale A experimental combat aircraft

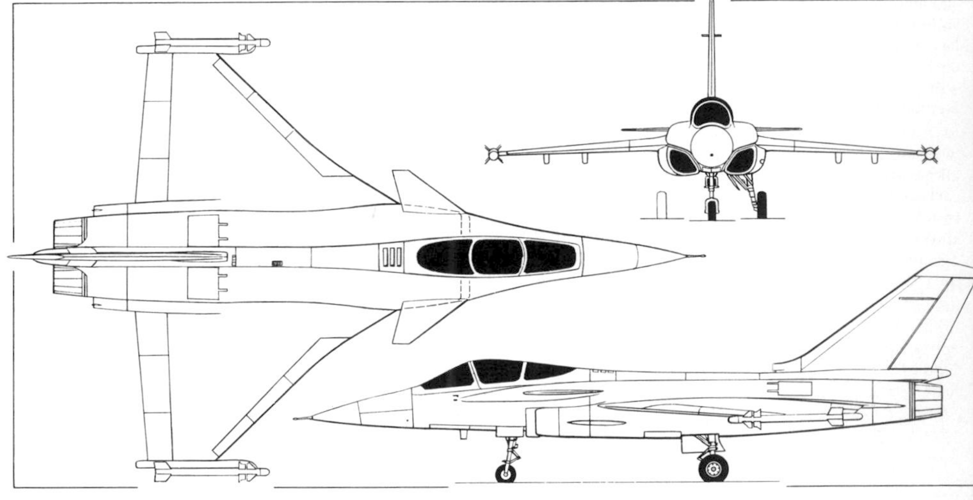

Dassault-Breguet Rafale A experimental combat aircraft *(Pilot Press)*

Essential characteristics of the Rafale A were revealed in the early weeks of 1983, at the time of Dassault-Breguet's decision to build it. On the basis of an airframe with overall dimensions little greater than those of the Mirage 2000, the company set out to produce a multi-role aircraft able to destroy everything from supersonic fighters to a helicopter in an air-to-air role, and able to deliver at least 3,500 kg (7,715 lb) of modern weapons on targets up to 350 nm (650 km; 400 miles) from its base. The ability to carry, and fire in rapid succession, at least six air-to-air missiles was considered essential, together with the ability to launch electro-optically guided and advanced 'fire and forget' standoff air-to-surface weapons.

High manoeuvrability, high angle-of-attack flying capability under combat conditions, and optimum low-speed performance for short take-off and landing were basic design aims. This led to choice of a compound-sweep delta wing, a large active canard foreplane mounted higher than the mainplane, twin engines, air intakes of new design in a semi-ventral position, and a single fin. To ensure a thrust-to-weight ratio far superior to one, it was decided to make extensive use of composites, such as carbon and Kevlar fibres, and aluminium-lithium alloys throughout the airframe, as well as the latest manufacturing techniques such as superplastic forming/diffusion bonding of titanium components.

Ergonomic cockpit studies suggested that the pilot's seat should be reclined at an angle of 30° to 40° during flight testing, and that equipment should include a side-stick controller, a wide angle holographic head-up display, an eye-level display collimated to infinity (avoiding the need to refocus from the HUD to the instrument panel), and lateral multi-function colour displays.

The digital fly by wire control system will embody automatic self-protection functions to prevent the aircraft from exceeding its limits at all times. Functional reconfiguration of the system in case of failure, and anti-turbulence functions, will be embodied. Provisions will be made for the introduction of fibre optics to enhance nuclear hardening, and of voice-activated controls and voice warning systems.

A full scale mockup of the original ACX design was exhibited at the 1983 Paris Air Show, and construction of the Rafale A began in March 1984. Compared with the mockup, it embodies a number of significant refinements. In particular, Dassault-Breguet was able to achieve improved flow into the engine air intakes, and greater efficiency at high angles of attack, by modifying the lower fuselage cross-section to a V shape, enabling it to dispense with centre-bodies and other moving parts. The size of the fin was also greatly reduced.

Rafale A was rolled out of the Saint-Cloud assembly plant on 14 December 1985, and exceeded Mach 1·3 during its first test flight on 4 July 1986. Mach 1·8 was achieved during the sixth flight, by which time the aircraft had been subjected to load factors of +6*g* in supersonic flight and +8*g* in subsonic flight, and angles of attack up to 23°.

TYPE: Single-seat twin-engined experimental combat aircraft.

WINGS: Cantilever multi-spar mid-wing monoplane of compound delta planform. Most of wing components made from carbonfibre, including three-segment full-span elevons on each trailing-edge. Wing spar/fuselage attachment fittings of aluminium-lithium alloy. Elevons can be deflected identically or differentially. Full-span three-segment leading-edge slats on each wing operate automatically with the elevons to alter wing camber and provide high lift. Slats made from titanium. Wing root tip fairings of aramid fibre. All movable surfaces actuated by fly by wire control system, via hydraulic actuators.

Dassault-Breguet Super Etendard with inert ASMP nuclear missile under its starboard wing *(Brian M. Service)*

FUSELAGE: Conventional semi-monocoque structure; 50 per cent carbonfibre, including entire front fuselage and dorsal spine fairings. Aramid fibre nosecone and jetpipe fairings. Most centre and rear fuselage skin panels of aluminium-lithium alloy. Wheel doors and engine doors of carbonfibre. Dorsal spine fairing from rear of canopy to jet nozzles. Forward hinged door type airbrake above engine duct on each side of fin leading-edge.

FOREPLANES: Shoulder-mounted active foreplanes of sweptback planform, actuated hydraulically by fly by wire control system. Made primarily of carbonfibre with honeycomb core and aramid fibre tips.

TAIL UNIT: Fin and inset rudder only, of sweptback form, made primarily of carbonfibre, with honeycomb core in rudder. Aramid fibre fin tip. Air intake in base of fin leading-edge. Rudder actuated hydraulically by fly by wire control system. No tabs.

LANDING GEAR: Hydraulically retractable tricycle type supplied by Messier-Hispano-Bugatti, with single wheel on each unit. Hydraulically steerable nosewheel. All wheels retract forward. Designed for impact at vertical speed of 4 m (13 ft)/s, without flare-out. Michelin radial tyres. Mainwheel tyres size 810 × 275-15, pressure 16·0 bars (232 lb/sq in). Carbon brakes on all three wheels, controlled by fly by wire system. Brake-chute for emergency use in cylindrical container at base of rudder.

POWER PLANT: Two General Electric F404-GE-400 augmented turbofan engines, in 71·2 kN (16,000 lb st) class, mounted side by side in rear fuselage. Kidney shape plain air intakes, with splitter plates, mounted low on centre-fuselage. Integral tanks in fuselage and wings for more than 4,250 kg (9,370 lb) of fuel. Inboard underwing pylons able to carry two 2,000 litre (440 Imp gallon; 528 US gallon) drop tanks. Provision for flight refuelling.

ACCOMMODATION: Pilot only, on Martin-Baker Mk 10 zero/zero ejection seat, reclined at angle of 30-40°. One-piece blister windscreen/canopy, hinged to open sideways, to starboard. HOTAS (hands on throttle and stick) controls, with sidestick controller on starboard console and small-travel throttle lever.

SYSTEMS: Bootstrap cockpit air-conditioning system. Dual hydraulic circuits, pressure 280 bars (4,000 lb/sq in), each with two Messier-Hispano-Bugatti pumps. Variable frequency electrical system, with two 30/40kVA Auxilec alternators. Triplex digital plus one dual analog fly by wire flight control system, integrated with engine controls and linked with weapons system. Eros oxygen system.

AVIONICS AND EQUIPMENT: Provision for more than 780 kg (1,720 lb) of avionics equipment and racks, including Thomson-CSF RDX lookdown/shootdown radar with acquisition range in 50 nm (92 km; 57 mile) class, able to track up to eight targets simultaneously, with automatic threat assessment and allocation of priority. (Radar and some other advanced equipment are not installed initially.) Sagem Uliss 52X INS. Digital CRT display of fuel, engine, hydraulic, electrical, oxygen and other systems information. Wide-angle diffractive optics HUD, collimated eye-level display and lateral multi-function colour displays by Thomson-CSF/SFENA. TRT com; SOCRAT VOR/ILS. Crouzet voice activated radio controls and voice alarm warning system. LMT IFF. Internal ECM suite.

ARMAMENT: One 30 mm DEFA 554 gun in side of port engine duct. Twelve external stores attachments: four under fuselage, four under wings, two at wingtips, and two below engine air intakes for sensors. Basic armament of four fuselage mounted Matra Mica medium-range air-to-air missiles and two wingtip mounted Matra Magic close-range air-to-air missiles for air defence role, with provision for four additional Micas under wings.

DIMENSIONS, EXTERNAL:
Wing span 11·2 m (36 ft 9 in)
Length overall 15·8 m (51 ft 10 in)

AREA:
Wings, gross 47·0 m² (506·0 sq ft)

WEIGHTS:
Weight empty 9,400-9,500 kg (20,725-20,945 lb)
Combat weight, with 4 Mica and 2 Magic missiles 14,000 kg (30,865 lb)

PERFORMANCE (estimated):
Max level speed Mach 2 (800 knots; 1,480 km/h; 920 mph IAS)
Approach speed under 120 knots (223 km/h; 138 mph)
T-O run: at 14,000 kg (30,865 lb) AUW 400 m (1,313 ft)
at 20,000 kg (44,100 lb) AUW under 700 m (2,300 ft)
g limit +9

DASSAULT-BREGUET RAFALE B

Rafale B is the planned production version of Rafale A, to replace French Air Force Mirage III-Es and Jaguars, and French Navy Crusaders and Étendard IV-Ps, in the mid-1990s. It is intended to be slightly smaller overall than the Rafale A, although the general configuration will be identical except for deletion of the air intake at the base of the tail fin. Differences in the naval version (ACM) compared with the Air Force version (ACT) will include a reinforced main landing gear able to cope with rates of sink up to 6 m (19·7 ft)/s; a modified nose gear for nose gear catapult launch and possible use of a mini ski-jump T-O technique; and added arrester hook.

The proposed development programme for Rafale B envisages design freeze by early 1987, followed by construction of four ACT prototypes and two ACM prototypes, with flight testing to start in 1990. Other features of Rafale B announced in Summer 1986 are as follows:

POWER PLANT: Two SNECMA M88 turbofan engines, each rated at approx 50 kN (11,240 lb st) dry and 75 kN (16,860 lb st) with afterburning. Internal fuel capacity more than 4,000 kg (8,818 lb).

AVIONICS: Thomson-CSF RDX multi-function radar to permit terrain following/terrain avoidance/threat avoidance flight at low altitude, with simultaneous air-to-air search/track of multiple targets; and fire control of Mica and AMRAAM air-to-air missiles. Self protection ECM. Communications via SINTAC/JTIDS. Autonomous navigation, supplemented by use of GPS/Navstar satellite systems.

DIMENSIONS, EXTERNAL (calculated):
Wing span over missiles 10·75 m (35 ft 3¼ in)
Length overall 14·20 m (46 ft 7 in)

AREA:
Wings, gross 44·0 m² (474·0 sq ft)

WEIGHTS:
Avionics more than 780 kg (1,720 lb)
Target operational weight, empty 8,500 kg (18,740 lb)

Updated Breguet Alizé (see 1985-86 *Jane's*) with directional ESM antennae on the wing leading-edge nacelles and tailcone, and omnidirectional antenna (not visible) on port bomb-bay door

DASSAULT-BREGUET/DORNIER ALPHA JET

Details of the Alpha Jet programme can be found in the International section of this edition.

DASSAULT-BREGUET/BAe JAGUAR

Details of the Jaguar programme can be found under 'SEPECAT' in the International section of this edition.

DASSAULT-BREGUET ATLANTIQUE 2 (ATL2)

The Atlantique 2, or ATL2 (formerly ANG—Atlantique Nouvelle Génération), is a twin-turboprop maritime patrol aircraft derived directly from the earlier Atlantic that was produced in 1964-73 for operation by the armed services of France (40, of which 3 were sold subsequently to Pakistan), the German Federal Republic (20, including 5 special-purpose ECM aircraft), Italy (18) and the Netherlands (9). Design definition of the ATL2 was initiated by the French government in July 1977, with the aim of providing a replacement for the first generation Atlantic (now known retrospectively as the Atlantic 1) during the period from 1988 to 1996. This led to launch of the development phase of the ATL2 programme in September 1978.

Two ATL2 prototypes were produced by modification of Atlantic 1 airframes. Work started in January 1979, and the first prototype flew for the first time in its new form on 8 May 1981, followed by the second on 26 March 1982. Series production was authorised on 24 May 1984, and two production aircraft had been ordered by mid-1985. The first of these is scheduled to fly in July 1988, enabling deliveries to begin in 1989. The French Navy requirement is for 42 aircraft, of which three more are expected to be ordered in 1986, five in 1987 and six in 1988. The work is being shared by most members of the European SECBAT (Société d'Etude et de Construction du Breguet Atlantic) consortium that was responsible for the earlier programme, with some modification of the work-split to reflect varying national interests in the ATL2 aircraft. Companies involved, under Dassault-Breguet direction, are SABCA and Sonaca of Belgium, MBB and Dornier of Federal Germany, Aeritalia of Italy and Aérospatiale of France. The Tyne engines are being produced by SNECMA of France, Rolls-Royce of the UK, FN of Belgium and MTU of Federal Germany; and propellers by Ratier of France and British Aerospace.

Structural changes by comparison with the Atlantic 1 include use of a refined bonding technique, improved anti-corrosion protection, better sealing between skin panels, and design improvements offering longer fatigue life and more economical maintenance. These are intended to ensure increased serviceability, with 75 per cent of squadron aircraft permanently available for operations; readiness to take off within 30 minutes of an order to go; and an aircraft life of 30 years.

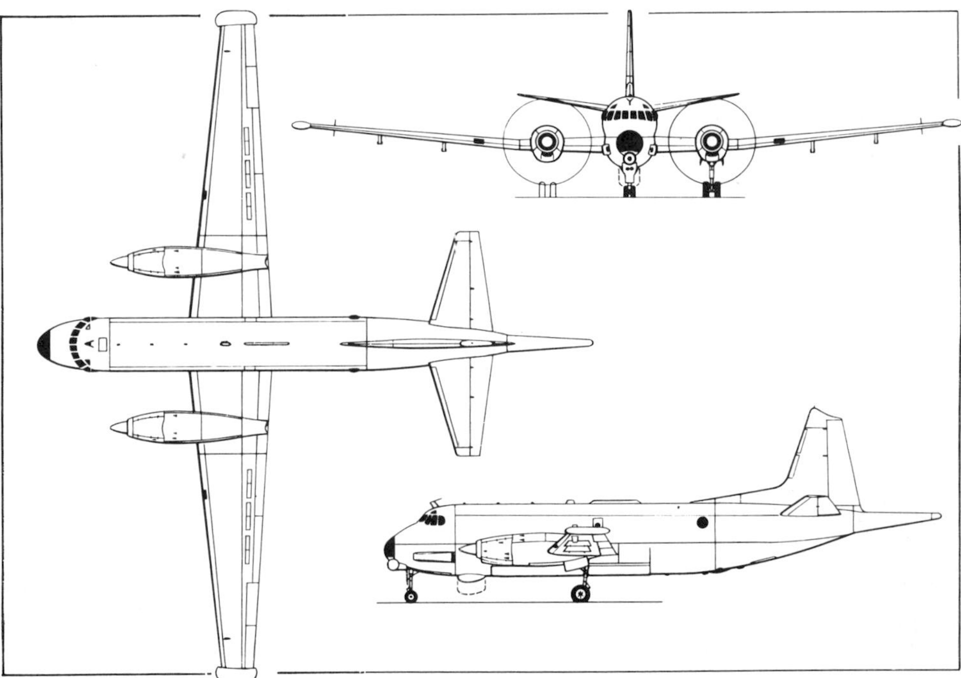

Dassault-Breguet Atlantique 2 (ATL2) twin-turboprop maritime patrol aircraft *(Pilot Press)*

Second prototype of the Dassault-Breguet Atlantique 2 (ATL2) maritime patrol aircraft

The basic mission performance requirements envisaged for the ATL2 are similar to those of the Atlantic 1: a high cruising speed to the operational area, quick descent from cruising altitude to patrol height, lengthy patrol endurance at low altitude, and a high degree of manoeuvrability at sea level. It is able to carry a wide variety of weapons and equipment for finding and attacking both submarines and surface targets in all weathers. In particular, its Thomson-CSF Iguane search radar can detect large ships at a range of 150-200 nm (275-370 km; 170-230 miles), and small targets such as submarine schnorkels over 'several dozen nautical miles' in rough seas.

Like the original Atlantic, the ATL2 is able to perform minelaying, logistic support, and passenger and freight transport missions. It could be adapted for advanced AEW duties, and is suitable for civilian tasks such as air/sea rescue and patrol of offshore fishing and oil interests.

Type: Twin-turboprop maritime patrol aircraft.

Wings: Cantilever mid-wing monoplane, with streamlined ECM pods on tips. Wing section NACA 64 series. Dihedral 6° on outer panels only. Incidence 3°. Tapered planform, with 9° sweepback on leading-edge. All-metal three-spar fail-safe structure, with bonded light alloy honeycomb skin panels on torsion box and on main landing gear doors. Two conventional all-metal ailerons on each wing, actuated by SAMM twin-cylinder jacks. All-metal slotted flaps, with bonded light alloy honeycomb filling, in three segments on each wing, over 75 per cent of span. Three hinged spoilers on upper surface of each outer wing, forward of flaps. Metal airbrake above and below each wing. No trim tabs. Air Equipement/Kléber-Colombes pneumatic de-icing system on leading-edges.

Fuselage: All-metal 'double-bubble' fail-safe structure, with bonded honeycomb sandwich skin on pressurised central section of upper lobe, upward sliding weapons bay doors and nosewheel door. Larger air intake and duct for air-conditioning system on each side of nose.

Tail Unit: Cantilever all-metal structure, with bonded honeycomb sandwich skin panels on torsion boxes. Slightly bulged housing for ESM antennae at top of fin leading-edge. Fixed incidence tailplane, with dihedral. Control surfaces operated through SAMM twin-cylinder jacks. No trim tabs. Air Equipement/Kléber-Colombes pneumatic de-icing system on leading-edges.

Landing Gear: Retractable tricycle type, supplied by Messier-Hispano-Bugatti, with twin wheels on each unit. Hydraulic retraction, nosewheels rearward, main units forward into engine nacelles. Kléber-Colombes or Dunlop tyres; size 39 × 13-20 on mainwheels, pressure 12 bars (170 lb/sq in), 26 × 8-13 on nosewheels, pressure 6·5 bars (94 lb/sq in). New Messier-Hispano-Bugatti disc brakes with higher braking energy, and Modistop anti-skid units.

Power Plant: Two 4,225 kW (5,665 shp) Rolls-Royce Tyne RTy.20 Mk 21 turboprop engines, each driving a four-blade Ratier/British Aerospace constant-speed metal propeller type PD 249/476/3 on prototypes. Four pressure-refuelled integral fuel tanks in wings, with total capacity of 23,120 litres (5,085 Imp gallons; 6,108 US gallons). Updated gauging system. Oil capacity 100 litres (22 Imp gallons; 26·5 US gallons).

Accommodation: Normal flight crew of 12, comprising observer in glazed nose; pilot, co-pilot and flight engineer on flight deck; a radio-navigator, ESM-ECM-MAD operator, radar-IFF operator, tactical co-ordinator and two acoustic sensor operators at stations on the starboard side of the tactical compartment; and two observers in beam positions at the rear. Provision for carrying relief crew, or 12 other personnel. Rest compartment, with eight seats, in centre fuselage, forward of crew room with tables and seats, galley, toilet and wardrobe. Primary access via extending airstair door in bottom of rear fuselage. Emergency exits above and below flight deck and on each side of fuselage, above wing trailing-edge.

Systems: Air-conditioning system supplied by two compressors driven by gearboxes. Heat exchangers and bootstrap system for cabin temperature control. Duplicated hydraulic system, to operate flying controls, landing gear, flaps, weapons bay doors and retractable radome. Three basic electrical systems: variable frequency three phase 115/200V AC system, with two 60/80kVA Auxilec alternators and modernised control and protection equipment; fixed frequency three phase 115/200V 400Hz AC system, with four 15kVA Auxilec Auxivar generators, two on each engine; 28V DC system, with four 6kW transformer-rectifiers supplied from the variable frequency AC system, and one 40Ah battery. One 60kVA emergency AC generator, driven at constant speed by APU. Individual oxygen bottles for emergency use. Electric anti-icing for engine air intake lips, propeller blades and spinners. Turboméca/ABG/SEMCA Astadyne gas turbine APU for engine starting, emergency electrical supply, and air-conditioning on ground.

Armament, Avionics and Operational Equipment: Main weapons bay in unpressurised lower fuselage can accommodate all NATO standard bombs, depth charges, up to eight Mk 46 homing torpedoes or two air-to-surface missiles (typical load comprises three torpedoes and one AM39 Exocet missile). Four underwing attachments for up to 3,500 kg (7,716 lb) of stores, including rockets, air-to-surface missiles or containers. More than 100 sonobuoys, with Alkan pneumatic launcher, in compartment aft of weapons bay, where whole of upper and lower fuselage provides storage for sonobuoys and marker flares. SAT/TRT forward looking infra-red sensor in turret under nose. Thomson-CSF Iguane retractable radar immediately forward of weapons bay, with integrated LMT IFF interrogator and SECRE decoder. Omera cameras in starboard side of nose and in bottom of rear fuselage. Crouzet MAD in lengthened tail sting. Thomson-CSF Arar 13A radar detector for ESM. Thomson-CSF Sadang system for processing active and passive acoustic detection data. A distributed data processing system around a data bus, with a CIMSA Mitra 125X tactical computer (512K words memory), two ESD bus computers, two Sagem magnetic bubble mass memories and Thomson-CSF display subsystem. Other equipment includes LMT NRAI 9A IFF responder and HF/BLU 400W transceiver, HF com, Tacan and DME by Thomson-CSF, VHF/AM com by Socrat, VOR/ILS by EAS, TRT radio altimeter, Collins MF radio compass, ADF, HSI and autopilot/flight director by SFENA, dual Sagem Uliss 53 inertial navigation systems coupled to a Navstar receiver, Sagem high-speed printer and terminal display, Crouzet geographical display and air data computer.

Dimensions, external:
- Wing span, incl wingtip pods — 37·42 m (122 ft 9¼ in)
- Wing aspect ratio — 11·63
- Length overall — 32·63 m (107 ft 0¾ in)
- Height overall — 10·89 m (35 ft 8¾ in)
- Fuselage: Max depth — 4·00 m (13 ft 1½ in)
- Tailplane span — 12·31 m (40 ft 4½ in)
- Wheel track — 9·00 m (29 ft 6¼ in)
- Wheelbase — 9·45 m (31 ft 0 in)
- Propeller diameter — 4·88 m (16 ft 0 in)
- Distance between propeller centres — 9·00 m (29 ft 6¼ in)
- Main weapons bay: Length — 9·00 m (29 ft 6¼ in)
  - Width — 2·10 m (6 ft 10¾ in)

Dimensions, internal:
- Cabin, incl rest compartment, galley, toilet, aft observers' stations: Length — 18·50 m (60 ft 8½ in)
  - Max width — 3·60 m (11 ft 9½ in)
  - Max height — 2·00 m (6 ft 6¾ in)
  - Floor area — 155 m² (1,668 sq ft)
  - Volume — 92 m³ (3,250 cu ft)

Areas:
- Wings, gross — 120·34 m² (1,295·3 sq ft)
- Ailerons (total) — 5·26 m² (56·62 sq ft)
- Flaps (total) — 26·80 m² (288·48 sq ft)
- Spoilers (total) — 1·66 m² (17·87 sq ft)
- Vertical tail surfaces (total) — 16·64 m² (179·11 sq ft)
- Rudder — 5·96 m² (64·15 sq ft)
- Horizontal tail surfaces (total) — 33·00 m² (355·21 sq ft)
- Elevators — 8·30 m² (89·34 sq ft)

Weights and Loadings:
- Weight empty, equipped, standard mission — 25,700 kg (56,659 lb)
- Military load:
  - ASW or ASSW mission — 3,000 kg (6,600 lb)
- Max fuel — 18,500 kg (40,785 lb)
- Mission T-O weight:
  - ASW or ASSW mission — 44,200 kg (97,440 lb)
  - combined ASW/ASSW mission — 45,000 kg (99,200 lb)
- Max overload T-O weight — 46,200 kg (101,850 lb)
- Max zero-fuel weight — 32,500 kg (71,650 lb)
- Normal design landing weight — 36,000 kg (79,365 lb)
- Max landing weight — 46,000 kg (101,400 lb)
- Max wing loading — 385 kg/m² (78·96 lb/sq ft)
- Max power loading — 5·07 kg/kW (8·34 lb/ehp)

Performance (with metal propellers, at T-O weight of 45,000 kg; 99,200 lb except where indicated):
- Never-exceed speed — Mach 0·73
- Max level speed at optimum height — 350 knots (648 km/h; 402 mph)
- Max level speed at S/L — 320 knots (592 km/h; 368 mph)
- Max cruising speed at 7,200 m (25,000 ft) — 300 knots (555 km/h; 345 mph)
- Normal patrol speed, S/L to 1 525 m (5,000 ft) — 170 knots (315 km/h; 195 mph)
- Stalling speed, flaps down — 90 knots (167 km/h; 104 mph)
- Max rate of climb at S/L, AUW of 30,000 kg (66,140 lb) — 884 m (2,900 ft)/min
- Max rate of climb at S/L, AUW of 40,000 kg (88,185 lb) — 610 m (2,000 ft)/min
- Rate of climb at S/L, one engine out, AUW of 30,000 kg (66,140 lb) — 365 m (1,200 ft)/min
- Rate of climb at S/L, one engine out, AUW of 40,000 kg (88,185 lb) — 213 m (700 ft)/min
- Service ceiling — 9,145 m (30,000 ft)
- Runway LCN at max T-O weight — 60
- T-O to 10·5 m (35 ft) — 1,840 m (6,037 ft)
- Landing from 15 m (50 ft) — 1,500 m (4,922 ft)
- 170 knot turning radius at AUW of 40,000 kg (88,185 lb) at:
  - 30° bank — 1,380 m (4,530 ft)
  - 45° bank — 800 m (2,625 ft)
  - 60° bank — 460 m (1,510 ft)

Typical mission profiles, with reserves of 5% total fuel, 5% of fuel consumed and 20 min hold-off:

Anti-ship mission: T-O with max fuel and one AM39 missile; fly 1,800 nm (3,333 km; 2,071 miles) to target area; descend for two-hour search and attack at 90 m (300 ft); return to base

Anti-submarine mission: T-O at 44,300 kg (97,665 lb) AUW with 15,225 kg (33,565 lb) of fuel, four Mk 46 torpedoes, 78 sonobuoys, and a full load of markers and flares; cruise to search area at 290 knots (537 km/h; 333 mph) at 7,620 m (25,000 ft); descend for 8 h low altitude patrol at 600 nm (1,110 km; 690 miles) from base, or 5 h patrol at 1,000 nm (1,850 km; 1,150 miles) from base; return to base at 9,145 m (30,000 ft). Total mission time 12 h 31 min

Ferry range with max fuel 4,900 nm (9,075 km; 5,635 miles)

Max endurance, no reserves 18 h

DASSAULT-BREGUET MYSTÈRE-FALCON 200

The Mystère-Falcon 200 is the latest in a family of twin-turbofan light transports based on the Mystère 20 design, which was first flown in prototype form on 7 May 1963. Production is undertaken jointly by Aérospatiale, which builds the fuselage and tail unit, and Dassault-Breguet's Mérignac works, which manufactures the wings and has responsibility for final assembly.

Manufacture of the Mystère-Falcon 200 began with aircraft c/n 401, concurrent with the production rundown of the earlier Mystère-Falcon 20F series, the last of which (c/n 486) came off the assembly line in late 1983. The model 200 had been introduced, originally as the Mystère-Falcon 20H, at the 1981 Paris Air Show, with Garrett turbofans in place of the F's General Electric CF700s, larger integral fuel tankage in the rear fuselage, redesigned wing root fairings, automatic slat extension, and many important systems changes. Like the earlier Mystère-Falcon 20 series, it can be modified for specific duties, as follows:

Calibration: Ten Mystère-Falcons, in several different variants, have been delivered to the French DGAC, French Air Force, and authorities in France, Spain, Indonesia and Iran, for navaid calibration. Most are equipped with Dassault designed high/low level navigation facility calibration systems, some in the form of a removable console.

Airline crew training: Mystère-Falcon 20s have been used by Air France to train pilots for its jet airliners, with up to five aircraft being used simultaneously. Japan Air Lines also bought three of this version.

Quick-change and cargo: A quick-change kit, consisting of an assembly of nets and supports, keeps the centre aisle free and allows direct access to nine freight compartments. Total usable volume of these compartments is 6·65 m³ (235 cu ft), and transformation from executive configuration to cargo configuration, or vice versa, takes less than one hour. A different specific cargo conversion was performed on 33 aircraft in the USA. For both versions an increase of the maximum zero-fuel weight from 8,900 kg (19,600 lb) to 9,980 kg (22,000 lb) allows an increased payload of up to 3,000 kg (6,615 lb).

Target towing: A Mystère-Falcon 20 is used by the French Air Force for target towing missions. It carries a Secapem target on an inboard hardpoint under each wing and a pod containing a winch and cable on each of two outboard hardpoints. Missions of up to 2 h duration can be flown, cruising at up to 300 knots (555 km/h; 345 mph) at 450 m (1,500 ft) or 270 knots (500 km/h; 310 mph) at 4,500 m (15,000 ft). The hardpoints (650 kg; 1,433 lb inboard, 750 kg; 1,650 lb outboard) can be used to carry alternative stores if required. Several former Federal Express cargo aircraft operated in this form by Flight Refuelling Ltd of the UK, with a variety of targets.

Aerial photography: This version has two ventral camera bays fitted with optical glass windows. It is operated for high altitude photography, survey and scientific research in several countries. The camera installation can be supplemented by a multispectral scanner and other scientific loads.

Systems trainer: Several aircraft fitted with the combat radar and navigation systems of various Mirage types are in service with the French Air Force for training its combat and reconnaissance pilots.

Ambulance: Up to three stretchers can be accommodated, together with a large supply of oxygen and equipment for intensive care and monitoring of patients. Cabinets near the door are removed to facilitate the loading of stretchers.

Electronic warfare: Norway, Canada and Morocco have been followed by several other nations in operating Mystère-Falcon 20 aircraft modified for ECM duties such as radar and communications intelligence and jamming. Threat simulation missions are among the roles for which 10 former Federal Express Mystère-Falcon 20s were acquired by Flight Refuelling Ltd of the UK, for duties in support of the Royal Navy's Fleet Requirements and Air Direction Unit (FRADU).

The following data apply to the standard Mystère-Falcon 200 executive transport:

TYPE: Twin-turbofan executive transport.

WINGS: Cantilever low-wing monoplane. Thickness/chord ratio varies from 10·5 to 8%. Dihedral 2°. Incidence 1° 30′. Sweepback at quarter-chord 30°. All-metal (copper bearing alloys) fail-safe torsion box structure with machined stressed skin. Ailerons are each operated by Dassault twin-body actuators, from dual hydraulic systems, and have artificial feel. Non-slotted slats inboard of fence, and slotted slats outboard, on each wing, with automatic extension and retraction. Hydraulically actuated airbrakes forward of the hydraulically actuated two-section single-slotted flaps. Leading-edges anti-iced by engine bleed air.

Dassault-Breguet Mystère-Falcon 200 (two Garrett ATF 3-6A-4C turbofan engines)

FUSELAGE: All-metal semi-monocoque structure of circular cross section, built on fail-safe principles.

TAIL UNIT: Cantilever all-metal structure, with electrically controlled variable incidence tailplane mounted halfway up fin. Elevators and rudder each actuated by twin hydraulic servos. No trim tabs.

LANDING GEAR: Retractable tricycle type, by Messier-Hispano-Bugatti, with twin wheels on all three units. Hydraulic retraction, main units inward, nosewheels forward. Oleo-pneumatic shock absorbers. Steerable and self centering nosewheels. Tyres size 26 × 6·6 in on main units, 14·5 × 5·5 in on nosewheels. Tyre pressure 11·5 bars (166 lb/sq in) on mainwheels, 10·4 bars (151 lb/sq in) on nosewheels. Goodyear disc brakes and anti-skid units.

POWER PLANT: Two Garrett ATF 3-6A-4C turbofan engines (each rated at 23·13 kN; 5,200 lb st). Optional thrust reversers are produced by Hurel-Dubois. Fuel in two integral tanks in wings and large integral tank in rear fuselage, with total capacity of 6,000 litres (1,320 Imp gallons; 1,585 US gallons).

ACCOMMODATION: Flight deck for crew of two, with airline type instrumentation. Jump seat and crew wardrobe. Airstair door, with handrail, on port side. On starboard side, opposite door, is a galley with oven and hot beverage containers. Main cabin normally seats nine passengers in three pairs of facing chairs, separated by tables, and an inward facing three-seat sofa, with a central 'trench' aisle. Alternative arrangement provides 12 compact seats at a pitch of 76 cm (30 in). Wardrobe immediately aft of door on port side. Externally serviced toilet compartment aft of main cabin on port side, with a baggage bay opposite on starboard side. Main heated, non-pressurised, baggage compartment in rear fuselage with external access on port side.

SYSTEMS: Duplicated air-conditioning and pressurisation system, supplied with air bled from both engines. Pressure differential 0·607 bars (8·8 lb/sq in). Cooling by bootstrap system. Two independent hydraulic systems, pressure 207 bars (3,000 lb/sq in), actuate primary flying controls, flaps, landing gear, wheel brakes, spoilers and nosewheel steering. No. 1 system is powered by one engine driven hydraulic pump and, in emergency, by a motor pump package driven by No. 2 system hydraulic pressure and by an electric standby pump. No. 2 system is powered by one engine driven hydraulic pump and, in emergency, by the electric standby pump. Hydraulic reservoir pressure 1·47 bars (21 lb/sq in). Electrical system includes a 9kW 28V DC starter/generator on each engine, three 750VA inverters and two 36Ah batteries. Solar T40 APU optional. Wing leading-edges and engine air inlets anti-iced with LP compressor bleed air. Windscreen, pitot and temperature probes anti-iced electrically.

AVIONICS AND EQUIPMENT: Collins FCS-80 flight control system standard, with dual Collins EFIS-86C electronic flight instrument system using colour CRTs. System includes four identical CRTs plus one multi-function display used for weather radar, navigation display or checklist. Standard optional avionics include duplicated VHF, VOR, ADF, DME and ATC transponder, one weather radar and one radio altimeter. Optional equipment includes HF, VLF/Omega navigation system and laser inertial reference system.

DIMENSIONS, EXTERNAL:

Wing span 16·30 m (53 ft 6 in)
Wing chord (mean) 2·85 m (9 ft 4 in)
Wing aspect ratio 6·5
Length overall 17·15 m (56 ft 3 in)
Length of fuselage 15·55 m (51 ft 0 in)
Height overall 5·32 m (17 ft 5 in)
Tailplane span 6·74 m (22 ft 1 in)
Wheel track 3·69 m (12 ft 1¼ in)
Wheelbase 5·74 m (18 ft 10 in)
Passenger door: Height 1·52 m (5 ft 0 in)
Width 0·80 m (2 ft 7½ in)
Height to sill 1·09 m (3 ft 7 in)
Emergency exits (each side, over wing):
Height 0·66 m (2 ft 2 in)
Width 0·48 m (1 ft 7 in)

DIMENSIONS, INTERNAL:

Cabin, incl fwd baggage space and rear toilet:
Length 7·26 m (23 ft 10 in)
Max width 1·79 m (5 ft 10½ in)
Max height 1·70 m (5 ft 7 in)
Volume 20·0 m³ (700 cu ft)
Baggage space (cabin) 0·65 m³ (23 cu ft)
Baggage compartment (rear fuselage) 0·80 m³ (28·2 cu ft)

AREAS:

Wings, gross 41·00 m² (440 sq ft)
Horizontal tail surfaces (total) 11·30 m² (121·6 sq ft)
Vertical tail surfaces (total) 7·60 m² (81·8 sq ft)

WEIGHTS:

Weight empty, equipped 8,250 kg (18,190 lb)
Payload with max fuel 1,265 kg (2,790 lb)
Max fuel 4,845 kg (10,680 lb)
Max T-O and ramp weight 14,515 kg (32,000 lb)
Max zero-fuel weight 10,200 kg (22,500 lb)
Max landing weight 13,100 kg (28,800 lb)

PERFORMANCE:

Max operating Mach No. 0·865
Max operating speed at S/L 350 knots (648 km/h; 402 mph) IAS
Max operating speed at 6,100 m (20,000 ft) 380 knots (704 km/h; 438 mph) IAS
Max cruising speed at 9,150 m (30,000 ft) at AUW of 11,340 kg (25,000 lb) 470 knots (870 km/h; 541 mph)
Econ cruising speed at 12,500 m (41,000 ft) 420 knots (780 km/h; 485 mph)
Stalling speed 84 knots (156 km/h; 97 mph)
Service ceiling 13,715 m (45,000 ft)
FAR 25 balanced field length with 8 passengers and full fuel 1,420 m (4,660 ft)
FAR 121 landing distance with 8 passengers, FAR 121 reserves 1,130 m (3,710 ft)
Range with max fuel and 8 passengers at long range cruising speed, FAR 121 reserves 2,370 nm (4,390 km; 2,730 miles)

DASSAULT-BREGUET GARDIAN

Based on engineering experience acquired with the HU-25A Guardian programme (see 1985-86 *Jane's*), this specialised maritime surveillance aircraft is an adaptation of the Mystère-Falcon 200 (which see). The first order, for five Gardians, was placed by the French Navy, to replace Lockheed P-2H Neptunes in the Pacific area. The first of these aircraft flew for the first time on 15 April 1981, and was delivered to the French Navy on 14 April 1983. All five Gardians flew to their operational bases at Faaa, Tahiti, and Tontouta, New Caledonia, during July 1984.

Several variants of the Gardian are available, with different standards of equipment. Changes in the basic version, by comparison with the Mystère-Falcon 200, can be summarised as follows:

POWER PLANT: Two Garrett ATF 3-6A-3C turbofan engines, each rated at 24·20 kN (5,440 lb st).

ACCOMMODATION: Crew of two side by side on flight deck; two observers seated behind very large lookout windows in the front of the cabin, with a navigator and a radar operator at the rear. The centre part of the cabin can be equipped, alternatively, with two four-seat couches for personnel transport; four seats and two removable tables in a VIP configuration; a two-section compartment for freight transport; or two stretchers and resuscitation kits for ambulance missions. Between the observers' seats is a hatch for airdropping lifeboats, packages or personnel. Four underwing attachments are capable of carrying 750 kg (1,650 lb) on the inner stations or 650 kg (1,430 lb) on the outer stations.

AVIONICS AND EQUIPMENT: In addition to a standard Mystère-Falcon 200 installation, comprising FCS-80, two VHF, two VOR/ILS, ADF, two DME and ATC transponder, the Gardian has a VHF-FM, UHF, V/UHF gonio, HF, VLF/Omega nav system, nav table, high performance Thomson-CSF Varan radar designed for maritime detection, and a hand held camera linked to the nav system for automatic data annotation.

DIMENSIONS: As Mystère-Falcon 200

WEIGHTS:

Weight empty, equipped	8,700 kg (19,180 lb)
Operating weight empty	8,880 kg (19,575 lb)
Max fuel	4,820 kg (10,625 lb)
Max payload	1,637 kg (3,610 lb)
Payload with max fuel	1,520 kg (3,350 lb)
Max T-O weight	15,200 kg (33,510 lb)
Max landing weight	13,100 kg (28,880 lb)
Max zero-fuel weight	10,500 kg (23,150 lb)

PERFORMANCE:

Max cruising speed at 9,150 m (30,000 ft) 470 knots (870 km/h; 541 mph)

Balanced field length at max T-O weight 1,680 m (5,512 ft)

FAR 25 landing distance at typical landing weight 625 m (2,050 ft)

Range with six crew, complete avionics and reserves of 5% total fuel and for 30 min at S/L 2,425 nm (4,490 km; 2,790 miles)

Dassault-Breguet Gardian 2 carrying two Exocet missiles, a Thomson-CSF Barem self-protection jamming pod and a Matra Sycomor chaff dispensing pod on underwing pylons *(Air Portraits)*

DASSAULT-BREGUET GARDIAN 2

The Gardian 2 is a simplified version of the maritime surveillance Gardian in service with the French Navy. In its basic form it is a Falcon 200 fitted with a Thomson-CSF Varan radar designed for maritime detection, a Crouzet Omega navigation system and four underwing hardpoints. With additional equipment, it can perform the following missions:

Target designation: This includes over-the-horizon targeting for maritime forces or coastal missile batteries; missile midcourse retargeting; control of surface operations; and strike guidance against surface ships or land objectives. Equipment includes a navigation table, UHF modem to transmit data, V/UHF DF, and IFF interrogator. Options include ESM, search windows, inertial platform, VHF/FM, HF and track-while-scan radar system.

AM39 Exocet attack: As well as two Exocet sea-skimming air-to-surface missiles, this requires an inertial platform, Omega/INS interface, AM39 interface and controls, and IFF interrogator. Options are track-while-scan, navigation table and ESM.

Electronic surveillance and countermeasures: This requires either Thomson-CSF DR 2000 ESM and navigation table, or an integrated system including a Thomson-CSF DR 4000 ESM, a computer, the Varan radar, an inertial platform and tactical visualisation elements from the Atlantique 2 system. Options include an IFF interrogator, AM39 installation, track-while-scan, countermeasures or decoy pods, elint equipment, HF/VHF/UHF comint equipment and V/UHF DF.

Light attack: Equipped with a weapon sight and two AMD-BA CC 420 30 mm gun pods; two AMD-BA/ECX 260 pods each containing two 12·7 mm machine-guns; two AMD-BA CEM 1 multi-store containers (rockets or machine-gun plus grenade launcher) and two Matra BLG 66 cluster bombs; or four Matra 155 (18 × 68 mm) or Matra F2 (6 × 68 mm) rocket packs.

Target towing: As for Falcon 200.

In all cases, the cabin can be arranged to permit secondary transport missions.

DASSAULT-BREGUET MYSTÈRE-FALCON 100

The Mystère-Falcon 100 is the latest version of the Mystère-Falcon 10 series, which it has replaced in production. Like its predecessors, it is a small executive 'jet' for five to eight passengers, with compound swept wings fitted with high-lift devices, and powered by Garrett TFE731-2 turbofan engines.

Details of the early history of the Mystère-Falcon 10 series can be found in the 1982-83 *Jane's*. By March 1985, a total of 204 Mystère-Falcon 10s and 100s had been delivered. Fuselages are provided by the Potez works at Aire-sur-Adour, which assembles components built by Sogerma, Socea and Socata. Wings come from CASA of Spain; tail units and nose assemblies from IAM of Italy; and many other components such as tail fins, doors and emergency exits from Latécoère's Toulouse works.

By comparison with the Mystère-Falcon 10, the model 100 has an increase of 225 kg (496 lb) in max T-O weight and higher max ramp weight; a fourth cabin window on the starboard side, opposite the door; a larger heated, unpressurised rear baggage compartment; and an optional Collins five-CRT EFIS-85 instrument package.

Under a state sponsored research and development programme, Aérospatiale and Dassault-Breguet have manufactured a set of resin-impregnated carbonfibre wings for a Falcon 10 designated **V10F**. Dassault-Breguet made the port wing, Aérospatiale the starboard wing, retaining the aerodynamic form of the standard metal wings. The V10F (F-WVPR, c/n 5) flew for the first time on 21 May 1985 and received DGAC certification on 16 December 1985. It made a total of 40 test flights and was building up flying hours as one of the aircraft in the charter fleet of Europe Falcon Service, at Le Bourget, in mid-1986.

The following details apply to the standard production Mystère-Falcon 100:

TYPE: Twin-turbofan executive transport.

WINGS: Cantilever low-wing monoplane with increased sweepback on inboard leading-edges. All-metal torsion box structure, with leading-edge slats and double-slotted trailing-edge flaps and plain ailerons. Two-section spoilers above each wing, forward of flaps.

FUSELAGE: All-metal semi-monocoque structure, designed to fail-safe principles.

TAIL UNIT: Cantilever all-metal structure, similar to that of Falcon 200.

LANDING GEAR: Retractable tricycle type, manufactured by Messier-Hispano-Bugatti, with twin wheels on each main gear unit, single wheel on nose gear. Hydraulic retraction, main units inward, nosewheel forward. Oleo-pneumatic shock absorbers. Mainwheel tyres size 22 × 5·75 in, pressure 9·31 bars (135 lb/sq in). Nosewheel tyre size 18 × 5·75 in, pressure 6·48 bars (94 lb/sq in).

POWER PLANT: Two Garrett TFE731-2 turbofan engines (each 14·4 kN; 3,230 lb st), pod mounted on sides of rear fuselage. Fuel in two integral tanks in wings and two integral feeder tanks in rear fuselage, with total capacity of 3,340 litres (735 Imp gallons; 882 US gallons). Separate fuel system for each engine, with provision for cross-feeding. Pressure refuelling system.

ACCOMMODATION: Crew of two on flight deck, with dual controls and airline type instrumentation. Provision for third crew member on a jump seat. Seating arrangements differ from aircraft to aircraft in accordance with customer preference. All have a two/three-place sofa in the rear of the cabin, with further seats for a total of up to eight passengers. There is an internal baggage compartment behind the sofa, and a small galley and toilet forward of the passenger accommodation. Clamshell door at the front, on the port side, with built-in steps.

SYSTEMS: Duplicated air-conditioning and pressurisation systems supplied with air bled from both engines. Pressure differential 0·61 bars (8·8 lb/sq in). Two independent hydraulic systems, each of 207 bars (3,000 lb/sq in) pressure and with twin engine driven pumps and emergency electric pump, to actuate primary flight controls, flaps, landing gear, wheel brakes, spoilers, yaw damper and nosewheel steering. Plain hydraulic reservoir, pressurised at 1·47 bars (21 lb/sq in). 28V DC electrical system with a 9kW DC starter/generator on each engine, three 750VA 400Hz 115V inverters and two 23Ah batteries. Automatic emergency oxygen system.

AVIONICS AND EQUIPMENT: Standard avionics include duplicated VHF and VOR/glideslope, dual ADF, marker beacon receiver, ATC transponder, autopilot, intercom system and duplicated blind-flying instrumentation. Optional avionics include Collins EFIS-85, duplicated DME and flight director, Global GNS 1000 flight management system, weather radar, radio altimeter and Global GNS 500 VLF/Omega long-range navigation system.

DIMENSIONS, EXTERNAL:

Wing span	13·08 m (42 ft 11 in)
Wing chord (mean)	2·046 m (6 ft 8½ in)
Wing aspect ratio	7·1
Length overall	13·86 m (45 ft 5¾ in)
Length of fuselage	12·47 m (40 ft 11 in)
Height overall	4·61 m (15 ft 1½ in)
Tailplane span	5·82 m (19 ft 1 in)
Wheel track	2·86 m (9 ft 5 in)
Wheelbase	5·30 m (17 ft 4¾ in)
Passenger door: Height	1·47 m (4 ft 10 in)
Width	0·80 m (2 ft 7 in)
Height to sill	0·884 m (2 ft 10¾ in)
Emergency exit (stbd side, over wing):	
Height	0·914 m (3 ft 0 in)
Width	0·508 m (1 ft 8 in)

DIMENSIONS, INTERNAL:

Cabin, excl flight deck: Length	4·70 m (15 ft 5 in)
Max width	1·55 m (5 ft 1 in)
Max height	1·45 m (4 ft 9 in)
Volume	7·11 m³ (251 cu ft)
Baggage compartment volume:	
cabin	0·72 m³ (25·4 cu ft)
rear	0·81 m³ (28·6 cu ft)

AREAS:

Wings, gross	24·1 m² (259·4 sq ft)
Horizontal tail surfaces (total)	6·75 m² (72·65 sq ft)
Vertical tail surfaces (total)	4·54 m² (48·87 sq ft)

WEIGHTS:

Weight empty, equipped	5,055 kg (11,145 lb)
Max payload	1,305 kg (2,875 lb)
Max fuel	2,680 kg (5,910 lb)
Max T-O weight	8,755 kg (19,300 lb)
Max zero-fuel weight	6,540 kg (14,420 lb)
Max landing weight	8,000 kg (17,640 lb)

PERFORMANCE:

Never-exceed speed at S/L 350 knots (648 km/h; 402 mph)

Max operating Mach No. 0·87

Max cruise Mach No. at 10,670 m (35,000 ft) 0·84

Dassault-Breguet Mystère-Falcon 100 (two Garrett TFE731-2 turbofan engines)

Max cruising speed at 7,620 m (25,000 ft)
492 knots (912 km/h; 566 mph)
Approach speed 100 knots (185 km/h; 115 mph)
FAR 25 balanced T-O field lengths with four passengers and fuel for a 1,000 nm (1,850 km; 1,150 mile) stage, 45 min reserves 960 m (3,150 ft)
FAR 25 balanced T-O field length, with four passengers and max fuel 1,325 m (4,350 ft)
FAR 121 landing field length, with four passengers and 45 min reserves 1,065 m (3,495 ft)
Range with four passengers and 45 min reserves
1,880 nm (3,480 km; 2,160 miles)

DASSAULT-BREGUET MYSTÈRE-FALCON 50

The Mystère-Falcon 50 three-turbofan executive transport has the same external fuselage cross section as the Mystère-Falcon 200, but is an entirely new design, featuring area ruling and advanced wing aerodynamics. Normal layout is for a crew of two or three and eight or nine passengers, with provision for up to twelve passengers. Since 1980 an ambulance version has also been available, with the interior laid out for three stretchers (or two stretchers and heavy medical equipment) and two doctors.

The original prototype (F-WAMD) flew for the first time on 7 November 1976, followed by a second prototype (F-WINR) on 18 February 1978 and the third (and sole pre-production) aircraft on 13 June 1978. DGAC certification was received on 27 February 1979, followed by FAA type approval on 7 March. Falcon 50 c/n 4, flown on 2 March 1979, was the first built on Dassault-Breguet's Mérignac assembly line and became Falcon Jet's US demonstrator. Deliveries began in July 1979 and totalled 147 aircraft, registered in 26 countries, by March 1985. Since delivery of the fifth aircraft to the Armée de l'Air's GLAM (Groupe de Liaisons Aériennes Ministérielles) in early 1980, for use by the President of the French Republic, Mystère-Falcon 50s have been purchased for state VIP transportation in West Germany, Iraq, Jordan, Libya, Morocco, South Africa, Spain and Yugoslavia. Two supplied to the Italian Air Force are equipped for both VIP and air ambulance duties.

On 31 March 1979 a Falcon 50 set the current straight-line distance record for Class C1h (business aircraft of 12,000-16,000 kg AUW) in the USA, by flying 3,293·69 nm (6,099·91 km; 3,790·31 miles). Two current records in Class C1i (16,000-20,000 kg) were set in France on 24 April 1980, with a sustained level flight at 13,716 m (45,000 ft), which qualified also as the altitude record in this class.

Fuselages for the Mystère-Falcon 50 are produced at Aérospatiale's Saint-Nazaire works, wings at the Colomiers plant of Dassault-Breguet, tail units by Aérospatiale at Méaulte, and cowlings by Hurel-Dubois at Vélizy-Villacoublay.

TYPE: Three-turbofan executive transport.

WINGS: Cantilever low-wing monoplane, with compound leading-edge sweepback and optimised section. Each wing is attached to the central box structure by multiple bolts and forms an integral fuel tank. Full span leading-edge slats, of which the outboard sections are slotted. Double-slotted trailing-edge flaps and ailerons, latter with carbonfibre skin. Three-section two-position air-brakes on top surface of each wing.

FUSELAGE: All-metal semi-monocoque structure of circular cross-section, with aft baggage compartment included in pressure cell.

TAIL UNIT: Cantilever all-metal structure. Horizontal surfaces, with anhedral, mounted partway up fin. Tailplane incidence adjustable by screwjack, driven by two electric motors controlled by 'normal' and 'emergency' controls located respectively on the control wheels and pedestal.

LANDING GEAR: Retractable tricycle type by Messier-Hispano-Bugatti, with twin wheels on each unit. Hydraulic retraction, main units inward, nosewheels forward. Mainwheel tyres size 26 × 6·6-14 in, pressure 14·34 bars (208 lb/sq in). Nosewheel tyres size 14·5 × 5·5-6 in, pressure 8·96 bars (130 lb/sq in). Four-disc brakes designed for 400 landings with normal energy braking.

POWER PLANT: Three Garrett TFE731-3 turbofan engines, each rated at 16·5 kN (3,700 lb st) for take-off. Two engines pod mounted on sides of rear fuselage, the third attached by two top mounts. Thrust reverser on centre engine. Fuel in wing and fuselage tanks, with total capacity of 8,765 litres (1,928 Imp gallons; 2,315 US gallons). Single point pressure fuelling.

ACCOMMODATION: Crew of two side by side on flight deck, with full dual controls and airline type instrumentation. Third seat to rear of co-pilot. Various cabin configurations available, based on two alternative toilet locations. An aft cabin toilet allows an eight/nine-passenger arrangement, with four chairs in forward cabin, facing each other in pairs, and a three-place sofa and two facing chairs in the rear cabin. A wardrobe, galley and crew toilet are located forward, in the entrance area. Alternatively, a forward toilet, facing the door, makes possible a lounge in the rear cabin, furnished with a four/five-place angle sofa and a chair. This rear lounge is separated from the forward cabin by either a wardrobe and refreshment/recreation console, or by two additional seats, raising the cabin accommodation to twelve persons. The rear baggage compartment is pressurised and air-conditioned, and has a capacity of 1,000 kg (2,200 lb). Access is by a separate door on the port side.

SYSTEMS: Air-conditioning system utilises bleed air from all three engines. Max pressure differential 0·61 bars (8·8 lb/sq in). Pressurisation maintains a max cabin altitude of 2,440 m (8,000 ft) to a flight altitude of 13,700 m (45,000 ft). Two independent hydraulic systems, pressure 207 bars (3,000 lb/sq in), with three engine driven pumps and one emergency electric pump, actuate primary flying controls, flaps, slats, landing gear, wheel brakes, air-brakes and nosewheel steering. Plain reservoir, pressurised by bleed air at 1·47 bars (21 lb/sq in). 28V DC electrical system, with a 9kW 28V DC starter/generator on each engine and two 23Ah batteries. Automatic emergency oxygen system. Optional 9kW Garrett APU.

AVIONICS: Standard items include Omega, inertial navigation system, duplicated VHF and VOR, ADF, DME, ATC and HF, radio altimeter and weather radar. Basic aircraft includes Collins autopilot and two FCS-80 flight directors. Latest versions have advanced symbology Collins 86C EFIS and dual Honeywell ring laser inertial reference platforms.

DIMENSIONS, EXTERNAL:

Wing span	18·86 m (61 ft 10½ in)
Wing chord (mean)	2·84 m (9 ft 3¾ in)
Wing aspect ratio	7·6
Length overall	18·50 m (60 ft 8½ in)
Length of fuselage	17·66 m (57 ft 11 in)
Height overall	6·97 m (22 ft 10½ in)
Tailplane span	7·74 m (25 ft 4¾ in)
Wheel track	3·98 m (13 ft 0¾ in)
Wheelbase	7·24 m (23 ft 9 in)

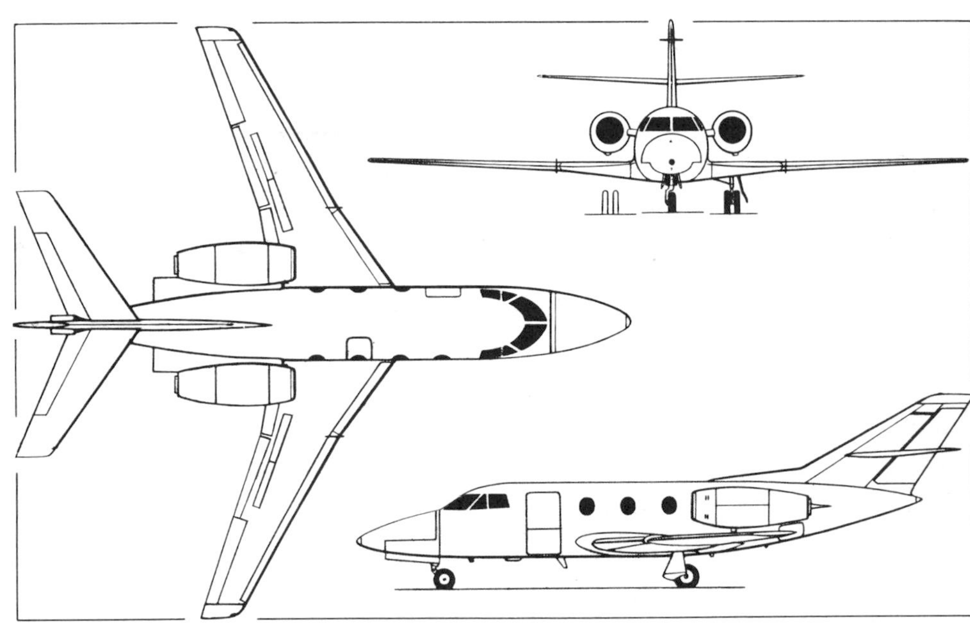

Dassault-Breguet Mystère-Falcon 100 four/eight-passenger executive transport *(Pilot Press)*

Dassault-Breguet Mystère-Falcon 50 supplied to the Italian Air Force

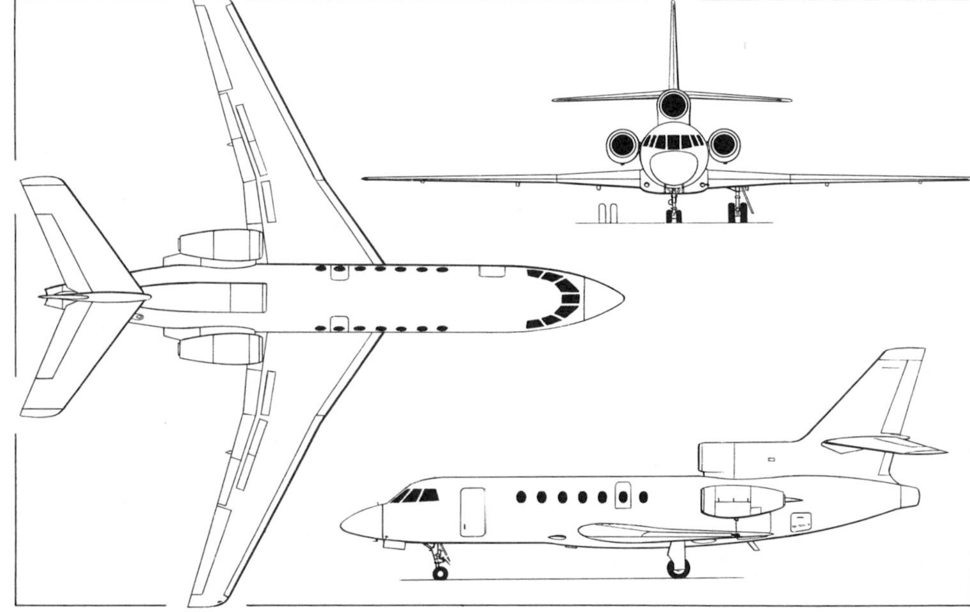

Dassault-Breguet Mystère-Falcon 50 long-range three-turbofan executive transport *(Pilot Press)*

Passenger door: Height 1·52 m (4 ft 11¾ in)
Width 0·80 m (2 ft 7½ in)
Height to sill 1·30 m (4 ft 3¼ in)
Emergency exits (each side, over wing):
Height 0·92 m (3 ft 0¼ in)
Width 0·51 m (1 ft 8 in)

DIMENSIONS, INTERNAL:
Cabin, incl forward baggage space and rear toilet:
Length 7·16 m (23 ft 6 in)
Max width 1·86 m (6 ft 1¼ in)
Max height 1·79 m (5 ft 10½ in)
Volume 20·0 m³ (706 cu ft)
Baggage space 0·75 m³ (26·5 cu ft)
Baggage compartment (rear) 2·55 m³ (90 cu ft)

AREAS:
Wings, gross 46·83 m² (504·1 sq ft)
Horizontal tail surfaces (total) 13·35 m² (143·7 sq ft)
Vertical tail surfaces (total) 9·82 m² (105·7 sq ft)

WEIGHTS:
Weight empty, equipped 9,150 kg (20,170 lb)
Max payload 2,120 kg (4,675 lb)
Max fuel 7,040 kg (15,520 lb)
Max T-O and ramp weight:
standard 17,600 kg (38,800 lb)
optional 18,500 kg (40,780 lb)
Max zero-fuel weight: standard 11,000 kg (24,250 lb)
optional 11,600 kg (25,570 lb)
Max landing weight 16,200 kg (35,715 lb)

PERFORMANCE:
Max operating Mach No. 0·86
Max operating speed at S/L
350 knots (648 km/h; 402 mph) IAS
Max operating speed at 7,225 m (23,700 ft)
370 knots (685 km/h; 425 mph) IAS
Max cruising speed
Mach 0·82 or 475 knots (880 km/h; 546 mph)
Service ceiling 14,935 m (49,000 ft)
FAR 25 balanced field length with 8 passengers and fuel for 3,500 nm (6,480 km; 4,025 miles)
1,430 m (4,690 ft)
FAR 121 landing distance with 8 passengers and 45 min LR reserves 1,080 m (3,545 ft)
Range at Mach 0·75 with 8 passengers and 45 min LR reserves 3,500 nm (6,480 km; 4,025 miles)

DASSAULT-BREGUET MYSTÈRE-FALCON 900

On 27 May 1983, at the Paris Air Show, Dassault-Breguet announced a programme to develop an intercontinental three-turbofan executive transport to be known as the Mystère-Falcon 900. The prototype (F-WIDE *Spirit of Lafayette*) was rolled out on 18 May 1984 and made its first flight on 21 September 1984. By 1 June 1985, it had accumulated 275 flying hours in 134 flights, and an airframe was undergoing static tests at the CEAT, Toulouse. The second development aircraft (F-WFJC) flew on 30 August 1985. In the following month it made a nonstop flight of 4,305 nm (7,973 km; 4,954 miles) from Paris to Little Rock, Arkansas, USA, for demonstration at the NBAA Convention and at 30 other locations. The return transatlantic flight from Teterboro, New Jersey, to Istres, France, was made at Mach 0·84.

Approval for full production was given on 18 May 1984. Sales totalled 51 aircraft by Spring 1986; DGAC certification was received on 14 March 1986, and FAA type approval on 21 March. Deliveries were planned to start in the second half of 1986, and to reach the rate of four a month by September 1987.

As can be seen in the accompanying illustrations, the Mystère-Falcon 900 is similar in configuration to the Mystère-Falcon 50, but with increased overall dimensions, notably a larger fuselage. Design and manufacturing programmes are computer assisted, and extensive use is made of carbonfibre and aramid composite (Kevlar) materials. Certification will be to FAR Pt 25 and 55 requirements, including qualification of the entire airframe to 'damage tolerance' standards. A secondary pressure bulkhead, while allowing in-flight access to the large baggage compartment at the rear, isolates the latter in the event of pressure loss. In a belly landing, the bottom fuselage fuel tanks would be protected by ventral skids and energy absorbing honeycomb pads which form an integral part of the fuselage structure.

TYPE: Three-turbofan executive transport.

WINGS: Cantilever low-wing monoplane, with profile optimised for Mach 0·84 cruise. Dihedral 0° 30′. Sweepback at quarter-chord 29° inboard, 24° 30′ on outer panels. Conventional two-spar light alloy torsion box structure, forming integral fuel tank in each wing, and attached to fuselage centre-section by multiple bolts. Full-span leading-edge slats in two segments on each wing, controlled manually. Outer segments are slotted and also operate automatically under the control of an angle of attack sensor. Two-segment hydraulically actuated double-slotted flaps and carbonfibre aileron on trailing-edge of each wing. Three airbrakes forward of flaps on each wing. Glassfibre wingtip fairings. Leading-edges anti-iced by engine bleed air.

FUSELAGE: All-metal semi-monocoque damage tolerant structure. Use of thicker skins than those of Falcon 50 has permitted number of frames to be reduced (35 compared with 43), with less riveting. Kevlar nosecone over radar. Kevlar fairing on each side of fuselage in area of wingroots.

TAIL UNIT: Cantilever structure, with horizontal surfaces mounted partway up fin at anhedral of 8°. All surfaces sweptback. Tailplane incidence adjustable by screwjack, driven by two electric motors controlled by 'normal' and 'emergency' controls located respectively on the pilots' control wheels and pedestal. All-metal construction, except for rear portion of fin below rudder, and tailcone, which are of Kevlar. Rudder and elevators operated hydraulically.

LANDING GEAR: Retractable tricycle type by Messier-Hispano-Bugatti, with twin wheels on each unit. Hydraulic retraction, main units inward, nosewheels forward. Oleo-pneumatic shock absorbers. Mainwheels fitted with Michelin radial tyres size 29 × 7·7-15, pressure 12·8 bars (183 lb/sq in). Nosewheel tyres size 17·5 × 5·75-8, pressure 9·8 bars (140 lb/sq in). Hydraulic nosewheel steering. MHB triple-disc carbon brakes. Nosewheel doors of Kevlar; mainwheel doors of carbonfibre.

POWER PLANT: Three Garrett TFE731-5A turbofan engines, each rated at 20 kN (4,500 lb st). Thrust reverser on centre engine. Fuel in two integral tanks in wings, centre-section tank, and two tanks under floor of forward and rear fuselage. Total fuel capacity 10,735 litres (2,361 Imp gallons; 2,835 US gallons). Kevlar air intake trunk for centre engine, and rear cowling for side engines. Carbonfibre central cowling around all three engines.

ACCOMMODATION: Provision of a type 3 emergency exit on the starboard side of the cabin permits a wide range of layouts for up to 19 passengers. The basic configuration has two crew side by side on the flight deck, with a jumpseat behind the pedestal. The flight deck is separated from the cabin by a door, with a crew wardrobe and baggage locker on either side. At the front of the main cabin, on the starboard side opposite the main cabin door, is a galley. The passenger area is divided into three lounges. The forward zone has four armchairs in facing pairs, separated by two tables. The centre zone contains a four-place sofa on the port side, facing a longitudinal table. On the starboard side, a bar cabinet contains a foldaway longitudinal bench, allowing five to six persons to be seated around the table for dinner, while leaving the emergency exit clear. In the rear zone, an inward facing settee on the starboard side converts into a bed. On the port side, two armchairs are separated by a table. At the rear of the cabin, a door leads to the toilet compartment, on the starboard side, and a second structural plug door to the large rear baggage area. The baggage door is electrically actuated. Other interior configurations include Dreyfuss 'human engineered' designs in the USA and IDEI 'travel ergonomics' concepts in France. The Dreyfuss interior features patented seating and galley innovations. It includes a crew lavatory forward, a transverse table with four chairs and two stowable lateral seats in a central conference area, a sofa bed on the port side and an executive work station opposite. An alternative eight-passenger configuration has a bedroom at the rear and three personnel seats in the forward zone. A 15-passenger layout divides a VIP area at the rear from six (three-abreast) chairs forward. The 18-passenger scheme has four rows of three-abreast airline type seats forward, and a VIP lounge with two chairs and a settee aft. Many optional items, including stereo, video and hot running water, are available. Windscreens anti-iced electrically.

SYSTEMS: Air-conditioning system uses engine bleed air or air from Garrett GTCP36-150 APU installed in rear fuselage. Softair pressurisation system, with max differential of 0·64 bars (9·3 lb/sq in), maintains sea level cabin environment to a height of 7,620 m (25,000 ft), and a cabin equivalent of 2,440 m (8,000 ft) at 15,550 m (51,000 ft). Cold air supply is by a single oversize air cycle unit. Two independent hydraulic systems, pressure 207 bars (3,000 lb/sq in), with three engine driven pumps and one emergency electric pump, actuate primary flying controls, flaps, slats, landing gear retraction, wheel brakes, airbrakes, nosewheel steering and thrust reverser. Bootstrap hydraulic reservoirs. DC electrical system

Dassault-Breguet Mystère-Falcon 50 eight/twelve-passenger executive transport

Dassault-Breguet Mystère-Falcon 900 three-turbofan executive transport for up to 19 passengers

supplied by three 9kW 28V Auxilec starter/generators and two 23Ah batteries. Eros (SFIM/Intertechnique) oxygen system.

AVIONICS AND EQUIPMENT: Dual bi-directional Sperry ASCB digital databus operating in conjunction with dual SPZ 800 flight director/autopilot and EFIS. Dual Sperry FMZ 605 flight management system, associated with two AZ 810 air data computers and Honeywell laser gyro inertial platforms. Collins Pro Line II ARINC 429 series com/nav receivers.

DIMENSIONS, EXTERNAL:
- Wing span: 19·33 m (63 ft 5 in)
- Wing chord: at root: 4·08 m (13 ft 4¾ in)
  - at tip: 1·12 m (3 ft 8 in)
- Wing aspect ratio: 7·62
- Length overall: 20·21 m (66 ft 3¾ in)
- Fuselage: Max diameter: 2·50 m (8 ft 2½ in)
- Height overall: 7·55 m (24 ft 9¼ in)
- Tailplane span: 7·74 m (25 ft 4¾ in)
- Wheel track: 4·44 m (14 ft 7 in)
- Wheelbase: 7·90 m (25 ft 11 in)
- Passenger door: Height: 1·72 m (5 ft 7¾ in)
  - Width: 0·80 m (2 ft 7½ in)
  - Height to sill: 1·79 m (5 ft 10½ in)
- Emergency exit (overwing, stbd):
  - Height: 0·91 m (2 ft 11¾ in)
  - Width: 0·53 m (1 ft 8¾ in)

DIMENSIONS, INTERNAL:
- Cabin, excl flight deck, incl toilet and baggage compartments:
  - Length: 11·90 m (39 ft 0½ in)
  - Max width: 2·34 m (7 ft 8 in)
  - Width at floor: 1·86 m (6 ft 1¼ in)
  - Max height: 1·87 m (6 ft 1½ in)
  - Volume: 39·5 m³ (1,395 cu ft)
- Rear baggage compartment volume: 3·60 m³ (127 cu ft)
- Flight deck volume: 3·75 m³ (132 cu ft)

AREAS:
- Wings, gross: 49·03 m² (527·75 sq ft)
- Horizontal tail surfaces (total): 13·35 m² (143·7 sq ft)
- Vertical tail surfaces (total): 9·82 m² (105·7 sq ft)

WEIGHTS:
- Weight empty, equipped: 10,240 kg (22,575 lb)
- Operating weight empty: 10,615 kg (23,402 lb)
- Max payload: 1,815 kg (4,000 lb)
- Max fuel: 8,620 kg (19,003 lb)
- Max T-O weight: 20,640 kg (45,500 lb)
- Max landing weight: 19,050 kg (42,000 lb)
- Normal landing weight: 12,250 kg (27,000 lb)
- Max zero-fuel weight:
  - standard: 12,430 kg (27,400 lb)
  - optional: 14,000 kg (30,865 lb)

PERFORMANCE (estimated at AUW of 12,250 kg; 27,000 lb, except where indicated):
- Max cruising speed: Mach 0·84
- Econ cruising speed: Mach 0·75
- Stalling speed: clean: 104 knots (193 km/h; 120 mph)
  - landing configuration: 82 knots (152 km/h; 95 mph)
- Approach speed, eight passengers and fuel reserves: 106 knots (196 km/h; 122 mph)
- Max cruising height: 15,550 m (51,000 ft)
- Balanced T-O field length with full tanks, eight passengers and baggage: 1,515 m (4,970 ft)
- FAR 91 landing field length at AUW of 12,250 kg (27,000 lb): 700 m (2,300 ft)
- Range with max payload, NBAA IFR reserves: 2,400 nm (4,444 km; 2,760 miles)
- Range at Mach 0·75 with max fuel and NBAA IFR reserves:
  - 15 passengers: 3,660 nm (6,780 km; 4,210 miles)
  - 8 passengers: 3,800 nm (7,035 km; 4,370 miles)

HERMES AEROSPACECRAFT

Dassault-Breguet is responsible for all work required to achieve successful flight within the atmosphere by the Hermes aerospacecraft, of which brief details can be found under the Aérospatiale entries in this section.

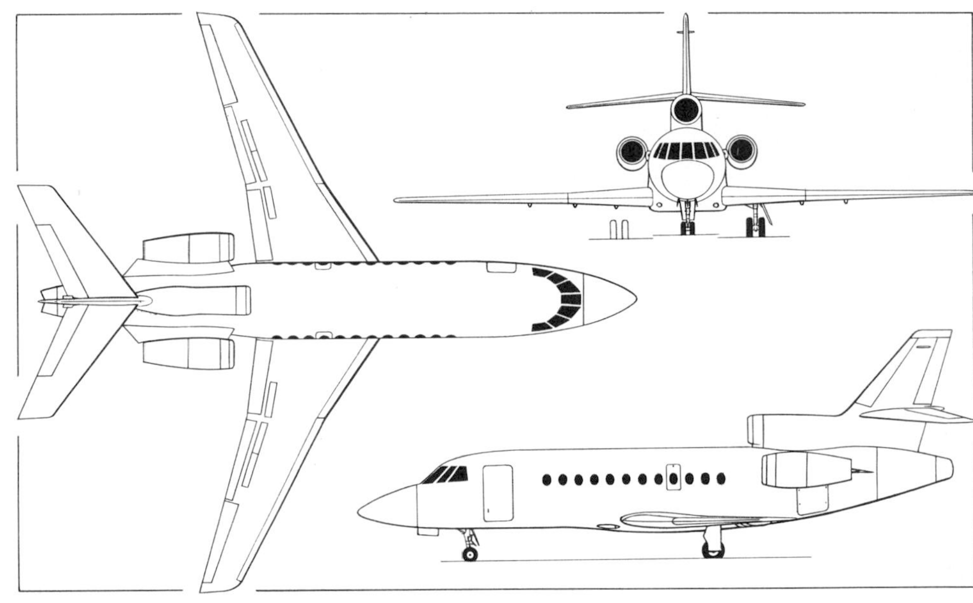

Dassault-Breguet Mystère-Falcon 900 (three Garrett TFE731-5A turbofan engines) *(Pilot Press)*

HELICOP-JET

HELICOP-JET PROJECT MANAGEMENT

30 avenue Georges V, Paris

Telephone: 47 23 78 08

PROJECT MANAGEMENT:
505 West Dorchester Boulevard, Suite 310, Montreal, Canada H2Z 1A8
Telephone: (514) 879 1671
Telex: 055 61075

VICE-PRESIDENT, MARKETING: Louis Thiffault

Helicop-Jet Project Management has been formed to progress towards series manufacture of the Helicop-Jet type of 'cold-jet' tip-driven light helicopter which has been under development in France, by M Charles Déchaux, for many years. The aircraft is described under the company's entry in the Canadian section of this edition.

MICROJET

MICROJET SA (Member company of Groupe Creuzet)

Aérodrome de Marmande-Virazeil, 47200 Marmande
Telephone: 53 64 53 50
Telex: 550 777
CHAIRMAN: Robert Creuzet

MICROJET 200 B

The early history of the Microjet programme was recorded in the 1984-85 and previous editions of *Jane's*. Aim of the programme is to offer economies in military pilot training by use of very small high-performance jet aircraft with comparatively low initial and operating costs.

First flight of a pre-production aircraft (F-WDMT) took place on 19 May 1983. Together with the earlier, wooden, prototype, it then underwent technical evaluation by pilots of the CEV, but was lost while flying over the sea on 13 March 1985. The second pre-production Microjet (F-WDMX), manufactured entirely by Marmande Aéronautique, flew for the first time on 5 January 1985 and has special significance in that it is the first Microjet with underwing hardpoints for expanded military applications. A third pre-production aircraft has since flown. The fourth pre-production airframe will be used for static tests at the CEAT, Toulouse.

The following description applies to the planned initial production version of the Microjet 200 B. Take-off rating of each engine will be increased progressively to 1·80 kN (405 lb st), to improve performance and payload, with particular emphasis on the aircraft's potential in an anti-helicopter combat role.

TYPE: Two-seat lightweight training aircraft.

WINGS: Cantilever low-wing monoplane of tapered planform. Wing section RA 16·303. Thickness/chord ratio 16%. Dihedral 5° 2′ constant from roots. Incidence 3°. Sweepback 0° at 30 per cent chord. Wings, Frise ailerons and electrically operated single-slotted trailing-edge flaps all of glassfibre/epoxy, with carbonfibre wing spars. Small airbrake forward of outer end of flap on upper surface of each wing. Ailerons embody adjustable artificial feel. Ground adjustable tab on starboard aileron.

FUSELAGE: Conventional light alloy semi-monocoque structure. NACA flush engine air intake on each side of fuselage aft of cockpit; exhaust through lateral jetpipes forward of tail unit.

TAIL UNIT: Cantilever V type, comprising interchangeable fixed surfaces and elevators of glassfibre/epoxy, with carbonfibre spars. Sweepback 26° at 50 per cent chord. Included angle 110°. Controllable tab at root end of each elevator. Shallow ventral fin.

LANDING GEAR: Retractable tricycle type, with single wheel on each unit. Electric retraction, nosewheel rearward, main units inward into fuselage. Manual emergency extension. All wheels fully enclosed by doors when retracted. Microjet oleo-pneumatic shock absorber in all three units. Nosewheel offset 149 mm (6 in) to starboard. Goodyear wheels, tyres and two-disc hydraulic brakes. Mainwheel tyres size 386 × 172-150, pressure 4·2 bars (61 lb/sq in); nosewheel tyre size 361 × 120-125, pressure 1·8 bars (26 lb/sq in). Parking brake.

POWER PLANT: Two Microturbo TRS 18-1 turbojet engines, each rated at 1·30 kN (293 lb st) for normal operation, uprated automatically to the T-O rating of 1·45 kN (326 lb st) on surviving engine after failure of the other during take-off. Ratings will be increased to 1·60 kN (360 lb st) and 1·80 kN (405 lb st) respectively for series production aircraft. Fuel in two structural tanks behind cockpit and one in each wing, with total capacity of 440 litres (97 Imp gallons; 116 US gallons). Two refuelling points, aft of cockpit on each side. Total oil capacity 1·6 litres (0·35 Imp gallon; 0·42 US gallon).

ACCOMMODATION: Pilot and instructor on side by side adjustable seats, under one-piece rearward hinged jettisonable tinted transparent canopy. Starboard (instructor's) seat staggered 55 cm (1 ft 9¾ in) aft of port seat. Adjustable rudder pedals. Cockpit heated and ventilated by ram air and exhaust heat exchanger, but not pressurised.

SYSTEMS: Electrical system comprises two 1·6kW engine driven generators and a 15Ah nickel-cadmium battery which actuate the landing gear and flaps through non-reversible mechanical jacks. Gaseous oxygen supply for two crew for four hours, from one 1,400 litre (50 cu ft) bottle.

Pre-production Microjet 200 B lightweight training aircraft (foreground) with the prototype

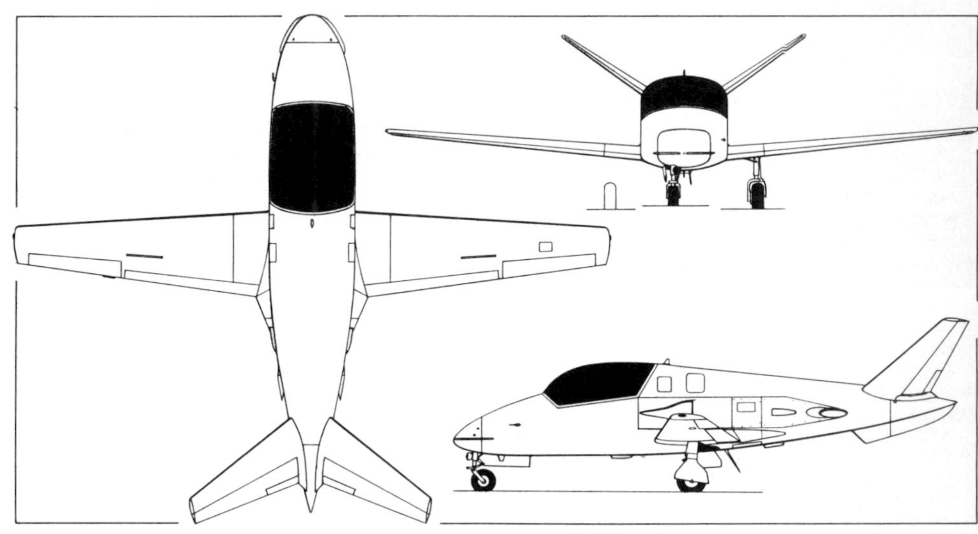
Microjet 200 B in production configuration *(Pilot Press)*

AVIONICS AND EQUIPMENT: Blind-flying instrumentation and avionics for IFR flight standard, including ADI, HSI and RMI. Typical installation would include VHF, VOR, ILS, DME, marker beacon receiver, transponder, ADF and intercom. Military version would have UHF, Tacan and IFF.

DIMENSIONS, EXTERNAL:

Wing span	7·56 m (24 ft 9¾ in)
Wing chord at root	0·85 m (2 ft 9½ in)
Wing aspect ratio	9·3
Length overall	6·665 m (21 ft 10½ in)
Length of fuselage	6·56 m (21 ft 6¼ in)
Width of fuselage	1·10 m (3 ft 7¼ in)
Height overall	2·27 m (7 ft 5½ in)
Tailplane span	3·07 m (10 ft 1 in)
Wheel track	1·92 m (6 ft 3½ in)
Wheelbase	2·64 m (8 ft 8 in)

AREAS:

Wings, gross	6·12 m² (65·87 sq ft)
Ailerons (total)	0·446 m² (4·80 sq ft)
Trailing-edge flaps (total)	0·69 m² (7·43 sq ft)
Tail surfaces (total)	2·50 m² (26·91 sq ft)

WEIGHTS AND LOADINGS:

Weight empty	770 kg (1,698 lb)
Max fuel	340 kg (750 lb)
Max T-O weight: Aerobatic	1,140 kg (2,513 lb)
Utility	1,300 kg (2,866 lb)
Max ramp weight	1,300 kg (2,866 lb)
Max zero-fuel weight	960 kg (2,116 lb)
Max landing weight	1,280 kg (2,822 lb)
Max wing loading	212·4 kg/m² (43·5 lb/sq ft)
Max power loading	448 kg/kN (4·40 lb/lb st)

PERFORMANCE (at max T-O weight with 1·45 kN engines):

Never-exceed speed	300 knots (555 km/h; 345 mph)
Max level speed and max cruising speed at 5,500 m (18,000 ft)	250 knots (463 km/h; 287 mph)
Econ cruising speed	210 knots (389 km/h; 241 mph)
Stalling speed, flaps down, engines idling	72 knots (134 km/h; 83 mph)
Max rate of climb at S/L	520 m (1,705 ft)/min
Rate of climb at S/L, one engine out	120 m (390 ft)/min
Service ceiling	9,150 m (30,000 ft)
Service ceiling, one engine out	3,050 m (10,000 ft)
T-O run	850 m (2,800 ft)
T-O to 15 m (50 ft)	1,180 m (3,870 ft)
Landing from 15 m (50 ft)	510 m (1,674 ft)
Landing run	390 m (1,280 ft)
Range with max internal fuel, 20 min hold	470 nm (870 km; 541 miles)
Max endurance	2 h
g limits:	+7/−3·5 Aerobatic
	+4/−1·8 Utility

MUDRY

AVIONS MUDRY et CIE

Aérodrome de Bernay, BP 47, 27300 Bernay
Telephone: 32 43 47 34
Telex: MUDRY 180 587 F
DIRECTOR: Auguste Mudry

Mudry Aviation Ltd

Dutchess County Airport, Wappingers Falls, NY 12590, USA
PRESIDENT: Daniel Heligoin

M Auguste Mudry established this company in 1958 in the works of the former Société Aéronautique Normande at Bernay, and operated it in parallel with his other aircraft manufacturing company, C.A.A.R.P. of Beynes (see 1977-78 *Jane's*). All activities of C.A.A.R.P. were subsequently combined with those of Avions A. Mudry, at Bernay.

MUDRY CAP 10 B

Developed from the Piel Emeraude two-seat light aircraft (see Homebuilts section), via the prototype C.P. 100 aerobatic version built by C.A.A.R.P., the CAP 10 is intended for use as a training, touring or aerobatic aeroplane. The prototype was flown for the first time in August 1968, and certification of the CAP 10 was granted on 4 September 1970. Later production aircraft, with ventral fin and enlarged rudder, are designated **CAP 10 B**. Construction is to French AIR 2052 (CAR 3) Category A standards for aerobatic flying. FAA certification for day and night VFR operation was received in 1974.

A total of 214 CAP 10/10 Bs had been delivered to customers in 21 countries by June 1985 including 56 for the French Air Force and six for the French Navy. Some are in service with the Air Force's Equipe de Voltige Aérienne (EVA) at Salon-de-Provence, others with its basic flying training schools at Clermont-Ferrand-Aulnat and Cognac, and the Navy's pilot selection centre at St Raphaël. Overseas operators include the Mexican Air Force's flying training school, whose 20 aircraft are equipped almost to IFR standard, and the Royal Moroccan Air Force, which has two.

To extend the potential market for the CAP 10, Mudry is

now offering a version equipped for glider towing under the designation **CAP 10 R** (for remorqueur).

TYPE: Two-seat aerobatic light aircraft.

WINGS: Cantilever low-wing monoplane. Wing section NACA 23012. Dihedral 5° from roots. Incidence 0°. No sweepback. All-spruce single-spar torsion box structure, with trellis ribs, rear auxiliary spar and okoumé plywood covering, with outer skin of polyester fabric. Inner section of each wing is rectangular in plan, outer section semi-elliptical. Wooden trailing-edge plain flaps and slotted ailerons.

FUSELAGE: Conventional spruce girder structure, built in two halves and joined by three main frames. Of basically rectangular section with rounded top decking. Polyester fabric covering. Forward section also has an inner plywood skin for added strength. Engine cowling panels of non-inflammable laminated plastics.

TAIL UNIT: Conventional cantilever structure. All-wood single-spar fin, integral with fuselage, and tailplane. All surfaces covered with both plywood and polyester fabric. Tailplane incidence adjustable on ground. Trim tab in each elevator. Automatic rudder trim. Small ventral fin.

LANDING GEAR: Non-retractable tailwheel type. Mainwheel legs of light alloy, with ERAM type 9 270 C oleo-pneumatic shock absorbers. Single wheel on each main unit, tyre size 380 × 150. Solid tailwheel tyre, size 6 × 200. Tailwheel is steerable by rudder linkage but can be disengaged for ground manoeuvring. Hydraulically actuated mainwheel disc brakes (controllable from port seat) and parking brake. Streamline fairings on mainwheels and legs.

POWER PLANT: One 134 kW (180 hp) Avco Lycoming AEIO-360-B2F flat-four engine, driving a Hoffmann two-blade fixed-pitch wooden propeller. Standard fuel tank aft of engine fireproof bulkhead, capacity 72 litres (16 Imp gallons; 19 US gallons). Optional auxiliary tank, capacity 75 litres (16·5 Imp gallons; 20 US gallons), beneath baggage compartment. Fuel and oil systems modified to permit periods of inverted flying.

ACCOMMODATION: Side by side adjustable seats for two persons, with provision for back parachutes, under rearward sliding and jettisonable moulded transparent canopy. Special aerobatic shoulder harness standard. Space for 20 kg (44 lb) of baggage aft of seats in training and touring models.

SYSTEMS: Electrical system includes Delco-Rémy 40A engine driven alternator and SAFT 12V DC nickel-cadmium battery.

AVIONICS AND EQUIPMENT: CSF 262 12-channel VHF radio and *g* meter fitted. Optional equipment includes starboard brake pedals; Narco, Jolliet or Badin VHF; Narco VOR; radio compass; IFR instrumentation; navigation and landing lights; and heated pitot.

DIMENSIONS, EXTERNAL:
Wing span	8·06 m (26 ft 5¼ in)
Wing aspect ratio	5·96
Length overall	7·16 m (23 ft 6 in)
Height overall	2·55 m (8 ft 4½ in)
Tailplane span	2·90 m (9 ft 6 in)
Wheel track	2·06 m (6 ft 9 in)
DIMENSION, INTERNAL:	
Cabin: Max width	1·054 m (3 ft 5½ in)
AREAS:	
Wings, gross	10·85 m² (116·79 sq ft)
Ailerons (total)	0·79 m² (8·50 sq ft)
Vertical tail surfaces (total)	1·32 m² (14·25 sq ft)
Horizontal tail surfaces (total)	1·86 m² (20·0 sq ft)
WEIGHTS (A: Aerobatic, U: Utility):	
Weight empty, equipped: A, U	540 kg (1,190 lb)
Fuel load: A	54 kg (119 lb)
U	108 kg (238 lb)
Max T-O weight: A	760 kg (1,675 lb)
U	830 kg (1,829 lb)
PERFORMANCE (at max T-O weight):	
Never-exceed speed	183 knots (340 km/h; 211 mph)
Max level speed at S/L	146 knots (270 km/h; 168 mph)
Max cruising speed (75% power)	135 knots (250 km/h; 155 mph)
Stalling speed:	
flaps up	54 knots (100 km/h; 62 mph) IAS
flaps down	46 knots (85 km/h; 53 mph) IAS
Max rate of climb at S/L	over 360 m (1,180 ft)/min
Service ceiling	5,000 m (16,400 ft)
T-O run	350 m (1,149 ft)
T-O to 15 m (50 ft)	450 m (1,477 ft)
Landing from 15 m (50 ft)	600 m (1,968 ft)
Landing run	360 m (1,182 ft)
Range with max fuel	647 nm (1,200 km; 745 miles)
g limits	+6/−4·5

MUDRY CAP 21

The CAP 21 is a single-seat aerobatic competition aircraft which retains the fuselage and tail unit of the earlier CAP 20LS-200, but has cantilever main landing gear legs and an entirely new wing, with a computer developed section, different planform and built by a new production method. This wing has improved the rate of roll to 180°/s at 135 knots (250 km/h; 155 mph) by comparison with the CAP 20L's 130°/s, and facilitates the execution of snap manoeuvres.

CAP 10 B two-seat aerobatic light aircraft of the French Air Force

The prototype (F-WZCH) was displayed at the 1979 Paris Air Show. It flew for the first time on 23 June 1980, and work was started on a first batch of ten production CAP 21s, for customers in Belgium, Brazil, France and Italy. Deliveries began in May 1982, and Mudry began manufacture of a second series in 1983. By early 1986, a total of 11 CAP 21s had been delivered, of which one (I-SIVM) had been retrofitted, easily and successfully, with a 194 kW (260 hp) engine by its Italian owner, Sig Sergio Dallan.

Known as the **CAP 21-260**, the Italian aircraft embodies several other modifications, including a main wing spar which permits load factors of ±10*g*; larger wing root fairings on both the leading- and trailing-edges; longer exhaust pipes which reduce noise; repositioned main landing gear legs with root fairings to reduce airflow disturbance at the wingroot leading-edge; a larger rudder; improved aileron control linkage; substitution of a one-piece canopy; movement of the pilot's seat further aft, and use of an inclined backrest to offset the effect on CG of a heavier power plant; replacement of the standard 40 litre (8·8 Imp gallon) fuel tank with a 60 litre (13·2 Imp gallon) tank; and installation of a ferry tank under the pilot's seat.

The following details apply to the standard CAP 21 production aircraft:

TYPE: Single-seat aerobatic light aircraft.

WINGS: Cantilever low-wing monoplane. Wing section V16F. Thickness/chord ratio 16%. Dihedral 1° 30′. No twist. All-wood single-spar structure, with flaps. Automatic tab in each aileron to reduce stick forces.

FUSELAGE: Conventional all-wood structure, of basically triangular section with rounded top decking. Wood covering, except for laminated plastics engine cowling.

TAIL UNIT: Cantilever all-wood structure. Trim tab in each elevator.

LANDING GEAR: Non-retractable tailwheel type. Cantilever glassfibre main legs, with streamline fairings over wheels. Disc brakes.

POWER PLANT: One 149 kW (200 hp) Avco Lycoming AEIO-360-A1B flat-four engine, driving a two-blade Hartzell variable-pitch propeller. Fixed-pitch propeller optional. Normal fuel tank capacity 40 litres (8·8 Imp gallons; 10·5 US gallons). Max fuel capacity 75 litres (16·5 Imp gallons; 20 US gallons), with 15 litre (3·3 Imp gallon; 4 US gallon) gravity tank for inverted flying.

ACCOMMODATION: Single glassfibre seat under rearward sliding transparent canopy. Special aerobatic shoulder harness.

DIMENSIONS, EXTERNAL:
Wing span	8·08 m (26 ft 6 in)
Wing aspect ratio	6·95
Length overall	6·46 m (21 ft 2½ in)
Height overall	1·52 m (5 ft 0 in)
AREA:	
Wings, gross	9·2 m² (99·0 sq ft)
WEIGHTS AND LOADINGS:	
Weight empty	500 kg (1,103 lb)
Max T-O weight (Aerobatic)	620 kg (1,367 lb)
Max wing loading (Aerobatic)	67·4 kg/m² (13·8 lb/sq ft)
Max power loading (Aerobatic)	4·16 kg/kW (6·84 lb/hp)
PERFORMANCE:	
Never-exceed speed	205 knots (380 km/h; 236 mph)
Max cruising speed (75% power)	143 knots (265 km/h; 165 mph)
Stalling speed	46 knots (85 km/h; 53 mph)
Max rate of climb at S/L	840 m (2,755 ft)/min
Endurance with max fuel	2 h
g limits	+6/−5

MUDRY CAP X

In early 1981, Avions Mudry announced its intention to develop a side by side two-seat training aircraft powered by its new MB-4-80 engine. Known as the **CAP X**, it is a low-wing monoplane, designed for low initial cost, minimum maintenance requirements and a fuel consumption of 17-18 litres (3·75-4 Imp gallons) per hour. Composite materials are used in its construction.

The prototype (F-WZCJ) flew for the first time on 10 September 1982. After completing its first phase flight testing with the MB-4-80 engine on 10 March 1983, it was re-engined with an 85 kW (115 hp) Avco Lycoming flat-four engine, with which it resumed flying on 5 May 1983 as the **CAP X Super**. The CAP X 002 pre-production aircraft flew for the first time on 13 June 1985, with an 83·5 kW (112 hp) Avco Lycoming O-235 engine, a modified structure entirely of wood, a new wing section, modified canopy, increased fuel (73 litres; 16 Imp gallons; 19·3 US gallons) and increased *g* limits to permit aerobatic flying. This CAP X was expected to complete its certification programme by early 1986.

The following details apply to the CAP X prototype with MB-4-80 engine, except where indicated:

TYPE: Two-seat low-cost basic flying trainer.

Mudry CAP 21 (Avco Lycoming AEIO-360-A1B engine) *(Austin J. Brown)*

WINGS: Cantilever low-wing monoplane. Wing section ONERA OAAG 04. Thickness/chord ratio 12%. Dihedral 5° from roots. No sweep at quarter-chord. Wood construction, with carbonfibre spar, and honeycomb sandwich ailerons and flaps.

FUSELAGE: Conventional wood structure.

TAIL UNIT: Cantilever wood structure, with sweptback fin and rudder. Small fixed tab on rudder. All-moving horizontal surfaces, with full span tab each side.

LANDING GEAR: Non-retractable tricycle type. Cantilever glassfibre main legs. Streamline fairing over each wheel. Small tailskid. JPX disc brakes and parking brake.

POWER PLANT: One 59 kW (80 hp) Mudry-Buchoux MB-4-80 flat-four engine, driving a two-blade fixed-pitch propeller. Fuel capacity 55 litres (12 Imp gallons; 14·5 US gallons). Oil capacity 4·5 litres (1 Imp gallon; 1·2 US gallons).

ACCOMMODATION: Two persons side by side under large forward sliding transparent canopy (rearward sliding canopy and fixed windscreen on 002).

DIMENSIONS, EXTERNAL:

Wing span	8·00 m (26 ft 3 in)
Wing aspect ratio	7·1
Length overall	5·90 m (19 ft 4½ in)
Height overall	2·05 m (6 ft 8¾ in)
Fuselage: Max width	1·08 m (3 ft 6½ in)
Propeller diameter	1·55 m (5 ft 1 in)

AREA:

Wings, gross	9·00 m² (96·9 sq ft)

WEIGHTS (A: CAP X prototype, B: CAP X 002):

Weight empty: A	340 kg (750 lb)
B	410 kg (904 lb)
Max T-O weight: A	530 kg (1,168 lb)
B	600 kg (1,322 lb)

PERFORMANCE (CAP X 002, estimated):

Max cruising speed	113 knots (210 km/h; 130 mph)
Econ cruising speed	89 knots (165 km/h; 102 mph)
Max rate of climb at S/L	300 m (985 ft)/min
Endurance with max fuel at max cruising speed	3 h

Mudry CAP X Super two-seat training aircraft (Avco Lycoming engine) *(Air Portraits)*

Prototype Mudry CAP 230 single-seat aerobatic aircraft *(Austin J. Brown)*

MUDRY CAP 230

The CAP 230 is a new version of the CAP 21 powered by a 224 kW (300 hp) Avco Lycoming AEIO-540 flat-six engine of the kind fitted to the Aérospatiale Epsilon. Its development was announced in January 1985, simultaneously with news of an initial order for four CAP 230s to equip the Royal Moroccan Air Force's aerobatic team. Three have been ordered for the French Air Force's Équipe de Voltige Aérienne (EVA) at Salon-de-Provence, to replace the team's current CAP 20s. The first of these was delivered on 13 June 1986.

The following details apply to the prototype (F-WZCH), which flew for the first time on 8 October 1985:

DIMENSIONS, EXTERNAL:

Wing span	8·08 m (26 ft 6 in)
Length overall	6·75 m (22 ft 1¾ in)
Height overall	1·80 m (5 ft 11 in)

WEIGHTS:

Weight empty	620 kg (1,366 lb)
Max T-O weight	700 kg (1,543 lb)

PERFORMANCE:

Never-exceed speed	215 knots (400 km/h; 248 mph)
Max cruising speed	172 knots (320 km/h; 198 mph)
Range with max fuel	405 nm (750 km; 466 miles)
g limits	±10

REIMS AVIATION

REIMS AVIATION SA

Aérodrome de Reims-Prunay, BP 2745, 51062 Reims Cédex
Telephone: 26 06 96 55
Telex: REMAVIA 830754

PRESIDENT DIRECTOR-GENERAL AND PRODUCTION DIRECTOR: Jean Pichon
FINANCIAL CONTROLLER: L. S. McCaffrey
FINANCIAL DIRECTOR: Jean-Luc Varga
ADMINISTRATIVE DIRECTOR: Armand Blang
PUBLIC RELATIONS: Lucien Benard

Reims Aviation is the successor to the former Société Nouvelle des Avions Max Holste, which had been founded in 1956. It has the right to manufacture under licence Cessna designs for sale in Europe, Africa and Asia; but the suspension of Cessna production of piston engined aircraft will apply also to Reims Aviation once the supply of airframes currently in hand is exhausted. By 1 January 1985 Reims had assembled a total of 6,294 aircraft of all types.

As an extension of its collaboration with Cessna, Reims Aviation developed and is manufacturing a twin-turboprop light transport aircraft known as the Reims-Cessna F 406.

Reims Aviation is a subcontractor to Dassault-Breguet in the Mystère-Falcon 100, 200, 50 and 900 programmes; and a subcontractor to Aérospatiale in the Transall programme and for miscellaneous parts. It had 520 employees in 1985. Its offices and factory at Reims-Prunay Airport have an area of 25,900 m² (278,785 sq ft).

REIMS/CESSNA F 152 and FA 152 AÉROBAT

Standard and aerobatic versions of the Cessna 152 assembled under licence by Reims Aviation are designated **F 152** and **FA 152 Aérobat** respectively.

Details of the Cessna 152 series in the US section of the 1984-85 *Jane's* apply also to aircraft assembled by Reims Aviation, except that conical camber wingtips are standard on the F 152 and FA 152, which have the following empty weights:

WEIGHTS: As Cessna 152 and Aerobat, except:

Weight empty: F 152	515 kg (1,136 lb)
FA 152	530 kg (1,169 lb)

REIMS/CESSNA F 172 SKYHAWK/100

Cessna Skyhawk and Skyhawk II aircraft assembled under licence by Reims Aviation are designated **F 172 Skyhawk/100** and **Skyhawk/100 II** respectively.

Details of the Cessna Skyhawk series in the US section of the 1985-86 *Jane's* apply also to aircraft assembled by Reims Aviation.

REIMS-CESSNA F 406/CARAVAN II

It was announced in mid-1982 that, with financial support from the French government, Reims Aviation and Cessna were collaborating in the development of an unpressurised twin-turboprop transport known as the **F 406** in France and **Caravan II** in the USA. Intended for business and utility use, it is a variant of Cessna's 400 series of light twins. A prototype (F-WZLT), constructed by Reims Aviation, was exhibited at the Paris Air Show prior to its first flight on 22 September 1983. Certification was achieved on 21 December 1984, and the F 406 is now being manufactured and marketed exclusively by Reims, using wings supplied by Cessna. Six production aircraft were completed in 1985 and 12 were scheduled for delivery in 1986.

The first production F 406 (F-GDRK) flew for the first time on 20 April 1985 and will be used as Cessna's US demonstrator following FAA certification. Next to fly, on 3 May, was c/n 4 (F-ZBEO), one of two F 406s for the French Customs Service, equipped with full King Gold Crown IFR avionics, a Crouzet Nadir navigation computer and a Bendix 1500 radar with 360° scan in an underbelly radome.

TYPE: Twin-turboprop light business and utility transport.

WINGS: Identical to those of the Cessna Conquest II, except where changes are necessary to mate with the fuselage and engine nacelles. Dihedral 3° 30′ on centre-section, 4° 55′ outboard of engine nacelles. Incidence 2° at root, −1° at tip. Goodrich pneumatic de-icing of leading-edges optional.

FUSELAGE: Basically similar to that of the Cessna Titan, strengthened locally.

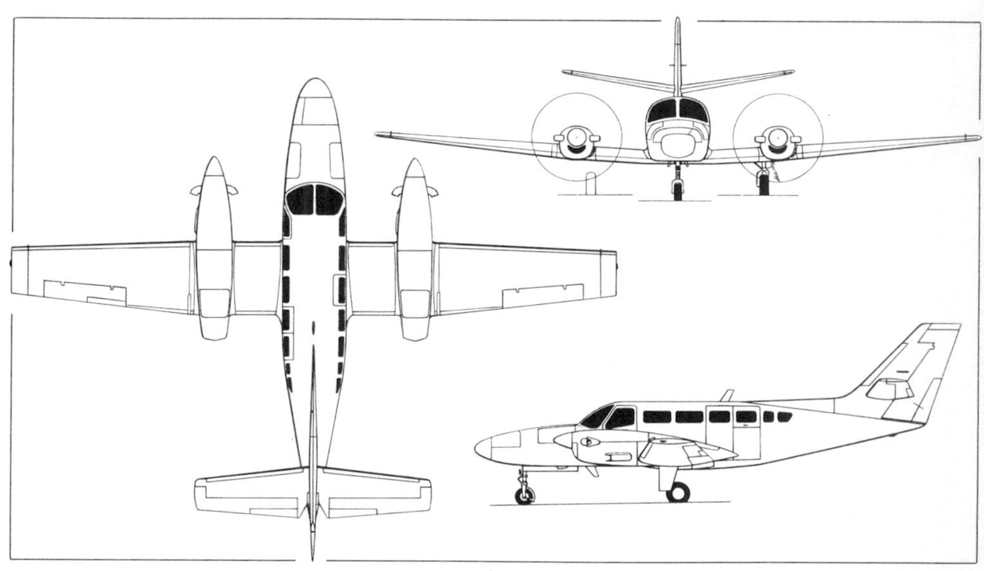
Reims-Cessna F 406/Caravan II light business and utility transport *(Pilot Press)*

Reims-Cessna F 406 for French Customs Service, with underbelly Bendix 1500 radar

Tail Unit: Cantilever all-metal two-spar structure, with horizontal surfaces mounted on sweptback fin. Fin offset 1° to port to counter torque of non-handed engines. Tailplane dihedral 9°. Goodrich pneumatic de-icing of leading-edges optional.

Landing Gear: As Cessna Conquest I and II, but strengthened for operation into and from unpaved strips.

Power Plant: Two Pratt & Whitney Canada PT6A-112 turboprop engines (each 373 kW; 500 shp), driving McCauley 3GFR34C701/93KB-0 three-blade reversible-pitch and automatically feathering metal propellers. Nacelles similar to those of Cessna Conquest I. Fuel capacity 1,798 litres (395 Imp gallons; 475 US gallons).

Accommodation: Crew of two and up to 12 passengers, in pairs, facing forward, with centre aisle, except at rear of cabin in 12/14-seat versions. Alternative basic configurations for six VIP passengers in reclining seats in executive version, and for operation in mixed passenger/freight role. Executive version has a partition between cabin and flight deck, and toilet on starboard side at rear. Split main door immediately aft of wing, on port side, with built-in airstair in downward hinged lower portion. Optional cargo door forward of this door to provide single large opening. Overwing emergency exit on each side. Passenger seats removable for cargo carrying, or for conversion to ambulance, air photography, maritime surveillance and other specialised roles. Baggage compartments in nose, with three doors, at rear of cabin and in rear of each engine nacelle. Electrical windscreen de-icing optional.

Systems: Air-conditioning, fuel and electrical systems generally similar to those of Cessna Conquest I.

Avionics and Equipment: To customer's individual requirements. Provision for equipment to FAR Pt 135A standards, including full controls and instrumentation for co-pilot, IFR com/nav, Bendix RDR-160XD weather radar and additional emergency exit.

Dimensions, external:	
Wing span	15·08 m (49 ft 5¾ in)
Wing aspect ratio	9·68
Length overall	11·89 m (39 ft 0 in)
Height overall	4·01 m (13 ft 2 in)
Tailplane span	5·87 m (19 ft 3 in)
Wheel track	4·28 m (14 ft 0½ in)
Wheelbase	3·81 m (12 ft 5⅞ in)
Propeller diameter	2·36 m (7 ft 9 in)
Cabin door: Height	1·27 m (4 ft 2 in)
Width	0·58 m (1 ft 10¾ in)
Cargo double door (optional): Total width	1·24 m (4 ft 1 in)
Dimensions, internal:	
Cabin (incl flight deck): Length	5·71 m (18 ft 8¾ in)
Max width	1·42 m (4 ft 8 in)
Max height	1·31 m (4 ft 3¼ in)
Min height (at rear)	1·21 m (3 ft 11½ in)
Width of aisle	0·29 m (11½ in)
Volume	8·64 m³ (305 cu ft)
Baggage compartment volume	2·22 m³ (78·5 cu ft)
Area:	
Wings, gross	23·50 m² (253 sq ft)
Weights:	
Weight empty, equipped	2,283 kg (5,033 lb)
Max payload	1,563 kg (3,446 lb)
Max fuel	1,444 kg (3,183 lb)
Max ramp weight	4,280 kg (9,435 lb)
Max T-O and landing weight	4,246 kg (9,360 lb)
Max zero-fuel weight	3,856 kg (8,500 lb)
Performance:	
Max operating Mach No.	0·52
Max operating speed	229 knots (424 km/h; 263 mph) IAS
Max cruising speed	246 knots (455 km/h; 283 mph)
Econ cruising speed	200 knots (370 km/h; 230 mph)
Max rate of climb at S/L	564 m (1,850 ft)/min
Rate of climb at S/L, one engine out	121 m (397 ft)/min
Stalling speed: 'clean'	94 knots (174 km/h; 108 mph) IAS
wheels and flaps down	81 knots (150 km/h; 93 mph) IAS
Service ceiling	9,145 m (30,000 ft)
Service ceiling, one engine out	4,935 m (16,200 ft)
T-O run	526 m (1,725 ft)
T-O to 15 m (50 ft)	773 m (2,536 ft)
Landing from 15 m (50 ft), without reverse pitch	674 m (2,212 ft)
Range with max fuel, at max cruising speed, 45 min reserves	1,027 nm (1,902 km; 1,181 miles)

ROBIN

AVIONS PIERRE ROBIN

BP 87, Aérodrome de Dijon Val-Suzon, Darois, 21121 Fontaine-les-Dijon Cédex
Telephone: 80 35 61 01
Telex: 350 818 Robin F

President Director General: Pierre Robin
Commercial Manager: Thérèse Robin
Production Director: Philippe Estassy
Technical Director: Daniel Muller
Public Relations: Jacques Bigenwald

This company was formed in October 1957 as Centre Est Aéronautique to design, manufacture and sell touring aircraft. It has since built some 2,600 aircraft at Dijon-Darois. In 1969 the name of the company was changed to Avions Pierre Robin.

Since 1973, Avions Pierre Robin has manufactured the DR 400 series of wooden light aircraft, which represent highly refined developments of the company's earlier Jodel designs and were first flown in prototype form in 1972. They are described in detail, together with the company's new ATL personal and club aircraft, and the R 3000 series of all-metal light aircraft, which is marketed by Socata under an agreement effective from 1 September 1983. Production of the DR 400 series is expected to end after Socata has sold 80 R 3000s. By mid-1986 a total of 17 R 3000s had been sold.

The company's works cover an area of about 11,000 m² (118,400 sq ft) and it employed 114 people in January 1985.

ROBIN DR 400/120 DAUPHIN

Robin DR 400/120 Dauphin three/four-seat light aircraft *(Kenneth Munson)*

The prototype of this DR 400 series lightplane flew for the first time on 15 May 1972 and received DGAC certification on the 10th of that month, followed by CAA certification in December 1972. The original version had a 93 kW (125 hp) engine and was manufactured as the DR 400/125 Petit Prince. It was superseded in 1975 by the DR 400/120 Petit Prince, with 88 kW (118 hp) engine, as described in the 1979-80 *Jane's*. The current version has a fine-pitch propeller and new instrument panel, and entered production in 1979 as the Dauphin. Seven were sold in France in 1985 and three exported.

Type: Three/four-seat light training and touring aircraft.

Wings: Cantilever low-wing monoplane. Wing section NACA 23013·5 (modified). Centre-section has constant chord and no dihedral; outer wings have a dihedral of 14°. All-wood one-piece structure, with single box spar. Leading-edge plywood covered; Dacron covering overall. Wooden ailerons, covered with Dacron. Aluminium alloy flaps. Ailerons and flaps interchangeable port and starboard. Manually operated airbrake under spar outboard of landing gear on each side. Picketing ring under each wingtip.

Fuselage: Wooden semi-monocoque structure of basic rectangular section, plywood covered.

Tail Unit: Cantilever all-wood structure, covered with Dacron. Sweptback fin and rudder. All-moving one-piece horizontal surface, with tab.

Landing Gear: Non-retractable tricycle type, with oleo-pneumatic shock absorbers and Manu hydraulically actuated drum brakes. All three wheels and tyres are size 380 × 150, pressure 1·57 bars (22·8 lb/sq in) on nose unit, 1·77 bars (25·6 lb/sq in) on main units. Nosewheel steerable via rudder bar. Fairings over all three legs and wheels. Tailskid with damper. Parking brake.

Power Plant: One 83·5 kW (112 hp) Avco Lycoming O-235-L2A flat-four engine, driving a Sensenich 72 CKS 6-0-56 two-blade fixed-pitch metal propeller, or Hoffmann two-blade fixed-pitch wooden propeller. Fuel tank in fuselage, usable capacity 100 litres (22 Imp gallons; 26·5 US gallons); optional 50 litre (11 Imp gallon; 13·2 US gallon) auxiliary tank. Oil capacity 5·7 litres (1·25 Imp gallons; 1·5 US gallons).

Accommodation: Enclosed cabin, with seats for three or four persons, in pairs, up to a max weight of 154 kg (340 lb) on front pair and 136 kg (300 lb), including baggage, at rear. Access via forward sliding jettisonable transparent canopy. Dual controls standard. Cabin heated and ventilated. Baggage compartment with internal access.

Systems and Equipment: Standard equipment includes a 12V 50A alternator, 12V 32Ah battery, push-button starter, audible stall warning, and windscreen de-icing. Radio, blind-flying equipment, and navigation, landing and anti-collision lights, to customer's requirements.

Dimensions, external:	
Wing span	8·72 m (28 ft 7¼ in)
Wing chord: centre-section (constant)	1·71 m (5 ft 7½ in)
at tip	0·90 m (3 ft 0 in)
Wing aspect ratio	5·6
Length overall	6·96 m (22 ft 10 in)
Height overall	2·23 m (7 ft 3¾ in)
Tailplane span	3·20 m (10 ft 6 in)
Wheel track	2·60 m (8 ft 6¼ in)
Wheelbase	5·20 m (17 ft 0¾ in)
Propeller diameter	1·78 m (5 ft 10 in)
Dimensions, internal:	
Cabin: Length	1·62 m (5 ft 3¾ in)
Max width	1·10 m (3 ft 7¼ in)
Max height	1·23 m (4 ft 0½ in)
Baggage, volume	0·39 m³ (13·75 cu ft)
Areas:	
Wings, gross	13·60 m² (146·39 sq ft)
Ailerons, total	1·15 m² (12·38 sq ft)
Flaps, total	0·70 m² (7·53 sq ft)
Fin	0·61 m² (6·57 sq ft)
Rudder	0·63 m² (6·78 sq ft)
Horizontal tail surfaces, total	2·88 m² (31·00 sq ft)
Weights and Loadings:	
Weight empty, equipped	530 kg (1,169 lb)
Max baggage	40 kg (88 lb)
Max T-O and landing weight	900 kg (1,984 lb)
Max wing loading	66·2 kg/m² (13·56 lb/sq ft)
Max power loading	10·23 kg/kW (16·8 lb/hp)
Performance (at max T-O weight):	
Never-exceed speed	166 knots (308 km/h; 191 mph)
Max level speed at S/L	130 knots (241 km/h; 150 mph)
Max cruising speed at 2,250 m (7,400 ft)	116 knots (215 km/h; 133 mph)

Econ cruising speed at 3,000 m (9,840 ft) 105 knots (195 km/h; 121 mph)
Stalling speed: flaps up 51 knots (94 km/h; 59 mph)
flaps down 45 knots (82 km/h; 51 mph)
Max rate of climb at S/L 183 m (600 ft)/min
Service ceiling 3,650 m (12,000 ft)
T-O run 235 m (771 ft)
T-O to 15 m (50 ft) 535 m (1,755 ft)
Landing from 15 m (50 ft) 460 m (1,510 ft)
Range with standard fuel at max cruising speed, no reserves 464 nm (860 km; 534 miles)

ROBIN DR 400/160 MAJOR

The first DR 400/160 flew on 29 June 1972. It was awarded DGAC certification on 6 September 1972, and CAA certification in December of the same year, and was manufactured as the Chevalier (see 1979-80 *Jane's*). The current version, with wing root fuel tanks, a baggage hold door, a propeller of finer pitch and a new instrument panel based on experience with the Aiglon, has been in production since 1980 as the Major. A total of 98 had been built by January 1986, including three sold in France and two exported during 1985.

TYPE: Four-seat light aircraft.

WINGS, FUSELAGE, TAIL UNIT, LANDING GEAR: Generally as for DR 400/120, but with external baggage door aft of cabin, in top of fuselage on port side.

POWER PLANT: One 119 kW (160 hp) Avco Lycoming O-320-D flat-four engine, driving a Sensenich two-blade metal fixed-pitch propeller. Fuel tank in fuselage, capacity 110 litres (24 Imp gallons; 29 US gallons), and two tanks in wing root leading-edges, giving total capacity of 190 litres (41·75 Imp gallons; 50 US gallons), of which 182 litres (40 Imp gallons; 48 US gallons) are usable. Provision for auxiliary tank, raising total capacity to 240 litres (52·75 Imp gallons; 63·5 US gallons). Oil capacity 7·5 litres (1·6 Imp gallons; 2 US gallons).

ACCOMMODATION: Seating for four persons, on two side by side adjustable front seats (max load 154 kg; 340 lb total) and rear bench seat (max load 154 kg; 340 lb total). Forward sliding transparent canopy gives access to all seats. Up to 40 kg (88 lb) of baggage can be stowed aft of rear seats when four occupants are carried.

SYSTEMS AND EQUIPMENT: As for DR 400/120.

DIMENSIONS AND AREAS: As for DR 400/120, except:
Propeller diameter 1·83 m (6 ft 0 in)
Baggage door: Height 0·47 m (1 ft 6½ in)
Width 0·55 m (1 ft 9½ in)
Wing area 14·20 m² (152·8 sq ft)

WEIGHTS AND LOADINGS:
Weight empty, equipped 570 kg (1,257 lb)
Max T-O and landing weight 1,050 kg (2,315 lb)
Max wing loading 74·2 kg/m² (15·20 lb/sq ft)
Max power loading 8·82 kg/kW (14·47 lb/hp)

PERFORMANCE (at max T-O weight):
Never-exceed speed 166 knots (308 km/h; 191 mph)
Max level speed at S/L 146 knots (271 km/h; 168 mph)
Max cruising speed (75% power) at 2,440 m (8,000 ft) 132 knots (245 km/h; 152 mph)
Econ cruising speed (65% power) at 3,200 m (10,500 ft) 130 knots (241 km/h; 150 mph)
Stalling speed: flaps up 56 knots (103 km/h; 64 mph)
flaps down 50 knots (93 km/h; 58 mph)
Max rate of climb at S/L 255 m (836 ft)/min
Service ceiling 4,115 m (13,500 ft)
T-O run 300 m (985 ft)
T-O to 15 m (50 ft) 500 m (1,640 ft)
Landing from 15 m (50 ft) 545 m (1,788 ft)
Landing run 250 m (820 ft)
Range with standard fuel at econ cruising speed, 45 min reserves 693 nm (1,285 km; 798 miles)

ROBIN DR 400/180 RÉGENT

First flown on 27 March 1972, this most powerful, four/five-seat member of the wooden DR 400 series received DGAC certification on 10 May 1972, and CAA certification in December 1972. A total of 168 had been built by January 1986, including four sold in France and six exported during 1985.

Robin DR 400/180RP Remorqueur glider towing aircraft, fitted experimentally with a Porsche PFM 3200 engine *(Air Portraits)*

A DR 400/180 delivered to the UK in mid-1985 was the 1,000th aircraft of the DR 400 series to be manufactured. It was equipped with a hook for glider towing.

The DR 400/180 is generally similar to the DR 400/160 Major, except in the following details:

POWER PLANT: One 134 kW (180 hp) Avco Lycoming O-360-A flat-four engine. Fuel tankage as for DR 400/160.

ACCOMMODATION, SYSTEMS AND EQUIPMENT: Basically as for DR 400/160, but optional seating for three persons on rear bench seat. Baggage capacity 55 kg (121 lb).

DIMENSIONS AND AREAS: As for DR 400/160, except:
Propeller diameter 1·93 m (6 ft 4 in)

WEIGHTS AND LOADINGS:
Weight empty, equipped 600 kg (1,322 lb)
Max T-O and landing weight 1,100 kg (2,425 lb)
Max wing loading 77·7 kg/m² (15·91 lb/sq ft)
Max power loading 8·21 kg/kW (13·47 lb/hp)

PERFORMANCE (at max T-O weight):
Never-exceed speed 166 knots (308 km/h; 191 mph)
Max level speed at S/L 150 knots (278 km/h; 173 mph)
Max cruising speed (75% power at 2,440 m (8,000 ft) 144 knots (267 km/h; 166 mph)
Econ cruising speed (60% power) at 3,660 m (12,000 ft) 134 knots (249 km/h; 155 mph)
Stalling speed: flaps up 57 knots (105 km/h; 65 mph)
flaps down 52 knots (95 km/h; 59 mph)
Max rate of climb at S/L 252 m (825 ft)/min
Service ceiling 4,720 m (15,475 ft)
T-O run 315 m (1,035 ft)
T-O to 15 m (50 ft) 610 m (2,000 ft)
Landing from 15 m (50 ft) 530 m (1,740 ft)
Landing run 249 m (817 ft)
Range with standard fuel at 65% power, no reserves 783 nm (1,450 km; 900 miles)

ROBIN DR 400/180R REMORQUEUR

The DR 400/180R is a member of the DR 400 range designed for use as a glider towing aircraft, although it can also be flown as a normal four-seat tourer. The prototype first flew on 6 November 1972 and received DGAC certification on the 28th of that month. A total of 207 had been built by January 1986, including four sold in France and ten exported during 1985.

An experimental version, designated **DR 400/180RP** (F-WEIQ, DR 400 c/n 999), has been fitted with a Porsche PFM 3200 aircooled flat-six engine, with fan forced cooling and derated to 134 kW (180 hp) in this application. This aircraft had flown only four hours before being exhibited at the 1985 Paris Air Show, but had already demonstrated a rate of climb of 420 m (1,378 ft)/min at max T-O weight, and a cruising speed of 146 knots (270 km/h; 168 mph) at 75% power. This would offer a range of 607 nm (1,125 km; 700 miles) at that speed, with a fuel consumption of 35 litres (7·7 Imp gallons; 9·25 US gallons)/h. Considerable interest has been shown by clubs in the potential of this aircraft for glider towing. However, no decision to put a Porsche engined DR 400 into production had been made by mid-1986.

Specification details of the standard DR 400/180R are generally the same as for the DR 400/180 Régent, except for the following items:

FUSELAGE: No external baggage door. The baggage compartment is covered with transparent Plexiglas as an extension of the canopy, allowing optimum rearward view.

POWER PLANT: One 134 kW (180 hp) Avco Lycoming O-360-A flat-four engine, driving (for glider towing) a Sensenich 76 EM 8S5 058 or Hoffmann HO-27-HM-180/138 two-blade propeller. For touring, a Sensenich 76 EM 8S5 064 propeller of the same diameter is fitted. Fuel capacity as for DR 400/120.

DIMENSIONS AND AREAS: As for DR 400/120, except:
Propeller diameter 1·83 m (6 ft 0 in)

WEIGHTS AND LOADINGS:
Weight empty, equipped 560 kg (1,234 lb)
Max T-O and landing weight 1,000 kg (2,205 lb)
Max wing loading 73·5 kg/m² (15·05 lb/sq ft)
Max power loading 7·46 kg/kW (12·25 lb/hp)

PERFORMANCE (glider tug, at max T-O weight):
Never-exceed speed 166 knots (308 km/h; 191 mph)
Max level speed at S/L (70% power) 124 knots (230 km/h; 143 mph)
Max cruising speed at 2,440 m (8 000 ft) 124 knots (230 km/h; 143 mph)
Econ cruising speed (56% power) at 3,660 m 12,000 ft) 122 knots (226 km/h; 140 mph)
Stalling speed: flaps up 54 knots (99 km/h; 62 mph)
flaps down 47 knots (87 km/h; 54 mph)
Max rate of climb at S/L towing Bijave sailplane 210 m (690 ft)/min
Service ceiling 6,000 m (19,685 ft)
T-O run 205 m (673 ft)
T-O to 15 m (50 ft) 400 m (1,313 ft)
Landing from 15 m (50 ft) 470 m (1,542 ft)
Landing run 220 m (722 ft)
Range at econ cruising speed, max fuel, no reserves 444 nm (825 km; 512 miles)

ROBIN R 3000 SERIES

Development of this series of all-metal light aircraft began in 1978, to replace types then in production. Two prototypes were built, with the designation R 3140. The first of these to fly, on 8 December 1980, had conventional unswept constant chord wings. The second, flown on 2 June 1981, introduced the tapered outer panels (later with upturned tips) that are now standard. Of the ten projected versions listed in the 1983-84 *Jane's*, the first three to be certificated for production are as follows:

R 3000/100. With 74·5 kW (100 hp) derated Avco Lycoming O-235-N2A or -L2A engine and two seats. First flown on 31 October 1984. Certificated by DGAC on 24 July 1985.

R 3000/120 (formerly R 3120 2 + 2). Powered by 86 kW (116 hp) Avco Lycoming O-235 engine. Seats for three adults, or two adults and two children. Certificated by DGAC on 12 December 1984. Five delivered in 1985.

R 3000/140 (formerly R 3140E). Generally similar to R 3000/120, except for 104 kW (140 hp) derated Avco Lycoming O-320-D2A engine, driving a Sensenich 74DMS5-2-64 propeller. Full four-seater. Certificated by DGAC on 13 October 1983. Two delivered in 1985.

One other version has flown but is not yet in production:

R 3000/180R. Glider towing version, with 134 kW (180 hp) Avco Lycoming O-360 engine. Dihedral reduced to 4°. First flown on 30 January 1985.

Robin is investigating the practicability of replacing the present engines of the R 3000 series with engines based on the more modern and fuel-efficient 89-119 kW (120-160 hp)

Robin DR 400/180 Régent (Avco Lycoming O-360-A engine)

PRV six-cylinder engines built in France for Peugeot, Renault and Volvo motor cars. First aircraft to be fitted with a PRV engine was an R 3140, which flew for the first time in this form on 2 August 1983. The basic motorcar engine was adapted for aircraft use by the École Nationale des Ingénieurs de St-Etienne (ENISE) in collaboration with Robin. Initial test results were promising and a company named Société France Aéromoteur has been established to produce an aviation certificated PRV engine.

In November 1981, Aérospatiale announced that its light aircraft subsidiary, Socata, would undertake the marketing of aircraft of this series. To avoid duplicating types of aircraft already produced by Socata (e.g. Tobago, Trinidad), it was agreed that Robin would concentrate on versions of the R 3000 with engines of 119 kW (160 hp) or less, except for the R 3000/180R glider/banner towing version with a 134 kW (180 hp) engine.

Seventeen R 3000s had been sold by mid-1986, with forecasts of 12 sales in that year, 15 in 1987 and 20 in 1988.

The following details apply to the R 3000/120 and 140, except where indicated:

TYPE: Three/four-seat all-metal light aircraft.

WINGS: Cantilever low-wing monoplane, with upturned tips. Wing section NACA 43013·5 on constant chord inner wings, NACA 43010·5 at tip of each tapered outer panel. Dihedral 6° from roots (4° on R 3000/180R). Incidence 3°. No sweep at quarter-chord. Conventional single-spar aluminium alloy structure. Entire trailing-edge of each constant chord panel comprises an electrically controlled slotted flap. Ailerons and flaps of aluminium alloy construction.

FUSELAGE: Conventional aluminium alloy semi-monocoque structure, except for quickly removable glassfibre engine cowling.

TAIL UNIT: Cantilever T tail of aluminium alloy construction, with dorsal fin. Elevator trim with anti-tabs.

LANDING GEAR: Non-retractable tricycle type. Nosewheel, steerable via rudder pedals, is self-centering and locks automatically after take-off. Robin long-stroke low pressure oleo-pneumatic shock absorbers. Mainwheel tyres size 380 × 150-6. Nosewheel tyre size 5·00-5. Cleveland disc brakes. Streamline polyester fairings on all three legs and wheels. Hydraulic disc brakes. Parking brake.

POWER PLANT: One Avco Lycoming flat-four engine, driving a two-blade fixed-pitch metal propeller, as described in individual model listings. Two integral fuel tanks in wing leading-edges, with total capacity of 120 litres (26·4 Imp gallons; 31·7 US gallons), or optionally 160 litres (35·2 Imp gallons; 42·25 US gallons), in R 3000/120; 160 litres (35·2 Imp gallons; 42·25 US gallons) standard, or 200 litres (44 Imp gallons; 52·8 US gallons) optional, in R 3000/140. Oil capacity 7·5 litres (1·6 Imp gallons; 2 US gallons).

ACCOMMODATION: Four seats in pairs in enclosed cabin, with dual controls and brakes. Adjustable front seats, with inertia reel safety belts. Removable rear seats, with belts. Carpeted floor. Forward sliding jettisonable and tinted transparent canopy, with safety lock, accessible from both sides. Automatically retracting step on each side. Baggage capacity 40 kg (88 lb). Cabin heated and ventilated. Windscreen demister.

SYSTEM: Electrical system includes 12V 60A alternator and 12V 32Ah battery.

AVIONICS AND EQUIPMENT: Standard equipment includes hour meter, audible stall warning system and towbar. Three standards of optional avionics and equipment available. Series I includes horizon and directional gyros with vacuum pump, type 9100 electric turn co-ordinator, rate of climb indicator, C 2400 magnetic compass (exchange for standard C 2300), position lights and two beacons, anti-collision light and instrument panel lighting. Series II adds to Series I either Becker AR 2009/25 720-channel VHF, with NR 2029 VOR/LOC receiver and indicator; or King KX 155/08 nav/com with audio and KI 203 VOR indicator. Series III adds to Series II either a Becker ATC 2000 transponder and type 2079 ADF; or King KT 76 A transponder and KR 87 digital ADF.

DIMENSIONS, EXTERNAL:	
Wing span	9·81 m (32 ft 2¼ in)
Wing chord: at root	1·72 m (5 ft 7¾ in)
at tip	0·655 m (2 ft 1¾ in)
Wing aspect ratio	6·65
Length overall	7·51 m (24 ft 7¾ in)
Height overall	2·66 m (8 ft 8¾ in)
Tailplane span	3·20 m (10 ft 6 in)
Wheel track	2·64 m (8 ft 8 in)
Wheelbase	1·74 m (5 ft 8½ in)
Propeller diameter	1·83 m (6 ft 0 in)
Propeller ground clearance	0·30 m (11¾ in)
DIMENSIONS, INTERNAL:	
Cabin: Length	2·70 m (8 ft 10¼ in)
Max width	1·14 m (3 ft 8¾ in)
Max height	1·20 m (3 ft 11¼ in)
Floor area	2·60 m² (28 sq ft)
Volume (incl baggage space)	2·4 m³ (84·75 cu ft)
Baggage space	0·43 m³ (15·2 cu ft)
AREAS:	
Wings, gross	14·47 m² (155·75 sq ft)
Ailerons (total)	1·32 m² (14·21 sq ft)
Trailing-edge flaps (total)	2·02 m² (21·74 sq ft)
Vertical tail surfaces (total)	1·30 m² (14·00 sq ft)
Horizontal tail surfaces (total)	2·44 m² (26·26 sq ft)

WEIGHTS AND LOADINGS (A: R 3000/100, B: R 3000/120, C: R 3000/140):	
Weight empty: A	575 kg (1,268 lb)
B	580 kg (1,279 lb)
C	600 kg (1,323 lb)
Max T-O and landing weight: A, B	900 kg (1,984 lb)
C	1,050 kg (2,315 lb)
Max wing loading: A, B	62·2 kg/m² (12·74 lb/sq ft)
C	72·6 kg/m² (14·86 lb/sq ft)
Max power loading: A	12·08 kg/kW (19·84 lb/hp)
B	10·47 kg/kW (17·10 lb/hp)
C	10·10 kg/kW (16·54 lb/hp)

PERFORMANCE (at max T-O weight, A, B and C as above):	
Max level speed at S/L:	
A	118 knots (220 km/h; 136 mph)
B	124 knots (230 km/h; 143 mph)
C	135 knots (250 km/h; 155 mph)
Max cruising speed (75% power) at optimum height:	
A	108 knots (200 km/h; 124 mph)
B	113 knots (210 km/h; 130 mph)
C	130 knots (240 km/h; 149 mph)
Econ cruising speed (65% power):	
B	108 knots (200 km/h; 124 mph)
C	119 knots (220 km/h; 136 mph)
Stalling speed, flaps down:	
A, B	45 knots (83 km/h; 52 mph)
C	47 knots (87 km/h; 54 mph)
Max rate of climb at S/L: A, B	180 m (590 ft)/min
C	258 m (846 ft)/min
Service ceiling: A, B	3,960 m (13,000 ft)
C	4,265 m (14,000 ft)
T-O run: B,C	280 m (920 ft)
T-O to 15 m (50 ft): B	510 m (1,673 ft)
C	525 m (1,725 ft)
Landing from 15 m (50 ft): B	425 m (1,395 ft)
C	490 m (1,610 ft)
Landing run: B, C	190 m (625 ft)
Range with max standard fuel, no reserves:	
B, 75% power	550 nm (1,020 km; 633 miles)
C, 75% power	605 nm (1,120 km; 696 miles)
B, 65% power	605 nm (1,120 km; 696 miles)
C, 65% power	640 nm (1,185 km; 736 miles)
Range with max optional fuel, no reserves:	
B, 75% power	734 nm (1,360 km; 845 miles)
C, 75% power	756 nm (1,400 km; 870 miles)
B, 65% power	766 nm (1,420 km; 882 miles)
C, 65% power	799 nm (1,480 km; 919 miles)

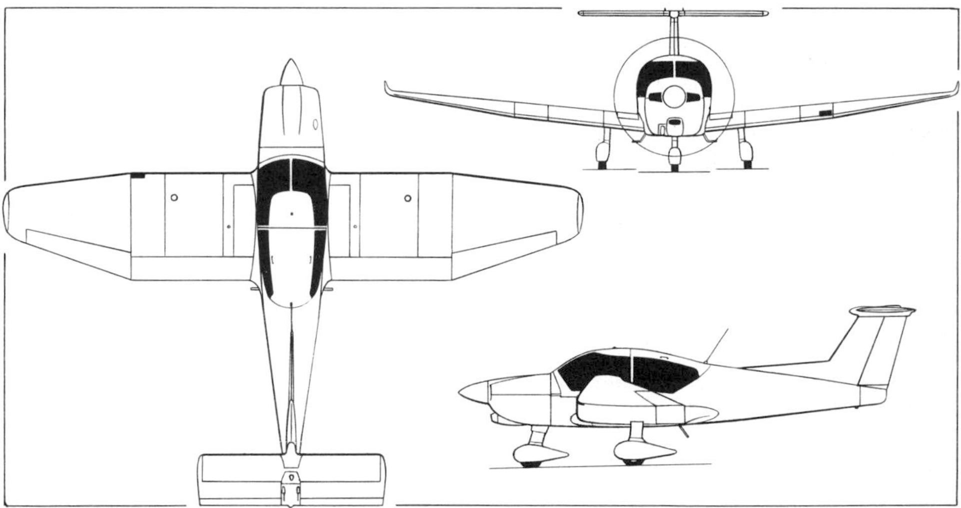

Photograph and three-view drawing *(Pilot Press)* **of Robin R 3000/140 four-seat light aircraft (Avco Lycoming O-320-D2A engine)**

ROBIN ATL

In the first half of 1981, Avions Pierre Robin began design of the ATL (avion très léger) to meet the requirement of French flying clubs for a very lightweight two-seat monoplane that would, in the tradition of the veteran Jodel D.112, be economical to buy and to operate. The prototype (F-WFNA) flew initially, on 17 June 1983, with a 35 kW (47 hp) JPX PAL 1300 three-cylinder aircooled radial two-stroke engine. To speed certification, it was re-engined subsequently with a 41·5 kW (56 hp) JPX converted 1,835 cc Volkswagen motorcar engine, and a 2,050 cc version of this engine is the current standard power plant of production ATLs. The increased power plant weight necessitated sweeping the wings forward to maintain an acceptable CG.

A first order, for 30, was placed by the French National Aeronautical Federation (FNA) on 28 November 1983.

A second ATL flew for the first time on 7 December 1984. Deliveries began on 27 April 1985, when the Coulommiers Aero Club received a production ATL (F-WFNC). Twenty-five more were delivered (one to Australia) with an F-W registration and DGAC 'laissez-passer' before certification was received on 15 January 1986. All of these aircraft were to be called back to Dijon for modification to full certification standards and re-registration in F-G sequence.

By 11 September 1986, a total of 80 ATLs had been delivered to 76 French flying clubs, and had logged more than 15,000 flying hours. Two others had been exported to Switzerland, where certification was received on 20 August 1986. The current production model is known as **ATL Club** in France and **Bijou** in the UK. Certification of the planned **ATL Voyage**, with 56 kW (75 hp) engine and more extensive equipment for longer cross-country flights and night VFR flying, has been deferred.

TYPE: Two-seat very light personal and club aircraft.

WINGS: Cantilever mid-wing monoplane. Wing section NACA 43015 modified. Dihedral 6° from roots. Incidence 3° at root, −1° at tip. Sweepforward at front spar 7° 30′. Conventional wood single-spar structure in two halves, with plywood covered leading-edge torsion box, light auxiliary rear spar, girder ribs and Dacron covering. Frise ailerons, actuated by cables, and electrically actuated flaps of light alloy along entire trailing-edges. No tabs.

FUSELAGE: Pod and boom configuration, made of glassfibre/Nomex honeycomb/epoxy sandwich.

TAIL UNIT: Cantilever V structure, with fixed surfaces of Dacron covered wood, and rod actuated light alloy control surfaces. Spring trim in elevator control.

LANDING GEAR: Non-retractable tricycle type. Cantilever main legs. Nosewheel has rubber shock absorption and is steerable via rudder pedals. Mainwheel tyres size 300-130, pressure 2·2 bars (32 lb/sq in); nosewheel tyre size 270-100, pressure 1·6 bars (23 lb/sq in). Hydraulic disc brakes on mainwheels. Parking brake.

POWER PLANT: One JPX 4T 60A (converted 2,050 cc Volkswagen) aircooled flat-four engine, rated at 48 kW (65 hp) and driving an EVRA two-blade wooden propeller. Optionally, one 56 kW (75 hp) JPX 4T 75B (converted Volkswagen) engine with electronic ignition. Fuel tank in each wingroot; total usable capacity 42 litres (9·25 Imp gallons; 11 US gallons).

ACCOMMODATION: Two glassfibre seats side by side under large transparent canopy which hinges upward and forward. Dual controls, with adjustable rudder pedals, cabin heating and ventilation standard.

SYSTEM: Electrical system includes 12V alternator and 12V 15Ah battery. Anti-collision, navigation, cabin and instrument lights optional.

AVIONICS AND EQUIPMENT: Optional avionics include 720 channel VHF transceiver, VOR, ADF and transponder. Standard equipment includes basic instruments, safety belts and tiedown rings. Optional items include horizon and directional gyros, rate of climb indicator, turn co-ordinator, outside air temperature gauge, hourmeter, exhaust gas temperature gauge, four-strap safety harness, tinted canopy, leather furnishing, faired main landing gear legs and canopy cover.

DIMENSIONS, EXTERNAL:

Wing span	10·25 m (33 ft 7½ in)
Wing mean aerodynamic chord	1·25 m (4 ft 1¼ in)
Wing aspect ratio	8·65
Length overall	6·72 m (22 ft 0½ in)
Height overall	2·00 m (6 ft 6¾ in)
Tailplane span	3·82 m (12 ft 6½ in)
Wheel track	3·00 m (9 ft 10 in)

AREA:

Wings, gross	12·15 m² (130·8 sq ft)

WEIGHTS AND LOADINGS (JPX 4T 60A engine):

Weight empty	360 kg (794 lb)
Max T-O weight	580 kg (1,278 lb)
Max wing loading	47·7 kg/m² (9·77 lb/sq ft)
Max power loading	12·1 kg/kW (19·7 lb/hp)

PERFORMANCE (A: ATL Club with JPX 4T 60A engine, B: estimated data for ATL Voyage, at max T-O weight):

Max level speed at S/L:	
A	100 knots (185 km/h; 115 mph)
B	111 knots (206 km/h; 128 mph)
Max cruising speed (75% power) at 2,440 m (8,000 ft):	
A	94 knots (175 km/h; 108 mph)
B	106 knots (196 km/h; 122 mph)
Econ cruising speed (50% power) at 2,440 m (8,000 ft):	
A	76 knots (142 km/h; 88 mph)
B	88 knots (163 km/h; 101 mph)
Stalling speed, flaps down:	
A	41 knots (75 km/h; 47 mph)
B	42 knots (77 km/h; 48 mph)
Max rate of climb at S/L: A	168 m (550 ft)/min
B	198 m (650 ft)/min
Service ceiling: A	3,960 m (13,000 ft)
B	4,420 m (14,500 ft)
T-O to 15 m (50 ft): A	420 m (1,378 ft)
B	400 m (1,313 ft)
Landing from 15 m (50 ft): A	380 m (1,247 ft)
B	390 m (1,280 ft)
Range with max fuel, at max cruising speed, no reserves:	
A	351 nm (650 km; 404 miles)
B	561 nm (1,040 km; 646 miles)
Range with max fuel at econ cruising speed, no reserves:	
A	426 nm (790 km; 490 miles)
B	702 nm (1,300 km; 807 miles)

Robin ATL Club very light two-seat personal and club aircraft *(Michel Isaac)*

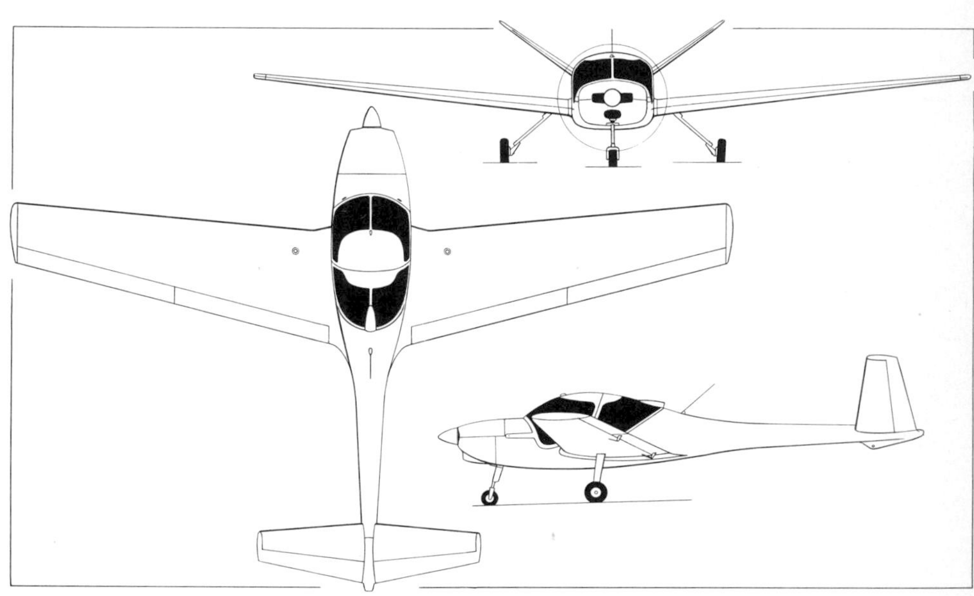

Robin ATL Club (JPX 4T 60A converted Volkswagen engine) *(Pilot Press)*

SELLET/PELLETIER

SELLET/PELLETIER HÉLICOPTÈRES

Lange SA, 28 rue de Naples, 75008 Paris
Telephone: 45 22 66 68
Telex: 290 959

M Christian Sellet and M Jacques Pelletier, engineers, are responsible for a small helicopter known as the Grillon 120, of which the single-seat prototype was exhibited in public for the first time at the 1985 Paris Air Show. This aircraft was designed and built by M Sellet. His partner is handling the administrative, commercial and public relations aspects of the project.

SELLET/PELLETIER GRILLON 120

The general appearance of the Grillon 120 (Cricket) is shown in an accompanying illustration. It was designed primarily to provide a means of training helicopter pilots at much reduced cost by comparison with other aircraft. Thus, although the prototype has been completed in single-seat form, production Grillons could have one or two seats, with single or dual controls.

Design of the Grillon began in August 1984; construction of the prototype started three months later. It was almost complete when exhibited at the Paris Air Show, and was expected to fly for the first time in March 1986.

TYPE: Prototype light helicopter.

ROTOR SYSTEM: Three-blade fully articulated main rotor and two-blade tail rotor, both of AU4GT aluminium alloy construction. Boeing Vertol blade section. Main rotor/engine rpm ratio 1:8·4. Tail rotor/engine rpm ratio 1:2·1.

FUSELAGE: Extensively glazed cabin pod, with aluminium alloy structure and minimal aluminium alloy skin. Tail rotor carried on aluminium alloy tube supported by mast structure at rear of cabin.

TAIL UNIT: Ventral fin only, under extremity of tailboom.

LANDING GEAR: Prototype was exhibited at Paris Air Show with a single Goodyear 10-A go-kart wheel on each unit of a non-retractable tricycle gear. The wheels, without brakes, were carried on aluminium alloy tube supports. Production aircraft are expected to have skid landing gear, as installed on prototype for initial flight testing.

POWER PLANT: One 89·5 kW (120 hp) Mazda twin-rotor engine, mounted above cabin, forward of main rotor mast. Fuel tank under seat; capacity 50 litres (11 Imp gallons; 13·2 US gallons) on prototype, 100 litres (22 Imp gallons; 26·4 US gallons) planned for production aircraft. Oil capacity 6 litres (1·3 Imp gallons; 1·6 US gallons) for engine; 2 litres (0·44 Imp gallons; 0·53 US gallons) for main gearbox.

ACCOMMODATION: Prototype has single semi-reclining seat and conventional helicopter controls, comprising collective and cyclic sticks and rudder pedals. Provision for second seat and dual controls. Large fully transparent door panel on each side. Heater standard.

DIMENSIONS, EXTERNAL:

Main rotor diameter	5·00 m (16 ft 4¾ in)
Tail rotor diameter	1·00 m (3 ft 3½ in)
Distance between rotor centres	3·10 m (10 ft 2 in)

Prototype of the Sellet/Pelletier Grillon 120 light helicopter

Main rotor blade chord 0·18 m (7 in)
Length overall, rotors turning 5·10 m (16 ft 9 in)
Length of fuselage, excl rotors 4·60 m (15 ft 1¼ in)
Width, excl rotors 1·40 m (4 ft 7¼ in)
Height to top of rotor hub 2·30 m (7 ft 6½ in)
Height overall 2·35 m (7 ft 8½ in)
AREAS:
Main rotor blades (each) 0·32 m² (3·44 sq ft)
Tail rotor blades (each) 0·034 m² (0·366 sq ft)
Main rotor disc 19·6 m² (211 sq ft)
Tail rotor disc 0·65 m² (7 sq ft)
WEIGHTS:
Weight empty 250 kg (551 lb)
Max T-O weight 530 kg (1,168 lb)
PERFORMANCE (estimated):
Max level speed at S/L 108 knots (200 km/h; 124 mph)
Max cruising speed at S/L 89 knots (165 km/h; 102 mph)
Econ cruising speed at S/L 62 knots (115 km/h; 71 mph)
Max rate of climb at S/L 300 m (985 ft)/min
Service ceiling 3,500 m (11,500 ft)
Range with max fuel 243 nm (450 km; 280 miles)
Range with max payload 191 nm (355 km; 220 miles)

SOCATA

SOCIÉTÉ DE CONSTRUCTION D'AVIONS DE TOURISME ET D'AFFAIRES
(Subsidiary of Aérospatiale)

3 Quai Léon Blum, 92150 Surèsnes
SALES MANAGEMENT: 12 rue Pasteur, 92150 Surèsnes
Telephone: (1) 45 06 37 60
Telex: SOCATAS 614 549 F
WORKS AND AFTER-SALES SERVICE: Aérodrome de Tarbes-Ossun-Lourdes, BP 38, 65001 Tarbes Cédex
Telephone: 62 93 97 30
Telex: SOCATA 520 828 F
FLYING SCHOOL: Aérodrome de Toussus-le-Noble, 78117 Chateaufort
Telephone: (1) 39 56 21 00
PRESIDENT AND DIRECTOR GENERAL: Pierre Gautier
GENERAL MANAGER: Didier Godechot
TECHNICAL DIRECTOR: Claude Lelaie
SALES MANAGER: A. Aubry
MANAGER, PROMOTION AND COMMUNICATION: Gérard Maoui

This company, formed in 1966, is a subsidiary of Aérospatiale, responsible for producing all of the group's piston engined light aircraft. As well as those described in this entry, Socata manufactures the Aérospatiale Epsilon military primary/basic trainer, described under the Aérospatiale heading in this section. During 1985, it delivered 112 light aircraft of its TB series, 43 of them to customers in Europe, 51 in the USA and 18 in other countries.

Socata also produces components for the A300 Airbus, ATR 42, Mystère-Falcon 100, 200 and 50 business aircraft, and Super Puma, Dauphin and Ecureuil helicopters. It is responsible for overhaul and repair of MS 760 Paris light jet aircraft.

Under an agreement effective from 26 May 1983, Socata markets in France and throughout the world the R 3000 series aircraft produced by Avions Pierre Robin.

Socata's works cover an area of 56,000 m² (602,775 sq ft), and employed a total of 950 people in 1985.

SOCATA R 235 GABIER

Production of this high-performance four-seat light aircraft, with STOL capability, has ended. It was described fully in the 1985-86 and earlier editions of *Jane's*.

SOCATA R 235 GUERRIER

This military aircraft (known also as the Rallye 235 G) has four Alkan 663 underwing stores pylons which enable it to be used for a variety of armed and support missions. The pylons are connected to a weapon selection box installed centrally on the radio panel in the cockpit.

Customers for the Guerrier include Rwanda and Senegal. Deliveries totalled 14 by 1 January 1985.

TYPE: Light general-purpose STOL military aircraft.

WINGS: Cantilever low-wing monoplane. Wing section NACA 63A416 (modified). Dihedral 7°. Incidence 4°. All-metal single-spar structure. Wide chord slotted ailerons. Full span automatic slats. Long span slotted flaps. Ailerons and flaps have corrugated metal skin. Ground adjustable aileron tabs. No anti-icing equipment.

FUSELAGE: All-metal semi-monocoque structure.

TAIL UNIT: Cantilever all-metal structure with corrugated skin on the mass balanced control surfaces. Fixed incidence tailplane. One automatic tab and one controllable tab on elevator. One controllable tab on rudder.

LANDING GEAR: Non-retractable tricycle type, with single wheel on each unit. Oleo-pneumatic shock absorbers. Castoring nosewheel. Cleveland mainwheels with tyres size 6·00-6, pressure 1·8 bars (26·1 lb/sq in); nosewheel tyre size 5·00-4, pressure 1·4 bars (20·3 lb/sq in). Cleveland hydraulic disc brakes.

POWER PLANT: One 175 kW (235 hp) Avco Lycoming O-540-B4B5 flat-six engine, driving a Hartzell HC-C2YK-1/8468-6 two-blade constant-speed metal propeller. Fuel in two metal tanks in wings, with total capacity of 282 litres (62 Imp gallons; 74·5 US gallons). Refuelling points above wings. Oil capacity 12 litres (2·6 Imp gallons; 3·2 US gallons).

ACCOMMODATION: Two side by side seats, with dual controls, enabling aircraft to be used for basic and operational training, as well as combat missions. Rear bench seat can be installed to permit the carriage of two passengers and a quantity of baggage or freight. Provision for carrying stretcher patient on casevac missions.

SYSTEM: 12V electrical system includes 32Ah battery and 55A alternator.

ARMAMENT AND OPERATIONAL EQUIPMENT: Underwing pylons can carry Matra F2 rocket launchers, each containing six 68 mm rockets; Type AA 52 pods, each containing two 7·62 mm machine-guns with 500 rds/gun, and large enough to retain all spent cartridge cases and links after firing; 50 kg operational or smaller practice bombs; rescue packs for airdropping over water, desert, jungle or polar regions; flares for use during operational or rescue missions by night; a surveillance pack containing a TV camera and transmitter to send images to a ground station. The camera is fitted with a zoom lens, and can scan to 45° on each side of the aircraft, with a vertical scan of 110°. The pilot has a control box (normal and zoom), and a monitor on which to check precisely the images the camera is viewing. All underwing loads can be jettisoned in an emergency.

DIMENSIONS, EXTERNAL:
Wing span 9·74 m (31 ft 11 in)
Wing chord (constant) 1·30 m (4 ft 3 in)
Wing aspect ratio 7·57
Length overall 7·25 m (23 ft 9½ in)
Height overall 2·80 m (9 ft 2¼ in)
Tailplane span 3·67 m (12 ft 0½ in)
Wheel track 2·01 m (6 ft 7 in)
Wheelbase 1·71 m (5 ft 7¼ in)
DIMENSIONS, INTERNAL:
Cabin: Length 2·25 m (7 ft 4 in)
Width 1·13 m (3 ft 8½ in)
AREAS:
Wings, gross 12·76 m² (137·3 sq ft)
Trailing-edge flaps (total) 2·40 m² (25·83 sq ft)
Vertical tail surfaces (total) 1·74 m² (18·73 sq ft)
Horizontal tail surfaces (total) 3·48 m² (37·50 sq ft)
WEIGHTS AND LOADINGS:
Weight empty 710 kg (1,565 lb)
Max T-O weight 1,350 kg (2,976 lb)
Max wing loading 105·8 kg/m² (21·68 lb/sq ft)
Max power loading 7·71 kg/kW (12·66 lb/hp)
PERFORMANCE:
Range/endurance:
armed reconnaissance with 2 gun pods at 70% power, 30 min fuel reserves 5 h or 556 nm (1,030 km; 640 miles)
armed reconnaissance with 4 rocket launchers at 70% power, 30 min fuel reserves 2 h 40 min or 286 nm (530 km; 329 miles)
ground support with 2 gun pods at 75% power at 915 m (3,000 ft), 30 min fuel reserves, 10 min over target 243 nm (450 km; 280 miles)
ground support with 4 rocket launchers at 75% power at 915 m (3,000 ft), 30 min fuel reserves, 10 min over target 130 nm (240 km; 149 miles)
ground support with 2 rocket launchers and 2 gun pods at 75% power at 915 m (3,000 ft), 15 min fuel reserves, 10 min over target 43 nm (80 km; 50 miles)
unarmed reconnaissance with TV pod at 70% power, 30 min fuel reserves 545 nm (1,010 km; 627 miles)

Socata Guerrier in ground support configuration, with two F2 rocket packs and bombs on underwing attachments

SOCATA TB 9 TAMPICO AND TB 10 TOBAGO

The prototype for this series of all-metal light aircraft was the original TB 10 (F-WZJP), of which design was initiated by Socata's Research and Development Department in February 1975. Construction began in February 1976, and it made a 25 min first flight at Tarbes on 23 February 1977, powered by a 119 kW (160 hp) Avco Lycoming O-320-D2A engine. The second prototype of the TB 10 was fitted with a 134 kW (180 hp) Lycoming engine.

Current production versions are as follows:

TB 9 Tampico FP. Four-seater, with 119 kW (160 hp) Avco Lycoming O-320-D2A engine, Sensenich fixed-pitch propeller, fuel capacity of 158 litres (34·75 Imp gallons; 41·75 US gallons), and non-retractable landing gear. Options include 210 litre (46 Imp gallon; 55·5 US gallon) fuel tanks (replacing standard tanks). Sales by 1 January 1986 totalled 114, of which 112 had been delivered.

TB 9 Tampico CS. As Tampico FP, but with Hartzell constant-speed propeller. Sales included in total under Tampico FP listing.

TB 10 Tobago. Four/five-seater, with 134 kW (180 hp) engine and non-retractable landing gear. DGAC certification received on 26 April 1979, followed by FAA approval on 27 November 1985. Sales by 1 January 1986 totalled 366, of which 283 had been delivered, some to customers in the USA. Eight are used by SFACT to provide flying training for French air traffic control officers.

The aerobatic TB 11 Tobago, listed in the 1983-84 *Jane's*, is not currently available. The more powerful **TB 20/21 Trinidad**, with retractable landing gear, is described separately.

The following description applies specifically to the TB 10 Tobago, but the Tampico is generally similar in basic construction.

TYPE: Four/five-seat all-metal light aircraft.

WINGS: Cantilever low-wing monoplane. Wing section RA 16·3C3. Thickness/chord ratio 16%. Dihedral 4° 30' from roots. No incidence at root. No sweep. Conventional light alloy single-spar structure of constant chord, with glassfibre tips. Balanced ailerons and electrically actuated slotted flaps, of light alloy. Ground adjustable tabs.

FUSELAGE: Light alloy semi-monocoque structure. Shallow strake under each side of fuselage immediately aft of wing root fillet. Glassfibre engine cowlings.

TAIL UNIT: Cantilever all-metal type, with sweptback vertical surfaces and constant chord all-moving horizontal surfaces mounted at extreme tail, aft of rudder. Ground adjustable tab at top of rudder. Anti-tab in horizontal surfaces.

LANDING GEAR: Non-retractable tricycle type, with steerable nosewheel. Oleo-pneumatic shock absorber in all three units. Mainwheel tyres size 6·00-6, 6-ply rating, pressure 2·3 bars (33 lb/sq in). Glassfibre wheel fairings on all three units. Hydraulic disc brakes. Parking brake.

Power Plant: One 134 kW (180 hp) Avco Lycoming O-360-A1AD flat-four engine, driving a Hartzell two-blade constant-speed propeller with spinner. Two integral fuel tanks in wing leading-edges; total capacity 210 litres (46 Imp gallons; 55·5 US gallons), of which 204 litres (45 Imp gallons; 54 US gallons) are usable. Oil capacity 7·5 litres (1·6 Imp gallons; 2 US gallons).

Accommodation: Four/five seats in enclosed cabin, with dual controls. Adjustable front seats with inertia reel seat belts. Removable rear bench seat with safety belts. Sharply inclined low-drag windscreen. Access via upward hinged window/doors of glassfibre. Baggage compartment aft of cabin, with external door on port side. Cabin carpeted, soundproofed, heated and ventilated. Windscreen defrosting standard.

Systems: Electrical system includes 12V 60A alternator and 12V 32A battery, landing and navigation lights, four individual cabin lights and instrument panel lighting. Hydraulic system for wheel brakes only.

Avionics and Equipment: Avionics to customer's specification. Current aircraft are equipped without extra charge with a basic nav pack that includes a rate of climb indicator, electric turn and bank indicator, horizontal and directional gyro, true airspeed indicator, EGT and outside air temperature indicator. Standard equipment includes armrests for all seats, map pockets, anti-glare visors, stall warning indicator, tiedown fittings and towbar.

Dimensions, external (Tampico and Tobago):
- Wing span: 9·76 m (32 ft 0¼ in)
- Wing chord (constant): 1·22 m (4 ft 0 in)
- Wing aspect ratio: 8
- Length overall: 7·63 m (25 ft 0½ in)
- Height overall: 3·20 m (10 ft 6 in)
- Tailplane span: 3·20 m (10 ft 6 in)
- Wheelbase: 1·96 m (6 ft 5 in)
- Propeller diameter: 1·88 m (6 ft 2 in)
- Propeller ground clearance: 0·10 m (4 in)
- Cabin doors (each): Width: 0·90 m (2 ft 11½ in)
  - Height: 0·76 m (2 ft 6 in)
- Baggage door: Width: 0·64 m (2 ft 1¼ in)
  - Height: 0·44 m (1 ft 5¼ in)

Dimensions, internal (Tampico and Tobago):
- Cabin: Length, firewall to rear bulkhead: 2·53 m (8 ft 3½ in)
  - Length, panel to rear bulkhead: 2·00 m (6 ft 6¾ in)
  - Max width, at rear seats: 1·28 m (4 ft 2¼ in)
  - Max width, at front seats: 1·15 m (3 ft 9¼ in)
  - Max height, floor to roof: 1·12 m (3 ft 8 in)

Areas:
- Wings, gross: 11·90 m² (128·1 sq ft)
- Ailerons (total): 0·91 m² (9·80 sq ft)
- Trailing-edge flaps (total): 3·72 m² (40·04 sq ft)
- Fin: 0·88 m² (9·47 sq ft)
- Rudder: 0·63 m² (6·78 sq ft)
- Horizontal tail surfaces (total): 2·56 m² (27·56 sq ft)

Weights (A: Tampico FP, B: Tampico CS, C: Tobago):
- Weight empty, with unusable fuel and oil:
  - A: 650 kg (1,433 lb)
  - B: 660 kg (1,455 lb)
  - C: 670 kg (1,477 lb)
- Baggage: C: 45 kg (100 lb)
- Max T-O weight: A, B: 1,060 kg (2,340 lb)
  - C: 1,150 kg (2,535 lb)

Performance (at max T-O weight, A, B and C as above):
- Max level speed: A: 122 knots (226 km/h; 140 mph)
  - B: 126 knots (234 km/h; 145 mph)
  - C: 133 knots (247 km/h; 153 mph)
- Max cruising speed (75% power):
  - A, B: 121 knots (225 km/h; 140 mph)
  - C: 127 knots (235 km/h; 146 mph)
- Econ cruising speed (65% power):
  - A, B: 108 knots (201 km/h; 125 mph)
  - C: 117 knots (217 km/h; 135 mph)
- Stalling speed, flaps up:
  - A, B: 58 knots (107 km/h; 67 mph)
  - C: 61 knots (112 km/h; 70 mph)
- Stalling speed, flaps down:
  - A, B: 48 knots (89 km/h; 56 mph)
  - C: 52 knots (97 km/h; 60 mph)
- Max rate of climb at S/L: A: 201 m (660 ft)/min
  - B: 231 m (760 ft)/min
  - C: 240 m (790 ft)/min
- Service ceiling: A: 3,810 m (12,500 ft)
  - B: 4,205 m (13,800 ft)
  - C: 3,960 m (13,000 ft)
- T-O run: A: 355 m (1,165 ft)
  - B: 286 m (938 ft)
  - C: 325 m (1,066 ft)
- T-O to 15 m (50 ft): A: 565 m (1,853 ft)
  - B: 426 m (1,398 ft)
  - C: 505 m (1,657 ft)
- Landing from 15 m (50 ft): A, B: 405 m (1,329 ft)
  - C: 425 m (1,395 ft)
- Landing run: A, B, C: 190 m (623 ft)
- Range with max standard fuel, allowances for T-O, climb, econ power cruise and descent, 45 min reserves:
  - A, B: 496 nm (920 km; 571 miles)
  - C: 653 nm (1,210 km; 752 miles)
- Range with max optional fuel, conditions as above:
  - A, B: 696 nm (1,290 km; 801 miles)

Socata TB 10 Tobago four/five-seat all-metal light aircraft

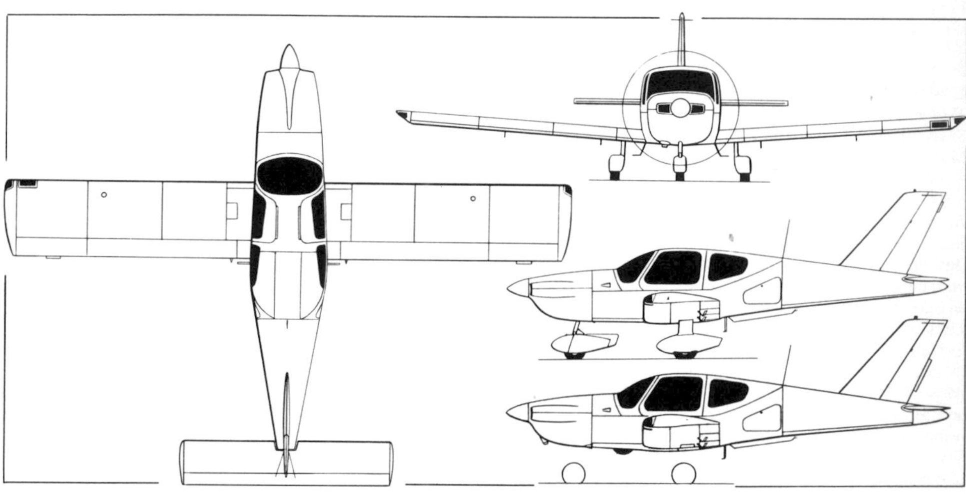

Socata Tobago, with additional side view (bottom) of Trinidad *(Pilot Press)*

SOCATA TB 20/21 TRINIDAD

The Trinidad is a four/five-seat touring and IFR training aircraft, basically similar to the TB 10 Tobago (which see) but with a more powerful engine and retractable landing gear. The prototype (F-WDBA) flew for the first time, at Tarbes, on 14 November 1980. French certification was received on 18 December 1981, and the first production Trinidad (F-WDBB) was delivered on 23 March 1982. FAA type approval was obtained on 27 January 1984. Orders totalled 206 by 1 January 1986, including 24 for the SFACT for commercial airline pilot training. Others have been supplied to civilian aviation training centres in Australia, India (eight) and Tunisia.

There are two current versions of the Trinidad, as follows:

TB 20 Trinidad. Basic version with 186 kW (250 hp) Avco Lycoming IO-540-C4D5D engine.

TB 21 Trinidad TC. Turbocharged version, first flown on 24 August 1984, with 186 kW (250 hp) Avco Lycoming TIO-540-AB1AD engine and oxygen system. DGAC certification received on 23 May 1985, followed by FAA type approval on 5 March 1986. The first production Trinidad TC (F-GENI), displayed at the 1985 Paris Air Show, was the 500th aircraft of the TB 9/10/20/21 series produced by Socata.

The description of the Tobago applies also to both versions of the Trinidad, except as follows:

Wings: Dihedral 6° 30′ from roots. Flap preselector standard.

Tail Unit: Span and chord of horizontal tail surfaces increased. Mechanical rudder trim standard.

Landing Gear: Hydraulically retractable tricycle type, with single wheel on each unit. Free fall emergency extension. Steerable nosewheel retracts rearward. Main units retract inward into fuselage. Hydraulic disc brakes. Parking brake.

Power Plant: One Avco Lycoming flat-six engine, as described in individual model listings, driving a Hartzell HC-C2YK-1BF/F8477-4 two-blade metal propeller. Fuel tanks in wings; total usable capacity 326 litres (71·75 Imp gallons). Oil capacity 12·6 litres (2·8 Imp gallons).

Systems: Self-contained electro-hydraulic system for landing gear actuation. Eros oxygen system is standard in TB 21.

Equipment: In addition to basic nav pack described in the Tampico/Tobago entry, current aircraft have as standard equipment a heated pitot, emergency static vent, cylinder head temperature gauge, emergency lighting systems, tinted windows and a storm window.

Dimensions:
- As for Tobago, except:
  - Length overall: 7·71 m (25 ft 3½ in)
  - Height overall: 2·85 m (9 ft 4¼ in)
  - Tailplane span: 3·64 m (11 ft 11¼ in)

Socata TB 21 Trinidad TC, with retractable landing gear *(G. Maoui)*

Wheelbase 1·91 m (6 ft 3¼ in)
Propeller diameter 2·03 m (6 ft 8 in)
AREAS:
As for Tobago, except:
Horizontal tail surfaces (total) 3·06 m² (32·94 sq ft)
WEIGHTS (A: TB 20, B: TB 21):
Weight empty: A 791 kg (1,744 lb)
B 815 kg (1,797 lb)
Max baggage: A, B 65 kg (143 lb)
Max ramp weight: A 1,341 kg (2,956 lb)
Max T-O weight: A 1,335 kg (2,943 lb)
B 1,400 kg (3,086 lb)
PERFORMANCE (at max T-O weight, A, B and C as above):
Max level speed: A 167 knots (310 km/h; 192 mph)
B at 4,575 m (15,000 ft) 200 knots (370 km/h; 230 mph)
Max cruising speed (75% power) at 2,440 m (8,000 ft):
A 164 knots (303 km/h; 188 mph)
Best power cruising speed (75% power) at 7,620 m (25,000 ft): B 187 knots (346 km/h; 215 mph)
Econ cruising speed (65% power):
A at 3,660 m (12,000 ft) 160 knots (296 km/h; 184 mph)
B at 7,620 m (25,000 ft) 170 knots (315 km/h; 195 mph)
Stalling speed: flaps up:
A 64 knots (118 km/h; 74 mph)
B 66 knots (121 km/h; 75 mph)
flaps and wheels down:
A 54 knots (99 km/h; 62 mph)
B 55 knots (101 km/h; 63 mph)
Rate of climb: A at S/L 384 m (1,260 ft)/min
B at 610 m (2,000 ft) 332 m (1,090 ft)/min
B at 5,180 m (17,000 ft) 244 m (800 ft)/min
Service ceiling: A 6,100 m (20,000 ft)
Certification ceiling: B 7,620 m (25,000 ft)
T-O run: A 295 m (968 ft)
B 330 m (1,083 ft)
T-O to 15 m (50 ft): A 479 m (1,572 ft)
B 540 m (1,772 ft)
Landing from 15 m (50 ft): A 530 m (1,739 ft)
B 540 m (1,772 ft)
Landing run: A 230 m (755 ft)
Range with max fuel, allowances for T-O, climb, cruise at best econ setting and descent, 45 min reserves:
A at 75% power at 2,135 m (7,000 ft) 885 nm (1,640 km; 1,019 miles)
A at 65% power at 3,050 m (10,000 ft) 963 nm (1,785 km; 1,109 miles)
Range with max fuel, no reserves:
B at 75% power at 7,620 m (25,000 ft) 890 nm (1,648 km; 1,024 miles)
B at 65% power at 7,620 m (25,000 ft) 1,030 nm (1,907 km; 1,185 miles)
Max ferry range at 6,100 m (20,000 ft):
A 1,158 nm (2,145 km; 1,332 miles)

GERMANY
(FEDERAL REPUBLIC)

CLAUDIUS DORNIER

CLAUDIUS DORNIER SEASTAR GmbH & Co KG

Werksflugplatz Oberpfaffenhofen, 8031 Wessling
Telephone: (08153) 2076/2079
Telex: 734282

Prof Dipl Ing Claudius Dornier Jr, who died on 30 April 1986, was the eldest son of the aviation pioneer Prof Claude Dornier. He worked closely with his father until the latter's death in 1969, and was Chairman of the Board of Dornier GmbH until 31 December 1981. The first product of this new company which he founded is the Seastar utility amphibian, of which design was initiated in January 1982. Construction of the VT 01 first prototype (D-ICDS) began in January 1983, at the Lufthansa facility in Hamburg, and the first flight was made on 17 August 1984. More than 80 hours of flying had been logged by mid-1985, when the aircraft was retired after being damaged. Certification, using a PT 01 production prototype, is to be gained under FAR Part 23, and initial deliveries of production aircraft are planned for 1988.

Practical evaluation of the design was made by using a one-fifth scale radio controlled flying model. This demonstrated excellent on-water performance, which results from adoption of the basic configuration developed for the famous Dornier Wal. However, the new hull is constructed of composite materials, their corrosion resistant characteristics and light weight being ideal for application to a flying-boat hull.

As a basic transport aircraft the Seastar will provide accommodation for two pilots and 12 passengers. It is suitable for a variety of missions, including feeder transport from water bases to airports; missions for which helicopters would be restricted by range, economics or safety factors; search and rescue; law enforcement; air ambulance (with five to six stretchers); and civil or military special missions, accommodating four persons over a range of 1,000 nm (1,850 km; 1,150 miles). The Seastar's ability to operate from land, water, snow or ice also enables it to perform such other roles as aerial surveillance, sightseeing and hunting tours, fire control and firefighting.

Claudius Dornier Seastar first prototype (two P&WC PT6A-11 turboprops) during sea trials in the Baltic

CLAUDIUS DORNIER SEASTAR

The Seastar VT 01 prototype was described in full in the 1984-85 *Jane's*. The following description applies to the production version, the prototype of which was due to fly by the end of 1986:

TYPE: Twin-engined utility amphibian.

WINGS: Cantilever parasol monoplane. Wing section NACA 23015 (modified). The high-lift glassfibre wing incorporates single-slotted trailing-edge flaps.

HULL: Conventional unpressurised flying-boat hull with structure of composite materials, primarily of glassfibre.

TAIL UNIT: Conventional tail unit, constructed of composite materials, and incorporating a variable incidence tailplane. Control surfaces horn balanced. Trim tab in each elevator and rudder.

LANDING GEAR: Hydraulically retractable tricycle type, with twin wheels on each main unit and single nosewheel. Main units retract forward into hull sponsons, nose unit forward into bow of hull.

POWER PLANT: Two 373 kW (500 shp) Pratt & Whitney Canada PT6A-112 turboprop engines mounted over the wing in tandem in a continuous nacelle, the forward and rear engines driving a tractor and pusher propeller respectively. Each is a four-blade Hartzell constant-speed propeller with spinner. Tank in each sponson for a combined max 1,288 kg (2,840 lb) of fuel.

ACCOMMODATION: Max accommodation for two pilots and 12 passengers in four rows of three. Dual controls standard. Door to flight deck on port side. Cabin has door at forward end on starboard side, and at rear of cabin on port side. The rear door has an optional airstair incorporated in the adjacent sponson structure. Baggage compartment at rear of cabin, with external door on port side which can be used also for loading long items such as stretchers into main cabin. Accommodation is heated and ventilated; air-conditioning optional. Alternative layouts for nine passengers, or six executives in VIP seating, have provision for a lavatory and toilet at rear of cabin and in the baggage compartment respectively. All passenger facilities can be removed to provide unobstructed cabin for cargo carrying.

SYSTEMS: Hydraulic system for landing gear actuation. Electrical system. Pneumatic de-icing system for wing and tail unit leading-edges, and for engine intakes.

AVIONICS: Complete IFR avionics installation.

DIMENSIONS, EXTERNAL:
Wing span 15·50 m (50 ft 10¼ in)
Wing chord, mean 1·89 m (6 ft 2½ in)
Wing aspect ratio 8·44
Length overall 12·46 m (40 ft 10½ in)
Fuselage width: Cabin (max) 1·90 m (6 ft 2¾ in)
Over sponsons 4·20 m (13 ft 9½ in)
Height overall 4·60 m (15 ft 1 in)
Tailplane span 5·56 m (18 ft 3 in)
Wheel track 2·45 m (8 ft 0½ in)
Propeller diameter: front 2·40 m (7 ft 10½ in)
rear 2·35 m (7 ft 8½ in)
Crew door: Height 0·85 m (2 ft 9½ in)
Width 0·70 m (2 ft 3½ in)
Passenger doors (two, each):
Height 1·00 m (3 ft 3¼ in)
Width 1·15 m (4 ft 11 in)
Rear cargo door (optional):
Height 0·50 m (1 ft 7¾ in)
Width 0·90 m (2 ft 11½ in)
DIMENSIONS, INTERNAL:
Cabin, excl flight deck and rear baggage compartment:
Length 5·00 m (16 ft 5 in)
Max width 1·62 m (5 ft 3¾ in)
Max height 1·40 m (4 ft 7 in)
Floor area 6·30 m² (67·8 sq ft)
Volume 8·30 m³ (293·1 cu ft)
Rear baggage compartment volume 1·70 m³ (60·0 cu ft)
AREAS:
Wings, gross 28·48 m² (306·6 sq ft)
Vertical tail surfaces (total) 3·15 m² (33·9 sq ft)
Horizontal tail surfaces (total) 6·32 m² (68·0 sq ft)
WEIGHTS:
Weight empty, equipped (standard) 2,400 kg (5,291 lb)
Max payload 1,460 kg (3,218 lb)
Max fuel weight 1,288 kg (2,840 lb)
Max T-O and landing weight 4,200 kg (9,259 lb)
PERFORMANCE (estimated, at 4,000 kg; 8,818 lb AUW):
Max cruising speed at 3,000 m (9,840 ft) 184 knots (341 km/h; 212 mph)
T-O to and landing from 15 m (50 ft) on land or water 580 m (1,905 ft)
Landing from 15 m (50 ft) on land 470 m (1,545 ft)
Range with 9 passengers 539 nm (1,000 km; 621 miles)
Range with max fuel, max range cruising speed 1,009 nm (1,870 km; 1,162 miles)
Max endurance 8 h

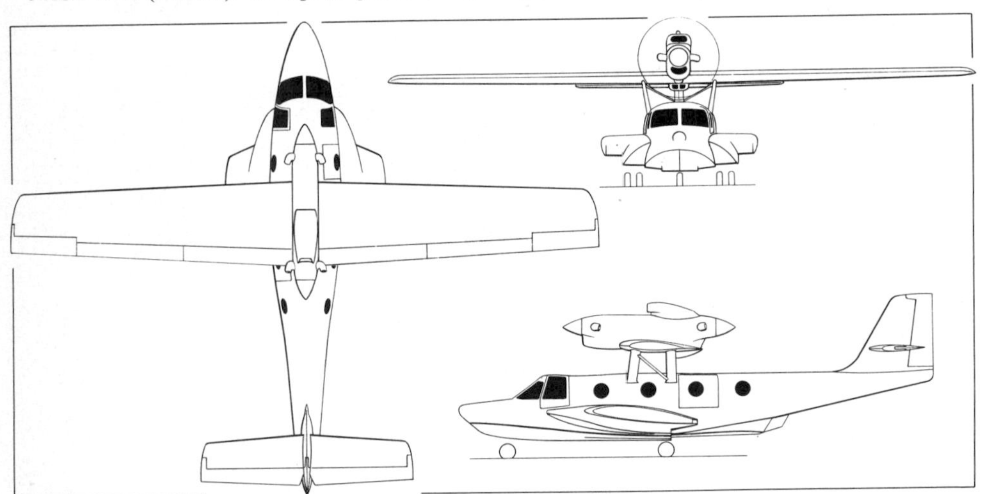

Claudius Dornier Seastar in its intended production form *(Pilot Press)*

DEUTSCHE AIRBUS

DEUTSCHE AIRBUS GmbH
(Subsidiary of MBB)

Arabellastrasse 30, Postfach 810260, 8000 München 81
Telephone: (089) 92 63 291/2
Telex: 5215149
CHAIRMAN OF THE SUPERVISORY BOARD:
Dr Franz Josef Strauss
PRESIDENT: Dipl Kfm Rolf Siebert
EXECUTIVE VICE-PRESIDENT: Dr Paul Hadrys
PUBLIC RELATIONS: Jochen H. Eichen

This company is the West German partner in the consortium formed for development and production of the A300, A310 and A320 transport aircraft described under the Airbus heading in the International section. It is a wholly owned subsidiary of MBB (which see).

DORNIER

DORNIER GmbH

Postfach 1420, 7990 Friedrichshafen/Bodensee
Telephone: Immenstaad (07545) 81+
Telex: 0734 209-0
WORKS:
Research and Development:
7990 Friedrichshafen/Bodensee
Production: Postfach 2160, Trimburgstrasse, 8000 München 66
AIRFIELD AND FLIGHT TEST CENTRE:
8031 Oberpfaffenhofen, near München
BONN OFFICE: Heussallee 2-10, 5300 Bonn
SUPERVISORY BOARD:
Edzard Reuter (Chairman)
Alois Laus (Deputy Chairman)
Fritz Bentenrieder
Silvius Dornier
Dr-Ing Rudolf Hörnig
Dr rer pol Gerhard Liener
Rudolf Merz
Konrad Messerschmid
Dipl-Ing Klaus Messmer
Dr-Ing E. h. Werner Niefer
Oscar Pauli
BOARD OF MANAGING DIRECTORS:
Johann Schäffler (Chairman)
Hans Ambos
Rainer Hainich
Werner Kresin
Dr-Ing Fritz Mader
PUBLIC RELATIONS: Gerhard Patt
Postfach 2160, 8000 München 66
Telephone: 089 87 153480
Telex: 52 35 43

Dornier GmbH, formerly Dornier-Metallbauten, was formed in 1922 by the late Professor Claude Dornier as the successor to the 'Do' division of the former Zeppelin Werke, Lindau, GmbH. It has been operated in the form of a Gesellschaft mit beschränkter Haftung since 22 December 1972. Of nearly 8,500 employees in the Dornier group, approximately 43% are production staff, 32% in research and development, and 25% engaged in technical and logistic support. Approval was gained on 15 May 1985 for Daimler-Benz AG to acquire a majority holding (65·5%) in Dornier GmbH. The remaining stock is held by Silvius Dornier and the State of Baden-Württemberg.

Member companies, in addition to Dornier GmbH, include Dornier-Reparaturwerft GmbH, at Oberpfaffenhofen (aircraft servicing and maintenance), Dornier System GmbH of Friedrichshafen (spaceflight, new technologies, electronics, management consultancy and contract research) and Dornier Medizintechnik GmbH of Munich.

The Dornier 128-6 twin-turboprop STOL transport and utility aircraft continues in production, as does the larger twin-turboprop Dornier 228. Available in several versions, the 228 embodies Dornier's TNT advanced technology wing. This type of wing is also fitted to the Dornier Do ATT (Amphibian Technology Testbed), described in the 1984-85 *Jane's*. Details of the TNT testbed aircraft have also been given in earlier editions of *Jane's*; it continues in use for basic flight test programmes of new technologies for general aviation.

Dornier is active in development of various types of RPV (see RPVs and Targets section), and continues to develop and produce the Alpha Jet training/light attack aircraft, described in the International section, in partnership with the Dassault-Breguet group in France.

Dornier is participating, under subcontract from Deutsche Airbus GmbH, in the manufacturing and development programmes for the Airbus A300-600, A310 and A320. It was responsible for integrating the operational avionics in the 18 Boeing E-3A Sentry AWACS aircraft (see US section) acquired by NATO for use in Europe.

Dornier is responsible for technical and logistic servicing of the Breguet Br 1150 Atlantic 1 aircraft operated by the Federal German Navy. Under a contract awarded by the German Federal Procurement Agency, it is also prime contractor for modernisation of the German Atlantics.

Dornier is one of the European aerospace companies which are defining and developing the multi-nation Eurofighter (see International section).

DORNIER Do 28 D-2 SKYSERVANT

Dornier has equipped two Do 28 D-2 Skyservants of the German naval air arm as airborne surveillance systems for the detection of oil pollution at sea. This task was financed equally by the Federal Ministry of Transport and the governments of the coastal states. The operating and maintenance costs are borne by the Federal Ministry of Defence.

The latest state-of-the-art systems are integrated into these aircraft for oil-spill detection. The major components of the systems package, developed by Swedish Space Corporation (SSC), include an Ericsson SLAR (side looking airborne radar) under the fuselage for the initial detection of oil pollution; a Daedalus IR/UV scanner for obtaining indications at short ranges of oil pollution in the wake of ships, or determination of oil leaks in the event of ship accidents; an Ericsson microwave radiometer (MWR) for registration of large oil quantities; and a tilting JAI TV camera with light amplifier and video recorder to identify and record ships by night. (A small handheld Nikon camera with a data-fade-in capability is used for daylight operation.)

Control and evaluation of the sensor signals is achieved via an SSC data processing system. Signals from the SLAR, IR/UV scanner and MWR, as well as from the LLLTV camera, can be presented selectively and in certain combinations on a TV screen. Navigation data is based on a Decca system, in which position lines are converted into geographic co-ordinates in a navigation computer. The aircraft are able to communicate additionally, on Collins HF-230, Collins ARC-182, VHF/UHF and AM/FM, with ships and land based operational units. The modified Skyservants have a cruising speed of 147 knots (272 km/h; 169 mph) at 3,050 m (10,000 ft) and a max range of 1,551 nm (2,875 km; 1,786 miles).

DORNIER 128-6

The first turboprop development of the Skyservant was the Do 28 D-5X prototype, which first flew on 9 April 1978 with two 447 kW (600 shp) Avco Lycoming LTP 101-600-1As derated to 298 kW (400 shp). It was redesignated Dornier 128-6X when refitted with Pratt & Whitney Canada PT6A-110 turboprops, and made its first flight with this power plant on 4 March 1980.

Except for reinforced landing gear and strengthening of the engine support structure, the airframe of the Dornier 128-6 is generally similar to that of the piston engined 128-2, and the aircraft is available also in maritime patrol (MPA) form with a large undernose radome.

Certification by the LBA was granted in March 1981; the first production Dornier 128-6, an aircraft for Lesotho Airways, was delivered in July 1981. A small number of 128-6MPAs, equipped with MEL Marec radar, was ordered by the Cameroun Air Force for maritime patrol, and in 1982 a contract for 18 Dornier 128-6 utility aircraft was placed by the Nigerian Air Force. No subsequent sales have been announced, but the aircraft remains available to order.

One Dornier 128-6, named *Polar 1*, was specially equipped to support the German Polar research organisation. It has wheel-ski landing gear, weather radar, a de-icing system and a survival kit for 20 days. It is used primarily to transport field teams to unprepared sites, and to ferry equipment such as sleds and skidoos.

A full description of the Dornier 128-6 has appeared in many previous editions of *Jane's*, most recently in the 1985-86 edition. The following is a shortened version of that description:

TYPE: Twin-turboprop STOL transport and utility aircraft.

AIRFRAME: See 1985-86 *Jane's*.

POWER PLANT: Two Pratt & Whitney Canada PT6A-110 turboprop engines, each derated to 298 kW (400 shp), mounted on stub wings and each driving a Hartzell B3TN-3D/T10282B-9·5 three-blade constant-speed and fully-feathering metal propeller with spinner. Fuel tanks in rear of engine nacelles, with total usable capacity of 893 litres (196·5 Imp gallons). Provision for two underwing auxiliary fuel tanks with combined capacity of 474 litres (104 Imp gallons).

ACCOMMODATION: Pilot and either co-pilot or passenger side by side on flight deck. Dual controls standard. Main cabin equipped normally to carry ten passengers in pairs, with centre aisle, or five stretchers and five folding seats, all layouts including toilet and/or baggage compartment and/or darkroom for aerial survey missions aft of cabin. Alternatively, cabin can be stripped for cargo carrying. Door on each side of flight deck. Emergency exit on starboard side of cabin. Combined two-section passenger and freight door on port side of cabin, at rear.

AVIONICS AND EQUIPMENT: See 1985-86 *Jane's*.

DIMENSIONS, EXTERNAL:
Wing span	15·85 m (52 ft 0 in)
Length overall (in flying attitude)	11·41 m (37 ft 5¼ in)
Height overall (static)	3·90 m (12 ft 9½ in)
Tailplane span	6·61 m (21 ft 8¼ in)
Wheel track	3·52 m (11 ft 6 in)
Wheelbase	8·63 m (28 ft 3¾ in)
Propeller diameter	2·36 m (7 ft 9 in)

DIMENSIONS, INTERNAL:
Cabin, excl flight deck and rear baggage compartment:	
Max length	3·97 m (13 ft 0½ in)
Max width	1·37 m (4 ft 6 in)
Max height	1·52 m (4 ft 11¾ in)
Floor area	5·30 m² (57·05 sq ft)
Volume	8·00 m³ (282·5 cu ft)
Baggage compartment volume	0·90 m³ (31·8 cu ft)

Dornier Do 28 D-2 Skyservant of the German Navy, converted for oil-spill detection duties

AREA:
Wings, gross 29·00 m² (312·2 sq ft)
WEIGHTS:
Weight empty 2,540 kg (5,600 lb)
Max payload 1,273 kg (2,806 lb)
Max T-O weight 4,350 kg (9,590 lb)
Max landing weight 4,140 kg (9,127 lb)
PERFORMANCE (at max T-O weight except where indicated):
Max level speed 183 knots (339 km/h; 211 mph)
Max cruising speed at 3,050 m (10,000 ft) 178 knots (330 km/h; 205 mph)
Cruising speed, 75% power at 3,050 m (10,000 ft) 165 knots (305 km/h; 190 mph)
Max rate of climb at S/L 384 m (1,260 ft)/min
Rate of climb at S/L, one engine out 54 m (177 ft)/min
Service ceiling 9,935 m (32,600 ft)
T-O to 15 m (50 ft) 554 m (1,820 ft)
Landing from 15 m (50 ft) at max landing weight 503 m (1,650 ft)
Range with 805 kg (1,774 lb) payload, no reserves 788 nm (1,460 km; 907 miles)
Range with max fuel at max range power 985 nm (1,825 km; 1,134 miles)

DORNIER 228

The Dornier 228 is a larger utility and commuter transport than the 128-6, and is available in the following versions:

228-100. Basic version, with the Dornier new technology (TNT) wing, Garrett turboprop power plant, and standard accommodation for 15 passengers in airline seats at 76 cm (30 in) pitch. German (LBA) certification awarded on 18 December 1981. Deliveries began in February 1982; entered service, with A/S Norving Flyservice in Norway, in late Summer of 1982. Suitable for a wide range of other duties, including freight or mixed cargo/passenger transport, executive travel, air taxi service, photogrammetry, airways calibration, training, ambulance or search and rescue operations, and paramilitary missions. Main fuselage segments, cabin door and cockpit equipment standardised with those of Dornier 128.

228-101. Identical to 228-100 except for reinforced fuselage and different mainwheel tyres, to permit higher operating weights, and installation of engine fire extinguishing system to conform to SFAR Pt 41b. Introduced in 1984. One specially equipped -101 delivered in 1985 to DFVLR for meteorological (remote sensing) and environmental forestry and pollution control work. Modifications include ventral camera/scanner apertures and numerous attachments for special sensors and other equipment under the wings and fuselage. A second, similar aircraft was due to be delivered in Summer 1986.

228-200. Lengthened fuselage, providing standard accommodation for 19 passengers at 76 cm (30 in) seat pitch and a larger rear baggage compartment, but otherwise generally similar to 228-100. Certificated by German LBA on 6 September 1982.

228-201. Identical to 228-200 except for changes noted under 228-101. Introduced in 1984. One being evaluated by German Navy and Air Force during 1986.

228 Maritime Patrol. Described separately.

The design of the Dornier 228 complies with US FAR Pt 23 requirements, including Amendment 23, and Appendix A of FAR Pt 135. One prototype of each initial version was built; the first of these, the Dornier 228-100 (D-IFNS) made its first flight on 28 March 1981. The 228-200 (D-ICDO) flew for the first time on 9 May 1981. A static test airframe of the 228-200 was also completed.

British CAA and American FAA certification were granted on 17 April and 11 May 1984 respectively, followed by Australian certification on 11 October 1985; in addition, LBA certification has been accepted by the licensing authorities of Bhutan, India, Japan, Malaysia, Nigeria, Norway, Sweden and Taiwan. Firm orders totalled 108 by September 1986, from 39 different customers in 23 countries. At that time 90 had been delivered, with production continuing at the rate of three and a half aircraft per month.

In addition, on 29 November 1983 contracts were signed covering the transfer of technology in a progressive programme to manufacture versions of the Dornier 228 under licence in India, by the Kanpur Division of Hindustan Aeronautics Ltd. A production run of about 150 aircraft is envisaged, for various Indian organisations and customers, and was prefaced by the delivery of a 228-200 to Vayudoot, the Indian regional airline, on 15 November 1984. Following this, Dornier began delivery of complete sets of aircraft assemblies for final assembly at HAL's Kanpur facility in early 1985. Subsequently, seven shipsets of major assemblies, ten shipsets of subassemblies and ten component shipments for the phased licence production programme of HAL in India are to be completed by the Dornier plants at Munich. Indian licence production is based on a monthly production rate of two Dornier 228 aircraft. In order to meet urgent needs of some customers in India, such as Vayudoot, a few additional flyaway aircraft were obtained directly from Dornier.

The Indian Coast Guard and Navy are among early customers for the 228, the former's aircraft being maritime surveillance versions (see separate description) fitted with MEL Marec 2 search radar. They are operated by No. 750 Squadron at Daman. Indian Navy 228s (24 are reportedly on order) are expected to be armed with anti-shipping missiles.

Two Dornier 228-100s, named *Polar 2* and *Polar 4*, are specially equipped for the German Alfred-Wegener Institute of Polar Research (AWI) at Bremerhaven. They are fitted with wheel-ski landing gear, and are equipped for geophysical survey duties as detailed in the 1984-85 *Jane's*. In ski configuration, with a max T-O weight of 6,800 kg (14,990 lb), they can carry a max payload of 1,000 kg (2,205 lb) and have a range of up to 1,000 nm (1,853 km; 1,151 miles). Together with a specially equipped Dornier 128-6, also with wheel-ski gear, they began their successful work with German Antarctic expeditions in the South Polar Summer of 1983/84. On 19 November 1984 *Polar 2* and *Polar 3* became the first German aircraft to land at the South Pole. *Polar 4* succeeded *Polar 3*, which was reported by the Polisario rebels to have been shot down over the western Sahara on 24 February 1985.

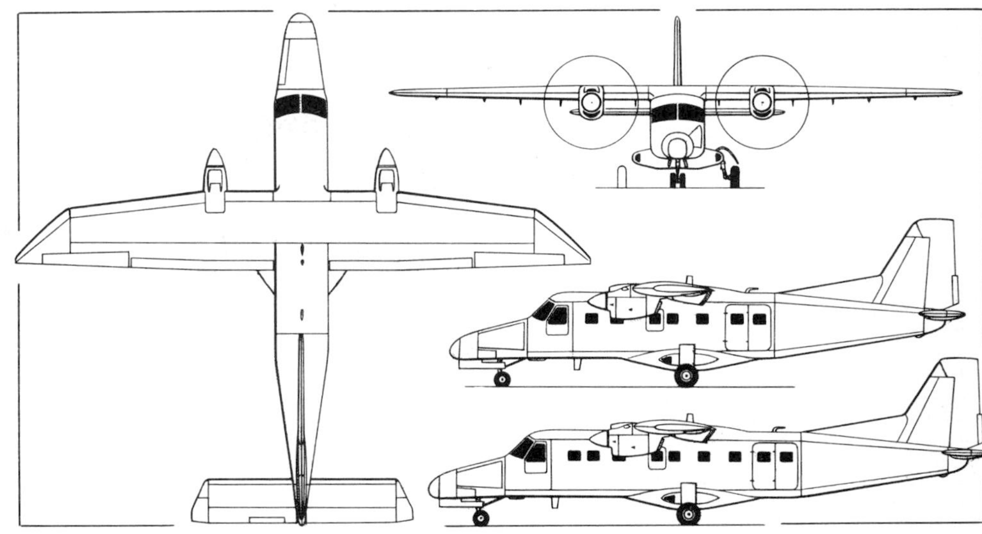
Dornier 228-100 light transport, with additional side view (bottom) of 228-200 *(Pilot Press)*

TYPE: Twin-turboprop light transport.

WINGS: Cantilever high-wing monoplane, comprising two-spar rectangular centre-section and two tapered outer panels ending in raked tips. Dornier Do A-5 supercritical wing section. No dihedral or anhedral. Sweepback on leading-edge of outer panels 8°. Wing leading-edge and raked wingtips of glassfibre/Kevlar composites. Remainder of wing of light alloy construction. Fowler single-slotted trailing-edge flaps and ailerons of carbonfibre composites. Ailerons can be drooped symmetrically to augment trailing-edge flaps, and are operated differentially to serve as conventional ailerons. Trim coupling of flaps and tailplane optional.

FUSELAGE: Conventional stressed skin unpressurised structure of light alloy, built in five sections. Glassfibre nose- and tailcones.

TAIL UNIT: Cantilever all-metal structure, with rudder and horizontal surfaces partly Eonnex covered. All-moving tailplane, with horn balanced elevators. Trim tab in rudder.

LANDING GEAR: Retractable tricycle type, with single wheel on each unit. Main units retract forward and inward into fairings built on to the lower fuselage. Hydraulically steerable nosewheel retracts forward. Goodyear wheels and tyres, size 8·50-10 on mainwheels (12 ply rating on 228-100, 10 ply rating on 228-200); size 6·00-6, 6 ply rating, on nosewheel. Low pressure tyres optional. Goodyear brakes on mainwheels.

POWER PLANT: Two 533 kW (715 shp) Garrett TPE331-5-252D turboprop engines, each driving a Hartzell HC-B4TN-5ML/LT10574 four-blade constant-speed fully-feathering reversible-pitch metal propeller. Primary wing box forms an integral fuel tank with a total usable capacity of 2,386 litres (525 Imp gallons).

The 19-passenger Dornier 228-201 twin-engined commuter and utility transport (two Garrett TPE331-5-252D turboprop engines)

ACCOMMODATION: Crew of two, and 15 or 19 passengers as described under model listings (16 passengers in -100 for Botswana, 20 in -200s for Bhutan and Taiwan), or 21 or 25 seats respectively in troop transport configuration. Pilots' seats adjustable fore and aft. Individual seats down each side of the cabin with a central aisle. Combined two-section passenger and freight door, with integral steps, on port side of cabin at rear. One emergency exit on port side of cabin, two on starboard side. Baggage compartment at rear of cabin, accessible externally and from cabin. Enlarged baggage door optional. Additional baggage space in fuselage nose. Modular units for rapid changes of role.

SYSTEMS: Entire accommodation heated and ventilated. Air-conditioning system optional. Heating by engine bleed air. Hydraulic system, pressure 207 bars (3,000 lb/sq in), for landing gear, brakes and nosewheel steering. Handpump for emergency landing gear extension. Primary 28V DC electrical system, supplied by two 28V 250A engine driven starter/generators and two 24V 25Ah nickel-cadmium batteries. Two 350VA inverters supply 115/26V 400Hz AC system. APU optional. Air intake anti-icing standard. De-icing system optional for wing and tail unit leading-edges, windscreen and propellers.

AVIONICS AND EQUIPMENT: Instrumentation for IFR flight standard. Autopilot optional, to permit single-pilot IFR operation. Standard avionics include dual King KY 196 VHF com, KN 53 VOR/ILS and KN 72 VOR/LOC converters; single KMR 675 marker beacon receiver, KR 87 ADF and KT 76A transponder; Aeronetics 7137 RMI; two Sperry GH14B gyro horizons; two King KPI 552 HSIs; Becker audio selector and intercom. Standard equipment includes complete internal and external lighting, hand fire extinguisher, first aid kit, gust control locks and tiedown kit. Wide range of optional avionics and equipment available. Equipment for a version to support oil pollution location and dispersal is under development.

DIMENSIONS, EXTERNAL:

Wing span	16·97 m (55 ft 8 in)
Wing aspect ratio	9·0
Length overall: 100	15·04 m (49 ft 4⅛ in)
200	16·56 m (54 ft 4 in)
Height overall	4·86 m (15 ft 11½ in)
Tailplane span	6·45 m (21 ft 2 in)
Wheel track	3·30 m (10 ft 10 in)
Wheelbase: 100	5·53 m (18 ft 1¾ in)
200	6·29 m (20 ft 7½ in)
Propeller diameter	2·73 m (8 ft 11½ in)
Passenger door (port, rear):	
Height	1·34 m (4 ft 4¾ in)
Width	0·64 m (2 ft 1¼ in)
Height to sill	0·60 m (1 ft 11½ in)
Freight door (port, rear):	
Height	1·34 m (4 ft 4¾ in)
Width, incl passenger door	1·28 m (4 ft 2½ in)
Emergency exits (each): Height	0·66 m (2 ft 2 in)
Width	0·48 m (1 ft 7 in)
Baggage door (nose): Height	0·50 m (1 ft 7½ in)
Width	1·32 m (4 ft 4 in)
Standard baggage door (rear):	
Height	0·76 m (2 ft 6 in)
Width	0·54 m (1 ft 9¼ in)

DIMENSIONS, INTERNAL:

Cabin, excl flight deck and rear baggage compartment:	
Length: 100	6·33 m (20 ft 9 in)
200	7·08 m (23 ft 2¾ in)
Max width	1·346 m (4 ft 5 in)
Max height	1·55 m (5 ft 1 in)
Floor area: 100	8·50 m² (91·49 sq ft)
200	9·56 m² (102·9 sq ft)
Volume: 100	13·00 m³ (459·1 cu ft)
200	14·70 m³ (519·1 cu ft)
Rear baggage compartment volume:	
100, standard	1·20 m³ (42·4 cu ft)
100, optional; 200, standard	2·60 m³ (91·8 cu ft)
Nose baggage compartment volume	0·89 m³ (31·4 cu ft)

AREAS:

Wings, gross	32·00 m² (344·3 sq ft)
Ailerons (total)	2·708 m² (29·15 sq ft)
Trailing-edge flaps (total)	5·872 m² (63·21 sq ft)
Fin, incl dorsal fin	4·50 m² (48·44 sq ft)
Rudder, incl tab	1·50 m² (16·15 sq ft)
Horizontal tail surfaces (total)	8·33 m² (89·66 sq ft)

WEIGHTS AND LOADINGS:

Weight empty, standard: 100	2,980 kg (6,570 lb)
101	2,990 kg (6,592 lb)
200	3,086 kg (6,803 lb)
201	3,096 kg (6,825 lb)
Operating weight empty: 100	3,413 kg (7,524 lb)
101	3,423 kg (7,546 lb)
200	3,547 kg (7,820 lb)
201	3,557 kg (7,842 lb)
Max payload: 100	2,127 kg (4,689 lb)
101	2,117 kg (4,667 lb)
200	1,993 kg (4,394 lb)
201	2,033 kg (4,482 lb)
Max ramp weight: 100, 200	5,730 kg (12,632 lb)
101, 201	6,010 kg (13,250 lb)
Max T-O weight: 100, 200	5,700 kg (12,566 lb)
101, 201	5,980 kg (13,183 lb)
Max landing weight: 100, 101, 200	5,700 kg (12,566 lb)
201	5,750 kg (12,676 lb)
Max wing loading:	
100, 200	178·1 kg/m² (36·48 lb/sq ft)
101, 201	186·9 kg/m² (38·28 lb/sq ft)
Max power loading:	
100, 200	5·35 kg/kW (8·79 lb/shp)
101, 201	5·61 kg/kW (9·22 lb/shp)

Dornier 228 German Polar research aircraft, fitted with various items of geophysical survey equipment

PERFORMANCE (at max T-O weight, S/L, ISA, except where indicated):

Max diving speed (all)	255 knots (472 km/h; 293 mph) IAS
Max cruising speed at 3,050 m (10,000 ft) (all)	231 knots (428 km/h; 266 mph)
Max cruising speed at S/L (all)	199 knots (370 km/h; 230 mph)
Stalling speed, flaps up:	
100	79 knots (146 km/h; 91 mph) IAS
200	81 knots (150 km/h; 93 mph) IAS
Stalling speed, flaps down:	
100	63 knots (117 km/h; 73 mph) IAS
200	67 knots (124 km/h; 77 mph) IAS
Max rate of climb at S/L:	
100, 200	618 m (2,025 ft)/min
101, 201	582 m (1,910 ft)/min
Rate of climb at S/L, one engine out:	
100, 200	162 m (531 ft)/min
101, 201	138 m (450 ft)/min
Service ceiling, 30·5 m (100 ft)/min rate of climb:	
100, 200	9,020 m (29,600 ft)
101, 201	8,535 m (28,000 ft)
Service ceiling, one engine out, 30·5 m (100 ft)/min rate of climb: 100, 200	4,265 m (14,000 ft)
T-O run: 100, 200	411 m (1,350 ft)
101, 201	442 m (1,450 ft)
T-O to 15 m (50 ft): 100, 200	564 m (1,850 ft)
101, 201	592 m (1,945 ft)
Landing from 15 m (50 ft) at max landing weight:	
100, 200	600 m (1,968 ft)
Range at 3,050 m (10,000 ft) with max passenger payload, max cruising speed:	
100	724 nm (1,343 km; 834 miles)
101	939 nm (1,740 km; 1,081 miles)
200	323 nm (600 km; 372 miles)
201	539 nm (1,000 km; 621 miles)
Max range at 3,050 m (10,000 ft) at econ cruising speed, 45 min reserves (all versions)	1,460 nm (2,704 km; 1,680 miles)

DORNIER 228 MARITIME PATROL

Dornier has developed two specialised versions of the Dornier 228-100 for maritime patrol. Designated Version A and Version B, they are equipped for particular roles as follows:

Dornier 228 Maritime Patrol Version A: Intended for surveillance of domestic and foreign fisheries; territorial tasks and activities of national safety relating to infiltration, prohibited border traffic and smuggling; and SAR. Ordered by Indian Coast Guard (three 228-101s). Primary surveillance sensor is an underfuselage MEL Marec 2 radar with 360° scan. The interior of the cabin is laid out to accommodate two observers, each with a forward facing seat adjacent to a bubble window at the forward end of the cabin; a radar operator's station is situated on the port side in a mid-cabin position. There are storage positions for a hand held camera and a crew liferaft. Two additional liferafts, each with capacity for 20 persons, are optional. There is a double entry door with airstair on the port side, just to the rear of the radar operator's position; a toilet towards the rear of the cabin on the starboard side; and, to its rear, storage and a deployment chute for marine markers, smoke floats and flares. Two 300A Lear Siegler starter/generators are standard to supply power for specialised equipment which, in addition to the Marec 2 radar, includes Global Navigation GNS-500A-3B VLF/Omega, Collins HF 220 HF com, Collins RT 1327/ARC VHF/AF-FM com, and Becker EB 3100 interphone. Additional equipment in the radar operator's console includes an airspeed indicator, altimeter and clock; Aeronetics Model 7137 RMI; VLF/Omega control unit; and a Becker ASI-3100 interphone. A Spectrol Sk-15 Nightscan steerable searchlight, mounted externally, is optional.

Dornier 228 Maritime Patrol Version B: Intended for surveillance of coastal waters to locate oil spills, survey sea traffic and protect fisheries. Secondary tasks include the detection of other pollution and the support of SAR missions. No orders announced up to mid-1986. Primary surveillance source is an Ericsson/Swedish Space Corporation SLAR. Standard cabin layout provides for the SLAR operator, adjacent to a bubble window on the port side of the cabin; an instrument console almost opposite the SLAR operator on the starboard side with, behind it, a desk and crew rest seat. There is stowage for a crew liferaft, and a toilet as in Version A, but the space behind it is available for installation of an optional Swedish Space Corporation SSP-1100 IR/UV scanner system. Other optional equipment includes Bendix RDR-1400 forward looking radar, Decca-Racal Mk 19 nav system with TANS, or Type 72 Doppler nav system with TANS, plus the additional equipment in the radar operator's console as detailed for Version A.

WEIGHTS (A: Version A; B: Version B):

Weight empty, standard:	
A, B	2,960 kg (6,526 lb)
Operating weight empty: A	3,935 kg (8,675 lb)
B	4,015 kg (8,852 lb)
Fuel weight: A, B	1,885 kg (4,155 lb)
Max T-O weight: A, B	5,980 kg (13,183 lb)
Typical zero-fuel weight:	
A, B	4,095 kg (9,028 lb)

PERFORMANCE (A and B at max T-O weight, ISA):

Average speed for max range	165 knots (305 km/h; 190 mph)
Average speed for max endurance	100 knots (185 km/h; 115 mph)
*Search time, max range cruise speed at 610 m (2,000 ft), search area adjacent to base	7 h 45 min
*Search time, max range cruise speed at 610 m (2,000 ft), search area 400 nm (740 km; 460 miles) from base	3 h 45 min
*Search time, max endurance cruise speed at 610 m (2,000 ft), search area adjacent to base	9 h 45 min
*Search time, max endurance cruise speed at 610 m (2,000 ft), search area 400 nm (740 km; 460 miles) from base	4 h 45 min

**Search time increased by approx 1 h 30 min if optional auxiliary fuel tank installed*

EQUATOR

EQUATOR AIRCRAFT GESELLSCHAFT FÜR FLUGZEUGBAU mbH ULM

Benzstrasse 15, D-7904 Erbach

Telephone: (073) 04 6116 and 05 6116

Telex: 712492

PRESIDENT: Günther H. Pöschel

This company was known until 1974 as Pöschel Aircraft GmbH. Its President designed and built the prototype P-300 Equator five/six-seat light STOL aircraft. This flew for the first time on 8 November 1970, powered by a 216 kW (290 hp) Avco Lycoming IO-540 flat-six engine, and was last described in the 1972-73 *Jane's*. A turboprop powered version of the design was then built as the P-400 Turbo-Equator STOL amphibian (see Addenda to 1977-78 *Jane's*). The configuration was subsequently changed extensively, and a common basic airframe is still being developed for a family of different models, as described in the 1984-85 *Jane's*.

EXTRA

EXTRA-FLUGZEUGBAU

Flugplatz Dinslaken, 4224 Hünxe
Telephone: 02858 6851
MANAGING DIRECTOR: Walter Extra

EXTRA 230

This single-seat aerobatic monoplane was designed for high performance competition work, to the requirements of leading pilots of the Swiss Aero-Club. The prototype (D-EHLE) was built by Walter Extra at Dinslaken, West Germany, under the patronage of the Thommen company, a Swiss manufacturer of precision and aircraft instruments, and was first flown in 1983.

Production is under way, and EA230s won seven of the first 28 places, including 3rd place, in the 1985 European Aerobatic Championships.

TYPE: Single-seat aerobatic aircraft.

WINGS: Cantilever mid-wing monoplane. Tapered wings, with square-cut tips and thick trailing-edge. Root and tip aerofoil sections of MA 15S and MA 12S respectively, resulting in a wing with virtually no curvature except on leading-edge. Incidence 0°. Structure comprises a box spar of high strength Polish pine, with pine capstrips and 'solid' ribs, covered with Dacron fabric and doped with an acrylic urethane paint. Long span ailerons (±26° deflection) occupy approx three-quarters of each trailing-edge. No flaps.

FUSELAGE: Steel tube mainframe, with aluminium alloy skin at front and on top-decking. Rear section covering similar to that of wings.

TAIL UNIT: Conventional wire braced structure of steel tube and bent sheet metal ribs; all parts fabric covered. Horn balanced rudder. Trim tab and servo tab in elevators. All control surfaces ±26° deflection.

LANDING GEAR: Non-retractable tailwheel type, with main-wheel units essentially similar to those of Christen Pitts Special, and Haigh steerable tailwheel. Mainwheel fairings optional.

POWER PLANT: One 171·5 kW (230 hp) Avco Lycoming AEIO-360 flat-four engine (DeMars modification). Mühlbauer two-blade constant-speed propeller, with composites-skinned wooden blades, McCauley hub, and large spinner. 12V battery for electric engine starting. Fuel capacity 80 litres (17·5 Imp gallons).

ACCOMMODATION: Single seat, under one-piece canopy which opens sideways to starboard.

DIMENSIONS, EXTERNAL:

Wing span	7·40 m (24 ft 3⅓ in)
Length overall	5·82 m (19 ft 1¼ in)
Height overall	1·73 m (5 ft 8¼ in)

WEIGHT:

Max T-O weight	550 kg (1,212 lb)

PERFORMANCE:

Never-exceed speed	220 knots (407 km/h; 253 mph)
Max level speed	190 knots (352 km/h; 218 mph) IAS
Stalling speed	38 knots (71 km/h; 44 mph) IAS
Roll rate at 160 knots (296 km/h; 184 mph) IAS	320°/s
Endurance with max fuel	2 h 30 min
g limits	±10

Extra 230 high performance aerobatic monoplane *(Wolfgang Wagner)*

Extra 230, owned by Swiss aerobatic champion Eric Müller *(Aviodata)*

GROB

BURKHART GROB FLUGZEUGBAU (Division of Grob-Werke GmbH & Co KG)

Postfach 150, 8948 Mindelheim
Telephone: 082 68 411
Telex: 5 39 623

Grob Flugzeugbau became established as a manufacturer of sailplanes in 1972, building the Schempp-Hirth Standard Cirrus under licence from that date until 1975. Since then the company has developed a family of sailplanes and the G 109B and G 111 motor gliders of its own design, of which details can be found in the Sailplanes section. Grob employed about 180 people in early 1986, by which time it had built 2,800 aircraft.

The Grob G 112 programme has been halted, and the Ranger will not go into production. All known details of these light aircraft were given in the 1985-86 *Jane's*.

GROB G 115

A prototype of this new light aircraft made its first flight in November 1985, powered by an 86·5 kW (116 hp) engine with fixed-pitch propeller. The second prototype, which flew in the Spring of 1986, was similarly powered, but introduced a taller fin and rudder and relocated tailplane. The third prototype, due to fly in the Summer of 1986, has a 119 kW (160 hp) engine and constant-speed propeller, and production aircraft will offer the same choice of engines and propellers. A constant-speed propeller for the lower-powered model is to be offered later.

The G 115 is being certificated to FAR Pt 23 standards, and the trials programme for LBA certification was well advanced by mid-1986, when nearly 90 hours had been flown by the first two prototypes.

TYPE: Two-seat light aircraft.

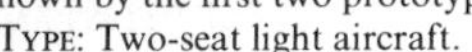

Prototype Grob G 115 two-seat light aircraft

AIRFRAME: Cantilever low-wing monoplane with non-retractable tricycle landing gear (speed fairings on 160 hp version). Construction mainly of GRP.

POWER PLANT: One 86·5 kW (116 hp) Avco Lycoming O-235 flat-four engine with two-blade fixed-pitch propeller with spinner; or one 119 kW (160 hp) Avco Lycoming O-320 with constant-speed propeller. Fuel capacity 100 litres (22 Imp gallons).

ACCOMMODATION: Two seats side by side under one-piece rearward sliding framed canopy, with dual controls. Baggage space behind seats.

AVIONICS: To customer's requirements. Instrument panel will accommodate full IFR instrumentation.

DIMENSIONS, EXTERNAL:
- Wing span 10·00 m (32 ft 9¾ in)
- Wing aspect ratio 8·19
- Length overall 7·36 m (24 ft 1¾ in)
- Height overall 2·75 m (9 ft 0¼ in)

AREA:
- Wings, gross 12·21 m² (131·4 sq ft)

WEIGHTS AND LOADINGS (A: 116 hp, B: 160 hp):
- Weight empty: A 550 kg (1,212 lb)
- B 580 kg (1,278 lb)
- Fuel weight: A 72 kg (159 lb)
- B 108 kg (238 lb)
- Max T-O weight: A 850 kg (1,874 lb)
- B 900 kg (1,984 lb)
- Max wing loading: A 69·61 kg/m² (14·26 lb/sq ft)
- B 73·71 kg/m² (15·10 lb/sq ft)
- Max power loading: A 9·83 kg/kW (16·15 lb/hp)
- B 7·55 kg/kW (12·40 lb/hp)

PERFORMANCE (at max T-O weight, A and B as above):
- Max level speed: A 129 knots (240 km/h; 149 mph)
- B 167 knots (310 km/h; 192 mph)
- Cruising speed, 75% power:
- A 121 knots (225 km/h; 140 mph)
- B 151 knots (280 km/h; 174 mph)
- Stalling speed: A 46 knots (85 km/h; 53 mph)
- B 48 knots (88 km/h; 55 mph)
- Max rate of climb at S/L: A 246 m (807 ft)/min
- B 300 m (984 ft)/min
- T-O run: A 210 m (689 ft)
- B 200 m (656 ft)
- T-O to 15 m (50 ft): A 410 m (1,345 ft)
- B 390 m (1,280 ft)
- Range with max fuel:
- A 540 nm (1,000 km; 621 miles)
- B 755 nm (1,400 km; 870 miles)

GYROFLUG

GYROFLUG INGENIEURGESELLSCHAFT mbH

Flughafen, 7570 Baden-Baden/Oos
Telephone: (07221) 65061
Telex: 781 300 LEMEG
PRESIDENT: Dipl-Ing Justus Dornier
MANAGING DIRECTOR: Dr-Ing Christian Hoseit
DIRECTOR, SALES AND MARKETING: Klaus Heege

Gyroflug was formed in August 1978 to develop, manufacture and market the two-seat SC 01 Speed Canard light aircraft. Its founders had flown, in April 1977, the first Rutan VariEze completed in Europe (D-EEEZ). Unlike the VariEze (see Rutan entry in Homebuilts section of 1985-86 *Jane's*), the Speed Canard is a ready to fly certificated production aircraft. Gyroflug became a member company of the Justus Dornier Group in late 1984.

GYROFLUG SC 01 B SPEED CANARD

As well as being slightly larger overall than the Rutan VariEze, from which it is basically derived, the Speed Canard differs in a number of important details. Its 22° swept wing retains the NASA winglets that have proved so successful on the original design, but utilises a new Eppler E793 aerofoil section (E1231 on foreplane) which is claimed to reduce drag by 30 per cent. Instead of retaining the glassfibre/foam core structure of the VariEze, the Speed Canard is made of GRP and CFRP laid up in female moulds, giving a lighter structure optimised for series production. The forward fuselage embodies a flush canopy similar to that of the Grob Twin Astir, with the rear seat raised to ensure a good field of view for both occupants, and there is space for 15 kg (33 lb) of baggage aft of the rear seat. The cockpit can be equipped to full IFR standards, including autopilot, and is heated and ventilated. The tricycle landing gear has fixed main units of glassfibre, with size 5·00-5 wheels enclosed in speed fairings; the 10 × 3·5-4 nosewheel is electrically retractable. The wings are detachable for transport and storage.

Standard power plant is an 86·5 kW (116 hp) Avco Lycoming O-235-P2A flat-four engine, driving a Hoffmann HO-V113B-L/LD 150+2A three-blade constant-speed pusher propeller with spinner. Two integral fuel tanks in the wing centre-section strakes have a combined capacity of 160 litres (35·2 Imp gallons).

The first pre-production prototype (D-EEEX) made its first flight on 2 December 1980, and a second (D-EEEW) was flown on 17 April 1983. German LBA certification was granted on 30 September 1983.

By early 1986 orders for more than 30 Speed Canards had been received, and production was at the approximate rate of one per month. Wings and other glassfibre components are manufactured by Glaser-Dirks; final assembly is by Gyroflug.

Manufacture of the initial SC 01 production version ended in September 1985 with c/n 23, the 20th production aircraft. Current production version in 1986 was the **SC 01 B**, which has enlarged winglets and minor improvements. This version can be powered optionally by a 119 kW (160 hp) Avco Lycoming O-320-D1A engine with an MT-Propeller MTV-6-C/LD152-07 propeller, considerably increasing take-off and climb performance. In this form it is known as the **SC 01 B-160**. Ten B/B-160s had been completed by May 1986, and a number of earlier examples had been modified to B standard.

Gyroflug SC 01 B-160 Speed Canard two-seat light aircraft

A decision on whether to proceed with a four-seat version was expected before the end of 1986.

DIMENSIONS, EXTERNAL:
- Wing span 7·77 m (25 ft 6 in)
- Foreplane span 3·60 m (11 ft 9¾ in)
- Foreplane chord (constant) 0·34 m (1 ft 1¾ in)
- Wing aspect ratio 7·70
- Foreplane aspect ratio 10·62
- Length overall 4·70 m (15 ft 5 in)
- Length of fuselage 4·40 m (14 ft 5¼ in)
- Max width of fuselage 0·74 m (2 ft 5 in)
- Height overall 1·81 m (5 ft 11¼ in)
- Wheel track 1·66 m (5 ft 5⅓ in)
- Wheelbase 2·47 m (8 ft 1¼ in)
- Propeller diameter 1·52 m (5 ft 0 in)

DIMENSIONS, INTERNAL:
- Cockpit: Max length 2·80 m (9 ft 2¼ in)
- Max width 0·64 m (2 ft 1¼ in)
- Max height 0·99 m (3 ft 3 in)

AREAS:
- Wings, gross 7·84 m² (84·39 sq ft)
- Foreplane, gross 1·22 m² (13·13 sq ft)
- Ailerons (total) 0·376 m² (4·05 sq ft)
- Winglets (total) 2·20 m² (23·68 sq ft)
- Rudders (total) 0·168 m² (1·81 sq ft)
- Elevators (total) 0·66 m² (7·10 sq ft)

WEIGHTS AND LOADINGS:
- Weight empty: B 420 kg (926 lb)
- B-160 440 kg (970 lb)
- Max fuel (both) 115 kg (253 lb)
- Max payload: B 188 kg (414·5 lb)
- B-160 204 kg (450 lb)
- Max T-O weight: B 680 kg (1,499 lb)
- B-160 715 kg (1,576 lb)
- Max landing weight: B, B-160 680 kg (1,499 lb)
- Max wing/foreplane loading:
- B 75·05 kg/m² (15·38 lb/sq ft)
- B-160 78·92 kg/m² (16·16 lb/sq ft)
- Max power loading: B 7·86 kg/kW (12·92 lb/hp)
- B-160 5·01 kg/kW (9·85 lb/hp)

PERFORMANCE (at max T-O weight):
- Never-exceed speed (both) 197 knots (365 km/h; 226 mph) IAS
- Max level speed at S/L:
- B 146 knots (270 km/h; 168 mph)
- B-160 159 knots (295 km/h; 183 mph)
- Max cruising speed, 75% power:
- B at 1,830 m (6,000 ft) 143 knots (265 km/h; 165 mph)
- B-160 at 2,135 m (7,000 ft) 153 knots (283 km/h; 176 mph)
- Econ cruising speed, 65% power:
- B at 3,050 m (10,000 ft) 138 knots (257 km/h; 160 mph)
- B-160 at 3,350 m (11,000 ft) 148 knots (275 km/h; 171 mph)
- Stalling speed (both) 57 knots (105 km/h; 66 mph) IAS
- Max rate of climb at S/L: B 300 m (985 ft)/min
- B-160 396 m (1,300 ft)/min
- Service ceiling: B 4,420 m (14,500 ft)
- B-160 5,640 m (18,500 ft)
- T-O run: B 450 m (1,475 ft)
- B-160 350 m (1,150 ft)
- T-O to 15 m (50 ft): B 700 m (2,300 ft)
- B-160 540 m (1,770 ft)
- Landing from 15 m (50 ft) (both) 700 m (2,300 ft)
- Landing run (both) 300 m (985 ft)
- Range at S/L with max fuel, 45 min reserves:
- 75% power: B 728 nm (1,350 km; 839 miles)
- B-160 553 nm (1,025 km; 637 miles)
- 45% power: B 1,011 nm (1,875 km; 1,165 miles)
- B-160 715 nm (1,325 km; 823 miles)
- *g* limits +4·4/−2·2

MBB

MESSERSCHMITT-BÖLKOW-BLOHM GmbH

Postfach 801109, 8000 München 80
Telephone: (089) 6000 0
Telex: 5287-310 mbb d

PRESIDENT AND GENERAL MANAGER:
Dr-Ing Hanns Arnt Vogels

EXECUTIVE VICE-PRESIDENT (EXTERNAL AFFAIRS AND SALES) AND DEPUTY GENERAL MANAGER: Sepp Hort

EXECUTIVE VICE-PRESIDENTS:
Dr Johannes Broschwitz
Dr Carl Peter Fichtmüller
Dr-Ing Othmar Heise
Ulrich Jacubowski
Günther Kuhlo
Hartmut Mehdorn

CHAIRMAN OF THE SUPERVISORY BOARD: Dr h.c. Max Streibl
PUBLIC RELATIONS: Hans-Ulrich Pieper

In May 1969 the former Messerschmitt-Bölkow GmbH and Hamburger Flugzeugbau GmbH (see 1968-69 *Jane's*) merged to form a new group known as Messerschmitt-Bölkow-Blohm GmbH. Subsequently, in 1980, the Federal German government expressed its wish that MBB and VFW should merge, to strengthen the capabilities and competitive position of the two companies, and to help improve the structure of the German aerospace industry. Following approval by the shareholders of both companies, MBB acquired all shares of VFW on 1 January 1981. Shareholders in the company are Bayerisch-Hamburgische Beteiligungsgesellschaft mbH (35·28%), Fides Industrie-Beteiligungsgesellschaft mbH (20%), ABM Beteiligungs-gesellschaft mbH (19·02%), BD Industrie-Beteiligungs-gesellschaft mbH (10%), the State of Bavaria (7·02%), the Willy and Lilly Messerschmitt Foundation (7%), Dr-Ing h.c. Ludwig Bölkow (1%), and the Blohm family (0·68%). The MBB group employed a total of 36,915 people at the end of 1985.

Integration of the two companies has taken place progressively. Aerospace and defence activities are now handled by the individual divisions listed in this entry. Diversified non-aerospace activities are undertaken by the Industrial Products Group and the Energy and Process Technology Division.

HELICOPTER AND MILITARY AIRCRAFT GROUP
(Helicopter Division and Military Aircraft Division)

Postfach 801160, 8000 München 80
Telephone: (089) 6000 3444
Telex: 5287-710/740 mbb d

WORKS: Ottobrunn, Donauwörth, Augsburg, Manching, Laupheim and Speyer
GROUP PRESIDENT: Dr Carl Peter Fichtmüller
GROUP SENIOR VICE-PRESIDENT, MARKETING:
Kurt Pfleiderer
GROUP VICE-PRESIDENTS:
Oskar Friedrich (Senior V-P, Military Aircraft Division)
Volker von Tein (V-P, Helicopter Division)

Helicopter activities of this Group include the manufacturing of civil and military versions of the MBB BO 105 helicopter, the MBB/Kawasaki BK 117 and Eurocopter programmes (described in the International section), and the ALH programme in co-operation with Hindustan Aeronautics Ltd (see Indian section). Main production centre for the BO 105 and BK 117 is MBB's Donauwörth factory. The Division also assumed the former VFW responsibility for overhaul and repair of Sikorsky CH-53G and Westland Sea King Mk 41 helicopters in service with the West German armed forces, and is currently upgrading 22 German Navy Sea Kings with Ferranti Seaspray Mk 3 radar, a Ferranti Link II target data transformer, AEG ALR-69 radar warning receiver, Tracor M130 chaff/flare dispenser and four BAe Sea Skua missiles. Under study, with the company designation BO 125, is a light transport helicopter (LTH) for service in the 1990s. International collaboration on this programme is planned.

Major military aircraft activities of the Group involve the Panavia Tornado (see International section), for which MBB is the German prime contractor; weapon system leadership for F-104G Starfighters of the Luftwaffe; modifications to improve the combat capability of Luftwaffe F-4F and RF-4E Phantoms; development of control configured vehicle (CCV) technology, using a modified F-104G aircraft; and participation in the European manufacturing programme for the General Dynamics F-16 combat aircraft.

In the Tornado programme, MBB is building centre-fuselages for all production aircraft, and is responsible for final assembly and flight testing of the aircraft required by the Luftwaffe and Marineflieger. Improvements are currently being made to the optical and electronic reconnaissance equipment in the Luftwaffe's RF-4E Phantoms, which are being armed to enable them to be used also in a fighter-bomber role. An enhancement programme for the F-4F tactical fighter is also under way.

The company has been engaged for a considerable time in intensive studies to define a new generation tactical fighter aircraft for the Luftwaffe and other European air forces in the 1990s (see Eurofighter entry in International section). In addition, it is conducting research and development programmes concerned with carbonfibre technology, and the creation of more simple, more reliable aircraft subsystems.

TRANSPORT AIRCRAFT GROUP

Postfach 950109, 2103 Hamburg 95
Telephone: (040) 7437 1
Telex: 21950-0 mbbh d

WORKS: Hamburg-Finkenwerder, Bremen, Einswarden, Varel, Lemwerder and Stade

GROUP PRESIDENT: Hartmut Mehdorn

MBB's Transport Aircraft Group, with 13,600 employees in six factories in northern Germany, is involved in manufacture and development of several international European collaborative programmes, its workload being divided between the Airbus A300/310/320 programmes (68%), Fokker 100 (5%), Transall C-160 (6%), Panavia Tornado (15%), and miscellaneous programmes (6%). Maintenance and conversion work on Airbus and other aircraft, for customers throughout the world, is carried out at Lemwerder as part of MBB's product support activities. Airspares in Hamburg provides a worldwide 24 h spares service for the company.

MBB is working intensively on the development and application of carbonfibre reinforced plastics (CFRP). Spoilers and rudders of this material are produced for Airbus aircraft, and a fin box for the Swissair A310-300, designed and manufactured by MBB, is currently the largest CFRP aircraft component made in Europe. The A320 is fitted with CFRP horizontal and vertical tail surfaces, which save 25 per cent in weight compared to metal equivalents and also minimise corrosion. Compared with 2,000 detail parts in the metal version, a CFRP tail-fin has only 99.

DEFENCE SYSTEMS GROUP
(Dynamics Division and Marine and Special Products Division)

DYNAMICS DIVISION:
Postfach 801149, 8000 München 80
Telephone: (089) 6000 6056
Telex: 5287-0 mbb d
MARINE AND SPECIAL PRODUCTS DIVISION:
Postfach 107845, 2800 Bremen 1
Telephone: (0421) 538-1
Telex: 245821 mbb d
WORKS: Ottobrunn, Bremen, Kassel, Nabern/Teck and Schrobenhausen
GROUP PRESIDENT: Günther Kuhlo
GROUP SENIOR VICE-PRESIDENT:
Dr Hans-Jürgen Blankenagel

Dynamics Division is engaged in a number of missile programmes including those for the MBB Kormoran, Euromissile Hot and Aérospatiale/MBB ANS described in the Air-Launched Missiles section. Others include Armbrust, Jupiter, Milan, MLRS, Patriot, Roland and RAM.

Since 1966, MBB has been developing a special type of conventional weapon system, designated **MW-1**, which is carried by the Tornado. A derivative MDS (Modular Dispenser System) can be carried by such other aircraft as the F-4, F-5, F/A-18 and Mirage. Now in production, the MW-1 consists of a dispenser carried under the aircraft's belly, from which a large number of small munitions can be ejected pyrotechnically. For use against tanks, the munitions may be shaped-charge bombs which detonate on impact or mines that are set off when the tanks run over them. They can be of types designed to destroy airfield runways, splinter mines with fuses triggered by aircraft movements, and for the future a type designed to destroy aircraft inside shelters.

The submunitions developed for the MW-1 are used also in other families of air-to-surface weapons, such as Apache/CWS. Further details can be found in the Air-Launched Missiles section of this edition.

Marine and Special Products Division was formed in April 1981 to continue the maritime programmes of VFW, and to initiate new activities. The Division is involved extensively in RPV development and production, as described under the MBB entry in the appropriate section of this edition; and in diversified MBB activities which include airborne subsystems, training systems and simulators, measuring and tracking systems, test and automation systems, and logistics.

SPACE SYSTEMS GROUP (MBB/ERNO)

Postfach 105909, 2800 Bremen 1
Telephone: (0421) 539 4348
Telex: 245548a erno d

Postfach 801169, 8000 München 80
Telephone: (089) 6000 3738
Telex: 5287-0 mbb d

WORKS: Bremen and Ottobrunn

GROUP PRESIDENT: Dr-Ing Othmar Heise
GROUP SENIOR VICE-PRESIDENT, MARKETING:
H. E. W. Hoffmann
GROUP VICE-PRESIDENTS, TECHNICAL OPERATIONS:
Klaus Berge (Bremen)
Ernst Högenauer (Ottobrunn)

Space programmes in which MBB/ERNO is or has recently been involved include orbital systems (Spacelab, Columbus, SPAS, Eureca, Polar Platform); communications satellites (DFS-Kopernikus, ECS, Marecs, Intelsat V and VI, TV-Sat/TDF-1, Tele-X, Spacebus); scientific and applications satellites (Exosat, Giotto, Hipparcos, ISO, Cluster/Soho, Meteosat, ERS 1 and 2, Seres, Navsat/Granas); payloads; launchers (including Ariane) and propulsion systems; space services; and ground stations. Details of many of the spacecraft mentioned can be found in the Spaceflight section of the 1983-84 and earlier editions of *Jane's*, or in *Jane's Spaceflight Directory*.

INDUSTRIAL PRODUCTS GROUP

Postfach 801109, 8000 München 80
GROUP PRESIDENT: Dr Gerhard Widl

This Group is responsible for all activities which are not part of MBB's aerospace and defence work. It consists of six product divisions for data technology, industrial electronics, automation technology, transportation technology, high-performance composite materials technology, and medical technology.

ENERGY AND PROCESS TECHNOLOGY DIVISION

Postfach 801109, 8000 München 80
DIVISION PRESIDENT: Karl-Heinz Brachthäuser

Activities of this Division include biotechnology, solar energy systems, wind energy plants, vacuum superinsulation systems, photovoltaics, and special instrumentation and control systems.

MBB/KAWASAKI BK 117

MBB has developed and is building in conjunction with Kawasaki of Japan an 8/11-seat multi-purpose helicopter known as the BK 117. A description of this aircraft can be found in the International section.

MBB/IPTN BN-109

The BN-109 is a small four-seat helicopter being developed in collaboration with the Indonesian aircraft industry (see NTT entry in International section).

MBB BO 105

Design of this light utility helicopter was started in July 1962 and construction of prototypes began in 1964, under Federal German government contract. The first BO 105 prototype was fitted with an existing conventional rotor and two Allison 250-C18 turboshaft engines; subsequent aircraft, of which the first one flew in February 1967, have had a rotor system based on a rigid titanium hub, with feathering hinges only, and hingeless flexible glassfibre blades. From the Spring of 1970 'droop-snoot' rotor blades of MBB design have been standard.

Details of prototypes, early BO 105C and D production helicopters and special variants can be found in previous editions of *Jane's*. Production of 100 BO 105 M (VBH) and 212 BO 105 P (PAH-1) military versions for the Federal German Army ended in 1984, and details of these versions can be found in the 1985-86 edition. By 1 January 1986 a total of 1,148 BO 105s of all models had been delivered, to 37 countries in five continents. Current models are as follows:

BO 105 CB. Standard production version since 1975, with two Allison 250-C20B engines, operable in air temperatures ranging from −45° to +54°C. LBA certification received in November 1976.

BO 105 CBS. Version with increased seating or cargo capacity in a 0·25 m (10 in) longer fuselage. Available in five-seat executive or six-seat high density configurations. Identified by small additional window aft of rear door on each side. Marketed in the USA, by MBB Helicopter Corporation, under the name **Twin Jet II**. Certificated in early 1983 by FAA for IFR operation in accordance with SFAR Pt 29-4, requiring two pilots, radar, Loran-C and a separate battery, but not a stability augmentation system, though SAS is available as an option.

BO 105 LS. Produced in Canada since 1985 and described separately under MBB entry in Canadian section. Five pre-production models produced in Germany during 1984.

Twelve Mexican Navy BO 105s are used for maritime patrol, fishery protection, anti-smuggling, and search and rescue duties from shore bases and corvettes of the 'Halcón' class. First BO 105s operated from ships designed especially for the purpose, these aircraft are equipped with search radar, flotation gear, a system to wash salt deposits from the engines, special deck lashing fixtures, and folding rotor blades to permit stowage in the shipboard hangars.

Twenty BO 105 CBs, equipped with Saab/Emerson

Helitow TOW missile systems, and Saab Helios sights providing night vision and laser capability, were ordered in July 1984 by the Swedish procurement agency FMV, for anti-tank operation by the Swedish Army. Deliveries of these are to begin in early 1987. In April 1985 the same agency ordered four BO 105 CBSs, in IFR search and rescue configuration, for use by the Swedish Air Force. All four were delivered in late 1985 and early 1986.

In Indonesia, IPTN (which see) is participating in a licence assembly programme for the BO 105. A contract for 60 BO 105 CBs was signed by the Spanish Ministry of Defence in late June 1979. Fifty-seven of these aircraft were assembled in Spain, including some parts manufacture, by CASA. They are operated by Spanish Army aviation units for armed reconnaissance (18), observation (14) and anti-tank (28) missions. CASA is now assembling further BO 105s, and had delivered a total of 100 to its customers by the end of 1985.

The description which follows applies to the BO 105 CB except where indicated:

Type: Five-seat light helicopter.

Rotor System: Four-blade main rotor, comprising rigid titanium head and GRP blades, with titanium anti-erosion strip forming leading-edge and vibration damper on each blade. MBB designed 'droop-snoot' blades of NACA 23012 asymmetrical section, having a specially designed trailing-edge giving improved control in pitching moment. Flexible tension/torsion blade retention, to take up centrifugal forces. Roller bearings for pitch change. Main rotor blade folding optional. Two-blade semi-rigid tail rotor; blades of GRP, with stainless steel anti-erosion strip on leading-edge. Main rotor rpm 424. Tail rotor rpm 2,220.

Rotor Drive: Main transmission utilises two bevel gear input stages with freewheeling clutches and a spur collector gear stage. Planetary reduction gear; three auxiliary drives for accessories. Main transmission rated for twin-engine input of 257 kW (345 shp) per engine, or a single engine input of 283 kW (380 shp). Main rotor brake standard. Tail rotor gearbox on fin. Main rotor/engine rpm ratio 1 : 14·2. Tail rotor/engine rpm ratio 1 : 2·7.

Fuselage: Conventional light alloy semi-monocoque structure of pod and boom type. Glassfibre reinforced cowling over power plant. Titanium sheet engine deck.

Tail Unit: Horizontal stabiliser of conventional light alloy construction with small endplate fins.

Landing Gear: Skid type, with cross-tubes designed for energy absorption by plastic deformation in the event of a heavy landing. Inflatable emergency floats can be attached to skids.

Power Plant: Two 313 kW (420 shp) Allison 250-C20B turboshaft engines, each with a max continuous rating of 298 kW (400 shp). Bladder fuel tanks under cabin floor, capacity 580 litres (127·5 Imp gallons), of which 570 litres (125·3 Imp gallons) are usable. Fuelling point on port side of cabin. Auxiliary tanks in freight compartment available optionally. Oil capacity: engine 12 litres (2·6 Imp gallons), gearbox 11·6 litres (2·55 Imp gallons).

Accommodation: Pilot and co-pilot or passenger on individual longitudinally adjustable front seats with safety belts and automatic locking shoulder harnesses. Optional dual controls. Bench seat at rear for three persons, removable for cargo and stretcher carrying. Both cabin and cargo compartment have panelling, sound insulation and floor covering. Entire rear fuselage aft of seats and under power plant available as freight and baggage space, with access through two clamshell doors at rear. Two standard stretchers can be accommodated side by side in ambulance role. One forward opening hinged and jettisonable door and one sliding door on each side of cabin. Ram air and electrical ventilation system. Heating system optional.

Systems: Tandem fully redundant hydraulic system, pressure 103·5 bars (1,500 lb/sq in), for powered main rotor controls. System flow rate 6·2 litres (1·36 Imp gallons)/min. Bootstrap/oil reservoir, pressurised at 1·7 bars (25 lb/sq in). Electrical system powered by two 150A 28V DC starter/generators and a 24V 25Ah nickel-cadmium battery; external power socket.

Avionics and Equipment: Standard equipment includes basic flight instruments, engine instruments, heated pitot, tiedown rings in cargo compartment, cabin and cargo compartment dome lights, position lights and collision warning lights. A wide range of optional avionics and equipment is available, including stability augmentation system, Doppler navigation, search radar, dual controls, heating system, windscreen wiper, rescue winch, landing light, searchlight, externally mounted loudspeaker, fuel dump valve, external load hook, settling protectors, snow skids, and main rotor blade folding. GEC Avionics AD 2780 Tacan in aircraft of Royal Netherlands Air Force. A completely equipped ambulance version is available.

Armament (military versions): Provision for a variety of alternative military loads, including six Hot or eight TOW anti-tank missiles and associated stabilised sight, or a Saab-Emerson Helitow installation (see accompanying photograph).

Dimensions, external:

Main rotor diameter 9·84 m (32 ft 3½ in)

MBB BO 105 CB offshore helicopter operated in Antarctica

BO 105 CB anti-tank helicopter with Saab-Emerson Helitow missile system

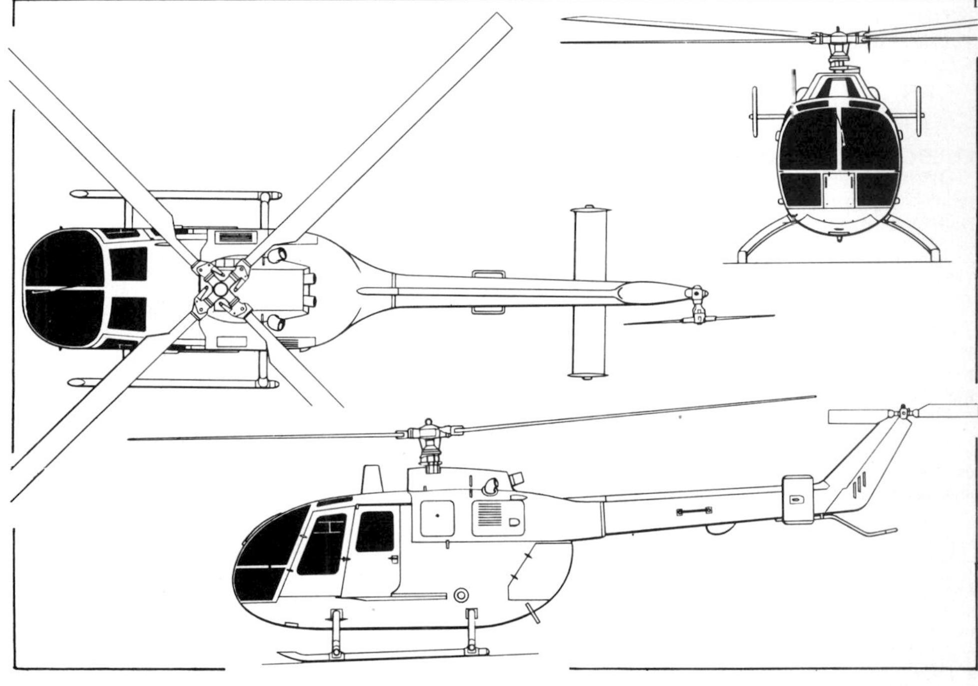

BO 105 CB five-seat light helicopter (two Allison 250-C20B turboshaft engines) *(Pilot Press)*

Tail rotor diameter	1·90 m (6 ft 2¾ in)
Main rotor blade chord	0·27 m (10⅝ in)
Tail rotor blade chord	0·18 m (7 in)
Distance between rotor centres	5·95 m (19 ft 6¼ in)
Length, incl main and tail rotors	11·86 m (38 ft 11 in)
Length, excl rotors: CB	8·56 m (28 ft 1 in)
CBS	8·81 m (28 ft 11 in)
Length of fuselage pod: CB	4·30 m (14 ft 1 in)
CBS	4·55 m (14 ft 11 in)
Height to top of main rotor head	3·00 m (9 ft 10 in)
Width over skids: unladen	2·53 m (8 ft 3½ in)
laden	2·58 m (8 ft 5½ in)
Rear loading doors: Height	0·64 m (2 ft 1 in)
Width	1·40 m (4 ft 7 in)

DIMENSIONS, INTERNAL:

Cabin, incl cargo compartment:	
Max width	1·40 m (4 ft 7 in)
Max height	1·25 m (4 ft 1 in)
Volume	4·80 m³ (169 cu ft)
Cargo compartment: Length	1·85 m (6 ft 0¾ in)
Max width	1·20 m (3 ft 11¼ in)
Max height	0·57 m (1 ft 10½ in)
Floor area	2·25 m² (24·2 sq ft)
Volume	1·30 m³ (45·9 cu ft)

AREAS:

Main rotor disc	76·05 m² (818·6 sq ft)
Tail rotor disc	2·835 m² (30·5 sq ft)

WEIGHTS AND LOADING:

Weight empty, basic: CB	1,276 kg (2,813 lb)
CBS	1,301 kg (2,868 lb)
Standard fuel (usable)	456 kg (1,005 lb)
Fuel, incl auxiliary tanks	776 kg (1,710 lb)
Standard T-O weight	2,400 kg (5,291 lb)
Max T-O weight	2,500 kg (5,511 lb)
Max disc loading	32·9 kg/m² (6·74 lb/sq ft)

PERFORMANCE (A at 2,400 kg; 5,291 lb gross weight, B at 2,500 kg; 5,511 lb max T-O weight):

Never-exceed speed at S/L:	
A	145 knots (270 km/h; 167 mph)
B	131 knots (242 km/h; 150 mph)
Max cruising speed at S/L:	
A, B	131 knots (242 km/h; 150 mph)
Best range speed at S/L:	
A, B	110 knots (204 km/h; 127 mph)
Max rate of climb at S/L, max continuous power:	
A	480 m (1,575 ft)/min
B	419 m (1,375 ft)/min
Vertical rate of climb at S/L, T-O power:	
A	183 m (600 ft)/min
B	91 m (300 ft)/min
Max operating altitude: A	5,180 m (17,000 ft)
B	3,050 m (10,000 ft)
Service ceiling, one engine out (30·5 m; 100 ft/min climb reserve, T-O power): A	890 m (2,920 ft)
Hovering ceiling IGE, T-O power:	
A	2,560 m (8,400 ft)
B	1,525 m (5,000 ft)
Hovering ceiling OGE, T-O power:	
A	1,615 m (5,300 ft)
B	457 m (1,500 ft)
Range with standard fuel and max payload, no reserves:	
at S/L: A	310 nm (575 km; 357 miles)
B	307 nm (570 km; 354 miles)
at 1,525 m (5,000 ft): A	355 nm (657 km; 408 miles)
B	321 nm (596 km; 370 miles)
Ferry range with auxiliary tanks, no reserves:	
at S/L: A	540 nm (1,000 km; 621 miles)
B	537 nm (995 km; 618 miles)
at 1,525 m (5,000 ft):	
A	600 nm (1,112 km; 691 miles)
B	550 nm (1,020 km; 634 miles)
Endurance with standard fuel and max payload, no reserves:	
at S/L: A	3 h 30 min
B	3 h 24 min

CBS version of the BO 105 in executive configuration

MBB VFW 614 ATTAS

Conversion has been completed at Bremen and Lemwerder of a twin-turbofan VFW 614 transport as a research aircraft for the DFVLR, the West German aerospace research establishment. The aircraft (c/n G 17, D-ADAM), is to be used in developing and evaluating future flight control concepts for civil air transports; the acronym ATTAS stands for advanced technologies testing aircraft system.

Delivery of the ATTAS aircraft to the DFVLR took place in the late Autumn of 1985. After about a year spent in implementing the data processing system, followed by flight testing, it was expected to be ready for service in late 1986. Primarily, this service will consist of:

(1) Testing and evaluating the new concept for use within integrated digital flight control systems, including navigation and air traffic control, in particular using a microwave landing system and position-finding and navigation systems;

(2) Testing of flight and systems characteristics by in-flight simulation; and

(3) Study of aerodynamic questions, in particular in connection with the boundary layer and fast-moving flaps.

The flight deck is equipped with separate controls for the safety pilot and the evaluating pilot, together with an artificial feel system for the latter. It also has experimental instrumentation and monitoring equipment for the fly by wire system. The main cabin has control consoles for various tasks and data acquisition, conditioning and processing equipment racks. The control system features error-detecting electric and electrohydraulic controls for the control surfaces and their actuators. It involves the elevators, rudder, tailerons, engines, direct lift flaps and landing flaps, with varying degrees of magnification.

MBB F-4F ICE PROGRAMME

Under a German Defence Ministry programme known as ICE (improved combat efficiency), 75 Luftwaffe F-4F Phantom IIs of fighter wings JG 71 and JG 74 are to be upgraded to give them a lookdown/shootdown capability against multiple targets. The programme, for which MBB is the prime contractor, was initiated in late 1983 and reached the end of the definition phase some two years later. It was expected to enter the full scale development phase in 1986, with first flight planned for late 1987/early 1988 and initial operational capability in 1991.

Main ingredient of this retrofit programme involves replacement of the existing Westinghouse APQ-120 radar with the all-digital multi-mode Hughes APG-65, built under licence in Germany by AEG. This advanced X band system has 30 air-to-air and air-to-ground modes, with a ten-target track-while-scan capability, of which eight can be displayed simultaneously. APG-65 subsystems include a low sidelobe planar array antenna, a 16-bit (256 K) memory, and a radar data processor with advanced ECCM. Armament capability of the ICE Phantoms will be extended to include up to four Hughes AIM-120 (AMRAAM) air-to-air missiles. Other new avionics in the full ICE package are to include a new AEG radar control console, optimisation (by Hughes) of the cockpit display, installation of a new Litef digital fire control computer, Honeywell H-423 laser inertial platform, GEC Avionics CPU-143/A digital air data computer, new IFF system, a new guided missile launcher, a MIL-1553 digital data bus with advanced operational software, and improved resistance to electronic jamming and other countermeasures.

About 90 other Luftwaffe F-4s, serving in the fighter-bomber role with JaboGs 35 and 36, are expected to undergo partial update (INS and ADC only, initially), with the option of a full ICE installation later.

RFB

RHEIN-FLUGZEUGBAU GmbH (Subsidiary of MBB)

Flugplatz (Postfach 408), 4050 Mönchengladbach 1
Telephone: (02161) 6820
Telex: 852 506

OTHER WORKS: Köln/Bonn, Lübeck-Blankensee, Dahlem and Hamburg

PRESIDENTS:
Dipl Kfm Wolfgang Kutscher
Dipl Ing Alfred Schneider

This company, founded in 1956, is part of MBB. It is continuing to function as an independent subsidiary; its own two former subsidiaries, Sportavia-Pützer of Dahlem and Elektro-Mechanischer Fluggerätebau of Hamburg, became branches of RFB in 1981.

RFB has specialised in the development and manufacture of airframe structural components, with particular reference to wings and fuselages made entirely of glassfibre reinforced plastics. Recent programmes included series and individual production of aircraft components and assemblies made of light alloy, steel and GRP, for aircraft in quantity production by other West German companies, as well as spare parts and ground equipment.

Under contract to the Federal German government, RFB is servicing military aircraft, and is providing target towing flights and other services with special aircraft. It has Luftfahrt-Bundesamt (LBA) approval as an organisation

RFB Fantrainer 600 two-seat trainer in the insignia of the Royal Thai Air Force *(Chris Pocock)*

for aircraft development, manufacture, maintenance and overhaul. It also operates a factory certificated service centre for aircraft manufactured by Piper, Partenavia and Mitsubishi, as well as for avionics produced by Bendix, Becker and King. General servicing of other types of all-metal aircraft is undertaken.

In the aircraft propulsion field, RFB has been engaged for some years in the development of specialised applications for ducted propellers, leading to the Fantrainer multi-purpose training aircraft.

RFB FANTRAINER 400 and 600

In March 1975 the Federal German Defence Ministry awarded RFB a contract to develop and build two Fantrainer prototypes. The first, designated AWI-2, flew for the first time on 27 October 1977, powered by two 112 kW (150 hp) Wankel engines. The ATI-2 second prototype (D-EATI) flew for the first time on 31 May 1978 and had one Allison 250-C20B turboshaft engine, as now fitted to the production **Fantrainer 400**. In June 1980 it was fitted with an Allison 250-C30 turboshaft and redesignated **Fantrainer 600**.

In August 1982 RFB received a contract covering the production of 47 Fantrainers for the Royal Thai Air Force: 31 Fantrainer 400s and 16 Fantrainer 600s. The first two aircraft were built in Germany and delivered to Thailand in October 1984; the remainder, of which nine had been delivered by the beginning of 1986, are being assembled in Thailand, initially with glassfibre wings, eventually with locally manufactured all-metal wings. Changes from the prototype include an enlarged canopy with improved all-round view, relocation of the engine air intakes above the wings, a 15 cm (6 in) longer fuselage, and an improved fan reduction gearbox permitting the full thrust of the engine to be utilised. About 92 per cent of the airframe is common to the 400 and the 600.

The first German built production Fantrainer, a 600, flew for the first time on 12 August 1984. This aircraft and one prototype were allocated to the certification programme, and LBA type approval of the 600 was granted on 23 May 1985.

One Fantrainer 400 and two 600s underwent a 241 hour flight evaluation by the Luftwaffe in July-September 1985, as a result of which some modifications to the design were recommended, including a revised cockpit instrument layout. The fan blades were also modified to have sweptback and slightly twisted tips, to reduce still further the already low noise level of the installation. First flight with the modified fan was made on 16 May 1986. The Fantrainer is being considered by the Luftwaffe as a possible replacement for its ageing Piaggio P.149Ds. RFB also planned to demonstrate a possible civil version in North America during the Summer of 1986.

TYPE: Two-seat primary and basic training aircraft (IFR).

WINGS: Cantilever mid-wing monoplane. Wing section Eppler 502. Thickness/chord ratio 15·7%. Dihedral 3°. No incidence. Sweepforward 2° 30′ at quarter-chord. German built aircraft have wings constructed mainly of glassfibre and plastics tube sandwich; Thai built Fantrainers will have all-metal wings. Conventional ailerons and electrically actuated trailing-edge split flaps. No tabs.

FUSELAGE: The load-carrying fail-safe structure of the forward and centre-fuselage is of light alloy, with non-load-bearing glassfibre skin, sections of which are removable for servicing purposes. Cruciform metal rear fuselage is connected to the centre-fuselage at three points. The integral fan duct is free of structural loads. Large airbrake on each side of fan duct, operation of which causes no lift or stability changes.

TAIL UNIT: All-metal T tail of light alloy, with conventional rudder and elevator. Servo tab in trailing-edge of each elevator. Trim tab in rudder.

LANDING GEAR: Retractable tricycle type, with single wheel on each unit. Hydraulic actuation, with manual emergency extension. Nosewheel retracts forward, main units inward and upward into wing roots. Steel tube legs, acting as torsional/bending springs. Cleveland mainwheels, size 15 × 6·00-6, tyre pressure 4·7 bars (68 lb/sq in). Goodyear nosewheel, size 5·00-5, tyre pressure 3·45 bars (50 lb/sq in). Cleveland wheel brakes.

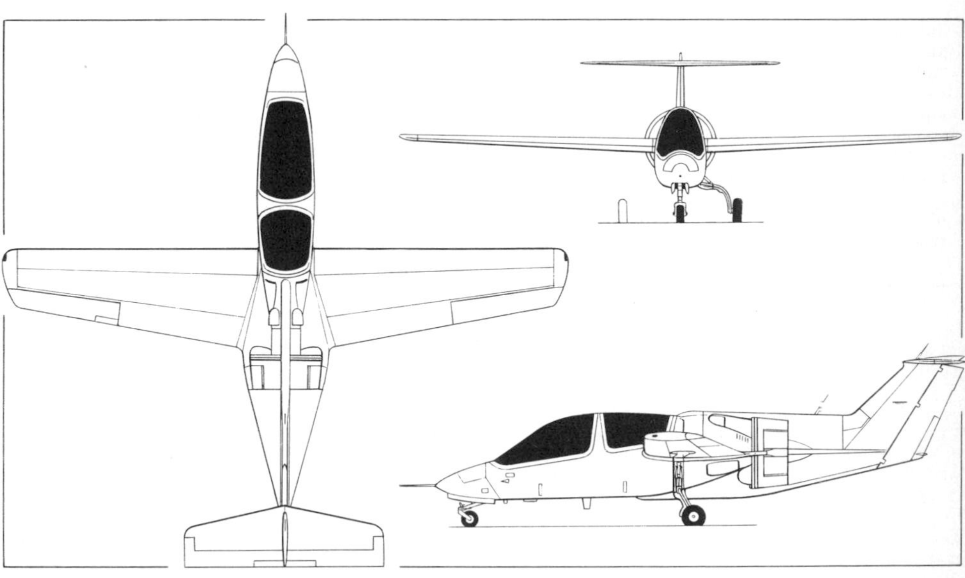
RFB Fantrainer 600 (Allison 250-C30 turboshaft engine) *(Pilot Press)*

POWER PLANT: One turboshaft engine, driving a Hoffmann five-blade constant-speed ducted fan. Fantrainer 400 has a 313 kW (420 shp) Allison 250-C20B, Fantrainer 600 a 485 kW (650 shp) Allison 250-C30. Engine air intakes above wing leading-edges. Four integral fuel tanks in wings, with combined capacity of 475 litres (104·5 Imp gallons). Refuelling points on wing upper surface. Both versions able to carry 420 litres (92·4 Imp gallons) of auxiliary fuel externally. Oil capacity 16 litres (3·5 Imp gallons).

ACCOMMODATION: Two seats in tandem cockpit, meeting US MIL specifications in terms of dimensions and layout. Seats and rudder pedals adjustable. Stencel Ranger zero/zero rocket assisted escape system standard; ejection seats optional. Fighter type side consoles. Canopy over each seat hinges sideways (to starboard) independently. Accommodation heated and ventilated.

SYSTEMS: Electrical system includes a starter/generator and battery. Hydraulic system for operation of landing gear and airbrakes.

AVIONICS: King Gold Crown avionics standard in RTAF aircraft.

DIMENSIONS, EXTERNAL:
- Wing span: 9·70 m (31 ft 10 in)
- Wing chord: at root: 1·89 m (6 ft 2½ in)
  - at tip: 1·02 m (3 ft 4 in)
- Wing aspect ratio: 6·72
- Length overall: 9·48 m (31 ft 1¼ in)
- Height overall: 3·00 m (9 ft 10 in)
- Tailplane span: 3·59 m (11 ft 9½ in)
- Wheel track: 1·94 m (6 ft 4¼ in)
- Wheelbase: 3·80 m (12 ft 5½ in)
- Fan diameter: 1·20 m (3 ft 11¼ in)

AREAS:
- Wings, gross: 14·00 m² (150·7 sq ft)
- Ailerons (total): 1·68 m² (18·08 sq ft)
- Trailing-edge flaps (total): 1·22 m² (13·13 sq ft)
- Rudder, incl tab: 0·87 m² (9·36 sq ft)
- Tailplane: 3·12 m² (33·58 sq ft)
- Elevators, incl tab: 0·92 m² (9·90 sq ft)

WEIGHTS AND LOADINGS (A: Aerobatic; U: Utility category):
- Weight empty: 400: A, U: 1,114 kg (2,456 lb)
  - 600: A, U: 1,160 kg (2,557 lb)
- Fuel weight: 400: A: 240 kg (529 lb)
  - U, internal fuel only: 340 kg (750 lb)
  - U, with drop tanks: 640 kg (1,411 lb)
  - 600: A: 190 kg (419 lb)
  - U, internal fuel only: 340 kg (750 lb)
  - U, with drop tanks: 640 kg (1,411 lb)
- Max T-O weight: 400: A: 1,600 kg (3,527 lb)
  - U: 1,800 kg (3,968 lb)
  - 600: A: 1,600 kg (3,527 lb)
  - U: 2,300 kg (5,070 lb)
- Max landing weight: 600: A: 1,600 kg (3,527 lb)
  - U: 2,000 kg (4,409 lb)
- Max wing loading: 400: 128·6 kg/m² (26·34 lb/sq ft)
  - 600: 164·3 kg/m² (33·65 lb/sq ft)
- Max power loading: 400: 5·75 kg/kW (9·45 lb/shp)
  - 600: 4·74 kg/kW (7·80 lb/shp)

PERFORMANCE (at max Aerobatic T-O weight, S/L, ISA, except where indicated):
- Never-exceed speed:
  - 400, 600: 300 knots (555 km/h; 345 mph)
- Max operating speed:
  - 400, 600: 250 knots (463 km/h; 288 mph)
- Max level speed:
  - 400 at 3,050 m (10,000 ft): 200 knots (370 km/h; 230 mph)
  - 600 at 5,490 m (18,000 ft): 225 knots (417 km/h; 259 mph)
- Cruising speed at 3,050 m (10,000 ft):
  - 400: 175 knots (325 km/h; 201 mph)
  - 600: 200 knots (370 km/h; 230 mph)
- Stalling speed:
  - 400, 600: 61 knots (113 km/h; 71 mph)
- Max rate of climb at S/L: 400: 472 m (1,550 ft)/min
  - 600: 914 m (3,000 ft)/min
- Service ceiling: 400: 6,100 m (20,000 ft)
  - 600: 7,620 m (25,000 ft)
- T-O run: 400: 280 m (920 ft)
  - 600: 250 m (820 ft)
- Landing run: 400, 600: 250 m (820 ft)
- Range with max internal fuel, optimum cruising speed at 3,050 m (10,000 ft), no reserves:
  - 400: 950 nm (1,750 km; 1,093 miles)
  - 600: 750 nm (1,390 km; 863 miles)
- Endurance, conditions as above: 400: 6 h 18 min
  - 600: 4 h 42 min
- *g* limits: 400: A: +6/−3
  - B: +4·4/−1·76
  - 600: A: +6/−3
  - B: +3·8/−1·52

VALENTIN

VALENTIN FLUGZEUGBAU GmbH

Flugplatzstrasse 18 (Postfach 26), 8728 Hassfurt
Telephone: (09521) 4730

DIRECTORS:
Dipl-Ing Bernard Valentin (Managing)
Günther Haas

HEAD OFFICE AND OTHER WORKS: Germanenstrasse 2 (Postfach 1165), 8901 Königsbrunn
Telephone: (08231) 4033/4

VALENTIN TAIFUN 12E

First flown in 1985 and displayed at an exhibition in Friedrichshafen in the Spring of that year, the 12E is a short-span version of the Taifun 17E motor glider (see Sailplanes section) which is being developed by Valentin for the private flying market. Initial plans are to certificate a basic version first, subsequently extending the certification to FAR Pt 23 standards.

The prototype (D-EDHB, a modified Taifun 17E) retains the fuselage, tail unit and retractable tricycle landing gear of

Prototype Valentin Taifun 12E two-seat light aircraft *(Wolfgang Wagner)*

the motor glider virtually unchanged, but has a new wing of Horstmann-Quast HQ 38 aerofoil section with smaller trailing-edge flaps and no airbrakes. It was powered originally with the Taifun 17E engine, a 59 kW (80 hp) Limbach L 2000 flat-four, but at the end of Summer 1985 this was replaced by a 65 kW (87 hp) L 2400 EB1B with a Mühlbauer MTV-1-A/L160-3 variable-pitch propeller, and it is intended to offer production aircraft with a choice of this latter engine or a 75 kW (100 hp) Continental O-200 with a Hoffmann constant-speed propeller. Trials with the O-200 were expected to take place during 1986. Fuel capacity of 90 litres (19·8 Imp gallons) remains unchanged.

It was hoped to begin series production of the 'basic' Taifun 12E by the end of 1986. This would have non-folding wings and non-retractable landing gear; the Continental powered version would have wing folding and landing gear retraction available as customer options.

DIMENSIONS, EXTERNAL:
- Wing span: approx 11·80 m (38 ft 8½ in)
- Wing aspect ratio: approx 9·95
- Length overall: 7·782 m (25 ft 6½ in)
- Height overall: 2·30 m (7 ft 6½ in)

AREA:
- Wings, gross: approx 14·00 m² (150·7 sq ft)

WEIGHTS:
- Basic weight empty: approx 550 kg (1,212 lb)
- Max fuel weight: 66 kg (145·5 lb)
- Max T-O weight: approx 850 kg (1,874 lb)

PERFORMANCE (at max T-O weight, 87 hp engine):
- Max cruising speed at 4,575 m (15,000 ft), 75% power: 124 knots (230 km/h; 143 mph)
- Service ceiling: 4,575 m (15,000 ft)
- T-O run: 350 m (1,148 ft)

GREECE

HAI

HELLENIC AEROSPACE INDUSTRY

Athens Tower, Messogion 2-4, GR-115 270 Athens
Telephone: (01) 77 99 678
Telex: 219528 HAI GR
WORKS: Tanagra, PO Box 23, GR-320 09 Schimatari
Telephone: (0262) 5200
Telex: 299306 HAI GR
CHAIRMAN OF THE BOARD AND MANAGING DIRECTOR:
Prof Pan Fotilas
DIRECTORS:
A. Pantazis (Materiel)
C. Economidis (Production & Maintenance)
Th. Spathopoylos (Engineering, Research & Development)
L. Dragogiannis (Quality Assurance/Quality Control)
Th. Stergiou (Administration)
MARKETING MANAGER: D. Sarlis
PUBLIC RELATIONS MANAGER: Spiros M. Xenos

Hellenic Aerospace Industry is Greece's most technologically developed industrial complex. It is owned 100% by the Greek government, headed by a board of directors, and operates as a Société Anonyme. A total of 3,200 people was employed in 1986.

HAI has recently been reorganised and now not only covers Greece's own needs for manufacture and repair in both military and civil aviation fields but is proving its capability in the international market by signing contracts with such customers as Dassault-Breguet, Dornier, Airbus Industrie, USAFE, British Aerospace, the RAF, Aeritalia, Agusta and Jordan. These include production of flaps for the BAe ATP, fuselage components for the Agusta A 109A, and components for the Dassault Mirage 2000, Dornier 228 and Aeritalia G222.

The HAI facility comprises an Aircraft Division, Engine Division, Electronics/Avionics Division and Manufacturing Division. A complete spectrum of additional depots, utilities and ancillary buildings and capabilities supports all company activities in every field. Special emphasis has been given to the Directorate of Quality Assurance/Quality Control. The Directorate of Engineering, Research and Development has also proved successful in the support, maintenance and modification of equipment as well as in the production of new electronic and aeronautical systems.

INDIA

HAL

HINDUSTAN AERONAUTICS LIMITED

Indian Express Building, Dr Ambedkar Veedhi, PO Box 5150, Bangalore 560 001
Telephone: 76901 (8 lines)
Telex: 845-266 HAL IN
CHAIRMAN: Air Marshal M. S. D. Wollen
DIRECTORS:
D. C. Bajpai
Prof K. Balaraman
P. R. Chari
C. L. Chaudhry
I. M. Chopra
S. K. Mehra
C. V. Nagendra
Dr R. Narasimha
K. P. Rabindranathan
Prof C. N. R. Rao
H. K. Singh
Vivek R. Sinha
GROUP EXECUTIVES:
S. K. Ohri (Group Executive, Kanpur Division)
J. N. Karan (Additional Group Executive, Quality Assurance & Staff Inspection)
GENERAL MANAGERS:
Bangalore Complex:
K. K. Ganapathy (Aircraft Division)
K. N. Murthy (Helicopter Division)
A. C. Sood (Engine Division)
J. R. Kapur (Overhaul Division)
C. G. Krishnadas Nair (Foundry and Forge Division)
K. P. Mukundan (Services Division)
Design & Development Complex:
T. V. Vareed (Chief Designer, Engine Design Bureau)
A. K. Kundu (Additional Chief Designer, Aircraft Design Bureau)
D. H. Sivamurthy (Additional Chief Designer, LCA)
S. R. Telang (Additional Chief Designer, Helicopter Design Bureau)
Accessories Complex:
R. N. Sharma (Hyderabad Division)
R. Sundar (Lucknow Division)
MiG Complex:
Wg Cdr A. K. Sar (Koraput Division)
H. K. L. Anand (Nasik Division)
Kanpur Division:
S. K. Ohri (Group Executive)
CORPORATE OFFICE (BANGALORE):
K. R. Natarajan (Chief of Planning)
B. S. Jaswal (Chief of Marketing)
D. P. Srivastava (Chief of Product Support)
S. C. Kochhar (Chief of Personnel)
K. Ganeshan (Chief of Finance)

Hindustan Aeronautics Limited (HAL) was formed on 1 October 1964, and has 11 Divisions, five at Bangalore and one each at Nasik, Koraput, Hyderabad, Kanpur, Lucknow and Korwa, plus a Design and Development Complex. The total workforce is about 42,000. The new factory at Korwa, set up to manufacture inertial navigation systems, was commissioned on 3 April 1986.

HAL is currently manufacturing and overhauling a variety of aircraft, helicopters, aero engines, avionics, instruments and accessories. It is also manufacturing components for the Indian Space Research Organisation (ISRO).

The Bangalore Complex is engaged in the manufacture of military aircraft, helicopters and aero engines, both under licence and of indigenous design. These include the SEPECAT Jaguar International combat aircraft and its Adour engine, and the Kiran Mk II armed jet trainer. The Complex also undertakes repair and overhaul of airframes, engines, and allied instruments and accessories. The Foundry and Forge Division supplies castings and forgings for the aircraft and engines.

Until recently, Kanpur Division was engaged mainly in the manufacture of different versions of the British Aerospace HS 748 under licence. It is now producing the HPT-32 trainer, designed by the Aircraft Design Bureau, and the Ardhra sailplane designed by the DGCA Technical Centre (see Sailplanes section). Kanpur is also assembling, under licence, the Dornier 228.

Nasik and Koraput Divisions are manufacturing airframes and engines of the Soviet MiG-21 and MiG-27 in collaboration with the USSR. Hyderabad Division manufactures avionics for all aircraft produced by HAL, as well as airport radars.

Lucknow Division is producing aircraft accessories under licence from various manufacturers in the UK (including Dowty, Dunlop, Ferranti, NGL and Smiths), France (including Badin, Jaeger, SFENA and SFIM) and the USSR. These accessories include wheels and brakes, ejection seats, instruments, fuel accessories, air-conditioning and pressurisation equipment. The Division has successfully developed a number of electrical and hydraulic accessories which have entered production.

Korwa Division production of sophisticated INS and laser systems, intended to give India an indigenous capability in these fields, had not started by September 1986.

In addition to its manufacturing programmes, HAL is pursuing design and development activities relating to aircraft, helicopters, small jet engines, avionics and accessories. The Aircraft Design Bureau at Bangalore is developing an HTT-34 turboprop version of the HPT-32 piston engined trainer. A Light Combat Aircraft (LCA) programme has been approved by the Indian government, and discussions are being held with a number of countries for design collaboration in selected areas. Selection of MBB as HAL's partner in the Advanced Light Helicopter (ALH) programme was made in 1984. HAL will also be taking up feasibility studies for an Advanced Jet Trainer (AJT) to meet the requirements of the Indian Air Force from the early 1990s.

The Engine Design Bureau at Bangalore has designed a 3·43 kN (350 kg; 771 lb st) engine, the PTAE-7, for the Pilotless Target Aircraft (PTA) built by the Aeronautical Development Establishment in Bangalore (see ADE entry in the RPVs and Targets section).

The Avionics Design Department at Hyderabad has designed and developed an IFF system (BAT), an ADF, a VHF COM-104A radio, a radio altimeter, and a V/UHF radio, all of which are in production. Under design and development are a VHF/UHF-AM/FM and UHF standby in hybrid technology, a ground proximity warning system, data transmission on voice channels, and improved air route surveillance radar and phased array precision approach radar.

BANGALORE COMPLEX

Vimanapura Post, Bangalore 560 017 (Karnataka State)
Telephone: 561020 and 565201
Telex: 0845 234
MANAGING DIRECTOR, BANGALORE COMPLEX: I. M. Chopra
MANAGING DIRECTOR, DESIGN AND DEVELOPMENT:
Prof K. Balaraman

The Bangalore Complex of HAL consists essentially of the former Hindustan Aircraft Limited, the activities of which, since its formation in 1940, have been described in previous editions of *Jane's*. The Complex is subdivided into an Aircraft Division, Helicopter Division, Engine Division, Overhaul Division, Foundry and Forge Division, and Design and Development Complex.

Bangalore Complex is engaged in producing aircraft designed and developed by the Aircraft Design Bureau, and also in manufacturing various aircraft and aero engines under licence. The Helicopter Division continues to manufacture Chetak (Alouette III) and Cheetah (Lama) helicopters, under licence from Aérospatiale of France. The Engine Division's activities are described in the appropriate section of this edition.

The Overhaul Division of Bangalore Complex repairs and overhauls Canberra, C-119, HT-2, Devon, Ajeet, C-47, Caribou and other types of aircraft; and various types of piston engine, including the Pratt & Whitney R-1830, R-2000-7M2 and R-1340-AN2, the Cirrus Major, and the de Havilland Gipsy Queen. Turbine engines, such as the Orpheus, Avon, Dart and Artouste IIIB, are overhauled at the Engine Division. The branch factory at Barrackpore near Calcutta continues to concentrate on repair and overhaul of C-47/DC-3s of the Indian Air Force and non-scheduled operators.

HAL (SEPECAT) JAGUAR INTERNATIONAL

The Bangalore Complex is responsible for the assembly and/or licence construction of SEPECAT Jaguar International combat aircraft (see International section) for the Indian Air Force. Current orders are for 76 aircraft. The first UK built airframe components for final assembly in India were delivered to HAL in 1981, and the first Indian assembled Jaguar (JS136) made its initial flight on 31 March 1982. Deliveries totalled 15 by mid-1985, the latest date for which details have been provided.

LIGHT COMBAT AIRCRAFT

The Indian government has confirmed a requirement for an air superiority and light close air support aircraft for service in the 1990s. Known as the LCA (light combat aircraft), it will be designed with assistance from a Western aerospace company but probably manufactured entirely in

India. It is expected to embody composite materials in its construction, and to have a fly by wire flight control system. Empty and max T-O weights were originally believed to be in the order of 6,000 kg (13,230 lb) and 10,500 kg (23,150 lb), but the latter has reportedly now risen to 12,500 kg (27,558 lb). An indigenous afterburning engine of about 83·4 kN (18,740 lb st), designated GTX-35, entered development by the Gas Turbine Research Establishment at Bangalore, but an existing foreign engine (the RB199 and/or F404 have been suggested) may be utilised until this is ready. The project definition phase is currently under way, but a first flight is not expected before the early 1990s.

HAL HJT-16 KIRAN Mk II

This version of the Kiran, for armament training and counter-insurgency duties, was developed from the Mks I/IA (1982-83 *Jane's*) by the Aircraft Design Bureau at Bangalore. The first prototype made its initial flight on 30 July 1976. A second prototype was flown in February 1979. Principal differences include improved weapon carrying capability, a more powerful engine, updated avionics and an improved hydraulic system. The Rolls-Royce Orpheus 701-01 turbojet, replacing the Viper engine of the Mks I/IA, gives the Kiran Mk II improved maximum speed, climb and manoeuvrability.

The design and development phase was completed by March 1983. Fifty-seven Kiran Mk IIs had been ordered by the Indian Air Force by June 1985, deliveries of which began in April 1984. Sixteen had been delivered by mid-1985, with others intended to follow at the rate of 18 a year. More than 100 may be ordered eventually.

Type: Two-seat jet trainer and light attack aircraft.

Wings: Cantilever low-wing monoplane. Wing section NACA 23015 at root, NACA 23012 at tip. Dihedral 4° from roots. Incidence 0° 30′ at root. Sweepback 7° 28′ at quarter-chord. Conventional all-metal three-spar structure of aluminium/copper alloy. Frise differential ailerons, with balance tab in each aileron and ground adjustable tab on port aileron. Hydraulically actuated trailing-edge split flaps. Two full-chord boundary layer fences on upper surface of each wing.

Fuselage: All-metal semi-monocoque fail-safe structure of light alloy. Hydraulically actuated door type airbrake under centre of fuselage, in line with flaps.

Tail Unit: Cantilever all-metal structure of aluminium/copper alloy. Electrically operated variable incidence tailplane, with elevators. Ground adjustable tab on rudder.

Landing Gear: Retractable tricycle type, of HAL manufacture. Hydraulic actuation. Main units retract inward into fuselage; self-centering twin-contact non-steerable nosewheel retracts forward. HAL oleo-pneumatic shock absorbers. Dunlop mainwheel tyres size 19 × 6·25-9, pressure 8·96 bars (130 lb/sq in). Nosewheel tyre size 15·4 × 4·6, pressure 6·90 bars (100 lb/sq in). Dunlop hydraulic brakes.

Power Plant: One Rolls-Royce Orpheus 701-01 turbojet engine, derated to 18·68 kN (4,200 lb st). Internal fuel in flexible main saddle tank in fuselage (625 litres; 137·5 Imp gallons), one 282 litre (62 Imp gallon) collector tank in wing centre-section, and two outboard integral wing tanks (each 218 litres; 48 Imp gallons), giving total internal fuel capacity of 1,345 litres (295·5 Imp gallons). Provision for two underwing tanks with total capacity of 454 litres (100 Imp gallons). One refuelling point in each outer wing and two in fuselage. Oil capacity 11·4 litres (2·5 Imp gallons).

Accommodation: Crew of two side by side in air-conditioned and pressurised cockpit, on Martin-Baker H4HA zero-altitude fully automatic ejection seats. Clamshell type canopy, hinged at rear and opening upward. Dual controls and duplicated blind-flying instruments.

Systems: Bootstrap type air-conditioning system, max pressure differential of 0·12 bars (1·75 lb/sq in). Dowty hydraulic system, pressure 207 bars (3,000 lb/sq in), actuates landing gear, flaps, airbrake and wheel brakes, electro-hydraulic servo yaw damper, and canopy emergency release. System flow rate 16 litres (3·5 Imp gallons)/min. Non-separated reservoir, pressurised at 1 bar (14·5 lb/sq in) by engine bleed air. Accumulator for manual emergency system. Electrical system is of 28V DC single-wire earth return type, with 5·1kW generator, 40Ah nickel-cadmium battery for standby power, and 250V inverter for AC power to supply avionics, instruments and other ancillary systems. High pressure demand type gaseous oxygen system.

Avionics and Equipment: HAL VUC 201 V/UHF multi-channel com transceiver; HAL COM 150A four-channel standby UHF; HAL ARC-610A ADF; HAL IFF Mk 10 (BAT). Blind-flying instrumentation standard. Landing light in nose.

Armament: Two 7·62 mm machine-guns in nose, with 150 rds/gun; G90 gun camera, and Ferranti ISIS gunsights with Teledyne camera. Two pylons under each outer wing, each with an ejector release unit capable of carrying a 227 litre (50 Imp gallon) drop tank, a 250 kg bomb, a reusable pod containing eighteen 68 mm SNEB rockets, or a CBLS-200 carrier with four 25 lb practice bombs.

Dimensions, external:
- Wing span: 10·70 m (35 ft 1¼ in)
- Wing chord: at root: 2·35 m (7 ft 8½ in)
- at tip: 1·02 m (3 ft 4 in)
- Wing aspect ratio: 6·03
- Length overall: 10·60 m (34 ft 9½ in)
- Fuselage: Max width: 1·36 m (4 ft 5½ in)
- Height overall: 3·635 m (11 ft 11 in)
- Tailplane span: 3·90 m (12 ft 9½ in)
- Wheel track: 2·42 m (7 ft 11 in)
- Wheelbase: 3·50 m (11 ft 6 in)

Dimensions, internal:
- Cockpit: Length: 1·94 m (6 ft 4¼ in)
- Max width: 1·06 m (3 ft 5¾ in)
- Max height: 1·41 m (4 ft 7½ in)

Areas:
- Wings, gross: 19·00 m² (204·5 sq ft)
- Ailerons (total, incl tabs): 1·169 m² (12·58 sq ft)
- Flaps (total): 2·34 m² (25·19 sq ft)
- Fin, incl dorsal fin: 1·576 m² (16·96 sq ft)
- Rudder, incl tab: 0·714 m² (7·69 sq ft)
- Tailplane: 2·58 m² (27·77 sq ft)
- Elevators (total): 1·14 m² (12·27 sq ft)

Weights and Loading:
- Weight empty, equipped: 2,995 kg (6,603 lb)
- Max fuel load: 1,775 kg (3,913 lb)
- Normal T-O weight 'clean': 4,250 kg (9,369 lb)
- Max T-O weight: 5,000 kg (11,023 lb)
- Normal landing weight: 4,300 kg (9,480 lb)
- Max wing loading: 263·1 kg/m² (53·9 lb/sq ft)

Performance (at max T-O weight, ISA):
- Never-exceed speed: 421 knots (780 km/h; 484 mph)
- Max level speed at S/L: 363 knots (672 km/h; 418 mph)
- Max cruising speed at 4,575 m (15,000 ft): 335 knots (621 km/h; 386 mph) IAS
- Econ cruising speed at 4,575 m (15,000 ft): 225 knots (417 km/h; 259 mph) IAS

SEPECAT Jaguar International, assembled by HAL for the Indian Air Force

HAL Kiran Mk II armament training and counter-insurgency aircraft

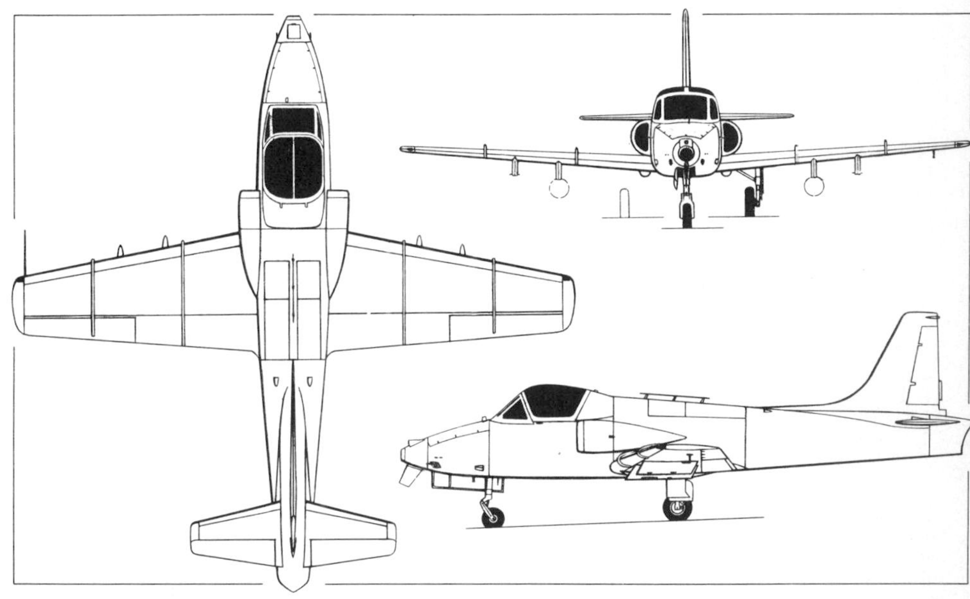

HAL Kiran Mk II weapon training and COIN aircraft *(Pilot Press)*

Stalling speed:
flaps and landing gear up
100 knots (185 km/h; 115 mph) IAS
flaps and landing gear down
85 knots (158 km/h; 98 mph) IAS
Max rate of climb at S/L 1,600 m (5,250 ft)/min
Service ceiling 12,000 m (39,375 ft)
Min ground turning radius 6·55 m (21 ft 6 in)
Runway LCN 6
T-O run 540 m (1,772 ft)
T-O to 15 m (50 ft) 730 m (2,395 ft)
Landing from 15 m (50 ft) 1,440 m (4,725 ft)
Range at 6,000 m (19,680 ft) with max internal fuel
397 nm (735 km; 457 miles)

HAL AJEET TRAINER

A description of the single-seat Ajeet (Invincible) lightweight fighter/ground attack aircraft last appeared in the 1982-83 *Jane's*. This tandem two-seat trainer version retains the four underwing hardpoints and full combat capability of the single-seater but has sections 0·70 m (2 ft 3½ in) long inserted in the fuselage fore and aft of the wings. Two of the single-seater's fuselage fuel tanks are deleted to make room for the second cockpit, although this can be offset by deleting the Aden cannon to make space for an additional 273 litres (60 Imp gallons) of internal fuel. In the latter event, provision is made for carrying a 7·62 mm gun pod on each of the inboard wing pylons.

The first prototype of the Ajeet Trainer made its initial flight on 20 September 1982, but was lost in an accident in December of that year. A second prototype (E2427) was flown on 7 September 1983, at which time the Indian Air Force had a stated requirement for 18 and the Indian Navy wanted twelve. Production of these was reportedly resumed in the Autumn of 1986. At about the same time British Aerospace announced the receipt of a contract for 16 of its SCR-300 flight data recorders for the Ajeet Trainer, with a possibility of other orders to come.

The following is the latest available description of the Ajeet Trainer:

TYPE: Tandem two-seat operational trainer.

WINGS: Cantilever shoulder-wing monoplane. Sweptback wings, of modified RAE 102 section. Thickness/chord ratio 8% at root and tip. Anhedral 5°. Incidence 0°. Sweepback 40° at quarter-chord. One-piece wing of two-spar thick-skin light alloy safe-life construction, fitting into recess in top of fuselage and secured by bolts at four points. Inboard ailerons, powered by Automotive Products hydraulic actuators, droop 22° to serve as flaps when the landing gear is lowered. Provision for alternative manual operation of ailerons. Ground adjustable tab on port aileron.

FUSELAGE: Light alloy semi-monocoque safe-life structure, with pressed frames and extruded stringers.

TAIL UNIT: Cantilever all-metal structure. Three-spar sweptback fin, integral with fuselage. One-piece three-spar variable incidence tailplane, powered by Lucas Aerospace hydraulic actuators. Rear portions of tailplane can be unlocked to perform as elevators; or locked to provide the functions of an all-moving tailplane. Ground adjustable tab on rudder. Electric datum trim.

LANDING GEAR: Retractable tricycle type, all units retracting rearward hydraulically into fuselage. Dowty Rotol oleo-pneumatic shock absorber struts. Wheel well fairings attached to individual landing gear units serve as airbrakes when landing gear is partly lowered, the relative movements of the airbrakes being so adjusted that no change of trim occurs at any speed. Dunlop mainwheel tyres size 542 × 146 × 279 mm, pressure 10·34 bars (150 lb/sq in); twin Dunlop nosewheel tyres, size 430 × 87 × 279 mm, pressure 5·65 bars (82 lb/sq in). Dunlop hydraulic disc brakes and Maxaret anti-skid units on mainwheels. GQ Mk 4 or Mk 6 brake-chute, diameter 2·29 m (7 ft 6 in), in fairing at base of fin.

POWER PLANT: One Rolls-Royce Orpheus 701-01AT non-afterburning turbojet engine, rated at 21·57 kN (4,850 lb st). Air intakes in sides of fuselage. Five flexible tanks in fuselage, and two 227 litre (50 Imp gallon) integral wing tanks. Total internal fuel capacity 900 litres (198 Imp gallons). Refuelling point in fuselage and one in each wing. Provision for two 136·5 litre (30 Imp gallon) underwing drop tanks. Oil capacity 5·1 litres (9 Imp pints).

ACCOMMODATION: Instructor and pupil in tandem, on Martin-Baker GF4 zero-height/90 knot (167 km/h; 104 mph) lightweight ejection seats. Pressurised, heated and air-conditioned cockpits, with individual canopies which are hinged at rear and open upward.

SYSTEMS: HAL (Lucknow Divn) bootstrap type air-conditioning and Semca pressurisation system, max differential 0·25 bars (3·6 lb/sq in) above 13,100 m (43,000 ft). Hydraulic system of 207 bars (3,000 lb/sq in) pressure, with variable-delivery pump, for aileron, landing gear, mainwheel brake and tailplane actuation. No pneumatic system. 28V DC electrical system, with 5·1kW generator, 40Ah nickel-cadmium battery and 4Ah Globe standby battery. BOC gaseous oxygen system. No de-icing provisions or APU.

AVIONICS AND EQUIPMENT: V/UHF main and standby com radio; HAL ADF and Mk 10 IFF. Blind-flying instrumentation and dual controls standard.

Prototype of the tandem two-seat HAL Ajeet Trainer

ARMAMENT: Two 30 mm Aden Mk 4 cannon in air intake fairings, one on each side of fuselage. Ferranti ISIS gunsight (front cockpit only), Vinten gun camera and Teledyne recording camera. Each inboard underwing pylon capable of carrying a Type 122 practice rocket pod, one pod of 57 mm rockets, one cluster bomb, or one CBLS with four 25 lb practice bombs. With a 136·5 litre (30 Imp gallon) drop tank on each outboard pylon, a 250 kg bomb can be carried on each inboard attachment.

DIMENSIONS, EXTERNAL:
Wing span 6·731 m (22 ft 1 in)
Wing chord: at c/l 2·583 m (8 ft 5¾ in)
at tip 1·175 m (3 ft 10¼ in)
Wing aspect ratio 3·58
Length overall 10·45 m (34 ft 3½ in)
Length of fuselage 10·055 m (33 ft 0 in)
Fuselage: Max width 1·483 m (4 ft 10¼ in)
Height overall 2·575 m (8 ft 5½ in)
Tailplane span 2·845 m (9 ft 4 in)
Wheel track 1·552 m (5 ft 1¼ in)
Wheelbase 3·069 m (10 ft 0¾ in)

AREAS:
Wings, gross 12·646 m² (136·12 sq ft)
Ailerons/flaps (total) 1·230 m² (13·24 sq ft)
Fin 0·936 m² (10·08 sq ft)
Rudder, incl tab 0·206 m² (2·22 sq ft)
Tailplane 2·967 m² (31·94 sq ft)
Elevators (total) 0·540 m² (5·81 sq ft)

WEIGHTS AND LOADINGS:
Basic weight empty, incl crew 2,940 kg (6,482 lb)
Max internal fuel 703 kg (1,550 lb)
Max external stores 850 kg (1,874 lb)
Max T-O weight 4,536 kg (10,000 lb)
Max landing weight 3,330 kg (7,341 lb)
Max wing loading 358·7 kg/m² (73·47 lb/sq ft)
Max power loading 210·2 kg/kN (2·06 lb/lb st)

PERFORMANCE (at max T-O weight):
Never-exceed speed at S/L
661 knots (1,225 km/h; 761 mph)
Max level speed at S/L
577 knots (1,070 km/h; 665 mph)
Max cruising speed at 11,000 m (36,000 ft)
Mach 0·95 (540 knots; 1,000 km/h; 621 mph)
Econ cruising speed at 11,000 m (36,000 ft)
Mach 0·80 (459 knots; 850 km/h; 528 mph)
Stalling speed, ailerons/flaps down, engine idling
133 knots (246 km/h; 153 mph)
Max rate of climb at S/L 3,240 m (10,625 ft)/min
Service ceiling 14,000 m (45,925 ft)
Min ground turning radius 6·00 m (19 ft 8¼ in)
Runway LCN 5·5
T-O run 725 m (2,380 ft)
T-O to 15 m (50 ft) 1,130 m (3,705 ft)
Landing from 15 m (50 ft) 1,400 m (4,595 ft)
Landing run 900 m (2,955 ft)
Range with max internal fuel, 136·5 litres (30 Imp gallons) reserves 485 nm (900 km; 559 miles)

HAL (AÉROSPATIALE) SA 315B LAMA

Indian name: Cheetah

The Bangalore Complex's Helicopter Division continues to build the French Aérospatiale SA 315B Lama five-seat general purpose helicopter (which see), under a licence granted in September 1970; it is known in India as the Cheetah. The first Indian assembled example flew for the first time on 6 October 1972, and production from locally manufactured components began in 1976-77.

Civil versions of the Cheetah are produced for VIP transport and cropspraying duties in addition to more general roles, and are equipped with Indian avionics which include VHF and V/UHF com radios and ADF by Hindustan Aeronautics, and an intercom system and optional gyromagnetic compass by Southern Electronics Ltd of Bangalore. The agricultural version can be equipped for seed sowing or the dispersal of liquid or dry chemicals.

The following Cheetah details differ from those given for the SA 315B in the French section:

HAL Cheetah, Indian built version of the Aérospatiale SA 315B Lama helicopter

HAL manufactured Aérospatiale Alouette III (Chetak) helicopter in Indian military insignia

WEIGHTS:

Max T-O weight	1,750 kg (3,858 lb)
Max zero-fuel weight	1,043 kg (2,299 lb)

PERFORMANCE (at max T-O weight):

Max cruising speed	102 knots (190 km/h; 118 mph)
Max rate of climb at S/L	318 m (1,043 ft)/min
Service ceiling	6,375 m (20,915 ft)
Range:	
at S/L, with max payload	264 nm (490 km; 304 miles)
at optimum speed and altitude, with max fuel	334 nm (620 km; 385 miles)

HAL (AÉROSPATIALE) SA 316B ALOUETTE III

Indian name: Chetak

The Bangalore Complex's Helicopter Division is building the French Aérospatiale SA 316B Alouette III under a licence granted in June 1962. The first Indian assembled Alouette III (Indian name Chetak) was flown for the first time on 11 June 1965.

By March 1983, the latest date for which precise details were received, 257 Alouette IIIs had been manufactured by HAL; customers have included state governments in India, the Royal Nepal Army, the government of the Seychelles, and the USSR.

An armed version of the Chetak was developed by HAL for the Indian Air Force, carrying four air-to-surface missiles on laterally mounted booms. Target identification and fire control are via a monocular periscopic sight on the cabin roof. A version for the Indian Navy, for detecting and attacking small surface craft such as torpedo boats, is equipped with a quick-mooring deck harpoon for instant and automatic mooring on landing and before take-off, a nosewheel locking system, and folding main rotor blades. This version has a Sfena AP-14G three-axis stabilisation system, and provisions for carrying two Mk 44 homing torpedoes under the fuselage, or one torpedo and a magnetic anomaly detector.

Combined production of the Chetak and Cheetah now exceeds 400, mostly for military and naval use.

MBB/HAL ADVANCED LIGHT HELICOPTER

In July 1984, the Indian government and MBB signed a contract for the development of an advanced twin-turboshaft light helicopter (ALH), initially for Indian national requirements, which are said to be in the order of 200 for the armed forces and coastguard. Development of the ALH basic version will be by HAL of Bangalore with MBB collaboration. MBB will provide support during design, development and the necessary preparations for production of the helicopter in Bangalore.

The preliminary design phase for ALH started on 1 November 1984 and has been completed. Configuration has been 'frozen' (see accompanying drawing), and overall design of critical components has also been completed. Power plant will be two 750 kW (1,000 shp) class turboshaft engines. Maximum take-off weight is four to five tonnes (8,818-11,023 lb), with seating capacity for up to 14 persons, including a crew of two; emphasis is on excellent 'hot and high' performance. Other details so far released are that the ALH will have an MBB four-blade all-composites FEL (fibre/elastomerics) bearingless main rotor with integrated drive system, fully retractable tricycle landing gear, and capability to carry sling loads. A version with skid landing gear is under consideration. Performance requirements are reported to include a sea level range of 216 nm (400 km; 248 miles), service ceiling of 6,000 m (19,685 ft) and hovering ceiling of 3,000 m (9,845 ft). First flight of the ALH is scheduled for early 1989.

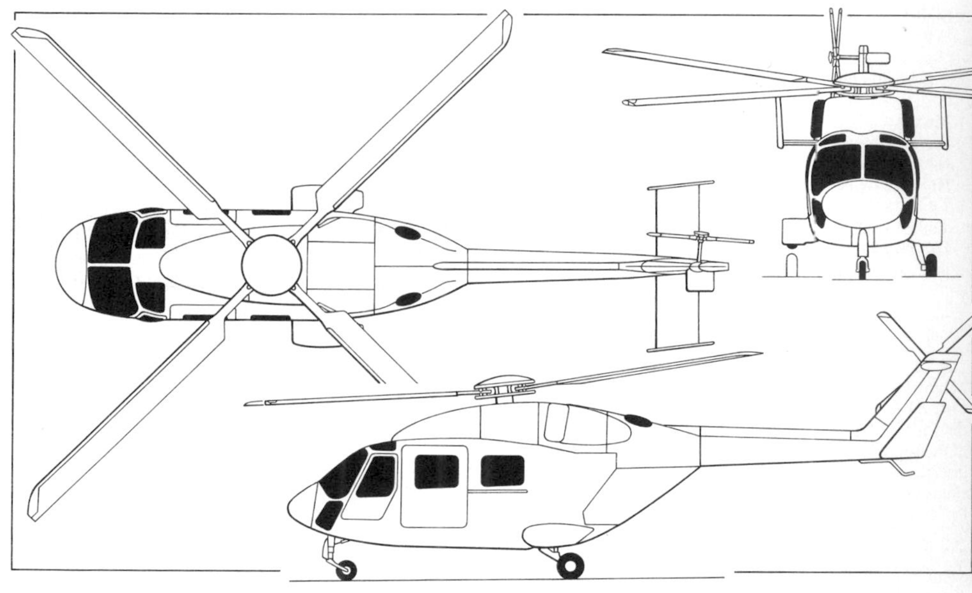

MBB/HAL Advanced Light Helicopter *(Jane's/Mike Keep)*

KANPUR DIVISION

Chakeri, Kanpur
Telephone: HAL PABX 62471-4
Telex: HAL 032 245

HAL (DORNIER) 228

Under a contract signed on 29 November 1983, HAL's Kanpur Division is undertaking licence assembly and manufacture of approximately 150 Dornier 228 twin-turboprop utility transports in a ten-year programme. Up to 350 Garrett TPE331-5 engines for these aircraft will be produced by the Engine Division.

The Dornier 228 was chosen to fulfil the Indian government's LTA (light transport aircraft) requirement, and will be used for a wide variety of duties within the country. In the Indian Air Force they will replace Otters, Devons and C-47s for a range of transport and other roles; the Indian Navy, Oil and Natural Gas Commission and other operators will employ them for maritime surveillance and reconnaissance, target towing, search and rescue, observer training, communications and logistic support; the Coast Guard will employ 228s equipped with a MEL Marec 2 Super Searcher surveillance radar, air-to-surface missiles, advanced navigation equipment, pollution sensors and SAR kits for coastal patrol, environmental control and anti-smuggling operations. Other operators include the regional domestic airline Vayudoot and the DGCA.

By 31 March 1986 a total of ten Dornier 228-201s, including five completed at Kanpur, had been delivered to Vayudoot, and one 228-101 to the ONGC. Further details of the technology transfer arrangements are given in the Dornier entry in the German section.

HAL (BAe) 748

HAL is reported to be in the project definition stage of an AEW version of the HAL built BAe 748, using a BEL antenna pylon mounted within an ADE radome.

HAL HPT-32

The HPT-32 is a fully aerobatic piston engined basic trainer, with side by side seats for instructor and pupil. Design began in March 1976. The aircraft can be used for a wide range of ab initio training, including instrument, navigation, night flying and formation flying; for armed patrol; for observation, liaison or sport flying; or for weapon training, light strike duties, supply dropping, search and rescue, reconnaissance, or glider or target towing. The airframe, which is of all-metal construction, is designed to FAR Pt 23, and is expected to have a fatigue life of 6,500 h.

The first prototype (X2157) made its initial flight on 6 January 1977. The second was flown on 12 March 1979; the third, flown on 31 July 1981, represents the production version, substantially lighter in weight and with aerodynamic refinements. Thirty-two had been delivered to the Indian Air Force by March 1986.

First Dornier 228-201 assembled by the Kanpur Division of Hindustan Aeronautics

HAL HPT-32 two-seat basic training aircraft in Indian Air Force insignia

The following description applies to the production version:

TYPE: Two-seat ab initio, aerobatic, night flying, instrument flying and navigation trainer.

WINGS: Cantilever low-wing monoplane. Wing section NACA 64A$_1$-212. Dihedral 5° from roots. Incidence 2° 30′ at root. No sweepback. Light alloy safe-life wings, of tapered planform, with stressed skin. Light alloy plain ailerons and plain trailing-edge flaps. Balance tab in, and ground adjustable tab on, each aileron. Pitot static tube can be heated.

FUSELAGE: Semi-monocoque safe-life structure of light alloy, with stressed skin.

TAIL UNIT: Cantilever light alloy stressed skin structure, with sweptback vertical surfaces. One-piece elevator. Trim tabs in rudder and starboard half of elevator; balance tabs in rudder and port half of elevator.

LANDING GEAR: Non-retractable tricycle type, with HAL oleo-pneumatic shock absorber in each unit. Dunlop UK single mainwheels and nosewheel. Dunlop UK mainwheel tyres, size 446 × 151 × 166 mm, pressure 3·10 bars (45 lb/sq in); Dunlop India nosewheel tyre, size 361 × 126 × 127 mm, pressure 2·41 bars (35 lb/sq in). Dunlop UK aircooled hydraulic disc brakes on mainwheels.

POWER PLANT: One 194 kW (260 hp) Avco Lycoming AEIO-540-D4B5 flat-six engine, driving a Hartzell two-blade constant-speed metal propeller with spinner. Total of 220 litres (48·4 Imp gallons) of fuel in four flexible tanks (two in each wing), plus a 9 litre (2 Imp gallon) metal collector tank in fuselage. Total fuel capacity 229 litres (50·4 Imp gallons). Overwing refuelling points. Oil capacity 13·6 litres (3 Imp gallons).

ACCOMMODATION: Side by side seats for two persons under rearward sliding jettisonable framed canopy. Seats adjustable in height by 127 mm (5 in). Full dual controls, and adjustable rudder pedals, for instructor and pupil. Cockpits ventilated.

SYSTEMS: Hydraulic system for brakes only. Electrical system (28V DC earth return type) powered by 70A alternator, with SAFT 24V nickel-cadmium standby battery. No air-conditioning, pneumatic, de-icing or oxygen systems.

AVIONICS: HAL (Hyderabad Divn) COM-150 main UHF and COM-104A standby VHF com; directional gyro. No blind-flying instrumentation.

DIMENSIONS, EXTERNAL:

Wing span	9·50 m (31 ft 2 in)
Wing chord: at root	2·24 m (7 ft 4¼ in)
at tip	0·92 m (3 ft 0¼ in)
Wing aspect ratio	6·02
Length overall	7·72 m (25 ft 4 in)
Fuselage: Max width	1·25 m (4 ft 1¼ in)
Height overall	2·88 m (9 ft 5½ in)
Tailplane span	3·60 m (11 ft 9¾ in)
Wheel track	3·45 m (11 ft 4 in)
Wheelbase	2·10 m (6 ft 10¾ in)
Propeller diameter	2·03 m (6 ft 8 in)
Propeller ground clearance (static)	0·23 m (9 in)

AREAS:

Wings, gross	15·00 m² (161·5 sq ft)
Ailerons (total)	1·04 m² (11·19 sq ft)
Trailing-edge flaps (total)	1·82 m² (19·59 sq ft)
Vertical tail surfaces (above fuselage reference line)	2·06 m² (22·17 sq ft)
Rudder (aft of hinge line), incl tabs	0·869 m² (9·35 sq ft)
Tailplane	3·024 m² (32·55 sq ft)
Elevator (aft of hinge line), incl tabs	1·34 m² (14·42 sq ft)

WEIGHTS AND LOADINGS:

Basic weight empty	890 kg (1,962 lb)
Fuel and oil (guaranteed minimum)	164 kg (361 lb)
Max T-O and landing weight	1,250 kg (2,756 lb)
Max wing loading	83·33 kg/m² (17·07 lb/sq ft)
Max power loading	6·44 kg/kW (10·60 lb/hp)

HAL HTT-34 prototype (converted HPT-32) *(Brian M. Service)*

PERFORMANCE (at max T-O weight, ISA):

Never-exceed speed (structural)	240 knots (445 km/h; 276 mph)
Max level speed at S/L	143 knots (265 km/h; 164 mph) IAS
Max cruising speed at 3,050 m (10,000 ft)	115 knots (213 km/h; 132 mph)
Econ cruising speed	95 knots (176 km/h; 109 mph)
Stalling speed, 20° flap, engine idling	60 knots (110 km/h; 69 mph)
Max rate of climb at S/L	335 m (1,100 ft)/min
Service ceiling	5,500 m (18,045 ft)
T-O run	345 m (1,132 ft)
T-O to 15 m (50 ft)	545 m (1,788 ft)
Landing from 15 m (50 ft)	487 m (1,598 ft)
Landing run	220 m (720 ft)
Min ground turning radius	6·50 m (21 ft 4 in)
Range at 3,050 m (10,000 ft) at econ cruise power	401 nm (744 km; 462 miles)
g limits	+6/−3

HAL HTT-34

Exhibited publicly for the first time at the 1984 Farnborough International air show, the HTT-34 is a private venture development of the piston engined HPT-32. First flown on 17 June 1984, the prototype is the third HPT-32 (X2335) refitted with an Allison 250-B17D turboprop engine. The airframe is virtually unchanged aft of the firewall.

The HTT-34 is designed to FAR 23 standards, is fully aerobatic, and can be used for a wide range of ab initio training duties. In addition, it can be used for instrument, night and formation flying training, or for reconnaissance, observation, liaison or sport flying.

Programme status for 1986 was not stated, but earlier plans for an optional third seat and retractable landing gear appear to have been dropped.

TYPE: Two-seat ab initio trainer.

WINGS: Cantilever low-wing monoplane. Wing section NACA 64A-212. Dihedral 5° from roots. Incidence 2° 30′ at root. No sweepback. Light alloy safe-life wings, of tapered planform, with stressed skin. Light alloy plain ailerons and plain trailing-edge flaps. Balance tab in, and ground adjustable tab on, each aileron.

FUSELAGE: Semi-monocoque safe-life structure of light alloy, with stressed skin.

TAIL UNIT: Cantilever light alloy stressed skin structure, with sweptback vertical surfaces. One-piece elevator. Trim tab in rudder and starboard half of elevator; balance tab in rudder and port half of elevator.

LANDING GEAR: Non-retractable tricycle type, with HAL oleo-pneumatic shock absorber in each unit. Dunlop tyres on all wheels (mainwheel size 6·00-6·5, nose size 5·00-5); pressure 2·76-3·10 bars (40-45 lb/sq in) on main units, 2·07-2·41 bars (30-35 lb/sq in) on nose unit. Hydraulic disc brakes on mainwheels.

POWER PLANT: One 313 kW (420 shp) Allison 250-B17D turboprop engine, driving a Hartzell three-blade constant-speed fully-feathering propeller with reverse pitch capability. Total of 220 litres (48·4 Imp gallons) of fuel in four flexible tanks (two in each wing), plus a 9 litre (2 Imp gallon) collector tank in fuselage. Total fuel capacity 229 litres (50·4 Imp gallons).

ACCOMMODATION: Side by side seats for two persons in front, with provision at rear for 20 kg (44 lb) of baggage with tiedown facilities. Rearward sliding jettisonable framed canopy. Seats adjustable in height by 127 mm (5 in). Full dual controls, and adjustable rudder pedals, for instructor and pupil. Cockpits ventilated.

AVIONICS: VHF and UHF com radio; ADF and pictorial navigation.

DIMENSIONS, EXTERNAL: As for HPT-32, except:

Length overall	8·07 m (26 ft 5¾ in)
Propeller diameter	2·13 m (7 ft 0 in)
Propeller ground clearance (static)	0·24 m (9½ in)

AREAS: As for HPT-32, except:

Rudder (aft of hinge line), incl tabs	0·75 m² (8·07 sq ft)
Tailplane	3·02 m² (32·51 sq ft)
Elevators (aft of hinge line), incl tabs	1·08 m² (11·63 sq ft)

WEIGHTS AND LOADINGS:

Weight empty	866 kg (1,909 lb)
Max T-O weight	1,220 kg (2,689 lb)
Max wing loading	81·3 kg/m² (16·7 lb/sq ft)
Max power loading	3·89 kg/kW (6·40 lb/shp)

PERFORMANCE (prototype at max T-O weight, ISA):

Max level speed:	
at S/L	167 knots (310 km/h; 192 mph)
at 3,000 m (9,845 ft)	143 knots (266 km/h; 165 mph)
Stalling speed, engine idling:	
flaps up	63 knots (116 km/h; 73 mph)
flaps down	58 knots (108 km/h; 67 mph)
Max rate of climb at S/L	650 m (2,132 ft)/min
Service ceiling	7,620 m (25,000 ft)
T-O to 15 m (50 ft)	265 m (870 ft)
Landing from 15 m (50 ft):	
without propeller reversal	465 m (1,526 ft)
with propeller reversal	200 m (656 ft)
Range with max fuel at 3,000 m (9,845 ft)	332 nm (615 km; 382 miles)
Endurance with max fuel at 3,000 m (9,845 ft)	3 h 8 min
g limits	+6/−3

MiG COMPLEX

The MiG Complex was originally formed with the Nasik, Koraput and Hyderabad Divisions of HAL, which, under an agreement concluded in 1962, built respectively the airframes, power plants and avionics of MiG-21 series fighters under licence from the USSR. Nasik had a workforce of 8,019 in September 1986. The Hyderabad Division is now a part of the Accessories Complex.

HAL (MIKOYAN) MiG-21bis

NATO reporting name: Fishbed-N

Several versions of the MiG-21 have been supplied to or, since 1966, manufactured in India. These have included the MiG-21F (IAF designation Type 74) and MiG-21PF (Type 76) of which details can be found in the 1976-77 *Jane's*; the MiG-21FL (Type 77) and MiG-21U (Types 66-400 and 66-600), as described in the 1977-78 *Jane's*; and the MiG-21M (Type 96) and MF (160 built: 1982-83 *Jane's*). The current production version is:

MiG-21bis ('Fishbed-N'). Deliveries of 75 Soviet built examples of this version, initially for service with No. 21 Squadron of the IAF, were reported in 1977. Indian production of 220 MiG-21bis (initially from knocked-down components) and their Tumansky R-25 engines had begun by the end of 1979, and the 21bis superseded the MiG-21M as the current production version in 1981.

HAL assembled Mikoyan MiG-21bis of the Indian Air Force

Indian production of MiG-21s was reported to be at the rate of about 30 per year in 1981-82. It is due to be phased out in 1986-87, as production of the MiG-27M 'Flogger-J' increases. Details of the MiG-21 appear in the USSR section of this edition.

HAL (MIKOYAN) MiG-27M

Indian Air Force name: Bahadur (Valiant)
NATO reporting name: Flogger-J

Licence assembly of some 165 MiG-27Ms (see USSR section) began at HAL in 1984, and the first example completed by HAL was rolled out in October of that year. These aircraft supplement Soviet built MiG-23s and MiG-27s already supplied to the Indian Air Force, and are the first MiG-27s to be assembled outside the USSR. From 1988-89, MiG-27Ms assembled at Nasik are expected to incorporate components manufactured in India. First IAF unit to receive Bahadurs was No. 32 ('Tiger Sharks') Squadron, the type being formally inducted into IAF service on 11 January 1986.

POWER PLANT: One Tumansky R-29B turbofan engine, rated at 78·45 kN (17,635 lb st) dry and 112·76 kN (25,350 lb st) with afterburning.

ARMAMENT: One 23 mm rotary cannon and up to 3,000 kg (6,614 lb) of external stores which can include 500 kg bombs, 57 mm S-24 rockets, two 'Kerry' air-to-surface or four R-60 air-to-air missiles.

WEIGHT:
Max T-O weight 18,000 kg (39,685 lb)

PERFORMANCE:
T-O run at S/L 800 m (2,625 ft)
Combat radius (low level) 210 nm (390 km; 242 miles)
Ferry range 1,349 nm (2,500 km; 1,553 miles)

INDONESIA

AKASAMITRA

AKASAMITRA HOMEBUILT AIRCRAFT ASSOCIATION

PO Box 167, Jakarta

CHAIRMAN: Air Vice-Marshal (Retd) J. Salatun, MP
DESIGNER: Dipl Ing Suharto

In addition to its work on a variety of aircraft for amateur flying, Akasamitra designed and built the prototype of a two-seat sporting and training aircraft designated ST-220 with financial support from the Indonesian Department of Defence and Security. Details of this aircraft can be found in the 1985-86 *Jane's*.

IPTN

INDUSTRI PESAWAT TERBANG NUSANTARA (Indonesian Aircraft Industries)

PO Box 563, Jalan Pajajaran 154, Bandung
Telephone: Bandung (022) 613662 and 611081
Telex: 28295 NUR BDG
HEAD OFFICE: PO Box 3752, 8 Jalan M.H. Thamrin, Jakarta
Telephone: (021) 322395 and 336651
Telex: 46141 ATP JAKARTA
PRESIDENT DIRECTOR: Prof Dr-Ing B. J. Habibie
DIRECTORS:
Mr Suwondo (General Affairs)
Drs Wisnubroto (Vice-Director, General Affairs)
Ir S. Paramajuda (Commercial and Product Support)
Ir H. D. Pusponegoro (Technology)
Ir Yuwono (Facilities Development and Construction)
Ir Sutadi Suparlan (Production)
ASSISTANTS TO PRESIDENT DIRECTOR:
Dr Sujana Sapi'ie (Computer Support)
Ir Budiarta Suradiningrat (Chief Engineer)
Drs Bambang Ekoyono (Finance)
Dr Parlin Napitupulu (Inspectorate)
Ir Djermani Sanjaya (Programme Management and Feasibility)
Ir Sundoro (Quality Assurance)
Ir Mangatur Pardede (Material)
Tatang Endan (Security)
HEADS OF DIVISIONS:
Ir Eddy Susilo (Fixed-wing Production)
Ir Yuliswar (Rotary-wing Production)
Ir Sutadi Suparlan (Fabrication)
Ir Hari Laksono (Aircraft Services)
Ir H. Erawan Lambri (Weapon Systems)
H. Pribadi (Flight Operations)
Ir S. Paramajuda (Universal Engine Maintenance Centre)
Ir Drs Pasaribu (Production Engineering)
Ir Indra Hasbi (Industrial Engineering)
Suripto Sugondo (Public Relations Manager)

This company was officially inaugurated as PT Industri Pesawat Terbang Nurtanio (Nurtanio Aircraft Industry Ltd) on 23 August 1976, when the government of Indonesia implemented a decision of 5 April 1976 to centralise all existing facilities in the establishment of a single new aircraft industry under the direction of Prof Dr-Ing B. J. Habibie. The original capital was provided by combining the assets of Pertamina's Advanced Technology and Aeronautical Division with those of the former Nurtanio Aircraft Industry (LIPNUR: see 1977-78 *Jane's*), which was pioneered by the late Air Marshal Nurtanio Pringgoadisurjo. The present name of the company was adopted in late 1985.

IPTN has a weapons system division, located in Menang Tasikmalaya, West Java, which develops and produces the weaponry fitted to aircraft built by the company for military customers.

IPTN is jointly responsible with CASA of Spain for development and production of the Airtech CN-235 (see International section), as well as continuing licence manufacture of the NC-212 Aviocar, NBO-105, NAS-332 Super Puma, NBell-412 and MBB/Kawasaki NBK-117, as described in the following entries. It also expects to undertake subcontract work for Boeing. The company had a workforce of approx 13,000 employees in late 1986.

With MBB of West Germany, IPTN has set up a new joint company known as NTT (New Transport Technologies), with its headquarters in Munich. Its first venture is a small helicopter (the BN-109). In January 1986 a memorandum of understanding was signed with MBB and Boeing, for joint development of a 100/135-seat transport aircraft known at present as the NTTC-285.

AIRTECH (CASA/IPTN) CN-235

IPTN and CASA (see Spanish section) are developing and manufacturing jointly a 40/44-passenger transport

IPTN NC-212 Srs 200 Aviocar twin-turboprop transport aircraft

IPTN NBO-105 helicopter, operated by the Indonesian Air Force for search and rescue duties

NAS-332 Super Puma assembled by IPTN

aircraft of their own design, known as the CN-235. Details of this aircraft can be found under the Airtech heading in the International section.

IPTN (CASA) NC-212 AVIOCAR

The C-212 Aviocar twin-turboprop multi-purpose transport aircraft has been manufactured in Indonesia since 1976, under licence from CASA of Spain (which see). Indonesian built Aviocars have the designation NC-212.

IPTN built 29 NC-212-100 series Aviocars before switching production to the NC-212-200 version, of which 88 had been delivered by mid-1986 for duties which include civil passenger and cargo carrying, LAPES airdropping (low altitude parachute extraction system), military transport, search and rescue, maritime patrol, medical evacuation, photographic, survey, and rainmaking. Domestic and foreign operators were listed in the 1985-86 *Jane's*.

IPTN (MBB) NBO-105

The BO 105 helicopter has been manufactured in Indonesia since 1976, under licence from MBB of the Federal Republic of Germany (which see). Indonesian designation is NBO-105.

By the beginning of 1986 a total of 105 NBO-105s had been delivered, and production was continuing with the NBO-105 S, which has a 25 cm (10 in) longer fuselage and optional radar. Customers are the Indonesian Army, Navy and Air Force, Pelita Air Service, the Indonesian Forestry Department, Indonesian Immigration Department, Indonesian Search and Rescue Agency, Gudang Garam, Gunung Madu, and the Indonesian Civil Aviation Training Centre.

IPTN (MBB/KAWASAKI) NBK-117

Under a contract signed with MBB in November 1982, IPTN is to manufacture the BK 117 helicopter (see International section) under licence. Indonesian aircraft, which have been ordered by government agencies and private operators, are to be designated NBK-117.

MBB/IPTN BN-109

Under this designation, MBB and IPTN are developing a small four-seat helicopter. All known details are given under the NTT heading in the International section.

IPTN-Bell NBell-412 twin-turbine helicopter

IPTN (AÉROSPATIALE) NAS-332 SUPER PUMA

IPTN began assembling the NSA 330J Puma in 1981, switching production to the AS 332 Super Puma in early 1983.

Rollout of the first IPTN assembled NAS-332 for Pelita Air Service took place on 22 April 1983. Total orders for the NAS-332 had reached 69 by the beginning of 1984, from the Indonesian armed forces, Forestry Department, Pelita and Derazona. IPTN had reportedly completed 17 by mid-1986.

IPTN (BELL) NBELL-412

A licence agreement for IPTN to manufacture the Bell Model 412 (see US section) was signed in November 1982. It covers the partial manufacture and assembly of more than 100 Bell 412s. Orders have been placed by the Indonesian armed forces and private operators. IPTN built aircraft, the first of which was nearing completion in early 1986, are designated NBell-412.

INTERNATIONAL PROGRAMMES

AERITALIA/AERMACCHI/ EMBRAER

PARTICIPATING COMPANIES:

Aeritalia (Combat Aircraft Group), Corso Marche 41, 10146 Turin, Italy
Telephone: (011) 33321
Telex: 221076 AERITOR

Aermacchi SpA, Via Sanvito Silvestro 80 (Casella Postale 246), 21100 Varese, Italy
Telephone: (0332) 254111
Telex: 380070 AERMAC I

EMBRAER (Empresa Brasileira de Aeronáutica SA), Av Brig Faria Lima 2170, Caixa Postal 343, 12200 São José dos Campos, SP, Brazil
Telephone: (123) 21 5400
Telex: (391) 1133589 EBAE BR or (391) 1133917 EBAE BR

AMX PROGRAMME MANAGER:
Ing Domenico Covelli (Aeritalia)

AMX INTEGRATION MANAGER:
Ing Giorgio Danieli (Aeritalia)

AMX

Brazilian Air Force designation: A-1

The AMX, when it enters service in 1988, will represent the outcome of an Italian Air Force specification drawn up eleven years earlier. By that date the Aeronautica Militare Italiana's G91Rs, G91Ys and F-104Gs are expected to have reached the end of their useful life, so that the AMI's two basic front line combat types will be the Tornado in the interdictor/strike and reconnaissance roles, and the Aeritalia built F-104S for all-weather interception. To complement these types, the AMI decided that a need existed for a small tactical fighter-bomber, optimised for direct air reconnaissance and weapons support of friendly ground and naval forces but capable also, when required, of carrying out missions which would otherwise require use of both the Tornado and F-104S.

Responding to this AMI specification, design studies were initiated by Aeritalia in 1977. Earlier that year the Brazilian Air Force (Força Aérea Brasileira) had made known a broadly similar requirement, called A-X, for a single-seat attack aircraft to supplement its AT-26 Xavantes (Brazilian built Aermacchi MB-326GBs). Collaboration between EMBRAER and Aermacchi on this project, involving an Aermacchi design known as the MB-340, had been discussed during the first half of 1977, and a decision on whether to go ahead with it was expected by the end of that year.

In the meantime, the AMI issued its own attack aircraft specification, an early result of which was the conclusion of a co-operation agreement between Aeritalia and Aermacchi in mid-1978, marking the beginning of an 18-month project definition phase of the AMX. In October 1978 the Italian Air Force selected the Rolls-Royce Spey Mk 807 turbofan engine as the power plant for the AMX. In March 1980, soon after completion of the definition phase, the Brazilian government confirmed its intention of taking part in the AMX programme, and four months later EMBRAER became an industrial partner of the two Italian manufacturers. The development phase, initiated in January 1981, was followed by an initial memorandum of understanding between the two air forces concerned. A second MoU, signed in October 1981, covered the joint development and production phases of the AMX on a fully collaborative basis; a third was signed during 1983, laying down the terms of that collaboration during the development phase.

Six prototypes have been completed, plus one airframe (built by Aeritalia at Turin) for static testing, which was completed by the Spring of 1985. In addition, selected components for fatigue testing have been completed by each of the three manufacturers.

The Aeritalia-assembled A01 first prototype made its initial flight on 15 May 1984. On 1 June, on its fifth flight, it was lost in a crash. The second prototype (A02), completed by Aermacchi, made its first flight on 19 November 1984. These aerodynamic prototypes were followed by the Aeritalia-assembled A03 avionics testbed, which flew for the first time on 28 January 1985. Next to fly was a replacement for A01, designated A11, which made its initial flight on 24 May 1985. First Brazilian assembled (YA-1) prototype to fly, on 16 October 1985, was A04; this was followed by the Aermacchi-assembled A05, in mid-1986, and the second Brazilian aircraft, A06, was due to fly in October 1986. A total of 1,400 flight hours is due to be completed during the development phase, with the main flight test programme ending in the closing months of 1987.

Based on present stated requirements for the air forces of Italy and Brazil, series production of the AMX is expected to continue until 1990. Manufacture of the first 30 production aircraft began, on schedule, in July 1986, and the first of these will fly in 1987. Deliveries are planned to begin to the Italian Air Force in the Spring of 1988 and the Brazilian Air Force in the Spring of 1989. The work split gives Aeritalia, the programme leader, 46·7 per cent (fuselage centre-section, nose radome, fin and rudder, elevators, flaps, ailerons and spoilers); Aermacchi has 23·6 per cent (forward fuselage, including gun and avionics integration, canopy, and tailcone); and EMBRAER 29·7 per cent (air intakes, wings, wing leading-edge slats, tailplane, wing pylons, external fuel tanks and reconnaissance pallets). There is single source component manufacture only, but there are final assembly lines in both Italy and Brazil. To co-ordinate and oversee the programme the three industrial partners formed a Comitato Direttivo Congiunto (joint management committee), within which are three key groups devoted to programme management, technical integration, and flight operations.

The series production phase entails building 266 aircraft — 187 for the Aeronautica Militare Italiana and 79 for the Força Aérea Brasileira. In the Italian Air Force the AMX is intended to take over duties performed at present by the G91R, due to be phased out of its close air support role by 1986-87; the G91Y interdictor, also due for phase-out by 1986-87; and the F-104G and S Starfighter, scheduled for replacement in the strike role by 1987-88. The close air support and interdiction tasks will be undertaken fully by

A04 first Brazilian prototype of the AMX single-seat multi-purpose combat aircraft

the AMX, while counter-air duties will be shared with the longer-range Tornado; the 187 aircraft to be ordered will be sufficient to equip eight squadrons.

The Brazilian Air Force aircraft differ primarily in avionics and weapon delivery systems, and have two internally mounted 30 mm cannon instead of the single multi-barrel 20 mm weapon of the Italian version.

The AMX will be capable of carrying out missions at high subsonic speed and very low altitude, by day and night, in poor visibility, and if necessary from bases with poorly equipped or partially damaged runways. Basic requirements included good take-off and landing performance, good penetration capability, and a proven, in-production power plant requiring a minimum of adaptation to the AMX airframe. The primary flying control surfaces have manual reversion, to provide a fly-home capability even if both of the two independent hydraulic systems become inoperative.

The aircraft's modular design, coupled with sophisticated avionics and other airborne systems, give it the flexibility to undertake additional roles. Definition has been completed of a two-seat version, with a second cockpit in tandem replacing the forward fuselage fuel tankage, and this is seen as suitable for advanced training, operational conversion, all-weather day/night tactical fighter, maritime, electronic warfare or standoff weapon carrying roles.

The following description applies to the single-seat AMX:

TYPE: Single-seat close air support, battlefield interdiction, anti-shipping and reconnaissance aircraft, with secondary capability for offensive counter-air.

WINGS: Cantilever shoulder-wing monoplane, with sweepback of 31° on leading-edges, 27° 30′ at quarter chord, and thickness/chord ratio of 12%. Three-spar torsion box structure, machined from solid aluminium alloy with integrally stiffened skins. Three-point attachment of each wing to fuselage main frames. Leading-edge slats (two segments each side) over most of span, and two-segment double-slotted Fowler flaps over approx two-thirds of each trailing-edge, are operated electrically and actuated hydraulically. Forward of each pair of flaps is a pair of hydraulically actuated spoilers, deployed separately in inboard and outboard pairs. These are controlled electronically by Aeritalia/GEC Avionics flight control computer, and serve also as airbrakes/lift dumpers. Hydraulically actuated ailerons, with manual reversion. No tabs.

FUSELAGE: Conventional semi-monocoque oval-section structure, built chiefly of aluminium alloy. Forward section incorporates main avionics and equipment bays, airborne systems, gun(s), nose landing gear and cockpit; central section includes engine air intake ducts, main landing gear and engine bay. Extreme rear fuselage, complete with tailplane, is detachable for access to engine.

TAIL UNIT: Sweptback fin (of carbonfibre) and rudder. Variable incidence tailplane, mid-mounted on fuselage. Tailplane and rudder movement controlled electronically by Aeritalia/GEC Avionics flight control computer. Hydraulically actuated carbonfibre elevators, with manual reversion. No elevator or rudder tabs.

LANDING GEAR: Hydraulically retractable tricycle type, of Messier-Hispano-Bugatti levered suspension design, built in Italy by Magnaghi (nose unit) and ERAM (main units). Single wheel and oleo-pneumatic shock absorber on each unit. Nose unit retracts forward; main units retract forward and inward, turning through approx 90° to lie almost flat in underside of engine air intake trunks. Nosewheel is hydraulically steerable (60° to left and right), self-centering, and fitted with anti-shimmy device. Mainwheel tyres size 670 × 210-12, pressure 9·65 bars (140 lb/sq in); nosewheel tyre size 18 × 5·5-8. Hydraulic brakes and anti-skid system. No brake-chute. Prototypes fitted with runway arrester hook.

POWER PLANT: One 49·1 kN (11,030 lb st) Rolls-Royce Spey Mk 807 non-afterburning turbofan engine, built under licence in Italy by Fiat, Piaggio and Alfa Romeo, with Brazilian participation. Fuel in compartmented fuselage tank and two integral wing tanks. Auxiliary underwing fuel tanks of up to 1,000 litres (220 Imp gallons) capacity can be carried on each of the inboard underwing pylons, and up to 500 litres (110 Imp gallons) on each of the outboard pylons. Single-point pressure or gravity refuelling of internal and external tanks. Provision for in-flight refuelling.

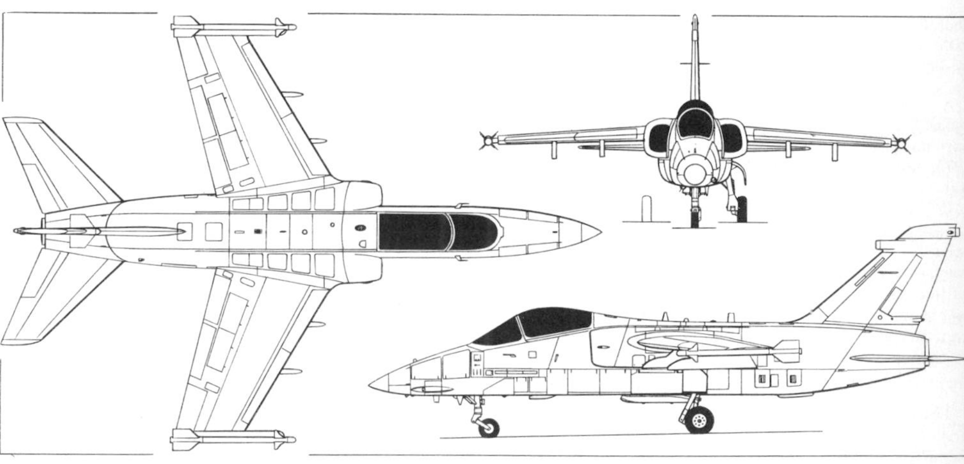

Aeritalia/Aermacchi/EMBRAER AMX, under development for the air forces of Italy and Brazil *(Pilot Press)*

ACCOMMODATION: Pilot only, on Martin-Baker Mk 10L zero/zero ejection seat; 18° downward view over nose. One-piece wraparound windscreen; one-piece hinged canopy, opening sideways to starboard. Cockpit pressurised and air-conditioned. Tandem two-seat combat trainer/special missions version under development.

SYSTEMS: Microtecnica environmental control system (ECS) provides air-conditioning of cockpit, avionics and reconnaissance pallets, cockpit pressurisation, air intake and inlet guide vane anti-icing, windscreen demisting, and anti-*g* systems. Duplicated redundant hydraulic systems, driven by engine gearbox, operate at pressure of 207 bars (3,000 lb/sq in) for actuation of primary flight control system, flaps, spoilers, landing gear, wheel brakes, anti-skid system, nosewheel steering and gun operation. Primary electrical system AC power (115/200V at fixed frequency of 400Hz) supplied by two 30kVA IDG generators, with two transformer-rectifier units for conversion to 28V DC; 36Ah nickel-cadmium battery for emergency use, to provide power for essential systems in the event of primary and secondary electrical system failure. Fiat FA 150 Argo auxiliary power unit for engine starting. Liquid oxygen system.

AVIONICS AND EQUIPMENT: Avionics and equipment are divided into six main subsystems: (1) UHF and VHF com, and IFF; (2) navigation (Litton Italia inertial system, with Tacan and standby AHRS, for Italian Air Force; VOR/ILS for Brazil); (3) Litton computer based weapons aiming and delivery, incorporating an Elta/FIAR range-only radar and OMI/Selenia stores management system; (4) digital data display (OMI/Selenia head-up, multi-function head-down, and weapons/nav); (5) data processing, with Microtecnica digital air data computer; and (6) Elettronica active and passive ECM, including fin mounted radar warning receiver. The ranging radar, known as Pointer, is an I/J band set modified from the Elta (Israel) EL/M-2001B and built in Italy by FIAR. In terms of redundancy and monitoring, the avionics are designed to permit successful completion of mission, even in the event of initial failure. Modular design and space provisions within the aircraft permit retrofitting of alternative systems if and when required. All avionics/equipment packages are pallet mounted to facilitate removal and replacement, and are positioned to allow rapid access for routine maintenance and change of configuration.

ARMAMENT AND OPERATIONAL EQUIPMENT: One M61A1 multi-barrel 20 mm cannon, with 350 rds, in port side of lower forward fuselage (one 30 mm DEFA 554 cannon on each side in aircraft for Brazilian Air Force). Single twin-pylon stores attachment point under fuselage, on centreline, plus two attachments under each wing, and wingtip rails for two AIM-9L Sidewinder or similar infra-red air-to-air missiles (MAA-1 Piranha on Brazilian aircraft). Fuselage and inboard underwing hardpoints each stressed for loads of up to 907 kg (2,000 lb), outboard underwing points for 454 kg (1,000 lb) each. Total external stores load 3,800 kg (8,377 lb). Attack weapons can include free-fall or retarded Mk 82/83/84 bombs, cluster bombs, air-to-surface missiles (including area denial, anti-radiation and anti-shipping weapons), electro-optical precision guided munitions, and rocket launchers. For reconnaissance missions, three alternative and interchangeable pallet mounted photographic systems (panoramic, TV and photogrammetric) can be carried, installed internally in forward fuselage; an external infra-red/optronics pod can be carried on the centreline pylon. Each of these systems is fully compatible with the aircraft, and will not affect operational capability; the aircraft will therefore be able to carry out reconnaissance missions without effect upon its normal navigation/attack and self defence capabilities. Camera bay is in lower starboard side of fuselage, forward of mainwheel bay.

DIMENSIONS, EXTERNAL:
- Wing span:
  - excl wingtip missiles and rails — 8·874 m (29 ft 1½ in)
  - over missiles — 10·00 m (32 ft 9¾ in)
- Wing aspect ratio — 3·75
- Wing taper ratio — 0·5
- Length overall — 13·575 m (44 ft 6½ in)
- Length of fuselage — 12·55 m (41 ft 2 in)
- Height overall — 4·576 m (15 ft 0¼ in)
- Tailplane span — approx 5·20 m (17 ft 0¾ in)
- Wheel track — 2·15 m (7 ft 0¾ in)
- Wheelbase — 4·74 m (15 ft 6½ in)

AREA:
- Wings, gross — 21·00 m² (226·04 sq ft)

WEIGHTS AND LOADINGS:
- Operational weight empty — 6,700 kg (14,770 lb)
- Max external stores load — 3,800 kg (8,377 lb)
- T-O weight 'clean' — 9,600 kg (21,164 lb)
- Typical mission T-O weight — 10,750 kg (23,700 lb)
- Max T-O weight — 12,500 kg (27,558 lb)
- Normal landing weight — 7,000 kg (15,432 lb)
- Combat wing loading ('clean') — 385 kg/m² (78·9 lb/sq ft)
- Max wing loading — 595·2 kg/m² (122·0 lb/sq ft)
- Max power loading — 254·77 kg/kN (2·5 lb/lb st)

PERFORMANCE (A: at 10,750 kg; 23,700 lb mission T-O weight, B: at max T-O weight, ISA in both cases):
- Max level speed — Mach 0·86
- Service ceiling — 13,000 m (42,650 ft)
- T-O run at S/L: A — 750 m (2,461 ft)
  - B — 950 m (3,120 ft)
- T-O to 15 m (50 ft) at S/L: B — 1,525 m (5,000 ft)
- Min ground turning radius:
  - A, B — 11·00 m (36 ft 1 in)
- Attack radius, with allowance for 5 min combat over target and 10% fuel reserves:
  - A with 907 kg (2,000 lb) of external stores:
    - hi-lo-hi — 480 nm (890 km; 550 miles)
    - lo-lo-lo — 300 nm (555 km; 345 miles)
  - B with 2,720 kg (6,000 lb) of external stores:
    - hi-lo-hi — 280 nm (520 km; 320 miles)
    - lo-lo-lo — 200 nm (370 km; 230 miles)
- Ferry range with two 1,000 litre (220 Imp gallon) drop tanks, 10% reserves:
  - A — 1,700 nm (3,150 km; 1,957 miles)
- *g* limits — +8/−4

AIRBUS

AIRBUS INDUSTRIE

Avenue Lucien Servanty, BP No. 33, 31707 Blagnac Cédex, France
Telephone: (33) 61 93 33 33
Telex: AIRBU 530526 F
PARIS OFFICE: 12bis avenue Bosquet, 75007 Paris, France
Telephone: (33) 145 51 40 95

AIRFRAME PRIME CONTRACTORS:

Aérospatiale, 37 boulevard de Montmorency, 75781 Paris Cédex 16, France

Deutsche Airbus GmbH, 8000 München 81, Arabellastrasse 30, Postfach 810260, Federal Republic of Germany

British Aerospace PLC, Richmond Road, Kingston upon Thames, Surrey KT2 5QS, England

CHAIRMAN OF SUPERVISORY BOARD: Dr Franz-Josef Strauss
VICE-CHAIRMAN OF SUPERVISORY BOARD: Henri Martre
PRESIDENT AND CHIEF EXECUTIVE OFFICER: Jean Pierson
EXECUTIVE VICE-PRESIDENT AND GENERAL MANAGER: Heribert Flosdorff
SENIOR VICE-PRESIDENTS:
Gérard Blanc (Customer Support)
Jean Roeder (Technology and New Product Development)
Stuart Iddles (Commercial)
Jürgen Thomas (Industrial and Programmes)
Angel Hurtado (Purchasing)
Robert Whitfield (Finance)
Bernard Ziegler (Engineering)

Airbus Industrie was set up in December 1970 as a Groupement d'Intérêt Economique to manage the development, manufacture, marketing and support of a twin-engined large-capacity short/medium-range transport aircraft known as the A300. This management now extends to the A300-600, A310 and A320 included in this entry. Airbus Industrie is responsible for all work on these programmes by the partner companies, made up of Aérospatiale of France, which has a 37·9% interest in Airbus Industrie, MBB (through Deutsche Airbus) of West Germany (37·9%), British Aerospace PLC (20%), and CASA of Spain (4·2%). Fokker (Netherlands) is an associate in the A300 and A310 programmes; and Belairbus (Belgium) in the programme for the A310. Some of the Deutsche Airbus work on the A300/A310 is subcontracted to the Italian aerospace industry, and some BAe work to the Australian industry.

Large, fully equipped and inspected, airframe sections are flown from their places of manufacture in Europe to the final assembly line in Toulouse on board Super Guppy outsize cargo aircraft. After assembly, painting in customers' colour scheme is carried out at Toulouse. Aircraft are then flown to Hamburg for installation of interior furnishings and cabin and cargo hold equipment before returning to Toulouse for final customer acceptance.

Projected Airbus developments include the A330 and A340. Work on refining these aircraft, in association with major world airlines, continues.

AIRBUS A300-600

The early history of the A300 programme has appeared in previous editions of *Jane's*.

The first A300, a B1 (F-WUAB, later F-OCAZ) made its first flight on 28 October 1972, and was followed by the second B1 (F-WUAC) on 5 February 1973. The B1 was described in detail in the 1971-72 *Jane's*.

Detailed descriptions of the B2-100 (30 built), B2-200 (24 built), B2-300, B4-100 (66 built, plus four converted from B2-300s) and B4-200 (100 built) can be found in the 1984-85 and earlier editions. A300B4 production ended in Autumn 1984.

The major production versions since early 1984 are:

A300-600. Advanced version of B4-200, first flown (F-WZLR) on 8 July 1983 and certificated (with JT9D-7R4H1 engines) on 9 March 1984. French certification for Category IIIB take-offs and landings awarded on 26 March 1985. Incorporates a number of improvements, including increased passenger and freight capacity. Modifications include use of rear fuselage developed for A310, shorter by two frame pitches in unpressurised section than that of 100/200 series A300s, with 0·52 m (1 ft 9 in) extension of parallel section of fuselage to restore tail moment arm. Passenger capacity thus increased by two seat rows for increase in overall length equivalent to only one frame pitch. Other improvements include forward facing two-man cockpit with CRT displays, new digital avionics, new braking control system, and new APU.

An extensive weight reduction programme, including simplified systems and the use of composite materials for some secondary structural components, allows greater payload capacity with very little change in empty weight. Performance improvements, offering better payload/range capability and greater fuel economy, result from a comprehensive 'drag clean-up' programme.

Definition of the -600 was completed in 1980 and the first order, from Saudi Arabian Airlines for 11 A300-600s (with JT9D-7R4H1 engines), was received in December of that year. First delivery (to Saudia) was made on 26 March 1984. September 1985 certification was obtained for the improved version (first flown on 20 March 1985) with CF6-80C2 engines, carbon brakes, wingtip fences and two-crew flight deck. This version has been ordered by Thai Airways International (eight), the Abu Dhabi Royal Flight (two), Korean Air (three) and Lufthansa (seven); first delivery (to Thai Airways) was made on 26 September 1985.

A300-600R. Extended range version of -600 (formerly known as -600ER), for introduction in 1988. Wingtip fences, additional fuel/trim tank in tailplane, carbon brakes, radial tyres, greater use of composites, and Porsche-styled cockpit standard. First flight due Autumn 1987.

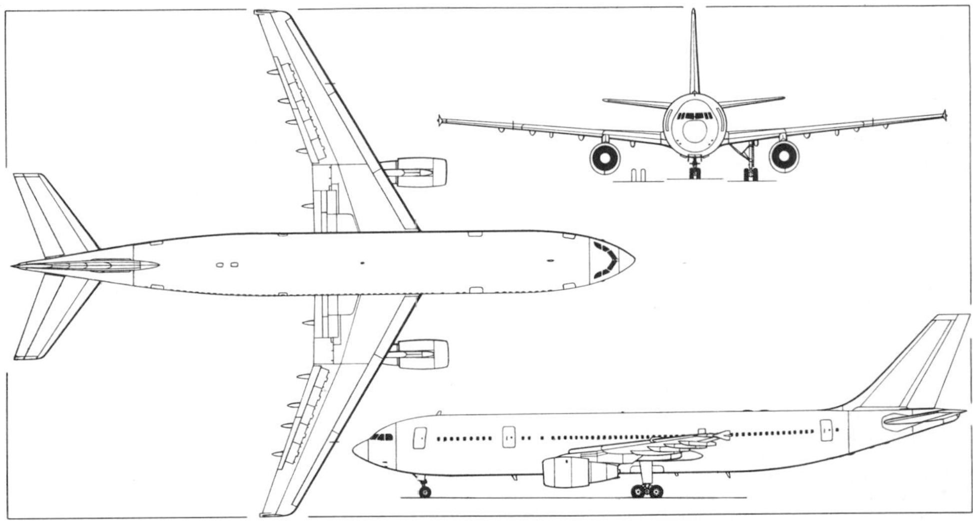

Airbus A300-600 wide-bodied medium-range transport (JT9D engines) *(Pilot Press)*

A300C and F. Convertible and freighter versions of the A300-600; described separately.

By 15 August 1986 a total of 281 A300s (all versions) had been ordered, of which 265 had been delivered.

Aérospatiale is responsible for manufacturing the entire nose section (including the flight deck), lower centre fuselage and engine pylons, and for final assembly. MBB is responsible for manufacturing the forward fuselage, between the flight deck and wing box, the upper centre fuselage, the rear fuselage and the vertical tail surfaces. British Aerospace has design responsibility for the wings, builds the wing fixed structures, and is working in collaboration with Fokker, which is building the wingtips and wing moving surfaces. Wing assembly is done by MBB. CASA manufactures the horizontal tail surfaces, the port and starboard forward passenger doors and the landing gear doors.

The following description applies to the A300-600:

Type: Large-capacity wide-bodied medium/long-range transport.

Wings: Cantilever mid-wing monoplane. Thickness/chord ratio 10·5%. Sweepback 28° at quarter-chord. Primary two-spar box structure, integral with fuselage and incorporating fail-safe principles, built of high strength aluminium alloy except for spoilers, flap track fairings and wing/fuselage fairings, which are of composite materials. Third spar across inboard sections. Machined skin with open-sectioned stringers. Each wing has three-section leading-edge slats (no slat cutout over the engine pylon), and three cambered tabless flaps on trailing-edge; a Krueger flap on the leading-edge wing root; and an all-speed aileron between inboard flap and outer pair. Two spoilers (outboard) and five airbrakes forward of flaps, all of which can be used as lift dumpers. The flaps extend over 84 per cent of each half span, and increase the wing chord by 25 per cent when fully extended. The all-speed aileron is deflected downward automatically 9° 2′ on each side when the flaps are operated. Drive mechanisms for flaps and slats are similar to one another, each powered by twin motors driving ball screwjacks on each surface with built-in protection against asymmetric operation. Two slat positions for take-off and landing. Pre-selection of the airbrake/lift dump lever allows automatic extension of the lift dumpers on touchdown. Primary control surfaces (ailerons, elevators and rudder) are fully powered by mechanically controlled hydraulic servos (three per surface); secondary control surfaces (spoilers, airbrakes, flaps and slats) fully hydraulically powered, with electrical control. Anti-icing of wing leading-edges, outboard of engine pods, is by hot air bled from engines.

Fuselage: Semi-monocoque pressurised structure of circular cross-section, with frames and open Z-section stringers. Built mainly of high strength aluminium alloy, with steel or titanium for some major components. Skin panels integrally machined in areas of high stress. Honeycomb panels or restricted glassfibre laminates for secondary structures.

Tail Unit: Cantilever structure, with sweepback on all surfaces. Construction mainly of metal except for fin leading/trailing-edges, fin tip, fin/fuselage fairings, rudder, tailplane trailing-edge and elevator leading-edge panels, tailplane and elevator tips, and access panels to elevator actuator, which are made of composites. Fin also of composites on A300-600R from mid-1987. Variable incidence tailplane is actuated by a fail-safe ball screwjack, driven by two independent hydraulic motors which are electrically controlled with an additional mechanical input. No anti-icing of leading-edges.

Landing Gear: Hydraulically retractable tricycle type, of Messier-Hispano-Bugatti design, with Messier-Hispano-Bugatti/Liebherr/Dowty shock absorbers and wheels standard. Twin-wheel nose unit retracts forward, main units inward into fuselage. Free-fall extension. Nosewheel doors and mainwheel leg fairing doors are of composite materials. Nose gear is structurally identical to -100/200 series; main gear is generally reinforced, with a new-design hinge arm and a new pitch damper hydraulic and electrical installation. Each four-wheel main unit comprises two tandem mounted bogies, interchangeable left with right. Standard bogie size is 927 × 1,397 mm (36½ × 55 in); wider bogie of 978 × 1,524 mm (38½ × 60 in) is optional. Mainwheel tyres size 49 × 17-20 (standard) or 49 × 19-20 (wide bogie), with respective pressures of 12·4 and 11·1 bars (180 and 161 lb/sq in). Nosewheel tyres size 40 × 14-16, pressure 9·4 bars (136 lb/sq in). Steering angles 65°/95°. Messier-Hispano-Bugatti/Liebherr/Dowty hydraulic disc brakes standard on all mainwheels. Normal braking powered by 'green' hydraulic system, controlled electrically through two master valves and monitored by a brake system control box to provide anti-skid protection. Standby braking (powered automatically by 'yellow' hydraulic system if normal 'green' system supply fails) controlled through a dual metering valve; anti-skid protection is ensured

Airbus A300-600 twin-turbofan transport for Thai Airways, with General Electric CF6-80C2 engines. This version was certificated in September 1985

through same box as normal system, with emergency pressure supplied to brakes by accumulators charged from 'yellow' system. Automatic braking system optional. Duplex anti-skid units fitted, with a third standby hydraulic supply for wheel brakes. Bendix or Goodrich wheels and brakes available optionally.

Power Plant: Underwing location of the power plant enables the A300-600 to use any advanced technology turbofan engine in the 222·5 kN (50,000 lb st) class. It has currently been ordered and is available with the following engines: Two 249 kN (56,000 lb st) Pratt & Whitney JT9D-7R4H1 or PW4156; or two 258 kN (58,000 lb st) PW4158; or two 263·8 kN (59,300 lb st) General Electric CF6-80C2-A1 engines. General Electric engines are assembled under licence by Rolls-Royce and SNECMA; some components are also licence built by SNECMA (France) and MTU (West Germany). Nacelles for GE and Pratt & Whitney engines are subcontracted to Rohr (California). Fuel in two integral tanks in each wing, and fifth tank in centre-section, giving standard usable capacity of 62,000 litres (13,638 Imp gallons). Additional 6,100 litre (1,342 Imp gallon) fuel/trim tank in tailplane (-600R only) can increase this total to 68,100 litres (14,980 Imp gallons). Optional extra fuel cell in aft cargo hold can increase totals to 69,000 litres (15,178 Imp gallons) in -600 or 73,000 litres (16,058 Imp gallons) in -600R. Two standard refuelling points beneath starboard wing; similar pair optional under port wing.

Accommodation: Crew of two on flight deck, plus two observer's seats. Seating for up to 375 passengers in main cabin in six, seven, eight or nine-abreast layout with two aisles. Typical layouts include one galley and two toilets forward, two galleys in mid-cabin, and one galley and four toilets at rear. Typical mixed class layout has 267 seats (20 first class and 247 economy), six/eight abreast at 96/86 cm (38/34 in) seat pitch. Typical economy class layout for 289 passengers eight-abreast at 86 cm (34 in) pitch. Up to 345 passengers can be carried at 76 cm (30 in) seat pitch in nine-abreast single-class high density layout. Closed overhead baggage lockers on each side (total capacity 10·48 m³; 370 cu ft) and in double-sided central installation (total capacity 8·27 m³; 292 cu ft), giving 0·04 to 0·07 m³ (1·3 to 2·32 cu ft) per passenger in typical economy layout. Two outward parallel-opening Type A plug type passenger doors ahead of wing leading-edge on each side, and one on each side at rear. Type I emergency exit on each side aft of wing. Underfloor baggage/cargo holds fore and aft of wings, with doors on starboard side. Forward hold will accommodate twelve LD3 containers, or four 2·24 × 3·17 m (88 × 125 in) or, optionally, 2·43 × 3·17 m (96 × 125 in) pallets, or engine modules. Rear hold will accommodate ten LD3 containers. Additional bulk loading of freight provided for in an extreme rear compartment with usable volume of 17·3 m³ (611 cu ft). Alternatively, the rear hold can be arranged optionally to carry eleven LD3 containers, with bulk cargo capacity reduced to 8·6 m³ (303 cu ft). The bulk cargo compartment can be used for the transport of livestock. Entire accommodation is pressurised, including freight, baggage and avionics compartments.

Systems: Air supply for air-conditioning system taken from engine bleed and/or APU via two high pressure points. Conditioned air can also be supplied direct to cabin by two low pressure ground connections. Ram air inlet for fresh air ventilation when packs not in use. Pressure control system (max differential 0·574 bars; 8·32 lb/sq in) consists of two identical, independent, automatic systems (one active, one standby). Switchover from one to the other is automatic after each flight and in case of active system failure. In each system, pressure is controlled by two electric outflow valves, its function depending on pre-programmed cabin pressure altitude and rate of change of cabin pressure, aircraft altitude, and preselected landing airfield elevation. Automatic pre-pressurisation of cabin before take-off is provided, to prevent noticeable pressure fluctuation during take-off. Hydraulic system comprises three fully independent circuits, operating simultaneously. Each system includes a reservoir of the direct air/fluid contact type, pressurised at 3·5 bars (51 lb/sq in); fluid used is a fire resistant phosphatester type. Nominal output flow of 136 litres (30 Imp gallons)/min is delivered at pressure of 207 bars (3,000 lb/sq in). 'Blue' and 'yellow' systems have one pump each, 'green' system has two pumps. The three circuits provide triplex power for primary flying controls; if any circuit fails, full control of the aircraft is retained without any necessity for action by the crew. All three circuits supply the ailerons, rudder and elevators; 'blue' circuit additionally supplies spoiler 7, spoiler/airbrake 4, airbrake 1, yaw damper and slats; 'green' circuit additionally supplies spoiler 6, flaps, Krueger flaps, slats, landing gear, wheel brakes, steering, tailplane trim, artificial feel, and roll/pitch/yaw autopilot; 'yellow' circuit additionally supplies spoiler 5, spoiler/airbrake 3, airbrake 2, flaps, wheel brakes, cargo doors, artificial feel, yaw damper, tailplane trim, and roll/pitch/yaw autopilot. Ram air turbine driven pump provides standby hydraulic power should both engines become inoperative. Main electrical power is supplied under normal flight conditions by two integrated drive generators, one on each engine. A third (auxiliary) generator, driven by the APU, can replace either of the main generators, having the same electromagnetic components but not the constant-speed drive. Each generator is rated at 90kVA, with overload ratings of 112·5kVA for 5 min and 150kVA for 5 s. The APU generator is driven at constant speed through a gearbox. Three unregulated transformer-rectifier units (TRUs) supply 28V DC power. Three 25Ah nickel-cadmium batteries are used for emergency supply and APU starting. Emergency electrical power taken from main aircraft batteries and an emergency static inverter, providing single-phase 115V 400Hz output for flight instruments, navigation, communications and lighting when power is not available from normal sources. Hot air anti-icing of engines, engine air intakes, and outer segments of leading-edge slats. Electrical heating for anti-icing flight deck front windscreens, demisting flight deck side windows, and for sensors, pitot probes and static ports, and waste water drain masts. Garrett GTCP 331-250F APU in tailcone, exhausting upward. The installation incorporates APU noise attenuation. Fire protection system is self-contained, and firewall panels protect main structure from an APU fire. APU provides bleed air to pneumatic system, and drives an auxiliary AC generator during ground and in-flight operation. APU drives a 90kVA oil spray cooled generator, and supplies bleed air for main engine start or air-conditioning system. For future deliveries of A300-600, APU has an improved relight capability, with starting capability throughout the flight envelope. Modular box system provides passenger oxygen to all installation areas. For new A300-600s, two optional modifications are offered for compliance with full extended-range twin-engine operations (ETOPS) requirements: a hydraulically driven fourth generator and an increased cargo hold fire suppression capability.

Avionics and Equipment: Standard communications avionics include two VHF sets, one HF, one Selcal system, interphone and passenger address systems, groundcrew call system, and voice recorder. Radio navigation avionics include two DME interrogators, two VOR receivers, two ATC transponders, one ADF, two marker beacon receivers, two ILS receivers, weather radar, and two radio altimeters. Full provisions for second weather radar and GPWS; space provisions for one or two HF, third VHF; structural provision for such future systems as a discrete address beacon system. Two Sperry digital air data computers standard. Most other avionics are to customer's requirements, only those related to the blind landing system (ILS and radio altimeter) being selected and supplied by the manufacturer. Six identical and interchangeable CRT electronic displays (four EFIS and two ECAM: electronic flight instrument system and electronic centralised aircraft monitor), plus digitalised electromechanical instruments with liquid crystal displays. The basic digital AFCS comprises a single flight control computer (FCC) for flight director and autopilot functions, a single thrust control computer (TCC) for speed and thrust control, and two flight augmentation computers (FACs) to provide yaw damping, electric pitch trim, and flight envelope monitoring and protection. Options include second FCC (for Cat. III automatic landing); second TCC; two flight management computers (FMCs) and two control display units for full flight management system; windscreen guidance display by adding optical device in glareshield; and addition of delayed flap approach (DFA) to TCC for decelerated approach. Basic aircraft is also fitted with an ARINC 717 data recording system, comprising a digital flight data acquisition unit, digital flight data recorder, three-axis linear accelerometer, and flight data entry panel. An optional speed reference system with built-in windshear protection is available. Dual automatic landing system provides coupled approach and automatic landing facilities suitable for Category II operation.

Dimensions, external:
Wing span 44·84 m (147 ft 1 in)
Wing aspect ratio 7·73
Length overall 54·08 m (177 ft 5 in)
Length of fuselage 53·30 m (174 ft 10½ in)
Fuselage: Max diameter 5·64 m (18 ft 6 in)
Height overall 16·62 m (54 ft 6½ in)
Tailplane span 16·26 m (53 ft 4 in)
Wheel track 9·60 m (31 ft 6 in)
Wheelbase (c/l of shock absorbers) 18·60 m (61 ft 0 in)
Passengers doors (each): Height 1·93 m (6 ft 4 in)
 Width 1·07 m (3 ft 6 in)
 Height to sill: fwd 4·60 m (15 ft 1 in)
  centre 4·80 m (15 ft 9 in)
  rear 5·50 m (18 ft 0½ in)
Emergency exits (each): Height 1·60 m (5 ft 3 in)
 Width 0·61 m (2 ft 0 in)
 Height to sill 4·87 m (15 ft 10 in)
Underfloor cargo door (fwd):
 Height 1·71 m (5 ft 7½ in)
 Width 2·69 m (8 ft 10 in)
 Height to sill 3·07 m (10 ft 1 in)
Underfloor cargo door (rear):
 Height 1·71 m (5 ft 7½ in)
 Width 1·81 m (5 ft 11¼ in)
 Height to sill 3·41 m (11 ft 2¼ in)
Underfloor cargo door (extreme rear):
 Height (projected) 0·95 m (3 ft 1 in)
 Width 0·95 m (3 ft 1 in)
 Height to sill 3·56 m (11 ft 8 in)

Dimensions, internal:
Cabin, excl flight deck:
 Length 40·21 m (131 ft 11 in)
 Max width 5·28 m (17 ft 4 in)
 Max height 2·54 m (8 ft 4 in)
Underfloor cargo hold:
 Length: fwd 10·60 m (34 ft 9¼ in)
  rear 7·95 m (26 ft 1 in)
  extreme rear 3·40 m (11 ft 2 in)
 Max height 1·76 m (5 ft 9 in)
 Max width 4·20 m (13 ft 9¼ in)
Underfloor cargo hold volume:
 fwd 75·1 m³ (2,652 cu ft)
 rear 55·0 m³ (1,942 cu ft)
 extreme rear 17·3 m³ (611 cu ft)

Areas:
Wings, gross 260·0 m² (2,798·6 sq ft)
Leading-edge slats (total) 30·30 m² (326·15 sq ft)
Krueger flaps (total) 1·115 m² (12·00 sq ft)
Trailing-edge flaps (total) 47·30 m² (509·13 sq ft)
All-speed ailerons (total) 7·06 m² (75·99 sq ft)
Spoilers (total) 5·396 m² (58·08 sq ft)
Airbrakes (total) 12·59 m² (135·52 sq ft)
Fin 45·20 m² (486·53 sq ft)
Rudder 13·57 m² (146·07 sq ft)
Horizontal tail surfaces (total) 64·0 m² (688·89 sq ft)

Weights and Loadings (A: JT9D-7R4H1 engines; B: CF6-80C2-A1s; C: PW4156s):
Manufacturer's weight empty:
 A (600) 77,764 kg (171,440 lb)
 B (600) 78,083 kg (172,143 lb)
 B (600R) 77,551 kg (170,970 lb)
 C (600) 78,024 kg (172,013 lb)
 C (600R) 77,492 kg (170,840 lb)
Operating weight empty:
 A (600) 86,408 kg (190,497 lb)
 B (600) 86,727 kg (191,200 lb)
 B (600R) 86,210 kg (190,060 lb)
 C (600) 86,668 kg (191,070 lb)
 C (600R) 86,151 kg (189,930 lb)
*Max payload (structural):
 A (600) 43,592 kg (96,104 lb)
 B (600) 43,273 kg (95,400 lb)
 B (600R) 43,790 kg (96,540 lb)
 C (600) 43,332 kg (95,530 lb)
 C (600R) 43,849 kg (96,670 lb)
Underfloor cargo capacity (A, B and C):
 containerised 31,300 kg (69,005 lb)
 bulk 2,800 kg (6,173 lb)
Max usable fuel:
 600: standard 49,790 kg (109,768 lb)
  with optional cargo hold tank 55,407 kg (122,151 lb)
 600R: standard 54,600 kg (120,372 lb)
  with optional cargo hold tank 58,619 kg (129,232 lb)
Max T-O weight (A, B and C):
 600 165,000 kg (363,765 lb)
 600R 170,500 kg (375,885 lb)
Max ramp weight (A, B and C):
 600 165,900 kg (365,745 lb)
 600R 171,400 kg (377,870 lb)
Max landing weight (A, B and C):
 600 138,000 kg (304,240 lb)
 600R 140,000 kg (308,645 lb)
Max zero-fuel weight (A, B and C):
 600, 600R 130,000 kg (286,600 lb)
Max wing loading (A, B and C):
 600 635 kg/m² (130·0 lb/sq ft)
 600R 656 kg/m² (134·4 lb/sq ft)
Max power loading:
 56,000 lb st engines 331·6 kg/kN (3·25 lb/lb st)
 58,000 lb st engines 320·4 kg/kN (3·14 lb/lb st)

* *with typical 289-seat all-economy layout*

Performance (at max T-O weight except where indicated: A, B and C as for 'Weights'):
Max operating speed (VMO) from S/L to 8,075 m (26,500 ft) 345 knots (639 km/h; 397 mph) CAS
Max operating Mach number (MMO) above 8,075 m (26,500 ft) 0·82
Max cruising speed at 7,620 m (25,000 ft) 480 knots (890 km/h; 553 mph)
Typical high-speed cruise at 9,145 m (30,000 ft) Mach 0·82 (484 knots; 897 km/h; 557 mph)
Typical long-range cruising speed at 9,450 m (31,000 ft) Mach 0·80 (472 knots; 875 km/h; 543 mph)
Approach speed at max landing weight 134 knots (248 km/h; 154 mph)
Max operating altitude 12,200 m (40,000 ft)
Min ground turning radius (wingtips) 33·51 m (109 ft 11¼ in)
Runway LCN (X: flexible pavement of 51 cm; 20 in thickness, Y: rigid pavement of 76 cm; 30 in radius of relative stiffness):
 49 × 17-20 tyres, standard bogie:
  600: X 84

Y 75
600R: X 89
Y 80
49 × 19-20 tyres, wide bogie option:
600: X 77
Y 68
600R: X 82
Y 73

T-O field length at S/L, ISA + 15°C:
600: A, C 2,347 m (7,700 ft)
B 2,438 m (8,000 ft)
600R: B 2,713 m (8,900 ft)
C 2,652 m (8,700 ft)

Landing field length at max landing weight:
600: A, B and C 1,536 m (5,040 ft)
600R: B and C 1,555 m (5,100 ft)

Range with 267 passengers and baggage, reserves for 200 nm (370 km; 230 miles):
600: A 3,500 nm (6,486 km; 4,030 miles)
B 3,670 nm (6,800 km; 4,226 miles)
C 3,700 nm (6,857 km; 4,260 miles)
600R: B 4,180 nm (7,746 km; 4,813 miles)
C 4,210 nm (7,802 km; 4,848 miles)

OPERATIONAL NOISE LEVELS (A300-600, ICAO Annex 16, Chapter 3):
T-O: A 91·5 EPNdB (96·2 limit)
B 91·3 EPNdB (96·2 limit)
Sideline: A 98·8 EPNdB (99·8 limit)
B 97·1 EPNdB (99·8 limit)
Approach: A 100·8 EPNdB (103·3 limit)
B 99·1 EPNdB (103·3 limit)

AIRBUS A300C and A300F

The **A300C** is a convertible version of the A300-600, with the same range of power plant options. Main differences are a large forward upper deck cargo door, a reinforced cabin floor, a smoke detection system in the main cabin, and an interior trim adaptable to the freighter role. The upper deck cargo door is on the opposite side to that of the forward underfloor hold, enabling loading or unloading to be carried out simultaneously at all positions. The first operator is Kuwait Airways (three -600Cs).

The **A300F** freighter is similar to the C, but with all passenger provisions removed completely and the cabin windows replaced by metal blanking plates. First customer is Korean Air, which ordered two A300Fs in October 1985.

The A300C can be converted to passenger or mixed passenger/cargo configuration. Typical options include accommodation (in mainly eight-abreast seating) for up to 297 passengers on the upper deck; or 145 passengers (seven/eight abreast) plus six 2·44 × 3·17 m (96 × 125 in) pallets; or 83 passengers plus nine 96 × 125 in pallets; up to twenty 2·24 × 3·17 m (88 × 125 in) pallets; or five 88 × 125 in plus nine 96 × 125 in pallets. Standard upper deck configurations for the A300F include fifteen 88 × 125 in or fourteen 96 × 125 in pallets, or six of the former plus nine of the latter. In an optional configuration, the F can carry up to twenty-one 88 × 125 in pallets on the upper deck. The loading system, consisting of ball mats, roller tracks and electrical drive units, is fitted to the existing seat rails, and a 9*g* barrier net is installed in the front of the cabin.

DIMENSIONS, EXTERNAL: As A300-600, plus:
Upper deck cargo door (fwd, port):
Height (projected) 2·57 m (8 ft 5¼ in)
Width 3·58 m (11 ft 9 in)
Height to sill 4·91 m (16 ft 1 in)

DIMENSIONS, INTERNAL:
Cabin upper deck usable for cargo (convertible, except where indicated):
Length 33·45 m (109 ft 9 in)
Min height 2·01 m (6 ft 7 in)
Max height 2·22 m (7 ft 3½ in)
Volume:
A300C 192-203 m³ (6,780-7,169 cu ft)
A300F 231-245 m³ (8,158-8,652 cu ft)

WEIGHTS (basic. A: A300C with JT9D-7R4H1 engines, B: A300C with CF6-80C2-A1s, C: A300F with CF6-80C2-A1s):
Manufacturer's weight empty:
A, passenger mode 80,259 kg (176,940 lb)
B, passenger mode 80,578 kg (177,644 lb)
A, freight mode 81,258 kg (179,143 lb)
B, freight mode 81,577 kg (179,846 lb)
C 78,547 kg (173,166 lb)
*Operating weight empty:
A, passenger mode 88,903 kg (195,997 lb)
B, passenger mode 89,222 kg (196,700 lb)
A, freight mode 82,286 kg (181,409 lb)
B, freight mode 82,605 kg (182,112 lb)
C 79,305 kg (174,837 lb)
Max payload (structural):
A, passenger mode 41,097 kg (90,603 lb)
B, passenger mode 40,778 kg (89,900 lb)
A, freight mode 47,714 kg (105,191 lb)
B, freight mode 47,395 kg (104,488 lb)
C 50,695 kg (111,763 lb)
Max T-O weight (A, B and C) 165,000 kg (363,765 lb)
Max landing weight (A, B and C) 138,000 kg (304,240 lb)
Max zero-fuel weight (A, B and C) 130,000 kg (286,600 lb)

**incl weight of underfloor cargo hold containers and pallets*

PERFORMANCE:
Range with max (structural) payload, allowances for 30 min hold at 460 m (1,500 ft) and 200 nm (370 km; 230 mile) diversion 2,300 nm (4,262 km; 2,648 miles)

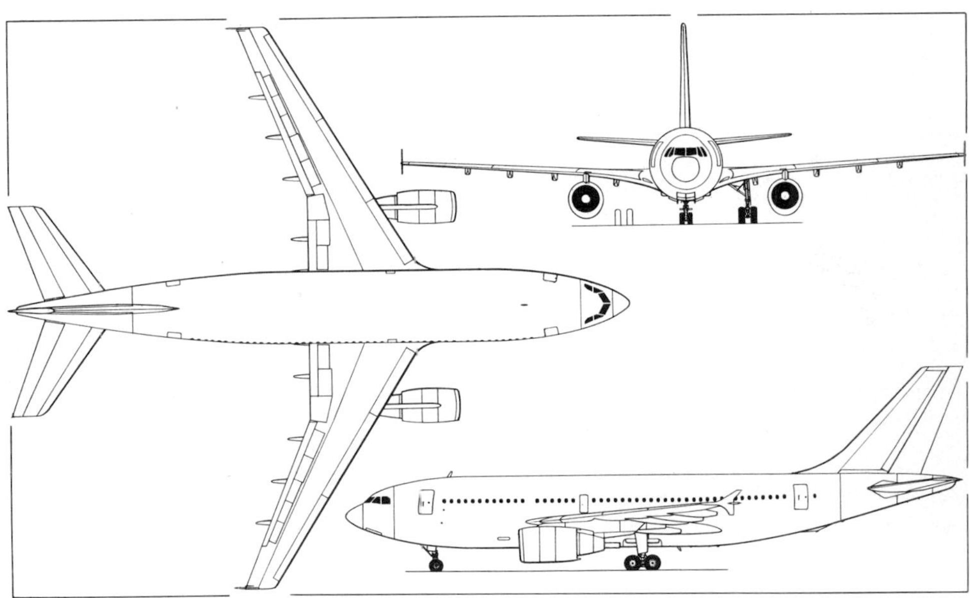

Airbus A310 medium-range transport aircraft *(Pilot Press)*

AIRBUS A310

The A310 was launched in July 1978. Compared with the A300B2/B4-100 and 200 series, the cabin is shorter by 11 frames and the overall fuselage by 13 frames. The cabin thus normally seats from 210–250 passengers, although the aircraft is certificated for up to 280 persons. The A310 retains the same fuselage cross-section as the A300, thus being able to carry standard LD3 containers two abreast, and/or standard pallets installed crosswise. Convertible and freighter versions are available.

The A310 also has new, advanced technology wings, of reduced span and area; new and smaller horizontal tail surfaces; common pylons able to support all types of General Electric and Pratt & Whitney engines offered; and landing gear modified to cater for these changes in size and weight. It features Airbus Industrie's advanced digital two-man flight deck.

Manufacturing breakdown of the A310 differs in minor respects from that of the A300. Aérospatiale builds the nose section (including flight deck), lower centre-fuselage and wing box, engine pylons and CFRP airbrakes, and is responsible for final assembly. MBB is responsible for the forward passenger cabin, upper centre-fuselage, rear fuselage, fin and rudder, flaps and flap tracks, CFRP spoilers and lift dumpers, for wing assembly, and for commercial installation. BAe Chester produces the wing fixed structures. CASA's contribution includes the horizontal tail surfaces, nose-gear and mainwheel doors, and forward passenger doors. Fokker manufactures the CFRP main landing gear leg doors, wingtips, all-speed ailerons, and CFRP flap track fairings. The wing leading-edge slats and wing/fuselage fairings are produced by Belairbus. Landing gear is by Messier-Hispano-Bugatti.

The prototype A310 (F-WZLH) flew for the first time on 3 April 1982. This aircraft, and the second A310 (F-WZLI, first flight 13 May 1982), are powered by JT9D-7R4 engines; the third A310, which flew for the first time on 5 August 1982, has CF6-80A3 engines. Simultaneous French and German certification was awarded on 11 March 1983, UK certification in January 1984 and FAA type approval in early 1985. The first aircraft (for Lufthansa and Swissair) were handed over on 29 March 1983, entering service on 12 and 21 April respectively. Certification to JAR Category IIIA was awarded by the French and German authorities on 28 and 29 September 1983, and Category IIIB on 28 November 1984.

The following versions have been announced:

A310-200. Basic passenger version. Wingtip fences introduced as standard from Spring 1986 (first delivery: Thai Airways on 7 May).

A310-200C. Convertible version; first delivered to Martinair on 29 November 1984.

A310-200F. Freighter version.

A310-300. Extended-range version. First flown on 8 July 1985 with JT9D-7R4E engines; certificated with these engines on 5 December 1985 and delivered to launch customer Swissair on 17 December. First member of Airbus family to introduce as standard the delta shaped wingtip fences (for drag reduction) developed by BAe and test flown in 1983 on an A310-200 testbed. Version with CF6-80C2 engines first flew on 6 September 1985, followed by certification and first delivery (to Balair) in March 1986. Extra range is provided by an increased basic max T-O weight (150,000 kg; 330,695 lb) and greater fuel capacity. Higher max T-O weight optional. The standard extra fuel capacity is in the tailplane, which allows flight phase CG control for added fuel efficiency; for extra long range, additional fuel can be stored in part of the cargo hold. Ordered by Swissair (four), Pan American (12), Air-India (six), Kenya Airways (two), Lufthansa (six), Singapore Airlines (two), Austrian Airlines (two) and Balair (one).

By 15 August 1986 firm orders for 127 A310s had been received, of which 87 had been delivered.

TYPE: Large-capacity wide-bodied medium/extended-range transport.

WINGS: Cantilever mid-wing monoplane. Thickness/chord ratio 15·2% at root, 11·8% at 'break' in trailing-edge, and 10·8% at tip. Dihedral at trailing-edge 11° 8′ (inboard) and 4° 3′ (outboard). Incidence 5° 3′ at root. Sweepback 28° at quarter-chord. Wing box is two-spar multi-rib structure of high strength light alloy, with top and bottom load-carrying skins. Three-section leading-edge slats on each wing over almost full span, with no cutout over engine pylon; Krueger flap between inboard slat and wing root. Fowler trailing-edge flap on outboard section of each wing; vaned Fowler flap inboard. All-speed aileron between flaps on each wing. Electrically signalled spoilers for roll control. Two independent computer systems with different software provide redundancy and operational safety. Two airbrakes between root and engine, two airbrakes outboard of engine, and three spoilers outboard of outer airbrakes, on each wing; all 14 surfaces are used also as lift dumpers. Delta shaped wingtip fences

First dedicated Airbus freighter, an A300F for Korean Air

Airbus A310-200 in the livery of Thai Airways. Wingtip fences are now standard on both the -200 and -300

now standard. Outer slat leading-edges de-iced by engine bleed air.

FUSELAGE: Generally similar to A300B4, except for reduced length (see introductory copy), resulting in deletion of two passenger doors. Redesigned rear fuselage, between parallel section and tailcone, allowing pressure bulkhead to be moved rearward.

TAIL UNIT: Vertical surfaces as for A300; horizontal surfaces as for A300-600. A310-300 fin box made of CFRP from December 1985, and for -200 from Spring 1986.

LANDING GEAR: Hydraulically retractable tricycle type. Twin-wheel steerable nose unit (steering angle 65°/95°) as for A300. Main gear by Messier-Hispano-Bugatti, each bogie comprising two tandem mounted twin-wheel units. Retraction as for A300. Undertail bumper beneath rear fuselage, to protect structure against excessive nose-up attitude during T-O and landing. Standard tyre sizes: main, 46 × 16-20, pressure 11·2 bars (163 lb/sq in); nose, 40 × 14-16, pressure 9·0 bars (131 lb/sq in). Two options for low-pressure tyres on main units: (1) size 49 × 17-20, pressure 9·8 bars (143 lb/sq in); (2) size 49 × 19-20, pressure 8·9 bars (129 lb/sq in). Messier-Hispano-Bugatti brakes and anti-skid units standard; Bendix type optional on A310-200. Carbon brakes on A310-300 (and, from Spring 1986, A310-200).

POWER PLANT: Currently ordered or available with the following turbofan engines:

Two 213·5 kN (48,000 lb st) Pratt & Whitney JT9D-7R4D1; or two 222·4 kN (50,000 lb st) General Electric CF6-80C2-A2, or Pratt & Whitney JT9D-7R4E1; or two 231·2 kN (52,000 lb st) Pratt & Whitney PW4152. Total usable fuel capacity 55,000 litres (12,098 Imp gallons) in A310-200. Increased to 61,100 litres (13,440 Imp gallons) in A310-300, with additional fuel in tailplane trim tank. Further 7,000 litres (1,540 Imp gallons) can be carried by both versions in forward part of aft cargo hold. Two refuelling points, one beneath each wing outboard of engine.

ACCOMMODATION: Crew of two on flight deck. Provision for third and fourth crew seats. Standard cabin arranged for 210-265 seats in six/seven/eight/nine-abreast layout, at pitch of 96·5-103 cm (38-40 in) first class, 76, 81 or 86 cm (30, 32 or 34 in) economy class. Nine-abreast seating at 76 cm (30 in) pitch for 280 passengers in high-density configuration. Standard layout has galley and toilet at forward end of cabin, plus larger galley and four toilets at rear. Depending upon customer requirements, a second toilet and galley can be added forward, and an additional galley aft. Toilets and galleys can be located at the forward end at the class divider position. Overhead baggage stowage as for A300, rising to average of 0·07 m³ (2·33 cu ft) per passenger with optional central stowage in 212-seat layout. Four passenger doors, one forward and one aft on each side. Type I emergency exit over wing on each side. Underfloor baggage/cargo holds fore and aft of wings, each with door on starboard side. Forward hold will accommodate eight LD3 containers or three 2·24 × 3·17 m (88 × 125 in) standard pallets; the enlarged upper deck cargo door, optional on the A300C/F, is standard on the A310, enabling 2·44 × 3·17 m (96 × 125 in) pallets to be loaded. Rear hold will accommodate six LD3 containers, with an optional seventh LD3 or LD1 position.

SYSTEMS: Garrett GTCP 331-250 APU. Air-conditioning system, powered by compressed air from engines, APU, or a ground supply unit, comprises two separate packs; air is distributed to flight deck, three separate cabin zones, electrical and electronic equipment, avionics bay and bulk cargo compartment. Ventilation of forward cargo compartments optional. Pressurisation system has a max normal differential of 0·57 bars (8·25 lb/sq in). Air supply for wing ice protection, engine starting and thrust reverser system is bled from various stages of the engine compressors, or supplied by the APU or a ground supply unit. Hydraulic system (three fully independent circuits operating at 207 bars; 3,000 lb/sq in: details as described for A300-600). Electrical system, similar to that of A300-600, consists of a three-phase 115/200V 400Hz constant frequency AC system and a 28V DC system. Two 90kVA engine driven brushless generators for normal single-channel operation, with automatic transfer of busbars in the event of a generator failure. Each has an overload rating of 135kVA for 5 min and 180kVA for 5 s. A third (identical) AC generator, directly driven at constant speed by the APU, can be used during ground operations, and also in flight to compensate for the loss of one or both engine driven generators. Current production A310s have APU with improved relight capability, which can be started and operated throughout the flight envelope. Any one generator can provide sufficient power to operate all equipment and systems necessary for an indefinite period of safe flight. DC power is generated via three 150A transformer-rectifiers. Three nickel-cadmium batteries are supplied. Flight crew oxygen system fed from re-chargeable pressure bottle of 2,166 litres (76·5 cu ft) capacity. Standard options are a second 76·5 cu ft bottle, a 3,256 litre (115 cu ft) bottle, and an external filling connection. Emergency oxygen sets for passengers and cabin attendants. Anti-icing of outer wing leading-edge slats and engine air intakes by hot air bled from engines; and of pitot probes, static ports and plates, and sensors, by electric heating. For current production A310s, two optional modifications are offered for full compliance with extended-range twin-engine operations (ETOPS) requirements: a hydraulically driven fourth generator and an increased cargo hold fire suppression capability.

AVIONICS AND EQUIPMENT: Basic standard flight deck displays include flight guidance, navigation, configuration and engine management/monitoring information presented by electro-mechanical indicators, and an electronic centralised aircraft monitoring (ECAM) system unique to Airbus Industrie; warning information presented by conventional warning lights and on a master warning CRT; system information presented on a system CRT. Electronic flight instrument system comprises a CRT primary flight display, replacing the ADI and radio altimeter, and a CRT navigation display replacing the HSI and weather radar. The latter displays data from the flight management system (map mode, flight data display). A flight data recorder is also installed. Head-up display is optional. The basic aircraft is fitted with an AIDS (airborne integrated data system) providing a basic 80-parameter system (40 mandatory plus 40 additional) with an option to extend the system to 160 parameters. Standard com system includes HF radio (ARINC 719) (full provision); two VHF transceivers and space provision for a third (all to ARINC 716); Selcal system (ARINC 714); passenger address system (the amplifier conforming to ARINC 715); audio systems, comprising service interphone, audio integrating and flight interphone systems, and a ground crew call circuit. Digital navigation system, to ARINC 429 and ARINC 600, includes ADF (ARINC 712); two radio altimeters (ARINC 707); two DME (ARINC 709); two ATC transponders (ARINC 718); two VOR, one including marker beacon receiver (ARINC 711); weather radar (ARINC 708); two ILS (ARINC 710); and three AHRS (ARINC 705). Options include a second ADF; two or three IRS (ARINC 704); Omega system; and a second weather radar. The digital automatic flight control system (AFCS), in its basic definition, comprises a single flight control computer (FCC) for automatic flight control (to ARINC 701); a single thrust control computer (TCC) for speed and thrust control (to ARINC 703); and a duplicated flight augmentation computer (to ARINC 701). The flight management system (to ARINC 702) comprises a computer unit and control display unit. The FCC, functioning as autopilot, flight director and speed reference system, has the following basic modes: pitch hold, heading/roll altitude hold, altitude hold, altitude acquire, level change, vertical speed select and hold, heading select, VOR, heading, take-off and go-around. The installation of a second FCC will provide Cat. III autolands. The TCC provides the following functions: permanent computation of N1 or EPR limits, auto-throttle functions, throttle pusher with windshear protection, speed and angle of attack protection, and a test function. A delayed flap approach mode is available as an option.

DIMENSIONS, EXTERNAL:

Wing span	43·89 m (144 ft 0 in)
Wing chord: at root	8·38 m (27 ft 6 in)
at tip	2·18 m (7 ft 1¾ in)
Wing aspect ratio	8·8
Length overall	46·66 m (153 ft 1 in)
Length of fuselage	45·13 m (148 ft 0¾ in)
Fuselage: Max diameter	5·64 m (18 ft 6 in)
Height overall	15·80 m (51 ft 10 in)
Tailplane span	16·26 m (53 ft 4¼ in)
Wheel track	9·60 m (31 ft 6 in)
Wheelbase (c/l of shock absorbers)	15·21 m (49 ft 10¾ in)
Passenger door (fwd, port):	
Height	1·93 m (6 ft 4 in)
Width	1·07 m (3 ft 6 in)
Height to sill at OWE	4·54 m (14 ft 10¾ in)
Passenger door (rear, port):	
Height	1·93 m (6 ft 4 in)
Width	1·07 m (3 ft 6 in)
Height to sill at OWE	4·85 m (15 ft 11 in)
Servicing doors (fwd and rear, stbd)	as corresponding passenger doors
Upper deck cargo door (A310C/F)	as A300C/F
Emergency exits (overwing, port and stbd, each):	
Height	1·39 m (4 ft 6¾ in)
Width	0·67 m (2 ft 2½ in)
Underfloor cargo door (fwd):	
Height	1·71 m (5 ft 7½ in)
Width	2·69 m (8 ft 10 in)
Height to sill at OWE	2·611 m (8 ft 6¾ in)
Underfloor cargo door (rear):	
Height	1·71 m (5 ft 7½ in)
Width	1·81 m (5 ft 11¼ in)
Height to sill at OWE	2·72 m (8 ft 11 in)
Underfloor cargo door (aft bulk hold):	
Height	0·95 m (3 ft 1½ in)
Width	0·95 m (3 ft 1½ in)
Height to sill at OWE	2·751 m (9 ft 0¼ in)

DIMENSIONS, INTERNAL:

Cabin, excl flight deck:	
Length	33·24 m (109 ft 0¾ in)
Max width	5·28 m (17 ft 4 in)
Max height	2·33 m (7 ft 7¾ in)
Volume	210·0 m³ (7,416·1 cu ft)
Fwd cargo hold: Length	7·63 m (25 ft 0½ in)
Max width	4·18 m (13 ft 8½ in)
Height	1·71 m (5 ft 7¼ in)
Volume	50·3 m³ (1,776·3 cu ft)
Rear cargo hold: Length	5·033 m (16 ft 6¼ in)
Max width	4·17 m (13 ft 8¼ in)
Height	1·67 m (5 ft 5¾ in)
Volume	34·5 m³ (1,218·4 cu ft)
Aft bulk hold: Volume	17·3 m³ (610·9 cu ft)
Total overall cargo volume	102·1 m³ (3,605·6 cu ft)

AREAS:

Wings, gross	219 m² (2,357·3 sq ft)
Leading-edge slats (total)	28·54 m² (307·20 sq ft)
Trailing-edge flaps (total)	36·68 m² (394·82 sq ft)

Ailerons (total) 6·86 m² (73·84 sq ft)
Spoilers (total) 7·36 m² (79·22 sq ft)
Airbrakes (total) 6·16 m² (66·31 sq ft)
Fin 45·20 m² (486·53 sq ft)
Rudder 13·57 m² (146·07 sq ft)
Tailplane 44·80 m² (482·22 sq ft)
Elevators (total) 19·20 m² (206·67 sq ft)

WEIGHTS (A: CF6-80C2-A2 engines; B: JT9D-7R4E1s; C: PW4152s):
*Operating weight empty:
200: A 76,747 kg (169,198 lb)
B 76,424 kg (168,485 lb)
C 76,714 kg (169,125 lb)
300: A 77,037 kg (169,837 lb)
B 76,713 kg (169,123 lb)
C 77,003 kg (169,762 lb)
*Max payload (structural):
200: A 35,253 kg (77,719 lb)
B 35,576 kg (78,431 lb)
C 35,286 kg (77,792 lb)
300: A 35,963 kg (79,284 lb)
B 36,287 kg (79,999 lb)
C 35,997 kg (79,359 lb)
Max fuel:
200: standard 44,160 kg (97,356 lb)
with optional cargo hold tank 49,781 kg (109,748 lb)
300: standard 49,050 kg (108,136 lb)
with optional cargo hold tank 54,674 kg (120,535 lb)
Max T-O weight:
200: basic 138,600 kg (305,560 lb)
optional 142,000 kg (313,055 lb)
300: basic 150,000 kg (330,695 lb)
optional 153,000 kg (337,305 lb)
Max landing weight: 200 122,000 kg (268,965 lb)
300 123,000 kg (271,170 lb)
Max zero-fuel weight: 200 112,000 kg (246,915 lb)
300 113,000 kg (249,120 lb)
including optional extra fuel tank in cargo bay

PERFORMANCE (at max T-O weight except where indicated; engines A, B and C as under 'Weights'):
Typical long-range cruising speed at 11,280 m (37,000 ft):
A, B and C Mach 0·80 (459 knots; 851 km/h; 529 mph)
Approach speed at max landing weight:
A, B and C 135 knots (250 km/h; 155 mph)
T-O field length at S/L, ISA + 15°C:
200: A 1,911 m (6,270 ft)
B 1,881 m (6,170 ft)
300: A 2,440 m (8,000 ft)
B 2,530 m (8,300 ft)
Landing field length at S/L, at max landing weight:
200: A 1,510 m (4,950 ft)
B 1,540 m (5,050 ft)
300: A 1,525 m (5,000 ft)
B 1,555 m (5,100 ft)
Runway LCN (X: flexible pavement of 51 cm; 20 in thickness, Y: rigid pavement of 76 cm; 30 in radius of relative stiffness):
46 × 16-20 tyres, standard bogie:
200: X 72
Y 65
300: X 81
Y 74
49 × 19-20 tyres, wide bogie option:
200: X 60
Y 54
300: X 68
Y 62

Airbus A300 fly by wire demonstrator, fitted with sidestick controllers and other equipment destined for the A320 *(Air Portraits)*

Range at typical airline OWE plus 218 passengers and baggage, international reserves, 200 nm (370 km; 230 mile) diversion:
200 at basic MTOGW:
A 3,710 nm (6,875 km; 4,272 miles)
B 3,600 nm (6,671 km; 4,145 miles)
C 3,790 nm (7,023 km; 4,364 miles)
200 at optional MTOGW:
A 4,020 nm (7,450 km; 4,629 miles)
B 3,900 nm (7,227 km; 4,491 miles)
C 4,110 nm (7,616 km; 4,732 miles)
300 at basic MTOGW:
A 4,560 nm (8,450 km; 5,251 miles)
B 4,400 nm (8,154 km; 5,066 miles)
C 4,650 nm (8,617 km; 5,354 miles)
300 at optional MTOGW with cargo hold fuel tank:
A 4,930 nm (9,136 km; 5,677 miles)
B 4,780 nm (8,858 km; 5,504 miles)
C 5,040 nm (9,340 km; 5,803 miles)

OPERATIONAL NOISE LEVELS (ICAO Annex 16, Chapter 3):
T-O: 200 (B) 89·7 EPNdB (95·1 limit)
300 (A, estimated) 92·7 EPNdB (95·6 limit)
Sideline: 200 (B) 95·4 EPNdB (99·1 limit)
300 (A, estimated) 95·7 EPNdB (99·4 limit)
Approach: 200 (B) 100·6 EPNdB (102·7 limit)
300 (A, estimated) 98·6 EPNdB (102·9 limit)

AIRBUS A320

The A320 is an entirely new short/medium-range, single-aisle, twin-turbofan commercial transport aircraft, making optimum use of advanced design concepts, modern production techniques, new materials, advanced digital avionics, and efficient systems design. Among a number of technological 'firsts', it will be the first subsonic commercial aircraft to have control by fly by wire (FBW) throughout normal flight; a centralised maintenance system (BITE and FIDS: built-in test equipment and fault identification and detection system); side-stick controls in the cockpit, in place of control columns; and composite materials for major elements of primary structure, including the fin and horizontal tailplane. Wing design incorporates the latest advances in technology, as well as experience from the wing of the A310, and the A320 will offer significant commonality with other Airbus Industrie aircraft where this is cost-effective.

Compared with existing single-aisle aircraft, the fuselage cross-section is significantly increased, permitting the use of wider triple seats to provide higher standards of passenger comfort; five-abreast business class seating provides a standard equal to that offered as first class on major competitive aircraft. In addition, the wider aisle permits quicker turnrounds. Overhead stowage space is superior to that available on existing aircraft of similar capacity, and provides ample carry-on baggage space; best use of the underseat space for baggage is provided by improved seat design and optimised positioning of the seat rails. The fuselage double-bubble cross-section provides increased baggage/cargo hold volume and working height, and the ability to carry containers derived from the standard interline LD3 type. As the base is the same as that of the LD3, all existing wide-body aircraft and ground handling equipment can accept these containers without modification.

Full go-ahead to develop and build the A320 was confirmed on 2 March 1984. Two versions are available initially, with **(A320-200)** and without **(A320-100)** a wing centre-section fuel tank. Convertible and all-freight versions, with a large upper deck cargo door, are being considered.

Four aircraft are to be used in the flight test programme, the first of which (in final assembly in mid-1986) is due to fly in March 1987; one static test and one fatigue test airframe will also be completed. Certification, anticipated for February 1988, will be for two-crew operation and Category IIIB all-weather landings. Entry into service will follow in the Spring of 1988. Aérospatiale is building the front fuselage (forward of the wing leading-edge), the centre wing box, engine pylons, and is responsible for final assembly. The centre and rear fuselage, wing flaps, fin, rudder, and commercial furnishing are undertaken by MBB. British Aerospace builds the complete wings, including all moving surfaces except the flaps, assisted by Belairbus, which produces the leading-edge slats. CASA is responsible for the tailplane, elevators, main landing gear doors, and sheet metal work for parts of the rear fuselage.

Airbus A310-300 in the insignia of launch customer Swissair

Firm orders for the A320 totalled 134 by 15 August 1986, from the following operators:

Air France	25
Air Inter (France)	10
Alia	6
Ansett	8
Australian Airlines	9
British Caledonian Airways	7
Cyprus Airways	4
GATX Air	10
Indian Airlines	19
Inex-Adria (Yugoslavia)	5
Lufthansa	15
Pan American World Airways	16

Type: Twin-turbofan short/medium-range transport.

Wings: Cantilever low/mid-wing monoplane, with 5° 6′ 36″ dihedral and 25° sweepback at quarter-chord. Five-segment leading-edge slats (one inboard and four outboard of engine pylon) over almost full span. These and most of fixed portion of wing are of aluminium alloy construction. Composite materials are used for the fixed leading/trailing-edge panels, trailing-edge flaps, flap fairings, spoilers, ailerons, and wing/fuselage fairings. Roll spoilers, in four segments on each wing, are located forward of the outboard flaps; the inner pair of spoilers on each side act also as lift dumpers. There are two-segment speed brakes forward of each inboard flap. Ailerons, spoilers, flaps, slats and speed brakes are controlled electrically by the fly by wire control system, acting via hydraulic actuators. Slat and flap controls by Liebherr and Lucas.

Fuselage: Semi-monocoque pressurised structure, of 'double bubble' cross-section.

Tail Unit: Cantilever structure, with sweepback on all surfaces (35° on fin, 28° on tailplane) and 6° dihedral on tailplane. Entire vertical and horizontal surfaces are fabricated from composite materials. Elevators are controlled and tailplane trimmed electrically, with hydraulic actuation, by the FBW system; if elevator control is lost through electrical failure, the tailplane can be trimmed mechanically to act as a backup pitch control surface. Rudder is excluded from FBW system, in order to provide directional control by conventional mechanical means if ailerons are lost due to FBW system failure. Electric rudder trim.

Landing Gear: Hydraulically retractable tricycle type, with twin wheels and oleo-pneumatic shock absorber on each unit. Dowty main units retract inward into wing/body fairing; steerable Messier-Hispano-Bugatti nose unit retracts forward. Main landing gear doors and fairings are of composite materials. Radial tyres, size 45 × 16-R20 on main units and 30 × 88-R15 on nose unit, are standard. Size 49 × 19-R20 radial tyres with 36 × 11 bogie, or conventional crossply tyres (46 × 16-20 or 49 × 19-20) with 36 × 11-XX bogie, are optional on main units; size 32 × 11·5-15 tyres optional for nose unit. Carbon brakes standard.

Power Plant: Two 104·5-111·2 kN (23,500-25,000 lb st) class CFM International CFM56-5 turbofan engines for first aircraft delivery in Spring 1988, or IAE V2500 engines for first aircraft delivery in Spring 1989. Rohr nacelles and thrust reversers for CFM56 engines. Dual-channel FADEC (full authority digital engine control) system on each engine standard. Standard fuel capacity of 15,588 litres (3,429 Imp gallons) for CFM56-5 engines and 15,354 litres (3,377 Imp gallons) for V2500 engines; A320-200 has additional 8,078 litres (1,777 Imp gallons) in wing centre-section tank. Composite materials used in construction of engine cowlings and pylon fairings.

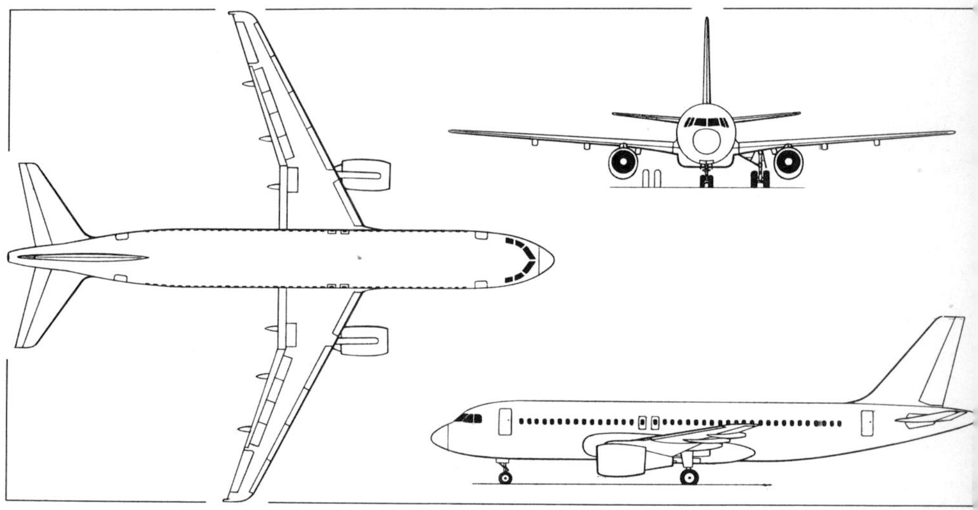

Airbus A320-200 twin-turbofan single-aisle 150/179-seat transport *(Pilot Press)*

Accommodation: Standard crew of two on flight deck, with one (optionally two) forward-facing folding seats for additional crew members; seats for four cabin attendants. Seating for up to 179 passengers, depending upon layout, with locations at front and rear of cabin for galley(s) and toilet(s). Typical mixed class 150-passenger layout would have 12 seats four-abreast at 91·5 cm (36 in) pitch in 'super first' and 138 six-abreast at 81 cm (32 in) pitch economy class; or 152 six-abreast seats (84 business + 68 economy) at 86 and 78 cm (34 and 31 in) pitch respectively. Single class economy layout could offer 164 seats at 81 cm (32 in) pitch, or up to 179 in high-density configuration. Passenger doors at front and rear of cabin on port side, forward one having optional integral airstairs; service door opposite each of these on starboard side. Two overwing emergency exits each side. Forward and rear underfloor baggage/cargo holds, plus overhead lockers; with 164 seats, overhead stowage space per seat is 0·059 m³ (2·1 cu ft). Mechanised cargo loading system available, allowing up to seven LD3-46 (LD3 base) containers to be carried in freight holds.

Systems: The A320 is the first subsonic commercial aircraft to be equipped for fly by wire (FBW) control throughout the entire normal flight regime, and the first to have a side-stick controller (one for each pilot) instead of a control column and hand wheel. The Thomson-CSF/Sfena quadruplex FBW system operates, via hydraulic jacks, all primary and secondary flight controls, except for the rudder and tailplane trim. The pilot's pitch and roll commands are applied through the side-stick controller via two different types of computer. These have a redundant architecture to provide safety levels as least as high as those of the mechanical systems they replace. The Sperry/Sfena flight control system incorporates flight envelope protection features to a degree that cannot be achieved with conventional mechanical control systems, and the systems's computers will not allow the aircraft's structural and aerodynamic limitations to be exceeded: even if the pilot pushes the side-stick fully forward, it is impossible to go beyond the aircraft's maximum design speed. Similarly, the A320 will have angle of attack protection: if the pilot pulls the side-stick fully back, he will just achieve maximum lift from the wing and no more, and therefore will be unable to stall the aircraft. Other systems include Liebherr/ABG-Semca air-conditioning, Nord-Micro/ABG-Semca pressurisation, hydraulic, Lucas electrical, oxygen and fire detection systems, and a new and more efficient AiResearch APU. Primary electrical system is powered by two Lucas Aerospace 75/90kVA constant frequency generators, providing 115/200V three-phase AC at 400Hz. A third generator of the same type, directly driven at constant speed by the APU, can be used during ground operations and, if required, during flight.

Avionics: Fully equipped digital avionics fit, to ARINC 700 series specification, including advanced digital automatic flight control and flight management systems. Each pilot has two Thomson-CSF electronic flight instrumentation system (EFIS) displays: a primary flight display and a navigation display. Between these two pairs of displays are two VDO electronic centralised aircraft monitor (ECAM) displays unique to Airbus Industrie and developed from the ECAM systems on the A310 and A300-600. The larger size of the A320 displays allows the upper one to incorporate engine performance and warnings. The lower display carries warning and system synoptic diagrams. Honeywell air data and inertial reference system.

Dimensions, external:

Wing span	33·91 m (111 ft 3 in)
Wing aspect ratio	9·39
Length overall	37·57 m (123 ft 3 in)
Fuselage: Max width	3·95 m (12 ft 11½ in)
Max depth	4·14 m (13 ft 7 in)
Height overall	11·80 m (38 ft 8½ in)
Tailplane span	12·45 m (40 ft 10 in)
Wheel track (c/l of shock struts)	7·59 m (24 ft 11 in)
Wheelbase	12·63 m (41 ft 5 in)
Passenger doors (port, fwd and rear), each:	
Height	1·83 m (6 ft 0 in)
Width	0·81 m (2 ft 8 in)
Height to sill	3·415 m (11 ft 2½ in)
Service doors (stbd, fwd and rear), each:	
Height	1·83 m (6 ft 0 in)
Width	0·81 m (2 ft 8 in)
Height to sill	3·415 m (11 ft 2½ in)
Overwing emergency exits (two port and two stbd), each:	
Height	1·02 m (3 ft 4¼ in)
Width	0·51 m (1 ft 8 in)
Underfloor baggage/cargo hold doors (stbd, fwd and rear), each: Height	1 249 m (4 ft 1¼ in)
Width	1 82 m (5 ft 11½ in)

Dimensions, internal:

Cabin: Max width	3·696 m (12 ft 1½ in)
Max height	2·22 m (7 ft 4 in)
Baggage/cargo hold volume:	
front	13·87 m³ (490 cu ft)
rear	26·16 m³ (924 cu ft)

Areas:

Wings, gross	122·4 m² (1,317·5 sq ft)
Leading-edge slats (total)	12·64 m² (136·1 sq ft)
Trailing-edge flaps (total)	21·10 m² (227·1 sq ft)
Ailerons (total)	2·74 m² (29·49 sq ft)
Spoilers (total)	8·64 m² (93·00 sq ft)
Airbrakes (total)	2·35 m² (25·30 sq ft)
Vertical tail surfaces (total)	2[illegible]·5 m² (231·4 sq ft)
Horizontal tail surfaces (total)	3[illegible]·0 m² (333·7 sq ft)

Weights and Loadings (A: CFM56-5 engines, B: V2500s):

Operating weight empty:	
A: basic	37,788 kg (83,308 lb)
optional	38,328 kg (84,498 lb)

First Airbus A320 in final assembly in mid-1986

B: basic	38,181 kg (84,175 lb)
optional	38,721 kg (85,365 lb)
Max payload (structural):	
A: basic	19,212 kg (42,355 lb)
optional	20,672 kg (45,574 lb)
B: basic	18,819 kg (41,488 lb)
optional	20,279 kg (44,707 lb)
Max fuel:	
A: basic	12,515 kg (27,590 lb)
optional	19,000 kg (41,888 lb)
or	18,812 kg (41,473 lb)
B: basic	12,327 kg (27,176 lb)
optional	18,812 kg (41,473 lb)
Max T-O weight:	
A and B: basic	66,000 kg (145,505 lb)
optional	72,000 kg (158,730 lb)
Max landing weight:	
A and B: basic	61,000 kg (134,480 lb)
optional	63,000 kg (138,890 lb)
Max zero-fuel weight:	
A and B: basic	57,000 kg (125,665 lb)
optional	59,000 kg (130,070 lb)
Max wing loading:	
A and B: basic	539 kg/m² (110·4 lb/sq ft)
optional	588 kg/m² (120·4 lb/sq ft)

PERFORMANCE (estimated, at max T-O weight except where indicated; engines A and B as for 'Weights'):

T-O distance at S/L, ISA + 15°C:	
A	1,707 m (5,600 ft)
B	1,722 m (5,650 ft)
Landing distance at max landing weight:	
A and B	1,448 m (4,750 ft)

Runway LCN (X: flexible pavement of 51 cm; 20 in thickness; Y: rigid pavement of 76 cm; 30 in radius of relative stiffness):

45 × 16-R20 tyres, standard bogie:	
A and B at basic MTOGW: X	60
Y	69
A and B at optional MTOGW: X	74
Y	79

Range with 150-seat mixed class layout, typical international reserves and 200 nm (370 km; 230 mile) diversion:

A	1,930 nm (3,576 km; 2,222 miles)
B	2,010 nm (3,725 km; 2,315 miles)

OPERATIONAL NOISE LEVELS (ICAO Annex 16, Chapter 3):

T-O: A	85·4 EPNdB (90·1 limit)
B	83·6 EPNdB (90·1 limit)
Sideline: A	92·7 EPNdB (96·3 limit)
B	92·4 EPNdB (96·3 limit)
Approach: A	97·6 EPNdB (100·1 limit)
B	95·3 EPNdB (100·1 limit)

AIRBUS A330 and A340

A series of presentations to world airlines has helped Airbus Industrie to identify possible launch customers for the A330 and A340 (formerly known as projects TA9 and TA11), and to anticipate a possible programme go-ahead in late 1986 or early 1987.

The A330 and A340 are versions of one basic aircraft, and feature the same fuselage, tail unit and advanced-technology wing; only the engines and their associated systems are different. The very-long-range four-engined A340 is being offered with seating for around 260 passengers in a typical long-haul layout of first, business and economy classes (or some 310 passengers in a two-class medium-haul arrangement). The high-capacity medium- to long-range A330 has only two engines, but will typically carry 300-330 passengers. Both aircraft would enter service in the early 1990s, the A330 following about six months after the A340.

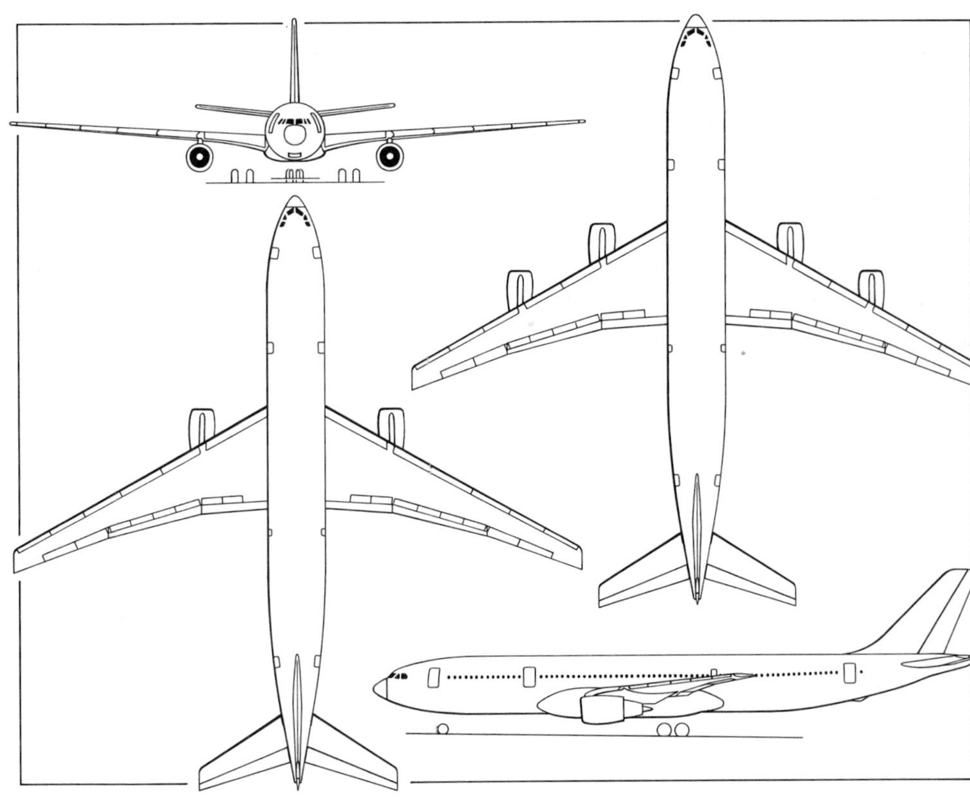

Airbus A330 twin-turbofan transport, with additional plan view of four-engined A340 (top right) *(Jane's/Mike Keep)*

The A340 is planned to link secondary cities, alleviating congestion at major airports and reducing the journey times of provincial passengers. It will also allow more non-stop flights on trunk routes, by eliminating the intermediate stops now made to augment passenger traffic in Boeing 747s.

In giving the A330 two engines and about the same passenger capacity as today's TriStar and DC-10/MD-11, Airbus Industrie brings twin-engine economy to the class of high-capacity, medium- to long-haul aircraft currently powered by three engines. It will thus be tailored to high-density medium-haul routes, such as coast-to-coast services in the USA, but equally suitable for long-range trans-Atlantic flights.

For the A340, the four engines will be either International Aero Engines V2500s or CFM International CFM56-5s, developed from those offered on the A320. Similar engine commonality exists for the twin-engined A330, which will have higher thrust versions of the General Electric CF6-80C2 or Pratt and Whitney PW4000 currently available on the A310 and A300-600.

Both new aircraft will retain many proven features of the Airbus family, including the wide-body fuselage cross-section. A key feature is their advanced aerodynamic wing, which will be the first on an airliner to derive the benefits of variable camber. As envisaged by Airbus Industrie, variable camber would use small movements of the trailing-edge flaps—normally used only during take-off and landing—to re-shape the aerodynamic profile of the wing during cruise. This 'tailoring' optimises the wing for the weight and altitude of the aircraft, thereby reducing drag and saving fuel. The new wing will also have a higher aspect ratio than that of other aircraft in its class. In addition to the new wing, the A330 and A340 will build upon many of the state-of-the-art technologies embodied in Airbus Industrie's current family, including the computer driven fly by wire (FBW) controls, sidestick controllers and integrated displays of the A320, as well as a weight-saving carbonfibre reinforced plastics (CFRP) fin and drag-saving tailplane trim tank.

The A330 and A340 fuselage will be about ten frame pitches, or 5·0 m (15 ft 5 in), longer than that of the A300-600. The passenger cabin will allow airlines to alter seating, toilet and galley layouts to suit the needs of their markets. The aircraft will be able to carry up to 24 LD3 containers in their underfloor cargo holds, or a mixture of the largest pallets and containers.

AIRTECH

AIRCRAFT TECHNOLOGY INDUSTRIES

Rey Francisco 4, Apartado 193, 28008 Madrid, Spain

PRESIDENT: Prof Dr-Ing B. J. Habibie

VICE-PRESIDENT: Dr Carlos Marin Ridruejo

PARTICIPATING COMPANIES:

Construcciones Aeronauticas SA, Rey Francisco 4, Apartado 193, 28008 Madrid, Spain
Telephone: (91) 247 25 00
Telex: 27418 CASA E

IPTN (Industri Pesawat Terbang Nusantara), PO Box 563, Jalan Pajajaran 154, Bandung, Indonesia
Telephone: Bandung (022) 613662 and 611081
Telex: 28295 NUR BDG

Airtech is a joint company formed by CASA of Spain and IPTN of Indonesia to develop a 40/44-passenger twin-turboprop transport aircraft known as the CN-235. Design and production work is shared 50-50 between the two companies. Market research is under way for an enlarged 60/70-seat version, under the designation CN-260.

AIRTECH (CASA/IPTN) CN-235

Preliminary design of the CN-235 was initiated in January 1980. Detail design work began a year later, and prototype construction started in May 1981. Two prototypes were built, one in each country (ECT-100 and PK-XNC), plus static and fatigue test airframes. Simultaneous rollouts were made on 10 September 1983, and first flights took place on 11 November (CASA) and 30 December 1983 (IPTN). The two prototypes had carried out 1,350 hours of flying by the end of April 1986 (approx 1,000 hours by the Spanish aircraft and 350 hours in Indonesia), and the initial flight of the first production CN-235 was made on 19 August 1986. Certification by the Spanish and Indonesian authorities had been received by that date, and by the end of 1986 type approval by the FAA was anticipated, thus fully certificating the CN-235 to FAR Pts 25 and 36, JAR 25, and ICAO Annex 16. CASA markets the aircraft in America and Europe, IPTN in Asia, with other markets shared as appropriate.

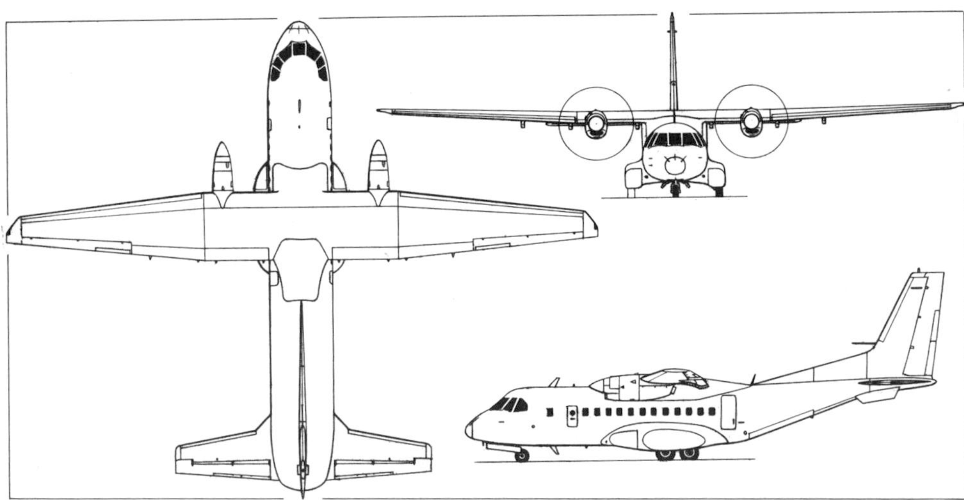

Airtech (CASA/IPTN) CN-235 twin-turboprop commuter transport *(Pilot Press)*

CASA builds the wing centre-section, inboard flaps, forward and centre fuselage; the outer wings, outboard flaps, ailerons, rear fuselage and tail surfaces are built by IPTN. Numerical control machinery is used extensively in the CN-235's manufacture. Design has been optimised for short-haul operations, enabling the CN-235 to fly four 100 nm (185 km; 115 mile) stage lengths, with reserves, before needing to refuel, and to operate from either paved runways or unprepared strips. The general configuration provides for extending the fuselage, if required in the future, to carry 60 passengers.

By June 1986, firm orders for the CN-235 totalled 110, for the Indonesian operators Deraya Air Taxi (10), Merpati Nusantara Airlines (14) and Pelita Air Service (10); the Indonesian Air Force (32) and Navy (18); the Spanish airline Aviaco (22); and the Royal Saudi Air Force (4). Options were then held by Merpati (14), Prinair of Puerto Rico (5), and Automotores Salta of Argentina (4).

TYPE: Twin-turboprop commuter and utility transport.

WINGS: Cantilever high-wing monoplane. NACA 65_3-218 wing section. Constant chord centre-section, without dihedral; 3° dihedral on tapered outer panels. Incidence 3°. No sweepback at quarter-chord. Three main assemblies each consist of a machined fail-safe main box structure of aluminium/copper alloy, with main spars at 15 and 55 per cent chord, plus leading- and trailing-edge structures. Inboard flaps on centre-section, outboard flap segments and ailerons on outer panels. Fail-safe attachment of centre-section to top of fuselage; large wing/fuselage fairing, made of composites. Chemically milled skins. Leading-edges each made up of a false spar, ribs and skin panels. Flap segments each have a machined aluminium spar, two sheet metal ribs of aluminium/zinc alloy, and leading/trailing-edges of composite materials (glassfibre laminates with honeycomb core). Inboard and outboard pairs are interchangeable port/starboard. Flaps are single-slotted and actuated hydraulically by Dowty Rotol irreversible jacks. Ailerons, of similar construction to flaps, are statically and dynamically balanced and have duplicated flight controls. Mechanically operated servo tab and electrically actuated trim tab in each aileron. Raked wingtips are of glassfibre. Pneumatic boot anti-icing of leading-edges outboard of engine nacelles.

FUSELAGE: Conventional fail-safe pressurised semi-monocoque structure (including baggage compartment), built mainly of aluminium/copper and aluminium/zinc alloy longerons, frames, stringers and skin panels. Flattened circular cross-section, upswept at rear. Glassfibre nose radome, reinforced with glassfibre/Nomex honeycomb/glassfibre sandwich, forward of front pressure bulkhead. Forward pressurised section includes flight deck and bulkhead at front of passenger cabin. Central (passenger cabin) section is 19 frames long, at 508 mm (20 in) pitch. Rear fuselage, 15 frames long, includes rear cargo ramp and door, baggage compartment, and the tailcone, which incorporates the rear pressure bulkhead. Composite fairings on fuselage sides house some equipment and systems, in addition to retracted main landing gear.

TAIL UNIT: Cantilever structure, comprising sweptback fin and statically and dynamically balanced rudder, large dorsal fin, two small ventral fins, and non-swept fixed incidence tailplane with statically and dynamically balanced elevators. Main fin and tailplane boxes are two-spar aluminium/copper alloy structures, with detachable leading-edges and glassfibre tips. Rudder and elevators have glassfibre skin and Nomex honeycomb core. Rudder and elevators actuated mechanically. Mechanically operated servo tab and electrically actuated trim tab in rudder and each elevator. Pneumatic boot anti-icing of fin and tailplane leading-edges.

LANDING GEAR: Messier-Hispano-Bugatti retractable tricycle type with levered suspension, suitable for operation from semi-prepared runways. Electrically controlled hydraulic extension/retraction, with mechanical backup system for emergency extension. Oleo-pneumatic shock absorber in each unit. Each main unit comprises two wheels in tandem, retracting rearward into fairing on side of fuselage. Mainwheels semi-exposed when retracted. Single steerable nosewheel retracts forward into unpressurised bay under flight deck. Dunlop 28 × 9·00-12 (12 ply rating) tubeless mainwheel tyres standard, pressure 5·17 bars (75 lb/sq in); low pressure mainwheel tyres optional, size 11·00-12/10, pressure 3·45 bars (50 lb/sq in). Dunlop 24 × 7·7 (12 ply rating) tubeless nosewheel tyre, pressure 5·65 bars (82 lb/sq in). Dunlop hydraulic differential disc brakes; Dunlop anti-skid units on main gear.

POWER PLANT: Two General Electric CT7-7A turboprop engines, each flat rated at 1,268 kW (1,700 shp) (S/L, to 29°C) for take-off and driving a Hamilton Standard 14-RF21 four-blade constant-speed propeller with full feathering and reverse-pitch capability. Blades are of glassfibre, with metal spar and urethane foam core. Fuel in two 1,042 litre (229 Imp gallon; 275 US gallon) integral main tanks in wing centre-section and two 1,592 litre (350 Imp gallon; 421 US gallon) integral outer-wing tanks; total fuel capacity 5,268 litres (1,158 Imp gallons; 1,392 US gallons), of which 5,128 litres (1,128 Imp gallons; 1,355 US gallons) are usable. Single pressure refuelling point in starboard main landing gear fairing; gravity filling point in top of each tank. Propeller braking permits engine to be used as an on-ground APU. Oil capacity 13·97 litres (3·07 Imp gallons; 3·69 US gallons).

ACCOMMODATION: Crew of two on flight deck, plus cabin attendant. Accommodation in commuter version for up to 44 passengers in four-abreast seating, at 76 cm (30 in) pitch, with 22 seats each side of central aisle. Toilet, galley and overhead luggage bins standard. Pressurised baggage compartment at rear of cabin, aft of movable bulkhead; additional stowage in overhead lockers. Can also be equipped as mixed passenger/cargo combi (eg, 18 passengers and two LD3 containers), or for all-cargo operation, carrying four standard LD3 containers, five LD2s, or two 2·24 m (88 in) wide pallets; or for military duties, carrying up to 48 troops or 41 paratroops. Other options include layouts for aeromedical (24 stretchers and four medical attendants), ASW/maritime patrol (with 360° search radar and Exocet missiles or Mk 46 torpedoes), electronic warfare, geophysical survey or aerial photographic duties. Main passenger door, outward opening with integral stairs, aft of wing on port side, serving also as a Type I emergency exit. Type III emergency exit facing this door on starboard side. Service door (forward, starboard) has built-in stairs, and serves also as a Type I emergency exit, or as passenger door in combi version; a second Type III exit is provided, opposite this door, on the port side. Wide ventral door/cargo ramp in underside of upswept rear fuselage, for loading of bulky cargo. Accommodation fully air-conditioned and pressurised.

SYSTEMS: Hamilton Standard air-conditioning system, using engine compressor bleed air. Garrett electro-pneumatic pressurisation system (max differential 0·25 bars; 3·6 lb/sq in) giving cabin environment of 2,440 m (8,000 ft) up to operating altitude of 5,485 m (18,000 ft). Hydraulic system, operating at nominal pressure of 207 bars (3,000 lb/sq in), comprises two engine driven, variable displacement axial electric pumps, a self pressurising standby mechanical pump, and a modular unit incorporating connectors, filters and valves; system is employed for actuation of wing flaps, landing gear extension/retraction, wheel brakes, emergency and parking brakes, nosewheel steering, cargo ramp and door, and propeller braking. Accumulator for backup braking system. No pneumatic system. DC primary electrical system powered by two 400A Auxilec engine driven starter/generators, with two 37Ah nickel-cadmium batteries for engine starting and 30 min (minimum) emergency power for essential services. Constant frequency single-phase AC power (115/26V) provided at 400Hz by three 600VA static inverters (two for normal operation plus one standby); two three-phase engine driven alternators for 115V variable frequency AC power. Fixed oxygen installation for crew of three (single cylinder at 124 bars; 1,800 lb/sq in pressure); three portable units and individual masks for passengers. Pneumatic boot anti-icing of wing (outboard of engine nacelles), fin and tailplane leading-edges. Electric anti-icing of propellers, engine air intakes, flight deck windscreen, pitot tubes and angle of attack indicators. No APU: starboard engine, with propeller braking, can be used to fulfil this function. Hand type fire extinguishers on flight deck (one) and in passenger cabin (two); smoke detector in baggage compartment. Engine fire detection and extinguishing system.

AVIONICS AND EQUIPMENT: Standard avionics include two Collins VHF-22 com radios, one Avtech DADS crew interphone, one Collins TDR-90 ATC transponder, two Collins VIR-32 VOR/ILS/marker beacon receivers, one Collins DME-41, one Collins ADF-60A, one Collins WXR-300 weather radar, two Collins 332D-11T vertical gyros, two Collins MCS-65 directional gyros, two Collins EADI-85 ADI, two Collins EHSI-85 HSI, two Collins ERMI-85 RMI, one Collins ADS-65, one Collins ALT-55B radio altimeter, one Collins FGS-65 flight director, one Fairchild F-800 flight data recorder, and one Fairchild A-100A cockpit voice recorder. CRT displays for ADIs and HSIs optional. Other options include second TDR-90, DME-41, and ADF-60A, plus Collins HF-220 com radio, Avtec PACIS PA system, Collins RNS-300 radar and Litton LTN-72 inertial navigation, and one Collins APS-65 digital autopilot. Space provisions for GPWS and altitude presentation. Navigation lights, anti-collision strobe lights, 600W landing light in front end of each main landing gear fairing, taxi lights, ice inspection lights, emergency door lights, flight deck and flight deck emergency lights, cabin and baggage compartment lights, individual passenger reading lights, and instrument panel white lighting, are all standard.

ARMAMENT (military version): Two fuselage hardpoints for torpedoes or missiles, plus two attachment points under each wing. Max weapon load 3,500 kg (7,716 lb).

DIMENSIONS, EXTERNAL:

Wing span	25·81 m (84 ft 8 in)
Wing chord: at root	3·00 m (9 ft 10 in)
at tip	1·20 m (3 ft 11¼ in)
Wing aspect ratio	9·13
Length overall	21·353 m (70 ft 0¾ in)
Length of fuselage	20·90 m (68 ft 7 in)
Fuselage: Max width	2·90 m (9 ft 6 in)
Max depth	2·615 m (8 ft 7 in)
Height overall	8·177 m (26 ft 10 in)
Tailplane span	11·00 m (36 ft 1 in)
Wheel track (c/l of mainwheels)	3·90 m (12 ft 9½ in)
Wheelbase	6·919 m (22 ft 8½ in)
Propeller diameter	3·35 m (11 ft 0 in)
Propeller ground clearance	1·528 m (5 ft 0¼ in)
Distance between propeller centres	7·00 m (22 ft 11½ in)
Passenger door (port, rear) and service door (stbd, fwd):	
Height	1·70 m (5 ft 7 in)
Width	0·73 m (2 ft 4¾ in)
Height to sill	1·22 m (4 ft 0 in)

The Spanish assembled prototype of the Airtech (CASA/IPTN) CN-235 commuter and utility transport aircraft

Ventral upper door (rear): Length 2·366 m (7 ft 9¼ in)
Width 2·349 m (7 ft 8½ in)
Height to sill 1·22 m (4 ft 0 in)
Ventral ramp/door (rear): Length 3·042 m (9 ft 11¾ in)
Width 2·349 m (7 ft 8½ in)
Height to sill 1·22 m (4 ft 0 in)
Type III emergency exits (port, fwd, and stbd, rear):
Height 0·91 m (3 ft 0 in)
Width 0·51 m (1 ft 8 in)

Dimensions, internal:
Cabin, excl flight deck: Length 9·65 m (31 ft 8 in)
Max width 2·70 m (8 ft 10½ in)
Width at floor 2·366 m (7 ft 9 in)
Max height 1·90 m (6 ft 2¾ in)
Floor area 22·822 m² (245·65 sq ft)
Volume 44·68 m³ (1,577·9 cu ft)
Baggage compartment volume, incl overhead bins 7·0 m³ (247·2 cu ft)

Areas:
Wings, gross 73·00 m² (785·8 sq ft)
Ailerons (total, incl tabs) 3·071 m² (33·06 sq ft)
Trailing-edge flaps (total) 10·87 m² (117·0 sq ft)
Fin, incl dorsal fin 7·12 m² (76·64 sq ft)
Rudder, incl tabs 3·98 m² (42·8 sq ft)
Tailplane 21·20 m² (228·2 sq ft)
Elevators (total, incl tabs) 4·25 m² (45·74 sq ft)

Weights and Loadings:
Operating weight empty:
passengers 9,400 kg (20,725 lb)
cargo 8,600 kg (18,960 lb)
Max fuel load 4,100 kg (9,039 lb)
Max payload: passengers 4,200 kg (9,260 lb)
cargo 5,000 kg (11,025 lb)
Max T-O weight 14,400 kg (31,745 lb)
Max ramp weight 14,450 kg (31,855 lb)
Max landing weight 14,200 kg (31,305 lb)
Max zero-fuel weight 13,600 kg (29,980 lb)
Max wing loading 197·26 kg/m² (40·40 lb/sq ft)
Max power loading 5·68 kg/kW (9·34 lb/shp)

Performance (civil version at max T-O weight, ISA, except where indicated):
Max operating speed at S/L 240 knots (445 km/h; 276 mph) IAS
Max cruising speed at 4,575 m (15,000 ft) 244 knots (452 km/h; 280 mph)
Stalling speed at S/L 77 knots (143 km/h; 89 mph) IAS
Max rate of climb at S/L 465 m (1,527 ft)/min
Rate of climb at S/L, one engine out 128 m (420 ft)/min
Service ceiling 8,110 m (26,600 ft)
Service ceiling, one engine out 4,550 m (14,925 ft)
T-O run 554 m (1,818 ft)
T-O to 10·7 m (35 ft) at S/L 687 m (2,254 ft)
Landing from 15 m (50 ft) at S/L 585 m (1,920 ft)
Min ground turning radius 18·974 m (62 ft 3 in)
Range at 5,485 m (18,000 ft), reserves for 87 nm (161 km; 100 mile) diversion and 45 min hold:
with max payload 208 nm (385 km; 239 miles)
with max fuel 2,110 nm (3,910 km; 2,429 miles)

Performance (military version, estimated at max T-O weight, ISA, except where indicated):
As for civil version except:
Service ceiling, one engine out 4,725 m (15,500 ft)
T-O run 453 m (1,487 ft)
T-O to 15 m (50 ft) 660 m (2,166 ft)
Landing from 15 m (50 ft), with propeller reversal 577 m (1,893 ft)
Landing run, with propeller reversal 286 m (939 ft)
Range with 45 min reserves:
with max payload, max cruising speed at 5,485 m (18,000 ft) 324 nm (600 km; 373 miles)
with max fuel and 1,800 kg (3,963 lb) payload, long-range cruising speed at 6,100 m (20,000 ft) 2,547 nm (4,720 km; 2,933 miles)

ATR

AVIONS DE TRANSPORT RÉGIONAL

316 route de Bayonne, Toulouse, France
Postal Address: BP 31107, 31026 Toulouse Cédex, France
Telephone: (61) 49 11 22
Telex: SNIAS 531 546 F

Board of Directors:
Henri Martre (Aérospatiale) (alternate Chairman, and Chief Executive Officer)
Renato Bonifacio (Aeritalia) (alternate Chairman, and Managing Director)
Yves Barbé (Aérospatiale) (Executive Vice-President)
Fausto Cereti (Aeritalia) (General Manager)

Management Committee:
Jacques Plenier (Aérospatiale) (Chief Executive Officer, Aircraft Group)
Jean-Paul Perrais (Aérospatiale) (Vice-President, ATR 42 Programme)
Giovanni Sarzotti (Aeritalia) (Joint General Manager and ATR 42 Consortium President)
Massimo Rizzo (Aeritalia) (General Secretary)

Commercial Manager: Henri-Paul Puel

Launching of the ATR 42 programme was announced at the beginning of November 1981, following a simultaneous decision on 29 October by Aérospatiale (France) and Aeritalia (Italy) to go ahead with this new twin-turboprop transport aircraft. The decision was confirmed on 4 November 1981 by a new co-operative agreement for equal sharing of ATR 42 programme work and costs, and for setting up a Groupement d'Intérêt Economique (pooling of common economic interest) to manage the programme. This GIE was formally established on 5 February 1982, and has its headquarters in Toulouse.

ATR corresponds to the initial letters of the French and Italian words for 'regional transport aircraft', and 42 to the seating capacity of the basic aircraft at 81 cm (32 in) pitch. A combined Aérospatiale/Aeritalia design group is working at Toulouse to complete the development of the aircraft; computer aided design and manufacturing techniques are being used throughout.

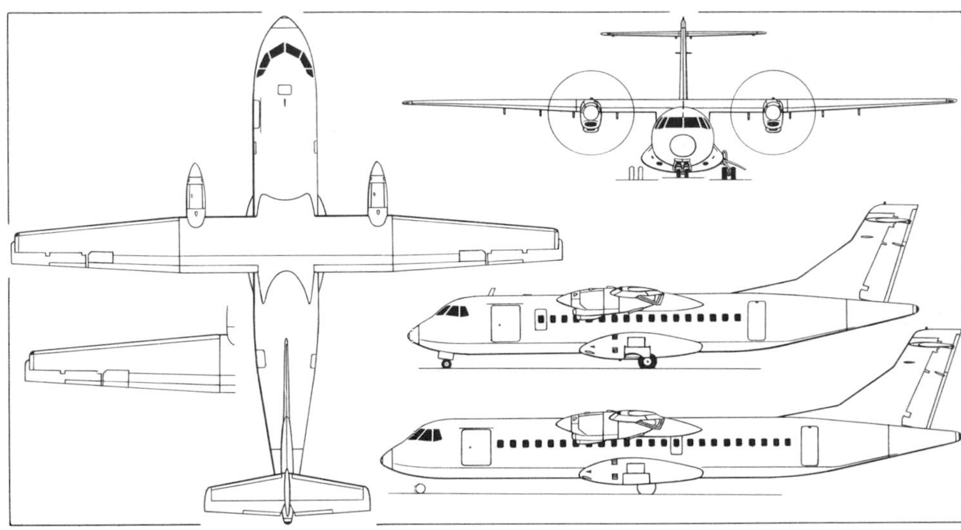

Aérospatiale/Aeritalia ATR 42 twin-turboprop regional transport aircraft, with added side view (bottom) and extended outer wing of ATR 72 *(Pilot Press)*

ATR 42

The ATR 42 is a high-wing twin-turboprop transport aircraft embodying a number of advanced technology features in the fields of aerodynamics, structures and equipment. Design is to FAR Pt 25 and to European Joint Airworthiness Requirement JAR 25 for the certification of transport aircraft. Choice of the Pratt & Whitney Canada PW120 turboprop as the aircraft's power plant was announced on 8 June 1981.

Aeritalia is responsible for the entire fuselage, including the tail unit and installation of the landing gear; and for the hydraulic, air-conditioning and pressurisation systems. Aérospatiale undertakes design and construction of the wings; layout of the flight deck and cabin; and is also responsible for power plant, electrical system, flight controls and de-icing system installation, and for final assembly and flight testing of the civil passenger versions. Aeritalia will assemble and flight test any cargo/military variants with a rear loading ramp.

Two development aircraft were built, plus airframes for static and fatigue test. First flight was made by F-WEGA on 16 August 1984, with the second aircraft (F-WEGB) following on 31 October 1984. The first production aircraft (F-WEGC) made its initial flight on 30 April 1985. French DGAC certification of the ATR 42-200 and -300 to JAR 25 was granted on 24 September 1985, with concurrent type approval by the Italian RAI. The three aircraft used in the programme had then accumulated a total of 1,236 flying hours in 747 flights. FAA certification (FAR Pt 25) followed on 25 October 1985. Deliveries began on 3 December 1985 with the fourth aircraft (to Air Littoral), and services with this airline began six days later. Construction of the first 50 aircraft has been authorised, and provisioning for the next 25 was authorised in September 1984. Production, running at three aircraft per month in the Summer of 1986, is scheduled to reach four per month by mid-1987.

Initial production is centred on the basic **ATR 42-200**, and on the essentially similar **ATR 42-300** which has minor structural changes to increase maximum take-off weight and payload/range capability. Beyond these two models, the following variants have been or are being studied:

ATR 42-F. Commercial freighter version, capable of carrying 3,800 kg (8,377 lb) or 42 passengers over 1,250 nm (2,316 km; 1,439 miles). Modified interior, reinforced cabin floor, port side flight-openable cargo/airdrop door.

ATM 42-R. Military cargo version, with rear ramp and payload of 4,000-5,000 kg (8,818-11,023 lb) in 11 m (36 ft) long hold.

ATR 42-S. Maritime patrol version fitted with specific equipment for radio communications, detection, search, observation and, if required, an air-to-surface weapon system. Patrol time of 3 h 30 min at 600 nm (1,112 km; 691 miles) from base.

SAR 42. Search and rescue/maritime surveillance version for public utility missions, with 4 hour search endurance at 600 nm (1,112 km; 691 miles) from base. Search radar, survival equipment, ship or shore communications link.

ATR 72. 'Stretched' version, launched in mid-1985. Described separately.

By 31 August 1986, a total of 63 firm orders had been received for the ATR 42. Customers include Air Calédonie, Air Guam, Air Littoral (France), Air Mauritius, Air Queensland, Alitalia (ATI), Britair (France), Holland Aero Lines (Netherlands), Cimber Air (Denmark), Finnair, Command Airways (USA), Ransome Airlines (USA) and Simmons Airlines (USA). A total of 18 ATR 42s had been delivered by 31 August 1986.

Type: Twin-turboprop regional transport aircraft.

Wings: Cantilever high-wing monoplane. Aérospatiale RA-XXX-43 wing section, derived from NACA 43 series, with thickness/chord ratio of 18% at root and 13% at tip. Two-spar fail-safe wings, constructed mainly of aluminium alloys, with leading-edges of Kevlar/Nomex sandwich, and skin panels of Kevlar/Nomex with carbon reinforcement on upper surface aft of rear spar. Constant chord centre-section and tapered outer panels. Dihedral 2° 30′ on outer panels. No sweepback at quarter-chord. Two-segment double-slotted single-rotation flaps, each segment with its own Ratier-Figeac hydraulic actuator, on each trailing-edge. Spoiler forward of outer end of each outer flap segment. Ailerons actuated mechanically by cables and push/pull rods; no servos. Flaps and ailerons of carbonfibre/Nomex and carbon/epoxy construction respectively, with aluminium frames and spars. Electrically actuated automatic trim tab in each aileron. Kléber-Colombes pneumatic de-icing of leading-edges outboard of engine nacelles.

Fuselage: Conventional semi-monocoque fail-safe structure mainly of light alloy unit construction, employing main and secondary frames and longitudinally disposed skin panels. Nosecone, tailcone, wing/body fairings, nosewheel doors and main landing gear fairings of Kevlar/Nomex sandwich. Basically circular cross-section throughout most of length. Crew, passenger and baggage/cargo compartments pressurised.

Tail Unit: Cantilever structure, with sweptback vertical surfaces (attached to rearmost fuselage frame) and nonswept horizontal surfaces. Fixed incidence tailplane mounted near tip of fin. Fin and tailplane construction mainly of aluminium alloys, with dorsal fin of Kevlar/Nomex and glassfibre/Nomex sandwich. Mechanically actuated mass balanced rudder and elevators, of carbonfibre/Nomex sandwich construction. Electrically actuated automatic trim tab in rudder and each elevator. Kléber-Colombes pneumatic de-icing of tailplane leading-edges.

Landing Gear: Hydraulically retractable tricycle type, of Messier-Hispano-Bugatti/Magnaghi/Nardi trailing-arm design, with twin wheels and oleo-pneumatic shock absorber on each unit. Nose unit retracts forward, main units inward into fuselage and large underfuselage fairing. Goodyear multi-disc brakes and Hydro-Aire antiskid units on main gear. No brake cooling. Goodyear mainwheels and tubeless tyres, size 32 × 8·8-10PR, pressure 7·17 bars (104 lb/sq in). Low pressure tyres optional, requiring modification to underfuselage fairing.

Goodyear nosewheels and tubeless tyres, size 450 × 190-5TL, pressure 4·14 bars (60 lb/sq in).

Power Plant: Two Pratt & Whitney Canada PW120 turboprop engines, each flat rated at 1,342 kW (1,800 shp) and driving a Hamilton Standard 14SF four-blade constant-speed fully-feathering and reversible-pitch propeller with metal spars and glassfibre/polyurethane skins. Fuel in two integral tanks formed by wing spar box, total capacity 5,700 litres (1,254 Imp gallons; 1,506 US gallons). Single pressure refuelling point in starboard wing leading-edge. Gravity refuelling points in wing upper surface. Oil capacity 40 litres (8·8 Imp gallons). Cowlings of carbonfibre/Nomex and Kevlar/Nomex sandwich, reinforced with carbonfibre in nose and underside.

Accommodation: Crew of two on flight deck, with optional third seat for observer. Seating for 42 passengers at 81 cm (32 in) pitch; or 46, 48 or 50 passengers at 76 cm (30 in) pitch, in four-abreast layout with central aisle. Passenger door, with integral steps, at rear of cabin on port side. Main baggage/cargo compartment between flight deck and passenger cabin, with access from inside cabin and separate loading door on port side. Rear baggage/cargo compartment, toilet, galley, wardrobe, and seat for cabin attendant, aft of passenger cabin, with service door on starboard side. Additional baggage space provided by overhead bins and underseat stowage. Entire accommodation, including baggage/cargo compartments, pressurised and air-conditioned. Passenger/cargo version (42 passengers or five LD3 containers) fitted with ball transfer plates aft, roller tracks, and anti-crash net at front of cabin. Emergency escape hatch for crew in roof of flight deck. Emergency exit via rear passenger and service doors, and by additional exits on each side at front of cabin.

Systems: Garrett air-conditioning and Softair pressurisation systems, utilising engine bleed air. Pressurisation system (nominal differential 0·41 bars; 6·0 lb/sq in) provides cabin altitude of 2,000 m (6,560 ft) at flight altitudes of up to 7,620 m (25,000 ft), and a sea level cabin environment at flight levels up to 4,025 m (13,200 ft). Two independent hydraulic systems, each at system pressure of 207 bars (3,000 lb/sq in), driven by an electrically operated Abex pump and separated by an interconnecting valve controlled from the flight deck. One system actuates wing flaps, spoilers, propeller braking, emergency wheel braking and nosewheel steering; second system for landing gear and normal braking system. Kléber-Colombes pneumatic system for de-icing of outer wing leading-edges, tailplane leading-edges and engine air intakes. Main electrical system is 28V DC, supplied by two Auxilec 12kW engine driven starter/generators and two nickel-cadmium batteries (27Ah and 16Ah) with two solid state static inverters for 115/26V single-phase AC supply, and a third (standby) inverter for 115V only. A 115/200V three-phase supply from two 20kVA frequency-wild engine driven alternators is used for anti-icing of windscreen, flight deck side windows, stall warning and airspeed indicator pitots, pitot tubes, propeller blades and control surface horns. Eros/Puritan oxygen system. Garrett APU optional.

Avionics: King Gold Crown III com/nav equipment standard, Collins Pro Line II optional. Other standard avionics include Sperry DFZ-600 autopilot/flight director, Sperry P-800 weather radar, dual Sperry AZ-800 digital air data computers and dual AH-600 attitude/heading reference systems with ASCB (avionics standard communication bus), GPWS, radio altimeter, and digital flight deck recorder. EDZ-820 electronic flight instrumentation system (R/Nav, microwave landing system, Omega nav and HF com) optional. Standard avionics package includes two VHF, two VOR/ILS/marker beacon receivers, radio compass, radio altimeter, DME, ATC transponder, cockpit voice recorder, intercom, PA system, and equipment to FAR Pt 121.

Dimensions, external:
Wing span 24·57 m (80 ft 7½ in)
Wing chord: at root 2·57 m (8 ft 5¼ in)
at tip 1·41 m (4 ft 7½ in)
Wing aspect ratio 11·08
Length overall 22·67 m (74 ft 4½ in)
Fuselage: Max width 2·865 m (9 ft 4½ in)
Height overall 7·586 m (24 ft 10¾ in)
Elevator span 7·31 m (23 ft 11¾ in)
Wheel track (c/l of shock struts) 4·10 m (13 ft 5½ in)
Wheelbase 8·78 m (28 ft 9¾ in)
Propeller diameter 3·96 m (13 ft 0 in)
Distance between propeller centres 8·10 m (26 ft 7 in)
Propeller/fuselage clearance 0·82 m (2 ft 8¼ in)
Passenger door (rear, port):
Height 1·75 m (5 ft 9 in)
Width 0·75 m (2 ft 5½ in)
Height to sill (at OWE) 1·375 m (4 ft 6¼ in)
Service door (rear, stbd): Height 1·22 m (4 ft 0 in)
Width 0·61 m (2 ft 0 in)
Height to sill 1·375 m (4 ft 6¼ in)
Cargo/baggage door (fwd, port):
Height 1·52 m (5 ft 0 in)
Width 1·275 m (4 ft 2¼ in)
Height to sill (at OWE) 1·15 m (3 ft 9¼ in)
Emergency exits (fwd, each):
Height 0·91 m (3 ft 0 in)
Width 0·51 m (1 ft 8 in)
Crew emergency hatch (flight deck roof):
Length 0·51 m (1 ft 8 in)
Width 0·483 m (1 ft 7 in)

Dimensions, internal:
Cabin:
Length (excl flight deck, incl baggage compartments) 13·85 m (45 ft 5¼ in)
Max width 2·57 m (8 ft 5¼ in)
Max width at floor 2·263 m (7 ft 5⅛ in)
Max height 1·91 m (6 ft 3¼ in)
Volume 44·8 m³ (1,582 cu ft)
Baggage/cargo compartment volume:
front (max) 6·2 m³ (219 cu ft)
front (50 passengers) 3·5 m³ (123·6 cu ft)
rear (max) 2·9 m³ (102·4 cu ft)
overhead bins 1·5 m³ (53 cu ft)

Areas:
Wings, gross 54·5 m² (586·6 sq ft)
Vertical tail surfaces (total, excl dorsal fin) 12·5 m² (134·5 sq ft)
Horizontal tail surfaces (total) 10·3 m² (110·9 sq ft)

Weights and Loadings:
Operating weight empty (incl FAR 121 equipment):
200, 300 9,973 kg (21,986 lb)
Max fuel load: 200, 300 4,500 kg (9,920 lb)
Max payload: 200 4,527 kg (9,980 lb)
300 4,827 kg (10,641 lb)
Max T-O weight: 200 15,750 kg (34,725 lb)
300 16,150 kg (35,605 lb)
Max ramp weight: 200 15,770 kg (34,765 lb)
300 16,170 kg (35,648 lb)
Max zero-fuel weight: 200 14,500 kg (31,965 lb)
300 14,800 kg (32,628 lb)
Max landing weight: 200 15,500 kg (34,171 lb)
300 16,000 kg (35,274 lb)
Max wing loading: 200 289·0 kg/m² (59·19 lb/sq ft)
300 296·3 kg/m² (60·69 lb/sq ft)
Max power loading: 200 5·87 kg/kW (9·64 lb/shp)
300 6·02 kg/kW (9·89 lb/shp)

Performance (at max T-O weight, to FAR Pt 25, incl Amendment 42, ISA, except where indicated):
Max cruising speed at 5,180 m (17,000 ft):
200 268 knots (497 km/h; 309 mph)
300 267 knots (495 km/h; 307 mph)
Normal max operating speed: 200, 300
Mach 0·55 (250 knots; 463 km/h; 288 mph CAS)
Stalling speed, flaps up:
200 96 knots (178 km/h; 111 mph)
300 97 knots (180 km/h; 112 mph)
Stalling speed, 45° flap:
200 72 knots (133 km/h; 83 mph)
300 73 knots (136 km/h; 84 mph)
Max rate of climb at S/L, AUW of 15,000 kg (33,069 lb):
200, 300 640 m (2,100 ft)/min
Rate of climb at S/L, one engine out, AUW as above:
200, 300 191 m (625 ft)/min
Cruise ceiling: 200, 300 7,620 m (25,000 ft)
Service ceiling, one engine out, at 97% of max T-O weight, ISA + 10°C:
200 3,094 m (10,150 ft)
300 2,819 m (9,250 ft)
T-O balanced field length:
at S/L: 200 1,090 m (3,575 ft)
300 1,140 m (3,740 ft)
at 915 m (3,000 ft), ISA + 10°C:
200 1,290 m (4,235 ft)
300 1,350 m (4,430 ft)
Landing field length at S/L at max landing weight:
200 960 m (3,150 ft)
300 980 m (3,215 ft)
Min ground turning radius 17·08 m (56 ft 0½ in)
Max range with 46 passengers, reserves for 87 nm (161 km; 100 mile) diversion and 45 min hold:
200 645 nm (1,195 km; 742 miles)
300 890 nm (1,649 km; 1,025 miles)
Range with max fuel, reserves as above:
max cruising speed:
200, 300 2,490 nm (4,614 km; 2,867 miles)
long-range cruising speed:
200, 300 2,750 nm (5,096 km; 3,166 miles)
Block time for 200 nm (370 km; 230 mile) stage length at max cruising speed at 6,100 m (20,000 ft), IFR reserves 58 min
Block fuel for above 469 kg (1,034 lb)

ATR 72

Go-ahead for this 'stretched' version of the ATR 42 was announced at the 1985 Paris Air Show. Powered by 1,790 kW (2,400 shp) PW124 engines with Hamilton Standard 14SF-11 four-blade propellers, it will have a greater wing span and area, and the lengthened fuselage will accommodate 66-74 passengers. Customers have a choice of passenger or cargo door at front on the port side. First flight is planned for Summer 1988, with deliveries starting in May 1989. The launch customer is Finnair, which has ordered five with another three on option.

Aérospatiale/Aeritalia ATR 42 short-haul commuter transport (two PW120 turboprop engines) in the insignia of Holland Aero Lines

WINGS: Generally as described for ATR 42 except for increased span, with wing spar box of new outer panels manufactured from carbonfibre/epoxy.

FUSELAGE: As described for ATR 42, but of increased length.

TAIL UNIT: As described for ATR 42.

LANDING GEAR: Of improved type, fitted with carbon brakes.

ACCOMMODATION: Crew of two on flight deck. Cabin seating for 64, 66, 70 or (high density) 74 passengers, at respective seat pitches of 81/79/76/76 cm (32/31/30/30 in), plus cabin attendant's seat. Single baggage compartment at rear of cabin; one or two at front, depending on seating layout and type of port forward door fitted. This can be a passenger or cargo door, with a service door opposite on starboard side. Second passenger door at rear of cabin, also with service door opposite. Two overwing emergency exits (one each side); both rear doors also serve as emergency exits. All doors are of plug type. Passenger cabin equipped with folding tables on seats, individual air outlets and reading lights, and increased-capacity air-conditioning system.

AVIONICS AND EQUIPMENT: Flight deck equipment and layout generally as for ATR 42. Additions/improvements include engine monitoring mini-aids, and fuel repeater on refuelling panel.

DIMENSIONS, EXTERNAL:

Wing span	27·05 m (88 ft 9 in)
Wing aspect ratio	11·99
Length overall	27·166 m (89 ft 1½ in)
Height overall	7·65 m (25 ft 1¼ in)
Wheel track	4·10 m (13 ft 5½ in)
Wheelbase	10·70 m (35 ft 1¼ in)
Propeller diameter	3·96 m (13 ft 0 in)
Passenger door (fwd, port): Height	1·75 m (5 ft 9 in)
Width	0·82 m (2 ft 8¼ in)
Alternative cargo door (fwd, port):	
Height	1·53 m (5 ft 0¼ in)
Width	1·275 m (4 ft 2½ in)

DIMENSIONS, INTERNAL:

Cabin:	
Length (excl flight deck, incl baggage compartments)	19·21 m (63 ft 0¼ in)
Cross-section	as for ATR 42
Baggage volume (total, incl overhead bins and stowage):	
74 pass	8·10 m³ (286 cu ft)
70 pass	11·05 m³ (390 cu ft)
66 pass, front pass door	11·60 m³ (410 cu ft)
66 pass, front cargo door	12·95 m³ (457 cu ft)
64 pass, front pass door	12·00 m³ (424 cu ft)
64 pass, front cargo door	13·05 m³ (461 cu ft)

AREA:

Wings, gross	61·0 m² (656·6 sq ft)

WEIGHTS (A: basic, B: optional):

Operating weight empty:	
front passenger door (A, B)	12,200 kg (26,896 lb)
front cargo door (A, B)	12,170 kg (26,830 lb)
Max payload:	
front passenger door: A	7,150 kg (15,763 lb)
B	7,500 kg (16,535 lb)
front cargo door: A	7,180 kg (15,829 lb)
B	7,530 kg (16,600 lb)
Max fuel weight: A, B	5,000 kg (11,023 lb)
Max T-O weight: A	19,990 kg (44,070 lb)
B	21,500 kg (47,400 lb)
Max zero-fuel weight: A	19,350 kg (42,660 lb)
B	19,700 kg (43,430 lb)
Max landing weight: A	19,900 kg (43,872 lb)
B	21,350 kg (47,068 lb)

PERFORMANCE (estimated, at max basic T-O weight except where indicated):

Max cruising speed	286 knots (530 km/h; 329 mph)
Max operating cruise altitude	7,620 m (25,000 ft)
Service ceiling, one engine out, at 97% MTOW and ISA + 10°C	3,385 m (11,100 ft)
T-O balanced field length: S/L, ISA	1,270 m (4,167 ft)
915 m (3,000 ft), ISA + 10°C	1,510 m (4,955 ft)
Landing field length at S/L, ISA	1,010 m (3,314 ft)

Still air range at max optional T-O weight (ISA), reserves for 87 nm (161 km; 100 mile) diversion and 45 min continued cruise:

max optional payload	650 nm (1,204 km; 748 miles)
66 passengers	1,500 nm (2,780 km; 1,727 miles)
max fuel and zero payload	2,400 nm (4,447 km; 2,763 miles)

DASSAULT-BREGUET/DORNIER

AIRFRAME PRIME CONTRACTORS:

Avions Marcel Dassault-Breguet Aviation, 27 rue du Professeur Victor Pauchet, BP 32, 92420 Vaucresson, France
Telephone: (1) 741 79 21
Telex: AMADAS 203944 F

Dornier GmbH, Postfach 2160, 8000 München 66, Federal Republic of Germany
Telephone: (089) 87 15 3480
Telex: 52 35 43

On 22 July 1969 the French and Federal German governments announced a joint requirement for a new subsonic basic/advanced training and light attack aircraft to enter service with their armed forces in the 1970s. Each government had a potential requirement for up to 200 such aircraft, to replace Magister, Lockheed T-33A and Mystère IV-A trainers, and Fiat G91 attack aircraft, then in service.

On 24 July 1970, it was announced that the Alpha Jet had been selected to meet the requirement. The programme received joint French-West German government approval in late 1972; approval to proceed with the production phase was announced on 26 March 1975.

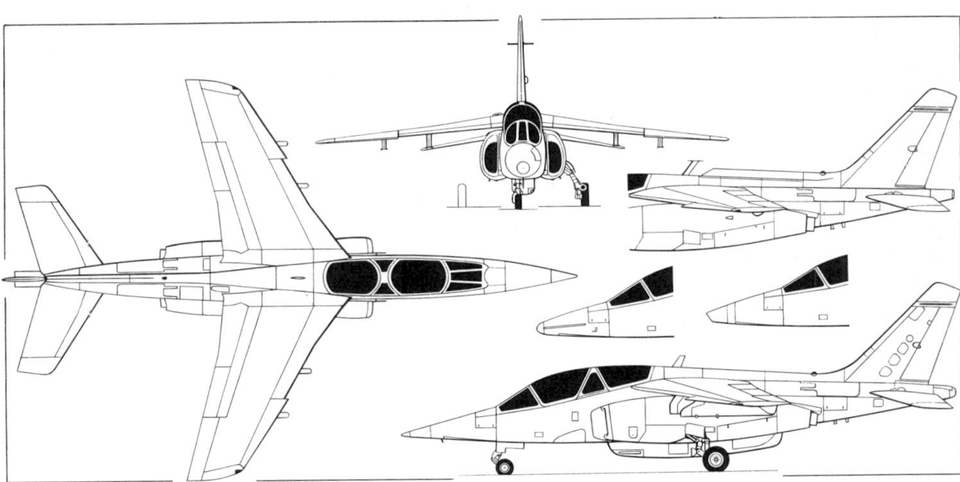

Alpha Jet close support version, with scrap views showing noses of advanced trainer/light attack version (centre left) and MS2 (centre right), plus rear fuselage with dorsal fin antenna fairing *(Pilot Press)*

DASSAULT-BREGUET/DORNIER ALPHA JET

Dassault-Breguet and Dornier are jointly producing the Alpha Jet, with Dassault-Breguet as main contractor and Dornier as industrial collaborator, the total workload being shared primarily between the two groups.

All production Alpha Jets have identical structure, power plant, landing gear and standard equipment; there are assembly lines in France, West Germany and Egypt. The outer wings, tail unit, rear fuselage, landing gear doors and cold-flow exhaust are manufactured in West Germany; the forward and centre fuselage (with integrated wing centre-section) are manufactured in France. Fuselage nosecones and wing flaps are manufactured in Belgium by SABCA. The power plant prime contractors are Turboméca and SNECMA in France, and MTU and KHD in West Germany; and, for the landing gear, Messier-Hispano-Bugatti in France and Liebherr Aero Technik in West Germany.

Four flying prototypes were built, plus two airframes for static and fatigue testing. The 01 made its first flight, at Istres, on 26 October 1973; all four had flown by the end of 1974. Details of the prototypes can be found in the 1978-79 and earlier editions of *Jane's*, and of Dornier's DSFC and TST national experimental programmes in the 1982-83 edition. Existing prototypes continue to be used as testbeds for various programmes, including armament testing, a CFRP wing, and development of the Larzac 04-C20 engine.

There are five versions of the Alpha Jet, as follows:

Advanced trainer/light attack version (formerly known as Alpha Jet E). Ordered for the air forces of France, Belgium (33), Egypt (30, designated **MS1**), Ivory Coast (7), Morocco (24), Nigeria (24), Qatar (6) and Togo (5). Those for Nigeria are from German assembly line, others from French production; 26 of Egyptian MS1s assembled in Egypt by AOI (which see). First production aircraft (E1 for French Air Force) flown on 4 November 1977; deliveries, starting with E2, began in the Summer of 1978. In service by 1 January 1985 with Groupement-École 314 at Tours (57 aircraft); the Patrouille de France (12 aircraft) at Salon de Provence; three aircraft at Mont-de-Marsan; and 37 with the 8e Escadre de Transformation at Cazaux to replace Mystère IV-As in the weapons training role. The 176th French Air Force Alpha Jet was delivered in 1985. Aircraft for Belgian Air Force, assembled by SABCA and delivered in 1978-80, serve with Nos. 7, 9 and 11 Squadrons.

Close support version (formerly known as Alpha Jet A). Ordered for Federal German Luftwaffe (175). First flown (A1) on 12 April 1978; deliveries began in mid-March 1979 and were completed on 26 January 1983. These aircraft now equip Jagdbombergeschwader (fighter-bomber groups) JaboG 49 at Fürstenfeldbruck (from 20 March 1980), JaboG 43 at Oldenburg (from January 1981), and JaboG 41 at Husum (from January 1982), replacing Fiat G91Rs in the close support and reconnaissance roles. Each of these units is allocated 51 aircraft. Eighteen others were assigned to the Luftwaffe base at Beja in Portugal for weapons training; these are earmarked to form an additional combat unit (JaboG 44) in the event of an emergency. An ICE (improved combat efficiency) update programme for the armament and avionics of Luftwaffe Alpha Jets is currently being devised by Dornier; under a separate programme, these aircraft are to be refitted with Larzac 04-C20 engines.

Alternative close support version, developed by Dassault-Breguet and first flown on 9 April 1982. Equipped with new nav/attack system which includes inertial platform, head-up display, laser rangefinder in modified nosecone, and radar altimeter. Ordered by Egypt (15) and Cameroun (6) by mid-1985. Egyptian Air Force version, designated **MS2**, was co-produced with Aircraft Factory No. 36 at Helwan, near Cairo (see AOI entry in Egyptian section): eleven were co-produced, following delivery in 1983 of four French built MS2s. Egyptian MS2s are to be upgraded to NGEA standard (see next paragraph) with Larzac 04-C20 engines and Magic missile capability.

Alpha Jet NGEA (Nouvelle Génération pour l'Ecole et l'Appui). Improved attack version, incorporating the nav/attack system developed for the MS2; uprated Larzac 04-C20 engines, developing 7-13 per cent more power than C6 version of earlier Alpha Jets; capability of carrying Magic 2 air-to-air missiles, plus auxiliary fuel tanks of up to 625 litres (137·5 Imp gallons) on inboard underwing stations and 450 litres (99 Imp gallons) on inboard or outboard stations. Egyptian MS2s (see previous paragraph) to be upgraded to this standard.

Alpha Jet Lancier. Extended capability version, derived from NGEA, for day/night attack, anti-shipping strike, airspace denial and self defence, and anti-helicopter missions. Incorporates fully tested core systems of NGEA (inertial platform and multiplex databus); added capabilities (a FLIR system providing a thermal image on the head-up display, Thomson-CSF/ESD Agave multifunction radar in a lengthened nose and a CP 2084 computer with corresponding extension of capability); wider variety of weapons including anti-ship all-weather missiles, laser guided bombs and missiles; internal passive and active ECM; and greater external fuel capacity. No orders announced up to mid-1986.

By early 1986 more than 480 of the 500 Alpha Jets then on order had been delivered, including 36 in 1984 and 21 in 1985.

TYPE: Tandem two-seat basic, low-altitude and advanced jet trainer and close support and battlefield reconnaissance aircraft.

WINGS: Cantilever shoulder-wing monoplane, with 6° anhedral from roots. Thickness/chord ratio 10·2% at root, 8·6% at tip. Sweepback 28° at quarter-chord. All-metal numerically or chemically milled structure, consisting of two main wing panels bolted to a centre frame. Extended chord on outer wings. Hydraulically actuated Fowler slotted flaps on each trailing-edge. Ailerons actuated by double-body irreversible hydraulic servo, with trimmable artificial feel system.

FUSELAGE: All-metal semi-monocoque structure, numerically or chemically milled, of basically oval cross-section. Built in three sections: nose (including cockpit), centre-section (including engine air intake trunks and main landing gear housings) and rear (including engine mounts and tail assembly). Narrow strake on each side of nose of aircraft with no nav/attack system. Pointed nose, with pitot probe, on Luftwaffe close support version. Electrically controlled, hydraulically actuated airbrake on each side of rear upper fuselage, of carbonfibre reinforced epoxy resin.

TAIL UNIT: Cantilever type, of similar construction to wings, with 45° sweepback on fin leading-edge and 30° on tailplane leading-edge. Dorsal spine fairing between cockpit and fin. Aircraft equipped with radio compass have a long, narrow strake above the dorsal spine fairing to house the antenna for this equipment. All-flying tailplane, with trimmable and IAS-controlled artificial feel system. Glassfibre fin tip and tailplane tips. Double-body irreversible hydraulic servo-actuated rudder, with trimmable artificial feel system. Yaw damper on close support versions. A rudder and tailplane of CFRP have been developed and flight tested.

Landing Gear: Forward retracting tricycle type, of Messier-Hispano-Bugatti/Liebherr design. All units retract hydraulically, main units into underside of engine air intake trunks. Single wheel and low-pressure tyre (approx 4 bars; 58 lb/sq in at normal T-O weight) on each unit. Tyre sizes 615 × 255-10 on main units, 380 × 150-4 on nose unit. Steel disc brakes and anti-skid units on main gear (Minispad or Modistop). Emergency braking system. Hydraulic nosewheel steering and arrester hook on close support version. Nosewheel offset to starboard to permit ground firing from gun pod.

Power Plant: Standard installation of two SNECMA/Turboméca Larzac 04-C6 turbofan engines, each rated at 13·24 kN (2,976 lb st), mounted on sides of fuselage. Alternative option (on any Alpha Jet) for 14·12 kN (3,175 lb st) Larzac 04-C20 turbofans, which are standard on the NGEA version. Splitter plate in front of each intake. Fuel in two integral tanks in outer wings, one in centre-section and three fuselage tanks. Internal fuel capacity 1,900 litres (418 Imp gallons) or 2,040 litres (449 Imp gallons). Provision for 310 or 450 litre (68 or 99 Imp gallon) capacity drop tank on each outer wing pylon, plus (on NGEA) a 450 or 625 litre (99 or 137·5 Imp gallon) tank on each inboard wing pylon. Pressure refuelling standard for all tanks, including drop tanks. Gravity system for fuselage tanks and drop tanks. Pressure refuelling point near starboard engine air intake. Fuel system incorporates provision for inverted flying.

Accommodation: Two persons in tandem, in pressurised cockpit under individual upward opening canopies. Dual controls standard. Rear seat (for instructor in trainer versions) is elevated. French trainer versions fitted with Martin-Baker AJRM4 ejection seats, operable (including ejection through canopy) at zero height and speeds down to 90 knots (167 km/h; 104 mph). Martin-Baker B10N zero/zero seats in aircraft for Belgium, E10N in those for Egypt and Q10N in those for Qatar. Aircraft for West Germany fitted with licence built (by MBB) Stencel S-III-S3AJ zero/zero ejection seats. Baggage compartment in tailcone, with door on starboard side.

Systems: Cockpit air-conditioning and demisting system. Cabin pressure differential 0·30 bars (4·3 lb/sq in). Two independent and redundant hydraulic systems, each 207 bars (3,000 lb/sq in), with engine driven pumps (emergency electric pump on one circuit), for actuating control surfaces, landing gear, brakes, flaps, airbrakes, and (when fitted) nosewheel steering. Pneumatic system, for cockpit pressurisation and air-conditioning, occupants' pressure suits and fuel tank pressurisation, is supplied by compressed air from engines. Main electric power supplied by two 28V 9kW starter/generators, one on each engine. Circuit includes a 36Ah nickel-cadmium battery for self-starting and two static inverters for supplying 115V AC power at 400Hz to auxiliary systems. External ground DC power receptacle in port engine air intake trunk. Hydraulic and electrical systems can be sustained by either engine in the event of the other engine becoming inoperative. Liquid film anti-icing system; de-icing by electrical heater mats. Oxygen mask for each occupant, supplied by liquid oxygen converter of 10 litres (2·2 Imp gallons) capacity. Emergency gaseous oxygen bottle for each occupant.

Avionics and Equipment: Large avionics bays in rear fuselage, containing most of the radio and navigation equipment. Standard avionics, according to version, include V/UHF and VHF or UHF transceivers, IFF/SIF, VOR/ILS/marker beacon receiver, Tacan, radio compass, gyro platform and intercom. Landing light on starboard mainwheel leg, taxying light on port leg. Basic French version has SFIM 550 gyro platform, LMT micro-Tacan, EAS 720 VOR/ILS/marker beacon receiver, TEAM com radio and intercom, and ESD 3300 IFF/SIF. West German version has Kaiser/VDO KM 808 head-up display, TRT AHV 6-18 radar altimeter, Lear Siegler LSI 6000 E attitude and heading reference system, and Litef LDN Doppler navigation system with LR-1416 navigation computer, Litef ABE control unit and Teledyne Ryan speed sensor, Elettronica (Italy) ECM, SEL Mitac/Setac Tacan with ILS, Siemens STR 700 IFF/SIF, Becker VCS 220 intercom, Rohde und Schwarz XT 3011 com radio, and EAS IMT 565 BDHI. NGEA version has Sagem Uliss 81 inertial platform (replacing SFIM 550), Thomson-CSF VE 110C head-up display (VEM 130 in Lancier), Thomson-CSF TMV 630 laser rangefinder, TRT AHV 9 radar altimeter and ESD Digibus digital multiplexed avionics databus.

Armament and Operational Equipment: More than 75 different basic weapon configurations for training and tactical air support missions have been qualified for Alpha Jet users. For armament training and close support, the Alpha Jet can be equipped with an underfuselage jettisonable pod containing a 30 mm DEFA or 27 mm Mauser cannon with 150 rds; or an underfuselage pylon for one 250 kg bomb, one 400 kg modular bomb, or a target towing system. Provision also for two hardpoints under each wing, with non-jettisonable adaptor pylons. On these can be carried M155 launchers for eighteen 68 mm rockets; HE or retarded bombs of 50, 125, 250 or 400 kg; 625 lb cluster dispensers; 690 or 825 lb special purpose tanks; practice launchers for bombs or rockets; Dassault-Breguet CC-420 underwing 30 mm gun pods, each with 180 rds; or two 310, 450 or 625 litre (68, 99 or 137·5 Imp gallon) drop tanks (see Power Plant paragraph). Provision for air-to-air or air-to-surface missiles such as Magic or Maverick, or reconnaissance pod. Total load for all five stations more than 2,500 kg (5,510 lb). Dassault-Breguet CEM-1 (combined external multistore) carriers can be attached to inboard underwing pylons, permitting simultaneous carriage of mixed fuel/bomb/rocket loads, including six rockets and four practice bombs, or eighteen rockets with one 500 lb bomb, or six penetration bombs, or grenades or other stores. A special version of the CEM-1 allows carriage of a reconnaissance pod containing four cameras (three Omera 61 cameras and an Omera 40 panoramic camera) and a decoy launcher. Luftwaffe aircraft equipped with ML Aviation twin stores carriers, CBLS 200 practice bomb and rocket launcher carriers, and ejector release units. Fire control system for air-to-air or air-to-ground firing, dive bombing and low-level bombing. Firing by trainee pilot (in front seat) is governed by a safety interlock system controlled by the instructor, which energises the forward station trigger circuit and illuminates a fire clearance indicator in the trainee's cockpit. Thomson-CSF 902 sight and film or video gun camera in French version; Kaiser/VDO KM 808 sight and gun camera in West German attack version; Thomson-CSF gun camera in NGEA version.

Dassault-Breguet/Dornier Alpha Jet testbed for Lancier, without Agave radar

Dimensions, external:
Wing span	9·11 m (29 ft 10¾ in)
Wing aspect ratio	4·8
Length overall: trainer	12·29 m (40 ft 3¾ in)
close support version, incl probe	13·23 m (43 ft 5 in)
Height overall (at normal T-O weight)	4·19 m (13 ft 9 in)
Tailplane span	4·33 m (14 ft 2½ in)
Wheel track	2·71 m (8 ft 10¾ in)
Wheelbase	4·72 m (15 ft 5¾ in)

Areas:
Wings, gross	17·50 m² (188·4 sq ft)
Ailerons (total)	1·04 m² (11·19 sq ft)
Trailing-edge flaps (total)	2·86 m² (30·78 sq ft)
Airbrakes (total)	0·74 m² (7·97 sq ft)
Fin	2·97 m² (31·97 sq ft)
Rudder	0·62 m² (6·67 sq ft)
Horizontal tail surfaces (total)	3·94 m² (42·41 sq ft)

Weights:
Weight empty, equipped:	
trainer	3,345 kg (7,374 lb)
close support version	3,515 kg (7,749 lb)
Fuel load (internal)	1,520 kg (3,351 lb)
	or 1,630 kg (3,593 lb)
Fuel load (external)	500 kg (1,102 lb)
	or 720 kg (1,587 lb)
	or 1,440 kg (3,174 lb)
Max external load	more than 2,500 kg (5,510 lb)
Normal T-O weight:	
trainer, 'clean'	5,000 kg (11,023 lb)
Max T-O weight:	
with external stores	8,000 kg (17,637 lb)

Performance (at normal 'clean' T-O weight, except where indicated):
Max level speed at 10,000 m (32,800 ft):	
Larzac 04-C6	Mach 0·85
Larzac 04-C20	Mach 0·86
Max level speed at S/L:	
Larzac 04-C6	540 knots (1,000 km/h; 621 mph)
Larzac 04-C20	560 knots (1,038 km/h; 645 mph)
Max speed for flap and landing gear extension	200 knots (370 km/h; 230 mph)
Approach speed	110 knots (204 km/h; 127 mph)
Landing speed at normal landing weight	92 knots (170 km/h; 106 mph)
Stalling speed: flaps and landing gear up	116 knots (216 km/h; 134 mph)
flaps and landing gear down	90 knots (167 km/h; 104 mph)
Max rate of climb at S/L	3,420 m (11,220 ft)/min
Rate of climb at S/L, one engine out, at 4,782 kg (10,542 lb) AUW, in landing configuration	330 m (1,085 ft)/min
Time to 9,145 m (30,000 ft)	less than 7 min
Service ceiling	14,630 m (48,000 ft)
T-O run	370 m (1,215 ft)
Landing run at usual landing weight	approx 500 m (1,640 ft)
Low altitude radius of action (trainer):	
'clean', max internal fuel	291 nm (540 km; 335 miles)
with external tanks	361 nm (670 km; 416 miles)
High altitude radius of action (trainer), reserves of 15% internal fuel:	
'clean', max internal fuel	664 nm (1,230 km; 764 miles)
with external tanks	782 nm (1,450 km; 901 miles)
Lo-lo-lo mission radius (close support version), incl combat at max continuous thrust and 54 nm (100 km; 62 mile) dash:	
with belly gun pod and underwing weapons	210 nm (390 km; 242 miles)
with belly gun pod, underwing weapons and external tanks	340 nm (630 km; 391 miles)
Hi-lo-hi mission radius (close support version), incl combat at max continuous thrust and 54 nm (100 km; 62 mile) dash:	
with belly gun pod and underwing weapons	315 nm (583 km; 363 miles)
with belly gun pod, underwing weapons and external tanks	580 nm (1,075 km; 668 miles)
Ferry range (internal fuel and four 450 litre external tanks)	more than 2,160 nm (4,000 km; 2,485 miles)
Endurance (internal fuel only):	
low altitude	more than 2 h 30 min
high altitude	more than 3 h 30 min
g limits	+12/−6·4 ultimate

EHI

EH INDUSTRIES LIMITED

Granville House, 132-135 Sloane Street, London SW1X 9BB, England
Telephone: 01 730 7243
Telex: 291600 EHILON
DIRECTORS:
Dott R. Teti
Sir John Cuckney
Dott Ing A. Antichi
Sir John Treacher
Dott Ing B. Lovera
D. K. Berrington
V. A. B. Rogers
Dott E. Striano
MANAGING DIRECTOR: Dott Ing L. Ferrante
MARKETING DIRECTOR: P. M. H. Ryan
DEPUTY MARKETING DIRECTOR: R. Rovere
SECRETARY: A. Moorhead
PARTICIPATING COMPANIES:
Agusta SpA, Via Caldera 21, 20153 Milan, Italy
Telephone: (2) 452751
Telex: 333280 AGUMI I
Westland Helicopters Ltd, Yeovil, Somerset BA20 2YB, England
Telephone: Yeovil (0935) 75222
Telex: 46277

This company was formed in June 1980 by Westland Helicopters and Agusta to undertake the joint development, production and marketing of a new anti-submarine warfare helicopter, for which the Royal Navy and Italian Navy both have a requirement. Such a programme was initiated by Westland in the UK in 1977 in response to Naval Staff Requirement 6646, leading to the WG 34 helicopter described under that company's heading in the 1979-80 *Jane's*.

The EH 101 is now being developed to meet the detailed requirements of both navies, and for other civil, military and naval roles. British and Italian government approval for the nine-month project definition phase was given on 12 June 1981, and full programme go-ahead was announced by the two governments on 25 January 1984. A formal contract for the naval version was signed on 7 March 1984. The programme is being handled on behalf of both governments by the British Ministry of Defence. Technical responsibility rests with Westland Helicopters and Agusta, each of which has a 50% interest in EHI. Westland has design leadership for the commercial version, and Agusta for the rear loading utility version; the naval version is being developed jointly by the two companies for their respective navies.

EH INDUSTRIES EH 101

In the Spring of 1977 the MoD (Navy) completed a series of feasibility studies for a new ASW helicopter, and to examine what sensors and performance standards it would require.

Westland's WG 34 design, marginally smaller than the Sea King but with substantially more payload capability, was selected by the MoD (Navy) for development in the late Summer of 1978. The Italian Navy, although it would place emphasis more on shore-based than shipboard operation, has a requirement broadly similar to that of the Royal Navy, and in 1980 Westland and Agusta decided to combine forces in a joint design, the EH 101, to meet the requirements of both services and for other military and civil applications. Development of this helicopter is now proceeding in three basic versions: naval, commercial transport, and utility. The commercial version is expected to enter service first, in 1990, followed shortly afterwards by the naval version.

The EH 101 will have three engines, and will incorporate composite materials, plus the latest available electronics and data handling systems. The physical dimensions of the helicopter are limited by frigate hangar size. Extensive market research showed that this also matches the requirement for civil use, especially for the offshore support role, and systems developed for operation to and from the pitching deck of a frigate at sea are equally valid for the pitching deck of an offshore platform.

The naval EH 101 is designed for fully autonomous all-weather day and night operations, and will operate from land bases, large and small vessels (including merchant ships), and oil rigs. It will be capable of launch and recovery from a frigate of 3,445 tonnes (3,500 tons), in sea state 6, with the ship on any heading and in wind speeds, from any direction, of up to 50 knots (93 km/h; 57 mph).

Primary roles of the maritime version will be anti-submarine warfare, anti-ship surveillance and tracking, anti-surface-vessel, amphibious operations, and search and rescue. Other roles include airborne early warning, vertical replenishment, and electronic countermeasures (deception, jamming and missile seduction). For the Royal Navy, the EH 101 has been specified as equipment for its Type 23 general purpose frigates; it has also been announced that the helicopter will operate from 'Invincible' class aircraft carriers, Royal Fleet Auxiliaries and other ships, as well as from land bases. Initial requirements are reportedly 50 for the Royal Navy and 38 for the Italian Navy.

It is envisaged that a commercial EH 101 would be operated by a crew of three, including a steward, and carry 30 passengers. The utility version, in a logistic transport configuration, would incorporate a rear loading ramp for the direct in-loading of vehicles and cargo, and would be able to airlift a payload of almost six tons: alternatively, a total of 35 troops could be carried. The design philosophy of the EH 101 is aimed at providing significant improvements in safety, availability, operating costs and performance. This is achieved through the use of three engines and higher power margins, damage tolerant airframe and dynamic structure, greater system redundancy, and onboard health monitoring systems. One major capability is zero-scheduled take-off field length to full Category A rules for much of the weight, altitude and temperature range. This will enable new applications to be exploited in congested areas.

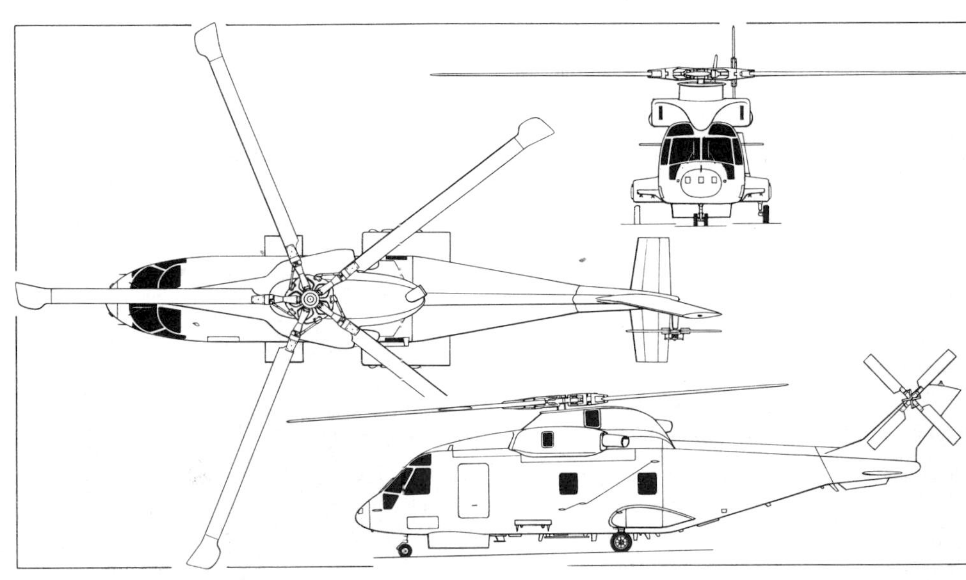

Basic naval ASW version of the EH 101 multi-role helicopter *(Pilot Press)*

Ten pre-production aircraft are planned, one of which will be used for ground tests. Of the other nine, four (PP1, 2, 4 and 7) will be used to qualify the basic aircraft, the first one being scheduled to make its initial flight at Yeovil in early 1987. A fifth EH 101 (PP3) is due to fly in Spring 1987 and will be used by Westland to speed the award of civil certification, planned for late 1989. Aircraft PP5 and PP6 will be devoted respectively to development of the Royal Navy and Italian Navy versions; PP8 and PP9 will be used for reliability proving and will serve as demonstrators for the commercial and utility versions. Metal for the first two aircraft was first cut in March 1985, and all nine are expected to fly within about two years of the first flight. First deliveries of the commercial version are planned for 1990, followed by deliveries to both navies. Aircraft will be produced by single source manufacture of components, with a final assembly line in each country. Major design responsibilities at present include Westland for the front fuselage and main rotor blades; Agusta for the rear fuselage, rotor head and drive system, hydraulic system and part of the electrical system.

TYPE: Multi-role helicopter.

ROTOR SYSTEM: Five-blade main rotor, hub of which is designed on multiple load path concept, incorporating fail-safe principles, and is formed from composite materials surrounding a metal core. Blades, also of composite construction, have an advanced aerofoil section, special high-speed tips resulting from British Experimental Rotor Programme (BERP), and are attached to hub by multi-path loading including elastomeric bearings. Naval version has fully automatic powered folding of main rotor blades (optional on other versions) and tail rotor pylon, with manual system for emergency backup. Electric de-icing of main and tail rotor blades (Lucas system) standard on naval version, optional on other versions. Four-blade tail rotor, mounted on port side of tail rotor pylon.

ROTOR DRIVE: Front drive directly into main gearbox from all three engines, with all gears straddle mounted for greater rigidity. External driveshaft to tail rotor gearbox.

FUSELAGE AND TAIL UNIT: For general appearance, see accompanying three-view drawing. Metal skinned front and centre fuselage common to all three versions. Modified rear fuselage and slimmer tailboom on utility version, to accommodate rear-loading ramp/door in underside. Tailcone and tail rotor pylon of composite construction; on naval version, this folds forward and downward so that starboard half of tailplane passes underneath rear fuselage. Small ventral fin under tailcone.

LANDING GEAR: Hydraulically retractable tricycle type, with single mainwheels and steerable twin-wheel nose unit, designed and manufactured by AP Precision Hydraulics in association with Officine Meccaniche Aeronautiche. Main units retract into fairings on sides of fuselage. Goodrich wheels, tyres and brakes.

POWER PLANT: Three General Electric CT7-2A (T700-GE-401A) turboshaft engines in pre-production aircraft (assembled by Alfa Romeo), currently rated at 1,289 kW (1,729 shp) max contingency, 1,262 kW (1,693 shp) intermediate and 1,071 kW (1,437 shp) max continuous. Engine for commercial version will be the CT7-6. A possible alternative engine is the Rolls-Royce Turboméca RTM 322. Computerised fuel management system. Dunlop electric anti-icing of engine air intakes, which are of Kevlar reinforced with aero-web honeycomb.

ACCOMMODATION: One or two pilots on flight deck (naval versions will be capable of single-pilot operation). ASW version will normally also carry observer and acoustic systems operator. Martin-Baker crew seats in naval version. Commercial version able to accommodate 30 passengers, four abreast at approx seat pitch of 76 cm (30 in), plus cabin attendant, with toilet, galley and baggage facilities (including overhead bins). Utility version can accommodate up to 28 combat-equipped troops or equivalent cargo. Main passenger door/emergency exit at front on port side (commercial and utility versions), with additional emergency exit on each side of cabin at rear, above main landing gear sponson. Large sliding door at mid-cabin position on starboard side, with inset emergency exit. Baggage bay aft of cabin on commercial transport version, with external access via door on each side. Cargo loading ramp/door at rear of cabin on utility version.

SYSTEMS: Microtecnica air-conditioning system. Triple redundant integrated hydraulic system, providing first and second failure survival for main flying controls. Nos. 1, 2 and 3 systems each supply fluid at 207 bars (3,000 lb/sq in) nominal working pressure, with flow rates of 49, 53 and 55 litres (10·8, 11·7 and 12·1 Imp gallons)/min respectively. Hydraulic system reservoir is a piston load pressurised type, with a nominal pressure of 0·97 bars (14 lb/sq in). Primary electrical system is 115/200V three-phase AC, powered by two Lucas brushless, oilspray-cooled generators (45 or 90 kVA, depending on version) driven by accessory gearbox, plus a third, separately driven standby alternator. Normalair-Garrett APU for main engine starting, and to provide electric and hydraulic power without running main engines. Fire detection and suppression systems by Graviner and Walter Kidde respectively.

AVIONICS: Avionics system is based on two MIL-STD-1553B multiplex data buses which link the basic aircraft management and mission systems. Main processing element of the management system is a dual redundant aircraft management computer, which carries out navigation, control and display management, performance, 'health' and usage monitoring computation; it also controls the basic bus. Other basic aircraft system elements are the dual duplex digital AFCS; a complex military communications subsystem; and Doppler, inertial, global positioning and other navigation sensors. Advanced flight deck makes extensive use of colour CRTs for flight navigation and systems display, and features multi-function keyboard control. Main processing element of the naval version mission system is the dual redundant mission computer, which carries out tracking, sensor management, control and display management, and controls the mission bus. AFCS will include electronic ADI and HSI. Avionics will wherever possible conform to ARINC 700 and 429 standards. Suppliers so far announced include British Aerospace for the ring laser gyro inertial navigation system, Smiths/OMI (automatic flight control system), Plessey/Elettronica (PA 5015 J-band radar altimeter), MEL (pilot's mission display units), GEC Avionics (air data system), Racal/Fiar (Doppler velocity sensor), Selenia/Ferranti (aircraft management computer) and Litton Italia (LISA-4000 strapdown AHRS).

ARMAMENT AND OPERATIONAL EQUIPMENT (naval and military utility versions): Naval version able to carry up to four homing torpedoes (probably Marconi Sting Ray in RN version) or other weapons. ASW version will have 360° search radar (Ferranti Blue Kestrel in RN aircraft) in a 'chin' radome, plus dipping sonar, two sonobuoy dispensers, advanced sonobuoy processing equipment, Racal ESM and an external rescue hoist. GEC Avionics' AQS-903 ASW system and Fairey Hydraulics deck lock have been selected for Royal Navy aircraft. ASST (anti-ship surveillance and tracking) version will carry equipment for tactical surveillance and OTH (over the horizon) targeting, to locate and relay to a co-operating frigate the position of a target vessel, and for midcourse guidance of the frigate's missiles. On missions involving the patrol of an exclusive economic zone it can also, with suitable radar, monitor every hour all surface contacts within an area of 77,700 km² (30,000 sq miles); can patrol an EEZ 400 × 200 nm (740 × 370 km; 460 × 230 miles) twice in one sortie; and can effect boarding and inspection of surface vessels during fishery protection and anti-smuggling missions. ASV version is designed to carry air-to-surface missiles and other weapons, for use as appropriate, from strikes against major units using sea-skimming anti-ship missiles to small-arms deterrence of smugglers. Various duties in amphibious operations could include personnel/stores transportation (eg, 24 combat-equipped troops and their stores over a 200 nm; 370 km; 230 mile radius), casualty evacuation, surveillance over the beachhead, and logistic support. In logistic support the EH 101 can carry internal loads or up to 4,536 kg (10,000 lb) on an external sling.

Mockup of the EH 101 naval version at the 1986 Farnborough International air show *(Kenneth Munson)*

DIMENSIONS, EXTERNAL:
- Main rotor diameter 18·59 m (61 ft 0 in)
- Tail rotor diameter 4·01 m (13 ft 2 in)
- Length overall, both rotors turning 22·94 m (75 ft 3 in)
- Length, main rotor and tail pylon folded 15·85 m (52 ft 0 in)
- Width, main rotor and tail pylon folded 5·49 m (18 ft 0 in)
- Height overall, both rotors turning 6·50 m (21 ft 4 in)
- Height, main rotor and tail pylon folded 5·18 m (17 ft 0 in)
- Passenger door (fwd, port):
  - Height 1·54 m (5 ft 0½ in)
  - Width 0·94 m (3 ft 1 in)
- Sliding door (stbd):
  - Height 1·54 m (5 ft 0½ in)
  - Width 1·96 m (6 ft 5 in)
- Baggage doors (port and stbd, each):
  - Height 1·22 m (4 ft 0 in)
  - Width 0·74 m (2 ft 5 in)

DIMENSIONS, INTERNAL:
- Cabin: Length 6·50 m (21 ft 4 in)
  - Max width 2·50 m (8 ft 2½ in)
  - Width at floor 2·39 m (7 ft 10 in)
  - Max height 1·83 m (6 ft 0 in)

AREAS:
- Main rotor disc 271·72 m² (2,924·8 sq ft)
- Tail rotor disc 12·57 m² (135·3 sq ft)

WEIGHTS (A: naval version, B: commercial version, C: utility version):
- Basic weight empty: A 7,195 kg (15,862 lb)
  - B 7,315 kg (16,126 lb)
  - C 7,662 kg (16,891 lb)
- Operating weight empty: A 9,275 kg (20,448 lb)
  - B 8,562 kg (18,876 lb)
  - C 8,545 kg (18,838 lb)
- Max fuel weight (internal tanks only):
  - A, B, C 3,447 kg (7,599 lb)
- Payload: A (four torpedoes) 960 kg (2,116 lb)
  - B (30 passengers) 2,721 kg (5,999 lb)
  - C (24 troops) 2,721 kg (5,999 lb)
- Max T-O weight: A 13,000 kg (28,660 lb)
  - B, C 14,290 kg (31,500 lb)

PERFORMANCE (estimated):
- Never-exceed speed at 915 m (3,000 ft), ISA 174 knots (322 km/h; 200 mph)
- Normal operating limit speed at S/L, ISA 160 knots (296 km/h; 184 mph)
- Cruising speed at max continuous power 150 knots (278 km/h; 173 mph)
- T-O distance at max T-O weight (Category A rules) approx 213 m (700 ft)
- Range with zero take-off distance (Category A rules), IFR reserves:
  - B, 30 passengers 250 nm (463 km; 288 miles)
- Still air range, with reserves:
  - B, 30 passengers 550 nm (1,020 km; 633 miles)
  - B, 20 passengers 750 nm (1,390 km; 863 miles)
- Ferry range 1,000 nm (1,850 km; 1,150 miles)
- Time on station for dunking cycle with full weapon and mission load: A 5 h

EUROCOPTER

Eurocopter GIE

2-20 avenue Marcel Cachin, 93126 La Courneuve, France
Telephone: (1) 838 41 19
Telex: ECOPTER 232 743 F

Eurocopter GmbH

Arabellastrasse 18/V, 8000 München 81, Federal Republic of Germany
Telephone: (089) 9218 633
Telefax: (089) 9218 666

MANAGEMENT BOARD (both Eurocopter companies):
- Dieter Halff (MBB) (Chief Executive Officer and Spokesman)
- Bernard Darrieus (Aérospatiale) (Joint Chief Executive)
- Dr Carl-Peter Fichtmüller (MBB)
- Michel Thomas (Aérospatiale)
- Dr Fritz Ramjoue (MBB)
- Jean-Claude Sieffer (Aérospatiale)

PARTICIPATING COMPANIES:

Messerschmitt-Bölkow-Blohm GmbH, Helicopter and Military Aircraft Group, Postfach 801160, 8000 München 80, Federal Republic of Germany
Telephone: (089) 6000 3444
Telex; 5287 710/740 mbb d

Aérospatiale, 37 boulevard de Montmorency, 75781 Paris Cédex 16, France
Telephone: 524 43 21
Telex; AISPA 620059 F

Following approval of a Franco-German co-operation programme on the basis of industry proposals, the defence ministers of West Germany and France signed on 29 May 1984 a memorandum of understanding covering the development of a new anti-tank helicopter for service with their two armies in the 1990s. Leadership and work will be shared between MBB and Aérospatiale on an equal basis. Eurocopter GIE is the instrument of co-operation in the field of helicopters between Aérospatiale and MBB. For the purpose of managing the Franco/German battlefield helicopter programme, Eurocopter GmbH was established in Munich on 18 September 1985 as a wholly owned subsidiary of Eurocopter GIE in Paris.

Executive authority for the battlefield helicopter programme is the Bundesamt für Wehrtechnik und Beschaffung (German federal defence technology and procurement agency).

EUROCOPTER HAP/PAH-2/HAC-3G

The co-operation programme, which will involve a total of 400 or more aircraft for the two countries, utilises a single basic helicopter design, from which three versions will be developed. These are:

HAP (Hélicoptère d'Appui et de Protection). Escort and fire support version for French Army for delivery from 1993. Armed with a 30 mm GIAT AM-30781 automatic cannon in undernose turret, with 150-450 rds of ammunition. Releasable weapons, mounted on stub-wings, comprise four Matra Mistral infra-red homing air-to-air missiles and two pods each with twenty-two 68 mm SNEB rockets. Roof mounted TV, FLIR, laser rangefinder and direct-optics sensors.

PAH-2 (Panzerabwehr Hubschrauber, 2nd generation). Anti-tank version for West German Army, for delivery from 1995. No gun turret. Underwing pylons for up to eight Hot 2 anti-tank missiles (inboard) and four Stinger 2 air-to-air missiles for self-defence (outboard). Combined nose-mounted sight for pilot and gunner. Will have later, as alternative to Hot, the capability to carry up to eight Euromissile Dynamics Group ATGW-3 (third generation anti-tank guided weapons) long-range 'fire and forget' infra-red homing missiles.

HAC-3G (Hélicoptère Anti-Char with 3rd generation anti-tank missiles). Anti-tank version for French Army, for delivery from 1996. Wing pylons for up to eight ATGW-3s

Model of the Eurocopter HAP (left) and mockup of the PAH-2 armed helicopters for the armies of France and West Germany respectively

inboard. Mast mounted TV/FLIR/tracker/laser rangefinder sighting system for gunner. Retains nose mounted night vision sensor for pilot.

Seven development aircraft are expected to be built, including four unarmed aerodynamic prototypes to flight test the common basic airframe. First flight is expected to take place in early 1988. Requirements have been estimated at 212 PAH-2s for Germany, 75 HAPs and 140 HAC-3Gs for France.

TYPE: Twin-engined anti-tank helicopter.

ROTOR SYSTEM AND DRIVE: Four-blade semi-rigid main rotor, with composite blades; no flapping or lead-lag hinges; elastomeric pitch bearings. Rotor head consists of two fibre composite starplates bolted together with a titanium spacer, a configuration which permits almost unrestricted installation of a mast mounted sight. Main features are a compact, robust construction, low aerodynamic drag, a very small number of parts, and ease of maintenance. Development of new blade aerofoil sections and geometries promises performance improvements of about 10 per cent over most present-day systems, and will provide the agility needed in typical anti-tank missions, ie in extreme nap-of-the-earth flights. Three-blade composite tail rotor, mounted on starboard side. Principal features of main transmission are separate load paths, high dry-run capability (up to 30 min), and compatibility with the mast mounted sight.

WINGS, FUSELAGE AND TAIL UNIT: Conventional semi-monocoque structures, meeting criteria for safety, crash resistance (to MIL-STD-1290 standards), and damage tolerance (survivable against hits from weapons of up to 23 mm calibre). Stub wings, with anhedral on outer panels, for releasable weapons. Sweptback fin/tail rotor pylon and underfin; horizontal stabiliser, with endplates, mounted low on main fin.

LANDING GEAR: Non-retractable tailwheel type, with single wheel on each unit.

POWER PLANT: Two 962 kW (1,290 shp) MTU/Turboméca MTM 385-R turboshaft engines, mounted side by side above centre-fuselage. Self-sealing crashworthy fuel tanks, with explosion suppression.

ACCOMMODATION: Crew of two in tandem, with pilot (France) or weapons system operator (Germany) in front according to national preference. Armoured, impact-absorbing seats. Stepped cockpits, with flat-plate transparencies.

SYSTEMS: Mechanical primary control; redundant hydraulics.

AVIONICS: Essential characteristics will be common to both French and German versions, and mainly European in origin. Systems architecture will be based on integrated digital avionics incorporating a 1553B data bus, multiple cockpit displays, two symbol generators, a central operating unit, and a decentralised computer. Four-axis autopilot. Comprehensive ECM, including radar/laser warning receivers.

ARMAMENT: As listed under model descriptions.

DIMENSIONS, EXTERNAL:
- Main rotor diameter: 13·00 m (42 ft 7¾ in)
- Tail rotor diameter: 2·70 m (8 ft 10¼ in)

AREAS:
- Main rotor disc: 132·7 m² (1,428·7 sq ft)
- Tail rotor disc: 5·72 m² (61·63 sq ft)

WEIGHTS:
- Mission T-O weight: approx 5,200 kg (11,464 lb)
- Design max T-O weight: 5,400 kg (11,905 lb)

PERFORMANCE (estimated):
- Cruising speed: HAP: 151 knots (280 km/h; 174 mph)
  - PAH-2: 135 knots (250 km/h; 155 mph)
  - HAC-3G: 135-151 knots (250-280 km/h; 155-174 mph)
- Max rate of climb at S/L: 600 m (1,970 ft)/min
- Hovering ceiling OGE:
  - HAP, HAC-3G, 25°C: 1,000 m (3,280 ft)
  - PAH-2, ISA + 10°C: 2,000 m (6,560 ft)
- Endurance, incl 20 min reserves: 2 h 50 min

EUROFIGHTER

EUROFIGHTER/JAGDFLUGZEUG GmbH

Arabellastrasse 16, 8000 München 81, Federal Republic of Germany

PRESIDENT (1986-88): Carl-Peter Fichtmüller (MBB)

MANAGEMENT:
- G. Willox (BAe) (Managing Director)
- F. Mexia (CASA) (Deputy Managing Director)
- M. Friemer (MBB) (Technical Director)
- P. Scarafiotti (Aeritalia) (Operations Director)
- S. Ward (BAe) (Commercial Director)
- H. Wenzel (MBB) (Product Support Director)

EUROPEAN FIGHTER AIRCRAFT (EFA/JF-90)

The air chiefs of staff of five European nations—France, West Germany, Italy, Spain and the UK—agreed and issued in December 1983 an outline staff target for a new combat aircraft to enter service with all five air forces in the mid-1990s. France withdrew from this partnership in July 1985, participation by the remaining four countries then being set at 33% each for Great Britain and Germany, 21% for Italy and 13% for Spain. National design teams from MBB (with Dornier as co-contractor), Aeritalia, CASA and British Aerospace are collaborating in developing and harmonising individual national requirements, incorporating some of the design aspects and technology that will become available via the BAe EAP programme (see UK section). The initial feasibility study, launched in July 1984, was followed in August 1985 by start of the project definition phase. In June 1986 Eurofighter GmbH, with headquarters in Munich, was formed to manage the EFA programme. Eurojet Engines GmbH was formed shortly afterwards to manage the engine programme.

The European air staff requirement was agreed in December 1985, and the project definition stage was completed in September 1986. Assuming an early 1987 go-ahead from the four governments, the full scale engineering development stage should begin shortly afterwards, leading to a first flight in 1990, the start of series production in 1992 and initial deliveries in 1995. Eight FSED prototypes are expected to be built. This development phase will be supervised by an International Project Office independent of, but co-located with, the NAMMA (NATO Management Agency) for the Panavia Tornado, based in Munich.

The EFA will be configured primarily for the air defence role, but with a secondary capability for air-to-surface attack. Some 800 aircraft are expected to be required by the partner nations, in the approximate ratio of 250 for Germany, 200 for Italy, 100 for Spain and 250 for Great Britain; a proportion of two-seat trainer versions would be included in these totals. Export orders are also anticipated.

TYPE: Single-seat, extremely agile STOL-capable fighter, optimised for air-to-air roles, with secondary ground attack capability.

AIRFRAME: Cantilever low-wing monoplane, of canard delta configuration, having fixed foreplanes, with elevators, and a single all-moving fin. Wings are of low aspect ratio, with straight leading-edges having 53° sweepback. Airframe will incorporate 'stealth' technologies, and a substantial proportion of it will be built of CFRP materials, in conjunction with new lightweight metal alloys, using advanced manufacturing techniques such as superplastic forming and diffusion bonding. Manufacture of major components will be single-source throughout the member countries, but there will be a final assembly line in each country.

POWER PLANT: Choice of engine for early EFA prototypes not yet made (Turbo Union RB199 and General Electric F404 are possible candidates). Later prototypes and the production aircraft will be powered by two Eurojet EJ200 advanced technology turbofans (90 kN; 20,250 lb st class with afterburning), mounted side by side in rear fuselage with ventral intakes. Provision for external fuel tanks and in-flight refuelling.

Artist's impression of 1986 concept of the European Fighter Aircraft (EFA)

ENGINE AIR INTAKES: Side by side intakes in underfuselage box, each having a fixed upper wedge/ramp and a variable-position lower cowl lip (vari-cowl).

SYSTEMS: Full-authority four-channel ACT (active control technology) fly by wire flight control system, combined with mission adaptive configuring and the aircraft's natural longitudinal instability, will provide the EFA with the required 'carefree' handling, gust alleviation and high sustained manoeuvrability throughout the flight envelope. Pitch control effected via foreplane/elevators ACT to provide artificial longitudinal stability; yaw control via all-moving tail-fin. The quadruplex AFCS, which will operate through a NATO standard databus, is designed to ensure that pilot cannot exceed aircraft's flying limits. Utilities systems controlled by microcomputer.

AVIONICS: Primary sensor will be a multi-mode pulse-Doppler radar with an interception range of 50-80 nm (92·5-148 km; 57·5-92 miles), able to acquire at least 85 per cent of probable targets (including eight targets simultaneously), and to direct lookdown/shootdown and snap-up weapons against them. Other radar requirements include velocity and single-target search, track-while-scan and range-while-scan, target priority processing, automatic weapons selection, and recommended combat tactics display. In attack mode, will have capability for ground mapping/ranging and terrain avoidance, but not terrain following. Proposals include Emerald, an adaptation of the F/A-18's APG-65 radar developed by Hughes Aircraft Company with GEC Avionics (UK) and AEG (Germany); and an all-new radar known as ECR 90 by Ferranti (UK), Fiar (Italy) and Inisel (Spain). Radar will form part of a comprehensive avionics suite which also includes extensive communications, and an advanced integrated defensive system (AIDS) housed in wingtip pods with an excellent all-round view. All avionics, flight control and utilities control systems will be integrated through NATO standard databus highways with appropriate redundancy levels and full use of microprocessors. Special attention has been given to reducing pilot workload. New cockpit techniques will simplify flying the aircraft safely and effectively to the limits of the flight envelope while monitoring and managing the aircraft and its operational systems, and detecting/identifying/attacking desired targets while remaining safe from enemy defences. This will be achieved through a high level of system integration and automation, together with three large multi-function colour displays.

ARMAMENT: Interceptor will have an internally mounted cannon, plus a mix of AIM-120 AMRAAM and short-range (AIM-132 ASRAAM or Sidewinder) air-to-air missiles carried externally, four of the former being mounted in tandem pairs in a semi-recessed underfuselage installation similar to that of the ADV Tornado. The short-range missiles are carried on underwing pylons. The EFA will, if necessary, be able to carry a considerable overload of air-to-air weapons. For air-to-surface weapons, and/or auxiliary fuel tanks, it will have a total of 15 external attachment points.

DIMENSIONS, EXTERNAL:
- Wing span: 10·50 m (34 ft 5½ in)
- Wing aspect ratio: 2·205
- Length overall: approx 15·75 m (51 ft 8 in)

AREA:
- Wings, gross: 50·0 m² (538·2 sq ft)

WEIGHTS (approx):
- Weight empty: 9,750 kg (21,495 lb)
- Internal fuel load: 4,000 kg (8,818 lb)
- External stores load (weapons and/or fuel): 4,500 kg (9,920 lb)
- Max T-O weight: 17,000 kg (37,480 lb)

DESIGN PERFORMANCE:
- Max level speed: more than Mach 1·8
- T-O and landing distance with full internal fuel and two AMRAAM plus two ASRAAM or Sidewinder missiles, ISA + 15°C: 500 m (1,640 ft)
- Combat radius (estimated): 250-300 nm (463-556 km; 288-345 miles)
- *g* limits with full internal fuel and two AMRAAM missiles: +9/−3

FIMA

FUTURE INTERNATIONAL MILITARY/CIVIL AIRLIFTER

FIMA is the acronym for a study group set up in December 1982 to work towards development of a late-1990s replacement for the Lockheed C-130 Hercules and Transall C-160 transport aircraft with increased payload capacity, enhanced performance and reduced operating costs. Four companies (British Aerospace, Lockheed-Georgia, Aérospatiale and MBB) are taking part in the programme, and in January 1986 agreed to extend, without change, their memorandum of understanding on the FIMA. No firm configuration has yet emerged, but a four-propfan propulsion system is one option being studied.

GATES/PIAGGIO — *see Piaggio in Italian section*

MBB/CATIC

Participating Companies:

Messerschmitt-Bolköw-Blohm (Transport Aircraft Group), Postfach 950109, 2103 Hamburg 95, Federal Republic of Germany
Telephone: (040 7437 1
Telex: 21950-0 mbbh d

China National Aero-Technology Import and Export Corporation, 67 Jiao Nan Street (PO Box 1671), Beijing, People's Republic of China
Telephone: 44 2444
Telex: 22318 AEROT CN

MBB/CATIC MPC 75

MBB and CATIC signed a memorandum of understanding on 3 October 1985 to explore together the possible development of a 60/80-seat regional transport aircraft. On 6 June 1986 the partnership was taken a stage further with the signing of an agreement to open a joint office in Hamburg tasked with pursuing the feasibility study and co-ordinating contacts with potential customers and equipment suppliers. The same day, MBB also signed an MOU with General Electric, under which the German and US companies will explore the advantages of powering such an aircraft with two unducted fan (UDF) engines. Max T-O weight has been estimated at approx 28,000 kg (61,730 lb).

By the end of 1987 MBB and CATIC expect to have defined the objectives and scope of the MPC 75 programme, calculated the market potential, and laid down basic details of future collaboration on the aircraft. MBB will be programme leader; the Chinese industrial partner is Shanghai Aviation Industrial Corporation.

Artist's impression of a possible MPC 75 powered by two rear-mounted UDF engines

MBB/KAWASAKI

Airframe Prime Contractors:

Messerschmitt-Bölkow-Blohm GmbH, Helicopter and Military Aircraft Group, Postfach 801160, 8000 München 80, Federal Republic of Germany
Telephone: (089) 6000 3444
Telex: 5287-710/470 mbb d

Kawasaki Heavy Industries Ltd, World Trade Center Building, 4-1 Hamamatsu-cho 2-chome, Minato-ku, Tokyo, Japan
Telephone: Tokyo (03) 435 2971
Telex: 242 4371 KAWASAKI HEAVY TOKYO

MBB/KAWASAKI BK 117 A-3

MBB and Kawasaki agreed on 25 February 1977 to develop jointly a multi-purpose helicopter known as the BK 117. This superseded two earlier, separate projects known as the MBB BO 107 and the Kawasaki KH-7.

The BK 117 has a number of components and accessories interchangeable with those of the MBB BO 105. Its rotor head is almost identical to that of the BO 105, from which aircraft the principle of the hydraulic boost system is also adapted. The transmission is based on that developed by Kawasaki for its earlier KH-7 design.

Development costs are shared equally between the two companies, with support for MBB in the form of a loan from the West German government. MBB is responsible for production of the main and tail rotor systems, tailboom and tail unit, skid landing gear, hydraulic system, engine firewall and cowlings, power-amplified controls and systems integration; Kawasaki is responsible for the fuselage, transmission, fuel and electrical systems, and standard items of equipment.

Four prototypes were built. Initial flight testing was undertaken by the second and third, which flew for the first time, in Germany and Japan respectively, on 13 June 1979 (D-HBKA) and 10 August 1979 (JQ-0003). An S-01 pre-production aircraft (D-HBKB) made its first flight on 6 March 1981. The first production BK 117 to fly was a Kawasaki-built aircraft (JQ1001), which flew for the first time on 24 December 1981. The first aircraft from the MBB production line (D-HBKC) flew on 23 April 1982. German LBA type certification was granted on 9 December 1982, followed by Japanese certification on 17 December 1982. Certification is to FAR Pt 29, Category A and B, including Amendments 29-1 to 29-16. FAA certification was granted on 29 March 1983. Customer deliveries, from both production lines, began in early 1983. By early 1986 Kawasaki had delivered 13; MBB delivery figures were not provided.

On 15 March 1985 the German LBA certificated the **BK 117 A-3** version with max T-O weight increased from 2,850 kg (6,283 lb) to 3,200 kg (7,055 lb). Japanese JCAB and Canadian DoT certification of this version was received in July 1985, followed by FAA type approval on 10 September that year. One feature contributing to this improvement is a new-design tail rotor with twisted blades of wider chord and increased diameter. From January 1987 a **BK 117 A-4** model (certificated by the LBA on 29 July 1986) becomes available. This has an increased transmission limit at T-O power, conferring improved climb rate and IGE/OGE hover ceilings, an improved tail rotor head, and 80 kg (176 lb) more internal fuel. The initial production version, now known as the **BK 117 A-1**, was detailed fully in the 1984-85 *Jane's*; the description in this edition is amended where necessary to apply to the A-3 model.

The BK 117 is manufactured by the single source method, each company producing the components which it has developed, which are then exchanged. There are two final assembly lines, one at the MBB plant in Donauwörth and one at Kawasaki's Gifu factory. On behalf of, and subsidised by, the German Federal Ministry of Defence, MBB is developing an entire helicopter airframe of fibre reinforced composite materials in a 3½ year research programme. A BK 117 will serve as the test rig. An agreement was signed with MBB in November 1982 whereby IPTN (formerly Nurtanio) of Indonesia (which see) will eventually manufacture the BK 117.

Type: Twin-turbine multi-purpose helicopter.

Rotor System: Four-blade 'System Bölkow' rigid main rotor; head almost identical to that of BO 105; main rotor blades similar to those of BO 105, but larger. Two-blade teetering tail rotor. Main rotor has a titanium head, to which are attached hingeless, fail-safe GRP blades of NACA 23012/23010 (modified) section with a stainless steel anti-erosion strip on each leading-edge. Optional folding of two blades of main rotor. Main rotor rpm: 383. Two-blade semi-rigid (teetering) tail rotor, mounted on port side of vertical fin and rotating clockwise when viewed from that side. Blades are of GRP, with high impact resistance and MBB-S102E performance/noise-optimised section. Tail rotor rpm: 2,169.

Rotor Drive: Each engine has separate drive input into Kawasaki KB 03 main transmission via single bevel gear and collector. Transmission rated at 632 kW (848 shp) for twin-engine take-off and max continuous operation; and, for single-engine operation, at 442 kW (592 shp) for 2½ min, 405 kW (543 shp) for 30 min, and 368 kW (493 shp) max continuous. Auxiliary drives for accessories. Dual redundant lubrication system.

Fuselage: Of typical pod shaped configuration, comprising flight deck, cabin, cargo compartment and engine deck. Structure, designed to fulfil requirements of FAR Pt 29, is generally similar to that of BO 105, main components being of semi-monocoque riveted aluminium construction with single curvature sheets and bonded aluminium sandwich panels. Secondary components are compound curvature shells with sandwich panels and Kevlar skins. Floor extends throughout cockpit, cabin and cargo compartment at same level. Engine deck forms roof of cargo compartment and, adjacent to engine bays, is of titanium to serve as a firewall.

Tail Unit: Semi-monocoque tailboom, of tapered conical section, attached integrally to engine deck at forward end. Rear end, which is detachable, carries main fin/tail rotor support, and horizontal stabiliser with endplate fins set at an offset angle. General design similar to that of BO 105, except for shape of outer fins.

Landing Gear: Non-retractable tubular skid type, of

IFR equipped two-pilot BK 117 A-3 in service with Helitransport of Zürich

aluminium construction, similar to that of BO 105. Skids are detachable from cross-tubes. Ground handling wheels standard. Emergency flotation gear, settling protectors and snow skids available optionally.

POWER PLANT: Two Avco Lycoming LTS 101-650B-1 turboshaft engines, each rated at 441 kW (592 shp) for take-off and 410 kW (550 shp) max continuous power. Fuel in four flexible bladder tanks (forward and aft main tanks, with two supply tanks between), in compartments under cabin floor. Two independent fuel feed systems for the engines and a common main fuel tank. Total standard fuel capacity 608 litres (133·75 Imp gallons). Two 200 litre (44 Imp gallon) auxiliary tanks and an additional enlarged main fuel tank of 100 litres (22 Imp gallons) available optionally, raising total capacity to 1,108 litres (243·75 Imp gallons).

ACCOMMODATION: Pilot and up to six (executive version) or seven passengers (standard version). High-density layouts available for up to ten passengers in addition to pilot. Provision for two-pilot operation at customer's option. Jettisonable forward hinged door on each side of cockpit, pilot's door having an openable window. Jettisonable rearward sliding passenger door on each side of cabin, lockable in open position. Fixed steps on each side. Two hinged, clamshell doors at rear of cabin, providing access to cargo compartment. Rear cabin window on each side. Aircraft can be equipped, according to mission, for offshore, medical evacuation (pilot, plus one or two stretchers side by side and two attendants), firefighting, search and rescue, law enforcement, cargo transport or other operations.

SYSTEMS: Ram air and electrical ventilation system. Fully redundant tandem hydraulic boost system (one operating and one standby), pressure 103·5 bars (1,500 lb/sq in), for flight controls. System flow rate 8·1 litres (1·78 Imp gallons)/min. Bootstrap/oil reservoir, pressure 1·7 bars (25 lb/sq in). Main DC electrical power from two 150A 28V starter/generators (one on each engine) and a 24V 25Ah nickel-cadmium battery. AC power can be provided optionally by two independent inverters. Emergency busbar provides direct battery power to essential services in event of a double generator failure. External DC power receptacle.

AVIONICS AND EQUIPMENT: Basic aircraft has instrumentation for single-pilot VFR operation, including airspeed indicator (IAS) with electrically heated pitot tube and static ports, barometric altimeter, attitude indicator, turn and bank indicator, vertical speed indicator, gyro magnetic heading system, magnetic compass and clock. Optional for Kawasaki aircraft (standard for MBB) are a 10 cm (4 in) self-contained gyro horizon with inclinometer, 7·6 cm (3 in) standby artificial horizon, and HSI. Dual controls and dual VFR instrumentation available optionally. Com/nav and other avionics available to customer's requirements, including VHF-AM/FM, UHF and HF transceivers, ADF, nav, R/Nav, Loran, Decca, VLF/Omega, LDNS and AHRS systems, radar altimeter, ATC/IFF transponder, encoding altimeter, DME, multi-mode radar, IFR instrumentation packages, and pitch/roll stability augmentation system. Standard basic equipment includes rotor brake and yaw CSAS (both optional only on Kawasaki aircraft), annunciator panel, master caution light, rotor rpm/engine fail warning control unit, fuel quantity indicator and low level sensor, outside air temperature indicator, engine and transmission oil pressure and temperature indicators, two exhaust temperature indicators, dual torque indicator, triple tachometer, two NI tachometers, mast moment indicator, instrument panel lights, cockpit/cabin/cargo compartment dome lights, utility lights, emergency exit lights, position lights, anti-collision warning light, retractable landing light, portable flashlight, ground handling wheels, pilot's and co-pilot's windscreen wipers, floor covering, interior panelling and sound insulation, ashtrays, map/document case, tiedown rings in cabin and cargo compartment, engine compartment fire warning indicator, engine fire extinguishing system, portable fire extinguisher, first aid kit, and single colour exterior paint scheme. Optional equipment includes high-density seating arrangement, bleed air heating system, fuel dump valve, two long-range fuel tanks, emergency flotation gear, settling protectors, snow skids, main rotor blade folding kit, non-retractable landing light, dual pilot operation kit, stretcher installation, external cargo hook, rescue hoist, SX 16 remotely controlled searchlight, external loudspeaker, and sand filter. Special optional equipment, including special mission kits for rescue, law enforcement and VIP transport, available at customer's request.

DIMENSIONS, EXTERNAL:
- Main rotor diameter: 11·00 m (36 ft 1 in)
- Tail rotor diameter: 1·956 m (6 ft 5 in)
- Main rotor blade chord: 0·32 m (1 ft 0½ in)
- Length overall, main and tail rotors turning: 13·00 m (42 ft 8 in)
- Length of fuselage, tail rotor blades vertical: 9·91 m (32 ft 6¼ in)
- Fuselage: Max width: 1·60 m (5 ft 3 in)
- Height overall, main and tail rotors turning: 3·85 m (12 ft 7½ in)
- Height to top of main rotor head: 3·36 m (11 ft 0¼ in)
- Tailplane span (over endplate fins): 2·70 m (8 ft 10¼ in)
- Tail rotor ground clearance: 1·90 m (6 ft 2¾ in)
- Width over skids: 2·50 m (8 ft 2½ in)

DIMENSIONS, INTERNAL:
- Combined cabin and cargo compartment:
  - Max length: 3·02 m (9 ft 11 in)
  - Max width: 1·49 m (4 ft 10½ in)
  - Min width: 1·21 m (3 ft 11½ in)
  - Max height: 1·28 m (4 ft 2½ in)
  - Min height: 0·99 m (3 ft 3 in)
  - Useful floor area: 3·70 m² (39·83 sq ft)
  - Volume: 5·00 m³ (176·6 cu ft)

AREAS:
- Main rotor disc: 95·03 m² (1,022·9 sq ft)
- Tail rotor disc: 3·00 m² (32·24 sq ft)

WEIGHTS:
- Basic weight empty: 1,660 kg (3,660 lb)
- Fuel: standard usable: A-3: 478 kg (1,054 lb)
  - A-4: 558 kg (1,230 lb)
  - incl auxiliary tanks: 878 kg (1,936 lb)
- Max T-O weight (A-3 and A-4):
  - internal payload: 3,200 kg (7,055 lb)
  - external payload: 3,000 kg (6,614 lb)

PERFORMANCE (ISA; A at gross weight of 2,700 kg: 5,952 lb, B at 2,900 kg; 6,393 lb, C at 3,100 kg; 6,834 lb, D (A-4 only) at 3,200 kg; 7,055 lb):
- Never-exceed speed at S/L:
  - A, B, C: 150 knots (278 km/h; 172 mph)
- Max cruising speed at S/L:
  - A: 136 knots (252 km/h; 157 mph)
  - B: 135 knots (250 km/h; 155 mph)
  - C: 134 knots (248 km/h; 154 mph)
- Max forward rate of climb at S/L:
  - A: 606 m (1,990 ft)/min
  - B: 540 m (1,770 ft)/min
  - C: 480 m (1,575 ft)/min
  - D: 632 m (2,075 ft)/min
- Max operating altitude: A, B: 4,575 m (15,000 ft)
  - C: 3,050 m (10,000 ft)
- Service ceiling, one engine out, 46 m (150 ft)/min climb reserve: A: 3,020 m (9,900 ft)
  - B: 2,345 m (7,700 ft)
  - C: 1,675 m (5,500 ft)
- Hovering ceiling IGE (zero wind):
  - A: 3,960 m (13,000 ft)
  - B: 3,200 m (10,500 ft)
  - C: 2,500 m (8,200 ft)
- Hovering ceiling IGE (17 knot; 32 km/h; 20 mph crosswind): A: 3,050 m (10,000 ft)
  - B: 2,470 m (8,100 ft)
  - C: 1,800 m (5,900 ft)
  - D: approx 2,440 m (8,000 ft)
- Hovering ceiling OGE: A: 3,505 m (11,500 ft)
  - B: 2,500 m (8,200 ft)
  - C: 610 m (2,000 ft)
  - D: 1,980 m (6,500 ft)
- Range at S/L with standard fuel, no reserves:
  - A: 272 nm (505 km; 314 miles)
  - B: 270 nm (500 km; 310 miles)
  - C: 267 nm (495 km; 307 miles)
- Ferry range at S/L with 500 litres (110 Imp gallons) max auxiliary fuel, no reserves:
  - B: 499 nm (925 km; 574 miles)
  - C: 496 nm (920 km; 571 miles)
- Endurance at S/L, standard fuel, no reserves:
  - A: 3 h 0 min
  - B: 2 h 57 min
  - C: 2 h 54 min

MBB BK 117 A-3M

Shown publicly for the first time at the 1985 Paris Air Show, the A-3M multi-role military version of the BK 117 is a purely German development by MBB. The airframe and

BK 117 A-3M multi-role military helicopter, equipped with undernose gun turret, roof and mast mounted sights, and eight Hot 2 anti-tank missiles. Kawasaki is not associated with this version

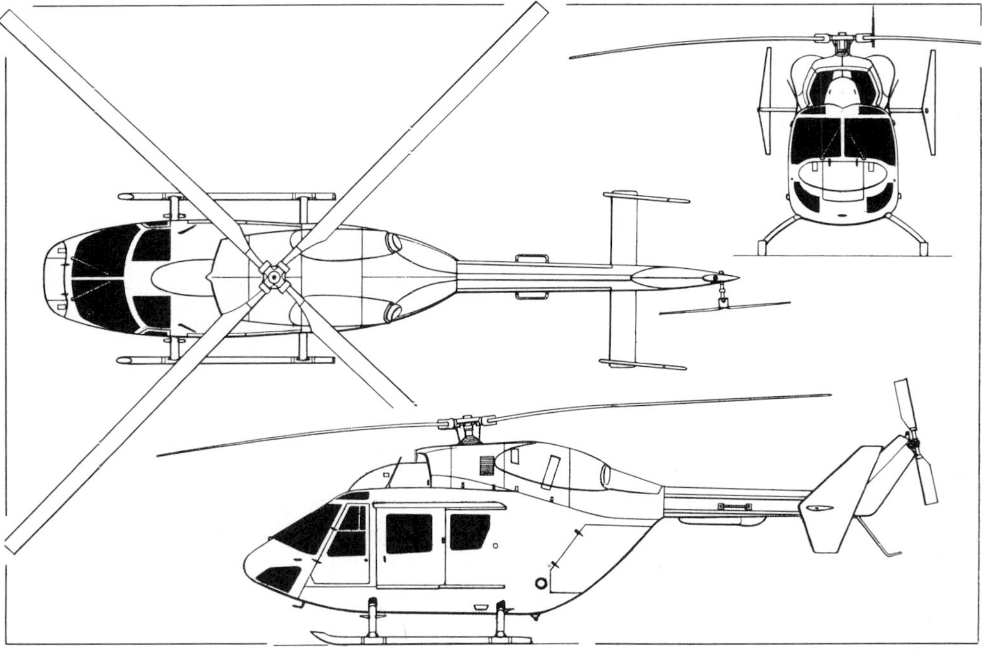

MBB/Kawasaki BK 117 twin-turboshaft multi-purpose helicopter *(Pilot Press)*

power plant are virtually unchanged from the commercial 117 A-3, except for a new high-skid landing gear to provide clearance for an underfuselage Lucas turret housing a 0·50 in or 12·7 mm Browning automatic machine-gun, with 450 rounds of ammunition, controlled by a helmet mounted sight. Typical weapons load is eight Hot 2 anti-tank missiles, mounted on outrigger pylons (four missiles each side of cabin), with which are associated a SFIM APX-M397 stabilised roof mounted sight and digital weapons control avionics. Provisions exist for a mast mounted sight of up to 120 kg (264 lb) weight, infra-red jamming and chaff/flare ECM, a Racal Prophet radar warning system, and a Racal RAMS 3000 Series avionics management system which uses a dual MIL-STD-1553B databus and multi-function cockpit displays. In this configuration the BK 117 A-3M has an empty equipped weight of 2,560 kg (5,644 lb), carries a crew of two and 460 kg (1,014 lb) of fuel, for a max T-O weight of 3,200 kg (7,055 lb). Alternative ordnance can include TOW anti-tank missiles, air-to-air missiles, unguided rockets, machine-gun pods, fixed forward-firing cannon, or a doorway gunner's position with a 0·50 in machine-gun. The capacity to serve instead as an 11-troop or cargo transport helicopter is the same as for the commercial BK 117 A-3.

Market studies and customer reactions were still being evaluated by MBB in mid-1986. No orders had been announced up to that time.

MCDONNELL DOUGLAS/BAe

AIRFRAME PRIME CONTRACTORS:

McDonnell Douglas Corporation, Box 516, St Louis, Missouri 63166, USA
Telephone: (314) 232 0232
Telex: 44-857

British Aerospace PLC, Richmond Road, Kingston upon Thames, Surrey KT2 5QS, England
Telephone: 01 546 7741
Telex: 23726

VICE-PRESIDENT AND GENERAL MANAGER, AV-8:
Edwin A. Harper (McDonnell Douglas)

PROGRAMME MANAGER, T45TS: Sterling D. Stalford

MCDONNELL DOUGLAS/BRITISH AEROSPACE HARRIER II

US Marine Corps designations: AV-8B and TAV-8B
RAF designation: Harrier GR. Mk 5
Spanish Navy designation: EAV-8B

Initial enthusiasm of the US Marine Corps for an advanced version of the AV-8A Harrier resulted in Anglo-American studies as long ago as 1973. After these foundered in 1975, McDonnell Douglas and Hawker Siddeley/British Aerospace at first pursued their own separate lines of development, both aimed broadly at doubling the payload/radius capability of the Harrier/AV-8A without departing too radically (or expensively) from the existing airframe/engine combination. The two companies subsequently joined forces in the current Harrier II programme, initially for the US Marine Corps (**AV-8B** and **TAV-8B**) and the Royal Air Force (**Harrier GR. Mk 5**).

As a first step, McDonnell Douglas and the USMC modified two AV-8As as prototype YAV-8Bs, these flying for the first time on 9 November 1978 and 19 February 1979. Four full scale development (FSD) AV-8Bs were ordered on 12 April 1979, and the first of these made its initial flight on 5 November 1981. The remaining three first flew on 17 April, 9 April and 4 June 1982 respectively. Two airframes were built for structural and fatigue testing.

The decision to commit the AV-8B to production was announced on 24 August 1981, at which time the British Ministry of Defence and the main industrial partners in the programme indicated initial requirements of 257 for the USMC and 60 for the RAF. The total current USMC requirement is for 328 production aircraft (300 AV-8Bs and 28 two-seat TAV-8Bs), of which the first 12 (pilot production) AV-8Bs were ordered in FY 1982. The first of these made its initial flight on 29 August 1983. Subsequent orders were placed in FYs 1983 (21 aircraft), 1984 (27, including one TAV-8B), 1985 (32, including two TAV-8Bs) and 1986 (46); funding for a further 42 aircraft was requested in FY 1987, and production is planned to continue into the early 1990s. The AV-8B is intended to re-equip three fleet operational AV-8A/C squadrons (VMA-331, VMA-542 and VMA-513), one training squadron (VMAT-203) and five A-4 Skyhawk squadrons by 1989. The first pilot production AV-8B was delivered to the USMC in October 1983. The first operational AV-8B squadron, VMA-331, was commissioned at MCAS Cherry Point, North Carolina, on 30 January 1985. Initial operational capability (IOC) was achieved in August 1985, and full operational readiness with 15 AV-8Bs was expected by mid-1986. VMA-231, the second operational AV-8B squadron, began receiving its aircraft in the Autumn of 1985, and the third (VMA-457) in mid-1986. Total deliveries to the USMC were more than 50 by 31 August 1986.

First flight of the two-seat TAV-8B occurred on 21 October 1986, to be followed by initial deliveries to VMAT-203 in March 1987. This version has a longer forward fuselage and 0·43 m (1 ft 5 in) taller vertical tail than the AV-8B, with two cockpits in tandem. For weapons training it is able to carry Mk 76 practice bombs, LAU-68 rocket launchers or 1,135 litre (300 US gallon) external fuel tanks. BAe is the major subcontractor for the TAV-8B.

Deliveries of the GR. Mk 5 to the Royal Air Force, scheduled to begin in 1987, are being preceded by two development aircraft for weapons system certification flying, plus—since most GR. Mk 5s are expected to be based in RAF Germany—a fatigue test airframe to clear the aircraft for the rigorous central European low-level operating environment. First flight by a GR. Mk 5 (ZD318) was made on 30 April 1985; the second (ZD319) was flown on 31 July 1985. In July 1986 it was announced that the RAF's current requirement for 62 GR. Mk 5s would be followed by orders for 18 to 27 additional aircraft, for which long lead production items were being authorised.

First export customer for the Harrier II is the government of Spain, which is acquiring 12 **EAV-8Bs**, assembled by McDonnell Douglas, to supplement its carrier-based AV-8A Matadors. Deliveries are due to begin in late 1987.

US Marine Corps AV-8B of VMAT-203 in hovering flight

A programme to develop a night attack version of the Harrier II was announced by McDonnell Douglas in November 1984, and a USMC prototype of this version should fly in May 1987, with production deliveries starting in September 1989; the RAF night attack version will be undertaken as a retrofit programme. Changes include the addition of a GEC Avionics FLIR system, use of night vision goggles, changes in cockpit lighting, and use of modified versions of the standard Smiths Industries head-up display (HUD) and display processor which provides information for the HUD and drives the aircraft's multi-purpose colour CRT displays. The changes will enable the HUD to display both raster and cursive symbology, as well as increasing the pilot's instantaneous field of view by about 45 per cent. During night operations the HUD will be able to present symbology superimposed on a FLIR image, and will be compatible with night vision goggles because of its use of refractive optics of novel design.

Simulator tests by McDonnell Douglas have shown that radars such as the Emerson Electric APG-69 could provide the AV-8B with the ability to attack enemy aircraft and identify ground targets at night or in adverse weather. No contract for such installation had been announced by mid-1986.

Features of the AV-8B include the use of graphite epoxy (carbonfibre) composite materials for the wings, and parts of the fuselage and tail unit; adoption of a supercritical section wing; addition of lift improvement devices (LIDs) comprising fuselage mounted or under-gun-pod strakes and a retractable fence panel forward of the pods, to augment lift for vertical take-off; larger wing trailing-edge flaps and drooped ailerons; redesigned forward fuselage and cockpit; redesigned engine air intakes to provide more VTO/STO thrust and more efficient cruise; and the Hughes Angle Rate Bombing Set. The leading-edge root extensions (LERX) developed originally by British Aerospace for the UK designed Big Wing Harrier (see 1980-81 *Jane's*) have also been adopted as standard, although they are now only 64 per cent of the size originally proposed. This feature adds considerably to the AV-8B's instantaneous turn rate, enhancing still further its air combat capability. The landing gear is strengthened to cater for the higher operating weights and greater external stores loads made possible by these changes.

Work split on the airframe for the AV-8B and EAV-8B is 60 per cent to McDonnell Douglas and 40 per cent to British Aerospace; the GR. Mk 5 work split is 50 per cent to each manufacturer. On any future third party orders McDonnell Douglas would make 75 per cent of the aircraft deliveries and British Aerospace 25 per cent. Each manufacturer is responsible for the systems in those parts of the airframe which are its concern, and for their installation. British Aerospace provides the complete reaction control system for all aircraft in the programme, and undertakes final assembly of aircraft for the RAF. McDonnell Douglas assembles the aircraft for the USMC and Spain. Planned peak production rates are four US and two UK aircraft per month.

Pratt & Whitney manufactures up to 25 per cent by value of the engines for the USMC aircraft; Rolls-Royce builds the remainder. The production engine is the F402-RR-406 (Pegasus Mk 105), an improved version of the Pegasus 11 with new features designed to offer substantially increased engine life and reduced peacetime operating costs. Beyond the current production engine, growth engines may offer some 13·3 kN (3,000 lb) more thrust, and Rolls-Royce began testing an uprated Pegasus known as the XG-15 in late 1985. Growth engines will also form the basis of a

Model of the TAV-8B two-seat training version of the Harrier II

supersonic engine using plenum chamber burning (PCB), and all four major airframe/engine partners are engaged in jointly funded R&D for the eventual development of a supersonic V/STOL combat aircraft. A digital engine control system (DECS) for the F402 is under development by Dowty and Smiths Industries; full production testing of this began in July 1986.

The following description applies to the production AV-8B and the Harrier GR. Mk 5:

TYPE: Single-seat V/STOL close support and (RAF only) reconnaissance aircraft.

WINGS: Cantilever shoulder-wing monoplane. Low aspect ratio sweptback wings, with non-swept inboard trailing-edges and curved leading-edge root extensions (LERX). Span and area increased by approx 20 per cent and 14·5 per cent respectively compared with Harrier/AV-8A. Supercritical aerofoil section, with thickness/chord ratio of 11·5% at root, 7·5% at tip. Leading-edge sweep 10° less than that of Harrier/AV-8A. Marked anhedral. One-piece structure, of mixed construction, with extensive use of graphite epoxy (carbonfibre) and other composite materials in the main multi-spar torsion box, ribs, skins, flaps, ailerons, LERX, and outrigger pods and fairings. Leading-edges (reinforced against bird strikes) and wing-tips of aluminium alloy. Wide chord single-slotted trailing-edge flaps, with flap slot closure doors. Drooping ailerons, actuated by Fairey hydraulic jacks. Jet reaction control valve at each wingtip. LERX for RAF aircraft manufactured by BAe; all other wing manufacture and assembly by McDonnell Douglas.

FUSELAGE: Conventional semi-monocoque safe-life structure of frames and stringers, generally similar to that of AV-8A, but longer, due to provision of a new forward fuselage built largely of graphite epoxy composite material. Centre and rear fuselage mainly of aluminium alloy, except for forward and rear underfuselage heat-shields, and small area immediately forward of the windscreen, which are of titanium. Lift augmenting underfuselage devices consist of a fixed strake on each of the two ventral gun packs, plus a retractable fence between forward edges of gun packs, just aft of forward main landing gear unit. During VTOL modes the 'box' formed by these surfaces, which are made of composite materials, traps the cushion of air bounced off the ground by the engine exhaust, providing sufficient additional lift to enable the AV-8B to take off vertically at a gross weight equal to its maximum hovering gross weight. Access to engine through top of fuselage, immediately ahead of wing. Large forward hinged airbrake beneath fuselage, aft of rear main landing gear bay. Jet reaction control valves in nose and tailcone. McDonnell Douglas is responsible for manufacture of all forward and forward centre-fuselages, including nosecones, air intakes, heat-shields, engine access doors, and forward fuel tanks; and for the underfuselage fences and strakes. British Aerospace builds, for all aircraft, the rear centre and rear fuselages, including blast and heatshields, centre and rear fuel tanks, dorsal air intakes, and tail bullets. Fuselage assembly is by McDonnell Douglas for USMC and by BAe for RAF aircraft.

TAIL UNIT: One-piece variable incidence tailplane, with marked anhedral, differing in planform from that of AV-8A in having constant sweep on leading-edges and reduced sweep on trailing-edges. Tailplane is built mainly of graphite epoxy, with aluminium alloy tips and leading-edges, and is operated by Fairey tandem irreversible hydraulic jacks. Aluminium alloy fin, with dielectric tip; manually operated graphite epoxy composite rudder, with inset trim tab. Dorsal airscoop, at base of fin, for equipment bay cooling system. Ventral fin under rear fuselage. Fins and rudders for all aircraft, and tailplanes for RAF aircraft, built by BAe; tailplanes for USMC aircraft built by McDonnell Douglas.

LANDING GEAR: Retractable bicycle type of Dowty Rotol design, permitting operation from rough unprepared surfaces of very low CBR (California Bearing Ratio). Hydraulic actuation, with nitrogen bottle for emergency extension. Single steerable nosewheel retracts forward, twin coupled mainwheels rearward, into fuselage. Small outrigger units, at approx mid span between flaps and ailerons, retract rearward into streamline pods. Telescopic oleo-pneumatic main and outrigger gear; levered suspension nosewheel leg. Dunlop wheels, tyres, multi-disc carbon brakes and anti-skid system. Mainwheel tyres (size 26·0 × 7·75-13·00) and nosewheel tyre (size 26·0 × 8·75-11) all have pressure of 8·62 bars (125 lb/sq in). Outrigger tyres are size 13·5 × 6·00-4·00, pressure 10·34 bars (150 lb/sq in). McDonnell Douglas responsible for entire landing gear system.

POWER PLANT: One 95·86 kN (21,550 lb st) Rolls-Royce F402-RR-406 (Pegasus 11-21) vectored-thrust turbofan engine in production AV-8B; one 96·75 kN (21,750 lb st) Pegasus Mk 105 in Harrier GR. Mk 5. Redundant digital engine control system (DECS), with mechanical backup, standard from late 1986. Zero-scarf front nozzles. Air intakes have an elliptical lip shape, leading-edges reinforced against bird strikes, and a single row of auxiliary intake doors. Integral fuel tanks in wings; total internal fuel capacity (fuselage and wing tanks) 4,163 litres (1,100 US gallons; 915 Imp gallons). Retractable in-flight refuelling probe. Each of the four inner underwing stations capable of carrying a 1,135 litre (300 US gallon; 250 Imp gallon) auxiliary fuel tank.

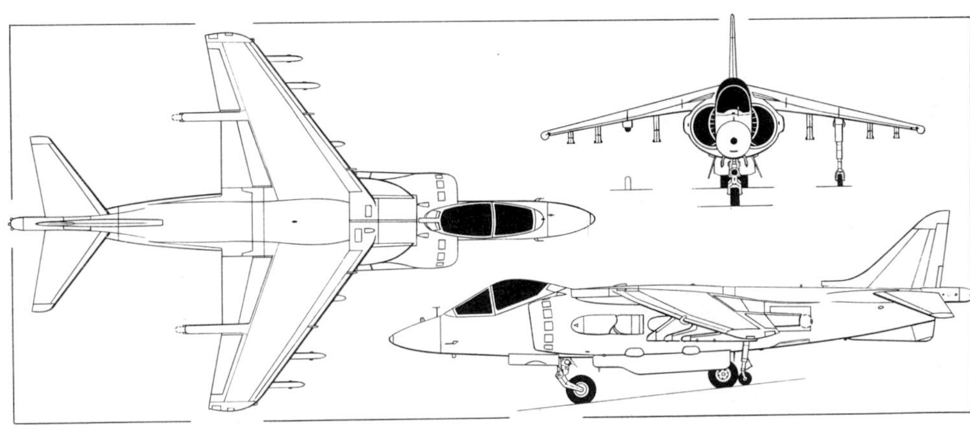

McDonnell Douglas/BAe AV-8B Harrier II V/STOL close support aircraft *(Pilot Press)*

First Harrier GR. Mk 5 for the Royal Air Force

ACCOMMODATION: Pilot only, on zero/zero ejection seat (Stencel for USMC, Martin-Baker for RAF), in pressurised, heated and air-conditioned cockpit. AV-8B cockpit raised approx 30·5 cm (12 in) by comparison with AV-8A/YAV-8B, with redesigned one-piece wraparound windscreen (thicker on RAF aircraft than on those for USMC) and rearward sliding bubble canopy, to improve all-round field of view. Windscreen de-icing and windscreen wiper. Windscreens and canopies for all aircraft manufactured by McDonnell Douglas.

SYSTEMS: Full details not yet announced, but generally similar to those of Harrier/Sea Harrier (see UK section). No. 1 hydraulic system has a flow rate of 43 litres (9·5 Imp gallons; 11·4 US gallons)/min; flow rate of No. 2 system is 27·25 litres (6·0 Imp gallons; 7·2 US gallons)/min. Reservoirs are nitrogen pressurised at 2·76-5·52 bars (40-80 lb/sq in). Other announced systems include Westinghouse variable speed constant frequency (VSCF) solid state electrical system, Lucas Mk 4 gas turbine starter/APU, Clifton Precision onboard oxygen generating system (OBOGS), and Graviner Firewire fire detection system.

AVIONICS AND EQUIPMENT: Include dual Collins RT-1250A/ARC U/VHF com (GEC Avionics AD3500 U/VHF-AM/FM in GR. Mk 5), R-1379B/ARA-63 all-weather landing receiver, RT-1159A/ARN-118 Tacan, RT-1015A/APN-194(V) radar altimeter, Sperry CV-3736/A com/nav/identification data converter, Bendix RT-1157/APX-100 IFF, Litton AN/ASN-130A inertial navigation system, Garrett AiResearch CP-1471/A digital air data computer, Smiths Industries SU-128/A dual combining glass head-up display and CP-1450/A display computer, IP-1318/A CRT Kaiser digital display indicator, and (RAF aircraft only) Ferranti moving map display. Litton AN/ALR-67(V)2 fore/aft looking radar warning receiver, and Goodyear flare/chaff dispenser (in lower rear fuselage). Primary weapon delivery sensor system for AV-8B and GR.Mk 5 is the Hughes Aircraft AN/ASB-19(V)2 Angle Rate Bombing Set, mounted in the nose and comprising a dual-mode (TV and laser) target seeker/tracker. This system functions in conjunction with the CP-1429/AYK-14(V) mission computer, the Lear Siegler AN/AYQ-13 stores management system, the display computer and its associated cockpit displays, the head-up display, and the digital display indicator. Flight controls that interface with the reaction control system are provided by the Sperry AN/ASW-46(V)2 stability augmentation and attitude hold system currently being updated to the high AOA capable configuration. RAF aircraft will have an accident data recorder. Backup standby mechanical instrumentation includes airspeed indicator, altimeter, angle of attack indicator, attitude indicator, cabin pressure altitude indicator, clock, flap position indicator, horizontal situation indicator, standby compass, turn and slip indicator, and vertical speed indicator. Other equipment includes anti-collision, approach, formation, in-flight refuelling, landing gear position, auxiliary exterior lights, and console, instrument panel and other internal lighting.

ARMAMENT AND OPERATIONAL EQUIPMENT: Two underfuselage gun/ammunition packs, mounting a five-barrel 25 mm cannon based on the General Electric GAU-12/U, with 300 rounds, in the AV-8B; or two 25 mm Royal Ordnance Factories cannon with 200 rds (derived from the 30 mm Aden) in the GR. Mk 5. Single 258 kg (570 lb) stores mount on fuselage centreline, between gun packs. Three stores stations under each wing on AV-8B, the inner one capable of carrying a 907 kg (2,000 lb) store, the centre one 454 kg (1,000 lb), and the outer one 286 kg (630 lb). The four inner wing stations are 'wet', permitting the carriage of auxiliary fuel tanks. Including fuel, stores, weapons and ammunition, and water injection for the engine, the maximum useful load for vertical take-off is approximately 3,062 kg (6,750 lb), and for short take-off nearly 7,710 kg (17,000 lb). Typical weapons include two or four AIM-9L Sidewinder, Magic or AGM-65E Maverick missiles; up to sixteen 500 lb general purpose bombs, 12 cluster bombs, ten Paveway laser guided bombs, eight fire bombs, ten rocket pods, six chaff or flare pods, or (in addition to the underfuselage gun packs) two underwing gun pods. ML Aviation BRU-36/A bomb release units standard on all versions. Provision for AN/ALQ-164 defensive ECM pod on centreline pylon (AV-8B). RAF aircraft will have two additional underwing weapon stations, for Sidewinder air-to-air missiles, ahead of the outrigger wheel fairings; a nose-mounted infra-red reconnaissance sensor; and a Marconi Defence Systems Zeus internal ECM system comprising an advanced radar warning receiver, and a multi-mode jammer with a Northrop RF transmitter.

DIMENSIONS, EXTERNAL:

Wing span	9·25 m (30 ft 4 in)
Wing aspect ratio	4·0
Length overall (flying attitude)	14·12 m (46 ft 4 in)
Height overall	3·55 m (11 ft 7¾ in)
Tailplane span	4·24 m (13 ft 11 in)
Outrigger wheel track	5·18 m (17 ft 0 in)

AREAS:

Wings, excl LERX, gross	21·37 m² (230 sq ft)
LERX (total)	0·81 m² (8·7 sq ft)
Ailerons (total)	1·15 m² (12·4 sq ft)
Trailing-edge flaps (total)	2·88 m² (31·0 sq ft)
Ventral fixed strakes (total)	0·51 m² (5·5 sq ft)
Ventral retractable fence (LIDs)	0·24 m² (2·6 sq ft)
Ventral airbrake	0·42 m² (4·5 sq ft)
Fin	2·47 m² (26·6 sq ft)
Rudder, excl tab	0·49 m² (5·3 sq ft)
Tailplane	4·51 m² (48·5 sq ft)

WEIGHTS:

Basic operating weight empty:	
AV-8B	5,936 kg (13,086 lb)
GR. Mk 5	6,258 kg (13,798 lb)
Max fuel: internal only	3,519 kg (7,759 lb)
internal and external	7,180 kg (15,829 lb)
Max external stores	4,173 kg (9,200 lb)

Basic flight design gross weight for 7*g* operation
10,410 kg (22,950 lb)
Max T-O weight:
500 m (1,640 ft) STO 14,061 kg (31,000 lb)
S/L VTO, ISA 8,595 kg (18,950 lb)
S/L VTO, 32°C 8,142 kg (17,950 lb)
Design max landing weight 11,340 kg (25,000 lb)
Max vertical landing weight 8,459 kg (18,650 lb)

PERFORMANCE:
Max Mach number in level flight:
at S/L 0·85 (562 knots; 1,041 km/h; 647 mph)
at altitude 0·91
STOL T-O run at max T-O weight 500 m (1,640 ft)
Operational radius with external loads shown:
short T-O (366 m; 1,200 ft), twelve Mk 82 Snakeye bombs, internal fuel, 1 h loiter
90 nm (167 km; 103 miles)
hi-lo-hi, short T-O (366 m; 1,200 ft), seven Mk 82 Snakeye bombs, external fuel tanks, no loiter (payload of 1,814 kg; 4,000 lb)
480 nm (889 km; 553 miles)
Combat air patrol endurance at 100 nm (185 km; 115 miles) from base 3 h
Unrefuelled ferry range, with four 300 US gallon external tanks 2,120 nm (3,929 km; 2,441 miles)
g limits +7/−3

MCDONNELL DOUGLAS/BRITISH AEROSPACE T45TS

US Navy designation: T-45A Goshawk

In November 1981 the US Navy selected the Douglas Aircraft Company division of McDonnell Douglas Corporation as prime contractor for its VTXTS programme, since renamed as the T45 Training System (T45TS). This is an integrated training system to replace the current intermediate and advanced system which includes use of T-2C Buckeye and TA-4J Skyhawk aircraft. The T45TS system features aircraft, academics, simulators, an integration system, and logistics support. British Aerospace (BAe) is principal subcontractor to Douglas for the T-45A aircraft (building the wings, rear fuselage, windscreen, canopy and flight controls), and Sperry for simulators. Final assembly and manufacture of some major components of the T-45A Goshawk will take place at the Douglas factory in Long Beach, California. The programme entered the full scale development phase in October 1984. The first of two prototypes is scheduled to fly in late 1987, with service entry due in 1990. A fixed-price contract for the first three production lots, including 60 aircraft and 15 flight simulators during FYs 1988-90, was signed on 16 May 1986.

The T-45A Goshawk is a derivative of the BAe Hawk (see UK section), and the US Navy has a production requirement for 300. To meet USN specifications, the T-45A will have a new main and nose landing gear, an arrester hook, and airframe strengthening to provide the capability to operate from aircraft carriers. The nose gear will have a catapult launch bar (nosewheel tow) and will be steerable. The T-45A will also have two fuselage side airbrakes, instead of the original Hawk underfuselage installation. The original twin ventral strakes are replaced by a single ventral surface, used also to fair the arrester hook. Avionics and cockpit displays will be modified for carrier-compatible operation, and weapons delivery capability for the advanced training role will be incorporated.

TYPE: Two-seat basic and advanced jet trainer.

WINGS: Similar to BAe Hawk, but redesigned and strengthened.

FUSELAGE: Similar to BAe Hawk, but with large airbrake on each side of rear fuselage aft of wing, and underfuselage arrester hook.

TAIL UNIT: Similar to BAe Hawk, but with single ventral fin at arrester hook attachment point.

LANDING GEAR: Hydraulically retractable tricycle type, with single wheel on each main unit and twin-wheel steerable nose unit. Articulated main gear by AP Precision Hydraulics, with folding side-stay. Nose gear by Cleveland Pneumatic, with Sterer steering system. Main units retract inward into wing, forward of front spar; nose unit retracts forward. Wheel doors close after gear lowering. Goodrich wheels, tyres and brakes. Mainwheel tyres size 24 × 7·7-10, pressure 20·69 bars (300 lb/sq in). Nosewheel tyres size 19 × 5·25-10, pressure 22·06 bars (320 lb/sq in). Dunlop adaptive anti-skid braking system.

Artist's impression of the US Navy T-45A Goshawk derivative of the British Aerospace Hawk

POWER PLANT: One 24·24 kN (5,450 lb st) Rolls-Royce Turboméca Adour Mk 861-49 non-afterburning turbofan engine (US Navy designation F405-RR-400). Air intakes and engine starting as described for BAe Hawk. Fuel system similar to BAe Hawk, but with revision for carrier operation. Capacities are 840 litres (185 Imp gallons; 222 US gallons) in fuselage bag tank and 863 litres (190 Imp gallons; 228 US gallons) in integral wing tank, giving total internal capacity of 1,703 litres (375 Imp gallons; 450 US gallons). Provision for carrying one 591 litre (130 Imp gallon; 156 US gallon) drop tank on each inboard underwing pylon.

ACCOMMODATION: Similar to BAe Hawk, except that ejection seats are of Martin-Baker NACES (Navy aircrew common ejection seat) zero/zero rocket assisted type.

SYSTEMS: Air-conditioning and pressurisation systems, using engine bleed air. Duplicated hydraulic systems, each 207 bars (3,000 lb/sq in), for actuation of control jacks, flaps, airbrakes, landing gear and anti-skid wheel brakes. No. 1 system has a flow rate of 36 litres (8·0 Imp gallons; 9·6 US gallons)/min, No. 2 system a rate of 23 litres (5·0 Imp gallons; 6 US gallons)/min. Reservoirs are nitrogen pressurised at 2·76-5·52 bars (40-80 lb/sq in). Hydraulic accumulator for emergency operation of wheel brakes. No pneumatic system. DC electrical power from single brushless generator, with two static inverters to provide AC power and two batteries for standby power. Onboard oxygen generating system (OBOGS). Pop-up Dowty Rotol ram air turbine in upper rear fuselage provides emergency power for flying controls in the event of an engine or No. 2 pump failure.

AVIONICS AND EQUIPMENT: Not yet finalised. GEC Avionics yaw damper computer.

DIMENSIONS: As for two-seat BAe Hawk except:
Length overall, incl nose probe 11·97 m (39 ft 3⅛ in)
Length of fuselage 10·89 m (35 ft 9 in)
Height overall 4·12 m (13 ft 6⅛ in)
Wheel track (c/l of shock struts) 3·90 m (12 ft 9½ in)
Wheelbase 4·29 m (14 ft 1 in)

AREAS: As for BAe Hawk except:
Airbrakes (total) 0·79 m² (8·55 sq ft)

WEIGHTS (estimated):
Weight empty 4,261 kg (9,394 lb)
Max T-O weight 5,787 kg (12,758 lb)

PERFORMANCE (estimated at max T-O weight):
Design limit diving speed at 1,000 m (3,280 ft)
610 knots (1,130 km/h; 702 mph)
Max Mach number in dive 1·1
Max level speed at 2,440 m (8,000 ft)
538 knots (997 km/h; 620 mph)
Max level speed Mach number at 9,145 m (30,000 ft) 0·85
Max rate of climb at S/L 2,128 m (6,982 ft)/min
Time to 9,145 m (30,000 ft), 'clean' 7 min 12 s
Service ceiling 12,875 m (42,250 ft)
T-O to 15 m (50 ft) 1,141 m (3,744 ft)
Landing from 15 m (50 ft) 1,189 m (3,900 ft)
Ferry range, 'clean' 950 nm (1,760 km; 1,094 miles)
g limits +7·33/−3

NH 90

Following a January 1985 memorandum of understanding initialled by the defence ministers of France, Germany, Italy, Netherlands and (later) the UK, a new helicopter is being proposed for the armed services of these five countries. Known provisionally as the NH 90 (NATO Helicopter for the '90s), it will be in the 8,000-9,000 kg (17,635-19,840 lb) gross weight class and powered by twin turboshaft engines (RTM 322s or T700s) in the 1,491 kW (2,000 shp) class.

One manufacturer from each country (Aérospatiale, MBB, Agusta, Fokker and Westland) was designated to form an industrial group to carry out a 'pre-definition feasibility study' by late 1986 to establish a common basic configuration for the NH 90, leading to a project definition phase to begin in 1987. Two major versions are foreseen at present: an NFH 90 (NATO frigate helicopter) for ASW, surface attack and SAR duties, and a land based tactical transport version known as the TTH 90. Estimated total requirements by the armed forces of the five participating nations are 200 and 500 respectively; this total could be doubled if full export potential is realised.

The leading technology features of the helicopter have been defined as: (a) a four-blade main rotor and four-blade anti-torque tail rotor, utilising composite blades of advanced aerofoil sections and tip planform; (b) twin-engined, semi-pod arrangement; (c) higher harmonic control; (d) tricycle landing gear to meet crashworthiness requirements; (e) high level of composites utilisation in the fuselage structure; (f) design features for low vulnerability and detectability; (g) flexible system layout for mission equipment.

The naval variant will offer autonomy in ASW operations, and will be designed for an all-weather, severe ship-motion environment. The payload capacity will meet a wide range of national requirements in respect of naval mission fits. The army/air force variant will offer a defensive weapons suite and low pilot workload.

NTT

NEW TRANSPORT TECHNOLOGIES LTD

Postfach 801304, 8000 München 80, Federal Republic of Germany
Telephone: (089) 6000 3444
Telex: 5287-740 mbb d

It was announced in April 1984 that MBB (West Germany) and IPTN (Indonesia) had signed an agreement to carry out a development study (still in progress in 1986) for a small, four-seat light helicopter to be known as the BN-109. Furthermore, it was agreed to set up a joint company, NTT, with headquarters in Munich, in which MBB and IPTN each hold 50 per cent of the shares. Objectives of NTT will be to develop, produce and market aircraft, such as the BN-109 and a light training aircraft, and special equipment. MBB also provides technical support in the flight test and certification of the Airtech (CASA/IPTN) CN-235.

NTT BN-109

The BN-109 is being designed for a variety of roles which include light transport, surveillance, search and rescue, casualty evacuation, police patrol and training. It will have an advanced three-blade main and two-blade tail rotor system, and will be powered by an engine in the 230-260 kW (308-348 hp) range. Certification will be under FAR Pt 27.

A go-ahead decision was expected in 1986; the following provisional data have been released:

TYPE: Four-seat multi-purpose light helicopter.

ROTOR SYSTEM AND DRIVE: Three-blade main and two-blade tail rotor, turning at 473 and 2,865 rpm respectively. Three-stage main gearbox. Mechanical controls, without hydraulics. Main rotor/engine rpm ratio 16·9:1.

AIRFRAME: Of conventional pod and boom configuration (see accompanying illustration), with skid landing gear. Two hinged doors on each side of cabin.

POWER PLANT: One Porsche motorcar engine (TAG modification), derated to 230 kW (308 hp), or an Allison turboshaft of 260 kW (348 shp). Fuel tank under cabin floor.

ACCOMMODATION: Cabin space for pilot, three passengers and up to 30 kg (66 lb) of baggage.

DIMENSIONS, EXTERNAL:
- Main rotor diameter: 8·40 m (27 ft 6¾ in)
- Main rotor blade chord: 0·27 m (10·6 in)
- Tail rotor diameter: 1·40 m (4 ft 7 in)
- Length overall, excl rotors: 7·41 m (24 ft 3¾ in)
- Fuselage: Max width: 1·15 m (3 ft 9¼ in)

AREAS:
- Main rotor disc: 55·42 m² (596·5 sq ft)
- Tail rotor disc: 1·54 m² (16·57 sq ft)

WEIGHTS AND LOADING:
- Weight empty: 640 kg (1,411 lb)
- Fuel weight: 190 kg (419 lb)
- Payload: 370 kg (815 lb)
- Max T-O weight: 1,200 kg (2,645 lb)
- Max disc loading: 21·65 kg/m² (4·44 lb/sq ft)

PERFORMANCE (estimated):
- Max cruising speed at S/L: 108 knots (200 km/h; 124 mph)
- Hovering ceiling OGE (ISA + 25°C): 2,500 m (8,200 ft)
- Range with max fuel: 264 nm (490 km; 304 miles)

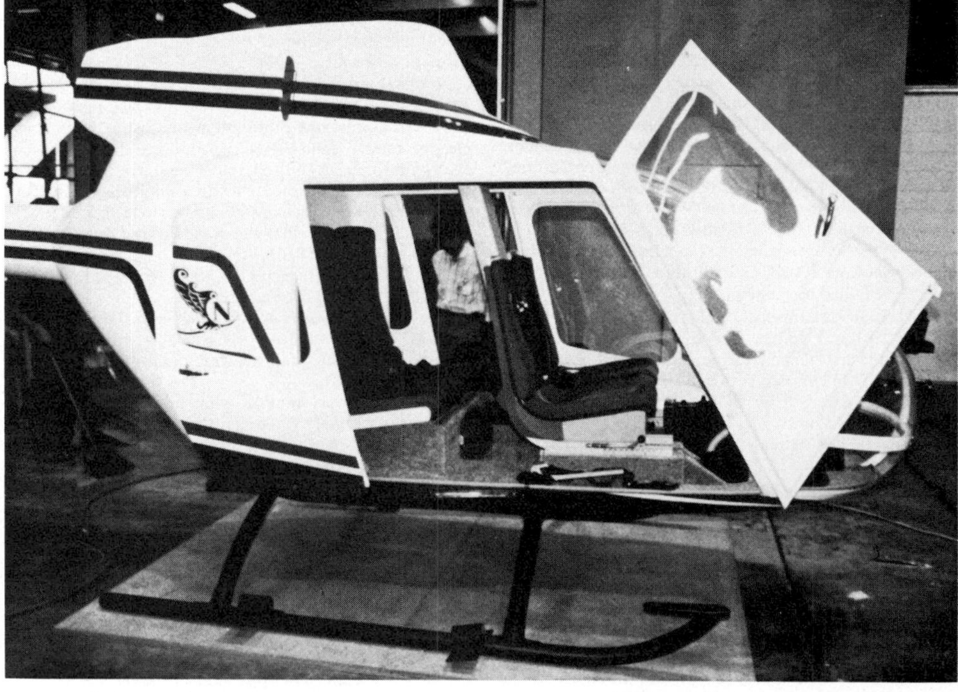

Full size mockup of the proposed NTT BN-109, displayed by IPTN at Jakarta in August 1985

PANAVIA

PANAVIA AIRCRAFT GmbH

8 München 86, Postfach 860629, Arabellastrasse 16, Federal Republic of Germany
Telephone: (089) 92171
Telex: 05 29 825

Panavia was formed on 26 March 1969 to design, develop and produce an all-weather combat aircraft for the air forces of the United Kingdom, the Federal Republic of Germany and Italy, and the Federal German Navy. The name Tornado for this aircraft was adopted officially in March 1976. This programme is one of the largest European industrial programmes ever undertaken. The three component companies of Panavia are British Aerospace PLC (42·5% participation), MBB (42·5%) and Aeritalia (15%).

The Federal German, British and Italian governments set up a joint organisation known as NAMMO (NATO MRCA Management and production Organisation). This has its executive agency NAMMA (NATO MRCA Management Agency) in the same building as Panavia, in Munich.

On 29 July 1976 the three governments signed a memorandum of understanding for the production of 809 Tornados, enabling the three partner countries to embark upon the production programme.

PANAVIA TORNADO IDS

RAF designation: Tornado GR. Mk 1

The Tornado is a twin-engined two-seat supersonic aircraft capable of fulfilling the agreed operational requirements of its three sponsoring countries. The use of a variable geometry wing, and avionics which enable the aircraft to fly 'blind' in all weathers, day and night, at very low level, with automatic terrain following, give it the necessary flexibility to achieve all-weather penetration.

The aircraft is intended to fulfil six major requirements, some of which are shared by more than one of the partners. These are:

(a) Close air support/battlefield interdiction
(b) Interdiction/counter air strike
(c) Air superiority
(d) Interception/air defence
(e) Naval strike
(f) Reconnaissance

Design of the Tornado was completed in August 1972. Nine flying prototypes were built—four in the UK, three in West Germany and two in Italy. The first prototype (D-9591), assembled by MBB, made its first flight at Manching, West Germany, on 14 August 1974. Details of all nine prototypes can be found in the 1978-79 and earlier editions of *Jane's*, and of the six pre-series Tornados in the 1980-81 and earlier editions.

The first 809 production aircraft ordered for the participating nations comprise 644 of the IDS (interdictor strike) version, and 165 examples of the ADV (air defence variant, described separately) for the RAF. These were ordered under six contracts with respective new-production totals of 43, 110, 164, 162, 171 and 155. Four of the early IDS pre-series batch will eventually be brought up to production standard (one for Great Britain, two for Germany, one for Italy) to make up the original 809 three-nation programme production total. A total of 643 will be operational aircraft, and 163 will be dual control trainers with full operational capability. Revised annual production rates announced in 1982 were: UK 44, West Germany 42, and Italy (unchanged) 24. These are not affected by subsequent orders. A seventh Tornado production contract, for 124 aircraft, was signed on 10 June 1986. This figure, bringing the overall total (excluding the four pre-series aircraft) to 929, is made up of 72 for the Royal Saudi Air Force (48 IDS and 24 ADV), eight ADV for the Sultan of Oman's Air Force, nine more GR. Mk 1s for the RAF, and 35 of the ECR variant (also described separately) for the Federal German Luftwaffe. The first two IDS Tornados for the RSAF arrived in Saudi Arabia on 27 March 1986, and six had been delivered by the following August.

The RAF is to have 229 Tornados of the GR. Mk 1 interdictor/strike version, including 48 trainers. Squadron deliveries began on 6 January 1982 to No. IX Squadron (formerly flying Vulcans) at RAF Honington, Suffolk, which became Strike Command's first operational Tornado squadron on 1 June 1982. It now also equips Nos. 27 and 617 at Marham (UK), Nos. XV, 16 and 20 at Laarbruch (West Germany), and Nos. 14, 17 and 31 at Brüggen (Germany). A total of seven Tornado GR. Mk 1 strike/attack squadrons and a further GR. Mk 1 reconnaissance squadron will eventually be based in RAF Germany. In 1984, RAF GR. Mk 1s based in West Germany began being

Tornado GR. Mk 1s of No. 31 Squadron, RAF Germany, based at Brüggen

modified to carry tactical nuclear weapons; they are also the first RAF Tornados to be equipped with the Hunting JP 233 anti-airfield weapon.

The Luftwaffe is to receive 212 IDS Tornados, to replace the Lockheed F-104G in the battlefield interdiction, counter air and close air support roles. Six squadrons, two each with JaboG 31 at Nörvenich, JaboG 32 at Lechfeld and JaboG 33 at Büchel, were operational by January 1986. The 112 for Marinefliegergeschwader 1 and 2 of the Federal German Navy are being equipped for strike missions against sea and coastal targets, and for reconnaissance. Two squadrons of IDS Tornados are in service with MFG. 1 at Jagel, and two MFG.2 squadrons were converting in 1986.

The Italian Air Force will receive 100 Tornados (99 production aircraft plus the No. 14 pre-series Tornado brought up to production standard). Of these, 54 will be used to replace F/RF-104G aircraft in the air superiority, ground attack and reconnaissance roles. Of the remainder, 34 will be kept in reserve and 12 will be equipped as dual control trainers. First unit to be equipped was the 154° Gruppo (Squadron) of 6° Stormo (Wing) at Brescia-Ghedi, which received its first Tornados in August 1982. By January 1986 the second unit, the 156° Gruppo (36° Stormo) at Gioia del Colle (Bari), and the third, the 155° Gruppo, also at Ghedi, had been equipped.

The first British production Tornado made its initial flight on 10 July 1979, the first West German on 27 July 1979, and the first Italian on 25 September 1981. About 550 production Tornados had been delivered by August 1986.

Fifty of these were delivered to the Tri-national Tornado Training Establishment (TTTE) at RAF Cottesmore in 1981-82. Weapons training is carried out at two Tornado Weapons Conversion Units (TWCU) at RAF Honington (UK) and JaboG 38 at Jever (West Germany).

By August 1986 the Tornado services of four nations had accumulated more than 220,000 hours of operational flying. In addition, over 10,200 hours had been flown by the industrial flight test crews from the three Panavia partner companies. Development flying has been virtually completed. A special low level flight test programme (JET), carried out by a tri-national team of service and industrial aircrews, included 98 sorties with heavy external stores at the lowest set altitude of 61 m (200 ft) and with a maximum speed of Mach 0·9. The first flight of a Tornado carrying ALARM missiles took place in early 1985, and German Air Force Tornados have proved the compatibility of the Dornier DATS-3 aerial target with the aircraft. The first flight of the RAF camera-less reconnaissance version of Tornado took place in Autumn 1985. This version is identifiable by a small underbelly blister fairing, immediately behind the laser rangefinder pod, containing a BAe sideways looking infra-red (SLIR) system, BAe Linescan 4000 infra-red surveillance system and Computing Devices Company signal processing and video recording system. Also in 1985, an initial technology demonstration was completed by an RAF Tornado equipped with BAe's Terprom (terrain profile matching) self-contained navigation system, and a contract was awarded to GEC Avionics for a night vision FLIR system for the Tornado GR. Mk 1. The FLIR sensor is installed in the undernose fairing used currently to house a laser rangefinder.

By Summer 1986, RAF Squadrons Nos. IX, 27 and 617 were SACEUR declared, RAF Germany Squadrons Nos. XV and 16 were strike declared, and the six squadrons at German MFG. 1 and JaboGs 31 and 32 were NATO assigned. The first operational batch of MW-1 weapons systems had been delivered to JaboG 32; and joint take-off and landing trials by RAF Germany and the Luftwaffe had been performed successfully on a motorway in north Germany.

In 1984 RAF crews from No. 617 Squadron won, for the first time ever with aircraft from outside the USA, the Curtis E. LeMay and John C. Meyer trophies during the 'Giant Voice'/'Prairie Vortex' strategic and tactical bombing competitions in the USA. This success was repeated by No. 27 Squadron in the 1985 competition, with even higher scores. In Winter 1985-86 ten Tornados from MFG.1 and JaboG 31 achieved another notable success with trans-Atlantic flights to Gander and Goose Bay in Canada respectively. The flights covered a distance of some 8,095 nm (15,000 km; 9,320 miles) and included 'buddy' refuelling and an intermediate stop on the Azores.

Nominal max weapons load of the IDS Tornado is approx 9,000 kg (19,840 lb), carried on seven fuselage and wing hardpoints: one centreline pylon fitted with a single ejection release unit (ERU), two fuselage shoulder pylons each with three ERUs, and, under each wing, one inboard and one outboard pylon each with a single ERU. The BAe Sea Eagle air-to-surface missile can be carried by the RAF's GR. Mk 1. Primary armament of the Federal German Navy Tornados is four MBB Kormoran anti-shipping missiles. Italy's Tornados are expected to be equipped with the Selenia Aspide 1A air-to-air missile.

The following details apply to the basic IDS production version:

TYPE: Twin-engined all-weather multi-purpose combat aircraft.

WINGS: Cantilever shoulder-wing monoplane. All-metal wings, of variable geometry, the outer panels having a leading-edge sweep of 25° in the fully forward position and 67° when fully swept. Fixed inboard portions have a leading-edge sweep of 60°. Wing carry-through box is of electron-beam-welded titanium alloy; majority of remaining wing structure is of aluminium alloy, with integrally stiffened skin. There is a Krueger flap on the leading-edge of each wing glove box. The wings each pivot hydraulically, on Teflon plated bearings, from a point in the centre-section just outboard of the fuselage. The root of the outer wing mates with the pivot pin through attachment members made of titanium alloy and fixed to the upper and lower light alloy panels of the outer wing box, and a so-called 'round rib', also of titanium alloy, transmitting the normal aerodynamic force. Sweep actuators are of the ballscrew type, with hydraulic motor drive. In the event of wing sweep failure, the aircraft can land safely with the wings fully swept. High-lift devices on the outer wings include full span leading-edge slats (three sections on each side), full span double-slotted fixed-vane trailing-edge flaps (four sections each side), and spoilers (two on upper surface on each side). Spoilers give augmented roll control at unswept and intermediate wing positions at low speed, and also act as lift dumpers after touchdown. All flying control surfaces actuated by electrically controlled tandem hydraulic jacks. No ailerons. Entire outer wings, including control surfaces, are Italian built, Aeritalia having prime responsibility for final assembly and production, assisted by Aermacchi, Aeronavali Venezia, Piaggio, Saca and SIAI-Marchetti as subcontractors. Microtecnica (Italy) is prime subcontractor for the wing sweep system.

FUSELAGE: Conventional all-metal semi-monocoque structure, mainly of aluminium alloy, built in three main sections. MBB is prime contractor for the centre fuselage section, including the engine air intake ducts and wing centre-section box and pivot mechanism. This task includes responsibility for the surface interface between the movable wing and the fixed portion, to ensure both a smooth and slender external contour and proper sealing against aerodynamic pressure over a range of wing sweep positions. The design uses fibre reinforced plastics in these areas, and an elastic seal between the outer wings and the fuselage sides. Responsibility for the front fuselage, including both cockpits, and for the rear fuselage, including the engine installation, is undertaken by BAe (Warton). Radar-transparent nosecone by AEG-Telefunken, assisted by Aeritalia and BAe, hinges sideways to starboard to provide access to ground mapping and terrain following radar antennae. Slice of fuselage immediately aft of nosecone also hinges sideways to starboard, to provide access to forward avionics bay and/or rear of radar. Door type airbrake on each side at top of rear fuselage.

TAIL UNIT: Cantilever all-metal structure, consisting of single sweptback two-spar fin and rudder, and low-set all-moving horizontal surfaces ('tailerons') which operate together for pitch control and differentially for roll control, assisted by use of the wing spoilers when the wings are not fully swept. Rudder and tailerons actuated by electrically controlled tandem hydraulic jacks. Passive ECM antenna fairing near top of fin. Ram air intake for heat exchanger at base of fin. Entire tail unit is the responsibility of BAe. Four tailerons of carbonfibre composite, 17 per cent lighter than the standard metal ones, have been developed by MBB and BAe. Two were for structural and fatigue testing; the other pair began flight testing on prototype P07 on 8 November 1982.

LANDING GEAR: Hydraulically retractable tricycle type, with forward retracting twin-wheel steerable nose unit. Single-wheel main units retract forward and upward into centre section of fuselage. Emergency extension system, using nitrogen gas pressure. Development and manufacture of the complete landing gear and associated hydraulics is headed by Dowty Rotol (UK). Dunlop aluminium alloy wheels, hydraulic multi-disc brakes and low-pressure tyres (to permit operation from soft, semi-prepared surfaces) and Goodyear anti-skid units. Main-wheel tyres size 30 × 11·50-14·5, Type VIII (24 or 26 ply); nosewheel tyres size 18 × 5·5, Type VIII (12 ply). Runway arrester hook beneath rear of fuselage.

POWER PLANT: Two Turbo-Union RB199-34R Mk 101 turbofan engines in initial production aircraft, each rated at more than 40·0 kN (9,000 lb st) dry and more than 71·2 kN (16,000 lb st) with afterburning, fitted with bucket type thrust reversers and installed in rear fuselage with downward opening doors for servicing and engine change. Mk 103 engines, offering approx 5 per cent more thrust, introduced on to production line from engine number 761 in May 1983; 100 modification kits ordered by RAF in 1983 to upgrade its Mk 101 engined aircraft to Mk 103 standard. All integral fuel in multi-cell Uniroyal self-sealing integral fuselage tanks and/or wing box tanks, all fitted with press-in fuel sampling and water drain plugs, and all refuelled from a single-point NATO connector. Detachable and retractable in-flight refuelling probe can be mounted on starboard side of fuselage, adjacent to cockpit. System also designed to accept a buddy-to-buddy refuelling pack. Provision for drop tanks to be carried beneath fuselage (1,500 litres; 330 Imp gallons) and on inboard underwing pylons (1,500 or 2,250 litres; 330 or 495 Imp gallons). Dowty Fuel Systems/Lucas/Microtecnica afterburning fuel control system. AEG-Telefunken intake de-icing system.

ACCOMMODATION: Crew of two on tandem Martin-Baker Mk 10A zero/zero ejection seats under Kopperschmidt/

Two Panavia Tornado IDS aircraft of the Royal Saudi Air Force

AIT one-piece canopy, which is hinged at rear and opens upward. Flat centre armoured windscreen panel and curved side panels, built by Lucas Aerospace, incorporate Sierracote electrically conductive heating film for windscreen anti-icing and demisting. Canopy (and windscreen in emergency) demisted by engine bleed air. Windscreen is hinged at front and can be opened forward and upward, allowing access to back of pilot's instrument panel. Seats provide safe escape at zero altitude and at speeds from zero up to 630 knots (1,166 km/h; 725 mph) IAS.

SYSTEMS: Cockpit air-conditioned and pressurised (max differential 0·36 bars; 5·25 lb/sq in) by Normalair-Garrett conventional air cycle system (with bootstrap cold air unit) using engine bleed air with ram air precooler, Marston intercooler, and Teddington temperature control system. Nordmicro/BAe/Microtecnica air intake control system, and Dowty Boulton Paul/Liebherr Aerotechnik engine intake ramp control actuators. Two independent hydraulic systems, each of 276 bars (4,000 lb/sq in pressure), are supplied from two separate, independently driven Vickers pumps, each mounted on an engine accessory gearbox. Each system is supplied from a separate bootstrap type reservoir. Systems provide fully duplicated power for primary flight control system, tailerons, rudder, flaps, slats, wing sweep, pitch Q-feel system, and refuelling probe. Left system also supplies power for Krueger flaps, inboard spoilers, port air intake ramps, canopy, and wheel brakes; right system for airbrakes, outboard spoilers, starboard air intake ramps, landing gear, nosewheel steering, and radar stabilisation and scanning. Main system includes Dowty accumulators and Teves power pack. Fairey Hydraulics system for actuation of spoilers, rudder and taileron control. Provision for reversion to single-engine drive of both systems, via a mechanical cross-connection between the two engine auxiliary gearboxes, in the event of a single engine failure. In the event of a double engine flameout, an emergency pump in No. 1 system has sufficient duration for re-entry into the engine cold relight boundary. Flying control circuits are protected from loss of fluid due to leaks in other circuits by isolating valves which shut off the utility circuits if the reservoir contents drop below a predetermined safety limit level. Electrical system consists of a 115/200V AC three-phase 400Hz constant-frequency subsystem and a 28V DC subsystem. Power is generated by two automatically controlled oil-cooled brushless AC generators integrated with a constant speed drive unit and driven by the engines via an accessory gearbox. Normally, each engine drives its own accessory gearbox, but provision is also made for either engine to drive the opposite gearbox through a cross-drive system. In the event of a generator failure, the remaining unit can supply the total aircraft load. Both gearboxes and generators can be driven by APU when aircraft is on ground. The generators supply two main AC busbars and an AC essential busbar. DC power is provided from two fan-cooled TRUs (power being derived from the main AC system), these feeding power to two main DC busbars, one essential DC busbar and a battery busbar. Either TRU can supply total aircraft DC load. A fifth DC busbar is provided for maintenance purposes only. Battery is a rechargeable nickel-cadmium type, and provides power for basic flightline servicing and for starting APU. In the event of main electrical system or double TRU failure, it is connected automatically to the essential services busbar to supply essential electrical loads. Normalair-Garrett/Draegerwerk/OMI demand type oxygen system, using a 10 litre (2·2 Imp gallon) lox converter. Emergency oxygen system installed on each seat. KHD accessory drive gearboxes and Rotax/Lucas/Siemens integrated drive generator. GEC Avionics flow metering system. Eichweber fuel gauging system and Flight Refuelling flexible couplings. Graviner fire detection and extinguishing systems. Rotax contactors. Smiths engine speed and temperature indicators.

AVIONICS AND EQUIPMENT: Communications equipment includes Plessey PTR 1721 (UK and Italy) or Rohde und Schwarz (West Germany) UHF/VHF transceiver; AEG-Telefunken UHF/ADF (UK and West Germany only); SIT/Siemens emergency UHF with Rohde und Schwarz switch; BAe HF/SSB aerial tuning unit; Rohde und Schwarz (UK and West Germany) or Montedel (Italy) HF/SSB radio; Ultra communications control system; GEC Avionics central suppression unit (CSU); Epsylon voice recorder; Chelton UHF communications and landing system aerials.

Primary self-contained nav/attack system includes Texas Instruments multi-mode forward looking ground mapping radar; Ferranti FIN 1010 three-axis digital inertial navigation system (DINS) and combined radar display; Decca Type 72 Doppler radar system, with Kalman filtering of the Doppler and inertial inputs for extreme navigational accuracy; Microtecnica air data computer; Litef Spirit 3 64K central digital computer; Aeritalia radio/radar altimeter; Smiths/Teldix/OMI electronic head-up display with Davall camera; Ferranti nose mounted laser rangefinder and marked target seeker; GEC Avionics TV tabular display, produced in partnership with AEG and Selenia; Astronautics (USA) bearing distance heading indicator and contour map display. Defensive equipment includes Siemens (West Germany) or Cossor SSR-3100 (UK) IFF transponder; Elettronica passive warning radar.

Flight control system includes a GEC Avionics/Bodenseewerk triplex command stability augmentation system (CSAS), incorporating fly by wire and autostabilisation; GEC Avionics/Aeritalia autopilot and flight director (APFD), using two self-monitoring digital computers; GEC Avionics triplex transducer unit (TTU), with analog computing and sensor channels; GEC Avionics terrain following E-scope (TFE), produced in partnership with Selenia; Fairey/GEC Avionics quadruplex electro-hydraulic actuator; and Microtecnica air data set. The APFD provides preselected attitude, heading or barometric height hold, heading and track acquisition, and Mach number or airspeed hold with autothrottle. Flight director operates in parallel with, and can be used as backup for, the autopilot, as a duplex digital system with an extensive range of modes. Automatic approach, terrain following and radio height-holding modes are also available. Other instrumentation includes Smiths horizontal situation indicator, vertical speed indicator and standby altimeter; Lital standby attitude and heading reference system; SEL (with Setac) or (in UK aircraft) GEC Avionics AD2770 (without Setac) Tacan; Cossor CILS 75 ILS; Bodenseewerk attitude director indicator; Dornier System flight data recorder.

Overall responsibility for the avionics rests with Panavia, with EASAMS (UK) as the avionics prime contractor, and ESG (Germany) and SIA (Italy) as subcontractors. The avionics systems, while standardised as far as possible, retain the flexibility necessary to perform the various roles required. They provide accurate low- and high-level navigation; precision visual attack on ground targets in blind and poor weather conditions; air-to-ground and air-to-air attack with a wide variety of weapons; manually controlled and automatic attack; and comprehensive onboard checkout and mission data recording; with minimisation of ground support facilities at bases and the front line.

ARMAMENT: Fixed armament comprises two 27 mm IWKA-Mauser cannon, one in each side of the lower forward fuselage, with 180 rds/gun. Other armament varies according to version, with emphasis on the ability to carry a wide range of advanced non-nuclear weapons on three underfuselage attachments and up to four swivelling hardpoints beneath the outer wings. A GEC Avionics/Selenia stores management system is fitted; Sandall Mace 355 and 762 mm (14 and 30 in) ejector release units, and ML Aviation CBLS 200 practice bomb carriers, are standard. The battlefield interdiction version is capable of carrying weapons for 'hard' or 'soft' targets. Naval and interdictor strike versions have provision for carrying additional, externally mounted fuel tanks. For German Navy and Italian Air Force Tornados, MBB has developed (first flight 14 April 1981) a multi-sensor reconnaissance pod to be carried on the centreline pylon. Some RAF Tornados will be fitted with infra-red cameras in ammunition bay. Among the weapons already specified for, or suitable for carriage by, the IDS Tornado are the Sidewinder air-to-air, and ALARM or HARM anti-radiation missiles; JP 233 low-altitude airfield attack munition dispenser, Paveway laser guided bomb, AS.30, Maverick, GBU-15, Sea Eagle and Kormoran air-to-surface missiles; napalm; BL755 Mks 1 and 2 600 lb cluster bombs; MW-1 munitions dispenser; Mk 83 or other 1,000 lb bombs; 'smart' or retarded bombs; BLU-1B 750 lb fire bombs; Matra 250 kg ballistic and retarded bombs; Lepus flare bombs; LAU-51A and LR-25 rocket launchers; Marconi Skyshadow (jamming/deception) and BOZ 107 (chaff/flare) ECM pods; Pave Spike pods; data link pods; and chaff/flare dispensers. External fuel tanks (see 'Power Plant' paragraph) can also be carried.

Panavia Tornado IDS multi-role combat aircraft *(Pilot Press)*

Trials installation of sensors for the RAF's Tornado reconnaissance system: windows for side-looking IR in sides of fuselage, and linescan aperture beneath

DIMENSIONS, EXTERNAL:

Wing span: fully spread	13·91 m (45 ft 7½ in)
fully swept	8·60 m (28 ft 2½ in)
Length overall	16·72 m (54 ft 10¼ in)
Height overall	5·95 m (19 ft 6¼ in)
Tailplane span	6·80 m (22 ft 3½ in)
Wheel track	3·10 m (10 ft 2 in)
Wheelbase	6·20 m (20 ft 4 in)

WEIGHTS AND LOADING:

Weight empty, equipped	14,091 kg (31,065 lb)
Max external fuel	5,806 kg (12,800 lb)
Nominal max weapon load	approx 9,000 kg (19,840 lb)
Max T-O weight:	
'clean', full internal fuel	20,411 kg (45,000 lb)
with external stores	approx 27,215 kg (60,000 lb)

PERFORMANCE:

Max Mach number in level flight at altitude, 'clean'	2·2
Max level speed, 'clean'	above 800 knots (1,480 km/h; 920 mph) IAS
Max level speed with external stores	Mach 0·92 (600 knots; 1,112 km/h; 691 mph)
Landing speed approx	115 knots (213 km/h; 132 mph)
Time to 9,145 m (30,000 ft) from brake release	less than 2 min
Automatic terrain following	down to 61 m (200 ft)
Required runway length	less than 900 m (2,950 ft)
Landing run	370 m (1,215 ft)
Max 360° rapid roll clearance with full lateral control	4g
Radius of action with heavy weapons load, hi-lo-lo-hi	750 nm (1,390 km; 863 miles)
Ferry range	approx 2,100 nm (3,890 km; 2,420 miles)
g limit	+7·5

TORNADO MID-LIFE IMPROVEMENT PROGRAMME

In order to retain effective mission capability and survivability in the face of the increased threat in the 1990s, a mid-life improvement programme is currently being developed by the Tornado air arms and industry. It will confer more accurate navigation for 'blind' attacks, improved sortie generation capability, increased range for better target coverage, increased target acquisition capability, reduced penetration altitude, covert operation, improved electronic self-defence, improved threat suppression, and greater reliability and maintainability.

The first avionics upgrade modifications are already incorporated in the sixth Tornado production batch. They include a MIL-1553B databus, upgraded radar warning equipment and active ECM, an improved missile control unit, a 128K main computer, and integration of the Texas Instruments HARM anti-radar guided missile. A HARM-equipped Tornado began flight testing on 5 December 1985, following the first flight of ALARM on a Tornado, made on 13 February 1985.

PANAVIA TORNADO ECR

The Federal German Luftwaffe has selected an ECR (electronic combat and reconnaissance) version of the IDS Tornado to replace tactical reconnaissance aircraft already in operation and to complement or supersede such NATO airborne electronic warfare types as the F-4G Phantom.

Retaining its air-to-surface role, except for the removal of the two 27 mm guns, the ECR Tornado is intended for standoff reconnaissance and border control, reconnaissance via image-forming and electronic means, electronic support, and employment of anti-radar guided missiles. For this purpose, it is to be equipped with a direction-finding system for ground-based radar installations (emitter locator); infra-red imaging system (IIS), onboard systems for processing, storing and transmitting reconnaissance data; and advanced tactical displays for the pilot and weapons officer. The external load stations on fuselage and wings may be used in ECR or fighter-bomber missions, or a combination of both.

The ECR version will normally be configured to carry two HARMs, two Sidewinders, an active ECM pod, chaff/flare dispenser pod, and two 1,500 litre (330 Imp gallon) underwing fuel tanks.

The seventh Tornado production contract, signed on 10 June 1986, included an order for 35 Tornado ECRs, deliveries of which are due to be made in 1989-90. Pre-production Tornado P16 is being equipped for initial ECR flight trials, which will begin at Manching in 1987.

MBB artist's impression of Luftwaffe Tornado in ECR configuration, with typical external stores load

First production Tornado F. Mk 3 air defence variant for the Royal Air Force

PANAVIA TORNADO ADV

RAF designation: Tornado F. Mks 2, 2A and 3

A possible air defence role for the Tornado was considered by the RAF when the interdictor/strike (IDS) programme was inaugurated in 1968, and low-key studies leading to an air defence variant (ADV) were initiated in the following year. These were given impetus in 1971, when the Ministry of Defence issued Air Staff Target (AST) 395 covering the development of an interceptor with a new advanced technology radar and XJ521 Sky Flash air-to-air missiles. Changes from the IDS Tornado were to be minimal, and costs kept as low as possible.

It soon became clear that a configuration using the existing RB199 engines and having the four Sky Flash missiles on underwing pylons would have too high a drag factor and would not meet the performance requirement. The solution adopted was therefore to semi-submerge the Sky Flash in tandem pairs under the fuselage, and to anticipate further performance benefits from ongoing development of the RB199 engine.

Full scale development of the Tornado ADV was authorised on 4 March 1976, and the RAF includes 165 of this long-range interceptor model, designated F. Mk 2 and F. Mk 3, in its total procurement of 394 Tornados, to re-equip two Lightning squadrons and seven squadrons of Phantoms. These have all been ordered, in batches comprising 3 (prototypes), 18, 52 and 92 aircraft.

Most of the ADV Tornados will be based in the United Kingdom (including two squadrons at Leuchars in Scotland, two plus an OCU at Coningsby, Lincolnshire, and three at Leeming, Yorkshire), for air defence of the UK and to protect the northern and western approaches of NATO. Equipped with a tactical display that can cover the entire North Sea, they will also fulfil the RAF's commitments to provide long-range air defence of Britain's maritime forces, over a wide UK defence region extending from the Atlantic approaches to the Baltic and from Iceland to the English Channel; and to contribute towards air defence in the Central Region of Europe. The F. Mk 2/3 can loiter on patrol for several hours, using in-flight refuelling when necessary, and can detect, identify and destroy enemy aircraft approaching at supersonic speeds at high, medium or low altitudes, using its snap-up/snap-down missiles. Its fire control system is able to engage multiple targets in rapid succession; its weapons systems are highly resistant to enemy ECM; and it can operate from damaged airfields by virtue of its good short-field performance. Supersonic acceleration is better than that of the IDS version. A genuine long-range autonomous capability enables it to operate more than 350 nm (645 km; 400 miles) from its base at night, in bad weather, in heavy ECM conditions, against multiple targets at low level.

Two main airframe modifications distinguish the ADV from the IDS version. The principal one is an increase in fuselage length forward of the front cockpit, to accommodate the longer radome of the GEC Avionics AI-24 Foxhunter radar, and a small 'stretch' aft of the rear cockpit to allow the four Sky Flash missiles to be carried in two tandem pairs. The other is that the fixed inboard portions of the wings are extended forward at the leading-edges (sweep angle 67° instead of 60°), to give increased chord and compensate for the shift in the CG. These changes also benefit performance by reducing drag, especially at supersonic speed, compared with the IDS version. Extension of the fuselage provides additional space for avionics and for an additional 10 per cent of internal fuel (909 litres; 200 Imp gallons).

Other changes include deletion of one of the two IWKA-Mauser 27 mm cannon; installation of RB199 Mk 103 engines in the first 18 production aircraft **(F. Mk 2)** and, thereafter **(F. Mk 3)**, Mk 104 engines with extended nozzles, increased reheat combat thrust, and a Lucas DECU 500 digital engine control unit; fitting of a ram air turbine, radar-dedicated cold air unit, and an internally mounted retractable in-flight refuelling probe; addition of a head-down display for the pilot, and replacement of the navigator's wet-film head-down display recorder with a displayed data video recorder; fitment of a second Ferranti 1010 INS platform; integration with the radar of a new Cossor IFF interrogator; incorporation (when its development is completed) of a Singer-Kearfott data link system; and introduction of new cockpit displays and redesign of symbology, together with an increase in computer storage capacity. The F. Mk 3 also introduced automatic wing sweep (AWS) and automatic manoeuvre device system (AMDS).

The F. 2s are scheduled to be returned to BAe and largely upgraded to F. 3 standard except for the Mk 104 engines, which could not be retrofitted without structural alterations to the rear fuselage. After upgrading, these F. 2s will be redesignated **F. Mk 2A**.

Although possessing some 80 per cent commonality with the IDS version, the Tornado ADV was sufficiently different for the initial production contract to include funding for three prototypes of the fighter version. These were identified by the manufacturer as the A01 to A03, making their first flights on 27 October 1979, 18 July 1980 and 18 November 1980. Their roles were discussed in some detail in the 1984-85 *Jane's*. Flight development has included successful guided firings of the Sky Flash and Sidewinder air-to-air missiles, and completion and service clearance of the rapid rolling programme. By February 1986 a total of 2,750 flying hours had been completed, 1,460 by British Aerospace and 1,290 by the RAF; the latter figure had passed 3,000 by August 1986.

The first two production F. Mk 2s (RAF serial numbers ZD899/900), are conversion trainers, and were rolled out on 28 March 1984. First flights were made on 12 April and 5 March 1984 respectively. They were delivered to the Aeroplane and Armament Experimental Establishment at Boscombe Down in the Summer of 1984, and were followed on 5 November by the first two aircraft (AT003 and 005) for No. 229 Operational Conversion Unit at RAF Coningsby, Lincolnshire, to which that unit's full complement of 16 aircraft had been delivered by October 1985. Deliveries of the F. Mk 2 were completed by December 1985, and in February 1986 deliveries began of the F. Mk 3, which flew for the first time (ZE154) on 20 November 1985.

The first export order for the ADV Tornado, for eight aircraft for the Sultan of Oman's Air Force, was announced on 14 August 1985. Six weeks later, on 26 September, an order for 24 was announced by the Saudi Arabian government. These aircraft are included in the seventh Tornado production contract which was signed on 10 June 1986.

TYPE: Twin-engined all-weather air defence interceptor.

WINGS: Similar to IDS version except that fixed inboard portions also have a leading-edge sweep of 67° and the Krueger leading-edge flaps are deleted. F. Mk 3 fitted with automatic wing sweep (AWS) and automatic manoeuvre device system (AMDS). With AWS, four different wing sweeps can be scheduled (25° at speeds up to Mach 0·73, 45° from there up to Mach 0·88, 58° up to Mach 0·95, and 67° above Mach 0·95), enabling specific excess power at transonic speeds and turning capability at subsonic speeds to be maximised. Buffet-free handling can be maintained, to the limits defined by the SPILS, by use of the AMDS, which schedules with wing incidence to deploy either flaps and slats at 25° sweep angle or slats only at 45° sweep. Beyond 45°, both flaps and slats are scheduled 'in'.

FUSELAGE: Generally as for IDS version, but lengthened forward of front cockpit and aft of rear cockpit. Nose-cone hinged in two places, providing access to front and rear of Foxhunter radar.

TAIL UNIT: As IDS version. On F. Mk 3, with extended afterburner nozzles, base of rudder is recontoured to clear the repositioned thrust reversers, and tailerons to clear the revised rear fuselage outline.

LANDING GEAR: As IDS version. Nosewheel steering augmentation system to minimise 'wander' on landing.

POWER PLANT: Two Turbo-Union RB199-34R Mk 103 afterburning turbofan engines in F. Mk 2/2A; F. Mk 3 has Mk 104 engines with 360 mm (14 in) extension to afterburner nozzles to increase reheat thrust. Compared with Mk 101 engine in early production IDS Tornados, the Mk 103 increases both dry and reheat thrust by 5 to 10 per cent; reheat combat thrust of the Mk 104 engine is increased by 7 per cent compared with that of the Mk 103. Max internal fuel capacity increased by 10 per cent compared with IDS version. Internally mounted, fully retractable in-flight refuelling probe in port side of nose, adjacent to cockpit. Provision for drop tanks of 1,500 or 2,250 litres (330 or 495 Imp gallons) capacity, as on IDS version.

ACCOMMODATION: As for IDS version.

SYSTEMS: Generally as described for IDS version, with the addition of a radar-dedicated cold air unit to cool the Foxhunter radar, and a pop-up ram air turbine to assist recovery in the event of engine flameout at high altitude in a zoom climb.

AVIONICS AND EQUIPMENT: Among those in the IDS Tornado which are retained in the ADV are the communications equipment (Plessey VHF/UHF transceiver, SIT/Siemens emergency UHF, Rohde und Schwarz HF/SSB, Ultra communications control system and Epsylon cockpit voice recorder); GEC Avionics triplex fly by wire command stability augmentation system and autopilot/flight director system (modified for increased roll rate and reduced pitch stick forces); Litef Spirit 3 central digital computer (with capacity increased from 64K to 128K) and data transmission system; Smiths electronic head-up and navigator's head-down display; Ferranti FIN 1010 inertial navigation system (to which is added a second 1010 to monitor the head-up display); GEC Avionics Tacan; Cossor ILS; and Cossor IFF transponder. Those deleted include the Texas Instruments nose radar, Decca 72 Doppler radar with terrain following, Ferranti laser rangefinder and marked target seeker, and Lital standby attitude and heading reference system.

The ADV's primary airborne interception system is based on a nose-mounted GEC Avionics AI-24 Foxhunter multi-mode track-while-scan pulse-Doppler radar with FMICW (frequency modulated interrupted continuous wave), with which is integrated a new Cossor IFF-3500 interrogator and a radar signal processor to suppress ground clutter. This system enables the aircraft to detect targets more than 100 nm (185 km; 115 miles) away, and to track several targets simultaneously. A ground mapping mode for navigation backup is also available. Ferranti is subcontractor for the Foxhunter transmitter and aerial scanning mechanism. A pilot's head-down display is added, a Ferranti displayed data video recorder (DDVR) replaces the navigator's wet-film display recorder, and an MSDS Hermes modular radar homing and warning receiver (RHWR) is added. Head-up/head-down displays are on front instrument panel only, radar control and data link presentations on rear panel only; both panels have weapon control and RHWR displays. A Ferranti FH 31A AC driven 3 in horizon gyro in the rear cockpit, in addition to providing an attitude display for the navigator, feeds pitch and roll signals to other avionics systems in the aircraft in certain modes. Analog electronic engine control unit on F. Mk 2 replaced by Lucas digital unit (DECU 500) on F. Mk 3. ESM (electronic surveillance measures) and ECCM are standard; a Singer-Kearfott ECM-resistant data link system, interoperable with other NATO systems, is under development for installation later. Because of its comprehensive avionics the Tornado ADV can contribute significantly to the transfer of vital information over the entire tactical area and can, if necessary, partially fulfil the roles of both AEW and ground based radar.

ARMAMENT AND OPERATIONAL EQUIPMENT: Fixed armament of one 27 mm IWKA-Mauser cannon in starboard side of lower forward fuselage. Four BAe Sky Flash semi-active radar homing medium-range air-to-air missiles are semi-recessed under the centre-fuselage, carried on internally mounted Frazer-Nash launchers; one or two European built NWC AIM-9L Sidewinder infra-red homing short-range air-to-air missiles on each of the inboard underwing stations. All four underwing stations are 'wet' for the carriage of auxiliary fuel tanks. Smiths Industries/Computing Devices Company missile management system (MMS), which also controls tank jettison, has provision for pilot override, optimised for visual attack. The Sky Flash missiles, each fitted with an MSDS monopulse seeker head, can engage targets at high altitude or down to 75 m (250 ft), in the face of heavy ECM, and at standoff ranges of more than 25 nm (46 km; 29 miles). Release system, designed specially for Sky Flash, permits the missile to be fired over the Tornado's full flight envelope. Furthermore, the missile is highly capable of tracking targets in a ground clutter environment, and of discriminating between closely spaced targets. A Thorn EMI active proximity fusing system allows these benefits to be realised fully in snap-down attacks against targets flying at very low level. For the future, the ADV will be able to carry, instead of Sky Flash and Sidewinder, up to six Hughes AIM-20 AMRAAM medium-range and four BAe/Bodenseewerk ASRAAM short-range air-to-air missiles; studies being undertaken for a 1553B multiplex digital data bus associated with these weapons.

DIMENSIONS, EXTERNAL: As for IDS version, except:
- Length overall 18·082 m (59 ft 3⅓ in)

WEIGHTS (approx):
- Operational weight empty 14,500 kg (31,970 lb)
- Max external fuel 5,806 kg (12,800 lb)
- Nominal max weapon load 8,500 kg (18,740 lb)
- Max T-O weight 27,986 kg (61,700 lb)

PERFORMANCE:
- Max Mach number in level flight at altitude, 'clean' 2·2
- Max level speed, 'clean' 800 knots (1,480 km/h; 920 mph) IAS
- Rotation speed, depending on AUW 145-160 knots (269-297 km/h; 167-184 mph)
- Normal touchdown speed 115 knots (213 km/h; 132 mph)
- Demonstrated roll rate at 750 knots (1,390 km/h; 864 mph) and up to 4*g* 180°/s
- Operational ceiling approx 21,335 m (70,000 ft)
- T-O run:
  - with normal weapon and fuel load 760 m (2,500 ft)
  - ferry configuration (four 1,500 litre drop tanks and full weapon load) approx 1,525 m (5,000 ft)
- T-O to 15 m (50 ft) under 915 m (3,000 ft)
- Landing from 15 m (50 ft) approx 610 m (2,000 ft)
- Landing run with thrust reversal 370 m (1,215 ft)
- Intercept radius:
  - supersonic more than 300 nm (556 km; 345 miles)
  - subsonic more than 1,000 nm (1,853 km; 1,151 miles)
- *Endurance
  - 2 h combat air patrol at 300-400 nm (555-740 km; 345-460 miles) from base, incl time for interception and 10 min combat
- *g* limit attained (to Spring 1985) 7·5

* *Prototype, using 1,500 litre drop tanks and having more than 5% of internal fuel left at end of mission, has demonstrated a CAP of 2 h 20 min at 325 nm (602 km; 374 miles) from base, in a total flight time of 4 h 13 min without in-flight refuelling*

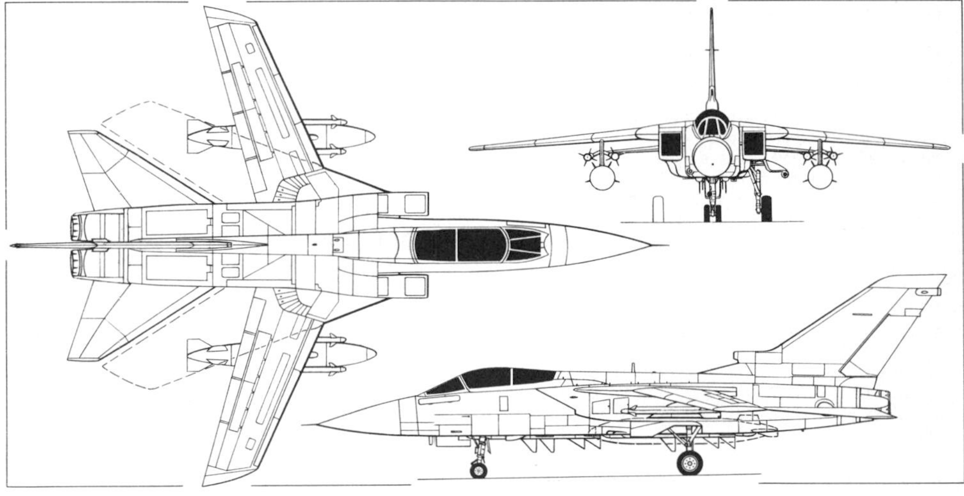

Panavia Tornado F. Mk 3, with lengthened afterburner nozzles *(Pilot Press)*

SAAB-FAIRCHILD — *see Saab-Scania in Swedish section*

SEPECAT

SOCIÉTÉ EUROPÉENNE DE PRODUCTION DE L'AVION E.C.A.T.

AIRFRAME COMPANIES:

British Aerospace PLC, Richmond Road, Kingston upon Thames, Surrey KT2 5QS, England
Telephone: 01 546 7741

Avions Marcel Dassault-Breguet Aviation, BP 32, 92420 Vaucresson, France
Telephone: 741 79 21

DIRECTORS:
I. R. Yates (President)
P. E. Jaillard (Vice-President)
J. Bonnet
C. Edelstenne
M. Berjon
R. H. Evans
J. Glover

PUBLIC RELATIONS:
G. B. Hill (BAe)

This Anglo-French company was formed in May 1966 by Breguet Aviation and British Aircraft Corporation, to design and produce the Jaguar supersonic strike fighter/trainer. The Jaguar project was initiated by the Defence Ministries of Britain and France on 17 May 1965. The two governments appointed an official Jaguar Management Committee to look after their interests. SEPECAT is the complementary industrial organisation.

SEPECAT JAGUAR INTERNATIONAL

All 402 Jaguars from the original orders for the Royal Air Force (202) and Armée de l'Air (200) had been delivered by the end of 1981, as described in the 1982-83 and earlier editions of *Jane's*; one additional two-seat Jaguar B for the RAF was delivered in late 1982. These aircraft were delivered with 22·75/32·5 kN (5,115/7,305 lb st) Adour Mk 102 turbofan engines. Between 1978 and 1984, RAF Jaguars were refitted with uprated Adour Mk 104 engines, equivalent to the Mk 804 which powered early Jaguar Internationals.

Jaguar International is the export version, the first example of which (G27-266) made its initial flight on 19 August 1976. It has Adour Mk 804 or more powerful Mk 811 engines, which give improved combat performance with substantially enhanced manoeuvrability and acceleration in the low-level speed range. Other customer options include overwing pylons compatible with Matra R.550 Magic or similar dogfight missiles; a multi-purpose radar such as the Thomson-CSF Agave; up to four anti-shipping weapons such as Sea Eagle, Harpoon, Exocet and Kormoran on the underwing and underfuselage hardpoints; and night sensors such as low light level TV.

Orders were placed by the Sultan of Oman's Air Force (two batches of 12) and Ecuadorean Air Force (12), each order including two two-seaters. The first 12 aircraft for Oman and those for Ecuador were powered by Adour Mk 804 engines; the second SOAF batch have Mk 811 Adours. SOAF aircraft are fitted with a GEC Avionics 920ATC NAVWASS computer and carry AIM-9P Sidewinder air-to-air missiles on the outboard underwing pylons. In 1985 BAe Warton was carrying out a major servicing of the first 12 SOAF Jaguars, including fitment of a Ferranti FIN 1064 inertial navigation system. Second batch Omani Jaguars are also scheduled to receive this system.

An initial batch of 40 Jaguar Internationals with Adour Mk 804 engines was purchased from Britain by the Indian government; deliveries of these were completed in 1982. The 1979 agreement provides for a further 45 (with Mk 811 engines) to be assembled in India from European built components, leading eventually to full manufacture of 31 additional aircraft under licence by Hindustan Aeronautics Ltd, Bangalore. The first Jaguar assembled at Bangalore (JS136) made its initial flight on 31 March 1982. The Indian Air Force's first Jaguar squadron (No. 14) was operational by the Summer of 1980, and the second (No. 5) in August 1981. Jaguars assigned to anti-shipping duty will have nose mounted Agave radar and air-to-surface missiles.

The most recent customer for the Jaguar International was the Nigerian Air Force, which ordered 18 in 1983 (13 single-seat and five two-seaters). Deliveries were completed by June 1985. Total Jaguar sales amount to 573.

TYPE: Single-seat tactical support aircraft and two-seat operational or advanced trainer.

AIRFRAME: As described in 1985-86 and earlier *Jane's*.

POWER PLANT: Two Rolls-Royce Turboméca Adour Mk 804 turbofan engines, rated at 23·7 kN (5,320 lb st) dry and 35·75 kN (8,040 lb st) with afterburning, in aircraft for Ecuador, India (first 40) and Oman (first 12). Adour Mk 811, rated at 24·6 kN (5,520 lb st) dry and 37·4 kN (8,400 lb st) with afterburning, in remaining aircraft for India, second 12 for Oman and those for Nigeria. Fixed geometry air intake on each side of fuselage aft of cockpit. Fuel in six tanks, one in each wing and four in fuselage. Total internal fuel capacity 4,200 litres (924 Imp gallons). Armour protection for critical fuel system components. In basic tactical sortie the loss of fuel from one tank at halfway point would not prevent aircraft from regaining its base. Provision for carrying three auxiliary drop tanks, each of 1,200 litres (264 Imp gallons) capacity, on fuselage and inboard wing pylons. Provision for in-flight refuelling, with retractable probe forward of cockpit on starboard side.

ACCOMMODATION (trainer): Crew of two in tandem on Martin-Baker 9B Mk II zero/zero ejection seats. Individual rearward hinged canopies. Rear seat 38 cm (15 in) higher than front seat. Windscreen bulletproof against 7·5 mm rifle fire.

ACCOMMODATION (single-seater): Enclosed cockpit for pilot, with rearward hinged canopy and Martin-Baker E9B (Ecuador), O9B (Oman) or IN9B (India) ejection seat as in two-seaters. Bulletproof windscreen, as in two-seat version.

SYSTEMS: As detailed in 1985-86 *Jane's*.

AVIONICS AND OPERATIONAL EQUIPMENT: Differ according to individual customer requirements; details are generally still classified, but first 40 for India have a Smiths head-up display similar to that in RAF Jaguars. Indian assembled Jaguars will have a raster cursive head-up display, Sagem inertial navigation and weapon aiming system, and a Ferranti COMED 2045 combined map and electronic display.

ARMAMENT: Two 30 mm Aden or DEFA 553 cannon in lower fuselage aft of cockpit in single-seater; single Aden gun on port side in two-seater. One stores attachment on fuselage centreline and two under each wing. Centreline and inboard wing points can each carry up to 1,134 kg (2,500 lb) of weapons, outboard underwing points up to 567 kg (1,250 lb) each. Maximum external stores load, including overwing loads, 4,763 kg (10,500 lb). Typical alternative loads include one Martel AS.37 anti-radar missile and two 1,200 litre (264 Imp gallon) drop tanks; eight 1,000 lb bombs; various combinations of free-fall and retarded bombs, Hunting BL755 or Belouga cluster bombs, Matra R.550 Magic missiles and air-to-surface rockets, including the 68 mm SNEB rocket; a reconnaissance camera pack; or two drop tanks. Jaguar International can also carry two Matra Magic air-to-air missiles on overwing pylons; aircraft for Oman carry two AIM-9P Sidewinders on outboard underwing pylons.

Two-seat Jaguar International in the insignia of the Nigerian Air Force

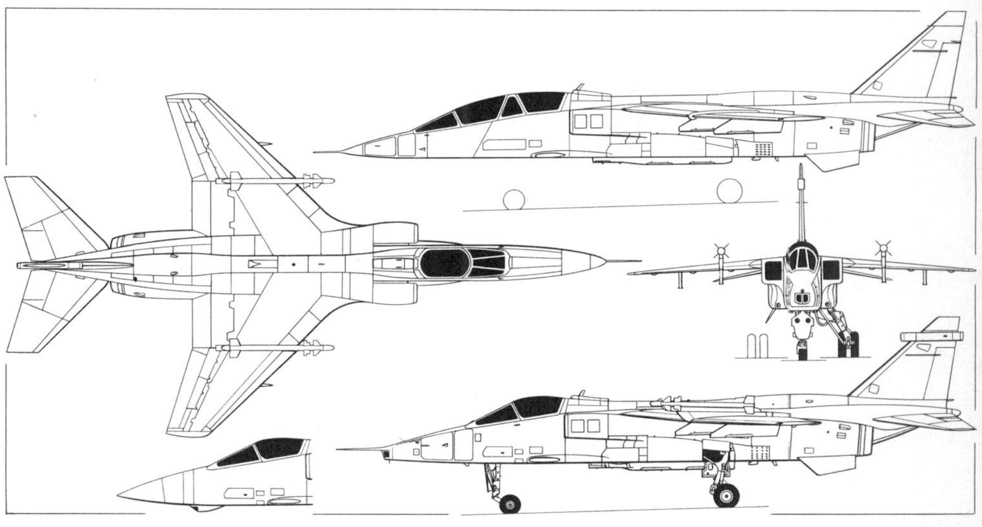
SEPECAT Jaguar International single-seat strike aircraft, with additional side view (top) of two-seat version and scrap view of version with Agave nose radar and Ferranti 105 laser *(Pilot Press)*

DIMENSIONS, EXTERNAL:
- Wing span: 8·69 m (28 ft 6 in)
- Length overall, incl probe:
  - single-seat: 16·83 m (55 ft 2½ in)
  - two-seat: 17·53 m (57 ft 6¼ in)
- Height overall: 4·89 m (16 ft 0½ in)
- Wheel track: 2·41 m (7 ft 11 in)
- Wheelbase: 5·69 m (18 ft 8 in)

AREA:
- Wings, gross: 24·18 m² (260·27 sq ft)

WEIGHTS AND LOADINGS:
- Typical weight empty: 7,000 kg (15,432 lb)
- Normal T-O weight (single-seater, with full internal fuel and ammunition for built-in cannon): 10,954 kg (24,149 lb)
- Max T-O weight with external stores: 15,700 kg (34,612 lb)
- Max wing loading: 649·3 kg/m² (133 lb/sq ft)
- Max power loading:
  - Adour Mk 804: 219·6 kg/kN (2·15 lb/lb st)
  - Adour Mk 811: 209·9 kg/kN (2·06 lb/lb st)

PERFORMANCE:
- Max level speed at S/L: Mach 1·1 (729 knots; 1,350 km/h; 840 mph)
- Max level speed at 11,000 m (36,000 ft): Mach 1·6 (917 knots; 1,699 km/h; 1,056 mph)
- Landing speed: 115 knots (213 km/h; 132 mph)
- T-O run: 'clean': 565 m (1,855 ft)
  - with four 1,000 lb bombs: 880 m (2,890 ft)
  - with eight 1,000 lb bombs: 1,250 m (4,100 ft)
- T-O to 15 m (50 ft) with typical tactical load: 940 m (3,085 ft)
- Landing from 15 m (50 ft) with typical tactical load: 785 m (2,575 ft)
- Landing run:
  - normal weight, with brake-chute: 470 m (1,540 ft)
  - normal weight, without brake-chute: 680 m (2,230 ft)
  - overload weight, with brake-chute: 670 m (2,200 ft)
- Typical attack radius, internal fuel only:
  - hi-lo-hi: 460 nm (852 km; 530 miles)
  - lo-lo-lo: 290 nm (537 km; 334 miles)
- Typical attack radius with external fuel:
  - hi-lo-hi: 760 nm (1,408 km; 875 miles)
  - lo-lo-lo: 495 nm (917 km; 570 miles)
- Ferry range with external fuel: 1,902 nm (3,524 km; 2,190 miles)
- *g* limits: +8·6/+12 ultimate

SOKO/CNIAR

PARTICIPANTS:

SOKO, Mostar, Yugoslavia

Centrul National al Industriei Aeronautice Române, 39 Bulevardul Aerogarii, Sector 1, Bucharest, Romania

SOKO J-22 ORAO (EAGLE)/CNIAR IAR-93

This twin-jet close support and ground attack aircraft is in production to meet a joint requirement of the air forces of Romania and Yugoslavia. In the latter country it is known as the J-22 Orao (Eagle); in Romania it is known as the IAR-93. The joint programme is known as 'Yurom' (from *Yu*goslavia-*Rom*ania).

The Orao/IAR-93 was designed jointly by Yugoslav engineers from the Vazduhoplovno Tehnicki Institut in Zarkovo, near Belgrade, and by Romanian engineers from the Institutul de Mecanica Fluidelor si Constructii Aerospatiale in Bucharest. Design began in 1970, and manufacture of a single-seat prototype was started simultaneously in the two countries in 1972. A first flight in each country was made on 31 October 1974. SOKO and CNIAR each then completed a two-seat prototype, these making simultaneous first flights on 29 January 1977. In that year construction began in each country of a pre-production batch of 15 aircraft, the first of these making their initial flights in 1978. The IAR-93 entered the series production phase in 1979, and the Orao about a year later.

The following production versions have been announced:

IAR-93A. Romanian version with non-afterburning Rolls-Royce Viper Mk 632 turbojet engines, first flown in 1981. Twenty ordered for Romanian Air Force, of which eight completed by Spring 1982 (no later figure received). Total includes single- and two-seat versions, the latter having almost the same operational capabilities despite a 0·41 m (1 ft 4¼ in) longer front fuselage.

IAR-93B. Romanian version with Viper Mk 633 engines and licence built afterburners. Total of 165 said to be ordered by Romanian Air Force, including two-seaters. First flight of production version made in 1985.

Orao 1. Yugoslav non-afterburning equivalent of IAR-93A, produced both as single-seat tactical reconnaissance aircraft and two-seat operational conversion trainer.

Orao 2. Yugoslav afterburning version, in production as single-seat attack aircraft. First flight (aircraft serial number 25101) 20 October 1983. Increased external stores load. Fuel system and capacities differ slightly from other versions.

TYPE: Single-seat close support, ground attack and tactical reconnaissance aircraft, with secondary capability as low level interceptor. Combat capable two-seat versions used also for advanced flying and weapon training.

WINGS: Cantilever shoulder-wing monoplane, of NACA 65A-008 (modified) section and low aspect ratio. Anhedral 3° 30′ from roots. Incidence 0°. Sweepback 35° at quarter-chord and approx 43° on outer leading-edges. Inboard leading-edges extended forward (sweepback approx 70°) on production single- and two-seaters, but not on prototypes or pre-production aircraft. Two-spar structure of aluminium alloy, with ribs, stringers and partially machined skin. Wing spar box forms integral fuel tanks on IAR-93B/Orao 2; IAR-93A/Orao 1 have rubber fuel cells, forward of which are sandwich panels. Hydraulically actuated (EEMCO system) two-segment aluminium alloy leading-edge slats. Two small boundary layer fences on upper surface of each wing. Hydraulically operated wide chord plain ailerons and semi-Fowler trailing-edge flaps, all of aluminium alloy; ailerons have Dowty servo-actuators. No tabs.

FUSELAGE: Conventional all-metal, partially fail-safe semi-monocoque structure of aluminium alloy. Hydraulically actuated door type perforated airbrake under fuselage on each side, forward of mainwheel bays. Narrow strake on each side of nose (not on prototypes). Dorsal spine fairing houses circuits, systems and flight controls. 'Pen nib' fairing above exhaust nozzles. Rear portion of fuselage is detachable to facilitate access for engine maintenance and removal.

TAIL UNIT: Cantilever all-metal structure, with sweepback on all surfaces. Low-set all-moving tailplane. Small dorsal fin. Auxiliary ventral fin on each side beneath rear fuselage (single-seat production versions). Conventional stressed skin construction, of aluminium alloy on development aircraft and early production versions; current aircraft have honeycomb rudder and tailplane. Development and early production aircraft have anti-flutter weights on tailplane tips; these were intended to be deleted on definitive production models. Tailplane and rudder controlled by Dowty servo-actuators. Trim tab in rudder on prototypes, deleted on pre-production and production models.

Landing Gear: Hydraulically retractable tricycle type of Messier-Hispano-Bugatti design, with single-wheel hydraulically steerable nose unit and twin-wheel main units. All units retract forward into fuselage. Two-stage oleo-pneumatic shock absorber in each unit. Mainwheels and tubeless tyres on all versions are size 615 × 225 × 254 mm, pressure 5·2 bars (75·4 lb/sq in). Nosewheel and tubeless tyre are size 551 × 250 × 152·4 mm, pressure 3·1 bars (45·0 lb/sq in), on IAR-93A/Orao 1; and size 451 × 190 × 127 mm, pressure 3·8 bars (55·1 lb/sq in), on afterburning versions. Hydraulic disc brakes on each mainwheel unit, and electrically operated anti-skid system. Bullet fairing at base of rudder contains a hydraulically deployed 4·2 m (13 ft 9½ in) diameter braking parachute.

Power Plant (non-afterburning versions): Two 17·79 kN (4,000 lb st) Turbomecanica/ORAO (licence built Rolls-Royce) Viper Mk 632-41R turbojets, mounted side by side in rear fuselage; air intake on each side of fuselage, below cockpit canopy. Fuel normally in seven fuselage tanks and two collector tanks, with combined capacity of 2,480 litres (545·5 Imp gallons) and two 235 litre (51·75 Imp gallon) wing tanks, giving total internal fuel capacity of 2,950 litres (649 Imp gallons). Orao 2 has six fuselage and two collector tanks, with two fuselage and both wing tanks enlarged, giving total internal capacity of 3,100 litres (682 Imp gallons). Provision for carrying three 540 litre (119 Imp gallon) auxiliary fuel tanks, one on underfuselage stores attachment and one inboard under each wing. Pressure refuelling point in fuselage; gravity refuelling points in fuselage and each external tank.

Power Plant (afterburning versions): Two Turbomecanica/ORAO (licence built Rolls-Royce) Viper Mk 633-41 turbojets, each rated at 17·79 kN (4,000 lb st) dry and 22·24 kN (5,000 lb st) with afterburning.

Accommodation: Single-seat or tandem two-seat cockpit(s), with Martin-Baker zero/zero seat for each occupant (RU10J in IAR-93, YU10J in Orao), capable of ejection through canopy. Canopy of single-seat IAR-93A and Orao 1/2 is hinged at rear and actuated electrically to open upward; single-seat IAR-93B, and all two-seaters, have manually opened canopies opening sideways to starboard. All accommodation pressurised, heated and air-conditioned. Dual controls in two-seat versions.

Systems: Bootstrap type environmental control system for cockpit pressurisation (max differential 0·214 bars; 3·1 lb/sq in), air-conditioning, and windscreen de-icing/demisting. Two independent hydraulic systems, each of 207 bars (3,000 lb/sq in) pressure, for actuation of leading-edge slats, trailing-edge flaps, ailerons, tailplane, rudder, airbrakes, landing gear extension/retraction, mainwheel brakes, nosewheel steering, brake-chute, and afterburner nozzles. No pneumatic system. Main electrical system is 28V DC, supplied by two Lucas BC-0107 9kW engine driven starter/generators through two voltage regulators and a switching system, and a 36Ah battery; two 700VA static inverters for AC power at 400Hz. Oxygen system for crew.

Avionics and Equipment: Standard avionics include VHF/UHF air-to-air and air-to-ground com radio (20W transmission power); gyro unit, radio altimeter, radio compass and marker beacon receiver; IFF; and GEC Avionics three-axis stability augmentation system, incorporating a basic bank/attitude hold autopilot and emergency wings-level facility. Orao 1 and 2 also have Collins VIR-30 VOR/ILS and Collins DME-40; Orao 2 fitted with Iskra SO-1 radar warning receiver. Landing light under nose, forward of nosewheel bay; taxying light on nosewheel shock strut.

Armament (IAR-93 and Orao 1): Two 23 mm GSh-23L twin-barrel cannon in lower front fuselage, below engine air intakes, with 200 rds/gun. Gun camera and Ferranti D282 gyro gunsight. Five external stores stations, of which the inboard underwing pair and the fuselage centreline station are each stressed for loads up to 500 kg (1,102 lb); outboard underwing stations stressed for up to 300 kg (661 lb) each, giving a max external stores load of 1,500 kg (3,307 lb). Typical weapon loads can include two or three 500 kg bombs; four or five 250 kg bombs; four multiple carriers each with three 100 kg or 50 kg bombs; two such multiple carriers plus two L-57-16MD launchers each with sixteen 57 mm rockets; four L-57-16MD launchers; four launchers each with two 122 mm, one 128 mm or one 240 mm rocket (122 and 240 mm not used on Orao); a GSh-23L cannon pod with four L-57-16MD rocket launchers; four 160 kg KPT-150 or similar munition dispensers; or (Romanian aircraft only) four L-57-32 launchers each with thirty-two 57 mm rockets. Centreline and inboard underwing points are each plumbed to carry a 540 litre (119 Imp gallon) drop tank; centreline point also capable of carrying a camera or infra-red reconnaissance pod or (not yet available for Orao) a night illumination pod.

Armament (Orao 2): Guns, gun camera, drop tanks and centreline camera or infra-red reconnaissance pod as for Orao 1. Thomson-CSF VE-120T head-up display. All four wing stations stressed for 500 kg (1,102 lb), and fuselage station for 800 kg (1,763 lb), giving a max external stores capacity of 2,800 kg (6,173 lb). Typical weapon loads include five 50 kg, 100 kg, 250 kg or 500 kg bombs; four multiple carriers for a total of twelve 50 or 100 kg or eight 250 kg bombs; four PLAB-340 napalm bombs (each 360 kg; 794 lb); five BL755 bomblet dispensers, or eight on four multiple carriers; sixteen BRZ-127 5 in HVAR rockets; four pods of L-57-16MD or L-128-04 (4 × 128 mm) rockets, or eight pods on multiple carriers; five 500 kg AM-500 sea mines; or two launch rails for AGM-65B Maverick air-to-surface missiles. The 100 kg and 250 kg bombs can be parachute retarded.

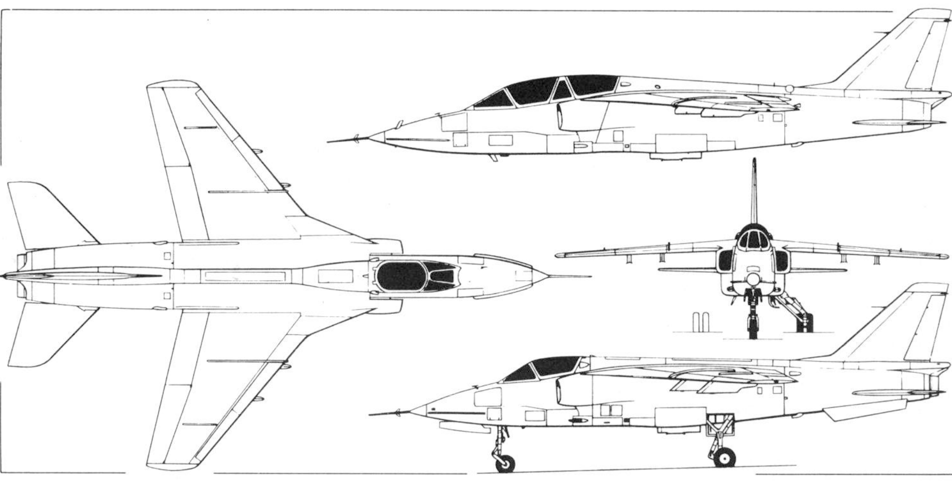

Single-seat IAR-93B close support/ground attack aircraft, with additional side view (top) of two-seat version of the IAR-93A *(Pilot Press)*

Romanian two-seat IAR-93A, showing the wing leading-edge root extensions and absence of ventral fins

Second production single-seat SOKO Orao 2 attack aircraft of the Yugoslav Air Force

Dimensions, external:

Wing span	9·62 m (31 ft 6¾ in)
Wing chord: at root	4·20 m (13 ft 9⅜ in)
at tip	1·40 m (4 ft 7⅛ in)
Wing aspect ratio	3·56
Length overall, incl probe:	
single-seater	14·90 m (48 ft 10⅝ in)
two-seater	15·38 m (50 ft 5½ in)
Length of fuselage:	
single-seater	13·96 m (45 ft 9⅝ in)
two-seater	14·44 m (47 ft 4½ in)
Fuselage: Max width	1·68 m (5 ft 6⅛ in)
Height overall	4·45 m (14 ft 7¼ in)
Tailplane span	4·72 m (15 ft 5⅞ in)
Wheel track (c/l of shock struts)	2·50 m (8 ft 2½ in)
Wheelbase: single-seater	5·42 m (17 ft 9⅜ in)
two-seater	approx 6·50 m (21 ft 4 in)

Areas:

Wings, gross	26·00 m² (279·86 sq ft)
Ailerons (total)	1·92 m² (20·67 sq ft)
Trailing-edge flaps (total)	3·13 m² (33·69 sq ft)
Leading-edge slats (total)	1·56 m² (16·79 sq ft)
Fin	2·67 m² (28·74 sq ft)
Rudder, incl tab	0·88 m² (9·47 sq ft)
Tailplane	7·62 m² (82·02 sq ft)

WEIGHTS AND LOADINGS (A: IAR-93A, B: IAR-93B, C: Orao 2):
- Weight empty, equipped: A 6,150 kg (13,558 lb)
  - B 5,700 kg (12,566 lb)
  - C 5,750 kg (12,676 lb)
- Max internal fuel: A 2,457 kg (5,416 lb)
  - B 2,450 kg (5,401 lb)
  - C 2,450 kg (5,401 lb)
- Max external stores load: A 1,500 kg (3,307 lb)
  - B, C 2,800 kg (6,173 lb)
- Basic operating weight: A 8,826 kg (19,458 lb)
  - B 8,400 kg (18,519 lb)
- Max T-O weight: A 10,326 kg (22,765 lb)
  - B 11,200 kg (24,692 lb)
  - C 11,250 kg (24,800 lb)
- Max landing weight: A 8,826 kg (19,458 lb)
  - B 9,360 kg (20,635 lb)
- Max wing loading: A 397 kg/m² (81·3 lb/sq ft)
  - B 430·7 kg/m² (88·3 lb/sq ft)
- Max power loading: A 289·8 kg/kN (2·84 lb/lb st)
  - B 251·8 kg/kN (2·47 lb/lb st)

PERFORMANCE (A at max T-O weight; B and C at 8,450 kg; 18,629 lb T-O weight):
- Max level speed at S/L:
  - A 577 knots (1,070 km/h; 665 mph)
  - B, C 626 knots (1,160 km/h; 721 mph)
- Max cruising speed:
  - A at 7,000 m (22,965 ft) 394 knots (730 km/h; 453 mph)
  - B at 9,000 m (29,525 ft) 354 knots (656 km/h; 407 mph)
- Stalling speed at S/L: A 130 knots (241 km/h; 150 mph)
  - B, C 148 knots (274 km/h; 171 mph)
- Max rate of climb at S/L: A 2,040 m (6,693 ft)/min
  - B, C 4,200 m (13,780 ft)/min
- Service ceiling: A 10,500 m (34,450 ft)
  - B, C 13,500 m (44,300 ft)
- Min ground turning radius 7·00 m (22 ft 11½ in)
- T-O run: A 1,500 m (4,921 ft)
  - B, C 500 m (1,640 ft)
- T-O to 15 m (50 ft): A 1,600 m (5,249 ft
  - B, C 820 m (2,690 ft
- Landing from 15 m (50 ft): A 1,650 m (5,413 ft
  - B, C 1,500 m (4,920 ft
- Landing run: A 720 m (2,362 ft
  - B, C 1,050 m (3,445 ft
- Landing run with brake chute: A, B, C 670 m (2,200 ft
- Mission radius, B, C:
  - lo-lo-lo with four rocket launchers, 5 min over target 140 nm (260 km; 161 miles
  - hi-hi-hi patrol with three 500 kg (1,102 lb) auxiliary fue tanks, 45 min over target 205 nm (380 km; 236 miles
  - lo-lo-hi with two rocket launchers, six 100 kg bomb and one 500 kg auxiliary fuel tank, 10 min ove target 243 nm (450 km; 280 miles
  - hi-hi-hi with four 250 kg bombs and one 500 k auxiliary fuel tank, 5 min over target 286 nm (530 km; 329 miles
- *g* limits: A, B, C +8/−4·

TRANSALL

ARBEITSGEMEINSCHAFT TRANSALL

AIRFRAME COMPANIES:

Aérospatiale, 37 boulevard de Montmorency, 75781 Paris Cédex 16, France
Telephone: 524 43 21
Telex: 620059 F

MBB, Postfach 950109, 2103 Hamburg 95, Federal Republic of Germany
Telephone: (040) 7437 1
Telex: 21950-0 mbbh d

TRANSALL C-160 (Second Series)

The Transall (Transporter Allianz) group was formed in January 1959 by MBB, Aérospatiale and VFW, and undertook development and production of the C-160 twin-turboprop transport for the air forces of France (50), Germany (90), South Africa (9) and Turkey (20). This initial production was shared between the three participating companies and ended in 1972, as described in earlier editions of *Jane's*.

Production of a second series was authorised in 1977 to meet an additional French order and requests from other countries. The main improvements in this second production series are updated avionics, and extended range resulting from a reinforced wing with an optional additional fuel tank in the centre-section.

First flight of the first aircraft of the new series took place at Toulouse on 9 April 1981. The French Air Force placed an initial order for 25 (increased to 29 in 1982), and deliveries of these were completed in mid-1985. Ten were fitted at the outset with in-flight refuelling equipment (hose reel and drogue type) in the port main landing gear fairing to permit their operation as tankers; five others incorporate provisions for this equipment and are capable of rapid adaptation to the tanker role if needed. All have a 4·00 m (13 ft 2 in) receiver boom mounted above and behind the flight deck. They are capable of refuelling carrier based aircraft of the French Navy, as well as French Air Force combat aircraft.

French Air Force second-series Transalls are in service with Escadrons 1/64 'Béarn' and 2/64 'Anjou' of the 64e Escadre de Transport at Evreux. Two of the four additional aircraft ordered in 1982 are for operation as communications relay aircraft on behalf of the nation's nuclear deterrent forces from 1987. To ensure maximum survivability and effectiveness in a nuclear combat environment, the aircraft are equipped as flight refuelling tankers/receivers. They are designated **Astarté** (Avion-station-relais de transmissions exceptionelles) and operated under the overall Ramses (réseau amont maillé stratégique et de survie) programme. Equipment includes a US built Collins VLF system, installed by Thomson-CSF, of the kind fitted to Tacamo EC-130s of the US Navy. The final two will be equipped as electronic intelligence (elint) aircraft, and are designated **Gabriel**.

In addition to the French order, six second-series Transalls were delivered to the Indonesian government, and are operated by Pelita Air Service to assist in the country's transmigration of inhabitants from Java to less heavily populated islands.

Conversion kits or modifications are being offered for maritime surveillance (**C-160S**) and electronic surveillance (**C-160SE**) versions (both described in the 1984-85 and earlier editions of *Jane's*), photographic reconnaissance (with vertical and oblique cameras), airborne command, VIP transport, firefighting and anti-pollution missions (with a 12 ton liquid dropping capability), and for aeromedical duties. An airborne early warning version, designated **C-160AAA** (avion d'alerte avancée), has also been proposed. This would have nose and tail radomes similar to those of the British Aerospace Nimrod AEW. Mk 3. No orders for any of these variants had been announced up to mid-1986.

The following shortened description applies to the standard second-series tanker/transport version; a more detailed description can be found in the 1985-86 *Jane's*.

Transall C-160 Astarté communications relay and flight refuelling tanker/receiver of the French Air Forc *(Aviodata)*

Transall C-160 (second series), one of six delivered to Pelita Air Service of Indonesia

TYPE: Twin-engined turboprop transport.

AIRFRAME: See 1985-86 *Jane's*.

POWER PLANT: Two 4,549 kW (6,100 ehp) Rolls-Royce Tyne RTy.20 Mk 22 turboprop engines, each driving a Ratier Forest built BAe 4/8000/6 four-blade constant-speed fully-feathering reversible-pitch propeller. Single-point pressure refuelling; gravity refuelling available optionally. Fuel in four integral wing tanks with total capacity of 19,050 litres (4,190 Imp gallons). Additional wing centre-section tank optional, capacity 9,000 litres (1,980 Imp gallons). Boom for in-flight refuelling. Hose reel and drogue type in-flight refuelling tanker equipment optional. Water-methanol usable capacity 318·5 litres (70 Imp gallons). Oil capacity (total) 68·4 litres (15 Imp gallons).

ACCOMMODATION: Pressurised accommodation for crew of three, comprising pilot, co-pilot and flight engineer. Typical payloads include 93 troops or 61-88 fully equipped paratroops; 62 stretchers and four attendants; armoured vehicles, tanks and tractors not exceeding max permissible payload weight. Flight deck and cargo compartment air-conditioned and pressurised in flight and on the ground. Power assisted controls. Paratroop door o each side immediately aft of the landing gear fairings hydraulically operated rear loading ramp. The floor an all doors are at truckbed height. The floor is provide with lashing points of 5,000 kg (11,023 lb) capacity arranged in a 51 cm (20 in) grid, and 12,000 kg (26,455 lb capacity on the sidewalls, and is stressed to carry larg military vehicles. Loads which cannot be driven in can b taken on board rapidly by an automatic translation an stowing system. Individual loads of up to 8,000 kg (17,63 lb) can be airdropped, including drops at low altitud (3-9 m; 10-30 ft) or during touch-and-go.

SYSTEMS, AVIONICS AND EQUIPMENT: As listed in 1985-8 *Jane's*.

DIMENSIONS, EXTERNAL:
- Wing span 40·00 m (131 ft 3 in
- Length overall, excl probe 32·40 m (106 ft 3½ in
- Fuselage: Max diameter 4·30 m (14 ft 1¼ in
- Height overall 11·65 m (38 ft 2¾ in
- Tailplane span 14·50 m (47 ft 7 in
- Wheel track 5·10 m (16 ft 9 in

Wheelbase 10·48 m (34 ft 4½ in)
Propeller diameter 5·49 m (18 ft 0 in)
Crew door (fwd, port): Height 1·22 m (4 ft 0 in)
Width 0·62 m (2 ft 0½ in)
Paratroop door (each side):
Height 1·90 m (6 ft 2½ in)
Width 0·90 m (3 ft 0 in)
Rear loading ramp: Length 3·70 m (12 ft 1½ in)
Width 3·15 m (10 ft 3½ in)

DIMENSIONS, INTERNAL:
Cabin, excl flight deck and ramp:
Length 13·51 m (44 ft 4 in)
Max width 3·15 m (10 ft 3½ in)
Max height 2·98 m (9 ft 8½ in)
Floor area 42·6 m² (458·5 sq ft)
Volume 115·0 m³ (4,061 cu ft)
Cabin, incl ramp: Length 17·21 m (56 ft 6 in)
Floor area 54·25 m² (584 sq ft)
Volume 139·9 m³ (4,940 cu ft)

AREA:
Wings, gross 160·00 m² (1,722 sq ft)

WEIGHTS AND LOADINGS:
Min operating weight empty 28,000 kg (61,730 lb)
Typical operating weight empty 29,000 kg (63,935 lb)
Max fuel load: standard 15,295 kg (33,720 lb)
optional 22,520 kg (49,648 lb)
Max payload 16,000 kg (35,275 lb)
Max T-O weight 51,000 kg (112,435 lb)
Max zero-fuel weight 45,000 kg (99,210 lb)
Max landing weight 47,000 kg (103,615 lb)
Max wing loading 319 kg/m² (65·34 lb/sq ft)
Max power loading 5·61 kg/kW (9·22 lb/ehp)

PERFORMANCE (at max T-O weight except where indicated):
Never-exceed speed:
at 4,875-9,145 m (16,000-30,000 ft) Mach 0·64
below 4,875 m (16,000 ft) 320 knots (593 km/h; 368 mph)
Max level speed at 4,875 m (16,000 ft) 277 knots (513 km/h; 319 mph)
Stalling speed, flaps down 95 knots (177 km/h; 110 mph)
Max rate of climb at S/L 396 m (1,300 ft)/min
Rate of climb at S/L, one engine out 91 m (300 ft)/min
Service ceiling at 45,000 kg (99,210 lb) AUW 8,230 m (27,000 ft)
Service ceiling, one engine out at 45,000 kg (99,210 lb) AUW 3,050 m (10,000 ft)
T-O run, 20° flap 715 m (2,346 ft)
T-O to 10·5 m (35 ft), 20° flap 990 m (3,248 ft)
Landing from 15 m (50 ft), 40° flap, at max landing weight without propeller reversal 869 m (2,850 ft)
Landing run, normal 550 m (1,800 ft)
Min ground turning radius 28·60 m (93 ft 10 in)
Range, reserve of 5% initial fuel, allowance for 30 min hold at S/L, OWE of 29,000 kg (63,935 lb):
with 8,000 kg (17,640 lb) payload 2,750 nm (5,095 km; 3,166 miles)
with 16,000 kg (35,275 lb) payload 1,000 nm (1,853 km; 1,151 miles)
Max ferry range with centre-section wing tank 4,780 nm (8,858 km; 5,504 miles)

ISRAEL

IAI

ISRAEL AIRCRAFT INDUSTRIES LTD

Ben-Gurion International Airport, 70100 Lydda (Lod)
Telephone: 03 9713 111
Telex: Isravia 371102, 371114 and 371133
PRESIDENT: Moshe Keret
CHAIRMAN OF THE BOARD: David Ivri
EXECUTIVE VICE-PRESIDENTS:
Dr M. Dvir (Planning and Business Development)
A. Ostrinsky
VICE-PRESIDENTS:
M. Ortasse (General Manager, Electronics Division)
I. Geva (General Manager, Bedek Aviation Division)
M. Blumkine (General Manager, Engineering Division)
Y. Ben-Bassat (General Manager, Aircraft Manufacturing Division)
Y. Shapira (General Manager, Combined Technologies Division)
N. Hassid (Finance)
D. Onn (Marketing)
Mrs. H. Ron (General Counsel)
Y. Ben-Zvi (Internal Auditor)
MANAGER, CORPORATE COMMUNICATIONS: Doron Suslik

This company was established in 1953 as Bedek Aircraft Company. The change of name, to Israel Aircraft Industries, was made on 1 April 1967.

IAI employs approx 21,000 people in all its facilities, which occupy a total covered floor area of 500,000 m² (5,381,950 sq ft). It is licensed by the Israel Civil Aviation Administration, US Federal Aviation Administration, British Civil Aviation Authority and the Israeli Air Force, among others, as an approved repair station and maintenance organisation.

Israel Aircraft Industries underwent a major reorganisation in the latter part of 1977, and now comprises five divisions, as follows:

Bedek Aviation Division, incorporating Turbochrome, is an internationally approved multi-faceted single-site civil and military aircraft service centre. Present programmes include the turnaround inspection, overhaul, repair, retrofitting, outfitting and testing of more than 30 types of aircraft, including the Boeing 707, 727, 737, 747, 767, McDonnell Douglas DC-8, DC-9, DC-10, Lockheed C-130, and F-4, F-15 and F-16 fighters; 30 types of civil and military engines, including the JT3D, JT8D, J79, F100, T56 and T53; and 10,000 types of components, accessories and systems. Offshore workload includes the supply of total technical support to several international operators. The division holds warranty and/or approved service centre approvals from many of the world's leading component manufacturers. Bedek has refurbished and resold numerous Boeing 707/720s, often after conversion from passenger to cargo, sigint, hose refuelling tanker or other configurations.

Bedek Aviation has a total floor area of some 83,613 m² (900,000 sq ft). Its workforce comprises about 4,000 technicians, engineers and supporting personnel.

The **Aircraft Manufacturing Division** produces the Kfir and Lavi fighters, the Arava STOL transport, the turbofan powered Westwind I and 2 and Astra business aircraft, and mini-RPVs. In addition, it is engaged in the manufacture of a vast variety of spares and assemblies for aircraft and jet engines, to meet Israeli Air Force requirements. As a subcontractor to many US and European aircraft manufacturers, the Division produces major aircraft structures, flight control surfaces, cargo loading systems and spares.

The **Engineering Division**, the largest establishment of its kind in Israel, employs some 1,800 technical, scientific and other skilled personnel. It is responsible for engineering research, design, development and testing of aerospace systems. It provides engineering support in system analysis, aerodynamics, materials and processing, landing and control systems, and in structural, flight and environmental testing. The Division performed modification and production support for the manufacture of the Magister jet trainer for the IAF. It designed and developed the Arava STOL transport aircraft and developed the 1123 and 1124 Westwind.

The Division's recent programmes have included development of the Astra business jet, a fly by wire system for flight testing in the Kfir, and research into materials, structures and electronic countermeasures. It is now developing the Lavi strike fighter.

The **Electronics Division** incorporates Elta Electronics Industries, MBT Weapons Systems, Tamam Precision Instruments, and MLM Systems Engineering and Integration, together employing nearly 6,500 people in facilities totalling 142,560 m² (1,534,500 sq ft). It specialises in the design, development and production of sophisticated electronic equipment such as airborne, ground and shipborne communications and radars, transceivers and navigational aids, general communications equipment, automatic test systems, and such electronic medical devices as cardiac resuscitation instruments. MBT participated in the development of the Division's Gabriel shipborne surface-to-surface missile system, among others, as well as of an electronic warning fence and an audible bomb release altimeter. Tamam manufactures and assembles high precision electromechanical components and servo-systems for such mechanisms as aerosystems, torque motors and gyroscopes.

Ramta Structures and Systems, Servo-Hydraulics Lod (SHL), MATA Helicopters, and Golan Industries, make up the **Technologies Division**. This designs, develops and manufactures hydraulic and fuel system components, hydraulic flight control servo-systems, landing gears and brake systems; produces air actuated chucks, miniature gears, clutches and brakes; manufactures ground support equipment, stainless steel tanks, the Dabur and Dvora patrol boats and the RBY armoured vehicle; manufactures high precision metal products for the aircraft and military industries; and produces electronic assemblies and sub-assemblies for aircraft.

Through its **Military Aircraft Marketing Group**, IAI offers a number of services to foreign customers, based on the considerable capability of its five main divisions. Among these are combat aircraft upgrading, a retrofit package that can include improved systems, engines, avionics, design configuration and structures. This has proved a successful export item, and programmes are available for Mirage, Skyhawk, Hunter, Phantom, Northrop F-5 and other types. In 1984-85 IAI had converted one Argentine Air Force Boeing 707 for ECM/sigint duties and was modifying two

Boeing 707 sigint/tanker with wingtip refuelling pods. The radome under the forward fuselage may house an Elta Electronics Industries automatic missile detection radar; onboard equipment includes Elta's EL/L-8300 computerised sigint system

others as in-flight refuelling tankers. Under a contract known as 'Finger II', IAI has installed a system called SINT (Sistema Integrado de Navigación y Tiro) to upgrade the nav/attack capability of the Fuerza Aérea Argentina's Dagger fighter-bombers (IAI modified Dassault Mirage IIIs, of which 48 were acquired) with modern avionics which include an Elta 2001 radar and a cockpit head-up display.

IAI AMIT FOUGA

Israeli Air Force name: Tzukit (Thrush)

The AMIT Fouga (Advanced Multi-mission Improved Trainer) was engineered by the Bedek Division of IAI to Israeli Air Force requirements, to remain as the standard IAF trainer during the 1980s. It is, in effect, completely rebuilt and modernised, and is a dedicated trainer with all armament removed, although it retains capability for patrol and aerial photographic missions.

Some 250 modifications are incorporated, including a full overhaul and 5,000 hour life extension of the airframe, including corrosion protection; easier maintainability and greater reliability; better braking; improved instrumentation and avionics (VHF, UHF, audio, Tacan/DME and IFF as standard, others to customer's requirements); renewal of wiring; installation of anti-collision lights and (optionally) a coloured smoke system; a redesigned cockpit and instrument layout; improved environmental control system; automatic starting system; new electrical power supply; liquid oxygen system (gaseous system optional); and an improved warning and failure simulation system. Two prototypes were flight tested in 1981, and deliveries to the IAF (reportedly of eight aircraft) were nearing completion in early 1986.

IAI MIRAGE MODIFICATIONS

IAI is marketing a retrofit kit designed to increase, at relatively low cost, the combat capability and survivability of Mirage III/5 aircraft. The basic airframe modifications consist of installation of Kfir type foreplanes and Kfir standard landing gear, the former permitting either a substantial reduction (305-457 m; 1,000-1,500 ft) in T-O run or a 907 kg (2,000 lb) increase in T-O gross weight, and the latter an increase in max T-O weight to 16,330 kg (36,000 lb). The foreplanes also offer a marked improvement in air turning radius (from 1,036 m; 3,400 ft to 610 m; 2,000 ft at 4,575 m; 15,000 ft altitude); improved sustained turn, a vastly extended usable angle of attack and low-speed envelope; and much improved handling qualities. By reducing air loads on the wings and fuselage, they extend the fatigue life of the airframe.

An additional fuselage fuel tank can be installed aft of the cockpit, and a Kfir type nose provides additional space for avionics such as control and stability augmentation systems. Other avionics include a radar warning system, with omnidirectional threat analysis and cockpit display, and a WDNS-391 fully inertial weapon delivery and navigation system with head-up operation in all air-to-surface and air-to-air modes. Additional external stores stations are provided, and flare/chaff dispensers can be installed under the rear fuselage.

IAI PHANTOM MODIFICATIONS

Israeli Air Force approval has been given for an airframe and avionics upgrade programme for the service's F-4 Phantoms. Four prototypes were to be modified during 1986 with structural improvements, new (probably conformal) external fuel tanks, and possibly the addition of Kfir-type canard surfaces. New or upgraded avionics are expected to include a new Elta pulse-Doppler radar (derived from the EL/M-2021); Elbit ACE-3 radar data processor; Elop (Kaiser licence) wide-angle diffractive optics head-up display; Astronautics multi-function CRT displays; an avionics interface computer; and a multiplex digital databus. Elbit is overall integrator for the avionics refit. The programme is expected to involve about 140 Phantoms still in IAF service.

Beyond this, though not yet given an official go-ahead, is a proposal to re-engine the IAF's F-4s with Pratt & Whitney PW1120 turbofans. A decision is likely to await results from flight testing of one F-4, with one of its J79 turbojets replaced by a PW1120, which is currently being used as an engine testbed in the Lavi development programme. This F-4 (IAF serial number 334) made its first flight on 30 July 1986. It was due to have both J79s replaced by PW1120s at the end of 1986, and to complete its test programme in late 1987.

IAI SKYHAWK MODIFICATIONS

Major airframe improvements offered by IAI's Skyhawk retrofit programme (already applied to Israeli Air Force A-4s) include a life extension overhaul, replacement of all wiring, provision of dual disc brakes on the mainwheels, a steerable nosewheel, addition of wing lift spoilers, an extra hardpoint under each wing, extension of the tailpipe (to change the heat signature and make the tailpipe more survivable and easier to repair), and addition of a brake-chute in a fairing beneath the rear fuselage. The wing root cannon are of increased calibre (30 mm instead of 20 mm), and a weapons delivery and navigation system (WDNS) similar to that in the Mirage package is installed. Additional space for lighter-weight avionics is made available in an extended nose compartment and in the 'saddleback' hump aft of the cockpit. As with the Mirage, flare and chaff dispensers can be installed under the rear fuselage, forward of the brake-chute fairing.

IAI AMIT Fouga (Tzukit) of the Israeli Air Force

IAI LAVI (YOUNG LION)

In the 1990s the Lavi is expected to become the workhorse of the Israeli Air Force, which has a requirement for at least 300, including about 60 combat-capable two-seat trainers. Emphasis will be on the close air support and interdiction roles, with a secondary capability for air-to-air self-defence to and from the target. Design characteristics include high-speed penetration, high manoeuvrability, first-pass bombing accuracy, and battle damage tolerance for safe recovery.

The Lavi is slightly smaller than the General Dynamics F-16, and has close-coupled delta main wings and canard surfaces, incorporating proven state of the art technology. Approx 22 per cent of the structure, by weight, is built of composite materials. This includes many components made from graphite epoxy (carbonfibre), such as wing skins and substructure, the vertical tail, the all-moving foreplanes, control surfaces, and various doors and panels. In most cases, development and initial production of such advanced technology components is taking place in the USA, before series manufacture is transferred to Israel. Production of composites will be undertaken eventually by MMCA Ltd, a new subsidiary of IAI based at Beer-Sheva.

Deliveries of the Lavi are planned to begin in 1990 initially to replace the Israeli Air Force's A-4 Skyhawks an later the Kfir-C2/C7. Initial operational capability is set fc 1992. The two-seat version will replace Skyhawks and F- Phantoms at present used in the training role. Serie production is intended to be at the initial rate of one pe month, increasing to 30-36 per year by the mid-1990s.

The Lavi (known earlier as Super Kfir and Arye) receive programme go-ahead, after a number of design changes, i February 1980, and the PW1120 turbojet engine wa selected as power plant in June 1981. Prototype construc tion was authorised by the Israeli government in early 1982 and the basic design was frozen later that year, full scal development starting in October 1982. Six flight develop ment aircraft are being built, including two-seaters, plus static test article. By May 1986 two prototypes were nearin completion, with a third in major subassembly. First fligh was expected in late 1986, with the second aircraft du to fly about six months later. The flight test programm is scheduled to last for three years. Recent changes ar understood to include an increase in control surface areas to counter any stability problems that might arise once fligh testing begins.

The following details apply to the single-seat Lavi:

TYPE: Single-seat close air support and interdiction aircraf with secondary capability for air defence.

Rollout of the first prototype IAI Lavi multi-role combat aircraft on 21 July 1986

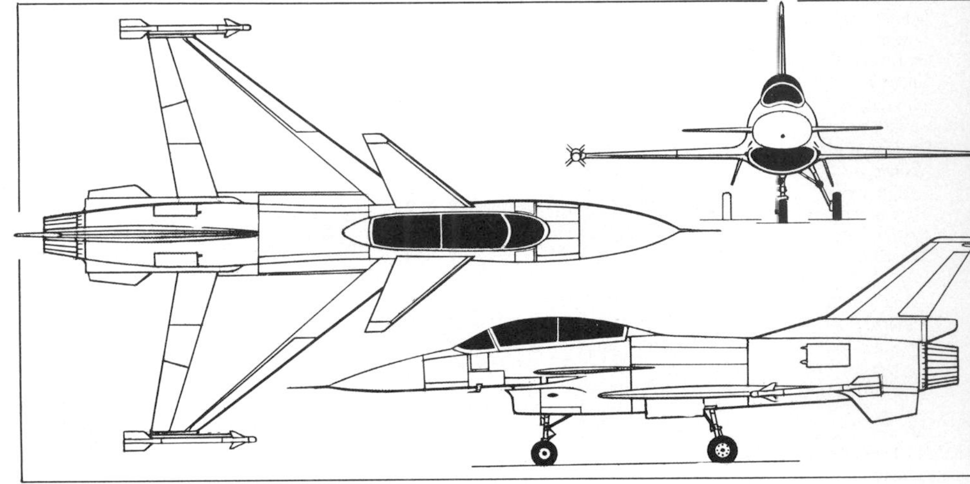

IAI Lavi close support, strike and air defence fighter *(Pilot Press)*

WINGS AND FOREPLANES: Cantilever low-wing monoplane. Close coupled 'swept delta' main wings (54° on leading-edges), plus all-moving foreplanes of similar planform. Leading-edge flaps over outer half of each wing. Inboard and outboard elevon on each trailing-edge. Substructure and skins of carbonfibre. First eight shipsets of wings designed, developed and produced by Grumman Aerospace Corporation.

FUSELAGE: Conventional semi-monocoque structure, 'waisted' in accordance with area rule and incorporating composite materials as well as metal.

TAIL UNIT: Sweptback fin and rudder; Grumman producing first six carbonfibre fins. No horizontal tail surfaces.

LANDING GEAR: SHL retractable tricycle type, with single wheel on each unit. Goodyear wheels, tyres and brakes.

POWER PLANT: One 91·7 kN (20,620 lb st) Pratt & Whitney PW1120 afterburning turbojet engine, most of which is expected to be manufactured under licence by Bet Shemesh Engines Ltd. Ventral single-shock intake based on that of General Dynamics F-16. Max fuel capacity 3,330 litres (732 Imp gallons; 880 US gallons) in integral wing tanks, 5,095 litres (1,121 Imp gallons; 1,346 US gallons) externally.

ACCOMMODATION: Pilot only, on ejection seat, under 'tear-drop' cockpit canopy.

SYSTEMS: Garrett AiResearch environmental control system for air-conditioning, pressurisation and engine bleed air control. Pneudraulics bootstrap type hydraulic system, pressure 207 bars (3,000 lb/sq in), with Abex pumps. Electrical system powered by Sundstrand 60kVA integrated drive generator, for single-channel AC power at 400Hz. SAFT main and Marathon standby battery. Garrett AiResearch EPU and Garrett Turbine Engine Co secondary power system.

AVIONICS: Electronic warfare self-protection system, by Elta Electronics, to provide rapid threat identification (IFF) and flexible response (ECM). This computer-based, fully automatic system will use active and passive countermeasures, including internal and externally podded power-managed noise and deception jammers. Elbit Computers Ltd is prime contractor for the integrated display system, which includes a Hughes Aircraft wide angle holographic head-up display, three multi-function displays (two monochrome and one colour), display computers, and communications controller. Pilot will operate most systems through a single El-Op up-front control. Lear Siegler/MBT quadruple-redundant digital fly by wire flight control system, with stability augmentation, MBT control unit and Moog servo-actuators. No mechanical backup. Sundstrant actuation system, with geared rotary actuators, for leading-edge flaps. Cockpit is designed to minimise pilot workload in high *g* and dense threat environment, and full HOTAS (hands on throttle and stick) operation. New Elta multi-mode pulse-Doppler radar, developed from the EL/M-2021B, will include automatic target acquisition and track-while-scan in the air-to-air mode, and beam-sharpened ground mapping/terrain avoidance and sea search in the air-to-surface mode. The radar's coherent transmitter and stable multi-channel receiver will ensure reliable lookdown performance over a broad band of frequencies, as well as high resolution mapping. Elta programmable signal processor, backed by a network of distributed, embedded computers, will provide optimum allocation of computer power and considerable flexibility for algorithm updating and system growth. Advanced versions of Elbit ACE-4 mission computer (128K memory) and SMS-86 stores management systems, both compatible with MIL-STD-1553B databus; SMS-86 capable of managing both conventional and 'smart' weapons and sensors. Elta fully computerised onboard communications system, Elisra radar warning receiver and Astronautics air data computer. Tamam advanced inertial navigation system.

ARMAMENT: Internally mounted 30 mm cannon, with helmet sight. Four underwing hardpoints for air-to-surface missiles, bombs, rockets and other stores; inboard pair 'wet' for carriage of auxiliary fuel tanks. Seven underfuselage stores attachments (three tandem pairs plus one on centreline). Infra-red air-to-air missile at each wingtip.

DIMENSIONS, EXTERNAL:

Wing span	8·78 m (28 ft 9⅔ in)
Length overall	14·57 m (47 ft 9⅔ in)
Height overall	4·78 m (15 ft 8¼ in)
Wheel track	2·31 m (7 ft 7 in)
Wheelbase	3·86 m (12 ft 8 in)

AREA:

Wings, gross	33·05 m² (355·75 sq ft)

WEIGHTS AND LOADING:

Max fuel: internal	2,721 kg (6,000 lb)
external	4,164 kg (9,180 lb)
Max ordnance (excl air-to-air missiles)	2,721 kg (6,000 lb)
Max external load	7,257 kg (16,000 lb)
T-O weight: basic	9,990 kg (22,024 lb)
max	19,277 kg (42,500 lb)
Max wing loading	523 kg/m² (107 lb/sq ft)
Combat thrust/weight ratio	1·07

PERFORMANCE (estimated):

Max level speed above 11,000 m (36,000 ft)	
	Mach 1·8 or 800 knots (1,482 km/h; 921 mph) CAS
Low-altitude penetration speed:	
two infra-red missiles and eight 750 lb M 117 bombs	538 knots (997 km/h; 619 mph)
two infra-red missiles and two 2,000 lb Mk 84 bombs	597 knots (1,106 km/h; 687 mph)
Air turning rate at Mach 0·8 at 4,575 m (15,000 ft):	
sustained	13·2°/s
max	24·3°/s
T-O run	approx 305 m (1,000 ft)
Combat radius:	
air-to-ground, lo-lo-lo	600 nm (1,112 km; 691 miles)
air-to-ground, hi-lo-hi with two Mk 84 or six Mk 82 bombs	1,150 nm (2,131 km; 1,324 miles)
air-to-air, combat air patrol	1,000 nm (1,853 km; 1,151 miles)
g limit	+9

IAI KFIR (LION CUB)

US Navy and Marine Corps designation: F-21A

A prototype of the Kfir (a modified Nesher airframe adapted to the J79 engine) was first flown in June 1973, following almost three years of flight tests of this engine in a Mirage III-B. Existence of the Kfir was made public officially for the first time on 14 April 1975, when the first production example was displayed at Ben-Gurion Airport.

The Kfir utilises a basic airframe similar to that of the Dassault Mirage 5, the main changes being a shorter but larger-diameter rear fuselage, to accommodate the J79 engine; an enlarged and flattened undersurface to the forward portion of the fuselage; introduction of four small fuselage airscoops, plus a larger dorsal airscoop in place of the triangular dorsal fin, to provide cooling air for the afterburner; and a strengthened landing gear, with longer-stroke oleos. Internal changes include a redesigned cockpit layout, addition of Israeli built avionics, and revised fuel tankage compared with the Mirage 5. Intended for both air defence and ground attack roles, the Kfir retains the standard Mirage fixed armament of two 30 mm DEFA cannon, and can carry a variety of external weapons including Rafael Shafrir 2 air-to-air missiles. Two squadrons of the Israeli Air Force were equipped with this initial version, which flew its first combat mission in 1977.

A modified version known as the **Kfir-C2** was made public on 20 June 1976, having begun flight testing in 1974. This has a number of changes, including non-retractable, sweptback foreplanes just aft of the engine air intakes; a small strake on each side of the extreme nose; and extended wing leading-edges, created by increasing the chord on approximately the outer 40 per cent of each wing. The foreplanes can be detached for missions not requiring high manoeuvrability.

The modifications were designed to improve the aircraft's dogfighting manoeuvrability at the lower end of the speed range and to enhance take-off and landing performance. It is claimed that, in particular, they give a better sustained turning performance, with improved lateral, longitudinal and directional control; contribute to a very low gust response at all operational altitudes, especially at very low level; offer improved handling qualities at all angles of attack, high *g* loadings, and low speeds; reduce take-off and landing distances, and landing speeds; and permit a more stable (and, if required, a steeper) approach, with a flatter angle of approach and touchdown. Later versions of the C2 have Elta EL/M-2001B nose radar in an extended nose, increasing the overall length by 0·80 m (2 ft 7½ in). According to Israeli official sources, most of the "some hundreds" of Kfirs produced were C2s, and many of the earlier models were later retrofitted to C2 configuration.

A two-seat version, known as the **Kfir-TC2**, was flown for the first time in February 1981, and is now in service. Overall dimensions, power plant and performance are similar to those of the single-seat version, except for the insertion of a 0·84 m (2 ft 9 in) plug in the forward fuselage to accommodate a second cockpit in tandem. The nose is drooped in order to maintain a good field of view from both seats, and the second cockpit accommodates additional systems not present in the single-seat version. Further details of the C2 and TC2 can be found in the 1983-84 and earlier editions of *Jane's*.

Early in the series production of the Kfir, when the C2 version was anticipated, reinforced structure was built into the airframe so that it could subsequently be fitted with the C2 modifications. Those Kfirs that had already entered service without this reinforcement were later fitted with smaller canards, which were able to withstand the added aerodynamic stress while providing some increase in performance. These aircraft also carry strakes on the nose, but do not have the saw-tooth wing extensions. It is 12 aircraft of this version which, from April 1985, the US Navy has leased for three years under the designation **F-21A**, for use with its VF-43 'Aggressor' squadron based at NAS Oceana, Virginia, as interim equipment pending delivery of the General Dynamics F-16N. Weights currently quoted for this version

Early production Kfir, with reduced-size canards, as supplied to US Navy in 1985 as F-21A 'aggressor' aircraft

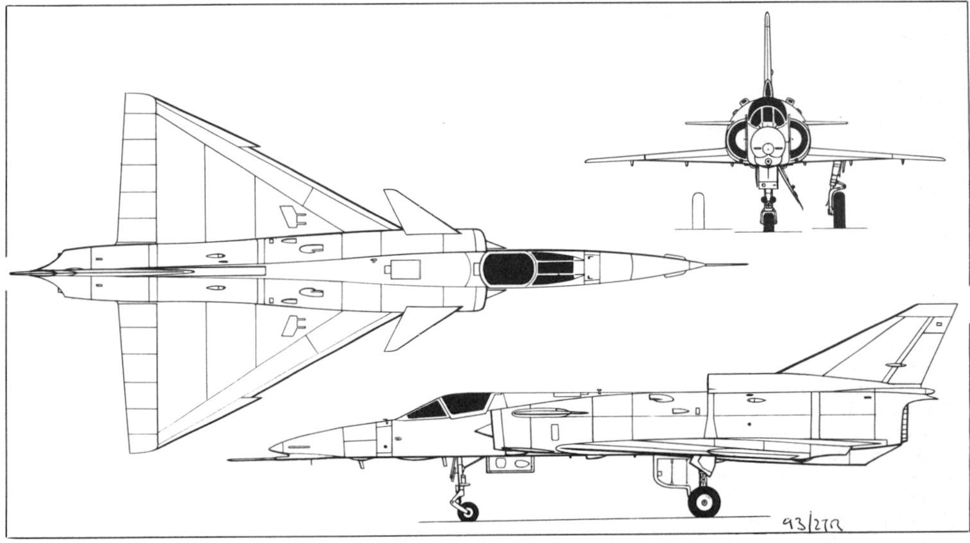

IAI Kfir-C2 (General Electric J79-J1E afterburning turbojet engine) *(Pilot Press)*

are: T-O 'clean', 10,390 kg (22,905 lb); max T-O, 14,700 kg (32,408 lb). Lease of a further 13 Kfirs by the US Marine Corps, for use in a similar role at MCAS Yuma, Arizona, was announced in the Summer of 1986.

Deliveries to the IAF began in Summer 1983 of the **Kfir-C7**, an improved version of the C2 in which the principal differences are higher augmented thrust, two additional hardpoints for increased payload/range capability, and a new HOTAS (hands on throttle and stick) cockpit installation facilitated by new avionics. The C7 and two-seat **TC7** are now the principal IAF versions. IAI continues to overhaul and retrofit the Kfir, upgrading the C2 to C7 configuration, and the assembly line can be stepped up for series production at short notice.

The following description applies to the Kfir-C7:

TYPE: Single-seat strike, ground attack and fighter aircraft.

WINGS: Cantilever low-wing monoplane of delta planform, with conical camber. Thickness/chord ratio 4·5% to 3·5%. Anhedral 1°. Incidence 1°. Sweepback on leading-edges 60° 35′. All-metal torsion box structure, with stressed skin of machined panels with integral stiffeners. Two-section elevons on each trailing-edge, with smaller elevator/trim flap inboard of inner elevon. Elevons powered by hydraulic jacks; trim flaps are servo-assisted. Small, hinged plate type airbrake above and below each wing, near leading-edge. Extended chord on outer leading-edges. Small leading-edge fence on some aircraft, at approx one-third span.

FOREPLANES: Detachable sweptback canard surface above and forward of each wing, near top lip of engine air intake.

FUSELAGE: All-metal semi-monocoque structure, 'waisted' in accordance with area rule. Cross-section of forward fuselage has a wider and flatter undersurface than that of Mirage 5. Nosecone built of locally developed composite materials, with a small horizontal strake or 'body fence' on each side near the tip. UHF antenna under front of fuselage, forward of nosewheel door. Enlarged diameter rear fuselage, compared with Mirage 5, with approx 0·61 m (2 ft) shorter tailpipe. Ventral fairing under rear of fuselage.

TAIL UNIT: Cantilever all-metal fin; rudder powered by hydraulic jack, with servo-assisted trim. UHF antenna in tip of fin. Triangular-section dorsal airscoop forward of fin, to provide cold air for afterburner cooling. No horizontal tail surfaces.

LANDING GEAR: Retractable tricycle type, with single SHL wheel on each unit. Electrically operated hydraulic actuation, nose unit retracting rearward, main units inward into fuselage. Longer-stroke oleos than on Mirage 5, and all units strengthened to permit higher operating weights. Low-pressure tubeless tyres on all units. Main-gear leg fairings shorter than on Mirage; inner portion of each main-leg door is integral with fuselage mounted wheel door. Steerable nosewheel, with anti-shimmy damper. Oleo-pneumatic shock absorbers, SHL hydraulic disc brakes and anti-skid units. Braking parachute in bullet fairing below rudder.

POWER PLANT: One General Electric J79-J1E turbojet engine (modified GE-17), built by IAI's Bedek Division, with variable area nozzle, rated at 52·89 kN (11,890 lb st) dry and 83·41 kN (18,750 lb st) with afterburning. Air intakes enlarged, compared with Mirage 5, to allow for higher mass flow. Adjustable half-cone centrebody in each air intake. Internal fuel in five fuselage and four integral wing tanks. Total internal capacity 3,243 litres (713·4 Imp gallons). Refuelling point on top of fuselage, above forward upper tank. Wet points for the carriage of one drop tank beneath each wing (inboard), and one under fuselage; these tanks may be of 500, 600, 825, 1,300 or 1,700 litres (110, 132, 181·5, 286 or 374 Imp gallons) capacity; max external fuel capacity 4,700 litres (1,034 Imp gallons). Provision for boom/receptacle or probe/drogue in-flight refuelling system, and for single-point pressure refuelling.

ACCOMMODATION: Pilot only, on Martin-Baker IL10P zero/zero ejection seat, under rearward hinged upward opening canopy. Cockpit pressurised, heated and air-conditioned. Two seats in tandem in TC7.

SYSTEMS: Two separate environmental control systems (ECS), one (using engine bleed air) for cockpit heating, pressurisation and air-conditioning, and one for avionics compartments. Two independent hydraulic systems, probably of 207 bars (3,000 lb/sq in) pressure. No. 1 system actuates flying control surfaces and landing gear; No. 2 actuates flying controls, airbrakes, landing gear, wheel brakes and utilities. Fully redundant primary AC electrical system, with two 15kVA (115V 400Hz) alternators, each driven by a CSD (constant speed drive) unit, and a 750VA Oram static inverter connected for split-bus non-synchronised operation. DC system includes two Elta 200A 28V transformer-rectifiers and a 24V 40Ah nickel-cadmium battery. External AC and DC power receptacles. Oxygen system for pilot.

AVIONICS AND EQUIPMENT: C2 fitted with MBT twin-computer flight control system (ASW-41 control augmentation and ASW-42 stability augmentation systems), with Tamam inertial measurement unit (IMU), angle of attack transmitter and indicator, and accelerometer indicator.

IAI Kfir-TC2 two-seater, with drooped and lengthened nose

IAI Kfir-C7 multi-mission combat aircraft, armed with Shafrir air-to-air missiles

Elbit S-8600 multi-mode navigation (Singer-Kearfott licence) and weapons delivery system or IAI/Elbit WDNS-141 or -341 weapons delivery and navigation system, Tamam central air data computer, Elta EL-2001 X-band air-to-air and air-to-surface pulse-Doppler ranging radar, IFF/SIF and fire control, Electro-Optics head-up display and automatic gunsight. Two Elta AN/ARC-51 UHF transceivers. Twin landing lights on nosewheel leg; anti-collision light in fin leading-edge. C7 differs in having an improved HOTAS (hands on throttle and stick) cockpit installation, facilitated by avionics which include a WDNS-391 as standard, an Elbit System 82 computerised stores management and release system, video subsystems, 'smart weapons' delivery capability, and updated electronic warfare systems. The EL-2001 ranging radar is replaced by an Elta EL/M-2001B advanced pulse-Doppler fire control radar, with lookup/lookdown capability, Doppler beam-sharpened mapping, terrain avoidance/following and sea search modes.

ARMAMENT: Fixed armament of one IAI built 30 mm DEFA 552 cannon in underside of each engine air intake (140 rds/gun). Nine hardpoints (five under fuselage and two under each wing) for up to 5,775 kg (12,730 lb) of external weapons, ECM pods or drop tanks. For interception duties, one Sidewinder, Python 3 or Shafrir 2 infra-red homing air-to-air missile can be carried under each outer wing. Ground attack version can carry a 3,000 lb M118 bomb, two 800 or 1,000 lb bombs, up to four 500 lb bombs, or a Shrike, Maverick or GBU-15 air-to-surface weapon under the fuselage, and two 1,000 lb or six 500 lb bombs (conventional, 'smart' or 'concrete dibber' type) under the wings. Alternative weapons can include Mk 82/83/84 and M117/118 bombs; CBU-24/49 and TAL-1/2 cluster bombs; LAU-3A/10A/32A rocket launchers; napalm, flares, chaff, ECM and other podded systems.

DIMENSIONS, EXTERNAL:
- Wing span: 8·22 m (26 ft 11½ in)
- Wing chord at root: 8·04 m (26 ft 4½ in)
- Wing aspect ratio: 1·94
- Foreplane span: 3·73 m (12 ft 3 in)
- Length overall, incl probe: C7: 15·65 m (51 ft 4¼ in)
  - TC7: 16·36 m (53 ft 8 in)
- Height overall: 4·55 m (14 ft 11¼ in)
- Wheel track: 3·20 m (10 ft 6 in)
- Wheelbase: C7: 4·87 m (15 ft 11¾ in)
  - TC7: 4·50 m (14 ft 9 in)

AREAS:
- Wings, gross: 34·8 m² (374·6 sq ft)
- Foreplanes (total): 1·66 m² (17·87 sq ft)

WEIGHTS AND LOADING:
- Weight empty (interceptor, estimated): 7,285 kg (16,060 lb)
- Max usable fuel: internal: 2,572 kg (5,670 lb)
  - external: 3,727 kg (8,217 lb)
- Typical combat weight:
  - interceptor, 50% internal fuel, two Shafrir missiles: 9,390 kg (20,700 lb)
  - interceptor, two 500 litre drop tanks, two Shafrir missiles: 11,603 kg (25,580 lb)
  - combat air patrol, three 1,300 litre drop tanks, two Shafrir missiles: 14,270 kg (31,460 lb)
  - ground attack, two 1,300 litre drop tanks, seven 500 lb bombs, two Shafrir missiles: 14,670 kg (32,340 lb)
- Max 'clean' T-O weight: 10,415 kg (22,961 lb)
- Max combat T-O weight: 16,500 kg (36,376 lb)
- Wing/foreplane loading at 9,390 kg (20,700 lb) combat weight: 257·5 kg/m² (52·8 lb/sq ft)
- Thrust/weight ratio at 9,390 kg (20,700 lb) combat weight: 1·1

PERFORMANCE:
- Max level speed above 11,000 m (36,000 ft): over Mach 2·3 (1,317 knots; 2,440 km/h; 1,516 mph)
- Max sustained level speed at height, 'clean': Mach 2·0
- Max level speed at S/L, 'clean': 750 knots (1,389 km/h; 863 mph)
- Max rate of climb at S/L: 14,000 m (45,930 ft)/min
- Time to 15,240 m (50,000 ft), full internal fuel, two Shafrir missiles: 5 min 10 s
- Height attainable in zoom climb: 22,860 m (75,000 ft)
- Stabilised ceiling (combat configuration): 17,680 m (58,000 ft)
- T-O run at max T-O weight: 1,450 m (4,750 ft)
- Landing from 15 m (50 ft) at 11,566 kg (25,500 lb) landing weight: 1,555 m (5,100 ft)
- Landing run at 11,566 kg (25,500 lb) landing weight: 1,280 m (4,200 ft)
- Combat radius, 20 min fuel reserves:
  - interceptor, one 825 litre and two 1,300 litre drop tanks, two Shafrir missiles: 419 nm (776 km; 482 miles)
  - combat air patrol, one 1,300 litre and two 1,700 litre drop tanks, two Shafrir missiles, incl 60 min loiter: 476 nm (882 km; 548 miles)
  - ground attack, hi-lo-hi, two 800 lb and two 500 lb bombs, two Shafrir missiles, one 1,300 litre and two 1,700 litre drop tanks: 640 nm (1,186 km; 737 miles)
- Ferry range:
  - three 1,300 litre drop tanks: 1,614 nm (2,991 km; 1,858 miles)
  - one 1,300 litre and two 1,700 litre drop tanks: 1,744 nm (3,232 km; 2,008 miles)
- *g* limit: +7·5

IAI ARAVA

Design of the Arava light STOL transport started in 1966, and construction of a prototype began towards the end of that year. This airframe was used for structural testing; it was followed by two flying prototypes, of which the first (4X-IAI) made its initial flight on 27 November 1969 and the second (4X-IAA) on 8 May 1971.

The Arava was first certificated as a civil aircraft, by the FAA in April 1972. This version, designated IAI 101, did not go into production, but formed the basis for the initial production IAI 102 (civil) and IAI 201 (military) transport versions.

More than 90 Aravas had been delivered by mid-1985, most of these being military IAI 201s and the majority of military and civil sales being to customers in Latin America. At that time, contracts for another 20 aircraft were said to be imminent, for customers in Africa, Central America and elsewhere. Contrary to previous reports, Israeli official sources now say that, apart from brief and successful use in the 1973 and subsequent conflicts, the Israeli Air Force continued to operate its Douglas C-47s in the main transport and trainer roles. Only in 1984 did it begin to replace these elderly aircraft with Aravas (a mixture of IAI 201s and 202s), deliveries of which were continuing in 1985. Duties include that of multi-engined trainer for transport pilots.

The following models of the Arava are currently available:

IAI 101B. Updated version, with PT6A-36 engines and accommodation for 19 passengers or more than 2,360 kg (5,200 lb) of cargo. Improved cabin interior, and enhanced performance at higher ambient temperatures. Certificated by FAA under SFAR Pt 41 on 17 November 1980 and SFAR Pt 41C in October 1982. Intended primarily for US commuter market. First customer was Airspur of Los Angeles, which ordered a cargo version (marketed in USA as **Cargo Commuterliner**) in June 1981, and the first of these entered service in March 1982. Four had been delivered to Airspur by September 1983.

IAI 102. Initial production civil transport version, based on IAI 101; certificated by Israel Civil Aviation Administration in April 1976. Accommodation for 20 passengers in airline-standard four-abreast configuration, with toilet. Available also in a VIP configuration for up to 12 passengers, as an all-cargo transport, as a medical clinic for flying doctor services, and in versions for mapping, mining research, rainmaking and bridge construction, as flying laboratories for agriculture and health ministries, and for supplying oil prospecting units. Total of 15 sold by September 1983, including eight in Argentina and five in Africa. One of the Argentine Aravas (LV-MRR) was adapted in that country by CATA to a water bomber configuration, with a 209 kg (461 lb) self-transportable water tank installation loaded into the cabin via the fuselage tailcone. The installation can deliver approx 2·72 tonnes (3 US tons) of water in 4 s.

IAI 201. Military transport version, based on IAI 101. Prototype (4X-IAB) first flew on 7 March 1972. Three lease-operated by Israeli Air Force in October 1973, others being delivered 1984-85. Standard equipment enables a wide variety of missions to be undertaken. Total of at least 68 sold by Spring 1985, including some equipped for maritime surveillance duties, fitted with either an AD-9 modification to extend the range and detection capability of the standard search/weather radar, or a more advanced detection system. Available also in several electronic warfare configurations, with various pallet-mounted elint and ESM packages, ventral or fuselage-side 'dustbin' radome, rearward facing scanners mounted on the fuselage tailcone, a 60kVA APU for additional electrical power generation, and numerous blade and whip type antennae above and below fuselage, on top of tailbooms, and elsewhere. According to independent survey published in Israel in 1985, export sales (not confirmed by IAI) have been made to the Bolivian Air Force (6), Colombian Air Force (3), Ecuadorean Army (6) and Navy (4), Guatemalan Air Force (10-17), Honduran Air Force (6), Liberian Air Force (4), Mexican Air Force (10), Nicaraguan Air Force (2), Papua New Guinea Defence Force (3), Paraguayan Air Force (6), Salvadorean Air Force (11-25), Swaziland (1), Thailand (3) and Venezuelan Army (3).

Israeli Air Force IAI 202 Arava, with winglets *(Ivo Sturzenegger)*

IAI 202. Modified version, flight tested (4X-IAO) in 1976-77. Differs principally in being longer, and in having a fully 'wet' wing containing approx 726 kg (1,600 lb) more fuel, wingtip winglets, and a boundary layer fence just inboard of each tip. Powered by 559 kW (750 shp) PT6A-36 engines; single-point pressure refuelling system. The winglet modification (but not the increased fuel capacity) is available as a retrofit modification of existing Aravas. Several IAI 202s operate in South America, and 1984-85 deliveries to the Israeli Air Force include some of this version. An improved version of the 202, with new engines and seats for up to 30 passengers, was under study in 1985.

The following description applies to the IAI 201, except where otherwise indicated:

TYPE: Twin-turboprop STOL light military transport.

WINGS: Braced high-wing monoplane, with single streamline section strut each side. Wing section NACA 63(215)A 417. Dihedral 1° 30′. Incidence 0° 27′. No sweepback. Light alloy two-spar torsion box structure. Frise light alloy ailerons. Electrically operated double-slotted light alloy flaps. Scoop type light alloy spoilers, for lateral control, above wing at 71 per cent chord. Electrically actuated trim tab in port aileron. Endplate winglets of NASA (Whitcomb) profile standard on IAI 202, optional for other models.

FUSELAGE: Conventional semi-monocoque light alloy structure of stringers, frames and single-skin panels. Of increased length on IAI 202.

TAIL UNIT: Cantilever light alloy structure, with twin fins and rudders, carried on twin booms extending rearward from engine nacelles. Fixed incidence tailplane. Geared tab and electrically actuated trim tab in elevator and geared trim tab in each rudder. Tailbooms are built by IAI Combined Technologies Division.

LANDING GEAR: Non-retractable tricycle type, of Servo-Hydraulics Lod manufacture, with single mainwheels and steerable nosewheel. Mainwheels carried on twin struts, incorporating oleo-pneumatic shock absorbers. Mainwheels size 11·00-12, tyre pressure 3·31 bars (48 lb/sq in); nosewheel size 9·00-6, tyre pressure 2·90 bars (42 lb/sq in). Disc brakes on main units.

POWER PLANT: Two 559 kW (750 shp) Pratt & Whitney Canada PT6A-34 turboprop engines, each driving a Hartzell HC-B3TN three-blade hydraulically actuated fully-feathering reversible-pitch metal propeller. (PT6A-36 engines of same T-O rating in IAI 101B and IAI 202.) Electric de-icing of propellers optional. Two integral fuel tanks in each wing, with total usable capacity (except IAI 202) of 1,663 litres (366 Imp gallons). Four overwing refuelling points. Optional pressure refuelling point (standard on IAI 202) behind fuselage/strut fairing. Two cabin mounted tanks, each of 1,022 litres (225 Imp gallons), are available optionally for self-ferry flights.

ACCOMMODATION: Crew of one or two on flight deck, with door on starboard side. Airline type seating for up to 20 passengers in IAI 102 (19 in IAI 101B, 24 in IAI 202), plus toilet. IAI 201 can accommodate 24 fully equipped troops (30 in IAI 202), or 16 paratroops and 2 dispatchers (20 + 3 in IAI 202). Outward opening door at rear of cabin, opposite which, at floor level, is an emergency exit/baggage door on the starboard side. Rear doors are built by IAI Combined Technologies Division. Fuselage tailcone is hinged to swing sideways through more than 90° to provide unrestricted access to main cabin. Alternative interior configurations available for ambulance role (12 stretchers and 2 medical attendants in IAI 201; 12 stretchers and 5 medical attendants/sitting patients in IAI 202); as all-freight transport carrying (typically) a Jeep mounted recoil-less rifle and its four-man crew; or as a maritime patrol aircraft fitted with search radar and other special equipment (see IAI 201 model listing paragraph). Emergency exit on each side, forward of wing leading-edge.

SYSTEMS: Hydraulic system (pressure 172 bars; 2,500 lb/sq in) for brakes and nosewheel steering only. Electrical system includes two 28V 170A DC engine driven starter/generators, a 28V 40Ah nickel-cadmium battery, and two 250VA 115/26V 400Hz static inverters.

AVIONICS AND EQUIPMENT: Blind-flying instrumentation standard. Optional avionics include VHF, VOR/ILS, ADF, marker beacon receiver, weather radar and PA system.

AVIONICS (electronic warfare version): Elta EL/L-8310 manually operated elint/ESM (electronic intelligence/surveillance) system (L-8311 or L-8312 systems optional); Elta EL/K-7010 jamming system; plus 60kVA auxiliary generator to provide necessary additional electrical power. See also photograph on page 136.

ARMAMENT: Optional 0·50 in Browning machine-gun pack on each side of fuselage, above a pylon for a pod containing six 82 mm rockets. Rearward firing machine-gun optional. Librascope gunsight.

DIMENSIONS, EXTERNAL:

Wing span: 201	20·96 m (68 ft 9 in)
202	21·63 m (70 ft 11½ in)
Wing chord (constant)	2·09 m (6 ft 10½ in)
Wing aspect ratio	10
Length overall: 201	13·03 m (42 ft 9 in)
202	13·47 m (44 ft 2¼ in)
Length of fuselage pod: 201	9·33 m (30 ft 7 in)
202	10·23 m (33 ft 6¾ in)
Diameter of fuselage	2·50 m (8 ft 2 in)
Height overall: 201	5·21 m (17 ft 1 in)
202	5·22 m (17 ft 1½ in)
Tailplane span (c/l of tailbooms)	5·21 m (17 ft 1 in)
Wheel track	4·01 m (13 ft 2 in)
Wheelbase: 201	4·62 m (15 ft 2 in)
202	5·12 m (16 ft 9½ in)
Propeller diameter	2·59 m (8 ft 6 in)
Propeller ground clearance	1·75 m (5 ft 9 in)
Crew door (fwd, stbd): Height	0·93 m (3 ft 0½ in)
Width	0·48 m (1 ft 7 in)
Passenger door (rear, port):	
Height	1·57 m (5 ft 2 in)
Width	0·62 m (2 ft 0½ in)
Airdrop opening, tailcone removed:	
Height	1·75 m (5 ft 9 in)
Width	2·33 m (7 ft 8 in)
Emergency/baggage door (rear, stbd):	
Height	1·12 m (3 ft 8 in)
Width	0·61 m (2 ft 0 in)

IAI 201 Arava twin-turboprop STOL light military transport *(Pilot Press)*

Electronic warfare versions of the Arava have been completed in various configurations. This one is equipped with an Elta EL/L-8310 elint system, the canister shaped antenna for which can be seen below the first cabin window. In flight, this is lowered to an underfuselage position where it can rotate through 360° to detect radar threat signals from any direction. An alternative EW configuration, with numerous blade antennae sprouting from the wings, tailbooms and flight deck roof, was illustrated in the 1985-86 edition

Emergency window exits (each):
- Height: 0·66 m (2 ft 2 in)
- Width: 0·48 m (1 ft 7 in)

DIMENSIONS, INTERNAL:
- Cabin, excl flight deck and hinged tailcone:
  - Length: 201: 3·87 m (12 ft 8 in)
  - 202: 4·77 m (15 ft 7¾ in)
  - Max width: 2·33 m (7 ft 8 in)
  - Max height: 1·75 m (5 ft 9 in)
  - Floor area: 201: 7·16 m² (77·07 sq ft)
  - 202: 8·83 m² (95·05 sq ft)
  - Volume: 201: 12·7 m³ (449·2 cu ft)
  - 202: 16·3 m³ (575·6 cu ft)
- Baggage compartment volume: 2·60 m³ (91·8 cu ft)
- Tailcone volume: 3·20 m³ (113 cu ft)

AREAS:
- Wings, gross: 43·68 m² (470·2 sq ft)
- Ailerons (total): 1·75 m² (18·84 sq ft)
- Trailing-edge flaps (total): 8·80 m² (94·72 sq ft)
- Spoilers (total): 0·85 m² (9·2 sq ft)
- Fins (total): 4·86 m² (52·31 sq ft)
- Rudders (total, incl tabs): 3·44 m² (37·03 sq ft)
- Tailplane: 9·36 m² (100·75 sq ft)
- Elevator, incl tabs: 2·79 m² (30·03 sq ft)

WEIGHTS AND LOADINGS:
- Basic operating weight empty:
  - 201: 3,999 kg (8,816 lb)
  - 202: 4,111 kg (9,063 lb)
- Max payload: 201: 2,351 kg (5,184 lb)
  - 202: 2,500 kg (5,511 lb)
- Max T-O weight: 201: 6,804 kg (15,000 lb)
  - 202: 7,711 kg (17,000 lb)
- Max landing weight: 201: 6,804 kg (15,000 lb)
  - 202: 7,416 kg (16,349 lb)
- Max zero-fuel weight: 201: 6,350 kg (14,000 lb)
- Max wing loading: 201: 153·5 kg/m² (31·44 lb/sq ft)
  - 202: 176·5 kg/m² (36·15 lb/sq ft)
- Max power loading: 201: 6·08 kg/kW (10·00 lb/shp)
  - 202: 6·90 kg/kW (11·33 lb/shp)

PERFORMANCE (at max T-O weight; 201 except where indicated):
- Never-exceed speed: 215 knots (397 km/h; 247 mph)
- Max level speed at 3,050 m (10,000 ft): 176 knots (326 km/h; 203 mph)
- Max cruising speed at 3,050 m (10,000 ft): 172 knots (319 km/h; 198 mph)
- Econ cruising speed at 3,050 m (10,000 ft):
  - 201: 168 knots (311 km/h; 193 mph)
  - 202: 150 knots (278 km/h; 173 mph)
- Stalling speed: flaps up: 75 knots (140 km/h; 87 mph)
  - flaps down: 62 knots (115 km/h; 72 mph)
- Max rate of climb at S/L: 393 m (1,290 ft)/min
- Rate of climb at S/L, one engine out: 55 m (180 ft)/min
- Service ceiling: 7,620 m (25,000 ft)
- Service ceiling, one engine out: 2,375 m (7,800 ft)
- STOL T-O run: 201: 293 m (960 ft)
  - 202: 400 m (1,315 ft)
- STOL T-O to 15 m (50 ft): 463 m (1,520 ft)
- STOL landing from 15 m (50 ft): 469 m (1,540 ft)
- STOL landing run: 250 m (820 ft)
- Range with max payload, 45 min reserves:
  - 201: 151 nm (280 km; 174 miles)
  - 202: 340 nm (630 km; 392 miles)
- Range with max fuel, 45 min reserves:
  - 201: 570 nm (1,056 km; 656 miles)
  - 202, 1,450 kg (3,197 lb) payload: 870 nm (1,612 km; 1,002 miles)

IAI 1124 WESTWIND

Israeli Navy designation: 1124N Sea Scan

The Westwind had its origins in the Jet Commander designed in the USA by Mr Ted Smith and flown for the first time on 27 January 1963. Production was transferred in 1968 to Israel Aircraft Industries, which has continued to develop and market successively improved versions.

A total of 186 early model Jet Commander/Commodore Jet/1123 Westwind executive aircraft, with General Electric CJ610 turbojet engines, were built by Aero Commander in the USA (150) and IAI (36). Details of these have appeared in previous editions of *Jane's*. Aircraft from c/n 187 onwards have Garrett TFE731 turbofan engines and are designated as follows:

1124 Westwind. Initial turbofan powered production version (53 built), introduced in 1975. Described in detail in 1978-79 *Jane's*.

1124 Westwind I. Basic turbofan powered production version since 1978, introduced from c/n 240 onwards. Improved version of 1124 Westwind, differing chiefly in having optional 317 kg (700 lb) increase in fuel load in removable tank in forward baggage compartment; increase of approx 5 per cent in cabin useful volume, achieved by relocation of some avionics and by lowering floor in toilet compartment; RCA Primus 400 colour weather radar as standard; and improved fuel and environmental control systems. Four of this version, operated by Rhein-Flugzeugbau, equipped for target towing on behalf of West German armed forces.

1124N Sea Scan. Maritime version. Three delivered to Israeli Navy in 1977 for coastal patrol, tactical support and anti-terrorist duties were later brought up to 1124N standard and equipped with thrust reversers, single-point pressure refuelling, anti-corrosion protection, fuselage-side stores pylons, bubble windows, Litton APS-504(V)2 360° search radar, Global GNS-500A VLF/Omega navigation system, operators' consoles, galley, and toilet. A low-altitude search range of 1,379 nm (2,555 km; 1,588 miles), and search endurance of more than 6 h 30 min, enables the Sea Scan to cover a search area of 82,740 nm² (268,056 km²; 103,496 sq miles) along a 60 nm (111 km; 69 mile) search band at a height of 915 m (3,000 ft). Increased search range and endurance to 2,500 nm (4,633 km; 2,878 miles) and over 8 h can be attained at altitudes up to 13,715 m (45,000 ft). Operational equipment to customer's specification.

Preliminary design and evaluation studies of a second generation Sea Scan have been completed by IAI. No sales of either version have been reported to *Jane's*, although Honduras and Panama are each reported to operate one 'Westwind reconnaissance aircraft'. In addition to routine anti-terrorist low-level maritime patrol functions, the new Sea Scan could be deployed for ASW, signal intelligence (sigint) and anti-shipping air-to-surface missile attack operations. In the ASW role, search, detection, tracking, identification and attack would be carried out using high performance maritime search radar, ESM, sonobuoys, onboard signal analysis, colour multi-purpose displays (MPDs), trailing MAD, long-range gyro stabilised sighting system (GSSS), and torpedos. Search, localisation and attack at 100 nm (185 km; 115 miles) from base could be performed for approx 5 h, enabling a landing back at base with 45 min reserve fuel. Replacing torpedos with Gabriel Mk III air-to-surface missiles, and removing some specific ASW mission equipment (sonobuoys, MAD etc), would allow anti-shipping missile attacks to be made from a standoff range of 32 nm (60 km; 37 miles) at distances greater than 1,000 nm (1,853 km; 1,151 miles) from base. Comint, elint and IDF equipment installed in the aircraft would permit long-range high-altitude sigint operations with an endurance of more than 8 h.

1124A Westwind 2. Developed version of Westwind I for improved 'hot and high' field performance, range and economy of operation. Prototype (4X-CMK, c/n 239, converted from early production 1124 Westwind) flown for first time on 24 April 1979. Certificated by Israeli CAA on 11 December 1979 and by FAA on 17 April 1980. New modified 'Sigma' wing of IAI section, NASA type winglets above tip tanks, flat (instead of 'trenched') cabin floor, increased seated headroom, airline type flushing toilet, relocated overhead passenger service units, and other improvements. First delivery (of the prototype, to Helicol of Colombia) made on 16 May 1980. In production. More than 50 delivered.

Deliveries of turbofan powered Westwinds (all versions) totalled approximately 250 by the beginning of 1986, with combined production then reportedly one aircraft per month. The following description applies to both the 1124 Westwind I and 1124A Westwind 2, except where a specific version is indicated:

TYPE: Twin-turbofan business transport.

WINGS: Cantilever mid-wing monoplane. Wing section NACA 64A212 on Westwind I, IAI modified Sigma 1 on Westwind 2. Dihedral 2°. Incidence 1° at root, −1° at tip. Sweepback 4° 37′ at quarter-chord. Aluminium alloy flush riveted two-spar fail-safe structure. Manually operated all-metal ailerons. Electrically operated all-metal double-slotted Fowler trailing-edge flaps. Drooped and cambered glassfibre covered leading-edges (Westwind I only). Electrically operated trim tab in port aileron. Hydraulically actuated speed brake and two lift dumpers above each wing, forward of flap. All skins chemically milled and fully sealed. All primary control surfaces, including aileron tab, are fully mass balanced. Goodyear pneumatic de-icing boots standard. Permanently attached wingtip fuel tanks, with (Westwind 2 only) NASA type winglet on upper surface.

FUSELAGE: All-metal semi-monocoque flush riveted structure of aluminium alloy and steel sheet, with chemically milled skins. Built in two main sections and joined at rear pressure bulkhead. Forward section, except for nosecone, is fully pressurised and fail-safe.

TAIL UNIT: Cantilever all-metal structure, with 28° sweepback at tailplane quarter-chord and 35° sweepback at fin quarter-chord. Variable incidence tailplane, actuated

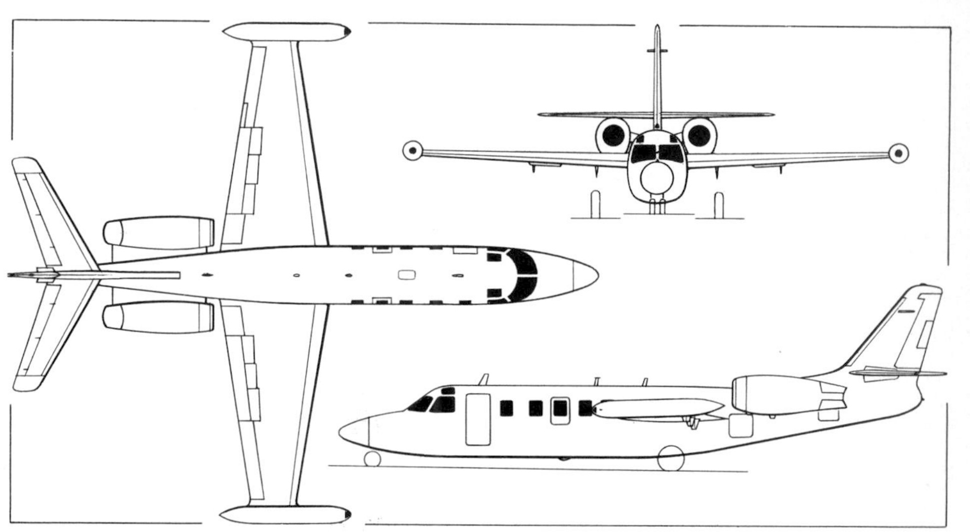

IAI 1124 Westwind I twin-turbofan executive light transport *(Pilot Press)*

electrically. Manually operated statically balanced elevators and rudder. Electrically operated trim tab in rudder. Goodyear pneumatic de-icing boots on tailplane leading-edges.

LANDING GEAR: Hydraulically retractable tricycle type, mainwheels retracting outward into wings, twin nosewheels rearward. No doors over mainwheels when retracted. Oleo-pneumatic shock absorbers. Single wheels on main units, pressure (Westwind I) 10·69 bars (155 lb/sq in). Nose unit steerable and self-centering. Nosewheel tyre pressure (Westwind I) 3·45 bars (50 lb/sq in). Westwind 2 has Goodyear wheels, with size 16 × 4·4 (main) and 24 × 9·50-10·5 tyres (nose), pressures 9·86 and 3·79 bars (143 and 55 lb/sq in) respectively. Goodyear multiple-disc brakes, with Hydro-Aire fully modulated anti-skid system having automatic computer/sensor to prevent wheel lock and maintain brake effectiveness. Parking brake.

POWER PLANT: Two 16·46 kN (3,700 lb st) Garrett TFE731-3-100G turbofan engines, with Grumman thrust reversers, pod mounted on sides of rear fuselage. 85 per cent of wing area forms an integral fuel tank, and additional fuel is carried separately in wingtip tanks and single rear fuselage tank. Total usable capacity (Westwind I) of 4,920 litres (1,082 Imp gallons; 1,300 US gallons), including wingtip tanks. Increased weight option permits additional 317 kg (700 lb) of fuel (397 litres; 87 Imp gallons; 105 US gallons) to be carried in a removable tank in forward baggage compartment. Capacity increased on Westwind 2, with 2,089 litres (460 Imp gallons; 552 US gallons) in each main wing tank, 428 litres (94 Imp gallons; 113 US gallons) in each wingtip tank, and 379 litres (83 Imp gallons; 100 US gallons) in rear fuselage auxiliary tank, giving total usable capacity of 5,413 litres (1,191 Imp gallons; 1,430 US gallons). Single-point pressure refuelling on starboard side of fuselage; gravity points in each wing upper surface, each tip tank, and for fuselage auxiliary tank. Oil capacity 5·7 litres (1·25 Imp gallons; 1·5 US gallons) per engine.

ACCOMMODATION: Standard seating for pilot, co-pilot and seven passengers, or up to a maximum of ten passengers, in pressurised and air-conditioned cabin. Elliptical cabin section in Westwind 2 increases seated headroom and allows a flat rather than 'trenched' cabin floor, an airline type flushing toilet, and improved placing of the overhead passenger service units. Standard passenger layout comprises six individual tracked and swivelling seats, with two tables, plus a one-person divan. Fully enclosed toilet compartment at rear of cabin on starboard side. Plug type door, at front on port side, provides access to both cabin and flight deck. Emergency exit on each side, forward of wing. Pressurised baggage compartment in rear of cabin, adjacent to toilet; two heated but unpressurised compartments for up to 476 kg (1,050 lb) of baggage in rear of fuselage, each with separate external access on port side.

SYSTEMS: Garrett three-spool freewheeling turbine air-conditioning system: pressurisation differential 0·61 bars (8·8 lb/sq in) normal, 0·62 bars (9·0 lb/sq in) maximum. Primary hydraulic system, pressure 138 bars (2,000 lb/sq in), operates through two engine driven pumps to actuate landing gear, wheel brakes, nosewheel steering, speed brakes, lift dumpers and thrust reversers. Electrically operated emergency system, pressure 69 bars (1,000 lb/sq in), for brakes only. Pneumatic system, using engine bleed air, for wing and tailplane de-icing boots only. DC electrical system with two 350A 28V engine driven starter/generators and two 28V 37Ah long life nickel-cadmium batteries. One main bus for each generator, connected to the central battery bus. Two 1kVA solid state static inverters provide 115V AC power at 400Hz, each being independently capable of supplying the entire AC load if required. Engine air intakes anti-iced by engine bleed air. Oxygen system supplied by pressurised cylinder of 1·36 m^3 (48 cu ft) capacity. Electrically heated windscreen, pitot system and angle of attack sensor. Engine fire extinguishing system. No APU.

AVIONICS AND EQUIPMENT (Westwind I): Full dual IFR instrumentation standard, including Collins dual VHF-20A com, dual VIR-30A nav, dual DME-40 and ADF-60A. Other avionics include Collins NCS-31A radar navigation and control system (Global Navigation NS-500A VLF in Sea Scan), RCA Primus 400 weather radar, and dual Sperry C-14 compass system. Collins FCS-105 flight control system (FD-109Z flight director and AP-105 autopilot). Canadian Marconi CMA-734 Omega navigation system approved for use in US and North Atlantic airspace.

AVIONICS AND EQUIPMENT (Westwind 2): Standard avionics and equipment (all Collins except where indicated) include dual VHF-20A VHF com, dual VIR-30A VHF nav, IAI nav switching system, FCS-80 flight control system, FDS-85 flight director, APS-80 autopilot, ADS-80 air data system, FMS-90 navigation system, DME-40 DME, ADF-60A ADF, dual RMI-36 RMIs, dual TDR-90 transponders, ALT-50A radio altimeter, ALI-80A encoding altimeter (pilot), Kollsman B4420 digital altimeter (co-pilot), MSI-80C Mach/airspeed indicator (pilot), IDC Mach/airspeed indicator (co-pilot), VNI-80A vertical nav indicator (pilot), Teledyne SLZ-9706-DGLE vertical nav indicator (co-pilot), PRE-80A preselector/alerter, dual 346B-3 audio systems, RNS-300 radar navigation system, WXR-300 weather radar, Teledyne SLZ-9618-5 angle of attack system, dual Sperry C-14 compasses, HSI-84 co-pilot's HSI, Sperry GH-14B co-pilot's attitude gyro, J.E.T. A1-804 standby attitude gyro, and Davco 811-B digital clock. Landing light in nose of each wingtip tank. Optional avionics include dual VHF-20B (instead of VHF-20A) and single VHF-251 VHF com; HF-718U-5 and HF-220 HF com; Litton LTN-211, Collins LRN-85 or Global GNS-500A-2 VLF/Omega nav; Collins EFIS-85A; Global GNS-1000 airborne flight information system (AFIS); second FDS-85, second ADC-80J for co-pilot's FDS-85, and comparator warning annunciator system; second ADF-60A, second DME-40, FPA-80 Flight Profile ADV, Collins TAI-80A SAT/TAS indicator, DRI-55 digital radio altimeter, ALT-55B (instead of ALT-50A) radio altimeter; Fairchild 5424-501 flight data recorder; Fairchild A-100 cockpit voice recorder; Kollsman ALT B4515 co-pilot's encoding altimeter (instead of B4420); Davco 811-B co-pilot's digital clock, Hobbs hour meter, Dorne and Margolin ELT-6 emergency locator transmitter, Devore Tel-Tail lights, Wulfsberg Flitefone III system, and ICD cabin display.

DIMENSIONS, EXTERNAL:
Wing span: incl tip tanks 13·65 m (44 ft 9½ in)
excl tip tanks 13·16 m (43 ft 2 in)
Wing chord: at root 3·20 m (10 ft 6 in)
at tip: Westwind I 1·07 m (3 ft 6 in)
Westwind 2 1·17 m (3 ft 10¼ in)
Wing aspect ratio 6·51
Length overall 15·93 m (52 ft 3 in)
Fuselage: Max width 1·57 m (5 ft 2 in)
Max depth 1·83 m (6 ft 0 in)
Height overall 4·81 m (15 ft 9½ in)
Tailplane span 6·40 m (21 ft 0 in)
Wheel track 3·35 m (11 ft 0 in)
Wheelbase 7·79 m (25 ft 6¾ in)
Passenger door: Height 1·32 m (4 ft 4 in)
Width 0·61 m (2 ft 0 in)
Height to sill 0·51 m (1 ft 8 in)
Baggage compartment door (main):
Height 0·61 m (2 ft 0 in)
Width 0·56 m (1 ft 10 in)
Height to sill 0·91 m (3 ft 0 in)
Baggage compartment door (rear):
Height 0·38 m (1 ft 3 in)
Width 0·51 m (1 ft 8 in)
Height to sill 1·27 m (4 ft 2 in)
Emergency exits (each):
Height 0·66 m (2 ft 2 in)
Width 0·51 m (1 ft 8 in)

DIMENSIONS, INTERNAL:
Cabin, incl flight deck and toilet:
Length (Westwind 2) 6·08 m (19 ft 11¼ in)
Cabin, excl flight deck:
Length: Westwind I 4·72 m (15 ft 6 in)
Westwind 2 4·74 m (15 ft 6½ in)
Max width 1·45 m (4 ft 9 in)
Max height 1·50 m (4 ft 11 in)
Floor area 6·52 m^2 (70·2 sq ft)
Volume 9·83 m^3 (347 cu ft)
Baggage compartments: fwd (main) 1·13 m^3 (40 cu ft)
rear 0·40 m^3 (14 cu ft)
cabin 0·25 m^3 (9 cu ft)

AREAS (A: Westwind I, B: Westwind 2):
Wings, gross 28·64 m^2 (308·26 sq ft)
Ailerons (total) 1·43 m^2 (15·40 sq ft)
Trailing-edge flaps (total): A 3·86 m^2 (41·58 sq ft)
B 3·85 m^2 (41·40 sq ft)
Speed brakes/lift dumpers (total) 1·37 m^2 (14·80 sq ft)
Fin: A 3·52 m^2 (37·94 sq ft)
B 3·02 m^2 (32·52 sq ft)
Rudder, incl tab: A 0·99 m^2 (10·66 sq ft)
B 1·02 m^2 (11·00 sq ft)
Tailplane: A 4·87 m^2 (52·42 sq ft)
B 4·86 m^2 (52·28 sq ft)
Elevators (total) 1·64 m^2 (17·66 sq ft)

WEIGHTS AND LOADINGS (A: Westwind I, B: Westwind 2):
Weight empty, equipped: A 5,578 kg (12,300 lb)
Basic operating weight empty:
A (typical) 5,760 kg (12,700 lb)
B 6,010 kg (13,250 lb)
Max fuel: B 4,345 kg (9,580 lb)
Max payload: A 1,496 kg (3,300 lb)
A (optional) 1,542 kg (3,400 lb)
B 1,474 kg (3,250 lb)
Max T-O weight: A 10,365 kg (22,850 lb)
A (optional), B 10,660 kg (23,500 lb)
Max ramp weight: A 10,430 kg (23,000 lb)
A (optional), B 10,725 kg (23,650 lb)
Max landing weight: A, B 8,620 kg (19,000 lb)
Max zero-fuel weight: A, B 7,485 kg (16,500 lb)
Max cabin floor loading 976 kg/m^2 (200 lb/sq ft)
Max wing loading: A 361·73 kg/m^2 (74·13 lb/sq ft)
A (optional), B 372·02 kg/m^2 (76·23 lb/sq ft)
Max power loading: A 314 kg/kN (3·09 lb/lb st)
A (optional), B 324 kg/kN (3·18 lb/lb st)

PERFORMANCE (Westwind I, at max T-O weight of 10,365 kg; 22,850 lb, except where indicated):
Max level speed, S/L to 5,900 m (19,400 ft) 471 knots (872 km/h; 542 mph)
Max operating speed, S/L to 5,900 m (19,400 ft) 360 knots (666 km/h; 414 mph) IAS
Max operating Mach No. from 5,900 m (19,400 ft) to 13,725 m (45,000 ft) Mach 0·765
Econ cruising speed at 12,500 m (41,000 ft) 400 knots (741 km/h; 460 mph)
Stalling speed, flaps and landing gear down, at max landing weight 99 knots (183 km/h; 114 mph) CAS
Max rate of climb at S/L 1,524 m (5,000 ft)/min
Max operating altitude 13,715 m (45,000 ft)
FAA T-O balanced field length 1,495 m (4,900 ft)
T-O balanced field length at 8,165 kg (18,000 lb) AUW 945 m (3,100 ft)
Landing distance from 15 m (50 ft) at max landing weight, with thrust reversal 625 m (2,050 ft)
Landing distance from 15 m (50 ft) at 6,350 kg (14,000 lb) AUW, with thrust reversal 518 m (1,700 ft)
Range with 7 passengers and baggage, IFR reserves more than 2,150 nm (3,983 km; 2,475 miles)
Max range with 2 passengers and baggage, 45 min reserves more than 2,600 nm (4,815 km; 2,993 miles)
Range with long-range fuel tank, 5 passengers and baggage, IFR reserves, at T-O weight of 10,660 kg (23,500 lb) 2,400 nm (4,446 km; 2,763 miles)
Range with long-range fuel tank, 2 passengers and baggage, 45 min reserves, at T-O weight of 10,660 kg (23,500 lb) 2,900 nm (5,373 km; 3,339 miles)

PERFORMANCE (Westwind 2, at max T-O weight except where indicated):
Never exceed, max level and max cruising speed at 8,840 m (29,000 ft) 469 knots (868 km/h; 539 mph)
Econ cruising speed between 11,890 and 12,500 m (39,000-41,000 ft) 390 knots (723 km/h; 449 mph)
Stalling speed at max landing weight, flaps down, engines idling 99 knots (184 km/h; 114 mph) CAS
Max rate of climb at S/L 1,524 m (5,000 ft)/min
Rate of climb at S/L, one engine out 250 m (820 ft)/min
Max certificated ceiling 13,715 m (45,000 ft)
Service ceiling, one engine out:
at 9,072 kg (20,000 lb) gross weight 6,400 m (21,000 ft)
at 7,030 kg (15,500 lb) gross weight 9,450 m (31,000 ft)
Min ground turning radius 14·50 m (47 ft 7 in)
T-O run 1,218 m (3,995 ft)
T-O balanced field length 1,600 m (5,250 ft)
Landing from 15 m (50 ft) at max landing weight 747 m (2,450 ft)
Landing run at max landing weight 534 m (1,750 ft)
Range, NBAA VFR reserves:
with max payload (10 passengers) 2,390 nm (4,430 km; 2,750 miles)

IAI 1124A Westwind 2, with 'Sigma' wings, tip tanks and winglets

with max fuel and 4 passengers
2,905 nm (5,385 km; 3,345 miles)

OPERATIONAL NOISE LEVELS (FAR Pt 36 at max T-O weight):

T-O: Westwind I, normal MTOW	84·2 EPNdB
Westwind 2	85·1 EPNdB
Approach: Westwind I, normal MTOW	93·0 EPNdB
Westwind 2	92·8 EPNdB
Sideline: Westwind I, normal MTOW	88·4 EPNdB
Westwind 2	88·5 EPNdB

IAI 1125 ASTRA

Known originally as the 1125 Westwind, the Astra is a more fuel-efficient, environmentally acceptable aircraft in the Westwind mould, featuring an improved standard of passenger comfort. In effect, only the tail unit and engine nacelles remain virtually unchanged from the Westwind airframe. The major difference is in the wings, which have a new-design aerofoil section, are sweptback, and are mounted low on the fuselage. Whereas the Westwind's mid-mounted wings pass through the rear of the passenger cabin, those of the Astra pass beneath the cabin floor, so avoiding interruption of the available internal space. This relocation results in a deeper fuselage profile, allowing 25 cm (8 in) more cabin headroom than in the Westwind 2. The cabin is nearly 0·61 m (2 ft) longer and 5 cm (2 in) wider than in the Westwind, but otherwise the fuselage is little changed structurally except for a 50·8 cm (20 in) longer nose providing more space for avionics.

Design of the Sigma 2 wing section, a computer-assisted improvement by IAI of the Sigma 1 section employed in the Westwind 2, is intended to provide more efficient high-subsonic cruising flight over long ranges, with reduced operating costs. Construction makes wider use than the Westwind of composite materials, notably for the control surfaces.

Development plans for the Astra were announced at the NBAA show in 1979. Work on a full scale mockup began in 1980, and on the first of two flying prototypes in April 1982. The second of these (4X-WIN, c/n 4002) was the first to fly, on 19 March 1984, being followed by c/n 4001 (4X-WIA) in August 1984. The third airframe was for static and fatigue testing. First flight by a production Astra (4X-CUA) was made on 20 March 1985, and FAA certification to FAR Pt 25 was received on 29 August of that year. Customer deliveries were expected to begin in February 1986. Up to mid-1986, orders had been placed by IAI's North American distributor, Atlantic Aviation, for ten Astras.

TYPE: Twin-turbofan business transport.

WINGS: Cantilever low-wing monoplane, with sweptback leading-edges (34° inboard, 25° on outer panels) and outboard trailing-edges. Thin, high-efficiency Sigma 2 aerofoil section, of IAI design. One-piece fail-safe structure, mainly of aluminium alloys, incorporates machined ribs and wing skin panels and is attached to underfuselage by four main and five secondary frames. Wing/fuselage fairings are of Kevlar, wingtips and inboard leading-edges of Kevlar and Nomex. Automatic leading-edge slats (outboard), interconnected with mechanically actuated trailing-edge flaps. Spoilers/lift dumpers forward of flaps. Ailerons of carbonfibre with Nomex honeycomb core, are operated manually with hydraulic boost. No winglets or tip tanks.

FUSELAGE: Generally similar structurally to that of Westwind 2 except in wing carry-through area. Constant cross-section throughout passenger cabin. Nosecone of composite materials, flight deck windows of laminated polycarbonate.

TAIL UNIT: Generally similar to that of Westwind 2. No dorsal fin. Manually operated (by pushrod) elevators and rudder. Geared tab in rudder; electric trim for elevators, linked to flap operation.

LANDING GEAR: Retractable tricycle type, of SHL (Servo Hydraulics) design, with twin wheels on each unit. Tyre sizes 23 × 7 in (main), 16 × 4·4 in (nose). Hydraulic extension, retraction and nosewheel steering; hydraulic multi-disc anti-skid brakes.

POWER PLANT: Two 16·23 kN (3,650 lb st) Garrett TFE731-3B-200G turbofan engines, with Grumman hydraulically actuated thrust reversers, pod-mounted in Grumman nacelle on each side of rear fuselage. Standard fuel load of 4,588 litres (1,009 Imp gallons; 1,212 US gallons) contained in integral tank in wing centre-section (624·5 litres; 137·5 Imp gallons; 165 US gallons), two outer-wing tanks (combined capacity 2,180·5 litres; 479·5 Imp gallons; 576 US gallons), and upper and lower tanks in centre-fuselage (combined capacity 1,783 litres; 392 Imp gallons; 471 US gallons). Additional fuel can be carried in two 189 litre (41·5 Imp gallon; 50 US gallon) tanks in upper forward area of baggage compartment. Single-point pressure refuelling.

ACCOMMODATION: Crew of two on flight deck. Standard accommodation in pressurised cabin for six persons, two in forward facing seats at front and four in 'club' layout; galley, coatrack and toilet at rear. Maximum accommodation for nine passengers. Trenched aisle and domed roof give increase of 25 cm (8 in) in cabin max height. Plug type airstair door at front on port side; emergency exit over wing on each side. Heated baggage compartment aft of passenger cabin, with external access. Polycarbonate windscreen. Cabin soundproofing improved compared with Westwind 2.

First production IAI Astra twin-turbofan business transport

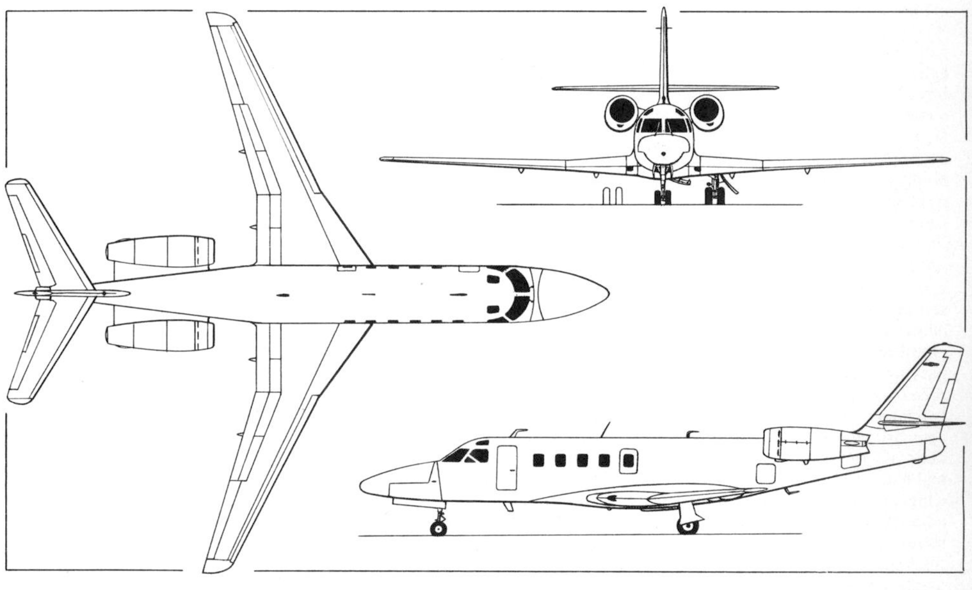

IAI 1125 Astra business transport (two Garrett TFE731-3B-200G turbofan engines) *(Pilot Press)*

SYSTEMS: Garrett environmental control system, with normal pressure differential of 0·615 bars (8·9 lb/sq in). Main and backup hydraulic systems, pressure 207 bars (3,000 lb/sq in), supply power via two engine driven pumps and electrically driven standby pump for actuation of brakes, landing gear, nosewheel steering, spoilers/lift dumpers, aileron boosters and thrust reversers. Either system alone is sufficient for manoeuvring the aircraft, and flight can be maintained manually even after total loss of hydraulic power. Electrical system comprises two 28V 300A starter/generators, two 1kVA solid state inverters and two 24Ah nickel-cadmium batteries; 28V DC external power receptacle standard.

AVIONICS AND EQUIPMENT: Collins EFIS-85 electronic flight instrument system, Collins Pro Line II com/nav, Collins APS-80 autopilot, single (optionally dual) Collins FMS-90 or Global GNS-1000 flight management system, weather radar, VLF/Omega navigation system and full IFR instrumentation standard.

DIMENSIONS, EXTERNAL:

Wing span	16·05 m (52 ft 8 in)
Wing aspect ratio	8·76
Length overall	16·94 m (55 ft 7 in)
Fuselage: Max width	1·57 m (5 ft 2 in)
Max depth	1·905 m (6 ft 3 in)
Height overall	5·54 m (18 ft 2 in)
Tailplane span	6·40 m (21 ft 0 in)
Wheel track (c/l of shock struts)	2·77 m (9 ft 1 in)
Wheelbase	7·34 m (24 ft 1 in)
Passenger door (fwd, port): Height	1·37 m (4 ft 6 in)
Width	0·66 m (2 ft 2 in)
Overwing emergency exits (each):	
Height	0·69 m (2 ft 3 in)
Width	0·48 m (1 ft 7 in)

DIMENSIONS, INTERNAL:

Cabin: Length: incl flight deck	6·86 m (22 ft 6 in)
excl flight deck	5·23 m (17 ft 2 in)
Max width	1·45 m (4 ft 9 in)
Max height	1·70 m (5 ft 7 in)
Baggage compartment volume	1·78 m³ (63 cu ft)

AREA:

Wings, gross	29·40 m² (316·6 sq ft)

WEIGHTS (A: without/B: with, long-range fuel tanks):

Basic operating weight empty (typical):	
A	5,747 kg (12,670 lb)
B	5,793 kg (12,770 lb)
Max usable fuel: A	3,901 kg (8,600 lb)
B	4,205 kg (9,270 lb)
Fuel with max payload: A, B	3,470 kg (7,650 lb)
Max payload: A	1,510 kg (3,330 lb)
B	1,465 kg (3,230 lb)
Payload with max fuel: A	1,080 kg (2,380 lb)
B	730 kg (1,610 lb)
Max ramp weight	10,727 kg (23,650 lb)
Max T-O weight	10,659 kg (23,500 lb)
Max landing weight	9,389 kg (20,700 lb)
Max zero-fuel weight	7,257 kg (16,000 lb)

PERFORMANCE (at max T-O weight ISA with long-range fuel tanks except where indicated):

Max cruising speed at 10,670 m (35,000 ft)
473 knots (876 km/h; 545 mph)

Max operating speed
Mach 0·855 or 360 knots (667 km/h; 414 mph)

Stalling speed at max landing weight:

flaps and gear up	111 knots (206 km/h; 128 mph)
flaps and gear down	92 knots (171 km/h; 106 mph)
Max rate of climb at S/L	1,085 m (3,560 ft)/min
Rate of climb at S/L, one engine out	335 m (1,100 ft)/min
Max certificated altitude	13,715 m (45,000 ft)
Service ceiling, one engine out	5,485 m (18,000 ft)
T-O balanced field length	1,518 m (4,980 ft)
Landing field length at max landing weight	806 m (2,645 ft)

Range with max fuel and 4 passengers, 45 min reserves:

at Mach 0·80	2,510 nm (4,651 km; 2,890 miles)
at Mach 0·72	3,110 nm (5,763 km; 3,581 miles)

OPERATIONAL NOISE LEVELS (FAR Pt 36 at max T-O weight, estimated):

T-O	88 EPNdB
Approach	92 EPNdB
Sideline	88 EPNdB

ITALY

AERITALIA

AERITALIA—SOCIETÀ AEROSPAZIALE ITALIANA p.A.

Piazzale Vincenzo Tecchio 51A (Casella Postale 3065), 80125 Naples
Telephone: (081) 7252111
Telex: N. 710370 AERIT
HONORARY CHAIRMAN: Amb Egidio Ortona
CHAIRMAN OF THE BOARD:
Ing Renato Bonifacio
DEPUTY CHAIRMAN AND MANAGING DIRECTOR:
Ing Fausto Cereti
GENERAL MANAGER: Dott Michele Crosio
DEPUTY GENERAL MANAGERS:
Ing Giandomenico Cantele (Combat Aircraft Group)
Dott Franco Capanna (Economics and Finance)
Ing Amedeo Caporaletti (Transport Aircraft Group)
Ing Roberto Mannu (Commercial)
Ing Carlo Scaglia (Avionics Systems and Equipment Group)
Ing Ernesto Vallerani (Space Systems Group)
SECRETARY GENERAL: Dott Massimo Rizzo
BOARD OF DIRECTORS:
Ing Renato Bonifacio
Ing Fausto Cereti
Dott Fabrizio Antonini
Dott Alfonso Cecere
Dott Antonio De Carlo
Dott Fabiano Fabiani
Ing Francesco La Via
Prof Roberto Marrama
Dott Umberto Nordio
Prof Carlo Pace
Gen Fulvio Ristori
Ing Beppe Sacchi
Prof Lucio Sicca
Dott Silvano Verzelli
EXECUTIVE DIRECTORS:
Ing Stefano Abbà (Research and Development)
Dott Eusebio Brancatisano (Finance)
Dott Gianni Cantini (Controller)
Ing Ciro Cirillo (Strategic Planning)
Ing Federico Dalla Volta (External Relations)
Ing Nino D'Angelo (Overhaul, Modification and Maintenance Group)
Ing Giovanni Gazzaniga (International Sales)
Ing Cesare Gianni (New Programmes Development)
Dott Claudio Gobbi (Personnel)
Ing Franco Lupidi (Domestic Sales)
Dott Filippo Martino (Organisation Planning and EDP Systems)
Ing Giuseppe Napoli (Asst General Manager)
Dott Nino Pusateri (General Affairs)
Ing Carlo Rosini (General Aviation Group)
Ing Ugo Sacerdote (Special International Agreements)
Ing Marcello Scolaris (Quality Assurance)
PRESS RELATIONS MANAGER: Dott Alfredo Mingione

Aeritalia is a joint stock company which was formed on 12 November 1969 by an equal shareholding of Fiat and IRI-Finmeccanica, to combine Fiat's aerospace activities (except those which concerned aero engines) with those of Aerfer and Salmoiraghi of the Finmeccanica group. The company became fully operational under the new title on 1 January 1972. On 28 September 1976 IRI-Finmeccanica purchased the Aeritalia stock owned by Fiat, thus acquiring complete control of the company's stock capital. In the Summer of 1981, following a general reorganisation of the Italian aerospace industry, Aeritalia acquired shareholdings of 100% in Aeronavali Venezia, 60% in Partenavia, and 50% in Meteor. A 25% holding in Aeronautica Macchi was acquired in 1983. Aeritalia has a total workforce of approx 14,500.

Aeritalia's organisation is based upon a centralised general management and seven operational groups: Combat Aircraft Group; Transport Aircraft Group; Avionics Systems and Equipment Group; Space Systems Group; Overhaul, Modification, Maintenance and General Aviation Group; RPVs and Missiles Group; and Alfa Romeo Avio (see Aero Engines section).

Aeritalia and Aermacchi (which see) are continuing, with EMBRAER of Brazil, the development phase of the AMX strike fighter, under an Italian Defence Ministry contract. Aeritalia is responsible for designing and manufacturing components for the Boeing 767 airframe, including nosecones, wing leading-edge slats, spoilers, outboard ailerons and trailing-edge flaps, and the elevators, fin and rudder. It is also a 50-50 partner with Aérospatiale of France in the ATR 42 regional transport aircraft programme, described in the International section.

COMBAT AIRCRAFT GROUP

HEADQUARTERS AND TURIN WORKS: Corso Marche 41, 10146 Turin
Telephone: (011) 33321
Telex: N. 221076 (AERITOR)
CASELLE WORKS: Turin Airport, 10100 Turin
Telephone: (011) 991362
Telex: 210095

The Turin area factories are engaged in the design, manufacture and testing of the AMX combat aircraft; design and manufacture of outer (movable) wings, final assembly and flight testing of the Panavia Tornado; definition, design and development of the Eurofighter European fighter aircraft, in partnership with other European companies; design and construction of wing for the EAP (Experimental Aircraft Programme) in collaboration with British Aerospace (see entry in UK section); manufacture of space vehicles; manufacture of carbonfibre structural components (ailerons and rudders) for the Boeing 767; and design, development, manufacture and testing of an improved weapon system for the F-104S. Other activities include extensive research in various fields of aerodynamics and advanced technologies (eg weapon dispensers and STOL aircraft), and the repair, overhaul and maintenance of F-104G, TF-104G and F-104S aircraft.

TRANSPORT AIRCRAFT GROUP

HEADQUARTERS AND NAPLES AREA WORKS: Viale dell' Aeronautica, 80038 Pomigliano d'Arco, Naples
Telephone: (081) 8451111
Telex: N. 710082 and 710522 (AERITPOM)
CAPODICHINO WORKS: Via del Riposo alla Doganella, Aeroporto di Capodichino, 80144 Naples
Telephone: (081) 7817111
Telex: N. 710356
CASORIA WORKS: Strada Statale 87 km 8·7, 80026 Casoria
Telephone: (081) 7583222
FOGGIA WORKS: Zona ASI, Localita Incoronata
Telephone: (0881) 38951
Telex: 810213

Aeritalia's principal activities in the Naples area comprise construction of the complete series of fuselage structural panels and moving surfaces for the McDonnell Douglas MD-80; fuselage upper panels and vertical tail surfaces for the DC-10 commercial airliner and KC-10A aerial tanker; engine support pylons for the Boeing 747; numerous components for the Boeing 767 (see earlier paragraph in this introduction); fuselages, outboard ailerons, trailing-edge flaps, spoilers and fins, and manufacture, assembly and flight testing, of the Aeritalia G222. Activities also include design and manufacture of the complete fuselage and tail unit of the ATR 42 regional transport aircraft.

The Foggia Works is dedicated mainly to the manufacture of structural components in carbonfibre, aramid fibre and other composite materials.

AVIONICS SYSTEMS AND EQUIPMENT GROUP

HEADQUARTERS AND CASELLE WORKS: 10072 Caselle, Turin
Telephone: (011) 991362
Telex: AITCEA 210086
NERVIANO WORKS: Viale Europa, 20014 Nerviano, Milan
Telephone: (0331) 587330
Telex: AITNER 330675

Since its creation within the Fiat Aircraft Division, and subsequent merger with Filotecnica Salmoiraghi, the activities of this Group have been extended to include research, development, production and integration of avionic systems and aircraft subsystems, ranging from nav/attack to computing and defensive aids. It has full capability to design and manufacture advanced analog and digital airborne equipment including main computer and databus controllers, flight control computers, armament controls and utility control systems. The Group is active in producing and integrating components and subsystems for the Hawk and other air defence missiles, and has developed customised turnkey flight inspection systems for both military (G222RM) and civil customers (Cessna Citation IIRM). Other activities include development and manufacturing of airborne and spaceborne electronic equipment, and instrumentation for Aeritalia's vehicles and for the international market. The Group also produces optical, optronic and electronic equipment and sensors, both for the military market (RPVs and other battlefield surveillance systems) and for civil (eg ecological mapping and biomedical) applications. The Group's own repair and overhaul facilities provide support for its products.

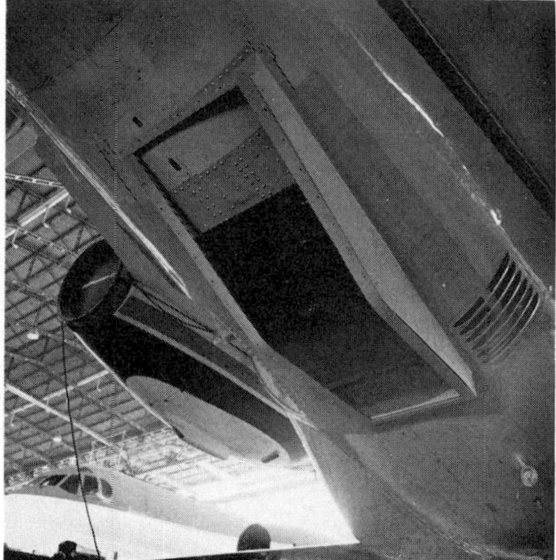

Underfuselage TV installation, for in-flight calibration of ground nav/com facilities, fitted by Aeritalia's Avionics Systems and Equipment Group to an Italian civil Cessna Citation IIRM of the Azienda Autonoma di Assistenza al Volo

SPACE SYSTEMS GROUP

HEADQUARTERS AND TURIN WORKS: Corso Marche 41, 10146 Turin
Telephone: (011) 33321
Telex: 221235

This Group is responsible for Aeritalia's space activities, taking part as a full partner in the international programmes of the European Space Agency (ESA), and is involved in national programmes, sponsored by the Ministry for Scientific Research and the National Research Council (CNR). The Turin factory's installations are capable of serving as an integration centre for major space systems, and the Group is European specialist in 'made for space' structures and thermal control, including work on such programmes as the ECS and Hipparcos satellites, the Olympus platform, the Eureca 'free flyer', and two flight models of the pressurised module for Spacelab. It leads the European industrial team producing pressurised modules for the Columbus programme, and is constructor of the Italian satellites Tethered, Lageos II, Sax and Iris. Further details of these programmes are given in *Jane's Spaceflight Directory*.

OVERHAUL, MODIFICATION, MAINTENANCE AND GENERAL AVIATION GROUP

HEADQUARTERS: Via Cupa Principe 102, 80144 Naples
Telephone: (081) 7817111
Telex: 722089
VENICE WORKS: Via Triestina 214, 30030 Tessera, Venice
Telephone: (041) 964044
Telex: 410446
CAPODICHINO WORKS: Via del Riposo alla Doganella, Capodichino, 80144 Naples
Telephone: (081) 7817111
CASELLE WORKS: Caselle Turin Airport, 10072 Caselle, Turin
Telephone: (011) 991362
Telex: 220411
CASORIA WORKS: Via Cava, 80026 Casoria (Naples)
Telephone: (081) 7596311
Telex: 720199 PARTNA I

This Group is responsible for providing full product support for aircraft built by Aeritalia; overhaul and conversion, through Officine Aeronavali Venezia's factory, in Venice, of aircraft not manufactured by Aeritalia; and support services, such as training of crew members and technicians, and field service, required by Aeritalia customers. On 1 September 1986, with an appropriate change of name, it took over the activities of the former General Aviation Group, centred upon the Partenavia plant at Casoria. These concern aircraft for the general aviation market, and for civil protection (eg, anti-pollution, patrol and fire observation). Design and production activities are undertaken by Partenavia, under which heading descriptions of current aircraft can be found.

RPVs and MISSILES GROUP

HEADQUARTERS: Piazzale Tecchio 51A, 80125 Naples
Telephone: (081) 7252111
Telex: 710370 AERIT I

Activities include those of Meteor SpA (which see).

ALFA ROMEO AVIO

HEAD OFFICE: Viale dell' Aeronautica, 80038 Pomigliano d'Arco, Naples
Telephone: (081) 8430111
Telex: 710082 AITPOM I

EUROFIGHTER

Aeritalia is collaborating in the design of this new generation fighter, all available details of which can be found in the International section.

AMX

A description and illustration of this joint Italian-Brazilian attack aircraft programme, involving Aeritalia, Aermacchi and EMBRAER, can be found in the International section of this edition.

ATR 42/72

Aeritalia is an equal partner with Aérospatiale of France in developing these new regional transport aircraft, descriptions and illustrations of which appear under the ATR heading in the International section.

TORNADO

Aeritalia has a 15% participation in the manufacturing programme for the Panavia Tornado (see International section), for which it is responsible for the radomes, the entire outer wings, including control surfaces, and the final assembly of aircraft for the Italian Air Force.

AERITALIA G222

Designed by Ing Giuseppe Gabrielli, the Aeritalia (originally Fiat) G222 was conceived in four separate configurations, three of which were halted at the research project stage. Two unpressurised prototypes were built of the military transport version, of which the first (MM582) made its initial flight on 18 July 1970 and the second (MM583) on 22 July 1971. The first prototype was handed over to the Italian Air Force on 21 December 1971 for operational evaluation. One airframe was completed for static and one for fatigue testing.

Several major Italian airframe companies share in the construction programme, including Aermacchi (outer wings); Piaggio (wing centre-section); SIAI-Marchetti (tail unit); CIRSEA (landing gear); and IAM (miscellaneous airframe components). Wing flaps are contributed by Hellenic Aerospace Industries. Fuselages are built by Aeritalia's Transport Aircraft Group, in the Pomigliano d'Arco Works near Naples; final assembly takes place at the Capodichino Works, Naples.

The following versions have been built:

G222. Standard military transport, to which the detailed description mainly applies. First delivery of a production G222 was made in November 1976 to the air force of Dubai, which ordered one. This was followed in 1977 by the first of three for the Argentine Army, and in early 1981 by two for the Somali Air Force. Two others originally ordered by Somalia were later cancelled. This version also ordered by Venezuelan Army (two) and Air Force (six), and Nigerian Air Force (five); deliveries to these countries were completed in 1985. Principal customer is the Italian Air Force, which has ordered 44 (30 standard transports, 8 G222SAA, 4 G222RM and 2 G222GE), of which 43 have been delivered. The first G222 for the Italian Air Force (MM62101) flew on 23 December 1975, and deliveries began on 21 April 1978. These aircraft are in service with the 46a Aerobrigata at Pisa-San Giusto, and are operated primarily in the roles of troop, paratroop and cargo transport, or for aeromedical duties. Six quick-change kits, produced by Aeritalia, are held by the Italian Air Force for in-the-field conversions to the aeromedical configuration. This latter version has been used in recent years in support of Red Cross relief operations in Kampuchea, Peru and elsewhere. Five G222s have been ordered by the Italian Ministry for Civil Defence, to create a rapid-intervention squadron for firefighting, aeromedical evacuation, and airlift of supplies to earthquake and other disaster areas. One of these aircraft had been delivered by the Spring of 1986.

G222RM. Flight inspection version (radiomisure), specially equipped for in-flight calibration of ground radio navigation and communication facilities (VOR, ILS, Tacan, NDB, AVHF and UHF). The automatic flight inspection system, based on an inspection programme recorded in a central computer, determines the exact aircraft position, mixing the information from an inertial reference unit with data from a DME or with visual fixes performed with a vertical TV, and processes signals from a set of dedicated receivers to provide the parameters of facilities under inspection. These parameters are available on CRT displays and on a paper recorder and printer. Only one flight inspector is necessary, in addition to the two-man flight crew, and ample space remains in the rear of the hold to carry a Jeep type vehicle for ground based operations. First flight of a G222RM took place in October 1982; the Italian Air Force ordered four, two being delivered in 1983 and two in 1984. They are operated from Pratica di Mare by the 8° Gruppo Sorveglianza Elettronica. Dimensions, weights and performance are similar to those of the standard troop transport.

G222SAA. Firefighting version (Sistema Aeronautico Antincendio), with specially designed modular dispersal system for water or retardant (see 'Equipment' paragraph later), testing of which was completed in 1976. Eight delivered to Italian Air Force, which has used them extensively and successfully in many parts of Italy.

G222T. Version with Rolls-Royce Tyne turboprop engines (see under 'Power Plant' for details), larger-diameter propellers and higher operating weights; other differences noted under 'Systems' and 'Performance' in main description. Twenty built, including two in VIP transport configuration, for Libyan Arab Air Force, by whom it is known as **G222L**, to overcome US embargo on export of General Electric engines to that country. Flown for the first time on 13 May 1980; delivered 1981-83.

G222VS (Versione Speciale). Electronic warfare version, first flown in prototype form on 9 March 1978. Carrying a pilot, co-pilot and up to ten systems operators, it has a modified cabin fitted with racks and consoles for detection, signal processing and data recording equipment, and an electrical system providing up to 40kW of power for its operation. Externally distinguishable by small 'thimble' radome beneath the nose and a larger 'doughnut' radome on top of the tail fin. Two ordered by Italian Air Force, of which the first was delivered in 1983; in service with the 71° Gruppo Guerra Elettronica at Pratica di Mare. IAF designation is **G222GE** (Guerra Elettronica). Second aircraft not delivered by Spring 1986. Dimensions, weights and performance similar to those of the standard troop transport.

Of the total of 88 G222s ordered (all versions), 83 had been delivered by 1 January 1986, with production continuing.

In addition to the foregoing, Aeritalia is actively studying further versions of the G222. The first of these is a 'light' **early warning/airborne warning and control** version which could be fitted with a GEC Avionics APY 922 AEW system in nose and tail mounted installations similar to those of the BAe Nimrod AEW. Mk 3 and Lockheed C-130 AEW. The second is a version for **maritime patrol** and possible **ASW/ASV** missions, and the third is a **launch aircraft for RPVs**. This last project, known as **Quiver**, would have a dorsal radome similar to (but smaller than) that of the AEW&C version, and would be able to carry up to six Meteor Mirach-100 jet powered RPVs beneath the outer wings (see photograph in RPVs & Targets section of 1985-86 *Jane's*). Two versions are being studied of a G222 **air tanker**, for in-flight refuelling of either two or one combat aircraft, capable (with minimum modifications to the basic transport) of transferring up to 5,000 kg (11,023 lb) of fuel. A kit enabling the basic aircraft itself to be refuelled in flight is also being studied. The G222 tanker is not a dedicated version, and could be reconfigured for the basic transport role in a very short time.

The prototype of a **marine oil spill control** version, with an easily installed and removed tank holding 6,000 litres (1,320 Imp gallons) of oil dispersant, was demonstrated at the 1986 Farnborough Air Show. Basic role of this version is the spraying of oil dispersant chemical, from a spraybar mounted above its tailplane, on to spillage pollutions at sea, although its use for spraying agricultural insecticide is also foreseen. Aeritalia is also studying an **Earth resources** version, equipped with an integrated aerial reconnaissance system for remote sensing of the environment. Possible applications include mapping of mineral and hydrological resources and glaciers, and identification of polluted areas, archaeological areas and vegetal diseases.

The following description applies to the standard G222 transport version, except where indicated:

TYPE: Twin-turboprop general purpose transport aircraft.

WINGS: Cantilever high-wing monoplane, with max thickness/chord ratio of 15%. Dihedral 2° 30′ on outer panels. Aluminium alloy three-spar fail-safe box structure, built in three portions. One-piece constant chord centre-section fits into recess in top of fuselage and is secured by bolts at six main points. Outer panels tapered on leading- and trailing-edges. Upper surface skins are of 7075-T6 alloy, lower surface skins of 2024-T3 alloy. All control surfaces have bonded metal skins with metal honeycomb core. Double-slotted flaps extend over 60 per cent of trailing-edge. Two-section hydraulically actuated spoilers ahead of each outboard flap segment, used also as lift dumpers on landing. Spoilers and flaps fully powered by tandem hydraulic actuators. Manually operated ailerons, each with inset servo tab. Pneumatically inflated de-icing boots on outer leading-edges, using engine bleed air.

FUSELAGE: Pressurised fail-safe structure of aluminium alloy stressed skin construction and circular cross-section. Easily removable stiffened floor panels.

TAIL UNIT: Cantilever safe-life structure of aluminium alloy, with sweptback three-spar fin and slightly swept two-spar variable incidence tailplane. Pneumatically inflated de-icing boots on fin and tailplane leading-edges, using engine bleed air. Rudder and elevators of metal honeycomb construction. Two tabs in each elevator; no rudder tabs. Rudder fully powered by tandem hydraulic actuators; elevators operated manually.

LANDING GEAR: Hydraulically retractable tricycle type, suitable for use from prepared runways, semi-prepared strips or grass fields. Messier-Hispano-Bugatti design, built under licence by CIRSEA (Nardi-Magnaghi). Steerable twin-wheel nose unit retracts forward. Main units, each consisting of two single wheels in tandem, retract into fairings on sides of fuselage. Oleo-pneumatic shock absorbers. Gear can be lowered by gravity in emergency, the nose unit being aided by aerodynamic action and the main units by the shock absorbers, which

Aeritalia G222RM flight inspection aircraft, operated by the 8° Gruppo (14° Stormo) of the Italian Air Force *(Aviodata)*

remain compressed in the retracted position. Oleo pressure in shock absorbers is adjustable to permit variation in height and attitude of cabin floor from ground. Low-pressure tubeless tyres on all units, size 37·91 × 12·35 in (Type III) on mainwheels, 27·56 × 10·51 in (Type III) on nosewheels. Tyre pressures 4·41 bars (64 lb/sq in) on main units, 3·92 bars (56·88 lb/sq in) on nose unit. Hydraulic multi-disc brakes.

Power Plant (except G222T): Two Fiat built General Electric T64-GE-P4D turboprop engines, each flat rated at 2,535 kW (3,400 shp) at ISA + 25°C and driving a Hamilton Standard 63E60-27 three-blade variable- and reversible-pitch propeller with spinner. Fuel in integral tanks: two in the outer wings, combined capacity 6,800 litres (1,495 Imp gallons), and two centre-section tanks, combined capacity 5,200 litres (1,143 Imp gallons), with cross-feed provision to either engine. Total overall fuel capacity 12,000 litres (2,638 Imp gallons). Single pressure refuelling point in starboard main landing gear fairing. Overwing gravity refuelling point above each tank.

Power Plant (G222T): Two 3,624 kW (4,860 shp) Rolls-Royce Tyne RTy.20 Mk 801 turboprop engines, with BAe 4/7000/6 four-blade variable-pitch propellers. Fuel system and capacity as for standard version.

Accommodation: Normal crew of three (two pilots and radio operator/flight engineer) on flight deck. Provision for loadmaster or jumpmaster when required. Standard troop transport version has 32 foldaway sidewall seats and 21 stowable seats for 53 fully equipped troops, and carries also two 20-man life rafts stowed in the wing/fuselage fairing and a single 9-man life raft in the cargo compartment. Paratroop transport version can carry up to 40 fully equipped paratroops, and is fitted with the 32 sidewall seats and life rafts as in the troop transport version, plus eight stowable seats, door jump platforms and static lines. Five-person VIP lounge plus seats for 16 other passengers in VIP transport version. Cargo transport version can accept standard pallets of up to 2·24 m (7 ft 4 in) wide, and can carry up to 9,000 kg (19,840 lb) of freight. Provision is made for 135 cargo tiedown points, on a 51 cm (20 in) square NATO standard grid, and a 1,500 kg (3,306 lb) capacity cargo hoist. Typical Italian military equipment loads can include two CL-52 light trucks; one CL-52 with a 105 mm L4 howitzer or one-ton trailer; Fiat AR-59 Campagnola reconnaissance vehicle with 106 mm recoilless gun or 250 kg (550 lb) trailer; or five standard A-22 freight containers. In the aeromedical role the G222 can accommodate 36 stretchers and four medical attendants. A second toilet can be installed, and provision can be made to increase the water supply and to install electrical points and hooks for medical treatment bottles. In this version, the cabin oxygen system is available to all stretcher positions. Crew door is forward of cabin on port side. Passenger doors, at front and rear of main cabin on starboard side and at rear on port side, can be used also as emergency exits. Two emergency hatches in cabin roof, forward and aft of wing carry-through structure. Hydraulically operated rear loading ramp and upward opening door in underside of upswept rear fuselage, which can be opened in flight for airdrop operations. In cargo version, five pallets of up to 1,000 kg (2,205 lb) each can be airdropped from rear opening, or a single pallet of up to 5,000 kg (11,023 lb). Paratroop jumps can be made either from this opening or from the rear side doors. Windscreens and quarter-light panels are de-iced and demisted electrically. Wipers and screen wash for both windscreens. Entire accommodation pressurised and air-conditioned.

Systems: Pressurisation system maintains a cabin differential of 0·41 bars (5·97 lb/sq in), giving a 1,200 m (3,940 ft) environment at altitudes up to 6,000 m (19,680 ft). Air-conditioning system uses engine bleed air (air supplied by centrifugal compressor in G222T) during flight; on ground, it is fed by compressor bleed air from APU to provide cabin heating to a minimum of 18°C. Garrett 113·3 kW (152 hp) APU, installed in starboard main landing gear fairing, provides power for engine starting, hydraulic pump and alternator actuation, air-conditioning on ground, and all hydraulic and electrical systems necessary for loading and unloading on ground. Two independent hydraulic systems, each of 207 bars (3,000 lb/sq in) pressure. No. 1 system actuates flaps, spoilers, rudder, wheel brakes and (in emergency only) landing gear extension; No. 2 system actuates flaps, spoilers, rudder, wheel brakes, nosewheel steering, landing gear extension and retraction, rear ramp/door and windscreen wipers. Auxiliary hydraulic system, fed by APU powered pump, can take over from No. 2 system in flight, if both main systems fail, to operate essential services. In addition, a standby handpump is provided for emergency use to lower the landing gear and, on the ground, to operate the ramp/door and parking brakes. Three 45kVA alternators (60kVA in G222T), one driven by each engine through constant-speed drive units and one by the APU, provide 115/200V three-phase AC electrical power at 400Hz. 28V DC power is supplied from the main AC buses via two transformer-rectifiers, with 24V 34Ah nickel-cadmium battery and static inverter for standby and emergency power. External AC power socket. Electric de-icing of spinners (except G222T) and propeller leading-edges. Engine intakes anti-iced by electrical/hot air system. Liquid oxygen system for crew and passengers (with cabin wall outlets); this system can be replaced by a gaseous oxygen system if required. Emergency oxygen system available for all occupants in the event of a pressurisation failure.

Flight demonstration of Aeritalia G222 equipped for marine oil spill control *(Brian M. Service)*

Aeritalia G222 twin-turboprop general purpose military transport aircraft *(Pilot Press)*

Avionics and Equipment: Standard communications equipment includes 3,500-channel UHF, two 1,360-channel VHF-AM, 920-channel VHF-FM, 28,000-channel HF/SSB, crew intercom and PA system. Navigation equipment includes Omega system, with TAS computer, autopilot, flight director, two compasses, and two vertical gyros; and an integrated ground based system incorporating two VOR, marker beacon receiver, two ILS, ADF, two Tacan or DME, and horizontal situation indicator. Other avionics include Meteo weather radar, with secondary terrain mapping mode; radar altimeter; and IFF/ATC transponder including altitude reporting. Provision for head-up display. Landing light on nosewheel leg.

Equipment (G222SAA): Modular palletised firefighting pack can be installed in under two hours without any modification to the basic transport aircraft. The module consists of a 6,000 litre (1,320 Imp gallon) tank and four pressurised air containers to activate the pneumatic actuators and discharge the retardant through the rear ramp/door opening via two nozzles. Length of area covered averages 300 m (985 ft).

Dimensions, external:

Wing span	28·70 m (94 ft 2 in)
Wing chord: at root	3·40 m (11 ft 1¾ in)
at tip	1·685 m (5 ft 6¼ in)
Wing aspect ratio	9·15
Length overall	22·70 m (74 ft 5½ in)
Height overall	9·80 m (32 ft 1¾ in)
Fuselage: Max diameter	3·55 m (11 ft 7¾ in)
Tailplane span	12·40 m (40 ft 8¼ in)
Wheel track	3·668 m (12 ft 0½ in)
Wheelbase (to c/l of main units)	6·23 m (20 ft 5¼ in)
Propeller diameter:	
except G222T	4·42 m (14 ft 6 in)
G222T	4·88 m (16 ft 0 in)
Distance between propeller centres	9·50 m (31 ft 2 in)
Rear-loading ramp/door: Width	2·45 m (8 ft 0½ in)
Height	2·25 m (7 ft 4½ in)

DIMENSIONS, INTERNAL:
Main cabin: Length 8·58 m (28 ft 1¾ in)
Width 2·45 m (8 ft 0½ in)
Height 2·25 m (7 ft 4½ in)
Floor area: excl ramp 21·00 m² (226·0 sq ft)
incl ramp 25·68 m² (276·4 sq ft)
Volume 58·0 m³ (2,048 cu ft)

AREAS:
Wings, gross 82·00 m² (882·6 sq ft)
Ailerons (total) 3·65 m² (39·29 sq ft)
Trailing-edge flaps (total) 18·40 m² (198·06 sq ft)
Spoilers (total) 1·65 m² (17·76 sq ft)
Fin (incl dorsal fin) 12·19 m² (131·21 sq ft)
Rudder 7·02 m² (75·56 sq ft)
Tailplane 19·09 m² (205·48 sq ft)
Elevators (total) 4·61 m² (49·62 sq ft)

WEIGHTS AND LOADINGS (standard version except where indicated):
Weight empty 14,590 kg (32,165 lb)
Weight empty, equipped 15,400 kg (33,950 lb)
Operating weight empty:
standard and SAA 15,700 kg (34,610 lb)
G222T 18,000 kg (39,685 lb)
Max payload (cargo) 9,000 kg (19,840 lb)
Equipment module (SAA) 2,200 kg (4,850 lb)
Retardant (SAA) 6,800 kg (14,990 lb)
Max fuel load 9,400 kg (20,725 lb)
Fuel (SAA) 3,330 kg (7,340 lb)
Max T-O weight:
standard and SAA 28,000 kg (61,730 lb)
G222T 29,000 kg (63,935 lb)
Max landing weight:
standard and SAA 26,500 kg (58,420 lb)
G222T 27,200 kg (59,965 lb)
Max zero-fuel weight 24,400 kg (53,790 lb)
Max cargo floor loading 750 kg/m² (155 lb/sq ft)
Max wing loading 341·5 kg/m² (69·9 lb/sq ft)
Max power loading:
except G222T 5·52 kg/kW (9·08 lb/shp)
G222T 4·00 kg/kW (6·58 lb/shp)

PERFORMANCE (standard G222 transport, at max T-O weight except where indicated):
Max level speed:
G222 at 4,575 m (15,000 ft) 291 knots (540 km/h; 336 mph)
G222T at 9,150 m (30,000 ft) 310 knots (574 km/h; 357 mph)
Long-range cruising speed:
G222 at 6,000 m (19,680 ft) 237 knots (439 km/h; 273 mph)
G222T at 9,150 m (30,000 ft) 300 knots (556 km/h; 345 mph)
Airdrop speed (paratroops or cargo) 110-140 knots (204-259 km/h; 127-161 mph) IAS
Drop speed (G222SAA, T-O configuration) 120 knots (222 km/h; 138 mph)
Stalling speed, flaps and landing gear down 84 knots (155 km/h; 97 mph)
Time to height:
G222 to 4,500 m (14,760 ft) 8 min 35 s
G222T to 4,575 m (15,000 ft) 6 min 48 s
Max rate of climb at S/L 520 m (1,705 ft)/min
Rate of climb at S/L, one engine out:
G222 125 m (410 ft)/min
G222T 305 m (1,000 ft)/min
Service ceiling 7,620 m (25,000 ft)
Service ceiling, one engine out:
G222 5,000 m (16,400 ft)
G222T 4,725 m (15,500 ft)
Optimum height above ground during drop (G222SAA) 50-100 m (165-330 ft)
T-O run: G222 662 m (2,172 ft)
G222T 649 m (2,130 ft)
T-O to 15 m (50 ft):
G222, G222T 1,000 m (3,280 ft)
Landing from 15 m (50 ft): G222 775 m (2,543 ft)
G222T 655 m (2,150 ft)
Landing run at max landing weight:
G222 545 m (1,788 ft)
G222T 378 m (1,240 ft)
Accelerate/stop distance 1,200 m (3,937 ft)
Min ground turning radius 20·80 m (68 ft 3 in)
Range with max payload, optimum cruising speed and height: G222 740 nm (1,371 km; 852 miles)
G222T 1,020 nm (1,890 km; 1,174 miles)
Range with 36 stretchers and 4 medical attendants:
G222 1,349 nm (2,500 km; 1,553 miles)
Range with max retardant load:
G222SAA 540 nm (1,000 km; 621 miles)
Ferry range with max fuel:
G222 2,500 nm (4,633 km; 2,879 miles)
G222T 2,750 nm (5,096 km; 3,166 miles)
g limit +2·5

Aeritalia F-104S ASA with upgraded weapons systems and equipment

Freighter conversion of a McDonnell Douglas DC-8 Super Sixty, carried out by Aeronavali Venezia

AERITALIA (LOCKHEED) F-104S ASA

Aeritalia production of the F-104S ended in March 1979 after the manufacture of 246 aircraft, including 40 for the Turkish Air Force. The remainder were then in service with the 4°, 5°, 9°, 36°, 51° and 53° Stormi (Wings) of the Italian Air Force. Development was initiated in 1982 of a weapons system updating programme for the latter aircraft, to increase their capability in the interception and interdiction/strike roles.

Now known as ASA (Aggiornamento Sistemi d'Arma), this programme is planned to include improved air-to-air self-defence and interception capability by the introduction of a Fiar R21G/M1 Setter radar; advanced ECM; improved IFF and altitude reporting system; improved electrical power generation and distribution system; lookdown capability against low-flying targets; improved weapons delivery (armament computer and time delay unit); and a new automatic pitch control computer.

An F-104S ASA demonstrator began flight testing in March 1985. Deliveries of production modification kits were due to start in Spring 1986.

AERITALIA (MCDONNELL DOUGLAS) DC-8 FREIGHTER CONVERSION

Under a programme launched at Tulsa works in February 1976, McDonnell Douglas began modifying DC-8 passenger transports into specialised freighters at a rate of up to nine aircraft per year. First to be converted were two DC-8-43 series airliners, which were also re-engined with Pratt & Whitney JT3D turbofans, under contract from Frederick B. Ayer and Associates. Subsequent orders for a total of eight conversions were received from Intercontinental Airways, International Air Leases Inc, International Air Service, Overseas National Airways and Transmeridian Air Cargo. Since 1982 responsibility for the DC-8 freighter conversion programme has been held by Aeritalia's wholly owned subsidiary, Officine Aeronavali Venezia SpA. A total of 20 conversions were made by McDonnell Douglas; Aeronavali Venezia delivered its first conversion, one of two for Air Canada, in February 1986. Three others were then on order for United Parcel Service of the USA.

Modification includes removal of passenger installations and fitting a production freighter seven-track floor, and a 2·16 m × 3·56 m (85 × 140 in) main deck cargo door. Cabin windows are replaced by metal plugs, and a cargo loading system is installed. The aircraft are then recertificated at a new max T-O weight of 161,025 kg (355,000 lb). Conversion to turbofan power is optional for turbojet models.

AERONAUTICA MACCHI

AERONAUTICA MACCHI SpA

Corso Vittorio Emanuele 15, 20122 Milan
Telephone: (02) 792696 and 702020
OFFICES: Via Don Tornatore 6, 21100 Varese
Telephone: (0332) 287700
Telex: 380070

PRESIDENT: Dott Fabrizio Foresio
VICE-PRESIDENT: Ing Renato Bonifacio
VICE-PRESIDENT AND MANAGING DIRECTOR:
Gen Ing Mario Matacotta

The original Macchi company was founded in 1913 in Varese, and its first aeroplane was built in that year. On 1 January 1981 the Aeronautica Macchi group reorganised its structure, transforming itself into a holding company and transferring all of its operating activities to a newly formed, wholly owned company known as Aermacchi SpA. The group includes, besides Aermacchi SpA, the subsidiary companies SICAMB (airframe and equipment manufacturing, including licence production of Martin-Baker ejection seats), OMG (precision machining), and Vega (electronic data processing). Aeronautica Macchi, the holding company, co-ordinates the corporate strategies in finance, commercial and industrial investments. A 25% holding in Aeronautica Macchi was acquired by Aeritalia in 1983.

AERMACCHI

AERMACCHI SpA (Subsidiary of Aeronautica Macchi SpA)

Via Sanvito Silvestro 80, CP 246, 21100 Varese
Telephone: (0332) 254111
Telex: 380070 AERMAC I
PRESIDENT: Dott Fabrizio Foresio
MANAGING DIRECTORS:
Dott Ing Ermanno Bazzocchi
Gen Ing Mario Matacotta
DIRECTOR GENERAL: Dott Ing Giulio Cesare Valdonio
COMMERCIAL DIRECTOR: Dott Ing Giovanni Cattaneo
TECHNICAL MANAGER: Dott Ing Alberto Notari
EXTERNAL RELATIONS: Paola Del Ponte

Aermacchi is the aircraft manufacturing company of the Aeronautica Macchi group. The company plants at Venegono airfield occupy a total area of 270,000 m² (2,906,260 sq ft), including 33,000 m² (355,210 sq ft) of covered space; the flight test centre has covered space of 5,100 m² (54,900 sq ft) in a total area of 28,000 m² (301,390 sq ft). Total workforce at the beginning of 1986 was approximately 2,500.

The MB-339A two-seat trainer is in series production for the Italian Air Force and for export. A single-seat version, the MB-339K Veltro 2, is also in production. Other activities include the manufacture of wings for the Aeritalia G222 transport aircraft and underwing pylons for the Panavia Tornado; Aermacchi is also active in the field of aerospace ground equipment, with a complete line of hydraulic, electric and pneumatic ground carts for servicing civil and military aircraft.

AMX

Aermacchi is teamed with Aeritalia and EMBRAER in developing the AMX combat aircraft (see International section) for the Italian and Brazilian air forces.

AERMACCHI MB-339A

The MB-339A is a tandem two-seat trainer/ground attack aircraft, powered by a Piaggio built Rolls-Royce Viper 632 engine.

The first of two MB-339X flying prototypes (MM588) was flown for the first time on 12 August 1976. The second aircraft (MM589), which made its first flight on 20 May 1977, was built to pre-production standard; the third airframe was used for static and fatigue testing. The first production aircraft made its initial flight on 20 July 1978, and the first of an initial series of 51 aircraft for the Italian Air Force were handed over for pre-service trials on 8 August 1979. In addition to MB-339A trainers, this series included four **MB-339RM** (radiomisure) calibration aircraft delivered to 8° Gruppo Sorveglianza Elettronica of the 14° Stormo Radiomisure at Pratica de Mare from 16 February 1981, and fifteen **MB-339PAN**s (Pattuglia Acrobatica Nazionale) delivered to the Italian Air Force aerobatic team, the Frecce Tricolori, which began using the type on 27 April 1982. The PAN aircraft have the wingtip tanks deleted (to facilitate formation keeping) and a smoke generating system installed, but are otherwise similar to the standard MB-339A. At least two more MB-339As have since been converted to MB-339PAN standard to offset attrition. In September 1982 the Italian Air Force received the first of the second production batch of 30 aircraft, which are camouflaged and are to be used as an emergency close air support force. A total of 85 MB-339s had been delivered to the Italian Air Force by the beginning of 1986, out of a planned total of 100 scheduled for completion in early 1987.

Ten MB-339As were delivered to the Argentine Navy in 1980, 16 to the Peruvian Air Force in 1981-82, 12 to the Royal Malaysian Air Force in 1983-84, two to Dubai in 1984, and 12 to Nigeria in 1985.

TYPE: Two-seat basic and advanced trainer and ground attack aircraft.

AIRFRAME: Structural design criteria based on MIL-A-8860A; 8*g* limit load factor in 'clean' configuration. Cockpit designed for 40,000 pressurisation cycles. Service life requirement 12,000 flying hours and 24,000 landings in the training role. Entire structure specially treated to prevent corrosion.

WINGS: Cantilever low/mid-wing monoplane. Wing section NACA 64A-114 (mod) at centreline, NACA 64A-212 (mod) at tip. Leading-edge swept back 11° 18′. Sweepback at quarter-chord 8° 29′. All-metal stressed skin structure, with single main spar and auxiliary rear spar, built in two portions and bolted to fuselage. Skin stiffened by spanwise stringers, closely spaced ribs, and false ribs. Wingtip tanks permanently attached. Single fence on each wing at approx two-thirds span. Servo powered ailerons embody 'Irving' type aerodynamic balance provisions, and are statically balanced along their entire span. Balance tabs facilitate reversion to manual operation in the event of servo failure. Hydraulically actuated single-slotted flaps, operated by push/pull rods.

FUSELAGE: All-metal semi-monocoque structure, built in two main portions: forward (nose to engine mounting bulkhead), and rear (engine bulkhead to tailcone). Forward portion built of C section frames, four C section spars, longitudinal L section stringers, and skin panels. Rear section manufactured entirely from aluminium alloy except for firewall and most of tailcone, which are of stainless steel; four-bolt attachment to forward fuselage to facilitate access to engine. Hydraulically actuated, electrically controlled airbrake under centre of fuselage, just forward of CG.

TAIL UNIT: Cantilever all-metal structure, of similar construction to wings. Slightly sweptback vertical surfaces. Rudder and elevators are statically balanced, each having an electrically actuated dual-purpose balance and trim tab. Two auxiliary fins under rear fuselage.

LANDING GEAR: Hydraulically retractable tricycle type, with oleo-pneumatic shock absorbers; suitable for operation from semi-prepared runways. Nosewheel retracts forward, main units outward into wings. Hydraulically steerable nosewheel. Low-pressure mainwheel tubeless tyres size 545 × 175-10 (12 ply rating); nosewheel tubeless tyre size 380 × 150-4 (6 ply rating). Emergency extension system. Hydraulic disc brakes with anti-skid system.

POWER PLANT: One Rolls-Royce Viper Mk 632-43 turbojet engine, rated at 17·8 kN (4,000 lb st). Engines built in Italy under Rolls-Royce licence; final assembly by Piaggio. Fuel in two-cell rubber fuselage tank, capacity 781 litres (172 Imp gallons), and two integral wingtip tanks, combined capacity 632 litres (139 Imp gallons). Total internal capacity 1,413 litres (311 Imp gallons) usable. Single-point pressure refuelling receptacle in port side of fuselage, below wing trailing-edge. Gravity refuelling points on top of fuselage and each tip tank. Provision for two drop tanks, each of 325 litres (71·5 Imp gallons) capacity, on centre underwing stations. Anti-icing system for engine air intakes.

ACCOMMODATION: Crew of two in tandem, on Martin-Baker IT10F zero/zero ejection seats in pressurised cockpit. Rear seat elevated 32·5 cm (12¾ in). Rearview mirror for each occupant. Two-piece moulded transparent canopy, opening sideways to starboard.

SYSTEMS: Pressurisation system max differential 0·24 bars (3·5 lb/sq in). Bootstrap type air-conditioning system, which also provides air for windscreen and canopy demisting. Hydraulic system, pressure 172·5 bars (2,500 lb/sq in), for actuation of flaps, aileron servos, airbrake, landing gear, wheel brakes and nosewheel steering. Backup system for wheel brakes and emergency extension of landing gear. Main electrical DC power from one 28V 9kW engine driven starter/generator and one 28V 6kW secondary generator. Two 24V 22Ah nickel-cadmium batteries for engine starting. Fixed frequency 115/26V AC power from two 600VA single phase static inverters. External power receptacle. Low pressure demand type oxygen system, operating at 28 bars (400 lb/sq in).

AVIONICS AND EQUIPMENT: Typical avionics installation includes Collins AN/ARC-159(V)-2, or Magnavox AN/ARC-150(V), or Magnavox AN/ARC-164(V) UHF transceiver; Collins AN/ARC-186(V) VHF/AM and FM transceiver; Collins ICS-200 interphone; Collins AN/ARN-118(V) Tacan or King KDM 706A DME; Collins 51RV-4B or Bendix RNA-34A VOR/ILS and MKI-3 marker beacon receiver; Collins DF-206 ADF; GEC Avionics AD-620C computerised area and dead reckoning navigation system; and Bendix AN/APX-100(V) or Italtel SIT 421A IFF. Standard instrumentation includes ARU-2B/A attitude director indicator, AQU-6/A HSI, Sperry AS-339 attitude and heading reference system, AG-5 standby attitude indicator, and flight director system. Retractable landing light beneath port wing; taxying light on nosewheel leg.

ARMAMENT AND OPERATIONAL EQUIPMENT: Up to 1,815 kg (4,000 lb) of external stores can be carried on six underwing hardpoints, the inner four of which are stressed for loads of up to 454 kg (1,000 lb) each and the outer two for up to 340 kg (750 lb) each. Provisions are made, on the two inner stations, for the installation of two Macchi gun pods, each containing either a 30 mm DEFA 553 cannon with 120 rds, or a 12·7 mm AN/M-3 machine-gun with 350 rds. Other typical loads can include two Matra 550 Magic or AIM-9 Sidewinder air-to-air missiles on the two outer stations; four 1,000 lb or six 750 lb bombs; six SUU-11A/A 7·62 mm Minigun pods with 1,500 rds/pod; six Matra 155 launchers, each for eighteen 68 mm rockets; six Matra F-2 practice launchers, each for six 68 mm rockets; six LAU-68/A or LAU-32G launchers, each for seven 2·75 in rockets; six Aerea AL-25-50 or AL-18-50 launchers, each with twenty-five or eighteen 50 mm rockets respectively; six Aerea AL-12-80 launchers, each with twelve 81 mm rockets; four LAU-10/A launchers, each with four 5 in Zuni rockets; four Thomson-Brandt 100-4 launchers, each with four 100 mm Thomson-Brandt rockets; six Aerea BRD bomb/rocket dispensers; six Aermacchi 11B29-003 bomb/flare dispensers; six Thomson-Brandt 14-3-M2 adaptors, each with six 100 mm anti-runway bombs or 120 mm tactical support bombs; or two 325 litre (71·5 Imp gallon) drop tanks; or a photographic pod with four 70 mm Vinten cameras; or a single underwing Elettronica ECM pod, combined with a flare/chaff dispenser, onboard RHAW receiver and indicators. Provision for Aeritalia 8.105.924 fixed reflector sight or Saab RGS 2 gyroscopic gunsight; a gunsight can also be installed in rear cockpit, to enable instructor to evaluate manoeuvres performed by student pilot. All gunsights can be equipped with fully automatic Teledyne TSC 116-2 gun camera. Provision for towing type A-6B (1·83 × 9·14 m; 6 × 30 ft) aerial banner target; tow attachment point on inner surface of ventral airbrake.

DIMENSIONS, EXTERNAL:
Wing span over tip tanks — 10·858 m (35 ft 7½ in)
Wing aspect ratio — 5·26
Length overall — 10·972 m (36 ft 0 in)
Height overall — 3·994 m (13 ft 1¼ in)
Elevator span — 4·08 m (13 ft 4¾ in)
Wheel track — 2·483 m (8 ft 1¾ in)
Wheelbase — 4·369 m (14 ft 4 in)

AREAS:
Wings, gross — 19·30 m² (207·74 sq ft)
Ailerons (total) — 1·328 m² (14·29 sq ft)
Trailing-edge flaps (total) — 2·21 m² (23·79 sq ft)
Airbrake — 0·68 m² (7·32 sq ft)
Fin — 2·37 m² (25·51 sq ft)
Rudder, incl tab — 0·61 m² (6·57 sq ft)
Tailplane — 3·38 m² (36·38 sq ft)
Elevators (total, incl tabs) — 0·979 m² (10·54 sq ft)

WEIGHTS AND LOADING:
Weight empty, equipped — 3,125 kg (6,889 lb)
Basic operating weight empty — 3,136 kg (6,913 lb)
Fuel load (internal, usable) — 1,100 kg (2,425 lb)
T-O weight, 'clean' — 4,400 kg (9,700 lb)
Typical T-O weights with armament indicated:
A: four Mk 82 bombs and two drop tanks — 5,895 kg (13,000 lb)
B: six Mk 82 bombs — 5,895 kg (13,000 lb)
C: two Macchi 30 mm gun pods, two LR-25-0 rocket launchers and two drop tanks — 5,808 kg (12,805 lb)
D: four LR-25-0 launchers and two drop tanks — 5,642 kg (12,440 lb)
E: six LR-25-0 launchers — 5,323 kg (11,735 lb)
Max T-O weight with external stores — 5,895 kg (13,000 lb)
Wing loading (50 per cent fuel) — 205 kg/m² (42·00 lb/sq ft)

PERFORMANCE (at 'clean' T-O weight, ISA, except where indicated):
IAS limit/Mach limit — Mach 0·85 (500 knots; 926 km/h; 575 mph)
Max level speed at S/L — 485 knots (898 km/h; 558 mph) IAS
Max level speed at 9,150 m (30,000 ft) — Mach 0·77 (441 knots; 817 km/h; 508 mph)
Max speed for landing gear extension — 175 knots (324 km/h; 201 mph) IAS
T-O speed — 100 knots (185 km/h; 115 mph)
Approach speed over 15 m (50 ft) obstacle — 98 knots (182 km/h; 113 mph) IAS
Landing speed — 89 knots (165 km/h; 103 mph) IAS
Stalling speed — 80 knots (149 km/h; 93 mph)
Max rate of climb at S/L — 2,010 m (6,595 ft)/min

Camouflaged MB-339A of the Italian Air Force, for light close air support duties

Time to 9,150 m (30,000 ft) 7 min 6 s
Service ceiling (30·5 m; 100 ft/min rate of climb) 14,630 m (48,000 ft)
Min ground turning radius 8·45 m (27 ft 8¾ in)
T-O run at S/L:
'clean' T-O weight 465 m (1,525 ft)
max T-O weight 915 m (3,000 ft)
Landing run at S/L, ISA 415 m (1,362 ft)
Max range without drop tanks 950 nm (1,760 km; 1,094 miles)
Max ferry range with two underwing drop tanks, 10% reserves 1,140 nm (2,110 km; 1,310 miles)
Max endurance without drop tanks 2 h 50 min
Max endurance at 7,620 m (25,000 ft) with two underwing drop tanks, 10% reserves 3 h 45 min
g limits +8/−4

PERFORMANCE (armed configuration, at T-O weights given earlier):
Radius of action, hi-lo-hi (no run-in or run-out):
A 320 nm (593 km; 368 miles)
B 212 nm (393 km; 244 miles)
C 275 nm (510 km; 317 miles)
D 305 nm (565 km; 351 miles)
E 165 nm (306 km; 190 miles)
Radius of action, lo-lo-lo (no run-in or run-out):
A 200 nm (371 km; 230 miles)
B 146 nm (271 km; 168 miles)
C 190 nm (352 km; 219 miles)
D 193 nm (358 km; 222 miles)
E 123 nm (228 km; 142 miles)

AERMACCHI MB-339B and C

Aermacchi introduced two new two-seat variants of the MB-339 in 1985, both powered by the Viper 680 engine. Details are as follows:

MB-339B. Advanced jet trainer, with enhanced light close air support capability compared with MB-339A. Fuel capacity increased by use of enlarged wingtip tanks.

MB-339C. Improved trainer/close air support version, with digital nav/attack system and other advanced avionics. Engine and enlarged wingtip tanks as MB-339B. Modified nose shape. Intended for effective pilot training in modern mission management techniques. Design and development began in 1982-83; prototype (I-AMDA) flew for the first time on 17 December 1985; flight testing continuing in 1986.

No orders for either version had been announced up to mid-1986. The description of the MB-339A applies also to the two new models except for the following details:

Aermacchi MB-339K Veltro 2 light close air support aircraft, developed from the two-seat MB-339A

POWER PLANT (B and C): One 19·79 kN (4,450 lb st) Rolls-Royce Viper Mk 680-43 turbojet engine. Fuselage fuel capacity as for MB-339A, but capacity of each integral tip tank increased to 500 litres (110 Imp gallons), giving total usable capacity of 1,781 litres (392 Imp gallons). Provision retained for two 325 litre (71·5 Imp gallon) drop tanks on centre underwing stations.

AVIONICS AND EQUIPMENT (C): Typical avionics installation includes Collins AN/ARN-118(V) type RT-1159/A Tacan or King KDM 706A DME; Collins 51RV-4B VOR/ILS and MKI-3 marker beacon receiver; Collins ADF-6A ADF/LF; Collins DF-301E VHF/UHF ADF (optional); GEC Avionics AD-660 Doppler radar integrated with a Litton LR-80 inertial platform; GEC Avionics 620K navigation computer; Kaiser Sabre head-up display/weapons aiming computer; Aeritalia CRT multifunction display; Aeritalia/Honeywell HG7505 radar altimeter; Fiar P 0702 laser rangefinder; ELT-156 radar warning system; Logic stores management system; Bendix AN/APX-100 IFF; Astronautics ARU-50/A attitude director indicator; Astronautics AQU-13 HSI; Fairchild Weston video camera; HOTAS (hands on throttle and stick) controls; Tracor AN/ALE-40 chaff/flare dispensers; and Elettronica ELT-555 active ECM pod.

ARMAMENT (B): Loads on six underwing hardpoints as for MB-339A. The aircraft is cleared for operation with rockets of 50 mm (SNIA), 68 mm, 81 mm (SNORA), 100 mm (Thomson-Brandt), 2·75 in and 5 in calibre, and with 500 lb Mk 82 and R bombs, 100 mm Thomson-Brandt runway demolition bombs, 120 mm close air support bombs, 250 lb Expal BPR bombs, 500 lb Matra bombs, and air-to-air infra-red missiles (AIM-9L and Matra Magic).

ARMAMENT (C): Nav/attack system makes possible the employment of air-to-air infra-red missiles (AIM-9L and Matra Magic), AGM-65 Maverick air-to-ground missiles and Marte Mk II sea skimming anti-ship missiles.

DIMENSIONS, EXTERNAL: As for MB-339A except:
Wing span over tip tanks: B, C 11·22 m (36 ft 9¾ in)
Length overall: C 11·24 m (36 ft 10½ in)

WEIGHTS (B):
Weight empty, equipped 3,158 kg (6,962 lb)
Max internal fuel (usable) 1,388 kg (3,060 lb)
T-O weight (training configuration) 4,472 kg (9,859 lb)
Max T-O weight with external stores 6,350 kg (14,000 lb)

PERFORMANCE (B at training configuration T-O weight, ISA):
Max level speed at S/L 487 knots (902 km/h; 560 mph)
Max rate of climb at S/L 2,225 m (7,300 ft)/min
Time to 9,150 m (30,000 ft) 6 min 42 s
Combat radius with four 500 lb Mk 82 bombs, internal fuel only:
lo-lo-lo 170 nm (315 km; 196 miles)
hi-lo-hi 270 nm (500 km; 311 miles)
Max range:
without drop tanks 1,060 nm (1,965 km; 1,221 miles)
ferry, with two underwing drop tanks, 10% reserves 1,187 nm (2,200 km; 1,367 miles)
Max endurance: without drop tanks 3 h 15 min
with two underwing drop tanks, 10% reserves 3 h 55 min

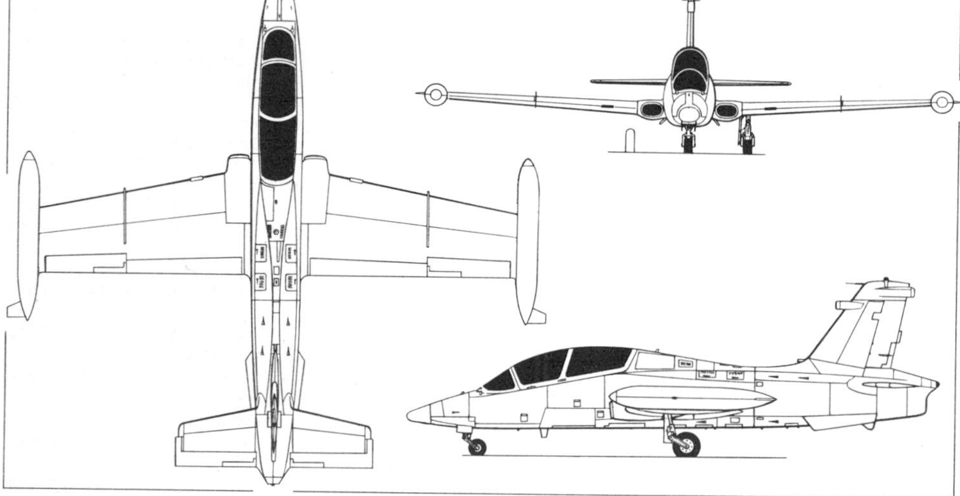
Aermacchi MB-339C, showing new nose and vertical tail configuration *(Pilot Press)*

Prototype MB-339C, equipped with a digital nav/attack system

AERMACCHI MB-339K VELTRO 2 (GREYHOUND)

The Veltro 2, which perpetuates the name of the Macchi MC 205V fighter of the second World War, is a single-seat development of the MB-339A, optimised for the roles of light close air support and operational training. The MB-339K private venture prototype (I-BITE) flew for the first time on 30 May 1980, powered by a 17·8 kN (4,000 lb st) Viper Mk 632 engine, and has since undertaken successfully many weapon firing and compatibility trials. According to Aermacchi, construction of an initial production batch has been launched, but no orders for the K version had been announced at the time of going to press.

The airframe of the MB-339A is retained, except for a new forward fuselage with redesigned single-seat cockpit, internally mounted cannon armament, auxiliary fuselage fuel tank and enlarged wingtip tanks. The other major changes in the production MB-339K concern the power plant, and the avionics and equipment relevant to the different roles performed by the Veltro 2. Flight testing with the Viper Mk 680 engine in the second prototype MB-339A took place between the Spring of 1983 and Summer of 1984, and this engine became available for the production MB-339K from early 1986. The following description applies to the basic MB-339K; operational capability can, at customer's option, be extended by adopting such additional features as a head-up display, cockpit TV display, ECM, and other improved avionics. (For further details of these, see Aermacchi MB-339C entry.)

TYPE: Single-seat ground attack aircraft and operational trainer.

AIRFRAME: Structural design criteria based on MIL-A-8860 series of specifications; +8/−4*g* limit load factor in 'clean' configuration. With a fatigue spectrum based on the ground attack role only, service life will be more than 9,000 flying hours with 18,000 landings. Entire structure is specially treated to prevent corrosion.

WINGS: As MB-339A.
FUSELAGE: As MB-339A, except for modified forward section.
TAIL UNIT: As MB-339A.
LANDING GEAR: Similar to MB-339A.
POWER PLANT: One 19·8 kN (4,450 lb st) Rolls-Royce Viper Mk 680 turbojet engine. Fuel in one fuselage tank, consisting of three rubber cells with a total capacity of 1,030 litres (226·5 Imp gallons), and two constant section integral wingtip tanks with a combined capacity of 1,020 litres (224·5 Imp gallons). Total usable internal fuel capacity 2,050 litres (451 Imp gallons).
ACCOMMODATION: Pilot only, on Martin-Baker IT10LK zero/zero ejection seat in pressurised cockpit. Rearview mirror standard. One-piece moulded transparent canopy, opening sideways to starboard.
SYSTEMS: As MB-339A.
AVIONICS AND EQUIPMENT: Typical avionics as listed for MB-339A, plus Collins DF-301E VHF/UHF DF. Standard instrumentation includes Astronautics ARU-2B/A attitude director indicator; AQU-6/A horizontal situation indicator and flight director system; Sperry AS-339 attitude and heading reference system; and Microtecnica AG-5 standby attitude indicator. Retractable landing light beneath port wing; taxying light on nosewheel leg.
ARMAMENT AND OPERATIONAL EQUIPMENT: Two 30 mm DEFA cannon, with 120 rds/gun, mounted internally in lower forward fuselage, with external fairings. Firing rate 1,200 rds/min. Loads on six underwing hardpoints generally as for MB-339A. Aircraft is cleared for operation with rockets of 50 mm (SNIA), 68 mm, 81 mm (SNORA), 100 mm (Thomson-Brandt), 2·75 in and 5 in calibre, and with 500 lb Mk 82 and R bombs, 100 mm Thomson-Brandt special runway demolition bombs, 120 mm close air support bombs, 250 lb Expal BPR bombs and 500 lb Matra bombs. Elettronica ELT555 airborne deception jamming and warning pod can be carried underwing. Under study are two additional 30 mm guns in pods and a Sidewinder missile installation. Saab-Scania RGS 2 gunsight, with gyro lead computer; gunsight can be equipped with a fully automatic Teledyne TSC 116-2 gun camera. Provision for towing type A-6B (1·83 × 9·14 m; 6 × 30 ft) aerial banner target.
DIMENSIONS, EXTERNAL: As for MB-339A except:
Wing span over tip tanks 11·22 m (36 ft 9¾ in)
Length overall 10·85 m (35 ft 7 in)
AREAS: As for MB-339A
WEIGHTS:
Weight empty, equipped 3,245 kg (7,154 lb)
Fuel load (internal, usable, with circular-section tip tanks) 1,582 kg (3,488 lb)
Max external stores load 1,935 kg (4,266 lb)
T-O weight 'clean', incl ammunition for internal guns 5,050 kg (11,133 lb)
Max T-O weight with external stores 6,350 kg (14,000 lb)
PERFORMANCE (with full gun ammunition load):
Max limiting Mach number 0·85
Never-exceed speed 500 knots (927 km/h; 575 mph)
Max level speed at S/L 486 knots (900 km/h; 560 mph) IAS
Landing speed 95 knots (176 km/h; 109 mph) IAS
Max rate of climb at S/L 2,400 m (7,875 ft)/min
Service ceiling 14,000 m (46,000 ft)
T-O run: 'clean' 580 m (1,900 ft)
at max T-O weight of 6,350 kg (14,000 lb) 910 m (2,985 ft)
Landing run 450 m (1,475 ft)
Combat radius with two 30 mm cannon (125 rds/gun) and four 500 lb Mk 82 bombs (total military load 1,088 kg; 2,400 lb):
lo-lo-lo 205 nm (380 km; 236 miles)
hi-lo-hi 340 nm (630 km; 391 miles)
g limits +8/−4

AGUSTA
AGUSTA SpA

21017 Cascina Costa di Samarate (VA)

Telephone: (0331) 229111
Telex: 332569 AGUCA I

OFFICES:
Via Caldera 21, 20153 Milan
Telephone: (02) 452751
Telex: 333280 AGUMI I
Via Abruzzi 11, 00187 Rome
Telephone: (06) 49801
Telex: 614398 AGURO I
Via Sicilia 43, 00187 Rome
Telephone: (06) 49801
Telex: 614398 AGURO

PRESIDENT AND CHAIRMAN OF THE BOARD:
Dott Raffaello Teti

SENIOR VICE-PRESIDENTS:
Dott Ing Arnaldo Antichi
Dott Domenico Tatangelo

Formed originally in 1977, the Agusta Group (see 1980-81 *Jane's*) completely reorganised its structure from 1 January 1981 under a new holding company known as Agusta SpA. It is part of the Italian public holding agency EFIM, and has three main divisions employing nearly 10,000 people in 12 factories in various parts of Italy.

Agusta International SA
Avenue Louise 523, Boite 9, 1050 Brussels, Belgium (aviation support services)
Telephone: (02) 6485515
Telex: 63349 AGINT B
Agusta Aviation Corporation (marketing and support in North and Central America)
2655 Interplex Drive, Trevose, Pennsylvania 19047, USA

DIVISIONE ELICOTTERI (Helicopter Division)
MANAGING DIRECTOR: Dott Ing Bruno Lovera
Costruzioni Aeronautiche Giovanni Agusta SpA
See following entry
EM (Elicotteri Meridionali SpA)
See page 153
EH Industries Ltd (50% holding)
See International section
EH Industries Inc, Wilmington, Delaware, USA
BredaNardi Costruzioni Aeronautiche SpA
See page 158

DIVISIONE AEROPLANI (Aircraft Division)
MANAGING DIRECTOR: Dott Ing Paolo Bellavita
SIAI-Marchetti SpA
See pages 153-157
Industria Aeronautica Meridionale SpA
Contrada Santa Teresa Pinti, 72100 Brindisi (aircraft co-production, and overhaul of aircraft and helicopters)
Telephone: (0831) 8911
Telex: 860026 IAMBR I
Caproni Vizzola Costruzioni Aeronautiche SpA
See pages 157-158

DIVISIONE SISTEMI ED ATTIVITÀ VARIE (Diversified Activities and Systems Division)
MANAGING DIRECTOR: Dott Ing Giuseppe Bertolazzi
Agusta Sistemi SpA
Via Caldera 21, 20153 Milan
Telephone: (02) 452751
Telex: 333280 AGUMI I
OMI (Ottico Meccanica Italiana SpA)
Via della Vasca Navale 79/81, 00145 Rome
Telephone: (06) 55421
Telex: 610137 SAROMI I
OMICA (OMI Corporation of America)
1319 Powhatan Street, Alexandria, Virginia 22314, USA
Telephone: (730) 549 4064
Telex: 809141 OMICA ALE
FOMB (Fonderie ed Officine Meccaniche di Benevento SpA)
Contrada Ponte Valentino, 82100 Benevento
Telephone: (0824) 43477
Telex: 710667 FOMBEN I
MV (Meccanica Verghera SpA)
Viale Adriatico 50, 21010 Verghera di Samarate (VA) (product support for MV Agusta motorcycles)
Telephone: (0331) 228200
SISDA (Società Italiana Sistemi d'Addestramento pA)
Aeroporto Ciampino, 00040 Rome (maintenance, overhaul and training systems for aircraft and helicopters, in equal partnership with Aeritalia and Elettronica)
Telephone: (06) 600281 and 600282

COSTRUZIONI AERONAUTICHE GIOVANNI AGUSTA SpA

21017 Cascina Costa di Samarate (VA)
Telephone: (0331) 229111
Telex: 332569 AGUCA I
COMMERCIAL OFFICES:
Via Caldera 21, 20153 Milan
Telephone: (02) 452751
Telex: 333280 AGUMI I
PRESIDENT AND CHAIRMAN OF THE BOARD:
Dott Raffaello Teti
GENERAL MANAGER: Dott Ing Michele Ferraioli

This company was established in 1907 by Giovanni Agusta and built many experimental and production aircraft before the Second World War.

In 1952 Agusta acquired a licence to manufacture the Bell Model 47 helicopter and the first Agusta built Model 47G made its initial flight on 22 May 1954.

In addition to the A 109A and A 129 of its own design, Agusta is producing under licence the Bell Models 205, 206 and 212. It collaborated with Bell Helicopter Textron (see US section) in developing the Model 412 version of the Bell 212, and has developed its own multi-role military version of this aircraft (the Griffon). Both of these are also in production. Under licence from Sikorsky, production of S-61A and SH-3D helicopters began in 1967, and manufacture of the HH-3F (S-61R) started in 1974; Agusta is now the sole production source of these aircraft. Agusta is developing its own AS-61N1 short-fuselage derivative of the civil Sikorsky S-61N, produces under licence the Boeing Vertol CH-47C Chinook helicopter, and is collaborating with Westland Helicopters of the UK in developing the EH 101 three-turboshaft helicopter (see under EHI in the International section).

AGUSTA A 109A Mk II

The basic version of the Agusta A 109A high-speed, high-performance twin-engined helicopter accommodates a pilot and seven passengers, and has a large baggage compartment in the rear of the fuselage. Alternatively, the A 109A can be adapted for freight carrying, as an ambulance, or for search and rescue and other duties. Military and naval versions are described separately.

The first of three A 109 flying prototypes flew for the first time on 4 August 1971. RAI and FAA certification for VFR operation was announced on 1 June 1975, and deliveries of the original A 109A production version started in early 1976. Certification for IFR single-pilot operation was obtained on 20 January 1977. Certification has also been granted in Canada, France, West Germany, the Philippines,

Agusta A 109A Mk II general purpose helicopter in 'wide-body' configuration

Sweden, Switzerland and the UK. Approximately 150 of this initial version, described in the 1981-82 *Jane's*, were built.

Deliveries of the uprated A 109A Mk II began in September 1981. This has an increase in transmission rating, a new tail rotor driveshaft, increased tail rotor blade life and reliability, new self-damping engine mounts, integral-design oil coolers and blowers, a structurally redesigned tailboom, higher-pressure hydraulic system, improved avionics and instrument layout, and a removable floor in the baggage compartment. In 1983 Agusta introduced a utility version of the Mk II, with less sophisticated interior and instrumentation. Under a 1983 agreement, Hellenic Aerospace Industries (see Greek section) is manufacturing major fuselage components for 77 Mk IIs during 1984-87.

In 1985 Agusta introduced a 'wide-bodied' version of the Mk II, with a more roomy and comfortable cabin created by modifying the shape of the underfloor fuel tanks and using bulged fuselage side panels similar to those of the medevac version. These changes do not affect either the basic structure or aerodynamic characteristics of the helicopter.

Agusta had delivered 90 A 109A Mk IIs by 1 January 1986. Of the overall sales total of approx 240, some 77 have been sales of VIP or medevac versions (see 'Accommodation' paragraph) to customers in the USA. One VIP 'wide-body' has been delivered to the President of Italy, for operation by the 31° Stormo of the Italian Air Force.

The following description applies to the standard A 109A Mk II:

TYPE: Twin-engined general purpose helicopter.

ROTOR SYSTEM: Fully articulated four-blade single main rotor and port side two-blade semi-rigid delta-hinged tail rotor. Main rotor blades have a 'droop snoot' aerofoil section, with thickness/chord ratios of 11·3% at root and 6% at tip, and are attached to hub by tension/torsion straps. They are of aluminium alloy bonded construction, with a honeycomb core, have swept tips, stainless steel tip caps and leading-edge strips, and are protected against corrosion. A manual blade folding capability and rotor brake are optional. Tail rotor blades are of aluminium alloy, bonded at the trailing-edge, with a Nomex honeycomb core and stainless steel leading-edge strip.

ROTOR DRIVE: Main transmission assembly housed in fairing above passenger cabin, driving main rotor through a coupling gearbox and 90° two-stage (15·62:1) main reduction gearbox. Take-off drive from coupling gearbox drives tail rotor via an output shaft and tail rotor gearbox. Transmission ratings 552 kW (740 shp) for take-off and max continuous twin-engined operation, with max contingency rating of 607 kW (814 shp) for 6 s. Ratings for single-engined operation are 336 kW (450 shp) for take-off (5 min limit), 313 kW (420 shp) max continuous, and 336 kW (450 shp) max contingency for 10 s. Main rotor/engine rpm ratio 1:15·62; tail rotor/engine rpm ratio 1:2·80.

FUSELAGE AND TAIL UNIT: Pod and boom type, of aluminium alloy construction, built in four main sections: nose, cockpit, passenger cabin and tailboom. Sweptback vertical fins (above and below tailboom). Non-swept elevator, mid-mounted on tailboom forward of fins, is linked to collective pitch control.

LANDING GEAR: Retractable tricycle type, with oleo-pneumatic shock absorber in each unit. Single mainwheels and castoring (45° each side of centre), self-centering nosewheel. Hydraulic retraction, nosewheel forward, mainwheels upward into fuselage. Hydraulic emergency extension and locking. Disc brakes on mainwheels. All tyres are of tubeless type, and of same size (650 × 6) and pressure (5·9 bars; 85 lb/sq in). Tailskid under ventral fin. Emergency pop-out flotation gear and fixed snow skis optional.

POWER PLANT: Two Allison 250-C20B turboshaft engines (each 313 kW; 420 shp for 5 min for T-O, 298 kW; 400 shp max continuous power, 276 kW; 370 shp max cruise power, derated to 258 kW; 346 shp for twin-engine operation), mounted side by side in upper rear fuselage and separated from passenger cabin and from each other by firewalls. Two bladder fuel tanks in lower rear fuselage, combined capacity 560 litres (123 Imp gallons), of which 550 litres (121 Imp gallons) are usable. Refuelling point in each side of fuselage, near top of each tank. Oil capacity 7·7 litres (1·7 Imp gallons) for each engine and 12 litres (2·6 Imp gallons) for transmission. Provision for internal auxiliary tank containing up to 170 litres (37·4 Imp gallons) of fuel.

ACCOMMODATION: Crew of one or two on flight deck, with pilot seated on right. Dual controls optional. Main cabin seats up to six passengers on three forward or rearward facing seats in centre, plus three forward facing seats at rear. A seventh passenger can be carried in lieu of second crew member. Four/five-seat VIP layout available, with refreshment and music centre. Forward opening crew door and passenger door on each side. Large space at rear of cabin for up to 150 kg (331 lb) of baggage, with access via forward opening door on port side. Centre row of seats removable to permit use as freight transport. Medevac version can accommodate one stretcher installed crosswise (by replacing standard doors with 'bubble' doors), and complete medical equipment including oxygen cylinders (enough for three hours' use),

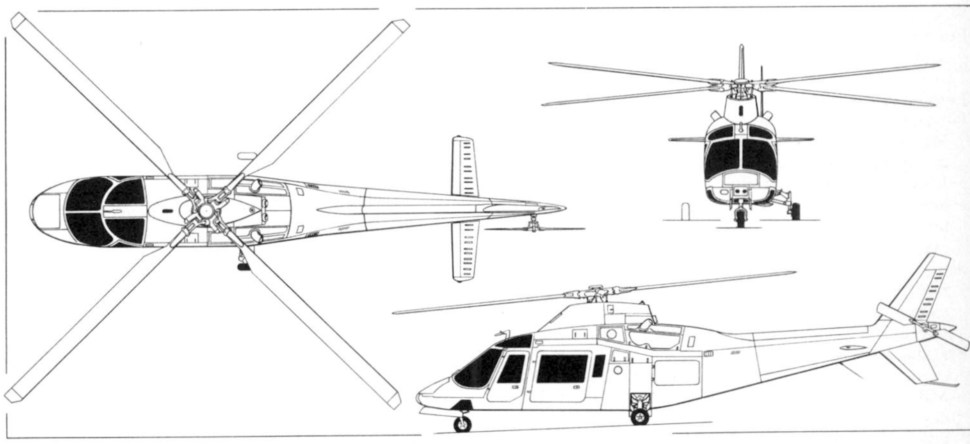

Agusta A 109A Mk II twin-engined general purpose helicopter *(Pilot Press)*

Agusta A 109A Mk II multi-role military version, armed with four TOW missiles

oxygen/air-oxygen respirator with flowmeter humidifier, ECG with monitoring equipment, and equipment for intensive care. A quick-change emergency medical service (EMS) unit is available which enables the standard transport configuration to be changed to air ambulance layout within a few minutes. The EMS configuration accommodates a pilot and three medical attendants, a longitudinally placed stretcher, and a cardio-circulatory and respiratory intensive care system. A second stretcher patient can be carried if necessary. In a cargo role, external freight can be transported on a CG hook. Sliding doors can be installed for rescue missions.

SYSTEMS: Two identical independent Magnaghi hydraulic systems, pressure 107 bars (1,550 lb/sq in), supply dual flight servo-controls and provide emergency power in the event of engine failure. A utility system connected to No. 2 servo-hydraulic system provides power to actuate landing gear, wheel and rotor braking, nosewheel locking, and emergency backup. 28V DC electrical system, using two 30V 150A engine driven starter/generators, and one 24V 13Ah nickel-cadmium battery (22Ah heavy duty battery on IFR version). Single phase AC power at 400Hz supplied by two 115/26V 250VA solid state static inverters. Third inverter as emergency backup on IFR version. External power receptacle. Engine anti-icing system, using engine bleed air.

AVIONICS: Standard instrumentation, plus Collins avionics for VFR or IFR operation, to customer's requirements, including VHF-20A VHF-AM com (dual in IFR version), AG-06 intercom, VIR-31A VOR/ILS with VOR/LOC, glideslope and marker beacon receiver, TDR-90 ATC transponder, ADF-60A and DME-40. Optional avionics include Sperry AA-300 radio altimeter with LGSC, Helcis II flight director and autotrim, AFCS, pilot's navigation instruments, co-pilot's flight and navigation instruments, standby attitude indicator, two- or three-axis autopilot, Bendix/FIAR RDR-1500 or Sperry Primus 300SL weather radar, and Loran or Omega navigation system, depending on requirement.

EQUIPMENT: Depending upon mission, may include internal cargo platform, external cargo sling, externally mounted rescue hoist, first aid kit, stretchers, Chadwick water bomber container for 208 or 584 litres (45·75 or 128·5 Imp gallons) of water or fire retardant, or equipment for exploration, thermal mapping, survey, or powerline control duties.

DIMENSIONS, EXTERNAL:

Main rotor diameter	11·00 m (36 ft 1 in)
Tail rotor diameter	2·03 m (6 ft 8 in)
Length overall, rotors turning	13·05 m (42 ft 9¾ in)
Length of fuselage	10·706 m (35 ft 1½ in)
Fuselage:	
Max width (except 'wide-body')	1·42 m (4 ft 8 in)
Height over tail fin	3·30 m (10 ft 10 in)
Elevator span	2·88 m (9 ft 5½ in)
Width over mainwheels	2·45 m (8 ft 0½ in)
Wheelbase	3·535 m (11 ft 7¼ in)
Passenger doors (each): Height	1·06 m (3 ft 5¾ in)
Width	1·15 m (3 ft 9¼ in)
Height to sill	0·65 m (2 ft 1½ in)
Baggage door (port, rear): Height	0·51 m (1 ft 8 in)
Width	1·00 m (3 ft 3¼ in)

DIMENSIONS, INTERNAL:

Cabin, excl flight deck: Length	1·63 m (5 ft 4¼ in)
Max width	1·32 m (4 ft 4 in)
Max height	1·28 m (4 ft 2½ in)
Volume	2·82 m³ (100 cu ft)
Baggage compartment volume	0·52 m³ (18·4 cu ft)

AREAS:

Main rotor blades (each)	1·84 m² (19·8 sq ft)
Tail rotor blades (each)	0·203 m² (2·185 sq ft)
Main rotor disc	95·03 m² (1,022·9 sq ft)
Tail rotor disc	3·24 m² (34·87 sq ft)

WEIGHTS AND LOADINGS:

Basic weight empty, equipped:	
standard	1,418 kg (3,126 lb)
offshore oil support (IFR)	1,604 kg (3,536 lb)
ambulance (IFR)	1,647 kg (3,631 lb)
firefighting	1,596 kg (3,518 lb)
Max external slung load	907 kg (2,000 lb)
Max baggage	150 kg (331 lb)
Typical T-O weight:	
offshore oil support (IFR)	2,596 kg (5,723 lb)
ambulance (IFR)	2,409 kg (5,311 lb)
Max certificated T-O weight	2,600 kg (5,732 lb)
Max disc loading	27·4 kg/m² (5·60 lb/sq ft)
Max power loading	4·15 kg/kW (6·82 lb/shp)

PERFORMANCE (S/L, ISA, except where indicated. A: AUW of 2,250 kg; 4,960 lb, B: AUW of 2,450 kg; 5,400 lb, C: AUW of 2,600 kg; 5,732 lb):

Never-exceed speed:	
A, B, C	168 knots (311 km/h; 193 mph)
Max cruising speed:	
A	154 knots (285 km/h; 177 mph)
B, C	150 knots (278 km/h; 172 mph)
Econ cruising speed:	
A, B, C	126 knots (233 km/h; 145 mph)
Max rate of climb at S/L: A	643 m (2,110 ft)/min
B	555 m (1,820 ft)/min
C	503 m (1,650 ft)/min

Rate of climb at S/L, one engine out:
- A 152 m (500 ft)/min
- B 108 m (355 ft)/min
- C 78 m (255 ft)/min

Service ceiling, 30·5 m (100 ft)/min rate of climb, at max continuous power: A, B 4,575 m (15,000 ft)
- C 4,450 m (14,600 ft)

Service ceiling, one engine out, 30·5 m (100 ft)/min rate of climb, at max continuous power:
- C 1,675 m (5,500 ft)

Hovering ceiling IGE: A 3,750 m (12,300 ft)
- B 2,985 m (9,800 ft)
- C 2,410 m (7,900 ft)

Hovering ceiling OGE: A 2,880 m (9,450 ft)
- B 2,072 m (6,800 ft)
- C 1,493 m (4,900 ft)

Range with max standard fuel, no reserves:
- A 350 nm (648 km; 402 miles)
- B 341 nm (631 km; 392 miles)
- C 332 nm (615 km; 382 miles)

Endurance with max fuel, no reserves: A 3 h 12 min
- B 3 h 2 min
- C 2 h 57 min

AGUSTA A 109A Mk II (MILITARY, NAVAL and POLICE VERSIONS)

Several non-commercial versions of the A 109A have been developed by Agusta. In general, their configuration, structure and power plant are similar to those of the standard civil versions, although specially modified versions can be made available if required. Features of some or all military and naval versions include, as standard, dual controls and instrumentation; rotor brake; tail rotor control magnetic brake; sliding doors; environmental control system; emergency flotation gear; armoured seats; heavy duty battery; particle separator; external cargo hook; multi-purpose universal supports for external stores; rescue hoist; and high-load cargo floor. The naval versions, specially configured for shipboard compatibility, can be equipped with four-axis AFCS, radar altimeter, internal auxiliary fuel tanks, non-retractable landing gear, search radar, anchorage points for deck lashings, and an automatic navigation system.

The principal military, naval and other non-commercial versions were listed in some detail in the 1984-85 *Jane's*. The following is an abbreviated description:

Aerial scout. Can be armed with a flexibly mounted 7·62 mm or 12·7 mm machine-gun, with stabilised sight, plus two XM157 launchers (each with seven 2·75 in rockets). Normal crew of three.

Light attack against tanks and other hard-point targets. Has been demonstrated with Hughes M65 TOW system incorporating undernose telescopic sight unit, plus four or eight TOW missiles. Normal crew of two. Argentine Army is adapting its A 109s to carry Mathogo anti-tank missiles.

Light attack against soft-point targets. Various combinations of armament include a pintle mounted 7·62 mm machine-gun in each doorway; a flexible, remotely controlled externally mounted 7·62 mm gun; twin trainable, remotely controlled externally mounted 7·62 mm guns; two external machine-gun pods; or two gun pods and two rocket launchers. Normal crew of two.

Command and control. For target designation and direction of helicopter attack force. Can be armed with combination of rockets and flexible machine-guns, as described in preceding paragraph.

Utility. For up to seven troops; two stretcher patients and two medical attendants; externally mounted rescue hoist; or underfuselage hook for slung load.

Mirach. Version carrying two Mirach-100 RPVs for battlefield surveillance, reconnaissance, target acquisition, elint, ECM, attack on ground or naval targets, and enemy defence saturation or decoy.

ESM/ECM. Electronic warfare version, for military and naval use. Available with passive ESM only, plus weapon systems if required; and with passive ESM plus modularised active ECM (jamming), plus any required weapons. Provision for chaff dispenser to be mounted on tailboom.

Naval. Primary naval missions are anti-surface vessel, electronic warfare, standoff missile guidance, reconnaissance, and anti-submarine classification. Secondary capabilities for search and rescue, troop transportation, ambulance, flying crane, coastguard patrol, and inter-ship liaison duties. Configurations for electronic warfare and utility roles generally similar to those described in preceding 'Utility' and 'ESM/ECM' paragraphs. For the ASW role, specialised equipment includes MAD, one or two homing torpedoes and six marine markers. For the ASV role the naval A 109 carries a high performance long-range search radar with high discrimination in rough sea conditions. The surface attack is performed with air-to-surface wire-guided missiles. For the TG-2 (standoff missile guidance) mission, the helicopter is equipped with a special system to control and guide a ship-launched Otomat missile. For armed patrol, the naval A 109 is equipped with a search radar and armament to customer's requirements. The coastguard patrol configuration includes a search radar, a special installation for external high efficiency loudspeakers, and a searchlight.

Police and other patrol duties. For patrol (including armed patrol) and surveillance, search and rescue, firefighting, and similar utility missions. Principal SAR equipment includes search radar, rescue hoist, stretcher/first aid kits, radar altimeter, skis or emergency flotation gear, AFCS, and flare/smoke grenades. For aerial patrol it can include 360° radar, automatic stability control system, external loudspeakers, FLIR, pollution monitoring equipment, system for spraying chemical retardants, and other items depending upon requirements of mission.

ROTOR DRIVE: As for civil A 109A Mk II, except for twin-engined max contingency rating of 638 kW (856 shp) and 5 min single-engined T-O rating of 313 kW (420 shp).

TYPICAL WEIGHTS (military Mk II):

Basic weight empty 1,418 kg (3,126 lb)

Weight empty, equipped:
- utility 1,560 kg (3,439 lb)
- ESM/ECM 1,627 kg (3,587 lb)
- ambulance 1,630 kg (3,594 lb)
- scout, attack, air defence 1,650 kg (3,638 lb)
- anti-tank 1,790 kg (3,946 lb)

Armament/equipment/payload:
- ambulance (1 medical attendant) 80 kg (176 lb)
- air defence (8 missiles) 150 kg (331 lb)
- anti-tank (8 missiles) 196 kg (432 lb)
- ESM/ECM (radar warning, deception jammer, noise jammer, ESM equipment) 270 kg (595 lb)
- scout (2 podded 12·7 mm and 2 pintle mounted 7·62 mm machine-guns) 287 kg (633 lb)
- attack (2 podded 12·7 mm machine-guns and 14 rockets in pods) 344 kg (758 lb)
- utility (7 equipped troops) 630 kg (1,389 lb)

T-O weight: ambulance 2,330 kg (5,136 lb)
- air defence 2,500 kg (5,512 lb)
- scout, attack, anti-tank, Mirach, ESM/ECM, utility (= max T-O weight) 2,600 kg (5,732 lb)

PERFORMANCE (S/L, ISA, except where indicated. A: AUW of 2,250 kg; 4,960 lb, B: AUW of 2,450 kg; 5,400 lb, C: AUW of 2,600 kg; 5,732 lb): As civil Mk II except:

Max cruising speed: A 155 knots (287 km/h; 178 mph)
- B 150 knots (278 km/h; 173 mph)
- C 147 knots (272 km/h; 169 mph)

Econ cruising speed:
- A 126 knots (233 km/h; 145 mph)
- B 125 knots (232 km/h; 144 mph)
- C 124 knots (230 km/h; 143 mph)

Max rate of climb at S/L: A 640 m (2,100 ft)/min

Service ceiling, 30·5 m (100 ft)/min rate of climb, at max continuous power: A 5,485 m (18,000 ft)
- B 4,575 m (15,000 ft)
- C 4,450 m (14,600 ft)

Range with max standard fuel, no reserves:
- A 320 nm (593 km; 368 miles)
- B 310 nm (574 km; 357 miles)
- C 300 nm (556 km; 345 miles)

Range with max standard fuel, 10 min reserves:
- Mirach 360 nm (667 km; 414 miles)

Endurance with max standard fuel, no reserves:
- A 3 h 43 min
- B 3 h 30 min
- C 3 h 15 min

Endurance with max standard fuel, 10 min reserves:
- Mirach 4 h 30 min

AGUSTA A 109 EOA

Twenty-four examples of this new version of the A 109 have been ordered by the Italian Army as advanced observation helicopters. Deliveries were due to begin at the end of 1986.

The EOA has the lengthened nose and fixed, raised landing gear of the A 109K (see following entry), but is powered by uprated Allison 250-C20R engines, offering better 'hot and high' performance than the -C20Bs in the standard A 109A Mk II. Other features of the EOA include sliding cabin doors, crashworthy self-sealing fuel tanks, missile launchers and a 12·7 mm machine-gun, a SFIN gyro-stabilised sight, and electronic warfare equipment.

AGUSTA A 109K

Agusta developed this multi-role 'hot and high' variant of the A 109A Mk II, aimed specifically at the military market in the Middle East and Africa. The A 109K has two 539 kW (723 shp) Turboméca Arriel IK turboshafts (instead of the A 109's usual 313 kW; 420 shp Allisons), an uprated transmission, a new main rotor hub made of composites, elastomeric bearings, composites blades with a hard surface coating that is resistant to abrasion by sand and hard dust, a new tail rotor of Wortmann blade section, a longer nose to house additional avionics, and a taller and non-retractable high shock absorption landing gear.

Intended for operation by a pilot and gunner in its primary combat role, the A 109K proved its capability during firing trials in Belgium. The first prototype flew for

Agusta A 109K multi-role 'hot and high' variant of the A 109A Mk II

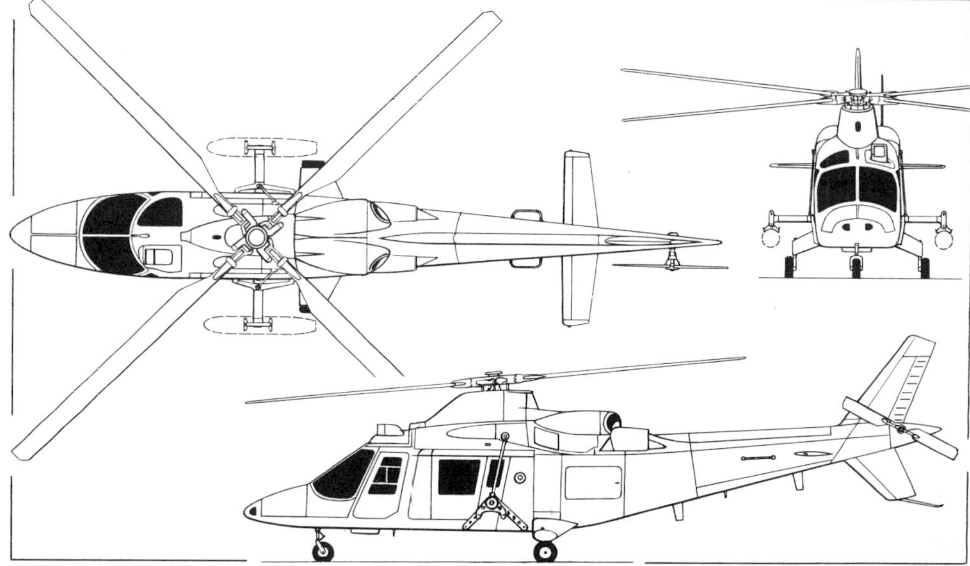

Agusta A 109K, with uprated engines and transmission, non-retractable landing gear and other changes *(Pilot Press)*

the first time in April 1983, and differed from the basic A 109A only in having the standard Allison 250-C20B turboshaft engines replaced by Arriel IKs. The second prototype, which began flying in March 1984, was fully representative of the planned production version.

Differences by comparison with the standard A 109A Mk II are as follows:

TYPE: Twin-engined multi-role helicopter.

ROTOR SYSTEM: Composites main rotor blades and hub, with elastomeric bearings, and special blade surface coating, for greater corrosion/abrasion resistance. New tail rotor of slightly reduced diameter, with high-efficiency Wortmann aerofoil section.

ROTOR DRIVE: Main transmission uprated to 608 kW (816 shp) for take-off and max continuous twin-engined operation. Ratings for single-engined operation are 410 kW (550 shp) for 2·5 minutes, and 373 kW (500 shp) max continuous.

FUSELAGE: Nose lengthened by 40 cm (15¾ in) and fitted with an upward hinged door on each side, for access to avionics. Provision for ECM or other sensors on nose.

LANDING GEAR: Non-retractable tricycle type, giving increased clearance between fuselage and ground. Changes restricted to replacement of nose leg actuator by a fixed strut, and replacement of each main leg actuator by a fixed strut and a V support frame.

POWER PLANT: Two Turboméca Arriel IK turboshaft engines, each rated at 539 kW (723 shp) for 2·5 minutes, 522 kW (700 shp) for take-off (5 minutes) and 436 kW (585 shp) max cruise power. Engine particle separator added. Standard fuel capacity 700 litres (154 Imp gallons).

ACCOMMODATION: Normal crew of two for combat missions, comprising pilot (on right) and gunner. Up to six passengers in cabin of utility version. Smaller instrument panel to improve forward view.

SYSTEMS: Lighter-weight hydraulic and electrical systems. 28V DC electrical system supplied by two 160A starter/generators, with 27Ah nickel-cadmium battery and external power socket. Three-phase AC power at 400Hz supplied by 6kVA 115V engine driven alternator and single-phase AC by a 250VA solid state inverter. Second alternator optional.

AVIONICS: Basic installation comprises dual UHF/VHF AM-FM, Collins AN/ARN-126 VOR/LOC/ILS, Collins ADF-60, AG-06 intercom, SIT 421 IFF transponder, Sperry three-axis AFCS and AN/ASN-75 nav compass system.

ARMAMENT (optional): Total of four stores attachments, two on each side of cabin, on outriggers. Typical loads include two 7·62 mm or 12·7 mm gun pods or up to eight TOW anti-armour missiles (with roof mounted sight), plus a 7·62 or 12·7 mm side-firing gun in cabin.

DIMENSIONS, EXTERNAL:
- Tail rotor diameter: 2·00 m (6 ft 6¾ in)
- Length of fuselage: 11·106 m (36 ft 5¼ in)

AREA:
- Tail rotor disc: 3·143 m² (33·83 sq ft)

WEIGHTS AND LOADINGS:
- Weight empty: 1,595 kg (3,517 lb)
- Max T-O weight: 2,850 kg (6,283 lb)
- Max disc loading: 30·0 kg/m² (6·15 lb/sq ft)
- Max power loading: 2·64 kg/kW (4·34 lb/shp)

PERFORMANCE (at max T-O weight except where indicated):
- *Max level speed at S/L, 'clean':
  - ISA: 138 knots (255 km/h; 159 mph)
  - ISA + 20°C: 140 knots (259 km/h; 161 mph)
- *Max cruising speed at S/L, at average weight, 'clean':
  - ISA: 141 knots (261 km/h; 162 mph)
  - ISA + 20°C: 144 knots (266 km/h; 166 mph)
- **Econ cruising speed at S/L, at average weight, 'clean':
  - ISA: 128 knots (237 km/h; 147 mph)
  - ISA + 20°C: 131 knots (243 km/h; 151 mph)
- Max rate of climb at S/L:
  - ISA: 530 m (1,740 ft)/min
  - ISA + 20°C: 509 m (1,670 ft)/min
- Rate of climb at S/L, one engine out:
  - ISA or ISA + 20°C: 167 m (550 ft)/min
- Service ceiling:
  - ISA or ISA + 20°C: 6,100 m (20,000 ft)
- Service ceiling, one engine out:
  - ISA: 2,770 m (9,100 ft)
  - ISA + 20°C: 1,950 m (6,400 ft)
- Hovering ceiling IGE at average weight, 'clean':
  - ISA: 5,640 m (18,500 ft)
  - ISA + 20°C: 4,970 m (16,300 ft)
- Hovering ceiling OGE at average weight, 'clean':
  - ISA: 3,350 m (11,000 ft)
  - ISA + 20°C: 2,680 m (8,800 ft)
- Max range at S/L, 'clean':
  - ISA: 290 nm (537 km; 333 miles)
  - ISA + 20°C: 284 nm (526 km; 326 miles)

* *reduced by 9 knots (17 km/h; 11 mph) with two gun pods fitted*

** *reduced by 6 knots (11 km/h; 7 mph) with two gun pods fitted*

AGUSTA A 129 MANGUSTA (MONGOOSE)

The Italian Army first made known its requirements for a light anti-armour helicopter in 1972, and the initial proposal, based on a derivative of the A 109A, was made in the following year. This was superseded by an all-new design, the A 129, which received Italian Army go-ahead in March 1978 and underwent several changes of configuration before reaching its final form in 1980. The first A 129 (MM 590/E.I. 901) made an official first flight on 15 September 1983, following two earlier 'unofficial' flights of which the first took place on 11 September.

Initially, the A 129 is intended for service with the Italian Army, primarily for specialised attack against armoured targets with anti-tank or area suppression weapons, and will have full night/bad weather combat capability. It is also suitable for advanced scouting and other roles.

The development programme, including the building of five flying prototypes, has been fully funded (70 per cent by the Italian Army and 30 per cent by Agusta). First flights of the second and third prototypes took place on 1 July and 5 October 1984; the fourth was flown on 27 May 1985, and the fifth on 1 March 1986. By September 1986 all scheduled test flying of the five prototypes had been completed.

Italian government approval has been given for an initial production batch of 60 A 129s, to equip two Italian Army Aviation operational squadrons. A requirement exists for an additional 30 aircraft, plus reserves, to equip a third operational squadron. Manufacture of the first 15 Mangustas for the Italian Army was under way by mid-1986, and the first production example was expected to be completed by early 1987, permitting deliveries to start in the third quarter of that year. Twenty Mangustas have been ordered by the Dutch Army; they will be operated on behalf of the Army by the Royal Netherlands Air Force.

TYPE: Light anti-tank, attack and advanced scout helicopter.

ROTOR SYSTEM: Fully articulated four-blade main rotor and two-blade semi-rigid delta-hinged tail rotor, each with elastomeric bearings and low-noise tips (various tip designs evaluated before production). Main rotor blades, which have a very low vibration level, each consist of a carbonfibre and Kevlar spar, Nomex honeycomb leading- and trailing-edge, stainless steel leading-edge abrasion strip, frangible tip, and skin of composite materials. They are designed to have a ballistic tolerance against hits from 12·7 mm ammunition, but are expected also to have considerable tolerance against 23 mm hits. The hub has the same ballistic tolerance; all mechanical linkages and moving parts are housed inside the rotor mast to eliminate foreign object damage, decrease icing problems, and reduce radar signature. There are no lubricated bearings in the rotor head. Tail rotor blades are also of composite materials, with a stainless steel leading-edge, and are tolerant to 12·7 mm hits.

ROTOR DRIVE: Transmission rating 969 kW (1,300 shp) (two engines), 704 kW (944 shp) for single-engined operation, with emergency rating of 759 kW (1,018 shp); power input into transmission is at 27,000 rpm. All driveshafts, components and couplings ballistically tolerant to 12·7 mm hits. Main transmission has integral independent oil cooling system; intermediate and tail rotor gearboxes are grease lubricated. Transmission and gearboxes are designed to continue to operate safely for at least 30 min without oil (45 min already demonstrated). Accessory gearbox forward of main transmission. In normal operation, accessories are driven by main gear train, but on ground they can be engaged by a pilot actuated clutch which connects No. 1 engine to the accessory section without engaging the rotors. Rotor brake fitted, to stop rotors quickly while the two engines run at ground idle, one driving the accessories.

WINGS: Cantilever mid mounted stub wings, built of composite materials, aft of rear cockpit in plane of main rotor mast.

FUSELAGE: Conventional semi-monocoque structure of aluminium alloy longerons and frames. Honeycomb panels in centre-fuselage and fuel tank areas. Composite materials, making up 45 per cent of total fuselage weight (excluding engine) and 16·1 per cent of total empty weight, are used for nosecone, tailboom, tail rotor pylon, engine nacelles, canopy frame and maintenance panels. Total 'wetted' surface area of airframe (excl blades and hub) is 50 m² (538·2 sq ft), of which 35 m² (376·7 sq ft) (70 per cent) are of composite materials. Small and narrow frontal area. Rollover bulkhead in nose and rollover bar in forward fuselage for crew protection; armour protection for vital areas of power plant. Overall infra-red-absorbing paint finish. Airframe has a ballistic tolerance against 12·7 mm armour-piercing ammunition, and meets the crashworthiness standards of MIL-STD-1290 (vertical velocity changes of up to 11·2 m; 36·75 ft/s and longitudinal changes of up to 13·1 m; 43 ft/s).

TAIL UNIT: Sweptback main fin, with tail rotor mounted near top on port side. Small underfin, serving also as mount for tailwheel. Tailplane mid-mounted on tailboom in line with fin leading-edge. All tail surfaces built of composite materials.

LANDING GEAR: Non-retractable tailwheel type, with single wheel on each unit. Hydraulic shock strut in each main unit. Gear designed to withstand hard landings at descent rates in excess of 10 m (32·8 ft)/s.

POWER PLANT: Two Rolls-Royce Gem 2 Mk 1004D turboshaft engines, each with a max continuous rating of 615 kW (825 shp) for normal twin-engined operation; intermediate contingency rating of 657 kW (881 shp) for 1 h; a max contingency rating of 704 kW (944 shp) for 2½ min; and an emergency rating (S/L, ISA) of 759 kW (1,018 shp) for 20 s. Production aircraft have engines licence built in Italy by Piaggio. Two separate fuel systems, with cross-feed capability; interchangeable self-sealing and crash resistant tanks, self-sealing lines, and digital fuel feed control. Tanks can be foam-filled for fire protection. Single-point pressure refuelling. Infra-red exhaust suppression system and low engine noise levels. Separate independent lubrication oil cooling system for each engine. Provision for auxiliary (self-ferry) fuel tanks on inboard underwing stations.

ACCOMMODATION: Pilot and co-pilot/gunner in separate cockpits in tandem. Elevated rear (pilot's) cockpit. Each cockpit has a flat plate low-glint canopy with upward hinged door panels on starboard side, blow-out side panel for exit in emergency, and armoured crashworthy seat.

SYSTEMS: Hydraulic system includes three main circuits dedicated to flight controls and two independent circuits for rotor and wheel braking. Main system operates at pressure of 207 bars (3,000 lb/sq in) and is fed by three independent power groups, two integrated and driven mechanically by the main transmission, the third integrated and driven by the tail rotor gearbox. Dual actuators are provided for main and tail rotor flight controls. Hydraulic system flow rate 23·6 litres (5·2 Imp gallons)/min in each main group. Spring type reservoirs, pressurised at 0·39 bars (5·6 lb/sq in). Electrical system includes fly by wire system as backup for mechanical control system. Full automatic stabilisation equipment, integrated with computerised IMS central management system. Automatic fire extinguishing system.

AVIONICS AND OPERATIONAL EQUIPMENT: All main functions of the helicopter are handled and monitored by a fully integrated digital multiplex system, or IMS (first installation in prototype 904), which controls com, nav, flight director, autopilot, fly by wire, transmission and engine condition monitoring, fuel/hydraulic/electrical

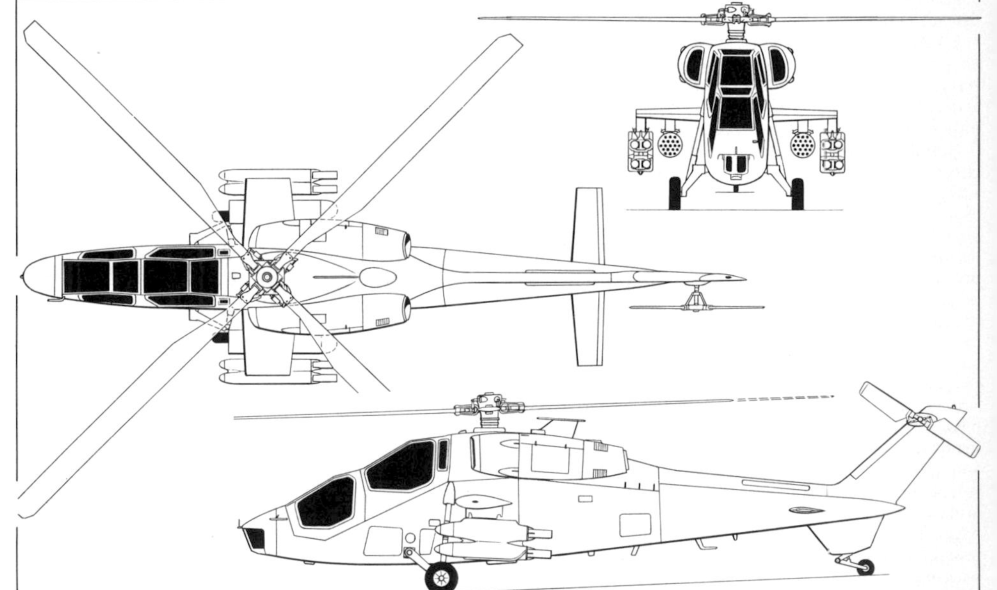

Agusta A 129 light anti-tank, attack and advanced scout helicopter *(Pilot Press)*

Agusta A 129 armed attack helicopter (first prototype)

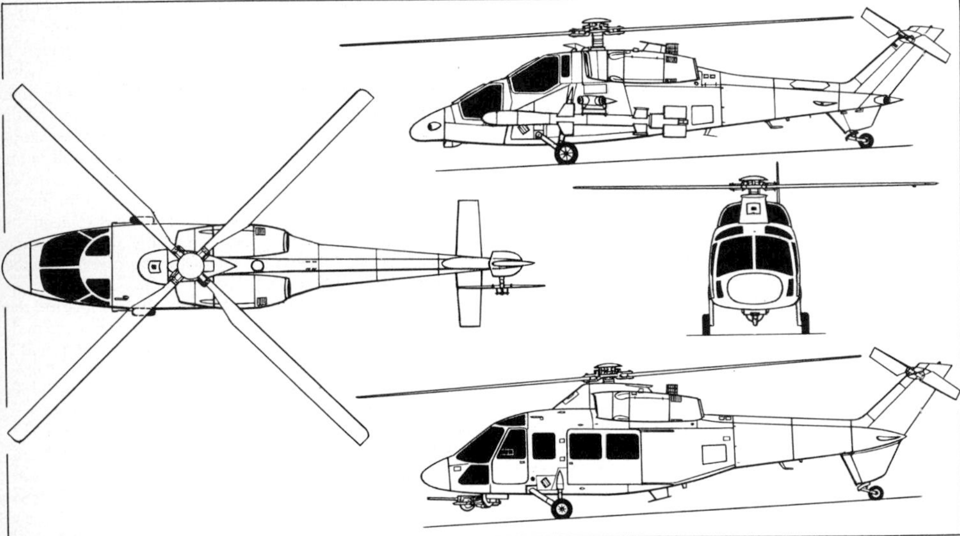

Three-view drawing of the proposed battlefield support version of the Agusta A 129, with additional side view (top) of the projected naval version *(Pilot Press)*

systems monitoring, aircraft performance, caution and warning systems, and rocket fire control. The IMS is managed by two redundant central computers, each capable of operating the system independently. They are backed by two interface units which pick up outputs from sensors and avionic equipment and transfer them, via a system of redundant 1553B data buses, to the main computers for real-time processing. Processed information is presented to the pilot and co-pilot/gunner on separate graphic/alphanumeric head-down multi-function displays (MFDs) with standard multi-function keyboards for easy access to information, including area navigation and synthetic waypoint map, weapons status and selection, radio tuning and mode selection, caution and warning, and display of aircraft performance. The IMS computer can store up to 100 waypoints, or a maximum of ten flight plans with ten waypoints each, and 100 pre-set frequencies for HF, VHF and UHF radio management. Navigation is controlled by the navigation computer of the IMS coupled to a Doppler radar and a radar altimeter. Synthetic map presentation of waypoints, target areas and dangerous areas is shown on the pilot's or co-pilot's MFD.

The A 129 has a full day/night operational capability, with equipment designed to give both crew members a view outside the helicopter irrespective of light conditions. A pilot's night vision system allows nap-of-the-earth (NOE) flight by night, a picture of the world outside being generated by the FLIR system inside the 'nose' of the pilot's night vision system (which is mounted at the nose of the aircraft) and presented to the pilot through the monocle of his integrated helmet and display sighting system (IHADSS). Symbology containing the information required for the flight is superimposed onto the image, giving a true head-up reference. The co-pilot/gunner is also equipped with an IHADSS. For night anti-tank engagements, the TOW target acquisition and missile guidance unit will be augmented by a FLIR. This vision equipment can also be used during daylight, especially the integrated helmet sight, which provides automatic weapon aiming and reduces reaction time against unexpected targets. An omnidirectional air data system is also installed.

As requested by the Italian Army, the A 129 has provision to install a mast mounted sight (MMS) for target acquisition, TOW missile tracking, laser ranging, laser designation (eg for Hellfire launch), and automatic laser tracking of targets designated by other air or ground lasers. An MMS would give the A 129 greater flexibility and survivability by allowing it to aim and fire from behind trees or other terrain features. Feasibility studies for an MMS have been carried out successfully.

Active and passive self-protection systems (ECCM and ECM) will be standard on the Italian Army A 129. Passive electronic warfare systems will include a radar warning receiver, and a laser warning receiver, which can detect enemy radars or lasers locked on to the helicopter and signal them to the crew for evasive action or the appropriate use of active countermeasures. The latter may include a radar jammer and infra-red jammer, and a chaff/flare dispenser.

ARMAMENT: Four underwing attachments, inner pair stressed for loads of up to 300 kg (661 lb) each, outer pair (at wingtips) also for 300 kg each. All stations incorporate articulation which allows pylon to be elevated 2° and depressed 10° from armament datum line. They are aligned with the aircraft automatically, with no need for boresighting. Initial armament of up to eight TOW wire guided anti-tank missiles (two, three or four in pod suspended from each wingtip station); with these can be carried, on the inboard stations, either two 7·62, 12·7 or 20 mm gun pods, or two launchers each for seven air-to-surface rockets. For general attack missions, rocket launchers can be carried on all four stations (two nineteen-tube plus two seven-tube). Alternatively, is able to carry six Hellfire anti-tank missiles (three beneath each wingtip); two Stinger type air-to-air missiles; eight Hot missiles; two gun pods plus two nineteen-tube rocket launchers; or grenade launchers. A 'chin' turret for a 0·50 in or 12·7 mm gun may be mounted under the nose.

DIMENSIONS, EXTERNAL:

Main rotor diameter	11·90 m (39 ft 0½ in)
Tail rotor diameter	2·24 m (7 ft 4¼ in)
Wing span	3·20 m (10 ft 6 in)
Width over TOW pods	3·60 m (11 ft 9¾ in)
Length overall, both rotors turning	14·29 m (46 ft 10½ in)
Fuselage: Length	12·275 m (40 ft 3¼ in)
Max width	0·95 m (3 ft 1½ in)
Height:	
over tail fin, tail rotor horizontal	2·65 m (8 ft 8¼ in)
over tail, tail rotor turning	3·315 m (10 ft 10½ in)
to top of rotor head	3·35 m (11 ft 0 in)
Tailplane span	3·00 m (9 ft 10 in)
Wheel track	2·20 m (7 ft 3½ in)
Wheelbase	6·955 m (22 ft 9¾ in)

AREAS:

Main rotor disc	111·2 m² (1,196·95 sq ft)
Tail rotor disc	3·94 m² (42·42 sq ft)

WEIGHTS AND LOADINGS:

Weight empty, equipped	2,529 kg (5,575 lb)
Max internal fuel load	750 kg (1,653 lb)
Max external weapons load	1,000 kg (2,205 lb)
Max T-O weight	4,100 kg (9,039 lb)
Max disc loading	33·3 kg/m² (6·8 lb/sq ft)
Max power loading	3·05 kg/kW (5·0 lb/shp)

PERFORMANCE:

At mission T-O weight of 3,700 kg (8,157 lb), at 2,000 m (6,560 ft), ISA + 20°C, except where indicated, the A 129 is designed to meet the following performance requirements:

Dash speed	170 knots (315 km/h; 196 mph)
Max level speed at S/L	140 knots (259 km/h; 161 mph)
Max rate of climb at S/L	637 m (2,090 ft)/min
Hovering ceiling: IGE	3,290 m (10,800 ft)
OGE	2,390 m (7,850 ft)

Basic 2 h 30 min mission profile with 8 TOW and 20 min fuel reserves

Fly 54 nm (100 km; 62 miles) to battle area, mainly in NOE mode, 90 min loiter (incl 45 min hovering), and return to base

Max endurance, no reserves	3 h 0 min
g limit	+3·5

AGUSTA A 129 (DEVELOPED VERSIONS)

Three possible variants of the A 129 Mangusta are being promoted by Agusta, which released first details at the 1985 Paris Air Show. The first of these, now named **Tonal** after an ancient Aztec deity, is an advanced multi-mission version to meet the requirements of the British, Dutch, Spanish and Italian armies. An agreement for a joint study was signed by Agusta, Westland and Fokker in 1985, with CASA joining in 1986. On 4 September 1986 the three original partners agreed to set up a new Joint European Helicopter company in Italy to carry out a technical and cost study for the Tonal, with CASA to sign shortly afterwards. Shareholdings are 38% each to Agusta and Westland, 19% to Fokker and 5% to CASA. Air-to-air, scout and anti-tank versions of the Tonal are planned.

Second proposed version is a ship or shore based **naval** development for anti-shipping and maritime support roles, with nose mounted radar, and an armament of two Marte Mk 2 or four Sea Skua missiles in the anti-shipping role or Mavericks, TOWs or rocket pods for maritime support.

The third proposal is for an **LBH** (light battlefield helicopter) tactical support version which would combine the Mangusta's rotor system, power plant and landing gear with an entirely new and larger fuselage having side by side crew seating and a cabin able to accommodate an eight-man assault squad, or six stretchers and two medical attendants. Provisions would be made for a 'chin' mounted gun turret, a 272 kg (600 lb) capacity rescue hoist, side looking airborne radar, and gun or rocket pods on the wing pylons.

AGUSTA-BELL 205

The Agusta-Bell 205 is a multi-purpose utility helicopter, corresponding to the UH-1D/UH-1H versions described under the Bell heading in the US section. It is fitted with IFR and night flying instruments, and for normal operation only one pilot is needed. Power plant is a 1,044 kW (1,400 shp) Avco Lycoming T53-L-13B turboshaft engine, flat rated at 820 kW (1,100 shp) for take-off.

The AB 205 is in service with the Italian armed forces and has been ordered by many other countries. Production was continuing in 1986.

WEIGHTS: As Bell Model 205 except:

Weight empty (standard)	2,177 kg (4,800 lb)

PERFORMANCE (at max T-O weight, ISA):

Max level speed at S/L	120 knots (222 km/h; 138 mph)
Cruising speed	110 knots (204 km/h; 127 mph)
Max rate of climb at S/L	512 m (1,680 ft)/min
Service ceiling	4,575 m (15,000 ft)

Italian Army Agusta-Bell 205 utility helicopter

Max range, standard tanks, no reserves
312 nm (580 km; 360 miles)
Max endurance, standard tanks, no reserves
3 h 48 min

AGUSTA-BELL 206B JETRANGER III

The JetRanger has been manufactured under licence from Bell since the end of 1967; deliveries began in 1972 of the Agusta-Bell 206B JetRanger II, and of the JetRanger III at the end of 1978. A description of the JetRanger III appears under the Bell entry in the US section. Approx 1,000 JetRangers have been built by Agusta, and production is expected to continue at least until 1990.

A new version of the JetRanger III, which became available in 1984, incorporates a modified Allison engine (250-C20J), offering lower cabin and external noise levels; new fuel system, increasing capacity by 64 litres (17 US gallons); roomier cabin with lowered seats and bulged windows; max range at 1,525 m (5,000 ft) with max fuel and max payload (no reserves) of 386 nm (715 km; 444 miles).

AGUSTA-BELL 212

The Agusta-Bell 212 is a twin-engined utility transport helicopter particularly suited to military or civilian passenger transport duties. Its general configuration is similar to that of the Bell Model 212 Twin Two-Twelve, described in the US section.

Recent customers for the AB 212 have included the Spanish Army (four), Morocco (five), Austrian Army (24), Somali Air Force (four), Italian Army, and government agencies of other countries.

The extensively modified AB 212ASW naval version is described separately.

DIMENSIONS, EXTERNAL: As Bell Model 212 except:
Main rotor diameter 14·63 m (48 ft 0 in)
Length overall, rotors turning 17·40 m (57 ft 1 in)
AREA:
Main rotor disc 168·1 m² (1,809·5 sq ft)
WEIGHTS: As Bell Model 212 except:
Weight empty (standard) 2,630 kg (5,800 lb)
PERFORMANCE (at AUW of 4,536 kg; 10,000 lb, ISA):
Cruising speed at S/L 110 knots (204 km/h; 127 mph)
Max rate of climb at S/L 567 m (1,860 ft)/min
Service ceiling 5,180 m (17,000 ft)
Hovering ceiling: IGE 3,960 m (13,000 ft)
OGE 3,050 m (10,000 ft)
Max range at 1,525 m (5,000 ft) with standard fuel, no reserves:
on two engines 267 nm (494 km; 307 miles)
on one engine 318 nm (589 km; 366 miles)

AGUSTA-BELL 212ASW

The AB 212ASW is an extensively modified version of the AB 212, intended primarily for anti-submarine search and attack missions, and for attacks on surface vessels, but suitable also for search and rescue and utility roles. A new SAR version has been developed recently with such additional features as a hydraulically operated external hoist and a four-channel Sperry autopilot. The 212 ASW benefits from considerable naval operational experience gained with the single-engined AB 204AS, and can operate from the same small ship decks. More than 100 are in service worldwide; recent customers have included the Greek Navy (12, including some in electronic warfare configuration), Iraqi Navy (5) and Turkish Navy (12 in both ASW and ASV configurations).

Apart from some local strengthening and the provision of deck mooring equipment, the airframe structure remains essentially similar to that of the commercial Model 212 and military UH-1N, described under the Bell entry in the US section. Main differences from the civil Agusta-Bell 212 are as follows:

TYPE: Twin-engined anti-submarine and anti-surface-vessel helicopter.

POWER PLANT: One Pratt & Whitney Canada PT6T-6 Turbo Twin Pac, rated at 1,398 kW (1,875 shp). Protection against salt water corrosion. Provision for one internal or two external auxiliary fuel tanks.

ACCOMMODATION: Normal crew of three or four. Volume of cabin is 6·1 m³ (215 cu ft), with floor area of 5·0 m² (54 sq ft). With sonar installed, volume is reduced to 5·1 m³ (180 cu ft). Naval 212 can accommodate two pilots and seven passengers; or two pilots, four stretcher patients and attendant. Single sliding door, with jettisonable emergency exit panel, on each side.

SYSTEMS: Standard duplicated hydraulic systems for flight controls, as in AB 212. The hydraulic system operates the automatic flight control system. Self-contained hydraulic system for operation of sonar, rescue hoist and other utilities. Electrical system capacity increased to cater for higher power demand (28V DC, and three phase 200/115V or single phase 26V AC at 400Hz); the two standard generators are integrated with a 20kVA alternator.

AVIONICS AND EQUIPMENT: Complete instrumentation for day and night sea operation in all weathers. Avionics installed are UHF transceiver, HF transceiver, and Agusta AG-03-M intercom, for communications; ADF, Tacan and homing UHF, for navigation assistance; radar altimeter, Doppler radar, ASW navigation computer and automatic flight control system with General Electric SR-3 gyro platform, Sperry four-axis autopilot with AATH (automatic approach to hover) mode for automatic navigation; IFF/SIF transponder; search radar and radar transponder; data link; and Bendix AN/AQS-13B/F sonar for ASW search.

ARMAMENT AND OPERATIONAL EQUIPMENT: Weapons may consist of two Motofides 244 AS or two Mk 44/46 homing torpedoes, or two Marte Mk 2 or Sea Skua type air-to-surface missiles. Rescue hoist, capacity 270 kg (600 lb) standard. Provisions for auxiliary installations such as a 2,270 kg (5,000 lb) capacity cargo sling, inflatable emergency pontoons, internal and external auxiliary fuel tanks, according to mission.

ASW MISSION: Basic sensor system for ASW search and attack is a Bendix AN/AQS-13B/F low-frequency variable depth sonar, with a max operating depth of 137 m (450 ft). Automatic navigation system permits positioning of helicopter over any desired 'dip' point of a complex search pattern. Position of helicopter, computed by automatic navigation system, is integrated with sonar target information in radar tactical display where both surface and underwater tactical situations can be continuously monitored. Additional navigation and tactical information provided by UHF direction finding equipment, from an A/A mode-capable Tacan and a radar transponder. Automatic flight control system (AFCS) integrates basic automatic stabilisation equipment with signal output from radar altimeter, Doppler radar, sonar cable angle signals, and outputs from dry cable transducer. Effectiveness of this system results in hands-off flight from cruise condition to sonar hover in all weathers and under rough sea conditions. Specially designed cockpit display shows pilots all flight parameters for each phase of ASW operation. Attack mission is carried out with two homing torpedoes, or with depth charges.

ASV MISSION: For this mission AB 212ASW carries a Ferranti Seaspray long-range search radar, with very efficient scanner design and installation possessing high discrimination in rough sea conditions. Provisions made to permit incorporation of future radar system developments. Automatic navigation systems and search radar are integrated to permit continuously updated picture of tactical situation. Provisions also incorporated for installation of the most advanced ECM systems (Selenia or Elettronica is system most commonly used). Surface attack is performed with air-to-surface missiles of the Marte Mk 2 or Sea Skua type.

STANDOFF MISSILE GUIDANCE MISSION: In this mission the AB 212ASW, with special equipment, can provide mid-course passive guidance for the ship launched Otomat 2 surface-to-surface missile. Equipment includes an SMA/APS series 360° search radar and a TG-2 real-time target data transmission system for guidance of the missile.

DIMENSIONS, EXTERNAL: As AB 212, except:
Max width: with torpedoes 3·95 m (12 ft 11½ in)
with missiles 4·17 m (13 ft 8¼ in)
WEIGHTS (A: ASW mission with Mk 46 torpedoes; B: ASV mission with AS.12 missiles; C: search and rescue mission; all at S/L, ISA):
Weight empty, equipped:
A, B, C 3,420 kg (7,540 lb)
Crew of three: A, B, C 240 kg (529 lb)
Mission equipment:
A (two Mk 46 torpedoes) 490 kg (1,080 lb)
B (AS.12 installation and XM-58 sight)
180 kg (396 lb)

Agusta-Bell 212ASW in the insignia of the Italian Navy

C (rescue hoist) 40 kg (89 lb)
Full fuel (normal tanks) 1,021 kg (2,250 lb)
Auxiliary external tanks 32 kg (70 lb)
Auxiliary fuel 356 kg (785 lb)
Mission T-O weight: A 5,070 kg (11,176 lb)
B 4,973 kg (10,961 lb)
C 4,937 kg (10,883 lb)

PERFORMANCE (at max T-O weight except where indicated, ISA):
Never-exceed speed 130 knots (240 km/h; 150 mph)
Max level speed at S/L 106 knots (196 km/h; 122 mph)
Max cruising speed with armament 100 knots (185 km/h; 115 mph)
Max rate of climb at S/L: A 396 m (1,300 ft)/min
Rate of climb at S/L, one engine out:
A 61 m (200 ft)/min
Hovering ceiling IGE: A 3,200 m (10,500 ft)
Hovering ceiling OGE:
A at AUW of 4,763 kg (10,500 lb) 396 m (1,300 ft)
Search endurance (A) with 50% at 90 knots (167 km/h; 103 mph) cruise and 50% hovering OGE, 10% reserve fuel 3 h 12 min
Search range (B) with 10% reserve fuel 332 nm (615 km; 382 miles)
Endurance (B), no reserves 4 h 7 min
Endurance (C) at 90 knots (167 km/h; 103 mph) search speed 5 h 4 min
Max range with auxiliary tanks, 100 knots (185 km/h; 115 mph) cruise at S/L, 15% reserves 360 nm (667 km; 414 miles)
Max endurance with auxiliary tanks, no reserves 5 h 0 min

Agusta-Bell 412 of the Italian Carabinieri *(Aviodata)*

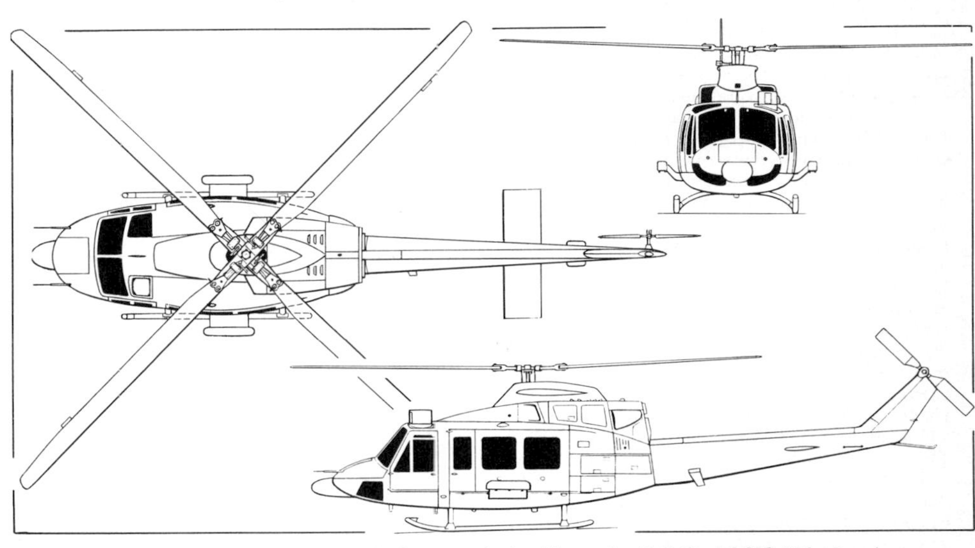

Agusta-Bell Griffon military helicopter, derived from the Bell Model 412 *(Pilot Press)*

AGUSTA-BELL 412 and GRIFFON

The first Bell prototype of the Model 412 was flown for the first time in August 1979, and customer deliveries began in January 1981. Licence production by Agusta was initiated later that year, and civil versions for a variety of applications are now available from the Italian manufacturer. A description of the basic civil Model 412 can be found under the Bell entry in the US section of this edition.

Agusta has also developed its own multi-purpose military version of the helicopter, known as the **Griffon**, for such applications as direct fire support, area suppression, scouting and reconnaissance, air defence, assault transport, combat equipment transport, and battlefield support. Special features include high-energy-absorbing landing gear, energy attenuating seats for crew and troops (the former also armour protected), and crash resistant self-sealing fuel tanks. Other survivability options can include passive (radar and laser warning, and missile detection) and active (ECM, radar jammer and decoy) systems, and a variety of ordnance can be carried. The Griffon is capable of performing medevac, tactical support, logistic transport, maritime surveillance, pollution monitoring, search and rescue, and patrol duties, and of being used effectively against surface ships, tanks and other armoured vehicles.

A prototype of the Griffon was flown for the first time in August 1982, and deliveries began in January 1983. Customers include the Italian Army, Zimbabwe Air Force (10), Ugandan Army, and Finnish border guard (3). The Griffon differs from the standard civil Model 412 in the following respects:

TYPE: Multi-purpose military helicopter.

ROTOR SYSTEM AND DRIVE: As for civil Model 412.

AIRFRAME: Generally similar to civil Model 412, but with reinforced impact-absorbing landing gear and armour protection in selected areas.

POWER PLANT: One 1,342 kW (1,800 shp) Pratt & Whitney Canada PT6T-3B Turbo Twin Pac (single-engine ratings 764 kW; 1,025 shp for 2½ min and 723 kW; 970 shp for 30 min), as in civil Model 412. Fuel system and capacity as for Model 412 (821 litres; 217 US gallons), but fuel is contained in crash resistant self-sealing tanks, three aft of cabin and two under cabin floor. Single-point refuelling. Two 76 or 341 litre (20 or 90 US gallon) auxiliary fuel tanks optional.

ACCOMMODATION: One or two pilots on flight deck, on energy-absorbing, armour protected seats. Fourteen crash-attenuating troop seats in main cabin in personnel transport roles, six patients and two medical attendants in ambulance version, or up to 1,814 kg (4,000 lb) of cargo or other equipment. Space for 181 kg (400 lb) of baggage in tailboom. Total of 51 fittings in cabin floor for attachment of seats, stretchers, internal hoist or other special equipment.

SYSTEMS: Generally as for Bell 212/412. Electrical system supplied by two independent 30V 200A DC starter/generators (derated to 150A) and 34Ah nickel-cadmium battery, with three 250VA single-phase solid state inverters for AC power.

AVIONICS AND EQUIPMENT: Typical avionics can include UHF/VHF (FM-AM) and HF secure voice com, ADF, VHF/UHF-DF, radar altimeter, IFF, DME, Tacan, VOR, navigation system, radar, Doppler radar, and four-axis AFCS. Optional avionics include AN/APR-39 radar warning receiver, laser warning receiver and pulse-Doppler radar missile detector system for passive warning of threats; active countermeasures options include AN/ALQ-144 ECM set, AN/ALQ-136 radar jammer, and ECM decoy system. A 272 kg (600 lb) capacity external rescue hoist can be fitted for search and rescue mission, and an external hook for cargo, battlefield support and other duties. Other optional equipment includes auxiliary fuel tanks, emergency floats, rotor brake, heavy duty heater, heated windscreen, loudspeakers, spectrolab, and searchlight, depending upon mission.

ARMAMENT: A variety of external weapon options for the Griffon includes two 25 mm Oerlikon cannon, four or eight TOW anti-tank missiles, two launchers each with nineteen 2·75 in SNORA rockets, two 12·7 mm machine-gun pods, four air-to-air or air defence suppression missiles, or, for attacking surface vessels, four Sea Skua or similar air-to-surface missiles.

WEIGHTS:
Weight empty, equipped (standard configuration) 2,841 kg (6,263 lb)
Max T-O weight 5,261 kg (11,600 lb)

PERFORMANCE (at max T-O weight, ISA):
Never-exceed speed at S/L 140 knots (259 km/h; 161 mph)
Max level speed at S/L 122 knots (226 km/h; 140 mph)
Econ cruising speed:
at S/L 122 knots (226 km/h; 140 mph)
at 1,500 m (4,920 ft) 125 knots (232 km/h; 144 mph)
at 3,000 m (9,840 ft) 123 knots (228 km/h; 142 mph)
Max rate of climb at S/L 438 m (1,437 ft)/min
Rate of climb at S/L, one engine out 168 m (551 ft)/min
Service ceiling, 30 m (100 ft)/min climb rate 5,180 m (17,000 ft)
Service ceiling, one engine out, 30 m (100 ft)/min climb rate 2,320 m (7,610 ft)
Hovering ceiling: IGE 1,250 m (4,100 ft)
OGE 670 m (2,200 ft)
Range with max standard fuel at appropriate econ cruising speed (see above), no reserves:
at S/L 220 nm (407 km; 253 miles)
at 1,500 m (4,920 ft) 249 nm (461 km; 287 miles)
at 3,000 m (9,840 ft) 269 nm (498 km; 310 miles)
Range with auxiliary internal fuel, no reserves 420 nm (778 km; 483 miles)
Max endurance: at S/L 2 h 30 min
at 1,500 m (4,920 ft) 2 h 42 min

AGUSTA-SIKORSKY AS-61 and ASH-3H

During 1967, Agusta began the construction under licence of Sikorsky S-61 and SH-3D helicopters. Deliveries of anti-submarine ASH-3Ds to the Italian Navy began in 1969. Additional orders have since been placed, both for the Italian armed forces and for other navies, in various configurations including ASW, VIP transport and rescue. Recent customers include the navies of Brazil (four) and Argentina (two). The VIP transport version, designated **SH-3D/TS** (Trasporto Speciale), serves with the 31° Stormo of the Italian Air Force and with some foreign air forces. Current production naval versions are to **SH-3H** standard.

Apart from some local strengthening, uprated engines and an improved horizontal tail surface, the Agusta built airframe remains essentially similar to that of the Sikorsky built SH-3D/H (see 1982-83 *Jane's*), of which production has ended. The Agusta SH-3H is capable of operation in the roles of anti-submarine search, classification and strike; anti-surface-vessel (ASV); anti-surface-missile defence (ASMD); electronic warfare (EW); tactical troop lift; search and rescue (SAR); vertical replenishment; and casualty evacuation.

Starting in mid-1987, an SH-3 is to be the first airborne testbed for the BAe/Bendix HELRAS long-range high resolution dipping sonar intended for naval versions of the Anglo-Italian EH 101 Sea King replacement helicopter.

The following description applies to the ASH-3H:

TYPE: Twin-engined amphibious all-weather anti-submarine helicopter.

ROTOR SYSTEM: Five-blade main and tail rotors. All-metal fully articulated oil lubricated main rotor. Flanged cuffs on blades bolted to matching flanges on all-steel rotor head. Main rotor blades are interchangeable and are provided with an automatic folding system. Rotor brake standard. All-metal tail rotor.

ROTOR DRIVE: Both engines drive through freewheel units and rotor brake to main gearbox. Steel driveshafts. Tail rotor shaft driven through intermediate and tail gearboxes. Accessories driven by power take-off on tail rotor shaft. Main rotor/engine rpm ratio 1:93·43. Tail rotor/engine rpm ratio 1 : 16·7.

FUSELAGE: Single-step boat hull of all-metal semi-monocoque construction. Tail section folds to reduce stowage requirements.

TAIL SURFACE: Fixed strut braced stabiliser on starboard side of tail section.

LANDING GEAR: Amphibious. Land gear consists of two twin-wheel main units, which are retracted rearward hydraulically into stabilising floats, and non-retractable tailwheel. Oleo-pneumatic shock absorbers. Mainwheels and tubeless tyres size 6·50-10 type III, pressure 4·83 bars (70 lb/sq in). Tailwheel and tyre size 6·00-6. Hydraulic disc brakes. Boat hull and pop-out flotation bags in stabilising floats permit emergency operation from water.

POWER PLANT: Two 1,118 kW (1,500 shp) General Electric T58-GE-100 turboshaft engines, mounted side by side above the cabin. An optional anti-ice/sand shield can be provided. Fuel in underfloor bag tanks with a total capacity of 3,180 litres (840 US gallons). Internal auxiliary fuel tank may be fitted for long-range ferry purposes. Pressure and gravity refuelling points.

ACCOMMODATION: Crew of four in ASW role (pilot, co-pilot and two sonar operators); accommodation for up to 31 paratroops in troop lift role, 15 stretchers and a medical attendant in casualty evacuation configuration, and up to 25 survivors in SAR role. Dual controls. Crew door at rear of flight deck on port side. Large loading door at rear of cabin on starboard side.

SYSTEMS: Three main hydraulic systems. Primary and auxiliary systems operate main rotor control. Utility system for landing gear, winches and blade folding, pressure 207 bars (3,000 lb/sq in). Electrical system includes two 20kVA 200V three phase 400Hz engine driven generators, a 26V single phase AC supply fed from the aircraft's 22Ah nickel-cadmium battery through an inverter, and DC power provided as a secondary system from two 200A transformer-rectifier units.

ARMAMENT AND OPERATIONAL EQUIPMENT (ASW/ASV roles): As equipped for these roles the ASH-3H is a fully integrated all-weather weapons system, capable of operating independently of surface vessels, and has the following equipment and weapons to achieve this task: low-frequency 360° depth AQS-18/AQS-13F sonar; Doppler radar and ASW automatic navigation system; SMA/APS-707 radar with one or two transceivers, with 'chin' radome for 360° coverage; radio altimeter; AFCS; marine markers and smoke floats; two or four homing torpedoes (A 244 AS, Mk 44 or Mk 46); or four depth charges. The AFCS provides three-axis stabilisation in pilot-controlled manoeuvres, attitude hold, heading hold and height hold in cruising flight; controlled transition manoeuvres to and from hover; automatic height control and plan position control in the hover; and trim facility. According to the threat, the Agusta SH-3H can be equipped with medium-range (four AS.12 air-to-surface wire-guided) missiles or long-range (two Marte Mk 2 or Exocet AM39/Harpoon type) missiles. The Oto Melara Marte Mk 2 is an all-weather day and night 'fire and forget' anti-ship missile with a range of 13·5 nm (25 km; 15·5 miles); guidance: sea skimming in elevation, terminal radar active homing in azimuth. The SMA/APS-707 radar has been specially designed to operate in a dense electronic emission environment and has a special interface to draw out target data to feed the computer for the long-range missiles. Provisions are also incorporated for the installation of MAD and advanced EW systems.

OPERATIONAL EQUIPMENT (Search and rescue and transport roles): Search radar, and variable speed hydraulic rescue hoist of 272 kg (600 lb) capacity mounted above starboard side cargo door.

DIMENSIONS, EXTERNAL:

Main rotor diameter	18·90 m (62 ft 0 in)
Main rotor blade chord	0·46 m (1 ft 6¼ in)
Tail rotor diameter	3·23 m (10 ft 7 in)
Distance between rotor centres	11·10 m (36 ft 5 in)
Length overall, both rotors turning	21·91 m (71 ft 10·7 in)
Length of fuselage	16·69 m (54 ft 9 in)
Length, main rotor and tail pylon folded	14·40 m (47 ft 3 in)
Width (over sponsons), rotors folded	4·98 m (16 ft 4 in)
Height to top of rotor head	4·74 m (15 ft 6½ in)
Height overall, main rotor and tail pylon folded	4·93 m (16 ft 2 in)
Height overall, tail rotor turning	5·23 m (17 ft 2 in)
Wheel track	3·96 m (13 ft 0 in)
Wheelbase	7·18 m (23 ft 6½ in)
Crew door (fwd, port): Height	1·68 m (5 ft 6 in)
Width	0·91 m (3 ft 0 in)
Height to sill	1·14 m (3 ft 9 in)
Main cabin door (stbd): Height	1·52 m (5 ft 0 in)
Width	1·73 m (5 ft 8 in)
Height to sill	1·14 m (3 ft 9 in)

AREAS:

Main rotor blades (each)	4·14 m² (44·54 sq ft)
Tail rotor blades (each)	0·22 m² (2·38 sq ft)
Main rotor disc	280·5 m² (3,019 sq ft)
Tail rotor disc	8·20 m² (88·30 sq ft)
Stabiliser	1·86 m² (20·00 sq ft)

WEIGHTS:

Internal load capacity (cargo)	2,720 kg (6,000 lb)
Max external load capacity (with low response sling)	3,630 kg (8,000 lb)
Max T-O weight	9,525 kg (21,000 lb)

PERFORMANCE (at max T-O weight):

Never-exceed speed	144 knots (267 km/h; 165 mph)
Typical cruising speed	120 knots (222 km/h; 138 mph)
Max rate of climb at S/L	670 m (2,200 ft)/min
Service ceiling	3,720 m (12,200 ft)
Hovering ceiling: IGE	2,500 m (8,200 ft)
OGE	1,130 m (3,700 ft)
Range with 31 troops	314 nm (582 km; 362 miles)
Range with max standard fuel	630 nm (1,166 km; 725 miles)

Agusta-Sikorsky ASH-3D ASW helicopter of the Italian Navy *(Aviodata)*

Agusta-Sikorsky AS-61N1 Silver (two General Electric CT58-140-1/2 turboshaft engines)

AGUSTA-SIKORSKY AS-61N1 SILVER

Manufacture by Sikorsky of the S-61L and S-61N commercial helicopters ended in 1980, after completion of 13 of the former and 123 of the latter model. Production rights to the S-61N have been acquired by Agusta, which has developed a modified version, designated AS-61N1 Silver.

Agusta's research suggested a market for a version with greater range and slightly less seating capacity than the standard S-61N, and these factors account for the two principal differences in the AS-61N1 version. The fuselage is shortened by 1·27 m (4 ft 2 in), reducing maximum seating capacity from 30 passengers to 28, and internal fuel capacity is increased to 3,482 litres (766 Imp gallons; 920 US gallons). The Silver is tailored primarily to carry 24 passengers over distances of up to 550 nm (1,019 km; 633 miles). Initially, the standard S-61N power plant of two 1,119 kW (1,500 shp) General Electric CT58-140-1/2 turboshaft engines is retained. Italian RAI and US FAA certification was expected during 1986.

The prototype flew for the first time on 25 July 1984. Three others, configured for offshore oil rig support, are under construction, and the second Silver was due to be completed in September 1986.

DIMENSIONS, EXTERNAL:

Main rotor diameter	18·90 m (62 ft 0 in)
Length of fuselage	17·97 m (58 ft 11½ in)
Height over tail rotor	5·24 m (17 ft 2¼ in)
Width over sponsons	5·82 m (19 ft 1⅓ in)

DIMENSIONS, INTERNAL:

Cabin, excl flight deck: Length	8·26 m (27 ft 1⅛ in)
Baggage compartment volume	2·26 m³ (80 cu ft)

AREA:

Main rotor disc	280·5 m² (3,019 sq ft)

WEIGHTS:

Max useful load (offshore configuration)	3,560 kg (7,850 lb)
Max T-O weight: internal payload	9,525 kg (21,000 lb)
with slung load	10,205 kg (22,500 lb)

PERFORMANCE (A at average gross weight of 8,618 kg; 19,000 lb, B at 9,525 kg; 21,000 lb, C at 9,979 kg; 22,000 lb):

Never-exceed speed at S/L: A	131 knots (242 km/h; 151 mph) IAS
B	115 knots (213 km/h; 132 mph) IAS
C	103 knots (191 km/h; 118 mph) IAS
Cruising speed at S/L: A	121 knots (224 km/h; 139 mph) IAS
Max rate of climb at S/L, max continuous power: A	396 m (1,300 ft)/min
B	320 m (1,050 ft)/min
Hovering ceiling IGE: A	2,135 m (7,000 ft)
B	1,130 m (3,700 ft)
C	335 m (1,100 ft)
Range at S/L, 3,482 litres (920 US gallons) of fuel, incl 30 min reserves at cruising speed: A	553 nm (1,025 km; 637 miles)
B	526 nm (974 km; 605 miles)

AGUSTA-SIKORSKY HH-3F (S-61R)

Agusta began production of this multi-purpose search and rescue helicopter in 1974, and deliveries began in 1976. Twenty were built initially for the Italian Air Force and a further 15 for the same customer are currently being produced. Sikorsky manufacture of the S-61R has ended.

TYPE: Twin-engined amphibious helicopter.

ROTOR SYSTEM: Five-blade fully articulated main rotor of all-metal construction. Flanged cuffs on blades bolted to matching flanges on rotor head. Control by rotating and stationary swashplates. Blades do not fold. Rotor brake standard. Conventional tail rotor with five aluminium blades.

ROTOR DRIVE: Twin turbines drive through freewheeling units and rotor brake to main gearbox. Steel driveshafts. Tail rotor shaft driven through intermediate gearbox and tail gearbox. Main rotor/engine rpm ratio 1 : 93·43. Tail rotor/engine rpm ratio 1 : 16·7.

FUSELAGE: All-metal semi-monocoque structure of pod and boom type. Cabin of basic square section.

TAIL SURFACE: Strut braced horizontal stabiliser on starboard side of tail rotor pylon.

LANDING GEAR: Hydraulically retractable tricycle type, with twin wheels on each unit. Mainwheels retract forward into sponsons, each of which provides 2,176 kg

(4,797 lb) of buoyancy and, with boat hull, permits amphibious operation. Oleo-pneumatic shock absorbers. All wheels and tyres tubeless Type III rib, size 22·1 × 6·50-10, pressure 6·55 bars (95 lb/sq in). Hydraulic disc brakes.

POWER PLANT: Two 1,118 kW (1,500 shp) General Electric T58-GE-5 turboshaft engines, mounted side by side above cabin, immediately forward of main transmission. Fuel in two bladder tanks beneath cabin floor; forward tank capacity 1,204 litres (318 US gallons), rear tank capacity 1,226 litres (324 US gallons). Total fuel capacity 2,430 litres (642 US gallons). Refuelling point on port side of fuselage. Total oil capacity 26·5 litres (7 US gallons).

ACCOMMODATION: Crew of two side by side on flight deck, with dual controls. Provision for flight engineer or attendant. Accommodation for up to 15 stretchers or 2,270 kg (5,000 lb) of cargo. Jettisonable sliding door on starboard side at front of cabin. Internal door between cabin and flight deck. Hydraulically operated rear loading ramp, in two hinged sections, giving opening with minimum width of 1·73 m (5 ft 8 in) and headroom of up to 2·21 m (7 ft 3 in).

SYSTEMS: Primary and auxiliary hydraulic systems, pressure 103·5 bars (1,500 lb/sq in), for flying control servos. Utility hydraulic system, pressure 207 bars (3,000 lb/sq in), for landing gear, rear ramp and winches. Pneumatic system, pressure 207 bars (3,000 lb/sq in), for emergency blow-down landing gear extension. Electrical system includes 24V 22Ah battery, two 20kVA 115V AC generators and one 300A DC generator. APU standard.

Agusta-Sikorsky HH-3F (S-61R) search and rescue helicopter of the Italian Air Force

DIMENSIONS, EXTERNAL:	
Main rotor diameter	18·90 m (62 ft 0 in)
Main rotor blade chord	0·46 m (1 ft 6¼ in)
Tail rotor diameter	3·15 m (10 ft 4 in)
Distance between rotor centres	11·22 m (36 ft 10 in)
Length overall, excl radome	22·25 m (73 ft 0 in)
Length of fuselage	17·45 m (57 ft 3 in)
Width over landing gear	4·82 m (15 ft 10 in)
Height to top of rotor head	4·90 m (16 ft 1 in)
Height overall	5·51 m (18 ft 1 in)
Wheel track	4·06 m (13 ft 4 in)
Wheelbase	5·21 m (17 ft 1 in)
Cabin door (fwd, stbd): Height	1·65 m (5 ft 4¾ in)
Width	1·22 m (4 ft 0 in)
Height to sill	1·27 m (4 ft 2 in)
Rear ramp: Length	4·29 m (14 ft 1 in)
Width	1·85 m (6 ft 1 in)
DIMENSIONS, INTERNAL:	
Cabin (excl flight deck):	
Length	7·89 m (25 ft 10½ in)
Max width	1·98 m (6 ft 6 in)
Max height	1·91 m (6 ft 3 in)
Floor area	approx 15·16 m² (168 sq ft)
Volume	approx 29·73 m³ (1,050 cu ft)
AREAS:	
Main rotor blades (each)	3·71 m² (39·9 sq ft)
Tail rotor blades (each)	0·22 m² (2·35 sq ft)
Main rotor disc	280·5 m² (3,019 sq ft)
Tail rotor disc	7·80 m² (83·9 sq ft)
Stabiliser	2·51 m² (27·0 sq ft)
WEIGHTS:	
Weight empty	6,010 kg (13,255 lb)
Normal T-O weight	9,635 kg (21,247 lb)
Max T-O weight	10,000 kg (22,050 lb)
PERFORMANCE (at normal T-O weight):	
Max level speed at S/L	141 knots (261 km/h; 162 mph)
Cruising speed for max range	125 knots (232 km/h; 144 mph)
Max rate of climb at S/L	400 m (1,310 ft)/min
Service ceiling	3,385 m (11,100 ft)
Hovering ceiling IGE	1,250 m (4,100 ft)
Min ground turning radius	11·29 m (37 ft 0½ in)
Runway LCN at max T-O weight	approx 4·75
Range with max fuel, 10% reserves	404 nm (748 km; 465 miles)

EM (ELICOTTERI MERIDIONALI SpA)

Via Giovanni Agusta 1, 03100 Frosinone
Telephone: (0775) 82801
Telex: 611377 ELMEF I
PRESIDENT: Dott Raffaello Teti
GENERAL MANAGER: Dott Ing Italo Omero Romiti

This company was formed with assistance from Agusta and began to operate in October 1967. Initially, its activities consisted of overhauling helicopters of the Italian armed forces and other organisations, and the manufacture of helicopter components and subassemblies. In 1968 EM acquired rights to the co-production, marketing and servicing of the Boeing Vertol CH-47C Chinook transport helicopter for customers in Italy and several foreign countries. Italian production of the CH-47C airframe is undertaken by SIAI-Marchetti.

EM, whose works occupy a total area of more than 300,000 m² (3,229,170 sq ft), participates in the manufacturing programmes for the Agusta A 109A Mk II and A 129, Agusta-Bell 205, 206B and 212, and Agusta-Sikorsky SH-3H helicopters. It has complete facilities for overhaul, repair and field assistance. EM is the designated overhaul organisation for all types of Italian Army helicopter, and is also distributor in Italy for the Allison 250 series of turboshaft engines.

A new factory was completed in August 1983 at Anagni, 25 km (15·5 miles) from the main facilities at Frosinone. It has a total area of 218,000 m² (2,346,550 sq ft), including 18,000 m² (193,750 sq ft) of covered space, and is intended entirely for the production of composite materials, especially rotor blades and other structure for helicopters.

Italian built Boeing Vertol CH-47C of the Italian Army

EM (BOEING VERTOL) CH-47C CHINOOK

Italian manufacture of the CH-47C began in the Spring of 1970, initially to meet an order for Italian Army Aviation. By Spring 1986, sales totalled 164, customers including the armed forces of Greece (10), Italy (32), Libya (20) and Morocco (9). Only 24 of the 50 ordered in 1977 by the Imperial Iranian Air Force had been delivered before the change of regime two years later and the subsequent embargo on the sale of US military equipment to that country. Of the remainder, 15 were subsequently sold to Egypt; the other 11 were temporarily taken on charge by the US Army, which released them to Iran in 1985.

Agusta has developed, jointly with Hosp Ital SpA (a division of Cogefar) of Milan, an ESFC (emergency surgery flying centre) version of the Chinook for use as a mobile hospital. Details of the ESFC can be found in the 1983-84 *Jane's*. The first ESFC Chinook, ordered by the Italian Army, was to be delivered during 1986. The Italian Army's entire fleet of Chinooks is being overhauled at the rate of three a year by Meridionali, which redelivered the first of 23 then-operational aircraft in March 1986. These aircraft are widely used for firefighting duties, in which configuration they are equipped with a 5,000 litre (1,100 Imp gallon) metal tank for retardant.

Simultaneously with the overhaul programme, an upgrading programme will take place, to fit new engines, composite rotor blades and a more advanced transmission system.

SIAI-MARCHETTI SpA (Subsidiary of Agusta SpA)

Via Indipendenza 2, 21018 Sesto Calende (VA)
Telephone: (0331) 924421
Telex: 332601 SIAIAV I
PRESIDENT: Dott Raffaello Teti
MANAGING DIRECTOR: Ing Luigi Passini
AERODROME AND MAIN WORKS: Vergiate (Varese)
OTHER WORKS: Sesto Calende (Varese) and Malpensa

Founded in 1915, the SIAI-Marchetti company produced a wide range of military and civil landplanes and flying-boats, including the trans-Atlantic S.55 flying-boat of the 1930s and the S.M. 79 torpedo-bomber of the Second World War. Its current products include a full range of military trainers (the piston engined SF.260M/W, turboprop powered SF.260TP and turbofan engined S.211), plus aircraft for general aviation (SF.260C/D) and utility transport (the twin-turboprop SF.600). Since the 1970s it has been engaged in the co-production with Agusta of licence built Boeing Vertol CH-47C, Bell 204/205/212/412, and Sikorsky S-61A, SH-3D/H and HH-3F helicopters.

SIAI-Marchetti is also engaged in the overhaul and repair of various types of aircraft (notably the C-130 Hercules, DHC-5 Buffalo and Cessna Citation II). It participates in national or multi-national programmes, producing parts for the Aeritalia G222, Panavia Tornado, AMX, Airbus A310, Dassault-Breguet Falcon 100 and Atlantique 2.

The company's works at Sesto Calende, Vergiate and Malpensa total 1,370,267 m² (14,749,416 sq ft) in area, of which 119,494 m² (1,286,221 sq ft) are covered, and employed nearly 2,300 people in 1986.

SIAI-MARCHETTI SF.260

The prototype for the SF.260 series, known as the F.250, was designed by Dott Ing Stelio Frati and built by Aviamilano. Flown for the first time on 15 July 1964, it was powered by a 186·5 kW (250 hp) Avco Lycoming engine and was certificated for aerobatic flying. A description appeared in the 1965-66 *Jane's*.

The version developed initially, for civil production, was manufactured, at first under licence from Aviamilano, by SIAI-Marchetti, and is designated SF.260. It received FAA type approval on 1 April 1966. Subsequently SIAI-Marchetti became the official holder of the type certificate and of all manufacturing rights in the SF.260.

Descriptions of the civil SF.260A and SF.260B can be found in the 1980-81 and earlier editions of *Jane's*, and of the SF.260C in the 1985-86 edition. Current models are as follows:

SF.260D. Improved and updated civil version, replacing SF.260C, with aerodynamic and structural improvements developed for military SF.260M. Certificated by RAI on 14 December 1985; FAA certification expected in 1986.

SF.260M. Two/three-seat military trainer, developed from civil SF.260A and first flown on 10 October 1970. Introduced a number of important structural and aerodynamic improvements, many of which were subsequently applied to later models. Meets requirements for basic flying training; instrument flying; aerobatics, including deliberate spinning and recovery; night flying; navigation flying; and formation flying. Detailed customer list in 1984-85 and earlier editions of *Jane's*.

SF.260W Warrior. Trainer/tactical support version of SF.260M, first flown (I-SJAV) in May 1972. Two or four underwing pylons, for up to 300 kg (661 lb) of external stores, and cockpit stores selection panel. Able to undertake a wide variety of roles, including low-level strike; forward air control; forward air support; armed reconnaissance; and liaison. Also meets same requirements as SF.260M for use as a trainer. Customers as listed in 1984-85 and earlier *Jane's*. One aircraft (described in 1980-81 and earlier editions) completed as **SF.260SW Sea Warrior** surveillance/SAR/supply version.

SF.260TP. Turboprop powered development. Described separately.

By early 1986 more than 800 SF.260s of all models had been delivered, mainly for export, and production of the piston engined models was continuing. Military trainer variants are operated by more than 20 armed forces worldwide.

The following description is generally applicable to all piston engined models unless otherwise stated:

Type: Two/three-seat fully aerobatic military light aircraft.

Wings: Cantilever low-wing monoplane. Wing section NACA 64_1-212 (modified) at root, NACA 64_1-210 (modified) at tip. Dihedral 6° 20′ from roots (5° on SF.260D). Incidence 2° 45′ at root, 0° at tip. No sweepback. All-metal light alloy safe-life structure, with single main spar and auxiliary rear spar, built in two portions bolted together at centreline and attached to fuselage by six bolts. Press-formed ribs, with dimpled stiffening holes. Skin, which is butt joined and flush riveted, stiffened by stringers between main and rear spars. Differentially operating Frise light alloy mass balanced ailerons, and electrically actuated light alloy single-slotted flaps. Flaps operated by torque tube and mechanical linkage, ailerons by pushrods and cables. Servo tab in each aileron.

Fuselage: Semi-monocoque safe-life structure of frames, stringers and flush riveted skin, exclusively of light alloy except for welded steel tube engine mounting, glassfibre front panel of engine cowling, stainless steel firewall and detachable glassfibre tailcone.

Tail Unit: Cantilever light alloy safe-life structure, with sweptback vertical surfaces, fixed incidence tailplane and one-piece elevator. Two-spar fin and one-piece tailplane, bolted to fuselage; single-spar elevator, statically and aerodynamically balanced, and balanced rudder. Rudder and elevator operated by cables. Controllable trim tab in starboard half of elevator; ground adjustable tab on rudder.

Landing Gear: Electrically retractable tricycle type, with manual emergency actuation. Inward retracting main gear, of trailing arm type, and rearward retracting nose unit, each embodying Magnaghi oleo-pneumatic shock absorber (type 2/22028 in main units). Each welded steel tube main leg is hinged to the main and rear spars. Nose unit is of leg and fork type, with coaxial shock absorber and torque strut. Cleveland P/N 3080A mainwheels, with size 6·00-6 tube and tyre (6-ply rating), pressure 2·45 bars (35·5 lb/sq in). Cleveland P/N 40-77A nosewheel, with size 5·00-5 tube and tyre (6-ply rating), pressure 1·96 bars (28·4 lb/sq in). Cleveland P/N 3000-500 independent hydraulic single-disc brake and parking brake on each mainwheel. Nosewheel steering (20° to left or right) is operated directly by the rudder pedals, to which it is linked by pushrods. Up-lock secures main gear in retracted position during flight; anti-retraction system prevents main gear from retracting whenever strut is compressed by weight of aircraft.

Power Plant: One 194 kW (260 hp) Avco Lycoming O-540-E4A5 flat-six engine, driving a Hartzell HC-C2YK-1BF/8477-8R two-blade constant-speed metal propeller with spinner. IO-540 engine available optionally. Fuel in two light alloy tanks in wings, capacity of each 49·5 litres (10·9 Imp gallons); and two permanent wingtip tanks, capacity of each 72 litres (15·85 Imp gallons). Total internal fuel capacity 243 litres (53·5 Imp gallons), of which 235 litres (51·7 Imp gallons) are usable. Individual refuelling point on top of each tank. In addition, SF.260W may be fitted with two 80 litre (17·5 Imp gallon) auxiliary tanks on underwing pylons. Oil capacity (all models) 11·4 litres (2·5 Imp gallons).

SIAI-Marchetti SF.260M of the Italian Air Force *(Aviodata)*

Accommodation (SF.260D): Three seats in enclosed cockpit, two side by side in front, one at rear. Two children with a combined weight not exceeding 113 kg (250 lb) may occupy rear seat. One-piece fully transparent rearward sliding Plexiglas canopy, with rubber cord canopy release. Baggage compartment, capacity 40 kg (88 lb), behind rear seat. Cabin carpeted, heated and ventilated; walls thermally insulated and soundproofed by a glassfibre lining. Slots at base of windscreen admit air for windscreen defrosting.

Accommodation (SF.260M; W similar): Side by side front seats (for instructor and pupil in SF.260M), with third seat centrally at rear. Front seats individually adjustable fore and aft, with forward folding backs and provision for back type parachute packs. Dual controls standard. All three seats equipped with lap belts and shoulder harnesses. Baggage compartment aft of rear seat. Upper portion of canopy tinted. Emergency canopy release handle for each front seat occupant. Steel tube windscreen frame for protection in the event of an overturn.

Systems (SF.260M; other models generally similar): Hydraulic equipment for mainwheel brakes only. No pneumatic system. 24V DC electrical system of single-conductor negative earth type, including 70A Prestolite engine mounted alternator/rectifier and 24V 24Ah Varley battery, for engine starting, flap and landing gear actuation, fuel booster pumps, electronics and lighting. Sealed battery compartment in rear of fuselage on port side. Connection of an external power source automatically disconnects the battery. Heating system for carburettor air intake. Emergency electrical system for extending landing gear if normal electrical actuation fails; provision for mechanical extension in the event of total electrical failure. Cabin heating, and windscreen de-icing and demisting, by heat exchanger using engine exhaust air. Additional manually controlled warm air outlets for general cabin heating. Oxygen system optional.

Avionics and Equipment (SF.260M; W generally similar): Basic instrumentation and military equipment to customer's requirements. Blind-flying instrumentation and communications equipment optional: typical selection includes dual Collins 20B VHF com; Collins VIR-31A VHF nav; Collins ADF-60A; Collins TDR-90 ATC transponder; Collins PN-101 compass; ID-90-000 RMI; and Gemelli AG04-1 intercom. Landing light in nose, below spinner. Instrument panel can be slid rearward to provide access to rear of instruments.

Armament (SF.260W): Two or four underwing hardpoints, able to carry external stores on NATO standard pylons up to a maximum of 300 kg (661 lb) when flown as a single-seater. Typical alternative loads can include one or two SIAI gun pods, each with one or two 7·62 mm FN machine-guns and 500 rds; two Aerea AL-8-70 launchers each with eight 2·75 in rockets; two LAU-32 launchers each with seven 2·75 in rockets; two Aerea AL-18-50 launchers each with eighteen 2 in rockets; two Aerea AL-8-68 launchers each with eight 68 mm rockets; two Aerea AL-6-80 launchers each with six 81 mm rockets; two LUU-2/B parachute flares; two SAMP EU 32 125 kg general purpose bombs or EU 13 120 kg fragmentation bombs; two SAMP EU 70 50 kg general purpose bombs; Mk 76 11 kg practice bombs; two cartridge throwers for 70 mm multi-purpose cartridges, F 725 flares, or F 130 smoke cartridges; one or two photo-reconnaissance pods with two 70 mm automatic cameras; two supply containers; or two 80 litre (17·5 Imp gallon) auxiliary fuel tanks.

Dimensions, external:
- Wing span over tip tanks: 8·35 m (27 ft 4¾ in)
- Wing chord: at root: 1·60 m (5 ft 3 in
  - mean aerodynamic: 1·325 m (4 ft 4¼ in
  - at tip: 0·784 m (2 ft 6⅞ in
- Wing aspect ratio (excl tip tanks): 6·3
- Wing taper ratio: 2·2
- Length overall: 7·10 m (23 ft 3½ in
- Fuselage: Max width: 1·10 m (3 ft 7¼ in
  - Max depth: 1·042 m (3 ft 5 in
- Height overall: 2·41 m (7 ft 11 in
- Elevator span: 3·01 m (9 ft 10½ in
- Wheel track: 2·274 m (7 ft 5½ in
- Wheelbase: 1·66 m (5 ft 5¼ in
- Propeller diameter: 1·93 m (6 ft 4 in
- Propeller ground clearance: 0·32 m (1 ft 0½ in

Dimensions, internal:
- Cabin: Length: 1·66 m (5 ft 5¼ in
  - Max width: 1·00 m (3 ft 3¼ in
  - Height (seat cushion to canopy): 0·98 m (3 ft 2½ in
  - Volume: 1·50 m³ (53 cu ft
- Baggage compartment volume: 0·18 m³ (6·36 cu ft

Areas:
- Wings, gross: 10·10 m² (108·70 sq ft
- Ailerons (total, incl tabs): 0·762 m² (8·20 sq ft
- Trailing-edge flaps (total): 1·18 m² (12·70 sq ft
- Fin: 0·76 m² (8·18 sq ft
- Dorsal fin: 0·16 m² (1·72 sq ft
- Rudder, incl tab: 0·60 m² (6·46 sq ft
- Tailplane: 1·46 m² (15·70 sq ft
- Elevator, incl tab: 0·96 m² (10·30 sq ft

Weights and Loadings:
- Manufacturer's basic weight empty:
  - M: 755 kg (1,664 lb
  - W: 770 kg (1,697 lb
- Weight empty, equipped: D: 755 kg (1,664 lb
  - M: 815 kg (1,797 lb
  - W: 830 kg (1,830 lb
- Fuel:
  - in-wing and wingtip tanks (all versions): 169 kg (372·5 lb
  - underwing tanks (W only): 114 kg (251·5 lb
- Typical mission weights:
  - M, trainer ('clean'): 1,140 kg (2,513 lb
  - W, two 47 kg (103·5 lb) machine-gun pods and full internal fuel: 1,163 kg (2,564 lb
  - W, one Alkan 500B cartridge thrower, one two-camera reconnaissance pod and full internal fuel: 1,182 kg (2,605 lb
  - W, trainer with 94 kg (207 lb) external stores: 1,249 kg (2,753 lb
  - W, self-ferry with two 80 litre (17·5 Imp gallon underwing tanks: 1,285 kg (2,833 lb
  - W, two 125 kg bombs and 150 kg (331 lb) internal fuel: 1,300 kg (2,866 lb
  - W, two AL-8-70 rocket launchers and 160 kg (353 lb internal fuel: 1,300 kg (2,866 lb
- Max T-O weight:
  - D, M, Aerobatic: 1,100 kg (2,425 lb
  - D, Utility: 1,100 kg (2,425 lb
  - M, Utility: 1,200 kg (2,645 lb
  - W, max permitted: 1,300 kg (2,866 lb
- Max wing loading: D: 109 kg/m² (22·4 lb/sq ft
  - M: 119 kg/m² (24·4 lb/sq ft
  - W: 129 kg/m² (26·4 lb/sq ft
- Max power loading: D: 5·68 kg/kW (9·33 lb/hp
  - M: 6·19 kg/kW (10·17 lb/hp
  - W: 6·70 kg/kW (11·01 lb/hp

Performance (C at AUW of 1,102 kg; 2,430 lb, M at AUW of 1,200 kg; 2,645 lb, W at 1,300 kg; 2,866 lb, except where indicated):
- Never-exceed speed:
  - D, M: 235 knots (436 km/h; 271 mph
- Max level speed at S/L:
  - D: 187 knots (347 km/h; 215 mph
  - M: 180 knots (333 km/h; 207 mph
  - W: 165 knots (305 km/h; 190 mph
- Max cruising speed (75% power):
  - D at 3,050 m (10,000 ft): 178 knots (330 km/h; 205 mph

M at 1,500 m (4,925 ft) 162 knots (300 km/h; 186 mph)
W at 1,500 m (4,925 ft) 152 knots (281 km/h; 175 mph)
Stalling speed, flaps and landing gear up:
M 74 knots (137 km/h; 86 mph)
W 88 knots (163 km/h; 102 mph)
Stalling speed, flaps and landing gear down:
D 60 knots (111 km/h; 70 mph)
M 68 knots (126 km/h; 79 mph)
W 72 knots (134 km/h; 83 mph)
Max rate of climb at S/L: D 546 m (1,791 ft)/min
M 457 m (1,500 ft)/min
W 381 m (1,250 ft)/min
Time to 1,500 m (4,925 ft): M 4 min 0 s
W 6 min 20 s
Time to 2,300 m (7,550 ft): M 6 min 50 s
W 10 min 20 s
Time to 3,000 m (9,850 ft): M 10 min 0 s
W 18 min 40 s
Service ceiling: D 5,790 m (19,000 ft)
M 4,665 m (15,300 ft)
W 4,480 m (14,700 ft)
T-O run at S/L: D 480 m (1,575 ft)
M 384 m (1,260 ft)
T-O to 15 m (50 ft) at S/L: M 606 m (1,988 ft)
W 825 m (2,707 ft)
Landing from 15 m (50 ft) at S/L:
D 445 m (1,460 ft)
M 539 m (1,768 ft)
W 645 m (2,116 ft)
Landing run at S/L: D, M 345 m (1,132 ft)
Operational radius:
W, 6 h 25 min single-seat armed patrol mission at 1,163 kg (2,564 lb) AUW, incl 5 h 35 min over operating area, 20 kg (44 lb) fuel reserves 50 nm (92 km; 57 miles)
W, 3 h 38 min single-seat strike mission, incl two 5 min loiters over separate en-route target areas, 20 kg (44 lb) fuel reserves 250 nm (463 km; 287 miles)
W, 4 h 54 min single-seat strike mission, incl 5 min over target area, 20 kg (44 lb) fuel reserves 300 nm (556 km; 345 miles)
W, 4 h 30 min single-seat photo-reconnaissance mission at 1,182 kg (2,605 lb) AUW, incl three 1 h loiters over separate en-route operating areas, 20 kg (44 lb) fuel reserves 150 nm (278 km; 172 miles)
W, 6 h 3 min two-seat self-ferry mission with two 80 litre (17·5 Imp gallon) underwing tanks, at 1,285 kg (2,833 lb) AUW, 30 kg (66 lb) fuel reserves 926 nm (1,716 km; 1,066 miles)
Range with max fuel:
D (two-seat) 805 nm (1,490 km; 925 miles)
M (two-seat) 890 nm (1,650 km; 1,025 miles)
g limits (M):
at max Aerobatic T-O weight +6/−3
at max Utility T-O weight without external load +4·4/−2·2

SIAI-MARCHETTI SF.260TP

First flown in July 1980, the SF.260TP is a turboprop powered development of the SF.260M/W, the airframe remaining virtually unchanged aft of the firewall except for substitution of an inset rudder trim tab and provision of an automatic fuel feed system.

More than 60 SF.260TPs have been ordered by military customers, the most recent being the air force of Sri Lanka (6) in 1985.

Airframe: As SF.260M/W, except for increased overall length and provision of trim tab in rudder.

Power Plant: One Allison 250-B17C turboprop engine, flat rated at 261 kW (350 shp) and driving a Hartzell HC-B3TF-7A/T10173-25R three-blade constant-speed fully-feathering and reversible-pitch propeller with spinner. Fuel capacity as for SF.260M/W; automatic fuel feed system. Oil capacity 7 litres (1·5 Imp gallons).

Accommodation, Systems, Avionics and Equipment: Generally as for SF.260.

Dimensions, external and internal, and Areas:
As for SF.260 except:
Length overall 7·40 m (24 ft 3¼ in)

Weights and Loadings: As for SF.260M/W except:
Weight empty, equipped 750 kg (1,654 lb)
Max power loading:
trainer 4·60 kg/kW (7·56 lb/shp)
Warrior 4·98 kg/kW (8·19 lb/shp)

Performance (at trainer Utility T-O weight of 1,200 kg; 2,645 lb, ISA):
Never-exceed speed 236 knots (437 km/h; 271 mph)
Max level speed at 3,050 m (10,000 ft) 228 knots (422 km/h; 262 mph)
Max cruising speed at 2,440 m (8,000 ft) 216 knots (400 km/h; 248 mph)
Econ cruising speed at 4,575 m (15,000 ft) 170 knots (315 km/h; 195 mph)
Stalling speed at S/L, flaps down, power off 68 knots (126 km/h; 79 mph)
Max rate of climb at S/L 661 m (2,170 ft)/min
Service ceiling 8,535 m (28,000 ft)
T-O run 298 m (978 ft)
T-O to 15 m (50 ft) 467 m (1,532 ft)

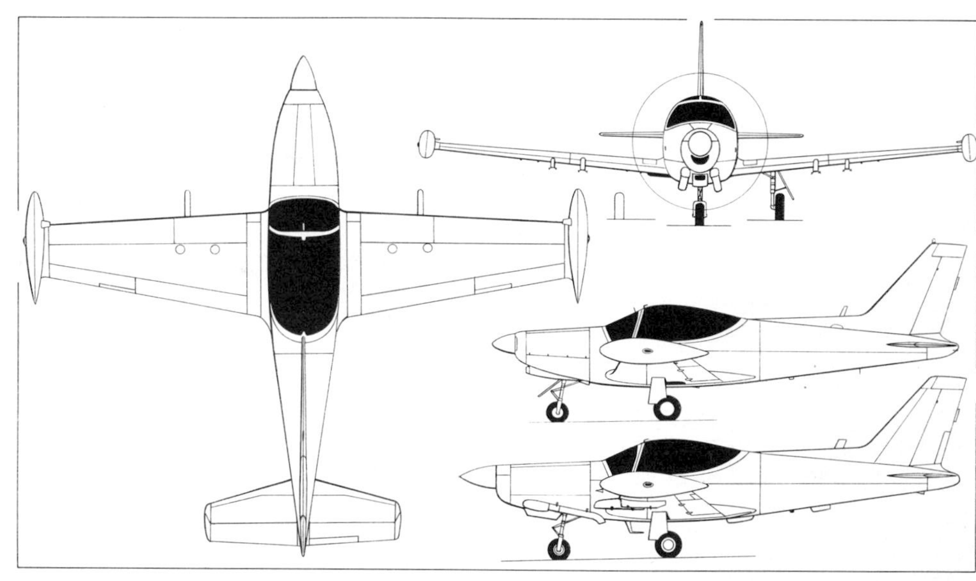

SIAI-Marchetti SF.260TP turboprop trainer, with additional side view (centre) of piston engined SF.260M *(Pilot Press)*

SIAI-Marchetti SF.260TP (Allison 250-B17C turboprop engine)

Landing from 15 m (50 ft) 533 m (1,749 ft)
Landing run, without reverse pitch 307 m (1,007 ft)
Range at 4,575 m (15,000 ft) with max fuel, 30 min reserves 512 nm (949 km; 589 miles)

SIAI-MARCHETTI S.211

This lightweight, low-cost basic trainer and light attack aircraft was first revealed in the form of a model at the Paris Air Show in May/June 1977. Two flying prototypes were built initially, and the first of these (I-SITF) made its initial flight on 10 April 1981.

Deliveries of production S.211s began in November 1984, and orders for 40 had been placed by July 1985. Deliveries totalled 22 by February 1986, at which time further orders were being negotiated. Customers include the air forces of Singapore (30) and Haiti (4). The first six S.211s for Singapore were delivered in component knocked-down form for reassembly; subsequent aircraft are in kit form for assembly by SAMCO, a subsidiary of Singapore Aircraft Industries (which see).

Features of the S.211 are its safe stalling and spinning characteristics, and the very low airframe weight, made possible by the fact that some 61 per cent of the external surfaces are made from composite materials.

In order to improve the S.211's operational capabilities a special nav/attack version, equipped with an advanced lightweight head-up display and navigation computer, is under development. No further details were available at the time of closing for press.

The following description applies to the current production S.211:

Type: Two-seat basic trainer and light attack aircraft.

Wings: Cantilever shoulder-wing monoplane, with supercritical section developed by computer with the assistance of the US universities of New York and Kansas. Thickness/chord ratio 15% at root, 13% at tip. Incidence 2° 13′ at root, −1° 17′ at tip. Anhedral 2° from roots. Sweepback 15° 30′ at quarter-chord. Two-spar metal torsion box structure, forming integral fuel tank; attached to fuselage by four bolts. Upper and lower skins each

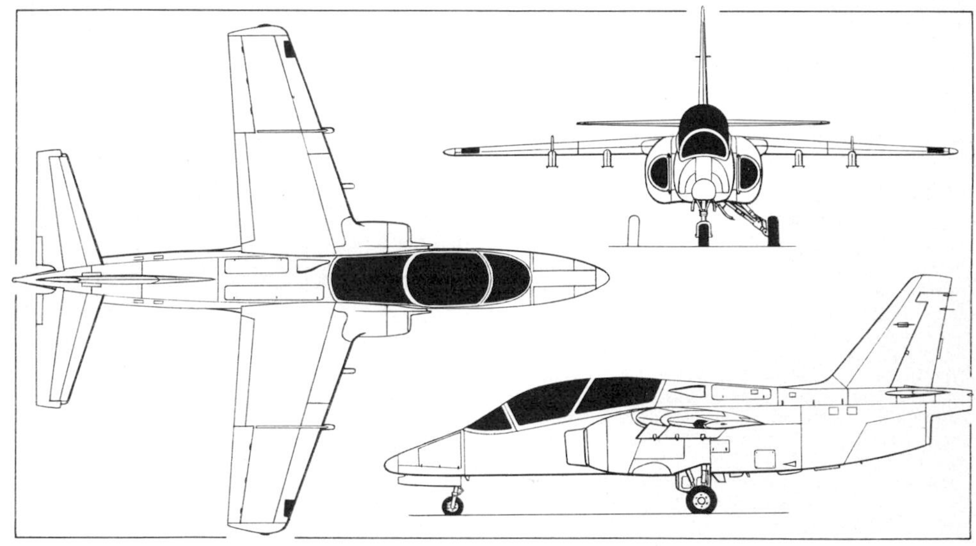

SIAI-Marchetti S.211 basic trainer and light attack aircraft *(Pilot Press)*

formed by two one-piece panels joined along centreline and to the spars. Hydraulically actuated ailerons and large area electrically actuated Fowler flaps on trailing-edges. Trim tab in each aileron; servo tab in port aileron.

FUSELAGE: Conventional metal and glassfibre semi-monocoque structure. Hydraulically actuated airbrake under centre-fuselage. Equipment bay in nose. Large quick-disconnect panel at rear, for rapid engine access or removal.

TAIL UNIT: Cantilever metal structure. Sweptback fin and horn balanced rudder; electrically actuated variable incidence tailplane has sweptback leading-edge. Horn balanced elevators, each with inset trim tab.

LANDING GEAR: Hydraulically retractable tricycle type, of Messier-Hispano-Bugatti/Magnaghi design. Oleo-pneumatic shock absorber in each unit. All units retract forward into fuselage (main units turning through 90° to lie flat in undersides of engine air intake trunks). Nosewheel steerable 18° left and right. Mainwheels size 6·50-8; nosewheel size 5·00-5. Designed for sink rate of 4 m (13 ft)/s. Wheel brakes actuated hydraulically, independently of main hydraulic system. Provision for emergency free-fall extension.

POWER PLANT: One 11·12 kN (2,500 lb st) Pratt & Whitney Canada JT15D-4C non-afterburning turbofan engine (-4 in first prototype), mounted in rear of fuselage; lateral intake each side of fuselage, with splitter plate. Fuel in 650 litre (143 Imp gallon) integral wing tank and 150 litre (33 Imp gallon) fuselage tank; total capacity 800 litres (176 Imp gallons). Single gravity refuelling point in top surface of starboard wing. Electric fuel pump for engine starting and emergency use. Fuel and oil systems permit inverted flight. Provision for two 350 litre (77 Imp gallon) drop tanks on inboard underwing stores points. Oil capacity 10 kg (22 lb).

ACCOMMODATION: Seats for two persons in tandem in pressurised and air-conditioned cockpit under one-piece framed canopy opening sideways to starboard: pupil in front, instructor on rear seat elevated 28 cm (11 in). Internal transparent screen between seats. Martin-Baker Mk 10 lightweight zero/zero ejection seats for both occupants.

SYSTEMS: Environmental control system for cockpit pressurisation and air-conditioning, using engine bleed air for heating, freon vapour for cooling. Max pressure differential 0·29 bars (4·2 lb/sq in). Hydraulic system, pressure 207 bars (3,000 lb/sq in), for actuation of airbrake, landing gear, freon compressor and aileron boost, and independent actuation of wheel brakes. Primary electrical system is 28V DC, using an engine driven starter/generator; nickel-cadmium battery; two static inverters supply AC power for instruments and avionics. External power receptacle in port side of lower fuselage aft of wing. Demand type main oxygen system, at 124 bars (1,800 lb/sq in) pressure, sufficient to supply both occupants for 4 hours, plus bottles for emergency oxygen supply.

AVIONICS AND EQUIPMENT: To customer's requirements. Communications system has, as standard, dual U/VHF and one HF/SSB, all with dual control. BAe AN16/D suppressed HF antenna. Choice of ADF, DME, Tacan, VOR/ILS or R/Nav; IFF, flight director and radio altimeter standard. Provision for Doppler radar, nose-mounted attack radar, head-up display, radar warning system and ECM. Landing and taxying lights (in inboard wing leading-edges of first two prototypes) relocated near wingtips on production aircraft.

ARMAMENT: Four underwing hardpoints, stressed for loads of up to 330 kg (727·5 lb) inboard, 165 kg (364 lb) outboard; max external load 660 kg (1,455 lb). Typical loads can include four single- or twin-gun 7·62 mm machine-gun pods, four 12·7 mm gun pods, or (inboard only) two 20 mm gun pods; four AL-18-50 (18 × 50 mm), Matra F2 (6 × 68 mm), LAU-32 (7 × 2·75 in), or AL-6-80 (6 × 81 mm) rocket launchers, or (inboard only) two Matra 155 (18 × 68 mm), SNORA RWK-020 (12 × 81 mm) or 100 mm rocket launchers; four bombs or practice bombs of up to 150 kg size, or (inboard only) two bombs or napalm containers of up to 300 kg; four 74 mm cartridge throwers; or (inboard only) two photo-reconnaissance pods each with four cameras and infra-red linescan; or (inboard only) two 350 litre (77 Imp gallon) auxiliary fuel tanks.

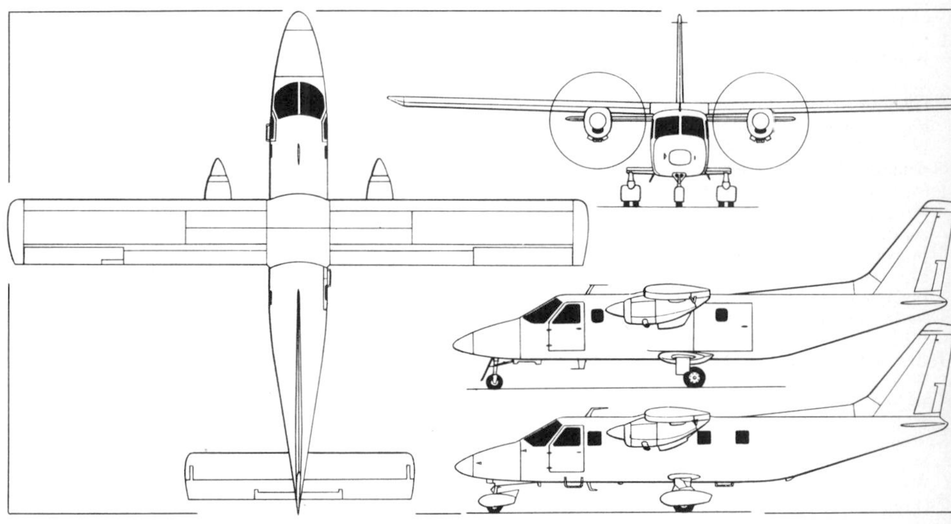

Basic SIAI-Marchetti SF.600TP, with additional side view (centre) of version with retractable landing gear
(Pilot Press)

DIMENSIONS, EXTERNAL:
- Wing span — 8·43 m (27 ft 8 in)
- Wing chord: at root — 2·151 m (7 ft 0¾ in)
  - at tip — 1·00 m (3 ft 3¼ in)
  - mean aerodynamic — 1·646 m (5 ft 4¾ in)
- Wing aspect ratio — 5·08
- Length overall — 9·31 m (30 ft 6½ in)
- Height overall — 3·80 m (12 ft 5½ in)
- Tailplane span — 3·96 m (13 ft 0 in)
- Wheel track — 2·29 m (7 ft 6 in)
- Wheelbase — 4·02 m (13 ft 2¼ in)

AREAS:
- Wings, gross — 12·60 m² (135·63 sq ft)
- Airbrake — 0·42 m² (4·52 sq ft)
- Vertical tail surfaces (total) — 2·01 m² (21·64 sq ft)
- Horizontal tail surfaces (total) — 3·378 m² (36·36 sq ft)

WEIGHTS:
- Weight empty, equipped — 1,645 kg (3,626 lb)
- Max usable fuel: internal — 622 kg (1,371 lb)
  - external — 390 kg (860 lb)
- Max T-O weight: trainer, 'clean' — 2,700 kg (5,952 lb)
  - armed version — 3,100 kg (6,834 lb)

PERFORMANCE (at T-O weight of 2,500 kg; 5,511 lb except where indicated):
- Never-exceed speed — Mach 0·80 (400 knots; 740 km/h; 460 mph EAS)
- Max cruising speed at 7,620 m (25,000 ft) — 360 knots (667 km/h; 414 mph)
- Rotation speed — 90 knots (167 km/h; 104 mph)
- Stalling speed, flaps down — 74 knots (138 km/h; 86 mph)
- Max rate of climb at S/L — 1,280 m (4,200 ft)/min
- Time to 6,100 m (20,000 ft) — 6 min 12 s
- Service ceiling — 12,200 m (40,000 ft)
- T-O run (S/L, ISA) — 390 m (1,280 ft)
- T-O to 15 m (50 ft) — 512 m (1,680 ft)
- Landing from 15 m (50 ft) — 705 m (2,313 ft)
- Landing run (S/L, ISA) — 361 m (1,185 ft)
- Min air turning radius at S/L — less than 305 m (1,000 ft)
- Typical attack radius with four rocket launchers, AUW of 3,100 kg (6,834 lb):
  - hi-lo-hi, out and back at 265 knots (491 km/h; 305 mph) at 9,145 m (30,000 ft), 2 h 50 min mission (incl 5 min over target), 60 kg (132 lb) of fuel remaining — 300 nm (556 km; 345 miles)
  - lo-lo-lo, out and back at 250 knots (463 km/h; 288 mph) at less than 305 m (1,000 ft), 1 h 5 min mission (incl 5 min over target), 60 kg (132 lb) of fuel remaining — 125 nm (231 km; 144 miles)
- Max range on internal fuel, 30 min reserves — 900 nm (1,668 km; 1,036 miles)
- Ferry range (AUW of 3,100 kg; 6,834 lb, max internal and external fuel) at 270 knots (500 km/h; 311 mph) at 9,145 m (30,000 ft), 90 kg (198 lb) of fuel remaining — 1,340 nm (2,483 km; 1,543 miles)
- Endurance, 30 min reserves — 3 h 50 min
- Sustained *g* limit at 4,575 m (15,000 ft) — 3·4
- *g* limits: — +6/−3 'clean'
  - +5/−2·5 with external stores

SIAI-MARCHETTI SF.600TP CANGURO (KANGAROO)

The prototype F.600 Canguro (I-CANG), built by General Avia and then powered by 261 kW (350 hp) Avco Lycoming TIO-540-J flat-six piston engines, made its first flight on 30 December 1978. This aircraft was described under the General Avia heading in the 1979-80 *Jane's*.

The basic production aircraft is now offered with Allison turboprop engines and non-retractable landing gear; major options include retractable landing gear and a swing-tail rear fuselage. The aircraft can be adapted for a variety of roles which include passenger or cargo transport, paratroop transport, air ambulance, maritime surveillance, electronic intelligence, and agricultural duties. The retractable gear version, offering better performance, is considered especially suitable for a maritime surveillance role, equipped with an underfuselage radome and other appropriate avionics and equipment.

Certification by the RAI was expected during 1986. An initial production batch of nine aircraft has been started, for possible deliveries beginning in early 1987. In September 1986 SIAI-Marchetti reported prospects of serious interest in the Canguro for civil defence duties.

TYPE: Twin-turboprop passenger, cargo, ambulance and general utility transport.

WINGS: Cantilever high-wing monoplane. Wing section NASA GAW-1, with 17% thickness/chord ratio. Dihedral 2°. Incidence (constant) 1° 30'. All-metal riveted structure in aluminium alloy, with stressed skin. Centre-section has main spar and two auxiliary spars; outboard of engines, wings have two spars. All-metal ailerons and electrically operated double-slotted flaps. Electrically operated trim tab in port aileron.

FUSELAGE: Aluminium alloy semi-monocoque structure of frames, stringers, bulkheads and stressed skin. Swing-tail rear fuselage available optionally.

TAIL UNIT: Cantilever all-metal stressed skin structure. Trim tabs in rudder (actuated mechanically) and each

SIAI-Marchetti S.211 (Pratt & Whitney Canada JT15D-4C turbofan engine)

elevator (electrically/mechanically operated). Small dorsal fin.

Landing Gear: Choice of retractable or non-retractable tricycle gear, of trailing arm type, with oleo-pneumatic shock absorber in each unit. Twin-wheel main units, mounted on small stub-wings attached to fuselage floor; single steerable nose unit. All five wheels and tyres same size, 7·00-6, tyre pressure 2·48 bars (36 lb/sq in). Hydraulic disc brakes on main units.

Power Plant: Two 313 kW (420 shp) Allison 250-B17C turboprop engines, each driving a Hartzell three-blade constant-speed fully-feathering reversible-pitch propeller. Fuel in four identical outer-wing tanks, total capacity 1,100 litres (242 Imp gallons). Self-sealing tanks optional on military versions. Provision for underwing tanks, total capacity 600 litres (132 Imp gallons). Oil capacity 11·4 litres (2·5 Imp gallons).

Accommodation: Pilot and co-pilot or passenger on flight deck. Dual controls standard. Cabin accommodates up to nine passengers at 100 cm (40 in) seat pitch (2-2-2-3); six passengers in VIP version, with reclining seats, folding tables, bar and toilet; or 12 paratroops; or four stretcher patients and two medical attendants; or freight. Baggage compartment at rear of cabin in standard passenger version; in centre of cabin, opposite toilet, in VIP version; rear compartment used to store folding passenger seats when converted for cargo use. Forward door on port side for crew. Wider, sliding door at rear on port side for passenger and freight loading and paratroop dropping, with smaller forward opening door opposite this on starboard side. Cargo version can accept three 1·30 × 1·15 × 1·07 m (51 × 45 × 42 in) containers, or two of size 2·20 × 1·15 × 1·07 m (87 × 45 × 42 in).

Systems: Standard cabin heating/defrosting system uses engine bleed air; ventilation is provided by ram air; freon air-conditioning system optional. Primary electrical system is 28V DC, powered by two 150A engine driven starter/generators, with a 24V 22Ah nickel-cadmium battery for independent engine starting and emergencies. AC power, 115V at 400Hz, is provided when required by a static inverter. Pneumatic de-icing system for wings and tail unit, and electric de-icing of propellers, are optional.

Avionics: Wide range of IFR com/nav avionics available, to customer's requirements. Typical installation includes VHF, UHF and HF com, ADF, VOR/LOC/ILS, DME and ATC transponder. Options include Omega nav system, weather radar, three-axis autopilot and flight director.

Equipment: Can be provided with pylons for external stores, two under outer wings and two under mainwheel stub-wings at junction with fuselage. Each inboard pylon is stressed for a 300 kg (661 lb) load, each outboard one for 100 kg (220 lb). Twelve inward facing seats in troop transport/parachutist version. Can be equipped for target towing, with floor mounted winch, 2,000 m (6,560 ft) of cable, electric power unit (100A/28V DC), and miss-distance indicator system; with undertail hook for towing one or more gliders; with one or two Wild or Zeiss type photogrammetric automatic cameras (plus additional avionics at customer's option); with equipment for in-flight inspection and calibration of ground radio/navigation aids; or with appropriate sensors, radar warning receiver and underwing chaff dispensers for elint, sigint or other ECM missions. Other specialised applications include agricultural duties (two underwing chemical tanks or single underfuselage tank, plus bubble type and additional lower windows in pilot's door, windscreen and nose-gear wire cutters, ceiling mounted airscoop, and anti-corrosion paint finish). The maritime surveillance version can be equipped with nose mounted 360° scan Bendix RDR-1400 search and navigation radar, underfuselage side/down-looking surveillance radar, belly mounted panoramic camera and forward looking oblique camera, FLIR or low light level TV camera under fuselage or in an underwing pod, Omega-VLF area navigation system, advanced compass system, periscopic sextant, bubble side windows for observers, and a searchlight. External stores can include auxiliary fuel tanks, weapons and survival gear.

Third SIAI-Marchetti SF.600TP, with retractable landing gear

Dimensions, external:
- Wing span: 15·00 m (49 ft 2½ in)
- Wing chord (constant): 1·60 m (5 ft 3 in)
- Wing aspect ratio: 9·375
- Length overall: 12·15 m (39 ft 10½ in)
- Height overall: 4·60 m (15 ft 1 in)
- Tailplane span: 5·89 m (19 ft 4 in)
- Wheel track: 2·40 m (7 ft 10½ in)
- Wheelbase: 4·88 m (16 ft 0 in)
- Propeller diameter: 2·03 m (6 ft 8 in)
- Crew door (fwd, port): Height: 1·14 m (3 ft 9 in)
  - Width: 0·86 m (2 ft 10 in)
  - Height to sill: 0·90 m (2 ft 11½ in)
- Cargo door (rear, port):
  - Height: 1·13 m (3 ft 8½ in)
  - Width: 1·49 m (4 ft 10¾ in)
  - Height to sill: 0·90 m (2 ft 11½ in)

Dimensions, internal:
- Cabin, excl flight deck: Length: 5·05 m (16 ft 6¾ in)
  - Width: 1·23 m (4 ft 0½ in)
  - Height: 1·27 m (4 ft 2 in)
  - Floor area: 6·0 m² (64·6 sq ft)
  - Volume: 7·90 m³ (279 cu ft)

Areas:
- Wings, gross: 24·00 m² (258·3 sq ft)
- Fin: 1·69 m² (18·19 sq ft)
- Rudder: 1·35 m² (14·53 sq ft)
- Tailplane: 3·68 m² (39·61 sq ft)
- Elevator: 2·76 m² (29·71 sq ft)

Weights and Loadings:
- Weight empty (standard utility version): 1,875 kg (4,133 lb)
- Max T-O weight: 3,400 kg (7,495 lb)
- Max cargo floor loading: 400 kg/m² (81·93 lb/sq ft)
- Max wing loading: 141·7 kg/m² (29·0 lb/sq ft)
- Max power loading: 5·43 kg/kW (8·92 lb/shp)

Performance (at max T-O weight, ISA):
- Max cruising speed at 1,525 m (5,000 ft): 165 knots (306 km/h; 190 mph)
- Cruising speed (75% power) at 3,050 m (10,000 ft): 155 knots (287 km/h; 178 mph)
- Stalling speed, flaps down: 59 knots (109 km/h; 68 mph)
- Max rate of climb at S/L: 451 m (1,480 ft)/min
- Rate of climb at S/L, one engine out: 152 m (500 ft)/min
- Service ceiling: 7,315 m (24,000 ft)
- Service ceiling, one engine out: 3,050 m (10,000 ft)
- T-O run: 287 m (940 ft)
- T-O to 15 m (50 ft): 408 m (1,340 ft)
- Landing from 15 m (50 ft):
  - without propeller reversal: 479 m (1,570 ft)
  - with propeller reversal: 396 m (1,300 ft)
- Landing run:
  - without propeller reversal: 280 m (920 ft)
  - with propeller reversal: 204 m (670 ft)
- Range at 3,050 m (10,000 ft), 10% reserves:
  - with max payload: 324 nm (600 km; 372 miles)
  - with max fuel and 500 kg (1,102 lb) payload: 853 nm (1,580 km; 981 miles)

CAPRONI VIZZOLA COSTRUZIONI AERONAUTICHE SpA (Subsidiary of Agusta SpA)

Via Per Tornavento 15, 21019 Somma Lombardo
Telephone: (0331) 230 826
Telex: 332554 CAVIZ I
General Manager: Ing Marcello Puppi

The Caproni company, formed in 1910, is the oldest Italian aircraft manufacturer. Its works at Vizzola Ticino have approx 30,000 m² (322,917 sq ft) of covered space, and are adjacent to Malpensa Airport. They are equipped to manufacture complete structural subassemblies for helicopters and medium-sized fixed-wing aircraft. Caproni Vizzola designed and built the C22J described in this entry, and also produces ground support equipment for General Electric T64/CT64, J79, J85 and CF6 and Turbo Union RB.199 turbojet and turbofan engines.

A 100% holding in Caproni Vizzola was acquired by Agusta in 1983.

CAPRONI VIZZOLA C22J VENTURA

The C22J is a two-seat lightweight training aircraft, developed by Caproni Vizzola as a private venture. Its configuration bears a close resemblance to that of the company's A-21SJ Calif jet powered sailplane (see 1983-84 and earlier *Jane's*); construction is largely of metal, with the forward fuselage skin, some fairings and other unstressed areas of glassfibre. A prototype (I-CAVJ), powered by 1·0 kN (220 lb st) TRS 18-046 engines, made its first flight on 21 July 1980.

Intended primarily for student pilot screening, basic and proficiency training, the C22J is also suitable for ECM evaluation, ground and air navaid calibration, ecological survey and high-speed liaison. It can be converted easily for photographic survey duties, or for use as an RPV.

The first pre-series C22J (I-GIAC) made its initial flight on 17 February 1983, and differs from the prototype in having shorter span wings, with tip tanks, and more powerful TRS 18-1 engines. RAI certification under FAR Pt 23 was expected by the end of 1986, with series production scheduled to start in early 1987.

The following description applies to the production C22J:

Type: Two-seat basic training aircraft.

Wings: Cantilever shoulder-wing monoplane. Constant chord wings, of Wortmann FX-67K-170 section. Dihedral 2°. Incidence 1° 9'. No sweepback. Single-spar structure, built as two panels and joined on centreline, with aluminium alloy skin and extruded leading-edge. Electrically actuated trailing-edge plain flaps can be set in any position throughout their full range of movement. Flaps operate in conjunction with aluminium alloy airbrakes/spoilers, of which there is one in the upper surface of each wing, forward of the flap. Airbrakes are opened manually, but move with the flaps to provide balanced control. Aerodynamically balanced ailerons operate differentially and are drooped to provide additional flap area. All movable surfaces are of extruded aluminium alloy, and are operated by push/pull rods. No tabs.

Fuselage: Tadpole shaped structure, designed as a laminar lifting body. Primary load-bearing keel and wing spar pickup cross-structure is of light alloy, inside moulded glassfibre shell. NACA type flush engine air inlet of glassfibre in top of fuselage, aft of cockpits. Tailboom is of light alloy.

Tail Unit: Cantilever T tail, tailplane being of light alloy stressed skin construction. Full span balanced elevator is a chemically milled extrusion, and has spring trim, actuated by an Industria electrical system located in the fin. All-metal two-spar stressed skin fin, bolted to tailboom. All control surfaces operated by push/pull rods. No tabs. Rudder pedals adjustable in flight.

Landing Gear: Retractable tricycle type, actuated electrically with manual backup. All units retract forward into fuselage. Cantilever sprung main legs, of glassfibre epoxy; rubber-in-torsion shock absorption on nose unit. Cleveland mainwheels, with Goodyear size 5·00-5 tyres (6 ply rating), pressure 3·0 bars (43·5 lb/sq in). Tost nosewheel, with Tost tyre size 260 × 85 mm (4 ply rating), pressure 2·5 bars (36·3 lb/sq in). Cleveland independent hydraulic disc brakes on mainwheels. Steerable nosewheel, linked to rudder pedals. Safety lock for up and down positions. Electrical warning system.

Power Plant: Two Microturbo TRS 18-1 turbojet engines, each rated at 1·45 kN (326 lb st) for take-off and 1·28 kN (288 lb st) max continuous, mounted side by side in fuselage aft of cockpits. Integral fuel tank in each wing leading-edge, combined capacity 290 litres (64 Imp gallons), and two 70 litre (15·5 Imp gallon) wingtip tanks. Total fuel capacity 430 litres (95 Imp gallons). Fuel system incorporates fuselage collector tank which permits inverted flight. Refuelling point at each wingtip. Provision for two 112 litre (24·5 Imp gallon) underwing drop tanks. Oil capacity 0·8 litres (1·4 Imp pints).

Accommodation: Seats for two persons side by side under jettisonable canopy which is hinged at rear and opens upward. Seats are semi-supine. Dual controls on production version. Single instrument panel and centre console, eliminating need for dual instruments and avionics. Cockpit heated, ventilated and demisted.

Systems: Hydraulic system for mainwheel brakes only. No pneumatic system. Electrical system is 28V DC, incorporating two Microturbo 1·5kW or KHD 1·2kW starter/generators and a 24V 18Ah lead-acid battery. Cockpit ventilation and demisting by heat exchangers on jetpipes. Demand type low-pressure oxygen system, capacity 8·5 litres (0·3 cu ft), for each occupant.

Avionics and Equipment: Avionics bay in top of fuselage, aft of cockpits. Collins Micro Line nav/com radio, Pro

Line flight director, navigation, landing and anti-collision lights, standard.

ARMAMENT: Provision for two standard NATO underwing pylons, for a wide range of stores (max external load 250 kg; 551 lb) for gunnery/weapon training, photographic reconnaissance and target towing missions. Typical loads include one auxiliary fuel tank and one three-camera pod; two auxiliary fuel tanks; two 7·62 mm gun pods and 500 rds of ammunition; two Simpres AL-18-50 pods with eighteen 2 in rockets; four SAMP EU70 50 kg general purpose bombs; four Mk 70 11 kg or M38-A2 50 kg practice bombs; or two Dornier DATS 1 50 kg towed targets.

DIMENSIONS, EXTERNAL:

Wing span	9·20 m (30 ft 2¼ in)
Wing chord (constant)	0·90 m (2 ft 11½ in)
Wing aspect ratio	11·06
Length overall	6·26 m (20 ft 6½ in)
Fuselage: Max width	1·228 m (4 ft 0½ in)
Height overall	1·88 m (6 ft 2 in)
Tailplane span	2·66 m (8 ft 8¾ in)
Wheel track	1·81 m (5 ft 11¼ in)
Wheelbase	1·81 m (5 ft 11¼ in)

AREAS:

Wings, gross	7·65 m² (82·35 sq ft)
Ailerons (total)	0·718 m² (7·73 sq ft)
Trailing-edge flaps (total)	0·824 m² (8·87 sq ft)
Airbrakes/spoilers (total)	0·572 m² (6·16 sq ft)
Fin	0·808 m² (8·70 sq ft)
Rudder	0·225 m² (2·42 sq ft)
Tailplane	1·40 m² (15·07 sq ft)
Elevator	0·338 m² (3·64 sq ft)

WEIGHTS AND LOADING:

Weight empty	738 kg (1,627 lb)
Max fuel load	360 kg (794 lb)
Max T-O and landing weight	1,255 kg (2,767 lb)
Max wing loading	164·0 kg/m² (33·59 lb/sq ft)

PERFORMANCE (at max T-O weight):

Max permissible diving speed	325 knots (602 km/h; 374 mph)
Max operating speed	300 knots (556 km/h; 345 mph)
Max cruising speed at S/L	260 knots (482 km/h; 299 mph)
Max design manoeuvring speed	234 knots (433 km/h; 269 mph)
Max diving speed with airbrakes fully deployed	214 knots (396 km/h; 246 mph)
Econ cruising speed at 3,050 m (10,000 ft)	175 knots (324 km/h; 202 mph)
Max speed for landing gear extension	157 knots (290 km/h; 180 mph)
Stalling speed, flaps down, power off	74 knots (137 km/h; 85 mph) EAS
Max rate of climb at S/L	600 m (1,970 ft)/min
Rate of climb at S/L, one engine out	177 m (580 ft)/min
Time to climb to 5,000 m (16,400 ft)	10 min
Max operating altitude	7,620 m (25,000 ft)
Service ceiling	10,000 m (32,800 ft)
Service ceiling, one engine out	5,500 m (18,045 ft)
T-O run at S/L, ISA, zero wind	650 m (2,133 ft)
T-O to 15 m (50 ft), conditions as above	880 m (2,887 ft)
T-O to 15 m (50 ft) at 1,500 m (4,920 ft), ISA, zero wind	1,000 m (3,280 ft)
Max range with wingtip tanks	700 nm (1,296 km; 805 miles)
Max endurance	3 h
g limits	+7/−3·5

Caproni Vizzola C22J Ventura, equipped as standard with wingtip tanks

BREDANARDI COSTRUZIONI AERONAUTICHE SpA (Subsidiary of Agusta SpA)

Monteprandone (AP), Casella Postale 108, 63039 San Benedetto del Tronto (Ascoli Piceno)
Telephone: (0735) 801721
Telex: 560165 BRENAR I
PRESIDENT: Dott Raffaello Teti

At Monteprandone (AP) BredaNardi continues to produce, under licence from their US manufacturers, the NH-300C and NH-500D light helicopters. Descriptions of the Model 500 series can be found under the McDonnell Douglas Helicopters heading in the US section of this edition, and of the Model 300C under the Schweizer heading.

Sales continue for agricultural work (mainly of the NH-300C) and training. Recent sales included two NH-300s to the Greek Air Force flying school, the first BredaNardi helicopters to be sold overseas.

NH-500D built by BredaNardi

GENERAL AVIA

GENERAL AVIA COSTRUZIONI AERONAUTICHE SRL

Via Trieste 22-24, 20096 Pioltello, Milan
Telephone: (02) 9266774
Fax: (02) 9260395

TECHNICAL DIRECTOR: Dott Ing Stelio Frati
SECRETARY-TREASURER: Lamberto Frati
TECHNICAL: Renato Cairo
PUBLIC RELATIONS: Carla Bielli

Dott Ing Stelio Frati is well known for the many successful light aircraft which, as a freelance designer, he has developed since 1950. These have been built in prototype and production series by several Italian manufacturers, and have included the Procaer F15 Picchio and the F.250, now manufactured by SIAI-Marchetti as the SF.260.

General Avia was established by Dott Ing Frati in early 1970, primarily to develop prototypes of his own design for production by other companies. These have included the F15F, a derivative of the Procaer F15E Picchio, and the F.20 Pegaso, both of which were described in the 1981-82 *Jane's*. General Avia developed and built the prototype of the Canguro transport aircraft described under the Agusta (SIAI-Marchetti) heading in this section. In 1983 it developed for SIAI-Marchetti a retractable landing gear version of the Canguro.

Latest prototype to be constructed is the F1300 Jet Squalus. Its design was commissioned by the Belgian company Promavia, which will manufacture the production version.

GENERAL AVIA JET SQUALUS F1300 NGT

The Jet Squalus (Latin for 'Shark') was designed to cover all stages of flying training, from ab initio to part of the advanced syllabus, and to be powered by a small, modern, fuel-efficient and quiet turbofan engine. A side by side seating arrangement was chosen for instructor and trainee, and the aircraft is provided with four underwing attachment points enabling it also to undertake weapons training or light tactical missions.

Two prototypes are being built, the first of which made its public debut as a static exhibit at the Farnborough International air show in September 1986. It was expected to make its first flight in October or November 1986. Fatigue, flutter and other testing of major components has been completed, as have drawings for the production version, which will be manufactured by the Belgian company Promavia (which see), with Sonaca of Belgium as principal subcontractor. Marketing and product support, including training programmes, will be provided by Promavia.

In its initial configuration the first Jet Squalus prototype is powered by a derated Garrett TFE109-1 turbofan engine, of the kind developed for the twin-engined T-46A, and is not fitted with ejection seats. The more powerful Williams International FJ44 will be installed in the second prototype, and the first aircraft's TFE109 will eventually be uprated to a comparable thrust level. Possible future options include Martin-Baker ejection seats and cockpit pressurisation.

The following description applies to the first prototype, except where indicated:

TYPE: Two-seat basic training aircraft.

AIRFRAME: Composite materials are used for fairings and some non-structural components; otherwise the aircraft is basically of metal construction throughout.

WINGS: Cantilever low-wing monoplane, with GAW-2 wing section. Dihedral 5° from roots. Incidence 1° at root, −1° 30′ at tip. All-metal single-spar structure in light alloy with flush riveted stressed skin. Differentially operated all-metal ailerons and hydraulically operated metal trailing-edge flaps.

FUSELAGE: All-metal semi-monocoque structure with flush riveted aluminium alloy skin. Hydraulically operated two-piece airbrake in lower central part of fuselage, in line with flaps. Avionics and equipment bay in nose. Large quick-disconnect panel in lower rear fuselage permits rapid engine access or removal. Small auxiliary aerofoil surface mid-mounted on each air intake trunk (Promavia calls these 'spinners'), to smooth out turbulence at wing/fuselage junction and delay onset of stall.

TAIL UNIT: Cantilever all-metal structure with flush riveted skin. Sweptback fin and rudder (42° on fin leading-edge). Non-swept, fixed incidence tailplane. Trim tab in port elevator.

LANDING GEAR: Retractable tricycle type, with single wheel and oleo-pneumatic shock absorber on each unit. Mainwheels retract inward, nosewheel rearward. Hydraulic actuation, with built-in emergency system. Nosewheel steerable 18° left and right. Mainwheels and tyres size 6·00-6, nosewheel 5·00-5. Goodyear brakes.

POWER PLANT: One Garrett TFE109-1 (F109-GA-100) turbofan engine in first prototype, for initial flight trials, mounted in rear fuselage and derated to 5·92 kN (1,330 lb st); will later be progressively uprated, first to 6·67 kN (1,500 lb st) and later to 8·23 kN (1,850 lb st). Second prototype will have an 8·01 kN (1,800 lb st) Williams International FJ44 turbofan. Semi-integral fuel tank in centre-fuselage, max usable capacity 720 litres (158 Imp gallons) in prototypes, 800 litres (176 Imp gallons) in production aircraft. Single gravity refuelling point on top of fuselage. Electric fuel pump for engine starting and emergency use.

ACCOMMODATION: Side by side seats for two persons in non-pressurised air-conditioned cockpit. One-piece framed canopy is hinged at rear and opens upward hydraulically. Provision for pressurisation to 0·28 bars (4·0 lb/sq in), and for optional Martin-Baker Mk 11 lightweight ejection seats for both occupants, capable of operation at altitudes up to 12,200 m (40,000 ft) and at any speed between 60 and 400 knots (111-741 km/h; 69-461 mph), including ejection through canopy.

SYSTEMS: Environmental control system for cockpit air-conditioning. Hydraulic system (operating pressure 107 bars; 1,550 lb/sq in) for actuation of airbrake, landing gear, flaps and canopy. System incorporates electrically driven oil pump, with two air/oil accumulators (one for normal and one for emergency operation); separate standby system for emergency lowering of landing gear. Electrical system is 28V DC, using an engine driven starter/generator and nickel-cadmium or lead-acid battery. Negretti Aviation oxygen system.

AVIONICS AND EQUIPMENT: Include dual Collins EFIS avionics and radio equipment.

ARMAMENT: Four underwing attachment points for such weapons or other stores as 0·50 in/12·7 mm machine-gun pods, seven-round 2·75 in rocket launchers, practice bombs or auxiliary fuel tanks.

DIMENSIONS, EXTERNAL:
- Wing span: 9·04 m (29 ft 8 in)
- Wing chord: at root: 1·90 m (6 ft 2¾ in)
  - at tip: 1·00 m (3 ft 3¼ in)
  - mean aerodynamic: 1·575 m (5 ft 2 in)
- Wing aspect ratio: 6·02
- Length overall: 9·36 m (30 ft 8½ in)
- Height overall: 3·60 m (11 ft 9¾ in)
- Tailplane span: 3·80 m (12 ft 5½ in)
- Wheel track: 3·59 m (11 ft 9¼ in)
- Wheelbase: 3·58 m (11 ft 9 in)

AREAS:
- Wings, gross: 13·58 m² (146·17 sq ft)
- Vertical tail surfaces (total): 2·04 m² (21·96 sq ft)
- Horizontal tail surfaces (total): 3·67 m² (39·50 sq ft)

Prototype General Avia F.20 TP Condor (two Allison 250-B17B turboprop engines) *(Aviodata)*

WEIGHTS AND LOADINGS (A: initially derated engine, B: uprated engines):
- Weight empty: A: 1,200 kg (2,645 lb)
  - B: 1,400 kg (3,086 lb)
- Max T-O weight: A (Aerobatic): 2,000 kg (4,409 lb)
  - A (Normal), B: 2,400 kg (5,291 lb)
- Max wing loading:
  - A (Aerobatic): 147·27 kg/m² (30·18 lb/sq ft)
  - A (Normal), B: 176·73 kg/m² (36·21 lb/sq ft)
- Max power loading:
  - A (Aerobatic): 337·75 kg/kN (3·31 lb/lb st)
  - A (Normal), B (TFE109-1): 291·83 kg/kN (2·86 lb/lb st)
  - A (Normal), B (FJ44): 300·00 kg/kN (2·94 lb/lb st)

PERFORMANCE (estimated at max T-O weight, A and B as above):
- Max permissible diving speed:
  - A: 380 knots (704 km/h; 437 mph)
- Never-exceed speed in level flight:
  - A: Mach 0·70 (345 knots; 638 km/h; 397 mph)
- Max level speed at 4,265 m (14,000 ft):
  - A: 315 knots (584 km/h; 363 mph)
- Normal operating speed:
  - A: Mach 0·60 (300 knots; 556 km/h; 345 mph)
- Design manoeuvring speed:
  - A: 210 knots (389 km/h; 242 mph)
- Max speed for landing gear extension:
  - A: 150 knots (278 km/h; 173 mph)
- Max speed for flap extension (landing position):
  - A: 130 knots (241 km/h; 150 mph)
- Stalling speed, flaps down:
  - A: 67 knots (124 km/h; 77 mph)
- Max rate of climb at S/L: A: 975 m (3,200 ft)/min
  - B: 1,219 m (4,000 ft)/min
- Service ceiling: A: 11,280 m (37,000 ft)
  - B: 12,800 m (42,000 ft)
- Max operating ceiling: A: 7,620 m (25,000 ft)
- T-O run at S/L, ISA: A: 366 m (1,200 ft)
  - B: 305 m (1,000 ft)
- Landing run at S/L, ISA: A: 336 m (1,100 ft)
- Radius of action with four Mk 81 underwing bombs:
  - A: 250 nm (463 km; 288 miles)
- Ferry range at 6,100 m (20,000 ft), max internal fuel:
  - A: 1,000 nm (1,850 km; 1,150 miles)
- *g* limits (A):
  - sustained, at 3,050 m (10,000 ft): +2·8
  - aerobatic: +7/−3·5

GENERAL AVIA F.20 TP CONDOR

Developed from the F.20 Pegaso six-seat light business twin (1981-82 *Jane's*), the Condor is a four-seat turboprop powered aircraft intended for such military applications as weapon training, long-range maritime surveillance, search and rescue, anti-armour, and ground attack. It can be equipped with two stores pylons under each wing, the outer one on each side being capable of carrying a 300 litre (66 Imp gallon) auxiliary fuel tank.

The prototype (I-GEAC) flew for the first time on 7 May 1983, and shortly afterwards was granted a special airworthiness certificate, enabling it to appear at the Paris Air Show later that month. The programme for full certification was continuing in May 1985, but was later delayed in order to give priority to the Jet Squalus programme.

TYPE: Twin-turboprop general purpose military aircraft.

WINGS: Cantilever low-wing monoplane. Wing section NACA 65_2-415. Dihedral 5° from roots. Incidence 1° 45'. All-metal single-spar structure in light alloy, with flush riveted stressed skin. Differentially operated all-metal ailerons and electrically actuated double-slotted metal trailing-edge flaps. Anti-icing optional.

FUSELAGE: All-metal semi-monocoque structure, with flush riveted aluminium alloy skin.

TAIL UNIT: Cantilever all-metal structure with flush riveted skin. Fixed incidence tailplane. Trim tabs in rudder and each elevator. Anti-icing optional.

LANDING GEAR: Retractable tricycle type, with single wheel on each unit. Nosewheel steerable 18° to left and right. Electric actuation, with manual backup. Oleo-pneumatic shock absorbers. Mainwheels and tyres size 7·00-6, pressure 3·24 bars (47 lb/sq in); nosewheel and tyre size 6·00-6, pressure 1·86 bars (27 lb/sq in). Cleveland brakes.

POWER PLANT: Two 298 kW (400 shp) Allison 250-B17B turboprop engines, each driving a Hartzell HC-B3TF-7A/T10173-21R three-blade propeller with spinner. Total internal fuel capacity 600 litres (132 Imp gallons); provision for a further 600 litres (132 Imp gallons) to be carried in two underwing auxiliary tanks. Oil capacity 16 litres (3·5 Imp gallons).

ACCOMMODATION: Normal seating for four persons, including pilot, in two pairs under rearward sliding moulded transparent canopy. Space for baggage in rear fuselage and rear of each engine nacelle. Cabin heated, ventilated, and soundproofed with glass-wool insulation.

AVIONICS AND EQUIPMENT: IFR instrumentation and dual controls standard; other installations to customer's requirements.

DIMENSIONS, EXTERNAL:
- Wing span over tip tanks: 10·34 m (33 ft 11 in)
- Wing chord: at root: 1·65 m (5 ft 5 in)
  - at tip: 1·50 m (4 ft 11 in)
- Wing aspect ratio: 6·67
- Length overall: 8·925 m (29 ft 3¼ in)
- Height overall: 3·50 m (11 ft 5¾ in)
- Tailplane span: 4·80 m (15 ft 9 in)
- Wheel track: 3·50 m (11 ft 5¾ in)
- Wheelbase: 2·40 m (7 ft 10½ in)
- Propeller diameter: 2·03 m (6 ft 8 in)
- Min propeller ground clearance: 0·18 m (7 in)
- Distance between propeller centres: 3·42 m (11 ft 2½ in)

DIMENSIONS, INTERNAL:
- Cabin: Max length: 3·66 m (12 ft 0 in)
  - Max width: 1·17 m (3 ft 10 in)
  - Max height: 1·13 m (3 ft 8½ in)

AREAS:
- Wings, gross: 16·02 m² (172·4 sq ft)
- Ailerons (total): 1·42 m² (15·28 sq ft)
- Trailing-edge flaps (total): 1·59 m² (17·13 sq ft)
- Fin: 1·24 m² (13·35 sq ft)
- Rudder, incl tab: 0·79 m² (8·50 sq ft)
- Tailplane: 2·88 m² (31·00 sq ft)
- Elevators, incl tabs: 2·28 m² (24·54 sq ft)

WEIGHTS AND LOADINGS (A: without external stores; B: with external stores):
- Weight empty, equipped: A: 1,400 kg (3,086 lb)
- Max T-O and landing weight: A: 2,400 kg (5,291 lb)
  - B: 2,700 kg (5,952 lb)
- Max wing loading: A: 149·8 kg/m² (30·68 lb/sq ft)
  - B: 168·5 kg/m² (34·51 lb/sq ft)
- Max power loading: A: 4·03 kg/kW (6·61 lb/shp)
  - B: 4·53 kg/kW (7·44 lb/shp)

Prototype Jet Squalus F1300 jet trainer at Farnborough International air show in September 1986, prior to its first flight *(Jay Miller/Aerofax)*

PERFORMANCE (estimated at max T-O weight, without external stores except where indicated):

Never-exceed speed	280 knots (519 km/h; 322 mph)
Max level speed at S/L	248 knots (460 km/h; 286 mph)
Max cruising speed (75% power) at 3,050 m (10,000 ft)	234 knots (435 km/h; 270 mph)
Econ cruising speed (60% power) at 3,050 m (10,000 ft)	210 knots (390 km/h; 242 mph)
Stalling speed, flaps down	70 knots (130 km/h; 81 mph)
Max rate of climb at S/L	900 m (2,950 ft)/min
Rate of climb at S/L, one engine out	300 m (985 ft)/min
Service ceiling	8,500 m (27,900 ft)
Service ceiling, one engine out	3,600 m (11,800 ft)
T-O run: without external stores	180 m (590 ft)
with external stores	220 m (720 ft)
Landing run	260 m (853 ft)
Combat radius with 900 kg (1,984 lb) of external stores	216 nm (400 km; 248 miles)
Range: without external stores	836 nm (1,550 km; 963 miles)
with external stores	1,673 nm (3,100 km; 1,926 miles)

GENERAL AVIA F.3500 SPARVIERO (HAWK)

Design of this twin-turbofan commuter transport began in 1983. The possibility of a manufacturing partnership was still being explored in mid-1986, but prototype construction had not then begun. Brief specification details and a three-view drawing can be found in the 1985-86 *Jane's*.

PARTENAVIA

PARTENAVIA COSTRUZIONI AERONAUTICHE SpA

Via G. Pascoli 7, 80026 Casoria (Naples)
Telephone: (081) 7596311
Telex: 720199 PARTNA I

BOARD OF DIRECTORS:
Ing Giulio Ciampolini
Ing Beppe Sacchi
Ing Giovanni Sarzotti
Dott Franco Capanna
Ing Carlo Rosini
Gen Fulvio Ristori
Ing Ermanno Raffetto

GENERAL MANAGER AND EXECUTIVE DIRECTOR:
Ing Carlo Rosini

This company was founded in 1957 by Prof Ing Luigi Pascale and his brother, Ing Nino Pascale, and has since built a series of light aircraft designed by Prof Ing Pascale. It came under the control of Aeritalia, through the latter's General Aviation Group, in July 1981.

Since 1974 Partenavia has occupied a 12,000 m² (129,165 sq ft) facility on Capodichino Airport, Naples, where it is concentrating on production of the P.68C and P.68C-TC twin-engined seven-seat light aircraft, a derivative known as the Observer, and the new turboprop powered Spartacus and Viator.

Partenavia P.68C-TC six/seven-seat light aircraft *(Aviodata)*

PARTENAVIA P.68

The original P.68, designed by Prof Ing Luigi Pascale in 1968, was described in the 1975-76 *Jane's*. From it was developed the P.68B Victor twin-engined light transport, which entered production in Partenavia's factory at Naples Airport in the Spring of 1974.

Details of the P.68B, P.68C-R, P.68 floatplane/amphibian and P.68R can be found in the 1980-81 and earlier editions of *Jane's*. The following versions are currently in production:

P.68C. Improved version of P.68B, with lengthened nose, increased fuel capacity, and several internal changes. Detailed description applies primarily to this version (also known formerly as the Victor), which superseded the P.68B (1979-80 *Jane's*) in late 1979.

P.68C-TC. Similar to P.68C, but powered currently by Avco Lycoming TIO-360-A1C6D turbocharged engines with fuel injection. Certificated in June 1980. In production; 42 delivered by beginning of 1986. Available as landplane or with twin amphibious floats. (Latter version first flown from land and water on 26 and 27 June 1985 respectively.) Floatplane-only version being studied.

P.68 Observer. Special observation version; described separately.

By the beginning of 1986 Partenavia had delivered 400 aircraft of the P.68 series, most of them for export to operators in more than 20 countries.

TYPE: Six/seven-seat light transport and trainer.

WINGS: Cantilever high-wing monoplane. Wing section NACA 63-3,515. Dihedral 1°. Incidence 1° 30′. No sweepback. Stressed skin two-spar torsion box structure of aluminium alloy. All-metal ailerons and electrically operated single-slotted trailing-edge flaps. Hoerner GRP wingtips. No tabs.

FUSELAGE: Conventional all-metal semi-monocoque structure of frames and longerons, with four main longerons and stressed skin covering. Fuselage/wing intersection mainly of GRP.

TAIL UNIT: Cantilever stressed skin metal structure. All-moving tailplane, in two symmetrical halves joined by steel cross-tube and of constant chord except for increase at leading-edge roots. Balance tab in tailplane trailing-edge, over 80 per cent of span. Sweptback fin and rudder, with small dorsal fin. Trim tab in rudder.

LANDING GEAR: Non-retractable tricycle type, with steerable nosewheel. Cantilever spring steel main legs. Oleo-pneumatic shock-absorber on nosewheel. Cleveland mainwheels, type 40-96, with Pirelli eight-ply tyres size 6·00-6. Goodyear six-ply nosewheel tyre, size 5·00-5. Cleveland type 30-61 hydraulic disc brakes. Parking brake. Streamline wheel fairings standard. C-TC version available optionally with De Vore PK twin-float gear having retractable ground wheels.

POWER PLANT (P.68C): Two 149 kW (200 hp) Avco Lycoming IO-360-A1B6 flat-four engines, each driving a Hartzell HC-C2YK-2C/C-7666A-4 two-blade constant-speed fully-feathering propeller with spinner. Integral fuel tank in each wing, total capacity 538 litres (118 Imp gallons), of which 520 litres (114 Imp gallons) are usable. Refuelling point above each wing. Oil capacity 15 litres (3·3 Imp gallons).

ACCOMMODATION: Seating for seven persons in cabin, including pilot, in two rows of two seats and a rear bench seat for three persons. A 'club' seating arrangement is available optionally, having the two middle seats facing rearward with a folding table between them and the bench seat. Front seats are of the adjustable sliding type. Access to all seats via large forward opening car type door on port side at front of cabin. Up to 181 kg (400 lb) of baggage can be carried in compartment aft of rear bench seat. Access to baggage compartment from inside cabin, or via large forward hinged door on starboard side at rear, which serves also as emergency exit. Two stretchers or other loads can be carried when all passenger seats are removed. Dual controls, cabin heating, ventilation and soundproofing standard.

SYSTEMS: Electrical power supplied by two 24V 70A alternators and a 24V 17Ah battery. No hydraulic system. Goodrich pneumatic de-icing system optional.

AVIONICS AND EQUIPMENT (P.68C): Wide range of Collins Micro Line or King Silver Crown avionics, and Edo-Aire Mitchell Century III autopilot, to customer's requirements. Provision for SunAir ASB 100 HF radio. Standard equipment includes airspeed indicator, gyro horizon, directional gyro, two cylinder head temperature gauges, clock, exhaust gas temperature gauge, outside air temperature gauge, rate of climb indicator, sensitive altimeter, electrical turn rate indicator, inertia reel shoulder harness for pilot and co-pilot, stall warning system, four upholstered seats with back pockets, and one bench seat with folding back (with safety belts on all seats), cabin fire extinguisher, six individual fresh air outlets and six floor warm air vents, windscreen defrosters, cabin soundproofing, annunciator panel warning lights, two map lights, individual reading lights, individual instrument panel floodlights with rheostat, anti-collision strobe light, two landing/taxying lights, navigation lights, anti-static kit, external power receptacle, oil coolers with thermostatic control, quick drain fuel and oil valves, and towbar. Optional equipment includes Janitrol 45,000 BTU combustion heater, wing and tail pneumatic de-icing system, electrothermal propeller de-icing system, 0·46 × 0·58 m (18 × 23 in) floor panel for photogrammetric camera, including periscope sight hatch, second airspeed indicator, second gyro horizon, chronometer, second altimeter, pilot's and co-pilot's vertically adjustable seats, alcohol windscreen de-icing, heated stall warning indicator, all-leather interior, forced ventilation blower, ice light and second oil cooler.

DIMENSIONS, EXTERNAL:

Wing span	12·00 m (39 ft 4½ in)
Wing chord (constant)	1·55 m (5 ft 1 in)
Wing aspect ratio	7·742
Length overall	9·55 m (31 ft 4 in)
Height overall	3·40 m (11 ft 1¾ in)
Tailplane span	3·90 m (12 ft 9½ in)
Wheel track	2·40 m (7 ft 10½ in)
Wheelbase	3·50 m (11 ft 5¾ in)
Propeller diameter	1·88 m (6 ft 2 in)
Distance between propeller centres	4·10 m (13 ft 5½ in)
Baggage door, stbd: Height	0·80 m (2 ft 7½ in)
Width	0·80 m (2 ft 7½ in)

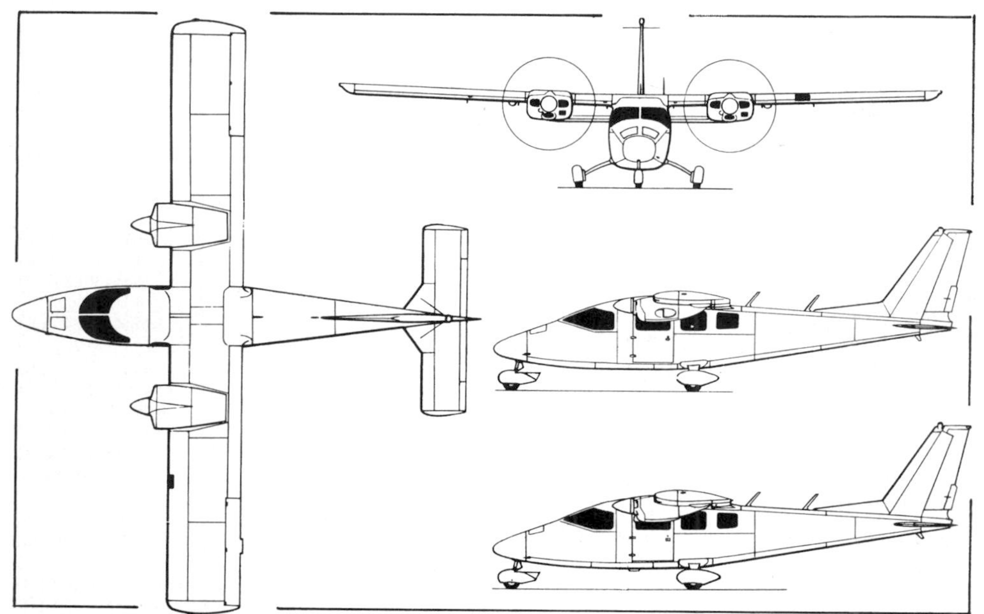

Partenavia P.68C, with additional side view (centre) of P.68C-TC *(Pilot Press)*

DIMENSIONS, INTERNAL:
Cabin: Length 3·58 m (11 ft 9 in)
Max width 1·16 m (3 ft 9½ in)
Max height 1·20 m (3 ft 11¼ in)
Baggage space 0·56 m³ (20 cu ft)
AREAS:
Wings, gross 18·60 m² (200·2 sq ft)
Ailerons (total) 1·79 m² (19·27 sq ft)
Trailing-edge flaps (total) 2·37 m² (25·51 sq ft)
Fin 1·59 m² (17·11 sq ft)
Rudder, incl tab 0·44 m² (4·74 sq ft)
Tailplane, incl tab 4·41 m² (47·47 sq ft)
WEIGHTS AND LOADINGS:
Weight empty: C 1,230 kg (2,711 lb)
C-TC 1,300 kg (2,866 lb)
*Max T-O weight: C, C-TC 1,990 kg (4,387 lb)
Max landing weight: C, C-TC 1,890 kg (4,166 lb)
Max wing loading: C, C-TC 107 kg/m² (21·9 lb/sq ft)
Max power loading: C 6·68 kg/kW (10·97 lb/hp)
C-TC 6·36 kg/kW (10·45 lb/hp)
* *C-TC amphibian 317 kg (700 lb) heavier*
PERFORMANCE (at max T-O weight):
Max level speed:
C at S/L 174 knots (322 km/h; 200 mph)
C-TC at 5,335 m (17,500 ft) 195 knots (361 km/h; 224 mph)
Max cruising speed (75% power):
C at 2,290 m (7,500 ft) 166 knots (307 km/h; 191 mph)
C-TC at 6,100 m (20,000 ft) 183 knots (339 km/h; 211 mph)
C-TC at 3,660 m (12,000 ft) 172 knots (318 km/h; 198 mph)
Cruising speed (65% power):
C at 3,350 m (11,000 ft) 161 knots (298 km/h; 185 mph)
C-TC at 3,050 m (10,000 ft) 158 knots (293 km/h; 182 mph)
Cruising speed (55% power):
C at 3,660 m (12,000 ft) 150 knots (278 km/h; 173 mph)
C-TC at 3,050 m (10,000 ft) 147 knots (272 km/h; 169 mph)
Stalling speed, flaps up:
C, C-TC 65 knots (120 km/h; 75 mph)
Stalling speed, flaps down:
C, C-TC 58 knots (106 km/h; 66 mph)
Max rate of climb at S/L: C 457 m (1,500 ft)/min
C-TC 472 m (1,550 ft)/min
Rate of climb at S/L, one engine out:
C 82 m (270 ft)/min
C-TC 88 m (290 ft)/min
Service ceiling: C 5,850 m (19,200 ft)
C-TC 7,620 m (25,000 ft)
Service ceiling, one engine out:
C 2,100 m (6,900 ft)
C-TC 4,420 m (14,500 ft)
T-O run: C, C-TC 230 m (755 ft)
T-O to 15 m (50 ft): C 396 m (1,300 ft)
C-TC 385 m (1,263 ft)
Landing from 15 m (50 ft):
C, C-TC 488 m (1,600 ft)
Landing run: C, C-TC 215 m (705 ft)
Accelerate/stop distance: C 473 m (1,550 ft)
C-TC 510 m (1,673 ft)
Optimum cruising range (C), 45 min reserves:
75% power at 2,290 m (7,500 ft) 1,050 nm (1,945 km; 1,209 miles)
65% power at 3,350 m (11,000 ft) 1,140 nm (2,112 km; 1,312 miles)
55% power at 3,660 m (12,000 ft) 1,210 nm (2,242 km; 1,393 miles)
Optimum cruising range (C-TC) at 3,660 m (12,000 ft), 45 min reserves:
75% power 775 nm (1,436 km; 892 miles)
65% power 940 nm (1,742 km; 1,082 miles)
55% power 1,020 nm (1,890 km; 1,175 miles)
Range with max fuel (C-TC):
65% power at 6,400 m (21,000 ft) 1,100 nm (2,037 km; 1,266 miles)

PARTENAVIA P.68 OBSERVER

Developed originally in collaboration with Sportavia-Pützer of West Germany, the Observer has a forward and downward view for the crew equal to that of a helicopter. The Plexiglas nose, cockpit and associated structure were designed by Sportavia-Pützer; the prototype (D-GERD) was constructed at that company's Dahlemer-Binz factory, and first flew on 20 February 1976.

With its good low-speed handling characteristics, the Observer is considered to be capable of performing many roles allocated normally to helicopters. It is intended particularly for patrol and observation operations.

The first Partenavia built Observer was flown in the Spring of 1980, and certification was obtained in June of that year. Improvements have since been made to the flight deck and instrument panel. By the beginning of 1986 a total of 25 Observers had been delivered, to customers in Africa, Australia, western Europe, and North and South America. The Observer was then being evaluated by a number of potential customers in several countries for such specific duties as anti-pollution patrol, traffic surveillance and fish shoal location.

Italian Police Observer (one of five ordered in early 1986) equipped with Electronique Aérospatiale ATAL television surveillance system

DIMENSIONS, EXTERNAL: As P.68C except:
Length overall 9·35 m (30 ft 8 in)
Wheelbase 3·80 m (12 ft 5½ in)
WEIGHTS AND LOADINGS:
Weight empty 1,280 kg (2,822 lb)
Max T-O weight 1,960 kg (4,321 lb)
Max wing loading 105·3 kg/m² (21·58 lb/sq ft)
Max power loading 6·58 kg/kW (10·80 lb/hp)
PERFORMANCE (at max T-O weight):
Max level speed at S/L 174 knots (322 km/h; 200 mph)
Cruising speed:
75% power at 2,285 m (7,500 ft) 165 knots (306 km/h; 190 mph)
65% power at 3,350 m (11,000 ft) 160 knots (296 km/h; 184 mph)
55% power at 3,660 m (12,000 ft) 149 knots (276 km/h; 171 mph)
Stalling speed: flaps up 64 knots (118 km/h; 74 mph)
flaps down 56 knots (101 km/h; 64 mph)
Max rate of climb at S/L 488 m (1,600 ft)/min
Rate of climb at S/L, one engine out 98 m (320 ft)/min
Service ceiling 6,100 m (20,000 ft)
Service ceiling, one engine out 2,375 m (7,800 ft)
T-O run 229 m (750 ft)
T-O to 15 m (50 ft) 387 m (1,270 ft)
Landing from 15 m (50 ft) 479 m (1,570 ft)
Landing run 210 m (690 ft)
Accelerate/stop distance 473 m (1,550 ft)
Optimum cruising range, 45 min reserves:
75% power at 2,285 m (7,500 ft) 1,060 nm (1,964 km; 1,220 miles)
65% power at 3,350 m (11,000 ft) 1,140 nm (2,112 km; 1,312 miles)
55% power at 3,660 m (12,000 ft) 1,200 nm (2,224 km; 1,382 miles)

PARTENAVIA AP 68TP-300 SPARTACUS

This eight/nine-seat turboprop derivative of the P.68, known originally as the P.68 Turbo, was developed by Partenavia in a joint programme with Aeritalia. A six-seat prototype (I-PAIT, known as the AP 68TP) flew for the first time on 11 September 1978. Certification of this aircraft, which had a retractable landing gear, was obtained on 8 June 1981. The second and third aircraft (I-RAIO and I-RAIP), with eight/nine seats and non-retractable gear, were designated AP 68TP-100; this version made its initial flight on 20 November 1981 and was certificated on 12 July 1982. Both of these aircraft, which had all-moving tailplanes, were lost during flight testing, and were superseded by the AP 68TP-300, subsequently named Spartacus, with non-retractable gear, fixed tailplane and separate elevators; two examples had been completed by the Spring of 1983. The first of these (I-RAIK) made its initial flight on 1 April 1983. Italian RAI certification was obtained in the following December.

The Spartacus is intended as a multi-role aircraft with low operating costs. The spectrum of possible missions includes air taxi, liaison, executive, cargo transport, coastal patrol, aerial survey, ambulance, and training. Underwing hardpoints are available on request.

The following description applies to the fixed-gear Spartacus; the retractable-gear AP 68TP-600, known initially as the Spartacus 10 and now as the Viator, is described separately.

TYPE: Twin-turboprop general purpose transport.

WINGS: As described for P.68C Victor. Trim tab in starboard aileron. Goodrich pneumatic boot de-icing of leading-edges optional.

FUSELAGE: Similar to P.68C, but slightly longer.

TAIL UNIT: Vertical surfaces similar to P.68C, but of increased chord. Fixed incidence tailplane with separate elevators; geared tab in port elevator. Pneumatic boot de-icing of leading-edges.

LANDING GEAR: Non-retractable tricycle type, with single wheel on each unit. Oleo-dynamic shock absorption on nose unit, leaf springs on main gear, both of Partenavia manufacture. Cleveland wheels, sizes 40-77B (nose) and 40-163EA (main). Nosewheel tyre size 5·00-5 (6 ply), pressure 1·93 bars (28 lb/sq in); mainwheel tyres size 6·50-8 (8 ply), pressure 4·13 bars (60 lb/sq in). Cleveland 30-139 brakes.

POWER PLANT: Two Allison 250-B17C turboprop engines, each flat rated at 244·5 kW (328 shp) for T-O and max continuous operation. Hartzell HC-B3TF-7A/T10173B-21R three-blade constant-speed fully-feathering reversible-pitch metal propellers with spinners. Fuel in two 380 litre (83·6 Imp gallon) tanks in wings and a 40 litre (8·8 Imp gallon) tank in each engine nacelle. Total capacity 840 litres (185 Imp gallons). Two 100 litre (22 Imp gallon) underwing tanks optional. Refuelling point at each wingtip. Oil capacity 11·4 litres (2·5 Imp gallons) per engine.

ACCOMMODATION: Seating for eight or nine persons, including pilot. Forward opening doors on starboard side of flight deck (crew), on port side at centre of cabin (passengers), and at rear of cabin on starboard side (passengers and emergency exit). Dual controls, cabin

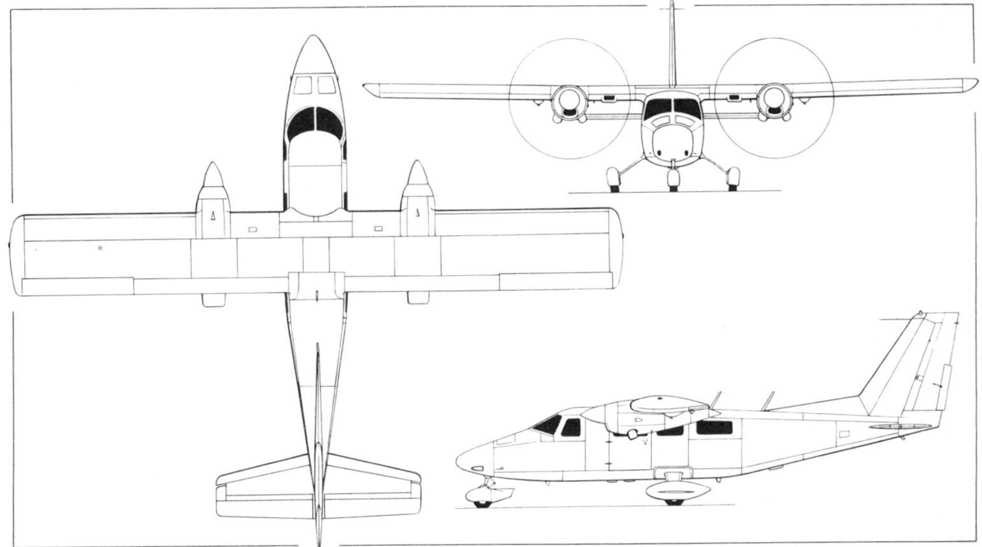
Partenavia Spartacus twin-turboprop general purpose transport *(Pilot Press)*

Partenavia AP 68TP-300 Spartacus (two Allison 250-B17C turboprop engines)

heating, ventilation and soundproofing standard. Air-conditioning optional.

SYSTEMS: Primary electrical power supplied by two 150A 28V DC starter/generators and two voltage regulators. In the event of primary electrical failure, power is supplied by a 24V 29Ah lead-acid battery (self-sufficient for engine starting), and an inverter for 115/26V AC power. Electric de-icing of engine air intakes standard; de-icing of propellers, pitot and stall detector, pneumatic boot de-icing of outer wing leading-edges, and oxygen system, are optional. No hydraulic or pneumatic system.

AVIONICS: Collins Micro Line or King Silver Crown, to customer's requirements. Typical installations include HF com, DME, weather radar (Sperry or Bendix), autopilot, and Narco ELT.

ARMAMENT AND OPERATIONAL EQUIPMENT (military version): Two underwing hardpoints, each of 181 kg (400 lb) capacity, with standard NATO MA-4A racks. Typical loads may include two SUU-11B/A 7·62 mm Minigun pods, four LAU-32B/A rocket launchers (each containing seven rockets), two 400 lb bombs, flare dispensers, air-to-surface missiles, supply containers, or auxiliary fuel tanks.

DIMENSIONS, EXTERNAL:
- Wing span: 12·00 m (39 ft 4½ in)
- Wing chord, constant: 1·55 m (5 ft 1 in)
- Wing aspect ratio: 7·742
- Length overall: 9·90 m (32 ft 5¾ in)
- Length of fuselage: 8·71 m (28 ft 7 in)
- Fuselage: Max width: 1·20 m (3 ft 11¼ in)
- Height overall: 3·65 m (11 ft 11¾ in)
- Tailplane span: 4·01 m (13 ft 2 in)
- Wheel track: 2·40 m (7 ft 10½ in)
- Wheelbase: 3·80 m (12 ft 5½ in)
- Propeller diameter: 2·03 m (6 ft 8 in)
- Propeller ground clearance: 0·74 m (2 ft 5 in)
- Distance between propeller centres: 4·03 m (13 ft 2¾ in)
- Passenger door (port): Height: 1·03 m (3 ft 4½ in)
  - Width: 0·80 m (2 ft 7½ in)
  - Height to sill: 0·65 m (2 ft 1½ in)
- Passenger/emergency door (stbd):
  - Height: 0·95 m (3 ft 1½ in)
  - Width: 0·90 m (2 ft 11½ in)
  - Height to sill: 0·65 m (2 ft 1½ in)

DIMENSIONS, INTERNAL:
- Cabin:
  - Length, excl flight deck and baggage compartment: 2·95 m (9 ft 8 in)
  - Max width: 1·12 m (3 ft 8 in)
  - Max height: 1·20 m (3 ft 11¼ in)
  - Floor area: 3·30 m² (35·52 sq ft)
  - Volume: 4·00 m³ (141·26 cu ft)
- Baggage compartment volume: 0·55 m³ (19·42 cu ft)

AREAS:
- Wings, gross: 18·60 m² (200·2 sq ft)
- Ailerons (total): 1·76 m² (18·94 sq ft)
- Trailing-edge flaps (total): 2·42 m² (26·05 sq ft)
- Fin: 2·90 m² (31·22 sq ft)
- Rudder, incl tab: 1·64 m² (17·65 sq ft)
- Tailplane: 3·76 m² (40·47 sq ft)
- Elevators (total): 1·30 m² (13·99 sq ft)

WEIGHTS AND LOADINGS:
- Weight empty, equipped: 1,490 kg (3,285 lb)
- Max fuel load: 640 kg (1,411 lb)
- Max payload: 834 kg (1,838 lb)
- Max T-O weight: 2,600 kg (5,732 lb)
- Max ramp weight: 2,625 kg (5,787 lb)
- Max landing weight: 2,470 kg (5,445 lb)
- Max zero-fuel weight: 2,404 kg (5,300 lb)
- Max wing loading: 139·8 kg/m² (28·6 lb/sq ft)
- Max power loading: 5·32 kg/kW (8·73 lb/shp)

PERFORMANCE (at max T-O weight):
- Max operating speed: 200 knots (370 km/h; 230 mph) IAS
- Max level and max cruising speed at 3,050 m (10,000 ft): 210 knots (389 km/h; 242 mph)
- Econ cruising speed at 4,575 m (15,000 ft): 172 knots (319 km/h; 198 mph)
- Stalling speed: flaps up: 80 knots (149 km/h; 93 mph)
  - flaps down: 66 knots (123 km/h; 76 mph)
- Max rate of climb at S/L: 627 m (2,057 ft)/min
- Rate of climb at S/L, one engine out: 158 m (520 ft)/min
- Service ceiling: 7,620 m (25,000 ft)
- Service ceiling, one engine out: 4,575 m (15,000 ft)
- T-O run: 232 m (760 ft)
- T-O to 15 m (50 ft): 387 m (1,270 ft)
- Landing from 15 m (50 ft): 436 m (1,430 ft)
- Landing run: 241 m (790 ft)
- Range at 180 knots (333 km/h; 207 mph) at 3,660 m (12,000 ft), allowances for start, taxi, take-off, descent, and 45 min reserves at long-range power:
  - with max payload: 340 nm (630 km; 391 miles)
  - with max fuel: 870 nm (1,612 km; 1,002 miles)

PARTENAVIA AP 68TP-600 VIATOR (WAYFARER)

The first retractable landing gear version of the Spartacus (I-RAIZ, c/n 6) made its initial flight in early July 1984. It was followed on 29 March 1985 by a prototype of the Viator (I-RAIL, previously known as the Spartacus 10), which has a longer fuselage than the fixed-gear AP 68TP-300, seating two additional passengers.

Certification of the Viator was expected in the Summer of 1986, and initial orders for seven have been placed.

The Spartacus description applies also to the Viator, except where indicated:

TYPE: Twin-turboprop general purpose transport.

WINGS, FUSELAGE AND TAIL UNIT: As for AP 68TP-300, except for lengthened fuselage.

LANDING GEAR: Retractable tricycle type, with electrically controlled hydraulic actuation. Oleo-pneumatic shock absorber in each unit. Nosewheel retracts forward, mainwheels inward into fuselage fairing. Wheels as for AP 68TP-300, but with McCreary 8-ply tyres, sizes 6·50-8 (main) and 6·00-6 (nose). Mainwheel tyre pressure 4·83 bars (70 lb/sq in). Cleveland disc brakes. No anti-skid units.

POWER PLANT: As for AP 68TP-300.

ACCOMMODATION: Standard club seating for pilot and nine passengers, in four rows of two seats (second and fourth rows rearward facing) plus a rear bench seat for two persons. Forward opening door on starboard side of flight deck, and for second/third row passengers on port side at centre of cabin. Double door (starboard, rear) provides access for rear seat passengers, and to 181 kg (400 lb) capacity baggage compartment aft of rear bench seat, and serves also as an emergency exit. With all passenger seats removed and special kits installed, up to 12 parachutists, or two stretcher patients plus two medical attendants, can be carried in cabin. Dual controls, and cabin heating, ventilation and soundproofing, are standard. Hot air for cabin heating and windscreen de-icing is provided by a Janitrol 45,000 BTU combustion heater installed in the fuselage nose.

Partenavia Viator, a 'stretched' version of the Spartacus with retractable landing gear

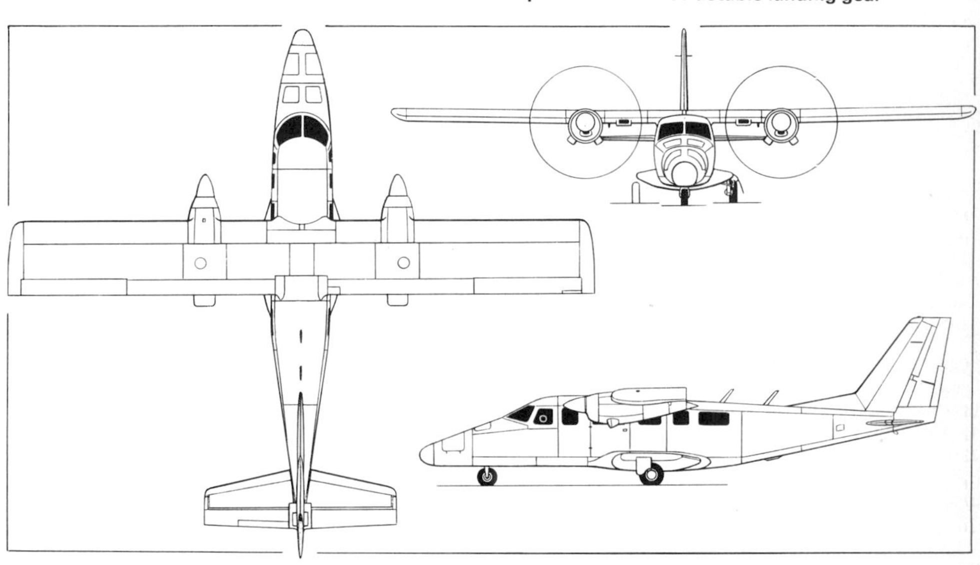

Partenavia Viator ten-seat twin-turboprop light transport *(Pilot Press)*

SYSTEMS, AVIONICS AND EQUIPMENT: As described for AP 68TP-300.

ARMAMENT (optional): As described for AP 68TP-300, plus two 7·62 mm machine-guns installed on the landing gear pods.

DIMENSIONS, EXTERNAL: As for AP 68TP-300 Spartacus, except:

Length overall	10·85 m (35 ft 7¼ in)
Length of fuselage	9·66 m (31 ft 8¼ in)
Height overall	3·64 m (11 ft 11¼ in)
Wheel track	2·167 m (7 ft 1¼ in)
Wheelbase	3·51 m (11 ft 6¼ in)
Propeller ground clearance	0·725 m (2 ft 4½ in)
Passenger door (port):	
Height to sill	0·71 m (2 ft 4 in)
Passenger/emergency door (stbd):	
Height (mean)	0·91 m (2 ft 11½ in)
Width	1·10 m (3 ft 7¼ in)
Height to sill	0·79 m (2 ft 7 in)

DIMENSIONS, INTERNAL:

Cabin, excl flight deck and baggage compartment:	
Length	3·60 m (11 ft 9¾ in)
Floor area	4·00 m² (43·06 sq ft)
Volume	4·70 m³ (165·98 cu ft)
Baggage compartment volume	0·65 m³ (22·95 cu ft)

AREAS: As for AP 68TP-300 Spartacus

WEIGHTS AND LOADINGS:

Basic weight empty	1,640 kg (3,615 lb)
Max fuel load (usable)	680 kg (1,499 lb)
Max payload	910 kg (2,006 lb)
Max T-O and landing weight	2,850 kg (6,283 lb)
Max ramp weight	2,875 kg (6,338 lb)
Max zero-fuel weight	2,550 kg (5,622 lb)
Max wing loading	153·23 kg/m² (31·38 lb/sq ft)
Max power loading	5·83 kg/kW (9·58 lb/shp)

PERFORMANCE (at max T-O weight):

Max operating speed	200 knots (370 km/h; 230 mph) IAS
Max level and max cruising speed at 3,660 m (12,000 ft)	220 knots (408 km/h; 253 mph)
Econ cruising speed at 3,660 m (12,000 ft)	170 knots (315 km/h; 196 mph)
Stalling speed, power off:	
flaps up	81 knots (151 km/h; 94 mph)
flaps down	70 knots (130 km/h; 81 mph)
Max rate of climb at S/L	589 m (1,932 ft)/min
Rate of climb at S/L, one engine out	131 m (430 ft)/min
Max operating altitude	7,620 m (25,000 ft)
Service ceiling, one engine out	3,355 m (11,000 ft)
T-O run	275 m (900 ft)
T-O to 15 m (50 ft)	460 m (1,510 ft)
Landing from 15 m (50 ft)	500 m (1,640 ft)
Landing run	250 m (820 ft)
Min ground turning radius	10·36 m (34 ft 0 in)
Range at long-range power, allowances for start, taxi, take-off, descent, and 45 min reserves:	
with max payload	445 nm (824 km; 512 miles)
with max fuel	860 nm (1,594 km; 990 miles)

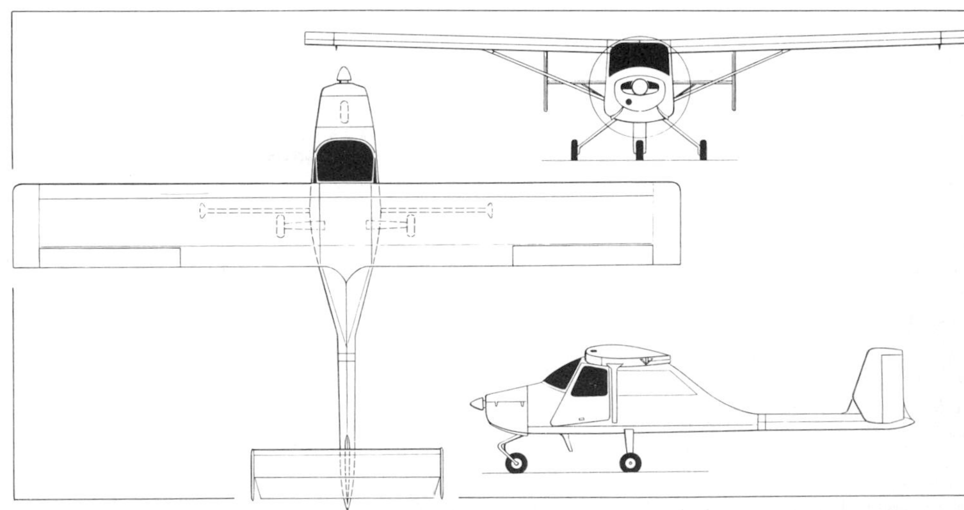

Drawing *(Pilot Press)* **and photograph of the Partenavia P.86 Mosquito two-seat light aircraft**

PARTENAVIA P.86 MOSQUITO

A prototype of this new Partenavia design flew for the first time on 27 April 1986, just over a year after the initiation of design work. Powered by a KFM 112M engine, it has side by side seats for two persons and it is designed to conform to FAR Pt 23 in the Utility category. Partenavia hopes to secure a production order from the Aero Club d'Italia.

Production aircraft will have a more powerful Limbach engine, and the following details apply to the aircraft with this power plant:

TYPE: Two-seat light aircraft.

WINGS: Braced high-wing monoplane, with single streamline section strut each side. Constant chord non-swept wings, of NACA 63A-416 (modified) section, with 1° 30′ dihedral and 3° incidence. Two-spar torsion box structure of 2024-T3 aluminium alloy, including trailing-edge split flaps and plain ailerons. Flared-up wingtips. No tabs.

FUSELAGE: Semi-monocoque forward fuselage and tubular rear tailboom, all of aluminium alloy.

TAIL UNIT: Cantilever all-metal stressed skin structure of 2024-T3 aluminium alloy, with front and rear channel section spars. Fixed incidence tailplane, mounted above tailboom on short pylon. Endplate fins and rudders. No rudder tabs; trim tab in centre of elevator.

LANDING GEAR: Non-retractable tricycle type, with Partenavia leaf spring shock absorption. McCreary wheel size 5·00-5 and tyre size 360 × 120-165 mm (5 ply) on each unit; tyre pressures 1·72 bars (25 lb/sq in) on main gear, 1·03 bars (15 lb/sq in) on nose unit. Cleveland 30-18 brakes.

POWER PLANT: One 59 kW (80 hp) Limbach L 2000 flat-four engine, driving a Hoffmann two-blade fixed-pitch propeller with spinner. Also available with 59 kW (80 hp) Avco Lycoming O-160 engine. Single integral fuel tank in wings, capacity 70 litres (15·4 Imp gallons). Refuelling point on inboard section of starboard wing. Oil capacity 2·5 litres (0·55 Imp gallons).

ACCOMMODATION: Side by side seats for pilot and one passenger, with baggage space behind seats. Upward opening door, with window, on each side of cabin. Cabin ventilated via ram air intake on wing leading-edge.

AVIONICS: King or Collins VHF com/nav radio, ADF and ATC transponder.

DIMENSIONS, EXTERNAL:

Wing span	10·00 m (32 ft 9¾ in)
Wing chord, constant	1·25 m (4 ft 1¼ in)
Wing aspect ratio	8·0
Length overall	6·775 m (22 ft 2¾ in)
Fuselage: Max width	1·22 m (4 ft 0 in)
Height overall	1·923 m (6 ft 3¾ in)
Tailplane span	2·80 m (9 ft 2¼ in)
Wheel track	2·00 m (6 ft 6¾ in)
Wheelbase	1·567 m (5 ft 1½ in)
Propeller diameter	1·65 m (5 ft 5 in)
Propeller ground clearance	0·325 m (1 ft 0¾ in)
Cabin doors (each): Height	0·90 m (2 ft 11½ in)
Max width	0·60 m (1 ft 11½ in)
Height to sill	0·975 m (3 ft 2½ in)

DIMENSIONS, INTERNAL:

Cabin: Length	0·90 m (2 ft 11½ in)
Max width	1·00 m (3 ft 3¼ in)
Max height	1·00 m (3 ft 3¼ in)
Floor area	0·86 m² (9·26 sq ft)
Volume	0·82 m³ (28·96 cu ft)
Baggage compartment: Volume	0·42 m³ (14·83 cu ft)

AREAS:

Wings, gross	12·50 m² (135·2 sq ft)
Ailerons (total)	1·028 m² (11·07 sq ft)
Rudders (total)	0·61 m² (6·57 sq ft)
Tailplane	1·34 m² (14·42 sq ft)
Elevator	0·80 m² (8·61 sq ft)

WEIGHTS AND LOADINGS:

Basic weight empty	320 kg (705 lb)
Max fuel weight	50 kg (110 lb)
Max T-O and landing weight	540 kg (1,190 lb)
Max wing loading	43·2 kg/m² (8·85 lb/sq ft)
Max power loading	9·15 kg/kW (14·88 lb/hp)

PERFORMANCE (at max T-O weight):

Never-exceed speed	150 knots (278 km/h; 172 mph)
Max level speed at S/L	97 knots (180 km/h; 112 mph)
Max cruising speed at S/L	86 knots (160 km/h; 99 mph)
Econ cruising speed at S/L	80 knots (148 km/h; 92 mph)
Stalling speed: flaps up	41 knots (76 km/h; 47 mph)
flaps down	36 knots (67 km/h; 42 mph)
Max rate of climb at S/L	235 m (770 ft)/min
Service ceiling	3,995 m (13,100 ft)
T-O run	149 m (490 ft)
T-O to 15 m (50 ft)	311 m (1,020 ft)
Landing from 15 m (50 ft)	120 m (395 ft)
Range with max fuel at econ cruising speed, allowances for start, taxi, T-O and 30 min reserves	340 nm (630 km; 391 miles)

PIAGGIO

INDUSTRIE AERONAUTICHE E MECCANICHE RINALDO PIAGGIO SpA

Via Cibrario 4, 16154 Genoa
Telephone: (010) 600831
Telex: 270695 AERPIA I

BRANCH OFFICE: Via A. Gramsci 34, Rome

WORKS: Genoa and Finale Ligure

CHAIRMAN AND MANAGING DIRECTOR:
Dott Rinaldo Piaggio

VICE-PRESIDENT: Ing Umberto Barnato

DIRECTOR OF INTERNATIONAL PROGRAMMES:
Ing Bruno Mori

DIRECTOR OF OPERATIONS: Ing Roberto Vianson

TECHNICAL DIRECTOR, AIRCRAFT: Ing Alessandro Mazzoni

MARKETING DIRECTOR: Commander G. B. Pizzinato

The original Piaggio company began the construction of aeroplanes in its Genoa-Sestri plant in 1916, and later in the Finale Ligure works. The present company was formed on 29 February 1964, and has since operated as an independent concern. It employs about 1,500 people and has a total covered works area (Genoa-Sestri and Finale Ligure) of approx 100,000 m² (1,076,390 sq ft). In addition to building aircraft of its own design, Piaggio is producing components for the Aeritalia G222, Panavia Tornado, Boeing 767 and McDonnell Douglas DC-10.

The company is organised into two production Divisions: the activities of the Aero-Engine Division are described in the appropriate section of this edition.

PIAGGIO AVANTI

First details of this new turboprop powered business aircraft were announced in October 1983, at the NBAA annual meeting at Dallas, Texas. A major change since that date was to specify Pratt & Whitney PT6A-66 engines to

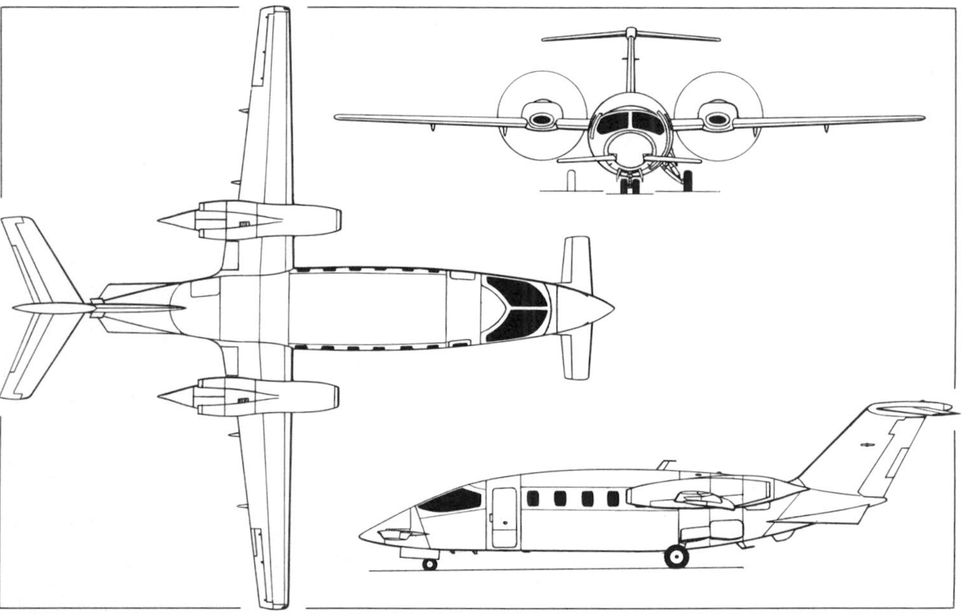

Piaggio Avanti twin-turboprop corporate transport *(Pilot Press)*

Prototype of the six/ten-passenger Avanti executive transport

power the aircraft, instead of the lower rated PT6A-61s originally selected. This was done to improve and ensure the initial performance goals, including particularly the aircraft's speed in a climb.

All research and development leading to the present design was begun by Piaggio in 1979. Gates Learjet became a partner in the programme in 1983, but announced the termination of its involvement with the Avanti, for economic reasons, on 13 January 1986. All of Gates' tooling, together with the forward fuselages of the first three development aircraft, were transferred to Piaggio.

As can be seen from the accompanying three-view drawing, the Avanti is of advanced aerodynamic configuration, the major design features being the adoption of a 'three lifting surfaces' concept, to reduce cruise drag and fuel consumption, and placement of the engines aft of the rear bulkhead to minimise engine noise levels in the cabin.

Primary lifting surface is the main wing, which is situated just above the mid position (to avoid drag-inducing bulges in the circular-section fuselage) and, by virtue of the 'pusher' engine installation, has an unbroken leading-edge except for the nacelle inlets. The second lifting surface is the horizontal T tailplane and elevator, which provides orthodox control from a conventional location. The third is the foreplane, which serves as a forward wing rather than a traditional canard surface, by producing a positive component of lift which not only assists the main wing in supporting the aircraft but allows the latter to be reduced in size, thereby also reducing cruise drag and fuel consumption.

While most of the Avanti is of conventional metal construction, the nosecone, tailcone, tail unit, engine nacelles, wing moving surfaces and landing gear doors are built of composite materials: graphite/epoxy (carbonfibre) in areas of high stress and Kevlar/epoxy elsewhere. Most of these parts of the airframe—48 components in all, representing about 10 per cent of the aircraft's operating weight empty—are manufactured under subcontract by Sikorsky Aircraft. Wing moving surfaces and foreplane (including flaps) are Italian built.

The first Avanti, assembly of which began at Piaggio's Finale Ligure plant in late 1984, made its first flight on 23 September 1986.

Current plans are to achieve certification in the third quarter of 1987, enabling customer deliveries to begin shortly afterwards.

TYPE: Twin-turboprop corporate transport.

WINGS: Cantilever non-swept mid-wing monoplane, tapered on leading- and trailing-edges. Piaggio PE 1491 G (modified) section at root, PE 1332 G section at tip; thickness/chord ratio 13%. Dihedral 2° from roots. Incidence 0°. Sweep 0° at 15 per cent chord. Integrally machined skins and spars of aluminium alloy; main spar forms an integral fail-safe structural unit with rear pressure bulkhead and main landing gear. Trailing-edge flaps (outboard of engine nacelles) and balanced ailerons are of all-composite construction. Trim tab in starboard aileron. Hot air anti-icing of outboard leading-edges.

FOREPLANES: All-composite fail-safe fixed incidence (+3°) foreplane at tip of nose, with 5° anhedral, fitted with all-composite single-slotted auxiliary trailing-edge flaps. Foreplane has Piaggio PE 1300 G aerofoil section, thickness/chord ratio 13%, and 0° sweep at 50 per cent chord. Electrical anti-icing of foreplane leading-edges. Auxiliary flaps do not control the aircraft in pitch, but are primarily to assist lift, being coupled with the main wing flaps and deflecting with them to offset changes in trim.

FUSELAGE: Circular-section pressurised fail-safe structure of mainly metal construction (machined and bonded aluminium alloy), with rear pressure bulkhead in line with wing main spar. Nosecone, baggage door and landing gear doors are built of composite materials. Two small metal ventral fins under tailcone.

TAIL UNIT: All-sweptback, all-composite T tail, with anhedral tailplane and balanced elevators and rudder. Trim tab in rudder and each elevator. No tail unit anti-icing.

LANDING GEAR: Hydraulically retractable tricycle type, with single-wheel main units and twin-wheel nose unit. Main units retract rearward into sides of fuselage; nose unit retracts forward. Dowty hydraulic shock absorbers. Tyre sizes 6·50-10 (main) and 5·00-4 (nose). Carbon brakes.

POWER PLANT: Two 597 kW (800 shp) (flat rated) Pratt & Whitney Canada PT6A-66 turboprop engines, each mounted above the wing in an all-composite nacelle and driving a Hartzell four-blade fully-feathering reversible-pitch pusher propeller with spinner. Propeller blades de-iced by engine exhaust. Fuel in two fuselage tanks totalling 700 litres (154 Imp gallons; 185 US gallons) and two 450 litre (99 Imp gallon; 119 US gallon) wing tanks; total fuel capacity 1,600 litres (352 Imp gallons; 423 US gallons). Dual gravity refuelling point in upper part of fuselage.

ACCOMMODATION: Crew of one or two on flight deck. Seating in main cabin for five to nine passengers, with galley, toilet and storage area. Rectangular cabin windows, including one emergency exit on starboard side. Passenger door at front on port side. Baggage compartment aft of rear pressure bulkhead, with door immediately aft of wing on port side. Entire accommodation pressurised and air-conditioned.

SYSTEMS: AiResearch bleed air environmental control system, with max pressure differential of 0·62 bars (9·0 lb/sq in). Single hydraulic system, driven by electric motor, with handpump for emergency backup. Electrical system powered by two starter/generators and a nickel-cadmium battery. Basic version has 0·62 m³ (22 cu ft) oxygen system. Hot air anti-icing of main wing outer leading-edges; electrical anti-icing for foreplane and windscreen.

AVIONICS AND EQUIPMENT: Standard com/nav equipment (Collins Pro Line or other, to customer's requirements). Collins APS-65 digital autopilot systems. Blind-flying instrumentation standard.

DIMENSIONS, EXTERNAL:

Wing span	13·84 m (45 ft 5 in)
Foreplane span	3·281 m (10 ft 9¼ in)
Wing chord: at root	1·79 m (5 ft 10½ in)
at tip	0·63 m (2 ft 0¾ in)
Foreplane chord: at root	0·786 m (2 ft 7 in)
at tip	0·55 m (1 ft 9⅔ in)
Wing aspect ratio	11·8
Foreplane aspect ratio	4·9
Length overall	14·168 m (46 ft 5¾ in)
Length of fuselage	12·528 m (41 ft 1¼ in)
Fuselage: Max width	1·95 m (6 ft 4¾ in)
Height overall	3·892 m (12 ft 9¼ in)
Tailplane span	4·184 m (13 ft 8¾ in)
Wheel track	2·845 m (9 ft 4 in)
Wheelbase	5·792 m (19 ft 0 in)
Propeller diameter	2·159 m (7 ft 1 in)
Propeller ground clearance	0·778 m (2 ft 6⅔ in)
Distance between propeller centres	4·13 m (13 ft 6½ in)
Passenger door (fwd, port): Height	1·30 m (4 ft 3¼ in)
Width	0·61 m (2 ft 0 in)
Height to sill	0·577 m (1 ft 10¾ in)
Baggage door (rear, port): Height	0·64 m (2 ft 1¼ in)
Width	0·70 m (2 ft 3½ in)
Height to sill	1·383 m (4 ft 6½ in)
Emergency exit (stbd): Height	0·665 m (2 ft 2¼ in)
Width	0·485 m (1 ft 7 in)

DIMENSIONS, INTERNAL:

Cabin: Length	6·00 m (19 ft 8¼ in)
Max width	1·83 m (6 ft 0 in)
Max height	1·75 m (5 ft 9 in)
Volume	10·48 m³ (370 cu ft)
Baggage compartment volume	1·19 m³ (42 cu ft)

AREAS:

Wings, gross	15·76 m² (169·64 sq ft)
Ailerons (total, incl tab)	0·66 m² (7·10 sq ft)
Trailing-edge flaps (total)	1·601 m² (17·23 sq ft)
Foreplane	1·607 m² (17·30 sq ft)
Foreplane flaps (total)	0·585 m² (6·30 sq ft)
Fin	3·681 m² (39·62 sq ft)
Rudder, incl tab	1·05 m² (11·30 sq ft)
Tailplane	2·485 m² (26·75 sq ft)
Elevators (total, incl tabs)	1·349 m² (14·52 sq ft)

WEIGHTS AND LOADINGS (estimated):

Weight empty, equipped	2,812 kg (6,200 lb)
Operating weight empty	2,903 kg (6,400 lb)
Max fuel load	1,215 kg (2,680 lb)
Max payload	907 kg (2,000 lb)
Payload with max fuel	367 kg (810 lb)
Max T-O weight	4,445 kg (9,800 lb)
Max ramp weight	4,486 kg (9,890 lb)
Max landing weight	4,223 kg (9,310 lb)
Max zero-fuel weight	3,810 kg (8,400 lb)
Max wing loading	282·04 kg/m² (57·8 lb/sq ft)
Max power loading	3·73 kg/kW (6·12 lb/shp)

PERFORMANCE (estimated, at max T-O weight except where indicated):

Max operating Mach number	0·67
Max operating speed	260 knots (482 km/h; 299 mph) IAS
Max level and max cruising speed at 8,230 m (27,000 ft)	400 knots (740 km/h; 460 mph)
Econ cruising speed at 12,500 m (41,000 ft)	320 knots (593 km/h; 368 mph)
Stalling speed, power off: flaps up	105 knots (195 km/h; 121 mph) CAS
flaps down	90 knots (167 km/h; 104 mph) CAS
Max rate of climb at S/L	1,112 m (3,650 ft)/min
Rate of climb at S/L, one engine out	381 m (1,250 ft)/min
Service ceiling	12,495 m (41,000 ft)
Service ceiling, one engine out	9,750 m (32,000 ft)
T-O to 15 m (50 ft)	736 m (2,415 ft)
Landing from 15 m (50 ft) at max landing weight	732 m (2,400 ft)
Range with 4 passengers, NBAA reserves, at 320 knots (593 km/h; 368 mph)	2,100 nm (3,892 km; 2,418 miles)

R. PIAGGIO P.166-DL3

The P.166 has been produced in several basic versions, of which the original piston engined P.166 was described in the 1963-64 *Jane's*; the P.166M, P.166B Portofino and P.166C

R. Piaggio P.166-DL3 twin-turboprop light transport and aircrew trainer

in the 1971-72 *Jane's*; the P.166S in the 1974-75 *Jane's*; and the P.166-DL2 in the 1978-79 *Jane's*.

Current version is the turboprop powered P.166-DL3, which flew for the first time on 3 July 1976, and received FAA and RAI certification in 1978. It can be configured and equipped for a wide variety of duties, including executive transport (EXC); transport and dropping of up to ten paratroops (PAR); air ambulance for two stretchers and two medical attendants (AMB); multi-engine aircrew training (MTR); light tactical transport (LTT); armed military counter-insurgency, field support, and search and rescue (AML); maritime reconnaissance (MAR); environmental control and geophysical survey (ECS); aerophotogrammetry (APH); and aerial firefighting (AFF). Piaggio is currently building a batch of 16 P.166-DL3s, of which 12 had been completed by February 1985: two for Alitalia, four for the Somali Air Force, and six (in APH configuration) for the Aeronautica Militare Italiana.

TYPE: Twin-turboprop light transport.

WINGS: Shoulder gull-wing cantilever monoplane. NACA 230 wing section. Dihedral 21° 30′ on inner portion, 2° 30′ on outer wings. Incidence 2° 43′ at root. Sweepback 7° 30′ at quarter-chord. Aluminium alloy flush riveted torsion box structure, with single main spar and auxiliary rear spar. All-metal slotted ailerons, with geared and trim tab in starboard aileron. All-metal hydraulically actuated slotted flaps. Rubber boot leading-edge de-icing optional.

FUSELAGE: Aluminium alloy flush riveted semi-monocoque structure of frames and L section extruded stringers: no longerons.

TAIL UNIT: Cantilever aluminium alloy structure, with flush riveted smooth skin on fixed surfaces and beaded skin on control surfaces. Rudder and elevators statically and dynamically balanced. Geared and trim tabs in elevators; trim tab in rudder. Rubber boot leading-edge de-icing of fin and tailplane optional.

LANDING GEAR: Retractable tricycle type. Magnaghi oleo-pneumatic shock absorbers in all units. Hydraulic actuation. Nosewheel retracts rearward, main units upward. Goodyear 24 × 7·7 mainwheels with size 8·50-10 tyres, pressure 3·79 bars (55 lb/sq in). Goodyear steerable and self-centering nosewheel with size 6·00-6 tyre, pressure 2·90 bars (42 lb/sq in). Goodyear or Magnaghi hydraulic brakes.

POWER PLANT: Two Avco Lycoming LTP 101-700 turboprop engines, each flat rated at 447·5 kW (600 shp) and driving a Hartzell HC-B3TN-3DL/LT10282-9·5 three-blade constant-speed fully-feathering metal pusher propeller. Fuel in two 212 litre (46·5 Imp gallon) outer-wing main tanks, two 323 litre (71 Imp gallon) wingtip tanks, and a 118 litre (26 Imp gallon) fuselage collector tank; total standard internal fuel capacity 1,188 litres (261 Imp gallons). Auxiliary fuel system available optionally, comprising a 236 litre (52 Imp gallon) fuselage tank, transfer pump and controls; with this installed, total usable fuel capacity is increased to 1,424 litres (313 Imp gallons). Gravity refuelling points in each main tank and tip-tank. Provision for two 177 or 284 litre (39 or 62·5 Imp gallon) underwing drop tanks. Air intakes and propeller blades de-iced by engine exhaust.

ACCOMMODATION: Crew of two on raised flight deck, with dual controls. Aft of flight deck, accommodation consists of a passenger cabin, utility compartment and baggage compartment. Access to flight deck is via passenger/cargo double door on port side, forward of wing, or via individual crew door on each side of flight deck. External access to baggage compartment via port side door aft of wing. Passenger cabin extends from rear of flight deck to bulkhead at wing main spar; fitting of passenger carrying, cargo or other interiors is facilitated by two continuous rails on cabin floor, permitting considerable flexibility in standard or customised interior layouts. Standard seating for eight passengers, with individual lighting, ventilation and oxygen controls. Flight deck can be separated from passenger cabin by a screen. Door in bulkhead at rear of cabin provides access to utility compartment, in which can be fitted a toilet, bar, or mission equipment for certain roles. Entire accommodation is heated, ventilated and soundproofed. Emergency exit forward of wing on starboard side. Windscreen hot-air demisting standard. Windscreen wipers, washers and methanol spray de-icing optional.

SYSTEMS: Hydraulic system, pressure 127 bars (1,840 lb/sq in), for landing gear, flap and brake actuation, nosewheel steering and lock, and (on APH version) actuation of ventral door. Handpump for emergency extension of landing gear. Standard electrical system is 28V DC, supplied by two engine driven starter/generators and a nickel-cadmium battery. External power receptacle. Static or rotary inverters, to supply AC power for avionics and instruments, available optionally. Oxygen system.

AVIONICS: Standard avionics packages available to individual customer's requirements: minimum recommended package includes two VHF com, two VHF nav (VOR/ILS), ADF, ATC transponder, compass system and intercom. Optional avionics include radar, autopilot, navigation system and synthesiser type HF radio.

EQUIPMENT: According to mission configuration. Quickly interchangeable individual seats of various types, bench

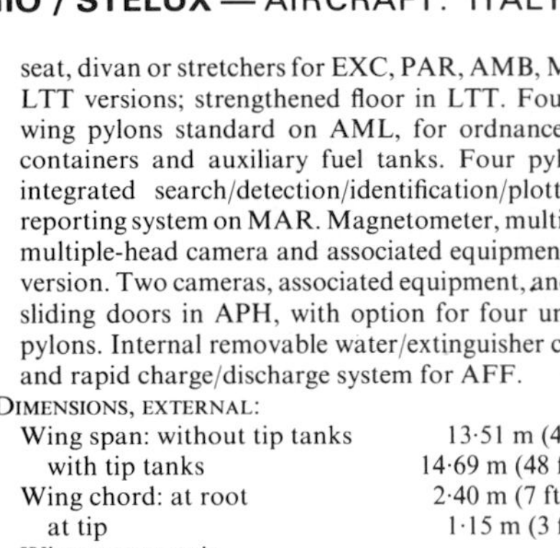

seat, divan or stretchers for EXC, PAR, AMB, MTR and LTT versions; strengthened floor in LTT. Four underwing pylons standard on AML, for ordnance, supply containers and auxiliary fuel tanks. Four pylons and integrated search/detection/identification/plotting and reporting system on MAR. Magnetometer, multiscanner, multiple-head camera and associated equipment in ECS version. Two cameras, associated equipment, and ventral sliding doors in APH, with option for four underwing pylons. Internal removable water/extinguisher container and rapid charge/discharge system for AFF.

DIMENSIONS, EXTERNAL:

Wing span: without tip tanks	13·51 m (44 ft 4 in)
with tip tanks	14·69 m (48 ft 2½ in)
Wing chord: at root	2·40 m (7 ft 10½ in)
at tip	1·15 m (3 ft 9¼ in)
Wing aspect ratio	7·3
Length overall	11·88 m (39 ft 0 in)
Height overall	5·00 m (16 ft 5 in)
Tailplane span	5·10 m (16 ft 9 in)
Wheel track	2·66 m (8 ft 9 in)
Wheelbase	4·71 m (15 ft 5½ in)
Propeller diameter	2·36 m (7 ft 9 in)
Cabin door: Height	1·38 m (4 ft 6 in)
Width	1·28 m (4 ft 2 in)

DIMENSIONS, INTERNAL:

Cabin, incl flight deck: Length	3·20 m (10 ft 6 in)
Max width	1·57 m (5 ft 2 in)
Max height	1·76 m (5 ft 9 in)
Floor area	5·14 m² (55·3 sq ft)
Volume	6·63 m³ (234·1 cu ft)
Utility compartment: Length	0·65 m (2 ft 1½ in)
Max width	1·52 m (5 ft 0 in)
Max height	1·70 m (5 ft 7 in)
Volume	2·27 m³ (80·2 cu ft)
Baggage compartment volume	1·80 m³ (63·6 cu ft)

AREAS:

Wings, gross	26·56 m² (285·9 sq ft)
Ailerons (total)	1·95 m² (21·00 sq ft)
Trailing-edge flaps (total)	2·38 m² (25·60 sq ft)
Fin	1·62 m² (17·44 sq ft)
Rudder, incl tab	1·23 m² (13·24 sq ft)
Tailplane	3·50 m² (37·67 sq ft)
Elevators, incl tabs	1·29 m² (13·88 sq ft)

WEIGHTS AND LOADINGS:

Weight empty, equipped	2,650 kg (5,842 lb)
Max fuel	1,139 kg (2,511 lb)
Max payload	1,073 kg (2,365 lb)
Max T-O weight	4,300 kg (9,480 lb)
Max ramp weight	4,320 kg (9,524 lb)
Max zero-fuel weight	3,800 kg (8,377 lb)
Max landing weight	3,800 kg (8,377 lb)
Max wing loading	162 kg/m² (33·2 lb/sq ft)
Max power loading	4·81 kg/kW (7·9 lb/shp)

PERFORMANCE (at max T-O weight except where indicated):

Never-exceed speed
220 knots (407 km/h; 253 mph) CAS

Max level and max cruising speed at 3,050 m (10,000 ft)
215 knots (400 km/h; 248 mph)

Econ cruising speed at 3,660 m (12,000 ft)
162 knots (300 km/h; 186 mph)

Stalling speed:
flaps and landing gear up
86 knots (160 km/h; 99 mph) CAS
flaps and landing gear down
75 knots (139 km/h; 87 mph) CAS

Max rate of climb at S/L	670 m (2,200 ft)/min
Rate of climb at S/L, one engine out	177 m (580 ft)/min
Service ceiling	8,535 m (28,000 ft)
Service ceiling, one engine out	4,270 m (14,000 ft)
T-O to 15 m (50 ft)	665 m (2,180 ft)
Landing from 15 m (50 ft) at max landing weight	457 m (1,500 ft)

Range, VFR:

with max payload	750 nm (1,390 km; 863 miles)
with max fuel	1,125 nm (2,084 km; 1,295 miles)

STELUX

STELUX AIRCRAFT CORPORATION (Division of Spartaria)

Via Crescini 82c, 35100 Padua
Telephone: (049) 753521
TECHNICAL DIRECTOR: Dipl Spartaco Trevisan
DESIGNER: Ing Sergio Stefanutti, Via Giovanni Severano 33, 00179 Rome
Telephone: (06) 425057

This company is building the prototype of a two-seat glider towing aircraft known as the Trenzo. Its designer is Ing Sergio Stefanutti, well known for his pioneering work in 'tail-first' configurations featuring a nose mounted foreplane with positive incidence and a rear mounted main wing with zero incidence. Elevators of symmetrical section are mounted independently beneath the trailing-edge of the foreplane. This configuration was first tested in 1938 on the small SS.2 and SS.3 lightplanes built by Stabilimento Costruzioni Aeronautiche of Guidonia. Evaluation of these led to the Ambrosini SS.4, the world's first all-metal 'canard' fighter, which first flew in May 1939 and later achieved a maximum speed of 291 knots (540 km/h; 335 mph) on the power of a 716 kW (960 hp) inverted V engine. The Trenzo is Ing Stefanutti's fifth aircraft to have a canard configuration.

STELUX 3esse3 TRENZO

Design of the Trenzo was started in 1979, in response to a request by Dipl Spartaco Trevisan on behalf of the Centro Nazionale di Volo a Vela at Rieti. Ing Sergio Stefanutti proposed a design of canard configuration, named Trenzo after Mr Trevisan and the founder of the US Information Service library in Italy, Mr Renzo. Construction and development was assigned entirely to Mr Trevisan, who was responsible for the completion of a one-quarter scale solid mockup. This subsequently received design approval from the RAI, which on 20 June 1985 authorised construction of a full size prototype. Work on this was initiated in September 1985, and a first flight was anticipated in late 1986 or early 1987.

TYPE: Tandem two-seat light aircraft.

WINGS: Rear-mounted mid-wings of NACA 23012 aerofoil section, with tapered leading-edge and non-swept trailing-edge, have 0° incidence and approx 5° dihedral. Wings, ailerons and endplate fins/winglets are of CFRP.

FOREPLANES: Cantilever CFRP fixed foreplanes, of NACA 64_2-415 section and near-delta planform, at extreme tip of nose, set at 3° incidence with approx 5° anhedral. Elevator (NACA 0009 section; 0° dihedral) below and behind each foreplane trailing-edge.

FUSELAGE: Oval-section semi-monocoque of laminated wood construction, with three main longerons.

LANDING GEAR: Tricycle type, with fully retractable nosewheel and semi-retractable mainwheels. Hydraulic actuation. Cleveland wheels, with tyres size 6·00-6 (main) and 5·00-5 (nose) and Parker disc brakes. Van Sickle (USA) shock absorbers. Mainwheels retract upward into underwing 'trouser' fairings. Inset rudder in rear of each fairing, split vertically to function also as airbrake.

POWER PLANT: One 75 kW (100 hp) Avco Lycoming flat-four engine, mounted at rear of fuselage and driving a Hamilton Standard pusher propeller. Fuel in two fuselage tanks between second cockpit and engine.

ACCOMMODATION: Seats for two persons in tandem under individual framed canopies which open sideways to starboard. Cockpits ventilated.

DIMENSIONS, EXTERNAL:

Wing span	10·50 m (34 ft 5½ in)
Foreplane span	4·00 m (13 ft 1½ in)
Length overall	6·85 m (22 ft 5¾ in)
Fuselage: Length	6·50 m (21 ft 4 in)
Max width	0·70 m (2 ft 3½ in)
Propeller diameter	1·60 m (5 ft 3 in)

AREA:

Wings/foreplane, gross	18·00 m² (193·75 sq ft)

WEIGHT:

Max T-O weight	750 kg (1,653 lb)

PERFORMANCE: No details received

Quarter-scale mockup of the Stefanutti (Stelux) Trenzo two-seat light aircraft

JAPAN

FUJI

FUJI HEAVY INDUSTRIES LTD (Fuji Jukogyo Kabushiki Kaisha)

Subaru Building, 7-2, 1-chome, Nishi-shinjuku, Shinjuku-ku, Tokyo
Telephone: Tokyo (03) 347 2515
Telex: 0 232 2268

CHAIRMAN OF THE BOARD: Sadamichi Sasaki

PRESIDENT: Toshihiro Tajima

UTSUNOMIYA MANUFACTURING DIVISION: 1-11, Yonan 1-chome, Utsunomiya, Tochigi 320
Telephone: (0286) 58 1111

UTSUNOMIYA MANUFACTURING DIVISION MANAGEMENT:

Aircraft Division

Yoshio Akiyama (Executive Managing Director)
Yasuo Kaneta (Director, and General Manager of Aircraft Division)
Johei Manda (General Manager, Commercial Business)
Yasuyuki Kogure (General Manager, Marketing and Sales, Defence Programmes)

Utsunomiya Manufacturing Division

Yasumasa Honda (General Manager of Aircraft Plant)
Akitoshi Nagao (General Manager, Aircraft Engineering Division)

Fuji Heavy Industries Ltd was established on 15 July 1953. It is a successor to the Nakajima aircraft company, which was established in 1917 and built 25,935 aircraft up to the end of the Second World War.

The present Utsunomiya Manufacturing Division (Aircraft and Rolling Stock Plants) occupies a site of 488,138 m² (5,254,270 sq ft) including a floor area of 172,158 m² (1,853,090 sq ft) and in 1986 employed 3,041 people.

Under licence from Cessna, Fuji produced 22 L-19E Bird Dog observation aircraft for the Japan Ground Self-Defence Force. Under licence from Beech, it built also the Beechcraft Mentor, and several modified versions of the Mentor designated LM-1 Nikko, LM-2, KM, KM-2, KM-2B and TL-1, as detailed in previous editions of *Jane's*. The KM-2D, a turboprop version of the KM-2, is under development.

Fuji is currently producing the Bell Model 204/205 series and AH-1S HueyCobra helicopters, as described in this entry. It is building wing main assemblies for the Lockheed P-3C Orion maritime patrol aircraft being manufactured under licence in Japan for the JMSDF, and main landing gear doors and some titanium airframe parts for Japanese built McDonnell Douglas F-15J fighters delivered to the JASDF. As a part of Japan's YX civil transport aircraft programme, Fuji is responsible, under subcontract through the JADC (Japan Aircraft Development Corporation), for building wing/fuselage body fairings and main landing gear doors for the Boeing 767 jet transport.

FUJI FA-200 AERO SUBARU

Production of the FA-200 began in March 1968, and 299 had been completed by 18 March 1985, of which more than 170 were for export. No further examples had been sold by early 1986, but the aircraft remains available to order. A full description of all versions can be found in the 1979-80 *Jane's*.

FUJI KM-2D

In 1984 Fuji refitted a company owned KM-2 with an Allison 250-B17D turboprop in place of the Avco Lycoming IGSO-480 piston engine. First flight in KM-2D form took place on 28 June 1984, and JCAB certification (Aerobatic and Utility categories) was gained in February 1985. Thirty-two KM-2Bs are currently in service with the JMSDF, and Fuji is proposing that this fleet be re-engined with turboprops for redelivery from 1988.

Fuji KM-2D prototype conversion of KM-2 to turboprop power

The KM-2B tandem two-seat trainer was last described in full in the 1981-82 *Jane's*; the prototype KM-2D (see accompanying photograph) has the four-seat cabin of the original KM-2, which was described in the 1969-70 edition. Main differences in the KM-2D are as follows:

POWER PLANT: One Allison 250-B17D turboprop engine, flat rated at 261 kW (350 shp), driving a Hartzell HC-B3TF-7A/T10173-18 three-blade propeller. Total fuel capacity 266 litres (70 US gallons), comprising one 95 litre (25 US gallon) and one 38 litre (10 US gallon) tank in each wing. Oil capacity 10 litres (2·7 US gallons).

SYSTEM: Electrical system (30V DC) powered by 150A starter/generator and a 24V 22Ah nickel-cadmium battery.

AVIONICS: King VHF, VOR, ADF, ATC transponder and DME.

DIMENSIONS, EXTERNAL:

Wing span	10·04 m (32 ft 11¼ in)
Length overall	8·43 m (27 ft 8 in)
Height overall	2·96 m (9 ft 8½ in)
Propeller diameter	2·12 m (6 ft 11½ in)

AREAS: As for KM-2 except:

Fin	2·00 m² (21·53 sq ft)
Rudder, incl tab	0·66 m² (7·10 sq ft)

WEIGHTS AND PERFORMANCE:
No details received

FUJI-BELL 204B-2 and UH-1H

Japanese designation: HU-1H

Fuji is manufacturing Bell Model 204B-2 and UH-1H helicopters under sublicence from Mitsui and Co Ltd, Bell's Japanese licensee. The first 204B arrived in Japan in kit form in May 1962 for assembly, and 34 commercial 204Bs were built before being replaced by the current B-2 model in 1974.

Fuji developed the higher powered Model 204B-2 in October 1973. Powered by a 1,044 kW (1,400 shp) Kawasaki built Avco Lycoming KT5313B turboshaft engine, it has the same basic airframe and dynamic components as the 204B, but has a tractor tail rotor. The first example of this version was delivered in early 1974, and 18 had been built by March 1986.

Following the delivery of 90 HU-1Bs (Japanese military version of the 204B) to the Japan Ground Self-Defence Force by early 1973, Fuji production continued with the UH-1H (military version of the Bell 205 and known in Japan as the HU-1H), of which the first example flew for the first time on 17 July 1973; 94 had been ordered by March 1986, and a further four had been approved in the FY 1986 budget.

The Fuji-Bell HU-1H has the same airframe and dynamic components as the Bell built UH-1H, but like the Fuji 204B-2 has a tractor tail rotor and 1,044 kW (1,400 shp) Kawasaki built Avco Lycoming T53-K-13B engine.

The following details apply to the standard Fuji-Bell 204B-2 and HU-1H:

DIMENSIONS, EXTERNAL:

Main rotor diameter	14·63 m (48 ft 0 in)
Tail rotor diameter	2·59 m (8 ft 6 in)
Length overall, tail rotor turning:	
204B-2	13·61 m (44 ft 8 in)
HU-1H	13·67 m (44 ft 10 in)
Length of fuselage: 204B-2	12·31 m (40 ft 4¾ in)
HU-1H	12·37 m (40 ft 7 in)
Height overall, tail rotor turning	4·42 m (14 ft 6 in)
Height to top of rotor head:	
204B-2	3·18 m (10 ft 5¼ in)
HU-1H	3·98 m (13 ft 0¾ in)
Max width over landing skids:	
204B-2	2·64 m (8 ft 8 in)
HU-1H	2·60 m (8 ft 6½ in)
Tailplane span	2·84 m (9 ft 4 in)

AREAS:

Main rotor disc	168·1 m² (1,809·5 sq ft)
Tail rotor disc	5·27 m² (56·75 sq ft)

WEIGHTS AND LOADINGS:

Weight empty: 204B-2	2,177 kg (4,800 lb)
HU-1H	2,390 kg (5,270 lb)
Max T-O weight:	
204B-2, internal load	3,855 kg (8,500 lb)
204B-2, external load	4,309 kg (9,500 lb)
HU-1H	4,309 kg (9,500 lb)
Max disc loading	25·6 kg/m² (5·25 lb/sq ft)
Max power loading	4·13 kg/kW (6·78 lb/shp)

PERFORMANCE (at max T-O weight):

Max level and max cruising speed
110 knots (204 km/h; 127 mph)

Max rate of climb at S/L:

204B-2	591 m (1,940 ft)/min
HU-1H	488 m (1,600 ft)/min
Service ceiling: 204B-2	5,790 m (19,000 ft)
HU-1H	3,840 m (12,600 ft)
Hovering ceiling IGE: 204B-2	4,635 m (15,200 ft)
HU-1H	4,145 m (13,600 ft)
Hovering ceiling OGE: 204B-2	3,200 m (10,500 ft)
HU-1H	335 m (1,100 ft)
Range at S/L: 204B-2	207 nm (383 km; 238 miles)
HU-1H	252 nm (467 km; 290 miles)

FUJI-BELL AH-1S

In FY 1982 Fuji was selected as prime contractor for a licence manufacturing programme for Bell AH-1S HueyCobra anti-armour helicopters for the JGSDF; Kawasaki is delivering the T53-K-703 engines for these aircraft. The JGSDF had previously purchased two Bell built examples in 1977 and 1978 for operational evaluation.

Current JGSDF plans are to purchase a total of 73 AH-1S. These will equip four anti-tank helicopter squadrons, with a surplus to provide attrition replacements and aircraft for training. Orders have so far been placed for 38 aircraft (12 in FY 1982, 5 in 1983, 5 in 1984, 8 in 1985 and 8 in 1986) of which the first was flown for the first time on 2 July 1984. All 38 are expected to be delivered by the end of FY 1988. The first squadron is based at Obihiro on Hokkaido.

Latest version of Fuji built AH-1S HueyCobra for the JGSDF *(Katsumi Hinata)*

KAWASAKI

KAWASAKI JUKOGYO KABUSHIKI KAISHA (Kawasaki Heavy Industries Ltd)

1-18 Nakamachi-Dori, 2-chome, Chuo-ku, Kobe

TOKYO AND AIRCRAFT GROUP OFFICE: World Trade Center Building, 4-1, Hamamatsu-cho 2-chome, Minato-ku, Tokyo

Telephone: Tokyo (03) 435 2971

Telex: 242-4371 KAWASAKI HEAVY TOKYO

CHAIRMAN: Zenji Umeda

PRESIDENT: Kenko Hasegawa

EXECUTIVE VICE-PRESIDENTS:
Yutaka Onishi
Teruaki Yamada

Aircraft Group

EXECUTIVE MANAGING DIRECTOR AND SENIOR GENERAL MANAGER: Masahiko Iwata

DIRECTOR AND DEPUTY SENIOR GENERAL MANAGER: Kanji Sonoda

WORKS: Gifu

With effect from 1 April 1969, Kawasaki Aircraft Co Ltd was amalgamated with the Kawasaki Dockyard Co Ltd and the Kawasaki Rolling Stock Mfg Co Ltd, to form Kawasaki Heavy Industries Ltd. The Aircraft Division of the former Kawasaki Aircraft Co Ltd, which employs some 3,700 people, continues its activities as the Aircraft Group of this company. Kawasaki has a 30·2% holding in Nippi (which see).

In addition to extensive overhaul work, Kawasaki has built many US aircraft under licence since 1955, including 48 Lockheed P2V-7 (P-2H) Neptune anti-submarine aircraft and 239 Bell Model 47 helicopters, plus another 211 Model KH-4 helicopters developed from the Bell 47 by its own design staff. From the Neptune it developed the P-2J anti-submarine aircraft, of which it delivered one prototype and 82 production examples (see 1978-79 *Jane's*). Two P-2Js have been converted to UP-2J configuration with equipment for target towing, ECM training and drone launch operations (see illustration in 1985-86 *Jane's*). Two others have been converted as EP-2J electronic intelligence (elint) aircraft, equipped with HLR-105 and HLR-106 systems. All four serve with No. 81 Squadron (3rd Fleet Air Wing) at Iwakuni. One P2V-7 was converted by Kawasaki, under Japan Defence Agency contract, as an experimental variable-stability aircraft (see 1981-82 *Jane's*).

Kawasaki is developing, as prime contractor, the Japan Defence Agency's new T-4 intermediate trainer to succeed both the Lockheed T-33A (of which Kawasaki built 210 under licence in 1956-59) and the Fuji T-1. The company has developed, jointly with MBB of West Germany, the BK 117 twin-engined multi-purpose helicopter described in the International section.

Kawasaki is prime contractor for licence production of the Lockheed P-3C/Update II Orion, 100 of which are to be purchased by the JMSDF. Sixty have so far been ordered. The first three (US built) P-3Cs were handed over to the JMSDF in April 1981. The next four were assembled by Kawasaki from knocked-down assemblies; the first of these made its initial flight on 17 March 1982, and was delivered on 27 May that year to Fleet Squadron 51 at Atsugi Air Base, where two squadrons are now based, each with eight aircraft. The remaining 53 are being built almost entirely in Japan, and the third P-3C squadron, at Hachinoe, was due to be equipped in 1985. Kawasaki is responsible for building the centre-fuselages, and for final assembly and flight testing. Participants in the programme include Fuji, Mitsubishi, Nippi and Shin Meiwa for the airframe, and IHI for the engines. Kawasaki is also a subcontractor for rear fuselages, wings and tail units of the McDonnell Douglas F-15J Eagles being licence built in Japan by Mitsubishi (which see). As a part of Japan's YX civil transport aircraft programme, Kawasaki is subcontracted to build forward and mid fuselage sections, and wing ribs, for the Boeing 767 jet transport. The company has been nominated by the JASDF as prime contractor for maintenance and support of its Grumman E-2C Hawkeye AEW and Lockheed C-130 Hercules transport aircraft.

Kawasaki has exclusive rights to manufacture and sell the twin-engined Boeing Vertol 107 Model II helicopter and its own KV107IIA development of it. McDonnell Douglas MD 500 series light observation helicopters are also being manufactured by Kawasaki under a licence agreement concluded in October 1967. By 1 April 1986 a total of 147 KV107 helicopters had been delivered to customers in Japan and other countries including Saudi Arabia, Sweden, Thailand and the USA; and approx 240 MD 500s to government and commercial operators in Japan. The company is also now co-producing Boeing Vertol CH-47 Chinooks for the Japanese armed forces, as described in this entry.

Kawasaki and Fuji are prime contractors for Japanese assembly of engines and airframes respectively for Bell AH-1S gunship helicopters for the JGSDF, as detailed under the Fuji entry in this section.

Kawasaki is engaged in missile development and production; its aero engine activities are described in the appropriate section of this edition.

KAWASAKI C-1 MODIFICATIONS

The National Aerospace Laboratory (see NAL entry) has built an experimental quiet STOL aircraft known as the **Asuka**, utilising the airframe of a C-1. Another JASDF C-1 was retrofitted by the Technical Research and Development Institute of the Japan Defence Agency as a flying testbed which was used from August 1982 to flight test the XF3 turbofan engine for the Kawasaki XT-4. The same aircraft was to be used to flight test the FJR710 high bypass turbofan engine which powers the NAL Asuka.

Under a March 1983 Defence Agency contract, Kawasaki has modified the 21st production C-1 (JASDF 78-1021) for evaluation as an ECM training aircraft. Known as the **C-1ECM**, it first flew on 3 December 1984 and was handed over to the JASDF's Air Proving Wing in late January 1985 for evaluation. Beginning on 17 April 1985 and continuing until March 1986, the Air Proving Wing expected to conduct about 100 test flights before transferring the C-1ECM to the JASDF's Electronic Warfare Training Unit. Equipped with a domestically built TRDI/Mitsubishi Electric XJ/ALQ-5 ECM system, the C-1ECM has large flat bulbous nose and tail radomes, a blister on each side of the forward fuselage aft of the flight deck side windows, others on each side of the rear fuselage, and two antennae beneath the fuselage.

A full description of the standard C-1 transport can be found in the 1981-82 *Jane's*.

KAWASAKI T-4

Kawasaki was named by the Japan Defence Agency on 4 September 1981 as the prime contractor to develop a new intermediate trainer to replace Lockheed T-33As and Fuji T-1A/Bs in service with the JASDF. The designation XT-4 was allocated officially to the type during its development.

Current plans call for procurement of about 200 production T-4s, for pilot training, liaison and other duties. Funding was approved in the FY 1983 defence budget to procure three flying prototypes and a static test aircraft. A fourth prototype and fatigue test aircraft were approved for FY 1984. The first 12 production aircraft were approved in the FY 1986 defence budget.

The T-4 is based on Kawasaki's KA-850 design, by an engineering team led by Mr Kohki Isozaki. Mitsubishi (centre fuselage and engine air intakes) and Fuji (rear fuselage, wings and tail unit) each have a 30 per cent share in the production programme. Kawasaki, as prime contractor, builds the forward fuselage, and is responsible for final assembly and flight test.

The T-4 was required to have high subsonic manoeuvrability, and to be able to carry external loads under the wings and fuselage. Basic design studies were completed in October 1982, and detail design by the Spring of 1984. Subassembly of the first XT-4 prototype began in April 1984, followed by the second, third and fourth in July, August and December 1984. The first of these (56-5601) was rolled out on 17 April 1985 and made its first flight on 29 July; the prototypes were delivered in December 1985, and February, May and July 1986. The static test aircraft was delivered in February 1985 and the fatigue test aircraft

Kawasaki C-1ECM electronic warfare training aircraft *(S. Akatsuka)*

in the following October. Flight testing and operational evaluation will continue until March 1988. Production was due to begin during FY 1986.

Type: Tandem two-seat intermediate jet trainer and liaison aircraft.

Wings: Cantilever mid-wing monoplane, of supercritical section, with anhedral from roots. Sweepback 27° 30′ at quarter-chord. Extended chord on outer panels, giving leading-edge 'dog-tooth'. Flaps of advanced design. Teijin aileron servo-actuators.

Fuselage: Conventional semi-monocoque fail-safe structure, mainly of aluminium alloy, with minimal use of titanium in critical areas. Twin airbrakes at rear.

Tail Unit: Cantilever structure, with sweepback on all surfaces. All-moving anhedral tailplane, mid-mounted on rear fuselage, has aluminium alloy spars, ribs and skins (except for trailing-edge skins of CFRP) and a Nomex honeycomb core. Fin and rudder are of CFRP construction. Rudder and tailplane servo-actuators by Mitsubishi.

Landing Gear: Sumitomo hydraulically retractable tricycle type, with oleo-pneumatic shock absorber in each unit. Single wheel and low pressure tyre on each unit. Main units have Bendix (Kayaba) wheels and brakes, and Hydro-Aire (Sumitomo) anti-skid units, and retract forward and inward. Steerable Kayaba nose unit retracts forward.

Power Plant: Two 16·28 kN (3,660 lb st) Ishikawajima-Harima XF3-30 turbofan engines, mounted side by side in centre-fuselage. Internal fuel (total 2,271 litres; 600 US gallons) in wing tanks and three Japanese built Goodyear rubber bag tanks in fuselage. Provision to carry one 454 litre (120 US gallon) Shin Meiwa drop tank on each underwing pylon.

Accommodation: Crew of two in tandem in pressurised and air-conditioned cockpit with wraparound windscreen and one-piece sideways (to starboard) opening canopy. Dual controls standard; rear (instructor's) seat elevated 27 cm (10·6 in). Stencel SIIIS-3ER ejection seats and Teledyne McCormick Selph canopy severance system, licence built by Daicel Chemical Industries. Baggage compartment in centre of fuselage, with external access via door on port side.

Systems: Shimadzu air-conditioning system; cockpit pressurisation system; flight control system with Lucas (Sumitomo) Q-feel; hydraulic system; Clifton Precision (Tokyo Aircraft Instruments) onboard oxygen generating system.

Avionics: Kaiser head-up display, Sperry air data computer, Honeywell AHRS, Teledyne Electronics SIF, all built under licence in Japan. Domestic avionics include Mitsubishi Electric UHF com, Nippon Electric Tacan, and Nagano intercom.

Armament: No built-in armament. Two Nippi pylons under each wing, and one under fuselage, for carriage of drop tanks, target towing equipment, or ECM/chaff dispenser/air sampling pods. In weapons training role, can carry a gun pod, three or four 500 lb practice bombs, or infra-red homing air-to-air missiles.

Dimensions, external (approx):
- Wing span: 9·90 m (32 ft 5¾ in)
- Length overall: 13·00 m (42 ft 8 in)
- Height overall: 4·60 m (15 ft 1 in)

Area (approx):
- Wings, gross: 21·6 m² (232·5 sq ft)

Weights:
- Weight empty: 3,700 kg (8,157 lb)
- T-O weight, 'clean': 5,500 kg (12,125 lb)
- Max design T-O weight: 7,500 kg (16,535 lb)

Performance (estimated, in 'clean' configuration. A: at weight of 4,700 kg; 10,361 lb with 50% fuel; B: at T-O weight of 5,500 kg; 12,125 lb):
- Max level speed: A — Mach 0·9
- Max level speed at S/L: A — 560 knots (1,038 km/h; 645 mph)
- Cruising speed: B — Mach 0·75
- Stalling speed: A — 90 knots (167 km/h; 104 mph)
- Max rate of climb at S/L: B — 3,050 m (10,000 ft)/min
- Service ceiling: B — 15,240 m (50,000 ft)
- T-O run, 35°C: B — 549 m (1,800 ft)
- Landing run: B — 670 m (2,200 ft)
- Range (B) at Mach 0·75 cruising speed:
  - internal fuel only — 700 nm (1,297 km; 806 miles)
  - with two 120 US gallon drop tanks — 900 nm (1,668 km; 1,036 miles)
- *g* limits: +7·33/−3

KAWASAKI (BOEING VERTOL) KV107IIA

Kawasaki has exclusive rights to manufacture and sell the Boeing Vertol 107 Model II helicopter. The first KV107 to be produced by Kawasaki under this licence agreement flew for the first time in May 1962.

In 1965, Kawasaki obtained worldwide sales rights in the helicopter from The Boeing Company's Vertol Division. In November 1965, it was awarded a type certificate for the KV107 by the FAA. Details of the initial production KV107II models have been given in the 1984-85 and earlier editions of *Jane's*.

The improved KV107IIA, introduced in 1968, is powered by General Electric CT58-140-1 or Ishikawajima-Harima CT58-IHI-140-1 turboshaft engines which give improved

Lockheed P-3C Orion for the JMSDF, assembled by Kawasaki

First prototype Kawasaki XT-4 twin-turbofan intermediate trainer

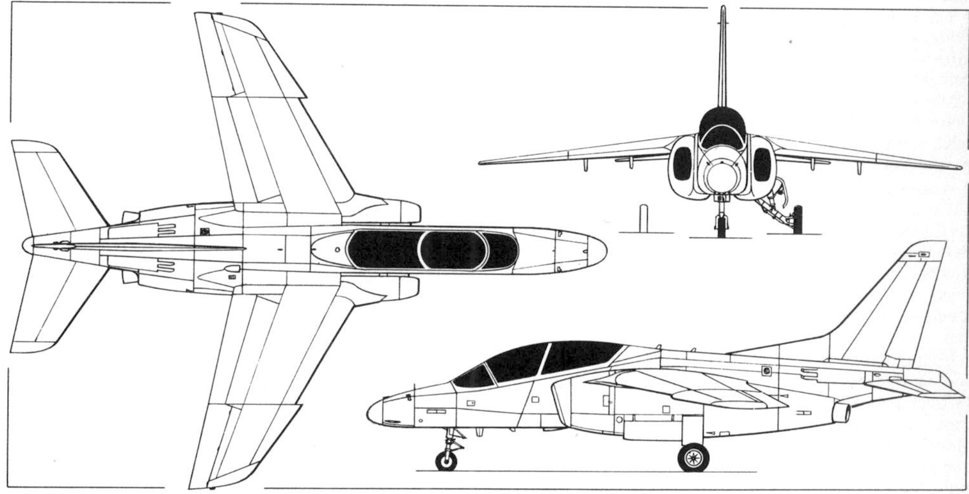
Kawasaki T-4 trainer (two Ishikawajima-Harima XF3-30 turbofans) *(Pilot Press)*

Camouflaged Kawasaki KV107IIA-4 of the JGSDF, with extended-range fuel tanks on fuselage sides

performance during VTOL and in 'hot and high' conditions. A prototype (JA9509) was converted from a standard KV107II-2 and first flown on 3 April 1968. Type approval was granted by the JCAB on 26 September 1968 and by the FAA on 15 January 1969.

The following versions of the KV107IIA have been produced:

KV107IIA-2. Basic airline helicopter. Prototype currently used as a company test aircraft. Two delivered (May 1969 and January 1980) to Aircraft Inc.

KV107IIA-3. Mine countermeasures (MCM) helicopter for JMSDF with minesweeping and retrieval equipment, extended range fuel tanks, towing hook and cargo sling. Seven delivered to 111th Air Wing of the JMSDF.

KV107IIA-4. Tactical cargo/troop transport for JGSDF, with foldable seats for 26 troops or 15 casualty litters. Strengthened floor for carrying heavy vehicles. Total of 18 delivered, including four fitted with extended-range fuel tanks.

KV107IIA-5. Long range search and rescue helicopter for JASDF. Total of 22 delivered by early 1986; five more approved in FY 1985 budget and four in FY 1986. Extended-range fuel tank each side of fuselage, making total capacity 3,785 litres (1,000 US gallons). Extensive nav/com equipment, four searchlights, domed observation window and rescue hoist. Eighteen aircraft have a Kawasaki/Boeing automatic flight control system.

KV107IIA-17. Long range passenger and cargo transport version for Metropolitan Police Department; one delivered in February 1973. Cabin divided into two compartments: front section with 12 passenger seats, rear section capable of accommodating 2,268 kg (5,000 lb) of cargo, six stretcher patients or 12 passengers.

KV107IIA-SM-1. Firefighting version for Saudi Arabian Ministry of the Interior; seven delivered. All can be fitted with specially designed equipment for various forms of firefighting (foam agent, chemical powder, water, and co-ordinated firefighting). For self-ferry flights the SM-1, 2 and 4 can be fitted with an internally mounted 1,893 litre (500 US gallon) auxiliary fuel tank.

KV107IIA-SM-2. Rescue and aeromedical version for Saudi Arabian Ministry of the Interior, with external rescue hoist, medical equipment, stretcher kit and other rescue gear; 303 litre (80 US gallon) additional fuel tank can be mounted on each side of fuselage. Four delivered.

KV107IIA-SM-3. De luxe VIP transport version for Saudi Arabian Ministry of the Interior. Two delivered.

KV107IIA-SM-4. Air ambulance version for Saudi Arabian Ministry of the Interior, with survival and first aid equipment. Three delivered.

The description which follows applies to the commercial KV107IIA-2, except where indicated:

TYPE: Twin-engined transport helicopter.

ROTOR SYSTEM: Two three-blade rotors in tandem, rotating in opposite directions. Each blade is made up of a steel D spar to which is bonded a trailing-edge box constructed of aluminium ribs and glassfibre or aluminium skin.

ROTOR DRIVE: Power is transmitted from each engine through individually-overrunning clutches into the rear transmission, which combines the engine outputs, thereby providing a single power output to the interconnecting shaft which enables both rotors to be driven by either engine.

FUSELAGE: Basically square-section semi-monocoque structure built primarily of high strength bare and Alclad aluminium alloy. Transverse bulkheads and built-up frames support transmission, power plant and landing gear. Loading ramp forms undersurface of upswept rear fuselage on utility and military models. Baggage container replaces ramp on airliner version. Fuselage is sealed to permit operation from water.

LANDING GEAR: Non-retractable tricycle type, with twin wheels on all three units. Oleo-pneumatic shock absorbers. Tubeless tyres, size 18 × 5·5, pressure 10·34 bars (150 lb/sq in), on all wheels. Disc brakes. Wheel/ski gear optional.

POWER PLANT: Two 1,044 kW (1,400 shp) General Electric CT58-140-1 or Ishikawajima-Harima CT58-IHI-140-1 turboshaft engines (max continuous rating 932 kW; 1,250 shp), mounted side by side at base of rear rotor pylon. Fuel tanks in sponsons, capacity 1,324 litres (350 US gallons) standard. Extended-range fuel tank on each side of fuselage of KV107IIA-4/5, increasing total capacity to 3,785 litres (1,000 US gallons). Other versions have provision for 632 litre (167 US gallon) auxiliary tank or 3,929 litre (1,038 US gallon) extended range tank in cabin.

ACCOMMODATION: Standard accommodation for two pilots, stewardess and 25 passengers in airliner version. Seats in eight rows, in pairs on port side and single seats on starboard side (two pairs at rear of cabin) with central aisle. Airliner fitted with parcel rack and a rollout baggage container, with capacity of approximately 680 kg (1,500 lb), located in underside of rear fuselage. Ramp of utility model is power operated on the ground or in flight and can be removed or left open to permit carriage of extra-long cargo.

AVIONICS AND EQUIPMENT: Standard avionics include stability augmentation system (SAS) and automatic speed trim system (AST). Optional avionics include automatic stabilisation equipment (ASE); automatic flight control system (AFCS); Doppler radar; radio altimeter; HF, VHF and UHF radio; ADF; VOR/ILS; Tacan; compass system and attitude director indicator system; and intercom system.

DIMENSIONS, EXTERNAL:
- Rotor diameter (each) — 15·24 m (50 ft 0 in)
- Length overall, both rotors turning — 25·40 m (83 ft 4 in)
- Length of fuselage — 13·59 m (44 ft 7 in)
- Height to top of rear rotor head — 5·13 m (16 ft 10 in)
- Wheel track (c/l of shock struts) — 3·94 m (12 ft 11 in)
- Width over mainwheels — 4·42 m (14 ft 6 in)
- Wheelbase — 7·59 m (24 ft 11 in)
- Passenger door (fwd): Height — 1·60 m (5 ft 3 in)
  - Width — 0·91 m (3 ft 0 in)

DIMENSIONS, INTERNAL:
- Cabin, excl flight deck:
  - Length — 7·37 m (24 ft 2 in)
  - Normal width — 1·83 m (6 ft 0 in)
  - Max width — 2·01 m (6 ft 7 in)
  - Max height — 1·83 m (6 ft 0 in)
  - Floor area — 13·47 m² (145 sq ft)
  - Volume (usable) — 24·5 m³ (865 cu ft)

AREAS:
- Rotor blades (each) — 3·48 m² (37·50 sq ft)
- Rotor discs (total) — 364·6 m² (3,925 sq ft)

WEIGHTS AND LOADINGS:
- Weight empty, equipped — 5,250 kg (11,576 lb)
- Max payload (at 8,618 kg; 19,000 lb T-O and landing weight) — 3,172 kg (6,993 lb)
- Fuel weight:
  - standard sponson tanks — 1,032 kg (2,275 lb)
  - auxiliary tank — 493 kg (1,087 lb)
  - extended range tank — 3,061 kg (6,748 lb)
- Max T-O and landing weight — 8,618 kg (19,000 lb) *or* 9,706 kg (21,400 lb)
- Cabin floor loading (cargo):
  - standard — 976 kg/m² (200 lb/sq ft)
  - optional — 1,464 kg/m² (300 lb/sq ft)
- Max disc loading — 23·6 kg/m² (4·84 lb/sq ft)
- Max power loading — 4·62 kg/kW (7·6 lb/shp)

PERFORMANCE (A: KV107IIA-2 at 8,618 kg; 19,000 lb AUW):
- Never-exceed speed — 146 knots (270 km/h; 168 mph)
- Max speed at S/L, normal rated power — 137 knots (254 km/h; 158 mph)
- Cruising speed at 1,525 m (5,000 ft) — 130 knots (241 km/h; 150 mph)
- Max rate of climb at S/L — 625 m (2,050 ft)/min
- Max vertical rate of climb at S/L — 381 m (1,250 ft)/min
- Service ceiling — 5,180 m (17,000 ft)
- Service ceiling, one engine out — 1,740 m (5,700 ft)
- Hovering ceiling: IGE — 3,565 m (11,700 ft)
  - OGE — 2,680 m (8,800 ft)
- Min landing area: Length — 38 m (126 ft)
  - Width — 23 m (75 ft)
- T-O to 15 m (50 ft) — 131 m (430 ft)
- Landing from 15 m (50 ft), one engine out — 84 m (275 ft)
- Range: standard fuel — 192 nm (357 km; 222 miles)
  - max fuel — 592 nm (1,097 km; 682 miles)

KAWASAKI (BOEING VERTOL) CH-47 CHINOOK

JASDF/JGSDF designation: CH-47J

The FY 1984 defence budget approved the purchase of three Boeing Vertol CH-47 Chinook helicopters: two for the JGSDF and one for the JASDF, which have eventual requirements for 39 and 15 respectively. The first two aircraft, delivered in Spring 1986, were US built, the third was delivered in CKD (component knocked down) form for assembly in Japan. Kawasaki has been granted a licence for local manufacture of Chinooks ordered for the Japanese services; the Japanese version is generally similar to the CH-47D, and is designated CH-47J. Seven more CH-47Js (three for the JASDF and four for the JGSDF) were approved in the FY 1986 defence budget.

KAWASAKI (MCDONNELL DOUGLAS) MODEL 500D

JGSDF/JMSDF designation: OH-6D

The first Model 369D (500D) built by Kawasaki under licence from Hughes (now McDonnell Douglas) Helicopters was flown for the first time on 2 December 1977; JCAB Normal category certification was awarded on 20 April 1978. Eight Model 500Ds had been delivered for civil operation in Japan by March 1986. The JGSDF ordered 65 as OH-6Ds, 58 of which had been delivered by the end of March 1986; purchase of a further 12 approved for FY 1986. The OH-6D was also selected by the JMSDF to replace its Bell 47G-2As in the training role. Five were ordered, all of which had been delivered by 1 January 1986.

Boeing Vertol CH-47J Chinook, now being assembled under licence by Kawasaki

Kawasaki (McDonnell Douglas) OH-6D light helicopter of the JGSDF

MITSUBISHI

MITSUBISHI JUKOGYO KABUSHIKI KAISHA (Mitsubishi Heavy Industries Ltd)

5-1, Marunouchi 2-chome, Chiyoda-ku, Tokyo 100
Telephone: Tokyo (03) 212 3111
Telex: J22282 and J22443
NAGOYA AIRCRAFT WORKS: 10, Oye-cho, Minato-ku, Nagoya 455
CHAIRMAN OF BOARD OF DIRECTORS: Masao Kanamori
PRESIDENT: Yotaro Iida
EXECUTIVE VICE-PRESIDENTS:
Nobuaki Kunimura
Riichiro Kuroki
Toshio Sakashita
MANAGING DIRECTOR AND GENERAL MANAGER OF AIRCRAFT AND SPECIAL VEHICLE HEADQUARTERS: Yoshio Sasaki
DEPUTY GENERAL MANAGER OF AIRCRAFT AND SPECIAL VEHICLE HEADQUARTERS: Shigeichi Tanaka
GENERAL MANAGER, AIRCRAFT AND SPECIAL VEHICLE ADMINISTRATION DEPARTMENT: Hiroshi Shibata
GENERAL MANAGER, AIRCRAFT DEPARTMENT: Toshiro Murai
GENERAL MANAGER, AIRCRAFT EQUIPMENT DEPARTMENT: Masaya Fujusaki
GENERAL MANAGER, GUIDED WEAPON SYSTEM DEPARTMENT: Mitsuo Tomita
GENERAL MANAGER, SPACE SYSTEM DEPARTMENT: Masahiko Hamada
GENERAL MANAGER, SPECIAL VEHICLE DEPARTMENT: Taizo Yoshida
GENERAL MANAGER, BUSINESS AIRCRAFT DEPARTMENT: Seiichiro Goto
GENERAL MANAGER, NAGOYA AIRCRAFT WORKS: Takaaki Yamada

Mitsubishi F-15J Eagle of 204 Sqn, 7th Air Wing, Japan Air Self-Defence Force *(Katsumi Hinata)*

Mitsubishi T-2 tandem-seat advanced trainer from Hyakuri Air Base *(Katsumi Hinata)*

Mitsubishi began the production of aircraft in the present Oye plant of its Nagoya Engineering Works in 1921, and manufactured a total of 18,000 aircraft of approximately 100 different types during the 24 years prior to the end of the Second World War in 1945. The company was also one of the leading aero engine manufacturers in Japan, and produced a total of 52,000 engines in the 1,000-2,500 hp range. The conclusion of the Peace Treaty in 1952 enabled the aircraft industry in Japan to recommence, and in December of that year the company constructed its present Komaki South plant. This factory, together with Mitsubishi's Oye, Daiko and Komaki North plants, was later consolidated as Nagoya Aircraft Works, with a combined floor area of 552,463 m² (5,946,666 sq ft).

By 1990 the Japan Defence Agency plans to procure a total of 187 McDonnell Douglas F-15 Eagles, including 14 US built aircraft (two single-seat F-15Js and 12 two-seat F-15DJs) supplied as Foreign Military Sales. The first two US built F-15s were followed by eight assembled in Japan from US supplied knocked-down assemblies. First aircraft of the latter batch flew on 26 August 1981 and was delivered on 11 December that year. First JASDF F-15 squadron was No. 202 (5th Air Wing) at Nyutabaru, which was activated in December 1982 with 20 F-15J/DJs. Other units now equipped are No. 203 Squadron of the 2nd Air Wing at Chitose, Hokkaido; No. 204 (7th Air Wing, at Kyakuri); and No. 205. Mitsubishi is building the forward and centre-fuselages, and is responsible for final assembly and flight testing. Participants in the programme include Fuji (landing gear doors), Kawasaki (wings and tail assembly), Nippi (pylons and missile launchers), Shin Meiwa (drop tanks), Sumitomo (landing gear), and IHI (engines). The J/ALQ-8 ECM and radar warning systems of all these aircraft are of Japanese design and manufacture. A total of 136 F-15J/DJs had been funded up to FY 1986; approx 60 had been delivered by the Spring of 1986.

Mitsubishi holds licence agreements to manufacture the Sikorsky S-61, S-61B (HSS-2/2A/2B) and S-61A helicopters. Between 1 April 1984 and 31 March 1985 Mitsubishi delivered five HSS-2Bs (for ASW) to the JMSDF. By the latter date it had delivered to the JMSDF, for ASW and rescue, 138 helicopters of the HSS-2 series and 11 S-61As, out of a total order for 154 HSS-2/2A/2B/S-61As. Thirteen HSS-2Bs and one S-61A were approved in the FY 1986 budget. Under the FY 1985 budget, Mitsubishi received funding to begin design work on the XSH-60J, a development of the Sikorsky SH-60B Seahawk ASW helicopter for the JMSDF.

Mitsubishi is prime contractor for the T-2 supersonic trainer and F-1 close support combat aircraft for the JASDF, with Fuji, Nippi and Shin Meiwa as principal subcontractors. It is producing forward and rear fuselages for the Lockheed P-3C Orions ordered by the JMSDF, under subcontract to Kawasaki (which see). As a part of Japan's YX civil transport aircraft programme, Mitsubishi is subcontracted, through the JADC, to build rear passenger cabin sections of the Boeing 767 jet transport. Part of this work is, in turn, subcontracted by Mitsubishi to Shin Meiwa. Mitsubishi also manufactures tailcones for the McDonnell Douglas DC-10 and wing trailing-edges for the MD-80 series of transports.

Mitsubishi's aero engine activities are described in the appropriate section of this edition.

MITSUBISHI MU-2

The prototype of the MU-2 twin-turboprop STOL multipurpose transport was flown for the first time on 14 September 1963. By 1 January 1986, total orders for the MU-2 series had reached 755, including 698 for export and 57 for Japanese customers. Fifteen versions have been announced, of which details have appeared in the 1965-66 and subsequent editions of *Jane's*.

The two final versions were the Marquise and Solitaire, detailed descriptions of which last appeared in the 1985-86 *Jane's* under the MAI (Mitsubishi Aircraft International) heading in the US section. Production of both ended in March 1986, at which time 171 Marquises and 111 Solitaires had been produced and sold.

Mitsubishi built Sikorsky HSS-2 of the JMSDF *(Katsumi Hinata)*

MITSUBISHI MU-300

The MU-300 was marketed worldwide (except in Japan), under the name **Diamond**, by Mitsubishi Aircraft International in the USA. A full description of the Diamond I and IA, of which 85 had been sold by 1 January 1986, can be found under the MAI entry in the US section of the 1985-86 *Jane's*.

As recorded under the MAI entry in this edition, the Diamond II programme has now been acquired by Beech Aircraft Corporation (which see), whose version is known as the **Beechjet**. Six Diamond IIs had been sold by 1 January 1986.

MITSUBISHI F-4EJKai

In co-operation with Kawasaki as subcontractor, Mitsubishi was the JDA's prime contractor in producing F-4EJ Phantom tactical fighters for the JASDF, under licence from McDonnell Douglas Corporation. The last of 140 F-4EJs was delivered to the JASDF on 20 May 1981; Mitsubishi is engaged currently in a major programme to update F-4EJ equipment and weapon systems. The prototype F-4EJKai (07-8431) was first flown on 17 July 1984 and delivered on the following 13 December. It has a Westinghouse AN/APG-66J fire control system, advanced avionics which include a Litton LN-39 INS, head-up display, and J/APR-4Kai radar warning receiver, look-down/shootdown capability with AIM-7F/M Sparrows or AIM-9L Sidewinders, and can carry two ASM-1 anti-shipping missiles. Current plans are to convert 110 of the JASDF's 125 remaining F-4EJs to F-4EJKai configuration and the other 15 to RF-4EJ reconnaissance-fighters.

MITSUBISHI T-2

The T-2, the first supersonic aircraft developed by the Japanese aircraft industry, is a twin-engined two-seat jet trainer designed to meet the requirements of the JASDF.

Mitsubishi was selected as prime contractor for the development programme in September 1967. Design, under the leadership of Dr Kenji Ikeda, was followed by the completion of four XT-2 flying prototypes plus static and fatigue test airframes. The first XT-2 (19-5101) flew for the first time on 20 July 1971, the second (29-5102) on 2 December 1971, and the third and fourth on 28 April and 20 July 1972.

Production orders have been placed for 92 T-2s (28 **T-2** advanced trainers, 62 **T-2A** combat trainers, plus two development aircraft for the F-1 close support fighter version, described separately). A total of 88 T-2/2As had been delivered by 31 March 1986, to the 4th Air Wing at Matsushima. In 1982, the JASDF's Blue Impulse aerobatic team received six of these T-2As in place of its F-86F Sabres.

Mitsubishi, as prime contractor, is responsible for fuselage construction, final assembly and flight testing of production aircraft. Major programme subcontractors were Fuji (wings and tail unit), Nippi (pylons and launchers) and Shin Meiwa (drop tanks).

Under contract to the Technical Research and Development Institute, Mitsubishi converted one T-2 as a CCV (control configured vehicle). This aircraft is described separately.

The following description applies to the standard production T-2/2A:

TYPE: Two-seat supersonic jet trainer.

WINGS: Cantilever all-metal shoulder-wing monoplane. Wing section NACA 65 series (modified). Thickness/chord ratio 4·66%. Anhedral 9° from roots. Sweepback on leading-edges 68° at root, 42° 29′ inboard of extended chord outer panels and 36° on outer panels; basic sweepback at quarter-chord 35° 47′. Multi-spar torsion box machined from tapered thick panels and constructed mainly of 7075 aluminium alloy. Electrically actuated aluminium honeycomb leading-edge flaps, the outer portions of which have extended chord. Electrically actuated all-metal single-slotted flaps, with aluminium honeycomb trailing-edges over 70 per cent of each half span. No conventional ailerons. Lateral control by hydraulically actuated all-metal two-section slotted spoilers ahead of flaps.

FUSELAGE: Conventional all-metal semi-monocoque structure, mainly of 7075 aluminium alloy. Approx 10 per cent of structure, by weight, is of titanium, mostly around engine bays. Two hydraulically actuated door type airbrakes under centre of fuselage, aft of mainwheel bays.

TAIL UNIT: Cantilever all-metal structure. One-piece hydraulically actuated all-moving swept tailplane, with 15° anhedral. Inner leading-edges of titanium; outer leading-edges of aluminium. Trailing-edges of aluminium honeycomb construction. Small ventral fin under each side of fuselage at rear. Hydraulically actuated rudder.

LANDING GEAR: Hydraulically retractable tricycle type, with pneumatic backup for emergency extension. Main units retract forward into fuselage, nose unit rearward. Single wheel on each unit. Nosewheel steerable through 72°. Oleo-pneumatic shock absorbers. Nosewheel tyre size 18 × 5·5 Type VII (14 ply rating), max pressure 14·82 bars (215 lb/sq in); mainwheel tyres size 25 × 6·75 Type VII (18 ply rating), max pressure 20·69 bars (300 lb/sq in). Hydraulic brakes and Hydro-Aire anti-skid units. Runway arrester hook beneath rear fuselage. Brake parachute in tailcone.

POWER PLANT: Two Rolls-Royce Turboméca Adour Mk 801A turbofan engines, each rated at 22·75 kN (5,115 lb st) dry and 32·49 kN (7,305 lb st) with afterburning, mounted side by side in centre of fuselage. (Engines licence built by Ishikawajima-Harima, under designation TF40-IHI-801A.) Fixed geometry air intake, with auxiliary 'blow-in' intake doors, on each side of fuselage aft of rear cockpit. Fuel in seven fuselage tanks with total capacity of 3,823 litres (841 Imp gallons; 1,010 US gallons). Pressure refuelling point in starboard side of fuselage, forward of mainwheel bay. Three 821 litre (180 Imp gallon; 217 US gallon) auxiliary fuel tanks can be carried beneath the wings and fuselage.

ACCOMMODATION: Crew of two in tandem on Daiseru built Weber ES-7J zero/zero ejection seats in pressurised and air-conditioned cockpits, separated by windscreen. Rear seat elevated 28 cm (11 in) above front seat. Individual manually operated rearward hinged jettisonable canopies.

SYSTEMS: Cockpit air-conditioning system. Two independent hydraulic systems, each 207 bars (3,000 lb/sq in), for flight controls, landing gear and utilities. Pneumatic bottle for landing gear emergency extension. Primary electrical power from two 12/15kVA AC generators.

AVIONICS AND EQUIPMENT: Mitsubishi Electric J/ARC-51 UHF. Nippon Electric J/ARN-53 Tacan and Toyo Communication J/APX-101 SIF/IFF. Mitsubishi Electric J/AWG-11 search and ranging radar in nose, with Mitsubishi Electric (Thomson-CSF) head-up display in cockpit. Lear Siegler 5010BL attitude and heading reference system. Liquid oxygen equipment.

ARMAMENT (combat trainer version): One Vulcan JM61 multi-barrel 20 mm cannon in lower fuselage, aft of cockpit on port side. Attachment point on underfuselage centreline and two under each wing for drop tanks or other stores. Wingtip attachments for air-to-air missiles.

DIMENSIONS, EXTERNAL:

Wing span	7·88 m (25 ft 10¼ in)
Wing chord: at root	4·172 m (13 ft 8¼ in)
at tip	1·133 m (3 ft 8½ in)
Wing aspect ratio	3
Wing taper ratio	3·7
Length overall, incl probe	17·86 m (58 ft 7 in)
Length of fuselage	17·31 m (56 ft 9½ in)
Height overall	4·39 m (14 ft 5 in)
Tailplane span	4·33 m (14 ft 2½ in)
Wheel track	2·82 m (9 ft 3 in)
Wheelbase	5·72 m (18 ft 9 in)

AREAS:

Wings, gross	21·17 m² (227·9 sq ft)
Airbrakes (total)	0·952 m² (10·25 sq ft)
Vertical tail surfaces (total, excl ventral fins)	5·00 m² (53·82 sq ft)
Horizontal tail surfaces (total)	6·70 m² (72·12 sq ft)

WEIGHTS:

Operational weight empty	6,307 kg (13,905 lb)
Max T-O weight	12,800 kg (28,219 lb)

PERFORMANCE (in 'clean' configuration except where indicated):

Max level speed	Mach 1·6
Max rate of climb at S/L	10,670 m (35,000 ft)/min
Service ceiling	15,240 m (50,000 ft)
T-O run	610 m (2,000 ft)

Mitsubishi experimental control configured vehicle (CCV) conversion of a T-2 trainer

MITSUBISHI T-2CCV

The Technical Research and Development Institute of the Japan Defence Agency selected the T-2 in 1978 for use as a testbed with which to develop active flight control technologies and to obtain engineering data on them. Redesign of the T-2 testbed (29-5103) to control configured vehicle (CCV) configuration was started by Mitsubishi in April of that year.

Modifications included installation of triplex digital fly by wire computers, flight control actuators, manoeuvring flaps, and canard surfaces of carbonfibre reinforced plastics. Five CCV modes were investigated: control augmentation, relaxed static stability, manoeuvre load control, direct lift control, and direct side force control.

First flight was made on 9 August 1983. The CCV was delivered to the JDA on 26 March 1984. Between 17 May 1984 and 20 March 1986 a total of 138 flight test sorties was flown at Gifu Air Base by a joint team from the TRDI and the Air Proving Wing of the JASDF.

A description of the T-2CCV testbed can be found in the 1985-86 *Jane's*. Max T-O weight, not recorded in that edition, was 10,326 kg (22,765 lb).

MITSUBISHI F-1

Following the JASDF's decision to develop a single-seat close air support fighter from the T-2 supersonic trainer, design of this aircraft began in 1972. The second and third production T-2 trainers (59-5106 and 59-5107) were converted as prototypes, in which form they made their first flights on 7 and 3 June 1975 respectively. They were delivered to the JASDF Air Proving Wing at Gifu in July and August 1975, and after a year of flight test and evaluation the aircraft was type approved in November 1976 and officially designated F-1.

Production orders had been placed by March 1986 for 77 F-1s, of which 74 had been delivered. The first production F-1 (70-8201) made its first flight on 16 June 1977, and was delivered to the JASDF on 26 September 1977. F-1s serve with the 3rd Squadron of the 3rd Air Wing at Misawa and the 8th Air Wing at Tsuiki.

TYPE: Single-seat close support fighter.

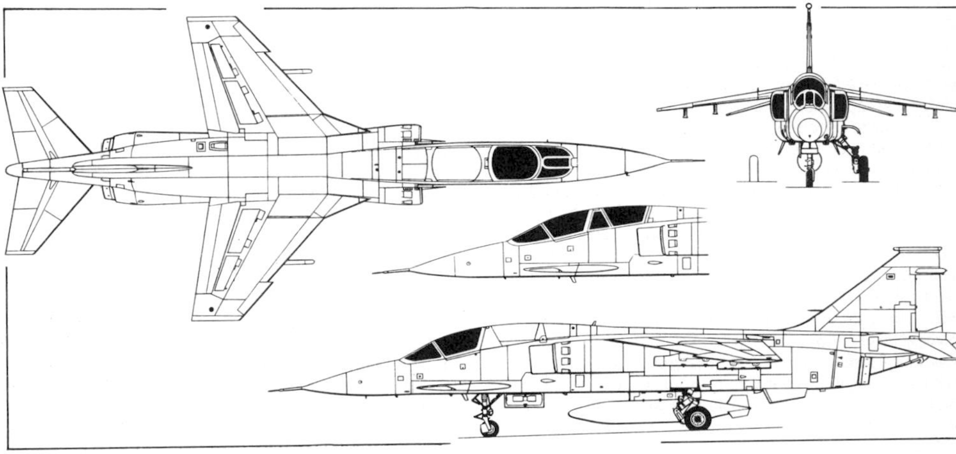

Mitsubishi F-1 (two Rolls-Royce Turboméca Adour turbofan engines), with additional scrap view of two-seat nose of T-2 trainer *(Pilot Press)*

Mitsubishi F-1 single-seat close support fighters of the JASDF

AIRFRAME, POWER PLANT AND SYSTEMS: Generally similar to T-2, but with the rear cockpit area modified as avionics compartment for bombing computer, inertial navigation system and radar warning system.

ACCOMMODATION: Generally similar to T-2, but without rear seat and with 'solid' fairing in place of second canopy.

AVIONICS AND EQUIPMENT: Dual UHF; Tacan; IFF/SIF; Mitsubishi Electric J/AWG-12 nose mounted air-to-air and air-to-ground radar, with Mitsubishi Electric (Thomson-CSF) head-up display; Ferranti 6TNJ-F inertial navigation system; radio altimeter; air data computer; Mitsubishi Electric J/ASQ-1 fire control system and bombing computer (replacing original fire control and bombing computer from January 1982, for compatibility with ASM-1 missile); strike camera system; radar homing and warning system; attitude and heading reference system.

ARMAMENT: Single JM61 multi-barrel 20 mm cannon. One underfuselage and four underwing hardpoints, as in T-2, with detachable multiple ejector racks. Primary weapon is the Mitsubishi ASM-1 air-to-surface missile, of which two can be carried on underwing stations. Bombs of 500 or 750 lb can be carried on all five external stations, up to a maximum weight of 2,721 kg (twelve 500 lb bombs). Infra-red and laser guidance systems for free-fall 500 and 750 lb bombs were reported to be under development by the JASDF in 1983-84. The four underwing stations can each be used for rocket pods such as the JLAU-3A (with nineteen 70 mm), RL-7 (seven 70 mm) and RL-4 (four 125 mm). For air-to-air combat the F-1 can carry up to four AIM-9 Sidewinder missiles, one at each wingtip and one on each of the outboard underwing hardpoints. For long-range missions, the F-1 can carry up to three auxiliary fuel tanks (see 'Power Plant' paragraph for the T-2).

DIMENSIONS AND AREAS: As for T-2

WEIGHTS:

Operational weight empty	6,358 kg (14,017 lb)
Max T-O weight	13,700 kg (30,203 lb)

PERFORMANCE:

Generally similar to T-2 'clean', except for:

T-O run at max T-O weight	1,280 m (4,200 ft)

MITSUBISHI (SIKORSKY) XSH-60J

Detailed design work on this developed version of the Sikorsky SH-60B Seahawk anti-submarine helicopter, to meet the specific requirements of the JMSDF, was funded under the FY 1985 budget. Japanese avionics and equipment, including ring laser gyro AHRS, data link, tactical data processing and automatic flight management systems, will be integrated by the Technical Research and Development Institute of the Japan Defence Agency. The first of two prototype XSH-60Js, based on imported airframes, is expected to fly in 1987.

NAL

NATIONAL AEROSPACE LABORATORY

7-44-1 Jindaijihigashi-machi, Chofu City, Tokyo 182
Telephone: Musashino (0422) 47 5911
DIRECTOR-GENERAL: Hideo Nagasu
DEPUTY DIRECTOR-GENERAL: Tadao Torisaki
DIRECTOR OF FLIGHT RESEARCH DIVISION:
Dr Goro Beppu
DIRECTOR OF V/STOL AIRCRAFT RESEARCH GROUP:
Dr Kazuyuki Takeuchi

The National Aerospace Laboratory (NAL) is a government establishment responsible for research and development in the field of aeronautical and space sciences. Since 1962 it has extended its activity in the field of V/STOL techniques.

NAL ASUKA QSTOL RESEARCH AIRCRAFT

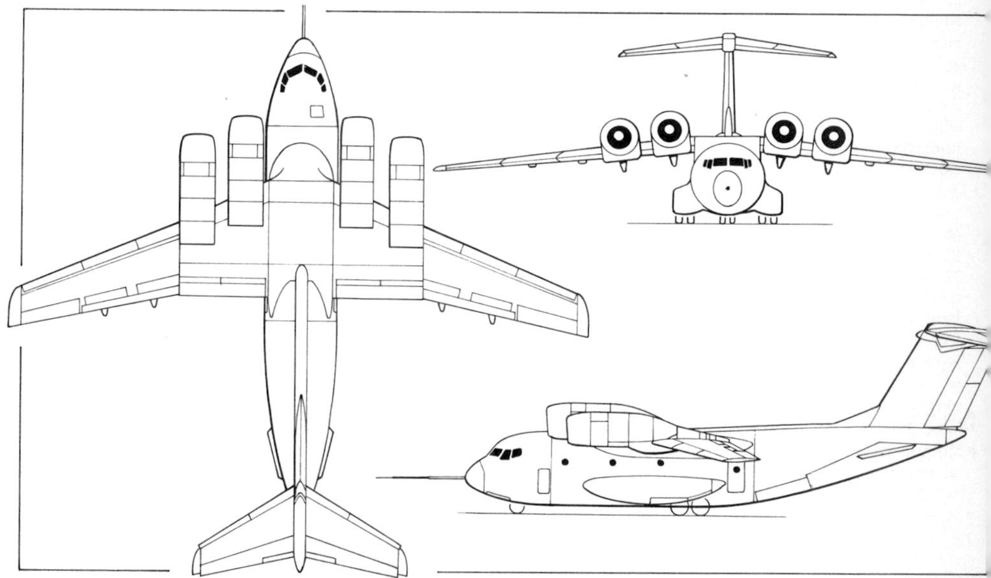

NAL Asuka QSTOL research aircraft, based on a Kawasaki C-1 airframe *(Michael A. Badrocke)*

The NAL was allotted Y3,709 million in the FY 1985 budget for continuation of a 12-year programme to develop a large experimental quiet STOL transport aircraft. This is based upon the airframe of the Kawasaki C-1 tactical transport, with the following modifications: replacement of the two Pratt & Whitney JT8D engines by four MITI/NAL FJR710/600S high bypass ratio turbofan engines, installed above and far ahead of the wing leading-edges in nacelles with upper surface blowing (USB), as on the Boeing YC-14 prototype STOL transport (see 1978-79 *Jane's*); installation of wing leading-edge and aileron boundary layer control systems; replacement of the existing inboard flaps by USB flaps; structural strengthening of the fuselage and landing gear; and installation of a digital stability and control augmentation system.

Modification began in 1979, and the aircraft (JQ8501) was named Asuka (after an ancient capital city of Japan) when it made its first public appearance, at the Japan International Aerospace Show, at Gifu in October 1983. At that time only the inboard engines had been installed, and it was expected that the first flight would take place in June 1984. However, inlet redesign and other problems associated with the power plant installation caused this to be postponed. After overcoming these problems the aircraft was rolled out in its complete form on 11 April 1985, and made its first flight on 28 October that year at Gifu. A series of experimental flights is scheduled to be carried out during 1985-88.

Total cost of the development programme is estimated at Y37,500 million, including flight testing. Data obtained from this programme will, it is hoped, enable NAL to develop, in co-operation with the Japanese aerospace industry, a commercial STOL transport aircraft able to operate from 800 m (2,625 ft) runways with 150 passengers.

TYPE: Four-turbofan experimental 'quiet STOL' transport.

WINGS: Cantilever high-wing monoplane. Aerofoil sections YX-12641-M-097MOD at root, YX-1135-N-2000MOD at tip, with respective thickness/chord ratios of 12% and 11%. Wings have 20° sweepback at quarter-chord, with slightly increased leading-edge sweep on the inboard portions. Anhedral 5° 30' from centre-section. Incidence 4°. Two-spar fail-safe basic structure of aluminium alloy; upper surface of inner panels covered with thermal sheilding panels of glass-polyimide honeycomb sandwich. Major elements of powered high lift device (PHLD) system are the fore and main USB flaps, aft of the engine nacelles, which are manufactured from titanium and aluminium alloys and glass-polyimide FRP. They are actuated by two independent Kayaba hydraulic actuators on each wing, the inner one powered by No. 2 and the outer by No. 3 hydraulic system. Outboard of the USB flaps the C-1's outer quadruple-slotted flaps and drooping ailerons are retained, as are the four spoilers and three of the four sections of leading-edge slats. All these surfaces are actuated hydraulically, with actuators by Sumitomo (screwjacks), Mitsubishi, Teijin and Shimazu (screwjacks) respectively. Slotted flaps, ailerons, spoilers and slats are all of aluminium alloy construction. BLC flow of engine bleed air is directed over USB flaps and ailerons by vortex generators forward of these surfaces on top of wing.

FUSELAGE: Conventional semi-monocoque fail-safe structure of aluminium alloy, with a circular cross-section. Major part of fuselage is pressurised.

TAIL UNIT: Aluminium alloy cantilever T tail, with sweepback on all surfaces (30° at fin quarter-chord, 25° at tailplane quarter-chord). Variable incidence tailplane has 5° anhedral and FRP slats on leading-edge. Balance tab in each elevator and anti-balance tabs in rudder. Elevators and rudder are each operated by two independent Mitsubishi hydraulic actuator systems: tailplane actuated hydraulically via Sumitomo screwjack, with electric actuation available as emergency backup.

LANDING GEAR: Hydraulically retractable tricycle type, of Sumitomo design. Each main unit has two pairs of wheels in tandem, retracting forward into fairings built on to the sides of the fuselage. Forward retracting nose unit has twin wheels. All units have Sumitomo oleo shock absorbers, Kayaba wheels and Dunlop tyres. Mainwheel tyres size 35 × 10·7-16, nosewheel tyres size 28 × 9-12; tyre pressure (all units) 6·21 bars (90 lb/sq in). Kayaba three-rotor hydraulic brakes and Sumisei anti-skid units.

POWER PLANT: Four 47·07 kN (10,582 lb st) MITI/NAL FJR710/600S turbofan engines, mounted in nacelles above and forward of wing centre-section. Six integral

National Aerospace Laboratory Asuka QSTOL research aircraft

wing fuel tanks with total capacity of 15,414 litres (3,391 Imp gallons). Single pressure refuelling point for all tanks, plus overwing gravity refuelling point for each tank. Oil capacity 117 litres (25·7 Imp gallons). Air intakes have aluminium alloy acoustic panels.

ACCOMMODATION: Crew of three, comprising pilot, co-pilot and flight engineer. Accommodation in main cabin for up to seven technical personnel to monitor test equipment and instrumentation. Escape hatch in flight deck roof on starboard side. Flight deck and main cabin pressurised and air-conditioned by engine bleed air. Access to flight deck via downward opening door, with built-in stairs, on port side of forward fuselage. Emergency exit on each side of fuselage, aft of wing trailing-edge.

SYSTEMS: Pressurisation and air-conditioning systems utilise middle-stage engine bleed air at pressure of 6·21 bars (90 lb/sq in). No APU. Three independent hydraulic systems, each 207 bars (3,000 lb/sq in). No. 1 system actuates elevators, tailplane, rudder, starboard aileron, outboard spoilers, and signal actuators (output actuators of stability and control augmentation system); No. 2 actuates elevators, rudder, port aileron, inboard spoilers, signal actuators, slats, outboard flaps, USB flap inboard actuators, landing gear, nosewheel steering and brakes; No. 3 system actuates both ailerons, signal actuators, slats (alternate), outboard flaps (alternate), USB flap outboard actuators, and emergency brakes. Leading-edge and aileron BLC, and engine intake anti-icing system, utilise final stage engine bleed air at pressure of 11·72 bars (170 lb/sq in). Electrical power supplied by four engine driven 40kVA AC generators. DC power is obtained from AC source through a transformer-rectifier. Three 24V 34Ah nickel-cadmium batteries for emergency DC power. Three 30V 7·8Ah nickel-cadmium batteries for IRU and SCAS backup DC power. 5 litre (1·1 Imp gallon) liquid oxygen converter for flight crew; seven portable gaseous oxygen bottles for occupants of main cabin.

AVIONICS AND EQUIPMENT: Avionics include radio altimeter, VHF and UHF radio, ADF, marker beacon receiver, VOR/ILS, Tacan, ATC transponder, triple IRS and flight director system. Special equipment includes telemetry, radar transponder, and stability and control augmentation system (SCAS).

DIMENSIONS, EXTERNAL:
- Wing span: 30·60 m (100 ft 4¾ in)
- Wing chord: at root: 6·30 m (20 ft 8 in)
  - at tip: 2·00 m (6 ft 6¾ in)
- Wing aspect ratio: 7·77
- Length overall: 33·154 m (108 ft 9¼ in)
- Fuselage: Length: 26·50 m (86 ft 11¼ in)
  - Max diameter: 3·80 m (12 ft 5½ in)
- Height overall: 10·175 m (33 ft 4½ in)
- Tailplane span: 11·30 m (37 ft 1 in)
- Wheel track (c/l of shock struts): 4·40 m (14 ft 5¼ in)
- Wheelbase: 9·33 m (30 ft 7¼ in)
- Passenger doors: Height: 1·34 m (4 ft 4¾ in)
  - Width: 0·63 m (2 ft 0¾ in)
  - Height to sill: 1·25 m (4 ft 1¼ in)
- Emergency exits: Height: 1·75 m (5 ft 9 in)
  - Width: 0·91 m (3 ft 0 in)
- Escape hatch: Length: 0·56 m (1 ft 10 in)
  - Width: 0·56 m (1 ft 10 in)

DIMENSIONS, INTERNAL:
- Cabin: Length: 10·80 m (35 ft 5¼ in)
  - Max width: 3·60 m (11 ft 9¾ in)
  - Max height: 2·55 m (8 ft 4½ in)
  - Floor area: 28·60 m² (308·0 sq ft)
  - Volume: 73·80 m³ (2,606·0 cu ft)

AREAS:
- Wings, gross: 120·50 m² (1,297·0 sq ft)
- Ailerons (total): 4·76 m² (51·24 sq ft)
- Trailing-edge flaps (total): USB: 12·70 m² (136·70 sq ft)
  - outboard: 10·58 m² (113·88 sq ft)
- Leading-edge slats (total): 9·23 m² (99·35 sq ft)
- Spoilers (total): 4·30 m² (46·28 sq ft)
- Fin: 22·77 m² (245·09 sq ft)
- Rudder, incl tabs: 6·88 m² (74·06 sq ft)
- Tailplane, incl slat: 30·10 m² (323·99 sq ft)
- Elevators (total, incl tabs): 7·60 m² (81·81 sq ft)

WEIGHTS AND LOADING:
- Weight empty: 32,372 kg (71,368 lb)
- Max fuel weight: 12,628 kg (27,840 lb)
- Max T-O weight: STOL: 38,700 kg (85,320 lb)
  - CTOL: 45,000 kg (99,210 lb)
- Max ramp weight: 45,000 kg (99,210 lb)
- Max zero-fuel weight: 35,150 kg (77,490 lb)
- Max wing loading: 373·4 kg/m² (76·5 lb/sq ft)

PERFORMANCE (at max T-O weight except where indicated):
- Never-exceed speed: 320 knots (593 km/h; 368 mph) CAS
- Max cruising speed: 260 knots (482 km/h; 299 mph) CAS
- Stalling speed at S/L, ISA, landing configuration, at landing weight of 36,860 kg (81,260 lb): 49 knots (91 km/h; 57 mph) CAS
- Service ceiling, ISA, AUW of 38,700 kg (85,320 lb): 8,535 m (28,000 ft)
- Min ground turning radius: 26·70 m (87 ft 7¼ in)
- STOL T-O to 15 m (50 ft): 823 m (2,700 ft)
- STOL landing from 15 m (50 ft): 853 m (2,800 ft)
- Range with max fuel, CTOL max T-O weight of 45,000 kg (99,210 lb): 720 nm (1,334 km; 829 miles)

OPERATIONAL NOISE LEVELS:
- T-O, at 3·5 nm (6·5 km; 4 miles) from start of T-O run: 93·8 EPNdB
- Approach, at 1·0 nm (1·8 km; 1·1 miles) from landing threshold on 6° glideslope: 100·6 EPNdB
- Sideline, at 0·35 nm (0·65 km; 0·4 miles) from runway c/l: 87·1 EPNdB

NIPPI

NIHON HIKOKI KABUSHIKI KAISHA (Japan Aircraft Manufacturing Co Ltd)

3175 Showa-machi, Kanazawa-ku, Yokohama 236
Telephone: Yokohama (045) 771 1251
Telex: (3822) 267 Nippi J
OTHER WORKS: Atsugi
PRESIDENT: Ritsuo Nakagawa
PUBLIC RELATIONS MANAGER: Atsumasa Kubota

Nippi's Sugita plant has a floor area of 48,946 m² (526,850 sq ft) and employs about 820 persons. The Atsugi plant, which employs about 670 persons, has a floor area of 37,372 m² (402,268 sq ft). Kawasaki has a 30·2% holding in Nippi.

The Atsugi plant is engaged chiefly in the overhaul, repair and maintenance of various types of aircraft and helicopters, including those of the Japan Defence Agency and Maritime Safety Agency, and carrier based aircraft of the US Navy. The Sugita plant manufactures in-spar ribs for the Boeing 767; components and assemblies for the Mitsubishi T-2, F-1, F-15J (pylons and launchers), Kawasaki built P-3C (engine nacelles), and Shin Meiwa US-1A; airframe and dynamic components for the Kawasaki KV107; dynamic components for the Fuji-Bell HU-1H and Kawasaki-McDonnell Douglas OH-6D; body structures for Japanese satellites; tail units for Japanese built rocket vehicles; and targets for the Japan Defence Agency.

SHIN MEIWA

SHIN MEIWA INDUSTRY CO LTD

Nippon Building, 6-2, Otemachi 2-chome, Chiyoda-ku, Tokyo 100
Telephone: Tokyo (03) 245 6611
Telex: 222 2431 SMIC T J
HEAD OFFICE: 1-5-25, Kosone-Cho, Nishinomiya-Shi, Hyogo-Ken
Telephone: Nishinomiya (0798) 47 0331
Telex: 5644493
WORKS (AIRCRAFT DIVISION): Konan and Tokushima
CHAIRMAN: Yoshio Yagi
PRESIDENT: Shinji Tamagawa
EXECUTIVE MANAGING DIRECTOR, AND GENERAL MANAGER, AIRCRAFT DIVISION: Susumu Ishimoto
BOARD DIRECTOR, DEPUTY GENERAL MANAGER AND KONAN WORKS MANAGER: Yosinobu Kasu
DIRECTOR AND ASST GENERAL MANAGER: Motohiro Matsushita (Tokyo Office)
SALES MANAGER AND PUBLIC RELATIONS: Junpei Matsuo (Tokyo Office)

The former Kawanishi Aircraft Company became Shin Meiwa in 1949 and established itself as a major overhaul centre for Japanese and US military and commercial aircraft.

Shin Meiwa's principal current activities concern production of the US-1 medium-range STOL search and rescue amphibian for the JMSDF, and overhaul work on flying-boats and amphibians. It manufactured six experimental drop tanks for use on the Kawasaki XT-4 trainer prototypes, and is performing design work to modify Gates Learjet 36As into U-36A naval fleet training support aircraft for the JMSDF. The first U-36A is due to be delivered in March 1987.

Shin Meiwa is also engaged in the manufacture of components for other aircraft, including underwing drop tanks for the Mitsubishi T-2 supersonic jet trainer and F-1 close support fighter, and Mitsubishi built McDonnell Douglas F-15J Eagle jet fighters; nose and tail cones, ailerons and trailing-edge flaps for Kawasaki licence built examples of the Lockheed P-3C. Shin Meiwa is also taking part in co-production of the Boeing 767, under subcontract to Mitsubishi.

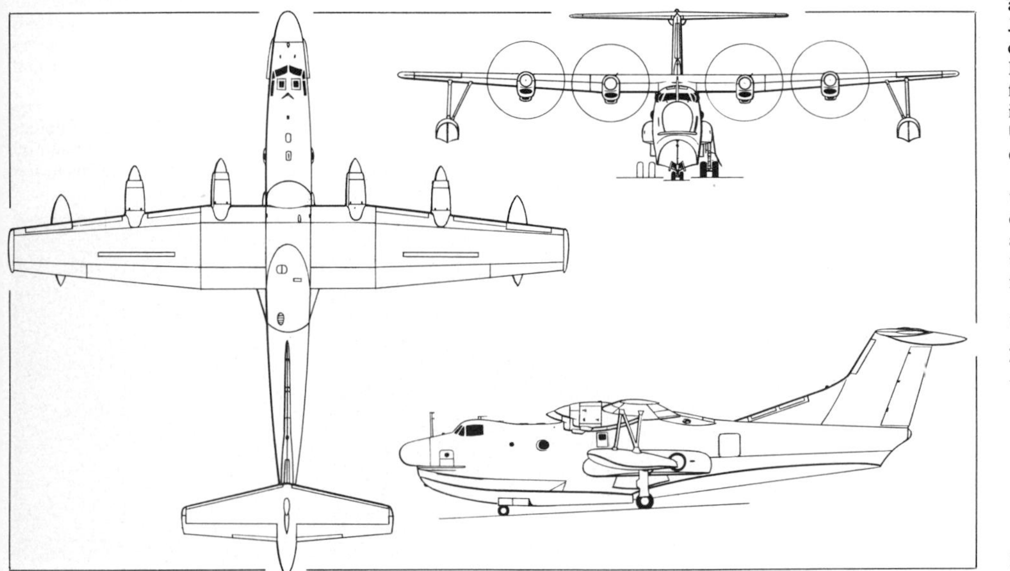

Shin Meiwa US-1A search and rescue amphibian, developed from the PS-1 *(Pilot Press)*

SHIN MEIWA SS-2A

JMSDF designation: US-1A

The **US-1** (manufacturer's designation SS-2A) is an amphibious adaptation of the PS-1 (SS-2) flying-boat (1980-81 *Jane's*), configured for search and rescue duties with the JMSDF.

Design of the US-1 began in June 1970; the first example (9071) made its first flight, following a waterborne take-off, on 16 October 1974, and its first flight from a land base on 3 December 1974. The first US-1 was delivered on 5 March 1975, and eight had been delivered by March 1983. These aircraft are in service with No. 71 SAR Squadron of the JMSDF, based at Iwakuni and Atsugi. A ninth aircraft was due for delivery in October 1985; a tenth was to follow in December 1986. The seventh and subsequent aircraft are fitted with T64-IHI-10J turboprops, offering a 14 per cent increase in power available for take-off, and are designated **US-1A**. The earlier aircraft are being retrofitted with these engines.

To make possible very low landing and take-off speeds, the US-1 has both a boundary layer control system and extensive flaps for propeller slipstream deflection. Control and stability in low-speed flight are enhanced by 'blowing' the rudder, flaps and elevators, and by use of an automatic flight control system.

The following data apply to the US-1A. Details of the US-1 can be found in the 1985-86 and earlier editions of *Jane's*.

TYPE: Four-turboprop STOL air/sea rescue amphibian.

WINGS: Cantilever high-wing monoplane. Conventional all-metal two-spar structure with rectangular centre-section and tapered outer panels. High-lift devices include outboard leading-edge slats extending over nearly 17 per cent of the span and large outer and inner blown trailing-edge flaps deflecting 60° and 80° respectively. Two spoilers in front of outer flap on each wing. Powered ailerons. Leading-edge de-icing boots.

FUSELAGE: All-metal semi-monocoque hull, with high length/beam ratio. V shaped single-step planing bottom, with curved spray suppression strakes along sides of nose

Shin Meiwa US-1A air/sea rescue amphibian (four Ishikawajima/General Electric T64-IHI-10J turboprop engines)

and spray suppressor slots in fuselage undersides aft of inboard propeller line. Double-deck interior.

TAIL UNIT: Cantilever all-metal T tail. Large dorsal fin. Tailplane has slats and de-icing boots on leading-edge. Blown rudder and elevators. Tab in each elevator.

LANDING GEAR: Flying-boat hull, plus hydraulically retractable Sumitomo tricycle landing gear with twin wheels on all units. Steerable nose unit. Oleo-pneumatic shock absorbers. Main units, which retract rearward into fairings on hull sides, have size 40 × 14-22 (Type VII) tyres, pressure 7·79 bars (113 lb/sq in). Nosewheel tyres size 25 × 6·75-18 (Type VII), pressure 20·69 bars (300 lb/sq in). Three-rotor hydraulic disc brakes. No anti-skid units.

POWER PLANT: Four 2,602 kW (3,490 ehp) Ishikawajima built General Electric T64-IHI-10J turboprop engines, each driving a Sumitomo built Hamilton Standard 63E60-19 three-blade constant-speed reversible-pitch propeller. Additionally, one 1,014 kW (1,360 shp) Ishikawajima built General Electric T58-IHI-10-M2 gas turbine is housed in the upper centre portion of the fuselage to provide power for boundary layer control system on rudder, flaps and elevators. Fuel in five wing tanks, with total usable capacity of 10,851 litres (2,387 Imp gallons) and two rear fuselage tanks (11,649 litres; 2,563 Imp gallons); total capacity 22,500 litres (4,950 Imp gallons). Pressure refuelling point on port side, near bow hatch. Oil capacity 152 litres (33·4 Imp gallons). The aircraft can be refuelled on open sea, either from a surface vessel or from another US-1/1A fitted with detachable at-sea refuelling equipment.

ACCOMMODATION: Crew of nine and 20 seated survivors or 12 stretchers, one auxiliary seat and two observers' seats. Sliding rescue door on port side of fuselage, aft of wing.

SYSTEMS: Cabin air-conditioning system. Two independent hydraulic systems, each 207 bars (3,000 lb/sq in). No. 1 system actuates ailerons, outboard flaps, spoilers, elevators, rudder and control surface 'feel'; No. 2 system actuates ailerons, inboard and outboard flaps, wing leading-edge slats, elevators, rudder, landing gear extension/retraction and lock/unlock, nosewheel steering, mainwheel brakes and windscreen wipers. Emergency system, also of 207 bars (3,000 lb/sq in), driven by 24V DC motor, for actuation of inboard flaps, landing gear extension/retraction and lock/unlock, and mainwheel brakes. Oxygen system for all crew and stretcher stations. Garrett GTCP85-131J APU provides power for starting main engines and shaft power for 40kVA emergency AC generator. BLC system includes a C-2 compressor, driven by T58-IHI-10-M2 gas turbine, which delivers compressed air at 14 kg (30·9 lb)/s and pressure of 1·86 bars (27 lb/sq in) for ducting to inner and outer flaps, rudder and elevators. Electrical system includes 115/200V three-phase 400Hz constant frequency AC and three transformer-rectifiers to provide 28V DC. Two 40kVA AC generators, driven by Nos. 2 and 3 main engines. Emergency 40kVA AC generator driven by APU. 24V emergency DC power from two 34Ah nickel-cadmium batteries. Anti-icing, air-conditioning, fire detection and extinguishing systems standard.

AVIONICS AND EQUIPMENT: HIC-3 interphone, HRC-107 HF, N-CU-58/HRC antenna coupler, HGC-102 teletypewriter, HRC-106 radio, HRC-110 radio, HRN-101 ADF, AN/ARA-50 UHF/DF, HRN-105 Tacan, HRN-104 Loran, HRA-4 Loran signal processor, HRN-106 ILS marker beacon receiver, AN/APN-171 (N2) radar altimeter, HPN-101B wave height meter, AN/APN-187C Doppler radar, AN/AYK-2 navigation computer, A/A24G-9 TAS transmitter, N-PT-3 dead reckoning plotting board, N-OA-35/HSA tactical plotter group, AN/APS-80N search radar, AN/APA-125N indicator group, AN/APX-68N IFF transponder, RRC-15 emergency transmitter and N-ID-66/HRN BDHI.

OPERATIONAL EQUIPMENT: Marker launcher, 10 marine markers, 6 green markers, 2 droppable message cylinders, 10 float lights, pyrotechnic pistol, parachute flares, 2 flare storage boxes, binoculars, 2 rescue equipment kits, 2 droppable liferaft containers, rescue equipment launcher, lifeline pistol, lifeline, 3 lifebuoys, loudspeaker, hoist unit, rescue platform, lifeboat with outboard motor, camera, and 12 stretchers. Stretchers can be replaced by troop seats.

DIMENSIONS, EXTERNAL:
Wing span — 33·15 m (108 ft 9 in)
Wing chord: at root — 5·00 m (16 ft 4¾ in)
at tip — 2·39 m (7 ft 10 in)
Wing aspect ratio — 8
Length overall — 33·46 m (109 ft 9¼ in)
Height overall — 9·95 m (32 ft 7¾ in)
Tailplane span — 12·36 m (40 ft 8½ in)
Wheel track — 3·56 m (11 ft 8¼ in)
Wheelbase — 8·33 m (27 ft 4 in)
Propeller diameter — 4·42 m (14 ft 6 in)
Rescue hatch, (port side, rear fuselage):
Height — 1·58 m (5 ft 2¼ in)
Width — 1·46 m (4 ft 9½ in)

AREAS:
Wings, gross — 135·82 m^2 (1,462·0 sq ft)
Ailerons (total) — 6·40 m^2 (68·90 sq ft)
Inner flaps (total) — 9·40 m^2 (101·18 sq ft)
Outer flaps (total) — 14·20 m^2 (152·85 sq ft)
Leading-edge slats (total) — 2·64 m^2 (28·42 sq ft)
Spoilers (total) — 2·10 m^2 (22·60 sq ft)
Fin — 17·56 m^2 (189·0 sq ft)
Dorsal fin — 6·32 m^2 (68·03 sq ft)
Rudder — 7·01 m^2 (75·50 sq ft)
Tailplane — 23·04 m^2 (248·0 sq ft)
Elevators, incl tab — 8·78 m^2 (94·50 sq ft)

WEIGHTS AND LOADINGS (search and rescue):
Manufacturer's weight empty — 23,300 kg (51,367 lb)
Weight empty, equipped — 25,500 kg (56,218 lb)
Usable fuel: JP-4 — 17,518 kg (38,620 lb)
JP-5 — 18,397 kg (40,560 lb)
Max oversea operating weight — 36,000 kg (79,365 lb)
Max T-O weight: from water — 43,000 kg (94,800 lb)
from land — 45,000 kg (99,200 lb)
Max wing loading — 331·4 kg/m^2 (67·9 lb/sq ft)
Max power loading — 4·32 kg/kW (7·10 lb/ehp)

PERFORMANCE (US-1A search and rescue, at max T-O weight from land, except where indicated):
Max level speed — 276 knots (511 km/h; 318 mph)
Max level speed at 3,050 m (10,000 ft), AUW of 36,000 kg (79,365 lb) — 282 knots (522 km/h; 325 mph)
Cruising speed at 3,050 m (10,000 ft) — 230 knots (426 km/h; 265 mph)
Max rate of climb at S/L — 488 m (1,600 ft)/min
Max rate of climb at S/L, AUW of 36,000 kg (79,365 lb) — 713 m (2,340 ft)/min
Service ceiling — 7,195 m (23,600 ft)
Service ceiling, AUW of 36,000 kg (79,365 lb) — 8,655 m (28,400 ft)
T-O to 15 m (50 ft) on land, 30° flap, BLC on — 655 m (2,150 ft)
T-O distance on water, AUW of 43,000 kg (94,800 lb), 40° flap, BLC on — 555 m (1,820 ft)
Landing from 15 m (50 ft) on land, AUW of 36,000 kg (79,365 lb), 50° flap, BLC on, with reverse pitch — 810 m (2,655 ft)
Landing distance on water, AUW of 36,000 kg (79,365 lb), 60° flap, BLC on — 220 m (722 ft)
Min ground turning radius:
self-powered — 21·20 m (69 ft 6¾ in)
towed — 18·80 m (61 ft 8¼ in)
Runway LCN requirement at AUW of 43,000 kg (94,800 lb) — 42
Max range at 230 knots (426 km/h; 265 mph) at 3,050 m (10,000 ft) — 2,060 nm (3,817 km; 2,372 miles)

KOREA
(REPUBLIC)

KA

KOREAN AIR

KAL Building, CPO Box 864, Seoul
Telephone: 771 66 and 771 67
Telex: KALHO K27526

PRESIDENT OF KOREAN AIR LINES: C. H. Cho

SENIOR VICE-PRESIDENT, SPECIAL PROJECT DEVELOPMENT: W. B. Lee

Following delivery by Hughes Helicopters of the USA of 34 Model 500MD Defender light helicopters to the Republic of Korea Air Force, Korean Air (a division of Korean Air Lines) began assembling Model 500 fuselages under licence in 1976 at its Kim Hae factory, and had assembled more than 200 by late 1984. The fuselages are shipped to the USA for final assembly, customer outfitting, flight test and delivery. Under a new 1984 offset agreement associated with the sale of Model 500MD Scouts to Korea (see 1984-85 edition), Korean Air will assemble fuselages from US kits for the MD 500E and 530F commercial helicopters, and military Model 500s. It is also manufacturing main rotor blades and some other components for these aircraft. Descriptions of the MD 500 and 530 can be found under the McDonnell Douglas Helicopters entry in the US section.

In 1981 KA began to assemble under licence 68 Northrop F-5E Tiger IIs and F-5F combat trainers (48 and 20 respectively), ordered for the Republic of Korea Air Force. Deliveries of completed aircraft began in the Autumn of 1982 and were due for completion in 1986. Korean name for the F-5F is **Chegoong-Ho (Air Master)**.

Northrop F-5E fighter of the Republic of Korea Air Force, licence assembled by KA as the Chegoong-Ho (Air Master)

KBHC

KOREA BELL HELICOPTER COMPANY (Subsidiary of United Industries International)

President: Kyu S. Rim

Formation of KBHC, by Bell Helicopter Textron Inc (see US section) and Korea Technologies Corporation, was followed on 31 July 1986 by announcement of a memorandum of agreement between Bell, KBHC and SPI (Samsung Precision Industries Company Ltd) to co-produce Bell helicopters in the Republic of Korea. KBHC is already licensed to repair, overhaul and modify Bell types, and to manufacture some components, and SPI's activities include manufacture of turbine engine parts. In support of the new agreement, SPI is building an 11,148 m² (120,000 sq ft) factory, to be completed in early 1987, for component manufacture and assembly of light and medium helicopters for the South Korean armed forces.

NETHERLANDS

FOKKER

FOKKER BV

Corporate Headquarters: PO Box 12222, 1100 AE Amsterdam-Zuidoost
Telephone: (020) 5649111
Telex: (General) 10687 FHK NL +, (Marketing) 11526 FOM NL +

Other Factories and Companies:
Fokker Schiphol; Fokker Drechtsteden, with plants at Papendrecht and Dordrecht; Fokker Ypenburg at Ypenburg Air Base, near the Hague; Fokker Woensdrecht at Woensdrecht Air Base, near Bergen op Zoom; and Fokker Hoogeveen in the north-east of the Netherlands
Trading Company Avio-Diepen BV

Supervisory Board:
Mr drs H. Langman (Chairman)
ir A. Meijer (Vice-Chairman)
R. E. Grovert
H. G. Buiter
Prof Dr W. H. J. Reynaerts
drs M. C. van der Harst
ir L. J. van Ameyden

Board of Management:
F. Swarttouw (President and Chairman)
D. Krook (Deputy Chairman; Marketing and Sales)
R. C. van den Heuvel (Finance)
F. Nel (Technology)

Vice-President, Corporate Affairs: ir P. van Lent
Director of Corporate Relations: H. Byvanck
Manager, Corporate Communications: G. W. Knook

Fokker, which is a private company without Dutch government financial holdings, forms the main aircraft industry in the Netherlands, with six plants. It employs some 10,000 people, including 1,400 at the corporate headquarters. Fokker delivered its 1,000th short/medium-range transport aircraft, an F27, to Busy Bee of Norway on 17 April 1986.

Fokker has an important share in the European manufacturing programme for the General Dynamics F-16 fighter, being responsible for component production and assembly of F-16s for the Netherlands (213) and Denmark (12). Seventy-two F-16s for Norway were delivered between January 1980 and June 1984 (see earlier editions of *Jane's*). Deliveries to the RNethAF began in June 1979, following the first flight by a Dutch assembled F-16 (J-259) on 3 May 1979. Deliveries to the RNethAF totalled 137 by mid-March 1986, and will begin to the Royal Danish Air Force in December 1987. The 200th Fokker built F-16 was delivered on 24 July 1985. Altogether, Fokker is producing 1,286 centre-fuselages, 1,246 wing moving surfaces, 1,007 main landing gear doors, 506 main landing gear legs, 262 horizontal stabilisers, 658 rudders and 597 fin leading-edges (for Fokker's own assembly line, as well as for a similar line in Belgium and for General Dynamics, which manufactures F-16s for the USAF and for 'third nation' sales).

In September 1986, Fokker joined IPTN of Indonesia, Boeing of USA and MBB of Germany in a joint venture memorandum of understanding study to determine the feasibility of an advanced technology medium-range regional transport in the 100-seat class for marketing in 1992-95.

Some 4,745 people are employed at the Fokker Schiphol plant, Amsterdam, which accommodates the Fokker 50 and 100 and F-16 assembly lines and test flying facilities. Production of the F27 and F28 ended in 1986. Wing moving surfaces are being produced for Airbus Industrie. Also at Schiphol are the design offices, spare parts stores, research and development department, numerically controlled milling department, metal bonding department, electronics division, space division and scientific and administrative computer facilities.

The Drechtsteden plant, formed by the integrated production facilities at Dordrecht and Papendrecht, employs 1,513 people. Most of these are engaged on detail production and component assembly for the Fokker 50 and 100, F-16, Airbus A300/A310 and Shorts 330/360 and Sherpa; other work includes the manufacture of specialised products.

At Ypenburg the installation of F-16 centre-fuselages is carried out by a workforce of 946 people. Composite material components for the Fokker 50, Fokker 100 and Airbus A300/A310, and radomes and fairings for the Westland Lynx helicopter, are manufactured at Ypenburg.

Woensdrecht, which has a current workforce of 953, specialises in the maintenance, overhaul, repair and modification of F27s, F28s, F-16s and a wide variety of other military aircraft, and in the incorporation of customers' requirements in such aircraft. Component production for the Patriot missile began in mid-1985. Also at Woensdrecht the ELMO division produces electrical and electronic systems and cable harnesses.

Hoogeveen is engaged in the manufacture of parts for the aerospace and other industries, including components for the Ariane launch vehicle. Quantity production of aluminium shelters and refurbishing of fuel tanks are also undertaken in this factory. A new facility became operational in 1982, producing carbonfibre composite tail components for the F-16, and Airbus A310 hinge and leg fairing doors. Hoogeveen employs 447 people.

FOKKER F27 FRIENDSHIP

The first of two F27 prototypes made its first flight on 24 November 1955, and the second on 29 January 1957. Deliveries by Fokker began in November 1958, and have been continuous for more than 27 years. Details of the 205 F-27 and FH-227 models produced by Fairchild in the USA can be found in the 1974-75 and earlier editions of *Jane's*. Many other versions have been built by Fokker, full details of the most recent Mks 200, 400M and 500 last appearing in the 1985-86 edition. Production of the F27 came to an end in 1986. An order for two by the Royal Thai Navy, announced on 23 June 1986, brought the overall sales total to 786 at that date, to 168 customers in 63 countries. These last two aircraft were due for delivery in late 1986 and early 1987.

FOKKER 50

At the end of November 1983, coinciding with the 25th anniversary in airline service of the twin-turboprop F27 Friendship, Fokker announced follow-on developments of both the F27 and the twin-turbofan F28 Fellowship, to be known respectively as the Fokker 50 and Fokker 100. Both aircraft build on successfully proven airframes, but with significant design and structural changes, allied to more efficient (and more fuel-efficient) power plants, increased use of composite materials, greater passenger comfort and convenience, advanced digital avionics, and improved airport handling characteristics. In consequence, more than 80 per cent of the component parts of the Fokker 50 are new or modified by comparison with those of the F27.

The two prototypes of the Fokker 50 utilise modified F27 fuselages rather than the redesigned fuselage of the production aircraft. The first of them (PH-OSO) flew for the first time on 28 December 1985, and the second (PH-OSI) on 30 April 1986; certification was expected by November 1986.

In the production aircraft, differences from the F27 include new-technology engines, in redesigned nacelles, with six-blade propellers; use of carbon, aramid and glassfibre composites in such areas as the wings, tailplane, fin, radome, engine nacelles and propellers; passenger door relocated at the front of the aircraft, and the large cargo door deleted; more windows in the passenger cabin; pneumatic system replaced by a hydraulic system; and a cruising speed some 12 per cent higher than that of the F27. Seating range is 46-58, with 50 as standard, but the cabin offers considerable flexibility for other layouts, including ample accommodation for baggage and freight.

Firm orders for 39 Fokker 50s had been received by September 1986, from Ansett of Australia (15), Austrian Airlines (2), Busy Bee of Norway (4), Corsair of USA (7), DLT of West Germany (7) and Maersk Air of Denmark (4). First delivery, to Ansett, was scheduled for December 1986.

Type: Twin-turboprop short-haul transport.

Wings: Cantilever high-wing monoplane. Wing section NACA 64_4-421 (modified) at root, NACA 64_2-415 (modified) at tip. Outer panels have 2° 30′ dihedral and 2° washout. Incidence 3° 30′. No sweepback. All-metal riveted and metal-bonded two-spar stressed skin primary structure, consisting of centre-section and two detachable outer wings. Detachable AFRP leading-edges with rubber boot de-icers. Trailing-edge skins are of composites material, supported by ribs of composites or metal construction. Single-slotted all-metal trailing-edge flaps (two segments per wing, divided by engine nacelle), operated by spindle/drive-nut. Flaps are actuated hydraulically, with electrical backup system, and are mechanically interconnected. Aileron structure is formed by bonded skin/stringer assemblies riveted to front, centre and rear spars and ribs, with leading-edges of composites material. Ailerons are actuated mechanically via cables. Each has an inboard spring tab and outboard geared/balance tab; starboard balance tab serves also as an electrically operated trim tab. Horn balance, known as Foklet, of metal reinforced composites, at each wingtip to increase lateral stability when turning.

Fuselage: All-metal stressed skin primary structure, built to fail-safe principles, with cylindrical portions metal bonded and conical part riveted. Pressurised between rear

Prototype of the Fokker 50 twin-turboprop transport (two Pratt & Whitney Canada PW124 engines), which made its first flight on 28 December 1985

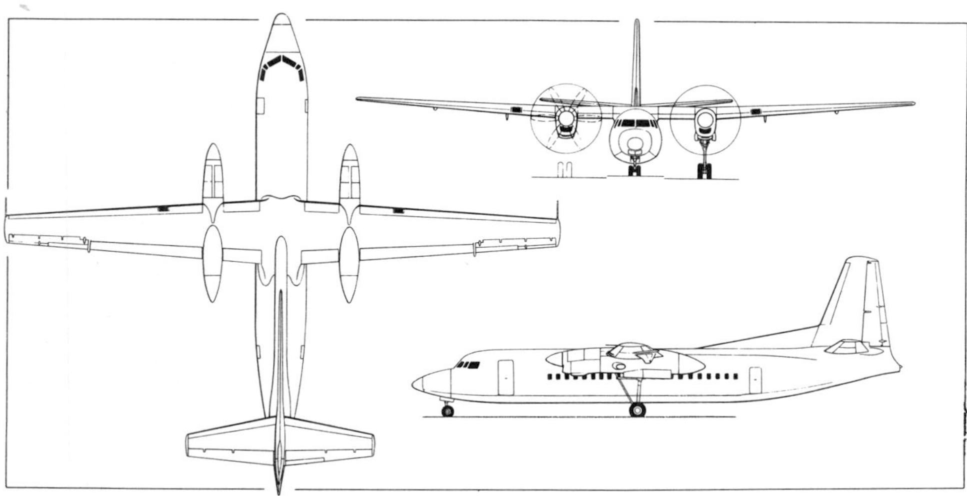

Fokker 50 twin-turboprop short-haul transport *(Pilot Press)*

bulkhead of nosewheel compartment and circular pressure bulkhead aft of baggage compartment. Nosecone, fairings, nosewheel doors, access doors and cabin floor are of composites materials.

TAIL UNIT: Cantilever fin and fixed incidence tailplane of all-metal primary construction. Leading-edges are made of composites and have integral pneumatic de-icing boots; part of dorsal fin also of composites material. Elevators and rudder (both built by Fuji in Japan) are cable actuated. Elevators are mechanically interconnected, with a fixed tab in each elevator and trim tab in starboard elevator. Rudder is provided with a trim tab, geared balance tab and horn balance.

LANDING GEAR: Retractable tricycle type of Dowty Rotol manufacture, with twin wheels on all units. Main units are attached to wings, retracting rearward hydraulically into rear extension of engine nacelle; nosewheels retract forward. Long-stroke oleo-pneumatic shock absorber in each unit (single-stage on nose unit, double-acting on main units). Goodyear wheels and tyres on all units. Standard main unit tyres are size 34 × 10·75-16, with pressure of 5·52 bars (80 lb/sq in); size 37 × 11·75-16 low-pressure tyres (4·00 bars; 58 lb/sq in) are optional. Nosewheel tyres are size 24 × 7·7-10, with pressure of 3·10 bars (45 lb/sq in). Goodyear hydraulic brakes, incorporating anti-skid system. Hydraulic nosewheel steering (±73°); free-castoring angle of ±130° available for towing.

POWER PLANT: Two 1,611 kW (2,160 shp) Pratt & Whitney Canada PW124 turboprop engines, each driving a Dowty Rotol six-blade propeller with spinner. Propellers have all-composite blades and Beta control. Lucas Aerospace 8·2 kW (11 hp) electric motor for engine starting. Composites materials used in construction of engine air intakes and nacelle cowlings. Fuel in two structural tanks located between the two spars of the central spar box outboard of the engine nacelle, with total standard capacity of 5,136 litres (1,130 Imp gallons). Single-point pressure refuelling. Engine air intakes, propeller blades and spinners de-iced electrically.

ACCOMMODATION: Crew of two on flight deck, plus two cabin attendants. Standard commuter layout seats 50 passengers, four-abreast with central aisle, at 81 cm (32 in) pitch. Alternative layouts include 46 business class passengers at 86 cm (34 in) pitch, 54 tourist class at 76 cm (30 in), or 58 in high-density arrangement, also at 76 cm (30 in). All layouts mentioned have overhead stowage bins and forward and rear main baggage/cargo compartments as standard, with toilet and carry-on baggage areas forward and galley at rear of cabin. Downward opening airstair door at front on port side; service door at rear on same side; baggage/cargo door opposite each of these on starboard side. All four doors serve also as Type I emergency exits. Entire accommodation pressurised and air-conditioned. Windscreens anti-iced electrically, flight deck side windows demisted by hot air.

SYSTEMS: Hamilton Standard air-conditioning system. Max pressure differential 0·38 bars (5·47 lb/sq in). Garrett digital cabin pressure control system. Hydraulic system, operating at 207 bars (3,000 lb/sq in) pressure via two engine driven Abex pumps, for landing gear actuation, brakes, nosewheel steering and flap drive. Pneumatic de-icing of wing, fin and tailplane leading-edges, using engine bleed air. Primary electrical system powered by a Sundstrand 30/40kVA integrated drive generator mounted on propeller gearbox of each engine, supplying 115/200V three-phase AC at 400Hz, with two 300A transformer-rectifiers and two 30/40kVA nickel-cadmium batteries for 28V DC power. Optional third (30/40kVA) generator driven by APU. External power socket. 30/40kVA APU optional (in rear cone of starboard engine nacelle), for additional electrical power and bleed air for air-conditioning.

AVIONICS: Flight deck has dual Sperry EDZ-801 electronic flight instrument system (EFIS) with CRT displays for primary flight and navigation information, and space provisions for a central multifunction display. Standard avionics include Sperry SPZ-600 AFCS with Cat. I landing; Sperry FZ-500 dual flight director systems; dual Bendix Series III VHF com; single Bendix Series III ADF and DME (latter including frequency hold facility); Bendix Series III ATC transponder; Sperry Primus P-650 weather radar with dual presentation on EFIS; dual Bendix Series III VHF nav with VOR, ILS and marker beacon receiver; TRT AHV-530A (ARINC 552A) radio altimeter with dual presentation on EFIS; dual Litton LTR 81·01 AHRS; Sundstrand Mk II GPWS (ARINC 549); Sperry AZ-800 air data computer; Fairchild A100 (ARINC 557) cockpit voice recorder; Collins 346-2B (ARINC 560) PA system; Sundstrand 980-4100 DXUS (ARINC 573) flight data recorder, incl underwater locator beacon and flight data entry panel; and Teledyne Model 70-275 flight data acquisition unit. Full provisions for Cat. II landing on AFCS and single Collins 628T-2A HF com to ARINC 559A2; space provisions for second ADF, second DME, second ATC transponder, Omega/VLF nav system, and Dorne & Margolin ELT.

DIMENSIONS, EXTERNAL:
Wing span 29·00 m (95 ft 1¾ in)
Wing chord: at root 3·464 m (11 ft 4½ in)
at tip 1·40 m (4 ft 7 in)
Wing aspect ratio 12·01
Length overall 25·247 m (82 ft 10 in)
Fuselage: Max width 2·70 m (8 ft 10¼ in)
Height overall (static) 8·317 m (27 ft 3½ in)
Tailplane span 9·746 m (31 ft 11¾ in)
Wheel track 7·20 m (23 ft 7½ in)
Wheelbase 9·70 m (31 ft 10 in)
Propeller diameter 3·66 m (12 ft 0 in)
Propeller ground clearance 1·162 m (3 ft 9¾ in)
Propeller/fuselage clearance 0·593 m (1 ft 11¼ in)
Passenger door (fwd, port): Height 1·78 m (5 ft 10 in)
Width 0·76 m (2 ft 6 in)
Service door (rear, port) and cargo door (fwd, stbd), each:
Height 1·27 m (4 ft 2 in)
Width 0·61 m (2 ft 0 in)
Cargo door (rear, stbd): Height 1·27 m (4 ft 2 in)
Width 0·86 m (2 ft 9¾ in)

DIMENSIONS, INTERNAL:
Cabin, excl flight deck: Length 15·96 m (52 ft 4 in)
Width at floor 2·11 m (6 ft 11 in)
Max width 2·50 m (8 ft 2½ in)
Max height 1·96 m (6 ft 5¼ in)
Floor area (excl toilet) 30·2 m^2 (325·0 sq ft)
Baggage/cargo volume (standard commuter version):
main compartments 7·82 m^3 (276 cu ft)
carry-on compartment 0·82 m^3 (29 cu ft)
overhead bins 2·22 m^3 (78·4 cu ft)

AREA:
Wings, gross 70·0 m^2 (753·5 sq ft)

WEIGHTS:
Typical operating weight empty 12,633 kg (27,850 lb)
Max fuel load 4,123 kg (9,090 lb)
Max payload 5,670 kg (12,500 lb)
Max ramp weight: standard 19,100 kg (42,110 lb)
optional 20,820 kg (45,900 lb)
Max T-O weight: standard 18,990 kg (41,865 lb)
optional 20,820 kg (45,900 lb)
Max landing weight: standard 18,990 kg (41,865 lb)
optional 19,731 kg (43,500 lb)
Max zero-fuel weight 18,303 kg (40,350 lb)

PERFORMANCE (estimated):
Max operating Mach number 0·507
Typical cruising speed 287 knots (532 km/h; 330 mph)
Typical climb speed
200 knots (370 km/h; 230 mph) IAS
Typical descent speed
227 knots (420 km/h; 261 mph) IAS
Max operating altitude 7,620 m (25,000 ft)
Service ceiling, one engine out, AUW of 18,250 kg (40,234 lb), ISA 4,110 m (13,485 ft)
Min ground turning radius 18·10 m (59 ft 4¾ in)
Runway LCN (51 cm; 20 in flexible pavement):
standard tyres 17·5
low-pressure tyres 14·2
T-O field length at S/L, ISA:
standard MTOW, 16·5° flap 1,055 m (3,460 ft)
optional MTOW, 0° flap 1,760 m (5,775 ft)
Landing field length at S/L, ISA:
standard MLW, 40° flap 1,022 m (3,355 ft)
optional MLW, 40° flap 1,060 m (3,480 ft)
Range with 50 passengers and baggage, reserves 10% flight fuel, 30 min hold at 457 m (1,500 ft) and 130 nm (241 km; 149 mile) diversion:
at standard MTOW:
high-speed procedure 498 nm (923 km; 573 miles)
min fuel procedure 603 nm (1,117 km; 694 miles)
at optional MTOW:
high-speed procedure
1,223 nm (2,266 km; 1,408 miles)
min fuel procedure
1,486 nm (2,753 km; 1,711 miles)

OPERATIONAL NOISE LEVELS (estimated):
T-O 81 EPNdB
Approach 96 EPNdB
Sideline 85 EPNdB

FOKKER 50 MARITIME AND SURVEILLANCE VERSIONS

A maritime patrol version of the F27, designed to meet the requirements of various coastal agencies throughout the world which require a cost-effective surveillance aircraft for coastal patrol, fishery protection, search and rescue, and similar offshore duties, was defined in July 1975, and shortly afterwards Fokker began converting an ex-airline F27 to serve as a prototype/demonstration aircraft (PH-FCX). This prototype made its first flight in February 1976. Production F27 Maritime aircraft were ordered by the Peruvian Navy (two), and air forces of Angola (one), Netherlands (two), Nigeria (four), Philippines (three) and Spain (three). Four others, for Royal Thai Navy, are equipped to carry armament, but are not to full Maritime Enforcer standard.

Fokker F27 Maritime in the insignia of the Royal Thai Navy

The F27 Maritime is now replaced in production by the following maritime and surveillance aircraft based on the Fokker 50:

Fokker Maritime Mk 2. Basic unarmed maritime patrol version of Fokker 50, for duties which include coastal surveillance, search and rescue, and environmental control. It is operated by a crew of up to six persons.

Maritime Enforcer Mk 2. Similar to Fokker Maritime Mk 2, but equipped for armed surveillance, anti-submarine and anti-shipping warfare, with enhanced avionics and provisions for carrying external stores (armament chosen and installed by operator).

Sentinel Mk 2. Border surveillance and standoff reconnaissance version. Primary sensor is a Motorola AN/APS-135(V) side looking airborne radar (SLAR), mounted in an underfuselage pod. Equipped with Doppler moving target indication, this can detect large targets at up to 80 nm (148 km; 92 miles) distant, or smaller targets at up to 48 nm (90 km; 56 miles). Onboard data processing via colour CRT display. Standoff photography with Litton/Itek KA-102 long-range oblique photography (LOROP) system, or a Vinten pod containing 70 mm vertical and oblique cameras or an infra-red linescan. Options include an automatic computerised COMINT (communications intelligence) system to intercept, record and analyse radio signals in the 20-1,000MHz frequency band.

King Bird Mk 2. Proposed AEW version, with Thorn EMI Skymaster surveillance radar in retractable ventral radome. Capability includes pulse-Doppler search and acquisition modes (for all aircraft within a 120 nm; 222 km; 138 mile radius). ESM to detect and identify radar-emitting targets within surveillance area. Reduced fuel load.

The following description applies specifically to the Maritime Enforcer Mk 2, Sentinel Mk 2 and King Bird Mk 2, based on the Fokker 50 airframe:

TYPE: Twin-turboprop maritime patrol aircraft.

WINGS, FUSELAGE AND TAIL UNIT: As described for Fokker 50, except that airframe is heavily treated with anti-corrosive measures; in tail unit, only the port elevator has a trim tab.

LANDING GEAR: As described for Fokker 50, but with tyre pressures of 5·52 bars (80 lb/sq in) on main units and 3·80 bars (55 lb/sq in) on nose unit. With long-stroke main gear fitted, pressure in the low-pressure mainwheel tyres is 4·50 bars (65 lb/sq in), and in tyre on the levered suspension nose unit is 3·80 bars (55 lb/sq in).

POWER PLANT: Two turboprop engines, as described in main Fokker 50 entry. Six-blade Dowty Rotol propellers. Integral fuel tanks in outer wings, total capacity 5,136 litres (1,130 Imp gallons). Overwing (gravity) and pressure refuelling. Additional centre-wing tank of 2,310 litres (508 Imp gallons) capacity, and two 938 litre (206·5 Imp gallon) tanks on underwing pylons, giving overall total fuel capacity of 9,322 litres (2,051 Imp gallons). Methyl bromide fire extinguishing system, with flame detectors.

ACCOMMODATION: Flight compartment seats two pilots side by side, with folding seat for third crew member if required. Main cabin of Fokker Maritime Mk 2 fitted out as tactical compartment (for two to four operators), containing advanced avionics, galley, toilet and crew rest area. Maritime Enforcer accommodates crew of seven including two pilots: tactical co-ordinator (Tacco) responsible for off-airways navigation and overall efforts of mission crew; acoustic sensor operator (ASO) to handle active and passive sonobuoys, acoustic receivers and processor display system; non-acoustic sensor operator (NASO) controlling search radar and electronic surveillance subsystem; and two observers. Bubble windows for observers are provided at rear of main cabin. Rear cabin door is openable in flight. Standard cargo door at front on port side, with sill at truckbed height. Cargo holds forward and aft of main cabin.

SYSTEMS: Generally as described for Fokker 50, except that cabin pressure differential is 0·38 bars (5·5 lb/sq in) and oxygen system includes individual supply for each tactical crew member.

AVIONICS AND EQUIPMENT: Com/nav equipment comprises Collins 628T-3 HF transceiver, two Bendix VCS-4 VHF transceivers, Collins AN/ARC-182 VHF/UHF transceiver (three in Enforcer), interphone, crew address system, Litton LTN-92 inertial navigation system, IDC air data computer, Bendix DFS-43 radio compass, two TRT AHV-530 radio altimeters, Collins DF-301E VHF/UHF direction finder, two Bendix VNS-41 VOR/ILS/marker beacon receivers, Sperry AD2-S01 EFIS, Teledyne AN/APX-101 IFF transponder, dual Sperry SPZ-600 AFCS, weather radar, low altitude warning system (Enforcer), and Tacan (Sentinel and King Bird).

OPERATIONAL EQUIPMENT (Maritime Mk 2 and Maritime Enforcer Mk 2): Both versions fitted with Litton 360° search radar in ventral radome: AN/APS-140(V) or AN/APS-504(V)5. Additional mission equipment in Enforcer Mk 2 includes GEC Avionics central tactical computer and display system, radar detection and display system, on-top position indicator/receiver, dual sonobuoy signal receivers, GEC Avionics AQS 902 (LAPADS) sonar, and sonobuoy processing system. Both passive and active sonobuoys are carried (up to 40 of SSQ-36, SSQ-41B or SSQ-47B type, up to 120 smaller buoys, or a mixture of both sizes), and launched from the internal stores area in the rear of the cabin. Argo Systems AR-700 electronic surveillance and monitoring equipment to detect radar transmissions, which can be classified and recorded and their bearings transferred to the tactical display. Infra-red detection system (IRDS). MAD. A data link with available ground or shipborne systems can be provided. Searchlight pod optional, on central starboard wing pylon.

F28 Fellowship prototype (PH-JHG) rewired and reconfigured as an avionics testbed for the Fokker 100

ARMAMENT (Maritime Enforcer Mk 2): Fokker only installs provisions for armament; weapon mix and purchase is up to customer. Alkan stores management system. Two 907 kg (2,000 lb) stores attachments on the fuselage and three under each wing (capacities 295 kg; 650 lb inboard, 680 kg; 1,500 lb in centre, and 113 kg; 250 lb outboard). Typical ASW armament can include two or four Mk 44, Mk 46, Sting Ray or A244/S torpedoes and/or depth bombs. For anti-shipping warfare, two AM39 Exocet, AGM-65F Maverick, AGM-84A Harpoon, Sea Skua, Sea Eagle or similar air-to-surface missiles can be carried. Auxiliary fuel tanks can be carried on the central underwing pylons.

DIMENSIONS: As for Fokker 50

WEIGHTS AND LOADINGS (A: Maritime Mk 2, B: Maritime Enforcer Mk 2, C: Sentinel Mk 2, D: King Bird Mk 2):

Manufacturer's weight empty:
- A: 12,519 kg (27,600 lb)
- B: 14,088 kg (31,060 lb)

Operating weight empty:
- A: 13,314 kg (29,352 lb)
- B (typical): 14,796 kg (32,620 lb)
- C: 14,515 kg (32,000 lb)
- D: 15,422 kg (34,000 lb)

Max fuel (incl pylon tanks):
- A: 7,257 kg (16,000 lb)
- B: 7,511 kg (16,560 lb)
- C: 7,484 kg (16,500 lb)
- D: 5,978 kg (13,180 lb)

Normal T-O weight: all 20,820 kg (45,900 lb)
Max T-O weight: all 21,545 kg (47,500 lb)
Emergency overload T-O weight:
- B: 22,680 kg (50,000 lb)

Max landing weight: all 19,730 kg (43,500 lb)
Max zero-fuel weight: all 18,144 kg (40,000 lb)
Max wing loading: all 291·6 kg/m² (59·75 lb/sq ft)
Max power loading: all 6·39 kg/kW (10·5 lb/shp)

PERFORMANCE (at normal T-O weight except where indicated):

Normal cruising speed 282 knots (522 km/h; 325 mph)
Typical search speed at 610 m (2,000 ft) 150 knots (277 km/h; 172 mph)
Service ceiling: all 7,620 m (25,000 ft)
Service ceiling, one engine out: A 3,565 m (11,700 ft)
Runway LCN (42 per cent tyre deflection) at 15,875 kg (35,000 lb) AUW: A
- rigid pavement, L = 76·2 cm (30 in): 10·4
- flexible pavement, h = 25·4 cm (10 in): 11·4
- flexible pavement, h = 12·7 cm (5 in): 9·0

Runway LCN (42 per cent tyre deflection) at 20,410 kg (45,000 lb) AUW: A
- rigid pavement, L = 76·2 cm (30 in): 16·0
- flexible pavement, h = 25·4 cm (10 in): 14·8
- flexible pavement, h = 12·7 cm (5 in): 12·0

Runway CBR, unpaved soil, h = 25·4 cm (10 in), 3,000 passes: A
- AUW of 15,875 kg (35,000 lb): 6·2%
- AUW of 20,410 kg (45,000 lb): 7·8%

T-O run at S/L, AUW of 21,320 kg (47,000 lb):
- ISA: 1,525 m (5,000 ft)
- ISA + 20°C: 1,700 m (5,575 ft)

Landing distance (unfactored, ISA at S/L), landing weight of 15,422 kg (34,000 lb) 560 m (1,837 ft)
Max radius of action with 1,814 kg (4,000 lb) mission load 1,200 nm (2,224 km; 1,382 miles)
Max range, no reserves 3,680 nm (6,820 km; 4,237 miles)
Max endurance, reserves for 30 min hold, 5% fuel remaining 14 h 42 min

FOKKER F28 FELLOWSHIP

First flight of the first prototype F28 (PH-JHG) was made on 9 May 1967, and two other prototypes flew later that year. The first delivery (of the fourth aircraft, to LTU) was made on 24 February 1969. Several versions were produced, the final ones being the Mks 3000 and 4000, a full description of which can be found in the 1985-86 *Jane's*.

Production of the F28 came to an end in 1986. By 23 June 1986, orders for all versions had totalled 241 from 59 customers in 39 countries. The last to be ordered, a Mk 4000 for Linjeflyg of Sweden, is due for delivery in mid-1987.

The following F28 airframe description is retained until a full description of the Fokker 100 becomes available:

WINGS: Cantilever low/mid-wing monoplane. Wing section NACA 0000-X 40Y series with camber varying along span. Thickness/chord ratio up to 14% on inner panels, 10% at tip. Dihedral 2° 30'. Sweepback at quarter-chord 16°. Single-cell two-spar light alloy torsion box structure, comprising centre-section, integral with fuselage, and two outer panels. Fail-safe construction. Lower skin made of three planks. Taper rolled top skin. Forged ribs in centre-section, built-up ribs in outer panels. Double skin leading-edge with ducts for hot air de-icing. Irreversible hydraulically operated ailerons. Emergency manual operation of ailerons, through tabs. Hydraulically operated Fowler double-slotted flaps over 70 per cent of each half span with electric emergency extension. Five-section hydraulically operated lift dumpers in front of flaps on each wing. Trim tab in each aileron.

FUSELAGE: Circular-section semi-monocoque light alloy fail-safe structure, made up of skin panels with Redux-bonded Z stringers. Bonded doubler plates at door and window cutouts. Quickly detachable sandwich (metal/end-grain balsa) floor panels. Hydraulically operated petal airbrakes form aft end of fuselage.

TAIL UNIT: Cantilever light alloy structure, with hydraulically actuated variable incidence T tailplane. Electric emergency actuation of tailplane. Hydraulically boosted elevators. Hydraulically operated rudder with duplicated actuators and emergency manual operation. Honeycomb sandwich skin panels used extensively, in conjunction with multiple spars. Double skin leading-edges for hot air de-icing.

FOKKER 100

Announced simultaneously with the Fokker 50, the Fokker 100 was due to fly for the first time in the fourth quarter of 1986. Certification is due in the Autumn of 1987. It is powered by Rolls-Royce Tay turbofan engines, and will comply with the Stage 3 requirements of FAR Pt 36 which were due to come into operation in 1986. The collaboration agreements with MBB (Germany) and Shorts (UK), set up for the F28 programme, continue with the Fokker 100.

The Fokker 100 is based generally on the airframe of the F28 Mk 4000, but has a longer fuselage, enabling it to accommodate 107 passengers at 81 cm (32 in) pitch in standard configuration, compared with 85 at 74 cm (29 in) pitch in the F28 Mk 4000. The extended and much-redesigned wings are claimed to be 30 per cent more efficient aerodynamically than those of the F28.

By September 1986 firm orders for 45 Fokker 100s had been placed, by Swissair (8), USAir (20) and KLM (10), with 31 more (6, 20 and 5 respectively) on option, plus an order for 7 from International Lease Finance Corporation. Deliveries, to Swissair, are scheduled to begin in the Autumn of 1987.

TYPE: Twin-turbofan short/medium-haul transport.

WINGS, FUSELAGE, TAIL UNIT: Generally based on F28 Mk 4000, but with extensive design and structural changes including use of aramid and carbonfibre composites. Wings (built by Shorts) have 1·5 m (4 ft 11 in) extension of each tip; new leading-edges, with reduced kink; new trailing-edges, including new flaps; and a different outer-wing aerofoil section. These changes have the effect also of altering the overall wing profile, providing an increase of approx 18 per cent in area and some 30 per cent in aerodynamic efficiency. The basic wing central box structure remains virtually unchanged. Flaps and ailerons are of carbonfibre, spoilers and aileron trim tabs of aluminium alloy. Fuselage is 5·74 m (18 ft 10 in) longer than that of the F28 Mk 4000, and tailplane span is extended by 1·4 m (4 ft 7 in). Aramid and carbonfibre used with aluminium alloys for fuselage and tail unit;

components built of composites include nosecone, wing/body fairings and floor panels, nacelle cowl doors, rudder, and dorsal fin. Thermal anti-icing of wing and tail leading-edges and external antennae. Menasco powered controls for ailerons, elevators and rudder.

LANDING GEAR: Hydraulically retractable tricycle type, with twin wheels on each unit. Main units retract inward into wing/body fairing; nosewheel retracts forward. Dowty Exports shock absorber in each unit. Goodyear tyres, size H40 × 14-19 on main units (pressure 8·96 bars; 130 lb/sq in), size 24 × 7·7-10 (pressure 5·86 bars; 85 lb/sq in) on nose unit. Goodyear multiple-disc carbon brakes, with anti-skid system. Steerable nose unit (effective angle ±73°).

POWER PLANT: Two 61·6 kN (13,850 lb st) Rolls-Royce Tay Mk 620-15 turbofan engines, with thrust reversers, pylon mounted on sides of rear fuselage. Nacelles and pylons manufactured from composite materials. Fuel in 4,870 litre (1,071 Imp gallon) main tank in each wing and 3,300 litre (726 Imp gallon) tank (seven flexible cells) in wing centre-section, giving total standard internal capacity of 13,040 litres (2,868 Imp gallons). Refuelling point under starboard wing, near wing/fuselage belly fairing. Oil capacity (two engines) 23 kg (51 lb).

ACCOMMODATION: Crew of two on flight deck; two cabin attendants. Standard accommodation for 107 passengers, in five-abreast seating (3 + 2) at 81 cm (32 in) pitch. Optional layouts include 12 first class seats (four-abreast) at 91 cm (36 in) pitch plus 85 economy class (five-abreast) at 32 in; 55 business class at 86 cm (34 in) plus 50 economy class, all five-abreast; or 119 tourist class passengers at 74 cm (29 in) pitch. Reduced galley and stowage space in 119 seat layout. Aircraft for Swissair configured for 84 passengers (8 first class, 53 business class and 23 economy). Standard layout includes two galleys, two toilets, two wardrobes, two other stowage/wardrobe compartments, and carry-on baggage compartment. Outward opening passenger door at front of cabin on port side, with outward opening service/emergency door opposite on starboard side. Auxiliary service door on starboard side near rear galley. Two overwing emergency exits (inward opening plug type) each side. Two underfloor baggage/cargo holds (one forward of wing, one aft), each with downward opening door on starboard side. Entire accommodation air-conditioned.

SYSTEMS: Garrett air-conditioning and pressurisation system. Two fully independent hydraulic systems for actuation of flight control surfaces, landing gear, brakes and nosewheel steering. Garrett pneumatic system. Sundstrand electrical system. Oxygen system for flight crew and passengers. Garrett thermal anti-icing system for wings and tail unit. Electric anti-icing of flight deck windows, pitot tubes, static vents, angle of attack vanes and ice detector probe. Garrett GTCP 36-150 APU.

AVIONICS: Standard avionics include dual VHF com (to ARINC 716), PA system (ARINC 715), ATC transponder (ARINC 718), triple AHRS (ARINC 705), dual radio altimeters (ARINC 707), dual VOR with marker beacon receiver (ARINC 711), dual ILS (ARINC 710), dual ADF (ARINC 712), dual DME (ARINC 709), Collins primary flight display (PFD) and navigation display (ND) for each pilot, dual digital air data systems (ARINC 706) with computer driven instruments, weather radar (ARINC 708 on ND), dual flight management control system (FMCS) plus full flight regime autothrottle system, and Collins digital automatic flight control and augmentation system (AFCAS) for Cat. IIIA automatic landing. Optional avionics include single or dual HF com (ARINC 719), third VHF com, Selcal (ARINC 714), second ATC, third ILS, third radio altimeter, dedicated display for weather radar, and Cat. IIIB autoland capability.

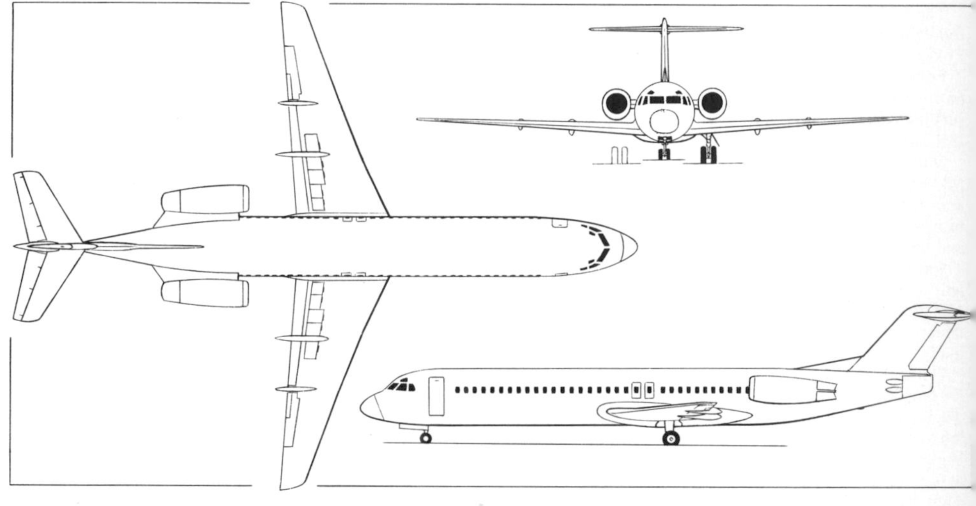

Fokker 100 'stretched' development of the F28 (two Rolls-Royce Tay turbofan engines) *(Pilot Press)*

DIMENSIONS, EXTERNAL:
- Wing span: 28·08 m (92 ft 1½ in)
- Wing chord: at root: 5·57 m (18 ft 3¼ in)
- at tip: 1·09 m (3 ft 7 in)
- Wing aspect ratio: 8·43
- Length overall: 35·53 m (116 ft 6¾ in)
- Fuselage: Length: 32·50 m (106 ft 7½ in)
- Max diameter: 3·30 m (10 ft 10 in)
- Height overall: 8·50 m (27 ft 10½ in)
- Tailplane span: 10·04 m (32 ft 11¼ in)
- Wheel track: 5·04 m (16 ft 6½ in)
- Wheelbase: 14·00 m (45 ft 11¼ in)
- Passenger door (fwd, port): Height: 2·21 m (7 ft 3 in)
- Width: 0·86 m (2 ft 9¾ in)
- Service door (fwd, stbd): Height: 1·28 m (4 ft 2½ in)
- Width: 0·61 m (2 ft 0 in)
- Cargo compartment doors (fwd and rear, stbd):
  - Height (each): 0·95 m (3 ft 1½ in)
  - Width (each): 0·90 m (2 ft 11½ in)
  - Height to sill (MTOW):
    - fwd door at front: 1·35 m (4 ft 5¼ in)
    - fwd door at rear: 1·41 m (4 ft 7½ in)
    - rear door: 1·56 m (5 ft 1½ in)
- Overwing emergency exits (four, each):
  - Height: 0·91 m (3 ft 0 in)
  - Width: 0·51 m (1 ft 8 in)

DIMENSIONS, INTERNAL:
- Cabin, excl flight deck: Length: 21·19 m (69 ft 6¼ in)
  - Max length of seating area: 18·80 m (61 ft 8¼ in)
  - Max width: 3·10 m (10 ft 2 in)
  - Width at floor: 2·89 m (9 ft 5¾ in)
  - Max height: 2·01 m (6 ft 7¼ in)
  - Max floor area: 58·48 m² (629·5 sq ft)
  - Max volume: 107·58 m³ (3,799 cu ft)
- Overhead stowage bins (total): 5·23 m³ (184·7 cu ft)
- Additional baggage space (total): 3·00 m³ (105·9 cu ft)
- Underfloor compartment volume:
  - fwd: 9·8 m³ (346 cu ft)
  - rear: 7·36 m³ (260 cu ft)

AREAS:
- Wings, gross: 93·5 m² (1,006·4 sq ft)
- Ailerons (total): 3·528 m² (37·98 sq ft)
- Trailing-edge flaps (total): 17·00 m² (182·99 sq ft)
- Spoilers (total): 2·65 m² (28·52 sq ft)
- Rudder: 2·30 m² (24·76 sq ft)
- Elevators (total): 7·68 m² (82·67 sq ft)

WEIGHTS:
- Typical operating weight empty (107 passengers): 23,800 kg (52,470 lb)
- Max payload (weight-limited): 11,350 kg (25,022 lb)
- Max fuel: 34,269 kg (75,550 lb)
- Max ramp weight: 43,320 kg (95,500 lb)
- Max T-O weight: 43,090 kg (95,000 lb)
- Max landing weight: 38,780 kg (85,500 lb)
- Max zero-fuel weight: 35,150 kg (77,500 lb)

PERFORMANCE (estimated):
- Max operating speed: Mach 0·75 (320 knots; 593 km/h; 368 mph CAS)
- Design approach speed at max landing weight: 129 knots (239 km/h; 149 mph)
- Max rate of climb at S/L: 152 m (500 ft)/min
- Service ceiling: 10,670 m (35,000 ft)
- FAR T-O field length at max T-O weight (S/L, ISA): 1,990 m (6,529 ft)
- FAR landing field length at max landing weight (S/L, ISA): 1,360 m (4,462 ft)
- Range with 107 passengers and baggage, Mach 0·73 cruise: 1,320 nm (2,446 km; 1,520 miles)

OPERATIONAL NOISE LEVELS (FAR Pt 36, estimated):
- Flyover: 85·4 EPNdB
- Approach: 97·0 EPNdB
- Sideline: 93·6 EPNdB

NEW ZEALAND

AERO TRADER

AERO TRADER LTD

16 Cliff Road, Torbay, Auckland

MANAGING DIRECTOR: A. Water

Aero Trader was reported in 1985 to be building a prototype two-seat training/touring aircraft, intended to obtain FAA certification under FAR Pt 25 Appendix A. Of conventional low-wing monoplane appearance, with mechanically actuated oleo-pneumatic landing gear, it was to be powered initially by an 1,850 cc VW engine, with fuel for six hours' flying; but a 2·3 litre engine is planned for the pre-production version. Performance with the prototype engine is expected to include a cruising speed of nearly 143 knots (266 km/h; 165 mph) and the ability to take off and land over a 15 m (50 ft) obstacle within 366 m (1,200 ft). Further details were requested, but no reply was received.

PAC

PACIFIC AEROSPACE CORPORATION LIMITED

Private Bag, Hamilton Airport, Hamilton
Telephone: (071) 436 144
Telex: NZ21242 PACORP

CHAIRMAN: Sir Richard Bolt
CHIEF EXECUTIVE: A. Hyde
CHIEF DESIGNER: M. G. McGregor
ENGINEERING MANAGER: H. C. Clarkson
SECRETARY: J. D. Linch

The former New Zealand Aerospace Industries Ltd (see 1982-83 and previous editions of *Jane's*) was reconstituted on 1 July 1982 as Pacific Aerospace Corporation Ltd, following its acquisition by the Aviation Corporation of New Zealand. PAC maintains full spares support of Airtrainer CT4A and Fletcher FU24-950 series aircraft in service, and is continuing to market the FU24-954 and Cresco agricultural monoplanes against firm orders.

Lockheed Corporation of Burbank, California, USA, has a 24·9% holding in Pacific Aerospace Corporation.

PAC FLETCHER FU24-954

The US built FU24 prototype flew in July 1954, followed by the first production aircraft five months later, as recorded in earlier editions of *Jane's*. Type certification was granted on 22 July 1955. All manufacturing and sales rights were transferred to New Zealand in 1964, and an initial production series of 100 was delivered to New Zealand operators. By April 1986 a total of 292 Fletcher FU24 series aircraft had been completed, including 56 for export to Australia, Bangladesh, Dubai, Iraq, Pakistan, Thailand, Uruguay and the USA. No further sales had been made by Spring 1986, but marketing and support are continuing.

Activities in the past year have centred around a methanol (methyl alcohol) fuelled variant of the aircraft, with about 400 hours' flying completed by April 1986 and certification expected by mid-year.

A full description of the current standard production version, the FU24-954, can be found in the 1985-86 *Jane's*. The following is an abbreviated version of that entry:

TYPE: Agricultural and general purpose aircraft.

AIRFRAME: See 1985-86 *Jane's*.

POWER PLANT: One 298 kW (400 hp) Avco Lycoming IO-720-A1A or A1B flat-eight engine, driving a Hartzell HC-C3YR-1R/847SR three-blade constant-speed variable-pitch metal propeller with spinner. Fuel tanks in wing leading-edges; total usable capacity 254 litres (67 US gallons) normal, 481 litres (127 US gallons) with optional long-range tanks.

ACCOMMODATION (agricultural models): Enclosed cockpit for pilot and one passenger on side by side seats under rearward sliding canopy. Cockpit reinforced for overturn/crash protection. Large port side cargo door. Optional features include additional cargo floor area and dual controls.

ACCOMMODATION (utility models): Enclosed cabin for pilot and up to seven passengers or equivalent freight. Dual controls optional. Rearward sliding hood over front two seats. Large passenger/cargo door on port side.

AGRICULTURAL EQUIPMENT: Glassfibre hopper aft of cockpit, capacity 1,211 litres (266 Imp gallons; 320 US gallons) of liquid, 1,066 kg (2,350 lb) of dry chemicals. Hopper outlets for spreading of solids (fertiliser, dry ice, poison bait etc). Transland Swathmaster for topdressing, seeding and high-volume spraying. Transland Boommaster for liquid spraying with booms, nozzles, fan driven pump, etc, for low- and high-volume spraying. Micronair spraying equipment with electrically or fan driven pump, varied control systems, side loading valve for liquids, and special adaptor plate for interchangeability of equipment.

OPTIONAL EQUIPMENT (all models): Full blind-flying instrumentation with ADF, VHF, VOR and DME. Full dual controls; dual mainwheels and brakes, wheel and leg fairings; long-range fuel tanks; cabin heating and air-conditioning systems; metric instrumentation.

DIMENSIONS, EXTERNAL:

Wing span	12·81 m (42 ft 0 in)
Length overall	9·70 m (31 ft 10 in)
Height overall	2·84 m (9 ft 4 in)
Wheel track	3·71 m (12 ft 2 in)
Wheelbase	2·28 m (7 ft 6 in)
Propeller diameter	2·18 m (7 ft 2 in)

DIMENSIONS, INTERNAL:

Cabin: Length	3·18 m (10 ft 5 in)
Max width	1·22 m (4 ft 0 in)
Max height	1·27 m (4 ft 2 in)
Floor area	3·87 m² (41·7 sq ft)
Volume aft of hopper	3·37 m³ (119·0 cu ft)
Hopper volume	1·22 m³ (43·0 cu ft)

AREA:

Wings, gross	27·31 m² (294·0 sq ft)

WEIGHTS AND LOADINGS:

Weight empty, equipped	1,188 kg (2,620 lb)
Max payload (agricultural)	1,052 kg (2,320 lb)
Normal max T-O weight	2,204 kg (4,860 lb)
Max agricultural T-O weight	2,463 kg (5,430 lb)
Cabin floor loading	1,885 kg/m² (386 lb/sq ft)
Normal wing loading	80·6 kg/m² (16·5 lb/sq ft)
Normal power loading	7·40 kg/kW (12·15 lb/hp)

PERFORMANCE (at Normal max T-O weight):

Never-exceed speed	143 knots (265 km/h; 165 mph)
Max level speed at S/L	126 knots (233 km/h; 145 mph)
Max cruising speed (75% power)	113 knots (209 km/h; 130 mph)
Operating speed for spraying (75% power)	90-115 knots (167-212 km/h; 104-132 mph)
Stalling speed: flaps up	55 knots (102 km/h; 64 mph)
flaps down	49 knots (91 km/h; 57 mph)
Max rate of climb at S/L	280 m (920 ft)/min
Service ceiling	4,875 m (16,000 ft)
T-O run	244 m (800 ft)
T-O to 15 m (50 ft)	372 m (1,220 ft)
Landing from 15 m (50 ft)	390 m (1,280 ft)
Landing run	207 m (680 ft)
Swath width (agricultural models): oily	23 m (75 ft)
aqueous	21·3-24·4 m (70-80 ft)
dust	7·6-15·2 m (25-50 ft)
Range with max normal fuel, 45 min reserves	383 nm (709 km; 441 miles)

PAC CRESCO 08-600

PAC Cresco 08-600 agricultural aircraft being used in a firefighting role

Design of this turboprop development of the FU24 began in 1977. Construction of a prototype started in the following year, and this aircraft (ZK-LTP) first flew on 28 February 1979. The Cresco has many components interchangeable with the FU24-954. Use of the LTP 101 engine, together with some structural refinements, permits a reduction in empty weight and a substantial increase in agricultural max T-O weight. The name Cresco is Latin for 'I grow'. The first production Cresco was flown in early 1980, and the type entered service in January 1982. Five, all for domestic customers, had been built by April 1986. Production, as with the FU24-954, was then at a standstill, but the aircraft continues to be actively marketed and supported.

The description of the FU24-954 applies also to the Cresco, except in the following respects:

TYPE: Turboprop powered agricultural and general purpose aircraft.

WINGS: As FU24-954, constructed mainly of 2014, 2024 and 6061 light alloys. Ground adjustable tab in each aileron.

FUSELAGE: Similar to FU24-954, with slight increase in length.

TAIL UNIT: Aerodynamically and mass balanced rudder and elevator. Electrically actuated trim tab in elevator, ground adjustable tab on rudder.

LANDING GEAR: Tyres size 8·50-6 on nosewheel and size 8·50-10 on mainwheels.

POWER PLANT: One Avco Lycoming LTP 101-700A-1A turboprop engine, flat rated at 447 kW (600 shp) and driving a Hartzell HC-B3TN-3D/T10282 three-blade constant-speed metal propeller with spinner. Four fuel tanks in wing centre-section, total capacity 545·5 litres (120 Imp gallons; 144 US gallons). Two refuelling points in upper surface of each wing. Oil capacity 5·5 litres (1·2 Imp gallons). Chin mounted engine air intake, fitted with Centrisep filter panel.

ACCOMMODATION: Pilot only, or crew of two side by side, under rearward sliding bulged cockpit hood. Tinted windscreen and canopy side panels standard. Dual controls available optionally. Large forward hinged door, with window, aft of wing on port side. Generous cargo space immediately aft of hopper. Cockpit ventilated; heating system optional.

SYSTEMS: No air-conditioning, pressurisation, hydraulic, pneumatic or oxygen systems. Electrical system powered by 24V 150A Auxilec starter/generator and two 24V 25Ah lead-acid batteries.

AVIONICS: Range of Narco or Becker avionics available, including VHF, VOR, ADF and transponder. Stall warning system standard.

AGRICULTURAL EQUIPMENT: Generally similar to FU24-954, except for substantially larger hopper, increasing capacity to 1,893 litres (416 Imp gallons; 500 US gallons) of liquid or 1,814 kg (4,000 lb) of dry chemical. Range of dispersal systems available to customer's requirements, from ultra-high-volume solids dispersal to ultra-low-volume spray.

DIMENSIONS, EXTERNAL:

Wing span	12·81 m (42 ft 0 in)
Wing chord, constant	2·13 m (7 ft 0 in)
Wing aspect ratio	6·00
Length overall	11·06 m (36 ft 3¼ in)
Length of fuselage	10·74 m (35 ft 2¾ in)
Height overall	3·42 m (11 ft 2½ in)
Tailplane span	4·95 m (16 ft 3 in)
Wheelbase	2·77 m (9 ft 1¼ in)
Propeller diameter	2·59 m (8 ft 6 in)
Propeller ground clearance (static)	0·38 m (1 ft 3 in)
Cargo door (port): Height	0·94 m (3 ft 1 in)
Width	0·94 m (3 ft 1 in)
Height to sill	0·91 m (3 ft 0 in)

DIMENSIONS, INTERNAL:

Cargo compartment volume (aft of hopper)	3·40 m³ (120·0 cu ft)
Hopper volume	1·77 m³ (62·5 cu ft)

AREAS:

Wings, gross	27·31 m² (294·0 sq ft)
Ailerons (total)	2·08 m² (22·4 sq ft)
Trailing-edge flaps (total)	3·06 m² (32·9 sq ft)
Fin, incl dorsal fin	1·89 m² (20·3 sq ft)
Rudder, incl tab	0·63 m² (6·8 sq ft)
Tailplane	3·47 m² (37·38 sq ft)
Elevators, incl tab	2·62 m² (28·25 sq ft)

WEIGHTS AND LOADINGS:

Weight empty, equipped	1,247 kg (2,750 lb)
Max disposable load (Agricultural, incl fuel)	1,851 kg (4,080 lb)
Max fuel load	435 kg (960 lb)
Max T-O weight: Normal	2,925 kg (6,450 lb)
Agricultural	3,175 kg (7,000 lb)
Max landing weight	2,925 kg (6,450 lb)
Max wing loading: Normal	107·07 kg/m² (21·94 lb/sq ft)
Agricultural	116·19 kg/m² (23·81 lb/sq ft)
Max power loading: Normal	6·54 kg/kW (10·75 lb/shp)

PERFORMANCE (at max Normal T-O weight, ISA, except where indicated):

Never-exceed speed	177 knots (328 km/h; 204 mph)
Max level speed at S/L	148 knots (274 km/h; 170 mph)
Max cruising speed (75% power)	135 knots (250 km/h; 155 mph)
Stalling speed at 2,767 kg (6,100 lb) AUW, flaps down, power off	52 knots (97 km/h; 60 mph)
Max rate of climb at S/L	321 m (1,054 ft)/min
Service ceiling	6,400 m (21,000 ft)
T-O to 15 m (50 ft)	436 m (1,430 ft)
Landing from 15 m (50 ft)	500 m (1,640 ft)
Range with max fuel, no reserves	467 nm (865 km; 537 miles)

PAKISTAN

PAC

PAKISTAN AERONAUTICAL COMPLEX

Kamra, District Attock

WORKS: F-6 Rebuild Factory, Mirage Rebuild Factory, and Aircraft Manufacturing Factory (all at Kamra)

Telephone: (92) 051 65961/4

Telex: 5601 PAC PK

DIRECTOR GENERAL:
Air Vice-Marshal M. Ajmal Khan

MANAGING DIRECTORS:
Air Cdre Maqsood Ahmed (F-6 RF)
Air Cdre Mehni M. Islam (MRF)
Air Cdre M. A. B. Subhani (AMF)

Located approximately midway between Islamabad and Peshawar, the Pakistan Aeronautical Complex is an organ of the Pakistan Ministry of Defence. It comprises three factories, as follows:

The **F-6 Rebuild Factory,** or F-6 RF, was established in 1980 for the primary purpose of overhauling the Pakistan Air Force's Chinese Shenyang F-6 aircraft and its airframe accessories. It is authorised to manufacture about 4,000 spares items for that aircraft, and also produces the 1,140 litre (250 Imp gallon) auxiliary fuel tanks fitted to the F-6. Current capacity (1985-86) is for 24 aircraft a year. Engines for the F-6 are rebuilt at Faisal Shaheed, a Pakistan Air Force base near Karachi. The F-6 RF possesses modern technical facilities for various engineering processes such as surface treatment, heat treatment, forging, casting, non-destructive testing, and other machine tools required to manufacture items from raw materials. In due course, the F-6 RF is expected to assume responsibility also for Chinese FT-5, FT-6 and A-5 aircraft in PAF service.

The **Mirage Rebuild Factory** (MRF) at Kamra, opened in 1978, can accomplish complete overhaul of Mirage III/5 aircraft, Atar 9C turbojet engines, and associated components and accessories, and has a current capacity of eight aircraft and over 30 engines per year. The MRF has a site area of some 810,000 m² (8,715,000 sq ft) and a workforce of nearly 1,600.

The **Aircraft Manufacturing Factory** came into operation in mid-1981, as the licence production centre for Saab Safari/Supporter two/three-seat light aircraft, which have the Pakistani name **Mushshak** (Urdu for 'proficient'). Progressive assembly of the first 90 of these aircraft (last described in detail in the 1978-79 *Jane's*) began in 1976 from semi-knocked-down and completely knocked-down kits, and it is now being manufactured at Kamra from raw materials. By mid-1985 about 130 examples of the Mushshak were in service with various units of the Pakistan Army and Air Force, with output continuing at the rate of 15 a year. The AMF is also reportedly modifying Mushshaks with extended span outer wings, to improve STOL performance, and considering the future installation of a more powerful Avco Lycoming or Continental engine.

Major facilities at the AMF include a 25,000-ton Swedish ASEA hydraulic press, and equipment to manufacture all GRP components of the Mushshak. Engines, instruments, electrical equipment and radios are imported, but almost all other items are manufactured locally.

Pakistan Air Force Mushshak (Saab Safari/Supporter), built under licence by PAC

PHILIPPINES

PADC
PHILIPPINE AEROSPACE DEVELOPMENT CORPORATION

MIA Road, Pasay, Metro Manila

Postal Address: PO Box 7395, Airmail Exchange Office, MIA 3120

Telephone: 832 27 41 to 49

Telex: 66019 PADC PN

President: Oscar M. Alejandro

Executive Vice-President: Jose L. Bustamante

Marketing Director: Antonio S. Duarte

Subsidiaries:

Philippine Helicopter Services Inc (PHSI) (maintenance and overhaul of BO 105 and Bell helicopters; overhaul and repair of Hughes/McDonnell Douglas helicopter blades; and repair of Zahnradfabrik Friedrichshafen AG products). President: Rodolfo A. Cacdac

Philippine Resource Helicopters Inc (PRHI) (short and long term charters of twin-engined helicopters and STOL aircraft in support of oil exploration and production, mineral and geological surveys, external lift operations, and tourist/executive transport)

PADC is a government owned corporation established in 1973 for the purpose of undertaking business and development projects in the aviation and aerospace industry in the Philippines.

PADC is engaged in the assembly and manufacture of **BO 105** helicopters and **Islander** light transport aircraft, under 1974 licence agreements with MBB of West Germany and Pilatus Britten-Norman of the UK respectively. By early 1986, PADC had assembled 44 BO 105s and 62 Islanders (including 22 Islanders for the Philippine Air Force), and had manufactured the GRP components for both types of aircraft.

PADC is also engaged in the maintenance and overhaul of lightweight aircraft, parts and components, and the sale of aircraft/engine related accessories and spare parts.

PADC is the appointed area service centre for the Islander, Cessna (Caravan I/II, Conquest and Citation) and Piper light aircraft, King Radio Corporation com/nav equipment, and Allison 250 series turboprop engines. It is also an authorised customer service facility of Bell Helicopter Asia (Pte) Ltd, providing maintenance, repair, overhaul and spare parts to owners and operators of Bell Model 204, 205 and 214 series helicopters.

POLAND

PZL
ZRZESZENIE WYTWÓRCÓW SPRZETU LOTNICZEGO I SILNIKOWEGO PZL (Association of Aircraft and Engine Industry)

ul. Miodowa 5, 00-251 Warszawa

Telephone: Warszawa 261441

Telex: 814281

President: Ing Tadeusz Ryczaj, MSc

Director: Col Jan Stojanowicz, MSc

The manufacture of aircraft in Poland began in 1910. In 1928 an industrial syndicate was established, grouping the existing aircraft factories into the Panstwowe Zaklady Lotnicze (State Aviation Works) to produce aircraft to meet domestic and export needs.

More than half a century of tradition in design and manufacture resulted in the production of several tens of thousands of aircraft, helicopters and gliders of various types, as well as of aero engines and equipment.

Until 1981, when new legislation made industrial unions illegal in Poland, the aviation industry was organised under control of the ZPLS-PZL (Aircraft and Engine Industry Union). In 1982 (see earlier editions of this annual) its activities came under the control of the Bureau of Ministers Plenipotentiary for the Aircraft and Engine Industry, and it is currently organised as the Zrzeszenie Wytwórców Sprzetu Lotniczego i Silnikowego PZL (Association of Aircraft and Engine Industry), managed by a council representing all factories which are members of the Association. Production plants within the Association are self-dependent.

Other members of the Association include the BTNU (Biuro Techniczne Nowych Uruchomień: Engineering Office for the Implementation of New Projects), and the PPT (Przedsiebiorstwo Projektowo-Technologiczne: Design and Production Methods Enterprise). The Instytut Lotnictwa (which see) is not a member, but is directly subordinated to the Ministry of Heavy and Machine Building Industry.

The Polish aviation industry currently comprises 24 factories, scientific and development units, technical and commercial organisations, which between them employ about 86,000 qualified workers. Its work has a broad base which includes research, design, development, manufacture, foreign trade, agricultural aviation services, and technical support for its own products which are operated by other countries.

Production by the Polish aviation industry relies substantially on aircraft, engines and equipment of its own design, as well as on co-operation and co-production with leading foreign aircraft manufacturers in both the East and the West. These programmes currently include the multi-purpose PZL-104 Wilga, the PZL-106 Kruk and M-18 Dromader low/medium-capacity agricultural aircraft; wing and tail component assembly (deliveries of which began in March 1979) for the Soviet Il-86 wide-bodied transport aircraft; the TS-11 Iskra, PZL-110 Koliber and M-20 Mewa light multi-purpose, training and sporting aircraft; local service passenger transports such as the Soviet designed An-2 and An-28; the Mi-2, Kania and Sokól low/medium-capacity helicopters for agricultural, medical and transport operations; sailplanes, including the Jantar series and Puchacz; piston, turbojet and turboprop engines; plus aircraft military equipment, propellers, and ground equipment for agricultural aircraft and helicopters.

The export sales of all Polish aviation products are handled by Pezetel Foreign Trade Enterprise, which became a limited company on 10 February 1983.

Pezetel Foreign Trade Enterprise Co Ltd

Aleja Stanów Zjednoczonych 61, PO Box 6, 00-991 Warszawa 44

Telephone: 10 80 01

Telex: 813314 PZL PL

Director and General Manager: Jerzy Krezlewicz, MA

Manager of Aviation Department: Kazimierz Niepsuj

Manager of Publicity Department: Ing Janusz Matuszewski

IL
INSTYTUT LOTNICTWA (Aviation Institute)

Al. Krakowska 110/114, 02-256 Warszawa-Okecie

Telephone: 460011 and 460993

Telex: 813537

General Manager: Prof Dr Ing Zbigniew Dżygadło

Chief Consultant for Scientific and Technical Co-operation: Dipl Ing Jerzy Grzegorzewski

Chief of Scientific, Technical and Economic Information Division: Dr Ing Tadeusz Kostia

The Instytut Lotnictwa was founded in 1926. It is directly subordinate to the Ministry of Heavy and Machine Building Industry. The IL is responsible for all research and development work in the Polish aviation industry. It conducts scientific research, including the investigation of problems associated with low-speed and high-speed aerodynamics, static and fatigue tests, development and testing of aero-engines, flight instruments, space science instrumentation, and other equipment, flight tests, and materials technology. It is also responsible for the construction of experimental aircraft and aero engines.

WSK-PZL KROSNO
WYTWÓRNIA SPRZETU KOMUNIKACYJNEGO-PZL KROSNO (Transport Equipment Manufacturing Centre, Krosno)

38-400 Krosno n. Wislokiem

Telephone: 229 11

Telex: 065236

General Manager: Ing Jan Czarnecki

PZL KROSNO KR-02

Described by a November 1982 issue of *Polish Daily* as "one of the world's smallest aircraft", the KR-02 was designed by Stanislaw Kustronie and Kazimierz Jarzab and is powered by a 45 kW (60 hp) PZL-Franklin flat-twin engine. First flight was made in late 1982 from the airfield of the research centre at WSK Mielec. Of metal construction, with a tricycle landing gear, the KR-02 is aerobatic and is suitable for both sport flying and training duties.

Flight testing has been suspended in order to give priority to the Puchatek glider (see Sailplanes section), but it was intended to resume the KR-02 programme once production of the Puchatek was under way.

Dimensions, external:

Wing span	8·80 m (28 ft 10½ in)
Length overall	4·95 m (16 ft 3 in)
Height overall	1·35 m (4 ft 5¼ in)

Performance:

Max level speed	155 knots (288 km/h; 179 mph)
Cruising speed	88 knots (163 km/h; 101 mph)

WSK-PZL MIELEC

WYTWÓRNIA SPRZETU KOMUNIKACYJ-NEGO-PZL MIELEC (Transport Equipment Manufacturing Centre, Mielec)

ul. Ludowego Wojska Polskiego 3, 39-300 Mielec
Telephone: Mielec 7000
Telex: 0632293
GENERAL MANAGER: Ing Tadeusz Ryczaj, MSc

Largest and best equipped aircraft factory in Poland, the PZL factory at Mielec was founded in 1938, and had produced 12,000 aircraft by the Spring of 1983. It was engaged mainly in licence production of MiG-15/17 single-seat jet fighters for several years, as detailed in earlier editions of *Jane's*, and in 1956 began production of 240 TS-8 Bies basic trainers, described in the 1962-63 *Jane's*. Four years later, the Soviet designed An-2 general utility biplane went into production at Mielec. In parallel production with the An-2 are the An-28 twin-turboprop light general purpose transport, the M-18 Dromader agricultural aircraft and the TS-11 Iskra jet trainer and light attack aircraft. In 1977 Mielec began to manufacture components, including fins, tailplanes, engine pylons, ailerons, and wing slats and flaps, for the Ilyushin Il-86 Soviet wide-bodied transport. By 1 January 1986 Mielec had completed 159 shipsets of Il-86 components. The Polish press has reported that Mielec will undertake production of the Antonov An-3 (see USSR section), a turboprop powered development of the An-2.

PZL MIELEC (ANTONOV) An-2 ANTEK

NATO reporting name: Colt

The prototype of the An-2, designed to a specification of the Ministry of Agriculture and Forestry of the USSR, made its first flight on 31 August 1947. In 1948 the aircraft went into production in the USSR as the An-2, with a 746 kW (1,000 hp) ASh-62 engine.

By 1960, more than 5,000 An-2s had been built in the Soviet Union for service with the Soviet armed forces, Aeroflot and other civilian organisations; the various Soviet built versions have been fully described in previous editions of *Jane's*. Many were exported, to all of the Socialist States, and to Greece, Afghanistan, Mali, Nepal, India and Cuba. Licence rights were granted to China, where the first locally produced An-2 was completed in December 1957, as the Yunshuji-5 or Y-5 (which see). Limited production continues in China.

Since 1960, apart from a few dozen Soviet built An-2Ms (1971-72 *Jane's*), continued production of the An-2 has been primarily the responsibility of PZL Mielec, the original licence arrangement providing for two basic versions: the An-2T transport and An-2R agricultural version. The first Polish built An-2 was flown on 23 October 1960. Mielec has since built about 12,000 An-2s for domestic use and for export to the USSR (more than 8,400), Bulgaria, Czechoslovakia, Egypt, France, the German Democratic Republic, Hungary, North Korea, Mongolia, the Netherlands, Romania, Sudan, Tunisia and Yugoslavia. They include approx 6,000 An-2Rs, and improvements made by Mielec to the airframe of the An-2R resulted in an increase in TBO from 900 h in 1961 to 1,500 h in 1970 and 2,000 h in 1973.

Polish production is continuing on a limited basis, partly to provide some fuselage components to the Antonov factory at Kiev in the USSR, where conversion of An-2s to turboprop powered An-3s is now under way. A description of the An-3 appears in the USSR section of this edition.

Polish built versions have different designations from those built in the USSR. They include the An-2 Geofiz; An-2LW; An-2P, PK, P-Photo and PR; An-2R; An-2S; An-2T, TD and TP. Further details of these can be found in the 1983-84 and earlier editions of *Jane's*.

The following details apply to the PZL Mielec An-2P:

TYPE: Single-engined general purpose biplane.

WINGS: Unequal span single-bay biplane. Wing section RPS 14% (constant). Dihedral, both wings, approx 2° 48'. All-metal two-spar structure, fabric covered aft of front spar. I type interplane struts. Differential ailerons and full span automatic leading-edge slots on upper wings, slotted trailing-edge flaps on both upper and lower wings. Flaps operated electrically, ailerons mechanically by cables and push/pull rods. Electrically operated trim tab in port aileron.

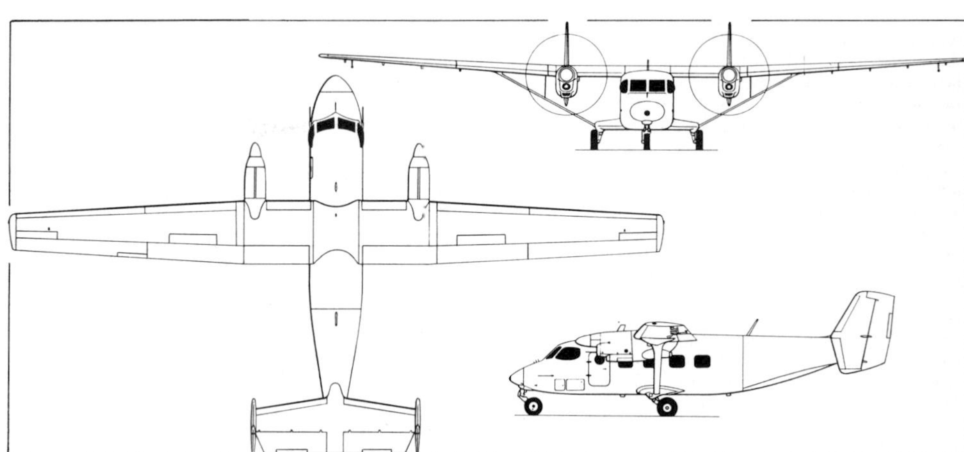

Antonov An-28 light transport, produced in Poland by WSK-PZL Mielec *(Pilot Press)*

FUSELAGE: All-metal stressed skin semi-monocoque structure of circular section forward of cabin, rectangular in the cabin section and oval in the tail section.

TAIL UNIT: Braced metal structure. Fin integral with rear fuselage. Fabric covered tailplane. Elevators and rudder operated mechanically by cables and push/pull rods. Electrically operated trim tab in rudder and port elevator.

LANDING GEAR: Non-retractable split axle type, with long stroke oleo shock absorbers. Mainwheel tyres size 800 × 260 mm, pressure 2·25 bars (32·7 lb/sq in). Pneumatic shoe brakes on main units. Fully castoring and self-centering PZL Krosno tailwheel, size 470 × 210, with electro-pneumatic lock. For rough field operation the oleo-pneumatic shock absorbers can be charged from a compressed air cylinder installed in the rear fuselage. Interchangeable ski landing gear available optionally.

POWER PLANT: One 746 kW (1,000 hp) PZL Kalisz ASz-62IR nine-cylinder radial aircooled engine, driving an AW-2 four-blade variable-pitch metal propeller. Six fuel tanks in upper wings, with total capacity of 1,200 litres (264 Imp gallons). Oil capacity 120 litres (26·4 Imp gallons).

ACCOMMODATION: Crew of two on flight deck, with access via passenger cabin. Standard accommodation for 12 passengers, in four rows of three with centre aisle. Two foldable seats for children in aisle between first and second rows, and infant's cradle at front of cabin on starboard side. Toilet at rear of cabin on starboard side. Overhead racks for up to 160 kg (352 lb) of baggage, with space for coats and additional 40 kg (88 lb) of baggage between rear pair of seats and toilet. Emergency exit on starboard side at rear. Walls of cabin are lined with glass-wool mats and inner facing of plywood to reduce internal noise level. Cabin floor is carpeted. Cabin heating and starboard windscreen de-icing by engine bleed air; port and centre windscreens are electrically de-iced. Cabin ventilation by ram air intakes on underside of top wings.

SYSTEMS: Compressed air cylinder, of 8 litres (490 cu in) capacity, for pneumatic charging of shock absorbers and operation of tailwheel lock at 49 bars (711 lb/sq in) pressure and operation of mainwheel brakes at 9·80 bars (142 lb/sq in). Contents of cylinder are maintained by AK-50 M engine driven compressor, with AD-50 automatic relief device to prevent overpressure. DC electrical system is supplied with basic 27V power (and 36V or 115V where required) by an engine driven generator and a storage battery. CO_2 fire extinguishing system with automatic fire detector.

AVIONICS AND EQUIPMENT: Dual controls and blind-flying instrumentation standard. R-842 short wave and R-860 ultra short wave lightweight radio transceivers, RW-UM radio altimeter, ARK-9 radio compass, MRP-56P marker beacon receiver, GB-1 gyro compass, GPK-48 gyroscopic direction indicator and SPU-7 intercom.

DIMENSIONS, EXTERNAL:

Wing span: upper	18·18 m (59 ft 7¾ in)
lower	14·24 m (46 ft 8½ in)
Wing chord (constant): upper	2·45 m (8 ft 0½ in)
lower	2·00 m (6 ft 6¾ in)
Wing aspect ratio: upper	7·57
lower	7·12
Wing gap	2·17 m (7 ft 1½ in)
Length overall: tail up	12·74 m (41 ft 9½ in)
tail down	12·40 m (40 ft 8¼ in)
Height overall: tail up	6·10 m (20 ft 0 in)
tail down	4·01 m (13 ft 2 in)
Tailplane span	7·20 m (23 ft 7½ in)
Wheel track	3·36 m (11 ft 0¼ in)
Wheelbase	8·19 m (26 ft 10½ in)
Propeller diameter	3·60 m (11 ft 9¾ in)
Propeller ground clearance	0·69 m (2 ft 3¼ in)
Cargo door (port): Mean height	1·55 m (5 ft 1 in)
Mean width	1·39 m (4 ft 6¾ in)
Emergency exit (stbd, rear):	
Height	0·65 m (2 ft 1½ in)
Width	0·51 m (1 ft 8 in)

DIMENSIONS, INTERNAL:

Cargo compartment: Length	4·10 m (13 ft 5½ in)
Max width	1·60 m (5 ft 3 in)
Max height	1·80 m (5 ft 11 in)

AREAS:

Wings, gross: upper	43·54 m² (468·7 sq ft)
lower	27·98 m² (301·2 sq ft)
Ailerons (total)	5·90 m² (63·5 sq ft)
Trailing-edge flaps (total)	9·60 m² (103 sq ft)
Fin	3·20 m² (34·4 sq ft)
Rudder, incl tab	2·65 m² (28·52 sq ft)
Tailplane	7·56 m² (81·4 sq ft)
Elevators (total, incl tab)	4·72 m² (50·81 sq ft)

WEIGHTS AND LOADINGS:

Weight empty	3,450 kg (7,605 lb)
Max T-O weight	5,500 kg (12,125 lb)
Max landing weight	5,250 kg (11,574 lb)
Max wing loading	76·82 kg/m² (15·7 lb/sq ft)
Max power loading	7·38 kg/kW (12·13 lb/hp)

PERFORMANCE (at AUW of 5,250 kg; 11,574 lb):

Max level speed at 1,750 m (5,740 ft)	139 knots (258 km/h; 160 mph)
Econ cruising speed	100 knots (185 km/h; 115 mph)
Min flying speed	49 knots (90 km/h; 56 mph)
T-O speed	43 knots (80 km/h; 50 mph)
Landing speed	46 knots (85 km/h; 53 mph)
Max rate of climb at S/L	210 m (689 ft)/min
Service ceiling	4,400 m (14,425 ft)
Time to 4,400 m (14,425 ft)	30 min
T-O run: hard runway	150 m (492 ft)
grass	170 m (558 ft)
T-O to 15 m (50 ft): hard runway	475 m (1,558 ft)
grass	495 m (1,624 ft)
Landing from 15 m (50 ft): hard runway	427 m (1,401 ft)
grass	432 m (1,417 ft)
Landing run: hard runway	170 m (558 ft)
grass	185 m (607 ft)
Range at 1,000 m (3,280 ft) with 500 kg (1,102 lb) payload	485 nm (900 km; 560 miles)

PZL Mielec (Antonov) An-2R aircraft operated by Aeroflot

PZL MIELEC (ANTONOV) An-28

NATO reporting name: Cash

The prototype of this enlarged turboprop version of the piston-engined An-14 light general purpose transport (SSSR-1968), initially designated An-14M, flew for the first time in the USSR in September 1969, powered by two 604 kW (810 shp) Isotov TVD-850 turboprop engines. It was described in the Soviet section of the 1974-75 and previous editions of *Jane's*; differences from the original An-14, and subsequent design changes, have been recorded in the 1983-84 and earlier editions.

Official Soviet flight testing was completed in 1972, and the production designation An-28 was allocated during 1973. The first pre-production An-28 (SSSR-19723) originally retained the same engines as the prototype, but in April 1975 (re-registered SSSR-19753) it flew for the first time with 716 kW (960 shp) Glushenkov TVD-10 turboprops, which are installed also in production An-28s.

The Antonov design bureau developed the An-28 for service on Aeroflot's shortest routes, particularly those operated by An-2 biplanes into places which are relatively inaccessible to other types of fixed-wing aircraft. The turboprop engines make possible full-payload operation under high temperature conditions and in mountainous regions; and the An-28 is suitable for carrying passengers, cargo and mail, for scientific expeditions, geological surveying, forest fire patrol, air ambulance or rescue operations, and parachute training.

The late Mr Oleg Antonov stated that Aeroflot pilots will begin their flying careers on the An-28, which will not stall, even with the control column held in the extreme rearward position, because of the action of its automatic slots. If an engine fails, the upper surface spoiler forward of the aileron on the opposite wing is opened automatically; as a result, the wing bearing the 'dead' engine drops only 12° in 5 s instead of the 30° that it would drop through loss of lift without the action of the Antonov patented spoiler. The fixed tailplane slot, also patented, improves handling during a high angle of attack climbout. Under icing conditions, if the normal anti-icing system fails, ice collects on the slat rather than the tailplane, to retain controllability.

Following Polish-Soviet talks in February 1978, it was announced that series production of the An-28 was to be entrusted to PZL Mielec. A temporary type certificate, under Soviet NLGS-2 regulations, was awarded on 4 October 1978 to the second Soviet built pre-production aircraft (originally SSSR-19754, later SSSR-48105), which was displayed at the Paris Air Show in June 1979.

Polish manufacture is beginning with an initial batch of 15 aircraft, of which four (three for flight and operational trials, plus a static test airframe) had been completed by the beginning of 1985. First flight by a Polish built An-28 (SSSR-28800) was made on 22 July 1984, and the following description applies to this version, which received its Polish type certificate on 7 February 1986:

TYPE: Twin-turboprop short-range transport aircraft.

WINGS: Braced high-wing monoplane, with single streamline section bracing strut each side. Wing section TsAGI P-II-14 (thickness/chord ratio 14%). Constant chord, non-swept no-dihedral centre-section, set at 4° incidence; tapered outer panels have 2° dihedral, negative incidence and 2° sweepback at quarter-chord. Conventional two-spar all-duralumin torsion box structure, with steel attachment fittings. Duralumin automatic leading-edge slats over full span of outer panels. Entire trailing-edges hinged, the single-slotted mass and aerodynamically balanced ailerons being designed to droop with the large, two-segment double-slotted flaps. Unpowered ailerons and hydraulically actuated flaps are of duralumin, with fabric and carbon plastics skins respectively; port aileron has a carbon plastics trim tab. Slab type spoiler, also of carbon plastics, forward of each aileron and each outer flap segment at 75 per cent chord. Thermal anti-icing of wing leading-edges by engine bleed air. Short stub-wing extends from each side of the lower fuselage, carrying the main landing gear unit and providing lower attachment for the wing bracing strut.

FUSELAGE: Conventional all-metal semi-monocoque non-pressurised structure. Underside of rear fuselage upswept and incorporating clamshell doors for passenger and cargo loading.

TAIL UNIT: Cantilever all-metal structure. Twin fins and rudders, mounted vertically on an inverted-aerofoil, no-dihedral fixed incidence tailplane. Fixed leading-edge slat under full span of tailplane leading-edge. Electrically actuated trim tab in each rudder and each elevator; main controls are unpowered. Thermal (engine bleed air) anti-icing of tailplane and fin leading-edges.

LANDING GEAR: Non-retractable tricycle type, with single Soviet built wheel and PZL oleo-pneumatic shock absorber on each unit. Main units have wide tread balloon tyres of Soviet manufacture, size 720 × 320 × 248 mm, pressure 3·5 bars (51 lb/sq in), and are mounted on small stub-wings which curve forward and downward at front to serve as mudguards. Steerable (50° left and right) and self-centering nosewheel, with size 595 × 185 × 280 mm Stomil (Poland) tyre, pressure 3·5 bars (51 lb/sq in). Soviet multi-disc hydraulic brakes on main units, and Soviet inertial anti-skid units.

POWER PLANT: Two 716 kW (960 shp) PZL Rzészow TVD-10S turboprop engines, each driving a PZL AW-24AN three-blade automatic propeller with full feathering and reversible-pitch capability. Two centre-section and two outer-wing integral fuel tanks in wing spar boxes, with total capacity of 1,960 litres (431 Imp gallons). Refuelling point on each tank. Oil capacity 16 litres (3·5 Imp gallons) per engine. Air intakes lined with epoxy laminate and anti-iced by engine oil; propellers, spinners and pitot heads anti-iced electrically.

ACCOMMODATION: Pilot and co-pilot on flight deck, which has bulged side windows and electric anti-icing for windscreens, and is separated from main cabin by a bulkhead with connecting door. Dual controls standard. Jettisonable emergency door at front on port side. Standard cabin layout of passenger version has seats for 17 people, with six single seats on port side, one single seat and five double seats on starboard side of aisle, at 72 cm (28 in) pitch. Aisle width 34·5 cm (13·5 in). Five passenger windows in each side of cabin. Seats fold back against walls when aircraft is operated as a freighter or in mixed passenger/cargo role, the seat attachments providing cargo tiedown points. Entire cabin heated, ventilated and soundproofed. Outward/downward opening clamshell double door, under upswept rear fuselage, for passenger and cargo loading. Emergency exit at rear of cabin on port side.

SYSTEMS: No air-conditioning, pressurisation or pneumatic systems. Hydraulic system for flap and spoiler actuation, mainwheel brakes and nosewheel steering, with emergency backup system for spoiler extension and mainwheel braking. Primary electrical system is three-phase AC, with two engine driven alternators providing 200/115V power for heating systems, engine vibration monitoring, fuel pump, radio, recorders, and instrument lights. Transformer-rectifiers on this system provide 36V AC power for pressure gauges, artificial horizon, navigation and recording equipment, and 27V DC for control systems and signalling, internal and external lighting, firefighting system, propeller pitch control and feathering, radio, and engine starting and monitoring systems. In emergency, 36V AC can be provided by a static inverter and 27V DC by two 25Ah batteries. Thermal (engine bleed air) anti-icing of outer-wing, fin and tailplane leading-edges. Electrical anti-icing of flight deck windscreens, propellers, spinners and pitot heads. Oxygen system (for crew plus two passengers) optional. No APU.

AVIONICS: Standard avionics include Baklan-5 (USSR) VHF com radio, R-855UM (USSR) VHF emergency locator transmitter, ARK-15 radio compass, MRP-66 marker beacon receiver, RW-5 or A-037 radio altimeter, Grebien-1 navigation unit, BUR-1-2A flight recorder, and SGU-6 intercom. Blind-flying instrumentation standard.

DIMENSIONS, EXTERNAL:
Wing span 22·07 m (72 ft 5 in)
Wing chord: at root 2·20 m (7 ft 2½ in)
mean aerodynamic 1·886 m (6 ft 2¼ in)
at tip 1·10 m (3 ft 7¼ in)
Wing aspect ratio 12·25
Length overall 13·10 m (42 ft 11¾ in)
Fuselage: Length 12·68 m (41 ft 7¼ in)
Max width 2·14 m (7 ft 0¼ in)
Max depth 1·90 m (6 ft 2¾ in)
Height overall 4·90 m (16 ft 1 in)
Tailplane span 5·14 m (16 ft 10¼ in)
Wheel track 3·405 m (11 ft 2 in)
Wheelbase 4·44 m (14 ft 6¾ in)
Propeller diameter 2·80 m (9 ft 2¼ in)
Propeller ground clearance 1·25 m (4 ft 1¼ in)
Distance between propeller centres 5·20 m (17 ft 0¾ in)
Rear clamshell doors: Length 2·40 m (7 ft 10½ in)
Total width: at top 1·00 m (3 ft 3¼ in)
at sill 1·40 m (4 ft 7 in)
Emergency exit (port, rear):
Height 0·91 m (3 ft 0 in)
Width 0·51 m (1 ft 8 in)

DIMENSIONS, INTERNAL:
Cabin, excl flight deck: Length 5·26 m (17 ft 3 in)
Max width 1·74 m (5 ft 8½ in)
Max height 1·60 m (5 ft 3 in)
Floor area approx 7·5 m² (80·73 sq ft)
Volume approx 14·0 m³ (494·4 cu ft)

AREAS:
Wings, gross 39·72 m² (427·5 sq ft)
Ailerons (total) 4·33 m² (46·61 sq ft)
Trailing-edge flaps (total) 7·986 m² (85·96 sq ft)
Spoilers (total) 1·922 m² (20·69 sq ft)
Fins (total) 10·00 m² (107·64 sq ft)
Rudders (total, incl tabs) 4·00 m² (43·06 sq ft)
Tailplane 8·85 m² (95·26 sq ft)
Elevators (total, incl tabs) 2·56 m² (27·56 sq ft)

WEIGHTS AND LOADINGS:
Weight empty, equipped 3,750 kg (8,267 lb)
Max fuel load 1,567 kg (3,454 lb)
Max payload 2,000 kg (4,409 lb)
Max T-O and landing weight 6,500 kg (14,330 lb)
Normal wing loading 153·5 kg/m² (31·5 lb/sq ft)
Max power loading 4·64 kg/kW (7·62 lb/shp)

PERFORMANCE (at max T-O weight):
Never-exceed speed 210 knots (390 km/h; 242 mph)
Max level and max cruising speed at 3,000 m (9,850 ft) 189 knots (350 km/h; 217 mph)
Econ cruising speed at 3,000 m (9,850 ft) 181 knots (335 km/h; 208 mph)
Lift-off speed 73 knots (135 km/h; 84 mph)
Approach speed 70 knots (130 km/h; 81 mph)
Landing speed, flaps down 68 knots (125 km/h; 78 mph)
Max rate of climb at S/L 705 m (2,315 ft)/min
Rate of climb at S/L, one engine out 210 m (689 ft)/min
Service ceiling above 6,000 m (19,685 ft)
Min ground turning radius 16·00 m (52 ft 6 in)
T-O run 260 m (853 ft)
T-O to 10·7 m (35 ft) 360 m (1,180 ft)
Landing from 15 m (50 ft) 315 m (1,035 ft)
Landing run 170 m (558 ft)
Range:
max payload, no reserves 302 nm (560 km; 348 miles)
max fuel and 1,000 kg (2,205 lb) payload, 30 min reserves 736 nm (1,365 km; 848 miles)
g limit +3·8

PZL MIELEC TS-11 ISKRA-BIS (SPARK)

Designed in 1957 under the supervision of Docent Ing T. Soltyk, the TS-11 Iskra two-seat jet trainer was produced as

Polish built Antonov An-28 light general purpose transport (two PZL Rzészow TVD-10S turboprop engines)

a replacement for the piston engined TS-8 Bies. Four prototypes were built during 1958-59, the first of these being used for static testing. First flight, on 5 February 1960, was made by the second aircraft, followed later in the same year by the third and fourth prototypes. Type approval was received in mid-1961, and quantity production began at Mielec in 1963. The formal handing over of the first Iskra to the Polish Air Force took place in March 1963, and the aircraft entered service in 1964.

Early production aircraft were powered by a 7·66 kN (1,720 lb st) HO-10 Polish designed axial flow turbojet engine. In April 1964, flight testing began using the intended power plant, the more powerful SO-1; from 1967 production Iskras were powered by the 9·81 kN (2,205 lb st) SO-1, the modified but similarly rated SO-3 being introduced in 1969. The current Iskra-Bis DF has the uprated SO-3W.

About 500 Iskras had been built by mid-1979. Production was then halted until 1982, when manufacture was resumed of the **Iskra-Bis DF**, which is now the only version being built. Details of the earlier versions can be found in the 1981-82 and previous editions of *Jane's*.

The following description applies to the Iskra-Bis DF:

TYPE: Fully aerobatic two-seat combat and reconnaissance trainer.

WINGS: Cantilever mid-wing monoplane. Wing section NACA 64209 at root, NACA 64009 at tip. Sweepback at quarter-chord 7°. Marked dihedral. All-metal torsion box structure with two steel main spars and duralumin stressed skin. Hydraulically servo-assisted, aerodynamically balanced ailerons. Hydraulically actuated two-section double-slotted flaps and airbrakes (max deflection 87°). One boundary layer fence on each wing. Anti-flutter weight fairing projecting from each wing near tip.

FUSELAGE: All-metal semi-monocoque structure of pod and boom type.

TAIL UNIT: Cantilever all-metal structure. Two-spar fin, integral with fuselage. Variable incidence two-spar tailplane, actuated electrically. Mass and aerodynamically balanced elevators and rudder. Anti-flutter weight fairing projecting from each half of tailplane at tip. Ground adjustable tab on rudder; fixed balance tab in port elevator.

LANDING GEAR: Retractable tricycle type with single wheel on each unit. Nosewheel retracts forward, mainwheels inward into wing root air intake trunks. Hydraulic actuation, with pneumatic emergency extension. Mainwheels size 600 × 180, tyre pressure 5·38 bars (78 lb/sq in). Nosewheel size 380 × 150, tyre pressure 3·45 bars (50 lb/sq in). Oleo-pneumatic shock absorbers. Disc brakes on mainwheels. Castoring and self-centering nosewheel, with shimmy damper.

POWER PLANT: One 10·79 kN (2,425 lb st) IL SO-3W turbojet engine, mounted in fuselage aft of cockpit section, with nozzle under tailboom. Fuel in two 315 litre (69 Imp gallon) integral wing tanks, one rubber 500 litre (110 Imp gallon) fuselage main tank (700 litre; 154 Imp gallon in single-seaters) and one rubber 70 litre (15·5 Imp gallon) fuselage collector tank. Total fuel capacity 1,200 litres (264 Imp gallons). Fuel and oil systems permit up to 40 s of inverted flight.

ACCOMMODATION: Crew of two in tandem, on lightweight ejection seats, under a one-piece hydraulically actuated rearward hinged upward opening jettisonable canopy. Rear seat slightly raised. Cockpit pressurised and air-conditioned.

SYSTEMS: Hydraulic system, pressure 138 bars (2,000 lb/sq in), for actuation of ailerons, flaps, airbrakes, landing gear, canopy, and mainwheel brakes. Pneumatic system, pressure 118 bars (1,710 lb/sq in), for cockpit pressurisation, canopy anti-icing and gun charging. Emergency pneumatic system for landing gear extension, flaps and emergency braking. Electrical power provided by 28·5V GSR-ST-6000A generator and 24V 28Ah battery, for engine starting, instruments, lights and armament control system; 115V converter for AC power. Air-conditioning, oxygen, windscreen ethyl alcohol anti-icing and CO_2 fire extinguishing systems standard.

Two-seat Iskra-Bis DF reconnaissance trainer version of the PZL Mielec TS-11

AVIONICS AND EQUIPMENT: Full dual controls and instrumentation, including blind-flying panels. Standard avionics include R-800, R-802G, R-802W or RS-6102/R VHF com; ARK-9 or ARL-1601 radio compass; RW-UM radio altimeter; MRP-56P marker beacon receiver; SPU-2P intercom; and IFF.

ARMAMENT: Forward firing 23 mm cannon in nose on starboard side, with S-13 gun camera. Four attachments for a variety of underwing stores, including bombs of up to 100 kg (220 lb), eight-barrel rocket pods and 7·62 mm gun pods. Provision for three cameras: one in each air intake fairing and one in fuselage floor beneath rear cockpit.

DIMENSIONS, EXTERNAL:
- Wing span: 10·06 m (33 ft 0 in)
- Wing chord: at root: 2·254 m (7 ft 4¾ in)
- at tip: 1·162 m (3 ft 9¾ in)
- Wing aspect ratio: 5·71
- Length overall: 11·15 m (36 ft 7 in)
- Height overall: 3·50 m (11 ft 5½ in)
- Tailplane span: 3·84 m (12 ft 7¼ in)
- Wheel track: 3·47 m (11 ft 4½ in)
- Wheelbase: 3·37 m (11 ft 0½ in)

AREAS:
- Wings, gross: 17·50 m^2 (188·37 sq ft)
- Ailerons (total): 1·48 m^2 (15·93 sq ft)
- Trailing-edge flaps (total): 1·74 m^2 (18·73 sq ft)
- Fin: 1·55 m^2 (16·68 sq ft)
- Rudder (incl tab): 0·70 m^2 (7·53 sq ft)
- Tailplane: 2·38 m^2 (25·62 sq ft)
- Elevators (incl tab): 1·16 m^2 (12·48 sq ft)

WEIGHTS AND LOADINGS:
- Weight empty: 2,565 kg (5,655 lb)
- Normal T-O weight with 570 litres (125·5 Imp gallons) internal fuel: 3,243 kg (7,150 lb)
- Normal T-O weight with 1,200 litres (263·5 Imp gallons) internal fuel: 3,734 kg (8,232 lb)
- T-O weight (reconnaissance): 3,787 kg (8,349 lb)
- Max T-O weight with full external armament: 3,840 kg (8,465 lb)
- Max wing loading: 219 kg/m^2 (44·85 lb/sq ft)
- Max power loading: 355·9 kg/kN (3·5 lb/lb st)

PERFORMANCE (at normal T-O weight with full internal fuel, except where indicated):
- Never-exceed speed: Mach 0·8 (404 knots; 750 km/h; 466 mph)
- Max level speed at 5,000 m (16,400 ft): 415 knots (770 km/h; 478 mph)
- Normal cruising speed: 324 knots (600 km/h; 373 mph)
- Unstick speed: 106 knots (197 km/h; 122 mph)
- Landing speed: 100 knots (184 km/h; 115 mph)
- Stalling speed, power off, flaps down: 99 knots (183 km/h; 114 mph)
- Max rate of climb at S/L: 1,164 m (3,820 ft)/min
- Time to 5,000 m (16,400 ft): 6 min 36 s
- Time to 11,000 m (36,000 ft): 26 min 0 s
- Service ceiling: 11,500 m (37,725 ft)
- T-O run: 655 m (2,150 ft)
- T-O to 15 m (50 ft), flaps down: 1,090 m (3,575 ft)
- Landing from 15 m (50 ft), flaps down: 1,190 m (3,904 ft)
- Landing run: 710 m (2,330 ft)
- Range at 7,000 m (22,975 ft) with 570 litres fuel: 243 nm (450 km; 280 miles)
- Range with 1,200 litres fuel: 680 nm (1,260 km; 783 miles)
- *g* limits: +8/−4 ultimate

PZL Mielec Iskra-Bis D two-seat trainer, with four underwing pylons *(Pilot Press)*

PZL MIELEC M-18 DROMADER (DROMEDARY)

Although superficially similar to the PZL Warszawa-Okecie PZL-106 Kruk, the M-18 Dromader is an entirely different and much larger agricultural aircraft, and is designed to meet the requirements of FAR Pt 23. Particular attention was paid in the design to pilot safety, and all parts of the structure exposed to contact with chemicals are treated with polyurethane or epoxy enamels, or manufactured from stainless steel.

Design began in 1974. The M-18 was first flown on 27 August 1976, and a second flying prototype followed on 2 October 1976; a third was completed for static tests. The M-18 made its public debut at the Paris Air Show in May/June 1977. The prototypes were followed by ten pre-series aircraft, of which two were used for static and fatigue testing. The remainder were employed for operating trials, two of them spraying and dusting cotton in Egypt during the Summer of 1978, prior to the award of a Polish type certificate on 27 September 1978. The Dromader has also been certificated in Canada, France, the German Democratic Republic, the USA and Yugoslavia. A firefighting version was flown for the first time on 11 November 1978. Series production began in 1979, and a total of 301 production M-18s had been built by the beginning of 1985, of which 90 per cent were for export. Customers include operators in Bulgaria, Canada, Cuba, Czechoslovakia, the German Democratic Republic, Greece (30 for firefighting), Hungary, Morocco, Nicaragua, Poland, Swaziland, Trinidad, Turkey, the USA, Venezuela and Yugoslavia. Two Dromaders were evaluated in the Soviet Union in 1981.

A number of improvements have been incorporated in the design, and a dual control version for pilot training was being built in Poland in 1985. In addition, Melex USA (which see), a US subsidiary of PZL, is developing a turboprop powered version with an 895 kW (1,200 shp) Pratt & Whitney Canada PT6A-45AG engine and Hartzell propeller, known as the **T45 Turbine Dromader**. An amphibious water bomber floatplane version is also under consideration.

The following description refers to the standard M-18 agricultural version:

TYPE: Single-seat agricultural aircraft.

WINGS: Cantilever all-metal low-wing monoplane, of constant chord, with 1° 25′ dihedral on centre-section and 6° on outer panels. Wing sections NACA 4416 at root, NACA 4412 at end of centre-section, and NACA 4412 on outer panels. Incidence 3°. Single steel capped duralumin spar. All-metal two-section trailing-edge slotted flaps, actuated hydraulically. All-metal slotted ailerons, mass and aerodynamically balanced, actuated by pushrods. Trim tab in each aileron.

FUSELAGE: All-metal structure. Main frame, of helium-arc welded chrome-molybdenum steel tube, oiled internally against corrosion. Duralumin side panels, detachable for airframe inspection and cleaning. Fixed stainless steel bottom covering.

TAIL UNIT: All-metal structure, with braced tailplane. Corrugated skin. Aerodynamically and mass balanced rudder and elevators. Elevator actuated by pushrods; rudder by cables. Trim tab on rudder and each elevator.

LANDING GEAR: Non-retractable tailwheel type. Oleo-pneumatic shock absorber in each unit. Main units have tyres size 800 × 260 mm, and are fitted with hydraulic disc brakes, parking brake and wire cutters. Fully castoring tailwheel, lockable for take-off and landing, with size 360 × 150 mm tyre.

POWER PLANT: One 746 kW (1,000 hp) PZL Kalisz ASz-62IR nine-cylinder radial aircooled supercharged engine, driving a PZL Warszawa AW-2-30 four-blade constant-speed aluminium propeller. Integral fuel tank in each outer wing panel, combined usable capacity 400 or 712 litres (88 or 156·6 Imp gallons; 105·7 or 188 US gallons). Gravity feed header tank in fuselage.

ACCOMMODATION: Single adjustable seat in fully enclosed, sealed and ventilated cockpit which is stressed to withstand 40*g* impact. Glassfibre cockpit roof and rear fairing. Adjustable shoulder type safety harness. Adjustable rudder pedals. Baggage compartment aft of seat. Quick-opening door on each side; port door jettisonable.

SYSTEMS: Hydraulic system, pressure 98-137 bars (1,421-1,987 lb/sq in), for flap actuation, disc brakes and dispersal system. Electrical system powered by 28·5V 100A generator, with 24V 25Ah nickel-cadmium battery and overvoltage protection relay.

AVIONICS AND EQUIPMENT: RS6102 (Polish built), King KX 175B or KY 195B com transceiver, KI 201C nav receiver, VOR-OBS indicator, gyro compass, radio compass, stall warning, landing lights, taxi light and night working light optional. Navigation lights, cockpit light, instrument panel lights, and two rotating beacons standard. Built-in jacking and tiedown points in wings and rear fuselage; towing lugs on main landing gear. Cockpit fire extinguisher and first aid kit.

AGRICULTURAL AND OTHER EQUIPMENT: Glassfibre epoxy hopper, with stainless steel tube bracing, forward of cockpit; capacity 2,500 litres (550 Imp gallons; 660 US gallons) of liquid or 2,000 kg (4,409 lb) of dry chemical. Deflector cable from cabin roof to fin. The M-18 can be fitted optionally with several different types of agricultural and firefighting systems, as follows: spray system with 54/96 nozzles on sprayboms; dusting system with standard, large or extra large spreader; atomising system with six atomisers; water bombing installation; and fire-bombing installation with foaming agents. Aerial application roles can include seeding, fertilising, weed or pest control, defoliation, forest and bush firefighting, and patrol flights. Special wingtip lights permit agricultural flights at night, and the aircraft can operate in both temperate and tropical climates.

DIMENSIONS, EXTERNAL:
- Wing span — 17·70 m (58 ft 0¾ in)
- Wing chord (constant) — 2·286 m (7 ft 6 in)
- Wing aspect ratio — 7·83
- Length overall — 9·47 m (31 ft 1 in)
- Height over tail fin — 3·70 m (12 ft 1¾ in)
- Height overall (flying attitude) — 4·60 m (15 ft 1 in)
- Tailplane span — 5·60 m (18 ft 4½ in)
- Wheel track — 3·48 m (11 ft 5 in)
- Propeller diameter — 3·30 m (10 ft 10 in)
- Propeller ground clearance (tail up) — 0·23 m (9 in)

AREAS:
- Wings, gross — 40·00 m² (430·5 sq ft)
- Ailerons (total) — 3·84 m² (41·33 sq ft)
- Trailing-edge flaps (total) — 5·69 m² (61·25 sq ft)
- Vertical tail surfaces (total) — 2·65 m² (28·5 sq ft)
- Horizontal tail surfaces (total) — 6·50 m² (70·0 sq ft)

WEIGHTS AND LOADINGS:
- Basic weight empty — 2,610 kg (5,754 lb)
- Weight empty, equipped — 2,670-2,760 kg (5,886-6,085 lb)
- Payload: FAR 23 — 1,050-1,350 kg (2,315-2,976 lb)
  - CAM 8 — 1,550-1,850 kg (3,417-4,078 lb)
- Max T-O weight: FAR 23 — 4,200 kg (9,259 lb)
  - CAM 8 — 4,700 kg (10,362 lb)
- Max landing weight — 4,200 kg (9,259 lb)
- Max wing loading (FAR 23) — 105·0 kg/m² (21·51 lb/sq ft)
- Max power loading (FAR 23) — 5·63 kg/kW (9·26 lb/hp)

PERFORMANCE (at 4,200 kg; 9,259 lb T-O weight, ISA. A: without agricultural equipment; B: with spreader equipment):
- Never-exceed speed:
  - A — 151 knots (280 km/h; 174 mph)
- Max level speed: A — 138 knots (256 km/h; 159 mph)
  - B — 128 knots (237 km/h; 147 mph)
- Cruising speed at S/L:
  - A — 110 knots (205 km/h; 127 mph)
  - B — 102 knots (190 km/h; 118 mph)
- Normal operating speed:
  - A — 124 knots (230 km/h; 143 mph)
  - B — 108 knots (200 km/h; 124 mph)
- Stalling speed, power off, flaps up:
  - A, B — 65 knots (119 km/h; 74 mph)
- Stalling speed, power off, flaps down:
  - A, B — 59 knots (109 km/h; 68 mph)

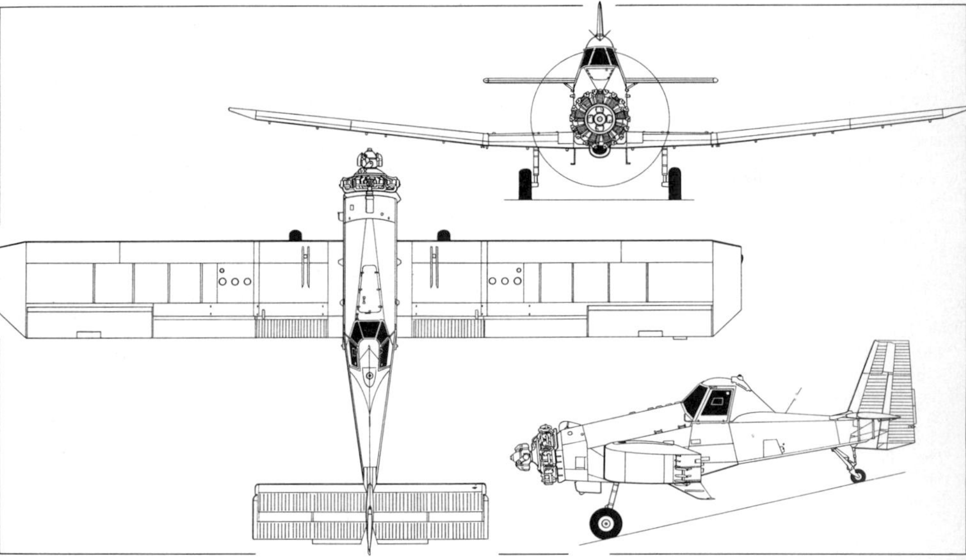

Three-view drawing *(Pilot Press)* **and photograph** *(Neil A. Macdougall)* **of the PZL Mielec M-18 Dromader**

- Max rate of climb at S/L: A — 414 m (1,360 ft)/min
  - B — 340 m (1,115 ft)/min
- Service ceiling: A — 6,500 m (21,325 ft)
- T-O run: A — 180-200 m (590-656 ft)
  - B — 210-245 m (689-805 ft)
- Landing run: A, B — 260-300 m (853-984 ft)
- Max range, no reserves:
  - A, 400 litres (88 Imp gallons) fuel — 291 nm (540 km; 335 miles)
  - A, 712 litres (156·6 Imp gallons) fuel — 523 nm (970 km; 602 miles)
- *g* limits: FAR 23 — +3·4/−1·4
  - CAM 8 — +3·0/−1·2

PZL MIELEC M-18A DROMADER

Until 1983 the M-18 had been produced only as a single-seater; the M-18A has been designed for operators requiring to transport a ground mechanic/loader to provisional airstrips. An additional cabin is located behind the cockpit and separated from it by a wall. The cabin is equipped with a rigid seat, with protective padding and safety belt, a port-side jettisonable door, windows (port and starboard), fire extinguisher, and ventilation valve. Communication with the pilot is provided via a window in the dividing wall, and by intercom.

Five M-18As were built during 1983, and in Spring 1984 were undergoing experimental operation in the German Democratic Republic. A supplementary Polish type certificate was awarded to the M-18A on 14 February 1984, and by the end of that year 14 M-18As had been exported to East Germany.

All other data are as for the M-18 except:

WEIGHTS:
- Basic weight empty — 2,690 kg (5,930 lb)
- Weight empty, equipped — 2,750-2,860 kg (6,063-6,305 lb)

PZL MIELEC M-20 (PZL-118) MEWA (GULL)

The M-20 Mewa six/seven-seat twin-engined aircraft is the Polish version of the Piper PA-34 Seneca (see US section), developed and assembled or manufactured by the Polish aircraft industry under an agreement made with Piper Aircraft Corporation in early 1977. It is designed for passenger transport, training, liaison and ambulance duties, and is certificated to FAR Pt 23. The Mewa can be operated from concrete runways or grass strips with a length of about 700 m (2,300 ft), and differs chiefly from the US built Seneca in being powered by Polish built Franklin engines.

Adaptation of the PA-34-200T Seneca II airframe to accept this power plant occupied the first half of 1978, and the first Polish prototype made its initial flight on 25 July 1979. The Mewa has been produced in three versions, any of which can be configured for passenger carrying or as an air ambulance:

PZL Mielec M-20 Mewa, a version of the Piper Seneca II with PZL F engines

M-20.00. Assembled from Piper built PA-34-200T kits with PZL F engines. First prototype was of this version. Four examples built during 1980 (no subsequent figures received). Polish (CACA) type certificate issued 22 September 1983.

M-20.01. Polish built airframe and PZL F engines. Construction of first example began in June 1980, and this aircraft flew for the first time on 22 September 1982. Five built (in ambulance configuration) in 1983-early 1984. Production reportedly to be resumed after manufacture of PZL F engines started at WSK-PZL Debica in 1986.

M-20.02. First flown in late 1985. No other details known.

The description of the Seneca in the US section applies generally also to the M-20 Mewa, except in the following respects:

LANDING GEAR: Disc brakes: Cleveland on M-20.00, PZL on M-20.01.

POWER PLANT: Two 153 kW (205 hp) PZL F (Franklin) 6A-350CIL/R 'handed' flat-six engines, each driving a Hartzell two-blade constant-speed propeller with spinner and (optionally) electric blade de-icing; PZL Warszawa-Okecie US-134 three-blade propellers optional. Propellers are contra-rotating. Fuel tanks as for Seneca (371 litres; 93 US gallons standard, 484·5 litres; 128 US gallons with auxiliary in-wing tanks). Oil capacity 10 litres (2·64 US gallons) per engine.

ACCOMMODATION: Passenger version seats one or two pilots plus four passengers (three rows of two), with optional seventh seat in third row. Baggage space aft of rear seats. Ambulance version can carry one stretcher patient, two medical attendants and one other person in addition to the pilot. The stretcher rack replaces the right hand centre seat and, like the seat, can be quickly and easily removed. The rack has special guides which can be connected to the door threshold to facilitate stretcher loading; they can be folded back when the stretcher is on board and locked. There are hooks in the cabin ceiling for suspending a transfusion set, and the aircraft carries an oxygen installation for the patient. The doctor's seat (centre, left) has an earphone and microphone, enabling him to contact the ground for assistance if required, and there is a nurse's seat at the rear. A modified electrical system permits an incubator to be installed.

SYSTEMS: Electrical system powered by two 12V 70A alternators and two 12V 35Ah batteries. Oxygen system standard in ambulance version.

AVIONICS: Multi-channel VOR/LOC radio and blind-flying instrumentation standard. Radio rangefinder, radio marker, radio compass and three-axis autopilot optional.

DIMENSIONS, EXTERNAL:
Cabin door (stbd, fwd):
Height 0·85 m (2 ft 9½ in)
Max width 0·96 m (3 ft 1¾ in)
Height to sill 0·85 m (2 ft 9½ in)
Baggage door (port, fwd):
Height 0·67 m (2 ft 2¼ in)
Width 0·52 m (1 ft 8½ in)
Height to sill 0·67 m (2 ft 2¼ in)
Baggage door (port, nose):
Max height 0·63 m (2 ft 0¾ in)
Width 0·62 m (2 ft 0½ in)
Max height to sill 0·63 m (2 ft 0¾ in)

WEIGHTS AND LOADINGS:
Weight empty (standard) 1,290 kg (2,844 lb)
Max T-O weight 2,070 kg (4,563 lb)
Max landing weight 1,970 kg (4,343 lb)
Max zero-fuel weight 1,810 kg (3,990 lb)
Max wing loading 107·9 kg/m² (22·10 lb/sq ft)
Max power loading 6·86 kg/kW (11·13 lb/hp)

PERFORMANCE (at max T-O weight):
Never-exceed speed 194 knots (360 km/h; 223 mph)
Max level and max cruising speed at 1,500 m (4,920 ft) 148 knots (275 km/h; 171 mph)
Econ cruising speed at 1,500 m (4,920 ft) 140 knots (260 km/h; 162 mph)
Stalling speed: flaps up 69 knots (128 km/h; 80 mph)
flaps down 59 knots (108 km/h; 68 mph)
Max rate of climb at S/L 384 m (1,260 ft)/min
Rate of climb at S/L, one engine out 54 m (177 ft)/min
Service ceiling 4,000 m (13,125 ft)
Service ceiling, one engine out 900 m (2,950 ft)
T-O to 15 m (50 ft), concrete runway, 25° flap 460 m (1,510 ft)
Landing from 15 m (50 ft) 655 m (2,150 ft)
Range with max standard fuel, 45 min reserves 550 nm (1,020 km; 634 miles)
Range with max standard and auxiliary fuel 734 nm (1,360 km; 845 miles)

PZL MIELEC M-21 DROMADER MINI

This reduced capacity version of the Dromader was developed in response to a need expressed by many users of the M-18 for a smaller version of the aircraft, with a less powerful engine and reduced chemical load. Such a version, it was felt, would form part of a mixed fleet, providing an operator with greater flexibility and improved operating costs. As a result, the Research and Development Centre for Transport Industry (Osrodek Badawczo-Rozwojowy Sprzetu Komunikacyjnego) at WSK Mielec began design work on the M-21 in January 1980.

Prototype of the PZL Mielec M-21 Dromader Mini agricultural aircraft

Construction of two flying prototypes and static testing of the airframe started in August 1981, and the first prototype (SP-PDM) flew for the first time on 18 June 1982, powered by a PZL-3S engine. First flight of the same aircraft with a PZL-3SR engine was made on 20 October 1983, and the second prototype, also with the -3SR engine, made its initial flight on 21 March 1985. Completion of operational testing, and certification, were expected during 1986.

Some 70 per cent of parts are common to both the M-18 and M-21, among them the outer wing panels (including flaps and ailerons); rear fuselage (including cockpit and tailwheel); mainwheels and brakes; upper surface of hopper, including hood; parts of the fuel, oil, hydraulic and electrical systems; and some of the agricultural equipment. New to the M-21 are the PZL-3SR engine and its propeller, wing centre-section, enlarged tail surfaces, main landing gear legs, lower part of hopper, and forward fuselage. Some standard subassemblies are, however, used in the new assemblies.

AIRFRAME: Generally similar to M-18, but starboard aileron has ground adjustable tab, forward fuselage has glass-fibre/epoxy laminate skin panels, tailwheel tyre is size 380 × 150 mm.

POWER PLANT: One 447 kW (600 hp) PZL-3SR seven-cylinder aircooled radial engine, driving a US 133 000 three-blade propeller. Fuel capacity as for M-18; oil capacity 75 litres (16·5 Imp gallons).

SYSTEMS: Hydraulic system pressure 153 bars (2,220 lb/sq in). Electrical system powered by 1·5 kW alternator and 18Ah battery.

AVIONICS: RS 6201 Unimor very short wave com transceiver.

DIMENSIONS, EXTERNAL:
Wing span 14·51 m (47 ft 7¼ in)
Wing aspect ratio 6·46
Length overall 9·48 m (31 ft 1¼ in)
Height overall 3·11 m (10 ft 2½ in)
Tailplane span 5·60 m (18 ft 4½ in)
Wheel track 2·70 m (8 ft 10¼ in)
Wheelbase 5·86 m (19 ft 2¾ in)
Propeller diameter 3·10 m (10 ft 2 in)
Propeller ground clearance 0·30 m (11¾ in)

AREAS:
Wings, gross 32·60 m² (350·9 sq ft)
Ailerons (total) 3·84 m² (41·33 sq ft)
Trailing-edge flaps (total) 2·78 m² (29·92 sq ft)
Fin 1·80 m² (19·38 sq ft)
Rudder, incl tab 1·44 m² (15·50 sq ft)
Tailplane 3·86 m² (41·55 sq ft)
Elevators (total, incl tabs) 3·42 m² (36·81 sq ft)

WEIGHTS AND LOADINGS:
Basic weight empty 2,060 kg (4,541 lb)
Weight empty, equipped 2,120-2,200 kg (4,674-4,850 lb)
Payload: FAR 23 900 kg (1,984 lb)
FAR 21.25 1,200 kg (2,645 lb)
Max T-O and landing weight:
FAR 23 3,300 kg (7,275 lb)
FAR 21.25 3,600 kg (7,936 lb)
Max wing loading:
FAR 23 101·2 kg/m² (20·73 lb/sq ft)
FAR 21.25 110·4 kg/m² (22·62 lb/sq ft)
Max power loading:
FAR 23 7·38 kg/kW (12·12 lb/hp)
FAR 21.25 8·05 kg/kW (13·23 lb/hp)

PERFORMANCE (at 3,300 kg; 7,275 lb T-O weight, ISA):
Never-exceed speed 145 knots (270 km/h; 167 mph)
Max level speed 113 knots (210 km/h; 130 mph)
Normal operating speed 84-97 knots (155-180 km/h; 97-112 mph)
Stalling speed, power off:
flaps up 65 knots (120 km/h; 75 mph)
flaps down 59 knots (108 km/h; 67 mph)
Max rate of climb at S/L 300 m (985 ft)/min
Service ceiling 4,000 m (13,125 ft)
T-O to 15 m (50 ft) 590 m (1,936 ft)
Landing from 15 m (50 ft) 550 m (1,805 ft)
Landing run 270 m (886 ft)
Range with max fuel, no reserves 378 nm (700 km; 435 miles)
Endurance, 30 min reserves 3 h 36 min
g limits +3·5/−1·4

PZL MIELEC M-24 DROMADER SUPER

Last mentioned in the 1983-84 *Jane's*, the M-24 prototype was still under construction in early 1986. It is expected to be powered initially by a 746 kW (1,000 hp) ASz-62IR radial engine. Hopper capacity is now said to have been increased to around 3,000 litres (660 Imp gallons; 792·5 US gallons) or 1,800 kg (3,968 lb), and other features to include wings increased in span to about 21 m (69 ft) and having a new aerofoil section. A turboprop version is also planned.

PZL MIELEC M-26 ISKIERKA (LITTLE SPARK)

The Iskierka (see accompanying illustrations) is a single-piston-engined aircraft, designed to FAR Pt 23 and intended for civil pilot training and pilot selection for military training. Selected parts and assemblies of the M-20 Mewa were used in the design of the wings, tail unit, landing gear, power plant, and electrical and power systems. Chief designer is Mr Krzysztof Piwek.

First flight of the **M-2600** Iskierka prototype (SP-PIA) was made on 18 July 1986. An **M-2601** version, with 224 kW (300 hp) Avco Lycoming engine, has been projected. The following details apply to the M-2600 prototype, except where indicated:

TYPE: Tandem two-seat training aircraft.

WINGS: Cantilever low-wing monoplane. NACA 65_2-415 section constant chord wings, with 7° dihedral from roots and 2° incidence. Sweptforward leading-edges at root. Safe-life semi-monocoque structure of aluminium alloy, including the Frise ailerons and single-slotted trailing-edge flaps. No spoilers, airbrakes or tabs.

FUSELAGE: Semi-monocoque safe-life structure of aluminium alloy.

TAIL UNIT: Conventional cantilever type, of similar construction to wings, with sweptback vertical and non-swept horizontal surfaces. Fixed incidence tailplane. Trim tab in starboard elevator.

LANDING GEAR: Retractable tricycle type, actuated hydraulically, with single wheel and oleo strut on each unit. Mainwheels retract inward into wings, nosewheel rearward. Cleveland 6·00-6 wheels and Goodrich 445 × 160 mm tyres on all three units; tyre pressures 3·43 bars (50 lb/sq in) on main units, 2·16 bars (31 lb/sq in) on nose unit. Cleveland disc brakes.

POWER PLANT: One 153 kW (205 hp) PZL F 6A-350C1 flat-six engine, driving a PZL Warszawa-Okecie US 142 two-blade variable-pitch propeller with pointed spinner. One 93 litre (20·5 Imp gallon) fuel tank in each wing leading-edge, plus a 10 litre (2·2 Imp gallon) fuselage tank, to give total capacity of 196 litres (43·2 Imp gallons). Gravity fuelling point in top of each tank. Oil capacity 10 litres (2·2 Imp gallons).

ACCOMMODATION: Tandem seats for pupil (in front) and instructor, under one-piece framed canopy which opens sideways to starboard. Rear seat is elevated. Baggage compartment aft of rear seat. Both cockpits heated and ventilated.

SYSTEMS: Two independent hydraulic systems, one operating at 154 bars (2,233 lb/sq in) for landing gear extension/retraction and the other at 103 bars (1,494 lb/sq in) for wheel braking. DC electrical power supplied by a 24V 50A alternator and 28Ah SAM-28 battery. No pneumatic or oxygen systems or de-icing provisions.

AVIONICS AND EQUIPMENT: Polish made ARL 1601 radio compass and CG 121 gyro compass standard; RS 6102 radio optional. No blind-flying instrumentation. Landing light in port wing leading-edge.

DIMENSIONS, EXTERNAL:

Wing span	8·60 m (28 ft 2½ in)
Wing chord: at root	1·88 m (6 ft 2 in)
at tip	1·60 m (5 ft 3 in)
Wing aspect ratio	5·28
Length overall	8·28 m (27 ft 2 in)
Length of fuselage	7·685 m (25 ft 2½ in)
Height overall	2·96 m (9 ft 8½ in)
Tailplane span	3·80 m (12 ft 5½ in)
Wheel track	2·93 m (9 ft 7¼ in)
Wheelbase	1·925 m (6 ft 3¾ in)
Propeller diameter	1·90 m (6 ft 2¾ in)
Propeller ground clearance	9 cm (3½ in)

DIMENSIONS, INTERNAL:

Cockpit: Length	2·91 m (9 ft 6½ in)
Max width	0·88 m (2 ft 10½ in)
Max height	1·30 m (4 ft 3¼ in)
Floor area	2·30 m² (24·76 sq ft)
Volume	2·30 m³ (81·22 cu ft)
Baggage compartment volume	0·20 m³ (7·06 cu ft)

AREAS:

Wings, gross	14·00 m² (150·7 sq ft)
Ailerons (total)	1·172 m² (12.62 sq ft)
Trailing-edge flaps (total)	1·06 m² (11·41 sq ft)
Fin	1·965 m² (21·15 sq ft)
Rudder	0·89 m² (9·58 sq ft)
Tailplane	3·30 m² (35·52 sq ft)
Elevators (total, incl tab)	1·15 m² (12·38 sq ft)

WEIGHTS AND LOADINGS (A: M-2600, B: M-2601):

Basic operating weight empty: A	900 kg (1,984 lb)
B	960 kg (2,116 lb)
Max fuel weight: A	140 kg (308 lb)
Max T-O and landing weight: A	1,250 kg (2,756 lb)
B	1,400 kg (3,086 lb)
Max wing loading: A	89·3 kg/m² (18·3 lb/sq ft)
B	100·0 kg/m² (20·5 lb/sq ft)
Max power loading: A	8·18 kg/kW (13·44 lb/hp)
B	6·26 kg/kW (10·29 lb/hp)

PERFORMANCE (estimated at max T-O weight, A and B as above):

Never-exceed speed: A	215 knots (400 km/h; 248 mph)
Max level speed at S/L:	
A	143 knots (265 km/h; 165 mph)
B	183 knots (340 km/h; 211 mph)
Max cruising speed at 1,500 m (4,920 ft):	
A	135 knots (250 km/h; 155 mph)
Stalling speed, flaps down:	
A	53 knots (98 km/h; 61 mph)
Max rate of climb at S/L: A	258 m (846 ft)/min
B	480 m (1,575 ft)/min
Service ceiling: A	4,000 m (13,125 ft)
T-O to 15 m (50 ft): A	470 m (1,542 ft)
B	570 m (1,870 ft)
Landing from 15 m (50 ft): A	460 m (1,510 ft)
B	640 m (2,100 ft)
Range with max fuel, 30 min reserves:	
A	507 nm (940 km; 584 miles)
B	863 nm (1,600 km; 994 miles)
g limits	+6/−3

Prototype PZL Mielec M-26 Iskierka (153 kW; 205 hp PZL F 6A-350C1 engine)

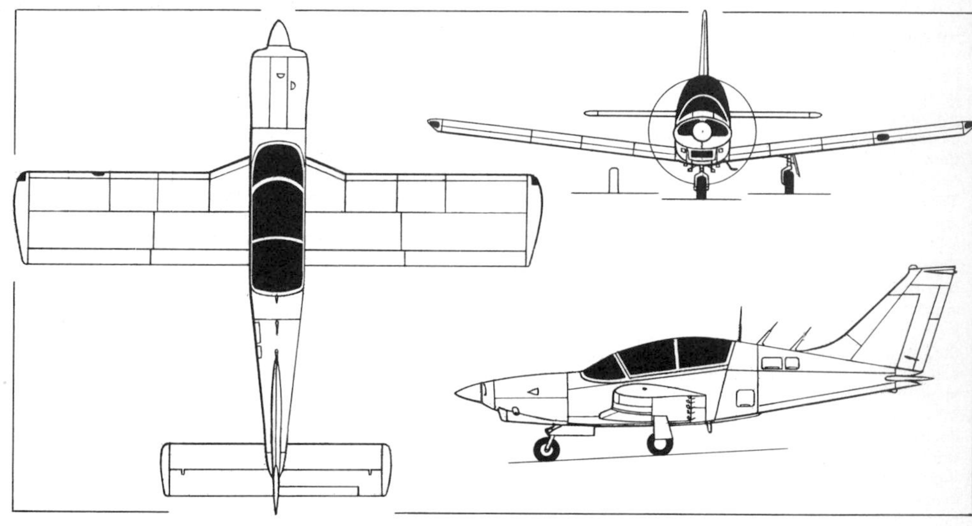

PZL Mielec M-26 Iskierka tandem two-seat primary trainer *(Pilot Press)*

WSK-PZL SWIDNIK

WYTWÓRNIA SPRZETU KOMUNIKACYJNEGO Im. ZYGMUNTA PULAWSKIEGO-PZL SWIDNIK (Zygmunt Pulawski Transport Equipment Manufacturing Centre, Swidnik)

21-040 Swidnik k/Lublina
Telephone: Lublin 12061, 12071, 13061 and 13071
Telex: 0642301 WSK PL

GENERAL MANAGER: Andrzej Zeh, MScEng

DIRECTOR OF RESEARCH AND DEVELOPMENT, AND CHIEF DESIGNER: Stanisław Kaminski

The factory at Swidnik was established in 1951 and was engaged initially in manufacturing components for the LiM-1 (MiG-15) jet fighter.

In 1955, when the manufacture of combat aircraft was drastically reduced in Poland, the WSK at Swidnik began licence production of the Soviet designed Mi-1 helicopter, some 1,700 of which were built under the designation SM-1, followed by 450 examples of the Swidnik developed SM-2. A design office was formed at the factory to work on variants and developments of the basic SM-1 design and on original projects such as the SM-4 Latka.

In September 1957, the Swidnik works was named after the famous pre-war PZL designer Zygmunt Pulawski, and currently employs about 10,000 people. Production is concentrated at present on various developments of the Soviet designed Mil Mi-2 turbine powered helicopter, and manufacture of wing and tailplane slats for the PZL Mielec (Antonov) An-28.

Swidnik, together with other PZL factories at Mielec and Kalisz, is manufacturing components for the Soviet Ilyushin Il-86 wide-bodied airliner.

PZL SWIDNIK (MIL) Mi-2

NATO reporting name: Hoplite

The Mil Mi-2, first flown in September 1961, was designed in the USSR by the Mikhail L. Mil bureau. It retains the basic configuration of Mil's earlier Mi-1 helicopter, but has a larger cabin and, instead of a single piston engine, has two Isotov turboshaft engines mounted side by side above the cabin.

Development of the two Mi-2 prototypes continued in the USSR until the helicopter had completed its initial State trials programme of flying. Then, in accordance with an agreement signed in January 1964, further development, production and marketing of the Mi-2 were assigned exclusively to the Polish aircraft industry, which flew its own first example of the Mi-2 on 4 November 1965.

Series production began in 1965, and Swidnik has since

PZL Swidnik Mi-2 in agricultural configuration

built more than 4,700 for various civil and military operators; the majority of these have been exported. Among the operators of the Mi-2 are the air forces of East Germany, Hungary, Nicaragua, North Korea, Libya, Poland, Syria and the USSR, and civil operators in European and various developing countries.

During the course of production the Mi-2 has undergone continuous improvement and upgrading, with versions for new applications being developed to meet specific customers' requirements. A full list of these can be found in the 1984-85 and earlier *Jane's*; the principal versions being produced in 1985 were as follows:

(a) Convertible passenger/cargo transport;
(b) Ambulance and rescue versions;
(c) Agricultural version, for dusting or conventional and ultra-low-volume spraying. In service in Bulgaria, Czechoslovakia, Egypt, Iran, Iraq, Libya, Poland, Sudan and USSR;
(d) Freighter version, with external cargo sling and electric hoist;
(e) Training version;
(f) Aerial photography versions, able to carry photographic, photogrammetric, thermal imaging or TV cameras for oblique or vertical pictures;
(g) Armed versions.

The following details apply specifically to the basic Mi-2, except where indicated:

TYPE: Twin-turbine general purpose light helicopter.

ROTOR SYSTEM: Three-blade main rotor fitted with hydraulic blade vibration dampers. All-metal blades, of NACA 230-12M section. Flapping, drag and pitch hinges on each blade. Main rotor blades and those of two-blade tail rotor each consist of an extruded duralumin spar with bonded honeycomb trailing-edge pockets. Anti-flutter weights on leading-edges, balancing plates on trailing-edges. Hydraulic boosters for longitudinal, lateral and collective pitch controls. Coil spring counterbalance mechanism in main and tail rotor systems. Pitch change centrifugal loads on tail rotor carried by ribbon type steel torsion elements. Rotors do not fold. Electric blade de-icing system for main and tail rotors. Rotor brake fitted.

ROTOR DRIVE: Main rotor shaft driven via gearbox on each engine; three-stage WR-2 main gearbox, intermediate gearbox and tail rotor gearbox. Main rotor/engine rpm ratio 1 : 24·6; tail rotor/engine rpm ratio 1 : 4·16. Main gearbox provides drive for auxiliary systems and take-off for rotor brake. Freewheel units permit disengagement of a failed engine and also autorotation.

FUSELAGE: Conventional semi-monocoque structure of pod and boom type, made up of three main assemblies: the nose (including cockpit), central section, and tailboom. Construction is of sheet duralumin, bonded and spot welded or riveted to longerons and frames. Main load bearing joints are of steel alloy.

TAIL UNIT: Variable incidence horizontal stabiliser controlled by collective pitch lever.

LANDING GEAR: Non-retractable tricycle type, plus tailskid. Twin-wheel nose unit. Single wheel on each main unit. Oleo-pneumatic shock absorbers in all units, including tailskid. Main shock absorbers designed to cope with both normal operating loads and possible ground resonance. Mainwheel tyres size 600 × 180, pressure 4·41 bars (64 lb/sq in). Nosewheel tyres size 400 × 125, pressure 3·45 bars (50 lb/sq in). Pneumatic brakes on mainwheels. Metal ski landing gear optional.

POWER PLANT: Two 298 kW (400 shp) Polish built Isotov GTD-350 turboshaft engines, mounted side by side above cabin. Fuel in single rubber tank, capacity 600 litres (131 Imp gallons), under cabin floor. Provision for carrying a 238 litre (52·4 Imp gallon) external tank on each side of cabin. Refuelling point in starboard side of fuselage. Oil capacity 25 litres (5·4 Imp gallons). Engine air intake de-icing by engine bleed air.

ACCOMMODATION: Normal accommodation for one pilot on flight deck (port side). Seats for up to eight passengers in air-conditioned cabin, comprising back to back bench seats for three persons each, with two optional extra starboard side seats at the rear, one behind the other. All passenger seats are removable for carrying up to 700 kg (1,543 lb) of internal freight. Access to cabin via forward hinged doors on each side at front of cabin and aft on port side. Pilot's sliding window jettisonable in emergency. Ambulance version has accommodation for four stretchers and a medical attendant, or two stretchers and two sitting casualties. Side by side seats and dual controls in pilot training version. Cabin heating, ventilation and air-conditioning standard. Electric de-icing of windscreen.

SYSTEMS: Cabin heating, by engine bleed air, and ventilation; heat exchangers warm atmospheric air for ventilation system during cold weather. Hydraulic system, pressure 65 bars (940 lb/sq in), for cyclic and collective pitch control boosters. Hydraulic fluid flow rate 7·5 litres (1·65 Imp gallons)/min. Vented reservoir, with gravity feed. Pneumatic system, pressure 49 bars (710 lb/sq in), for mainwheel brakes. AC electrical system, with two STG-3 3kW engine driven starter/generators and 208V 16kVA three-phase alternator. 24V DC system, with two 28Ah lead-acid batteries.

AVIONICS AND EQUIPMENT: Standard equipment includes two transceivers (MF/HF), gyro compass, radio compass, radio altimeter, intercom system and blind-flying panel. Electrically operated wiper for pilot's windscreen. Fire extinguishing system, for engine bays and main gearbox compartment, is generally similar to, but simpler than, the freon system fitted to the Soviet Mil Mi-8, and can be actuated automatically or manually.

Passenger transport version of the PZL Swidnik (Mil) Mi-2 twin-turbine helicopter

OPERATIONAL EQUIPMENT: Agricultural version carries a hopper on each side of the fuselage (total capacity 1,000 litres; 220 Imp gallons of liquid or 750 kg; 1,650 lb of dry chemical) and either a spraybar to the rear of the cabin on each side or a distributor for dry chemicals under each hopper. Swath width covered by the spraying version is 40-45 m (130-150 ft). As a search and rescue aircraft, an electric hoist, capacity 120 kg (264 lb), is fitted. In the freight role an underfuselage hook can be fitted for suspended loads of up to 800 kg (1,763 lb). Nose and tail warning radar fitted to some military versions.

ARMAMENT: Some Mi-2s of the Polish Air Force are equipped with rocket pods or 'Sagger' air-to-surface missiles mounted on pylons on each side of the cabin.

DIMENSIONS, EXTERNAL:
Main rotor diameter 14·50 m (47 ft 6⅞ in)
Main rotor blade chord (constant, each) 0·40 m (1 ft 3¾ in)
Tail rotor diameter 2·70 m (8 ft 10¼ in)
Length overall, rotors turning 17·42 m (57 ft 2 in)
Length of fuselage 11·40 m (37 ft 4¾ in)
Height to top of rotor head 3·75 m (12 ft 3½ in)
Stabiliser span 1·85 m (6 ft 0¾ in)
Wheel track 3·05 m (10 ft 0 in)
Wheelbase 2·71 m (8 ft 10¾ in)
Tail rotor ground clearance 1·59 m (5 ft 2¾ in)
Cabin door (port, rear):
Height 1·065 m (3 ft 5¾ in)
Width 1·115 m (3 ft 8 in)
Cabin door (stbd, front):
Height 1·11 m (3 ft 7¾ in)
Width 0·75 m (2 ft 5½ in)
Cabin door (port, front): Height 1·11 m (3 ft 7¾ in)
Width 0·78 m (2 ft 6¾ in)

DIMENSIONS, INTERNAL:
Cabin:
Length: incl flight deck 4·07 m (13 ft 4¼ in)
excl flight deck 2·27 m (7 ft 5½ in)
Mean width 1·20 m (3 ft 11¼ in)
Mean height 1·40 m (4 ft 7 in)

AREAS:
Main rotor blades (each) 2·40 m² (25·83 sq ft)
Tail rotor blades (each) 0·22 m² (2·37 sq ft)
Main rotor disc 166·4 m² (1,791·11 sq ft)
Tail rotor disc 5·73 m² (61·68 sq ft)
Horizontal stabiliser 0·70 m² (7·53 sq ft)

WEIGHTS AND LOADING:
Weight empty, equipped:
passenger version 2,402 kg (5,295 lb)
cargo version 2,372 kg (5,229 lb)
ambulance version 2,410 kg (5,313 lb)
agricultural version 2,372 kg (5,229 lb)
Basic operating weight empty:
single-pilot versions 2,365 kg (5,213 lb)
dual control version 2,424 kg (5,344 lb)
Max payload, excl pilot, oil and fuel 800 kg (1,763 lb)
Normal T-O weight (and max T-O weight of agricultural version) 3,550 kg (7,826 lb)
Max T-O weight (special versions) 3,700 kg (8,157 lb)
Max disc loading 22·4 kg/m² (4·6 lb/sq ft)

PERFORMANCE (at 3,550 kg; 7,826 lb T-O weight):
Never-exceed speed at 500 m (1,640 ft):
agricultural version 84 knots (155 km/h; 96 mph)
other versions 113 knots (210 km/h; 130 mph)
Max cruising speed at 500 m (1,640 ft):
agricultural version (without agricultural equipment) 102 knots (190 km/h; 118 mph)
other versions 108 knots (200 km/h; 124 mph)

Armed version of the PZL Swidnik Mi-2, with four pylon mounted 'Sagger' air-to-surface missiles

Max level speed with agricultural equipment
(agricultural version) 84 knots (155 km/h; 96 mph)
Econ cruising speed:
for max range at 500 m (1,640 ft) 102 knots (190 km/h; 118 mph)
for max endurance at 500 m (1,640 ft) 54 knots (100 km/h; 62 mph)
Max rate of climb at S/L 270 m (885 ft)/min
Time to 1,000 m (3,280 ft) 5 min 30 s
Time to 4,000 m (13,125 ft) 26 min 0 s
Service ceiling 4,000 m (13,125 ft)
Hovering ceiling: IGE approx 2,000 m (6,560 ft)
OGE approx 1,000 m (3,280 ft)
Min landing area 30 × 30 m (100 × 100 ft)
Range at 500 m (1,640 ft):
max payload, 5% fuel reserves 91 nm (170 km; 105 miles)
max internal fuel, no reserves 237 nm (440 km; 273 miles)
max internal and auxiliary fuel, 30 min reserves 313 nm (580 km; 360 miles)
max internal and auxiliary fuel, no reserves 430 nm (797 km; 495 miles)
Endurance at 500 m (1,640 ft), no reserves:
max internal fuel 2 h 45 min
max internal and auxiliary fuel 5 h 0 min
Endurance (agricultural version), 5% reserves:
spraying 40 min
dusting 50 min

PZL SWIDNIK Mi-2B

The PZL Mi-2B differs from the Mi-2 in having a different electrical system and more modern navigation aids. It has been manufactured in the same versions (except agricultural) as the Mi-2, and has the same flight performance. Empty equipped weights are 2,300 kg (5,070 lb) for the passenger version and 2,293 kg (5,055 lb) for the cargo version; T-O weight remains unchanged at 3,550 kg (7,826 lb). Rotor blade de-icing is not available on the Mi-2B.

PZL SWIDNIK KANIA/KITTY HAWK

In collaboration with Allison in the USA, PZL Swidnik developed the Kania or Kitty Hawk, powered by two Allison 250-C20B turboshaft engines. Two examples were converted from Mi-2 airframes, and the first of these (SP-PSA) made its initial flight on 3 June 1979.

Certification of the Kania was carried out in two stages. The first took place in 1979-81 and resulted, on 1 October 1981, in a supplementary type certificate to that of the Mi-2. The second stage, concerning a considerably improved **Kania Model 1** version, was carried out during 1982-86 under the leadership of Stanisław I. Markisz. Improvements included, among others, redesigned cockpit and cabin layout, engine and flight controls, engine and transmission cowlings. On 21 February 1986 this version of the Kania was granted a separate type certificate as an FAR Pt 29 (Transport Category B) day and night SVFR multipurpose utility helicopter with Category A engine isolation. Deliveries were due to begin in August 1986. An improved (Category B) version, for 'hot and high' operation, is expected to follow in late 1987.

The Kania Model 1 is offered in a number of versions and configurations. These include passenger transport (with standard, executive or customised interiors), cargo transport (internal or slung load), agricultural (LV and ULV spraying, spreading and dusting), medical evacuation, training, rescue, and aerial surveillance. Flight testing of advanced rotor blades and other new equipment on the two prototypes is continuing.

TYPE: Twin-turboshaft multi-purpose light helicopter.

ROTOR SYSTEM: Three-blade fully articulated main rotor and two-blade seesaw tail rotor. Glassfibre/epoxy blades on both rotors. Three hydraulic boosters for longitudinal, lateral and collective pitch control augmentation. Electric de-icing of rotor blades (incl icing and 'system out' warnings) optional.

ROTOR DRIVE: Transmission includes main rotor, intermediate and tail rotor gearboxes, each with individual lubrication system. Main gearbox equipped with freewheel units, oil cooling system, oil temperature and pressure gauges and switches, tacho-generator with low and high rpm warning, air compressor, and a spare power pad of 19·1 kW (25·6 shp) at 8,000 rpm. Steel engine driveshafts, each with two crowned tooth couplings. Tail rotor driveshaft of duralumin tube, with similar crowned tooth couplings and anti-friction bearings.

FUSELAGE AND TAIL UNIT: Conventional semi-monocoque fuselage and circular-section tailboom. Glassfibre/epoxy horizontal stabiliser at end of tailboom. Hoist and cargo sling attachment points standard.

LANDING GEAR: Non-retractable tricycle type, plus tailskid. Twin-wheel castoring nose unit; single wheel on each main unit. Pneumatic brakes on mainwheels.

POWER PLANT: Two Allison 250-C20B turboshaft engines, mounted side by side above cabin; each rated at 313 kW (420 shp) for T-O, 30 min and one engine out max continuous power, and 276 kW (370 shp) for normal cruise. Automatic and manual torque sharing control systems standard. Two separate fuel boost systems, each with fuel filter bypass switch, fuel pressure gauge and switch, connected by crossfeed. Standard usable fuel capacity of 600 litres (131 Imp gallons), with provision for additional 423 litres usable (93 Imp gallons) in optional auxiliary tanks. Fuel quantity gauge and fuel reserve warning. Two separate oil systems, each with oil cooling, temperature and pressure gauges, oil filter bypass pop-up and chip warning. Each engine equipped with starter/generator, engine fuel pump effective for cruise after both boost pumps out, N1 and N2 tacho-generators, TOT gauge and switch, start counter, and 'engine out' warning. Dual engine inlet de-icing standard. Each engine compartment equipped with fire detection system and with automatic and manual fire extinguishing systems.

ACCOMMODATION: Pilot (port side), and co-pilot or passenger, on adjustable and removable front seats, each fitted with safety belt. Dual controls optional. Accommodation for up to eight more persons, on two three-person bench seats and a single or double seat at rear of cabin, all with safety belts. Seats removable for carriage of cargo (up to 1,200 kg; 2,645 lb), stretchers, agricultural or other specialised equipment. Access to cabin via jettisonable door on each side at front (port door of sliding type) and larger passenger/cargo door at rear on port side. Pilot's windscreen wiper standard, co-pilot's optional. Cargo and stretcher tiedown points in cabin floor. Cabin soundproofing and ventilation standard; heating, carpets, double pane windows, pilot's heated windscreen, all optional. Baggage compartment at rear of cabin. Cockpit and cabin lighting standard.

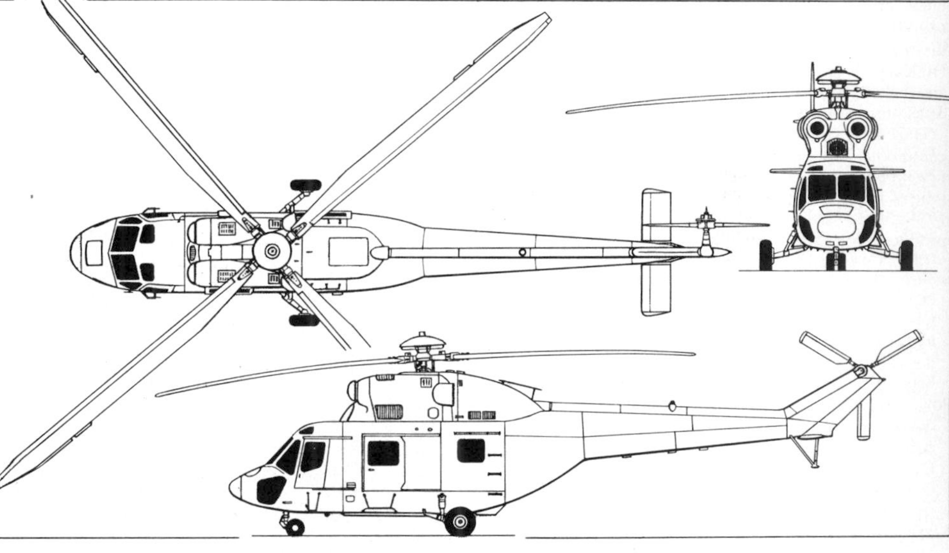

PZL Swidnik W-3 Sokól twin-turboshaft helicopter *(Pilot Press)*

SYSTEMS: Hydraulic system, with pressure gauge and switch, standard. Compressed air system, with accumulator and system gauges, standard. Ventilation standard, with individually controllable fresh air outlets; Casey cabin heaters optional, with individual control of hot air flow and central control of overall cabin air temperature. DC electrical system based on two 28V 150A starter/generators and a 25Ah nickel-cadmium battery, with ground power receptacle. Ground/battery power, battery overtemperature and 'generator out' warnings standard. A 16kVA AC generator and/or 115V 250A static inverter are optional; this AC system is equipped with AC generator and AC 115V warnings. Dual fire detection and extinguishing systems for engines standard.

AVIONICS AND EQUIPMENT: Primary instrumentation includes attitude, altitude, airspeed, turn and slip, and rate of climb indicators; magnetic compass and gyro compass; HSI; clock; VHF com transceiver; and full range of power plant and systems control, monitoring and warning instruments. Optional radio-navigation avionics include ADF (VOR 1) or R/Nav (VOR 2), audio panel, VOR/LOC/glideslope converter, transponder, altitude encoder, marker beacon receiver, DME, second VHF com transceiver, HF com transceiver, and radar altimeter. Standard equipment includes dual anti-collision lights, navigation lights, portable fire extinguisher, tool kit and first aid kit. Fluorescent tube cabin lighting and/or individual lights optional.

OPERATIONAL EQUIPMENT: According to mission, the Kania can be equipped with an 800 kg (1,763 lb) capacity stabilised cargo sling; 120 kg (265 lb) capacity hoist (275 kg; 606 lb hoist under test in 1986); stretchers and casualty care equipment; or equipment for a variety of agricultural duties.

DIMENSIONS, EXTERNAL:
Main rotor diameter 14·558 m (47 ft 9¼ in)
Tail rotor diameter 2·70 m (8 ft 10¼ in)
Length overall, rotors turning 17·35 m (56 ft 11 in)
Length of fuselage 12·10 m (39 ft 8½ in)
Height to top of rotor head 3·75 m (12 ft 3½ in)
Stabiliser span 1·84 m (6 ft 0½ in)
Wheel track 3·05 m (10 ft 0 in)
Wheelbase 2·71 m (8 ft 10¾ in)

DIMENSIONS, INTERNAL:
Cabin: Length, incl flight deck 4·07 m (13 ft 4¼ in)
Max width 1·50 m (4 ft 11 in)
Max height 1·62 m (5 ft 3¾ in)
Floor area 5·68 m² (61·1 sq ft)
Volume 7·76 m³ (274·0 cu ft)
Baggage compartment volume 0·45 m³ (15·89 cu ft)

AREAS:
Main rotor disc 166·50 m² (1,792·2 sq ft)
Tail rotor disc 5·725 m² (61·6 sq ft)

WEIGHTS:
Basic weight empty 2,000 kg (4,409 lb)
Normal T-O weight 3,350 kg (7,385 lb)
Max T-O weight 3,550 kg (7,826 lb)
Max load in cabin 1,200 kg (2,645 lb)
Max cargo sling load 800 kg (1,763 lb)

PERFORMANCE ('clean' aircraft at S/L, ISA, zero wind, at normal T-O weight):
Max cruising speed 116 knots (215 km/h; 134 mph)
Econ cruising speed 102 knots (190 km/h; 118 mph)
Max rate of climb (T-O power) 525 m (1,725 ft)/min
Rate of climb, one engine out 65 m (212 ft)/min
Service ceiling 4,000 m (13,125 ft)
Hovering ceiling: IGE 2,500 m (8,200 ft)
OGE 1,375 m (4,510 ft)
Range at econ cruising speed:
standard fuel, 30 min reserves 217 nm (402 km; 250 miles)
standard fuel, no reserves 257 nm (476 km; 296 miles)
max fuel, 30 min reserves 383 nm (710 km; 441 miles)
max fuel, no reserves 420 nm (779 km; 484 miles)

PZL SWIDNIK W-3 SOKÓL (FALCON)

Development of this all-new Polish helicopter took place in the second half of the 1970s, and the first flight was made on 16 November 1979 by one of five prototypes, which subsequently underwent a wide range of tiedown tests. The remaining prototypes were completed embodying changes made as a result of these tests, the manufacturer's flight trials being resumed on 6 May 1982 by the second aircraft (SP-PSB). Certification trials with two other aircraft have been carried out in a wide range of operating conditions, including extreme temperatures of −60°C and +50°C. The design team was headed by Stanislav Kaminski. Larger than the Mi-2/Kania, the Sokól accommodates a crew of two, and 12 passengers or a maximum 2,100 kg (4,630 lb) of internal cargo.

The Sokól is intended to be Swidnik's major production helicopter during the second half of the 1980s; series manufacture began in 1985.

TYPE: Twin-turboshaft medium weight multi-purpose helicopter.

ROTOR SYSTEM: Four-blade fully articulated main rotor and three-blade tail rotor. Main rotor has a pendular Salomon type vibration absorber, providing smooth flight and low vibration levels. Blades of both rotors constructed of laminated glassfibre impregnated with epoxy resin. Main rotor blades have tapered tips. Three hydraulic boosters for longitudinal, lateral and collective pitch control of main rotor, and one booster for tail rotor

PZL Swidnik Kania twin-turboshaft light helicopter

control. Blade anti-icing by electrically heated elements. Rotor brake fitted.

ROTOR DRIVE: Transmission driven via main rotor, intermediate and tail rotor gearboxes. Tail rotor driveshaft of duralumin tube with splined couplings.

FUSELAGE AND TAIL UNIT: Conventional light alloy semi-monocoque structure, with circular section monocoque tailboom. Fin integral with tailboom structure and fitted with glassfibre trailing-edge panels. Horizontal stabiliser, under end of tailboom, has a single continuous spar, is built up of laminated glassfibre impregnated with epoxy resin, and is not interconnected with the main rotor control system.

LANDING GEAR: Non-retractable tricycle type, plus tailskid beneath tailboom. Twin-wheel castoring nose unit; single wheel on each main unit. Oleo-pneumatic shock absorber in each unit. Mainwheel tyres size 700 × 250 mm; nosewheel tyres size 400 × 140 mm. Hydraulic disc brakes on mainwheels. Metal ski landing gear optional.

POWER PLANT: Two PZL-10W turboshaft engines (Polish developed helicopter version of Glushenkov TVD-10), each with rating of 662 kW (888 shp) for T-O and 30 min OEI, and emergency ratings of 735 kW (986 shp) and 845·5 kW (1,134 shp) for 8 min and 2½ min OEI respectively. Particle separators on engine intakes, and inlet de-icing, are standard. Power plant is equipped with advanced electronic fuel control system for maintaining rotor speed at pilot-selected value amounting to ± 5 per cent of normal rpm, and also for torque sharing as well as for supervising engine limits during start-up and normal or OEI operation. Engines and main rotor gearbox are mounted on a bed frame, eliminating any drive misalignment due to deformations of the fuselage structure. It is intended to investigate the potential of reducing noise and vibration by attaching this frame to the fuselage by elastomeric pads. Bladder fuel tanks beneath cabin floor, with combined capacity of 1,700 litres (374 Imp gallons). Auxiliary tanks, total capacity 1,100 litres (242 Imp gallons), optional.

ACCOMMODATION: Pilot (port side), and co-pilot or flight engineer, side by side on flight deck, on adjustable seats with safety belts. Dual controls and dual flight instrumentation optional. Accommodation for 12 passengers in main cabin. Seats removable for carriage of internal cargo. Ambulance version will carry four stretcher cases and a medical attendant. Baggage space at rear of cabin. Door on each side of flight deck; large sliding door for passenger and/or cargo loading on port side at forward end of cabin; second sliding door at rear of cabin on starboard side. Optically flat windscreens, improving view and enabling wipers to sweep a large area. Accommodation soundproofed, heated (by engine bleed air) and ventilated.

SYSTEMS: Two independent hydraulic systems, working pressure 90 bars (1,300 lb/sq in), for controlling main and tail rotors, unlocking collective pitch control lever, and feeding damper of directional steering system. Flow rate 11 litres (2·4 Imp gallons)/min in each system. Vented gravity feed reservoir, at atmospheric pressure. Pneumatic system for actuating hydraulic mainwheel brakes. Electrical system providing both AC and DC power. Automatic power control system linking power plant and rotor pitch for optimum performance. Fire detection/extinguishing system. Air-conditioning and oxygen systems optional. Neutral gas system optional, for inhibiting fuel vapour explosion.

AVIONICS AND EQUIPMENT: Standard IFR nav/com avionics permit adverse weather operation by day or night. Weather radar optional. Stability augmentation system

PZL Swidnik W-3 Sokól (two PZL-10W turboshaft engines)

standard. Cargo version equipped with 2,100 kg (4,630 lb) capacity external hook and 150 kg (331 lb) capacity rescue hoist; 300 kg (661 lb) capacity hoist to become available in near future.

DIMENSIONS, EXTERNAL:
- Main rotor diameter: 15·70 m (51 ft 6 in)
- Tail rotor diameter: 3·03 m (9 ft 11¼ in)
- Length overall, rotors turning: 18·85 m (61 ft 10⅛ in)
- Length of fuselage: 14·21 m (46 ft 7½ in)
- Height to top of rotor head: 4·12 m (13 ft 6¼ in)
- Stabiliser span: 3·45 m (11 ft 3¾ in)
- Wheel track: 3·40 m (11 ft 2 in)
- Wheelbase: 3·55 m (11 ft 7¾ in)
- Passenger/cargo doors:
  - Height (each): 1·20 m (3 ft 11¼ in)
  - Width: port 0·95 m (3 ft 1½ in)
  - starboard 1·25 m (4 ft 1¼ in)

DIMENSIONS, INTERNAL:
- Cabin: Length 3·20 m (10 ft 6 in)
  - Max width 1·55 m (5 ft 1 in)
  - Max height 1·40 m (4 ft 7 in)

AREAS:
- Main rotor disc: 193·6 m² (2,083·8 sq ft)
- Tail rotor disc: 7·2 m² (77·6 sq ft)

WEIGHTS:
- Minimum basic weight empty: 3,300 kg (7,275 lb)
- Basic operating weight empty (multi-purpose versions): 3,630 kg (8,002 lb)
- Max payload, internal or external: 2,100 kg (4,630 lb)
- Normal T-O weight: 6,100 kg (13,448 lb)
- Max T-O weight: 6,400 kg (14,110 lb)

PERFORMANCE (at normal T-O weight at 500 m; 1,640 ft, ISA, except where indicated):
- Never-exceed speed: 145 knots (270 km/h; 167 mph)
- Max level speed: 138 knots (255 km/h; 158 mph)
- Max cruising speed: 127 knots (235 km/h; 146 mph)
- Econ cruising speed: 119 knots (220 km/h; 137 mph)
- Max rate of climb at S/L: 510 m (1,673 ft)/min
- Rate of climb at S/L, one engine out:
  - at 30 min rating: 30 m (100 ft)/min
  - at 8 min emergency rating: 96 m (315 ft)/min
  - at 2½ min emergency rating: 186 m (610 ft)/min
- Service ceiling:
  - at normal T-O weight: 5,100 m (16,725 ft)
  - at T-O weight below normal: up to 6,000 m (19,680 ft)
- Service ceiling, one engine out:
  - at 30 min rating: 500 m (1,640 ft)
  - at 8 min emergency rating: 1,800 m (5,905 ft)
  - at 2½ min emergency rating: approx 2,300 m (7,545 ft)
- Hovering ceiling: IGE 3,000 m (9,845 ft)
  - OGE 2,100 m (6,890 ft)
- Range:
  - standard fuel, 5% reserves: 367 nm (680 km; 422 miles)
  - standard fuel, no reserves: 386 nm (715 km; 444 miles)
  - with auxiliary fuel, 5% reserves: 626 nm (1,160 km; 721 miles)
  - with auxiliary fuel, no reserves: 661 nm (1,225 km; 761 miles)
- Endurance:
  - standard fuel, 5% reserves: 3 h 50 min
  - standard fuel, no reserves: 4 h 5 min
  - with auxiliary fuel, 5% reserves: 6 h 41 min
  - with auxiliary fuel, no reserves: 7 h 5 min

PZL SWIDNIK SW-4

Development of this 4/5-seat single-engined multi-purpose light helicopter began in 1985. No official details were available for publication at the time of going to press.

WSK-PZL WARSZAWA-OKECIE

WYTWÓRNIA SPRZETU KOMUNIKACYJNEGO-PZL WARSZAWA-OKECIE (Transport Equipment Manufacturing Centre, Warsaw-Okecie)

Al. Krakowska 110/114, 02-256 Warszawa-Okecie
Telephone: Warszawa 461173 and 460031
Telex: 814649

MANAGERS:
Jerzy Milczarek, Eng MSc (General Manager)
Lech Fronczak, Eng MSc (Technical)
Franciszek Sobczak, Eng MSc (Sales)

PUBLIC RELATIONS: Przemysław Siehen, Eng MSc

The Okecie factory, founded in 1928, is responsible for light aircraft development and production, and for the design and manufacture of associated agricultural equipment for its own aircraft and for those built at other factories in the Polish aviation industry.

PZL-104 WILGA (THRUSH) 35 and 80

The PZL-104 Wilga is a light general purpose aircraft intended for a wide variety of general aviation and flying club duties. The prototype Wilga 1 flew for the first time on 24 April 1962. This aircraft, and other early models, were described in the 1968-69 *Jane's*.

The Wilga 35 (first flight 28 July 1967) with a 194 kW (260 hp) AI-14R engine, and Wilga 32 (first flown 12 September 1967) with a 171·5 kW (230 hp) Continental O-470-K, -L or

Italian registered PZL-104 Wilga 80 (PZL AI-14RA-KAF engine) *(Aviodata)*

-R engine and shorter landing gear, introduced improved cabin comfort, redesigned landing gear and a glassfibre tailwheel leg. Production began in 1968, and both received a Polish type certificate on 31 March 1969; the Wilga 32 was described in the 1974-75 *Jane's*, and its Indonesian built modified version, the Lipnur Gelatik, in the 1975-76 edition. Details of the experimental Wilga 40 and 43 were given in the 1972-73 *Jane's*, and of the Wilga 80/1400 prototype in the 1983-84 edition.

The aircraft is currently manufactured in two basic versions: the **Wilga 35**, which meets the requirements of British BCAR regulations, and the **Wilga 80**, which conforms to US FAR Pt 23 requirements. The latter has the carburettor air intake located further aft. Aeroclub versions (Wilga 35A and 80A) are fitted with a glider towing hook; Wilgas with agricultural equipment are designated 35R and 80R, and aircraft with twin Airtech (Canada) LAP-3000 floats are known as Wilga 35H and 80H. The first Wilga 80 was flown on 30 May 1979.

Examples of the Wilga have been sold to customers in Austria, Belgium, Bulgaria, Canada, Cuba, Czechoslovakia, Denmark, Egypt, Germany (Democratic Republic), Germany (Federal Republic), Hungary, Indonesia, Italy, Poland, Romania, Spain, Switzerland, Turkey, the UK, the USA, the USSR (more than 500), Venezuela and Yugoslavia.

Total sales of the Wilga (all versions) had reached 843 by 1 January 1986. A six-seat **Wilga 88** is in the design stage.

The following description applies to the Wilga 35 and 80, except where a specific version is indicated:

TYPE: Single-engined general purpose monoplane.

WINGS: Cantilever high-wing monoplane. Wing section NACA 2415. Dihedral 1°. All-metal single-spar structure, with leading-edge torsion box and beaded metal skin. Each wing attached to fuselage by three bolts, two at spar and one at forward fitting. All-metal aerodynamically and mass balanced slotted ailerons, with beaded metal skin. Ailerons can be drooped to supplement flaps during landing. Manually operated all-metal slotted flaps with beaded metal skin. Fixed metal slat on leading-edge along full span of wing and over fuselage. Tab on starboard aileron.

FUSELAGE: All-metal semi-monocoque structure in two portions, riveted together. Forward section incorporates main wing spar carry-through structure. Rear section is in the form of a tailcone. Beaded metal skin. Floor in cabin is of metal sandwich construction, with a paper honeycomb core, covered with foam rubber.

TAIL UNIT: Braced all-metal structure, with sweptback vertical surfaces. Stressed skin single-spar tailplane attached to fuselage by a single centre fitting and supported by a single aluminium alloy strut on each side. Stressed skin two-spar fin structure of semi-monocoque construction. Rudder and one-piece elevator are aerodynamically horn balanced and mass balanced. Trim tab at centre of elevator trailing-edge.

LANDING GEAR: Non-retractable tailwheel type. Semi-cantilever main legs, of rocker type, have oleo-pneumatic shock absorbers. Low-pressure tyres size 500 × 200 mm on mainwheels. Hydraulic brakes. Steerable tailwheel, tyre size 255 × 110 mm, carried on rocker frame with oleo-pneumatic shock absorber. Metal ski landing gear, and Airtech Canada LAP-3000 twin-float landing gear, optional.

POWER PLANT: One 194 kW (260 hp) PZL AI-14RA nine-cylinder supercharged radial aircooled engine (AI-14RA-KAF in Wilga 80), driving a PZL US-122000 two-blade constant-speed wooden propeller. Two removable fuel tanks in each wing, with total capacity of 195 litres (43 Imp gallons). Refuelling point on each side of fuselage, at junction with wing. Oil capacity 16 litres (3·5 Imp gallons).

ACCOMMODATION: Passenger version accommodates pilot and three passengers, in pairs, with adjustable front seats. Baggage compartment aft of seats, capacity 35 kg (77 lb). Upward opening door on each side of cabin, jettisonable in emergency. In the parachute training version the starboard door is removed and replaced by two tubular uprights with a central connecting strap, and the starboard front seat is rearward facing. Jumps are facilitated by a step on the starboard side and by a parachute hitch. A controllable towing hook can be attached to the tail landing gear permitting the Wilga, in this role, to tow a single glider of up to 650 kg (1,433 lb) weight or two or three gliders with a total combined weight of 1,125 kg (2,480 lb).

SYSTEMS: Hydraulic system pressure 39 bars (570 lb/sq in). Engine starting is effected pneumatically by a built-in system of 7 litres (427 cu in) capacity with a pressure of 49 bars (710 lb/sq in). Electrical system powered by DC generator and 24V 10Ah battery.

AVIONICS AND EQUIPMENT: Standard avionics and equipment include VHF transceiver and blind-flying instrumentation. Optional avionics and equipment include RS-6102 (of Polish design), R-860 II, R860 IIM, King KY 195 or Bendix radio; and ARL-1601 VHF, ARK-9, King KR 85 or Bendix AV-200 ADF, GB-1 gyro compass, K2-715 airspeed and altitude recorder, sun visors, exhaust silencer and windscreen wiper.

DIMENSIONS, EXTERNAL:

Wing span: 35	11·12 m (36 ft 5¾ in)
80	11·13 m (36 ft 6¼ in)
Wing chord (constant)	1·40 m (4 ft 7¼ in)
Wing aspect ratio	7·95
Length overall: 35	8·10 m (26 ft 6¾ in)
80	8·03 m (26 ft 4¼ in)
Height overall	2·96 m (9 ft 8½ in)
Tailplane span	3·70 m (12 ft 1¾ in)
Wheel track	2·75 m (9 ft 0¼ in)
Wheelbase	6·70 m (21 ft 11¾ in)
Propeller diameter	2·65 m (8 ft 8 in)
Passenger doors (each): Height	1·00 m (3 ft 3¼ in)
Width	1·50 m (4 ft 11 in)

DIMENSIONS, INTERNAL:

Cabin: Length	2·20 m (7 ft 2½ in)
Max width	1·20 m (3 ft 10 in)
Max height	1·50 m (4 ft 11 in)
Floor area	2·20 m² (23·8 sq ft)
Volume	2·40 m³ (85 cu ft)
Baggage compartment	0·50 m³ (17·5 cu ft)

AREAS:

Wings, gross	15·50 m² (166·8 sq ft)
Ailerons (total)	1·57 m² (16·90 sq ft)
Trailing-edge flaps (total)	1·97 m² (21·20 sq ft)
Fin	0·97 m² (10·44 sq ft)
Rudder	0·92 m² (9·90 sq ft)
Tailplane	3·16 m² (34·01 sq ft)
Elevator, incl tab	1·92 m² (20·67 sq ft)

WEIGHTS AND LOADINGS (Wilga 35A and 80):

Weight empty, equipped	870 kg (1,918 lb)
Max T-O and landing weight	1,300 kg (2,866 lb)
Max wing loading	83·9 kg/m² (17·18 lb/sq ft)
Max power loading	6·70 kg/kW (11·02 lb/hp)

PERFORMANCE (Wilga 35A, at max T-O weight):

Never-exceed speed	150 knots (279 km/h; 173 mph)
Max level speed	105 knots (194 km/h; 120 mph)
Cruising speed (75% power)	85 knots (157 km/h; 97 mph)
Cruising speed for max range	74 knots (137 km/h; 85 mph)
Stalling speed: flaps up	35 knots (65 km/h; 41 mph)
flaps down	30 knots (56 km/h; 35 mph)
Max rate of climb at S/L	276 m (905 ft)/min
Time to 1,000 m (3,280 ft)	3 min
Service ceiling	4,040 m (13,250 ft)
T-O run (grass)	121 m (397 ft)
Landing run	106 m (348 ft)
Range with max fuel, 30 min reserves	275 nm (510 km; 317 miles)

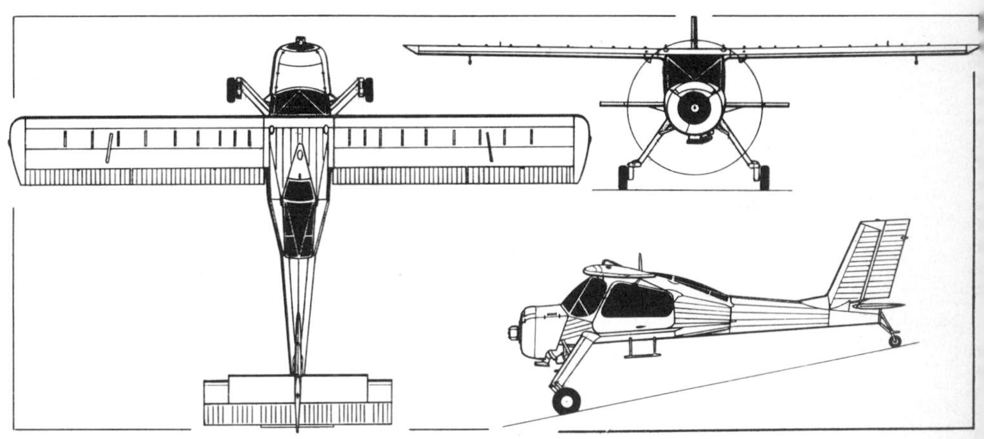

PZL-104 Wilga 35 general purpose monoplane *(Pilot Press)*

PZL-106B KRUK (RAVEN)

The PZL-106 was designed in early 1972 by a team led by Andrzej Frydrychewicz. The first prototype (SP-PAS) flew for the first time on 17 April 1973, powered by a 298 kW (400 hp) Avco Lycoming IO-720 engine. It was followed in

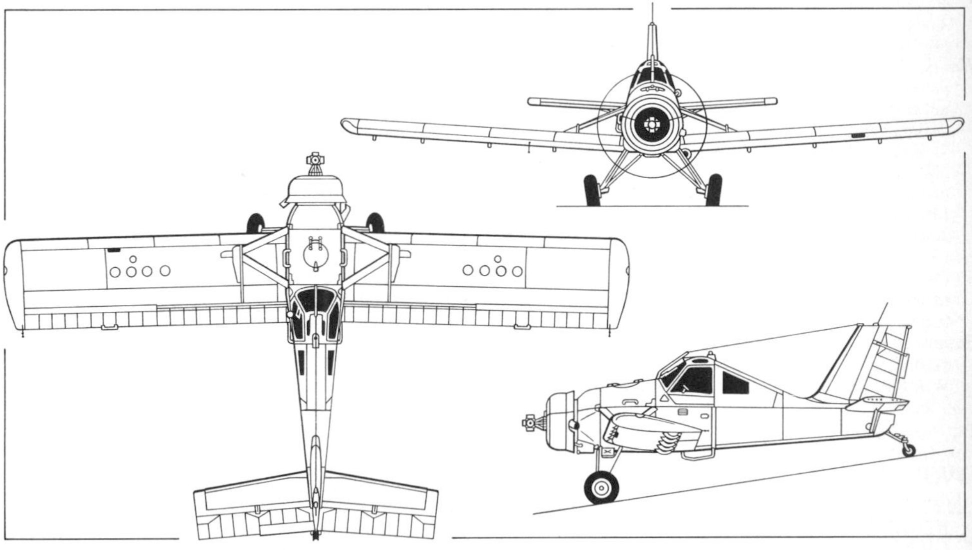

PZL-106BR Kruk single-seat agricultural aircraft *(Jane's/Mike Keep)*

Prototype PZL-106BT, first version of the Kruk with a Czechoslovak turboprop engine

October of that year by a second Avco Lycoming engined prototype (SP-PBG) and, from October 1974, by four prototypes fitted with the 441 kW (592 hp) PZL-3S radial engine that powers the PZL-106A and B. These production versions also have a low-mounted tailplane instead of the earlier T tail, and a greater chemical load in a larger hopper. Manufacture of some 600 aircraft for the member countries of the CMEA (Council for Mutual Economic Aid) is anticipated. A total of more than 165 (all versions) had been built by Spring 1986, including 144 PZL-106As produced between 1976-81. Details of the PZL-106A, and of the AR and AT prototypes, can be found in the 1985-86 and earlier editions of *Jane's*.

The following versions of the Kruk were current in 1986:

PZL-106AS. To increase the performance of more than 60 PZL-106A Kruks operated by Pezetel in Egypt and the Sudan, PZL Warszawa-Okecie adapted the design to take a 746 kW (1,000 hp) PZL (Shvetsov) ASz-62IR nine-cylinder radial engine instead of the standard 441 kW (592 hp) PZL-3S. The prototype of this version (SP-PBD) flew for the first time on 19 August 1981. First ten re-engined in 1982, total of 45 converted by early 1986. Hopper load reduced to 750 kg (1,653 lb) initially, due to heavier engine. May later be re-certificated at higher (Restricted) max T-O weight of 3,600 kg (7,936 lb). New-production aircraft with this engine are to PZL-106BS standard (which see).

PZL-106B. Prototypes for improved series, having re-designed wings with a new aerofoil section, increased span and area, trailing-edge flaps, and shortened V bracing struts. First prototype (SP-PKW) flew for the first time on 15 May 1981. Two further prototypes made their first flights in July and September 1981. Weights and performance data in 1985-86 and earlier *Jane's*.

PZL-106BR. Version with geared PZL-3SR engine; first flown on 8 July 1983. Entered series production (initial batch of 15) in 1985. Tested also with wingtip vanes (three at each tip).

PZL-106BS. The prototype (SP-PBK) of this uprated version of the Kruk, with a PZL (Shvetsov) ASz-62IR radial engine, flew for the first time on 8 March 1982. Production expected to start in 1986 with initial batch of 14. For Restricted category operation, with higher max T-O weight and increased load of chemical.

PZL-106BT Turbo-Kruk. Version with Czechoslovak Walter M 601 D turboprop engine, 6° wing sweepback and taller fin. Prototype (SP-PAA) first flown on 18 September 1985. Chemical load further increased.

The following description applies generally to the PZL-106B series, except where a specific version is indicated:

TYPE: Single-engined agricultural aircraft. Structure is corrosion resistant, and is additionally protected by an external finish of polyurethane enamel.

WINGS: Braced low-wing monoplane with upward cambered tips. NACA 2415 wing section throughout span. Dihedral 4° from roots. Incidence 6° 6′. Sweepback 1° at quarter-chord on B/BR/BS, 6° on BT. All-metal two-spar duralumin structure, of constant chord. Metal and polyester fabric covering. Glassfibre wingtips, with upswept undersurfaces. Full span four-segment fixed leading-edge slats on each wing, of glassfibre sandwich construction with foam core. Slotted ailerons of duralumin, with polyester fabric covering. Trailing-edge flaps of similar construction. Ground adjustable tab on each aileron. Duralumin streamline section V bracing struts, with jury struts.

FUSELAGE: Welded steel tube structure, protected by several coats of polyurethane enamel and covered with quickly removable panels of light alloy and GRP. Steel tube structure can be pressure tested for crack detection.

TAIL UNIT: Conventional duralumin structure, with single tailplane bracing strut each side. Fixed surfaces metal covered; rudder and mass balanced elevators are polyester fabric covered. Trim tab in port elevator, automatic tab on rudder. Enlarged fin on BT.

LANDING GEAR: Non-retractable tailwheel type, with oleo-pneumatic shock absorber in each unit. Mainwheels, with low-pressure tyres size 800 × 260 mm, each carried on side V and half-axle. Mainwheel tyre pressure 2·0 bars (29 lb/sq in). Pneumatically operated hydraulic disc brakes on mainwheels. Parking brake. Steerable tailwheel, with tubeless tyre size 350 × 135 mm, pressure 2·5 bars (36·25 lb/sq in).

POWER PLANT: *(PZL-106BR):* One 448 kW (600 hp) PZL-3SR seven-cylinder radial aircooled geared and supercharged engine, driving a PZL US-132000/A four-blade constant-speed metal propeller. *(PZL-106BS):* One 746 kW (1,000 hp) PZL (Shvetsov) ASz-62IR nine-cylinder radial aircooled engine. *(PZL-106BT):* One 544 kW (730 shp) Walter M 601 D turboprop engine, with Avia V 503 D propeller. Fuel in two integral wing tanks, total capacity 300 litres (66 Imp gallons); can be increased to total of 540 litres (119 Imp gallons) by using hopper as auxiliary fuel tank. Gravity refuelling point on each wing; semi-pressurised refuelling point on starboard side of fuselage. Oil capacity 54 litres (11·9 Imp gallons) max, 7 litres (1·54 Imp gallons) min. Carburettor air filter fitted.

ACCOMMODATION: Single vertically adjustable seat in enclosed, ventilated and heated cockpit with steel tube overturn structure. Provision for instructor's cockpit with basic dual controls, forward of main cockpit and offset to starboard, for training of pilots in agricultural duties. Optional rearward facing second seat (for mechanic) to rear. Jettisonable window/door on each side of cabin. Pilot's seat and seat belt designed to resist 40*g* impact.

SYSTEMS: Pneumatic system, rated at 49 bars (710 lb/sq in), for brakes and agricultural equipment. Electrical power, from 3kW 27·5V DC generator and 24V 15Ah battery, for engine starting, pneumatic system control, aircraft lights, instruments, VHF transceiver and semi-pressurised refuelling. Cockpit air-conditioning system optional.

EQUIPMENT: VHF com transceiver standard. Easily removable non-corrosive (GRP) hopper/tank, forward of cockpit, can carry more than 1,000 kg (2,205 lb) (see under 'Weights and Loadings' paragraph) of dry or liquid chemical, and has a maximum capacity of 1,400 litres (308 Imp gallons). Turnround time, with full load of chemical, is in the order of 28 s. The hopper has a quick-dump system that can release 1,000 kg of chemical in 5 s or less. A pneumatically operated intake for the loading of dry chemicals is optional. Distribution system for liquid chemical (jets or atomisers) is powered by a fan-driven centrifugal pump. A precise and reliable dispersal system, with positive on/off action for dry chemicals, gives effective swath widths of 30-35 m (100-115 ft). For ferry purposes, hopper can be used to carry additional fuel instead of chemical. When the Kruk is converted into a two-seat trainer (see 'Accommodation' paragraph), standard hopper can be replaced easily by a special container with reduced capacity tank for liquid chemical. Steel cable cutter on windscreen and each mainwheel leg; steel deflector cable runs from top of windscreen cable cutter to tip of fin. Windscreen washer and wiper standard. Other equipment includes 720-channel ultra short wave transceiver (optional), artificial horizon, gyro compass, engine hour meter, clock, rearview mirror, second (mechanic's) seat (optional), cockpit air-conditioning (optional), cockpit heating and ventilation, landing light, anti-collision light, and night working lights (optional).

DIMENSIONS, EXTERNAL:
Wing span: except BT — 14·90 m (48 ft 10½ in)
BT — 15·00 m (49 ft 2½ in)
Wing chord (constant): except BT — 1·90 m (6 ft 2¾ in)
Wing aspect ratio: except BT — 6·9
BT — 7·1
Length overall: except BT — 9·10 m (29 ft 10¼ in)
BT — 10·24 m (33 ft 7¼ in)
Height overall: except BT — 3·32 m (10 ft 10¾ in)
BT — 3·82 m (12 ft 6½ in)
Tailplane span — 5·77 m (18 ft 11¼ in)
Wheel track — 3·10 m (10 ft 2¼ in)
Wheelbase — 7·41 m (24 ft 3¾ in)
Propeller diameter: except BT — 2·62 m (8 ft 7 in)
BT — 2·50 m (8 ft 2½ in)
Propeller ground clearance (tail up):
except BT — 0·63 m (2 ft 0¾ in)
Crew doors (each): Height — 0·91 m (2 ft 11¾ in)
Width — 1·06 m (3 ft 5¾ in)
Baggage door: Height — 0·70 m (2 ft 3½ in)
Width — 0·60 m (1 ft 11¾ in)

DIMENSIONS, INTERNAL:
Cabin: Length — 1·37 m (4 ft 6 in)
Max width — 1·25 m (4 ft 1¼ in)
Max height — 1·30 m (4 ft 3¼ in)
Floor area — 1·12 m² (12·05 sq ft)
Rear cockpit/baggage compartment:
Length — 1·40 m (4 ft 7 in)
Width — 1·00 m (3 ft 3¼ in)
Depth — 0·60 m (1 ft 11¾ in)

AREAS:
Wings, gross: except BT — 32·18 m² (346·4 sq ft)
BT — 31·69 m² (341·1 sq ft)
Ailerons (total) — 2·46 m² (26·50 sq ft)
Fin: except BT — 1·26 m² (13·56 sq ft)
BT — 1·82 m² (19·59 sq ft)
Rudder, incl tab — 1·62 m² (17·44 sq ft)
Tailplane — 3·34 m² (35·95 sq ft)
Elevators, incl tab — 4·22 m² (45·42 sq ft)

WEIGHTS AND LOADINGS:
Weight empty, equipped: B — 1,670 kg (3,681 lb)
BT — 1,680 kg (3,704 lb)
Max chemical payload: BR — 1,050 kg (2,315 lb)
BS — 1,200 kg (2,645 lb)
BT — 1,300 kg (2,866 lb)
Max T-O and landing weight: BR — 3,000 kg (6,614 lb)
BS — 3,600 kg (7,936 lb)
BT — 3,300 kg (7,275 lb)
Max wing loading: BR — 93·2 kg/m² (19·10 lb/sq ft)
BS — 111·9 kg/m² (22·92 lb/sq ft)
BT — 104·1 kg/m² (21·34 lb/sq ft)
Max power loading: BR — 6·71 kg/kW (11·02 lb/hp)
BS — 4·83 kg/kW (7·94 lb/hp)
BT — 6·07 kg/kW (9·97 lb/shp)

PERFORMANCE (at max T-O weight):
Never-exceed speed:
all — 145 knots (270 km/h; 167 mph)
Max level speed at S/L (without agricultural equipment):
BR — 123 knots (229 km/h; 142 mph)
BS — 140 knots (260 km/h; 161 mph)
BT — 133 knots (247 km/h; 153 mph)
Max level speed at S/L (with agricultural equipment):
BR — 109 knots (203 km/h; 126 mph)
BS — 124 knots (230 km/h; 143 mph)
BT — 118 knots (219 km/h; 136 mph)
Operating speed with max chemical load:
BR, BT — 81-86 knots (150-160 km/h; 93-99 mph)
BS — 86 knots (160 km/h; 99 mph)
Stalling speed at S/L:
BR, BT — 49 knots (90 km/h; 56 mph)
BS — 54 knots (99 km/h; 62 mph)
Max rate of climb at S/L (with agricultural equipment):
BR — 228 m (748 ft)/min
BS — 372 m (1,220 ft)/min
BT — 360 m (1,180 ft)/min
T-O run (with agricultural equipment):
BR — 200 m (656 ft)
BS — 120 m (394 ft)
BT — 160 m (525 ft)
Landing run (with agricultural equipment):
BR, BS — 160 m (525 ft)
BT — 120 m (395 ft)
Range with max standard fuel:
BS — 540 nm (1,000 km; 621 miles)
BR — 593 nm (1,100 km; 683 miles)
BT — 404 nm (750 km; 466 miles)

PZL-140 GASIOR

Under this designation, Warszawa-Okecie has proposed a biplane version of the Kruk, to be used in a firefighting role carrying 2,000 kg (4,410 lb) of retardant. It would have a wing span of 14·67 m (48 ft 1½ in), Restricted category max T-O weight of 5,700 kg (12,566 lb), and normal operating speed of 129 knots (240 km/h; 149 mph). Present status of this project is not known.

PZL-110 KOLIBER (HUMMING-BIRD)

Under this designation, PZL Warszawa-Okecie is producing under licence a two/four-seat version of the Socata Rallye 100 ST, the lowest powered model in the Rallye light aircraft family, and one which is no longer in production in France. The first PZL-110, modified to receive an 86·5 kW (116 hp) PZL Franklin engine, made its initial flight on 18 April 1978.

The first production PZL-110 was flown on 8 May 1979, and ten Series I aircraft were built during that year. A Polish type certificate was awarded on 24 August 1979.

Although suitable for touring and liaison duties, the Koliber is intended primarily for basic and refresher flying training. Series II production aircraft (built 1983-84) are approved for limited aerobatics, and are for use only by Polish aeroclubs. The first five were delivered to Polish aero clubs in 1984; production of the next 20 was under way in

PZL-110 Koliber Series II, Polish built version of the Socata Rallye 100 ST

1985. A third series (30 aircraft) was due for completion in mid-1986.

An agricultural version, with hopper capacity for 100 kg (220 lb) of liquid chemical, is under study. The following description applies to the current production version:

TYPE: Two/three-seat light aircraft.

WINGS: Cantilever low-wing monoplane. Wing section NACA 63A416 (modified). Dihedral 7°. Incidence 4°. All-metal single-spar structure. Wide chord slotted ailerons. Full span automatic leading-edge slats. Long span electrically actuated trailing-edge slotted flaps. Ailerons and flaps have corrugated metal skin. Ground adjustable aileron tabs. No anti-icing.

FUSELAGE: All-metal semi-monocoque structure.

TAIL UNIT: Cantilever all-metal structure, with corrugated skin on mass balanced control surfaces. Fixed incidence tailplane. One controllable tab on elevator; ground adjustable tab on rudder.

LANDING GEAR: Non-retractable tricycle type, with oleo-pneumatic shock absorption. Castoring nosewheel. Hydraulic disc brakes.

POWER PLANT: One 86·5 kW (116 hp) PZL F 4A-235B1 flat-four engine, driving a PZL US 135 two-blade fixed-pitch propeller. Fuel in two metal tanks in wings, with total capacity of 95 litres (20·9 Imp gallons). Refuelling points above wings. Oil capacity 6 litres (1·3 Imp gallons).

ACCOMMODATION: Two side by side seats, plus bench seat at rear, under large rearward sliding canopy. Dual controls. Heating and ventilation standard.

SYSTEMS AND EQUIPMENT: 12V electrical system, with alternator and 18Ah battery. Equipment optional for Series I and standard for Series II includes VHF transceiver, ADF, electrically powered gyro attitude indicator, turn and bank indicator, and directional gyro. Equipment for the training role includes pupil's window blinds for instrument training, front seat backrests suitable for use with back type parachutes, safety belts, and accelerometers.

DIMENSIONS, EXTERNAL:

Wing span	9·74 m (31 ft 11½ in)
Wing chord (constant)	1·30 m (4 ft 3 in)
Length overall	7·15 m (23 ft 5½ in)
Height overall	2·80 m (9 ft 2¼ in)
Tailplane span	3·67 m (12 ft 0½ in)
Wheel track	2·01 m (6 ft 7¼ in)
Wheelbase	1·71 m (5 ft 7¼ in)
Propeller diameter	1·78 m (5 ft 10 in)

AREAS:

Wings, gross	12·66 m² (136·3 sq ft)
Ailerons (total)	1·56 m² (16·79 sq ft)
Trailing-edge flaps (total)	2·40 m² (25·83 sq ft)
Vertical tail surfaces (total)	1·74 m² (18·73 sq ft)
Horizontal tail surfaces (total)	3·48 m² (37·50 sq ft)

WEIGHTS AND LOADINGS:

Weight empty, equipped	535 kg (1,179 lb)
Max T-O weight: Utility	770 kg (1,697 lb)
Normal	820 kg (1,808 lb)
Max wing loading:	
Utility	60·82 kg/m² (12·46 lb/sq ft)
Normal	64·77 kg/m² (13·27 lb/sq ft)
Max power loading: Utility	8·90 kg/kW (14·63 lb/hp)
Normal	9·49 kg/kW (15·59 lb/hp)

PERFORMANCE (at 770 kg; 1,697 lb Utility max T-O weight except where indicated):

Never-exceed speed	145 knots (270 km/h; 167 mph)
Max level speed at S/L	102 knots (190 km/h; 118 mph)
Max cruising speed at S/L	92 knots (170 km/h; 106 mph)
Stalling speed: flaps up	48 knots (89 km/h; 56 mph)
flaps down	41 knots (76 km/h; 48 mph)
Max rate of climb at S/L	180 m (590 ft)/min
Service ceiling	3,500 m (11,480 ft)
T-O run at S/L	155 m (509 ft)
T-O to 15 m (50 ft) at S/L	380 m (1,247 ft)
Landing from 15 m (50 ft) at S/L	275 m (902 ft)
Landing run at S/L	110 m (361 ft)
Range at 500 m (1,640 ft) with max fuel, no reserves	394 nm (730 km; 453 miles)

PZL-130 ORLIK (EAGLET)

The Orlik is one of three elements, together with a flight simulator and an electronic diagnostic system, in a new Polish system now being developed for the training of future military and civilian pilots. It is intended to use the aircraft for a wide range of duties, including preselection training, basic handling, aerobatics, instrument flying, navigation training, formation flying, aerial combat training, air gunnery and ground attack, reconnaissance and target acquisition, and target towing. Cockpit instruments and displays are installed in modular units similar to those of modern combat aircraft to permit quick changes of avionics and equipment and enable the Orlik to perform as a 'flying operational simulator' for jet powered military aircraft.

Initial proposals for the PZL-130 were prepared in 1980, and detail design began in the Autumn of 1981 under the leadership of Mr Andrzej Frydrychewicz. Prototype construction started in the Spring of 1983. Two prototypes began flight testing in 1984: SP-PCA (c/n 002) on 12 October and SP-PCC on 29 December, followed by SP-PCB on 12 January 1985; a static test aircraft has also been completed. The Orlik was designed and built to FAR Pt 23 standards and will be certificated in all three categories (Normal, Utility, and Aerobatic). Construction of pre-production aircraft also started in 1985. A turboprop powered **Turbo Orlik** prototype (described separately) was due to fly in mid-1986; future plans include a version with extended wingtips, increasing span to 9·00 m (29 ft 6⅓ in).

Second flying prototype of the PZL-130 Orlik tandem two-seat trainer

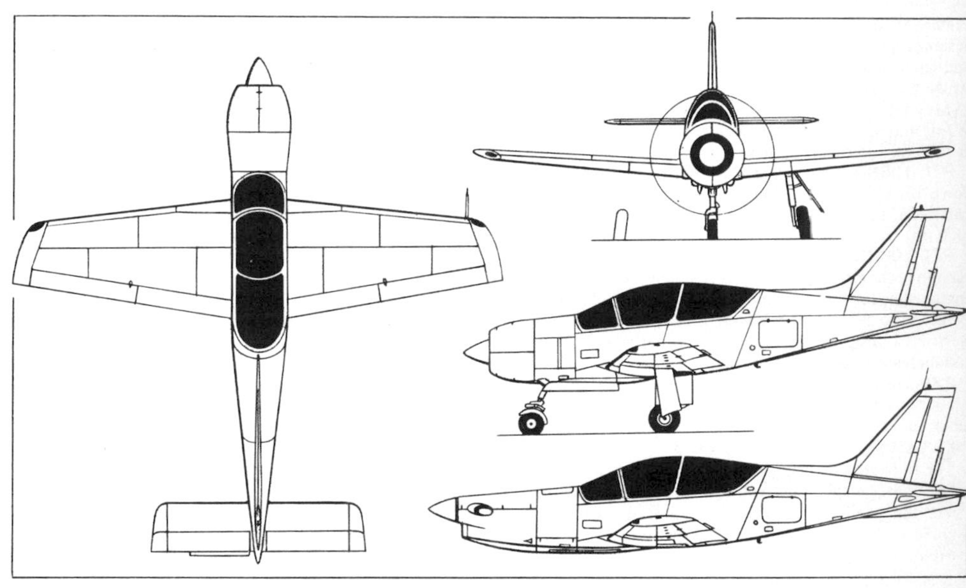

PZL-130 Orlik (Vedeneyev M-14Pm engine), with additional side view (bottom) of Turbo Orlik *(Pilot Press)*

The following description applies to the piston engined prototypes:

TYPE: Tandem two-seat primary, basic and multi-purpose trainer.

WINGS: Cantilever low-wing monoplane. Wing section NACA $64_{2}215$ (modified). Dihedral 5° from roots. Incidence 0° at root, −3° at tip. One-piece all-metal (light alloy) multi-spar torsion box structure, forming integral fuel tankage. Tapered planform, with raked tips of glassfibre/epoxy. Leading-edges are detachable; trailing-edge skin panels are electrically spot welded. All-metal constant chord single-slotted trailing-edge flaps, actuated electrically (max deflection 40°). Frise differential ailerons (20° up/12° down) are also all-metal and of constant chord, actuated mechanically via pushrods and torque tube in fuselage. Electrically actuated trim tab on port aileron. No slats, spoilers or airbrakes. Provision for anti-icing system.

FUSELAGE: All-metal (light alloy) unpressurised semi-monocoque structure, with electrically spot welded engine cowling and skin panels.

TAIL UNIT: Cantilever light alloy structure, with sweptback vertical and non-swept horizontal surfaces. Small, curved dorsal fin; shallow ventral strake under fuselage tailcone. Fixed incidence tailplane. Elevators aerodynamically and mass balanced, controlled by rods and cables; electrically actuated trim tab on port elevator. Aerodynamically and mass balanced rudder, also with electrically actuated trim tab, is cable controlled. Provision for anti-icing system.

LANDING GEAR: Pneumatically retractable type, all three units retracting into fuselage (mainwheels inward, nosewheel rearward). Oleo-pneumatic shock absorber in each unit (mainwheels on rockers, nosewheel on semi-fork with shimmy damper and centering device). Low pressure tubeless tyres, size 500 × 200 (main) and 400 × 140 (nose). Hydraulic disc brakes, operated pneumatically. No brake cooling or anti-skid units.

POWER PLANT: One 268 kW (360 hp) Vedeneyev M-14Pm (m = modified) nine-cylinder radial aircooled engine, driving a PZL US 146 three-blade constant-speed metal propeller with pointed spinner. Four integral fuel tanks (two of 110 litres; 24·2 Imp gallons and two of 100 litres; 22·0 Imp gallons capacity) in wing torsion box, plus a 10 litre (2·2 Imp gallon) collector tank in fuselage; total internal fuel capacity 430 litres (94·6 Imp gallons). Overwing refuelling point for each wing tank. No provision for external fuel tanks. Oil capacity 26 litres (5·7 Imp gallons). Fuel and oil systems adapted for aerobatics, including up to 60 s of inverted flight. Electrically adjustable exhaust flaps for engine cooling air.

ACCOMMODATION: Tandem seating for trainee and instructor under one-piece framed canopy, which opens sideways to starboard. Rear (instructor's) seat slightly elevated. Both seats are adjustable electrically, can accommodate back type and seat type parachutes, and are fitted with seat belts/harnesses. Full dual controls standard; rudder pedals are adjustable (three positions). Windscreen and canopy frames are of glassfibre/epoxy; windscreen is removable, canopy jettisonable. Cockpits heated (electric heater with blower) and ventilated. Baggage compartment aft of rear seat.

SYSTEMS: Two independent pneumatic systems, each at 49 bars (711 lb/sq in) pressure: main system for engine starting, landing gear extension/retraction, and wheel braking/steering; emergency system for all of these except landing gear retraction. External source connector. No hydraulic system. Electrical power (24/28V DC) supplied by 3kW generator and 18Ah battery; system includes voltage regulator with overvoltage relay, and external DC power socket. Provision for oxygen bottles and individual masks. Provision also for anti-icing of wing and tail leading-edges.

AVIONICS AND EQUIPMENT: One RS-6102 720-channel UHF com (UNIMOR), one ARL-1601 ADF (RADMOR) and blind-flying instrumentation are standard; nav VOR/ILS, transponder and radio altimeter are optional.

ARMAMENT: No installed armament. Two underwing pylons for practice bombs, gun pods or other weapon training stores. Provision for gunsight, gun camera and armament control system.

DIMENSIONS, EXTERNAL:

Wing span	8·00 m (26 ft 3 in)
Wing chord: at root	2·00 m (6 ft 6¾ in)

mean aerodynamic	1·62 m (5 ft 3¾ in)
Wing aspect ratio	5·2
Length overall	8·45 m (27 ft 8¾ in)
Fuselage: Max width	0·90 m (2 ft 11½ in)
Height overall (incl fin tip antenna)	4·00 m (13 ft 1½ in)
Tailplane span	3·50 m (11 ft 5¾ in)
Wheel track	3·10 m (10 ft 2 in)
Wheelbase	2·22 m (7 ft 3½ in)
Propeller diameter	2·00 m (6 ft 6¾ in)
Propeller ground clearance	0·27 m (10½ in)

DIMENSIONS, INTERNAL:

Cabin: Length	2·95 m (9 ft 8¼ in)
Max width	0·71 m (2 ft 4 in)
Baggage compartment volume	0·17 m³ (6·0 cu ft)

AREAS:

Wings, gross	12·30 m² (132·4 sq ft)
Ailerons (total, incl tab)	1·38 m² (14·85 sq ft)
Trailing-edge flaps (total)	1·37 m² (14·75 sq ft)
Fin	1·46 m² (15·71 sq ft)
Rudder, incl tab	0·65 m² (6·97 sq ft)
Tailplane	1·81 m² (19·48 sq ft)
Elevators (total, incl tab)	0·94 m² (10·12 sq ft)

WEIGHTS AND LOADINGS:

Weight empty, standard	1,110 kg (2,447 lb)
Max fuel weight	310 kg (683 lb)
Aerobatic T-O weight	1,450 kg (3,196 lb)
Max T-O weight	1,600 kg (3,527 lb)
Max wing loading	130·08 kg/m² (26·64 lb/sq ft)
Max power loading	5·96 kg/kW (9·80 lb/hp)

PERFORMANCE (S/L, at Aerobatic T-O weight except where indicated):

Never-exceed speed	234 knots (434 km/h; 269 mph) EAS
Max level speed	197 knots (365 km/h; 227 mph) EAS
Max cruising speed	174 knots (322 km/h; 200 mph) EAS
Max manoeuvring speed	185 knots (344 km/h; 214 mph)
Stalling speed: flaps up	74 knots (137 km/h; 85 mph) EAS
flaps down	60 knots (111 km/h; 69 mph) EAS
Max rate of climb at S/L	480 m (1,575 ft)/min
Service ceiling	5,200 m (17,060 ft)
T-O run (concrete)	340 m (1,115 ft)
Landing run (concrete)	400 m (1,312 ft)
Range with max fuel	765 nm (1,417 km; 881 miles)
Max endurance at max T-O weight	6 h 6 min
g limits: at Aerobatic T-O weight	+6/−3
at max T-O weight	+4·4/−1·76

PZL-130T TURBO ORLIK

Developed in collaboration with Airtech of Canada (which see), the Turbo Orlik is powered by a 410 kW (550 shp) Pratt & Whitney Canada PT6A-25 turboprop engine with Hartzell HC-B3TN-3B/T10173B-11 three-blade propeller, and was due to fly for the first time in mid-1986. The pneumatic system is deleted, landing gear being actuated hydraulically. King IFR com/nav equipment and an oxygen system are installed, and the underwing attachments are increased to four, on which a total load of 640 kg (1,411 lb) can be carried. Other details are as follows:

DIMENSIONS, EXTERNAL: As for PZL-130 except:

Length overall	8·68 m (28 ft 5¾ in)
Propeller diameter	2·29 m (7 ft 6 in)

WEIGHTS AND LOADINGS (estimated):

Weight empty, standard	1,100 kg (2,425 lb)
Max T-O weight with external stores	1,977 kg (4,358 lb)
Max wing loading	160·73 kg/m² (32·92 lb/sq ft)
Max power loading	4·82 kg/kW (7·92 lb/shp)

PERFORMANCE (estimated, at T-O weight of 1,450 kg; 3,196 lb except where indicated):

Max level speed: at S/L	236 knots (438 km/h; 272 mph)
at 3,050 m (10,000 ft)	269 knots (499 km/h; 310 mph)
Rate of climb: at S/L	955 m (3,135 ft)/min
at 3,050 m (10,000 ft)	888 m (2,915 ft)/min
Service ceiling	10,300 m (33,800 ft)
T-O run at S/L (on concrete)	250 m (820 ft)
T-O to 15 m (50 ft) at S/L	410 m (1,345 ft)
Landing from 15 m (50 ft) at S/L	570 m (1,870 ft)
Landing run at S/L (on concrete)	370 m (1,214 ft)
Range at 3,050 m (10,000 ft), T-O weight of 1,600 kg (3,527 lb), no reserves	695 nm (1,288 km; 800 miles)
Max range with external tanks, max T-O weight of 1,977 kg (4,358 lb)	1,198 nm (2,220 km; 1,379 miles)

PZL (ANTONOV) An-3M

Polish production of the An-3 turboprop conversion of the An-2 biplane is planned to be undertaken at PZL Mielec, as mentioned under that factory's entry. The An-3M (for modified) is an alternative version which has been proposed by PZL Warszawa-Okecie as a co-operative venture between the two factories, with Mielec supplying fuselages, complete with their 1,059 kW (1,420 shp) TVD-20 turboprop engines, and vertical tail units. Okecie's contribution would consist primarily of a new set of wings, new horizontal tail surfaces, and new, frameless 'bug-eye' cockpit transparencies.

Wings of the An-3M would be similar in planform to those of the PZL-106B series Kruk, with slight sweepback, full span flaps and ailerons on all four wings, and slightly greater span on the lower wings. The wide span tailplane/elevator unit would also be slightly sweptback, with square-cut tips.

Exact status of the An-3M proposal was not known at the time of going to press, but the following data for this version were published in the Polish press in the Spring of 1986:

DIMENSIONS, EXTERNAL:

Wing span (lower)	16·10 m (52 ft 10 in)
Length overall	14·39 m (47 ft 2½ in)
Height overall	5·19 m (17 ft 0¼ in)

DIMENSIONS, INTERNAL:

Volume: flight deck	3·1 m³ (109·5 cu ft)
main cabin	11·4 m³ (402·5 cu ft)
chemical tank	2·4 m³ (84·75 cu ft)

AREA:

Wings, gross	66·3 m² (713·6 sq ft)

WEIGHTS (estimated):

Weight empty (transport version)	3,200 kg (7,055 lb)
Max T-O weight: Normal category	5,250 kg (11,574 lb)
Restricted category	5,700 kg (12,566 lb)

PERFORMANCE (estimated):

Never-exceed speed	146 knots (270 km/h; 168 mph)
Normal operating speed	129 knots (240 km/h; 149 mph)
Max rate of climb	285 m (935 ft)/min

PORTUGAL

OGMA

OFICINAS GERAIS DE MATERIAL AERONÁUTICO (General Aeronautical Material Workshops)

2615 Alverca
Telephone: 2580 786; 2581 293/803/979; and 2582 748/749
Telex: 14479 OGMA P

DIRECTOR:
Lt-Gen Eng Rui do Carmo da Conceição Espadinha

PRODUCTION MANAGER:
Col Eng Victor M. F. Albuquerque

COMMERCIAL MANAGER: Col Eng Aristides Leitão

OGMA was founded in 1918 and has been in continuous operation since then. It is the department of the Portuguese Air Force responsible for maintenance and repair, at depot level, of its aircraft, avionics, engines, ground communications and radar equipment, and can undertake similar work for civil or military national or foreign customers. OGMA has a total covered area of 116,000 m² (1,248,612 sq ft), and a workforce of approx 2,500 people.

Under a contract signed in 1959, OGMA undertakes IRAN, refurbishing and rehabilitation, periodic inspection and emergency maintenance and crash repair of US Air Force and US Navy aircraft. For Aérospatiale of France, OGMA has manufactured main and tail structures for the SA 315B Lama and some components for other helicopters.

OGMA's engine repair and maintenance facility, with a covered area of 28,000 m² (301,390 sq ft), overhauls military and commercial turbojets and turbofans (up to 146·8 kN; 33,000 lb st), and turboprop and turboshaft engines of up to 5,667 kW (7,600 shp). In addition to two fully computerised test cells, this facility is equipped with plasma spray, two vacuum furnaces, complete cleaning and electroplating facilities, non-destructive testing, shot-peening and other specific equipment. Besides work for the Portuguese Air Force, OGMA also overhauls, under contract, Artouste III and Turmo IV turboshaft engines for Turboméca of France and T56 engines and gearboxes for the USAF and other customers.

OGMA currently performs major maintenance on C-130/L-100 Hercules transport aircraft as a Lockheed Service Center, and on such helicopters as the Alouette II/III, Puma and Ecureuil as an Aérospatiale Station-Service.

The Avionics Division has new premises covering an area of approx 6,400 m² (68,900 sq ft), fully equipped to the latest demands in the field of maintenance for new generation avionics, communications systems, test equipment and calibration laboratories. OGMA is licensed by Litton Systems of Canada to carry out level 2 and 2A maintenance on LTN-72 INS equipment, and is currently doing work for that company.

ROMANIA

CNIAR

CENTRUL NATIONAL AL INDUSTRIEI AERONAUTICE ROMÂNE (National Centre of the Romanian Aeronautical Industry)

39 Bulevardul Aerogarii, Sector 1, Bucharest
Telephone: 50 27 14
Telex: 11648 AEROM

DIRECTOR GENERAL: Dipl Eng Ion Petroaica
COMMERCIAL DIRECTOR: Dipl Eng Vasile Racovitan

Romania has had a tradition of aviation since the earliest days of flying, dating from the first monoplane built in France in early 1906 by the Romanian engineer Traian Vuia, the original monoplane of Aurel Vlaicu which, in Bucharest on 17 June 1910, became the first nationally designed aeroplane to be flown in Romania, and the aeroplanes designed and built in France and Britain by Henri Coanda in 1910-14.

Since that time the Romanian aircraft industry (IAR) has produced some 90 different types of landplane, including helicopters (of which 80 were Romanian designed), and about 40 different types of sailplane. Many other achievements in the fields of theoretical and experimental aerodynamics have been made by teams of Romanian engineers, led by Prof Elie Carafoli, Prof Ion Stroiescu, Prof Ion Grosu, Dipl Eng Radu Manicatide, Dipl Eng Iosif Silimon and others, using latterly the Canadian licensed trisonic wind tunnel at INCREST in Bucharest.

The foundations for the present industry were laid at Brasov in 1926, and details of its history from then until the late 1960s can be found in the 1983-84 and earlier editions of *Jane's*.

The industry was reorganised in 1968, and its activities are now undertaken, within the Ministry of Machine Building Industry, by the CNIAR, which combines the activities of the former CIAR and GAB (see 1979-80 *Jane's*). Major activities are carried out in seven factories. The two main aircraft factories are the ICA at Brasov and IAv Bucuresti. The latter was enlarged in the late 1970s to cater for the Rombac 1-11 manufacturing programme. A third factory, IAv Bacau, builds the Soviet Yak-52 under licence and manufactures various components for the IAR-823 and IAR-316B. Romanian versions of the SOKO/CNIAR Orao/IAR-93 (see International section) are manufactured at IAv Craiova. Viper 632 and 633 engines for the IAR-93, Spey 512-14DW engines for the Rombac 1-11, and Turmo IV CA engines for the IAR-330 (Puma) helicopter, are built by the Turbomecanica Enterprise in Bucharest. Aerofina Bucharest is a new dedicated factory for manufacture of avionics and airborne equipment; forgings and castings for the aviation industry are manufactured at IMRA (Intreprinderea Metalurgica Romana Pentru Aeronautica), also in Bucharest.

Exports and imports of aircraft and aero engines are the responsibility of the CNA (see next entry), formed in 1979; avionics and electronic equipment sales are dealt with by Electronum and Electroexportimport. Aeronautical research and development are undertaken by INCREST (formerly IMFCA), the Aerospace Research and Design Institute at Bucharest. INCREST also designs and manufactures aerospace equipment, including anti-skid brakes, engine stands, fuel monitoring equipment, intercoms and various aviation raw materials. The flight test centre is the CIIAR (Centrul de încercari in zbor) at Craiova.

The Baneasa area of Bucharest is being developed as the headquarters and main centre for CNIAR activities, and for the laboratories and design offices of INCREST.

CNA

CENTRUL NATIONAL AERONAUTIC (Intreprindere de Comert Exterior) (National Centre for Aeronautical Foreign Trade)

Bulevardul Dacia 13, Casuta Postala 22-149, R-70185 Bucharest
Telephone: 12 08 78
Telex: 10660 CNAER

DIRECTOR GENERAL: Dipl Eng Aurel Adăscălitei
DEPUTY DIRECTOR: Dipl Ec Emil Boitan
FINANCIAL DIRECTOR: Dipl Ec Gheorghe Dumitru
PUBLICITY: Dipl Ec Eugenia Irina Boros

IAv BACAU

INTREPRINDEREA DE AVIOANE BACAU (Bacau Aircraft Enterprise)

Bacau

DIRECTOR GENERAL: Dipl Eng Eugen Pascariu

DEPUTY DIRECTORS:
Dipl Eng Eduard Ardeleanu
Dipl Eng Ion Geosanu

This factory, originally an aircraft repair centre known as URA (later IRA), now manufactures hydraulic, pneumatic, air-conditioning, fuel system and landing gear components for the IAv Bucuresti Rombac 1-11 jet transport, the ICA IAR-823 light aircraft and IAR-316B helicopter, and the IAR-93 close support fighter. It is building under licence the Soviet Yakovlev Yak-52 two-seat light aircraft, and is expected to manufacture the single-seat Yak-53 (see Soviet section).

IAv BACAU (YAKOVLEV) Yak-52

Announced in late 1978, the Yak-52 is a tandem-cockpit variant of the Yak-50, with unchanged span and length, but with a semi-retractable tricycle landing gear. Although aesthetically unattractive, this last feature is intended to reduce damage in a wheels-up landing.

The Yak-52 is a replacement for the Yak-18, which has been the standard ab initio trainer for Soviet pilots since the mid-1940s. Alexander Yakovlev has believed for many years that aeroplanes to be flown by young people should be designed by members of the Komsomol youth brigades and light aircraft enthusiasts, under experienced leadership. The enthusiasm engendered by this policy led to first flight of the prototype Yak-52 less than a year after its design was started. Flight testing was then undertaken by pilots qualified as Soviet Masters of Sport, as well as professional test pilots. Production was entrusted to the Romanian aircraft industry, under the Comecon (Council for Mutual Economic Assistance) programme.

Manufacture began at Bacau in 1979, and the aircraft is in series production; it does not have an IAR designation number. IAv Bacau delivered its 500th Yak-52 in 1983, and production was continuing in 1986.

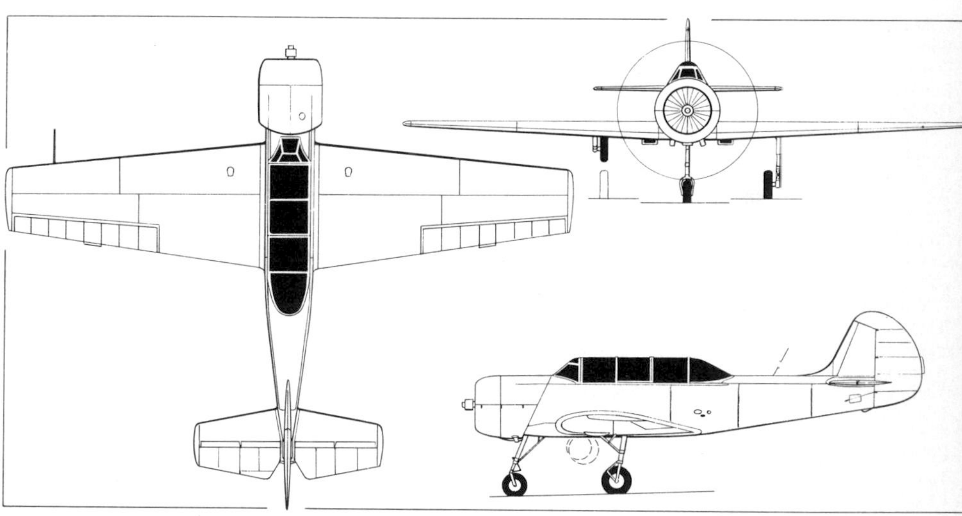

Yakovlev Yak-52 tandem two-seat primary trainer *(Pilot Press)*

Yakovlev Yak-52 primary trainer, of which more than 500 have been built in Romania by IAv Bacau

TYPE: Tandem two-seat piston engined primary trainer.

WINGS: Cantilever low-wing monoplane of single-spar stressed skin all-metal construction. Clark YN wing section, with thickness/chord ratio of 14·5% at root, 9% at tip. Dihedral 2° from roots. Incidence 2°. No sweepback: each wing comprises a single straight-tapered panel, attached directly to the side of the fuselage. Fabric covered slotted ailerons. Light alloy trailing-edge split flaps. Ground adjustable tab on each aileron.

FUSELAGE: Conventional light alloy semi-monocoque structure.

TAIL UNIT: Cantilever light alloy structure. Fin and fixed incidence tailplane metal covered; control surfaces fabric covered. Horn balanced rudder, with ground adjustable tab. Mass balanced elevators. Controllable tab in port elevator.

LANDING GEAR: Semi-retractable tricycle type, with single wheel on each unit. Pneumatic actuation, nosewheel retracting rearward, main units forward. All three wheels remain fully exposed to airflow, against the undersurface of the fuselage and wings respectively, to offer greater safety in the event of a wheels-up emergency landing. Oleo-pneumatic shock absorbers. Mainwheel tyre size 500 × 150; nosewheel tyre size 400 × 150. Tyre pressure (all units) 3·0 bars (43 lb/sq in). Pneumatic brakes. Skis can be fitted in place of wheels for Winter operations, permissible at temperatures down to −42°C.

POWER PLANT: One 268 kW (360 hp) Vedeneyev M-14P nine-cylinder aircooled radial engine, driving a two-blade variable-pitch propeller type V-530TA-D35, without spinner. Louvres in front of cowling to regulate cooling. Two-part cowling, split on horizontal centreline. Two fuel tanks, in wing roots forward of spar, each with capacity of 61 litres (13·5 Imp gallons). Collector tank in fuselage of 5·5 litres (1·25 Imp gallons) capacity supplies engine during inverted flight. Total internal fuel capacity 122 litres (27 Imp gallons). Oil capacity 22·5 litres (5 Imp gallons).

ACCOMMODATION: Tandem seats for pupil and instructor (at rear) under long 'glasshouse' canopy, with separate rearward sliding hood over each seat. Seats and dual flying controls are adjustable. Sides of cockpit have a soft synthetic lining. Heating and ventilation standard.

SYSTEMS: No hydraulic system. Independent main and emergency pneumatic systems, pressure 50 bars (725 lb/sq in), for flap actuation, landing gear actuation, engine starting, and wheel brake control. Pneumatic systems supplied by two compressed air bottles, mounted behind rear seat and recharged in flight by an AK-50T compressor. GSR-3000M 28·5V engine driven generator and (in port wing) 25V Varley battery for DC electric power; two static inverters in fuselage for 36V AC power at 400Hz.

AVIONICS AND EQUIPMENT: Dual engine and flying instruments. Equipment includes GMK-1A gyro compass, ARK-15M automatic radio compass, Baklan-5 VHF com and SPU-9 intercom. Oxygen system optional.

DIMENSIONS, EXTERNAL:
Wing span — 9·30 m (30 ft 6¼ in)
Wing chord: at root — 1·997 m (6 ft 6¾ in)
at tip — 1·082 m (3 ft 6½ in)
Wing aspect ratio — 5·77
Length overall — 7·745 m (25 ft 5 in)
Fuselage: Max width — 0·90 m (2 ft 11½ in)
Height overall — 2·70 m (8 ft 10¼ in)
Tailplane span — 3·16 m (10 ft 4½ in)
Wheel track — 2·715 m (8 ft 10¾ in)
Wheelbase — 1·86 m (6 ft 1¼ in)
Propeller diameter — 2·40 m (7 ft 10½ in)
Propeller ground clearance — 0·36 m (1 ft 2¼ in)

DIMENSIONS, INTERNAL:
Cockpit: Max width — 0·736 m (2 ft 5 in)
Max height — 1·12 m (3 ft 8 in)

AREAS:
Wings, gross — 15·00 m² (161·5 sq ft)
Ailerons (total) — 1·98 m² (21·31 sq ft)
Trailing-edge flaps (total) — 1·03 m² (11·09 sq ft)
Fin — 0·609 m² (6·55 sq ft)
Rudder — 0·871 m² (9·37 sq ft)
Tailplane — 1·325 m² (14·26 sq ft)
Elevators (total, incl tab) — 1·535 m² (16·52 sq ft)

WEIGHTS AND LOADINGS:
Weight empty — 1,000 kg (2,205 lb)
Max fuel load — 100 kg (220 lb)
Max T-O weight — 1,290 kg (2,844 lb)
Max wing loading — 86·0 kg/m² (17·61 lb/sq ft)
Max power loading — 4·80 kg/kW (7·90 lb/hp)

PERFORMANCE:
Never-exceed speed — 194 knots (360 km/h; 223 mph)
Max level speed at 500 m (1,640 ft) — 162 knots (300 km/h; 186 mph)
Max cruising speed at 1,000 m (3,280 ft) — 145 knots (270 km/h; 167 mph)
Econ cruising speed at 1,000 m (3,280 ft) — 102 knots (190 km/h; 118 mph)
Stalling speed:
flaps up — 60 knots (110 km/h; 69 mph)
flaps down, power on — 54-57 knots (100-105 km/h; 62-66 mph)
flaps down, engine idling — 46-49 knots (85-90 km/h; 53-56 mph)
Max rate of climb at S/L — 420 m (1,378 ft)/min
Service ceiling:
without oxygen — 4,000 m (13,125 ft)
with oxygen — 6,000 m (19,685 ft)
Min ground turning radius — 6·22 m (20 ft 5 in)
T-O run — 170 m (558 ft)
Landing run — 300 m (984 ft)
Range with max fuel — 297 nm (550 km; 341 miles)
Endurance with max fuel — 2 h 50 min
g limits — +7/−5

IAv BUCURESTI

INTREPRINDEREA DE AVIOANE BUCURESTI (Bucharest Aircraft Enterprise)

44 Bulevardul Ficusului, Baneasa Airport, Bucharest
Telephone: Bucharest 336260

DIRECTOR GENERAL: Dipl Eng Teodor Zanfirescu

CHIEF ENGINEER: Dipl Eng Mirka Dimitrescu

IAv Bucuresti's predecessor, IRMA, was formed in 1959 from part of the former URMV-3 at Brasov (see 1979-80 and earlier editions of *Jane's*). The present title was adopted in 1980. The factory is currently responsible for manufacture of the BAe One-Eleven (components and complete aircraft) and the Pilatus Britten-Norman Islander. It specialises in the development and manufacture of commercial and agricultural aircraft; in the repair and overhaul of various large and small aircraft; is agent and repair centre for Avco Lycoming engines; and manufactures aircraft equipment.

IAv BUCURESTI ROMBAC 1-11 (BAe ONE-ELEVEN)

IAv Bucuresti is the Romanian prime contractor for the licence manufacture of BAe One-Eleven twin-turbofan transports, which have the Romanian designation Rombac 1-11. A corresponding programme provides for Romanian manufacture of the Rolls-Royce Spey engines.

Five commercial versions of the One-Eleven were produced formerly by BAe/BAC. Details of the Series 200 (56 built), 300 (nine built) and 400 (69 built) can be found in the UK section of the 1974-75 *Jane's*, and of the Series 475 (nine built) and 500 (87 built) in the 1981-82 edition.

In May 1979, BAe concluded an agreement with CNIAR for the Series 475 and 500 to be built under licence in Romania to cover Romanian domestic requirements and for export. To initiate the transfer education process, a Srs 487 freighter and two Srs 525/1s were delivered as complete aircraft by BAe in 1981-82, as detailed in earlier *Jane's*.

Third Romanian assembled Rombac 1-11 Series 560 (two Rolls-Royce Spey Mk 512-14DW turbofan engines), which has a VIP interior

industrial transfer to the Romanian aircraft industry, due to be completed by 1986, has been undertaken in seven stages by means of a reducing scale of UK supplied kits of parts for an initial batch of 22 aircraft. In the first of these stages, delivery was completed in April 1981 of three sets of wings, fuselages and other major British built components, and the first flight by a Romanian assembled Srs 560 (YR-BRA) was made on 18 September 1982. This aircraft was handed over to Tarom, the Romanian state airline, on 24 December 1982, and entered service in January 1983. Four had been completed by mid-1985, and three more were due for completion by the end of that year.

Romanian versions are designated as follows:

Series 495. Combines standard fuselage and accommodation of British built Series 400 with wings and power plant of Series 560 and a modified landing gear system, using low-pressure tyres, to permit operation from secondary low-strength runways with poorer grade surfaces. None yet completed.

Series 560. Derived from British built Series 300/400, this version has a lengthened fuselage (2·54 m; 100 in fwd of wing, 1·57 m; 62 in aft) which accommodates up to 109 passengers, with a flight crew of two. Wingtip extensions increase span by 1·52 m (5 ft). Take-off performance improved by increased wing area and by installation of two Rolls-Royce Spey Mk 512-14DW turbofans, each rated at 55·8 kN (12,550 lb st). Main landing gear strengthened and heavier wing planks used to cater for increased AUW.

It was confirmed in mid-1985 that Romania is to undertake a Tay powered updated version of the Rombac 1-11, to achieve certification in 1988.

The following description applies to the currently available Series 495 and 560:

TYPE: Twin-turbofan short/medium-range transport.

WINGS: Cantilever low-wing monoplane. Modified NACA cambered wing section. Thickness/chord ratio 12½% at root, 11% at tip. Dihedral 2°. Incidence 2° 30′. Sweepback 20° at quarter-chord. All-metal structure of copper based aluminium alloy, built on fail-safe principles. Three-fihear-web torsion box with integrally machined skin/stringer panels. Ailerons of Redux bonded light alloy honeycomb, manually operated through servo tabs. Port servo tab used for trimming. Hydraulically operated light alloy Fowler flaps. Light alloy spoiler/airbrakes on upper surface of wing, operated hydraulically. Hydraulically actuated lift dumpers, inboard of spoilers. Flaps on Series 495 have a glassfibre coating. Thermal de-icing of wing leading-edges with engine bleed air.

FUSELAGE: Conventional circular-section all-metal fail-safe structure with continuous frames and stringers. Skin made from copper based aluminium alloy.

TAIL UNIT: Cantilever all-metal fail-safe structure, with variable incidence T tailplane, controlled through duplicated hydraulic units. Fin integral with rear fuselage. Elevators and rudder actuated hydraulically through tandem jacks. Leading-edges of fin and tailplane de-iced by engine bleed air.

LANDING GEAR: Retractable tricycle type, with twin wheels on each unit. Hydraulic retraction, nose unit forward, main units inward. Oleo-pneumatic shock absorbers. Hydraulic nosewheel steering. Wheels have tubeless tyres, 5-plate heavy duty hydraulic disc brakes, and anti-skid units. Mainwheel tyres size 40 × 12 on Srs 560, pressure 11·03 bars (160 lb/sq in); size 44 × 16 on Srs 495, pressure 5·72 bars (83 lb/sq in). Nosewheel tyres size 24 × 7·25 on Srs 560, pressure 7·58 bars (110 lb/sq in); size 24 × 7·7 on Srs 495, pressure 7·24 bars (105 lb/sq in). All tyre pressures are for aircraft at mid-CG position and max taxi weight.

POWER PLANT: Two Rolls-Royce Spey Mk 512-14DW turbofan engines, each rated at 55·8 kN (12,550 lb st), pod-mounted on sides of rear fuselage. Fuel in integral wing tanks with usable capacity of 10,160 litres (2,235 Imp gallons) and centre-section tank of 3,968 litres (873 Imp gallons) usable capacity; total usable fuel 14,129 litres (3,108 Imp gallons). Executive versions can be fitted with auxiliary fuel tanks of up to 5,791 litres (1,274 Imp gallons) usable capacity. Pressure refuelling point in fuselage forward of wing on starboard side. Provision for gravity refuelling. Oil capacity (total engine oil) 13·66 litres (3 Imp gallons) per engine. Engine hush kits standard.

ACCOMMODATION (Srs 495): Crew of two on flight deck and up to 89 passengers in main cabin. Single class or mixed class layout, with movable divider bulkhead to permit any first/tourist ratio. Typical mixed class layout has 16 first class (four abreast) and 49 tourist (five abreast) seats. Galley units normally at front on starboard side. Coat space available on port side aft of flight deck. Ventral entrance with hydraulically operated airstair. Forward passenger door on port side incorporates optional power operated airstair. Galley service door forward on starboard side. Two baggage and freight holds under floor, fore and aft of wings, with doors on starboard side. Upward opening forward freight door available at customer's option. Entire accommodation air-conditioned.

ACCOMMODATION (Srs 560): Crew of two on flight deck and up to 109 passengers in main cabin. Two additional overwing emergency exits, making two on each side. One toilet on each side of cabin at rear. Otherwise generally similar to Srs 495.

SYSTEMS: Fully duplicated air-conditioning and pressurisation systems. Air bled from engine compressors through heat exchangers. Max pressure differential 0·52 bars (7·5 lb/sq in). Hydraulic system, pressure 207 bars (3,000 lb/sq in), operates flaps, spoilers, rudder, elevators, tailplane, landing gear, brakes, nosewheel steering, ventral and forward airstairs and windscreen wipers. No pneumatic system. Electrical system utilises two 30kVA AC generators, driven by constant speed drive and starter units, plus a similar generator mounted on the APU and shaft driven. Gas turbine APU in tailcone to provide ground electric power, air-conditioning and engine starting, also some system checkout capability. APU is run during take-off to eliminate performance penalty of bleeding engine air for cabin air-conditioning.

AVIONICS AND EQUIPMENT: Communications and navigation avionics generally to customers' requirements. Typical installation includes dual VHF com to ARINC 546, dual VHF nav to ARINC 547A, including glideslope receivers, marker beacon receiver, flight/service interphone system, ADF, ATC transponder to ARINC 532D, DME, weather radar. Compass system and flight director system (dual) are also installed. Autopilot system. Provision on the Srs 560 for additional equipment, including automatic throttle control, for low weather minima operation.

DIMENSIONS, EXTERNAL:

Wing span	28·50 m (93 ft 6 in)
Wing chord: at root	5·00 m (16 ft 5 in)
at tip	1·61 m (5 ft 5 in)
Wing aspect ratio	8·5
Length overall: Srs 495	28·50 m (93 ft 6 in)
Srs 560	32·61 m (107 ft 0 in)
Length of fuselage: Srs 495	25·55 m (83 ft 10 in)
Srs 560	29·67 m (97 ft 4 in)
Height overall	7·47 m (24 ft 6 in)
Tailplane span	8·99 m (29 ft 6 in)
Wheel track	4·34 m (14 ft 3 in)
Wheelbase: Srs 495	10·08 m (33 ft 1 in)
Srs 560	12·62 m (41 ft 5 in)
Passenger door (fwd, port):	
Height	1·73 m (5 ft 8 in)
Width	0·84 m (2 ft 9 in)
Height to sill	2·08 m (6 ft 10 in)
Ventral entrance, bulkhead door:	
Height	1·83 m (6 ft 0 in)

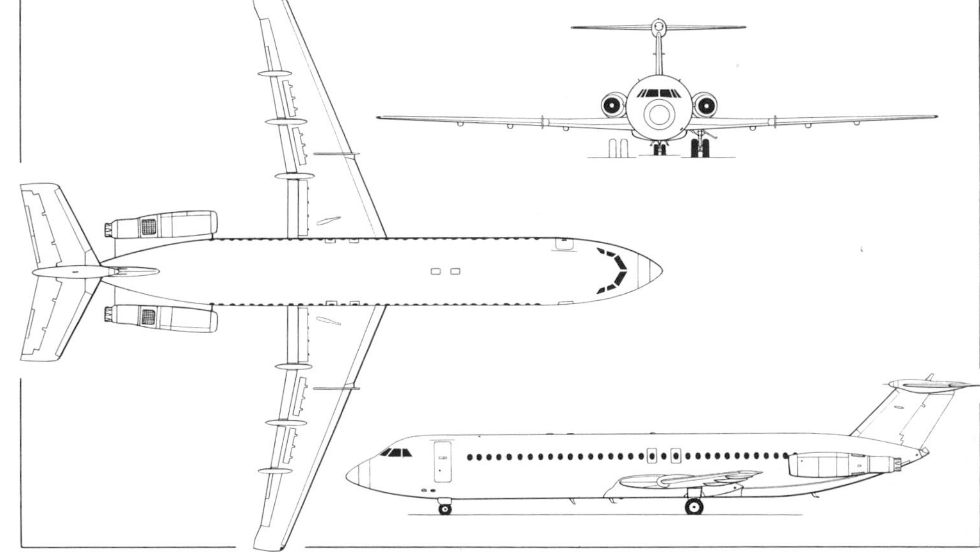

Rombac 1-11 (BAe One-Eleven) Series 560 twin-turbofan short/medium-range airliner *(Pilot Press)*

Width 0·66 m (2 ft 2 in)
Height to sill 2·08 m (6 ft 10 in)
Freight door (fwd, starboard):
Height (projected) 0·79 m (2 ft 7 in)
Width 0·91 m (3 ft 0 in)
Height to sill 1·04 m (3 ft 5 in)
Freight door (rear, starboard):
Height (projected) 0·71 m (2 ft 4 in)
Width 0·91 m (3 ft 0 in)
Height to sill 1·17 m (3 ft 10 in)
Freight door, main deck (optional, fwd, Srs 495):
Height 1·85 m (6 ft 1 in)
Width 3·05 m (10 ft 0 in)
Galley service door (fwd, starboard):
Height (projected) 1·22 m (4 ft 0 in)
Width 0·69 m (2 ft 3 in)
Height to sill 2·08 m (6 ft 10 in)

DIMENSIONS, INTERNAL (Srs 495):
Cabin, excl flight deck:
Length 17·32 m (56 ft 10 in)
Max width 3·15 m (10 ft 4 in)
Max height 1·98 m (6 ft 6 in)
Floor area approx 47·4 m² (510 sq ft)
Freight hold, fwd 10·02 m³ (354 cu ft)
Freight hold, rear 4·42 m³ (156 cu ft)

DIMENSIONS, INTERNAL (Srs 560):
Cabin, excl flight deck:
Length 21·44 m (70 ft 4 in)
Total floor area approx 59·5 m² (640 sq ft)
Freight holds (total volume) 19·45 m³ (687 cu ft)

AREAS (Srs 495, 560):
Wings, gross 95·78 m² (1,031·0 sq ft)
Ailerons (total) 2·86 m² (30·8 sq ft)
Flaps (total) 16·26 m² (175·0 sq ft)
Spoilers (total) 2·30 m² (24·8 sq ft)
Vertical tail surfaces (total) 10·91 m² (117·4 sq ft)
Rudder, incl tab 3·05 m² (32·8 sq ft)
Horizontal tail surfaces (total) 23·97 m² (258·0 sq ft)
Elevators, incl tab 6·54 m² (70·4 sq ft)

WEIGHTS AND LOADINGS:
Operating weight empty, typical:
Srs 495 (89 seats) 23,286 kg (51,339 lb)
Srs 560 (109 seats) 25,267 kg (55,704 lb)
Max payload, typical:
Srs 495 10,733 kg (23,661 lb)
Srs 560 11,474 kg (25,296 lb)
Max T-O weight:
Srs 495 41,730-44,679* kg (92,000-98,500* lb)
Srs 560 45,200-47,400* kg (99,650-104,500* lb)
Max ramp weight:
Srs 495 41,957-44,906* kg (92,500-99,000* lb)
Srs 560 45,450-47,627* kg (100,200-105,000* lb)
Max landing weight:
Srs 495 38,102-39,463* kg (84,000-87,000* lb)
Srs 560 39,463 kg (87,000 lb)
Max zero-fuel weight:
Srs 495 33,112-34,019* kg (73,000-75,000* lb)
Srs 560 36,741 kg (81,000 lb)
Max wing loading:
Srs 495 466·3 kg/m² (95·5 lb/sq ft)
Srs 560 495·1 kg/m² (101·4 lb/sq ft)
Max power loading:
Srs 495 400·2 kg/kN (3·92 lb/lb st)
Srs 560 424·5 kg/kN (4·16 lb/lb st)
*optional

PERFORMANCE (at standard max T-O weight):
Design diving speed (S/L) 410 knots (760 km/h; 472 mph) EAS
Max level and cruising speed at 6,400 m (21,000 ft) 470 knots (870 km/h; 541 mph)
Econ cruising speed at 10,670 m (35,000 ft) 410 knots (760 km/h; 472 mph)
Stalling speed (landing flap setting, at standard max landing weight):
Srs 495 98 knots (182 km/h; 113 mph) EAS
Srs 560 100 knots (186 km/h; 115 mph) EAS
Rate of climb at S/L at 300 knots (555 km/h; 345 mph) EAS: Srs 495 786 m (2,580 ft)/min
Srs 560 722 m (2,370 ft)/min
Max cruising height 10,670 m (35,000 ft)
Min ground turning radius (to outer wingtip):
Srs 495 15·24 m (50 ft 0 in)
Srs 560 17·07 m (56 ft 0 in)
Runway LCN, rigid pavement (l = 30):
Srs 495 32
Srs 560 53
T-O run at S/L, ISA: Srs 495 1,676 m (5,500 ft)
Srs 560 1,981 m (6,500 ft)
Balanced T-O to 10·7 m (35 ft) at S/L, ISA:
Srs 495 1,798 m (5,900 ft)
Srs 560 2,225 m (7,300 ft)
Landing distance (BCAR) at S/L, ISA, at standard max landing weight: Srs 495 1,440 m (4,725 ft)
Srs 560 1,455 m (4,775 ft)
Max still air range, ISA, with reserves for 200 nm (370 km; 230 mile) diversion and 45 min hold:
Srs 495 1,933 nm (3,582 km; 2,226 miles)
Srs 560 1,897 nm (3,515 km; 2,184 miles)
Still air range with typical capacity payload, ISA, reserves as above:
Srs 495 at 44,679 kg (98,500 lb) 1,454 nm (2,694 km; 1,674 miles)
Srs 560 at 47,400 kg (104,500 lb) 1,327 nm (2,459 km; 1,528 miles)
Srs 495 executive aircraft with additional 5,602 litres (1,232 Imp gallons) fuel and ten passengers 2,875 nm (5,325 km; 3,308 miles)

IAv BUCURESTI (PILATUS BRITTEN-NORMAN) ISLANDER

The Pilatus Britten-Norman Islander (see UK section) has been manufactured under licence in Romania, originally by IRMA, for several years. The first Romanian built example flew for the first time at Baneasa Airport, Bucharest, on 4 August 1969, and the initial commitment to build 215 Islanders was completed in 1976. A total of 395 had been delivered to Pilatus Britten-Norman by the Spring of 1985.

IAv CRAIOVA
INTREPRINDEREA DE AVIOANE CRAIOVA (Craiova Aircraft Enterprise)

Craiova
DIRECTOR GENERAL: Dipl Eng Dumitru Stanescu
DEPUTY DIRECTORS:
Dipl Eng Ion Bratu
Dipl Eng Iancu Pentes

This factory is responsible for Romanian manufacture of the IAR-93 close support and ground attack aircraft and operational trainer built in collaboration with Yugoslavia. Series production of the IAR-93 for the Romanian Air Force is now under way. A detailed description of the aircraft appears under the SOKO/CNIAR heading in the International section. Craiova's latest product is the IAR-99 Soim jet trainer.

IAR-99 SOIM (HAWK)

The existence of this new Romanian designed advanced jet trainer/light ground attack aircraft first became known during the 1983 Paris Air Show, at which time it was said to be still undergoing flight testing. It was designed and built at Craiova, and is powered by a version of the non-afterburning Rolls-Royce Viper Mk 632 turbojet engine that is installed in the IAR-93A. It was registered to appear at the 1985 Paris Salon, but failed to do so.

TYPE: Tandem two-seat advanced jet trainer and light ground attack aircraft.

WINGS: Cantilever low-wing monoplane, with non-swept tapered leading- and trailing-edges and approx 3° dihedral from roots. Trim tab in each aileron.

FUSELAGE: Conventional all-metal semi-monocoque structure, of oval cross-section.

TAIL UNIT: Sweptback fin, with dorsal fin, and balanced rudder. Non-swept, no-dihedral tailplane, mounted above tailpipe, with balanced elevators. Trim tab in rudder and each elevator.

LANDING GEAR: Retractable tricycle type, with single wheel and oleo-pneumatic shock absorber on each unit. Mainwheels retract inward, nosewheel forward, all wheels being fully enclosed by doors when retracted. Landing light in port wing root leading-edge.

POWER PLANT: One 17·8 kN (4,000 lb st) Rolls-Royce Viper Mk 632-41 turbojet engine, mounted in rear fuselage. Lateral air intake, with splitter plate, on each side of fuselage abreast of rear cockpit.

ACCOMMODATION: Crew of two in tandem, with elevated rear seat. One-piece wraparound windscreen; single framed canopy over both seats.

ARMAMENT: Four underwing attachments for weapons and other stores.

DIMENSIONS, EXTERNAL:
Wing span 9·85 m (32 ft 3¾ in)
Wing aspect ratio 5·18
Length overall 10·88 m (35 ft 8¼ in)
Height overall 3·89 m (12 ft 9 in)

AREA:
Wings, gross 18·71 m² (201·4 sq ft)

WEIGHTS AND LOADINGS:
Weight empty 3,120 kg (6,878 lb)
Max T-O weight 5,476 kg (12,072 lb)
Max wing loading 292·7 kg/m² (59·95 lb/sq ft)
Max power loading 307·76 kg/kN (3·02 lb/lb st)

PERFORMANCE (at max T-O weight):
Max level speed at S/L 467 knots (865 km/h; 537 mph)
Max rate of climb at S/L 2,190 m (7,185 ft)/min
Service ceiling 13,900 m (45,600 ft)
T-O run 790 m (2,590 ft)
Landing run 750 m (2,460 ft)

Romania's new advanced jet trainer, the IAR-99 Soim *(Pilot Press drawing)*

ICA
INTREPRINDEREA DE CONSTRUCTII AERONAUTICE (Aeronautical Construction Enterprise)

Casuta Postala 198, 2200 Brasov
Telephone: 92114037
Telex: 61 266

ICA, created in 1968, continues the work that was begun in 1926 by IAR-Brasov and was then undertaken in 1950-59 as URMV-3 Brasov. Today, it manufactures the Romanian designed IAR-28MA, IAR-823, IAR-825, IAR-827/828 and IAR-831 series of light aircraft; the Alouette III and Puma helicopters under licence from Aérospatiale of France (as the IAR-316B and IAR-330 respectively); and the IS-28/29 series of Romanian sailplanes and motor gliders. It is developing its own IAR-317 version of the Alouette III, and also produces aircraft components and equipment.

ICA IAR-28MA

As indicated in the Sailplanes section, the IAR-28MA side by side two-seat light aircraft is derived from the IS-28M2 motor glider, with which it shares a common uselage, tail unit and flying controls. It has a new-design ving, fitted with split flaps and ailerons, and is powered by a 50 kW (80 hp) Limbach L2000 EOI flat-four engine driving a Hoffmann HO-V-62R two-blade variable-pitch propeller vith spinner.

An initial batch of ten, for training duties with the Romanian Air Force, was delivered in 1984, and production was continuing in the Spring of 1985, the latest date for which information has been received.

DIMENSIONS, EXTERNAL:
- Wing span: 10·40 m (34 ft 1½ in)
- Wing aspect ratio: 7·73
- Length overall: 7·50 m (24 ft 7¼ in)
- Height overall: 1·90 m (6 ft 2¾ in)

AREA:
- Wings, gross: 14·00 m² (150·7 sq ft)

WEIGHTS AND LOADINGS:
- Weight empty: 520 kg (1,146 lb)
- Max T-O weight: 760 kg (1,675 lb)
- Max wing loading: 54·3 kg/m² (11·12 lb/sq ft)
- Max power loading: 12·7 kg/kW (20·9 lb/hp)

PERFORMANCE (at max T-O weight):
- Never-exceed speed: 135 knots (250 km/h; 155 mph)
- Max level speed: 103 knots (190 km/h; 118 mph)
- Econ cruising speed: 78 knots (145 km/h; 90 mph)
- Stalling speed: 44 knots (80 km/h; 50 mph)
- Max rate of climb at S/L: 120 m (394 ft)/min
- Service ceiling: 5,000 m (16,400 ft)
- T-O run (grass): 382 m (1,253 ft)
- T-O to 15 m (50 ft) (grass): 525 m (1,722 ft)
- Landing run (grass): 300 m (985 ft)
- Range with max fuel: 378 nm (700 km; 435 miles)
- *g* limits: +5·3/−2·65
- Best glide ratio at 62 knots (115 km/h; 72 mph): 15
- Min rate of sink at 50 knots (93 km/h; 58 mph), power off: 1·90 m (6·23 ft)/s

ICA IAR-823

Design of the IAR-823 two/five-seat training and touring light aircraft was started at IMFCA in May 1970, by a team led by Dipl Eng Radu Manicatide. Construction of a prototype began at ICA-Brasov in the Autumn of 1971, and this aircraft made its first flight in July 1973. Construction and testing were in compliance with FAR Pt 23, and the aircraft is certificated for Aerobatic, Utility and Normal category operation. The first production aircraft flew in 1974, and 87 had been delivered to the Romanian Air Force and Romanian flying clubs by the Summer of 1982, the latest date for which a figure has been supplied. Production was continuing in 1985.

As a two-seater, the IAR-823 is fully aerobatic and is intended for training duties. With a rear bench seat for up to three more persons it is suitable as an executive, taxi or touring aircraft. Provision is made for two underwing pylons for the carriage of drop tanks or practice weapons.

TYPE: Two/five-seat cabin monoplane.

WINGS: Cantilever low-wing monoplane. Wing section NACA 23012 (modified). Dihedral 7° from roots. Incidence 3° at root, 1° at tip. Conventional all-metal structure, with single main spar and rear auxiliary spar; three-point attachment to fuselage. Riveted spars, ribs and skin of corrosion-proof aluminium alloy. Leading-edges riveted, and sealed to ribs and main spar to form main torsion box and integral fuel tanks. Electrically actuated fabric covered metal single-slotted flaps and fabric covered Frise slotted metal ailerons. Ground adjustable tab on each aileron.

FUSELAGE: All-metal semi-monocoque structure. Glassfibre engine cowling.

TAIL UNIT: Cantilever metal structure. Two-spar duralumin covered fin and tailplane; fabric covered duralumin horn balanced rudder and elevators. Electrically actuated automatic trim tab in each elevator; controllable tab in rudder.

LANDING GEAR: Retractable tricycle type, with steerable nosewheel. Electrical retraction, main units inward, nose unit rearward. Emergency manual actuation. Oleo-pneumatic shock absorbers. Mainwheel tyres size 6·00-6, pressure 2·93 bars (42·5 lb/sq in). Nosewheel tyre size 355 × 150 mm. Independent hydraulic mainwheel brakes, pedal controlled from left front seat. Shimmy damper on nose unit. No wheel doors.

POWER PLANT: One 216 kW (290 hp) Avco Lycoming IO-540-G1D5 flat-six engine, driving a Hartzell HC-92WK-1D/W 9350-4·6 two-blade constant-speed metal propeller. Fuel in four integral wing tanks, total capacity 360 litres (79 Imp gallons). Provision for two 70 litre (15·4 Imp gallon) drop tanks on underwing pylons.

ACCOMMODATION: Fully enclosed cabin, seating two persons side by side on individual adjustable front seats, with removable bench seat at rear for up to three more people. Dual controls standard in training version, optional in other versions. Upward hinged window/door (optionally jettisonable) on each side of cabin, which is soundproofed, heated and ventilated. Compartment at rear of cabin for up to 40 kg (88 lb) of baggage. Equipment and layout can be varied for use as air taxi, executive or freight transport, ambulance, liaison or photographic aircraft.

SYSTEMS AND AVIONICS: Electrical system, including 50A alternator and 24V 30Ah battery, for engine starting, elevator tab and landing gear actuation, radio communications, landing and navigation lights, and cabin and instrument lighting. Standard avionics include VFR instrumentation and TR 800 transceiver. Optional equipment, according to mission, includes blind-flying instrumentation and, in civil transport version, marker beacon receiver, nav/com radio, VOR/ILS, ADF and autopilot.

ICA IAR-28MA two-seat light aircraft for the Romanian Air Force

DIMENSIONS, EXTERNAL:
- Wing span: 10·00 m (32 ft 9¾ in)
- Wing chord: at c/l: 2·00 m (6 ft 6¾ in)
  - at tip: 1·00 m (3 ft 3¼ in)
- Wing aspect ratio: 6·66
- Length overall: 8·315 m (27 ft 3½ in)
- Height overall: 2·86 m (9 ft 4¾ in)
- Wheel track: 2·48 m (8 ft 1¾ in)
- Wheelbase: 1·86 m (6 ft 1¼ in)
- Propeller diameter: 2·23 m (7 ft 4 in)

AREAS:
- Wings, gross: 15·00 m² (161·5 sq ft)
- Ailerons (total): 1·20 m² (12·92 sq ft)
- Trailing-edge flaps (total): 1·78 m² (19·16 sq ft)
- Horizontal tail surfaces (total): 3·30 m² (35·52 sq ft)
- Vertical tail surfaces (total): 1·50 m² (16·15 sq ft)

WEIGHTS AND LOADINGS (A: Aerobatic; U: Utility; N: Normal category):
- Weight empty: A: 910 kg (2,006 lb)
  - U: 930 kg (2,050 lb)
  - N: 950 kg (2,094 lb)
- Max T-O weight: A: 1,190 kg (2,623 lb)
  - U: 1,380 kg (3,042 lb)
  - N: 1,500 kg (3,307 lb)
- Max wing loading: A: 79·3 kg/m² (16·24 lb/sq ft)
  - U: 92·0 kg/m² (18·85 lb/sq ft)
  - N: 100·0 kg/m² (20·48 lb/sq ft)
- Max power loading: A: 5·51 kg/kW (9·05 lb/hp)
  - U: 6·39 kg/kW (10·49 lb/hp)
  - N: 6·94 kg/kW (11·40 lb/hp)

PERFORMANCE (at Aerobatic max T-O weight):
- Max level speed at S/L: 162 knots (300 km/h; 186 mph)
- Max cruising speed at S/L:
  - 75% power: 154 knots (285 km/h; 177 mph)
  - 60% power: 140 knots (260 km/h; 162 mph)
- Stalling speed: flaps up: 61 knots (112 km/h; 70 mph)
  - flaps down, power off: 55 knots (102 km/h; 64 mph)
- Max rate of climb at S/L: 420 m (1,380 ft)/min
- Service ceiling: 5,600 m (18,375 ft)
- T-O run: 160 m (525 ft)
- T-O to 15 m (50 ft): 300 m (984 ft)
- Landing from 15 m (50 ft): 250 m (820 ft)
- Landing run: 200 m (656 ft)
- Range: 701 nm (1,300 km; 807 miles)
- *g* limits: +6/−3

PERFORMANCE (at 1,400 kg; 3,086 lb AUW except where indicated):
- Never-exceed speed: 215 knots (400 km/h; 248 mph)
- Max level speed at S/L: 162 knots (300 km/h; 186 mph)
- Max cruising speed (75% power) at 1,750 m (5,750 ft): 162 knots (300 km/h; 186 mph)
- Econ cruising speed (60% power) at 3,050 m (10,000 ft): 156 knots (290 km/h; 180 mph)
- Landing speed: 57 knots (105 km/h; 65 mph)
- Stalling speed: flaps up: 63 knots (115 km/h; 72 mph)
  - flaps down, power off: 49 knots (90 km/h; 56 mph)
- Max rate of climb at S/L: 420 m (1,380 ft)/min
- Time to 1,000 m (3,280 ft): 2 min 20 s
- Service ceiling: 5,600 m (18,375 ft)
- T-O run: 160 m (525 ft)
- T-O to 15 m (50 ft): 300 m (985 ft)
- Landing from 15 m (50 ft): 250 m (820 ft)
- Landing run: 200 m (656 ft)
- Range, according to mission and payload, 1 h reserves: 431-970 nm (800-1,800 km; 497-1,118 miles)
- Endurance, according to mission and payload: 3-6 h

IAR-823 two/five-seat light aircraft

ICA IAR-825TP TRIUMF

The Romanian aerospace industry exhibit at Farnborough International 1982 included the first public appearance of the IAR-825TP, a turboprop powered tandem-seat aircraft which has been developed to FAR Pt 23 standards as an economical multi-role trainer for the Romanian Air Force. Construction of the prototype (YR-IGB) started on 22 September 1981, and it flew for the first time on 12 June 1982, with a 507 kW (680 shp) P&WC PT6A-15AG engine. Series production with a more powerful engine, as described under 'Power Plant', was due to begin in 1986.

The IAR-825 has some features in common with the earlier IAR-823, utilising essentially the same wings, which are strengthened for the carriage of practice weapons in the armament training role but interchangeable with those of the IAR-823. Fuselage, landing gear and tail unit are of new design.

TYPE: Turboprop powered military trainer.

WINGS: Generally as described for IAR-823, but flaps and ailerons have metal skins.

FUSELAGE: Conventional semi-monocoque structure. Small bumper under tailcone.

TAIL UNIT: Cantilever metal structure. Two-spar duralumin covered sweptback fin and non-swept tailplane; horn balanced control surfaces; otherwise as described for IAR-823.

LANDING GEAR: Generally as described for IAR-823. Mainwheel tyres size 500 × 180 mm.

POWER PLANT: One 559 kW (750 shp) Pratt & Whitney Canada PT6A-25C turboprop engine, driving a Hartzell HC-B3TN-3/T10173-13R three-blade constant-speed reversible-pitch metal propeller. Wings incorporate four integral fuel tanks, as in IAR-823. Two streamlined auxiliary tanks above wingtips optional.

ACCOMMODATION: Seats for two persons in tandem, under one-piece framed canopy which opens sideways to starboard. Dual controls standard.

DIMENSIONS, EXTERNAL:

Wing span, excl tip tanks	10·00 m (32 ft 9¾ in)
Wing aspect ratio	6·66
Length overall	8·99 m (29 ft 6 in)
Height overall	3·20 m (10 ft 6 in)
Wheel track	2·45 m (8 ft 0½ in)

DIMENSIONS, INTERNAL:

Cockpit: Max length	2·65 m (8 ft 8¼ in)
Max width	0·87 m (2 ft 10¼ in)

AREA:

Wings, gross	15·00 m² (161·5 sq ft)

WEIGHTS (A: Aerobatic, U: Utility category):

Weight empty	1,250 kg (2,756 lb)
Max T-O weight: A	1,700 kg (3,748 lb)
U	2,300 kg (5,070 lb)

PERFORMANCE (at Aerobatic max T-O weight):

Never-exceed speed	296 knots (550 km/h; 341 mph)
Max level speed at 4,000 m (13,125 ft)	254 knots (470 km/h; 292 mph)
Max cruising speed at 4,000 m (13,125 ft)	237 knots (440 km/h; 273 mph)
Stalling speed, power off: flaps down	57 knots (105 km/h; 66 mph)
Max rate of climb at S/L	960 m (3,150 ft)/min
Service ceiling	9,000 m (29,525 ft)
T-O to 15 m (50 ft)	250 m (820 ft)
Landing from 15 m (50 ft)	300 m (985 ft)
Range with max fuel, 30 min reserves	755 nm (1,400 km; 870 miles)
Endurance, conditions as above	3 h
g limits	+6/−3

ICA IAR-827A

Design of the basic IAR-827, to FAR Pt 23 standards, began in the early part of 1973. The objective was to develop an agricultural aircraft with an airframe life of 4,000 h (equivalent to 22,000 flights) and able to carry a useful load equivalent to 2 kg (4·4 lb) for every horsepower. Particular attention was paid to minimising corrosion problems.

Early flight testing, which began in July 1976, revealed the need for a more powerful engine, and the original 298 kW (400 hp) Avco Lycoming IO-720-DA1B flat-eight engine in the first prototype (YR-MGA, c/n 01) was replaced by a 447 kW (600 hp) PZL-3S radial. The second prototype (YR-MGB) was also powered by a PZL-3S engine. The certification programme with these two aircraft began in 1977, and the IAR-827A, as the radial-engined version is known, was certificated in 1979.

Five pre-series IAR-827As (YR-MGC to 'MGG), and the prototypes, were all built by IAv Bucuresti. The production IAR-827A, manufacture of which began in late 1981, is built by the ICA at Brasov. An initial batch of 15 has been completed.

TYPE: Single/two-seat agricultural aircraft.

WINGS: Cantilever low-wing monoplane. Wing section NACA 23015. Constant chord safe-life structure, with 6° dihedral from roots. Welded chrome-molybdenum steel tube centre-section with duralumin skin. All-metal single-spar outer panels. Plain slotted ailerons. Electrically operated all-metal single-slotted Fowler flaps. Automatic trim tab in each aileron.

FUSELAGE: Forward structure of welded chrome-molybdenum steel tube, with duralumin and glassfibre skin panels attached by quick-release fastenings. Rear fuselage is a light alloy monocoque.

TAIL UNIT: Cantilever all-metal structure, with slightly sweptback fin and rudder. Balanced elevators. Automatic trim tab in port elevator, ground adjustable tab on rudder, and manually controlled tab in starboard elevator.

LANDING GEAR: Non-retractable tailwheel type. Main units comprise 140 mm stroke hydraulic shock struts and side Vs, and are fitted with Dunlop wheels (tyre size 615 × 225) and brakes. Gear is of Romanian design and is designed to withstand a vertical velocity of 6 m (19·5 ft)/s or a free drop of 1·2 m (3 ft 11¼ in).

POWER PLANT: One 447 kW (600 hp) PZL-3S seven-cylinder radial aircooled engine, driving a PZL US-132000/A four-blade constant-speed metal propeller. Fuel tank in each wing leading-edge, each of 230 litres (50·5 Imp gallons) capacity.

ACCOMMODATION: Side by side seats for pilot and mechanic in fully enclosed cockpit, with window/door on each side. Dual controls and emergency door jettison optional. Seat height and rudder pedals adjustable. Crash pylon in fairing aft of seats. Heated and ventilated cockpit is sealed and slightly pressurised to exclude dust.

EQUIPMENT: Glassfibre hopper in forward fuselage, with a volume of 1·23 m³ (43·44 cu ft). Hopper stressed for loads of up to 1,000 kg (2,205 lb), but normal max load is 900 kg (1,984 lb) of dry or 1,200 litres (264 Imp gallons) of liquid chemical. Hopper has a jettison system.

DIMENSIONS, EXTERNAL:

Wing span	14·00 m (45 ft 11¼ in)
Wing aspect ratio	6·67
Length overall	8·80 m (28 ft 10½ in)
Height overall	2·60 m (8 ft 6½ in)
Tailplane span	4·90 m (16 ft 1 in)
Wheel track	3·42 m (11 ft 2¾ in)
Wheelbase	6·20 m (20 ft 4 in)
Propeller diameter	2·62 m (8 ft 7 in)

AREA:

Wings, gross	29·40 m² (316·46 sq ft)

WEIGHTS:

Weight empty, with agricultural equipment	1,660 kg (3,660 lb)
Max T-O weight	2,800 kg (6,173 lb)

PERFORMANCE (with agricultural equipment, at max T-O weight):

Max level speed	113 knots (210 km/h; 130 mph)
Cruising speed	104 knots (193 km/h; 120 mph)
Operating speed range	78-97 knots (145-180 km/h; 90-112 mph)
Stalling speed, 10° flap, power off	60 knots (110 km/h; 69 mph)
Max rate of climb at S/L	210 m (690 ft)/min
Service ceiling	4,500 m (14,775 ft)
T-O run	100 m (328 ft)
T-O to 15 m (50 ft)	550 m (1,805 ft)
Landing run	150 m (492 ft)
Range with max fuel	350 nm (650 km; 404 miles)
Endurance (agricultural operations)	1 h 30 min
Max endurance	2 h 30 min

ICA IAR-828TP

The original IAR-827 prototype (YR-MGA) was retrofitted with a 533 kW (715 shp) Pratt & Whitney Canada PT6A-15AG turboprop engine and Hartzell HC-B3TN-3/T10282R propeller. Known then as the **IAR-827TP**, it flew for the first time on 7 September 1981, and was displayed publicly at the Bucharest Trade Fair in October of that year. Hopper load under FAR Pt 23 is 1,100 kg (2,425 lb); under CAM 8 regulations, this can be increased to 1,500 kg (3,307 lb).

Prototype of the ICA Brasov IAR-825TP Triumf tandem-seat military trainer

IAR-827A single/two-seat agricultural aircraft

IAR-828TP prototype, with spraybars under wings

Flight testing of this aircraft, now redesignated **IAR-28TP**, was continuing towards certification in the Spring f 1985. It can be fitted alternatively with a Walter 601 M ırboprop engine. Fuel capacity is 450 litres (99 Imp allons). Weight and performance figures which follow pply to the PT6A-15AG version:

IMENSIONS, EXTERNAL

Wing span	13·96 m (45 ft 9½ in)
Length overall	9·07 m (29 ft 9 in)
Height overall	3·79 m (12 ft 5¼ in)
Wheel track	3·408 m (11 ft 2¼ in)

REA:

Wings, gross	29·40 m² (316·46 sq ft)

VEIGHTS:

Weight empty	1,450 kg (3,196 lb)
Max T-O weight	2,800 kg (6,173 lb)

ERFORMANCE (with agricultural equipment, at max T-O weight):

Max permitted speed with spraygear	135 knots (250 km/h; 155 mph)
Cruising speed, 75% power	128 knots (238 km/h; 148 mph)
Operating speed range	87-128 knots (160-238 km/h; 100-148 mph)
Stalling speed, flaps down, power off	60-62 knots (110-115 km/h; 69-72 mph)
Max rate of climb at S/L	468 m (1,535 ft)/min
Service ceiling	7,000 m (22,975 ft)
T-O run	140 m (460 ft)
Landing run	150 m (492 ft)
Ferry range	464 nm (860 km; 534 miles)

ICA IAR-831 PELICAN

The Pelican, the prototype of which (YR-IGA) made its irst public appearance at the 1983 Paris Air Show, is ssentially a combination of the IAR-825TP airframe with he piston engine power plant of the IAR-823. No indication of its development status has been given by ICA.

ACCOMMODATION: As for IAR-825TP.

DIMENSIONS, EXTERNAL AND INTERNAL: As for IAR-825TP except:

Wing span	10·00 m (32 ft 9¾ in)
Wing aspect ratio	6·67

WEIGHTS AND LOADINGS (A: Aerobatic category, U: Utility):

Weight empty	950 kg (2,094 lb)
Max T-O weight: A	1,200 kg (2,645 lb)
U	1,500 kg (3,307 lb)
Max wing loading: A	80·0 kg/m² (16·39 lb/sq ft)
U	100·0 kg/m² (20·48 lb/sq ft)
Max power loading: A	5·56 kg/kW (9·12 lb/hp)
U	6·94 kg/kW (11·40 lb/hp)

PERFORMANCE (at Aerobatic max T-O weight except where indicated):

Never-exceed speed	270 knots (500 km/h; 310 mph)
Max level speed	172 knots (320 km/h; 199 mph)
Max cruising speed, 75% power at S/L	159 knots (295 km/h; 183 mph)
Stalling speed, flaps up	60 knots (110 km/h; 69 mph)
Max rate of climb at S/L	420 m (1,380 ft)/min
Service ceiling	5,600 m (18,375 ft)
T-O to 15 m (50 ft)	300 m (984 ft)
Landing from 15 m (50 ft)	250 m (820 ft)
Range with max fuel	701 nm (1,300 km; 807 miles)
g limits: A	+6/−3
U	+3·8/−1·9

ICA (AÉROSPATIALE) IAR-316B ALOUETTE III

ICA and Aérospatiale concluded an agreement in 1971 for manufacture in Romania of SA 316B Alouette III helicopters. Production totalled more than 185 by the Spring of 1985. Romanian built components have also been supplied for French built Alouette IIIs.

The first French built SA 316B made its initial flight on 27 June 1968, and deliveries began in 1970. The sale of Alouette IIIs to India, Romania and Switzerland included licence agreements for manufacture of the aircraft in those countries, the quantities involved being 250, 180 and 60 respectively. Production continues in India and Romania.

Prototype of the IAR-831 Pelican multi-role trainer

TYPE: Turbine driven general purpose helicopter.

ROTOR SYSTEM: Three-blade main and anti-torque rotors. All-metal main rotor blades, of constant chord, on articulated hinges, with hydraulic drag-hinge dampers. Main rotor brake and blade folding standard.

ROTOR DRIVE: Main rotor driven through planetary gearbox, with freewheel for autorotation. Take-off drive for tail rotor at lower end of main gearbox, from where a torque shaft runs to a small gearbox which supports the tail rotor and houses the pitch change mechanism. Cyclic and collective pitch controls are powered.

FUSELAGE: Welded steel tube centre-section, carrying the cabin at the front and a semi-monocoque tailboom.

TAIL UNIT: Cantilever all-metal fixed tailplane, with twin endplate fins, mounted on tailboom.

LANDING GEAR: Non-retractable tricycle type, manufactured under Messier-Hispano-Bugatti licence. Hydraulic shock absorption. Nosewheel is fully castoring. Provision for skis or emergency pontoon landing gear.

POWER PLANT: One 649 kW (870 shp) Turboméca Artouste IIIB turboshaft engine, derated to 410 kW (550 shp) for max continuous operation. Fuel in single tank in fuselage centre-section, with capacity of 575 litres (126·5 Imp gallons), of which 573 litres (126 Imp gallons) are usable.

ACCOMMODATION: Normal accommodation for pilot and six persons, with three seats in front and a four-person folding seat at the rear of the cabin. Two baggage holds in centre-section, on each side of the welded structure and enclosed by the centre-section fairings. Provision for carrying two stretchers athwartships at rear of cabin, and two other persons, in addition to pilot. All passenger seats removable to enable aircraft to be used for freight carrying. Can also be adapted for cropspraying or aerial survey roles. Provision for external sling for loads of up to 750 kg (1,650 lb). One forward opening door on each side, immediately in front of two rearward sliding doors. Dual controls and cabin heating optional.

OPERATIONAL EQUIPMENT (military version): In the assault role, the Alouette III can be equipped with a wide range of weapons. A 7·62 mm machine-gun (with 1,000 rds) can be mounted athwartships on a tripod behind the pilot's seat, firing to starboard, either through a small window in the sliding door or through the open doorway with the door locked open. The rear seat is removed to allow the gun mounting to be installed. In this configuration, max accommodation is for pilot, co-pilot, gunner and one passenger, although normally only the pilot and gunner would be carried. Alternatively, a 20 mm cannon (with 480 rds) can be carried on an open turret-type mounting on the port side of the cabin. For this installation all seats except that of the pilot are removed, as is the port side cabin door, and the crew consists of pilot and gunner. Instead of these guns, the Alouette III can be equipped with two or four wire-guided missiles on external jettisonable launching rails, a gyro-stabilised sight, or 68 mm rocket pods.

DIMENSIONS, EXTERNAL:

Main rotor diameter	11·02 m (36 ft 1¾ in)
Main rotor blade chord (each)	0·35 m (13·8 in)
Tail rotor diameter	1·912 m (6 ft 3¼ in)
Spraybar span (agricultural version)	10·00 m (32 ft 9¾ in)
Length overall, rotors turning	12·84 m (42 ft 1½ in)
Length of fuselage, tail rotor turning	10·17 m (33 ft 4½ in)
Width overall, blades folded	2·60 m (8 ft 6¼ in)
Height to top of rotor head	2·97 m (9 ft 9 in)
Wheel track	2·602 m (8 ft 6½ in)

AREAS:

Main rotor disc	95·38 m² (1,026·6 sq ft)
Tail rotor disc	2·87 m² (30·9 sq ft)

WEIGHTS:

Weight empty: standard version	1,050 kg (2,315 lb)
agricultural version	1,300 kg (2,866 lb)
Max payload (agricultural version)	685 kg (1,510 lb)
Max T-O weight	2.200 kg (4,850 lb)

PERFORMANCE (standard version at max T-O weight, except where indicated):

Never-exceed speed at S/L	113 knots (210 km/h; 130 mph)
Max cruising speed at S/L	100 knots (185 km/h; 115 mph)
Operating speed (agricultural version)	32-76 knots (60-140 km/h; 37-87 mph)
Max rate of climb at S/L	260 m (850 ft)/min
Service ceiling	3,200 m (10,500 ft)
Hovering ceiling: IGE	2,850 m (9,350 ft)
OGE	1,500 m (4,920 ft)
Range with max fuel at S/L	267 nm (495 km; 307 miles)
Range at optimum altitude	290 nm (540 km; 335 miles)
Swath width (agricultural version)	30-40 m (98-131 ft)

ICA built IAR-316B Alouette III (left) and IAR-330L Puma helicopters

ICA IAR-317 AIRFOX

Exhibited publicly for the first time at the 1985 Paris Air Show, the IAR-317 first prototype had then accumulated about 100 hours of flying since it first flew in April 1984. Completion of two more prototypes was planned by the end of 1985; production, initially for the Romanian armed forces had not begun by May 1986.

Developed under the leadership of Dipl Ing Gheorghe Mitrea, the IAR-317 is modified from an IAR-316B Alouette III. It is intended primarily as a light ground attack, training and military liaison helicopter, although civil versions can also be produced to meet specific customer requirements. The modifications occur mainly ahead of the main rotor mast, the new cabin contours being considerably slimmer with tandem seating for a crew of two, the rear cockpit being elevated to improve the pilot's field of view. In the combat version, armour protection is provided for crew seats and fuel tank, toughened material is used in the cockpit transparencies, and attachments are provided for up to six external weapons.

TYPE: Tandem two-seat light attack and training helicopter.

ROTOR SYSTEM AND DRIVE: Generally as described for Alouette III. Rotor brake and main rotor blade folding standard.

FUSELAGE AND TAIL UNIT: Similar to Alouette III except for modified front section of fuselage (of duralumin) and glassfibre tail surfaces.

LANDING GEAR: Similar to Alouette, but has steerable nosewheel with optional locking device. Metal ski gear, floats and emergency flotation gear optional.

POWER PLANT: One 640 kW (858 shp) Turboméca Artouste IIIB turboshaft engine, as in Alouette III. Standard usable fuel capacity 573 litres (126 Imp gallons); one or two auxiliary fuel tanks optional, each of 125 litres (27·5 Imp gallons) capacity.

ACCOMMODATION: Crew of two in tandem, with elevated rear (pilot's) cockpit. Seats are of bucket type, adjustable vertically and horizontally, removable, and armoured in military versions. Windscreens and lower portions of side window/doors are flat-plate and of toughened material; forward and rear window/doors on each side can be jettisoned for escape in an emergency. Dual controls standard. Both cockpits heated and ventilated; air-conditioning is optional.

SYSTEM: Electrical system (28·5V DC) supplied by 4kW starter/generator and a 40Ah nickel-cadmium battery. Ground power receptacle.

AVIONICS AND EQUIPMENT: Standard avionics include TR-800A VHF nav, AHV-6 radio altimeter, radio compass, marker beacon receiver, intercom, and pilot's gyro horizon, directional gyro and sideslip indicator. Pilot's main and secondary panels include altimeter, airspeed indicator, VSI, magnetic compass, tachometer, voltmeter, collective pitch indicator, temperature indicator, fuel gauge, oil pressure and temperature indicator, outside air temperature indicator, and clock. Pilot's main instruments (altimeter, airspeed indicator, variometer and collective pitch indicator) are repeated on co-pilot's panel; option also for co-pilot's gyro horizon and directional gyro. Standard equipment includes gunsight, roof mounted missile sight, position lights, anti-collision light, pilot's instrument failure warning lights, instrument and panel lights, windscreen heating/demisting, windscreen wiper, retractable landing light, rotor brake, alternative static source, mission selector and cockpit fire extinguisher. Optional equipment includes agricultural spraygear, external cargo sling, rescue sling seat, 175 kg (386 lb) capacity rescue hoist, deck-lock harpoon, fuel quick drain, sand filter and flares.

ARMAMENT: Fixed armament of two 7·62 mm machine-guns, one on each side of lower front fuselage. Load carrying beam aft of rear cockpit, with two (optionally three) weapon attachment points on each side. Typical stores loads, up to a maximum of 750 kg (1,653 lb), can include four rocket launchers (each with four or twelve 57 mm rockets), four twin-gun machine-gun pods, four 50 kg or 100 kg bombs, or '2+2' combinations of these weapons; four cartridge launchers or flare pods; four air-to-surface missiles; or six small 'Sagger' type anti-tank missiles. Naval weapons and stores can also be carried. RAD weapon aiming system, with PKV gyrostabilised sight, in front cockpit.

DIMENSIONS, EXTERNAL: As for Alouette III except:

Length overall, main rotor blades folded: 10·845 m (35 ft 7 in)

Length of fuselage: 9·80 m (32 ft 1¾ in)

WEIGHTS:

Weight empty	1,150 kg (2,535 lb)
Max usable fuel: standard	453 kg (998 lb)
auxiliary tanks (two, total)	200 kg (441 lb)
Max T-O and landing weight	2,200 kg (4,850 lb)

PERFORMANCE (prototype: A at 1,700 kg; 3,748 lb gross weight, B at max T-O weight, no external stores, both in ISA zero wind conditions):

Never-exceed speed, and max level speed* at S/L:

A, B	118 knots (220 km/h; 136 mph)

*Max cruising speed at S/L:

A	108 knots (200 km/h; 124 mph)
B	102 knots (190 km/h; 118 mph)

First prototype of the IAR-317 Airfox gunship helicopter *(Brian M. Service)*

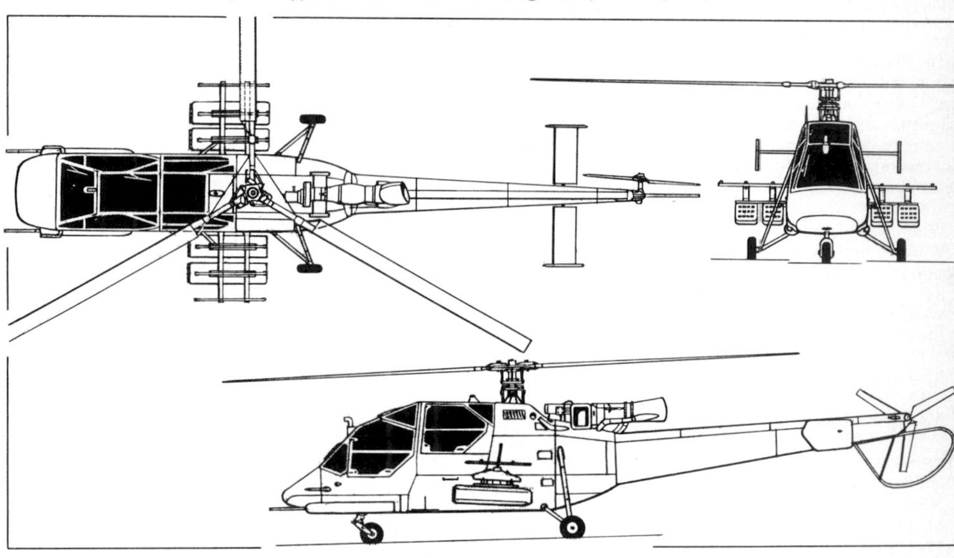

IAR-317 Airfox armed with four rocket packs and two machine-guns *(Pilot Press)*

Prototype Kamov Ka-126, a turbine powered development of the Ka-26

First conversion of a Ka-26 to 'production' standard Ka-126 (copied from *Flieger-Revue*)

Max rate of climb at S/L: A	510 m (1,673 ft)/min
B	270 m (886 ft)/min
Service ceiling: A	6,300 m (20,670 ft)
B	3,200 m (10,500 ft)
Hovering ceiling IGE: A	5,950 m (19,520 ft)
B	2,850 m (9,350 ft)
Hovering ceiling OGE: A	5,600 m (18,375 ft)
B	1,500 m (4,920 ft)
*Max range at S/L:	
with standard fuel: A	294 nm (545 km; 338 miles)
B	283 nm (525 km; 326 miles)
with auxiliary tanks: A	469 nm (870 km; 540 miles)
B	437 nm (810 km; 503 miles)

* *Reduced by 10% with external stores*

ICA (AÉROSPATIALE) IAR-330L PUMA

An agreement for licence production of the Aérospatiale SA 330 Puma in Romania was concluded in 1977, an initial quantity of 100 being involved. A total of 112 had been delivered by Spring 1985, most of them (and most Alouette IIIs) reportedly to the Romanian Air Force.

ICA (KAMOV) Ka-126

A photograph of the prototype of this helicopter was published in a book entitled *Soviet Aviation on the World Market* presented to *Jane's* by Aviaexport at the 1981 Paris Air Show. The aircraft appeared to be identical to the Ka-26 except for the two very small closely cowled turboshaft engines which replaced the latter's M-14V-26 radial piston engines.

At the 1985 Paris Air Show, it was stated that conversion of Ka-26s to Ka-126 standard would be undertaken by ICA at Brasov in Romania. Five pre-series aircraft were to be completed in 1986, with deliveries to the Soviet Union, for agricultural and utility operation, scheduled to begin in 1987. Production Ka-126s are powered by a single 537 kW (720 shp) TVD-100 turboshaft engine, centrally mounted on top of the cabin.

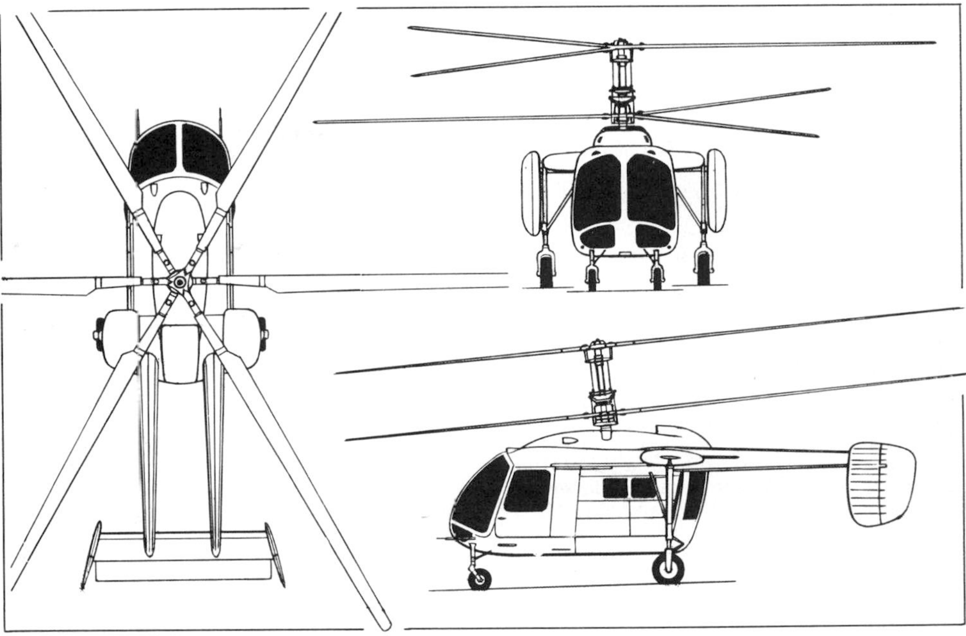

Kamov Ka-126 twin-turboshaft helicopter, being converted in Romania by ICA Brasov *(Pilot Press)*

WEIGHTS:	
Max payload	1,000 kg (2,205 lb)
Max T-O weight	3,238 kg (7,138 lb)
PERFORMANCE:	
Max range	325 nm (603 km; 375 miles)
Endurance	2 h

SINGAPORE

SAI

SINGAPORE AIRCRAFT INDUSTRIES PTE LTD

SAI Building, 540 Airport Road, Paya Lebar, Singapore 1953
Telephone: 2871111
Telex: RS 51158 SAI
Fax: (65) 2809713
MARKETING MANAGER: Teo Yong Hwee
WHOLLY OWNED SUBSIDIARIES:

Singapore Aerospace Maintenance Co Pte Ltd (SAMCO), West Camp, Seletar Airbase, Singapore 2879
Telephone: 4815955
Telex: RS 25507 SAMAIR
Fax: (65) 4820245

Singapore Electronic and Engineering Pte Ltd (SEEL)

Singapore Aerospace Manufacturing Pte Ltd (SAM), 503 Airport Road, Singapore 1953
Telephone: 2846255
Telex: RS 38216 SAMPL
Fax: (65) 2880965

Singapore Aero-Components Overhaul Pte Ltd (SACO), SAI Building, 540 Airport Road, Singapore 1953
Telephone: 2872222
Telex: RS 34100 SACOMP
Fax: (65) 2809713

Singapore Aerospace and Warehousing Supplies Pte Ltd (SAWS), SAWS Building, 540 Airport Road, Singapore 1953
Telephone: 2872033
Telex: RS 56128 SAWS
Fax: (65) 2809713

OTHER SUBSIDIARIES:

Singapore Aero-Engine Overhaul Pte Ltd (SAEOL) (co-owned with Singapore International Airlines), 501 Airport Road, Singapore 1953
Telephone: 2851111
Telex: RS 33268 SAEOL
Fax: (65) 2809713

Samaero Co Pte Ltd (co-owned with Aérospatiale, France)

SAI was formed in early 1982 as a government owned industrial group under control of the Ministry of Defence's Sheng-Li Holding Company Pte Ltd. It has a combined workforce of more than 2,600, in five wholly owned and two jointly owned subsidiaries, of which the largest are SAMCO and SEEL. SAMCO was formed in 1975, initially to maintain and overhaul aircraft of the Republic of Singapore Air Force (RSAF), and began operating in April 1976, on both fixed-wing aircraft and helicopters.

SIAI-Marchetti S.211 in Republic of Singapore Air Force colour scheme

Major programmes undertaken since that time have included rebuilding, refurbishing and A-4 to TA-4 conversion of Skyhawk aircraft for the RSAF and other air forces, and depot level maintenance, overhaul, repair and refurbishment of many types of aircraft including the C-130 Hercules, F-5E/F Tiger II, Hunter, Strikemaster, and several models of Bell and Aérospatiale helicopters. Most of this work has been carried out at Seletar, but a new 15,000 m² (161,450 sq ft) factory at Paya Lebar was opened in October 1983 and was due to be completed by the end of 1986. SAI's other subsidiaries have a substantial capability in the fields of aircraft and engine overhaul, maintenance and repair, component and equipment manufacture for civil and military aircraft and aero engines, external stores equipment, and defence avionics.

In late 1983, SAI began evaluating potential aircraft licence assembly and manufacturing programmes, and the first outcome of this is the assembly of 30 SIAI-Marchetti S.211 jet trainers (which see) for the RSAF, using kits supplied by the Italian manufacturer. It has also been reported that SAI will assemble 17 of the 22 Super Pumas ordered from Aérospatiale. In due course, SAI is expected to be involved in production programmes for aircraft selected to replace the RSAF's Hunters and Strikemasters.

SAI A-4 CONVERSIONS

SAI is re-engining each of two Douglas A-4S-1 Skyhawk combat aircraft of the Singapore Air Force with a General Electric F404-GE-100D non-afterburning turbofan engine. The first of them was scheduled to make its first flight with the new power plant in September 1986. If flight testing shows major improvements, all of the Air Force's A-4S aircraft may undergo similar conversion, followed by a possible avionics update.

SOUTH AFRICA

ATLAS

ATLAS AIRCRAFT CORPORATION OF SOUTH AFRICA (PTY) LIMITED

PO Box 11, Atlas Road, 1620 Kempton Park, Transvaal
Telephone: (011) 927 9111
Telex: 742403
GENERAL MANAGER: G. W. Ward
DIVISIONAL MANAGER (COMMERCIAL): G. Eckermann
MANAGER, PRODUCT SALES: A. O. Burger

Atlas Aircraft Corporation, which was founded in 1963, built two versions of the Impala (MB-326) under licence from Aermacchi. These programmes have now been completed.

Atlas continues to manufacture, under licence, components for Dassault Mirage F1-AZ and -CZ multi-purpose combat aircraft currently in service with Nos. 1 and 3 Squadrons respectively of the South African Air Force. It also undertakes maintenance and overhaul of SAAF aircraft. The company has developed the Cheetah combat aircraft for the SAAF, by modifying and upgrading the radar and other avionics of the service's Mirage IIIs. It has also developed a light attack helicopter, the Alpha XH-1, based on the French Alouette III.

ATLAS CHEETAH

The South African Air Force has given the name Cheetah to a redesigned and upgraded version of the Mirage III which is now undergoing modification by Atlas Aircraft Corporation. The new name, justified by the extensive changes, commemorates the fact that South Africa's first Mirage IIIs entered service, in March 1963, with the SAAF's No. 2 'Cheetah' Squadron.

Unveiled by Prime Minister P. W. Botha in Pretoria on 16 July 1986, the Cheetah's configuration invites immediate comparison with the Israel Aircraft Industries Kfir, although official South African statements imply that no outside assistance was given in its design. According to the SAAF, the modification is a mid-life update aimed at increasing the aircraft's operational life, made necessary by the continuing escalation of hostile forces on South Africa's borders (notably between northern Namibia and southern Angola) and the country's inability to procure modern front-line aircraft from elsewhere since the United Nations embargo on the sale of arms to South Africa in November 1977. Since then, and increasingly since the ending of Impala Mk 2 production, Atlas has been charged with maintaining and updating the existing aircraft of the SAAF.

South Africa received some 74 Mirage IIIs from France between 1963 and the mid-1970s, and the majority of these remain in service. No. 2 Squadron at Hoedspruit in the Eastern Transvaal operates a mixture of the single-seat Mirage III-CZ, two-seat III-BZ trainer and reconnaissance III-RZ/R2Z models, while No. 85 Combat Flying School at Pietersburg flies mainly the III-EZ single-seater and III-DZ/-D2Z two-seat combat trainer versions. Most of these are powered by 60·8 kN (13,670 lb st) Snecma Atar 9C afterburning turbojet engines, but the later D2Z and R2Z have the higher rated (70·6 kN; 15,873 lb st) Atar 9K-50. In the mid-1970s Atlas acquired a licence to manufacture the latter engine, which also powers the SAAF's Mirage F1s, and refit with the 9K-50 may be an ingredient of the Cheetah modification.

According to the SAAF, the Cheetah programme includes new performance levels, and the replacement of many structural components and upgrading of flight systems, about 50 per cent of the existing airframe being reconstructed and equipped with the latest navigation and weapons systems. The Cheetah chosen for the July 1986 rollout was a two-seat III-D2Z (SAAF serial number 845), and exhibited many outward similarities to the TC2/TC7 two-seat versions of the Kfir, including the sweptback, intake mounted fixed foreplanes, small nose side-strakes, curved lower-fuselage side-strakes, and 'dog-tooth' wing leading-edges. The nose extension appears to be shorter than that of the Kfir TC, and has rather more droop, but is large enough to accommodate a multi-mode radar. Beneath the nose mounted pitot probe are box and blister shaped fairings which suggest the presence of such equipment as a Doppler or terrain following radar and an infra-red seeker. Retention of the Atar engine is confirmed by absence of the Kfir's large dorsal airscoop (for its bigger, heavier J79 engine) and also of the smaller, rearmost pair of over-fuselage airscoops of the Israeli aircraft. Cheetah 845 also retains the upward opening framed canopy of the two-seat Mirage.

Sum total of the changes may be expected to confer upon the Cheetah the same kind of performance benefits as those claimed for the Kfir, namely improvements in dogfighting agility, especially in instantaneous and sustained turn rates (19°/s and 9·5°/s respectively in the case of the Kfir); handling and control at higher angles of attack; gust response, especially at low level; and take-off and landing distances. Other general performance figures are likely to remain similar to those of the Mirage III.

In addition to the pair of built-in 30 mm DEFA cannon, recent armament of SAAF Mirage IIIs has consisted primarily of Matra R.550 Magic or AIM-9 Sidewinder air-to-air missiles, medium-range Matra R.530 missiles, Matra JL-100 combined fuel/missile pods, and Nord AS 30 air-to-surface missiles. The Magic has already begun to be replaced by the domestic Armscor V3B infra-red homing missile, and it has been stated officially that all weaponry for the Cheetah is totally of South African origin.

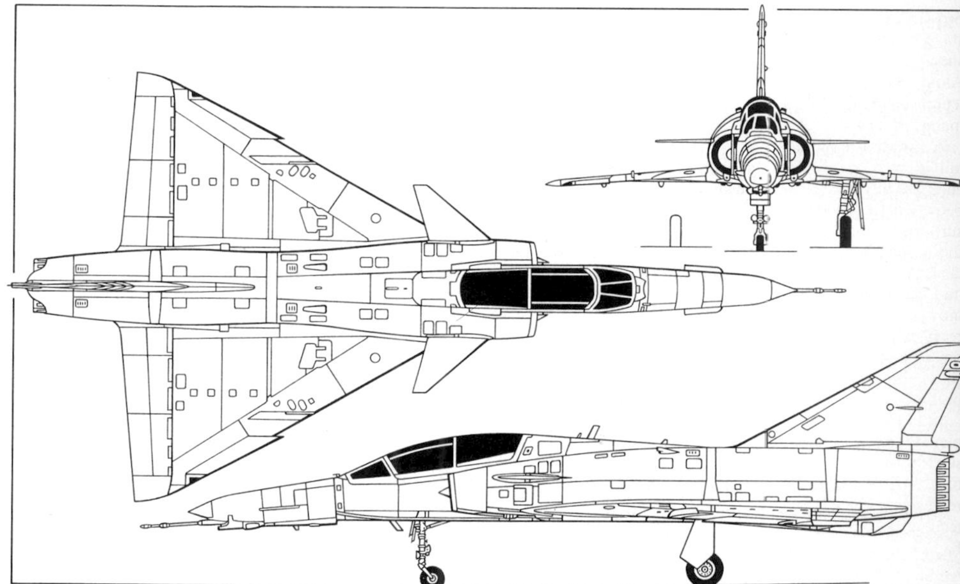

Three-view drawing *(Jane's/Mike Keep)* **and photograph of the Cheetah multi-role fighter developed by Atlas from the Mirage III**

ATLAS ALPHA XH-1

Revealing the existence of the Alpha XH-1 at a press conference in Johannesburg on 9 March 1986, the head of the South African Air Force, Lt Gen Dennis Earp, described this light attack helicopter prototype as "entirely locally designed to SAAF specifications, using what the South African industry can provide". In fact, this was a slight overstatement, since the XH-1 is based on the three-blade non-folding main and tail rotor and transmission systems, and almost certainly the power plant, of the French Aérospatiale SA 316B Alouette III, albeit with many engine, gearbox and rotor system components manufactured in South Africa.

The Alpha XH-1 was developed under a SAAF contract awarded to Atlas in March 1981. Construction began in January 1983, and the XH-1 made its first flight on 3 February 1985, more than a year before its public disclosure. Although exhibiting some outward signs of its Alouette ancestry, it clearly does embody a considerable degree of new design. This is chiefly apparent in the almost all-new fuselage, which probably has no more than the tailboom and horizontal stabiliser in common with the Alouette III. In place of the latter's three-abreast cabin, the XH-1 has two single cockpits in tandem, resulting in a much narrower fuselage. The central portion has a mainframe of welded steel tube with metal skin, while the front portion is a semi-monocoque structure using components of both metal and composite materials. The hemispherical nosecone,

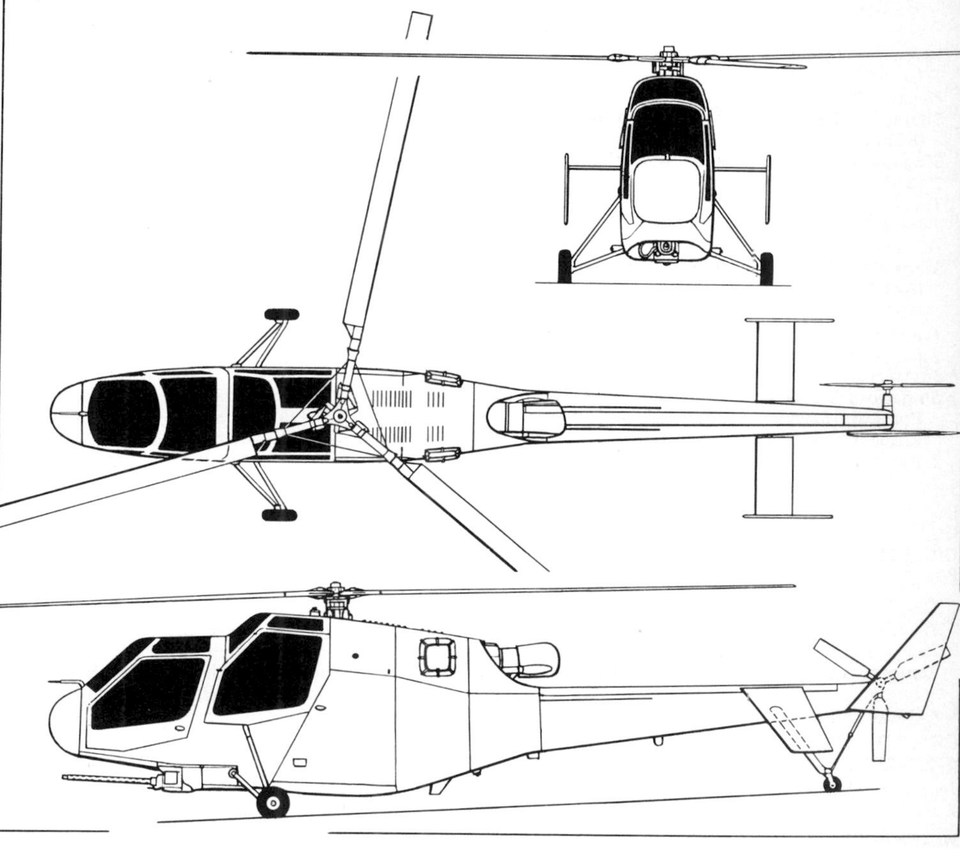

Atlas Alpha XH-1 (Turboméca Artouste IIIB turboshaft engine) *(Pilot Press)*

probably containing only flight test instrumentation at this stage of the aircraft's development, could be of different shape on the production version. Compared with the Alouette III the max T-O weight is unchanged, and fuselage length probably differs very little, but the empty weight is increased by a little over 20 per cent.

A sweptback fin has been added to the port side of the tailboom opposite the three-blade tail rotor, and new endplate fins attached to the stabiliser are angular, swept-back structures with most of their area below the horizontal surface. To give clearance for the undernose gun which is the Alpha XH-1's main feature, the non-retractable tricycle landing gear of the Alouette has had to be replaced by a 'tailsitter' type. In this, the mainwheel units have been moved much further forward, to a position level with the rear cockpit instrument panel, while the tailwheel is carried on long V struts beneath the tailplane with a telescopic shock strut to the rear. The mainwheels are fitted with disc brakes.

Initial flight testing of the Alpha XH-1 has been completed, and some modifications were planned before the start of the next stage of flight trials, which are aimed not only at further XH-1 development but also at conducting requirement studies and expanding the degree of local technology involved. According to General Earp, "we will be testing a wide range of airframe/engine/systems in the future, and technology derived from this programme will be tested on other helicopters in the SAAF inventory". These plans are expected to include provision of outriggers or stub-wings for the carriage of anti-tank guided weapons and unguided rockets.

TYPE: Experimental light attack helicopter.

POWER PLANT (SA 316B): One 649 kW (870 shp) Turbomeca Artouste IIIB turboshaft engine, derated to 425 kW (570 shp). Refuelling point in port side of rear fuselage.

ACCOMMODATION (XH-1): Two seats in tandem, with step down from rear (pilot's) cockpit to front cockpit occupied by weapons operator. Each cockpit has a forward opening door each side with very deep transparencies, giving an excellent field of view sideways and downward.

Atlas Alpha XH-1 prototype light attack helicopter

ARMAMENT (XH-1): Single-barrel GA1 20 mm cannon, with up to 1,000 rds of ammunition and max firing rate of 600 rds/min, in a servo controlled undernose turret. Gun is aimed by gunner's helmet mounted sight, and flexible mounting permits it to be traversed 120° to left and right and +10°/−60° in elevation. Installation can accept alternative weapons, including a grouping of four 7·62 mm machine-guns.

DIMENSIONS, EXTERNAL (SA 316B):
- Main rotor diameter — 11·02 m (36 ft 1¾ in)
- Tail rotor diameter — 1·91 m (6 ft 3¼ in)
- Length overall, rotors turning — 12·84 m (42 ft 1½ in)
- Height to top of rotor head — 2·97 m (9 ft 9 in)

WEIGHTS (XH-1):
- Weight empty — 1,400 kg (3,086 lb)
- Max T-O weight — 2,200 kg (4,850 lb)

PERFORMANCE (XH-1 at S/L, estimated):
- Max level speed — 113 knots (210 km/h; 130 mph)
- Max cruising speed — 100 knots (185 km/h; 115 mph)
- Max rate of climb — 244 m (800 ft)/min
- Combat radius — 148 nm (275 km; 171 miles)

ATLAS IMPALA Mk 2

The name Impala is given to two South African versions of the Aermacchi MB-326. Details of the two-seat Impala Mk 1 can be found in the 1983-84 and earlier *Jane's*. The single-seat MB-326KC Impala Mk 2 light ground attack aircraft is based on the MB-326K (1980-81 *Jane's*). South African manufacture began with the assembly of seven aircraft from Italian built components, the first of which made its initial flight on 13 February 1974. Production of the Mk 2 has now ended. It is believed that approx 100 Mks 1/2 are in SAAF service, with about the same number in the Reserve.

CAI

COMPOSITE AIRCRAFT INDUSTRIES

Pretoria

PRESIDENT: J. Israel Harris

Mr Harris, an aeronautical engineer, businessman and former Israeli Air Force transport pilot, formed CAI to design, develop and market a new business aircraft known as the SE-86.

CAI SE-86

Announced at the Aviation Africa '86 air show at Rand Airport, Germiston, in March 1986, the SE-86 is an eight-seat (two crew and six passengers) executive aircraft suitable also for air ambulance and other roles. Its advanced configuration broadly resembles that of the Beechcraft Starship, except that the foreplane is fixed and non-swept, the twin engines are pod mounted on overwing pylons, and the SE-86 has a single conventional vertical tail instead of the Starship's winglet/fins. The design also incorporates airbrakes, but no wing flaps.

The SE-86 was exhibited in the form of a wind tunnel model; and tunnel testing, by the National Institute for Aeronautics and Systems Technology and the Council for Scientific and Industrial Research, was completed in April 1986. Construction of a prototype, almost entirely of glassfibre, carbonfibre and Kevlar, was due to begin shortly afterwards, and first flight is planned for April 1987. Certification to FAR Pt 23, and completion of the first production aircraft, are scheduled for October 1988. European and US interest in licence manufacture has been shown.

The SE-86 is to be offered in both piston and turboprop powered forms, the former with two 261 kW (350 hp) Avco Lycoming TIO-540 turbocharged engines and the latter with 447 kW (600 shp) Allison 250-C30s.

DIMENSIONS, EXTERNAL:
- Wing span — 15·30 m (50 ft 2½ in)
- Foreplane span — 8·60 m (28 ft 2½ in)

DIMENSION, INTERNAL:
- Cabin: Max width — 1·80 m (5 ft 11 in)

AREA:
- Wings and foreplane, gross — 27·7 m² (298·2 sq ft)

WEIGHTS (A: piston engines, B: turboprops):
- Fuel weight: A — 900 kg (1,984 lb)
- B — 1,100 kg (2,425 lb)
- Max T-O weight: A — 3,700 kg (8,157 lb)
- B — 3,900 kg (8,598 lb)

PERFORMANCE (estimated at max T-O weight, A and B as above):
- Max level speed:
  - A at 4,575 m (15,000 ft) — 200 knots (370 km/h; 230 mph)
  - B at 7,620 m (25,000 ft) — 275 knots (509 km/h; 316 mph)
- Max cruising speed (75% power):
  - A at 4,575 m (15,000 ft) — 175 knots (324 km/h; 201 mph)
  - B at 7,620 m (25,000 ft) — 238 knots (441 km/h; 274 mph)
- Stalling speed: A — 70 knots (130 km/h; 81 mph)
- B — 73 knots (136 km/h; 85 mph)
- Service ceiling: A — 9,450 m (31,000 ft)
- B — 10,050 m (33,000 ft)
- Range at normal cruise power, IFR reserves:
  - A — 1,600 nm (2,965 km; 1,842 miles)
  - B — 1,500 nm (2,780 km; 1,727 miles)

SPAIN

AISA

AERONAUTICA INDUSTRIAL SA

Cuatro Vientos (Carretera del Aeroclub Carabanchel Alto), Apartado 984, Madrid 28044

Telephone: (91) 208 75 40

Telex: 23593 E Madrid

PRESIDENT: Gonzalo Suárez

GENERAL MANAGER: José A. Delgado

DESIGN MANAGER: Juán del Campo

PLANT MANAGER: Carlos Herraiz

This company was founded in 1923 by Ing Jorge Loring Martinez, assuming its present title in 1935. Its design office has, since the Second World War, been responsible for several liaison, training and sporting aircraft for the Spanish Air Force and aeroclub flying schools, including the I-11, I-11B, AVD-12, and I-115. The Cuatro Vientos factory has a covered area of 8,000 m² (86,110 sq ft) and employs about 170 persons.

AISA is engaged in repair and general overhaul of US aircraft, in particular the Beechcraft B55 Baron and F33 Bonanza aircraft operated by the Spanish Air Force and the National School of Aeronautics. It is also engaged in the repair and overhaul of Bell 47, 204, 205 and 206, and Boeing Vertol CH-47 helicopters, and their dynamic components, for the Spanish Army, Spanish Air Force and civilian operators. As a subcontractor to Messier-Hispano-Bugatti, it is producing landing gear shock absorbers and hydraulic actuators for the Dassault Mirage F1 and 2000 and Falcon series, Dassault-Breguet/Dornier Alpha Jet, and other European aviation programmes. Under subcontract to CASA, it produces structural components for the C-212 Aviocar and Airbus programmes; and, in offset programmes, helicopter structures and hydraulic components for Aérospatiale and Agusta.

AISA's most recent project to reach the hardware stage was the GN autogyro, which was completed in 1981 and described fully in the 1983-84 *Jane's*.

CASA

CONSTRUCCIONES AERONAUTICAS SA

Rey Francisco 4, Apartado 193, 28008 Madrid

Telephone: (1) 247 25 00

Telex: 27418 CASA E

WORKS: Getafe, Ajalvir, Tablada, San Pablo and Cádiz

PRESIDENT AND GENERAL MANAGER: Fernando de Caralt

COMMERCIAL DIRECTOR: Pablo de Bergia

ENGINEERING DIRECTOR: Alberto Elvira

PRODUCTION DIRECTOR: Alberto Fernández

PROGRAMME DIRECTOR: Luis Muñoz

SALES DIRECTOR: Juan A. Alonso

PUBLIC RELATIONS AND PRESS MANAGER: José de Sanmillán

This company was formed on 3 March 1923 for the primary purpose of producing metal aircraft for the Spanish Air Force. It began by building under licence the Breguet XIX and has since manufactured many other aircraft of foreign design, recent examples including the Northrop F-5 fighter. It assembled 57 MBB BO 105 helicopters ordered by the Spanish Army, and delivered 24 armed BO 105s to the air force of Iraq. Output of BO 105s continued with a further 32 aircraft in 1984. CASA also produces glassfibre doors and some rotor head components for the German BO 105 production line. Under an agreement signed with Sikorsky Aircraft on 13 June 1984, CASA is producing components (tailcones, tail rotor pylons and horizontal stabilisers) for S-70 helicopters. The agreement allows also for final assembly and flight testing of S-70s purchased by the Spanish armed forces, and development of additional helicopter marketing, product support, research and development, and other forms of collaboration. CASA will also assemble six of the 12 Aérospatiale AS 332B₁ Super Pumas ordered in 1986 for the Spanish Army.

CASA's own Project Office has designed several aircraft under contract to the Spanish Air Ministry, including the C-212 Aviocar transport and the C-101 Aviojet jet trainer, both of which are currently in production. In order to promote sales in the Far East, CASA established a C-212 assembly line in Indonesia, as well as full after-sales suppo

CASA assembled MBB BO 105 S (for Spain) *(Antonio Camarasa)*

in that area (see IPTN entry in Indonesian section). As described in the International section, it is collaborating with IPTN to develop and manufacture the Airtech CN-235 transport aircraft.

Under contract to Dassault-Breguet (which see), CASA is responsible for manufacturing outer wings for the Falcon 100 light business aircraft and centre fuselages for the Mirage F1 combat aircraft. As a full member (4·2%) of Airbus Industrie (see International section), it manufactures the horizontal tail surfaces, landing gear doors and forward passenger doors for the Airbus A300/310/320 family of wide-bodied transport aircraft. It also manufactures glassfibre honeycomb components, including underwing fillets for McDonnell Douglas DC-10s, outboard flaps for the Boeing 757, and components for the MD-80 and Canadair CL-215.

CASA undertakes maintenance and modernisation work for the Spanish Air Force and Navy, and for the US Air Force in Europe. Its principal current activities of this kind concern maintenance and specific modifications to the McDonnell Douglas F-15, and overhaul and maintenance of McDonnell Douglas F-4 and BAe Matador (Harrier) combat aircraft and Bell 47G, 204 and 205 helicopters.

CASA has five factories, employing about 9,600 people. Including production by the former Hispano Aviación SA, which it absorbed in 1972, the company has manufactured more than 3,500 aircraft and overhauled approx 6,250. CASA has a total covered area in the region of 200,000 m² (2,152,780 sq ft). Majority shareholder in the company is the INI (Instituto Nacional de Industria); other shareholders include Northrop Corporation of the USA (13%) and MBB of the German Federal Republic (11%).

AIRTECH (CASA-IPTN) CN-235

Details of this programme can be found in the International section.

CASA C-212 SERIES 200 AVIOCAR

The standard version of the Aviocar since 1979, the Series 200 is an improved version of the original C-212-5 Series 100 (1981-82 and earlier *Jane's*), of which 135 examples (including ten development aircraft) were built by CASA and 29 by Nurtanio (IPTN) in Indonesia. The Srs 200 has more powerful TPE331-10 engines and increased max T-O weight. Aircraft c/n 138 and 139 served as prototypes for this version, making their first flights on 30 April and 20 June 1978 respectively.

Certificated in March 1979 under FAR Pt 25, the Series 200 can be operated under FAR Pt 121 and Pt 135 conditions, and is well within the noise requirements of FAR Pt 36.

By February 1986 total sales of the Aviocar (all versions) had reached 390 (197 civil and 193 military), of which more than 300 had been delivered by CASA and IPTN, with production continuing. Recent civil customers have included Transair of the USA (6) and Hawa Air of Belgium (1); recent military and maritime orders have included 8 for the Angolan Army, 10 for the Mexican Navy, 1 for the Swedish Navy and 2 for the Swedish Coastguard.

ASW/maritime patrol and elint/ECM versions of the Aviocar are available, and are described separately, as is the more recent **Series 300**, which becomes the standard version from early 1987. The following description applies to the Series 200 transport:

TYPE: Twin-turboprop STOL utility transport.

WINGS: Cantilever high-wing monoplane. Wing section NACA 65_3-218. Incidence 2° 30′. No dihedral or sweepback. All-metal light alloy fail-safe structure. Light alloy ailerons and double-slotted trailing-edge flaps. Trim tab in port aileron. Pneumatic de-icing of leading-edges (rubber boots and engine bleed air). Glassfibre extended wingtips optional.

FUSELAGE: Semi-monocoque non-pressurised fail-safe structure of light alloy construction.

TAIL UNIT: Cantilever two-spar all-metal structure, with dorsal fin. Fixed incidence tailplane, mid mounted on rear of fuselage. Trim tab in rudder and each elevator. Pneumatic de-icing of leading-edges (rubber boots and engine bleed air).

LANDING GEAR: Non-retractable tricycle type, with single mainwheels and single steerable nosewheel. CASA oleo-pneumatic shock absorbers. Goodyear wheels and tyres, main units size 11·00-12 Type III (10-ply rating), nose unit size 24-7·7 Type VII (8-ply rating). Tyre pressure 3·86 bars (56 lb/sq in) on main units, 3·65 bars (53 lb/sq in) on nose unit. Goodyear hydraulic disc brakes on mainwheels. No brake cooling. Anti-skid system optional.

POWER PLANT: Two Garrett TPE331-10R-511C turboprop engines, each flat rated at 671 kW (900 shp) and driving a Dowty Rotol R-313 four-blade constant-speed fully-feathering reversible-pitch propeller (Hartzell propellers on aircraft built before July 1983). Fuel in four integral wing tanks, with total capacity of 2,040 litres (449 Imp gallons), of which 2,000 litres (440 Imp gallons) are usable. Gravity refuelling point above each tank. Additional fuel can be carried in one 1,000 litre or two 750 litre (220 or 165 Imp gallon) optional ferry tanks inside cabin, and/or two 500 litre (110 Imp gallon) auxiliary underwing tanks. Single pressure refuelling point in starboard wing leading-edge; gravity point for each integral wing tank. Oil capacity 6·5 litres (1·43 Imp gallons) per engine.

ACCOMMODATION: Crew of two on flight deck; cabin attendant in civil version. For troop transport role, main cabin can be fitted with 21 inward facing seats along cabin walls, plus three forward facing seats, to accommodate 23 paratroops with an instructor/jumpmaster; or seats for 24 fully equipped troops. As an ambulance, cabin is normally equipped to carry 12 stretcher patients and up to four medical attendants. As a freighter, up to 2,770 kg (6,107 lb) of cargo can be carried in main cabin, including two LD1, LD727/DC-8 or three LD3 pallets, or light vehicles. Photographic version is equipped with two Wild RC-10A vertical cameras and a darkroom. Navigation training version has individual desks for instructor and five pupils, in two rows, with appropriate instrument installations. Civil passenger transport version has standard seating for up to 26 persons in mainly four-abreast layout at 72 cm (28·5 in) pitch, with provision for quick change to all-cargo or mixed passenger/cargo interior. Toilet, galley and 400 kg (882 lb) capacity baggage compartment standard. VIP transport version can be furnished to customer's requirements. Forward and outward opening door on port side immediately aft of flight deck; passenger door on port side aft of wing; inward opening emergency exit opposite each door on starboard side. Additional emergency exits in roof and floor of flight deck. A two-section underfuselage loading ramp/door aft of main cabin is openable in flight for discharge of paratroops or cargo, and is fitted with external wheels, to allow door to remain open during ground manoeuvring. Interior of rear loading door can be used for additional baggage stowage. Final production examples of Series 200 have the new toilet/galley kit, and rear baggage compartment (without ramps), as introduced for the Series 300. Entire accommodation heated and ventilated; air-conditioning optional.

SYSTEMS: Engine bleed air or Garrett freon cycle air-conditioning system optional. Hydraulic system, pressure 138 bars (2,000 lb/sq in), provides duplicated circuit via electric pump for mainwheel brakes, flaps, nosewheel steering and ventral cargo ramp/door. Handpump for emergency use in case of electric failure. Electrical system is supplied by two 9kW starter/generators, three batteries and three static converters. Pneumatic boot de-icing of wing and tail unit leading-edges, electric anti-icing of propellers and windscreens. Oxygen system for crew (incl cabin attendant); two portable oxygen cylinders for passenger supply. Engine and cabin fire protection systems.

AVIONICS AND EQUIPMENT: Standard avionics include King or Collins VHF com, VOR/ILS, ADF, DME, ATC transponder, radio altimeter, intercom (with Gables control) and PA system; King directional gyro; Sperry flight director; and Bendix weather radar. Blind-flying instrumentation standard. Optional avionics include second King or Collins ADF and transponder; Collins HF com; Collins flight director; Global Omega nav; Sperry autopilot; Sperry weather radar; Martech emergency radio beacon; and Fairchild flight data and cockpit voice recorders.

ARMAMENT (military versions, optional): Two machine-gun pods or two rocket launchers, or one launcher and one gun pod, on hardpoints on fuselage sides (capacity 250 kg; 551 lb each).

DIMENSIONS, EXTERNAL:

Wing span (standard, without optional glassfibre extended tips)	19·00 m (62 ft 4 in)
Wing chord: at root	2·49 m (8 ft 2 in)
at tip	1·50 m (4 ft 11 in)
Wing aspect ratio	9
Length overall	15·15 m (49 ft 8½ in)
Fuselage: Max width	2·30 m (7 ft 6½ in)
Height overall	6·30 m (20 ft 8 in)
Tailplane span	8·40 m (27 ft 6¾ in)
Wheel track	3·10 m (10 ft 2 in)
Wheelbase	5·55 m (18 ft 2½ in)
Propeller diameter: Hartzell	2·79 m (9 ft 2 in)
Dowty	2·74 m (9 ft 0 in)
Propeller ground clearance (min)	1·32 m (4 ft 4 in)
Distance between propeller centres	5·30 m (17 ft 4¾ in)
Passenger door (port, rear):	
Max height	1·58 m (5 ft 2¼ in)
Max width	0·70 m (2 ft 3½ in)
Crew and servicing door (port, fwd):	
Max height	1·10 m (3 ft 7¼ in)
Max width	0·58 m (1 ft 10¾ in)
Rear loading door: Max length	3·66 m (12 ft 0 in)
Max width	1·70 m (5 ft 7 in)
Max height	1·80 m (5 ft 11 in)
Emergency exit (stbd, fwd): Height	1·10 m (3 ft 7¼ in)
Width	0·58 m (1 ft 10¾ in)
Emergency exit (stbd, rear): Height	0·94 m (3 ft 1 in)
Width	0·55 m (1 ft 9¾ in)

CASA C-212 Series 200 Aviocar twin-turboprop STOL utility transport

Dimensions, internal:
Cabin (excl flight deck and rear loading door):
Length 6·50 m (21 ft 4 in)
Max width 2·10 m (6 ft 10¾ in)
Max height 1·80 m (5 ft 11 in)
Floor area 11·33 m² (121·95 sq ft)
Volume 23·0 m³ (812·2 cu ft)
Cabin: volume incl flight deck and rear loading door 27·0 m³ (953·5 cu ft)
Baggage compartment volume 2·9 m³ (102·4 cu ft)

Areas:
Wings, gross (standard) 40·0 m² (430·56 sq ft)
Ailerons (total, incl tab) 2·44 m² (26·26 sq ft)
Trailing-edge flaps (total) 7·47 m² (80·41 sq ft)
Fin, incl dorsal fin 6·27 m² (67·49 sq ft)
Rudder, incl tab 2·05 m² (22·07 sq ft)
Tailplane 11·90 m² (128·09 sq ft)
Elevators, incl tabs 4·36 m² (46·93 sq ft)

Weights and Loadings:
Manufacturer's weight empty 3,780 kg (8,333 lb)
Weight empty, equipped (cargo) 4,115 kg (9,072 lb)
Max payload (cargo) 2,770 kg (6,107 lb)
Max fuel: standard 1,600 kg (3,527 lb)
optional 2,180 kg (4,806 lb)
Max T-O weight 7,450 kg (16,424 lb)
Max ramp weight 7,500 kg (16,534 lb)
Max landing weight 7,350 kg (16,204 lb)
Max zero-fuel weight 7,050 kg (15,542 lb)
Max cabin floor loading 732 kg/m² (150 lb/sq ft)
Max wing loading 186·2 kg/m² (38·1 lb/sq ft)
Max power loading 5·55 kg/kW (9·12 lb/shp)

Performance (at max T-O weight, ISA):
Max operating speed (VMO) 202 knots (374 km/h; 232 mph) IAS
Max cruising speed at 3,050 m (10,000 ft) 197 knots (365 km/h; 227 mph)
Normal cruising speed at 3,050 m (10,000 ft) 187 knots (346 km/h; 215 mph)
Stalling speed, T-O configuration 78 knots (145 km/h; 90 mph)
Max rate of climb at S/L 474 m (1,555 ft)/min
Rate of climb at S/L, one engine out 108 m (355 ft)/min
Service ceiling 8,535 m (28,000 ft)
Service ceiling, one engine out 3,505 m (11,500 ft)
T-O run 440 m (1,445 ft)
T-O distance (FAR Pt 25, unfactored) 610 m (2,000 ft)
T-O to 15 m (50 ft) 630 m (2,065 ft)
Landing from 15 m (50 ft) 505 m (1,655 ft)
Landing distance (FAR Pt 25, unfactored) without propeller reversal 550 m (1,805 ft)
Landing run 200 m (656 ft)
Min ground turning radius 14·99 m (49 ft 3¼ in)
Range at max cruising speed, no reserves:
with max payload 220 nm (408 km; 253 miles)
with max fuel 950 nm (1,760 km; 1,094 miles)
g limits +3/−1·2

CASA C-212 Srs 200 Aviocar in Spanish Air Force maritime search and rescue configuration

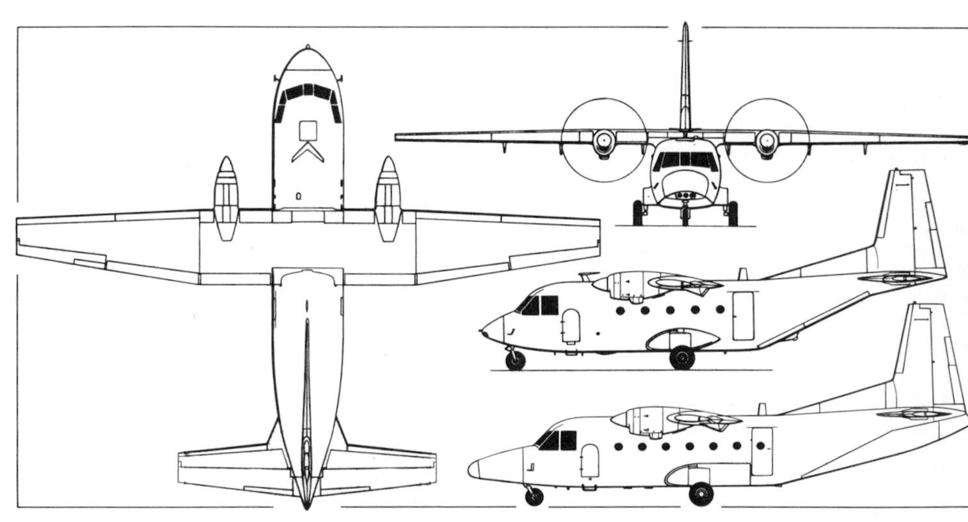
CASA C-212 Series 200 Aviocar, with additional side view (bottom) of Series 300 *(Pilot Press)*

CASA C-212 SERIES 200 AVIOCAR (ASW and MARITIME PATROL VERSION)

Swedish Navy designation: TP89

For service with the Spanish Air Force, and for certain foreign countries, CASA has developed a version of the C-212 Srs 200 equipped for anti-submarine and maritime patrol duties. Nine have been ordered by the Spanish Air Force for SAR duties, three by the Spanish Ministry of Finance, one ASW version by the Swedish Navy, two for maritime patrol (with a SLAR and IR/UV search equipment) by the Swedish Coastguard, four by the Venezuelan Navy, two by Sudan and one by the Uruguayan Air Force.

The principal external differences from the transport version are the addition of a nose radome and the appearance of various antennae on the fuselage and tail fin. Two fuselage hardpoints are provided for the carriage of torpedoes, rocket pods and other weapons.

Type: Twin-turboprop ASW and maritime patrol aircraft.

Airframe: Generally similar to standard C-212 Srs 200 except for addition of nose radome and various external antennae.

Power Plant: As for standard C-212 Srs 200. Auxiliary fuel tanks, total capacity 1,400 litres (308 Imp gallons).

Accommodation (ASW version): Pilot and co-pilot on flight deck, with OTPI and additional central console for radar repeater; control for radio navigation, Doppler, DME, ADF, UHF/DF, Omega and VOR/ILS; weapons delivery controls; and intervalometer for rockets. Avionics rack on port side, aft of pilot, for com/nav equipment; second rack on starboard side, aft of co-pilot, contains avionics for mission equipment (radar, sonobuoys, MAD and ESM). Immediately aft of the latter rack, along the starboard side of the cabin, are three control consoles for the mission crew members. The first console has the radar control and display, ESM control and display, and intercom switch control. The second has the tactical display and control, MAD recorder and control, and intercom switch. The rearmost of the three incorporates intercom switch, sonobuoy receiver control unit, acoustic control panel, and acoustic control and display units.

Accommodation (maritime patrol version): Pilot and co-pilot on flight deck, with central console for radar repeater; control for radio navigation, Doppler, DME, ADF, UHF/DF, Omega, VOR/ILS and searchlight. Avionics rack on port side, aft of pilot, for com/nav and radar equipment. On starboard side of cabin is a console for the radar operator that incorporates radar PPI and ICS controls. Posts for two observers are located at the rear of the cabin.

Avionics: Communications equipment includes two HF and two VHF transceivers, single UHF, and interphone. Navigation equipment includes automatic flight control system, flight director, VOR/ILS (including VOR/LOC), glideslope and marker beacon receiver, DME, two ADF, UHF/DF, radar altimeter, Doppler radar, VLF/Omega, autopilot and compass.

Operational Equipment (ASW version): Underfuselage search radar with 360° scan, electronic support measures (ESM), sonobuoy processing system (SPS), OTPI, MAD, tactical processing system (TPS), IFF/SIF transponder, sonobuoy and smoke marker launcher, torpedoes, rockets and other weapons.

Operational Equipment (maritime patrol version): Nose mounted AN/APS-128 100kW search radar with 270° scan, searchlight, FLIR (optional), smoke markers and camera.

Armament: Includes option to carry torpedoes such as Mk 46 and Sting Ray, and light air-to-surface missiles such as Sea Skua and AS 15TT.

Weights (ASW version):
Max T-O weight 8,400 kg (18,519 lb)
Max landing weight 7,350 kg (16,204 lb)

Performance (at max T-O weight, ISA):
Max cruising speed at 3,050 m (10,000 ft) 190 knots (353 km/h; 219 mph)
Loiter speed at 457 m (1,500 ft) 105 knots (195 km/h; 121 mph)
Service ceiling 7,315 m (24,000 ft)
Max range 1,650 nm (3,055 km; 1,898 miles)
Max endurance more than 12 h

CASA C-212 SERIES 200 AVIOCAR (ELINT/ECM VERSION)

A version of the Srs 200 Aviocar for electronic intelligence and electronic countermeasures duties entered development in 1981, at which time four had been ordered by an export customer. Two more have since been ordered by an undisclosed customer, and two C-212s already delivered to the Portuguese Air Force have been modified retrospectively for elint/ECM duties.

The elint/ECM version carries equipment for automatic signal interception, classification and identification in dense signal environments, data from which enable a map to be drawn plotting the position and characteristics of hostile radars. Emitters for the jamming part of the mission are also carried.

CASA C-212 SERIES 300 AVIOCAR

First flown in September 1984, the Series 300 Aviocar is essentially a modified Series 200 with higher max T-O weight, increased range with max payload, and other performance improvements. Structural changes include redesigned glassfibre wingtips (optional also for late-production Series 200), a modified nose with increased baggage volume, and, for customers not requiring use of the rear-loading facility, a new rear baggage compartment (also optional for Series 200), retaining the same external fuselage form, and a new external baggage door is provided. At the rear of the passenger cabin, new galley and toilet facilities are provided, as improved passenger amenities. Passenger accommodation can seat up to 26 people at a pitch of 86 cm (34 in). Engines are Garrett TPE331-10R-513Cs, with Dowty Rotol R33414-82F/13 propellers and synchrophasers as standard; ratings are 690 kW (925 shp) for T-O and landing (with optional APR on), and 671 kW (900 shp) for max continuous operation. Oil capacity 6·5 litres (1·43 Imp gallons). Nosewheel tyre pressure increased to 3·72 bars (54 lb/sq in). Pressure refuelling point under starboard wing. Military or special versions can carry two 500 litre (110 Imp gallon) auxiliary underwing fuel tanks. Third 9kW starter/generator added. Additional crew door/emergency exit on starboard side. King Gold Crown III or Collins Pro Line II avionics package standard; Sperry SPZ-4500 digital AFCS optional. Certification of the Series 300 is to FAR Pts 25, 121 and 135 (Appendix A). All C-212s produced from early 1987 will be to Series 300 standard.

Accommodation: Cabin seating for 23 passengers three-abreast, or maximum of 26 four-abreast, plus galley, toilet and seat for cabin attendant. Additional compartment for up to 150 kg (330 lb) of baggage in lengthened nose. Otherwise similar to that described for Series 200. Cargo version can accommodate two LD1, two LD727/DC8 or three LD3 containers.

Dimensions, external: As for Series 200 except:
Wing span 20·25 m (66 ft 5¼ in)
Length overall 16·15 m (52 ft 11¾ in)
Wheelbase 5·46 m (17 ft 11 in)
Propeller diameter 2·79 m (9 ft 2 in)
Baggage door: Height 1·25 m (4 ft 1¼ in)
Width 1·70 m (5 ft 7 in)

Series 300 version of the C-212 Aviocar, showing the lengthened nose and optional rear ramp/door fairing

DIMENSIONS, INTERNAL:
- Cabin (excl flight deck and rear baggage compartment):
  - Length: 7·275 m (23 ft 10½ in)
  - Cross-section: as for Srs 200
  - Floor area: 13·35 m² (143·7 sq ft)
  - Volume: passengers: 23·82 m³ (841 cu ft)
  - cargo (incl rear ramp): 26·40 m³ (932 cu ft)
- Baggage compartment volume:
  - nose: 1·0 m³ (35·3 cu ft)
  - rear: 2·5 m³ (88·3 cu ft)

AREAS: As for Series 200 except:
- Wings, gross: 41·00 m² (441·3 sq ft)

WEIGHTS AND LOADINGS:
- Weight empty, equipped:
  - passengers: 4,850 kg (10,692 lb)
  - cargo: 4,280 kg (9,436 lb)
- Max payload: passengers: 2,250 kg (4,960 lb)
  - cargo: 2,820 kg (6,217 lb)
- Max fuel weight: standard: 1,600 kg (3,527 lb)
  - optional: 2,400 kg (5,291 lb)
- Max T-O weight: 7,700 kg (16,975 lb)
- Max overload T-O weight: 8,000 kg (17,637 lb)
- Max ramp weight: 7,750 kg (17,085 lb)
- Max landing weight: 7,450 kg (16,424 lb)
- Max zero-fuel weight: 7,100 kg (15,653 lb)
- Max wing loading: 187·8 kg/m² (38·46 lb/sq ft)
- Max power loading: 5·74 kg/kW (9·43 lb/shp)

PERFORMANCE (at max T-O weight. A: passenger version, B: freighter, C: military version at 8,000 kg; 17,637 lb AUW):
- Max operating speed (VMO):
  - A, B: 200 knots (370 km/h; 230 mph) IAS
- Max cruising speed at 3,050 m (10,000 ft):
  - A, B: 198 knots (367 km/h; 228 mph)
- Econ cruising speed at 3,050 m (10,000 ft):
  - A, B: 166 knots (308 km/h; 191 mph)
- Stalling speed in T-O configuration:
  - A, B: 79 knots (147 km/h; 91 mph)
- Max rate of climb at S/L: A, B: 474 m (1,555 ft)/min
- Rate of climb at S/L, one engine out:
  - A, B: 104 m (341 ft)/min
- Service ceiling: A: 7,955 m (26,100 ft)
  - B: 8,655 m (28,400 ft)
- Service ceiling, one engine out: A: 3,015 m (9,900 ft)
  - B: 3,415 m (11,200 ft)
- T-O run: A: 584 m (1,916 ft)
  - B: 548 m (1,798 ft)
- T-O distance: A to 10·7 m (35 ft): 649 m (2,130 ft)
  - B to 10·7 m (35 ft): 580 m (1,903 ft)
  - C to 15 m (50 ft): 560 m (1,838 ft)
- Landing from 15 m (50 ft) with propeller reversal:
  - A: 510 m (1,673 ft)
  - B: 462 m (1,516 ft)
  - C: 460 m (1,510 ft)
- Landing run:
  - B, C: 285 m (935 ft)
- Range at 3,050 m (10,000 ft), ISA, no reserves:
  - A with max payload: 330 nm (611 km; 380 miles)
  - A with max fuel: 1,025 nm (1,899 km; 1,180 miles)
  - B with max payload: 345 nm (639 km; 397 miles)
  - B with max fuel: 952 nm (1,764 km; 1,096 miles)

CASA C-101 AVIOJET

Spanish Air Force designation: E.25 Mirlo (Blackbird)

Chilean Air Force designations: T-36 and A-36 Halcón

CASA and the Spanish Ministerio del Aire signed a contract for this basic and advanced military jet trainer aircraft on 16 September 1975. The contract covered the construction of four flying prototypes (first flights 27 June and 30 September 1977, 26 January and 17 April 1978) and two static and fatigue test airframes. MBB (West Germany) and Northrop (USA) collaborated in the design, the latter company providing design assistance with the inlets and the 'Norcasa' wing section.

To minimise cost and maintenance, the C-101 is built on modular lines, with ample space within the airframe for equipment for any training mission likely to be required. The C-101 is fully aerobatic, and is able to carry out such additional duties as ground attack, reconnaissance, escort, weapons training, electronic countermeasures (ECM), and photographic missions. Manufacture is entirely by CASA except for the nosewheel unit, which is produced in the UK by Dowty Rotol. Wings and main landing gear units are built at Getafe and fuselages at Seville. Aircraft for Chile are assembled and partially manufactured locally by ENAER. Spanish production started at the beginning of 1978, and the first production aircraft made its initial flight on 8 November 1979.

The following versions have been announced:

C-101EB. Initial production trainer version for Spanish Air Force, with 15·57 kN (3,500 lb st) TFE731-2-2J engine. Total of 88 delivered from 17 March 1980; now in service with the Academia General del Aire at San Javier and the 41° Grupo at Zaragoza. Described in 1983-84 *Jane's*.

C-101BB. Armed export version, with 16·46 kN (3,700 lb st) TFE731-3-1J engine, ordered by air forces of Chile (17 **BB-02**) and Honduras (four **BB-03**, similar except for avionics, with options on eight more). All except first four BB-02s are for licence assembly and partial local manufacture in Chile (see ENAER entry in Chilean section), which has options on 23 more. Known as **T-36 Halcón** in Chilean service.

C-101CC. Light attack version, with more powerful TFE731-5-1J engine (normal rating 19·13 kN; 4,300 lb st, military power reserve (MPR) rating 20·91 kN; 4,700 lb st), and other modifications. First of two prototypes flown on 16 November 1983. Twenty **CC-02** ordered by Chile, including 19 for assembly and partial manufacture by ENAER as **A-36 Halcón**, and 16 **CC-04** ordered by Royal Jordanian Air Force.

C-101DD. Enhanced training version, announced in 1984 and flown for the first time on 20 May 1985. Additional avionics include Ferranti head-up display, weapon aiming computer and inertial AHRS, and GEC Avionics AD 6601 Doppler velocity sensor. Power plant as for C-101CC. No orders announced up to mid-1986.

The following description applies to the standard C-101CC except where indicated:

TYPE: Tandem two-seat basic and advanced trainer and light tactical aircraft.

WINGS: Cantilever low-wing monoplane. Wing section Norcasa 15, thickness/chord ratio 15%. Dihedral 5°. Incidence 1°. Sweepback at quarter-chord 1° 53'. All-metal (aluminium alloy) three-spar fail-safe stressed-skin structure, with six-bolt attachment to fuselage. Plain ailerons and slotted trailing-edge flaps, of glassfibre/honeycomb sandwich construction. Flap track guides of titanium. Ailerons actuated hydraulically, with electrically actuated artificial spring feel and manual backup. Ground adjustable tab on port aileron.

FUSELAGE: All-metal semi-monocoque fail-safe structure. Hydraulically operated aluminium honeycomb airbrake under centre of fuselage.

TAIL UNIT: Cantilever all-metal structure, with electrically actuated variable incidence tailplane. Aluminium honeycomb rudder and elevators, actuated manually via push/pull rods. Electrically actuated trim tab in rudder. Twin ventral strakes under jetpipe on armed versions.

LANDING GEAR: Hydraulically retractable tricycle type, with single wheel and oleo-pneumatic shock absorber on each unit. Forward retracting Dowty Rotol nose unit, with non-steerable nosewheel and chined tubeless tyre size 457 × 146 (18 × 5·75-8). Inward retracting mainwheels with tubeless tyres size 622 × 216 (24·5 × 8·5-10) and hydraulically actuated multi-disc brakes.

POWER PLANT: One Garrett TFE731 non-afterburning turbofan engine (see model listings for details), with lateral intake on each side of fuselage abreast of second cockpit. Fuel in one 1,155 litre (254 Imp gallon) fuselage bag tank, one 575 litre (126·5 Imp gallon) integral tank in wing centre-section, and two outer wing integral tanks, for ferry missions, each of 342 litres (75·25 Imp gallons). Total usable internal fuel capacity 1,730 litres (380·5 Imp gallons) normal, 2,414 litres (531 Imp gallons) maximum. Fuel system permits up to 30 s of inverted flight. Pressure refuelling point beneath port air intake; gravity fuelling point for each tank. No provision for external fuel tanks. Oil capacity 8·5 litres (1·8 Imp gallons).

ACCOMMODATION: Crew of two in tandem, on Martin-Baker Mk 10L zero/zero ejection seats, under individual canopies which open sideways to starboard and are separated by internal screen. Rear (instructor's) seat elevated 32·5 cm (12¾ in). Cockpit pressurised and air-conditioned by engine bleed air. Dual controls standard.

SYSTEMS: Hamilton Standard three-wheel bootstrap type air-conditioning and pressurisation system, differential 0·28 bars (4·07 lb/sq in), using engine bleed air. Single hydraulic system, pressure 207 bars (3,000 lb/sq in), for

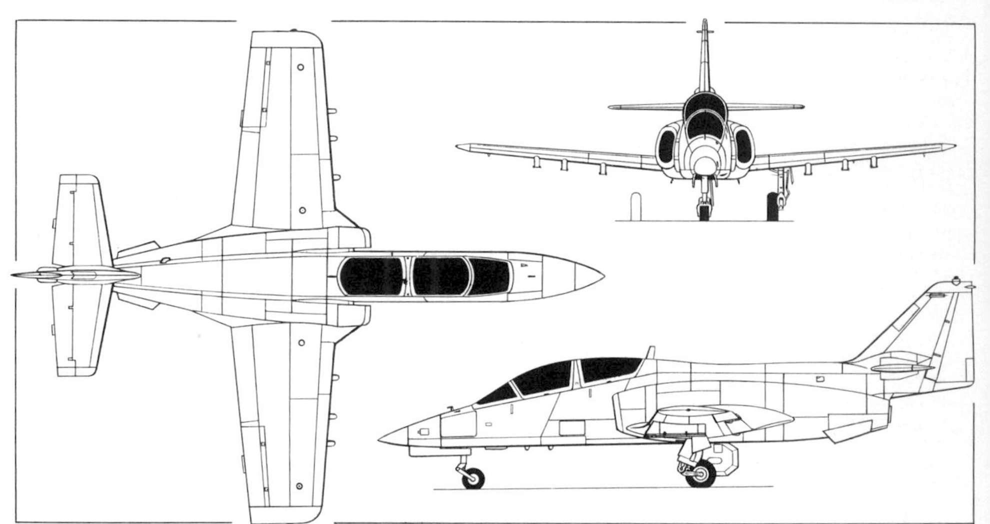

CASA C-101CC Aviojet light attack aircraft *(Pilot Press)*

landing gear, ailerons, flaps, airbrake, anti-skid units and wheel brakes. Backup system comprising compressed nitrogen bottle for landing gear extension and accumulator for aileron boosters and emergency braking. Pneumatic system for air-conditioning, pressurisation and canopy seal. Electrical system includes 28V 9kW DC starter/generator, two 700VA static inverters for 115/26V single phase AC power, and two 24V 23Ah nickel-cadmium batteries for emergency DC power and engine starting. High pressure gaseous oxygen system.

Avionics and Equipment: C-101EB and BB as listed in earlier *Jane's*. Standard C-101CC equipped with Magnavox AN/ARC-164 UHF com, Collins 21B VHF com, Collins VIR-31A VOR/ILS, Collins DME-40, Collins ADF-60, Andrea AN/AIC-18 interphone, Teledyne/CASA AN/APX-101 IFF/SIF, Sperry ZC-222 flight director, Sperry AS-339 gyro platform, ADI-500C, RD-550A HSI, Avimo RGS2 gunsight (front and rear cockpit), and CASA SCAR-81 armament control system. Wide range of alternative avionics and equipment available for export versions, including a Maverick pod, and (in the DD), a Ferranti FD4503 head-up display and weapon aiming computer, Ferranti FIN 1100 AHRS, General Instrument AN/ALR-66 radar warning receiver, GEC Avionics AD 6601-12 Doppler velocity sensor, TRT AHV-8 radio altimeter, Collins AN/ARC-182(V) UHF/VHF-AM/FM com, Ferranti FD 5000 video camera, Vinten Vicon 78 chaff and flare dispenser and Ferranti FD2062 rear seat monitor.

Armament and Operational Equipment: Large bay below rear cockpit suitable for quick-change packages, including 30 mm DEFA cannon pod, a twin 12·7 mm M3 machine-gun pod, reconnaissance camera, ECM package or laser designator. Six underwing hardpoints, capacities 500 kg (1,102 lb) inboard, 375 kg (827 lb) centre and 250 kg (551 lb) outboard; total external stores load 2,250 kg (4,960 lb). Typical armament can include one 30 mm cannon with up to 130 rds, or two 12·7 mm guns, in the fuselage; and four LAU-10 pods of 5 in rockets, six 250 kg BR250 bombs, four LAU-3/A rocket launchers, four 125 kg BR125 bombs and two LAU-3/A launchers, two AGM-65 Maverick missiles, or four BIN200 napalm bombs.

Dimensions, external:
Wing span 10·60 m (34 ft 9⅜ in)
Wing chord: at c/l 2·36 m (7 ft 9 in)
at tip 1·41 m (4 ft 7½ in)
Wing aspect ratio 5·6
Length overall 12·50 m (41 ft 0 in)
Height overall 4·25 m (13 ft 11¼ in)
Tailplane span 4·32 m (14 ft 2 in)
Wheel track (c/l of shock struts) 3·18 m (10 ft 5¼ in)
Wheelbase 4·77 m (15 ft 7¾ in)

Areas:
Wings, gross 20·00 m² (215·3 sq ft)
Ailerons (total) 1·18 m² (12·70 sq ft)
Trailing-edge flaps (total) 2·50 m² (26·91 sq ft)
Fin 2·10 m² (22·60 sq ft)
Rudder 1·10 m² (11·84 sq ft)
Tailplane 3·44 m² (37·03 sq ft)
Elevators 1·00 m² (10·76 sq ft)

Weights and Loadings:
Weight empty, equipped 3,340 kg (7,666 lb)
Max fuel weight 1,932 kg (4,260 lb)
Max external stores load 2,250 kg (4,960 lb)
T-O weight:
trainer, 'clean': BB, CC 4,850 kg (10,692 lb)
DD 4,570 kg (10,075 lb)

CASA C-101CC Aviojet (Garrett TFE731-5 turbofan engine) *(Air Portraits)*

ground attack: BB 5,600 kg (12,345 lb)
CC, DD 6,300 kg (13,890 lb)
Max landing weight:
3·66 m (12 ft)/s sink rate 4,700 kg (10,361 lb)
3·05 m (10 ft)/s sink rate 5,400 kg (11,905 lb)
Wing loading:
trainer, 'clean': BB, CC 242·5 kg/m² (46·69 lb/sq ft)
DD 228·5 kg/m² (46·82 lb/sq ft)
ground attack: BB 280·0 kg/m² (57·38 lb/sq ft)
CC, DD 315·0 kg/m² (64·55 lb/sq ft)
Power loading:
trainer 'clean': BB 294·9 kg/kN (2·89 lb/lb st)
CC (normal) 254·1 kg/kN (2·49 lb/lb st)
CC (with MPR) 231·6 kg/kN (2·27 lb/lb st)
DD (normal) 238·8 kg/kN (2·34 lb/lb st)
DD (with MPR) 218·4 kg/kN (2·14 lb/lb st)
ground attack: BB 340·8 kg/kN (3·34 lb/lb st)
CC, DD (normal) 329·6 kg/kN (3·23 lb/lb st)
CC, DD (with MPR) 301·0 kg/kN (2·95 lb/lb st)

Performance (C-101BB at 4,400 kg; 9,700 lb AUW, C-101CC and DD at 4,500 kg; 9,921 lb):
Max limiting Mach No. (all) Mach 0·80
Never-exceed speed (all)
450 knots (834 km/h; 518 mph) IAS
Max level speed at S/L:
BB 373 knots (691 km/h; 430 mph)
CC 415 knots (769 km/h; 478 mph)
Max level speed at height:
BB at 7,620 m (25,000 ft)
430 knots (797 km/h; 495 mph)
CC and DD at 6,100 m (20,000 ft)
435 knots (806 km/h; 501 mph)
CC and DD at 4,575 m (15,000 ft) with MPR
450 knots (834 km/h; 518 mph)
Econ cruising speed at 9,145 m (30,000 ft) (all)
Mach 0·60 (354 knots; 656 km/h; 407 mph)
Unstick speed (all) 115 knots (213 km/h; 132 mph)
Touchdown speed (all) 95 knots (176 km/h; 109 mph)
Stalling speed (all):
flaps up 99 knots (183 km/h; 114 mph) IAS
flaps down 88 knots (164 km/h; 102 mph) IAS
Max rate of climb at S/L: BB 1,152 m (3,780 ft)/min
CC and DD (normal) 1,494 m (4,900 ft)/min
CC and DD (with MPR) 1,859 m (6,100 ft)/min
Time to 7,620 m (25,000 ft): BB 8 min 30 s
CC, DD 6 min 30 s
Service ceiling: BB 12,200 m (40,000 ft)
CC, DD 12,800 m (42,000 ft)
T-O run: BB 630 m (2,065 ft)
CC, DD 560 m (1,835 ft)
T-O to 15 m (50 ft): BB 850 m (2,790 ft)
CC, DD 750 m (2,460 ft)
Landing from 15 m (50 ft) (all) 800 m (2,625 ft)
Landing run (all) 480 m (1,575 ft)
Typical interdiction radius (lo-lo-lo) with four 250 kg bombs and 30 mm gun:
CC and DD, 3 min over target, 30 min reserves
280 nm (519 km; 322 miles)
Typical close air support radius (lo-lo-lo):
CC and DD with four 19 × 2·75 in rocket launchers and 30 mm gun, 50 min loiter over battle area, 8 min over target, 30 min reserves
200 nm (370 km; 230 miles)
CC and DD, load as above plus two 125 kg bombs, 30 min loiter, 10 min attack (MPR thrust) and 7% reserves 170 nm (315 km; 196 miles)
CC and DD with two Maverick missiles and 30 mm gun, 8 min over target, 30 min reserves
325 nm (602 km; 374 miles)
Typical ECM radius:
BB and CC, 3 h 15 min loiter over target, 30 min reserves 330 nm (611 km; 380 miles)
Typical photo-reconnaissance radius (hi-lo-lo):
BB and CC, 30 min reserves
520 nm (964 km; 599 miles)
Armed patrol, no underwing stores, 100 nm (185 km; 115 mile) transit from base to patrol area:
BB, CC and DD with one 30 mm or two 12·7 mm guns, 45 min reserves
3 h 30 min at 200 knots (370 km/h; 230 mph) at S/L
Ferry range (all), 30 min reserves
2,000 nm (3,706 km; 2,303 miles)
Typical training mission endurance (all):
two 1 h 10 min general handling missions, incl aerobatics, with 20 min reserves after second mission
Max endurance (all) 7 h
g limits (all):
at 4,800 kg (10,582 lb) AUW +7·5/−3·9
at 6,300 kg (13,890 lb) AUW +5·5/−1

CASA E.26 TAMIZ (SIEVE)

Spanish Air Force designation: E.26 Tamiz

Under a reciprocal agreement with ENAER of Chile (which see), CASA is assembling 40 T-35C Pillán trainers (generally similar to the T-35A) ordered for the Spanish Air Force in 1984. These are known as the E.26 Tamiz in Spanish Air Force service.

SWEDEN

FIBRA

FIBRA AB

Ellesta, S-610 56 Vrena
Managing Director: Göran Ulfvengren
Public Relations: Richard Ulfvengren

FIBRA 8

This tandem two-seat design by Mr Sven-Olof Ridder was publicised at the 1985 Paris Air Show as a 'proficiency trainer', powered by a 559 kW (750 shp) turboprop engine of unspecified type. Intended to be built almost entirely of fibre composites, it bears some resemblance to the Windex 1100 motor glider (see Radab entry in the Sailplanes section), but has 32° sweptback, 4° anhedral wings, sweptback anhedral horizontal tail surfaces, a swept fin and rudder, and a small underfin. The engine drives a propeller mounted concentrically on a driveshaft in the rear of the fuselage, just forward of the tail unit.

The project was still in the R & D stage in early 1986, but the following brief details have been quoted:

Dimensions, external:
Wing span 8·00 m (26 ft 3 in)
Wing chord: at root 1·943 m (6 ft 4½ in)

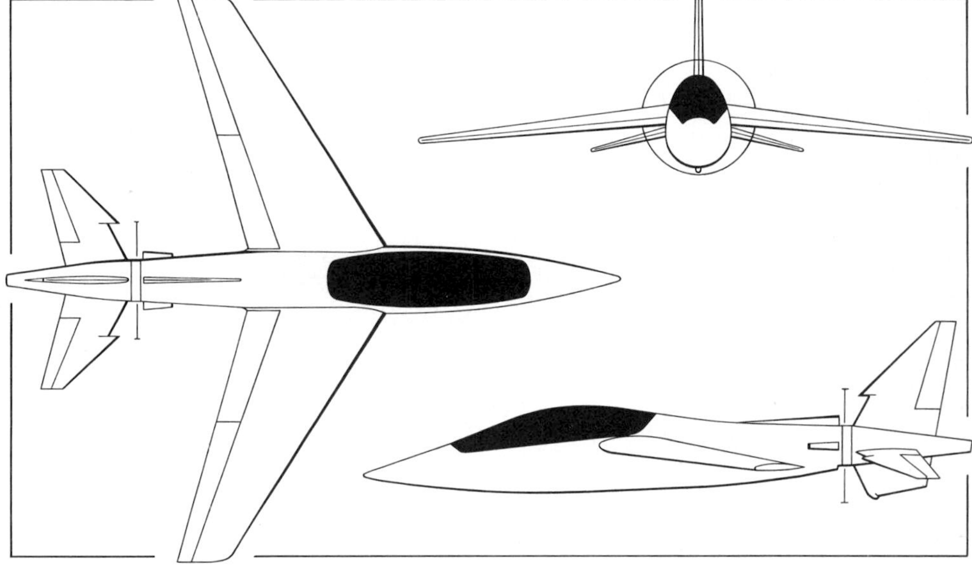

Provisional drawing of the proposed Fibra 8 proficiency trainer *(Jane's/Mike Keep)*

at tip	0·70 m (2 ft 3½ in)
Wing aspect ratio	5·98
Length overall	8·40 m (27 ft 6¾ in)
Height overall	2·40 m (7 ft 10½ in)

AREA:

Wings, gross	10·70 m² (115·2 sq ft)

WEIGHT:

Max T-O weight	1,000 kg (2,205 lb)

PERFORMANCE (estimated):

Max level speed	351 knots (650 km/h; 404 mph)
Stalling speed	65 knots (120 km/h; 75 mph)
T-O run	75 m (246 ft)

NYGE-AERO

AB NYGE-AERO

Box 321, S-611 27 Nyköping
Telephone: 0155 176 00
Telex: 64004
DIRECTOR: Åke Svensson

NYGE-AERO VLA-1 SPARROW

Prototype Nyge-Aero VLA-1 Sparrow two-seat light aircraft

The VLA-1 (Very Light Aircraft) was announced in early 1984 as a lightweight, economical two-seater for training and sport flying. Production was expected to start in 1985.

TYPE: Tandem two-seat light aircraft.

WINGS: Strut braced high-wing monoplane. Constant chord all-metal wings, with conventional control surfaces.

FUSELAGE: Semi-monocoque all-metal structure of pod and boom configuration. Centre-fuselage of rugged frame construction to absorb loads from landing gear, wings and power plant.

TAIL UNIT: Conventional all-metal cruciform surfaces. Rectangular planform tailplane and elevators; angular fin, dorsal fin and rudder.

LANDING GEAR: Non-retractable tricycle type, plus tailskid under rear fuselage. Main units have rubber cord shock absorption and are mounted on cantilever steel tube legs, attached to centre-fuselage frame. Hydraulic disc brakes on mainwheels. Castoring nosewheel, with plate spring shock absorption.

POWER PLANT: One 59·6 kW (80 hp) Duncan-Wankel SR-120R watercooled rotating-piston engine in prototype, installed above and behind cockpits and driving a two-blade pusher propeller. Dual electronic ignition system, with Bosch electric starter, and fuel injection. Change of engine anticipated in production version. Fuel capacity 49 litres (11 Imp gallons; 13 US gallons); engine can run on automotive fuel. An Eberspächer fuel heater (which can also be used to pre-heat the engine) is optional.

ACCOMMODATION: Seats for two persons in tandem under sideways opening framed Plexiglas canopy. One-piece wraparound windscreen. Seats are shaped from sheet metal and fitted with removable upholstery. Cockpits heated by air from engine cooling system.

EQUIPMENT: 35A Mazda alternator to power engine starting system.

DIMENSIONS, EXTERNAL:

Wing span	10·44 m (34 ft 3 in)
Length overall	7·32 m (24 ft 0 in)
Fuselage: Max width	0·76 m (2 ft 6 in)
Height overall	2·54 m (8 ft 4 in)

WEIGHTS:

Standard weight empty	385 kg (848 lb)
Max T-O weight	590 kg (1,300 lb)

PERFORMANCE (prototype, preliminary):

Cruising speed (75% power)	70 knots (130 km/h; 80 mph)
Stalling speed	40 knots (74 km/h; 46 mph)
Max rate of climb at S/L	183 m (600 ft)/min
T-O run	152 m (500 ft)
T-O to 15 m (50 ft)	305 m (1,000 ft)
Landing from 15 m (50 ft)	244 m (800 ft)
Landing run	122 m (400 ft)

SAAB-SCANIA

SAAB-SCANIA AKTIEBOLAG

S-581 88 Linköping
Telephone: 46 13 18 00 02
Telex: 50040 SAABLG S
PRESIDENT: Georg Karnsund

Saab Aircraft Division
Telephone: 46 13 18 00 02
GENERAL MANAGER OF DIVISION: Harald Schröder
DIRECTOR OF COMMERCIAL AIRCRAFT SECTOR: Thure Svensson
DIRECTOR OF MILITARY AIRCRAFT SECTOR: Tommy Ivarsson
DIRECTOR OF COLLABORATIVE PROGRAMMES SECTOR: Stellan Eklöf
PROJECT LEADER, JAS 39: Ingemar Nycander
PROGRAMME DIRECTOR, SF 340: Tomy Hjorth
DIRECTOR, SF 340 PRODUCT SUPPORT: K. Ahlborg
SENIOR CONSULTANT, PUBLIC RELATIONS: Hans G. Andersson
PUBLIC AFFAIRS MANAGER: Rolf Erichs
WORKS: Linköping, Malmö, Ödeshog, Norrköping and Kramfors
SF 340 MARKETING:
Saab Aircraft International Ltd, Leworth House, 14-16 Sheet Street, Windsor, Berkshire SL4 1BG, England
Telephone: (0753) 859991
Telex: 847 815 SFIWIN G
Saab Aircraft of America Inc, 200 Fairbrook Drive, Herndon, Virginia 22070, USA
Telephone: (703) 478 9720
Telecopier: (703) 478 9727
VICE-PRESIDENT, PUBLIC RELATIONS AND PROMOTIONAL SERVICES: Mike Savage

The original Svenska Aeroplan AB was founded at Trollhättan in 1937 for the production of military aircraft. In 1939 this company was amalgamated with the Aircraft Division (ASJA) of the Svenska Järnvägsverkstäderna rolling stock factory in Linköping. Following this merger, Saab moved its head office and engineering departments to Linköping, which is now the main aerospace factory. The company's name was changed to Saab Aktiebolag in May 1965.

Post-war expansions include a bombproof underground factory in Linköping, as well as important new production and engineering facilities in Linköping, Jönköping, Trollhättan and Gothenburg.

During 1968 Saab merged with Scania-Vabis, to strengthen the two companies' position in automotive product development, production and export. Malmö Flygindustri (MFI) was acquired in the same year.

Saab-Scania has more than 47,000 employees, organised in three operating divisions and two major subsidiaries (Saab-Scania Combitech and Saab-Scania Enertech). Of these, nearly 6,500 are employed by the Saab Aircraft Division, including 5,500 at Linköping.

Saab-Scania's current aerospace activities include production of the JA 37 Viggen supersonic STOL combat aircraft and SF 340A airliner, and development of the Saab JAS 39 Gripen multi-role combat aircraft. Since 1949 the company has delivered more than 2,000 military jet aircraft to the air forces of four nations, and in 1985 received an order to refurbish 24 former Swedish Air Force Saab 35 Drakens for delivery to the Austrian Air Force. It has also delivered more than 1,500 piston engined aircraft to military and civil customers around the world. Since 1962, Saab-Scania has had a dealership for McDonnell Douglas (Hughes) helicopters in Scandinavia and Finland. Since 1978, it has manufactured inboard wing flaps and vanes for the McDonnell Douglas MD-80 series, and now also produces composite spoilers for the MD-82/83; it is currently also manufacturing tailplanes, elevators, rudders, ailerons and spoilers for the British Aerospace 146 four-turbofan feederliner.

In January 1980 Saab-Scania and Fairchild Industries announced that they had signed an agreement to jointly develop, produce and market a new transport aircraft. Known originally as the Saab-Fairchild 340A, it was the first collaborative venture of this kind between members of the European and US aerospace industries, and is certificated to both FAR and JAR standards. Following a major restructuring of Fairchild's aircraft manufacturing activities, Saab-Scania took over complete control of the programme in November 1985. Fairchild, which had previously been responsible for the wings and tail unit, is, however, remaining in the programme as a subcontractor until early 1987, up to and including the 108th production aircraft. In 1986 Saab was preparing to take over the manufacture of the whole aircraft, now known as the Saab SF 340A. A 25,000 m² (269,100 sq ft) factory at Linköping, for final assembly of the SF 340A, was completed in July 1982; an extension to this facility, to accommodate also the wing and tail unit production, was inaugurated on 26 June 1986.

Saab-Scania has greatly expanded its activities in the electronics field in recent years. Current production items include computer systems, autopilots, fire control and bombing systems for piloted aircraft, and electronics for guided missiles. A major production programme is the airborne computer for the Saab 37. The Saab RGS2 lead-computing optical sighting system was selected for the Royal Netherlands Air Force Northrop NF-5A, the Italian Air Force Aermacchi MB-339A, and British Aerospace Hawks for the Finnish Air Force. Spaceborne computers, optronic fire control systems and field artillery computer systems are also under development and in production.

Saab-Scania's guided missile activities are now conducted by its subsidiary, Saab Missiles AB. The RBS 15 anti-ship weapon is now in quantity production.

SAAB SF 340A

First details of this twin-turboprop transport aircraft were announced in January 1980. Engine selection was announced in June, and the project definition phase was completed in September 1980, when agreement was reached for a full go-ahead on joint design, development, production and marketing programmes.

Design emphasis is on simplicity of systems, operation and maintenance, with quick turnarounds made possible by a number of built-in features to make the aircraft independent of ground handling equipment. It is designed specially for short-haul low-density routes, and is available in both airliner and corporate transport versions, with General Electric CT7-5A2 engines.

Flight testing of the CT7 engine and Dowty Rotol composite propellers began in September 1982, in a Gulfstream I testbed aircraft. The first prototype SF 340 (SE-ISF) made its first flight on 25 January 1983; it was followed on 11 May by the second prototype (SE-ISA), and by the third aircraft (SE-ISB) on 25 August 1983. Static and fatigue test airframes were completed in the USA and Sweden respectively.

The fourth (first production) SF 340A (SE-E04) flew for the first time on 5 March 1984, and Swedish type certification was awarded on 30 May 1984. The certification was ratified by nine other European countries and the US FAA on 29 June 1984. First delivery, of the fifth aircraft, was to Crossair of Switzerland, with whom the 340A entered scheduled service on 14 June 1984; the sixth aircraft was delivered in July to Comair, the first US customer, and entered service in August 1984. The first corporate 340A was delivered, to Mellon Bank of Pittsburgh, Pennsylvania, in November 1985. Meanwhile, engine power rating was increased from 1,215 kW (1,630 shp) to 1,294 kW (1,735 shp) from mid-1985, and aircraft already delivered are being modified to the new standard, with propellers of increased diameter. Market studies for a possible 'stretched' version were being undertaken in 1986.

By 13 June 1986 firm orders totalled 97, of which approximately half were from US customers; the remainder were from operators in Europe, the Middle East, Asia/Australasia and Latin America. A total of 65 SF 340As had been delivered by 30 September 1986, and were in service with eight airlines and three corporate customers.

TYPE: Twin-turboprop transport aircraft.

WINGS: Cantilever low-wing monoplane. Basic wing section NASA MS(1)-0313 with thickness/chord ratios of 16% and 12% at root and tip respectively. Dihedral 7° from roots. Incidence 2° at root. Sweepback 3° 36′ at quarter-chord. Tapered two-spar wings embodying fail-safe principles. Stringers and skins of 2024/7075 aluminium alloy. Wing-root/fuselage fairings of Kevlar sandwich. Hydraulically actuated single-slotted trailing-edge flaps with aluminium alloy spars, honeycomb panels faced with aluminium sheet, and leading/trailing-edges of

Saab SF 340A twin-turboprop transport in the insignia of Crossair of Switzerland, seen here flying over Hong Kong

Kevlar. Ailerons have Kevlar skins and glassfibre leading-edges. Electrically operated geared/trim tab in each aileron. Pneumatic boot de-icing of leading-edges.

FUSELAGE: Conventional fail-safe/safe-life semi-monocoque pressurised metal structure, of circular cross-section. Built in three portions: nose (incl flight deck), passenger compartment, and tail section (incorporating baggage compartment). All doors of aluminium honeycomb. Nosecone of Kevlar; cabin floor of carbonfibre sandwich.

TAIL UNIT: Cantilever structure, with sweptback vertical and non-swept horizontal surfaces, the latter having marked dihedral. Fin integral with fuselage. Construction similar to that of wings, with tailplane and fin of aluminium honeycomb. Rudder and elevators have Kevlar skins and glassfibre leading-edges. Geared/trim tab in each elevator; spring/trim tab in rudder. Pneumatic boot de-icing of fin and tailplane leading-edges.

LANDING GEAR: Retractable tricycle type, of AP Precision Hydraulics design and manufacture, with twin Goodyear wheels and oleo-pneumatic shock absorber on each unit. Hydraulic actuation. All units retract forward, main units into engine nacelles. Mainwheel doors of Kevlar sandwich. Hydraulically steerable nose unit (60° to left and right), with shimmy damper. Mainwheel tyres size 24 × 7·7-10, pressure 6·89 bars (100 lb/sq in); nosewheel tyres size 18 × 6·0-6, pressure 3·79 bars (55 lb/sq in). Independent Goodyear carbon hydraulic disc brakes on main units, with anti-skid control.

POWER PLANT: Two General Electric CT7-5A turboprop engines, each rated at 1,215 kW (1,630 shp) initially; CT7-5A2 engines rated at 1,294 kW (1,735 shp) since mid-1985. Dowty Rotol four-blade slow-turning constant-speed propellers, each with spinner and glassfibre/polyurethane foam/carbonfibre moulded blades. Fuel in two integral tanks in each outer wing; total capacity 3,220 litres (708 Imp gallons). Single-point pressure refuelling inlet in starboard outer wing panel. Overwing gravity refuelling point in each wing.

ACCOMMODATION: Two pilots and provision for observer on flight deck; attendant's seat (forward, port) in passenger cabin. Main cabin accommodates up to 35 passengers, in eleven rows of three, with aisle, and two rearward facing seats on starboard side at front. One rearward facing seat can be replaced by an optional galley module or baggage/wardrobe module; the two modules can replace both seats. Seat pitch 76 cm (30 in). Standard provision for galley, wardrobe or storage module on port side at front of cabin, regardless of installations on starboard side. Movable bulkhead aft of last row of seats. Toilet at front or rear of cabin. Aircraft can be converted quickly to various passenger/freight combinations (eg, 15 passengers and 1,814 kg; 4,000 lb of cargo). A corporate/executive version is also in production. Passenger door at front of cabin on port side, with separate airstair. Type II emergency exit opposite this on starboard side; Type III emergency exit over wing on each side. Overhead crew escape hatch in flight deck roof. Baggage space under each passenger seat; overhead storage bins. Main baggage/cargo compartment aft of passenger cabin, with large door on port side. Entire accommodation pressurised, including baggage compartment.

SYSTEMS: Hamilton Standard environmental control system (max pressure differential 0·48 bars; 7·0 lb/sq in) maintains a S/L cabin environment up to an altitude of 3,660 m (12,000 ft) and a 1,525 m (5,000 ft) environment up to the max cruising altitude of 7,620 m (25,000 ft). Single on-demand hydraulic system, operating between 138 and 207 bars (2,000-3,000 lb/sq in), for actuation of landing gear, wheel and propeller braking, nosewheel steering and wing flaps. System is powered by single 28V DC electric motor driven pump, rated delivery 9·5 litres (2·1 Imp gallons)/min. Self-pressurising main reservoir with 5·08 litres (310 cu in) capacity, operating at pressure of 1·79-2·69 bars (26-39 lb/sq in). Hydraulic backup via four accumulators and pilot operated handpump, working via an emergency reservoir of 2·5 litres (150 cu in) capacity. Electrical power supplied by two 28V 400A DC engine driven starter/generators, each connected to a separate busbar. One main solid state inverter provides fixed frequency 26/115V AC power at 400Hz. Two 43Ah nickel-cadmium batteries for ground power and engine starting. Pneumatic boot de-icing of wing and tail unit leading-edges, using engine bleed air. Flight deck windows have electric anti-icing and electrically driven windscreen wipers. Electric anti-icing is provided also for engine air intakes, propellers and pitot heads. Demisting by means of air-conditioning system. Plug-in connections for oxygen masks. Kidde engine fire detection system. Duncan/Garrett GTCP 36-150W APU kit certificated for installation as optional extra, to provide standby and emergency electrical power, main engine starting assistance, ground pre-heating and pre-cooling, and other power support functions.

AVIONICS AND EQUIPMENT: Standard avionics include all equipment required for FAR Pt 121 operations. The aircraft is equipped with King Gold Crown III or Collins Pro Line II com/nav radios, and a Collins integrated digital flight guidance and autopilot system (FGAS) consisting of attitude and heading reference units, electronic (CRT) flight display units, fail-passive autopilot/flight director system, colour weather radar, air data system with servo instruments, and radio altimeter. Lucas Aerospace electroluminescent flight deck instrument panel array. Dowty Electronics microprocessor-based flight deck central warning system. Rosemount pitot static tubes, total temperature sensors and stall warning system. Provision for additional avionics to customer's requirements. Landing light in each wing leading-edge.

DIMENSIONS, EXTERNAL:

Wing span	21·44 m (70 ft 4 in)
Wing chord: at root	2·837 m (9 ft 3·7 in)
at tip	1·0645 m (3 ft 5·9 in)
Wing aspect ratio	11
Length overall	19·72 m (64 ft 8½ in)
Fuselage: Max diameter	2·31 m (7 ft 7 in)
Height overall	6·86 m (22 ft 6 in)
Wheel track	6·71 m (22 ft 0 in)
Wheelbase	7·14 m (23 ft 5 in)
Propeller diameter: initially	3·20 m (10 ft 6 in)
current	3·35 m (11 ft 0 in)
Propeller ground clearance	0·58 m (1 ft 11 in)
Distance between propeller centres	6·71 m (22 ft 0 in)
Passenger door: Height	1·60 m (5 ft 3 in)
Width	0·69 m (2 ft 3 in)
Height to sill	1·63 m (5 ft 4 in)
Cargo door: Height	1·30 m (4 ft 3¼ in)
Width	1·35 m (4 ft 5 in)
Height to sill	1·68 m (5 ft 6¼ in)
Emergency exit (fwd, stbd):	
Height	1·32 m (4 ft 4 in)
Width	0·51 m (1 ft 8 in)
Emergency exits (overwing, each):	
Height	0·91 m (3 ft 0 in)
Width	0·51 m (1 ft 8 in)

DIMENSIONS, INTERNAL:

Cabin, excl flight deck, incl toilet and galley:	
Length	10·39 m (34 ft 1 in)
Max width	2·16 m (7 ft 1 in)
Width at floor	1·70 m (5 ft 7 in)
Max height	1·83 m (6 ft 0 in)
Baggage/cargo compartment volume	6·8 m³ (240·0 cu ft)

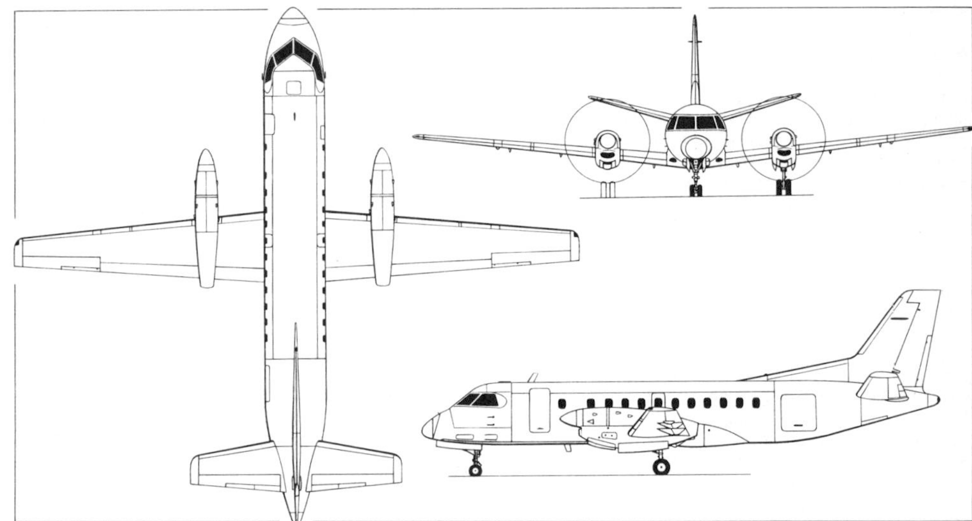

Saab SF 340A airliner (two General Electric CT7-5A2 turboprop engines) *(Pilot Press)*

AREAS:

Wings, gross	41·81 m² (450·0 sq ft)
Ailerons (total)	2·12 m² (22·84 sq ft)
Trailing-edge flaps (total)	8·07 m² (86·84 sq ft)
Fin, incl dorsal fin	10·53 m² (113·38 sq ft)
Rudder, incl tab	2·76 m² (29·71 sq ft)
Tailplane	13·30 m² (143·16 sq ft)
Elevators (total, incl tabs)	3·29 m² (35·40 sq ft)

WEIGHTS AND LOADINGS:

Typical operating weight empty	7,899 kg (17,415 lb)
Max payload (weight limited)	3,440 kg (7,585 lb)
Max fuel load	2,581 kg (5,690 lb)
Max ramp weight	12,383 kg (27,300 lb)
Max T-O weight	12,372 kg (27,275 lb)
Max landing weight	12,020 kg (26,500 lb)
Max zero-fuel weight	11,340 kg (25,000 lb)
Max wing loading	295·8 kg/m² (60·61 lb/sq ft)
Max power loading	4·78 kg/kW (7·86 lb/shp)

PERFORMANCE (at max T-O weight, ISA, except where indicated):

Max operating speed (VMO) 250 knots (463 km/h; 288 mph) IAS

Max operating Mach No. (MMO) 0·5

Max cruising speed at 4,575 m (15,000 ft), AUW of 11,793 kg (26,000 lb) 272 knots (504 km/h; 313 mph)

Best range cruising speed at 7,620 m (25,000 ft) 250 knots (463 km/h; 288 mph)

Stalling speed: 0° flap 104 knots (193 km/h; 120 mph)

T-O flap setting 93 knots (173 km/h; 107 mph)

approach flap setting 87 knots (162 km/h; 101 mph)

landing flap setting 82 knots (152 km/h; 95 mph)

Max rate of climb at S/L 548 m (1,800 ft)/min

Rate of climb at S/L, one engine out 167 m (550 ft)/min

Service ceiling 7,620 m (25,000 ft)

Service ceiling, one engine out (net) 3,475 m (11,400 ft)

FAR Pt 25 required T-O field length:

at S/L, ISA 1,215 m (3,980 ft)

at S/L, ISA +15°C 1,295 m (4,250 ft)

at 1,525 m (5,000 ft), ISA 1,495 m (4,900 ft)

at 1,525 m (5,000 ft), ISA +15°C 1,935 m (6,350 ft)

FAR Pt 25 landing field length at max landing weight, ISA: at S/L 1,140 m (3,740 ft)

at 1,525 m (5,000 ft) 1,262 m (4,140 ft)

Min ground turning radius 15·85 m (52 ft 0 in)

Runway LCN: flexible pavement 8

rigid pavement 10

Range with 35 passengers and baggage, reserves for 45 min hold at 1,525 m (5,000 ft) and 100 nm (185 km; 115 mile) diversion 500 nm (926 km; 576 miles)

TYPICAL MISSION PERFORMANCE (200 nm; 370 km; 230 mile stage with 35 passengers and baggage, T-O weight of 11,791 kg; 25,995 lb):

Block speed at 5,180 m (17,000 ft) 210 knots (389 km/h; 242 mph)

Required T-O field length (S/L, ISA) 1,075 m (3,525 ft)

Block fuel 424 kg (935 lb)

Reserve fuel for 100 nm (185 km; 115 mile) diversion and 45 min hold 461 kg (1,016 lb)

Block time 57 min

OPERATIONAL NOISE LEVELS (FAR Pt 36 and ICAO Annex 16):

T-O (with cutback)	77·1 EPNdB
Sideline	86·0 EPNdB
Approach	84·2 EPNdB

SAAB JAS 39 GRIPEN (GRIFFIN)

In June 1980 the Swedish government approved funding for project definition and initial development during 1980-82 of a Viggen replacement to enter service from about 1992. Known officially as the JAS 39 (Jakt/Attack/Spaning: fighter/attack/reconnaissance), this multi-role combat aircraft is intended to replace, successively, the AJ/SH/SF/JA 37 versions of the Viggen. A similar financial commitment was made by Industri Gruppen JAS, a Swedish aerospace industry group formed in 1980 by Saab-Scania, Volvo Flygmotor, Ericsson and FFV.

On 3 June 1981 the group submitted to the Swedish Defence Materiel Administration (FMV) its detailed proposals for an aircraft to meet the JAS requirement. The airframe then had the Saab project design number 2105 (since superseded by the slightly modified Saab 2110), and will be powered by a single General Electric F404J afterburning turbofan engine in the 80 kN (18,000 lb thrust) class developed and produced, as the RM12, in collaboration with Volvo Flygmotor.

Of similar aerodynamic configuration to the Viggen (see accompanying illustrations), with delta wings and all-moving foreplanes, the airframe will use some 30 per cent of composite materials, permitting weight savings of up to 25 per cent and enabling the normal T-O weight to be kept down to approx 8,000 kg (17,635 lb). Performance will include supersonic speed at all altitudes and, like the Viggen, the JAS 39 will be adapted to the specific Swedish defence profile, using ordinary roads as air bases as well as requiring only simple maintenance with turnaround service handled mainly by conscripts.

The FMV evaluated the Swedish industry proposals against aircraft from other countries, and recommended adoption of the Saab design. A procurement programme was agreed on 30 April 1982 between Industri Gruppen JAS and the FMV, and approved by the Swedish government on 6 May 1982. This covers the development and procurement of 140 aircraft by the year 2000. A JAS go-ahead was given by the Swedish parliament on 4 June 1982 as part of the next five-year (1982-87) defence plan, and a contract for the first 30 aircraft was signed on 30 June 1982. On 14 September 1982 a JA 37 Viggen testbed aircraft made its first flight equipped with the triplex fly by wire flight control system intended for the JAS 39. A second Viggen will join the programme as testbed for avionics and weapons systems. Overall programme go-ahead was confirmed in the Spring of 1983, and prototype construction began in 1984. First wing/fuselage mating was taking place in September 1986.

Five Gripen prototypes are being built, with first flight scheduled to take place in 1987, and entry into service in 1992.

The following description applies to the prototypes:

TYPE: Single-seat all-weather, all-altitude fighter, attack and reconnaissance aircraft.

AIRFRAME: Close-coupled canard configuration, with extensive use of composites in its construction. Cropped delta main wings, mid-mounted on fuselage, with leading-edge 'dog-tooth' and inboard and outboard elevons; swept-back all-moving foreplanes, mounted on upper sides of engine air intake trunks. BAe is collaborating with Saab-Scania on design and construction of the carbonfibre wings, and is manufacturing those for the first two prototypes. Fin and rudder; no horizontal tail surfaces. AP Precision Hydraulics retractable tricycle landing gear, mainwheels retracting forward and inward into fuselage; steerable twin nosewheel unit retracts rearward, turning through 90° to lie flat in underside of fuselage. Goodyear wheels, tyres, carbon disc brakes and anti-skid units.

POWER PLANT: One General Electric/Volvo Flygmotor RM12 (F404J) turbofan engine, rated in the 80 kN (18,000 lb st) class with afterburning. Wedge-shape intakes, each with splitter plate. Fuel in self-sealing main tank and collector tank in fuselage. Intertechnique fuel management system.

ACCOMMODATION: Pilot only, on Martin-Baker S10LS zero/zero ejection seat under 'teardrop' canopy. Canopy and one-piece wraparound windscreen by Lucas Aerospace. Design study for two-seat version, if required, has been carried out.

SYSTEMS: BAe environmental control system, for cockpit air-conditioning and pressurisation and cooling of avionics. Hughes-Treitler heat exchanger. Abex/Dowty hydraulic system. Sundstrand main electrical power generating system (40 kVA constant speed, constant frequency at 400Hz) comprises an integrated drive generator, generator control unit and current transformer assembly. Lear Siegler triple-redundant digital fly by wire flight control system, with Moog servo-actuators for primary flight control surfaces, Lucas Aerospace rotary actuators ('geared hinges') for leading-edge flaps, and Saab Combitech aircraft motion sensors and throttle actuator subsystem. Lucas Aerospace auxiliary and emergency power system, comprising a gearbox mounted turbine, hydraulic pump and AC generator. In emergency role, the turbine is driven by engine bleed or APU air; if this is not available the stored energy mode, using pressurised oxygen and methanol, is selected automatically. Microturbo TGA 15 APU and DA 15 air turbine starter. Two main and one auxiliary hydraulic systems, with Abex pumps.

AVIONICS: Bofors Aerotronics AMR 345 VHF/UHF-AM/FM com transceiver. Honeywell laser inertial navigation system. Advanced EP 17 electronic display system in cockpit, using one Hughes Aircraft diffraction optics head-up and three Ericsson head-down displays, with a Ferranti FD 5040 video camera, plus a minimum of conventional instruments for backup purposes only. The head-up display, using advanced diffraction optics, will present vital information within the pilot's line of vision. Left hand head-down display normally replaces all conventional flight instruments. Central display shows a computer generated map of the area surrounding the aircraft (indicating land, lakes, rivers, roads, population centres, and obstacles to low-level flying), on which tactical information is superimposed. Right hand presentation is a multi-sensor display for information from the radar and FLIR. An Ericsson D 80 onboard digital computer is part of the overall SDS 80 computing system which controls the aircraft's central computer, radar, electronic displays and other computer controlled systems, and allows for multi-mode use and flexibility for further development.

OPERATIONAL EQUIPMENT: Ericsson/Ferranti PS-05/A multi-mode pulse-Doppler target search and acquisition system, comprising a nose mounted radar and pod mounted forward-looking infra-red equipment (FLIR). For fighter missions, this system provides target search, and tracking of several targets at long range; wide angle quick-scanning and lock-on at short ranges; and fire control for missiles and cannon. In the attack and reconnaissance roles its operating functions are search against sea and ground targets; mapping, with normal and high resolution; fire control for missiles and other attack weapons; and obstacle avoidance and navigation. The pulse-Doppler radar is only some 60 per cent as large as current Swedish fighter radars but has three times the number of functions, is designed to detect targets at all altitudes and at longer ranges, and will have improved resistance to enemy ECM. It includes modes for surface surveillance, and is the basic part of the system for attack

Full scale mockup of the Saab JAS 39 Gripen multi-role air defence and attack aircraft

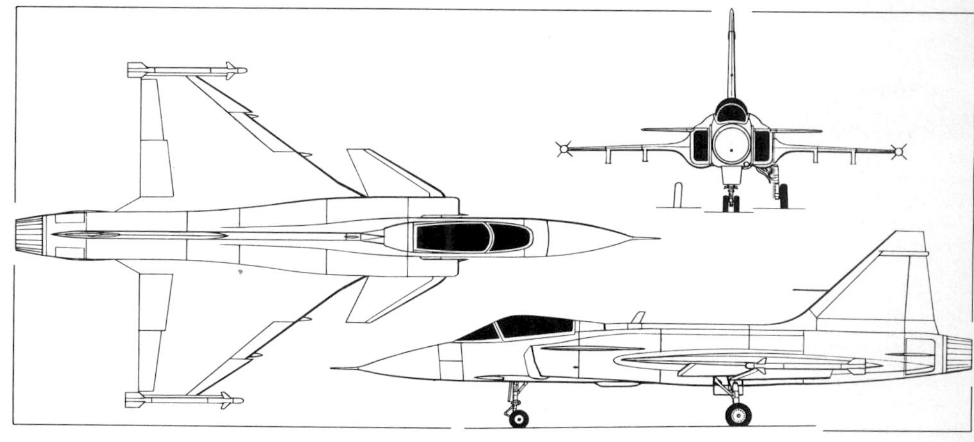

Saab JAS 39 Gripen multi-role combat aircraft for the Swedish Air Force *(Pilot Press)*

and reconnaissance missions. The FLIR pod, carried externally under the starboard engine air intake trunk, forward of the wing leading-edge, is used for attack and reconnaissance missions at night, providing a 'heat picture' of the target on the cockpit right hand electronic display. The JAS 39 will also carry advanced ECM, both built-in and externally.

ARMAMENT: Internally mounted 27 mm Mauser BK27 automatic cannon in fuselage. External attachment for FLIR pod under starboard intake (see preceding paragraph). Six other external hardpoints (two under each wing and one at each wingtip). Sidewinder, Sky Flash or other advanced infra-red or radar homing air-to-air missile on each wingtip station. Underwing stores can include Saab RBS 15F or other heavy anti-shipping missiles, electro-optically guided air-to-surface missiles and bombs, area weapons, or a day/night reconnaissance pod.

DIMENSIONS, EXTERNAL (approx):
Wing span 8·00 m (26 ft 3 in)
Length overall 14·00 m (45 ft 11 in)

WEIGHT (approx):
Normal max T-O weight 8,000 kg (17,635 lb)

PERFORMANCE:
Max level speed supersonic at all altitudes
T-O and landing strip length well below 1,000 m (3,280 ft)

SAAB JA 37 VIGGEN (THUNDERBOLT)

The Saab 37 Viggen multi-mission combat aircraft has been produced to fulfil the primary roles of attack, interception, reconnaissance and training. Its STOL characteristics enable it to operate from narrow runways of about 500 m (1,640 ft) length. By early 1986 Viggens (all versions) equipped 12 of the planned total of 17 Swedish Air Force squadrons.

The first of seven prototypes flew for the first time on 8 February 1967, and by April 1969 all six single-seat prototypes were flying. The seventh was the prototype for the two-seat SK 37 operational trainer.

Production deliveries of the AJ 37, SF 37, SH 37 and SK 37 versions, totalling 180 aircraft, have been completed. Details of these, and of the Saab 37X proposed export version, can be found in the 1980-81 and earlier editions of *Jane's*. The following version of the Viggen continues in production:

JA 37. Single-seat interceptor, with more powerful Volvo Flygmotor RM8B engine. Improved performance, and secondary capability for attack missions. Four elevon hydraulic actuators under each wing, instead of three as on other versions, and a modified, taller tail fin similar to that of the SK 37. Total of 149 ordered, to re-equip eight Draken fighter squadrons of the Swedish Air Force: two squadrons each of Wings F4, F16 and F21, and one each of F13 and F17. First flight by a production JA 37 (serial No. 301) was made on 4 November 1977. Deliveries, to a squadron of F13 Wing at Norrköping, began in 1979, and the 100th JA 37 was delivered on 20 August 1985. Improvements added since the JA 37's entry into service include new generation AIM-9L Sidewinder missiles, effective also against head-on targets, and an aircraft-to-aircraft communications system known as fighter link which makes possible efficient liaison between aircraft, even at night and in IMC conditions, regardless of their relative positions. Production is due to end in 1988.

TYPE: Single-seat all-weather multi-purpose combat aircraft.

WINGS: Tandem arrangement of delta foreplane, with trailing-edge flaps, and a rear mounted delta main wing with two-section hydraulically actuated powered elevons on each trailing-edge, which can be operated differentially or in unison. Main wing has compound sweep on leading-edge. Outer sections have extended leading-edge. Extensive use of metal bonded honeycomb panels for wing control surfaces, foreplane flaps and main landing gear doors.

FUSELAGE: Conventional all-metal semi-monocoque structure, using light metal forgings and heat resistant plastics bonding. Local use of titanium for engine firewall and other selected areas. Four plate type airbrakes, one on each side and two below fuselage. Metal bonded honeycomb construction is used to a large extent. Quick-release handle permits nosecone to be pulled forward on tracks to give access to radar compartment.

TAIL UNIT: Vertical surfaces only, comprising main fin and powered rudder, supplemented by a small ventral fin. Rudder of metal bonded honeycomb construction. The main fin can be folded downward to port. More than 20 fins for JA 37s are being made of composite materials, to gain experience in preparation for the JAS 39 programme.

LANDING GEAR: Retractable tricycle type of Saab origin, built by Motala Verkstad and designed for a max rate of sink of 5 m (16·4 ft)/s. Power steerable twin-wheel nose unit retracts forward. Each main unit has two mainwheels in tandem and retracts inward into main wing and fuselage. Main oleos shorten during retraction. Nosewheel tyres size 18 × 5·5, pressure 10·7 bars (155 lb/sq in). Mainwheel tyres size 26 × 6·6, pressure 14·8 bars (215 lb/sq in). Goodyear wheels and brakes. Dunlop anti-skid system.

POWER PLANT: One Volvo Flygmotor RM8B (supersonic development of the Pratt & Whitney JT8D-22) turbofan engine, fitted with a Swedish developed afterburner and thrust reverser. This engine is rated at 72·1 kN (16,203 lb st) dry and 125 kN (28,108 lb st) with afterburning. Thrust reverser doors are actuated automatically by compression of the oleo as the nose gear strikes the runway, the thrust being deflected forward via three annular slots in the ejector wall. The ejector is normally kept open at subsonic speeds to reduce fuselage base drag; at supersonic speeds, with the intake closed, the ejector serves as a supersonic nozzle. Fuel is contained in one tank in each wing, a saddle tank over the engine, one tank in each side of the fuselage, and one aft of the cockpit. Electrically powered pumps deliver fuel to the engine from the central fuselage tank, which is kept filled continuously from the peripheral tanks. Pressure refuelling point beneath starboard wing. Provision for jettisonable external auxiliary tank on underfuselage centreline pylon.

ACCOMMODATION: Pilot only, on Saab-Scania fully adjustable rocket assisted zero/zero ejection seat beneath rearward hinged clamshell canopy. Cockpit pressurisation, heating and air-conditioning by engine bleed air, via Delaney Gallay heat exchangers, cooling turbines and water separator. Birdproof windscreen.

SYSTEMS: Two independent hydraulic systems, each of 207 bars (3,000 lb/sq in) pressure, each with engine driven pump; bootstrap reservoir; auxiliary electrically operated standby pump for emergency use. Three-phase AC electrical system supplies 210/115V 400Hz power via a Westinghouse 75kVA liquid-cooled brushless generator, which also provides 28V DC power via 24V nickel-cadmium batteries and rectifier. Emergency standby power from 6kVA turbogenerator, which is extended automatically into the airstream in the event of a power failure. External power receptacle on port side of fuselage. Graviner fire detection system.

AVIONICS AND FLIGHT EQUIPMENT: Altogether, about 50 avionics units, with a total weight of approx 600 kg (1,323 lb), are installed in the Viggen. Flight equipment includes an automatic speed control system, a Smiths electronic head-up display, Bofors Aerotronics aircraft attitude instruments, radio and fighter link equipment, Singer-Kearfott SKC-2037 central digital computer, Garrett LD-5 digital air data computer, Singer-Kearfott KT-70L inertial measuring equipment, Honeywell/Saab-Scania SA07 digital automatic flight control system, Honeywell radar altimeter, Decca Doppler Type 72 navigation equipment, SATT radar warning system, Ericsson radar display system and electronic countermeasures, and AIL Tactical Instrument Landing System (TILS), a microwave scanning beam landing guidance system. Most avionics equipment is connected to the central digital computer, which is programmed to check out and monitor these systems both on the ground and during flight. Ram air intake on underfuselage centreline, for cooling avionics compartment.

ARMAMENT AND OPERATIONAL EQUIPMENT: Permanent underbelly pack, offset to port side of centreline, containing one 30 mm Oerlikon KCA long-range cannon with 150 rounds, a muzzle velocity of 1,050 m (3,445 ft)/s, a rate of fire of 1,350 rds/min, and a projectile weight of 0·36 kg (0·79 lb). Improved fire control equipment. This gun installation permits retention of the three underfuselage stores attachment points, in addition to the four underwing hardpoints. Advanced target search and acquisition system, based on a high performance long-range L.M. Ericsson UAP-1023 I/J-band pulse-Doppler radar which is unaffected by variations of weather and

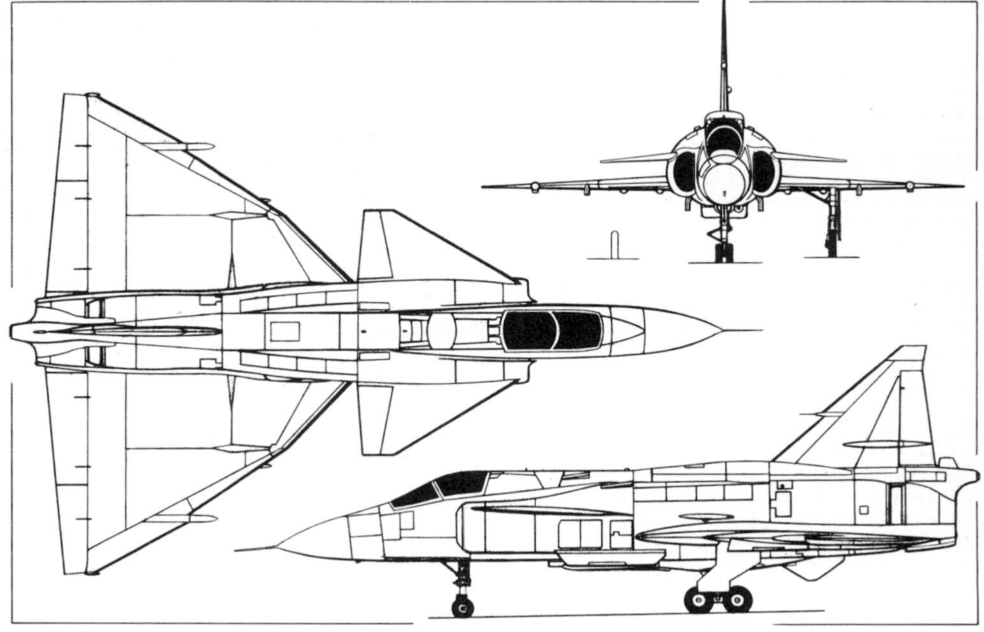

Saab JA 37 Viggen single-seat interceptor *(Pilot Press)*

Saab JA 37 Viggens of F13 Wing, Swedish Air Force, at Norrköping, in new blue-grey finish

altitude. This radar is not disturbed by ground clutter, and is highly resistant to ECM. Armament can include two BAe Sky Flash (Swedish designation RB71) and six AIM-9L Sidewinder (RB74) air-to-air missiles. For air-to-surface attack, a total of twenty-four 135 mm rockets can be carried in four pods.

DIMENSIONS, EXTERNAL:
- Main wing span: 10·60 m (34 ft 9¼ in)
- Main wing aspect ratio: 2·45
- Foreplane span: 5·45 m (17 ft 10½ in)
- Length overall (incl probe): 16·40 m (53 ft 9¾ in)
- Length of fuselage: 15·58 m (51 ft 1½ in)
- Height overall: 5·90 m (19 ft 4¼ in)
- Height overall, main fin folded: 4·00 m (13 ft 1½ in)
- Wheel track: 4·76 m (15 ft 7½ in)
- Wheelbase (c/l of shock absorbers): 5·69 m (18 ft 8 in)

AREAS:
- Main wings, gross: 46·00 m² (495·1 sq ft)
- Foreplanes, outside fuselage: 6·20 m² (66·74 sq ft)

WEIGHTS (approx):
- T-O weight: 'clean': 15,000 kg (33,070 lb)
- with normal armament: 17,000 kg (37,478 lb)

PERFORMANCE:
- Max level speed: at high altitude: above Mach 2
- at 100 m (300 ft): Mach 1·2
- Approach speed: approx 119 knots (220 km/h; 137 mph)
- Time to 10,000 m (32,800 ft) from brakes off, with afterburning: less than 1 min 40 s
- T-O run: approx 400 m (1,310 ft)
- Landing run: approx 500 m (1,640 ft)
- Required landing field length:
  - conventional landing: 1,000 m (3,280 ft)
  - no-flare landing: 500 m (1,640 ft)
- Tactical radius with external armament:
  - hi-lo-hi: over 540 nm (1,000 km; 620 miles)
  - lo-lo-lo: over 270 nm (500 km; 310 miles)

SAAB J 32E LANSEN

Details of this extensively modified electronic warfare and countermeasures version of the Lansen were released in 1985. It equips F13M target flying squadron of the Swedish Air Force, which is based at Malmslätt, near Linköping, but operates throughout Sweden and provides target flying services for other nations such as Switzerland. Currently, F13M consists of two flying units. Flying unit 85 performs most of the Air Force's signal reconnaissance missions, using two specially equipped TP 85 Caravelles, supported by a Fairchild Metro for flight training. Flying unit 32 has 14 J 32E (for electronic) Lansens, six J 32D Lansen target tugs and three dual-control J 32B Lansens for training and radioactive sampling. The J 32Es can be used for a variety of missions, including jamming and countermeasures training, and 'aggressor' flying for SwAF combat squadrons.

The J 32E is a conversion of the standard J 32B, fitted with new flight instrumentation, a civil and military transponder, modernised autopilot and a range of specialised mission equipment, including:

Ingeborg, a micro-computer signal homing receiver for the S, C and part of L band, which works in parallel with the Adrian and G 24 systems to make possible optimum jamming. Its three antennae are inside the aircraft's dielectric nosecone. The control unit replaces the original radar scope in the navigator's cockpit.

G 24, a nose mounted jamming transmitter which exists in three versions, covering the L, S and C bands, and is for use against ground and ship radars.

Boz 3 chaff dispenser pods, usually carried on each of the two outboard underwing pylons. Operator can select different dispensing programmes covering various radar bands.

Petrus jamming pod is intended mainly for use against X band fighter, attack aircraft and anti-aircraft radars. Microcomputer control equipment can transmit camouflage (roar) and disguise jamming, and generate radar signatures within wide ranges, ahead and rearward, and also warns of attacks from the rear. Petrus is carried on the J 32E's inboard underwing pylons.

Adrian jamming pod. Externally similar to, and interchangeable with, Petrus. Used mainly against ground and ship S and C band radars. Has forward and rearward pointing antennae.

Mera is a computerised radio jamming equipment and homing receiver for the VHF and UHF bands. Jamming can take place at several frequencies, such as FM/AM (roar), pulse and oscillating roar. Using a tape-recorded disguise, replay of commands and music can be transmitted. The jamming operator can also transmit misleading commands on a selected frequency.

The Lansen was last described fully in the 1962-63 *Jane's*.

One of the two TP 85 Caravelle elint aircraft operated by SwAF Squadron F13M *(Swedish Air Force)*

Saab J 32E Lansen ECM/aggressor aircraft of SwAF Squadron F13M *(Swedish Air Force)*

SAAB J 35J DRAKEN

Under the revised designation J 35J (originally J 35F Mod), 64 Draken fighters of F10 Wing of the Swedish Air Force, based near Ängelholm in southern Sweden, are being updated to extend their service life to the mid-1990s. Two additional inboard underwing stores pylons enable these aircraft to operate with four external fuel tanks and two missiles, or four missiles and two fuel tanks. The infra-red target seeker associated with the missile armament is updated. An altitude warning system and transponder are added, and instrument changes include a new horizon system. The aircraft's primary radar and IFF transponders are also modified.

Only F10 Wing will operate the J 35J, which will continue in first-line service for three years after JAS 39 Gripens have begun to enter service with other units of the Swedish Air Force.

The J 35F was last described fully in the 1969-70 *Jane's*.

Additional underwing stores pylons identify this J 35J Draken fighter of F10 Wing *(Swedish Air Force)*

SACAB
SCANDINAVIAN AIRCRAFT CONSTRUCTION AB

PO Box 43, S-23032 Malmö-Sturup
Telephone: (0) 40 500220
Telex: 8305192
PRESIDENT: Peter Ahrens

SACAB, which is owned by a consortium of Scandinavian companies, was formed in 1984 by Mr Peter Ahrens. His Puerto Rico based Ahrens Aircraft Corporation built four prototypes of a square-fuselage turboprop transport known as the AR-404 before ceasing operations in 1982; this aircraft has been described in previous editions of *Jane's*.

SACAB's first venture, much of which was designed by Mr Ahrens' son Kim, is the four-turboprop KM-180.

SACAB KM-180

A full scale fuselage mockup of the KM-180 was completed in 1985, and in early 1986 construction was under way of a flying prototype and static test airframe. First flight was anticipated in December 1986, with certification under FAR Pt 25 expected about a year later. Two versions are projected initially, the following description applying to the standard KM-180. A higher gross weight version, designated **KM C-180**, is aimed at government customers, both civil and military.

Features of the KM-180 include unrestricted fuselage cross-section, with provision for future pressurisation if required, and a rear-loading tailgate. Intended as a feederliner and short-haul utility transport, it has a useful load (payload plus fuel) in the cargo configuration of some 5,942 kg (13,100 lb).

TYPE: Turboprop powered utility transport.

WINGS: Cantilever high-wing monoplane. Wing section NACA 64_3-418. Dihedral 2° 30'. Constant chord wings, of high aspect ratio and with tapered tips, built as single unit. Three-spar fail-safe main structure of 2024-T3 aluminium alloy, with 4130 chromoloy steel for engine mounts and 303 stainless steel for engine cowlings, firewalls and other fire risk areas. Conventional trailing-edge flaps and ailerons. B. F. Goodrich pneumatic de-icing boots on leading-edges.

FUSELAGE: Unpressurised fail-safe semi-monocoque structure, mainly of 2024-T3 aluminium alloy. Circular cross-section throughout most of length, and standard jet airliner type windows and doors, to facilitate subsequent development of pressurised version. Upswept rear fuselage, with rear-loading ramp/door in underside.

TAIL UNIT: Conventional cantilever fail-safe structure. Angular sweptback fin and rudder, with small dorsal fin; constant chord non-swept tailplane and elevators (former with leading-edge root extensions), mounted on top of fuselage. Trim tabs in rudder and each elevator.

LANDING GEAR: Retractable tricycle type, with hydraulic actuation. Main units are of trailing-arm type, with oleo-pneumatic shock absorption. Each consists of two independent 670 × 210 × 12 wheels in tandem, retracting upward into large fairing on fuselage side. Steerable twin-wheel nose unit (wheel size 650 × 10) retracts forward. Mechanical or free-fall emergency extension in event of hydraulic failure. B. F. Goodrich wheels, tyres and brakes.

POWER PLANT: Four 559 kW (750 shp) Avco Lycoming LTP 101-750 turboprop engines, derated to 447 kW (600 shp), each driving a Hartzell four-blade variable- and reversible-pitch propeller with spinner. Fuel in four equal-volume integral wing tanks, combined capacity 3,028 litres (666 Imp gallons). Provision for external auxiliary fuel tanks.

ACCOMMODATION: Pilot and co-pilot side by side on flight deck, with provision for third crew member if required. Cabin can be configured for up to 50 passengers, in mainly four-abreast seating with central aisle, with a typical layout for 40 passengers plus a cabin attendant. In all-cargo role, up to five standard LD3 containers can be accommodated. Passenger/crew door at front of cabin on port side. Two-door tailgate in underside of rear fuselage, lower portion serving as loading/unloading ramp for cargo, upper portion opening upward and inward. Additional payload can be carried on tailgate. Emergency exit on each side at rear of cabin. Entire accommodation heated (mixture of engine bleed air and combustion heater) and air-conditioned.

SYSTEMS: Freon type air-conditioning system. Hydraulic system, pressure 103·5 bars (1,500 lb/sq in), for landing gear extension/retraction, nosewheel steering, brakes, and tailgate actuation. Pneumatic system, using engine bleed air, for de-icing system and standby instruments. Electrical system (28V DC) powered by four 200A engine driven starter/generators, with voltage regulators, and lead-acid batteries. Converter for AC power available optionally. Aircooled diesel APU for on-demand power to drive one starter/generator, hydraulic pump and air-conditioning system.

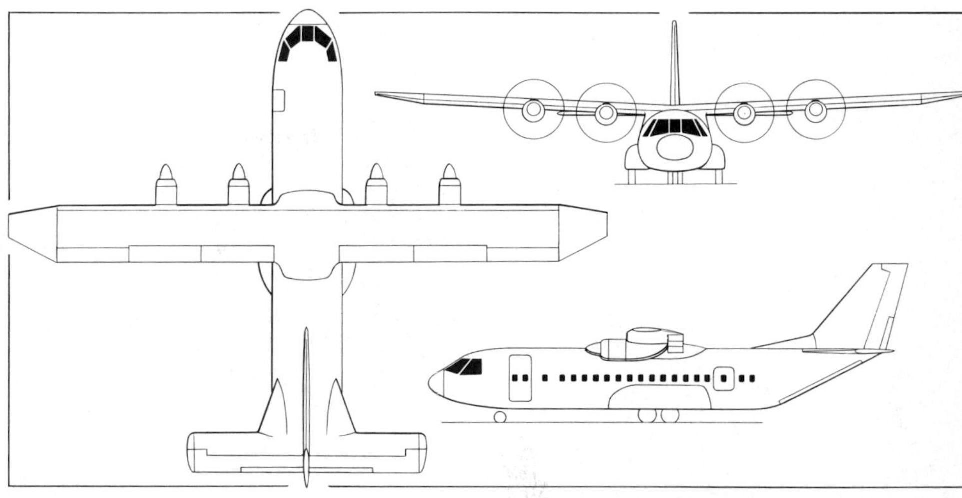

SACAB (Ahrens) KM-180 four-turboprop utility transport *(Pilot Press)*

DIMENSIONS, EXTERNAL:	
Wing span	21·34 m (70 ft 0 in)
Wing chord, constant portion	2·16 m (7 ft 1 in)
Wing aspect ratio	9·61
Length overall	18·44 m (60 ft 6 in)
Fuselage: Max diameter	2·74 m (9 ft 0 in)
Height overall	6·25 m (20 ft 6 in)
Tailplane span	8·00 m (26 ft 3 in)
Wheel track	3·23 m (10 ft 7 in)
Wheelbase	5·49 m (18 ft 0 in)
Propeller diameter	2·34 m (7 ft 8 in)
Propeller/fuselage clearance	0·305 m (1 ft 0 in)
Propeller ground clearance	1·52 m (5 ft 0 in)
Passenger/crew door: Height	1·83 m (6 ft 0 in)
Width	0·81 m (2 ft 8 in)
Emergency exits (each): Height	0·91 m (3 ft 0 in)
Width	0·51 m (1 ft 8 in)
Lower tailgate: Length	1·93 m (6 ft 4 in)
Width	1·93 m (6 ft 4 in)
Upper tailgate: Length	3·05 m (10 ft 0 in)
Width	1·93 m (6 ft 4 in)
DIMENSIONS, INTERNAL:	
Cabin: Length	10·06 m (33 ft 0 in)
Max width	2·59 m (8 ft 6 in)
Max flat floor width	1·93 m (6 ft 4 in)
Tailgate opening width	1·93 m (6 ft 4 in)
Volume	41·06 m³ (1,450 cu ft)
AREAS:	
Wings, gross	47·38 m² (510·0 sq ft)
Ailerons (total)	2·42 m² (26·0 sq ft)
Trailing-edge flaps (total)	6·78 m² (73·0 sq ft)
Fin, incl dorsal fin	13·47 m² (145·0 sq ft)
Rudder	2·69 m² (29·0 sq ft)
Tailplane	11·15 m² (120·0 sq ft)
Elevator	5·30 m² (57·0 sq ft)
WEIGHTS AND LOADING:	
Weight empty, equipped:	
38-passenger configuration	5,443 kg (12,000 lb)
cargo configuration	4,944 kg (10,900 lb)
Max tailgate load: on ground	1,542 kg (3,400 lb)
in flight	635 kg (1,400 lb)
*Max T-O weight	10,886 kg (24,000 lb)
Max landing weight	9,072 kg (20,000 lb)
Max cabin floor loading	976 kg/m² (200 lb/sq ft)
*12,700 kg (28,000 lb) for KM C-180	
PERFORMANCE (estimated at max T-O weight, S/L, ISA):	
Max level speed for normal operation	200 knots (370 km/h; 230 mph)
Econ cruising speed	180 knots (333 km/h; 207 mph)
Cruising speed, one engine out	175 knots (324 km/h; 201 mph)
Stalling speed, flaps and landing gear down	75 knots (139 km/h; 87 mph)
Max rate of climb (4 engines)	548 m (1,800 ft)/min
Rate of climb, one engine out	274 m (900 ft)/min
Service ceiling	7,925 m (26,000 ft)
T-O run	488 m (1,600 ft)
T-O to 15 m (50 ft)	915 m (3,000 ft)
Landing run: normal	732 m (2,400 ft)
with brakes and propeller reversal	183 m (600 ft)
Balanced field length for T-O and landing	915 m (3,000 ft)

SWITZERLAND

ALR

ARBEITSGRUPPE FÜR LUFT- UND RAUMFAHRT (Aerospace Task Group)

Gotthardstrasse 54, CH-8002 Zürich
Telephone: (01) 202 93 88
Telex: 56970 FEYER

PRESIDENT: Jean-Pierre Klaiber
PROGRAMME MANAGER: Dr Ing Georges Bridel

ALR PIRANHA 6

This group of Swiss scientists started work on the design of the Piranha in September 1977, in an attempt to develop a new-generation lightweight supersonic combat aircraft at a cost that could be afforded by the world's less affluent air forces. Details were given in the 1981-82 *Jane's* of four basic proposed single-seat versions: the Piranha 2C and 2D (single Adour engine), 4 (twin Larzac) and 5 (twin TFE 1042). Latest known details of the Piranha 6, with RB199 engine, were given in the 1985-86 edition. Updating of the design continues.

DÄTWYLER

MDC MAX DÄTWYLER AG

Flugplatz, CH-3368 Bleienbach-Langenthal
Telephone: (063) 22 83 83
Telex: 68218 mdc ch
PRESIDENT OF THE BOARD: Max Dätwyler

Dätwyler has specialised for many years in the repair and modification of light aircraft, and was responsible for the MDC-Trailer glider towing aircraft described in the 1966-67 *Jane's*. It has also manufactured components for the Pilatus Porter/Turbo-Porter STOL transport aircraft and B4-PC11 sailplane, and for the Dassault Mercure jet transport. Its latest design is the MD-3 Swiss Trainer.

DÄTWYLER MD-3 SWISS TRAINER

Dätwyler announced preliminary details of a two-seat basic training aircraft called the Swiss Trainer in the late 1960s, and a description of this aircraft appeared in the 1974-75 *Jane's*. Since then the general configuration has undergone little change, but considerable effort has been made by Mr Dätwyler to make the design genuinely modular in nature, to facilitate its manufacture by possible licensees in countries without a developed aircraft industry. In particular the ailerons, two-segment flaps, elevators and rudder constitute nine control surfaces which are all basically identical and interchangeable. The same is true of the tailplane halves and fin; fin and tailplane tips; wing leading-edge sections (four per aircraft); and the central inner and outer portions of the wings. Stock-keeping is thus also simplified, as well as manufacture.

The MD-3 prototype (HB-HOH) made its first flight, with Mr Dätwyler at the controls, on 12 August 1983. An Experimental category C of A was being sought in 1985, to be followed by full FAR Pt 23 certification allowing production to begin.

Two versions of the Swiss Trainer are planned, as follows:

MD-3-115. Two-seat primary training version, powered by an 82 kW (110 hp) Avco Lycoming O-235-N2A flat-four engine. Not yet flown; to become available after certification of MD-3-160.

MD-3-160. With more powerful Avco Lycoming O-320-D2A engine; particularly suitable for glider towing. Prototype is of this version. Changes made subsequent to first flight include an increase in wing dihedral, increased max flap deflection, electric flap actuation instead of mechanical, replacement of the original spring trim by an elevator trim tab, and substitution of a McCauley metal propeller for the original and smaller wooden type.

The following description applies to the MD-3-160, except where indicated:

TYPE: Two-seat primary training aircraft, of modular construction.

WINGS: Cantilever mid-wing monoplane. Wing section NACA $64_2$15414 (modified). Thickness/chord ratio 14%. Dihedral 5° 30′. Incidence 2°. No sweepback. All-metal structure, with single main spar, consisting of five different modules of which the largest measures 3·45 × 0·67 × 0·21 m (136 × 26·4 × 8·3 in). All-metal electrically operated two-segment flaps, max deflection 45°; single-slotted mass balanced ailerons. Flap, aileron, rudder and elevator segments identical.

FUSELAGE: Mainly metal semi-monocoque structure, with glassfibre fairings and cowling. Tailboom detachable from fuselage aft of wing.

TAIL UNIT: Sweptback horizontal and vertical surfaces of all-metal two-spar construction, assembled from three equal modules. Dorsal fin. Mass balanced rudder and elevators, modules of which are identical to those of ailerons and flaps. Trim tab in elevator.

LANDING GEAR: Non-retractable tricycle type with steerable nosewheel. Main-gear legs are cantilever steel struts, descending at 45° from fuselage main bulkhead. Nose gear fitted with oleo-pneumatic shock absorber. Cleveland 6·00-6 mainwheels and 5·00-5 nosewheel. Tyre pressure 2·41 bars (35 lb/sq in) on all units. Independent hydraulically operated Cleveland disc brake on each mainwheel. Speed fairings on all three wheels.

POWER PLANT: One 119 kW (160 hp) Avco Lycoming O-320-D2A flat-four engine in MD-3-160, driving a McCauley 1-C160-F6M-7462 two-blade fixed-pitch metal propeller with spinner (82 kW; 110 hp O-235-N2A in MD-3-115). Exhaust system can optionally be extended full length under fuselage to extreme rear of tailcone,

Prototype Dätwyler MD-3-160 Swiss Trainer

exhaust gases being emitted through a narrow slot running along the pipe. (Aircraft meets noise requirements with short or long exhaust.) One integral fuel tank in each wing: total capacity 140 litres (36 US gallons). Refuelling point above each wing. Oil capacity 7·6 litres (2 US gallons).

ACCOMMODATION: Side by side adjustable seats for pilot and one passenger. Five-point fixed seat belts. Forward sliding canopy. Space behind seats for 50 kg (110 lb) of baggage. Dual controls, cabin ventilation and heating standard.

SYSTEMS: Hydraulic system for brake actuation only. One 28V 60A engine driven alternator and one 24V 30Ah battery provide electrical power for engine starting, lighting, instruments, communications and navigation installations.

AVIONICS AND EQUIPMENT: Provision for VHF radio, VOR, ADF, transponder or other special equipment at customer's option. Equipment for glider towing optional.

DIMENSIONS, EXTERNAL:

Wing span	10·00 m (32 ft 9¾ in)
Wing chord, constant	1·50 m (4 ft 11 in)
Wing aspect ratio	6·67
Length overall	6·98 m (22 ft 10¾ in)
Height overall	2·92 m (9 ft 7 in)
Tailplane span	3·00 m (9 ft 10 in)
Wheel track	2·00 m (6 ft 6¾ in)
Wheelbase	1·56 m (5 ft 1½ in)
Propeller diameter	1·88 m (6 ft 2 in)

DIMENSIONS, INTERNAL:

Cabin, from firewall to rear bulkhead:

Length	1·30 m (4 ft 3¼ in)
Max width	1·12 m (3 ft 8 in)
Max height	1·08 m (3 ft 6½ in)

AREAS:

Wings, gross	15·00 m² (161·5 sq ft)
Ailerons (total)	1·22 m² (13·13 sq ft)
Trailing-edge flaps (total)	1·96 m² (21·10 sq ft)
Vertical tail surfaces (total)	1·44 m² (15·50 sq ft)
Rudder	0·51 m² (5·49 sq ft)
Horizontal tail surfaces (total)	2·56 m² (27·56 sq ft)
Elevators (total)	1·04 m² (11·19 sq ft)

WEIGHTS AND LOADINGS (A: Aerobatic, U: Utility):

Weight empty	633 kg (1,395 lb)
Max T-O and landing weight: A	840 kg (1,852 lb)
U	920 kg (2,028 lb)
Max wing loading: A	56·0 kg/m² (11·47 lb/sq ft)
U	61·3 kg/m² (12·56 lb/sq ft)
Max power loading: A	7·06 kg/kW (11·58 lb/hp)
U	7·73 kg/kW (12·68 lb/hp)

PERFORMANCE (MD-3-160 at T-O weight of 815 kg; 1,796 lb):

Never-exceed speed	169 knots (313 km/h; 195 mph)
Max manoeuvring speed	133 knots (246 km/h; 153 mph)
Max cruising speed (75% power) at 1,525 m (5,000 ft)	124 knots (230 km/h; 143 mph)
Econ cruising speed (66% power) at 1,525 m (5,000 ft)	117 knots (217 km/h; 135 mph)
Stalling speed, engine idling: flaps up	56 knots (104 km/h; 65 mph)
flaps down	46 knots (85 km/h; 53 mph)
Max rate of climb at S/L	420 m (1,378 ft)/min
Max rate of climb (75% power) towing 365 kg (805 lb) sailplane	104 m (341 ft)/min
T-O run	108 m (354 ft)
Landing run	130 m (426 ft)
Range with max fuel, no reserves	588 nm (1,090 km; 677 miles)

FFA

FFA FLUG- und FAHRZEUGWERKE AG (and sister company REPAIR AG)

CH-9423 Altenrhein
Telephone: (071) 43 01 01
Telex: 77 230 ffa ch
Telefax: (071) 42 53 66

CHAIRMAN OF THE BOARD: Dr L. Caroni
PRESIDENT: Oskar Ronner
CHIEF ENGINEER AND MARKETING: Dipl Ing P. Spalinger
SALES MANAGER, COMPONENTS: P. Hohl

This company had its origin in AG für Dornier Flugzeuge, which was formed as the Swiss branch of the West German Dornier company. In 1948 it became an entirely Swiss company named FFA (Flug- und Fahrzeugwerke AG).

Current activities, besides production of the AS 202 Bravo piston-engined basic trainer, consist of subcontracting for various aircraft manufacturers throughout the world, and licence production of components for Swiss built Northrop F-5E/F Tiger IIs.

Overhaul, servicing and maintenance for the Swiss Air Force and for general aviation are also done at Altenrhein. The two companies have about 900 employees, approximately one-quarter of whom are engaged in aviation activities.

FFA AS 202 BRAVO

Following an agreement concluded with SIAI-Marchetti of Italy, FFA is engaged in production and development of the AS 202 Bravo light trainer and sporting aircraft.

The first Bravo to fly was a Swiss assembled AS 202/15 prototype (HB-HEA), which flew for the first time on 7 March 1969. The Italian built second prototype flew on 7 May 1969. The third aircraft (HB-HEC) made its first flight on 16 June 1969, and the first production aircraft on 22 December 1971. A total of 155 Bravos had been sold by January 1983, in Switzerland and to foreign customers including Royal Air Maroc (five AS 202/18A), the Royal Flight of Oman (two AS 202/18A), the Uganda Central Flying School (eight AS 202/18A1), and the air forces of Indonesia (40 AS 202/18A3), Iraq (48 AS 202/18A2, some of which were transferred to the Royal Jordanian Air Force), and Morocco (10 AS 202/18A1).

The following three versions of the AS 202 Bravo remain available:

AS 202/15. Two/three-seat initial production version, with 112 kW (150 hp) Avco Lycoming O-320-E2A engine. Optional third seat. Swiss certification granted on 15 August 1972; FAA certification awarded on 16 November 1973. Production totalled 34; details in 1981-82 and earlier editions of *Jane's*.

AS 202/18A. Two/three-seat aerobatic version with a 134 kW (180 hp) Avco Lycoming engine, Hartzell constant-speed propeller and inverted oil system. First example (HB-HEY) flew for the first time on 22 August 1974. Swiss certification granted on 12 December 1975; FAA certification awarded on 17 December 1976. Deliveries totalled 121 by early 1986; further 11 ordered in October 1986 for delivery in 1987-88 to British Aerospace Flying College at Prestwick, Scotland.

AS 202/26A. First flown in 1978. No further examples yet built. Details in 1985-86 and earlier *Jane's*.

FFA AS 202/18A2 Bravo of the Iraqi Air Force Academy at Tikret *(Ivo Sturzenegger)*

The following description applies to the AS 202/18A:

TYPE: Two/three-seat light aircraft.

WINGS: Cantilever low-wing monoplane. Wing section NACA 63_2618 (modified) at centreline, 63_2415 at tip. Thickness/chord ratio 17·63% at root, 15% at tip. Dihedral 5° 43′ from roots. Incidence 3°. Sweepback at quarter-chord 0° 40′. Conventional aluminium single-spar fail-safe structure, with riveted honeycomb laminate skin. Aluminium single-slotted flaps and single-slotted ailerons. Ground adjustable tab on each aileron.

FUSELAGE: Conventional aluminium semi-monocoque fail-safe structure, with engine cowling and several fairings of glassfibre.

TAIL UNIT: Cantilever aluminium single-spar structure with sweptback vertical surfaces. Rudder mass balanced, with provision for anti-collision beacon. Fixed incidence tailplane. Two-piece elevator with full span trim tab on starboard half. Ground adjustable tab on rudder.

LANDING GEAR: Non-retractable tricycle type, with steerable nosewheel. Rubber cushioned shock absorber struts of SIAI-Marchetti design. Mainwheel tyres size 6·00-6; nosewheel tyre size 5·00-5. Tyre pressure (all units) 2·41 bars (35 lb/sq in). Independent hydraulically operated disc brake on each mainwheel.

POWER PLANT: One 134 kW (180 hp) Avco Lycoming AEIO-360-B1F flat-four engine, driving a Hartzell HC-C2YK-1BF/F7666A-2 two-blade constant-speed propeller with spinner. Hoffmann three-blade propeller optional. Two wing leading-edge rubber fuel tanks with total capacity of 170 litres (37 4 Imp gallons). Refuelling point above each wing. Starboard tank has additional flexible fuel intake for aerobatics. Christen 801 fully aerobatic oil system, capacity 7·6 litres (1·6 Imp gallons).

ACCOMMODATION: Seats for two persons side by side, in Aerobatic versions, under rearward sliding jettisonable transparent canopy. Space at rear in Utility versions for a third seat or 100 kg (220 lb) of baggage. Dual controls, cabin ventilation and heating standard.

SYSTEMS: Hydraulic system for brake actuation. One 12V 60A engine driven alternator and one 25Ah battery provide electrical power for engine starting, lighting, instruments, communications and navigation installations. 28V electrical system optional.

AVIONICS AND EQUIPMENT: Provision for VHF radio, VOR, ADF, Nav-O-Matic 200A autopilot, blind-flying instrumentation or other special equipment at customer's option. Clutch and release mechanism for glider towing optional.

DIMENSIONS, EXTERNAL:

Wing span	9·75 m (31 ft 11¾ in)
Wing chord: at root	1·88 m (6 ft 2 in)
at tip	1·16 m (3 ft 9½ in)
Wing aspect ratio	6·51
Length overall	7·50 m (24 ft 7¼ in)

Length of fuselage	7·15 m (23 ft 5½ in)
Height overall	2·81 m (9 ft 2¾ in)
Tailplane span	3·67 m (12 ft 0½ in)
Wheel track	2·25 m (7 ft 4½ in)
Wheelbase	1·78 m (5 ft 10 in)
Propeller diameter	1·88 m (6 ft 2 in)
Propeller ground clearance	0·31 m (1 ft 0¼ in)
DIMENSIONS, INTERNAL:	
Cabin: Max length	2·15 m (7 ft 0½ in)
Max width	1·02 m (3 ft 4¼ in)
Max height	1·10 m (3 ft 7¼ in)
Floor area	2·15 m² (23·14 sq ft)
AREAS:	
Wings, gross	13·86 m² (149·2 sq ft)
Ailerons (total)	1·09 m² (11·7 sq ft)
Trailing-edge flaps (total)	1·49 m² (16·04 sq ft)
Fin	0·45 m² (4·84 sq ft)
Rudder, incl tab	0·94 m² (10·12 sq ft)
Tailplane	1·88 m² (20·24 sq ft)
Elevators, incl tab	0·76 m² (8·18 sq ft)
WEIGHTS AND LOADINGS:	
Weight empty, equipped	700 kg (1,543 lb)
Max useful load (incl fuel): Aerobatic	172 kg (379 lb)
Utility	258 kg (568 lb)
Max T-O and landing weight:	
Aerobatic	950 kg (2,094 lb)
Utility	1,050 kg (2,315 lb)
Max wing loading: Utility	75·8 kg/m² (15·52 lb/sq ft)
Max power loading: Utility	7·84 kg/kW (12·86 lb/hp)
PERFORMANCE (Utility category at max T-O weight):	
Never-exceed speed	173 knots (320 km/h; 199 mph)
Max level speed at S/L	130 knots (241 km/h; 150 mph)
Max cruising speed (75% power) at 2,440 m (8,000 ft)	122 knots (226 km/h; 141 mph)
Econ cruising speed (55% power) at 3,050 m (10,000 ft)	109 knots (203 km/h; 126 mph)
Stalling speed, engine idling:	
flaps up	62 knots (114 km/h; 71 mph)
flaps down	49 knots (90 km/h; 56 mph)
Max rate of climb at S/L	276 m (905 ft)/min
Service ceiling	5,490 m (18,000 ft)
T-O run at S/L	210 m (689 ft)
T-O to 15 m (50 ft) at S/L	400 m (1,312 ft)
Landing from 15 m (50 ft)	465 m (1,525 ft)
Landing run	210 m (690 ft)
Range with max fuel, no reserves	521 nm (965 km; 600 miles)
Max endurance	5 h 30 min

PILATUS

PILATUS FLUGZEUGWERKE AG

CH-6370 Stans, near Lucerne
Telephone: (041) 63 61 11
Telex: 866202
Telefax: (041) 613351

BOARD OF DIRECTORS:
W. Gubler (Chairman and General Manager)
D. C. Klöckner (Marketing and Programmes)
P. Ebner (Finance and Administration)
W. Zbinden (Production)

MANAGERS:
W. Odermatt (Sales and Sales Support)
O. L. P. Masefield (Research and Development)
K. G. Trautmann (Projects)
W. Volkart (Product Support)

PUBLIC RELATIONS: Ulrich Wenger

Pilatus Flugzeugwerke AG was formed in December 1939; details of its early history can be found in previous editions of *Jane's*. It is part of the Oerlikon-Bührle Group.

Current Pilatus products are the PC-6 Turbo-Porter single-engined utility transport, the PC-7 Turbo-Trainer and PC-9 turboprop trainer.

On 24 January 1979 Pilatus purchased the assets of Britten-Norman (Bembridge) Ltd of the UK, which has operated since then under the name Pilatus Britten-Norman Ltd (which see) as a subsidiary of Pilatus Aircraft Ltd.

PILATUS PC-6 TURBO-PORTER

US Army designation: UV-20A Chiricahua

The Pilatus PC-6 is a single-engined multi-purpose utility aircraft, with STOL characteristics permitting operation from unprepared strips under harsh environmental and terrain conditions. The aircraft can be converted rapidly from a pure freighter to a passenger transport, and can be adapted for a great number of different missions, including supply dropping, search and rescue, ambulance, aerial survey and photography, parachuting, cropspraying, water bombing, rainmaking and glider or target towing as well as operation from soft ground, snow, glacier or water, and long-range operations.

The first of five PC-6 piston engined prototypes made its first flight on 4 May 1959, and 20 pre-series PC-6s, with 253·5 kW (340 hp) Avco Lycoming engines, had been delivered by the Summer of 1961. Subsequent versions have included the piston engined PC-6 and PC-6/350 Porters; and the PC-6/A, A1, A2, B, B1, B2 and C2-H2 Turbo-Porters, with various turboprop power plants. Descriptions of all of these can be found in the 1974-75 and earlier editions of *Jane's*.

The B1 and B2 versions can be fitted with an air inlet filter for operation in desert conditions and for agricultural applications.

Pilatus also markets a Q-STOL (Quiet STOL) conversion kit for the B1 and B2 Turbo-Porters fitted with PT6A-20 or -27 turbine engines. This includes a system whereby propeller speed can be altered independently of the engine power setting, and is claimed to reduce the noise level by more than 10 dB for T-O and 20 dB for landing.

The standard production version in recent years has been the **PC-6/B2-H2 Turbo-Porter**, certificated on 30 June 1970 and powered by a PT6A-27 turboprop engine.

Flight testing ended in 1986 of a new version, designated **PC-6/B2-H4**, in which for CAR.3 operations (commercial operations with fare paying passengers) the maximum take-off weight is increased by 600 kg (1,323 lb), resulting in a payload increase of 570 kg (1,257 lb). This was achieved by improving the aerodynamic efficiency of the wings with new tip fairings, enlarging the dorsal fin, installing uprated mainwheel shock absorbers and a new tailwheel assembly, and a slight strengthening of the airframe. While the H4 modification can be retrofitted to all existing PC-6/B1-H2 and B2-H2 models equipped with electrically operated longitudinal trim, all new-production Porters from mid-1985 are of the H4 version only.

By the Summer of 1986 more than 465 PC-6 aircraft, of all models, had been delivered (including US licence manufacture), and were operating in more than 50 countries. Military operators include the air forces of Angola, Argentina, Australia, Austria, Bolivia, Burma, Chad, Ecuador, Iran, Oman, Peru, Sudan, Switzerland and Thailand, and the US Army. Recent customers for the civil version have been based in Austria, Colombia, England, Guatemala, Hungary, Malaysia, New Zealand, Switzerland, the USA and Zaïre.

The structural description which follows is applicable to the B2-H2 and -H4 versions except where indicated. Details of the agricultural Turbo-Porter are given separately.

TYPE: Single-engined STOL utility transport.

WINGS: Braced high-wing monoplane, with single streamline-section bracing strut each side. Wing section NACA 64-514 (constant). Dihedral 1°. Incidence 2°. Single-spar all-metal structure. Entire trailing-edge hinged, inner sections consisting of electrically operated all-metal double-slotted flaps and outer sections of all-metal single-slotted ailerons. No airbrakes or de-icing equipment. Trim tabs and/or Flettner tabs on ailerons optional; ground adjustable tabs are mandatory if these are not fitted. Span-increasing tip fairings on H4.

FUSELAGE: All-metal semi-monocoque structure.

TAIL UNIT: Cantilever all-metal structure. Variable incidence tailplane. Flettner tabs on elevator. Enlarged dorsal fin on H4.

LANDING GEAR: Non-retractable tailwheel type. Oleo shock absorbers of Pilatus design in all units. Steerable/lockable tailwheel. Goodyear Type II mainwheels and GA 284 tyres size 24 × 7 or 7·50 × 10 (pressure 2·21 bars; 32 lb/sq in); oversize Goodyear Type III wheels and tyres optional, size 11·0 × 12, pressure 0·88 bars (12·8 lb/sq in). Goodyear tailwheel with size 5·00-4 tyre. Goodyear disc brakes. Pilatus wheel/ski gear or Edo 58-4580 or 679-4930 floats optional.

POWER PLANT (PC-6/B2-H2 and B2-H4): One 507 kW (680 shp) Pratt & Whitney Canada PT6A-27 turboprop engine (flat rated at 410 kW; 550 shp at S/L), driving a Hartzell HC-B3TN-3D/T-10178 C or CH, or T10173 C or CH constant-speed fully-feathering reversible-pitch propeller with Beta mode control. Standard fuel in integral wing tanks, usable capacity 480 litres (127 US gallons; 105·5 Imp gallons) normal, 644 litres (170 US gallons; 142 Imp gallons) maximum. Two underwing auxiliary tanks, each of 190 or 245 litres (50 or 65 US gallons; 42 or 54 Imp gallons), available optionally. Oil capacity 12·5 litres (2·75 Imp gallons; 3·3 US gallons).

ACCOMMODATION: Cabin has pilot's seat forward on port side, with one passenger seat alongside, and is normally fitted with six quickly removable seats, in pairs, to the rear of these for additional passengers. Up to 11 persons, including the pilot, can be carried in 2-3-3-3 high density layout; or up to eight parachutists, who can be dropped from heights up to 7,620 m (25,000 ft); or two stretchers plus three attendants in ambulance configuration. Floor is level, flush with door sill, and is provided with seat rails. Forward opening door beside each front seat. Large rearward sliding door on starboard side of main cabin. Double doors, without central pillar, on port side. Hatch in floor 0·58 × 0·90 m (1 ft 10¾ in × 2 ft 11½ in), openable from inside cabin, for aerial camera or for supply dropping. Hatch in cabin rear wall 0·50 × 0·80 m (1 ft 7 in × 2 ft 7 in) permits stowage of six passenger seats or accommodation of freight items up to 5·0 m (16 ft 5 in) in length. Walls lined with lightweight soundproofing and heat insulation material. Adjustable heating and ventilation systems provided. Dual controls optional.

SYSTEMS: Cabin heated by engine bleed air. Scott 8500 oxygen system optional. 200A 30V starter/generator and 24V 34Ah (optionally 40Ah) nickel-cadmium battery.

EQUIPMENT: Generally to customer's requirements, but can include stretchers for ambulance role, aerial photography and survey gear, agricultural equipment (see separate description) or an 800 litre (176 Imp gallon; 211 US

Pilatus PC-6/B2-H2 at Stans prior to delivery to the Iranian Islamic Air Force *(Ivo Sturzenegger)*

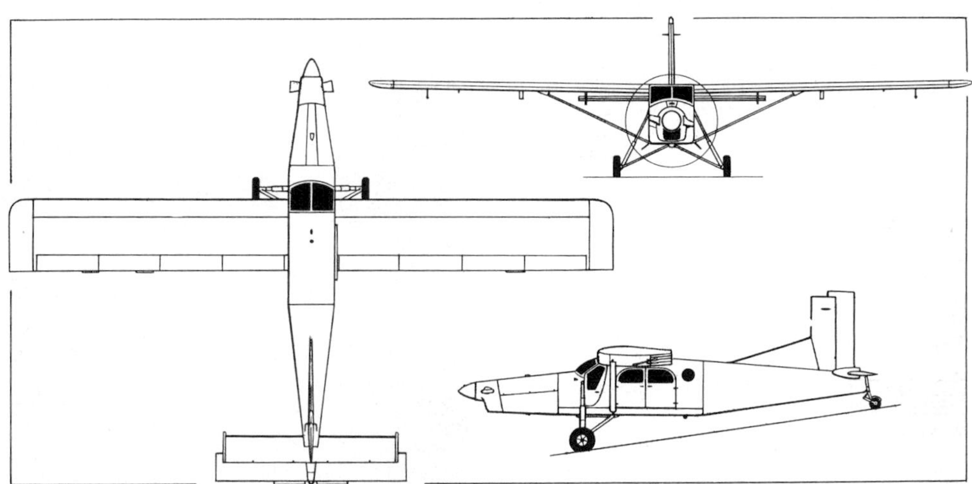

Pilatus PC-6/B2-H4 Turbo-Porter, with new wingtips, enlarged dorsal fin and other changes *(Pilot Press)*

gallon) water tank in cabin, with quick release system, for firefighting role. The 1,330 litre tank (see under description of agricultural versions) can also be used in the firebombing role.

DIMENSIONS, EXTERNAL (H4):

Wing span	15·87 m (52 ft 0¾ in)
Wing chord (constant)	1·90 m (6 ft 3 in)
Wing aspect ratio	8·35
Length overall	11·00 m (36 ft 1 in)
Height overall (tail down)	3·20 m (10 ft 6 in)
Elevator span	5·12 m (16 ft 9½ in)
Wheel track	3·00 m (9 ft 10 in)
Wheelbase	7·87 m (25 ft 10 in)
Propeller diameter	2·56 m (8 ft 5 in)
Cabin double door (port) and sliding door (starboard):	
Max height	1·04 m (3 ft 5 in)
Width	1·58 m (5 ft 2¼ in)

DIMENSIONS, INTERNAL:

Cabin, from back of pilot's seat to rear wall:	
Length	2·30 m (7 ft 6½ in)
Max width	1·16 m (3 ft 9½ in)
Max height (at front)	1·28 m (4 ft 2½ in)
Height at rear wall	1·18 m (3 ft 10½ in)
Floor area	2·67 m² (28·6 sq ft)
Volume	3·28 m³ (107 cu ft)

AREAS (H4):

Wings, gross	30·15 m² (324·5 sq ft)
Ailerons (total)	3·83 m² (41·2 sq ft)
Flaps (total)	3·76 m² (40·5 sq ft)
Fin	1·70 m² (18·3 sq ft)
Rudder, incl tab	0·96 m² (10·3 sq ft)
Tailplane	4·03 m² (43·4 sq ft)
Elevator, incl tab	2·11 m² (22·7 sq ft)

WEIGHTS AND LOADINGS (H4):

Weight empty, equipped	1,270 kg (2,800 lb)
Max fuel load	508 kg (1,120 lb)
Max T-O weight, Normal (CAR 3):	
wheels (standard)	2,800 kg (6,173 lb)
skis	2,600 kg (5,732 lb)
Max landing weight: wheels	2,660 kg (5,864 lb)
skis	2,600 kg (5,732 lb)
Max cabin floor loading	488 kg/m² (100 lb/sq ft)
Max wing loading (Normal):	
wheels	92·87 kg/m² (19·03 lb/sq ft)
skis	86·23 kg/m² (17·67 lb/sq ft)
Max power loading (Normal):	
wheels	6·83 kg/kW (11·22 lb/shp)
skis	5·13 kg/kW (8·43 lb/shp)

PERFORMANCE (H4 at max T-O weight, ISA, Normal category):

Never-exceed speed	151 knots (280 km/h; 174 mph) IAS
Econ cruising speed at 3,050 m (10,000 ft)	115 knots (213 km/h; 132 mph)
Stalling speed, power off, flaps down	52 knots (96 km/h; 60 mph)
Max rate of climb at S/L	287 m (941 ft)/min
Max operating altitude	7,620 m (25,000 ft)
T-O run at S/L	197 m (646 ft)
Landing run at S/L	127 m (417 ft)
Max range, no reserves, with external fuel	811 nm (1,503 km; 934 miles)
g limits	+3·72/−1·5

PILATUS PC-6 TURBO-PORTER (AGRICULTURAL VERSIONS)

The Turbo-Porter can, if required, be equipped for agricultural duties, the necessary equipment being easily removable when not required, to permit the use of the aircraft for other work. Approx 40 Turbo-Porters have been completed in agricultural configuration: these are in service in Indonesia, Sudan, Switzerland, Thailand and Zaïre.

For liquid spraying, a stainless steel tank (capacity 1,330 litres; 292·5 Imp gallons; 351·5 US gallons) is installed behind the two front seats, and 46- or 62-nozzle spraybooms are fitted beneath the wings. In this configuration the aircraft can cover a swath width of 45 m (148 ft). An ultra-low-volume system, using four to six atomisers or two to six Micronairs, is also available, permitting increase in swath width up to 400 m (1,310 ft).

For dusting with granulated materials, the lower part of the standard tank can be replaced by a discharge and dispersal door permitting coverage of a swath width of up to 20 m (66 ft). A Transland spreader can be fitted for dust application (swath up to 30 m; 100 ft). Effective swath width of these versions is 13-40 m (43-131 ft), the optimum being approx 20 m (66 ft).

Both versions are fitted with small doors in the fuselage sides, giving access to the tank/hopper for servicing, removal or replenishment, and two single seats or a bench seat for three persons can be installed aft of the tank. Optional items include an engine air intake screen and a loading door for chemical in the top of the fuselage.

AVIONICS AND EQUIPMENT: Optional avionics include Decca Mk 8A navigator, Decca Hi-Fix radio, Decca Doppler 72 radar, gyrosyn CL-11 compass and SR 54A radio altimeter.

WEIGHTS (liquid spray system):

Weight empty, incl spray system, oil and pilot	1,440 kg (3,170 lb)
Fuel	380 kg (837 lb)
Chemical	950 kg (2,093 lb)
Max T-O weight	2,770 kg (6,100 lb)
Max landing weight	2,200 kg (4,850 lb)

Pilatus PC-6/B2-H4 Turbo-Porter for the Malaysian Police

PERFORMANCE (liquid spray version, PT6A-27 engine, at max T-O weight):

Never-exceed speed	120 knots (222 km/h; 138 mph)
Operating speed	approx 90 knots (167 km/h; 104 mph)
Operating height	6-8 m (20-26 ft)
Stalling speed, power off, flaps down	49 knots (91 km/h; 57 mph)
T-O run	180 m (590 ft)
T-O to 15 m (50 ft)	390 m (1,280 ft)
Landing from 15 m (50 ft)	345 m (1,132 ft)
Landing run	130 m (427 ft)
Spraying duration with full spraytank	6 min

PILATUS PC-7 TURBO-TRAINER

Swiss Air Force designation: PC-7/CH

The PC-7 Turbo-Trainer is a fully aerobatic two-seat training aircraft, powered by a 410 kW (550 shp) Pratt & Whitney Canada PT6A-25A turboprop engine. It can be used for basic, transition and aerobatic training, and, with suitable equipment installed, for IFR and tactical training. It received FAA certification to FAR Pt 23 (Aerobatic and Utility categories) on 12 August 1983, and also meets the requirements of a selected group of US military specifications (Trainer category). As a single-seater, it is flown from the front seat. The PC-7 also holds type certificates from the Swiss Federal Office for Civil Aviation (5 December 1978/6 April 1979) and the French DGAC (16 May 1983).

The first production PC-7 was flown on 18 August 1978, and deliveries began in December of that year. Sales totalled more than 380 by 1 September 1986, of which more than 370 had been delivered. Customers include the air forces of Abu Dhabi (24), Angola (18), Austria (16), Bolivia (36), Burma (17), Chile (10 for Navy), Guatemala (12), Iran, Iraq (52), Malaysia (44), Mexico (75), Switzerland (40) and undisclosed countries; other customers include CIPRA of France (2), Swissair (1), Contraves (1) and two US private owners (1 each).

The PC-7 is available with new, lightweight Mk 15 ejection seats developed in collaboration with Martin-Baker. These offer safe escape for both occupants at speeds between 60 knots on the runway and 300 knots in the air (111-556 km/h; 69-345 mph), and at altitudes up to 9,750 m (32,000 ft).

TYPE: Single-engined single/two-seat training aircraft.

WINGS: Cantilever low-wing monoplane. Wing section NACA 64_2A-415 at root, NACA 64_1A-612 at tip. Dihedral 7° on outer panels. Sweepback 1° at quarter-chord. One-piece all-metal single-spar structure, with auxiliary spar, ribs and stringer-reinforced skin. Constant chord centre-section and tapered outer panels. Alclad aluminium alloy (2022 or 2024) skin, reinforced by stringers. Some fairings of GRP. Mass balanced Frise ailerons; trailing-edge split flaps, extending under fuselage. Flaps actuated electrically, ailerons mechanically by pushrods. Trim tab in port aileron.

FUSELAGE: All-metal semi-monocoque structure, with stringers, bulkheads and aluminium alloy skin. Some fairings of GRP.

TAIL UNIT: Cantilever all-metal structure, of similar construction to wings. Dorsal fin; small ventral fin under tailcone. Forward strakes on inboard leading-edges of tailplane. Trim tab in starboard half of elevator; anti-servo tab in rudder. All control surfaces mass balanced and cable operated.

LANDING GEAR: Electrically actuated retractable tricycle type, with emergency manual extension. Mainwheels retract inward, nosewheel rearward. Oleo-pneumatic shock absorber in each unit. Castoring nosewheel, with shimmy dampers. Goodrich mainwheels and tyres, size 6·50-8, pressure 4·5 bars (65 lb/sq in). Goodrich nosewheel and tyre, size 6·00-6, pressure 2·75 bars (40 lb/sq in). No mainwheel doors. Goodrich hydraulic disc brakes on mainwheels. Parking brake.

POWER PLANT: One 485 kW (650 shp) Pratt & Whitney Canada PT6A-25A turboprop engine, flat rated at 410 kW (550 shp at S/L), driving a Hartzell HC-B3TN-2/T10173C-8 three-blade constant-speed fully-feathering propeller with spinner. Fuel in integral tanks in outer wing leading-edges, total usable capacity 474 litres (104 Imp gallons). Overwing refuelling point on each tank. Fuel system permits up to 30 s of inverted flight. Provision for two 152 or 240 litre (33·5 or 52·75 Imp gallon) underwing drop tanks. Oil capacity 16 litres (3·5 Imp gallons).

ACCOMMODATION: Adjustable seats for two persons in tandem (instructor at rear), beneath rearward sliding jettisonable Plexiglas canopy. Martin-Baker Mk 15 lightweight ejection seats available optionally. Dual controls standard. Cockpits ventilated and heated by engine bleed air, which can also be used for windscreen de-icing. Space for 25 kg (55 lb) of baggage aft of seats, with external access.

SYSTEMS: Freon air-conditioning system standard. Hydraulic system for mainwheel brakes only. No pneumatic system. 28V DC operational (24V nominal) electrical system, incorporating Lear Siegler 30V 200A starter/generator and Marathon 36Ah or 42Ah nickel-cadmium battery; two static inverters for AC power supply. Ground power receptacle in fuselage forward of port wing root. Goodrich propeller de-icing system optional.

AVIONICS AND EQUIPMENT: Basic flight and navigation instrumentation in both cockpits, except for magnetic compass (front cockpit only). Additional nav and com equipment to customer's requirements. Other optional equipment includes IFR training shield to screen rear cockpit, and oxygen system. Landing/taxying light on each mainwheel leg.

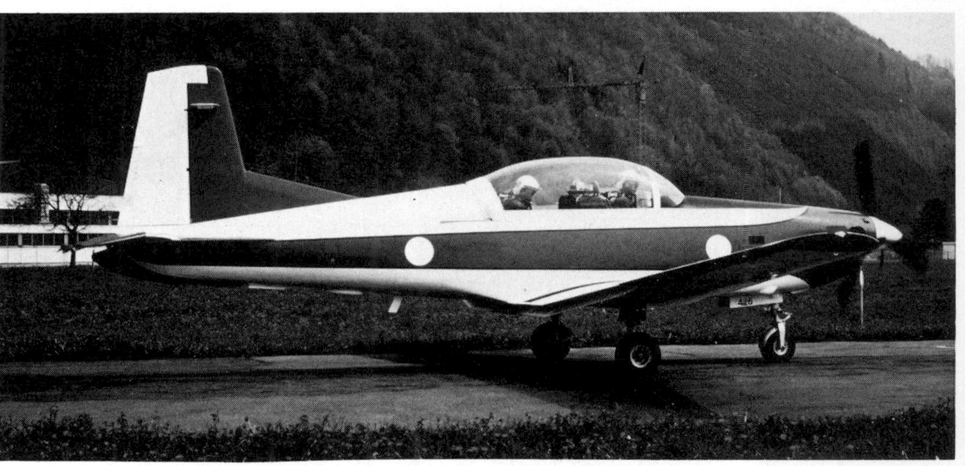

PC-7 Turbo-Trainer of the Iranian Islamic Air Force *(Ivo Sturzenegger)*

DIMENSIONS, EXTERNAL:
- Wing span: 10·40 m (34 ft 1½ in)
- Wing chord: mean aerodynamic: 1·64 m (5 ft 4½ in)
  - mean geometric: 1·596 m (5 ft 2·8 in)
- Wing aspect ratio: 6·52
- Length overall: 9·775 m (32 ft 0¾ in)
- Height overall: 3·21 m (10 ft 6½ in)
- Tailplane span: 3·40 m (11 ft 2 in)
- Wheel track: 2·60 m (8 ft 6½ in)
- Wheelbase: 2·58 m (8 ft 5½ in)
- Propeller diameter: 2·36 m (7 ft 9 in)

AREAS:
- Wings, gross: 16·60 m² (178·7 sq ft)
- Ailerons (total): 1·621 m² (17·45 sq ft)
- Trailing-edge flaps (total): 2·035 m² (21·90 sq ft)
- Fin, incl dorsal fin: 1·062 m² (11·43 sq ft)
- Rudder, incl tab: 0·959 m² (10·32 sq ft)
- Tailplane: 1·783 m² (19·19 sq ft)
- Elevators, incl tab: 1·395 m² (15·02 sq ft)

WEIGHTS AND LOADINGS:
- Basic weight empty: 1,330 kg (2,932 lb)
- Max T-O weight: Aerobatic: 1,900 kg (4,188 lb)
  - Utility: 2,700 kg (5,952 lb)
- Max ramp weight: Utility: 2,711 kg (5,976 lb)
- Max landing weight:
  - Aerobatic (military specification): 1,804 kg (3,977 lb)
  - Aerobatic (FAR Pt 23): 1,900 kg (4,188 lb)
  - Utility: 2,565 kg (5,655 lb)
- Max zero-fuel weight: 1,664 kg (3,668 lb)
- Max wing loading:
  - Aerobatic: 114·5 kg/m² (23·44 lb/sq ft)
  - Utility: 162·7 kg/m² (33·31 lb/sq ft)
- Max power loading:
  - Aerobatic: 4·63 kg/kW (7·61 lb/shp)
  - Utility: 6·59 kg/kW (10·82 lb/shp)

PERFORMANCE (at max T-O weight, ISA, except where indicated. A: Aerobatic category, B: Utility category):
- Never-exceed speed:
  - A, B: 270 knots (500 km/h; 310 mph) EAS
- Max operating speed:
  - A, B: 270 knots (500 km/h; 310 mph) EAS
- Max cruising speed at 6,100 m (20,000 ft):
  - A: 222 knots (412 km/h; 256 mph)
  - B: 196 knots (364 km/h; 226 mph)
- Econ cruising speed at 6,100 m (20,000 ft):
  - A: 171 knots (317 km/h; 197 mph)
  - B: 165 knots (305 km/h; 190 mph)
- Manoeuvring speed:
  - A: 175 knots (325 km/h; 202 mph) EAS
  - B: 181 knots (335 km/h; 208 mph) EAS
- Max speed with flaps and landing gear down:
  - A, B: 135 knots (250 km/h; 155 mph) EAS
- Stalling speed, flaps and landing gear up, power off:
  - A: 71 knots (131 km/h; 82 mph) EAS
  - B: 83 knots (154 km/h; 96 mph) EAS
- Stalling speed, flaps and landing gear down, power off:
  - A: 64 knots (119 km/h; 74 mph) EAS
  - B: 74 knots (138 km/h; 86 mph) EAS
- Max rate of climb at S/L: A: 610 m (2,000 ft)/min
  - B: 364 m (1,195 ft)/min
- Time to 5,000 m (16,400 ft): A: 9 min
  - B: 17 min
- Service ceiling: A: 9,755 m (32,000 ft)
  - B: 7,925 m (26,000 ft)
- T-O run at S/L: A: 240 m (787 ft)
  - B: 780 m (2,560 ft)
- T-O to 15 m (50 ft) at S/L: A: 400 m (1,312 ft)
  - B: 1,180 m (3,870 ft)
- Landing from 15 m (50 ft) at S/L at max landing weight:
  - A: 510 m (1,675 ft)
  - B: 800 m (2,625 ft)
- Landing run at S/L at max landing weight:
  - A: 295 m (968 ft)
  - B: 505 m (1,655 ft)
- Max range at cruise power at 5,000 m (16,400 ft), 5% fuel plus 20 min reserves:
  - A: 647 nm (1,200 km; 745 miles)
  - B: 1,420 nm (2,630 km; 1,634 miles)
- Endurance at 6,100 m (20,000 ft), with reserves:
  - A, at max speed: 3 h 0 min
  - A, for max range: 4 h 22 min
  - B, at max speed: 2 h 36 min
  - B, for max range: 3 h 45 min
- *g* limits: A: +6/−3
  - B: +4·5/−2·25

PILATUS PC-9

Design of the PC-9, as an advanced, high performance turboprop trainer suitable for all aspects from basic through to advanced flying, began in May 1982. Despite an external similarity to the PC-7, it has only about 10 per cent structural commonality with that aircraft, differences including a more powerful engine, 'stepped' tandem cockpits with ejection seats, a ventral airbrake, modified wing profiles and tips, new ailerons, a longer dorsal fin, mainwheel doors, and larger wheels with high pressure tyres. The PC-9 complies with the requirements of FAR Pt 23 in the Aerobatic and Utility categories, and with a selected group of US military specifications in the Trainer category.

Flight testing of major components, and aerodynamic optimisation of the new design, were completed during 1982-83 on a PC-7 technology demonstration aircraft, and were followed by the manufacture of two pre-production PC-9s. The first of these (HB-HPA) made its initial flight, fitted temporarily with a Hartzell three-blade propeller, on 7 May 1984. The second (HB-HPB), first flown on 20 July 1984, was more fully representative of the production version.

The two flight test aircraft had flown more than 350 hours by the end of May 1985, enabling certification to be obtained on 19 September 1985, three months ahead of schedule. First customer for the PC-9 was the Union of Burma Air Force, which ordered four. It was followed by the Royal Saudi Air Force, which ordered 30 on 26 September 1985. On 16 December 1985 the Australian Defence Minister announced his government's decision to order PC-9s for the RAAF in preference to the domestic A 10B Wamira design, and a contract for 67 aircraft, to be co-produced by Hawker de Havilland and Government Aircraft Factories, was signed on 10 July 1986. By the end of that month total orders also included approx 25 more PC-9s from two undisclosed customers. For the Australian order, Pilatus will supply two complete aircraft, six in kit form, and major components for a further 11; the remaining 48 will be built by HDH and GAF.

TYPE: Single/two-seat training aircraft.

WINGS: Cantilever low-wing monoplane. Wing section PIL15M825 at root, PIL12M850 at tip. Dihedral 7° on outer panels. Incidence 1° at root, washout −2° at tip. Sweepback 1° at quarter-chord. One-piece all-metal single-spar primary structure with auxiliary spar, ribs, and stringer-reinforced skin. Constant chord centre-section and tapered outer panels. Alclad aluminium alloy (2024) skin, reinforced by stringers; some fairings of GRP. Mass balanced plain ailerons; trailing-edge split flaps extending under fuselage with plate type airbrake at centre. Flaps and airbrake actuated hydraulically, ailerons mechanically by pushrods. Aileron trim is by an electrically actuated, variable load centering spring on the control column.

FUSELAGE: All-metal semi-monocoque structure with stringers, bulkheads and aluminium alloy skin. Some fairings of GRP.

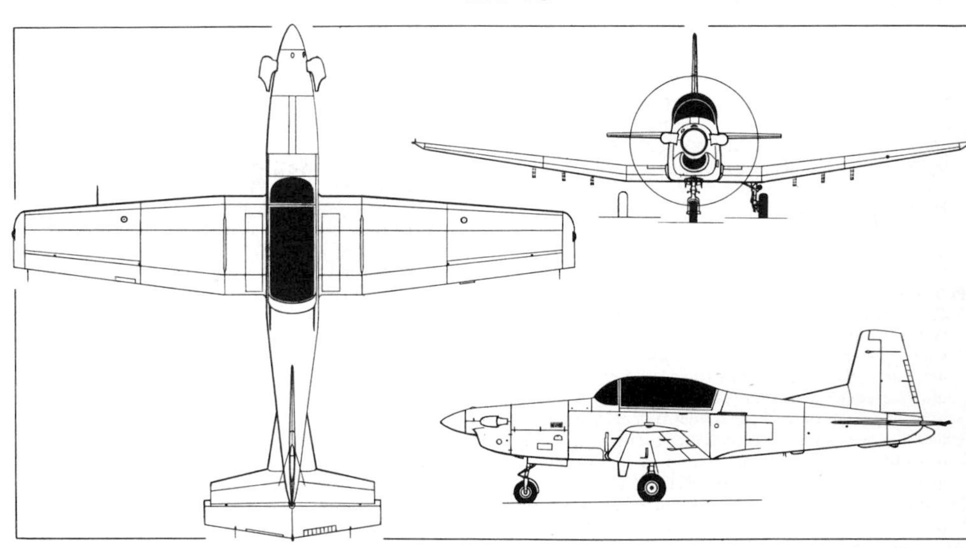

Pilatus PC-7 Turbo-Trainer (Pratt & Whitney Canada PT6A-25A turboprop engine) *(Pilot Press)*

First series production Pilatus PC-9 turboprop powered training aircraft

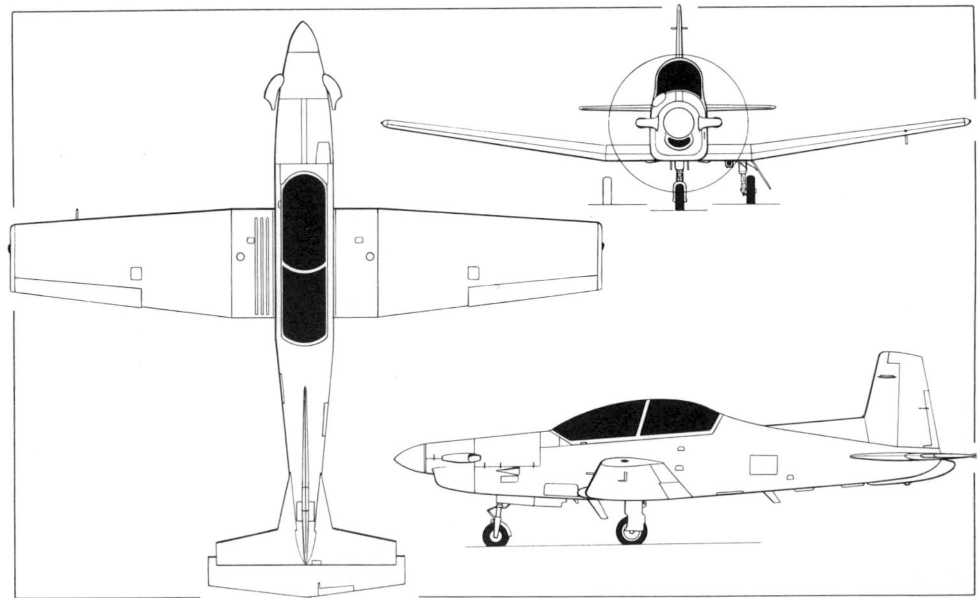

Pilatus PC-9 basic/advanced trainer (Pratt & Whitney Canada PT6A-62 turboprop engine) *(Pilot Press)*

Tail Unit: Cantilever all-metal structure with mass balanced cable operated rudder and elevator. Trim tab in starboard half of elevator, and trim/anti-balance tab in rudder, both mass balanced and electrically actuated.

Landing Gear: Retractable tricycle type, with hydraulic actuation in both normal and emergency modes. Mainwheels retract inward into wing centre-section, nosewheel rearward; all units enclosed by doors when retracted. Oleo-pneumatic shock absorber in each leg unit. Hydraulically actuated nosewheel steering. Goodrich wheels and tyres, with Goodrich multi-piston hydraulic disc brakes on mainwheels. Parking brake.

Power Plant: One 857 kW (1,150 shp) Pratt & Whitney Canada PT6A-62 turboprop engine, flat rated at 708 kW (950 shp), driving a Hartzell HC-D4N-3/D9512 four-blade constant-speed fully-feathering propeller with spinner. Fuel in two integral tanks in wing leading-edges, total usable capacity 508 litres (112 Imp gallons). Overwing refuelling point on each side. Fuel system includes a 12 litre (2·6 Imp gallon) aerobatics tank in fuselage, forward of front cockpit, which permits up to 60 s of inverted flight. Provision for two 152 or 240 litre (33·4 or 52·8 Imp gallon) drop tanks on the centre underwing attachment points. Total oil capacity 16 litres (3·5 Imp gallons).

Accommodation: Martin-Baker Mk CH 11A adjustable ejection seats for two persons, in 'stepped' tandem arrangement with rear seat elevated 15 cm (6·3 in). Seats operable, through canopy, at zero height and speeds down to 60 knots (112 km/h; 70 mph). One-piece acrylic Perspex windscreen; one-piece framed canopy, incorporating rollover bar, opens sideways to starboard. Dual controls standard. Cockpit heating, ventilation and canopy demisting standard. Space for 25 kg (55 lb) of baggage aft of seats, with external access.

Systems: Normalair-Garrett environmental control system, using air cycle and engine bleed air, for cockpit heating/ventilation and canopy demisting. Fairey Systems hydraulic system, pressure 207 bars (3,000 lb/sq in), for actuation of landing gear, mainwheel doors, nosewheel steering and airbrake; system max flow rate 18·8 litres (4·14 Imp gallons)/min. Bootstrap oil/oil reservoir, pressurised at 3·45-207 bars (50-3,000 lb/sq in). Oil/nitrogen accumulator, also charged to 207 bars (3,000 lb/sq in), provides emergency hydraulic power for flaps and landing gear. Primary electrical system (28V DC operational, 24V nominal) powered by a Lear Siegler 30V 200A starter/generator and a 24V 40Ah battery; two static inverters supply 115/26V AC power at 400Hz. Ground power receptacle provided. Electric anti-icing of pitot tube, static ports and AOA transmitter standard; electric de-icing of propeller blades optional. Diluter demand oxygen system, selected and controlled individually from a panel in each cockpit.

Avionics and Equipment: Both cockpits fully instrumented to standard customer specifications, with Kratos computer operated instrument system (COINS). Single or dual system VHF, UHF and/or HF to customer's requirements. Audio integrating system controls audio services from com, nav and interphone systems. Customer-specified equipment provides flight environmental, attitude and direction data, and ground-transmitted position determining information. Retractable 250W landing/taxying light in each main landing gear leg bay. Optional equipment includes Collins or Bendix CRT displays (electronic ADI and HSI), J.E.T. head-up displays, emergency battery, encoding altimeter, emergency locator transmitter, IFR hood, anti-*g* system, propeller electric de-icing, and underwing drop tanks.

Dimensions, external:

Wing span	10·192 m (33 ft 5¼ in)
Wing chord: mean aerodynamic	1·64 m (5 ft 4½ in)
mean geometric	1·61 m (5 ft 3½ in)
Wing aspect ratio	6·38
Length overall	10·175 m (33 ft 4¾ in)
Height overall	3·26 m (10 ft 8⅓ in)
Wheel track	2·54 m (8 ft 4 in)
Propeller diameter	2·44 m (8 ft 0 in)

Areas:

Wings, gross	16·29 m^2 (175·3 sq ft)
Ailerons (total)	1·57 m^2 (16·90 sq ft)
Trailing-edge flaps (total)	1·77 m^2 (19·05 sq ft)
Airbrake	0·30 m^2 (3·23 sq ft)
Fin	0·86 m^2 (9·26 sq ft)
Rudder, incl tab	0·90 m^2 (9·69 sq ft)
Tailplane	1·80 m^2 (19·38 sq ft)
Elevator, incl tab	1·60 m^2 (17·22 sq ft)

Weights and Loadings (A: Aerobatic, U: Utility):

Basic weight empty	approx 1,620 kg (3,571 lb)
Weight empty, equipped	1,685 kg (3,715 lb)
Max T-O weight: A	2,250 kg (4,960 lb)
U	3,200 kg (7,055 lb)
Max ramp weight: A	2,260 kg (4,982 lb)
U	3,210 kg (7,077 lb)
Max landing weight: A	2,250 kg (4,960 lb)
U	3,100 kg (6,834 lb)
Max zero-fuel weight: A	1,900 kg (4,188 lb)
Max wing loading: A	138·1 kg/m^2 (28·3 lb/sq ft)
U	196·4 kg/m^2 (40·2 lb/sq ft)
Max power loading: A	3·18 kg/kW (5·22 lb/shp)
U	4·52 kg/kW (7·42 lb/shp)

Performance (at appropriate max T-O weight, ISA, propeller speed 2,000 rpm):

Max permissible diving speed:
A — Mach 0·73 (360 knots; 667 km/h; 414 mph EAS)
U — Mach 0·55 (300 knots; 556 km/h; 345 mph EAS)

Max operating speed:
A — Mach 0·68 (320 knots; 593 km/h; 368 mph EAS)
U — Mach 0·50 (270 knots; 500 km/h; 311 mph EAS)

Max level speed:
A at S/L — 268 knots (496 km/h; 308 mph)
A at 6,100 m (20,000 ft) — 300 knots (556 km/h; 345 mph)

Max cruising speed:
A at 6,100 m (20,000 ft) — 300 knots (556 km/h; 345 mph)

Manoeuvring speed:
A — 210 knots (389 km/h; 242 mph) EAS
U — 200 knots (370 km/h; 230 mph) EAS

Max speed with flaps and/or landing gear down:
A and U — 150 knots (278 km/h; 172 mph) EAS

Stalling speed, engine idling:
A, flaps and landing gear up — 79 knots (147 km/h; 91 mph) EAS
U, flaps and landing gear up — 94 knots (175 km/h; 109 mph) EAS
A, flaps and landing gear down — 70 knots (130 km/h; 81 mph) EAS
U, flaps and landing gear down — 83 knots (154 km/h; 96 mph) EAS

Max rate of climb at S/L: A	1,247 m (4,091 ft)/min
Time to 4,575 m (15,000 ft): A	4 min 30 s
Max operating altitude	7,620 m (25,000 ft)
Service ceiling	11,580 m (38,000 ft)
T-O run at S/L: A	240 m (788 ft)
T-O to 15 m (50 ft) at S/L: A	440 m (1,444 ft)
Landing from 15 m (50 ft) at S/L A	530 m (1,739 ft)
Landing run at S/L: A	260 m (853 ft)

Max range at cruise power at 6,100 m (20,000 ft), 5% fuel plus 20 min reserves — 830 nm (1,538 km; 955 miles)

Endurance (typical mission power settings) — 2 sorties of 1 h duration plus 20 min reserves

g limits: A — +7/−3·5
U — +4·5/−2·25

SWISS FEDERAL AIRCRAFT FACTORY (F+W)

EIDGENÖSSISCHES FLUGZEUGWERK—FABRIQUE FÉDÉRALE D'AVIONS—FABBRICA FEDERALE D'AEROPLANI

CH-6032 Emmen
Telephone: (041) 59 41 11
Telex: 868 505
Telefax: (041) 55 25 88
Director: Lucien Othenin-Girard
Deputy Director and Commercial Manager:
Dr Peter Burkhardt
Manager, Research and Development:
Hansjürg Kobelt
Head of Production: Hanspeter Arnold
Head of Quality Assurance: Dr Claus Utz

F+W is the Swiss government's official aircraft establishment for research, development, production, maintenance and modification of military aircraft and guided missile systems. It employs about 700 people in its works at Emmen, near Lucerne, which cover 35,300 m^2 (380,000 sq ft). Research and Development is divided into four departments. Aerodynamics and thermodynamics, with appropriate test facilities which include four wind tunnels for speeds of up to Mach 4·5, test cells for piston and turbojet engines with or without afterburners, all equipped with computerised data acquisition and processing; structural and systems engineering for aircraft, helicopters and space hardware, with a speciality in fatigue analysis and testing of entire aircraft structures; electronics and missile systems, covering all system aspects of aircraft and helicopter avionics, missiles and RPVs; prototype and test, covering prototype fabrication, flight test instrumentation and system and environmental testing.

The Production Department covers the whole field of production capabilities, from mechanical and sheet metal parts to composite parts and subassemblies (including leading-edge slats for the McDonnell Douglas MD-80 series and rudders for the Northrop F-5E/F); electronics, electrical, electro-mechanical and electro-optical subassemblies; final assembly of missiles, missile systems, aircraft and helicopters. Recent major activities have included licence manufacture of aircraft, helicopters and missile systems, and fabrication of the shroud of the Ariane space launcher (designed by F+W with Contraves as main contractor). In March 1985 F+W delivered to the Swiss Air Force the last of 110 Northrop Tiger IIs (98 F-5Es and 12 F-5Fs) ordered from the USA under two 'Peace Alps' contracts. All except the first 19 of these aircraft (13 Es and six Fs) were assembled and partially manufactured by F+W.

Since 1977 F+W has manufactured under licence the tracker, its field test equipment and appropriate training equipment for the MDAC Dragon anti-tank weapon system, and has assembled the missile itself for the Swiss government since 1981. In 1980 it became general manager of a Swiss industry programme to produce Rapier surface-to-air missiles under licence from BAe.

Under a $10·7 million USAF contract awarded jointly to Northrop and F+W in October 1984, the two companies are manufacturing more than 230 sets of new horizontal tail surfaces for the Northrop T-38 Talon supersonic jet trainer.

F+W conducts wind tunnel tests for foreign aircraft manufacturers, ground transportation developers and users, and for the building industry. It performs development and integration of internal stores and other modification work on military aircraft, including, currently, adding canard surfaces to Swiss Air Force Mirages, the first of which first flew in this configuration on 23 August 1983. F+W has also developed a low-level dispenser bombing system which is already integrated on Swiss Air Force Hunter and Tiger II aircraft. The system utilises aerodynamically retarded bomblets, carried in underwing pods and ejected by ram air. Integration on other types of aircraft is under way.

F+W offers proprietary products which include acoustic systems for failure and flight envelope warning; all-electronic linear angle of attack and *g* indicators; scoring indicators for air-to-air or ground-to-air shooting, with a microcomputer based ground station; multi-component strain gauge balances for testing purposes, covering forces from a few hundred grammes to several tons; water separators for aircraft conditioning; and POHWARO hot water rockets. (Details of these rockets can be found in the 1977-78 *Jane's*.) Co-operative development led to the Farner KZD 85 target drone described in the RPVs & Targets section of this edition. Services are also offered for environmental testing, especially high-shock long-duration testing on a newly designed sled type shock test installation.

F+W MIRAGE IMPROVEMENT PROGRAMME

The Swiss government approved funding at the end of 1985 for a retrofit programme for Mirage III aircraft of the Swiss Air Force, which currently has 52 of these aircraft (30 III-S, 18 III-RS, two III-BS and two III-DS) in its inventory. Main ingredients of this programme are the fitting of non-moving canard surfaces just aft of the engine air intakes, and addition of a very slim strake on each side of the extreme nose, the former to improve manoeuvrability and low-speed handling and eliminate buffeting, the latter

Swiss Air Force Mirage III-S evaluation aircraft, modified by F+W with nose strakes and fixed foreplane surfaces

to increase stability in yaw near the upper limit of the flight envelope. F + W began flight testing this configuration on a Swiss Air Force Mirage III-S (J-2301) on 23 August 1983, and a second aircraft (J-2302) was later converted for operational evaluation by Swiss Air Force pilots. The canards are of similar size and shape to those on the Mirage 3 NG, and have a span about one-third that of the wings. The nose strakes, which extend along part of the nose pitot and the tip of the radome, are approx 0·5 m (1 ft 7¾ in) long and less than 5 cm (1·97 in) wide.

Other improvements forming part of the upgrading package include new audible warning and visual angle of attack monitoring systems, to alert the pilot when approaching limits of the flight envelope; substitution of Martin-Baker Mk 4 ejection seats in place of the present Mk 6 seats; addition of infra-red and passive/active ECM; provision of more powerful VHF radios; wing strengthening; ability to carry two underwing 500 litre (110 Imp gallon) IMI auxiliary fuel tanks and a 730 litre (160·5 Imp gallon) centreline tank; mounting of improved blast deflectors for the two internal guns, to allow firing at high angles of attack; and a new camouflage paint scheme. The retrofit programme is planned to be undertaken over the period 1986-1990.

TAIWAN

AIDC

AERO INDUSTRY DEVELOPMENT CENTER

PO Box 8676, Taichung, Taiwan 400
Telephone: Taichung (042) 523051 and 523052
Telex: 51140 AIDC
OTHER WORKS: Kang-Shan
DIRECTOR: Dr Hsichun M. Hua
DEPUTY DIRECTORS:
Dr Shih-sen Wang (Research and Engineering)
Y. L. Chang (Manufacturing)

The Aero Industry Development Center was established on 1 March 1969 as a successor to the Bureau of Aircraft Industry (BAI), which was formed in 1946 in Nanking and moved to Taiwan in 1948. AIDC, which employs more than 3,000 people, is now a subsidiary of the Chung Shan Institute of Science and Technology.

In October 1968 the Aeronautical Research Laboratory, then a branch of BAI, constructed the first Chinese built PL-1A (see 1970-71 *Jane's*), a slightly modified version of the US Pazmany PL-1 which flew for the first time on 26 October 1968. After further modifications, 55 PL-1B Chienshou production models were built by AIDC in 1970-74. The PL-1B was described and illustrated in the 1975-76 *Jane's*.

Between 1969 and 1976, the AIDC produced in Taiwan 118 Bell UH-1H (Bell Model 205) helicopters under licence for the Chinese Nationalist Army.

The AIDC is currently engaged in licence building 248 Northrop F-5E Tiger II tactical fighter aircraft (see US section) and 36 two-seat F-5Fs for the Chinese Nationalist Air Force. The first Chinese-built F-5E (CAF name **Chung Cheng**) was rolled out on 30 October 1974, and most of these had been delivered by the beginning of 1986.

The AIDC designed and produced the T-CH-1 turboprop basic trainer for the Chinese Nationalist Air Force, and has since developed and put into production the twin-turbofan AT-3.

AIDC FIGHTER

Preliminary design was reportedly nearing completion in mid-1986 of a supersonic lightweight air defence fighter to replace the Lockheed F-104 and Northrop F-5E in Chinese Nationalist Air Force service in the 1990s. According to Taiwan's Defence Minister in late 1985, a development/production budget of $1,000 million had been approved for this programme, which is expected to lead to an aircraft with similar performance characteristics to the Northrop F-20A Tigershark, the sale of which to Taiwan has been forbidden by the US government. US technological assistance in developing an indigenous fighter is not, however, subject to the same restrictions, and AIDC is reported to have received such assistance from General Dynamics (airframe), Garrett (power plant) and Lear Siegler (avionics), the fighter being likely to be powered by two 37·14 kN (8,350 lb st) Garrett TFE1042 turbofan engines. First flight is tentatively planned for 1989.

AIDC AT-3

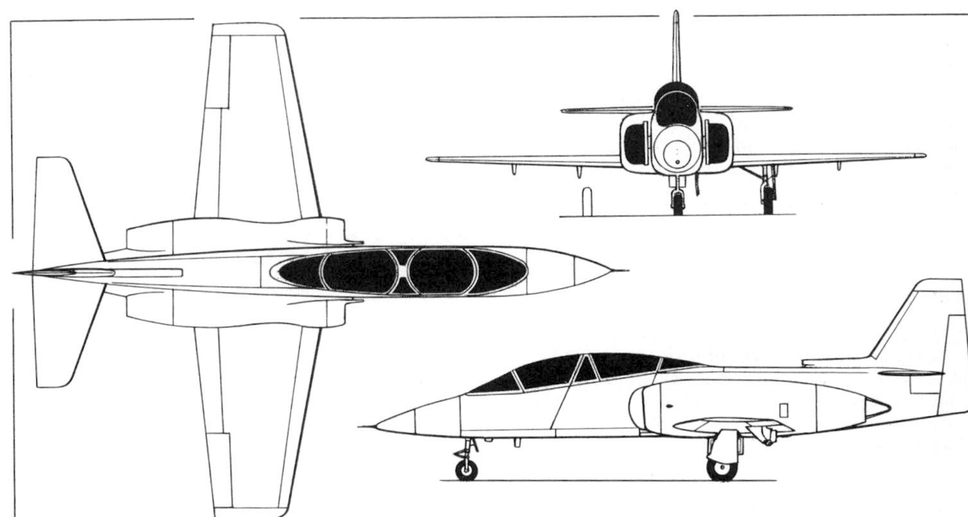

AIDC AT-3 twin-turbofan military basic and advanced trainer *(Pilot Press)*

In July 1975, AIDC was awarded a contract to design and develop prototypes of a new basic and advanced military jet training aircraft, designated XAT-3. Construction of two prototypes (0801 and 0802) began in January 1978, and these flew for the first time on 16 September 1980 and 30 October 1981 respectively. Following receipt of a contract for more than 50 production aircraft, AIDC began the manufacture of these, under the CAF designation AT-3, in March 1982. The first production aircraft (0803) made its initial flight on 6 February 1984, and deliveries began in the following month. The AT-3 became available for export in mid-1985, but no orders had been announced at the time of going to press.

TYPE: Tandem two-seat twin-turbofan military trainer.

WINGS: Cantilever low-wing monoplane of supercritical section. Thickness/chord ratio 10%. Dihedral 0° 46′. Incidence 1° 30′. Sweepback at quarter-chord 7° 20′. One-piece carry-through wing, with a machined torsion box, attached to fuselage by six bolts. Multi-spar light alloy structure, with heavy plate machined skin. Hydraulically powered light alloy honeycomb sealed-gap ailerons. Electrically operated light alloy single-slotted trailing-edge flaps. No anti-icing system.

FUSELAGE: Light alloy semi-monocoque basic structure, with steel, magnesium and graphite/epoxy used in certain areas. Built in three sections: forward fuselage, including cockpit; centre fuselage, including nacelles; and rear fuselage, including vertical and horizontal tail assembly. Two electrically controlled hydraulically actuated airbrakes, of laminated graphite/epoxy construction, mounted on fuselage undersurface forward of mainwheel wells. Fail-safe structure in pressurised cockpit section.

TAIL UNIT: Cantilever all-metal structure, integral with rear fuselage. One-piece all-moving tailplane; incidence varied by tandem hydraulic actuator. Dual hydraulic actuators for rudder, with yaw stability augmentation. No trim tabs.

LANDING GEAR: Hydraulically retractable tricycle type, with single wheel on each unit. Main units retract inward into fuselage, nosewheel forward. Oleo-pneumatic shock absorber in each unit. Two-position extending nose leg increases static angle of attack by 3° 30′, to reduce T-O run, and is shortened automatically during retraction. Emergency extension by gravity. Mainwheels and tyres size 24 × 8·00-13, pressure 8·96 bars (130 lb/sq in). Hydraulically steerable nose unit, with wheel and tyre size 18 × 6·50-8, pressure 5·51 bars (80 lb/sq in). All-metal multi-disc brakes.

POWER PLANT: Two Garrett TFE731-2-2L non-afterburning turbofan engines (each 15·57 kN; 3,500 lb st), installed in nacelle on each side of fuselage. Inclined ram air intakes, each with splitter plate, abreast of rear cockpit. Engine starting by onboard battery or ground power. All fuel carried in fuselage, in two equal-size rubber impregnated nylon bladder tanks, with combined capacity of 1,630 litres (358·5 Imp gallons). Two independent fuel systems, one for each engine, with crossfeed to allow fuel from either or both systems to be fed to either or both engines. Pressure fuelling point forward of, and below, port air intake for internal and external tanks. A 568 litre (125 Imp gallon) auxiliary drop tank can be carried on each inboard underwing pylon. Oil capacity 5·7 litres (1·25 Imp gallons) total, 1·9 litres (0·42 Imp gallons) usable. Fire warning and extinguishing systems for each engine bay.

ACCOMMODATION: Crew of two in tandem on zero/zero ejection (through canopy) seats, under individual manually operated canopies which open sideways to starboard. Crew separated by internal windscreen. Independent miniature detonation cord (MDC) system to break each canopy for ground and in-flight emergency egress. MDC can be operated from outside cockpit on ground. Rear seat elevated 30 cm (12 in). Dual controls standard.

SYSTEMS: Garrett bootstrap air cycle environmental control system, for cockpit air-conditioning and pressurisation (max differential 0·34 bars; 5 lb/sq in), canopy seal, demisting, and pressurisation of *g* suits, hydraulic reservoirs and external fuel tanks. Two independent hydraulic systems, pressure 207 bars (3,000 lb/sq in), with engine driven pumps (flow rate 34·4 litres; 7·57 Imp gallons/min). Air type reservoir, pressurised at 2·41 bars (35 lb/sq in). Flight control hydraulic system provides power only for operation of primary flying control surfaces. Utility system serves primary flying control surfaces, landing gear, landing gear doors, airbrakes, wheel brakes, nosewheel steering, and stability augmentation system. Primary electrical power supplied by two 28V 12kW DC starter/generators, one on each engine. One 40Ah nickel-cadmium battery for engine starting. Two static inverters supply AC power at 400Hz. External DC power socket on starboard side of centre fuselage. Hydraulic and electrical systems can be sustained by either engine. Liquid oxygen system, capacity 5 litres (1·1 Imp gallons), for crew.

AVIONICS AND EQUIPMENT: Most radio and nav equipment located in large avionics bays in forward fuselage. Standard avionics include UHF com, intercom, IFF/SIF, Tacan, panel mounted VOR/ILS/marker beacon indicator, attitude and heading reference system and angle of attack system, plus full blind-flying instrumentation. Wide range of optional avionics available.

ARMAMENT AND OPERATIONAL EQUIPMENT: Manually adjustable gunsight and camera in forward cockpit, for armament training. Large weapons bay beneath rear cockpit can house variety of stores, including quick-change semi-recessed machine-gun packs. Disposable

AIDC AT-3 tandem two-seat trainer (two Garrett TFE731 turbofan engines)

weapons can be carried on a centreline pylon (stressed for 907 kg; 2,000 lb load), two inboard underwing pylons (each 635 kg; 1,400 lb and capable of accepting triple ejector racks), two outboard underwing pylons (each 272 kg; 600 lb), and wingtip launch rails (each of 91 kg; 200 lb capacity), subject to a max external stores load of 2,721 kg (6,000 lb). Weapons that can be carried include GP, SE, cluster and fire bombs; SUU-25A/A, -25C/A and -25E/A flare dispensers; LAU-3/A, -3A/A, -3B/A, -10/A, -10A/A, -60/A, -68A/A and -68B/A rocket launchers; wingtip infra-red air-to-air missiles; and rocket pods, practice bombs, and bomb or rocket training dispensers. The aircraft can also be equipped with an A/A37U-15TTS aerial target system, carried on the centreline pylon.

Dimensions, external:
Wing span 10·46 m (34 ft 3¾ in)
Wing chord: at root 2·80 m (9 ft 2¼ in)
at tip 1·40 m (4 ft 7 in)
Wing aspect ratio 5
Length overall, incl nose probe 12·90 m (42 ft 4 in)
Height overall 4·36 m (14 ft 3¾ in)
Tailplane span 4·83 m (15 ft 10¼ in)
Wheel track 3·96 m (13 ft 0 in)
Wheelbase 5·49 m (18 ft 0 in)

Areas:
Wings, gross 21·93 m^2 (236·05 sq ft)
Ailerons (total) 1·33 m^2 (14·32 sq ft)
Trailing-edge flaps (total) 2·53 m^2 (27·23 sq ft)
Fin 3·45 m^2 (37·14 sq ft)
Rudder 1·15 m^2 (12·38 sq ft)
Tailplane 5·02 m^2 (54·04 sq ft)

Weights and Loadings:
Weight empty, equipped 3,855 kg (8,500 lb)
Max fuel: internal 1,270 kg (2,800 lb)
external 884 kg (1,950 lb)
Max external stores load 2,721 kg (6,000 lb)
Normal T-O weight:
trainer, 'clean' 5,216 kg (11,500 lb)
Max T-O weight with external stores 7,938 kg (17,500 lb)
Max landing weight 7,360 kg (16,225 lb)
Max wing loading 362 kg/m^2 (74·14 lb/sq ft)
Max power loading 254·9 kg/kN (2·5 lb/lb st)

Performance (at max T-O weight):
Max limiting Mach No. 1·05
Max level speed:
at S/L 485 knots (898 km/h; 558 mph)
at 11,000 m (36,000 ft) Mach 0·85 (488 knots; 904 km/h; 562 mph)
Max cruising speed at 11,000 m (36,000 ft) Mach 0·83 (476 knots; 882 km/h; 548 mph)
Stalling speed:
flaps and landing gear up 100 knots (185 km/h; 115 mph)
flaps and landing gear down 90 knots (167 km/h; 104 mph)
Max rate of climb at S/L 3,078 m (10,100 ft)/min
Service ceiling 14,625 m (48,000 ft)
T-O run 458 m (1,500 ft)
T-O to 15 m (50 ft) 671 m (2,200 ft)
Landing from 15 m (50 ft) 945 m (3,100 ft)
Landing run 671 m (2,200 ft)
Range with max internal fuel 1,230 nm (2,279 km; 1,416 miles)
Endurance with max internal fuel 3 h 12 min

THAILAND

RTAF (SWDC)

ROYAL THAI AIR FORCE (Science and Weapon Systems Development Centre)

Office of Aeronautical Engineering, Directorate of Aeronautical Engineering (DAE), No. 1 Pradipath Street, Dusit, Bangkok 10300
Telephone: 2412885
Director of DAE: Air Marshal Banyat Wongthongsuk
Director of SWDC: Air Marshal Sak Tareechat
Chief Designer: Gp Capt Preecha Wannabhoom

The RTAF-1, the first design for which engineers of the Royal Thai Air Force were responsible after the end of the second World War, was followed by the RTAF-2 utility aircraft, now in the RTAF Museum at Don Muang, near Bangkok. No details of the RTAF-3 are known, except that a model underwent wind tunnel testing in Japan. Details of the RTAF-4 Chandra, a conversion of the DHC-1 Chipmunk, were given in the 1983-84 *Jane's*.

The Office of Aeronautical Engineering was set up in 1975, and has been responsible for all subsequent design activity.

RTAF-5

Most ambitious product of the DAE to date, the RTAF-5 is a turboprop trainer and FAC aircraft designed and built entirely in Thailand. Design started in February 1975, and construction of the first of two prototypes began on 26 May 1976. This aircraft made a successful 12 min first flight at Don Muang Air Base on 5 October 1984, with minimum fuel and the landing gear fixed in the down position. Following the second test flight, on 18 December 1984, the aircraft was to have undergone modifications which included fitment of the landing gear retraction mechanism, but design difficulties have prevented this from being accomplished successfully.

Work on the RTAF-5 has been temporarily suspended until the wing manufacturing programme for the RFB Fantrainer has been completed (see German section), which should be in 1987. After that, design and development work will continue on the second RTAF-5 prototype, embodying lessons learnt during building and flying the first example.

The following description applies to the first prototype:

Type: Tandem two-seat advanced trainer and forward air control aircraft.

Wings: Cantilever mid-wing monoplane, with constant chord centre-section and slightly tapered outer panels, with provision for small wingtip fuel tanks. Wing section NACA 63_2A415 at root, NACA 63_1A412 at tip. Dihedral 3° on outer panels, none on centre-section. Incidence 3° at root. Conventional aluminium alloy (7075 main spars and 2024-T3) two-spar fail-safe structure. Manually operated ailerons, each with inset balance tab. Electrically operated single-slotted Fowler trailing-edge flaps, in two sections on each wing separated by tailbooms.

Fuselage: Pod type central nacelle, suspended from wing, of conventional aluminium alloy (2024-T3) semi-monocoque fail-safe construction. Forward section contains equipment bay and crew accommodation, under large glazed canopy. Rear section houses wing carry-through structure and power plant.

Tail Unit: Cantilever all-metal (2024-T3) structure carried on twin booms of semi-monocoque construction. Horizontal tailplane, with one-piece elevator, mounted between tips of sweptback vertical fins. Manually operated rudders and elevator. Adjustable trim tabs in elevator only. Tailskid below boom under each fin.

Landing Gear: Tricycle type, with twin wheels on main units and single nosewheel (fixed down for preliminary flight test). Oleo-pneumatic shock absorber in nose unit. Mainwheel legs have rubber in compression shock absorbers. Steerable nosewheel with tyre size 5·00-5, pressure 3·10 bars (45 lb/sq in). Mainwheel tyres size 7·00-6, pressure 3·45 bars (50 lb/sq in). Bendix hydraulic disc brakes on mainwheels.

Power Plant: One 313 kW (420 shp) Allison 250-B17C turboprop engine, driving a Hartzell three-blade constant-speed pusher propeller with spinner. Integral fuel tank in wing centre-section, capacity 76 litres (16·5 Imp gallons; 20 US gallons); 113 litre (25 Imp gallon; 30 US gallon) fuselage tank and 30 litre (6·5 Imp gallon; 8 US gallon) collector tank. Total internal fuel capacity 219 litres (48 Imp gallons; 58 US gallons). Refuelling points in top of wing centre-section and (for fuselage tank) underneath wing. Provision for wingtip tanks, total capacity 95 litres (21 Imp gallons; 25 US gallons). Oil capacity 11·4 litres (2·5 Imp gallons; 3 US gallons).

Accommodation: Pilot and co-pilot (pupil at front, instructor at rear in trainer version) in tandem under large framed canopy which opens sideways to port. Rear seat elevated 7·5 cm (3 in). Dual controls standard. Accommodation ventilated.

Electrical System: 28V DC (150Ah battery).

Avionics and Equipment: VHF nav/com, UHF, transponder, ADF, intercom, rotating beacon, navigation and position lights, instrument and warning lights are all standard. Gunsight can be installed above front instrument panel.

Armament: Four weapon attachment points under wings, with capacity of 68 kg (150 lb) on each inner hardpoint and 45 kg (100 lb) on each outer point.

Dimensions, external:
Wing span 9·55 m (31 ft 4 in)
Wing span over tip tanks 9·86 m (32 ft 4¼ in)
Wing chord: at root 1·65 m (5 ft 5 in)
at tip 1·44 m (4 ft 8½ in)
Wing aspect ratio (incl tip tanks) 6·18
Length overall (incl nose probe) 9·96 m (32 ft 8 in)
Fuselage: Length 6·71 m (22 ft 0 in)
Max width 1·14 m (3 ft 9 in)
Height overall 3·05 m (10 ft 0 in)
Tailplane span 3·66 m (12 ft 0 in)
Wheel track 3·76 m (12 ft 4 in)
Wheelbase 2·84 m (9 ft 4 in)
Propeller diameter 2·29 m (7 ft 6 in)
Propeller ground clearance (static) 15·25 cm (6 in)

Areas:
Wings, gross (incl tip tanks) 15·67 m^2 (168·7 sq ft)
Ailerons (total) 1·49 m^2 (16·00 sq ft)
Trailing-edge flaps (total) 1·50 m^2 (16·13 sq ft)
Fins (total) 2·42 m^2 (26·03 sq ft)
Rudders (total) 0·84 m^2 (9·00 sq ft)
Tailplane 2·84 m^2 (30·60 sq ft)
Elevator (incl tabs) 1·11 m^2 (12·00 sq ft)

Weights and Loadings:
Weight empty 1,645 kg (3,628 lb)
Fuel weight (284 litres; 62·5 Imp gallons; 75 US gallons) 236 kg (520 lb)
Max ramp weight 2,177 kg (4,800 lb)
Max T-O weight 2,154 kg (4,750 lb)
Max zero-fuel weight 1,746 kg (3,850 lb)
Max landing weight 2,086 kg (4,600 lb)
Max wing loading 137·4 kg/m^2 (28·16 lb/sq ft)
Max power loading 6·88 kg/kW (11·3 lb/shp)

Performance (preliminary flight test):
Cruising speed at S/L 115 knots (213 km/h; 132 mph)
Min flying speed at S/L 85 knots (158 km/h; 98 mph)
Stalling speed, 30° flap 80 knots (149 km/h; 93 mph)
Max rate of climb at S/L 91 m (300 ft)/min
T-O run (hot day) 549 m (1,800 ft)
T-O to 15 m (50 ft) (hot day) 701 m (2,300 ft)
Landing from 15 m (50 ft) (hot day) 915 m (3,000 ft)

First prototype of the RTAF-5 trainer/FAC aircraft, designed and built by the Royal Thai Air Force

TURKEY

TAI

TUSAŞ HAVACILIK VE UZAY SANAYİİ AS (Turkish Aerospace Industries Inc)

Head Office: Tahran Cad. 3 (PO Box 18), Mimhan, 06690 Kavaklidere, Ankara
Telephone: (90 41) 671170/5
Telex: 46065 THUS TR
Telefax: 671177

Directors:
J. Jones (Managing)
M. O. Kiciman, PhD (Research and Development)

TUSAŞ (see 1985-86 and previous editions of *Jane's*) was officially established on 11 July 1973, with joint funding by the Turkish government and the Turkish Air Force Foundation, with the objective of creating an aircraft manufacturing industry in Turkey. An area of 5 million m^2 (1·93 sq miles) at Mürted, near Ankara, was allocated for an aircraft manufacturing facility and auxiliary buildings.

Following selection of the General Dynamics F-16 in 1983 as the new fighter aircraft for the Turkish Air Force, TAI was established on 15 May 1984 as the corresponding industrial organisation, owned jointly by Turkish interests (51%), General Dynamics (42%) and General Electric (7%). Construction of the new facility began in the same year, and this was due to come into operation in late 1986. Co-production will include aircraft assembly, test, and airframe manufacture. A total of 160 F-16Cs and Ds are involved in the programme, of which the first eight will be US built. Initial assembly by TAI will be from kits supplied by General Dynamics, progressing gradually towards local manufacture. Deliveries are planned to begin in 1988 and be completed by 1994.

UNION OF SOVIET SOCIALIST REPUBLICS

ANTONOV

OLEG K. ANTONOV DESIGN BUREAU

General Designer: Pyotr V. Balabuev

This design bureau, based at Kiev, is named after its founder, Oleg Konstantinovich Antonov who, after establishing his reputation with a series of successful glider and sailplane designs, became one of the Soviet Union's leading designers of transport aircraft, particularly those types intended for short field operation. He died on 4 April 1984, at the age of 78.

ANTONOV An-2

NATO reporting name: Colt

Following manufacture of the An-2M specialised agricultural version of this large single-engined biplane, in the mid-sixties, production of the An-2 came to an end at Kiev in the Soviet Union. Details of the various versions that were built can be found in the 1971-72 *Jane's*.

Several versions of the An-2 continued in production under licence in Poland in 1985 (see WSK-PZL Mielec entry). Others have been built at Harbin and elsewhere, in China, under the Chinese designation Y-5.

ANTONOV An-3

It was first reported in the Spring of 1972 that the Antonov design bureau was engaged on design studies for a turboprop development of the An-2 biplane (see WSK-PZL Mielec in Polish section). Designated An-3, the aircraft was intended specifically for agricultural duties and was then expected to compete with the Polish turbofan engined WSK-Mielec M-15 as the next generation agricultural aircraft for use throughout the countries of eastern Europe and the Soviet Union.

At the 1979 Paris Air Show, Mr Oleg Antonov emphasised his continued interest in agricultural aircraft, and confirmed that a prototype of the An-3 had been produced by retrofitting an An-2 with a Glushenkov turboprop engine, driving a slow turning large-diameter three-blade propeller optimised for an aircraft operating speed of 75-97 knots (140-180 km/h; 87-112 mph). He added that an important feature was the ability of the turboprop to ensure adequate cockpit air-conditioning, with clean air at 18-20°C, during operation in ambient temperatures of 40-45°C.

A photograph of the An-3 prototype (SSSR-30576) under test was released to the East European press in 1979 and was reproduced in the 1982-83 and previous editions of *Jane's*. The production standard aircraft shown in an accompanying illustration differs externally from the standard An-2 in having a longer and slimmer nose, housing a 1,081 kW (1,450 shp) Glushenkov TVD-20 turboprop, and short plugs inserted immediately fore and aft of the wings to lengthen the fuselage. The cockpit is further forward, and is sealed and air-conditioned. Instrumentation, electrical and fuel systems are all new, and the former multi-panelled starboard cockpit windows are replaced by a single large blister window. When equipped for agricultural duties, access to the cockpit is via a small door on the port side. When the aircraft is to be used only for transport duties, this door is omitted and access is via the main cabin door and through the airtight door leading from the cabin to the flight deck.

Antonov An-12 modified as testbed for advanced avionics

The An-3 can be equipped for either dusting or spraying. The chemical spraytank has a capacity of 2,200 litres (484 Imp gallons; 581 US gallons), representing an increase of more than 50 per cent over that of the An-2; the cost of spraying each hectare of land is reduced by 25 to 30 per cent. A total of 1,200 litres (264 Imp gallons; 317 US gallons) of fuel is carried in six tanks in the upper wings.

State trials of the An-3 were conducted with renewed urgency in 1982-83, under the project leadership of Mr V. J. Zadrozhnyi, following rejection of the M-15 in the Soviet Union. At their conclusion, a plant in Kiev was assigned the task of converting piston engined An-2s to An-3 standard, using some fuselage components produced by WSK-PZL Mielec. A repair plant for An-3s will be operated at Bulharsk.

Six payload-to-height records were set by an An-3 in 1985. On 12 December, piloted by Vladimir Lysenko, it lifted a record 2,583 kg (5,694 lb) to 2,000 m and set two further Class C1f records by climbing to 6,100 m (20,013 ft) with a payload of 2,000 kg, qualifying also for the record with 1,000 kg. On the following day, piloted by Sergei Gorbik, it lifted 2,375 kg (5,236 lb) to 2,000 m and set two further Class C1e records for 1,000 and 2,000 kg lifted to 6,150 m (20,177 ft).

Dimensions, external: As for An-2, except:
Length overall 14·33 m (47 ft 0 in)

Weight:
Max T-O weight 5,800 kg (12,787 lb)

Performance:
Normal cruising speed 97 knots (180 km/h; 112 mph)
Rate of climb at S/L with max payload 240 m (785 ft)/min

ANTONOV An-3M

Details of this much changed agricultural version of the An-3 can be found under the heading of its design organisation, WSK-PZL Warszawa-Okecie (see Polish section).

ANTONOV An-12

NATO reporting name: Cub

More than 900 An-12 freighters were built for military and civil use before production ended in the Soviet Union in 1973. Versions in service with the Soviet air forces, and identified by NATO reporting names, are as follows:

Cub. Standard Soviet military paratroop and freight transport since 1959. At peak strength, many hundreds of 'Cubs' could carry two full army divisions, totalling 14,000 men and their equipment, over a radius of 651 nm (1,207 km; 750 miles). In 1986, about 260 'Cubs', designated **An-12BP** in the USSR, continued in service with the VTA (Military Transport Aviation) force, although replacement with Ilyushin Il-76s started in 1974. Another 200 An-12s and Il-76s are operated nominally by Aeroflot, forming an immediately available reserve military transport force. An-12s are also operated by the air forces of Algeria, China, Czechoslovakia, Ethiopia, India, Iraq, Malagasy Republic, Poland and Yugoslavia. Some Soviet Air Force An-12s have a larger undernose radome than that originally fitted. Civil An-12s serve with CAAC (China), Balkan Air and Air Guinée, as well as Aeroflot. 'Cub' has a tail gunner's position. In the refined commercial production version, first demonstrated at the 1965 Paris Air Show, the turret is removed and replaced by a streamline fairing.

China is building, at the Hanzhong factory near Xian, its own version of the An-12BP. Known as the **Y-8**, this is listed in the Chinese section, together with a specialised maritime surveillance version of the Y-8.

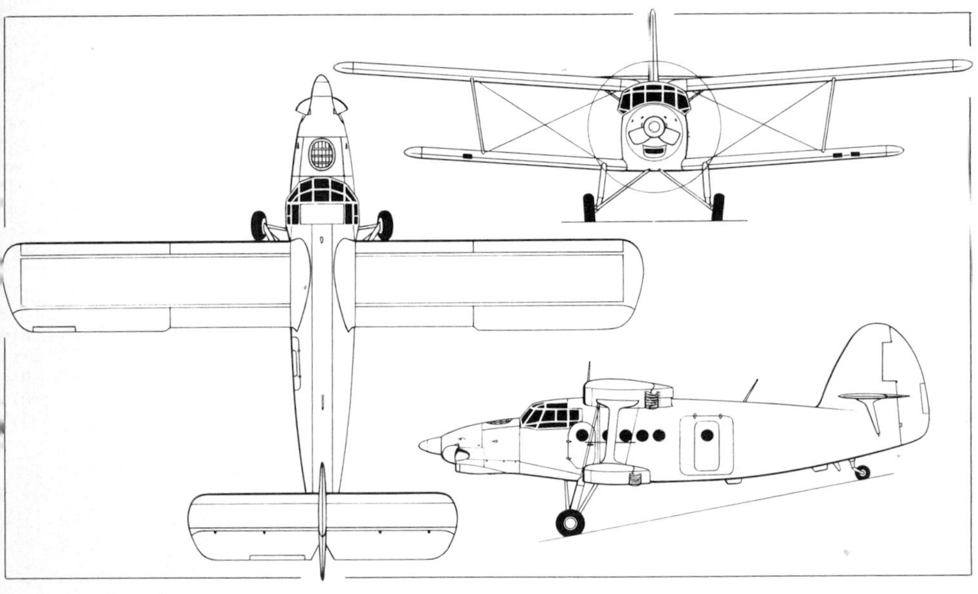

Antonov An-3 turboprop agricultural aircraft, with original flight deck side windows *(Pilot Press)*

Antonov An-3 agricultural biplane (Glushenkov TVD-20 turboprop engine)

Electronic intelligence version of the Antonov An-12 known to NATO as 'Cub-B', with investigating F-104G of Royal Norwegian Air Force

Cub-A. Electronic intelligence (elint) version. Generally similar to basic 'Cub' but with blade aerials on front fuselage, aft of flight deck, and other changes.

Cub-B. Conversion of 'Cub' transport for elint duties with Soviet Naval Air Force. Examples photographed over international waters by the crews of Swedish and Norwegian combat aircraft each had two additional blister fairings under forward and centre fuselage, plus other antennae. About 10 produced.

Cub-C. ECM variant carrying several tons of electrical generation, distribution and control gear in cabin, and palletised jammers for at least five wavebands faired into belly, plus ECM dispensers. Glazed nose and undernose radar of transport retained. An ogival 'solid' fuselage tailcone, housing electronic equipment, is fitted in place of the usual gun position.

Cub-D. This further variant of the An-12 reflects the huge efforts being made by the Soviet Union to ensure effective handling of every conceivable ECM task. Equipment differs from that of 'Cub-C', to handle different active countermeasures duties. Up to 40 'Cub-C and D' aircraft are believed to serve with the Soviet Air Force and Navy.

In addition to these operational variants, An-12s have been modified extensively as testbeds for advanced avionics. One example, fitted with MAD and radar for ASW duties, has been illustrated in previous editions of *Jane's*. Another, shown in the 1985-86 *Jane's*, had special electronics under a large blister fairing on each side of the fuselage forward of the landing gear fairing, and in other housings under the front of the loading ramp/door and rear turret. The avionics testbed illustrated this year has a large box under the rear fuselage, with what appear to be flush dielectric panels covering most of the flat lower face. This aircraft also has a long ogival tailcone similar to that fitted on the ASW testbed mentioned above.

The following abbreviated details apply to the standard Soviet built military An-12BP transport. A full description can be found in the 1979-80 *Jane's*.

TYPE: Four-engined cargo transport.

POWER PLANT: Four 2,983 kW (4,000 ehp) Ivchenko AI-20K turboprops, driving AV-68 four-blade reversible-pitch propellers. All fuel in 22 bag tanks in wings, total normal capacity 13,900 litres (3,058 Imp gallons; 3,672 US gallons). Max capacity 18,100 litres (3,981 Imp gallons; 4,781 US gallons).

ACCOMMODATION: Pilot and co-pilot side by side on flight deck. Engineer's station on starboard side, behind co-pilot. Radio operator in well behind pilot, facing outward. Navigator in glazed nose compartment. Rear gunner in tail turret. Crew door on port side forward of wing. No integral rear loading ramp. Access to freight hold via large door under upswept rear fuselage, comprising two longitudinal halves which can be hinged upward inside cabin to provide access for direct loading of freight from trucks. Undersurface of fuselage aft of this door is formed by a further, rear-hinged, door which retracts upward into fuselage to facilitate loading and unloading. Equipped to carry 90 troops or 60 paratroops, all of whom can be despatched in under one minute, with rear door panels folded upward.

ARMAMENT: Two 23 mm NR-23 guns in tail turret.

DIMENSIONS, EXTERNAL:

Wing span	38·00 m (124 ft 8 in)
Wing chord (mean)	3·452 m (11 ft 4 in)
Wing aspect ratio	11·85
Length overall	33·10 m (108 ft 7¼ in)
Height overall	10·53 m (34 ft 6½ in)
Tailplane span	12·20 m (40 ft 0¼ in)
Wheel track	5·42 m (17 ft 9½ in)
Wheelbase	10·82 m (35 ft 6 in)
Propeller diameter	4·50 m (14 ft 9 in)
Rear loading hatch: Length	7·70 m (25 ft 3 in)
Width	2·95 m (9 ft 8 in)

DIMENSIONS, INTERNAL:

Cargo hold: Length	13·50 m (44 ft 3½ in)
Max width	3·50 m (11 ft 5¾ in)
Max height	2·60 m (8 ft 6¼ in)
Volume	97·2 m³ (3,432·6 cu ft)

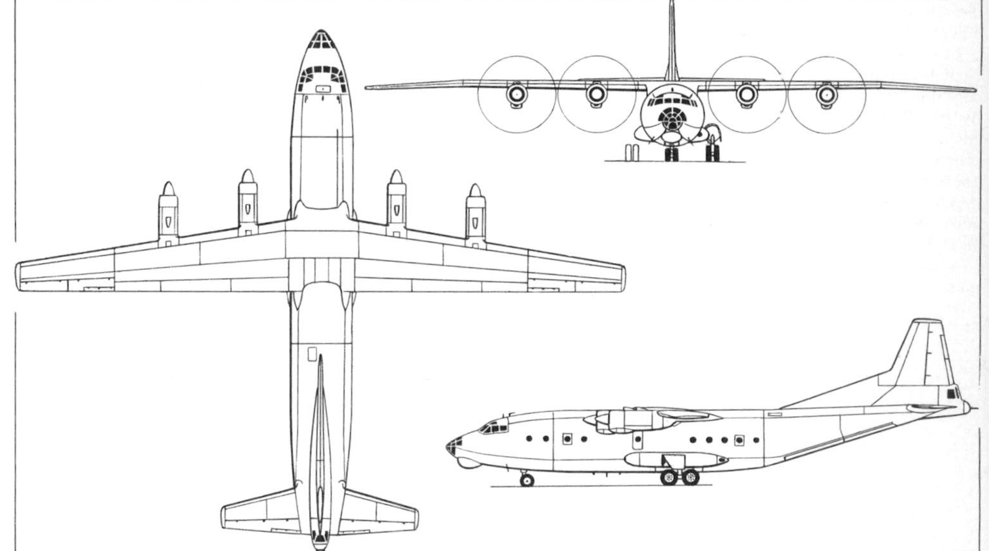

Antonov An-12BP ('Cub') four-turboprop general purpose military transport aircraft *(Pilot Press)*

ECM version of the Antonov An-12 ('Cub-C'), operated temporarily in Egyptian Air Force insignia

AREA:

Wings, gross	121·70 m² (1,310 sq ft)

WEIGHTS:

Weight empty	28,000 kg (61,730 lb)
Max payload	20,000 kg (44,090 lb)
Normal T-O weight	55,100 kg (121,475 lb)
Max T-O weight	61,000 kg (134,480 lb)

PERFORMANCE:

Max level speed	419 knots (777 km/h; 482 mph)
Max cruising speed	361 knots (670 km/h; 416 mph)
Min flying speed	88 knots (163 km/h; 101 mph)

Landing speed 108 knots (200 km/h; 124 mph)
Max rate of climb at S/L 600 m (1,970 ft)/min
Service ceiling 10,200 m (33,500 ft)
T-O run 700 m (2,300 ft)
Landing run 500 m (1,640 ft)
Range with max payload
1,942 nm (3,600 km; 2,236 miles)
Range with max fuel
3,075 nm (5,700 km; 3,540 miles)

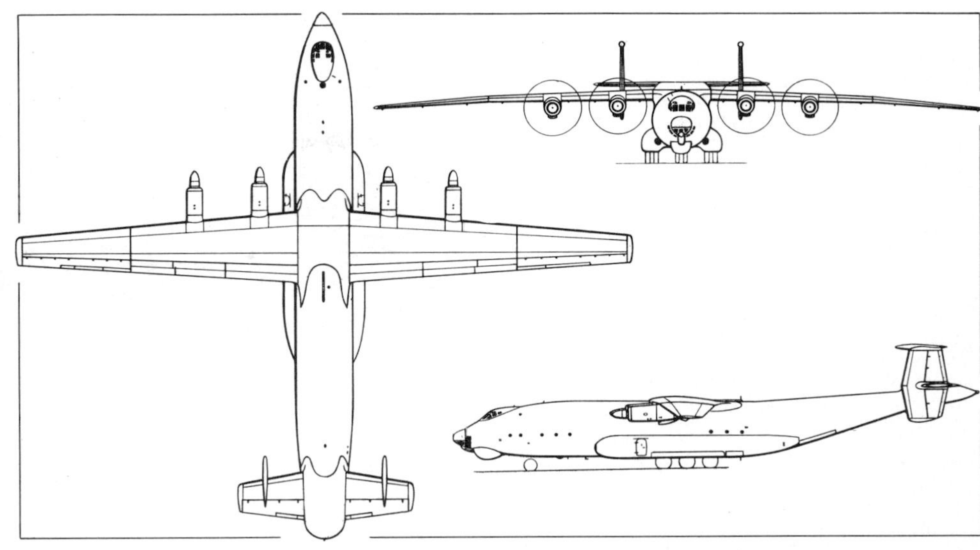

Antonov An-22 Antheus long-range heavy transport aircraft *(Pilot Press)*

ANTONOV An-22 ANTHEUS

NATO reporting name: Cock

The prototype of this very large transport aircraft flew for the first time on 27 February 1965. About 55 production An-22s remain in service with the Soviet Air Force and Aeroflot, which uses the aircraft primarily for military support duties. Deliveries were completed during 1974, but the diminishing force of An-22s provided the only Soviet transports capable of airlifting tanks as large as the T-62, pending the introduction into service of the An-124 (NATO 'Condor'). A structural description can be found in the 1982-83 and earlier editions.

TYPE: Long-range heavy turboprop transport.

POWER PLANT: Four 11,186 kW (15,000 shp) Kuznetsov NK-12MA turboprop engines, each driving a pair of four-blade contra-rotating propellers.

ACCOMMODATION: Crew of five or six. Navigator's station in nose. Cabin for 28-29 passengers aft of flight deck, separated from main cabin by bulkhead containing two doors. Uninterrupted main cabin, with reinforced titanium floor, tiedown fittings and rear loading ramp. When ramp lowers, a large door which forms the underside of the rear fuselage retracts upward inside fuselage to permit easy loading of tall vehicles. Rails in roof of cabin for four travelling gantries continue rearward on underside of this door. Two winches, used in conjunction with the gantries, each have a capacity of 2,500 kg (5,500 lb). Door in each landing gear fairing, forward of wheels, for crew and passengers.

DIMENSIONS, EXTERNAL:
Wing span 64·40 m (211 ft 4 in)
Length overall approx 57·92 m (190 ft 0 in)
Height overall 12·53 m (41 ft 1½ in)
Propeller diameter 6·20 m (20 ft 4 in)

DIMENSIONS, INTERNAL:
Main cabin: Length 33·0 m (108 ft 3 in)
Max width 4·4 m (14 ft 5 in)
Max height 4·4 m (14 ft 5 in)

AREA:
Wings, gross 345 m² (3,713 sq ft)

WEIGHTS:
Weight empty, equipped 114,000 kg (251,325 lb)
Max payload 80,000 kg (176,350 lb)
Max fuel 43,000 kg (94,800 lb)
Max T-O weight 250,000 kg (551,160 lb)

PERFORMANCE:
Max level speed 399 knots (740 km/h; 460 mph)
T-O run 1,300 m (4,260 ft)
Landing run 800 m (2,620 ft)
Range with max fuel and 45,000 kg (99,200 lb) payload 5,905 nm (10,950 km; 6,800 miles)
Range with max payload
2,692 nm (5,000 km; 3,100 miles)

ANTONOV An-24

NATO reporting name: Coke

Production of the An-24 in the Soviet Union ended in 1978, after about 1,100 had been delivered. A version known as the **Y-7** (which see) continues in production at Xian in China.

ANTONOV An-26

NATO reporting name: Curl

First displayed in public at the 1969 Paris Air Show, the An-26 is generally similar to the earlier An-24RT specialised freighter, with an auxiliary turbojet in the starboard engine nacelle, but has more powerful AI-24T turboprop engines and a completely redesigned rear fuselage of the 'beaver-tail' type. This embodies Oleg Antonov's special type of loading ramp, which forms the underside of the rear fuselage when retracted, in the usual way, but can be slid forward under the rear of the cabin to facilitate direct loading, or when the cargo is to be airdropped.

There are two versions:

An-26. Original version, with electrically/manually operated conveyor built in flush with cabin floor to facilitate movement of freight.

An-26B. Improved version, announced in 1981. Equipped to carry three standard freight pallets, each 2·438 m (8 ft) long, 1·46 m (4 ft 9½ in) wide and 1·60 m (5 ft 3 in) high, with a total weight of 5,500 kg (12,125 lb). Rollgangs on floor, mechanism to move the pallets, and moorings, enable two men to load and unload all three pallets in 30 min. Rollgangs can be stowed against sides of cabin when not required.

Although intended primarily for cargo carrying, the An-26 can be adapted easily for passenger, ambulance or paratroop transport duties.

An-26s have been delivered to the Afghan, Algerian, Angolan, Bangladesh, Benin, Bulgarian, Chinese, Congolese, Cuban, Czechoslovak, East German, Ethiopian, Guinea-Bissau, Hungarian, Iraqi, Lao, Malagasy, Mozambique, Nicaraguan, Peruvian, Polish, Romanian, Somali, Syrian, Tanzanian, Yugoslav, Zambian and Soviet Air Forces. Those operated by the Angolan government forces are reported to have been used also for bombing missions, and one of the Mozambique An-26s has been photographed with a bomb rack on the fuselage below each wingroot trailing-edge. Aeroflot has more than 200, which are available to supplement the military An-26s assigned to air commands in regiments and squadrons; Cubana has nine, Aero Caribbean of Cuba has four, Syrianair has four and Tarom of Romania seven.

TYPE: Twin-turboprop pressurised short-haul transport.

WINGS: Cantilever high-wing monoplane, with 2° anhedral on outer panels. Incidence 3°. Sweepback at quarter-chord on outer panels 6° 50′. All-metal two-spar structure, built in five sections: centre-section, two inner wings and two detachable outer wings. Wing skin is attached by electrical spot welding. Mass balanced servo compensated ailerons, with large trim tabs of glassfibre construction. Hydraulically operated, tracked and slotted TsAGI flaps along entire wing trailing-edges inboard of unpowered ailerons; single-slotted flaps on centre-section, double-slotted outboard of nacelles. Servo tab and electrically operated trim tab in each aileron. Bleed-air thermal de-icing system.

FUSELAGE: All-metal semi-monocoque structure in front, centre and rear portions, of bonded/welded construction. Skin on lower portion of fuselage is made of 'bimetal' (duralumin-titanium) sheet for protection during operations from unpaved airfields. Blister on each side forward of rear loading ramp, carrying tracks to enable ramp to slide forward under fuselage.

TAIL UNIT: Cantilever all-metal structure, with ventral fin strake on each side of rear ramp. 9° dihedral on tailplane. All controls manually operated. Manually operated trim tab in each elevator. Electrically operated combined trim/servo tab in rudder. All leading-edges incorporate bleed-air thermal de-icing system.

LANDING GEAR: Hydraulically retractable tricycle type, with twin wheels on each unit. Emergency extension by gravity. All units retract forward. Shock absorbers of oleo-nitrogen type on main units; nitrogen-pneumatic type on nose unit. Mainwheel tyres size 1,050 × 400, pressure 3·93 bars (57 lb/sq in). Nosewheel tyres size 700 × 250, pressure 4·41 bars (64 lb/sq in). Mainwheels fitted with hydraulic disc brakes and anti-skid units. Nosewheels can be steered hydraulically through 45° each side while taxying and are controllable through ± 10° during take-off and landing.

POWER PLANT: Two 2,103 kW (2,820 ehp) Ivchenko AI-24VT turboprop engines, each driving a four-blade constant-speed fully-feathering propeller. Electric de-icing system for propeller blades and hubs; hot air system for engine air intakes. One 7·85 kN (1,765 lb st) RU 19A-300 auxiliary turbojet in starboard nacelle for use, as required, at take-off, during climb and in level flight, and for self-contained starting of main engines. Fuel load 5,500 kg (12,125 lb), contained in integral tanks in inner wings and ten bag tanks in centre-section. Pressure refuelling socket in starboard engine nacelle. Gravity fuelling point above each tank area. Carbon dioxide inert gas system to create fireproof condition inside fuel tanks.

ACCOMMODATION: Basic crew of five (pilot, co-pilot, radio operator, flight engineer and navigator), with station at rear of cabin on starboard side for loading supervisor or load dispatcher. Optional domed observation window for navigator on port side of flight deck. Electric de-icing system for windscreens. Toilet on port side aft of flight deck; crew door, small galley and oxygen bottle stowage on starboard side. Emergency escape hatch in door immediately aft of flight deck. Large downward hinged rear ramp/door, hinged to an anchorage mounted on tracks running forward under the blister fairings. This enables ramp/door to slide forward under fuselage for direct loading on to cabin floor or for airdropping of freight. When doing so, its rear is supported by the

Antonov An-22 Antheus long-range heavy transport aircraft (four Kuznetsov NK-12MA turboprop engines) *(Tass)*

pivoted swinging arm on each side which also raises and lowers door in the alternative fixed-hinge mode. Electrically powered mobile winch, capacity 2,000 kg (4,409 lb), hoists crates through rear entrance and runs on a rail in the cabin ceiling to position payload in cabin. Electrically and manually operated conveyor, capacity 4,500 kg (9,920 lb), built-in flush with cabin floor of original An-26, facilitates loading and airdropping of freight. An-26B has removable rollgangs, mechanism for moving pallets inside hold, and moorings (see introductory notes). Both versions can accommodate a variety of motor vehicles, including GAZ-69 and UAZ-469 military vehicles, or cargo items up to 1·50 m (59 in) high by 2·10 m (82·6 in) wide. Height of rear edge of cargo door surround above the cabin floor is 1·50 m (4 ft 11 in). Cabin is pressurised and air-conditioned, and can be fitted with a row of tip-up seats along each wall to accommodate a total of 38 to 40 persons. Conversion to troop transport role, or to an ambulance for 24 stretcher patients and a medical attendant, takes 20 to 30 min in the field.

SYSTEMS: Air-conditioning system uses hot air tapped from the 10th compressor stage of each engine, with a heat exchanger and turbocooler in each nacelle. Cabin pressure differential 0·29 bars (4·27 lb/sq in). Main and emergency hydraulic systems, pressure 151·7 bars (2,200 lb/sq in), for landing gear retraction, nosewheel steering, flaps, brakes, windscreen wipers, propeller feathering and operation of cargo ramp and emergency escape doors. Handpump to operate doors only and build up pressure in main system. Electrical system includes two 27V DC starter/generators on engines, a standby generator on the auxiliary turbojet, and three storage batteries for emergency use. Two engine driven alternators provide 115V 400Hz single-phase AC supply, with standby inverter. Basic source of 36V 400Hz three-phase AC supply is two inverters, with standby transformer. Permanent oxygen system for pilot, installed equipment for other crew members and three portable bottles for personnel in cargo hold.

AVIONICS AND EQUIPMENT: Standard com/nav avionics comprise two VHF transceivers, HF, intercom, two ADF, radio altimeter, glidepath receiver, glideslope receiver, marker beacon receiver, weather/navigation radar, directional gyro and flight recorder. Optional equipment includes a flight director system, astrocompass and autopilot. Standard operational equipment includes parachute static line attachments and retraction devices, tiedowns, jack to support ramp sill, flight deck curtains, sun visors and windscreen wipers. Optional items include OPB-1R sight for pinpoint dropping of freight, medical equipment, and liquid heating system.

Antonov An-26 in the insignia of Cubana *(Paul R. Duffy)*

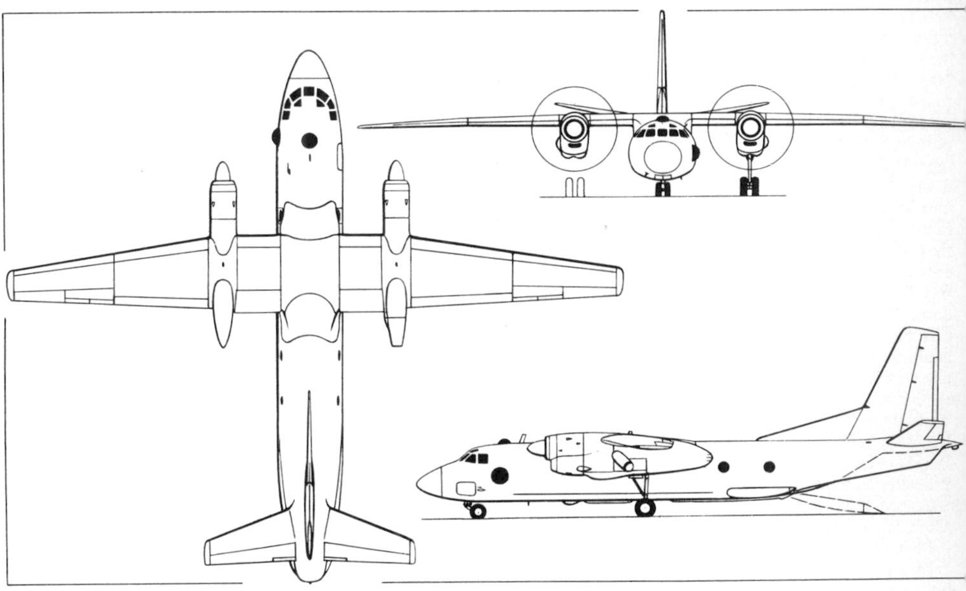
Antonov An-26 twin-turboprop short-haul transport *(Pilot Press)*

DIMENSIONS, EXTERNAL:
Wing span 29·20 m (95 ft 9½ in)
Wing aspect ratio 11·7
Length overall 23·80 m (78 ft 1 in)
Height overall 8·575 m (28 ft 1½ in)
Width of fuselage 2·90 m (9 ft 6 in)
Depth of fuselage 2·50 m (8 ft 2½ in)
Tailplane span 9·973 m (32 ft 8¾ in)
Wheel track (c/l shock struts) 7·90 m (25 ft 11 in)
Wheelbase 7·651 m (25 ft 1¼ in)
Propeller diameter 3·90 m (12 ft 9½ in)
Propeller ground clearance 1·227 m (4 ft 0¼ in)
Crew door (stbd, front): Height 1·40 m (4 ft 7 in)
Width 0·60 m (1 ft 11¾ in)
Height to sill 1·47 m (4 ft 9¾ in)
Loading hatch (rear): Length 3·40 m (11 ft 1¾ in)
Width at front 2·40 m (7 ft 10½ in)
Width at rear 2·00 m (6 ft 6¾ in)
Height to sill 1·47 m (4 ft 9¾ in)
Height to top edge of hatchway 3·014 m (9 ft 10¾ in)
Emergency exit (in floor at front):
Length 1·02 m (3 ft 4¼ in)
Width 0·70 m (2 ft 3½ in)
Emergency exit (top):
Diameter 0·65 m (2 ft 1½ in)
Emergency exits (one each side of hold):
Height 0·60 m (1 ft 11¾ in)
Width 0·50 m (1 ft 7½ in)

DIMENSIONS, INTERNAL:
Cargo hold: Length of floor 11·50 m (37 ft 8¾ in)
Width of floor 2·40 m (7 ft 10½ in)
Max height 1·91 m (6 ft 3 in)

AREAS:
Wings, gross 74·98 m² (807·1 sq ft)
Horizontal tail surfaces (total) 19·83 m² (213·45 sq ft)
Vertical tail surfaces (total, incl dorsal fin) 15·85 m² (170·61 sq ft)

WEIGHTS:
Weight empty 15,020 kg (33,113 lb)
Normal payload 4,500 kg (9,920 lb)
Max payload 5,500 kg (12,125 lb)
Normal T-O and landing weight 23,000 kg (50,706 lb)
Max T-O and landing weight 24,000 kg (52,911 lb)

PERFORMANCE (at normal T-O weight):
Cruising speed at 6,000 m (19,675 ft) 237 knots (440 km/h; 273 mph)
T-O speed 108 knots (200 km/h; 124 mph) CAS
Landing speed 102 knots (190 km/h; 118 mph) CAS
Max rate of climb at S/L 480 m (1,575 ft)/min
Service ceiling 7,500 m (24,600 ft)
T-O run, on concrete 780 m (2,559 ft)
T-O to 15 m (50 ft) 1,240 m (4,068 ft)
Landing from 15 m (50 ft) 1,740 m (5,709 ft)

Antonov An-26 transport of the Czechoslovak Air Force with rear loading ramp lowered

Landing run, on concrete	730 m (2,395 ft)
Min ground turning radius	22·3 m (73 ft 2 in)
Range with max payload, no reserves	594 nm (1,100 km; 683 miles)
Range with max fuel, no reserves	1,376 nm (2,550 km; 1,584 miles)

ANTONOV An-28

NATO reporting name: Cash

Responsibility for An-28 production has been allocated to the WSK-PZL Mielec works in Poland (see Polish section).

ANTONOV An-30

NATO reporting name: Clank

The An-30 aerial survey aeroplane was developed from the An-24RT and An-26 twin-turboprop transports, to which it is generally similar. The major modifications are made to the nose, which is extensively glazed to give the navigator a wide field of view, and to the flight deck, which is raised to provide access to the navigator's compartment. There are fewer windows in the main cabin, which contains a darkroom and film storage cupboard, as well as survey cameras and a control desk. Other amenities include a toilet, buffet and crew rest area with armchairs and couches. All accommodation is pressurised and air-conditioned.

Photography can be automatic or semi-automatic if required, but two photographer/surveyors are normally carried, in addition to a flight crew of five (pilot, co-pilot, flight engineer, radio operator and navigator).

For the primary task of air photography for map-making, the An-30 is equipped with large survey cameras. These are mounted in the cabin above glazed apertures, of which there are five, each covered by a door. A crew photographer uncovers the apertures, as required, by remote control from his desk in the aircraft.

Standard equipment includes radio topographic distance measuring equipment and a radio altimeter, with recording units. The pre-programmed flight path of the aircraft over the area to be photographed is fed into an onboard computer, controlled from the navigator's station, which maintains the correct speed, altitude and direction of flight throughout the mission. The cartographic An-30 has an AFA-41/7·5 wide-angle camera, in a TAU-M gyro-stabilised mounting, over No. 1 aperture; and an A54/50-FK long focal length camera over No. 3 aperture, each mounted vertically. Two further A54/50-FK cameras take oblique photographs at 28° to the vertical, port and starboard, through Nos. 4 and 5 apertures, and an SU-5 lightmeter is positioned over No. 2 window. One photogrammetric version has a vertically mounted AFA-41/7·5 camera in a TAU-M mount and an AFA-41/10 or AFA-41/20 camera in a fixed vertical mount. Another has the same installation without the gyroscopic mounting. A fourth variation offers an AFA-41/7·5 and an AFA-42/20, both in fixed mountings.

If required, the cameras can be replaced by other kinds of survey equipment, such as those used for mineral prospecting or for microwave radiometer survey, which measures the heat emission of land and ocean to obtain data on ocean surface characteristics, sea and lake ice, snow cover, flooding, seasonal vegetation changes, and soil types.

The power plant comprises two 2,103 kW (2,820 ehp) Ivchenko AI-24VT turboprop engines, with water injection, each driving an AV-72T four-blade constant-speed fully-feathering and reversible-pitch propeller. Main engines are supplemented by a 7·85 kN (1,765 lb st) RU 19A-300 auxiliary turbojet in the rear of the starboard engine nacelle. The latter is used for engine starting, and for take-off, climb and cruise power in the event of failure of the primary power plant. Max fuel capacity is 6,200 litres (1,364 Imp gallons; 1,638 US gallons).

Antonov An-30 aerial survey development of the An-24 twin-turboprop transport *(M. D. West)*

The An-30 can be converted into a transport aircraft by placing cover plates over the camera apertures. It retains the standard An-24 cabin door, on the port side of the fuselage at the rear, together with the standard forward freight compartment door on the starboard side and the load hoisting/conveying system. A version designated **An-30M** has been mentioned in the Soviet press, equipped for 'cloud seeding' to protect vulnerable areas from heavy rainfall.

The prototype An-30 flew for the first time in 1974. Operators include Balkan Bulgarian Airlines and the Romanian Air Force, which has three. At least ten have been reported in Aeroflot markings.

DIMENSIONS, EXTERNAL:	
Wing span	29·20 m (95 ft 9½ in)
Wing aspect ratio	11·4
Length overall	24·26 m (79 ft 7 in)
Height overall	8·32 m (27 ft 3½ in)
Tailplane span	9·09 m (29 ft 10 in)
Fuselage, nominal diameter	2·90 m (9 ft 6¼ in)
Wheel track (c/l of oleos)	7·90 m (25 ft 11 in)
Wheelbase	7·65 m (25 ft 1¼ in)
Propeller diameter	3·90 m (12 ft 9½ in)
Propeller ground clearance	1·20 m (3 ft 11¼ in)
AREAS:	
Wings, gross	74·98 m² (807·1 sq ft)
Horizontal tail surfaces (total)	17·23 m² (185·46 sq ft)
Vertical tail surfaces (total, incl dorsal fin)	15·85 m² (170·61 sq ft)
WEIGHTS:	
Basic operating weight	15,590 kg (34,370 lb)
Weight of aerial photography equipment	650 kg (1,433 lb)
Max T-O and landing weight	23,000 kg (50,706 lb)
PERFORMANCE:	
Max level speed	291 knots (540 km/h; 335 mph)
Cruising speed at 6,000 m (19,685 ft)	232 knots (430 km/h; 267 mph)
Landing speed	95 knots (175 km/h; 109 mph)
Service ceiling:	
with APU operating	8,300 m (27,230 ft)
without APU	7,300 m (23,950 ft)
T-O run on concrete	710 m (2,330 ft)
Landing run on concrete	670 m (2,198 ft)
Range with max fuel, no reserves	1,420 nm (2,630 km; 1,634 miles)

ANTONOV An-32

Indian Air Force name: Sutlej

NATO reporting name: Cline

This pressurised short/medium-range transport, of which first details were released in May 1977, is a developed version of the An-26, with a generally similar airframe, except for having triple-slotted trailing-edge flaps, automatic leading-edge slats, much enlarged ventral fins and a full span slotted tailplane.

Two versions are available, differing only in the type of Ivchenko AI-20M turboprop engine fitted, as follows:

An-32/AI-20M. With two AI-20M engines, each rated at 3,128 kW (4,195 ehp), for operation in moderate climatic conditions.

An-32/AI-20DM. With two AI-20DM engines, each rated at 3,862 kW (5,180 ehp), for operation under high temperature conditions, or from high altitude airfields.

The large increase in power compared with the An-26 is intended specifically to improve take-off performance, service ceiling and payload. Thus, the 'hot and high' version with AI-20DM engines is able to operate from airfields 4,000-4,500 m (13,125-14,750 ft) above sea level in an ambient temperature of ISA+ 25°C, and can transport 3 tonnes of freight over a 594 nm (1,100 km; 683 mile) stage length, with fuel reserves. The overwing location of the engines requires nacelles of considerable depth, as the main landing gear units continue to retract into the underwing portions. The nacelles terminated at mid-chord above the wing on the prototype, but extend to the trailing-edge on production An-32s.

A rear loading hatch and forward-sliding ramp-door, similar to those of the An-26, are retained, as well as a hoist, capacity 2,000 kg (4,409 lb), to facilitate handling of the maximum payload of more than 6 tonnes of freight. Cargo or vehicles can be airdropped by parachute. The air-conditioned and pressurised accommodation enables alternative payloads to include 39 passengers or 30 parachutists, on a row of tip-up seats along each cabin wall, or 24 stretcher patients and a medical attendant; the normal crew of five comprises pilot, co-pilot, navigator, radio operator and flight engineer.

Low pressure tyres (of the same sizes as those on the An-26) permit operation from unpaved strips; and the high position of the engines reduces the possibility of stone or debris ingestion. A TG-16M APU, housed in the rear of the starboard landing gear fairing, helps to make the An-32 independent of ground servicing equipment by providing onboard engine starting capability at airfields up to 4,500 m (14,750 ft) above sea level.

The prototype An-32 was exhibited at the 1977 Paris Air Show. At the 1979 Show, Mr Antonov commented that production would be undertaken only if sufficient orders were received in advance to justify such a move. The first order was foreshadowed in December 1980, when India's Prime Minister, Mrs Indira Gandhi, stated in answer to a parliamentary question that An-32s would replace C-119s in the Indian Air Force. At that stage, it was anticipated that many of the required total of 95 An-32s (with the more powerful AI-20DM engines) would be manufactured by

Antonov An-32/AI-20DM of the Indian Air Force, by which it is known as the Sutlej *(Franz Knuchel)*

HAL at Kanpur. By the time the order was confirmed by the Indian parliament, in early 1982, it had been decided to acquire all the aircraft directly from the USSR, with only instruments and avionics of Indian manufacture. Deliveries began on 11 July 1984, when three An-32s (named **Sutlej** after a Punjabi river) were delivered to Agra for use by the paratroop training school. Five medium transport squadrons of the Indian Air Force were also to be re-equipped with An-32s during 1984-86. Other orders are reported to have been received from Cape Verde, Sao Tome and Principe, and Tanzania.

The ability of the An-32 to lift heavy payloads at high altitudes was demonstrated by flights which set 14 official records for Group II (turboprop) aircraft in the Autumn of 1985. A climb to 11,760 m (38,583 ft) on 25 October set payload to height records with payloads of 1,000 and 2,000 kg in Classes C1 and C1j. On 5 November, further records in these Classes were set by a climb to 11,230 m (36,844 ft) with a 5,000 kg payload. A Class C1j height record of 12,010 m (39,403 ft) was set on 24 October, and a Class C1j record of 11,530 m (37,828 ft) for sustained height in horizontal flight on 21 October. Six records in Class C1k were for a climb to 10,940 m (35,892 ft) on 24 October; a sustained height of 10,420 m (34,186 ft) in horizontal flight on 21 October; climbs to 11,120 m (36,483 ft) with 1,000 kg payload and to 10,890 m (35,728 ft) with 2,000 kg on 28 October, and to 10,510 m (34,482 ft) with 5,000 kg on 4 November; and a record payload of 7,256 kg (15,996 lb) lifted to 2,000 m on 4 November. The flights, near Kiev, were made by various two-man teams of test pilots Alexander Tkachenko, Vladimir Lysenko, Petr Kiritchuk, Yuri Kurlin and Georgi Pobol.

DIMENSIONS, EXTERNAL AND INTERNAL:
As for An-26, except:

Length overall	23·68 m (77 ft 8¼ in)
Height overall	8·75 m (28 ft 8½ in)
Tailplane span	10·24 m (33 ft 7 in)
Propeller diameter	4·70 m (15 ft 5 in)

WEIGHTS:

Max payload	6,700 kg (14,770 lb)
Max T-O weight	27,000 kg (59,525 lb)

PERFORMANCE (AI-20DM engines):

Normal cruising speed	286 knots (530 km/h; 329 mph)
Optimum cruising height	8,000 m (26,250 ft)
Service ceiling	9,000 m (29,525 ft)
Service ceiling, one engine out	5,000 m (16,400 ft)
T-O run	760 m (2,495 ft)
Landing run	470 m (1,542 ft)
Range with max payload, 45 min reserves	432 nm (800 km; 497 miles)
Range with max fuel, 45 min reserves	1,188 nm (2,200 km; 1,367 miles)

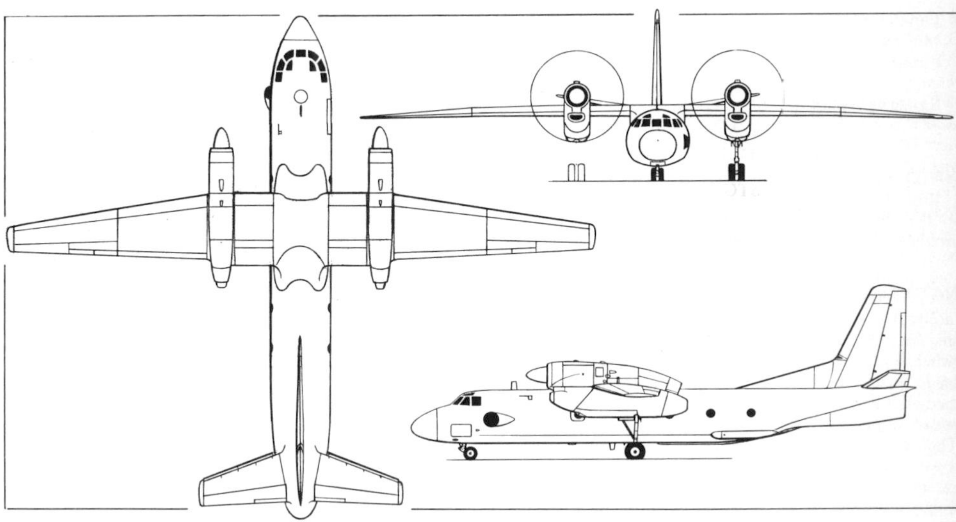

Antonov An-32 short/medium-range transport in production form with lengthened nacelles *(Pilot Press)*

ANTONOV An-72

NATO reporting name: Coaler

Two prototypes of this twin-turbofan STOL transport were built, plus a third airframe for static testing. First photographs of one of these aircraft (SSSR-19774) were released by the Soviet Tass news agency shortly after the first flight of an An-72 on 22 December 1977. By the time of the 1979 Paris Air Show the two An-72s had logged a total of just over 1,000 h in about 300 flights, and were described by the late Mr Antonov as "progressing faster than the An-28", which was itself to enter production at Mielec in Poland.

Design features of the An-72 make it uniquely suited to its primary role, as a STOL replacement for the turboprop An-26, with the emphasis on freight carrying. Its low pressure tyres and multi-wheel landing gear enable it to operate from unprepared airfields, or from surfaces covered with ice or snow; and the high-set engines avoid problems caused by foreign object ingestion. The exhaust efflux is ejected over the upper surface of the wing and down over the very large multi-slotted flaps. By taking advantage of the so-called 'Coanda effect', which causes the airflow to 'attach to' the extended flaps, a considerable increase in lift can be achieved.

Aircraft exhibited to date in the West have been fitted with deflector doors on each side at the rear of each engine nacelle, to 'spread' the exhaust flow for maximum effectiveness during take-off and landing. Mr Antonov was not convinced that so small a transport had much to gain from such complications, and suggested that they might be omitted from production An-72s. This appears to have been confirmed by the first appearance in the west of the developed An-74 (which see), and it seems likely that this aircraft represents or shares the production configuration of the An-72.

To ensure optimum versatility and efficiency, the rear loading doors have undergone considerable refinement since 1977. The original prototype (see 1978-79 *Jane's*) had two large outward canted ventral fins, one on each side at the rear of its ramp-door, aft of which the fuselage tailcone was made up of two petal airbrakes. By comparison, the An-72 (SSSR-83966) shown in Paris in 1979 had a flattened 'beaver tail' aft of two outward hinged clamshell doors and a simple downward hinged ramp-door (see 1980-81 *Jane's*). This arrangement was superseded on a later demonstrator by a special ramp/door of the kind fitted to the An-26 and An-74, which can be hinged down conventionally to allow wheeled or tracked vehicles to be driven into the hold or, alternatively, can slide forward under the fuselage to permit direct loading from a truck.

Particular care was taken to ensure easy handling of the An-72 in the air, and the designer commented that the aircraft had proved outstanding in this respect. Its Doppler based automatic navigation system, linked to an onboard computer, is preprogrammed before take-off on a push-button panel to the right of the large cockpit map display. Failure warning panels above the windscreen display red lights for critical failures, yellow lights for non-critical failures, to minimise the time that needs to be spent on monitoring instruments and equipment.

During November/December 1983, three pilots, Marina Popovich, Alexander Galunenko and Sergei Maksimov, operating in pairs, set a total of 17 official records in an An-72. In class C1j (20,000-25,000 kg), they climbed to 3,000 m in 2 min 2·7 s, to 6,000 m in 4 min 53·1 s, to 9,000 m in 9 min 38 s, to 12,000 m in 18 min 1·2 s, to an absolute record height of 13,440 m (44,095 ft), to 13,080 m (42,913 ft) with a 1,000 kg payload, 13,090 m (42,946 ft) with 2,000 kg, and with a record payload of 3,528 kg (7,778 lb) to a height of 2,000 m. They also set a sustained height record of 12,980 m (42,585 ft). Corresponding records in class C1k (25,000-35,000 kg) included climb to 3,000 m in 2 min 33·6 s, to 6,000 m in 5 min 9 s, to 9,000 m in 10 min 54·3 s, to 12,000 m in 27 min 25·4 s, to a record height of 12,400 m (40,682 ft) with a 1,000 kg payload, to 12,270 m (40,256 ft) with 2,000 kg, 11,380 m (37,336 ft) with 5,000 kg, and with a record payload of 8,064 kg (17,778 lb) to a height of 2,000 m. The D-36 turbofans fitted to the record breaking aircraft were each said to be rated at only 58·84 kN (13,227 lb st).

Three closed circuit speed records for Group III (turbojet) aircraft were set by test pilots Georgi Pobol, Vladimir Tkachenko and Sergei Gorbik in an An-72, near Kiev. On 7 November 1985 they achieved 360·68 knots (667·99 km/h; 415·07 mph) around 1,000 km in Class C1k. In the same Class an average speed of 368.14 knots (681·80 km/h; 423·65 mph) was recorded over 2,000 km on 28 November. On 3 January 1986 a Class C1j record of 363·41 knots (673·03 km/h; 418·20 mph) was set over a 2,000 km circuit. Again

Antonov An-72 twin-turbofan STOL transport in landing configuration

The thrust of the engines was quoted at only 58·84 kN (13,227 lb st).

The last An-72s seen in the West (CCCP-19795 at the 1981 Paris Air Show and CCCP-72000 at Farnborough in 1984) were prototypes or pre-series aircraft, renumbered for the occasion. The following details apply to the version described at that time in publicity brochures from Aviaexport:

TYPE: Twin-turbofan light STOL transport.

WINGS: Cantilever high-wing monoplane, with 17° sweepback on leading-edges and straight trailing-edges. Multi-spar structure. Short constant chord centre-section, without dihedral or anhedral, mounted above fuselage to avoid encroaching on internal space. Approx 10° anhedral on outer panels. Wing upper surface blowing requires engines to be mounted above and forward of wings, to exhaust over upper surface. Aft of nacelles, wing skin, spoilers and flaps made of titanium. Hydraulically actuated full span leading-edge flaps outboard of nacelles, embodying thermal anti-icing. Wide span trailing-edge flaps, double-slotted inboard in exhaust efflux, triple-slotted on outer panels. Normal T-O flap setting 25-30°; max deflection 60°. Five-section spoilers forward of flaps on each side; some sections opened automatically on touchdown by sensors actuated by weight on main landing gear. Conventional ailerons outboard of flaps, with tab in port aileron.

FUSELAGE: Conventional all-metal semi-monocoque structure of circular cross-section. Underside of upswept rear fuselage formed by ramp-door, which can hinge downward conventionally or slide forward under fuselage to permit direct loading of hold from truck. One-piece 'beaver tail' bottom section (replacing original clamshell doors) drops and moves backward slightly to release ramp.

TAIL UNIT: Cantilever all-metal T tail, with wide chord sweptback vertical surfaces and variable incidence tailplane. Double-hinged rudder, with tab in lower portion of two-section aft panel. During normal flight only the lower rear segment is used. Both rear segments are used during low-speed flight. The forward segment is actuated automatically to offset thrust asymmetry. Tailplane leading-edge sweep slightly greater than that of wings, with straight trailing-edge on horn balanced and aerodynamically balanced elevators. Two tabs in each elevator. Leading-edges of fin and tailplane are de-iced. Tapered fairing forward of fin/tailplane junction. Two outward canted ventral fins near extreme tip of fuselage (not on pre-series aircraft, but shown on latest Aviaexport drawing).

LANDING GEAR: Hydraulically retractable tricycle type. Twin wheels on rearward retracting steerable nose unit. Each main unit comprises two trailing-arm legs in tandem, each with a single wheel, retracting inward through 90° so that wheels lie horizontally in bottom of large fairings, outside fuselage pressure cell. Oleo-pneumatic shock absorber in each unit. Low pressure tyres, size 720 × 310 on nosewheels, 1050 × 400 on mainwheels. Hydraulic disc brakes. Telescopic strut is hinged downward, from rear of each side fairing, to support fuselage during direct loading of hold with ramp-door under fuselage.

POWER PLANT: Two Lotarev D-36 high bypass ratio turbofan engines, each rated at 63·74 kN (14,330 lb st). Integral fuel tanks between spars of outer wings. Thrust reversers standard.

ACCOMMODATION: Pilot and co-pilot/navigator side by side on very roomy flight deck, with heated windows. Two windscreen wipers. Flight engineer's seat, at rear on starboard side, slides forward on tracks to position between and slightly aft of pilots, to give access to controls on central console. Main cabin designed primarily for freight, but with folding seats for 32 passengers along side walls and provision for carrying 24 casualties and attendant in ambulance configuration. Flight deck and cabin pressurised and air-conditioned. Large downward hinged and forward sliding rear ramp-door for loading trucks and tracked vehicles, and for direct loading of hold from trucks, as described under An-26 entry. Mobile winch, capacity 2,500 kg (5,511 lb), assists loading of containers up to 1·90 × 2·44 × 1·46 m (6 ft 3 in × 8 ft × 4 ft 9½ in) in size, pallets 1·90 × 2·42 × 1·46 m (6 ft 3 in × 7 ft 11 in × 4 ft 9½ in) in size, and other bulky items. Cargo straps and nets are stowed in lockers on each side of hold when not in use. Provision for building roller conveyors into floor. Main crew and passenger door at front of cabin on port side. Small emergency exit and servicing door at rear of cabin on starboard side.

SYSTEMS: Air-conditioning system provides comfortable environment to altitude of 10,000 m (32,800 ft), with independent temperature control in flight deck and main cabin areas. It can be used to refrigerate main cabin when perishable goods are carried. Hydraulic system for actuating landing gear, flaps, ailerons, variable incidence tailplane and ramp. Electrical system powers auxiliary systems, flight deck equipment, lighting and mobile hoist. Thermal de-icing system for leading-edges of wings and tail unit, engine air intakes and cockpit windows.

AVIONICS AND EQUIPMENT: Large radome over navigation/weather radar in nose. Doppler based automatic navigation system, with map display on flight deck.

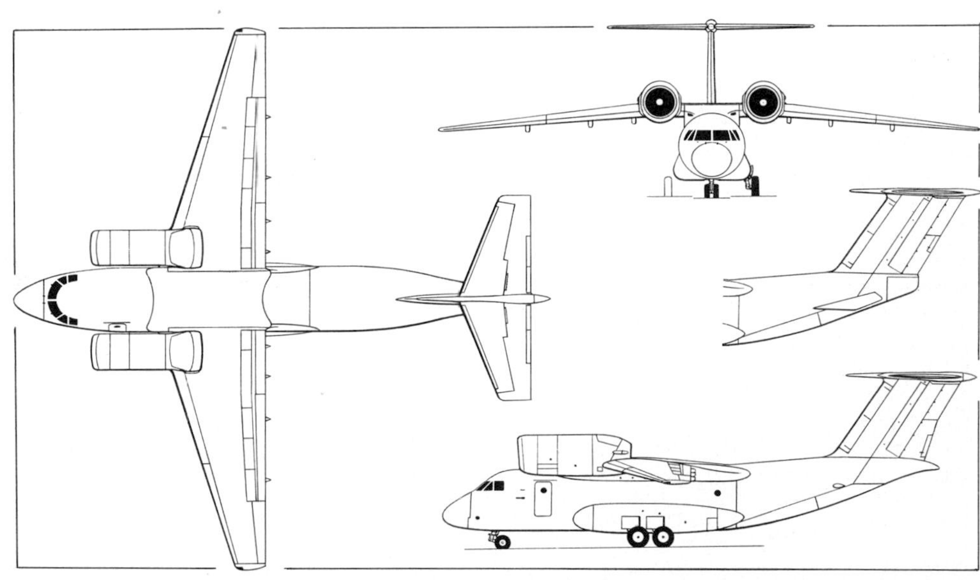

Second prototype of the Antonov An-72 (two Lotarev D-36 turbofan engines), with scrap view of rear fuselage of first prototype *(Pilot Press)*

An-72 after touchdown, with thrust reversers erected and flaps extended *(Air Portraits)*

DIMENSIONS, EXTERNAL:
- Wing span: 25·83 m (84 ft 9 in)
- Wing aspect ratio: 7·4
- Length overall: 26·576 m (87 ft 2¼ in)
- Height overall: 8·235 m (27 ft 0¼ in)

DIMENSIONS, INTERNAL:
- Main cabin: Length: 9·00 m (29 ft 6¼ in)
  - Width at floor level: 2·10 m (6 ft 10¾ in)
  - Height: 2·20 m (7 ft 2½ in)

AREA:
- Wings, gross: approx 90 m^2 (969 sq ft)

WEIGHTS:
- Max payload: Normal: 10,000 kg (22,045 lb)
  - STOL: 3,500 kg (7,715 lb)
- Max T-O weight: from 1,000 m (3,280 ft) runway: 26,500 kg (58,420 lb)
  - from 1,200 m (3,935 ft) runway: 30,500 kg (67,240 lb)
  - from 1,500 m (4,925 ft) runway: 33,000 kg (72,750 lb)

PERFORMANCE:
- Max level speed: 410 knots (760 km/h; 472 mph)
- Max cruising speed: 388 knots (720 km/h; 447 mph)
- T-O speed with light load: 81 knots (150 km/h; 94 mph)
- T-O speed with heavier load: 97 knots (180 km/h; 112 mph)
- Landing speed: 89 knots (165 km/h; 103 mph)
- Service ceiling: 11,000 m (36,100 ft)
- Normal operating height: 8,000-10,000 m (26,250-32,800 ft)
- T-O run: 470 m (1,542 ft)
- T-O run, one engine out: 1,200 m (3,940 ft)
- Range with max payload, 30 min reserves: 540 nm (1,000 km; 620 miles)
- Range with max fuel, 30 min reserves: 2,050 nm (3,800 km; 2,360 miles)

ANTONOV An-74

In February 1984, the Soviet newspaper *Pravda* referred to a new transport aircraft, designated An-74, which had been built for operation in the Arctic and Antarctic regions. It stated that, unlike the Il-18D turboprop transports used

Antonov An-74 twin-turbofan light STOL transport *(David O'Mahony)*

The lengthened fuselage of the An-74, compared with the An-72, is evident in this view *(Paul R. Duffy)*

to carry men and equipment between Leningrad and the Antarctic base of Molodejnaya, the An-74 can have a wheel-ski landing gear for operation on snow and ice landing strips. It was described as an all-weather aircraft, equipped with the latest available radio navigation aids, and with de-icing equipment on the wings, tail unit and engine air intakes. In the Polar regions, its duties will include assistance in setting up scientific stations on Arctic ice floes, airdropping supplies to motorised trans-Antarctic expeditions, and reconnaissance to observe changes in the icefields. It was assumed to be a development of the An-72, and this was confirmed on 28 July 1986, when an An-74 (SSSR-58642, c/n 0202) made its first appearance in the west, at Shannon Airport, Ireland, en route to the Expo 86 exhibition in Vancouver, Canada. Major changes by comparison with the An-72 are as follows:

WINGS: The span has been extended considerably, with two new tapered outer panels displaying reduced leading-edge sweepback and modest trailing-edge sweepback. Leading-edge flaps on inner wing panels only.

FUSELAGE: This is lengthened, both forward and aft of the wings, but is otherwise generally similar to that of An-72.

TAIL UNIT AND LANDING GEAR: Generally as for An-72. Wheel-skis optional.

POWER PLANT: Lotarev D-36 turbofans, as An-72. Large deflector doors on each side at the rear of each engine nacelle have been eliminated, as forecast by the late Mr Oleg Antonov.

ACCOMMODATION: Crew of four: pilot, co-pilot, navigator and engineer. Lengthened cabin. Loading doors and provisions unchanged. Able to carry eight passengers in combi role, in two rows of seats, with tables, and with two bunks installed, one on each side of cabin aft of seats. Bulged observation windows on port side for navigator and hydrologist. Provision for wardrobe and galley. Movable bulkhead between passenger and freight compartments. Freight can be airdropped.

DIMENSIONS, EXTERNAL:
- Wing span — 31·89 m (104 ft 7½ in)
- Length overall — 28·07 m (92 ft 1¼ in)
- Height overall — 8·65 m (28 ft 4½ in)

DIMENSIONS, INTERNAL:
- Cabin: Length — 10·50 m (34 ft 5¼ in)
  - Width at floor level — 2·15 m (7 ft 0½ in)
  - Height — 2·20 m (7 ft 2½ in)

WEIGHTS:
- Max payload: Normal — 10,000 kg (22,045 lb)
- Max T-O weight, from 1,800 m (5,905 ft) runway — 34,500 kg (76,060 lb)

PERFORMANCE:
- Max level speed — 380 knots (705 km/h; 438 mph)
- Normal cruising speed at 8,000-10,000 m (26,250-32,800 ft) — 297 knots (550 km/h; 342 mph)
- Service ceiling — 10,500 m (34,450 ft)
- Range with 1,500 kg (3,307 lb) payload and 2 h reserves — 2,430 nm (4,500 km; 2,796 miles)
- Range, cargo version, with 1 h reserves:
  - with 10,000 kg (22,045 lb) payload — 620 nm (1,150 km; 715 miles)
  - with 5,000 kg (11,023 lb) payload — 1,781 nm (3,300 km; 2,050 miles)
  - with max fuel and 2,300 kg (5,070 lb) payload — 2,537 nm (4,700 km; 2,920 miles)

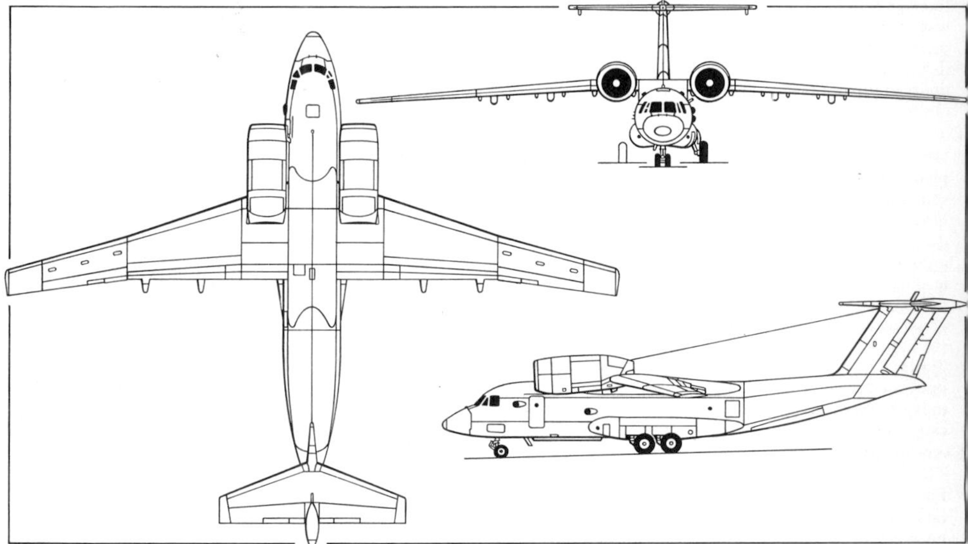

Antonov An-74 (two Lotarev D-36 turbofan engines) *(Jane's/Mike Keep)*

ANTONOV An-124

NATO reporting name: Condor

Following an interview with the late Oleg K. Antonov at the 1977 Paris Air Show, *Jane's* was able to report in its 1977-78 edition "that the Antonov design bureau was working on a new, very large, turbofan powered transport in the class of the USAF's Lockheed C-5 Galaxy . . . intended as a replacement for the turboprop powered An-22 strategic freighter, of which production was terminated in 1974". The new transport was listed under the provisional designation of An-40. This had changed to An-400 by 1984, when it became possible to produce for the 1984-85 edition of *Jane's* a reasonably representative three-view drawing and estimated dimensions which proved to be accurate to within 1·5 m (5 ft) in the case of overall length. NATO had, meanwhile, allocated to the aircraft the reporting name Condor, after the world's largest flying bird. Its range of likely loads had expanded over the years from the largest Soviet army tanks to complete SS-20 nuclear missile systems, Siberian oil well equipment and earth movers.

In May/June 1985 the second prototype of this transport (SSSR-82002 *Ruslan*, named after the giant hero of Russian folklore immortalised by Pushkin) was exhibited in public for the first time at the Paris Air Show, where it arrived under the command of Antonov's chief test pilot, Vladimir Terski, and co-pilot Yuri Pobol. Its service designation was revealed as An-124, and it was confirmed as the largest aircraft currently flying, in terms of wing span, with the heaviest max take-off weight of any aeroplane yet built. Three An-124s had flown by mid-1985. First flight of the original prototype had been made by Vladimir Terski on 26 December 1982, and the number of aircraft flown had increased to five when SSSR-82005 was exhibited at the 1986 Farnborough show. Operational flying was said to have started in January 1986 when units of a US/Canadian

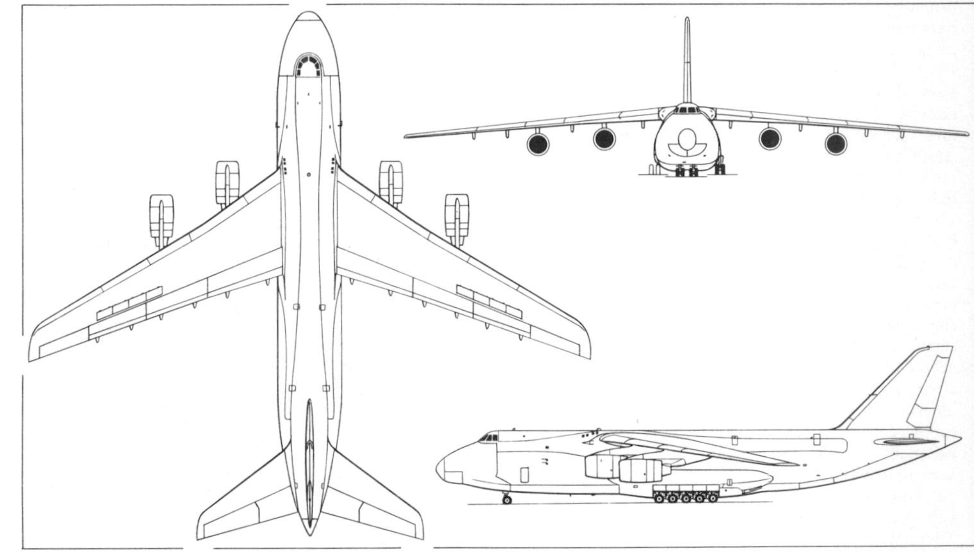

Antonov An-124 (four Lotarev D-18T turbofan engines) *(Pilot Press)*

World's largest transport aircraft, the An-124, in landing configuration

Nose of the An-124 opens upward around the flight deck *(Anna T. Hogg)*

Euclid 154 tonne dumper truck were transported for use by Yakut diamond miners.

Except for having a low mounted tailplane, the general configuration of the An-124 is similar to that of its US counterpart, the Lockheed C-5 Galaxy. It has an upward hinged visor type nose, and rear fuselage ramp-door, for simultaneous front and rear loading/unloading. Advanced features include a 100 per cent fly-by-wire control system, titanium floor throughout the main hold, and 5,500 kg (12,125 lb) of composites, making up 1,500 m² (16,150 sq ft) of its surface area and giving a weight saving of 1,800 kg (3,968 lb). The 24-wheel landing gear enables the An-124 to operate from unprepared fields, hard packed snow and ice covered swampland.

On 26 July 1985, an An-124 lifted a payload of 171,219 kg (377,473 lb) to a height of 10,750 m (35,269 ft). This exceeded by 53 per cent the previous official record for maximum payload lifted to 2,000 m, set by a Lockheed C-5A Galaxy, and also qualified for a total of 20 other FAI approved records with payloads from 75,000 to 170,000 kg. The pilot was Vladimir Terski, with Alexander Galunenko as co-pilot.

TYPE: Long-range heavy-lift freight transport.

WINGS: Cantilever shoulder-wing monoplane, of supercritical section, with anhedral. Sweepback approx 35° on inboard leading-edge, 32° over most of span. Conventional light alloy construction, with one-piece root-to-tip upper surface extruded skin panel on each wing. Strip of carbonfibre skin panels on undersurface forward of trailing-edge control surfaces. Glassfibre wingtips. Each wing has two-section aileron, three-section single-slotted Fowler flaps, and six-section full-span leading-edge flaps. Small slot inset in lower surface of two inner flap segments on each side, at inboard leading-edge, to optimise aerodynamics. Front and rear portions of each flap guide fairing made of glassfibre; centre portion of carbonfibre. Eight spoilers on upper surface of each wing, forward of trailing-edge flaps. No fences, vortex generators, or tabs. All moving surfaces hydraulically operated, with hydraulic flutter dampers on ailerons. Bleed air anti-icing of wing leading-edges.

FUSELAGE: Conventional semi-monocoque light alloy structure of basic double-bubble form. Hard chine between sides and shallow-section bottom surface. Central frames each made up of four large forgings. Visor type nose door and rear ramp-door described under Accommodation heading. Fairings over intersection of fuselage lobes, in line with wing, from rear of flight deck to plane of fin leading-edge, made primarily of glassfibre with central, and lower underwing, portions of carbonfibre. Other carbonfibre components include nose and main landing gear doors, some service doors, and clamshell doors aft of rear loading ramp. Glassfibre components include most of bottom skin panels forming underfuselage blister fairing between main landing gear legs, plus nosecone and tailcone. All control runs and other services are channelled along roof of fuselage.

TAIL UNIT: Cantilever all-metal structure, except for glassfibre tips of fixed-incidence tailplane and strip of carbonfibre skin panels forward of each control surface. Rudder and each elevator in two sections, without tabs. Control surfaces hydraulically operated, with hydraulic flutter dampers. Fence at mid-point on fin leading-edge. Electro-impulse de-icing of fin and tailplane leading-edges.

LANDING GEAR: Hydraulically retractable nosewheel type. Nose gear comprises two independent forward retracting twin-wheel units, side by side. Each main gear comprises five independent inward retracting twin-wheel units. Each mainwheel bogie is enclosed by separate upper and lower doors when retracted. Nosewheel doors and lower mainwheel doors close when gear is extended. All wheel doors are of carbonfibre. Nosewheels are steerable, with front pair of mainwheels on each side. Rear pair of mainwheels on each side is castoring. Main gear bogies can be retracted individually for repair or wheel change. Mainwheel tyres size 1270 × 510. Nosewheel tyres size 1120 × 450. Aircraft can 'kneel', by retracting nosewheels and settling on two extendable 'feet', giving floor of hold a 3·5° slope to assist loading and unloading. Rear of cargo hold can be lowered by compressing main gear oleos. Carbon brakes are normally toe operated, via rudder pedals. For severe braking, pedals are depressed by both toes and heels.

POWER PLANT: Four Lotarev D-18T turbofan engines, each rated at 229·5 kN (51,590 lb st). Thrust reversers standard. Engine cowlings of glassfibre; pylons have carbonfibre skin at rear end. All fuel in ten integral tanks in wings.

ACCOMMODATION: All crew and passenger accommodation on upper deck; freight and/or vehicles on lower deck. Flight crew of six, in pairs, on flight deck, with place for loadmaster in lobby area. Pilot and co-pilot on fully adjustable seats, which rotate for improved access. Two flight engineers, on wall-facing seats on starboard side, have complete control of master fuel cocks, detailed systems instruments, and digital integrated data system with CRT monitor. Behind pilot are the navigator and communications specialist, also on wall-facing seats. Between flight deck and wing carry-through structure, on

Antonov An-124 heavy freight transport, with landing gear partially extended *(Brian M. Service)*

port side, are toilets, washing facilities, galley, equipment compartment, and two cabins for total of up to six relief crew, with table and facing bench seats convertible into bunks. Aft of wing carry-through is a passenger cabin for up to 88 persons. Flight deck and passenger cabin are each accessible from cargo hold by means of an hydraulically folding ladder, operated automatically with manual override. Rearward sliding and jettisonable window on each side of flight deck. Primary access to flight deck via airstair door, with ladder extension, forward of wing on port side. Smaller door forward of this and slightly higher. Door from main hold aft of wing on starboard side. Upper deck doors at rear of flight deck on starboard side and at rear of passenger cabin on each side. Emergency exit from upper deck aft of wing on each side. Hydraulically operated visor type upward hinged nose takes 7 min to open fully, with simultaneous extension of folding nose loading ramp. When open, nose is steadied by reinforcing arms against wind gusts. No hydraulic, electrical or other system lines are broken when nose is open. Radar wiring passes through hollow tube in hinge. Hydraulically operated rear loading doors take 3 min to open, with simultaneous extension of three-part folding ramp. This can be locked in intermediate position for direct loading from truck or loading galley. Aft of ramp, centre panel of fuselage undersurface hinges upward; clamshell door to each side opens downward. Completely unobstructed lower deck freight hold has titanium floor, attached 'mobilely' to lower fuselage structure to accommodate changes of temperature, with rollgangs and retractable attachments for cargo tiedowns. Folding canvas seats along sidewalls are not normally used in flight, because of low pressurisation of hold. Two electric travelling cranes in roof of hold, each with two lifting points, offer total lifting capacity of 20,000 kg (44,100 lb). Two winches each have a 3,000 kg (6,614 lb) capacity.

SYSTEMS: Entire interior of aircraft is pressurised and air-conditioned. Max pressure differential 0·55 bars (7·8 lb/sq in) on upper deck, 0·25 bars (3·55 lb/sq in) on lower deck. Four independent hydraulic systems. Quadruple redundant fly-by-wire flight control system, with mechanical emergency fifth channel to hydraulic control servos. Special secondary bus electrical system. Landing lights under nose and at front of each main landing gear fairing. APU in rear of each landing gear fairing is used for engine starting, and can be operated in the air or on the ground to open loading doors for airdrop from rear or normal ground loading/unloading, as well as for supplying electric, hydraulic and air conditioning systems.

AVIONICS AND EQUIPMENT: Aircraft displayed at 1985 Paris Air Show has comprehensive but conventional flight deck equipment, including large radar screen and moving map display forward of throttle and thrust reverse levers on centre console. No electronic flight displays. Two dielectric areas of nose visor enclose forward looking weather radar and downward looking ground mapping/navigation radar. Hemispherical dielectric fairing above centre fuselage for satellite navigation receiver. Quadruple INS, plus Loran and Omega. Small two-face mirror, of V form, enables pilots to adjust their seating position until their eyes are reflected in the appropriate mirror, which ensures an optimum field of view from the flight deck.

DIMENSIONS, EXTERNAL:
- Wing span: 73·30 m (240 ft 5¾ in)
- Length overall: 69·10 m (226 ft 8½ in)
- Height overall: 20·78 m (68 ft 2¼ in)

DIMENSIONS, INTERNAL:
- Cargo hold: Length: 36·0 m (118 ft 1¼ in)
  - Max width: 6·4 m (21 ft 0 in)
  - Max height: 4·4 m (14 ft 5¼ in)

AREA:
- Wings, gross: 628·0 m² (6,760·0 sq ft)

WEIGHTS:
- Max payload: 150,000 kg (330,693 lb)
- Max fuel: 230,000 kg (507,063 lb)
- Max T-O weight: 405,000 kg (892,872 lb)

PERFORMANCE:
- Max cruising speed: 467 knots (865 km/h; 537 mph)
- Normal cruising speed at 10,000-12,000 m (32,800-39,370 ft) 432-459 knots (800-850 km/h; 497-528 mph)
- Approach speed: 124-140 knots (230-260 km/h; 143-162 mph)
- T-O balanced field length at max T-O weight: 3,000 m (9,850 ft)
- Landing run at max landing weight: 800 m (2,625 ft)
- Range with max payload: 2,430 nm (4,500 km; 2,795 miles)
- Range with max fuel: 8,900 nm (16,500 km; 10,250 miles)

OPERATIONAL NOISE LEVELS:
- Stated to meet ICAO requirements

BERIEV

This design bureau is named after Georgi Mikhailovich Beriev, whose death at the age of 77 was reported in July 1979. Based at Taganrog, it has been the centre for all Soviet seaplane development since 1945.

BERIEV Be-12 (M-12) TCHAIKA (SEAGULL)

NATO reporting name: Mail

This twin-turboprop medium-range anti-submarine and maritime reconnaissance amphibian flew for the first time in 1960 and made its initial public appearance in the 1961 Aviation Day flypast at Tushino Airport, Moscow. Subsequently, during the period 23-27 October 1964, it established six international height records in Class C3 Group II. Data submitted in respect of these records revealed that the designation of the aircraft was M-12 (changed subsequently to Be-12) and the power plant two 4,000 shp Ivchenko AI-20D turboprop engines. The aircraft was also, clearly, able to lift a payload of around 10 tons under record conditions.

The 1964 records have never been bettered. Subsequent record attempts ensured that the Be-12 retained all 22 FAI records listed in Class C3 Group II for turboprop amphibians, and all 22 current records in Class C2 Group II, for turboprop flying-boats. All of these records have been listed in previous editions of *Jane's*. Some of the more important ones are included among the Official Records listed on an early page of this edition. Two further records were set by Nikolai Shlikov and Sergei Tyukavkin (pilot and co-pilot respectively), for distance in a straight line, in 1983. They covered a distance of 2,647·634 km (1,645·163 miles) between Morskoy and Sukhoputny on 30 October to claim the class C3/II record. On the following day, they covered a precisely similar distance between Severny and Morskoy to claim the class C2/II record.

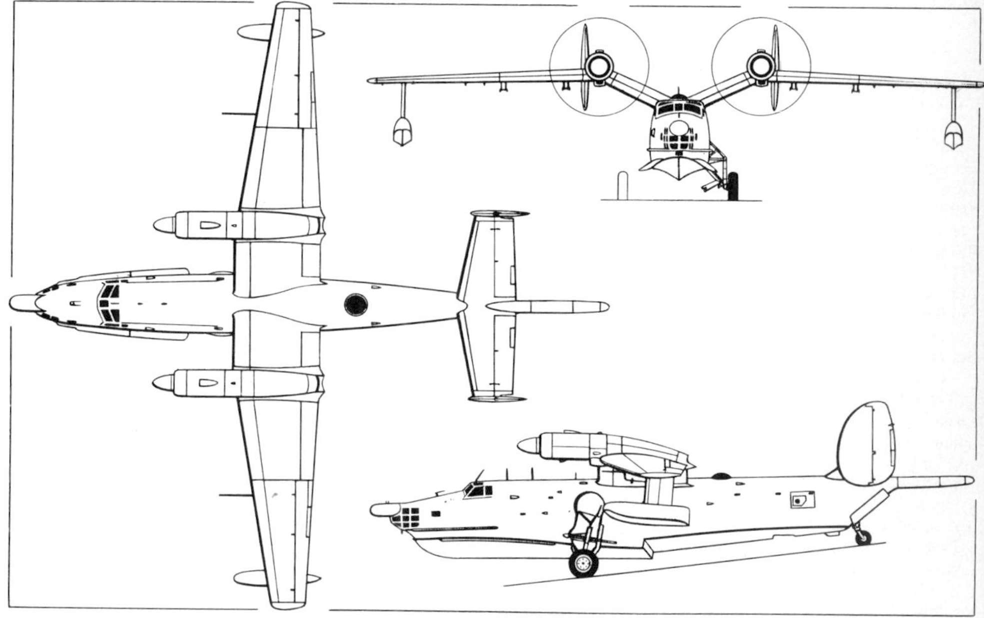

Beriev Be-12 Tchaika twin-turboprop maritime reconnaissance amphibian *(Pilot Press)*

Production started in 1964, and when three Be-12s took part in the 1967 air display at Domodedovo, the commentator said that the unit to which they belonged was "one of those serving where the country's military air force began", implying that the aircraft were then in operational service. Be-12s have subsequently formed standard equipment at coastal air bases of the Soviet Northern and Black Sea Fleets, for anti-submarine and surveillance duties out to some 200 nm (370 km; 230 miles) from shore, and were operational for a period from bases in Egypt, in Egyptian insignia. Production is believed to have totalled 100, of which about 95 remain in service.

Beriev Be-12 Tchaika anti-submarine and maritime patrol amphibian flying-boat of the Soviet Naval Air Force *(Swedish Air Force)*

TYPE: Twin-turboprop anti-submarine and maritime patrol amphibian.

WINGS: Cantilever high-wing monoplane of sharply cranked configuration to raise propellers clear of water. Unswept constant chord centre-section; tapered outer panels. All-metal two-spar structure. Hydraulically boosted ailerons actuated by push-rods. Two electrically operated tabs in each aileron. Hydraulically actuated trailing-edge flaps in two sections on each wing, from aileron to centre-section (passing under engine) and on centre-section.

FUSELAGE: Single-step all-metal semi-monocoque hull of high length to beam ratio. Two long strakes, one above the other, on each side of front fuselage to prevent spray from enveloping the propellers at take-off.

TAIL UNIT: All-metal structure. Considerable dihedral on two-spar tailplane, which has two endplate fins and horn balanced rudders at tips. Control surfaces actuated by push-rods, with hydraulic boost. Electrically operated trim tab in each elevator and each rudder.

LANDING GEAR: Hydraulically retractable tailwheel type, comprising single-wheel main units which retract upward through 180° to lie flush within sides of hull, and a rearward retracting steerable tailwheel. Oleo-pneumatic mainwheel shock absorbers. Except for top of each mainwheel, all units are fully enclosed by doors when retracted. Non-retractable wingtip floats.

POWER PLANT: Two Ivchenko AI-20D turboprop engines, each rated at 3,124 kW (4,190 ehp) and driving an AV-681 four-blade variable-pitch propeller. Metal cowlings open downward in halves, permitting their use as servicing platforms. Fuel tanks, between spars in wings and in fuselage, with total capacity of approx 11,000 litres (2,420 Imp gallons; 2,905 US gallons).

ACCOMMODATION: Crew of five on flight deck. Glazed navigation and observation station in nose. Astrodome observation station in top of rear fuselage. Side hatches in rear fuselage permit loading while afloat.

SYSTEMS: Hydraulic system actuates flaps and landing gear. Two engine driven generators power 28V DC electrical system.

AVIONICS AND EQUIPMENT: No details available of com/nav systems or IFF. Radome above nose glazing. MAD (magnetic anomaly detection) 'sting' extends rearward from tail. APU exhausts through aperture in port side of rear fuselage.

ARMAMENT: Internal weapons bay in bottom of hull aft of step. One large and one smaller external stores pylon under each outer wing panel, for torpedoes, depth charges, mines and other stores.

DIMENSIONS, EXTERNAL:

Wing span	29·71 m (97 ft 5¾ in)
Wing aspect ratio	8·4
Length overall	30·17 m (99 ft 0 in)
Height overall	7·00 m (22 ft 11½ in)
Propeller diameter	4·85 m (16 ft 0 in)

AREA:

Wings, gross	105 m² (1,130 sq ft)

WEIGHTS:

Max operational load	10,000 kg (22,045 lb)
Max T-O weight	31,000 kg (68,345 lb)

PERFORMANCE:

Max level speed	328 knots (608 km/h; 378 mph)
Normal operating speed	172 knots (320 km/h; 199 mph)
Rate of climb at S/L	912 m (2,990 ft)/min
Service ceiling	11,280 m (37,000 ft)
Range with max fuel	4,050 nm (7,500 km; 4,660 miles)

ILYUSHIN

DESIGN BUREAU HEADQUARTERS: Moscow Central Airport, Khodinka, Moscow

GENERAL DESIGNER: G. Novozhilov

This design bureau is named after its former leader, Sergei Vladimirovich Ilyushin, who died on 9 February 1977, at the age of 83. Aircraft designed by Ilyushin and still in service include the Il-14 piston engined light transport and four-turboprop Il-18 transport, of which details have been given in earlier editions of *Jane's*, and the Il-28 twin-jet bomber, produced also in China (which see). More recent types from the Ilyushin bureau are as follows:

ILYUSHIN Il-18

The **Il-18DORR** conversion of an Il-18 airliner was first mentioned in the Soviet press in 1986. It was described as a long range ocean fishery reconnaissance aircraft. No details are known.

Another previously unknown variant of the Il-18D is aircraft SSSR-75442 of the Soviet Meteorological Institute shown in an accompanying illustration. It was photographed at Shannon, Ireland, en route to Havana, Cuba. Note the many protrusions and canisters.

Previously unknown variant of Il-18D seen in 1986 and described as a meteorological aircraft *(David O'Mahony)*

ILYUSHIN Il-20

NATO reporting name: Coot

The Il-18 prototype flew for the first time on 4 July 1957 and production models entered service with Aeroflot in 1959. Production exceeded 700 aircraft, of which more than 100 were exported for use by commercial airlines; a few were delivered for military and government use, usually as VIP transports. Those still in civilian and military use include former passenger carrying Il-18s converted into freighters for Aeroflot by Factory 402 at Moscow/Bykovo. Modifications include installation of a freight door 3·50 m (11 ft 6 in) wide in the rear fuselage and a strengthened cabin floor.

An anti-submarine derivative, the **Il-38** (NATO reporting name 'May'), is in service and is described separately. Another military variant of the Il-18, seen for the first time in 1978, is the **Il-20** elint/reconnaissance aircraft, known to NATO as **Coot-A** and shown in an accompanying illustration. In this case, the airframe appears to be basically unchanged by comparison with the transport. It carries under its fuselage a container about 10·25 m long and 1·15 m deep (33 ft 7½ in × 3 ft 9 in), which is assumed to house side looking radar. There is a further container, about 4·4 m long and 0·88 m deep (14 ft 5 in × 2 ft 10½ in) on each side of the forward fuselage, containing a door over a camera or other sensor. Numerous other antennae and blisters can be seen, about eight of them on the undersurface of the centre and rear fuselage, with two large plates projecting above the forward fuselage.

A detailed description of the commercial airliner versions of the Il-18 can be found in the 1979-80 and earlier editions of *Jane's*. The following abbreviated details of the Il-18D are retained as an indication of likely features of the military Il-20:

POWER PLANT: Four 3,169 kW (4,250 ehp) Ivchenko AI-20M turboprop engines, each driving an AV-68I four-blade reversible-pitch propeller. Ten flexible fuel tanks in inboard panel of each wing and integral tank in outboard panel, with a total capacity of 23,700 litres (5,213 Imp gallons; 6,261 US gallons). Some Il-18 airliners have additional bag tanks in centre-section, giving a total capacity of 30,000 litres (6,600 Imp gallons; 7,925 US gallons).

DIMENSIONS, EXTERNAL:

Wing span	37·42 m (122 ft 9¼ in)
Wing chord: at root	5·61 m (18 ft 5 in)
at tip	1·87 m (6 ft 2 in)
Wing aspect ratio	10
Length overall	35·9 m (117 ft 9 in)
Height overall	10·17 m (33 ft 4 in)
Tailplane span	11·80 m (38 ft 8½ in)
Wheel track	9·00 m (29 ft 6 in)
Wheelbase	12·78 m (41 ft 10 in)
Propeller diameter	4·50 m (14 ft 9 in)
Cabin doors (each): Height	1·40 m (4 ft 7 in)
Width	0·76 m (2 ft 6 in)
Height to sill	2·90 m (9 ft 6 in)

DIMENSIONS, INTERNAL:

Flight deck: Volume	9·36 m³ (330 cu ft)
Cabin, excl flight deck: Length	approx 24·0 m (79 ft 0 in)
Max width	3·23 m (10 ft 7 in)
Max height	2·00 m (6 ft 5¾ in)
Volume	238 m³ (8,405 cu ft)

AREA:

Wings, gross	140 m² (1,507 sq ft)

WEIGHTS (Il-18D airliner):

Max payload	13,500 kg (29,750 lb)
Max T-O weight	64,000 kg (141,100 lb)

PERFORMANCE (Il-18D airliner, at max T-O weight):

Max cruising speed	364 knots (675 km/h; 419 mph)
Econ cruising speed	337 knots (625 km/h; 388 mph)
Operating height	8,000-10,000 m (26,250-32,800 ft)
T-O run	1,300 m (4,265 ft)
Landing run	850 m (2,790 ft)
Range with max fuel, 1 h reserves	3,508 nm (6,500 km; 4,040 miles)
Range with max payload, 1 h reserves	1,997 nm (3,700 km; 2,300 miles)

ILYUSHIN Il-38

NATO reporting name: May

The airframe of this shore-based anti-submarine/maritime patrol aircraft was developed from that of the Il-18 airliner in the same way that the US Navy's P-3 Orion was based on the Lockheed Electra transport. The fuselage is lengthened, and the complete wing assembly is much farther forward than on the Il-18, to cater for the effect on the CG position of internal equipment and stores.

Il-38s of the Soviet Naval Air Force are encountered frequently over the Baltic and North Atlantic. A Treaty of Friendship and Co-operation signed with the People's Democratic Republic of Yemen permits patrols over the Red Sea, Gulf of Aden, Arabian Sea and Indian Ocean

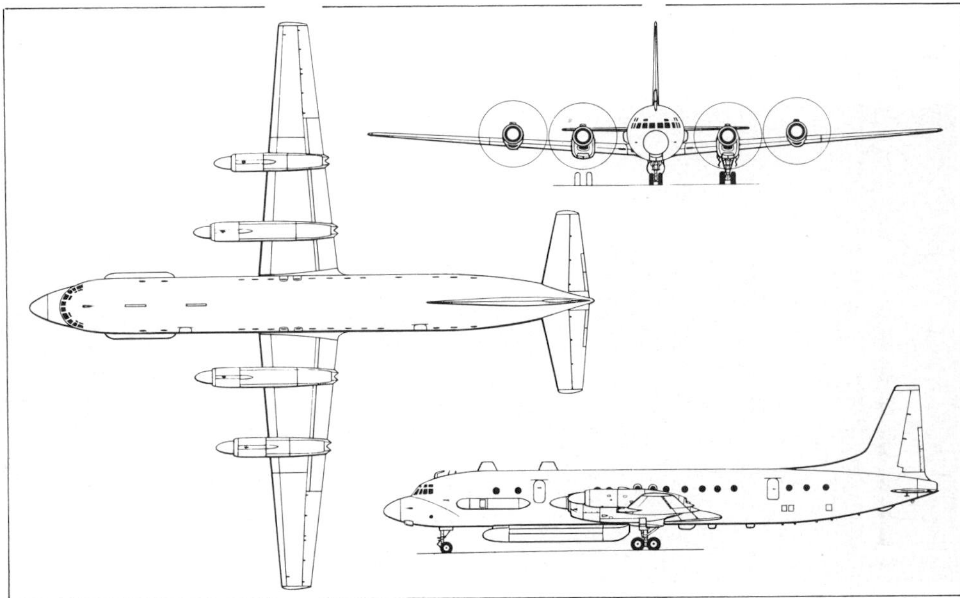

Ilyushin Il-20 (NATO 'Coot-A') elint/reconnaissance development of the Il-18 airliner *(Pilot Press)*

Ilyushin Il-20 (NATO 'Coot-A') electronic intelligence (elint) and reconnaissance aircraft *(Royal Navy)*

from a base in that country. Other Il-38s are deployed periodically to Libya, Tiyas in Syria, and Mozambique.

In 1975, the Indian Navy ordered an initial batch of three refurbished ex-Soviet Navy Il-38s, which equip INAS 315 at Dabolim, Goa. About 50 are believed to be operational with Soviet naval units.

TYPE: Four-turboprop maritime patrol aircraft.

WINGS: Cantilever low-wing monoplane. Dihedral 3° from roots. Mean thickness/chord ratio 14%. All-metal structure. Three spars in centre-section, two in outer wings. All-metal ailerons are mass and aerodynamically balanced, and fitted with electrically actuated trim tabs. Flying controls cable actuated. Hydraulically actuated double-slotted flaps. Electro-thermal de-icing.

FUSELAGE: Circular-section all-metal semi-monocoque structure of fail-safe type, with rip stop doublers around window cutouts, door frames and the more heavily loaded skin panels.

TAIL UNIT: Cantilever all-metal structure. Electrically actuated trim tabs in rudder and elevators. Additional spring tab in rudder. Flying controls cable actuated and power assisted. Electro-thermal de-icing.

LANDING GEAR: Retractable tricycle type, strengthened by comparison with that of Il-18. Hydraulic actuation. Four-wheel bogie main units, with 930 mm × 305 mm tyres and hydraulic brakes. Steerable (45° each way) twin nosewheel unit, with 700 mm × 250 mm tyres. Hydraulic brakes and nosewheel steering. Pneumatic emergency braking.

POWER PLANT: Four Ivchenko AI-20M turboprops, each rated at 3,169 kW (4,250 shp), driving AV-68I four-blade reversible-pitch metal propellers. Multiple bag type fuel tanks in centre-section and in inboard panel of each wing, and integral tank in outboard panel, with a total capacity of 30,000 litres (6,600 Imp gallons; 7,925 US gallons). Pressure fuelling through four international standard connections in inner nacelles. Provision for overwing fuelling. Oil capacity 58·5 litres (12·85 Imp gallons; 15·45 US gallons) per engine. Engines started electrically.

ACCOMMODATION: Pilot and co-pilot side by side on flight deck, with dual controls; flight engineer to rear. Number of operational crew believed to be nine, but unconfirmed. Flight deck is separated from main cabin by a pressure bulkhead to reduce hazards following sudden decompression of either. Main cabin has few windows and contains search equipment, electronic equipment and crew stations appropriate to role. Door is on starboard side at rear of cabin (location of Il-18 service door).

SYSTEMS: Cabin pressurised to max differential of 0·49 bars (7·1 lb/sq in). Electrical system includes eight engine driven generators for 28V DC and 115V 400Hz AC supply. Hydraulic system, pressure 207 bars (3,000 lb/sq in), for landing gear retraction, nosewheel steering, brakes, elevator and rudder actuators, flaps, weapon bay doors and radar antennae.

AVIONICS AND EQUIPMENT: Navigation/weather radar in nose. Search radar in undernose radome. MAD tail 'sting'. Forward weapons bay occupied by avionics equipment, under a second, larger, blister fairing, on one aircraft illustrated. Automatic navigation equipment, radio compasses and radio altimeter probably similar to those of Il-18.

ARMAMENT: Two weapons/stores bays forward and aft of wing carry-through structure on most aircraft, to accommodate a variety of attack weapons and sonobuoys.

DIMENSIONS, EXTERNAL:
As listed under Il-20 entry, except:
- Length overall: 39·60 m (129 ft 10 in)
- Height overall: 10·16 m (33 ft 4 in)

WEIGHTS:
- Weight empty: 36,000 kg (79,367 lb)
- Max T-O weight: 63,500 kg (140,000 lb)

PERFORMANCE:
- Max level speed at 6,400 m (21,000 ft): 390 knots (722 km/h; 448 mph)
- Max cruising speed at 8,230 m (27,000 ft): 330 knots (611 km/h; 380 mph)
- Patrol speed at 600 m (2,000 ft): 216 knots (400 km/h; 248 mph)
- Min flying speed: 103 knots (190 km/h; 118 mph)
- T-O run: 1,300 m (4,265 ft)
- Landing run with reverse thrust: 850 m (2,790 ft)

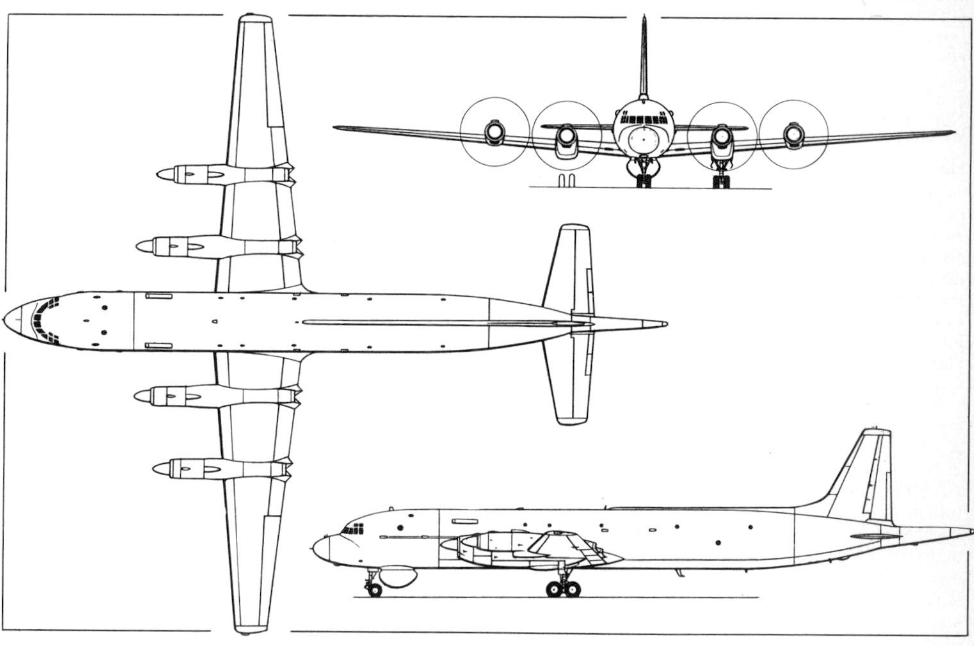

Ilyushin Il-38 anti-submarine/maritime patrol derivative of the Il-18 airliner *(Pilot Press)*

Close-up of side-looking radar pod and other elint features of 'Coot-A' *(Royal Air Force)*

Version of Il-38 with second radome replacing forward weapons bay doors

Ilyushin Il-38 anti-submarine/maritime patrol aircraft (four Ivchenko AI-20M turboprop engines) *(US Department of Defense)*

Range with max fuel
3,887 nm (7,200 km; 4,473 miles)
Patrol endurance with max fuel 12 h

ILYUSHIN Il-62

NATO reporting name: Classic

Brief details of the early history of this rear-engined four-turbofan long-range airliner can be found in the 1982-83 *Jane's*. The standard Kuznetsov engines were not ready in time for the first flight of the first prototype, which took place in January 1963 with four 73·55 kN (16,535 lb st) Lyulka AL-7 engines installed. Aeroflot introduced the Il-62 on to its Moscow-Montreal service on 15 September 1967, as a replacement for the Tu-114. Production is reported to have totalled more than 200, including developed Il-62M/MKs (described separately). Current operators of Il-62s and Il-62M/MKs include Aeroflot (about 150), CAAC of China, Choson Minhang of North Korea, CSA Czechoslovak Airlines, Cubana, Interflug of East Germany, Polish Airlines LOT, Tarom of Romania and the Czechoslovak government for VIP operation.

Type: Four-turbofan long-range airliner.

Wings: Cantilever low-wing monoplane. Sweepback 32° 30′ at quarter-chord. Extended chord leading-edge on outer two-thirds of each wing. All-metal structure, with four spars inboard, two at tip. Removable leading-edge. Each wing fitted with three-section manually operated ailerons, electrically actuated slotted flaps and two hydraulically operated spoiler sections forward of flaps. Trim tab and spring loaded servo tab in each centre aileron, spring loaded servo tab in each inner aileron. Hot air anti-icing of leading-edges.

Fuselage: Conventional all-metal semi-monocoque structure. Frames are duralumin stampings and pressings. Integrally pressed skin panels at highly stressed areas. Floors are sandwich panels with foam plastics filler. Nosecone hinges upward for access to radar.

Tail Unit: Cantilever all-metal structure, with electrically actuated variable incidence T tailplane. All surfaces sweptback. Manually operated rudder, fitted with yaw damper, trim tab and spring servo tab. Manually operated elevators have two automatic trim tabs and two manual trim tabs. Hot air leading-edge anti-icing system.

Landing Gear: Hydraulically retractable tricycle type. Forward retracting twin-wheel steerable nose unit. Emergency extension by gravity. Oleo-nitrogen shock absorber in each unit. Each main unit carries a four-wheel bogie and retracts inward into wing roots. Mainwheel tyres size 1450 × 450, pressure 9·31 bars (135 lb/sq in). Nosewheel tyres size 930 × 305, pressure 7·86 bars (114 lb/sq in). Hydraulic disc brake and inertia type electric anti-skid unit on each mainwheel, supplemented by large tail parachute. Parking brakes. Hydraulic twin-wheel strut is extended downward to support rear fuselage during loading and unloading.

Power Plant: Four Kuznetsov NK-8-4 turbofan engines, each rated at 103 kN (23,150 lb st), mounted in horizontal pairs on each side of rear fuselage. Thrust reverser on each outboard engine. Hot air anti-icing system for engine intakes. Automatically controlled fuel system, with seven integral tanks, three in wing centre-section, two in each outer panel. Each engine has its own independent fuel system, with cross-feed. Total fuel capacity 100,000 litres (21,998 Imp gallons; 26,417 US gallons). Four standard international underwing pressure refuelling points. Eight gravity refuelling sockets. Total oil capacity 204 litres (45 Imp gallons; 54 US gallons).

Accommodation: Crew of five (two pilots, navigator, radio operator and flight engineer) on flight deck. Provision for two supernumerary pilot/navigators. Basic two-cabin layout, and galley, toilet and wardrobe facilities, are unchanged in the three main versions, only the width and pitch of the seats being varied. In the 186-passenger version, there are 72 seats in the forward cabin and 114 in the rear cabin, all six-abreast and all at a seat pitch of 86 cm (34 in). In the 168-seat configuration, increased pitch reduces capacity to 66 in the forward cabin and 102 in the rear cabin. The 114-passenger version has 45 seats in the forward cabin and 69 in the rear cabin, all five-abreast, except for four-abreast rear row by door. A first class/de luxe version for 85 passengers is available, with 45 seats in forward cabin and 40 four-abreast sleeperette chairs with footrests in rear cabin. Passenger doors forward of front cabin and between cabins on port side. Total of five toilets, opposite forward door, between cabins (starboard) and aft of rear cabin (both sides). Electrically powered galley/pantry amidships and wardrobes in each version. Pressurised baggage and freight compartments under cabin floor, forward and aft of wing. Unpressurised baggage/cargo compartment at extreme rear of fuselage. All compartments have tiedown fittings and rails in floor, and removable nets to restrain cargo.

Systems: Air-conditioning and pressurisation system maintains sea level conditions up to 7,000 m (23,000 ft) and gives equivalent of 2,100 m (6,900 ft) at 13,000 m (42,600 ft). Pressure differential 0·62 bars (9·0 lb/sq in). Hydraulic system, pressure 207 bars (3,000 lb/sq in), for landing gear retraction, nosewheel steering, brakes, spoilers and windscreen wipers. Emergency hydraulic system, powered by electric motor, for nosewheel steering, mainwheel extension and spoiler control. Three-phase 200/115V AC electrical supply from four 40kVA engine driven generators (optional 27V DC system with eight 18kW engine driven generators). Four transformer-rectifiers and four batteries for DC supply. Electric windscreen de-icing. TA-6 APU in tailcone.

Avionics: Standard avionics include two-channel autopilot, navigation computer, air data system, HF and UHF radio, VOR/ILS, RMI, Doppler, radio altimeter and weather radar. Polyot automatic flight control system optional.

Dimensions, external:

Wing span	43·20 m (141 ft 9 in)
Length overall	53·12 m (174 ft 3½ in)
Length of fuselage	49·00 m (160 ft 9 in)
Height overall	12·35 m (40 ft 6¼ in)
Tailplane span	12·23 m (40 ft 1½ in)
Fuselage height	4·10 m (13 ft 5½ in)
Fuselage width	3·75 m (12 ft 3½ in)
Wheel track	6·80 m (22 ft 3½ in)
Wheelbase	24·49 m (80 ft 4½ in)
Passenger doors (each): Height	1·83 m (6 ft 0 in)
Width	0·86 m (2 ft 9¾ in)
Height to sill	3·55 m (11 ft 8 in)
Emergency exit (galley service) door:	
Height	1·38 m (4 ft 6¼ in)
Width	0·61 m (2 ft 0 in)
Emergency exits (overwing):	
Height	0·91 m (2 ft 11¾ in)
Width	0·51 m (1 ft 8 in)
Front cargo hold door: Height	1·31 m (4 ft 3½ in)
Width	1·26 m (4 ft 1½ in)
Height to sill	1·90 m (6 ft 3 in)
Second cargo hold door: Height	1·00 m (3 ft 3¼ in)
Width	1·26 m (4 ft 1½ in)
Height to sill	1·90 m (6 ft 3 in)
Third cargo hold door: Height	0·70 m (2 ft 3½ in)
Width	0·70 m (2 ft 3½ in)
Height to sill	2·26 m (7 ft 5 in)

Ilyushin Il-62M long-range airliner (four Soloviev D-30KU turbofan engines) of CSA Czechoslovak Airlines *(Anton Wettstein)*

Ilyushin Il-62M (NATO 'Classic') long-range four-turbofan transport *(Pilot Press)*

Rear cargo hold door: Height 1·15 m (3 ft 9 in)
Width 1·07 m (3 ft 6 in)
Height to sill 3·68 m (12 ft 0¾ in)

DIMENSIONS, INTERNAL:
Cabin: Max height 2·12 m (6 ft 11½ in)
Max width 3·49 m (11 ft 5¼ in)
Volume 163 m³ (5,756 cu ft)
Total volume of pressure cell 396 m³ (13,985 cu ft)
Cargo hold volume: Front 22·7 m³ (801 cu ft)
Second 12·6 m³ (445 cu ft)
Third 6·9 m³ (243 cu ft)
Rear 5·8 m³ (205 cu ft)

AREAS:
Wings, gross 279·55 m² (3,009 sq ft)
Ailerons (total) 16·25 m² (174·9 sq ft)
Spoilers (total) 9·54 m² (102·7 sq ft)
Flaps (total) 43·48 m² (468·0 sq ft)
Horizontal tail surfaces (total) 40·00 m² (430·5 sq ft)
Vertical tail surfaces (total) 35·60 m² (383·2 sq ft)

WEIGHTS AND LOADING:
Weight empty 66,400 kg (146,390 lb)
Operating weight empty 69,400 kg (153,000 lb)
Max payload 23,000 kg (50,700 lb)
Max fuel 83,325 kg (183,700 lb)
Max ramp weight 167,000 kg (368,000 lb)
Max T-O weight 162,000 kg (357,150 lb)
Max landing weight 105,000 kg (231,500 lb)
Max zero-fuel weight 93,500 kg (206,130 lb)
Max wing loading 572 kg/m² (117·2 lb/sq ft)

PERFORMANCE (at max T-O weight):
Normal cruising speed
442-486 knots (820-900 km/h; 509-560 mph)
Normal cruising height
10,000-12,000 m (33,000-39,400 ft)
Landing speed
119-129 knots (220-240 km/h; 137-149 mph)
Max rate of climb at S/L 1,080 m (3,540 ft)/min
FAR T-O field length:
ISA at S/L 3,250 m (10,660 ft)
ISA + 20°C at S/L 3,915 m (12,840 ft)
FAR landing field length:
ISA at S/L 2,800 m (9,185 ft)
ISA + 20°C at S/L 2,950 m (9,680 ft)
Range with max payload, 66,700 kg (147,050 lb) fuel, 1 h fuel reserves 3,612 nm (6,700 km; 4,160 miles)
Range with 80,000 kg (176,370 lb) fuel and 10,000 kg (22,045 lb) payload, 1 h fuel reserves
4,963 nm (9,200 km; 5,715 miles)

ILYUSHIN Il-62M/MK

NATO reporting name: Classic

First displayed publicly at the 1971 Paris Air Show, the **Il-62M** is a developed version of the Il-62, with no dimensional changes to the airframe. It is fitted with more powerful turbofans, of a different type, with clamshell thrust reversers on the outboard engine of each pair, offering a lower approach speed and improved airflow over the rear of the nacelles. An additional fuel tank is installed in the tail fin, contributing (with the improved specific fuel consumption of the engines) to the longer range of this version.

Revised layout of the flight deck equipment, and improved navigation and radio communications equipment, are features of the Il-62M. Control wheels of different design allow the pilots a better field of view, and the aircraft's automatic flight control system permits automatic landings in ICAO Category II conditions, with planned extension to Category III. The wing spoilers of this version can be utilised differentially to enhance roll control.

Additional emergency and rescue equipment is installed on the Il-62M. Unlike the Il-62, it has a containerised baggage and freight system, with mechanised loading and unloading.

The Il-62M exhibited in Paris in 1971 and 1973 was the prototype (SSSR-86673). Production models entered service on Aeroflot's Moscow-Havana route in 1974 and took over progressively all of the airline's very long distance services.

A variant announced in 1978 is the **Il-62MK**, still dimensionally unchanged and with the same power plant as the Il-62M, but with strengthened wings, wider main landing gear bogies, lower-pressure tyres, improved brakes, and revised spoilers which deploy automatically at touchdown. Max T-O weight is increased to 167,000 kg (368,170 lb) and max landing weight to 110,000 kg (242,500 lb), permitting the carriage of up to 195 passengers. To ensure adequate cabin service with so many passengers, the interior was redesigned to permit the more efficient use of service trolleys. It has a 'wide-body look', with enclosed overhead baggage racks and indirect lighting. Range with max fuel and 10,000 kg (22,045 lb) payload is 5,180 nm (9,600 km; 5,965 miles). Max payload is 25,000 kg (55,115 lb).

In 1985, the Il-62M and Il-62MK were being updated by improvements to the navigation system, based on a new triplex INS, and by changes to the turbofans and pods to reduce noise and air pollution,

The basic structural description of the Il-62 applies also to the Il-62M. The main innovations are as follows:

POWER PLANT: Four Soloviev D-30KU turbofan engines, each rated at 107·9 kN (24,250 lb st), mounted in horizontal pairs on each side of rear fuselage. Clamshell thrust reverser on each outboard engine. Remainder of power plant basically as for Il-62, but additional fuel tank in tail fin, giving total capacity of 105,300 litres (23,162 Imp gallons; 27,817 US gallons).

ACCOMMODATION: Alternative configurations for up to 174 economy class, 168 tourist class or 140 mixed class passengers. In the basic tourist class version there are two toilets opposite the forward door, on the starboard side, aft of the flight deck. The forward cabin contains 66 seats, all six-abreast in threes with centre aisle. Galley/pantry, coat stowage and toilet amidships. Rear cabin contains 102 seats, six-abreast in threes with centre aisle. Two toilets and wardrobe to rear of this cabin. Doors as on Il-62. Two emergency exits on each side, over wing. Forward underfloor baggage and freight hold accommodates nine containers, each weighing approximately 45 kg (100 lb) empty and with a capacity of 600 kg (1,322 lb) and 1·6 m³ (56·5 cu ft). Rear hold accommodates five similar containers. Two compartments for non-containerised cargo. Total baggage and freight capacity 48 m³ (1,695 cu ft)

SYSTEMS AND EQUIPMENT: See introductory notes.

AVIONICS: Duplicated SAU-1T automatic flight control system provides for automatic control from a height of 200 m (660 ft) after take-off to a height of 30 m (100 ft) on the approach to land; DISS-013 Doppler indicator and NV-PB-1 navigation computer; TKS-P course sensing system; TsGV-10P vertical master gyros; SVS-PN-15 air data system; Kurs-MP-2 radio navigation system, utilising VOR, ILS or SP-50 beacons; GROZA radar; SD-67 DME; ARK-15 ADF; RV-5 radio altimeter; SO-70 IFF transponder; MIKRON 2-24MHz HF radio; LANDASH 118-135MHz VHF radio; VESHANIE public address and in-flight entertainment system.

DIMENSIONS AND AREAS:
Same as for Il-62

WEIGHTS (Il-62M):
Max payload 23,000 kg (50,700 lb)
Max T-O weight 165,000 kg (363,760 lb)
Max landing weight 105,000 kg (231,500 lb)
Max zero-fuel weight 94,600 kg (208,550 lb)

PERFORMANCE (Il-62M, at max T-O weight):
Normal cruising speed
442-486 knots (820-900 km/h; 509-560 mph)
Normal cruising height
10,000-12,000 m (33,000-39,400 ft)
Balanced T-O distance (ISA, S/L) 3,300 m (10,830 ft)
Landing run (ISA, S/L) 2,500 m (8,200 ft)
Range with max payload, with 5,100 kg (11,240 lb) fuel reserves 4,210 nm (7,800 km; 4,846 miles)
Range with 10,000 kg (22,045 lb) payload, with reserves 5,400 nm (10,000 km; 6,215 miles)

ILYUSHIN Il-76

NATO reporting name: Candid
Indian Air Force name: Gajaraj

Towards the end of the 1960s, the Ilyushin design bureau, under the leadership of Mr G. V. Novozhilov, began design of a heavy transport to replace the turboprop An-12. Nominal task for the aircraft was to transport 40 tonnes of freight for a distance of 2,700 nm (5,000 km; 3,100 miles) in less than six hours. It had to be capable of operation from short unprepared airstrips, in the most difficult weather conditions experienced in Siberia, the north of the Soviet Union and the Far East, while being much simpler to service and able to fly much faster than the An-12.

The prototype of the new transport, known as the Il-76 (SSSR-86712), flew for the first time on 25 March 1971 and made its public debut at the 29th Salon de l'Aéronautique et de l'Espace in Paris in May 1971. Test flying continued until 1975, when the Il-76 entered series production. Subsequent operation in the most difficult weather and ground conditions of Central and Eastern Siberia revealed operating costs more than 25 per cent lower per tonne/km

Ilyushin Il-76TD freight transport (four Soloviev D-30KP-1 turbofan engines) in Aeroflot service *(Martin Fricke)*

than for the An-12. This suggested that the Il-76 would be competitive with river transport, even during Summer months.

It was clear from the start that the Il-76 had considerable potential as a military transport. Evaluation by the Soviet Air Force had reached an advanced stage by 1974, when an official film depicted Il-76s with twin-gun rear turrets in use as vehicles for Soviet airborne troops, presumably with a development squadron.

Since that time, development of the Il-76 has continued, and the following major production versions can now be identified:

Il-76 (Candid-A). Initial basic production version.

Il-76T (Candid-A). Developed version, with additional fuel tankage in wing centre-section, above fuselage, and heavier payload. No armament.

Il-76M (Candid-B). As Il-76T, but for military use, with rear gun turret containing two 23 mm NR-23 guns, and small ECM fairings between centre windows at front of navigator's compartment, on each side of front fuselage, and on each side of rear fuselage. Turret and ECM not always fitted on export Il-76Ms. Up to 140 troops or 125 paratroops can be carried as an alternative to freight.

Il-76TD (Candid-A). Unarmed version, generally similar to Il-76T. First identified in November 1982, when an example registered SSSR-76467 passed through Shannon Airport in Ireland. Fully operational from July 1983, this version has Soloviev D-30KP-1 engines which maintain full power up to ISA + 27°C against ISA + 15°C for earlier models. Max T-O weight and payload are increased. An increase of 10,000 kg (22,046 lb) in max fuel capacity provides an increase of 648 nm (1,200 km; 745 miles) in range with max fuel.

One Il-76TD has been equipped to transport members of Soviet Antarctic expeditions between Maputo in Mozambique and Molodezhnaya Station in Antarctica. The hold has been soundproofed and contains seats, a buffet kitchen, toilet and working facilities. Baggage is carried in containers. First flight from Maputo was made on 25 February 1986, replacing the Il-18D used on the service for five years.

Il-76MD (Candid-B). Military version, generally similar to Il-76M but with same improvements as Il-76TD.

About 300 military Il-76s and Il-76M/MDs have been delivered to first-line squadrons of the Soviet Transport Aviation force, as An-12 replacements, from the assembly plant at Tashkent. Other customers for the military version include the air forces of Iraq, Czechoslovakia and Poland. India ordered an initial batch of 20 Il-76Ms to meet its Heavy Transport Aircraft requirement; deliveries began on 20 February 1985, to replace the An-12s of Nos. 25 and 44 Squadrons of the Indian Air Force, and the first five were accepted into service formally on 17 July 1985, with the Indian Air Force name of Gajaraj.

India is reported to be considering the conversion of some of its standard Il-76s for AEW duties. A specialised AEW&C version of the Il-76, known to NATO as 'Mainstay', is described separately, as is a flight refuelling tanker version known as 'Midas'.

It was announced in 1978 that, following extensive testing of the commercial Il-76T in Siberia, the type was to be introduced into service on the Moscow-Japan route of Aeroflot. This airline now has more than 50 Il-76s, including Il-76Ts and Il-76Ms, which form an immediately available military reserve. More than 50 civil and military Il-76s have been exported. Of these, Iraqi Airways has received a total of 16 Il-76Ts and Il-76Ms (one has been shot down), which are operated on behalf of the military services; Jamahiriyan Air Transport of Libya has six Il-76Ts; Syrianair has two Il-76Ms and two Il-76Ts; Bakhtar Afghan Airlines had one Il-76 on loan from Aeroflot in 1986. The guns are removed from the rear turret of Il-76Ms in airline service.

The first of at least two Il-76MDs delivered to Cubana, in November 1984, has no tail turret. Its date of manufacture was given as September of that year.

In July 1975, the Il-76 set a total of 25 officially recognised records for speed and altitude with payload. Fifteen of them, for speed with payload over 1,000 km and 2,000 km, have since been beaten by an Il-86; that for the greatest payload lifted to a height of 2,000 m has been beaten by an Antonov An-124. Details of the old records can be found in the 1981-82 *Jane's*; those still held by the Il-76 in mid-1986 are as follows: Piloted by Yakov I. Vernikov, on 4 July 1975, it reached an altitude of 11,875 m (38,960 ft) with payloads of 60,000 kg, 65,000 kg and 70,000 kg. On 10 July, Alexander Turumine averaged 440·305 knots (815·968 km/h; 507·019 mph) around a 5,000 km circuit, claiming records with 15,000 kg, 20,000 kg, 25,000 kg, 30,000 kg, 35,000 kg and 40,000 kg payloads.

In specialised roles, Il-76s have served as a testbed for the power plant of the Il-86 and as aircraft in which Soviet cosmonauts have been able to experience several tens of seconds of weightlessness during training.

Production was at the rate of more than 30 aircraft a year in 1986. The following description applies to the Il-76T:

TYPE: Four-turbofan medium/long-range freight transport.

WINGS: Cantilever monoplane, mounted above fuselage to leave interior unobstructed, and with constant anhedral from junction with centre-section on each side. Sweepback 25° at quarter-chord. All-metal five-piece structure, comprising centre-section, two inner panels carrying engines, and two outer panels. Leading-edge sweepback constant. Trailing-edge sweep increases outboard of joint between each inner and outer panel. Multi-spar fail-safe construction. Centre-section integral with fuselage. Mass balanced ailerons, with balance/trim tabs. Two-section triple-slotted flaps over approx 75 per cent of each semi-span, from wing root to inboard edge of aileron. Upper surface spoilers forward of flaps in 16 segments, four on each inner and outer wing panel. Ten-segment leading-edge slats over almost entire span, two on each inner panel, three on each outer panel.

Ilyushin Il-76MD Gajaraj of No. 44 Squadron, Indian Air Force

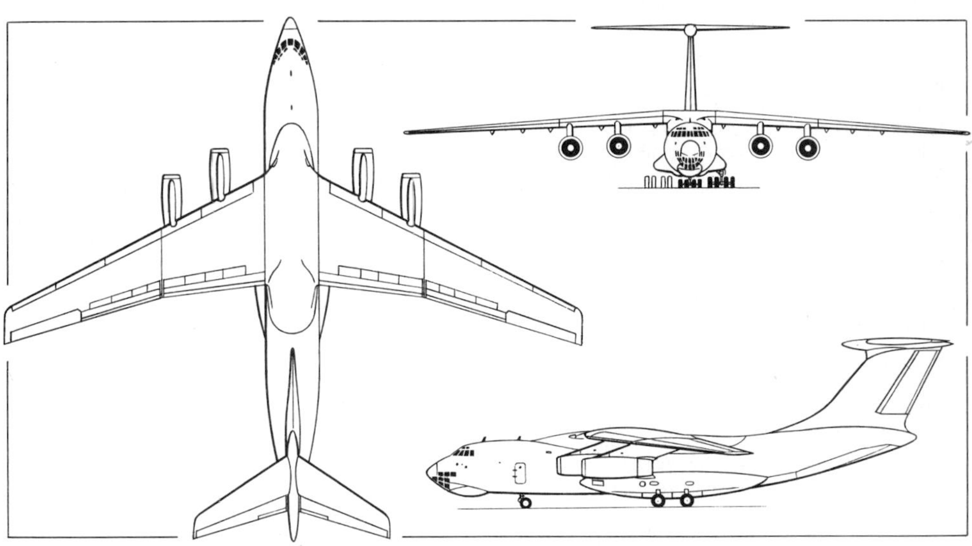

Ilyushin Il-76T four-turbofan heavy freight carrying transport *(Pilot Press)*

FUSELAGE: All-metal semi-monocoque fail-safe structure of basically circular section. Underside of upswept rear fuselage made up of two outward hinged clamshell doors, upward hinged panel between these doors, and downward hinged loading ramp.

TAIL UNIT: Cantilever all-metal structure, with variable incidence T tailplane. All surfaces sweptback. All control surfaces aerodynamically balanced. Tabs in rudder and each elevator.

LANDING GEAR: Hydraulically retractable tricycle type, designed for operation from prepared and unprepared runways. Nose unit made up of two pairs of wheels, side by side, with central oleo. Main gear on each side is made up of two units in tandem, each unit with four wheels on a single axle. Low-pressure tyres size 1,300 × 480 on mainwheels, 1,100 × 330 on nosewheels. Nosewheels retract forward. Main units retract inward into two large ventral fairings under fuselage, with an additional large fairing on each side of lower fuselage over actuating gear. During retraction mainwheel axles rotate around leg, so that wheels stow with axles parallel to fuselage axis (ie: wheels remain vertical but at 90° to direction of flight). All doors on wheel wells close when gear is down, to prevent fouling of legs by snow, ice, mud, etc. Oleo-pneumatic shock absorbers. Tyre pressure can be varied in flight from 2·5 to 5 bars (36-73 lb/sq in) to suit different landing strip conditions. Hydraulic brakes on mainwheels.

POWER PLANT: Four Soloviev D-30KP turbofan engines, each rated at 117·7 kN (26,455 lb st), in individual underwing pods. Each pod is carried on a large forward-inclined pylon and is fitted with a clamshell thrust reverser. Integral fuel tanks between spars of inner and outer wing panels. Total fuel capacity reported to be 81,830 litres (18,000 Imp gallons; 21,617 US gallons).

ACCOMMODATION: Crew of seven, including two freight handlers. Conventional side by side seating for pilot and co-pilot on spacious flight deck. Station for navigator below flight deck in glazed nose. Forward hinged door on each side of fuselage forward of wing. Two windows on each side of hold serve as emergency exits. Hold has reinforced floor of titanium alloys, with folding roller conveyors, and is loaded via rear ramp. Entire accommodation is pressurised, and advanced mechanical handling systems are provided for containerised and other freight, which can include standard ISO containers, each 12 m (39 ft 4½ in) long, building machinery, heavy crawlers and mobile cranes. Typical loads include six containers measuring either 2·99 × 2·44 × 2·44 m (9 ft 9¾ in × 8 ft × 8 ft) or 2·99 × 2·44 × 1·90 m (9 ft 9¾ in × 8 ft × 6 ft 2¾ in) and with loaded weights of 5,670 kg (12,500 lb) or 5,000 kg (11,025 lb) respectively; or twelve containers measuring 1·46 × 2·44 × 1·90 m (4 ft 9¼ in × 8 ft × 6 ft 2¾ in) and each weighing 2,500 kg (5,511 lb) loaded; or six pallets measuring 2·99 × 2·44 m (9 ft 9¾ in × 8 ft) and each weighing 5,670 kg (12,500 lb); or twelve pallets measuring 1·46 × 2·44 m (4 ft 9¼ in × 8 ft) and each weighing 2,500 kg (5,511 lb). Quick configuration changes can be made by the use of modules, each able to accommodate 30 passengers in four-abreast seating, litter patients and medical attendants, or cargo. Three such modules can be carried, each approx 6·10 m (20 ft) long, 2·44 m (8 ft) wide and 2·44 m (8 ft) high. They are loaded through the rear doors by means of two overhead travelling cranes, and are secured to the cabin floor with cargo restraints. Cranes can utilise two hoists, each with capacity of 3,000 kg (6,615 lb), or four hoists, each with capacity of 2,500 kg (5,510 lb). Ramp can be used as additional hoist, with capacity of up to 30,000 kg (66,140 lb) to facilitate loading of large vehicles and those with caterpillar tracks. Pilot's and co-pilot's windscreens can each be fitted with two wipers, top and bottom.

SYSTEMS: Hydraulic system includes servo motors and motors to drive the flaps, slats, landing gear and its doors, ramp, rear fuselage clamshell doors and load hoists. Flying control boosters are supplied by electric pumps and are independent of the central hydraulic supply. Manual control is possible after booster failure. Electrical system includes engine driven generators, auxiliary generators driven by an APU, DC converters and batteries. It powers the pumps for the flying control system boosters, radio and avionics, and lighting systems.

AVIONICS AND EQUIPMENT: Full equipment for all-weather

operation by day and night, including a computer for automatic flight control and automatic landing approach. Large meteorological and ground mapping radar in undernose radome. APU in port side landing gear fairing for engine starting and to supply all aircraft systems on ground, making aircraft independent of ground facilities.

DIMENSIONS, EXTERNAL:
- Wing span: 50·50 m (165 ft 8 in)
- Wing aspect ratio: 8·5
- Length overall: 46·59 m (152 ft 10¼ in)
- Height overall: 14·76 m (48 ft 5 in)
- Rear loading aperture:
  - Width: 3·40 m (11 ft 1¾ in)
  - Height: 3·45 m (11 ft 4 in)

DIMENSIONS, INTERNAL:
- Cabin: Length, excl ramp: 20·00 m (65 ft 7½ in)
  - Length, incl ramp: 24·50 m (80 ft 4½ in)
  - Width: 3·40 m (11 ft 1¾ in)
  - Height: 3·46 m (11 ft 4¼ in)
  - Volume: 235·3 m³ (8,310 cu ft)

AREA:
- Wings, gross: 300·0 m² (3,229·2 sq ft)

WEIGHTS AND LOADINGS (A: Il-76T, B: Il-76TD):
- Max payload: A: 40,000 kg (88,185 lb)
  - B: 48,000 kg (105,820 lb)
- Max T-O weight: A: 170,000 kg (374,785 lb)
  - B: 190,000 kg (418,875 lb)
- Permissible axle load (vehicles)
  - A: 7,500-11,000 kg (16,535-24,250 lb)
- Permissible floor loading
  - A: 1,450-3,100 kg/m² (297-635 lb/sq ft)
- Max wing loading: A: 566·7 kg/m² (116·05 lb/sq ft)
  - B: 633·3 kg/m² (129·72 lb/sq ft)
- Max power loading: A: 361 kg/kN (3·54 lb/lb st)
  - B: 403·6 kg/kN (3·95 lb/lb st)

PERFORMANCE (Il-76T):
- Max level speed: 459 knots (850 km/h; 528 mph)
- Cruising speed: 405-432 knots (750-800 km/h; 466-497 mph)
- T-O speed: 114 knots (210 km/h; 131 mph)
- Approach and landing speed: 119-130 knots (220-240 km/h; 137-149 mph)
- Normal cruising height: 9,000-12,000 m (29,500-39,370 ft)
- Absolute ceiling: approx 15,500 m (50,850 ft)
- T-O run: 850 m (2,790 ft)
- Landing run: 450 m (1,475 ft)
- Nominal range with 40,000 kg (88,185 lb) payload: 2,700 nm (5,000 km; 3,100 miles)
- Max range, with reserves: 3,617 nm (6,700 km; 4,163 miles)

ILYUSHIN Il-76 (AEW&C)

NATO reporting name: Mainstay

This AEW&C (airborne early warning and control system) version of the Il-76 has been under development since the 1970s as a replacement for the Tu-126s operated by the Soviet Voyska PVO home defence force and tactical air forces. Known to NATO as 'Mainstay', it is said by the US Department of Defense to provide the Soviet forces with the capability to detect aircraft and cruise missiles flying at low altitude over land and water; to help direct fighter operations over European and Asian battlefields; and to enhance air surveillance and defence of the USSR.

'Mainstay' has a conventionally located rotating 'saucer' radome, lengthened fuselage forward of the wings, and flight refuelling probe. The first examples are operational and a production rate of at least five aircraft per year is to be expected.

ILYUSHIN Il-76 (FLIGHT REFUELLING TANKER)

NATO reporting name: Midas

A version of the Il-76 has been under development since the mid-1970s as a probe-and-drogue flight refuelling tanker to replace the modified Myasishchev M-4 ('Bison') aircraft currently serving in this role. Nearing deployment in early 1986, it will support both tactical and strategic aircraft, and will improve significantly the ability of Soviet aircraft to conduct longer-range operations.

ILYUSHIN Il-86

NATO reporting name: Camber

The early history of this four-turbofan wide-bodied passenger transport was outlined in the 1982-83 and previous editions of *Jane's*. Construction of two prototypes was started in 1974. On 22 December 1976, piloted by Hero of the Soviet Union A. Kuznetsov, the first of these (SSSR-86000) made a first flight of about 40 min after taking off in 1,700 m (5,575 ft) from a 1,820 m (5,970 ft) runway at the old Moscow Central Airport of Khodinka, where the Ilyushin Bureau has its headquarters, to the official flight test centre.

Aircraft SSSR-86002, which flew for the first time at Voronezh on 24 October 1977, was described as the first production Il-86. Aeroflot took delivery of its first Il-86 (SSSR-86004) on 24 September 1979, and scheduled services began on 26 December 1980, operating three times each week between Moscow's Vnukovo Airport and Tashkent. Services between Moscow and Mineralnye Vody were being operated with Il-86s by Spring 1981, at which time Aeroflot planned to introduce the type on to 27 other major

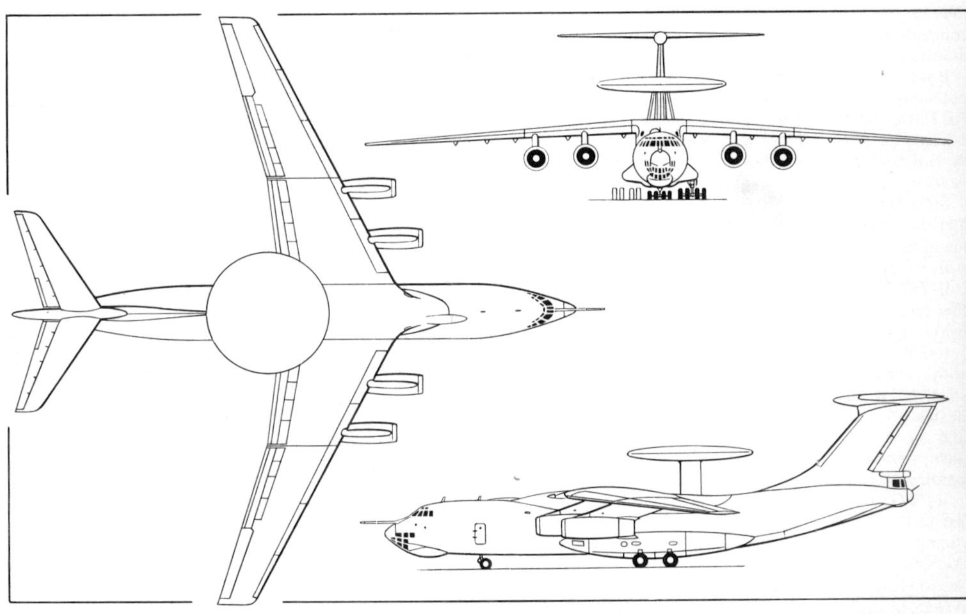

Provisional three-view drawing of AEW&C version of Il-76, known to NATO as 'Mainstay' *(Pilot Press)*

domestic routes, including those to Simferopol and Sochi. First international service operated by Il-86 was Moscow-East Berlin, from 3 July 1981. At that time, about 20 Il-86s had flown.

On 22 September 1981, an Il-86 piloted by G. Volokhov averaged 526·6 knots (975·3 km/h; 606 mph) over a 2,000 km closed circuit, carrying a payload of 65,000 kg. This flight set seven records, for payloads from 35,000 to 65,000 kg. Two days later, the same pilot averaged 519·4 knots (962 km/h; 597·8 mph) over 1,000 km, setting 11 records for payloads from 30,000 to 80,000 kg.

For production aircraft, wing slats, pylons to carry the engine pods, the tail fin and tailplane are being manufactured in Poland by PZL Mielec, which had delivered more than 130 sets by mid-1985. Final assembly is centred at Voronezh. The airframe is believed to be designed for 40,000 flying hours or 20,000 landings.

The following description applies to the initial production Il-86. The aircraft is said to have "passed through a redesign cycle" since 1980, during which the max T-O weight has increased to 208,000 kg (458,560 lb). The anticipated longer range commercial version is now believed to be designated Il-96.

TYPE: Four-turbofan wide-bodied passenger transport.

WINGS: Cantilever monoplane of all-metal construction (fixed surfaces made at Voronezh). Wings mounted in low-mid position on fuselage. Dihedral from roots. Sweepback 35° at quarter-chord. Three spars in inner wings, two in each outer panel. Large double-slotted trailing-edge flaps, in two sections along entire span of each wing inboard of aileron. Multi-section spoilers and airbrakes in top surface, forward of all four flap sections. Full span leading-edge slats, with small cutaway to clear each inboard engine pylon. Shallow fence on top surface in line with each pylon.

FUSELAGE: Conventional semi-monocoque light alloy pressurised structure of circular cross section. Floors of main and lower decks of honeycomb and carbonfibre reinforced plastics.

TAIL UNIT: Conventional sweptback cantilever structure, with tailplane dihedral. Variable incidence tailplane. Each control surface in two sections.

LANDING GEAR: Retractable four-unit type. Forward retracting steerable twin-wheel nose unit, and three four-wheel bogie main units. Two of the latter retract inward into the wing root fairings; the third unit is mounted centrally under the fuselage, slightly forward of the others, and retracts forward. (Main landing gear made at Kuibyshev.) Mainwheel tyres size 1300 × 480; nosewheel tyres size 1120 × 450.

POWER PLANT: Four Kuznetsov NK-86 turbofan engines, each rated at 127·5 kN (28,660 lb st), mounted on pylons forward of wing leading-edges. Engines fitted with combined thrust reversers/noise attenuators. Integral fuel tanks in wings, capacity 70,000-80,000 litres (15,398-17,597 Imp gallons; 18,492-21,133 US gallons).

ACCOMMODATION: Standard flight crew comprises two pilots and a flight engineer, with provision for a navigator if required. Flight engineer's seat normally faces to starboard, aft of co-pilot, but can pivot to central forward-facing position to enable the engineer to operate the throttles. Upper deck, on which all seats are located, is divided into three separate cabins by wardrobes, a serving area connected by elevator to the lower deck galley, and cabin staff accommodation, with a total of eight toilets at front (2) and rear (6) of the aircraft. Cabins feature unusually large windows, indirect lighting in walls and in ceiling panels, and enclosed baggage lockers at top of side walls. Preponderance of metal and natural fibre materials rather than plastics throughout cabins to enhance safety in an emergency. Up to 350 passengers in basic nine-abreast seating throughout, with two aisles, each 55 cm (21·6 in) wide. Suggested mixed class alternative layout provides for 28 passengers six-abreast in the front cabin, and 206 passengers eight-abreast in the other two cabins. Passengers enter via three airstair doors (made in Kharkov), which hinge down from the port side of the lower deck. One of these doors is forward of the wing; the others are aft of the wing. Four further doors at upper deck level on each side, for emergency use (using dual inflatable escape slides) and for use at airports where the utilisation of high level boarding steps or bridges is preferred. Coats and hand baggage are stowed on the lower deck before passengers climb one of three fixed staircases to the main deck. (A version of the Il-86 is available without the lower deck airstair doors and staircases, reducing operating weight empty by 3,000 kg; 6,610 lb and permitting installation of 25 more seats on

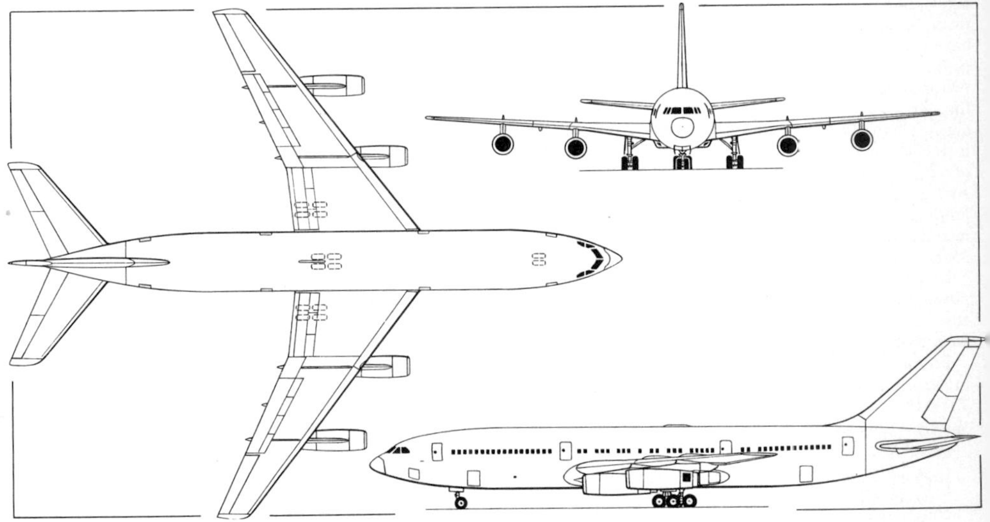

Ilyushin Il-86 four-turbofan wide-bodied passenger transport *(Pilot Press)*

Ilyushin Il-86 wide-bodied transport (four Kuznetsov NK-86 turbofans) in Aeroflot markings *(Anton Wettstein)*

upper deck.) Cargo holds on the lower deck are designed to accommodate heavy or registered baggage and freight in 8 standard LD3 containers, or 16 LD3 containers if some of the carry-on baggage racks are omitted. Access is via upward hinged doors forward of the starboard wing root leading-edge and at the side of the rear hold. Containers can be loaded and unloaded by means of a self-propelled truck with built-in roller conveyor. Films can be shown in flight, and there is a choice of 12 tape recorded audio programmes. A bar-buffet can be provided on the lower deck in place of the baggage and freight accommodation in the forward vestibule.

SYSTEMS: Four completely self-contained hydraulic systems, each operated by one of the engines, for actuation of flying control surfaces, tailplane variable incidence, spoilers, airbrakes, slats, flaps, landing gear, nosewheel steering, wheel brakes, anti-skid system, and upper level doors when passenger gangways are used. No provision for manual operation of primary flying control surfaces after failure of powered systems. All hot pipelines of air-conditioning system, and all fuel supply lines, outside pressure cell. Primary 200/155V 400Hz AC electrical system, powered by four 40kVA engine driven generators. Secondary 36V three-phase AC and 27V DC systems. Five accumulators and static transformer. Smoke detection system, with sensors in baggage, freight and equipment stowage areas. Pulse generating de-icing system consuming 500 times less energy than a conventional hot air or electrical system. APU in tailcone.

AVIONICS: All avionics equipment located within pressurised part of fuselage. Flight control and nav systems provide for automatic climb to the selected height, control of the rate of climb and automatic descent, and permit automatic landing in ICAO Cat IIIA conditions. Pre-programmable Doppler nav system with readout display screen on flight deck, on which microfilmed maps can be projected. Position of aircraft is indicated by cursor, driven by system computer. Nav system is updated automatically by inputs from VOR or VOR/DME radio beacons.

DIMENSIONS, EXTERNAL:
- Wing span: 48·06 m (157 ft 8¼ in)
- Length overall: 59·54 m (195 ft 4 in)
- Length of fuselage: 56·10 m (184 ft 0¾ in)
- Diameter of fuselage: 6·08 m (19 ft 11½ in)
- Height overall: 15·81 m (51 ft 10½ in)
- Tailplane span: 20·57 m (67 ft 6 in)
- Wheel track (c/l of outer shock struts): 11·15 m (36 ft 7 in)
- Wheelbase: 21·34 m (70 ft 0 in)

DIMENSIONS, INTERNAL:
- Main cabins: Height: 2·61 m (8 ft 7 in)
  - Max width: approx 5·70 m (18 ft 8½ in)

AREA:
- Wings, gross: 320 m² (3,444 sq ft)

WEIGHTS:
- Max payload: 42,000 kg (92,600 lb)
- Max fuel: 86,000 kg (189,600 lb)
- Max T-O weight (dependent on size and type of runway): 190,000-206,000 kg (418,875-454,150 lb)
- Max landing weight: 175,000 kg (385,800 lb)

PERFORMANCE (estimated):
- Normal cruising speed at 9,000-11,000 m (30,000-36,000 ft): 486-512 knots (900-950 km/h; 559-590 mph)
- Approach speed: 130-141 knots (240-260 km/h; 149-162 mph)
- Field length for take-off and landing: 2,300-2,600 m (7,550-8,530 ft)
- * Range with 40,000 kg (88,185 lb) payload: 1,944 nm (3,600 km; 2,235 miles)
- * Range with max fuel: 2,480 nm (4,600 km; 2,858 miles)

* *Reports suggest that these design ranges are not being achieved. The East German airline Interflug quotes a max range of 1,350 nm (2,500 km; 1,550 miles) in its sales literature*

ILYUSHIN Il-96-300

The longer-range derivative of the Il-86, to which reference was first made in the 1982-83 *Jane's*, is now known to be designated Il-96-300. It bears a superficial resemblance to the Il-86 but is, in fact, a new design. Advanced structural materials and state of the art technology are intended to make practicable a service life of 60,000 hours and 12,000 landings. The power plant will comprise four high bypass ratio turbofan engines, each rated at about 157 kN (35,300 lb st).

The entirely new wings of the Il-96 will have a supercritical section, winglets, an increased span compared with those of the Il-86 and reduced sweepback of 30° at quarter-chord. The control surfaces are enlarged, to improve stability after an engine failure. The fuselage will be basically unchanged in form, with lighter and more comfortable seats for 235 to 300 passengers, eight or nine abreast, and a three-man (two pilots and flight engineer) flight deck. Conventional standby instruments will be retained, but primary flight information will be presented on dual twin-screen colour CRTs, fed by triplex INS, a satellite navigation system and other sensors. Triplex flight control and flight management systems, together with a head-up display, will permit fully automatic en-route control and operations in ICAO Category III minima. Duplex engine and systems monitoring and failure warning systems will feed in-flight information to both the flight engineer's station and monitors on the ground. Another electronic system will provide real-time automatic weight and CG situation data.

The Il-96 is designed to conform with ICAO Chapter 3 Supplement 16 noise requirements. First flight is expected to be made before the end of 1990.

DIMENSIONS, EXTERNAL:
- Wing span: 57·66 m (189 ft 2 in)
- Wing aspect ratio: 9·5
- Length overall: 55·35 m (181 ft 7¼ in)
- Length of fuselage: 51·15 m (167 ft 9¾ in)
- Diameter of fuselage: 6·08 m (19 ft 11½ in)
- Height overall: 17·57 m (57 ft 7¾ in)

AREA:
- Wings, gross: 350·0 m² (3,767·4 sq ft)

WEIGHTS:
- Max payload: 42,000 kg (92,595 lb)
- Max T-O weight: 230,000 kg (507,060 lb)
- Max landing weight: 175,000 kg (385,810 lb)

PERFORMANCE (estimated):
- Normal cruising speed at 9,000-12,000 m (29,525-39,370 ft): 459-486 knots (850-900 km/h; 528-559 mph)
- Landing speed: 135-146 knots (250-270 km/h; 155-168 mph)
- Range:
  - with max payload: 4,050 nm (7,500 km; 4,660 miles)
  - with 30,000 kg (66,140 lb) payload: 4,860 nm (9,000 km; 5,590 miles)
  - with 15,000 kg (33,070 lb) payload: 5,940 nm (11,000 km; 6,835 miles)

ILYUSHIN Il-114

The Il-114 is the smallest of the new generation of transport aircraft that will be developed and produced jointly by various Comecon nations and Yugoslavia for operation at the turn of the century. Intended to replace aircraft in the class of the An-24, it is being designed for short-haul and feeder services from both paved and grass surfaces. Equipment will be to the latest standards for ICAO Category I and II operations. Service life is intended to be 30,000 hours and 30,000 landings.

TYPE: Twin-turboprop short range passenger and freight transport.

WINGS: Cantilever low-wing monoplane. Dihedral from roots. Conventional all-metal structure. Double-slotted flaps, inboard and outboard of engine nacelle, and aileron occupy entire trailing-edge of each wing. Airbrake forward of each flap section. Two tabs in each aileron.

FUSELAGE: Conventional metal semi-monocoque structure of circular section.

TAIL UNIT: Conventional cantilever metal structure, with sweptback vertical surfaces. Two tabs in rudder; one in each elevator.

LANDING GEAR: Retractable tricycle type, with twin wheels on each unit, manufactured by WSK-PZL Krosno. Hydraulic retraction, with emergency extension by gravity. Oleo-pneumatic shock absorber in each unit. Nosewheels steerable ±55°. Brakes on mainwheels. All wheel doors remain closed except during retraction or extension of the landing gear.

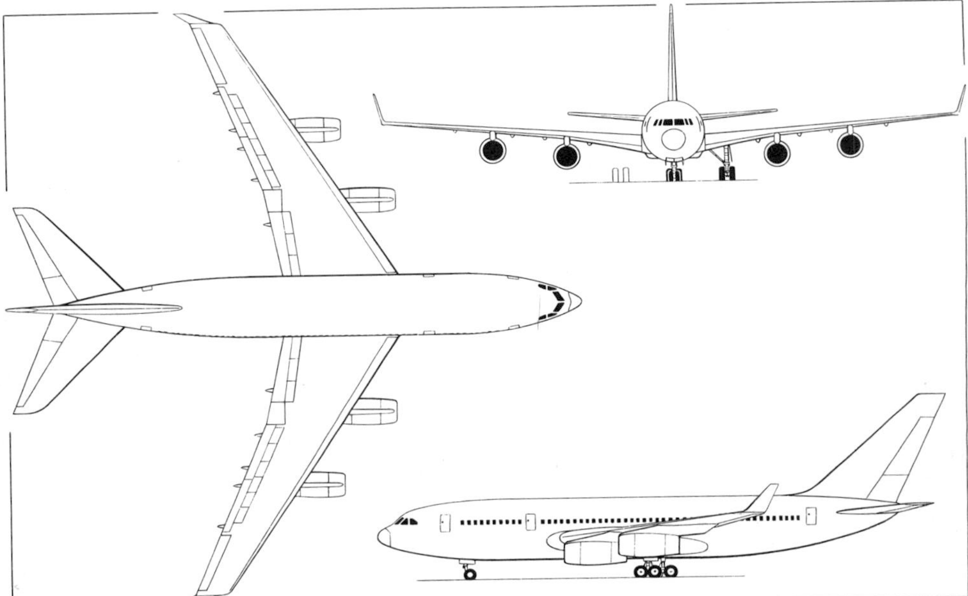

Ilyushin Il-96-300 four-turbofan long range transport *(Pilot Press)*

Artist's impression of Ilyushin Il-114 twin-turboprop airliner *(Jane's/Mike Keep)*

Power Plant: Two 1,864 kW (2,500 shp) turboprop engines, each driving a six- or eight-blade WSK-PZL Warszawa-Okecie propeller with spinner.

Accommodation: Flight crew of two, plus stewardess. Four abreast seats for 60 passengers in main cabin, at 75 cm (29·5 in) seat pitch, with central aisle. Airstair type passenger door at front of cabin on port side. Galley, cloakroom and toilet at rear, with emergency escape slide by door on starboard side. Emergency exit over each wing. Baggage hold door at front of cabin on starboard side. Optional large carry-on baggage shelves in lobby by main door at front of cabin.

Avionics: Digital avionics for automatic or manual control by day or night, including automatic approach and landing in limiting weather conditions (ICAO Category I and II).

Dimensions, external:
- Wing span: 30·00 m (98 ft 5¼ in)
- Length overall: 25·46 m (83 ft 6½ in)
- Diameter of fuselage: 2·80 m (9 ft 2¼ in)
- Height overall: 8·60 m (28 ft 2½ in)
- Propeller diameter: 3·60 m (11 ft 9¾ in)

Weights:
- Weight empty: 13,000 kg (28,660 lb)
- Max payload: 6,000 kg (13,227 lb)
- Max T-O weight: 20,250 kg (44,640 lb)

Performance (estimated):
- Max cruising speed: 270 knots (500 km/h; 310 mph)
- Approach speed: 97-102 knots (180-190 km/h; 112-118 mph)
- Optimum cruising height: 6,000-8,000 m (19,685-26,250 ft)
- Balanced field length: paved 1,400 m (4,600 ft)
- unpaved 1,650 m (5,415 ft)
- Range, with reserves:
  - with 5,400 kg (11,905 lb) payload: 540 nm (1,000 km; 621 miles)
  - with 3,500 kg (7,715 lb) payload: 1,538 nm (2,850 km; 1,770 miles)

KAMOV

Chief of Design Bureau: S. V. Mikheyev

This design bureau continues the work of Nikolai I. Kamov, a leading designer of rotating wing aircraft since the late 1920s, who died on 24 November 1973, aged 71.

KAMOV Ka-25

NATO reporting name: Hormone

The prototype of this military helicopter was first shown in public in the Soviet Aviation Day flypast over Tushino Airport, Moscow, in July 1961. It was allocated the NATO code name 'Harp', but this was changed to 'Hormone' for the production versions, of which about 460 were built in 1966-75. Together with the newer Mil helicopters known to NATO as 'Haze-A', these replaced piston engined Mi-4s in the Soviet Navy's ship and shore based force of around 250 helicopters. About 190 of them remain operational. In addition, five ex-Soviet Navy Ka-25s equip INAS 333 of the Indian Navy, for deployment on three 'Krivak' class destroyers. Nine are operated on coastal anti-submarine duties by the Syrian Arab Air Force and others by Yugoslavia and Viet-Nam (17).

As well as serving as an anti-submarine and missile support aircraft, the Ka-25 fulfils a number of other military roles. Three versions are identified by NATO reporting names:

Hormone-A. Basic ship-based anti-submarine version, operated from cruisers of 'Kresta II' and 'Kara' classes, the nuclear powered guided missile cruiser *Kirov*, carrier/cruisers *Kiev* and *Minsk*, each of which can carry about 19 'Hormone-As' and 'Bs', and helicopter carrier/cruisers *Moskva* and *Leningrad*, each of which accommodates about 18 'Hormone-As'. Some have an underfuselage weapon bay. Search radar in undernose radome, diameter 1·25 m (4 ft 1 in); dipping sonar housed in compartment at rear of cabin. Canister for sonobuoys can be mounted to rear of main landing gear on starboard side. A major shortcoming is said to be lack of night and all-weather sonar dipping capability. Being replaced by Ka-27 ('Helix-A').

Hormone-B. Special electronics variant, able to provide over-the-horizon target acquisition for long-range cruise missiles launched from ships. These are believed to include SS-N-3 (NATO 'Shaddock') missiles launched from 'Kresta I' cruisers, SS-N-12 ('Sandbox') missiles from 'Kiev' class carrier/cruisers, and SS-N-19 missiles from the battle cruisers *Kirov* and *Frunze*. Larger undernose radome with more spherical undersurface. Cylindrical radome under rear of cabin. Data link equipment.

Hormone-C. Utility and search and rescue model, generally similar to 'Hormone-A' but with inessential operational equipment and weapons removed. This version sometimes has a yagi aerial mounted on the nose; it has been photographed in non-operational red and white paint finish.

Type: Twin-turbine anti-submarine, missile support and general purpose helicopter.

Rotor System: Two three-blade coaxial contra-rotating rotors. Automatic blade folding.

Fuselage: Conventional all-metal semi-monocoque structure of pod and boom type.

Tail Unit: Cantilever all-metal structure, with central fin, ventral fin and twin endplate fins and rudders which are toed inward.

Landing Gear: Four-wheel type. Oleo-pneumatic shock absorbers. Nosewheels are smaller than mainwheels and are of castoring type. Each wheel can be enclosed in an inflatable pontoon surmounted by inflation bottles to provide flotation in event of an emergency alighting on water. Rear legs are pivoted to retract upward about their wishbone supports, so that the wheels can be moved to a position where they offer least interference to signals from the nose radar.

Power Plant: Two 671 kW (900 shp) Glushenkov GTD-3F turboshaft engines, mounted side by side above cabin, forward of rotor driveshaft, on early aircraft. Later aircraft have 738 kW (990 shp) GTD-3BM turboshafts. Independent fuel supply to each engine. Provision for carrying external fuel tank on each side of cabin.

Accommodation: Pilot and co-pilot side by side on flight deck, with rearward sliding door on each side. Entry to main cabin is via a rearward sliding door to rear of main landing gear on port side. Cabin accommodates two or three systems operators in ASW role, but is large enough to contain 12 folding seats for passengers.

Avionics and Equipment: Equipment available for all versions includes autopilot, navigational system, radio compass, radio communications installations, lighting system for all-weather operation by day or night, and hoist mounted above cabin door. IFF antennae (NATO 'Odd Rods') above nose and alongside central tail fin. Dipping sonar housed in compartment at rear of main cabin, immediately forward of tailboom, and search radar under nose of anti-submarine version, which can have a canister of sonobuoys mounted externally aft of the starboard main landing gear. Some aircraft have a

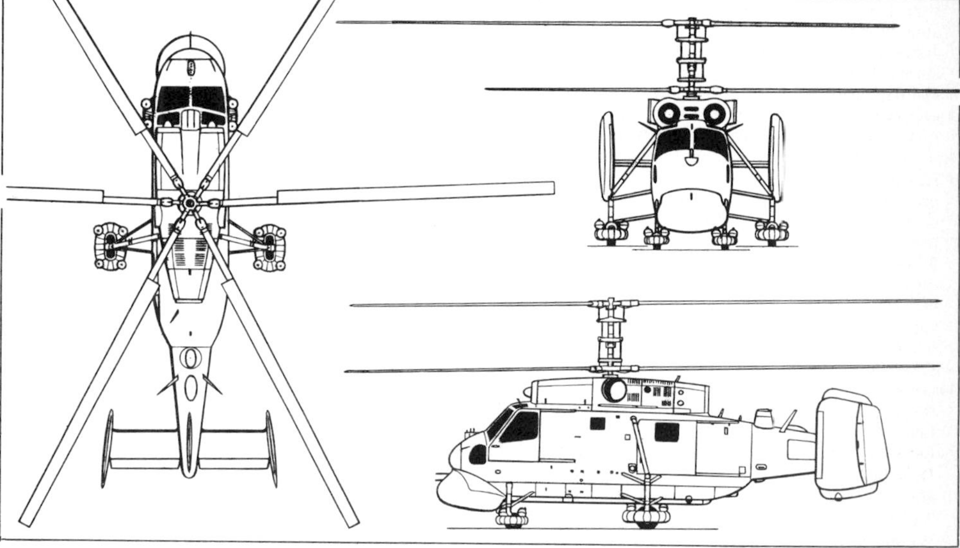
'Hormone-A' anti-submarine version of the Kamov Ka-25 helicopter *(Pilot Press)*

Ka-25 ('Hormone-A') anti-submarine helicopter, equipped with sonobuoy canister and dye markers

blister fairing over equipment mounted at the base of the centre tail fin; others have a cylindrical housing with a transparent top above the tailboom, probably for ESM, and a window in the undersurface of the boom, with a shallow blister fairing to the rear of the cylindrical housing.

ARMAMENT: Doors under the fuselage of some aircraft enclose a weapons bay for two 450 mm (18 in) ASW torpedoes, nuclear depth charges and other stores. Bay was extended downward by a long underbelly container on one aircraft, see 1985-86 *Jane's*, reportedly to house wire guided torpedoes.

DIMENSIONS, EXTERNAL:
- Rotor diameter (each) 15·74 m (51 ft 7¾ in)
- Length of fuselage 9·75 m (32 ft 0 in)
- Height to top of rotor head 5·37 m (17 ft 7½ in)
- Width over tail-fins 3·76 m (12 ft 4 in)
- Wheel track: front 1·41 m (4 ft 7½ in)
  - rear 3·52 m (11 ft 6½ in)
- Cabin door: Height 1·10 m (3 ft 7¼ in)
  - Width 1·20 m (3 ft 11¼ in)

DIMENSIONS, INTERNAL:
- Cabin, excl flight deck:
  - Length 3·95 m (12 ft 11½ in)
  - Max width 1·50 m (4 ft 11 in)
  - Max height 1·25 m (4 ft 1¼ in)

WEIGHTS (approx):
- Weight empty 5,000 kg (11,025 lb)
- Max T-O weight 7,500 kg (16,535 lb)

PERFORMANCE:
- Max level speed 119 knots (220 km/h; 136 mph)
- Normal cruising speed 104 knots (193 km/h; 120 mph)
- Service ceiling 3,500 m (11,500 ft)
- Range with standard fuel, with reserves 217 nm (400 km; 250 miles)
- Range with external tanks, with reserves 351 nm (650 km; 405 miles)

KAMOV Ka-26

NATO reporting name: Hoodlum

First details of this twin-engined light helicopter were announced in January 1964, and the prototype flew for the first time in the following year. Kamov described it as an ideal helicopter for agriculture, possessing all the virtues of the Ka-15 (which was used in about a dozen countries) but able to lift three times as much chemical payload, and the Ka-26 entered large scale service as an agricultural aircraft in the Soviet Union in 1970, being used primarily over orchards and vineyards. It is also used widely on Aeroflot's air ambulance services and is suitable for many other applications, including cargo and passenger transport, forest firefighting, mineral prospecting, pipeline construction, laying transmission lines, and a number of military duties, including search and rescue.

The space aft of the cabin, between the main landing gear units and under the rotor transmission, is able to accommodate a variety of interchangeable payloads. For agricultural work the chemical hopper (capacity 900 kg; 1,985 lb) and dust spreader or spraybars are fitted in this position, on the aircraft's centre of gravity. This equipment is quickly removable and can be replaced by a cargo/passenger pod accommodating four or six persons, with provision for a seventh passenger beside the pilot. Alternatively, the Ka-26 can be operated with either an open platform for hauling freight or a hook for slinging bulky loads at the end of a cable or in a cargo net.

A version for geophysical survey has an electromagnetic pulse generator in the cabin and is encircled by a huge 'hoop' antenna. It carries on the port side of the fuselage a mounting for the receiver 'bird' which is towed at the end of a cable, beneath the helicopter, when in use. The receiver is lowered by an electric winch and the cable is cut by automatic shears if its traction should exceed the authorised limit.

An aerial survey model is available with an AFA-31-MA camera mounted in the cabin. This aircraft can photograph 5 km² (2 sq miles) per hour at a scale of 1 : 10,000.

As an air ambulance, the Ka-26 can carry two stretcher patients, two seated casualties and a medical attendant. A winch, with a capacity of up to 150 kg (330 lb), enables it to be used for search and rescue duties. Ka-26s used in this role in Soviet coastal areas are each fitted with three large inflatable pontoons, to permit operation from water. Items of equipment carried inside the cabin can include lifejackets and MLAS-1 inflatable dinghies for individual rescues, LAC-5 dinghies each able to carry five persons, PSN-1 rafts and emergency radio beacons. During tests, the hoist has been used to tow boats in sea state 5 conditions.

When operating as an agricultural sprayer, the Ka-26 originally discharged its chemical payload at 1·5-12 litres/s (0·33-2·65 Imp gallons/s). The rate of discharge in a dusting role was 1·5-12 kg/s (3·3-26·5 lb/s). Up to 120 hectares (296 acres) could be sprayed during each flying hour at the rate of 50 kg/ha (44·5 lb/acre). As a duster, 140 ha (346 acres) could be treated at the same discharge rate. 50 ha (123 acres) could be topdressed with chemical fertilisers each flying hour, at a rate of 100 kg/ha (89 lb/acre). These work rates were improved substantially by the introduction of an atomiser for liquid chemicals in 1978, followed by a centrifugal spreader for granular chemicals and dust in 1979.

Kamov Ka-26 fitted with open platform for freight transport *(Peter J. Bish)*

To protect the pilot against toxic chemicals in the agricultural role, the cabin is lightly pressurised by a blower and air filter system which ensures that the cabin air is always clean. The flying and navigation equipment is adequate for all-weather operation, by day and night. VHF and HF radio are fitted, together with a radio compass and radio altimeter.

Because of its small size and manoeuvrability, the Ka-26 can be operated from platforms on small ships such as whalers and icebreakers, and a Soviet fishing boat operating in the North Atlantic in early 1970 carried a Ka-26 for fish spotting duties. This aircraft was equipped with inflated pontoons to permit alighting on the water.

In mid-1969, a Ka-26 was tested in Siberia and the north-west USSR in a forest protection version able to deliver six firemen and their equipment speedily to the site of a forest fire. In the Spring of 1972, Ka-26s joined Mi-1, Mi-2 and Mi-4 helicopters in operations to clear ice from Soviet rivers, by landing demolition teams on thick ice floes and destroying thinner ice fields from the air.

More than 600 Ka-26s were produced by 1977. They are in civilian service in 15 countries, including Bulgaria, East Germany, West Germany, Hungary, Japan, Romania and Sweden, as well as in the USSR. Military operators include the air forces of Bulgaria and Hungary. Some are now being converted to turbine powered Ka-126 standard by ICA Brasov (see Romanian section).

TYPE: Twin-engined general purpose light helicopter.

ROTOR SYSTEM: Contra-rotating coaxial three-blade rotor system, with hydraulic dampers fitted to each rotor head and rotor shafts inclined forward at 6° to the vertical. Blades, made of glass-textolyte (plastics) materials, weigh 25 kg (55 lb) each, are interchangeable, and are equipped with an anti-icing system.

FUSELAGE: Small extensively glazed crew cabin forward of rotor mast, and two tapered cylindrical plastics tailbooms.

TAIL UNIT: Tailplane, mounted at extremity of tailbooms; twin endplate fins and rudders, toed inward at 15°.

LANDING GEAR: Non-retractable four-wheel landing gear. Main units, at rear, carried by stub wings. All four units embody oleo-pneumatic shock absorbers. Forward wheels of castoring type, not fitted with brakes. Rear wheels fitted with pneumatically operated brakes. Tyres size 595 × 185 on mainwheels, 300 × 125 on forward wheels. Provision for large inflatable pontoons, across front of aircraft forward of nosewheels and under each mainwheel unit.

POWER PLANT: Two 242·5 kW (325 hp) Vedeneyev M-14V-26 aircooled radial piston engines, mounted in pods on short stub wings at top of fuselage. Each engine is cooled by a fan in the front of its pod, which absorbs about 18·6 kW (25 hp) from engine output. Dust filters in air delivery ducts, to protect engines, each of which is connected to the rotor transmission by a shaft and two flexible couplings. Both rotors can be driven by either engine if the other fails; disengagement of the failed engine is automatic.

ACCOMMODATION: Fully enclosed cabin, with door on each side, fitted out normally for operation by single pilot; second seat and dual controls optional. Cabin warmed and demisted by air from combustion heater, which also heats passenger compartment when fitted. Air filter on nose of agricultural version. Details of alternative payload arrangements given in introductory copy.

SYSTEMS: Powered controls, actuated by single hydraulic system, with manual override in case of system failure. Anti-icing system for rotor blades and windscreen is activated automatically by radioisotope ice warning device and utilises an alcohol glycerine mixture.

DIMENSIONS, EXTERNAL:
- Rotor diameter (each) 13·00 m (42 ft 8 in)
- Vertical separation between rotors 1·17 m (3 ft 10 in)
- Length of fuselage 7·75 m (25 ft 5 in)
- Height overall 4·05 m (13 ft 3½ in)
- Width over engine pods 3·64 m (11 ft 11½ in)
- Width over agricultural spraybars 11·20 m (36 ft 9 in)
- Tailplane span 4·60 m (15 ft 1 in)
- Wheel track: mainwheels 2·42 m (7 ft 11½ in)
  - nosewheels 0·90 m (2 ft 11½ in)
- Wheelbase 3·48 m (11 ft 5 in)
- Passenger pod door: Height 1·40 m (4 ft 7 in)
  - Width 1·25 m (4 ft 1¼ in)

Kamov Ka-26 fitted with cabin pod for four passengers *(Peter J. Bish)*

DIMENSIONS, INTERNAL:
Passenger pod:
Length, floor level 1·83 m (6 ft 0 in)
Width, floor level 1·25 m (4 ft 1¼ in)
Headroom 1·40 m (4 ft 7 in)

WEIGHTS:
Operating weight, empty:
stripped 1,950 kg (4,300 lb)
cargo/platform 2,085 kg (4,597 lb)
cargo/hook 2,050 kg (4,519 lb)
passenger 2,100 kg (4,630 lb)
agricultural 2,216 kg (4,885 lb)
Fuel weight: transport 360 kg (794 lb)
other versions 100 kg (220 lb)
Payload: transport 900 kg (1,985 lb)
agricultural duster 1,065 kg (2,348 lb)
agricultural sprayer 900 kg (1,985 lb)
with cargo platform 1,065 kg (2,348 lb)
flying crane 1,100 kg (2,425 lb)
Normal T-O weight: transport 3,076 kg (6,780 lb)
agricultural 2,980 kg (6,570 lb)
Max T-O weight: all versions 3,250 kg (7,165 lb)

PERFORMANCE (at max T-O weight):
Max level speed 91 knots (170 km/h; 105 mph)
Max cruising speed 81 knots (150 km/h; 93 mph)
Econ cruising speed
49-59 knots (90-110 km/h; 56-68 mph)
Agricultural operating speed range
16-62 knots (30-115 km/h; 19-71 mph)
Service ceiling 3,000 m (9,840 ft)
Service ceiling, one engine out 500 m (1,640 ft)
Hovering ceiling at AUW of 3,000 kg (6,615 lb):
IGE 1,300 m (4,265 ft)
OGE 800 m (2,625 ft)
Range with 7 passengers, 30 min fuel reserves
215 nm (400 km; 248 miles)
Max range with auxiliary tanks
647 nm (1,200 km; 745 miles)
Endurance at econ cruising speed 3 h 42 min

Kamov Ka-32S under automatic control, with no crew on flight deck

KAMOV Ka-27

NATO reporting name: Helix

Ka-27 is the Soviet designation for military versions of the helicopter known as the Ka-32 in its civil forms. The basic airframe, power plant, systems and equipment of the Ka-27 and Ka-32 are identical. Furnishings, avionics and mission equipment vary accordingly to role.

First reference to a military version of this helicopter appeared in a 1981 document on *Soviet Military Power*, published by the US Department of Defense, which referred to "Hormone variant" helicopters that could be carried in a telescoping hangar on the new 'Sovremennyy' class of Soviet guided missile destroyers, for secondary ASW missions. Photographs of such helicopters were released to the technical press after two of them had been seen on the stern platform of the *Udaloy*, first of a new class of Soviet ASW guided missile destroyers, during the Zapad-81 (West-81) series of exercises in the Baltic in September 1981. The fact that one was finished in Aeroflot markings suggested that development of the military version might then have been at an early stage. The US Department of Defense first referred to the ASW helicopter as Ka-27 in 1982. At least 16 were observed on board the 'Kiev' class carrier/cruiser *Novorossiysk* during its maiden deployment in 1983.

Three versions of the Ka-27 have been identified by unclassified NATO reporting names:

Helix-A. Basic ASW version, as shown in accompanying illustrations. Probable crew of three. Operational since 1982. About 50 in Soviet Naval Aviation service in 1986. Eight ordered for Indian Navy.

Helix-B. Infantry assault transport. Different undernose equipment. No photographs released by Summer 1986.

Helix-C. Search and rescue and plane guard helicopter, first seen on the *Novorossiysk*. Features include an external fuel tank on each side of the cabin, as on the civil Ka-32, and a winch beside the port cabin door.

'Helix-A' follows closely the configuration of 'Hormone' but has a longer and more capacious fuselage pod, no central tail fin, and different undernose radome. The overall dimensions of the two aircraft are generally similar, enabling 'Helix' to be stowed on board ship in hangars and via deck lifts built for its predecessor.

The general description of the Ka-32 (which see) applies also to the Ka-27. The IFF (NATO 'Odd Rods'), radar warning antennae and directional ESM radomes fitted to prototype SSSR-31000 are standard on the Ka-27. The rectangular containers on each side of the bottom centre fuselage may be used to house sonobuoys. Torpedoes and other stores are carried in the ventral weapons bay.

'Helix-A' being wheeled into port hangar of guided missile destroyer *Udaloy*, with rotor blades folded

Kamov Ka-27 anti-submarine helicopter (NATO 'Helix-A') *(US Department of Defense)*

KAMOV Ka-32

NATO reporting name: Helix

It was announced in early 1981 that a new civilian helicopter, designed under the leadership of Mr S. V. Mikheyev and known as the Ka-32, was to be put on display in the permanent Exhibition of Achievements of the National Economy (VDNKL) in Moscow. Primary applications for the aircraft were said to be surveillance, search and rescue, by day and night in all weathers, from ships that would include the atomic powered icebreakers *Lenin, Sibir, Arktika* and *Rossiya*.

The Ka-32 was not identified officially until the first prototype (SSSR-04173) was exhibited in public with other Soviet and Polish aircraft at Minsk Airport, in late 1981, during the fourth CMEA scientific/technical conference on the use of aircraft in the national economy. As expected, it proved to be a demilitarised counterpart to the Ka-27 (NATO 'Helix-A') naval helicopter already observed on the Soviet ASW guided missile destroyer *Udaloy*. Major applications of the civil Ka-32 shown at Minsk were said to be for construction/assembly and flying crane duties, and it carried a truck as a slung load during the flying display. It was claimed to be able to lift up to 5,000 kg (11,023 lb) as an external slung load, and to have a range of 100 nm (185 km; 115 miles) with such a load.

A detailed appraisal of the Ka-32 became possible in June 1985, when a prototype of the utility version (SSSR-31000), converted from an ASW Ka-27, was exhibited at the Paris Air Show. Its designer explained that there are two civil versions:

Ka-32. As displayed in Paris. Basic transport and flying crane, with limited avionics. Duties include transport of internal and external freight, and passengers, to offshore drilling rigs.

Ka-32S (maritime). Equipped with more comprehensive avionics, including undernose radar, for operation to full IMC standards from icebreakers in adverse weather conditions. Duties include ice patrol, unloading and loading ships, and maritime search and rescue.

According to Mr Mikheyev, the Ka-32 was conceived as a completely autonomous 'compact truck', able to stow in much the same space as the Ka-25 with its rotors folded, despite its much greater power and capability, and able to operate independently of ground support equipment. Titanium and composite materials are used extensively throughout the airframe, with particular emphasis on resistance to corrosion. Special attention was also paid to ease of handling, with a single pilot. Yaw control is by differential collective pitch applied through the rudder pedals. A 'mix' in the collective control system maintains constant total rotor thrust during turns, to reduce the pilot's workload when landing on a pitching deck, and to simplify transition into hover and landing. The twin rudders are intended mainly to improve control in autorotation, but are effective in co-ordinating turns in normal cruising flight. Being a 'workhorse' the helicopter is not designed for negative *g* loading.

Flight can be maintained on one engine at maximum take-off weight. The effectiveness of the automatic control system is illustrated by an accompanying photograph of a Ka-32S in flight. Both crew doors are open, to show that there is nobody on the flight deck; the crew can be seen in the rear doorway of the main cabin.

Flying alternately as pilot and co-pilot, two women instructors from the Yegoryevsk flying club, near Moscow, set a number of officially confirmed feminine records in the Ka-32 that was exhibited at the Paris Air Show in 1985. Nadezhda Yeremina piloted the helicopter to set a time to height record by climbing to 3,000 m in 2 min 11·1 s on 12 May 1983. On the previous day Tatyana Zuyeva, flying as pilot, had climbed to 6,000 m in 4 min 46·5 s and set a record of 6,552 m for sustained height in level flight. The time to height records had been held previously by a Mil A-10 (Mi-24 'Hind'). Take-off weight of the Ka-32 was 7,251 kg (15,986 lb) on 11 May and 7,156 kg (15,776 lb) on 12 May. On 29 January 1985 Miss Zuyeva was pilot on a flight which set a women's height record of 8,250 m (27,067 ft) in a Ka-32, and raised the sustained height record to 8,215 m (26,952 ft). Miss Yeremina piloted the Ka-32 to 7,305 m (23,966 ft) with a 1,000 kg payload, and to 6,400 m (20,997 ft) with 2,000 kg on the same day.

The description which follows applies specifically to the Ka-32 displayed at the 1985 Paris Air Show, but is generally applicable also to the Ka-32S and the military Ka-27:

TYPE: Twin-turbine utility helicopter.

ROTOR SYSTEM: Two fully articulated three-blade coaxial contra-rotating rotors. Blades of all-composites construction, with carbonfibre and glassfibre main spars, pockets (13 per blade) of a material similar to Kevlar, and a filler similar to Nomex. As in all Soviet helicopters, blades have a non-symmetrical aerofoil section. Each blade is fitted with a ground adjustable tab. The three lower blades each carry an adjustable vibration damper, comprising two dependent weights, mounted on the root section, and there are further vibration dampers in the fuselage. Tip light on each blade of upper rotor. Blades fold manually outboard of all control mechanisms, to a folded width within the track of the main landing gear. Electrothermal de-icing of the entire profiled portion of each blade, operating at all times when engines are running. Heat generated by rotor head prevents icing of droop stops. Main rotor hub is 50 per cent titanium/50 per cent steel. Rotor brake standard.

FUSELAGE: Conventional all-metal semi-monocoque structure of pod and boom type, making extensive use of titanium for primary components. Tailcone of composites material. Lower fuselage sealed for flotation.

TAIL UNIT: Braced structure, comprising fixed incidence tailplane, elevators, twin endplate fins and rudders, with aluminium alloy structure and composite skins. Single bracing strut under each side of tailplane. Fins toe inward approx 25°. Fixed leading-edge slat on each fin prevents airflow over fin stalling in crosswinds or at high yaw angles.

LANDING GEAR: Four-wheel type. Oleo-pneumatic shock absorbers. Nosewheels are smaller than mainwheels and of castoring type. Rear legs are pivoted on some versions, to retract upward about their wishbone supports so that the wheels can be moved to a position where they offer least interference to emissions from the undernose radar. Mainwheel tyres size 600 × 180. Nosewheel tyres size 400 × 150.

POWER PLANT: Two 1,660 kW (2,225 shp) Isotov TV3-117V turboshaft engines, with automatic synchronisation system, mounted side by side above cabin, forward of rotor driveshaft. Main gearbox brake standard. Oil cooler fan aft of gearbox. Electrothermal intake anti-icing. Cowlings hinge downward for use as maintenance platforms. All standard fuel in tanks under cabin floor and inside container on each side of centre fuselage. Provision for auxiliary tanks in cabin. Refuelling point behind small forward hinged door on port side, where bottom of tailboom meets rear of cabin. APU in rear of engine bay fairing on starboard side, for engine starting and to power all essential hydraulic and electrical services on the ground, eliminating need for GPU.

ACCOMMODATION: Pilot and navigator side by side on large air-conditioned flight deck, in fully adjustable seats. Rearward sliding jettisonable door with blister window on each side. Seat behind navigator, on starboard side, for observer, loadmaster or rescue hoist operator. Electric windscreen anti-icing. Direct access to cabin from flight deck. Heated and ventilated main cabin can accommodate freight or 16 passengers, on three folding seats at rear, six along port sidewall and seven along starboard sidewall. Lifejackets under seats. Fittings to carry stretchers. No provisions for toilet or galley. Pyramid structure can be fitted on floor beneath rotor driveshaft to prevent swinging of external cargo sling loads. Rearward sliding door aft of main landing gear on port side, with steps below. Emergency exit door opposite. Door to avionics compartment on port side of tailboom.

SYSTEMS: Dual hydraulically powered flight control systems without manual reversion. Spring stick trim.

AVIONICS AND EQUIPMENT: Include electro-mechanical flight director controlled from autopilot panel, Doppler hover indicator, two HSI and air data computer. Autopilot is capable of providing automatic approach and hover on predetermined course, using Doppler. Radar altimeter. Doppler box under tailboom. Doors at rear of fuel tank bay provide access to small compartment for auxiliary fuel, or liferafts which eject during descent in emergency, by command from flight deck. Container on each side of fuselage, under external fuel containers, for emergency flotation bags (not fitted to prototype shown in Paris). Rescue hoist, capacity 300 kg (661 lb), can be installed between top of door opening and landing gear. Optional external load sling, with automatic release and integral load weighing and stabilisation systems. Equipment on prototype (not necessarily standard on production Ka-32s) included IFF, two radar warning antennae above tailplane, and two ESM radomes above rear fuselage and tail.

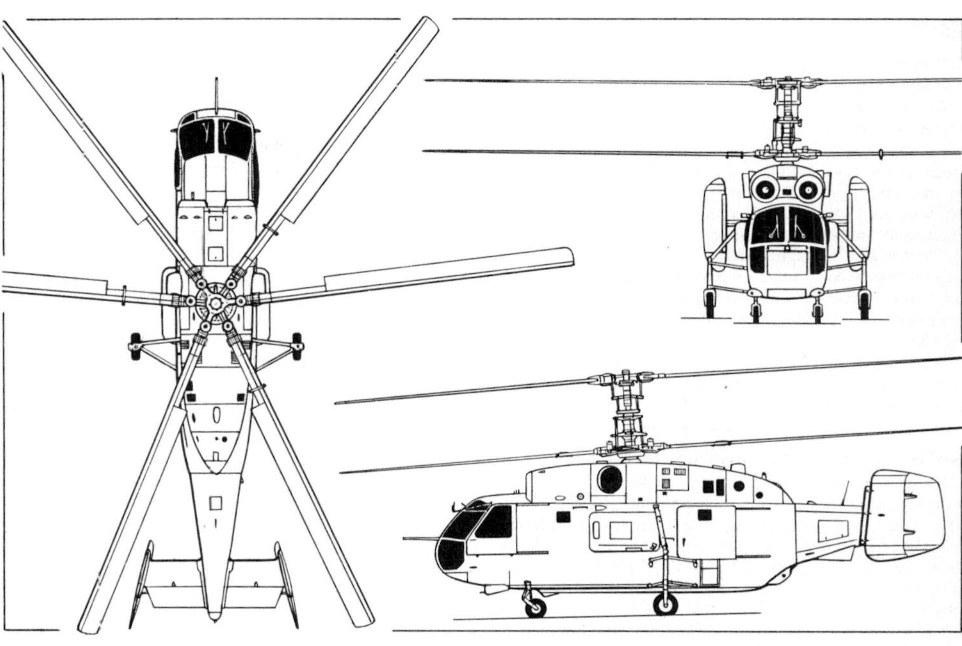

Kamov Ka-32 utility helicopter (two Isotov TV3-117V turboshaft engines) *(Pilot Press)*

DIMENSIONS, EXTERNAL:
- Rotor diameter (each): 15·90 m (52 ft 2 in)
- Length overall: excl rotors: 11·30 m (37 ft 1 in)
  - rotors folded: 12·25 m (40 ft 2¼ in)
- Width, rotors folded: 4·00 m (13 ft 1½ in)
- Height to top of rotor head: 5·40 m (17 ft 8½ in)
- Wheel track: mainwheels: 3·50 m (11 ft 6 in)
  - nosewheels: 1·40 m (4 ft 7 in)
- Wheelbase: 3·02 m (9 ft 11 in)
- Cabin door: Height: approx 1·20 m (3 ft 11¼ in)
  - Width: approx 1·20 m (3 ft 11¼ in)

DIMENSIONS, INTERNAL:
- Cabin: Length: 4·52 m (14 ft 10 in)
  - Max width: 1·30 m (4 ft 3 in)
  - Max height: 1·32 m (4 ft 4 in)

WEIGHTS:
- Max payload: internal: 4,000 kg (8,818 lb)
  - external: 5,000 kg (11,023 lb)
- Normal T-O weight: 11,000 kg (24,250 lb)
- Max flight weight with slung load: 12,600 kg (27,775 lb)

PERFORMANCE (at AUW of 11,000 kg; 24,250 lb):
- Max level speed: 135 knots (250 km/h; 155 mph)
- Max cruising speed: 124 knots (230 km/h; 143 mph)
- Service ceiling at normal T-O weight: 6,000 m (19,685 ft)
- Hovering ceiling OGE: 3,500 m (11,480 ft)
- Range with max fuel: 432 nm (800 km; 497 miles)
- Endurance with max fuel: 4 h 30 min

KAMOV Ka-126

Responsibility for converting piston engined Ka-26 helicopters to turbine powered Ka-126 standard has been allocated to ICA Brasov (see Romanian section).

KAMOV Ka-

NATO reporting name: Hokum

It became known in Summer 1984 that the Kamov bureau had begun flight testing a new combat helicopter which has the NATO reporting name 'Hokum'. No details are available except that it has co-axial contra-rotating main rotors, a take-off weight in the 5,450 kg (12,000 lb) class, and two-man crew in tandem, with elevated rear seat. Duties include attack and air-to-air anti-helicopter intercept. Survivability is enhanced by use of infra-red suppressors, infra-red decoy dispensers and armour.

A crude side elevation drawing of what purports to be 'Hokum' is included in the 1986 edition of the US Department of Defense's *Soviet Military Power* document. It shows an aircraft with a conventional fuselage, three tail fins and retractable tricycle landing gear. Wide vertical separation of the contra-rotating rotors implies a conventional drive system, as opposed to anything as advanced as Sikorsky's ABC system. However, the DoD comments that "Hokum will give the Soviets a significant rotary-wing air superiority capability. The system has no current Western counterpart".

DIMENSIONS, EXTERNAL:
- Rotor diameter (each): 14·0 m (45 ft 10 in)
- Length overall, excl nose probe and gun: 13·5 m (44 ft 3½ in)
- Height overall: 5·4 m (17 ft 8 in)

PERFORMANCE (estimated):
- Max level speed: 189 knots (350 km/h; 217 mph)
- Combat radius: 135 nm (250 km; 155 miles)

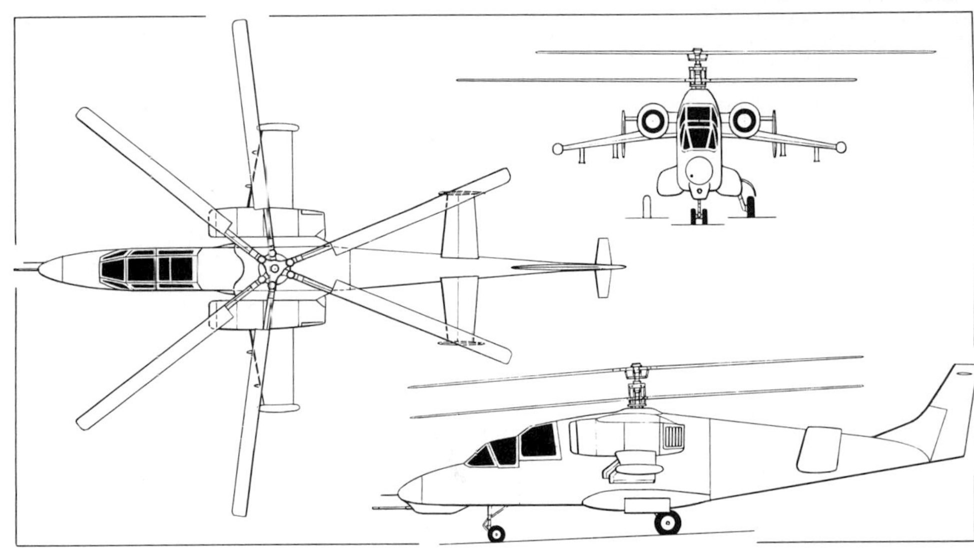

Provisional drawing of Kamov combat helicopter known to NATO as 'Hokum' *(Pilot Press)*

MiG

General Designer in Charge of Bureau:
Rostislav A. Belyakov

Colonel-General Artem I. Mikoyan, who died on 9 December 1970 at the age of 65, was head of the design bureau responsible for the MiG series of fighter aircraft from 1940. With Mikhail I. Gurevich (1893-1976), a mathematician, he collaborated in the design of the first really modern Soviet jet fighter, the MiG-15, which began to enter squadron service in numbers in 1949.

The MiG-17, a progressive development of the MiG-15, was first observed in Soviet squadrons in 1953 or 1954, and was followed into service by the supersonic MiG-19, which appeared in 1955 and has been manufactured also in large numbers in China (which see).

All available details of aircraft designed by the Mikoyan bureau which are currently in production or known to be under development follow:

MiG-21bis ('Fishbed-N') armed with two radar homing 'Atolls' outboard and two 'Aphids' inboard

MIKOYAN MiG-21

NATO reporting names: Fishbed and Mongol

MiG-21s continue to be flown by at least 37 air forces worldwide, but replacement with later fighters has left about 780 in first-line units of the Soviet tactical air forces, including 60 of the reconnaissance models known to NATO as 'Fishbed-H'. Early MiG-21F/PF/PFM variants (NATO 'Fishbed-C/D/F') are flown by various Warsaw Pact air forces; details of their individual features can be found in the 1985-86 and earlier editions of *Jane's*. The major versions currently deployed with Soviet air forces of the military districts (MDs) and groups of forces, and variants of these basic versions, are as follows:

MiG-21PFMA (Fishbed-J). Multi-role version with Tumansky R-11-300 turbojet, rated at 38·25 kN (8,598 lb st) dry and 60·8 kN (13,668 lb) with afterburning. Deeper dorsal spine fairing than on earlier versions, containing fuel tankage above fuselage, giving straight line from top of canopy to fin. Improved radar (NATO 'Jay Bird'). Four underwing pylons, instead of former two, for a variety of ground attack weapons and stores, as alternative or supplementary to two or four air-to-air missiles. Able to carry two underwing tanks in addition to standard underbelly tank, offsetting reduced internal fuel capacity. Small boat shape fairing with angle of attack indicator added on port side of nose.

MiG-21R. Generally similar to MiG-21PFMA, but belly gun replaced by a pack of three reconnaissance cameras mounted on a side-hinged (to starboard) door which protrudes from underfuselage, immediately aft of nosewheel leg. Operated by Egyptian Air Force.

MiG-21R (Fishbed-H). Tactical reconnaissance version, basically similar to MiG-21PFMA. Equipment includes an external pod for forward facing or oblique cameras, or elint sensors, on fuselage centreline pylon. Suppressed ECM antenna at mid-point on dorsal spine and optional radar warning receivers in wingtip fairings.

MiG-21MF (Fishbed-J). Generally similar to MiG-21PFMA but re-engined with a Tumansky R-13-300 turbojet, lighter in weight and with higher performance ratings. Debris deflector beneath each suction relief door forward of wingroot. Entered service with Soviet Air Force in 1969.

MiG-21M. Export variant of MiG-21MF. Generally similar to MiG-21PFMA, but with R-11F2S-300 engine. Superseded MiG-21FL on Hindustan Aeronautics production line in India, with IAF designation Type 96. First Indian built MiG-21M handed over officially to IAF on 14 February 1973; HAL production ended 1981.

MiG-21RF (Fishbed-H). Tactical reconnaissance version of MiG-21MF. Equipment as for MiG-21R. Total of 60 'Fishbed-Hs' of both models estimated in service with Soviet tactical air forces in 1986.

MiG-21SMB (Fishbed-K). Similar to MiG-21MF, except for having deep dorsal spine extended rearward as far as brake parachute housing, to provide maximum possible fuel tankage and optimum aerodynamic form. Deliveries to Warsaw Pact air forces reported to have begun in 1971. Like the MiG-21PFMA and MiG-21MF, this version can carry K-13A 'Atoll' infra-red missiles and/or radar homing 'Advanced Atolls'.

MiG-21bis (Fishbed-L). Third generation multi-role air combat/ground attack version, with Tumansky R-25 turbojet engine, rated at 73·6 kN (16,535 lb st) with afterburning, updated avionics and generally improved construction standards. Wider and deeper dorsal fairing than MiG-21MF. Max fuel capacity of seven internal self-sealing tanks 2,900 litres (638 Imp gallons; 766 US gallons).

MiG-21bis (Fishbed-N). Advanced version of 'Fishbed-L' with further improved avionics, indicated by 'Swift Rod' ILS antennae under nose and on fin tip. Standard equipment in Soviet Air Force. Empty weight reported to be 6,000 kg (13,225 lb), 'clean' T-O weight 8,500 kg (18,740 lb). Rate of climb at AUW of 6,800 kg (15,000 lb), with 50% fuel and two 'Atoll' missiles, is 17,700 m (58,000 ft)/min. Now carries two radar homing 'Atolls' outboard, two 'Aphids' inboard. Produced also by HAL from 1980, expected to phase out in 1987.

MiG-21U (Mongol). Two-seat training versions. Initial version, 'Mongol-A', is generally similar to the MiG-21F but has two cockpits in tandem with sideways hinged (to starboard) double canopy, larger mainwheels and tyres of MiG-21PF, one-piece forward airbrake, and pitot boom repositioned above intake. Cannon armament is deleted. Later models, 'Mongol-B', have the broader-chord vertical tail surfaces and under-rudder brake parachute housing of the later operational variants, with a deeper dorsal spine and no dorsal fin fillet.

MiG-21US (Mongol-B). Similar to later MiG-21U but with provision for SPS flap-blowing, and retractable periscope for instructor in rear seat. Max internal fuel capacity 2,400 litres (528 Imp gallons).

MiG-21UM (Mongol-B). Two-seat trainer counterpart of MiG-21MF with R-13 turbojet and four underwing stores pylons.

In addition to these Soviet developed versions, the Chinese aircraft industry (which see) is producing fighters based on the MiG-21, under the designation **Xian J-7/F-7**.

The following details refer to the MiG-21MF ('Fishbed-J'):

Type: Single-seat multi-role fighter.

Wings: Cantilever mid-wing monoplane of clipped delta planform, with 2° anhedral from roots. TsAGI section; thickness/chord ratio 5% at root, 4·2% at tip. No leading-edge camber. Sweepback on leading-edges 57°. Small pointed fairing on each side of fuselage forward of wing root leading-edge. Small boundary layer fence above each wing near tip. All-metal structure, with two primary spars and one auxiliary spar. Inset ailerons, hydraulically boosted. Large 'blown' plain trailing-edge flaps, actuated hydraulically.

Fuselage: Circular section all-metal semi-monocoque structure. Ram air intake in nose, with three-position movable centrebody. Forward hinged door in top of nose gives access to avionics. Large dorsal spine fairing along top of fuselage from canopy to fin, housing control pushrods, avionics, single-point refuelling cap and fuel tank. Forward hinged door type airbrake on each side of underfuselage below wing leading-edge. A further forward hinged airbrake under fuselage forward of ventral fin. All airbrakes actuated hydraulically. Blister fairings above and below wing on each side to accommodate mainwheels when retracted.

Tail Unit: Cantilever all-metal structure, with all surfaces sharply swept. Conventional fin and hydraulically boosted rudder. Hydraulically boosted one-piece all-moving horizontal surface, mass balanced at tips, with two gearing ratios for use at varying combinations of altitude and airspeed. Tailplane trim switch on control column. No trim tabs. Single large ventral fin.

Landing Gear: Hydraulically retractable tricycle type, with single wheel on each unit; all units housed in fuselage when retracted. Forward retracting non-steerable nosewheel unit, tyre size 500 × 180; inward retracting mainwheels which turn to stow vertically inside fuselage. Size 800 × 200 tyres on mainwheels, inflated to approximately 7·93 bars (115 lb/sq in), ruling out normal operation from grass runways. Pneumatic disc brakes on all three wheels, supplied from compressed air bottles. Steering by differential mainwheel braking. Wheel doors remain open when legs are extended. Brake parachute housed inside acorn fairing at base of rudder.

Power Plant: One Tumansky R-13-300 turbojet engine, rated at 40 kN (9,000 lb st) dry and 64·73 kN (14,550 lb st) with afterburning. Fuel tanks in fuselage, and two integral tanks in each wing, with total capacity of 2,600 litres (572 Imp gallons; 687 US gallons), of which approx 1,800 litres (396 Imp gallons; 475 US gallons) are usable within CG limits at low speed. Provision for carrying one finned external fuel tank, capacity 490 litres (108 Imp gallons; 130 US gallons) or 800 litres (176 Imp gallons; 211 US gallons), on underfuselage pylon and two 490 litre drop tanks on outboard underwing pylons. Two jettisonable solid propellant JATO rockets can be fitted under rear fuselage, aft of wheel doors.

Accommodation: Pilot only, on zero/zero ejection seat with spring loaded arm at top which ensures that seat cannot be operated unless hood is closed. Canopy is sideways hinged, to starboard, and is surmounted by a small rearview mirror. Flat bulletproof windscreen. Cabin air-conditioned. Armour plating forward and aft of cockpit.

Systems: Duplicated hydraulic system, supplied by engine driven pump, with backup by battery powered electric pump, and emergency electric tailplane trim and manual operation of flying controls. Autostabilisation in pitch and roll only.

Avionics and Equipment: Search and track radar (NATO 'Jay Bird') in intake centrebody, with search range of 10·8 nm (20 km; 12·5 miles). Other standard avionics include VOR, ARK automatic radio-compass, IFF and Sirena 3 radar warning system with an indicator marked in 45° sectors in front of and behind the aircraft. Gyro gunsight maintains precision up to 2·75*g*. Automatic ranging can be fed into gunsight. Full blind-flying instrumentation, with attitude and heading indicators driven by remote central gyro platform.

Armament: One twin-barrel 23 mm GSh-23 gun, with 200

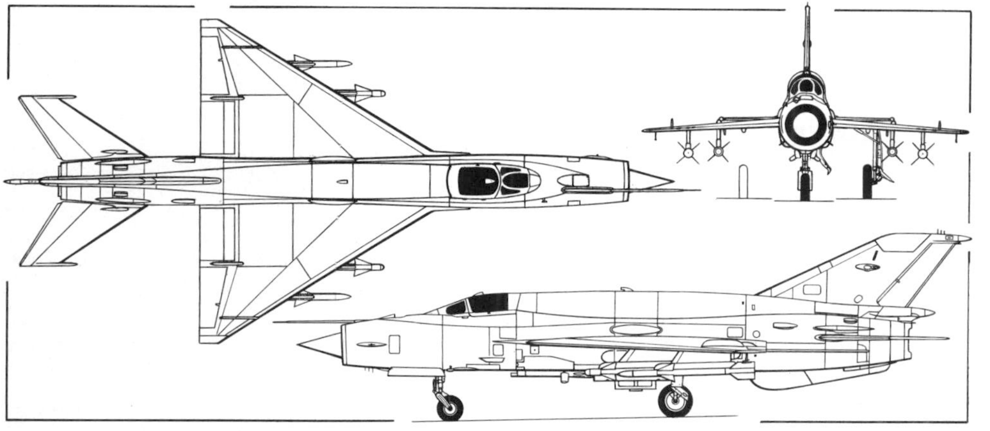

Mikoyan MiG-21SMB ('Fishbed-K') single-seat multi-role fighter *(Pilot Press)*

rounds, in belly pack. Four underwing pylons for weapons or drop tanks. Typical loads for interceptor role include two K-13A 'Atoll' air-to-air missiles on inner pylons and two radar homing 'Advanced Atolls' or two UV-16-57 rocket packs (each sixteen 57 mm rockets) on outer pylons; four K-13As/'Advanced Atolls'; or two drop tanks and two K-13As or 'Advanced Atolls'. Typical loads for ground attack role are four UV-16-57 rocket packs; two 500 kg and two 250 kg bombs; or four S-24 240 mm air-to-surface rockets.

DIMENSIONS, EXTERNAL (MiG-21MF):
Wing span 7·15 m (23 ft 5½ in)
Length, incl pitot boom 15·76 m (51 ft 8½ in)
Fuselage length, intake lip to jetpipe nozzle 12·30 m (40 ft 4¼ in)
Height overall 4·00 m (14 ft 9 in)
Tailplane span 3·70 m (12 ft 8 in)
Wheel track 2·69 m (8 ft 10 in)
Wheelbase 4·81 m (15 ft 9½ in)

AREA:
Wings, gross 23 m² (247 sq ft)

WEIGHTS (MiG-21MF):
T-O weight:
with four K-13A missiles 8,200 kg (18,078 lb)
with two K-13A missiles and two 490 litre (108 Imp gallon) drop tanks 8,950 kg (19,730 lb)
with two K-13As and three drop tanks 9,400 kg (20,725 lb)

PERFORMANCE (MiG-21MF):
Max level speed above 11,000 m (36,000 ft) Mach 2·1 (1,203 knots; 2,230 km/h; 1,385 mph)
Max level speed at low altitude Mach 1·06 (701 knots; 1,300 km/h; 807 mph)
Landing speed 146 knots (270 km/h; 168 mph)
Design ceiling 18,000 m (59,050 ft)
Practical ceiling about 15,250 m (50,000 ft)
T-O run at normal AUW 800 m (2,625 ft)
Landing run 550 m (1,805 ft)
Combat radius (hi-lo-hi):
with four 250 kg bombs, internal fuel 200 nm (370 km; 230 miles)
with two 250 kg bombs and drop tanks 400 nm (740 km; 460 miles)
Range, internal fuel only 593 nm (1,100 km; 683 miles)
Ferry range, with three external tanks 971 nm (1,800 km; 1,118 miles)

PERFORMANCE (MiG-21US, 'clean'):
Max level speed above 12,200 m (40,000 ft) Mach 2·02 (1,159 knots; 2,150 km/h; 1,335 mph)
Max level speed at S/L Mach 1·06 (701 knots; 1,300 km/h; 807 mph)
Max rate of climb at S/L 6,400 m (21,000 ft)/min
Rate of climb at 11,000 m (36,000 ft) 3,050 m (10,000 ft)/min
Time to 1,500 m (4,920 ft) 20 s
Turn rate at 4,570 m (15,000 ft):
instantaneous (Mach 0·5) 11·1°/s
instantaneous (Mach 0·9) 13·4°/s
sustained (Mach 0·9) 7·5°/s
T-O run 700 m (2,297 ft)

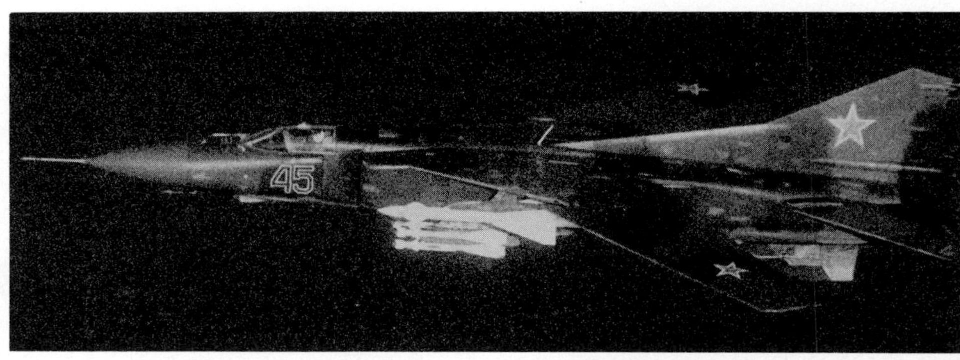
MiG-23MF 'Flogger-B' single-seat variable geometry air combat fighter of the Soviet Air Force armed with two AA-7 'Apex' and four AA-8 'Aphid' air-to-air missiles *(Swedish Air Force)*

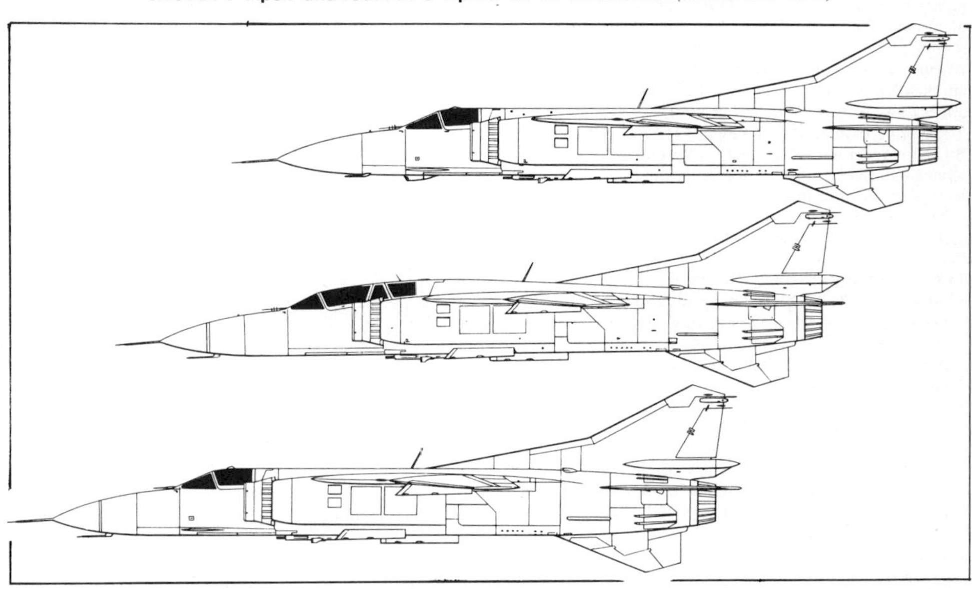
Top to bottom: Side views of the 'Flogger-B', 'Flogger-C' and 'Flogger-E' variants of the MiG-23 series *(Pilot Press)*

The two-seat MiG-23UM, identical to the early MiG-23M except for second cockpit

MIKOYAN MiG-23

NATO reporting names: Flogger-A, B, C, E, F, G, H and K

The prototype of this variable geometry air combat fighter was displayed in public for the first time on 9 July 1967, during the Aviation Day flypast at Domodedovo Airport, Moscow, soon after its first flight. Pre-series aircraft were delivered to the Soviet Air Force in 1970, followed by initial series production MiG-23 interceptors in 1973. Two Soviet fighter regiments, with a total of about 75 aircraft, were deployed to East Germany in 1973-74; since then the MiG-23 and related MiG-27 have superseded the MiG-21 progressively as primary equipment of the Soviet tactical air forces and Voyska PVO home defence interceptor force, with production continuing at the rate of several hundred a year. MiG-23s are flown by all of the Warsaw Pact air forces, and have been exported to ten other air forces.

US press reports suggest that former Egyptian operated MiG-23s are being flown by the US Air Force from an air base in the western USA, alongside MiG-21s, for realistic air-to-air combat training of USAF and allied pilots. At least one other was presented to China in a technology transfer deal.

There have been twelve versions of the MiG-23 of which details can be published in 1986:

MiG-23 (Flogger-A). Prototype shown at Domodedovo on 9 July 1967. One Lyulka AL-7F-1 afterburning turbojet, rated at 98·1 kN (22,046 lb st). Illustrated in 1973-74 and preceding editions of *Jane's*.

MiG-23S (Flogger-A). Pre-production version, with AL-7F-1 engine. Issued to complete fighter regiment in 1971 for development.

MiG-23SM (Flogger-A). As MiG-23S, but with four APU-13 pylons for external stores added under engine air intake ducts and fixed inboard wing panels.

MiG-23U. Tandem two-seat training counterpart of MiG-23S.

MiG-23M (Flogger-B). First series production version. Single-seat air combat fighter with Tumansky R-27 turbojet, rated at 68·65 kN (15,430 lb st) dry and 100·0 kN (22,485 lb st) with afterburning. Wings moved forward about 61 cm (2 ft) to compensate for lighter engine, increasing gap between wing and tailplane. Length of rear fuselage reduced; size of dorsal fin increased; wing chord increased on movable panels, giving large dogtooth. Deliveries began in 1972.

MiG-23MF (Flogger-B). Improved version of MiG-23M, with more powerful R-29 engine and uprated equipment, including more modern radar, ECM in fairings forward of starboard underwing pylon and above rudder, Doppler, and a small infra-red sensor pod under the cockpit. The US *Military Posture* statement for FY 1979 described 'Flogger-B' as "the first Soviet aircraft with a demonstrated ability to track and engage targets flying below its own altitude". Standard version for Soviet Air Force from about 1975, and for other Warsaw Pact air forces from 1978.

MiG-23UM (Flogger-C). Tandem two-seat version suitable for both operational training and combat use. Individual canopy over each seat. Rear seat slightly higher than forward seat, with retractable periscopic sight for occupant. Dorsal spine fairing of increased depth aft of rear canopy. Otherwise identical to MiG-23M with R-27 turbojet. In service with Soviet and Warsaw Pact air forces and those of other countries, including Cuba, Egypt, India and Libya.

MiG-23MS (Flogger-E). Export version of 'Flogger-B', equipped to a lower standard. Smaller radar (NATO 'Jay Bird': search range 15 nm; 29 km; 18 miles, tracking range 10 nm; 19 km; 12 miles) in shorter nose radome. No infra-red sensor or Doppler navigation equipment. Armed with 'Atoll' missiles and GSh-23 gun. In service in Algeria, Cuba, Iraq, North Korea and Libya.

MiG-23BN (Flogger-F). Export single-seat fighter-bomber. Has the nose shape, raised seat, cockpit external armour plate and larger, low pressure tyres of Soviet Air Force's MiG-27 ('Flogger-D'), but retains the power plant, variable geometry intakes and GSh-23 twin-barrel gun of the MiG-23MF interceptor. Laser rangefinder instead of target seeking radar. Operated by Algerian, Cuban, Egyptian, Ethiopian, Iraqi, Libyan, Syrian and Vietnamese air forces.

MiG-23 (Flogger-G). First identified when six aircraft from Kubinka air base made goodwill visits to Finland and France in the Summer of 1978. Although basically similar to 'Flogger-B' version of MiG-23MF, these aircraft had a much smaller dorsal fin. Absence of operational equipment, such as underwing pylons and infra-red and tracking pods, suggested initially that only a few aircraft had been modified to this standard for improved aerobatic capability as a display team. 'Flogger-G' has since been confirmed as a standard Soviet operational variant which has also been exported, to the German Democratic Republic and Syria. The radar is lighter in weight, and the undernose sensor pod on some aircraft is of new design.

MiG-23BN (Flogger-H). As 'Flogger-F' but with small avionics pod on each side at bottom of fuselage, immediately forward of nosewheel doors. Operated by Bulgarian, Czechoslovak and Polish air forces. Total of 80 delivered to Indian Air Force, beginning December 1980 with completion in 1982, to re-equip Nos. 10, 220 and 221 Squadrons. Has also been used by Soviet Air Force.

MiG-23 (Flogger-K). Photographed from F-4 of US Navy 100 nm off Vietnamese coast, near Cam Ranh Bay, in 1986. Identified by dog-tooth notch at junction of wing glove leading-edge and intake trunk on each side, to generate vortices to improve stability in yaw at high angles of attack. This compensates for use of smaller ventral folding fin and small 'Flogger-G' type dorsal fin. New IFF antenna forward of windscreen. AA-11 close-range air-to-air missiles on fuselage pylons. Pivoting weapon pylons under outer wings.

In Spring 1986, it was estimated that about 430 'Flogger-B/G' interceptors served with the 1,250-strong Soviet strategic air defence interceptor force, and a further 1,750 in tactical air force regiments.

The following description refers specifically to the single-seat MiG-23MF ('Flogger-G') as supplied to the Soviet Air Force:

TYPE: Single-seat variable geometry air combat fighter.

WINGS: Cantilever shoulder-wing monoplane of conventional light alloy construction, with front and rear main spars and auxiliary centre spar. Sweepback of main panels variable in flight or on the ground by manual control, at 16°, 45° or 72°. Two hydraulic wing sweep motors driven separately by main and control booster systems. If one system fails, wing sweep system remains effective at 50 per cent normal angular velocity. Extended chord (dogtooth) on outer panels visible when wings are swept. Fixed triangular inboard panels, with leading-edges swept at 72°. Welded steel pivot box carry-through structure. Full span hydraulically actuated trailing-edge single-slotted flaps, each in three sections, permitting independent actuation of outboard sections when wings are fully swept. No ailerons. Two-section hydraulically actuated upper surface spoilers/lift dumpers, forward of mid and inner flap sections on each side, operate differentially in conjunction with horizontal tail surfaces (except when disengaged at 72° sweep), and collectively for improved runway adherence and braking after touch-down. Hydraulically actuated leading-edge flap on outboard two-thirds of each main (variable geometry) panel, coupled to trailing-edge flaps.

FUSELAGE: Conventional semi-monocoque structure of basic circular section; flattened on each side of cockpit, forward of lateral air intake trunks which blend into circular shape of rear fuselage. Large flat splitter plate, with boundary layer bleeds, forms inboard face of each intake. Two small rectangular suction relief doors in each trunk, under inboard wing leading-edge. Perforations under rear fuselage, aft of mainwheel bays, are pressure relief vents. Four hydraulically actuated door type air-brakes, mounted two on each side of rear fuselage above and below horizontal tail surface. Rear fuselage detachable between wing and tailplane for engine servicing.

TAIL UNIT: Hydraulically actuated all-moving horizontal surfaces, swept back at 57° on leading-edge, operate both differentially and symmetrically to provide aileron and elevator function respectively. Conventional fin, swept back at 65° on leading-edge, with inset rudder. Fin and forward portion of each horizontal surface of conventional light alloy construction with spars and ribs. Rudder and rear of each horizontal surface have honeycomb core. Large dorsal fin. Ground adjustable tab on each horizontal surface at inboard trailing-edge. Large ventral fin in two portions. Lower portion is hinged to fold to starboard when landing gear is extended, to increase ground clearance.

LANDING GEAR: Hydraulically retractable tricycle type, with single wheel on each main unit and steerable twin-wheel nose unit. Main units retract inward into rear of air intake trunks. Main fairings to enclose these units are attached to legs. Small inboard fairing for each wheel bay hinged to fuselage belly. Nose unit, fitted with small mudguard over each wheel, retracts rearward. Mainwheels fitted with brakes and anti-skid units. Brake parachute, area 21 m² (226 sq ft), housed in cylindrical fairing at base of rudder with split conic doors.

POWER PLANT: One Tumansky R-29B turbojet engine, rated currently at up to 122 kN (27,500 lb st) with max afterburning in aircraft for Soviet Air Force. Water injection system, capacity 28 litres (6·15 Imp gallons; 7·4 US gallons). Four fuel tanks in fuselage, aft of cockpit, and two in wings. Max internal fuel capacity 5,750 litres (1,265 Imp gallons; 1,519 US gallons). Variable geometry air intakes and variable nozzle. Provision for carrying jettisonable external fuel tank, capacity 800 litres (176 Imp gallons; 211 US gallons), on underfuselage centreline pylon, and two more under fixed wing panels. Two additional external tanks of same capacity may be carried on non-swivelling pylons under outer wings for ferry flights, with wings in fully forward position. Attachment for assisted take-off rocket on each side of fuselage aft of landing gear.

ACCOMMODATION: Pilot only, on zero/zero ejection seat in air-conditioned and pressurised cockpit, under small hydraulically actuated rearward hinged canopy. Bulletproof windscreen. Small electrically heated rearview mirror on top of canopy.

AVIONICS AND EQUIPMENT: J band radar dish (NATO 'High Lark': search range 46 nm; 85 km; 53 miles, tracking range 29 nm; 54 km; 34 miles) behind dielectric nosecone. ILS antennae (NATO 'Swift Rod') under radome and at tip of fin trailing-edge; suppressed UHF antennae form tip of fin and forward fixed portion of ventral fin; yaw vane above fuselage aft of radome; angle of attack sensor on port side. SRO-2 (NATO 'Odd Rods') IFF antenna immediately forward of windscreen. Undernose infra-red sensor pod, Sirena 3 radar warning system, and Doppler equipment standard on Soviet Air Force version. Sirena 3 antennae in horns at inboard leading-edge of each outer wing and below ILS antenna on fin. Retractable landing/taxying light under each engine air intake.

ARMAMENT: One 23 mm GSh-23L twin-barrel gun in fuselage belly pack, with large flash eliminator around muzzles. One pylon under centre-fuselage, one under each engine air intake duct, and one under each fixed inboard wing panel, for rocket packs, air-to-air missiles or other external stores. Use of twin launchers under air intake ducts permits carriage of four R-60 ('Aphid') missiles, plus two R-23 ('Apex') on underwing pylons.

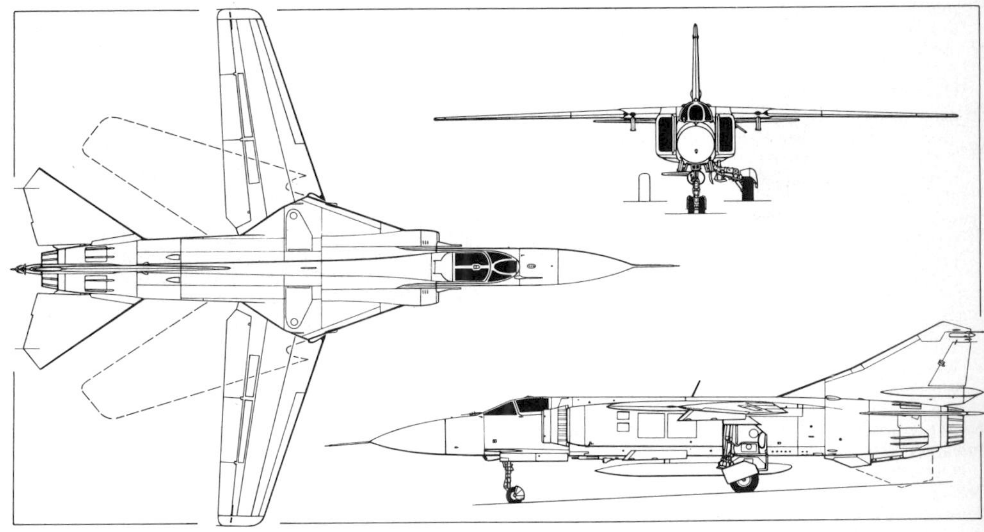

A shorter dorsal fin identifies the 'Flogger-G' version of the MiG-23 *(Pilot Press)*

'Flogger-H' can be distinguished from 'Flogger-F' by the avionics pods near the nosewheel doors, and from the MiG-27 ('Flogger-D') by its variable geometry intakes *(Letectvi + Kosmonautika)*

Notches in wing gloves identify the new MiG-23 ('Flogger-K') *(US Navy)*

DIMENSIONS, EXTERNAL:

Wing span: fully spread	14·25 m (46 ft 9 in)
fully swept	8·17 m (26 ft 9½ in)
Length overall	18·15 m (59 ft 6½ in)
Height overall	5·50 m (18 ft 0½ in)

AREA:

Wings, gross (spread)	27·30 m² (293·8 sq ft)

WEIGHTS:

Weight empty	8,200 kg (18,075 lb)
Max external weapon load	2,000 kg (4,410 lb)
T-O weight	16,000-18,900 kg (35,275-41,670 lb)

PERFORMANCE:

Max level speed: at height	Mach 2·35
at S/L	Mach 1·2
Service ceiling	20,000 m (65,600 ft)
T-O and landing run	900 m (2,950 ft)
Combat radius	485-700 nm (900-1,300 km; 560-805 miles)

MIKOYAN MiG-27

NATO reporting names: Flogger-D and J
Indian Air Force name: Bahadur

Although the single-seat ground attack aircraft known to NATO as 'Flogger-D/J' have many airframe features in common with the MiG-23, they differ in important respects and are designated MiG-27. Their use of fixed air intakes and a fixed nozzle is consistent with the primary requirement of transonic speed at low altitude. Two versions are operational in Soviet tactical air force regiments:

Flogger-D. Initial version for Soviet tactical air forces, introduced in second half of the 1970s. Forward portion of fuselage completely redesigned by comparison with interceptor versions of MiG-23. Instead of having an ogival radome, 'Flogger-D' nose is sharply tapered in side elevation, with a radar ranging antenna and a small sloping window covering laser rangefinder and marked target seeker. Additional armour on flat sides of cockpit. Seat and canopy raised to improve view from cockpit. Six-barrel 30 mm Gatling type underbelly gun replaces GSh-23 of interceptor. Bomb rack under each side of rear fuselage in addition to five pylons for external stores, including tactical nuclear weapons and, probably, the air-to-surface missile known to NATO as 'Kerry'. Typical external load comprises six 500 kg bombs and two 800 litre (176 Imp gallon; 211 US gallon) jettisonable fuel tanks. Bullet shape antenna above each glove pylon.

Flogger-J. Identified in 1981. New nose shape, with lip at top and blister fairing below. Bullet shape antennae above wingroot glove pylons deleted. Wingroot leading-edge extensions on some aircraft. Armament includes two gun pods on underwing pylons, with gun barrels that can be depressed for attacking ground targets. MiG-27M export version is being built under licence by HAL in India as the Bahadur (Valiant) (see Indian section).

A total of about 790 'Flogger-Ds' and 'Js' is deployed with the Soviet tactical air forces, plus at least one squadron with the East German Air Force. The somewhat similar aircraft known to NATO as 'Flogger-F and H' are members of the MiG-23 series, with variable geometry intakes and a GSh-23 twin-barrel gun, although having the nose shape, raised seat and larger, low pressure tyres of 'Flogger-D'. Both versions have been operated by Soviet units; but the 'F' and 'H' are basically export counterparts of 'Flogger-D', with lower standards of equipment and performance, and are described under the MiG-23 entry.

The following data are estimated for the MiG-27 'Flogger-D':

POWER PLANT: Generally similar to MiG-23MF, but R-29B engine rated at 78·45 kN (17,635 lb st) dry and 112·8 kN (25,350 lb st) with max afterburning.

DIMENSIONS, EXTERNAL: As MiG-23, plus:

Wing aspect ratio (spread)	7·45
Length overall	16·00 m (52 ft 6 in)
Tailplane span	5·75 m (18 ft 10¼ in)

AREA:

Horizontal tail surfaces	6·88 m² (74·06 sq ft)

WEIGHTS:

Max external load	4,500 kg (9,920 lb)
Max T-O weight, 'clean'	15,500 kg (34,170 lb)
Max T-O weight	20,100 kg (44,313 lb)

PERFORMANCE (estimated):

Max level speed: at height	Mach 1·7
at S/L	Mach 1·1
Service ceiling	16,000 m (52,500 ft)
T-O to 15 m (50 ft) at AUW of 15,700 kg (34,600 lb)	800 m (2,625 ft)
Combat radius, with underbelly fuel tank, four 500 kg bombs and two 'Atoll' missiles, lo-lo-lo	210 nm (390 km; 240 miles)
Max ferry range with three external tanks	1,350 nm (2,500 km; 1,550 miles)

MIKOYAN MiG-25 (E-266)

NATO reporting name: Foxbat

Development of the MiG-25 interceptor was initiated as a high priority programme to counter the threat of the US Air Force's Mach 3 B-70 strategic bomber, for which North American Aviation Inc was chosen as prime contractor in December 1957. When the B-70 was cut back to a research project by President Kennedy, in March 1961, work on the MiG-25 continued, with increased emphasis on the reconnaissance potential of the design.

First indication that the prototype had flown came with a Soviet claim, in April 1965, that a twin-engined aircraft designated Ye-266 had set a 1,000 km closed circuit speed record of 1,251·9 knots (2,320 km/h; 1,441·5 mph), carrying a 2,000 kg payload. Photographs of the Ye-266 issued subsequently in the Soviet Union identified it as the twin-finned single-seat fighter of which four examples had taken part in the Aviation Day display at Domodedovo Airport, Moscow, in July 1967; the designation MiG-25 was confirmed later. NATO had, meanwhile, allocated the reporting name 'Foxbat' to the type.

The aircraft's performance in level flight was demonstrated further on 5 October 1967, when M. Komarov set a speed record of 1,608·83 knots (2,981·5 km/h; 1,852·61 mph) over a 500 km closed circuit. Other speed and height records followed, of which details can be found in the 1982-83 *Jane's*. Three time-to-height records established by the Ye-266 on 4 June 1973 were beaten by the McDonnell Douglas F-15 *Streak Eagle* in January-February 1975; but two of them were recaptured by a Ye-266M (with uprated power plant) on 17 May 1975. The late Alexander Fedotov climbed to 25,000 m in 2 min 34·2 s and P. Ostapenko reached 30,000 m in 3 min 9·85 s. Fedotov also set a new record by climbing to 35,000 m in 4 min 11·7 s.

The current absolute height record was set by Fedotov on 31 August 1977, when he climbed to 37,650 m (123,524 ft) in a Ye-266M. He had, on 22 July, climbed to 37,080 m (121,654 ft) carrying a 2,000 kg payload, qualifying also for the record with 1,000 kg.

Four MiG-25 reconnaissance aircraft were deployed with Soviet Air Force units in Egypt in the Spring of 1971, having been airlifted to that country in An-22 transports. First foreign operators, in 1979, were the Algerian and Syrian air forces, followed by the air forces of Iraq, Libya and India.

MiG-27 ('Flogger-D') landing, with wings extended and ventral fin folded *(Flug Revue)*

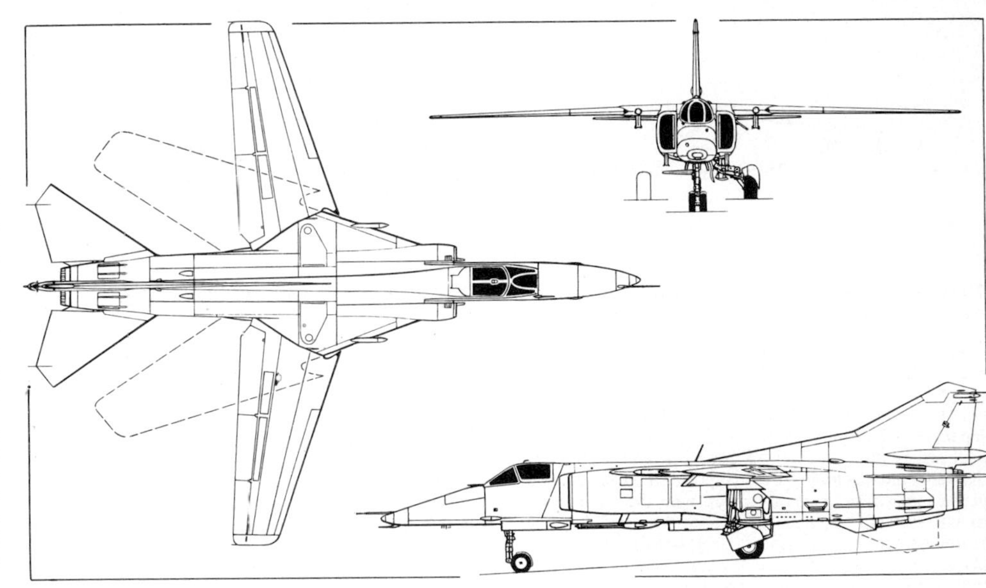
MiG-27 ('Flogger-D') single-seat ground attack aircraft *(Pilot Press)*

Comparison of this photograph of a MiG-27 'Flogger-J' with that of a 'Flogger-D' shows the restyled nose, absence of bullet shape antennae on the wing gloves, addition of wingroot leading-edge extensions and depressed barrel of gun in port underwing pod

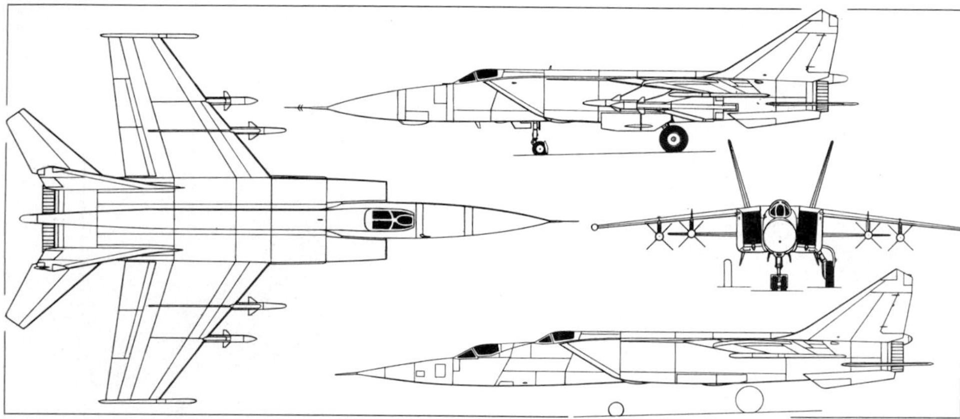

Mikoyan MiG-25M single-seat fighter (NATO 'Foxbat-E') with additional side view (bottom) of two-seat MiG-25U *(Pilot Press)*

The reconnaissance version of the MiG-25 known to NATO as 'Foxbat-B' in service with the Libyan Arab Air Force. Note the camera-carrying nose and dielectric panel *(US Navy)*

The first opportunity to study the MiG-25 interceptor outside the Soviet Union came when Lt Viktor Belenko defected in one from the Soviet air base of Sikharovka, 200 km (120 miles) from Vladivostok, to Hakodate airport, Japan, on 6 September 1976. Statements attributed to this pilot suggest that more than 400 MiG-25s had been built by that time, and that his particular aircraft left the production line less than three years earlier. Japanese and US military technicians who examined the aircraft reported that the airframe is constructed mainly of steel, with titanium only in places subjected to extreme heating such as the wing leading-edges. The inevitable weight penalty restricts the amount of equipment that can be carried. Belenko said that the aircraft took a considerable time to accelerate to high speeds, which were then difficult to maintain.

Examination of the aircraft is said to have shown that the fuselage weighs about 13,600 kg (30,000 lb) with the wings, tail surfaces and afterburners removed; the fire control system is bulky and lacking in advanced technology, with its very high power (600kW) devoted to anti-jamming capability rather than range, and with vacuum tubes rather than solid state circuitry throughout the avionics. The number of cockpit instruments was described as 50 per cent of those in F-4EJ Phantoms of the JASDF, with a smaller and less versatile weapon sight; and the Machmeter has a 'red line' limit at Mach 2·8, which almost certainly represents a never-exceed speed when carrying missiles and pylons rather than the maximum speed of which the 'clean' aircraft is capable. Of particular interest is the aircraft's high quality airborne computer which, in conjunction with a ground based flight control system, enables the interceptor to be vectored automatically on to its target over long ranges.

There are five variants of the MiG-25, as follows:

MiG-25 (Foxbat-A). Basic interceptor, with large radar (NATO 'Fox Fire') in nose and armed with four air-to-air missiles on underwing attachments. Slightly reduced wing leading-edge sweep towards tips. ECM and CW target illuminating radar in wingtip anti-flutter bodies. Production cut back in 1977-78, reflecting new emphasis on interception of low flying targets. Most 'Foxbat-As' in service in the Soviet Union are being converted progressively to 'Foxbat-E' standard. 'Foxbat-As' remain operational in Algeria, Iraq, Libya and Syria.

MiG-25R (Foxbat-B). Basic reconnaissance version, with five camera windows and various flush dielectric panels aft of very small dielectric nosecap for radar. Equipment believed to include Doppler navigation system and side looking airborne radar (SLAR). No armament. Slightly reduced span. Wing leading-edge sweep constant from root to tip. Operated by Soviet tactical air forces, and in Algeria, Libya (one squadron, including 'Foxbat-Ds') and Syria. Eight delivered from Summer 1981 to replace Canberras of No. 106 Squadron, Indian Air Force.

MiG-25U (Foxbat-C). Trainer, of which first photographs were published towards the end of 1975. Generally similar to operational versions, but with new nose, containing separate cockpit with individual canopy, forward of standard cockpit and at a lower level. No search radar or reconnaissance sensors in nose. In service with air forces of Soviet Union and India (two). The aircraft designated **Ye-133** in which Svetlana Savitskaya set a women's world speed record of 1,448·942 knots (2,683·44 km/h; 1,667·412 mph) on 22 June 1975 is believed to have been a MiG-25U. She has since set a women's sustained height record of 21,209·9 m (69,586 ft) in a Ye-133 on 31 August 1977, a women's speed record of 1,331·70 knots (2,466·31 km/h; 1,532·49 mph) around a 500 km closed circuit on 21 October 1977, and a women's speed record of 1,259·7 knots (2,333 km/h; 1,449·6 mph) around a 1,000 km circuit on 12 April 1978.

MiG-25R (Foxbat-D). Generally similar to 'Foxbat-B', but with larger SLAR (side looking airborne radar) dielectric panel, further aft on side of nose, and no cameras. Operated by Soviet Air Force and in Libya.

MiG-25M (Foxbat-E). Converted 'Foxbat-A' with changes to radar and equipment to provide limited look-down/shootdown capability comparable with that of 'Flogger-B'. Undernose sensor pod. Engines uprated to 137·3 kN (30,865 lb st). Developed via aircraft known as the **Ye-266M**, which set three time-to-height records in 1975 and also holds the absolute height record.

About 300 'Foxbat' interceptors served with the 1,250-strong Soviet home defence interceptor force in 1986; a further 130 interceptors and 170 reconnaissance MiG-25s served with the tactical air forces. Most 'Foxbat-As' in Soviet service are being converted progressively to 'Foxbat-E' standard. Some Libyan aircraft have been converted.

The following description applies to the MiG-25 ('Foxbat-A') interceptor except where indicated:

TYPE: Single-seat interceptor.

WINGS: Cantilever high-wing monoplane. Anhedral 4° from roots. Sweepback on leading-edge approx 40° inboard, 38° outboard of each outer missile attachment. Sweepback at quarter-chord 32°. Wing structure basically of arc-welded nickel steel, with titanium leading-edge. Upper surface fence in line with each inboard weapon attachment; shorter shallow fence in line with each outer attachment. Long anti-flutter body (max diameter 30 cm; 11·8 in) at each wingtip, housing avionics. Light alloy aileron at centre of each semi-span, with simple light alloy flap on inboard 37 per cent of trailing-edge. No other movable wing surfaces.

FUSELAGE: Basic fuselage is quite slim, but is blended into the rectangular air intake trunks, which have wedge inlets. Inner walls of intakes are curved at top and do not run parallel with outer walls; a hinged panel forms the lower lip of each intake, enabling intake area to be varied electronically. Airbrake beneath jetpipes, between ventral fins. Structure mainly of arc-welded nickel steel.

TAIL UNIT: Cantilever structure comprising twin outward canted fins with inset rudders, and all-moving horizontal surfaces. All surfaces sweptback (tailplane 50°, fins 60°), without tabs. Main structures of arc-welded nickel steel, with titanium leading-edges and light alloy rear sections. Two outward canted ventral fins, with retractable sprung tailskids. Large areas of each main and ventral fin form flush antennae.

LANDING GEAR: Retractable tricycle type. Single wheel, with high pressure tyre of 1·20 m (47·25 in) diameter, on each forward retracting main unit. Wheel stows vertically between air intake duct and outer skin of each trunk. Twin-wheel forward retracting nose unit. Twin brake-chutes in fairing above and between jet nozzles.

POWER PLANT: Two Tumansky R-31 (R-266) single-shaft turbojet engines, each rated at 91·18 kN (20,500 lb st) dry, and 120 kN (27,010 lb st) with afterburning. Water-methanol injection standard. Fuel in two structural tanks in fuselage, between cockpit and engine bay, in saddle tanks around intake ducts, and in integral tank in each wing, filling almost the entire volume inboard of outer fence. Total fuel capacity approx 14,000 kg (30,865 lb) or 17,410 litres (3,830 Imp gallons; 4,600 US gallons).

ACCOMMODATION: Pilot only, on KM-1 zero-height, 80 knot (150 km/h; 93 mph) ejection seat similar to that fitted to

MiG-25M ('Foxbat-E') interceptor of the Libyan Arab Air Force, armed with 'Acrid' and 'Aphid' air-to-air missiles *(US Navy)*

This photograph shows clearly the tandem cockpits in the nose of the MiG-25U ('Foxbat-C')

some versions of MiG-21. Canopy hinged to open sideways, to starboard.

AVIONICS AND EQUIPMENT: Main fire control radar (NATO 'Fox Fire': range believed to be 45 nm; 85 km; 52 miles) in nose, forward of avionics compartment housing navigation radar. SRZO-2 (NATO 'Odd Rods') IFF and SOD-57M ATC/SIF, with antennae in starboard fin tip. Sirena 3 360° radar warning system with receivers in centre of each wingtip anti-flutter body and starboard fin tip. Unidentified ECCM, decoys and jammers. RSB-70/RPS HF, RSIU-5 VHF, R-831 UHF communications equipment, SP-50 (NATO 'Swift Rod') ILS, MRP-56P marker beacon receiver and ARK-15 radio compass. Retractable landing light under front of each intake trunk.

ARMAMENT: Four air-to-air missiles on underwing attachments. These may comprise one infra-red and one radar homing example of the missile known to NATO as 'Acrid' under each wing. Alternatively, one 'Apex' and a pair of AA-11s or 'Aphids' can be carried under each wing. Backup optical weapon sight.

DIMENSIONS, EXTERNAL:
- Wing span: 'Foxbat-A' — 13·95 m (45 ft 9 in)
  - 'Foxbat-B' — 13·40 m (44 ft 0 in)
- Wing aspect ratio: 'Foxbat-A' — 3·4
- Length overall — 23·82 m (78 ft 1¾ in)
- Length of fuselage — 19·40 m (63 ft 7¾ in)
- Height overall — 6·10 m (20 ft 0¼ in)

AREA:
- Wings, gross: 'Foxbat-A' — 56·83 m² (611·7 sq ft)

WEIGHTS (estimated):
- Basic operating weight, empty:
  - 'Foxbat-A' — at least 20,000 kg (44,100 lb)
  - 'Foxbat-B' — 19,600 kg (43,200 lb)
- Max T-O weight: 'Foxbat-A' — 37,425 kg (82,500 lb)
  - 'Foxbat-B' — 33,400 kg (73,635 lb)

PERFORMANCE (estimated):
- Max level speed at height:
  - 'Foxbat-B', 'clean' — Mach 3·2
- Never-exceed combat speed: 'Foxbat-A', with four 'Acrid' missiles and 50% fuel — Mach 2·83
- Max level speed at low altitude: 'Foxbat-A', with four 'Acrid' missiles and 50% fuel — Mach 0·85
- Landing speed:
  - 'Foxbat-A' — 146 knots (270 km/h; 168 mph)
- Max rate of climb at S/L:
  - 'Foxbat-A' — 12,480 m (40,950 ft)/min
- Time to 11,000 m (36,000 ft) with afterburning:
  - 'Foxbat-A' — 2 min 30 s
- Service ceiling: 'Foxbat-A' — 24,400 m (80,000 ft)
  - 'Foxbat-B, D' — 27,000 m (88,580 ft)
- T-O run: 'Foxbat-A' — 1,380 m (4,525 ft)
- Landing run: 'Foxbat-A' — 2,180 m (7,150 ft)
- Normal operational radius:
  - 'Foxbat-A' — 610 nm (1,130 km; 700 miles)
  - 'Foxbat-B, D' — 485 nm (900 km; 560 miles)
- Max combat radius, econ power:
  - 'Foxbat-A' — 780 nm (1,450 km; 900 miles)

MIKOYAN MiG-29

NATO reporting name: Fulcrum

Operational since early 1985, the MiG-29 is a twin-engined aircraft comparable in size to the US F/A-18 Hornet. It is fitted with a large pulse Doppler lookdown/shootdown radar which gives it day and night all-weather operating capability against low-flying targets, as well as freedom from the outmoded ground control interception techniques that restricted Soviet air defence effectiveness in the past. Like other new Soviet air superiority fighters, it also has an infra-red search/track sensor, mounted inside a transparent dome in front of the windscreen, offset to starboard. It is expected to replace MiG-21s, Su-21s and some MiG-23s in Soviet service.

References to this fighter first appeared in the Western press in 1979, after a prototype had been identified on photographs taken over Ramenskoye flight test centre by a US reconnaissance satellite. NATO allocated the reporting name 'Fulcrum' when it became clear that the MiG was intended as a production aircraft.

From the start, it was plain that 'Fulcrum' represented a concerted effort by the Soviet Union to close the technology gap with the West. Its sustained turn rate is much improved over earlier Soviet fighters, and thrust-to-weight ratio is better than 1. Although intended primarily as a single-seat counter-air fighter, it is likely to have a full dual-role air combat/attack capability, and a combat capable two-seater is also in production.

Production is centred at a factory in Moscow. Its status and scale are evident from the fact that export of the first of 80 aircraft to Syria appeared imminent in the Autumn of 1986, and that the Indian government is acquiring MiG-29s (in flyaway form for the first 40; for licence manufacture later) to meet its requirement for aircraft to match Pakistan's F-16s. Deliveries of an initial batch of single- and two-seaters are expected to begin in the Spring of 1987. Meanwhile, more than 150 MiG-29s were already operational with Soviet units stationed in East Germany, in the Soviet Union west of the Urals and in the far eastern USSR by mid-1986.

On 1 July 1986, a detachment of six, from Kubinka air base, near Moscow, made a goodwill visit to Kuopio-Rissala air base in Finland. As the nosewheel of each aircraft made contact with the runway, doors were triggered to blank off the underslung engine air intakes. This surprising technique was adopted by the aircraft's designers to overcome problems caused by ingestion of stones, snow, slush, ice and foreign objects into the engine ducts during take-off and landing on the kind of runways used by Warsaw Pact front-line air forces, especially in Winter. When the intake trunks are closed, engine air is taken in through a series of lateral louvres in the upper surface of the aircraft's deep wingroot leading-edge extensions.

There was nothing on the MiG-29s in Finland to suggest that the Soviet Union is yet equipping its fighters to refuel in flight. Also, although the MiG-29 has a high-set cockpit, giving its pilot a reasonable forward view over the sloping nose, he lacks the all-round field of view offered to the pilots of western fighters such as the F-15 and F-16 through 360° low-sill canopies. Nor can the bulky head-up display, IR sensor, and large wing leading-edge extensions be helpful in this respect.

Comparison of the general configurations of the MiG-29 Fulcrum and Su-27 Flanker prompts the thought that some authority, perhaps the TsAGI Central Aerodynamics and Hydrodynamics Institute, may be exerting a greater influence on design than was the case in the era of the late Artem Mikoyan and Pavel Sukhoi. The Sukhoi fighter maintains the tradition of being larger and seemingly less sophisticated than the MiG, but the two designs are strikingly similar in most respects, even in such detail as current tail fin location and the manner in which the mainwheels retract into the wingroots.

TYPE: All-weather counter-air fighter, with attack capability.

WINGS: Cantilever low-wing monoplane. Leading-edge sweepback approx 42° on outer wings, with very large ogival root extensions. Anhedral approx 2°. Leading-edge manoeuvring flaps over full span except for tips. Plain flap and aileron on trailing-edge of each wing. No tabs.

FUSELAGE: Semi-monocoque all-metal structure, sharply tapered and downswept aft of flat-sided cockpit area, with ogival dielectric nosecone.

TAIL UNIT: Cantilever structure, comprising twin fins, small inset rudders, and all-moving horizontal surfaces, all carried on slim booms alongside engine nacelles. Vertical surfaces sweptback at approx 40° and canted outward at 7°, each with dorsal fin that extends forward as an overwing fence. Horizontal surfaces sweptback at approx 50°. No tabs.

LANDING GEAR: Retractable tricycle type, with single wheel on each main unit and twin nosewheels. Mainwheels

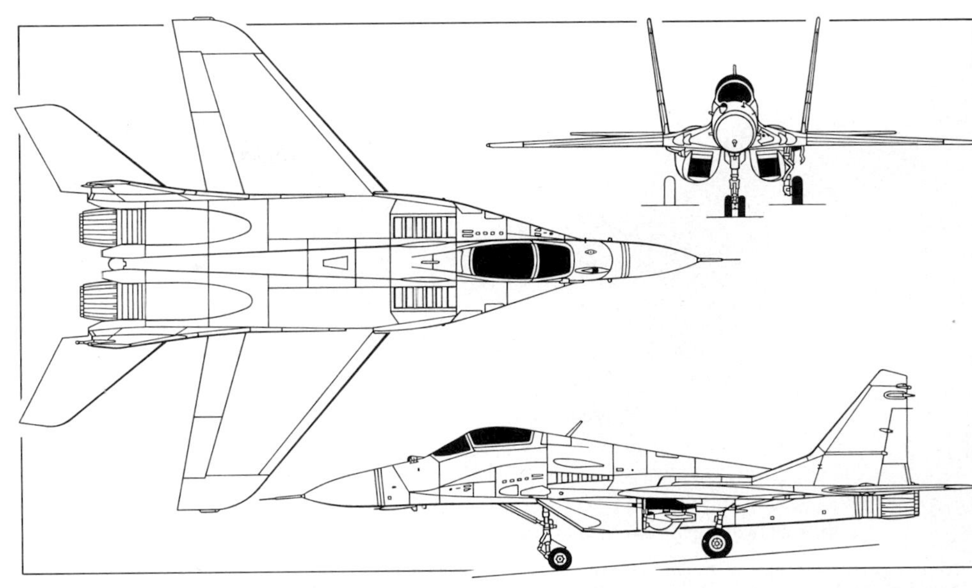

MiG-29 counter-air fighter (two Tumansky R-33D afterburning turbofan engines) *(Jane's/Mike Keep)*

Two photographs taken during the MiG-29's first appearance outside the Warsaw Pact countries, in Finland in July 1986 *(Hasse Vallas)*

MiG-29 taking off from Kuopio-Rissala air base, Finland *(Press Association)*

retract forward into wingroots, turning through 90° to lie flat above leg. Nosewheels, on trailing-link oleo, retract rearward between engine air intakes. Mainwheel tyre size 770 × 200; nosewheel tyre size 530 × 100. Container for cruciform brake-chute recessed in centre of boat-tail between engine nozzles.

POWER PLANT: Two Tumansky R-33D turbofan engines, each rated at 50 kN (11,240 lb st) dry and 81·4 kN (18,300 lb st) with afterburning. Engine ducts are canted at approx 9° and have wedge intakes, sweptback at approx 35°, under wingroot leading-edge extensions. Doors inside each intake close the duct while the nosewheels are in contact with the runway, to prevent ingestion of foreign objects, ice, or snow. Air is then fed to each engine through louvres in top of wingroot leading-edge extension.

ACCOMMODATION: Pilot only (tandem two-seater to follow), under rearward hinged transparent blister canopy in high-set cockpit. Sharply inclined one-piece curved windscreen.

ARMAMENT AND OPERATIONAL EQUIPMENT: Six medium-range radar homing AA-10 and/or close-range AA-11 air-to-air missiles, bombs, rocket pods or other stores, on three pylons under each wing. One six-barrel 30 mm Gatling type gun in port wingroot leading-edge extension. Equipment includes pulse Doppler engagement radar, IR sensor, SRZO-2 (NATO Odd Rods) IFF, Sirena-3 360° radar warning system, and head-up display.

DIMENSIONS, EXTERNAL:

Wing span	11·50 m (37 ft 8¾ in)
Wing chord: on centreline	5·45 m (17 ft 10½ in)
at tip	1·40 m (4 ft 7 in)
Length overall, incl nose probe	17·20 m (56 ft 5 in)
Height overall	4·40 m (14 ft 5¼ in)
Tailplane span	7·75 m (25 ft 5 in)
Wheel track	3·00 m (9 ft 10 in)
Wheelbase	3·60 m (11 ft 9¾ in)

WEIGHTS (estimated):

Operating weight empty	7,825 kg (17,250 lb)
Normal T-O weight (interceptor)	16,500 kg (36,375 lb)

PERFORMANCE (estimated):

Max level speed: at height
Mach 2·2 (1,260 knots; 2,335 km/h; 1,450 mph)
at S/L Mach 1·06 (700 knots; 1,300 km/h; 805 mph)
Combat radius 620 nm (1,150 km; 715 miles)

MIKOYAN MiG-31

NATO reporting name: Foxhound

Evidence that the Mikoyan design team was developing an improved interceptor based on the general configuration of the MiG-25 (NATO 'Foxbat') came first from Lt Viktor Belenko, the Soviet pilot who defected to Japan in a 'Foxbat-A' in September 1976. He said that the airframe of the new fighter was strengthened to permit supersonic flight at low altitude; more powerful engines were fitted, each giving 137·3 kN (30,865 lb st) with afterburning; the avionics were improved; and fuselage mountings had been added to enable the aircraft to carry six air-to-air missiles.

In mid-1982 it became known that NATO had allocated the reporting name 'Foxhound' to what the technical press referred to as 'Super Foxbat' and which was subsequently identified as the MiG-31. A three-view was displayed publicly for the first time in September of the following year, during briefings at the annual AFA Convention in Washington DC, enabling the aircraft to be illustrated in the Addenda to the 1983-84 *Jane's*. The drawing showed significant new features, including tandem seating for a two-man crew, much enlarged engine air intakes, rearward extension of the jet nozzles, and wingroot leading-edge extensions on wings that were little changed in size and shape from those of the MiG-25. Its general accuracy was confirmed in the Autumn of 1985 when the pilot of an F-16 of the Royal Norwegian Air Force intercepted a MiG-31 off the coast of Eastern Finnmark in Northern Norway and took the photographs which accompany this entry.

The MiG-31's radar is said to embody technology found in the Hughes AN/APG-65 digital radar fitted in the US Navy's F/A-18 Hornet, providing true lookdown/shoot-down and multiple target engagement capability for the first time in a Soviet interceptor. Other equipment includes active countermeasures dispensers, and an infra-red search/track sensor.

Deployment of MiG-31s with Voyska PVO air defence regiments had begun by early 1983, and more than 100 were known to be operational by the Spring of 1986, deployed from the Arkhangelsk area near the USSR's western borders to Dolinsk on Sakhalin Island, north of Japan. Of these, about 24 are said by US official sources to be assigned to strategic reconnaissance missions. Production is centred at the Gorkiy airframe plant.

The detailed description which follows must be regarded as provisional. It is not yet possible, for example, to confirm that the arc-welded nickel steel structure of the MiG-25 has been retained on what has to be seen as a new design. The better heat resistant characteristics of steel are not essential at the reduced maximum speed of the MiG-31; but a switch to light alloy construction would have required extensive redesign of such well proven features as the basic wing structure, as well as major manufacturing changes. It is doubtful if these would have been considered worthwhile.

TYPE: Two-seat all-weather interceptor.

WINGS: Cantilever high-wing monoplane. Anhedral 4° from roots. Sweepback on leading-edge approx 40°, at quarter-chord 32°, with small sharply-swept wingroot extensions. Upper surface fence in line with each inboard weapon pylon. Aileron and flap on each wing, of greater span than those of MiG-25. No wingtip fairings or mountings.

FUSELAGE: Basic fuselage is slim, but is blended into wide rectangular air intake trunks, which have wedge inlets. Inner wall of each inlet is curved and does not run parallel with outer wall. Hinged panel forms lower lip of each inlet, and there is a large door towards the forward part of each top surface.

TAIL UNIT: Twin outward canted fins, with inset rudders, and all-moving one-piece horizontal surfaces. All surfaces sharply sweptback, without tabs. Two outward canted ventral fins. Large areas of each main and ventral fin form flush antennae. Aerodynamic fairings between base of each fin and engine duct, extending well forward of leading-edge.

LANDING GEAR: Retractable tricycle type. Single wheel on each main unit, retracting forward into air intake trunk. Twin nosewheels.

POWER PLANT: Two Tumansky turbojet engines, each

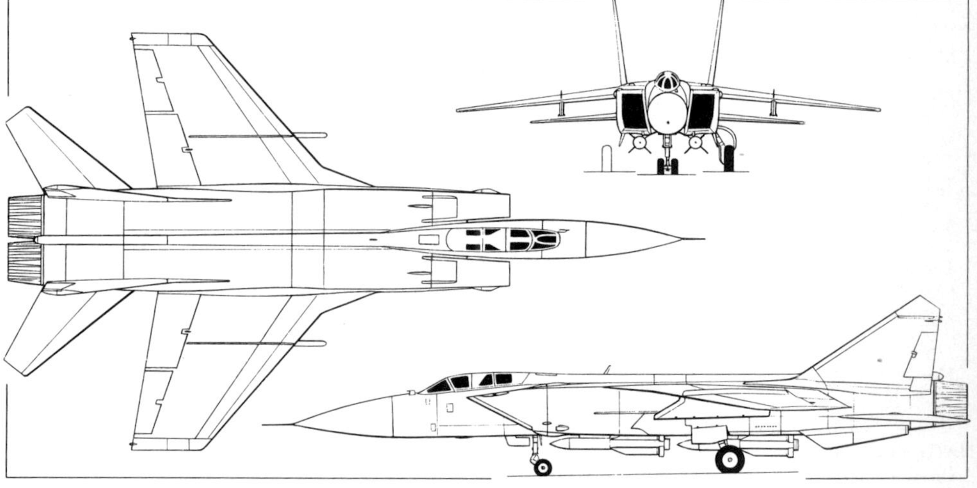

Mikoyan MiG-31 (NATO 'Foxhound') all-weather interceptor *(Pilot Press)*

Two views of the MiG-31 photographed by a Royal Norwegian Air Force pilot in Autumn 1985

reportedly rated at 137·3 kN (30,865 lb st) with afterburning. Fuel tankage probably similar to that of MiG-25, which has two structural tanks in fuselage, between cockpit and engine bay, saddle tanks around intake ducts, and integral tank in each wing, filling almost the entire volume inboard of outer stores pylon, with total capacity of approx 17,410 litres (3,830 Imp gallons; 4,600 US gallons). Provision for two large external fuel tanks on outer underwing pylons.

ACCOMMODATION: Pilot and weapon systems operator in tandem. Canopy has only limited side glazing for rear cockpit, and blends into shallow dorsal spine fairing which extends to forward edge of jet nozzles.

AVIONICS AND EQUIPMENT: Main fire control radar of pulse-Doppler lookdown/shootdown type in nose, with reported search range of 165 nm (305 km; 190 miles) and tracking range of 145 nm (270 km; 167 miles). Infra-red sensor in bottom of front fuselage. Radar warning receivers, active IR and electronic countermeasures.

ARMAMENT: Aircraft illustrated has four AA-9 (NATO 'Amos') semi-active radar homing long-range air-to-air missiles in pairs under fuselage, and twin mounts for smaller stores such as AA-8 (NATO 'Aphid') air-to-air missiles on one large pylon under each wing. These pylons, and outer underwing pylons (not fitted when photographs were taken) can probably increase the number of AA-9s carried by MiG-31 to reported total of eight.

DIMENSIONS, EXTERNAL (estimated):
- Wing span: 14·00 m (45 ft 11¼ in)
- Length of fuselage, nosecone tip to end of jetpipe: 21·50 m (70 ft 6½ in)

WEIGHTS (estimated):
- Weight empty: 21,825 kg (48,115 lb)
- Max T-O weight: 41,150 kg (90,725 lb)

PERFORMANCE (estimated):
- Max level speed at height: Mach 2·4 (1,375 knots; 2,550 km/h; 1,585 mph)
- Max combat radius: 1,135 nm (2,100 km; 1,305 miles)

MIL

GENERAL DESIGNER IN CHARGE OF BUREAU:
Marat N. Tishchenko

Mikhail L. Mil was connected with Soviet gyroplane and helicopter development from at least 1930 until his death on 31 January 1970. His original Mi-l, which was designed in 1949, first flown in 1950 and introduced into squadron service in 1951, was the first helicopter to enter series production in the Soviet Union. Current products of the design bureau named after him are as follows:

MIL Mi-2 (V-2)

Built exclusively in Poland and described under Polish aircraft industry entry for WSK-PZL Swidnik.

MIL Mi-6

NATO reporting name: Hook

Announced in the Autumn of 1957, the Mi-6 was then the world's largest helicopter. From it were developed the Mi-10 and Mi-10K flying crane helicopters, and its dynamic components were used in duplicated form on the V-12 (Mi-12) of 1967, which remains the largest helicopter yet flown anywhere in the world.

Five Mi-6s are reported to have been built for development testing, followed by an initial pre-series of 30 and subsequent manufacture of more than 800 for military and civil use. About 450 serve currently with Soviet ground forces. Others serve currently with the Algerian, Iraqi, Peruvian and Vietnamese air forces. A full structural description can be found in the 1983-84 and previous editions of *Jane's*.

TYPE: Heavy transport helicopter.

POWER PLANT: Two 4,101 kW (5,500 shp) Soloviev D-25V (TV-2BM) turboshaft engines, mounted side by side above cabin, forward of main rotor shaft. Eleven internal fuel tanks, with total capacity of 6,315 kg (13,922 lb), and two external tanks, on each side of cabin, with total capacity of 3,490 kg (7,695 lb). Provision for two additional ferry tanks inside cabin, with total capacity of 3,490 kg (7,695 lb).

ACCOMMODATION: Crew of five, consisting of two pilots, navigator, flight engineer and radio operator. Four jettisonable doors and overhead hatch on flight deck. Electro-thermal anti-icing system for glazing of flight deck and navigator's compartment. Equipped normally for cargo operation, with easily removable tip-up seats along side walls. When these seats are supplemented by additional seats installed in centre of cabin, 65-90 passengers can be carried, with cargo or baggage in the aisles. Normal military seating is for 70 combat equipped troops. As an air ambulance, 41 stretcher cases and two medical attendants on tip-up seats can be carried. One of attendant's stations is provided with intercom to flight deck, and provision is made for portable oxygen installations for the patients. Cabin floor is stressed for loadings of 2,000 kg/m² (410 lb/sq ft), with provision for cargo tiedown rings. Rear clamshell doors and ramps are operated hydraulically. Standard equipment includes an electric winch of 800 kg (1,765 lb) capacity and pulley block system. Central hatch in cabin floor for cargo sling system for bulky loads. Three jettisonable doors, fore and aft of main landing gear on port side and aft of landing gear on starboard side.

AVIONICS AND EQUIPMENT: Standard equipment includes VHF and HF communications radio, intercom, radio altimeter, radio compass, three-channel autopilot, marker beacon receiver, directional gyro and full all-weather instrumentation.

ARMAMENT: Some military Mi-6s are fitted with a 12·7 mm machine-gun in the fuselage nose.

DIMENSIONS, EXTERNAL:
- Main rotor diameter: 35·00 m (114 ft 10 in)
- Tail rotor diameter: 6·30 m (20 ft 8 in)
- Length overall, rotors turning: 41·74 m (136 ft 11½ in)
- Length of fuselage, excl nose gun and tail rotor: 33·18 m (108 ft 10½ in)
- Height overall: 9·86 m (32 ft 4 in)
- Wing span: 15·30 m (50 ft 2½ in)
- Wheel track: 7·50 m (24 ft 7¼ in)
- Wheelbase: 9·09 m (29 ft 9¾ in)
- Rear loading doors: Height: 2·70 m (8 ft 10¼ in)
  - Width: 2·65 m (8 ft 8¼ in)
- Passenger doors:
  - Height: front door: 1·70 m (5 ft 7 in)
  - rear doors: 1·61 m (5 ft 3½ in)
  - Width: 0·80 m (2 ft 7½ in)
  - Sill height: front door: 1·40 m (4 ft 7¼ in)
  - rear doors: 1·30 m (4 ft 3¼ in)
- Central hatch in floor: 1·44 m (4 ft 9 in) × 1·93 m (6 ft 4 in)

DIMENSIONS, INTERNAL:
- Cabin: Length: 12·00 m (39 ft 4½ in)
  - Max width: 2·65 m (8 ft 8¼ in)
  - Max height: at front: 2·01 m (6 ft 7 in)
  - at rear: 2·50 m (8 ft 2½ in)
  - Cabin volume: 80 m³ (2,825 cu ft)

WEIGHTS:
- Weight empty: 27,240 kg (60,055 lb)
- Max internal payload: 12,000 kg (26,450 lb)
- Max slung cargo: 8,000 kg (17,637 lb)
- Fuel load: internal: 6,315 kg (13,922 lb)
  - with external tanks: 9,805 kg (21,617 lb)
- Max T-O weight with slung cargo at altitudes under 1,000 m (3,280 ft): 38,400 kg (84,657 lb)
- Normal T-O weight: 40,500 kg (89,285 lb)
- Max T-O weight for VTO: 42,500 kg (93,700 lb)

PERFORMANCE (at max T-O weight for VTO):
- Max level speed: 162 knots (300 km/h; 186 mph)
- Max cruising speed: 135 knots (250 km/h; 155 mph)
- Service ceiling: 4,500 m (14,750 ft)
- Range with 8,000 kg (17,637 lb) payload: 334 nm (620 km; 385 miles)
- Range with external tanks and 4,500 kg (9,920 lb) payload: 540 nm (1,000 km; 621 miles)
- Max ferry range (tanks in cabin): 781 nm (1,450 km; 900 miles)

MIL Mi-8 (V-8)

NATO reporting name: Hip

This turbine powered helicopter was shown in public for the first time during the 1961 Soviet Aviation Day display. Since then, more than 10,000 Soviet built Mi-8s and uprated Mi-17s (described separately) have been delivered for military and civil use from two plants in Kazan and Ulan Ude, and production continues. Component production of the Mi-8 has also taken place at Harbin and Nanchang in China.

An estimated total of 1,750 Mi-8s and Mi-17s support Soviet armies in the field, in a variety of forms, some carrying extremely heavy weapon loads. Many others are operated by Soviet air forces, and military Mi-8s have been supplied to at least 39 other air forces, as listed in previous editions of *Jane's*.

The commercial Mi-8, with larger, square windows in place of the circular cabin windows of the military version, is in service with Aeroflot for transport and air ambulance duties, and is operated by this airline in support of Soviet activities in the Antarctic. Standard Mi-8s are used there for ice patrol and reconnaissance, for rescue operations, and for carrying supplies and equipment to Vostok Station, near the South Pole. Details of an official evaluation of the aircraft for heavy-lift agricultural duties were given in the 1985-86 and previous editions of *Jane's*. Aeroflot Mi-8s are available as a military reserve, with provision for carrying strap-on weapons and operational equipment.

The original prototype (NATO **Hip-A**) had a single 2,013 kW (2,700 shp) Soloviev turboshaft engine and four-blade main rotor. When fitted with the five-blade rotor that became standard on subsequent aircraft, it was redesignated **Hip-B**. The second prototype, which flew for the first time on 17 September 1962, introduced the now-standard Isotov twin-turbine power plant and became **Hip-C** to NATO in both civil and military forms.

There are three civil transport versions, as follows:

Mi-8. Passenger version, with standard seating for 28-32 persons in main cabin.

Mi-8T. General utility version, equipped normally to carry internal or external freight, but able to accommodate 24 tip-up passenger seats along the cabin walls.

Mi-8 Salon. De luxe version. Main cabin is furnished normally for eleven passengers, with an eight-place couch facing inward on the port side, and two chairs and a swivelling seat on the starboard side. There is a table on the starboard side. An air-to-ground radio telephone and removable ventilation fans are standard equipment. Forward of the main cabin is a compartment for a hostess, with buffet and crew wardrobe. Aft of the main cabin are a toilet (port) and passenger wardrobe (starboard), to each side of the entrance. An alternative nine-passenger layout is available. The Mi-8 Salon has a max T-O weight of 10,400 kg (22,928 lb) and range of 205 nm (380 km; 236 miles) with 30 min fuel reserve. In other respects it is similar to the standard Mi-8.

Military versions are identified by the following NATO reporting names:

Hip-C. Basic assault transport. Twin-rack for stores on each side of cabin, able to carry total of 128 × 57 mm rockets in four packs, or other weapons.

Hip-D. For airborne communications role. Generally similar to 'Hip-C' but with canisters of rectangular section on outer stores racks and added antennae.

Hip-E. Standard equipment of Soviet army support

Mil Mi-6 heavy general purpose helicopter (two Soloviev D-25V turboshaft engines) *(Denis Hughes)*

'Hip-D' has additional antennae as well as the canisters to which reference is made in the accompanying copy. It has an airborne communications role

'Hip-K' communications jamming variant of the Mi-8

forces. One flexibly mounted 12·7 mm machine-gun in nose. Triple stores rack on each side of cabin, able to carry up to 192 rockets in six suspended packs, plus four 'Swatter' homing anti-tank missiles on rails above racks.

Hip-F. Export counterpart of 'Hip-E'. Missile armament changed to six 'Saggers'.

Hip-G. Airborne communications version with rearward inclined antennae projecting from rear of cabin and from undersurface of tailboom, aft of box for Doppler radar.

Hip-H. See separate entry on Mi-17. Some Mi-8s being updated to this standard.

Hip-J. Additional small boxes on sides of fuselage, fore and aft of main landing gear legs, identify this ECM version.

Hip-K. Communications jamming ECM version with large antenna array on each side of cabin, of the kind seen previously on the Mi-4 ('Hound-C'). No Doppler radar box under tailboom.

TYPE: Twin-engined transport helicopter.

ROTOR SYSTEM: Five-blade main rotor and three-blade tail rotor. Transmission comprises a type VR-8 two-stage planetary main reduction gearbox giving main rotor shaft/engine rpm ratio of 0·016 : 1, intermediate and tail gearboxes, main rotor brake and drives off the main gearbox for the tail rotor, fan, AC generator, hydraulic pumps and tachometer generators. Main rotor shaft inclined forward at 4° 30′ from vertical. All-metal main rotor blades of basic NACA 230 section; solidity 0·0777. Each main blade is made up of an extruded light alloy spar carrying the blade root fitting, 21 trailing-edge pockets and the blade tip. Pockets are honeycomb filled. Main rotor blades are fitted with balance tabs, embody a spar failure warning system, and are interchangeable. Their drag and flapping hinges are a few inches apart, and they are carried on a machined spider. Control system utilises irreversible hydraulic boosters. Main rotor collective pitch control is interlocked to throttle controls. All-metal tail rotor blades, each made up of a spar and honeycomb filled trailing-edge. Automatically controlled electro-thermal de-icing system on all blades. In an emergency, the rotor blades of the Mi-8 and intermediate and tail gearboxes are interchangeable with those of the piston-engined Mi-4, although this prevents use of the de-icing system.

FUSELAGE: Conventional all-metal semi-monocoque structure of pod and boom type.

TAIL UNIT: Tail rotor support acts as small vertical stabiliser. Horizontal stabiliser near end of tailboom.

LANDING GEAR: Non-retractable tricycle type, with steerable twin-wheel nose unit, which is locked in flight, and single wheel on each main unit. All units embody oleo-pneumatic (gas) shock absorbers. Mainwheel tyres size 865 × 280; nosewheel tyres size 595 × 185. Pneumatic brakes on mainwheels. Pneumatic system can also recharge tyres in the field, using air stored in main landing gear struts. Optional mainwheel fairings.

POWER PLANT: Two 1,267 kW (1,700 shp) Isotov TV2-117A turboshaft engines. Main rotor speed governed automatically, with manual override. Single flexible internal fuel tank, capacity 445 litres (98 Imp gallons; 117·5 US gallons), and two external tanks, one each side of cabin, with capacity of 745 litres (164 Imp gallons; 197 US gallons) in the port tank and 680 litres (149·5 Imp gallons; 179·5 US gallons) in the starboard tank. Total standard fuel capacity 1,870 litres (411·5 Imp gallons; 494 US gallons). Provision for carrying one or two additional ferry tanks in cabin, raising max total capacity to 3,700 litres (814 Imp gallons; 977 US gallons). Fairing over starboard external tank houses optional cabin air-conditioning equipment at front. Engine cowling side panels form maintenance platforms when open, with access via hatch on flight deck. Engine air intake de-icing standard. Total oil capacity 60 kg (132 lb).

ACCOMMODATION: Two pilots side by side on flight deck, with provision for a flight engineer's station. Windscreen de-icing standard. Basic passenger version is furnished with 28 four-abreast track mounted tip-up seats at a pitch of 72-75 cm (28-29·5 in), with a centre aisle 32 cm (12·5 in) wide, a wardrobe and baggage compartment; or 32 seats without wardrobe. Seats and bulkheads of basic version are quickly removable for cargo carrying. Mi-8T has cargo tiedown rings in floor, a winch of 200 kg (440 lb) capacity and pulley block system to facilitate the loading of heavy freight, an external cargo sling system (capacity 3,000 kg; 6,614 lb), and 24 tip-up seats along the side walls

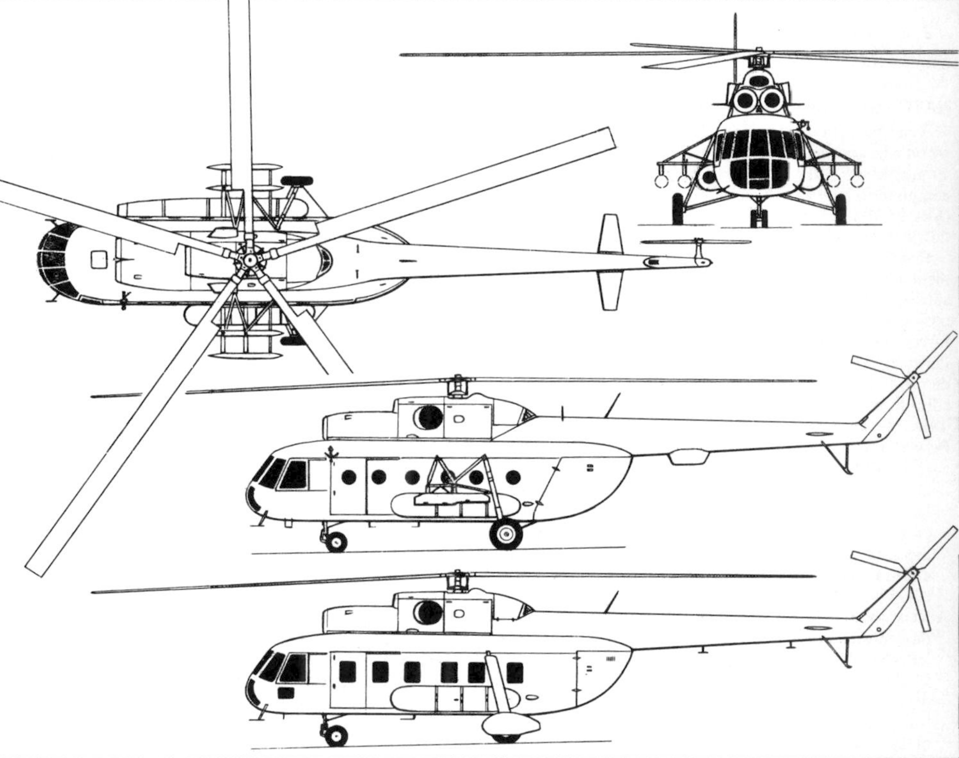

'Hip-C' military version of Mil Mi-8 twin-turbine helicopter, with additional side view (bottom) of commercial version *(Pilot Press)*

Mil Mi-8 ('Hip-E') military helicopter. This differs from the commercial version in having circular cabin windows, an optional nose gun, and weapon carriers on outriggers

of the cabin. All versions can be converted for air ambulance duties, with accommodation for 12 stretchers and a tip-up seat for a medical attendant. The large windows on each side of the flight deck slide rearward. The sliding, jettisonable main passenger door is at the front of the cabin on the port side. An electrically operated rescue hoist (capacity 150 kg; 330 lb) can be installed at this doorway. The rear of the cabin is made up of clamshell freight loading doors, which are smaller on the commercial versions, with a downward hinged passenger airstair door inset centrally at the rear. Hook-on ramps are used for vehicle loading.

SYSTEMS: Standard heating system can be replaced by full air-conditioning system. Two independent hydraulic systems, each with own pump; operating pressure 44-64 bars (640-925 lb/sq in). DC electrical supply from two 27V 18kW starter/generators and six 28Ah storage batteries. AC supply for de-icing system and some radio equipment supplied by 208/115/36/7·5V 400Hz generator, with 36V three-phase standby system. Provision for oxygen system for crew and, in ambulance version, for patients. Freon fire extinguishing system in power plant bays and service fuel tank compartments, actuated automatically or manually. Two portable fire extinguishers for use in cabin.

AVIONICS AND EQUIPMENT: Standard equipment includes a type R-842 HF transceiver with frequency range of 2 to 8MHz and range of up to 540 nm (1,000 km; 620 miles), type R-860 VHF transceiver operating on 118 to 135·9MHz over ranges of up to 54 nm (100 km; 62 miles), intercom, radio telephone, type ARK-9 automatic radio compass, type RV-3 radio altimeter with 'dangerous height' warning, and four-axis autopilot to give yaw, roll and pitch stabilisation under any flight conditions, stabilisation of altitude in level flight or hover, and stabilisation of pre-set flying speed, navigation equipment and instrumentation for all-weather flying by day and night, including two gyro horizons, two airspeed indicators, two main rotor speed indicators, turn indicator, two altimeters, two rate of climb indicators, magnetic compass, radio altimeter, radio compass and astrocompass for Polar flying. Doppler radar in box under forward part of tailboom. Military versions can be fitted with infra-red suppressors and infra-red decoy dispensers.

ARMAMENT: See individual model descriptions of military versions.

DIMENSIONS, EXTERNAL:
- Main rotor diameter: 21·29 m (69 ft 10¼ in)
- Tail rotor diameter: 3·91 m (12 ft 9⅞ in)
- Distance between rotor centres: 12·65 m (41 ft 6 in)
- Length overall, rotors turning: 25·24 m (82 ft 9¾ in)
- Length of fuselage, excl tail rotor: 18·17 m (59 ft 7⅜ in)
- Width of fuselage: 2·50 m (8 ft 2½ in)
- Height overall: 5·65 m (18 ft 6½ in)
- Wheel track: 4·50 m (14 ft 9 in)
- Wheelbase: 4·26 m (13 ft 11¾ in)
- Fwd passenger door: Height: 1·41 m (4 ft 7¼ in)
  - Width: 0·82 m (2 ft 8¼ in)
- Rear passenger door: Height: 1·70 m (5 ft 7 in)
  - Width: 0·84 m (2 ft 9 in)
- Rear cargo door: Height: 1·82 m (5 ft 11½ in)
  - Width: 2·34 m (7 ft 8¼ in)

DIMENSIONS, INTERNAL:
- Passenger cabin: Length: 6·36 m (20 ft 10¼ in)
  - Width: 2·34 m (7 ft 8¼ in)
  - Height: 1·80 m (5 ft 10¾ in)
- Cargo hold (freighter):
  - Length at floor: 5·34 m (17 ft 6¼ in)
  - Width: 2·34 m (7 ft 8¼ in)
  - Height: 1·80 m (5 ft 10¾ in)
  - Volume: approx 23 m³ (812 cu ft)

AREA:
- Main rotor disc: 356 m² (3,832 sq ft)

WEIGHTS:
- Weight empty:
  - civil passenger version: 6,799 kg (14,990 lb)
  - civil cargo version: 6,624 kg (14,603 lb)
  - military versions (typical): 7,260 kg (16,007 lb)
- Max payload: internal: 4,000 kg (8,820 lb)
  - external: 3,000 kg (6,614 lb)
- Fuel: standard tanks: 1,450 kg (3,197 lb)
  - with 2 auxiliary tanks: 2,870 kg (6,327 lb)
- Normal T-O weight: 11,100 kg (24,470 lb)
- T-O weight with 28 passengers, each with 15 kg (33 lb) of baggage: 11,570 kg (25,508 lb)
- T-O weight with 2,500 kg (5,510 lb) of slung cargo: 11,428 kg (25,195 lb)
- Max T-O weight for VTO: 12,000 kg (26,455 lb)

PERFORMANCE:
- Max level speed at 1,000 m (3,280 ft):
  - normal AUW: 140 knots (260 km/h; 161 mph)
- Max level speed at S/L:
  - normal AUW: 135 knots (250 km/h; 155 mph)
  - max AUW: 124 knots (230 km/h; 142 mph)
  - with 2,500 kg (5,510 lb) of slung cargo: 97 knots (180 km/h; 112 mph)
- Max cruising speed:
  - normal AUW: 122 knots (225 km/h; 140 mph)
  - max AUW: 97 knots (180 km/h; 112 mph)

'Hip-J' ECM variant of the Mi-8

- Service ceiling: 4,500 m (14,760 ft)
- Hovering ceiling at normal AUW:
  - IGE: 1,900 m (6,235 ft)
  - OGE: 800 m (2,625 ft)
- Ranges:
  - cargo version at 1,000 m (3,280 ft), with standard fuel, 5% reserves:
    - normal AUW: 251 nm (465 km; 289 miles)
    - max AUW: 240 nm (445 km; 276 miles)
  - with 28 passengers at 1,000 m (3,280 ft), with 20 min fuel reserves: 270 nm (500 km; 311 miles)
  - ferry range of cargo version, with auxiliary fuel, 5% reserves: 647 nm (1,200 km; 745 miles)

MIL Mi-10 and Mi-10K

NATO reporting name: Harke

The original **Mi-10** (V-10) flying crane development of the Mi-6 was demonstrated at the 1961 Soviet Aviation Day display at Tushino, having flown for the first time in the previous year. Above the line of the cabin windows the two helicopters were almost identical, but the depth of the fuselage was reduced considerably on the Mi-10, and the tailboom was deepened so that the flattened undersurface ran unbroken to the tail. The Mi-10 also lacked the fixed wings of the Mi-6, and was fitted with a tall long-stroke quadricycle landing gear, with wheel track exceeding 6·0 m (19 ft 8 in) and clearance under the fuselage of 3·75 m (12 ft 3½ in) with the aircraft fully loaded. This enabled the Mi-10 to taxi over a load it was to carry and to accommodate loads as bulky as a prefabricated building.

A developed version of this flying crane, known as the **Mi-10K**, was displayed in public for the first time, in Moscow, on 26 March 1966. It embodied a number of important design changes, most apparent of which were a reduction in the height of the landing gear and a more slender tail rotor support structure.

The Mi-10K can be operated by a crew of only two pilots. This is made possible by provision of an additional cockpit gondola under the front fuselage, with full flying controls and a rearward facing seat. By occupying this seat, one of the pilots can control the aircraft in hovering flight and, at the same time, have an unrestricted view of cargo loading, unloading and hoisting, which are also under his control.

In the Mi-10K, the maximum slung payload was initially 11,000 kg (24,250 lb) but was expected to be increased to 14,000 kg (30,865 lb) by using Soloviev D-25VF turboshaft engines, uprated to 6,500 shp each.

A detailed description of the original Mi-10 can be found in the 1982-83 and earlier editions of *Jane's*. A total of about 55 of both versions had been delivered by 1977, when production was resumed briefly, at a modest rate, after a six-year break. Most production helicopters are thought to be Mi-10Ks, to which the following data apply. A more extensive description can be found in the 1983-84 and previous editions of *Jane's*.

TYPE: Heavy flying-crane helicopter.

POWER PLANT: Two 4,101 kW (5,500 shp) Soloviev D-25V turboshaft engines in early production aircraft, mounted side by side above cabin, forward of main rotor driveshaft. Fuel capacity, in standard internal and two external tanks, on sides of cabin, 9,000 litres (1,980 Imp gallons; 2,377 US gallons). Provision for ferry tanks in cabin.

ACCOMMODATION: Two pilots on flight deck, which has bulged side windows to provide an improved downward view. Flight deck is heated and ventilated and has provision for oxygen equipment. Additional cockpit gondola under front fuselage (see introductory notes). Crew door is immediately aft of flight deck on port side. Main cabin can be used for freight and/or passengers, 28 tip-up seats being installed along the side walls. Freight is loaded into this cabin through a door on the starboard side, aft of the rear landing gear struts, with the aid of a boom and 200 kg (440 lb) capacity electric winch. External sling gear standard, with hatch in the cabin floor, directly beneath main rotor shaft.

DIMENSIONS, EXTERNAL:
- Main rotor diameter: 35·00 m (114 ft 10 in)
- Tail rotor diameter: 6·30 m (20 ft 8 in)
- Length overall, rotors turning: 41·89 m (137 ft 5½ in)
- Length of fuselage: 32·86 m (107 ft 9¾ in)
- Height overall: 7·80 m (25 ft 7 in)
- Wheel track (c/l of shock struts): 5·00 m (16 ft 4¾ in)
- Wheelbase: 8·74 m (28 ft 8 in)
- Freight loading door: Height: 1·56 m (5 ft 1½ in)
  - Width: 1·26 m (4 ft 1½ in)
  - Height to sill: 1·82 m (5 ft 11½ in)
- Cabin floor hatch: Diameter: 1·00 m (3 ft 3¼ in)

DIMENSIONS, INTERNAL:
- Cabin: Length: 14·04 m (46 ft 0¾ in)
  - Width: 2·50 m (8 ft 2½ in)

Mil Mi-10K preparing to lift a 10-tonne sheet steel drum to the top of a tower at the Sinarski pipe works in Kamensk-Uralskii *(Tass)*

Height 1·68 m (5 ft 6 in)
Volume approx 60 m³ (2,120 cu ft)
WEIGHTS:
Weight empty 24,680 kg (54,410 lb)
Max fuel load with ferry tanks in cabin 8,670 kg (19,114 lb)
Max T-O weight with slung cargo 38,000 kg (83,775 lb)
PERFORMANCE:
Cruising speed, empty 135 knots (250 km/h; 155 mph)
Max cruising speed with slung load 109 knots (202 km/h; 125 mph)
Service ceiling 3,000 m (9,850 ft)
Ferry range with auxiliary fuel 428 nm (795 km; 494 miles)

MIL Mi-14 (V-14)

NATO reporting name: Haze

The Mi-14 shore-based amphibious helicopter flew for the first time in 1973 and subsequently entered service with the Soviet Navy in anti-submarine form, as a replacement for the Mi-4. Clearly derived from the Mi-8, it is known to NATO as 'Haze'.

Comparison of photographs of this aircraft and the Mi-8 shows that the Mi-14 has shorter engine nacelles, with the intakes positioned above the mid-point of the sliding cabin door. Such nacelles, found also on the Mi-24 'Hind' and Mi-17, house Isotov TV3-117 turboshaft engines in place of the lower rated TV2s of the Mi-8. Overall dimensions and dynamic components of the Mi-14 are generally similar to those of the Mi-8, except that the tail rotor is on the port side of the vertical stabiliser. New features to suit it for its role include a boat hull planing bottom on the fuselage, a sponson on each side at the rear, and a small float under the tailboom, to confer a degree of amphibious capability. The fully retractable landing gear comprises two single-wheel nose units and two twin-wheel main units. There is a Doppler radar box under the forward part of the tailboom. Operational anti-submarine equipment can be seen to include a large undernose radome, a retractable sonar unit housed in the starboard rear of the planing bottom, forward of what appear to be two sonobuoy or signal flare chutes, and a towed magnetic anomaly detection (MAD) 'bird' stowed against the rear of the fuselage pod. Weapons include torpedoes and depth charges, carried in an enclosed bay in the bottom of the hull.

More than 100 Mi-14s are currently operated by the Soviet Naval Air Force. Two versions may be identified by NATO reporting names, as follows:

Haze-A. Basic ASW version, with crew of four or five, as described above. About 100 operational in 1986.

Haze-B. Mine countermeasures version, identified by fuselage strake and pod on starboard side of cabin, and deletion of MAD. Aircraft illustrated has also a second equipment box under the centre of the tailboom. About 10 in service with Soviet Navy.

Three Mi-14s have been exported to Bulgaria, four to Cuba, twelve to Libya, at least four to Poland, six to Romania and eight to the German Democratic Republic. Production was continuing in 1986.

DIMENSIONS, EXTERNAL:
Main rotor diameter 21·29 m (69 ft 10¼ in)
Length overall, rotors turning 25·30 m (83 ft 0 in)
Height overall 6·90 m (22 ft 7¾ in)
WEIGHT:
Max T-O weight 13,000 kg (28,660 lb)
PERFORMANCE:
Max level speed 124 knots (230 km/h; 143 mph)
Max cruising speed 108 knots (200 km/h; 124 mph)
Range with max fuel 500 nm (925 km; 575 miles)

MIL Mi-17

NATO reporting name: Hip-H

First displayed in public at the 1981 Paris Air Show, the Mi-17 combines the airframe of the Mi-8 with the uprated power plant of the Mi-14. The example exhibited at Le Bourget (SSSR-17718) had flown from Moscow to Paris, in short stages, in company with an Mi-26. Production had already started, and the basic civil and military version is known to NATO as 'Hip-H'. Many are operational side by side with Mi-8s in the Soviet armed forces, with the same armament options as the older aircraft. Export deliveries include 16 to Cuba in 1983, and others subsequently to India and Peru. Mi-8s can be updated to Mi-17 standard.

The general description of the Mi-8 applies also to the Mi-17, except that the tail rotor is on the port side of the vertical stabiliser (as on the Mi-14). Externally, the new power plant can be identified by the shorter nacelles, the air intakes extending forward only to the mid-point of the door on the port side at the front of the cabin. Also new is the small orifice on each side forward of the jetpipe. Take-off rating of each of the two Isotov TV3-117MT turboshafts is 1,417 kW (1,900 shp), which offers a considerable improvement in performance compared with the Mi-8. Correct rotor speed is maintained automatically by a system which also synchronises the output of the two engines. Loss of power by one engine is offset automatically by increasing the output of the other. Should one engine stop, the output of the other is increased to a contingency rating of 1,640 kW (2,200 shp), enabling the flight to continue. An APU is carried to start the turboshafts pneumatically. If required, the engine air

Mil Mi-14 anti-submarine helicopter ('Haze-A') with weapons bay doors open and MAD 'bird' under tow

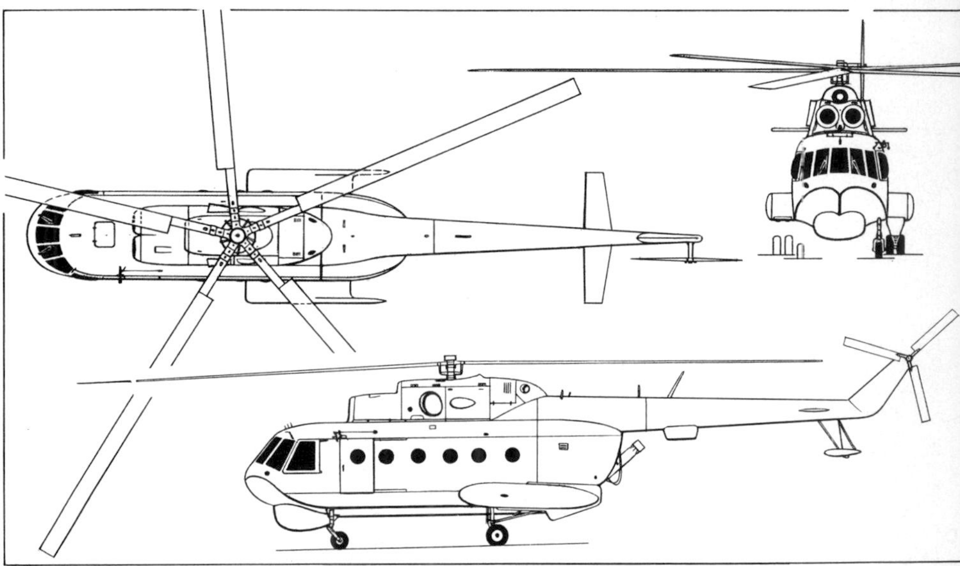
Mil Mi-14 (V-14) ASW helicopter (NATO 'Haze-A') *(Pilot Press)*

Mil Mi-14 ('Haze-B') twin-turboshaft mine countermeasures helicopter

intakes can be fitted with deflectors to prevent the ingestion of sand, dust or foreign objects at unprepared landing sites.

Cabin configuration and payloads are unchanged by comparison with the Mi-8; but the civilian Mi-17 is described by Aviaexport as essentially a cargo carrying helicopter, with secondary passenger transport role.

DIMENSIONS, EXTERNAL AND INTERNAL:
As for Mi-8, except:
Distance between rotor centres 12·661 m (41 ft 6½ in)
Length overall, rotors turning 25·352 m (83 ft 2 in)
Length of fuselage, excl tail rotor 18·424 m (60 ft 5⅜ in)
Height to top of main rotor head 4·755 m (15 ft 7¼ in)
Wheel track 4·510 m (14 ft 9½ in)
Wheelbase 4·281 m (14 ft 0½ in)
WEIGHTS:
Weight empty, equipped 7,100 kg (15,653 lb)

Max payload: internal 4,000 kg (8,820 lb)
external, on sling 3,000 kg (6,614 lb)
Normal T-O weight 11,100 kg (24,470 lb)
Max T-O weight 13,000 kg (28,660 lb)

PERFORMANCE (A at normal T-O weight; B at max T-O weight):
Max level speed: B 135 knots (250 km/h; 155 mph)
Max cruising speed: B 129 knots (240 km/h; 149 mph)
Service ceiling: A 5,000 m (16,400 ft)
B 3,600 m (11,800 ft)
Hovering ceiling OGE: A 1,760 m (5,775 ft)
Range with max standard fuel, 5% reserves:
A 267 nm (495 km; 307 miles)
B 251 nm (465 km; 289 miles)
Range with auxiliary fuel:
A 513 nm (950 km; 590 miles)

MIL Mi-24 (and A-10)

NATO reporting name: Hind

This assault helicopter was known to exist for two years before photographs became available to the technical press in 1974. The two versions shown in those first photographs (known to NATO as 'Hind-A and B') each carried a crew of three (with pilot and co-pilot side by side) and were designed to deliver a squad of eight combat-equipped troops into a battle area. They had attachments under their auxiliary wings for a variety of ordnance with which to clear a path past any tanks, anti-aircraft guns or other obstructions encountered on the way, and to keep down the heads of enemy troops in the drop zone.

At least two units of approximate squadron strength were based at Parchim and Stendal, northwest and west of Berlin, near the border with West Germany, by the Spring of 1974. Experience gained in training exercises soon led to a major change in tactics. Today, the Mi-24 is regarded as not only an effective anti-tank weapon, but capable itself of functioning as a high-speed nap-of-the-earth 'tank', and of destroying opposing helicopters in air-to-air combat. Other duties include escort of troop carrying Mi-8/17s and ground attack.

To exploit the Mi-24's potential, the Mil bureau first increased performance by replacing the original Isotov TV2-117 turboshaft engines with more powerful TV3-117s, at the same time transferring the tail rotor from the starboard to the port side of the tail fin. The front fuselage was then redesigned to give priority to the gunship role, with a two-man crew of weapon operator and pilot in tandem individual cockpits, while retaining the original transport capability. To reduce vulnerability to ground fire, steel and titanium were substituted for aluminium in critical components, and glassfibre skinned rotor blades replaced the original metal blade pocket design. The gunship (beginning with the version known to NATO as 'Hind-D') then superseded the original versions in production.

Deliveries of all models are known to exceed 2,300, from plants in Arsenyev and Rostov, with production continuing at a rate of more than 15 a month. At Soviet army level, there are some 20 helicopter attack regiments, each with up to 60 Mi-8s and Mi-24s. At division level, helicopter detachments are expanding to squadrons. Other operators include the Warsaw Pact air forces of Bulgaria, Czechoslovakia, East Germany, Hungary and Poland. Export deliveries, mostly of the gunship version, have been made to Afghanistan (at least 30), Algeria (37, including 'Hind-As'), Angola (12), Cuba (18), India (initial batch of 12), Iraq (41), Libya (26), Nicaragua (12), Viet-Nam (30) and South Yemen (15). Some of these are designated **Mi-25** (see separate entry). Many Mi-24s have been operated by Soviet forces in Afghanistan since December 1979, often in partnership with Sukhoi Su-25 fixed-wing ground attack aircraft.

Except for the crew accommodation, the basic airframe, power plant and transmission system appear to be common to all current versions of the Mi-24, with differences in armament, operational equipment and tail rotor location. Major variants of which details may be published are known by the following NATO reporting names:

Hind-A. Armed assault helicopter, with large enclosed flight deck for crew of three, comprising pilot, co-pilot/gunner and ground engineer, and places for up to eight fully equipped troops in main cabin. Access to flight deck via large rearward sliding blistered transparent panel which forms the aft flight deck window on the port side, and a large upward hinged window forward of this. Auxiliary wings, with considerable anhedral, carry total of four underwing pylons for UB-32 rocket pods, special bombs, or other stores, and rails for four AT-2 (NATO 'Swatter') anti-tank missiles under endplate pylons at wingtips. One 12·7 mm single-barrel DShK machine-gun in nose, slaved to undernose sighting system. Camera at top of port inner underwing pylon. Anti-torque rotor, originally on starboard side of offset tail pylon, repositioned to port side when original TV2-117 engines were replaced by TV3-117s on later and converted aircraft.

Hind-B. Similar to 'Hind-A' except that auxiliary wings have neither anhedral nor dihedral, and carry only the two inboard weapon stations on each side. This version preceded 'Hind-A' but was not built in large numbers.

Hind-C. Training version. Generally similar to late model 'Hind-A' but without nose gun and undernose blister fairing, and no missile rails at wingtips.

Mil Mi-17 ('Hip-H), a development of the Mi-8 with uprated engines *(Air Portraits)*

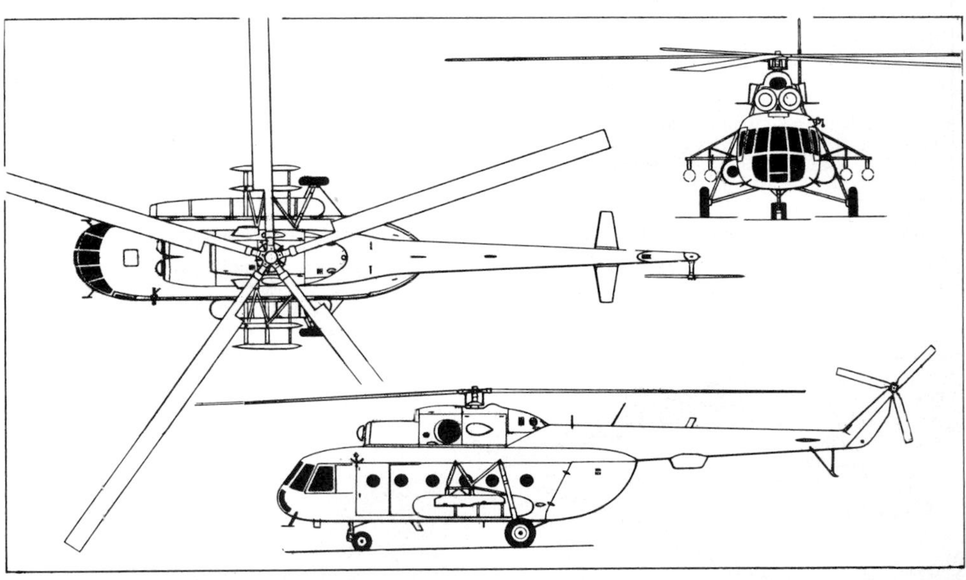

Mi-17 military general purpose helicopter, with external stores carriers *(Pilot Press)*

Hind-D. Basically similar to late model 'Hind-A', with TV3-117 engines and tail rotor on port side, but with completely new and heavily armoured accommodation for flight crew of two forward of the engine inlets and above the fuselage floor for primary gunship role. Weapon operator and pilot in tandem. Transport capability retained. Undernose Gatling type 12·7 mm machine-gun provides air-to-air as well as air-to-surface capability. Extended nosewheel leg to increase ground clearance of sensor pack; nosewheels semi-exposed when retracted. Weapons, equipment and other details listed in aircraft structural description.

Hind-E. As 'Hind-D', for Soviet armed forces, but with modified wingtip launchers and four underwing pylons for a total of up to twelve AT-6 radio guided tube-launched anti-tank missiles (NATO 'Spiral') in pairs, and enlarged undernose guidance pod on port side.

Hind-F. First shown in service with Soviet forces in photographs published in 1982. Generally similar to 'Hind-E' but with the nose gun turret replaced by a twin-barrel 30 mm cannon mounted inside a semi-cylindrical pack on the starboard side of the fuselage, and the bottom of the nose smoothly faired above and forward of sensors.

The helicopter known to the Soviet authorities as **A-10**, in which various FAI approved records in class E1 were set between 1975 and 1978 was an Mi-24. The records were listed in the 1985-86 *Jane's*. The women's speed records and general speed record over a 1,000 km closed circuit were unbeaten in mid-1986, but the remainder have been exceeded.

The following details apply to the 'Hind-D' gunship version:

TYPE: Gunship helicopter, with transport capability.

ROTOR SYSTEM: Dynamic components developed from those of Mi-8. Five-blade constant-chord main rotor, of NACA 230 blade section, and three-blade tail rotor; latter on port side of offset tail fin. Main rotor blades,

'Hind-A', first major production version of the Mil Mi-24 with original starboard side tail rotor

with titanium spars, glassfibre skin and honeycomb core, on forged and machined steel head, with conventional flapping, drag and pitch change articulation. Blade spars nitrogen pressurised for crack detection. Hydraulic lead/lag dampers. Balance tab and electric leading-edge de-icing on each blade. Main rotor brake standard. Aluminium alloy tail rotor blades.

FUSELAGE: Conventional all-metal semi-monocoque structure of pod and boom type. Forward portion, above shallow floor structure, embodies integral side armour.

AUXILIARY WINGS: All-metal cantilever shoulder wings of tapered planform, with about 16° anhedral and 20° incidence. No movable surfaces. Wings contribute about 25 per cent of total lift in cruising flight.

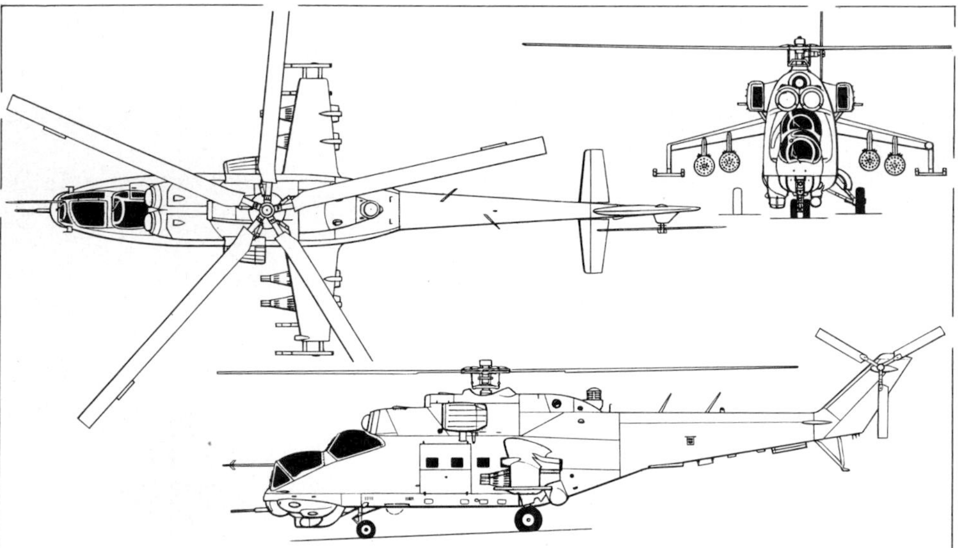

Mil Mi-24 gunship known to NATO as 'Hind-D', showing exhaust IR suppressor boxes *(Pilot Press)*

Artist's impression of chemical agents being released from underwing tanks on a Mil Mi-24 'Hind-D' *(US Department of Defense)*

Mil Mi-24 'Hind-F', with twin-barrel cannon in place of earlier nose turret

TAIL UNIT: Swept fin, offset at 3°, serves also as tail rotor pylon. Variable incidence horizontal stabiliser at base of fin.

LANDING GEAR: Tricycle type, with rearward retracting steerable twin-wheel nose unit, and single-wheel main units with oleo-pneumatic shock absorbers and low pressure tyres. Main units retract rearward and inward into the aft end of the fuselage pod, turning through 90° to stow almost vertically, discwise to the longitudinal axis of the fuselage, under prominent blister fairings. Tubular tripod skid assembly, with shock strut, protects tail rotor in a tail-down take-off or landing.

POWER PLANT: Two Isotov TV3-117 turboshaft engines, each with max rating of 1,640 kW (2,200 shp), mounted side by side above the cabin, with their output shafts driving rearward to the main rotor shaft through a combining gearbox. Main fuel tank in fuselage to rear of cabin, with bag tanks under cabin floor and provision for auxiliary tank in cabin. Optional deflectors and separators for foreign objects and dust in air intakes; and infra-red suppression exhaust mixer boxes over exhaust ducts. APU mounted transversely inside fairing aft of rotor head.

ACCOMMODATION: Pilot (at rear) and weapon operator on armoured seats in tandem cockpits under individual canopies. Front canopy hinged to open sideways, to starboard; footstep under starboard side of fuselage for access to pilot's rearward hinged door. Rear seat raised to give pilot an unobstructed forward view. Anti-fragment shield between cockpits. Main cabin can accommodate eight persons on folding seats, or four stretchers. At front of passenger cabin on each side is a door, divided horizontally into two sections which are hinged to open upward and downward respectively, with integral step on lower portion. Optically flat bulletproof glass windscreen, with wiper, for each crew member. Cockpits heated and ventilated.

SYSTEMS: Dual electrical system, with three generators. Stability augmentation system. Electro-thermal de-icing system for main and tail rotor blades. Cabin heating and ventilation systems.

AVIONICS AND EQUIPMENT: Include VHF and UHF radio, autopilot, radar altimeter, blind-flying instrumentation, and ADF navigation system with map display. Retractable landing/taxying light under nose. Navigation lights. Anti-collision light above tailboom. Air data sensor boom forward of top starboard corner of bulletproof windscreen at extreme nose. Undernose pods for electro-optics and missile guidance, including low light level TV. Gun camera on port wingtip. Many small antennae and blisters, including IFF (NATO 'Odd Rods') and radar warning antennae. Infra-red suppressor in 'flower pot' container above forward end of tailboom; decoy flare/chaff dispenser under tailboom forward of tailskid assembly.

ARMAMENT: One remotely controlled four-barrel Gatling type 12·7 mm machine-gun in undernose turret with range of movement in azimuth and elevation, and slaved to undernose sighting system. Rails for four AT-2 'Swatter' anti-tank missiles under endplate pylons at wingtips. Four underwing pylons for UV-32-57 rocket pods (each thirty-two S-5 type 57 mm rockets), up to 1,500 kg (3,300 lb) of chemical or conventional bombs, or other stores. Reflector gunsight for pilot. Provisions for firing AK-47 guns from cabin windows.

DIMENSIONS, EXTERNAL (estimated):
- Main rotor diameter — 17·00 m (55 ft 9 in)
- Tail rotor diameter — 3·90 m (12 ft 9½ in)
- Length overall:
  - excl rotors and guns — 17·50 m (57 ft 5 in)
  - rotors turning — 21·50 m (70 ft 6½ in)
- Height overall: rotors turning — 6·50 m (21 ft 4 in)

WEIGHTS (estimated):
- Weight empty — 8,400 kg (18,520 lb)
- Max external weapons — 1,500 kg (3,300 lb)
- Normal T-O weight — 11,000 kg (24,250 lb)

PERFORMANCE ('Hind-D'):
- Max level speed — 167 knots (310 km/h; 192 mph)
- Max cruising speed — 159 knots (295 km/h; 183 mph)
- Max rate of climb at S/L — 750 m (2,460 ft)/min
- Service ceiling — 4,500 m (14,750 ft)
- Hovering ceiling OGE — 2,200 m (7,200 ft)
- Combat radius with max military load — 86 nm (160 km; 99 miles)
- Range with max fuel — 405 nm (750 km; 466 miles)

MIL Mi-25

NATO reporting name: Hind

Some export variants of the Mi-24 ('Hind-E'), including those for India, are reportedly designated Mi-25. Such a change, presumably, signifies different equipment standards.

MIL Mi-26

NATO reporting name: Halo

Design of the Mi-26 heavy lift helicopter began in the early 1970s to meet the requirement for an aircraft of greater capability than the Mi-6 and Mi-10, for day and night operation in all weathers. Except for the four-engined twin-rotor Mi-12 (see 1977-78 *Jane's*), which did not progress beyond prototype testing, it is the heaviest helicopter yet

Mil Mi-26 heavy lift helicopter (two Lotarev D-136 turboshaft engines) *(Air Portraits)*

flown anywhere in the world. Its rotor diameter is smaller than that of the Mi-6 and Mi-10, but this is offset by the fact that the Mi-26 is the first helicopter to operate successfully with an eight-blade main rotor.

It has obvious military applications, with a payload and cargo hold very similar in size to those of a Lockheed C-130 Hercules. To meet also Soviet Ministry of Civil Aviation requirements, for operation in Siberia and northern swamp and tundra areas of the USSR, emphasis had to be placed on reliability, especially when operating into unprepared landing sites. According to Mr Marat Tishchenko, General Designer in charge of the Mil Bureau, this (plus, no doubt, the need to ensure torsional stiffness) explains why the main rotor blades have conventional steel spars.

Use of titanium for the rotor hub helped the Mil Bureau to meet the official requirement of an empty weight only 50 per cent of the aircraft's maximum permissible take-off weight. A further contribution to weight saving resulted from the decision to design the main gearbox in-house. The end product offers an impressive power to weight ratio, despite the need to absorb an unprecedented input from two Lotarev D-136 turboshaft engines. Nor does the Mi-26 need auxiliary wings, like the Mi-6, to achieve its required payload/range performance.

Representatives of the Mil Bureau claimed at the 1981 Paris Air Show that the Mi-26 had already undergone two years of flight development, and that D-136 engines had amassed more than 13,000 hours of running on the test-bench and in the air. The Mi-26 (SSSR-06141) exhibited at the Show was stated to be one of several prototypes or pre-production examples then flying. The Mi-26 began in-field evaluation, probably with a single air force development squadron, in early 1983 and was fully operational by 1985. The first export order, for ten, was placed by India, and two of these were delivered in June 1986.

During three days in February 1982, the Mi-26 set five world helicopter payload-to-height records, exceeding records established previously by the Sikorsky CH-54B Skycrane and Mil Mi-12. On 2 February, piloted by G. P. Karapetyan, it lifted a 10,000 kg payload to 6,400 m (20,997 ft). On 3 February, piloted by G. V. Alfeurov, it lifted a payload of 25,000 kg to 4,100 m (13,451 ft), and lifted a total mass of 56,768·8 kg (125,153·8 lb) to a height of 2,000 m. On 4 February, it lifted a payload of 15,000 kg to 5,600 m (18,373 ft), piloted by S. V. Petrov; and 20,000 kg to 4,600 m (15,092 ft), piloted by A. P. Kholoupov.

TYPE: Twin-turboshaft heavy transport helicopter.

ROTOR SYSTEM: Eight-blade main rotor, with flapping and drag hinges, droop stops and hydraulic drag dampers; five-blade tail rotor, mounted on starboard side of tail fin. Each main rotor blade consists of a one-piece tubular steel spar and 26 glassfibre aerofoil shape full chord pockets, Nomex-filled with ribs and stiffeners and non-removable titanium leading-edge abrasion strip. Blades have moderate twist, taper in thickness towards tip, and are attached to titanium hub of unconventional design. Ground adjustable tab on trailing-edge of each blade. Hydraulically powered cyclic and collective pitch controls actuated by small parallel jacks, with redundant autopilot and stability augmentation system inputs. Tail rotor blades made of glassfibre. Leading-edge of main and tail rotor blades heated electrically for anti-icing. Main rotor rpm 132.

ROTOR DRIVE: Conventional transmission. Tail rotor shaft runs inside roof of cabin. Main gearbox type VR-26, rated at 14,914 kW (20,000 hp), is fan cooled, with air intake above rear of engine cowlings.

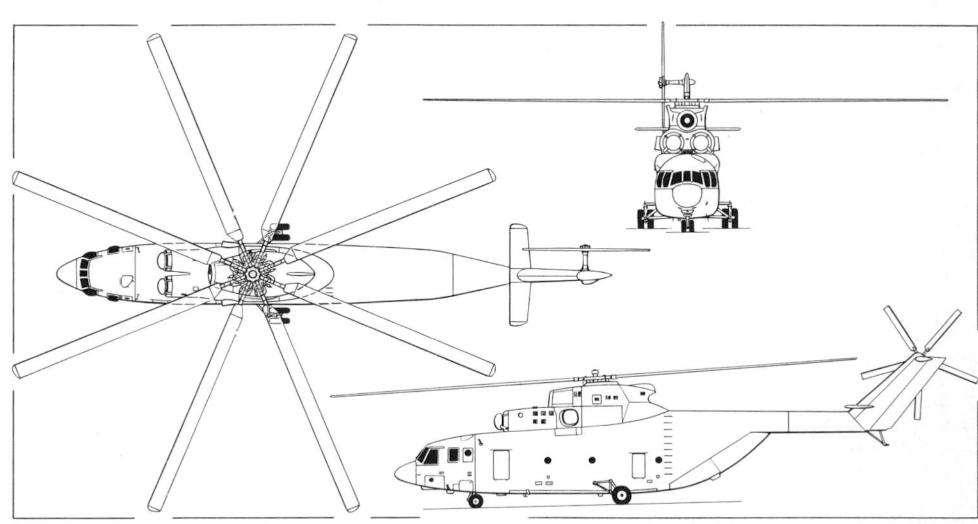

Mil Mi-26, first helicopter to operate successfully with an eight-blade main rotor *(Pilot Press)*

Unloading armoured vehicles from a military Mil Mi-26

FUSELAGE: Conventional all-metal riveted semi-monocoque structure of pod and boom type, with clamshell rear loading doors and ramp. Flattened undersurface to tailboom.

TAIL UNIT: Sweptback vertical stabiliser, carrying tail rotor, is offset to port. Ground adjustable variable incidence horizontal stabiliser mounted on leading-edge of vertical stabiliser, a short distance above the tailboom.

LANDING GEAR: Non-retractable tricycle type, with twin wheels on each unit. Mainwheel tyres size 1,120 × 450. Retractable tailskid at end of tailboom to permit unrestricted approach to rear cargo doors. Length of main legs can be adjusted hydraulically to facilitate loading through rear doors and to permit landing on varying surfaces. A device on the main gear indicates take-off weight to flight engineer at lift-off, on panel on shelf to rear of his seat.

POWER PLANT: Two 8,500 kW (11,400 shp) Lotarev D-136 free-turbine turboshaft engines, mounted side by side above cabin, forward of main rotor driveshaft. Air intakes designed to prevent foreign object ingestion, and provided with both electrical and bleed air anti-icing systems. Above and behind is a central oil cooler intake. System for synchronising the output of the engines and maintaining constant rotor rpm. If one engine fails, output of the other is increased to maximum automatically. Fuel in eight underfloor tanks, feeding into two header tanks above engines, which permit gravity feed for a period in emergencies. Two large panels on each side of main rotor mast fairing, aft of engine exhaust outlet, hinge downward as work platforms.

ACCOMMODATION: Crew of five, consisting of pilot (on port side) and co-pilot side by side, flight engineer behind pilot, navigator behind co-pilot on flight deck, and loadmaster in freight hold. Four-seat passenger compartment aft of flight deck. Loads that can be accommodated in hold include two airborne infantry combat vehicles. About 20 tip-up seats along each side wall of hold. Max military seating for about 85 combat equipped troops. Heated windscreen. Four large blistered side windows on flight deck. Forward pair swing open slightly outward and rearward. Downward hinged doors, with integral airstairs, at front of hold on port side, and on each side of hold aft of main landing gear units. Hold is loaded via a downward hinged lower door, with integral folding ramp, and two clamshell upper doors which form rear wall of hold when closed. Doors are opened and closed hydraulically, with backup handpump for emergency use. Two electric winches on overhead rails, each with capacity of 2,500 kg (5,511 lb), enable loads to be transported along cabin. Flight deck and hold fully air-conditioned.

SYSTEMS: Two hydraulic systems, operating pressure 210 kg/cm² (3,000 lb/sq in). (Much higher pressure than usual for Soviet helicopters, reflected by small size of jacks for rotor head controls.) APU under flight deck, with intake louvres (forming fuselage skin when closed) and exhaust on starboard side, supplies hydraulic, electrical and air-conditioning systems on ground. Only flight deck pressurised. Four-axis autostabilisation.

AVIONICS AND EQUIPMENT: All items necessary for day and night operations in all weathers are standard, including weather radar in the hinged (to starboard) nosecone, Doppler, map display, HSI, and automatic hover system. Attachment for sling loads in bottom of centre-fuselage. closed circuit TV cameras to observe slung payloads.

DIMENSIONS, EXTERNAL:

Main rotor diameter	32·00 m (105 ft 0 in)
Tail rotor diameter	7·60 m (24 ft 11¼ in)
Length overall, rotors turning	40·025 m (131 ft 3¾ in)
Length of fuselage, excl tail rotor	33·727 m (110 ft 8 in)
Height to top of rotor head	8·145 m (26 ft 8¾ in)
Width over mainwheels	8·15 m (26 ft 9 in)
Wheelbase	8·95 m (29 ft 4½ in)

DIMENSIONS, INTERNAL:

Freight hold:	
Length: ramp trailed	15·00 m (49 ft 2½ in)
excl ramp	12·00 m (39 ft 4¼ in)
Width	3·25 m (10 ft 8 in)
Height	2·95-3·17 m (9 ft 8 in to 10 ft 4¾ in)

WEIGHTS:

Weight empty	28,200 kg (62,170 lb)
Max payload, internal or external	20,000 kg (44,090 lb)
Normal T-O weight	49,500 kg (109,125 lb)
Max T-O weight	56,000 kg (123,450 lb)

PERFORMANCE:

Max level speed	159 knots (295 km/h; 183 mph)
Normal cruising speed	137 knots (255 km/h; 158 mph)
Service ceiling	4,600 m (15,100 ft)
Hovering ceiling OGE, ISA	1,800 m (5,900 ft)
Range with max internal fuel at max T-O weight, 5% reserves	432 nm (800 km; 497 miles)

MIL Mi-28

NATO reporting name: Havoc

The existence of this Soviet combat helicopter was confirmed in the 1984 edition of *Soviet Military Power*, published by the US Department of Defense. The 1985 edition contained the first detailed artist's impression of the Mi-28, which is reproduced in this entry, and the 1986 edition suggested that production might start during that year. Elimination of transport capability, by comparison with the Mi-24, should ensure much improved agility and survivability, as the result of a greatly reduced cross-section (almost certainly smaller than suggested by the DoD drawing). The following details should be regarded as provisional:

TYPE: Twin-engined combat helicopter.

ROTOR SYSTEM: Five-blade main rotor and three-blade tail rotor of new design. Tail rotor mounted on starboard side of tail fin, possibly at tip of small horizontal stabiliser.

WINGS: Cantilever mid-mounted wings of low aspect ratio, with sweptback leading-edge. No movable surfaces.

FUSELAGE: Conventional all-metal semi-monocoque structure, embodying integral armour around cockpit area.

TAIL UNIT: Sweptback fin with small horizontal stabiliser at tip.

LANDING GEAR: Non-retractable tailwheel type, with single wheel on each unit. Mainwheels carried on side Vs, embodying shock absorbers.

POWER PLANT: Two unidentified turboshaft engines, possibly related to TV3-117 engines of Mi-24, in pods mounted above each wing root. Upward deflected jetpipes. Deflectors for dust and foreign objects forward of air intakes.

ACCOMMODATION: Co-pilot/gunner in front cockpit; pilot behind, on elevated seat. Flat, non-glint transparencies. Glazed panels under nose, probably enclosing sensors such as low light level TV or laser designator and marked target seeker.

ARMAMENT AND OPERATIONAL EQUIPMENT: Heavy calibre gun in undernose turret. Pylon under each wing for external stores, including rocket packs. Wingtip pylons each capable of carrying two tube-launched missiles for air-to-air or air-to-ground use. Radar in small radome on nose. Infra-red suppressors and infra-red decoy dispensers fitted.

DIMENSIONS, EXTERNAL (estimated):

Main rotor diameter	17·00 m (55 ft 9 in)
Length overall, excl rotors	17·40 m (57 ft 1 in)

PERFORMANCE (estimated):

Max level speed	162 knots (300 km/h; 186 mph)
Combat radius	130 nm (240 km; 149 miles)

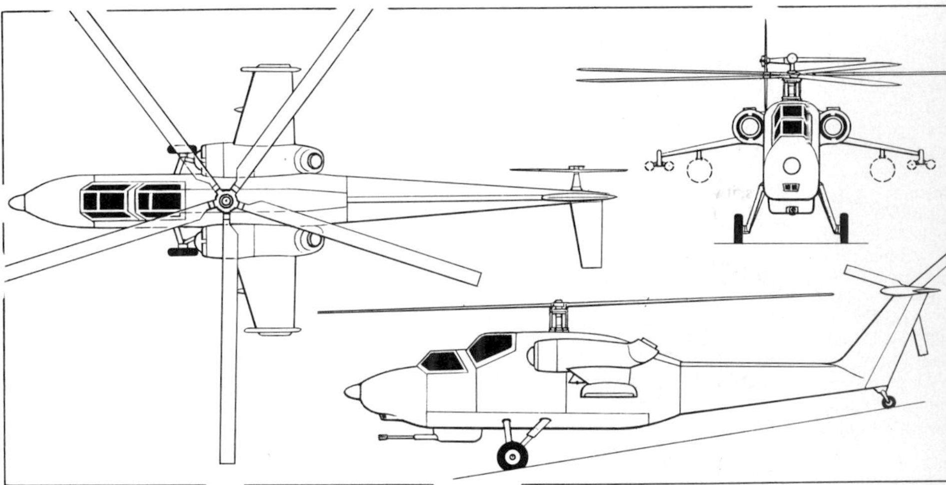

Mil Mi-28 combat helicopter (two turboshaft engines) *(Pilot Press, provisional)*

Artist's impression of Mil Mi-28 combat helicopters *(US Department of Defense)*

MYASISHCHEV

This design bureau was formed in 1951, under the leadership of Professor Vladimir Mikhailovich Myasishchev, who died on 14 October 1978, at the age of 76. Its first product was the four-jet M-4 bomber (known in the West by the reporting name of 'Bison') which remains in service as a strategic bomber, maritime reconnaissance aircraft and flight refuelling tanker.

Myasishchev M-4 ('Bison-B') maritime reconnaissance aircraft *(Royal Air Force)*

MYASISHCHEV M-4

NATO reporting name: Bison

Three major production versions of this four-jet aircraft were identified by NATO reporting names, as follows:

Bison-A. The Soviet Union's first operational four-jet strategic bomber, carrying free fall weapons only. Design began in 1951 and the prototype was displayed over Moscow on 1 May 1954. Comparable with early versions of Boeing B-52 Stratofortress, it was powered by four 85·3 kN (19,180 lb st) Mikulin AM-3D turbojets, buried in wing roots. Defensive armament of eight 23 mm NR-23 cannon in twin-gun turrets in tail, above fuselage forward of wing and under fuselage fore and aft of three weapons bays.

Bison-B. Maritime reconnaissance version, described in 1979-80 *Jane's*. Few remain.

Bison-C. Improved maritime reconnaissance version, described in 1979-80 *Jane's*. Few remain.

About 75 of these aircraft were available in 1986, as bombers for maritime and Eurasian missions and as probe-and-drogue flight refuelling tankers for the 'Backfire/Bear/Bison/Blinder' attack force. Pending replacement, the 'Bisons' were being phased out of service and placed in storage.

One M-4 has been adapted to carry on its back the large Soviet space shuttle orbiter vehicle. Most apparent change is replacement of the standard sweptback vertical tail surfaces by twin endplate fins and rudders of rectangular shape. In the Spring of 1986, preparations were under way for the first landing test of the orbiter after mid-air separation from the M-4 carrier.

DIMENSIONS, EXTERNAL ('Bison-A'):
- Wing span: 50·48 m (165 ft 7½ in)
- Length overall: 47·20 m (154 ft 10 in)
- Tailplane span: 15·00 m (49 ft 2½ in)

WEIGHT ('Bison-A'):
- Max T-O weight: 158,750 kg (350,000 lb)

PERFORMANCE ('Bison-A', estimated):
- Max level speed at 11,000 m (36,000 ft): 538 knots (998 km/h; 620 mph)
- Service ceiling: 13,700 m (45,000 ft)
- Max unrefuelled combat radius: 3,025 nm (5,600 km; 3,480 miles)
- Range at 450 knots (835 km/h; 520 mph) with more than 5,450 kg (12,000 lb) of bombs: 4,320 nm (8,000 km; 4,970 miles)

Artist's impression of M-4 ('Bison-C') adapted to carry the large Soviet space shuttle orbiter *(US Department of Defense)*

SUKHOI

CHIEF DESIGNER OF SUKHOI BUREAU: E. A. Ivanov

This design bureau is named after Pavel Osipovich Sukhoi, who headed it from 1953 until his death in September 1975. It remains one of the two primary Soviet centres for fighter and attack aircraft development.

SUKHOI Su-7B

NATO reporting names: Fitter-A and Moujik

The Su-7B single-seat ground attack fighter has been almost phased out of service in the Soviet air forces, but remains operational in the air forces of Afghanistan, Algeria, Czechoslovakia, Iraq, North Korea, Poland and Syria. Full details and illustrations can be found in the 1985-86 and previous editions of *Jane's*.

SUKHOI Su-17, Su-20 and Su-22

NATO reporting names: Fitter-C, D, E, F, G, H, J and K

The prototype of this variable geometry fighter series, designated S-22I or Su-7IG (Izmenyaemaya Geometriya; variable geometry), was an R & D aircraft first flown on 2 August 1966 and shown at the Soviet Aviation Day display at Domodedovo Airport, Moscow, in July 1967, after which it was allocated the NATO reporting name 'Fitter-B'. Only 4·2 m (13 ft 9 in) of each wing was pivoted, outboard of a very large fence. The remainder of the airframe was virtually identical with that of the earlier fixed-wing Su-7, although the inboard glove panels were deepened in section. An attachment for an external store was built into each wing fence, but the Lyulka AL-7 power plant was unchanged and there was no reason to expect 'Fitter-B' to form the basis of a production aircraft.

Discovery of two squadrons of 'improved Fitter-Bs' in service with the Soviet tactical air forces in 1972 came as a surprise, suggesting that even a small increase in range and endurance by comparison with the Su-7 was considered worthwhile. These aircraft still retained the AL-7 engine, had a Sirena 2 radar warning antenna on the fin tip and a parachute brake.

A more powerful AL-21F-3 engine and rearward hinged canopy were fitted to subsequent major production versions for the Soviet Air Forces, which were designated **Su-17** (S-32). Combined with the variable geometry wings, the new engine permitted a doubled external load to be lifted from strips little more than half as long as those needed by the Su-7, and to be carried about 30 per cent further. Added to new avionics, this made the variable geometry 'Fitters' so attractive that about 1,020 are deployed currently by Soviet tactical air forces, 65 more by Soviet Naval Aviation units assigned to anti-shipping strike and amphibious support roles in the Baltic Sea area, and a further Naval unit of indeterminate size in the Pacific theatre. All aircraft of this type in Soviet service are designated Su-17. Differences between the various versions are as follows:

Su-17 (Fitter-C). Basic single-seat attack aircraft for Soviet tactical air forces, with Lyulka AL-21F-3 turbojet and eight stores pylons. Manual wing sweep control. Additional wing fence on fixed centre-section each side. Curved dorsal fin between tail fin and dorsal spine fairing. Operational since 1971, in relatively small numbers. Serves also with Soviet Navy.

Su-17M (S-32M, Fitter-D). Generally similar to 'Fitter-C', but forward fuselage lengthened by about 0·25 m (10 in). Added undernose electronics pod for Doppler navigation radar. Laser rangefinder in intake centrebody.

Su-17UM (U-32, Fitter-E). Tandem two-seat trainer for Soviet Air Force. Generally similar to 'Fitter-D', without electronics pod, but entire fuselage forward of wing drooped slightly to improve pilot's view. Deepened dorsal spine fairing, almost certainly to provide additional fuel tankage. Port wingroot gun deleted.

Su-17 (Fitter-G). Two-seat trainer variant of 'Fitter-H', with combat capability. Deepened dorsal spine fairing and drooped front fuselage like 'Fitter-E'. Taller vertical tail surfaces. Shallow ventral fin (removable). Starboard gun only. Laser target seeker fitted in intake centrebody.

Su-17 (Fitter-H). Improved single-seater for Soviet air forces. Basically as 'Fitter-D', but with wide and deep dorsal fairing aft of canopy, like 'Fitter-E/G'. Doppler navigation radar fitted internally in deepened undersurface of nose. Taller fin like 'Fitter-G'. Removable ventral fin. Retains both wingroot guns. About 200 'Fitter-H/Ks' are equipped for tactical reconnaissance duties.

Su-17 (Fitter-K). Latest single-seat version for Soviet Air Forces, identified in 1984. Dorsal fin embodies small cooling air intake at front.

It was deduced for some years that certain export versions of the variable geometry 'Fitter' series had different engines from the Su-17 variants listed above. 'Fitter-C/D/E/G/H/K' operated by the Soviet Air Force and some other air forces have a rear fuselage of basically constant diameter and are powered by a Lyulka turbojet. Versions exported to Angola, Libya, Peru, Syria, Viet-Nam, and North and South Yemen were seen to have a more bulged rear fuselage, now known to house a Tumansky R-29BS-300 turbojet, as fitted in the MiG-27, with rearranged external air ducts, and a shorter plain metal shroud terminating the rear fuselage. This change of power plant, and/or variations in equipment standard, is covered by the following changes to the Soviet type designation:

Su-20 (Su-17MK, S-32MK, Fitter-C). Generally similar to Soviet Air Force 'Fitter-C', with Lyulka engine, but with reduced equipment standard. Supplied to Algeria, Czechoslovakia, Egypt, Iraq and Poland. Two former Egyptian aircraft were acquired by Federal German Luftwaffe for evaluation during 1985 by Erprobungsstelle 61 at Manching.

Su-22 (Fitter-F). Export counterpart of 'Fitter-D', with slightly modified undernose electronics pod. Tumansky R-29B turbojet, rated at 112·8 kN (25,350 lb st) with

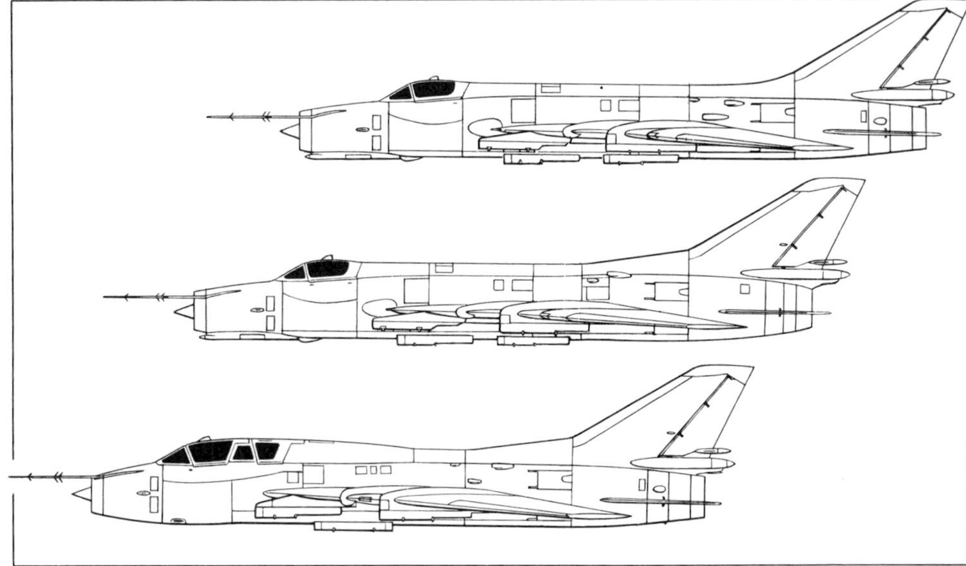

Top to bottom: The versions of the Su-17/20/22 series known to NATO as 'Fitter-D', 'Fitter-F' and 'Fitter-E' respectively. Tumansky powered versions can be identified by more bulged rear fuselage and single air intake by dorsal fin *(Pilot Press)*

afterburning, in increased diameter rear fuselage. Gun in each wingroot. Weapons include 'Atoll' air-to-air missiles. Aircraft supplied to Peru had Sirena 2 limited coverage radar warning receiver, virtually no navigation aids, and IFF incompatible with that nation's SA-3 (NATO 'Goa') surface-to-air missiles.

Su-22 (Fitter-G). Export counterpart of Su-17 'Fitter-G', with R-29B engine.

Su-22 (Fitter-J). Generally similar to 'Fitter-H' but with Tumansky engine. Internal fuel tankage 6,270 litres (1,379 Imp gallons; 1,656 US gallons). More angular dorsal fin. 'Atoll' air-to-air missiles. Supplied to Libya.

The following description applies to the Su-17 ('Fitter-C'):

TYPE: Single-seat ground attack fighter.

WINGS: Cantilever mid-wing monoplane, with wide span fixed centre-section and manually operated variable geometry outer panels, with min sweep angle of 28° and max sweep angle of approx 62°. Slight sweepback on trailing-edge of area-increasing centre-section flaps. Outboard of these flaps, centre-section trailing-edge is swept to align with trailing-edge of outer panels when they are fully swept. Full span leading-edge slats on movable panels. Trailing-edge of each movable panel made up of a slotted flap, operable only when the wings are spread, and a slotted aileron operable at all times. Large main fence on each side, at junction of fixed and movable panels, is square-cut at front and incorporates attachments for external stores. Shorter fence above centre-section on each side, inboard of main fence.

FUSELAGE: Conventional all-metal semi-monocoque structure of circular section. Large dorsal spine fairing along top of fuselage, from canopy to fin. Ram air intake in nose, with variable shock-cone centrebody. Four door type airbrakes, at top and bottom on each side of rear fuselage, forward of tailplane. Pitot on port side of nose; transducer to provide pitch and yaw data for fire control computer and antennae on starboard side.

TAIL UNIT: Cantilever all-metal structure, with sweepback on all surfaces. All-moving horizontal surfaces, with anti-flutter body projecting forward on each side near tip. Conventional rudder. No tabs.

LANDING GEAR: Retractable tricycle type, with single wheel on each unit. Nosewheel retracts forward, requiring blistered door to enclose it. Main units retract inward into centre-section. Container for twin brake-chutes between base of rudder and tailpipe.

POWER PLANT: One Lyulka AL-21F-3 turbojet engine, rated at 76·5 kN (17,200 lb st) dry and 110 kN (24,700 lb st) with afterburning. Fuel capacity increased to 4,550 litres (1,000 Imp gallons; 1,202 US gallons) by added tankage in dorsal spine fairing. Provision for carrying up to four 800 litre (176 Imp gallon; 211 US gallon) drop tanks on outboard wing pylons and under fuselage. When underfuselage tanks are carried, only the two inboard wing pylons may be used for ordnance, to a total weight of 1,000 kg (2,204 lb). Two solid propellant rocket units can be attached to rear fuselage to shorten T-O run.

ACCOMMODATION: Pilot only, on ejection seat, under rearward hinged transparent canopy. Rearview mirror above canopy.

AVIONICS AND EQUIPMENT: SRD-5M (NATO 'High Fix') I-band ranging radar in intake centrebody; ASP-5ND fire control system; Sirena 3 radar warning system providing 360° coverage, with antennae in slim cylindrical housing above brake-chute container and in each centre-section leading-edge, between fences; SRO-2M IFF; SOD-57M ATC/SIF, with transponder housing beneath brake-chute container; and RSIU-5/R-831 VHF/UHF.

ARMAMENT: Two 30 mm NR-30 guns, each with 70 rds, in wing root leading-edges. Total of eight weapon pylons (two tandem pairs under fuselage, one under each centre-section leading-edge, one under each main wing fence) for more than 3,175 kg (7,000 lb) of bombs, including nuclear weapons, rocket pods and guided missiles such as the air-to-surface AS-7 (NATO 'Kerry').

DIMENSIONS, EXTERNAL:

Wing span: fully spread	13·80 m (45 ft 3 in)
fully swept	10·00 m (32 ft 10 in)
Wing aspect ratio: fully spread	4·8
fully swept	2·7
Length overall, incl probes	18·75 m (61 ft 6¼ in)
Fuselage length	15·40 m (50 ft 6¼ in)
Height overall	5·00 m (16 ft 5 in)

AREAS (estimated):

Wings, gross: fully spread	40·0 m² (430·0 sq ft)
fully swept	37·0 m² (398·0 sq ft)

WEIGHTS (estimated):

Weight empty	10,000 kg (22,046 lb)
Max internal fuel	3,700 kg (8,157 lb)
T-O weight, 'clean'	14,000 kg (30,865 lb)
Max T-O weight	17,700 kg (39,020 lb)

PERFORMANCE (estimated for 'clean' aircraft, 60% internal fuel, except where indicated):

Max level speed: at height	Mach 2·09 (1,200 knots; 2,220 km/h; 1,380 mph)
at S/L	Mach 1·05 (693 knots; 1,285 km/h; 798 mph)
Touchdown speed	143 knots (265 km/h; 165 mph)
Max rate of climb at S/L	13,800 m (45,275 ft)/min
Service ceiling	18,000 m (59,050 ft)

Single-seat Su-17 ('Fitter-H') of Soviet Air Force, armed with underbelly rocket pods, 'Atoll' air-to-air missiles, and two AS-7 ('Kerry') air-to-surface missiles

A bulged rear fuselage and undernose electronics pod distinguish this Su-22 'Fitter-F' of the Libyan Arab Air Force *(US Navy)*

Sukhoi Su-17 ('Fitter-K') firing air-to-ground missiles

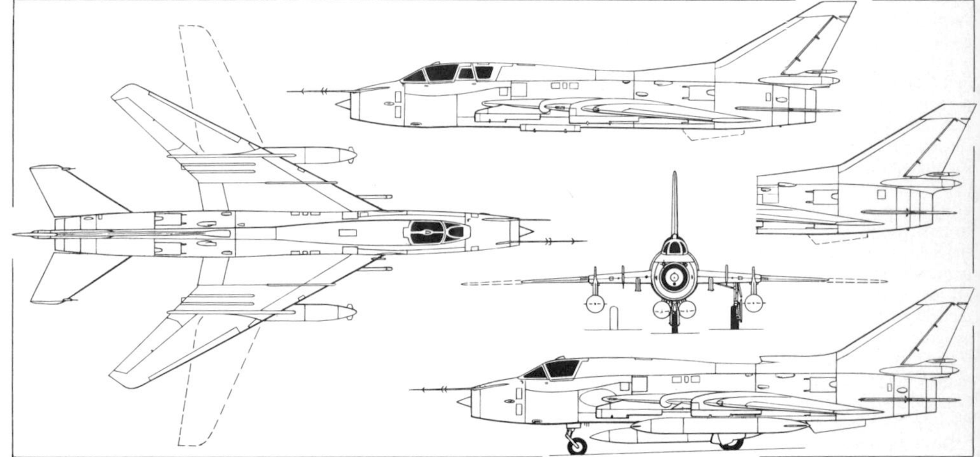

'Fitter-K', latest single-seat version of the Sukhoi Su-17 series, with added side elevation (top) of Su-17 'Fitter-G' and rear fuselage of Su-22 'Fitter-J' *(Pilot Press)*

T-O run at AUW of 17,000 kg (37,478 lb) 1,000 m (3,280 ft)
T-O to 15 m (50 ft) at AUW of 17,000 kg (37,478 lb) 1,400 m (4,600 ft)
Landing run 600 m (1,970 ft)
Combat radius with 2,000 kg (4,409 lb) external stores, incl fuel: hi-lo-hi 370 nm (685 km; 425 miles)
lo-lo-lo 240 nm (445 km; 275 miles)

SUKHOI Su-21

NATO reporting name: Flagon

Details of the initial versions of this twin-jet delta-wing interceptor, which were designated Su-15, can be found in the 1983-84 and previous editions of *Jane's*. The number of 'Flagons' in first-line home defence units is believed to have diminished to about 225, plus 340 in tactical units. Those remaining are of three variants, so different from early Su-15s that they are believed to be designated Su-21 in the USSR:

Flagon-E. Single-seat interceptor. Longer-span wings than those of earlier 'Flagon-A', with compound sweep. Tumansky R-13F-300 turbojets, each rated at 64·73 kN (14,550 lb st), and increased fuel capacity, giving increased speed and range. Uprated avionics (NATO 'Twin Scan' replacing 'Skip Spin' radar). Major production version, operational since second half of 1973.

Flagon-F. Last known production version. Ogival nose radome instead of conical type of earlier variants. Generally similar to 'Flagon-E', but with uprated engines.

Flagon-G. Two-seat training version of 'Flagon-F', with probable combat capability. Individual rearward hinged canopy over each seat. Periscope fitted above rear canopy for enhanced forward view.

The following details apply to 'Flagon-F':

TYPE: Single-seat twin-jet all-weather interceptor.

WINGS: Cantilever mid-wing monoplane. Basic wings are of simple delta form, similar to those of earlier Su-11, but with new and extended outer panels. Sweepback 60° on inner wings, 45° on outer panels. No dihedral or anhedral. All-metal structure. Single boundary layer fence above each wing at approx 70 per cent span. Large-chord flap extends from inboard end of aileron to fuselage on each side.

FUSELAGE: Cockpit section is basically circular with large ogival dielectric nosecone. Centre-fuselage is faired into rectangular section air intake ducts. Two door type airbrakes at top and bottom on each side of rear fuselage, forward of tailplane.

TAIL UNIT: Cantilever all-metal structure, with sweepback on all surfaces. All-moving tailplane, with anhedral, mounted slightly below mid position and fitted with anti-flutter bodies near tips. Conventional rudder. No trim tabs.

LANDING GEAR: Tricycle type, with single wheel on each main unit and twin nosewheels. Mainwheels retract inward into wings and intake ducts; nosewheels retract forward. Container for brake-chute between base of rudder and tailpipe.

POWER PLANT: Two turbojets, with variable area nozzles, mounted side by side in rear fuselage. These are reported to be Tumansky R-13F2-300s, each rated at 70·6 kN (15,875 lb st) with afterburning. Ram air intakes, with variable ramps on splitter plates, embodying vertical slots for boundary layer control. Blow-in auxiliary inlets between main intake and wing leading-edge in side of each duct.

ACCOMMODATION: Single seat in enclosed cockpit, with rearward sliding blister canopy. Rearview mirror above canopy of some aircraft.

ARMAMENT: Two pylons for external stores under each wing. Normal armament comprises one radar homing and one infra-red homing air-to-air missile (NATO 'Anab') on outboard pylons, and an infra-red homing close-range missile (NATO 'Aphid') on each inboard pylon. Side by side pylons under centre-fuselage for weapons, including GSh-23L 23 mm gun pods, or external fuel tanks.

AVIONICS AND EQUIPMENT: Large X-band radar (NATO 'Twin Scan') in nose, SOD-57M ATC/SIF nav system, SRO-2 (NATO 'Odd Rods') IFF, Sirena 3 radar warning system.

DIMENSIONS, EXTERNAL (estimated):
Wing span 10·53 m (34 ft 6 in)
Length overall 20·5 m (68 ft 0 in)

WEIGHT (estimated):
Max T-O weight 16,000 kg (35,275 lb)

PERFORMANCE (estimated):
Max level speed above 11,000 m (36,000 ft): with external stores Mach 2·1
Time to 11,000 m (36,000 ft) 2 min 30 s
Service ceiling 20,000 m (65,600 ft)
Combat radius 390 nm (725 km; 450 miles)

SUKHOI Su-24

NATO reporting name: Fencer

Although smaller and lighter than its USAF counterpart, the F-111, the variable geometry Su-24 brought entirely new capability to Soviet tactical air power. Lt Gen Donald R. Keith, former US Army Deputy Chief of Staff for Research, Development and Acquisition, said that 'Fencer' is credited with having terrain avoidance radar, in addition to nav/attack radar, and "has the capability to deliver ordnance in all weather within 55 m (180 ft) of its target". The radar dish appears to have a diameter of at least 1·25 m (49 in), and is reported to be of the pulse-Doppler type. Equipment includes a laser rangefinder and marked target seeker.

Four variants have been identified by NATO reporting names:

Fencer-A. Identifiable by rectangular rear fuselage box enclosing jet nozzles.

Fencer-B. Rear fuselage box around jet nozzles has deeply dished bottom skin between nozzles. Larger brake-chute housing.

Fencer-C. Introduced in 1981. Important equipment

'Flagon-G' tandem two-seat combat trainer based on the 'Flagon-F' interceptor

'Flagon-F' twin-jet interceptor, armed with 'Anab' missiles and gun pods *(Swedish Coast Guard/Air Patrol)*

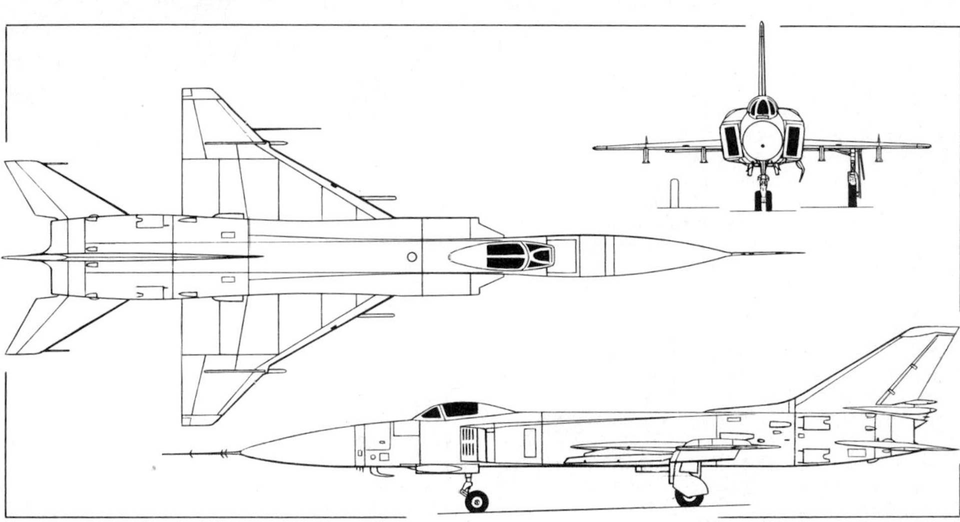

Sukhoi Su-21 ('Flagon-F') single-seat twin-jet all-weather interceptor *(Pilot Press)*

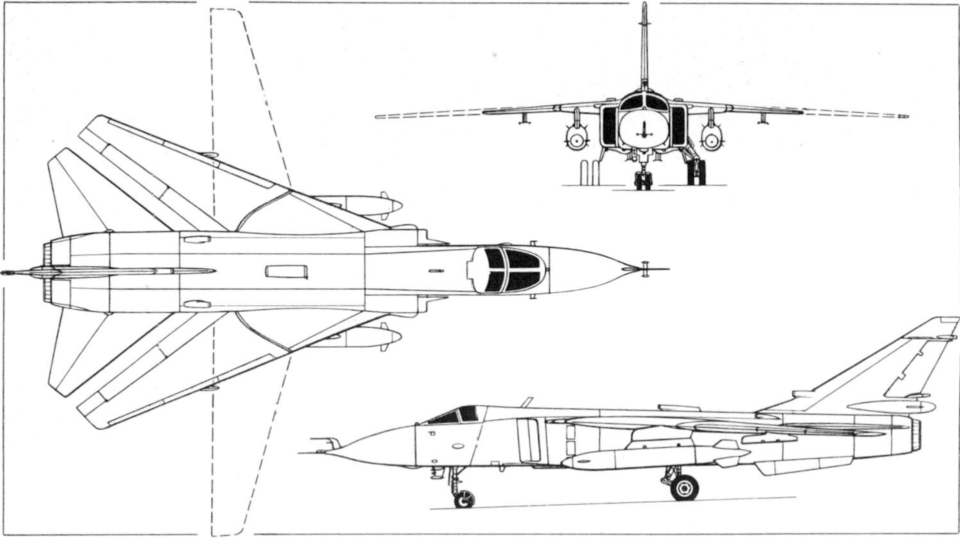

Sukhoi Su-24 ('Fencer-C') variable geometry attack aircraft *(Pilot Press)*

changes. Multiple fitting on nose instead of former simple probe. Triangular fairing forward of each fixed wing root, on side of air intake (presumably housing equipment of the kind seen on the fuselage sides, forward of the nosewheel doors, of ground attack MiG-23/27 'Floggers') and also on each side of fin, near tip.

Fencer-D. Introduced in 1983, with added flight refuelling capability. Slightly longer nose (approx 0·75 m; 2 ft 6 in) forward of windscreen; chord of lower part of tail fin extended, giving kinked leading-edge; large overwing fences integral with extended wingroot glove pylons, probably for AS-14 missiles in class of US Maverick; undernose aerials deleted; blister, probably for electro-optical sensor, added aft of nosewheel bay; and single long noseprobe. A reconnaissance variant of 'Fencer-D' has been reported.

It is likely that an electronic warfare version of Fencer will replace the Yak-28. Its reported, but unconfirmed, designation is 'Fencer-E'.

'Fencer' entered squadron service in December 1974, as a replacement for the Yak-28 (NATO 'Brewer'). In the Spring of 1986 nearly 650 were serving with first-line units, including two full regiments at Tukums in Latvia, near the Gulf of Riga, and at Chernyakhovsk, near Kaliningrad on the Soviet Baltic coast. There are two more at Starokonstantinov and Gorodok in the Ukraine, and a single regiment in the Soviet Far East. No 'Fencer' was allowed to fly outside the Soviet Union or its home waters until July 1979, when an Su-24 regiment was deployed briefly with the 16th Air Army, at Templin air base, north of Berlin in East Germany. Not until 1982 was the first fully operational unit of 30 Su-24s deployed to East Germany as a regular component of the Frontal Aviation air forces stationed in Europe. About 450 of the aircraft now in service are assigned to strategic missions.

The following details apply specifically to 'Fencer-C' but are generally applicable to all versions:

TYPE: Two-seat variable geometry attack aircraft.

WINGS: Cantilever shoulder-wing monoplane, each wing comprising a triangular fixed glove box and three-position pivoted outer panel of all-metal construction. Slight anhedral from roots. Leading-edge sweepback on outer panels estimated at 16° fully forward, and 68° fully swept, with an intermediate sweep angle of 45°. Full span leading-edge slats and almost full span two-section double-slotted trailing-edge flaps on the outer panels. Differential spoilers forward of flaps for roll control at low speeds and for use as lift dumpers on landing.

FUSELAGE: Conventional all-metal semi-monocoque structure of slab-sided rectangular section, with integral engine air intake trunks. Splitter plate and outer lip of each intake are inclined slightly downward. Variable intake ramps. Airbrake under each side of centre-fuselage, curved to follow shape of underbelly fairing.

TAIL UNIT: Cantilever all-metal structure, comprising single sweptback fin with inset rudder, and all-moving horizontal surfaces which operate together for pitch control and differentially for roll control, assisted by use of the wing spoilers when the wings are not fully swept. Two slightly splayed ventral fins, one each side of fuselage undersurface.

LANDING GEAR: Retractable tricycle type, with twin wheels on each unit. Main units retract forward and inward into air intake duct fairings; nose unit retracts rearward. Trailing link type of shock absorbers in main units and low pressure tyres for operation from semi-prepared fields. Mudguard on nosewheels.

POWER PLANT: Two afterburning engines side by side in rear fuselage. These are believed to be related to the Lyulka AL-21F turbojet, as fitted in Su-17. Internal fuel capacity, estimated at 13,000 litres (2,860 Imp gallons; 3,434 US gallons), can be supplemented by four large external tanks.

ACCOMMODATION: Crew of two (pilot and weapon systems officer) side by side on ejection seats.

AVIONICS: Latest photographs show a small avionics pod at top of engine air intake duct on each side, immediately aft of lip, and on each side of fin. These pods appear similar to those immediately forward of the nosewheel bay of ground attack versions of the MiG-23/27.

ARMAMENT: Eight pylons under fuselage, each wing root glove and outer wings for approx 11,000 kg (24,250 lb) of guided and unguided air-to-surface weapons, including nuclear weapons, missiles such as AS-7 (NATO 'Kerry'), AS-10 ('Karen') and AS-14 ('Kedge'), or external fuel tanks. Two pivoting underwing pylons were the first of their kind observed on a Soviet aircraft. No internal weapons bay. One six-barrel 30 mm Gatling type gun inside fairing on starboard side of fuselage undersurface. Unidentified fairing on other side.

DIMENSIONS, EXTERNAL (estimated):

Wing span: spread	17·50 m (57 ft 5 in)
swept	10·50 m (34 ft 5½ in)
Length overall, excl probe	21·29 m (69 ft 10 in)
Height overall	6·00 m (19 ft 8¼ in)
Wheel track	4·00 m (13 ft 1½ in)

WEIGHTS (estimated):

Weight empty, equipped	19,000 kg (41,885 lb)
Max T-O weight	41,000 kg (90,390 lb)

PERFORMANCE (estimated):

Max speed, 'clean': at height	Mach 2·18
at S/L	Mach 1·2
Service ceiling	16,500 m (54,135 ft)
Combat radius:	
lo-lo-lo	over 174 nm (322 km; 200 miles)
lo-lo-hi with 2,500 kg (5,500 lb) weapons	515 nm (950 km; 590 miles)
hi-lo-hi, with 3,000 kg (6,615 lb) weapons and two external tanks	700 nm (1,300 km; 805 miles)

This photograph of an Su-25 shows the wingtip airbrakes open *(Letectvi + Kosmonautika)*

Sukhoi Su-24 ('Fencer-C') two-seat attack aircraft *(Swedish Air Force)*

Sukhoi Su-24 ('Fencer-D') with wings fully spread and landing gear extended *(US Department of Defense)*

SUKHOI Su-25

NATO reporting name: Frogfoot

First photographs of this Soviet counterpart to the U Air Force's single-seat A-10 Thunderbolt II attack aircra became available in December 1982, following deployme of Su-25s to Afghanistan to support the Russian grour forces fighting in mountain terrain.

When first observed by satellite at Ramenskoye flight te centre in 1977, the Su-25 was given the provisional U designation Ram-J. The NATO reporting name 'Frogfoc was released in 1982, and the Su-25 had attained fu operational capability by 1984. The emphasis during ope ational use in Afghanistan is said to have been on techniqu for co-ordinating low level close support by fixed wir aircraft and Mi-24 helicopter gunships. About 75 Su-2 were operational with Soviet forces by Spring 1986, plus o squadron serving with the Czechoslovak Air Force. Othe have been exported to Iraq. Production is centred at t Tbilisi airframe plant.

TYPE: Single-seat close support aircraft.

WINGS: Cantilever shoulder-wing monoplane. Anhedr from roots. Approx 20° sweepback. Entire trailing-ed occupied by hydraulically actuated ailerons and doubl slotted two-section flaps. Multiple tabs in each ailero Full span leading-edge slats in two segments on ea wing. Extended chord leading-edge 'dogtooth' on out

Sukhoi Su-25 single-seat close support aircraft *(Pilot Press)*

50 per cent of each wing. Pods at wingtips each split at rear to form airbrakes which project above and below wing when extended, like those of Grumman A-6 Intruder. Retractable landing light in base of each pod, aft of dielectric nosecap for ECM.

FUSELAGE: Conventional semi-monocoque structure, with flat armoured sides around cockpit. Pitot on port side of nose; transducer to provide data for fire control computer on starboard side.

TAIL UNIT: Conventional cantilever structure. Variable incidence tailplane, with slight dihedral. Hydraulically actuated two-section inset rudder. Tabs in lower rudder segment and each elevator.

LANDING GEAR: Hydraulically retractable tricycle type. Mainwheels retract to lie horizontally in bottom of engine air intake trunks. Single wheel with low-pressure tyre on each levered suspension unit. Mudguard on forward retracting steerable nosewheel.

POWER PLANT: Two non-afterburning Tumansky R-13-300 turbojet engines in long nacelles at wingroots, each rated at 41·5 kN (9,340 lb st). Fuel tanks in fuselage between cockpit and wing front spar, and between rear spar and fin leading-edge, and in wing centre-section. Provision for external fuel tank on each inboard underwing pylon.

ACCOMMODATION: Single ejection seat under sideways hinged (to starboard) canopy, with small rearview mirror on top. Flat bulletproof windscreen.

AVIONICS: SRO-2 (NATO 'Odd Rods') IFF antennae forward of windscreen and under tail. Sirena 3 radar warning system antenna above fuselage tailcone.

ARMAMENT AND OPERATIONAL EQUIPMENT: One twin-barrel 30 mm gun in bottom of front fuselage on port side. Eight large pylons under wings for estimated 4,500 kg (9,920 lb) of air-to-ground weapons, including 57 mm and 80 mm rockets and 500 kg incendiary, anti-personnel and chemical cluster bombs. Two small outboard pylons for 'Atoll' or 'Aphid' air-to-air self-defence missiles. Laser rangefinder and marked target seeker under flat sloping window in nose. Chaff/flare dispenser in tailcone. Strike camera in top of nosecone.

DIMENSIONS, EXTERNAL:
- Wing span: 14·30 m (46 ft 11 in)
- Length overall: 15·40 m (50 ft 6¾ in)

AREA:
- Wings, gross: 33·7 m² (362·75 sq ft)

WEIGHTS:
- Weight empty: 9,500 kg (20,950 lb)
- Max T-O weight: 18,120-19,200 kg (39,950-42,330 lb)

PERFORMANCE (estimated):
- Max level speed: Mach 0·8 (530 knots; 980 km/h; 608 mph)
- Combat radius, hi-lo-hi, with 2,000 kg (4,410 lb) air-to-ground weapons and two external fuel tanks: 300 nm (556 km; 345 miles)

SUKHOI Su-26M

Among Soviet aircraft that participated in the World Aerobatic Championships in Hungary, in August 1984, were two examples of the hitherto unknown Sukhoi Su-26, which had flown for the first time in June of that year. Brief details of this initial version can be found in the 1985-86 *Jane's*. The three examples that participated in the 1986 World Aerobatic Championships in the UK (c/n 06, 07 and 08) were modified **Su-26Ms**, identified by a sharp-cornered (rather than rounded) rudder and reduced fuselage side glazing. The following description applies to these aircraft:

TYPE: Single-seat aerobatic competition aircraft.

WINGS: Cantilever mid-wing monoplane of tapered planform. Specially developed symmetrical wing section, variable along span; slightly concave in region of ailerons to increase their effectiveness; leading-edge somewhat sharper than usual to make aircraft more responsive to control surface movement. Thickness/chord ratio 18% at root, 12% at tip. No dihedral, incidence or sweep at quarter-chord. One-piece two-spar stressed skin structure, without ribs, covered with three-lamination glassfibre/epoxy (GFRP). Foam filled front box spar with carbonfibre reinforced plastics (CFRP) booms and wound glassfibre webs. Channel section rear spar of CFRP. Outer 67% of each wing trailing-edge formed by plain aileron with CFRP box spar, GFRP skin and foam filling. Each aileron, actuated by pushrods, has ground adjustable tab on trailing-edge and two suspended triangular balance tabs. No flaps.

FUSELAGE: Oval-section, with basic welded truss structure of VNS-2 high strength stainless steel tubing. Lower nose section of truss removable to facilitate detachment of wings. Three-lamination GFRP skin panels, with duralumin reinforcement, are all quickly removable for access to interior. Light alloy engine cowlings.

TAIL UNIT: Conventional cantilever fin and tailplane of similar construction to wings. Horn balanced rudder and elevators of similar construction to ailerons and each with ground adjustable tab. Elevators actuated by pushrods, rudder by cable.

LANDING GEAR: Non-retractable tailwheel type. Arched cantilever mainwheel legs of titanium alloy. Mainwheels size 350 × 135 mm, with hydraulic disc brakes. Sprung steerable tailwheel connected to rudder.

POWER PLANT: One 268 kW (360 hp) Vedeneyev M-14P

The above three photographs of Sukhoi Su-25 combat aircraft of the Czechoslovak Air Force are reproduced by courtesy of *Letectvi + Kosmonautika (Václav Jukl)*

Sukhoi Su-26M at 1986 World Aerobatic Championships *(Austin J. Brown)*

nine-cylinder radial engine, driving a three-blade Hoffmann variable-pitch metal propeller. Optional V-530TA-D35 two-blade variable-pitch propeller. Steel tube engine mounting. Fuel in glassfibre lined foam plastics tank bonded into each wingroot section between spars; total capacity 130 litres (28·5 Imp gallons; 34·3 US gallons). Port wing tank only is used in competition; starboard tank supplements it for ferry flights. Oil capacity 22·6 litres (5 Imp gallons; 6 US gallons). Fuel and oil systems adapted for inverted flight.

ACCOMMODATION: One-piece pilot's seat of GFRP, inclined at 45° and designed for use with PLP-60 back-pack parachute. Sideways hinged (to starboard) jettisonable canopy. Safety harness anchored to fuselage structure.

SYSTEM: Electrical system of 24/28V, with 3kW generator, batteries and external supply socket.

AVIONICS: Briz VHF radio.

DIMENSIONS, EXTERNAL:	
Wing span	7·80 m (25 ft 7 in)
Wing chord: at root	1·95 m (6 ft 4¾ in)
at tip	1·10 m (3 ft 7¼ in)
Wing aspect ratio	5·6
Length overall	6·82 m (22 ft 4½ in)
Height overall	2·78 m (9 ft 1½ in)
Tailplane span	2·95 m (9 ft 8¼ in)
Wheel track	2·20 m (7 ft 2½ in)
Wheelbase	5·05 m (16 ft 6¾ in)
Propeller diameter	2·40 m (7 ft 10½ in)
AREAS:	
Wings, gross	10·85 m² (116·8 sq ft)
Ailerons (total)	1·18 m² (12·70 sq ft)
Fin	0·34 m² (3·66 sq ft)
Rudder	0·89 m² (9·58 sq ft)
Tailplane	1·10 m² (11·84 sq ft)
Elevators (total)	1·53 m² (16·47 sq ft)
WEIGHT:	
Normal competition T-O weight	720 kg (1,587 lb)
PERFORMANCE:	
Max level speed	192 knots (355 km/h; 220 mph)
Normal cruising speed	140 knots (260 km/h; 161 mph)
Max rate of climb at S/L	1,008 m (3,307 ft)/min
g limits	+11/−9

SUKHOI Su-27

NATO reporting name: Flanker

Responsibility for the larger of two new-generation Soviet counter-air fighters, equivalent to the US F-15 Eagle, was assigned to the Sukhoi design bureau. It was first observed by reconnaissance satellite at Ramenskoye flight test centre in the late 1970s. Its Soviet designation of Su-27 was quoted by official sources in the West in 1982, and it received the NATO reporting name of 'Flanker'.

Like the MiG-29, it is described by the US Department of Defense as a supersonic all-weather counter-air fighter, with lookdown/shootdown weapon systems and beyond-visual-range air-to-air missiles, and with a possible secondary ground attack role. The Su-27's range, thrust-to-weight ratio and manoeuvrability are all said to be improved by comparison with earlier Soviet fighters. Its large pulse Doppler radar and heavy armament should also give it formidable potential against low flying aircraft and cruise missiles, particularly when it is deployed in partnership with the new Soviet AEW&C aircraft, based on the Il-76 transport and known to NATO as 'Mainstay'.

Release by the Soviet Union of the accompanying photographs, before the Su-27 is fully operational, suggests that the aircraft shown is a prototype or pre-series model. The single plan view drawing, based on material released officially in the USA, is believed to reflect better the form of the wingtips (with wingtip launchers for air-to-air missiles), outboard location of the tail fins, and tailcone extension on current production Su-27s.

Series production of the Su-27 is centred at a plant in Komsomolsk, Khabarovsk territory. The fighter was known to be in service with one Soviet air defence unit in 1986 and, with the MiG-31, is intended to replace many of the MiG-21, MiG-23/27, Su-21 and MiG-25 aircraft in the 17 tactical air forces assigned to Soviet military districts and groups of forces. It may also equip, in a navalised form, the large Soviet aircraft carrier now fitting out at Nikolayev.

TYPE: Single-seat all-weather counter-air fighter, with secondary ground attack capability.

WINGS: Cantilever mid-wing monoplane. Basic wing sweepback approx 40° on leading-edge, with long leading-edge root extensions sweptback at 77°. Anhedral approx 2° 30′. Leading-edge manoeuvring flaps. Flap and aileron (possibly flaperons) on trailing-edge of each wing. Two fences on upper surface of each wing of aircraft illustrated are deleted on later aircraft.

FUSELAGE: Short semi-monocoque all-metal structure of basically circular section, with cockpit high-set behind drooped nose. Large ogival dielectric nosecone.

TAIL UNIT: Cantilever structure, comprising uncanted twin fins and rudders, mounted on narrow decks outboard of engines, and all-moving horizontal surfaces, all sharply sweptback.

LANDING GEAR: Retractable tricycle type, with single wheel on each main unit. Mainwheels retract into wingroots, nosewheels rearward. Mudguard on nosewheel unit. Brake-chute housed in fuselage tailcone.

The above photographs and artist's impression *(US Department of Defense)* **show prototype or pre-series Sukhoi Su-27s. The curved wingtips, location of the fins above the engines, and absence of an extended tailcone will be noted**

POWER PLANT: Two unidentified turbofans, possibly related to the Tumansky R-31, each with estimated rating of 133·5 kN (30,000 lb st) with afterburning. Underwing engine ducts have bottom lip on their wedge inlets.

ACCOMMODATION: Pilot only, under rearward sliding transparent blister canopy.

AVIONICS: Track-while-scan radar with reported search range of 130 nm (240 km; 150 miles) and tracking range of 100 nm (185 km; 115 miles).

ARMAMENT: Basic interception armament of six medium-range radar homing AA-10 and/or close-range AA-11 air-to-air missiles under wings, and on wingtip launch-rails. Ability to carry up to 6,000 kg (13,225 lb) of external stores (e.g. twelve 500 kg bombs) for secondary attack role.

DIMENSIONS, EXTERNAL (estimated):

Wing span	14·50 m (47 ft 7 in)
Length overall, excl nose probe	21·00 m (69 ft 0 in)
Height overall	5·50 m (18 ft 0 in)
Tailplane span	9·75 m (32 ft 0 in)

WEIGHT (estimated):
Max T-O weight 20,000-27,200 kg (44,000-60,000 lb)

PERFORMANCE (estimated):
Max level speed: at height
Mach 2·0 (1,150 knots; 2,120 km/h; 1,320 mph)
at S/L Mach 1·1 (725 knots; 1,345 km/h; 835 mph)
Combat radius 810 nm (1,500 km; 930 miles)

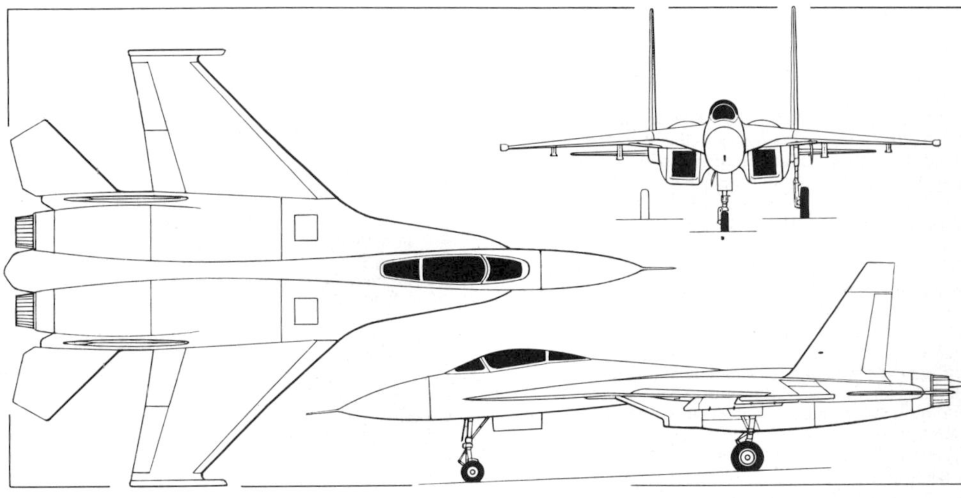

Sukhoi Su-27 twin-jet all-weather counter-air fighter in production form *(Pilot Press, provisional)*

TUPOLEV

CHIEF DESIGNERS: Dr Alexei A. Tupolev, L. L. Selyakov and Dmitry Markov

DEPUTY CHIEF OF BUREAU: Andrei Kandolov

Andrei Tupolev, born in 1888, was a leading figure in the Central Aero-Hydrodynamic Institute (TsAGI) in Moscow from the time when it was founded, in 1929, until his death on 23 December 1972. Current chief designers of the bureau which bears his name include his son, Dr Alexei A. Tupolev. The bureau has doubled in size during the past decade.

TUPOLEV Tu-16

NATO reporting name: Badger

The prototype of this intermediate-range bomber, which had the Tupolev design bureau designation Tu-88, was flown for the first time by N. Rybko in the Winter of 1952. The original strategic bomber version entered series production as the Tu-16 in 1953, and made its first major public appearance on 1 May 1954. An estimated 287 remained operational with the Soviet strategic bomber force in early 1986, equipped to carry both nuclear and conventional weapons. The bombers are supported by 20 Tu-16 in-flight refuelling tankers, more than 90 of various versions equipped for ECM duties, and 15 for reconnaissance. Soviet Naval Aviation had, in 1986, about 240 attack models of 'Badger', plus 75 tankers and up to 80 reconnaissance and ECM models.

The original 1981 edition of *Soviet Military Power* stated that "The prime strike force of Soviet Naval Aviation consists of . . . . 'Badger' and 'Blinder' aircraft which are fitted to carry one or two of several types of anti-ship cruise missiles with standoff ranges varying from 90 to over 300 km (48-162 nm; 56-186 miles). Some missiles have variable flight paths and various homing techniques to help penetrate ship defences. All these missiles are assessed to carry either a nuclear or a high explosive warhead of about 1,000 to 2,000 lb (450-900 kg) . . . In addition to naval aircraft armed with anti-ship missiles, certain 'Bear' and 'Badger' bombers of the Soviet strategic bomber force can be used for attacks against ships, and these aircraft regularly participate in naval exercises."

Early production Tu-16s had AM-3 turbojet engines. These were replaced in later aircraft by improved RD-3M (AM-3M) engines, which increased maximum speeds by up to 54 knots (100 km/h; 62 mph), and range with max fuel to 3,885 nm (7,200 km; 4,470 miles). Eleven versions of the Tu-16 have been identified by unclassified NATO reporting names. All remain in service, as follows:

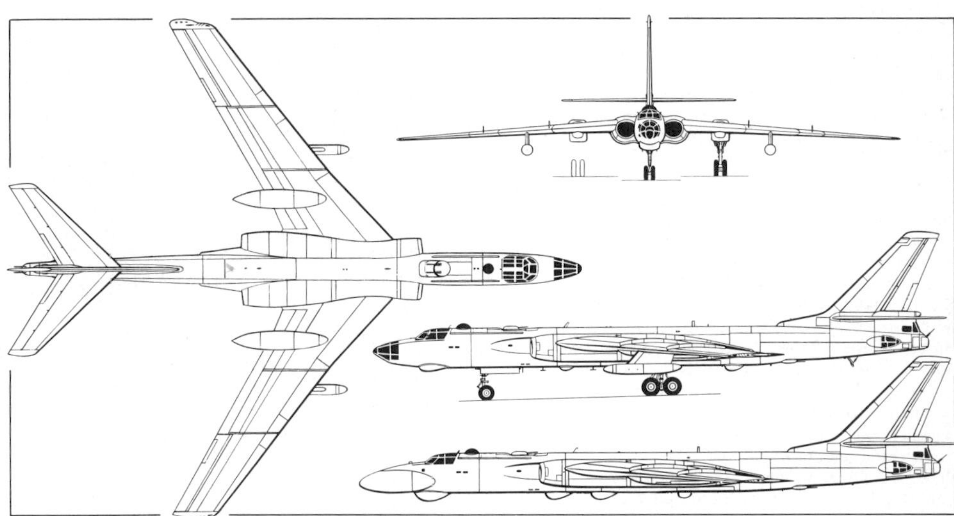

Tupolev Tu-16, in the form known to NATO as 'Badger-F', with additional side view (bottom) of 'Badger-D' *(Pilot Press)*

Badger-A. Basic strategic jet bomber, able to carry nuclear or conventional free-fall weapons. Glazed nose, with small undernose radome. Defensive armament of seven 23 mm cannon. Some equipped as flight refuelling tankers, using a unique wingtip-to-wingtip transfer technique to refuel other Tu-16s, or a probe-and-drogue system to refuel Tu-22s. About 120 operational with Chinese Air Force, and production continues in China under the designation Xian **H-6**.

Badger-B. Similar to 'Badger-A' but equipped originally to carry two turbojet powered aeroplane type anti-shipping missiles (NATO 'Kennel') underwing. Superseded by 'Badger-G' in missile role. Continues in service with Aviation Armies as conventional free-fall bomber.

Badger-C. Anti-shipping version, first seen at 1961 Soviet Aviation Day display. Large air-to-surface winged missile (NATO 'Kipper') carried in recess under fuselage ('Badger-C Mod' carries 'Kingfish' on underwing pylons). Wide nose radome (NATO 'Puff Ball'), in place of glazing and nose gun of 'Badger-A'. No provision for free-fall bombs. Operational with Soviet Northern, Baltic, Black Sea and Pacific Fleets in 1986.

Badger-D. Maritime/electronic reconnaissance version. Nose similar to that of 'Badger-C'. Larger undernose radome; three radomes in tandem under bomb bays.

Badger-E. Photographic and electronic reconnaissance version. Similar to 'Badger-A' but with cameras in bomb

Latest form of Tu-16 'Badger' flight refuelling tanker, photographed over the Baltic Sea *(Swedish Air Force)*

bay and two additional radomes under fuselage, larger one aft.

Badger-F. Basically similar to 'Badger-E' but with electronic intelligence pod on a pylon under each wing. No radomes under centre-fuselage.

Badger-G. Converted from 'Badger-B' with underwing pylons for two rocket-powered air-to-surface missiles (NATO 'Kelt') which can be carried over a range greater than 1,735 nm (3,220 km; 2,000 miles). Free-fall bombing capability retained. Majority serve with anti-shipping squadrons of Soviet Naval Air Force. A few have been transferred to Iraq.

Badger-G modified. Specially equipped carrier for 'Kingfish' air-to-surface missiles, of which first photograph was released, by Swedish Air Force (see Air-Launched Missiles section), in mid-1981. Large radome, presumably associated with missile operation, under centre-fuselage, replacing chin radome. Device mounted externally on glazed nose might help to ensure correct attitude of Tu-16 during missile launch. Total of about 85 standard and modified 'Badger-Gs' believed operational with Soviet Northern, Black Sea and Pacific Fleets.

Badger-H. Stand-off or escort ECM aircraft, with primary function of chaff dispensing to protect missile carrying strike force. The dispensers, with a total capacity of up to 9,075 kg (20,000 lb) of chaff, are located in the weapons bay area. Hatch aft of weapons bay. Two teardrop radomes, fore and aft of weapons bay. Two blade antennae aft of weapons bay. Glazed nose and chin radome.

Badger-J. Specialised ECM jamming/elint aircraft to protect strike force, with some equipment located in a canoe shape radome protruding from inside the weapons bay and surrounded by heat exchangers and exhaust ports. Anti-radar noise jammers operate in A to I bands inclusive. Glazed nose as 'Badger-A'. Some aircraft (as illustrated) have large flat-plate antennae at wingtips.

Badger-K. Electronic reconnaissance variant, with nose as 'Badger-A'. Two teardrop radomes, inside and forward of weapons bay; four small pods on centreline in front of rear radome.

Maritime reconnaissance versions of 'Badger' make regular flights over units of the US Navy and other NATO naval forces at sea in the Atlantic, Pacific and elsewhere. They also make electronic intelligence (elint) sorties around the coastlines of NATO and other countries. The 1984 edition of *Soviet Military Power* noted that about ten strike, tanker and ECM variants of 'Badger' had been deployed to Cam Ranh Bay, the former US Navy base in Viet Nam, during the previous year.

TYPE: Twin-jet medium bomber and maritime reconnaissance/attack aircraft.

WINGS: Cantilever high mid-wing monoplane, with marked anhedral and with 35° of leading-edge sweep on outer panels; 42° sweep on inboard panels. Thickness/chord ratio 12½%. Two-spar light alloy structure, with two fences on each wing. Entire trailing-edge made up of slotted flaps (max deflection 35°) and mass balanced ailerons, each with trim tab. Heavy engine nacelles form root fairings. Versions equipped for inflight refuelling have modified wingtips (see illustration of 'Badger-J').

FUSELAGE: All-metal semi-monocoque structure of oval cross-section, made in five sections. The nose section houses the navigator's pressure cabin with double-glazed nose panels in a magnesium alloy frame, the pilots' pressure cabin, the forward gunner's cabin, and radar equipment. The second and fourth sections house the aircraft's fuel tanks, with the weapon compartment between them; the tail section contains a pressure cabin for the radio operator and rear gunner. Skin panels made of 3 mm light alloy sheet.

TAIL UNIT: Cantilever all-metal structure, with 42° leading-edge sweepback on all surfaces. Trim tabs in rudder and each elevator.

LANDING GEAR: Retractable tricycle type. Twin-wheel nose unit retracts rearward. Main four-wheel bogies retract into housings projecting beyond the wing trailing-edge.

POWER PLANT: Early Tu-16s have two Mikulin AM-3 turbojet engines, each rated at 85·8 kN (19,285 lb st) at sea level. Later aircraft fitted with RD-3M (AM-3M) turbojets, each rated at 93·19 kN (20,950 lb st). Engines semi-recessed into sides of fuselage. Divided air intake ducts: main duct passes through wing torque box between spars; secondary duct passes under wing to feed into primary airflow in front of engine. Engines separated from wings and fuselage by firewalls. Jetpipes inclined outward 3° to shield fuselage from effects of exhaust gases. Fuel in wing and fuselage tanks, with total capacity of approx 45,450 litres (10,000 Imp gallons; 12,000 US gallons). Provision for underwing auxiliary fuel tanks and for flight refuelling. Tu-16 tankers trail hose from starboard wingtip; receiving equipment is in port wingtip extension.

ACCOMMODATION: Normal crew of six, with two pilots side by side on flight deck. Navigator, on seat with armoured sides and base, in glazed nose of all versions except 'Badger-C and D'. Manned tail position plus lateral observation blisters in rear fuselage under tailplane. Entry via two hatches in bottom of fuselage, in front and rear structural sections.

AVIONICS AND EQUIPMENT: Radio and radar aids probably include HF and VHF R/T equipment, as well as IFF and a radio compass and radio altimeter. Other equipment differs according to role.

Soviet Naval Air Force crew in front of a hitherto unknown version of the Tu-16 with nose radome *(copied from Aviation and Cosmonautics)*

'Badger-J' ECM jamming version of Tu-16 *(Swedish Air Force)*

ARMAMENT: Forward dorsal and rear ventral barbettes each containing two 23 mm NR-23 guns. Two similar guns in tail position controlled by an automatic gun ranging radar set. Seventh, fixed, gun on starboard side of nose of versions with nose glazing. Bomb load of up to 9,000 kg (19,800 lb) delivered from weapons bay 6·5 m (21 ft) long in standard bomber, under control of navigator. Naval versions can carry air-to-surface winged standoff missiles.

DIMENSIONS, EXTERNAL ('Badger-G'):
- Wing span: 32·93 m (108 ft 0½ in)
- Length overall: 36·25 m (118 ft 11¼ in)
- Height overall: 14·00 m (45 ft 11¼ in)
- Basic diameter of fuselage: 2·50 m (8 ft 2½ in)
- Tailplane span: 11·75 m (38 ft 6½ in)
- Wheel track: 9·775 m (32 ft 0¾ in)

AREA:
- Wings, gross: 164·65 m² (1,772·3 sq ft)

WEIGHTS ('Badger-G'):
- Weight empty, equipped: 37,200 kg (82,000 lb)
- Normal T-O weight: 75,000 kg (165,350 lb)

PERFORMANCE ('Badger-G', at max T-O weight):
- Max level speed at 6,000 m (19,700 ft): 535 knots (992 km/h; 616 mph)
- Service ceiling: 12,300 m (40,350 ft)
- Range with 3,790 kg (8,360 lb) bomb load: 3,200 nm (5,925 km; 3,680 miles)
- Max unrefuelled combat radius: 1,700 nm (3,150 km; 1,955 miles)

TUPOLEV Tu-95 and Tu-142

NATO reporting name: Bear

Documents issued in Washington concerning the SALT 2 negotiations, in 1979, revealed that the Soviet authorities use the designation **Tu-95** for the force of strategic attack 'Bears' that forms the major part of the long-range bombing force of the five Soviet strategic air armies, and for maritime reconnaissance 'Bear-Ds', but that the much changed 'Bear-Fs', used by the Soviet Naval Air Force are known as **Tu-142s.** The Naval aircraft, being employed only for reconnaissance and anti-submarine warfare, and being observably different from the bombers, have never been subject to SALT restrictions. Those air force and naval versions deployed to bases made available in Cuba and Angola are capable of covering the North and South Atlantic from the Mediterranean approaches westward to the US east coast, and southward to the Cape of Good Hope. Others operate regularly from Cam Ranh in Viet-Nam.

Long range and endurance are only two of the attributes that have kept these huge four-turboprop aircraft in production for 32 years, an unprecedented length of time for a combat aircraft. Their high speed, exceeding that once considered possible for propeller driven aircraft, eclipsed the contemporary four-jet Myasishchev M-4. Their size and payload potential enabled them to accommodate the largest air-to-surface missiles and radars yet carried by operational aircraft. Thus, production to offset attrition continued into the 1980s, and in 1984 was increased to equip operational units with the new 'Bear-H' version, built at Kuybyshev.

Details of the eight versions identified by NATO reporting names, all of which remain in service, with constantly updated equipment, are as follows:

Bear-A. Basic Tu-95 strategic bomber, first flown in late Summer of 1954 and shown in Aviation Day display at Tushino in July 1955. Internal stowage for two nuclear or a variety of conventional free-fall weapons. Fitted with chin radar, and defensive armament comprising three pairs of 23 mm cannon in remotely controlled rear dorsal and ventral barbettes and manned tail turret. Two glazed blisters on rear fuselage, under tailplane, are used for sighting by the gunner controlling all these weapons. The dorsal and ventral barbettes can also be controlled from a station aft of the flight deck. Max range with 11,340 kg (25,000 lb) bomb load is 8,000 nm (14,800 km; 9,200 miles). A small number remain in service.

'Bear-G' has two large pylons under the wingroots on which to carry 'Kitchen' missiles *(UK Ministry of Defence)*

Deep flight deck glazing and new undernose antennae are features of the 'Bear-H' cruise missile carrier *(US Department of Defense)*

Bear-B. First seen in 1961 Aviation Day flypast. As 'Bear-A' but able to carry a large air-to-surface aeroplane type missile (NATO reporting name 'Kangaroo') under fuselage, with associated radar (NATO 'Crown Drum') in wide undernose radome, replacing the original glazing. Defensive armament retained. A few 'Bear-Bs' operate in maritime reconnaissance role, with flight refuelling nose-probe and, sometimes, an elint blister fairing on the starboard side of the rear fuselage. Some carry a pointed canister under each wing, for air sampling.

Bear-C. Another strike version, able to carry 'Kangaroo'; first observed near NATO naval forces during Exercise Teamwork in September 1964. Generally similar to 'Bear-B' but with an elint blister fairing on *both* sides of rear fuselage. Refuelling probe standard. Has been observed with a faired tail housing special equipment, like that illustrated on a 'Bear-D'.

Bear-D. Identified in August 1967, this maritime reconnaissance version has a glazed nose, an undernose radar (NATO 'Short Horn'), a large underbelly radome for I band surface search radar (NATO 'Big Bulge'), an elint fairing on each side of the rear fuselage like 'Bear-C', a nose refuelling probe, and a variety of other blisters and antennae, including a streamlined fairing on each tailplane tip. The housing for I band tail warning radar above the tail turret is much larger than on previous versions. Tasks include pinpointing of maritime targets for missile launch crews on board ships and aircraft which are themselves too distant to ensure precise missile aiming and guidance. 'Bear-D' carries no offensive weapons.

A 'Bear-D' photographed in the second half of 1978, after interception by US Navy F-4s, had in place of the normal tail turret and associated radome a faired tail housing special equipment. A similar tail is now fitted to 'Bear-G'.

Bear-E. Reconnaissance version, basically similar in configuration to 'Bear-A' but with refuelling probe and rear fuselage elint fairings as on 'Bear-C'. Six camera windows in bomb bay, in pairs in line with the wing flaps, with a seventh window to the rear on the starboard side.

Bear-F. First deployed by the Soviet Naval air force in 1970, since when four variants have been seen, this much refined anti-submarine version re-entered production in the mid-1980s. Originally, it had enlarged and lengthened fairings aft of its inboard engine nacelles, but later aircraft reverted to standard size fairings. Some have no undernose radar; others have a radome in this position, but of considerably modified form compared with that of the maritime 'Bear-D'. On both models the main underfuselage J band radar housing is considerably farther forward than on 'Bear-D' and smaller in size; the forward portion of the fuselage is longer; the flight deck windscreens are deeper, giving increased headroom; there are no large blister fairings under and on the sides of the rear fuselage; and the nosewheel doors are bulged prominently, suggesting the use of larger or low pressure tyres. 'Bear-F' has two stores bays for sonobuoys, torpedoes and nuclear depth charges in its rear fuselage, one of them replacing the usual rear ventral gun turret and leaving the tail turret as the sole defensive gun position. Some examples have an MAD 'sting' projecting from the rear of the fin tip and no tailplane tip fairings (see illustration).

Bear-G. Generally similar to 'Bear-B/C' but reconfigured to carry two AS-4 ('Kitchen') air-to-surface missiles instead of one AS-3 ('Kangaroo'), on a large pylon under each wingroot. Other new features include a small thimble radome under the inflight refuelling probe and a solid tailcone, containing special equipment, similar in shape to that on some 'Bear-Ds'. Operational.

Bear-H. This new production version, based on the Tu-142 type airframe of 'Bear-F' but with a shorter fuselage, is equipped with pylons under the inboard wing panels to carry long-range cruise missiles, including the AS-15 (NATO 'Kent'). It achieved initial operational

'Bear-H' has a new fin tip fairing *(UK Ministry of Defence)*

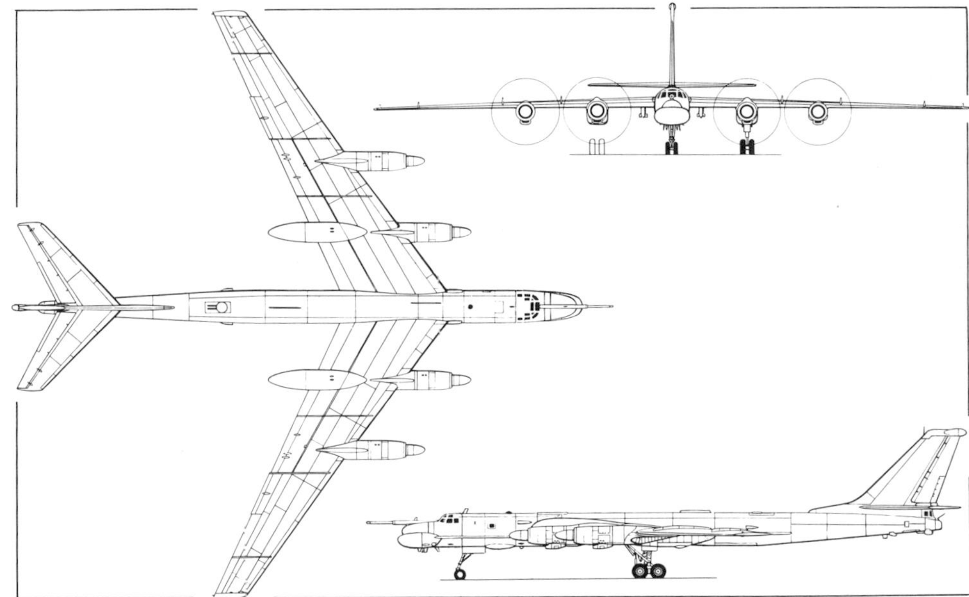

The version of the Tupolev Tu-95/142 known to NATO as 'Bear-H' *(Pilot Press)*

The Tu-95 'Bear-G' is a reconfigured 'Bear-B or C'. The underwing pods are not connected directly with operation of its 'Kitchen' missiles *(UK Ministry of Defence)*

Tupolev Tu-142 ('Bear-F') of the Soviet Naval Air Force with MAD 'sting' at the tip of its tail fin *(UK Ministry of Defence)*

capability in 1984 and about 40 were deployed by Spring 1986. Features include a larger and deeper radome built into the nose and a small fin-tip fairing. There are no elint blister fairings on the sides of the rear fuselage and the ventral gun turret is deleted.

Most of the 125 'Bears' now serving with the air armies are of the 'G' and 'H' models; Soviet Naval Aviation units have about 15 'Bear-Ds' and 60 'Bear-Fs'. Their duties include regular deployments to staging bases in Cuba and Angola, and eight are based permanently at Cam Ranh in Vietnam. 'Bears' are encountered frequently off the US east coast during transits between Murmansk and Cuba, and during elint missions from Cuba. 'Bear-Hs' also carry out simulated attack and training missions against the USA.

The Indian Navy is reported to have ordered three ex-Soviet Navy 'Bears' for maritime reconnaissance.

TYPE: Four-turboprop long-range bomber and maritime reconnaissance aircraft.

WINGS: Cantilever mid-wing monoplane. Slight anhedral. Sweepback 37° at quarter-chord on inner panels, 35° at quarter-chord on outer panels. All-metal structure, with four spars in inboard panels, three spars outboard. All-metal three-segment hydraulically powered ailerons and two-segment Fowler flaps on each wing. Trim tab in each inboard aileron segment. Spoilers in top surface of wing forward of inboard end of ailerons. Three boundary layer fences on top surface of each wing. Thermal anti-icing system in leading-edges.

FUSELAGE: All-metal semi-monocoque structure of circular section, containing three pressurised compartments. Those forward and aft of the weapons bay are linked by a crawlway tunnel. The tail gunner's compartment is not accessible from the other compartments.

TAIL UNIT: Cantilever all-metal structure, with sweepback on all surfaces. Adjustable tailplane incidence. Hydraulically powered rudder and elevators. Trim tabs in rudder and each elevator. Thermal anti-icing system in tailplane leading-edge.

LANDING GEAR: Hydraulically retractable tricycle type. Main units consist of four-wheel bogies, with tyres of approx 1·50 m (5 ft) diameter and hydraulic internal expanding brakes. Twin wheels on nose unit. All units retract rearward, main units into nacelles built on to wing trailing-edge. Retractable tail bumper consisting of two small wheels. Braking parachute may be used to reduce landing run.

POWER PLANT: Four Kuznetsov NK-12MV turboprop engines, each with max rating of 11,033 kW (14,795 ehp) and driving eight-blade contra-rotating reversible-pitch Type AV-60N propellers. Fuel in wing tanks, with normal capacity of 95,000 litres (20,900 Imp gallons; 25,100 US gallons).

ACCOMMODATION AND ARMAMENT: See notes applicable to individual versions and under 'Fuselage'.

OPERATIONAL EQUIPMENT ('Bear-D'): Large I band radar (NATO 'Big Bulge') in blister fairing under centre-fuselage, for reconnaissance and to provide data on potential targets for anti-shipping aircraft or surface vessels. In latter mode, PPI presentation is data linked to missile launch station. Four-PRF range J band circular and sector scan navigation radar (NATO 'Short Horn'). I band tail warning radar (originally NATO 'Bee Hind'; later 'Box Tail') in housing at base of rudder.

DIMENSIONS, EXTERNAL ('Bear-F', approx):
Wing span 51·10 m (167 ft 8 in)
Length overall 49·50 m (162 ft 5 in)
Height overall 12·12 m (39 ft 9 in)

WEIGHT ('Bear-F', estimated):
Max T-O weight 188,000 kg (414,470 lb)

PERFORMANCE:
Max level speed at 7,620 m (25,000 ft) 500 knots (925 km/h; 575 mph)
Over-target speed at 12,500 m (41,000 ft) 450 knots (833 km/h; 518 mph)
Max unrefuelled combat radius 4,475 nm (8 285 km; 5,150 miles)

TUPOLEV Tu-126

NATO reporting name: Moss

An officially released Soviet documentary film, shown in the West in 1968, included sequences depicting a military version of the Tu-114 four-turboprop transport (see 1972-73 *Jane's*), carrying above its fuselage a rotating 'saucer' type early warning radar with a diameter of about 11 m (36 ft). This was a logical development, as the Tu-114 had a fuselage of larger diameter than the military Tu-95, and could accommodate more easily the extensive avionic equipment and crew of 12 required by what was soon

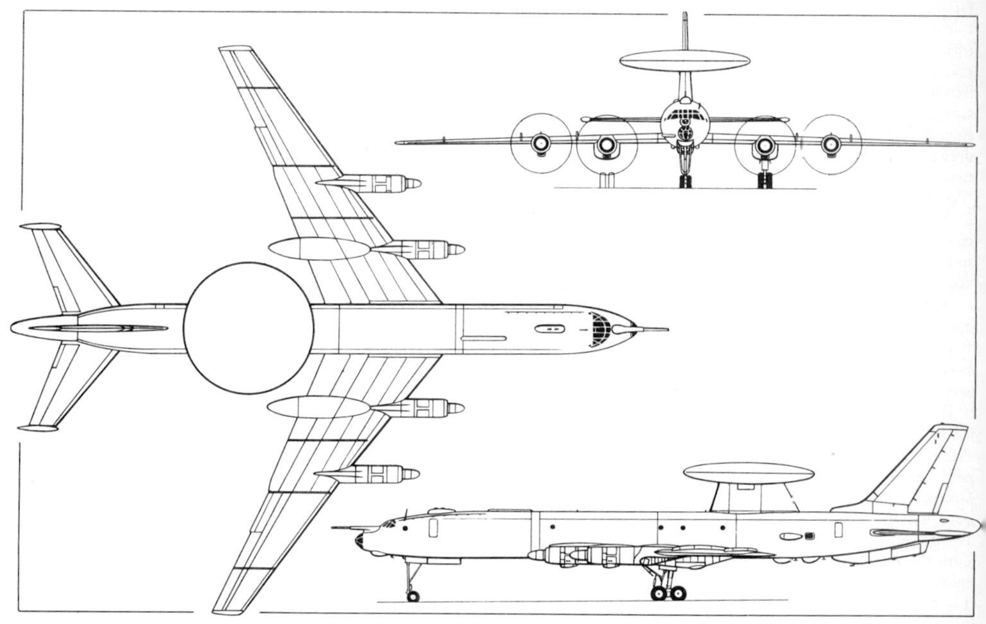

Tupolev Tu-126 (four Kuznetsov NK-12MV turboprop engines) *(Pilot Press)*

The Tu-126 airborne early warning and control system aircraft, known to NATO as 'Moss'

confirmed as the Soviet air forces' first generation airborne early warning and control system aircraft, with the designation Tu-126. It proved to have also wings similar to those of the Tu-114, with extended chord trailing-edge flaps, rather than the 'straight' trailing-edge of the Tu-95. The interior of the fuselage is fully air-conditioned. Few cabin windows are installed.

The general appearance of the Tu-126, which has the NATO reporting name 'Moss', is shown in the accompanying illustrations. It can be seen to have a flight refuelling nose-probe, ventral tail fin and numerous additional antennae and blisters for electronic equipment, including streamlined fairings and associated dielectric panels on the sides of the rear fuselage as on the Tu-95 'Bear-C/D'. The power plant comprises four 11,033 kW (14,795 ehp) Kuznetsov NK-12MV turboprop engines. Wing fuel tanks have a capacity of 60,800 kg (134,040 lb).

The Tu-126 is intended to work in conjunction with advanced interceptors. After locating incoming low-level strike aircraft, it would ideally direct towards them fighters armed with 'snapdown' air-to-air missiles able to be fired from a cruising height of 6,100 m (20,000 ft) or higher. It has a further, obvious application in assisting strike aircraft to elude enemy interceptors picked up by its radar.

About nine Tu-126s are operational with the Soviet air defence forces. They are said, by US defence experts, to have demonstrated some effectiveness in overwater exercises but to be ineffective over land.

DIMENSIONS, EXTERNAL:
- Wing span: 51·20 m (168 ft 0 in)
- Wing aspect ratio: 8·42
- Length overall: 55·20 m (181 ft 1 in)
- Fuselage diameter: 3·70 m (12 ft 1½ in)
- Height overall: 16·05 m (52 ft 8 in)
- Wheel track: 13·70 m (44 ft 11½ in)
- Propeller diameter: 5·60 m (18 ft 4½ in)

AREA:
- Wings, gross: 311·1 m² (3,349 sq ft)

WEIGHT (estimated):
- Max T-O weight: 170,000 kg (374,785 lb)

PERFORMANCE:
- Max level speed: 459 knots (850 km/h; 528 mph)
- Normal operating speed: 351 knots (650 km/h; 404 mph)
- Max range without flight refuelling: 6,775 nm (12,550 km; 7,800 miles)

TUPOLEV Tu-22

NATO reporting name: Blinder

First shown publicly in the 1961 Aviation Day flypast over Moscow, the Tu-22 was the first operational Soviet supersonic bomber. Of the ten examples which took part in that display, only one carried visible weapons, in the form of an air-to-surface missile (NATO reporting name 'Kitchen'), some 11 m (36 ft) long, semi-submerged in the underside of its fuselage. This aircraft had also a wider nose radome.

A total of 22 Tu-22s took part in the 1967 display at Domodedovo. One was escorted by six MiG-21PFs, permitting a more accurate calculation of its overall dimensions than had previously been possible. Most carried 'Kitchen' missiles; all had a partially retractable nose refuelling probe and the wide radome seen on the single missile-armed aircraft in 1961.

About 250 Tu-22s were built, in four versions, as follows:

Blinder-A. Basic reconnaissance bomber, with fuselage weapon bay for free-fall nuclear and conventional bombs. 'Blinder-A' entered limited service, its range being inadequate for the originally intended strategic role.

Blinder-B. Generally similar to 'Blinder-A' but equipped to carry air-to-surface nuclear missile (NATO reporting name 'Kitchen') recessed in weapons bay. Larger radar and partially retractable flight refuelling probe on nose.

Blinder-C. Maritime reconnaissance version, with six camera windows in weapons bay doors. Flight refuelling probe like 'Blinder-B'. Modifications to nosecone, dielectric panels, etc, on some aircraft suggest possible electronic intelligence role or equipment for electronic countermeasures (ECM) duties. About 60 delivered, of which 35 remain in service, for operation primarily over sea approaches to the Soviet Union, from bases in the Southern Ukraine and Estonia.

Blinder-D. Training version. Cockpit for instructor in raised position aft of standard flight deck, with stepped-up canopy. In service in the Soviet Union and Libya.

About 135 'Blinder-As' and 'Blinder-Bs' remain operational with the Soviet air armies, plus 15 equipped for reconnaissance. The Soviet Naval Air Force has about 35 bombers and 20 equipped for reconnaissance. The Libyan and Iraqi Air Forces each have about seven Tu-22s.

The following details apply to 'Blinder-A and B' but are generally applicable to all versions except as noted under model descriptions:

TYPE: Twin-jet supersonic bomber and maritime patrol aircraft.

WINGS: Cantilever mid-wing monoplane. Constant slight anhedral from roots. Sweepback approx 45° on leading-edge outboard of fence and 50° inboard of fence, increasing to acute sweep at roots. Conventional all-metal structure. Fully powered two-section ailerons, with tab in each inboard section. Flaps inboard and outboard of wheel pod on each wing trailing-edge.

FUSELAGE: All-metal semi-monocoque structure of circular section, with area rule 'waisting' at wing roots.

TAIL UNIT: Cantilever all-metal structure, with sweepback on all surfaces. Fully powered all-moving horizontal surfaces at bottom of fuselage. Aerodynamically balanced rudder, with inset tab.

LANDING GEAR: Retractable tricycle type. Wide track four-wheel bogie main units retract rearward into pods built on to wing trailing-edges. Oleo-pneumatic shock absorbers. Main legs designed to swing rearward for additional cushioning during taxying and landing on rough runways. Twin-wheel nose unit retracts rearward. Small retractable skid to protect rear fuselage in tail-down landing or take-off.

POWER PLANT: Two Koliesov VD-7 turbojet engines, each rated at 137·5 kN (30,900 lb st) with afterburning, mounted in pods above rear fuselage, on each side of tail fin. Lip of each intake is in the form of a ring which can be translated forward by jacks for take-off. Air entering ram intake is then supplemented by air ingested through annular slot between ring and main body of pod. Jetpipes have convergent-divergent nozzle inside outer fairing. Semi-retractable flight refuelling probe on nose of 'Blinder-B', with triangular guard underneath to prevent drogue damaging nosecone.

ACCOMMODATION: Crew of three in tandem. Row of windows in bottom of fuselage, aft of nose radome, at navigator/systems operator's station. Pilot has upward ejection seat; other crew members have downward ejection seats.

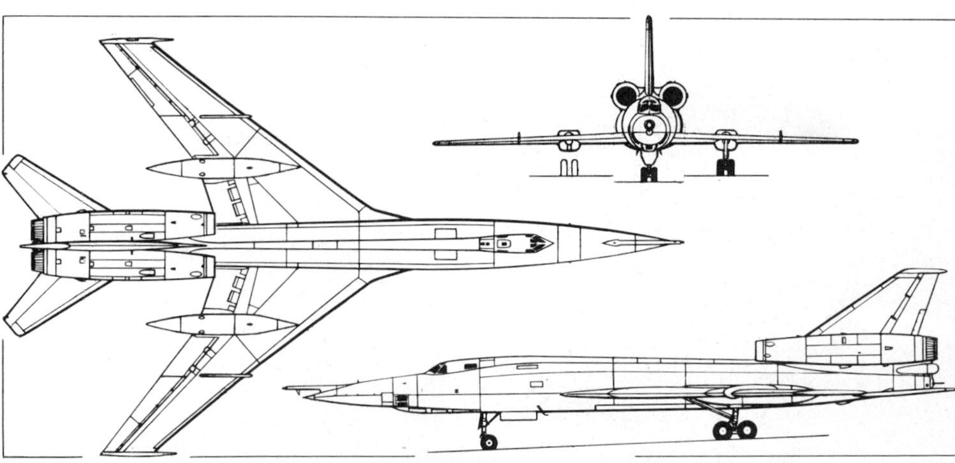

Tupolev Tu-22 twin-jet supersonic bomber ('Blinder-A') *(Pilot Press)*

ARMAMENT AND OPERATIONAL EQUIPMENT: Weapons bay in centre-fuselage, with double-fold doors on 'Blinder-A'. Special doors with panels shaped to accommodate recessed 'Kitchen' missile on 'Blinder-B'. Single 23 mm NR-23 gun in radar directed tail turret, beneath 'Bee Hind' tail warning radar antenna. Radar in nose. Chaff/flare countermeasures dispensers and bombing assessment cameras carried in rear of wheel pods of some aircraft.

DIMENSIONS, EXTERNAL (estimated):
- Wing span: 23·75 m (78 ft 0 in)
- Length overall: 40·53 m (132 ft 11½ in)
- Height overall: 10·67 m (35 ft 0 in)

WEIGHT (estimated):
- Max T-O weight: 83,900 kg (185,000 lb)

PERFORMANCE (estimated):
- Max level speed at 12,200 m (40,000 ft): Mach 1·4 (800 knots; 1,480 km/h; 920 mph)
- Service ceiling: 18,300 m (60,000 ft)
- Max unrefuelled combat radius: 1,565 nm (2,900 km; 1,800 miles)

TUPOLEV Tu-26 (Tu-22M)

NATO reporting name: Backfire

NATO first acknowledged the existence of a Soviet variable geometry medium bomber in the Autumn of 1969. Such an aircraft was not unexpected, as the Tu-22 (NATO 'Blinder') was incapable of fulfilling the bombing role for which it had been intended.

A prototype of the bomber was observed in July 1970, on the ground near the manufacturing plant at Kazan in Central Asia, and was confirmed subsequently as a twin-engined design by the Tupolev Bureau. At least two prototypes were built, and flight testing is believed to have started in 1971. Up to twelve pre-production models followed, for development testing, weapons trials and evaluation, by the beginning of 1973. Soviet delegates referred to the type as the **Tu-22M** during the SALT 2 treaty talks, but the current designation is believed to be **Tu-26**. The NATO reporting name allocated to the aircraft is 'Backfire'.

When drawing up the basic parameters for the bomber, the Tupolev Bureau is believed to have aimed at a maximum unrefuelled range of 4,775-5,200 nm (8,850-9,650 km; 5,500-6,000 miles) at high altitude. Unwillingness to depart from the Tupolev practice of retracting the main landing gear bogies into fairings on the wing trailing-edges limited the variable geometry to the outer wings, as on the Sukhoi Su-17/20/22. There is evidence to believe that the large size of these fairings, with the wheels stowed beneath the wing, caused excessive drag, so that 'Backfire's' range fell short of what had been planned. Redesign almost eliminated the fairings from later aircraft, after the main landing gear had been revised to retract inward into the fuselage.

Tupolev Tu-22 photographed from an investigating interceptor of the Royal Norwegian Air Force

'Backfire-B' version of the Tupolev Tu-26/Tu-22M with wings spread, photographed from an interceptor of the Swedish Air Force

By 1986, three versions of the Tu-26/Tu-22M had been identified by NATO reporting names:

Backfire-A. Initial version, with large landing gear fairing pods on the wing trailing-edges. Believed to have equipped only one squadron.

Backfire-B. Developed series production version, with increased wing span and landing gear fairing pods eliminated except for shallow underwing fairings, no longer protruding beyond the trailing-edge. Inward retracting main landing gear units. During the abortive SALT 2 treaty negotiations, 'Backfire-Bs' were seen with the standard flight refuelling nose probe removed, although the housing remained. This was assumed to stress Soviet assertions that the aircraft are intended for peripheral/theatre operations rather than long-range strategic use, and were therefore exempt from the restrictions that would have been imposed on intercontinental bombers by the treaty. External stores racks seen frequently under air intake trunks.

Backfire-C. This advanced production version with wedge type engine air intakes, like those of the MiG-25, was first reported in the 1980-81 *Jane's*. No photograph yet available.

'Backfire-B and C' are capable of performing nuclear strike, conventional attack, anti-ship and reconnaissance missions. Low-level penetration features make them more survivable than previous Soviet bombers, and they have adequate range to be employed against the contiguous United States on high-altitude subsonic missions, although such a flight profile would make them far more vulnerable. Their low altitude supersonic dash capability makes them formidable weapons with which to support military operations in Europe and Asia. A retractable flight refuelling nose probe makes possible extended-range missions.

About 250 'Backfire-Bs and Cs' are in service. Two-thirds of them oppose NATO in Europe and over the Atlantic, with the others in the far east of the Soviet Union. The latter are observed frequently over the Sea of Japan, and 30 of them are reportedly drawn from the 100 'Backfire-Bs and Cs' deployed in a maritime role by Soviet Naval Aviation. The FY 1979 Annual Report of the US Department of Defense stated: "There is increasing evidence that the Soviet bomber and cruise missile force may be overtaking their submarine force as a threat to our fleet and to our forces necessary for the resupply of Europe. They can concentrate aircraft, co-ordinate attacks with air, surface, or submarine launched missiles, and use new technology to find our fleet units, jam our defences and screen their approach".

It is expected that the 'Backfire' strategic/maritime force will be maintained eventually at a total of at least 400 aircraft. Production appears to be limited to the average rate of 30 aircraft a year which was specified by the unratified SALT 2 agreement. 'Backfires' have been used for development launches of new generation Soviet cruise missiles, but are not expected to become designated AS-15 carriers.

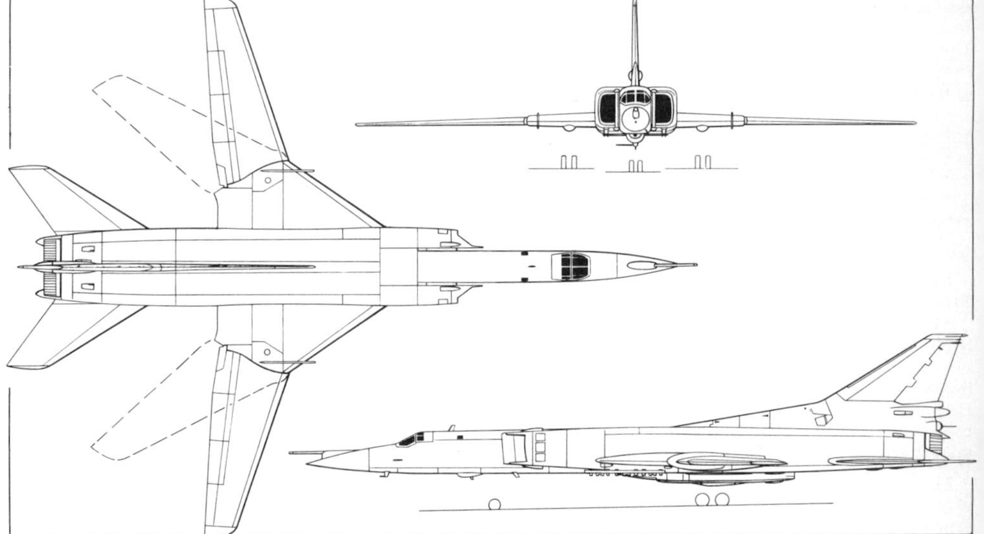

Tupolev Tu-26/Tu-22M (NATO 'Backfire-B') bomber and maritime reconnaissance/attack aircraft
(Pilot Press)

The following details refer specifically to 'Backfire-B':

TYPE: Twin-engined medium bomber and maritime reconnaissance/attack aircraft.

WINGS: Cantilever low mid-wing monoplane, made up of a large span fixed centre-section and two variable geometry outer panels. No anhedral or dihedral, but wing section is so thin that considerable flexing of the outer panels takes place in flight. Leading-edge fence towards tip of centre-section on each side. Each outer wing panel is believed to be fitted with a full span leading-edge slat, aileron, and slotted trailing-edge flaps aft of spoilers/lift dumpers. Wing sweep is believed to be variable from fully spread (20°) to fully swept (65°), rather than limited to one intermediate position as on the MiG-23.

FUSELAGE: Forward of wings, fuselage is basically circular with large ogival dielectric nosecone. Centre-fuselage is faired into rectangular section air intake trunks, each fitted with a large splitter plate and assumed to embody complex variable geometry ramps. There is no evidence to suggest external area rule 'waisting' of these trunks.

TAIL UNIT: Cantilever structure, with sweepback on all surfaces. All-moving horizontal surfaces; conventional inset rudder.

LANDING GEAR: Retractable tricycle type. Each main unit carries a multi-wheel bogie, which pivots inward from the vestigial fairing under the centre-section into the bottom of the adjacent intake trunk.

POWER PLANT: Two unidentified turbofan engines with afterburners, mounted side by side in the rear fuselage.

This 1984 photograph of the Tupolev Tu-26/Tu-22M (NATO 'Backfire-B'), taken over the Sea of Japan, shows two additional mounts for air-to-surface missiles under the fixed wing centre-section panels

Reported to be uprated versions of the Kuznetsov NK-144 engines (each 196·1 kN; 44,090 lb st) that were developed for Tupolev's Tu-144 supersonic transport. Fuel tankage is believed to include integral tanks in the entire fixed portion of the wings and much of the centre-fuselage above the weapon bay. Removable flight refuelling nose probe; after one observed refuelling, a 'Backfire' prototype remained airborne for a further 10 h.

ACCOMMODATION: Pilot and co-pilot side by side on flight deck. Two crew members further aft, as indicated by position of windows between flight deck and air intakes.

AVIONICS AND EQUIPMENT: Large bombing and navigation radar (NATO 'Down Beat') inside dielectric nosecone. Radar (NATO 'Bee Hind') for tail turret, above guns.

ARMAMENT: Primary armament of one 'Kitchen' air-to-surface missile semi-recessed in the underside of the centre-fuselage; or two 'Kitchens', carried under the fixed centre-section panel of each wing. Multiple racks for 12 to 18 bombs sometimes fitted under the air intake trunks. Alternative weapon loads include up to 12,000 kg (26,450 lb) of conventional bombs. US reports have suggested that the Soviet Union is developing decoy missiles to assist penetration of advanced defence systems, in addition to very advanced ECM and ECCM. Twin 23 mm guns in radar directed tail mounting.

DIMENSIONS, EXTERNAL (estimated):

Wing span: fully spread	34·45 m (113 ft 0 in)
fully swept	24·00 m (78 ft 9 in)
Length overall	42·5 m (140 ft 0 in)
Height overall	10·50 m (34 ft 6 in)

WEIGHTS:

Nominal weapon load	12,000 kg (26,450 lb)
Max T-O weight	130,000 kg (286,600 lb)

PERFORMANCE (estimated):

Max level speed at high altitude	Mach 2·0
Max level speed at low altitude	Mach 0·9
Max unrefuelled combat radius	2,160 nm (4,000 km; 2,485 miles)

NEW TUPOLEV BOMBER

NATO reporting name: Blackjack

Tupolev's variable geometry strategic bomber known to NATO as 'Blackjack' is the long expected supersonic successor to the M-4 'Bison' and Tu-95 'Bear-A'. Apart from artists' impressions prepared by the US Department of Defense, the only perspective picture of 'Blackjack' released by Spring 1985 is a poor quality reconnaissance photograph taken over Ramenskoye flight test centre on 25 November 1981 and reproduced in the 1982-83 *Jane's*. Showing the aircraft parked alongside two Tu-144 supersonic airliners, this enabled its length, including nose probe, to be calculated as around 50·6 m (166 ft). What this implies in terms of weapon load and fuel tankage is easy to estimate. 'Blackjack' is about 25 per cent longer than Tupolev's last operational bomber, the supersonic 'Backfire', 13 per cent larger than USAF's B-1B, and longer than even the Boeing B-52. It is in no way a simple scale-up of 'Backfire'. Common features include low mounted variable geometry wings, and large vertical tail surfaces with a massive dorsal fin; but 'Blackjack's' horizontal tail surfaces are mounted higher, at the intersection of the dorsal fin and main fin. The fixed root panel of each wing seems to be long and very sharply swept, like the inboard section of the Tu-144's delta wing. The engine installation also seems to resemble that of the now-retired airliner rather than 'Backfire'. However, it must be borne in mind that the two bombers are designed for a similar subsonic cruise/supersonic dash flight profile. As 'Blackjack's' max T-O weight is twice that of 'Backfire', it might have been logical to use four of the latter's turbofans. If the engines are mounted in pairs, inside two divided underwing ducts, as on the Tu-144, the gap between the ducts will determine the type and size of weapons that 'Blackjack' can carry.

Five prototype and pre-production 'Blackjacks' were undergoing advanced flight testing in 1986, and the US Department of Defense expects the Soviet Union to build a production series of at least 100 in a new complex added to the huge Kazan airframe plant, with an initial operational capability in 1988. 'Blackjack's' primary weapons will be the AS-15 'Kent' air-launched cruise missile and supersonic BL-10 missile, each with a range of 1,620 nm (3,000 km; 1,850 miles); but it will have provision for carrying bombs or a mix of missiles and bombs.

DIMENSIONS, EXTERNAL (initial estimates):

Wing span: fully spread	52·00 m (172 ft)
fully swept	33·75 m (110 ft)
Length overall	50·625 m (166 ft)
Height overall	13·75 m (45 ft)

WEIGHTS (initial estimates):

Max weapon load	16,330 kg (36,000 lb)
Max T-O weight	250,000 kg (551,150 lb)

PERFORMANCE (estimated):

Max level speed at high altitude	Mach 2·0
Max unrefuelled combat radius	3,940 nm (7,300 km; 4,535 miles)

TUPOLEV Tu-28P/Tu-128

NATO reporting name: Fiddler

Largest purpose-designed interceptor yet put into squadron service, this supersonic twin-jet aircraft was seen for the first time at Tushino in July 1961, with a large delta wing air-to-air missile (NATO 'Ash') mounted under each wing. It is thought to have the service designation Tu-28P (US Department of Defense has used Tu-128); its NATO reporting name is 'Fiddler'.

The Tu-28P has a large ogival nose radome and carries a crew of two in tandem. The shoulder intakes for its two afterburning turbojet engines have half-cone shock-bodies, and the jetpipes are side by side in the bulged tail. Each engine is estimated to have a max rating of about 120·1 kN (27,000 lb st).

The sharply swept wings are mid-set, with slight anhedral, and have considerably increased chord on the inboard panels, which have both increased sweep and a straight trailing-edge. The wide track main landing gear units, comprising four-wheel bogies, retract into large fairings built on to the wing trailing-edges.

The tail unit is also sharply swept, and the original two aircraft seen in 1961 **('Fiddler-A')** were each fitted with two ventral fins. These were missing on the three Tu-28Ps **('Fiddler-B')** which flew past at Domodedovo in July

Artist's impression of the new Tupolev strategic bomber known to NATO as 'Blackjack' *(US Department of Defense)*

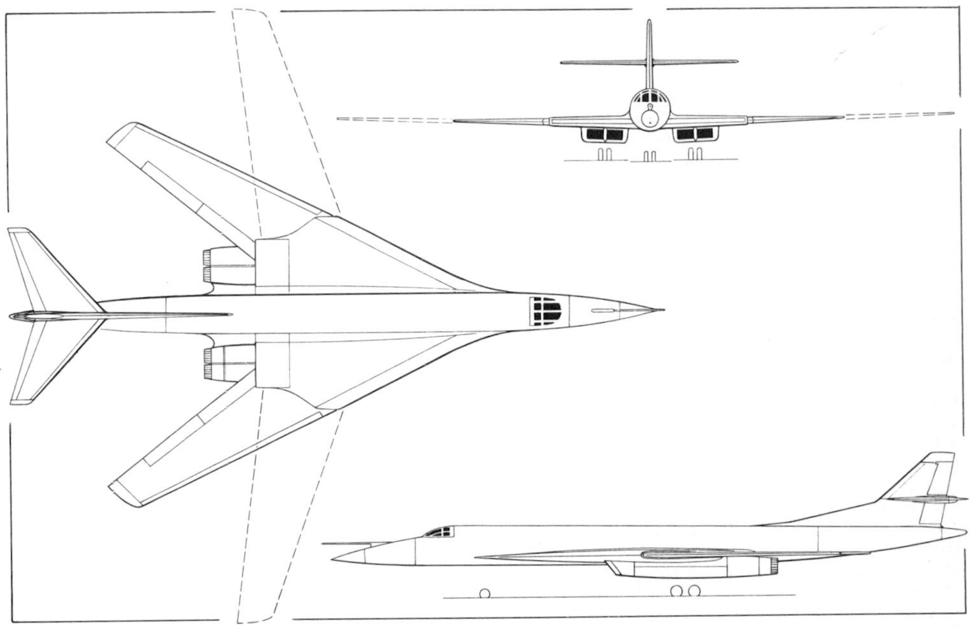

Provisional three-view drawing of Tupolev's new strategic bomber (NATO 'Blackjack') *(Pilot Press)*

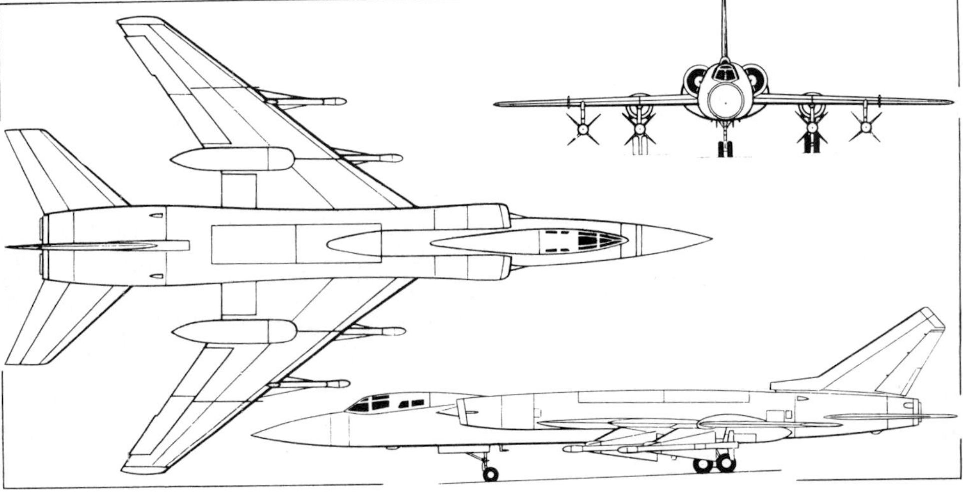

Tupolev Tu-28P supersonic twin-jet all-weather interceptor *(Pilot Press)*

Tupolev Tu-28P taking off, with underwing armament of two 'Ash' missiles

1967, as was the large bulged fairing fitted under the fuselage in 1961.

'Fiddler-B' proved to be the production configured version, with an armament double that seen in 1961, each aircraft being equipped to carry two 'Ash' missiles under each wing, one usually of the radar homing type and the other of the infra-red homing type. This was confirmed as the standard armament of first-line service aircraft in a film released in 1969, showing units of the Soviet armed forces taking part in defence exercises.

About 90 'Fiddler-Bs' are thought to remain in service with the Soviet Union's Voyska PVO home defence fighter force, plus 25 with tactical air forces.

DIMENSIONS, EXTERNAL (estimated):
- Wing span: 18·10 m (59 ft 4½ in)
- Length overall: 27·20 m (89 ft 3 in)

WEIGHT (estimated):
- Max T-O weight: 45,000 kg (100,000 lb)

PERFORMANCE (estimated):
- Max level speed at 11,000 m (36,000 ft): Mach 1·65 (950 knots; 1,760 km/h; 1,090 mph)
- Service ceiling: 20,000 m (65,620 ft)
- Combat radius with max internal fuel: 810 nm (1,500 km; 930 miles)

TUPOLEV Tu-154M

NATO reporting name: Careless

The basic three-engined **Tu-154**, announced in the Spring of 1966, was developed to replace the Tu-104, Il-18 and An-10 transport aircraft on Aeroflot's medium/long stage lengths of up to 3,240 nm (6,000 km; 3,725 miles). The first of six prototype and pre-production models flew for the first time on 4 October 1968. Regular passenger services began on 9 February 1972.

The Tu-154 was superseded in production successively by the **TU-154A**, **Tu-154B** and **Tu-154B-2**, with uprated turbofan engines and many refinements. Production of all four versions exceeded 350, of which more than 300 were delivered to Aeroflot and others to Balkan Bulgarian Airlines, Cubana, Malév and Tarom. Full descriptions of these aircraft can be found in the 1985-86 and previous editions of *Jane's*.

Following the development of the Tu-154B-2, the Tupolev Bureau decided that further improvement of the type would be impossible without more radical changes to the basic airframe and a switch to more modern engines. This led to development of the **Tu-154M**.

As the first step, a standard production Tu-154B-2 (SSSR-85317) was returned to the factory, where the original Kuznetsov NK-8-2U turbofans were removed. Soloviev D-30KU turbofans, as used on the Il-62M, were installed in their place, with the thrust rating of each engine (designated D-30KU-154-II in production form) reduced. The engine nacelles mounted on each side of the rear fuselage were developments of those fitted to the Il-62M, with the same type of clamshell thrust reverser on the engines they carried. To accommodate the centre engine, the TA-92 APU had to be transferred from its former position over the tail nozzle to the fuselage, and the air intake had to be enlarged to a circular form.

Flight testing began in 1982.

In its new configuration, as the prototype Tu-154M, SSSR-85317 had a redesigned tailplane; the slats were made smaller and the area of the spoilers was increased. The original three-crew flight deck and cabin layout for 169 passengers were retained, but the production Tu-154M offers alternative configurations for up to 180 economy class passengers. An executive version is available; and it is possible to remove all seats and utilise any version of the aircraft to carry light freight.

Production is centred in Kuybyshev, from where Aeroflot took delivery of its first two Tu-154Ms on 27 December 1984. Other customers include Balkan Bulgarian Airlines, CAAC of China, Cubana, LOT Polish Airlines and Syrianair. The Tu-154M is designed for a service life of 30,000 hours and 15,000 landings over a 15 year period.

TYPE: Three-turbofan medium range transport aircraft.

WINGS: Cantilever low-wing monoplane. Sweepback 35° at quarter-chord. Anhedral on outer panels. Geometric twist along span. Conventional all-metal riveted three-spar structure, centre spar extending to just outboard of inner edge of aileron in each wing. Hydraulically actuated ailerons, double-slotted flaps and four-section spoilers forward of flaps on each wing. Electrically actuated slats on outer 80 per cent of each wing leading-edge. Tab in each aileron. Hot air anti-icing of wing leading-edge. Slats electrically heated.

FUSELAGE: Conventional all-metal semi-monocoque fail-safe structure of circular section. Single pressure cell containing flight deck and two cabins separated by service compartments.

TAIL UNIT: Cantilever all-metal structure, with electrically actuated variable incidence T tailplane. Rudder and elevators of honeycomb sandwich construction. Sweepback of 40° at quarter-chord on horizontal surfaces, 45° on leading-edge of vertical surfaces. Control surfaces hydraulically actuated by irreversible servo controls. Tab in each elevator. Leading-edges of fin and tailplane and engine air intake anti-iced by hot air.

LANDING GEAR: Retractable tricycle type. Hydraulic actuation. Main units retract rearward into fairings on wing trailing-edge. Each consists of a bogie made up of three pairs of wheels in tandem. Rearward retracting anti-shimmy twin-wheel nose unit, steerable through ±63°. Disc brakes and anti-skid units on mainwheels.

POWER PLANT: Three Soloviev D-30KU-154-II turbofan engines, each rated at 103 kN (23,150 lb st), one in pod on each side of rear fuselage and one inside extreme rear of fuselage. Two lateral engines fitted with clamshell thrust reversers. Integral fuel tanks in wings: four tanks in centre-section and two in outer wings. For reasons of trim, all fuel is fed to a collector tank in the centre-section and thence to engines. Single-point refuelling. APU in rear fuselage.

ACCOMMODATION: Crew of three on flight deck, comprising two pilots and flight engineer, with provisions for navigator and five cabin staff. Alternative configurations for 180 economy class passengers, 164 tourist class with hot meal service, or 154 tourist/economy plus a separate first class cabin seating 8 to 24 persons. Mainly six-abreast seating with centre aisle. Washable non-flamable materials used for all interior furnishing. Fully enclosed luggage containers. Toilet, galley and wardrobe installations to customer's requirements. Executive and light cargo configurations available. Passenger doors are forward of the front cabin and between cabins on port side, with emergency and service doors opposite. All four doors open outward. Six emergency exits: two overwing and one immediately forward of engine nacelle on each side. Two pressurised baggage holds under floor of cabin, with two inward opening doors. Smaller unpressurised hold under rear of cabin.

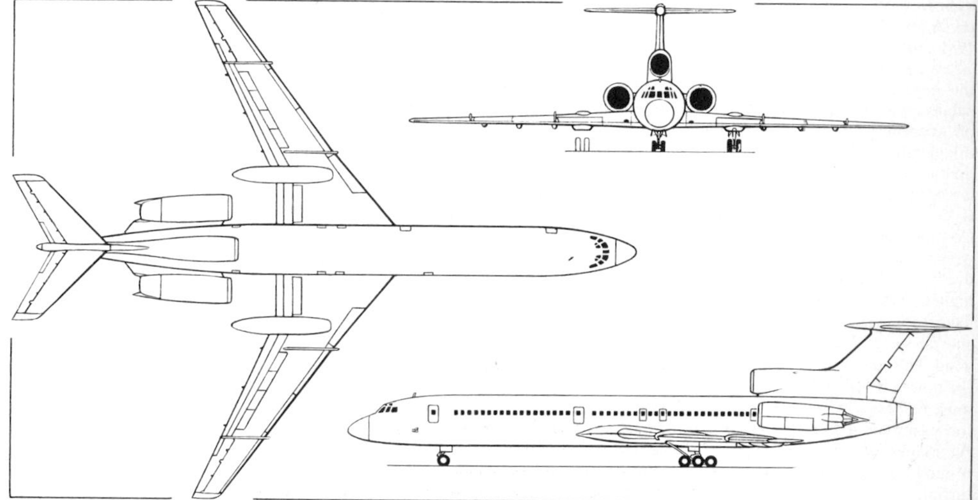

Tupolev Tu-154M medium-range three-turbofan transport aircraft *(Pilot Press)*

Tupolev Tu-154M medium range airliner (three Soloviev D-30KU-154-II turbofan engines) in service with Balkan Bulgarian Airlines *(Anton Wettstein)*

SYSTEMS: Air-conditioning system pressure differential 0·58 bars (8·4 lb/sq in). Three independent hydraulic systems, working pressure 207 bars (3,000 lb/sq in), powered by engine driven pumps. Nos 2 and 3 systems each have additional electric backup pump. Systems actuate landing gear retraction and extension, nosewheel steering, and operation of ailerons, rudder, elevators, flaps and spoilers. Three-phase 200/115V 400Hz AC electrical system supplied by three 40kVA alternators. Additional 36V 400Hz AC and 27V DC systems and four storage batteries. Engine fire-extinguishing system in each nacelle. Smoke detectors in baggage holds.

AVIONICS: Avionics meet ICAO standards for Cat II weather minima and include updated navigation system with triplex INS. Automatic flight control system operates throughout flight except during take-off to 400 m (1,312 ft) and landing from 30 m (100 ft). Automatic go-round and automatic speed control provided by autothrottle down to 10 m (33 ft) on landing. Weather radar, transponder, Doppler, dual HF and VHF com and emergency VHF, cockpit voice recorder and GPWS standard.

DIMENSIONS, EXTERNAL:

Wing span	37·55 m (123 ft 2½ in)
Length overall	47·90 m (157 ft 1¾ in)
Height overall	11·40 m (37 ft 4¾ in)
Diameter of fuselage	3·80 m (12 ft 5½ in)
Tailplane span	13·40 m (43 ft 11½ in)
Wheel track	11·50 m (37 ft 9 in)
Wheelbase	18·92 m (62 ft 1 in)
Passenger doors (each): Height	1·73 m (5 ft 7 in)
Width	0·80 m (2 ft 7½ in)
Height to sill	3·10 m (10 ft 2 in)
Servicing door: Height	1·28 m (4 ft 2½ in)
Width	0·61 m (2 ft 0 in)
Emergency door: Height	1·28 m (4 ft 2½ in)
Width	0·64 m (2 ft 1¼ in)
Emergency exits (each): Height	0·90 m (2 ft 11½ in)
Width	0·48 m (1 ft 7 in)
Main baggage hold doors (each):	
Height	1·20 m (3 ft 11¼ in)
Width	1·35 m (4 ft 5 in)
Height to sill	1·80 m (5 ft 11 in)
Rear (unpressurised) hold:	
Height	0·90 m (2 ft 11½ in)
Width	1·10 m (3 ft 7¼ in)
Height to sill	2·20 m (7 ft 2½ in)

DIMENSIONS, INTERNAL:

Cabin: Width	3·58 m (11 ft 9 in)
Height	2·02 m (6 ft 7½ in)
Volume	163·2 m³ (5,763 cu ft)
Main baggage holds: front	21·5 m³ (759 cu ft)
rear	16·5 m³ (582 cu ft)
Rear underfloor hold	5·0 m³ (176 cu ft)

AREAS:

Wings, gross	201·45 m² (2,169 sq ft)
Horizontal tail surfaces	42·20 m² (454·24 sq ft)

WEIGHTS:

Basic operating weight, empty	55,300 kg (121,915 lb)
Max payload	18,000 kg (39,680 lb)
Max fuel	39,750 kg (87,633 lb)
Max T-O weight	100,000 kg (220,460 lb)
Max landing weight	80,000 kg (176,370 lb)

PERFORMANCE:

Max cruising speed	513 knots (950 km/h; 590 mph)
Max cruising height	11,900 m (39,000 ft)
Range:	
with max payload	2,019 nm (3,740 km; 2,324 miles)
with max fuel and 5,450 kg (12,015 lb) payload	3,563 nm (6,600 km; 4,100 miles)

TUPOLEV Tu-154C

This freight carrying version of the Tu-154 was announced in the Autumn of 1982. It is being offered initially as a conversion of the Tu-154B, with an unobstructed cargo volume of 72 m³ (2,542 cu ft) in the main cabin. A freight door 2·80 m (9 ft 2¼ in) wide and 1·87 m (6 ft 1½ in) high is installed in the port side of the cabin, forward of the wing, with a ball mat inside and roller tracks the full length of the floor of the cabin. Typical loads include nine standard international pallets measuring 2·24 m × 2·74 m (88 in × 108 in), plus additional freight in the standard underfloor baggage holds which have a volume of 38 m³ (1,341 cu ft). Nominal range of the Tu-154C, with 20,000 kg (44,100 lb) of cargo, is 1,565 nm (2,900 km; 1,800 miles).

Artist's impression of the twin-turbofan Tupolev Tu-204, under development to replace the Tu-154 *(Jane's/Mike Keep)*

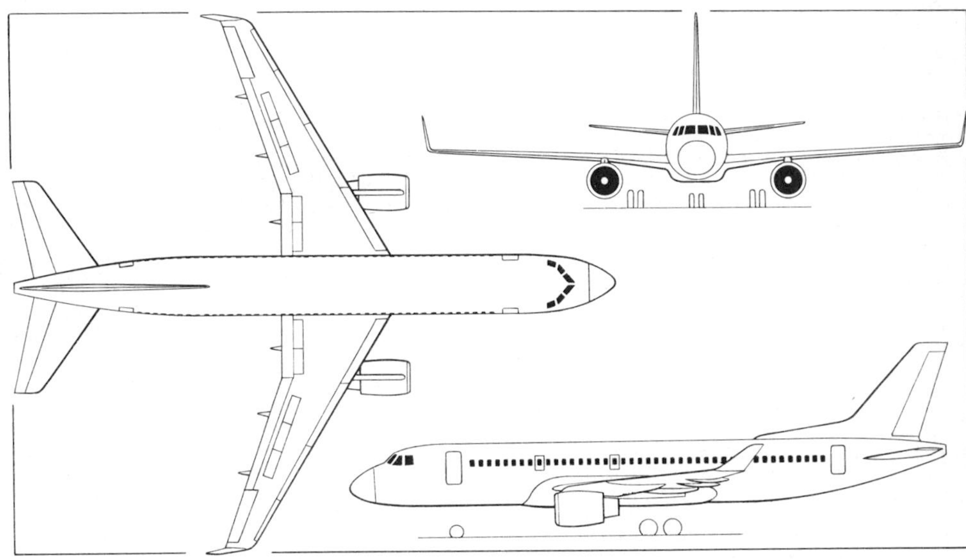
Tupolev Tu-204 medium range transport (two turbofans in 157 kN; 35,300 lb st class) *(Pilot Press)*

TUPOLEV Tu-204

It was announced in 1983 that the Tupolev Bureau was developing a new medium range transport aircraft, designated Tu-204, to replace the Tu-154. Preliminary details became available in Spring 1985.

The Tu-204 will be a low-wing monoplane, with two Soloviev turbofan engines of the type specified for the four-engined Il-96-300, pylon mounted in underwing pods. They will each be rated at 157 kN (35,300 lb st). The fuselage, of elliptical cross-section, will accommodate 170-219 passengers six-abreast. Two-crew operation will be permitted, but there will be provision for a flight engineer if required. New metals and composites will be used in the airframe; new generation equipment will include a dual EFIS with twin colour CRT displays for each pilot, a triplex automatic approach and landing system permitting operation in ICAO Category III minima, and a head-up display. The traditional control columns will be replaced by side-stick controllers similar to those on the Airbus A320. Noise levels will meet ICAO Chapter 3 Supplement 16 requirements.

The Tu-204 is being designed for a service life of 45,000 flight hours and 30,000 landings.

DIMENSIONS, EXTERNAL:

Wing span over winglets	42·00 m (137 ft 9½ in)
Length overall	45·00 m (147 ft 7¾ in)
Fuselage: Max depth	4·08 m (13 ft 4¾ in)
Max width	3·80 m (12 ft 5½ in)

DIMENSION, INTERNAL:

Cabin: Height	2·20 m (7 ft 2½ in)

WEIGHTS:

Weight empty	56,600 kg (124,780 lb)
Max payload	21,000 kg (46,300 lb)
Max T-O weight	94,000 kg (207,235 lb)

PERFORMANCE (estimated):

Max level speed	486 knots (900 km/h; 559 mph)
Cruising speed at 11,000-12,000 m (36,100-39,375 ft)	448 knots (830 km/h; 515 mph)
Landing speed	135 knots (250 km/h; 155 mph)
Range:	
with max payload	1,295 nm (2,400 km; 1,490 miles)
with 212 passengers	1,400 nm (2,600 km; 1,615 miles)
with 17,200 kg (37,920 lb) payload	1,890 nm (3,500 km; 2,175 miles)
with 15,600 kg (34,390 lb) payload	2,160 nm (4,000 km; 2,485 miles)

YAKOVLEV

GENERAL DESIGNER IN CHARGE OF BUREAU:
Alexander Sergeivich Yakovlev

Alexander Yakovlev is one of the most versatile Soviet designers, and products of his design bureau have ranged from transonic long-range fighters to the Yak-24 tandem-rotor helicopter, an operational VTOL carrier based fighter and a variety of training and transport aircraft. Types in current production and service are described hereafter.

YAKOVLEV Yak-18T

The first prototype of this extensively redesigned cabin version of the Yak-18 trainer flew for the first time in Summer 1967. It was powered, like the Yak-18A and -18PM, with a 224 kW (300 hp) Ivchenko AI-14RF nine-cylinder radial engine, driving a two-blade variable-pitch propeller, but this was superseded by a more powerful M-14P radial engine when the Yak-18T was ordered into full production at Smolensk. Details of the development programme can be found in the 1982-83 and earlier editions of *Jane's*.

Yakovlev Yak-18T ambulance aircraft (Vedeneyev M-14P engine)

By 1974 it was possible to train the complete intake of 100 pupil pilots at Sasov flying school on the new aircraft. Now, as the standard basic trainer at Aeroflot schools, the Yak-18T is used for circuits, instrument training and navigation training, and as a flying classroom for an instructor and three pupils. Only one pupil accompanies the instructor on aerobatic flights.

Second version to enter service, as a successor to the Yak-12, was the Yak-18T ambulance, with accommodation for a stretcher patient on the starboard side of the cabin and a medical attendant behind the pilot. Other current versions include a light communications transport for four persons, in pairs; and a freighter with the three passenger seats removed to enable cargo to be carried beside and behind the pilot and in the baggage compartment.

Designer responsible for this variant of the Yak-18 was Mr Yuri Yankievich.

TYPE: Four-seat multi-purpose light aircraft.

WINGS: Cantilever low-wing monoplane, in three sections: a constant chord centre-section, integral with the fuselage, and two tapered outer panels. Wing section Clark YH, with thickness/chord ratio of 14·5% at root and 9·3% at tip. Dihedral on outer panels only. Two-spar light alloy construction. Light alloy covering on centre-section and on leading-edges of outer panels; inboard 25% of outer panels covered with light alloy, remainder with fabric. Slotted ailerons of light alloy construction, each hinged at three points and partly fabric covered. Light alloy split flap across entire span of centre-section, actuated by two pneumatic servo motors. Fixed step at port wingroot trailing-edge, with corrugated upper surface walkway to door on each side. Ailerons operated by pushrods. Ground adjustable tab on each aileron.

FUSELAGE: Conventional light alloy semi-monocoque structure, of basically square section. Skin on rear fuselage spot welded to frames and stringers.

TAIL UNIT: Braced light alloy structure, with wire bracing above tailplane and wire and strut bracing below. All surfaces fabric covered. Control surfaces operated by both pushrods and cables. Controllable trim tab in each elevator.

LANDING GEAR: Fully retractable tricycle type, with single wheel on each unit. Pneumatic retraction, nosewheel rearward, main units inward into centre-section. No mainwheel doors. Oleo-nitrogen shock absorbers. Castoring but non-steerable self-centering nosewheel with shimmy damper. Mainwheel tyres size 500 × 150; nosewheel tyre size 400 × 150. Differential pneumatic brakes on mainwheels, with override button on instructor's control wheel.

POWER PLANT: One 269 kW (360 hp) Vedeneyev M-14P nine-cylinder aircooled radial engine, driving a two-blade variable-pitch metal propeller, without spinner. Louvres in front of cowling to regulate cooling. Two-part cowling, split on horizontal centreline. Fuel tank in each wingroot, combined capacity 208 litres (45·75 Imp gallons; 55 US gallons).

ACCOMMODATION: Car type cabin, seating four persons in pairs. Large forward hinged door on each side, jettisonable in emergency. Provision for upholstered or parachute type front seats. Rear bench seat removable for freight carrying. Ambulance configuration available, for pilot, stretcher patient and medical attendant. Large baggage compartment aft of rear seat, with external access on port side. Stretcher of ambulance version is loaded via baggage door. Cabin furnishings of non-inflammable synthetic materials. Dual control wheels. Glareshield above panel. Heating and ventilation standard.

SYSTEMS: Pneumatic system for actuating landing gear and flaps. Electrical system includes instrument panel red lighting, navigation and landing lights, and anti-collision beacon at top of fin.

AVIONICS AND EQUIPMENT: Standard equipment includes UHF radio, intercom, radio compass, radio altimeter and flight recorder.

DIMENSIONS, EXTERNAL:

Wing span	11·16 m (36 ft 7¼ in)
Length overall	8·35 m (27 ft 4¾ in)

AREA:

Wings, gross	18·75 m² (201·8 sq ft)

WEIGHTS AND LOADINGS (A, with instructor and one pupil; B, with instructor and three pupils):

Max payload: A	306 kg (675 lb)
B	436 kg (960 lb)
Max T-O weight: A	1,500 kg (3,307 lb)
B	1,650 kg (3,637 lb)
Max wing loading: A	80 kg/m² (16·4 lb/sq ft)
B	88 kg/m² (18·0 lb/sq ft)
Max power loading: A	5·59 kg/kW (11·0 lb/hp)
B	6·15 kg/kW (12·1 lb/hp)

PERFORMANCE (at max T-O weight: A, with instructor and one pupil; B, with instructor and three pupils):

Max level speed:	
A, B	159 knots (295 km/h; 183 mph)
Max cruising speed:	
B	135 knots (250 km/h; 155 mph)
Max rate of climb at S/L: B	300 m (985 ft)/min
Service ceiling: A, B	5,500 m (18,000 ft)
T-O run: A	330 m (1,085 ft)
B	400 m (1,315 ft)
Landing run: A	400 m (1,315 ft)
B	500 m (1,640 ft)
Range with max fuel, with reserves:	
A	350 nm (650 km; 403 miles)
B	485 nm (900 km; 560 miles)

Version of the Yak-28 known to NATO as 'Brewer-D' *(Flug Revue)*

Yak-28P ('Firebar') fitted with original short radome and carrying two 'Anab' missiles *(Flug Revue)*

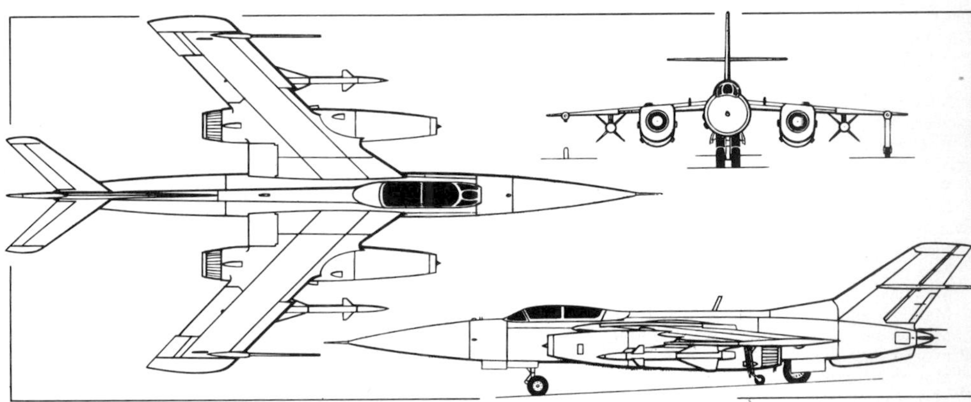

The long-nose version of the Yakovlev Yak-28P two-seat all-weather fighter ('Firebar') *(Pilot Press)*

YAKOVLEV Yak-28

NATO reporting names: Brewer, Firebar and Maestro

First seen in considerable numbers in the 1961 Soviet Aviation Day flypast were three successors to the Yak-25/27 series (see 1971-72 *Jane's*), described by the commentator as supersonic multi-purpose aircraft and identified subsequently by the designation Yak-28. Brief details of the two-seat tactical attack versions known to NATO as 'Brewer-A, B and C' can be found in earlier editions of *Jane's*. Versions still operational are as follows:

Brewer-D. Reconnaissance version, with cameras or other sensors, including side looking airborne radar, in bomb bay. Two-seater, with pilot under blister canopy and navigator in glazed nose. Blister radome under fuselage forward of wings. About 220 operational in 1986.

Brewer-E. First Soviet operational ECM escort aircraft, deployed in 1970. Active ECM pack built into bomb bay, from which it projects in cylindrical form. No radome under front fuselage, but many additional antennae and fairings. Attachment under each outer wing, outboard of external fuel tank, for a rocket pod, chaff dispenser or anti-radiation missile. About 102 in service in 1986, including some in the Soviet far east which have been seen over the Sea of Japan.

Firebar. Tandem two-seat all-weather fighter. No internal weapons bay. Armament comprises one 'Anab' air-to-air missile under each wing. Identified as **Yak-28P** (Perekhvatchik; interceptor), the suffix 'P' indicating that the design had been *adapted* for the fighter role. Longer dielectric nosecone fitted retrospectively on many Yak-28Ps in squadron service does not indicate any increase in radar capability or aircraft performance. About 105 Yak-28P 'Firebars' continue to operate with the Soviet Voyska PVO home defence interceptor force and tactical forces.

Maestro (Yak-28U). Trainer version of 'Firebar'. Normal cockpit layout replaced by two individual single-seat cockpits in tandem, each with its own canopy. Front canopy sideways hinged to starboard; rear canopy rearward sliding.

The following details refer specifically to the Yak-28P, but are generally applicable to the other versions of the Yak-28:

TYPE: Two-seat all-weather interceptor.

WINGS: Cantilever shoulder-wing monoplane of basically constant chord. Extended leading-edge on outer wings and also between fuselage and each engine nacelle. Outer extensions are drooped. Slotted flap, with unswept trailing-edge, between fuselage and each engine nacelle. Basic wing sweepback 45°. Anhedral from root. Single fence on upper surface of each wing, between fuselage and engine nacelle. Large trailing-edge flap and short aileron, with tab, outboard of nacelle on each wing. Balancer wheel fairings, inset from wingtips, are extended forward as lead filled wing balance weights.

FUSELAGE: All-metal semi-monocoque structure of basically circular section. Finely tapered dielectric nosecone over radar scanner.

TAIL UNIT: Cantilever all-metal structure. Variable incidence tailplane mounted midway up fin. All surfaces sweptback. Trim tab in rudder. Dorsal fin fairs into spine along top of fuselage. Shallow ventral stabilising fin.

LANDING GEAR: Two twin-wheel main units in tandem, retracting into fuselage. Front unit retracts forward, rear unit rearward. Small balancer wheel near each wingtip, retracting rearward under wing; fairing integral with leg.

POWER PLANT: Two afterburning turbojet engines, related to Tumansky R-11 fitted to some versions of MiG-21, with rating of 58·35 kN (13,120 lb st). Each fitted with centrebody shock cone. A pointed external fuel tank can be carried under the leading-edge of each wing, outboard of the engine nacelle.

ACCOMMODATION: Crew of two in tandem on ejection seats in pressurised cabin under long rearward sliding transparent blister canopy.

AVIONICS: Reported to include tail warning radar.

ARMAMENT: Two pylons under each outer wing. Normal armament comprises two air-to-air missiles (NATO 'Anab'), with alternative infra-red or semi-active radar homing heads.

DIMENSIONS, EXTERNAL (estimated):
Wing span 12·95 m (42 ft 6 in)
Length overall: Yak-28P (long nose) 23·00 m (75 ft 5½ in)
Height overall 3·95 m (12 ft 11½ in)

WEIGHT (estimated):
Max T-O weight: Yak-28P 20,000 kg (44,000 lb)

PERFORMANCE (Yak-28P, estimated):
Max level speed at 10,670 m (35,000 ft) Mach 1·88 (1,080 knots; 2,000 km/h; 1,240 mph)
Cruising speed 496 knots (920 km/h; 571 mph)
Service ceiling 16,750 m (55,000 ft)
Max combat radius 500 nm (925 km; 575 miles)

YAKOVLEV Yak-36MP/Yak-38

NATO reporting name: Forger

Known originally as the **Yak-36MP** (*Morskoy Palubnyi:* maritime carrier-borne), the **Yak-38** is the V/STOL combat aircraft deployed by a Soviet Navy development squadron on the *Kiev*, the first of its class of four 40,000 ton carrier/cruisers to put to sea in 1976, and subsequently on its sister ships, the *Minsk, Novorossiysk* and *Baku.* Two versions have been observed, as follows:

Forger-A. Basic single-seat combat aircraft, utilising a mixture of vectored thrust and direct jet lift. Prototype was completed in 1971 and production began in 1975. Twelve appear to be operational on each ship, in addition to 'Forger-Bs' and about 19 Kamov Ka-25 or Ka-27 anti-submarine and missile targeting helicopters. Primary operational roles assumed to be reconnaissance, strikes against small ships, and fleet defence against shadowing maritime reconnaissance aircraft.

Forger-B. Two-seat trainer, of which two are deployed on each carrier/cruiser. Second cockpit forward of normal cockpit, with ejection seat at a lower level, under a continuous transparent canopy. To compensate for the longer nose, a 'plug' is inserted in the fuselage aft of the wing, lengthening the constant-section portion without requiring modification of the tapering rear fuselage assembly. In other respects this version appears to be identical to 'Forger-A', but has no ranging radar or weapon pylons.

Observers of deck flying by 'Forger-As' report that the aircraft appear to be extremely stable during take-off and landing. Initially, take-off was always made vertically, with the vectored thrust nozzles up to 10° forward of vertical. This was followed by a smooth conversion about 5 to 6 m (15-20 ft) above the deck, achieved by lowering the aircraft's nose about 5° below the horizon and maintaining this attitude until the aircraft had accelerated to 30-40 knots (55-75 km/h; 35-46 mph). At this speed, a 5° nose-up attitude was assumed, and the accelerating transition was continued by vectoring aft the nozzles of the propulsion engine.

This VTO technique has been superseded by a STOL type of take-off, with a short forward run, made possible by an automatic control system which ensures 'that the lift engines are brought into use, and the thrust vectoring rear nozzles rotated, at the optimum point in the take-off run'. As in the case of the British Harrier, STOL take-off can be assumed to offer improved payload/range capability.

Landing procedure begins with a gradual descent from far astern, with the last 400 m (1,300 ft) flown essentially level, about 30 m (100 ft) above the water. The aircraft crosses the ship's stern with about a 5 knot (10 km/h; 6 mph) closure rate, 10-14 m (35-45 ft) above the flight deck, then flares gently to a hover and descends vertically. Precise landings are ensured by the automatic control system, perhaps in association with laser devices lining each side of the rear deck.

Development has been continuous throughout the period since the Yak-38 was first seen on the *Kiev*. Some early 'Forger-As' lacked the now standard auxiliary intake doors aft of each engine air intake. A fence has been added on each side of the hinged door above the liftjets, extending back to a station in line with the wingroot leading-edge, presumably to prevent ingestion of reflected exhaust efflux. Production is thought to have totalled some 70 aircraft by Spring 1986.

The following description applies to the single-seat 'Forger-A':

TYPE: Ship based V/STOL combat aircraft.

WINGS: Cantilever mid-wing monoplane, of very small area. Thickness/chord ratio estimated at 6% or less. Constant anhedral from roots. Sweepback on leading-edge approx 45°. Conventional light alloy structure. Each wing comprises two all-metal panels of approx equal span, of which the outer panel folds vertically upward for stowage on board ship. Inboard panel has unswept trailing-edge, occupied by a large single-slotted Fowler flap. Outer panel has a slightly sweptback trailing-edge, occupied almost entirely by an aileron with setback hinges and inset trim tab. No leading-edge flaps or slats. Jet reaction control valve with upper and lower slots in each wingtip.

FUSELAGE: Conventional semi-monocoque light alloy structure of oval cross-section. Integral engine air intake ducts, with boundary layer splitter plates and downward inclined lips forward of rear edge of transparent cockpit canopy. Row of small blow-in auxiliary intake doors a short distance aft of each intake. Rearward hinged door over liftjets, immediately aft of canopy, with 16 spring loaded louvres. Location of corresponding side-hinged underfuselage doors conforms with forward tilt of lift engines. Positions of these doors are controlled automatically during take-off and landing as part of control system. Fence on each side of door above liftjets. Small fence aft of each door beneath liftjets. Yaw reaction control nozzle to each side of small tailcone. No reaction control system in nose.

TAIL UNIT: Conventional light alloy structure, with sweepback on all surfaces and considerable tailplane anhedral. Rudder and each elevator have setback hinges and trim tab. Air intake at front of long duct extending forward from base of fin, to cool avionics bay in rear fuselage.

LANDING GEAR: Retractable tricycle type. Single wheel on each unit, with legs of trailing link type with oleo-pneumatic shock absorption. Nose unit retracts rearward, main units forward into fuselage. Small bumper under upward curving rear fuselage.

POWER PLANT: Primary power plant is a Lyulka AL-21 turbojet engine (approx 80 kN; 17,985 lb st), mounted in the centre-fuselage and exhausting through a single pair of vectoring side nozzles aft of the wings. No afterburner is fitted. Two Koliesov liftjet engines (each 35 kN; 7,875 lb st) in tandem, immediately aft of cockpit, exhausting downward, and used also to adjust pitch and trim. Fuel tanks in fuselage, forward and aft of main engine. Drop tanks, each estimated to have capacity of 600 litres (132

Yakovlev Yak-38 (NATO 'Forger-A') V/STOL combat aircraft on the carrier/cruiser *Novorossiysk*. **Note the underwing gun and rocket pods** *(Royal Navy)*

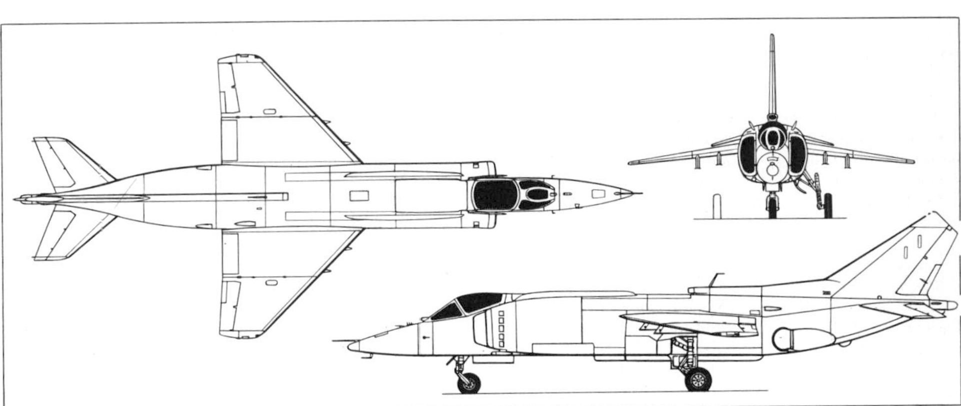

Yakovlev Yak-38 single-seat V/STOL carrier based combat aircraft (NATO 'Forger-A') *(Pilot Press)*

The two-seat training version of the Yak-38 ('Forger-B')

Yakovlev Yak-42 medium-range transport (three Lotarev D-36 turbofan engines) *(Brian M. Service)*

Imp gallons; 158 US gallons), can be carried on underwing pylons.

ACCOMMODATION: Pilot only, on zero-speed/zero-height ejection seat, under sideways hinged (to starboard) transparent canopy. Electronic system ejects pilot automatically if aircraft height and descent rate are sensed to indicate an emergency. Armoured glass windscreen.

AVIONICS: Ranging radar in nose. IFF (NATO 'Odd Rods') antennae forward of windscreen. Other avionics in rear fuselage. Fully automatic control system for use during take-off and landing, to ensure synchronisation of engine functioning, aerodynamic control operation, jet reaction nozzle operation, stabilisation and guidance.

ARMAMENT: No installed armament. Two pylons under fixed panel of each wing for 2,600-3,600 kg (5,730-7,935 lb) of external stores, including gun pods each containing a 23 mm twin-barrel GSh-23 cannon, rocket packs, bombs weighing up to 500 kg each, 'Kerry' short-range air-to-surface missiles, armour-piercing anti-ship missiles, 'Aphid' air-to-air missiles and auxiliary fuel tanks.

DIMENSIONS, EXTERNAL (estimated):
Wing span 7·32 m (24 ft 0 in)
Width, wings folded 4·88 m (16 ft 0 in)
Length overall: 'Forger-A' 15·50 m (50 ft 10¼ in)
'Forger-B' 17·68 m (58 ft 0 in)
Height overall 4·37 m (14 ft 4 in)
Tailplane span 3·81 m (12 ft 6 in)
Wheel track 2·90 m (9 ft 6 in)
Wheelbase 5·50 m (18 ft 0 in)

AREA:
Wings, gross 18·5 m² (199 sq ft)

WEIGHTS (estimated):
Basic operating weight, incl pilot(s):
'Forger-A' 7,485 kg (16,500 lb)
'Forger-B' 8,390 kg (18,500 lb)
Max T-O weight 11,700 kg (25,795 lb)

PERFORMANCE ('Forger-A', estimated, at max T-O weight):
Max level speed at height
Mach 0·95 (545 knots; 1,009 km/h; 627 mph)
Max level speed at S/L
Mach 0·8 (528 knots; 978 km/h; 608 mph)
Max rate of climb at S/L 4,500 m (14,750 ft)/min
Service ceiling 12,000 m (39,375 ft)
Combat radius:
with air-to-air missiles and external tanks, 75 min on station 100 nm (185 km; 115 miles)
with max weapons, lo-lo-lo 130 nm (240 km; 150 miles)
with max weapons, hi-lo-hi 200 nm (370 km; 230 miles)

YAKOVLEV Yak-42

NATO reporting name: Clobber

On the basis of experience with the Yak-40, the Yakovlev Design Bureau developed for Aeroflot this larger civil airliner with a similar three-engined layout. According to Alexander Yakovlev, the basic design objectives were simple construction, reliability in operation, economy, and the ability to operate in remote areas with widely differing climatic conditions. Up to 2,000 aircraft in this category are needed, for use particularly on feederline services extending north and south from the main east-west trans-Siberian trunk routes.

Three prototypes of the Yak-42 were ordered initially. The first of these (SSSR-1974) flew for the first time on 7 March 1975, with a wing sweepback of 11°, and was furnished as a 100-passenger local service version with carry-on baggage and coat stowage fore and aft of the cabin. The second prototype (SSSR-1975) had 23° of wing sweep, and cabin windows which extended further forward and rearward on each side, indicating that it was representative of the 120-seat version with three more rows of seats and no carry-on baggage areas. The third prototype (SSSR-1976; re-registered subsequently as SSSR-42303) differed from the second only in detail, having hot air de-icing on the tail surfaces as well as the wings; fairing discs over the mainwheels and longer leg fairings to improve airflow over the doorless main landing gear when retracted; and movement further forward of the overwing emergency exits.

It was made known that a decision on the degree of wing sweep to be standardised for production aircraft would be taken after simultaneous evaluation of the prototypes, in terms of high speed cruise, economy and low speed handling characteristics. The 23° wing showed itself superior, and aircraft No. SSSR-42303, exhibited at the 1977 Paris Salon, was generally typical of the first series of 200 production Yak-42s, which are being built at Smolensk to replace Tu-134s currently in Aeroflot service. Further changes introduced on production aircraft include the use of four-wheel main landing gear bogies instead of the twin-wheel units fitted to the prototypes.

The Yak-42 entered scheduled passenger service with Aeroflot in late 1980, operating first over the Moscow-Krasnodar route. Ten aircraft had been flown by mid-1981, and it was hoped to complete 20 more by the end of the year. A first export order, for seven, had been placed by Aviogenex of Yugoslavia.

An accident in 1982 is reported to have led to withdrawal of the Yak-42 from Aeroflot service until October 1984. It then began to re-enter service, starting with the Saratov-Leningrad and Moscow-Bykovo routes.

On 29 January 1981, a Yak-42 piloted by Valentin Mukhin set a record in FAI Class C1m (T-O weight 45,000-55,000 kg) by lifting a load of 20,186 kg (44,502 lb) to a height of 2,000 m (6,562 ft). In subsequent flights, the aircraft climbed to 3,000 m in 2 min 37·3 s, 6,000 m in 5 min 11·4 s, and 9,000 m in 9 min 31·1 s to claim Class C1l (35,000-45,000 kg) records; and to 3,000 m in 3 min 5·9 s, 6,000 m in 6 min 26·9 s, and 9,000 m in 11 min 48·2 s to claim Class C1m records. On 14-15 December 1981, a Yak-42 with Valentin Mukhin as pilot in command set a Class C1m straight line distance record of 3,317·94 nm (6,144·82 km; 3,818·21 miles) between Sheremetievo (Moscow) and Khabarovsk.

The Yak-42 is intended to use all three engines at cruise power during flight. It can, however, continue take-off after the failure of any one engine, and can maintain level cruising flight on a single engine.

Design is in accordance with the latest airworthiness standards of the Soviet civil authorities and US FAR 25 requirements. Special care has been taken during design to ensure that the D-36 engines conform with national and international limits on smoke and noise; and the Yak-42 is intended to operate in temperatures ranging from −50°C to +50°C. An APU is standard, for engine starting and ground services, making the aircraft independent of airport equipment. Airframe design life is 30,000 flying hours or 30,000 landings in 15 years. Engine life is 18,000 operating hours with two major overhauls.

The following details refer to the Yak-42 in its current production form, as exhibited at the 1985 Paris Air Show. Wing span is increased by 48 cm (1 ft 7 in) and max T-O weight by 500 kg (1,102 lb) by comparison with early aircraft.

TYPE: Three-turbofan short/medium-range passenger transport.

WINGS: Cantilever low-wing monoplane, consisting of a centre-section and two outer panels. No dihedral or anhedral. Sweepback 23° at quarter-chord. All-metal two-spar torsion box structure. Two-section aileron on each wing, with servo tab on inner section and trim tab on outer section. Two-section single-slotted trailing-edge flaps on each wing. Three-section spoilers forward of outer flaps. Full span leading-edge flaps. Ailerons and flaps actuated hydraulically.

FUSELAGE: All-metal riveted, bonded and welded semi-monocoque structure, of basic circular section, blending into an oval section rear fuselage.

TAIL UNIT: Cantilever all-metal T tail structure, with sweepback on all surfaces. One-piece tailplane; incidence variable from 4° upward to 8° downward. Trim tab in each elevator. Trim tab and spring servo tab in rudder. Control surfaces actuated hydraulically.

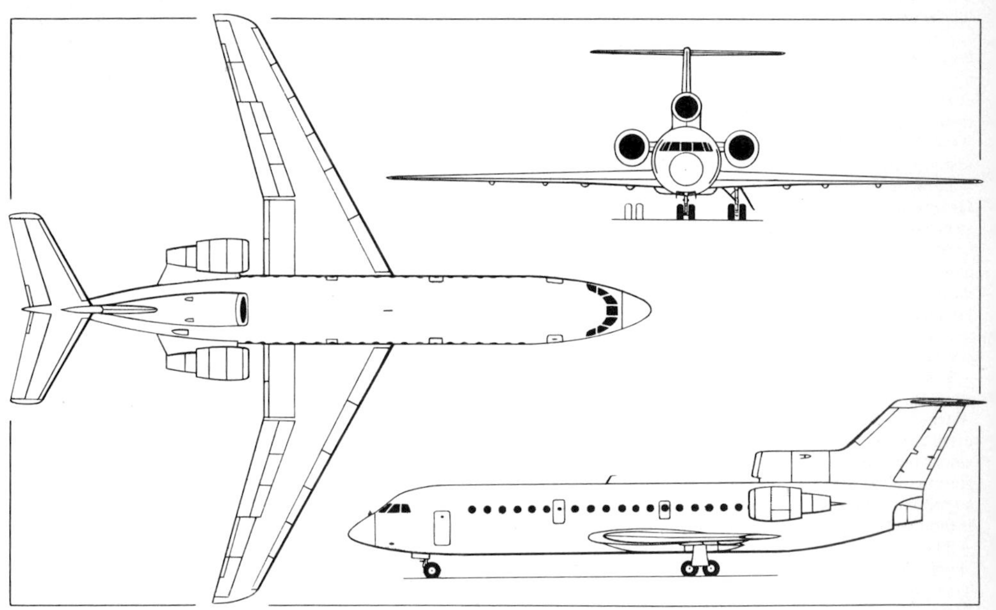

Yakovlev Yak-42 three-turbofan medium-range passenger transport *(Pilot Press)*

LANDING GEAR: Hydraulically retractable tricycle heavy-duty type. Four-wheel bogie main units retract inward into flattened fuselage undersurface. Twin nosewheels retract forward. Hydraulic backup system for extension only. Emergency extension by gravity. Oleo-nitrogen shock absorbers. Steerable nose unit of levered suspension type. Low pressure tyres; size 930 × 305 on nosewheels. Hydraulic disc brakes on mainwheels. Nosewheel brakes to stop wheel rotation after take-off.

POWER PLANT: Three Lotarev D-36 three-shaft turbofan engines, each rated at 63·74 kN (14,330 lb st). Centre engine, mounted inside rear fuselage, has S-duct air intake. Outboard engines are mounted in pod on each side of rear fuselage. No thrust reversers. Integral fuel tanks between spars in wings, capacity approx 23,175 litres (5,100 Imp gallons; 6,120 US gallons). APU standard, for engine starting, and for power and air-conditioning supply on ground and, if necessary, in flight.

ACCOMMODATION: Crew of two side by side on flight deck, with provision for flight engineer if required, and two or three cabin attendants. Single passenger cabin, with total of 120 seats in six-abreast rows, at pitch of 75 cm (29·5 in), with centre aisle, 45 cm (17·7 in) wide, in high-density configuration. Alternative 104-passenger (96 tourist, 8 first class) local service configuration, with carry-on baggage and coat stowage compartments fore and aft of cabin. Main airstair door hinges down from undersurface of rear fuselage. Second door forward of cabin on port side, with integral airstairs. Service door opposite. Galley and crew coat stowage between flight deck and front vestibule. Passenger coat stowage and toilet between vestibule and cabin. Second coat stowage and toilet at rear of cabin. Two underfloor holds for cargo, mail and baggage in standard containers, loaded through a large door on the starboard side, forward of wing. Chain-drive handling system for containers built into cabin floor. Forward hold accommodates six containers, each with capacity of 2·2 m³ (77·7 cu ft); rear hold takes three similar containers. Provision for convertible passenger/cargo interior, with enlarged loading door on port side of front fuselage. Two emergency exits overwing on each side. All passenger and crew accommodation pressurised and air-conditioned, and furnished with non-inflammable materials.

AVIONICS AND EQUIPMENT: Flight and navigation equipment for operation by day and night under adverse weather conditions, with landings on concrete or unpaved runways in ICAO Category II weather minima down to 40 m (131 ft) visibility at 300 m (985 ft). Type SAU-42 automatic flight control system and area navigation system standard.

DIMENSIONS, EXTERNAL:
- Wing span: 34·88 m (114 ft 5¼ in)
- Wing aspect ratio: 8·11
- Length overall: 36·38 m (119 ft 4¼ in)
- Fuselage diameter: 3·80 m (12 ft 5½ in)
- Height overall: 9·83 m (32 ft 3 in)
- Tailplane span: 10·80 m (35 ft 5 in)
- Wheel track: 5·63 m (18 ft 5¾ in)
- Wheelbase: 14·78 m (48 ft 6 in)
- Passenger door (fwd):
  - Height: 1·81 m (5 ft 11¼ in)
  - Width: 0·83 m (2 ft 8½ in)
- Passenger entrance (rear): Height: 1·78 m (5 ft 10 in)
  - Width: 0·81 m (2 ft 7¾ in)
- Cargo door (convertible version):
  - Height: 2·025 m (6 ft 7¾ in)
  - Width: 3·23 m (10 ft 7 in)
- Baggage/cargo hold door: Height: 1·35 m (4 ft 5 in)
  - Width: 1·145 m (3 ft 9 in)
  - Height to sill: 1·45 m (4 ft 9 in)

DIMENSIONS, INTERNAL:
- Cabin: Length: 19·89 m (65 ft 3 in)
  - Max width: 3·60 m (11 ft 9¾ in)
  - Height: 2·08 m (6 ft 9¾ in)
- Forward baggage compartment volume (100-seater): 19·8 m³ (700 cu ft)
- Rear baggage compartment volume (100-seater): 9·5 m³ (335 cu ft)

AREAS:
- Wings, gross: 150 m² (1,615 sq ft)
- Horizontal tail surfaces (total): 27·60 m² (297·1 sq ft)
- Vertical tail surfaces (total): 23·29 m² (250·7 sq ft)

WEIGHTS:
- Weight empty, equipped:
  - 120 passengers: 32,500 kg (71,650 lb)
  - 104 passengers: 34,000 kg (74,955 lb)
- Max payload: 120 passengers: 14,000 kg (30,865 lb)
  - 104 passengers: 11,600 kg (25,575 lb)
- Max fuel: 18,500 kg (40,785 lb)
- Max T-O weight: 54,000 kg (119,050 lb)
- Max landing weight: 50,000 kg (110,230 lb)

PERFORMANCE:
- Max cruising speed at 7,620 m (25,000 ft): 437 knots (810 km/h; 503 mph)
- Econ cruising speed: 405 knots (750 km/h; 466 mph)
- T-O speed: 124 knots (230 km/h; 143 mph) IAS
- Approach speed: 114 knots (210 km/h; 131 mph) IAS
- Max cruising height: 9,100 m (29,850 ft)
- T-O field length (30°C): 1,800 m (5,900 ft)
- Landing from 15 m (50 ft): 1,100 m (3,610 ft)
- Range at econ cruising speed, with 3,470 kg (7,650 lb) fuel reserves:
  - with 10,800 kg (23,810 lb) payload (120 seater): 940 nm (1,740 km; 1,080 miles)
  - with 9,360 kg (20,635 lb) payload (104 seater): 918 nm (1,700 km; 1,056 miles)
  - with max fuel and 3,300 kg (7,275 lb) payload (120 seater): 2,050 nm (3,800 km; 2,360 miles)
  - with max fuel and 1,800 kg (3,968 lb) payload (104 seater): 2,050 nm (3,800 km; 2,360 miles)

Yakovlev Yak-50 single-seat aerobatic and sporting aircraft

YAKOVLEV Yak-42M

This stretched version of the Yak-42 is scheduled to enter service with Aeroflot in 1987. The fuselage will be lengthened by 4·50 m (14 ft 9 in), to accommodate 156 to 168 passengers. The current D-36 engines will be replaced by three Lotarev D-436 turbofans, each rated at 73·6 kN (16,550 lb st). Navigation equipment will also be upgraded.

WEIGHT:
- Max T-O weight: 66,000 kg (145,505 lb)

PERFORMANCE (estimated):
- Balanced T-O field length:
  - at 62,000 kg (136,685 lb) AUW: 1,800 m (5,900 ft)
  - at max T-O weight: 2,300 m (7,550 ft)
- Range:
  - with 15,000 kg (35,275 lb) payload: 1,350 nm (2,500 km; 1,550 miles)
  - with 10,000 kg (22,050 lb) payload: 2,025 nm (3,750 km; 2,330 miles)
- Range with max fuel, with reserves: 2,160 nm (4,000 km; 2,485 miles)

YAKOVLEV Yak-50

First reference to this aircraft came in a Novosti Press Agency bulletin on 30 June 1975, which stated that tests of a new Yakovlev sporting aircraft, designated Yak-50, had been carried out near Arsenyev in the Soviet Far East. Mr Nikolai Sazykin, director of the Progress Engineering Works in which all Yakovlev sporting aircraft are assembled, was quoted as saying that the Yak-50 was intended to participate in the 1976 world aerobatic championships. Test pilot Anatoly Sergeyev stated only that it was more advanced than the familiar Yak-18 training and aerobatic monoplane, with a more powerful engine, better manoeuvrability, a speed of over 215 knots (400 km/h; 248 mph) in a dive, and the ability to perform all aerobatics with its landing gear retracted or extended.

When six Yak-50s participated in the 1976 world aerobatic championships at Kiev, their evolution from the Yak-18 was apparent, but with significant changes. Basic configuration is little different from that of the single-seat Yak-18PS, with tailwheel type landing gear. This was deliberate, to keep the handling characteristics of the two types as similar as possible. However, overall dimensions are reduced; control surface hinge lines have been moved to keep control forces light; and overall structural strength has been increased by switching entirely to metal covering. In particular, the fuselage is now semi-monocoque instead of steel tube with fabric covering to the rear of the cockpit. Designers responsible for these and other changes were Sergei Yakovlev (son of Alexander Yakovlev) and Yuri Yankievich.

The wings dispense with the Yak-18's centre-section, have 2° dihedral and 2° incidence, and retain an asymmetric section. To ensure a high power/weight ratio in a relatively large aerobatic aircraft, the power plant is a 268 kW (360 hp) Vedeneyev (Ivchenko) M-14P aircooled radial piston engine, driving a V-530TA-D35 two-blade variable-pitch propeller, instead of the 224 kW (300 hp) Ivchenko AI-14RF of the Yak-18PS. Mainwheel tyre size is 500 × 150, tailwheel tyre size 200 × 80. The main fuel tank, capacity 55 litres (12 Imp gallons; 14·5 US gallons), is aft of the engine firewall, the electrical system battery behind the pilot's seat. A Zyablik radio transceiver is standard.

Observers at the world championships at Kiev reported that the Yak-50s performed the all-important Aresti manoeuvres with smooth precision, their primary shortcoming being excessive directional stability. Yak-50s flown by V. Letsko and I. Egorov finished first and second in the men's competition. Others came fifth, seventh and ninth, to win the team prize. First five places in the women's championship were taken by Yak-50s.

The current world record in FAI Class C1b for climb to 3,000 m is held by Miss Svetlana Savitskaya, who set a time of 4 min 21·4 s in a Yak-50 on 17 January 1979.

DIMENSIONS, EXTERNAL:
- Wing span: 9·50 m (31 ft 2 in)
- Length overall: 7·676 m (25 ft 2¼ in)
- Tailplane span: 3·16 m (10 ft 4½ in)
- Wheel track: 2·00 m (6 ft 6¾ in)
- Wheelbase: 5·10 m (16 ft 8¾ in)
- Propeller diameter: 2·40 m (7 ft 10½ in)

AREAS:
- Wings, gross: 15·00 m² (161·5 sq ft)
- Ailerons (total): 1·95 m² (21·00 sq ft)
- Vertical tail surfaces (total): 1·48 m² (15·93 sq ft)
- Horizontal tail surfaces (total): 2·86 m² (30·78 sq ft)

WEIGHTS AND LOADINGS:
- Weight empty, equipped: 765 kg (1,686 lb)
- Max T-O weight: 900 kg (1,984 lb)
- Max wing loading: 60 kg/m² (12·29 lb/sq ft)
- Max power loading: 3·36 kg/kW (5·51 lb/hp)

PERFORMANCE:
- Never-exceed speed: 226 knots (420 km/h; 261 mph)
- Max level speed: 173 knots (320 km/h; 199 mph)
- T-O speed: 65 knots (120 km/h; 75 mph)

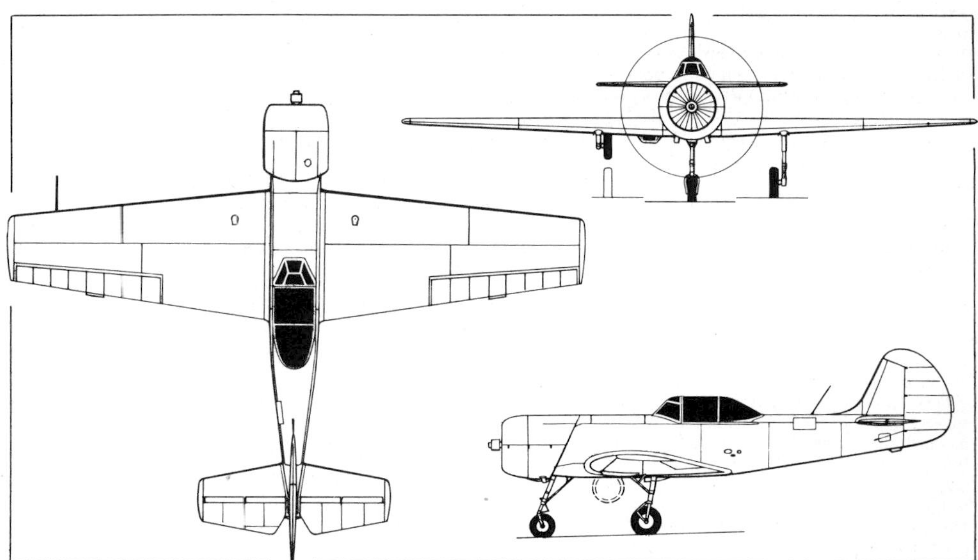

Yakovlev Yak-53 (Vedeneyev M-14P radial engine) *(Pilot Press)*

Rate of climb at S/L	960 m (3,150 ft)/min
Service ceiling	5,500 m (18,045 ft)
T-O run	200 m (657 ft)
Landing run	250 m (820 ft)
Max range at 1,000 m (3,280 ft), with 120 litres (26·4 Imp gallons; 31·7 US gallons) auxiliary fuel, reserve of 10 litres (2·2 Imp gallons; 2·6 US gallons)	267 nm (495 km; 307 miles)
Endurance at 500 m (1,640 ft) with 52 litres (11·4 Imp gallons; 13·7 US gallons) auxiliary fuel, reserve of 10 litres (2·2 Imp gallons; 2·6 US gallons)	48 min
g limits	+9/−6

YAKOVLEV Yak-52

Production of this tandem two-seat piston engined primary trainer was entrusted to the Romanian aircraft industry (which see), under the Comecon (Council for Mutual Economic Assistance) programme.

YAKOVLEV Yak-53

The Yak-53 is a single-seat fully aerobatic version of the Yak-52 two-seat primary trainer (see Romanian section). It retains the latter's pneumatically operated semi-retractable tricycle landing gear, but lacks the spring loaded controls of the Yak-52 and is stripped of non-essential equipment such as a radio compass and direction finder to enhance its agility. Power plant is a 268 kW (360 hp) Vedeneyev M-14P nine-cylinder aircooled radial piston engine, driving a two-blade variable-pitch propeller. Fuel capacity is 130 litres (28·5 Imp gallons; 34 US gallons), in two tanks forward of the main spar in the inner wings. The pilot sits under a rearward sliding canopy.

On 15 February 1982, a Yak-53 piloted by Vladimir Makagonov set a Class C1c time-to-height record, reaching 3,000 m in 5 min 5 s. On 23 February, piloted by Mikhail Molchanyuk, a prototype (c/n 06) climbed to 6,000 m in 13 min 54 s to set a second Class C1c record.

The Yak-53 is intended as a 'long life' aerobatic trainer, whereas the Yak-50 is a maximum-performance high *g* aircraft supplied exclusively to State Co-operatives. Production of the Yak-53 has started at the Progress Factory of the Soviet State Aviation Industry at Arsenyev, and is expected to be undertaken eventually by IAv Bacau in Romania, under licence.

DIMENSIONS, EXTERNAL:	
Wing span	9·50 m (31 ft 2 in)
Length overall	7·68 m (25 ft 2¼ in)
Height overall	2·95 m (9 ft 8¼ in)
Propeller diameter	2·40 m (7 ft 10½ in)
AREA:	
Wings, gross	15·00 m² (161·5 sq ft)
WEIGHTS:	
Weight empty	900 kg (1,985 lb)
Max T-O weight	1,060 kg (2,337 lb)
PERFORMANCE:	
Max permissible speed in dive	194 knots (360 km/h; 223 mph)
Max level speed	162 knots (300 km/h; 186 mph)
Cruising speed	124 knots (230 km/h; 143 mph)
Stalling speed	62 knots (115 km/h; 72 mph)
Max rate of climb at S/L	900 m (2,950 ft)/min
T-O run	150 m (492 ft)
Landing run	250 m (820 ft)
Endurance with max fuel	50 min

Yakovlev Yak-53 single-seat fully aerobatic light aircraft

Yakovlev's aerobatic Yak-55 (Vedeneyev M-14P engine) *(Flight International)*

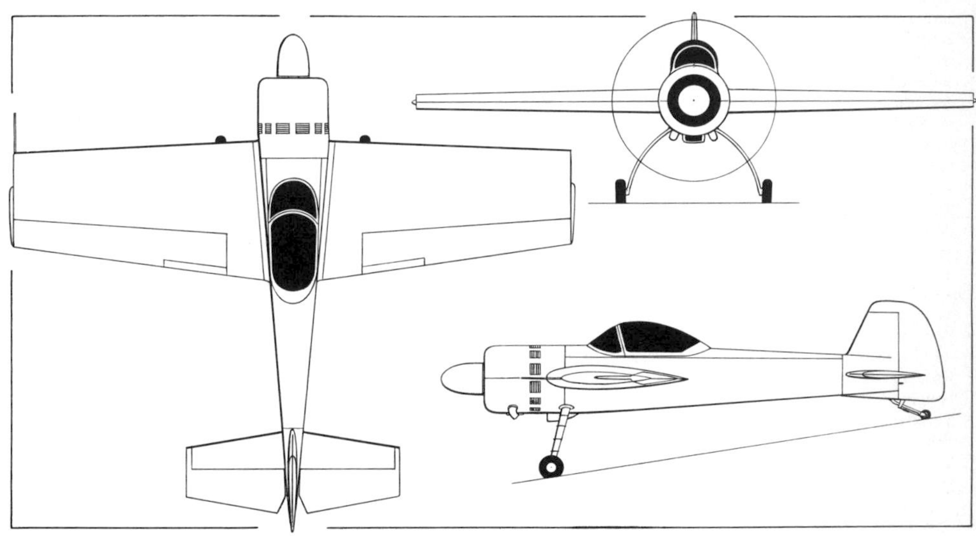
Yakovlev Yak-55 single-seat aircraft for competitive aerobatics *(Pilot Press)*

YAKOVLEV Yak-55

When a prototype of this Yakovlev single-seat competitive aerobatics monoplane made a surprise appearance at the 11th World Aerobatic Championships at Spitzerberg, Austria, in August 1982, it was described as the latest in the Yak-18/50 series. It is, however, smaller and almost entirely new, as can be seen in the accompanying illustration.

Construction of the Yak-55 is all-metal, with mid-mounted cantilever wings, originally of 18% t/c NACA 23 section and with a low aspect ratio. Inflight structural failures compelled redesign, and Yak-55s entered for the 1984 World Aerobatic Championships had new and stronger tapered wings of thinner section. Incidence and dihedral appear to be nil. All control surfaces are horn balanced; the only tabs appear to be on the inboard trailing-edge of the almost full span ailerons. The tail unit is unbraced, the tailwheel steerable, and the small mainwheels are carried on bowed cantilever spring steel legs. The blister canopy is rearward sliding. Power plant is a 268 kW (360 hp) Vedeneyev M-14P nine-cylinder aircooled radial engine, driving a two-blade controllable-pitch propeller. Wing fuel tanks, capacity 120 litres (26 Imp gallons; 31·5 US gallons).

DIMENSIONS, EXTERNAL:	
Wing span	8·20 m (26 ft 10¾ in)
Length overall	7·48 m (24 ft 6½ in)
Height	2·30 m (7 ft 6½ in)
AREA:	
Wings, gross	14·30 m² (153·9 sq ft)
WEIGHTS:	
Weight empty	640 kg (1,411 lb)
Max T-O weight	840 kg (1,852 lb)
PERFORMANCE:	
Max level speed	173 knots (320 km/h; 199 mph)
Cruising speed	140 knots (260 km/h; 161 mph)
Max rate of climb at S/L	960 m (3,150 ft)/min
T-O run	150 m (492 ft)
Landing run	200 m (656 ft)
g limits	+9/−6

AIRCRAFT OF UNKNOWN DESIGN

Ram-M. Among the new aircraft observed at Ramenskoye flight test centre, and allocated a provisional 'Ram' designation, is a high-altitude reconnaissance aircraft in the class of the USAF's Lockheed TR-1. Few details are known except that it has twin tail fins. It was first reported in mid-1982.

SOVIET AEROSPACECRAFT

Persistent unofficial reports over a period of many years suggested that the Soviet Union was developing a re-usable manned and winged space vehicle similar in concept to NASA's Space Shuttle Orbiter. These reports were given credence by Anatoli Y. Skripko, then Soviet science and technology attaché in Washington, who said that the Soviet Union was developing a system "to reduce considerably the cost of delivery of materials into orbit". According to Skripko, the Soviet goal is to reduce payload-to-orbit costs to one-tenth those of the US Space Shuttle.

In parallel, the Soviet Union appears to be developing a smaller aerospacecraft, known in the USA as the Soviet Reusable Space Plane.

REUSABLE SPACE PLANE

The Soviet spacecraft designated Cosmos 1374, launched from Kapustin Yar on 3 June 1982, was believed to be a small scale unmanned flight test version of a 'reusable space plane'. Weighing about 900 kg (2,000 lb), it was despatched on its flight of just over one orbit by a standard Soviet launcher based on the SS-5 (NATO 'Skean') intermediate range ballistic missile. After successful re-entry into the atmosphere, it was recovered from the Indian Ocean.

Cosmos 1445 was also recovered from the Indian Ocean, on 16 March 1983, after a flight of one orbit. On this occasion the recovery operation was photographed from a Royal Australian Air Force Orion aircraft. The resulting pictures, one of which is reproduced on page 277, show a slender delta winged and finned vehicle, similar to the USAF/Boeing X-20 Dyna-Soar project of the early 1960s (see 1962-63 *Jane's*). Cosmos 1517, launched on 27 December 1983, was the third test of the subscale shuttle. This vehicle was recovered from the Black Sea, as was Cosmos 1614 at the end of the fourth test flight on 19 December 1984. It is suggested that a full scale version could be used for military reconnaissance, crew transport to space stations, satellite repair and maintenance, satellite interception and /or destruction, and space station defence.

An accompanying drawing, from the US Department of Defense, suggests that the full scale 'reusable space plane' will have a wing span of about 9·4 m (30 ft 9 in) and length of 16·25 m (53 ft 3 in), including motors. Its launcher is expected to be capable of inserting a payload of more than 15,000 kg (33,000 lb) into a 180 km (112 mile) orbit.

SOVIET SHUTTLE ORBITER

Information and artist's impressions published in the 1985 edition of the Department of Defense's *Soviet Military Power* document suggest that the Soviet Union also has in the final stages of development a manned orbiter almost as large as NASA's Space Shuttle Orbiter and with a very similar configuration for both the vehicle and its new type launcher (large external tank, strap-on boosters and a piggy-back orbiter). The assembled launch vehicle is shown as being 65 m (213 ft) tall, compared with 56 m (184 ft) for the US Shuttle. Significant differences are said to be the use of liquid propellants for the strap-on boosters, and location of the liquid hydrogen main engines on the external tank rather than on the orbiter itself. (See also Myasishchev entry in this section.)

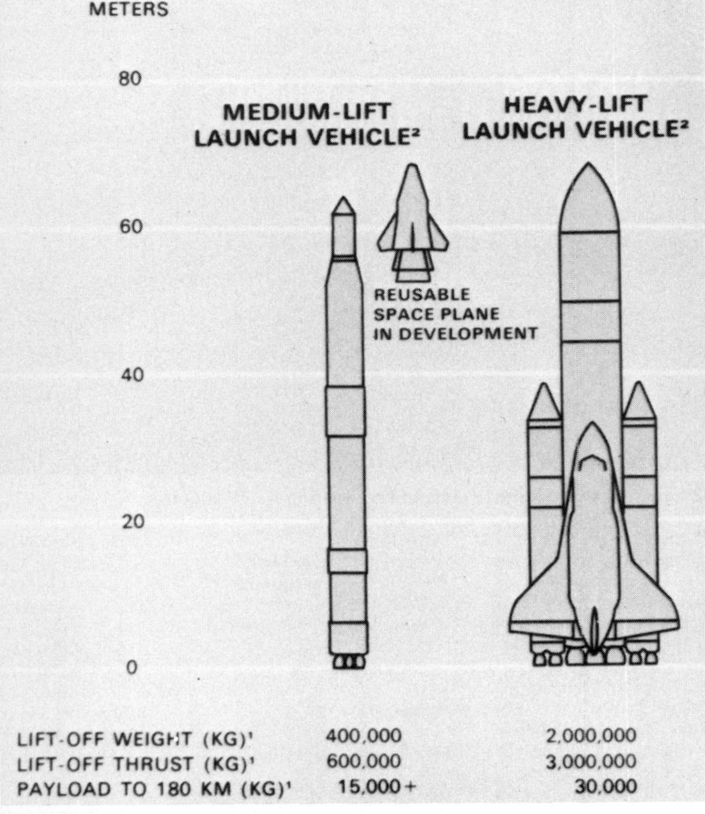

US Department of Defense drawing showing the Soviet reusable space plane and space shuttle orbiter, now under development

Soviet subscale reusable space plane, designated Cosmos 1445, recovered from the Indian Ocean *(Australian Department of Defence)*

UNITED KINGDOM

ARV

ARV AVIATION LTD

ARV Hangar, Sandown Airport, Isle of Wight PO36 9PJ
Telephone: 0983 406124/5
SALES OFFICE: Blackbushe Airport, Camberley, Surrey GU17 9LQ
Telephone: 0252 878675
CHAIRMAN AND MANAGING DIRECTOR: R. J. A. Noble, OBE
DIRECTORS:
M. F. Barrett (Production)
S. B. Giddings, MIED (Chief Designer)
J. N. Morton, BA (Design Office Manager and Secretary)
N. J. Sibley, BSc (Chief Engineer)
C. Wald, ACIS, AAAI, AIB, MIEx
A. V. Alexander
ASSOCIATE DIRECTOR: H. Kendall

ARV Aviation was formed by Mr R. Noble to design and produce the two-seat Super2 light aircraft, powered by a new British aero-engine developed by Hewland Engineering Ltd. Use is made of superplastically formed aluminium alloy pressings to save weight and to reduce manufacturing costs. The Super2 is designed to British Civil Aviation Airworthiness Requirements, Section K, with emphasis on the ability to operate from European grass strips.

ARV Super2 two-seat monoplane (Hewland Engineering AE 75 engine)

ARV SUPER2 (ARV-1)

The prototype Super2 (G-OARV) flew for the first time on 11 March 1985, piloted by Mr Hugh Kendall, and the second example (G-STWO) on 12 November. Before certification was obtained, in July 1986, the first eight production aircraft were supplied in kit form, 65 per cent complete, for completion by home builders under the auspices of the Popular Flying Association. Subsequent deliveries, of completed aircraft, began with the tenth production airframe which went to the Airborne School of Flying at Sandown, Isle of Wight. By September 1986, orders for 37 Super2s had been received from customers in Australia, Canada, the Netherlands, New Zealand and the UK. Production was then at the rate of four per month.

Potential developments include an aerobatic version, a long range version with wingtip tanks, alternative float landing gear, glider tug fittings, cropspraying equipment, and a version for photographic duties.

TYPE: Two-seat light cabin monoplane.

WINGS: Braced shoulder-wing monoplane with single streamline bracing strut each side. Wing section NACA 2415 (modified). Single-spar wing, of aluminium alloy construction, cold bonded and flush riveted, is swept forward 5° 6′ to optimise the CG and the structural merits of a single uncompromised main bulkhead carrying the wings, bracing struts, controls, seats, fuel tank and main landing gear. Mass balanced ailerons operated by torque tube through leading-edge of manually operated plain flaps. Wings readily detachable for road transportation by light trailer.

FUSELAGE: Rear fuselage of aluminium alloy construction, cold bonded and flush riveted, with single curvature skinning. Forward of the main bulkhead the structure is conventional double beam carrying the firewall, nose landing gear and engine. Between the firewall and the main bulkhead, the fuselage is skinned by four panels, superplastically formed in Supral 220/150 aluminium alloy.

TAIL UNIT: Conventional aluminium alloy structure, cold bonded and flush riveted, with three-spar fixed surfaces and single-spar mass balanced control surfaces. Trim tab on elevator.

LANDING GEAR: Non-retractable tricycle type. Cantilever main legs of tapered steel leaf spring. All three wheels size 3·50 × 6·0, with tyres size 13 × 4·00-6, pressure 1·72 bars (25 lb/sq in). Hydraulic disc brakes. Nose leg of leading link design, with rubber in tension springing, with damping by an adjustable Spax gas filled shock absorber. Wheels and brakes made by ARV.

POWER PLANT: One 57·4 kW (77 hp) Hewland Engineering AE 75 three-cylinder, 750 cc liquid cooled inline two-stroke engine, driving a two-blade, fixed-pitch Hoffmann propeller through 2·7:1 reduction gearing. Electronically variable ignition timing. Serck aluminium radiator in recessed duct in rear fuselage. Fuel capacity 55 litres (12 Imp gallons) in single fuselage tank. Refuelling point in top of fuselage.

ACCOMMODATION: Enclosed cabin seating two side by side. Seats are adjustable for height, and fold to reveal baggage compartment. Additional storage space under the seats. Rearward hinged canopy is one-piece Perspex moulding with GRP frame. Dual flying controls standard.

SYSTEMS: Wheel disc brakes operated hydraulically. Electrical system includes 11A generator.

AVIONICS AND EQUIPMENT: Standard equipment includes three basic flight instruments plus engine instruments. Optional vacuum instruments driven by a single venturi mounted under the front fuselage. Radio equipment to customers' requirements.

DIMENSIONS, EXTERNAL:
Wing span 8·69 m (28 ft 6 in)
Width, wings folded 2·54 m (8 ft 4 in)
Wing aspect ratio 8·8
Length overall 5·49 m (18 ft 0 in)
Height overall 2·31 m (7 ft 7 in)
Tailplane span 2·54 m (8 ft 4 in)
Wheel track 1·83 m (6 ft 0 in)
Wheelbase 1·74 m (5 ft 8½ in)
Propeller diameter 1·60 m (5 ft 3 in)
Propeller ground clearance 0·23 m (9 in)

DIMENSIONS, INTERNAL:
Cabin: Length 1·27 m (4 ft 2 in)
Max width 0·99 m (3 ft 3 in)
Max height 1·09 m (3 ft 7 in)

AREAS:
Wings, gross 8·59 m² (92·5 sq ft)
Ailerons (total) 0·60 m² (6·5 sq ft)
Trailing-edge flaps (total) 0·89 m (9·6 sq ft)
Fin 0·59 m² (6·4 sq ft)
Rudder 0·26 m² (2·8 sq ft)
Tailplane 1·23 m² (13·2 sq ft)
Elevators, incl tab 0·55 m² (5·9 sq ft)

WEIGHTS AND LOADINGS:
Weight empty 288 kg (635 lb)
Max fuel weight 40 kg (88 lb)
Max T-O and landing weight 499 kg (1,100 lb)
Max wing loading 58·1 kg/m² (11·9 lb/sq ft)
Max power loading 8·69 kg/kW (14·3 lb/shp)

PERFORMANCE (at AUW of 474 kg; 1,045 lb):
Never-exceed speed 137 knots (254 km/h; 158 mph)
Max level speed at 1,066 m (3,500 ft) 109 knots (202 km/h; 126 mph)
Max cruising speed at 1,066 m (3,500 ft) 96 knots (177 km/h; 110 mph)
Econ cruising speed at 1,066 m (3,500 ft) 87 knots (161 km/h; 100 mph)
Stalling speed, power off:
flaps up 51 knots (95 km/h; 59 mph)
flaps down 44·5 knots (83 km/h; 52 mph)
Rate of climb at S/L 244 m (800 ft)/min
T-O run 143 m (470 ft)
Range with max fuel 370 nm (685 km; 426 miles)

BAe

BRITISH AEROSPACE PUBLIC LIMITED COMPANY

HEADQUARTERS: 11 The Strand, London WC2N 5JT
Telephone: 01 930 1020
Telex: 919221
and
Brooklands Road, Weybridge, Surrey KT13 0SJ
Telephone: 0932 53444
Telex: 27111
BOARD OF DIRECTORS:
Sir Austin Pearce, CBE, PhD, FEng (Chairman)
Admiral Sir Raymond Lygo, KCB, RN (Retd) (Chief Executive)
I. R. Yates, CBE, BEng, CEng, FRAeS, FIMechE (Deputy Chief Executive, Engineering)
H. Metcalfe, OBE, BSc, ARCS, CEng, FRAeS (Deputy Chief Executive, Operations)
J. L. Glasscock, BA, FCIS (Commercial Director)
B. E. Friend, CBE, FCA (Financial Director)
NON-EXECUTIVE DIRECTORS:
K. M. Bevins, CBE, TD
Sir Kenneth Durham, BSc
D. O. Gladwin, CBE, JP
H. A. Hitchcock, DFC
Sir Jack Wellings, CBE
PERSONNEL DIRECTOR: D. Bucknall
SECRETARY/LEGAL ADVISER: B. Cookson, LLB, FRAeS
MARKETING DIRECTOR: L. A. Sanson, OBE
FINANCIAL COMPTROLLER: A. Smith
CORPORATE EXECUTIVE, PUBLIC AFFAIRS: Don McClen

In 1977 the former companies of British Aircraft Corporation (Holdings) Ltd, Hawker Siddeley Aviation Ltd, Hawker Siddeley Dynamics Ltd and Scottish Aviation Ltd were brought together through nationalisation. In January 1981 the structure of British Aerospace was changed from a corporation in public ownership to a public limited company in the private sector, and in May 1985 HM Government sold its remaining shareholding. The Gyroscope division of Sperry was acquired in May 1982, forming the basis of the Electronic Systems and Equipment Division.

During 1985-86 the divisions of British Aerospace were reorganised, and from January 1987 the Company will operate through six divisions, employing 76,000 people in the UK and overseas: Civil Aircraft Division, Military Aircraft Division, Air Weapons Division, Army Weapons Division, Space and Communications Division, and a new Division combining the former Naval Weapons and Electronic Systems and Equipment Divisions.

British Aerospace has the following principal overseas subsidiaries: British Aerospace Australia Ltd, British Aerospace Inc, and British Scandinavian Aviation AB; and the following UK subsidiaries: British Aerospace (Insurance) Ltd, British Aerospace (Insurance Brokers) Ltd, and British Aerospace (Pension Fund Trustees) Ltd.

Associated companies include SEPECAT (formed in May 1966 by BAC and Breguet Aviation to control the development and production of the Jaguar tactical strike fighter and trainer), Panavia Aircraft GmbH (formed in March 1969 by BAC, MBB and Aeritalia to manage the development and production of the Tornado all-weather combat aircraft), Dulles International Aeroservices Inc (formed in 1976 by BAC (USA) Inc and Rolls-Royce Inc to supply customers in North America with spares and engineering support), Arab-British Dynamics Co (inaugurated in 1977 by BAC Guided Weapons Division and the Egyptian government to manufacture the Swingfire missile in Egypt), and Frames Travel (Fylde) Ltd.

British Aerospace is a partner in the Airbus Industrie international consortium, with a 20% stake in the A300, A300-600 and A310 civil transports, and a 26% stake in the A320 programme. British Aerospace is also a partner in Euromissile Dynamics Group (EMDG), formed with MBB and Aérospatiale for the development and production of anti-tank missiles.

CIVIL AIRCRAFT DIVISION

HATFIELD: Hatfield, Hertfordshire AL10 9TL
Telephone: 07072 62345
Telex: 22411

CIVIL MARKETING OPERATIONS CENTRE: PO Box 35, Stevenage, Hertfordhire SG1 2DG
Telephone: 07072 68123
Telex: 826 876

BRISTOL: Filton House, Bristol BS99 7AR
Telephone: 0272 693831
Telex: 44163

CHADDERTON: Chadderton Works, Greengate, Middleton, Manchester M24 1SA
Telephone: 061 681 2020
Telex: 667015

CHESTER: Broughton, near Chester, Clwyd CH4 0DR
Telephone: 0244 535333
Telex: 61201

PRESTWICK: Prestwick Airport, Ayrshire KA9 2RW
Telephone: 0292 79888
Telex: 77432

WOODFORD: Woodford Aerodrome, Chester Road, Woodford, Cheshire CK7 1QR
Telephone: 061 439 5050
Telex: 668939/667545

DIVISIONAL MANAGEMENT COMMITTEE:
S. Gillibrand, MSc, CEng, FRAeS (Managing Director, Civil Aircraft Division)
G. J. Evans, BSc (Divisional Production Director)
J. B. Scott-Wilson, MA, FRAeS (Divisional Technical Director)
J. J. Hughes, FCA (Divisional Financial Director)
B. G. Thomas (Marketing Director, Civil Aircraft)
W. R. Lee (Divisional Personnel and Administration Director)
A. F. Smith (Divisional Commercial Director)
R. M. McKinlay, BSc (Hons), CEng, MRAeS, ARTC (Director, Filton and Chester, and General Manager, Filton)
C. B. G. Masefield, MA, MRAeS (Director, Hatfield, Prestwick and Manchester, and General Manager, Hatfield)
G. J. Curran, ACMA (Divisional Director and General Manager, Prestwick)
R. J. W. Fletcher (Divisional Director and General Manager, Manchester)
J. P. Gillbanks. MBIM (Divisional Director and General Manager, Chester)

SECRETARY: J. A. Watson
ASSISTANT SECRETARY: A. M. Goodall, BSc (Econ), ACIS
DIVISIONAL PUBLIC RELATIONS MANAGER:
D. A. Dorman
PUBLIC RELATIONS MANAGER, HATFIELD:
M. V. Brown
PUBLIC RELATIONS OFFICER, CHESTER:
Ms K Roden
PUBLIC RELATIONS MANAGER, PRESTWICK:
G. Lillistone
PUBLIC RELATIONS MANAGER, FILTON:
H. Berry
PUBLIC RELATIONS MANAGER, MANCHESTER:
H. Holmes

Civil Aircraft Division, centred at Hatfield, is responsible for design, development, production, marketing and support of the BAe 146 regional jet airliner, the BAe 125 business jet, the Jetstream 31 airliner, corporate and executive aircraft, the BAe 748 turboprop transport and the Advanced Turboprop (ATP) transport. The Division is also responsible for the Rombac 1-11 licence manufacturing programme with Romania, and for the design, development and production of wings for the A300, A310 and A320 versions of the European Airbus, VC10 conversion to the air to air refuelling role for the Royal Air Force and F-111 maintenance under USAF contract. The Division also supplies civil aircraft design, development, research, support, modification and refurbishing services. All marketing, sales and support activities are centred at the newly created Civil Marketing Operations Centre at Stevenage. Current research work includes investigations into the potential benefits and problems of open rotor technology, this generic term covering all types of propfan and unducted fan engines.

Under a technical co-operation agreement signed with the government of Mexico, the Division, in conjunction with the Mexican authorities, is preparing a study of the whole range of civil aviation and aerospace industrial activity in Mexico, to identify areas of common interest for future collaboration. The Division has also signed a major collaborative agreement with Hellenic Aerospace Industry (HAI) of Greece, planned to last well into the next century.

MILITARY AIRCRAFT DIVISION

WEYBRIDGE: Brooklands Road, Weybridge, Surrey KT13 0SF
Telephone: 0932 45522
Telex: 27111 BAEWEY G

BROUGH: Brough, North Humberside HU15 1EQ
Telephone: 0482 667121
Telex: 52634 BAEBRO G

DUNSFOLD: Dunsfold Aerodrome, Godalming, Surrey, GU8 4BS
Telephone: 0483 272121
Telex: 859475 BAEDUN G

HAMBLE: Kings Avenue, Hamble, Hampshire SO3 5NF
Telephone: 0703 453371
Telex: 47543 BAEHAM G

KINGSTON: Richmond Road, Kingston-upon-Thames, Surrey KT2 5QS
Telephone: 01 546 7741
Telex: 23726 BAEKIN G

PRESTON: Strand Road, Preston, Lancs PR1 8UD
Telephone: 0772 54722
Telex: 67616 BAEP G

SAMLESBURY: Samlesbury Aerodrome, Balderstone, Lancs BB2 7LF
Telephone: 025 481 2371
Telex: 63435 BAES G

WARTON: Warton Aerodrome, Preston, Lancashire PR4 1AX
Telephone: 0772 633333
Telex: 67627 BAEWAA G

DIVISIONAL MANAGEMENT COMMITTEE:
F. E. Roe, CBE, DIC, BSc, ACGI, CEng, FRAeS, DL (Managing Director)
R. H. Evans, CBE (Deputy Managing Director and Managing Director designate)
N. V. Barber, BA, MSc (Deputy Managing Director)
A. H. Baxter, CEng, MIProdE (Director and General Manager, Warton, Preston and Samlesbury)
Dr M. C. S. Dixson, BA, MA, DPhil(Oxon), MRAeS (Director in charge Saudi Arabian Operations)
M. Edwards, CEng, FRAeS (Director and General Manager, Brough)
D. Ethell, FCA, MRAeS (Personnel Director)
A. R. Keys, OBE, DFC, BSc (Director of Marketing and Product Support)
L. W. Milsom, BSc(Eng), CEng, MIMechE (Director of Projects, Weybridge)
J. E. Perry, MSc, CEng, FIMechE, FIProdE (Director and General Manager, Hamble)
R. B. Searle, CEng, MRAeS (Production Director)
R. D. Smith Wright (Finance Director)
M. J. Turner, BA, ACIS (Director and General Manager, Weybridge, Kingston and Dunsfold)
F. G. Willox, BSc(Hons), MSc(Aero), MIMechE, CEng, FRAeS (Director of Projects, Warton)
B. Young, BSc(Hons) (Technical Director)

DIVISIONAL PUBLIC RELATIONS MANAGER:
J. R. Gray, DFC, BA
PUBLIC RELATIONS MANAGER, WEYBRIDGE: N. A. Barfield, MSc, CEng, FRAeS, FIMechE, AFAIAA
PUBLIC RELATIONS MANAGER, BROUGH: E. Barker
PUBLIC RELATIONS MANAGER, KINGSTON: J. W. Coombs
PUBLIC AFFAIRS MANAGER, WARTON:
G. B. Hill, MBE, MBIM

Main activities of this Division include the development, in partnership with West Germany, Italy and Spain, of the new European Fighter Aircraft (EFA); design and development of an Experimental Aircraft Programme (EAP) technology demonstrator; design, development, production and support, with MBB and Aeritalia, of the Panavia Tornado; joint development and production, with Dassault-Breguet, of the SEPECAT Jaguar; design, development, production and support of the V/STOL Harrier and Sea Harrier and, with McDonnell Douglas, of the AV-8B/GR. Mk 5 Harrier and the T-45A Goshawk for the US Navy; design, development, production and support of the Hawk strike/advanced jet trainer and Hawk 200 single-seat lightweight fighter.

In addition to major contracts for the update of RAF Phantom and Buccaneer aircraft, the Division is responsible for joint design and manufacture, with Saab-Scania, of the carbonfibre wings of the JAS 39 Gripen combat aircraft. It undertakes conversion programmes for the Canberra bomber, and makes major contributions to the BAe 146, and Airbus A300, A310 and A320 family of airliners. Full product support services are provided for earlier aircraft still in service throughout the world.

In June 1986, BAe announced that it had signed a memorandum of understanding with Lockheed to evaluate the possibility of designing a military cargo variant of the BAe 146 commercial airliner.

The company's defence support services business is centred in the Military Aircraft Division, which additionally offers overseas and specialist training facilities covering a wide range of technical and management courses.

AIR WEAPONS DIVISION

HATFIELD: Manor Road, Hatfield, Hertfordshire AL10 9LL
Telephone: 07072 62300
Telex: 22324

LOSTOCK: Bolton, Lancashire BL6 4BR
Telephone: 0204 66551
Telex: 63134

MANAGING DIRECTOR: B. J. Rosser, BSc, CEng, FRAeS
PUBLIC RELATIONS MANAGER: S. Raynes

ARMY WEAPONS DIVISION

Six Hills Way, Stevenage, Hertfordshire SG1 2DA
Telephone: 0438 312422
Telex: 825125/6

MANAGING DIRECTOR: R. J. Parkhouse, CBE, MSc, BSc, CEng, FIProdE
PUBLIC RELATIONS MANAGER: P. Birtles

*NAVAL WEAPONS DIVISION

BRISTOL: PO Box No. 5, Filton, Bristol BS12 7QW
Telephone: 0272 693831
Telex: 449452

WEYMOUTH: 10 Cambridge Road, Granby Industrial Estate, Weymouth, Dorset DT4 9TJ
Telephone: 03057 74661
Telex: 417214

MANAGING DIRECTOR: D. Rowley, MA, CEng, FRAeS
PUBLIC RELATIONS MANAGER: T. C. Bickerton

SPACE AND COMMUNICATIONS DIVISION

STEVENAGE: Argyle Way, Stevenage, Hertfordshire SG1 2AS
Telephone: 0438 313456
Telex: 82130/82197

BRISTOL: PO Box No. 5, Filton, Bristol BS12 7QW
Telephone: 0272 693831
Telex: 449452

MANAGING DIRECTOR: J. A. Holt, MSc, BSc, CEng, MRAeS
PUBLIC RELATIONS MANAGER: J. Humby

*ELECTRONIC SYSTEMS AND EQUIPMENT DIVISION

BRACKNELL: Downshire Way, Bracknell, Berkshire RG12 1QL
Telephone: 0344 483222
Telex: 848129

PLYMOUTH: Clittaford Road, Southway, Plymouth, Devon PL6 6DE
Telephone: 0752 707951
Telex: 45564

MANAGING DIRECTOR: P. Brighton, CBE, BSc, FIEE, FRAeS, CBIM
PUBLIC RELATIONS MANAGER: P. Odds

* *These two Divisions to be amalgamated from 1 January 1987, with headquarters at Bristol and with Mr Brighton as Managing Director*

Details of the wide range of missiles for which the Weapons Divisions are responsible can be found in *Jane's Weapon Systems.* Other defence work includes development and manufacture of infra-red linescan systems which equip the Jaguar aircraft (see International section) and the Canadair CL-89 surveillance RPV (see RPVs section).

The Air Weapons Division is also responsible for BAe's work on propellers, and is engaged currently on the development of an advanced fuel-efficient low-noise propeller suitable for commuter/feeder/short-haul airliners with engines in the 1,850-2,250 kW (2,500-3,000 shp) range. Selected already for BAe's own ATP, this has six blades of composite construction and a diameter of 4·2 m (13 ft 9 in).

The Space and Communications Division is responsible for the Skynet 4 UK military communications satellite programme, civil communications satellites, and pallets for the US Space Shuttle.

Acquisition by BAe of the Gyroscope Division of Sperry Ltd was completed in May 1982. As the Electronic Systems and Equipment Division, this produces aircraft instruments, navigation systems, underwater weapons, mine countermeasures, naval weapon fire control systems, and missile equipment.

BAe JETSTREAM 31

Development of this current version of the Jetstream was announced by British Aerospace on 4 December 1978. A development aircraft (G-JSSD), converted from a Jetstream 1 built by Handley Page, flew for the first time on 28 March 1980. Full production go-ahead was given in January 1982, and the first production Jetstream 31 (G-TALL) made its first flight on 18 March 1982. On 29 June 1982 the Jetstream 31 was certificated to BCAR Section D in the UK. US certification under SFAR 41C followed on 30 November 1982. German (LBA) certification was gained in July 1983 and Australian (DOA) certification in early 1984. First deliveries, to customers in Germany and the UK, took place in December 1982, and the 100th delivery was made on 25 June 1986. Orders totalled 130 on 3 September 1986. The production rate is scheduled to be increased from 36 to 48 aircraft a year.

The following versions have been announced:

Airliner. Designed to carry 18/19 passengers. Able to operate up to 680 nm (1,260 km; 783 miles) stage length, without refuelling, with 18 passengers, baggage and full IFR reserves.

Corporate. Executive version, designed for eight to ten passengers, and able to carry nine passengers and baggage for 1,050 nm (1,945 km; 1,208 miles) with full IFR reserves. Typical interior has six fully reclining and swivelling chairs, a three-place divan, galley for hot and cold meal service, cocktail cabinet, wardrobe and washroom/toilet.

Executive Shuttle. Intended for the large company, shuttling its personnel between factories, or for the business charter market. With typical layout for 12 passengers, this version has a range of 1,050 nm (1,945 km; 1,208 miles) with full IFR reserves.

Special Role. Intended for various specialist applications such as military communications, casualty evacuation, multi-engine training, cargo operations, airfield calibration, resources survey and protection. A patrol version, designated **Jetstream 31EZ**, is available for operation in exclusive economic zones (ie offshore patrol and surveillance), with underbelly 360° scan radar, increased fuel, observation windows and searchlight.

Jetstream T. Mk 3. Training version, ordered by the Royal Navy. Eyebrow windows above flight deck windscreen to improve all-round view. Interior fitted with two observer training consoles with radar indicator, TANS computer and Doppler. Racal ASR 360 search radar mounted under the fuselage. Four ordered in April 1984, for operation by No. 750 Naval Air Squadron based at Culdrose, Cornwall, for helicopter observer training. All delivered by July 1986.

As part of the continuing programme of aircraft improvements, increases in design weights and engine ratings have been achieved. A quick change (QC) facility allows conversion from 18-seat to 12/10-seat layouts in just over one hour. A water methanol injection system has been developed for 'hot and high' conditions, and the Jetstream 31 has been cleared for use from unsealed runways.

TYPE: Light commuter/executive transport.

WINGS: Cantilever low-wing monoplane. Wing section NACA 63A418 at root, NACA 63A412 at tip. Dihedral 7° from roots. Incidence 2° at root, 0° at tip. Sweepback 0° 34′ at quarter-chord. Aluminium alloy fail-safe structure. Aluminium alloy manually operated Frise ailerons. Hydraulically operated aluminium alloy double-slotted flaps. No slats or leading-edge flaps. Trim tab in each aileron. Goodrich rubber boot de-icing system for leading-edges.

FUSELAGE: Conventional aluminium alloy semi-monocoque fail-safe structure, with chemically milled skin panels. Fully pressurised.

TAIL UNIT: Cantilever two-spar aluminium alloy structure. Fixed incidence tailplane. Manually operated control surfaces. Trim tabs in rudder and each elevator. Goodrich rubber boot de-icing system for leading-edges.

LANDING GEAR: Retractable tricycle type, with nosewheel steering. Hydraulic retraction, mainwheels inward into wings, twin nosewheels forward. British Aerospace oleo-pneumatic shock absorbers in all units. Dunlop wheels and tyres: mainwheel tyres size 28 × 9·00-12, pressure 3·93 bars (57 lb/sq in); nosewheel tyres size 6·00-6, pressure 2·34 bars (34 lb/sq in). No brake cooling. Anti-skid units.

POWER PLANT: Two 701 kW (940 shp) Garrett TPE331-10UG turboprop engines, each driving a Dowty Rotol four-blade variable- and reversible-pitch fully-feathering metal propeller. Fuel in integral tank in each wing, total capacity 1,718 litres (378 Imp gallons; 454 US gallons). Refuelling point on top of each outer wing. Water methanol injection optional.

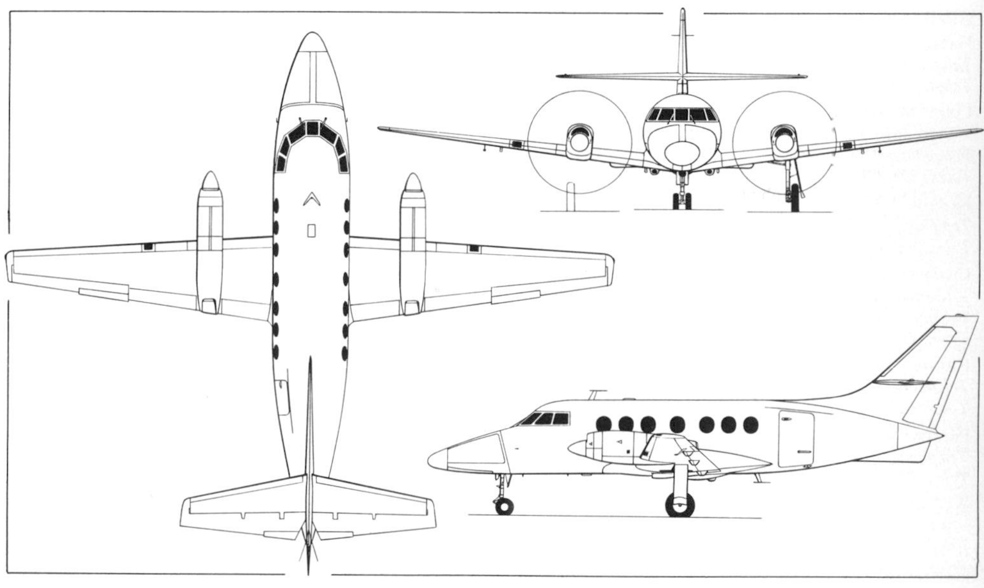

BAe Jetstream 31 twin-turboprop commuter/executive light transport *(Pilot Press)*

ACCOMMODATION: Two seats side by side on flight deck, with provision for dual controls, though aircraft can be approved (subject to local regulations) for single pilot operation. Main cabin can be furnished in commuter layout for up to 19 passengers at 76/79 cm (30/31 in) pitch, or with executive interior for 8/10 passengers, but optional layouts are available, including a QC (quick change) option enabling an operator to change from an 18-seat layout to 12-seat executive configuration in around 1¼ hours. Downward opening passenger door, with integral airstairs, at rear of cabin on port side. Emergency exit over wing on starboard side. Baggage compartment in rear of cabin, aft of main door. Entire accommodation pressurised, heated, ventilated and air-conditioned. Toilet standard; galley and bar optional.

SYSTEMS: Air-conditioning system with cabin pressurisation at max differential of 0·38 bars (5·5 lb/sq in), providing a 2,440 m (8,000 ft) cabin altitude at 7,620 m (25,000 ft). Single hydraulic system, pressure 138 bars (2,000 lb/sq in), with two engine driven pumps, each capable of supplying 20·7 litres (4·55 Imp gallons)/min. One pump is capable of supplying all hydraulic systems. Combined air/oil reservoir, pressurised to 1·24 bars (18 lb/sq in), for main and emergency supply, for actuation of flaps, landing gear, brakes and nosewheel steering. APU optional.

DIMENSIONS, EXTERNAL:

Wing span	15·85 m (52 ft 0 in)
Wing chord: at root	2·19 m (7 ft 2½ in)
at tip	0·80 m (2 ft 7¼ in)
Wing aspect ratio	10
Length overall	14·37 m (47 ft 1½ in)
Length of fuselage	13·40 m (43 ft 11½ in)
Height overall	5·32 m (17 ft 5½ in)
Fuselage: Max diameter	1·98 m (6 ft 6 in)
Tailplane span	6·60 m (21 ft 8 in)
Wheel track	5·94 m (19 ft 6 in)
Wheelbase	4·60 m (15 ft 1 in)
Propeller diameter	2·69 m (8 ft 10 in)
Passenger door: Height	1·42 m (4 ft 8 in)
Width	0·86 m (2 ft 10 in)
Emergency exit: Height	0·91 m (3 ft 0 in)
Width	0·56 m (1 ft 10 in)

DIMENSIONS, INTERNAL:

Cabin, excl flight deck: Length	7·39 m (24 ft 3 in)
Max width	1·85 m (6 ft 1 in)
Max height	1·80 m (5 ft 11 in)
Floor area	8·35 m² (90 sq ft)
Volume (trimmed aircraft)	16·92 m³ (598 cu ft)
Baggage compartment volume:	
Airliner	2·13-2·74 m³ (75·2-96·7 cu ft)
Corporate	1·34-1·48 m³ (47·2-52·2 cu ft)
Baggage pod (optional)	1·39 m³ (49 cu ft)

AREAS:

Wings, gross	25·20 m² (271·3 sq ft)
Ailerons, aft of hinge line (total)	1·52 m² (16·4 sq ft)
Trailing-edge flaps (total)	3·25 m² (35·0 sq ft)
Vertical tail surfaces (total)	7·72 m² (83·1 sq ft)
Horizontal tail surfaces (total)	7·80 m² (84·0 sq ft)

WEIGHTS AND LOADINGS:

Operating weight empty	4,360 kg (9,613 lb)
Max fuel	1,372 kg (3,024 lb)
Max payload	1,805 kg (3,980 lb)
Max T-O weight: standard	6,950 kg (15,322 lb)
US domestic	6,900 kg (15,212 lb)
Max ramp weight	7,000 kg (15,432 lb)
Max landing weight	6,600 kg (14,550 lb)
Max zero-fuel weight	6,300 kg (13,889 lb)
Max wing loading	275·8 kg/m² (56·5 lb/sq ft)
Max power loading	4·96 kg/kW (8·15 lb/shp)

PERFORMANCE (at max T-O weight, except where stated):

Max cruising speed at max cruise power at 4,570 m (15,000 ft)	263 knots (488 km/h; 303 mph)
Econ cruising speed at 7,620 m (25,000 ft)	230 knots (426 km/h; 264 mph)
Stalling speed, flaps down	86 knots (159 km/h; 99 mph)
Max rate of climb at S/L	635 m (2,080 ft)/min
Rate of climb at S/L, one engine out	119 m (390 ft)/min
Certificated ceiling	7,620 m (25,000 ft)
Service ceiling, one engine out	3,660 m (12,000 ft)
T-O field length: BCAR Section D	1,440 m (4,724 ft)
T-O to 15 m (50 ft): SFAR 41C	975 m (3,200 ft)
Landing field length, at max landing weight:	
BCAR Section D	1,235 m (4,052 ft)
SFAR 41C/FAR 135	1,165 m (3,820 ft)
Accelerate/stop distance:	
SFAR 41C	1,362 m (4,470 ft)
Range	see individual model listings

BAe Jetstream 31 light transport (two Garrett TPE331-10 turboprop engines) in service with the US feeder airline American Eagle

BAe 125 SERIES 800

The prototype (G-BKTF) of this advanced version of the BAe 125 made a 3 h 8 min first flight on 26 May 1983, during which it climbed to its max operating altitude of 13,100 m (43,000 ft). Like the earlier turbojet and turbofan powered versions of the 125, of which a total of 573 were sold, it is primarily a twin-engined business aircraft but can be used in a wide variety of other civil and military roles, including communications, air ambulance, airways inspection and airline crew training. The **Series 800A** is built by BAe's Civil Aircraft Division for the North American market, **Series 800B** for the rest of the world. Type certification was obtained on 4 May 1984 and the Certificate of Airworthiness, Public Transport Category, on 30 May 1984. By 3 September 1986, Series 800 sales totalled 67. The 600th BAe 125 of all series was delivered to Gillett Group of Nashville, Tennessee, in Spring 1985.

Airframe improvements compared with the Series 700 include a curved windscreen, sequenced nosewheel doors, extended fin leading-edge, larger ventral fuel tank, and an increased wing span which reduces induced drag, improves aerodynamic efficiency and accommodates additional fuel. The outboard 3·05 m (10 ft) of each wing has been redesigned.

Garrett TFE731-5R-1H turbofans have been introduced to improve airfield/climb performance and to increase both maximum speed and range. The interior has also been redesigned. Increased headroom has been achieved by relocating oxygen dropout units to the sidewall panels. Increased width results from sculpturing the sidewall panels around the fuselage frames, giving an extra 12·2 cm (4·8 in) at shoulder height. The flight deck incorporates a Collins EFIS-85 five-tube electronic flight instrument system. A key element of this is a centrally mounted multi-function display which can show flight plans and checklists.

TYPE: Twin-turbofan business transport aircraft.

WINGS: Cantilever low-wing monoplane. BAe wing sections. Thickness/chord ratio 14% at root, 8·35% at tip. Dihedral 2°. Incidence 2° 5′ 42″ at root, −3° 5′ 49″ at tip. Sweepback 20° at quarter-chord. Wings built in one piece and dished to pass under fuselage, to which they are attached by four vertical links, a side link and a drag spigot. All-metal two-spar fail-safe structure, with partial centre spar of approx two-thirds span, sealed to form integral fuel tankage which is divided into two compartments by centreline rib. Skins are single-piece units on each of the upper and lower semi-spans. Detachable leading-edges. Mass balanced ailerons, operated manually by cable linkage. Each aileron has a servo action geared tab; port tab trimmed manually via screwjack. Large four-position double-slotted flaps, actuated hydraulically via a screwjack on each flap. Mechanically operated hydraulic cutout prevents asymmetric operation of the flaps. Airbrakes above and below each wing, forming part of flap shrouds, provide lift dumping facility during landing, and have interconnected controls to prevent asymmetric operation. TKS liquid system, using porous stainless steel leading-edge panels, for de-icing or anti-icing.

FUSELAGE: All-metal semi-monocoque fail-safe structure, making extensive use of Redux bonding. Constant circular cross-section over much of its length.

TAIL UNIT: Cantilever all-metal structure, with fixed incidence tailplane mounted on fin. Small fairings on tailplane undersurface to eliminate turbulence around elevator hinge cutouts. Extended dorsal fin, enclosing air-conditioning intake duct. Control surfaces operated manually via cable linkage. Geared tabs in rudder and each elevator. TKS liquid de-icing or anti-icing of tailplane leading-edges.

BAe 125 Series 800 twin-turbofan business transport operated by Carlton and United Breweries of Australia

LANDING GEAR: Retractable tricycle type, with twin wheels on each unit. Hydraulic retraction; nosewheels forward, mainwheels inward into wings. Oleo-pneumatic shock absorbers. Fully castoring nose unit, steerable 45° to port and starboard. Dunlop mainwheels and 12-ply tubeless tyres, size 23 × 7-12. Dunlop nosewheels and 6-ply tubeless tyres, size 18 × 4·25-10. Dunlop triple-disc hydraulic brakes with Maxaret anti-skid units on all mainwheels.

POWER PLANT: Two 19·13 kN (4,300 lb st) Garrett TFE731-5R-1H turbofan engines, pod mounted on sides of rear fuselage, in pods designed and manufactured by Grumman Aerospace. Optional thrust reversers developed by Dee Howard Company. Engine intake anti-icing by engine bleed air. Integral fuel tanks in wings, with combined capacity of 4,820 litres (1,060 Imp gallons). Rear underfuselage tank of 854 litres (188 Imp gallons) capacity, giving total capacity of 5,674 litres (1,248 Imp gallons). Single pressure refuelling point at rear of ventral tank. Overwing refuelling point near each wingtip.

ACCOMMODATION: Crew of two on flight deck, which is fully soundproofed, insulated and air-conditioned. Dual controls standard. Seat for third crew member. Standard executive layout has seating for eight passengers, forward and rear baggage compartments, forward galley, wardrobe and toilet at rear. Individual recessed lights, air louvres and oxygen masks above each passenger position. Cabin styling offers the operator a choice of interchangeable furnishing units to suit individual requirements, with up to 14 seats. The wide seats swivel through 180°, are adjustable fore, aft and sideways, and can be reclined and used as a bed. Typical executive furnishing includes a rear couch for three persons, five individual seats, and individual foldaway wall tables. Outward opening door at front on port side, with integral airstairs. Emergency exit over wing on starboard side. Electric windscreen anti-icing. Optional heated baggage pannier in place of fuel tank in rear ventral section of fuselage, with bottom-hinged door on each side.

SYSTEMS: Garrett-AiResearch air-conditioning and pressurisation system. Max cabin differential 0·59 bars (8·55 lb/sq in). Oxygen system standard, with dropout masks for passengers. Hydraulic system, pressure 186-207 bars (2,700-3,000 lb/sq in), for operation of landing gear, mainwheel doors, flaps, spoilers, nosewheel steering, mainwheel brakes and anti-skid units. Two accumulators, pressurised by engine bleed air, one for main system pressure, the other providing emergency hydraulic power for wheel brakes in case of main system failure. Independent auxiliary system for lowering landing gear and flaps in the event of a main system failure. DC electrical system utilises two 30V 12kW engine driven starter/generators and two 24V 23Ah nickel-cadmium batteries. A 24V 4Ah battery provides separate power for standby instruments. AC electrical system includes two 1·25kVA static inverters, providing 115V 400Hz single-phase supplies, one 250VA standby static inverter for avionics, and two engine driven 208V 7·4kVA frequency-wild alternators for windscreen anti-icing. Ground power receptacle on starboard side at rear of fuselage for 28V external DC supply. Garrett GTCP-30-92 auxiliary power unit. Engine ice protection system supplied by engine bleed air. Graviner triple FD Firewire fire warning system and two BCF engine fire extinguishers. Stall warning system indicates approach to the stall, and an identification system operates a stick pusher to initiate a nose down pitching movement if the approach to the stall exceeds a predetermined rate.

AVIONICS AND EQUIPMENT: Digital avionics have been introduced. Standard avionics include dual Collins VHF-22A com transceivers, Collins 628T-3 HF com transceiver, dual Collins VIR-32 VHF nav receivers with marker beacon indicator, dual Collins ADF-60B, dual Collins AHS-85 attitude and heading reference systems, dual Collins DME-42 DME, dual Collins TDR-90 ATC transponders, Collins WXR-300 weather radar, dual Collins ADS-82 air data systems, Collins APS-85 autopilot, dual Collins EFIS-85B-2 electronic flight instrument systems, Collins ALT-55B radio altimeter, Baker M1045 audio system, Global GNS-1000 flight management system, Pioneer KE-8300 stereo tape and FM/AM radio.

DIMENSIONS, EXTERNAL:

Wing span	15·66 m (51 ft 4½ in)
Wing chord (mean)	2·29 m (7 ft 6¼ in)
Wing aspect ratio	7·06
Length overall	15·60 m (51 ft 2 in)
Height overall	5·36 m (17 ft 7 in)
Fuselage: Max diameter	1·93 m (6 ft 4 in)
Tailplane span	6·10 m (20 ft 0 in)
Wheel track (c/l of shock absorbers)	2·79 m (9 ft 2 in)
Wheelbase	6·41 m (21 ft 0½ in)

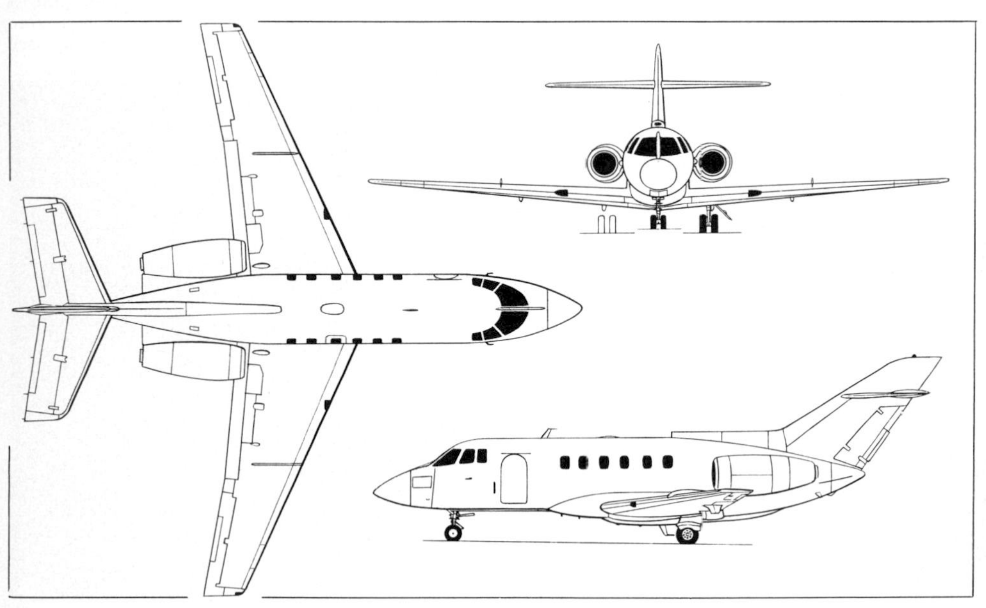

BAe 125 Series 800 (two Garrett TFE731-5R-1H turbofan engines) *(Pilot Press)*

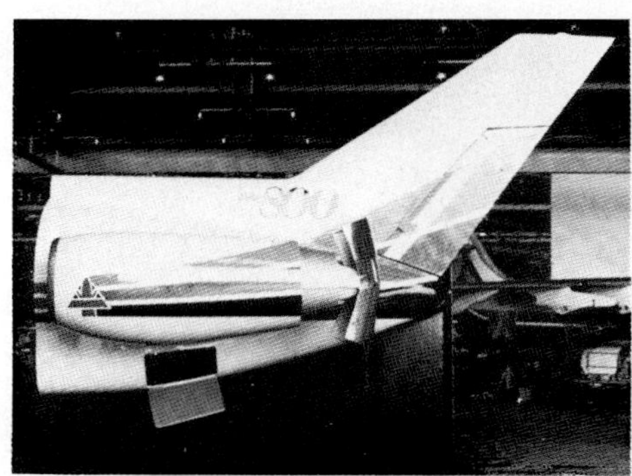

Mockup of optional rear baggage pannier and Dee Howard thrust reversers now available for BAe 125 Series 800

Passenger door (fwd, port):
- Height 1·30 m (4 ft 3 in)
- Width 0·69 m (2 ft 3 in)
- Height to sill 1·07 m (3 ft 6 in)

Emergency exit (overwing, stbd):
- Height 0·91 m (3 ft 0 in)
- Width 0·51 m (1 ft 8 in)

DIMENSIONS, INTERNAL:
- Cabin (excl flight deck): Length 6·50 m (21 ft 4 in)
  - Max width 1·83 m (6 ft 0 in)
  - Max height 1·75 m (5 ft 9 in)
  - Floor area 5·11 m² (55·0 sq ft)
  - Volume 17·10 m³ (604·0 cu ft)
  - Baggage compartments:
    - forward 0·74 m³ (26·0 cu ft)
    - rear 0·74 m³ (26·0 cu ft)
    - pannier (optional) 0·79 m³ (28·0 cu ft)

AREAS:
- Wings, gross 34·75 m² (374 sq ft)
- Ailerons (total) 2·05 m² (22·1 sq ft)
- Spoilers: upper (total) 0·74 m² (8·0 sq ft)
  - lower (total) 0·46 m² (5·0 sq ft)
- Trailing-edge flaps (total) 4·83 m² (52·0 sq ft)
- Fin (excl dorsal fin) 6·43 m² (69·2 sq ft)
- Rudder 1·32 m² (14·2 sq ft)
- Horizontal tail surfaces (total) 9·29 m² (100·0 sq ft)

WEIGHTS AND LOADING:
- Basic weight 6,676 kg (14,720 lb)
- Typical operating weight empty 6,858 kg (15,120 lb)
- Max payload 1,088 kg (2,400 lb)
- Max ramp weight 12,480 kg (27,520 lb)
- Max T-O weight 12,430 kg (27,400 lb)
- Max zero-fuel weight 7,950 kg (17,520 lb)
- Max landing weight 10,590 kg (23,350 lb)
- Max wing loading 357·69 kg/m² (73·26 lb/sq ft)

PERFORMANCE (provisional):
- Never-exceed speed Mach 0·87
- Max level speed and max cruising speed at 8,840 m (29,000 ft) 456 knots (845 km/h; 525 mph)
- Econ cruising speed at 11,900-13,100 m (39,000-43,000 ft) 400 knots (741 km/h; 461 mph)
- Stalling speed in landing configuration at typical landing weight 92 knots (170 km/h; 106 mph)
- Max rate of climb at S/L 945 m (3,100 ft)/min
- Time to 10,670 m (35,000 ft) 19 min
- Service ceiling 13,100 m (43,000 ft)
- T-O balanced field length at max T-O weight 1,713 m (5,620 ft)
- Landing from 15 m (50 ft) at typical landing weight (6 passengers and baggage) 1,372 m (4,500 ft)
- Range with max payload 2,870 nm (5,318 km; 3,305 miles)
- Range with max fuel, NBAA VFR reserves 3,000 nm (5,560 km; 3,454 miles)

BAe SUPER 748

Design of this short/medium range turboprop airliner started in January 1959, initially as the Avro 748. The first prototype flew on 24 June 1960, followed by a second on 10 April 1961. UK production of the Series 1 (18 built), Series 2 (including two Andover CC.Mk 2s for The Queen's Flight and four for Air Support Command), Series 2A and 2B, described in previous editions of *Jane's*, has been completed. Current models are as follows:

BAe Super 748. This latest version of the BAe 748 (first flight 30 July 1984) embodies all the improvements of the earlier Series 2B, together with significant new developments, including an advanced flight deck, new style galley, and engine hush kits. A new mark of engine, the Dart RDa.7 Mk 552, offers up to 12 per cent reduction in fuel consumption over previous marks. A system for dynamic balancing of the propellers to reduce cabin vibration and noise levels is optional. On the flight deck, push button selector/indicators replace old technology switches, and not only select the services required, but indicate the system status by a colour coded system of illumination. Baggage capacity is increased by 0·37 m³ (13 cu ft). Options include a large rear freight door with an opening of 2·67 m by 1·72 m (8 ft 9 in × 5 ft 7¾ in), together with a strengthened cabin floor capable of supporting an overall floor loading of 976 kg/m² (200 lb/sq ft).

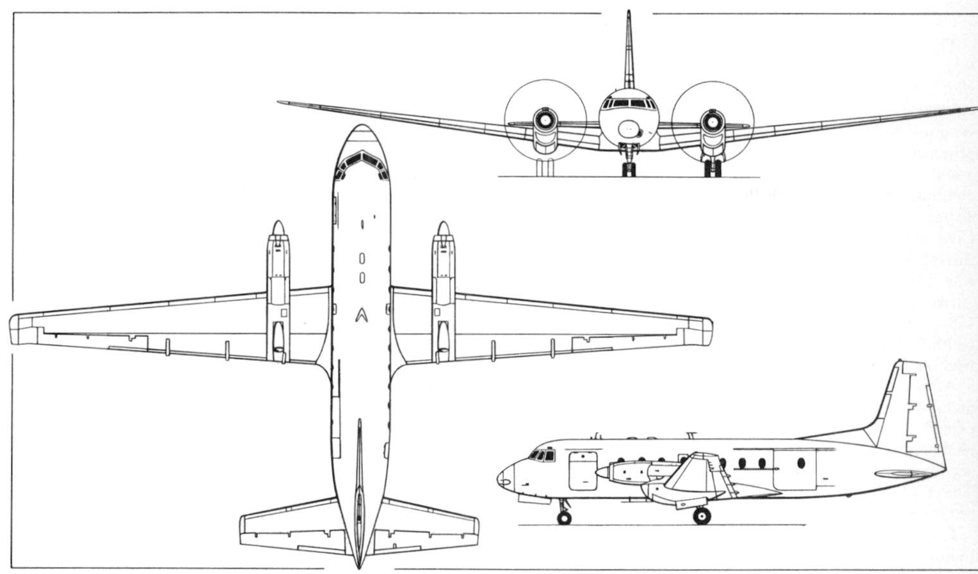
BAe Super 748 twin-turboprop transport aircraft. Large freight door is optional *(Pilot Press)*

BAe 748 Military Transport. The military transport version has the large rear freight door and strengthened floor that are available for the civil transport and has, in addition, fixed fittings to undertake a wide range of military roles. Optional military overload take-off and landing weights give improved payload/range capabilities. A total of 52 military BAe 748 Series 2As were exported, of which 18 were fitted with the rear freight door and strengthened floor. These were for the air forces of Belgium (3), Brazil (6), Ecuador (2), three undisclosed air forces (6), and the Nepal Royal Flight (1). The Colombian Air Force has a Series 2B military transport, operated for it by Satena.

Sales of all Series (including 31 Andover C. Mk 1s for the RAF: see 1968-69 *Jane's*) totalled 377, to 80 operators in 50 countries, by Summer 1986, the latest being two Super 748s to Cameroon Airlines.

The BAe 748 is the subject of a manufacturing agreement with the Indian government, and 89 aircraft (included in above overall total) were assembled from British built components by Hindustan Aeronautics Ltd (which see). Of these, 17 were for Indian Airlines and 72 for the Indian Air Force.

The following description applies to the current basic BAe Super 748, except where indicated:

TYPE: Twin-engined passenger and/or freight transport.

WINGS: Cantilever low-wing monoplane. Wing section NACA 23018 at root, NACA 4412 at tip. Dihedral 7°. Incidence 3°. Sweepback 2° 54′ at quarter-chord. All-metal two-spar fail-safe structure. No cutouts in spars for engines or landing gear. All-metal setback hinge, shielded horn balance, manually operated ailerons and electrically actuated Fowler flaps. Geared tab in each aileron. Trim tab in starboard aileron. Pneumatic leading-edge de-icing boots.

FUSELAGE: All-metal semi-monocoque riveted fail-safe structure, of circular section.

TAIL UNIT: Cantilever all-metal structure. Fixed incidence tailplane. Manually operated controls. Trim tabs in elevators and rudder. Spring tab in rudder.

LANDING GEAR: Retractable tricycle type, with hydraulically steerable nose unit. All wheels retract forward hydraulically. Mainwheels retract into bottom of engine nacelles forward of front wing spar. Dowty Rotol shock absorbers. Twin wheels, with Dunlop tyres, on all units. Mainwheels size 32 × 10·75-14. Nosewheels size 25·65 × 8·5-10. Standard tyre pressures: mainwheels 5·03 bars (73 lb/sq in); nosewheels 3·79 bars (55 lb/sq in). Minimum tyre pressures: mainwheels 4·48 bars (65 lb/sq in); nosewheels 3·45 bars (50 lb/sq in). Dunlop disc brakes with Maxaret anti-skid units. No brake cooling.

POWER PLANT: Two 1,700 kW (2,280 ehp) Rolls-Royce Dart RDa.7 Mk 552 turboprop engines, each driving a Dowty Rotol four-blade constant-speed fully-feathering propeller. Engine hush kits. Provision for automatic injection of water methanol into live engine in the event of an engine failure on take-off. Fuel in two integral wing tanks, with total capacity of 6,500 litres (1 440 Imp gallons). Underwing pressure refuelling and overwing gravity refuelling. Oil capacity 14·2 litres (25 Imp pints) per engine.

ACCOMMODATION (commercial): Crew of two on flight deck, and cabin attendant. Accommodation for 40-58 passengers in paired seats on each side of central gangway. Two baggage compartments forward of cabin. Galley, toilet and baggage compartment aft of cabin, with provision for steward's seat. Forward baggage compartments can be replaced by freight hold with moving partition between hold and passenger cabin. Main passenger door, on port side at rear, with smaller door on starboard side to serve as baggage door and emergency exit. Crew and freight door on port side at front. Hydraulically operated airstairs.

ACCOMMODATION (military transport): Up to 58 troops in airline type seats. Provision for forward and aft baggage compartments and hydraulically operated airstairs. In paratroop role up to 48 paratroops and dispatchers can be accommodated on sidewall folding seats with safety harness. Dropping by static line or free fall. For casualty evacuation up to 24 stretchers and nine nursing staff can be carried, with provision for medical supplies and

BAe Super 748 twin-turboprop transport (two Rolls-Royce Dart RDa.7 Mk 552 engines) for Cameroon Airlines

equipment. For supply dropping a guided roller conveyor system allows twelve 340 kg (750 lb) or six 680 kg (1,500 lb) loads to be dropped within six seconds. Large cargo door will accept items up to 1·42 m × 1·42 m × 3·66 m (4 ft 8 in × 4 ft 8 in × 12 ft) or small diameter pipes over 12 m (39 ft 4 in) in length. Onboard freight hoist and palletised freight system available. Quickly removable VIP cabin available, and a variety of VIP layouts, with separate toilet, telephone and wide range of options.

SYSTEMS: Normalair automatic pressurisation and air-conditioning system, giving equivalent altitude of 2,440 m (8,000 ft) at 7,620 m (25,000 ft). Pressure differential 0·38 bars (5·5 lb/sq in). Hydraulic system includes two Lockheed Mk 9 pumps, one driven by each engine accessory gearbox, providing 172 bars (2,500 lb/sq in) pressure and a flow rate of 13·6 litres (3 Imp gallons)/min for landing gear retraction and lowering, nosewheel steering, brakes and propeller brakes, and airstairs operation. Air/oil reservoirs, pressurised to 0·83 bars (12 lb/sq in). No pneumatic system. One 9kW 28V DC generator and one 22kVA alternator on each engine. Two 1,500VA static inverters.

AVIONICS AND EQUIPMENT: Collins or Bendix solid state avionics. Blind-flying instrumentation and Bendix RDR 1300 colour weather radar. Standard equipment by Sperry includes SPZ-500 multi-mode autopilot/flight director system, air data computer, flight director instruments, GH-14 vertical gyro and C-14 Gyrosyn compass systems. Provision for flight data recorder, flight deck voice recorder and GPWS.

DIMENSIONS, EXTERNAL (Super 748):

Wing span	31·24 m (102 ft 6 in)
Wing chord at root	3·49 m (11 ft 5¼ in)
Wing aspect ratio	12·668
Length overall	20·42 m (67 ft 0 in)
Fuselage: Max diameter	2·67 m (8 ft 9 in)
Height overall	7·57 m (24 ft 10 in)
Tailplane span	10·97 m (36 ft 0 in)
Wheel track	7·54 m (24 ft 9 in)
Wheelbase	6·30 m (20 ft 8 in)
Propeller diameter	3·66 m (12 ft 0 in)
Propeller ground clearance	0·61 m (2 ft 0 in)
Passenger door (port, rear):	
Height	1·57 m (5 ft 2 in)
Width	0·76 m (2 ft 6 in)
Height to sill	1·84 m (6 ft 0½ in)
Freight and baggage door (fwd):	
Height	1·37 m (4 ft 6 in)
Width	1·22 m (4 ft 0 in)
Height to sill	1·84 m (6 ft 0½ in)
Baggage door (rear, stbd):	
Height	1·24 m (4 ft 1 in)
Width	0·64 m (2 ft 1 in)
Height to sill	1·84 m (6 ft 0½ in)
Optional freight door (rear, port):	
Height	1·72 m (5 ft 7¾ in)
Width	2·67 m (8 ft 9 in)

DIMENSIONS, INTERNAL:

Cabin, excl flight deck: Length	14·17 m (46 ft 6 in)
Max width	2·46 m (8 ft 1 in)
Max height	1·92 m (6 ft 3½ in)
Floor area	27·5 m² (296 sq ft)
Volume	56·35 m³ (1,990 cu ft)
Max total freight holds	8·95 m³ (316 cu ft)

AREAS:

Wings, gross	77·00 m² (828·87 sq ft)
Ailerons (total)	3·98 m² (42·90 sq ft)
Trailing-edge flaps (total)	14·81 m² (159·40 sq ft)
Fin	9·81 m² (105·64 sq ft)
Rudder, incl tabs	3·66 m² (39·36 sq ft)
Tailplane	17·55 m² (188·90 sq ft)
Elevators, incl tabs	5·03 m² (54·10 sq ft)

WEIGHTS AND LOADINGS (A: Super 748; B: military transport):

Basic operating weight, incl crew:	
A	12,274 kg (27,059 lb)
B	11,630 kg (25,639 lb)
Max payload: A	5,189 kg (11,441 lb)
B	5,833 kg (12,861 lb)
B, optional overload	7,848 kg (17,302 lb)
Max fuel weight: A, B	5,225 kg (11,520 lb)
Max T-O weight: A, B	21,092 kg (46,500 lb)
B, optional overload	23,133 kg (51,000 lb)
Max zero-fuel weight: A, B	17,463 kg (38,500 lb)
B, optional overload	19,504 kg (43,000 lb)
Max landing weight: A, B	19,504 kg (43,000 lb)
B, optional overload	21,546 kg (47,500 lb)
Max wing loading: A	273·9 kg/m² (56·1 lb/sq ft)
Max power loading: A	6·20 kg/kW (10·2 lb/ehp)

PERFORMANCE (Super 748 at max T-O weight unless otherwise indicated):

Cruising speed at AUW of 17,236 kg (38,000 lb) 245 knots (454 km/h; 282 mph)

Max rate of climb at S/L at AUW of 17,236 kg (38,000 lb) 433 m (1,420 ft)/min

Service ceiling	7,620 m (25,000 ft)
Min ground turning radius	11·82 m (39 ft)
Runway LCN	9 to 18
T-O run (BCAR)	1,082 m (3,550 ft)
Balanced field length: BCAR	1,379 m (4,525 ft)

for 150 nm (278 km; 173 mile) sector, 48 passengers and reserves for 100 nm (185 km; 115 miles) diversion, plus 45 min hold at 3,050 m (10,000 ft) 777 m (2,550 ft)

Landing field length at max landing weight 1,024 m (3,360 ft)

Landing run 387 m (1,270 ft)

Range: with max payload, reserves for 100 nm (185 km; 115 miles) diversion and 45 min hold at 3,050 m (10,000 ft) 1,007 nm (1,865 km; 1,159 miles)

with 48 passengers (4,354 kg; 9,600 lb) 1,340 nm (2,481 km; 1,542 miles)

with max fuel and 3,593 kg (7,921 lb) payload 1,650 nm (3,055 km; 1,898 miles)

Ferry range 1,905 nm (3,528 km; 2,192 miles)

OPERATIONAL NOISE LEVELS (FAR Pt 36):

T-O	88·7 EPNdB
Approach	92·8 EPNdB
Sideline	93·3 EPNdB

BAe ATP

On 1 March 1984, British Aerospace announced the formal launch of the ATP programme. First flight took place on 6 August 1986, with first deliveries to airlines scheduled for September 1987. A launch order for two aircraft was placed by Leeward Islands Air Transport in June 1985, followed by an order for five aircraft by the British Midland Group.

Based on the BAe 748, the ATP retains the same cabin cross section but has a longer fuselage. Standard accommodation is for 64 passengers at a seat pitch of 79 cm (31 in), but various layouts are available for 60 to 72 passengers. There are separate forward and rear passenger doors, with integral airstairs at the forward door, and separate forward and rear baggage doors. The sill height of the forward passenger door allows the ATP to use jetways at regional airports. Certification will be to the latest JAR and FAR regulations.

TYPE: Twin-turboprop regional transport aircraft.

WINGS: Cantilever low-wing monoplane, with dihedral from centre-section. All-metal two-spar fail-safe structure, generally similar to that of BAe 748. Wing spars do not intrude into passenger cabin. Horn balanced ailerons and Fowler trailing-edge flaps; geared tab in each aileron. Pneumatic boot de-icing of leading-edges outboard of engine nacelles.

FUSELAGE: All-metal circular section semi-monocoque fail-safe structure, generally similar to BAe 748 but lengthened by 5·03 m (16 ft 6 in).

TAIL UNIT: Cantilever all-metal structure, with slightly swept vertical and non-swept horizontal surfaces. Power assisted rudder. Trim tab in each elevator; trim and spring tabs in rudder. Pneumatic boot de-icing of fin and tailplane leading-edges.

LANDING GEAR: Retractable tricycle type, of Dowty Rotol design, with twin-wheel main units and twin-wheel steerable nose unit. All units retract forward, main units into bottom of engine nacelles. All units incorporate oleo-pneumatic shock absorbers. Mainwheels fitted with 34 × 11·75-14 tubeless tyres. Nosewheels fitted with 22 × 6·75-10 tubeless tyres. Mainwheels have fusible plugs operating at 199°C. All wheels have 'roll on rim' capability. Dunlop carbon brakes and Maxaret anti-skid units on mainwheels. Inner and outer brakes on each leg supplied from two hydraulically independent systems via engine driven pump or standby DC pump.

POWER PLANT: Two 1,864 kW (2,500 shp) Pratt & Whitney Canada PW125 turboprop engines or 1,790 kW (2,400 shp) PW124 engines. BAe/Hamilton Standard slow-turning propellers, each having six blades of advanced aerodynamic profile and lightweight composite construction. Fuel in two integral wing tanks, with combined capacity of 6,364 litres (1,400 Imp gallons; 1,681 US gallons). Single pressure refuelling point underneath starboard outer wing.

ACCOMMODATION: Crew of two on flight deck; two cabin attendants. Main cabin has pressurised accommodation for 64 passengers as standard, at seat pitch of 79 cm (31 in), in four abreast layout with central aisle. Variations in layout available for 60 to 72 seats. Galley at rear of cabin on starboard side, forward toilet on port side. Separate passenger doors at front (with airstairs) and rear of cabin on port side. Compartment for carry-on baggage on port side of cabin, forward of front row of seats. Two baggage/freight compartments, one forward on starboard side and one aft of main cabin, both with external access. Overhead lockers above passenger seats. Total available baggage volume per passenger, excluding overhead lockers, is 0·18 m³ (6·2 cu ft). Forward cabin bulkhead can be moved on seat rails to permit flexibility for multi-sector or mixed passenger/cargo operations.

SYSTEMS: Hamilton Standard environmental control system with twin ECS packs using three-wheel air cycle machines with sub zero delivery temperature capability. Automatic pressurisation system, giving altitude equivalent to 2,440 m (8,000 ft) at 7,620 m (25,000 ft). Pressure differential 0·38 bars (5·5 lb/sq in). Each engine drives an Abex variable delivery hydraulic pump providing hydraulic power at a regulated pressure of 172 bars (2,500 lb/sq in) for landing gear actuation, nosewheel steering, brakes and airstairs. Auxiliary hydraulic power is supplied from a separate DC pump and reservoir for emergency operation of the landing gear and brakes. The system also provides hydraulic pressure for servicing purposes when the engines are not running. Main system has a flow rate of 41 litres (9 Imp gallons)/min controlled to 169 bars (2,450 lb/sq in); emergency system has a flow rate of 2·25 litres (0·5 Imp gallons)/min controlled to 145 bars (2,100 lb/sq in). Air/oil reservoirs pressurised to 1·25 bars (18 lb/sq in). Electrical power provided by Lucas 200V 30/45KVa variable frequency alternators, mounted on each engine. 28V DC subsystem from either two TRUs or two 35Ah nickel-cadmium batteries. Second subsystem provides 1·5KVa 200/115V constant frequency power from two static inverters. Garrett Model GTCP36-150 APU for air-conditioning on the ground, and electrical

BAe ATP regional transport aircraft (two Pratt & Whitney Canada PW125 turboprop engines)

power for battery charging, engine starting assist and other tasks.

AVIONICS AND EQUIPMENT: Digital avionics system using ARINC 429 data transmission, Smiths SDS-201 four-tube EFIS, Bendix avionics. Twin VHF com, twin VHF nav, scanning DME with additional frequency under R/Nav control, ADF, ATC transponder, CVR, FDR and digital GPWS. Bendix RDS-86 colour weather radar, with checklist facility, can display weather on EFIS nav display. Built-in test and recording facility. Dual AFCS, each with Litton LTR 81-01 AHRS and Smiths digital DADS. Options include second DME, second ADF, second transponder, R/Nav, MLS and single HF.

DIMENSIONS, EXTERNAL:

Wing span	30·63 m (100 ft 6 in)
Length overall	26·00 m (85 ft 4 in)
Height overall	7·14 m (23 ft 5 in)
Wheel track	8·46 m (27 ft 9 in)
Wheelbase	9·70 m (31 ft 9¾ in)
Propeller diameter	4·19 m (13 ft 9 in)
Propeller/fuselage clearance	0·80 m (2 ft 7½ in)
Passenger doors: Height	1·73 m (5 ft 8 in)
Width	0·71 m (2 ft 4 in)
Height to sill: fwd, door	2·09 m (6 ft 10 in)
aft door	1·71 m (5 ft 7½ in)

DIMENSIONS, INTERNAL:

Cabin: Length	19·20 m (63 ft 0 in)
Max width	2·49 m (8 ft 2 in)
Max height	1·92 m (6 ft 4 in)
Volume	75·1 m^3 (2,652 cu ft)
Baggage/freight compartment volume (three, total)	11·21 m^3 (396 cu ft)

WEIGHTS:

Operating weight empty	13,595 kg (29,970 lb)
Max payload	6,726 kg (14,830 lb)
Max ramp weight	22,590 kg (49,800 lb)
Max T-O weight	22,450 kg (49,500 lb)
Max landing weight	21,773 kg (48,000 lb)
Max zero-fuel weight	20,320 kg (44,800 lb)

PERFORMANCE (estimated):

Cruising speed at AUW of 19,051 kg (42,000 lb) at 4,575 m (15,000 ft) 268 knots (496 km/h; 308 mph)

T-O field length:

at max T-O weight 1,539 m (5,050 ft)

for 150 nm (278 km; 173 mile) sector, 64 passengers, reserves for 100 nm (185 km; 115 miles) diversion, plus 45 min hold at 3,050 m (10,000 ft) 1,097 m (3,600 ft)

Landing field length at max landing weight 1,097 m (3,600 ft)

Range, with reserves for 100 nm (185 km; 115 mile) diversion and 45 min hold at 3,050 m (10,000 ft):

with max payload 575 nm (1,065 km; 662 miles)

with 64 passengers (5,806 kg; 12,800 lb) 985 nm (1,825 km; 1,134 miles)

with max fuel and 3,778 kg (8,330 lb) payload 1,860 nm (3,444 km; 2,140 miles)

Ferry range 2,198 nm (4,070 km; 2,529 miles)

BAe 146

RAF designation: BAe 146 CC. Mk 2

In August 1973, Hawker Siddeley announced that it was to produce with government support a four-turbofan quiet operating transport aircraft known as the HS (now BAe) 146. Within a few months economic problems in the UK halted this programme, but research and design continued on a limited basis. With the absorption of Hawker Siddeley into British Aerospace in April 1977, BAe continued to provide limited funding to allow the manufacture of assembly jigs, systems test rigs, and continuing design and wind tunnel testing. On 10 July 1978, the British Aerospace Board's decision to give the 146 programme a full go-ahead was approved by the government. Production is undertaken in several BAe factories, including Brough (fin), Filton (centre fuselage), Manchester (rear fuselage), Weybridge (interior trim), Hamble (electric looms), Chester (nose fitting and completion) and Prestwick (engine pylons). Hatfield builds the front fuselage and flight deck, and is responsible for final assembly and flight testing.

Following the production decision, risk sharing agreements were signed with Avco Aerostructures (USA) for the manufacture of 20 sets of wing boxes; and with Saab-Scania (Sweden) for 20 sets of tailplanes and all movable control surfaces. Under an initial contract, Short Brothers (UK) manufactured 100 pods for the Avco Lycoming ALF 502 engines which power the 146. Follow-on production orders have been placed with each of these companies.

Three series are available:

Series 100. Four ALF 502R-5 turbofans, each rated at 31·0 kN (6,970 lb st). Designed to operate from short or semi-prepared airstrips with minimal ground facilities, with a normal seating capacity of 82-93. Rollout of the Series 100 prototype (G-SSSH) took place on 20 May 1981, and first flight was made on 3 September 1981. The second Series 100 (G-SSHH) flew on 25 January 1982, followed by the third (G-SSCH) on 2 April 1982. Transport category CAA certification of the Series 100 was obtained on 20 May 1983, with the first delivery, to Dan-Air, on 21 May 1983, and first scheduled operation on 27 May.

Series 200. Four ALF 502R-5 turbofans, each rated at 31·0 kN (6,970 lb st). For operation from paved runways only, with seating capacity of 82-109. Fuselage lengthened by five frame pitches (2·39 m; 7 ft 10 in). Increased maximum T-O weight and zero-fuel weight. Underfloor cargo volume increased by 35 per cent. The first Series 200 (G-WISC), made its initial flight on 1 August 1982 and the first production Series 200 (N601AW) was delivered to Air Wisconsin in June 1983. It operated its first scheduled service on 27 June, following receipt of FAA certification of both Series.

Series 300. Development of the Series 200 with lengthened fuselage to seat 100 passengers in standard form. Described separately.

146-QT Quiet Trader. Series 100 and 200 freighter versions. Cabin volume allows the 146-200 freighter to carry six standard 2·74 × 2·24 m (108 × 88 in) pallets, with space for an extra half pallet, or up to nine standard LD3 containers. Minor modifications to the standard floor make possible a maximum freight payload of 9,979 kg (22,000 lb), and the floor stressing permits a maximum individual pallet load of 2,721 kg (6,000 lb). Later versions, making use of further structural developments, will enable payloads of up to 12,973 kg (28,600 lb) to be carried.

The freight door is located in the rear fuselage, allowing normal passenger facilities to be retained at the front of the cabin for use in a Combi configuration; the rear passenger door is retained separately.

The first freighter conversion, a Series 200 aircraft (N146FT), was undertaken in the USA by Hayes International Corporation's Dothan, Alabama Division, which was responsible for the design, manufacture and installation of the door, the freight handling equipment, internal structure reinforcements and furnishings. Hayes will continue to undertake future conversions.

Statesman. British Aerospace has announced plans for

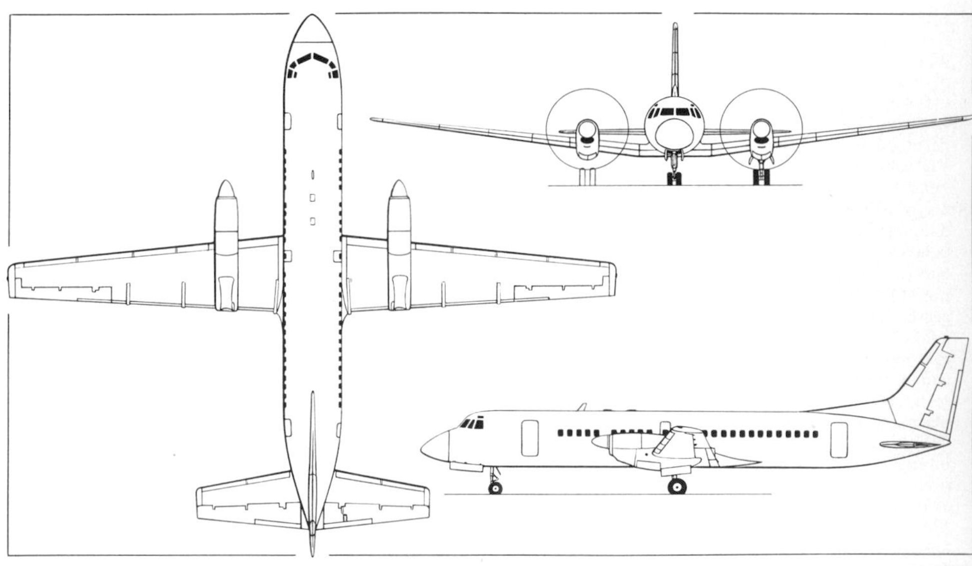

Three-view drawing of the twin-turboprop BAe ATP transport *(Pilot Press)*

BAe 146 CC. Mk 2 short range transport of The Queen's Flight

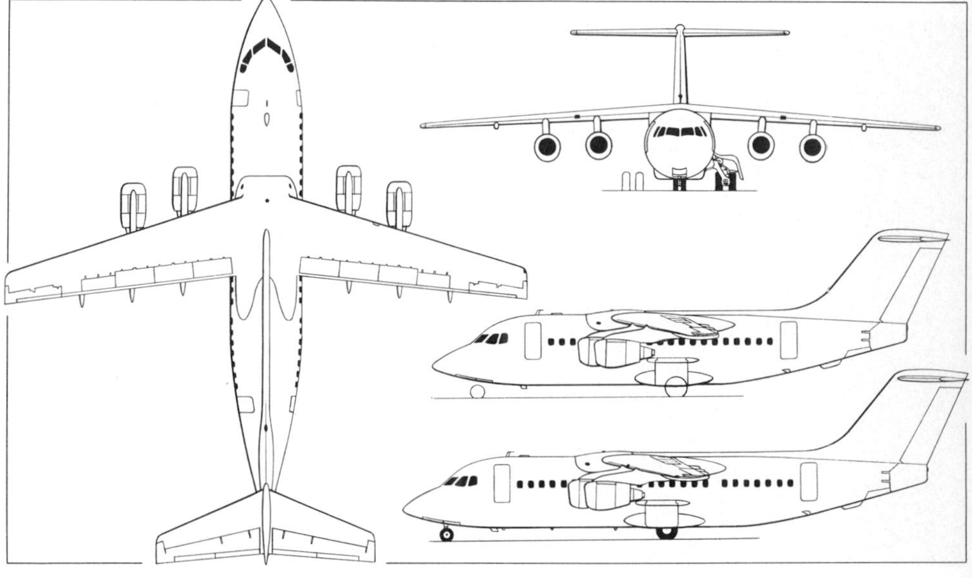

BAe 146 Series 200, with additional side view (centre right) of Series 100 *(Pilot Press)*

executive versions of Series 100 and 200 aircraft. The cabin area available allows flexibility of interior design. Staterooms, staff quarters, additional galley and wardrobe space can be provided. The first BAe 146 Statesman was delivered in mid-1986 for use in the Far East.

Orders for all versions totalled 78 by 6 October 1986, as follows:

	Orders	*(Series)*
AirCal	6	(200)
AirPac (Alaska)	1	(100)
Air Wisconsin	15*	(200)
Ansett	2	(200)
Aspen	2	(100)
British Caribbean Airways	2	(100)
CASC of China	10	(100)
Dan-Air	3	(100)
Government of Mali	1	(100)
Ministry of Defence (The Queen's Flight)	2	(100)
Pacific Southwest Airlines	24	(200)
Pelita	1	(200)
Presidential Airways	5	(200)
Royal West Airlines	3	(100)
Unannounced	1	

* *Five may be Series 300*

Fifty-five BAe 146s had been delivered by 6 October 1986.

The following description applies to the BAe 146 Series 100 and Series 200:

TYPE: Four-turbofan short range transport aircraft.

WINGS: Cantilever high-wing monoplane. British Aerospace high lift aerofoil section. Thickness/chord ratio 15·3% adjacent to fuselage, 12·2% at tip. Anhedral 3° at trailing-edge. Incidence 3° 6′ at fuselage side, 0° at tip. Sweepback 15° at quarter-chord. All-metal fail-safe structure of light alloy with machined skins, integrally machined spars and ribs. Single-section hydraulically actuated tabbed Fowler flaps of light alloy, spanning 78 per cent of each wing trailing-edge, with Dowty Rotol actuators. Mechanically actuated balanced ailerons, with hydraulically operated roll spoilers. Lift spoilers on upper surfaces. Trim and servo tab in each aileron. No leading-edge lift devices. Hot air anti-icing of leading-edges.

FUSELAGE: All-metal fail-safe pressurised semi-monocoque structure. Flight deck and tailcone areas free of stringers. Remainder of structure has 'top hat' stringers bonded to skins above keel area. Z section stringers 'wet' assembled with bonding agent and riveted to skin in keel area. Chemically etched skins of light alloy. Petal airbrakes form tailcone when closed.

TAIL UNIT: Cantilever sweptback T tail, of all-metal construction. Chemically etched light alloy skins bonded to 'top hat' section stringers. Fixed incidence tailplane. Manually operated balanced elevators, each with trim and servo tab. Powered rudder. Hot air anti-icing of tailplane leading-edges.

LANDING GEAR: Hydraulically retractable tricycle type, of Dowty Rotol design, with twin Dunlop wheels on each unit. Main units retract inward into fairings on fuselage sides; steerable nose unit retracts forward. Oleo-pneumatic shock absorbers with wheels mounted on trailing axle. Simple telescopic nosewheel strut. Mainwheel tyres size 12·50-16 Type III, pressure (Series 100) 8·42 bars (122 lb/sq in). Nosewheel tyres size 7·50-10 Type III, pressure (Series 100) 7·80 bars (113 lb/sq in). Low pressure tyres optional. Dunlop multi-disc carbon brakes operated by duplicated hydraulic systems. Anti-skid units in both primary and secondary brake systems.

BAe 146-QT Quiet Trader, with freight door open *(Air Portraits)*

POWER PLANT: Four Avco Lycoming ALF 502 turbofan engines (see aircraft Series listings for model), installed in pylon mounted underwing pods. No reverse thrust. Fuel in two integral wing tanks and integral centre-section tank (the latter with a vented and drained sealing diaphragm above passenger cabin), having a combined capacity of 11,728 litres (2,580 Imp gallons). Optional auxiliary tanks in wing root fairings, with combined capacity of 1,173 litres (258 Imp gallons), giving total capacity of 12,901 litres (2,838 Imp gallons). Single-point pressure refuelling, with coupling situated in starboard wing outboard of outer engine.

ACCOMMODATION: Crew of two pilots on flight deck, and two or three cabin staff. Optional observer's seat. Series 100 has accommodation in main cabin for 82 passengers with six-abreast seating at 84 cm (33 in) pitch, and up to 93 seats six-abreast at 74 cm (29 in) pitch. Series 200 has max capacity for 109 passengers with six-abreast seating at 74 cm (29 in) pitch. Various alternative layouts for mixed passenger/freight configurations. All seating layouts have two toilets and a forward galley as standard. One outward opening passenger door forward and one aft on port side of cabin. Built-in airstairs optional. Servicing doors, one forward and one aft, on starboard side of cabin. Freight and baggage holds under cabin floor. All accommodation air-conditioned. Windscreen electrical anti-icing and demisting standard. Rain repellent system optional.

SYSTEMS: BAe/Normalair-Garrett cabin air-conditioning and pressurisation system, using engine bleed air. Electro-pneumatic pressurisation control with discharge valves at fore and aft of cabin. Max differential 0·45 bars (6·5 lb/sq in). Hydraulic system, duplicated for essential services, for landing gear, flaps, rudder, roll and lift spoilers, airbrakes, nosewheel steering, brakes and auxiliary fuel pumps; pressure 207 bars (3,000 lb/sq in). Electrical system powered by two 40kVA integrated-drive alternators to feed 115/200V 3-phase 400Hz primary systems. 28V DC power supplied by transformer-rectifier in each channel. Hydraulically powered emergency electrical power unit. Garrett GTCP 36-100M APU for ground air-conditioning and electrical power generation. High pressure gaseous oxygen system, pressure 124 bars (1,800 lb/sq in). Stall warning and identification system, comprising stick shaker (warning) and stick force (identification) elements, providing soft and hard corrective stick forces at the approach of stall conditions. Series 100: stick force soft with flaps up; Series 200: force soft above 185 knots (343 km/h; 213 mph) regardless of configuration.

AVIONICS: Smiths SEP 10 automatic flight control and flight guidance system incorporates a simplex Cat I autopilot with a flight director display and separate attitude reference for each pilot. Addition of extra equipment and wiring permits coupled approaches to Cat II minima. Standard ARINC interface with radio nav system allows

BAe 146 Series 200 four-turbofan transport of AirCal of the USA

choice of radio equipment. Basic avionics include dual VHF com, audio system, passenger address system, cockpit voice recorder, dual compass systems, dual ADIs with separate attitude reference driven by single computer, marker beacon receiver, weather radar, dual radio altimeters, ground proximity warning system, dual DME, dual ATC transponders, dual VHF nav and dual ADF. Dowty-UEL flight deck warning system. Optional avionics include third VHF com, area navigation system, Selcal, tape reproducer, and single or dual HF com.

DIMENSIONS, EXTERNAL:
Wing span 26·34 m (86 ft 5 in)
Wing aspect ratio 8·97
Length overall: Series 100 26·19 m (85 ft 11 in)
Series 200 28·60 m (93 ft 10 in)
Height overall 8·61 m (28 ft 3 in)
Fuselage diameter 3·56 m (11 ft 8 in)
Tailplane span 11·09 m (36 ft 5 in)
Wheel track 4·72 m (15 ft 6 in)
Wheelbase: Series 100 10·09 m (33 ft 1½ in)
Series 200 11·20 m (36 ft 9 in)
Passenger doors (port, fwd and rear):
Height 1·83 m (6 ft 0 in)
Width 0·85 m (2 ft 9½ in)
Height to sill: fwd 1·88 m (6 ft 2 in)
rear 1·98 m (6 ft 6 in)
Servicing doors (stbd, fwd and rear):
Height 1·47 m (4 ft 10 in)
Width 0·85 m (2 ft 9½ in)
Height to sill: fwd 1·88 m (6 ft 2 in)
rear 1·98 m (6 ft 6 in)
Underfloor freight hold door (stbd, fwd):
Height 1·09 m (3 ft 7 in)
Width 1·35 m (4 ft 5 in)
Height to sill 0·78 m (2 ft 7 in)
Underfloor freight hold door (stbd, rear):
Height 1·04 m (3 ft 5 in)
Width 0·91 m (3 ft 0 in)
Height to sill 0·90 m (2 ft 11½ in)
Freight door (Freighter versions):
Height 1·98 m (6 ft 6 in)
Width: 146-100 2·92 m (9 ft 7 in)
146-200 3·30 m (10 ft 10 in)

DIMENSIONS, INTERNAL:
Cabin (excl flight deck, incl galley and toilets):
Length: Series 100 15·42 m (50 ft 7 in)
Series 200 17·81 m (58 ft 5 in)
Max width 3·38 m (11 ft 1 in)
Max height 2·02 m (6 ft 7½ in)
Floor area: Series 100 49·24 m² (530 sq ft)
Baggage/freight holds, underfloor:
Series 100 13·7 m³ (479 cu ft)
Series 200 18·3 m³ (645 cu ft)

AREAS:
Wings, gross 77·30 m² (832 sq ft)
Ailerons (total) 3·62 m² (39 sq ft)
Trailing-edge flaps (total) 19·51 m² (210 sq ft)
Spoilers (total) 10·03 m² (108 sq ft)
Fin 15·51 m² (167 sq ft)
Rudder 5·30 m² (57 sq ft)
Tailplane 15·61 m² (168 sq ft)
Elevators, incl tabs 10·03 m² (108 sq ft)

WEIGHTS AND LOADINGS:
Typical operating weight empty:
Series 100 22,226 kg (49,000 lb)
Series 200 22,861 kg (50,400 lb)
Max payload: Series 100 8,845 kg (19,500 lb)
Series 200 10,478 kg (23,100 lb)
Max fuel weight:
Series 100, 200 standard 9,362 kg (20,640 lb)
Series 100, 200, optional 10,298 kg (22,704 lb)
Max T-O weight:
Series 100 38,102 kg (84,000 lb)
Series 200 42,184 kg (93,000 lb)
Max ramp weight:
Series 100 38,329 kg (84,500 lb)
Series 200 42,410 kg (93,500 lb)
Max zero-fuel weight:
Series 100 31,071 kg (68,500 lb)
Series 200 33,339 kg (73,500 lb)
Max landing weight:
Series 100 35,153 kg (77,500 lb)
Series 200 36,741 kg (81,000 lb)
Max wing loading:
Series 100 493·0 kg/m² (101·0 lb/sq ft)
Series 200 545·7 kg/m² (111·8 lb/sq ft)
Max power loading:
Series 100, standard 307·3 kg/kN (3·01 lb/lb st)
Series 200 340·2 kg/kN (3·34 lb/lb st)

PERFORMANCE (at max standard T-O weight, except where indicated):
Max operating Mach No: Series 100 and 200 0·70
Max operating speed:
Series 100 300 knots (555 km/h; 345 mph CAS)
Series 200 295 knots (546 km/h; 339 mph CAS)
Econ cruising speed:
Series 100 and 200 at 9,145 m (30,000 ft) 383 knots (709 km/h; 440 mph)
Stalling speed, 30° flap:
Series 100 97 knots (180 km/h; 112 mph) EAS

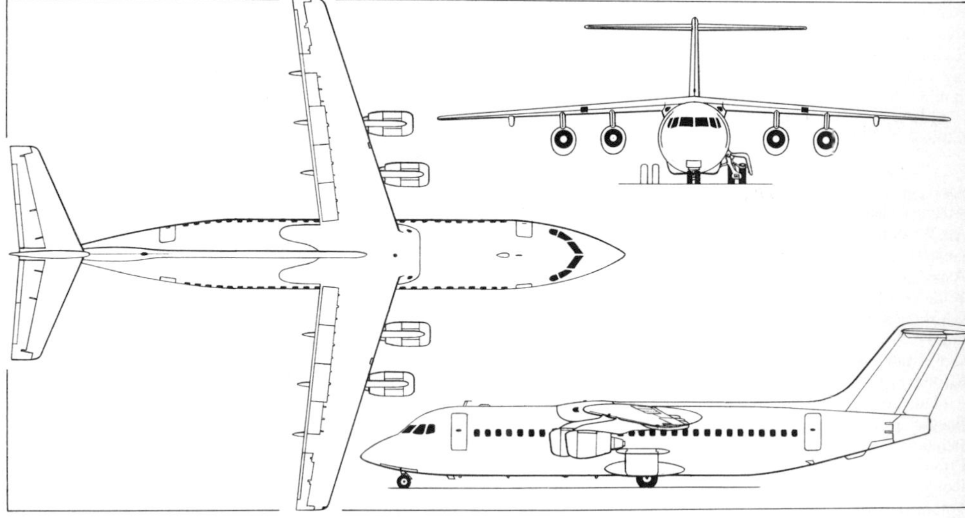

BAe 146 Series 300, the 'stretched' version of this short range transport *(Pilot Press)*

Series 200 102 knots (189 km/h; 118 mph) EAS
Stalling speed, 33° flap, at max landing weight:
Series 100 89 knots (165 km/h; 103 mph) EAS
Series 200 92 knots (170 km/h; 106 mph) EAS
T-O to 11 m (35 ft), S/L, ISA:
Series 100 1,219 m (4,000 ft)
Series 200 1,509 m (4,950 ft)
FAR landing distance from 15 m (50 ft), S/L, ISA, at max landing weight:
Series 100 1,067 m (3,500 ft)
Series 200 1,103 m (3,620 ft)
Range with max fuel, incl 86 kg (190 lb) fuel for ground manoeuvres, plus fuel for 150 nm (278 km; 173 mile) diversion and 45 min hold at 1,525 m (5,000 ft):
Series 100 1,672 nm (3,096 km; 1,924 miles)
Series 200 1,476 nm (2,733 km; 1,698 miles)
Range with max payload, allowances as above:
Series 100 935 nm (1,733 km; 1,077 miles)
Series 200 1,176 nm (2,179 km; 1,355 miles)

OPERATIONAL NOISE LEVELS (FAR Pt 36-12, certificated):
T-O: Series 100 83·0 EPNdB
Series 200 86·1 EPNdB
Approach: Series 100 95·6 EPNdB
Series 200 96·0 EPNdB
Sideline: Series 100 87·5 EPNdB
Series 200 87·2 EPNdB

BAe 146 Series 300

In July 1986 British Aerospace revealed plans for conversion of the Series 100 prototype (c/n 1001, G-SSSH) into an aerodynamic and structural prototype of the Series 300, with first flight programmed for the second quarter of 1987.

Original plans to produce a version with modified wings and uprated ALF 502R-7 engines, to seat up to 130 passengers, have been changed. Airline customers requested increased capacity with the same economy. So the Series 300 will now retain the ALF 502R-5s of the Series 200, and the same wings, and will operate at the same max T-O weight of 42,184 kg (93,000 lb). The fuselage is to be lengthened by some 2·44 m (8 ft) to 30·99 m (101 ft 8 in), by the insertion of two plugs of the same standard cross-section. This will enable 100 passengers to be carried in a highly comfortable five-abreast business class layout with scope for ample galley and wardrobe space.

BUCCANEER

It was announced in February 1985 that British Aerospace had been appointed prime contractor for a £40 million programme to update Buccaneer S.2Bs in service with the Royal Air Force, to improve the avionics, armaments and electronic countermeasures to meet Air Staff Requirement 1012.

A major element of the programme is the installation of a Ferranti FIN 1063 inertial navigation system. This is a derivative of the FIN 1064 which equips RAF Sepecat Jaguars, minus the weapon aiming system. Ferranti will also update the Blue Parrot attack radar, and Marconi Defence Systems will update the radar warning/ESM suite to Guardian Series 200 standard.

The aircraft are being updated for further service in the maritime role, and will be armed with BAe Sea Eagle and the TV guided Martel anti-ship missiles. Complementary with the avionics update is a full-scale fatigue test intended to extend the airframe life for many years. The update programme involves 60 of the RAF's Buccaneers.

BAe HAWK (TWO-SEAT VERSIONS)

RAF designation: Hawk T. Mk 1
US Navy designation: T-45 Goshawk

After examining designs submitted by BAC and Hawker Siddeley to meet an RAF requirement for a basic and advanced jet trainer, the Ministry of Defence announced in October 1971 that the Hawker Siddeley P1182 had been selected to meet this requirement. Selection of a non-afterburning version of the Rolls-Royce Turboméca Adour to power the aircraft was announced on 2 March 1972, and later in the same month the Ministry of Defence confirmed

British Aerospace Hawk carrying a Sea Eagle sea skimming anti-ship missile on its centreline pylon

an order for 176 HS P1182s, which were given the RAF name of Hawk T. Mk 1. These were to consist of one pre-production aircraft (XX154), which first flew on 21 August 1974, and 175 production Hawks.

There were no separate prototypes; instead, the first five production aircraft were allocated to the development programme. The first two production Hawks (XX162 and 163) were delivered to No. 4 Flying Training School at RAF Valley on 4 November 1976, and this basic version now serves also with Nos. 1 and 2 Tactical Weapons Units at Brawdy, Wales, and Chivenor, Devon, and with the RAF's premier aerobatic team, the Red Arrows.

The Hawk is fully aerobatic and is designed to have a safe fatigue life of 6,000 hours. It replaced the Jet Provost, Gnat Trainer and Hunter in RAF service for advanced flying training, and for radio, navigation and weapons training, and has since been adapted for airfield defence and limited attack duties. The design is capable of other operational roles, and has been developed through a succession of variants into a single-seat combat version, as follows:

Hawk T. Mk 1. Basic two-seater for RAF flying and weapon training. Adour 151 non-afterburning turbofan, rated at 23·13 kN (5,200 lb st). Two underwing hardpoints. Underbelly 30 mm gun pack. Simple weapon sight. Three-position flaps. No external fuel tanks.

Hawk T. Mk 1A. Eighty-eight RAF Hawks have been modified to this war role standard for airfield defence and limited attack, of which 72 have been formally declared to NATO. Capable of carrying two AIM-9L Sidewinder air-to-air missiles on underwing hardpoints.

Hawk 50 series. Initial export version, with Adour 851 turbofan, rated at 23·75 kN (5,340 lb st). Max operating weight increased by 30 per cent. Max disposable load increased by 70 per cent. Max range increased by 30 per cent. Revised tailcone shape to improve directional stability at high speed. Larger nose equipment bay. Two additional weapon pylons underwing. All four wing stations configured for single or twin store carriage; each pylon cleared to carry 515 kg (1,135 lb). 'Wet' inboard pylons for 455 litre (100 Imp gallon) fuel tanks. Improved nav/com. Improved cockpit, with angle of attack indication, fully aerobatic twin gyro AHRS, slim seat head boxes and weapon control panel. Optional brake-chute. Suitable for ground attack in day VMC, and armed reconnaissance with camera/sensor pod. Sold to Finland (50 **Mk 51** to replace Fouga Magisters. Construction of components for 46 aircraft, and final assembly, undertaken in Finland by Valmet); Kenya (12 **Mk 52**); and Indonesia (20 **Mk 53** ground attack/trainers). Deliveries began in 1980.

Hawk 60 series. Development of the 50 series with Adour 861 turbofan, rated at 25·35 kN (5,700 lb/st). Wing changes, including leading-edge devices and four-position flaps to improve lift capability. Low-friction nose leg, strengthened wheels and tyres, and adaptive anti-skid system. Drop tanks of 592 or 864 litre (130 or 190 Imp gallon) capacity. Provision for Sidewinder or Magic air-to-air missiles. Max operating weight increased by further 17 per cent compared with Mk 50 series, disposable load by 33 per cent and range by 30 per cent. Improved field performance, acceleration, rate of climb and turn rate. Sold to Zimbabwe (eight **Mk 60**), Dubai (eight **Mk 61**), Abu Dhabi (16 **Mk 63**), Kuwait (12 **Mk 64**) and Saudi Arabia (30 **Mk 65**). Entered service 1982.

T-45 Goshawk. In November 1981 the Hawk was selected, out of six designs, in the US Navy's VTXTS competition for an undergraduate jet pilot trainer, and is expected to replace the T-2C Buckeye and TA-4J Skyhawk. The US Navy's requirement is for more than 300 Hawks, designated T-45 Goshawk, without armament but compatible with carrier deck operation. McDonnell Douglas is prime contractor to the US Navy for the programme, with British Aerospace as principal subcontractor for the airframe and Sperry as principal subcontractor for simulators. Adour Mk 871 engine. Further brief details can be found under the McDonnell Douglas/BAe entry in the International section.

Two 60 series Hawks, one in ground attack configuration and the second with two 190 Imp gallon drop tanks and Sidewinder missiles for air defence

Hawk 100 series. To exploit the Hawk's five-pylon capability for carrying external stores, BAe announced this enhanced ground attack development of the 60 series in mid-1982. Still basically a two-seater, but likely to carry only a pilot on combat missions, the 100 series will have a Singer Kearfott SKN 2416 inertial navigation unit of the type used on the F-16, an advanced Smiths Industries head-up display/weapon aiming computer (HUD/WAC), and new air data sensor package, with optional laser ranging and FLIR; improved weapons management system allowing pre-selection during flight and displaying weapon status; manual or automatic weapon release; passive warning radar; HOTAS (hands on throttle and stick) controls; full colour multi-purpose CRT display in each cockpit; and provision for carrying an ECM pod. Max external load will be increased to 3,265 kg (7,200 lb); T-O run reduced by typically 20 per cent and landing run by 15 per cent; max ferry range increased by over 50 per cent with two 864 litre (190 Imp gallon) external tanks; and hi-lo-hi combat radius improved to 660 nm (1,222 km; 759 miles) with two 1,000 lb bombs or 275 nm (509 km; 316 miles) with seven 1,000 lb bombs. In a combat air patrol mission, the Hawk Series 100 will be able to loiter for 3½ h on station, 140 nm (260 km; 160 miles) from its base, armed with two Sidewinder type missiles and its 30 mm gun.

Hawk 200 series. Single-seat multi-role combat version. Described separately.

The following description applies to current UK production Hawks for export:

TYPE: Two-seat basic and advanced jet trainer, with capability for air defence and ground attack roles.

WINGS: Cantilever low-wing monoplane. Thickness/chord ratio 10·9% at root, 9% at tip. Dihedral 2°. Sweepback 26° on leading-edge, 21° 30′ at quarter-chord. One-piece wing, with six-bolt attachment to fuselage, employing a machined spars-and-skin torsion box, the greater part of which forms an integral fuel tank. Hydraulically operated double-slotted flaps and ailerons, latter operated by Automotive Products tandem actuators.

FUSELAGE: Conventional all-metal structure of frames and stringers, cut out to accept the one-piece wing. Large airbrake under rear fuselage, aft of wing.

TAIL UNIT: Cantilever all-metal structure, with sweepback on all surfaces. One-piece all-moving power operated anhedral tailplane, with Automotive Products tandem hydraulic actuator. Manually operated rudder, with electrically actuated trim tab. Two small ventral fins.

LANDING GEAR: Wide track hydraulically retractable tricycle type, with single wheel on each unit. Automotive Products oleos and jacks. Main units retract inward into wing, ahead of front spar; castoring nosewheel retracts forward. Dunlop mainwheels, brakes and tyres size 6·50-10, pressure 9·86 bars (143 lb/sq in). Nosewheel and tyre size 4·4-16, pressure 8·27 bars (120 lb/sq in). Tail bumper fairing under rear fuselage. Anti-skid wheel brakes. Tail braking parachute, diameter 2·64 m (8 ft 8 in), optional.

POWER PLANT: One Rolls-Royce Turboméca Adour non-afterburning turbofan engine, as described under individual series entries. Air intake on each side of fuselage, forward of wing leading-edge. Engine starting by integral gas turbine starter. Fuel in one fuselage bag tank of 868 litres (191 Imp gallons) capacity and integral wing tank of 836 litres (184 Imp gallons) capacity ; total fuel capacity 1,704 litres (375 Imp gallons). Pressure refuelling point near front of port engine air intake trunk. Provision for carrying one 455, 592 or 864 litre (100, 130 or 190 Imp gallon) drop tank on each inboard underwing pylon, according to series.

ACCOMMODATION: Crew of two in tandem under one-piece fully transparent sideways opening canopy. Fixed front windscreen and separate internal windscreen in front of rear cockpit. From March 1986 an improved front windscreen was being fitted retrospectively to RAF Hawks, able to withstand a 1 kg (2·2 lb) bird at 528 knots (978 km/h; 607 mph). Rear seat elevated. Martin-Baker Mk 10B zero/zero rocket assisted ejection seats, with MDC (miniature detonating cord) system to break canopy before seats eject. The MDC can also be operated from outside the cockpit for ground rescue. Dual controls standard. Entire accommodation pressurised, heated and air-conditioned.

SYSTEMS: BAe cockpit air-conditioning and pressurisation systems, using engine bleed air. Two hydraulic systems; flow rate: System 1, 36 litres (8 Imp gallons)/min; System 2, 22·7 litres (5 Imp gallons)/min. Systems pressure 207 bars (3,000 lb/sq in), for actuation of control jacks, flaps, airbrake, landing gear and anti-skid wheel brakes. Compressed nitrogen accumulators provide emergency power for flaps and landing gear at a pressure of 2·75 to 5·5 bars (40 to 80 lb/sq in). Hydraulic accumulator for emergency operation of wheel brakes. No pneumatic system. DC electrical power from single brushless generator, with two static inverters to provide AC power and two batteries for standby power. Gaseous oxygen system for crew. Pop-up Dowty Rotol ram air turbine in upper rear fuselage provides emergency power for flying controls in the event of an engine or No. 2 pump failure.

AVIONICS AND EQUIPMENT: The RAF standard of flight instruments includes Ferranti gyros and inverter, two Sperry Gyroscope RAI-4 4 in remote attitude indicators and a magnetic detector unit, and Louis Newmark compass system. Radio and navigation equipment includes Sylvania UHF and VHF, Cossor CAT.7000 Tacan, Cossor ILS with CILS.75/76 localiser/glideslope receiver and marker receiver, and IFF/SSR (Cossor 2720 Mk 10A IFF in aircraft for Finland).

ARMAMENT AND OPERATIONAL EQUIPMENT: Ferranti F.195 weapon sight and camera recorder in each cockpit of RAF, series 50 and 60 aircraft. (Saab RGS2 sighting system in aircraft for Finland.) Underfuselage centreline mounted 30 mm Aden gun and ammunition pack, and two or four hardpoints underwing, according to series. Provision for pylon in place of the ventral gun pack. In

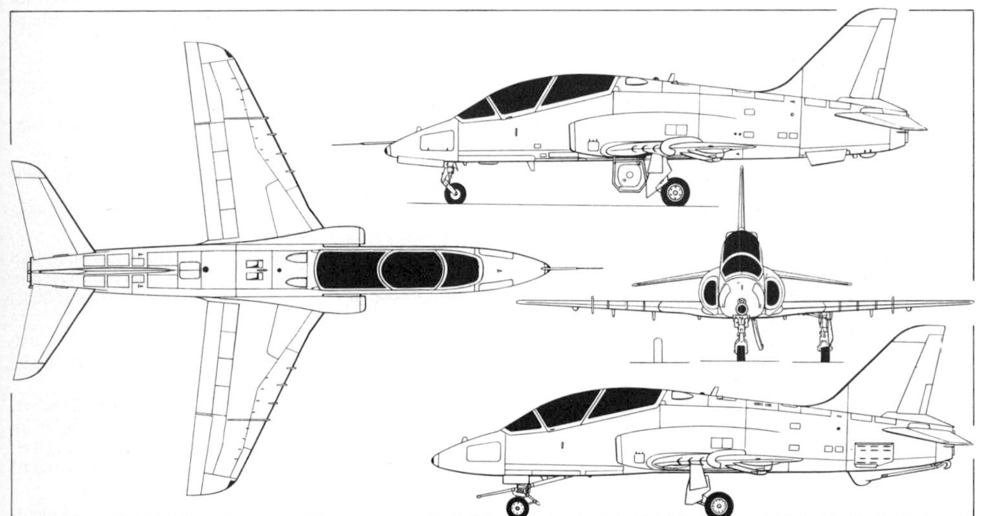

British Aerospace Hawk 60 series two-seat jet trainer/ground attack aircraft, with additional side view (bottom) of US Navy T-45 Goshawk *(Pilot Press)*

RAF training roles the normal max external load is about 680 kg (1,500 lb), but the uprated Hawk has demonstrated its ability to carry a total external load of 3,084 kg (6,800 lb). Typical weapon loadings on 60 series include a 30 mm or 12·7 mm centreline gun pod and four packs each containing eighteen 68 mm rockets; a centreline reconnaissance pod and four packs each containing twelve 81 mm rockets; seven 1,000 lb free fall or retarded bombs; four launchers each containing four 100 mm rockets; nine 250 lb or 250 kg bombs; thirty-six 80 lb runway denial or tactical strike bombs; five 600 lb cluster bombs; four Sidewinder/Magic air-to-air missiles; nine 50 Imp gallon napalm canisters; four CBLS 100/200 carriers each containing four practice bombs and four rockets; or two 130 Imp gallon drop tanks and two Stingray homing torpedoes. Maverick missiles could also be carried. A configuration demonstrated at the 1983 Paris Air Show included a Sea Eagle anti-ship missile on the centreline pylon, plus two Sidewinder missiles and two 864 litre (190 Imp gallon) drop tanks underwing.

DIMENSIONS, EXTERNAL:

Wing span	9·39 m (30 ft 9¾ in)
Wing chord: at root	2·65 m (8 ft 8¼ in)
at tip	0·90 m (2 ft 11½ in)
Wing aspect ratio	5·284
Length overall: excl probe	11·17 m (36 ft 7¾ in)
incl probe	11·86 m (38 ft 11 in)
Height overall	3·99 m (13 ft 1¼ in)
Tailplane span	4·39 m (14 ft 4¾ in)
Wheel track	3·47 m (11 ft 5 in)

AREAS:

Wings, gross	16·69 m² (179·6 sq ft)
Ailerons (total)	1·05 m² (11·30 sq ft)
Trailing-edge flaps (total)	2·50 m² (26·91 sq ft)
Airbrake	0·53 m² (5·70 sq ft)
Fin	2·51 m² (27·02 sq ft)
Rudder, incl tab	0·58 m² (6·24 sq ft)
Tailplane	4·33 m² (46·61 sq ft)

WEIGHTS:

Weight empty: 60 series	3,635 kg (8,015 lb)
100 series	3,855 kg (8,500 lb)
T-O weight:	
60 series trainer, 'clean'	5,150 kg (11,350 lb)
Max T-O weight: T. Mk 1	5,700 kg (12,566 lb)
50 series	7,350 kg (16,200 lb)
60, 100 series	8,570 kg (18,890 lb)
Max landing weight: T. Mk 1	4,649 kg (10,250 lb)
60 series	7,650 kg (16,865 lb)

PERFORMANCE:

Max speed in dive at height	575 knots (1,065 km/h; 661 mph)
Max Mach number in dive	1·2
Max level speed:	
50 series	535 knots (990 km/h; 615 mph)
60, 100 series	560 knots (1,037 km/h; 644 mph)
Max level speed Mach number	0·88
Max rate of climb at S/L	3,600 m (11,800 ft)/min
Time to 9,145 m (30,000 ft), 'clean'	6 min 6 s
Service ceiling	15,250 m (50,000 ft)
T-O run	550 m (1,800 ft)
Landing run	488 m (1,600 ft)
Combat radius:	
with 2,268 kg (5,000 lb) weapon load	538 nm (998 km; 620 miles)
with 908 kg (2,000 lb) weapon load	781 nm (1,448 km; 900 miles)
Ferry range 'clean'	1,313 nm (2,433 km; 1,510 miles)
Ferry range, 60 series, with two 864 litre (190 Imp gallon) drop tanks	2,200 nm (4,075 km; 2,530 miles)
Endurance, 100 nm (185 km; 115 miles) from base	approx 4 h 0 min
g limits	+8/−4

BAe HAWK 200 SERIES (SINGLE-SEATER)

On 20 June 1984, British Aerospace announced its intention to build as a private venture a demonstrator single-seat combat version of the Hawk, and this aircraft (ZG200) flew for the first time on 19 May 1986. It was lost, through no apparent aircraft fault, on 2 July 1986, and is being replaced by the first pre-production Hawk 200, scheduled to fly by mid-1987.

The Hawk 200 is virtually identical with the current production two-seater aft of the cockpit, giving 80 per cent airframe commonality. Built-in twin-cannon armament frees the centreline pylon for other stores, including a 592 litre (130 Imp gallon) external fuel tank. Each of the four underwing pylons is capable of carrying 907 kg (2,000 lb), within the max external load of 3,084 kg (6,800 lb). The wide range of missions that such capability permits include:

Airspace denial. Carrying two Sidewinder type missiles and two 864 litre (190 Imp gallon) drop tanks, the Hawk 200 could loiter for 3·5 hours on station at 9,150 m (30,000 ft), 100 nm (185 km; 115 miles) from base; or for one hour on station 550 nm (1,018 km; 633 miles) from base. Max intercept radius is 720 nm (1,333 km; 828 miles).

Close air support. Five 1,000 lb and four 500 lb bombs could be delivered with precision up to 104 nm (192 km; 120 miles) from base in a lo-lo mission.

Battlefield interdiction. In a hi-lo-hi operation, the Hawk 200 has a radius of action of 579 nm (1,072 km; 666 miles), with a 1,360 kg (3,000 lb) military load.

BAe Hawk 200 single-seat multi-role combat aircraft

Three-view drawing of the single-seat Hawk 200 Series *(Pilot Press)*

Long-range photo reconnaissance. A wide area of search is made possible by the mission range of 1,723 nm (3,190 km; 1,982 miles) offered by two external tanks, carried with a pod containing cameras and infra-red linescan. A rapid role change could then permit follow-up attack by the same aircraft. Lo-lo radius by day or night is 510 nm (945 km; 586 miles).

Long-range deployment. Ferry range with two 864 litre (190 Imp gallon) and one 592 litre (130 Imp gallon) external tanks is 1,950 nm (3,610 km; 2,244 miles), unrefuelled and with 864 litre tanks retained. Reserves would allow 10 min over destination at 150 m (500 ft).

Anti-shipping strike. Armed with a Sea Eagle sea skimming anti-ship missile, and carrying two 864 litre (190 Imp gallon) tanks, the Hawk 200 could attack a ship 800 nm (1,480 km; 920 miles) from base, and return with 10 per cent fuel reserves. This puts ships almost anywhere in the North Atlantic within range of the Hawk from shore bases. Weapon release could be beyond the target's radar envelope.

Three standards of equipment are envisaged, depending on the customer's mission requirements, as follows:

Day operation. The most simple equipment fit would comprise a gyro stabilised attack sight and attitude heading reference system, with navigation by radio aids. Navigation and weapon aiming capabilities could be extended by adding an inertial navigation system, head-up display and weapon aiming computer. Other options are HOTAS controls, laser rangefinder, IFF, radar warning receiver.

Night operation. With a FLIR and laser rangefinder mounted in a modified nosecone, the Hawk 200 could carry out precision ground attacks and tactical reconnaissance by day and night.

All-weather operation. Installation of an advanced multi-mode radar, such as the Sea Harrier's Ferranti Blue Fox, would add all-weather target acquisition and navigational fixing capabilities. Weapons like the anti-shipping Sea Eagle and air-to-air Sky Flash could also be employed.

Changes by comparison with the two-seat Hawk are as follows:

TYPE: Single-seat multi-role combat aircraft.

WINGS: As Hawk two-seater, except for detail modifications to leading-edge aerofoil section.

FUSELAGE: Modified to single-seat configuration. Unchanged design concept and criteria.

LANDING GEAR: Mainwheel tyres size 559 × 165-279, pressure 16·2 bars (235 lb/sq in). Nosewheel tyre size 457 × 140-203, pressure 7·24 bars (105 lb/sq in).

POWER PLANT: One Rolls-Royce Turboméca Adour Mk 871, with uninstalled rating of 26·0 kN (5,845 lb st).

ACCOMMODATION: Pilot only, on Martin-Baker Type 10L ejection seat, under side-hinged (to starboard) canopy.

SYSTEMS: Fairey Hydraulics yaw control system added, comprising rudder actuator and servo control system, incorporating an autostabiliser computer.

ARMAMENT: One or two internally mounted 25 mm Aden guns beneath cockpit floor. Ferranti ISIS sight or Smiths head-up display optional.

DIMENSIONS, EXTERNAL:

As Hawk two-seater, except:

Length overall	11·38 m (37 ft 4 in)
Height overall	4·16 m (13 ft 8 in)
Wheelbase	3·298 m (10 ft 10 in)

WEIGHTS:

Weight empty	4,128 kg (9,100 lb)
Max fuel: internal	1,360 kg (3,000 lb)
internal + three drop tanks	3,210 kg (7,080 lb)
Max weapon load	3,500 kg (7,700 lb)
Max T-O weight	9,101 kg (20,065 lb)

PERFORMANCE (estimated; no external stores or role equipment unless stated):

Never-exceed speed at height	Mach 1·2 (575 knots, 1,065 km/h; 661 mph)
Max level speed at S/L	560 knots (1,037 km/h; 644 mph)
Max cruising speed at S/L	550 knots (1,019 km/h; 633 mph)
Econ cruising speed at 12,500 m (41,000 ft)	430 knots (796 km/h; 495 mph)
Stalling speed, flaps down	106 knots (197 km/h; 122 mph) IAS
Max rate of climb at S/L	3,508 m (11,510 ft)/min
Service ceiling	15,250 m (50,000 ft)
Runway LCN: flexible pavement	15
rigid pavement	10
T-O run with max weapon load	1,585 m (5,200 ft)
T-O to 15 m (50 ft) with max weapon load	2,134 m (7,000 ft)
Landing from 15 m (50 ft) at landing weight of 4,550 kg (10,030 lb): with brake-chute	854 m (2,800 ft)
without brake-chute	1,250 m (4,100 ft)
Range:	
with internal fuel only	482 nm (892 km; 554 miles)
with internal fuel plus three drop tanks	1,950 nm (3,610 km; 2,244 miles)
g limits	+8/−4

BAe HARRIER

RAF designations: Harrier GR. Mk 3 and T. Mk 4/4A
USMC designations: AV-8A (Mk 50) and TAV-8A (Mk 54)
Spanish Navy designation: Matador (AV-8S and TAV-8S)

The Harrier was the world's first operational fixed-wing V/STOL strike fighter. The first of six single-seat prototypes (XV276) flew for the first time on 31 August 1966; the following versions have since been built:

Harrier GR. Mk 1, 1A and 3. Single-seat close support and tactical reconnaissance versions for the RAF. First of initial series of 78 production GR. Mk 1s (XV738) flew on 28 December 1967. No. 1 Squadron at RAF Wittering received its first aircraft (XV744) on 9 April 1969. Deliveries to No. 233 OCU, also at Wittering, began on 5 May 1969 (aircraft XV747). Delivered subsequently to Nos. 3, 4 and 20 Squadrons in West Germany. These aircraft were designated Harrier GR. Mk 1 when fitted initially with Pegasus 101 engines. When retrofitted subsequently with the Pegasus 102 they were redesignated GR. Mk 1A. Aircraft now in service have Pegasus 103 engines and are designated GR. Mk 3. A total of 120 GR. 1/3s has been delivered to the Royal Air Force. Fourteen of them took part in the Falklands campaign in 1982, as described in the 1984-85 and previous editions of *Jane's*.

A Harrier GR. Mk 1A, piloted by Sqn Ldr T. L. Lecky-Thompson, still holds two international time-to-height records after VTO, in Class H for jet lift aircraft, set on 5 January 1971. The aircraft reached 9,000 m (29,528 ft) in 1 min 44·7 s and 12,000 m (39,370 ft) in 2 min 22·7 s. The same RAF pilot also set a Class H altitude record of 14,040 m (46,063 ft) in a Harrier GR. Mk 1A on 2 January 1971.

Harrier T. Mk 2, 2A, 4 and 4A and Sea Harrier T. Mk 4RN. Two-seat versions, retaining the full combat capability of the single-seater in terms of equipment fit and weapon carriage. There is a large degree of commonality in structure and system components, ground support equipment and flight and ground crew training. Differences include a longer nose section forward of the wing leading-edge, with two cockpits in tandem; a tailcone approx 1·83 m (6 ft) longer than that of the single-seat model; and enlarged fin surfaces. The two-seat Harrier can be used operationally with the rear seat and compensating tail ballast removed, thus minimising the weight penalty over its single-seat counterpart. First of two development aircraft (XW174) flew on 24 April 1969, and the first of 21 production aircraft for the RAF (XW264) on 3 October 1969. The two-seater entered RAF service in July 1970.

The RAF Harrier T. Mk 2, like the GR. Mk 1, was powered originally by the Pegasus 101 engine. The designations T. Mk 2A and T. Mk 4 apply to aircraft retrofitted with, respectively, the Pegasus 102 and 103. The T. Mk 4A has a pointed nose, without LRMTS, to make it more suitable for training duties with No. 233 OCU at RAF Wittering because of decreased weight. Deliveries of T. Mk 2/4A aircraft totalled 23 by February 1984. Royal Navy two-seaters are designated Sea Harrier T. Mk 4RN; one was delivered in 1980 and three in 1983.

Harrier GR. Mk 5. Designation of AV-8B Harrier IIs ordered for the RAF. This version, which is being produced jointly for the US Marine Corps, the RAF and the Spanish Navy, is described under the McDonnell Douglas/BAe heading in the International section.

Harrier Mk 50 (USMC designation AV-8A). Single-seat close support and tactical reconnaissance version for the US Marine Corps, delivery of which began on 26 January 1971. Dimensionally as GR. Mk 3, but without laser ranger and marked target seeker, and with modifications to customer's specification, including provision for the carriage of Sidewinder missiles. Total of 102 ordered for US Marine Corps, plus eight Harrier **Mk 54s** (a two-seat version designated **TAV-8A**); all of those still in service now have F402-RR-402 or -402A (Pegasus 803) engines.

The AV-8As equip three US Marine Corps combat squadrons: VMA 513, VMA 542 and VMA 231; and training squadron VMA(T) 203, at Cherry Point, North Carolina.

In the period from 1979 until FY 1984, the US Marine Corps upgraded 47 of its AV-8As to **AV-8C** standard. This was a CILOP (conversion in lieu of procurement) programme under which the AV-8As were fitted with forward looking passive radar warning equipment at the wingtips, tail warning radar in the tail 'bullet' fairing, improved UHF com radio, a flare/chaff dispenser in the rear fuselage equipment bay, the LIDS (lift improvement devices: underfuselage strakes and forward flap) developed for the AV-8B, an onboard oxygen generating system, and KY 58 secure voice system. The ram air turbine of the AV-8A was removed. Conversion of the first few AV-8As to AV-8C standard was undertaken by McDonnell Douglas, from kits supplied by BAe. The remaining conversions were carried out by the US Marine Corps at NAS Cherry Point, North Carolina, using BAe kits.

Eleven AV-8As and two TAV-8As were ordered, through USA, for the Spanish Navy, by whom they are known as **Matadors** and designated **AV-8S** and **TAV-8S** respectively. The first batch of six Spanish AV-8s are Mk 50 aircraft; the second batch of five are **Mk 55** aircraft; the TAV-8Ss are Mk 54s. They equip the 8a Escuadrilla of the Spanish Navy at Rota, Cadiz, and operate from the aircraft carrier *Dedalo*. Like the AV-8As of the USMC, the Matador has a Sidewinder capability.

Harrier Mk 52. One aircraft built as a demonstrator using BAe and equipment suppliers' private funding. It is similar to the Harrier T. Mk 4, and is fitted with a Pegasus 103 engine; in recognition of its status as the first civil registered jet V/STOL aircraft in the UK, it was granted the civil registration G-VTOL. First flight was made on 16 September 1971, with a Pegasus 102 fitted initially.

Harrier T. Mk 60. Two-seat operational trainer version for Indian Navy. T. Mk 4 configuration, but with complete Sea Harrier avionics except for Blue Fox radar. Two ordered.

Sea Harrier FRS. Mks 1 and 51. Versions for Royal Navy and Indian Navy. Described separately.

Harrier Mk 80. Export version, based on Sea Harrier but with laser ranger/seeker of GR. Mk 3 instead of Blue Fox radar. None yet built or ordered.

The following details apply generally to the Harrier GR. Mk 3 and T. Mk 4/4A, except where a specific version is indicated:

TYPE: V/STOL close support and reconnaissance aircraft.

WINGS: Cantilever shoulder-wing monoplane. Wing section of BAe (HS) design. Thickness/chord ratio 10% at root, 5% at tip. Anhedral 12°. Incidence 1° 45'. Sweepback at quarter-chord 34°. One-piece aluminium alloy three-spar safe-life structure with integrally machined skins, manufactured by Brough factory of BAe, with six-point attachment to fuselage. Plain ailerons and flaps, of bonded aluminium alloy honeycomb construction. Ailerons irreversibly operated by Fairey tandem hydraulic jacks. Jet reaction control valve built into front of each outrigger wheel fairing. Entire wing unit removable to provide access to engine. For ferry missions, the normal 'combat' wingtips can be replaced by bolt-on extended tips to increase ferry range.

FUSELAGE: Conventional semi-monocoque safe-life structure of frames and stringers, mainly of aluminium alloy, but with titanium skins at rear and some titanium adjacent to engine and in other special areas. Access to power plant through top of fuselage, ahead of wing. Jet reaction control valves in nose and tailcone. Large forward hinged airbrake under fuselage, aft of mainwheel well.

TAIL UNIT: One-piece variable incidence tailplane, with 15°

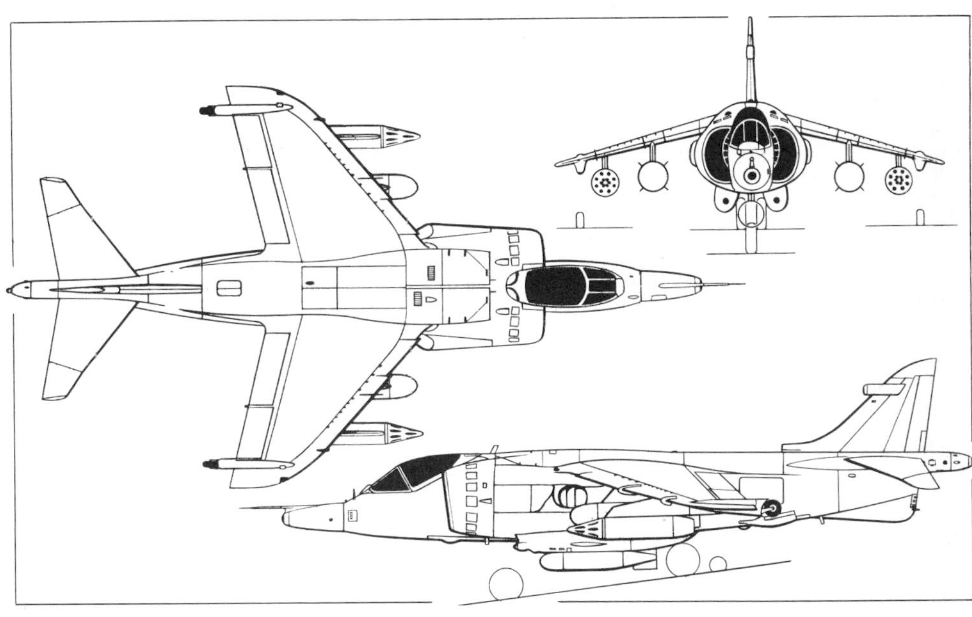

BAe Harrier GR. Mk 3 single-seat V/STOL close support and reconnaissance aircraft *(Pilot Press)*

Royal Air Force Harrier GR. Mk 3 taking off from its concealed dispersal site in Germany

BAe Sea Harrier T. Mk 4RN of No. 899 Naval Air Squadron *(HMS Heron)*

of anhedral, irreversibly operated by Fairey tandem hydraulic jack. Rudder and trailing-edge of tailplane are of bonded aluminium honeycomb construction. Rudder is operated manually. Trim tab in rudder. Ventral fin under rear fuselage. Fin tip carries suppressed VHF aerial.

Landing Gear: Retractable bicycle type of Dowty Rotol manufacture, permitting operation from rough unprepared surfaces of CBR as low as 3 to 5 per cent. Hydraulic actuation, with nitrogen bottle for emergency extension of landing gear. Single steerable nosewheel retracts forward, twin coupled mainwheels rearward, into fuselage. Small outrigger units retract rearward into fairings slightly inboard of wingtips. Nosewheel leg is of levered suspension Liquid Spring type. Dowty Rotol telescopic oleo-pneumatic main and outrigger gear. Dunlop wheels and tyres, size 26·00 × 8·75-11 (nose unit), 27·00 × 7·74-13 (main units) and 13·50 × 6·4 (outriggers). GR. Mk 3 tyre pressures 6·21 bars (90 lb/sq in) on nose and main units, 6·55 bars (95 lb/sq in) on outriggers. T. Mk 4 tyre pressures 6·90 bars (100 lb/sq in) on nose unit, 6·55 bars (95 lb/sq in) on main and outrigger units. Dunlop multi-disc brakes and Dunlop-Hytrol adaptive anti-skid system.

Power Plant: One Rolls-Royce Pegasus Mk 103 vectored thrust turbofan engine (95·6 kN; 21,500 lb st), with four exhaust nozzles of the two-vane cascade type, rotatable through 98·5° from fully aft position. Engine bleed air from HP compressor used for jet reaction control system and to power duplicated air motor for nozzle actuation. The low drag intake cowls each have eight automatic suction relief doors aft of the leading-edge to improve intake efficiency by providing extra air for the engine at low forward or zero speeds. A 227 litre (50 Imp gallon) tank supplies demineralised water for thrust restoration in high ambient temperatures for STO, VTO and vertical landings. Fuel in five integral tanks in fuselage and two in wings, with total capacity of approx 2,865 litres (630 Imp gallons). This can be supplemented by two 455 litre (100 Imp gallon) jettisonable combat tanks, or two 864 litre (190 Imp gallon) tanks, or two 1,500 litre (330 Imp gallon) ferry tanks on the inboard wing pylons. Ground refuelling point in port rear nozzle fairing. Provision for in-flight refuelling probe above the port intake cowl.

Accommodation: Crew of one (Mk 3) or two (Mk 4) on Martin-Baker Mk 9D zero/zero rocket ejection seats which operate through the miniature detonating cord equipped canopy of the pressurised, heated and air-conditioned cockpit. AV-8As of the US Marine Corps retrofitted with Stencel SIIIS-3 ejection seats. Manually operated canopy, rearward sliding on single-seat, sideways opening (to starboard) on two-seat versions. Bird-proof windscreen, with hydraulically actuated wiper. Windscreen washing system.

Systems: Three-axis limited authority autostabiliser for V/STOL flight. Pressurisation system of BAe design, with Normalair-Garrett and Marston major components; max pressure differential 0·24 bars (3·5 lb/sq in). Two hydraulic systems; flow rate: System 1, 36 litres (8 Imp gallons)/min; System 2, 23 litres (5 Imp gallons)/min. Systems, pressure 207 bars (3,000 lb/sq in), actuate Fairey flying control and general services and, except on AV-8C, include a retractable ram air turbine inside top of rear fuselage, driving a small hydraulic pump for emergency power. Hydraulic reservoirs nitrogen pressurised at 2·75 to 5·5 bars (40 to 80 lb/sq in). AC electrical system with transformer-rectifiers to provide required DC supply. One 12kVA Lucas generator. Two 28V 25Ah batteries, one of which energises a 24V motor to start Lucas gas turbine starter/APU. This unit drives a 6kVA auxiliary alternator for ground readiness servicing and standby. Normalair-Garrett liquid oxygen system of 5 litres (1 Imp gallon) capacity. Bootstrap cooling unit for equipment bay, with intake at base of dorsal fin.

Avionics and Equipment: Plessey U/VHF, Ultra standby UHF, GEC Avionics AD 2770 Tacan and Cossor IFF, Ferranti FE 541 inertial navigation and attack system (INAS), with Sperry C2G compass, Smiths electronic head-up display of flight information, and air data computer. Marconi ARI.18223 radar warning receiver. INAS can be aligned equally well at sea or on land. The weapon aiming computer provides a general solution for manual or automatic release of free fall and retarded bombs, and for the aiming of rockets and guns, in dive and straight-pass attacks over a wide range of flight conditions and very considerable freedom of manoeuvre in elevation. Communications equipment ranges through VHF in the 100-156MHz band to UHF in the 220-400MHz band. Ferranti Type 106 laser ranger and marked target seeker (LRMTS) retrofitted to all RAF single-seat and some two-seat Harriers.

Armament and Operational Equipment: Optically flat panel in nose, on port side, for F.95 oblique camera, which is carried as standard. A cockpit voice recorder with in-flight playback facility supplements the reconnaissance cameras, and facilitates rapid debriefing and mission evaluation. No built-in armament. Combat load is carried on four underwing and one underfuselage pylons, all with ML ejector release units. The inboard wing points and the fuselage point are stressed for loads of up to 910 kg (2,000 lb) each, and the outboard underwing pair for loads of up to 295 kg (650 lb) each; the two strake fairings under the fuselage can each be replaced by a 30 mm Aden gun pod and ammunition. The Harrier is cleared for operations with a maximum external load exceeding 2,270 kg (5,000 lb), and has flown with a weapon load of 3,630 kg (8,000 lb). It is able to carry 30 mm guns, bombs, rockets and flares of UK and US designs, and in addition to its fixed reconnaissance camera can also carry a five-camera reconnaissance pod on the underfuselage pylon. A typical combat load comprises a pair of 30 mm Aden gun pods, a 1,000 lb bomb on the underfuselage pylon, a 1,000 lb bomb on each of the inboard underwing pylons, and a Matra 155 launcher with 19 × 68 mm SNEB rockets on each outboard underwing pylon. A Sidewinder installation is provided in the AV-8A and Matador versions (and retrospectively on some GR. Mk 3s), to give the aircraft an effective air-to-air capability in conjunction with the two 30 mm Aden guns. A flare/chaff dispenser can be fitted.

Dimensions, external:
- Wing span: combat — 7·70 m (25 ft 3 in)
  - ferry — 9·04 m (29 ft 8 in)
- Wing chord: at root — 3·56 m (11 ft 8 in)
  - at tip — 1·26 m (4 ft 1½ in)
- Wing aspect ratio: combat — 3·175
  - ferry — 4·08
- Length overall: single-seat — 13·89 m (45 ft 7 in)
  - single-seat (laser nose) — 14·27 m (46 ft 10 in)
  - two-seat (laser nose) — 17·50 m (57 ft 5 in)
- Height overall: single-seat — 3·63 m (11 ft 11 in)
  - two-seat — 4·17 m (13 ft 8 in)
- Tailplane span — 4·24 m (13 ft 11 in)
- Outrigger wheel track — 6·76 m (22 ft 2 in)
- Wheelbase, nosewheel to mainwheels — approx 3·45 m (11 ft 4 in)

Areas:
- Wings, gross: combat — 18·68 m² (201·1 sq ft)
  - ferry — 20·1 m² (216 sq ft)
- Ailerons (total) — 0·98 m² (10·5 sq ft)
- Trailing-edge flaps (total) — 1·29 m² (13·9 sq ft)
- Fin (excl ventral fin): single-seat — 2·40 m² (25·8 sq ft)
  - two-seat — 3·57 m² (38·4 sq ft)
- Rudder, incl tab — 0·49 m² (5·3 sq ft)
- Tailplane — 4·41 m² (47·5 sq ft)

Weights and Loading:
- Basic operating weight, empty:
  - GR. Mk 3 — 6,140 kg (13,535 lb)
  - T. Mk 4 — 6,850 kg (15,100 lb)
- Internal fuel — 2,295 kg (5,060 lb)
- Max T-O weight:
  - single-seat — 11,430 kg (25,200 lb)
  - two-seat — 11,880 kg (26,200 lb)
- Max wing loading (single-seat): — 610 kg/m² (125 lb/sq ft)

Performance:
- Max speed at S/L — 635 knots (1,176 km/h; 730 mph)
- Max Mach number in a dive at height — 1·3
- Time to 12,200 m (40,000 ft) from vertical T-O — 2 min 23 s
- Service ceiling — 15,600 m (51,200 ft)
- T-O run: with 2,270 kg (5,000 lb) payload at max T-O weight — approx 305 m (1,000 ft)
- Range: hi-lo-hi with 1,995 kg (4,400 lb) payload — 360 nm (666 km; 414 miles)
  - lo-lo with 1,995 kg (4,400 lb) payload — 200 nm (370 km; 230 miles)
- Ferry range — 1,850 nm (3,425 km; 2,129 miles)
- Range with one in-flight refuelling — more than 3,000 nm (5,560 km; 3,455 miles)
- Endurance:
  - combat air patrol 100 nm (185 km; 115 miles) from base — 1 h 30 min
  - with one in-flight refuelling — more than 7 h
- *g* limits — +7·8/−4·2

BAe SEA HARRIER

RN designation: FRS. Mk 1/2

Indian Navy designation: FRS. Mk 51

On 15 May 1975, the British government announced its decision to proceed with full development of a maritime version of the Harrier, subsequently designated Sea Harrier **FRS. Mk 1**. The first Sea Harrier to fly (XZ450) made its first flight on 20 August 1978, and the first for the Royal Navy (XZ451) was handed over on 18 June 1979. The first Sea Harrier ship trials were carried out on board HMS *Hermes* during November 1979.

The initial Royal Navy order was for three development aircraft. Successive production orders for 21, 10, 14 and 9 had taken the total to 57 by Summer 1986. The Naval Intensive Flying Trials Unit for the Sea Harrier (No. 700A Squadron) was commissioned at RNAS Yeovilton on 19 September 1979. It became subsequently the shore based No. 899 HQ squadron, with eight aircraft. Front line units, each nominally with five aircraft, are Nos. 800 and 801 Squadrons, able to operate from the anti-submarine cruisers HMS *Invincible, Illustrious* and *Ark Royal*. Six similar Sea Harriers, designated **FRS. Mk 51**, ordered by the Indian Navy are now in service with No. 300 (White Tiger) Squadron and operate from INS *Vikrant*. Three standard, non-navalised T. Mk 4N two-seaters were delivered to the Royal Navy for land based training, and two T. Mk 60s to the Indian Navy. In November 1985 the Indian Government ordered 10 additional FRS Mk 51 Sea Harriers and one more T. Mk 60 two-seat trainer. A letter of intent to purchase eight more FRS Mk 51s was issued in September 1986, to equip the former HMS *Hermes* when it is transferred to the Indian Navy.

Following proposals by Lt Cdr D. R. Taylor, RN, tests were carried out successfully in 1977 with a 'ski-jump' launching ramp designed to boost the short take-off performance of vectored thrust aircraft. This technique makes possible substantial benefits in Harrier operation both at sea and ashore, and is a feature of Royal Navy ships in which Sea Harriers are based. A 7° ski-jump ramp is fitted to HMS *Invincible* and HMS *Illustrious*; that in HMS *Ark Royal* is more steeply angled, at 12°, permitting an increase of 1,135 kg (2,500 lb) in launch weight for the same T-O run, or a 50-60 per cent reduction in T-O run for the same weight.

Major changes compared with the Harriers in service with the RAF, Spanish Navy and US Marine Corps comprise the elimination of magnesium components, introduction of a raised cockpit, revised operational avionics, and installation of multi-mode Ferranti radar in a redesigned nose that folds to port for carrier stowage. Known by the name Blue Fox, this radar is a derivative of the frequency agile Seaspray radar fitted in the Royal Navy Lynx helicopter, but embodies changes to suit its different role, with air-to-air intercept and air-to-surface modes of operation.

The Royal Navy's Sea Harrier FRS. Mk 1 has a Rolls-Royce Pegasus 104 vectored thrust turbofan engine, with the same rating as the Pegasus 103 fitted to current RAF Harriers. The two variants differ little in design, except that the Pegasus 104 incorporates additional anti-corrosion features and has the capability to generate more electrical power.

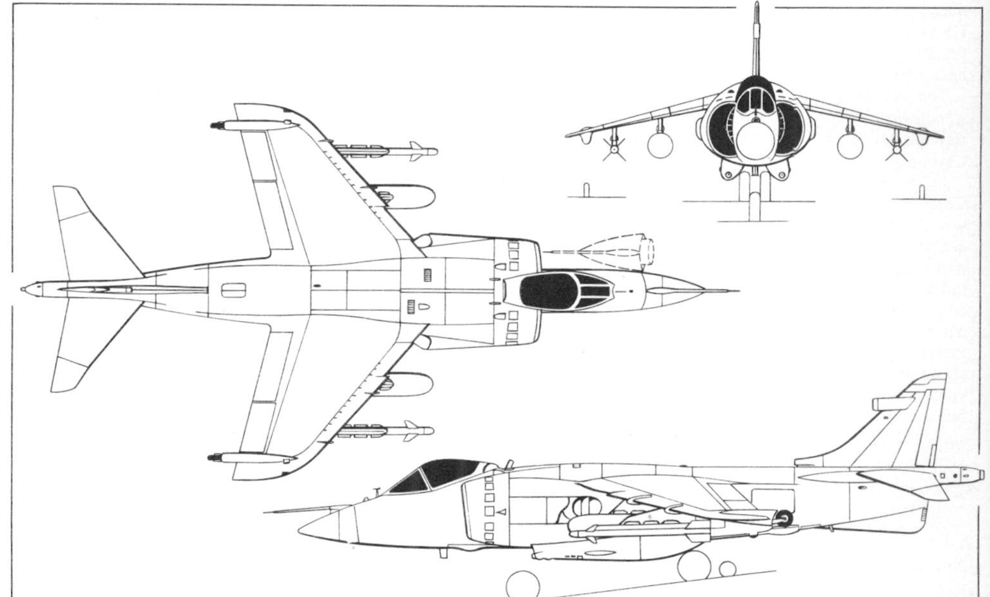

BAe Sea Harrier FRS. Mk 1 V/STOL fighter, reconnaissance and strike aircraft *(Pilot Press)*

BAe Sea Harrier FRS. Mk 1 of the Royal Navy, armed with four Sidewinder missiles

Detailed weights, loadings and performance figures are not available for the Sea Harrier. It was expected that the FRS. Mk 1 would operate at approximately the same weights as the GR. Mk 3, and would be capable of lifting a full military load with a 152 m (500 ft) flat deck run into an overdeck wind of 30 knots (55·5 km/h; 34·5 mph). It was first used operationally during the Falkland Islands campaign in 1982, from HMS *Hermes* and *Invincible*, when a total of 28 Sea Harriers flew more than 2,000 sorties. They destroyed at least 20 enemy aircraft in air-to-air combat without loss. Four Sea Harriers were lost in accidents and two to ground fire.

In January 1985 the UK Ministry of Defence awarded a contract to British Aerospace for the project definition phase of a mid-life update of Royal Navy Sea Harriers, of which 34 had been delivered by that time, with 23 more on order. The upgraded Sea Harriers, the first of which was to fly in 1986, will be designated **FRS. Mk 2**.

Operational Sea Harrier FRS. Mk 1s will be returned to BAe for conversion from early 1988, and will re-enter squadron service one year later. Delivery of new production FRS. Mk 2s could begin in 1990.

Externally, the Mk 2 will differ from the Mk 1 in having role change wingtip extensions that will increase the span by 61 cm (2 ft); a less pointed nose radome; a longer rear fuselage, resulting from insertion of a 35 cm (1 ft 1¾ in) plug aft of the wing trailing-edge; and revisions of the antennae and external stores.

Installation of Ferranti Blue Vixen pulse-Doppler radar, instead of the original Blue Fox, will give the Sea Harrier FRS. Mk 2 all-weather lookdown/shootdown capability, with inherent track-while-scan, multiple target engagement, greatly increased missile launch range, enhanced surface target acquisition, and improved ECCM performance. In addition to the wide range of weapons with which the current operational Sea Harrier is compatible, the FRS. Mk 2 will be equipped to carry the new air-to-air AIM-120 AMRAAM.

Improved systems will be built around a MIL 1553B databus. This uses a dual redundant data highway, allowing computerised time sharing of information processed in the databus control and interface unit.

Redesign of the cockpit will allow presentation of the total fleet defence picture, radar picture, threat data, target priority, and navigational information on dual multi-purpose displays. All time-critical weapon systems controls will be positioned on the up-front control panel, or on the throttle and stick.

Operational efficiency will be improved by the ergonomic integration of additional switches as part of the control column and throttle handle functions. HOTAS (hands on throttle and stick) controls will provide simultaneous control of the aircraft, radar, and weapons systems without the need to operate separate controls and switches.

The Sea Harrier FRS. Mk 2 will retain two external stores pylons under each wing, an underbelly centreline pylon, and mountings under the fuselage for two 30 mm Aden or new 25 mm gun packs, or AMRAAM missile pylons. Two 455 or 864 litre (100 or 190 Imp gallon) combat drop tanks, or 1,500 litre (330 Imp gallon) ferry tanks, can be carried on the inboard underwing pylons. Alternative loadings include five free-fall or retarded 1,000 lb bombs, five cluster bombs, six Matra 115/116 packs of 68 mm rockets, eight Bofors Lepus flares, four Sidewinder, Magic or AMRAAM air-to-air missiles, two Sea Eagle air-to-surface missiles, or two ALARM anti-radiation missiles. Other standard weapons with which the aircraft will be compatible include 250, 500, and 1,000 lb LDGP free-fall bombs, 250 and 500 lb Snakeye retarded bombs, LAU-10A, LAU-68A and LAU-69A rocket launchers, Mk 77 fire bombs, APAM cluster/Mk 7 dispensers, Rockeye 11 cluster/Mk 7 dispensers, and PMBR practice bomb racks.

The description of the GR. Mk 3 applies also to the FRS. Mk 1, except as follows:

TYPE: V/STOL fighter, reconnaissance and strike aircraft.

POWER PLANT: As GR. Mk 3, except one Rolls-Royce Pegasus Mk 104 vectored thrust turbofan engine of 95·6 kN (21,500 lb st). Internal fuel capacity and external combat fuel capacity as for GR. Mk 3, except that 864 litre (190 Imp gallon) drop tanks are in the regular RN inventory.

ACCOMMODATION: As GR. Mk 3, but with pilot raised 28 cm (11 in), on Martin-Baker Mk 10H zero/zero ejection seat.

SYSTEMS: As GR. Mk 3, except autopilot function on Fairey Hydraulics, giving throughput to aileron and tailplane power controls as well as to three-axis autostabs. Ram air turbine may be removed eventually. Pressurisation system of BAe design with major components from Normalair-Garrett and Delaney Gallay. Current production aircraft have two 15kVA generators instead of one 12kVA; earlier aircraft may be retrofitted. British Oxygen liquid oxygen system of 5 litres (1 Imp gallon) capacity in Royal Navy aircraft; those for Indian Navy have gaseous oxygen system. Lucas Mk 2 GTS/APU.

AVIONICS AND EQUIPMENT: Nose mounted Ferranti Blue Fox multi-mode radar, with TV raster daylight viewing tube which conveys flight information, as well as radar data, to pilot. New and larger Smiths electronic head-up display and 20,000 word digital weapon aiming computer. Autopilot, radar altimeter and Decca Doppler 72 radar. Ferranti self aligning attitude and heading reference platform and digital navigation computer. Radio navaids include UHF homing, GEC Avionics AD 2770 Tacan with offset facility and I band transponder. Radio com by multi-channel Plessey PTR 377 U/VHF, with VHF standby via D 403M transceiver. Passive electronic surveillance and warning of external radar illumination by receiver with forward and rear hemisphere antennae in fin and tailcone respectively.

ARMAMENT AND OPERATIONAL EQUIPMENT: As GR. Mk 3, except for standard addition of four AIM-9 Sidewinder missiles on the outboard underwing pylons (Matra Magic instead of Sidewinder on Indian Navy aircraft), and provision for two air-to-surface missiles of Sea Eagle or Harpoon type.

DIMENSIONS, EXTERNAL: As GR. Mk 3 except:

Wing span: FRS. Mk 1	7·70 m (25 ft 3 in)
FRS. Mk 2	8·31 m (27 ft 3 in)
Length overall: FRS. Mk 1	14·50 m (47 ft 7 in)
FRS. Mk 2	14·10 m (46 ft 3 in)
Length overall, nose folded:	
FRS. Mk 1	12·73 m (41 ft 9 in)
FRS. Mk 2	13·16 m (43 ft 2 in)
Height overall	3·71 m (12 ft 2 in)

WEIGHTS (FRS. Mk 1):

Operating weight empty	6,374 kg (14,052 lb)
Max fuel: internal	2,295 kg (5,060 lb)
external	2,404 kg (5,300 lb)
Max weapon load: STO	3,630 kg (8,000 lb)
VTO	2,270 kg (5,000 lb)
Max T-O weight	11,880 kg (26,200 lb)

PERFORMANCE (FRS. Mk 1):

Max Mach No. at high altitude 1·25

Max level speed at low altitude above 640 knots (1,185 km/h; 736 mph) EAS

Typical cruising speed:
high altitude, for well over 1 h on internal fuel above Mach 0·8
low altitude 350-450 knots (650-833 km/h; 404-518 mph), with rapid acceleration to 600 knots (1,110 km/h; 690 mph)

STO run at max T-O weight, without 'ski-jump' approx 305 m (1,000 ft)

Time from alarm to 30 nm (55 km; 35 miles) combat area under 6 min

High altitude intercept radius, with 3 min combat and reserves for VL 400 nm (750 km; 460 miles)

Strike radius 250 nm (463 km; 288 miles)

g limits +7·8/−4·2

COMBAT PROFILES (FRS. Mk 2, from carrier fitted with a 12° ski-jump ramp, at ISA + 15°C and with a 20 knot; 37 km/h; 23 mph wind over the deck):

Combat air patrol: Up to 1½ hours on station at a radius of 100 nm (185 km; 115 miles), carrying four AMRAAMs, or two AMRAAMs and two 30 mm guns, plus two 864 litre (190 Imp gallon; 228 US gallon) combat drop tanks.

Reconnaissance: Low-level cover of 28,000 nm² (96,000 km²; 37,065 sq miles) at a radius of 525 nm (970 km; 600 miles) from the carrier, with outward and return flights at medium/high level, carrying two 30 mm guns and two 864 litre (190 Imp gallon; 228 US gallon) combat drop tanks. Overall flight time 1 h 45 min.

Surface attack (hi-lo-hi): Radius of action to missile launch 200 nm (370 km; 230 miles), carrying two Sea Eagle missiles and two 30 mm guns.

Take-off deck run for the above missions is 137 m, 107 m and 92 m (450 ft, 350 ft and 300 ft) respectively, with vertical landing.

Interception: A typical deck-launched interception could be performed against a Mach 0·9 target at a radius of 116 nm (215 km; 133 miles), or a Mach 1·3 target at 95 nm (175 km; 109 miles), after initial radar detection of the approaching target at a range of 230 nm (425 km; 265 miles), with the Sea Harrier at 2 min alert status, carrying two AMRAAM missiles.

BAe EAP

British Aerospace exhibited at the 1982 Farnborough Air Show, and again at the 1983 Paris Air Show, a full scale mockup of what was then known as the Agile Combat Aircraft (**ACA**). It represented the result of several years of private venture research and development by BAe, with industry support from Rolls-Royce, Dowty, Ferranti, Lucas, GEC Avionics and Smiths Industries, at a total estimated cost of £25 million by mid-1983. MBB of Germany and Aeritalia of Italy had also contributed to the project.

No government support for the ACA was forthcoming but, at the 1982 Farnborough show, the UK government announced that it would make a financial contribution to an experimental aircraft programme (**EAP**) technology demonstrator based on the ACA design. The aims of the programme were to bring together a specific range of new

Artist's impression of Sea Harrier FRS. Mk 2s embodying mid-life update

BAe EAP advanced technology demonstrator photographed during its first flight

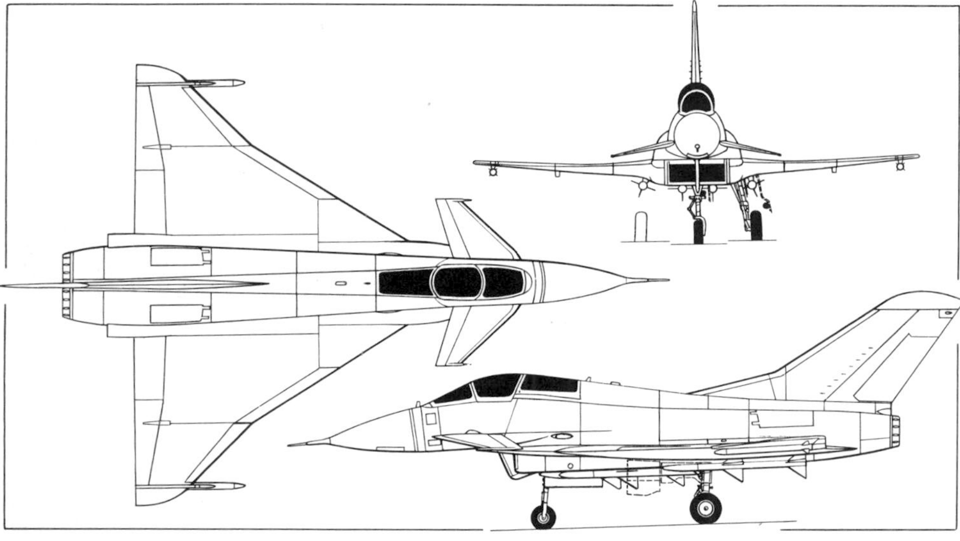

Three-view drawing of BAe EAP demonstrator *(Pilot Press)*

and advanced technologies being developed by BAe and other aerospace manufacturers in Europe.

On 26 May 1983, BAe announced that a contract had been signed with the Ministry of Defence for the design, development and construction of a single demonstrator aircraft which would be used to prove advanced technological features, including: advanced aerodynamics; active control technology for unstable aircraft; a digital databus system; advanced electronic cockpit; and advanced structural design including the extensive use of carbonfibre composites.

The EAP demonstrator was funded by the UK Ministry of Defence, BAe and its industrial partners. These included Aeritalia, which designed and manufactured the carbonfibre wings jointly with BAe, and equipment suppliers in Britain, Italy and West Germany. The remainder of the airframe was designed and manufactured by BAe.

With the UK committed to participation in the international programme for a European fighter aircraft (EFA, see International section), the relevance of the EAP is that it is designed to demonstrate a complete weapon system that would meet a generally similar requirement. During its first flight, on 8 August 1986, the EAP demonstrator (ZF534) accelerated to Mach 1·1 at 9,150 m (30,000 ft).

TYPE: Advanced technology demonstrator aircraft.

WINGS: Main wing aerofoil section varies from root to tip. Multi-spar carbonfibre composite co-bonded construction. Spars bonded to bottom skin; top skin bolted to spar flanges. Foreplanes of carbonfibre composite construction. Aerodynamic configuration provides high negative stability. The leading- and trailing-edge flight surfaces, and the foreplanes, are operated by a GEC Avionics computer controlled active control system, using technology developed in the Jaguar ACT programme. Dowty Boulton Paul actuators on the foreplane, rudder and flaperon control surfaces are operated via a pilot's stick sensor assembly (PSSA) which uses spring damping and viscous loading to give the required stick resistance, to allow full and accurate movement of the stick in relation to aircraft speed and attitude.

FUSELAGE: Front fuselage is conventional metal semi-monocoque structure with carbonfibre composite side skin panels. Engine air inlet duct of conventional aluminium alloy construction. Hinged forward lower lip. Centre and rear fuselage of conventional metal construction, using Tornado technology and components. Centre keel member of carbonfibre composite to save weight and space.

TAIL UNIT: Cantilever all-metal structure, consisting of single sweptback two-spar fin and rudder, essentially the same as those fitted to the Tornado.

LANDING GEAR: Hydraulically operated tricycle type, with single wheel on each unit. Rearward retracting nose unit. Operation of Dowty Rotol main landing gear involves rotary movement about the leg of each outboard wheel during retraction and lowering, to facilitate compact stowage and positive locking when the gear is fully down.

POWER PLANT: Two Turbo-Union RB199-34R Mk 104D turbofan engines, as fitted to the latest version of the IDS Tornado, rated in the 40·0 kN (9,000 lb st) class dry and 75·5 kN (17,000 lb st) class with afterburning. Installed in rear fuselage with downward opening doors for servicing and engine change. Lucas DECU 500 full authority digital engine control system, developed in conjunction with Rolls-Royce. Fuel is carried integrally in the wings and in 14 tanks in the fuselage.

ACCOMMODATION: Pilot only, on Martin-Baker zero-zero ejection seat, in pressurised cockpit embodying advanced avionic management systems designed to reduce substantially the pilot's workload. Equipment includes three colour multi-function display CRTs supplied by Smiths Industries, and an advanced GEC Avionics head-up display embodying holographic optics, and an additional raster (TV-like) display for night flying. Sensors control level of integrated internal illumination to cater automatically for varying external conditions.

AVIONICS AND EQUIPMENT: Racal Acoustics RA 800 series digital audio control system (IDACS). GEC Avionics AD 3400 VHF/UHF multimode radio. GEC Avionics AD 2780 Tacan system. GEC Avionics television sensor in cockpit records what the pilot sees during flight. Ferranti FIN 1070 inertial navigation system and BAe SCR 300E flight data recorder. Major avionics units mounted in an innovative avionics equipment module in the front fuselage behind the cockpit. Information supplied to cockpit multi-function displays by databus highways, replacing great lengths of multicored conventional wiring.

It is expected that the aircraft will be used for weapon system trials, and the avionics module will facilitate the evaluation of alternative equipment from other manufacturers.

DIMENSIONS, EXTERNAL:

Wing span	11·17 m (36 ft 7¾ in)
Length overall	14·70 m (48 ft 2¾ in)
Height	5·52 m (18 ft 1½ in)

AREA:

Wings, gross	52·0 m² (560 sq ft)

PERFORMANCE:

Max speed at height	Mach 2·0+

EUROFIGHTER (EFA)

Brief details of this military aircraft programme, in which British Aerospace is participating with companies from West Germany, Italy and Spain, can be found in the International section.

BAe NIMROD

The Nimrod was developed to replace the Shackleton maritime reconnaissance aircraft of RAF Strike Command, with which it is scheduled to serve until well into the 1990s. Design of the Nimrod, as the Hawker Siddeley 801, began in June 1964, and government authority to proceed was announced in June 1965.

Based substantially upon the airframe of the Hawker Siddeley (de Havilland) Comet 4C, the Nimrod is a new production aircraft with a 1·98 m (6 ft 6 in) shorter, modified pressurised fuselage; an unpressurised, underslung pannier for operational equipment and weapons; and Rolls-Royce Spey turbofan engines (instead of the Avon turbojets of the Comet), with wider air intakes to allow for the greater mass flow. Other external changes include enlarged flight deck main windows and 'eyebrow' windows; ESM and MAD equipment, in glassfibre fairings on top of the fin and in the tailboom respectively; and a searchlight in the starboard wing external fuel tank. The search radar is housed in a glassfibre fairing which forms the nose of the unpressurised lower fuselage.

The Nimrod was designed to combine the advantages of high altitude, fast transit speed with low wing loading and good low speed manoeuvring capabilities when operating in its primary roles of anti-submarine warfare, surveillance and anti-shipping strike. When required, two of the four Spey engines can be shut down to extend endurance, and the aircraft can cruise and climb on only one engine. A wide range of weapons can be carried in the 14·78 m (48 ft 6 in) long bomb bay, and large numbers of sonobuoys and markers can be carried and released from the pressurised rear fuselage area.

In addition to its surveillance and ASW roles, the Nimrod can be used for day and night photography. As supplied originally to the RAF, the aircraft had a standoff surface missile capability. This was subsequently deleted but was reactivated on some aircraft during the Falklands campaign in 1982. The Nimrod MR. Mk 1 can carry 16 additional personnel in the self-support role; the MR. Mk 2 can carry only 10 without the removal of equipment.

Two prototypes were built, utilising existing Comet 4C airframes. The first of these (XV148), fitted with Spey engines, flew for the first time on 23 May 1967 and was used for aerodynamic testing. The second (XV147) retained its original Avon engines, was first flown on 31 July 1967, and was used for development of the nav/tac system and special maritime equipment. Both are now in storage in interim MR. Mk 2 condition.

The following versions have been produced:

Nimrod MR. Mk 1. Initial production version. First flown on 28 June 1968. Forty-six delivered (XV226-263,

BAe Nimrod R. Mk 1 of No. 51 Squadron, RAF. Note the modified tailcone in place of the MAD boom and the revised contours of the wing leading-edge pods *(M. Barclay)*

XZ280-287). Eleven (XV259, XV261-263, XZ280-283 and XZ285-287) converted to AEW. Mk 3. Remainder upgraded to MR. Mk 2.

Nimrod R. Mk 1 and **1P.** Three aircraft (additional to the 46 MR. Mk 1s ordered for RAF Strike Command) were delivered to No. 51 Squadron at RAF Wyton. These aircraft (XW664-666), are employed for electronic intelligence (elint) missions, and can be identified by the absence of an MAD tailboom. XW664 now has a flight refuelling probe and is designated R. Mk 1P.

Nimrod MR. Mk 2 and **2P.** Thirty-five RAF Nimrod MR. Mk 1s have been refitted with new communications equipment, and advanced tactical sensor, ESM and navigation systems, under a programme which began in 1975 (one, XV256, has been lost subsequently through bird strike). Redelivery started on 23 August 1979 with XV236, the first completely refitted aircraft. After refit these aircraft were redesignated MR. Mk 2, and repainted in a NATO approved camouflage scheme. Equipment includes an advanced search radar, offering greater range and sensitivity coupled with a higher data processing rate; a new acoustic processing system, developed by GEC Avionics, which is compatible with a wide range of existing and projected sonobuoys, and Loral early warning support measures (EWSM) equipment in a pod at each wingtip. Aircraft deployed to Ascension Island during the Spring 1982 Falklands campaign were fitted with Sidewinder air-to-air missiles for self-defence, and were given an attack capability with bombs, Sting Ray torpedoes and, later, Harpoon missiles. Air-to-air refuelling probes were fitted at that time to 16 aircraft (redesignated MR. Mk 2P) making possible flights of up to 19 h with one additional pilot and navigator. Provision for such probes, and Sidewinder and Harpoon missile installations, have now been made on all MR. Mk 2 aircraft. Associated with these changes are an added ventral fin, small finlets above and below the tailplane on each side, and eleven vortex generators on the leading-edge of each outer wing.

Nimrod AEW. Mk 3. Airborne early warning version; described separately.

Ample space and power is available in the basic Nimrod design to accept additional or alternative sensors such as sideways looking radar, forward looking infra-red, infra-red linescan, low light level TV and digital processing of intercepted ESM signals.

The following description applies to the Nimrod MR. Mks 1 and 2:

TYPE: Four-turbofan maritime patrol aircraft.

WINGS: Cantilever low/mid-wing monoplane, of metal construction. Sweepback 20° at quarter-chord. All-metal two-spar structure, comprising a centre-section, two stub wings and two outer panels. Extensive use of Redux metal to metal bonding. All-metal ailerons, operated through duplicated hydraulic and mechanical units. Trim tab in each aileron. Plain flaps outboard of engines, operated hydraulically. Hot air anti-icing system.

FUSELAGE: All-metal semi-monocoque structure. The circular section cabin space is fully pressurised. Below this is an unpressurised pannier housing the bomb bay, radome and additional space for operational equipment. Segments of this pannier are free to move relative to each other, so that structural loads in the weapons bay are not transmitted to the pressure cell. Glassfibre nose radome and tailboom.

TAIL UNIT: Cantilever all-metal structure, with large dorsal and small ventral fin. Small finlets near leading-edge of tailplane on each side. Rudder and elevators operated through duplicated hydraulic and mechanical units. A glassfibre pod on top of the fin houses ESM equipment. Trim tab in each elevator. Hot air anti-icing system.

LANDING GEAR: Retractable tricycle type. Four-wheel tandem bogie main units, with size 36 × 10-18 Dunlop

Close-up of port wingtip of BAe Nimrod MR. Mk 2P, showing Loral EWSM pod and larger finlets on tailplane associated with this installation *(S. G. Richards)*

tyres, pressure 12·76 bars (185 lb/sq in). Twin-wheel nose unit, with size 30 × 9-15 Dunlop tyres, pressure 6·21 bars (90 lb/sq in).

POWER PLANT: Four Rolls-Royce RB168-20 Spey Mk 250 turbofan engines, each rated at 54 kN (12,140 lb st). Reverse thrust fitted on two outer engines. Fuel in fuselage keel tanks, integral wing tanks, and permanent external tank on each wing leading-edge, with total capacity of 48,780 litres (10,730 Imp gallons). Provision for up to six removable tanks in weapons bay. Flight refuelling probe over flight deck.

ACCOMMODATION: Normal crew of 12, comprising pilot, co-pilot, and flight engineer on flight deck; routine navigator, tactical navigator, radio operator, radar operator, two sonics systems operators, ESM/MAD operator, and two observers/stores loaders in main (pressurised) cabin, which is fitted out as a tactical compartment. In this compartment, from front to rear, are a toilet on the port side; stations for the two navigators (stbd), radio and radar operators (port), and sonics systems operators (stbd) in the forward section; ESM/MAD operator's station, galley, four seat dining area, rest quarters and sonobuoy stowage in the middle section; and buoy and marker launch area in the rear section. Three hemi-spherical observation windows forward of wings (one port, two stbd), giving 180° field of view. Two normal doors, emergency door, and four overwing emergency exits. Weapons bay can be utilised for additional fuel tanks (see under 'Power Plant') or for the carriage of cargo. Provision is made for a trooping role, in which configuration 45 passengers can be accommodated if some rear fuselage equipment is removed.

SYSTEMS: Air-conditioning by engine bleed air; Smith-Kollsman pressurisation system, with additional Normalair-Garrett conditioning pack on Mk 2 aircraft, max differential 0·603 bars (8·75 lb/sq in). Anti-icing and bomb bay heating by engine bleed air. Lockheed hydraulic system, pressure 172 bars (2,500 lb/sq in), for duplicated flying control power units, landing gear shock absorbers, steering and door jacks, weapons bay door jacks, camera aperture door jacks, and self-sealing couplings for water charging, ground test, engine bay and ancillary services. Lucas APU provides high pressure air for engine starting. Electrical system utilises four 60kVA engine driven alternators, with English Electric constant speed drives, to provide 200V 400Hz three-phase AC supply. Secondary AC comes from two 115V three-phase static transformers, with duplicate 115/26V two-phase static transformers which also feed a 1kVA frequency changer providing a 115V 1,600Hz single-phase supply for radar equipment. Emergency supplies for flight instruments are provided by a 115V single-phase static inverter. DC supply is by four 28V transformer-rectifier units backed up by two nickel-cadmium batteries.

AVIONICS AND EQUIPMENT (MR. Mk 1): Routine navigation by Decca Doppler Type 67M/GEC Avionics E3 heading reference system, with reversionary heading from a Sperry GM7 duplicated gyro compass system, operating in conjunction with a Ferranti routine dynamic display. Tactical navigation, and stores selection and release, by GEC Avionics nav/attack system utilising an 8K GEC Avionics 920B digital computer. Tactical display station provides continually updated information about aircraft position, with present and past track, sonobuoy positions, range circles from sonobuoys, ESM bearings, MAD marks, radar contacts and visual bearings. Course information can be displayed automatically to the pilots on the flight director system; alternatively, the computer can be coupled to the autopilot to allow the tactical navigator to direct the aircraft to a predicted target interception, weapon release point, or any other point on the tactical display. ASW equipment includes Sonics 1C sonar and a new long range sonar system; Thorn EMI ASV-21D surface vessel detection radar in nose; Thomson-CSF ESM (electronic support measures) equipment in pod on top of fin; and Emerson Electronics ASQ-10A MAD (magnetic anomaly detector) in extended tail-boom. Strong Electric 70 million candlepower searchlight at front of starboard external wing fuel tank. Aeronautical and General Instruments F.126 and F.135 cameras for day and night photography respectively, the latter having Chicago Aero Industries electronic flash equipment. Smiths SFS.6 automatic flight control system, embodying SEP.6 three-axis autopilot, integrated with the navigation and tactical system. Twin Plessey PTR 175 UHF/VHF, and GEC Avionics AD 470 HF,

BAe Nimrod MR. Mk 2P in latest configuration, with wingtip EWSM pods, flight refuelling probe and larger finlets on tailplane

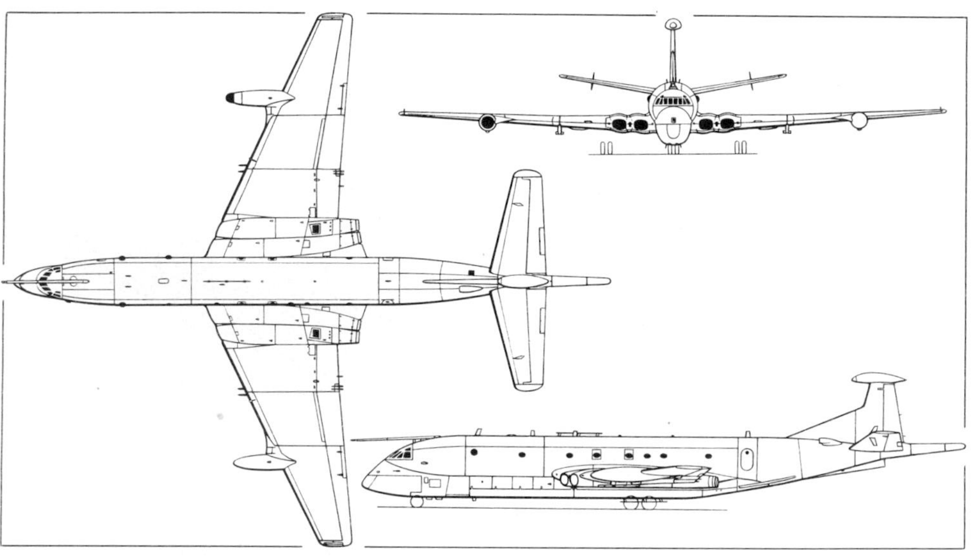

BAe Nimrod MR. Mk 2P four-turbofan maritime patrol aircraft *(Pilot Press)*

communications transceivers; twin GEC Avionics AD 260 VOR/ILS; GEC Avionics AD 2770 Tacan; Decca Loran C/A; GEC Avionics AD 360 ADF; Honeywell AN/APN-171(V) radar altimeter. Yaw damper and Mach trim standard.

Avionics and Equipment (MR. Mk 2): New and more flexible operational system, using three separate processors for tactical navigation, radar and acoustics. GEC Avionics central tactical system, based on a 920 ATC computer with a greater storage capacity than that of MR. Mk 1, to provide improved computing and display facilities and, in conjunction with a Ferranti inertial navigation system, improved navigation capabilities. Thorn EMI Searchwater long range surface vessel detection radar, with its own data processing subsystem incorporating a Ferranti FM 1600D digital computer. This system presents a clutter free picture, can detect and classify surface vessels, submarine snorts and periscopes at extreme ranges, can track several targets simultaneously is designed to operate in spite of countermeasures. Under a contract announced in May 1985, Thorn EMI is developing a colour display for Searchwater, which has previously used monochrome; the new display is scheduled to enter service in 1987. AQS 901 acoustics processing and display system, based on twin GEC Avionics 920 ATC computers, is compatible with a wide range of passive and active sonobuoys, either in existence or under development, including the Australian BARRA passive directional sonobuoy, the Canadian TANDEM, the US SSQ-41 and SSQ-53, and the Ultra A size X17255 command active multi-beam sonobuoy (CAMBS), with a performance similar to that of helicopter dipping sonars. Communications improved by the installation of twin GEC Avionics AD 470 HF transceivers (instead of the original single AD 470), and a radio teletype and encryption system. Loral EWSM equipment in two wingtip pods. Onboard crew training system developed by the Maritime Aircraft Systems Division of GEC Avionics Ltd. Known as ACT-1 (Airborne Crew Trainer Mk 1), it consists of a single exercise control unit comprising a control and display panel with push-buttons, and a reel of magnetic tape containing the software programme, by means of which the AQS 901 processing and display system can operate in a training mode. Using the ACT-1, which physically resembles a TV game, one crew member can 'play' the part of a submarine, trying to outwit his colleagues operating the AQS 901 detection system. Although not a replacement for ground based simulator training, the ACT-1 onboard system enables a Nimrod captain to train his crew in authentic operational conditions, without the expenditure of sonobuoys.

Armament (MR. Mk 2): 14·78 m (48 ft 6 in) long weapons bay, with two pairs of doors, in unpressurised lower fuselage pannier, able to carry up to six lateral rows of ASW weapons, including up to nine torpedoes as well as bombs. Alternatively, up to six auxiliary fuel tanks can be fitted in the weapons bay, or a combination of fuel tanks and weapons can be carried. To ensure weapon serviceability, the weapons bay is heated when the ambient temperature falls below + 5°C. Bay approx 9·14 m (30 ft) long in rear pressurised part of fuselage for storing and launching of active and passive sonobuoys and marine markers. Two rotary launchers, each capable of holding six size A sonobuoys, are used when the cabin is unpressurised; two single-barrel launchers are used when the aircraft is pressurised. A hardpoint is provided beneath each wing, just outboard of the mainwheel doors, on which can be carried two Sidewinder air-to-air missiles, a Harpoon air-to-surface missile, rocket or cannon pod, or mine, according to mission requirements.

Dimensions, external:
- Wing span: 35·00 m (114 ft 10 in)
- Wing chord: at root: 9·00 m (29 ft 6 in)
  - at tip: 2·06 m (6 ft 9 in)
- Wing aspect ratio: 6·2
- Length overall:
  - MR. Mk 2 excl refuelling probe: 38·63 m (126 ft 9 in)
  - MR. Mk 2 incl probe: 39·35 m (129 ft 1 in)
  - R. Mk 2 excl probe: 35·66 m (117 ft 0 in)
  - R. Mk 2 incl probe: 36·60 m (120 ft 1 in)
- Height overall: 9·08 m (29 ft 8½ in)
- Tailplane span: 14·51 m (47 ft 7¼ in)
- Wheel track: 8·60 m (28 ft 2½ in)
- Wheelbase: 14·24 m (46 ft 8½ in)

Dimensions, internal:
- Cabin (incl flight deck, navigation and ordnance areas, galley and toilet): Length: 26·82 m (88 ft 0 in)
  - Max width: 2·95 m (9 ft 8 in)
  - Max height: 2·08 m (6 ft 10 in)
  - Volume: 124·14 m³ (4,384 cu ft)

Areas:
- Wings, gross: 197·0 m² (2,121 sq ft)
- Ailerons (total): 5·63 m² (60·6 sq ft)
- Trailing-edge flaps (total): 23·37 m² (251·6 sq ft)
- Fin and rudder (above tailplane centreline): 10·96 m² (118 sq ft)
- Dorsal fin: 5·67 m² (61 sq ft)
- Tailplane: 40·41 m² (435 sq ft)
- Elevators (incl tabs): 12·57 m² (135·3 sq ft)

Weights (MR. Mk 1):
- Typical weight empty: 39,000 kg (86,000 lb)
- Max disposable load: 6,120 kg (13,500 lb)
- Fuel load: standard tanks: 38,940 kg (85,840 lb)
  - max with six auxiliary tanks in weapons bay: 45,785 kg (100,940 lb)
- Normal max T-O weight: 80,510 kg (177,500 lb)
- Max overload T-O weight: 87,090 kg (192,000 lb)
- Typical landing weight: 54,430 kg (120,000 lb)

Performance (MR. Mk 1):
- Max operational necessity speed, ISA + 20°C: 500 knots (926 km/h; 575 mph)
- Max transit speed, ISA + 20°C: 475 knots (880 km/h; 547 mph)
- Econ transit speed, ISA + 20°C: 425 knots (787 km/h; 490 mph)
- Typical low-level patrol speed (two engines): 200 knots (370 km/h; 230 mph)
- Operating height range: S/L to 12,800 m (42,000 ft)
- Min ground turning radius: 27·1 m (89 ft 0 in)
- Runway LCN at T-O weight of 82,550 kg (182,000 lb): 50
- T-O run at 80,510 kg (177,500 lb) AUW, ISA at S/L: 1,463 m (4,800 ft)
- Unfactored landing distance at 54,430 kg (120,000 lb) landing weight, ISA at S/L: 1,615 m (5,300 ft)
- Typical ferry range: 4,500-5,000 nm (8,340-9,265 km; 5,180-5,755 miles)
- Typical endurance: 12 h

BAe NIMROD AEW. Mk 3

This airborne early warning (AEW) version of the Nimrod was designed by Hawker Siddeley Aviation specifically for European defence. On 31 March 1977 the British Defence Secretary announced the government's intention to proceed with the procurement of 11 of the aircraft for the RAF, under the designation Nimrod AEW. Mk 3. These have been produced by the conversion of MR. Mk 1 airframes. Such a programme was made possible by the development by GEC Avionics of a new radar system which, in addition to an essential maritime capability, has the potential to satisfy also the air defence requirements of central Europe. Using this equipment, the Nimrod AEW. Mk 3 is intended to provide, at long range and at low or high altitude, detection, tracking and classification of aircraft, missiles and ships; interceptor control; direction of strike aircraft; air defence; air traffic control; and search and rescue facilities. In so doing, it was expected to be compatible with, and complementary to, the USAF's Boeing E-3 Sentry AWACS, and with the E-3As that are operated directly by NATO.

Designed specifically for installation in this modified version of the maritime reconnaissance Nimrod, the radar made necessary some modifications to the nose and tail to permit installation of the newly developed and identically shaped dual-frequency twisted cassegrain antennae in fore and aft positions. The aircraft's performance is affected only marginally by the structural changes, and a reduction in directional stability is compensated by a 0·91 m (3 ft 0 in) increase in fin height.

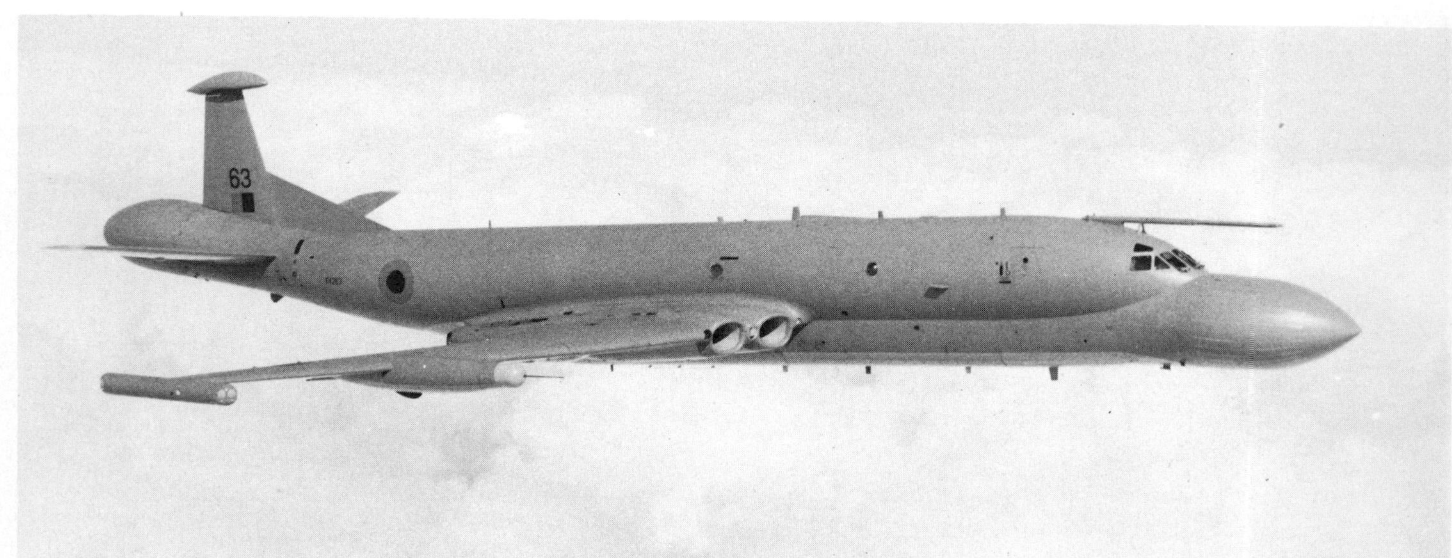

Production standard example (XV263) of the BAe Nimrod AEW. Mk 3 airborne early warning aircraft

Mounting the scanners at the extremities of the airframe ensures good all-round coverage, and they do not suffer from airframe obscuration effects. Designed for very low sidelobe level, each sweeps through 180° in azimuth, the dual Cossor Jubilee Guardsman IFF 3500 interrogators using the same scanners to aid correlation of IFF and radar returns.

The associated radar is a pulsed Doppler system that, in addition to the detection of aircraft, has a ship surveillance capability. The rate at which pulses are transmitted can be varied to provide maximum detection in differing terrain conditions or sea states. The system has also highly sophisticated anti-jamming features to cope with the growing efficiency of electronic countermeasures.

The radar passes target plots in terms of range, azimuth, radial velocity and altitude to the advanced digital data handling system; this is based on an airborne computer that controls the flow of data from the scanners and correlates track information between the AEW aircraft and a surface control station. Six operator consoles are provided. Each has a tactical situation display, showing the tracks selected by the operator, and a tabular display for the selective presentation of detailed track and control information. Much of the data control is fully automatic; thus, association of radar, IFF and EWSM, track initiation, tracking and data storage requires no action from the operator. Control of the data handling system is achieved by rolling ball and functionally arranged keyboards, the operator interfacing with the system to carry out system control, track classification, fighter control and data link management.

High standards of communications and navigation are essential to complement the advanced radar and data handling system. For communications the AEW Nimrod carries tactical UHF transceivers, SIMOP HF transceivers, pilot's U/VHF, RATT, secure voice com, LF receiver and data links. Primary navigation avionics consist of dual inertial navigation systems (INS), plus a gyro magnetic compass, air data computer, twin VOR/ILS, ADF, Tacan, autopilot and a flight director. Loral EWSM (early warning support measures) equipment is housed in the two pods at the wingtips. Other features of special significance for this role are the spacious cabin for avionics and crew, high transit speed and good low speed characteristics. An in-flight refuelling probe is standard.

The first of four development aircraft, a converted Comet 4C (XW626), made its first flight on 28 June 1977. This aircraft carried nose mounted radar only, and was used for communications trials; its part in the programme was completed in October 1980. The other three development aircraft were diverted from the batch of eight extra Nimrod MR. Mk 1s ordered in 1972, and were completed instead as AEW. Mk 3s. The first of these (XZ286), which made its initial flight on 16 July 1980, was the first aerodynamically representative AEW. Mk 3 airframe. This aircraft began its service trials in 1982. Radar trials with the second development aircraft started at the end of May 1982, and in the following August the third development AEW. Mk 3 (which, like the second, has full mission systems avionics) began its test programme. On completion of their flight development, all three will be brought up to full RAF production standard.

Meanwhile, on 9 March 1982 the first 'production' Nimrod AEW. Mk 3 made its initial flight. A first aircraft was delivered to the Joint Trials Unit (JTU) at RAF Waddington, Lincolnshire, in December 1984. Operator of this Nimrod version is intended to be No. 8 Squadron, based at Waddington. Initial operational capability is currently deferred, pending solution of technical problems concerning the avionics.

DIMENSIONS, EXTERNAL:

Wing span	35·08 m (115 ft 1 in)
Length overall	41·97 m (137 ft 8½ in)
Height overall	10·67 m (35 ft 0 in)

BAe VC10 K. Mk 3 flight refuelling tanker with all three hoses streamed

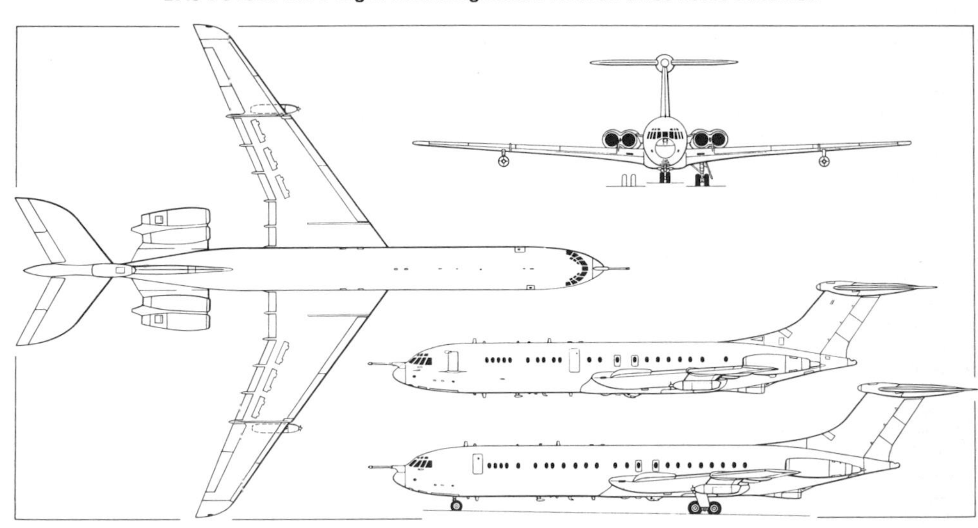

BAe VC10 K. Mk 3 flight refuelling tanker, with additional side view (upper) of K. Mk 2 *(Pilot Press)*

PERFORMANCE: Generally similar to Nimrod MR.Mk 2

Endurance	in excess of 10 h

BAe (BAC/VICKERS) VC10 K. Mk 2/Mk 3 TANKERS

In early 1978 it was announced in Parliament by the Under-Secretary of State for Defence that the Royal Air Force had a requirement for additional flight refuelling tankers, and that it was intended to investigate the feasibility of converting civil VC10s for this role. By April 1978 Air Staff Requirement 406 had been formulated, and a contract for the design study awarded to British Aerospace. This study was completed before the middle of the year, proving that the aircraft could be converted effectively for such operations, and leading to the award to British Aerospace of a contract for the work in July 1978. Valued at that time at some £40 million, it covered the conversion of nine aircraft to tanker configuration, with delivery during 1983-85.

The nine VC10s which were acquired to fulfil this programme comprise five of the 12 standard Model 1101s built during 1962-64 for service with British Overseas Airways Corporation, and four of the five Model 1154 Super VC10s that were delivered to East African Airways in the period 1966-70. RAF designations for the VC10 and Super VC10 tanker conversions are **VC10 K. Mk 2** (manufacturer's Model 1112) and **VC10 K. Mk 3** (manufacturer's Model 1164) respectively. The modification of these commercial transports to a tanker configuration was complicated by the fact that the RAF's No. 10 Squadron already operated a fleet of 13 VC10 multi-mission transports under the designation VC10 C. Mk 1. These differed in several ways from the standard civil transports, and it was desirable for these aircraft and the new tanker fleet to have generally similar configurations for both operating and engineering considerations.

The modification work was carried out by British Aerospace at Filton, and the first converted aircraft, a K. Mk 2 (ZA141), was flown for the first time on 22 June 1982. This aircraft was used for flight trials, followed by further trials at the Ministry of Defence A&AEE, Boscombe Down. First of the nine aircraft to be delivered, for No. 101 Squadron of RAF Strike Command, on 25 July 1983, was another K. Mk 2 (ZA140). The Squadron re-formed officially on 1 May 1984 at RAF Brize Norton, Oxfordshire. First flight of a K. Mk 3 was made on 4 July 1984, and this version entered service with No. 101 Squadron on 20 February 1985. The last of the nine tankers, having completed flight trials, was delivered in 1986.

A description of both the VC10 and Super VC10 can be found under the British Aircraft Corporation entry in the 1969-70 *Jane's*. Detailed here are the modifications required to make these commercial transports suitable for their new tanker role, as well as those needed to maintain an acceptable degree of commonality between these aircraft and the VC10 C. Mk 1s.

To supplement the nine K. Mk 2/3 tankers, when the RAF's earlier Victor tankers have to be retired, it is proposed to modify to the air-to-air tanker configuration further Model 1151 Super VC10s, purchased by MoD(PE) from British Airways.

TYPE: Military flight refuelling aircraft.

WINGS: As for VC10 and Super VC10, but pylons installed beneath the wings, at the inboard end of the ailerons, to carry Flight Refuelling Mk 32/2800 refuelling pods, each capable of transferring fuel at a rate of 1,270 kg (2,800 lb) per minute. Aircraft can be flown without these pods.

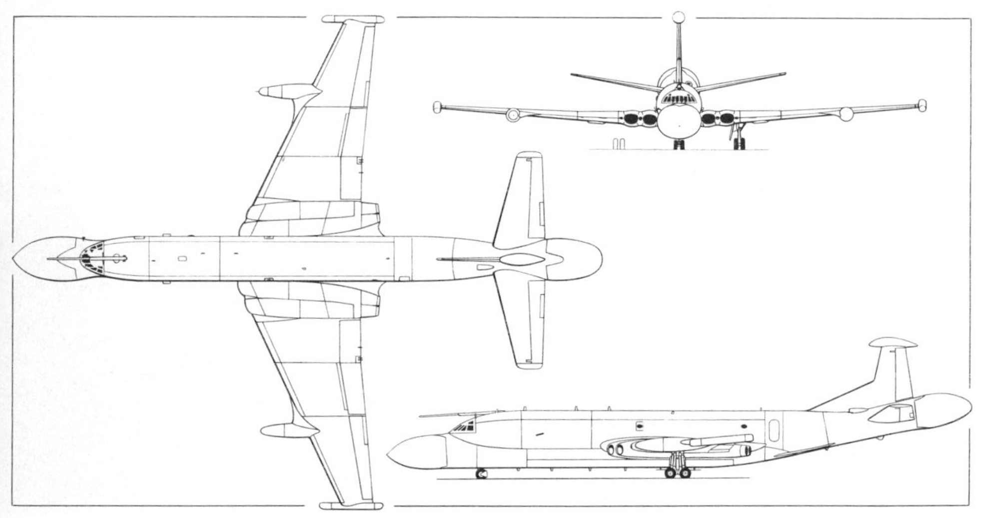

The AEW. Mk 3 version of the BAe Nimrod *(Pilot Press)*

Floodlights installed in each side of wing pylon fairings, and in the wing flap actuator fairings, illuminate the aircraft for night operations.

FUSELAGE: As for VC10 and Super VC10, but with flight refuelling probe on nose, directly above weather radar radome, to conform with installation in C. Mk 1s. Remotely controlled Flight Refuelling Mk 17B HDU (hose drum unit) installed in lower rear fuselage, involving the cutting of an aperture in the pressurised structure. This necessitates new pressure bulkheads fore and aft of the cutout, new sidewalls, and a pressure roof over the HDU. Other items incorporated in the underfuselage structure include a remotely operated closed circuit TV (CCTV) for monitoring receiver aircraft approach and contact, and floodlights in the rear fuselage to illuminate the engine nacelles.

TAIL UNIT AND LANDING GEAR: As for VC10 and Super VC10.

POWER PLANT: Four 97 kN (21,800 lb st) Rolls-Royce Conway Mk 301 or Mk 550B turbofan engines. Thrust reversers installed on outboard engines only. Basic fuel capacity of the VC10 K. Mk 2 is the same as that of the standard VC10; that of the K. Mk 3 is the same as in the Super VC10. Additional fuel for flight refuelling operations accommodated in five cylindrical tanks installed within the fuselage. Each consists of a double-walled metal container with an inner flexible bag tank, capacity 3,182 litres (700 Imp gallons), and each is mounted on two large beams and restrained from forward movement in the crash case by a heavy A frame in front of each tank. These supplementary tanks and the aircraft's basic fuel system are interconnected, giving a total capacity of 94,272 litres (20,737 Imp gallons) in the K. Mk 2 and 102,782 litres (22,609 Imp gallons) in the K. Mk 3. It is possible to transfer all but sufficient fuel for the tanker's mission requirement, or to take on board a similar volume via the nose mounted refuelling probe. Installation of these fuselage tanks in the standard VC10 requires a section of the fuselage upper surface to be cut out and replaced. In the case of the Model 1154s which were built for East African Airways, these incorporate a large freight door forward of the wing, on the port side, which is large enough to accept these tanks. Following installation, the freight door is sealed.

ACCOMMODATION: Primary flight crew of four, comprising pilot, co-pilot, navigator and flight engineer. Flight engineer's station, on starboard side of flight deck, equipped also for control of the air refuelling operation, has a cathode ray tube (CRT) display from the CCTV. At the forward end of the cabin, and separated from the tank bay by a bulkhead, limited seating is provided for airlift of essential ground personnel when the tanker is deployed away from its home base: K. Mk 2 seats 18 persons, K. Mk 3 has seats for 17. Cabin windows and overhead baggage racks retained in this passenger area, but half of the windows are blanked off in the tank bay, and all baggage racks removed. Access for crew and passengers through forward starboard door. Forward port door is modified with escape chute, only for emergency exit by parachute. Remaining cabin doors are sealed. Forward underfloor freight hold unchanged, and can be used to carry spares or accommodate refuelling pods during ferry flights.

SYSTEMS: Generally similar to those of C. Mk 1. A Rolls-Royce Turboméca Artouste Mk 520 APU is installed in the tailcone of both tanker versions to conform to the C. Mk 1s. This provides compressed air for engine starting, or essential electrical power when required on the ground.

AVIONICS AND EQUIPMENT: Avionics conform to those provided in VC10 C. Mk 1s, including dual VHF/UHF com, dual HF, ADF, IFF, Omega, Tacan and weather radar. A Smiths SFS6 flight system is standard. Equipment includes Flight Refuelling Mk 32/2800 pods and Mk 17B HDUs, one 10-man dinghy and one 26-man dinghy.

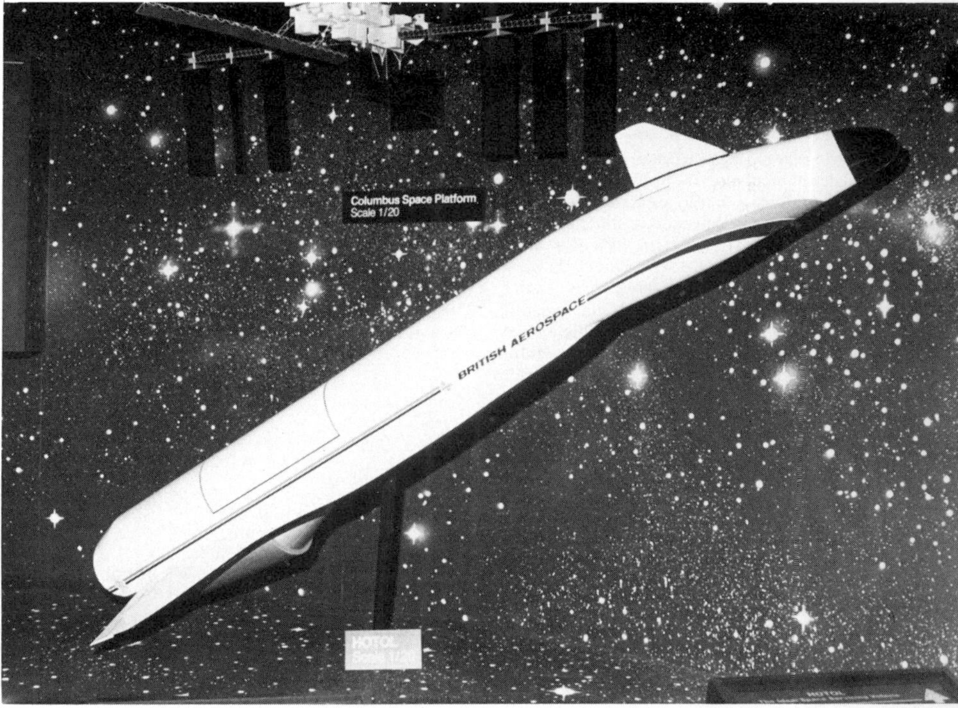

Latest configuration of HOTOL aerospacecraft displayed in model form at 1986 Farnborough Air Show *(Air Portraits)*

DIMENSIONS, EXTERNAL:

Wing span	44·55 m (146 ft 2 in)
Length overall:	
excl refuelling probe:	
K. Mk 2	48·36 m (158 ft 8 in)
K. Mk 3	52·32 m (171 ft 8 in)
incl refuelling probe:	
K. Mk 2	50·62 m (166 ft 1 in)
K. Mk 3	54·59 m (179 ft 1 in)
Height overall	12·04 m (39 ft 6 in)
Tailplane span	13·36 m (43 ft 10 in)
Wheel track	6·53 m (21 ft 5 in)
Wheelbase: K. Mk 2	20·08 m (65 ft 10½ in)
K. Mk 3	21·98 m (72 ft 1½ in)

WEIGHTS AND PERFORMANCE:
Normal operating weights and performance are similar to those of the commercial variants from which the tankers were derived.

HOTOL

HOTOL (horizontal take-off and landing) is the title of a space transport study being undertaken by the Space and Communications Division of British Aerospace. The initial objective is a space vehicle able to carry satellites into orbit for one fifth the cost of current procedures. The vehicle is claimed to be capable of development into an airliner which could carry passengers from Europe to Australia in one hour.

In February 1986 the British National Space Centre of the Department of Trade announced that it had allocated £375,000 to initiate a two-year proof of concept study costing £3 million. The initial funds cover the first six months of the study, in 1987; an equal amount is being made available by industry. If development studies can be completed by 1997, a first test flight in 1998-99 might be feasible.

HOTOL resembles Concorde superficially, and will take-off and land like a conventional aircraft. Novel features include a laser guided trolley for take-off, which would be left behind in the interests of weight saving. Landing would be on a relatively lightweight gear carried on board. This arrangement has been adopted because the take-off weight will be about five times the landing weight. The key to the HOTOL concept is a revolutionary hybrid power plant under study by Rolls-Royce. Known as the Swallow, this will act as an air-breathing turbofan engine in the atmosphere, and as an oxygen/hydrogen rocket engine in space.

Detail design is at an early stage, but BAe states that re-entry heat protection would be by a metal skin and not by tiles of the kind used on the US Space Shuttle. Titanium will be used on the upper surfaces.

As an airliner, a passenger compartment occupying the space of the cargo bay could accommodate up to 70 passengers.

DIMENSIONS (provisional):

Wing span	20·73 m (68 ft)
Length overall	61·00 m (200 ft)
Height overall	12·20 m (40 ft)

WEIGHTS (provisional):

T-O weight	196,000 kg (432,100 lb)
Landing weight	34,000 kg (74,950 lb)

PERFORMANCE (provisional):

Payload into low Earth orbit	7,000 kg (15,430 lb)
Landing speed	170 knots (315 km/h; 195 mph)
Landing run	1,145 m (3,750 ft)
Speed (airliner version)	Mach 9

CMC

CHICHESTER-MILES CONSULTANTS LTD

West House, The Old Rectory, Ayot St Lawrence, Welwyn, Hertfordshire AL6 9BT
Telephone: 0438 820341
CHAIRMAN: I. Chichester-Miles

CMC LEOPARD

Mr Ian Chichester-Miles, formerly Chief Research Engineer of British Aerospace Aircraft Division at Hatfield, Hertfordshire, established Chichester-Miles Consultants to develop a high performance light business jet. Design of the four-seat Leopard started in January 1981 and was sufficiently advanced for a mockup to be completed in early 1982. Detail design and construction of a prototype by Designability Ltd of Dilton Marsh, Wiltshire, began in July 1982, under contract to CMC. First flight of this aircraft was scheduled for the end of 1986. It will have lower-powered engines, and will lack the full pressurisation/air-conditioning system, avionics and instrumentation of the production aircraft.

TYPE: Four-seat light business aircraft.

WINGS: Cantilever mid-wing monoplane. ARA designed wing section and 3D profiles combining laminar flow and supercritical wing technology. Thickness/chord ratio

Prototype of CMC Leopard business jet *(Jay Miller/Aerofax)*

14% at root, 11% at tip. Sweepback at quarter-chord 25°. Two-spar structure, primarily of GRP, with some carbonfibre reinforcement. Full span electrically actuated trailing-edge plain flaps of carbonfibre, with deflections of ±45° for high drag landing and air-braking/lift dumping. No ailerons or spoilers. Liquid de-icing and decontamination system in leading-edge.

FUSELAGE: Built in three sections: unpressurised nose section accommodating avionics and nosewheel gear when retracted, pressurised cabin section, and unpressurised rear section providing a baggage bay, with fuel tanks below and equipment bays to rear. Basic monocoque structure, primarily of GRP with some carbonfibre reinforcement; fore and aft cabin bulkheads, engine and tailplane axle frames moulded in. Pressure cabin section divided approximately along aircraft horizontal datum, with upper section formed by electrically actuated upward opening canopy hinged at windscreen leading-edge. Multiple latches around canopy lower edge. Bonded-in acrylic side windows carry pressurisation tension. Nose opens for access to avionics.

TAIL UNIT: All-moving fin and tailplane of all-composites construction. Fin sternpost projects to bottom of rear fuselage. Low-set tailplane in two independent sections, each mounted on a steel axle projecting from side of rear fuselage. Tailplane panels are operated collectively for control in pitch and differentially for roll control. Fin and tailplane sections each have a carbonfibre geared anti-servo tab, adjustable for trim. Anti-icing as for wings.

LANDING GEAR: Electrically retractable tricycle type, main units retracting inward into wing root wells, nosewheels forward. Well closure doors linked mechanically to landing gear units. Gravity extension assisted by bias springs and aerodynamic drag. Long stroke shock absorber in each unit, using synthetic elastomers in compression. Main units, each with single Cleveland wheel, size 500 × 5, have tyres size 11 × 4, pressure 4·82 bars (70 lb/sq in) on prototype, 7·24 bars (105 lb/sq in) on production aircraft. Twin-wheel nose unit has wheels size 400 × 3 and tyres size 8·5 × 2·75 in on prototype; tyre pressure 2·75 bars (40 lb/sq in). Tyre pressure 3·8 bars (55 lb/sq in) on production aircraft. Hydraulic disc brakes. Parking brake.

POWER PLANT: Prototype has two Noel Penny Turbines NPT 301-3 turbojets each of nominal 1·42 kN (319 lb st) rating. Production aircraft will have two low-bypass Noel Penny Turbines NPT 904 turbofans, each of 3·56 kN (800 lb st). Each engine in nacelle, mounted from composite crossbeam located elastically in rear fuselage. Nacelles of composite construction, with stainless steel firewalls and liquid de-icing system for leading-edges. Fuel tanks in fuselage, below baggage bay. Prototype has total fuel capacity of 455 litres (100 Imp gallons). Production aircraft will have maximum capacity of 591 litres (130 Imp gallons). Refuelling point on upper surface of fuselage, near base of fin.

ACCOMMODATION: Cabin seats four, in two pairs, on semi-reclining (35°) seats beneath upward opening jettisonable canopy. Options include dual controls, and accommodation for pilot, stretcher and attendant in medevac role. Unpressurised baggage bay aft of cabin, capacity 54 kg (120 lb), with external door in upper surface of fuselage.

SYSTEMS (production aircraft): Air-conditioning and pressurisation (max differential 0·55 bars: 8 lb/sq in) by engine bleed air, with simple Normalair-Garrett air cycle cold air/dehumidifier unit. Electrical system powered by dual engine driven 3kVA starter/generators. Hydraulic system for brakes only.

AVIONICS AND EQUIPMENT (production aircraft): Full nav/com and weather radar systems. Avionics, mounted in nose bay, supply data to three CRTs in pilot's instrument panel and one below: they comprise EADI, EHSI, engine management display, and systems management display. CRT displays can be transferred in the failure mode. Reduced scale electromechanical standby flight instruments. All avionics systems fully integrated with digital autopilot.

DIMENSIONS, EXTERNAL:	
Wing span	7·16 m (23 ft 6 in)
Wing chord: at root	1·14 m (3 ft 9 in)
at tip	0·36 m (1 ft 2 in)
Wing aspect ratio	8·84
Length overall	7·52 m (24 ft 8 in)
Height overall	2·06 m (6 ft 9 in)
Height to canopy sill	0·76 m (2 ft 6 in)
Tailplane span	3·91 m (12 ft 10 in)
Wheel track	3·45 m (11 ft 4 in)
Wheelbase	3·20 m (10 ft 6 in)
DIMENSIONS, INTERNAL:	
Cabin: Length	2·74 m (9 ft 0 in)
Max width	1·14 m (3 ft 9 in)
Max height	0·94 m (3 ft 1 in)
Baggage bay volume	0·40 m³ (14 cu ft)
AREAS:	
Wings, gross	5·81 m² (62·5 sq ft)
Trailing-edge flaps	1·24 m² (13·3 sq ft)
Fin	0·86 m² (9·3 sq ft)
Tailplane (incl tabs)	2·14 m² (23·0 sq ft)

WEIGHTS AND LOADING (A: prototype, B: production aircraft, estimated):	
Weight empty, equipped: B	862 kg (1,900 lb)
Max fuel weight: A	367 kg (810 lb)
B	476 kg (1,050 lb)
Max T-O weight: A	1,088 kg (2,400 lb)
B	1,701 kg (3,750 lb)
Max zero-fuel weight: A	952 kg (2,100 lb)
B	1,224 kg (2,700 lb)
Max landing weight: A	1,088 kg (2,400 lb)
B	1,497 kg (3,300 lb)
Max wing loading: A	187·3 kg/m² (38·4 lb/sq ft)
B	292·9 kg/m² (60·0 lb/sq ft)

PERFORMANCE (production aircraft, estimated, ISA):

Never-exceed speed	Mach 0·81 (300 knots; 556 km/h; 345 mph) EAS
Max level speed at 9,450 m (31,000 ft)	469 knots (869 km/h; 540 mph)
Max and econ cruising speed at 13,100 m (43,000 ft)	434 knots (804 km/h; 500 mph)
Stalling speed, full flap, at AUW of 1,406 kg (3,100 lb)	82 knots (152 km/h; 95 mph)
Max rate of climb at S/L	1,370 m (4,500 ft)/min
Rate of climb at S/L, one engine out	365 m (1,200 ft)/min
Service ceiling	12,955 m (42,500 ft)
Service ceiling, one engine out	6,400 m (21,000 ft)
T-O to 15 m (50 ft)	727 m (2,385 ft)
Landing from 15 m (50 ft) at AUW of 1,406 kg (3,100 lb)	747 m (2,450 ft)
Range with max fuel, with reserves	1,500 nm (2,775 km; 1,725 miles)

CRANFIELD

CRANFIELD INSTITUTE OF TECHNOLOGY, COLLEGE OF AERONAUTICS

Cranfield, Bedford MK43 0AL
Telephone: 0234 750111
Telex: 825072 CITECH G
PROJECT MANAGER, HARRIER: J. H. Webb
PROJECT MANAGER, HAWK: D. Williams
PROJECT CO-ORDINATOR: P. Lawson

Under Ministry of Defence contracts, the College of Aeronautics at Cranfield has converted a BAe Harrier and a BAe Hawk for special research and training purposes. The converted Hawk is for use by the Empire Test Pilots School (ETPS), Boscombe Down, and the Harrier for the Royal Aircraft Establishment (RAE) at Bedford.

ASTRA HAWK

The BAe Hawk T. Mk 1 (XX341) conversion is known as the ASTRA (Advanced System Training Aircraft), and is intended to provide the Empire Test Pilots School (ETPS) with an advanced variable stability aircraft. It enables student test pilots to experience a wide range of aircraft handling characteristics, and demonstrates the effectiveness of integrated control systems and displays.

Principal features of the ASTRA Hawk (which is essentially an airborne simulator) are a sophisticated artificial feel system fitted to the trainee pilot's controls in the front cockpit, a digital simulation computer, a system controller, a flight safety monitor and primary flight control surface actuators.

The front cockpit is equipped with both the normal central flying control column and a sidestick controller, so that variable force stick characteristics can be demonstrated. The trainee pilot is also provided with a head-up display, programmed to give the usual flight and navigation information, and a multi-function display (MFD) on which basic instruments, or additional navigation or variable stability data, can be displayed. The front cockpit fly by wire controls are isolated from the normal flying control system.

The instructor occupies the rear cockpit, the controls of which are physically linked to the primary flight control surfaces at all times. The natural flying characteristics of the Hawk can be modified electronically to simulate the instructor's requirements. They can, for example reproduce the effects of varying the wing sweep angle on a Tornado. The aircraft is unique in providing the flight envelope and response characteristics of a high performance fighter aircraft, with the variable stability system operational at speeds up to 500 knots (925 km/h; 575 mph), heights up to 9,150 m (30,000 ft) and normal acceleration between $-2g$ and $+7g$.

The ASTRA Hawk was scheduled to fly for the first time in the Summer of 1986.

ASTRA Hawk advanced system training aircraft

VAAC Harrier research aircraft

VAAC HARRIER

This converted BAe two-seat Harrier is a research aircraft able to undertake experiments into the vertical take-off and landing (VTOL) flight envelope and applications of advanced control systems. The aircraft is known as the VAAC Harrier, standing for Vectored thrust Aircraft Advanced flight Control.

The Harrier (XW175) arrived at Cranfield in December 1983 and by mid-1984 had been dismantled prior to the installation of the new flight control system. When used for research, the VAAC Harrier is flown from the rear cockpit, in which the pitch, throttle and nozzle control inceptors are no longer connected mechanically and directly to the aircraft's control circuits, but interface with these circuits through a flight control computer. The computer is coupled to these aircraft control runs through new actuators and disconnecting devices.

The computer was supplied by Smiths Industries, and is based on a flight management control computer under development for the A310 Airbus. As well as being responsible for the controlling function, it contains a high level of both system monitoring and self monitoring, and will be able to disengage the flight control system automatically if unacceptable conditions are detected.

The controls in the front cockpit retain the conventional Harrier mechanically linked systems at all times. This arrangement enables the rear pilot to control the aircraft through the new system, while the other has the conventional system and can monitor the flight as safety pilot. Control reverts to the front pilot whenever the new system is disengaged. For a research aircraft this provides flexibility to alter the control characteristics through changes in the flight control computer software, without the same degree of exhaustive integrity testing for each change which would be required for a dedicated fly by wire system.

The first flight of the VAAC Harrier was made on 12 December 1985. The programme is being run by Cranfield's Flight Systems Department at RAE Bedford.

CRANFIELD A3

Mr Philip Scott, who is tetraplegic (paralysed in the lower arms, body and legs), has formed a company known as Operation Ability Ltd (The Meadows, Firgrove Road, Whitehill, Bordon, Hampshire GU35 9DY, *telephone* 04203 5062). Its first objective is a programme to enable a severely disabled man with 85% paralysis to gain a Private Pilot's Licence, and Mr Scott is the first tetraplegic to have passed a CAA medical examination accepting him as 'fit to learn'.

The Cranfield A3 is an aircraft designed specially to meet the needs of training a student who is unable to walk, stand or lift. These include providing an upward opening nose section, to enable the disabled trainee to enter the front cockpit by reversing his retractable-wheel wheelchair into it, and a 'tailored' cockpit design which meets the exact needs of the disabled pilot during all flight manoeuvres.

As envisaged in mid-1986, although the design had not then been 'frozen', the A3 would be a twin-boom 'pusher' engined low/mid-wing monoplane, with tandem seating and an elevated rear seat for the instructor. Advice on the design has been provided by the RAF Institute of Aviation Medicine; Westland Helicopters Ltd is providing ergonomic advice concerning cockpit controls layout; and Racal Avionics Ltd has provided, on long-term loan, a fully automatic navigation computer with a moving map display. Further sponsorship was being sought to enable detail design and prototype construction of the A3 to proceed, with a view to a possible first flight in 1987. Chief designer of the A3 is Mr James Webb.

EVERETT

R. J. EVERETT ENGINEERING LTD

Abbey Oaks, Sproughton, Nr Ipswich, Suffolk
Telephone: 0473 47685

EVERETT AUTOGYRO

The Everett autogyro was designed with knowledge gained from the Bensen and Campbell Cricket single-seat light autogyros (see 1975-76 *Jane's*). Detail design was by R. J. Everett Engineering Ltd, which was granted CAA Manufacturers Approval on 8 May 1985. The autogyro is marketed in ready for flight form, with alternative 1,600 cc or 1,830 cc converted Volkswagen motorcar engine. First flight of an Everett autogyro was made on 15 February 1984. Five of the initial batch of 25 production aircraft had been sold by the Spring of 1985, including one to the commissioner of police in Malawi.

DIMENSIONS, EXTERNAL:

Rotor diameter	6·63 m (21 ft 9 in)
Length overall	3·43 m (11 ft 3 in)
Height overall	2·08 m (6 ft 10 in)
Wheel track	1·59 m (5 ft 2½ in)

WEIGHTS:

Weight empty	139 kg (307 lb)
Max T-O weight	272 kg (600 lb)

PERFORMANCE:

Never-exceed speed	69 knots (129 km/h; 80 mph)
Max cruising speed	65 knots (120 km/h; 75 mph)
Normal cruising speed	56 knots (104 km/h; 65 mph)
Max rate of climb at S/L	182 m (600 ft)/min
T-O run: with spin-up	164 m (538 ft)
without spin-up	256 m (840 ft)
Landing run	2·5 m (8 ft)
Range with max fuel	130 nm (240 km; 150 miles)
Endurance with max fuel	approx 2 h 30 min

Everett single-seat light autogyro

FR

FR GROUP PLC

Brook Road, Wimborne, Dorset BH21 2BJ
Telephone: 0202 882121
Telex: 41247

CHAIRMAN: M. J. Cobham, CBE, MA, FRAeS, Barrister

FR Group (Flight Refuelling), founded by pioneer pilot/manufacturer Sir Alan J. Cobham in 1934, has remained a world leader in the development of techniques and equipment for refuelling in flight. Its products, described in previous editions of *Jane's*, are in standard use on many aircraft, including the VC10 and TriStar tankers and Harrier combat aircraft of the Royal Air Force.

LOCKSPEISER

LOCKSPEISER AIRCRAFT LTD

Royal Chambers, High Street, Weston-super-Mare, Avon BS23 1JT
Telephone: 0278 423008
MANAGING DIRECTOR: D. Lockspeiser, MRAeS
SECRETARY: Christopher E. Bean, FCA

The 1979-80 edition of *Jane's* contained an illustrated description of a utility aircraft known as the LDA-01 (Land Development Aircraft), designed by Mr David Lockspeiser. The prototype has undergone considerable refinement since that time, with particular emphasis on simplifying the control system.

LOCKSPEISER LDA-500 BOXER

The designation LDA-500, now applied to the prototype of Mr Lockspeiser's general utility aircraft, implies a disposable load of 500 kg (1,102 lb). Similarly, the name Boxer reflects its basic cargo carrying role. Variants will receive different names to indicate their primary use for duties that include passenger, freight and vehicle transport, agricultural, ambulance, survey, firefighting, military transport and battlefield support, in land and optional floatplane versions.

The basic concept of the LDA is that of an 'aerial Land-Rover', offering a wide variety of applications, low initial cost and economy of operation, and capable of being easily assembled, inspected and repaired. Many of the major components are interchangeable, and the aircraft can carry a set of its own spares, including a wing panel. A primary design consideration was ease of construction for licensed manufacture and assembly.

The following description applies to the LDA-500 prototype in its present form, as G-UTIL. The LDA-1000, with a 1,000 kg (2,205 lb) disposable load, is described separately.

TYPE: Single-engined general utility aeroplane.

WINGS: Strut braced main wings at rear and cantilever foreplane at front. Main wings and foreplane are of constant NACA 23012 section and constant chord. Dihedral 3° on main wings; 0° on foreplane. Main wing incidence 1°, foreplane 4° (adjustable on ground). Conventional light alloy construction, with parallel main and rear spars and pop-riveted stressed-skin covering. Built in three basically identical and interchangeable units, two forming the main wings and the third being used as the foreplane, with added tips housing landing lights. Each

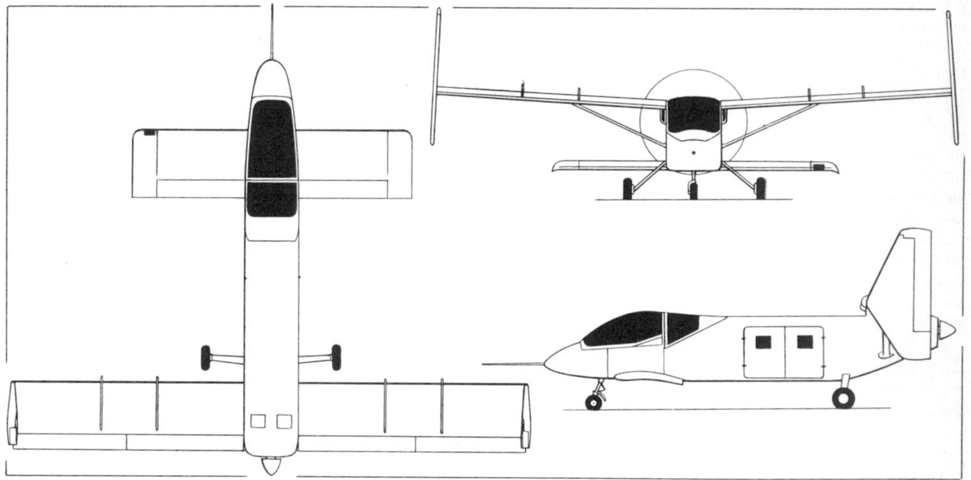

Lockspeiser LDA-500 Boxer utility aircraft *(Pilot Press)*

panel has four strongpoints at the centre. These serve as attachment points to the fuselage when the panel is positioned as a foreplane; when it is positioned as a port or starboard mainplane they serve as lift-strut attachments, picketing points and hardpoints on which to attach pylons for underwing stores. They can also be located on a 'luggage rack' under the fuselage when a wing panel is carried as a spare by an aircraft of the same type. Each panel fitted with two identical trailing-edge control surfaces. Those on each main wing function as an elevator/flap (inboard) and aileron (outboard). Those on the foreplane are used for pitch trim. Main wings each fitted with two fences to contain vortex disturbance from the foreplane tips.

FUSELAGE: Conventional box-shaped structure, consisting of a space frame of 19 mm (¾ in) square 22 gauge T.35 steel, welded on a flat jig and covered with light alloy. Nosecone and cowling panels are of glassfibre. On production aircraft, the centre portion will be a conventional light alloy semi-monocoque structure, with front and rear sections as prototype.

TAIL UNIT: Conventional cantilever light alloy fin and rudder at each wingtip.

LANDING GEAR: Non-retractable tricycle or four-wheel type, with cantilever main-gear legs (from a Cessna 150) at rear. Goodyear 6·00-6 mainwheels and tyres, pressure 2·07 bars (30 lb/sq in). Goodyear single or twin nosewheel(s) and tyre(s), size 5·00-5·5, pressure 1·035 bars (15 lb/sq in), steerable from rudder bar. Ackerman steering of nose units on four-wheel landing gear. Goodyear hydraulic brakes on mainwheels.

POWER PLANT: One 119 kW (160 hp) Lycoming O-320-D1A flat-four engine, at rear of fuselage, driving a Hoffmann HO-V-72 constant-speed pusher propeller with two composites blades and spinner. Two fuel tanks in fuselage, one forward and one aft of cargo bay, each of 69 litres (15·2 Imp gallons) capacity. Refuelling points on starboard side.

ACCOMMODATION: Pilot only, in enclosed cabin. Sideways opening canopy, hinged on port side. Side loading double doors, 1·98 m (6 ft 6 in) wide and 1·22 m (4 ft 0 in) in height, with optional additional access via the roof so that conventional loaders can be used when the aircraft is employed in an agricultural role. Proposed military version capable of carrying six soldiers and their equipment, or of being fitted with anti-tank missiles or machine-gun pods.

SYSTEMS: 12V electrical system. Rabat Type 35 battery.

AVIONICS: King KX 155 VHF/VOR nav/com, KT 76A transponder and KR 86 ADF.

DIMENSIONS, EXTERNAL:

Main wing span	9·00 m (29 ft 6 in)
Foreplane span	4·85 m (15 ft 11 in)
Main wing and foreplane chord, constant	1·14 m (3 ft 9 in)
Main wing aspect ratio	7·87
Foreplane aspect ratio	4·23
Length overall	7·14 m (23 ft 5¼ in)
Fuselage: Max width	0·91 m (3 ft 0 in)
Max depth	1·07 m (3 ft 6 in)
Height overall	3·20 m (10 ft 6 in)
Wheel track	2·59 m (8 ft 6 in)
Wheelbase	4·17 m (13 ft 8 in)
Propeller diameter	1·80 m (5 ft 11 in)
Fuselage floor/ground clearance	0·57 m (1 ft 10½ in)

DIMENSIONS, INTERNAL:

Payload compartment: Length	1·98 m (6 ft 6 in)
Width	0·91 m (3 ft 0 in)
Depth	1·07 m (3 ft 6 in)

AREAS:

Main wings, gross	10·27 m² (110·6 sq ft)
Foreplane, gross	5·56 m² (59·85 sq ft)
Mainplane flaps (total)	0·93 m² (10·0 sq ft)
Ailerons (total)	1·49 m² (16·0 sq ft)
Foreplane flaps (total)	0·93 m² (10·0 sq ft)
Fins (total)	2·66 m² (28·66 sq ft)
Rudders (total)	1·13 m² (12·12 sq ft)

WEIGHTS:

Basic weight empty	561 kg (1,236 lb)
Operating weight empty	635 kg (1,401 lb)
Max payload	500 kg (1,102 lb)
Normal T-O weight	733 kg (1,617 lb)
Design max T-O weight	1,043 kg (2,300 lb)

PERFORMANCE:

Cruising speed	115 knots (213 km/h; 132 mph)
Optimum climbing speed	75 knots (139 km/h; 87 mph)
Stalling speed	42 knots (78 km/h; 49 mph)
T-O run, flaps up	335 m (1,100 ft)
Landing run, flaps up	116 m (380 ft)
Range with max fuel	400 nm (740 km; 460 miles)

LOCKSPEISER LDA-1000 BOXER

The LDA-1000 is a projected scale-up of the basic LDA-500, with a nominal payload of 1,000 kg (2,205 lb). It could be fitted with a wide variety of engines in the 224-448 kW (300-600 hp) range, and has been defined with a 298 kW (400 hp) Avco Lycoming IO-720 flat-eight. Its development might coincide with availability of the new Avco Lycoming stratified charge rotary combustion engine of equivalent power, which is regarded as an ideal potential power plant for the LDA-1000.

Preliminary details of the LDA-1000 are as follows:

DIMENSIONS, EXTERNAL:

Main wing span	12·04 m (39 ft 6 in)
Main wing aspect ratio	7·43
Length overall	9·70 m (31 ft 10 in)

DIMENSIONS, INTERNAL:

Payload compartment: Length	3·81 m (12 ft 6 in)
Max width	1·22 m (4 ft 0 in)
Max height	1·52 m (5 ft 0 in)
Volume	7·08 m³ (250 cu ft)

AREA:

Main wings, gross	19·51 m² (210·0 sq ft)

WEIGHTS:

Basic empty weight	817 kg (1,800 lb)
Operating weight empty	921 kg (2,030 lb)
Normal T-O weight	1,815 kg (4,000 lb)
Design max T-O weight	2,040 kg (4,500 lb)

LUSCOMBE

LUSCOMBE AIRCRAFT LTD

Luscombe Aircraft was formed to design and build lightweight sporting aircraft for private operators. The first project, of which design was initiated in 1971, was the Luscombe Vitality. Subsequently, the company developed a lightweight military version of this aircraft, known as the Rattler, and an ultralight two-seat civil variant named the Valiant. Work on these three aircraft has ceased and the company is now developing a new family of tandem-wing aircraft known as the Ranger, Super Ranger and Twin Ranger, for light military and civil sport duties.

LUSCOMBE VALIANT

Development of this ultralight two-seat aircraft has now ceased. Details of the Valiant were given in the 1985-86 *Jane's*.

LUSCOMBE P3 RATTLER

Development of this single-seat ultralight aircraft has now ended. Details and a photograph can be found in the 1985-86 *Jane's*.

LUSCOMBE P3B VIPER

Work on this aircraft has now ceased; provisional details were given in the 1985-86 *Jane's*.

LUSCOMBE RANGER

The Ranger owes much to development work on tandem-wing aircraft performed by Luscombe over a fourteen-year period. Constructed almost entirely of Kevlar and GRP, with some carbonfibre, it combines strength with light weight, and is corrosion-proof. In addition, the sound deadening properties of the Nomex sandwich fuselage help to ensure crew comfort during very long flights. This was considered important in an aircraft intended to cover the entire spectrum from long distance cruising to military utility duties with STOL ability and low radar signature. The power plant is fully cowled with Kevlar panels and, if required, the engine heat and exhaust can be mixed with cold air and released above the wing to minimise IR emissions.

In addition to stores carried on two standard NATO 14 in underwing attachments, the Ranger can carry a variety of stores and equipment in a unique conformal pod attached beneath the floor of the cockpit on further NATO 14 in attachments. As well as making the pod quickly removable, and jettisonable, this feature enables the aircraft to carry 227 kg (500 lb) of bombs, mines or other stores under the fuselage when the conformal pod is not fitted. Versatility will be increased further in due course by the availability of retractable flotation equipment, permitting operation from land, water, ice or snow without major sacrifice of performance. The flotation gear will also provide platforms for stretcher carrying when the aircraft is used for military, police, maritime or search and rescue casevac duties.

TYPE: Two-seat tandem-wing general purpose aircraft.

WINGS: High-wing monoplane, with single streamline-section bracing strut each side. Centre-section and two main panels of composite construction, with moderate sweepback. No dihedral. Ailerons operate in conjunction with spoiler in upper surface of each wing. Split flap extends from each wingroot to inboard edge of aileron. Sweptback fin and rudder, of composite construction, mounted at each wingtip.

FOREPLANES: Cantilever all-moving surfaces of composite construction, mounted on each side of fuselage nose. No dihedral or sweep.

FUSELAGE: Short pod of Nomex sandwich construction, with removable and jettisonable conformal pod contoured to bottom lines. Pod can be airdropped by parachute or released during slow flight at minimum height above surface. Compartment for avionics or equipment in nose, which can have optically flat 45° window at front.

LANDING GEAR: Non-retractable tricycle type, with single wheel on each unit. Steerable nosewheel.

POWER PLANT: One 145 kW (195 hp) Continental O-360 flat-six engine, driving three-blade Hartzell constant-speed pusher propeller.

ACCOMMODATION: Pilot and passenger side by side in enclosed, heated and ventilated cabin.

OPERATIONAL EQUIPMENT: Provision for carrying laser target marker, IR or TV sensor in nose. Two hardpoints under each wing for standard NATO 14 in attachments, able to carry a maximum of 181 kg (400 lb) of rockets, bombs, armament or equipment pods, surveillance equipment, spraygear or other loads under each wing. Underfuselage conformal pod can house twin machine-guns and magazines; inflatable liferaft and survival equipment for sea rescue missions; tent, rations and survival equipment for overland SAR; medical supplies; additional fuel or spraying equipment. Instead of pod, aircraft can carry 227 kg (500 lb) of weapons under the fuselage.

DIMENSIONS, EXTERNAL:

Wing span	8·89 m (29 ft 2 in)
Foreplane span	3·71 m (12 ft 2 in)
Length overall	5·79 m (19 ft 0 in)
Height overall	2·95 m (9 ft 8 in)

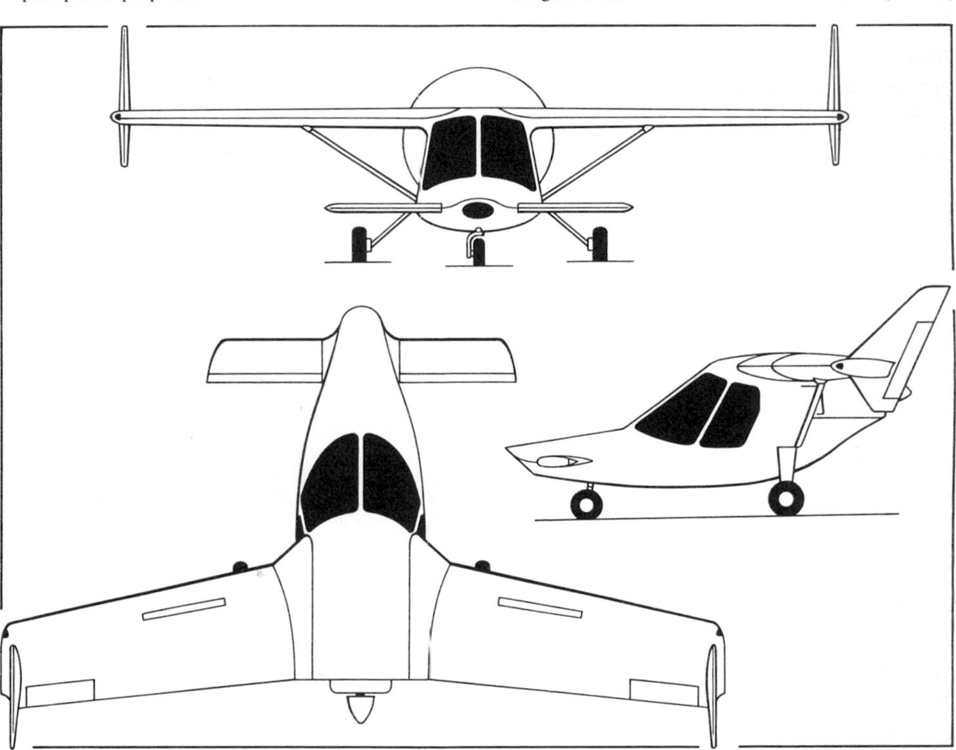

Luscombe Ranger two-seat general purpose light aircraft *(Jane's/Mike Keep)*

AREAS:

Wings, gross	9·01 m² (97·0 sq ft)
Foreplanes, gross	1·67 m² (18·0 sq ft)

WEIGHTS:

Weight empty	544 kg (1,200 lb)
Max T-O weight	1,088 kg (2,400 lb)

PERFORMANCE (estimated):

Max speed	156 knots (290 km/h; 180 mph)
Cruising speed	122 knots (225 km/h; 140 mph)
Loiter speed	43 knots (80 km/h; 50 mph)
Range:	
standard fuel	1,042 nm (1,931 km; 1,200 miles)
with auxiliary tanks	3,126 nm (5,793 km; 3,600 miles)
Endurance with standard fuel	11 hours

LUSCOMBE SUPER RANGER

Using 85 per cent of the components of the Ranger, the Super Ranger is a stretched variant with the fuselage lengthened to accommodate two additional seats. The extra space at the rear enables a retractable landing gear to be fitted.

The principal market for the Super Ranger is seen as 'long distance, comfortable cruising, with excellent economy'. The first Super Ranger is scheduled to be completed in August 1987.

The description and details of the Ranger apply also to the Super Ranger, except as follows:

TYPE: Four-seat lightweight tandem-wing aircraft.

WINGS: As for Ranger, but of slightly increased span.

FOREPLANES: As for Ranger, but of increased span.

FUSELAGE: As for Ranger, but with a 0·51 m (1 ft 8 in) plug inserted between rear of pilot/co-pilot seats and the rear stressed bulkhead. A glazed emergency escape panel is installed in the roof above the rear seats.

LANDING GEAR: Retractable tricycle type, with single wheel on each unit. Electro-hydraulic actuation.

POWER PLANT: One 142 kW (190 hp) Teledyne Continental IOL-300 liquid-cooled flat-six engine.

ACCOMMODATION: Pilot and passenger side by side, and two side by side passenger seats in enclosed, heated and air-conditioned cabin.

AVIONICS: Provision for comprehensive avionics, to customer's requirements.

DIMENSIONS, EXTERNAL (provisional):

Wing span	9·14 m (30 ft 0 in)
Length overall	6·30 m (20 ft 8 in)
Height overall	2·84 m (9 ft 4 in)

WEIGHTS (estimated):

Weight empty	726 kg (1,600 lb)
Max fuel load (normal)	159 kg (350 lb)
Max T-O weight	1,292 kg (2,850 lb)

PERFORMANCE (estimated):

Max range at econ cruising speed	1,736 nm (3,218 km; 2,000 miles)
Endurance	8 h

LUSCOMBE TWIN RANGER

The Twin Ranger is a twin-engined development of the Ranger with accommodation for six people. To provide adequate directional control, the wingtip fins and rudders are replaced by a single swept conventional fin and rudder on the rear fuselage. Many parts of the Twin Ranger are common with those of the Ranger and Super Ranger.

First flight of the Twin Ranger is scheduled for late 1987.

The description of the Ranger applies also to the Twin Ranger, except as follows:

TYPE: Six-seat lightweight tandem-wing aircraft.

WINGS: Outer wings as for the Ranger, except for winglet instead of fin and rudder on each wingtip.

FOREPLANES: As for Ranger, but of increased area.

FUSELAGE: Of Nomex sandwich construction. Front fuselage common with Ranger. Centre-section entirely new to accommodate the twin-engine power plant.

TAIL UNIT: Sweptback fin and horn balanced rudder at rear of fuselage pod.

LANDING GEAR: Retractable tricycle type. Twin wheels on nose unit, single wheel on each main unit. Electro-hydraulic actuation. Main units retract inward into fuselage.

POWER PLANT: Two 142 kW (190 hp) Teledyne Continental IOL-300 liquid-cooled flat-six engines, mounted on trailing-edge of centre-section. Fuel tanks in wingroots, total capacity 682 litres (150 Imp gallons).

ACCOMMODATION: Enclosed cabin seats six people, including the pilot. Passenger seats quickly detachable to provide usable payload volume of 4·2 m³ (148 cu ft), without severe restraints on loading due to CG considerations. Cabin soundproofed and air-conditioned.

DIMENSIONS, EXTERNAL (provisional):

Wing span	11·23 m (36 ft 10 in)
Length overall	8·08 m (26 ft 6 in)
Height overall	3·35 m (11 ft 0 in)

WEIGHTS (estimated):

Weight empty	862 kg (1,900 lb)
Max T-O weight	1,932 kg (4,260 lb)

PERFORMANCE (estimated):

Range, with reserves	2,952 nm (5,471 km; 3,400 miles)
Max endurance	over 14 h

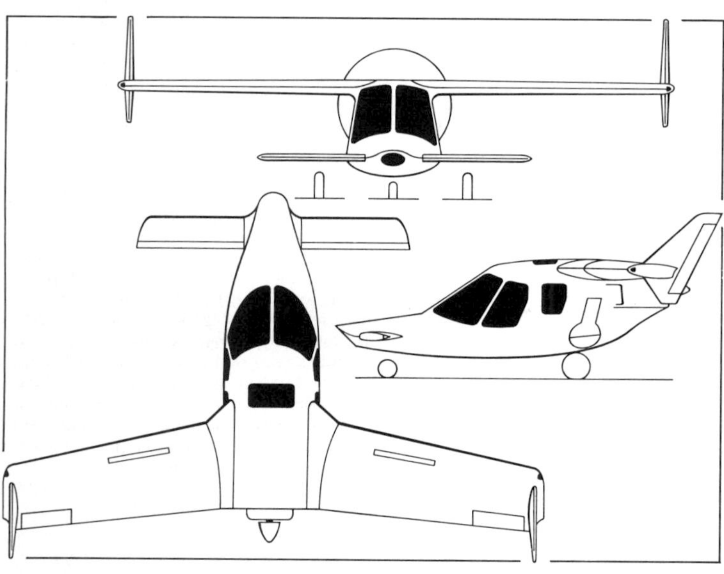

Provisional drawing of Luscombe Super Ranger four-seat general purpose light aircraft *(Jane's/Mike Keep)*

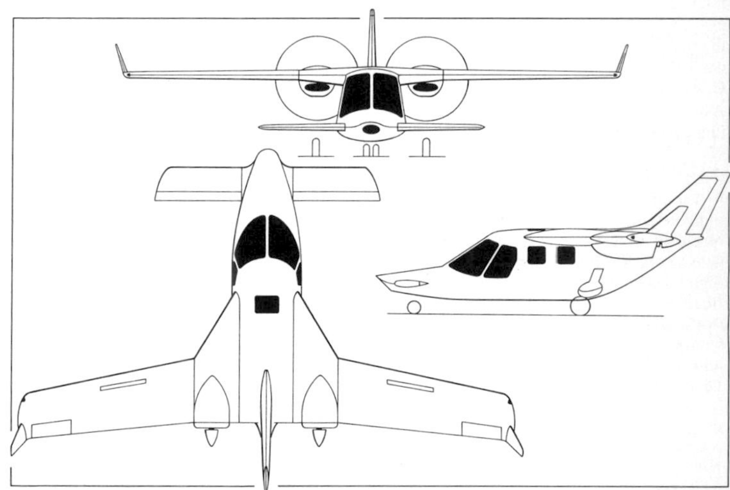

Provisional drawing of Luscombe Twin Ranger six-seat general purpose light aircraft *(Jane's/Mike Keep)*

MARSHALL

MARSHALL OF CAMBRIDGE (ENGINEERING) LTD (Aircraft Division)

Airport Works, Cambridge CB5 8RX
Telephone: 0223 61133
Telex: 81208

MANAGING DIRECTOR: Sir Arthur Marshall, OBE
EXECUTIVE DIRECTOR, COMMERCIAL: R. H. Pleace
EXECUTIVE DIRECTOR, ENGINEERING: R. O. Gates, OBE
SALES MANAGER: G. McA. Bacon
PUBLIC RELATIONS MANAGER: C. Buisseret

The Aircraft Division of this company (known as Marshalls Flying School Ltd until 1962) has specialised for many years in the modification, overhaul and repair of aircraft, including the design and installation of interior furnishing for executive transports and of avionics fits up to and including the complete outfitting of aircraft for calibration and electronic countermeasures roles.

The company's design and maintenance departments are approved by both CAA and MoD(PE). In addition, maintenance approvals are held for eight other countries, including the USA (FAA). The company is an approved service and repair centre for Lockheed C-130 and L-100, Gulfstream Aerospace Gulfstream and Cessna Citation aircraft. Its conversion, modification and overhaul facilities include some of the largest hangars in the UK, with design and workshop support to full aircraft construction standards. These resources have enabled Marshall to undertake successfully advanced programmes including the design and manufacture of Tornado avionics systems, trial installations in Buccaneers, and equipment for space, including an experimental sled successfully flown in the Space Shuttle in 1985. The company has specialised facilities for painting large aircraft; it has a full CAD capability, and has installed MODAS automatic analysis equipment to speed the assessment of flight trials.

Lockheed Hercules C. Mk 1K tanker, converted additionally for elint/sigint duties *(Paul Jackson)*

In 1966, Marshall was appointed the designated centre for Royal Air Force Hercules C. Mk 1 transport aircraft, and in 1973 the company completed the conversion of an RAF Hercules C. Mk 1 to W. Mk 2 configuration, as detailed in the 1979-80 and earlier editions of *Jane's*. It has since undertaken the conversion of Hercules into flight refuelling tanker/receivers, and the lengthening of RAF Hercules C. Mk 1 transports to C. Mk 3 standard. It now has a major contract to convert ex-airline TriStars into flight refuelling tankers and freighters for the RAF. The first converted TriStar was delivered to RAE Boscombe Down for service trials in September 1985. The second converted TriStar was handed over to the RAF (216 Squadron) on 24 March 1986.

In recent years the company has become involved increasingly in the modification of avionics systems in both fixed-wing aircraft and helicopters. To improve navigational accuracy and fuel efficiency, it has fitted revised autopilots and flight navigation systems to a variety of civil and military aircraft.

MARSHALL (LOCKHEED) HERCULES CONVERSIONS

It was announced in 1978 by the Ministry of Defence that a contract had been signed with Lockheed Corporation to modify 30 Hercules C. Mk 1s (C-130Ks) of the Royal Air Force to **Hercules C. Mk 3** configuration. The modification involves 'stretching' the fuselage by the insertion of a 2·54 m (8 ft 4 in) plug forward of the wings and a 2·03 m (6 ft 8 in) plug aft of the wings, thus producing the same fuselage dimensions and capacity as those of the L-100-30 Commercial Hercules (see US section). The first aircraft (XV223) was modified by Lockheed in Marietta, Georgia, in 1979; the remaining 29 were modified by Marshall of Cambridge, the programme being completed on 25 November 1985.

Examples of volumetric and load differences include:

Cabin volume, incl ramp:	
C. Mk 1	127·4 m³ (4,500 cu ft)
C. Mk 3	171·5 m³ (6,057 cu ft)
Palletised loads: C. Mk 1	5
C. Mk 3	7
Land-Rovers plus trailers: C. Mk 1	3 + 2
C. Mk 3	4 + 3

HERCULES C. Mk 1K TANKER and HERCULES C. Mk 1P/3P RECEIVER AIRCRAFT

Six Royal Air Force Lockheed Hercules C. Mk 1 aircraft have been converted by Marshall into flight refuelling tanker/receivers by fitting a Mk 17 hose drum unit (HDU) on the cargo compartment ramp, a drogue deployment box on the outside of the cargo bay door, four long-range fuel tanks in the cabin, and an in-flight refuelling probe over the flight deck. Modified in this way, each aircraft retains the availability of a pressurised cargo compartment for normal flight, but depressurises when operating with the drogue deployed. The first converted aircraft, designated Hercules **C. Mk 1K**, became operational with No. 1312 Flight from Ascension Island in early August 1982. The example illustrated (XV213) has been further modified by Marshall with a pod under each wingtip, presumably for elint/sigint duties. It also has low-observable camouflage and markings.

Sixteen other RAF Hercules C. Mk 1 aircraft have each been fitted with a probe to provide an in-flight refuelling capability, and are now designated **C. Mk 1P**. During the 1982 Falklands campaign, one of them remained in the air for 28 h on an operational mission, creating a new record for duration of flight in a Hercules. It is now intended that all C. Mk 1 and C. Mk 3 Hercules will be equipped with probes, and the first **C. Mk 3P** (XV214) was returned to RAF Lyneham in February 1986, after conversion.

Marshall, in co-operation with Flight Refuelling Ltd, is now marketing the Hercules tanker/receiver refuelling package to other military operators of this aircraft. It is possible to embody the conversion in such a way that cabin pressurisation is maintained while 'tanking', and reversion to the transport role is even easier than with the RAF conversion. Fuel transfer rate remains the same at 1,814 kg (4,000 lb)/min.

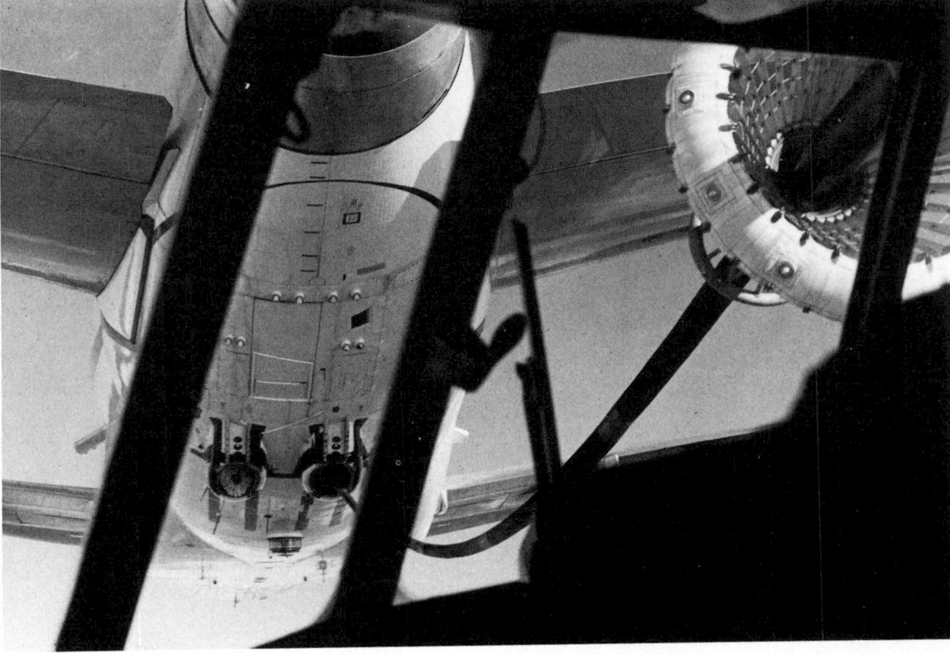

Lockheed TriStar K. Mk 1, equipped by Marshall as a flight refuelling tanker, passing fuel to an RAF Hercules

MARSHALL (LOCKHEED) TRISTAR TANKER CONVERSION

To meet a growing Royal Air Force requirement for flight refuelling tanker support, Marshall of Cambridge is converting to this role six Lockheed L-1011-500 TriStar transport aircraft purchased from British Airways in 1982. Work started in 1983 and the original package has been rescheduled to provide four TriStar K. Mk 1 tanker/passenger aircraft during 1985-86 and the first two tanker/passenger/freighter aircraft during 1986-87. Two of the first four tanker/passenger aircraft will be returned to Marshall to have a freight door fitted in 1987-88.

The first converted TriStar K. Mk 1 tanker/passenger aircraft (ZD950) flew for the first time on 9 July 1985. Its max T-O weight is increased to 244,940 kg (540,000 lb).

The tanker modification entails installation of twin in-flight refuelling hose drum units and fuel tanks in the fore and aft baggage compartments, to provide an additional 45,360 kg (100,000 lb) of fuel, giving a total aircraft fuel capacity of 136,080 kg (300,000 lb). The hose drum units deliver this fuel at a rate of 1,814 kg (4,000 lb)/min at 3·45 bars (50 lb/sq in). In addition, a Flight Refuelling Mk 32 refuelling pod will be fitted later under each wing, and these will be capable of delivering fuel at a rate of 1,134 kg (2,500 lb)/min at 3·45 bars (50 lb/sq in) simultaneously from each pod.

A flight refuelling probe is installed above the forward fuselage to provide a receiver capability. There is also a crew rest area for use by the non-operating crew on long sorties.

Total fuel management during refuelling and defuelling is controlled from a panel at the engineer's station. Closed circuit TV enables the crew to monitor all in-flight refuelling operations.

The other four TriStars will be operated in a tanker/freighter role. In addition to embodiment of the fuel system modifications, this requires the installation of a 2·64 m × 3·56 m (104 in × 140 in) cargo door on the port side, forward of the wing leading-edge, together with a cargo handling system. The passenger floor must also be strengthened to provide for the high density loadings. In these aircraft all items carried on the cabin floor will be mounted on pallets. Thus, passengers could be carried when seat equipped pallets were fitted. All four aircraft could therefore operate in the tanker/freighter/passenger role.

Three additional, ex-Pan Am, aircraft have been purchased. The first is being converted immediately to the tanker/passenger role. All three are expected to be operational as tankers by the early 1990s.

NAC

THE NORMAN AEROPLANE COMPANY LTD

Cardiff (Wales) Airport, Barry, South Glamorgan CF6 9AY, Wales

Telephone: 0446 711884

Telex: 497245 NORAC G; 497504 NORAC G

DIRECTORS:

R. W. Holder, MA (Chairman)

N. D. Norman, CBE, CEng, FRAeS (Managing Director)

Mrs B. E. Norman (Commercial Director and Deputy Managing Director)

P. M. H. Ryan

C. J. Breese, FCA

Mr N. D. Norman founded this company, as NDN Aircraft Ltd, in 1976. The company name was changed to The Norman Aeroplane Company with effect from 22 July 1985, simultaneously with a transfer of its manufacturing centre to Wales.

Aircraft for which The Norman Aeroplane Company is responsible are described in this entry. Production is taking place in a purpose-built factory at Cardiff (Wales) International Airport.

NAC FIRECRACKER

The development history of the Firecracker was last described under the Hunting Firecracker entry in the 1984-85 *Jane's*. Responsibility for the aircraft has now reverted to The Norman Aeroplane Company, which will build Firecrackers to order.

The prototype of the turbine-engined Firecracker (G-SFTR) flew for the first time on 1 September 1983 and was certificated on 23 March 1984. It is one of two aircraft of this type which were acquired subsequently by Specialist Flying Training Ltd for use in its training operations; the other is G-SFTS.

The following details apply to the aircraft in its certificated civil form, except where indicated. Military Firecrackers can be offered with a PT6A-25D engine, rated at 559 kW (750 shp), Stencel Ranger zero/zero rocket escape system, extra fuel (435 kg; 960 lb max) and air-conditioning.

TYPE: Two-seat turboprop powered training aircraft.

WINGS: Cantilever low-wing monoplane. Wing section NACA 23012, modified on centre-section, where forward extension of leading-edge reduces thickness/chord ratio at wingroot. Extended chord (dog-tooth) on leading-edge of outer panels of civil registered aircraft. Dihedral 5° on outer wing panels only. Incidence 3°. Leading-edge of inner wing panels swept back approximately 20°. Light alloy three-spar structure, with Frise ailerons and electrically operated single-slotted trailing-edge flaps. Trim tab in starboard aileron; balance tab in port aileron. All controls manually operated. No de-icing system.

FUSELAGE: Semi-monocoque stressed skin structure of light alloy. Hydraulically operated light alloy door type airbrake in fuselage undersurface, at wing trailing-edge.

TAIL UNIT: Cantilever stressed skin structure of light alloy. Fixed incidence tailplane. Trim tab in starboard half of elevator and in rudder. No de-icing system.

LANDING GEAR: Hydraulically retractable tricycle type with single wheel on each unit. Steerable nosewheel retracts rearward, main units inward. Tyres remain partially exposed when retracted, to reduce damage in wheels-up landing. Oleo-pneumatic shock absorber in each unit. Cleveland type 551-751 mainwheels with size 6·00-6 Goodyear tyres. Cleveland type 551-753 nosewheel, with size 5·00-5 Goodyear tyre. Cleveland Model 30-83A hydraulically operated disc brakes. Parking brake. Emergency extension of main units by free fall; nose unit is extended by CO_2 pressure from an emergency bottle.

POWER PLANT: One 533 ekW (715 eshp) Pratt & Whitney Canada PT6A-25A turboprop engine, flat rated at 410 kW (550 shp) at S/L, and driving a Hartzell type HC-B3TN-3/T10173-17 three-blade constant-speed fully-feathering and reversible-pitch metal propeller with spinner. Goodrich electric propeller de-icing standard. Two integral fuel tanks in each wing and a fuselage collector tank, with a combined capacity of 405 litres (89 Imp gallons). Two non-jettisonable auxiliary fuel tanks, each of 145 litres (32 Imp gallons), can be carried on underwing hardpoints. Overwing refuelling points for main fuel system. Oil capacity 13 litres (2·9 Imp gallons). Engine air intakes have a Centrisep particle separator for air cleaning/ice protection.

ACCOMMODATION: Two seats in tandem beneath sideways opening (to starboard) transparent canopy. Stencel crew ejection system available optionally. Canopy can be jettisoned in emergency. Rear seat is raised 10 cm (4 in) above level of forward seat for improved view. Baggage space (0·25 m³; 9 cu ft) aft of rear seat. Accommodation heated and ventilated.

SYSTEMS: Hydraulic system, pressure 103·5 bars (1,500 lb/sq in), supplied by electro-hydraulic pump with hand operated emergency pump. Gas bottle for emergency nosewheel extension. Electrical system powered by a Prestolite engine driven 28V 70A alternator. 12V 35Ah battery for aerobatics. Air-conditioning and oxygen systems optional.

AVIONICS: Include dual VHF nav/com, DME and glideslope receivers, Becker ADF 2079 ADF, ATC 2000 transponder, AL3B audio control centre and intercom.

ARMAMENT: Four underwing hardpoints, each of 181 kg (400 lb) capacity, for the carriage of two auxiliary fuel tanks and/or Portsmouth Aviation FN 7·62 mm or FFV Unipod 0·50 in gun pods; rocket launchers including Aerea AL 18-50, AL 8-70 and AL 6-80, Brandt, LAU 32, Matra F2, SNIA and SURA-D; SAMP EU 70 and EU 32 GP bombs, SAMP EU 13 fragmentation bombs; photo reconnaissance pods; and SAMAR, SATER and EMER. PACK survival kits. An SP.800 HUD can be installed in the cockpit to provide the pupil pilot with information relating to weapons aiming and vital aircraft systems failure warnings.

DIMENSIONS, EXTERNAL:
Wing span 7·92 m (26 ft 0 in)
Wing chord: at root 1·83 m (6 ft 0 in)
at tip 1·45 m (4 ft 9 in)
Wing aspect ratio 5·28
Length overall 8·33 m (27 ft 4 in)
Height overall 3·25 m (10 ft 8 in)
Tailplane span 3·35 m (11 ft 0 in)
Wheel track 3·05 m (10 ft 0 in)
Wheelbase 2·10 m (6 ft 10½ in)
Propeller diameter 2·13 m (7 ft 0 in)

AREAS:
Wings, gross 11·89 m² (128·0 sq ft)
Ailerons (total, incl tabs) 1·20 m² (12·89 sq ft)
Trailing-edge flaps (total) 1·23 m² (13·20 sq ft)
Fin 0·48 m² (5·13 sq ft)
Rudder, incl tab 0·66 m² (7·14 sq ft)
Tailplane 1·56 m² (16·77 sq ft)
Elevator, incl tab 1·27 m² (13·66 sq ft)
Dive brake 0·26 m² (2·75 sq ft)

WEIGHTS (A: civil version, B: military version):
Weight empty, equipped: A 1,066 kg (2,350 lb)
B 1,210 kg (2,667 lb)
Max T-O and landing weight: A 1,633 kg (3,600 lb)
B 1,832 kg (4,040 lb)
* Military overload T-O weight 1,927 kg (4,250 lb)
* *must be from smooth hard surface*

PERFORMANCE (civil version at max T-O weight, except where indicated):
Never-exceed speed 288 knots (533 km/h; 331 mph) EAS
Max level speed at 4,575 m (15,000 ft) 198 knots (367 km/h; 228 mph)
Econ cruising speed at 6,100 m (20,000 ft) 180 knots (333 km/h; 207 mph)
Stalling speed, flaps down and engine idling 60 knots (111 km/h; 69 mph) EAS
Max rate of climb at S/L 628 m (2,060 ft)/min
Service ceiling 8,260 m (27,100 ft)
T-O run 347 m (1,140 ft)
T-O to 15 m (50 ft) 500 m (1,640 ft)
Landing from 15 m (50 ft) at AUW of 1,451 kg (3,200 lb) with reverse thrust 677 m (2,220 ft)
Range with max fuel, incl external auxiliary tanks, no reserves 1,100 nm (2,038 km; 1,266 miles)
Range with max standard fuel, no reserves 625 nm (1,158 km; 720 miles)
g limits at normal max T-O weight +6/−3

PERFORMANCE (military version, estimated at max T-O weight, ISA):
Max level speed at S/L 223 knots (413 km/h; 257 mph)
Time to 4,575 m (15,000 ft) 6 min 15 s
T-O to 15 m (50 ft) 457 m (1,500 ft)
g limits +6·7/−3·5

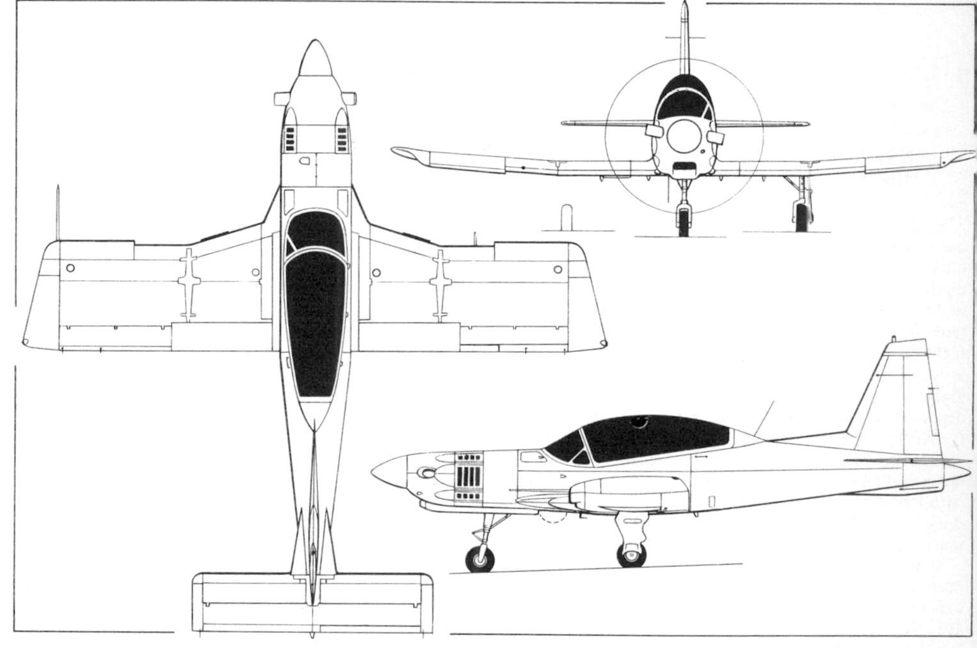

Three-view drawing *(Pilot Press)* **and photograph of the NAC Firecracker tandem-seat trainer**

NAC 6 FIELDMASTER

The NAC 6 Fieldmaster was designed by Mr Desmond Norman, with financial support from the UK National Research Development Corporation, specifically for agricultural, firefighting and oil pollution control work. Representing an entirely new approach to the design of agricultural aircraft, it has a titanium chemical hopper which is an integral part of the fuselage structure, its outer surface being contoured to serve as the skin of that fuselage section. The power plant is mounted on the front of this hopper, the aft fuselage to its rear, and the wings are attached directly to each side of the hopper's base. The cockpit, in the rear fuselage, is protected by a strong rollover structure, and is large enough to accommodate a second seat in tandem. Removable dual controls are available, to simplify flight training and checkout procedures. The wing is fitted with wide span auxiliary aerofoil trailing-edge flaps, embodying a liquid spray dispersal system that discharges directly into the downwash of the flaps, and so ensures that the spray droplets achieve the best possible crop penetration.

For the firefighting role the Fieldmaster can be fitted with a scoop gear enabling it to refill its water tank in flight. A retractable boom, extending rearward along the underside of the fuselage, can be lowered in flight to an angle of about 45°. A scoop at the rear end of the boom penetrates the surface when the aircraft's wheels are about 3 m (10 ft) above the water, and the dynamic pressure generated by the scoop's passage through the water refills the tank in less than one minute. Operation of a dump lever unlatches a 101·5 × 48·25 cm (40 × 19 in) door in the bottom of the tank to release the water load on to a fire zone, the door being closed electro-hydraulically after dumping.

The prototype Fieldmaster (G-NRDC) made its first flight at Sandown, Isle of Wight, on 17 December 1981, and by March 1986 had flown 300 hours during flight testing, demonstrations and in-service spraying trials by an agricultural operator. A programme has been established for certification in 1987 and production at the rate of 18 aircraft a year.

TYPE: Two-seat large capacity agricultural aircraft.

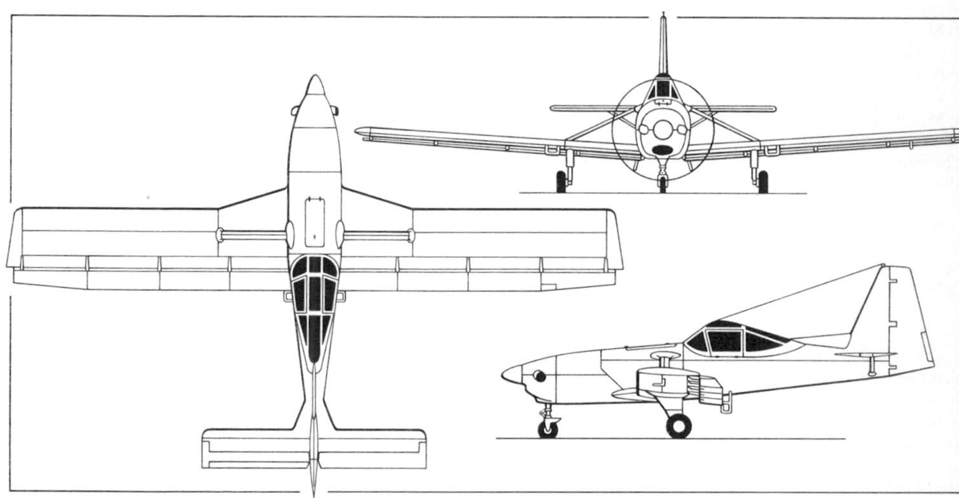

Photograph and three-view drawing *(Jane's/Mike Keep)* **of NAC 6 Fieldmaster agricultural aircraft prototype (Pratt & Whitney Canada PT6A-34AG turboprop engine). Photo shows aircraft in firefighting role**

WINGS: Low-wing monoplane, with an overwing streamline section bracing strut each side. Wing section NACA 23012, modified on inner panels, where forward extension of leading-edge reduces thickness/chord ratio to 8° 30′ at wing root. Dihedral 4° 15′. Incidence 4° 30′. Conventional all-metal structure with full corrosion proofing. Electrically actuated wide span auxiliary aerofoil trailing-edge flaps, which incorporate plumbing for 20 standard spray nozzles on each wing. The ailerons are also of auxiliary aerofoil type. Servo tab on starboard aileron, linked mechanically to rudder pedals, ensuring some bank with rudder movement.

FUSELAGE: Forward fuselage comprises structural titanium hopper with capacity of 2,032 kg (4,480 lb) dry, or 2,555 litres (562 Imp gallons) of liquid chemicals, and incorporating large access door, vent system, inspection windows, and light. Rear fuselage, attached to the rear of this hopper, is of semi-monocoque light alloy construction, fully corrosion proofed, and with easy access for cleaning and maintenance.

TAIL UNIT: Braced conventional structure of light alloy. Fixed incidence tailplane. Trim tab in port elevator. Servo tab on rudder controlled by stick movement, so that tab is moved automatically with bank.

LANDING GEAR: Non-retractable tricycle type, with single wheel on each unit. Nosewheel has alternative steerable or castoring facility. Main units of levered suspension type. Nosewheel tyre size 7·00-8, pressure 3·45 bars (50 lb/sq in); mainwheels have tubed tyres, diameter 736 mm (29 in), pressure 3·79 bars (55 lb/sq in). Cleveland hydraulic disc brakes. Landing gear incorporates wire cutters.

POWER PLANT: One 559 kW (750 shp) Pratt & Whitney Canada PT6A-34AG turboprop engine, driving a Hartzell type HC-B3TN-3/T10282+4 three-blade fully-feathering reversible-pitch metal propeller with spinner. Two integral fuel tanks in each wing, with combined capacity of 1,079 litres (237·5 Imp gallons). Oil capacity 13 litres (2·9 Imp gallons). Engine air intake has a Centrisep filtration system.

ACCOMMODATION: Standard accommodation for pilot and trainee/passenger on fully adjustable tandem seats in an enclosed cockpit, with rollover protective structure. Dual controls standard, those for pupil easily removable. Crew safety helmets with headsets optional. Baggage space in fuselage. Sideways hinged door on each side. Birdproof armoured glass windscreen, two-speed windscreen wiper and windscreen washer standard. Accommodation ventilated; air-conditioning and heating system optional. Wirecutters forward of windscreen, and cable deflecting wire from top of windscreen to tip of fin.

SYSTEMS: Electrical system includes 24V 300A starter/generator. Hydraulic system for brakes only. Central warning system standard, including engine fire warning.

AVIONICS AND EQUIPMENT: Intercom standard. Avionics, and IFR instrument package, to customer requirements. Standard equipment includes an external power socket. Optional equipment includes airframe and engine hour meter; instrument lighting, navigation lights, fin and wingtip strobe lights; two forward looking retractable work lights, each 765,000 candlepower; automatic flagman installation; firefighting dump door and water scoop (see introductory copy); Transland gatebox, high volume spreader, quick disconnect flange kit, and side loading system; and Micronair installation, with flowmeter and rpm indicator.

DIMENSIONS, EXTERNAL:

Wing span	16·33 m (53 ft 7 in)
Wing chord (excl flaps): at root	2·01 m (6 ft 7¼ in)
at tip	1·45 m (4 ft 9 in)
Wing aspect ratio	8·02
Length overall	10·97 m (36 ft 0 in)
Height overall	4·12 m (13 ft 6 in)
Wheel track	5·08 m (16 ft 8 in)
Wheelbase	3·35 m (11 ft 0 in)
Propeller diameter	2·69 m (8 ft 10 in)

DIMENSION, INTERNAL:

Hopper volume	2·64 m³ (93·3 cu ft)

AREA:

Wings, gross	33·25 m² (358·0 sq ft)

WEIGHTS AND LOADINGS:

Typical weight empty, equipped	2,154 kg (4,750 lb)
Hopper load: with max fuel	1,562 kg (3,443 lb)
max, with 336 litres (74 Imp gallons) fuel	2,032 kg (4,480 lb)
Max T-O weight: (BCAR Public Transport Category)	3,855 kg (8,500 lb)
UK CAA AN 90	4,535 kg (10,000 lb)
Max wing loading (AN 90)	136·37 kg/m² (27·93 lb/sq ft)
Max power loading (AN 90)	8·11 kg/kW (13·33 lb/shp)

PERFORMANCE ('clean', with main landing gear fairings installed, at max Public Transport Category T-O weight, S/L, ISA, except where indicated):

Never-exceed speed	167 knots (301 km/h; 192 mph)
Max level speed, clean:	
at S/L	143 knots (265 km/h; 165 mph)
at 1,830 m (6,000 ft)	147 knots (272 km/h; 169 mph)
Design manoeuvring speed	126 knots (233 km/h; 145 mph)
Stalling speed: flaps up	70 knots (129 km/h; 81 mph)
flaps down (30°)	60 knots (111 km/h; 69 mph)
Max rate of climb at S/L	294 m (955 ft)/min
T-O run	419 m (1,375 ft)
T-O to 15 m (50 ft)	625 m (2,050 ft)
Landing from 15 m (50 ft)	472 m (1,550 ft)
Landing run at typical landing weight of 2,720 kg (6,000 lb), with propeller reversal	152 m (500 ft)
Range at 3,050 m (10,000 ft) with two crew, 454 kg (1,000 lb) of equipment and max fuel, no reserves:	800 nm (1,482 km; 921 miles)
g limits	+3·4/−1·7

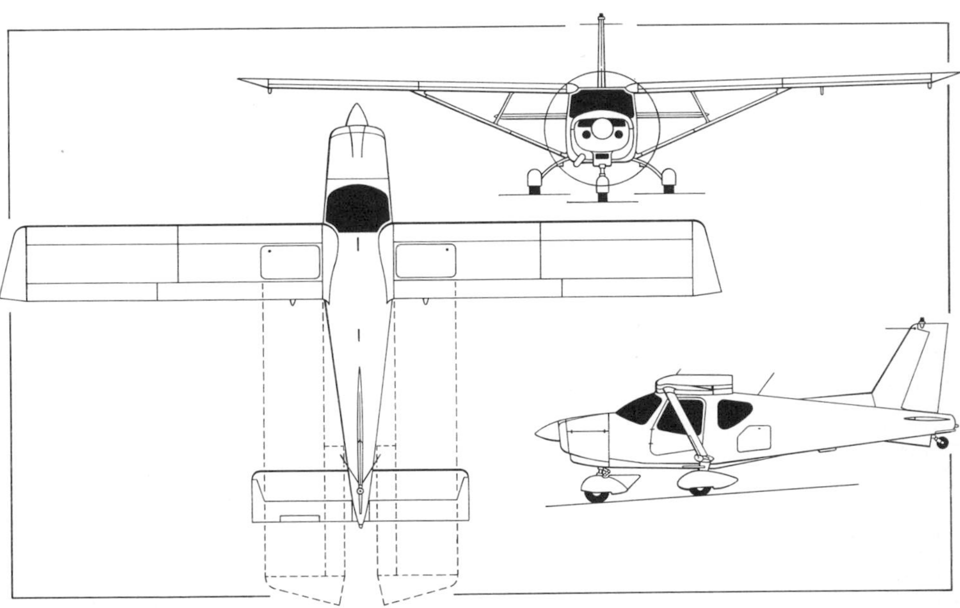

NAC1 Freelance four-seat utility aircraft *(Jane's/Mike Keep)*

Prototype NAC1 Freelance multi-purpose utility aircraft *(Air Portraits)*

NAC1 FREELANCE

The prototype Freelance (G-NACI) made its first flight on 29 September 1984. Production aircraft will have a wider fuselage, a larger glazed area and certain other features to maximise passenger comfort. Production has started and is expected to increase to a rate of 21 to 24 aircraft a year after certification in 1987.

The Freelance is intended to be suitable for a wide range of specialist tasks, including air ambulance, glider and banner towing, agricultural spraying, photography and parachutist duties, with interchangeable wheel, ski and float landing gear.

TYPE: Four-seat multi-purpose utility aircraft.

WINGS: Strut braced high-wing monoplane. Wing section NACA 23012 (modified). Dihedral 1° 30′ from roots. Incidence 3° 30′. No sweepback. Constant chord conventional two-spar all-metal structure of Alclad light alloy, including trailing-edge flaps and ailerons, braced on each side by single strut from fuselage floor line. No tabs. Wing folding system enables wings to be swung back, permitting aircraft to be stored within a 4 × 9 m (13 ft 1 in × 29 ft 6 in) space.

FUSELAGE: Conventional semi-monocoque structure of basically rectangular section, with frames, stringers and Alclad light alloy sheet covering. Composites engine cowling.

TAIL UNIT: Cantilever all-metal structure, with sweptback vertical surfaces and non-swept rectangular horizontal surfaces. Small dorsal fin. Trim tab in port elevator.

LANDING GEAR: Non-retractable tricycle gear standard. All three wheels same size; tyre size 600 × 6, pressure 2·07 bars (30 lb/sq in). Wheel/ski and float gear, and balloon tyres, available optionally.

POWER PLANT: One 134 kW (180 hp) Avco Lycoming O-360-A3A flat-four engine, driving a Sensenich two-blade fixed-pitch (optionally constant-speed) metal propeller with spinner. Avco Lycoming engines of 157 kW (210 hp) (turbocharged) and 175 kW (235 hp) to be available optionally. Fuel tank in each wing, combined capacity 280 litres (62 Imp gallons) usable. Refuelling point above each wing.

ACCOMMODATION: Individual seats for pilot and three passengers in fully enclosed cabin. Forward opening door on each side. Baggage space behind rear seats, with loading door on port side of fuselage. Rear (sliding) door optional, for paradropping. Cabin can be configured for one specially designed full-length stretcher, plus medical attendant, in addition to pilot.

SYSTEMS: Hydraulic system, pressure 34·5 bars (500 lb/sq in), for mainwheel brakes. DC electrical system includes 28V 60A alternator and 25Ah battery. Exhaust muff heater with punka louvres for cabin ventilation.

AVIONICS: Normal instrumentation for VFR and IFR flying. General Aviation Class 1 radio equipment optional.

EQUIPMENT: Wide variety of equipment options, according to role. These can include towing gear for sailplane (up to 907 kg; 2,000 lb AUW) or banners; passengers' ski carrying bin in rear fuselage; a 378·5 litre (100 US gallon) detachable belly spraytank, plus boom and nozzles or Micronair atomisers; outward opening cabin windows for aerial photography; rear (sliding) door for paradropping; and ambulance kit (see 'Accommodation' paragraph).

DIMENSIONS, EXTERNAL:

Wing span	12·25 m (40 ft 2½ in)
Wing chord, constant	1·32 m (4 ft 4 in)
Wing aspect ratio	9·51
Width, wings folded	3·66 m (12 ft 0 in)
Length overall	7·21 m (23 ft 7¾ in)
Height overall	2·90 m (9 ft 6 in)
Tailplane span	3·66 m (12 ft 0 in)
Wheel track	2·18 m (7 ft 2 in)
Wheelbase	2·08 m (6 ft 10 in)
Propeller diameter	1·93 m (6 ft 4 in)
Passenger door (port): Height	0·91 m (3 ft 0 in)
Width	0·86 m (2 ft 10 in)
Height to sill	0·76 m (2 ft 6 in)

DIMENSIONS, INTERNAL:

Cabin: Length	2·69 m (8 ft 10 in)
Max width	1·04 m (3 ft 5 in)
Max height	1·22 m (4 ft 0 in)

AREAS:

Wings, gross	15·79 m² (170·0 sq ft)
Ailerons (total)	1·38 m² (14·9 sq ft)
Trailing-edge flaps (total)	1·86 m² (20·0 sq ft)
Fin	0·72 m² (7·74 sq ft)
Rudder	0·53 m² (5·66 sq ft)
Tailplane	2·01 m² (21·6 sq ft)
Elevators (total)	1·24 m² (13·4 sq ft)

WEIGHTS AND LOADINGS:

Basic weight empty, equipped	709 kg (1,564 lb)
Max T-O and landing weight	1,225 kg (2,700 lb)
Max wing loading	77·96 kg/m² (15·98 lb/sq ft)
Max power loading	9·13 kg/kW (15·00 lb/hp)

PERFORMANCE (at max T-O weight):

Max level speed at S/L	124 knots (230 km/h; 143 mph)
Cruising speed at S/L (75% power)	119 knots (220 km/h; 137 mph)
Stalling speed, power off: flaps up	57 knots (105 km/h; 65 mph)
flaps down	52 knots (97 km/h; 60 mph)
Max rate of climb at S/L	203 m (667 ft)/min
Service ceiling	5,030 m (16,500 ft)
T-O run	298 m (976 ft)
T-O to 15 m (50 ft)	606 m (1,988 ft)
Landing from 15 m (50 ft)	431 m (1,415 ft)
Landing run	170 m (557 ft)

Max range at 75% power at 2,440 m (8,000 ft), with allowances for start, taxi, T-O, climb and 45 min reserves 808 nm (1,496 km; 930 miles)

Max range at 3,050 m (10,000 ft), allowances as above 1,056 nm (1,955 km; 1,215 miles)

NASH

NASH AIRCRAFT LTD (a subsidiary of Kinetrol Ltd)

Trading Estate, Farnham, Surrey GU9 9NU
Telephone: 0252 723688
Telex: 858567

DIRECTORS:
A. R. B. Nash (Managing)
Roy G. Procter
R. C. Nash

Mr Alan Nash acquired a controlling interest in Procter Aircraft Associates Ltd in early 1978, as a result of which the company was renamed Nash Aircraft Ltd in 1980. Its principal current activity is the development and manufacture of the Petrel two-seat light aircraft.

Company owned prototype of the Nash Petrel, now with upswept wingtips and leading-edge cuffs

NASH PETREL

The company prototype of the Petrel (G-AXSF) made its first flight on 8 November 1980. In initial glider towing trials, it towed Vega, Mini-Nimbus and Nimbus sailplanes to a height of 610 m (2,000 ft) in under 4 min. During 1982 the original Avco Lycoming O-320-D2A engine was replaced by a 134 kW (180 hp) Avco Lycoming O-360-A3A, to optimise aircraft performance in the glider towing and pilot training roles. During 1983 a new high tailplane was designed and fitted, to improve stability and spin recovery. In 1984 upswept tips were fitted to the wings to improve handling. Early in 1985 cuffs were fitted to the wing leading-edge, extending from 50 per cent span to the tips.

A pre-production batch of five Petrels is under construction. These will have either an O-320 or O-360 engine according to individual customer requirements.

TYPE: Two-seat light aircraft.

WINGS: Cantilever low-wing monoplane. Wing section NACA 3415. Dihedral 5° on outer panels. No sweepback or washout. All-metal constant chord structure, built in three sections: centre-section, integral with fuselage, to which outer panels are each attached with three bolts. Single main spar at 30 per cent chord and lightweight auxiliary spar at 66 per cent chord. Multiple ribs, with no spanwise stiffeners. All-metal NACA slotted flaps and Frise ailerons on outer panels. Flaps are operated manually by pushrod and torque tube; ailerons are operated by pushrods.

FUSELAGE: All-metal structure. Four longeron basic structure, with flat sides and bottom and single-curvature top decking. Integral wing centre-section forms seat and main landing gear attachment structure.

TAIL UNIT: Cantilever all-metal structure. Fixed incidence tailplane. Manually operated tab in starboard elevator. Tab on rudder. Control surfaces mass balanced. Rudder operated by cables; elevators by pushrods.

LANDING GEAR: Non-retractable tricycle type. Nose unit consists of a telescopic strut with elastomeric shock absorption, carrying a Goodyear 5·00-6 wheel, and is steerable from the rudder pedals. Main gear is of cantilever steel leaf spring type, with Goodyear 6·00-6 wheels and hydraulic disc brakes. Tyre pressure (all) 1·72 bars (25 lb/sq in).

POWER PLANT: One 134 kW (180 hp) Avco Lycoming O-360-A3A flat-four engine, driving a Sensenich two-blade fixed-pitch metal propeller with spinner. Provision for alternative engines of 88-134 kW (118-180 hp). Removable fuel tanks in wing centre-section leading-edges, capacity 104·5 litres (23 Imp gallons).

ACCOMMODATION: Two persons side by side, on seats with individually adjustable backs. One-piece rearward sliding bubble canopy. Dual controls standard. Baggage space aft of seats.

EQUIPMENT: Starter, generator and basic instrumentation. Radio, navigation and other equipment to customer's requirements.

DIMENSIONS, EXTERNAL:

Wing span	9·04 m (29 ft 8 in)
Wing chord, constant	1·37 m (4 ft 6 in)
Wing aspect ratio	6·3
Length overall	6·22 m (20 ft 5 in)
Height overall	2·23 m (7 ft 4 in)
Tailplane span	3·35 m (11 ft 0 in)
Wheel track	2·24 m (7 ft 4 in)
Wheelbase	1·52 m (5 ft 0 in)

AREA:

Wings, gross	13·00 m² (140·0 sq ft)

WEIGHTS:

Weight empty	544 kg (1,200 lb)
Max T-O weight	794 kg (1,750 lb)

PERFORMANCE (at max T-O weight):

Max level speed	115 knots (213 km/h; 132 mph)
Cruising speed	90 knots (167 km/h; 104 mph)
Stalling speed: flaps up	46 knots (86 km/h; 53 mph)
flaps down	40 knots (74 km/h; 46 mph)
Max rate of climb at S/L	350 m (1,150 ft)/min

OPTICA AVIATION

OPTICA INDUSTRIES LTD

Old Sarum Airfield, Salisbury, Wiltshire SP4 6BJ
Telephone: 0722 21812
Telex: 47106 AERODS G

DIRECTORS:
A. Haikney, CEng, MIMechE, FInstPET
C. F. Underwood, FAPA, FSCA

The original company responsible for the Optica, Edgley Aircraft Ltd, was formed in 1974 to design, build and market a specialised observation aircraft that would combine the all-round visibility of a helicopter with the lower operating costs of a fixed-wing aircraft.

Production of the Optica started in 1983 in the company's 6,505 m² (70,000 sq ft) premises at Old Sarum Airfield. The first production aircraft (c/n 003, G-BLFC) was rolled out and first flew on 4 August 1984. CAA type certification was granted on 8 February 1985, for day VFR flying and was extended to night and IFR clearance in time for the delivery of the first customer's aircraft in April 1985.

The company encountered financial difficulties, and was purchased from the receiver by A. Haikney of Aero-Docks Ltd in December 1985. The new company, Optica Industries Ltd, re-started production in January 1986. It is planned to produce 21 aircraft in 1986 and 46 in 1987.

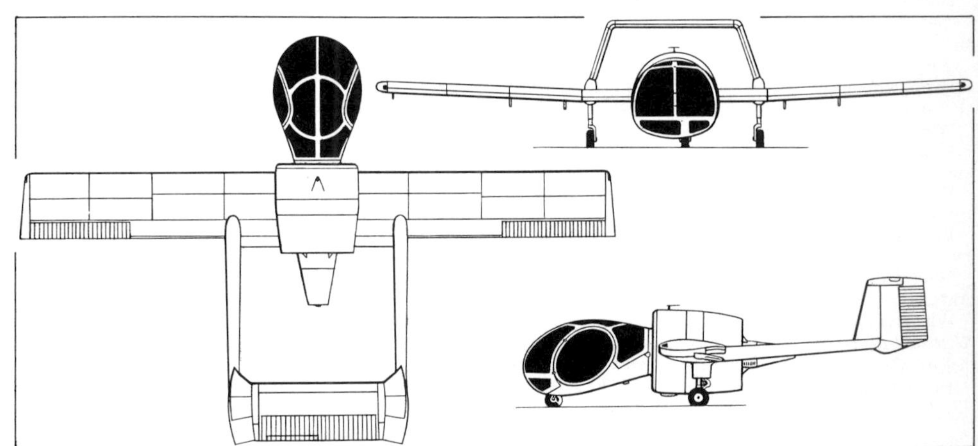
OA7 Optica (Avco Lycoming IO-540 engine) *(Pilot Press)*

OA7 OPTICA

First flown on 14 December 1979, the Optica is a three-seat observation aircraft, designed particularly for pipeline and powerline inspection; forestry and coastal patrol; police duties; frontier patrol; aerial photography; film, TV and press reporting; and touring. The cabin configuration is designed to give the best possible all-round view. Power plant is a ducted propulsor unit, offering quietness, both within the cabin and from the ground. A low wing loading, pre-set inboard flaps and a low stalling speed facilitate continuous en-route flight at low speeds. Generous flap area provides good field performance from both hard and soft strips. Stability increases at low speeds.

TYPE: Three-seat slow flying observation aircraft; stressed to BCAR Section K (non-aerobatic category) and FAR Pt 23 (Normal category).

WINGS: Cantilever mid-wing monoplane. Wing section NASA GAW-1; thickness/chord ratio 17%. Dihedral 3° on outer panels. Incidence 0°. Constant chord single-spar non-swept wings of aluminium alloy stressed skin construction. Wingtips (also fin/tailplane fillets, nosewheel mudguard and some power plant fairings) of glassfibre. Fowler trailing-edge flaps (29 per cent of total wing chord) inboard and outboard of tailbooms. Electrically actuated outboard flaps can be set at angles up to 50° for landing; inboard flaps set permanently at 10°, giving the effect of a slotted wing, for continuous low speed flying. Bottom hinged, mass balanced slotted ailerons outboard of outer flaps, operated by pushrods. No spoilers, airbrakes or tabs.

CABIN: 'Insect eye' shaped structure, built of aluminium alloy with Suntex vacuum formed acrylic windows. Cabin attached to fan shroud and rest of airframe by six stators of steel tube and aluminium alloy shear web construction. Steel tube and aluminium alloy nose beam supports cabin floor. Horizontal window frame member just above floor level, together with nosewheel box, is designed to withstand 9*g* impact. Tinted windows optional. Two movable 9 kg (20 lb) ballast weights may be positioned on the nose beam. Two lamps are also mounted in the nose beam, one as a landing lamp, the other as a taxi/standby landing lamp.

Tail Unit: Twin-tailboom configuration, of aluminium alloy stressed skin tubular construction. Tailboom pick-up points at extremities of wing centre-section. Angular, inward canted fins and balanced rudders. Fixed incidence tailplane, with elevator, bridging space between tops of fins. Inset trim tab occupies port half of elevator trailing-edge; no rudder tabs. Two movable 9 kg (20 lb) ballast weights may be positioned, one in each fin.

Landing Gear: Non-retractable tricycle type, with steerable nosewheel offset to port. Mainwheel legs embody rubber in compression shock absorption. Nosewheel shock absorption by bungee rubber in tension. Single wheel on each unit, tyre sizes 6·00-6 (main) and 5·00-5 (nose). Hydraulic disc brakes on mainwheels.

Power Plant: Ducted propulsor unit, with engine and fan forming a power pod separate from the main shroud. Pod is attached to fan shroud with four Lord rubber mountings, and supported by four stators of steel channel and aluminium alloy shear web construction, with steel tube engine bearers. Five-blade fixed-pitch fan, driven by a 194 kW (260 hp) Avco Lycoming IO-540 flat-six engine, mounted in a duct downstream of the fan. Fuel tank of 123 litres (27 Imp gallons) in each wing leading-edge, immediately outboard of tailbooms and forward of wing spar. Tanks are of full wing section, but are designed not to be stressed by wing bending and torsion. Total usable fuel capacity 246 litres (54 Imp gallons). Refuelling point in upper surface of each wing. Oil capacity 7·6 litres (1·7 Imp gallons).

Accommodation: Cabin designed to accommodate up to three persons side by side on fixed seats, with either single- or two-pilot operation (left hand and centre seats). Dual controls standard. Baggage space aft of seats. Single elliptical door on each side, hinged at front and opening forward. Can be flown with doors removed. Cabin heated, by hot air from engine, and ventilated. A Janitrol combustion heater is offered as an extra.

Systems: Hydraulics for mainwheel brakes only. Electrical system (24V) includes engine driven alternator and storage battery for engine starting and actuation of flaps.

Avionics and Equipment: Standard nav/com avionics by King (Silver Crown). Alternative avionics could be provided. Special equipment which has been tested successfully includes Barr & Stroud IR18 Mk II and an air-to-ground video relay. Other equipment such as FLIR, GEC Avionics TICM II, searchlights and loudspeakers is being assessed.

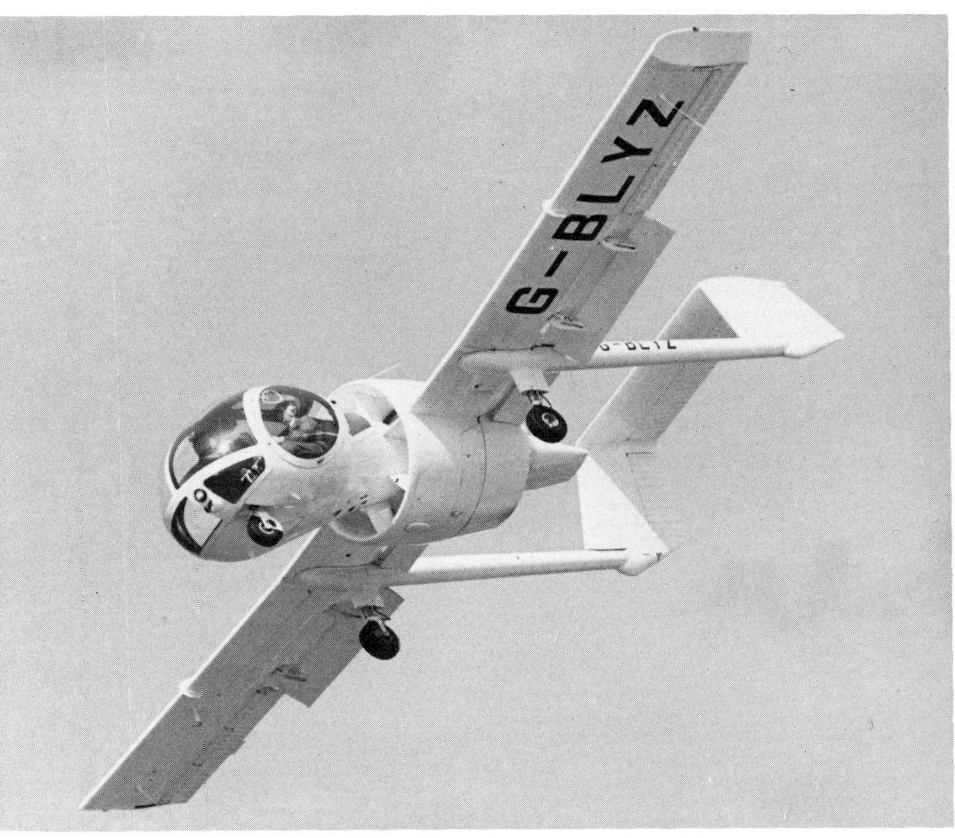

Optica Aviation OA7 Optica three-seat slow flying observation aircraft *(Air Portraits)*

Dimensions, external:

Wing span	12·00 m (39 ft 4 in)
Wing chord: basic, constant	1·32 m (4 ft 4 in)
over 10° fixed flaps	1·45 m (4 ft 9 in)
Wing aspect ratio	9·1
Length overall	8·15 m (26 ft 9 in)
Height over fan shroud (excl aerial)	1·98 m (6 ft 6 in)
Diameter of fan shroud	1·68 m (5 ft 6 in)
Diameter of fan	1·22 m (4 ft 0 in)
Shroud ground clearance	0·25 m (10 in)
Height over tailplane	2·31 m (7 ft 7 in)
Tailplane span:	
c/l of tailbooms	3·40 m (11 ft 2 in)
intersection fin chord	2·60 m (8 ft 6½ in)
Wheel track	3·40 m (11 ft 2 in)
Wheelbase	2·73 m (9 ft 0 in)
Doors (each): Long axis	1·35 m (4 ft 5 in)
Short axis	0·96 m (3 ft 1¾ in)
Height to sill	0·51 m (1 ft 8 in)

Dimensions, internal:

Cabin: Length	2·44 m (8 ft 0 in)
Max width (to door Perspex)	1·68 m (5 ft 6 in)
Max height	1.35 m (4 ft 5 in)
Floor area	0·72 m² (7·75 sq ft)

Areas:

Wings, gross	15·84 m² (170·5 sq ft)
Ailerons (total)	1·55 m² (16·68 sq ft)
Trailing-edge flaps:	
inboard (total)	0·61 m² (6·57 sq ft)
outboard (total)	1·59 m² (17·12 sq ft)
Fins (total)	1·98 m² (21·31 sq ft)
Rudders (total)	1·10 m² (11·84 sq ft)
Tailplane	1·62 m² (17·44 sq ft)
Elevator, incl tab	1·26 m² (13·56 sq ft)

Weights and Loadings:

Weight empty	944 kg (2,081 lb)
Max T-O weight	1,315 kg (2,899 lb)
Max wing loading	83·0 kg/m² (17·0 lb/sq ft)
Max power loading	6·78 kg/kW (11·2 lb/hp)

Performance (at 1,315 kg; 2,899 lb, forward limit CG):

Never-exceed speed	140 knots (259 km/h; 161 mph)
Max level speed	120 knots (222 km/h; 138 mph)
Cruising speed (55% power)	87 knots (161 km/h; 100 mph)
Recommended min patrol speed	65 knots (120 km/h; 75 mph)
Stalling speed: flaps up	56 knots (104 km/h; 64 mph)
50° flap	51 knots (95 km/h; 59 mph)
Max rate of climb at S/L	247 m (810 ft)/min
Service ceiling	4,275 m (14,000 ft)
T-O run	335 m (1,099 ft)
Landing run	255 m (837 ft)
Range with max fuel, at 55% power	500 nm (926 km; 576 miles)
Endurance: at patrol speed	7 h
at 55% power cruising speed	6 h

PILATUS BRITTEN-NORMAN

PILATUS BRITTEN-NORMAN LTD (Subsidiary of Oerlikon-Bührle Holding Ltd)

Bembridge Airport, Bembridge, Isle of Wight PO35 5PR
Telephone: 0983 872511
Telex: 86277 PBNBEM G

Directors:
Dr E. Haefliger (Managing)
P. G. Palmer (Marketing)
D. Fear (Production)
A. Larwood (Administration/Finance)
R. Wilson (Technical)

Public Relations: Alice Day

In 1979 Pilatus Aircraft Ltd of Switzerland acquired all assets of Britten-Norman (Bembridge) Ltd, including the facilities on the Isle of Wight and the former Fairey SA Islander/Trislander production hardware at Gosselies in Belgium.

The previous history of this company can be found in the 1978-79 and earlier editions of *Jane's*. It produces the Islander transport aircraft in a variety of forms; the Islander is manufactured in Romania by IAv Bucuresti (which see), and 395 had been delivered to Pilatus Britten-Norman from that source by the Spring of 1985. Romanian production was then continuing at the rate of 25 per year. In addition to the Bembridge and Romanian production lines, Philippine Aerospace Development Corporation had an Islander production line in Manila, for the production of 115 aircraft under licence in four phases during the period 1974-1980. Only 55 aircraft were built, but assembly of BN-2Bs is being continued in the Philippines by PADC (which see). A licence to manufacture the three-engined Trislander in the USA is held by International Aviation Corporation (see US section). The last Trislander produced by Pilatus Britten-Norman was delivered to the Botswana Defence Force in September 1984.

PILATUS BRITTEN-NORMAN BN-2B ISLANDER

Detail design of the Islander began in April 1964 and construction of the prototype (G-ATCT) was started in September of the same year. It flew for the first time on 13 June 1965, powered by two 157 kW (210 hp) Rolls-Royce Continental IO-360-B engines and with wings of 13·72 m (45 ft) span. Subsequently, the prototype was re-engined with more powerful Avco Lycoming O-540 engines, with which it flew for the first time on 17 December 1965. The wing span was also increased by 1·22 m (4 ft) to bring the prototype to initial production standard.

The production prototype BN-2 Islander (G-ATWU) flew for the first time on 20 August 1966. The Islander received its domestic C of A on 10 August 1967 and an FAA Type Certificate on 19 December 1967.

Deliveries of Islanders began in August 1967, and various models, including military Defenders, have been supplied to operators in approx 120 countries. By August 1985 deliveries totalled more than 1,060.

Initial production Islanders were designated **BN-2**. Those built from 1 June 1969 until 1978 had the designation **BN-2A**, as described in the 1977-78 *Jane's*. The current standard piston engined model is the **BN-2B** Islander, which has a higher max landing weight and improved interior design. It is available with a choice of two piston engine power plants and either standard fuel tanks or optional wingtip tanks. Features, compared with the BN-2A, include a range of passenger seats and covers, more robust door locks, improved door seals and stainless steel sills, redesigned fresh air system to improve ventilation in hot and humid climates, smaller diameter propellers to decrease cabin noise, and redesigned flight deck and instrument panel. The two basic versions are designated **BN-2B-26** (with O-540 engines) and **BN-2B-20** (with IO-540s); BN-2B-27 and BN-2B-21 versions are no longer available, but new improved tip tanks are available as options to the basic BN-2B-26 and BN-2B-20 aircraft. The **BN-2T Turbine Islander**, powered by two Allison 250-B17C turboprop engines, and the military **Defender** and **Maritime Defender**, are described separately.

A series of modification kits is available as standard or as an option for new production aircraft, and can also be supplied to operators in the field for retrospective fitting to existing aircraft. An extended nose, incorporating 0·62 m³ (22 cu ft) of additional baggage space, was introduced as an optional feature in 1972.

A Rajay turbocharging installation was developed in the United States by Jonas Aircraft, the New York based distributors for Pilatus Britten-Norman aircraft. The Rajay installation is a bolt-on unit, which can be fitted on to standard 194 kW (260 hp) engines.

The following description applies to the standard piston engined versions of the BN-2B:

Type: Twin-engined feederline transport.

Wings: Cantilever high-wing monoplane. NACA 23012 constant wing section. No dihedral. Incidence 2°. No sweepback. Conventional riveted two-spar torsion box structure in one piece, using L72 aluminium-clad aluminium alloys. Flared-up wingtips of Britten-Norman design. Wingtip fuel tanks optional. Slotted ailerons and single-slotted flaps of metal construction. Flaps operated electrically, ailerons by pushrods and cables. Ground adjustable tab on starboard aileron. BTR-Goodrich pneumatic de-icing boots optional.

FUSELAGE: Conventional riveted four-longeron semi-monocoque structure of pressed frames and stringers and metal skin, using L72 aluminium clad aluminium alloys.

TAIL UNIT: Cantilever two-spar structure, with pressed ribs and metal skin, using L72 aluminium-clad aluminium alloys. Fixed incidence tailplane and mass balanced elevator. Rudder and elevator are actuated by pushrods and cables. Trim tabs in rudder and elevator. Pneumatic de-icing of tailplane and fin optional.

LANDING GEAR: Non-retractable tricycle type, with twin wheels on each main unit and single steerable nosewheel. Cantilever main legs mounted aft of rear spar. All three legs fitted with oleo-pneumatic shock absorbers. All five wheels and tyres size 16 × 7-7, supplied by Goodyear. Tyre pressure: main 2·41 bars (35 lb/sq in); nose 2·00 bars (29 lb/sq in). Foot operated aircooled Cleveland hydraulic brakes on main units. Parking brake. Wheel/ski gear available optionally.

POWER PLANT: Two Avco Lycoming flat-six engines, each driving a Hartzell HC-C2YK-2B or -2C two-blade constant-speed feathering metal propeller. Propeller synchronisers optional. Standard power plant is the 194 kW (260 hp) O-540-E4C5, but the 224 kW (300 hp) IO-540-K1B5 can be fitted at customer's option. Optional Rajay turbocharging installation on 194 kW (260 hp) engines, to improve high altitude performance. Integral fuel tank between spars in each wing, outboard of engine. Total fuel capacity (standard) 518 litres (114 Imp gallons; 137 US gallons). With optional wingtip fuel tanks, total capacity is increased to 855 litres (188 Imp gallons; 226 US gallons). Additional pylon mounted underwing auxiliary tanks, each of 227 litres (50 Imp gallons; 60 US gallons) capacity, available optionally. Refuelling point in upper surface of wing above each internal tank. Total oil capacity 22·75 litres (5 Imp gallons).

ACCOMMODATION: Up to 10 persons, including pilot, on side by side front seats and four bench seats. No aisle. Seat backs fold forward. Access to all seats via three forward opening doors, forward of wing and at rear of cabin on port side and forward of wing on starboard side. Baggage compartment at rear of cabin, with port side loading door in standard versions. Exit in emergency by removing door windows. Special executive layouts available. Can be operated as freighter, carrying more than a ton of cargo; in this configuration the passenger seats can be stored in the rear baggage bay. In ambulance role, up to three stretchers and two attendants can be accommodated. Other layouts possible, including photographic and geophysical survey, parachutist transport or trainer (with accommodation for up to eight parachutists and a dispatcher), firefighting, public health spraying and crop spraying.

SYSTEMS: Southwind cabin heater standard. 45,000 BTU Stewart Warner combustion unit, with circulating fan, provides hot air for distribution at floor level outlets and at windscreen demisting slots. Fresh air, boosted by propeller slipstream, is ducted to each seating position for on-ground ventilation. Electrical DC power, for instruments, lighting and radio, from two engine driven 24V 50A self-rectifying alternators and a controller to main busbar and circuit breaker assembly. Emergency busbar is supplied by a 24V 17Ah heavy duty lead-acid battery in the event of a twin alternator failure. Ground power receptacle provided. Optional electric de-icing of propellers and windscreen, and pneumatic de-icing of wing and tail unit leading-edges. Intercom system, including second headset, and passenger address system are standard. Oxygen system available optionally for all versions.

AVIONICS AND EQUIPMENT: Standard items include blind-flying instrumentation, autopilot, dual flying controls and brake system, and a wide range of VHF and HF communications and navigation equipment.

DIMENSIONS, EXTERNAL:

Wing span	14·94 m (49 ft 0 in)
Wing chord (constant)	2·03 m (6 ft 8 in)
Wing aspect ratio	7·4
Length overall	10·86 m (35 ft 7¾ in)
Fuselage: Max width	1·21 m (3 ft 11½ in)
Max depth	1·46 m (4 ft 9¾ in)
Height overall	4·18 m (13 ft 8¾ in)
Tailplane span	4·67 m (15 ft 4 in)
Wheel track (c/l of shock absorbers)	3·61 m (11 ft 10 in)
Wheelbase	3·99 m (13 ft 1¼ in)
Propeller diameter	1·98 m (6 ft 6 in)
Cabin door (front, port): Height	1·10 m (3 ft 7½ in)
Width: top	0·64 m (2 ft 1¼ in)
Height to sill	0·59 m (1 ft 11¼ in)
Cabin door (front, starboard): Height	1·10 m (3 ft 7½ in)
Max width	0·86 m (2 ft 10 in)
Height to sill	0·57 m (1 ft 10½ in)
Cabin door (rear, port): Height	1·09 m (3 ft 7 in)
Width: top	0·635 m (2 ft 1 in)
bottom	1·19 m (3 ft 11 in)
Height to sill	0·52 m (1 ft 8½ in)
Baggage door (rear, port): Height	0·69 m (2 ft 3 in)

Pilatus Britten-Norman BN-2B Islander delivered to Falkland Island Government Air Services

DIMENSIONS, INTERNAL:

Passenger cabin, aft of pilot's seat: Length	3·05 m (10 ft 0 in)
Max width	1·09 m (3 ft 7 in)
Max height	1·27 m (4 ft 2 in)
Floor area	2·97 m² (32 sq ft)
Volume	3·68 m³ (130 cu ft)
Baggage space aft of passenger cabin	1·39 m³ (49 cu ft)
Freight capacity: aft of pilot's seat, incl rear cabin baggage space	4·70 m³ (166 cu ft)
with four bench seats folded into rear cabin baggage space	3·68 m³ (130 cu ft)

AREAS:

Wings, gross	30·19 m² (325·0 sq ft)
Ailerons (total)	2·38 m² (25·6 sq ft)
Flaps (total)	3·62 m² (39·0 sq ft)
Fin	3·41 m² (36·64 sq ft)
Rudder, incl tab	1·60 m² (17·2 sq ft)
Tailplane	6·78 m² (73·0 sq ft)
Elevator, incl tabs	3·08 m² (33·16 sq ft)

WEIGHTS AND LOADINGS (A: 194 kW; 260 hp engines, B: 224 kW; 300 hp engines):

Weight empty, equipped (without avionics): A	1,866 kg (4,114 lb)
B	1,925 kg (4,244 lb)
Max payload: A	929 kg (2,048 lb)
B	870 kg (1,918 lb)
Max fuel weight: standard: A, B	354 kg (780 lb)
with optional tip tanks: A, B	585 kg (1,290 lb)
Max T-O and landing weight: A, B	2,993 kg (6,600 lb)
Max zero-fuel weight (BCAR): A, B	2,855 kg (6,300 lb)
Max wing loading: A, B	99·1 kg/m² (20·3 lb/sq ft)
Max floor loading, without cargo panels: A, B	586 kg/m² (120 lb/sq ft)
Max power loading: A	7·71 kg/kW (12·7 lb/hp)
B	6·68 kg/kW (11·0 lb/hp)

PERFORMANCE (at max T-O weight. A and B as above):

Never-exceed speed: A, B	183 knots (339 km/h; 211 mph) IAS
Max level speed at S/L: A	148 knots (274 km/h; 170 mph)
B	151 knots (280 km/h; 173 mph)
Max cruising speed (75% power) at 2,135 m (7,000 ft): A	139 knots (257 km/h; 160 mph)
B	142 knots (264 km/h; 164 mph)
Cruising speed (67% power) at 2,750 m (9,000 ft): A	134 knots (248 km/h; 154 mph)
B	137 knots (254 km/h; 158 mph)
Cruising speed (59% power) at 3,660 m (12,000 ft): A	130 knots (241 km/h; 150 mph)
B	132 knots (245 km/h; 152 mph)
Stalling speed: flaps up: A, B	50 knots (92 km/h; 57 mph) IAS
flaps down: A, B	40 knots (74 km/h; 46 mph) IAS
Max rate of climb at S/L: A	262 m (860 ft)/min
B	344 m (1,130 ft)/min
Rate of climb at S/L, one engine out: A	44 m (145 ft)/min
B	61 m (200 ft)/min
Absolute ceiling: A	4,145 m (13,600 ft)
B	6,005 m (19,700 ft)
Service ceiling: A	3,445 m (11,300 ft)
B	5,240 m (17,200 ft)
Service ceiling, one engine out: A	1,525 m (5,000 ft)
B	1,980 m (6,500 ft)
Min ground turning radius	9·45 m (31 ft 0 in)
T-O run at S/L, zero wind, hard runway: A	278 m (913 ft)
B	264 m (866 ft)
T-O run at 1,525 m (5,000 ft): A	374 m (1,228 ft)
T-O to 15 m (50 ft) at S/L, zero wind, hard runway: A	371 m (1,218 ft)
B	352 m (1,155 ft)
T-O to 15 m (50 ft) at 1,525 m (5,000 ft): A	499 m (1,638 ft)
Landing from 15 m (50 ft) at S/L, zero wind, hard runway: A, B	299 m (980 ft)
Landing from 15 m (50 ft) at 1,525 m (5,000 ft): B	361 m (1,186 ft)
Landing run at 1,525 m (5,000 ft): B	171 m (560 ft)
Landing run at S/L, zero wind, hard runway: A, B	140 m (460 ft)
Range at 75% power at 2,135 m (7,000 ft): A	622 nm (1,153 km; 717 miles)
B	555 nm (1,028 km; 639 miles)
Range at 67% power at 2,750 m (9,000 ft): A	713 nm (1,322 km; 822 miles)
B	577 nm (1,070 km; 665 miles)
Range at 59% power at 3,660 m (12,000 ft): A	755 nm (1,400 km; 870 miles)
B	613 nm (1,136 km; 706 miles)

PILATUS BRITTEN-NORMAN DEFENDER

The Defender is a variant of the civil Islander which can be adapted for a wide variety of government and military roles such as search and rescue, internal security, long-range patrol, forward air control, troop transport, logistic support and casualty evacuation. It is available with the same choices of wing configuration as the current civil versions and can be equipped with a wide range of sophisticated avionics, including nose mounted weather radar, providing the aircraft with a marine search capability. For an electronic warfare role, equipment can range from a simple radar warning receiver to a comprehensive passive electronics intelligence gathering system, ESM, and ECM coupled to the ESM to provide radar jamming or defensive chaff/IR flare dispensing. Other optional equipment includes four NATO standard underwing pylons for a variety of external stores, the inboard pair each carrying up to 317·5 kg (700 lb) and the outboard pair up to 204 kg (450 lb).

Typical underwing loads include twin 7·62 mm machine-guns in pod packs, 250 lb or 500 lb GP bombs, Matra rocket packs, SURA rocket clusters, wire guided missiles, 5 in reconnaissance flares, anti-personnel grenades, smoke bombs, marker bombs and 227 litre (50 Imp gallon; 60 US gallon) drop tanks.

Internal capacity for passengers, stretcher cases or cargo is the same as that of the civil Islander.

Britten-Norman Defenders/Islanders are in service with the Abu Dhabi Defence Force, Belgian Army, Belize Defence Force, Botswana Defence Force, British Army Parachute Association, Ghana Air Force, Guyana Defence Force, Jamaica Defence Force, Malagasy Air Force, Presidential Flight of the Mexican Air Force, Royal Hong Kong Auxiliary Air Force, Panamanian Air Force, Sultan of Oman's Air Force, Suriname Air Force, Mauritania Islamic Defence Force, the Seychelles Ministry of Agriculture and Fisheries, the Malawi Army Air Wing and the Rwanda Air Force. Those operated by the air forces of Iraq, Israel and Qatar are military Islanders, and are not equipped to carry offensive weapons; those which serve with the Cyprus National Guard, Indian Navy and Philippine Navy are Maritime Islanders.

The description given for the BN-2B Islander applies also to the Defender, except as follows:

POWER PLANT: Two 224 kW (300 hp) Avco Lycoming IO-540-K1B5 flat-six engines standard.

AVIONICS: Typical installation comprises 720 channel VHF nav/com transceivers with VOR/LOC and VOR/ILS, ADF, marker beacon receiver, transponder, HF com transceiver, weather radar and full autopilot. Optional equipment includes RWR, ESM and ECM.

PILATUS BRITTEN-NORMAN MARITIME DEFENDER

Generally similar to the Defender, the Maritime Defender differs by having a modified nose with a larger (Bendix RDR-1400) search radar, capable of detecting a 100 m^2 (1,076 sq ft) target in sea state 4-5 at a range of 36 nm (67 km; 41·5 miles). Scanning 60° on each side of the flight path, the radar provides a search width of 60 nm (111 km; 69 miles) at optimum altitude. The interior layout provides for pilot and co-pilot, a radar operator at a mid-cabin position on the starboard side, and two observers in the rear of the cabin, one aft of the radar operator, and one adjacent to a window on the port side.

Intended for coastal patrol, fishery and oil rig protection duties, as well as search and rescue support, the Maritime Defender is suitable for all-weather operation, by day or night, and carries the equipment necessary to fulfil such roles. This can include compass/HSI, horizon gyro (radar stabilisation), autopilot, ground mapping and weather radar, VLF/Omega, radio altimeter, dual VHF com, dual VHF nav/ILS, VHF marine band com, ADF, transponder, DME, encoding altimeter and SSB HF com. Specialised equipment includes a searchlight installation and hand held camera; the four underwing pylons can be used to carry a loudspeaker pod, flares, parachute dinghy packs and a variety of weapons.

The description of the Defender applies also to the Maritime Defender, except that overall length is increased to 11·07 m (36 ft 3¾ in).

PILATUS BRITTEN-NORMAN BN-2T TURBINE ISLANDER and DEFENDER

On 2 August 1980 the prototype (G-BPBN) was flown of the BN-2T Turbine Islander, powered by two Allison 250-B17C turboprop engines. These enable the BN-2T to use available low cost jet fuel instead of scarce and costly Avgas, and offer a particularly low operating noise level.

British CAA certification of the Turbine Islander was received at the end of May 1981; FAR Pt 23 US type approval was granted on 15 July 1982. Full icing clearance to FAR Pt 25 was granted on 23 July 1984. The first production aircraft was delivered during December 1981. The company announced in January 1983 the receipt of an order for four BN-2T Turbine Islanders for service with Transportes e Trabalhos Aereos, the domestic airline of Mozambique. Eighteen aircraft had been delivered by 15 February 1985. Deliveries include one to RAF Weston-on-the-Green, incorporating an in-flight sliding parachute door.

The Turbine Islander is available for the same range of applications as the piston engined Islander, including a military **Turbine Defender**.

The description of the BN-2B Islander applies also to the BN-2T, except as follows:

Type: Twin-turboprop feederline transport.

Fuselage: Generally as for BN-2B.

Power Plant: Two 298 kW (400 shp) Allison 250-B17C turboprop engines, flat rated at 238·5 kW (320 shp), and each driving a Hartzell three-blade constant-speed fully-feathering metal propeller. Fuel capacity 814 litres (179 Imp gallons). Pylon mounted underwing tanks, each of 227 litres (50 Imp gallons) capacity, are available optionally for special purposes. Total oil capacity 5·7 litres (1·25 Imp gallons).

Accommodation: Generally as for BN-2B. In ambulance role can accommodate, in addition to the pilot, a single stretcher, one medical attendant, and five seated occupants; or two stretchers, one attendant, and three passengers; or three stretchers, two attendants, and one passenger. Other possible layouts include photographic and geophysical survey; parachutist transport or trainer (with accommodation for up to eight parachutists and a dispatcher); and pest control or other agricultural spraying. Maritime Turbine Islander/Defender versions available for fishery protection, coastguard patrol, pollution survey, search and rescue, and similar applications. Offered as an option is an in-flight sliding parachute door.

Avionics and Equipment: Standard avionics and equipment generally similar to BN-2B. Other equipment, according to mission, includes fixed tail 'sting' or towed 'bird' magnetometer, spectrometer, or electromagnetic detection/analysis equipment (geophysical survey); one or two cameras, navigation sights, and appropriate avionics (photographic survey); 188·7 litre (41·5 Imp gallon) Micronair underwing spraypods complete with pump and rotary atomiser (pest control/agricultural spraying versions); radar, VLF/Omega nav system, radar altimeter, marine band and VHF transceivers, dinghies, survival equipment, and special crew accommodation (maritime versions).

Dimensions, external:
- As for BN-2B, except
- Length overall: standard nose — 10·87 m (35 ft 7¾ in)
- weather radar nose — 11·07 m (36 ft 3¾ in)
- Propeller diameter — 2·03 m (6 ft 8 in)

Weights:
- Weight empty, equipped (incl pilot) — 1,914 kg (4,220 lb)
- Payload with max fuel — 608 kg (1,340 lb)
- Max T-O weight — 3,175 kg (7,000 lb)
- Max landing weight — 3,084 kg (6,800 lb)
- Max zero-fuel weight — 2,994 kg (6,600 lb)

Performance (standard aircraft and Turbine Defender, at max T-O weight, ISA, except where indicated):
- Max cruising speed at 3,050 m (10,000 ft) — 170 knots (315 km/h; 196 mph)
- Max cruising speed at S/L — 154 knots (285 km/h; 177 mph)
- Cruising speed, 72% power at 3,050 m (10,000 ft) — 150 knots (278 km/h; 173 mph)
- Cruising speed, 72% power at 1,525 m (5,000 ft) — 142 knots (263 km/h; 164 mph)
- Stalling speed, power off:
  - flaps up — 52 knots (97 km/h; 60 mph) IAS
  - flaps down — 45 knots (84 km/h; 52 mph) IAS
- Max rate of climb at S/L — 320 m (1,050 ft)/min
- Rate of climb at S/L, one engine out — 66 m (215 ft)/min
- Service ceiling — over 7,620 m (25,000 ft)
- Absolute ceiling, one engine out — 3,080 m (10,100 ft)
- T-O run — 255 m (837 ft)
- T-O to 15 m (50 ft) — 381 m (1,250 ft)
- Landing from 15 m (50 ft) — 340 m (1,115 ft)
- Landing run — 228 m (747 ft)
- Range (IFR) with max fuel, reserves for 45 min hold plus 10% — 590 nm (1,093 km; 679 miles)
- Range (VFR) with max fuel, no reserves — 728 nm (1,349 km; 838 miles)

Pilatus Britten-Norman BN-2T Defender delivered to Central Air Force of Dubai

Pilatus Britten-Norman BN-2T Turbine Islander with Micronair underwing spray system

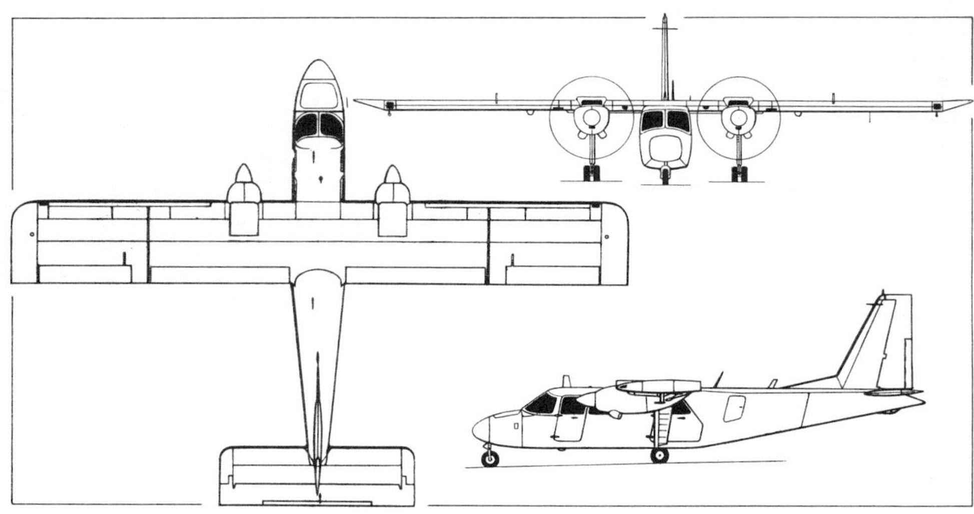
Pilatus Britten-Norman BN-2T Turbine Islander *(Pilot Press)*

PILATUS BRITTEN-NORMAN CASTOR ISLANDER

CASTOR (Corps Airborne STand-Off Radar) is the acronym for a British Ministry of Defence programme which is seeking to fulfil a requirement for an airborne surveillance radar to provide an overall picture of a battle area. It is intended to operate in conjunction with a battlefield reconnaissance RPV called Phoenix (see GEC Avionics entry in RPVs and Targets section), which would be sent in to obtain a closer look at any area or target shown by the CASTOR aircraft to be deserving of more detailed examination.

Two CASTOR aircraft have undergone development and evaluation, the one for the Royal Air Force (CASTOR C) involving a BAC/English Electric Canberra fitted with a modified Thorn EMI Searchwater radar. In parallel development for the Army is the CASTOR I, which is being used to evaluate a Ferranti radar. This was originally to have been helicopter mounted (the British Army is not authorised to operate aircraft of more than 4,536 kg; 10,000 lb gross weight), but in late 1983 it was decided to install it instead on a Turbine Islander testbed (G-DLRA, c/n 2140), which had been purchased by the Ministry of Defence for Army evaluation. This aircraft is now undergoing a three-year joint NATO demonstrator programme under the control of the MoD and US Department of Defense, prior to a production decision.

Pilatus Britten-Norman began work on the CASTOR Islander on 5 March 1984, and the converted aircraft made its first flight on 12 May, the undernose radome at that stage containing ballast only. As can be seen from the accompanying illustration, the radome and redesigned nose structure considerably alter the Islander nose shape, but this was considered the best location to provide optimum lookdown capability for the scanner. To provide ground clearance for the radar in this position, the nosewheel leg has been lengthened by 30·5 cm (12 in) and a Trislander landing gear fitted, and it is planned to re-certificate the CASTOR aircraft at a maximum take-off weight of 3,630 kg (8,000 lb), or 455 kg (1,000 lb) more than the standard Turbine Islander. Despite the ungainly appearance, flight tests have shown adequate performance and virtually unaltered handling characteristics.

The Ferranti Radar Systems CASTOR radar is a lightweight all-weather multi-mode I-band data acquisition system, designed to meet UK General and Air Staff Requirement 3956 and to provide primary intelligence information in the immediate battle zone and beyond, while operating well within friendly territory. It has full 360° scan, and offers a wide area of coverage against moving and fixed targets. The associated transmitter, receiver and processing equipment are housed in the fuselage of the Islander, which can be flown and operated by a two-man crew. Data acquired are processed and transmitted automatically, via an airborne link, to one or more ground stations.

The description of the standard BN-2T Turbine Islander applies also to the CASTOR Islander, except as follows:

TYPE: Twin-turboprop experimental battlefield surveillance aircraft.

FUSELAGE: Modified nose, as described in introductory paragraphs.

LANDING GEAR: Modified BN-2A Mk III Trislander main landing gear. Longer nosewheel leg to provide adequate ground clearance for radome. Main landing gear tyre size 6·50 × 8, pressure 2·4 bars (35 lb/sq in).

SYSTEMS AND AVIONICS: Ferranti multi-mode radar installed in nose, as described in introductory paragraphs. Other systems and avionics generally as described for Islander/Turbine Islander.

DIMENSIONS, EXTERNAL:

Wing span	14·94 m (49 ft 0 in)
Wing aspect ratio	7·4
Length overall	approx 11·89 m (39 ft 0 in)
Propeller diameter	2·03 m (6 ft 8 in)

WEIGHT:

Design max T-O weight	3,630 kg (8,000 lb)

PILATUS BRITTEN-NORMAN AEW, AEW/MR and ASW/ASV MARITIME DEFENDERS

To meet a need for a lightweight AEW system, Pilatus Britten-Norman asked Thorn EMI Electronics to collaborate in the installation of the latter company's Skymaster multi-role radar in the Turbine Islander airframe and so create the **AEW Defender**. As the accompanying illustration shows, the nose radome of the AEW Defender is deeper, more bulbous and less angular than that of the CASTOR aircraft, to house the Skymaster radar. In an AEW role this long-range radar, using pulse-Doppler processing, can acquire and track automatically large numbers of targets flying at all altitudes against a land or sea background. For maritime reconnaissance (MR) the operator selects a non-coherent, frequency agile mode of operation, optimising the radar for the detection of small surface targets in high sea states out to the radar horizon.

The Defender's STOL performance enables it to be operated from forward unprepared strips, and in the air the aircraft's low radar cross section aids survivability. The **AEW/MR Defender** is fitted with a second console to increase operational flexibility and target handling capacity. An air-to-air and air-to-ground data link, ESM, IFF and navigation equipments may be fully integrated with the radar display and control system.

Future developments will include a border surveillance role, with the radar optimised for the detection of moving targets at long range. A synthetic aperture mode would provide high resolution mapping video, which could be linked to provide ground commanders with an all-weather real-time display showing enemy dispositions and movements.

A further variant, the **ASW/ASV Maritime Defender**

Pilatus Britten-Norman BN-2T CASTOR Islander with Ferranti airborne surveillance radar in nose

Pilatus Britten-Norman ASV Maritime Defender with Sea Skua missiles and Seaspray radar

Pilatus Britten-Norman AEW Defender with nose-mounted Thorn EMI Skymaster radar *(Air Portraits)*

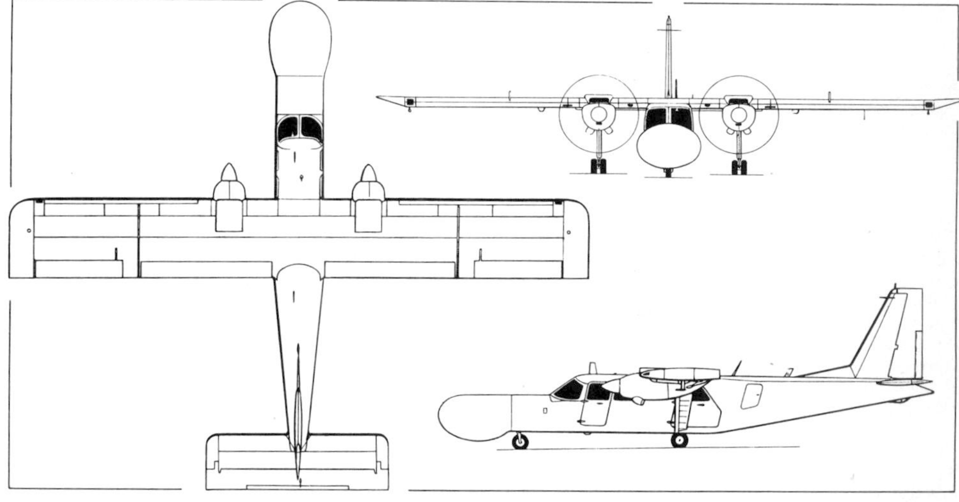

Pilatus Britten-Norman AEW Defender, a Turbine Islander development with Skymaster maritime surveillance radar *(Pilot Press)*

(G-OPBN, c/n 2034) made its first appearance at the Hanover Air Show in May 1984. This aircraft may be equipped to varying standards, to the customer's specification. Equipment can include a 360° radar, FLIR, sonobuoys, acoustic processing equipment, and a magnetic anomaly detector. Four underwing hardpoints can be used to carry two Sting Ray lightweight torpedoes, four Sea Skua missiles, depth charges, ECM and ESM pods, survival packs, rockets, gun pods or other stores. A crew of three is normal, with room for a trainee.

The UK Ministry of Defence has purchased Pilatus Britten-Norman's former Turbine Defender demonstrator (G-OPBN) for use by the Royal Navy's Directorate-General of Underwater Weapons torpedo trials unit. The design max T-O weight is 3,628 kg (8,000 lb).

SHORTS

SHORT BROTHERS PLC

PO Box 241, Airport Road, Belfast BT3 9DZ, Northern Ireland
Telephone: 0232 58444
Telex: 74688
Other Factories: Newtownards, Castlereagh, Belfast (3)
London Office: Berkeley Square House, Berkeley Square, London W1X 5LB
Chairman and Managing Director:
Sir Philip Foreman, CBE, DL
Deputy Chairman: Sir John Sparrow
Deputy Managing Director:
R. W. R. McNulty, BA, BComm, CA
Directors:
Sir Sidney Bacon, CB
A. R. Manvell, OBE
D. M. McCallum, CBE
A. F. C. Roberts, OBE
H. E. Trevan-Hawke
Secretary: R. Milnes
Executive Directors:
B. Carlin (Resources)
G. R. I. Heaton (Project Management)
A. R. Manvell, OBE (Engineering and Missile Systems)
R. W. R. McNulty (Deputy Managing)
A. F. C. Roberts, OBE (Sales and Marketing)
K. W. Tyson, OBE (Production)
M. I. Wild (Programme Management)
R. S. Williamson, BSc(Econ), FCA (Finance and Administration)
M. Wilson (Aircraft Engineering)
C. Raitt-Brown (Engineering—Missile Systems)
Senior Technical and Scientific Adviser:
Sir John Charnley, CB, MEng, FEng, FRAeS, FRIN

Short Brothers were first established, as aeronauts, in 1898, and in 1901 they began the manufacture of balloons at Hove, Sussex. Works were later established in London, first at premises off the Tottenham Court Road and, in 1906, at Battersea. In March 1909 Shorts opened the United Kingdom's first purpose built aircraft factory at Shellbeach, Isle of Sheppey. (The Short No. 1 had been ordered by F. T. McClean in January 1909.) The contract placed with Shorts by the Wright brothers in March 1909, for six Flyers, was the first aircraft series production contract to be placed in the UK. The main aircraft works moved to Eastchurch in 1909-10, and to Rochester in 1913-14.

In June 1936 Short Brothers, in collaboration with Harland & Wolff Ltd, formed a new company known as Short & Harland Ltd to build aircraft in Belfast, and in 1947 activities were concentrated in Belfast under the name Short Bros & Harland Ltd. The name Short Brothers Ltd was re-adopted on 1 June 1977.

The British government now owns, directly or indirectly, 100% of the issued shareholding. In 1985 the company received the Queen's Award to Industry for the 14th time. It had 7,000 employees in February 1986.

The company's current products include the 30-seat Shorts 330 and 36-seat Shorts 360 commuter airliners and the Skyvan turboprop STOL light transport, in use throughout the world for passenger, freight, survey, military and miscellaneous operations.

Important collaborative agreements between Shorts and EMBRAER of Brazil were announced in May 1984. As a first step, Shorts is marketing and manufacturing under licence a new version of the EMB-312 Tucano turboprop basic trainer, which was selected in March 1985 as the replacement for the Royal Air Force's Jet Provosts. The Tucano is being manufactured in the company's new Shorlac (Shorts Light Aircraft Company) facility, at the former Royal Naval Air Station Sydenham, Belfast.

Five Canberra PR. Mk 9 reconnaissance aircraft are undergoing major refurbishment for the UK Ministry of Defence, under a programme extending over several years and involving the design and embodiment of unspecified modifications.

Internationally, Shorts is collaborating as a risk sharing partner with Fokker BV in production of the Fokker F28 Fellowship transport and development of the new Fokker 100, with responsibility for the wings of both aircraft; and with Boeing in development and production of that company's projected Model 7J7 propfan airliner. Shorts also holds contracts to produce landing gear doors for the Boeing 747, inboard trailing-edge flap assemblies for the Boeing 757, and rudder assemblies for the Boeing 737-300.

Shorts is also quality approved subcontractor to many major US and UK aerospace companies. Conversely, production of the wings for the Shorts 330 is undertaken jointly by British Hovercraft and Fokker, and production of the 330 landing gear by Menasco in Canada.

During 1967, Shorts began the design and manufacture of pods for Rolls-Royce jet engines. It is currently podding RB211 engines for the Boeing 747 and 757, and has produced pods for more than 1,000 RB211s. Those produced for the 757 from mid-1983 utilise carbonfibre for the outer skin barrel of the nose cowl, offering a 25 per cent weight saving compared with aluminium alloy. The company also produces pods for the Avco Lycoming ALF 502 turbofans of the British Aerospace 146, and was responsible for the design and manufacture of the first flight test pod for the PW2037 turbofan engine chosen to power some Boeing 757s.

In September 1984 Shorts and Rohr Industries of the USA joined forces to offer a nacelle system for the advanced V2500 turbofan being developed by International Aero Engines AG for 150-seat jetliners; and in January 1985 it was announced that the Shorts/Rohr team had been selected to produce the pods for V2500 engines selected for the Airbus Industrie A320. The first of these pods is scheduled for delivery in September 1986.

In September 1986 Shorts and The de Havilland Aircraft of Canada Ltd signed an agreement under which the two companies are studying jointly the requirements for a new-generation transport aircraft for regional airline and corporate use.

In addition to its activities in the field of piloted aircraft, Shorts is engaged in missile development and production, production of supersonic target drones, and production to UK Ministry of Defence contract of the Skeet target drone (see RPVs and Targets section).

The company's Flying Services Division operates maintenance units and airfields for various civil and military organisations, and flies and maintains aircraft and target drones for the Ministry of Defence.

Short Brothers Air Services Limited, a subsidiary company, operates targets for the Ministry of Defence and provides a service for overseas countries.

SHORTS 330

The Shorts 330 (originally SD3-30) is a 30-passenger twin-turboprop transport aircraft designed primarily for commuter and regional air service operators whose current 18/20-seat aircraft require replacement by larger aircraft.

Design of the 330 is derived from that of the Skyvan STOL utility transport, and it retains many of the latter type's well proven characteristics, including the large cabin cross section. The same safe-life concept and design philosophy is employed in the structural components. The cabin, including the toilet and galley compartments, is 3·78 m (12 ft 5 in) longer than that of the Skyvan Srs 3.

Two prototypes and the first production aircraft were used for the development programme. The first prototype (G-BSBH) flew for the first time on 22 August 1974. Eight days earlier, the first order for the 330 was placed by Command Airways of Poughkeepsie, New York, for three aircraft. CAA certification to full Transport Category requirements was granted on 18 February 1976; this was followed on 18 June 1976 by US FAR Pt 25 and Pt 36 approval, and subsequently by approvals from the Canadian Dept of Transport, the West German LBA and the Australian Dept of Transport. The 330 conforms with CAB Pt 298 (US) and meets the noise requirements of FAR Pt 36 by a substantial margin. Initial deliveries began in June 1976; first to enter service, on 24 August 1976, was a Time Air 330.

By October 1986 orders for all variants of the 330 (including 330-UTT and Sherpa) totalled 123 aircraft, all of which had been delivered.

The first 26 Shorts 330s are powered by 862 kW (1,156 shp) PT6A-45A engines; the next 40 have PT6A-45B engines. Subsequent aircraft have more powerful PT6A-45R engines and a number of items as standard which were available only as options on the original version.

Three versions of the 330 are available:

330-200. Standard passenger version, as described in detail.

330-UTT. Military utility tactical transport version. Described separately.

Sherpa. Freighter version of 330-200, from which it differs mainly in having a ramp type full width rear loading door. In service with US Air Force under designation C-23A. Described separately.

In addition, the US Army has four ex-airline 330s, modified to military standards by Field Aircraft Services of Calgary, Alberta, for operation in the Kwajalein area of the Pacific.

The following description applies to the standard 330-200 passenger version:

Type: Twin-turboprop transport aircraft.

Wings: Braced high-wing monoplane, of all-metal safe-life construction, built in three sections. Wing sections NACA 63A series (modified). Thickness/chord ratio 18% at root, 14% on outer panels. Dihedral 3° on outer panels. Centre-section, integral with top of centre-fuselage, has taper on leading- and trailing-edges, and is a two-spar single-cell box structure of light alloy with conventional skin and stringers. The strut braced outer panels, which are pin jointed to the centre-section, are reinforced Skyvan constant chord units, built of light alloy, and each consists of a two-cell box having wing skins made up of a smooth outer skin bonded to a corrugated inner skin. All-metal single-slotted ailerons.

Shorts 330 regional airliner in the livery of Olympic Airways

Geared trim tabs in ailerons. All-metal single-slotted flaps, each in three sections. Primary control surfaces are rod actuated. Optional Goodrich pneumatic boot de-icing of leading-edges.

FUSELAGE: Light alloy structure, built in two main portions: nose (including flight deck, nosewheel bay and forward baggage compartment); and the centre (including main wing spar attachment frames and lower transverse beams which carry the main landing gear and associated fairings) and rear portion (including aft baggage compartment and tail unit attachment frames). The nose and rear underfuselage are of conventional skin/stringer design. The remainder is composed of a smooth outer skin bonded to a corrugated inner skin and stabilised by frames.

TAIL UNIT: Cantilever all-metal two-spar structure with twin fins and rudders, basically similar to that of the Skyvan. Fixed incidence tailplane, with reinforced leading-edge. Full span elevator, aerodynamically balanced by set-back hinges. Rudders each have an unshielded horn aerodynamic balance. Primary control surfaces are rod actuated. Geared trim tabs in elevator and starboard rudder (port rudder, trim only). Optional Goodrich pneumatic boot de-icing of leading-edges.

LANDING GEAR: Menasco retractable tricycle type, with single wheel on each unit. Main units carried on short sponsons, into which the wheels retract hydraulically. Oleo-pneumatic shock absorbers. Nosewheel is steerable. Mainwheel tyre size 34 × 10·75-16; nosewheel tyre size 9-6. Normal tyre pressures: main units 5·45 bars (79 lb/sq in), nose unit 3·79 bars (55 lb/sq in).

POWER PLANT: Two 893 kW (1,198 shp) Pratt & Whitney Canada PT6A-45R turboprop engines, each driving a Hartzell five-blade constant-speed fully-feathering metal low-speed propeller. Fuel tanks in wing centre-section/fuselage fairing; total usable capacity increased from original 2,182 litres (480 Imp gallons) to 2,546 litres (560 Imp gallons) in January 1985. Normal cross-feed provisions to allow for pump failure. Single-point pressure refuelling.

ACCOMMODATION: Crew of two on flight deck, plus cabin attendant. Dual controls standard. Standard seating for 30 passengers, in ten rows of three at 76 cm (30 in) pitch, with wide aisle. Seat rails fitted to facilitate changes in configuration. Galley, toilet and cabin attendant's seat at rear. Large overhead baggage lockers. Entire accommodation soundproofed and air-conditioned. Baggage compartments in nose (1·27 m³; 45 cu ft) and to rear of cabin (2·83 m³; 100 cu ft), each with external access and capable of holding a combined total of 500 kg (1,100 lb) of baggage. Passenger door is at rear of cabin on port side. Passenger version has two emergency exits on the starboard side, two on the port side (including passenger door) and one in the flight deck roof. Mixed traffic version has full access to these emergency exits. For mixed passenger/freight operation a partition divides the cabin into a rear passenger area (typically for 18 persons) and a forward cargo compartment, the latter being loaded through a large port side door, capable of admitting ATA 'D' type containers. In all-cargo configuration the cabin can accommodate up to seven 'D' type containers, with ample space around them for additional freight. Cabin floor is flat throughout its length, and is designed to support loadings of 181 kg (400 lb) per foot run at 610·3 kg/m² (125 lb/sq ft). Locally reinforced areas of higher strength are also provided. Seat rails can be used as cargo lashing points. Freight loading is facilitated by the low-level cabin floor.

SYSTEMS: Hamilton Standard air-conditioning system, using engine bleed air. Hydraulic system of 207 bars (3,000 lb/sq in), supplied by engine driven pumps, operates landing gear, nosewheel steering, flaps and brakes (at lower pressure) and includes emergency accumulators. Air/oil reservoir pressurised to 1·72 bars (25 lb/sq in) at 20°C. Main electrical system, for general services, is 28V DC and is of the split busbar type with cross-coupling for essential services. Lucas 28V 250A DC starter/generator for engine starting and aircraft services, with separate 1·5kW 200V AC output for windscreen anti-icing and demisting. Special AC sources of 115V and 26V available at 400Hz for certain instruments, avionics and fuel booster pumps. Anti-icing standard for engine intake ducts, inlet lips and propellers. Optional de-icing of wing and tailplane leading-edges.

AVIONICS AND EQUIPMENT: Passenger safety equipment standard. Wide range of radio and navigation equipment available to customer's requirements. Typical standard avionics comprise duplicated VHF communications and navigation systems, two glideslope/marker beacon receivers, two ILS repeaters, two radio magnetic indicators, one ADF, one transponder, one DME, PA system and weather radar. Flight data recorder and voice recorder available as standard options.

DIMENSIONS, EXTERNAL:

Wing span	22·76 m (74 ft 8 in)
Wing chord (standard mean)	1·85 m (6 ft 0·7 in)
Length overall	17·69 m (58 ft 0½ in)
Height overall	4·95 m (16 ft 3 in)
Tailplane span	5·68 m (18 ft 7¾ in)
Wheel track	4·24 m (13 ft 11 in)

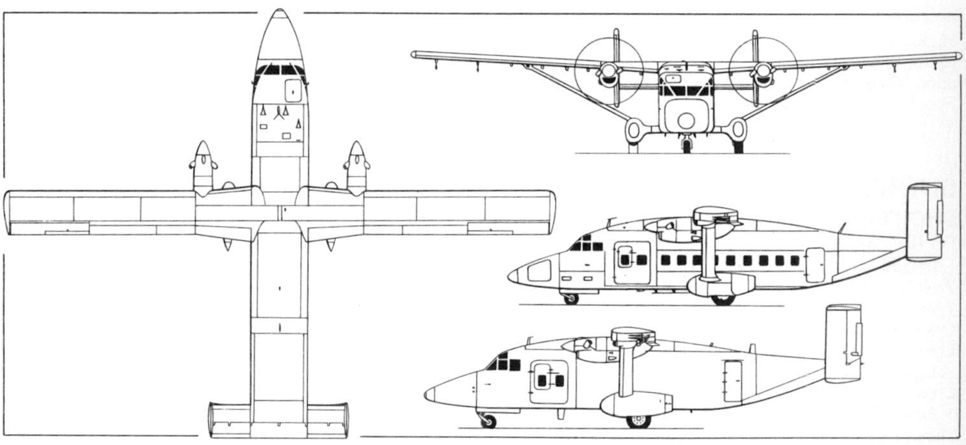

Shorts 330 twin-turboprop commuter and utility transport, with added side view (bottom) of Sherpa *(Pilot Press)*

Wheelbase	6·15 m (20 ft 2 in)
Propeller diameter	2·82 m (9 ft 3 in)
Propeller ground clearance	1·83 m (6 ft 0 in)
Cabin floor: Height above ground	0·94 m (3 ft 1 in)
Passenger door (port, rear):	
Height	1·57 m (5 ft 2 in)
Width	0·71 m (2 ft 4 in)
Height to sill	0·94 m (3 ft 1 in)
Cargo door (port, forward):	
Height	1·68 m (5 ft 6 in)
Width	1·42 m (4 ft 8 in)
Height to sill	0·94 m (3 ft 1 in)

DIMENSIONS, INTERNAL:

Cabin: Max length, incl toilet	9·47 m (31 ft 1 in)
Max width	1·93 m (6 ft 4 in)
Max height	1·93 m (6 ft 4 in)
Floor area	18·77 m² (202 sq ft)
Volume (all-cargo)	34·83 m³ (1,230 cu ft)
Baggage compartments volume (total usable)	4·11 m³ (145 cu ft)
Cabin overhead lockers (total)	1·13 m³ (40 cu ft)

AREAS:

Wings, gross	42·1 m² (453·0 sq ft)
Ailerons (total, aft of hinges)	2·55 m² (27·5 sq ft)
Trailing-edge flaps (total)	7·74 m² (83·3 sq ft)
Fins (total)	8·65 m² (93·1 sq ft)
Rudders (total, aft of hinges)	2·24 m² (24·1 sq ft)
Tailplane	7·77 m² (83·6 sq ft)
Elevator (total, aft of hinges)	2·55 m² (27·4 sq ft)

WEIGHTS AND LOADINGS:

Weight empty, equipped (incl crew of three):	
330-200 for 30 passengers	6,680 kg (14,727 lb)
Fuel	2,032 kg (4,480 lb)
Max payload for normal max T-O weight:	
30 passengers and baggage	2,653 kg (5,850 lb)
cargo	3,400 kg (7,500 lb)
Max T-O weight	10,387 kg (22,900 lb)
Max landing weight	10,251 kg (22,600 lb)
Max wing loading	246·8 kg/m² (50·55 lb/sq ft)
Max power loading	5·81 kg/kW (9·56 lb/shp)

PERFORMANCE (at max T-O weight, ISA at S/L, except where indicated):

Max cruising speed at 3,050 m (10,000 ft), AUW of 9,525 kg (21,000 lb) — 190 knots (352 km/h; 218 mph)

Econ cruising speed at 3,050 m (10,000 ft), AUW of 9,525 kg (21,000 lb) — 160 knots (296 km/h; 184 mph)

Stalling speed, flaps and landing gear up — 90 knots (167 km/h; 104 mph) EAS

Stalling speed at max landing weight, flaps and landing gear down — 73 knots (136 km/h; 85 mph) EAS

Max rate of climb at S/L — 360 m (1,180 ft)/min

Service ceiling, one engine out, AUW of 9,072 kg (20,000 lb) — 3,500 m (11,500 ft)

T-O distance (FAR Pt 25 and BCAR Gp A):

ISA	1,042 m (3,420 ft)
ISA + 15°C	1,295 m (4,250 ft)

Landing distance, AUW of 9,072 kg (20,000 lb):

BCAR	1,143 m (3,750 ft)
FAR	1,030 m (3,380 ft)
Runway LCN at max T-O weight	10·7

Range with max passenger payload, cruising at 3,050 m (10,000 ft), no reserves — 473 nm (876 km; 544 miles)

Range with max fuel, cruising at 3,050 m (10,000 ft), no reserves:

passenger version, 1,966 kg (4,335 lb) payload — 915 nm (1,695 km; 1,053 miles)

cargo version, 2,306 kg (5,085 lb) payload — 758 nm (1,403 km; 872 miles)

OPERATIONAL NOISE LEVELS (FAR Pt 36):

Take-off	88·9 EPNdB
Sideline	84·7 EPNdB
Approach	92·9 EPNdB

SHORTS 330-UTT

Shorts stated on 7 September 1982 that production had begun of this military utility tactical transport version of the Model 330. The Royal Thai Army took delivery of two (one in June 1984 and one in April 1985) and the Royal Thai Police took two (in October 1984 and March 1985).

The basic airframe and power plant remain unchanged, but max payload is increased to 3,630 kg (8,000 lb) and max operational necessity T-O weight to 11,158 kg (24,600 lb). Other changes include a strengthened cabin floor and reconfigured avionics panel. Cabin accommodation can be provided for up to 33 troops, 30 paratroops plus a jumpmaster (exit via inward opening rear door each side), or 15 stretchers plus four seated personnel.

PERFORMANCE (provisional, ISA conditions):

Cruising speed at 3,050 m (10,000 ft), AUW of 9,979 kg (22,000 lb):

high-speed cruise, max continuous power — 201 knots (372 km/h; 231 mph)

long-range cruise — 160 knots (296 km/h; 184 mph)

Max rate of climb at S/L at normal max T-O weight of 10,387 kg (22,900 lb):

two engines	381 m (1,250 ft)/min
one engine	89 m (290 ft)/min
STOL T-O run at S/L, 15° flap	415 m (1,360 ft)
STOL T-O to 15 m (50 ft), 15° flap	644 m (2,110 ft)

STOL landing from 15 m (50 ft) at AUW of 9,525 kg (21,000 lb), flaps down, propeller reversal — 488 m (1,600 ft)

STOL landing run, conditions as above — 235 m (770 ft)

Range with 30 fully armed assault troops — 600 nm (1,112 km; 691 miles)

SHORTS SHERPA

US Air Force designation: C-23A

The Sherpa is a freighter version of the Shorts 330-200. It retains many features of the all-passenger version, to allow utility passenger transport operations to be undertaken. The forward freight door and wide-body hold of the 330-200 are unchanged, but the Sherpa's design incorporates a full width rear cargo door, which permits through loading.

The hydraulically actuated rear ramp/door, which is operated from inside or outside the aircraft, can be lowered to a variety of positions to simplify loading from a wide range of ground equipment. The forward baggage compartment of the Shorts 330-200 is retained and this, being lockable, is suitable for high value cargo. Standard airline containers can be accommodated in the main cabin, up to the size of the LD3, making the Sherpa particularly suited for the operation of short-haul cargo feeder services. Typical loads can include two LD3 containers and nine passengers; four LD3 or seven CO8 containers; two half-ton vehicles in the class of the Land-Rover, using load spreaders; and a wide range of bulky cargo. The cabin is suitable for the installation of specialist role equipment and, for example, lends itself readily to onboard sorting of letters and small packages. Roller conveyor systems, including pallet locks which pick up on the aircraft's standard seat rails, are available optionally (standard on the C-23A).

The prototype of the Sherpa was flown for the first time on 23 December 1982. In March 1984 the US Air Force ordered 18 Sherpas for use by the 10th Military Airlift Squadron of Military Airlift Command in the EDSA (European Distribution System Aircraft) role. The fleet is based at Zweibrücken in West Germany, for the transport of high priority spares between more than 20 peacetime US Air Force bases in Europe. The initial contract included ten years' logistic support and servicing. In addition, the US Air Force took options on a further 48 aircraft.

The first Sherpa, designated C-23A in the EDSA role, made its first flight on 6 August 1984; with the second aircraft, it was delivered in November 1984. The remaining 16 C-23As were delivered by 6 December 1985. A civil Sherpa has been delivered to Venezuela.

TYPE: Twin-turboprop freight/utility aircraft.

AIRFRAME AND POWER PLANT: As described for Shorts 330-200 except for constant width rear fuselage with hydraulically actuated rear loading ramp/door.

ACCOMMODATION: Crew of two on flight deck, plus flight mechanic. Dual controls standard. Flight deck air-conditioned. Main cabin air-conditioning optional. Baggage

Shorts C-23A Sherpa, with rear ramp/door, for the US Air Force

compartment in nose (1·27 m³; 45 cu ft) with external access. Passenger door at rear of cabin on port side. Cargo door at front of cabin on port side. Hydraulically actuated full width rear loading ramp/door. In an all-cargo configuration the cabin can accommodate up to seven CO8 or four LD3 containers. Cabin floor is flat throughout its length and is designed to support 181 kg (400 lb) per foot run at 610·3 kg/m² (125 lb/sq ft). The locally reinforced centre cabin area is able to carry 272 kg (600 lb) per foot run at 732·4 kg/m² (150 lb/sq ft). A further 272 kg (600 lb) total load can be stowed on the ramp/door. Seat rails can be used as cargo lashing points. Freight loading is facilitated by the low-level cabin floor.

AVIONICS AND EQUIPMENT: Avionics on the C-23As for the US Air Force include single UHF and HF radios, dual VHF-AM/FM, two flight directors, dual VOR/ILS, a Litton LTN-96 ring laser gyro inertial navigation system, Tacan, dual ADF, flight data recorder, cockpit voice recorder, IFF transponder, GPWS, radar altimeter, and a Collins RNS-300 colour weather radar with terrain mapping.

DIMENSIONS, EXTERNAL: As for 330-200 plus:
- Rear loading door: Height — 1·98 m (6 ft 6 in)
  - Width — 1·98 m (6 ft 6 in)

DIMENSIONS, INTERNAL:
- Cabin: Max length — 9·09 m (29 ft 10 in)
  - Max width — 1·98 m (6 ft 6 in)
  - Max height — 1·98 m (6 ft 6 in)
  - Volume (all-cargo) — 35·68 m³ (1,260 cu ft)
- Baggage compartment (nose) — 1·27 m³ (45 cu ft)

WEIGHTS AND LOADINGS: As for 330-200, except:
- Max payload — 3,175 kg (7,000 lb)

PERFORMANCE (at max T-O weight, ISA, except where indicated):
- Max cruising speed at AUW of 9,525 kg (21,000 lb at 3,050 m (10,000 ft) — 190 knots (352 km/h; 218 mph)
- Econ cruising speed at AUW of 9,525 kg (21,000 lb) at 3,050 m (10,000 ft) — 157 knots (291 km/h; 181 mph)
- Max rate of climb at S/L — 360 m (1,180 ft)/min
- Service ceiling, one engine out, AUW of 9,072 kg (20,000 lb) — 3,930 m (12,900 ft)
- T-O distance (FAR Pt 25 and BCAR Gp A):
  - ISA — 1,042 m (3,420 ft)
  - ISA + 15°C — 1,295 m (4,250 ft)
- Landing distance at max landing weight:
  - BCAR: normal field — 1,225 m (4,020 ft)
  - short field — 960 m (3,150 ft)
  - FAR — 1,113 m (3,650 ft)
- Range with max fuel, reserves for 45 min hold and 43 nm (80 km; 50 mile) diversion:
  - with 3,175 kg (7,000 lb) payload — 195 nm (362 km; 225 miles)
  - with 2,268 kg (5,000 lb) payload — 669 nm (1,239 km; 770 miles)

SHORTS 360

On 10 July 1980, Shorts released first details of this 'stretched' development of the Model 330, seating six more passengers in a lengthened fuselage and having strengthened outer wing panels and bracing struts, and a new tail unit, as well as more powerful and more fuel-efficient engines.

Designed specifically for short haul airline operation, over typical commuter average stage lengths of about 120 nm (222 km; 138 miles), the Shorts 360 retains the basic configuration of the Model 330, the major external differences being the lengthened fuselage (a 0·91 m; 3 ft plug is inserted forward of the wings) and the introduction of a sweptback single fin and rudder instead of the latter's twin assembly. Power plant is a higher rated version of the proven PT6A turboprop engine.

Pressurisation was considered unnecessary in view of the short stage lengths over which the aircraft would operate, and this enables the Shorts 360 to retain the same 'walk-about' headroom, square section wide-bodied interior, seating comfort, air-conditioning and other amenities as its predecessor. The new rear fuselage/tail configuration is designed to reduce drag, improve fuel efficiency, and provide even greater baggage capacity. Considerable emphasis is placed on the 360's ability to provide more than 0·20 m³ (7 cu ft) of baggage space for each of its 36 passengers, a feature which Shorts claim is unique among today's commuter aircraft. The 360 won a UK Design Council award in the Spring of 1984.

The prototype (G-ROOM) made its first flight on 1 June 1981, some six months ahead of schedule, powered initially by PT6A-45 engines. The PT6A-65R power plant which had been selected for production aircraft was installed subsequently, and CAA certification was obtained on 3 September 1982, nearly one month ahead of schedule. FAA certification, to FAR Pt 25 and Pt 36, followed in early November 1982. The first production 360 made its first flight on 19 August 1982, and entered commercial service with Suburban Airlines of Pennsylvania on 1 December 1982.

An enhanced variant, known as the **Shorts 360 Advanced**, with more powerful PT6A-65AR engines, was introduced in November 1985. First customers for this were Thai Airways Company and Simmons Airlines of the USA.

By October 1986 orders and options for the Shorts 360 totalled 140, of which 100 had been delivered.

TYPE: Twin-turboprop commuter transport.

WINGS: Generally as for Shorts 330-200.

FUSELAGE: As Shorts 330-200, but lengthened by insertion of 0·91 m (3 ft) plug forward of wings. Rear fuselage modified to cater for redesigned tail unit.

TAIL UNIT: Cantilever all-metal two-spar structure, with single sweptback fin and rudder and constant chord non-swept tailplane. Trim tabs in each elevator.

LANDING GEAR: Similar to Shorts 330-200, but of Dowty design and with higher tyre pressures to cater for increased operating weights (7·72 bars; 112 lb/sq in on main units, 4·21 bars; 61 lb/sq in on nose unit). Maxaret anti-skid units standard.

POWER PLANT: Two 1,062 kW (1,424 shp) Pratt & Whitney Canada PT6A-65AR turboprop engines, each driving a Hartzell advanced technology five-blade constant-speed fully-feathering propeller with spinner. Fuel capacity 2,182 litres (480 Imp gallons).

ACCOMMODATION: Crew of two on flight deck, plus cabin attendant. Dual controls standard. Main cabin accommodation similar to Shorts 330-200, but seating a total of 36 passengers in 12 rows of three. Large overhead baggage lockers. Baggage compartments in nose and to rear of cabin, each with external access, giving equivalent of almost 0·17 m³ (6 cu ft) of baggage space per passenger (0·20 m³; 7·2 cu ft per passenger if locker space is included).

SYSTEMS: Generally as for Shorts 330-200 except for electrical system, which has Lear Siegler 28V 300A DC starter/generators and three 400VA single-phase static inverters for AC power. Full de-icing and anti-icing systems standard.

AVIONICS: Typical standard avionics comprise duplicated VHF com and nav systems (VOR/ILS and marker beacon receiver), two ATC transponders, one DME, one ADF, two gyromagnetic compass systems, two RMI, two ILS repeater indicators, dual flight director, HSI, weather radar, PA and stereo music systems, flight data recorder, voice recorder and GPWS. Options include Collins APS-65 digital AFCS.

DIMENSIONS, EXTERNAL: As for Shorts 330-200 except:
- Wing span — 22·81 m (74 ft 10 in)
- Length overall — 21·59 m (70 ft 10 in)
- Height overall — 7·21 m (23 ft 8 in)
- Tailplane span — 7·19 m (23 ft 7 in)
- Wheelbase — 7·06 m (23 ft 2 in)
- Propeller diameter — 2·82 m (9 ft 3 in)

DIMENSIONS, INTERNAL:
- Cabin: Length — 11·02 m (36 ft 2 in)
  - Max width — 1·93 m (6 ft 4 in)
  - Max height — 1·93 m (6 ft 4 in)
- Passenger compartment volume — 41·06 m³ (1,450 cu ft)
- Baggage compartment volume:
  - forward — 1·27 m³ (45 cu ft)

Shorts 360 Advanced commuter transport supplied to Thai Airways Company

rear 4·81 m^3 (170 cu ft)
lockers 1·47 m^3 (52 cu ft)

AREAS: As for Shorts 330-200 except:
- Vertical tail surfaces (total) 8·49 m^2 (91·4 sq ft)
- Horizontal tail surfaces (total) 9·85 m^2 (106·0 sq ft)

WEIGHTS:
- Operating weight empty:
  - 36 passengers 7,666 kg (16,900 lb)
  - cargo 7,183 kg (15,835 lb)
- Max payload:
  - 36 passengers and baggage 3,184 kg (7,020 lb)
  - cargo 3,765 kg (8,300 lb)
- Max fuel load 1,741 kg (3,840 lb)
- Max T-O weight 11,999 kg (26,453 lb)
- Max ramp weight 12,044 kg (26,553 lb)
- Max landing weight 11,839 kg (26,100 lb)

PERFORMANCE (at max T-O weight except where indicated):
- Cruising speed at max recommended cruise power 213 knots (394 km/h; 245 mph)
- T-O distance at S/L: ISA 1,280 m (4,200 ft)
  - ISA + 15°C 1,395 m (4,575 ft)
- Landing distance (BCAR) at S/L at max landing weight, ISA 1,262 m (4,140 ft)
- Runway LCN 14·1
- Range at 3,050 m (10,000 ft), cruising at 213 knots (394 km/h; 245 mph), no reserves:
  - with max passenger payload 530 nm (982 km; 610 miles)
  - with max fuel 900 nm (1,667 km; 1,036 miles)

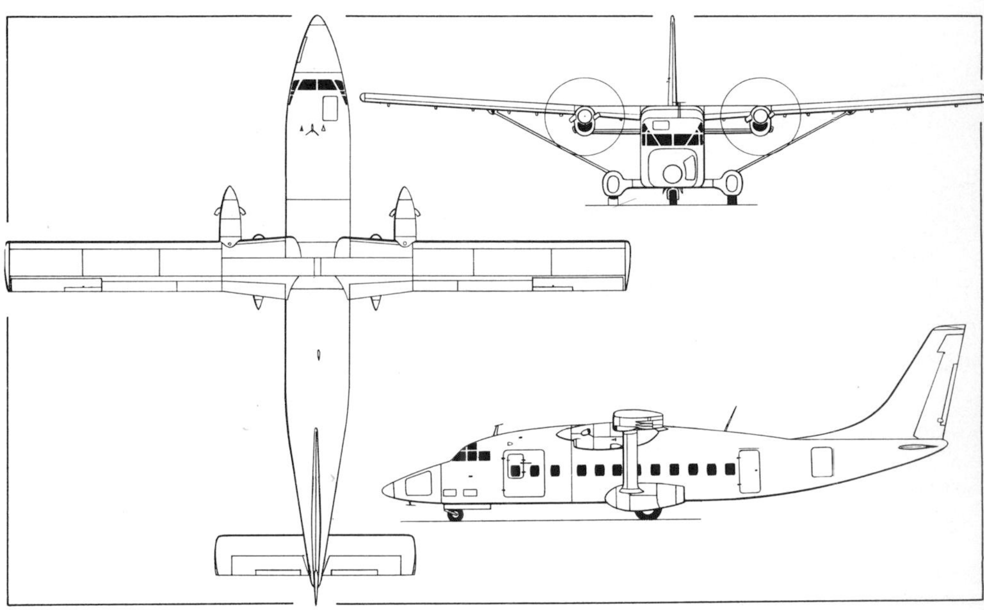

Shorts 360 commuter transport (two P&WC PT6A-65R turboprop engines) *(Pilot Press)*

SHORTS SC.7 SKYVAN Srs 3 and 3M

Design of the SC.7 Skyvan was started as a private venture in 1959, and construction of the first prototype began in 1960. This aircraft (G-ASCN) flew for the first time on 17 January 1963, with two 290 kW (390 hp) Continental GTSIO-520 piston engines, and completed its flight trials by mid-1963. It was then re-engined with 388 kW (520 shp) Astazou II turboprops and first flew in its new form on 2 October 1963. The change to Garrett TPE331 turboprops was made on the Skyvan Srs 3 in 1967.

Details of the Srs 1/1A/2/3A/Skyliner models appeared in the 1980-81 and previous editions of *Jane's*. The current versions are as follows:

Skyvan Srs 3. Current civil version, which superseded Srs 2 in 1968. First Srs 3 to fly was the second development aircraft, G-ASZI, which had been equipped originally with Astazous. The first flight with Garrett engines was made on 15 December 1967, and a second aircraft (G-ASZJ) re-engined with TPE331s flew on 20 January 1968. Recent customers include Air Group International (Colombia), the government of the Maldives, the government of Ciskei, and Aero Services Barbados (1982) Ltd.

Skyvan Srs 3M. Military version of Srs 3, modified internally to accept optional equipment for typical military missions. Prototype (G-AXPT) flew for the first time in early 1970. Suitable for paratrooping and supply dropping, assault landing, troop transport, casualty evacuation, staff transport, and vehicle or ordnance transport.

Skyvan Srs 3M-200. Following an engineering product review programme in early 1982, the Skyvan has been cleared for operations in non-civil applications at a max T-O weight of 6,804 kg (15,000 lb).

Thorn EMI has proposed an airborne early warning version with a large nose radome for its Skymaster I-band radar. Two additional tail fins, aligned with the sides of the fuselage, would maintain directional stability. Two or three radar operators could be housed in the cabin. Radar horizon would be about 100 nm (185 km; 115 miles) from the Skyvan's cruising height, and patrol time about 2 hours.

Orders for all versions of the Skyvan totalled 150 by October 1986, all of which had been delivered. In February 1970 the Skyvan became the first aircraft to be certificated under the British Air Registration Board's new Civil Airworthiness Requirements for STOL operations.

Fifty-eight Skyvans have been delivered to armed services, including the Argentinian Naval Prefectura (5), Austrian Air Force (2), Botswana Defence Force (2), Ecuador Army Air Force (1), Ghana Air Force (6), Guyana Defence Force (2), Indonesian Air Force (3), Lesotho Police (2), Malawi Police (1), Mauritanian Air Force (2), Royal Nepalese Army (3), No. 2 Squadron of the Sultan of Oman's Air Force (16), Panama National Guard (1), Singapore Air Force (6), Royal Thai Police (3), Yemen Arab Republic Air Force (2) and the Amiri Guard of Sharjah (1). Three of the Singapore aircraft are equipped for search and rescue duties. Those of the Indonesian Air Force are equipped to civil standard and operate social services on behalf of the Ministry of the Interior.

The following description applies to the standard current civil Series 3 and military Series 3M:

TYPE: Civil or military STOL utility light transport.

WINGS: Braced high-wing monoplane. Wing section NACA 63A series (modified). Thickness/chord ratio 14%. Dihedral 2° 2′. Incidence 2° 30′. Light alloy structure consisting of a two-cell box with wing skins made up of a uniform outer sheet bonded to a corrugated inner sheet. All-metal single-slotted ailerons. Geared tabs in port and starboard ailerons, with manual trim in starboard aileron. All-metal single-slotted flaps. Provision for sintered leading-edge de-icing system.

FUSELAGE: Light alloy structure. Nose and crew cabin section is of conventional skin/stringer design. Elsewhere, the fuselage structure consists of double skin panels (flat outer sheets bonded to inner corrugated sheets), stabilised by frames.

TAIL UNIT: Cantilever all-metal two-spar structure, with twin fins and rudders. Fixed incidence tailplane. Geared trim tabs in outer elevators and rudders. Provision for sintered leading-edge de-icing system.

LANDING GEAR: Non-retractable tricycle type. Single wheel on each unit. Steerable nosewheel. Main units carried on short sponsons. Electro-Hydraulics oleo-pneumatic shock absorbers. Mainwheel tyres size 11·00-12, nosewheel tyre size 7·50-10. Tyre pressure (all units, standard) 2·76 bars (40 lb/sq in). Hydraulically operated disc brakes, with differential braking for steering. Low pressure tyres (2·07 bars; 30 lb/sq in) available optionally.

POWER PLANT: Two 533 kW (715 shp) Garrett TPE331-2-201A turboprop engines, each driving a Hartzell HC-B3TN-5/T10282H three-blade variable-pitch propeller. Fuel in four tanks in pairs on top of fuselage between wing roots, each pair consisting of one tank of 182 litres (40 Imp gallons) capacity and one of 484 litres (106·5 Imp gallons) capacity. Total fuel capacity of 1,332 litres (293 Imp gallons). Provision for increase in total fuel capacity to 1,773 litres (390 Imp gallons) by installing four specially designed tanks in spaces between fuselage frames on each side, beneath main fuel tank. Oil capacity 7·73 litres (1·7 Imp gallons).

ACCOMMODATION: Crew of one, with provision for two. Accommodation (Srs 3) for up to 19 passengers, or 12 stretcher patients and attendants, or 2,085 kg (4,600 lb) of freight, vehicles or agricultural equipment. Srs 3M can accommodate 22 equipped troops; 16 paratroops and a dispatcher; 12 stretcher cases and two medical attendants; or 2,358 kg (5,200 lb) of freight. It carries its own lightweight vehicle loading ramps and has a one-piece door which leaves the fuselage threshold entirely clear of appendages. Executive version provides luxury accommodation and equipment for nine passengers. Full-width rear loading door, and forward door on each side of crew compartment. Rear door can be opened in flight to permit the parachuting of loads up to 1·37 m (4 ft 6 in) in height. Cockpit and cabin heated by engine bleed air mixed with fresh air from intake in nose. Cabin unpressurised. Some aircraft fitted with Rolamat cargo loading equipment.

SYSTEMS: Hydraulic system, pressure 172 bars (2,500 lb/sq in), operates flaps, wheel brakes and nosewheel steering. Bootstrap hydraulic reservoir. No pneumatic system. Electrical system utilises two busbars, operating independently, each connected to a 28V 125A DC starter/generator, a battery and a 115V 400Hz static inverter. General services are 28V DC; some radio and instruments 115V AC.

AVIONICS AND EQUIPMENT: Radio optional. Typical installation for operations in Europe and USA consists of duplicated VHF, duplicated VOR/ILS, marker beacon receiver and ADF. Provision for HF, DME, transponder, Bendix M4D autopilot and weather radar. Blind-flying instrumentation standard. Aircraft of Sultan of Oman's Air Force to be fitted in 1984 with Racal ASR 360 airborne surveillance radar, for use in offshore patrol, SAR and environmental protection roles.

EQUIPMENT (Srs 3M): Port side blister window for an air dispatcher; two anchor cables for parachute static lines; a guard rail beneath the tail to prevent control surface fouling by the static lines; inward facing paratroop seats with safety nets; parachute signal light; mounts for NATO stretchers; and roller conveyors for easy loading and paradropping of pallet mounted supplies.

DIMENSIONS, EXTERNAL:
- Wing span 19·79 m (64 ft 11 in)
- Wing chord (constant) 1·78 m (5 ft 10 in)
- Wing aspect ratio 11
- Length overall: without radome 12·21 m (40 ft 1 in)
  - with radome 12·60 m (41 ft 4 in)
- Height overall 4·60 m (15 ft 1 in)
- Tailplane span 5·28 m (17 ft 4 in)
- Wheel track 4·21 m (13 ft 10 in)
- Wheelbase 4·52 m (14 ft 10 in)
- Propeller diameter 2·59 m (8 ft 6 in)

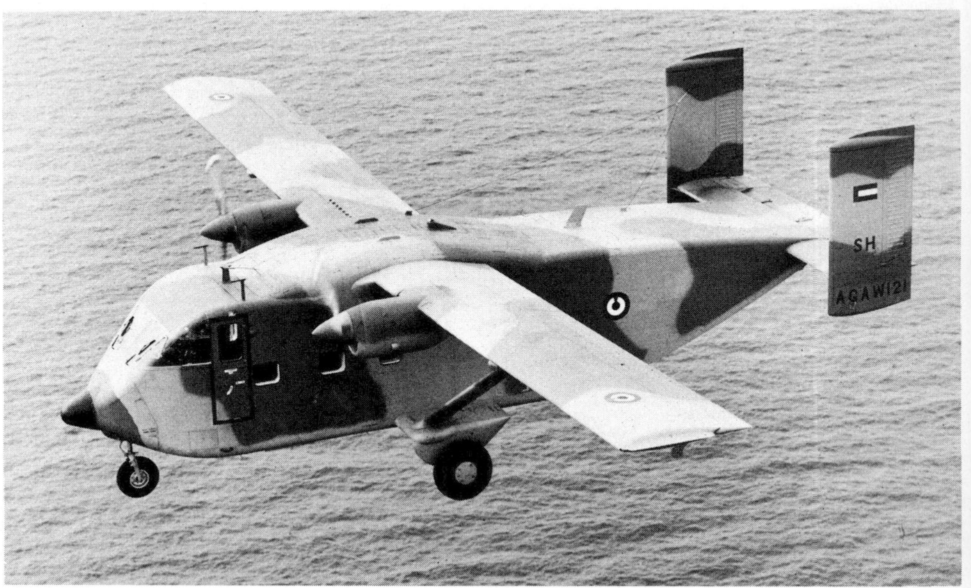

Shorts Skyvan operated by the Amiri Guard of Sharjah

Propeller ground clearance 1·52 m (5 ft 0 in)
Crew and passenger doors (fwd, port and stbd):
 Height 1·52 m (5 ft 0 in)
 Width 0·51 m (1 ft 8 in)
 Height to sill 1·14 m (3 ft 9 in)
Rear loading door: Height 1·78 m (5 ft 10 in)
 Width 1·98 m (6 ft 6 in)
 Height to sill 0·74 m (2 ft 5 in)

DIMENSIONS, INTERNAL:
Cabin, excl flight deck: Length 5·67 m (18 ft 7 in)
 Max width 1·98 m (6 ft 6 in)
 Max height 1·98 m (6 ft 6 in)
 Floor area 11·15 m² (120 sq ft)
 Volume 22·09 m³ (780 cu ft)

AREAS:
Wings, gross 35·12 m² (378 sq ft)
Ailerons (total) 3·00 m² (32·3 sq ft)
Trailing-edge flaps (total) 5·86 m² (63·1 sq ft)
Fins 7·62 m² (82·0 sq ft)
Rudders, incl tabs 2·41 m² (25·9 sq ft)
Tailplane 7·53 m² (81·0 sq ft)
Elevators, incl tabs 3·62 m² (39·0 sq ft)

WEIGHTS AND LOADINGS (with 1,332 litres; 293 Imp gallons of fuel):
Basic operating weight: 3 3,331 kg (7,344 lb)
 3M 3,356 kg (7,400 lb)
 3M-200, equipped 3,768 kg (8,307 lb)
Typical operating weight as freighter:
 3 3,447 kg (7,600 lb)
 3M 3,456 kg (7,620 lb)
Typical operating weight:
 3, with passengers 3,674 kg (8,100 lb)
 3M, with troops 3,778 kg (8,330 lb)
 3M-200 paratroop transport 3,943 kg (8,692 lb)
Max payload for normal T-O weight:
 3 2,086 kg (4,600 lb)
 3M, 3M-200 2,358 kg (5,200 lb)
Max payload for overload T-O weight:
 3M 2,721 kg (6,000 lb)
Max fuel weights: standard tanks 1,052 kg (2,320 lb)
 with additional tanks 1,415 kg (3,120 lb)
Max T-O weight: 3, normal 5,670 kg (12,500 lb)
 3M, normal 6,214 kg (13,700 lb)
 3M, overload 6,577 kg (14,500 lb)
 3M-200 6,804 kg (15,000 lb)
Max landing weight: 3 5,670 kg (12,500 lb)
 3M 6,123 kg (13,500 lb)
 3M-200 6,577 kg (14,500 lb)
Max wing loading: 3 163·6 kg/m² (33·5 lb/sq ft)
 3M 179·1 kg/m² (36·7 lb/sq ft)
 3M-200 196·3 kg/m² (40·2 lb/sq ft)
Max power loading: 3 5·32 kg/kW (8·74 lb/shp)
 3M 6·17 kg/kW (9·58 lb/shp)
 3M-200 6·38 kg/kW (10·49 lb/shp)

PERFORMANCE (at max T-O weight, except where noted, with 1,332 litres; 293 Imp gallons of fuel):
Never-exceed speed:
 3, 3M 217 knots (402 km/h; 250 mph) EAS
Max cruising speed at 3,050 m (10,000 ft):
 3, 3M at max continuous power 175 knots (324 km/h; 202 mph)
 3M-200 at max continuous power at AUW of 6,577 kg (14,500 lb) 174 knots (322 km/h; 200 mph)
 3, 3M at cruise power 168 knots (311 km/h; 193 mph)
 3M-200 at cruise power at AUW of 6,577 kg (14,500 lb) 166 knots (308 km/h; 191 mph)
Econ cruising speed at 3,050 m (10,000 ft):
 3, 3M 150 knots (278 km/h; 173 mph)
 3M-200 at AUW of 6,577 kg (14,500 lb) 150 knots (278 km/h; 173 mph)
Stalling speed, flaps down:
 3 60 knots (111 km/h; 69 mph) EAS
 3M 62 knots (115 km/h; 71 mph) EAS
Max rate of climb at S/L: 3 500 m (1,640 ft)/min
 3M 466 m (1,530 ft)/min
Service ceiling (30·5 m; 100 ft/min climb):
 3 6,858 m (22,500 ft)
 3M 6,705 m (22,000 ft)
Service ceiling, one engine out (15 m; 50 ft/min climb):
 3 3,810 m (12,500 ft)
 3M 2,895 m (9,500 ft)
Min ground turning radius 3·76 m (12 ft 4 in)
Runway LCN at AUW of 5,670 kg (12,500 lb):
 standard tyres 3·5
 low pressure tyres 3·0
T-O run, STOL, unfactored: 3 213 m (700 ft)
 3M 238 m (780 ft)
 3M-200 290 m (950 ft)
T-O run (normal): 3 (BCAR) 512 m (1,680 ft)
T-O to 10·7 m (35 ft), Transport Group A, ISA at S/L:
 3 1,020 m (3,350 ft)
T-O to 15 m (50 ft), STOL, unfactored:
 3 320 m (1,050 ft)
 3M 384 m (1,260 ft)
 3M-200 488 m (1,600 ft)
T-O to 15 m (50 ft):
 3 (BCAR, normal) 610 m (2,000 ft)
 3 (BCAR, STOL) 482 m (1,580 ft)
 3 (FAR Pt 23) 488 m (1,600 ft)

The Brazilian built prototype of the Shorts S312 Tucano, under test from Belfast

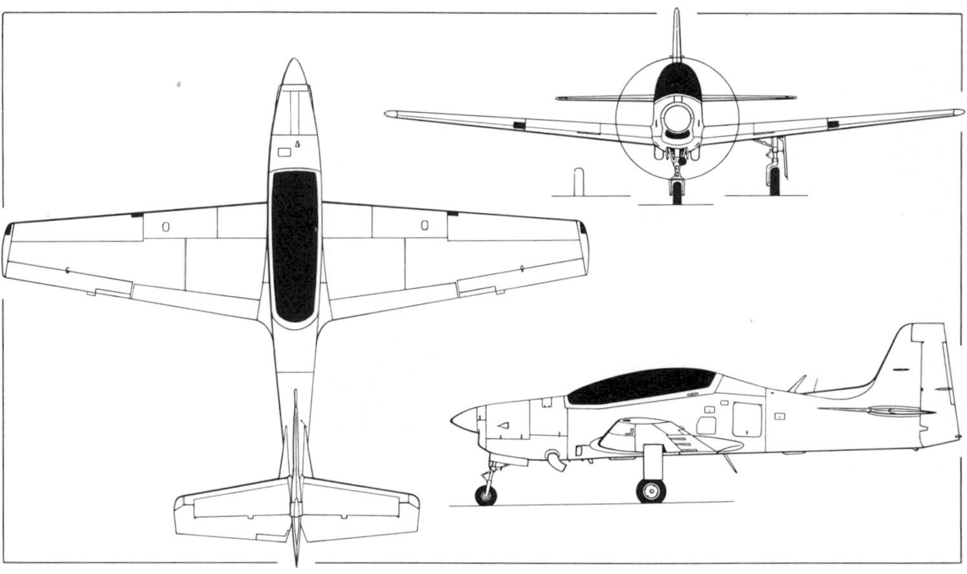
Shorts S312 Tucano basic trainer (Garrett TPE331-12B turboprop engine *(Pilot Press)*

Landing from 15 m (50 ft), at max landing weight:
 3 (BCAR, normal) 622 m (2,040 ft)
 3 (BCAR, STOL) 567 m (1,860 ft)
 3 (FAR Pt 23) 451 m (1,480 ft)
 3M (STOL, unfactored) 425 m (1,395 ft)
 3M-200 (STOL, unfactored) 457 m (1,500 ft)
Landing from 15 m (50 ft), Transport Group A, ISA at S/L, at max landing weight 1,010 m (3,320 ft)
Landing from 9 m (30 ft), at max landing weight:
 3 (STOL, unfactored) 351 m (1,150 ft)
 3 (BCAR, STOL) 500 m (1,640 ft)
Landing run, at max landing weight:
 3M (STOL, unfactored) 212 m (695 ft)
Range at long-range cruising speed, 45 min reserves:
 3 600 nm (1,115 km; 694 miles)
 3M 580 nm (1,075 km; 670 miles)
Range at long-range cruising speed, 45 min reserves:
 3 (typical freighter) with 1,815 kg (4,000 lb) payload, ISA 162 nm (300 km; 187 miles)
 3M (typical freighter) with 2,268 kg (5,000 lb) payload, ISA 208 nm (386 km; 240 miles)
 3M-200 with 1,815 kg (4,000 lb) payload, ISA + 10°C 540 nm (1,000 km; 621 miles)

SHORTS S312 TUCANO

RAF designation: Tucano T. Mk 1

Under the terms of a co-operation agreement between Shorts and EMBRAER of Brazil, announced in May 1984, Shorts undertook to develop from the basic EMB-312 Tucano (see EMBRAER entry in Brazilian section) a new version of the turboprop trainer that would meet or exceed all requirements of the UK Ministry of Defence Air Staff Target 412 for a Jet Provost replacement.

The UK Government announced on 21 March 1985 that the Shorts Tucano had been selected for this role. The decision ended a competition which had lasted two years. The decisive consideration, according to the UK Secretary of State for Defence, was the "cost factor", the Shorts offer being the least expensive "by a clear margin". Initially, 130 Tucanos are being built for the Royal Air Force. Deliveries are scheduled to begin in early 1987, and twelve aircraft will be in service by the end of that year.

To exceed Air Staff Target 412, the Shorts Tucano embodies significant modifications compared with the basic EMB-312. These include a changed power plant to improve speed, particularly at low altitude, and provide an increased rate of climb; a ventral airbrake to control speed during descent; structural strengthening for increased manoeuvre loads and fatigue life; a new cockpit layout to meet RAF requirements; wide use of UK equipment; and an optional armament and strike capability. The Shorts Tucano has a design fatigue life of 12,000 hours.

The first flight of a Tucano with a Garrett engine (PP-ZTC), as chosen for the RAF version, took place in Brazil on 14 February 1986. After completing some six hours of test flying there, it was airfreighted to the UK, reassembled in Belfast, and made its first flight with a British test flight serial (G-14-007) on 11 April 1986. During that flight it demonstrated its ability to fly at a sea level speed of 268 knots (496 km/h; 308 mph), as required by the RAF.

The main description of the Tucano can be found under the EMBRAER heading in the Brazilian section. The Shorts Tucano T. Mk 1 for the RAF differs in the following respects:

WINGS: Incidence 1° 13′. Aluminium alloy two-spar torsion box structure of 7075-T73511 and 2024-T3511 extrusions and 7075-T76 and 2024-T3 sheet. Electrically actuated trim tab in, and small ground adjustable tab on, each aileron.

FUSELAGE: Hydraulically actuated ventral airbrake.

LANDING GEAR: Nosewheel unit supplied by Fairey Hydraulics. Dunlop wheels and tyres, size 22 × 6·75-10 on mainwheels, 5·00-5 on nosewheel. Dunlop hydraulic single-disc brakes on mainwheels.

POWER PLANT: One 820 kW (1,100 shp) Garrett TPE331-12B turboprop engine, driving a Hartzell constant-speed fully-feathering reversible-pitch propeller with spinner. Two integral fuel tanks in wings, total capacity 694 litres (153 Imp gallons; 183 US gallons). Gravity refuelling point in each wing upper surface. Oil capacity 4·25 litres (0·94 Imp gallons; 1·13 US gallons).

ACCOMMODATION: Instructor and pupil in tandem, on Martin-Baker Mk 8LCP lightweight ejection seats.

SYSTEMS: Cockpit air-conditioning by engine bleed air plus recirculated cockpit air through a regenerative turbofan system. Single hydraulic system, pressure 207 bars (3,000 lb/sq in), for landing gear extension and retraction, and airbrake. Accumulator to lower landing gear in emergency. DC electrical power provided by a 28V 200A starter/generator and two 24Ah alkaline batteries. Static inverter for 115V and 26V AC power at 400Hz. Normalair-Garrett oxygen system supplied from a single bottle, capacity 2,250 litres (80 cu ft). Emergency oxygen bottle, capacity 70 litres (2·5 cu ft), mounted on each ejection seat. Engine air intake de-iced by engine bleed air; propeller, pitot head, static vents, and stall warning system de-iced electrically.

AVIONICS AND EQUIPMENT: Standard avionics include VHF/UHF/audio by Marconi, Plessey and Dowty; gyro-magnetic compass, VOR/ILS/marker beacon receiver, GEC Avionics AD2780 Tacan, and Narco transponder.

DIMENSIONS, EXTERNAL:
Wing span 11·28 m (37 ft 0 in)
Propeller diameter 2·39 m (7 ft 10 in)

AREAS:
Wings, gross 19·33 m² (208·08 sq ft)
Fin, excl dorsal fin 2·08 m² (22·40 sq ft)
Rudders, incl tab 1·46 m² (15·70 sq ft)
Tailplane, incl fillets 4·57 m² (49·20 sq ft)

WEIGHTS AND LOADINGS:
Basic weight empty 2,017 kg (4,447 lb)
Max internal fuel 555 kg (1,223 lb)
Max T-O weight 2,650 kg (5,842 lb)
Max wing loading 137·1 kg/m² (28·07 lb/sq ft)
Max power loading 3·23 kg/kW (5·31 lb/shp)

PERFORMANCE (estimated at max T-O weight):
Never-exceed speed 280 knots (518 km/h; 322 mph) EAS
Max level and cruising speed at 3,050-4,575 m (10,000-15,000 ft) 274 knots (507 km/h; 315 mph)
Econ cruising speed at 6,100 m (20,000 ft) 220 knots (407 km/h; 253 mph)
Stalling speed, power off:
flaps and landing gear down 69 knots (128 km/h; 80 mph) EAS
flaps and landing gear up 75 knots (139 km/h; 87 mph) EAS
Max rate of climb at S/L 1,070 m (3,510 ft)/min
Service ceiling 10,365 m (34,000 ft)
T-O run 290 m (950 ft)
T-O to 15 m (50 ft) 503 m (1,650 ft)
Landing from 15 m (50 ft) 500 m (1,640 ft)
Landing run 275 m (900 ft)
Range at 7,620 m (25,000 ft) with max fuel, 30 min reserves 900 nm (1,665 km; 1,035 miles)
Endurance at econ cruising speed at 7,620 m (25,000 ft), 30 min reserves 5 h 12 min

SLINGSBY

SLINGSBY AVIATION PLC

Ings Lane, Kirkbymoorside, North Yorkshire YO6 6EZ
Telephone: 0751 32474
Telex: 57597

DIRECTORS:
Air Marshal Sir Peter Wykeham, KCB, DSO, OBE, AFC, FRAeS, CBIM (Chairman)
James S. Tucker, BSc (Eng), CEng, MRAeS (Managing)
S. A. Cooper, BSc, CEng, MIMechE, ACIS
John W. Davy, MBIM, MITD, MRAeS

CHIEF DESIGNER: B. Mellers

SALES MANAGER AND PRESS CONTACT:
Roger C. Bull, BSc(Eng)

Slingsby has previously been recognised primarily as a manufacturer of sailplanes. This aspect of the company's activities has ended and Slingsby is concentrating on development and production of the T67 light aircraft. Slingsby also manufactures the gondola, propulsion ducts, flying controls and nosecone, and installs the engines, electrics and avionics of the Airship Industries Skyship 500 and 600 airships described in the Lighter than Air section of this edition. In conjunction with Ferranti Ltd, Slingsby designed and manufactured a development batch of Phoenix RPV airframes in composite materials (see RPVs and Targets section). In mid-1986 its covered works area was approx 9,290 m² (100,000 sq ft) and it had a workforce of 200.

SLINGSBY T67

The original T67A was a licence built version of the Fournier RF6B light aircraft. Production by Fournier, in France, was limited to 45 RF6B-100s and a single RF6B-120, which flew for the first time on 14 August 1980 and received FAR Pt 23 certification on 7 November 1980. Slingsby built ten T67As (similar to the RF6B-120), of which the first (G-BIOW) flew for the first time on 15 May 1981. This model, which was described in the 1982-83 *Jane's*, has been superseded by new versions, built primarily of GRP instead of wood, including the military T67M Firefly (described separately). To speed the T67M programme, a T67A (G-BJNG) was modified to Firefly 160 standard by installation of a 119 kW (160 hp) engine and constant-speed propeller for tests that included spinning trials at extreme CG limits.

Current versions for civil use are as follows:

T67B. Basic version, of GRP construction, as described in detail. Powered by an 86·5 kW (116 hp) Avco Lycoming O-235-N2A flat-four engine driving a two-blade fixed-pitch propeller with spinner.

T67C. As T67B, but with 119 kW (160 hp) Avco Lycoming engine, driving a metal fixed-pitch propeller, and with 24V 70A engine driven alternator and 24V 12Ah battery.

T67D. As T67C, but with constant-speed propeller.

By October 1986 a total of 43 civil and military T67s had been delivered, with a further 12 in production. The military versions are described separately.

The following details apply to the T67B:

TYPE: Two-seat aerobatic, training and sporting aircraft.

WINGS: Cantilever low-wing monoplane. Wing section NACA 23015 at root, NACA 23013 at tip. Dihedral 3° 30′. Incidence 3°. Wings, Frise ailerons and manually operated plain trailing-edge flaps all of GRP construction.

FUSELAGE: Oval section structure of GRP.

TAIL UNIT: Cantilever structure of GRP. Fixed incidence tailplane. Trim tab in port elevator. Spin strakes forward of tailplane roots.

LANDING GEAR: Non-retractable tricycle type. Oleo-pneumatic shock absorber in each unit. Steerable nose-wheel. Mainwheel tyres size 6·00-6, pressure 1·4 bars (20 lb/sq in). Nosewheel tyre size 5·00-5, pressure 2·5 bars (37 lb/sq in). Hydraulic disc brakes. Parking brake. GRP mainwheel fairings optional.

POWER PLANT: One flat-four engine as described in model listings. Fuselage fuel tank, immediately aft of firewall, capacity 114 litres (25 Imp gallons). Refuelling point on fuselage upper surface, forward of windscreen. Oil capacity 4 litres (0·88 Imp gallons). Oil system permits short periods of inverted flight.

ACCOMMODATION: Two seats side by side under one-piece transparent canopy, which swings upward and rearward for access to cockpit. Optional canopy has fixed windscreen, and upward hinged and rearward opening rear section. Dual controls standard. Adjustable rudder pedals. Cockpit heated and ventilated. Baggage space aft of seats.

SYSTEMS: Hydraulic system for brakes only. Vacuum system for blind-flying instrumentation. Electrical power supplied by 12V 60A engine driven alternator and 12V 25Ah battery.

AVIONICS AND EQUIPMENT: Standard equipment includes artificial horizon and directional gyro, with vacuum system and vacuum gauge, electric turn co-ordinator, rate of climb indicator, recording tachometer, stall warning system, clock, outside air temperature gauge, accelerometer; cabin fire extinguisher, heated pitot; instrument, landing, navigation and strobe lights; tie-down rings and towbar. Optional avionics, available to customer requirements, include equipment by Becker, King and Narco, up to full IFR standard.

DIMENSIONS, EXTERNAL:
Wing span 10·59 m (34 ft 9 in)
Wing chord: at root 1·53 m (5 ft 0¼ in)
at tip 0·83 m (2 ft 8¾ in)
Wing aspect ratio 8·88
Length overall 7·32 m (24 ft 0¼ in)
Height overall 2·51 m (8 ft 3 in)
Tailplane span 3·40 m (11 ft 1¾ in)
Wheel track 2·44 m (8 ft 0 in)
Wheelbase 1·50 m (4 ft 11 in)
Propeller diameter 1·83 m (6 ft 0 in)

DIMENSIONS, INTERNAL:
Cabin: Length 2·05 m (6 ft 8¾ in)
Max width 1·08 m (3 ft 6½ in)
Max height 1·08 m (3 ft 6½ in)

AREAS:
Wings, gross 12·63 m² (136·0 sq ft)
Ailerons (total) 1·24 m² (13·35 sq ft)
Trailing-edge flaps (total) 1·74 m² (18·73 sq ft)
Fin 0·80 m² (8·61 sq ft)
Rudder 0·81 m² (8·72 sq ft)
Tailplane 1·65 m² (17·76 sq ft)
Elevators (incl tab) 0·99 m² (10·66 sq ft)

WEIGHTS AND LOADINGS:
Weight empty (basic): T67B 610 kg (1,345 lb)
T67C 630 kg (1,390 lb)
T67D 635 kg (1,400 lb)
Max fuel: T67B, T67C 82 kg (181 lb)
T67D 114 kg (252 lb)
Max baggage: T67B 18 kg (40 lb)
T67C, T67D 30 kg (66 lb)
Max T-O and landing weight: T67B 862 kg (1,900 lb)
T67C, T67D 907 kg (2,000 lb)
Max wing loading: T67B 68·21 kg/m² (13·97 lb/sq ft)
T67C, T67D 71·82 kg/m² (14·71 lb/sq ft)
Max power loading: T67B 9·97 kg/kW (16·38 lb/hp)
T67C, T67D 7·62 kg/kW (12·50 lb/hp)

PERFORMANCE (at max T-O weight):
Never-exceed speed:
T67B 165 knots (305 km/h; 190 mph)
T67C, T67D 180 knots (333 km/h; 207 mph)
Max level speed at S/L:
T67B 115 knots (213 km/h; 132 mph)
T67C 135 knots (250 km/h; 155 mph)
T67D 138 knots (256 km/h; 159 mph)
Max cruising speed (75% power) at 2,440 m (8,000 ft):
T67B 110 knots (204 km/h; 126 mph)
T67C 125 knots (231 km/h; 144 mph)
T67D 128 knots (237 km/h; 147 mph)
Stalling speed, power off, flaps up:
T67B 55 knots (102 km/h; 64 mph)
Stalling speed, power off, flaps down:
T67B 46 knots (85 km/h; 53 mph)
T67C, T67D 49 knots (91 km/h; 57 mph)
Max rate of climb at S/L: T67B 201 m (660 ft)/min
T67C 320 m (1,050 ft)/min
T67D 350 m (1,150 ft)/min
Service ceiling: T67B 3,660 m (12,000 ft)
T-O run: T67B 223 m (733 ft)
T67C 201 m (660 ft)
T67D 190 m (623 ft)
T-O to 15 m (50 ft): T67B 537 m (1,760 ft)
T67C 442 m (1,450 ft)
T67D 402 m (1,319 ft)
Landing from 15 m (50 ft): T67B 521 m (1,710 ft)
T67C, T67D 533 m (1,750 ft)
Landing run: T67B 213 m (700 ft)
T67C, T67D 232 m (760 ft)
Range with max fuel (65% power at 2,440 m; 8,000 ft), allowances for T-O and climb, 45 min reserves at 45% power: T67B 451 nm (835 km; 519 miles)
T67C 360 nm (666 km; 414 miles)
T67D 565 nm (1,046 km; 650 miles)
g limits +6/−3

Slingsby T67M Firefly 160 two-seat military basic trainer with original one-piece canopy

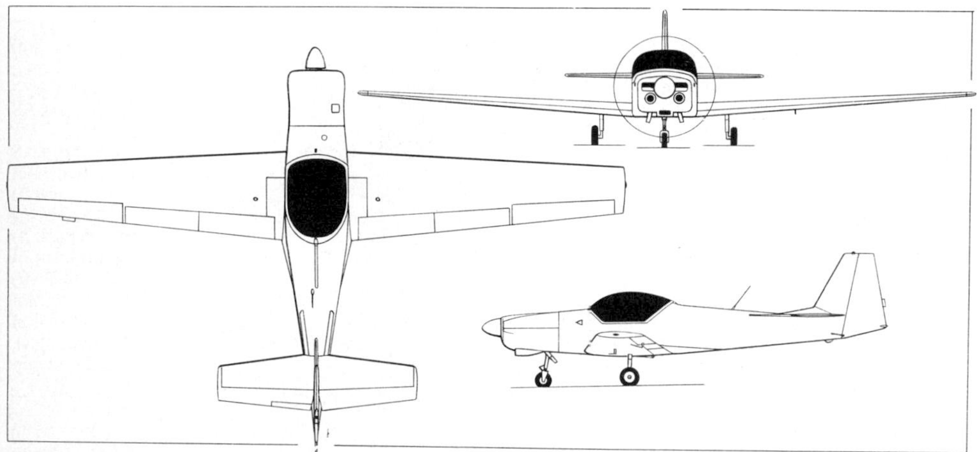

Slingsby T67M Firefly 160 (Avco Lycoming AEIO-320-D1B engine) with original canopy *(Pilot Press)*

Slingsby T67M200 Firefly with new canopy and windscreen *(Jay Miller/Aerofax)*

SLINGSBY T67M FIREFLY 160

This military basic trainer version of the T67 is based on the T67B of GRP construction. The description of the T67B applies also to the T67M, except as detailed below. A first flight of this version (G-BKAM), known as the Firefly 160, was made on 5 December 1982, and CAA certification was achieved in September 1983.

TYPE: Two-seat military basic trainer.

WINGS, FUSELAGE, TAIL UNIT AND LANDING GEAR: Generally as for T67B.

POWER PLANT: One 119 kW (160 hp) Avco Lycoming AEIO-320-D1B flat-four engine, driving a Hoffmann HO-V72 two-blade constant-speed wooden propeller with spinner. Fuel and oil systems suitable for inverted flight. Fuel tanks in leading-edge of wings, capacity 162 litres (35·5 Imp gallons). Refuelling point in upper wing surface. Oil capacity 7·7 litres (1·7 Imp gallons).

ACCOMMODATION AND SYSTEMS: As for T67B, except that current aircraft have new canopy with fixed windscreen and upward hinged and rearward opening rear section. Inertia reel lockable shoulder harness standard, and air-conditioning optional.

AVIONICS AND EQUIPMENT: Avionics to customer requirements. Prototype has Narco nav/com. Blind-flying instrumentation standard.

DIMENSIONS AND AREAS: As for T67B

WEIGHTS AND LOADINGS:

Weight empty, equipped	649 kg (1,430 lb)
Max fuel weight	114 kg (252 lb)
Max T-O, aerobatic and landing weight	907 kg (2,000 lb)
Max wing loading	71·82 kg/m² (14·71 lb/sq ft)
Max power loading	7·62 kg/kW (12·5 lb/hp)

PERFORMANCE (at max T-O weight):

Never-exceed speed	180 knots (333 km/h; 207 mph)
Max level speed at S/L	138 knots (256 km/h; 159 mph)
Max cruising speed, 75% power at 2,440 m (8,000 ft)	128 knots (237 km/h; 147 mph)
Stalling speed, power off, flaps down	49 knots (91 km/h; 57 mph)
Max rate of climb at S/L	350 m (1,150 ft)/min
Service ceiling	4,575 m (15,000 ft)
T-O run	190 m (623 ft)
T-O to 15 m (50 ft)	402 m (1,319 ft)
Landing from 15 m (50 ft)	533 m (1,750 ft)
Landing run	232 m (760 ft)
Range with max fuel at 75% power, allowances for T-O, climb and 45 min reserves at 45% power	529 nm (980 km; 608 miles)
g limits at 884 kg (1,950 lb) AUW	+6/−3

SLINGSBY T67M200 FIREFLY

A development of the T67M, this version has a 149 kW (200 hp) Avco Lycoming AEIO-360-A1E engine, driving a Hoffmann HO-V123 three-blade variable-pitch propeller. The description and dimensions of the T67M apply also to the T67M200; weight and performance data are given below. This version flew for the first time on 16 May 1985. First customer was the Turkish Aviation Institute at Ankara, to which five aircraft were delivered in 1985.

WEIGHTS AND LOADINGS:

Weight empty	685 kg (1,510 lb)
Max fuel	114 kg (252 lb)
Max baggage	30 kg (66 lb)
Max T-O and landing weight	975 kg (2,150 lb)
Max wing loading	77·20 kg/m² (15·81 lb/sq ft)
Max power loading	6·54 kg/kW (10·75 lb/hp)

PERFORMANCE:

Never-exceed speed	180 knots (333 km/h; 207 mph)
Max level speed at S/L	140 knots (259 km/h; 161 mph)
Max cruising speed (75% power, at 2,440 m; 8,000 ft)	133 knots (246 km/h; 153 mph)
Stalling speed, power off, flaps down	51 knots (95 km/h; 59 mph)
Max rate of climb at S/L	411 m (1,350 ft)/min
T-O run	168 m (550 ft)
T-O to 15 m (50 ft)	345 m (1,130 ft)
Landing from 15 m (50 ft)	549 m (1,800 ft)
Landing run	247 m (810 ft)
Range with max fuel (65% power at 2,440 m; 8,000 ft), allowances for T-O and climb, 45 min reserves at 45% power	500 nm (926 km; 575 miles)
g limits	+6/−3

SNIPE

SNIPE AIRCRAFT DEVELOPMENTS LTD

This company is now dormant.

TRAGO MILLS

TRAGO MILLS LTD (Aircraft Division)

Treswithick Farm, Cardinham, Bodmin, Cornwall PL30 4BU

Telephone: 020 882 485

CHIEF DESIGNER: Sydney A. Holloway

TEST PILOT AND PRESS CONTACT:
Air Vice-Marshal Geoffrey Cairns

Trago Mills has built the prototype of Mr Sydney Holloway's SAH-1 two-seat light aircraft. The company is CAA approved for light aircraft design, development, manufacture and testing, and has retained as design consultant Mr Frank H. Robertson, who has held engineering and senior design appointments with Vought Corporation in the USA, and with Miles, Saunders-Roe and Shorts in the UK.

TRAGO MILLS SAH-1

Design of the SAH-1 started in October 1977, and construction of a prototype began in January 1978. Both design and construction are to full CAA and FAR Pt 23 standards. The first flight of the prototype (G-SAHI) was made on 23 August 1983 and a full Certificate of Airworthiness, Public Transport Category, was obtained on 12 December 1985. In mid-1986 discussions were being held to obtain financial backing for a production programme.

In addition to the basic SAH-1, with O-235 engine, a more powerful version is expected to be made available, with a 119 kW (160 hp) Avco Lycoming AEIO-320-DB flat-four engine driving a constant-speed propeller. Estimated weights and performance for this model are included in the following specification of the basic version:

TYPE: Two-seat fully aerobatic light aircraft.

WINGS: Cantilever low-wing monoplane. Wing section NACA 2413·6 (constant). Dihedral 5° from roots. Incidence 3° at root, 1° at tip. Tapered, non-swept aluminium alloy wings, with L65 spar booms and L72 sheet skins, stabilised with PVC foam. Trailing-edge single-slotted flaps and slotted ailerons of similar construction.

FUSELAGE: Aluminium alloy stressed skin structure, with radiused corners, incorporating centre-section spars.

TAIL UNIT: Aluminium alloy cantilever structure, stabilised with PVC foam. Constant chord tailplane, attached to fuselage, with horn balanced elevators; full span trim tab in starboard elevator. Sweptback fin and horn balanced rudder. Ventral fin.

LANDING GEAR: Non-retractable tricycle type, with single wheel on each unit. Oleo-pneumatic shock absorber in nosewheel leg; spring steel main legs. Cleveland mainwheels and tyres size 6·00-6, pressure 1·24 bars (18·0 lb/sq in). Nosewheel and tyre size 5·00-5, pressure 1·03 bars (15 lb/sq in). Cleveland hydraulic brakes.

POWER PLANT: One 88 kW (118 hp) Avco Lycoming O-235-L2A flat-four engine, driving a two-blade fixed-pitch propeller with spinner. Integral fuel tank in each wing leading-edge, total capacity 114 litres (25 Imp gallons). Refuelling point in upper surface of each wing. Oil capacity 5·7 litres (1·25 Imp gallons).

ACCOMMODATION: Two seats side by side under rearward sliding bubble canopy. Baggage space aft of seats. Cockpit heated and ventilated.

SYSTEM: 60A engine driven alternator.

AVIONICS AND EQUIPMENT: Blind-flying instrumentation standard. Radio to customer's specification.

DIMENSIONS, EXTERNAL:

Wing span	9·36 m (30 ft 8·4 in)
Wing chord: at root	1·515 m (4 ft 11⅔ in)
at tip	0·81 m (2 ft 8 in)
Wing aspect ratio	7·5
Length overall	6·58 m (21 ft 7¼ in)
Height overall	2·38 m (7 ft 9·6 in)
Tailplane span	2·74 m (9 ft 0 in)
Wheel track	2·40 m (7 ft 10½ in)
Wheelbase	1·46 m (4 ft 9·6 in)
Propeller diameter	1·68 m (5 ft 6 in)
Propeller ground clearance	0·30 m (12 in)

DIMENSIONS, INTERNAL:

Cockpit: Length	1·52 m (5 ft 0 in)
Max width	1·21 m (3 ft 11½ in)
Baggage space	0·4 m³ (14·0 cu ft)

AREAS:

Wings, gross	11·15 m² (120·0 sq ft)
Ailerons (total)	0·89 m² (9·6 sq ft)
Trailing-edge flaps (total)	1·30 m² (14·0 sq ft)
Fin	0·96 m² (10·3 sq ft)
Rudder	0·63 m² (6·8 sq ft)
Tailplane	1·11 m² (12·0 sq ft)
Elevators, incl tab	0·93 m² (10·0 sq ft)

WEIGHTS AND LOADINGS (A, O-235 engine; B, AEIO-320 engine):

Weight empty, equipped: A	460 kg (1,014 lb)
B	571 kg (1,259 lb)
Max fuel load: A	85 kg (188 lb)
Max T-O weight: A	748 kg (1,649 lb)
B	870 kg (1,919 lb)
Max wing loading: A	67·06 kg/m² (13·74 lb/sq ft)
B	78·04 kg/m² (15·99 lb/sq ft)
Max power loading: A	8·50 kg/kW (13·97 lb/hp)
B	7·31 kg/kW (11·99 lb/hp)

PERFORMANCE (estimated at max T-O weight):

Never-exceed speed:	
A	202 knots (374 km/h; 232 mph) EAS
B	232 knots (430 km/h; 267 mph) EAS
Max level speed at S/L:	
A	121 knots (224 km/h; 139 mph)
B	140 knots (259 km/h; 161 mph)
Max cruising speed, 75% power at S/L:	
A	110 knots (204 km/h; 127 mph)
B	126 knots (233 km/h; 145 mph)
Econ cruising speed, 50% power at S/L:	
A	93 knots (172 km/h; 107 mph)
B	110 knots (204 km/h; 127 mph)
Stalling speed:	
flaps up: A	54 knots (100 km/h; 63 mph) EAS
B	57 knots (106 km/h; 66 mph) EAS
flaps down: A	47 knots (88 km/h; 55 mph) EAS
B	51 knots (95 km/h; 59 mph) EAS
Max rate of climb at S/L: A	279 m (915 ft)/min
B	393 m (1,290 ft)/min
Service ceiling: A	5,000 m (16,400 ft)
B	6,645 m (21,800 ft)
T-O run: A	247 m (812 ft)
B	223 m (730 ft)
T-O to 15 m (50 ft): A	374 m (1,228 ft)
B	315 m (1,033 ft)
Landing from 15 m (50 ft): A	290 m (953 ft)
B	315 m (1,033 ft)

Range with max fuel, 13·6 litres (3 Imp gallons) reserves:
A at 78 knots (145 km/h; 90 mph) at 1,525 m (5,000 ft) 620 nm (1,149 km; 714 miles)
B at 95 knots (175 km/h; 109 mph) at 3,050 m (10,000 ft) 490 nm (907 km; 564 miles)

Trago Mills SAH-1 side by side two-seat light aircraft

VINTEN

W. VINTEN LTD (Military Division)

Western Way, Bury St Edmunds, Suffolk IP33 3TB
Telephone: 0284 2121
Telex: 81176

In March 1981 a collaborative agreement was reached between Wg Cdr K. H. Wallis and W. Vinten Ltd, permitting the latter to take steps towards the manufacture of autogyros to Wallis designs for various military and commercial purposes. Two autogyros, known as Venom Mk 2 aircraft, were completed and flown in early 1986 under West German government contract. A version named Vindicator demonstrated its ability to operate as an RPV. Further information is not considered appropriate at this time.

WALLIS

WALLIS AUTOGYROS LTD

Reymerston Hall, Norfolk NR9 4QY
Telephone: 0362 850418
DIRECTORS:
Wg Cdr K. H. Wallis, CEng, FRAeS, FRSA, RAF (Retd)
D. A. Wallis
P. M. Wallis

The first Wallis single-seat ultralight autogyro introduced many patented features, including a rotor head with offset gimbal system to provide hands and feet off stability and to eliminate pitch-up and 'tuck-under' hazards; a high speed flexible rotor spin-up shaft with positive disengagement during flight; an automatic system of controlling rotor drive on take-off which allows power to be applied until the last moment; centrifugal stops to control rotor blade teetering; and a novel safe starting arrangement.

Many other Wallis autogyros have since been completed. However, Wallis Autogyros does not engage in production for public sale; it builds these aircraft only for operation within the company. Manufacture and marketing for the military and civil market is undertaken by W. Vinten Ltd (which see).

WALLIS WA-116 and WA-116-T

The WA-116 represents the original Wallis design, of which the prototype (G-ARRT) flew for the first time on 2 August 1961, powered by a 54 kW (72 hp) modified McCulloch 4318 piston engine. Four more WA-116s were built by Beagle and five by Wg Cdr Wallis, as described in the 1973-74 *Jane's*. The last of these was later dismantled for construction of the two-seat G-AXAS, a WA-116-T.

WA-116/Mc. The prototype (G-ARRT) is re-engined with a 67 kW (90 hp) McCulloch. This aircraft, and the 'James Bond' WA-116/Mc (G-ARZB), continue to perform well. The latter has appeared in more than 500 displays, as far afield as Australia and the USA.

WA-116/F. Designation applied following the refitting of G-ASDY in 1971 with a 44 kW (60 hp) Franklin 2A-120-A engine. It is currently fitted with a Franklin 2A-120-B engine, driving a specially designed two-blade propeller, and has carried out specialised aerial photographic work, as detailed in earlier editions of *Jane's*.

A particularly successful WA-116/F is G-ATHM which currently holds nine world rotorcraft records. This aircraft underwent more extensive conversion than its predecessors, mainly to increase fuel capacity and pilot comfort to fit it for special long range flights. It has a 50 litre (11 Imp gallon) internal fuel tank, and began test flying, for range, in April 1974. Fitted also with a 36 litre (8 Imp gallon) jettisonable long range ventral tank, it set up on 13 July 1974 new Class E3 and E3a world records, for nonstop distance in a closed circuit, of 361·91 nm (670·26 km; 416·48 miles). Additionally, this flight set new 100 km (Class E3a only) and 500 km (Class E3 and E3a) closed circuit speed records of 70·51 knots (130·67 km/h; 81·19 mph) and 68·07 knots (126·14 km/h; 78·38 mph) respectively. A 91 litre (20 Imp gallon) ventral tank was next fitted, and on 28 September 1975, with this tank containing some 70 litres (15·5 Imp gallons), Wg Cdr Wallis made a nonstop flight from Lydd, Kent, to Wick, Caithness. This flight set Class E3 and E3a records for nonstop distance in a straight line of 472·092 nm (874·315 km; 543·274 miles). The ventral tank was not jettisoned after being emptied, and G-ATHM landed with sufficient fuel remaining for a further 65 nm (121 km; 75 miles). Its time of 6 h 25 min is a record for duration in both Class E3 and Class E3a. On 14 October 1984 WA-116/F/S G-BLIK set new Class E3 and E3a speed records over 15 km of 102·365 knots (189·58 km/h; 117·80 mph). On 17 April 1985 it set new Class E3 and E3a world speed records over 100 km of 102·81 knots (190·41 km/h; 118·31 mph); and on 18 September 1986 new speed records over 3 km (subject to FAI homologation) of 104·7 knots (193·9 km/h; 120·48 mph). The suffix S denotes 'Special' because of the numerous cleaning up refinements embodied. Thus, WA-116s hold all the major autogyro world records for speed, range and endurance.

In 1982 a WA-116/Mc (G-ATTB), which incorporated many components of the ex-Army WA-116 XR944, was rebuilt to WA-116/F standard, finished in military colours and given again the XR944 registration. It has taken part in a succession of military exercises and, in 1984, was fitted with inert replicas of Oerlikon SURA D 81 mm unguided rockets for handling tests. The company already has some experience of firing rockets from its aircraft during film sequences.

WA-116-T/Mc. The McCulloch engined WA-116-T/Mc, G-AXAS, is a tandem two-seat autogyro which flew for the first time on 3 April 1969. It remains the lightest two-seater in the Wallis range, and is expected to improve even further upon the 3·14 : 1 ratio of all-up weight to empty weight, which it established at RAE Bedford in 1971. It made more than 130 flights in a programme of multispectral experiments by Plessey Radar on behalf of the Home Office, as described in the 1979-80 *Jane's*, and has been used for motion picture work. Recent activities include work utilising the slow flight and short take-off and landing capability, and also electrostatically charged spraying tests, employing a spray system that can be lowered beneath the lowest part of the aircraft in flight.

WEIGHTS (WA-116/F):

Weight empty	143 kg (316 lb)
Max T-O weight	317·5 kg (700 lb)

PERFORMANCE (WA-116/F):

Max level speed	not fully explored
Cruising speed without long-range tank	87 knots (161 km/h; 100 mph)
Max rate of climb at S/L	305 m (1,000 ft)/min
Max range with long-range tank (estimated)	651 nm (1,207 km; 750 miles)

WALLIS WA-116/X

In 1985 Wg Cdr Wallis began the development of a new autogyro for a particular reconnaissance role. The requirement calls for a day and night all-weather capability, together with very low vibration levels.

As part of the development programme a series of flight tests is being conducted with current and new technology engines. Current engines tested include a special version of the 59·6 kW (80 hp) Limbach L 2000, a 37 kW (50 hp) Fuji 440 cc two-cylinder aircooled two-stroke, and the 47·7 kW (64 hp) Rotax 520 Bombardier geared two-cylinder liquid cooled two-stroke engine. Modified engines include the Rootes Imp and a two-cylinder engine made from components of the Rolls-Royce Continental O-240. New technology engines in the programme include a special version of the Norton Motors twin-rotor Wankel type and a supercharged or turbocharged 1,360 cc automobile engine. The radiator for the Rotax and Norton engines is in the nose

Wallis WA-116/F/S which holds Class E3 and E3a speed records, showing fixed foreplane surfaces

of the cockpit nacelle, providing some cockpit heating in inclement weather conditions.

Airframes being used for these flight tests are a basic WA-116 (G-AVDG), with appropriate modifications, and a new one (G-BMJX) provisionally designated WA-116/X, the suffix X indicating the unknown quantity pending selection of a suitable engine.

First flight of the Wallis WA-116 testbed for an experimental Norton engine, 31 July 1986. Note nose air intake for radiator

VINTEN WALLIS WA-116 VENOM Mk 2

On 1 March 1981 Wg Cdr Wallis and W. Vinten Ltd, the well known manufacturer of airborne reconnaissance systems, reached a collaborative agreement to exploit the basic single-seat Wallis design for various civil and military applications such as agricultural duties, reconnaissance, powerline/pipeline inspection and border patrol. Details of one resulting aircraft, designated Venom Mk 2, can be found in the 1985-86 *Jane's*.

A radio controlled version (G-BKLZ) known as the **Vindicator**, described under the Vinten heading in the RPVs and Targets section of the 1985-86 *Jane's*, has also been flown.

WALLIS WA-117/R-R

Started in 1964, the WA-117 combines the proven features of the WA-116 airframe with a fully certificated engine, the 74 kW (100 hp) Rolls-Royce Continental O-200-B. An experimental test vehicle (G-ATCV) flew for the first time on 24 March 1965; this was later dismantled for the construction of a true WA-117 prototype (G-AVJV), which made its first flight on 28 May 1967. This aircraft has since undertaken considerable evaluation of infra-red linescan, such as the BAe Type 214, and low light level TV systems. It has also been fitted with a Vinten Type 751 panoramic camera, which can be used in the beam mode or in a cross-track mode. With its special silencers and four-blade 'quiet' propeller, G-AVJV is one of the quietest powered aircraft of any kind yet built.

WEIGHT:

Max T-O weight	approx 317·5 kg (700 lb)

PERFORMANCE:

Max level speed	104 knots (193 km/h; 120 mph)
Cruising speed	78 knots (145 km/h; 90 mph)
Max rate of climb	approx 305 m (1,000 ft)/min

WALLIS WA-118/M METEORITE

The WA-118 Meteorite flew for the first time on 6 May 1966, having at that time the registration G-ATPW. Its 89 kW (120 hp) supercharged Italian Meteor Alfa 1 engine was brought up to then current standards during 1969-70. The aircraft was also fitted with a bubble canopy, reclining cockpit and other modifications, and was rebuilt as G-AVJW, making its first flight in this form on 9 August 1969. Intended for a long term test programme, it was then completely redesigned and rebuilt with the latest features of the Wallis range. The aircraft has a partially stress bearing GRP cockpit nacelle capable of being used as an open cockpit or, in inclement weather, of accepting an optional hardtop (not yet tested). The nacelle is being tested for a planned Franklin powered autogyro of even better performance than the WA-116/F G-ATHM. The objective is to provide more space and comfort for the pilot, without sacrificing performance.

WALLIS WA-120/R-R

The WA-120 (G-AYVO) is powered by a 97 kW (130 hp) Rolls-Royce Continental O-240-A flat-four engine and cruises at a fuel consumption of 15·9 litres (3·5 Imp gallons)/h. Construction began under the original designation WA-117-S. It subsequently developed into more than a re-engined version of the WA-117, justifying the use of a new designation. It flew for the first time on 13 June 1971.

The WA-120 has a forward sliding transparent cockpit canopy, and can be flown at speeds of up to 60 knots (111 km/h; 69 mph) with this canopy partly open.

WALLIS WA-121

The WA-121 is the smallest and lightest Wallis autogyro to date. Three versions were projected: a high-speed **WA-121/Mc** with a Wallis-McCulloch engine of about 74 kW (100 hp); a cross-country **WA-121/F** with a 44·5 kW (60 hp) Franklin 2A-120-B engine; and a high-altitude **WA-121/M Meteorite 2** with a supercharged 89 kW (120 hp) Meteor Alfa 1 radial two-stroke engine and transistorised ignition.

The prototype WA-121/Mc (G-BAHH) has a high-mounted tailplane and an open cockpit, and made its first flight on 28 December 1972. It employs a number of improvements in control system design, resulting in greater stability at speed, better head resistance and greater pilot comfort. It set new Class E3 and E3a height records on 20 July 1982, when Wg Cdr Wallis flew it to a height of 5,643·7 m (18,516 ft) at Boscombe Down. Special features in the rotor head suspension, incorporated originally in the WA-117 prototype G-AVJV, are incorporated also in the WA-120 and WA-121. Now fitted with an improved oxygen system, and a wider track main landing gear to standardise

Rolls-Royce engined Wallis WA-117/R-R, with Vinten 751 panoramic camera pack

The Wallis WA-118/M, designed to fly at altitudes of more than 9,145 m (30,000 ft)

Wallis WA-121/Mc, which set Class E3 and E3a height records in July 1982

The two-seat Wallis WA-122/R-R

it with other autogyros in the Wallis range, the WA-121 is intended to undertake experimental flying using rotor blades designed for high speeds.

WALLIS WA-122/R-R

The basic layout of the open frame, two-seat WA-116-T proved very successful in providing a passenger with autogyro air experience. In addition, dual controls can be fitted when required, and other controls such as the throttle and spin-up drive lever can be reached by both occupants. However, the high noise level of the modified McCulloch engine would preclude the use of this aircraft for ab initio instruction, and reliability of this uncertificated engine could not be accepted for regular training use.

In consequence, a slightly larger two-seat aircraft (G-BGGW), known as the WA-122/R-R, was built, and began flight testing on 16 July 1980. Powered by a 119 kW (160 hp) Rolls-Royce Continental O-240 flat-four engine, the WA-122/R-R retains the main characteristics of the WA-116-T, keeping the tandem layout but with the rear seat placed higher than the one in front, more space between the seats, and dual controls. The WA-122/R-R was designed for a rotor of 7·0 m (23 ft 0 in) diameter, but flight testing with the standard 6·20 m (20 ft 4 in) rotor of the WA-116 has shown it to be entirely satisfactory for this two-seat version. The rotor blades, and also the landing gear legs, can be folded quickly, for ease of transportation in a container.

WESTLAND

WESTLAND plc

Yeovil, Somerset BA20 2YB
Telephone: 0935 75222
Telex: 46277 WHLYEO G
LONDON OFFICE: 4 Carlton Gardens, Pall Mall, SW1
Telephone: (01) 839 4061
CHAIRMAN: Sir John Cuckney
VICE-CHAIRMAN: Sir John Treacher, KCB, FRAeS
GROUP CHIEF EXECUTIVE: H. P. Stewart, LLB, FCA
FINANCE DIRECTOR: C. D. Verrall
MANAGING DIRECTOR, TECHNOLOGIES DIVISION:
W. T. C. Miller, OBE, MA, CEng, MIMechE, MInstM
DIRECTORS:
Lord Fanshawe, KCMG
Sir Maldwyn Thomas
Dr G. Boffetta (Fiat)
Sir Peter Carey (UTC)
Wesley A. Kuhrt (UTC)
SECRETARY: J. R. Bayley, LLB
GROUP EXECUTIVE, PUBLIC RELATIONS:
John Teague, CEng, MRAeS, MIM

Westland Aircraft Ltd (now Westland plc) was formed in July 1935, to take over the aircraft branch of Petters Ltd, known previously as the Westland Aircraft Works, which had been engaged in aircraft design and construction since 1915. It entered the helicopter industry in 1947 by acquiring a licence to build the US Sikorsky S-51, which it produced as the Westland Dragonfly. This technical association with Sikorsky Division of United Technologies has continued since the decision was taken to concentrate on the design, development and construction of helicopters.

In 1959, Westland acquired Saunders-Roe Ltd. In 1960 it acquired the Helicopter Division of Bristol Aircraft Ltd and Fairey Aviation Ltd, and has been subsequently the only major helicopter design and manufacturing organisation in the United Kingdom.

A shareholders' meeting in February 1986 approved a financial reconstruction package under which United Technologies (USA) and Fiat (Italy) acquired a minority holding in Westland plc.

Since 1 October 1966, the company's helicopter business has been conducted through a wholly owned company named Westland Helicopters Ltd.

In April 1983 the Aerospace Division of British Hovercraft Corporation was combined with the Westland Helicopters Industrial Division to form the Aerospace Division of Westland plc. In October 1985 three additional divisions were created: Helicopter Division, Helicopter Customer Support Division and Technologies Division.

Programmes on which the Aerospace Division is engaged include the production of centre wings for the Shorts 330 and 360 transport aircraft, composite engine cowlings for the de Havilland Canada Dash 8, missile and satellite structures, fuel pods and transmission components for Boeing Vertol Chinook helicopters, and gears and gearboxes for other aerospace companies. Its latest products include retrofit composite rotor blades for Sea King and Sikorsky S-61 helicopters.

One of Westland's subsidiary companies, Normalair-Garrett Ltd, specialises in the design, development and production of aircraft pressure control air-conditioning, oxygen breathing and hydraulic systems. Most British pressurised aircraft, civil and military, use Normalair-Garrett equipment, as do the Panavia Tornado and many aircraft of foreign design. In addition, this company produces data loggers, trace readers and hydraulic equipment for aircraft flying controls.

The collaboration between Westland and Agusta of Italy, already well established with the EH 101 programme (see International section), has been extended to include design, manufacture and marketing across the joint product range. It was announced in May 1985 that the two companies are studying a common feasibility and pre-definition study of a light attack helicopter for the British and Italian armies. This would be based on the A 129, developed by the Italians as the Mangusta anti-tank helicopter (see Agusta entry).

A joint Westland/Agusta marketing company, EHI Limited, has been set up in Milan, initially to support the EH 101 civil and military helicopter. EHI Inc is a subsidiary of EHI in the USA.

Westland Group activities in the USA, Central America and the Caribbean are represented by Westland Inc, a wholly owned subsidiary.

WESTLAND HELICOPTERS LTD

Yeovil, Somerset BA20 2YB
Telephone: 0935 75222
Telex: 46277 WHLYEO G
HELICOPTER DIVISION
MANAGING DIRECTOR:
D. K. Berrington, BA, CEng, MIMechE, MRAeS
PUBLIC RELATIONS MANAGER: Ian Woodward

Helicopters in current production at Yeovil are the Sea King, Commando, Army Lynx, Navy Lynx and Westland 30.

In an international programme, Westland Helicopters and Agusta of Italy have formed jointly a company named EH Industries Ltd to develop and produce the EH 101 naval, commercial and utility helicopter (see International section).

Work on advanced composite components is undertaken in a new production facility at Yeovil. Composite main rotor blades, based on carbonfibre and glassfibre materials, are in production as direct replacements for metal blades on S-61, SH-3 and Westland Sea King helicopters. Composite tail rotor blades are also in production for the Westland 30.

Advanced design composite main rotor blades have been successfully test flown on Lynx, Lynx 3 and the new Westland TT300. Development work is well advanced on composite rotor blades of similar form for the EH 101.

WESTLAND SEA KING

The Westland Sea King development programme stemmed from a licence agreement for the S-61 helicopter concluded originally with Sikorsky in 1959. This permitted Westland to utilise the basic airframe and rotor system of the Sikorsky SH-3 now described under Agusta in the Italian section. Considerable changes were made in the power plant and in specialised equipment, initially to meet a Royal Navy requirement for an advanced anti-submarine helicopter with prolonged endurance. The Sea King can also undertake secondary roles, such as search and rescue, tactical troop transport, casualty evacuation, cargo carrying and long-range self-ferry. A land based general purpose version, the Commando, is described separately.

Current versions of the Sea King are as follows:

Sea King Mk 2 AEW. Version developed in mid-1982 to provide Royal Navy with airborne early warning capability. Under a programme known as Project LAST (low altitude surveillance task), it was developed in only 11 weeks, using two converted HAS. Mk 2 Sea Kings (XV650 and XV651) as testbeds. These aircraft (which first embarked in HMS *Illustrious* in August 1982 for deployment to the South Atlantic) each have a Thorn EMI Searchwater maritime surveillance radar in an air pressurised 'kettledrum' container of Kevlar impregnated fabric carried on a swivel mounting on the starboard side of the fuselage, in line with the dorsal radome. The container is swung, hydraulically, forward and downward below wheel level when deployed. The scanner is pitch and roll stabilised, and offers full 360° scan.

Two radar operator positions are provided for search and target classification. Radar classification is by raster displays having three modes; PPI (plan), B-scope (selected plan sector enlarged) and A-scope (profile, showing contact shape). A multiple target track while scan capability permits tracking without interrupting search. A Cossor Electronics Jubilee Guardsman IFF interrogator is integrated with the radar. An MIR-2 electronic support measures suite provides 360° detection of radar emissions and classifies them against stored signatures for positive identification of radar contacts. A UHF radio link provides voice and data communications with the fleet, enabling warning of a target's course, speed, coded identity, range and bearing to be transmitted quickly. Targets can be detected at a range of more than 87 nm (161 km; 100 miles), from a normal service ceiling of 3,050 m (10,000 ft). A four-hour endurance can be extended by refuelling at the hover.

The two original Mk 2 AEW aircraft formed the basis of No. 849 Squadron, which was reformed at RNAS Culdrose, Cornwall, on 9 November 1984. Eight more AEW Sea Kings are being acquired by modification of HAS. Mk 2 aircraft; and the Squadron's 'A' Flight was commissioned with three helicopters on 31 May 1985, for service in HMS *Illustrious* in August 1985.

Sea King HAR. Mk 3. Uprated version for SAR duties with the Royal Air Force. Provision for flight crew of two pilots, air electronics/winch operator and loadmaster/winchman; up to six stretchers, or two stretchers and 11 seated survivors, or 19 persons. Nav system includes Decca TANS F computer, accepting inputs from Mk 19 Decca nav receiver and Type 71 Doppler. MEL radar. Sixteen ordered initially, to equip No. 202 Squadron at Lossiemouth, Scotland. First HAR. Mk 3 flew on 6 September 1977; deliveries of all 16 completed in 1979. Three more ordered in 1983 were delivered in 1985.

Sea King HC. Mk 4. Utility version of Commando Mk 2 (which see) for Royal Navy.

Sea King HAS. Mk 5. Updated ASW and SAR version for the Royal Navy. Thirty new-build aircraft ordered in three batches (17, 8 and 5), of which the first two (ZA126/127) were handed over officially on 2 October 1980. Delivery of the first batch was completed in September 1982; delivery of the next eight began in July 1984, and the final five were scheduled for delivery by May 1986. The nav/attack system of the Sea King HAS. Mk 5 utilises Tans G coupled to Decca 71 Doppler and MEL Sea Searcher radar. Also fitted are Racal MIR-2 ESM, passive sonobuoy dropping equipment, and associated GEC Avionics LAPADS acoustic processing and display equipment. The increased size of the rotating antenna has necessitated the Mk 5's larger dorsal radome.

Using this new equipment, the Sea King can pinpoint the position of an enemy submarine at far greater range than has been possible in the past, and attack it with torpedoes. In addition to monitoring signals from its own sonobuoys, the Sea King can handle information from buoys dropped by RAF Nimrod aircraft in a joint search. It can remain on station, up to 87 nm (160 km; 100 miles) from its parent ship, for long periods.

The Sea King HAS. Mk 5 carries a crew of four, with the dunking sonar operator also monitoring the LAPADS equipment at an additional crew station. To make room for the extra equipment, the cabin has been enlarged by moving the rear bulkhead nearly 1·83 m (6 ft 0 in) further into the

Westland Sea King Mk 2 AEW helicopter of the Royal Navy, with Searchwater maritime surveillance radar in retracted position

tail. Improvements envisaged for the future include the carriage of more powerful torpedoes and improved anti-submarine sensors.

Max T-O weight of the Sea King HAS. Mk 5 is 9,525 kg (21,000 lb), the same as that of the Mk 2. Royal Navy HAS. Mk 2s are being upgraded to this standard.

Sea King Mk 42. ASW version for Indian Navy. Original order for six, which are in service with No. 330 Squadron. Delivery of a further six was completed in 1974, and these are in service with Nos. 330 and 336 Squadrons. Follow-on order announced in June 1977 for three uprated aircraft, designated **Mk 42A**, with hauldown capability for small ship operation, which were delivered in March 1980.

Advanced Sea King. Version with 1,092 kW (1,465 shp) Rolls-Royce Gnome H.1400-1T engines, uprated main gearbox with emergency lubrication and strengthened main lift frames. Other changes include composite main and tail rotor blades, and improved search radar. Maximum AUW increased to 9,752 kg (21,500 lb) to give an improved payload/range performance. Through life costs reduced. Seven ordered for Royal Navy, armed with Sea Eagle missiles, and one for the UK Ministry of Defence Procurement Executive.

Sea King Mk 42B. ASW version of the Advanced Sea King of which 12 were ordered for the Indian Navy in July 1983, with an option on eight more. Features include GEC Avionics AQS-902 sonobuoy processor and tactical processing system; MEL Super Searcher radar; Alcatel HS-12 dipping sonar; Chelton 700 sonics homing; Marconi Hermes ESM; and ability to carry British Aerospace Sea Eagle long-range anti-ship missiles.

Sea King Mk 42C. Utility transport version of the Advanced Sea King of which six have been ordered for the Indian Navy. Navigation systems similar to HAR. Mk 3, except that the MEL radar is replaced by Bendix RDR 1400C, nose mounted; the ADF and IFF are produced by HAL.

Other versions, for which orders have been completed, were described in the 1983-84 *Jane's* and included the Sea King HAS. Mk 1 (Royal Navy), Sea King HAS. Mk 2 (Royal Navy), Sea King Mk 4X (Royal Aircraft Establishment), Sea King Mk 41 (Federal German Navy), Sea King Mk 43 (Norwegian Air Force), Sea King Mk 45 (Pakistan Navy), Sea King Mk 47 (Egyptian Navy), Sea King Mk 48 (Belgian Air Force) and Sea King Mk 50 (Royal Australian Navy).

A total of 305 Sea Kings and 79 Commandos had been ordered by January 1986, of which 269 had been delivered.

The following details apply to current production Advanced Sea Kings:

Airframe: Generally similar to Agusta-Sikorsky ASH-3H (see Italian section), but with main and tail rotor blades of composite materials. Stabiliser on starboard side of tail pylon is unbraced.

Power Plant: Two 1,238 kW (1,660 shp) (max contingency rating) Rolls-Royce Gnome H.1400-1T turboshaft engines, mounted side by side above cabin. Transmission rating 2,200 kW (2,950 shp). Fuel in six underfloor bag tanks, total capacity 3,714 litres (817 Imp gallons). Internal auxiliary tank, capacity 863 litres (190 Imp gallons) may be fitted for long range ferry purposes. Pressure refuelling point on starboard side, two gravity points on port side.

Accommodation: Crew of four in ASW role; accommodation for up to 22 survivors in SAR role; and up to 28 troops in utility role. Two-section airstair door at front on port side, cargo door at rear on starboard side. Entire accommodation heated and ventilated. Cockpit doors and windows, and two windows each side of cabin, can be jettisoned in an emergency.

Systems: Three main hydraulic systems. Primary and auxiliary systems operate main rotor control. System pressure 103·5 bars (1,500 lb/sq in); flow rate 22·7 litres/min at 87·9 bars (5 Imp gallons/min at 1,275 lb/sq in). Unpressurised reservoir. Utility system for main landing gear, sonar and rescue winches, blade folding and rotor brake. System pressure 207 bars (3,000 lb/sq in); flow rate 41 litres/min at 186·2 bars (9 Imp gallons/min at 2,700 lb/sq in). Unpressurised reservoir. Electrical system includes two 20kVA 200V three-phase 400Hz engine driven generators, a 26V single-phase AC supply fed from the aircraft's 22Ah nickel-cadmium battery through an inverter, and DC power provided as a secondary system from two 200A transformer-rectifier units.

Operational Equipment (ASW models): As equipped for this role, the Sea King is a fully integrated all-weather hunter/killer weapon system, capable of operating independently of surface vessels, and the following equipment and weapons can be fitted to achieve this task: Plessey Type 195, Bendix AN/AQS-13B or Alcatel HS-12 dipping sonar, GEC Avionics AD 580 Doppler navigation system, AW 391 search radar in dorsal radome, transponder beneath rear fuselage, Honeywell AN/APN-171 radar altimeter, Sperry GM7B Gyrosyn compass system, Louis Newmark Mk 31 automatic flight control system, two No. 4 marine markers, four No. 2 Mk 2 smoke floats, Ultra Electronics mini-sonobuoys, up to four Mk 46 homing torpedoes, or four Mk 11 depth charges or one Clevite simulator. Observer/navigator has tactical display on which sonar contacts are integrated with search radar and navigational information. Radio equipment comprises Plessey PTR 377 UHF/VHF and homer, Ultra D 403M standby UHF, Collins 618-T3 HF radio, Ultra UA 60M intercom, Telebrief system and IFF provisions. For secondary role a mounting is provided on the aft frame of the starboard door for a general purpose machine-gun. The Mk 31 AFCS provides radio altitude displays for both pilots; artificial horizon displays; three axis stabilisation in pilot controlled manoeuvres; attitude hold, heading hold and height hold in cruising flight; controlled transition manoeuvres to and from the hover; automatic height control and plan position control in the hover; and an auxiliary trim facility.

Operational Equipment (non-ASW models): A wide range of radio and navigation equipment may be installed, including VHF/UHF communications, VHF/UHF homing, radio compass, Doppler navigation system, radio altimeter, VOR/ILS, radar and transponder, of Collins, Plessey, Honeywell and GEC Avionics manufacture. A Sperry compass system and a Louis Newmark automatic flight control system are also installed. Sea Kings equipped for search and rescue have in addition a Breeze BL 10300 variable speed hydraulic rescue hoist of 272 kg (600 lb) capacity mounted above the starboard side cargo door. Automatic main rotor blade folding and spreading is standard; for shipboard operation the tail pylon can also be folded. With search radar fitted, a total of 18 survivors and medical staff can be carried; this total can be increased to 22 if the search radar is omitted. In the casualty evacuation role, the Sea King can accommodate up to 9 stretchers and two medical attendants, or intermediate combinations of seats and stretchers; a typical layout might provide for 15 seats and six stretchers. In the troop transport role, the Sea King can accommodate 28 troops. As a cargo transport, the aircraft has an internal capacity of 3,628 kg

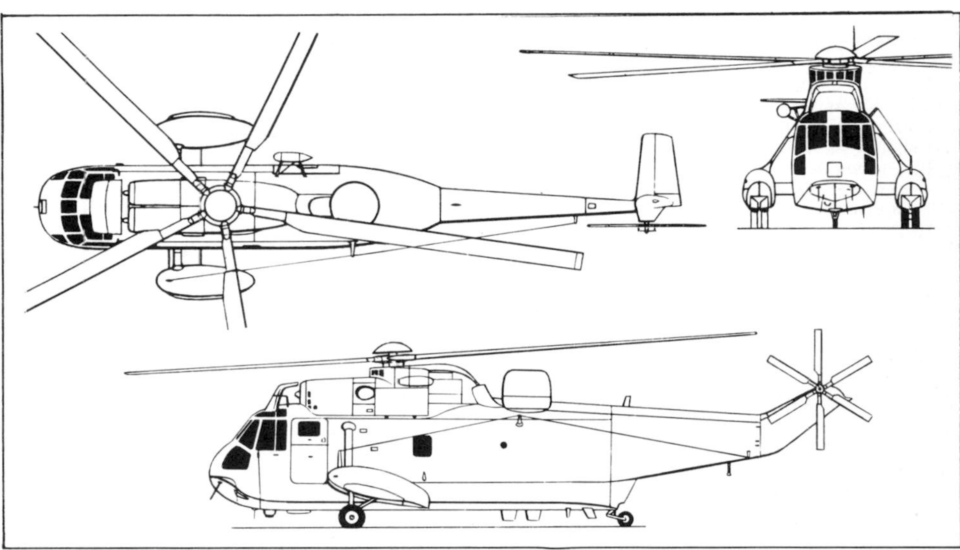

Westland Sea King HAS. Mk 5 anti-submarine helicopter *(Pilot Press)*

Westland Advanced Sea King carrying two Sea Eagle long-range anti-ship missiles

Westland main rotor blade of advanced design, using high performance aerofoil section and paddle shape tip. Blades of this type will be standard on production Westland 30 Series 300 and Lynx 3 helicopters, and available for Army Lynx and Navy Lynx. They are also specified for the EH 101 (see International section)

(8,000 lb) and the same max external load capacity when a low response sling is fitted.

DIMENSIONS, EXTERNAL:
Main rotor diameter 18·90 m (62 ft 0 in)
Tail rotor diameter 3·16 m (10 ft 4 in)
Length overall (rotors turning) 22·15 m (72 ft 8 in)
Length of fuselage 17·02 m (55 ft 10 in)
Length overall:
main rotor folded 17·42 m (57 ft 2 in)
rotors and tail folded 14·40 m (47 ft 3 in)
Height overall: rotors turning 5·13 m (16 ft 10 in)
rotors spread and stationary 4·85 m (15 ft 11 in)
Height to top of rotor head 4·72 m (15 ft 6 in)
Width overall (rotors folded):
with flotation bags 4·98 m (16 ft 4 in)
without flotation bags 4·77 m (15 ft 8 in)
Wheel track (c/l of shock absorbers) 3·96 m (13 ft 0 in)
Cabin door (port): Height 1·68 m (5 ft 6 in)
Width 0·91 m (3 ft 0 in)
Cargo door (stbd): Height 1·52 m (5 ft 0 in)
Width 1·73 m (5 ft 8 in)
Height to sill 1·14 m (3 ft 9 in)

DIMENSIONS, INTERNAL:
Cabin: Length: ASW 5·87 m (19 ft 3 in)
SAR 7·59 m (24 ft 11 in)
Max width 1·98 m (6 ft 6 in)
Max height 1·92 m (6 ft 3½ in)
Floor area (incl area occupied by radar, sonar etc):
ASW 12·08 m² (130 sq ft)
SAR 13·94 m² (150 sq ft)

AREAS:
Main rotor disc 280·6 m² (3,020·3 sq ft)
Tail rotor disc 7·8 m² (83·9 sq ft)

WEIGHTS AND LOADINGS (A: anti-submarine, B: anti-surface vessel, C: airborne early warning, D: SAR, E: troop transport, F: external cargo):
Basic weight (depending on version) approx 5,530 kg (12,194 lb)
Weight equipped (typical): A 6,236 kg (13,749 lb)
B 6,454 kg (14,229 lb)
C 6,929 kg (15,275 lb)
D 6,280 kg (13,844 lb)
E 5,438 kg (11,990 lb)
F 5,424 kg (11,958 lb)
Max T-O weight 9,752 kg (21,500 lb)
Max disc loading 34·75 kg/m² (7·12 lb/sq ft)
Max power loading 4·44 kg/kW (7·29 lb/shp)

PERFORMANCE (at max T-O weight, ISA):
Never-exceed speed (British practice) at S/L 122 knots (226 km/h; 140 mph)
Cruising speed at S/L 110 knots (204 km/h; 126 mph)
Max rate of climb at S/L 619 m (2,030 ft)/min
Max vertical rate of climb at S/L 246 m (808 ft)/min
Service ceiling, one engine out 1,220 m (4,000 ft)
Max contingency ceiling (1 hour rating) 1,067 m (3,500 ft)
Hovering ceiling: IGE 1,982 m (6,500 ft)
OGE 1,433 m (4,700 ft)
Range with max standard fuel, at 1,830 m (6,000 ft) 800 nm (1,482 km; 921 miles)
Ferry range with max standard and auxiliary fuel, at 1,830 m (6,000 ft) 940 nm (1,742 km; 1,082 miles)

PERFORMANCE (at typical mid-mission weight):
Never-exceed speed (British practice) at S/L 146 knots (272 km/h; 169 mph)
Cruising speed at S/L 132 knots (245 km/h; 152 mph)

WESTLAND COMMANDO

First flown on 12 September 1973, the Commando is a tactical helicopter based on the Sea King.

The payload/range performance and endurance capabilities of the Sea King have been optimised in the design of the Commando, which is intended to operate with maximum efficiency in the primary roles of tactical troop transport, logistic support and cargo transport, and casualty evacuation. In addition, the Commando can operate effectively in the secondary roles of air-to-surface strike and search and rescue.

The following versions have been announced:

Commando Mk 1. Designation of first five Commandos, ordered on behalf of the Egyptian Air Force by the Saudi Arabian government. Minimally modified version; essentially a standard Sea King Mk 41 aircraft, able to transport up to 21 troops. First two delivered to Egypt in January/February 1974.

Commando Mk 2. Major production version, to which detailed description applies. Flew for first time (G-17-12) on 16 January 1975. Saudi Arabian order included 17 Mk 2s and two VIP Mk 2Bs for the Egyptian Air Force. Four Mk 2s (three Mk 2As and one VIP Mk 2C) delivered to Qatar Emiri Air Force. The Egyptian Air Force also received in 1979-80 four Commando **Mk 2Es** equipped with Elettronica IHS-6 ECM/ESM for an electronic warfare role.

Commando Mk 3. Eight delivered to Qatar.

Sea King HC. Mk 4. Utility version of Commando Mk 2 for Royal Navy. Has folding main rotor blades and folding tail pylon of Sea King, but retains non-retractable wheeled landing gear of Commando. Designed to carry up to 28 fully equipped troops, or 2,720 kg (6,000 lb) of cargo, and to operate in Arctic and tropical conditions. Max slung load 3,628 kg (8,000 lb). Equipped for parachuting and abseiling. Revised avionics, including Decca TANS with chart display and Decca 71 Doppler navigation system. One cabin mounted 7·62 mm machine-gun. For service with Nos. 707, 845 and 846 (Naval Air Commando) Squadrons. First flight (by ZA290) 26 September 1979. Seventeen ordered initially, of which the first was handed over to the Royal Navy in November 1979. This figure of 17 includes two Sea King Mk 4X for supply to RAE Farnborough. In 1982, following the Falkland Islands campaign, it was announced that a further eight had been ordered for the Royal Navy. Four more were ordered in 1984 and delivered in 1985, and ten more in 1985, for delivery in 1986 and 1987. The 28th HC.Mk 4 (ZF115) was the first production Sea King to fly from the start with composites main rotor blades, on 14 November 1985, although others had been retrofitted.

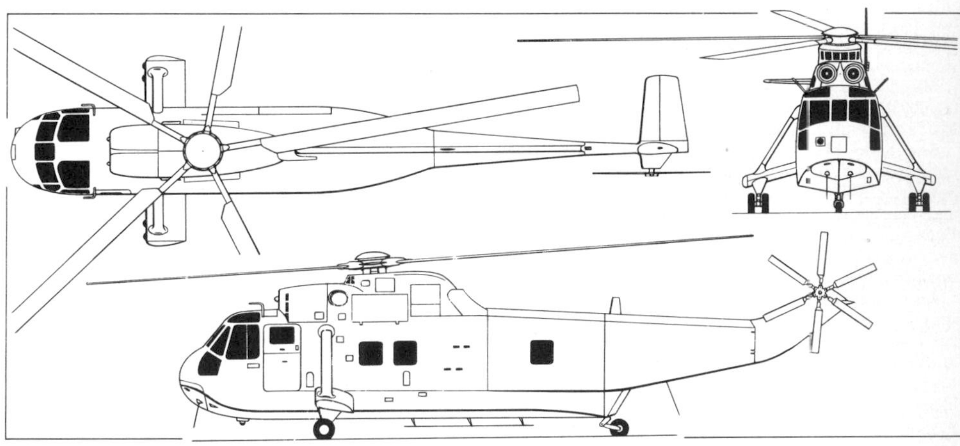

Westland Commando Mk 2 twin-turboshaft tactical military helicopter *(Pilot Press)*

Westland Sea King HC. Mk 4 logistic support version of the Commando for the Royal Navy *(RNAS Yeovilton)*

The following data apply to current production aircraft:

TYPE: Twin-turboshaft tactical military helicopter.

ROTOR SYSTEM: Five-blade main rotor and six-blade tail rotor, of composite construction. Main rotor blades, of NACA 0012 section, attached to hub by multiple bolted joint. Rotor brake fitted. Automatic folding of main rotor blades available as an option.

ROTOR DRIVE: Twin input four-stage reduction main gearbox, with single bevel intermediate and tail gearboxes. Main rotor/engine rpm ratio 93·43; tail rotor/engine rpm ratio: 15·26.

FUSELAGE: Light alloy stressed skin structure, unpressurised. Sea King sponsons replaced by stub wings.

TAIL UNIT: Similar to Advanced Sea King, with starboard side stabiliser at top of fixed tail rotor pylon. Folding tail pylon available as an option.

LANDING GEAR: Non-retractable tailwheel type, with twin-wheel main units. Oleo-pneumatic shock absorbers. Mainwheel tyres size 6·50-10, tailwheel tyre size 6·00-6.

POWER PLANT: As for current versions of Advanced Sea King.

ACCOMMODATION: Crew of two on flight deck. Seats along cabin sides, and single jump seat, for up to 28 troops. Two-piece airstair door at front on port side, cargo door at rear on starboard side. Entire accommodation heated and ventilated. Cockpit doors and windows, and two windows each side of main cabin, are jettisonable in an emergency.

SYSTEMS: Primary and secondary hydraulic systems for flight controls. No pneumatic system. Electrical system includes two 20kVA alternators.

AVIONICS AND EQUIPMENT: Wide range of radio, radar and navigation equipment available to customer's requirements. Cargo sling and rescue hoist optional.

ARMAMENT: Wide range of guns, missiles, etc may be carried, to customer's requirements.

DIMENSIONS, EXTERNAL:
Main rotor diameter 18·90 m (62 ft 0 in)
Tail rotor diameter 3·16 m (10 ft 4 in)
Distance between rotor centres 11·10 m (36 ft 5 in)
Main rotor blade chord 0·46 m (1 ft 6¼ in)
Length overall (rotors turning) 22·15 m (72 ft 8 in)
Length of fuselage 17·02 m (55 ft 10 in)
Height overall (rotors turning) 5·13 m (16 ft 10 in)
Height to top of rotor head 4·72 m (15 ft 6 in)
Wheel track (c/l of shock absorbers) 3·96 m (13 ft 0 in)
Wheelbase 7·21 m (23 ft 8 in)
Passenger door (fwd, port):
Height 1·68 m (5 ft 6 in)
Width 0·91 m (3 ft 0 in)
Cargo door (rear, stbd): Height 1·52 m (5 ft 0 in)
Width 1·73 m (5 ft 8 in)

DIMENSIONS, INTERNAL: As Advanced Sea King (SAR version)

AREAS: As for Advanced Sea King, plus:
Main rotor blades (each) 4·14 m² (44·54 sq ft)
Tail rotor blades (each) 0·23 m² (2·46 sq ft)
Tailplane 1·80 m² (19·40 sq ft)

WEIGHTS:
Operating weight empty (troop transport, 2 crew, typical) 5,620 kg (12,390 lb)
Max T-O weight 9,752 kg (21,500 lb)

PERFORMANCE (at max T-O weight): As given for Advanced Sea King, plus:
Range with max payload (28 troops), reserves for 30 min standoff 214 nm (396 km; 246 miles)

WESTLAND LYNX and SUPER LYNX

The Lynx is one of three types of aircraft (Puma, Gazelle and Lynx) covered by the Anglo-French helicopter agreement first proposed in February 1967 and confirmed on 2 April 1968. Westland has design leadership in the Lynx, which fulfils general purpose and naval roles.

The first of 13 Lynx prototypes (XW835) flew for the first

time on 21 March 1971 and was followed by XW837, the third prototype (second Lynx to fly), on 28 September 1971. Details of subsequent development aircraft can be found in the 1975-76 *Jane's*. Production versions are as follows:

Lynx AH. Mk 1. General purpose and utility version for British Army, with Gem 2 engines, for tactical troop transport, logistic support, armed escort of troop carrying helicopters, anti-tank strike, search and rescue, casualty evacuation, reconnaissance and command post duties. Max T-O weight 4,354 kg (9,600 lb). Total of 113 built. First production aircraft (XZ170) flown on 11 February 1977. All delivered by February 1984.

A Westland owned aircraft (G-LYNX, first flown in May 1979), demonstrated the helicopter's multi-role capability with a wide range of weapons which included Hughes TOW and Euromissile Hot anti-tank guided missiles; SURA 80 mm, SNEB 68 mm and FZ 2·75 in rockets; twin 7·62 mm machine-gun pods and 20 mm automatic cannon; Matra Magic 550 air-to-air missiles; an AN/ALE-39 counter-measures dispenser with ECM chaff; and ECM warning equipment. It can also carry mine dispensers, or anti-tank teams armed with Milan missiles. Sixty Lynx AH. Mk 1 have been equipped with TOW missiles, for service with BAOR in the anti-tank role. The first six of these were delivered in the Spring of 1981 to No. 654 Squadron of No. 4 Regiment, Army Aviation.

On 11 August 1986, the Lynx demonstrator G-LYNX set a new world's absolute speed record for helicopters by averaging 216·45 knots (400·87 km/h; 249·09 mph) over a 15/25 km course. Subject to confirmation, this exceeded the former record held by a Soviet A-10 (Mil Mi-24). For the attempt, the Lynx was fitted with Westland's new advanced technology BERP III main rotor blades, Westland 30 type horizontal and vertical tail surfaces, a water-methanol injection system and tuned jetpipes on the standard Gem 60 engines. The standard main gearbox was re-rated, and 32 kg (70 lb) of airframe drag removed by enhanced streamlining.

Lynx HAS. Mk 2. Version for Royal Navy, for advanced shipborne anti-submarine and other duties. Gem 2 engines. Ferranti Seaspray search and tracking radar in modified nose. Capable of operation on anti-submarine classification and strike, air to surface vessel search and strike, search and rescue, reconnaissance, troop transport, fire support, communication and fleet liaison, and vertical replenishment duties. Total of 60 delivered. First production aircraft (XZ229) flown on 10 February 1976. First operational RN unit, No. 702 Squadron, formed on completion of Navy intensive flight trials in December 1977. Able to carry Sea Skua anti-ship missiles.

Lynx HAS. Mk 3. Royal Navy aircraft with uprated power plant, comprising two 835 kW (1,120 shp) Rolls-Royce Gem 41-1 turboshaft engines. Delivery of original series of 20, plus three Falklands War replacements, began in March 1982 and has been completed. One was built for the Empire Test Pilots School. Seven more were ordered in July 1985. In May 1985, it was announced that Westland, with Racal Avionics as subcontractor, is developing a central tactical system (CTS) for the Lynx HAS. Mk 3. This will ease the crew's workload by centrally processing all sensor data and presenting mission information on a multi-function electronic display. First flight of the CTS is scheduled for 1987.

Lynx Mk 4. Second batch of 14 aircraft ordered for French Navy in May 1980 with Gem 41-1 engines and uprated transmission to permit an increase in AUW to 4,763 kg (10,500 lb). Deliveries began on 28 January 1983 and have been completed.

Lynx AH. Mk 5. Uprated aircraft for British Army. Similar to AH. Mk 1 but with Gem 41-1 turboshaft engines, three-pinion main gearbox and 4,535 kg (10,000 lb) AUW. Two trials aircraft built initially for RAE Bedford: AH. Mk 1/5 (ZD285), first flown 21 November 1984, with uprated three-pinion gearbox and Gem 2 engines; Mk 5X (ZD559), first flown 11 February 1985, with Gem 41-1s, uprated transmission and max T-O weight of 4,535 kg (10,000 lb). Nine AH Mk 5s ordered. Initial example (ZE375) flew on 23 February 1985 and was used for engine trials. Remainder transferred to AH.Mk 7 contract, although ZE376 flew initially as Mk 5 on 23 April 1986.

Prototype Westland Lynx AH. Mk 7 for British Army

Lynx AH. Mk 7. Uprated aircraft to meet GSR 3947 requirement for the British Army. As Mk 5 but with improved systems, reversed-direction (clockwise when seen from port side) tail rotor with composite blades, and 4,876 kg (10,750 lb) AUW. The more powerful tail rotor reduces noise and improves the ability to hover for extended periods at high weights, important during anti-tank operations. Eight transferred from AH.Mk 5 contract, plus five more ordered in 1985. First AH.Mk 7 (ZE376) flew for first time on 7 November 1985.

Lynx Mk 88. ASW version for use on board frigates of the Federal German Navy. Generally similar to HAS. Mk 2 but with Gem 41-2 engines, non-folding tail and Bendix AN/AQS-18 sonar. Original batch of 12 delivered. Two more ordered in 1984 for 1986 delivery. Another five ordered in February 1986 for delivery in 1988.

Other versions, for which orders have been completed (described in the 1983-84 *Jane's*), include Lynx Mk 2 (French Navy), Lynx Mk 21 (Brazilian Navy), Lynx Mk 23 (Argentine Navy), Lynx Mk 25 (Royal Netherlands Navy), Lynx Mk 27 (Royal Netherlands Navy), Lynx Mk 28 (State of Qatar Police), Lynx Mk 80 (Royal Danish Navy), Lynx Mk 81 (Royal Netherlands Navy), Lynx Mk 86 (Royal Norwegian Air Force) and Lynx Mk 89 (Nigerian Navy).

A total of 342 Lynx had been ordered by Summer 1986. Production is shared in the ratio of 70 per cent by Westland to 30 per cent by Aérospatiale.

Under development is a new version of the Navy Lynx known as **Super Lynx**, with extended range and payload and all-weather day/night capability, using advanced dipping sonar and MEL Super Searcher 360° radar. Powered by 835 kW (1,120 shp) Rolls-Royce Gem 42 engines, it will be fitted with a new high-efficiency tail rotor and, optionally, Westland's new advanced technology swept-tip composites main rotor blades. Weapons will include Penguin and Sea Skua missiles and Sting Ray torpedoes.

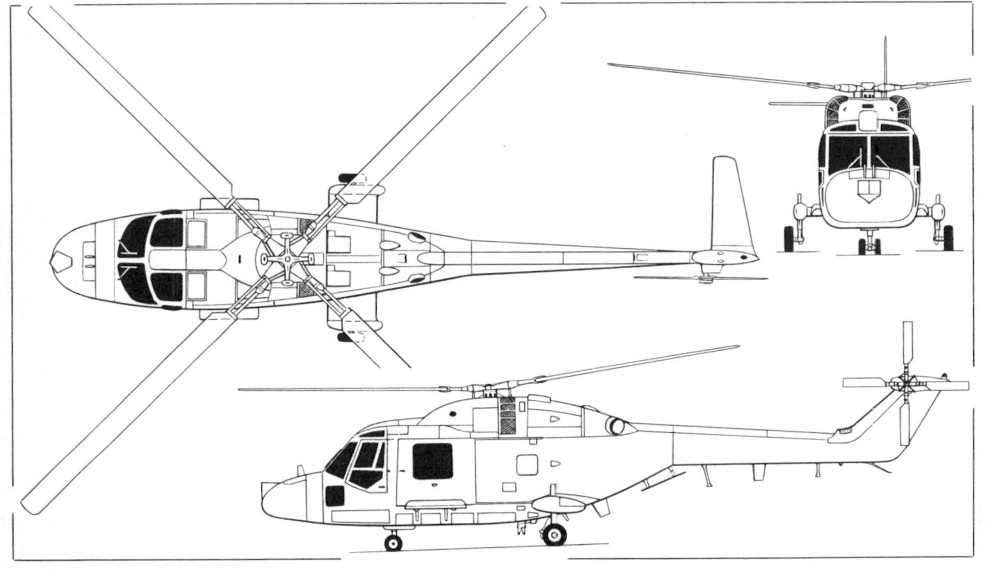

Westland Lynx HAS. Mk 2 anti-submarine helicopter for the Royal Navy *(Pilot Press)*

The following description applies to both the military general purpose and naval versions with the Gem 2 power plant, except where indicated:

TYPE: Twin-engined multi purpose helicopter.

ROTOR SYSTEM: Single four-blade semi-rigid main rotor and four-blade tail rotor. The main rotor blades, which are interchangeable, are of cambered aerofoil section and embody mass taper. Each blade consists of a two-piece, two-channel stainless steel D shaped box spar, to which is bonded a GRP rear skin stabilised by a Nomex plastics honeycomb core. Blade tips are of moulded GRP, with a stainless steel anti-erosion sheath forward of the 50 per cent chord line. Each blade is attached to the main rotor hub by titanium root attachment plates and a flexible arm. The rotor hub and inboard portions of the flexible arms are built as a complete unit, in the form of a titanium monobloc forging. Tail rotor blades have a light alloy spar, stainless steel leading-edge sheath, and rear section similar to that of main rotor blades. Main rotor blades of both versions can be folded.

ROTOR DRIVE: Drives are taken from the front of the engines into the main gearbox, which is mounted above the cabin forward of the engines. This gearbox interconnects the two engines, with speed reduction in two stages. In flight, the accessory gears, which are all at the front of the main gearbox, are driven by one of the two through shafts from the first stage reduction gears. For system checking on the ground without the rotor turning, the accessories can be driven by the port engine. Freewheel units are mounted in each engine gearbox shaft, and also within the accessory drive chain of gears. Rotor head controls are actuated by three identical tandem servo jacks, trunnion mounted from the main rotor gearbox and powered by two independent hydraulic systems. Control system incorporates a simple stability augmentation system. Provision is made for in-flight blade tracking. Each engine embodies an independent control system which provides full authority rotor speed governing, pilot control being limited to selection of the desired rotor speed range. In the event of an engine failure, this system will restore power up to single engine maximum contingency rating. On the naval versions, the main rotor can provide negative thrust to increase stability on deck after touchdown. Tail rotor drive is taken from the main ring gear. A hydraulically operated rotor brake is mounted on the main gearbox.

FUSELAGE AND TAIL UNIT: Conventional semi-monocoque pod and boom structure, mainly of light alloy. Glassfibre components used for access panels, doors and fairings. Single large window in each of the main cabin sliding doors. Provision for internally mounted defensive armament, and for universal flange mountings on each side of the exterior to carry weapons or other stores. Tailboom is a light alloy monocoque structure bearing the sweptback vertical fin/tail rotor pylon, which has a half tailplane near the tip on the starboard side. Tail pylon leading- and trailing-edges, and bullet fairing over tail rotor gearbox, are of glassfibre. Tail pylon of naval version can be folded and spread manually, to reduce overall length for stowage.

LANDING GEAR (general purpose military version): Non-retractable tubular skid type. Provision for a pair of adjustable ground handling wheels on each skid. Flotation gear optional.

LANDING GEAR (naval versions): Non-retractable oleo-pneumatic tricycle type. Single-wheel main units, carried on sponsons, are fixed at 27° toe-out for deck landing, and can be manually turned into line and locked fore and aft for movement of aircraft into and out of ship's hangar. Twin-wheel nose unit can be steered hydraulically through 90° by the pilot. Designed for high shock absorption to facilitate take-off from, and landing on, small decks under severe sea and weather conditions. Sprag brakes (wheel locks) fitted to each wheel prevent rotation on landing or inadvertent deck roll. These locks are disengaged hydraulically and will re-engage automatically in the event of hydraulic failure. Flotation gear, and hydraulically actuated harpoon deck lock securing system, optional.

POWER PLANT: Two Rolls-Royce Gem 2 turboshaft engines, each with max contingency rating of 671 kW (900 shp) in Lynx AH. 1, HAS. 2 and early export variants. Later versions have Gem 41-1 or 41-2 engines, each with max contingency rating of 835 kW (1,120 shp), or Gem 43-1 engines, each with max contingency rating of 846 kW (1,135 shp). Engines mounted side by side on top of the fuselage upper decking, aft of the main rotor shaft and gearbox, and separated from fuselage, transmission area and each other by firewalls. Engine air intakes de-iced electrically. Fuel in five crashproof bag tanks, all within the fuselage structure, comprising two main tanks each of 204 kg (450 lb) capacity, two side by side collector tanks each of 93 kg (204·5 lb) capacity, and a 148 kg (326 lb) capacity underfloor tank at the forward end of the cabin. Total fuel capacity 733 kg (1,616 lb). If required, ferry range can be increased by installing in rear of cabin two metal auxiliary tanks. Single-point pressure refuelling and defuelling; two points for gravity refuelling. A removable refuelling/defuelling pack can be fitted in the cabin and used to refuel aircraft from dump stocks on ground or containers suspended from hoist. It is also possible to raise fuel about 5 m (15 ft) while the aircraft is hovering. Fuel jettison capability for main and forward tanks. Provision for self-sealing of both collector tanks (except in Royal Navy versions). Engine oil tank capacity 6·8 litres (1·5 Imp gallons). Main rotor gearbox oil capacity 18 litres (4 Imp gallons).

ACCOMMODATION: Pilot and co-pilot or observer on side by side seats which are adjustable fore and aft and for height. Inertia reel shoulder harness for pilot and co-pilot. Dual controls optional. Additional crew members according to role. Individual forward hinged cockpit door and large rearward sliding cabin door on each side; all four doors jettisonable. Cockpit accessible from cabin area. Maximum high density layout (general purpose version) for one pilot and 10 armed troops or paratroops, on lightweight bench seats in soundproofed cabin. Alternative VIP layouts for four to seven passengers, with additional cabin soundproofing. Seats can be removed quickly to permit the carriage of up to 907 kg (2,000 lb) of freight internally. Tiedown rings are provided at approx 51 cm (20 in) intervals on main cabin floor, which is stressed for loads of up to 976 kg/m² (200 lb/sq ft). Alternatively, loads of up to 1,360 kg (3,000 lb) can be carried externally on freight hook mounted below the cabin floor and fitted, in naval version, with electrically operated emergency release system. In the casualty evacuation role, with a crew of two, the Lynx can accommodate three standard stretchers and a medical attendant. Both basic versions have secondary capability for search and rescue (up to nine survivors) and other roles.

SYSTEMS: Two independent hydraulic systems, pressure 141 bars (2,050 lb/sq in). A third hydraulic system, at the same pressure, is provided in the naval version when Alcatel sonar equipment, MAD or a hydraulic winch system is installed. When this third hydraulic system is installed, the deck lock harpoon is also operated by this system. When the Bendix AN/AQS-13 sonar is installed, a 207 bar (3,000 lb/sq in) 'utility' hydraulic system is used. No pneumatic system. 28V DC electrical power supplied by two 6kW engine driven starter/generators and an alternator. External power sockets. 24V 23Ah (optionally 40Ah) nickel-cadmium battery fitted for essential services and emergency engine starting. 200V three-phase AC power available at 400Hz from two 15kVA transmission driven alternators. Graviner Triple FD engine fire detection system; two separate fire suppression systems fitted. Optional cabin heating and ventilation system. Optional supplementary cockpit heating system. Electric anti-icing and demisting of windscreen, and electrically operated windscreen wipers, standard; windscreen washing system optional.

AVIONICS AND FLIGHT EQUIPMENT: All versions equipped as standard with navigation, cabin and cockpit lights; adjustable landing light under nose; anti-collision beacon; first aid kit(s); and hand fire extinguishers for cabin. Avionics common to all roles (general purpose and naval versions) include GEC Avionics duplex three-axis automatic stabilisation equipment; Sperry GM9 Gyrosyn compass system; Decca tactical air navigation system (TANS); Decca 71 Doppler, E2C standby compass; and S.G. Brown intercom system. Optional role equipment for both versions includes GEC Avionics automatic flight control system (AFCS); Plessey PTR 377 UHF/VHF with homing; Collins ARC-159 UHF with homing; Plessey PTR 1751 UHF; Ultra D 403M standby UHF; Collins ARC-182 VHF/UHF; AM/FM with homing;

Westland Super Lynx naval helicopter, armed with a Sting Ray torpedo *(Brian M. Service)*

Collins VHF-20B VHF/AM; GEC Avionics AD 120 VHF/FM; Chelton 7 homer; Collins VOR/ILS; DME; Collins ARN-118 Tacan; I-band transponder (naval version only); Plessey PTR 446, Collins APX-72, Siemens STR 700/375 or Italtel APX-77 IFF; GEC Avionics AD 370 and AD 380 radio compass; and vortex sand filter for engine air intakes. Additional units are fitted in naval version, when sonar is fitted, to provide automatic transition to hover and automatic Doppler hold in hover.

ARMAMENT AND OPERATIONAL EQUIPMENT: For armed escort, anti-tank or air-to-surface strike missions, general purpose version can be equipped with one 20 mm Oerlikon-Bührle KDA or similar cannon mounted in the cabin with 1,500 rds; or two 20 mm cannon mounted externally so as to permit the carriage also of anti-tank missiles or a pintle-mounted 7·62 mm GEC Minigun inside the cabin; or a side mounted 25 mm Oerlikon cannon; or a Minigun beneath cabin, in Emerson Minitat installation, with 3,000 rds. External pylon can be fitted on each side of cabin for a variety of stores, including two Minigun or other self-contained gun pods; two pods each carrying eighteen 68 mm SNEB, twelve 80 mm SURA, or nineteen 2·75 in rockets, the 2·75 in rockets containing illuminating flares if required; or up to six Aérospatiale AS.11, or eight Aérospatiale/MBB Hot, Rockwell Hellfire, Hughes TOW, or similar air-to-surface missiles. An additional six or eight missiles can be carried in cabin, for rearming in forward areas, and a stabilised sight is fitted for target detection and missile direction. British Army Lynx aircraft equipped with TOW missiles have roof mounted Hughes sight manufactured under licence by British Aerospace. The TOW roof sight is being upgraded under a £60 million mid-life improvement contract awarded to British Aerospace Army Weapons Division in 1986. The upgraded sight will have a night vision capability in the far infra-red waveband to increase operational versatility in low-light night conditions or poor daylight visibility. The Lynx can transport anti-tank teams of three gunners with missiles and launchers. For search and rescue role, with three crew, both versions can have a waterproof floor, eight 4 in flares in utility version (or six 4·5 in flares in naval version), and a 272 kg (600 lb) capacity electrically operated 'clip-on' hoist in starboard side of cabin. Alternative option of hydraulically operated hoist in naval version when third hydraulic system is installed. Optional equipment, according to role, can include lightweight sighting system with alternative target magnification, vertical and/or oblique cameras, up to six 4·5 in flares for night operation, low light level TV, infra-red linescan, searchlight, and specialised communications equipment. Naval version can carry out a number of these roles, but has specialised equipment for its primary duties. For ASW role, this includes two Mk 44, Mk 46 or Sting Ray homing torpedoes, one each on an external pylon on each side of fuselage, and six marine markers; or two Mk 11 depth charges. Detection of submarines is by means of either Alcatel DUAV 4 or Bendix AN/AQS-18 dipping sonars or Texas Instruments AN/ASQ-81 magnetic anomaly detector. The dipping sonars are operated by a hydraulically powered winch and cable hover mode facilities within the AFCS. Ferranti Seaspray lightweight search and tracking radar, for detecting small surface targets in low visibility/high sea conditions. Armament includes four BAe Sea Skua semi-active homing missiles for attacking light surface craft; alternatively, four AS.12 or similar wire guided missiles can be employed in conjunction with AF 530 or APX-334 lightweight stabilised optical sighting system.

DIMENSIONS, EXTERNAL (A: general purpose version; N: naval version):
Main rotor diameter (A, N) 12·80 m (42 ft 0 in)
Tail rotor diameter (A, N) 2·21 m (7 ft 3 in)
Main rotor blade chord (A, N, constant, each) 0·395 m (1 ft 3½ in)
Tail rotor blade chord (A, N, constant, each) 0·18 m (7·1 in)
Length overall:
A, N both rotors turning 15·163 m (49 ft 9 in)
A, main rotor blades folded 13·165 m (43 ft 2·3 in)
N, main rotor blades and tail folded 10·618 m (34 ft 10 in)
Length of fuselage, nose to tail rotor centre:
A 12·06 m (39 ft 6·8 in)
N 11·92 m (39 ft 1·3 in)
Width overall, main rotor blades folded:
A 2·94 m (9 ft 7¾ in)
N 3·75 m (12 ft 3¾ in)
Height overall, both rotors turning:
A 3·66 m (12 ft 0 in)
N 3·60 m (11 ft 9¾ in)
Height overall, both rotors stopped:
A 3·504 m (11 ft 6 in)
N 3·48 m (11 ft 5 in)
Height to top of rotor head: A 2·964 m (9 ft 8·7 in)
Height overall, main rotor blades and tail folded:
N 3·20 m (10 ft 6 in)
Tail rotor ground clearance: A 1·41 m (4 ft 7½ in)
N 1·38 m (4 ft 6·3 in)
Tailplane half-span (from fuselage c/l):
A, N 1·776 m (5 ft 9·9 in)
Skid track: A 2·032 m (6 ft 8 in)
Wheel track: N 2·778 m (9 ft 1·4 in)
Wheelbase: N 2·94 m (9 ft 7¾ in)
Cabin door openings (A, N, each):
Mean width 1·372 m (4 ft 6 in)
Height 1·194 m (3 ft 11 in)

DIMENSIONS, INTERNAL:
Cabin, from back of pilots' seats:
Min length 2·057 m (6 ft 9 in)
Max width 1·778 m (5 ft 10 in)
Width at rear 1·409 m (4 ft 7½ in)
Max internal floor width 1·715 m (5 ft 7½ in)
Max height 1·422 m (4 ft 8 in)
Floor area 3·72 m² (40·04 sq ft)
Volume 5·21 m³ (184 cu ft)

AREAS:
Main rotor disc 128·7 m² (1,385·4 sq ft)
Tail rotor disc 3·84 m² (41·28 sq ft)

WEIGHTS (A: general purpose version, N: naval version):
Manufacturer's empty weight: A 2,578 kg (5,683 lb)
N 2,740 kg (6,040 lb)
Manufacturer's basic weight: A 2,658 kg (5,860 lb)
N 3,030 kg (6,680 lb)

Operating weight empty, equipped:
A, troop transport (pilot and 10 troops) 2,787 kg (6,144 lb)
A, anti-tank strike (incl weapon pylons, firing equipment and sight) 3,072 kg (6,772 lb)
A, search and rescue (crew of three) 2,963 kg (6,532 lb)
N, anti-submarine strike 3,343 kg (7,370 lb)
N, reconnaissance (crew of two) 3,277 kg (7,224 lb)
N, anti-submarine classification and strike 3,472 kg (7,654 lb)
N, air to surface vessel search and strike (crew of two and four Sea Skuas) 3,414 kg (7,526 lb)
N, search and rescue (crew of three) 3,416 kg (7,531 lb)
N, dunking sonar search and strike 3,650 kg (8,047 lb)
Max T-O weight: A 4,535 kg (10,000 lb)
N 4,763 kg (10,500 lb)

PERFORMANCE (at normal max T-O weight at S/L, ISA, except where indicated. A: general purpose version; N: naval version):
Max continuous cruising speed:
A 140 knots (259 km/h; 161 mph)
N 125 knots (232 km/h; 144 mph)
A (ISA + 20°C) 130 knots (241 km/h; 150 mph)
N (ISA + 20°C) 114 knots (211 km/h; 131 mph)
Max continuous cruising speed (1 h), one engine out:
A 134 knots (248 km/h; 154 mph)
N 122 knots (225 km/h; 140 mph)
A (ISA + 20°C) 114 knots (211 km/h; 131 mph)
N (ISA + 20°C) 99 knots (184 km/h; 114 mph)
Speed for max endurance:
A, N (ISA and ISA + 20°C) 70 knots (130 km/h; 81 mph)
Min flying speed (max contingency rating, one engine out): A 19 knots (36 km/h; 22 mph)
N 23 knots (43 km/h; 27 mph)
A (ISA + 20°C) 32 knots (60 km/h; 37 mph)
N (ISA + 20°C) 39 knots (73 km/h; 45 mph)
Max forward rate of climb: A 756 m (2,480 ft)/min
N 661 m (2,170 ft)/min
A (ISA + 20°C) 536 m (1,760 ft)/min
N (ISA + 20°C) 469 m (1,540 ft)/min
Max forward rate of climb (1 h power), one engine out:
A 277 m (910 ft)/min
N 223 m (730 ft)/min
A (ISA + 20°C) 72 m (235 ft)/min
N (ISA + 20°C) 64 m (210 ft)/min
Max vertical rate of climb:
A 472 m (1,550 ft)/min
N 351 m (1,150 ft)/min
A (ISA + 20°C) 390 m (1,280 ft)/min
N (ISA + 20°C) 244 m (800 ft)/min
Hovering ceiling OGE: A 3,230 m (10,600 ft)
N 2,575 m (8,450 ft)
Typical range, with reserves:
A, troop transport 292 nm (540 km; 336 miles)
Radius of action, out and back at max sustained speed, allowances for T-O and landing, 30 min loiter in search area, 3 min hover for each survivor, and 10% fuel reserves at end of mission:
N, search and rescue (crew of 3 and 2 survivors) 115 nm (212 km; 132 miles)
N, search and rescue (crew of 3 and 7 survivors) 96 nm (178 km; 111 miles)
Time on station at 50 nm (93 km; 58 miles) radius, out and back at max sustained speed, with 2 torpedoes, smoke floats and marine markers, allowances for T-O and landing and 10% fuel reserves at end of mission:
N, anti-submarine classification and strike, loiter speed on station 2 h 0 min
N, anti-submarine strike, loiter on station 2 h 29 min
N, dunking sonar search and strike, 50% loiter speed and 50% hover on station 1 h 5 min
Time on station at 50 nm (93 km; 58 miles) radius, out and back at max sustained speed, with crew of 2 and 4 Sea Skuas, allowances and reserves as above:
N, air to surface vessel strike, en-route radar search and loiter speed on station 1 h 36 min
Max range: A 340 nm (630 km; 392 miles)
N 320 nm (593 km; 368 miles)
A (ISA + 20°C) 339 nm (628 km; 390 miles)
N (ISA + 20°C) 320 nm (593 km; 368 miles)
Max endurance: A 2 h 57 min
N (ISA + 20°C) 2 h 50 min
Max ferry range with auxiliary cabin tanks:
A 724 nm (1,342 km; 834 miles)
N 565 nm (1,046 km; 650 miles)

WESTLAND LYNX-3

The Lynx-3 is a dedicated anti-tank helicopter, derived from the earlier production Lynx and incorporating its dynamic systems. It has a gross weight some 27 per cent greater, is engineered to offer increased survivability and is able to mount greater firepower. Advanced avionics allow Lynx-3 to operate by day or night, and in adverse weather conditions. Night vision and target acquisition systems are available in optional nose, roof or rotor mast mounts. It can be equipped to carry and launch current and future versions of Euromissile Hot, Hughes TOW and Rockwell Hellfire air-to-surface missiles; for defence against air attack, it can be armed with General Dynamics Stinger missiles. A naval version has also been announced.

A Lynx-3 (ZE477) flew for the first time on 14 June 1984 fitted temporarily with a standard Lynx main rotor. It has since been retrofitted with the production standard BERP blades. The following details refer generally to the anti-armour version:

TYPE: Twin-engined anti-armour helicopter.

ROTOR SYSTEM: Advanced four-blade semi-rigid main rotor and four-blade tail rotor. Main rotor blades of Westland composite construction, incorporating BERP (British Experimental Rotor Programme) tips, which are claimed

Westland Navy Lynx armed with two Sea Skua missiles and a homing torpedo

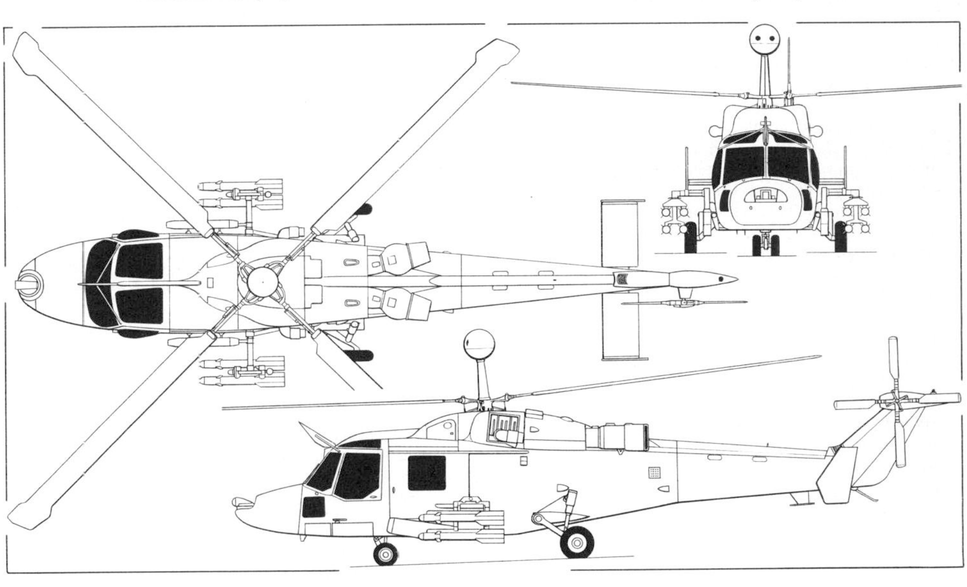

Westland Lynx-3 with mast mounted sight and Hellfire missiles *(Pilot Press)*

Mockup of naval version of Westland Lynx-3 showing new BERP rotor blade tips

to increase rotor efficiency by up to 40 per cent. Main rotor blade folding optional (standard on naval version). The tail rotor, which is generally similar to that of the Westland 30, also has blades of composite construction; it rotates in the opposite direction to that of the standard Lynx and is considerably quieter.

ROTOR DRIVE: Similar to that of standard Lynx, with drives taken from the front of the engines into the main gearbox, which is mounted above the cabin forward of the engines. In the event of an engine failure, the rotor drive system allows the surviving power unit to operate at its maximum contingency rating.

FUSELAGE AND TAIL UNIT: Conventional semi-monocoque pod and boom structure of light alloy frames and stringers. By comparison with the standard Lynx the fuselage has been lengthened by 30 cm (11·8 in) to provide increased cabin volume. This makes it possible to seat the two-man crew slightly further forward, thus enhancing their view to the rear. It also provides increased storage space for missile reloads and allows for larger cabin doors. The tailcone is a light alloy monocoque structure with integral sweptback vertical fin/tail rotor pylon, as for the Westland 30. (Tailcone will fold on naval version.) Fixed incidence tailplane of inverted aerofoil section.

LANDING GEAR: Non-retractable tricycle type, with single-wheel main units and twin-wheel nose unit. Shock absorption system designed to survive descent rates as high as 6·10 m (20 ft)/s.

POWER PLANT: Two Rolls-Royce Gem 60 turboshaft engines, each with a max continuous rating of 832 kW (1,115 shp) for normal twin-engined operation and a one-engine-inoperative max contingency rating of 1,004 kW (1,346 shp). Lateral engine air intakes incorporate particle filters. Engines, gearbox and rotor head mounted on vibration absorbing raft isolated from the main cabin by four elastomeric suspension units. Crash resistant fuel system. IR suppression optional.

ACCOMMODATION: Crew of two, side by side, in wide-view cockpit designed to meet the requirements of MIL-STD-1290. Crew seats have armour protection and are mounted on shock absorbing struts designed to ensure survival at descent rates tolerable to landing gear. Layout of the advanced cockpit, incorporating new tactical display and flight data management systems to minimise crew workload, is not yet finalised. Considerable space for storage of missile reloads, or to transport mobile anti-tank teams with missiles and launchers. Windscreen anti-icing, demisting and electrically operated wipers.

AVIONICS: Lynx-3 avionics are not yet finalised, but the inclusion of a mission avionics databus system, to MIL-STD-1553B, will allow integration of the latest systems, reduce wiring looms to a minimum, and simplify the introduction of alternative or new sensor and weapons fits. Navigation is likely to be based on the Sperry GM9 Gyrosyn compass system, Decca tactical air navigation system (TANS) and Decca Doppler. Mission avionics may include Martin Marietta target acquisition and designation system (TADS) and pilot's night vision sensor (PNVS), IFF, radar warning receivers, and IR jamming. Sensors for target acquisition, and enhanced viewing systems, will be mounted in optional positions including a mast mounted sight (MMS) or on the fuselage nose or roof. (Naval version will have 360° radar, MAD, dunking sonar, and active and passive sonobuoys).

ARMAMENT AND EQUIPMENT: Can be equipped with an Oerlikon or similar 20 mm cannon (25 mm cannon under evaluation); a pintle mounted 7·62 mm GEC Minigun inside the cabin; an 0·5 in machine-gun pod; air-to-surface missiles including Euromissile Hot, Hughes TOW and Rockwell Hellfire; air-to-air missiles including General Dynamics Stinger or Shorts Blowpipe; and SNEB, SNORA or SURA rockets. Goodyear chaff dispenser. Cable cutter mounted on roof, immediately above windscreen. (Naval version can carry Mk 44, Mk 46 or Sting Ray torpedoes; depth charges; and Sea Skua anti-ship missiles; and will have a harpoon deck lock and main rotor negative thrust capability to simplify deck recover.)

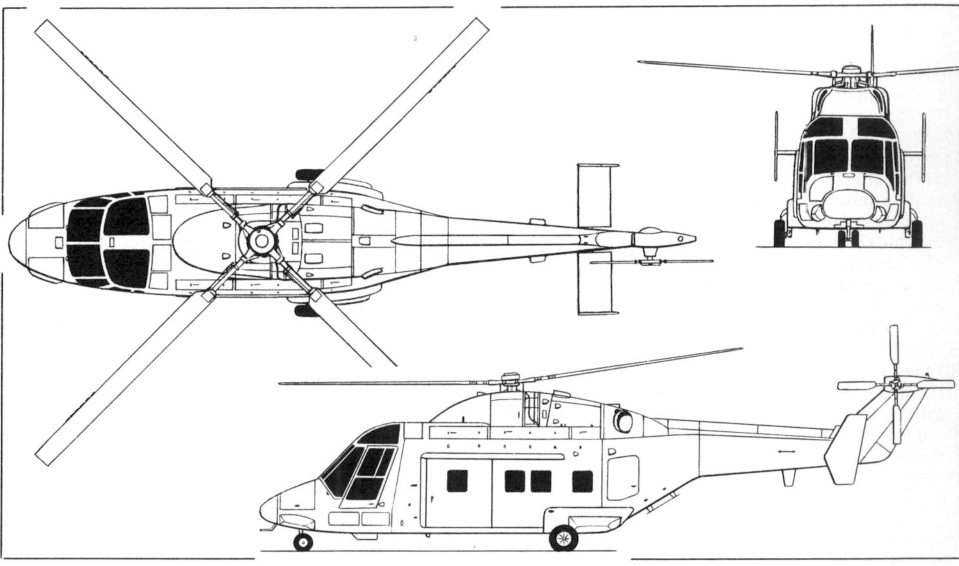

Westland 30 (TT30) twin-turboshaft general purpose military and civil helicopter *(Pilot Press)*

DIMENSIONS, EXTERNAL:	
Main rotor diameter	12·80 m (42 ft 0 in)
Tail rotor diameter	2·44 m (8 ft 0 in)
Length overall: rotors turning	15·47 m (50 ft 9 in)
main rotor folded	13·79 m (45 ft 3 in)
Width overall, main rotor folded	3·05 m (10 ft 0 in)
Height overall, rotors turning	3·30 m (10 ft 10 in)
AREAS:	
Main rotor disc	128·7 m² (1,385·4 sq ft)
Tail rotor disc	4·67 m² (50·27 sq ft)
WEIGHTS (estimated):	
Max fuel weight	1,000 kg (2,204 lb)
Payload	1,542 kg (3,400 lb)
Normal max T-O weight	5,896 kg (13,000 lb)
PERFORMANCE (estimated):	
Max level speed	165 knots (306 km/h; 190 mph)
Cruising speed	150 knots (278 km/h; 172 mph)
Range with max fuel, 20 min reserves	335 nm (620 km; 385 miles)
Endurance	3 h 30 min

WESTLAND 30 (TT30 and TT300)

Westland Helicopters first undertook studies leading to this enlarged, twin-engined development of the Lynx helicopter in early 1976. The first prototype (G-BGHF) made its first flight on 10 April 1979, two weeks ahead of schedule. British CAA type certification (VFR and IFR) was received in March 1982, and FAA certification in December of that year.

Pre-production Westland Lynx-3 armed with Hellfire missiles

Main differences from the Lynx are the completely new and more spacious fuselage; increased diameter main and tail rotor; a dynamic system developed from that of the Lynx and retaining more than 85 per cent of the proven system in that aircraft; increased fuel capacity; new automatic flight control system; and simplified electrical system. Payload/range capability is increased, but the controllability of the Lynx is retained.

The original designation of this helicopter was WG 30, but this was changed subsequently to Westland 30, and the current designations are TT30 and TT300. The version for the civil market can be equipped for passenger and/or cargo transport, executive and VIP use, and for offshore rig support. A military version is planned as a tactical transport, battlefield support and aeromedical helicopter.

The following versions have been announced:

Series 100 (TT30). Initial production version, flown for the first time in September 1981. Powered by Rolls-Royce Gem 41-1 engines, each rated at 846 kW (1,135 shp) max contingency.

Series 100-60 (TT30). Designation of later production version, powered by two Rolls-Royce Gem 60-3 engines, each rated at 940 kW (1,260 shp) max contingency. First flown on 19 January 1984.

Series 200 (TT30). Variant with more powerful General Electric CT7-2B turboshafts, each rated at 1,277 kW (1,712 shp) max contingency, 1,135 kW (1,522 shp) intermediate contingency, 1,205 kW (1,615 shp) for T-O, and 940 kW (1,260 shp) max continuous. These engines drive the same conformal main gearbox as that of the Series 100 but, due to the higher output speed of the CT7, via an additional reduction gearbox on each engine output shaft. The Series 200 is generally similar to the Series 100, except for new sideways facing engine air intakes, heated for anti-icing; new engine control system to match the CT7; and new DC electrical generation system. Visible external differences include the shape of the upper fuselage decking, which is lengthened to accommodate the longer raft upon which the engines and main gearbox are mounted. Manufacturer's bare weight 3,411 kg (7,520 lb); max T-O weight 5,806 kg (12,800 lb). Max payload 1,782 kg (3,928 lb). First flight (G-ELEC) 3 September 1983.

Series 300 (TT300). Variant with General Electric CT7s (and military equivalents. The prototype TT300 (G-17-22, G-HAUL) made its first flight on 5 February 1986 and combines the spacious accommodation of the standard Westland 30 cabin with improved payload/range and higher cruising speed. This is achieved by an increase in maximum AUW to 7,257 kg (16,000 lb) and the adoption of a five-blade main rotor with Westland's new BERP advanced technology composite blades. The rotor head and main gearbox are further developments of the proven Lynx/Westland 30 units. New standards of low noise and low vibration are offered, with a low tip speed, large diameter composite tail rotor, and a further refinement of the raft isolation concept already employed successfully on the Series 100. The TT300 is available in civil, utility and naval versions. With reserves, the civil version will carry a full complement of 17 passengers and their baggage at 144 knots (267 km/h; 166 mph) for 215 nm (398 km; 247 miles) or, with an easily installed long range tank, 13 passengers and their baggage for 360 nm (667 km; 414 miles). In a military role it can carry 20 troops or 1,360 kg (3,000 lb) of stores in the cabin. The cockpit is compatible with use of night vision goggles, and EFIS is available as an option. Flight in maximum continuous icing conditions is possible with optional blade de-icing.

Two Westland 30s were ordered by British Airways Helicopters in February 1981: these were delivered in January and October 1982, followed by a third in June 1983. Sixteen have gone to various operators in the USA.

In April 1986 the Helicopter Corporation of India confirmed an order for 21 Westland 30 Series 100-60s, for use in offshore energy exploration. The aircraft are being supplied under a £65 million overseas aid package from the UK Government.

The following details apply specifically to the Series 100-60:

TYPE: Twin-turboshaft general purpose military and civil helicopter.

ROTOR SYSTEM: Four-blade hingeless main rotor and four-blade articulated tail rotor. Main rotor blades are of constant chord and NPL9615 cambered section; each has a stainless steel spar and a bonded GRP rear skin. Forged titanium hingeless main rotor head. The tail rotor has composite blades, each with a glassfibre D spar and carbonfibre and glassfibre skinned, foam filled trailing-edge. Main rotor blades fold. Rotor brake standard.

ROTOR DRIVE: Engines drive directly into standard Lynx conformal main gearbox, thence by driveshafts to intermediate and tail rotor gearboxes. Main rotor shaft of titanium. Main rotor/engine rpm ratio 1:18·91. Tail rotor/engine rpm ratio 1:3·74.

FUSELAGE: Main cabin, which is of basically rectangular cross-section, is a conventional semi-monocoque structure of light alloy frames and stringers, with stringer spacing constant throughout the airframe. Two lift frames support vibration absorbing raft on which engines and main gearbox are mounted. Roof panels, fuel tank surrounds and bulkheads are of aluminium honeycomb, floor panels of Ciba-Geigy Fibrelam GRP.

LANDING GEAR: Non-retractable tricycle type, with oleo-pneumatic shock absorber in each unit and castoring nose unit. Single mainwheels with Goodyear tyres, size 651 × 221-254 mm, pressure 4·69 bars (68 lb/sq in). Twin self-centering nosewheels with Goodyear tyres, size 361 × 126-156 mm, pressure 3·80 bars (55 lb/sq in). Goodyear disc brakes.

POWER PLANT: Two Rolls-Royce Gem turboshaft engines, as detailed in model listings, mounted side by side above cabin. Fuel in two integral tanks, used as supports for front and rear seats in cabin. Capacity 663 litres (146 Imp gallons; 175 US gallons) in front tank; 656 litres (144 Imp gallons; 173 US gallons) in rear tank. Auxiliary tanks optional. Fuel booster pumps, with provision for cross-feed to either engine. Engine intakes anti-iced.

ACCOMMODATION: Crew of two on flight deck, with provision for one-pilot operation. Main cabin can accommodate, in military version, 14 troops each weighing 127 kg (280 lb) including full equipment, or 20 troops with less equipment. Aeromedical version can accommodate six stretchers plus sitting casualties/medical attendants. Civil passenger version can provide three/four-abreast seating for up to 17 persons in airline standards of comfort. This version, too, has a high density layout, in which up to 19 passengers can be accommodated. Various other civil layouts include executive/VIP transport (six/eleven seats, refreshment cabinet, table, toilet and galley unit), offshore oil support, all-cargo, and mixed passenger/cargo. Door on starboard side incorporating airstair. Large rearward sliding door (width 1·27 m; 4 ft 2 in) on each side of cabin optional. Baggage compartment in rear fuselage, aft of cabin, with external doors.

SYSTEMS: Two independent hydraulic systems (each 141 bars; 2,050 lb/sq in). System flow rate 14·5 litres/min at 117·2 bars (3·2 Imp gallons/min at 1,700 lb/sq in). Reservoir unpressurised. DC electrical system of 28V is powered by two 6kW engine driven starter/generators and storage battery. AC power provided by two 450VA static inverters, but 15 kVA alternators are available at customer's option.

AVIONICS AND EQUIPMENT: Nose compartment for avionics and radio. Standard equipment includes Collins Pro Line II nav/com and Sperry Primus 500 radar. Optional items include King Gold Crown nav/com, Bendix RDR 1400 radar and Racal/Decca R/Nav plus Doppler and HF radio. Louis Newmark duplex automatic flight control system for all three axes, with computer based control and duplex heading hold. Duplicated three-axis automatic stabilisation equipment.

Prototype of the Westland TT300, with General Electric CT7 turboshaft engines and advanced technology BERP main rotor blades

DIMENSIONS, EXTERNAL:
- Main rotor diameter: 13·31 m (43 ft 8 in)
- Main rotor blade chord (constant): 0·394 m (1 ft 3½ in)
- Tail rotor diameter: 2·44 m (8 ft 0 in)
- Length overall, rotors turning: 15·91 m (52 ft 2½ in)
- Height overall, rotors turning: 4·74 m (15 ft 6½ in)
- Wheel track: 2·44 m (8 ft 0 in)
- Wheelbase: 5·45 m (17 ft 10½ in)
- Standard airstair door (stbd, fwd):
  - Height: 1·40 m (4 ft 7 in)
  - Width: 0·71 m (2 ft 4 in)
  - Height to sill: 0·58 m (1 ft 11 in)

DIMENSIONS, INTERNAL:
- Cabin, excl flight deck: Length: 4·42 m (14 ft 6 in)
  - Width: 1·98 m (6 ft 6 in)
  - Height: 1·28 m (4 ft 2¼ in)
  - Volume: 13·03 m³ (460 cu ft)
- Baggage compartment volume (rear): 1·97 m³ (70 cu ft)

AREAS:
- Main rotor disc: 139·14 m² (1,497·7 sq ft)
- Tail rotor disc: 4·67 m² (50·3 sq ft)

WEIGHTS (A: Series 100; B: Series 100-60):
- Manufacturer's empty weight, with basic minimum equipment: A: 3,167 kg (6,982 lb)
  - B: 3,789 kg (8,353 lb)
- Max fuel load: 1,043 kg (2,300 lb)
- Max weight for hovering OGE, S/L, ISA + 10°C:
  - A: 5,511 kg (12,150 lb)
- Max T-O and landing weight: A: 5,602 kg (12,350 lb)
  - B: 5,806 kg (12,800 lb)
- Max weight up to ISA + 35°C and 4,575 m (15,000 ft):
  - B: 5,806 kg (12,800 lb)

PERFORMANCE (estimated, at max T-O weight except where indicated):
- Max level cruising speed at S/L, ISA:
  - A, B: 120 knots (222 km/h; 138 mph)
- Max level cruising speed at S/L, ISA + 20°C:
  - A: 120 knots (222 km/h; 138 mph)
  - B: 118 knots (219 km/h; 136 mph)
- Max level speed, one engine out at S/L, ISA:
  - A: 98 knots (182 km/h; 113 mph)
  - B: 105 knots (195 km/h; 121 mph)
- Min level speed, one engine out at S/L, ISA:
  - A: 41 knots (76 km/h; 48 mph)
  - B: 38 knots (71 km/h; 44 mph)
- Hovering ceiling IGE, ISA: A: 1,158 m (3,800 ft)
  - B: 792 m (2,600 ft)
- Hovering ceiling OGE, ISA: A: 792 m (2,600 ft)
  - B: 884 m (2,900 ft)
- Radius of action, offshore oil support, IFR, 45 min hold, 5% fuel reserves: A: 135 nm (250 km; 156 miles)
  - B: 145 nm (269 km; 167 miles)
- Range with 1,814 kg (4,000 lb) internal payload, no reserves: A: 190 nm (352 km; 219 miles)
  - B: 255 nm (472 km; 293 miles)
- Max ferry range, no reserves:
  - A: 405 nm (750 km; 466 miles)
  - B: standard fuel: 395 nm (732 km; 455 miles)
  - standard plus auxiliary fuel: 510 nm (945 km; 587 miles)

WESTLAND/AÉROSPATIALE GAZELLE

The Gazelle, described fully under the Aérospatiale heading in the French section, was a joint project in Britain and France under the same Anglo-French agreement as the Puma. A total of 212 Gazelle AH. Mk 1s was built for the British Army, 40 HT. Mk 2s for the Royal Navy, 33 HT. Mk 3s and one HCC. Mk 4 for the Royal Air Force.

WESTLAND/SIKORSKY WS 70

Following agreement of full partnership with United Technologies, Westland received US State Department approval to produce a version of the Sikorsky Black Hawk helicopter designated WS 70. The Westland board has set aside £3 million for production of a demonstrator, which will be assembled from a Sikorsky kit to US Army S-70A battlefield transport standards. It is scheduled to fly in April 1987, powered by two General Electric T700 turboshaft engines.

UNITED STATES OF AMERICA

AAI

AMERICAN AVIATION INDUSTRIES

16700 Roscoe Boulevard, Van Nuys, California 91406
Telephone: (818) 786 1921
Telex: 662903 ACI USA
Chief Executive Officer: Geoff Miller
Vice-President, Marketing: Don Sterling

Aviation Consultants Inc formed American Aviation Industries to re-engine Lockheed JetStar business jets with new turbofan engines. The modified aircraft is known as the FanStar. AAI is also considering re-engining programmes for several other types of business jet and commuter aircraft, including the Fairchild Swearingen Metro II. The Fan Commander project (1985-86 *Jane's*) has been abandoned.

AAI FANSTAR

The FanStar conversion involves the removal of the four 14·68 kN (3,300 lb st) Pratt & Whitney JT12 engines or the four 16·46 kN (3,700 lb st) AiResearch TFE731-3 turbofans from Lockheed JetStar I and II aircraft respectively, and replacing them with two General Electric CF34-3A high bypass turbofan engines, each rated at 40·70 kN (9,150 lb st), with automatic power reserve (APR), 38·48 kN (8,650 lb) without APR, installed in new translating sleeve, short-cowl nacelles with cascade type thrust reversers. Fuel capacity is 10,069 litres (2,660 US gallons) in four integral wing tanks and two non-removable external tanks. Other changes include replacement of the aircraft's DC electrical system by an AC system with power rectified into DC, with static inverters to supply regulated AC where needed. The inverters are of the dual split-bus type, with no load shedding, and permit operation of all AC components in the event of engine failure. A dual fuel pump system is installed if not already fitted to the aircraft. A new high-volume auxiliary power unit will be installed in each conversion.

Structural changes to the FanStar include the addition of a 0·61 m (2 ft 0 in) extension and 1·22 m (4 ft 0 in) high NASA (Whitcomb) winglet to each wingtip and a 0·76 m (2 ft 6 in) extension to the rudder below the tailplane for improved yaw control, connected to a rudder bias system for enhanced directional control in engine-out situations. A Collins APS-85 digital autopilot with heading and reference systems replaces all existing gyros and autopilot components. A full EFIS display and long-range navigation equipment are available.

AAI claims a reduction in direct operating costs of 34 per cent for the FanStar over the unconverted JetStar, with a 10-year extension of service life. A further advantage of the conversion is compliance with FAR Part 36 noise regulations. The first aircraft for conversion, a JetStar Dash 8, was delivered in May 1985 to General Electric's Mojave Flight Test Center in California, and made its first flight on 5 September 1986. AAI believes that a market exists for 75 to 110 FanStar conversions over a five-year period. FAA approval, by Supplemental Type Certificate, is anticipated in July 1987, with simultaneous start of production conversions.

American Aviation Industries FanStar conversion of Lockheed JetStar business jet

Dimensions, external:	
Wing span	18·79 m (61 ft 8 in)
Wing chord: at root	4·16 m (13 ft 7¾ in)
at tip	1·14 m (3 ft 9 in)
Wing aspect ratio	5·97
Length overall	18·41 m (60 ft 5 in)
Height overall	6·22 m (20 ft 5 in)
Tailplane span	7·54 m (24 ft 9 in)
Wheel track	3·75 m (12 ft 3½ in)
Wheelbase	6·68 m (20 ft 7 in)
Dimensions, internal:	
Cabin: Length	8·60 m (28 ft 2½ in)
Max width	1·89 m (6 ft 2½ in)
Max height	1·85 m (6 ft 1 in)
Floor area	15·33 m² (165 sq ft)
Volume	29·31 m³ (1,035 cu ft)
Areas:	
Wings, gross	52·72 m² (567·5 sq ft)
Ailerons (total)	4·53 m² (48·8 sq ft)
Trailing-edge flaps (total)	5·81 m² (62·6 sq ft)
Leading-edge slats (total)	3·16 m² (34·0 sq ft)
Winglets (total)	2·28 m² (24·5 sq ft)
Speed-brake	0·85 m² (9·2 sq ft)
Fin	8·73 m² (94·0 sq ft)
Rudder	1·50 m² (16·2 sq ft)
Tailplane	10·94 m² (117·8 sq ft)
Elevators (total)	2·90 m² (31·2 sq ft)
Weights and Loadings:	
Weight empty	10,511 kg (23,174 lb)
Max fuel weight	8,266 kg (18,224 lb)
Max T-O weight	20,185 kg (44,500 lb)
Max ramp weight	20,298 kg (44,750 lb)
Max zero-fuel weight	12,474 kg (27,500 lb)
Max landing weight	16,329 kg (36,000 lb)
Max wing loading	382·9 kg/m² (78·4 lb/sq ft)
Max power loading	249·4 kg/kN (2·44 lb/lb st)
Performance (estimated at max T-O weight except where indicated):	
Never-exceed speed	Mach 0·87
Max level speed at 7,010 m (23,000 ft)	479 knots (888 km/h; 551 mph)
Max cruising speed at 13,100 m (43,000 ft)	459 knots (851 km/h 528 mph)
Econ cruising speed at 12,500 m (41,000 ft)	418 knots (775 km/h; 481 mph)
Stalling speed, T-O flap setting	123 knots (228 km/h; 142 mph)
Max rate of climb at S/L	1,225 m (4,020 ft)/min
Rate of climb at S/L, one engine out	366 m (1,200 ft)/min
Service ceiling	13,105 m (43,000 ft)
Service ceiling, one engine out	6,400 m (21,000 ft)
T-O run	980 m (3,216 ft)
T-O to 15 m (50 ft)	1,707 m (5,600 ft)
Landing run	1,067 m (3,500 ft)
Range with max fuel	3,550 nm (6,579 km; 4,088 miles)
Operational Noise Levels (estimated):	
T-O	80·3 EPNdB
Approach	89·9 EPNdB
Sideline	86·0 EPNdB

ACA

ACA INDUSTRIES INC

28603 Trailriders Drive, Rancho Palos Verdes, California 90274
Telephone: (213) 539 7121
President: Dr Julian Wolkovitch

In 1974 Dr Julian Wolkovitch flew a proof-of-concept glider featuring his patented joined wing configuration which comprises two sets of wings arranged to form diamond shapes in plan and front views. The configuration was adopted subsequently for the Summit Aircraft Corporation Trident T-3 microlight aircraft (see Sport Aircraft section).

The Defense Advanced Research Project Agency (DARPA), NASA and the US Navy have supported research into the joined wing concept for application to aircraft and missiles. Claimed benefits of the configuration, drawn from wind tunnel tests and structural analyses, include lighter structural weight, greater stiffness, less induced drag, lower wave drag, higher trimmed maximum lift coefficient and inbuilt direct lift and sideforce capabilities.

Studies by NASA's Ames Research Center have shown that a joined wing weighs some 40 per cent less than aerodynamically equivalent conventional wing and tail surfaces. NASA has awarded ACA Industries Inc a Small Business Innovation Research contract to design a manned joined wing research aircraft. ACA is studying applications for joined wings, which may include transport and general aviation aircraft, fighters, VTOL aircraft, agricultural aircraft and RPVs, and is providing consultancy services to Rockwell International Corporation and to other manufacturers working on joined wing aircraft projects.

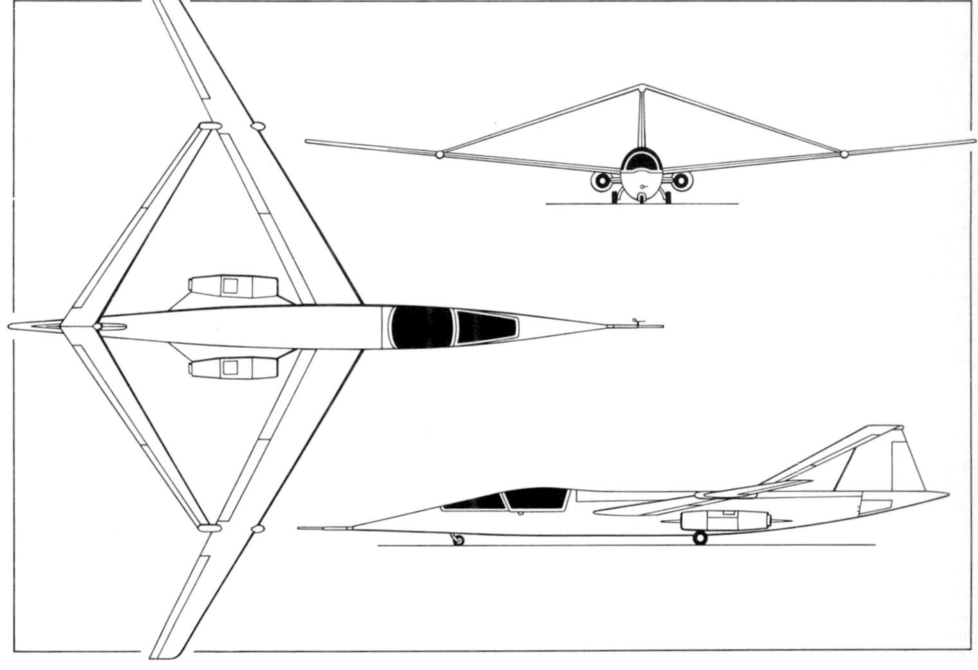

ACA JW-1, based on the Ames/NASA AD-1 airframe *(Jane's/Mike Keep)*

ACA JW-1, JW-2 and JW-3

In March 1986 ACA Industries began work on redesigning the Ames/NASA AD-1 oblique wing research aircraft (described in the 1981-82 *Jane's*) as a jointed wing technology demonstrator. It proposes to use the fuselage, engines and landing gear of the AD-1 mated to a new joined wing which will have removable tip panels, enabling the aircraft to be progressively modified to configurations with the wing joint located at 60 per cent, 80 per cent and 100 per cent of span. Initially the aircraft will be configured with the joint at 60 per cent span, and designated **JW-1**, in which form it will be used for a 10 hour flight test programme to assess basic flying qualities and performance. The tip panels will subsequently be removed in two phases to create the **JW-2** (joint at 80 per cent span) and **JW-3** (joint at 100 per cent span). The aircraft may also be tested in NASA wind tunnel facilities.

TYPE: Single-seat research aircraft.

WINGS: Front and rear wings in joined wing configuration. Two-spar fail-safe structure of composite materials. Wing section specially designed by NASA. Thickness/chord ratio 11·3% on front wing, 12·1% on rear wing. Dihedral 5° on front wing. Anhedral −20° on rear wing. Sweepback 30° 28′ on front wing. Sweepforward at quarter-chord 31° 50′ on rear wing. In JW-1 configuration front wing has eight trailing-edge control surfaces, rear wing four trailing-edge control surfaces, which can operate in a variety of combinations to provide pitch and roll control.

FUSELAGE: Fail-safe structure of composite construction. Single airbrake on each side of rear fuselage.

TAIL UNIT: Single vertical fin with rudder. Streamlined 'bullet' fairing at junction with rear wing.

LANDING GEAR: Non-retractable tricycle type. Retractable nosewheel may be incorporated during development programme.

POWER PLANT: Two Ames Industrial Corporation TRS-18-046 turbojet engines, each rated at 0·978 kN (220 lb st), mounted in pods aft of front wing/fuselage junction.

ACCOMMODATION: Pilot only, in enclosed cockpit with canopy. Cockpit is not pressurised.

DIMENSIONS, EXTERNAL (A: JW-1, B: JW-2, C: JW-3):

Wing span, front: A	12·19 m (40 ft 0 in)
B	9·84 m (32 ft 3½ in)
C	7·31 m (24 ft 0 in)
rear, all	7·31 m (24 ft 0 in)
Wing chord: at root: all	1·19 m (3 ft 11 in)
at tip: A	0·48 m (1 ft 6¾ in)
B	0·61 m (2 ft 0 in)
C	0·76 m (2 ft 6 in)
Wing aspect ratio, front: A	11·18
B	8·07
C	5·21

AREAS:

Wings, gross: A	13·29 m² (143·1 sq ft)
B	12·01 m² (129·3 sq ft)
C	10·27 m² (110·6 sq ft)
Front wing: A	10·17 m² (109·5 sq ft)
B	8·89 m² (95·7 sq ft)
C	7·15 m² (77·0 sq ft)
Rear wing: all	3·12 m² (33·6 sq ft)

WEIGHT AND LOADINGS:

Max T-O weight	973 kg (2,145 lb)
Max wing loading: A	73·21 kg/m² (14·99 lb/sq ft)
B	81·01 kg/m² (16·59 lb/sq ft)
C	94·74 kg/m² (19·39 lb/sq ft)

PERFORMANCE (provisional):

Max speed at 2,135 m (7,000 ft):	
A	276 knots (511 km/h; 318 mph)
B	283 knots (524 km/h; 326 mph)
C	291 knots (539 km/h; 335 mph)
Max rate of climb at S/L, ISA:	
A, B, C	518 m (1,700 ft)/min
Rate of climb at S/L, ISA, one engine out:	
A, B	152 m (500 ft)/min
C	91 m (300 ft)/min

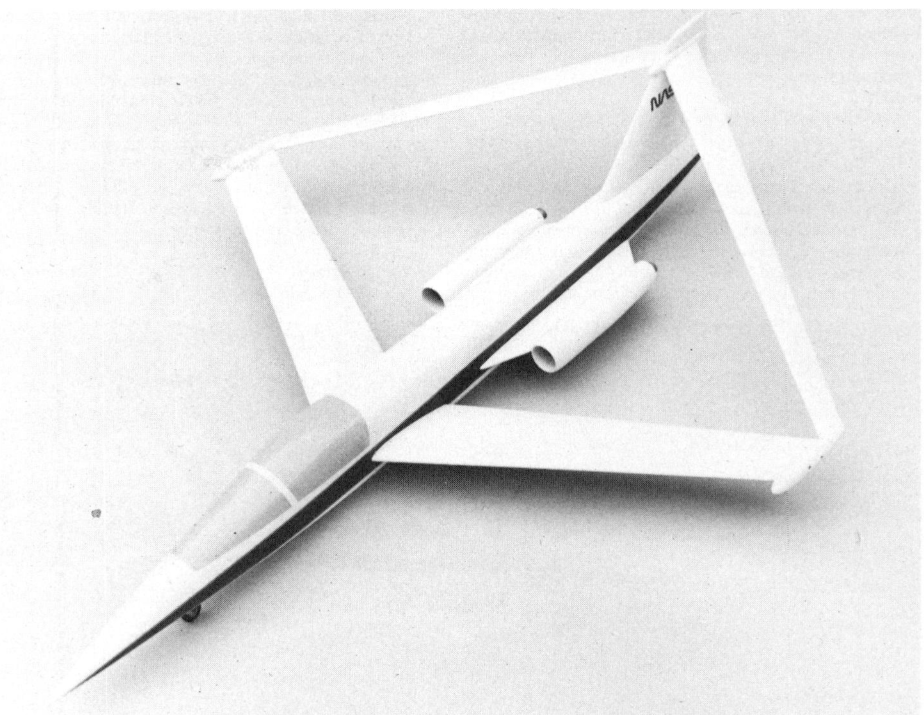

Model of ACA JW-3 short-span version of NASA's joined wing research aircraft

ADVANCED AIRCRAFT

ADVANCED AIRCRAFT CORPORATION

2016 Palomar Airport Road, Carlsbad, California 92008
Telephone: (619) 438 1964
Telex: 249075 (ATSD UR)
PRESIDENT: Neil F. Martin
CHAIRMAN: Robert Graf
GENERAL MANAGER: Leland L. Dimon III

This company was formed on 1 July 1983. It has acquired the production facilities of the former Riley Aircraft Manufacturing Inc (see 1983-84 *Jane's*).

ADVANCED AIRCRAFT TURBINE P-210

The basic Cessna Model 210 Centurion, and the variations for the Pressurised Centurion, have been described fully under the Cessna entry in previous editions of *Jane's*. The Advanced Aircraft Turbine P-210 (previously known as the Spirit 750) is a turboprop conversion of the Pressurised Centurion, developed by Riley Aircraft Manufacturing. The prototype Riley Turbine P-210, powered by a 507 kW (680 shp) Pratt & Whitney Canada PT6A-112 turboprop, flat rated at 373 kW (500 shp), made its first flight on 30 June 1982. Development was delayed subsequently during financial reorganisation of the Riley company, and manufacturing and marketing rights for the modification were acquired by Advanced Aircraft Corporation in 1983. Flight testing resumed in March 1984, but the prototype was lost on 18 May during spinning trials with a radar pod on the starboard wing. The pilot parachuted to safety. A second prototype began flying in November 1984, and an FAA Supplemental Type Certificate was granted during 1985.

The Turbine P-210 is powered by a 559 kW (750 shp) PT6A-135 turboprop engine, flat rated at 335·5 kW (450 shp) and driving a Hartzell three-blade constant-speed fully-feathering and reversible-pitch Q-tip propeller with spinner. The conversion includes modified control surfaces, the addition of a ventral fin, installation of a glassfibre aerodynamic cowling with inertial separator and electric induction air lip de-icing, electric propeller de-icing, a Lear Siegler 28V 200A starter/generator, a 28V 50A standby generator, Gill 639T heavy duty battery, fuel computer, a new engine instrument panel, a 24V electrical system to meet FAA requirements, Flint wingtip fuel tanks with a combined capacity of 62·5 litres (16·5 US gallons), and 3M Stormscope radar.

DIMENSIONS, EXTERNAL: As for Cessna Centurion, except:

Length overall	9·17 m (30 ft 1 in)
Propeller diameter	1·98 m (6 ft 6 in)

WEIGHTS AND LOADINGS:

Weight empty	1,199 kg (2,621 lb)
Max ramp weight	1,822 kg (4,016 lb)
Max T-O weight	1,814 kg (4,000 lb)
Max landing weight	1,723 kg (3,800 lb)
Max wing loading	102·53 kg/m² (21·0 lb/sq ft)
Max power loading	5·41 kg/kW (8·88 lb/shp)

PERFORMANCE (at max T-O weight except where indicated):

Max cruising speed at 7,010 m (23,000 ft)	253 knots (470 km/h; 292 mph)
Econ cruising speed	213 knots (394 km/h; 245 mph)
Stalling speed:	
flaps up	67 knots (125 km/h; 78 mph) IAS
30% flaps	63 knots (117 km/h; 73 mph) IAS
flaps down	58 knots (108 km/h; 67 mph) IAS
Max rate of climb at S/L	549 m (1,800 ft)/min
Service ceiling	above 7,010 m (23,000 ft)
T-O to 15 m (50 ft) at AUW of 1,542 kg (3,400 lb)	334 m (1,095 ft)
Landing from 15 m (50 ft) at AUW of 1,542 kg (3,400 lb)	394 m (1,291 ft)
Range with max fuel, ISA, max cruise power at 7,010 m (23,000 ft), allowances for start, taxi, take-off, climb and descent, 45 min reserves	1,008 nm (1,868 km; 1,160 miles)

ADVANCED AIRCRAFT REGENT 1500

Known formerly as the Riley Turbine Eagle 421, this modification unites the Cessna 421C Golden Eagle airframe with Pratt & Whitney Canada PT6A turboprop engines, mounted in new low-drag nacelles. Each of these engines has more than double the power output of the engine it replaces, yet weighs some 40 per cent less. The Riley

Advanced Aircraft Turbine P-210 turboprop conversion of Cessna Pressurised Centurion, before addition of ventral fin

prototype flew for the first time in late November 1979, at Palomar Airport, and the certification programme was completed during 1980. Eight Riley conversions had been delivered by February 1985, when three more were being produced.

A description of the Cessna 421C Golden Eagle appeared under the Cessna entry in the 1985-86 edition; it applies also to the Regent 1500 (421CP), except as follows:

Power Plant: Two Pratt & Whitney Canada PT6A-135 turboprop engines, each flat rated at 559 kW (750 shp), and driving Hartzell three-blade constant-speed auto-feathering reversible-pitch propellers with Q-tips and spinners. Standard fuel as for Cessna 421C, but auxiliary tanks in rear of nacelles with combined capacity of 568 litres (150 US gallons). Optionally, the rear nacelles can be replaced by new all-glassfibre fuel tanks which increase standard fuel capacity by a total of 605 litres (160 US gallons). Advanced aerodynamic cowlings incorporate inertial separators. Electric de-icing of propellers and air intakes.

Systems: Generally as for Cessna 421C, except bleed air unit for pressurisation system; electrical system with 200A starter/generators and heavy duty battery; engine fire detection system; and pneumatic leading-edge de-icing boots for wings and tail unit.

Weights:
- Weight empty — 2,404 kg (5,300 lb)
- Max T-O weight — 3,447 kg (7,600 lb)
- Max zero-fuel weight — 2,993 kg (6,600 lb)
- Max landing weight — 3,266 kg (7,200 lb)

Performance (at max T-O weight except where indicated):
- Max cruising speed, at max cruise power, AUW of 3,220 kg (7,100 lb):
  - at 8,230 m (27,000 ft) 315 knots (584 km/h; 363 mph)
  - at 6,705 m (22,000 ft) 278 knots (515 km/h; 320 mph)
  - at 4,875 m (16,000 ft) 251 knots (465 km/h; 289 mph)
- Max rate of climb at S/L:
  - at max T-O weight — 945 m (3,100 ft)/min
  - at 3,175 kg (7,000 lb) AUW — 1,310 m (4,300 ft)/min
- Service ceiling — 9,145 m (30,000 ft)
- Service ceiling, one engine out, at 3,175 kg (7,000 lb) AUW — 7,620 m (25,000 ft)
- T-O run — 462 m (1,517 ft)
- T-O to 15 m (50 ft) — 694 m (2,277 ft)
- Landing from 15 m (50 ft) with propeller reversal — 606 m (1,988 ft)
- Landing run with propeller reversal — 324 m (1,064 ft)
- Range with max fuel, ISA, allowances for start, taxi, take-off, climb and descent, 45 min reserves:
  - max cruise power:
    - at 4,875 m (16,000 ft) — 832 nm (1,542 km; 958 miles)
    - at 6,705 m (22,000 ft) — 987 nm (1,829 km; 1,136 miles)
    - at 8,230 m (27,000 ft) — 1,169 nm (2,166 km; 1,346 miles)
  - max range power:
    - at 5,485 m (18,000 ft) — 908 nm (1,682 km; 1,045 miles)
    - at 6,705 m (22,000 ft) — 1,112 nm (2,060 km; 1,280 miles)
    - at 8,230 m (27,000 ft) — 1,276 nm (2,364 km; 1,469 miles)

Advanced Aircraft Regent 1500, with Pratt & Whitney Canada PT6A-135 engines

AERODYNE

AERODYNE SYSTEMS ENGINEERING LTD

1140 19th Street NW, Suite 600, Washington, DC 20036
Telephone: (202) 223 9100
Telex: 46-6169

President: James J. Solano

In early 1985 Aerodyne Systems acquired the assets of the former Texas Helicopter company (see 1983-84 *Jane's*). The latter company's **Wasp** single-seat agricultural conversion of the Bell 47 continues to be available, and a development of the tandem two-seat M79T Jet Wasp is also in production as the **M79 Hornet**.

Aerodyne also manufactures the Pegasus CH-84 remotely piloted co-axial helicopter, described in the RPVs and Targets section of this edition.

AERODYNE ML74 WASP

The ML74 Wasp is an agricultural/utility conversion of the Bell 47G helicopter. The original Texas Helicopter versions, based on the military OH-13E (company designation **M74**) and OH-13H (**M74A**), received FAA certification on 3 May 1976 and 31 August 1977 respectively. By mid-1985 about fifty Wasps had been sold.

Type: Lightweight general utility helicopter.

Rotor System: Two-blade semi-rigid main rotor, with interchangeable blades of all-metal construction. Conventional swashplate assembly for cyclic pitch (hydraulically boosted) and collective pitch control. Blades do not fold. Two-blade all-metal tail rotor assembly, with blades of light alloy honeycomb, and tail rotor guard.

Rotor Drive: Through centrifugal clutch and two-stage planetary transmission. Steel shaft to tail rotor with 90° gearbox at rear end of tailboom. Main rotor/engine rpm ratio 1:9,009; tail rotor/engine rpm ratio 1:1·667.

Fuselage: In three sections: centre, rear fuselage and cabin. Centre section is welded 4130 steel tube structure to carry engine and cabin. Rear section of 4130 steel tube, triangular in cross-section, and supports tail rotor driveshaft.

Tail Unit: Small ventral fin constructed of light alloy honeycomb sandwich, with very small horizontal surface at forward end of fin.

Landing Gear: Tubular fixed skid type. Shock absorption by flexing of crosstubes. Removable ground handling wheels standard.

Power Plant: One 197·6 kW (265 hp) Avco Lycoming VO-435 flat-six engine, derated to 164 kW (220 hp) and mounted vertically. One fuel tank aft of engine with capacity of 110 litres (29 US gallons). Refuelling point at each side of tank. Oil capacity 7·6 litres (2 US gallons).

Accommodation: Pilot only, in blue-tinted Plexiglas bubble. Single door on each side, with sliding windows. Contoured seat cushions. Nylon safety belt and shoulder harness.

Systems: Hydraulic system, with manual backup, for operation of flight controls. Electrical system supplied by 28V 50A alternator, with 24V battery.

Equipment: Standard equipment includes airspeed indicator, compass, rotor tachometer, engine tachometer, fuel quantity gauge, altimeter, manifold pressure gauge, cylinder head temperature and engine/transmission oil temperature gauges, loadmeter, carburettor air temperature gauge, hour meter, main rotor tiedowns and Imron paint. Avionics, agricultural spraygear and sling load cargo hook are optional.

Dimensions, external:
- Main rotor diameter — 10·70 m (35 ft 1¼ in)
- Main rotor blade chord — 0·28 m (11 in)
- Tail rotor diameter — 1·73 m (5 ft 8¼ in)
- Length overall, excl main rotor — 9·59 m (31 ft 5½ in)
- Height to top of rotor head — 2·84 m (9 ft 3¾ in)
- Skid track — 2·29 m (7 ft 6 in)

Dimensions, internal:
- Cabin: Length — 1·40 m (4 ft 7 in)
  - Max width — 0·66 m (2 ft 2 in)
  - Max height — 1·35 m (4 ft 5 in)

Areas:
- Main rotor blades, each — 1·65 m² (17·71 sq ft)
- Tail rotor blades, each — 0·11 m² (1·2 sq ft)
- Main rotor disc — 90·02 m² (969·0 sq ft)
- Tail rotor disc — 2·35 m² (25·31 sq ft)
- Ventral fin — 0·36 m² (3·86 sq ft)
- Horizontal tail surface (total) — 0·19 m² (2·0 sq ft)

Weights and Loadings:
- Basic weight empty — 658 kg (1,450 lb)
- Max T-O weight — 1,293 kg (2,850 lb)
- Max disc loading — 14·36 kg m² (2·94 lb/sq ft)
- Max power loading — 7·88 kg/kW (12·95 lb/hp)

Performance (at max T-O weight except where indicated):
- Never-exceed and max level speed — 87 knots (161 km/h; 100 mph)
- Max cruising speed at S/L — 78 knots (145 km/h; 90 mph)
- Econ cruising speed at S/L — 68 knots (125 km/h; 78 mph)
- Max rate of climb at S/L — 152 m (500 ft)/min
- Hovering ceiling IGE, ISA + 20°C — 1,006 m (3,300 ft)
- Range with max fuel, no reserves — 130 nm (241 km; 150 miles)
- Endurance — 2 h 6 min

AERODYNE M79 HORNET

Aerodyne Systems has developed a two-seat version of the Wasp, originally known as the Texas Helicopter M79T Jet Wasp II. The prototype (N1001X) first flew in piston engined form on 6 January 1979. Redesignated M79 Hornet, and powered by an Allison 250-C20B turbine engine, the aircraft received FAA certification on 25 April 1985 and was subsequently exhibited at the Paris Air Show in June, at which time it had accumulated some 125 hours' flying.

The Hornet is intended as a low cost training helicopter for the crews of modern combat types such as the McDonnell Douglas AH-64A Apache. Airframe differences from

Aerodyne Wasp agricultural helicopter, based on the Bell 47 *(Brian M. Service)*

the standard single-seat ML74 Wasp include a redesigned front fuselage and cabin area with repositioned engine, variable incidence tailplane, and provision for armament on outriggers above the landing gear skids.

TYPE: Turbine powered light helicopter.

ROTOR SYSTEM AND DRIVE: As described for Wasp, except main rotor of increased diameter, with rotor/engine rpm ratio 1:16·666.

FUSELAGE: Centre section of welded 4130 steel tube carrying engine and cockpit structure. Rear section also of 4130 tube, of triangular section open framework construction, serving as support for tail rotor driveshaft.

TAIL UNIT: As for Wasp, plus variable incidence tailplane with small endplate fins.

LANDING GEAR: As for Wasp.

POWER PLANT: One 313 kW (420 shp) Allison 250-C20B turboshaft engine, derated to 194 kW (260 shp) with 600 series transmission, or to 201 kW (270 shp) with 900 series transmission. Fuel contained in two stub wing fuel tanks, one above each side of fuselage at base of rotor mast. Total capacity 284 litres (75 US gallons). Refuelling point at top of each tank.

ACCOMMODATION: Two seats, in tandem, in enclosed bubble cockpit. Two doors on starboard side. Dual controls and dual instrumentation standard. Contoured seat cushions, and nylon safety belts and shoulder restraints, standard.

DIMENSIONS, EXTERNAL: As for Wasp except:

Main rotor diameter	11·31 m (37 ft 1¼ in)
Length overall, excl main rotor	10·97 m (36 ft 0 in)

DIMENSIONS, INTERNAL:

Cabin: Length	2·74 (9 ft 0 in)
Max width	0·84 m (2 ft 9 in)
Max height	1·35 m (4 ft 5 in)

AREAS: As for Wasp except:

Main rotor blades (each)	1·73 m² (18·63 sq ft)
Main rotor disc	100·69 m² (1,083·87 sq ft)
Tailplane	0·42 m² (4·5 sq ft)

WEIGHTS AND LOADINGS:

Weight empty	780 kg (1,720 lb)
Max T-O weight:	
600 series transmission	1,338 kg (2,950 lb)
900 series transmission	1,451 kg (3,200 lb)
Max disc loading	14·41 kg/m² (2·95 lb/sq ft)
Max power loading (270 shp)	7·22 kg/kW (11·85 lb/shp)

PERFORMANCE (at max T-O weight of 1,338 kg; 2,950 lb):

Never-exceed speed and max level speed	92 knots (170 km/h; 106 mph)
Max cruising speed	85 knots (157 km/h; 98 mph)
Econ cruising speed	69 knots (128 km/h; 79 mph)
Max rate of climb at S/L	381 m (1,250 ft)/min
Max vertical rate of climb	296 m (970 ft)/min
Range with max fuel, no reserves	260 nm (482 km; 299 miles)

Aerodyne M79 Hornet tandem two-seat helicopter in armed configuration *(Brian M. Service)*

AEROFAN

AEROFAN AIRCRAFT MANUFACTURING CO

2834 Teal Club Road, Oxnard, California 93030

PRESIDENT: Ronald Smith

CHIEF DESIGN ENGINEER: Robert H Dunkelburger

AEROFAN SINGLETWIN

Conceived in the early 1970s, work began on the prototype Aerofan SingleTwin in 1980, and a first flight was expected during 1985 following initial taxying tests in the Autumn of 1984.

Two versions of the SingleTwin are planned. The **Model 700R** is powered by two rear-mounted 260·9 kW (350 hp) Avco Lycoming TIO-540 piston engines driving a single pusher propeller, and carries eight passengers in a basically unpressurised cabin. Construction is all-metal, flush-riveted, with retractable tricycle type landing gear, full span trailing-edge slotted flaps and full span leading-edge flaps to enhance short-field performance. Pressurisation of the cabin is optional. The prototype features a Y-shaped tail surface configuration, but production aircraft may have X shaped tail surfaces, with movable surfaces on all four rear flying surfaces providing pitch, roll and yaw control. In addition, production Model 700Rs will have an 0·4 m (1 ft 6 in) cabin 'stretch' to increase passenger capacity to eight, the prototype having accommodation for six.

The **SingleTwin Model 800J** would have 313·2 kW (420 shp) Allison 250 turbine engines and seat ten passengers in a pressurised cabin with a maximum pressure differential of 0·48 bars (7·0 lb/sq in).

Aerofan says that the SingleTwin will be certificated under FAR Pt 23, and that production aircraft could be available 18 months after some $11 million in certification and production funding has been obtained. There has been no further news of the programme during 1986.

Model of the Aerofan SingleTwin twin-engined business aircraft *(Howard Levy)*

DIMENSIONS, EXTERNAL:

Wing span	9·75 m (32 ft 0 in)
Wing chord (mean aerodynamic)	1·37 m (4 ft 6 in)
Length overall: prototype	11·28 m (37 ft 0 in)
production 700R	11·73 m (38 ft 6 in)

WEIGHTS (800J):

Weight empty	1,451 kg (3,200 lb)
Max T-O weight	2,721 kg (6,000 lb)

DESIGN PERFORMANCE:

Cruising speed, 75% power:	
700R at 5,485 m (18,000 ft)	260 knots (481 km/h; 299 mph)
800J at 7,315 m (24,000 ft)	300 knots (555 km/h; 345 mph)
Max rate of climb at S/L:	
800J	610 m (2,000 ft)/min
Max operating altitude:	
700R	6,705-7,315 m (22,000-24,000 ft)
800J	11,275 m (37,000 ft)

AERO MOD

AERO MOD GENERAL

Chelan Municipal Airport, Washington 98816

Telephone: (509) 682 5150

AERO MOD SUPER AG MAX

This company has developed a series of conversions of the Grumman/Schweizer Ag-Cat agricultural biplane which can be applied to A and B-series Ag-Cats and are known as the Super Ag Max. The modification consists basically of lengthening the fuselage by 0·84 m (2 ft 9 in) (0·61 m; 2 ft ahead of the cockpit, and 0·23 m; 9 in to the rear) to accommodate a 1,628 litre (430 US gallon) glassfibre hopper, replacement of wing spars with new units with heavier flanges, and an increase in wing span to 13·72 m (45 ft 0 in). Aero Mod claims that the Super Ag Max modifications applied to an Ag-Cat B provide a speed increase of about 13 knots (24 km/h; 15 mph) and a 27 per cent increase in fuel efficiency achieved through a greater hourly workload and wider swath width.

AERO MOD/AYRES THRUSH CONVERSION

Aero Mod has also developed a modification for the Ayres Thrush S2R (which see), which consists of new wingtip panels providing an additional 4·74 m² (51 sq ft) of wing area. The Aero Mod wingtips, which are supplied to operators in kit form, reduce take-off run by 91 m (300 ft) and reduce turning radius by up to 60 per cent at max T-O weight, while enabling lower power settings to be used, with attendant savings in fuel consumption. By the Summer of 1985 some 160 conversion kits had been installed on Thrush aircraft.

Aero Mod Super Ag Max conversion of the Ag-Cat *(Howard Levy)*

AERO UNION

AERO UNION CORPORATION

Municipal Airport, 1380 Invader, Chico, California 95926
Telephone: (916) 342 7577
Telex: 171359 AEROUNION CICO
PRESIDENT: Dale P. Newton
VICE-PRESIDENT AND SALES MANAGER: Richard E. Foy

This company was established in 1959 as an aerial firefighting operation, using converted war surplus aircraft for aerial retardant delivery. Aero Union developed a number of tank systems for aircraft such as the Boeing B-17, Douglas DC-4, DC-6 and DC-7, Fairchild C-119 and Grumman S-2. A description of the company's Douglas DC-3 aerial spraying system can be found in the 1984-85 *Jane's*. In 1980 the company received CAB certification as an all-cargo air service carrier using DC-4, Carvair and Guppy aircraft. Aero Union also manufactures a wide variety of equipment, including aircraft fuel tanks, airstairs, retardant delivery and aerial spraying systems, and dorsal fin assemblies.

AERO UNION MODULAR AIRBORNE FIRE FIGHTING SYSTEM (MAFFS)

Designed for cargo aircraft such as the Lockheed C-130 which use the Air Force 463L pallet system, the Aero Union Modular Airborne Fire Fighting System (MAFFS) comprises five retardant tank modules with a total capacity of 11,356 litres (3,000 US gallons), a control module, and a dispensing module with two retractable nozzles providing a retardant line 13-61 m (43-200 ft) wide, and 180-610 m (590-2,000 ft) long, depending on aircraft altitude and speed. The MAFFS, which has an installed weight, empty, of 2,177 kg (4,800 lb), is powered by compressed air stored in reservoirs at each tank module. The control module is battery powered. An installation time of less than one hour is claimed for the C-130 if the MAFFS is assembled on a loader outside the aircraft with a typical turnaround time of 15 minutes for replenishing the system in operational use. The MAFFS can be operated at altitudes of 30-150 m (98-492 ft) and at speeds of 130-140 knots (241-259 km/h; 150-161 mph).

AERO UNION C-130 AUXILIARY FUEL SYSTEM

Aero Union has developed an auxiliary fuel system for the Lockheed C-130 which can be used for inflight refuelling, extra fuel capacity, or fuel transportation. The system consists of a 6·1 m (20 ft) platform on which two cylindrical tanks are mounted by means of a pair of cradles. The plumbing is in compliance with MIL-F-17874 and offers a flow rate of 1,136 litres (300 US gallons)/minute. The unit interfaces with the Lockheed air refuelling manifold, and a passage is provided for crew access fore and aft of the tank installation. Tank capacity (total) 13,627 litres (3,600 US gallons); length 5·26 m (17 ft 3 in); width 3·0 m (9 ft 10¼ in); height, excluding plumbing, 1·68 m (5 ft 6 in); weight empty approx 1,542 kg (3,400 lb).

AERO UNION HELICOPTER EMERGENCY FIRE FIGHTING SYSTEM (HEFFS)

Designed for helicopters such as the Boeing Vertol CH-47C Chinook, the Aero Union Helicopter Emergency Fire Fighting System (HEFFS) consists of tank modules and a dispensing module with nozzle and hose fittings which can be installed in any appropriate helicopter that uses the standard military pallet cargo system. The CH-47C system comprises three retardant tanks, with a total capacity of 5,678 litres (1,500 US gallons) and a centre dispensing module providing a retardant line 12-24 m (40-80 ft) wide, and 24-427 m (80-1,400 ft) long. Coverage is up to 1·41 litres/m² (4 US gallons/sq ft). The HEFFS has an installed weight, empty, of 2,381 kg (5,250 lb) in CH-47C configuration, and may be used at altitudes of 9-137 m (30-450 ft), and at airspeeds of 0-110 knots (204 km/h; 127 mph). Aero Union claims an installation time of 20 minutes, with a typical turnaround time of five minutes.

AERO UNION (GRUMMAN) HU-16B ALBATROSS TANKER CONVERSION

Aero Union has developed a firefighting conversion of the standard HU-16B Albatross amphibian that enables the aircraft to carry 3,785 litres (1,000 US gallons) of water or retardant in two side by side tanks in the fuselage. The tanks can be filled from two retractable probes which extend into the water while the aircraft is planing on the step, or on land by a single filling point located on the side of the fuselage. The retardant tanks can be emptied individually or simultaneously, and can be refilled from a body of water within 10 seconds at a speed of 70 knots (130 km/h; 81 mph).

WEIGHTS:
- Weight empty — 9,956 kg (21,950 lb)
- Max T-O weight — 15,036 kg (33,150 lb)

PERFORMANCE:
- Max level speed — 220 knots (408 km/h; 253 mph)
- Cruising speed — 162 knots (300 km/h; 186 mph)

AIR AMERICA

AIR AMERICA INC

Wilkes Barre/Scranton International Airport, Avoca, Pennsylvania 18641
Telephone: (717) 457 6736
PRESIDENT: Richard Newell

AIR AMERICA (CESSNA P210) JAVELIN

Air America has developed a modification package for the Cessna Model P210 Pressurised Centurion (described under Cessna entry in 1985-86 *Jane's*) which involves replacement of the standard 231 kW (310 hp) Continental TSIO-520-AF engine with a 261 kW (350 hp) turbocharged Avco Lycoming TIO-540-V2AD engine, driving a four-blade Hartzell constant-speed Q-tip propeller. Other changes include modification and balancing of control surfaces, and installation of a Garrett pressurisation system, a large intercooler to reduce intake air temperatures, a new cowling with low-drag ducts, dual 70A alternators, dual vacuum pumps, pressurised magnetos, an Alcor engine analyser and a Hoskins fuel computer. Options include a 114 litre (30 US gallon) auxiliary fuel tank, speed brakes, air-conditioning, and a landing gear door removal modification. FAA certification of the modification, marketed under the name Air America Javelin, was granted on 23 May 1985. By 1 January 1986 a total of ten Javelin conversions had been completed.

Air America Javelin (turbocharged Avco Lycoming TIO-540-V2AD engine)

PERFORMANCE:
- Max cruising speed at 7,010 m (23,000 ft) — 224 knots (415 km/h; 257 mph)
- Cruising speed:
  - 75% power — 218 knots (403 km/h; 251 mph)
  - 60% power — 201 knots (371 km/h; 231 mph)
- Max rate of climb at S/L — 518 m (1,700 ft)/min

AIR AMERICA CESSNA 340/340A

Air America is developing a modification for the Cessna 340 and 340A pressurised twin-engined business aircraft (described in the 1984-85 *Jane's*) which involves replacement of the standard 212·5 kW (285 hp) or 231 kW (310 hp) Continental TSIO-520-K or TSIO-520-NB engines with two 261 kW (350 hp) turbocharged Avco Lycoming TIO/LTIO-540-V2AD engines. Certification of the modification was expected in June 1986.

AIRESEARCH

AIRESEARCH AVIATION COMPANY (Division of Garrett Corporation)

c/o Garrett General Aviation Services Company, Los Angeles International Airport, 6201 West Imperial Highway, Los Angeles, California 90045
Telephone: (213) 568 3700
VICE-PRESIDENT, MARKETING & SALES: Richard A. Graser

AiResearch Aviation is the Garrett General Aviation Services Company facility producing the 731 Hawker, a Garrett TFE731 engine retrofit programme for the HS 125. In January 1986 the company announced the transfer of this programme to Los Angeles International Airport, and termination of its other aircraft modification and completion activities at Long Beach Municipal Airport. The Long Beach facility was subsequently acquired by Gulfstream Aerospace Corporation.

AIRESEARCH AVIATION 731 HAWKER

The AiResearch Aviation 731 Hawker is a British Aerospace HS 125 Series 400 airframe retrofitted with two new Garrett TFE731-3 turbofan engines, enabling it to comply with FAR Pt 36 Stage III noise regulations. On the flight deck, the aircraft is equipped with a dual Collins EFIS 85B electronic flight instrumentation system, Collins ATS-80 autopilot, Collins WXR-270 colour radar display, and a Universal UNS-1JR flight management system with integral data base and Omega/VLF sensor. The main cabin has a new interior for seven passengers, with berthing seats, a private rear lavatory and a complete galley.

AiResearch Aviation Company's 731 Hawker conversion, from an HS 125-400 airframe

The first 731 Hawker was delivered to the Ayala Company of the Philippines in the Summer of 1985, for use as an executive transport. The retrofit is available also to existing owners of all Viper-engined HS 125s.

Details of the basic HS 125 Series 400 can be found in the 1972-73 *Jane's*.

AIRMASTER

AIRMASTER INC

840 West Perimeter Road, Renton, Washington 98055
Telephone: (206) 255 1422
Telex: 185195 AMAST UT
PRESIDENT: Lawrence Matanski
VICE-PRESIDENT: Walter H. Wainwright
MARKETING AND SALES MANAGER: Joe L. Brewer

Airmaster Inc was formed in 1980 to develop and manufacture the Avalon 680 and Twin Star turboprop amphibian aircraft. A prototype of the Avalon 680 was flown for the first time in 1983, and this aircraft is now available to order, together with a military/maritime patrol version known as the A-750 Guardian.

The original Twin Star 800 twin-engined variant of the same twin-boom airframe, described in the 1985-86 *Jane's*, will not be developed. Instead, Airmaster is putting its main effort into the much refined Avalon Twin Star 1000 and A-1200 Guardian with a more conventional flying-boat hull.

Airmaster Avalon 680 prototype amphibian

AIRMASTER AVALON 680

The Avalon 680 prototype (N767LB), which first flew on 1 October 1983, uses wings, strengthened tailbooms and the tailplane from a Cessna Model 337 Skymaster (described in 1980-81 *Jane's*). Production versions are intended to have new cantilever wings of increased area and parallel chord, larger fins and rudders, a 0·35 m (1 ft 2 in) fuselage stretch in the cabin area to provide seating for seven people, additional cabin windows, increased capacity in the main fuel tanks between the outrigger sponsons and the fuselage, a 189 litre (50 US gallon) auxiliary fuel tank in each wing, larger mainwheels, engine mounts and cowling, and side-mounted engine and oil cooler intakes.

TYPE: Single-engined seven-seat amphibian.

WINGS: Prototype uses wings from Cessna Model 337 Skymaster. Production aircraft are intended to have larger cantilever constant chord wings of conventional all-aluminium construction. Aerofoil section NACA 23015 (modified). Dihedral 2°. Incidence 4°. Frise ailerons. Fowler single-slotted trailing-edge flaps. Electrically actuated trim tabs. Pneumatic boot de-icing of leading-edges.

FUSELAGE: Conventional 2024T-3 fail-safe aluminium structure, with hull section comprising 14 watertight compartments.

TAIL UNIT: Prototype uses Cessna Skymaster tailbooms with structural strengthening, tailplane and fins/rudders, with additional dorsal and ventral fins to increase area. Trim tab on elevator and starboard rudder, actuated mechanically. Pneumatic boot de-icing of tailplane leading-edge.

LANDING GEAR: Tricycle type, with oleo shock absorption. Hydraulic retraction, nosewheel forward into hull, single mainwheels rearward into outrigger sponsons. Mainwheels, tyre size 7·00-6; steerable nosewheel, tyre size 6·00-6. Cleveland brakes. Steerable, hydraulically actuated retractable water rudder.

POWER PLANT: One 559 kW (750 shp) Pratt & Whitney Canada PT6A-34 turboprop engine, driving a Hartzell three-blade constant-speed reversible-pitch pusher propeller. Total fuel capacity 946 litres (250 US gallons); main tank in fuselage area between sponsons, capacity 568 litres (150 US gallons), with filler point above sponson; 189 litre (50 US gallon) auxiliary tank in each wing, each with single flush refuelling point in top of wing. Oil capacity 11·4 litres (3 US gallons). Engine air intake has heated lip for anti-icing.

ACCOMMODATION: Enclosed cabin, with seating for seven, including pilot. Forward and middle row of two seats each, with rear row of three seats. Dual controls standard. Single forward-hinged door on each side of forward cabin, incorporating boarding step in lower hinge-down section. Doors open 180°; starboard door serves as emergency exit. Accommodation is heated and ventilated, with freon air-conditioning optional.

SYSTEMS: Cabin pressurisation system with max differential of 0·27 bars (4·0 lb/sq in) optional; Freon air-conditioning system optional. Single hydraulic system, with emergency hand pump, pressurised at 83 bars (1,200 lb/sq in). 24V electrical system. Oxygen system, wing and tail surface de-icing boots and windscreen wipers/alcohol de-icing system optional.

AVIONICS AND EQUIPMENT: To customer's choice, including autopilot, fuel management computer, weather radar and 3M/Ryan Stormscope. Blind-flying instrumentation standard.

DIMENSIONS, EXTERNAL (proposed production version):
- Wing span: 13·41 m (44 ft 0 in)
- Wing aspect ratio: 7·3
- Length overall: 10·36 m (34 ft 0 in)
- Length of fuselage: 8·08 m (26 ft 6 in)
- Height overall (ground operation): 3·81 m (12 ft 6 in)
- Tailplane span: 3·53 m (11 ft 7 in)
- Wheel track: 3·35 m (11 ft 0 in)
- Wheelbase: 4·09 m (13 ft 5 in)
- Propeller diameter: 2·59 m (8 ft 6 in)
- Passenger doors:
  - Height: port 1·22 m (4 ft 0 in)
  - starboard 0·89 m (2 ft 11 in)
  - Width: port 0·84 m (2 ft 9 in)
  - starboard 0·81 m (2 ft 8 in)

DIMENSIONS, INTERNAL:
- Cabin: Max length 3·05 m (10 ft 0 in)
  - Max width 1·27 m (4 ft 2 in)
  - Max height 1·57 m (5 ft 2 in)

AREAS:
- Wings, gross: 24·53 m² (264·0 sq ft)
- Fins (total): 2·90 m² (31·2 sq ft)
- Rudders (total, incl tab): 1·45 m² (15·6 sq ft)
- Tailplane: 4·92 m² (53·0 sq ft)

WEIGHTS AND LOADING:
- Weight empty: 1,587 kg (3,500 lb)
- Max fuel weight: 680 kg (1,500 lb)
- Max T-O weight: 2,631 kg (5,800 lb)
- Max landing weight: 2,540 kg (5,600 lb)
- Max zero-fuel weight: 1,497 kg (3,300 lb)
- Max wing loading: 107·3 kg/m² (21·97 lb/sq ft)

PERFORMANCE (estimated at max T-O weight):
- Never-exceed speed: 217 knots (402 km/h; 250 mph)
- Max level speed and max cruising speed at 4,875 m (16,000 ft): 199 knots (370 km/h; 230 mph)
- Econ cruising speed: 174 knots (322 km/h; 200 mph)
- Stalling speed, flaps down, power on: 56 knots (105 km/h; 65 mph)
- Max rate of climb at S/L: 670 m (2,200 ft)/min
- Service ceiling: 7,925 m (26,000 ft)
- T-O run: on land 244 m (800 ft)
  - on water 366 m (1,200 ft)
- T-O to 15 m (50 ft) on land: 305 m (1,000 ft)
- Landing from 15 m (50 ft) on land: 290 m (950 ft)
- Landing run: on land 198 m (650 ft)
  - on water 213 m (700 ft)
- Range with max fuel:
  - at econ cruise power 955 nm (1,770 km; 1,100 miles)
  - at cruise power 781 nm (1,448 km; 900 miles)
- Min depth of water for operation: 0·56 m (1 ft 10 in)

AIRMASTER A-750 GUARDIAN

The A-750 Guardian is a proposed military/maritime patrol version of the Avalon 680 for multi-mission roles including SAR, fishery protection, pollution monitoring, oil and gas rig patrol and drug enforcement. It is intended to have provision for carrying lightweight rocket and grenade launchers, 7·62 mm machine-gun pods or mini torpedoes on standard NATO racks under the wings or on mounts above the aircraft's outrigger sponsons. Radar could be installed above the cabin section. The A-750 Guardian's dimensions, weights and estimated performance are as for the Avalon 680, with the exception of an empty weight of 1,451 kg (3,200 lb) and a maximum loiter range of 1,216 nm (2,253 km; 1,400 miles). Power plant is a 559 kW (750 shp) PT6A-135 turboprop; fuel capacities are 757 litres (200 US gallons) standard or 1,325 litres (350 US gallons) for long-range patrol.

AIRMASTER AVALON TWIN STAR 1000

The Twin Star 1000 is intended to be the basic model in Airmaster's family of modern turboprop amphibians. It has a conventional flying-boat hull, with twin-turboprop engines mounted in pusher configuration above the wings, instead of the coupled power plant and twin-boom tail unit of the original Twin Star 800 design. Construction of a prototype was started in February 1985.

TYPE: Twin-turboprop multi-purpose amphibian.

WINGS: Cantilever high-wing monoplane of constant chord. NACA 23015 (modified) wing section. Dihedral 2°. Incidence 4°. Aluminium alloy fail-safe structure, with Frise ailerons and Fowler single-slotted trailing-edge flaps over full span except for wingtips. Electric aileron trim. Pneumatic de-icing boots on wing leading-edge optional.

FUSELAGE: Conventional flying-boat hull of high length-to-beam ratio, with single step. Aluminium alloy (2024-T3) semi-monocoque structure, with 17 watertight compartments. Stabilising floats carried on cantilever aerofoil shape sponsons mid-mounted on hull beneath wings. Hull drains and manifold bilge pumping.

TAIL UNIT: Conventional cantilever structure of aluminium alloy, with unswept tailplane mounted on sweptback vertical surfaces, well above top of hull. Horn balanced rudder and elevators, each with electric trim. Large dorsal fin. Optional pneumatic de-icing boots on leading-edge of fin and tailplane.

LANDING GEAR: Hydraulically retractable tricycle type, with emergency manual backup. Nosewheel retracts forward, enabling tyre to serve as fender for nose. Main units retract rearward into stabilising floats. Oleo-pneumatic shock absorbers. Single wheel on each unit. Mainwheel tyres size 7·00-6; nosewheel tyre size 6·00-6. Cleveland brakes.

POWER PLANT: Two 373 kW (500 shp) Pratt & Whitney Canada PT6A-11 turboprop engines, each driving a Hartzell three-blade constant-speed fully-feathering and reversible-pitch metal propeller, with spinner. Main fuel tank in fuselage between sponsons, capacity 568 litres (150 US gallons), with refuelling point above sponson. Auxiliary tank, capacity 189 litres (50 US gallons), in each wing, with flush refuelling point in wing upper surface. Total fuel capacity 946 litres (250 US gallons). Oil capacity (total) 11·4 litres (3 US gallons). Engine air intakes each have heated lip for anti-icing. Propellers are anti-iced automatically by hot engine exhaust.

ACCOMMODATION: Pilot and six passengers in 2-2-3 forward facing seats in enclosed cabin, with forward hinged door on each side. Airstairs for land operation. Heating and ventilation standard. Pressurisation and freon air-conditioning optional. Baggage space behind rear seats. Optional alcohol de-icing system and wipers for windscreen.

SYSTEMS: Optional air-conditioning and pressurisation system, with max pressure differential of 0·24 bars (3·5 lb/sq in). Single electro-hydraulic system, with emergency hand pump. Pneumatic system pressure 82 bars (1,200 lb/sq in). 24V electrical system. Standby oxygen system optional.

AVIONICS AND EQUIPMENT: Blind-flying instrumentation standard. Avionics, autopilot, weather radar, stormscope and fuel management computer optional.

DIMENSIONS, EXTERNAL:
- Wing span: 13·41 m (44 ft 0 in)
- Wing aspect ratio: 7·33
- Length overall: 11·13 m (36 ft 6 in)
- Fuselage width: 1·42 m (4 ft 8 in)
- Height overall: 4·42 m (14 ft 6 in)
- Tailplane span: 4·67 m (15 ft 3½ in)
- Wheel track: 3·51 m (11 ft 6 in)
- Wheelbase: 4·63 m (15 ft 2½ in)
- Propeller diameter (each): 2·54 m (8 ft 4 in)
- Propeller ground clearance: 1·46 m (4 ft 9½ in)
- Distance between propeller centres: 3·60 m (11 ft 9½ in)
- Passenger doors:
  - Height: port 1·22 m (4 ft 0 in)
  - stbd 0·89 m (2 ft 11 in)
  - Width: port 0·84 m (2 ft 9 in)
  - stbd 0·81 m (2 ft 8 in)

DIMENSIONS, INTERNAL:
- Cabin: Length 3·05 m (10 ft 0 in)
  - Max width 1·27 m (4 ft 2 in)
  - Max height 1·57 m (5 ft 2 in)

AREAS:
- Wings, gross: 24·53 m² (264·0 sq ft)
- Ailerons (total): 2·16 m² (23·3 sq ft)
- Trailing-edge flaps (total): 4·74 m² (51·0 sq ft)
- Fin: 2·38 m² (25·6 sq ft)
- Rudder: 1·58 m² (17·0 sq ft)
- Tailplane: 3·81 m² (41·0 sq ft)
- Elevators: 2·55 m² (27·5 sq ft)

WEIGHTS AND LOADINGS:
- Weight empty: 1,769 kg (3,900 lb)
- Max T-O weight: 2,948 kg (6,500 lb)
- Max landing weight: 2,812 kg (6,200 lb)
- Max wing loading: 120·18 kg/m² (24·62 lb/sq ft)
- Max power loading: 3·95 kg/kW (6·50 lb/shp)

PERFORMANCE (estimated at max T-O weight):
- Never-exceed speed 217 knots (402 km/h; 250 mph)
- Max level speed and max cruising speed at 3,660 m (12,000 ft) 207 knots (383 km/h; 238 mph)
- Econ cruising speed 180 knots (333 km/h; 207 mph)
- Stalling speed, flaps down 58 knots (108 km/h; 67 mph)
- Max rate of climb at S/L 731 m (2,400 ft)/min
- Service ceiling 7,925 m (26,000 ft)
- Service ceiling, one engine out 3,810 m (12,500 ft)
- T-O run: on land 256 m (840 ft)
  - on water 336 m (1,100 ft)
- Landing run: on land 183 m (600 ft)
  - on water 198 m (650 ft)
- Range with max fuel:
  - at cruise power 695 nm (1,287 km; 800 miles)
  - at econ cruise power 869 nm (1,609 km; 1,000 miles)

AIRMASTER A-1200 GUARDIAN

The Airmaster A-1200 Guardian is basically similar to the Twin Star 1000, except for the installation of military or maritime patrol equipment and/or armament. It can be upgraded with two 507 kW (680 shp) PT6A-27 or 559 kW (750 shp) PT6A-34 turboprop engines to improve its STOL performance. Total fuel capacity can be increased to 1,514 litres (400 US gallons) to extend the patrol range to 1,216 nm (2,253 km; 1,400 miles) with standard PT6A-11 engines. JATO rockets can be attached on each side of the rear fuselage for emergency short take-off in rough water.

Operational equipment can include radar mounted in the nose of the port engine nacelle and a high intensity searchlight in the nose of the starboard nacelle. Six hardpoints under the wings can carry lightweight rocket launchers, grenade launchers, 7·62 mm machine-gun pods, or air-to-air missiles on standard NATO pylons. A Gatling type machine-gun can be pod mounted above the port stabilising float. Mini-torpedoes can be carried outboard of the stabilising floats.

DIMENSIONS, WEIGHTS AND PERFORMANCE:
Generally as for Twin Star 1000

Artist's impression of the Airmaster Twin Star 1000 (left) and A-1200 Guardian amphibians

AIR TRACTOR

AIR TRACTOR INC

PO Box 485, Municipal Airport, Olney, Texas 76374
Telephone: (817) 564 5616
Telex: 910 890 4792

PRESIDENT: Leland Snow

The Air Tractor series of agricultural aircraft are new designs embodying more than 25 years' experience by their designer, Mr Leland Snow, who designed, developed, certificated and put into production the earlier Snow S-2 series of agricultural aircraft. The latter, which later became the Rockwell S-2R Thrush, have been described in previous editions of *Jane's*.

Five versions of the Air Tractor series were available in 1986: the Models AT-301, AT-301A and AT-501 with Pratt & Whitney radial engine, the AT-400 with a Pratt & Whitney Canada PT6A-15AG turboprop engine, and the AT-503 with a Pratt & Whitney Canada PT6A-45R turboprop engine. Air Tractor delivered 54 aircraft during 1985.

AIR TRACTOR MODEL AT-301/301A AIR TRACTOR

Design of the Model **AT-301** Air Tractor was initiated in January 1971, and construction of the first prototype/preproduction aircraft started in August 1972. This aircraft flew for the first time in September 1973, and received FAA certification under FAR Pt 23 in November of that year. At that time the aircraft was also flight tested to meet FAR Pt 8 requirements. The Model **AT-301A**, introduced in 1980, is identical to the AT-301 except for the installation of a larger hopper, with a 0·97 m (3 ft 2 in) wide gatebox for high application rates of dry chemicals.

By 1 January 1986 a total of 690 AT-301/301As had been ordered, of which 640 had been completed, and production was continuing at a rate of four aircraft per month.

TYPE: Single-seat agricultural aircraft.

WINGS: Cantilever low-wing monoplane. Wing section NACA 4415. Dihedral 3° 30′. Incidence 2°. No sweepback. Conventional two-spar structure of 2024-T3 light alloy. Ailerons of light alloy construction, interconnected with trailing-edge flaps to droop 10° at maximum flap deflection of 30°. Electrically operated Fowler trailing-edge flaps of light alloy construction. No trim tabs. Wing ribs and skins zinc chromated before assembly. Wing roots and skin overlaps sealed against chemical entry.

FUSELAGE: Welded structure of 4130N steel tube, oven stress relieved and oiled internally. Quickly detachable skins of 2024-T3 light alloy, with Camloc fasteners. Rear fuselage lightly pressurised to prevent chemical ingress.

TAIL UNIT: Light alloy structure, with cantilever fin and strut braced tailplane. Fabric covered rudder and elevators. Trim tab in each elevator.

LANDING GEAR: Non-retractable tailwheel type. Cantilever spring steel main gear; flat spring suspension for castoring and lockable tailwheel. Cleveland mainwheels with tyres size 8·50-10 (8-ply), pressure 2·83 bars (41 lb/sq in). Tailwheel tyre size 12·50-4, pressure 2·42 bars (35 lb/sq in). Cleveland type 30-89 hydraulic disc brakes.

POWER PLANT: One 447 kW (600 hp) Pratt & Whitney R-1340 aircooled radial engine, driving a Hamilton Standard 12D40/6101A-12 two-blade constant-speed metal propeller without spinner, or a Pacific Propeller 22D40 constant-speed Hydromatic propeller. Fuel in two integral wing tanks with combined capacity of 477 litres (126 US gallons). Refuelling points on upper surface of wings at root. Oil capacity 30·3 litres (8 US gallons).

ACCOMMODATION: Single seat in enclosed cabin which is sealed to prevent chemical ingress. Downward hinged window/door on each side. Baggage compartment in bottom of fuselage, aft of cabin, with door on port side. Cabin ventilation by 0·10 m (4 in) diameter airscoop.

SYSTEMS: Agricultural dispersal system comprises a 1,211 litre (320 US gallon) glassfibre hopper, mounted in the forward fuselage for the AT-301, 1,325 litre (350 US gallon) hopper for the AT-301A; Transland gatebox; Agrinautics valve and strainer; 5 cm (2 in) Root Model 67 pump; 5 cm (2 in) stainless steel plumbing; and up to 69 nozzles in spraybars mounted below and just aft of wing trailing-edges. 24V electrical system, supplied by 60A engine driven alternator.

AVIONICS AND EQUIPMENT: Optional avionics include Narco Com 811 radio and Nav 825/Com 811 nav/com. Optional equipment includes 600W retractable landing light in port wingtip; night flying package of strobe/navigation, instrument, post and dome lights; night working lights; directional and attitude gyro instrument package; glassfibre engine cowling ring; Hydromatic propeller; Cleveland 29-11 wheels and high-flotation tyres; external power socket; and ferry fuel system. Alternative agricultural equipment includes Transland high volume and extra high volume spreader systems, and six- or eight-unit Micronair installations, and windscreen washer.

DIMENSIONS, EXTERNAL:
- Wing span 13·75 m (45 ft 1¼ in)
- Wing chord, constant 1·83 m (6 ft 0 in)
- Wing aspect ratio 7·5
- Length overall 8·23 m (27 ft 0 in)
- Height overall 2·59 m (8 ft 6 in)
- Propeller diameter 2·77 m (9 ft 1 in)

AREAS:
- Wings, gross 25·08 m² (270 sq ft)
- Ailerons (total) 3·55 m² (38·2 sq ft)
- Trailing-edge flaps (total) 3·34 m² (36·0 sq ft)
- Fin 0·90 m² (9·7 sq ft)
- Rudder 1·30 m² (14·0 sq ft)
- Tailplane 2·42 m² (26·0 sq ft)
- Elevators (incl tabs) 2·36 m² (25·4 sq ft)

WEIGHTS AND LOADINGS (A: AT-301; B: AT-301A):
- Weight empty, spray equipped:
  - A 1,723 kg (3,800 lb)
  - B 1,746 kg (3,850 lb)
- Certificated gross weight (FAR 23):
  - A, B 2,268 kg (5,000 lb)
- Typical operating weight (CAM 8):
  - A 3,356 kg (7,400 lb)
  - B 3,492 kg (7,700 lb)
- Max wing loading: A 133·8 kg/m² (27·4 lb/sq ft)
  - B 139·1 kg/m² (28·5 lb/sq ft)
- Max power loading: A 7·51 kg/kW (12·33 lb/hp)
  - B 7·81 kg/kW (12·83 lb/hp)

PERFORMANCE (at max T-O weight except where indicated):
- Max level speed at S/L:
  - A 146 knots (270 km/h; 168 mph)
  - B 142 knots (264 km/h; 164 mph)

Air Tractor Model AT-301 Air Tractor (Pratt & Whitney R-1340 engine)

Max level speed at S/L with dispersal equipment:
A 139 knots (257 km/h; 160 mph)
B 135 knots (251 km/h; 156 mph)
Cruising speed at 1,825 m (6,000 ft), spraypump removed for ferrying:
A 135 knots (249 km/h; 155 mph)
B 132 knots (245 km/h; 152 mph)
Typical working speed: A, B
104-121 knots (193-225 km/h; 120-140 mph)
Stalling speed, at 2,268 kg (5,000 lb) AUW:
flaps up, A, B 64 knots (118 km/h; 73 mph)
flaps down, A, B 53 knots (98 km/h; 61 mph)
Stalling speed as usually landed:
A, B 49 knots (90 km/h; 56 mph)
Max rate of climb at S/L, dispersal equipment installed, AUW of 2,268 kg (5,000 lb):
A 488 m (1,600 ft)/min
B 457 m (1,500 ft)/min
T-O run at AUW of 2,268 kg (5,000 lb):
A, B 244 m (800 ft)
T-O run at AUW of 3,175 kg (7,000 lb):
A, B 396 m (1,300 ft)
Landing run at normal landing weight:
A 91 m (300 ft)
Range with max fuel, no allowances:
A 469 nm (869 km; 540 miles)

AIR TRACTOR MODEL AT-302/302A AIR TRACTOR

Production of the 447 kW (600 shp) Avco Lycoming LTP-101-600A1A powered Air Tractor Models AT-302 and AT-302A has ceased. A total of 18 was delivered. A full description may be found in the 1985-86 edition of *Jane's*.

AIR TRACTOR MODEL AT-400 TURBO AIR TRACTOR

This version of the Air Tractor incorporates the 1,514 litre (400 US gallon) hopper and 0·97 m (3 ft 2 in) wide gatebox introduced on the AT-302A; is powered by a 507 kW (680 shp) Pratt & Whitney Canada PT6A-15AG turboprop engine, driving a Hartzell three-blade constant-speed reversible-pitch propeller; has steel alloy wing lower spar caps for indefinite fatigue life, and a reinforced leading-edge to prevent bird strike damage; size 29-11 high-flotation tyres and wheels as standard; and a 250A starter/generator and two 24V 21Ah batteries. Fuel capacity is 477 litres (126 US gallons). Optional equipment includes Transland extra high volume dispersal system.

Five Turbo Air Tractors were ferried from Olney, Texas, via the Arctic Circle to delivery points specified by the customer, Flug Service GmbH of Kapfenberg, Austria. One was delivered to the Austrian Civil Aviation Authority at Graz, Austria, the other four to El-Minya, Egypt. Flight time for each of the four latter aircraft was 53·5 hours for the 7,295 nm (13,520 km; 8,400 mile) journey from Texas. Current deliveries are made across the North Atlantic from Gander, Newfoundland, to Shannon, Ireland. A total of 83 AT-400s had been delivered by 1 January 1986.

WEIGHTS AND LOADINGS:
Weight empty, spray equipped 1,610 kg (3,550 lb)
Certificated gross weight (FAR 23) 2,721 kg (6,000 lb)
Typical operating weight (CAM 8) 3,538 kg (7,800 lb)
Max wing loading 141·1 kg/m² (28·9 lb/sq ft)
Max power loading 6·98 kg/kW (11·47 lb/shp)
PERFORMANCE (at max T-O weight except where indicated):
Max level speed at S/L, 'clean'
174 knots (322 km/h; 200 mph)
Max level speed at S/L with dispersal equipment
160 knots (298 km/h; 185 mph)
Cruising speed, 55% power at 2,440 m (8,000 ft), spraypump removed for ferrying
143 knots (265 km/h; 165 mph)
Typical working speed
113-126 knots (209-233 km/h; 130-145 mph)
Stalling speed at 2,721 kg (6,000 lb) AUW:
flaps up 66 knots (122 km/h; 76 mph)
flaps down 58 knots (106 km/h; 66 mph)
Stalling speed as usually landed
48 knots (89 km/h; 55 mph)
Max rate of climb at S/L, dispersal equipment installed, AUW of 2,721 kg (6,000 lb) 457 m (1,500 ft)/min
T-O run at AUW of 2,721 kg (6,000 lb)
305 m (1,000 ft)
Landing run as usually landed 152 m (500 ft)

AIR TRACTOR MODEL AT-501

Air Tractor displayed a prototype Model AT-500 at the National Agricultural Aircraft Association's convention at Las Vegas, Nevada, in December 1984. This aircraft, which was described briefly in the 1985-86 *Jane's*, was a market research prototype for a new series of larger Air Tractors, and resulted in the production AT-501 variant which was expected to become available in the Autumn of 1986. The Air Tractor AT-501 is powered by a 447 kW (600 hp) Pratt & Whitney R-1340-S1H1G radial engine, driving a three-blade Hydromatic propeller. Fuel capacity is 636 litres (168 US gallons); hopper capacity, 1,900 litres (502 US gallons).

DIMENSIONS, EXTERNAL:
Wing span 16·46 m (54 ft 0 in)
Wing chord, constant 2·03 m (6 ft 8 in)
Length overall 9·05 m (29 ft 8½ in)
Height overall 2·99 m (9 ft 9½ in)

Air Tractor Model AT-400 Turbo Air Tractor (P&WC PT6A-15AG turboprop engine)

Wheel track 3·11 m (10 ft 2½ in)
Propeller diameter 3·30 m (10 ft 10 in)
AREA:
Wings, gross 33·44 m² (360·0 sq ft)
WEIGHTS:
Weight empty 2,086 kg (4,600 lb)
Design gross weight 3,629 kg (8,000 lb)
Normal operating weight 4,173 kg (9,200 lb)
PERFORMANCE:
Max level speed, with spray equipment
139 knots (257 km/h; 160 mph)
Cruising speed 121 knots (225 km/h; 140 mph)
Working speed
104-121 knots (193-225 km/h; 120-140 mph)
Stalling speed at normal landing weight
45 knots (84 km/h; 52 mph)

AIR TRACTOR MODEL AT-503

Work began on the design of the Air Tractor Model 503 in September 1985 in response to a US State Department requirement for aerial application aircraft suitable for eradication of narcotics crops. The AT-503 is larger than previous Air Tractor models and is the company's first two-seat design. It is intended for special purpose operations such as fire-bombing, forest spraying in mountainous terrain and high-volume seeding or fertiliser applications, in addition to anti-drug enforcement operations. The prototype made its first flight on 25 April 1986, flown by its designer, Mr Leland Snow. A single-seat version, designated **AT-502**, was under development in the Spring of 1986. It will be powered by a 559 kW (750 shp) Pratt & Whitney Canada PT6A-34AG turboprop engine.

The description which follows applies to the Air Tractor AT-503:

TYPE: Two-seat agricultural aircraft.

WINGS: As for AT-301 except incidence 1° 30′.

FUSELAGE: As for AT-301, but with some steel tube members of larger diameter in landing gear area.

TAIL UNIT: As for AT-301, but elevator trim tabs actuated electrically.

LANDING GEAR: Non-retractable tailwheel type. Cantilever spring steel main units; flat spring suspension for castoring and lockable tailwheel. Cleveland mainwheels with Goodyear high flotation tyres, size 29-11, pressure 2·96 bars (43 lb/sq in). Cleveland disc brakes.

POWER PLANT: One Pratt & Whitney Canada PT6A-45R turboprop engine, flat rated at 820 kW (1,100 shp), driving a Hartzell five-blade feathering and reversible-pitch constant-speed metal propeller. Frakes Aviation 'Jet Thrust' exhaust outlets. Fuel in four integral wing tanks, total usable capacity 893 litres (236 US gallons).

ACCOMMODATION: Two seats in tandem in enclosed cabin, which is sealed to prevent chemical ingress and protected with overturn structure. Four downward hinged doors, two on each side, with 25·4 mm (1 in) square chromoly tube frames. Rear seat position windows are bulged to provide downward and forward view for observer/instructor. Separate ram airscoops for ventilation of each cockpit.

SYSTEMS: Integral chemical hopper, capacity 1,900 litres (502 US gallons).

DIMENSIONS, EXTERNAL:
Wing span 14·63 m (48 ft 0 in)
Wing chord, constant 1·83 m (6 ft 0 in)
Wing aspect ratio 8·0
Length overall 10·21 m (33 ft 6 in)
Height overall 2·99 m (9 ft 9½ in)
Wheel track 3·11 m (10 ft 2½ in)
Wheelbase 6·64 m (21 ft 9½ in)
Propeller diameter 2·82 m (9 ft 3 in)
AREAS:
Wings, gross 26·76 m² (288·0 sq ft)
Ailerons, total 3·53 m² (38·0 sq ft)
Trailing-edge flaps, total 3·40 m² (36·6 sq ft)
Fin 0·90 m² (9·70 sq ft)
Rudder 1·30 m² (14·0 sq ft)
Tailplane 2·41 m² (26·0 sq ft)
Elevators, incl tab 2·44 m² (26·3 sq ft)
WEIGHTS AND LOADINGS:
Weight empty, equipped 2,109 kg (4,650 lb)
Payload 2,644 kg (5,830 lb)
Max T-O weight (CAM 8) 4,754 kg (10,480 lb)
Max landing weight 3,629 kg (8,000 lb)
Max wing loading 177·65 kg/m² (36·39 lb/sq ft)
Max power loading 5·80 kg/kW (9·53 lb/shp)
PERFORMANCE (at max T-O weight):
Max level speed at S/L 204 knots (378 km/h; 235 mph)
Max cruising speed at 2,440 m (8,000 ft)
191 knots (340 km/h; 220 mph)
Ferry speed 156 knots (290 km/h; 180 mph)
Stalling speed, power off, flaps down, at max landing weight 63 knots (116 km/h; 72 mph)
Max rate of climb, no hopper load
1,280 m (4,200 ft)/min
Service ceiling 12,800 m (42,000 ft)
T-O run 85 m (280 ft)
Range with max fuel 695 nm (1,287 km; 800 miles)
g limit +3·8

Prototype Air Tractor Model AT-503 (P&WC PT6A-45R turboprop engine)

ALLISON

ALLISON GAS TURBINE OPERATIONS GMC

PO Box 420, Indianapolis, Indiana 46206-0420
Telephone: (317) 242 4567
Chief Project Engineer: Barry N. Rohm
Public Relations Officer: Don O'Brien

ALLISON TURBO FLAGSHIP ATF

Allison Gas Turbine Operations Division of General Motors Corporation has developed the Turbo Flagship ATF from the Convair Super 580 airliner (see Super 580 Corporation entry in this section), with engineering assistance from the Convair Division of General Dynamics Corporation. A prototype was under construction in early 1986 by Tracor Aviation of Santa Barbara, California.

The aircraft has an extended fuselage, created by the insertion of a 2·41 m (7 ft 11 in) 'plug' forward of the wing/fuselage junction, and a 1·93 m (6 ft 4 in) plug aft of the wing, offering standard seating for 72 passengers in 'wide-body' 86 cm (34 in) pitch seats, 76 passengers in an optional configuration, or provision for up to 8,618 kg (19,000 lb) of payload in all-cargo configuration, with port side rear cargo door. The Turbo Flagship ATF conversion includes installation of two 3,728 kW (5,000 shp) Allison 501-D22G Series III turboprop engines, driving Hamilton Standard 54H60-77 four-blade propellers, a new APU, improved cabin pressurisation control, an all-AC electrical system with lightweight electrical wiring, zero-timed airframe, single point refuelling under each wing, anti-skid braking, overhead baggage stowage bins, and a King Gold Crown Series III avionics package with dual Sperry flight director systems. Optional equipment includes a cabin door designed for both 'jetway' and self-contained airstair ground boarding, deluxe hot food galley, exterior strobe lighting, a 1·64 m³ (58 cu ft) baggage stowage space in the aft fuselage plug, a high speed landing light system, and a Collins avionics package, including EFIS and Pro Line II com/nav with dual digital flight director systems.

Standard fuel capacity of the Allison Turbo Flagship ATF is 6,549 litres (1,730 US gallons), with 7,790 litres (2,058 US gallons) and 11,008 litres (2,908 US gallons) available optionally. The all-cargo configuration can accommodate up to seven 2·23 × 2·74 m (88 × 108 in) pallets or up to nine LD-3 containers, and is equipped with a 9*g* cargo tiedown system.

Dimensions, external:
- Wing span: 32·11 m (105 ft 4 in)
- Length overall: 33·53 m (110 ft 0 in)
- Height overall: 8·58 m (28 ft 1⅔ in)
- Cargo door: Width: 3·66 m (12 ft 0 in)

Dimensions, internal:
- Cabin: Width: 2·69 m (8 ft 10 in)
  - Height: 1·98 m (6 ft 6 in)
  - Floor area: 48·1 m² (518 sq ft)
  - Volume: 87·6 m³ (3,096 cu ft)
- Baggage holds, volume:
  - Passenger: standard: 12·6 m³ (444 cu ft)
    - optional: 14·2 m³ (502 cu ft)
  - Cargo: standard: 4·2 m³ (150 cu ft)
    - optional: 5·9 m³ (208 cu ft)

Weights:
- Weight empty: Passenger: 17,236 kg (38,000 lb)
  - Cargo: 15,195 kg (33,500 lb)
- Max T-O weight: 27,215 kg (60,000 lb)
- Max landing weight: 26,308 kg (58,000 lb)
- Zero-fuel weight: 24,494 kg (54,000 lb)

Performance (estimated, at max T-O weight except where indicated):
- Max cruising speed: 305 knots (565 km/h; 351 mph)
- Max rate of climb at S/L: 746 m (2,450 ft)/min
- Service ceiling: 7,620 m (25,000 ft)
- Service ceiling, one engine out: 4,265 m (14,000 ft)
- T-O balanced field length, S/L, ISA: 1,600 m (5,250 ft)
- Landing field length, S/L, ISA, at max landing weight: 1,317 m (4,320 ft)
- Range with 72 passengers, 45 min reserves: 640 nm (1,185 km; 736 miles)

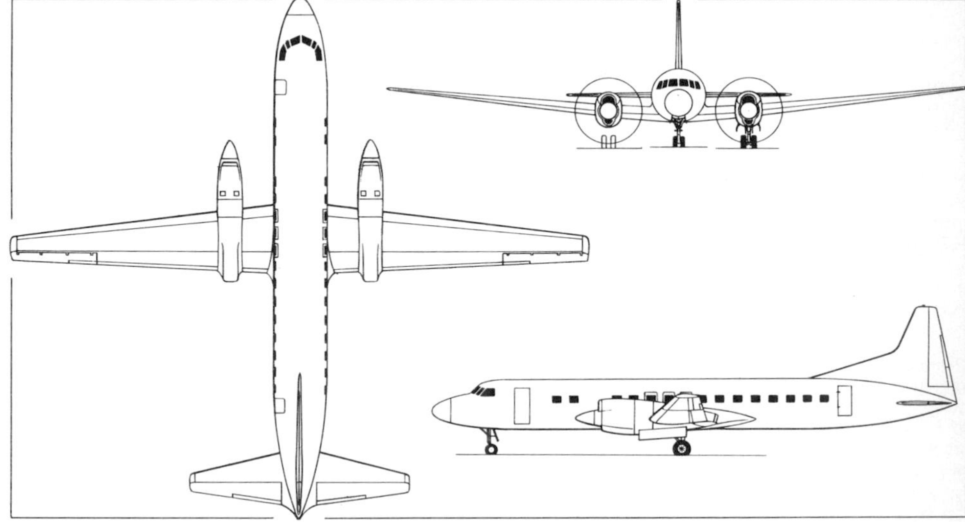

Allison Turbo Flagship ATF development of Convair Super 580 airliner *(Pilot Press)*

APOLLO

APOLLO HELICOPTER SERVICES

PO Box 1636, Yreka, California 96097
Telephone: (916) 459 5221
President: Wayne H. Mulgrew

Apollo Helicopter Services has developed the DTM-3 agricultural spraygear equipment for the Robinson R22 helicopter. The DTM-3 kit comprises a chemical tank with a capacity of 151 litres (40 US gallons), with 0·8 kW (1·1 hp) two-stroke pump and 7·31 m (24 ft 0 in) semi-tapered, semi-cantilevered sprayboom with 16 Flood Jet adjustable nozzles, optimised at a working pressure of 0·83-1·17 bars (12-17 lb/sq in). The equipment weighs 31·7 kg (70 lb), will deliver some 18·9 litres (5 US gallons) per acre at a working speed of 70-75 knots (130-139 km/h; 81-86 mph), with a swath width of 12·2 m (40 ft). Apollo claims that the DTM-3 kit can be attached to or removed from an R22 in 10 minutes. The DTM-3 is approved by the FAA and British Civil Aviation Authority.

Robinson R22 helicopter equipped with Apollo Helicopter Services DTM-3 spraygear

ARCTIC

ARCTIC AIRCRAFT COMPANY

PO Box 6-141, Anchorage, Alaska 99502
Telephone: (907) 243 1580
President: William A. Diehl
Secretary: Catherine J. Diehl

Arctic Aircraft is constructing and marketing, as the S1B2 Arctic Tern, an updated and improved version of the Interstate S1A, first flown more than 30 years ago. Built to CAR.04a (aerobatic) standard, it was certificated for operation on optional Edo floats on 20 January 1981.

ARCTIC AIRCRAFT INTERSTATE S1B2 ARCTIC TERN

Type: Two-seat sporting and general utility aircraft.

Wings: High-wing monoplane, with V bracing struts each side and auxiliary struts. Wing section NACA 23012. Dihedral 2°. Incidence 4°. Composite structure with Sitka spruce spars, light alloy ribs and Dacron covering. Hoerner glassfibre wingtips. Semi-Fowler single-slotted trailing-edge flaps. Plain inset ailerons.

Fuselage: Welded structure of 4130 chrome-molybdenum steel tube, Dacron covered. Two-piece engine cowling of glassfibre.

Tail Unit: Wire braced structure of welded 4130 steel tube with Dacron covering. Trim tab in elevator; ground adjustable tab on rudder.

Landing Gear: Non-retractable tailwheel type. Mainwheels carried in two side Vs and half-axles hinged to fuselage. Shock absorption by hydraulic/coil spring oleo unit. Cleveland mainwheels with US Uniroyal tyres size 8·50-6. Maule tailwheel, diameter 203 mm (8 in). Scott tailwheel optional. Scott toe-operated brakes. Parking brake optional. Peekay 1800 or Edo 2000 floats or 2500 skis optional.

Power Plant: One 112 kW (150 hp) Avco Lycoming O-320 flat-four engine, driving a McCauley two-blade

Arctic Aircraft Interstate S1B2 Arctic Tern *(Neil A. Macdougall)*

fixed-pitch metal propeller. One fuel tank in each wing, total capacity 151 litres (40 US gallons). Oil capacity 7·5 litres (2 US gallons). Underbelly auxiliary fuel tank optional.

ACCOMMODATION: Two seats in tandem; rear seat removable to provide additional space for cargo. Cabin door on starboard side, beneath wing. Cabin step. Baggage space in rear fuselage, with external door on starboard side, capacity 45 kg (100 lb). Tinted windows and cabin skylight optional. Safety belts and fittings standard. Dual controls standard. Cabin soundproofed, heated and ventilated. Windscreen de-icing by hot air. Cabin floor carpeted.

SYSTEM: Electrical system includes 55A engine driven alternator, 12V DC storage battery and engine starter.

AVIONICS AND EQUIPMENT: A range of radios is available. Standard features include epoxy priming, ground manoeuvring handles and engine quick oil drain. Optional items include Alcor exhaust gas analyser, folding front seat, shoulder harness, dome light, instrument lights, landing light, navigation lights, three-colour external paint scheme, underbelly cargo pack, lumber rack and salt water corrosion proofing.

DIMENSIONS, EXTERNAL:
Wing span 11·18 m (36 ft 8 in)
Wing chord (constant) 1·57 m (5 ft 2 in)
Length overall: landplane 7·01 m (23 ft 0 in)
seaplane 7·32 m (24 ft 0 in)
Height overall 2·13 m (7 ft 0 in)
Tailplane span 3·35 m (11 ft 0 in)

DIMENSIONS, INTERNAL:
Cabin: Max width 0·66 m (2 ft 2 in)
Volume 1·38 m³ (48·7 cu ft)
Baggage compartment volume 0·84 m³ (29·63 cu ft)

AREAS:
Wings, gross 17·30 m² (186·2 sq ft)
Flaps (total) 1·77 m² (19·02 sq ft)
Fin 0·74 m² (7·98 sq ft)
Rudder, incl tab 0·75 m² (8·10 sq ft)
Horizontal tail surfaces (total, incl tab) 2·67 m² (28·75 sq ft)

WEIGHTS AND LOADINGS (A: landplane; B: seaplane with Edo 2000 floats):
Weight empty: A 487 kg (1,073 lb)
B 521·5 kg (1,150 lb)
Max T-O weight: A 862 kg (1,900 lb)
B 965 kg (2,127 lb)
Max wing loading: A 49·8 kg/m² (10·2 lb/sq ft)
B 55·7 kg/m² (11·4 lb/sq ft)
Max power loading: A 7·7 kg/kW (12·67 lb/hp)
B 8·62 kg/kW (14·18 lb/hp)

PERFORMANCE:
Never-exceed speed:
A 152 knots (282 km/h; 175 mph)
Max cruising speed at S/L, 75% power:
A 102 knots (188 km/h; 117 mph)
B 91 knots (169 km/h; 105 mph)
Cruising speed, 65% power at optimum altitude:
A 96 knots (178 km/h; 111 mph)
Stalling speed, flaps down:
A, B 30 knots (55 km/h; 34 mph)
Max rate of climb at S/L, at max T-O weight:
A 389 m (1,275 ft)/min
B 305 m (1,000 ft)/min
Service ceiling: A, B 5,790 m (19,000 ft)
Absolute ceiling: A 6,400 m (21,000 ft)
T-O run at max T-O weight: A 99 m (325 ft)
T-O to 15 m (50 ft) at max T-O weight:
A 152 m (500 ft)
Landing from 15 m (50 ft): A 137 m (450 ft)
Range with max fuel, 45 min reserves:
A, 75% power 479 nm (888 km; 552 miles)
A, 65% power 566 nm (1,049 km; 652 miles)
Range with max fuel, no reserves:
B 499 nm (925 km; 575 miles)

ATAC

ADVANCED TECHNOLOGY AIRCRAFT CO INC

11755 Glendale Avenue, Hanford, California 93230

Telephone: (209) 584 1591
Telex: 754633 ATAC UD

PRESIDENT: R. David Record

ATAC MODEL 480 PREDATOR

The original Predator design (Rutan Model 59: see 1983-84 *Jane's*) was for a unique joined-wing strutless biplane, with the inner panels of the wings sweptback to unite with sweptforward inverted V tail surfaces; intended power plant was a 559 kW (750 shp) P&WC PT6A-34 turboprop engine.

Although this design was verified aerodynamically by NASA wind tunnel testing (completed in 1980), a simpler configuration has been adopted for the Model 480 Predator, the prototype of which (Model M120-9E, registration N480AG) was built for Advanced Technology Aircraft by Mr Rutan's Scaled Composites Inc (see SCI entry in this section) and flown for the first time on 17 September 1984. It had completed some 40 hours of test flying by early 1985, but was damaged in an accident later that year, since when no further information has been received. All known details of the Model 480, and an illustration, can be found in the 1985-86 *Jane's*.

AVTEK

AVTEK CORPORATION

4680 Calle Carga, Camarillo, California 93010
Telephone: (805) 482 2700
Telex: 910-336-1222 AVTEK-CAMA

PRESIDENT: Robert F. Adickes
EXECUTIVE VICE-PRESIDENT: Dr Leo J. Windecker
VICE-PRESIDENTS:
Niels Andersen (Engineering)
Matti Kankaanpää (Valmet)
Dorothy J. Sholer (Comptroller)
PUBLIC RELATIONS: Dr J. C. Adickes
DIRECTOR OF MARKETING: Robert D. Honeycutt

Avtek Corporation was established by a number of men with extensive experience in the aviation industry to develop and certificate a new all-composite twin-turboprop six/nine-seat business aircraft of canard configuration. Known as the Avtek Model 400, this was designed by Al W. Mooney, founder of Mooney Aircraft Corporation, and test pilot William W. Taylor. The company benefits also from the expertise of Leo Windecker, formerly of Windecker Industries and designer of the Windecker Eagle which was the first all-composite aircraft to gain FAA certification. A proposed twin-engined Eagle, known as the 'Tweagle', formed the basis for initial Avtek 400 design studies. Structural materials used in the Avtek 400 are primarily Nomex honeycomb sandwiched between outer and inner plies of unwoven biaxial or triaxial fabric of Kevlar aramid fibre. Where maximum stiffness is required, such as in spars, graphite is used in conjunction with the aramid fibre. Du Pont Co and Dow Chemicals Co of the USA, and Valmet of Finland, are investors in Avtek Corporation.

On 7 November 1985 Avtek concluded an agreement with the State of New Mexico for the establishment of a manufacturing facility at Albuquerque. Total employment at the facility is expected to be 750 people, with an initial production rate of 100 aircraft per year.

AVTEK MODEL 400

Design of the Avtek 400 was initiated in March 1981, and construction of the first prototype started on 1 January 1982. This proof of concept aircraft (N400AV) flew for the first time on 17 September 1984. By September 1985 it had completed 92 flights and accumulated 60 hours of flight time, as a result of which a number of modifications had been made to the airframe including the addition of a ventral fin, a 4° increase in foreplane angle of incidence, and a strengthened nose gear leg.

In the Spring of 1985 major development work was undertaken to define the production configuration of the Avtek 400. Among the changes were a fuselage 'stretch' of 0·20 m (8 in) forward and 0·76 m (2 ft 6 in) aft of the forward pressure bulkhead; an increase in cabin width; a new wing incorporating additional fuel capacity in large wingroot leading-edge extensions; a new foreplane of greater span and reduced chord; relocated main landing gear legs; 559 kW (750 shp) Pratt & Whitney PT6A-135M engines derated to 507 kW (680 shp) and mounted closer to the wing. This revised design was 'frozen' for production standard aircraft, and in late 1985 work was underway on

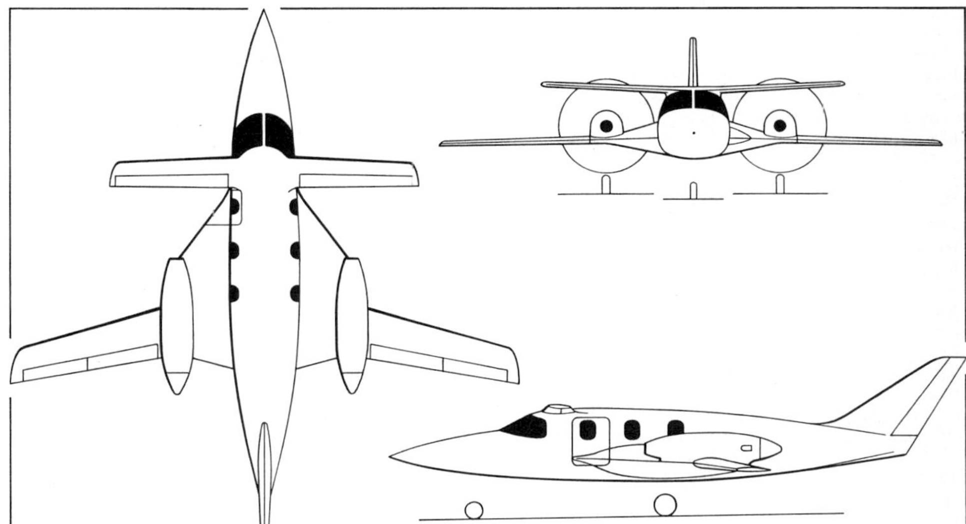

Avtek Model 400 composites business aircraft in production form *(Jane's/Mike Keep)*

two flying and two static test airframes for use in the FAA certification programme. Certification is now anticipated in late 1987.

The pre-moulded components which make up the Avtek 400's composites airframe will be manufactured by Avtek Far East in Osaka, Japan, and shipped to the United States for assembly.

On 20 March 1985 Valmet Corporation of Finland signed a licensing agreement with Avtek for the production of 'government' derivatives of the Avtek 400 for special missions such as maritime surveillance, liaison, coastal patrol, aerial survey, search and reconnaissance, and ESM, tailored to individual customer requirements. Production was expected to begin in Finland in 1987, though no decision had been taken on whether Valmet would manufacture composites components or assemble the aircraft from Avtek-supplied parts. Valmet will also distribute the Avtek 400 in Nordic countries.

A description of the proof of concept prototype can be found in the 1985-86 *Jane's*. This aircraft has been retrofitted and flown with PT6A-135M engines and four-blade propellers, but it is not otherwise planned to modify it to production configuration. The following details apply to the intended production version:

TYPE: Six/nine-seat business aircraft.

WINGS: Cantilever low-wing monoplane, with large wingroot leading-edge extensions. Wing section Avtek 12. Anhedral 2° on outer panels. Sweepback 50° inboard of nacelles, 15° 30′ outboard. All-composites fail-safe structure. Mass balanced two-section ailerons of composite construction, inner sections functioning as pitch trim stabilisers. All control surfaces operated through bellcranks and rigid pushrods. No trim tabs. No trailing-edge flaps. Pneumatic de-icing boots on leading-edges.

FOREPLANE: Cantilever structure of composite materials, located on upper fuselage above forward end of cabin. Conventional elevators, mass balanced and operated through bellcranks and pushrods. No trim tabs. Electric or engine bleed air de-icing of leading-edges.

FUSELAGE: All-composites fail-safe monocoque structure. Cabin and cabin baggage compartment pressurised.

TAIL UNIT: Conventional sweptback vertical surfaces only, of all-composites construction. Rudder mass balanced and operated through bellcranks and pushrods. No trim tab. Pneumatic de-icing of fin leading-edge. Ventral fin.

LANDING GEAR: Hydraulically retractable tricycle type, main units retracting inward and nosewheel forward. Emergency extension system. Oleo-pneumatic shock absorber in each unit. Single wheel on each unit, mainwheels size 6·00-6 with Goodyear tyres size 17·5-6·25 × 7·5, pressure 7·0 bars (102 lb/sq in). Steerable nosewheel unit with wheel size 5·00-5 and Goodyear tyre size 14·2-5·5 × 6·5, pressure 5·0 bars (73 lb/sq in). Cleveland hydraulic disc brakes.

POWER PLANT: Two 559 kW (750 shp) Pratt & Whitney Canada PT6A-135M turboprop engines, derated to 507 kW (680 shp), one mounted within nacelle above each wing, driving a Hartzell four-blade constant-speed fully-feathering reversible-pitch pusher propeller. Propellers have Q tips, automatic synchrophasing, full Beta control reversing and autofeathering. In-flight start capability. Integral fuel tanks, with 1,003 litres (265 US gallons) in each wingroot, and 182 litres (40 US gallons) in foreplane. Total fuel capacity 2,157 litres (570 US gallons).

Refuelling point in upper surface of each wing and in foreplane. Oil capacity 21 litres (4·6 US gallons). Dual anti-icing inlets for each engine.

ACCOMMODATION: Pilot and five to eight passengers according to interior layout. Optional configurations include eight-passenger Pullman or Salon; eight-passenger Lounge; six-passenger Conference; Ambulance with stretcher, medical equipment and seats for three ambulatory patients or medical attendants; and Cargo with seats for pilot and one passenger. Two-section door on port side of cabin, with step incorporated in lower half. Emergency exit on starboard side opposite cabin door. Baggage compartment at rear of cabin with internal access. Unpressurised baggage compartment in nose with external door on port side. Accommodation is pressurised, air-conditioned, heated and ventilated.

SYSTEMS: Garrett AiResearch bleed air pressurisation system with max differential of 0·48 bars (7·0 lb/sq in), and air cycle air-conditioning system. Electrically driven hydraulic pump provides pressure of 138 bars (2,000 lb/sq in) for landing gear actuation. Electrical system includes dual 28V 300A engine driven generators, dual 29Ah storage batteries and external power socket. Oxygen system of 1·39 m³ (49 cu ft) capacity, pressure 128 bars (1,850 lb/sq in), provides constant flow for passengers and demand flow for pilot. De-icing of windscreen and foreplane by engine bleed air or electrical system, of propellers by engine efflux; pneumatic de-icing of wing and fin leading-edges; electrically heated pitot. Engine fire extinguishing system optional.

AVIONICS AND EQUIPMENT: Wide range of optional avionics by Bendix, Collins and Sperry, including EFIS and EICAS, and colour radar by RCA. Full IFR instrumentation optional.

DIMENSIONS, EXTERNAL:

Wing span	10·50 m (34 ft 5½ in)
Foreplane span	6·35 m (20 ft 10 in)
Length overall	12·02 m (39 ft 5 in)
Length of fuselage	10·41 m (34 ft 2 in)
Height overall	3·27 m (10 ft 8¾ in)
Propeller diameter	1·93 m (6 ft 4 in)
Passenger door (port): Height	1·17 m (3 ft 10 in)
Width	0·76 m (2 ft 6 in)
Height to sill	0·76 m (2 ft 6 in)
Baggage door (port, nose): Height	0·51 m (1 ft 8 in)
Width	0·56 m (1 ft 10 in)
Height to sill	0·79 m (2 ft 7 in)
Emergency exit (stbd): Height	0·51 m (1 ft 8 in)
Width	0·67 m (2 ft 2½ in)

DIMENSIONS, INTERNAL:

Cabin: Max width	1·55 m (5 ft 1 in)
Max height	1·32 m (4 ft 4 in)

AREAS, WEIGHTS & LOADINGS, AND PERFORMANCE:
No details received

AYRES

AYRES CORPORATION

PO Box 3090, Albany, Georgia 31707
Telephone: (912) 883 1440
Telex: 547629 AYRESPORT ABN
SALES MANAGERS: Marvin H. Wilson (Domestic)
Bill Brodbeck (International)

AYRES THRUSH S2R-600

Ayres Corporation purchased the manufacturing and world marketing rights of the Rockwell Thrush Commander-600 and -800 from Rockwell International's General Aviation Division in late November 1977, and now offers six versions of this large agricultural aircraft.

Thrush S2R-600. Basic version with Pratt & Whitney R-1340 Wasp aircooled radial engine. Previously known as S2R-R1340. Available with one or two seats.

Bull Thrush S2R-R1820. As Thrush S2R-600, but with a Wright R-1820 engine. Described separately.

Turbo-Thrush S2R. As Thrush S2R-600, but with a Pratt & Whitney Canada PT6A-11, -15, -34 or -65R turboprop engine. Described separately.

By early 1986 a total of 1,630 piston engined Thrushes had been delivered.

The Thrush S2R-600 has a 1·50 m³ (53 cu ft) hopper able to contain up to 1,514 litres (400 US gallons) of liquid or 1,487 kg (3,280 lb) of dry chemicals. The aircraft has a corrosion-proof, polyurethane finish, and is certificated to both CAR 3 Normal category and CAM 8 Restricted category requirements.

The Canadian company Specialty Aircraft Sales of Vancouver (which see) obtained FAA type approval for a **Sea Thrush** water bombing version mounted on twin Edo floats and fitted with a drop door beneath the hopper. The prototype (C-GYXL), first flown in June 1983, was converted from a Thrush S2R-600, but the Canadian company planned to base its marketing effort on the Turbo-Thrush. An amphibious version was also under consideration.

The following details refer to the Ayres basic single-seat Thrush S2R-600, but are applicable also to the Bull Thrush, except as described in the separate entry for the latter aircraft.

TYPE: Single-seat (optionally two-seat) agricultural aircraft.

WINGS: Cantilever low-wing monoplane. Dihedral 3° 30′. Two-spar structure of light alloy throughout, except for main spar caps of 4130 chrome molybdenum steel. Leading-edge formed by heavy main spar and the nose skin. Light alloy plain ailerons. Electrically operated flaps. Wing roots sealed against chemical entry. Wing extensions, adding 2·79 m² (30 sq ft) of effective lifting surface, are standard on S2R-600, optional on Turbo-Thrush.

FUSELAGE: Welded chrome molybdenum steel tube structure covered with quickly removable light alloy panels. Underfuselage skin of stainless steel.

TAIL UNIT: Wire braced welded chrome molybdenum steel tube structure, fabric covered. Streamline section heavy duty stainless steel wire bracing and heavy duty stainless steel attachment fittings. Light alloy controllable trim tab in each elevator. Deflector cable from cockpit to fin tip.

LANDING GEAR: Non-retractable tailwheel type. Main units have rubber in compression shock absorption and 29 × 11·00-10 wheels with 10-ply tyres. Hydraulically operated disc brakes. Parking brakes. Wire cutters on main gear. Steerable, locking tailwheel, size 12·5 × 4·5 in.

POWER PLANT: One 447 kW (600 hp) Pratt & Whitney R-1340 Wasp nine-cylinder aircooled radial engine, driving a Hamilton Standard type 12D40/EAC AG-100-2 two-blade constant-speed metal propeller, is standard. Fuel contained in wing tanks with combined capacity of 401 litres (106 US gallons).

ACCOMMODATION: Single adjustable mesh seat in 'safety pod' sealed cockpit enclosure is standard, with steel tube overturn structure. Dual tandem seating optional, with forward or rear facing second seat. Dual controls optional with forward facing rear seat, for pilot training. Adjustable rudder pedals. Downward hinged door on each side. Tempered safety glass windscreen. Cockpit wire cutter. Dual inertia reel safety harness with optional second seat. Baggage compartment available on single-seat aircraft. Windscreen wiper and washer.

Ayres Thrush S2R-600 (600 hp Pratt & Whitney R-1340 Wasp engine)

SYSTEM: Electrical system powered by a 24V 200A generator. Lightweight 24V 35Ah battery.

AVIONICS AND EQUIPMENT: Transland glassfibre hopper forward of cockpit with capacity of 1·50 m³ (53 cu ft) or 1,514 litres (400 US gallons). Hopper has a 0·33 m² (3·56 sq ft) lid, openable by two handles, and cockpit viewing window. Standard equipment includes Universal spray system with external 50 mm (2 in) stainless steel plumbing, 50 mm pump with wooden fan, Transland gate, 50 mm valve, quick-disconnect pump mount and strainer. Streamlined spraybooms with outlets for 68 nozzles. Micro-adjust valve control (spray) and calibrator (dry). A 63 mm (2·5 in) side loading system is installed on the port side. Stainless steel rudder cables. Navigation lights, instrument lights and two strobe lights. Optional equipment includes a rear cockpit to accommodate aft facing crew member, or forward facing seat for passenger, or flying instructor if optional dual controls installed; space can be used alternatively for cargo. Other optional items are a Transland high-volume spreader, agitator installation, ten-unit AU5000 Micronair installation in lieu of standard booms and nozzles; Transland gatebox with stiffener casting; quick-disconnect flange and kit; night working lights including landing light and wingtip turn lights; cockpit fire extinguisher; and water bomber configuration. Optional avionics on request.

DIMENSIONS, EXTERNAL:

Wing span	14·48 m (47 ft 6 in)
Length overall (tail up)	8·95 m (29 ft 4½ in)
Height overall	2·79 m (9 ft 2 in)
Tailplane span	4·86 m (15 ft 11½ in)
Wheel track	2·72 m (8 ft 11 in)
Propeller diameter	2·74 m (9 ft 0 in)

AREA:

Wings, gross	33·13 m² (356·6 sq ft)

WEIGHTS AND LOADINGS:

Weight empty, equipped	1,678 kg (3,700 lb)
Max T-O weight: CAR 3	2,721 kg (6,000 lb)
CAM 8	3,130 kg (6,900 lb)
Max wing loading	103·0 kg/m² (21·1 lb/sq ft)
Max power loading	6·99 kg/kW (11·5 lb/hp)

PERFORMANCE (with spray equipment installed and at CAR 3 max T-O weight, except where indicated):

Max level speed	122 knots (225 km/h; 140 mph)
Max cruising speed, 70% power	108 knots (200 km/h; 124 mph)
Working speed, 70% power	91-100 knots (169-185 km/h; 105-115 mph)
Stalling speed: flaps up	58 knots (108 km/h; 67 mph)
flaps down	55 knots (101 km/h; 63 mph)
Stalling speed at normal landing weight:	
flaps up	47 knots (87 km/h; 54 mph)
flaps down	45 knots (84 km/h; 52 mph)
Max rate of climb at S/L	317 m (1,040 ft)/min
Service ceiling	4,575 m (15,000 ft)
T-O run	215 m (705 ft)
Landing run	139 m (455 ft)
Ferry range with max fuel at 70% power	350 nm (648 km; 403 miles)

AYRES BULL THRUSH S2R-R1820

Claimed by Ayres to be the most powerful production agricultural aircraft in the world, the Bull Thrush is generally similar to the Thrush S2R-600 except for the installation of a Wright R-1820 engine and a chemical hopper of increased capacity. The description of the Thrush S2R-600 applies also to the Bull Thrush, except as follows:

POWER PLANT: One 895 kW (1,200 hp) Wright R-1820 Cyclone nine-cylinder aircooled radial engine, driving a Hamilton Standard three-blade constant-speed metal propeller. Fuel system as for Thrush, but total usable fuel capacity 863 litres (228 US gallons).

AVIONICS AND EQUIPMENT: Generally as for Thrush, except that the chemical hopper is of 1·93 m³ (68·2 cu ft) or 1,930 litres (510 US gallons) capacity.

DIMENSIONS, EXTERNAL: As for Thrush, except:

Wing span	13·54 m (44 ft 5 in)
Length overall	9·60 m (31 ft 6 in)
Height overall	2·92 m (9 ft 7 in)
Wheel track	2·74 m (9 ft 0 in)

AREA:

Wings, gross	30·34 m² (326·6 sq ft)

WEIGHTS:

Weight empty, equipped	2,263 kg (4,990 lb)
Typical operating weight (CAM 8)	4,536 kg (10,000 lb)

PERFORMANCE (with spray equipment, at CAM 8 max T-O weight, except where indicated):

Max level speed	138 knots (256 km/h; 159 mph)
Cruising speed, 50% power	135 knots (249 km/h; 155 mph)
Working speed, 30-50% power	87-130 knots (161-241 km/h; 100-150 mph)
Stalling speed: flaps up	61 knots (113 km/h; 70 mph)
flaps down	58 knots (107 km/h; 66 mph)
Stalling speed at normal landing weight:	
flaps up	52 knots (95 km/h; 59 mph)
flaps down	50 knots (92 km/h; 57 mph)
Max rate of climb at S/L	620 m (2,033 ft)/min
Service ceiling	8,535 m (28,000 ft)
T-O run	168 m (550 ft)
Landing run at normal landing weight	290 m (950 ft)
Ferry range at 40% power	582 nm (1,078 km; 670 miles)

AYRES TURBO-THRUSH S2R

Four versions of the turbine engined Turbo-Thrush S2R are currently available:

Turbo-Thrush S2R-T11: Version with a 373 kW (500 shp) Pratt & Whitney Canada PT6A-11AG turboprop engine and available only with the standard 1,514 litre (400 US gallon) chemical hopper.

Turbo-Thrush S2R-T15: Version with a 507 kW (680 shp) Pratt & Whitney Canada PT6A-15AG turboprop engine, available with a 1,514 litre (400 US gallon) or, optionally, 1,930 litre (510 US gallon) chemical hopper.

Turbo-Thrush S2R-T34: This version has a 559 kW (750 shp) Pratt & Whitney Canada PT6A-34AG turboprop engine and is available with standard and optional chemical hoppers as above.

Turbo-Thrush NEDS: Ayres has developed a special version of the Turbo-Thrush, known as the Narcotics Eradication Delivery System (NEDS), for the US State Department. This aircraft is powered by a 1,026 kW (1,376 shp) Pratt & Whitney Canada PT6A-65R turboprop driving a five-blade propeller of 2·82 m (9 ft 3 in) diameter and features a two-seat cockpit and a 75·7 litre (20 US gallon) self-sealing auxiliary fuel tank mounted in a bulletproof structure. Nine aircraft were delivered to the US State Department during 1983-85.

With the exception of the Turbo-Thrush NEDS, in each case the turboprop engine drives a Hartzell three-blade constant-speed fully-feathering and reversible-pitch metal propeller with spinner. To compensate for the small size and light weight of the turboprop, it is mounted well forward of the firewall, in a slender cowling. Current installations have cowlings which comprise individual panels to improve access. Standard and optional equipment is generally as detailed for the basic Thrush. Total usable fuel capacity is 863 litres (228 US gallons).

Advantages claimed for this conversion include greatly improved take-off and climb performance; improved short landing capability; a 454 kg (1,000 lb) increase in payload due to reduced power plant weight; ability to operate on aviation turbine fuel, or diesel fuel; a TBO of 3,500 h; quieter operation; and the ability to feather the propeller during fuelling and loading operations without shutting down the engine, because of the free-turbine configuration.

By early 1986 a total of 261 Turbo-Thrushes had been delivered.

DIMENSIONS, EXTERNAL AND AREA: As for Bull Thrush S2R-R1820 except:
- Length overall — 10·06 m (33 ft 0 in)
- Height overall — 2·79 m (9 ft 2 in)

WEIGHTS AND LOADINGS (A: standard hopper; B: optional 1,930 litre; 510 US gallon hopper):
- Weight empty: A — 1,633 kg (3,600 lb)
- B — 1,769 kg (3,900 lb)
- Max T-O weight (CAR 3): A, B — 2,721 kg (6,000 lb)
- Typical operating weight (CAM 8):
  - A — 3,719 kg (8,200 lb)
  - B — 3,856 kg (8,500 lb)
- Max wing loading — 127·1 kg/m² (26·0 lb/sq ft)
- Max power loading — 7·6 kg/kW (14·17 lb/shp)

PERFORMANCE (A and B with PT6A-34AG power plant, at max T-O weight except where indicated):
- Max level speed with spray equipment — 138 knots (256 km/h; 159 mph)
- Cruising speed, 50% power — 130 knots (241 km/h; 150 mph)
- Working speed, 30-50% power — 82-130 knots (153-241 km/h; 95-150 mph)
- Stalling speed: flaps up — 61 knots (113 km/h; 70 mph)
  - flaps down — 57 knots (106 km/h; 66 mph)
- Stalling speed at normal landing weight:
  - flaps up — 51 knots (95 km/h; 59 mph)
  - flaps down — 50 knots (92 km/h; 57 mph)
- Max rate of climb at S/L — 530 m (1,740 ft)/min
- Service ceiling — 7,620 m (25,000 ft)
- T-O run — 183 m (600 ft)
- Landing run — 152 m (500 ft)
- Landing run with propeller reversal — 91 m (300 ft)
- Ferry range at 40% power — 664 nm (1,231 km; 765 miles)

Ayres Turbo-Thrush S2R-T34 with optional dual cockpit and spreader installation

BEECHCRAFT

BEECH AIRCRAFT CORPORATION (Subsidiary of Raytheon Company)

9709 East Central, Wichita, Kansas 67201-0085

Telephone: (316) 681 7111

BRANCH DIVISIONS: Salina, Kansas; and Boulder, Colorado

CHAIRMAN EMERITUS, AND CHAIRMAN OF BEECH AIRCRAFT FOUNDATION: Mrs Olive Ann (Walter H.) Beech

CHAIRMAN OF THE BOARD: Thomas L. Phillips

PRESIDENT AND CHIEF EXECUTIVE OFFICER:
James S. Walsh

EXECUTIVE VICE-PRESIDENTS:
Charles W. Dieker (Marketing)
Glenn Ehling (Operations)

SENIOR VICE-PRESIDENT:
John J. Funsch

VICE-PRESIDENTS:
Karl H. Berg (Product Marketing)
Max Bleck (Asst to the President)
Jack E. Braly (Manufacturing)
William R. Coughenour (Aerospace Programmes)
Harold W. Deets (Materiel and Production)
Max P. Eaton (Operations Administration)
Joseph T. Giardina (Controller)
Richard R. Griffiths (Industrial Relations)
Gary M. Hanssen (Procurement)
LeRoy P. LoPresti (Chief Engineer)
George D. Rodgers (Sales and Marketing Services)
Elbert L. Rutan
William G. Rutherford (Government Relations)
W. D. Wise (Quality Assurance)

CORPORATE SECRETARY: David S. Dwelley

ASST CONTROLLER AND CHIEF ACCOUNTANT:
D. C. Cullinane

TREASURER: Andrew F. Horvath

DIRECTOR OF CORPORATE COMMUNICATIONS:
William D. Mellon

Beech Aircraft Corporation was founded jointly in 1932 by Mrs Olive Ann Beech and the late Walter H. Beech, pioneer designer and builder of light aeroplanes in the USA. On 8 February 1980, Raytheon Company and Beech Aircraft Corporation completed the signing of closing merger documents under which Beech became a wholly owned subsidiary of Raytheon. It continues to operate as a separate entity, and is currently engaged in the production of civil and military aircraft, missile targets, aircraft and missile components, and cryogenic equipment for spacecraft.

Deliveries by Beech in 1985 were made up of 102 King Airs, 40 Barons, 99 Bonanzas, 5 Duchesses, 1 Sundowner and 21 Model 1900 Airliners. By 1 January 1986 Beech had delivered 5,012 pressurised aircraft since introducing the King Air 90 in 1964. Total production of Beech aeroplanes surpassed 47,817 by the beginning of 1986.

In 1986 Beech began its 20th consecutive year of manufacturing complete airframes for the Bell Helicopter Textron Model 206B JetRanger. These units, plus the military OH-58A observation helicopters built during the Viet-Nam conflict, then totalled 5,980. Present and future contractual commitments are expected to extend this programme for several more years. A contract to supply Beechcraft Model 1080 aerial refuelling units for USAF Boeing KE-3A tanker aircraft was announced in March 1984. These units have also been ordered by the Canadian Armed Forces and the Royal Saudi Air Force.

In October 1976 Beech established a wholly owned subsidiary, Beech Aerospace Services Inc (BASI), to provide worldwide logistic support of aerospace products. This company is currently responsible for total support of 226 Army/Air Force/Navy C-12s (plus additional 40 C-12Fs), and Beech MQM-107A targets, in more than 137 locations in 37 countries worldwide. BASI headquarters for administration, spare parts, publications central supply and training is based at Jackson, Mississippi.

Beech Aircraft had 7,935 employees worldwide at the end of 1985 and occupies 348,773 m² (3,754,286 sq ft) of plant area at its three major facilities in Wichita and Salina, Kansas; and Boulder, Colorado.

The plant at Selma, Alabama, formerly used for production of the C99 Airliner, and the King Air C90A and F90-1, was scheduled to close by September 1986. Production of these aircraft is now undertaken at Wichita.

The Salina division supplies all wings, non-metallic interior components, ventral fins, nosecones and tailcones used in Wichita production, and is responsible for manufacture and final assembly of the pressurised Baron 58P and the T-34C trainer.

Work at Boulder involves space vehicle or missile applications. The company's contracts on the Space Shuttle programme alone (details in 1980-81 *Jane's*) totalled $53·5 million by the beginning of 1983. Boulder also produces aircraft assemblies for other Beech divisions and missile target systems for the US Army and Navy (see RPVs and Targets section).

Wholly owned subsidiaries of the parent company include Scaled Composites Inc (which see), which was acquired in June 1985 to serve as an advanced development arm for the company; Beech Acceptance Corporation Inc, which is engaged in business aircraft retail finance and leasing; Beechcraft AG, which has its headquarters in Zurich, Switzerland, and supports in Europe the sales, liaison and other activities of the parent company; Travel Air Insurance Company Ltd, a Bermuda-based company organised during 1972 to provide aircraft liability insurance; Beech Holdings Inc, which provides marketing support to the parent company; Beech International Sales Corporation, Wichita, through which all Beech export sales are made; Beech Aerospace Services Inc, which provides worldwide support of Beech military aircraft, missile targets and related products; and the following sales outlets which are wholly owned subsidiaries of Beech Holdings Inc: Beechcraft East Inc, Farmingdale, New York, and Bedford, Massachusetts; Rocky Mountain Beechcraft, Engelwood, Colorado; Hangar One Inc, Atlanta, Hartsfield, DeKalb-Peachtree, and Fulton County, Georgia; Birmingham, Alabama; Chattanooga, Tennessee; and Opa Locka, Orlando and Tampa, Florida; United Beechcraft Inc, Wichita, Kansas; Beechcraft West, Ontario, Hayward, Van Nuys, Fresno and Orange County, California; Indiana Beechcraft Inc, Indianapolis, Indiana; Salt Lake Beechcraft, Salt Lake City, Utah; Ohio Aviation Co, Dayton, Cincinnati and Cleveland, Ohio; Hartzog Aviation, Rockford, Illinois; and Flightcraft Inc, Portland Oregon, and Seattle and Spokane, Washington.

BEECHCRAFT T-34C

US Navy designation: T-34C

In March 1953 the US Air Force selected the Beechcraft Model 45 as its new primary trainer, and a total of 450 was eventually acquired by USAF as the T-34A Mentor,

Beechcraft T-34C-1 in service with the Navy of Peru

powered by a 168 kW (225 hp) Continental O-470-13 flat-six engine. The US Navy subsequently received 423 similar Mentors as the T-34B.

Design of the upgraded T-34C, with a PT6A-25 turboprop engine and updated avionics, began under US Navy contract in March 1973, and the first of two YT-34C prototypes flew for the first time on 21 September 1973. Under initial US Navy contracts, Beech delivered 184 new-production T-34Cs to Naval Air Training Command (Training Air Wing 5) at NAS Whiting Field, Milton, Florida, between November 1977 and June 1981. Deliveries of a further 150 T-34Cs to the US Navy were completed in April 1984. An export civil version, known as the **Turbine Mentor 34C**, is in service at the Algerian national pilot training school, which received six in 1979.

A **T-34C-1** armament systems trainer version is also available and, in addition to its basic role, is capable of carrying out forward air control (FAC) and tactical strike training missions. Deliveries of 89 T-34C-1s, also completed in 1984, were made to Argentina (Navy 15), Ecuador (Air Force 20, Navy 3), Gabon (Presidential Guard 4), Indonesia (Air Force 25), Morocco (Air Force 12), Peru (Navy 7) and Uruguay (Navy 3).

TYPE: Two-seat turbine powered primary training and light strike training aircraft.

WINGS: Cantilever low-wing monoplane. Wing section NACA 23016·5 (modified) at root, NACA 23012 at tip. Dihedral 7°. Incidence 4° at root, 1° at tip. No sweepback. Conventional box beam structure of light alloy. Ailerons of light alloy construction. Single-slotted trailing-edge flaps of light alloy. Manually operated trim tab in port aileron. Servo tabs in both ailerons.

FUSELAGE: Semi-monocoque light alloy structure.

TAIL UNIT: Cantilever structure of light alloy. Fixed incidence tailplane. Manually operated trim tabs in elevators and rudder. Twin ventral fins under rear fuselage.

LANDING GEAR: Electrically retractable tricycle type. Main units retract inward, nosewheel aft. Beech oleo-pneumatic shock absorbers. Single wheel on each unit. Mainwheels size 7·00-8, pressure 6·20 bars (90·0 lb/sq in). Nosewheel and tyre size 5·00-5, pressure 4·83 bars (70·0 lb/sq in). Goodyear multiple-disc hydraulic brakes.

POWER PLANT: One 533 kW (715 shp) Pratt & Whitney Canada PT6A-25 turboprop engine, torque limited to 298 kW (400 shp), driving a Hartzell three-blade constant-speed fully-feathering metal propeller with spinner. Version of same engine derated to 410 kW (550 shp) is available optionally. Two bladder fuel cells in each wing, in inboard leading-edge and aft of main spar outboard of landing gear; total usable capacity 492 litres (130 US gallons). Oil capacity 15 litres (4 US gallons).

ACCOMMODATION: Instructor and pupil in tandem beneath rearward sliding cockpit canopy. Cockpit ventilated, heated by engine bleed air and air-conditioned. Dual controls standard. All armament controls in forward cockpit of T-34C-1.

SYSTEMS: Hydraulic system for brakes only. Pneumatic system for emergency opening of cockpit canopy. Diluter demand gaseous oxygen system, pressure 103·5 bars (1,500 lb/sq in). Electrical power supplied by 250A starter/generator. Freon air-conditioner for cockpit cooling.

AVIONICS AND EQUIPMENT: Standard avionics can include UHF or VHF com, VOR or Tacan nav, DME, transponder, angle of attack indicator, ADF, marker beacon receiver, compass and intercom system. R/Nav, Loran, HF and specialised tactical systems available to customer's requirements. US Navy T-34C has ARC-159V UHF com, VIR-30A VOR/Omni, dual 255Y-1 ICS/audio, TCN-40 Tacan and PN-101 remote compass, all by Collins; two TDR-950 transponders and a CIR-11-2 emergency locator transmitter. Blind-flying instrumentation standard. Electrically heated pitot.

ARMAMENT (T-34C-1): CA-513 fixed-reticle reflector gunsight. Four underwing hardpoints are provided for the carriage of stores. The inboard stations are rated at 272 kg (600 lb) each, the outboard stations at 136 kg (300 lb) each, with a maximum load of 272 kg (600 lb) each side and 544 kg (1,200 lb) total. Weapons which can be carried on MA-4 racks include AF/B37K-1 bomb containers with practice bombs or flares, LAU-32 or LAU-59 rocket pods, Mk 81 bombs, SUU-11 Minigun pods, BLU-10/B incendiary bombs, AGM-22A wire guided anti-tank missiles and TA8X towed target equipment.

DIMENSIONS, EXTERNAL:

Wing span	10·16 m (33 ft 3⅜ in)
Wing chord: at root	2·55 m (8 ft 4½ in)
at tip	1·05 m (3 ft 5¼ in)
Wing aspect ratio	6·22
Length overall	8·75 m (28 ft 8½ in)
Height overall	2·92 m (9 ft 7 in)
Tailplane span	3·71 m (12 ft 2⅛ in)
Wheel track	2·95 m (9 ft 8 in)
Wheelbase	2·41 m (7 ft 11 in)
Propeller diameter	2·29 m (7 ft 6 in)
Propeller ground clearance	0·29 m (11¼ in)

DIMENSIONS, INTERNAL:

Cabin: Length	2·74 m (9 ft 0 in)
Max width	0·86 m (2 ft 10 in)
Max height	1·22 m (4 ft 0 in)

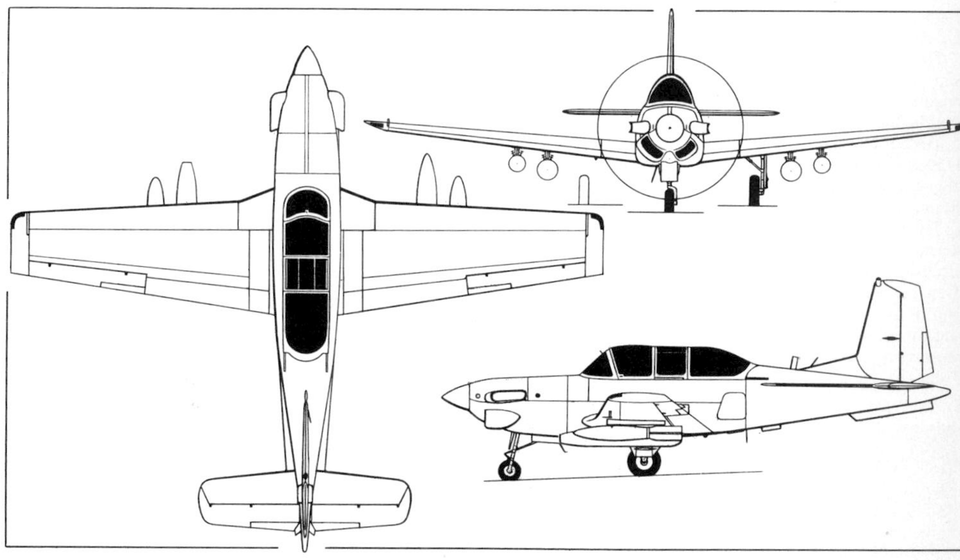

Beechcraft T-34C-1 turboprop powered training/light attack aircraft *(Pilot Press)*

AREAS:

Wings, gross	16·69 m² (179·6 sq ft)
Ailerons (total)	1·06 m² (11·4 sq ft)
Trailing-edge flaps (total)	1·98 m² (21·3 sq ft)
Fin	1·20 m² (12·9 sq ft)
Rudder, incl tab	0·64 m² (6·9 sq ft)
Tailplane	3·46 m² (37·2 sq ft)
Elevators, incl tabs	1·26 m² (13·6 sq ft)

WEIGHTS AND LOADING:

Weight empty: T-34C	1,342 kg (2,960 lb)
T-34C-1	1,356 kg (2,990 lb)
Max T-O and landing weight:	
T-34C	1,950 kg (4,300 lb)
T-34C-1, strike role	2,494 kg (5,500 lb)
Max ramp weight: T-34C	1,962 kg (4,325 lb)
Max wing loading: T-34C	108·3 kg/m² (22·2 lb/sq ft)

PERFORMANCE (T-34C, at T-O weight of 1,910 kg; 4,210 lb, except where indicated):

Never-exceed speed	280 knots (518 km/h; 322 mph)
Max cruising speed at 5,180 m (17,000 ft)	214 knots (396 km/h; 246 mph)
Stalling speed, flaps down, power off, at typical landing weight of 1,588 kg (3,501 lb)	53 knots (98 km/h; 61 mph)
Max rate of climb at S/L	451 m (1,480 ft)/min
Service ceiling	over 9,145 m (30,000 ft)
T-O run	352 m (1,155 ft)
T-O to 15 m (50 ft)	586 m (1,920 ft)
Landing from 15 m (50 ft)	547 m (1,795 ft)
Landing run	226 m (740 ft)
Range with max fuel:	
at 181 knots (335 km/h; 208 mph) at 305 m (1,000 ft)	427 nm (790 km; 491 miles)
at 202 knots (374 km/h; 232 mph) at 3,050 m (10,000 ft)	523 nm (968 km; 601 miles)
at 180 knots (333 km/h; 207 mph) at 6,100 m (20,000 ft)	708 nm (1,311 km; 814 miles)
g limits	+6/−3

PERFORMANCE (T-34C-1 with 410 kW; 550 shp engine, estimated. A with two stores at AUW of 2,222 kg; 4,900 lb. B with four stores at AUW of 2,494 kg; 5,500 lb, except where indicated):

Max level speed at 5,500 m (18,000 ft):	
A	209 knots (387 km/h; 241 mph)
B	206 knots (382 km/h; 237 mph)
Stalling speed, flaps down, idle power:	
A	65 knots (120 km/h; 75 mph) CAS
B	69 knots (128 km/h; 80 mph) CAS
Max rate of climb at S/L: A	540 m (1,771 ft)/min
B	436 m (1,431 ft)/min
Typical combat radius:	
FAC mission at AUW of 2,429 kg (5,355 lb), with four stores and optional max fuel, incl 2·6 h loiter over target and 20 min +5% reserves	100 nm (185 km; 115 miles)
Strike mission at AUW of 2,473 kg (5,452 lb), with four stores and optional max fuel, incl 20 min +5% reserves	300 nm (555 km; 345 miles)

BEECHCRAFT SUNDOWNER 180 and SIERRA 200

Production of the Sundowner 180 totalled 2,384, and of the Sierra 200, 1,146. A description of both models can be found in the 1984-85 *Jane's*.

BEECHCRAFT BONANZA MODEL V35B

Production of the V-tail Bonanza, first flown on 22 December 1945, ended in 1985 after 38 years of unbroken production. Total production of the V-tail models was 10,390.

BEECHCRAFT BONANZA MODEL F33A/C

The **F33A** version of the Bonanza is a four/five-seat single-engined executive aircraft, similar in general configuration to the Bonanza Model V35B, but distinguished by a conventional tail unit with sweptback vertical surfaces. The prototype flew for the first time on 14 September 1959, and the production models were known as Debonairs until 1967. The 1985 model introduced as standard equipment a large cargo door, measuring 0·96 m × 0·57 m (3 ft 2 in × 1 ft 10½ in), three-blade propeller, super soundproofing, and the avionics and equipment listed in the appropriate paragraphs, representing full IFR standard.

The aerobatic **F33C** is the subject of an order for 21 for the Mexican Air Force, to be delivered in 1986. In addition, a limited number of F33Cs, built to special order, were due to be delivered to civilian customers in the last quarter of 1986, after which no further production of the aerobatic variant was anticipated.

A total of 2,497 Model 33s had been built by 1 January 1986. They included 21 for pilot training by Lufthansa in West Germany; and 16 F33As for Pacific Southwest Airlines for airline crew training. Deliveries of F33As and aerobatic F33Cs to foreign air forces were as follows: Imperial Air Force of Iran, 16 F33Cs; Mexican Navy, 5 F33Cs; Netherlands Government Flying School, 16 F33Cs; and Spanish Air Ministry and Air Force, 74 F33s. In July 1986 Lufthansa ordered an additional three Model F33As for delivery in the Autumn of 1986.

Optional extras include the 'Magic Hand' automatic landing gear control system, air-conditioning system and a dual-duct fresh air system to increase cabin airflow. Safety features include single diagonal strap shoulder harness with inertia reel for all occupants as standard equipment. Three optional factory installed IFR avionics packages include dual communication, dual navigation, ADF, marker beacon receiver, glideslope, DME, and transponder. The packages meet FAA Technical Standard Order (TSO). Beech was in 1972 the first general aviation manufacturer to acquire approval for factory installation of area navigation equipment on production aircraft with IFR equipment. The large cargo door, air-conditioning and fifth seat are not available for the Bonanza F33C.

Recent options available on current F33As include Loran C, 3M/Ryan Stormscope, approach plate holder, new oxygen masks, and a communications frequency transfer switch on the control panel.

TYPE: Four/five-seat light cabin monoplane.

WINGS: Cantilever low-wing monoplane. Wing section Beech modified NACA 23016·5 at root, modified NACA 23012 at tip. Dihedral 6°. Incidence 4° at root, 1° at tip. Sweepback 0° at quarter-chord. Each wing is a two-spar semi-monocoque box-beam of conventional aluminium alloy construction. Symmetrical section ailerons and single-slotted three-position flaps of aluminium alloy construction. Ground adjustable trim tab in each aileron.

FUSELAGE: Conventional aluminium alloy semi-monocoque structure. Hat section longerons and channel type keels extend forward from cabin section, making the support structure for the engine and nosewheel an integral part of the fuselage.

TAIL UNIT: Conventional cantilever all-metal stressed-skin structure, primarily of aluminium alloy but with beaded magnesium skin on elevators. Large trim tab in each elevator. Fixed tab in rudder.

LANDING GEAR: Electrically retractable tricycle type, with steerable nosewheel. Mainwheels retract inward into wings, nosewheel rearward. Beech oleo-pneumatic shock absorbers in all units. Cleveland mainwheels, size 6·00-6, and tyres, size 7·00-6, pressure 2·28-2·76 bars (33-40 lb/sq in). Cleveland nosewheel and tyre, size 5·00-5, pressure

2·76 bars (40 lb/sq in). Cleveland ring-disc hydraulic brakes. Parking brake. 'Magic Hand' landing gear system optional.

POWER PLANT: One 212·5 kW (285 hp) Continental IO-520-BB flat-six engine, driving a McCauley three-blade constant-speed metal propeller with spinner. Manually adjustable engine cowl flaps. Two standard fuel tanks in wing leading-edges, with total usable capacity of 280 litres (74 US gallons). Refuelling points above tanks. Oil capacity 11·5 litres (3 US gallons).

ACCOMMODATION: Enclosed cabin with four individual seats in pairs as standard, plus optional forward facing fifth seat (F33A only). Baggage compartment and hat shelf aft of seats. Passenger door and baggage compartment door on starboard side. Heater standard. Large cargo door, on starboard side of fuselage, standard on F33A. F33C has removable seat cushions, to accommodate parachutes, and a quick-release passenger door.

SYSTEMS: Optional 12,000 BTU refrigeration type air-conditioning system comprises evaporator located beneath pilot's seat, condenser on lower fuselage and engine mounted compressor. Air outlets on centre console, with two-speed blower. Electrical system supplied by 28V 60A alternator, 24V 15·5Ah battery; a 100A alternator is available as an option, as is a standby generator. Hydraulic system for brakes only. Pneumatic system for instrument gyros and refrigeration type air-conditioning system optional. Oxygen system optional.

AVIONICS AND EQUIPMENT: Standard avionics include King KX 165-05 720-channel com transceiver, 200-channel nav/glideslope receiver/converter with KI 206 VOR/ILS indicator, King KY 165-04 720-channel com transceiver, 200-channel nav receiver/converter with KI 202 VOR/LOC indicator, KR 87 ADF with 227-00 indicator, KN 63 DME with KDI 572 indicator, DME hold and nav 1/nav 2 switching, KT 76A transponder, KMA 24-03 audio control/marker beacon receiver, microphone, headset, cabin speaker and static wicks. A wide range of optional avionics is available, by Collins and King. King and S-Tec autopilots, Sperry WeatherScout radar and 3M/Ryan Stormscope are optional. Standard equipment includes electric clock, exhaust gas temperature gauge, outside air temperature gauge, rate of climb indicator, sensitive altimeter, turn co-ordinator, 3 in horizon and directional gyros, four fore and aft adjustable and reclining seats, armrests, headrests, shoulder harness and lapbelts, pilot's storm window, sun visors, ultraviolet-proof windscreen and windows, emergency locator transmitter, stall warning device, alternate static source, heated pitot, rotating beacon, three light strobe system, carpeted floor, coat hooks, glove compartment, in-flight storage pockets, approach plate holder, utility shelf, cabin dome light, reading lights, instrument post lights, control wheel map light, electroluminescent sub-panel lighting, landing light, taxi light, full-flow oil filter, polyurethane exterior paint, external power socket and towbar. Optional equipment includes control wheel clock, dual controls, co-pilot's wheel brakes, fifth seat, large cargo door, super soundproofing, control wheel map lights, entrance door courtesy light, internally lit instruments and fresh air vent blower. Also available is a Beech designed 'Magic Hand' landing gear safety system. Designed to eliminate the possibility of wheels-up landing or inadvertent retraction of the landing gear on the ground, it lowers the gear automatically on approach when the engine manifold pressure falls below approximately 508 mm (20 in) and airspeed has been reduced to 104 knots (193 km/h; 120 mph). On take-off, it keeps the gear down until the aircraft is airborne and has accelerated to 78 knots (145 km/h; 90 mph) IAS. The system can be switched off by the pilot at will. F33C has accelerometer, second boost pump with indicator light, non-baffled fuel cells, heavy-gauge rudder cables and reinforced fuselage, wings and tail surfaces as standard.

DIMENSIONS, EXTERNAL:
- Wing span: 10·21 m (33 ft 6 in)
- Wing chord: at root: 2·13 m (7 ft 0 in)
  - at tip: 1·07 m (3 ft 6 in)
- Wing aspect ratio: 6·2
- Length overall: 8·13 m (26 ft 8 in)
- Height overall: 2·51 m (8 ft 3 in)
- Tailplane span: 3·71 m (12 ft 2 in)
- Wheel track: 2·92 m (9 ft 7 in)
- Wheelbase: 2·13 m (7 ft 0 in)
- Propeller diameter: two-blade: 2·13 m (7 ft 0 in)
  - three-blade: 2·03 m (6 ft 8 in)
- Passenger door: Height: 0·91 m (3 ft 0 in)
  - Width: 0·94 m (3 ft 1 in)
- Baggage compartment door:
  - Height: 0·57 m (1 ft 10½ in)
  - Width: 0·47 m (1 ft 6½ in)

DIMENSIONS, INTERNAL:
- Cabin, aft of firewall: Length: 3·07 m (10 ft 1 in)
  - Max width: 1·07 m (3 ft 6 in)
  - Max height: 1·27 m (4 ft 2 in)
  - Volume: 3·31 m³ (117 cu ft)
- Baggage space: 0·99 m³ (35 cu ft)

AREAS:
- Wings, gross: 16·80 m² (181 sq ft)
- Ailerons (total): 1·06 m² (11·4 sq ft)
- Trailing-edge flaps (total): 1·98 m² (21·3 sq ft)
- Fin: 0·93 m² (10·0 sq ft)
- Rudder, incl tab: 0·52 m² (5·6 sq ft)
- Tailplane: 1·75 m² (18·82 sq ft)
- Elevators, incl tabs: 1·67 m² (18·0 sq ft)

WEIGHTS AND LOADINGS:
- Weight empty: 981 kg (2,164 lb)
- Max T-O and landing weight: 1,542 kg (3,400 lb)
- Max T-O weight, F33C in Aerobatic category: 1,270 kg (2,800 lb)
- Max ramp weight: 1,548 kg (3,412 lb)
- Max wing loading: 91·8 kg/m² (18·8 lb/sq ft)
- Max power loading: 7·26 kg/kW (11·93 lb/hp)

PERFORMANCE (at max T-O weight, except cruising speeds at mid-cruise weight):
- Max level speed at S/L: 182 knots (338 km/h; 209 mph)
- Cruising speed:
  - 75% power at 1,830 m (6,000 ft): 172 knots (319 km/h; 198 mph)
  - 66% power at 3,050 m (10,000 ft): 168 knots (311 km/h; 193 mph)
  - 55% power at 3,660 m (12,000 ft): 157 knots (291 km/h; 181 mph)
  - 45% power at 2,440 m (8,000 ft): 136 knots (253 km/h; 157 mph)
- Stalling speed, power off:
  - flaps up: 64 knots (118 km/h; 74 mph) IAS
  - 30° flap: 51 knots (94 km/h; 59 mph) IAS
- Max rate of climb at S/L: 356 m (1,167 ft)/min
- Service ceiling: 5,443 m (17,858 ft)
- T-O run: 305 m (1,002 ft)
- T-O to 15 m (50 ft): 539 m (1,769 ft)
- Landing from 15 m (50 ft): 404 m (1,324 ft)
- Landing run: 233 m (763 ft)
- Range with 280 litres (74 US gallons) usable fuel, allowances for engine start, taxi, T-O, climb and 45 min reserves at 45% power:
  - 75% power at 1,830 m (6,000 ft): 716 nm (1,326 km; 824 miles)
  - 66% power at 3,050 m (10,000 ft): 777 nm (1,440 km; 894 miles)
  - 55% power at 3,660 m (12,000 ft): 838 nm (1,553 km; 964 miles)
  - 45% power at 2,440 m (8,000 ft): 889 nm (1,648 km; 1,023 miles)

Beechcraft Model F33A Bonanza four/five-seat cabin monoplane

BEECHCRAFT BONANZA MODEL A36

The current version of the A36, introduced on 3 October 1983, succeeded the earlier 212·5 kW (285 hp) Continental IO-520-BB powered model, and is a full six-seat utility aircraft developed from the Bonanza Model V35B but has a conventional tail unit with sweptback vertical surfaces, similar to that of the Bonanza F33 series. In addition, the A36 has large double doors on the starboard side of the fuselage aft of the wing root, to facilitate loading and unloading of bulky cargo when used in a utility role. The cabin volume is increased by 0·54 m³ (18·9 cu ft) compared with the F33, due to a fuselage extension of 0·25 m (10 in), and an increase of 0·28 m³ (10 cu ft) in the baggage compartment volume.

Like all Bonanzas, the Model A36 is licensed in the FAA Utility category at full gross weight, with no limitation of performance. The 1985-86 model has as standard a Continental IO-550-B engine, redesigned instrument panels with 40% more space for instruments and avionics, dual controls, throttle control power levers, exhaust gas temperature gauge, automatically-dimming landing gear and annunciator lights for night operation, a three-blade propeller and a standby vacuum system. Landing gear and flap controls have been repositioned to conform to GAMA recommendations. Optional extras include instrument post lights, internally-lit instruments, courtesy lights for entrance door and rear step, co-pilot's vertically adjusting seat, refrigeration type air-conditioning system and all other items mentioned under the Model F33A Bonanza entry, except for the large cargo door.

A total of 2,734 Model 36 Bonanzas had been delivered by 1 January 1986. In April 1985 Saudia (Saudi Arabian Airlines) took delivery of four Model A36 Bonanzas for the carrier's pilot training academy at Jeddah.

TYPE: Four/six-seat utility light cabin monoplane.

WINGS: As for Model F33A.

FUSELAGE: As for Model F33A but lengthened by 0·25 m (10 in).

TAIL UNIT: As for Model F33A.

LANDING GEAR: As for Model F33A, but without 'Magic Hand' system option.

POWER PLANT: One 224 kW (300 hp) Continental IO-550-B flat-six engine, driving a McCauley three-blade constant-speed propeller. The engine is equipped with an altitude-compensating fuel pump which automatically leans and enriches the fuel/air mixture during climb and descent respectively. Fuel capacity as for Model F33A.

ACCOMMODATION: Enclosed cabin seating four to six persons on individual seats. Pilot's seat is vertically adjustable. Dual controls standard. Two rear removable seats and two folding seats permit rapid conversion to utility configuration. Optional club seating with rear facing third and fourth seats, executive writing desk, refreshment cabinet, headrests for third and fourth seats, reading lights and fresh air outlets for fifth and sixth seats. Double doors of bonded aluminium honeycomb construction on starboard side facilitate loading of cargo. As an air ambulance, one stretcher can be accommodated with ample room for a medical attendant and/or other passengers. Extra windows provide improved view for passengers. Stowage for 181 kg (400 lb) of baggage.

SYSTEMS: Electrical system as for F33A. Hydraulic system for brakes only. Pneumatic system for instrument gyros, and refrigeration type air-conditioning system, optional.

AVIONICS AND EQUIPMENT: Standard avionics include King KX 155 720-channel nav/com, with KI 208 VOR/LOC Omni converter/indicator, but a wide range of optional avionics is available. An optional ground communication switch permits use of one com radio without turning on the battery master switch. Optional equipment is as detailed for the F33A Bonanza, except as noted.

DIMENSIONS, EXTERNAL AND AREAS: As for F33A except:
- Length overall: 8·38 m (27 ft 6 in)
- Height overall: 2·57 m (8 ft 5 in)
- Wheelbase: 2·39 m (7 ft 10¼ in)
- Rear passenger/cargo door:
  - Height: 1·02 m (3 ft 4 in)
  - Width: 1·14 m (3 ft 9 in)

DIMENSIONS, INTERNAL:
- Cabin, aft of firewall: Length, incl extended baggage compartment: 3·84 m (12 ft 7 in)
  - Max width: 1·07 m (3 ft 6 in)
  - Max height: 1·27 m (4 ft 2 in)
  - Volume: 3·85 m³ (135·9 cu ft)

WEIGHTS AND LOADINGS:
- Weight empty, standard: 1,019 kg (2,247 lb)
- Max T-O weight: 1,655 kg (3,650 lb)
- Max ramp weight: 1,661 kg (3,663 lb)
- Max wing loading: 98·6 kg/m² (20·2 lb/sq ft)
- Max power loading: 7·40 kg/kW (12·2 lb/hp)

PERFORMANCE (max speed at minimum weight; cruising speeds at mid-cruise weight):
- Max level speed: 184 knots (340 km/h; 212 mph)
- Max cruising speed:
  - 2,500 rpm at 1,830 m (6,000 ft): 176 knots (326 km/h; 202 mph)
  - 2,300 rpm at 2,440 m (8,000 ft): 167 knots (309 km/h; 192 mph)
  - 2,100 rpm at 1,830 m (6,000 ft): 160 knots (296 km/h; 184 mph)
  - 2,100 rpm at 3,050 m (10,000 ft): 153 knots (283 km/h; 176 mph)
- Stalling speed, power off:
  - flaps up: 68 knots (126 km/h; 78 mph) IAS
  - 30° flap: 59 knots (109 km/h; 68 mph) IAS

Max rate of climb at S/L 368 m (1,210 ft)/min
Service ceiling 3,638 m (18,500 ft)
T-O run: 0° flap 360 m (1,182 ft)
12° flap 296 m (971 ft)
T-O to 15 m (50 ft): 0° flap 666 m (2,185 ft)
12° flap 583 m (1,913 ft)
Landing from 15 m (50 ft) 449 m (1,473 ft)
Landing run 278 m (913 ft)
Range with 280 litres (74 US gallons) usable fuel, with allowances for engine start, taxi, T-O, climb and 45 min reserves at economy cruise power:
2,500 rpm at 3,660 m (12,000 ft) 876 nm (1,622 km; 1,009 miles)
2,300 rpm at 3,660 m (12,000 ft) 903 nm (1,672 km; 1,039 miles)
2,100 rpm at 1,830 m (6,000 ft) 914 nm (1,692 km; 1,052 miles)

BEECHCRAFT TURBO BONANZA MODEL B36TC

Beech introduced in 1979 a turbocharged version of the A36 Bonanza, following FAA certification on 7 December 1978, and 271 of the initial A36TC version were delivered. In 1982 Beech introduced the improved B36TC, with a wing of greater span and increased fuel capacity, and 444 of this model had been delivered by 1 January 1986. The B36TC is generally similar to the A36, except as follows:

WINGS: Wing section NACA 23010·5 at tip. Incidence 0° at tip.

POWER PLANT: One 223·7 kW (300 hp) Continental TSIO-520-UB turbocharged flat-six engine, driving a three-blade constant-speed metal propeller with spinner. Fixed engine cowl flaps. Two fuel tanks in each wing leading-edge, with total usable capacity of 386 litres (102 US gallons). Refuelling points above tanks. Oil capacity 11·5 litres (3 US gallons).

ACCOMMODATION AND SYSTEMS: Air-conditioning available as an option.

AVIONICS AND EQUIPMENT: As for Model A36, except that exhaust gas temperature gauge is not available. Turbine inlet temperature gauge is standard.

DIMENSIONS, EXTERNAL: As for Model A36, except:
Wing span 11·53 m (37 ft 10 in)
Wing chord at tip 0·91 m (3 ft 0 in)
Wing aspect ratio 7·6
Propeller diameter 1·98 m (6 ft 6 in)

DIMENSIONS, INTERNAL: As for Model A36

AREA:
Wings, gross 17·47 m² (188·1 sq ft)

WEIGHTS AND LOADINGS:
Weight empty, standard 1,057 kg (2,330 lb)
Max T-O and landing weight 1,746 kg (3,850 lb)
Max ramp weight 1,753 kg (3,866 lb)
Max wing loading 100·1 kg/m² (20·5 lb/sq ft)
Max power loading 7·81 kg/kW (12·8 lb/hp)

PERFORMANCE (at max T-O weight, except speeds are at mid-cruise weight):
Max level speed at 6,700 m (22,000 ft) 213 knots (394 km/h; 245 mph)
Cruising speed at 7,620 m (25,000 ft):
79% power 200 knots (370 km/h; 230 mph)
75% power 195 knots (361 km/h; 224 mph)
69% power 188 knots (348 km/h; 216 mph)
56% power 173 knots (320 km/h; 199 mph)
50% power 162 knots (300 km/h; 186 mph)
Stalling speed, power off:
flaps up 65 knots (120 km/h; 75 mph) IAS
30° flap 57 knots (106 km/h; 66 mph) IAS
Max rate of climb at S/L 319 m (1,049 ft)/min
Service ceiling over 7,620 m (25,000 ft)
T-O run, 15° flaps 314 m (1,030 ft)
T-O to 15 m (50 ft), 15° flaps 652 m (2,141 ft)
Landing run 298 m (976 ft)
Range with max fuel, allowances for engine start, taxi, T-O, cruise climb, descent, and 45 min reserves at 50% power:
79% power at 7,620 m (25,000 ft) 956 nm (1,770 km; 1,100 miles)
75% power at 7,620 m (25,000 ft) 984 nm (1,822 km; 1,132 miles)
69% power at 7,620 m (25,000 ft) 1,022 nm (1,892 km; 1,176 miles)
56% power at 6,100 m (20,000 ft) 1,092 nm (2,022 km; 1,256 miles)
50% power at 6,100 m (20,000 ft) 1,130 nm (2,092 km; 1,300 miles)

BEECHCRAFT DUCHESS 76

Production of the Duchess 76 four-seat twin-engined light aircraft has ceased. A total of 429 was built. A description of the aircraft appeared in the 1984-85 edition.

BEECHCRAFT BARON MODEL E55

The Baron Model E55 is no longer manufactured. Beech delivered a total of 1,201 of this Baron series. A description of the aircraft may be found in the 1984-85 *Jane's*.

BEECHCRAFT BARON MODEL 58

In late 1969 Beech introduced a new version of the Baron, designated Model 58. Developed from the Baron D55, it differed by having the forward cabin section extended by 0·254 m (10 in), allowing the windscreen, passenger door, instrument panel and front seats to be moved forward and so provide a more spacious cabin. This change was made without affecting the wing main spar location, but the wheelbase was extended by moving the nosewheel forward, to improve ground handling. New features included double passenger/cargo doors on the starboard side of the cabin, extended propeller hubs, redesigned engine nacelles to improve cooling, and a fourth window on each side of the cabin. The Model 58 Baron was licensed by the FAA in the Normal category on 19 November 1969.

Beechcraft turbocharged Model B36TC Turbo Bonanza (Continental TSIO-520-UB flat-six engine)

Beech had delivered 2,095 of this Baron series (including Baron 58Ps and 58TCs) by 1 January 1986.

TYPE: Four/six-seat cabin monoplane.

WINGS: Cantilever low-wing monoplane. Wing section NACA 23016-5 at root, NACA 23010-t at tip. Dihedral 6°. Incidence 4° at root, 0° at tip. No sweepback. Each wing is a two-spar semi-monocoque box beam of conventional aluminium alloy construction, with beaded skins. Electrically operated single-slotted light alloy trailing-edge flaps, with beaded skins. Manually operated trim tab in port aileron. Pneumatic rubber de-icing boots optional.

FUSELAGE: Semi-monocoque aluminium alloy structure. Hat section longerons and channel type keels extend forward from the cabin section, making the support structure for the forward nose section and nosewheel gear an integral part of the fuselage.

TAIL UNIT: Cantilever all-metal structure. Elevators have smooth magnesium alloy skins. Manually operated trim tab in each elevator and in rudder. Pneumatic rubber de-icing boots optional.

LANDING GEAR: Electrically retractable tricycle type. Main units retract inward into wings, nosewheel aft. Beech oleo-pneumatic shock absorbers in all units. Steerable nosewheel with shimmy damper. Cleveland wheels, with mainwheel tyres size 6·50-8, pressure 3·59-3·96 bars (52-56 lb/sq in). Nosewheel tyre size 5·00-5, pressure 3·79-4·14 bars (55-60 lb/sq in). Cleveland ring-disc hydraulic brakes. Heavy duty brakes optional. Parking brake.

POWER PLANT: Two 224 kW (300 hp) Continental IO-550-C flat-six engines, each driving a McCauley three-blade constant-speed fully feathering metal propeller with spinner. The standard fuel system has a usable capacity of 514 litres (136 US gallons), with optional usable capacity of 628 litres (166 US gallons). Optional 'wet wingtip' installation also available, increasing usable capacity to 734 litres (194 US gallons).

ACCOMMODATION: Standard model has four individual seats in pairs in enclosed cabin, with door on starboard side. Single diagonal strap shoulder harness with inertia reel standard on all seats. Vertically adjusting pilot's seat is standard. Vertically adjusting co-pilot's seat, folding fifth and sixth seats, or club seating comprising folding fifth and sixth seats and aft facing third and fourth seats, are optional. Executive writing desk available as option with club seating. Baggage compartment in nose, capacity 136 kg (300 lb). Double passenger/cargo doors on starboard side of cabin provide access to space for 181 kg (400 lb) of baggage or cargo behind the third and fourth seats. Pilot's storm window. Openable windows adjacent to the third and fourth seats are used for ground ventilation and as emergency exits. Cabin heated and ventilated. Windscreen defrosting standard.

SYSTEMS: Cabin heated by Janitrol 50,000 BTU heater, which serves also for windscreen defrosting. Oxygen system of 1·41 m³ (49·8 cu ft) or 1·87 m³ (66 cu ft) capacity optional. Electrical system includes two 28V 60A engine driven alternators with alternator failure lights and two 12V 25Ah batteries. Two 100A alternators optional. Hydraulic system for brakes only. Pneumatic pressure system for air driven instruments, and optional wing and tail unit de-icing system. Oxygen system optional. Cabin air-conditioning and windscreen electric anti-icing systems optional.

AVIONICS AND EQUIPMENT: Standard avionics include King KX 155-09 720-channel com transceiver with audio amplifier, 200-channel nav receiver with KI 208 VOR/LOC converter/indicator, KR 87 ADF with KI 227-00 indicator, King combined loop/sense antenna, microphone, headset, cabin speaker, nav and com antennae. Bendix, King and Sperry weather radars optional. Optional avionics by Collins, King and S-Tec. Standard equipment includes dual controls, blind-flying instruments, control wheel clock, outside air temperature

Beechcraft Baron Model 58 four/six-seat cabin monoplane

gauge, sensitive altimeter, turn co-ordinator, pilot storm window, sun visors, ultra violet-proof windscreen and cabin windows, armrests, adjustable rudder pedals (retractable on starboard side), emergency locator transmitter, heated pitot head, instrument panel floodlights, map light, lighted trim tab position indicator, step and entrance door courtesy lights, reading lights, navigation and position lights, steerable taxi light, dual landing lights, cabin carpeting and soundproofing, headrests, heated fuel vents, cabin dome light, door ajar warning light, nose baggage compartment light, heated fuel and stall warning vanes, external polyurethane paint finish, EGT and CHT gauges, synchroscope, engine winterisation kit, towbar and external power socket. Options include a true airspeed indicator, engine and flight hour recorders, instantaneous vertical speed indicator, alternate static source, internally illuminated instruments, rotating beacon, strobe lights, electric windscreen anti-icing, wing ice detection light, static wicks, cabin club seating, executive writing desk, refreshment cabinet, cabin fire extinguisher, ventilation blower, super soundproofing, and approach plate holder.

DIMENSIONS, EXTERNAL:
- Wing span — 11·53 m (37 ft 10 in)
- Wing chord: at root — 2·13 m (7 ft 0 in)
- at tip — 0·90 m (2 ft 11·6 in)
- Wing aspect ratio — 7·16
- Length overall — 9·09 m (29 ft 10 in)
- Height overall — 2·90 m (9 ft 6 in)
- Tailplane span — 4·85 m (15 ft 11 in)
- Wheel track — 2·92 m (9 ft 7 in)
- Wheelbase — 2·72 m (8 ft 11 in)
- Propeller diameter — 1·93 m (6 ft 4 in)
- Rear passenger/cargo doors:
  - Max height — 1·02 m (3 ft 4 in)
  - Width — 1·14 m (3 ft 9 in)
- Baggage door (fwd): Height — 0·56 m (1 ft 10 in)
  - Width — 0·64 m (2 ft 1 in)

DIMENSIONS, INTERNAL:
- Cabin, incl rear baggage area:
  - Length — 3·84 m (12 ft 7 in)
  - Max width — 1·07 m (3 ft 6 in)
  - Max height — 1·27 m (4 ft 2 in)
  - Floor area — 3·72 m² (40 sq ft)
  - Volume — 3·85 m³ (135·9 cu ft)
- Baggage compartment: fwd — 0·51 m³ (18 cu ft)

AREAS:
- Wings, gross — 17·47 m² (188·1 sq ft)
- Ailerons (total) — 1·06 m² (11·40 sq ft)
- Trailing-edge flaps (total) — 1·98 m² (21·30 sq ft)
- Fin — 1·46 m² (15·67 sq ft)
- Rudder, incl tab — 0·81 m² (8·75 sq ft)
- Tailplane — 4·95 m² (53·30 sq ft)
- Elevators, incl tabs — 1·84 m² (19·80 sq ft)

WEIGHTS AND LOADINGS:
- Weight empty — 1,579 kg (3,481 lb)
- Max T-O weight — 2,495 kg (5,500 lb)
- Max landing weight — 2,449 kg (5,400 lb)
- Max ramp weight — 2,506 kg (5,526 lb)
- Max wing loading — 143·4 kg/m² (27·6 lb/sq ft)
- Max power loading — 5·60 kg/kW (9·2 lb/hp)

PERFORMANCE (at max T-O weight, except cruising speeds at average cruise weight):
- Max level speed at S/L — 208 knots (386 km/h; 239 mph)
- Max cruising speed, 2,500 rpm at 1,525 m (5,000 ft) — 203 knots (376 km/h; 234 mph)
- Cruising speed, 2,500 rpm at 3,050 m (10,000 ft) — 198 knots (367 km/h; 228 mph)
- Econ cruising speed, 2,100 rpm at 3,660 m (12,000 ft) — 163 knots (302 km/h; 188 mph)
- Stalling speed, power off:
  - flaps up — 84 knots (156 km/h; 97 mph) IAS
  - flaps down — 74 knots (137 km/h; 85 mph) IAS
- Max rate of climb at S/L — 533 m (1,750 ft)/min
- Rate of climb at S/L, one engine out — 120 m (394 ft)/min
- Service ceiling — 6,306 m (20,688 ft)
- Service ceiling, one engine out — 2,220 m (7,284 ft)
- T-O run — 428 m (1,403 ft)
- T-O to 15 m (50 ft) — 723 m (2,371 ft)
- Landing from 15 m (50 ft) — 761 m (2,498 ft)
- Landing run — 439 m (1,439 ft)
- Range with 734 litres (194 US gallons) usable fuel, with allowances for engine start, taxi, T-O, climb and 45 min reserves at econ cruise power:
  - max cruising speed (power/altitude settings as above) — 1,150 nm (2,130 km; 1,324 miles)
  - cruising speed (power/altitude settings as above) — 1,411 nm (2,615 km; 1,625 miles)
  - econ cruising speed (power/altitude settings as above) — 1,575 nm (2,919 km; 1,814 miles)

BEECHCRAFT BARON MODEL 58P

Design of this pressurised version of the Model 58 Baron started in June 1972; the first flight of the prototype was made in August 1973. Certification under FAR Part 23 was received in May 1974; the first production aircraft flew later the same year. Examples of the Model 58P produced prior to 1979 are powered by two 231 kW (310 hp) Continental TSIO-520-L (or -LB) engines. Current production aircraft have more powerful TSIO-520-WB engines, and introduced propeller synchrophasers as standard equipment in 1981.

Beechcraft Baron Model 58P pressurised twin-engined business aircraft

Deliveries of production aircraft began in late 1975, and a total of 480 Baron 58Ps had been delivered by 1 January 1986. This total includes 18 Baron 58Ps delivered to the US Forest Service for use as lead aircraft in smoke jumping operations, reconnaissance, administration and cargo missions.

TYPE: Four/six-seat cabin monoplane.

WINGS: As for Model 58.

FUSELAGE: As for Model 58, except structural reinforcement to cater for pressurisation.

TAIL UNIT: As for Model 58.

LANDING GEAR: Electrically retractable tricycle type. Main units retract inward, nosewheel rearward; all three units have fairing doors. Beechcraft oleo-pneumatic shock absorbers. Goodrich mainwheels and tyres size 19·50 × 6·75-8 10-ply rating, pressure 5·24 to 5·66 bars (76 to 82 lb/sq in). Steerable nosewheel with shimmy damper, with tyre size 5·0-5, pressure 3·79-4·14 bars (55-60 lb/sq in). Goodrich single-disc hydraulic brakes. Parking brake.

POWER PLANT: Two 242 kW (325 hp) Continental TSIO-520-WB turbocharged flat-six engines, each driving a McCauley three-blade constant-speed fully-feathering metal propeller with spinner. Propeller synchrophasers standard, unfeathering accumulators optional. Electrically operated engine cowl flaps. Integral fuel tanks in wings, with standard capacity of 651 litres (172 US gallons) of which 628 litres (166 US gallons) are usable. Optional maximum capacity of 742 litres (196 US gallons) of which 719 litres (190 US gallons) are usable. Refuelling points in outboard leading-edge of wings and, for optional maximum fuel, in wingtips. Oil capacity 22·7 litres (6 US gallons). Electric anti-icing for propellers optional.

ACCOMMODATION: Standard accommodation has four individual seats in pairs, facing forward, with shoulder harness and inertia reel. Fifth and sixth seats optional, as is club layout. Doors on starboard side, adjacent to co-pilot, and at trailing-edge of wing on port side. Baggage space in aft cabin and in fuselage nose, with door on starboard side of nose. Openable storm window for pilot on port side. Cabin heated and pressurised. Air-conditioning optional. Windscreen defrosting by hot air. Windscreen electric anti-icing optional.

SYSTEMS: Garrett pressurisation system with max differential of 0·27 bars (3·9 lb/sq in), giving a 3,050 m (10,000 ft) cabin environment to a height of 6,705 m (22,000 ft). Beechcraft 14,000 BTU air-conditioning optional. Janitrol 35,000 BTU heater. Engine driven compressors supply air for flight instruments, pressurisation control and optional pneumatic de-icing boots. Electrical system powered by two 28V 60A alternators, with two 12V 25Ah storage batteries. Two 24V 100A alternators optional. Hydraulic system for brakes only. Oxygen system of 0·42 m³ (15 cu ft) optional.

AVIONICS AND EQUIPMENT: Standard avionics package comprises King KX 155 nav/com (720-channel com transceiver and 200-channel nav receiver) with KI 208 VOR/LOC converter-indicator, KR 87 ADF with KI 227 indicator, microphone, headset and cabin speaker. Optional avionics by Bendix, Collins, King and Sperry. Standard equipment as for Model 58, plus dual rotating beacons, and exterior urethane paint. Optional equipment includes engine and flight hour recorders, true airspeed indicator, electrically operated elevator trim, cabin fire extinguisher, executive writing desk, internally illuminated instruments, strobe lights, wing ice lights, and static wicks.

DIMENSIONS, EXTERNAL:
- Wing span — 11·53 m (37 ft 10 in)
- Wing chord: at root — 2·13 m (7 ft 0 in)
- at tip — 0·90 m (2 ft 11½ in)
- Length overall — 9·12 m (29 ft 11 in)
- Height overall — 2·79 m (9 ft 2 in)
- Tailplane span — 4·85 m (15 ft 11 in)
- Wheel track — 2·92 m (9 ft 7 in)
- Wheelbase — 2·72 m (8 ft 11 in)
- Propeller diameter — 1·98 m (6 ft 6 in)
- Propeller ground clearance — 0·28 m (10¾ in)
- Passenger door (stbd, fwd):
  - Height — 0·91 m (3 ft 0 in)
  - Width — 0·94 m (3 ft 1 in)
  - Height to sill — 0·51 m (1 ft 8 in)
- Passenger door (port, rear):
  - Height — 0·89 m (2 ft 11 in)
  - Width — 0·58 m (1 ft 11 in)
  - Height to sill — 0·79 m (2 ft 7 in)
- Baggage door (nose, stbd):
  - Height — 0·38 m (1 ft 3 in)
  - Width — 0·64 m (2 ft 1 in)

DIMENSIONS, INTERNAL: As for Model 58

AREAS: As for Model 58

WEIGHTS AND LOADINGS:
- Weight empty, equipped — 1,826 kg (4,026 lb)
- Max T-O and landing weight — 2,812 kg (6,200 lb)
- Max ramp weight — 2,830 kg (6,240 lb)
- Max zero-fuel weight — 2,585 kg (5,700 lb)
- Max wing loading — 161·1 kg/m² (33 lb/sq ft)
- Max power loading — 5·81 kg/kW (9·54 lb/hp)

PERFORMANCE (at max T-O weight, except cruising speeds at average cruise weight):
- Max level speed — 261 knots (483 km/h; 300 mph)
- Max cruising speed at approx 77% power:
  - at 4,575 m (15,000 ft) — 222 knots (412 km/h; 256 mph)
  - at 6,100 m (20,000 ft) — 232 knots (430 km/h; 267 mph)
  - at 7,620 m (25,000 ft) — 241 knots (447 km/h; 277 mph)
- Cruising speed at approx 75% power:
  - at 4,575 m (15,000 ft) — 220 knots (407 km/h; 253 mph)
  - at 6,100 m (20,000 ft) — 229 knots (425 km/h; 264 mph)
  - at 7,620 m (25,000 ft) — 237 knots (439 km/h; 273 mph)
- Cruising speed at approx 62% power:
  - at 4,575 m (15,000 ft) — 201 knots (372 km/h; 231 mph)
  - at 6,100 m (20,000 ft) — 210 knots (389 km/h; 242 mph)
  - at 7,620 m (25,000 ft) — 218 knots (404 km/h; 251 mph)
- Econ cruising speed at approx 53% power:
  - at 4,575 m (15,000 ft) — 185 knots (343 km/h; 213 mph)
  - at 6,100 m (20,000 ft) — 194 knots (359 km/h; 223 mph)
  - at 7,620 m (25,000 ft) — 202 knots (375 km/h; 233 mph)
- Stalling speed, power off:
  - flaps up — 84 knots (156 km/h; 97 mph)
  - flaps down — 78 knots (145 km/h; 90 mph)
- Max rate of climb at S/L — 450 m (1,475 ft)/min
- Rate of climb at S/L, one engine out — 68 m (223 ft)/min
- Service ceiling — above 7,620 m (25,000 ft)
- Service ceiling, one engine out — 3,725 m (12,220 ft)
- T-O run — 474 m (1,555 ft)
- T-O to 15 m (50 ft) — 806 m (2,643 ft)
- Landing from 15 m (50 ft) — 740 m (2,427 ft)
- Landing run — 420 m (1,378 ft)
- Range with 719 litres (190 US gallons) usable fuel, and allowances for engine start, taxi, T-O, climb and 45 min reserves at econ cruising speed:
  - at approx 77% power
    - at 4,575 m (15,000 ft) — 917 nm (1,699 km; 1,056 miles)
    - at 6,100 m (20,000 ft) — 960 nm (1,779 km; 1,105 miles)

at 7,620 m (25,000 ft)
1,013 nm (1,877 km; 1,166 miles)
at approx 75% power:
at 4,575 m (15,000 ft)
930 nm (1,723 km; 1,071 miles)
at 6,100 m (20,000 ft)
975 nm (1,807 km; 1,122 miles)
at 7,620 m (25,000 ft)
1,030 nm (1,908 km; 1,186 miles)
at approx 65% power:
at 4,575 m (15,000 ft)
1,098 nm (2,035 km; 1,264 miles)
at 6,100 m (20,000 ft)
1,122 nm (2,079 km; 1,292 miles)
at 7,620 m (25,000 ft)
1,160 nm (2,150 km; 1,335 miles)
at approx 53% power:
at 4,575 m (15,000 ft)
1,289 nm (2,182 km; 1,356 miles)
at 6,100 m (20,000 ft)
1,220 nm (2,261 km; 1,405 miles)
at 7,620 m (25,000 ft)
1,235 nm (2,288 km; 1,422 miles)

BEECHCRAFT BARON MODEL 58TC

This turbocharged version of the Baron Model 58, is no longer in production. A total of 149 Model 58TCs was produced. A description of the aircraft may be found in the 1984-85 edition.

BEECHCRAFT KING AIR MODEL C90A

The King Air C90A is a pressurised 6/10-seat twin-turboprop business aircraft which superseded the Models 90, A90, B90, C90 and C90-1 King Air. Performance is improved by new 'pitot' cowlings which improve engine efficiency and reduce drag. The air inlet area of the pitot cowlings is 387 cm² (60 sq in), compared with 748 cm² (116 sq in) on the King Air C90-1. The reduced air intake area and sealed ducting increase the ram air flow to the engines by 30 per cent. A flow-through exhaust-heated intake lip provides continuous anti-ice protection. Other improvements include aerodynamically faired exhaust stacks, dual-vane dual-motor inertial ice separators, hydraulically actuated landing gear retraction and extension, a three-bus electrical power distribution system with automatic load shedding capability and a rudder boost system for engine-out flight conditions.

The King Air C90A utilises the cabin pressurisation and heating system of the King Air F90-1. In the C90A, this provides a sea level cabin environment to an altitude of 3,370 m (11,065 ft) and a 3,050 m (10,000 ft) cabin altitude to a height of 8,075 m (26,500 ft).

A total of 1,116 commercial and 226 military King Air 90/A90/B90/C90/C90-1/C90As had been delivered by 1 January 1986.

TYPE: Six/ten-seat twin-turboprop business aircraft.

WINGS: Cantilever low-wing monoplane. Wing section NACA 23014·1 (modified) at root, NACA 23016·22 (modified) at outer end of centre-section, NACA 23012 at tip. Dihedral 7°. Incidence 4° 48′ at root, 0° at tip. No sweepback at quarter-chord. Two-spar aluminium alloy structure. All-metal ailerons of magnesium, with adjustable trim tab on port aileron. Single-slotted aluminium alloy flaps. Automatic pneumatic de-icing boots on leading-edges are standard.

FUSELAGE: Aluminium alloy semi-monocoque structure.

TAIL UNIT: Cantilever all-metal structure with sweptback vertical surfaces. Fixed incidence tailplane, with 7° dihedral. Trim tabs in rudder and each elevator. Automatic pneumatic de-icing boots on leading-edges of fin and tailplane are standard.

LANDING GEAR: Hydraulically retractable tricycle type. Nosewheel retracts rearward, mainwheels forward into engine nacelles. Mainwheels protrude slightly beneath nacelles when retracted, for safety in a wheels-up emergency landing. Fully castoring steerable nosewheel with shimmy damper. Beech oleo-pneumatic shock absorbers. Goodrich mainwheels with tyres size 8·50-10, pressure 3·79 bars (55 lb/sq in). Goodrich nosewheel with tyre size 6·50-10, pressure 3·59 bars (52 lb/sq in). Goodrich heat-sink and aircooled multi-disc hydraulic brakes. Parking brakes.

POWER PLANT: Two 410 kW (550 shp) Pratt & Whitney Canada PT6A-21 turboprop engines, each driving a Hartzell three-blade constant-speed fully-feathering propeller with spinner. Propeller electrothermal anti-icing, auto ignition system, environmental fuel drain collection system, and magnetic chip detector, standard. Automatic propeller feathering, and propeller synchrophaser, optional. Fuel in two tanks in engine nacelles, each with usable capacity of 231 litres (61 US gallons), and auxiliary bladder tanks in outer wings, each with capacity of 496 litres (131 US gallons). Total usable fuel capacity 1,454 litres (384 US gallons). Refuelling points in top of each engine nacelle and in wing leading-edge outboard of each nacelle. Oil capacity 13·2 litres (3·5 US gallons) per engine. Engine anti-icing system standard. Engine fire detection and extinguishing system optional.

ACCOMMODATION: Two seats side by side in cockpit with dual controls standard. Normally, four reclining seats in main cabin, in pairs facing each other fore and aft. Standard furnishings include cabin forward partition, with fore and aft partition curtain and coat rack, hinged nose baggage compartment door, seat belts and inertia reel shoulder harness for all seats. Optional arrangements seat up to eight persons, some with two- or three-place couch, lateral tracking chairs, and refreshment cabinets. Baggage racks at rear of cabin on starboard side, with optional toilet on port side. Door on port side aft of wing, with built-in airstairs. Emergency exit on starboard side of cabin. Entire accommodation pressurised and air-conditioned. Electrically heated windscreen, windscreen defroster and windscreen wipers standard.

SYSTEMS: Pressurisation by dual engine bleed air system with pressure differential of 0·34 bars (5·0 lb/sq in). Cabin heated by 45,000 BTU dual engine bleed air system and auxiliary electrical heating system. Hydraulic system for landing gear actuation. Electrical system includes two 28V 250A starter/generators, 24V 45Ah aircooled nickel-cadmium battery with failure detector. Complete de-icing and anti-icing equipment. Oxygen system, 0·62 m³ (22 cu ft), 1·39 m³ (49 cu ft) or 1·81 m³ (64 cu ft) capacity, optional. Vacuum system for flight instruments.

AVIONICS AND EQUIPMENT: Standard avionics package comprises dual Collins VHF-251 VHF transceivers; dual Collins VIR-351 Omni nav receivers; Collins AMR-350 audio system; Collins ADF-650A ADF; Collins marker beacon receiver integral with AMR-350, plus marker lights; dual Collins GLS-350 glideslope receivers; Collins DME-451, with Nav 1/Nav 2 switching and DME hold; Collins PN-101 compass system (pilot); Standard Electric gyro horizon (pilot); CF gyro horizon and directional gyro (co-pilot); dual Flite-Tronics PC-125 125VA inverters with failure light; avionics transient protection; dual flight instrumentation; sectional instrument panel; white lighting; radio accessories, static wicks and Beech metal radio panel; microphone key button in pilot and co-pilot control wheels; dual microphones, headsets and cockpit speakers; and avionics master switch. Optional avionics include a wide range of equipment by Bendix, Collins, King, Edo-Aire Mitchell, RCA and Sperry. Standard equipment includes dual blind-flying instrumentation with sensitive altimeters, standby magnetic compass, outside air temperature gauge, LCD digital clock/chronometer, vacuum gauge, de-icing pressure gauge, cabin rate of climb indicator, cabin altitude and pressure differential indicators, dual load meters, voltage meter with bus selector switch, propeller de-ice meter, pilot and co-pilot four-way adjustable seats with shoulder harness, map pockets, control locks, storm windows, tracked sun visors, automatic fuel heater system, emergency locator transmitter, heated pitots, heated stall warning transmitter, stall warning device, cabin windows with adjustable polarised shades, carpeted floor, internal corrosion proofing, 'No smoking—Fasten seat belt' sign, fresh air outlets, dual map lights, primary and secondary instrument light systems, indirect cabin lighting, two overhead cabin spotlights, entrance door light, adjustable reading lights, aft compartment lights, dual landing lights, taxi light, position lights, dual rotating beacons, wing ice lights, heated fuel vents, external power socket, static wicks, and external urethane paint. Optional equipment includes flight hour recorder, instantaneous vertical speed indicator, cockpit and cabin fire extinguishers, a range of cabin seats, cabinets, storage drawers and toilets, entrance door step lights, tail floodlights, strobe lights, and wingtip recognition lights.

DIMENSIONS, EXTERNAL:

Wing span	15·32 m (50 ft 3 in)
Wing chord: at root	2·15 m (7 ft 0½ in)
at tip	1·07 m (3 ft 6 in)
Wing aspect ratio	8·57
Length overall	10·82 m (35 ft 6 in)
Height overall	4·34 m (14 ft 3 in)
Tailplane span	5·26 m (17 ft 3 in)
Wheel track	3·89 m (12 ft 9 in)
Wheelbase	3·73 m (12 ft 3 in)
Propeller diameter	2·36 m (7 ft 9 in)
Propeller ground clearance	0·305 m (1 ft 0 in)
Passenger door: Height	1·30 m (4 ft 3½ in)
Width	0·69 m (2 ft 3 in)
Height to sill	1·17 m (3 ft 10 in)

DIMENSIONS, INTERNAL:

Total pressurised length	5·43 m (17 ft 10 in)
Cabin: Length	3·94 m (12 ft 11 in)
Max width	1·37 m (4 ft 6 in)
Max height	1·45 m (4 ft 9 in)
Floor area	6·50 m² (70 sq ft)
Volume	8·88 m³ (313·6 cu ft)
Baggage compartment, rear	1·51 m³ (53·5 cu ft)

AREAS:

Wings, gross	27·31 m² (293·94 sq ft)
Ailerons (total)	1·29 m² (13·90 sq ft)
Trailing-edge flaps (total)	2·72 m² (29·30 sq ft)
Fin	2·20 m² (23·67 sq ft)
Rudder, incl tab	1·30 m² (14·00 sq ft)
Tailplane	4·39 m² (47·25 sq ft)
Elevators, incl tabs	1·66 m² (17·87 sq ft)

WEIGHTS AND LOADINGS:

Weight empty	2,742 kg (6,045 lb)
Max T-O weight	4,377 kg (9,650 lb)
Max ramp weight	4,404 kg (9,710 lb)
Max landing weight	4,159 kg (9,168 lb)
Max wing loading	160·1 kg/m² (32·8 lb/sq ft)
Max power loading	5·34 kg/kW (8·8 lb/shp)

PERFORMANCE (at max T-O weight except where indicated):
Max cruising speed at AUW of 3,855 kg (8,500 lb):
at 3,660 m (12,000 ft)
242 knots (448 km/h; 278 mph)
at 4,880 m (16,000 ft)
247 knots (457 km/h; 284 mph)
at 6,400 m (21,000 ft)
243 knots (450 km/h; 280 mph)
Stalling speed, power off:
wheels and flaps up
89 knots (164 km/h; 102 mph) IAS
wheels and flaps down
76 knots (140 km/h; 87 mph) IAS
Max rate of climb at S/L 656 m (2,155 ft)/min
Rate of climb at S/L, one engine out
164 m (539 ft)/min
Service ceiling above 9,600 m (31,500 ft)
Service ceiling, one engine out 4,490 m (14,725 ft)
Min ground turning radius 10·82 m (35 ft 6 in)
Runway LCN 4
T-O run 497 m (1,629 ft)
T-O to 15 m (50 ft) 689 m (2,261 ft)
Accelerate/stop distance 1,066 m (3,498 ft)
Landing from 15 m (50 ft) at max landing weight:
without propeller reversal 613 m (2,010 ft)
with propeller reversal 510 m (1,672 ft)
Landing run at max landing weight:
without propeller reversal 328 m (1,075 ft)
with propeller reversal 225 m (737 ft)
Range with max fuel at max cruising speed, incl allowance for starting, taxi, take-off, climb, descent and 45 min reserves at max range power, ISA, at:
6,400 m (21,000 ft)
1,080 nm (2,001 km; 1,243 miles)
4,875 m (16,000 ft)
935 nm (1,733 km; 1,076 miles)
3,660 m (12,000 ft)
870 nm (1,612 km; 1,002 miles)

Beechcraft King Air C90A business aircraft with new 'pitot' cowlings

Max range at econ cruising power, allowances as above, at:
- 6,400 m (21,000 ft) — 1,317 nm (2,440 km; 1,516 miles)
- 4,875 m (16,000 ft) — 1,180 nm (2,187 km; 1,359 miles)
- 3,660 m (12,000 ft) — 1,070 nm (1,983 km; 1,232 miles)

BEECHCRAFT KING AIR MODEL F90-1

Deliveries of the original King Air F90 began in mid-1979. Basically, it combined the pressurised fuselage of the King Air 90 with reduced span wings similar to those of the King Air 100, and a T tail assembly similar to that of the Super King Air 200. Slow-turning four-blade propellers were fitted, to reduce airport and in-flight noise. Cabin pressurisation was increased to 0·34 bars (5·0 lb/sq in) to give a sea level environment at 3,375 m (11,065 ft), a 2,440 m (8,000 ft) environment at 7,050 m (23,120 ft), and a 3,050 m (10,000 ft) environment at an altitude of 8,075 m (26,500 ft).

The current King Air Model F90-1, announced by Beech on 13 June 1983, has improved performance, resulting from the use of PT6A-135A engines in low-drag 'pitot' cowlings as described for the Model C90A.

A total of 225 commercial King Air F90s and F90-1s had been delivered by 1 January 1986.

TYPE: Seven/ten-seat twin-turboprop business aircraft.

WINGS: Similar to King Air 100 (1983-84 *Jane's*). De-icing system standard.

FUSELAGE: Similar to King Air 90.

TAIL UNIT: Similar to Super King Air 200. Tailplane de-icing standard.

LANDING GEAR: Retractable tricycle type, with twin-wheel main units and single steerable nosewheel with shimmy damper. Electrical retraction, nosewheel rearward, main units forward into engine nacelles. Beech oleo-pneumatic shock absorbers. Mainwheel tyres size 18 × 5·5, pressure 7·10-7·37 bars (103-107 lb/sq in). Nosewheel tyre size 22 × 6·75-10, pressure 4·13-4·41 bars (60-64 lb/sq in). Single-disc hydraulic brakes. Optional high-flotation gear for use on unimproved airstrips.

POWER PLANT: Two Pratt & Whitney Canada PT6A-135A turboprop engines, each driving a Hartzell HC-B4TN-3A (or -3B)/T10173FK-10·5 four-blade constant-speed fully-feathering reversible-pitch metal propeller with spinner. Although flat rated at the same 559 kW (750 shp) as the PT6A-135 engines in the earlier Model F90, the -135A has an ISA rating of 660 kW (885 shp) at max continuous T-O power, instead of 634 kW (850 shp) for the -135 model. Propellers available optionally with reversible pitch. Usable fuel capacity 1,779 litres (470 US gallons). Automatic fuel transfer system, engine anti-icing, propeller de-icing, and ice-free fuel venting system, are standard. Oil capacity 13·2 litres (3·5 US gallons) per engine.

ACCOMMODATION: Two seats side by side on flight deck, with dual controls. Seats for five to eight persons in main cabin, in deep-cushioned chairs. Passengers screened from flight deck and toilet by partitions at front and rear of cabin. Space for 172 kg (380 lb) of baggage. Windscreen anti-icing standard.

SYSTEMS: Pressurisation system, differential 0·34 bars (5·0 lb/sq in); 16,000 BTU air-conditioning system. Electrical system includes two 28V 250A starter/generators and 45Ah aircooled nickel-cadmium battery. Oxygen system, 0·62 m³ (22 cu ft) capacity, with eight automatically deployed passenger masks and one first aid mask.

AVIONICS: Standard avionics package, by Collins, includes two VHF-20A transceivers, VIR-30MGM and VIR-30MG manual omnis, DB system Model 415 audio amplifier, ADF-650A ADF, marker beacon indicator, dual glideslope, DME-40, TDR-950 transponder, and PN-101 compass system. Full blind-flying instrumentation for pilot and co-pilot. Collins APS-80 autopilot, and large range of optional avionics available.

DIMENSIONS, EXTERNAL:	
Wing span	13·98 m (45 ft 10½ in)
Length overall	12·13 m (39 ft 9½ in)
Height overall	4·62 m (15 ft 1¾ in)
Tailplane span	5·61 m (18 ft 5 in)
Wheel track	3·96 m (13 ft 0 in)
Wheelbase	3·80 m (12 ft 5½ in)
Propeller diameter	2·34 m (7 ft 8 in)
Propeller ground clearance	0·32 m (1 ft 0¾ in)
Passenger door: Height	1·31 m (4 ft 3½ in)
Width	0·69 m (2 ft 3 in)
DIMENSIONS, INTERNAL:	
Cabin, excl flight deck: Length	3·86 m (12 ft 8 in)
Max width	1·37 m (4 ft 6 in)
Max height	1·45 m (4 ft 9 in)
Volume	8·88 m³ (313·6 cu ft)
Avionics compartment volume	0·45 m³ (16 cu ft)
Rear baggage compartment volume	1·51 m³ (53·5 cu ft)
AREA:	
Wings, gross	25·99 m² (279·74 sq ft)
WEIGHTS AND LOADINGS:	
Weight empty	3,041 kg (6,704 lb)
Max T-O and landing weight	4,966 kg (10,950 lb)
Max ramp weight	5,003 kg (11,030 lb)
Max wing loading	190·8 kg/m² (39·1 lb/sq ft)
Max power loading	4·4 kg/kW (7·3 lb/shp)

Beechcraft King Air F90-1 seven/ten-seat business aircraft, showing redesigned engine cowlings

PERFORMANCE (at max T-O weight except where indicated:	
Max cruising speed at average cruise weight:	
at 3,660 m (12,000 ft)	279 knots (517 km/h; 321 mph)
at 5,490 m (18,000 ft)	275 knots (510 km/h; 316 mph)
at 7,925 m (26,000 ft)	265 knots (491 km/h; 305 mph)
Max operating speed (VMO)	253 knots (469 km/h; 291 mph) IAS
Stalling speed, power off:	
flaps up	94 knots (174 km/h; 108 mph) IAS
32·5% flap	87 knots (162 km/h; 101 mph) IAS
100% flap	79 knots (147 km/h; 91 mph) IAS
Max rate of climb at S/L	748 m (2,455 ft)/min
Rate of climb at S/L, one engine out	192 m (632 ft)/min
Service ceiling	9,280 m (30,450 ft)
Service ceiling, one engine out	4,660 m (15,300 ft)
Min ground turning radius	10·06 m (33 ft 0 in)
T-O run, 32·5% flap	465 m (1,524 ft)
T-O to 15 m (50 ft), 32·5% flap	1,196 m (3,925 ft)
Landing from 15 m (50 ft):	
without propeller reversal	907 m (2,977 ft)
with propeller reversal	694 m (2,275 ft)
Landing run:	
without propeller reversal	578 m (1,895 ft)
with propeller reversal	364 m (1,194 ft)
Accelerate/stop distance, 32·5% flap	1,073 m (3,520 ft)
Cruising range at max cruise power, with reserves:	
at 3,660 m (12,000 ft)	961 nm (1,781 km; 1,106 miles)
at 5,490 m (18,000 ft)	1,156 nm (2,142 km; 1,331 miles)
at 7,925 m (26,000 ft)	1,439 nm (2,667 km; 1,657 miles)
Cruising range at max range power, with reserves:	
at 3,660 m (12,000 ft)	1,187 nm (2,200 km; 1,367 miles)
at 5,490 m (18,000 ft)	1,397 nm (2,589 km; 1,608 miles)
at 7,925 m (26,000 ft)	1,612 nm (2,987 km; 1,856 miles)

BEECHCRAFT SUPER KING AIR B200

Design of the **Super King Air 200** began in October 1970, construction of the first prototype and first pre-production aircraft starting simultaneously a year later. The first prototype (c/n BB1) flew for the first time on 27 October 1972, followed by the second aircraft (BB2) on 15 December 1972. Construction of the first production aircraft began in June 1973. FAA certification under FAR Part 23 was awarded on 14 December 1973, the aircraft satisfying also the icing requirements of FAR Part 25.

By comparison with the original King Air 100, the Super King Air 200 has increased wing span, basically the same fuselage, a T tail, more powerful engines, additional fuel capacity, increased cabin pressurisation and a higher gross weight. The cargo door fitted to some military versions became available as an option on civil Super King Airs in 1979; first deliveries were for air ambulance use in Libya and commuter operations in Australia.

In February 1977 Beech delivered to the French Institut Géographique National two specially modified Super King Airs. These have twin Wild RC-10 Superaviogon camera installations and Doppler navigation systems, and were the first Super King Airs to be equipped with optional wingtip fuel tanks, which increase the total usable fuel capacity from 2,059 litres (544 US gallons) to 2,460 litres (650 US gallons) to provide a max endurance of 10·3 h. Designated **Model 200T**, they are fitted with high-flotation main landing gear, and are being operated under a special French airworthiness certificate which allows max T-O and landing weights of 6,350 kg (14,000 lb) and 6,123 kg (13,500 lb) respectively. The aircraft can be operated with or without the wingtip tanks, for high-altitude photographic and weather observation missions.

Beechcraft Super King Air B200 eight/fifteen-seat pressurised transport

Beech announced on 25 April 1977 a specially equipped **Maritime Patrol** version of the Super King Air, which is described separately.

During 1978 Beech supplied to the Egyptian government a Super King Air which is being used to continue water, uranium and other natural resources exploration in the Sinai and Egyptian deserts which was originated by US ERTS-1 and Landsat satellites. This aircraft is equipped with remote sensing equipment, specialised avionics, and sophisticated cameras. In June 1978, Beech delivered to the government of Taiwan a Super King Air equipped to check ground based navigation systems; and Malaysia uses two Super King Airs for airways calibration and flight inspection. A second special mission aircraft was delivered to Taiwan's Ministry of the Interior in May 1979.

The **Super King Air B200**, introduced in March 1981, is generally similar to the Super King Air 200, except for the installation of Pratt & Whitney Canada PT6A-42 turboprop engines, which provide better cruise and altitude performance than the PT6A-41s in the original Super King Air 200. In addition, max zero-fuel weight is increased by 272 kg (600 lb) and cabin pressure differential is increased from 0·41 bars (6·0 lb/sq in) to 0·44 bars (6·5 lb/sq in). Design of the Super King Air B200 began in March 1980, the prototype being a modified Super King Air 200 (c/n BB343). Manufacture of production aircraft began in May 1980, and FAA certification was granted on 13 February 1981. Five versions are available:

Super King Air B200. Basic version, as detailed.

Super King Air B200C. As Super King Air B200, but with a 1·32 × 1·32 m (4 ft 4 in × 4 ft 4 in) cargo door.

Super King Air B200T. Generally similar to Maritime Patrol 200T, with standard provision to carry removable wingtip tanks to increase maximum fuel capacity by 401 litres (106 US gallons), to a total of 2,460 litres (650 US gallons). Span without tip-tanks 16·92 m (55 ft 6 in).

Super King Air B200CT. Version with both cargo door and wingtip tank provisions as standard.

Super King Air 300. Described separately.

By 1 January 1986 Beech had delivered 1,358 Super King Airs to commercial and private operators and 238 military versions (described separately) to the US Army, Air Force, Navy and Marine Corps.

A full description of the original Super King Air 200 can be found in the 1980-81 *Jane's*. The following description applies to the B200, which replaced it in production:

TYPE: Twin-turboprop passenger, cargo or executive light transport.

WINGS: Cantilever low-wing monoplane, with constant chord centre-section and tapered outer panels. Leading-edges extended forward just outboard of engine nacelles. Wing section NACA 23018·5 (modified) at root, NACA 23011·3 at tip. Dihedral 6°. Incidence 3°48′ at root, −1° 7′ at tip. No sweepback at quarter-chord. Two-spar light alloy structure. Conventional ailerons of light alloy construction, with trim tab in port aileron. Single-slotted trailing-edge flaps of light alloy construction. Pneumatic de-icing boots standard.

FUSELAGE: Light alloy semi-monocoque structure of safe-life design.

TAIL UNIT: Conventional cantilever T tail structure of light alloy with swept vertical and horizontal surfaces. Dorsal fin, and shallow ventral fin. Fixed incidence tailplane. Trim tab in each elevator. Anti-servo tab in rudder. Pneumatic de-icing boots standard, on leading-edge of tailplane only.

LANDING GEAR: Hydraulically retractable tricycle type, with twin wheels on each main unit. Single wheel on steerable nose unit, with shimmy damper. Main units retract forward, nosewheel rearward. Beech oleo-pneumatic shock absorbers. Goodrich mainwheels and tyres size 18 × 5·5, pressure 7·25 bars (105 lb/sq in). Oversize and/or 10-ply mainwheel tyres optional. Goodrich nosewheel size 6·50 × 10, with tyre size 22 × 6·75-10, pressure 3·93 bars (57 lb/sq in). Goodrich hydraulic multiple-disc brakes. Parking brake.

POWER PLANT: Two 634 kW (850 shp) Pratt & Whitney Canada PT6A-42 turboprop engines, each driving a Hartzell three-blade constant-speed fully-feathering reversible-pitch metal propeller with spinner. Bladder fuel cells in each wing, with main system capacity of 1,461 litres (386 US gallons) and auxiliary system capacity of 598 litres (158 US gallons). Total usable fuel capacity 2,059 litres (544 US gallons). Two refuelling points in upper surface of each wing. Wingtip tanks optional, providing an additional 401 litres (106 US gallons) and raising maximum usable capacity to 2,460 litres (650 US gallons). Oil capacity 29·5 litres (7·8 US gallons). Anti-icing of engine air intakes by hot air from engine exhaust is standard. Electrothermal anti-icing for propellers standard; automatic feathering and synchrophaser optional.

ACCOMMODATION: Pilot only, or crew of two side by side, on flight deck, with full dual controls and instruments as standard. Six cabin seats standard, each equipped with seat belts and inertia reel shoulder harness; alternative layouts for a maximum of 13 passengers in cabin and 14th beside pilot. Partition with sliding door between cabin and flight deck, and partition at rear of cabin. Door at rear of cabin on port side, with integral airstair. Large cargo door optional. Inward opening emergency exit on starboard side over wing. Lavatory and stowage for up to 249 kg (550 lb) baggage in aft fuselage. Maintenance access door in rear fuselage; radio compartment access doors in nose. Standard equipment includes reading lights and fresh air outlets for all passengers, triple cabin windows with polarised glare control, fully carpeted floor, 'No smoking—Fasten seat belt' sign, cabin coat rack, fluorescent cabin lighting, aisle and door courtesy lights. Electrically heated windscreens, hot air windscreen defroster, dual storm windows, sun visors, map pockets and windscreen wipers. Cabin is air-conditioned and pressurised, and can be provided with optional radiant heat panels.

SYSTEMS: Cabin pressurisation by engine bleed air, with a maximum differential of 0·44 bars (6·5 lb/sq in). Cabin air-conditioner of 34,000 BTU capacity. Auxiliary cabin heating by radiant panels optional. Oxygen system for flight deck, and 0·62 m³ (22 cu ft) oxygen system for cabin, with automatic drop-down face masks; standard system of 1·39 m³ (49 cu ft); 1·81 m³ (64 cu ft) or 2·15 m³ (76 cu ft) optional. Dual vacuum system for instruments. Hydraulic system for landing gear retraction and extension, pressurised to 171-191 bars (2,475-2,775 lb/sq in). Separate hydraulic system for brakes. Pneumatic system for wing and tailplane de-icing. Electrical system has two 250A 28V starter/generators and a 24V 45Ah aircooled nickel-cadmium battery with failure detector. AC power provided by dual 250VA inverters. Engine fire detection system standard; engine fire extinguishing system optional.

AVIONICS AND EQUIPMENT: Standard avionics include dual Collins VHF-20A VHF transceivers; Collins VIR-30AGM automatic Omni No. 1 with 331A-3G indicator; Collins VIR-30AG automatic Omni No. 2 with IND31C indicator; dual Omni range filters; Collins dual DB system Model 415 with dual Model 210 voice activated interphone, ADF voice/range filters and dual audio switches; Collins ADF-60A ADF, less indicator; Collins marker beacon receiver, integral with VIR-30 No. 1; dual Collins glideslopes, integral with VIR-30 No. 1 and No. 2; Sperry Primus 200 colour weather radar, Sperry C-14-A compass system, with servo amplifier (pilot); Collins RMI-30, with Nav 1/ADF on single needle, Nav 2/ADF on double needle; Collins TDR-90 transponder; Collins DME-40 with Nav 1/Nav 2 switching and DME hold; dual Flite-Tronics PC-250 250VA inverters with failure light; sectional instrument panel; dual flight instrumentation; Standard Electric gyro horizon (pilot); CF gyro horizon (co-pilot); Beech edge-lit radio panel, radio accessories, microphone key button in pilot's and co-pilot's control wheels, static wicks and white lighting; dual microphones, headsets and cockpit speakers; avionics master switch; and avionics overvoltage protection. A wide range of optional avionics by Bendix, Collins, King, RCA, Sperry and SunAir is available to customer's requirements, including a Collins EFIS with three colour CRT displays replacing the HSI, ADI and conventional radar screen; and Collins FMS-9C, flight management system, combining FMS-90 VLF/Omega, VOR/DME and R/Nav navigation functions. Also available is a two-CRT Sperry EFIS, and Sperry SPZ 4000 autopilot/flight control system with digital computer. Standard equipment is generally as listed for King Air C90A, plus dual max allowable airspeed indicators, control wheel mounted chronographs, toilet, fluorescent cabin lighting instead of indirect lighting, aisle courtesy light, transistor controlled blue/white cockpit lighting, passenger door light, rudder boost system, and yaw damper system. Optional equipment includes a flight hour recorder, instantaneous vertical speed indicator, cockpit and cabin fire extinguishers, a range of cabin chairs, cabinets and table, flushing toilet, aft cabin air-conditioning installation, passenger door step lights, wingtip recognition lights, strobe lights, and fin illumination lights.

DIMENSIONS, EXTERNAL:

Wing span	16·61 m (54 ft 6 in)
Wing chord: at root	2·18 m (7 ft 1¾ in)
at tip	0·90 m (2 ft 11⅝ in)
Wing aspect ratio	9·8
Length overall	13·34 m (43 ft 9 in)
Height overall	4·57 m (15 ft 0 in)
Tailplane span	5·61 m (18 ft 5 in)
Wheel track	5·23 m (17 ft 2 in)
Wheelbase	4·56 m (14 ft 11½ in)
Propeller diameter	2·50 m (8 ft 2½ in)
Propeller ground clearance	0·37 m (1 ft 2½ in)
Distance between propeller centres	5·23 m (17 ft 2 in)
Passenger door: Height	1·31 m (4 ft 3½ in)
Width	0·68 m (2 ft 2¾ in)
Height to sill	1·17 m (3 ft 10 in)
Cargo door (optional): Height	1·32 m (4 ft 4 in)
Width	1·32 m (4 ft 4 in)
Nose avionics service doors (port and stbd):	
Max height	0·57 m (1 ft 10½ in)
Width	0·63 m (2 ft 1 in)
Height to sill	1·37 m (4 ft 6 in)
Emergency exit (stbd): Height	0·66 m (2 ft 2 in)
Width	0·50 m (1 ft 7¾ in)

DIMENSIONS, INTERNAL:

Cabin (from forward to rear pressure bulkhead):	
Length	6·71 m (22 ft 0 in)
Max width	1·37 m (4 ft 6 in)
Max height	1·45 m (4 ft 9 in)
Floor area	7·80 m² (84 sq ft)
Volume	11·10 m³ (392 cu ft)
Baggage hold, rear of cabin:	
Volume	1·51 m³ (53·5 cu ft)

AREAS:

Wings, gross	28·15 m² (303 sq ft)
Ailerons (total)	1·67 m² (18·0 sq ft)
Trailing-edge flaps (total)	4·17 m² (44·9 sq ft)
Fin	3·46 m² (37·2 sq ft)
Rudder, incl tab	1·40 m² (15·1 sq ft)
Tailplane	4·52 m² (48·7 sq ft)
Elevators, incl tabs	1·79 m² (19·3 sq ft)

WEIGHTS AND LOADINGS:

Weight empty	3,419 kg (7,538 lb)
Max fuel load	1,653 kg (3,645 lb)
Max T-O and landing weight	5,670 kg (12,500 lb)
Max ramp weight	5,710 kg (12,590 lb)
Max zero-fuel weight	4,990 kg (11,000 lb)
Max wing loading	201·6 kg/m² (41·3 lb/sq ft)
Max power loading	4·47 kg/kW (7·35 lb/shp)

PERFORMANCE (at max T-O weight ISA, except where indicated):

Never-exceed speed
260 knots (482 km/h; 299 mph) IAS

Max operating Mach No. 0·52

Max level speed at 7,620 m (25,000 ft), average cruise weight 294 knots (545 km/h; 339 mph)

Max cruising speed at 7,620 m (25,000 ft), average cruise weight 289 knots (536 km/h; 333 mph)

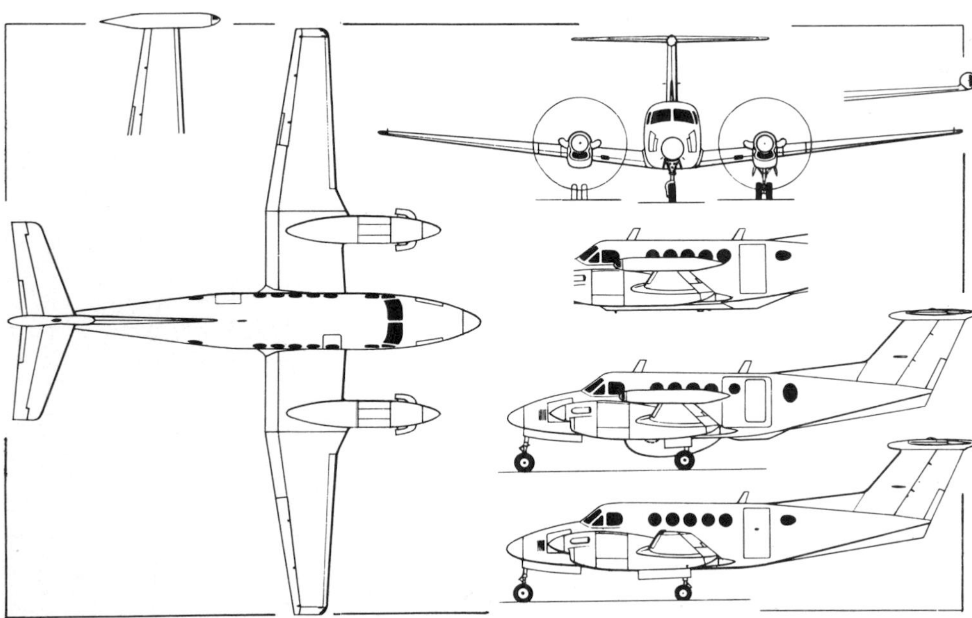

Beechcraft Super King Air B200 twin-turboprop transport, with additional side view of Maritime Patrol 200T (centre right); scrap views of wingtip tanks and centre-fuselage of photo survey aircraft for IGN
(Pilot Press)

Econ cruising speed at 7,620 m (25,000 ft), average cruise weight, normal cruise power
282 knots (523 km/h; 325 mph)
Stalling speed:
flaps up 99 knots (183 km/h; 114 mph) IAS
flaps down 76 knots (140 km/h; 87 mph) IAS
Max rate of climb at S/L 747 m (2,450 ft)/min
Rate of climb at S/L, one engine out
226 m (740 ft)/min
Service ceiling over 10,670 m (35,000 ft)
Service ceiling, one engine out 6,625 m (21,735 ft)
T-O run 592 m (1,942 ft)
T-O to 15 m (50 ft), 40% flap 786 m (2,579 ft)
Landing from 15 m (50 ft):
without propeller reversal 867 m (2,845 ft)
with propeller reversal 632 m (2,074 ft)
Landing run 536 m (1,760 ft)
Range with max fuel, allowances for start, taxi, climb, descent, and 45 min reserves at max range power, ISA:
max range power at:
5,485 m (18,000 ft)
1,192 nm (2,209 km; 1,372 miles)
7,620 m (25,000 ft)
1,461 nm (2,707 km; 1,682 miles)
9,450 m (31,000 ft)
1,766 nm (3,273 km; 2,033 miles)
10,670 m (35,000 ft)
1,972 nm (3,654 km; 2,271 miles)
econ cruise power at:
5,485 m (18,000 ft)
1,517 nm (2,811 km; 1,747 miles)
7,620 m (25,000 ft)
1,802 nm (3,339 km; 2,075 miles)
9,450 m (31,000 ft)
1,974 nm (3,658 km; 2,273 miles)
10,670 m (35,000 ft)
2,027 nm (3,756 km; 2,334 miles)

BEECHCRAFT MARITIME PATROL B200T

Beech announced on 9 April 1979 that it had begun to flight test a maritime patrol version of its Super King Air 200 twin-turboprop light transport, for FAA certification as the Maritime Patrol 200T.

In production form, the current B200T can be equipped for missions such as surface and subsurface monitoring of exclusive economic zones, detecting pollution, inspecting offshore installations, and conducting search and rescue flights. Special missions for which it could also be used include aerial photography, environmental and ecological research, airways and ground based navigation equipment checks, target towing, and ambulance duties.

Modifications to the standard Super King Air to adapt it to Maritime Patrol B200T configuration include fitting new outboard wing assemblies, with mountings for a 200·5 litre (53 US gallon) removable fuel tank at each wingtip; strengthened landing gear to cater for higher take-off and landing weights; two bubble observation windows in the rear cabin for visual search and photography; a hatch for dropping survival equipment; and a search radar with full 360° scan in a radome beneath the fuselage. Advanced navigation equipment is available; standard avionics include VLF/Omega which provides ground stabilisation and is coupled with the autopilot. This permits a search pattern to be programmed before take-off or en route. An integrated systems approach is utilised, with controls and displays located on the cabin operator's console.

Deliveries include 15 Maritime Patrol 200Ts to Japan's Maritime Safety Agency, two for the Algerian Ministry of Defence, three to Australia, one to Chile, three to Peru and one to the Uruguayan Navy.

The description of the Super King Air B200 applies also to the B200T, except as follows:

Type: Twin-turboprop maritime patrol or multi-mission aircraft.

Wings: As for Super King Air B200, except for new outboard wing panels redesigned to permit mounting of removable wingtip tanks. Optional wingtip ESM antennae.

Landing Gear: Strengthened to cater for higher operating weights.

Power Plant: As for Super King Air B200, including removable wingtip tanks which increase maximum usable fuel capacity by 401 litres (106 US gallons), to a total of 2,460 litres (650 US gallons).

Avionics and Equipment: Standard items as detailed in introductory description. Optional avionics include ESM integrated with INS, VHF-FM com, HF and VHF com, Northrop Seehawk FLIR, LLLTV, sonobuoys and processor, OTPI, multispectral scanner, tactical navigation computer, and two alternative search radar systems, both with 360° scan and weather avoidance capability, and integrated with INS.

Dimensions, external: As for Super King Air B200, except:
Wing span over tip tanks 17·25 m (56 ft 7 in)
Wing aspect ratio 10·5

Dimensions, internal: As for Super King Air B200, except:
Cabin: Length (excl flight deck) 5·08 m (16 ft 8 in)

Weights (A: Normal category; B: Restricted category):
Weight empty: A, B 3,744 kg (8,255 lb)
Max T-O weight: A 5,670 kg (12,500 lb)
B 6,350 kg (14,000 lb)

One of 15 Beechcraft Maritime Patrol 200Ts in service with Japan's Maritime Safety Agency

Max landing weight: A 5,670 kg (12,500 lb)
B 6,123 kg (13,500 lb)

Performance (at max T-O weight except where indicated):
Max cruising speed, AUW of 4,990 kg (11,000 lb) at 4,265 m (14,000 ft) 265 knots (491 km/h; 305 mph)
Typical patrol speed
140 knots (259 km/h; 161 mph)
Range with max fuel, patrolling at 227 knots (420 km/h; 261 mph) at 825 m (2,700 ft), 45 min reserves
1,790 nm (3,317 km; 2,061 miles)
Typical endurance at 140 knots (259 km/h; 161 mph), at 610 m (2,000 ft), 45 min reserves 6 h 36 min
Max time on station, with wingtip fuel tanks
9 h 0 min

BEECHCRAFT SUPER KING AIR 200/B200 (MILITARY VERSIONS)

US military designation: C-12

The first three production Super King Airs were acquired by the US Army in 1974 as **RU-21Js**, fitted with various types of electronic warfare equipment and an array of antennae resembling those of the current RC-12D. After serving as testbeds for some years, these aircraft were stripped of the special mission avionics and configured as VIP transports.

In August 1974, Beech received an initial military contract to build and support 34 modified versions of the Super King Air designated C-12A. Worldwide deployment of the C-12s began in July 1975. They are described as "standard off-the-shelf Super King Air types, modified slightly to meet military flight requirements and to orient the control systems for two-pilot operation which is standard military practice". Accommodation is provided for eight passengers, plus two pilots, with easy conversion to cargo missions. The large baggage area has provisions for storing survival gear.

The following versions of the C-12 have been announced:

C-12A. Initial Model A200 for US Army (60) and US Air Force (30), with two 559 kW (750 shp) Pratt & Whitney Canada PT6A-38 turboprop engines, each driving a Hartzell three-blade constant-speed fully-feathering reversible-pitch propeller. Wing span 16·61 m (54 ft 6 in); auxiliary tanks. Weights, loadings and performance given in 1980-81 *Jane's*. Army aircraft later refitted with PT6A-41 engines; USAF C-12As refitted with PT6A-42s are redesignated **C-12E**. Total of 91 built, including one for Foreign Military Sales. Entered service at Fort Monroe, Virginia, in July 1975.

UC-12B. US Navy/Marine Corps version (Model A200C), with 634 kW (850 shp) PT6A-41 turboprop engines, cargo door and high-flotation landing gear. Total of 66 (49 Navy, 17 Marine Corps) delivered by 31 May 1982. A further 12 aircraft ordered in August 1985 for delivery commencing in 1986, and 11 ordered in May 1986 for delivery starting in 1987.

C-12C. As C-12A, for US Army (14), but with PT6A-41 engines. Deliveries completed.

C-12D (Model A200CT). As C-12C, for US Army, but with cargo door, high flotation landing gear and provisions for tip tanks. Wing span (over tip tanks) 16·92 m (55 ft 6 in). Total of 33 ordered initially (including 13 modified to RC-12Ds, which see, and five for Foreign Military Sales), of which delivery was completed by March 1983. A further 12 aircraft ordered in August 1985 for delivery in 1986/1987, and five more ordered in May 1986.

UC-12D. Utility version, generally similar to C-12D, ordered in April 1983. Six for US Air Force; six for Army National Guard; all delivered in first half of 1984.

RC-12D Improved Guardrail V (Model A200CT). 'Special mission' US Army version, acquired to supplement earlier unpressurised RU-21H Guardrail V aircraft for battlefield duties in Europe and South Korea. The RC-12D serves as the aerial platform for the AN/USD-9 Improved Guardrail remotely controlled communications intercept and direction finding system, with direct reporting to tactical commanders at corps level and below. It is configured with an aircraft survivability equipment (ASE) suite, a Carousel IV-E inertial platform and Tacan set, and mission equipment including a radio data link, AN/ARW-83(V)5 airborne relay facility, associated antennae above and below the wings, and ECM in wingtip pods which increase overall span to 17·63 m (57 ft 10 in). Other system components are an AN/TSQ-105(V)4 integrated processing facility, AN/ARM-63(V)4 AGE flightline van, and AN/TSC-87 tactical commander's terminal. Thirteen RC-12Ds are included in total given for C-12D, with deliveries from Summer 1983. Further six delivered in 1985, under contract announced in May 1983; these are to B200 standard. Nine included in FY 1985 budget requests. Prime system contractor is ESL Inc, with Beech as mission equipment integrator. Max T-O weight of the RC-12D is 6,441 kg (14,200 lb).

C-12E. Upgraded C-12A for US Air Force, refitted with PT6A-42 engines.

C-12F. Operational support aircraft (OSA), generally similar to Model B200C, with hydraulically retractable landing gear. Forty aircraft for US Air Force purchased following initial five-year lease contract. First C-12F delivered in May 1984 to Military Airlift Command at Scott Air Force Base, Illinois. Cargo door standard.

Beechcraft C-12F operational support aircraft of USAF Military Airlift Command

C-12J. Variant of Beechcraft 1900C (which see), not Super King Air.

RC-12K Improved Guardrail V. Electronics special missions aircraft. Nine ordered by US Army in October 1985 for delivery from Spring 1988. Large cargo door and oversized landing gear standard.

BEECHCRAFT SUPER KING AIR 300

The Super King Air 300 is an improved version of the Model B200 with two 783 kW (1,050 shp) Pratt & Whitney Canada PT6A-60A engines, increased maximum take-off and landing weights to FAA SFAR 41C standards, redesigned 'pitot cowl' engine air inlets of 451 cm^2 (70 sq in) area compared with 567 cm^2 (88 sq in) on the B200, aerodynamically faired exhausts, a 12·7 cm (5 in) forward extension of the inboard wing leading-edges, 13·2 cm (5·2 in) forward extension of the propeller line, hydraulically actuated landing gear and numerous interior and equipment changes.

Design of the Super King Air 300 began in August 1980. A modified Model 200 testbed began flight trials in October 1981, and construction of a genuine prototype was started in November 1982. This production prototype made its first flight in September 1983 and was awarded FAA type certification on 24 January 1984. Customer deliveries of the Model 300 began in the Spring of 1984 and had totalled more than 60 by Autumn 1985.

The following description applies to those features of the Model 300 which differ from the Super King Air Model 200 series:

WINGS: Inboard leading-edges extended forward and fitted with strakes.

LANDING GEAR: Hydraulically retractable tricycle type. Goodrich mainwheels and tyres size 19 × 6·75-8, pressure 6·20 bars (90 lb/sq in) at max T-O weight. Goodrich nosewheel and tyre size 22 × 6·75-10, pressure 3·79-4·13 bars (55-60 lb/sq in). Beech brake de-icing system optional.

POWER PLANT: Two 783 kW (1,050 shp) Pratt & Whitney Canada PT6A-60A turboprop engines, each driving a Hartzell four-blade constant-speed fully-feathering reversible-pitch metal propeller with spinner. Bladder cells and integral tanks in each wing, with total capacity of 1,438 litres (380 US gallons); auxiliary tanks inboard of engine nacelles, capacity 601 litres (159 US gallons). Total fuel capacity 2,039 litres (539 US gallons). No provision for wingtip tanks. Oil capacity 30·2 litres (8 US gallons).

ACCOMMODATION: As for Model B200, except for additional emergency exit on port side of cabin, opposite starboard emergency exit and of the same dimensions. No pilot and co-pilot storm windows. Cabin features single-piece upper sidewall panels, indirect overhead lighting system with rheostat controls, stereo system with graphic equaliser and overhead speakers, larger executive tables incorporating magnetic game boards, seats with inflatable lumbar support adjustment, fore-and-aft, reclining and lateral tracking movement as standard. Crew seats have 2½° or 5° tilt positions. Emergency exit lighting standard. Electric heating on ground standard. Optional radiant heat panels on B200 not available.

SYSTEMS: As for Model B200, except for automatic bleed air type heating and 22,000 BTU cooling system with high capacity ventilation system; hydraulic landing gear retraction and extension system; two 300A 28V starter/generators with triple bus electrical distribution system.

AVIONICS AND EQUIPMENT: Dual Collins VHF-22A transceivers; dual Collins VIR-32 VOR/LOC/glideslope/marker beacon receivers, with dual 331A-3G indicators and CTL-32 controllers; dual DB system Model 415, with dual DB system Model 210 voice-activated interphone; Collins ADF-60A; dual Collins marker beacon receivers (included in VIR-32s), with marker lights; dual Collins glideslopes (included in VIR-32s); Sperry Primus 200 colour weather radar; Sperry C-14A compass system or Collins MCS-65 compass system; dual Collins RMI-30s with Nav 1/ADF on single needle, Nav 2/ADF on double needle; Collins TDR-90 transponder; IDC encoding altimeter; Collins DME-42; dual 250VA Flite-Tronics PC-250 inverters with failure light. Sectional instrument panel. Dual flight instrumentation, internally lighted. Pilot's Standard Electric gyro horizon; co-pilot's 3 in CF gyro horizon. Custom edge-lighted radio panel, microphone key button in pilot's and co-pilot's control wheels, static wicks, white lighting. Dual microphones, headsets and cockpit speakers. External interphone with jack plug in nosewheel bay, cabin paging and avionics master switch. Dual level electrically heated, safety plate glass windscreens, hot-air windscreen defroster; fail safe (dual pane) cockpit side windows; dual adjustable sun visors; map pocket; oxygen outlets and overhead-mounted diluter demand masks with microphones; pedestal mounted oxygen controls; dual cockpit speakers; fire extinguisher; two-speed bleed air system; POH storage container. Standard cabin equipment includes: fail safe (dual pane) cabin windows with polarised sun shades; six fully adjustable cabin chairs, each with shoulder harness, lap belt and retractable inboard arm rest; forward partition with sliding doors; aft partition with sliding doors; private lavatory; aft compartment retractable coat rods; airstair door with folding steps; airstair door courtesy light; emergency exit lights; wing ice lights; two landing lights; nosewheel taxi light; flush position lights; dual white rotating beacons; dual map lights; adjustable reading light for each cabin seat; indirect cabin lighting; two cockpit overhead floodlights; entrance door area illumination light; blue white cockpit lighting; cabin door inspection lights; aft compartment lights; primary and secondary instrument lighting systems.

Retouched photograph of US Army RC-12D in Improved Guardrail V configuration

DIMENSIONS, EXTERNAL: As for Model B200 except:
- Length overall: 13·36 m (43 ft 10 in)
- Height overall: 4·37 m (14 ft 4 in)
- Propeller diameter: 2·67 m (8 ft 9 in)
- Propeller ground clearance: 0·31 m (1 ft 0¼ in)

DIMENSIONS, INTERNAL: As for Model B200 except:
- Emergency exit doors (each side of cabin, above wing):
  - Height: 0·66 m (2 ft 2 in)
  - Width: 0·95 m (1 ft 7¾ in)

WEIGHTS AND LOADINGS:
- Weight empty: 3,760 kg (8,290 lb)
- Max baggage weight: 249 kg (550 lb)
- Max T-O and landing weight: 6,350 kg (14,000 lb)
- Max ramp weight: 6,396 kg (14,100 lb)
- Max zero-fuel weight: 5,216 kg (11,500 lb)
- Max wing loading: 225·6 kg/m^2 (46·2 lb/sq ft)
- Max power loading: 4·05 kg/kW (6·7 lb/shp)

PERFORMANCE (at max T-O weight, ISA):
- Never-exceed speed: 259 knots (480 km/h; 298 mph) IAS
- Max operating Mach No.: 0·58
- Max level speed: 317 knots (587 km/h; 365 mph)
- Max cruising speed: 315 knots (583 km/h; 363 mph)
- Econ cruising speed: 307 knots (568 km/h; 353 mph)
- Stalling speed:
  - flaps up: 100 knots (185 km/h; 115 mph) IAS
  - flaps down: 81 knots (150 km/h; 93 mph) IAS
- Max rate of climb at S/L: 867 m (2,844 ft)/min
- Rate of climb at S/L, one engine out: 264 m (867 ft)/min
- Max certificated ceiling: 10,670 m (35,000 ft)
- Service ceiling, one engine out: 6,970 m (22,875 ft)
- T-O run: flaps up: 622 m (2,042 ft)
  - 40% flap: 480 m (1,576 ft)
- T-O to 15 m (50 ft): flaps up: 854 m (2,803 ft)
  - 40% flap: 673 m (2,208 ft)
- Accelerate/stop distance, 40% flap: 1,122 m (3,682 ft)
- Landing from 15 m (50 ft): 886 m (2,907 ft)
- Landing run, without propeller reversal: 514 m (1,686 ft)
- Range with max fuel, allowances for start, taxi, T-O, climb, descent and 45 min reserves at max range power:
  - max cruise power at:
    - 5,485 m (18,000 ft): 1,055 nm (1,955 km; 1,215 miles)
    - 7,315 m (24,000 ft): 1,240 nm (2,298 km; 1,428 miles)
    - 8,535 m (28,000 ft): 1,400 nm (2,594 km; 1,612 miles)
    - 10,670 m (35,000 ft): 1,748 nm (3,235 km; 2,010 miles)
  - max range power at:
    - 5,485 m (18,000 ft): 1,429 nm (2,647 km; 1,645 miles)
    - 7,315 m (24,000 ft): 1,651 nm (3,059 km; 1,901 miles)
    - 8,535 m (28,000 ft): 1,795 nm (3,326 km; 2,067 miles)
    - 10,670 m (35,000 ft): 1,960 nm (3,632 km; 2,257 miles)

Beechcraft Super King Air 300 (Pratt & Whitney Canada PT6A-60A turboprop engines)

BEECHCRAFT C99 AIRLINER

The first aircraft in the Beechcraft 99 series, then known as a Commuter 99, was delivered on 2 May 1968, and a total of 164, comprising 99s, A99s, A99-As and B99s, had been delivered when production was discontinued in 1975. On 7 May 1979, Beech announced its intention to re-enter the commuter airliner market, initially with two aircraft designated Commuter C99 and Commuter 1900. A prototype of the Commuter C99, converted from a B99 airframe and powered by P&WC PT6A-34 turboprop engines, flew for the first time on 20 June 1980. Manufacture of production aircraft began in September 1980, and deliveries started on 30 July 1981, following FAA certification earlier in the same week. The name of the type was changed to C99 Airliner shortly afterwards.

TYPE: Twin-turboprop commuter/cargo transport.

WINGS: Cantilever low-wing monoplane. Wing section NACA 23018 at root, NACA 23016·5 at centre-section joint with outer panel, NACA 23012 at tip. Dihedral 7°. Incidence 4° 48′ at root, 0° at tip. Two-spar all-metal structure of aluminium alloy. Single-slotted trailing-edge flaps of aluminium alloy. All-metal ailerons of magnesium alloy. Trim tab in port aileron. Optional pneumatic de-icing boots for wing leading-edges.

FUSELAGE: All-metal semi-monocoque structure.

TAIL UNIT: Cantilever all-metal structure with sweptback vertical surfaces and a ventral stabilising fin. Variable incidence tailplane. Tailplane dihedral 7°. Trim tab in rudder. Pneumatic de-icing boots for fin and tailplane leading-edges optional.

LANDING GEAR: Hydraulically retractable tricycle type with single steerable nosewheel and twin wheels on each main unit. Nose unit retracts aft, main units forward into engine nacelles. Beech oleo-pneumatic shock absorbers. Goodrich wheels and tyres. Mainwheel tyres size 18 × 5·5, pressure 6·34-6·62 bars (92-96 lb/sq in). Nosewheel tyre size 6·50-10, pressure 3·45-3·79 bars (50-55 lb/sq in). Goodrich heat-sink and aircooled single-disc hydraulic brakes. Parking brake. Shimmy damper on nosewheel.

POWER PLANT: Two Pratt & Whitney Canada PT6A-36 turboprop engines, each flat rated at 533 kW (715 shp) and driving a Hartzell three-blade constant-speed fully-feathering reversible-pitch propeller. Five rubber fuel cells in each wing; total fuel capacity 1,412 litres (373 US gallons), of which 1,393 litres (368 US gallons) are usable. Refuelling points on each engine nacelle and at each wingtip. Oil capacity 26·5 litres (7 US gallons).

ACCOMMODATION: Crew of two side by side on flight deck, with dual controls and full blind-flying instrumentation as standard. Half-curtain or bulkhead between flight deck and cabin. Standard high density seating arrangement accommodates 15 passengers two-abreast with centre aisle; single seat opposite cabin door. Baggage compartment aft of rear seats, with external door. Nose baggage compartment with two external doors. An underfuselage baggage/cargo pod with a maximum cargo length of 3·31 m (10 ft 10½ in) and a volume of 1·68 m³ (59·4 cu ft) is available as an option. Airstair door at rear of cabin on port side, with forward hinged cargo door adjacent to and forward of the cabin door, to provide a large unobstructed opening for cargo loading. Emergency exit on each side at forward end of cabin. Pilot's door for flight deck optional.

SYSTEMS: Engine bleed air heating system of 68,800 BTU output. Freon air-conditioning system of 32,000 BTU optional. Hydraulic system, pressure 114 bars (1,650 lb/sq in), with duplicated lines and alternative reservoir for operation of landing gear and brakes. Electrical system includes two 28V 200A generators, 40Ah nickel-cadmium battery with failure detector, and dual solid state inverters.

AVIONICS AND EQUIPMENT: Dual nav/com, dual glideslope receivers and transponders, ADF, DME, marker beacon receiver, Bendix radar, encoding altimeter, and ELT.

DIMENSIONS, EXTERNAL:

Wing span	13·98 m (45 ft 10½ in)
Length overall	13·58 m (44 ft 6¾ in)
Height overall	4·37 m (14 ft 4¼ in)
Tailplane span	6·82 m (22 ft 4½ in)
Wheel track	3·96 m (13 ft 0 in)
Wheelbase	5·48 m (17 ft 11¾ in)
Propeller diameter	2·37 m (7 ft 9½ in)
Propeller ground clearance	0·34 m (1 ft 1½ in)
Cabin door (port, rearmost):	
Height	1·31 m (4 ft 3½ in)
Width	0·69 m (2 ft 3 in)
Height to sill	1·19 m (3 ft 11 in)
Cargo door (port, rear): Height	1·31 m (4 ft 3½ in)
Width, total incl cabin door	1·36 m (4 ft 5½ in)
Height to sill	1·19 m (3 ft 11 in)
Emergency exits (port and stbd, fwd):	
Height	0·71 m (2 ft 4 in)
Width	0·53 m (1 ft 9 in)

DIMENSIONS, INTERNAL:

Cabin, incl flight deck and rear baggage compartment:	
Length	7·73 m (25 ft 4½ in)
Max width	1·40 m (4 ft 7 in)
Max height	1·45 m (4 ft 9 in)
Volume	13·71 m³ (484·3 cu ft)
Cabin cargo volume	10·02 m³ (353·9 cu ft)
Baggage compartment volume:	
aft of cabin	0·48 m³ (17·0 cu ft)
nose	1·24 m³ (43·9 cu ft)

AREAS:

Wings, gross	25·98 m² (279·7 sq ft)
Vertical tail surfaces (total)	4·17 m² (44·9 sq ft)
Horizontal tail surfaces (total)	9·29 m² (100·0 sq ft)

WEIGHTS AND LOADINGS:

Basic operating weight empty	3,039 kg (6,700 lb)
Max payload	1,474 kg (3,250 lb)
Max fuel weight	1,118 kg (2,466 lb)
Max T-O and landing weight	5,125 kg (11,300 lb)
Max ramp weight	5,162 kg (11,380 lb)
Max wing loading	197·25 kg/m² (40·4 lb/sq ft)
Max power loading	4·81 kg/kW (7·9 lb/shp)

PERFORMANCE (at max T-O weight except where indicated):

Never-exceed speed	282 knots (522 km/h; 324 mph)
Max level speed at 2,440 m (8,000 ft)	268 knots (496 km/h; 308 mph)
Cruising speed at AUW of 4,536 kg (10,000 lb), at:	
2,440 m (8,000 ft)	249 knots (461 km/h; 287 mph)
3,660 m (12,000 ft)	248 knots (460 km/h; 286 mph)
4,875 m (16,000 ft)	245 knots (454 km/h; 282 mph)
Max rate of climb at S/L	677 m (2,221 ft)/min
Rate of climb at S/L, one engine out	164 m (539 ft)/min
Service ceiling	7,620 m (25,000 ft)
Service ceiling, one engine out	4,375 m (14,360 ft)
Range with max fuel, IFR reserves	910 nm (1,686 km; 1,048 miles)

BEECHCRAFT 1900C and KING AIR EXEC-LINER

US military designation: C-12J

Beech began design of the basic 1900 commuter airliner during 1979, and the construction of three flying prototypes, a static test airframe and a fuselage pressure cycle test airframe in 1981. The first flight of the performance prototype (UA-1) was made on 3 September 1982, followed by the systems prototype (UA-2) on 30 November 1982. The third prototype (UA-3) was used for function and reliability testing, equipment certification, and demonstration; it is now in operational service. FAA certification under SFAR Pt 41C was obtained on 22 November 1983, and included single pilot approval under FAR 135 Appendix A.

The Beech 1900 is offered in two variants: **Model 1900C** with cargo door, the first of which was delivered in February 1984; and **King Air Exec-Liner**, the first delivery of which (N34GT) was made to General Telephone Company of Illinois in the Summer of 1985. Recent orders for the Model 1900C include three for Pennsylvania Airlines of Middletown, Pennsylvania; one for Mesa Airlines of Farmington, New Mexico; four for Business Express of Bridgeport, Connecticut; and six aircraft configured for electronic surveillance missions for delivery to the Egyptian Air Force in 1988. The Egyptian aircraft will be equipped with a new 'wet' wing which will increase fuel capacity by nearly 60 per cent and extend range by some 85 per cent.

In March 1986 US Army Aviation Systems Command ordered six Model 1900Cs for delivery commencing September 1987. These aircraft, designated **C-12J**, will also have 'wet' wings and will serve as Air National Guard mission support aircraft, replacing Convair C-131s.

The description which follows applies to the commercial Model 1900C and King Air Exec-Liner:

TYPE: Twin-turboprop commuter/cargo airliner and executive transport.

WINGS: Cantilever low-wing monoplane. Wing section NACA 23000. Thickness/chord ratio 18% at root, 12% at tip. Dihedral 6°. Incidence 3° 29′ at root, − 1° 4′ at tip. No sweepback at quarter-chord. Semi-monocoque fail-safe structure of aluminium alloy, riveted and bonded, with a continuous main spar. Single-slotted trailing-edge flaps, in two sections on each wing, of aluminium alloy construction; symmetrical ailerons of similar construction. Trim tab at inboard end of port aileron. Pneumatic de-icing boots on wing leading-edges.

FUSELAGE: Semi-monocoque fail-safe pressurised structure of aluminium alloy, mainly of bonded construction but including some riveting. Small horizontal vortex generator on each side of fuselage, immediately forward of wing leading-edge.

TAIL UNIT: Aluminium alloy structure comprising a cantilever T tail with sweptback vertical and horizontal

Beechcraft C99 Airliner twin-turboprop commuter aircraft

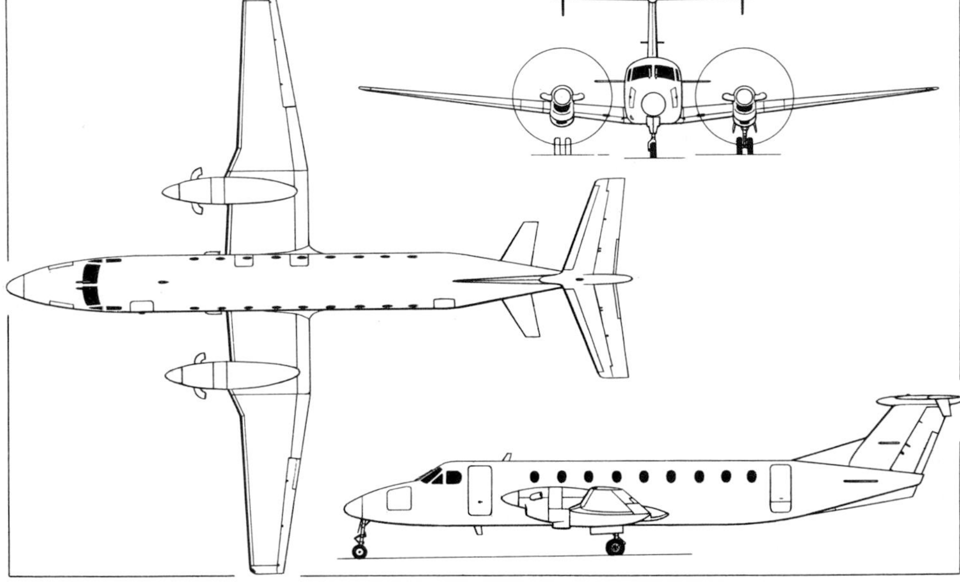

Beechcraft King Air Exec-Liner twin-turboprop executive transport *(Pilot Press)*

surfaces. Small fin (tail-let) beneath each side of tailplane, near tip; and auxiliary fixed horizontal tail surface (stabilon) on each side of rear fuselage. Trim tabs in elevators and rudder. Pneumatic de-icing boots on leading-edges of tailplane and stabilons.

LANDING GEAR: Hydraulically retractable tricycle type. Main units retract forward and nose unit rearward. Beech oleo-pneumatic shock absorber in each unit. Twin Goodyear wheels on each main unit, size 6·50 × 10, with Goodyear tyres size 22 × 6·75-10, pressure 6·07 bars (88 lb/sq in); Goodrich steerable nosewheel size 6·5 × 8, with Goodrich tyre size 19·5 × 6·75-8, pressure 6·07 bars (88 lb/sq in). Multiple-disc hydraulic brakes. Beech/Hydro-Aire anti-skid units and power steering optional.

POWER PLANT: Two Pratt & Whitney Canada PT6A-65B turboprop engines, each flat rated at 820 kW (1,100 shp) and driving a Hartzell four-blade constant-speed fully-feathering reversible-pitch composite propeller with spinner. Five bladder tanks and one integral fuel cell in each wing, all interconnected, with a total capacity in both wings of 1,627 litres (430 US gallons), of which 1,608 litres (425 US gallons) are usable. Refuelling point in each wing leading-edge, adjacent to tip. Oil capacity (total) 27·2 litres (7·2 US gallons).

ACCOMMODATION: Crew of one (FAR Pt 91) or two (FAR Pt 135) on flight deck, with standard accommodation in cabin of commuter version for 19 passengers, in single seats on each side of centre aisle. Forward and rear carry-on baggage lockers, underseat baggage stowage, rear baggage compartment and nose baggage compartment. Forward and rear doors, incorporating airstairs, on port side. Upward hinged cargo door instead of rear passenger door on model 1900C. Two emergency exits over wing on starboard side, plus one on port side (1900C only). Accommodation is air-conditioned, heated, ventilated and pressurised. Executive model has 12/18-passenger cabin with forward and rear compartments, combination lavatory/passenger seat and two beverage bars at cabin compartment division. Club seating optional. Customised interiors to customer choice.

SYSTEMS: Bleed air cabin heating and pressurisation, max differential 0·33 bars (4·8 lb/sq in). Air cycle and vapour cycle air-conditioning. Hydraulic system, pressure 207 bars (3,000 lb/sq in) for landing gear actuation. Electrical system includes two 300A engine starter/generators and one 22Ah nickel-cadmium battery. Constant flow oxygen system of 4·33 m³ (153 cu ft) capacity standard.

AVIONICS: Duplicated King com/nav, glideslope receiver, transponder, audio, ADF, DME, marker beacon receiver and Bendix RDR-160 weather radar. Sperry EFIS, and Collins autopilot and Pro Line II equipment, optional.

DIMENSIONS, EXTERNAL:

Wing span	16·61 m (54 ft 5¾ in)
Wing chord: at root	2·18 m (7 ft 1¾ in)
at tip	0·91 m (2 ft 11¾ in)
Wing aspect ratio	9·8
Length overall	17·63 m (57 ft 10 in)
Fuselage: Length	16·19 m (53 ft 1½ in)
Max diameter	1·79 m (5 ft 10½ in)
Height overall	4·54 m (14 ft 10¾ in)
Tailplane span	5·63 m (18 ft 5¾ in)
Wheel track	5·23 m (17 ft 2 in)
Wheelbase	7·25 m (23 ft 9½ in)
Propeller diameter	2·78 m (9 ft 1½ in)
Propeller ground clearance	0·35 m (1 ft 1¾ in)
Distance between propeller centres	5·23 m (17 ft 2 in)
Passenger doors (fwd and rear, port, each):	
Height	1·32 m (4 ft 4 in)
Width	0·69 m (2 ft 3 in)
Height to sill: fwd	1·28 m (4 ft 2½ in)
rear	1·15 m (3 ft 9¼ in)
Cargo door (rear, port): Height	1·32 m (4 ft 4 in)
Width	1·32 m (4 ft 4 in)
Height to sill	1·15 m (3 ft 9¼ in)
Baggage door (nose, port):	
Max height	0·56 m (1 ft 10 in)
Width	0·66 m (2 ft 2 in)
Height to sill	1·45 m (4 ft 9 in)
Emergency exits (two stbd; plus one port on 1900C only; all overwing): Height	0·70 m (2 ft 3½ in)
Width	0·51 m (1 ft 8 in)

DIMENSIONS, INTERNAL:

Cabin, incl flight deck and rear baggage compartment:	
Length	12·02 m (39 ft 5½ in)
Max width	1·37 m (4 ft 6 in)
Max height	1·45 m (4 ft 9 in)
Floor area	15·28 m² (164·5 sq ft)
Volume (excl baggage space)	16·79 m³ (593 cu ft)
Baggage space:	
Cabin:	
1900C, fwd: standard	0·42 m³ (15·0 cu ft)
optional	1·19 m³ (41·9 cu ft)
rear: Exec-Liner	2·18 m³ (77·0 cu ft)
1900C	4·36 m³ (154·0 cu ft)
Nose compartment	0·38 m³ (13·5 cu ft)

AREAS:

Wings, gross	28·15 m² (303·0 sq ft)
Ailerons (total)	1·67 m² (18·0 sq ft)
Trailing-edge flaps (total)	4·17 m² (44·9 sq ft)
Fin	3·42 m² (36·85 sq ft)
Rudder (incl tab)	1·106 m² (11·9 sq ft)
Tail-lets (total)	0·305 m² (3·28 sq ft)
Tailplane	4·52 m² (48·7 sq ft)
Elevator (incl tab)	1·79 m² (19·3 sq ft)
Stabilons (total, exposed)	1·44 m² (15·46 sq ft)

WEIGHTS AND LOADINGS:

Weight empty	3,947 kg (8,700 lb)
Max fuel weight (usable)	1,292 kg (2,848 lb)
Max payload	2,404 kg (5,300 lb)
Payload with max fuel	2,341 kg (5,162 lb)
Max baggage	880 kg (1,940 lb)
Max T-O weight	7,530 kg (16,600 lb)
Max ramp weight	7,580 kg (16,710 lb)
Max landing weight	7,302 kg (16,100 lb)
Max zero-fuel weight	6,350 kg (14,000 lb)
Max wing loading	267·5 kg/m² (54·8 lb/sq ft)
Max power loading	4·59 kg/kW (7·55 lb/shp)

PERFORMANCE (at max T-O weight except where indicated):

Max cruising speed at AUW of 6,350 kg (14,000 lb):
- at 2,440 m (8,000 ft): 256 knots (474 km/h; 295 mph)
- at 4,875 m (16,000 ft): 253 knots (468 km/h; 291 mph)
- at 7,620 m (25,000 ft): 235 knots (435 km/h; 271 mph)

T-O speed, 20° flap: 105 knots (194 km/h; 121 mph) CAS

Approach speed at max landing weight: 113 knots (209 km/h; 130 mph) CAS

Stalling speed at max T-O weight:
- wheels and flaps up: 101 knots (187 km/h; 116 mph) CAS
- wheels down and 20° flap: 95 knots (176 km/h; 109 mph) CAS

Stalling speed at max landing weight, wheels and flaps down: 87 knots (161 km/h; 100 mph) CAS

Max rate of climb at S/L	710 m (2,330 ft)/min
Rate of climb at S/L, one engine out	149 m (490 ft)/min
Service ceiling	exceeds certificated ceiling of 7,620 m (25,000 ft)
Service ceiling, one engine out	3,960 m (13,000 ft)
T-O run, 20° flap	671 m (2,200 ft)
T-O to 15 m (50 ft), 20° flap	991 m (3,250 ft)
Landing from 15 m (50 ft) at max landing weight	774 m (2,540 ft)
Landing run at max landing weight	466 m (1,530 ft)
Accelerate/stop distance, 20° flap	1,158 m (3,800 ft)

Range with max fuel in system using bladder tanks, with allowances for starting, taxi, T-O, climb, descent and 45 min reserves at max range speed:
- max cruise power:
  - at 2,440 m (8,000 ft): 531 nm (984 km; 611 miles)
  - at 4,875 m (16,000 ft): 663 nm (1,228 km; 763 miles)
  - at 7,620 m (25,000 ft): 794 nm (1,471 km; 914 miles)
- max range power:
  - at 2,440 m (8,000 ft): 596 nm (1,104 km; 686 miles)
  - at 4,875 m (16,000 ft): 712 nm (1,319 km; 820 miles)
  - at 7,620 m (25,000 ft): 794 nm (1,471 km; 914 miles)

Range with max fuel in 'wet' wings
- max range power, with IFR reserves: over 1,500 nm (2,775 km; 1,725 miles)

BEECHCRAFT MODEL 2000 STARSHIP 1

The first flight took place on 29 August 1983 of an 85 per cent scale proof of concept prototype of this new Beechcraft turboprop powered corporate aircraft. It was built by Mr 'Burt' Rutan's Scaled Composites Inc (which see, now a Beech subsidiary), and is providing data for the full size Starship 1. By early 1986 the scale version had completed over 500 flight hours with its initial power plant of 559 kW (750 shp) PT6A-135A engines. This aircraft was first flown with Pratt & Whitney Canada PT6A-67 engines on 29 August 1985.

Six pre-production Starship 1s are being built, three for flight testing and one each for static, damage tolerance and pressure cycle testing. Bell Aerospace has been contracted to manufacture the CFRP foreplanes for these aircraft. The first full-scale prototype (N2000S) made its first flight from Wichita on 15 February 1986, followed by a 'commemorative first flight' on 24 February. This aircraft was powered initially by PT6A-65A-4 engines pending delivery of the production standard PT6A-67 power plants. A second prototype, fitted with the Collins advanced integrated avionics system specified for production Starships, joined the flight test programme on 14 June 1986, at which time the first aircraft had completed 75 flight hours. Certification, to new FAA FAR Pt 23 requirements, is scheduled for late 1987, with first customer deliveries planned for the second quarter of 1988.

The description applies to the full size Starship 1:

TYPE: Eight/eleven-seat business aircraft.

WINGS: Cantilever mid/low-wing monoplane. Specially developed wing section. Dihedral 1° 18′ 36″. Incidence 2° at root. Sweepback 24° 24′ at quarter-chord. Continuous tip to tip structure of honeycomb and graphite/epoxy monocoque, semi-monocoque and honeycomb sandwich. Wingtip stabilisers (which the company terms tipsails) of composite construction, incorporating rudders and trim tabs. Elevons and Fowler flaps of

Beech Model 1900C in service with Business Express of Bridgeport, Connecticut

composite construction. Manual trim tabs on elevons; electric pitch trim optional; electric trim tab on each rudder. Leading-edge liquid anti-icing system standard.

FUSELAGE: Circular section fuselage of fail safe construction, using similar materials to wings, produced from a single filament wrapped around a form, or by manual lay-up method. A ventral fin has a movable surface for yaw trim/damping.

FOREPLANES: Low-set, electrically operated variable geometry foreplanes, of similar construction to wings, each with an elevator. Foreplane sweep is electronically interconnected with the flaps to counter pitch moment changes, over sweep range 4° forward to 30° back. Leading-edge liquid anti-icing system standard.

LANDING GEAR: Retractable tricycle type, hydraulically operated with emergency backup. Main units retract inboard, nose unit forward. Beech oleo-pneumatic shock absorbers. Twin Goodyear mainwheels with tyres size 19·5 × 6·75-10, pressure 5·38 bars (78 lb/sq in). Single Goodrich nosewheel with tyre size 19·5 × 6·75-8, pressure 5·38 bars (78 lb/sq in). Goodyear multi-disc brakes with carbon heat sink.

POWER PLANT: Two Pratt & Whitney Canada PT6A-67 turboprop engines, each flat rated at 820 kW (1,100 shp) and driving a four-blade fully-feathering and reversible-pitch composite pusher propeller with spinner. Fuel, total capacity 1,923 litres (508 US gallons), contained in integral wing tanks with flush refuelling point in upper surface of each wing.

ACCOMMODATION: To be certificated for single pilot operation, but provision for two crew on three-way adjustable seats on flight deck, separated from cabin by bulkhead with door. Two basic interior configurations to be offered, with other configurations available optionally. Typical configuration has seven swivelling, reclining, lateral tracking, and fore and aft adjustable seats. Individual stereo headset, ashtray/drink holder, indirect cabin lighting, reading light and fresh air vent by each seat. Sidewall console houses folding work tables and storage for cabin accessories. Forward toilet compartment opposite cabin entrance door, with hot/cold water and mirror; pull-out flushing toilet; privacy doors to cockpit and cabin enclose the forward baggage compartment, which has hang-up storage. Refreshment galley on rear port side of cabin with cold water, hot coffee dispenser, ice chest, beverage decanters and storage cabinet. The second basic cabin configuration has six passenger seats with a seventh seat/toilet at the rear, and a vanity unit on the opposite side. Refreshment cabinet aft of airstair door. Rear baggage compartment, accessible in flight via mirrored door in rear cabin bulkhead. Hi-fi speakers in one-piece cabin headliner. Cabin trim panels secured to isolation mounts to enhance acoustics and eliminate vibration. 'No smoking' and 'Fasten seat belt' signs. Cabin is bleed air heated, with electric augmentation, vapour cycle air-conditioned and blower ventilated.

SYSTEMS: Pressurisation system with max differential of 0·58 bars (8·5 lb/sq in) to provide a cabin altitude of 2,440 m (8,000 ft) at 12,495 m (41,000 ft). Freon vapour cycle cooling system. Engine bleed air provides pressurisation, heating and ventilation. 28V DC three-bus electrical system supplied by single aircooled 34Ah battery and starter/generator mounted on each engine and connected in parallel. Oxygen cylinder capacity 2·18 m³ (77 cu ft) rated at 124 bars (1,800 lb/sq in), mounted in nose, provides passenger oxygen supply automatically via drop-down masks until cabin altitude reaches 4,115 m (13,500 ft). Quick-donning masks for crew. Glycol anti-icing system, using porous titanium leading-edges on wings and foreplanes. De-icing and anti-icing systems for windscreen, engine air inlets, fuel vents, pitot static probes and stall warning sensor.

Full-scale prototype Beech Starship 1 landing after 'commemorative first flight' on 24 February 1986

AVIONICS AND EQUIPMENT: Collins integrated avionics package comprising 12 colour and two monochrome CRT displays in 'all glass' cockpit. Pilot and co-pilot have duplicated instrument panels, each with two 15·2 × 17·8 cm (6 × 7 in) EFIS displays for primary flight and navigation functions and two 10·2 × 10·2 cm (4 × 4 in) airspeed indicator and altitude/vertical speed indicator CRTs. Monochrome sensor display units (SDUs) provide heading bearings, DME and ILS functions and latitude/longitude information from a VLF/Omega long-range navigation system, and can be used as a primary navigation display in the event of EFIS failure. Dual control/display units (CDUs) control EFIS, weather radar, navigation radios and flight management functions. Engine indication caution and advisory system (EICAS) provides nearly 100 specific pieces of information in analog or digital form on a 15·2 × 17·8 cm (6 × 7 in) colour CRT display, with a priority message system to override extraneous information. Dual multi-function displays (MFDs) provide weather radar images, maps, checklists and diagnostic and maintenance data, and serve as backup to EICAS. Two radio tuning units provide gas discharge tube alphanumerics for displaying navigation and transponder frequencies and codes, and can be used for display of engine parameters if EICAS fails. Dual flight management system (FMS) keyboards control all navigation frequencies, selected from onboard microdisc storage which is updated every 28 days. Dual clocks, altitude awareness panels, a course heading panel, reversionary switching panels and standby electromagnetic airspeed indicator, gyro horizon and altimeter are provided. Information from sensors and data acquisition units located throughout the aircraft is available to all instruments through an ARINC 429 bus system.

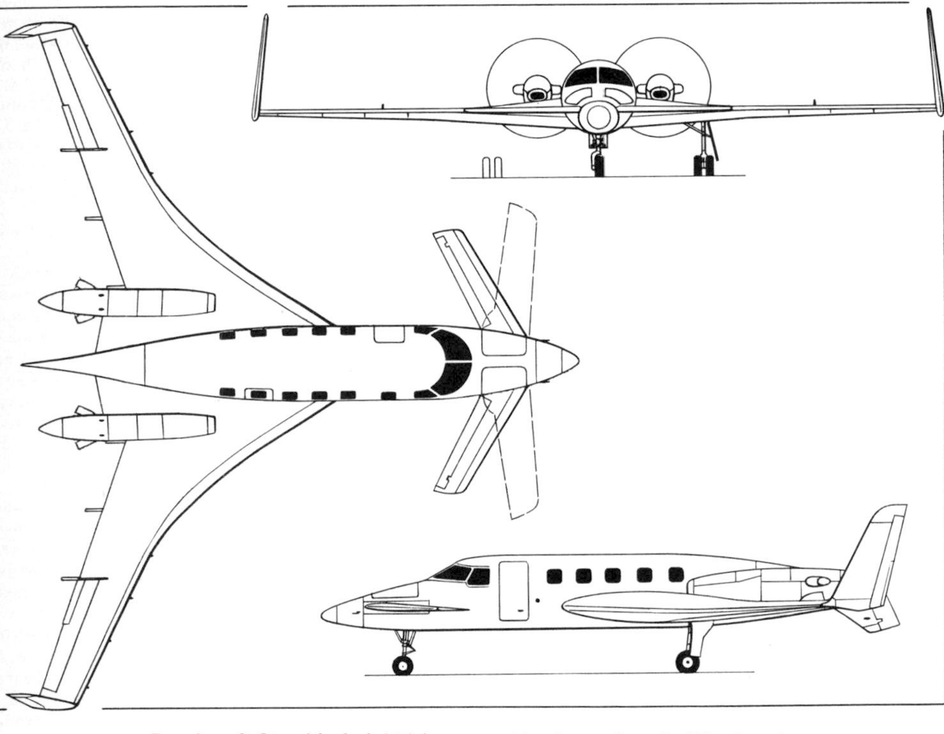

Beechcraft Starship 1 eight/eleven-seat business aircraft *(Pilot Press)*

DIMENSIONS, EXTERNAL:
- Wing span (reference) 16·46 m (54 ft 0 in)
- Winglet height, each 2·45 m (8 ft 0½ in)
- Foreplane span: sweptforward 7·30 m (23 ft 11½ in)
  - sweptback 6·37 m (20 ft 11 in)
- Length overall 14·05 m (46 ft 1 in)
- Fuselage: Length 13·67 m (44 ft 10 in)
  - Diameter (constant section) 1·78 m (5 ft 10 in)
- Height overall 3·91 m (12 ft 10 in)
- Wheel track 5·13 m (16 ft 10 in)
- Wheelbase 6·86 m (22 ft 6 in)
- Propeller diameter 2·54 m (8 ft 4 in)
- Propeller ground clearance 0·89 m (2 ft 11 in)
- Distance between propeller centres 3·07 m (10 ft 1 in)
- Passenger door: Height 1·88 m (4 ft 8 in)
  - Width 0·71 m (2 ft 4 in)
- Emergency exit: Height 0·56 m (1 ft 10 in)
  - Width 0·66 m (2 ft 2 in)

DIMENSIONS, INTERNAL:
- Cabin, excl flight deck: Length 4·88 m (16 ft 0 in)
  - Max width 1·68 m (5 ft 6 in)
  - Max height 1·66 m (5 ft 5½ in)
  - Floor area 5·94 m² (64 sq ft)
  - Volume (between pressure bulkheads) 15·57 m³ (550 cu ft)
- Baggage holds: forward 0·56 m³ (20 cu ft)
  - rear 0·99 m³ (35 cu ft)

AREAS:
- Wings, gross 26·09 m² (280·9 sq ft)
- Elevons (total) 1·59 m² (17·1 sq ft)
- Trailing-edge flaps (total) 4·78 m² (51·5 sq ft)
- Ventral fin 1·25 m² (13·5 sq ft)
- Foreplane (forward position) 5·67 m² (61·0 sq ft)
- Elevators (total) 1·01 m² (10·9 sq ft)
- Winglets (total) 4·92 m² (53·0 sq ft)
- Rudders, (total, incl tabs) 1·04 m² (11·2 sq ft)

WEIGHTS AND LOADINGS:
- Basic weight empty 3,992 kg (8,800 lb)
- Max payload 1,136 kg (2,505 lb)
- Max fuel weight 1,542 kg (3,400 lb)
- Max T-O weight 6,350 kg (14,000 lb)
- Max zero-fuel weight 4,899 kg (10,800 lb)
- Max landing weight 5,386 kg (11,875 lb)
- Max wing loading 243·4 kg/m² (49·84 lb/sq ft)
- Max power loading 3·87 kg/kW (6·36 lb/shp)

PERFORMANCE (estimated at AUW of 5,670 kg; 12,500 lb):
- Never-exceed speed Mach 0·76
- Max level speed and max cruising speed at 7,620 m (25,000 ft) 352 knots (652 km/h; 405 mph)
- Max cruising speed at 10,670 m (35,000 ft) 341 knots (631 km/h; 392 mph)
- Econ cruising speed 272 knots (504 km/h; 313 mph)
- Stalling speed, power off:
  - flaps up 94 knots (175 km/h; 109 mph)
  - flaps down 79 knots (147 km/h; 91 mph)
- Max rate of climb at S/L 990 m (3,250 ft)/min
- Rate of climb at S/L, one engine out 360 m (1,180 ft)/min
- Max operating altitude 11,885 m (39,000 ft)
- Service ceiling, one engine out 8,960 m (29,400 ft)
- T-O run 486 m (1,595 ft)
- T-O to 15 m (50 ft), flaps up 732 m (2,400 ft)
- Landing from 15 m (50 ft) 878 m (2,880 ft)
- Landing run 607 m (1,990 ft)
- Range with max fuel, long range cruise power, 45 min reserves 2,625 nm (4,860 km; 3,020 miles)
- Range with max payload, long range cruise power, 45 min reserves 1,127 nm (2,089 km; 1,298 miles)

BEECHCRAFT BEECHJET

In December 1985 Beech Aircraft Corporation acquired from Mitsubishi Heavy Industries and Mitsubishi Aircraft International the Diamond II business jet programme. The aircraft is now known as the Beechjet. Under the terms of the sale, Beech assembles the aircraft at Wichita from kits manufactured by MHI in Japan, with an option to transfer the entire manufacturing process to the United States in the future. Beech completes the aircraft, installing engines, interiors, avionics and other systems, and has worldwide marketing rights outside Japan. Mitsubishi Aircraft International (see MAI entry in this section) ceased all general aviation operations outside of Japan on 31 March 1986. Beech, through its dealer network, is providing support for existing Mitsubishi aircraft, including the MU-2 turboprop series and the Diamond I and IA business jets. A description of the development of the Mitsubishi Diamond series can be found under the MAI entry in the 1985-86 edition of *Jane's*.

Beech has introduced as standard on the Beechjet an extended range fuel tank, capacity 363 litres (80 Imp gallons; 96 US gallons), and a tailcone baggage compartment, both of which were optional on the Diamond II. No airframe or performance changes have been announced, but work was under way in early 1986 on a new interior design and new avionics options. The first Beech assembled aircraft was rolled out on 19 May 1986, and deliveries began in the following month. The company plans to manufacture two aircraft per month during 1987.

TYPE: Twin-turbofan business aircraft.

WINGS: Cantilever low-wing monoplane. Mitsubishi computer-designed wing sections: thickness/chord ratio 13·2% at root, 11·3% at tip. Dihedral from roots. Incidence 3° at root. Washout 6° 30'. Sweepback 20° at quarter-chord. Wings are of chemically milled aluminium alloy, and built in three portions: a centre-section and two outer panels. Each wing has two primary box beam spars, forming an integral fuel tank. Narrow chord Fowler type flaps over most of trailing-edges, actuated hydraulically and having double-slotted inboard and single-slotted outboard segments. Immediately forward of flaps are long span narrow chord spoilers, for roll control; these also serve as airbrakes, and can be used as lift dumpers to assist braking on touchdown. Outboard of each outer trailing-edge flap is a small, short span aileron for roll trim. Leading-edges are anti-iced by hot air.

FUSELAGE: Pressurised, fail-safe fatigue resistant semi-monocoque structure, of oval cross section with flattened cabin floor. Construction is mainly of aluminium alloy, using multiple load paths, bonded doublers and small skin panels in the principal load-bearing members. Built in three main portions: forward (including flight deck), centre and rear.

TAIL UNIT: Cantilever T tail, with sweepback on all surfaces; construction generally similar to that of wings. Curved dorsal fin, plus small underfin. A small horizontal strake is fitted on each side of rear fuselage, abreast of main fin, to assist airflow control. Trim tab in base of rudder. Small yaw damping control surface above rudder. Variable incidence tailplane, with elevators.

LANDING GEAR: Sumitomo retractable tricycle type, with single wheel and oleo-pneumatic shock absorber on each unit. Hydraulic actuation, controlled electrically. Emergency free-fall extension. Nosewheel, which is steerable by rudder pedals, retracts forward; main wheels retract inward into fuselage. Goodyear wheels, with Goodrich tyres, on all units. Goodyear brakes.

POWER PLANT: Two Pratt & Whitney Canada JT15D-5 turbofan engines, each rated at 12·9 kN (2,900 lb st) for take-off. Rohr thrust reversers optional. Total usable fuel capacity 3,134 litres (689 Imp gallons; 828 US gallons). One refuelling point in top of each wing, and one in rear fuselage for fuselage tank only, which can also be filled by transferring fuel from wing tanks using electric boost pump. Oil capacity 7·7 litres (2 US gallons).

ACCOMMODATION: Crew of two on flight deck. Standard layout seats seven passengers in pressurised cabin, with four tracking, reclining seats in facing pairs, each with integral headrest and armrest, and a three-place couch with reclining backrest. Side facing seat incorporating flushing toilet on starboard side at front. Baggage compartment at rear, capacity 272 kg (600 lb). Additional baggage space in tailcone area.

SYSTEMS: Pressurisation system, with max differential of 0·62 bars (9·0 lb/sq in). Backup pressurisation system, using engine bleed air, for use in emergency. Hydraulic system, pressure 103·5 bars (1,500 lb/sq in), for actuation of flaps, landing gear and other services. Each variable volume output engine driven pump has a maximum flow rate of 14·76 litres (3·9 US gallons)/min, and one pump can actuate all hydraulic systems. Reservoirs, capacity 4·16 litres (1·1 US gallons), pressurised by filtered engine bleed air at 1·03 bars (15 lb/sq in). All systems are, wherever possible, of modular conception: for example, entire hydraulic installation can be removed as a single unit. Stick shaker as backup stall warning device.

AVIONICS: Standard avionics include Sperry SPZ-900 integrated flight control system with pilot's AD-650A ADI and HSI with vertical gyro and gyro compass, AAR 3137 RMI, dual VHF-22A transceivers, dual VIR-32A VOR/ILS receivers, TDR-90 transponders, Collins ADF-60A, DME-42 and ALT-55B radio altimeter, Sperry Primus 300SL weather radar, and dual Gables G-6686 audio system. Optional avionics include second ADF-60A, second DME-42, Foster LNS-616A area navigation system with Loran C update, Global GNS-500A VLF/Omega navigation system, Sperry EDZ-601 flight director, Primus 400SL or Primus 800 weather radar, Sperry SPI-501 co-pilot's flight director, King KHF 950 HF transceiver, and Wulfsburg Flitefone VI.

Model of Beech's proof of concept eight-passenger light twin, now under development

Beechcraft Beechjet twin-turbofan business aircraft

DIMENSIONS, EXTERNAL:

Wing span	13·25 m (43 ft 6 in)
Wing aspect ratio	7·54
Length overall	14·75 m (48 ft 5 in)
Fuselage: Length	13·15 m (43 ft 2 in)
Max width	1·68 m (5 ft 6 in)
Max depth	1·85 m (6 ft 1 in)
Height overall	4·19 m (13 ft 9 in)
Tailplane span	5·00 m (16 ft 5 in)
Wheel track	2·84 m (9 ft 4 in)
Wheelbase	5·86 m (19 ft 3 in)
Crew/passenger door: Height	1·27 m (4 ft 2 in)
Width	0·71 m (2 ft 4 in)

DIMENSIONS, INTERNAL:

Cabin:	
Max length, incl flight deck	6·37 m (20 ft 11 in)
Length, excl flight deck	4·76 m (15 ft 7 in)
Max width	1·50 m (4 ft 11 in)
Max height	1·45 m (4 ft 9 in)
Volume: incl flight deck	11·33 m³ (400 cu ft)
excl flight deck	8·64 m³ (305 cu ft)
Baggage compartment volume	1·4 m³ (50 cu ft)

AREAS:

Wings, net	22·43 m² (241·4 sq ft)
Trailing-edge flaps (total)	5·22 m² (56·4 sq ft)
Spoilers (total)	0·57 m² (6·2 sq ft)
Fin, incl dorsal fin	5·91 m² (63·6 sq ft)
Rudder, incl yaw damper	1·12 m² (12·1 sq ft)
Tailplane	5·25 m² (56·5 sq ft)
Elevators, incl tab	1·56 m² (16·8 sq ft)

WEIGHTS AND LOADINGS:

Weight empty	4,202 kg (9,265 lb)
Basic operating weight, incl crew, avionics, interior fittings and typical options	4,502 kg (9,925 lb)
Max fuel weight	2,224 kg (4,904 lb)
Max T-O weight	7,157 kg (15,780 lb)
Max ramp weight	7,189 kg (15,850 lb)
Max zero-fuel weight	5,656 kg (12,470 lb)
Max landing weight	6,450 kg (14,220 lb)
Max wing loading	319·1 kg/m² (65·37 lb/sq in)
Max power loading	277·4 kg/kN (2·72 lb/lb st)

PERFORMANCE (at max T-O weight except where indicated):

Never-exceed speed	Mach 0·785
Max level speed at 8,840 m (29,000 ft)	461 knots (854 km/h; 531 mph)
Typical cruising speed at 11,890 m (39,000 ft)	439 knots (813 km/h; 505 mph)
Long-range cruising speed at 12,500 m (41,000 ft)	394 knots (730 km/h; 453 mph)
Stalling speed, flaps down, idling power	87 knots (161 km/h; 100 mph) IAS
Max operating altitude	12,500 m (41,000 ft)
FAA (FAR 25) T-O to 10·7 m (35 ft) at S/L, ISA	1,204 m (3,950 ft)
FAA landing distance from 15 m (50 ft) at S/L, ISA, max landing weight	893 m (2,930 ft)
Range with four passengers, max fuel, ISA, zero wind, with allowance for climb and descent, long-range cruise power:	
NBAA IFR reserves	1,550 nm (2,872 km; 1,785 miles)
NBAA VFR reserves	1,810 nm (3,354 km; 2,084 miles)
Range with seven passengers, ISA, zero wind, with allowance for climb and descent, long-range cruise power:	
NBAA VFR reserves	1,592 nm (2,952 km; 1,834 miles)

BEECH RESEARCH & DEVELOPMENT PROJECTS

Beech has announced brief details of research and development projects being undertaken by Burt Rutan and the Beech-owned subsidiary Scaled Composites Inc (see entry in this section). One is a medium-sized cabin class pressurised twin-engined design of pusher configuration which draws on technology developed for the Starship 1. It features composites construction and has a three-surface configuration with foreplane, swept wings with winglets and a swept T tail with ventral fin. Although intended initially to be powered by two piston engines in the 261 kW (350 hp) class, the airframe has been designed to be readily adaptable to rotary, turboprop or turbofan power plants. In piston engined form it would have a max T-O weight of approximately 3,402 kg (7,500 lb), carry eight passengers and have a cruising speed of 260 knots (482 km/h; 299 mph). A turbofan derivative, possibly powered by Williams turbofans of 8·00 kN (1,800 lb) thrust, would have a max T-O weight of 3,855 kg (8,500 lb) and a max cruising speed of Mach 0·72. In early 1986 a proof of concept prototype was under construction at SCI's Mojave, California, facility. A first flight is anticipated in early 1987 and a production decision could be taken before the end of that year, with customer deliveries commencing by 1989.

Also under development at Mojave in early 1986 was a prototype for an all-composite five-seat single piston engine aircraft, based on Mr Rutan's Design No. 81. The aircraft will be pressurised, seating the pilot alone ahead of two rows of passengers, and will also be of three-surface configuration. Power plant will be a 156·5 kW (210 hp) Avco Lycoming four-cylinder piston engine. Projected performance includes a cruising speed of 217 knots (402 km/h; 250 mph) at 7,620 m (25,000 ft) and range sufficient to fly from coast to coast across the United States unrefuelled. A prototype was expected to fly during 1986, with a production decision following in 1987.

ƷELL

ƷELL HELICOPTER TEXTRON INC (Subsidiary of Textron Inc)

'O Box 482, Fort Worth, Texas 76101
'elephone: (817) 280 2011

'RESIDENT: Leonard M. Horner
:XECUTIVE VICE-PRESIDENT: Webb F. Joiner
ENIOR VICE-PRESIDENTS:
Dwayne K. Jose (Corporate Relations)
Gainor J. Lindsey (Commercial Business, and General Manager, Customer Support and Service Division)
Robert R. Lynn (Research & Engineering)
Richard K. May (General Manager)
Charles R. Rudning (Government Business)
W. Clive Sloan (V-22 Programme Director)
'ICE-PRESIDENTS:
Charles E. Davis (Product Engineering)
Jan M. Drees (Technology)
George Galerstein (Law)
James A. Hamilton (Commercial Marketing)
Clifford J. Kalista (International Marketing)
James J. Kenna (Operations)
C. M. McKeen Jr (Materiel)
Stanley Martin (Development Engineering)
Phil C. Norwine (Market Development)
David Poster (Product Assurance)
Ray Swindell (Military Business Development)
Edmund Szol (Employee Relations)
George G. Troutman (Washington Operations)
)IRECTOR, PUBLIC AFFAIRS: Carl L. Harris
)IRECTOR, AMARILLO FACILITY: J. Alan Carmena Jr
ƷENERAL MANAGER, BELL HELICOPTER DE VENEZUELA CA: Ross Gutierrez
ΛANAGING DIRECTOR, BELL HELICOPTER ASIA LTD: William J. Maddox Jr

The business activities of Bell Helicopter Textron were onducted from 1970 until the end of 1981 as an unincorporated division of Textron Inc. Since 3 January 1982, the ame activities have been conducted by Bell Helicopter 'extron Inc, a wholly owned subsidiary of Textron Inc.

Available details of the range of military and commercial elicopters in current production, or under development, by ell Helicopter Textron are published in this entry. Several odels are also built under licence by Agusta in Italy and uji in Japan (which see). Korea Bell Helicopter Company KBHC, which see) will co-produce helicopters in the epublic of Korea with Bell Helicopter Textron and amsung Precision Industries Company.

In mid-1986 more than 7,500 people were employed by ell, which, with its licensees, has manufactured more than 0,000 helicopters. Of these, more than 9,000 were delivered r commercial use.

In October 1983 Bell Helicopter Canada (see entry in 'anadian section) was formed under a contract with the 'anadian government to establish a manufacturing plant at Airabel, near Montreal, Quebec. The Canadian facility will anufacture a new line of light twin-engined helicopters, eginning with the Model 400A/440 TwinRanger. The lant was due to be completed in early 1986. To make more pace available at Fort Worth for the V-22 Osprey rogramme, Bell intends to relocate its Model 206B JetRanger and Model 206L LongRanger production lines to Airabel. Completion of the transfer was expected by anuary 1987.

Bell Helicopter de Venezuela CA, a joint venture with Aaquinarias Mendoza CA and Aerotecnica SA, was established in early 1984, in Caracas, to provide marketing and ipport services in Venezuela. Bell Helicopter Asia Ltd, ormed in October 1983 in conjunction with Inchcape viation Corporation, is a Singapore-based company oviding marketing and support for the Southeast Asia egion.

BELL MODEL 205

'S military designations: UH-1D/H/V, EH-1H and HH-1H Iroquois

anadian military designation: CH-118 Iroquois

Although basically similar to the earlier Model 204 (see 971-72 *Jane's*), the Model 205 introduced a longer iselage, increased cabin space to accommodate a much rger number of passengers, and other changes. Details of e full range of military variants have been recorded in revious editions of *Jane's*. The final production version is e **UH-1H**. Deliveries of this version to the US Army egan in September 1967 and totalled 3,573. Production of e UH-1H continued subsequently to satisfy export orders, hich totalled 1,317 by Spring 1985. It ended temporarily in ecember 1980, but was restarted in order to build 55 for urkey. Deliveries of these will continue until October 987. The Model 205 is also manufactured by Agusta in aly, and (as the HU-1H) by Fuji in Japan. In addition, nder a licensing agreement, 118 UH-1Hs were produced r the Nationalist Chinese Army, with much of the anufacturing and assembly carried out by AIDC (which e).

Up to FY 1980, a total of $47 million was provided to odify UH-1Hs to **EH-1H** electronic countermeasures onfiguration, with the Quick Fix I airborne communications interception, emitter locating and jamming system, cluding an AN/APR-39V2 radar warning receiver,

Bell Model 205 Iroquois helicopter of the Indonesian Army

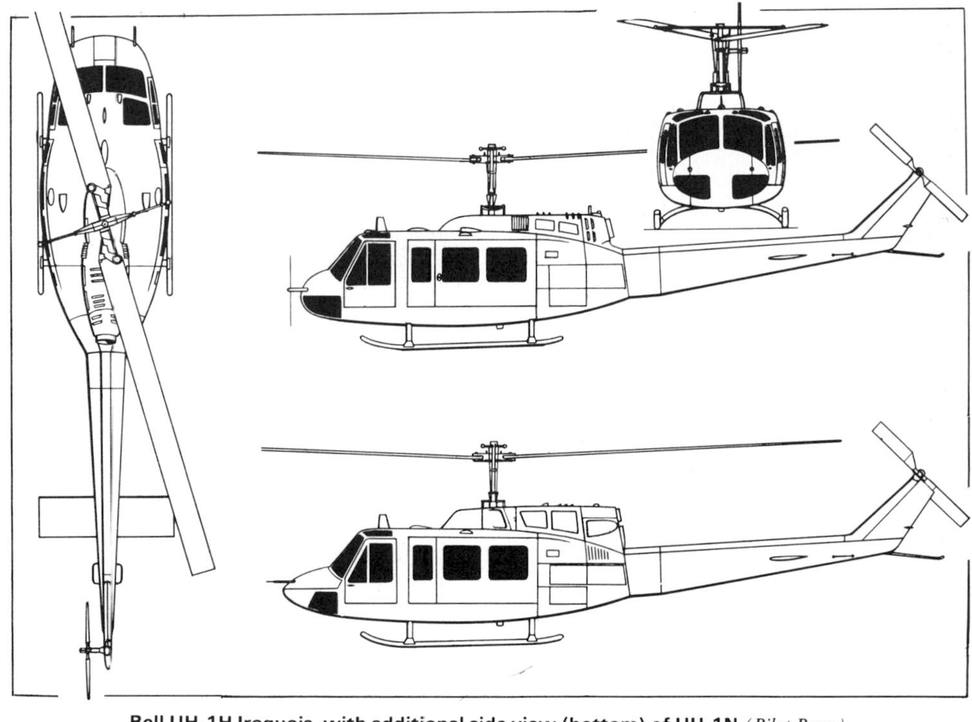
Bell UH-1H Iroquois, with additional side view (bottom) of UH-1N *(Pilot Press)*

XM130 chaff/flare dispenser and AN/ALQ-144 infra-red jammer. The FY 1981 budget added $5·1 million to convert initial Quick Fix IA systems in the EH-1H to Phase IB configuration, plus survivability equipment to protect the aircraft against known and postulated threats, including hot metal/plume suppression. By April 1981, three of the EH-1Hs had been delivered, with seven more to follow. However, the Quick Fix mission has been taken over by the much larger Sikorsky EH-60A version of the Black Hawk utility transport helicopter, which is able to carry an 816 kg (1,800 lb) electronics package.

About 220 UH-1Hs have been converted by US Army Electronics Command to **UH-1V** medevac configuration. Avionics and equipment in this version include a radio altimeter, AEL AN/ARN-124 DME, glideslope and rescue hoist.

The US Army plans to retain at least 2,700 improved UH-1Hs in service beyond the year 2000 to perform such operations as resupply, troop transport, command and control, electronic warfare, medical evacuation and minefield emplacement. To make such a plan realistic, a product improvement programme for the Army's UH-1H fleet introduced improved or new avionics and equipment including an AN/ALQ-144 infra-red jammer, AN/APN-209 radar altimeter, AN/APR-39 radar warning receiver, AN/ARC-164 UHF/AM radio, AN/ARN-124 DME, XM130 chaff/flare dispenser, NOE communications (FM/HF), communications security, infra-red suppressor (hot metal and plume), altimeter lighting (5V), crashworthy auxiliary fuel system, closed circuit refuelling, fuel tank vent, improved main input driveshaft, and main rotor mast plug. In addition, it is planned to introduce, as a minimum, new composite main rotor blades; improved stabiliser bar, tail rotor hub and servo cylinders; a split engine deck, and improved oil filtration; a night vision compatible cockpit; built-in Vibrex connections; an improved AN/ASN-43 gyro magnetic compass; and Doppler navigation.

A US Army Request for Proposal for composite main rotor blades for the UH-1H was issued on 16 November 1981. The Army's schedule called for a qualified blade to be ready for production after 32 months. Procurement of 6,000 blades is anticipated in 1985-89, at a cost of $20,000 or less per blade in FY 1981 dollars. Bell tendered a joint proposal with Boeing Vertol and this team was awarded a $19 million development contract during 1982 by the US Army Aviation Research and Development Command. Bell has designed the composite blade for the UH-1H, but both companies are fabricating test blades and supporting laboratory and flight testing to ensure compliance with Army requirements. Bell has provided manufacturing tools and fixtures and transferred specific manufacturing knowledge to Boeing Vertol, so that both companies are equally capable and qualified to manufacture production blades, for which contracts are expected to exceed $100 million. The first flight of the composite rotor blades on a UH-1H took place in early 1985. Production deliveries were scheduled to begin in 1986.

The following details apply to the military UH-1H in its current form:

TYPE: Single-rotor general purpose helicopter.

ROTOR SYSTEM: Two-blade semi-rigid main rotor. Interchangeable blades, built up of extruded aluminium spars and laminates, now being replaced by new composite blades, with unidirectional glassfibre roving spar, afterbody of glassfibre skin over a Nomex honeycomb core, unidirectional glassfibre roving trailing-edge, and a polyurethane leading-edge abrasion strip. A stainless steel sheath under this strip on the outboard portion of the blade reinforces the inertia weight attachment and enhances tree cutting capability. Stabilising bar above and at right angles to main rotor blades. Underslung feathering axis head. Two-blade all-metal tail rotor of honeycomb construction. Blades do not fold.

ROTOR DRIVE: Shaft drive to both main and tail rotors. Transmission rating 820 kW (1,100 shp). Main rotor rpm 294-324.

FUSELAGE: Conventional all-metal semi-monocoque structure.

TAIL SURFACE: Small synchronised elevator on rear fuselage is connected to the cyclic control to increase allowable CG travel.

LANDING GEAR: Tubular skid type. Lock-on ground handling wheels and inflated nylon float bags available.

POWER PLANT: One 1,044 kW (1,400 shp) Avco Lycoming T53-L-13 turboshaft engine, mounted aft of the transmission on top of the fuselage and enclosed in cowlings. Five interconnected rubber fuel cells, total capacity 844 litres (223 US gallons), of which 799 litres (211 US gallons) are usable. Overload fuel capacity of 1,935 litres (511 US gallons) usable, obtained by installation of kit comprising two 568 litre (150 US gallon) internal auxiliary fuel tanks interconnected with the basic fuel system.

ACCOMMODATION: Pilot and 11-14 troops, or six litters and a medical attendant, or 1,759 kg (3,880 lb) of freight. Crew doors open forward and are jettisonable. Two doors on each side of cargo compartment; front door is hinged to open forward and is removable, rear door slides aft. Forced air ventilation system.

AVIONICS AND EQUIPMENT: FM, UHF, VHF radio sets, IFF transponder, Gyromatic compass system, direction finder set, VOR receiver and intercom standard. Optional nav/com systems. Standard equipment includes bleed air heater and defroster, comprehensive range of engine and flight instruments, power plant fire detection system, 30V 300A DC starter/generator, navigation, landing and anti-collision lights, controllable searchlight, hydraulically boosted controls. Optional equipment includes external cargo hook, auxiliary fuel tanks, rescue hoist, 150,000 BTU muff heater.

DIMENSIONS, EXTERNAL:
Main rotor diameter — 14·63 m (48 ft 0 in)
Tail rotor diameter — 2·59 m (8 ft 6 in)
Main rotor blade chord — 0·53 m (1 ft 9 in)
Tail rotor blade chord — 0·213 m (8·4 in)
Length:
overall (main rotor fore and aft) — 17·62 m (57 ft 9⅝ in)
fuselage — 12·77 m (41 ft 10¾ in)
Height:
overall, tail rotor turning (excl fin tip antenna) — 4·41 m (14 ft 5½ in)
to top of main rotor head — 3·60 m (11 ft 9¾ in)
Stabiliser span — 2·84 m (9 ft 4 in)
Width over skids — 2·91 m (9 ft 6½ in)

DIMENSIONS, INTERNAL:
Cabin: Max width — 2·34 m (7 ft 8 in)
Max height — 1·25 m (4 ft 1¼ in)
Volume (excl flight deck) — approx 6·23 m³ (220 cu ft)

AREAS:
Main rotor disc — 168·11 m² (1,809·56 sq ft)
Tail rotor disc — 5·27 m² (56·7 sq ft)

WEIGHTS AND LOADINGS:
Weight empty, equipped — 2,363 kg (5,210 lb)
Basic operating weight (troop carrier mission) — 2,520 kg (5,557 lb)
Mission weight — 4,100 kg (9,039 lb)
Max T-O and landing weight — 4,309 kg (9,500 lb)
Max zero-fuel weight — 3,660 kg (8,070 lb)
Max disc loading — 25·6 kg/m² (5·25 lb/sq ft)
Max power loading — 4·13 kg/kW (8·63 lb/shp)

PERFORMANCE (at max T-O weight):
Never-exceed speed — 110 knots (204 km/h; 127 mph)
Max level and cruising speed — 110 knots (204 km/h; 127 mph)
Econ cruising speed at 1,735 m (5,700 ft) — 110 knots (204 km/h; 127 mph)
Max rate of climb at S/L — 488 m (1,600 ft)/min
Service ceiling — 3,840 m (12,600 ft)
Hovering ceiling: IGE — 4,145 m (13,600 ft)
OGE — 1,220 m (4,000 ft)
Range with max fuel, no allowances, no reserves, at S/L — 276 nm (511 km; 318 miles)

BELL MODEL 206B JETRANGER III

In the Summer of 1977, Bell began delivery of the Model 206B JetRanger III, which subsequently replaced in production the lower-powered JetRanger II, of which 1,619 were delivered.

Power plant of the JetRanger III is the Allison 250-C20 turboshaft, which Bell was able to install with minimal modification of the original airframe to meet requests for higher performance under hot day/high altitude conditions. This enables Bell to offer modification kits to convert JetRanger IIs to JetRanger III standard.

Under a succession of major contracts, Beech Aircraft has produced airframes for all US built commercial and military versions of the JetRanger, the first airframe being delivered to Bell on 1 March 1968. The work involves manufacture of the fuselage, skid gear, tailboom, spars, stabiliser and two rear fairing assemblies. Licence production of JetRangers is undertaken by Agusta in Italy.

By January 1986, Bell and its licensees had manufactured well over 7,000 helicopters of the Model 206 series, more than 4,600 of them for commercial customers. Recent orders include seven for the Royal Thai Army, which were delivered by August 1985, and 16 for the Brazilian Navy's pilot training school at the San Pedro São Padro D'Aldea Naval Air Base, deliveries of which were completed in December 1985. Manufacture of the Model 206B is scheduled for eventual transfer to the Mirabel facility in Canada, according to a Bell announcement in July 1986.

TYPE: Turbine powered general purpose light helicopter.

ROTOR SYSTEM: Two-blade semi-rigid seesaw type main rotor, employing pre-coning and underslinging to ensure smooth operation. Blades are of standard Bell 'droop snoot' section. They have a D-shape aluminium spar, bonded aluminium alloy skin, honeycomb core and a trailing-edge extension. Each blade is connected to the head by means of a grip, pitch change bearings and a tension-torsion strap assembly. Two tail rotor blades have bonded aluminium skin but no core. Main rotor blades do not fold, but modification to permit manual folding is possible. Rotor brake available as optional kit.

ROTOR DRIVE: Rotors driven through tubular steel alloy shafts with spliced couplings. Initial drive from engine through 90° spiral bevel gear to single-stage planetary main gearbox. Shaft to tail rotor single-stage bevel gearbox. Freewheeling unit ensures that main rotor continues to drive tail rotor when engine is disengaged. Main rotor/engine rpm ratio 1 : 15; main rotor rpm 374-394. Tail rotor/engine rpm ratio 1 : 2·3.

FUSELAGE: Forward cabin section is made up of two aluminium alloy beams and 25 mm (1 in) thick aluminium honeycomb sandwich. Rotor, transmission and engine are supported by upper longitudinal beams. Upper and lower structures are interconnected by three fuselage bulkheads and a centrepost to form an integrated structure. Intermediate section is of aluminium alloy semi-monocoque construction. Aluminium monocoque tailboom.

TAIL UNIT: Fixed stabiliser of aluminium monocoque construction, with inverted aerofoil section. Fixed vertical tail fin in sweptback upper and ventral sections, made of aluminium honeycomb with aluminium alloy skin.

LANDING GEAR: Aluminium alloy tubular skids bolted to extruded cross-tubes. Tubular steel skid on ventral fin to protect tail rotor in tail-down landing. Special high skid gear (0·25 m; 10 in greater ground clearance) available for use in areas with high brush. Pontoons or stowed floats, capable of in-flight inflation, available as optional kits.

POWER PLANT: One 313 kW (420 shp) Allison 250-C20J turboshaft engine, flat rated at 236 kW (317 shp). Rupture resistant fuel tank below and behind rear passenger seat, capacity 344 litres (91 US gallons). Refuelling point on starboard side of fuselage, aft of cabin. Oil capacity 5·2 litres (5·5 US quarts).

ACCOMMODATION: Two seats side by side in front and rear bench seat for three persons. Dual controls optional. Two forward hinged doors on each side, made of formed aluminium alloy with transparent panels (bulged on rear pair). Baggage compartment aft of rear seats, capacity 113 kg (250 lb), with external door on port side.

SYSTEMS: Hydraulic system, pressure 41·5 bars (600 lb/sq in), for cyclic, collective and directional controls. Maximum flow rate 7·57 litres (2 US gallons)/min. Open reservoir. Electrical supply from 150A starter/generator. One 24V 13Ah nickel-cadmium battery.

AVIONICS AND EQUIPMENT: Full range of avionics available in form of optional kits, including VHF communications and omni navigation kit, ADF, DME, R/Nav, transponder and intercom and speaker system. Standard equipment includes cabin fire extinguisher, first aid kit, door locks, night lighting, and dynamic flapping restraints. Optional items include clock, engine hour meter, turn and slip indicator, custom seating, internal litter kit, cabin heater, environmental control system, camera access door, high intensity night lights, engine fire detection system, and external cargo sling of 680 kg (1,500 lb) capacity.

DIMENSIONS, EXTERNAL:
Main rotor diameter — 10·16 m (33 ft 4 in)
Tail rotor diameter — 1·65 m (5 ft 5 in)
Main rotor blade chord — 0·33 m (1 ft 1 in)
Distance between rotor centres — 5·96 m (19 ft 6½ in)
Length: overall, rotors turning — 11·82 m (38 ft 9½ in)
fuselage, incl tailskid — 9·50 m (31 ft 2 in)
Height: over tail fin — 2·54 m (8 ft 4 in)
overall — 2·91 m (9 ft 6½ in)
Stabiliser span — 1·97 m (6 ft 5¾ in)
Width over skids — 1·92 m (6 ft 3½ in)

DIMENSIONS, INTERNAL:
Cabin: Length — 2·13 m (7 ft 0 in)
Max width — 1·27 m (4 ft 2 in)
Max height — 1·28 m (4 ft 3 in)
Volume — 1·13 m³ (40 cu ft)
Baggage compartment volume — 0·45 m³ (16 cu ft)

AREAS:
Main rotor blades (total) — 3·35 m² (36·1 sq ft)
Tail rotor blades (total) — 0·22 m² (2·37 sq ft)
Main rotor disc — 81·07 m² (872·7 sq ft)
Tail rotor disc — 2·14 m² (23·04 sq ft)
Stabiliser — 0·90 m² (9·65 sq ft)

WEIGHTS:
Weight empty, standard configuration — 742 kg (1,635 lb)
Max T-O weight — 1,451 kg (3,200 lb)

PERFORMANCE (at max T-O weight, ISA):
Never-exceed speed at S/L — 122 knots (225 km/h; 140 mph)
Max cruising speed:
at 1,525 m (5,000 ft) — 116 knots (216 km/h; 134 mph)
at S/L — 115 knots (214 km/h; 133 mph)
Max rate of climb at S/L — 384 m (1,260 ft)/min
Vertical rate of climb at S/L — 91 m (300 ft)/min
Service ceiling — 4,115 m (13,500 ft)
Hovering ceiling: IGE — 3,900 m (12,800 ft)
OGE — 2,680 m (8,800 ft)
Range with max fuel and max payload:
at S/L, no reserves — 364 nm (674 km; 419 miles)
at 1,525 m (5,000 ft), no reserves — 404 nm (748 km; 465 miles)

Bell Model 206B JetRanger III of the Chengdu Aviation Academy in the People's Republic of China

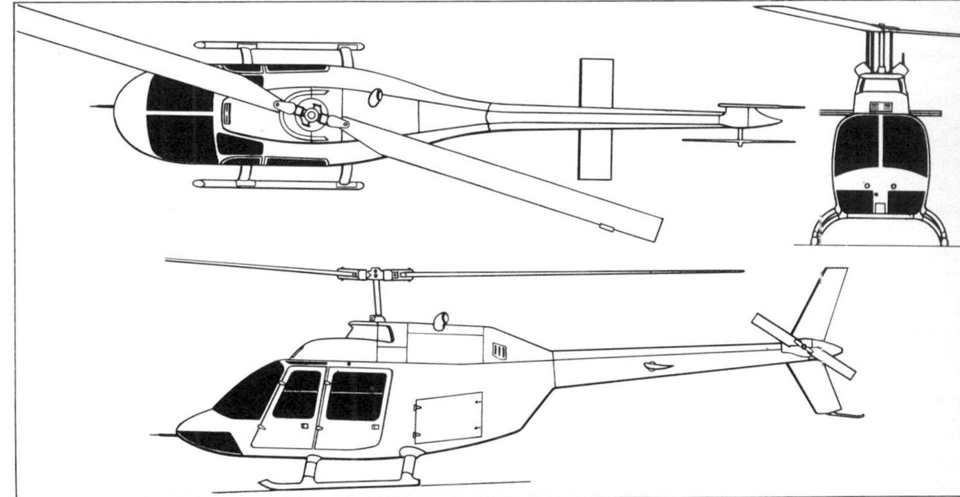

Bell 206B JetRanger III (Allison 250-C20J turboshaft engine) *(Pilot Press)*

BELL SEARANGER

US Navy designation: TH-57

The SeaRanger is a US Navy training version of the JetRanger. Three versions have been procured, as follows:

TH-57A. Designation of 40 'off the shelf' Model 206A JetRanger IIs (Allison 250-C18 engine), delivered in 1968 for primary training duties with Training Squadron HT-8 at NAS Whiting Field, Milton, Florida. Thirty-four still in service in 1982.

TH-57B. New production primary training version, based on Model 206B JetRanger III (see previous entry). Standard configuration includes 17Ah battery, force trim system, second anti-collision light, closed circuit refuelling, heavy duty skid shoes, modified tailskid, fire detection system, flashing nav light, VOR transceiver provision and equipment with Omni/LOC indicator, and guarded starter switch on collective pitch lever. Total of 51 ordered; deliveries completed in December 1985.

TH-57C. New production advanced instrument training version, also based on 206B JetRanger III. Configuration as for primary trainer, plus full IFR instrument panel, Sfena Ministab ASE, Parker Hannifin environmental control unit, dual electrical system, jettisonable doors, rotor brake, and provision for external cargo hook. Fifty-five ordered initially in January 1982, for service with Training Squadron HT-18 at NAS Whiting Field. Total subsequently increased to 89, of which all were delivered by December 1984.

WEIGHTS (A: TH-57A, C: TH-57C):

Weight empty: A — 699 kg (1,541 lb)
C — 840 kg (1,852 lb)
Max T-O weight:
A, internal load — 1,315 kg (2,900 lb)
C, internal load — 1,451 kg (3,200 lb)
C, external load — 1,519 kg (3,350 lb)

PERFORMANCE (TH-57C at 1,360 kg; 3,000 lb AUW, ISA):

Max cruising speed at S/L — 114 knots (211 km/h; 131 mph)
Max rate of climb at S/L — 469 m (1,540 ft)/min
Max vertical rate of climb at S/L — 213 m (700 ft)/min
Range with max fuel:
at S/L — 374 nm (693 km; 430 miles)
at 3,050 m (10,000 ft) — 458 nm (848 km; 527 miles)

BELL KIOWA

US Army designation: OH-58
Canadian military designation: CH-136

On 8 March 1968 the US Army named Bell as winner of its reopened light observation helicopter competition, and awarded the company the first increment of a total order for 2,200 **OH-58A** Kiowa aircraft, generally similar to the Model 206A and each powered by a 236·5 kW (317 shp) Allison T63-A-700 turboshaft engine. Major difference concerns the main rotor, that of the Kiowa having an increased diameter. There are also differences in the internal layout and avionics. The first OH-58A was delivered to the US Army on 23 May 1969 and deployment in Viet-Nam began in the early Autumn of 1969.

Seventy-four COH-58As, generally similar to the OH-58A, were delivered to the Canadian Armed Forces, and are now designated **CH-136**. Fourteen of them, used for basic helicopter pilot training at Portage la Prairie, Manitoba, were replaced by 14 new JetRanger IIIs from May 1981, and reissued to other units.

Under a co-production agreement with the Australian government 56 Model 206B-1 Kiowa military light observation helicopters (similar to the OH-58A) were delivered over an eight-year period. The initial 12 206B-1s were built by Bell. Commonwealth Aircraft Corporation was prime Australian licensee, with responsibility for final assembly of the remainder. Only the engines and avionics were supplied from US sources. Delivery of 12 **OH-58Bs** to the Austrian Air Force was completed in 1976.

Under a US Army development qualification contract placed on 30 June 1976, Bell converted an OH-58A to an improved standard, under the designation **OH-58C**. This involved installation of a flat glass canopy to reduce glint, an uprated Allison T63-A-720 turboshaft engine, and an IR reduction package. Two additional OH-58As were modified to OH-58C configuration, for pre-production flight testing by Bell and the US Army, and production modification of 435 OH-58As to OH-58C standard was completed in March 1985 at Bell Helicopter's Amarillo plant. An additional 150 modifications were carried out by Israel Aircraft Industries (IAI) for the US Army in West Germany. The final configuration includes a new instrument panel, modifications to reduce vulnerability in combat, CONUS (continental US) navigation equipment, day optics, improved avionics and improved maintenance features. The additional power significantly improves high-altitude, hot-weather performance.

In September 1985 Bell began to deliver to the US Army improved tail rotor configuration kits for installation in the OH-58A and OH-58C. The kit increases the amount of tail rotor thrust available, giving the pilot more capability to correct an uncommanded yaw at low speeds, as experienced during nap-of-the-earth flying.

Details of the US Army programme under which OH-58As are being converted to **OH-58D** near-term scout helicopter standard are given in a separate entry on the Bell Model 406 (AHIP).

The following details apply specifically to the OH-58C:

TYPE: Turbine powered light observation helicopter.

ROTOR SYSTEM: As described for JetRanger III.

ROTOR DRIVE: Transmission improvements include a four-pinion upper planetary, with new thrust bearing and 'fly dry' capability. Shaft to tail rotor single-stage bevel gearbox protected by cover. Main rotor/engine rpm ratio 1 : 17·44; main rotor rpm 354. Tail rotor/engine rpm ratio 1 : 2·353. Otherwise as described for JetRanger III.

FUSELAGE: As described for JetRanger III. A low-glare canopy design reduces the solar glint signature. The windscreens are slightly convex to assist rain removal and increase their strength.

TAIL UNIT AND LANDING GEAR: As described for JetRanger III.

POWER PLANT: One 313 kW (420 shp) Allison T63-A-720 turboshaft engine. 'Black Hole' exhaust stacks and hot metal shroud for infra-red suppression. Fuel tank below and behind aft passenger seat, total usable capacity 276 litres (73 US gallons). Refuelling point on starboard side of fuselage, aft of cabin. Oil capacity 5·6 litres (1·5 US gallons).

ACCOMMODATION: Forward crew compartment seats pilot and co-pilot/observer side by side. Entrance to this compartment is provided by single door on each side of fuselage. The cargo/passenger compartment, which has its own doors, one on each side, provides approximately 1·13 m³ (40 cu ft) of cargo space, or provision for two passengers by installation of two seat cushions, seat belts and shoulder harnesses. A redesigned instrument panel houses new avionics, and all flight instruments have been modified for night operations using night vision goggles. An improved defrost/defog air circulation system increases the aircraft's mission readiness.

SYSTEMS: As described for JetRanger III.

AVIONICS: C-6533/ARC intercommunication subsystem, AN/ARC-114 VHF-FM, AN/ARC-115 VHF-AM, AN/ARC-116 UHF-AM, AN/ARN-89 ADF, AN/ASN-43 gyro magnetic compass, AN/APX-100 IFF transponder, TSEC/KY-28 communications security set, C-8157/ARC control indication, MT-3802/ARC mounting, TS-1843/APX transponder test set and mounting, KIT-1A/TSEC computer and mounting, duplicate AN/ARC-114, AN/APR-39 radar warning, ID-1351 C/A HBI, ID-1347 C/ARN CDI; and provisions for AN/ARN-123(V)1 CONUS nav, AN/APN-209 radar altimeter and YG-1054 proximity warning.

ARMAMENT: Standard equipment is the M27 armament kit, utilising the 7·62 mm Minigun.

DIMENSIONS, EXTERNAL: As JetRanger III, except:

Main rotor diameter — 10·77 m (35 ft 4 in)
Length: overall, rotors turning — 12·49 m (40 ft 11¾ in)
fuselage — 9·93 m (32 ft 7 in)

AREAS: As JetRanger III, except:

Main rotor blades (total) — 3·55 m² (38·26 sq ft)
Main rotor disc — 90·93 m² (978·8 sq ft)

WEIGHTS AND LOADINGS (A: OH-58A; C: OH-58C):

Weight empty: A — 664 kg (1,464 lb)
C — 825 kg (1,818 lb)
Operating weight: A — 1,049 kg (2,313 lb)
C — 1,104 kg (2,434 lb)
Max T-O and landing weight: A — 1,360 kg (3,000 lb)
C — 1,451 kg (3,200 lb)
Max zero-fuel weight: A — 1,145 kg (2,525 lb)
C — 1,200 kg (2,646 lb)
Max disc loading: A — 14·9 kg/m² (3·07 lb/sq ft)
C — 15·9 kg/m² (3·27 lb/sq ft)

PERFORMANCE (A: OH-58A at observation mission gross weight of 1,255 kg; 2,768 lb, ISA, except where indicated; C: OH-58C at mission gross weight of 1,311 kg; 2,890 lb):

Never-exceed speed at S/L:
A, C — 120 knots (222 km/h; 138 mph)
Cruising speed for max range:
A, C — 102 knots (188 km/h; 117 mph)
Loiter speed for max endurance:
A, C — 49 knots (91 km/h; 56 mph)
Max rate of climb at S/L: A — 543 m (1,780 ft)/min
C — 549 m (1,800 ft)/min
Service ceiling: A — 5,760 m (18,900 ft)
C — 5,640 m (18,500 ft)
Hovering ceiling: IGE: A — 4,145 m (13,600 ft)
C — 4,025 m (13,200 ft)
OGE: A — 2,680 m (8,800 ft)
C — 2,955 m (9,700 ft)
OGE (armed scout mission):
A at 1,360 kg (3,000 lb) — 1,830 m (6,000 ft)
C at 1,451 kg (3,200 lb) — 2,500 m (8,200 ft)
Max range at S/L, 10% reserves:
A, C — 259 nm (481 km; 299 miles)
Max range at S/L, armed scout mission at 1,451 kg (3,200 lb), no reserves: C — 264 nm (490 km; 305 miles)
Endurance at S/L, no reserves: A, C — 3 h 30 min

BELL MODEL 406 (AHIP)

US Army designation: OH-58D

The US Army announced on 21 September 1981 that Bell's Model 406 proposal had been selected as winner of its Army Helicopter Improvement Program (AHIP) competition to develop a near-term scout helicopter. Its configuration includes a mast mounted sight developed by McDonnell Douglas Astronautics in association with Northrop's Electro-Mechanical Division, and a cockpit control and display subsystem by Sperry Flight Systems. The US Army plans to modify at least 578 existing OH-58A Kiowa helicopters in 1985-91, under the designation OH-58D, at an estimated cost of $2,000 million. This will provide the Army with a force of close combat aerial reconnaissance helicopters capable of intelligence gathering and surveillance as well as supporting attack helicopter missions and directing artillery fire. In addition, the OH-58D has demonstrated its capability in a helicopter air-to-air combat role, using the onboard defensive missiles.

Bell was awarded an initial $151 million development contract, and the first of five prototypes made its first flight on 6 October 1983. US Army development and operational test programmes began in July 1984, at Yuma and at Edwards AFB, California, and were completed in February 1985. A contract for long-lead items to convert the first 16 aircraft was received on 25 July 1983, followed by larger contracts which authorised procurement of these Lot 1 OH-58Ds and, successively, of Lot 2 (44 aircraft), for delivery between July 1986 and May 1987, and Lot 3 (56 aircraft) for delivery during FY 1987. A further 60 conversions are requested in the FY 1987 budget proposals. Two OH-58Ds were delivered in December 1985, with completion of deliveries of the first 16 helicopters anticipated in June 1986.

On 21 May 1984 Bell announced development of a lighter and simplified two/five-seat combat helicopter, with a four-blade soft-in-plane rotor and quick-change weapons systems, known as the **Model 406CS (Combat Scout)**. It flew for the first time in June 1984. This multi-mission helicopter omits the MMS, specialised avionics and integrated multiplex cockpit of the AHIP 406, but incorporates many OH-58D (AHIP) features including a 548 kW (735 shp) Allison 250-C34R engine, AHIP dynamics and drive train, mated to a damage-resistant, 10,000 hour fail-safe four-blade rigid rotor of composites construction and a high-thrust composites tail rotor. Armament can comprise four TOW 2 anti-tank missiles, or a mix of Stinger air-to-air missiles, 70 mm rockets and 7·62 mm or 0·50 in machine-guns. Empty and max T-O weights are 1,035 kg (2,283 lb) and 2,041 kg (4,500 lb); hovering ceilings are 4,360 m (15,200 ft) IGE and 3,290 m (10,800 ft) OGE; range is 213 nm (394 km; 245 miles), and endurance 2 h 30 min. Max and cruising speeds are 124 knots (230 km/h; 143 mph) and 120 knots (222 km/h; 138 mph) respectively.

The following specification applies to the OH-58D:

TYPE: Two-seat scout helicopter.

ROTOR SYSTEM: Four-blade soft-in-plane main rotor. Blade section BHTI M406183. Glassfibre composite blades, with hollow spar, and afterbody skins supported by Nomex honeycomb core. Main rotor head has glassfibre yoke and elastomeric bearings. Each blade attached to head by two side by side pins. Main rotor blades fold and have a bendable tab at 60 per cent radius. No rotor brake. Two-blade non-lubricated tail rotor on port side of tailboom; blades of glassfibre composite with nickel coated abrasion strip.

ROTOR DRIVE: Steel spiral bevel and planetary gear transmissions in aluminium and magnesium cast housings. Transmission rating 454 kW (609 shp) maximum, 339 kW (455 shp) continuous. Main gearbox beneath main rotor, tail rotor gearbox at tail rotor. Main rotor/engine rpm ratio 0·065668:1. Tail rotor/engine rpm ratio 0·39584:1.

Bell OH-58D (AHIP) with mast mounted sight

Fuselage: Stressed aluminium semi-monocoque fail-safe structure incorporating skins, longerons, two upper longitudinal roof beams and a lower curved honeycomb sandwich underfuselage panel. Tapered stressed aluminium semi-monocoque tailboom, composed of bulkheads and skins.

Tail Unit: Fixed stabiliser of aluminium monocoque construction with inverted aerofoil section on starboard side of tailboom. Fixed vertical fin in sweptback upper and ventral sections.

Landing Gear: Light alloy tubular skids bolted to extruded cross-tubes.

Power Plant: One Allison 250-C30R turboshaft engine, with an intermediate power rating of 485 kW (650 shp) at S/L ISA. One self-sealing crash resistant fuel cell, capacity 399 litres (105·4 US gallons) located aft of the cabin area. Refuelling point on starboard side of fuselage. Oil capacity 5·7 litres (1·5 US gallons).

Accommodation: Pilot and co-pilot/observer seated side by side. Door on each side of fuselage. Accommodation is heated and ventilated. Avionics in rear of cabin.

Systems: Single hydraulic system, pressure 69 bars (1,000 lb/sq in) for main and tail rotor controls and SCAS system. Maximum flow rate 11·36 litres (3 US gallons)/min. Open-type reservoir. Primary electrical power provided by 10kVA 400Hz three-phase 120/208V AC alternator with 200A 28V DC transformer/rectifier unit for secondary DC power. Backup power provided by 500VA 400Hz single-phase 115V AC solid state inverter and 200A 28V DC starter/generator.

Avionics and Equipment: Multi-function displays for vertical and horizontal situation indication, mast mounted sight day/night viewing and communications control, with selection via control column handgrip switches. Five com transceivers, data link and secure voice equipment. Doppler, strapdown INS. Equipped for day/night VFR. Mast mounted sight houses 12x magnification TV camera, auto-focusing IR thermal imaging sensor and laser rangefinder/designator, with automatic target tracking and in-flight automatic boresighting. Night vision goggles; AHRS; and airborne target handoff subsystem (ATHS).

Armament: Two Stinger air-to-air missiles in pack on starboard side of cabin. Provision for similar pack on port side.

Dimensions, external:

Main rotor diameter	10·67 m (35 ft 0 in)
Main rotor blade chord	0·24 m (9½ in)
Tail rotor diameter	1·65 m (5 ft 5 in)
Length: overall, rotors turning	12·85 m (42 ft 2 in)
fuselage, excl rotors	10·31 m (33 ft 10 in)
Width, rotors folded	1·97 m (6 ft 5½ in)
Height: to top of rotor head	2·59 m (8 ft 6 in)
overall	3·90 m (12 ft 9½ in)
Skid track	1·88 m (6 ft 2 in)
Cabin doors (port and stbd, each):	
Height	1·04 m (3 ft 5 in)
Width	0·91 m (3 ft 0 in)
Height to sill	0·66 m (2 ft 2 in)

Areas:

Main rotor blades (each)	1·30 m² (13·95 sq ft)
Tail rotor blades (each)	0·13 m² (1·43 sq ft)
Main rotor disc	89·37 m² (962·0 sq ft)
Tail rotor disc	2·14 m² (23·04 sq ft)
Fin	0·85 m² (9·1 sq ft)
Stabiliser (stbd)	0·90 m² (9·74 sq ft)

Weights and Loadings:

Weight empty	1,281 kg (2,825 lb)
Max fuel weight	321 kg (707 lb)
Max T-O and landing weight	2,041 kg (4,500 lb)
Max zero-fuel weight	1,711 kg (3,773 lb)
Max disc loading	22·95 kg/m² (4·7 lb/sq ft)
Max power loading	6·27 kg/kW (10·3 lb/shp)

Performance (at max T-O weight, 'clean'):

Never-exceed speed	130 knots (241 km/h; 149 mph)
Max level speed at 1,220 m (4,000 ft)	128 knots (237 km/h; 147 mph)
Max cruising speed at 610 m (2,000 ft)	120 knots (222 km/h; 138 mph)
Econ cruising speed at 1,220 m (4,000 ft)	110 knots (204 km/h; 127 mph)
Max rate of climb: at S/L, ISA	469 m (1,540 ft)/min
at 1,220 m (4,000 ft), 35°C (95°F)	over 152 m (500 ft)/min
Vertical rate of climb: at S/L, ISA	232 m (760 ft)/min
at 1,220 m (4,000 ft), 35°C (95°F)	over 152 m (500 ft)/min
Service ceiling	over 3,660 m (12,000 ft)
Hovering ceiling: IGE, ISA	over 3,660 m (12,000 ft)
OGE, ISA	3,415 m (11,200 ft)
OGE, 35°C (95°F)	1,735 m (5,700 ft)
Range with max fuel, no reserves	300 nm (556 km; 345 miles)
Endurance	2 h 30 min

BELL TWINRANGER

Full details of the Model 400A/440 TwinRanger programme can now be found under the Bell Helicopter Canada entry in the Canadian section.

Bell Model 406CS Combat Scout, armed with 70 mm rocket pack and pod containing two 7·62 mm machine-guns

BELL MODEL 206L-3 LONGRANGER III

Announced on 25 September 1973, Bell's LongRanger was intended to satisfy a requirement for a turbine powered general purpose light helicopter in a size and performance range between the five-seat JetRanger II and 15-seat Model 205A-1. It incorporates Bell's Noda-Matic cabin suspension system, which gives a substantial reduction in rotor-induced vibration and results in a standard of comfort comparable with that of turboprop powered fixed-wing aircraft.

The current production **Model 206L-3 LongRanger III**, developed during 1981, has a 485 kW (650 shp) Allison 250-C30P engine with a max continuous rating of 415 kW (557 shp). The transmission is rated at 324 kW (435 shp) for take-off, with a continuous rating of 276 kW (370 shp). 340 kW (456 shp) transmission optional. Main rotor rpm is 394. Fuel capacity is 416 litres (110 US gallons).

Cabin volume of the LongRanger III is 2·35 m³ (83 cu ft), representing a considerable increase over that of the original JetRanger, and utility is enhanced by innovations that allow maximum use of this space. For example, the port forward passenger seat has a folding back to allow loading of a container measuring 2·44 × 0·91 × 0·30 m (8 × 3 × 1 ft), making possible the carriage of such items as survey equipment, skis, and long components that cannot be accommodated in any other light helicopter. Double doors on the port side of the cabin provide an opening 1·52 m (5 ft 0 in) wide, for easy straight-in loading of litter patients or utility cargo; in an ambulance or rescue role two litter patients and two ambulatory patients/attendants may be carried. With a crew of two, the standard cabin layout accommodates five passengers in two canted rearward facing seats and three forward facing seats. An optional executive cabin layout has four individual passenger seats.

Detail improvements first introduced in the LongRanger II include a redesigned rear cabin to provide 0·05 m (2 in) more headroom for passengers in aft cabin seats; new cowlings, firewall, engine mountings, and engine deck area structure; new freewheeling unit, input shaft, forward tail rotor drive shaft, and increased-thrust tail rotor; a rupture resistant fuel system; new engine oil system, oil tank, cooler, and transition duct; deletion of the water/alcohol system required formerly; and increased capacity 17Ah battery. Optional kits include emergency flotation gear, a 907 kg (2,000 lb) cargo hook, and an engine bleed air environmental control system.

Standard avionics fit of Collins MicroLine equipment includes dual nav/com, ADF, DME, transponder and marker beacon receiver. R/Nav, radio altimeter and encoding altimeter are optional. A Collins AP-107H autopilot can be fitted, to provide single-pilot IFR capability. A Sfena autopilot is also available, featuring automatic heading, altitude navigation, approach and basic stabilisation modes of operation. By January 1986 a total of more than 960 LongRangers had been delivered. They have proved particularly popular in an ambulance role, far outnumbering any other type in the fleet of more than 130 helicopters used by 112 US emergency medical service (EMS) centres at that time.

Bell announced in July 1986 that it plans to transfer JetRanger and LongRanger production to the Bell Helicopter Canada facility in Mirabel, Quebec, in the near future.

The following details apply to the LongRanger III:

Dimensions, external:

Main rotor diameter	11·28 m (37 ft 0 in)
Tail rotor diameter	1·65 m (5 ft 5 in)
Length overall, both rotors turning	13·02 m (42 ft 8½ in)
Height: over tail fin	2·90 m (9 ft 6¼ in)
to top of rotor head	3·14 m (10 ft 3¾ in)
Fuselage: Max width	1·32 m (4 ft 4 in)
Stabiliser span	1·98 m (6 ft 6 in)

Dimension, internal:

Cabin volume	2·26 m³ (80 cu ft)

Areas:

Main rotor disc	99·89 m² (1,075·2 sq ft)
Tail rotor disc	2·14 m² (23·04 sq ft)

Weights:

Weight empty, standard	998 kg (2,200 lb)
Max external load	907 kg (2,000 lb)
Max T-O weight: normal	1,882 kg (4,150 lb)
external load	1,927 kg (4,250 lb)

Performance (at max normal T-O weight, ISA, except where indicated):

Never-exceed speed at 1,882 kg (4,150 lb) AUW:	
at S/L	130 knots (241 km/h; 150 mph)
at 1,525 m (5,000 ft)	133 knots (246 km/h; 153 mph)
Max cruising speed at 1,525 m (5,000 ft)	110 knots (203 km/h; 126 mph)
Max rate of climb at S/L	408 m (1,340 ft)/min
Service ceiling at max cruise power	6,100 m (20,000 ft)
Hovering ceiling: IGE	5,030 m (16,500 ft)
OGE	1,645 m (5,400 ft)
Range, no reserves:	
at S/L	320 nm (592 km; 368 miles)
at 1,525 m (5,000 ft)	360 nm (666 km; 414 miles)

Bell Model 206L-3 LongRanger III

BELL MODEL 209 HUEYCOBRA, SEACOBRA and SUPERCOBRA

US Army designations: AH-1G, AH-1Q and AH-1R
US Navy/Marine Corps designations: AH-1J, AH-1T and AH-1W

Bell Helicopter Textron initiated the Model 209 in March 1965 as a company funded development of the UH-1B/C Iroquois intended specifically for armed helicopter missions. The original design combined the basic transmission and rotor system and (in its standard form) the power plant of the UH-1C with a new, streamlined fuselage designed for maximum speed, armament load and crew efficiency. Relatively small, its low silhouette and narrow profile make it easy to conceal with small camouflage nets or to move under cover of trees. Tandem seating provides the best possible field of view for the crew of two.

The Model 209 prototype made its first flight on 7 September 1965, and the US Army's intention to order the aircraft was announced on 11 March 1966, the initial model being known as the AH-1G HueyCobra. Total orders to date for all versions of the HueyCobra/SeaCobra exceed 1,400.

Versions announced so far are as follows:

AH-1G HueyCobra. Original version for US Army, powered by a single 1,044 kW (1,400 shp) Avco Lycoming T53-L-13 turboshaft engine, derated to 820 kW (1,100 shp) for T-O and max continuous rating. Development contract for two pre-production aircraft placed on 4 April 1966, followed on 13 April by an initial order for 110 aircraft plus long-lead-time spares. Subsequent contracts raised the total US Army order to 1,075, deliveries of which began in June 1967. The US Marine Corps acquired 38 AH-1Gs during 1969, for transition training and initial deployment pending deliveries of the AH-1J. Six were supplied to Israel in 1974, and the Spanish Navy received eight (designated **Z.14**), for anti-shipping strike duties, giving an overall production total of 1,127 AH-1Gs. A number of AH-1Gs have been converted to **TH-1G** dual control trainers. Following the decision in 1977 to equip the HueyCobra with TOW missiles, 92 AH-1Gs were converted to interim AH-1Q standard; all of these, and 286 other AH-1Gs, had been converted to Mod AH-1S configuration by February 1984, completing contracts existing at that time. An order for 29 more conversions was announced in September 1984, followed by a contract for a further 29 in September 1985. One AH-1G was converted to **JAH-1G** as an armament testbed aircraft (details in 1985-86 *Jane's*). Two US Army AH-1Gs have been acquired for night interception missions by the US Customs Service.

AH-1J SeaCobra. Initial twin-turboshaft version for US Marine Corps, powered by a 1,342 kW (1,800 shp) Pratt & Whitney Canada T400-CP-400 coupled free-turbine turboshaft engine, a military version of the PT6T-3 Turbo Twin Pac. Engine and transmission flat rated at 820 kW (1,100 shp) continuous output, with increase to 932 kW (1,250 shp) available for T-O or 5 min emergency power. Total of 69 delivered to US Marine Corps between mid-1970 and February 1975, the last two being converted later as prototypes for the AH-1T. About 58 USMC AH-1Js remained operational in May 1982, when US Naval Air Systems Command awarded Bell a $4·7 million contract for phase 1 of a two-phase programme which calls for the company to integrate a Hellfire missile system and night vision cockpit in these helicopters. A further 202 TOW-capable AH-1Js were supplied to the Imperial Iranian Army Aviation from 1974, the US Army acting as purchasing agent.

AH-1Q HueyCobra. Interim anti-armour version for US Army, converted from AH-1G to fire Hughes TOW anti-tank missiles. Total of 92 converted; subsequently upgraded to Mod AH-1S standard. Details in 1982-83 and earlier *Jane's*.

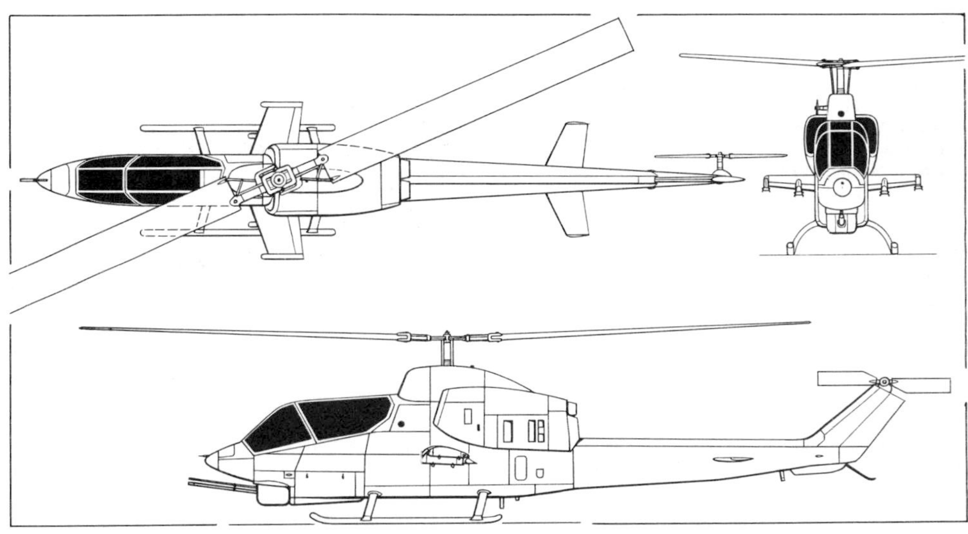

Bell AH-1T Improved SeaCobra (P&WC T400-WV-402 power plant) *(Pilot Press)*

Bell AH-1T twin-engined attack helicopter

AH-1S HueyCobra. Advanced and modernised TOW-capable version for US Army; described separately.

AH-1T Improved SeaCobra. Improved version of twin-engined AH-1J for US Marine Corps. Last two AH-1Js modified as prototypes under a US Army Aviation Systems Command contract, with uprated components for significantly increased payload and performance. Incorporates features of AH-1J airframe, but embodies dynamic system of Bell Model 214, some technology developed for Bell Model 309 Kingcobra, an upgraded power plant (1,469 kW; 1,970 shp T400-WV-402) and transmission capable of transmitting the full rated engine power. Initial contract for 10 announced on 23 June 1975; total of 57 built, of which 51 were subsequently modified to TOW configuration. First AH-1T (USN serial number 59228) flew on 20 May 1976, and was delivered to US Marine Corps on 15 October 1977.

AH-1W SuperCobra. During 1980, Bell flight tested successfully an AH-1T powered by two General Electric T700-GE-700 turboshaft engines with a combined output in excess of 2,386 kW (3,200 shp). This installation was made in an AH-1T loaned by the US Marine Corps, as part of an R & D programme to establish the specification of a helicopter with enhanced capability for future procurement. Improvements that were proposed for a qualification configuration, suitable for retrofit to existing AH-1Ts, included installation of General Electric T700-GE-401 turboshafts with a combined output of 2,423 kW (3,250 shp); a new combining gearbox; and a number of detail improvements. The T700-GE-401 has intermediate and contingency ratings of 1,260 kW (1,690 shp) and 1,285 kW (1,723 shp) respectively. The fuel system is designed to survive 23 mm shell damage.

A T700-GE-401 testbed helicopter, then designated AH-1T+, made its first flight on 16 November 1983 and was evaluated by the US Marine Corps, beginning in December 1983. Early in 1984 Congressional approval was given for the procurement of 44 production AH-1W SuperCobras, 22 each in FYs 1985 and 1986. The first AH-1W delivered, on 27 March 1986, was scheduled to undergo a seven-month test programme with Naval Air Systems Command. A second AH-1W began a three-month electromagnetic interference test programme in the Spring of 1986. Deliveries are due to continue at the rate of two per month until February 1988. The USMC also plans to update its fleet of approximately 40 AH-1Ts to AH-1W standard, with the first modification funded to begin in November 1986, for delivery in 1989. Missions assigned to the AH-1W include anti-armour, troop carrying helicopter escort, multiple weapon fire support, reconnaissance by fire, and search and target acquisition. The AH-1W is configured to carry seventy-six 2·75 in or sixteen 5 in Zuni rockets, or two GPU-2A self contained 20 mm gun pods, or two AIM-9L Sidewinder air-to-air missiles plus 750 rounds of 20 mm ammunition for its three-barrel M197 gun, or up to eight TOW or Hellfire missiles. For other missions, the AH-1W carries flare dispensers for night illumination and the M118 smoke grenade dispenser for marking targets. Equipment includes dual radar warning, infra-red jamming and dual chaff dispensing systems. Max cruising speed is increased by 25 knots (46 km/h; 29 mph) to 160 knots (296 km/h; 184 mph) at 915 m (3,000 ft) on a hot day.

TYPE: Single-engined (AH-1G/S) and twin-engined (AH-1J/T/W) close support and attack helicopters.

ROTOR SYSTEM AND DRIVE (AH-1G/J): Model 540 two-blade wide chord 'door hinge' main rotor, similar to that of UH-1C. Interchangeable blades, built up of extruded aluminium spars and laminates. Rotor brake fitted. Blades do not fold. Two-blade all-metal flex-beam tractor tail rotor on starboard side, of honeycomb construction; blade chord increased on AH-1J, which also has push/pull tail rotor controls. Shaft drive to both main and tail rotors. Main rotor rpm 294-324.

ROTOR SYSTEM AND DRIVE (AH-1T/W): Similar to that of Bell Model 214, with strengthened main rotor head incorporating Lord Kinematics Lastoflex elastomeric and Teflon faced bearings. Main rotor blades have increased chord, and swept tips which reduce noise and improve high-speed performance. Tail rotor also similar

TOW-armed Bell AH-1G HueyCobra of the United States Army

to that of Model 214, with increased diameter and blade chord. Main rotor/engine rpm ratio: 1 : 21·288. Tail rotor/engine rpm ratio 1 : 4·52.

WINGS: Small mid-mounted stub-wings, to carry armament and offload rotor in flight.

FUSELAGE: Conventional all-metal semi-monocoque structure, with low silhouette and narrow profile. AH-1T/W have forward fuselage lengthened by insertion of a 0·305 m (1 ft 0 in) plug, to accommodate tankage for additional 181·5 kg (400 lb) of fuel, and tailboom lengthened by 0·79 m (2 ft 7 in).

TAIL UNIT: Sweptback vertical fin/tail rotor pylon, strengthened on twin-engined models to cater for increased power. Elevator, of inverted aerofoil section, mid-mounted on tailboom forward of fin.

LANDING GEAR: Non-retractable tubular skid type. Ground handling wheels optional.

POWER PLANT: Single or twin turboshaft engines, as detailed under model listings. Fuel capacity: G and J, 1,014 litres (268 US gallons); T, two fuselage tanks, total capacity 1,158 litres (306 US gallons). (Fuel loads, where known, are given under 'Weights' heading.) Refuelling point in port side of fuselage, aft of cockpits. Oil capacity: T, 19 litres (5 US gallons).

ACCOMMODATION: Crew of two in tandem, with co-pilot/gunner in front seat and pilot at rear. Crew are protected by seats and side panels of Norton Co 'Noroc' armour; other panels protect vital areas of aircraft.

SYSTEMS: Hydraulic system, pressure 207 bars (3,000 lb/sq in), with Abex pumps, for flight controls and other services. Maximum flow rate (primary system) 30·3 litres (8 US gallons)/min, (utility system) 19 litres (5 US gallons)/min. Closed bootstrap reservoir. Battery powered 28V DC electrical system. Environmental control and fire detection systems.

AVIONICS (AH-1G): Communications equipment includes AN/ARC-54/131 FM radio; AN/ARC-51 and AN/ARC-134 voice com; KY-28 secure voice system.

AVIONICS (AH-1T): AN/ARC-159(V)1 UHF command set, AN/ARC-114A FM tactical set, AN/AIC-18 intercom, AN/ARN-84(V) Tacan, AN/ARA-50 UHF DF, AN/ASN-75B gyrosyn compass, AN/ARN-83 DF, AN/APN-171(V) radar altimeter, AN/APX-72 IFF transponder and AN/APN-154(V) radar beacon. Provision for TSEC/KY-28 com security unit and KIT-1A/TSEC Mk XII computer.

ARMAMENT AND OPERATIONAL EQUIPMENT (AH-1G): Initial production AH-1Gs were fitted with GAU-2B/A 7·62 mm Minigun in Emerson Electric TAT-102A undernose turret (see 1978-79 *Jane's*). This was superseded by an M28 turret, able to mount either two Miniguns (each with 4,000 rds), or two M129 40 mm grenade launchers (each with 300 rds), or one Minigun and one M129. The Miniguns in these turrets have two rates of fire, controlled by the gunner's trigger: 1,600 rds/min for searching or registry fire, or 4,000 rds/min for attack. The M129 fires at a single rate of 400 rds/min. Four external stores attachments under stub-wings can accommodate seventy-six 2·75 in rockets in four M159 launchers, 28 similar rockets in four M157 launchers, or two M18E1 Minigun pods. An initial batch of six AH-1Gs was delivered to the US Army in December 1969 equipped with a Bell/General Electric M35 armament subsystem. This unit consists of an M61 six-barrel 20 mm automatic cannon on the port inboard wing station, having a firing rate of 750 rds/min. Two ammunition boxes faired flush to the fuselage below the stub-wings each accommodate 500 rds, and total installed weight of the system is 531 kg (1,172 lb). A total of 350 M35 kits was ordered subsequently by the US Army. All wing stores are symmetrically or totally jettisonable. In normal operation, the co-pilot/gunner controls and fires the turret armament, and the pilot (aided by an M73 adjustable reflex rocket sight) normally fires the wing stores. The pilot can fire the turreted weapons only in the stowed (ie, dead ahead) position; the turret returns to the stowed position automatically when the gunner releases his grip on the slewing switch. The gunner also has the capability to fire the wing stores if required. Other operational equipment on the AH-1G includes an M130 chaff dispenser.

ARMAMENT (AH-1J): Electrically operated General Electric undernose turret, housing an M197 three-barrel 20 mm weapon (a lightweight version of the M61 cannon). A 750-rd ammunition container is located in the fuselage directly aft of the turret; firing rate is 750 rds/min, but a 16-round burst limiter is incorporated in the firing switch. Barrel length of 1·52 m (5 ft) makes it imperative that the M197 is centralised before wing stores are fired. Gun can be tracked 110° to each side, 18° upward, and 50° downward. Four attachments under stub-wings for various loads, including LAU-68A/A (seven-tube) or LAU-61A/A (19-tube) 2·75 in rocket launchers, or M18E1 Minigun pods. Total possible armament load 245 kg (542 lb) internal, 998 kg (2,200 lb) external.

ARMAMENT (AH-1T): Chin turret as AH-1J. Underwing attachments for four LAU-61A, LAU-68A, LAU-68A/A, LAU-68B/A or LAU-69A 2·75 in rocket pods; or two CBU-55B fuel-air explosive weapons; four SU-44 flare dispensers; two M118 grenade dispensers; Mk 45 parachute flares; or two Minigun pods. Alternative TOW or Hellfire air-to-surface missile installations.

Bell AH-1W SuperCobra armed with Hellfire missiles

DIMENSIONS, EXTERNAL:

Main rotor diameter: G, J	13·41 m (44 ft 0 in)
T, W	14·63 m (48 ft 0 in)
Main rotor blade chord: G, J	0·69 m (2 ft 3 in)
T	0·84 m (2 ft 9 in)
Tail rotor diameter: G, J	2·59 m (8 ft 6 in)
T	2·96 m (9 ft 8½ in)
Tail rotor blade chord: G	0·21 m (8·4 in)
J	0·29 m (11½ in)
T	0·305 m (1 ft 0 in)
Wing span (all)	3·23 m (10 ft 7 in)
Length overall, main rotor fore and aft:	
G	16·14 m (52 ft 11½ in)
J	16·26 m (53 ft 4 in)
T, W	17·68 m (58 ft 0 in)
Length of fuselage: G, J	13·59 m (44 ft 7 in)
T	14·68 m (48 ft 2 in)
Width of fuselage: G	0·965 m (3 ft 2 in)
J, T	0·98 m (3 ft 2½ in)
Height overall: G	4·12 m (13 ft 6¼ in)
J, W	4·15 m (13 ft 8 in)
T	4·32 m (14 ft 2 in)
Elevator span (all)	2·11 m (6 ft 11 in)
Width over skids (all)	2·13 m (7 ft 0 in)
Width over TOW missile pods:	
G	3·26 m (10 ft 8¾ in)

AREAS:

Main rotor disc: G, J	141·26 m² (1,520·53 sq ft)
T	168·11 m² (1,809·56 sq ft)
Tail rotor disc: G, J	5·27 m² (56·75 sq ft)
T	6·88 m² (74·03 sq ft)

WEIGHTS:

Operating weight empty, incl amounts shown for crew, fluids, avionics and armour:	
G (404 kg; 891 lb)	2,754 kg (6,073 lb)
J (398 kg; 877 lb)	3,294 kg (7,261 lb)
Weight empty: T	3,642 kg (8,030 lb)
W	4,627 kg (10,200 lb)
Operating weight empty: T	3,904 kg (8,608 lb)
Mission fuel load:	
G (871 litres; 230 US gallons)	680 kg (1,500 lb)
J	725 kg (1,600 lb)
T	944 kg (2,081 lb)
Max useful load (fuel and disposable ordnance):	
J	1,144 kg (2,523 lb)
T	2,445 kg (5,392 lb)
Mission weight: G	4,266 kg (9,407 lb)
J	4,523 kg (9,972 lb)
Max T-O and landing weight:	
G	4,309 kg (9,500 lb)
J	4,535 kg (10,000 lb)
T	6,350 kg (14,000 lb)
W	6,690 kg (14,750 lb)

PERFORMANCE (at max T-O weight, ISA):

Never-exceed speed:	
G	190 knots (352 km/h; 219 mph)
J	180 knots (333 km/h; 207 mph)
Max level speed at S/L:	
G, T	149 knots (277 km/h; 172 mph)
J	180 knots (333 km/h; 207 mph)
W	189 knots (350 km/h; 218 mph)
Max crosswind speed for hovering:	
J	40 knots (74 km/h; 46 mph)
Vertical rate of climb at S/L:	
T	92 m (301 ft)/min
Max rate of climb at S/L:	
G, normal rated power	375 m (1,230 ft)/min
J, normal rated power	332 m (1,090 ft)/min
T	544 m (1,785 ft)/min
Rate of climb at S/L, one engine out:	
W	over 244 m (800 ft)/min
Service ceiling:	
G, normal rated power	3,475 m (11,400 ft)
J, normal rated power	3,215 m (10,550 ft)
T, max cont power	2,255 m (7,400 ft)
Hovering ceiling IGE: G	3,015 m (9,900 ft)
J	3,794 m (12,450 ft)
W	4,495 m (14,750 ft)
Hovering ceiling OGE: T	365 m (1,200 ft)
W	914 m (3,000 ft)
Combat radius at 138 knots (255 km/h; 158 mph) at S/L:	
T	108 nm (200 km; 124 miles)
Range at S/L with max fuel, no reserves:	
G	325 nm (602 km; 374 miles)
J	335 nm (620 km; 385 miles)
T	310 nm (574 km; 356 miles)
W	343 nm (635 km; 395 miles)

BELL MODEL 209 HUEYCOBRA (MODERNISED VERSION)

US Army designations: AH-1S and TH-1S

The AH-1S is an advanced version of the single-engined TOW-capable HueyCobra for the US Army, with upgraded power plant, gearbox, transmission and many other improvements. The US Army's AH-1S fleet is being formed by procurement of new-production aircraft and by modification of AH-1Gs and other earlier models. Funds

Bell AH-1S HueyCobra of the Japan Ground Self-Defence Force

were provided in FY 1981 both to complete the new-production programme and to continue the conversions. A total of 1,066 AH-1Ss were manufactured and modified for US and foreign customers by the end of 1985.

The first of a succession of US Army contracts was placed in 1975, and orders to the beginning of 1984 were as follows:

Mod AH-1S. This designation (the 'Mod' in this case indicating 'Modified') applies to 378 AH-1Gs retrofitted with the TOW missile system, and with a 1,342 kW (1,800 shp) Avco Lycoming T53-L-703 turboshaft engine, and the same rotor system dynamics as the Production AH-1S. The total includes the 92 AH-1Gs previously converted to AH-1Qs, which were further modified by Bell and Dornier to Mod AH-1S. An additional 29 conversions from AH-1G were ordered in September 1984, and 29 more in September 1985. Ten Mod AH-1S have been converted to **TH-1S** by Northrop's Electro-Mechanical Division, under a programme known as Night Stalker, to train US Army pilots in operation of the Martin Marietta FLIR-based night vision system and Honeywell integrated helmet and display sighting system (IHADSS) fitted to AH-64 Apache helicopters. Deliveries began on 31 July 1984 and were to be completed in April 1985. Each TH-1S has a pilot's night vision sensor (PNVS) and associated visual and avionics systems. Blue instrument lighting makes the cockpit compatible with night vision goggles.

Production AH-1S. Under Step 1 of a three-step new-production programme, 100 Production AH-1S HueyCobras were built and delivered to the US Army between March 1977 and September 1978. These aircraft have a flat-plate canopy, improved nap-of-the-earth (NOE) instrument panel layout, continental United States (CONUS) navigation equipment, radar altimeter, improved communication radios, uprated engine and transmission, push/pull anti-torque controls, and (from the 67th aircraft onwards) Kaman developed composite rotor blades. First unit to receive this version, in August 1977, was the 82nd Airborne Division at Fort Bragg, North Carolina.

Up-gun AH-1S. The next 98 new-production aircraft (Step 2) have all the improvements detailed for the Production AH-1S, plus a universal 20/30 mm gun turret, an improved wing stores management system for the 2·75 in rockets, automatic compensation for off-axis gun firing, and a 10kVA alternator to provide the necessary additional electric power. Deliveries of this version began in September 1978 and were completed in October 1979.

Modernised AH-1S. This version, not to be confused with the 'Mod AH-1S' referred to earlier, represents the fully upgraded AH-1S, and became standard from the 199th new-production aircraft. To the improvements already mentioned for the two preceding stages are added, as Step 3, a new fire control subsystem (comprising a laser rangefinder and tracker, ballistics computer, low-airspeed sensor, and pilot's head-up display), air data system, Doppler navigation system, IFF transponder, infra-red jammer, hot metal and plume infra-red suppressor, closed circuit refuelling, new secure voice communications, and new composite rotor blades developed by Kaman. Total of 99 delivered to US Army. The Army National Guard has also acquired 27 Modernised AH-1Ss, with a further 23 to be added later.

Under a $13 million 1980 contract awarded by the US Army Missile Command, Hughes Aircraft Company manufactured 157 Laser Augmented Airborne TOW (LAAT) stabilised sights for installation in Modernised AH-1S aircraft, and subsequently manufactured a further 120 new sights. The very small (13 × 13 × 4 cm; 5 × 5 × 1·5 in) laser transmitter has been developed to fit within the existing sight turret of the AH-1S.

Three engineering development models of the LAAT were used for flight testing by Bell at Yuma Proving Grounds, Arizona. They demonstrated that the LAAT can significantly improve first-burst accuracy of gun and rocket fire. In use, the gunner sights a target and fires the laser. Reflected from the target, the returning beam provides accurate and almost instantaneous range information, enabling the aircraft's fire control computer to integrate range, wind and ammunition ballistics data to direct weapon firing with great accuracy.

To reduce the time taken by co-pilot/gunners to acquire targets and fire their missiles and guns, US Army AH-1S aircraft are to be fitted with an automatic airborne laser tracker (ALT) system produced by Rockwell. Delivery of 163 ALTs has been completed.

Hughes Aircraft has developed, as a further enhancement of the AH-1S TOW system, a FLIR-augmented Cobra TOW sight. This telescopic sight, mounted under the nose of the helicopter, enables the gunner to 'see' through darkness, smoke and haze, and offers a considerable improvement in round-the-clock combat capability. Delivery of the sight, now known as Cobra-Nite (C-Nite) began in mid-1986, with planned installation on some 500 AH-1Ss.

Thirty Modernised AH-1S, of a planned total of 54, have been ordered by the Japan Ground Self-Defence Force for delivery between 1985 and 1987. These are assembled under licence in Japan, with Fuji as prime contractor under sub-licence from Mitsui. Other deliveries of the Modernised AH-1S have included 24 for Jordan and 20 for Pakistan. The supply of an undisclosed number to Israel has been authorised.

The major differences between the current standard AH-1S and earlier single-engined HueyCobras may be summarised as follows:

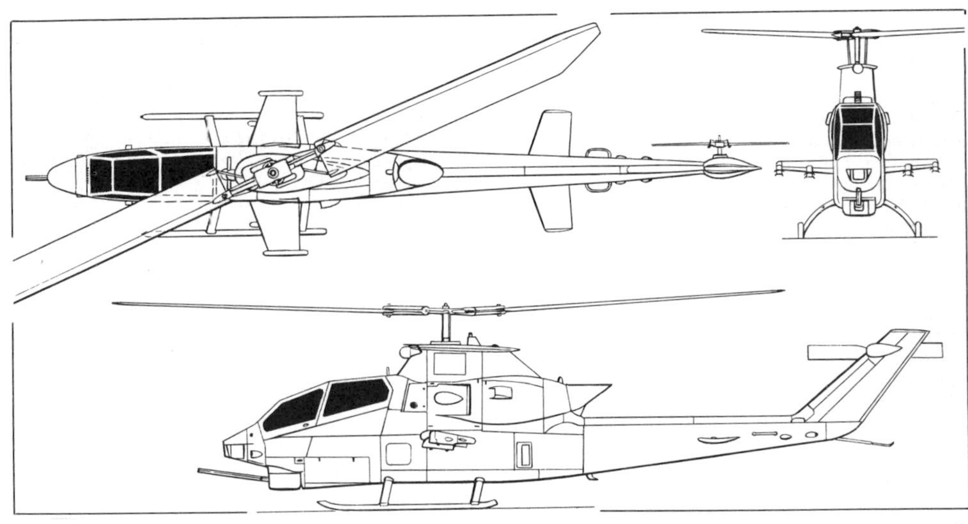

Bell AH-1S HueyCobra (Avco Lycoming T53-L-703 turboshaft engine) *(Pilot Press)*

TYPE: Anti-armour attack helicopter.

ROTOR SYSTEM AND DRIVE: Upgraded gearbox and transmission, the latter rated at 962 kW (1,290 shp) for take-off, 845 kW (1,134 shp) continuous. From 67th new-production AH-1S onward, main rotor blades of composite construction are fitted, developed by Kaman Aerospace Corporation and equipped with tungsten carbide bearing sleeves. The outer 15 per cent of these blades, which are tolerant of damage by weapons of up to 23 mm calibre, is tapered in both chord and thickness.

FUSELAGE: Tailboom strengthened to increase survivability against weapons of up to 23 mm calibre. Entire airframe has an anti-infra-red paint finish.

POWER PLANT: One 1,342 kW (1,800 shp) Avco Lycoming T53-L-703 turboshaft engine. Closed circuit refuelling on Modernised AH-1S. Fuel capacity 980 litres (259 US gallons).

ACCOMMODATION: New flat-plate canopy has seven planes of viewing surfaces, designed to minimise glint and reduce possibility of visual detection during nap-of-the-earth (NOE) flying; it also provides increased headroom for pilot. Improved instrument layout and lighting, compatible with use of night vision goggles. Improved, independently operating window/door ballistic jettison system to facilitate crew escape in emergency.

SYSTEMS: 10kVA 400Hz AC alternator with emergency bus added to electrical system. Hydraulic system pressure 103·5 bars (1,500 lb/sq in), maximum flow rate 22·7 litres (6 US gallons)/min. Open reservoir. Battery driven Abex standby pump, for use in event of main hydraulic system failure, can be used for collective pitch control and for boresighting turret and TOW missile system. Improved environmental control and fire detection systems.

AVIONICS AND EQUIPMENT: Standard lightweight avionics equipment (SLAE) includes AN/ARC-114 FM, AN/ARC-164 UHF/AM voice com, and E-Systems (Memcor Division) AN/ARC-115 VHF/AM voice com (compatible with KY-58 single-channel secure voice system). Other avionics include AN/ASN-128 Doppler nav system in Modernised AH-1S; APR-39 radar warning receiver; ALQ-144 infra-red jammer; HSI; VSI; radar altimeter; push/pull anti-torque controls for tail rotor; co-pilot's standby magnetic compass.

ARMAMENT AND OPERATIONAL EQUIPMENT: M65 system with eight Hughes TOW missiles, disposed as two two-round clusters on each of the outboard underwing stations. The inboard wing stations remain available for other stores. Beginning with the 101st new-production AH-1S (the first 'Up-gun' example), the M28 (7·62/40 mm) turret in earlier HueyCobras is replaced by a new electrically powered General Electric universal turret, designed to accommodate either a 20 mm or a 30 mm weapon and to improve stand-off capability. Initially, the 20 mm M197 three-barrel cannon (with 750 rds) is mounted in this turret. Rate of fire is 730 rds/min. Turret position is controlled by the pilot or co-pilot/gunner through helmet sights, or by the co-pilot using the M65 TOW missile system's telescopic sight unit. Field of fire is up to 110° to each side of aircraft, 20·5° upward and 50° downward. Also from the first 'Up-gun' AH-1S, the helicopter is equipped with a Baldwin Electronics M138 wing stores management subsystem, providing the means to select and fire, singly or in groups, any one of five types of external 2·75 in rocket store. These are mounted in launchers each containing from 7 to 19 tubes, and are additional to the TOW missile capability.

In addition to these installations the 199th new-built AH-1S (the first to full 'Modernised' standard) introduced a fire control subsystem which includes a Kaiser head-up display for the pilot, Teledyne Systems digital fire control computer for the turreted weapon and underwing rockets, omnidirectional airspeed system to improve cannon and rocket accuracy, Hughes laser rangefinder (accurate to 10,000 m; 32,800 ft), and provisions for a Rockwell AN/AAS-32 airborne laser tracker. Other operational equipment includes a Hughes LAAT stabilised sight (see introductory copy), a GEC Avionics M-143 air data subsystem, AN/APX-100 solid-state IFF transponder, Sanders AN/ALQ-144 infra-red jammer (above engine), suppressor for infra-red signature from engine hot metal and exhaust plume, and AN/APR-39 radar warning receiver.

DIMENSIONS, EXTERNAL: As AH-1G except:

Main rotor blade chord (from 67th new-production AH-1S)	0·76 m (2 ft 6 in)
Tail rotor blade chord	0·305 m (1 ft 0 in)
Wing span	3·28 m (10 ft 9 in)
Length overall, rotors turning	16·18 m (53 ft 1 in)
Width of fuselage	0·99 m (3 ft 3 in)
Height to top of rotor head	4·09 m (13 ft 5 in)
Width over TOW pods	3·56 m (11 ft 8 in)

WEIGHTS:

Operating weight empty	2,993 kg (6,598 lb)
Mission weight	4,524 kg (9,975 lb)
Max T-O and landing weight	4,535 kg (10,000 lb)

PERFORMANCE (at max T-O weight, ISA):

Never-exceed speed (TOW configuration)	170 knots (315 km/h; 195 mph)
Max level speed (TOW configuration)	123 knots (227 km/h; 141 mph)
Max rate of climb at S/L, normal rated power	494 m (1,620 ft)/min
Service ceiling, normal rated power	3,720 m (12,200 ft)
Hovering ceiling IGE	3,720 m (12,200 ft)
Range at S/L with max fuel, 8% reserves	274 nm (507 km; 315 miles)

BELL MODEL 212 TWIN TWO-TWELVE

US military designation: UH-1N

Canadian military designation: CH-135

Bell announced on 1 May 1968 that the Canadian government had approved development of a twin-engined UH-1 helicopter to be powered by a Pratt & Whitney Canada PT6T-3 power plant. Subsequently, the Canadian government ordered 50 of these aircraft (designated CUH-1N) for the Canadian Armed Forces. Simultaneously, orders totalling 141 aircraft for the US services were announced, comprising 79 for the US Air Force, 40 for the US Navy and 22 for the US Marine Corps, all having the designation **UH-1N**. Subsequent orders covered the delivery of 159 more UH-1Ns to the US Navy and Marine Corps in 1973-78.

Initial deliveries for the US Air Force began in 1970, when UH-1Ns joined UH-1Ps (modified UH-1Fs) in support of Special Operations Force counter-insurgency activities, psychological warfare and unconventional warfare operations worldwide. The first CUH-1N for the Canadian Armed Forces was handed over officially at Uplands Airport, Ottawa, on 3 May 1971; the Canadian order was completed one year later. Deliveries to the US Navy and US Marine Corps also began during 1971. Canadian aircraft are now designated **CH-135**. Six were delivered to the air force of Bangladesh in early 1977, and the Argentine Air Force ordered eight in 1978.

A commercial version, known as the Twin Two-Twelve, is in full scale production. This received FAA type certification with PT6T-3 power plant in October 1970, and FAA Transport Type Category A certification on 30 June 1971. The Model 212 can carry an external load of 2,268 kg (5,000 lb), and the military UH-1N a load of 1,814 kg (4,000 lb). The PT6T-3B engine was introduced in June 1980, offering improved single-engine performance and, consequently, additional safety margins.

The Twin Two-Twelve has been certificated for IFR operations by the FAA, UK's CAA, Norwegian DCA and

Canadian DoT. Conversion from VFR to IFR configuration requires a new avionics package, new instrument panel and aircraft stabilisation controls. In June 1977, the Model 212 became the first helicopter FAA certificated for single-pilot IFR operations with fixed floats.

An order for eight Model 212s, to support energy and natural resources development in China, was received in early 1979, and all were delivered by the end of the year. Operated by the Civil Aviation Administration of China (CAAC), they represented the first order received from the People's Republic of China by a US helicopter manufacturer. A ninth Model 212, in IFR configuration, with ADF, weather radar, automatic flight control system, environmental control unit, pop-out floats and auxiliary fuel tanks, was delivered in December 1981 for offshore petroleum missions in the South China Sea. Two Model 212s were delivered to the Panamanian Air Force during 1985.

TYPE: Twin-turbine utility helicopter.

ROTOR SYSTEM: Two-blade all-metal semi-rigid main rotor with interchangeable blades, built up of extruded aluminium spars and laminates. Stabilising bar above and at right angles to main rotor blades. Underslung feathering axis head. Two-blade all-metal tail rotor. Main rotor blades do not fold. Rotor brake optional.

ROTOR DRIVE: Shaft drive to both main and tail rotors.

FUSELAGE: Conventional all-metal semi-monocoque structure.

TAIL UNIT: Small fixed stabiliser on rear fuselage.

LANDING GEAR: Tubular skid type. Lock-on ground handling wheels, fixed floats and inflatable nylon float bags optional.

POWER PLANT: Pratt & Whitney Canada PT6T-3B Turbo Twin Pac, comprising two PT6 turboshaft engines coupled to a combining gearbox with a single output shaft. Producing 1,342 kW (1,800 shp), the Twin Pac is flat rated at 962 kW (1,290 shp) for T-O and 842 kW (1,130 shp) for continuous operation. In the event of an engine failure, the remaining engine can deliver 764 kW (1,025 shp) for 2·5 min, 723 kW (970 shp) for 30 min, or 596 kW (800 shp) continuously. Five interconnected rubber fuel cells, total usable capacity 814 litres (215 US gallons). Auxiliary fuel tanks optional, to provide a max total capacity of 1,495 litres (395 US gallons). Single-point refuelling on starboard side of cabin. Oil capacity 11·5 litres (3 US gallons) for engines, 8·5 litres (2·25 US gallons) for transmission.

ACCOMMODATION: Pilot and up to 14 passengers. In cargo configuration there is a total internal volume of 7·02 m³ (248 cu ft), including baggage space in tailboom. Exterior baggage compartment capacity 181 kg (400 lb). Forward door on each side of fuselage, opening forward. Two doors on each side of cabin; forward door hinged to open forward, rear door sliding aft. Accommodation heated and ventilated. Dual controls optional. Garrett air-cycle environmental control unit available optionally.

SYSTEMS: Dual hydraulic systems, pressure 69 bars (1,000 lb/sq in), maximum flow rate 22·7 litres (6 US gallons)/min. Open reservoir. 28V DC electrical system supplied by two completely independent 30V 200A starter/generators. Secondary AC power supplied by two completely independent 250VA single-phase solid state inverters. A third inverter can acquire automatically the load of a failed inverter. 34Ah nickel-cadmium battery.

AVIONICS AND EQUIPMENT: Optional IFR avionics include dual King KTR 900A com transceivers; dual King KNR 660A VOR/LOC/RMI receivers; King KDF 800 ADF; King KMD 700A DME; King KXP 750A transponder; King KGM 690 marker beacon/glideslope receiver; dual Sperry Tarsyn-444 three-axis gyro units; stability control augmentation system; and an automatic flight control system. Flight director and weather radar optional. Other optional equipment includes a litter kit, cargo hook, cargo sling, rescue hoist, fixed float gear, emergency pop-out flotation gear and high skid gear.

DIMENSIONS, EXTERNAL:
- Main rotor diameter (with tracking tips) 14·69 m (48 ft 2¼ in)
- Tail rotor diameter 2·59 m (8 ft 6 in)
- Main rotor blade chord 0·59 m (1 ft 11¼ in)
- Tail rotor blade chord 0·292 m (11½ in)
- Length:
  - overall (main rotor fore and aft) 17·46 m (57 ft 3¼ in)
  - fuselage 12·92 m (42 ft 4¾ in)
- Height: to top of rotor head 3·91 m (12 ft 10 in)
  - overall 4·53 m (14 ft 10¼ in)
- Width: over skids 2·64 m (8 ft 8 in)
  - overall (main rotor fore and aft) 2·86 m (9 ft 4½ in)
- Stabiliser span 2·86 m (9 ft 4½ in)
- Rear sliding doors (each): Height 1·24 m (4 ft 1 in)
  - Width 1·88 m (6 ft 2 in)
  - Height to sill 0·76 m (2 ft 6 in)
- Baggage compartment door: Height 0·53 m (1 ft 9 in)
  - Width 1·71 m (2 ft 4 in)
- Emergency exits (centre cabin windows, each):
  - Height 0·76 m (2 ft 6 in)
  - Width 0·97 m (3 ft 2 in)

DIMENSIONS, INTERNAL:
- Cabin, excl flight deck: Length 2·34 m (7 ft 8 in)
  - Max width 2·44 m (8 ft 0 in)
  - Max height 1·24 m (4 ft 1 in)
  - Volume 6·23 m³ (220 cu ft)
- Baggage compartment volume 0·78 m³ (28 cu ft)

AREAS:
- Main rotor disc 173·90 m² (1,871·91 sq ft)
- Tail rotor disc 5·27 m² (56·74 sq ft)

WEIGHTS:
- VFR empty weight plus usable oil 2,720 kg (5,997 lb)
- Max external load 2,268 kg (5,000 lb)
- Max T-O weight and mission weight 5,080 kg (11,200 lb)

PERFORMANCE (at max T-O weight):
- Never-exceed speed and max cruising speed at S/L 100 knots (185 km/h; 115 mph)
- Max rate of climb at S/L 402 m (1,320 ft)/min
- Service ceiling 3,960 m (13,000 ft)
- Max altitude for T-O and landing 1,430 m (4,700 ft)
- Hovering ceiling IGE 3,350 m (11,000 ft)
- Max range with standard fuel at S/L, no reserves 227 nm (420 km; 261 miles)

Bell Model 212 twin-turbine helicopter of the Brazilian operator Taxi Aereo Lider

BELL MODEL 412

Bell announced on 8 September 1978 its intention to develop this variant of the twin-turbine Model 212 with a four-blade main rotor of advanced design. The Model 412 is the first production helicopter with a four-blade rotor to be manufactured by Bell, although the company has flown many helicopters with multi-blade rotors for research purposes.

Introduction by Bell of the new rotor has not only improved performance and reduced noise, but has reduced vibration significantly without requiring a costly redesign of the fuselage structure to introduce nodal suspension. A pendulum absorber kit, to reduce internal vibration levels, became standard in mid-1984, and is available for retrofit to earlier Model 412s.

Two new fully certificated Model 212s were modified for use in the development and certification programme for the Model 412. The first of these began its flight trials in early August 1979, and the second in December 1979. FAA type approval, in accordance with FAR Pt 29, for VFR operation was received on 9 January 1981, and IFR certification on 13 February 1981. The first delivery to a customer was made to ERA Helicopters of Anchorage, Alaska, on 18 January 1981; this operator has since acquired 11 more Model 412s, supplementing 16 Model 212s and 52 other Bell helicopters. Two Model 412s are operated by the Venezuelan Air Force, two by the Public Security Flying Wing of the Bahrain Defence Force, four by Sri Lanka's armed forces and two by the Nigerian Police Air Wing. By June 1986 more than 125 Model 412s had been delivered.

The latest commercial version of the helicopter is known as the **Model 412SP** (Special Performance), and features an increased max T-O weight, new interior seating options and a 55% increase in standard fuel capacity.

Recent orders have been received from the Republic of Honduras for 10 Model 412SPs, delivery of which was expected to be completed by the end of 1986; and from the Royal Norwegian Air Force for 12 Model 412SPs. Eleven of the Norwegian aircraft will be assembled by Helikopter Services A/S of Stavanger, using subassemblies and components supplied by Bell.

In June 1986 Bell announced the **412AH** (Attack Helicopter) military counterpart, equipped with a 600 rds/min 0·50 in calibre machine-gun in a Lucas Aerospace undernose turret, guided by a Sperry Head Tracker helmet sight system similar to that used in the AH-1S. The installation carries 875 rounds of ammunition, weighs 188 kg (414 lb), including the helmet sight, and can be installed or removed in less than 30 minutes. With the turret, the 412H has a max level speed of 120 knots (222 km/h; 138 mph); in addition, it can be equipped with 19 air-to-ground rockets on each side of the aircraft.

Bell's Italian licensee, Agusta, has developed its own multi-role military version, known as the **Griffon**, capable of performing medical evacuation, armed tactical support, logistic transport, SAR and patrol missions. Details of the Griffon are given under the Agusta heading in the Italian section.

The description of the Model 212 applies also to the Model 412SP, except as follows:

ROTOR SYSTEM: Four-blade flex-beam soft-in-plane advanced technology main rotor. Blades are of similar construction to those described for the Model 214ST, but are interchangeable and have lightning protection mesh moulded into the structure and provisions for inclusion of de-icing heater elements. New design main rotor head of steel and light alloy construction, with elastomeric bearings and dampers. Main rotor can be folded. Rotor brake standard. Two-blade tail rotor of all-metal construction. Main rotor rpm 314.

ROTOR DRIVE: As for Model 212, except for shorter main rotor mast. Transmission rating 1,044 kW (1,400 shp) for T-O, 846 kW (1,134 shp) max continuous.

Bell Model 412AH with Lucas undernose gun turret

POWER PLANT: Pratt & Whitney Canada PT6T-3B-1 Turbo Twin Pac, comprising two 671 kW (900 shp) turboshaft engines, rated to produce a total of 1,044 kW (1,400 shp) for take-off and 843 kW (1,130 shp) for continuous operation. In the event of an engine failure the remaining engine can deliver up to 764 kW (1,025 shp) for 2½ min, or 723 kW (970 shp) for 30 min. Seven interconnected rupture resistant fuel cells, with automatic shut-off valves (breakaway fittings), have a combined capacity of 1,249 litres (330 US gallons). Optional auxiliary fuel tanks provide a maximum total capacity of 1,870 litres (494 US gallons). Single-point refuelling on starboard side of cabin.

AVIONICS AND EQUIPMENT: Optional IFR avionics include King Gold Crown III equipment and dual Sperry Automatic Flight Control Systems. Optional equipment includes a cargo sling, rescue hoist, emergency pop-out flotation gear and high skid gear.

DIMENSIONS, EXTERNAL:

Main rotor diameter	14·02 m (46 ft 0 in)
Tail rotor diameter	2·59 m (8 ft 6 in)
Main rotor blade chord: at root	0·40 m (1 ft 3·9 in)
at tip	0·22 m (8½ in)
Tail rotor blade chord	0·29 m (11½ in)
Length: overall (rotors turning)	17·07 m (56 ft 0 in)
fuselage (excl rotors)	12·92 m (42 ft 4¾ in)
Height: to top of rotor head	3·29 m (10 ft 9½ in)
overall, tail rotor turning	4·32 m (14 ft 2¼ in)
Stabiliser span	2·86 m (9 ft 4½ in)
Width over skids	2·59 m (8 ft 6 in)
Door sizes	as Model 212

AREAS:

Main rotor disc	154·40 m² (1,661·9 sq ft)
Tail rotor disc	5·27 m² (56·75 sq ft)

WEIGHTS:

Weight empty with utility seating, plus usable oil	2,935 kg (6,470 lb)
Max T-O weight	5,397 kg (11,900 lb)

PERFORMANCE (at max T-O weight except where indicated):

Never-exceed speed at S/L	140 knots (259 km/h; 161 mph)
Max cruising speed at S/L	124 knots (230 km/h; 143 mph)
Max rate of climb at S/L	411 m (1,350 ft)/min
Service ceiling	4,970 m (16,300 ft)
Max altitude for T-O and landing	427 m (1,400 ft)
Hovering ceiling: IGE	2,805 m (9,200 ft)
OGE, AUW of 4,762 kg (10,500 lb)	2,805 m (9,200 ft)
Range with max payload, standard fuel, at 118 knots (219 km/h; 136 mph) at 3,200 m (10,500 ft), 30 min fuel reserves	375 nm (695 km; 432 miles)
Max range with standard fuel at S/L, no reserves	354 nm (656 km; 408 miles)

BELL MODEL 214ST SUPERTRANSPORT

The Model 214ST was developed originally for major production and service in Iran. It was expected to serve primarily as a military transport helicopter; but Bell has since developed the 214ST as a commercial transport with multi-mission capability. Originally, the suffix ST indicated Stretched Twin: Bell is retaining these initials to represent SuperTransport.

The prototype 214ST flew for the first time in February 1977, and construction of three pre-production examples began in 1978. The decision to manufacture an initial series of 100 production 214STs was announced in November 1979. FAA and CAA certification for two-pilot IFR operation was obtained in 1982, and deliveries by Bell started soon afterwards, at a rate of three per month. Initial contracts included two 214STs for operation by the Venezuelan Air Force, and three for British Caledonian Helicopters for offshore support in the North Sea. To enhance the helicopter's value for such missions, on which it is now operated worldwide, the FAA approved a new configuration with seats for a crew of two and 18 (instead of the original 16) passengers in Spring 1982. The Peruvian Air Force has six 214STs; two were delivered to the Royal Thai Army in 1984. Other recent orders include four for the People's Republic of China, and one for the North Slope Borough Search and Rescue team based at Barrow, Alaska, equipped for emergency medical service and SAR duties. The Model 214ST has been certificated under transport category airworthiness requirements in Canada, Japan, the United Kingdom and United States. The CAA has approved it for flight into icing conditions with added icing kit.

TYPE: Twin-turboshaft commercial transport helicopter.

ROTOR SYSTEM: Two-blade advanced technology main rotor. Each blade has a unidirectionally laid glassfibre spar, with a ±45°-wound torque casing of glassfibre cloth. The trailing-edge is also of unidirectional glassfibre, and the space between spar and trailing-edge is filled by a Nomex honeycomb core. The entire blade is then bonded together by glassfibre wrapping, with the leading-edge protected by a titanium abrasion strip and the tip by a replaceable stainless steel cap. Two-blade tail rotor; interchangeable blades, each with a stainless steel leading-edge spar and covering, aluminium honeycomb core and glassfibre trailing-edge strip. Main rotor head incorporates elastomeric bearings. Second-generation Noda-Matic nodal suspension system. Nodal beam requires no lubrication. Main rotor brake standard.

Bell Model 214ST SuperTransport helicopter in service with British Caledonian Helicopters

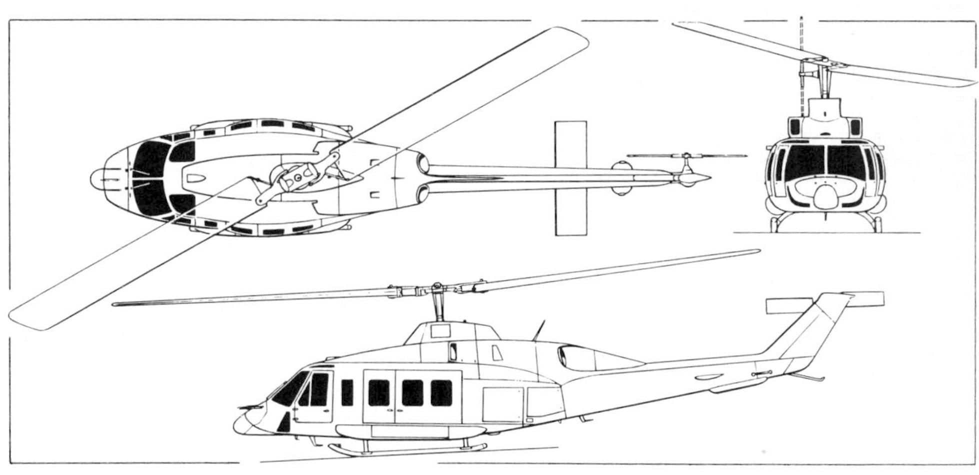
Bell Model 214ST SuperTransport in production configuration *(Pilot Press)*

ROTOR DRIVE: Main transmission has a maximum rating of 1,752 kW (2,350 shp), maximum continuous rating of 1,454 kW (1,950 shp), and single-engine rating of 1,286 kW (1,725 shp). Combining, intermediate and tail rotor gearboxes, each with one-hour run-dry capability.

FUSELAGE: Conventional all-metal semi-monocoque structure, incorporating rollover protection ring.

TAIL SURFACE: Electronically controlled elevator, which minimises trim changes with alterations of power and CG, and improves longitudinal stability.

LANDING GEAR: Energy absorbing non-retractable tubular skid type or tricycle type wheeled landing gear standard.

POWER PLANT: Two 1,212 kW (1,625 shp) General Electric CT7-2A turboshaft engines, connected to a combining gearbox. In the event of an engine failure, the remaining engine is capable of developing 1,286 kW (1,725 shp) to provide continued flight capability. Standard fuel capacity 1,647 litres (435 US gallons), contained in seven interconnected rupture resistant cells, arranged to provide two independent fuel systems as required by FAR Pt 29. Single-point refuelling. Auxiliary fuel system optional, consisting of two tanks in rear of cabin, each of 329 litres (87 US gallons) capacity; 95 litre (25 US gallon) underseat auxiliary fuel tanks also available. Engine anti-icing and inlet screens standard.

ACCOMMODATION: Standard seating for pilot, co-pilot and up to 18 passengers. Dual controls standard. Crew seats adjustable. Passenger seats in three rows across cabin plus a two-place bench seat on each side of rotor mast. Standard configuration offers utility or deluxe interiors with contemporary or energy attenuating seats. Jettisonable crew door each side. Large cabin door on each side for passengers or easy loading of cargo. Glass windscreens, with standard anti-icing system. Two emergency exits on each side. Baggage space aft of cabin, capacity 1·84 m³ (65 cu ft). Passenger seating removable to provide 9·23 m³ (326 cu ft) of cargo capacity. Cabin heated and ventilated.

SYSTEMS: Dual engine driven hydraulic pumps for fully redundant hydraulic power for flight control system; pressure 207 bars (3,000 lb/sq in), maximum flow rate 25·4 litres (6·7 US gallons)/min for primary control system; 19 litres (5 US gallons)/min for utility system. Closed bootstrap pressurised reservoirs. Third system operates oil cooler blower for transmission and combiner gearbox. Redundant electrical system with dual engine driven generators. Stability and control augmentation system (SCAS). Main rotor blade in-flight tracking system. Attitude/altitude retention system (AARS). Computer controlled fly by wire automatic elevator trim system.

AVIONICS AND EQUIPMENT: Standard avionics include dual com, dual nav, R/Nav, ADF, transponder, DME, air data computer, and standby attitude indicator to provide IFR capability. Avionics options include radar, nav coupling, and VLF nav system. Optional equipment includes anti-icing kit, emergency flotation gear, external cargo suspension system, internal rescue hoist, and two pneumatically ejected 10- or 12-person liferafts inside engine cowl fairing forward of rotor mast.

DIMENSIONS, EXTERNAL:

Main rotor diameter	15·85 m (52 ft 0 in)
Tail rotor diameter	2·95 m (9 ft 8 in)
Main rotor blade chord	0·84 m (2 ft 9 in)
Tail rotor blade chord	0·36 m (1 ft 2 in)
Length: overall, rotors turning	18·95 m (62 ft 2¼ in)
fuselage	15·02 m (49 ft 3½ in)
Height overall	4·84 m (15 ft 10½ in)
Skid track	2·64 m (8 ft 8 in)
Wheel track	2·83 m (9 ft 3½ in)

DIMENSIONS, INTERNAL:

Cabin: Length, instrument panel to centre rear bulkhead	3·42 m (11 ft 2¾ in)
Max length	4·13 m (13 ft 6¾ in)
Max width	2·41 m (7 ft 11 in)
Volume	8·95 m³ (316 cu ft)

AREAS:

Main rotor disc	197·30 m² (2,123·7 sq ft)
Tail rotor disc	6·82 m² (73·39 sq ft)

WEIGHT:

Max T-O weight: internal or external load	7,938 kg (17,500 lb)

PERFORMANCE (at max T-O weight except where indicated):

Normal cruising speed at S/L, at average cruise weight	140 knots (259 km/h; 161 mph)
Max cruising speed at 1,220 m (4,000 ft)	138 knots (256 km/h; 159 mph)
Max rate of climb at S/L, ISA	543 m (1,780 ft)/min
Service ceiling, one engine out, ISA	1,460 m (4,800 ft)
Hovering ceiling IGE	1,950 m (6,400 ft)
Range at 1,220 m (4,000 ft) with max standard fuel, no reserves	463 nm (858 km; 533 miles)
Range, ISA, VFR, standard fuel, no reserves	439 nm (813 km; 505 miles)
Ferry range with auxiliary fuel, pilot only, no payload, no reserves	over 550 nm (1,019 km; 633 miles)

BELL MODEL 222

In April 1974, Bell announced its intention of developing the Model 222, described as the first commercial light twin-engined helicopter to be built in the USA. Construction of five prototypes began on 1 September 1974 and the first of these flew for the first time on 13 August 1976. FAA certification for a Model 222 in pre-production configuration was received on 16 August 1979. The production 222 received approval for VFR operation on 20 December, and the first delivery, to Petroleum Helicopters Inc, was made on 16 January 1980. FAA certification for single-pilot IFR operations in Category I weather conditions was granted on 15 May 1980. A Model 222 delivered to Omniflight Helicopters on 18 January 1981 was the 25,000th Bell helicopter built; another is serving as a flying testbed for Bell's Model 680 rotor system (described separately).

Current production aircraft are available in the following configurations:

Basic 222B. Basic model, as described. On 29 July 1982 the 222B became the first transport category helicopter to be certificated by the FAA for single-pilot IFR flight without stability augmentation.

222B Executive. Fully equipped for both single and dual pilot IFR flight. Sperry coupled automatic flight control system to provide stability augmentation and automatic hold for attitude, altitude, heading and airspeed, plus VOR/LOC course and glideslope hold during approach. Collins Proline avionics include dual VHF com, dual VOR nav with glideslope, ADF, marker beacon receiver, transponder, DME and area navigation. Luxury accommodation for five or six passengers, with automatic temperature control, fluorescent and reading lights, window curtains and ceiling speakers. Optional stereo system and refreshment cabinet.

222UT (Utility Twin). Utility version of the Model 222, incorporating the improvements and power plant detailed for the Model 222B. Retractable tricycle landing gear replaced by tubular skid gear with lock-on ground handling wheels. Fuselage mounted flotation system optional. Standard seating for a pilot and six or seven passengers. Optional layout for a pilot and eight passengers. VFR and single-pilot IFR certification received in Spring 1983; customer deliveries began in September 1983. Customers include Lloyd Helicopters of Australia, which has six intended primarily for offshore oil support, the New York City Police Department, and the Port Authority of New York and New Jersey. This model is used widely for air ambulance duties.

By January 1986 a total of 146 Model 222s had been delivered.

The following details refer to the basic Model 222B, except where indicated:

TYPE: Twin-turbine light commercial helicopter.

ROTOR SYSTEM: Two-blade main rotor. Blade section Wortmann 090. Thickness/chord ratio 8%. Each blade comprises a stainless steel spar with bonded glassfibre safety straps to retard crack propagation and offer secondary load path; replaceable stainless steel leading-edge; and afterbody of Nomex honeycomb covered with glassfibre skin. Each blade is attached to the rotor head by two chordwise bolts. Small trim tab on each blade. Completely dry titanium main rotor hub has conical elastomeric bearings. Two-blade tail rotor of stainless steel construction, with preconing, underslung feathering axis and skewed flapping axis. Rotor blades do not fold. A rotor brake is standard.

ROTOR DRIVE: Rotors shaft driven through gearbox with two spiral bevel reductions and one planetary reduction. Transmission rating (two engines) 690 kW (925 shp). Single-engine rating 548 kW (735 shp). Main rotor/engine rpm ratio 1 : 27·4; tail rotor/engine rpm ratio 1 : 5·08.

SPONSONS: Short span cantilever sponson set low on each side of fuselage, serving as main landing gear housings, fuel tanks and work platforms. Section NACA 0035. Dihedral 3° 12′. Incidence 5°. Sweepback at quarter-chord 3° 30′. All-metal structure of light alloy sheet and honeycomb. No movable surfaces.

FUSELAGE: Semi-monocoque structure of light alloy, with limited use of light alloy honeycomb panels. Fail-safe structure in critical areas. One-piece nosecone tilts forward and down for access to avionics and equipment bay.

TAIL UNIT: Cantilever structure of light alloy. Fixed vertical fin in sweptback upper and lower sections. Tailplane, with slotted leading-edge and endplate fins, mounted midway along rear fuselage. Small skid below ventral fin for protection in tail-down landing.

LANDING GEAR: Hydraulically retractable tricycle type. All units retract forward, mainwheels into sponsons. Free-fall extension in emergency. Oleo-pneumatic shock absorbers, with scissored yoke. Self-centering nosewheel, swivelling through 360°. Single wheel and tyre on each unit. Mainwheel tyres size 6·00-6, pressure 5·18 bars (75 lb/sq in). Nosewheel tyre size 5·00-5, pressure 4·14 bars (60 lb/sq in). Hydraulic disc brakes. New type water-activated emergency 'pop-out' floats optional. Model 222UT has skid type landing gear and lock-on ground handling wheels, with fuselage mounted flotation system optional.

POWER PLANT: Two Avco Lycoming LTS 101-750C-1 turboshafts, each rated at 510 kW (684 shp) for take-off, mounted in a streamline housing above the cabin and aft of the rotor pylon. Bell focused pylon with nodalisation. Fuel contained in five crash resistant internal bladders, in fuselage and sponsons, with total capacity of 710 litres (187·5 US gallons) in Model 222B. Model 222UT has max fuel capacity of 931 litres (246 US gallons). Rear seat fuel tank, capacity 246 litres (65 US gallons), and parcel shelf fuel tank, capacity 181 litres (48 US gallons), optional on both models. Single-point refuelling on starboard side of fuselage. Oil capacity 3·2 litres (6·85 US quarts) per engine.

Bell Model 222B Executive twin-turbine helicopter

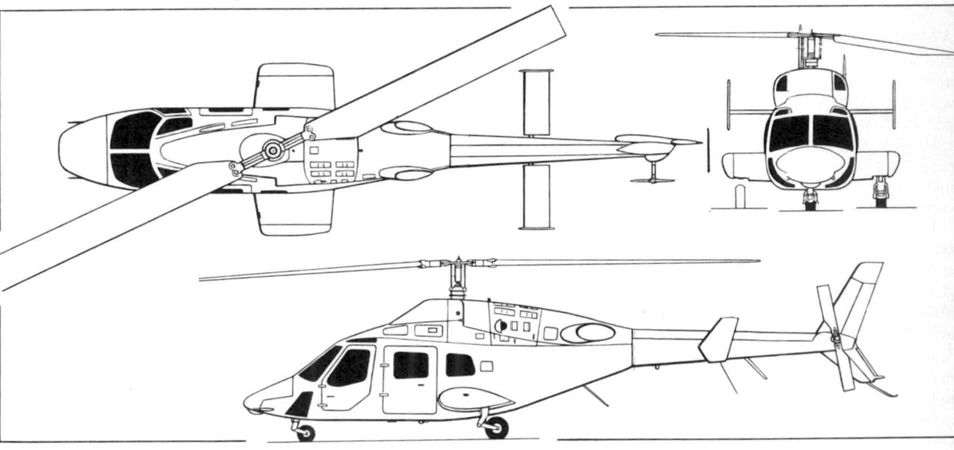

Bell Model 222B twin-turbine light commercial helicopter *(Pilot Press)*

ACCOMMODATION: Pilot and seven passengers in standard 2-3-3 layout; alternatively pilot, co-pilot and six passengers. Two additional passengers can be accommodated in a high-density 2-2-3-3 arrangement. Energy attenuating seats, all with shoulder harness in Model 222B. Crew door at forward end of cabin on each side; cabin door on each side immediately forward of wing. Space for 1·05 m³ (37 cu ft) of baggage aft of cabin, with external door on starboard side. Ventilation standard; air-conditioning and heating optional.

SYSTEMS: Dual hydraulic systems, pressure 103·5 bars (1,500 lb/sq in). Maximum flow rate 15·1 litres (4 US gallons)/min. Open reservoir. Electrical system of Model 222B supplied by dual 150A DC generators, dual 250VA AC inverters, and 17Ah nickel-cadmium storage battery. Dual inverters deleted in Model 222UT, and 17Ah battery replaced by one of 34Ah capacity.

AVIONICS AND EQUIPMENT: Standard avionics in 222B comprise VHF transceiver and intercom system. Collins ProLine and King Gold Crown Series III avionics optional. Sperry SPZ-7000 digital automatic flight control system approved for single-pilot IFR operation in 222UT. Other avionics, blind-flying instrumentation and equipment, including Sperry Helipilot System, Bendix RDR-1400 weather radar and 1,270 kg (2,800 lb) capacity cargo hook kit, to customer's requirements.

DIMENSIONS, EXTERNAL:

Main rotor diameter	12·80 m (42 ft 0 in)
Tail rotor diameter	2·10 m (6 ft 10½ in)
Main rotor blade chord	0·66 m (2 ft 2 in)
Tail rotor blade chord	0·254 m (10 in)
Sponson chord: at root	1·55 m (5 ft 1 in)
at tip	1·49 m (4 ft 10¾ in)
Length: overall, rotors turning	15·36 m (50 ft 4¾ in)
fuselage	12·85 m (42 ft 2 in)
Width overall	3·46 m (11 ft 4 in)
Height overall	3·51 m (11 ft 6 in)
Wheel track: 222B	2·77 m (9 ft 1 in)
Wheelbase: 222B	3·70 m (12 ft 1¾ in)
Passenger doors (each): Height	1·30 m (4 ft 3 in)
Width	0·99 m (3 ft 3 in)
Height to sill	0·46 m (1 ft 6 in)
Baggage door (stbd, rear): Height	0·62 m (2 ft 0½ in)
Width	0·89 m (2 ft 11 in)
Height to sill	1·14 m (3 ft 9 in)

DIMENSIONS, INTERNAL:

Cabin (passenger area): Length	2·01 m (6 ft 7 in)
Max width	1·41 m (4 ft 7½ in)
Max height	1·30 m (4 ft 3 in)
Volume, incl crew area	5·52 m³ (195 cu ft)
Baggage hold	1·05 m³ (37 cu ft)
Hatbox (aft of cabin seats)	0·14 m³ (5 cu ft)

AREAS:

Main rotor blades (each)	4·23 m² (45·50 sq ft)
Tail rotor blades (each)	0·23 m² (2·45 sq ft)
Main rotor disc	128·7 m² (1,385·4 sq ft)
Tail rotor disc	3·46 m² (37·2 sq ft)
Vertical tail surfaces (total)	1·44 m² (15·5 sq ft)
Horizontal tail surfaces (total)	1·37 m² (14·8 sq ft)

WEIGHTS AND LOADING: (A: 222B; B: 222UT):

Weight empty: A	2,223 kg (4,900 lb)
B	2,210 kg (4,874 lb)
Max T-O and landing weight:	
internal payload	3,742 kg (8,250 lb)
external payload	1,270 kg (2,800 lb)
Max disc loading:	
internal payload	29·1 kg/m² (5·95 lb/sq ft)

PERFORMANCE (at max T-O weight, ISA. A: 222B; B: 222UT):

Never-exceed speed:	
at S/L: A, B	150 knots (278 km/h; 172 mph)
at 1,220 m (4,000 ft):	
A, B	156 knots (289 km/h; 179 mph)
Econ cruising speed, S/L to 1,220 m (4,000 ft):	
A	140 knots (259 km/h; 161 mph)
B	133 knots (246 km/h; 153 mph)
Max rate of climb at S/L: A, B	512 m (1,680 ft)/min
Service ceiling: A, B	4,815 m (15,800 ft)
Service ceiling, one engine out:	
A, B	2,285 m (7,500 ft)
Hovering ceiling: IGE: A, B	2,165 m (7,100 ft)
OGE: A, B	1,950 m (6,400 ft)
Range with max fuel at 1,220 m (4,000 ft), 20 min reserves: A	287 nm (532 km; 330 miles)
B	373 nm (691 km; 429 miles)
Range with max fuel at S/L, 20 min reserves:	
A	255 nm (472 km; 294 miles)
B	330 nm (610 km; 380 miles)

BELL MODEL D292 (ACAP)

Under the US Army's Advanced Composite Airframe Program (ACAP), Bell Helicopter Textron has been awarded a contract valued at $37 million to design and develop the prototype of an advanced composite-airframe helicopter. Phase I, engineering design and design support testing, began on 1 April 1981 and was completed by the end of 1982. Phase II, the construction and testing of three airframes, began in October 1982. The first airframe built was a tool-proofing article (TPA) and was used for repairability demonstrations and ballistics testing. The second airframe became the flight test vehicle (FTV) after systems installation. The FTV, which made its initial hover flight on 30 August 1985, is being used for shake testing, controls proof loading and EMC testing, in addition to 15 hours of ground running and 50 hours of flight testing, of which 12 hours had been completed by mid-January 1986. A third airframe is serving as static test article (STA) in trials which began in March 1985. By January 1986 the STA had been tested in four critical flight conditions and in vertical landing impacts of up to 5·8 m (19 ft)/s.

The purpose of the ACAP programme is to achieve the

Bell Model D292 ACAP prototype, pictured on its first flight on 30 August 1985

Army's goal of reducing weight and cost, and improving military helicopter characteristics, by demonstrating the application of advanced composite materials. Goals are a weight reduction of 22 per cent in airframe structure, a 17 per cent saving in cost, survivability in a 13 m (42 ft)/s vertical crash, and reduced radar signature. Each competing manufacturer has also designed a duplicate aircraft in current conventional metal construction for baseline comparison against the composite-construction aircraft.

Bell's design, which has the designation D292, embodies the power plant, transmission and rotor system of the commercial Model 222, and carries a crew of two and two passengers in energy absorbing seats. It has a non-retractable tailwheel type landing gear, embodying special energy absorbing devices in addition to oleos; design gross weight is 3,413 kg (7,525 lb). Selection of a particular composite material for each component of the helicopter has been made on the basis of required strength, toughness, environment, ballistic tolerance, crashworthiness, cost, and manufacturing methods. Thus, graphite is specified for such areas as the fuselage beams and frames, compartment bulkheads, and the forward roof, where high strength and stiffness are needed. The fuselage shells are of Kevlar/epoxy; tailboom skin and cargo floor of glassfibre/epoxy; the nose, canopy frame, vertical fin, horizontal stabiliser, fuel compartment bulkheads and general flooring of Kevlar/graphite/epoxy hybrid; the engine firewalls of Nextel/polyimide; and the rear cabin roof of graphite and/or glassfibre/Bismaleimide. Grumman Aerospace was responsible for building 30 per cent of the airframe, and Menasco Inc supplied the landing gear.

BELL MODEL 301

US Army designation: XV-15

Bell Helicopter has been working on tilt-rotor technology since the late 1940s, proving the concept feasible with its XV-3 prototype, described in the 1962-63 *Jane's*. Since that time development of tilt-rotor systems has progressed steadily, leading to the Model 301 which Bell proposed to meet a 1973 NASA/US Army requirement. The two research aircraft, on which design work was started in July 1973, have the Army designation XV-15; US Navy funding was provided in 1979 and 1980. The two XV-15s are being used in a research programme to prove the concept, explore the limits of the operational flight envelope and assess its application to military and civil transport needs.

The first aircraft (702) made its first free hovering flight on 3 May 1977. Flight tests of the second XV-15 in helicopter mode began on 23 April 1979. The first full in-flight conversion to aeroplane mode was made by this second XV-15 (N703NA) on 24 July 1979.

Details of the earlier stages of this programme can be found in the 1980-81 and previous editions of *Jane's*. Test achievements by the end of 1982 were summarised in the 1984-85 edition, and 1983-84 progress in the 1985-86 *Jane's*. New rotor blades, built of carbonfibre, glassfibre and Nomex, and developed by Boeing Vertol as part of the V-22 Osprey programme, were being fitted in the Spring of 1986.

The XV-15 structure, tilt-rotor and control systems were described in detail in the 1983-84 *Jane's*. An abbreviated description follows:

Type: Tilt-rotor research aircraft.

Rotor System: Two three-blade rotors, spring restrained, stiff in plane and gimballed, with stainless steel blades of high-twist design attached to titanium head by tension/torsion straps and roller pitch bearings. Elastomeric flapping restraints to increase helicopter mode control power and damping. Blades do not fold. No rotor brake.

Rotor Drive: Each rotor is driven by individual engine via reduction gear, engine coupling, rotor planetary gear and shaft centrebox. Interconnected driveshafts and redundant tilting mechanisms permit single-engine operation and fail-operative tilt capability.

Wings: Cantilever all-metal high-wing monoplane. Wing section Bell-modified NACA 64A223. Dihedral 2°. Incidence 3°. Forward sweep at quarter-chord 6° 30′. Light alloy 'flaperon' outboard and plain flap inboard on each trailing-edge.

Fuselage: Semi-monocoque fail-safe structure of light alloy.

Tail Unit: Cantilever structure of light alloy, with endplate fin and rudder mounted at each tailplane tip. Tailplane incidence ground-adjustable. Elevators and rudders powered hydraulically. No tabs.

Landing Gear: Hydraulically retractable tricycle type, as used originally on Canadair CL-84, with twin wheels on each unit. Main units retract forward into fuselage mounted landing gear pods, nose unit aft.

Power Plant: Two 1,156 kW (1,550 shp) Avco Lycoming LTC1K-4K turboshaft engines, each with a two minute contingency rating of 1.343 kW (1,800 shp), wingtip mounted with tilt mechanism operated by SPECO interconnected double ballscrew actuators. Two fuel tanks in each wing, total capacity 867 litres (229 US gallons).

Accommodation: Pilot and co-pilot on Rockwell-Columbus LW-3B ejection seats, side by side on flight deck, with access to cabin. Currently in austere test configuration for research equipment; cabin could accommodate nine personnel.

Dimensions, external:	
Rotor diameter (each)	7·62 m (25 ft 0 in)
Wing span over engine nacelles	10·72 m (35 ft 2 in)
Wing aspect ratio	6·12
Width overall, rotors turning	17·42 m (57 ft 2 in)
Length: fuselage	12·50 m (41 ft 0 in)
overall	12·83 m (42 ft 1 in)
Height: over tail fins	3·86 m (12 ft 8 in)
overall, nacelles vertical	4·67 m (15 ft 4 in)
Tail unit span (incl fins)	3·91 m (12 ft 10 in)
Wheel track, c/l of shock absorbers	2·64 m (8 ft 8 in)
Wheelbase	4·80 m (15 ft 9 in)
Cabin door (stbd): Height	1·37 m (4 ft 6 in)
Width	0·81 m (2 ft 8 in)
Height to sill	0·56 m (1 ft 10 in)
Dimensions, internal:	
Cabin (excl flight deck):	
Length	4·53 m (14 ft 10½ in)
Max width	1·52 m (5 ft 0 in)
Max height	1·52 m (5 ft 0 in)
Floor area	5·40 m² (58·1 sq ft)
Volume	8·50 m³ (300 cu ft)
Areas:	
Rotor discs (each)	45·60 m² (490·9 sq ft)
Wings, gross	15·70 m² (169·0 sq ft)
Weights and Loading:	
Weight empty	4,341 kg (9,570 lb)
Max payload (STOL)	1,542 kg (3,400 lb)
Max fuel weight	676 kg (1,490 lb)
Design T-O weight (VTO)	5,897 kg (13,000 lb)
Max T-O weight (STO)	6,804 kg (15,000 lb)
Max disc loading	74·2 kg/m² (15·2 lb/sq ft)
Performance (at design T-O weight):	
Never-exceed speed	364 knots (674 km/h; 419 mph)
Max level speed at 5,180 m (17,000 ft)	332 knots (615 km/h; 382 mph)
Max cruising speed at 4,970 m (16,300 ft)	303 knots (561 km/h; 349 mph)
Econ cruising speed at 6,100 m (20,000 ft)	200 knots (371 km/h; 230 mph)
Max rate of climb at S/L	960 m (3,150 ft)/min
Service ceiling	8,840 m (29,000 ft)
Service ceiling, one engine out	4,570 m (15,000 ft)
Hovering ceiling: IGE	3,200 m (10,500 ft)
OGE	2,635 m (8,650 ft)
Min ground turning radius	6·83 m (22 ft 5 in)
Range with max fuel	445 nm (824 km; 512 miles)

BELL/BOEING VERTOL V-22 OSPREY

Bell is teamed with Boeing Vertol in a joint programme, based on the Model 301/XV-15, to meet the US government's Joint Services Advanced Vertical Lift Aircraft (formerly JVX) proposal, named V-22 Osprey in January 1985. The US Navy and US Air Force are currently participating in the programme, with the USN as executive service.

On 26 April 1983 the two companies received a US Naval Air Systems Command contract to proceed with preliminary design of the aircraft over the following 24 months. Two further contracts, totalling $17·5 million, were awarded in April 1985 for systems engineering, long-lead tooling, a V-22 mockup, and purchasing and design analysis for the aircraft's engine interface and avionics integration. Bell/Boeing Vertol, as prime contractors, have subcontracted Grumman to design and build the V-22's tail unit, General Electric for the digital fly by wire flight control system, Lockheed-Georgia for the wing control surfaces and fixed trailing-edge, and Menasco of Canada and Dowty of Canada respectively for nose and main landing gear. Boeing will build the fuselage and overwing fairing; Bell is responsible for wings, nacelles, drive system and prop-rotor assemblies.

In January 1984 Bell began a simulated V-22 flight test programme, using data from wind tunnel tests and analyses. Formal evaluation by military pilots, using NASA/Ames simulation, began in the following March. Boeing Vertol has built a two-thirds scale rotor/wing model to prove hover performance predictions. Testing of critical structural components was co-ordinated at Bell and Boeing Vertol.

In December 1985 the US Navy announced its selection of the 4,475 kW (6,000 shp) class Allison 501-M80C (T406) turboshaft engine for the V-22. Pratt & Whitney Government Products Division was named in April 1986 as second production source for the engine.

On 2 May 1986 Naval Air Systems Command awarded Bell/Boeing Vertol $497·3 million as the first instalment of a $1,714 million fixed price incentive award contract for a seven-year full scale development (FSD) programme for the V-22. This will include the manufacture of six flying prototypes, three to be completed by each partner, and three non-flying airframes for static, ground and fatigue testing. The V-22's first flight is scheduled for 18 June 1988, with production deliveries beginning in December 1991.

The V-22 Osprey has been conceived as a multi-mission aircraft. The US Marine Corps, which will receive the first production examples, has a requirement for 552 assault transport variants, designated **MV-22A**, to replace CH-46 and CH-53 helicopters. The MV-22A is required to carry 24 combat-equipped Marines at a speed of 250 knots (463 km/h; 288 mph) over an operational radius of 200 nm (370 km; 230 miles), with the ability to hover at 915 m (3,000 ft) at an ambient air temperature of 33°C. The US Navy has a requirement for up to 50 combat search and rescue aircraft, designated **HV-22A**, to replace HH-3 helicopters. In this role, the Osprey would be required to operate at 250

Bell XV-15 tilt-rotor research aircraft *(Aerofax/Jay Miller)*

knots (463 km/h; 288 mph) over a 460 nm (852 km; 530 mile) radius and hover mid-mission at 2,135 m (7,000 ft) OGE, with accommodation for four survivors. The US Navy has also expressed an interest in up to 300 V-22s for anti-submarine warfare duties.

The US Air Force requires 80 long-range special operations aircraft, designated **CV-22A**, to carry 12 special forces troops or up to 1,306 kg (2,880 lb) of internal cargo over a 700 nm (1,297 km; 806 mile) mission radius at 250 knots (463 km/h; 288 mph), with capability to hover OGE at 1,525 m (5,000 ft).

The US Army, although not involved in the development phase, currently has plans to procure 231 aircraft in the Marine Corps configuration for multi-mission transport duties, including utility operations, medical evacuation and corps area operations, making a total requirement for the US services of 1,213 aircraft.

Additional requirements specified by one or more of the services for the V-22 Osprey include an unrefuelled ferry range of 2,100 nm (3,892 km; 2,418 miles) for self-deployability; in-flight refuelling capability; ability to carry outsize external loads of up to 4,536 kg (10,000 lb); all-weather low-altitude capability; all-weather low-altitude navigation capability; self-protection; and low maintenance. To meet the Navy/Marine Corps requirement for operation from US Navy amphibious assault ships, the wing and rotor system must 'fold' in 90 seconds. After landing, the rotor blades are stopped and folded inboard automatically; nacelles are then rotated to the aeroplane mode, bringing the folded blades in line with the wing leading-edge; finally, the entire wing is rotated automatically by a Lucas Aerospace actuator and locking unit, to align it with the fuselage. The Ospreys for the Navy and US Air Force will be fitted with Texas Instruments AN/APQ-168 multi-mode radar.

The following data are provisional:

DIMENSIONS, EXTERNAL:

Rotor diameter (each)	11·58 m (38 ft 0 in)
Distance between rotor centres	14·19 m (46 ft 6¾ in)
Length overall	17·47 m (57 ft 4 in)
Height: over tail fins	5·28 m (17 ft 4 in)
overall, nacelles vertical	6·15 m (20 ft 2 in)
Tail unit span, incl fins	5·61 m (18 ft 5 in)
Width over mainwheels	4·64 m (15 ft 2½ in)
Nacelle ground clearance, nacelles vertical	1·58 m (5 ft 2½ in)

DIMENSIONS, INTERNAL:

Cabin: Length	7·32 m (24 ft 0 in)
Width	1·83 m (6 ft 0 in)
Height	1·83 m (6 ft 0 in)

AREA:

Rotor discs (each)	105·4 m² (1,134 sq ft)

WEIGHTS:

Max T-O weight:	
STOL (20° forward tilt)	26,762 kg (59,000 lb)
VTOL	21,546 kg (47,500 lb)

PERFORMANCE:

Max cruising speed at max STOL T-O weight	340 knots (630 km/h; 391 mph)
T-O run at max STOL T-O weight	less than 152 m (500 ft)

BELL MODEL 680 ROTOR

On 27 May 1982 Bell began test flying its new Model 680 composite bearingless rotor system, which promises significant improvements in performance, noise levels and ride quality. By May 1985, after more than 375 hours of flight testing in four-blade form on a Model 222, indications were that all basic goals had been achieved. The Model 680 system, intended for application to future rather than present Bell designs, consists of a one-piece glassfibre yoke with inboard flapping flexures and outboard feathering elements. Elastomeric shear pads for lead-lag damping and elastomeric shear restraints to control feathering motion are incorporated between the yoke and the cuff assemblies. All major components are of composite construction, with at least 50 per cent fewer parts and a weight reduction of 15 per cent.

Industrial co-operation is continuing, with Dornier GmbH of Germany as partner, to develop a higher-thrust version of the Model 680 known at present as 'Rotor 90'. Intended to be applicable to helicopters in the 8-ton class, Rotor 90 is a hingeless, bearingless design comprising only six basic parts, and was planned to be ready for flight test by mid-1986. Blade tooling is being developed by Bell and hub tooling by Dornier.

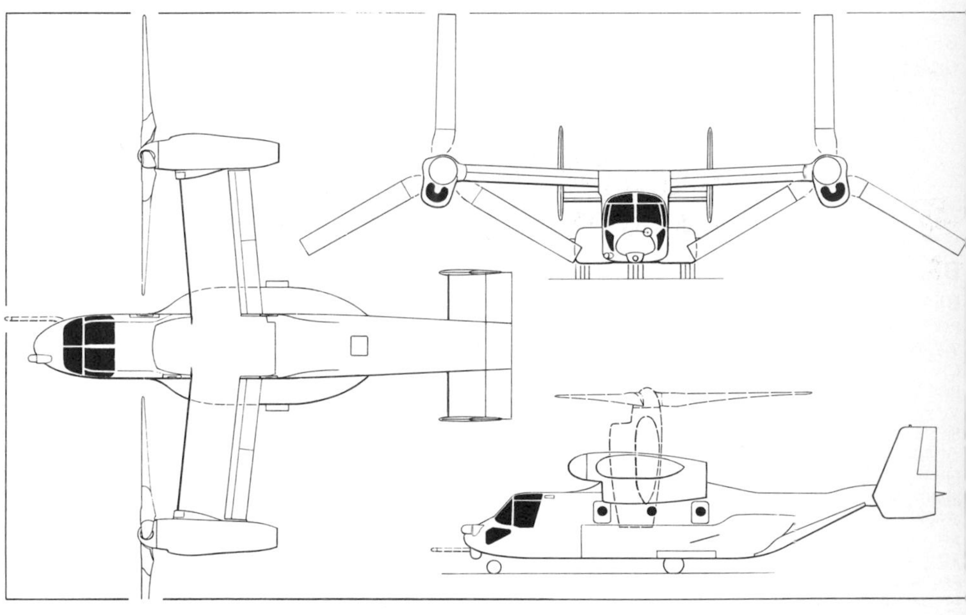

Bell/Boeing Vertol V-22 Osprey multi-mission tilt-rotor aircraft *(Pilot Press)*

BELL ARTI and LHX

In 1982 the US Army invited manufacturers to submit design concepts for its Light Helicopter Experimental (LHX) programme, representing a requirement for some 5,000 helicopters in two variants: scout/attack (SCAT) and utility, both using the same dynamic systems. Bell began a contracted study which included derivative variants of the UH-1 and AH-1, as well as new designs for helicopters and high-performance (tilt-rotor) craft. The US Army subsequently announced that a conventional helicopter rather than a tilt-rotor is wanted for the LHX requirement. Accordingly, Bell is concentrating on a single main rotor design incorporating the Model 680 bearingless main rotor system, composite materials adapted from the ACAP programme, a ring-fin tail rotor, and twin 895 kW (1,200 shp) T800 turboshaft engines. Specifications for the **LHX** design include main and tail rotor diameters of 11·58 m (38 ft) and 1·92 m (6·3 ft), max length with rotors turning of 14·02 m (46 ft), and width over landing gear of 2·29 m (7·5 ft). Primary mission gross weight is 3,402-3,855 kg (7,500-8,500 lb), with a fuel capacity of 700 litres (185 US gallons), and a speed of 170 knots (315 km/h; 196 mph) at max continuous power. In accordance with US Army specifications it will be designed to fire Hellfire and Stinger missiles, 2·75 inch rockets and a single-barrel 20 mm cannon.

A major supporting contract for the LHX is the Advanced Rotorcraft Technology Integration **(ARTI)** effort. In December 1983 Bell received a contract to design a single-pilot cockpit for the SCAT LHX, which will fly all-weather, day and night nap of the earth missions. The requirement calls for an aircraft that can fly itself while simultaneously seeking, identifying and assigning priority to targets. Bell is in partnership with Sperry Flight Systems, Honeywell Inc and Texas Instruments on the ARTI contract, and in early 1985 began conducting 'hands-off' flight tests of the digital fly by wire AFCS using the experimental YAH-1S four-blade Model 249 HueyCobra as the testbed aircraft. In fact, the FBW system is activated by 'hands-on' controls, but once selected the pilot can temporarily delegate his piloting task to the system while he performs navigation, target designation, weapon operating or other functions. He can interrupt the automatic flight mode and assume manual control at any time.

Bell artist's impression of possible LHX contender

Bell/Boeing Osprey in US Marine Corps MV-22A configuration

BELLANCA

BELLANCA AIRCRAFT ENGINEERING INC

Galena, Maryland 21635
Telephone: (301) 648 5172
PRESIDENT AND DESIGNER: August T. Bellanca

DIRECTOR OF CERTIFICATION: Millard F. Griffiths

TEST PILOT: Patrick J. Foley

The original Bellanca Aircraft Corporation of New Castle, Delaware, merged with companies not engaged in aircraft manufacture and lost its identity in 1959. The present company was formed by Mr August Bellanca, son of the late G. M. Bellanca, to initiate and develop a family of entirely new high-performance fuel-efficient single- and twin-engined aircraft. Full details of the first of these, the six-seat Model 25 Skyrocket light cabin monoplane, can be found in previous editions of *Jane's*.

BELLANCA

BELLANCA INC

PO Box 964, Alexandria, Minnesota 56308
Telephone: (612) 762 1501
CHAIRMAN OF THE BOARD: James M. Miller
PRESIDENT: Charles F. Holm
VICE-PRESIDENT: Marge Mitchell
SECRETARY/TREASURER: Gerald E. Sather

This company, then known as Viking Aviation, acquired in 1982 the assets of the former Bellanca Aircraft Corporation (see 1981-82 and earlier editions of *Jane's*), which went into liquidation in 1981. The executives of Viking Aviation were mainly from Miller Flying Service, Schiller & Associates, and Weber's Aero Repair, and they remain as executives of Bellanca Inc.

The company's initial activity was limited to provision of product support for the Bellanca Viking series of four-seat light business aircraft (of which 1,598 had been built by January 1979) and various 14 Series models; replacement parts for the Viking are being manufactured under FAA-PMA approval. Bellanca Inc holds the type certificates and production inventory for Models 14-19, 14-19-2, 14-19-3, 14-19-3A, 17-30, 17-31, 17-31TC, 17-30A, 17-31A and 17-31ATC. Production of the Bellanca Viking resumed in 1984. Sales are handled exclusively by Miller Flying Service, PO Box 190, Plainview, Texas 79072.

In 1984 Bellanca Inc also acquired the FAA type certificate and production jigs for the Eagle Aircraft Eagle agricultural biplane (see 1983-84 *Jane's*). Bellanca provides support for existing Eagles, but has no immediate plans to resume production. Eagle Aircraft built 96 of these biplanes, of which about 80 were in service at the beginning of 1985.

BELLANCA VIKING SERIES

There are three current aircraft in the Viking series, developed from the earlier Bellanca 260C and Standard Viking 300 (see 1971-72 *Jane's*), as follows:

Model 17-30A Super Viking 300A. Powered by a 224 kW (300 hp) Continental IO-520-K flat-six engine, driving a McCauley two- or three-blade metal constant-speed propeller.

Model 17-31A Super Viking 300A. This is identical to the foregoing version except for the installation of a 224 kW (300 hp) Lycoming IO-540-K1E5 engine, driving a Hartzell three-blade constant-speed propeller.

Model 17-31ATC Turbo Viking 300A. Powered by a 224 kW (300 hp) Lycoming IO-540-K1E5 engine with two Rajay turbochargers. Hartzell three-blade constant-speed propeller.

By early 1986 Bellanca had completed nine Vikings since production was resumed.

TYPE: Four-seat light business aircraft.

WINGS: Cantilever low-wing monoplane. Bellanca B wing section. Dihedral 4° 30′. Incidence 0° at root, −3° at tip. Structure consists of two laminated Sitka spruce spars, mahogany plywood and spruce ribs and mahogany plywood skin, covered with Dacron. Dacron covered wooden ailerons and electrically actuated flaps.

FUSELAGE: Welded 4130 steel tube structure, covered with Dacron. Two-piece glassfibre engine cowling, suspended from firewall.

TAIL UNIT: Strut braced welded 4130 steel tube structure, covered with Dacron. Sweptback vertical surfaces. Trim tab in port elevator.

LANDING GEAR: Tricycle type, with Auto-Axion electro-hydraulic retraction, which lowers gear automatically during approach if pilot omits to do so, and prevents accidental retraction on ground. Manual emergency extension. Nosewheel retracts rearward, mainwheels forward into underwing fairings, optionally enclosed by doors. Spring-air-oil shock absorbers. Mainwheel tyres size 6·00-6 six-ply. Steerable nosewheel. Goodyear type 2-747 hydraulic disc brakes. Parking brakes.

POWER PLANT: One flat-six engine (details given under model descriptions). Six fuel tanks in wings with total usable capacity of 257 litres (68 US gallons). Optional auxiliary fuel tank in fuselage, increasing max usable capacity to 314 litres (83 US gallons). Refuelling points above each wing and on starboard side of fuselage. Oil capacity 11·5 litres (3 US gallons).

Bellanca 17-30A Super Viking 300A *(Mike Jerram)*

ACCOMMODATION: Four seats in pairs in enclosed cabin. Dual controls standard, with brakes on port side only. Moulded glassfibre door on starboard side of cabin. Tinted glass. Baggage space, capacity 84 kg (186 lb) aft of rear seats, with glassfibre external door and in-flight access. Provision for tube carrying skis, max weight 9 kg (20 lb). Heating, ventilation and windscreen defrosting standard.

SYSTEMS: 12V electrical system, with Prestolite 60A alternator, solid-state regulator and 12V 33Ah battery. Hydraulic system for brakes only. Partial provisions for oxygen system.

AVIONICS AND EQUIPMENT: Standard equipment includes cylinder head temperature gauge, manifold pressure gauge, sensitive altimeter, internally-illuminated instruments with rheostat controls, stall warning system, anti-glare instrument panel cover, individually adjustable seats with shoulder harness, arm and headrests, pilot's storm window, tinted windows, map pockets, super soundproofing, dome light, map light, landing/taxi light, navigation lights, quick oil drain, tiedown rings and towbar. With factory installed radio equipment the following additional equipment is standard: Narco omni antenna, Electro Voice microphone, power cable, Narco VP-10 broad-band transmitting antenna and microphone jacks. Mitchell Century I, II or III autopilot optional, with optional accessories which include radio tracker, radio coupler and automatic trim for Century II or III, glideslope coupler for Century III, electric trim and switch kits. Optional radio and navigation equipment includes Bendix, Collins, King and Narco VHF transceivers, transponders and marker beacon receivers; Bendix, Collins, King, Kett and Narco ADF radio receivers; King and Narco DME and Narco course line computer. Miscellaneous optional equipment includes full blind-flying instrumentation, turn co-ordinator, outside air temperature gauge, vacuum gauge, 8-day clock, exhaust gas temperature gauge, strobe lights, heated pitot, emergency locator transmitter, boom microphone and control wheel switch, co-pilot brakes, cabin fire extinguisher, golf club/ski container, reclining front seats, inertia reel shoulder harness for each seat, cabin entry step, sun visor, external power socket, electrical operation of elevator trim, stereo tape player, Whelen strobe lights, Alcor engine analyser, Avicon digital engine analyser, Astrotech elapsed digital timer, alternate static source, altitude encoder, true airspeed indicator and Hobbs flight hour meter.

DIMENSIONS, EXTERNAL:
- Wing span — 10·41 m (34 ft 2 in)
- Length overall — 8·02 m (26 ft 4 in)
- Height overall — 2·24 m (7 ft 4 in)
- Tailplane span — 3·71 m (12 ft 2 in)
- Wheel track — 2·74 m (9 ft 0 in)
- Wheelbase — 2·24 m (7 ft 4 in)
- Propeller diameter — 2·03 m (6 ft 8 in)
- Cabin door: Height — 0·95 m (3 ft 1½ in)
  - Max width — 0·88 m (2 ft 10½ in)
- Baggage compartment door:
  - Height — 0·61 m (2 ft 0 in)
  - Width — 0·51 m (1 ft 8¼ in)

DIMENSIONS, INTERNAL:
- Cabin:
  - Length, firewall to rear wall — 3·10 m (10 ft 2 in)
  - Max width — 1·09 m (3 ft 7 in)
  - Max height — 1·19 m (3 ft 11 in)
- Baggage compartment volume — 0·34 m³ (12·08 cu ft)

AREAS:
- Wings, gross — 15·00 m² (161·5 sq ft)
- Ailerons (total) — 1·09 m² (11·77 sq ft)
- Trailing-edge flaps (total) — 1·50 m² (16·16 sq ft)

WEIGHTS (A: IO-520, B: IO-540, C: turbocharged IO-540):
- Weight empty: A — 991 kg (2,185 lb)
  - B — 1,019 kg (2,247 lb)
  - C — 1,076 kg (2,372 lb)
- Max T-O weight — 1,508 kg (3,325 lb)
- Max wing loading — 112·3 kg/m² (23·0 lb/sq ft)
- Max power loading — 5·88 kg/kW (9·65 lb/hp)

PERFORMANCE (at max T-O weight, A: IO-520, B: IO-540, C: turbocharged IO-540):
- Never-exceed speed:
  - A, B, C — 196 knots (363 km/h; 226 mph)
- Max level speed at S/L:
  - A — 181 knots (335 km/h; 208 mph)
  - B — 174 knots (322 km/h; 200 mph)
- Max cruising speed (75% power):
  - A — 175 knots (325 km/h; 202 mph)
  - B — 165 knots (306 km/h; 190 mph)
  - C at 7,315 m (24,000 ft) — 193 knots (357 km/h; 222 mph)
- Cruising speed (65% power):
  - A — 159 knots (295 km/h; 183 mph)
  - B — 163 knots (303 km/h; 188 mph)
  - C at 7,315 m (24,000 ft) — 175 knots (325 km/h; 202 mph)
- Stalling speed, wheels and flaps down:
  - A, B, C — 61 knots (113 km/h; 70 mph) CAS
- Max rate of climb at S/L: A — 369 m (1,210 ft)/min
  - B, C — 356 m (1,170 ft)/min
- Service ceiling: A — 6,100 m (20,000 ft)
  - B — 5,550 m (18,200 ft)
- Certificated ceiling — 7,315 m (24,000 ft)
- T-O to 15 m (50 ft): A, B, C — 433 m (1,420 ft)
- Landing from 15 m (50 ft): A, B, C — 409 m (1,340 ft)
- Max range with max optional fuel, cruise at 75% power, with allowances for start, taxi, S/L T-O, climb and descent, no reserves:
  - A — 929 nm (1,722 km; 1,070 miles)
  - B — 821 nm (1,521 km; 945 miles)
  - C — 802 nm (1,485 km; 923 miles)

BENSEN — *see Sport Aircraft section*

BOEING

THE BOEING COMPANY

PO Box 3707, Seattle, Washington 98124
Telephone: (206) 655 2121
ESTABLISHED: July 1916
CHAIRMAN OF THE BOARD: T. A. Wilson
VICE-CHAIRMAN: Malcolm T. Stamper
PRESIDENT AND CHIEF EXECUTIVE OFFICER:
Frank A. Shrontz
EXECUTIVE VICE-PRESIDENT & CHIEF FINANCIAL OFFICER:
Harold W. Haynes
SENIOR VICE-PRESIDENTS:
L. D. Alford
K. F. Holtby
W. M. Maulden
R. W. Tharrington
VICE-PRESIDENTS:
R. E. Bateman
D. P. Beighle (Contracts, General Counsel and Secretary)
R. B. Brown
D. J. Crispin
F. G. Coffey
D. D. Cruze
S. M. Little (Industrial and Public Relations)
A. H. Lowell (Controller)
B. Mishel (Washington DC Office)
J. H. Morrison
H. C. Munson
B. D. Pinick
John M. Swihart (Airplane Marketing Analysis)
TREASURER: J. B. L. Pierce
PUBLIC RELATIONS AND ADVERTISING DIRECTOR:
H. E. Carr

Operating components of The Boeing Company include:

Boeing Commercial Airplane Company
See following entry

Boeing Aerospace Company
See pages 376-378 of this section

Boeing Military Airplane Company
See pages 378-381 of this section

Boeing Vertol Company
See pages 381-386 of this section

In May 1961 The Boeing Airplane Company changed its proprietary name to The Boeing Company in recognition of its diversified interests. On 19 December 1972 three of its operating organisations were designated as companies, comprising Boeing Commercial Airplane Company, Renton, Washington; Boeing Aerospace Company, Kent, Washington; and Boeing Vertol Company, Philadelphia, Pennsylvania. The Boeing Military Airplane Company at Wichita, Kansas, was formed in Autumn 1979 to replace the former Boeing Wichita Company and to take over some aircraft programmes from Boeing Aerospace Company.

A factory with an area of 75,000 m² (807,300 sq ft) at St James-Assiniboia Airport, near Winnipeg, produces 747 components.

On 31 January 1986 The Boeing Company completed the purchase of de Havilland Canada Ltd from the Canadian government (see entry in Canadian section of this edition).

Total employment within The Boeing Company was approximately 97,500 at the beginning of 1986.

BOEING COMMERCIAL AIRPLANE COMPANY (BCAC)

PO Box 3707, Seattle, Washington 98124
Telephone: (206) 237 2121
PRESIDENT: Dean D. Thornton
EXECUTIVE VICE-PRESIDENTS:
R. R. Albrecht (Chairman, Boeing Canada and Sales, Marketing, Contracts, International Business and Customer Relations)
Philip M. Condit (Engineering, Manufacturing, Product Development and Customer Services)
Joseph F. Sutter (Special Assignments)
SENIOR VICE-PRESIDENT: Ernest V. Fenn
VICE-PRESIDENTS:
M. S. Belyamani (Middle East, Africa and Latin America Sales)
J. A. Blue (Quality Assurance)
Borge Boeskov (Europe Sales)
R. E. Brown (Product Development)
Ben A. Cosgrove (Engineering)
R. C. Gamrath (General Manager, Fabrication Division)
Bruce Gissing (Renton Division)
James T. Johnson (7J7 Division)
W. G. Loeken (Finance)
J. C. Longridge (Marketing)
R. E. McDonald (Computing Systems)
George D. Nible (Customer Services)
R. P. Norton (International Sales, Asia and Pacific)
Robert E. Perdue (US and Canada)
O. M. Roetman (Contracts)
W. L. Shineman (General Manager, Everett Division)
R. W. Taylor (Government Technical Liaison)
E. L. Webb (General Manager, Engineering Division)
R. B. Woodard (Materiel)
Brien S. Wygle (Flight Operations and Airline Technical Support)
Robert E. Wylie (US and Used Aircraft)
DIVISION COUNSEL: D. L. Clancy

The Boeing Commercial Airplane Company, with headquarters at the company's Renton, Washington, facility just south of Seattle, was reorganised in 1983 into three divisions. Renton Division is responsible for manufacture of 707, 727, 737 and 757 series aircraft; the Everett Division handles the 747 and 767 programmes; and the Fabrication Division serves the other operating groups with its massive NC machine capability. A separate Engineering Organisation, reporting to company headquarters, is responsible for such functions as technology, quality control and flight operations. A Materiel Division was created in 1984 to consolidate activities of purchasing, quality control and vendor supplies.

Including military derivatives, 3 Model 707s, 115 Model 737s, 24 Model 747s, 36 Model 757s and 25 Model 767s were delivered in 1985. Orders for 390 new air transports (282 of them Model 737s), valued at approximately $14,900 million, were announced by Boeing customers during the year. Deliveries during the first six months of 1986 comprised 1 Model 707, 11 Model 737-200s, 49 Model 737-300s, 17 Model 747s, 19 Model 757s and 12 Model 767s. Schedules called for the delivery of 5 Model 707s, 9 Model 737-200s, 69 Model 737-300s, 17 Model 747s, 16 Model 757s and 15 Model 767s during the remainder of 1986. Cumulative total of announced orders was 5,693 aircraft on 30 September 1986, of which 4,981 had been delivered. On 17 August 1986 Boeing rolled out its 5,000th commercial jet airliner, a Model 737-300 for KLM Royal Dutch Airlines. The company estimated that more than 5·6 billion passengers had been carried by that date on its jet airliners, which had collectively flown about 63·2 billion miles (101,700 million km), or the equivalent of 340 round trips between the Earth and the Sun.

In January 1986 The Boeing Commercial Airplane Company, Industri Pesawat Terbang Nurtanio (IPTN) of Indonesia and Messerschmitt-Bölkow-Blohm GmbH (MBB) of West Germany signed a memorandum of understanding for possible joint development of a future advanced technology passenger aircraft in the 100-seat class. Fokker BV of the Netherlands joined the team in September 1986.

BOEING MODEL 707

USAF designations: VC-137 and E-8A

The prototype for the Boeing Model 707, designated Model 367-80, was the first jet transport designed as such to be completed and flown in the United States. It made its first flight on 15 July 1954, and a developed version was ordered in large numbers as a flight refuelling tanker/transport for the US Air Force under the designation KC-135 (Boeing Model 717).

On 13 July 1955 Boeing was given clearance by the US Air Force to build commercial developments of the prototype concurrently with the production of KC-135s. These transport aircraft, with the basic designations of Boeing 707 and 720, were manufactured in many versions. Details can be found in the 1980-81 and earlier editions of *Jane's*. The last commercially configured example, a 707-320C for the Moroccan government, was delivered in March 1982.

Manufacture continued in 1985-86 solely to provide airframes for the USAF/NATO military AWACS and Saudi Arabian defence programmes, details of which can be found in the Boeing Aerospace Company section of this entry. Deliveries of all commercial and military models totalled 970 by 30 September 1986, when orders totalled 988 aircraft. Boeing Military Airplane Company is offering tanker/transport conversions of ex-airline 707s, as described under the BMAC entry. The Boeing 707 to be utilised for the Joint STARS attack radar system is designated **E-8A**.

BOEING MODEL 737-200, CORPORATE 77-32 and SURVEILLER

USAF designation: T-43A

The decision to build this short-range transport was announced by Boeing on 19 February 1965. Simultaneously, a first order for 21 aircraft was placed by Lufthansa.

The original Model 737 was designed to utilise many components and assemblies already in production for the Boeing 727. Design began on 11 May 1964, and the first Model 737 flew on 9 April 1967. Deliveries began before the end of 1967, following FAA certification on 15 December. Sales of all versions of the 737 totalled 1,724 by 30 September 1986; a total of 1,274 had been delivered by that date, including 19 Model 737-200s modified as T-43A navigation trainers for the US Air Force (see 1975-76 *Jane's*) and three maritime reconnaissance 737-200 Surveillers for Indonesia. The Boeing 737 was the third commercial transport to reach a sales total of one thousand.

Details of the early production versions of the Model 737, and of subsequent design development can be found in the 1974-75 *Jane's*. Versions currently available are as follows:

Advanced 737-200. Current standard model, with max ramp weight of 52,615 kg (116,000 lb) and max T-O weight of 52,390 kg (115,500 lb). JT8D-15A engines (each 68·9 kN; 15,500 lb st) standard; JT8D-17A (71·2 kN; 16,000 lb st) optional; basic fuel capacity of 19,532 litres (5,160 US gallons). Accommodation for 115 passengers and baggage, with 86 cm (34 in) pitch seating, or up to 130 passengers in 76 cm (30 in) pitch seating with no reduction in cabin facilities. Use of graphite composite in place of former aluminium honeycomb in the latest production aircraft reduces the weight of the rudder, elevators and ailerons. Coupled with further use of composites in a new advanced technology interior, this results in a total weight reduction of more than 454 kg (1,000 lb).

Advanced 737-200C/QC. Standard convertible passenger/cargo model with strengthened fuselage and floor, and a large two-position upper deck cargo door with effective opening of 2·15 m × 3·40 m (7 ft 0½ in × 11 ft 2 in). The quick change (QC) feature allows more rapid conversion by using palletised passenger seating and other special interior furnishings.

Corporate 77-32. Same as standard Advanced 737-200, except interiors are adapted to special business and executive luxury requirements. Executive interiors can be obtained from vendors. Additional fuel capacity offered by installation of fuel cells in lower cargo compartments. With max fuel this model can carry a 1,134 kg (2,500 lb) payload up to 4,000 nm (7,412 km; 4,606 miles).

Advanced 737-200 High Gross Weight Structure. Higher gross weight models of the Advanced 737-200/200C, for longer-range use, are available in two versions. One has a maximum taxi weight of 56,700 kg (125,000 lb) and a maximum T-O weight of 56,472 kg (124,500 lb) with JT8D-15A or JT8D-17A engines, and a fuel capacity of either 21,009 litres (5,550 US gallons) or 22,598 litres (5,970 US gallons). The additional capacity for increased range

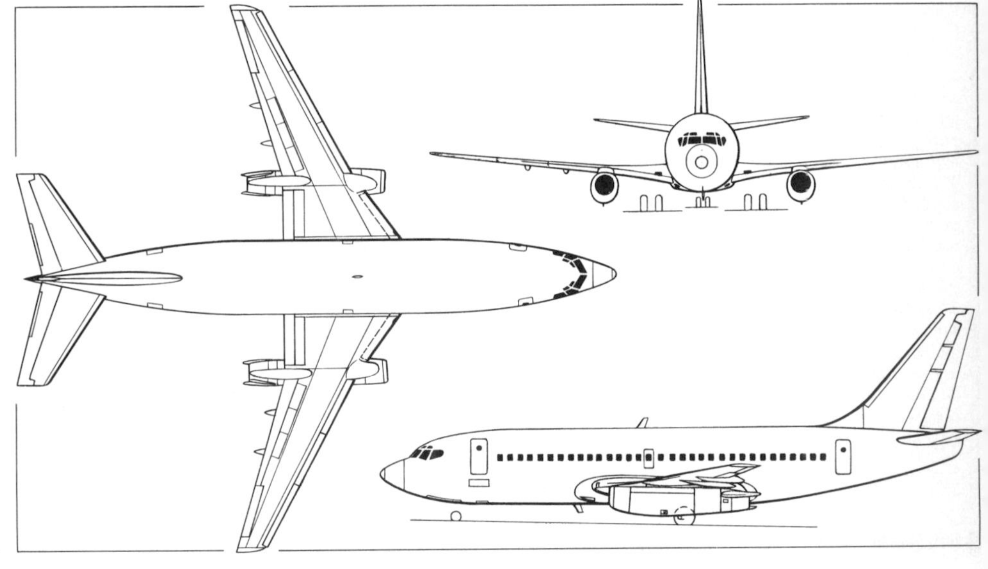

Boeing 737-200 twin-turbofan short-range transport *(Pilot Press)*

capability is provided by a 1,476 litre (390 US gallon) or a 3,066 litre (810 US gallon) fuel tank installed in the aft lower cargo compartment. The second version, with a maximum taxi weight of 58,332 kg (128,600 lb), maximum T-O weight of 58,105 kg (128,100 lb), design landing weight of 48,534 kg (107,000 lb), and maximum zero-fuel weight of 43,091 kg (95,000 lb), has approximately 650 nm (1,204 km; 748 miles) greater range capability than the standard Advanced 737-200. Sectors of 2,300 nm (4,262 km; 2,648 miles) can be served with a 130 passenger payload and typical fuel reserves. Aircraft is identical to the current Advanced 737-200 except for the auxiliary fuel tank, new wheels, tyres and brakes.

All 737-200 versions meet FAR Pt 36 and ICAO Annex 16 in respect of noise characteristics.

An FAA certificated kit is available which enables the Model 737 to operate from unpaved or gravel runways. The kit includes a vortex dissipator for each engine, consisting of a short hollow boom that protrudes from under each engine's forward edge. The boom is capped by a plug with downward facing orifices. Pressurised engine bleed air forced through these orifices destroys any ground level vortex and prevents small pieces of gravel being ingested by the engines. Other items include a gravel deflection 'ski' on the nosewheel, deflectors between the main landing gear wheels, protective shields over hydraulic tubing and speed brake cable on the main gear strut, glassfibre reinforcement of lower inboard flap surfaces, application of Teflon-base paint to fuselage and wing undersurfaces and provision of more robust DME, ATC and VHF antennae.

On 10 February 1980 British Airways began operations with the first of 44 Advanced 737s which the airline and its British Airtours subsidiary call 'Super 737s'. These aircraft are equipped with advanced flight deck avionics, including a Sperry SP-177 digital automatic flight control system. Lufthansa ordered 38 Advanced 737s with similar equipment. Category IIIA certification of these AFCS versions was granted on 2 December 1981.

Surveiller. Specially equipped 737-200 for use primarily in a maritime surveillance role. The specialised equipment consists of a Motorola high-resolution side-looking airborne modular multi-mission radar (SLAMMR), its console linked to two 5 m (16 ft) long blade antennae, mounted one on each side of the upper rear fuselage. This installation makes it possible to spot a small ship in heavy sea conditions at a range of 100 nm (185 km; 115 miles) on each side of the aircraft's flight path from a height of 9,150 m (30,000 ft). Three 737-200 Surveillers delivered to Indonesian Air Force each have 14 first class and 88 tourist class seats so that they can be used also for government transport purposes.

737-300. Developed from Advanced 737-200, and entered service in December 1984. Described separately.

Corporate 77-33. Corporate/executive transport version of 737-300. Described separately.

737-400. 'Stretched' version of 737-300: described separately.

The description which follows applies to the commercial versions of the 737-200 in current production:

TYPE: Twin-turbofan short-range transport.

WINGS: Cantilever low-wing monoplane. Special Boeing wing sections. Average thickness/chord ratio 12·89%. Dihedral 6°. Incidence 1° at root. Sweepback at quarter-chord 25°. Aluminium alloy dual-path fail-safe two-spar structure. Ailerons of graphite composite construction. Triple-slotted trailing-edge flaps of aluminium, with trailing-edges of aluminium honeycomb. Aluminium alloy Krueger flaps on leading-edge, inboard of nacelles. Three leading-edge slats of aluminium alloy with aluminium honeycomb trailing-edge on each wing from engine to wingtip. Two graphite composite flight spoilers on each outer wing serve both as airbrakes in the air and for lateral control, in association with ailerons. Two graphite composite ground spoilers on each wing, one outboard and one inboard of engine, are used only during landing. Ailerons are hydraulically powered by two hydraulic systems with manual reversion. Trailing-edge flaps are hydraulically powered, with electrical backup. Leading-edge slats and Krueger flaps are symmetrically powered by one hydraulic system normally, and by a second hydraulic system for alternate extension. Flight spoilers are symmetrically powered by the two main individual hydraulic systems. Engine bleed air for anti-icing supplied to engine nose cowls and all wing leading-edge slats.

FUSELAGE: Aluminium alloy semi-monocoque fail-safe structure.

TAIL UNIT: Cantilever aluminium alloy multi-spar structure, with graphite composite control surfaces. Variable incidence tailplane. Elevator has dual hydraulic power, with manual reversion. Rudder is powered by a dual actuator from two main hydraulic systems, with a standby hydraulic actuator and system. Tailplane trim has dual electric drive motors, with manual backup. Elevator control tabs for manual reversion are locked out during hydraulic actuation.

LANDING GEAR: Hydraulicaly retractable tricycle type, with free-fall emergency extension. Nosewheels retract forward, main units inward. No main-gear doors: wheels form wheel well seal. Twin wheels on each main and nose unit. Boeing oleo-pneumatic shock absorbers. Mainwheels and tyres size 40 × 14-16 (low-pressure 40 × 18-17 tyres, or C40 × 14-21/H40 × 14·5-19 tyres with heavy duty wheel brakes, are available optionally). Nosewheels and tyres size 24 × 7·7 (low-pressure 24·5 × 8·5 tyres available optionally). Bendix or Goodrich multi-disc brakes. Hydro-Aire Mk III anti-skid units and automatic brakes standard.

POWER PLANT: Two Pratt & Whitney JT8D turbofan engines (details under individual model listings), in underwing pods. High performance target type thrust reversers, with full sound attenuation quiet nacelles. All models have standard fuel capacity of up to 19,532 litres (5,160 US gallons), with integral fuel cells in wing centre-section as well as two integral wing tanks. Long-range version has auxiliary fuel tank in rear lower cargo compartment, giving max fuel capacity of 22,598 litres (5,970 US gallons). Single-point pressure refuelling through leading-edge of starboard wing. Fuelling rate 1,135 litres (300 US gallons)/min. Auxiliary overwing fuelling points. Total oil capacity 41·5 litres (11 US gallons).

ACCOMMODATION: Crew of two side by side on flight deck. Details of passenger accommodation given under individual model descriptions. Passenger versions are equipped with forward airstair; a rear airstair is optional. Convertible passenger/cargo versions have the rear airstair as standard and forward airstair optional. One plug type door at each corner of cabin, with passenger doors on port side and service doors on starboard side. Overwing escape hatches on each side. Basic passenger cabin has one lavatory and one galley at each end. Large-volume hand baggage overhead bins. Provision for a wide variety of interior arrangements. Freight holds forward and aft of wing, under floor.

SYSTEMS: Air-conditioning and pressurisation system utilises engine bleed air. Max differential 0·52 bars (7·5 lb/sq in). Two functionally independent hydraulic systems with a third standby system, using fire resistant hydraulic fluid, for flying controls, flaps, slats, landing gear, nosewheel steering and brakes; pressure 207 bars (3,000 lb/sq in). No pneumatic system. Electrical supply provided by engine driven generators. Garrett APU for air supply and electrical power in flight and on the ground, as well as engine starting.

AVIONICS AND EQUIPMENT: Equipment to satisfy FAA Category II low weather minimum criteria is standard, as well as a Lear Siegler performance data computer system. Autopilot, specially designed for ILS localiser and glide-slope control, with control wheel steering. Optional equipment will permit Category IIIA capability. Very low frequency (VLF-Omega) navigation systems, and a range of flight management systems with various levels of automation, including autothrottle and automatic flight control, are available as options.

DIMENSIONS, EXTERNAL:

Wing span	28·35 m (93 ft 0 in)
Wing chord: at root	4·71 m (15 ft 5·6 in)
at tip	1·60 m (5 ft 3 in)
Wing aspect ratio	8·83
Length overall	30·53 m (100 ft 2 in)
Length of fuselage	29·54 m (96 ft 11 in)
Height overall	11·28 m (37 ft 0 in)
Tailplane span	10·97 m (36 ft 0 in)
Wheel track	5·23 m (17 ft 2 in)
Wheelbase	11·38 m (37 ft 4 in)
Main passenger door (port, front):	
Height	1·83 m (6 ft 0 in)
Width	0·86 m (2 ft 10 in)
Height to sill	2·62 m (8 ft 7 in)
Passenger door (port, rear):	
Height	1·83 m (6 ft 0 in)
Width	0·76 m (2 ft 6 in)
Width with airstair	0·86 m (2 ft 10 in)
Height to sill	2·74 m (9 ft 0 in)
Galley service door (stbd, front):	
Height	1·65 m (5 ft 5 in)
Width	0·76 m (2 ft 6 in)
Height to sill	2·62 m (8 ft 7 in)
Service door (stbd, rear):	
Height	1·65 m (5 ft 5 in)
Width	0·76 m (2 ft 6 in)
Height to sill	2·74 m (9 ft 0 in)
Freight hold door (stbd, fwd):	
Height	1·30 m (4 ft 3 in)
Width	1·22 m (4 ft 0 in)
Height to sill	1·30 m (4 ft 3 in)
Freight hold door (stbd, rear):	
Height	1·22 m (4 ft 0 in)
Width	1·22 m (4 ft 0 in)
Height to sill	1·55 m (5 ft 1 in)

DIMENSIONS, INTERNAL:

Cabin, incl galley and toilet:	
Length	20·88 m (68 ft 6 in)
Max width	3·53 m (11 ft 7 in)
Max height	2·13 m (7 ft 0 in)
Floor area	63·8 m² (687 sq ft)
Volume	131·28 m³ (4,636 cu ft)
Freight hold (fwd) volume	10·48 m³ (370 cu ft)
Freight hold (rear) volume	14·30 m³ (505 cu ft)

AREAS:

Wings, gross	102·00 m² (1,098 sq ft)
Ailerons (total)	2·49 m² (26·8 sq ft)
Trailing-edge flaps (total)	16·87 m² (181·6 sq ft)
Slats (total)	6·52 m² (70·2 sq ft)
Ground spoilers (total)	3·68 m² (39·6 sq ft)
Flight spoilers (total)	2·64 m² (28·4 sq ft)
Fin	20·81 m² (224 sq ft)
Rudder	5·22 m² (56·2 sq ft)
Tailplane	28·99 m² (312 sq ft)
Elevators, incl tabs (total)	6·55 m² (70·5 sq ft)

WEIGHTS AND LOADINGS (standard aircraft at brake release weight of 52,390 kg; 115,500 lb except where indicated):

Operating weight empty (JT8D-17A engines):	
200	27,445 kg (60,507 lb)
200C all-passenger	28,828 kg (63,555 lb)
200C all-cargo	27,231 kg (60,034 lb)
200QC all-passenger	30,141 kg (66,450 lb)

Boeing 737-200 twin-turbofan short-range transport in the insignia of Federal Express

200QC all-cargo 27,500 kg (60,629 lb)
Max payload: 200 15,645 kg (34,493 lb)
200C all-passenger 14,263 kg (31,445 lb)
200C all-cargo 15,860 kg (34,966 lb)
200QC all-passenger 12,950 kg (28,550 lb)
200QC all-cargo 15,590 kg (34,371 lb)
Max T-O weight:
All models, basic 52,390 kg (115,500 lb)
Optional: 53,070 kg (117,000 lb)
or 56,472 kg (124,500 lb)
or 58,105 kg (128,100 lb)
Max ramp weight:
All models, basic 52,615 kg (116,000 lb)
Optional: 53,295 kg (117,500 lb)
or 56,700 kg (125,000 lb)
or 58,332 kg (128,600 lb)
Max zero-fuel weight:
All models, basic 43,091 kg (95,000 lb)
Optional for 200C 44,906 kg (99,000 lb)
Max landing weight:
All models, basic 46,720 kg (103,000 lb)
Optional: 47,627 kg (105,000 lb)
or 48,534 kg (107,000 lb)
Wing loading:
All models, basic 575·5 kg/m² (117·9 lb/sq ft)
Max optional 638·2 kg/m² (130·7 lb/sq ft)
Power loading (JT8D-17A engines):
All models, basic 368 kg/kN (3·61 lb/lb st)
Max optional 408 kg/kN (4·00 lb/lb st)

Weights and Loadings (at brake release weight of 56,472 kg; 124,500 lb):
Operating weight empty 27,574 kg (60,790 lb)
Max payload 15,517 kg (34,210 lb)
Max T-O weight 56,472 kg (124,500 lb)
Max ramp weight 56,700 kg (125,000 lb)
Max zero-fuel weight 43,091 kg (95,000 lb)
Max landing weight 48,534 kg (107,000 lb)
Max wing loading 620·24 kg/m² (127·04 lb/sq ft)
Max power loading (JT8D-17A engines) 397 kg/kN (3·9 lb/lb st)

Performance (ISA, with JT8D-17A engines):
Max operating speed, all models
Mach 0·84 (350 knots; 648 km/h; 402 mph EAS)
Max cruising speed, at an average cruise weight of 45,359 kg (100,000 lb) at 10,060 m (33,000 ft)
462 knots (856 km/h; 532 mph)
Econ cruising speed at 10,060 m (33,000 ft)
Mach 0·73
Stalling speed, flaps down, at 46,720 kg (103,000 lb) landing weight 102 knots (189 km/h; 117 mph)
Runway LCN (at max taxi weight of 52,615 kg; 116,000 lb, optimum tyre pressure and 20 in flexible pavement):
40 × 14-16 tyres 53
C40 × 14-21 tyres 53
C40 × 18-17 tyres 38
FAR T-O distance to 10·7 m (35 ft), 737-200 at 49,435 kg (109,000 lb) AUW and 28·9°C (84°F):
JT8D-9A engines 2,027 m (6,650 ft)
JT8D-17A engines 1,615 m (5,300 ft)
FAR landing distance from 15 m (50 ft), 737-200 at landing weight of 46,720 kg (103,000 lb)
1,372 m (4,500 ft)
Min ground turning radius 17·58 m (57 ft 8 in)
Range, JT8D-17A engines, FAR domestic reserves, cruising at 10,060 m (33,000 ft), at 52,615 kg (116,000 lb) ramp weight with 115 passengers and 19,533 litres (5,160 US gallons) fuel
1,855 nm (3,437 km; 2,136 miles)
Range, all conditions as above, except 58,332 kg (128,600 lb) ramp weight and 22,599 litres (5,970 US gallons) fuel 2,530 nm (4,688 km; 2,913 miles)
Range, conditions as above, with 130 passengers
2,255 nm (4,179 km; 2,596 miles)

Operational Noise Levels (JT8D-9 engines and nacelle acoustic treatment, FAR Pt 36):
T-O at 52,390 kg (115,500 lb) brake release weight
95·3 EPNdB
Sideline at 52,390 kg (115,500 lb) brake release weight 100·6 EPNdB
Approach at 46,720 kg (103,000 lb) max landing weight 101·1 EPNdB

BOEING MODEL 737-300 and CORPORATE 77-33

Work on this new short-range transport was started in early 1980. Lengthening of the fuselage, to accommodate additional passengers and underfloor freight, and the installation of new-generation turbofan engines, offer much reduced fuel consumption per seat-mile and lower noise levels compared with the earlier model.

Following production go-ahead in March 1981, work began in mid-1982 and a Class II mockup was completed early in 1983. Major assembly began in mid-1983 and the prototype 737-300 was rolled out ahead of schedule on 17 January 1984. This aircraft made its first flight on 24 February 1984. A second aircraft joined the flight test programme on 2 March. Certification was granted on 14 November 1984, with the first delivery (to US Air) on 28 November. The first revenue service with a 737-300 was flown by Southwest Airlines on 7 December 1984.

Boeing does not regard the 737-300 as a replacement for the 737-200, but as a complement to the existing Boeing range of aircraft. During 1985 the 737-300 set a world sales record for commercial jet airliners with 252 orders received during the year. Orders totalled 534 by 30 September 1986. Deliveries totalled 164 by that date.

The executive version of the 737-300 is designated **Corporate 77-33**. It is equipped typically for about 20 passengers, with conference room, bedroom, bathroom and full dining facilities.

The description of the 737-200 applies also to the 737-300, except as follows:

Wings: Generally similar to the 737-200 except: modified aerofoil section for leading-edge slats outboard of engine nacelles; revised trailing-edge flap sections and flap track fairings aft of engines; additional spoilers outboard; wing structure strengthened; and each wingtip extended by 0·28 m (11 in).

Fuselage: As for 737-200, but lengthened by a total of 2·64 m (8 ft 8 in), by insertion of a 1·12 m (3 ft 8 in) fuselage plug forward of the wing, and a 1·52 m (5 ft 0 in) plug aft of the wing carry-through structure. In addition to providing increased passenger capacity, this 'stretch' gives a lower freight hold volume which is greater by 5·47 m³ (193 cu ft) than that of the standard 737-200.

Tail Unit: As for 737-200, except dorsal fin area and tailplane span increased. Composite material rudders manufactured by Short Brothers (UK).

Landing Gear: Generally as for 737-200, but nose unit repositioned and modified to ensure adequate ground clearance for larger engine nacelles. Twin nosewheels have tyres size 27 × 7·75. Main units have heavy duty wheels, H40 × 14·5-19 heavy duty tyres, and Bendix or Goodrich heavy duty wheel brakes as standard. Mainwheel tyre pressure 13·45-14·00 bars (195-203 lb/sq in).

Power Plant: Two 89 kN (20,000 lb st) CFM International CFM56-3 turbofan engines, pylon-mounted one on each wing. Nacelles are forward of wings, and higher than those of 737-200; each is fitted with an aerodynamic fence. Standard fuel capacity up to 20,104 litres (5,311 US gallons), with integral fuel cells in wing centre-section and integral wing tanks. Single-point pressure refuelling through leading-edge of starboard wing.

Accommodation: Crew of two side by side on flight deck (unchanged from 737-200). Alternative cabin layouts seat from 110 to 149 passengers. Typical arrangements offer 8 first class seats four-abreast at 96·5 cm (38 in) pitch and 114 or 120 tourist class seats six-abreast at 86 cm (34 in) or 81 cm (32 in) respectively in mixed class; and 132, 140 or 149 all-tourist class at seat pitches of 86 cm (34 in), 81 cm (32 in) or 76 cm (30 in) respectively. One plug type door at each corner of cabin, with passenger doors on port side and service doors on starboard side. Airstair for forward cabin door optional. Overwing emergency exit on each side. One or two galleys and one lavatory forward, and one or two galleys and lavatories aft, depending on configuration. New lightweight interior, using advanced crushed core materials, providing total overhead baggage capacity of 6·80 m³ (240 cu ft), equivalent to 0·048 m³ (1·7 cu ft) per passenger. Underfloor freight holds, forward and aft of wing, with access doors on starboard side.

Systems: Generally as for 737-200. Garrett bleed air control

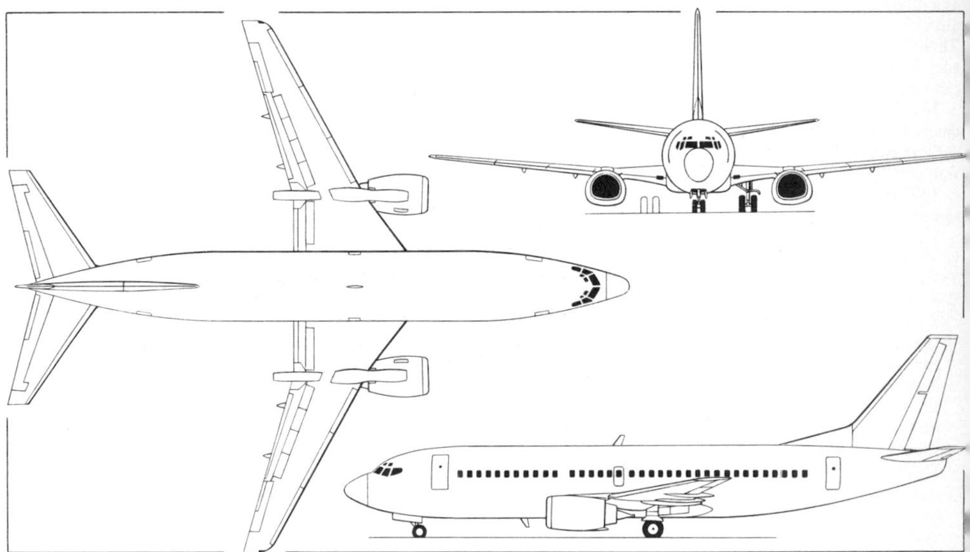

Boeing Model 737-300 (two CFM International CFM56-3 turbofan engines) *(Pilot Press)*

Boeing 737-300 short-range transport of Austrian carrier Lauda Air

system for air-conditioning and thermal anti-icing systems; Garrett GTCP 85-129(C) APU.

AVIONICS AND EQUIPMENT: Equipped to FAA Category II low weather minimum criteria as standard. Flight management computer system (FMCS), with performance and navigation functions, includes FAA Category II SP-300 digital autopilot with optional Category IIIA capability, inertial reference system (IRS) with laser gyros in lieu of gimbal type, 12·7 cm (5 in) electro-mechanical flight displays, 10 cm (4 in) electrical air data displays, dual digital air data computer, and full-range digital autothrottle. Other items include dual nav/com, VHF nav, colour digital radar, and digital autobrake. Optional equipment includes VLF/Omega nav system and dual INS. An EFIS installation received FAA certification on 24 July 1986.

DIMENSIONS, EXTERNAL:

Wing span	28·88 m (94 ft 9 in)
Wing chord at root	4·71 m (15 ft 5·6 in)
Length overall	33·40 m (109 ft 7 in)
Height overall	11·13 m (36 ft 6 in)
Tailplane span	12·70 m (41 ft 8 in)
Wheel track	5·23 m (17 ft 2 in)
Wheelbase	12·45 m (40 ft 10 in)
Main passenger door (port, fwd):	
Height	1·83 m (6 ft 0 in)
Width	0·86 m (2 ft 10 in)
Passenger door (port, rear):	
Height	1·83 m (6 ft 0 in)
Width	0·76 m (2 ft 6 in)
Emergency exit (overwing, port and stbd):	
Height	0·97 m (3 ft 2 in)
Width	0·51 m (1 ft 8 in)
Service doors (stbd, fwd and rear):	
Height	1·65 m (5 ft 5 in)
Width	0·76 m (2 ft 6 in)
Freight hold door (stbd, fwd):	
Height	1·22 m (4 ft 0 in)
Width	1·30 m (4 ft 3 in)
Freight hold door (stbd, rear):	
Height	1·22 m (4 ft 0 in)
Width	1·22 m (4 ft 0 in)

DIMENSIONS, INTERNAL:

Cabin, incl galley and toilet:	
Length	23·52 m (77 ft 2 in)
Max width	3·45 m (11 ft 4 in)
Max height	2·13 m (7 ft 0 in)
Freight hold (fwd) volume	12·03 m³ (425 cu ft)
Freight hold (rear) volume	18·21 m³ (643 cu ft)

AREAS:

Wings, gross	105·4 m² (1,135 sq ft)
Ailerons (total)	2·49 m² (26·8 sq ft)
Trailing-edge flaps (total)	16·87 m² (181·6 sq ft)
Slats (total)	7·23 m² (77·8 sq ft)
Ground spoilers (total)	5·00 m² (53·8 sq ft)
Flight spoilers (total)	2·64 m² (28·4 sq ft)
Fin	23·13 m² (249 sq ft)
Rudder	5·22 m² (56·2 sq ft)
Tailplane	31·31 m² (337 sq ft)
Elevators, incl tabs (total)	6·55 m² (70·5 sq ft)

WEIGHTS:

Operating weight empty	31,479 kg (69,400 lb)
Max payload: standard	16,148 kg (35,600 lb)
optional	16,828 kg (37,100 lb)
Max T-O weight: standard	56,472 kg (124,500 lb)
optional	62,822 kg (138,500 lb)
Max ramp weight: standard	56,700 kg (125,000 lb)
optional	63,049 kg (139,000 lb)
Max zero-fuel weight:	
standard	47,625 kg (105,000 lb)
optional	48,307 kg (106,500 lb)
Max landing weight	51,710 kg (114,000 lb)

PERFORMANCE: (A: at brake release weight of 56,472 kg; 124,500 lb. B: at optional BRW of 62,822 kg; 138,500 lb):

T-O field length, S/L, at 29°C (84°F):	
A	2,027 m (6,650 ft)
B	2,749 m (9,020 ft)
Wet landing field length, 40° flap, at max landing weight:	
A, B	1,603 m (5,260 ft)
Still air range with 141 passengers, T-O at S/L:	
A	1,615 nm (2,993 km; 1,860 miles)
B	2,590 nm (4,800 km; 2,982 miles)

BOEING MODEL 737-400

Details of this new variant were announced in June 1986. The Model 737-400 offers all the new technology of the 737-300, but has a fuselage lengthened by 2·90 m (9 ft 6 in) by means of two 'plugs', one of 1·68 m (5 ft 6 in) forward of the wing and one of 1·22 m (4 ft 0 in) aft. The aircraft will be powered by two General Electric CFM56-3B2 turbofans, each rated at 97·86 kN (22,000 lb st). The outer wings and landing gear will be strengthened to permit a maximum landing weight of 54,885 kg (121,000 lb). A tail bumper will be standard. In typical mixed-class configuration the 737-400 will seat 146 passengers; lower cargo hold volume is 38·51 m³ (1,360 cu ft).

Launch customer for the 737-400 was Piedmont Airlines, which has ordered 25 aircraft for delivery commencing September 1988 and continuing until December 1989, with options on a further 30 aircraft. GPA Group Ltd, of Shannon, Ireland, has ordered 30 737-400s, and International Lease Finance Corporation of Beverly Hills, California, has ordered three. The first 737-400 is scheduled for rollout in January 1988, with FAA certification expected to follow seven months later.

BOEING MODEL 747

First details of this wide-body commercial transport were announced on 13 April 1966, simultaneously with the news that Pan American had placed a $525 million contract for 25 Boeing 747s, including spares. Programme go-ahead date was officially 25 July 1966.

The first 747 (designated RA001) flew for the first time on 9 February 1969 and was retained by Boeing as an experimental flight test vehicle for airframe, avionics and systems technology development, evaluation, and certification. FAA certification of the basic 747 was granted on 30 December 1969. The first 747 to be delivered was received by Pan American on 12 December 1969, and this company inaugurated commercial service with the type on its New York/London route on 22 January 1970.

Orders for all versions of the 747, including military E-4s, totalled 750 at 30 September 1986. By that date a total of 654 had been delivered. The total 747 fleet operating in July 1986 carried more than 6·75 million passengers each month, and had flown more than 18·5 million hours in revenue service. The 630th Boeing 747 was delivered to UTA on 31 January 1986.

Versions of the Boeing 747 currently available are as follows:

747-100B. The original 747-100 (167 built) was introduced into commercial service in January 1970. This aircraft, in versions with gross weights up to 334,751 kg (738,000 lb), more than doubled passenger and cargo payload capabilities by comparison with any previous commercial air transport, and 167 were sold. (Two of these have since been converted to -200B Combis and are included in the total given for this version.) The current -100B incorporates strengthened wing, fuselage and landing gear structure. Initial order, with JT9D-7F engines, was placed by Iran Air in 1978, and this aircraft was delivered on 5 July 1979. Current versions, with max taxi weights of 323,411 kg (713,000 lb), 334,751 kg (738,000 lb), and 341,555 kg (753,000 lb), allow for the installation of a variety of optional engines in addition to the basic 206·8 kN (46,500 lb st) General Electric CF6-45A2. These include the 206·8 kN (46,500 lb st) CF6-50E2-F, 233·5 kN (52,500 lb st) CF6-50E2, 222·9 kN (50,100 lb st) Rolls-Royce RB211-524B2, and 229·5 kN (51,600 lb st) RB211-524C2. Nine ordered and delivered by 30 September 1986.

747SP. Lighter weight, shorter bodied derivative of the 747-100B. Described separately.

747SR. This short-range version of the 747-100B embodies structural changes required for high take-off and landing cycles. The 747SR is available at max taxi weights up to 341,555 kg (753,000 lb) with the same engines as available for the 747-100B. The initial purchase of four 747SRs by Japan Air Lines (later increased to seven) was announced on 30 October 1972. The JAL aircraft have max taxi weights of 273,515 kg (603,000 lb) and 237,225 kg (523,000 lb). The first 747SR flew on 4 September 1973 and was delivered on 26 September 1973. Total of 27 ordered and delivered by 30 September 1986.

747-200B. Passenger version, with same accommodation as 747-100B. First flown on 11 October 1970 and certificated on 23 December 1970; deliveries began on 15 January 1971. Basic version had max T-O weight of 351,535 kg (775,000 lb) and increased fuel capacity. Available now with 243·5 kN (54,750 lb st) JT9D-7R4G2 engines and max T-O weight of 377,840 kg (833,000 lb); 233·5 kN (52,500 lb st) CF6-50E2 engines and max T-O weight of 377,840 kg (833,000 lb); 222·9 kN (50,100 lb st) Rolls-Royce RB211-524B2 engines and max T-O weight of 371,945 kg (820,000 lb); 229·5 kN (51,600 lb st) RB211-524C2 engines and max T-O weight of 377,840 kg (833,000 lb); and 236·25 kN (53,110 lb st) RB211-524D4 engines and max T-O weight of 377,840 kg (833,000 lb). Total of 231 ordered and 216 delivered by 30 September 1986. Selected by US Air Force for Presidential transport to replace VC-137 aircraft (further details in BMAC entry, under 'Air Force One' heading.

747-200M Combi. A version of the basic 747-200B, incorporating a 3·12 × 3·40 m (123 × 134 in) cargo door in the port side of the fuselage, aft of the wing. This permits main deck layouts for passengers only, or for passengers and up to 12 main deck pallets/containers, with passenger and cargo areas separated by removable bulkhead. The first modification to Combi configuration was carried out on a Sabena 747-100, and redelivery was made in February 1974. The first 747-200B production Combi was delivered to Air Canada in March 1975. Total of 74 ordered and 70 delivered by 30 September 1986.

747-200C Convertible. Version of 747-200 which can be converted from all-passenger to all-cargo, or five combinations of both. The first 747-200C flew on 23 March 1973, was certificated on 17 April, and was delivered to World Airways on 27 April 1973. Max T-O weight of 377,840 kg (833,000 lb) with Pratt & Whitney JT9D-7R4G2 engines; 371,945 kg (820,000 lb) with Rolls-Royce RB211-524B2 engines; and 377,840 kg (833,000 lb) with General Electric CF6-50E2 or 263 kN (59,000 lb st) CF6-80C2 or Rolls-Royce RB211-524B2/C2/D4 engines. Thirteen ordered, 11 delivered by 30 September 1986.

747-200F Freighter. Version of the 747-200 capable of delivering 90,720 kg (200,000 lb) of palletised cargo over a range of 4,480 nm (8,300 km; 5,159 miles). Described separately.

747-300. Version with extended upper deck to increase passenger accommodation. Described separately.

747-400. Advanced version of 747-300; described separately.

747ASB. Proposed Advanced Short Body (ASB) aircraft with 300-seat capacity, offering maximum range of nearly 8,000 nm (14,825 km; 9,212 miles).

E-4. Advanced Airborne Command Post version of 747, developed for US Air Force. Four built. Described separately under Boeing Aerospace heading.

747 modification programmes. A major modification to enhance capability is now available to operators of 747-100 and -200B aircraft. Performed at Boeing facilities, it includes installation of a side cargo door. The side cargo door modification enables an operator to convert 747-100 or -200B passenger aircraft into a version with main deck cargo capability. Variations include an all-cargo Special Freighter, a 6- or 12-pallet Combi, and an all-passenger or all-cargo Convertible. Like the Combi, the Convertible configuration can also be operated in a mixed passenger/cargo mode. The major elements of the side door modification include installation of a 3·05 m (10 ft 0 in) high by 3·52 m (11 ft 2 in) long side cargo door, strengthened main deck floor, a fully powered or manual cargo handling system, and an option to increase certificated design weights of the aircraft. By early 1985 four side-cargo Combi models,

Boeing Model 747-200B for All Nippon Airways of Japan

and 24 all-freighter models had been delivered to nine airlines. The US Air Force and Pan American World Airways, with Boeing Military Airplane Company as modification contractor, have signed an agreement for the modification of nineteen 747s into the passenger/convertible configuration to support the CRAF (Civil Reserve Air Fleet) enhancement programme. The first converted aircraft was redelivered to Pan American on 31 May 1985. These aircraft are known by the military designation C-19A. (See also BMAC entry.)

The 747 can be fitted, or retrofitted, with a performance management system (PMS) developed by Boeing and Delco. The PMS computer memory is programmed with airline economic factors and the performance characteristics of the individual aircraft/engine combination, and receives continuous inputs of altitude, airspeed, air temperature, fuel flow, wind velocity and other data during flight. Using these data, coupled with existing autopilot, autothrottle and inertial navigation systems, the PMS calculates, displays and controls automatically the optimum or desired airspeed, engine power setting, attitude and flight path of the aircraft for minimum fuel burn and/or minimum operating cost. The first complete system was delivered for airline service in June 1982. Results of in-service airline evaluations show trip fuel burn reductions in excess of one per cent. Thirteen airlines had ordered a total of 149 Delco/Boeing 747 PMS units by early 1986.

The following details apply specifically to the basic Model 747-100B/200B passenger airliner:

Type: Four-turbofan heavy commercial transport.

Wings: Cantilever low-wing monoplane. Special Boeing wing sections. Thickness/chord ratio 13·44% inboard, 7·8% at mid-span, 8% outboard. Dihedral 7°. Incidence 2°. Sweepback 37° 30′ at quarter-chord. Aluminium alloy dual-path fail-safe structure. Low-speed outboard ailerons; high-speed inboard ailerons. Triple-slotted trailing-edge flaps. Six aluminium honeycomb spoilers on each wing, comprising four flight spoilers outboard and two ground spoilers inboard. Ten variable camber leading-edge flaps outboard and three-section Krueger flaps inboard on each wing leading-edge. All controls fully powered.

Fuselage: Conventional semi-monocoque structure, consisting of aluminium alloy skin, longitudinal stiffeners and circumferential frames. Structure is of fail-safe design, utilising riveting, bolting and structural bonding.

Tail Unit: Cantilever aluminium alloy dual-path fail-safe structure. Variable incidence tailplane. No trim tabs. All controls fully powered.

Landing Gear: Hydraulically retractable tricycle type. Twin-wheel nose unit retracts forward. Main gear comprises four four-wheel bogies: two, mounted side by side under fuselage at wing trailing-edge, retract forward; two, mounted under wings, retract inward. Cleveland Pneumatic oleo-pneumatic shock absorbers. All 18 wheels and tubeless tyres of Model 747-100B are size 46 × 16 Type VII. Tyre pressure: mainwheels 14·49 bars (210 lb/sq in), nosewheels 13·11 bars (190 lb/sq in). Mainwheels and tyres size 49 × 17 on 747-200B model, pressure 14·15 bars (205 lb/sq in). The high gross weight aircraft has 49 × 19 tyres at a pressure of 13·46 bars (195 lb/sq in). Disc brakes on all mainwheels, with individually controlled anti-skid units.

Power Plant: Four Pratt & Whitney, General Electric or Rolls-Royce turbofan engines, as detailed in model listings, in pods pylon-mounted on wing leading-edges. Fuel in seven integral tanks. Capacity of centre wing tank varies according to version: 747-100B: 49,966 litres (13,200 US gallons); 747-200: 64,973 litres (17,164 US gallons). Remaining tanks common to all versions: two inboard main tanks, each 47,492 litres (12,546 US gallons); two outboard main tanks, each 16,966 litres (4,482 US gallons); two inboard reserve tanks, each 2,021 litres (534 US gallons). Outboard mains are reduced by 1,234 litres (326 US gallons) when CF6-50E2 engines are installed. 747-200 also available with two outboard reserve tanks, each 2,983 litres (788 US gallons). Fuselage tank, capacity 6,511 litres (1,720 US gallons) optional. Total capacity, including manifolds, 747-100B: 183,380 litres (48,445 US gallons); 747-200: 204,355 litres (53,985 US gallons). Refuelling point on each wing between inboard and outboard engines. Total usable oil capacity 19 litres (5 US gallons).

Accommodation: Normal operating crew of three, on flight deck above level of main deck. Observer station and provision for second observer station are provided. Basic accommodation for 452 passengers, made up of 32 first class and 420 economy class, which includes a 32-passenger upper deck (extended on 747-300, which see). Alternative layouts accommodate 447 economy class passengers in nine-abreast seating or 516 ten-abreast, with 32 passengers on upper deck. All versions have two aisles. Five passenger doors on each side, of which two forward of wing on each side are normally used. Freight holds under floor, forward and aft of wing, with doors on starboard side. One door on forward hold, two on rear hold. Aircraft is designed for fully mechanical loading of baggage and freight. An optional side cargo door is available for passenger, convertible and freighter versions of the Model 747. Installed aft of door 4 on the port side of the fuselage, it allows the carriage of main deck cargo on passenger versions. Addition of this door to the freighter allows loads up to 3·05 m (10 ft) in height to be accommodated aft of the flight deck, and also makes possible simultaneous nose and side cargo handling.

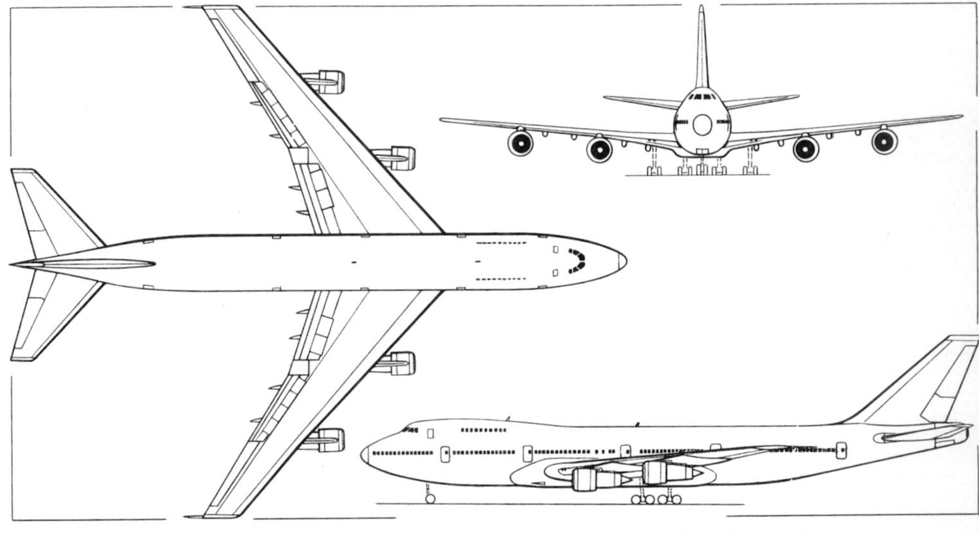

Boeing 747-200B four-turbofan heavy transport aircraft *(Pilot Press)*

Systems: Air cycle air-conditioning system. Pressure differential 0·61 bars (8·9 lb/sq in). Four independent hydraulic systems, pressure 207 bars (3,000 lb/sq in), maximum capacity 265 litres (70 US gallons)/min at 196·5 bars (2,850 lb/sq in), each with one engine driven and one pneumatically driven pump. The latter pumps supplement or substitute for engine driven pumps. Reservoir in each system, pressurised by engine bleed air via a pressure regulation module. Reservoir relief valve pressure is nominal 4·48 bars (65 lb/sq in). A small AC powered electric pump is installed to charge the brake accumulator during towing of the aircraft. Electrical supply from four aircooled 60kVA generators mounted one on each engine. Two 60kVA generators (supplemental cooling allows 90kVA each) mounted on APU for ground operation and to supply primary electrical power when engine mounted generators are not operating. Three-phase 400Hz constant frequency AC generators, 115/200V output. 28V DC power obtained from transformer-rectifier units. 24V 36Ah nickel-cadmium battery for selected ground functions and as in-flight backup. Gas turbine APU for pneumatic and electrical supplies.

Avionics and Equipment: Standard avionics include three ARINC 566 VHF communications systems, two ARINC 533A HF communications systems, one ARINC 531 Selcal, three ARINC 547 VOR/ILS navigation systems, two ARINC 570 ADF, marker beacon receiver, two ARINC 568 DME, two ARINC 572 ATC, three ARINC 552 low-range radio altimeters, two ARINC 564 weather radar units, three ARINC 561 inertial navigation systems, two heading reference systems, ARINC 412 interphone, ARINC 560 passenger address system, multiple passenger service and entertainment system, ARINC 573 flight recorder, ARINC 557 cockpit voice recorder, integrated electronic flight control system with autothrottle and rollout guidance to provide automatic stabilisation, path control and pilot assist functions for Category II and III landing conditions, two ARINC 565 central air data systems, stall warning system, central instrument warning system, ground proximity warning system, attitude and navigation instrumentation, and standby attitude indication.

Dimensions, external:

Wing span	59·64 m (195 ft 8 in)
Wing chord: at root	16·56 m (54 ft 4 in)
at tip	4·06 m (13 ft 4 in)
Wing aspect ratio	6·96
Length overall	70·66 m (231 ft 10 in)
Length of fuselage	68·63 m (225 ft 2 in)
Height overall	19·33 m (63 ft 5 in)
Tailplane span	22·17 m (72 ft 9 in)
Wheel track	11·00 m (36 ft 1 in)
Wheelbase	25·60 m (84 ft 0 in)
Passenger doors (ten, each):	
Height	1·93 m (6 ft 4 in)
Width	1·07 m (3 ft 6 in)
Height to sill	approx 4·88 m (16 ft 0 in)
Baggage door (front hold):	
Height	1·68 m (5 ft 6 in)
Width	2·64 m (8 ft 8 in)
Height to sill	approx 2·64 m (8 ft 8 in)
Baggage door (forward door, rear hold):	
Height	1·68 m (5 ft 6 in)
Width	2·64 m (8 ft 8 in)
Height to sill	approx 2·69 m (8 ft 10 in)
Bulk loading door (rear door on rear hold):	
Height	1·19 m (3 ft 11 in)
Width	1·12 m (3 ft 8 in)
Height to sill	approx 2·90 m (9 ft 6 in)
Optional cargo door (port):	
Height	3·05 m (10 ft 0 in)
Width	3·40 m (11 ft 2 in)

Dimensions, internal:

Cabin, incl toilets and galleys:	
Length	57·00 m (187 ft 0 in)
Max width	6·13 m (20 ft 1½ in)
Max height	2·54 m (8 ft 4 in)
Floor area, passenger deck	327·9 m² (3,529 sq ft)
Volume, passenger deck	789 m³ (27,860 cu ft)
Baggage hold (fwd, containerised) volume	78·4 m³ (2,768 cu ft)
Baggage hold (rear, containerised) volume	68·6 m³ (2,422 cu ft)
Bulk volume	28·3 m³ (1,000 cu ft)

Areas:

Wings, reference area	511 m² (5,500 sq ft)
Ailerons (total)	20·6 m² (222 sq ft)
Trailing-edge flaps (total)	78·7 m² (847 sq ft)
Leading-edge flaps (total)	48·1 m² (518 sq ft)
Spoilers (total)	30·8 m² (331 sq ft)
Fin	77·1 m² (830 sq ft)
Rudder	22·9 m² (247 sq ft)
Tailplane	136·6 m² (1,470 sq ft)
Elevators	32·5 m² (350 sq ft)

Weights (letters are used to denote engine installations as follows: (A) JT9D-7R4G2; (B) CF6-45A2; (C) CF6-50E2; (D) CF6-50E2-F; (E) CF6-80C2; (F) RB211-524B2; (G) RB211-524C2; and (H) RB211-524D4):

Operating weight empty (approx) for max available gross weights:	
747SR (550 pass):	
B, C, D	161,932 kg (357,000 lb)
F, G	164,654 kg (363,000 lb)
747-100B (452 pass):	
B, C, D	170,097 kg (375,000 lb)
F, G	172,818 kg (381,000 lb)
747-200B (452 pass):	
A	170,097 kg (375,000 lb)
C	171,911 kg (379,000 lb)
E	172,818 kg (381,000 lb)
F, G	174,633 kg (385,000 lb)
H	174,179 kg (384,000 lb)
747-200M Combi (238 pass and 12 pallets):	
A	170,097 kg (375,000 lb)
C	171,911 kg (379,000 lb)
E	172,818 kg (381,000 lb)
F, G	174,633 kg (385,000 lb)
H	174,179 kg (384,000 lb)
747-200C (452 pass):	
A	175,540 kg (387,000 lb)
C	177,354 kg (391,000 lb)
E	178,262 kg (393,000 lb)
F, G	180,076 kg (397,000 lb)
H	179,622 kg (396,000 lb)
747-200C (28 pallets):	
A	162,839 kg (359,000 lb)
C	164,200 kg (362,000 lb)
E	165,561 kg (365,000 lb)
F, H	166,922 kg (368,000 lb)
G	167,375 kg (369,000 lb)
Max fuel weight:	
747-100B, 747SR:	
B, C, D	147,181 kg (324,480 lb)
F, G	148,324 kg (327,000 lb)
747-200B, 747-200B Combi, 747-200C:	
A, F, G, H	160,463 kg (353,760 lb)
C, E	159,320 kg (351,240 lb)
Max payload:	
747SR (550 pass):	
B, C, D	58,060 kg (128,000 lb)
F, G	55,338 kg (122,000 lb)
747-100B (452 pass):	
B, C, D	68,719 kg (151,500 lb)

F, G	65,998 kg (145,500 lb)
747-200B (452 pass):	
A	68,719 kg (151,500 lb)
C	66,905 kg (147,500 lb)
E	65,998 kg (145,500 lb)
F, G	64,183 kg (141,500 lb)
H	64,637 kg (142,500 lb)
747-200M Combi (238 pass and 12 pallets):	
A	77,111 kg (170,000 lb)
C	75,296 kg (166,000 lb)
E	74,389 kg (164,000 lb)
F, G	72,575 kg (160,000 lb)
H	73,028 kg (161,000 lb)
747-200C (452 pass):	
A	92,079 kg (203,000 lb)
C	90,265 kg (199,000 lb)
E	89,358 kg (197,000 lb)
F, G	87,543 kg (193,000 lb)
H	87,997 kg (194,000 lb)
747-200C (28 pallets):	
A	104,780 kg (231,000 lb)
C	103,419 kg (228,000 lb)
E	102,058 kg (225,000 lb)
F, H	100,697 kg (222,000 lb)
G	100,244 kg (221,000 lb)

Max T-O weight:
747SR (initial aircraft):
B, C, D, F, G — 235,870 kg (520,000 lb) *or* 272,155 kg (600,000 lb)
747-100B, 747SR (optional):
B, C, D, F, G — 322,050 kg (710,000 lb) *or* 333,390 kg (735,000 lb) *or* 340,195 kg (750,000 lb)
747-200B, -200M Combi, -200C:
A, C, E, G, H — 362,875 kg (800,000 lb) *or* 371,945 kg (820,000 lb) *or* 377,840 kg (833,000 lb)
F — 362,875 kg (800,000 lb) *or* 371,945 kg (820,000 lb)

Max ramp weight:
747-100B, 747SR:
B, C, D, F, G — 341,555 kg (753,000 lb)
747-200B, -200M Combi, -200C:
A, C, G, H — 379,200 kg (836,000 lb)
F — 373,305 kg (823,000 lb)

Max zero-fuel weight:
747SR (initial aircraft):
B, C, D, F, G — 215,455 kg (475,000 lb) *or* 219,990 kg (485,000 lb)
747-100B, 747SR (optional):
B, C, D, F, G — 238,815 kg (526,500 lb)
747-200B:
A, C, E, F, G, H — 238,815 kg (526,500 lb)
747-200M Combi:
A, C, E, F, G, H — 247,205 kg (545,000 lb)
747-200C:
A, C, E, F, G, H — 267,620 kg (590,000 lb)

Max landing weight:
747SR (initial aircraft):
B, C, D, F, G — 229,065 kg (505,000 lb) *or* 238,135 kg (525,000 lb)
747-100B, 747SR (optional):
B, C, D, F, G — 255,825 kg (564,000 lb) *or* 265,350 kg (585,000 lb)
747-200B:
A, C, E, F, G, H — 255,825 kg (564,000 lb) *or* 265,350 kg (585,000 lb) *or* 285,765 kg (630,000 lb)
747-200M Combi:
A, C, E, F, G, H — 265,350 kg (585,000 lb) *or* 285,765 kg (630,000 lb)
747-200C:
A, C, E, F, G, H — 285,765 kg (630,000 lb)

PERFORMANCE (at max T-O weight except where indicated):
Max level speed:
747-100B, CF6-45A2 engines and AUW of 272,160 kg (600,000 lb) at 9,145 m (30,000 ft) — 527 knots (977 km/h; 607 mph)
747-200B, JT9D-7R4G2 engines and AUW of 317,515 kg (700,000 lb) at 9,145 m (30,000 ft) — 523 knots (969 km/h; 602 mph)
Cruise ceiling, all versions — 13,715 m (45,000 ft)
Min ground turning radius — 22·86 m (75 ft 0 in)
Runway LCN (W: 334,750 kg; 738,000 lb, X; 341,560 kg; 753,000 lb, Y: 366,500 kg; 808,000 lb, Z: 379,200 kg; 836,000 lb max taxi weight on h = 0·51 m; 20 in flexible pavement): W 81, X 83, Y 86, Z 88
Runway LCN (weights as above, on l = 1·02 m; 40 in rigid pavement): W 87, X 89, Y 93, Z 95
FAR T-O distance to 10·7 m (35 ft) at S/L, ISA:
747-100B, CF6-45A2 engines at BRW of 340,195 kg (750,000 lb) — 3,050 m (10,000 ft)
747-200B/C/F, JT9D-7R4G2 engines at BRW of 377,840 kg (833,000 lb) — 3,170 m (10,400 ft)
FAR landing field length, at max landing weights:
747-100B, -200B at 255,825 kg (564,000 lb) — 1,881 m (6,170 ft)
747-100B, -200B, at 265,350 kg (585,000 lb) — 1,942 m (6,370 ft)
747-200B/C/F, at 285,765 kg (630,000 lb) — 2,109 m (6,920 ft)
Range (long-range cruise, FAR 121.645 reserves):
747-100B, CF6-45A2 engines at T-O weight of 340,195 kg (750,000 lb), with 452 passengers and baggage — 4,800 nm (8,895 km; 5,527 miles)
747-200B, JT9D-7R4G2 engines at T-O weight of 377,840 kg (833,000 lb), with 452 passengers and baggage — 6,150 nm (11,397 km; 7,082 miles)
Ferry range (long-range cruise, FAR 121.645 reserves):
747-200B — 7,100 nm (13,158 km; 8,176 miles)

OPERATIONAL NOISE LEVELS (As per FAR Pt 36, A: RB211-524C2 engines at brake release weight (BRW) of 340,195 kg; 750,000 lb and landing weight of 265,350 kg; 585,000 lb, B: JT9D-7R4G2 at BRW of 377,840 kg; 833,000 lb and landing weight of 285,765 kg; 630,000 lb):
T-O: A — 104 EPNdB
B — 106 EPNdB
Approach: A — 107 EPNdB
B — 107 EPNdB
Sideline: A — 97 EPNdB
B — 99 EPNdB

BOEING MODEL 747-300 and CORPORATE 77-43

On 12 June 1980, Boeing announced an option for the Model 747 which incorporates structural changes to the aircraft's upper deck area to increase passenger carrying capacity. The upper forward fuselage is extended aft by 7·11 m (23 ft 4 in) to increase upper deck accommodation from 32 to 91 passengers in all-economy class configuration. Seating is six abreast, with a single aisle, and panniers between the outer seats and cabin wall are provided for hand baggage. Alternative configurations include 26 first class sleeper seats on the extended upper deck. In addition, seven additional seats can be accommodated on the main deck as a result of deleting the standard circular stairway. It is replaced by a new straight stairway at the rear of the upper deck area. Two new doors 1·83 m (6 ft 0 in) high and 1·07 m (3 ft 6 in) wide replace the existing 1·22 × 0·61 m (4 ft 0 in × 2 ft 0 in) upper deck exits. Other structural changes include the provision of a new emergency exit and additional windows. The extended upper deck option is available initially on existing aircraft of the 747-100 and -200 series, which then become known as **747-300s**; maximum take-off weights are unchanged, but operating weight empty is increased by about 4,220 kg (9,310 lb). Most efficient high speed cruise is increased from Mach 0·84 to Mach 0·85 by the revised upper contours. Flight testing with JT9D-7R4G2 engines began on 5 October 1982, followed on 10 December by the first 747-300 with CF6-50E2 engines, and FAA certification of the -300 was announced by Boeing on 7 March 1983. Initial deliveries were to Swissair and UTA, with whom the aircraft entered service on 28 March and 1 April 1983 respectively. Orders totalled 66, including two -300SR and 15 -300M Combis, by 30 September 1986, by which date deliveries totalled 53, including 12 Combis.

A Boeing 747-300 completed in VIP transport form for a head of state is designated **Corporate 77-43**.

The detailed specification for the Boeing 747-100B/200B applies also to the 747-300 except as follows:

WEIGHTS: ((A) JT9D-7R4G2; (B) CF6-50E2; (C) CF6-80C2; (D) RB211-524B2; (E) RB211-524C2; and (F) RB211-524D4):

Operating weight empty (approx) for max available gross weights:

747-300 (496 pass): A	174,179 kg (384,000 lb)
B	175,994 kg (388,000 lb)
C	176,901 kg (390,000 lb)
D	178,715 kg (394,000 lb)
E	179,169 kg (395,000 lb)
F	178,262 kg (393,000 lb)
747-300M Combi (278 pass and 12 pallets):	
A	174,179 kg (384,000 lb)
B	175,994 kg (388,000 lb)
C	176,901 kg (390,000 lb)
D, E	178,715 kg (394,000 lb)
F	178,262 kg (393,000 lb)

Max fuel weights — as for 747-200B

Max payload:

747-300 (496 pass):	
A	68,492 kg (151,000 lb)
B	66,678 kg (147,000 lb)
C	65,771 kg (145,000 lb)
D	63,956 kg (141,000 lb)
E	63,503 kg (140,000 lb)
F	64,410 kg (142,000 lb)
747-300M Combi (278 pass and 12 pallets):	
A	82,100 kg (181,000 lb)
B	80,286 kg (177,000 lb)
C	79,379 kg (175,000 lb)
D, E	77,564 kg (171,000 lb)
F	78,018 kg (172,000 lb)

Max T-O weight:
747-300, -300M Combi:
A, B, C, E, F — 351,535 kg (775,000 lb) *or* 356,070 kg (785,000 lb) *or* 362,875 kg (800,000 lb) *or* 371,945 kg (820,000 lb) *or* 377,840 kg (833,000 lb)
D — 362,875 kg (800,000 lb) *or* 371,945 kg (820,000 lb)

Max ramp weight:
747-300, -300M Combi:
A, B, C, E, F — 379,200 kg (836,000 lb)
D — 373,300 kg (823,000 lb)

Max zero-fuel weight:
747-300:
A, B, C, D, E, F — 242,670 kg (535,000 lb)
747-300M Combi:
A, B, C, D, E, F — 256,280 kg (565,000 lb)

Boeing Model 747-300 for Qantas, with extended upper deck

Boeing Model 747SP four-turbofan special performance long-range transport in the insignia of Air Malawi *(Peter J. Bish)*

Max landing weight:
747-300:
A, B, C, D, E, F 260,360 kg (574,000 lb)
or 265,350 kg (585,000 lb)
or 285,765 kg (630,000 lb)
747-300M Combi:
A, B, C, D, E, F 274,420 kg (605,000 lb)
or 285,765 kg (630,000 lb)

PERFORMANCE (at max T-O weight except where indicated):
Max level speed:
747-300: JT9D-7R4G2 engines and AUW of 317,515 kg (700,000 lb) at 9,145 m (30,000 ft) 530 knots (982 km/h; 610 mph)
FAR T-O distance to 10·7 m (35 ft) at BRW of 377,840 kg (833,000 lb), S/L, ISA:
747-300, JT9D-7R4G2 engines 3,185 m (10,450 ft)
FAR landing field length, at max landing weight:
747-300 at 265,350 kg (585,000 lb) 1,942 m (6,370 ft)
747-300 at 285,765 kg (630,000 lb) 2,109 m (6,920 ft)
Range (long-range cruise, FAR 121.645 reserves):
747-300, JT9D-7R4G2 engines, at T-O weight of 377,840 kg (833,000 lb), with 496 passengers and baggage 5,650 nm (10,463 km; 6,502 miles)

BOEING MODEL 747SP

The Boeing Company announced on 3 September 1973 that it intended to develop a lower-weight longer-range version of the basic Model 747, known as the 747SP (special performance), for use on lower-density routes.

Retaining a 90 per cent commonality of components with the standard Model 747, the major change is a reduction in overall length of 14·35 m (47 ft 1 in). Construction of the first production aircraft began in April 1974, with rollout on 19 May 1975, first flight on 4 July 1975, and FAA certification on 4 February 1976. First delivery was made on 5 March that year. By 30 September 1986, a total of 44 had been ordered and delivered.

On 23-24 March 1976, taking off at a gross weight of 323,547 kg (713,300 lb) with 50 passengers, the first 747SP for South African Airways made a delivery flight from Paine Field, Washington, to Cape Town of 8,913 nm (16,507 km; 10,257 miles), a world record for nonstop distance flown by a commercial aircraft. The aircraft landed with fuel remaining for a further 2 h 27 min of flight.

A 747SP of Pan American, commanded by Capt Walter H. Mullikin, set a round-the-world speed record of 436·95 knots (809·24 km/h; 502·84 mph), by circumnavigating the globe in 1 day 22 h 0 min 50 s on 1-3 May 1976. The same pilot circumnavigated the world via the North and South Poles in a 747SP on 28-31 October 1977, covering 22,926 nm (42,459 km; 26,382·75 miles) in 2 days 6 h 7 min 12 s at an average speed of 423·49 knots (784·31 km/h; 487·35 mph). Start and finish were at San Francisco, with en route landings at London, Cape Town and Auckland, New Zealand.

The description of the basic Model 747 applies also to the 747SP, except for the following details:

WINGS: As Model 747, except that trailing-edge flaps are of single-slotted variable pivot type, and wing structural materials are of reduced gauge. Large flap track fairings replaced by small link fairings. New wing/body fairings and leading-edge fillets.

FUSELAGE: As Model 747, except length reduced.

TAIL UNIT: Similar to 747, but tailplane span increased by 3·05 m (10 ft). Two-segment elevators. Height of fin increased by 1·52 m (5 ft 0 in). Double-hinged rudder.

LANDING GEAR: As Model 747, except structural weight reduced. Mainwheel tyres size 46 × 16, pressure 12·63 bars (183 lb/sq in). Nosewheel tyres size 49 × 17, pressure 13·8 bars (200 lb/sq in). Higher gross weight aircraft use 747-100 wheels and brakes. Modified 747-100 steel brakes by Bendix.

POWER PLANT: Four General Electric CF6-45A2 turbofan engines, each of 206·8 kN (46,500 lb st), or CF6-50E2-F engines, each of 206·8 kN (46,500 lb st); four Rolls-Royce RB211-524B2 turbofan engines, each of 222·8 kN (50,100 lb st), RB211-524C2 engines, each of 229·5 kN (51,600 lb st), or RB211-524D4 engines each of 236·25 kN (53,110 lb st). Fuel system and oil capacity as for Model 747-100B, except Model 747SP has an additional 5,966 litres (1,576 US gallons) reserve fuel, providing a total capacity of 190,625 litres (50,359 US gallons).

ACCOMMODATION: Normal operating crew of three on flight deck above level of main deck. Observer station and provision for second observer station are provided. Accommodation for 299 passengers on main deck, with 28 first class seats in forward area and ten-abreast seating throughout the major part of the main cabin. Seating for 32 passengers on upper deck, giving total capacity of 331 passengers. Max high-density accommodation for 440 passengers. Four doors on each side, two forward and two aft of the wing. Crew door on starboard side giving access to upper deck. Freight holds under floor, forward and aft of wing box, each with one door on starboard side.

SYSTEMS, AVIONICS AND EQUIPMENT: As for Model 747.

DIMENSIONS, EXTERNAL: As for Model 747 except:
Length overall 56·31 m (184 ft 9 in)
Height overall 19·94 m (65 ft 5 in)
Tailplane span 25·22 m (82 ft 9 in)
Wheelbase 20·52 m (67 ft 4 in)

DIMENSIONS, INTERNAL:
Cabin, incl toilets and galleys:
Length 42·27 m (138 ft 8 in)
Max width 6·13 m (20 ft 1½ in)
Max height 2·54 m (8 ft 4 in)
Floor area, passenger deck 253·2 m² (2,725 sq ft)
Volume, passenger deck 613·34 m³ (21,660 cu ft)
Baggage hold volume (fwd) 48·99 m³ (1,730 cu ft)
Baggage hold volume (rear, containerised) 48·99 m³ (1,730 cu ft)
Bulk compartment volume (rear) 11·33 m³ (400 cu ft)

AREAS: As for Model 747 except:
Ailerons (total) 20·37 m² (219·3 sq ft)
Trailing-edge flaps (total) 78·78 m² (848 sq ft)
Fin 82·22 m² (885 sq ft)
Tailplane 142·51 m² (1,534 sq ft)

WEIGHTS: (letters are used to denote engine installations as follows: (A) CF6-45A2; (B) CF6-50E2-F; (C) RB211-524B2; (D) RB211-524C2; and (E) RB211-524D4):
Operating weight empty (approx, with 331 passengers):
A, B 148,778 kg (328,000 lb)
C, D 151,500 kg (334,000 lb)
E 151,045 kg (333,000 lb)
Max fuel weight: A, B 153,024 kg (337,360 lb)
C, D, E 154,185 kg (339,920 lb)
Max payload: A, B 37,194 kg (82,000 lb)
C, D 34,473 kg (76,000 lb)
E 34,926 kg (77,000 lb)
Max T-O weight (dry engines):
A, B, C, D, E 285,765 kg (630,000 lb)
or 299,370 kg (660,000 lb)
or 303,905 kg (670,000 lb)
or 312,980 kg (690,000 lb)
or 315,700 kg (696,000 lb)
or 317,515 kg (700,000 lb)
Max ramp weight:
A, B, C, D, E 284,485 kg (636,000 lb)
or 302,090 kg (666,000 lb)
or 306,630 kg (676,000 lb)
or 315,700 kg (696,000 lb)
or 318,875 kg (703,000 lb)
Max zero-fuel weight:
A, B, C, D, E 185,975 kg (410,000 lb)
or 192,775 kg (425,000 lb)
C, D, E or 197,310 kg (435,000 lb)
Max landing weight:
A, B, C, D, E 204,115 kg (450,000 lb)
or 210,920 kg (465,000 lb)
C, D, E or 215,455 kg (475,000 lb)

PERFORMANCE (at max T-O weight, except where indicated):
Never-exceed speed Mach 0·92
Max level speed, AUW of 226,795 kg (500,000 lb) at 9,145 m (30,000 ft) 537 knots (995 km/h; 618 mph)
Service ceiling 13,745 m (45,100 ft)
Min ground turning radius over outer wingtip 22·25 m (73 ft 0 in)
Runway LCN (Y: 302,095 kg; 666,000 lb, Z: 317,515 kg; 700,000 lb max taxi weight on h = 0·51 m; 20 in flexible pavement): Y 70
Z 75
Runway LCN (weights as above, on l = 1·02 m; 40 in rigid pavement): Y 76
Z 80
FAR T-O distance to 10·7 m (35 ft) at S/L, ISA (317,515 kg; 700,000 lb max T-O weight) 2,423 m (7,950 ft)
FAR landing field length:
at 204,115 kg (450,000 lb) MLW 1,594 m (5,230 ft)
at 210,920 kg (465,000 lb) MLW 1,646 m (5,400 ft)
Range (long-range step cruise, FAR 121.645 reserves, with 331 passengers and baggage at 317,515 kg; 700,000 lb) 5,750 nm (10,656 km; 6,621 miles)
Ferry range (long-range step cruise, FAR 121.645 reserves) 7,300 nm (13,528 km; 8,406 miles)

BOEING MODEL 747-200F FREIGHTER

The Boeing Model 747-200F Freighter is a version of the standard Model 747-200, capable of delivering 90,720 kg (200,000 lb) of containerised or palletised main deck cargo over a range of 4,480 nm (8,300 km; 5,159 miles).

The first 747-200F flew for the first time on 30 November 1971. It was certificated on 7 March 1972 and delivered to Lufthansa two days later. A total of 56 had been ordered and 53 delivered by 30 September 1986.

To ensure maximum utilisation, the 747-200F has a special loading system that enables two men to handle and stow the maximum load of up to 113,400 kg (250,000 lb) in 30 min. This system was fully described in the 1977-78 *Jane's*.

The 747-200F can carry up to 29 containers measuring 3·05 m × 2·44 m × 2·44 m (10 ft long, 8 ft high and 8 ft wide), plus 30 lower-lobe containers, each of 4·90 m³ (173 cu ft) capacity, and 22·65 m³ (800 cu ft) of bulk cargo. The main deck can accommodate ANSI/ISO containers of up to

12·2 m (40 ft) in length, and many combinations of pallets and igloos. The lower hold can accommodate combinations of IATA-A1 or -A2, and ATA LD-1 or -3 half-width containers, full-width or main-deck baggage containers, and many combinations of pallets and igloos.

The nose loading door, which is hinged just below the flight deck to allow it to swing forward and upward, gives clear access to the main deck to facilitate the handling of long or large loads. A side cargo door is available as an option, allowing simultaneous nose and side loading. The side cargo door will accept palletised loads up to 3·05 m (10 ft 0 in) in height.

The description of the Model 747-200B applies also to the Model 747-200F except as follows:

TYPE: Four-turbofan heavy commercial freighter.

FUSELAGE: As for Model 747-200B, except nose cargo loading door, which is hinged at the top and opens forward and upward.

ACCOMMODATION: Normal operating crew of three on flight deck. Nose cargo loading door, hinged at top. Lower lobe cargo doors, on starboard side, one forward and one aft of wing. Bulk compartment cargo door, on starboard side, aft of lower lobe cargo door. Two doors for crew on port side of aircraft. Aircraft is designed for fully mechanical loading of freight.

DIMENSIONS, EXTERNAL: As for Model 747-200B except:
Crew doors (two, each): Height 1·93 m (6 ft 4 in)
Width 1·07 m (3 ft 6 in)
Height to sill approx 4·88 m (16 ft 0 in)
Nose cargo loading door: Height 2·49 m (8 ft 2 in)
Width at top (min) 2·67 m (8 ft 9 in)
Max width 3·81 m (12 ft 6 in)
Height to sill approx 4·90 m (16 ft 1 in)

DIMENSIONS, INTERNAL:
Main cargo deck: Height 2·54 m (8 ft 4 in)
Max width at floor level 5·92 m (19 ft 5 in)
Lower lobe: Width at floor level 3·18 m (10 ft 5 in)
Total cargo volume 687·0 m³ (24,260 cu ft)

AREAS: As for Model 747-200B

WEIGHTS (letters are used to denote engine installations as follows: (A) JT9D-7R4G2; (B) CF6-50E2; (C) CF6-80C2; (D) RB211-524B2; (E) RB211-524C2; and (F) RB211-524D4):
Operating weight empty (approx) for max available gross weights: A 154,675 kg (341,000 lb)
B 156,036 kg (344,000 lb)
C 157,396 kg (347,000 lb)
D, E 159,211 kg (351,000 lb)
F 158,757 kg (350,000 lb)
Max fuel weights:
as for 747-200B
Max payload (29 pallets): A 112,944 kg (249,000 lb)
B 111,584 kg (246,000 lb)
C 110,223 kg (243,000 lb)
D, E 108,408 kg (239,000 lb)
F 108,862 kg (240,000 lb)
Max T-O weight:
A, B, C, E, F 351,535 kg (775,000 lb)
or 356,070 kg (785,000 lb)
or 362,875 kg (800,000 lb)
or 371,945 kg (820,000 lb)
or 377,840 kg (833,000 lb)
D 362,875 kg (800,000 lb)
or 371,945 kg (820,000 lb)
Max ramp weight:
A, B, C, E, F 379,200 kg (836,000 lb)
D 373,305 kg (823,000 lb)

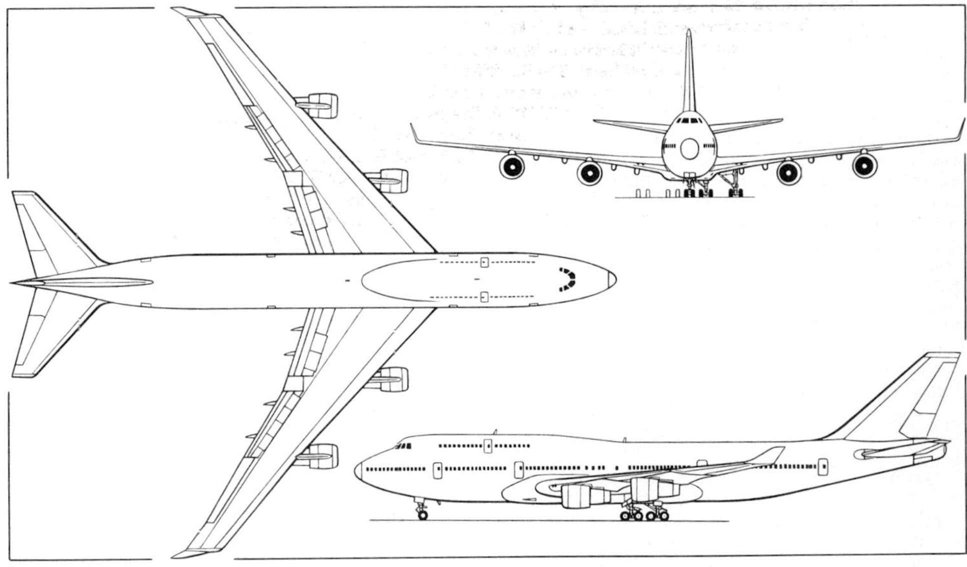

Boeing 747-400 advanced long-range version of the 747-300 *(Pilot Press)*

Max zero-fuel weight:
A, B, C, D, E, F 267,620 kg (590,000 lb)
Max landing weight:
A, B, C, D, E, F 285,765 kg (630,000 lb)

PERFORMANCE (at max T-O weight except where indicated, JT9D-7R4G2 engines):
Max level speed at AUW of 272,160 kg (600,000 lb), at 9,145 m (30,000 ft)
532 knots (986 km/h; 612 mph)
Cruise ceiling 13,715 m (45,000 ft)
Min ground turning radius 22·86 m (75 ft 0 in)
FAR T-O distance to 10·7 m (35 ft) at S/L, ISA, at BRW of 377,840 kg (833,000 lb) 3,185 m (10,450 ft)
FAR landing field length, at max landing weight
2,240 m (7,350 ft)
Range, long-range step cruise, FAR 121.645 reserves, with 90,720 kg (200,000 lb) payload:
T-O weight of 377,840 kg (833,000 lb)
4,480 nm (8,300 km; 5,159 miles)
Ferry range with max fuel, long-range cruise, FAR 121.645 reserves 7,770 nm (14,400 km; 8,947 miles)

BOEING MODEL 747-400

Boeing announced in May 1985 development of the Model 747-400, an advanced long-range version of the 747-300. Improvements include 266·9 kN (60,000 lb st) class CF6-80C2, PW4000 or RB211-524D4D engines, a modern two-crew digital flight deck, more flexible interior configurations, increased range and better fuel economy.

The 747-400 shares the extended upper deck fuselage of the 747-300. A 1·83 m (6 ft 0 in) extension has been added to each wingtip, with a 1·83 m (6 ft 0 in) winglet, canted outboard at an angle of 22° and swept back 60°, the combined tip extension and winglet installation offering a claimed increase in range of some three per cent. By employing advanced aluminium alloys developed for the Models 757 and 767 in the 747-400's wing structure, Boeing engineers have achieved a weight saving of 2,721 kg (6,000 lb). Substitution of carbon brakes for steel brakes, and new 0·56 m (1 ft 10 in) wide wheels with low-profile tyres, has provided a further weight saving of 816 kg (1,800 lb) in the aircraft's landing gear. New engine nacelles and support pylons have been designed, offering commonality with those of the Boeing 767. The 747-400's flight deck is configured for two-crew operation with digital avionics, sharing many common features with the 757/767 and resulting in a fifty per cent reduction in the number of instruments and gauges on the 747 flight deck. The final flight deck configuration may include a head-down display of fuel status on the engine indicating and crew alerting (EICAS) CRT displays rather than on overhead panels.

Improvements to the cabin area of the 747-400 include increased overhead storage facilities, alternative galley and toilet positions, a wireless cabin entertainment system in which audio and visual signals are picked up from floor mounted transmitters, and greater flexibility in interior design to permit airlines to react quickly to changes in market requirements which demand different mixes of first, business and economy class seating. A Combi cargo/passenger variant will be available.

A new feature of the 747-400 is the provision for the carriage of 11,356 litres (3,000 US gallons) of fuel in the horizontal tail surfaces, in tanks located between the front and rear spars. No provision is made for transferring this fuel as a means of adjusting longitudinal trim or maintaining aft centre of gravity. As a result of the increased fuel capacity, greater fuel economy of new generation engines and structural weight savings, the 747-400 will offer a 1,000 nm (1,853 km; 1,151 mile) increase in range over the 747-300. Maximum range, with a payload of 412 passengers in three class accommodation, will be more than 7,000 nm (12,970 km; 8,060 miles). Depending on the engines selected, the 747-400 is expected to burn 10-12 per cent less fuel than a 747-300 and to offer fuel burned per passenger seat reductions of up to 24 per cent over a 747-200. A Pratt & Whitney Canada APU will be installed in the tailcone.

Boeing Model 747-200F Freighter of Nippon Cargo Airlines

Design go-ahead for the 747-400 was granted in July 1985. Construction of the first aircraft was expected to begin in mid-1986 with rollout scheduled for early 1988 and FAA certification and first customer deliveries anticipated in the last quarter of that year. In October 1985 Northwest Orient Airlines became the launch customer for the 747-400 with an order for 10 aircraft, powered by PW4000 series engines. The Northwest Orient aircraft will be configured for 450 passengers. Delivery will take place during 1988-1990. British Airways has ordered 16 747-400s with RB211 engines and taken options on a further 12; Singapore Airlines has ordered 14; Lufthansa has ordered 6 with CF6 engines; KLM 6; Korean Air 3; Cathay Pacific 2 with RB211 engines; and UTA 2. At 30 September 1986 options had been taken for 39 aircraft.

WEIGHTS (letters are used to denote engine installations as follows: (A) PW4256; (B) CF6-80C2; (C) RB211-524D4D):

Operating weight empty (approx) for max available gross weights: A	176,990 kg (390,200 lb)
B	176,175 kg (388,400 lb)
C	178,170 kg (392,800 lb)
Max fuel weights: A, C	175,420 kg (386,740 lb)
B	174,245 kg (384,150 lb)
Max payload (412 passengers):	
A	65,680 kg (144,800 lb)
B	66,496 kg (146,600 lb)
C	64,500 kg (142,200 lb)
Max T-O weight	362,875 kg (800,000 lb)
	or 385,555 kg (850,000 lb)
Max ramp weight	364,235 kg (803,000 lb)
	or 386,915 kg (853,000 lb)
Max zero-fuel weight	242,670 kg (535,000 lb)
Max landing weight	260,360 kg (574,000 lb)

PERFORMANCE (estimated at max T-O weight except where indicated):

Max level speed, PW4256 engines and AUW of 317,515 kg (700,000 lb) at 9,145 m (30,000 ft) 530 knots (982 km/h; 610 mph)

FAR T-O distance to 10·7 m (35 ft) at BRW of 385,555 kg (850,000 lb), S/L, ISA, PW4256 engines 3,185 m (10,450 ft)

FAR landing field length, at max landing weight of 260,360 kg (574,000 lb) 1,905 m (6,250 ft)

Range, long-range cruising speed, PW4256 engines, at T-O weight of 385,555 kg (850,000 lb), 412 passengers and baggage, FAR 121.645 reserves 6,900 nm (12,785 km; 7,945 miles)

BOEING MODEL 757 and CORPORATE 77-52

In the early months of 1978, The Boeing Company announced a proposal to develop a new family of advanced technology commercial aircraft, to which it gave the Model designations 757, 767 and 777. The short/medium-range 757 was intended to differ considerably from the other two, being based on the Boeing 727 fuselage. Improved performance would come from two new high bypass engines and an advanced technology wing, with less sweepback than that of the Model 727.

On 31 August 1978 Eastern Air Lines and British Airways announced their intention to purchase 21 and 19 Model 757s respectively, the former taking an option on an additional 24, and the latter on 18. Following the signature in early 1979 of formal contracts by both of these airlines, Boeing announced on 23 March 1979 that the company had initiated full production of the Model 757; the first metal was cut for the new aircraft on 10 December 1979, and final assembly began in September 1981. The first 757 (N757A) was rolled out at Renton on 13 January, and made its first flight from there on 19 February 1982. This, and the next four aircraft off the production line, were used in the certification programme, which resulted in type certification by the FAA on 21 December 1982 and the UK CAA on 14 January 1983. Deliveries to Eastern Air Lines and British Airways began on 22 December 1982 and 25 January 1983, with respective revenue services being initiated on 1 January and 9 February 1983. Aircraft for these two airlines are designated **Model 757-200** and are powered initially by 166·4 kN (37,400 lb st) Rolls-Royce 535C turbofan engines. This was the first time that Boeing had launched a new airliner with a non-American engine. The 757s for Delta are fitted with Pratt & Whitney PW2037 turbofans, each rated at 170 kN (38,200 lb st). The first PW2037 engined 757 made its maiden flight on 14 March 1984; it was certificated in October and deliveries to Delta began on 5 November 1984. The first 757 with uprated Rolls-Royce 535E4 engines was delivered to Eastern on 10 October 1984. With the 535C engines, the 757-200 provides 53 per cent more seat miles per unit of fuel than earlier medium-range aircraft. With 535E4 and PW2037 engines the advantage was expected to be 76 per cent. A corporate/executive transport version is designated **Corporate 77-52**. An extended range variant is designated **Model 757ER**, the first example of which was delivered to Royal Brunei Airlines in May 1986.

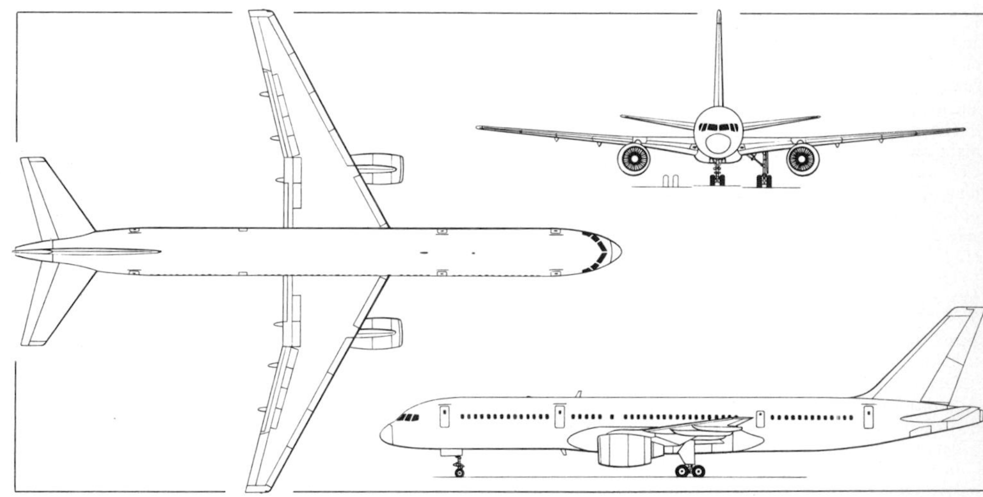

Boeing Model 757-200 twin-turbofan short/medium-range transport aircraft *(Pilot Press)*

Boeing announced in January 1986 a dedicated freighter version of the 757-200 designated Model **757-200PF** (Package Freighter). This aircraft features a large side cargo door in the forward fuselage, a single crew door and a windowless interior which will accept up to 15 standard 2·24 × 3·18 m (88 × 125 in) cargo containers on the main deck. United Parcel Service has ordered 20 Model 757-200PFs, with options on a further 15, for deliveries scheduled to commence in September 1987. The UPS aircraft will be powered by PW2037 engines.

In February 1986 Boeing announced the **Model 757-200 Combi**, which, unlike the 757-200PF, retains all passenger windows and doors but has a mixed cargo/passenger configuration with an upward opening 3·40 × 2·18 m (134 × 86 in) cargo door on the port side of the forward fuselage. The 757-200 Combi can carry up to three standard cargo containers and 123 to 148 passengers depending on cabin class and seating arrangments. Royal Nepal Airlines was the launch customer for the 757-200 Combi, with an order for a single aircraft scheduled for delivery in September 1988.

Fatigue testing equivalent to 100,001 flights over 40 years of commercial service was completed on a full size 757 airframe by early 1984.

On 16 July 1986 a Boeing 757 on delivery to Royal Air Maroc set a new distance record for the type, completing the 4,909 nm (9,098 km; 5,653 mile) journey from Seattle to Casablanca in 10 h 15 min.

By 30 September 1986 firm orders totalled 191; deliveries totalled 106.

The Model 757 retains the same fuselage cross-section as the 707/727/737 family. The original design provided for a T tail configuration, but as a result of wind tunnel testing it was decided to mount the tailplane on the fuselage.

TYPE: Twin-turbofan short/medium-range transport aircraft.

WINGS: Cantilever low-wing monoplane. Special Boeing wing sections. Dihedral 5°. Incidence 3° 12′. Sweepback at quarter-chord 25°. All aluminium alloy two-spar fail-safe wing box structure, manufactured by Boeing, with wing in-spar ribs by Hawker de Havilland of Australia. Centre-section continuous through fuselage. All-speed fully-powered ailerons outboard of double-slotted inboard and outboard trailing-edge flaps. Inboard flaps manufactured by Shorts of Northern Ireland; outboard flaps by CASA of Spain. High-lift full span leading-edge slats, in five sections on each wing, manufactured by Boeing Renton; fixed leading-edges by Boeing Vertol. Five flight spoilers and one ground spoiler on wing upper surface forward of trailing-edge flaps, manufactured by Grumman. Lateral control provided by ailerons, plus flight spoilers operated differentially. Spoilers operated collectively as speed brakes. Extensive use of honeycomb, and graphite composites and laminates, in construction of ailerons, flaps and spoilers. Thermal anti-icing of wing leading-edges. Wing/fuselage fairings and flap track fairings, of graphite/Kevlar, manufactured by Heath Tecna; wingtips by Schweizer.

FUSELAGE: All-metal semi-monocoque fail-safe structure, its cross-sectin based on two circular arcs of different radii, the larger above, and faired into a smooth contoured oval. Flight deck manufactured by BMAC at Wichita; main cabin sections by Boeing Renton; extreme rear fuselage by LTV.

TAIL UNIT: Tailplane consists of full span torque boxes of conventional light alloy construction, and is attached at pivot points and to an actuator. The fin comprises a three-spar dual-cell light alloy torque box attached to the fuselage. Elevators and rudder have graphite/epoxy honeycomb skins, supported by honeycomb and laminated spar and rib assemblies. Fin and tailplane manufactured by LTV; rudder and elevators of graphite by Boeing.

LANDING GEAR: Retractable tricycle type, with main and nose units manufactured by Menasco. Each main unit comprises a four-wheel bogie, fitted with Dunlop wheels, carbon brakes and tyres. Twin-wheel nose unit, also with Dunlop tyres. All landing gear doors of graphite/Kevlar.

POWER PLANT: Two 166·4 kN (37,400 lb st) Rolls-Royce 535C; 170 kN (38,200 lb st) Pratt & Whitney PW2037; or

Boeing Model 757-200 short/medium-range transport in the insignia of British Airways

178·4 kN (40,100 lb st) Rolls-Royce 535E4 turbofan engines, mounted in underwing pods. Engine support struts supplied by Rohr Industries. Fuel capacity 42,597 litres (11,253 US gallons).

ACCOMMODATION: Crew of two on flight deck, with provision for an observer. Five to seven cabin attendants. Nine standard interior arrangements for 178 (16 first class/162 tourist), 186 (16 first class/170 tourist), 201 (12 first class/189 tourist), 205 (12 first class/193 tourist) mixed class passengers, or 212, 218, 223, 224 or 239 all-tourist passengers. First class seats are four-abreast, at 96·5 cm (38 in) pitch; tourist seat pitch is 81 or 86 cm (32 or 34 in), basically six-abreast, in mixed class arrangements. Large overhead bins of Kevlar provide approximately 0·054 m³ (1·9 cu ft) of stowage per passenger. Choice of two cabin door configurations, with either three passenger doors and two overwing emergency exits on each side (used with 186, 205, 218 and 224 seat interiors); or four doors on each side (used with 178, 201, 212, 223 and 239 seat interiors). All versions have a galley at the front on the starboard side and another at the rear (two on 178 and 186 passenger versions and three on the 239 version plus one amidships); a toilet at the front on the port side and three more at the rear (186, 201, 205, 218, 224 passengers or two at the rear 239) or amidships (178, 212, 223 passengers). Coat closet at front of first class cabins and 212/218 passenger interiors.

SYSTEMS AND AVIONICS: Garrett environmental control system; General Electric engine thrust management system; Sperry-Vickers engine driven hydraulic pumps; four Abex electric hydraulic pumps. Hydraulic system maximum flow rate 140 litres (37 US gallons)/min at T-O power on engine driven pumps; 25·4-34·8 litres (6·7-9·2 US gallon)/min on electric motor pumps; 42·8 litres (11·3 US gallons)/min on ram air turbine. Independent reservoirs, pressurised by air from pneumatic system, maximum pressure 207 bars (3,000 lb/sq in) on primary pumps. Sundstrand electrical power generating system and ram air turbines; and Garrett GTCP331-200 APU. Collins FCS-700 autopilot flight director system (AFDS), EFIS-700 electronic flight instrument system, engine indication and crew alerting system (EICAS), RMI-743 radio distance magnetic indicator (RDMI) and optional radio magnetic indicator (RMI). Avionics also include a Honeywell inertial reference system (IRS). In this IRS, conventional mechanical gyroscopes are replaced by laser gyroscopes, and utilisation, in both the Models 757 and 767, represents their first commercial application. The IRS provides position, velocity and attitude information to flight deck displays, and the flight management computer system (FMCS) and digital air data computer (DADC) supplied by Sperry Flight Systems. The FMCS provides automatic en-route and terminal navigation capability, and also computes and commands both lateral and vertical flight profiles for optimum fuel efficiency, maximised by electronic linkage of the FMCS with automatic flight control and thrust management systems. Aircraft for British Airways and Monarch Airlines have Bendix ARINC 700 series avionics, including colour weather radar and seven digital com, nav and identification systems.

DIMENSIONS, EXTERNAL:
Wing span 38·05 m (124 ft 10 in)
Wing chord: at root 8·20 m (26 ft 11 in)
at tip 1·73 m (5 ft 8 in)
Wing aspect ratio 7·77
Length overall 47·32 m (155 ft 3 in)
Length of fuselage 46·96 m (154 ft 10 in)
Height overall 13·56 m (44 ft 6 in)
Tailplane span 15·21 m (49 ft 11 in)
Wheel track 7·32 m (24 ft 0 in)
Wheelbase 18·29 m (60 ft 0 in)
Passenger doors (two, fwd, port):
Height 1·83 m (6 ft 0 in)
Width 0·84 m (2 ft 9 in)
Passenger door (rear, port): Height 1·83 m (6 ft 0 in)
Width 0·76 m (2 ft 6 in)
Service door (fwd, stbd): Height 1·65 m (5 ft 5 in)
Width 0·76 m (2 ft 6 in)
Service door (stbd, opposite second passenger door):
Height 1·83 m (6 ft 0 in)
Width 0·84 m (2 ft 9 in)
Service door (rear, stbd): Height 1·83 m (6 ft 0 in)
Width 0·76 m (2 ft 6 in)
Emergency exits (four, overwing):
Height 0·97 m (3 ft 2 in)
Width 0·51 m (1 ft 8 in)
Emergency exits, optional (two, aft of wings):
Height 1·32 m (4 ft 4 in)
Width 0·61 m (2 ft 0 in)

DIMENSIONS, INTERNAL:
Cabin (aft of flight deck to rear pressure bulkhead):
Length 36·09 m (118 ft 5 in)
Max width 3·53 m (11 ft 7 in)
Max height 2·13 m (7 ft 0 in)
Floor area 116·04 m² (1,249 sq ft)
Passenger area volume 275·98 m³ (9,746 cu ft)
Underfloor cargo volume (bulk loading):
fwd 19·82 m³ (700 cu ft)
rear 30·87 m³ (1,090 cu ft)

AREAS:
Wings, gross 185·25 m² (1,994 sq ft)
Ailerons (total) 4·46 m² (48 sq ft)
Trailing-edge flaps (total) 30·38 m² (327 sq ft)
Leading-edge slats (total) 18·39 m² (198 sq ft)
Flight spoilers (total) 10·96 m² (118 sq ft)
Ground spoilers (total) 12·82 m² (138 sq ft)
Fin 34·37 m² (370 sq ft)
Rudder 11·61 m² (125 sq ft)
Tailplane 50·35 m² (542 sq ft)
Elevators (total) 12·54 m² (135 sq ft)

WEIGHTS AND LOADINGS (with 186 passengers. A: 535C engines; B: PW2037s; C: 535E4s):
Operating weight empty: A 57,438 kg (126,630 lb)
B 57,411 kg (126,570 lb)
C 57,551 kg (126,880 lb)
Max basic T-O weight:
A, B, C 99,790 kg (220,000 lb)
Max T-O weight (medium range):
A, B, C 104,325 kg (230,000 lb)
Max T-O weight (long range):
A, B, C 113,395 kg (250,000 lb)
Max landing weight: A, B, C 89,810 kg (198,000 lb)
Max zero-fuel weight:
A, B, C 83,460 kg (184,000 lb)
Max wing loading:
A, B, C at max basic T-O weight
538·5 kg/m² (110·3 lb/sq ft)
A, B, C at long range max T-O weight
587·8 kg/m² (120·4 lb/sq ft)
Max power loading:
at max basic T-O weight:
A 299·85 kg/kN (2·94 lb/lb st)
B 293·5 kg/kN (2·88 lb/lb st)
C 279·68 kg/kN (2·75 lb/lb st)
at long range max T-O weight:
A 327·1 kg/kN (3·21 lb/lb st)
B 320·18 kg/kN (3·14 lb/lb st)
C 305·1 kg/kN (3·00 lb/lb st)

PERFORMANCE (nominal, with 186 passengers, US mixed class operations; at max basic T-O weight, except where indicated, and with engines as above):
Max operating speed: A, B, C Mach 0·86
Cruising speed: A, B, C Mach 0·80
Approach speed at S/L, flaps down, max landing weight:
A, B, C 132 knots (245 km/h; 152 mph) EAS
*Initial cruising height: A 11,645 m (38,200 ft)
B 11,552 m (37,900 ft)
C 11,825 m (38,800 ft)
Min ground turning radius:
over wingtip 29·87 m (98 ft)
nose gear 21·64 m (71 ft)
Runway LCN at max basic T-O weight, optimum tyre pressure and subgrade C flexible pavement:
H40 × 14·5-19·0 tyres 34
T-O field length (S/L, 29°C):
at max basic T-O weight: A 1,817 m (5,960 ft)
B 1,770 m (5,810 ft)
C 1,640 m (5,380 ft)
at long range max T-O weight:
A 2,365 m (7,760 ft)
B 2,310 m (7,580 ft)
C 1,950 m (6,400 ft)
Landing field length at max landing weight:
A, B, C 1,400 m (4,600 ft)
Max range:
at max basic T-O weight:
A 2,390 nm (4,429 km; 2,752 miles)
B 2,880 nm (5,337 km; 3,316 miles)
C 2,710 nm (5,022 km; 3,120 miles)
at long range max T-O weight:
A 3,410 nm (6,319 km; 3,926 miles)
B 3,990 nm (7,394 km; 4,595 miles)
C 3,820 nm (7,079 km; 4,399 miles)

OPERATIONAL NOISE LEVELS (FAR Pt 36 stage 3):
T-O, at max basic T-O weight, full power:
A 91·8 EPNdB
B 90·4 EPNdB
C 89·8 EPNdB
T-O, at max basic T-O weight, cutback power:
A 85·5 EPNdB
B 86·2 EPNdB
C 82·2 EPNdB
Approach at max landing weight, 30° flaps:
A 100·3 EPNdB
B 97·7 EPNdB
C 95·0 EPNdB
Sideline: A, B 94·0 EPNdB
C 93·3 EPNdB

* *at max climb thrust, 92 m (300 ft)/min rate of climb*

BOEING MODEL 767 and CORPORATE 77-62

On 14 July 1978, Boeing announced its intention to launch full scale development of the twin-turbofan Model 767, following receipt of an order for 30 from United Air Lines. This airline had participated actively in defining the design of the Model 767, as it did with the design of the Model 727 in 1959-60. These aircraft, in service with twenty airlines by May 1986, are proving to be up to 40 per cent more fuel-efficient than the aircraft they replace, and comply also with the stringent noise regulations which came into force in 1985.

Construction of the first Model 767 began on 6 July 1979. It has a completely new airframe, with a fuselage 1·24 m (4 ft 1 in) wider than that of the Model 757, permitting a two-aisle seating layout. It was proposed initially in two forms, as the 767-100 with accommodation for approximately 180 passengers, and the 767-200MR with accommodation for up to 255 passengers. Subsequently, a 220-passenger version known as the **767-200** was finalised as the basic model. The first Model 767 (N767BA) was rolled out on 4 August 1981, and made its first flight on 26 September 1981. One airframe was built for static testing, which has been finished, and another was used for fatigue testing which was completed in October 1983. The fifth aircraft, and the first powered by CF6-80A engines, flew for the first time on 19

Boeing 767-200ER twin-turbofan transport operated by CAAC of China

First Boeing Model 767-300 for US carrier Delta Airlines

February 1982. A proposed corporate/executive transport version is designated **Corporate 77-62**.

As well as the basic model, an optional medium-range version of the 767-200 with reduced fuel capacity, and an optional higher gross weight version, certificated in June 1983, are available. In addition, an extended-range **767-200ER**, with still higher gross weight and increased fuel capacity, is available. The basic extended-range version, with gross weight increased to 156,490 kg (345,000 lb) and increased fuel capacity due to wing centre-section tanks, was first delivered, to Ethiopian Airlines on 1 June 1984. On 1 April 1986 a Boeing 767-200ER on delivery to Kuwait Airways set a new world distance record for commercial twin-jet aircraft with a nonstop flight of 6,854 nm (12,700 km; 7,892 miles) from Seattle to Kuwait. On 1 September 1986 a Boeing 767-200ER of LAN Chile operated the first revenue earning twin-jet service across the South Atlantic, flying from Rio de Janeiro, Brazil, to Madrid, Spain, with 193 passengers in 10 h 12 min. A higher gross weight version (159,211 kg; 351,000 lb with the same fuel capacity) is available as an option. Other higher gross weight versions are under study.

In February 1983 Boeing announced the addition to the line of a 269-seat **767-300**, with the same max T-O weight as the basic 767-200ER, strengthened main and nose landing gear, and additional metal thickness in certain areas of the fuselage and wing lower surface. The fuselage is extended by a 3·07 m (10 ft 1 in) plug forward of the wing, and a 3·35 m (11 ft) plug aft of the wing. Flight deck, cabin cross-section and systems are as for the other 767 models; power plant options are as for the 767-200ER. The first order for the 767-300 was received on 29 September 1983, when Japan Air Lines purchased four, followed by Delta Airlines, which has ordered nine, and All-Nippon Airways which has ordered 15 for delivery commencing in 1987. The first 767-300 flew for the first time on 30 January 1986, powered by JT9D-7R4D engines. A second aircraft, powered by CF6-80A2 engines and destined for Delta Airlines, is also taking part in a 430-hour flight test programme leading to first customer delivery to JAL in September 1986.

In January 1985 Boeing began development of an extended range, higher gross weight version of the 767-300, designated **767-300ER**. This version, with a gross weight of 172,365 kg (380,000 lb), and further enlarged wing centre-section fuel tanks, will be powered by advanced General Electric CF6-80C2 or Pratt & Whitney PW4000 series engines. A higher gross weight of 181,435 kg (400,000 lb) will be available as an option. Structural changes will be incorporated to accommodate the increased fuel capacity and higher gross weight. First deliveries of certificated aircraft are anticipated in 1987.

In July 1984 Boeing was awarded a $289·4 million contract by the US Army as part of its Airborne Optical Adjunct (AOA) programme which will include flight demonstrations of two long wavelength infra-red sensors designed to evaluate detection and tracking of incoming intercontinental ballistic missiles on re-entry to the Earth's atmosphere. Boeing has proposed the use of a modified Boeing 767 incorporating a new upper deck extending aft from above the flight deck to a position approximately adjacent to the wing root trailing-edge. This upper deck will house the infra-red sensors, which are being developed by Hughes Aircraft Company and Aerojet Electro Systems. The aircraft's main deck will house a Honeywell data processing system, and signal processing and control consoles for the sensors. The lower deck will be used to accommodate cryogenic systems for sensor cooling, and support equipment. The five-year research programme, which will lead to a two-year flight demonstration period, is being conducted by the US Army's Ballistic Missile Defense Systems Command.

Alternative engines for the Boeing 767-200, 767-200ER and 767-300 are the Pratt & Whitney JT9D-7R4D, rated at 212·6 kN (47,800 lb st), General Electric CF6-80A, rated at 213 kN (47,900 lb st), and the JT9D-7R4E and CF6-80A2, both in the 222·4 kN (50,000 lb st) class, and the PW4000 and CF6-80C2-B2/B6 series, all in the 222·4-273·6 kN (50,000-61,500 lb st) class.

A major change, following considerable flight testing, was Boeing's decision to modify the first 767s produced from a three-crew flight deck to the now basic two-crew layout, so that the latter was standard from the start of deliveries. The basic interior arrangements of all versions are identical.

FAA certification of the initial JT9D-7R4D version was received on 30 July 1982, and on 30 September 1982 for the CF6-80A version. Delivery of the first 767, to United Air Lines, was made on 19 August 1982, this airline operating its initial revenue service on 8 September. The first CF6-engined 767 was delivered to Delta on 25 October and entered service on 15 December 1982.

The 50th Model 767 was delivered on 4 June 1983, and the 100th was rolled out on 24 July 1984. By 30 September 1986, orders for the Model 767 (all versions) totalled 209, of which 146 had been delivered.

Boeing has awarded manufacturing subcontracts to Grumman Aerospace Corporation (wing centre-section, an adjacent lower fuselage section, and fuselage bulkheads); to LTV (horizontal tail); and to Canadair Ltd (rear fuselage). In two other major work-sharing programmes announced in August and September 1978, Boeing gave details of co-production agreements whereby Aeritalia of Italy and member companies of the Japanese aerospace industry participate as follows:

Aeritalia: Wing control surfaces, flaps and leading-edge slats; wingtips; elevators; fin, rudder; and nose radome.

Fuji: Wing fairings and main landing gear doors.

Kawasaki: Centre-fuselage body panels, exit hatches and wing in-spar ribs.

Mitsubishi: Rear-fuselage body panels, stringers, passenger and cargo doors, and dorsal fin.

The following details apply to the basic Model 767-200, except where indicated:

TYPE: Twin-turbofan medium-range commercial transport.

WINGS: Cantilever low-wing monoplane. Special Boeing wing sections. Thickness/chord ratio 15·1% at root, 10·3% at tip. Dihedral 6°. Incidence 4° 15′. Sweepback 31° 30′ at quarter-chord. Fail-safe structure of aluminium alloy. Plain inboard and outboard ailerons with extensive use of graphite hybrid composites. Single-slotted linkage-supported aluminium outboard trailing-edge flaps; double-slotted inboard flaps. Conventional inboard and outboard spoilers of graphite composite construction are provided for roll control, to act as airbrakes, and for lift dumping. Track mounted leading-edge slats of light alloy construction. Roll trim through spring feel system. All control surfaces are powered hydraulically. Anti-icing of outboard wing leading-edges.

FUSELAGE: Conventional semi-monocoque structure of aluminium alloy, consisting of skin, longitudinal stringers and circumferential frames. Structure is of fail-safe design, and is pressurised except for tailcone aft of passenger cabin, landing gear wheel wells and air cycle machine wells.

TAIL UNIT: Cantilever fail-safe structure of aluminium alloy and aluminium honeycomb. Variable incidence tailplane. Elevators of single hinge type with redundant parallel actuators. No trim tabs. All controls are powered hydraulically. Yaw trim through spring feel system. No anti-icing.

LANDING GEAR: Hydraulically retractable tricycle type. Menasco twin-wheel nose unit retracts forward. Cleveland Pneumatic main gear, comprising two four-wheel bogies which retract inward. Oleo-pneumatic shock absorbers. Bendix wheels and brakes. Mainwheel tyres size 45 × 17-20, pressure 12·6 bars (183 lb/sq in). Nosewheel tyres size 37 × 14-15, pressure 10·0 bars (145 lb/sq in). Steel disc brakes on all mainwheels. Electronically controlled anti-skid units.

POWER PLANT: Two high bypass turbofan engines (details in introductory copy), in pods pylon-mounted on the wing leading-edges. Fuel in one integral tank in each wing, and in a centre tank, with total capacity of 63,216 litres (16,700 US gallons) in 200/300; 767-200ER has additional 14,195 litres (3,750 US gallons) in a second centre-section tank, raising total capacity to 77,412 litres (20,450 US gallons). The 767-300ER has a further expanded wing centre-section tank, bringing total capacity to 91,039 litres (24,050 US gallons). Refuelling point in port outer wing. Anti-icing of engine air inlets.

ACCOMMODATION: Normal operating crew of two on flight deck, with third position optional. Basic accommodation in -200 models for 216 passengers, made up of 18 first class passengers forward in six-abreast seating at 96·5 cm (38 in) pitch, and 198 tourist class in mainly seven-abreast seating at 84 cm (33 in) pitch. Type A inward opening plug doors are provided at both the front and rear of the cabin on each side of the fuselage, with a Type III emergency exit over the wing on each side. A total of five toilets is installed, two centrally in the main cabin, two aft in the main cabin, and one forward in the first class section. Galleys are situated at forward and aft ends of the cabin. Alternative single class layouts provide for 230 tourist passengers, seated seven-abreast at 86 cm (34 in) pitch; 242 passengers seated seven-abreast at 81 cm (32 in) pitch; or 255 passengers mainly seven-abreast (two-three-two) at 76 cm (30 in) pitch, or eight-abreast (two-four-two) at 81 cm (32 in) pitch. Max seating capacity in -200 models (requiring additional overwing emergency exit) for 290 passengers, mainly eight-abreast, at 76 cm (30 in) pitch, or in -300 for 290 passengers seven-abreast. By installing an additional pair of Type A doors (optional), the seating capacity of the 767-300 can be increased to 330. The overwing exits are deleted in this configuration. Underfloor cargo holds of -200 versions can accommodate, typically, up to 22 LD2 or 11 LD1 containers. The 767-300 underfloor cargo holds can accommodate 30 LD2 or 15 LD1 containers. Forward and rear cargo doors of equal size are standard on the 767-200 and 767-300 but a larger (1·75 by 3·40 m; 5 ft 9 in by 11 ft 2 in) forward cargo door is standard on the 767-200ER and 767-300ER and optional on 767-200 and 767-300, to permit loading of Type 2 pallets, three such pallets being accommodated in the -200/200ER and four in the -300/300ER. Bulk cargo door at rear on port side. Overhead stowage for carry-on baggage. Cabin is air-conditioned, cargo holds heated.

SYSTEMS: Garrett dual air cycle air-conditioning system. Pressure differential 0·59 bars (8·6 lb/sq in). Electrical supply from two engine driven 90kVA three-phase 400Hz constant frequency AC generators, 115/200V output. 90 kVA generator mounted on APU for ground operation or for emergency use. Three hydraulic systems at 207 bars (3,000 lb/sq in), for flight control and utility functions, supplied from engine driven pumps and a Garrett bleed air powered hydraulic pump or APU. Maximum generating capacity of port and starboard systems is 163 litres (43 US gallons)/hour; centre system 185·5 litres (49 US gallons), at 196·5 bars (2,850 lb/sq in). Reservoirs pressurised by engine bleed air via a pressure regulation module. Reservoir relief valve pressure is nominally 4·48 bars (65 lb/sq in). An additional hydraulic motor driven generator, to provide essential functions for extended range operations, is standard on the 767-200ER and 767-300ER and optional on the 767-200 and 767-300. Nitrogen chlorate oxygen generators in passenger cabin, plus gaseous oxygen for flight crew. Anti-icing for air data sensors and windscreen. APU in tailcone to provide ground and in-flight electrical power and pressurisation.

AVIONICS AND EQUIPMENT: Standard avionics include ARINC 700 Series equipment (Bendix VOR/marker beacon receiver, ILS receiver, radio altimeter, transponder, DME, ADF and RDR-4A colour weather radar in aircraft for All Nippon, Britannia and Transbrasil). Collins caution annunciator, dual digital flight management systems, and triple digital flight control computers, including FCS-700 flight control system, EFIS-700 electronic flight instrument system and RMI-743 radio distance magnetic indicator. Honeywell IRS, and Sperry Flight Systems FMCS and DADC, as described in Boeing Model 757 entry.

DIMENSIONS, EXTERNAL:
Wing span 47·57 m (156 ft 1 in)
Wing chord: at root 8·57 m (28 ft 1¼ in)
at tip 2·29 m (7 ft 6 in)
Wing aspect ratio 7·9
Length overall: 200/200ER 48·51 m (159 ft 2 in)
300/300ER 54·94 m (180 ft 3 in)
Length of fuselage: 200/200ER 47·24 m (155 ft 0 in)
300/300ER 53·67 m (176 ft 1 in)
Fuselage: Max width 5·03 m (16 ft 6 in)
Height overall 15·85 m (52 ft 0 in)
Tailplane span 18·62 m (61 ft 1 in)
Wheel track 9·30 m (30 ft 6 in)
Wheelbase: 200/200ER 19·69 m (64 ft 7 in)
300/300ER 22·76 m (74 ft 8 in)
Passenger doors (two, fwd and rear, port):
Height 1·88 m (6 ft 2 in)
Width 1·07 m (3 ft 6 in)
Galley service door (two, fwd and rear, stbd):
Height 1·83 m (6 ft 0 in)
Width 1·07 m (3 ft 6 in)
Emergency exits (two, each):
Height 0·97 m (3 ft 2 in)
Width 0·51 m (1 ft 8 in)
Cargo doors (two, fwd and rear, stbd):
Height 1·75 m (5 ft 9 in)
Width 1·78 m (5 ft 10 in)
Optional cargo door (fwd, port):
Height 1·75 m (5 ft 9 in)
Width 3·40 m (11 ft 2 in)

DIMENSIONS, INTERNAL:
Cabin, excl flight deck:
Length: 200/200ER 33·93 m (111 ft 4 in)
300/300ER 40·36 m (132 ft 5 in)
Max width 4·72 m (15 ft 6 in)
Max height 2·87 m (9 ft 5 in)
Floor area: 200/200ER 154·9 m² (1,667 sq ft)
300/300ER 184·0 m² (1,981 sq ft)
Volume: 200/200ER 428·2 m³ (15,121 cu ft)
300/300ER 483·9 m³ (17,088 cu ft)
Volume, flight deck 13·5 m³ (478 cu ft)
Baggage holds (containerised), volume:
200/200ER 74·8 m³ (2,640 cu ft)
300/300ER 101·9 m³ (3,600 cu ft)
Bulk cargo hold volume:
All models 12·2 m³ (430 cu ft)
Combined baggage hold/bulk cargo hold volume:
200/200ER 87·0 m³ (3,070 cu ft)
300/300ER 114·1 m³ (4,030 cu ft)
Total cargo hold volume:
200/200ER 111·3 m³ (3,930 cu ft)
300/300ER 147·0 m³ (5,190 cu ft)

AREAS:
Wings, gross 283·3 m² (3,050 sq ft)
Ailerons (total) 11·58 m² (124·6 sq ft)
Trailing-edge flaps (total) 36·88 m² (397·0 sq ft)
Leading-edge slats (total) 28·30 m² (304·6 sq ft)
Spoilers (total) 15·83 m² (170·4 sq ft)
Fin 30·19 m² (325·0 sq ft)
Rudder 15·95 m² (171·7 sq ft)
Tailplane 59·88 m² (644·5 sq ft)
Elevators (total) 17·81 m² (191·7 sq ft)

WEIGHTS (A: 767-200 basic/JT9D-7R4D engines; B: 767-200 basic/CF6-80A; C: medium-range version/JT9D-7R4D; D: medium-range version/CF6-80A; E: higher gross weight version/JT9D-7R4D; F: higher gross weight version/CF6-80A; G: 767-200ER basic/JT9D-7R4E; H: 767-200ER basic/CF6-80A2; J: higher gross weight version/JT9D-7R4E; K: higher gross weight version/CF6-80A2; L: 767-300/JT9D-7R4E; M: 767-300/CF6-80A2; N: higher gross weight version/JT9D-7R4E; P: higher gross weight version/CF6-80A2; Q: 767-300ER/PW4056; R: 767-300ER/CF6-80C2-B4; S: higher gross weight version/PW4060; T: higher gross weight version/CF6-80C2-B6:
Manufacturer's weight empty:
A, C, E 74,390 kg (164,000 lb)
B, D, F 73,981 kg (163,100 lb)
G, J 75,432 kg (166,300 lb)
H, K 75,024 kg (165,400 lb)
L, N 78,789 kg (173,700 lb)

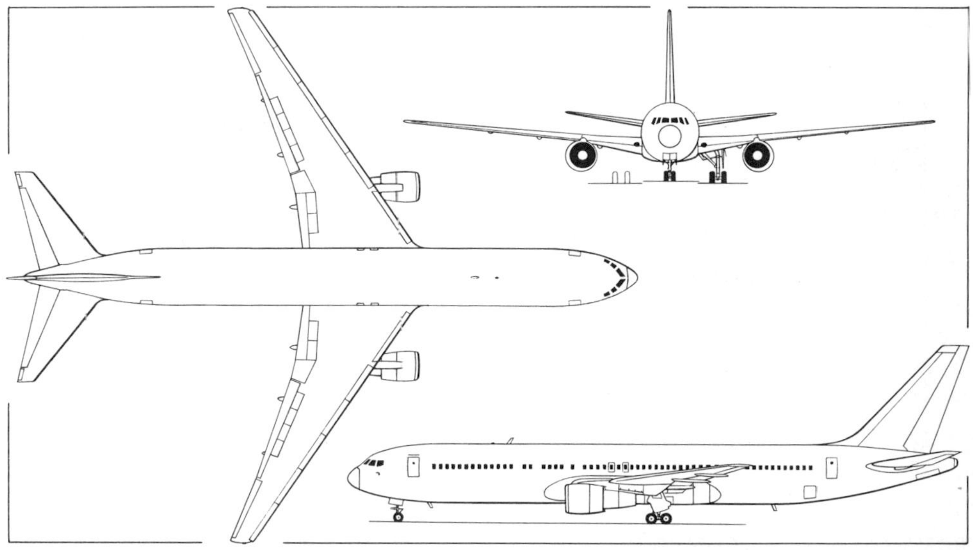

Boeing Model 767-300 wide-bodied medium-range commercial transport aircraft *(Pilot Press)*

M, P 78,381 kg (172,800 lb)
Q 80,330 kg (177,100 lb)
R 80,150 kg (176,700 lb)
S 80,920 kg (178,400 lb)
T 80,740 kg (178,000 lb)
Operating weight empty:
A, C, E 79,923 kg (176,200 lb)
B, D, F 79,515 kg (175,300 lb)
G, J 81,919 kg (180,600 lb)
H, K 81,510 kg (179,700 lb)
L, N 85,638 kg (188,800 lb)
M, P 85,230 kg (187,900 lb)
Q 87,997 kg (194,000 lb)
R 87,815 kg (193,600 lb)
S 88,585 kg (195,300 lb)
T 88,405 kg (194,900 lb)
Max payload (767-200, 220 passengers; 767-200ER, 216 passengers; 767-300, 269 passengers; 767-300ER, 261 passengers): A, B, C, D, E, F 19,958 kg (44,000 lb)
G, H, J, K 19,595 kg (43,200 lb)
L, M, N, P 24,403 kg (53,800 lb)
Q, R, S, T 23,677 kg (52,200 lb)
Max fuel weight:
A, B, E, F, L, M, N, P 51,131 kg (112,725 lb)
C, D 37,169 kg (81,945 lb)
G, H, J, K 62,613 kg (138,038 lb)
Q, R, S, T 73,635 kg (162,338 lb)
Max T-O weight: A, B 136,078 kg (300,000 lb)
C, D 127,913 kg (282,000 lb)
E, F 142,881 kg (315,000 lb)
G, H, L, M 156,489 kg (345,000 lb)
J, K, N, P 159,211 kg (351,000 lb)
Q, R 172,365 kg (380,000 lb)
S, T 181,435 kg (400,000 lb)
Max ramp weight: A, B 136,985 kg (302,000 lb)
C, D 128,820 kg (284,000 lb)
E, F 143,789 kg (317,000 lb)
G, H, L, M 157,396 kg (347,000 lb)
J, K, N, P 159,755 kg (352,200 lb)
Q, R 172,818 kg (381,000 lb)
S, T 181,890 kg (401,000 lb)
Max zero-fuel weight: A, B 112,491 kg (248,000 lb)
C, D 109,769 kg (242,000 lb)
E, F 113,398 kg (250,000 lb)
G, H, J, K 114,759 kg (253,000 lb)
L, M, N, P, Q, R 126,098 kg (278,000 lb)
S, T 130,635 kg (288,000 lb)
Max landing weight: A, B 122,470 kg (270,000 lb)
C, D 116,573 kg (257,000 lb)
E, F 123,377 kg (272,000 lb)
G, H, J, K 126,098 kg (278,000 lb)
L, M, N, P, Q, R 136,078 kg (300,000 lb)
S, T 145,150 kg (320,000 lb)

PERFORMANCE (in US mixed class operation, at max T-O weight except where indicated):
Normal cruising speed, all versions Mach 0·80
Approach speed at max landing weight:
A, B, E, F 136 knots (252 km/h; 157 mph)
C, D 133 knots (246 km/h; 153 mph)
G, H, J, K 138 knots (256 km/h; 159 mph)
L, M, N, P, S, T 145 knots (269 km/h; 167 mph)
Q, R 140 knots (259 km/h; 161 mph)
Initial cruise altitude: A 11,950 m (39,200 ft)
B 12,100 m (39,700 ft)
C 12,315 m (40,400 ft)
D 12,435 m (40,800 ft)
E 11,645 m (38,200 ft)
F 11,795 m (38,700 ft)
G 11,245 m (36,900 ft)
H 11,280 m (37,000 ft)
J, L 11,125 m (36,500 ft)
K, M 11,155 m (36,600 ft)
N 11,000 m (36,100 ft)
P 11,035 m (36,200 ft)
Q 10,850 m (35,600 ft)
R 10,880 m (35,700 ft)
S 10,455 m (34,300 ft)
T 10,545 m (34,600 ft)
Service ceiling, one engine out (weight for 1,000 nm; 1,850 km; 1,150 mile range):
A, B, C, D, E, F 7,070 m (23,200 ft)
G, H, J, K 7,130 m (23,400 ft)
L, N 6,430 m (21,100 ft)
M, P 6,460 m (21,200 ft)
Q, T 6,890 m (22,600 ft)
R 6,920 m (22,700 ft)
S 6,795 m (22,300 ft)
T-O field length (S/L, 29°C):
A, B 1,800 m (5,900 ft)
C, D 1,615 m (5,300 ft)

Model of proposed Boeing Model 7J7

E	1,951 m (6,400 ft)
F	1,981 m (6,500 ft)
G, H	2,375 m (7,800 ft)
J	2,499 m (8,200 ft)
K, M	2,560 m (8,400 ft)
L	2,530 m (8,300 ft)
N, Q, R	2,743 m (9,000 ft)
P	2,713 m (8,900 ft)
S, T	2,895 m (9,500 ft)
Design range: A	3,280 nm (6,078 km; 3,777 miles)
B	3,285 nm (6,088 km; 3,783 miles)
C	2,420 nm (4,485 km; 2,787 miles)
D	2,440 nm (4,522 km; 2,810 miles)
E	3,965 nm (7,348 km; 4,566 miles)
F	3,960 nm (7,339 km; 4,560 miles)
G	5,040 nm (9,340 km; 5,804 miles)
H	5,015 nm (9,294 km; 5,775 miles)
J	5,280 nm (9,785 km; 6,080 miles)
K	5,255 nm (9,738 km; 6,051 miles)
L	3,835 nm (7,107 km; 4,416 miles)
M	3,825 nm (7,088 km; 4,404 miles)
N	4,075 nm (7,551 km; 4,692 miles)
P	4,060 nm (7,523 km; 4,675 miles)
Q	5,225 nm (9,683 km; 6,017 miles)
R	5,170 nm (9,580 km; 5,953 miles)
S	5,825 nm (10,795 km; 6,707 miles)
T	5,835 nm (10,813 km; 6,719 miles)
OPERATIONAL NOISE LEVELS (FAR Pt 36, Stage 3):	
T-O at max basic T-O weight: B	87·1 EPNdB
H	90·4 EPNdB
Approach at max landing weight: B	101·6 EPNdB
H	101·7 EPNdB
Sideline: B	95·4 EPNdB
H	96·6 EPNdB

BOEING MODEL 7J7

In March 1986 The Boeing Company and the Japanese companies of Mitsubishi Heavy Industries, Kawasaki Heavy Industries, Fuji Heavy Industries and the Japan Aircraft Development Corporation signed a memorandum of understanding for the design, development and production of an advanced technology airliner known as the Model 7J7. The Japanese companies will have a 25 per cent equity share in the programme and will participate on a full partnership basis. SAAB-Scania of Sweden and Shorts of Belfast have also signed understandings with Boeing to participate as programme associates.

The 7J7 will be an entirely new design using very high bypass engines driving propfans, an advanced wing design, new structural materials, advanced avionics and digital communications equipment and fly by wire and fly by light technologies. The aircraft will be in the 150-seat class. A 100-110 seat Model 7J7 'Short' is also under consideration. Pratt & Whitney and the Allison Gas Turbine Division of General Motors are jointly developing a demonstrator engine for the 7J7 which will drive two counter-rotating propfans. The general configuration of the aircraft can be seen in the accompanying photograph.

Boeing expects to make a production decision on the 7J7 in mid-1988, with initial service entry anticipated during 1992. The company predicts a 45 per cent increase in fuel efficiency and a ten per cent reduction in direct operating costs for the aircraft when compared with the latest turbofan airliners which will be available at the end of the decade. Scandinavian Airlines System has indicated that it could become launch customer for the 7J7.

BOEING AEROSPACE COMPANY

Kent, Washington

PRESIDENT: M. K. Miller

EXECUTIVE VICE-PRESIDENT: B. D. Pinick

VICE-PRESIDENTS:
- C. P. Ekas (Defense Systems Division)
- R. W. Hager (Space Station)
- A. E. Hitsman (Operations)
- D. B. Jacobs (Space Division)
- H. Kennet (Research and Engineering)
- C. G. King (Information Systems Division)
- W. A. Nomer (Business Management)
- J. B. Sheridan (Ballistic Systems Division)
- J. R. Utterstrom (Advanced Development)

The Boeing Aerospace Company has its headquarters at the company's space centre at Kent, Washington, some 12 miles south of Seattle. It consists of four major divisions: Information Systems; Space Systems; Ballistic Systems and Defense Systems. Departments include Advanced Development, Business Development, Business Management, Operations, Technical Operations, and Research and Engineering. Subsidiary companies are: Boeing Agri-Industrial Company; Boeing Technical Operations; Boeing Technical and Management Services, and Boeing Petroleum Services. Major programmes and activities concern airborne warning and control, the E-4 advanced airborne command post, the E-6 Tacamo aircraft, the Inertial Upper Stage, Minuteman ICBM, Peacekeeper ICBM ground support system, air-launched cruise missile, ASW standoff weapon, and Roland. Responsible for much of Boeing's military and space effort, it has a labour force of approximately 17,900 employees.

BOEING E-3 SENTRY

USAF designations: EC-137D and E-3

The E-3 Sentry AWACS (Airborne Warning And Control System) is effectively a mobile, flexible, survivable and jamming-resistant high capacity radar station, command, control and communications centre, installed within a Boeing 707 airframe. It offers the potential of long-range high- or low-level surveillance of all air vehicles, manned or unmanned, and provides detection, tracking and identification capability within its surveillance capacity during all weathers and above all kinds of terrain. The radar system of later production aircraft also incorporates a maritime surveillance mode. Each of these aircraft is able to support a variety of tactical and/or air defence missions with no change in configuration. Its data storage and processing capability can provide real-time assessment of enemy action, and of the status and position of friendly resources.

In US Air Force service, the E-3 has a dual use: as a command and control centre to support quick-reaction deployment and tactical operations by Tactical Air Command units; and as a survivable early warning airborne command and control centre for identification, surveillance and tracking of airborne enemy forces, and for the command and control of NORAD (North American Air Defense) forces over the continental USA. The E-3 provides comprehensive surveillance out to a range of more than 200 nm (370 km; 230 miles) for low-flying targets, and still further for targets at higher altitudes.

Boeing's Aerospace Group, as it was then named, was awarded an initial contract as prime contractor and systems integrator for the AWAC system on 23 July 1970. In order to ensure that maximum effort and finance were devoted to the design and development of the most advanced radar and associated onboard systems, Boeing's design submission was based on the airframe of the Model 707-320B commercial jet transport. The only major change proposed for production E-3As was the installation of more powerful Pratt & Whitney TF33 turbofan engines, in lieu of the commercial turbofans then standard for the civil transport models. Two of these aircraft, with the prototype designation EC-137D, were modified initially for comparative trials with prototype downward looking radars designed by Hughes Aircraft Company and Westinghouse Electric Corporation. After several months of airborne tests, the Westinghouse radar was selected.

On 26 January 1973 the US Air Force announced approval for full scale AWACS development, and production received Congressional approval in the Spring of 1975. The name Sentry was given subsequently to the E-3. The full scale development test programme, completed at the end of 1976, involved a fleet of three aircraft completely equipped with mission avionics, and a fourth aircraft equipped for airworthiness testing. Thirty-five E-3s were delivered subsequently to the USAF, the last of them in June 1984. A further 18 were built for NATO.

These USAF and NATO AWACS have been developed and produced to four differing standards, as follows:

Core E-3A. Initial form of the first 24 production Sentries delivered to USAF. Equipped with pulse-Doppler radar capable of detecting high and low flying aircraft; CC-1 computer; nine situation display consoles (SDCs) which provide the mission crew with all display and control features required to carry out their surveillance, weapons directing, and battle staff functions; two auxiliary display units (ADUs) which support the communications, maintenance and data processing functions; and 13 available communications links (seven UHF, three VHF/AM, one VHF/FM, and two HF/SSB), many of them in clear voice.

E-3B. Under the USAF Block 20 modification programme, the two prototypes and 22 USAF core-configured

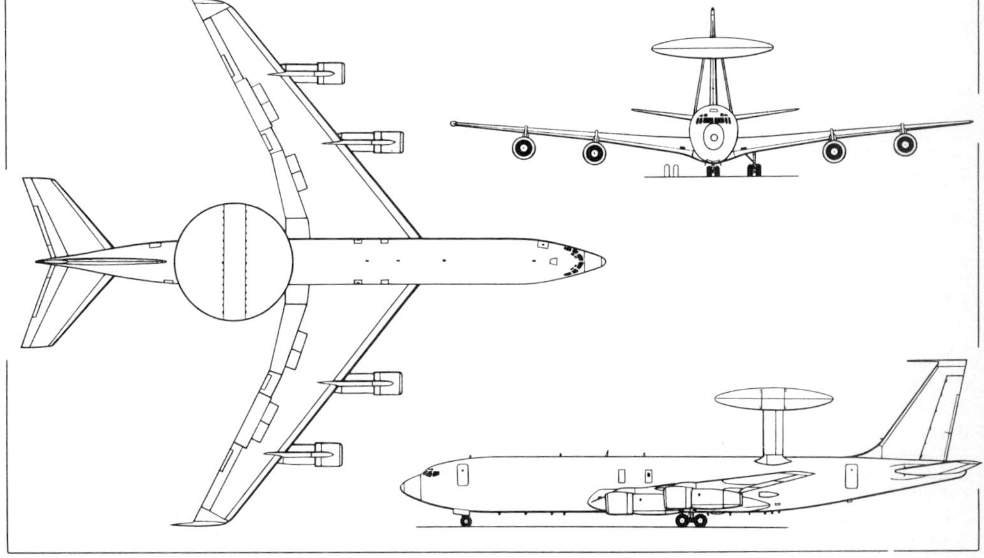

Three-view drawing *(Pilot Press)* **and photograph** *(S. G. Richards)* **of NATO Boeing E-3A Sentry AWACS aircraft**

E-3As (aircraft Nos. 4 to 9 and 11 to 26) are being updated to E-3B standard by the installation of ECM-resistant voice communications; one more HF and five more UHF radios; a new and faster IBM CC-2 computer with much expanded memory and greatly increased processing speed compared with the CC-1; five additional SDCs; and an austere maritime surveillance capability which Westinghouse developed for incorporation in the basic radar system. The E-3B also has provisions for Have Quick anti-jamming improvements to UHF radios, self defence, and a radio teletypewriter. First E-3B was re-delivered to USAF, after modification, on 18 July 1984. Remaining 23 are being modified by USAF at Tinker AFB, using Boeing kits.

US/NATO Standard E-3A. Original standard for USAF aircraft Nos. 27 to 35, of which delivery began in December 1981, and of the updated aircraft No. 3. Radar modified to embody full maritime surveillance capability; CC-2 computer; additional HF radios; ECM-resistant voice communications; radio teletypewriter; provisions for self defence and ECM. NATO aircraft are to this standard and retain E-3A designation.

E-3C. Under USAF Block 25 modification programme, begun in 1984, upgrading of the 10 USAF Standard E-3As to E-3C configuration is adding five more SDCs, five more UHF radios, and provisions for Have Quick anti-jamming improvements.

The USAF Electronic Systems Division has proposed a $425 million MSIP for the E-3, phased over five years, to give the radar greater 'detectability', add passive sensors, and make other improvements. Eventually, all USAF and NATO E-3s will be equipped with the Joint Tactical Information Distribution System (JTIDS) for anti-jam communications.

The first production core-configured E-3A Sentry was delivered on 24 March 1977 to Tactical Air Command's 552nd Airborne Warning and Control Wing (later Division), based at Tinker AFB, Oklahoma. E-3As achieved initial operational status in April 1978, and have since completed deployments to Alaska, Iceland, West Germany, Saudi Arabia, Sudan, the Mediterranean area, and the Pacific. E-3 aircraft are also employed in support of the US drug enforcement programme.

E-3As began to assume a role in US continental air defence on 1 January 1979, when NORAD personnel started to augment E-3A flight crews from TAC on all operational NORAD missions from Tinker AFB. The operating component was redesignated 552nd AWAC Wing in April 1985; it consists of several subordinate units. At Tinker, these include the 963rd and 964th AWAC Squadrons, the 966th AWAC Training Squadron, the 552nd Aircraft Generation Squadron (systems support), the 552nd Component Repair Squadron, and the 8th Tactical Deployment Control Squadron (flying EC-135/WC-135 aircraft). Overseas detachments of the 552nd AWACW include the 960th and 961st AWAC Support Squadrons. Based respectively at NAS Keflavik, Iceland, and Kadena AB, Okinawa, Japan, they provide command and control capability to CINCLANT (through the Commander, Iceland Defence Force) and CINCPAC.

Much of the avionics for NATO E-3As was produced in West Germany, with Dornier as systems integrator. NATO funded a third HF radio, to cover the maritime environment; a new data analysis and programming group; underwing hardpoints for self defence system stores; and a radio teletype to link the AWACS with the Organisation's maritime forces and commands. The first NATO production E-3A flew for the first time on 18 December 1980, from the manufacturing plant at Renton to Boeing Field, Seattle, where its rotodome and associated equipment were installed subsequently. It was delivered to Dornier's factory at Oberpfaffenhofen on 19 March 1981, and installation and checkout of mission avionics began on 1 April. Delivery of this first complete E-3A was made to NATO on 22 January 1982, and the final aircraft was delivered on 25 April 1985.

The NATO AWACS aircraft's main operating base is at Geilenkirchen in West Germany. Initial forward operating bases were at Oerland, Norway, and Konya, Turkey. Additional forward operating bases became operational during 1985 at Preveza, Greece and Trapani, Italy. The forward operating bases are manned by 20-35 NATO personnel, who provide turnaround maintenance services. E-3As are deployed periodically for training and surveillance missions. Eventually, aircraft are expected to be deployed to the forward bases nearly full-time.

The sale of five E-3 AWACS aircraft to the Royal Saudi Air Force was approved during October 1981, under a programme known as Peace Sentinel. Also included in the sale were six E-3 derivative tanker aircraft, which are designated **KE-3A**, and in 1984 the Saudi government exercised an option to increase the number of KE-3As to eight. In the same year, agreement was reached to equip the RSAF aircraft with CFM56-2 engines, fitted with Hispano-Suiza thrust reversers. The first Saudi E-3 was handed over on 30 June 1986, and deliveries of all 13 aircraft are due to be completed by mid-1987. Aircraft delivered to Saudi Arabia are not expected to be equipped with JTIDS, the latest-standard ECCM or Have Quick provisions.

The following details apply specifically to the USAF E-3A:

Type: Airborne early warning and command post aircraft.

Wings: Cantilever low-wing monoplane. Dihedral 7°. Incidence 2°. Sweepback at quarter-chord 35°. All-metal two-spar fail-safe structure. Centre-section continuous through fuselage. Normal outboard aileron, and small inboard aileron on each wing, built of aluminium honeycomb panels. Two tracked and slotted flaps and one fillet flap of aluminium alloy on each wing. Full span leading-edge flaps. Four hydraulically operated aluminium alloy spoilers on each wing, forward of flaps. Primary flying controls are aerodynamically balanced and manually operated through spring tabs. Lateral control at low speeds by all four ailerons, supplemented by spoilers which are interconnected with the ailerons. Lateral control at high speeds by inboard ailerons and spoilers only. Operation of flaps adjusts linkage between inboard and outboard ailerons to permit outboard operation with flaps extended. Spoilers may also be used symmetrically as speed brakes. Thermal anti-icing of wing leading-edges.

Fuselage: All-metal semi-monocoque fail-safe structure with cross-section made up of two circular arcs of diffferent radii, the larger above, faired into smooth-contoured oval. Structure strengthened by comparison with that of the commercial Model 707-320.

Tail Unit: Cantilever all-metal structure. Electrically and manually operated variable incidence tailplane. Powered rudder. Anti-balance tab and trim tab in rudder. Trim and control tabs in each elevator.

Landing Gear: Hydraulically retractable tricycle type. Main units are four-wheel bogies which retract inward into underside of thickened wing-root and fuselage. Twin-wheel nose unit retracts forward into fuselage. Landing gear doors close when legs fully extended. Boeing oleo-pneumatic shock absorbers. Mainwheels and tyres size 46 × 16. Nosewheels and tyres size 39 × 13. Multi-disc brakes by Goodyear. Hydro-Aire flywheel detector type anti-skid units.

Power Plant: Four Pratt & Whitney TF33-PW-100/100A turbofans, each rated at 93·4 kN (21,000 lb st), mounted in pods beneath the wings. Fuel contained in integral wing tanks. Provision for in-flight refuelling, with receptacle for boom over flight deck.

Accommodation: Basic operational crew of 20 includes a flight crew complement of four plus 16 AWACS specialists, though this latter number can vary for tactical and defence missions. Aft of flight deck, from front to rear of fuselage, are communications, data processing and other equipment bays; multi-purpose consoles; communications, navigation and identification equipment; and crew rest area, galley and parachute storage rack.

Systems: A liquid cooling system provides protection for the radar transmitter. An air cycle pack system, a draw-through system, and two closed loop ram-cooled environmental control systems ensure a suitable environment for crew and avionics equipment. Electrical power generation has a 600kVA capability. The distribution centre for mission equipment power and remote avionics is located in the lower forward cargo compartment. The aft cargo compartment houses the radar transmitter and an APU. External sockets allow intake of power when the aircraft is on the ground. Two separate and independent hydraulic systems power essential flight and mission equipment, but either system has the capability of satisfying the requirements of both equipment groups in an emergency.

Avionics and Equipment: Prominent feature is the elliptical cross-section rotodome of 9·14 m (30 ft) diameter and 1·83 m (6 ft) max depth, mounted 3·35 m (11 ft) above the fuselage. It comprises four essential elements: a turntable, strut mounted above the rear fuselage, that supports the rotary joint assembly to which are attached sliprings for electrical and waveguide continuity between rotodome and fuselage; a structural centre section of aluminium skin and stiffener construction which supports the AN/APY-1 surveillance radar and IFF/TADIL C antennae, radomes, auxiliary equipment for radar operation and environmental control of the rotodome interior; liquid cooling of the radar antennae; and two radomes constructed of multi-layer glassfibre sandwich material, one for the surveillance radar and one for the IFF/TADIL C array. For surveillance operations the rotodome is hydraulically driven at 6 rpm, but during non-operational flights it is rotated at only ¼ rpm, to keep the bearings lubricated. The Westinghouse radar operates in the S band and can function both as a pulse and/or a pulse-Doppler radar for detection of aircraft targets. A similar pulse radar mode with additional pulse compression and sea clutter adaptive processing is used to detect maritime/ship traffic. The radar is operable in six modes: PDNES (pulse-Doppler non-elevation scan), when range is paramount to elevation data; PDES (pulse-Doppler elevation scan), providing elevation data with some loss of range; BTH (beyond the horizon), giving long-range detection with no elevation data; Maritime, for detection of surface vessels in various sea states; Interleaved, combining available modes for all-altitude longer-range aircraft detection, or for both aircraft and ship detection; and Passive, which tracks enemy ECM sources without transmission-induced vulnerability. The radar antennae, spanning about 7·32 m (24 ft), and 1·52 m (5 ft) deep, scan mechanically in azimuth, and electronically from ground level up into the stratosphere. Heart of the data processing capability of the first 24 aircraft in their original core E-3A form is an IBM 4 Pi CC-1 high-speed computer, the entire group consisting of arithmetic control units, input/output units, main storage units, peripheral control units, mass memory drums, magnetic tape transports, punched tape reader, line printer, and an operator's control panel. Processing speed is in the order of 740,000 operations/s; main memory size is 114,688 words (expandable to 180,224), and mass memory size 802,816 words (expandable to 1,204,224). An interface adapter unit developed by Boeing is the key integrating element interconnecting functional data between AWACS avionics subsystems, the data processing functional group, radar, communications, navigation/guidance, display, azimuth and identification, and also provides the central timing system. From the 25th aircraft, the new and improved IBM CC-2 computer was installed from the start, with a main storage capacity of 665,360 words. Data display and control are provided by Hazeltine Corporation high resolution colour situation display consoles (SDC) and auxiliary display units (ADU). The core-configured E-3A carries nine SDCs and two ADUs. Navigation/guidance relies upon three principal sources of information: two Delco AN/ASN-119 Carousel IV inertial navigation platforms, a Northrop AN/ARN-120 Omega set which continuously updates the inertial platforms, and a Teledyne Ryan AN/APN-213 Doppler velocity sensor to provide airspeed and drift information. Communications equipment of the core-configured E-3As, supplied by Collins Radio, Electronic Communications Inc, E-Systems, and Hughes Aircraft, provides HF, VHF and UHF communication channels by means of which information can be transmitted or received in clear or secure mode, in voice or digital form. Identification is based on an AN/APX-103 interrogator set developed by Eaton Corporation's AIL Division. It is the first airborne IFF interrogator set to offer complete AIMS Mk X SIF air traffic control and Mk XII military identification friend or foe (IFF) in a single integrated system. Simultaneous Mk X and Mk XII multi-target and multi-mode operations allow the operator to obtain instantaneously the range, azimuth and elevation, code identification, and IFF status, of all targets within radar range. NATO E-3As carry, and USAF aircraft have provisions for, a radio teletype. All aircraft from c/n 25 have an inboard underwing hardpoint on each side. There is no immediate requirement for either USAF or NATO AWACS to carry weapons; but on NATO E-3As these hardpoints may be used to mount additional podded items of ECM equipment.

Dimensions, external:

Wing span	44·42 m (145 ft 9 in)
Length overall	46·61 m (152 ft 11 in)
Height overall	12·73 m (41 ft 9 in)

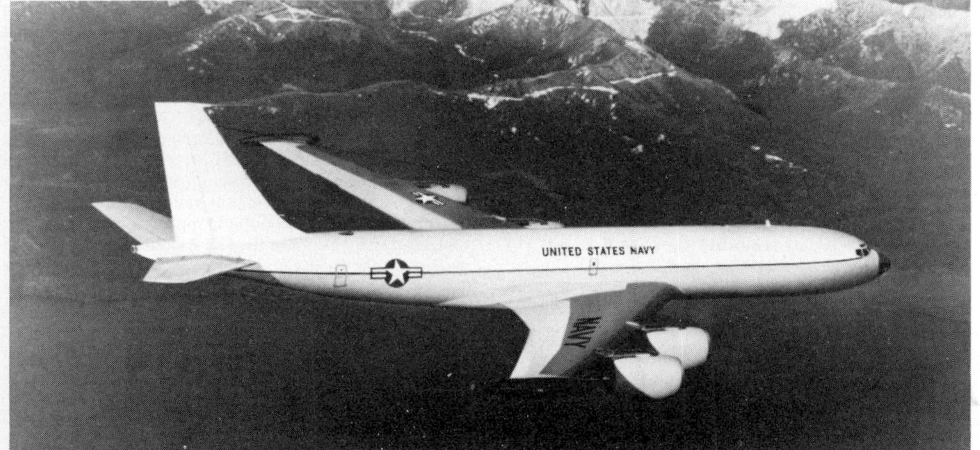

Retouched photograph of Boeing E-3/AWACS airframe with CFM56 engines, in E-6 Tacamo configuration

WEIGHT:
- Max T-O weight: 147,417 kg (325,000 lb)

PERFORMANCE:
- Max level speed: 460 knots (853 km/h; 530 mph)
- Service ceiling: over 8,850 m (29,000 ft)
- Endurance on station, 870 nm (1,610 km; 1,000 miles) from base: 6 h
- Max unrefuelled endurance: more than 11 h

BOEING ADVANCED AIRBORNE COMMAND POST

USAF designation: E-4

Four E-4s were produced to replace EC-135 Airborne Command Posts of the National Military Command System and Strategic Air Command. They are intended to provide the critical communications link between US National Command Authority and the nation's strategic retaliatory forces during and following a nuclear or conventional attack on the United States. They were described fully in the 1985-86 and previous editions of *Jane's*.

BOEING TACAMO

US Navy designation: E-6A

On 29 April 1983, Boeing Aerospace Company received a contract to develop a survivable airborne communications system to provide an on-station/all-ocean link between the US National Command Authority and the US Navy's Trident ballistic nuclear submarine (SSBN) fleet. To be designated E-6A, the new aircraft will replace the EC-130Q version of the Lockheed Hercules used currently for this mission, known as Tacamo (TAke Charge And Move Out).

The airframe of the E-6A will be almost identical with that of the E-3 Sentry, and will be assembled on the same production line. The prototype is scheduled to fly in February 1987. Initial operational capability is planned for November 1988, by which time six E-6As should have been delivered to the US Navy. At this point the Trident force will have increased to ten SSBNs, while the EC-130 Tacamo fleet will have been reduced to 12 aircraft. During 1989-91 it is intended to deliver a further eight E-6As, and the full Tacamo complement of 15 E-6As (including the refurbished prototype) and ten EC-130Qs is planned to be achieved by 1993, when all 14 Trident SSBNs will be in service.

Eight of the E-6As will be allocated to the Pacific Fleet, and the remainder to the Atlantic/Mediterranean. In each of these areas one E-6A will be required to be on station, in the air, at any given time, ready and able to relay emergency action messages to a high percentage of submarines, with an equally high chance of successful first-time reception. Another E-6A will be on standby alert, one on ready alert, and the remainder at dispersed bases or on maintenance or training.

The following details apply to the E-6A prototype:

TYPE: Long endurance communications relay aircraft.

AIRFRAME: Retains more than 75 per cent commonality with that of the E-3A, main differences being deletion of the dorsal radome and its support structure, the addition of wingtip ESM/Satcom pods and HF antenna fairings, and increased corrosion protection. Also retained is the nuclear/EMP (electromagnetic pulse) 'hardening' of the E-3A airframe. Additions include incorporation of the large forward freight door of the commercial Boeing 707-320C. Landing gear is identical to that of the E-3A.

POWER PLANT: Four 97·86 kN (22,000 lb st) CFM International F108-CF-100 (CFM56-2A-2) turbofan engines in individual underwing pods, as on E/KE-3As for Saudi Arabia. Fuel contained in integral tanks in wings, with single-point refuelling. In-flight refuelling via boom receptacle above flight deck.

ACCOMMODATION: Basic militarised interior sidewalls, ceilings and lighting are same as in E-3A. Interior divided into three main functional areas: forward of wings (flight deck and crew rest area), overwing (eight-man mission crew), and aft of wings (equipment). Forward crew area, 50 per cent common with that of E-3A, accommodates a four-man flight crew on flight deck. Compartment immediately aft of this contains food storage, galley, dining area, toilets, and an eight-bunk rest area for spare crew carried on extended or remote deployment missions. Crew enter by ladder and hatch in floor of this compartment. Then follows the C^3 overwing compartment with central and other consoles, their operators, and an airborne control officer (ACO). Through this is reached, to the rear, the compartment containing the R/T racks, transmitters, trailing wire antennae and their winches, parachutes, equipment spares, and a baggage storage area. There is a bale-out door at rear of this compartment on the starboard side.

SYSTEMS: Some 75 per cent of the E-6A's systems are the same as those in the E-3A. Among those retained are the liquid cooling system for the transmitters, the 'draw-through' cooling system for other avionics, the 600kVA electrical power generation system, the APU, the liquid oxygen system, and MIL specification hydraulic oil.

AVIONICS AND OPERATIONAL EQUIPMENT: Three Collins AN/ARC-182 VHF/UHF com transceivers, all with secure voice capability; two Collins AN/ARC-190 HF com (one transceiver, one receive only); and Hughes Aircraft AIC-29 crew intercom with secure voice capability. External aerials for Satcom UHF reception in each wingtip pod; fairings beneath each pod are antennae for standard HF reception. Navigation by triplex Litton LTN-90 ring laser gyro-based inertial reference system integrated with a Litton LTN-211 VLF/Omega system and duplex Smiths Industries SFM 102 digital/analog flight management computer system (FMCS). Bendix APS-133 colour weather radar, in nosecone, with capability for short range terrain mapping, tanker beacon homing, and waypoint display. Honeywell APN-222 high/low-range (0-15,240 m; 0-50,000 ft) radio altimeter, and Collins low-range (0-762 m; 0-2,500 ft) radio altimeter, with ILS and GPWS. General Instruments ALR-66(V)4 electronic support measures (ESM), in starboard wingtip pod, provide information on threat detection, identification, bearing and approximate range. In overwing compartment, overseen by ACO, are two banks of three consoles and a new communications central console, which incorporate ERCS (emergency rocket communications system) receivers, Satcom cryptographic equipment, new teletypes, tape recorders, and other C^3 equipment, all hardened against electromagnetic interference. In each operational area the E-6 links 'upward' with the airborne command posts and the Presidential E-4, to satellites, and to the ERCS; and 'downward' to VLF ground stations and the SSBN fleet. The main VLF antenna is a 7,925 m (26,000 ft) long trailing wire aerial (LTWA), with a 41 kg (90 lb) drogue at the end, which is winched out from the middle part of the rear cabin compartment through an opening in the cabin floor. The LTWA, with its drogue, weighs about 495 kg (1,090 lb) and creates some 907 kg (2,000 lb) of drag when fully deployed. Acting as a dipole is a much shorter (1,220 m; 4,000 ft) trailing wire (STWA), winched out from beneath the rear fuselage just forward of the tailplane. At patrol altitude, with the LTWA deployed, the aircraft enters a tight orbit and the drogue stalls, causing the wire to be almost vertical (70 per cent verticality is required for effective sub-sea communications) and the aircraft/wire combination acts like a lasso being whirled above the head, only in reverse: i.e., the path of the drogue is that of the hand holding the rope, while the orbit of the aircraft is the lasso. Signals transmitted through the trailing wire antennae use 200kW of power, and can be received by submerged SSBNs via a towed buoyant wire antenna. Mean time between failures of complete mission avionics is approx 20 h, but the E-6 is able to carry spares, and a spare crew, to permit extended missions of up to 72 h with in-flight refuelling, and/or deployment to remote bases.

ARMAMENT: None.

DIMENSIONS, EXTERNAL:
- Wing span: 44·42 m (145 ft 9 in)
- Length overall: 46·61 m (152 ft 11 in)
- Height overall: 12·93 m (42 ft 5 in)
- Wheel track: 6·73 m (22 ft 1 in)
- Wheelbase: 17·98 m (59 ft 0 in)
- Forward cargo door: Height: 2·34 m (7 ft 8 in)
  - Width: 3·40 m (11 ft 2 in)
  - Height to sill: 3·20 m (10 ft 6 in)

AREA:
- Wings, gross: 283·4 m² (3,050·0 sq ft)

WEIGHTS:
- Max payload: 25,855 kg (57,000 lb)
- Max fuel: 70,305 kg (155,000 lb)
- Max T-O weight: 155,128 kg (342,000 lb)

PERFORMANCE:
- Dash speed: 525 knots (972 km/h; 604 mph)
- Cruising speed at 12,200 m (40,000 ft): 445 knots (825 km/h; 512 mph)
- Patrol altitude: 7,620-9,150 m (25,000-30,000 ft)
- Ceiling: 12,800 m (42,000 ft)
- Range (unrefuelled) 6,700 nm (12,416 km; 7,715 miles)
- On-station endurance (unrefuelled): 16 h
- Max mission endurance (with in-flight refuelling): 72 h

BOEING MILITARY AIRPLANE COMPANY (BMAC)

PO Box 7730, Wichita, Kansas 67277-7730
Telephone: (316) 526 3153

PRESIDENT: A. M. S. Goo

VICE-PRESIDENTS:
- Donald R. Chesnut (B-52 Avionics and Weapon Systems Integration)
- Beverly N. Lancaster (Operations)
- Charles F. Tiffany (Research and Engineering)
- Frank Verginia (Advanced Military Aeroplane)
- John B. Walsh (Chief Scientist)

PUBLIC RELATIONS: Allen Hobbs

Boeing Military Airplane Company, the formation of which was announced on 23 October 1979, is responsible for all work on the B-52 Stratofortress bomber and KC-135 jet tanker-transport series, and the offensive avionics system of the Rockwell B-1B strategic bomber. It manufactures parts and assemblies for the Boeing Model 707, 727 and 737 series of commercial transports, and is producing the nose section and nacelles of the Models 757 and 767, and pylons for the 747 and 767. It also undertakes conversion of Boeing aircraft from passenger to freight carrying and other configurations, installs new interiors and embodies structural modifications. BMAC is avionics integrator for the Bell/Boeing V-22 Osprey programme (see Bell entry) and Boeing/Sikorsky's development work for the LHX helicopter competition, and has been awarded an R & D contract for the US National Aerospace Plane trans-atmospheric aircraft. The Wichita facility occupies an area of 376·5 hectares (930 acres), including 810,950 m² (8,729,000 sq ft) of covered space. BMAC also has facilities in Huntsville, Alabama, at Edwards AFB, California, and a major design and development centre in Seattle, Washington. At the beginning of 1986, BMAC had a total Kansas workforce of 18,500 persons.

Under a major US Air Force contract awarded in 1979, Boeing is developing a system known as the mission-adaptive wing. Instead of conventional flaps, this wing has a smooth and uninterrupted upper surface in all phases of flight, its camber being varied mechanically to bend, physically, flexible glassfibre skinned leading- and trailing-edges. The technology is expected to increase dramatically the performance of a wide variety of military aircraft, as part of the joint US Air Force/NASA Advanced Fighter Technology Integration (AFTI) programme, and it is anticipated that after the first year of testing the F-111 testbed will be further modified to incorporate an automatic flight control system.

In early 1985, BMAC was awarded a 26-month, $572,000 contract by the USAF to investigate the impact of advanced technologies on future fighter interceptors. BMAC will optimise aircraft configurations for continental air defence roles and conduct wind tunnel studies. BMAC is now teamed with General Dynamics and Lockheed-California in development work for the USAF's advanced tactical fighter (ATF) programme (which see, under USAF heading). In May 1985 the company was selected to design, develop and produce replacement wings for the US Navy's fleet of Grumman A-6 Intruder attack aircraft. Flight testing of the new wing is set for late 1987, and contracts are expected to involve up to 336 sets of new wings, which will be manufactured of graphite/epoxy, titanium and aluminium.

In July 1985 BMAC was awarded a $995,175 study contract by USAF Aeronautical Systems Division to investigate requirements for improved penetration of enemy air defences by strategic systems including the B-52, FB-111, SRAM and cruise missiles.

During 1986 BMAC assumed marketing responsibility for the Skyfox modification of the Lockheed T-33 military jet trainer, and now holds an exclusive licence to produce the aircraft.

BOEING B-52 STRATOFORTRESS

The early development history of the B-52 has been recorded in previous editions of *Jane's*, and a structural description can be found in the 1964-65 edition. The two versions in squadron service in 1986 are the B-52G and H, of which a combined total of 295 was built (193 and 102 respectively); 265 of these remain operational, serving with the 2nd, 7th, 42nd, 97th, 379th, 410th and 416th Bomb Wings of the Eighth Air Force; the 5th, 28th, 92nd, 93rd, 96th, 319th and 320th Bomb Wings of the Fifteenth Air Force; and the 43rd Strategic Wing of the 3rd Air Division of SAC.

Several programmes involving the **B-52G** and **H** have been undertaken or are now in progress to improve the avionics, equipment and operational capability. Under a 1971 contract, 281 of these two models were modified to carry 20 Boeing SRAMs (short range attack missiles), and the first of these became operational on 4 August 1972. Additionally, all B-52Gs and B-52Hs have been equipped with an AN/ASQ-151 Electro-optical Viewing System (EVS) to improve low level penetration capability. The EVS sensors are housed in two steerable, side by side chin turrets. The starboard turret houses a Hughes Aircraft AAQ-6 forward-looking infra-red (FLIR) scanner, while the port turret contains a Westinghouse AVQ-22 low light level TV camera.

The B-52Gs and Hs are being updated progressively with Phase VI avionics. This includes Motorola ALQ-122 SNOE (Smart Noise Operation Equipment) and Northrop AN/ALQ-155(V) advanced ECM; an AFSATCOM kit which permits worldwide communication via satellite; a Dalmo Victor ALR-46 digital radar warning receiver; Westinghouse ALQ-153 pulse-Doppler tail warning radar; and improved versions of the ITT Avionics ALQ-117 ECM system for the B-52G and ALQ-172 ECM system for the B-52H. Boeing is also producing an Offensive Avionics System (OAS) to upgrade the navigation and weapons delivery of the B-52G and H during low-level penetration missions. This is a digital (instead of analog) based, solid state system, and includes Tercom (terrain comparison) guidance. The first flight by an OAS-equipped B-52G was made on 3 September 1980, and the first use of the OAS to launch a live SRAM occurred on 10 June 1981. The new equipment includes a Teledyne Ryan Doppler radar, Honeywell AN/ASN-131 gimballed electrostatic airborne inertial navigation system (GEANS), IBM/Raytheon ASQ-38 analog bombing/navigation system with IBM digital processing, Lear Siegler attitude heading and reference system, Honeywell radar altimeter, Sperry controls and displays, and Norden Systems modernised strategic radar. Under Phase II of the programme, scheduled for completion by FY 1989, 168 B-52Gs and 96 Hs are being equipped with OAS, and contracts covering a total of 264 kits for B-52G and H aircraft had been placed by 1 January 1984.

A Collins Navstar Global Positioning System (GPS) was installed in a B-52G in late 1984 at Tinker AFB, prior to a 50-hour test flight programme carried out at the Yuma, Arizona, Proving Grounds test range.

A further major programme involves adaptation of the B-52G and B-52H force as carrier aircraft for AGM-86 air-launched cruise missiles. Full scale development of B-52 carrier aircraft equipment began in early 1978, and three B-52Gs were modified for use in the fly-off programme at Edwards AFB, California. The current programme calls for 99 B-52Gs and 96 B-52Hs each to be modified to carry 12 AGM-86s externally (six on each inboard underwing pylon), in addition to an internal load of SRAMs and other weapons. The first B-52G with OAS and equipped to carry cruise missiles was delivered to the US Air Force in August 1981. SAC's 416th Bombardment Wing at Griffiss AFB, NY, became the first unit to attain operational capability with the AGM-86 in December 1982, with 12 missiles on each of its 14 B-52Gs. It was followed by the 379th Wing at Wurtsmith AFB, Michigan. Other stations equipping with ALCM-equipped B-52s are Blytheville AFB, Arkansas; Grand Forks AFB, North Dakota, Fairchild AFB, Washington, and Barksdale AFB, Louisiana. Towards the end of the 1980s, the B-52H will be further modified to carry SRAMs, ALCMs, advanced cruise missiles or free-fall nuclear weapons on a common strategic rotary launcher (CSRL). Development of this internal carrying capability was initiated in 1982, and the first CSRL began flight testing in September 1985. A $44·5 million contract to initiate CSRL production was awarded to BMAC in February 1986.

Cruise missile carrying B-52Gs are being fitted with a distinctive fairing (known as a 'strakelet') at the leading-edge of each wing root to give these aircraft a recognisable appearance in accordance with provisions of the unratified SALT II agreement. B-52Hs will not need 'strakelets', as all will carry cruise missiles and are already recognisably different from other versions of the Stratofortress.

Those B-52Gs not scheduled for use as cruise missile carriers will replace B-52Ds in a conventional maritime support role. First test launches of Harpoon anti-ship missiles from B-52s in Spring 1983 all met their specified objectives, one after release at a height of 9,145 m (30,000 ft). Two squadrons of Harpoon-equipped B-52s were to be operational by December 1984.

On 11 February 1986 the US Air Force Aeronautical Systems Division began flight tests of an integrated conventional stores management (ICSM) software system in a B-52G at McConnell AFB, Kansas. The ICSM has been developed by BMAC for installation on 69 B-52Gs which will not be configured as ALCM carrier aircraft, permitting aircraft normally configured for the carriage of nuclear weapons to carry conventional weapons by rearranging data stored in the weapons systems computer by means of a pre-programmed removable software cassette. IOC for ICSM-equipped B-52Gs is planned for 1988.

The following details apply to the B-52G and B-52H:

Power Plant (B-52G): Eight 61·2 kN (13,750 lb st) J57-P-43WB turbojet engines. Fuel capacity 174,130 litres (46,000 US gallons) internally, plus two 2,650 litre (700 US gallon) underwing drop tanks.

Power Plant (B-52H): Eight 75·6 kN (17,000 lb st) Pratt & Whitney TF33-P-3 turbofan engines. Fuel capacity as for B-52G.

Boeing C-135FR of the French Air Force, re-engined with CFM56-2B-1 turbofans *(Michel Isaac)*

Accommodation (B-52G/H): Crew of six (pilot and co-pilot, side by side on flight deck, navigator, radar navigator, ECM operator and gunner).

Armament (B-52G): Four 0·50 in machine-guns in tail turret, remotely operated by AGS-15 fire control system, remote radar control, or closed circuit TV. Up to 20 Boeing AGM-69 SRAM short-range attack missiles: eight on rotary launcher in internal weapons bay, and six under each wing, plus nuclear free-fall bombs; ability to carry AGM-86 cruise missiles being introduced progressively on large proportion of fleet.

Armament (B-52H): As B-52G, except for single 20 mm Vulcan multi-barrel cannon in tail turret instead of four machine-guns.

Dimensions, external:
- Wing span: 56·39 m (185 ft 0 in)
- Wing area, gross: 371·6 m² (4,000 sq ft)
- Length overall: 49·05 m (160 ft 10·9 in)
- Height overall: 12·40 m (40 ft 8 in)
- Wheel track (c/l of shock struts): 2·51 m (8 ft 3 in)
- Wheelbase: 15·48 m (50 ft 3 in)

Dimension, internal:
- Weapons bay volume: 29·53 m³ (1,043 cu ft)

Weight:
- Max T-O weight: more than 221,350 kg (488,000 lb)

Performance:
- Max level speed at high altitude: Mach 0·90 (516 knots; 957 km/h; 595 mph)
- Cruising speed at high altitude: Mach 0·77 (442 knots; 819 km/h; 509 mph)
- Penetration speed at low altitude: Mach 0·53 to 0·55 (352-365 knots; 652-676 km/h; 405-420 mph)
- Service ceiling: 16,765 m (55,000 ft)
- T-O run: G: 3,050 m (10,000 ft)
- H: 2,900 m (9,500 ft)
- Range with max fuel, without in-flight refuelling:
  - G: more than 6,513 nm (12,070 km; 7,500 miles)
  - H: more than 8,685 nm (16,093 km; 10,000 miles)

BOEING KC-135 STRATOTANKER

The first of 732 **KC-135A** tanker-transports built by Boeing for the US Air Force flew on 31 August 1956. About 650 remain operational to support Strategic Air Command aircraft and those of other US Air Force commands, the US Navy and Marine Corps, and other nations.

Since 1975 Boeing at Wichita has been engaged in a programme to extend the flying life of each KC-135A by 27,000 hours, by replacing sections of the lower wing skins. This will enable the aircraft to remain fully operational well past the year 2020, and justified a programme to retrofit modern technology engines, to improve fuel economy and reduce noise. Selection of the 97·86 kN (22,000 lb st) CFM International CFM56-2B-1 turbofan (military designation F108-CF-100) for evaluation on a KC-135A testbed aircraft was announced in early 1980, and retrofit during FY 1983-95 of some 630 KC-135As, plus 11 French Air Force C-135Fs, by Boeing Military Airplane Company is anticipated. The re-engined aircraft, the first of which (61-0293) made its first flight on 4 August 1982, have the new USAF designation **KC-135R**. Electrical, hydraulic, performance and fuel management, and flight control systems are also undergoing modification, the main landing gear is being strengthened, and dual APUs are being installed for quick engine starting. The first nine KC-135R 'production' conversions for the USAF were funded in the FY 1982 budget, 19 in FY 1983, 30 in FY 1984, 43 in FY 1985 and 43 in FY 1986. The USAF plans to acquire a total of 389 modification kits by FY 1990. Deliveries to the 384th Air Refueling Wing at McConnell AFB began in July 1985. Other KC-135Rs are now in service at Robins AFB, Georgia (19th ARW), and Ellsworth AFB, South Dakota. Eleven **C-135FR** conversions have also been funded for the French Air Force; the first of these arrived at BMAC for conversion on 12 June 1985, flew for the first time with its new engines on 3 August, and was returned to service officially on 26 August.

Compared with the standard turbojet KC-135A, Boeing estimated that the KC-135R would be able to offload 65 per cent more fuel over a 1,500 nm (2,775 km; 1,725 mile) radius at average T-O gross weight, and 150 per cent more at 2,500 nm (4,630 km; 2,875 mile) radius. Increased thrust enables it to take off to 762 m (2,500 ft) before a KC-135A could leave the ground. Its noise footprint is 98 per cent smaller in terms of a 90 EPNdB landing/take-off contour. Max take-off weight of the KC-135R is 146,285 kg (322,500 lb), compared with 136,800 kg (301,600 lb) for the KC-135A. Max fuel load is 92,210 kg (203,288 lb) compared with the KC-135A's 86,047 kg (189,702 lb).

In a parallel programme, intended to satisfy the near-term critical requirements for replacing the turbojet engines of Air National Guard and Air Force Reserve KC-135s with turbofans, the US Air Force has acquired many retired commercial Boeing 707-100B/720B/320B/320C airliners, together with spare JT3D-3B turbofans. The airliners are flown to the Military Aircraft Storage and Disposition Center, Tucson, Arizona, to be stripped of their engines, pylons, tailplanes and other components intended for overhaul/refurbishment and transfer to the Air Force's KC-135 aircraft.

The initial US Air Force programme for the replacement of turbojet engines by JT3D turbofans involved 18 special-purpose -135 aircraft, comprising three C-135Es, one KC-135E, two NKC-135Es, five EC-135Hs, two EC-135Ks, two EC-135Ns, two EC-135Ps, and one RC-135T. These re-engined special purpose aircraft were redelivered to the Air Force between January and July 1981 and continue in service for airborne command post and other special communications missions. Three more have since been re-engined.

Follow-on contracts to Boeing Military Airplane Company cover the retrofit of five special purpose -135s, and 104 Air National Guard and 24 Air Force Reserve KC-135 aircraft with JT3D engines. Simultaneously with this modification, five-rotor wheel brakes and a Mark II/III anti-skid system are installed. The first re-engined **KC-135E** for the ANG (57-1496) was delivered to Phoenix, Arizona, on 26 July 1982, for service with the 161st Aerial Refueling Group, and subsequent deliveries were made to ANG units in Tennessee, Utah and Wisconsin. The 99th aircraft was redelivered in February 1985, by which time re-engined KC-135s were serving also with ANG units in Arkansas, Illinois, Kansas, Maine, New Hampshire, New Jersey, Ohio, Pennsylvania and Washington.

By comparison with the J57 turbojets they replace, the JT3D-3B turbofans provide 30 per cent thrust increase, and 14 per cent fuel savings, with resulting decreases in environmental factors (85 per cent noise and 90 per cent emission).

Boeing B-52G Stratofortress, armed with AGM-86B air-launched cruise missiles

With all the ANG KC-135Es equipped with JT3D engines, the annual fuel saving should be in excess of 30 million litres (8 million US gallons). Compared with the turbojet powered KC-135A, the KC-135E will be able to offload 37 per cent more fuel over a 1,500 nm (2,780 km; 1,727 mile) radius at normal T-O weight, and 82 per cent more over a 2,500 nm (4,633 km; 2,879 mile) radius.

USAF KC-135s and special-purpose -135s are also being retrofitted in service with a combined performance management system and integrated fuel management system for which Delco Electronics Division of General Motors is prime contractor. The prototype system, installed in 1982, is being followed by an initial quantity of 371 systems, including spares. Options cover the eventual supply of a total of more than 700 systems.

BOEING C-18A

Eight former American Airlines Boeing 707-323C transports are to be modified as airborne platforms for the Joint Surveillance Target Attack Radar System (Joint STARS) under a US Air Force Systems Command (Electronic Systems Division) programme. Grumman Corporation is prime contractor. Boeing Military Airplane Company is modifying the airframes to accept an airborne multi-mode radar built by Norden. Grumman will then integrate and install subsystems and conduct the test programme. The first aircraft to be modified arrived at BMAC's Wichita facility in January 1986, and is scheduled for delivery to Grumman in June 1987. A second Boeing 707-323C is expected to arrive at BMAC for modification in February 1987, for delivery to Grumman two months later.

BOEING EC-18B ARIA

In 1982 Aeronautical Systems Division of the US Air Force procured six former American Airlines Boeing 707-320C transport aircraft of which four will replace EC-135N Advanced Range Instrumentation Aircraft (ARIA) operated by its 4950th Test Wing. Like the ARIA EC-135Ns, each of the 707s will be converted to house the world's largest airborne steerable antenna in a bulbous nose, will have a probe antenna on each wingtip, and will embody a totally new cockpit configuration, with navigation station, a new flight director, modified electrical system and improved environmental control system. Designated EC-18B after conversion, the aircraft will have a greater payload capability than the EC-135Ns they replace, making them better able to support the expanding ARIA mission. This includes support of unmanned space launches, cruise missile tests, Army and Navy ballistic missile tests, and the Space Transportation System (Shuttle) programme.

The first EC-18B made its first flight after conversion on 27 February 1985 and entered operational service in January 1986. All four are expected to be fully operational by 1988. A future modification will incorporate the sonobuoy missile impact location system (SMILS) currently installed on some US Navy P-3 Orion aircraft. The USAF Aeronautical Systems Division was expected to award an EC-18B SMILS contract during 1985, with the first installation taking place in 1987.

BOEING E-8A (J/STARS)

On 27 September 1985, Grumman Corporation received a $657 million contract for full scale development of the USAF/US Army Joint Surveillance Target Attack Radar System (J/STARS). Boeing is modifying two C-18 (707-320) airframes as vehicles for the airborne equipment. This will include a Norden multi-mode side looking radar antenna, some 7·62 m (25 ft) long, faired into the belly of each aircraft. The radar will operate in synthetic aperture radar (SAR) mode to detect and locate stationary objects such as parked tanks, and will alternate between SAR and Doppler to locate slow moving targets. The J/STARS system will then direct attack on the targets, via the Joint Tactical Information Distribution System (JTIDS).

The first J/STARS aircraft, designated E-8A, will fly for the first time in late 1988. The demonstration programme is scheduled for completion by 1991, when a decision will be taken on whether to proceed to production of an initial batch of about ten operational E-8As.

BOEING 707 TANKER/TRANSPORT

Royal Saudi Air Force designation: KE-3A

In 1982 BMAC initiated a programme to demonstrate the use of the commercial Model 707-320 Intercontinental airframe modified as an aerial refuelling tanker. A former TWA 707-320C was converted as a demonstration aircraft, making its first flight in this form in early 1983. This aircraft is equipped with three hose and drogue refuelling points, one on the fuselage centreline and one at each wingtip, the latter being housed in pods similar to those used on earlier tanker modifications of the Model 707 for such operators as the Canadian Armed Forces and the Royal Moroccan Air Force. The centreline station is a new modification.

This is seen as a method of acquiring air refuelling capability at a fraction of the cost of a new tanker and, at the same time, to gain a large capacity aircraft which can be converted easily into an all-passenger, all-cargo, or combination passenger/cargo transport, and with special interiors for VIP or aeromedical transport. Seats, cargo handling equipment, as well as most executive interior partitions and furnishings, are mounted on permanently installed tracks with quick disconnect fittings.

Boeing EC-18B ARIA of USAF's 4950th Test Wing

A variety of refuelling system options is available, including a probe or receptacle in the nose, Beech or Sargent-Fletcher wingtip pods deploying a hose and drogue, a Sargent-Fletcher rear fuselage centreline hose and drogue installation, or a Boeing centreline boom refuelling installation of the type developed for the USAF's KC-135 tanker/transports. These can be combined to customer requirements, enabling the Boeing 707 tanker/transport to be equipped in a configuration that is compatible with any type of Western fighter. Increased fuel capacity can be provided by the installation of an optional 19,040 litre (5,030 US gallon) tank in the rear lower cargo hold. With this, the 707-320's standard 90,299 litre (23,855 US gallon) wing fuel tanks, and triple refuelling points, the tanker can rendezvous with fighters 1,000 nm (1,853 km; 1,151 miles) from its base and transfer 55,878 kg (123,190 lb) of fuel.

In addition to installation of the refuelling pods or boom, basic modifications include the provision of a refuelling control panel at the flight engineer's station; improved hydraulic system and fuel pumps; strengthening of the outer wing; the introduction of new wingtips, military avionics and a TV scanner; and the installation of either a boom operator's or pod observer's station. Military avionics which are installed include dual UHF with DF, Tacan, IFF, weather radar, rendezvous radar, and dual INS. Boeing emphasises that the quick-change capability of the interior installations of the 707 tanker/transport make it easily adaptable for a range of military roles including coastal patrol, electronic countermeasures, maritime missions, and tactical command and control (C^2). By the installation of wing hardpoints or dispensing bays, the aircraft could also be used as a weapons platform for the deployment of sonobuoys or other ASW sensors, mines and bombs, air-to-air or standoff missiles, and chaff or flares.

Twenty-five 707 tanker/transports were in, or scheduled for, service in four countries by January 1987. These are in various hose-drogue, boom, or combined boom/hose-drogue configurations. Depending on the configuration selected by the customer, Boeing can deliver 707 tanker/transports within 12 to 18 months from order, and can provide all required support to allow effective utilisation of the multi-role capabilities of these aircraft. Orders were announced in September 1985 from the Brazilian Air Force (four tanker-only aircraft) and Spanish Air Force (two, each with a VIP interior for about 66 passengers).

The eight tankers ordered for the Royal Saudi Air Force, simultaneously with five E-3A Sentry AWACS aircraft, are designated **KE-3A**. They differ from standard 707 tankers in having CFM56 turbofan engines, fitted with Hispano-Suiza thrust reversers, to provide commonality with the RSAF's E-3As. Deliveries will be made in 1986-87.

A description of the Model 707-320C can be found in the 1980-81 and earlier editions of *Jane's*.

BOEING C-25A 'AIR FORCE ONE'

The US Air Force has selected two Boeing 747-200Bs to provide airlift for the President of the United States. Scheduled for delivery in November 1988 and May 1989, they will replace the current Boeing 707-320Cs which entered the presidential fleet on 12 October 1962 and 4 August 1972, and will be designated C-25A.

The main airframes of the C-25As will be built in Everett, Washington, and flown to BMAC for configuration as 'Air Force One', the radio call sign used by the 89th Military Airlift Wing at Andrews AFB for an aircraft carrying the President.

Powered by four 252·4 kN (56,750 lb st) General Electric CF6-80C2B1 engines, the C-25As will have a fuel capacity of 202,940 litres (53,611 US gallons), providing an unrefuelled range in excess of 6,000 nm (11,120 km; 6,910 miles). Self-sufficiency will be enhanced by utilising self-contained airstairs in the lower lobe and the addition of a second Garrett GTCP331-200 APU in the tail.

The new aircraft will have complete onboard state-of-the-art communications equipment, including secure voice terminals and cryptographic equipment for writing and deciphering classified messages. E-Systems will provide the mission communication system kits, which Boeing will instal along with normal aircraft communications equipment. Each C-25A will accommodate 80 passengers and 23 crew, including ground crew required to travel with the aircraft.

Extensively modified to meet presidential requirements, the 371·6 m² (4,000 sq ft) of interior floor space of each 'Air Force One' will include an executive suite with presidential office, stateroom and lavatory; two galleys, each capable of providing food for 50 persons; an emergency treatment medical facility; and work and rest areas for the presidential staff, news media representatives and USAF crew.

WEIGHTS:

Long-range mission T-O weight	364,552 kg (803,700 lb)
Max zero-fuel weight	238,816 kg (526,500 lb)
Design mission zero-fuel weight	202,302 kg (446,000 lb)
Max landing weight	285,763 kg (630,000 lb)

BOEING 747 CRAF PROGRAMME

Under the CRAF (Civil Reserve Air Fleet) programme, initiated in 1952, BMAC is modifying 19 Boeing 747s of Pan American World Airways to supplement military transport forces by providing airlift of bulk and oversize cargo during emergencies. The main deck floor of each aircraft is being strengthened, and a cargo handling system and side cargo door installed. Empty weight of the aircraft is increased by 5,900 kg (13,000 lb), for which the airline receives compensation during commercial operations. Boeing 747s so modified are known by the military designation **C-19A**.

The first modified 747 (N655PA) was returned to Pan American on 31 May 1985 and continues to operate in all-passenger configuration. Fourteen conversions had been funded at that time, with the last five requested in the FY 1986 budget. The programme is scheduled for completion by February 1988.

BOEING (MCDONNELL DOUGLAS) MODERNISED F-4 PHANTOM

In February 1986 the US Air Force's Aeronautical Systems Division suspended development of Boeing Military Airplane company's modernisation scheme for F-4 Phantom fighter aircraft, details of which may be found in

Boeing Model 707 tanker/transport demonstrator with its three hose and drogue refuelling systems deployed

the 1985-86 *Jane's*. The company has, however, a \$22·6 million 1986 contract from the Ogden Air Logistics Center at Hill AFB, Utah, to modify the navigation and weapons delivery system on up to 600 F-4s of the USAF and Air National Guard. It includes production options extending up to 1990. Flight testing is due to begin in mid-1987, with production of conversion kits starting in early 1988.

BOEING USAF/NASA MISSION ADAPTIVE WING

Under a US Air Force contract awarded in 1979, Boeing Military Airplane Company has modified the wings of NASA's General Dynamics F-111A (63-9778) to Mission Adaptive Wing (MAW) configuration. Instead of utilising flaps, slats, ailerons or spoilers, this is designed to alter wing camber to satisfy a variety of flight conditions and yet maintain a smooth, uninterrupted upper surface. Mechanisms built inside the MAW act upon flexible single-segment leading- and three-segment trailing-edge surfaces to change wing camber during flight. The smooth, flexible surface of this unique wing is made of glassfibre, and its contours are altered by internal link driven by power hinges. The leading-edge has a range of movement from 1° up to 20° down; the trailing-edge can be varied from 1° up to 18° down, and can also twist spanwise. The resulting variations in curvature produce extremely efficient airflow over and under the wing. In addition to demonstrating the performance improvements of smooth variable camber wings, the programme is intended to check and validate the deformable portion of the glassfibre structure, and to evaluate the agility and increased buffet-free envelope of the aircraft with the MAW as part of the F-111's continuing AFTI (advanced fighter technology integration) programme.

The MAW offers six control modes: roll, manoeuvre camber, cruise camber, manoeuvre load, gust alleviation and manoeuvre enhancement. Six mission modes are expected to provide tighter manoeuvring radii for evasive action and survivability; increased fatigue life; improved handling; greater weapons platform stability; and a more comfortable ride with reduced crew fatigue.

The first flight of the AFTI F-111 MAW took place from Edwards AFB, California, on 18 October 1985 and was followed by a second flight on 22 November. Wing sweep was fixed at 26° for these flights. The flight test programme will be divided into two year-long phases totalling some 30 flights which will cover performance improvements of the MAW over the standard F-111 wing; determination of optimum camber for all phases of flight; verification of wing loadings at specific flight conditions; determination of MAW handling characteristics; and confirmation of anticipated improvements in the buffet envelope. Phase 1, scheduled for completion during 1986, was conducted with the MAW operating in manual mode. Further development in Phase 2 will lead to an automatic flight control system with several modes of control.

NASA's AFTI F-111/MAW testbed aircraft, modified by Boeing Military Airplane Company

BOEING SKYFOX

The Skyfox is a two-seat twin-turbine tactical trainer, designed and developed initially by Flight Concepts Inc and Skyfox Corporation (see 1985-86 *Jane's*) as a derivative of the Lockheed T-33. Known popularly as the 'T-Bird', the T-33 was itself based on the single-seat F-80C Shooting Star fighter which was given a fuselage 'stretch' of 0·98 m (3 ft 2½ in) to accommodate a second cockpit in tandem, with a new canopy covering both cockpits, and was stripped of all armament. It remained in production for more than ten years as the USAF's standard jet trainer, and was also built under licence in Canada and Japan. When production ended, 5,800 had been built, including 649 for the US Navy and 1,058 for the US Military Aid Program; it is estimated that more than 700 are still in service with various armed forces worldwide.

Although not recognisably related to the T-33 in its new form, the Skyfox retains some 70 per cent of the original basic structure, including the centre fuselage, wings and landing gear. The conversion transforms it into a new, advanced performance tactical combat trainer, embodying modern engines, avionics and equipment. Using interchangeable nose modules, the aircraft could be used for a variety of other military duties, including ECM, target-towing, tactical support and reconnaissance.

Production would be based upon the use of available T-33 airframes, refurbished, updated, and provided with a new power plant and the latest commercially available systems and subsystems. By combining the proven T-33 airframe with innovative new design and economical remanufacturing techniques, air forces would be able to procure the Skyfox at significantly lower costs than other current generation turbine powered trainer aircraft. The prototype Skyfox flew for the first time on 23 August 1983.

The original power plant of the T-33 comprised a single Allison J33 turbojet mounted within the centre-fuselage. This is replaced in the Skyfox by two 16·46 kN (3,700 lb st) Garrett TFE731-3A turbofan engines pylon-mounted in pods, one on each side of the rear fuselage. For compatibility with this installation the tail unit has been redesigned, and now has sweptback vertical surfaces with the tailplane mounted about midway up the fin to ensure that it is clear of efflux from the turbofans. The elevators are enlarged and two tail strakes added. New wingtips are fitted, with downward canted winglets; and elimination of the lateral engine intakes from the fuselage has made it possible to give the composite construction forward fuselage completely new aerodynamically clean contours. Fuel is contained in eight wing cells with a total capacity of 976 litres (258 US gallons), one fuselage tank of 359 litres (95 US gallons) capacity, and two duct tanks of 806 litres (213 US gallons) each. Up to 2,720 kg (6,000 lb) of external stores can be carried on underwing hardpoints. Stencel Mk 3 zero/zero ejection seats and a one-piece windscreen are installed; the standard avionics package consists of Collins Pro Line II flight instruments and displays, with Canadian Marconi engine and instrument displays.

BMAC began flight testing the Skyfox prototype in early 1985, and later acquired the exclusive licence to produce the aircraft. World market interest was being canvassed in the Summer of 1986, and a development/production decision will be taken based on the results of that survey.

DIMENSIONS, EXTERNAL:
- Wing span: 11·84 m (38 ft 10 in)
- Wing chord: at root: 2·79 m (9 ft 2 in)
- at tip: 1·06 m (3 ft 5¾ in)
- Wing aspect ratio: 6·68
- Length overall: 14·02 m (46 ft 0 in)
- Height overall: 3·76 m (12 ft 4 in)
- Tailplane span: 4·83 m (15 ft 10 in)
- Wheel track: 2·67 m (8 ft 9 in)

AREA:
- Wings, gross: 22·22 m² (239·2 sq ft)

WEIGHTS:
- Weight empty: 4,665 kg (10,284 lb)
- Normal T-O weight (clean): 7,365 kg (16,235 lb)
- Max T-O weight: 9,070 kg (20,000 lb)

PERFORMANCE (at normal T-O weight):
- Max level speed at S/L: 505 knots (935 km/h; 581 mph)
- Max level speed at optimum altitude: Mach 0·80
- Approach speed: 105 knots (195 km/h; 121 mph)
- Landing speed: 95 knots (176 km/h; 109 mph)
- Max rate of climb at S/L: over 2,285 m (7,500 ft)/min
- Time to 9,145 m (30,000 ft): 8 min
- Service ceiling: 15,240 m (50,000 ft)
- T-O to 15 m (50 ft): 670 m (2,200 ft)
- Landing from 15 m (50 ft): 1,097 m (3,600 ft)
- Landing run: 488 m (1,600 ft)
- Range, internal fuel only, with reserves: 1,960 nm (3,630 km; 2,255 miles)
- Ferry range, with reserves: 2,947 nm (5,458 km; 3,391 miles)
- *g* limits: +7·33/−3·5

Boeing Skyfox prototype twin-turbofan tactical trainer, derived from the Lockheed T-33

BOEING VERTOL COMPANY

PO Box 16858, Ridley Park, Philadelphia, Pennsylvania 19142
Telephone: (215) 522 2121
Telex: 845 205
PRESIDENT: Joseph Mallen
EXECUTIVE VICE-PRESIDENT: Donald R. Chesnut
VICE-PRESIDENTS:
C. W. Ellis (V-22 Programme)
Kenneth I. Grina (Research and Engineering)
William P. Jones (Customer Support and Business Development)

Boeing Vertol Company, established in 1960, has produced and delivered some 2,500 tandem-rotor helicopters to the US military services, as well as to many foreign nations. The CH-47 Chinook is the company's current production helicopter for the US Army, and is in service also with the armed forces of 13 other nations. A development, the Model 234 Commercial Chinook, is also in production.

Boeing Vertol is teamed with Bell Helicopter Textron to develop and produce the V-22 Osprey, as described under the Bell entry in this section. The airframe of the V-22 is based on that of Bell's Model 301/XV-15 research aircraft, and Boeing Vertol is developing, under a three-year NASA contract, 7·62 m (25 ft) diameter advanced technology graphite/glassfibre rotor blades, which will be test flown in place of the existing metal blades of the XV-15. First flight with the new blades was scheduled for mid-1986.

On 3 June 1985 Boeing Vertol signed a memorandum of understanding with Sikorsky Aircraft to enter a joint design to meet the US Army's new LHX light helicopter requirement, with BMAC responsible for the avionics integration. The Boeing Vertol/Sikorsky contender will have a gross weight of approx 3,629 kg (8,000 lb).

Boeing Vertol also produces parts and assemblies for Model 727, 737 and 747 commercial transports, and the fixed portions of the wing leading-edges of the 757 and 767.

Employment within Boeing Vertol Company stood at 6,100 at the end of December 1985, a 22 per cent increase over the 1984 average.

BOEING VERTOL XCH-62

Activity on development of a heavy lift helicopter, suspended in 1975, was reinstituted in 1980 following the receipt of a contract from NASA for transmission development work. Two subsequent contracts covered continuation of this work into 1984, using the aft and combiner transmissions of the company's XCH-62 helicopter (stored since 1975 in uncompleted form; see 1975-76 *Jane's*) to test large, high-power spiral bevel and planetary gears. In March 1983 more than 100 hours of testing (50 of them at 100 per cent of design rated power) were completed successfully on the XCH-62's aft transmission, validating design changes and establishing the feasibility of high power gearboxes for large helicopters.

On 14 August 1984, DARPA, NASA and the US Army signed a memorandum of understanding to complete and fly the XCH-62 as a one-aircraft heavy lift research vehicle (HLRV) programme. However, funding for the project was rejected from FY 1986 budget proposals, although support for the HLRV programme continues.

The XCH-62 was intended to have a max T-O weight of 67,130 kg (148,000 lb) and design payload of 20,410 kg (45,000 lb). Other data: fuselage length 27·2 m (89 ft 3 in); overall length, rotors turning 49·45 m (162 ft 3 in); rotor diameter 28·04 m (92 ft 0 in); height overall 12·20 m (38 ft 7½ in); wheel track 9·67 m (29 ft 10 in).

BOEING VERTOL MODEL 107

USN and USMC designation: CH-46/UH-46 Sea Knight

Details of the Boeing Vertol Model 107, of which production by Boeing Vertol ended some years ago, can be found in the 1971-72 *Jane's*. A derivative, the KV107IIA, is being produced under licence in Japan by Kawasaki (which see).

A total of 624 basically similar CH/UH-46 aircraft was delivered to the US Marine Corps and US Navy in the 1964-1971 period. With a view to modernising the Marine Corps' fleet of CH-46s, two were modified by Boeing Vertol in 1975. From 1977, following test and evaluation of these, the US Marine Corps updated 273 CH-46s to **CH-46E** configuration, with 1,394 kW (1,870 shp) General Electric T58-GE-16 turboshaft engines and other modifications (see 1985-86 and earlier editions of *Jane's*).

In April 1975 Boeing Vertol received a contract from Naval Air Systems Command to initiate the development of glassfibre main rotor blades for the H-46 fleet. Following bench, whirl, and flight testing of the first sets of glassfibre blades, by Boeing Vertol and the US Marine Corps, in 1977-78, the first production order was issued by the US Navy in December 1977; follow-on orders have been programmed, to maintain deliveries of glassfibre blades up to the end of 1986.

During 1981 Boeing Vertol received three separate contracts to provide glassfibre rotor blades for other existing Model 107-II aircraft. They cover 96 blades for Canadian Armed Forces CH-113/113A helicopters, with delivery over a three-year period beginning in January 1983; 33 blades for Columbia Helicopters Inc, for delivery between April 1983 and March 1984 (this contract including provisions for FAA certification testing); and 103 blades for Swedish HKP-4s, with delivery beginning in the second quarter of 1983 and scheduled for completion in mid-1986.

In December 1980 the Naval Air Systems Command awarded Boeing Vertol an initial contract, followed by further contracts in December 1981, December 1982, February 1984 and July 1986, for a multi-year US Navy/Marine Corps helicopter improvement programme. Known as the safety, reliability and maintainability (SR&M) programme, this will reduce the operating costs of HH-46A, CH-46D and CH-46E helicopters beyond the end of this century. Improvements involve an aircraft retrofit kit which Boeing Vertol manufactures for installation by the Navy. During the eight-year programme, 358 modification kits are being supplied. SR&M is a two-phase programme. The first (completed) phase involved design, development and testing of a prototype SR&M modified CH-46E, which flew for the first time on 23 November 1983. The production phase began during the first quarter of 1984, with delivery to the Navy of the first production kit in July 1985. Service deliveries of CH-46Es with SR&M improvements began in December 1985 from MCAS Cherry Point, North Carolina. Production of kits will continue until January 1989, at a current rate of ten per month.

Development testing of rapid-inflating emergency flotation bags for CH-46Es was completed during 1985. When deflated, the bags are stowed in fuselage side panels measuring approximately 1·78 m × 0·81 m (5 ft 10 in × 2 ft 8 in). All US Navy and US Marine Corps CH-46Es are to be fitted with the equipment, commencing in late 1987.

First Boeing Vertol updated CH-46E for the US Marine Corps with SR&M improvements

BOEING VERTOL MODELS 114 and 414

US Army designation: CH-47 Chinook
Canadian Armed Forces designation: CH-147
Royal Air Force designation: Chinook HC. Mk 1

Development of the CH-47 Chinook began in 1956, to meet a US Army requirement for an all-weather medium transport helicopter. The first of five YCH-47As made its initial hovering flight on 21 September 1961.

Details of the initial production **CH-47A** (354 for US Army and four for Royal Thai Air Force) and **CH-47B** (108 for US Army) can be found in the 1974-75 edition of *Jane's*. Transmissions of all existing US Army As and Bs were later uprated to CH-47C standard.

Current domestic and export versions are as follows:

CH-47C. Increased performance from a combination of strengthened transmissions, two 2,796 kW (3,750 shp) T55-L-11A engines and increased integral fuel capacity. First flight of original CH-47C made 14 October 1967; deliveries of 270 to US Army began in Spring 1968. First deployed in Viet-Nam in September 1968. Total of 182 US Army CH-47Cs undergoing retrofit with glassfibre rotor blades; this programme was continuing in 1986.

A crashworthy fuel system and an integral spar inspection system (ISIS) were made available during 1973. Incorporation of the crashworthy fuel system on US Army CH-47Cs was accomplished by retrofit kits, deliveries of which began in March 1973. Chinooks delivered to Australia have this system, which provides a total fuel capacity of 3,944 litres (1,042 US gallons). Nine CH-47Cs, designated **CH-147**, were delivered to Canada from September 1974. Details of these, eight of which are still in service with Nos. 447 and 450 Squadrons, can be found in the 1985-86 and earlier editions. There is a full description of the CH-47C in the 1980-81 edition. Ten of the Spanish Army's 18 Chinooks are CH-47Cs.

CH-47D. Under a 1976 US Army contract Boeing Vertol modified three earlier model CH-47s (one A, one B and a C) as D standard prototypes, the first one being flown on 11 May 1979. In October 1980 the first CH-47D 'production' modernisation contract was awarded by the US Army. Eighty-eight were funded by annual contracts by 1984, and in April 1985 Boeing Vertol was awarded a multi-year contract to modernise an additional 240 CH-47A/B/Cs in FYs 1985-1989. The first 'production' CH-47D made its initial flight in its new form on 26 February 1982. It was handed over to the US Army on 20 May 1982, as the first of a planned total of 436 aircraft which are to be remanufactured to this much-modified and modernised standard, extending the service life of the Army's Chinook fleet into the next century. Of this total, 328 had been funded by Spring 1986. Initial operational capability for the CH-47D was achieved on 28 February 1984, with the aircraft first equipping the 101st Airborne Division, followed by other units of the Rapid Deployment Force. Deliveries totalled 111 by April 1986 and are scheduled to continue until 1993, at a current rate of four per month.

The CH-47D remanufacturing programme involves stripping the Chinooks down to their basic airframes before refitting them with improved components and systems to bring them up to the new standard. Any necessary body or other repairs are done at the same time.

Thirteen major improvements are involved in the conversion. Avco Lycoming T55-L-712 turboshafts, with standard

Boeing Vertol CH-47D Chinook of the US Army with fuel containers slung from external cargo hooks

and emergency ratings of 2,796 kW (3,750 shp) and 3,356 kW (4,500 shp) respectively, replace the lower-rated T55-L-7C or -11 engines of earlier models. Rotor transmission rating is increased to 5,593 kW (7,500 shp), with integral lubrication and cooling, and composite rotor blades are fitted. The flight deck is reconfigured to reduce pilot workload. Other changes include redundant and improved electrical systems, modular hydraulic systems, an advanced flight control system, improved avionics, aircraft survivability equipment, and night vision goggle compatibility. A Solar T62-T-2B auxiliary power unit runs the accessory gear drive, thereby operating all hydraulic and electrical systems, and a single-point pressure refuelling system and triple cargo hooks are installed. Some 10-15 per cent (by weight) of the CH-47D airframe is of composite construction. The basic airframe structure, landing gear, and seats are the only major components that are not replaced or rebuilt. Some 300 subcontractors are engaged in the conversion programme.

At a max gross weight of 22,680 kg (50,000 lb) the CH-47D has more than double the useful load capability of the CH-47A (10,334 kg; 22,783 lb compared with 4,990 kg; 11,000 lb). Its versatility covers a variety of combat and support missions, including troop movement, artillery emplacement, and battlefield resupply. It is the prime mover for the Army's new M198 towed 155 mm howitzer; this artillery piece, plus 32 rounds of ammunition and an 11-man gun crew, represents a combined internal/external load of approx 9,980 kg (22,000 lb). It is the only Army helicopter capable of lifting, using the centre underfuselage hook, the 11,225 kg (24,750 lb) D5 caterpillar bulldozer. It is able to airlift Army Milvans (supply containers) at speeds of up to 138 knots (256 km/h; 159 mph), and carry (using all three hooks) up to seven 1,893 litre (500 US gallon), 1,587 kg (3,500 lb) rubber fuel blivets in a single mission. According to the US Army, the CH-47D offers more than 100 per cent increase in performance over the A model Chinook when operated in a standard European climate, and a 68 per cent increase in 'hot and high' conditions.

On 4 August 1985 a CH-47D operated by the US Army Aviation Engineering Flight Activity unit based at Edwards AFB, California, conducted in-flight refuelling trials with a US Air Force HC-130 tanker aircraft. The CH-47D was equipped with an 11·6 m (38 ft) retractable refuelling probe mounted on its lower right side and made 35 successful hook-ups to the tanker's drogue units while flying at approximately 120 knots (222 km/h; 138 mph) and 1,525 m (5,000 ft). Refuelling was conducted at the rate of 568 litres (150 US gallons)/min, permitting the CH-47D to be refuelled completely in six minutes.

Chinook HC. Mk 1. Version for Royal Air Force, which ordered 33 in 1978. First example (ZA670) made its initial flight on 23 March 1980. Generally similar to Canadian CH-147, with Avco Lycoming T55-L-11E turboshaft engines, but with provision for glassfibre/carbonfibre rotor blades and three external cargo hooks (capacity 12,700 kg; 28,000 lb on centre hook, or 9,072 kg; 20,000 lb total on forward and rear hooks); accommodation for up to 44 troops or 24 standard NATO stretchers; and other airframe and equipment changes as detailed in the 1985-86 and earlier *Jane's*. The RAF's No. 18 Squadron, its first all-Chinook squadron, was formed at Odiham, Hampshire, on 4 August 1981. A second RAF squadron (No. 7) became equipped with HC. Mk 1s at Odiham during 1982. Work was started in June 1982, by the Royal Navy's Aircraft Yard at Fleetlands, Gosport, Hants, to retrofit the first 14 RAF Chinooks with glassfibre rotor blades and a single-point pressure fuelling system. Radar warning receivers are being added in another retrofit programme. Eight more HC. Mk 1s, with uprated T55-L-712 engines as in the CH-47D (beginning ZD574), were ordered later; three were delivered in 1984 and the remaining five by March 1986. It is planned eventually that all RAF Chinooks will be powered by the T55-L-712 engine.

Model 234. Commercial version, described separately.

Model 414. International military version of CH-47C, described in 1985-86 *Jane's*. Now superseded by CH-47D International Chinook (which see). Two ordered in 1980 for Spanish Army Aviation's 5th Helicopter Transport Battalion (Bheltra-V) at Colmenar Viejo, Madrid.

CH-47D International Chinook. New name for Model 414, starting with aircraft for Japan and including also the six ordered by Spanish Army (FAMET) in December 1984. Japanese programme began in Spring 1984 when the Japan Defence Agency approved the purchase of two International CH-47Ds for the JGSDF and one for the JASDF. The first production International CH-47D (N7425H) made its first flight in January 1986, and, with the second, was shipped to Kawasaki Heavy Industries of Japan in April 1986 for avionics and interior installation. Five more are being shipped to Japan in knocked-down form for assembly prior to a co-production arrangement in which Kawasaki will manufacture eight CH-47Ds using some Boeing Vertol-supplied components and some locally produced assemblies. The first Kawasaki assembled aircraft made its initial flight on 4 July 1986. It is expected that licence manufacture by Kawasaki will equip the JGSDF and JASDF with a total of 54 International Chinooks, which in Japanese service will have the designation **CH-47J**. Initial deliveries of CH-47Js to the JGSDF and JASDF were planned for November and December 1986 respectively. Deliveries of the six International Chinooks for Spain are being made in batches of two aircraft each in July and October 1986 and April 1987. These aircraft are fitted with nose mounted Bendix RDR-1400 weather radar.

Total US Army procurement of CH-47A/B/C models was 732. Other military customers for US built Chinooks include Argentina (5), Australia (12), Canada (9), Japan (2), Spain (19), Thailand (4), and the UK (41). Orders for Agusta/EM built CH-47Cs have been received from Egypt (15), Greece (10), Iran (35), Italy (28), Libya (20) and Morocco (9).

The following data apply generally to the CH-47D and International CH-47D, except where a specific version is indicated:

TYPE: Twin-engined medium transport helicopter.

ROTOR SYSTEM: Two three-blade rotors in tandem, rotating in opposite directions and driven through interconnecting shafts which enable both rotors to be driven by either engine. Rotor blades, of glassfibre, have Boeing Vertol VR7 and VR8 aerofoil sections, cambered leading-edge, D shaped glassfibre spar, and a fairing assembly consisting of Nomex honeycomb core with crossply glassfibre laminates for skin. Blades can survive hits by 22 mm API and HEI munitions and still provide a 'fly home' capability. All blades can be folded manually. Rotor

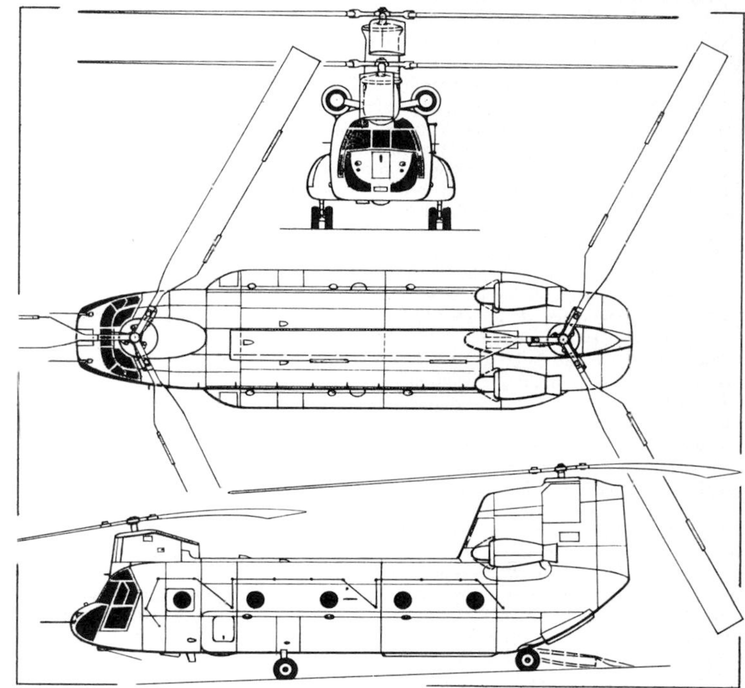

Boeing Vertol CH-47D military helicopter. Broken lines show rear loading ramp lowered *(Pilot Press)*

CH-47D CHINOOK WEIGHTS AND PERFORMANCE

	Condition 1	Condition 2	Condition 3	Condition 4
Take-off condition				
Altitude	1,220 m (4,000 ft)	Sea level	1,220 m (4,000 ft)	Sea level
Temperature	35°C (95°F)	15°C (59°F)	35°C (95°F)	15°C (59°F)
Empty weight	10,500 kg (23,149 lb)	10,500 kg (23,149 lb)	10,423 kg (22,980 lb)	10,265 kg (22,630 lb)
T-O weight	19,459 kg (42,900 lb)	22,679 kg (50,000 lb)	19,958 kg (44,000 lb)	22,679 kg (50,000 lb)
Payload: external	7,348 kg (16,200 lb)	10,446 kg (23,030 lb)	—	—
internal	—	—	6,680 kg (14,728 lb)	—
Max level speed, S/L, ISA, max continuous power, no external load	159 knots (295 km/h; 183 mph)	159 knots (295 km/h; 183 mph)	150 knots (278 km/h; 173 mph)	—
Average cruising speed	120 knots (222 km/h; 138 mph)	130 knots (241 km/h; 150 mph)	130 knots (241 km/h; 150 mph)	138 knots (256 km/h; 159 mph)
Max rate of climb, S/L, ISA, intermediate rated power	595 m (1,950 ft)/min	406 m (1,333 ft)/min	605 m (1,980 ft)/min	455 m (1,485 ft)/min
Hovering ceiling OGE, ISA, max power	3,200 m (10,500 ft)	1,705 m (5,600 ft)	3,050 m (10,000 ft)	1,830 m (6,000 ft)
Mission radius	30 nm (55·5 km; 34·5 miles)	30 nm (55·5 km; 34·5 miles)	100 nm (185 km; 115 miles)	—
Ferry range	—	—	—	1,111 nm (2,059 km; 1,279 miles)

Condition 1
T-O weight is gross weight for 61 m (200 ft)/min vertical rate of climb to hover OGE at 1,220 m/35°C (4,000 ft/95°F). External payload is carried outbound only. Fuel reserve is 30 min cruise fuel. Max speed shown is at T-O weight less external payload.

Condition 2
T-O gross weight is max structural T-O weight for which vertical climb capability at S/L, ISA is 271 m (890 ft)/min. Otherwise same as Condition 1.

Condition 3
T-O weight is gross weight for hover OGE at 1,220 m/35°C (4,000 ft/95°F). Radius is with inbound payload 50 per cent of outbound internal payload. Fuel reserve is 30 min cruise fuel. Max speed shown is at T-O weight.

Condition 4
T-O weight is max structural T-O weight. Max ferry range (internal and internal auxiliary fuel). Optimum cruise climb to 2,440 m (8,000 ft) and complete cruise at 2,440 m (8,000 ft). Fuel reserve is 10 per cent of initial fuel.

heads fully articulated with pitch, flapping and drag hinges. All bearings submerged completely in oil. Provisions for optional rotor brake.

ROTOR DRIVE: Power transmitted from each engine through individual overrunning clutches, into the combiner transmission, thereby providing a single power output to the interconnecting shafts. Rotor/engine rpm ratio 1 : 64.

FUSELAGE: Semi-monocoque mainly metal structure comprising flight deck, cabin, rear fuselage, and pylon sections. The cabin is of constant cross-section, with the lower half sealed during manufacture to form a watertight compartment that provides water landing capability. The rear of the fuselage contains the cargo ramp and door.

LANDING GEAR: Non-retractable quadricycle type, with twin wheels on each forward unit and single wheels on each rear unit. Oleo-pneumatic shock absorbers in all units. Rear units fully castoring and steerable; power steering installed on starboard rear unit. All wheels are size 24 × 7·7-VII, with tyres size 8·50-10-III, pressure 4·62 bars (67 lb/sq in). Two single-disc hydraulic brakes. Provision for fitting detachable wheel-skis.

POWER PLANT: Two Avco Lycoming T55-L-712 turboshaft engines, pod-mounted on sides of the rear pylon, and each with a standard power rating of 2,796 kW (3,750 shp) and emergency rating of 3,356 kW (4,500 shp). Combined transmission rating 5,593 kW (7,500 shp) in CH-47D, 5,033 kW (6,750 shp) at 225 rpm and 95 per cent torque in International; single-engine transmission emergency rating of 3,430 kW (4,600 shp), in CH-47D, at 225 rpm and 129 per cent torque. Self-sealing pressure refuelled crashworthy fuel tanks in external fairings on sides of fuselage. Total fuel capacity 3,899 litres (1,030 US gallons). Oil capacity 14 litres (3·7 US gallons).

ACCOMMODATION: Two pilots on flight deck, with dual controls. Jump seat for crew chief or combat commander. Jettisonable door on each side of flight deck. Depending on seating arrangement, 33 to 44 troops can be accommodated in main cabin, or 24 litters plus two attendants, or vehicles and freight. Rear loading ramp can be left completely or partially open, or can be removed to permit transport of extra-long cargo and in-flight parachute or free-drop delivery of cargo and equipment. Main cabin door, at front on starboard side, comprises upper hinged section which can be opened in flight, and lower section with integral steps. Lower section is jettisonable. Triple external cargo hook system, as on Model 234, with centre hook able to carry max load of 12,700 kg (28,000 lb). Provisions are installed for a power-down ramp and water dam to permit ramp operation on water; for forward and aft cargo hooks, ferry fuel tanks, external rescue hoist, and windscreen washers.

SYSTEMS: Cabin heated by 200,000 BTU heater/blower. Hydraulic system provides pressure of 207 bars (3,000 lb/sq in) for flying controls. Max flow rate 53·0 litres (14 US gallons) per minute. Spherical hydraulic reservoir, volume 5,326 cm³ (325 cu in), pressurised to 1·72 bars (25 lb/sq in). Utility hydraulic system, pressure 231 bars (3,350 lb/sq in), max flow rate 51·5 litres (13·6 US gallons) per minute. Piston type reservoir, volume 7,014 cm³ (428 cu in), of which 5,326 cm³ (325 cu in) are usable, pressurised to 3·86 bars (56 lb/sq in). Electrical system includes two 40kVA aircooled alternators driven by transmission drive system. Solar T62-T-2B APU runs accessory gear drive, thereby operating all hydraulic and electrical systems.

AVIONICS AND EQUIPMENT (International CH-47D: US Army CH-47D assumed to be generally similar. Avionics for RAF HC. Mk 1 listed in 1985-86 and earlier editions): Standard avionics include ARC-102 HF com radio, Collins ARC-186 UHF/AM-FM, Magnavox ARC-164 UHF/AM com; C-6533 intercom; Bendix APX-100 IFF; APN-209 radar altimeter; ARN-89B ADF; ARN-123 VOR/glideslope/marker beacon receiver; and ASN-43 gyromagnetic compass. Flight instruments are standard for IFR, and include an AQU-6A horizontal situation indicator. AFCS maintains helicopter stability, eliminating the need for constant small correction inputs by the pilot to maintain desired attitude. The AFCS is a redundant system using two identical control units and two sets of stabilisation actuators. Standard equipment includes a hydraulically powered winch for rescue and cargo handling, rearview mirror, plus integral work stands and step for maintenance. Provisions for static lines, and maintenance davits for removal of major components.

DIMENSIONS, EXTERNAL:
- Rotor diameter (each) — 18·29 m (60 ft 0 in)
- Rotor blade chord (each) — 0·81 m (2 ft 8 in)
- Distance between rotor centres — 11·94 m (39 ft 2 in)
- Length overall, rotors turning — 30·18 m (99 ft 0 in)
- Length of fuselage — 15·54 m (51 ft 0 in)
- Width, rotors folded — 3·78 m (12 ft 5 in)
- Height to top of rear rotor head — 5·68 m (18 ft 7·8 in)
- Wheel track (c/l of shock absorbers) — 3·20 m (10 ft 6 in)
- Wheelbase — 6·86 m (22 ft 6 in)
- Passenger door (fwd, stbd):
  - Height — 1·68 m (5 ft 6 in)
  - Width — 0·91 m (3 ft 0 in)
  - Height to sill — 1·09 m (3 ft 7 in)
- Rear loading ramp entrance:
  - Height — 1·98 m (6 ft 6 in)
  - Width — 2·31 m (7 ft 7 in)
  - Height to sill — 0·79 m (2 ft 7 in)

DIMENSIONS, INTERNAL:
- Cabin, excl flight deck: Length — 9·20 m (30 ft 2 in)
  - Width (mean) — 2·29 m (7 ft 6 in)
  - Width at floor — 2·51 m (8 ft 3 in)
  - Height — 1·98 m (6 ft 6 in)
  - Floor area — 21·0 m² (226 sq ft)
  - Usable volume — 41·7 m³ (1,474 cu ft)

AREAS:
- Rotor blades (each) — 7·43 m² (80·0 sq ft)
- Rotor discs (total) — 525·3 m² (5,655 sq ft)

WEIGHTS (CH-47D):
- Internal payload over 100 nm (185 km; 115 mile) radius at 1,220 m (4,000 ft), hovering OGE at T-O — 6,512 kg (14,356 lb)
- External payload over 30 nm (55·5 km; 34·5 mile) radius at 1,220 m (4,000 ft), 61 m (200 ft)/min vertical climb at T-O, 35°C — 7,192 kg (15,856 lb)
- *Gross weight, hovering OGE at S/L, ISA — 24,766 kg (54,600 lb)

**Current MTOGW authorised for US Army operation is 22,680 kg (50,000 lb)*

WEIGHTS (International CH-47D):
- Weight empty — 10,184 kg (22,452 lb)
- Internal payload over 100 nm (185 km; 115 mile) radius at 1,525 m (5,000 ft), hovering OGE at 20,616 kg (45,450 lb), ISA + 20°C — 8,164 kg (18,000 lb)
- External payload over 30 nm (55·5 km; 34·5 mile) radius, other conditions as above — 9,389 kg (20,700 lb)
- Design gross weight — 14,968 kg (33,000 lb)
- Alternative design gross weight — 20,865 kg (46,000 lb)
- Max T-O weight — 22,680 kg (50,000 lb)

PERFORMANCE (CH-47D):
- As in accompanying table, plus:
- Max level speed at S/L, ISA, at AUW of 14,968 kg (33,000 lb) — 157 knots (291 km/h; 181 mph)
- Service ceiling, one engine out, at 14,968 kg (33,000 lb) AUW, ISA — 3,900 m (12,800 ft)

PERFORMANCE (International CH-47D at max continuous power, ISA, at gross weights of A: 22,680 kg; 50,000 lb; B: 20,865 kg; 46,000 lb, C: 14,968 kg; 33,000 lb):
- Max level speed at S/L:
  - A — 145 knots (269 km/h; 167 mph)
  - B — 150 knots (278 km/h; 173 mph)
  - C — 160 knots (297 km/h; 184 mph)
- Service ceiling, max continuous power:
  - A — 2,590 m (8,500 ft)
  - B — 3,140 m (10,300 ft)
  - C — 4,570 m (15,000 ft)
- Hovering ceiling OGE, T-O power:
  - A — 1,035 m (3,400 ft)
  - B — 2,680 m (8,800 ft)
  - C — 4,570 m (15,000 ft)

BOEING VERTOL MODEL 234 COMMERCIAL CHINOOK

Announced in the late Summer of 1978, this development of the military CH-47 Chinook is being produced for use as a commercial passenger transport, as a cargo carrier, and for specialised tasks such as servicing offshore oil and natural gas rigs, remote resources exploration and extraction, logging, and construction work.

The airframe of the Model 234 is based on that of the latest military Chinook, but has many new features. These include the use of wide chord glassfibre rotor blades, instead of the usual metal blades; redesign of the fuselage side fairings; a lengthened nose to accommodate the weather radar antenna; and repositioning further forward of the front landing gear units.

Three basic versions of the commercial Model 234 are offered:

Long-range model (234 LR). Identified by continuous fuselage-side fairings, approximately twice as large as those of the military Chinook and containing large fuel tanks. Equipped to airline standards as a passenger, passenger/freight 'combi', or all-cargo transport. Received FAA certification on 19 June 1981 for passenger operations and a max gross weight of 22,000 kg (48,500 lb).

Extended-range model (234 ER). Version of 234 LR with two internal auxiliary fuel tanks and fewer seats. Typical configuration is that ordered by Arco Alaska, with 17 seats for passengers and fuel for a range of up to 875 nm (1,621 km; 1,008 miles). This version of the Model 234 can also be configured for 32 passengers and a single internal fuel tank where maximum range is not required. FAA certification was granted in May 1983 for operation with internal and external loads at the max T-O weights listed.

Utility model (234 UT). Fuselage side fuel tanks replaced by two drum shaped internal tanks, mounted longitudinally side by side at the front of the cabin. Fuselage-side fairings removed, leaving only an individual blister around each landing gear mounting. As well as reducing weight, this enhances the helicopter's lifting capability by reducing the airframe surface area on which the rotor downwash impinges. The 234 UT received supplemental type certification from the FAA in October 1981 at a max gross weight of 23,133 kg (51,000 lb) for external cargo lift operations. The FAA approval included also the carriage of 24 passengers, external loads of up to 12,700 kg (28,000 lb) on the aircraft's single cargo hook, and external cargo lift missions at altitudes of up to 3,660 m (12,000 ft) under max gross weight conditions.

Multi-purpose long-range model (234 MLR). Similar to 234 LR but with airline standard interior replaced by utility interior. Three delivered to a Far East government operator in 1985.

Conversion from one configuration of the Model 234 to another is estimated to take eight hours, and requires four persons to handle the fuel tanks of the utility model and the ramp baggage bins of the passenger carrying helicopter.

Initial order for the Model 234 was placed by British Airways Helicopters, which ordered three of the long-range model in 1978 (later increased to six), primarily for North Sea oil rig support operations. First flight was made on 19 August 1980. FAA and UK CAA certification was received on 19 and 26 June 1981 respectively. The first BAH Model

Boeing Vertol CH-47D helicopter pictured during in-flight refuelling trials in August 1985

234 LR (which had been delivered in January) went into service on 1 July 1981, and all six had been delivered by 1 June 1982. FAA and CAA certification of the 234 LR 'combi' was received in the Summer of 1982. In July 1985 one of BAH's Model 234 LRs became the first example of the type to complete 6,000 flight hours.

Helikopter Service A/S of Norway ordered two Model 234 LRs in 1982; it took up an option on a third in December 1985, this helicopter having been leased from the manufacturer in the Summer of 1984. Two 234 ERs were leased in 1983 to Arco Alaska, for use in offshore oil rig support operations. In March 1985 ERA Helicopters of Anchorage, Alaska, leased a 234 ER (with option to purchase) for offshore oil support duties in the Navarin Basin area of the Bering Sea. Columbia Helicopters of Aurora, Oregon, took delivery of two former British Airways Helicopters Model 234s in the Autumn of 1984.

TYPE: Twin-turbine commercial transport helicopter.

ROTOR SYSTEM: Two three-blade rotors in tandem, turning in opposite directions and driven through interconnecting shafts which enable both rotors to be driven by either engine. Wide chord glassfibre blades, with VR7 section over inboard 85 per cent of span, and VR8 section on outer 15 per cent of span; thickness/chord ratio 12% and 8% respectively. Overall blade twist 12°. Each blade comprises a laminated glassfibre skin over a glassfibre D spar, forming the front half of the section, and with the rear half filled with Nomex honeycomb. An aluminium screen inserted in the skin provides lightning protection, discharging strikes via the titanium leading-edge. Outboard 25 per cent of leading-edge capped with replaceable nickel section. Blade balancing by tracking weights in tips. Two blades of each rotor can be folded manually. Heads fully articulated, with pitch, flapping and drag hinges. All bearings submerged completely in oil. Blades embody electric de-icing blankets, permitting addition of a de-icing kit if required. Rotor rpm 225.

ROTOR DRIVE: Power is transmitted from each engine through individual overrunning clutches, into the combiner transmission, thereby providing a single power output to the interconnecting shafts. Auxiliary transmission lubrication system enables flight to be completed after total loss of oil in primary system.

FUSELAGE: All-metal semi-monocoque structure of basically square section. Loading ramp forms undersurface of upswept rear fuselage. External fuel pods of long-range model made of advanced composites, including glassfibre, graphite/epoxy and Nomex nylon honeycomb. These fairing pods provide flotation capability adequate to meet British airworthiness requirements applicable to a sea state seven (9·15 m; 30 ft waves. Wave length-to-height ratio 15) without added flotation gear.

LANDING GEAR: Non-retractable quadricycle type, with twin wheels on each forward unit and single wheels on each rear unit. All tyres size 8·50-10, Type III (12 ply), pressure 8·55 bars (124 lb/sq in) on forward gear, 7·20 bars (104·4 lb/sq in) on rear gear. Oleo-pneumatic shock absorbers in all units. Rear units fully castoring and steerable. Hydraulic disc brakes.

POWER PLANT: Two Avco Lycoming AL 5512 turboshaft engines, pod-mounted on sides of rear rotor pylon. Each engine has max T-O rating of 3,039 kW (4,075 shp), max continuous rating of 2,218·5 kW (2,975 shp), and 30 min contingency rating of 3,247 kW (4,355 shp). Transmission rated at 5,033 kW (6,750 shp) at 225 rotor rpm, and 3,430 kW (4,600 shp) for single-engine operation. Long-range model has two fuel tanks, one in each fuselage side fairing, with total capacity of 7,949 litres (2,100 US gallons). Utility model has two drum-shape internal tanks, with total capacity of 3,702 litres (978 US gallons). Extended-range model has both fuselage side and internal drum tanks. Single-point pressure refuelling.

ACCOMMODATION: Two pilots side by side on flight deck, with dual controls. Passenger cabin of long-range model seats up to 44 persons four-abreast, with centre aisle. Each seat has overhead bin and underseat stowage for carry-on baggage; larger items are stowed over the rear ramp in the main baggage compartment. Galley, with cabin attendant's seat, and toilet, are standard, between flight deck and cabin. Basic FAA/CAA approved 'combi' versions offer 8-32 passenger seats, with cargo at rear of cabin, loaded via rear ramp; or 22-32 passenger seats, with cargo stowed on only one side of cabin's centre aisle. All passenger facilities can be removed, and heavy duty floor installed, for freight-only service. Passenger door at front of cabin on starboard side. Crew door on each side of flight deck. Cabin floor supported by dynamically tuned fittings to reduce vibration. Hydraulically powered cargo ramp can be stopped at any intermediate position to match the level of the loading vehicle being used. Single central cargo hook is standard on utility model for carrying external loads of up to 12,700 kg (28,000 lb). Optional dual tandem hooks for precision operations and for load stability in high-speed flight; or three tandem hooks for delivering multiple loads.

SYSTEMS: Heating and ventilation systems maintain comfortable flight deck/cabin temperature in ambient temperatures down to −32°C. Duplicated flying control, hydraulic and electrical systems, as described for CH-47D/Model 414. Solar T62T-2B APU, rated at 71 kW (95 shp), drives auxiliary gearbox on rear transmission to start engines and provide power for two flying control system hydraulic pumps and two alternators. All critical systems heated to inhibit ice build-up.

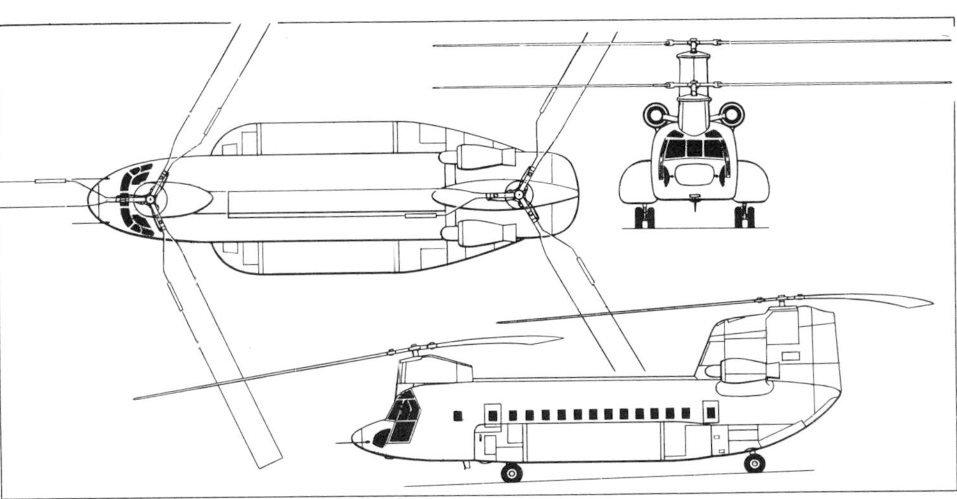

Boeing Vertol Model 234 LR long-range Commercial Chinook *(Pilot Press)*

Boeing Vertol 234 ER of Helikopter Service A/S of Norway

AVIONICS AND EQUIPMENT: Duplicated full blind-flying instrumentation, weather radar, and dual four-axis automatic flight control system with built-in test equipment, provide all-weather capability. Optional equipment includes passenger interior furnishings for the utility model, 'combi' interior, downward-shining cargo load light, rescue hoist of 272 kg (600 lb) capacity, glassfibre wheel-skis, an ice detector probe, and ditching equipment that includes two liferafts, each with an overload capacity of 36 persons. Standard items include integral work platforms, and a maintenance panel that allows 26 separate checks to be made from a single ground-level position.

DIMENSIONS, EXTERNAL:
- Rotor diameter (each) — 18·29 m (60 ft 0 in)
- Rotor blade chord (constant) — 0·813 m (2 ft 8 in)
- Length overall, rotors turning — 30·18 m (99 ft 0 in)
- Length of fuselage — 15·87 m (52 ft 1 in)
- Height overall — 5·68 m (18 ft 7·8 in)
- Width over fuselage side fairings — 4·78 m (15 ft 8 in)
- Wheel track:
  - fwd landing gear — 3·20 m (10 ft 6 in)
  - rear landing gear — 3·40 m (11 ft 2 in)
- Wheelbase — 7·87 m (25 ft 9·9 in)

DIMENSIONS, INTERNAL:
- Passenger cabin: Length — 9·19 m (30 ft 2 in)
  - Max width — 2·51 m (8 ft 3 in)
  - Max height — 1·98 m (6 ft 6 in)
- Baggage compartment volume — 4·42 m³ (156 cu ft)
- Utility model, cargo hold volume — 41·03 m³ (1,449 cu ft)

WEIGHTS:
- Manufacturer's weight empty:
  - LR — 11,748 kg (25,900 lb)
  - ER — 12,020 kg (26,500 lb)
  - MLR — 11,113 kg (24,500 lb)
  - UT — 9,797 kg (21,600 lb)
- Operating weight empty:
  - LR — 12,292 kg (27,100 lb)
  - ER — 12,406 kg (27,350 lb)
  - MLR — 11,317 kg (24,950 lb)
  - UT — 10,002 kg (22,050 lb)
- Fuel load: LR, MLR — 6,391 kg (14,091 lb)
  - ER — 9,368 kg (20,653 lb)
  - UT — 2,976 kg (6,562 lb)
- Max payload: LR, MLR, internal — 9,072 kg (20,000 lb)
  - ER, UT, internal — 8,731 kg (19,250 lb)
  - ER, MLR, R, UT, external — 12,700 kg (28,000 lb)
- Max T-O weight:
  - ER, LR, MLR, internal load — 22,000 kg (48,500 lb)
  - UT, internal load — 19,051 kg (42,000 lb)
  - ER, LR, MLR, UT, external load — 23,133 kg (51,000 lb)

PERFORMANCE:
- Never-exceed speed:
  - ER, LR, MLR — 150 knots (278 km/h; 173 mph)
  - UT — 140 knots (259 km/h; 161 mph)
- Max cruising speed at 610 m (2,000 ft):
  - ER, LR, MLR, internal load, at 22,000 kg (48,500 lb) AUW — 145 knots (269 km/h; 167 mph)
  - UT, internal load, at 19,051 kg (42,000 lb) AUW — 140 knots (259 km/h; 161 mph)
- Cruising speed for optimum range, at 610 m (2,000 ft):
  - ER, LR, MLR, UT, internal load, at all gross weights — 135 knots (250 km/h; 155 mph)
- Max rate of climb at S/L at max T-O weight:
  - ER, LR, MLR, internal load — 360 m (1,180 ft)/min
  - UT, internal load — 457 m (1,500 ft)/min
- Operational ceiling:
  - ER, LR, MLR, UT — 4,570 m (15,000 ft)
- Hovering ceiling IGE:
  - ER, LR, MLR, internal load — 2,590 m (8,500 ft)
  - UT, internal load — 4,085 m (13,400 ft)
- Hovering ceiling OGE:
  - ER, LR, MLR, internal load — 820 m (2,700 ft)
  - UT, internal load — 3,505 m (11,500 ft)
- Range with 45 min IFR reserves:
  - LR, 44 passengers — 530 nm (982 km; 610 miles)
  - ER, 17 passengers — 830 nm (1,538 km; 956 miles)
  - LR, MLR, with max fuel — 620 nm (1,149 km; 714 miles)
  - ER with max fuel — 1,035 nm (1,918 km; 1,192 miles)

UT with max internal load 229 nm (424 km; 264 miles)
UT with max external load 145 nm (269 km; 167 miles)
Max endurance:
LR, MLR, internal load 5 h 18 min
ER, internal load 8 h 25 min
UT, external load 2 h 18 min

BOEING VERTOL MODEL 360

Boeing Vertol has designed and is building as a private venture the prototype of a twin-turboshaft twin-rotor cargo helicopter known as the Model 360. Similar in size to the CH-46/UH-46 Sea Knight, it makes extensive use of composites materials in the fuselage, rotor hubs, upper controls and drive system components. An advanced flight control and flight management system will be installed. Shake testing to verify the airframe's dynamic characteristics, and proof-load testing, have been completed. The prototype was in final assembly by August 1986 and the first flight was due at the end of that year.

TYPE: Twin-turbine medium-size cargo/utility helicopter.

ROTOR SYSTEM: Two four-blade rotors in tandem, turning in opposite directions and linked through interconnecting shafts to enable both rotors to be driven by either engine. All-composites rotor blades of new VR12 and VR15 aerofoil section, which will improve hovering efficiency and high speed performance. Rotor head is constructed almost entirely of glassfibre and carbon composites, with elastomeric bearings. Automatic blade-folding motors and linkages are integrated with the lead-lag damping system. Many transmission and control system components made of carbonfibre or glassfibre, including rotor driveshafts and rotor swashplates.

FUSELAGE: Basic structure of graphite fuselage frames and longerons, covered by preformed panels of Kevlar diagonal-weave skins with Nomex honeycomb core; graphite reinforcement is provided at the panel edges and for all cut-outs. Panels attached to structure by combination of cold bonding and metallic fasteners. The floor is formed as a separate assembly incorporating the fuel tanks and cargo handling roller system, and is suspended on sprung counterweights to isolate it from vibration; the entire flight deck is mounted similarly. The rear of the fuselage, containing the one-piece cargo ramp and door, is of new drag-reducing design.

Artist's impression of Boeing Vertol Model 360 helicopter with all-composites airframe and rotors

LANDING GEAR: Retractable tricycle type with twin wheels on each unit. The landing gear structure is of carbonfibre composites.

POWER PLANT: Two Avco Lycoming T55-L-712 turboshaft engines, mounted one on each side of the rear fuselage just forward of the rear pylon, each with a standard power rating of 3,579 kW (4,800 shp).

SYSTEMS: Hydraulic and electrical system components are modular in nature, and grouped to allow systems and structure to be integrated during construction.

AVIONICS AND EQUIPMENT: Full nav/com equipment. Doppler radar and optional remote map reader. Bendix integrated flight control and flight management system incorporates computer controlled EADI and EHSI displays for pilot and co-pilot, linked to a heading and attitude reference system via a multiplex data bus.

DIMENSIONS, EXTERNAL:
Length of fuselage 15·54 m (51 ft 0 in)
Height overall 5·91 m (19 ft 4¾ in)
Wheel track 3·96 m (13 ft 0 in)

WEIGHT (estimated):
Design T-O weight 13,834 kg (30,500 lb)

PERFORMANCE (estimated):
Normal cruising speed 200 knots (370 km/h; 230 mph)

BELL/BOEING V-22 OSPREY

Boeing Vertol is teamed with Bell Helicopter Textron to develop a tilt-rotor aircraft to meet the US government's Joint Services Vertical Lift Aircraft requirement. This programme, formerly known as JVX, has been officially designated V-22 and the tilt-rotor aircraft under development has been given the name of Osprey. A full description of the aircraft appears under the Bell entry in this section.

BOEING VERTOL ADOCS PROGRAMME

Under contract to the US Army's Aviation Applied Technology Directorate at Fort Eustis, Virginia, Boeing Vertol is conducting a helicopter research programme known as ADOCS (Advanced Digital/Optical Control System). Intended to demonstrate an advanced fibre optic ('fly by light') system as part of the Army's LHX programme, ADOCS achieves control solely by optical signal paths, using Teledyne Ryan Electronics optical transducers, and a Lear Siegler four-axis sidestick controller. Other ADOCS subcontractors include Bendix (actuators) and Honeywell (digital flight processors). The system made its first flight on 7 November 1985 in a Sikorsky UH-60A Black Hawk testbed, validating the safety system's ability to transfer control back to the normal mechanical system. On this flight it was flown to a maximum height of 1,220 m (4,000 ft) and a speed of 125 knots (232 km/h; 144 mph). A further six months of flight testing was planned, to refine handling characteristics and evaluate the digital/optical hardware performance.

BOEING VERTOL ARTI PROGRAMME

In 1984 Boeing Vertol began flight testing an advanced rotorcraft technology integration (ARTI) testbed, using a modified Agusta A 109A helicopter. The A 109A's cockpit and cabin were reconfigured to provide a second pilot station in the passenger cabin from which all direct external view has been eliminated. Three 38·1 cm (15 in) colour CRT displays provide a 126° field of view via nose mounted video cameras. The remote cockpit station has conventional mechanical flight controls linked to those at the safety pilot's position in the A 109A's right hand cockpit seat. The first test stage, which began in November 1984, included evaluation of a wide field of view cockpit panoramic display, voice controls, digital map display and finger-on-glass control switches. Subsequent testing included measurement of pilot workload during simulated nap-of-the-earth (NOE) missions and evaluation of evolving hardware/software modifications. Testing has now been completed.

Sikorsky UH-60A 'Light Hawk' testbed for US Army/Boeing Vertol ADOCS fly by light control system

BRANSON

BRANSON AIRCRAFT CORPORATION

3790 Wheeling Street, Denver, Colorado 80239
Telephone: (303) 371 9112
Telex: 45-4577 BRANSON DVR
VICE-PRESIDENT, MARKETING: Dan Preble

CITATION I AUXILIARY TANK

Branson Aircraft Corporation has received an FAA FAR Pt 25 supplemental type certificate for its 454 litre (120 US gallon) auxiliary fuel tank installation in the Cessna Citation I business jet. The tank installation and associated structural work permit a 295 kg (650 lb) increase in the aircraft's maximum gross weight, enabling Citation I operators to carry an additional three passengers, plus 27 kg (60 lb) of baggage, for an additional 350 nm (648 km; 403 miles). The first of these installations, which takes two weeks to complete, was made in January 1985.

DIAMOND I LONG-RANGE TANK

Branson Aircraft Corporation has developed a 363 litre (96 US gallon) long-range fuel tank for the Mitsubishi Diamond I and IA business jets. The tank mounts in the aircraft's fuselage against the rear pressure bulkhead. Also available for the Diamond is a transfer system for filling the aircraft's fuselage fuel tank from the port wing tank, eliminating the need for manual filling of the fuselage tank. A Branson tailcone baggage compartment, capacity 0·93 m³ (33 cu ft), maximum load 204 kg (450 lb), is also available for retrofit to Diamond IA aircraft.

LEARJET 55 LONG-RANGE TANKS

Branson has developed long-range auxiliary fuel tanks for the Gates Learjet Model 55 business jet which provide an additional 378 litres (100 US gallons) or 757 litres (200 US gallons) of fuel. The installation takes approximately four weeks for the 378 litre tank, and five weeks for the 757 litre tank, which extends the aircraft's range by 400 nm (741 km; 461 miles)

BUSH

BUSH CONVERSIONS INC

Box 431, Udall, Kansas 67146
Telephone: (316) 782 3851
VICE-PRESIDENT: Barbara Williams

BOLEN 'TAILDRAGGER' CONVERSIONS

Bush Conversions Inc is offering the 'Taildragger' conversions which the former Ralph Bolen Inc designed as a tailwheel landing gear conversion for application to Cessna 150/152, 172/Skyhawk and 175 aircraft. Flight testing has indicated an average 8·5-10·5 knots (16-19·5 km/h; 10-12 mph) increase in speed resulting from removal of the nosewheel unit; but this change in landing gear configuration is intended also to improve performance from short ields and rough surfaces, to permit a tighter turn radius on narrow strips, and to simplify operation on floats or skis when this is desirable.

The conversion is carried out by the addition of two bulkheads in the front fuselage and a new main landing gear attachment box, just forward of the existing box, to which new cantilever main-gear legs are installed in the case of Cessna Models 172 and 175. Cessna 150 series F, G, H, J and K, and Cessna 152s, retain their existing main-gear legs, but these are removed from their original mounting and attached to the new forward box. Earlier versions require new legs of the design fitted to Cessna 150s of the above series, so that the now-standard wheel with 15 × 6·00-6 tyre and wheel brakes can be installed. The remainder of the conversion covers the removal of the nose gear, and the installation of a new tailwheel unit that includes a Scott 3200 wheel. This unit is attached by stress plates and stringers, so that the tailwheel assembly becomes an integral part of the fuselage structure. No skin removal is required for the conversion.

The 'Taildragger' modification of the landing gear system has been so designed that on completion there is no shift in the CG position. The STC for most of the Cessna Model 150/152 series, and for the Model 172, covers operation on Fluidyne snow skis, and similar approval is being sought for the Model 175. No weight penalty results from conversion of Model 150/152 aircraft; the longer and stronger main gear units introduced on the Models 172/175, and accompanying structure, increase weight by 13·6 kg (30 lb).

Bolen 'Taildragger' conversion of a Cessna Model 150 *(Mike Jerram)*

CALIFORNIA HELICOPTER

CALIFORNIA HELICOPTER PARTS INC

2935 Golf Course Drive, Ventura, California 93003
Telephone: (805) 644 5800
Telex: 6831165 CHI UW
PRESIDENT: Gary A. Podolny
VICE-PRESIDENT AND GENERAL MANAGER:
W. E. (Jake) Dangle

CALIFORNIA HELICOPTER (SIKORSKY) S-58T

On 22 December 1981, California Helicopter acquired from Sikorsky the rights to the S-58T helicopter, a twin-turbine (Pratt & Whitney Canada PT6T-6) conversion of the piston engined Sikorsky S-58. Details of the conversion can be found under the Sikorsky entry in the 1978-79 and earlier editions of *Jane's*. FAA certification for VFR flight was awarded to Sikorsky in April 1971, followed by IFR certification in mid-1973, and that company had delivered approximately 146 converted aircraft and/or conversion kits when negotiations with California Helicopters were finalised in 1981. These covered rights to manufacture turbine conversion kits and spare parts, and support of the worldwide fleet of S-58/S-58T aircraft.

California Helicopter is currently manufacturing conversion kits and offers remanufactured H-34 helicopter airframes for use with the kits, together with a component exchange programme. The company's subsidiary, California Helicopter International Inc at San Antonio, Texas, is responsible for international sales and export of the finished aircraft, conversion kits and remanufactured airframes.

The S-58T is operated commercially on a variety of services ranging from passenger transport to heavy lift external cargo. The FAA and British Civil Aviation Authority have approved the aircraft for IFR operation.

New York Airways uses two S-58Ts with 14-passenger configuration on its shuttle operation from Manhattan to the New York Metropolitan Airports. Others are operated throughout the world.

California Helicopter conversion of Sikorsky S-58 to twin-turbine S-58T configuration

The Indonesian Air Force has converted and delivered to its own units a total of twelve S-58Ts, with the purchase of four more planned. The Royal Thai Air Force has acquired 18 S-58Ts. Two additional S-58Ts have been acquired by the Thai Ministry of Agriculture as VIP transports, and California Helicopter has received a number of enquiries from agencies of the Thai government for S-58Ts to be used in applications that include cargo and troop transport, search and rescue, and multi-role operation.

WEIGHTS AND LOADINGS:

Weight empty	3,437 kg (7,577 lb)
Max T-O and landing weight	5,896 kg (13,000 lb)
Max disc loading	25·8 kg/m² (5·29 lb/sq ft)
Max power loading	4·72 kg/kW (7·76 lb/shp)

PERFORMANCE (at max T-O weight. A: PT6T-3; B: PT6T-6):

Max level speed at S/L:	
A, B	120 knots (222 km/h; 138 mph)
Cruising speed:	
A, B	110 knots (204 km/h; 127 mph)
Hovering ceiling OGE: A	1,433 m (4,700 ft)
B	1,980 m (6,500 ft)
Single-engine absolute ceiling: A	640 m (2,100 ft)
B	1,280 m (4,200 ft)
Min ground turning radius: A, B	12·50 m (41 ft 0 in)
Runway LCN: A, B	approx 3·7
Range with 1,071 litres (283 US gallons) usable fuel, including 20 min reserves at cruising speed:	
A	260 nm (481 km; 299 miles)
B	242 nm (447 km; 278 miles)

CAMMACORP

PO Box 987, 360 N Sepulveda Boulevard, El Segundo, California 90245
Telephone: (213) 640 1710
Telex: 182507
PRESIDENT: Jackson R. McGowen
EXECUTIVE VICE-PRESIDENT: Leroy Cooper
VICE-PRESIDENTS:
Richard A. Bibee (Finance)
William Gelfand (Assistant to the President)
William E. Jenne (Cost Control and Financial Analysis)
Jesse L. Jones (Manufacturing and Quality Assurance)
Walter J. Wayman (Contracts)
DIRECTOR, ENGINEERING: James Hong
DIRECTOR, FLIGHT OPERATIONS: Donald L. Mullin

Cammacorp was formed in 1977 as programme manager for a project to re-engine DC-8 Srs 61, 62 and 63 aircraft with CFM International (General Electric/SNECMA) CFM56 turbofan engines under the respective designations of DC-8 Super 71, 72 and 73. The contractor team handling the programme included McDonnell Douglas, Long Beach, for engineering, flight test and product support; and McDonnell Douglas, Tulsa, which performed 44 aircraft modifications up to 1983. Air Canada (9), Delta Air Lines (48) and UTA (9) completed all other aircraft modifications, using Cammacorp kits. A total of 110 conversions was completed, the last being a Delta conversion delivered to NASA's Ames Research Center in the Spring of 1986.

Following this delivery, Cammacorp planned to cease operations before the end of 1986.

CAMMACORP/McDONNELL DOUGLAS DC-8 SUPER 71, 72 and 73

The first modification completed under the Cammacorp programme was that of a DC-8 Srs 61; the resulting Super 71 made its first flight on 15 August 1981. FAA certification was received in April 1982, followed by Super 73 and Super 72 certification in June and September 1982 respectively. Similar conversions were made to both passenger and freight versions of Srs 61, 62 and 63 aircraft.

By mid-1986, Super 70s were in passenger or cargo service with Air Canada (six Super 73F), Delta Air Lines (13 Super 71), Emery Worldwide (7 Super 73F), Evergreen International (4 Super 73F), German Cargo Services, a Lufthansa subsidiary (4 Super 73F and one Super 73CF), Minerve (one Super 73), National Airlines (1 Super 71), United Air Lines (29 Super 71), United Parcel Service (8 Super 71F and 19 Super 73F), and Transamerica (7 Super 73CF). In addition, three Super 72CFs are operated by the French Air Force as VIP/executive jet transports; three Super 72s and three Super 73s are in service with corporate operators or as VIP aircraft, and one Super 72 is operated by NASA's Ames Research Center at Moffett Field, California.

Full details of the Super Seventy series can be found in the 1985-86 and earlier editions of *Jane's*.

CESSNA

CESSNA AIRCRAFT COMPANY (Subsidiary of General Dynamics Corporation)

PO Box 1521, Wichita, Kansas 67201
Telephone: (316) 685 9111
Telex: 417 400
CHAIRMAN OF THE BOARD AND CHIEF EXECUTIVE OFFICER: Russell W. Meyer Jr
PRESIDENT AND CHIEF OPERATING OFFICER:
R. W. Van Sant
SENIOR VICE-PRESIDENTS:
Brian E. Barents (Aircraft Marketing Division)
William A. Boettger (New Business Development)
John E. Moore (Personnel and Community Relations)
Russell R. Roth (Finance)
VICE-PRESIDENTS:
Homer G. Nester (Treasurer)
Bruce Peterman (Product Engineering and Planning)
Joseph J. Solomon (Product Support)
Walter B. Voisard (McCauley Accessory Division)
Thaine L. Woolsey (Fluid Power Division)
SECRETARY: David R. Edwards
DIRECTOR OF PUBLIC RELATIONS: H. Dean Humphrey

Cessna Aircraft Company was founded by the late Clyde V. Cessna, a pioneer in US aviation in 1911, and was incorporated on 7 September 1927. Its former Pawnee and

Turboprop powered Cessna Model 208 Caravan I amphibian of Royal Canadian Mounted Police

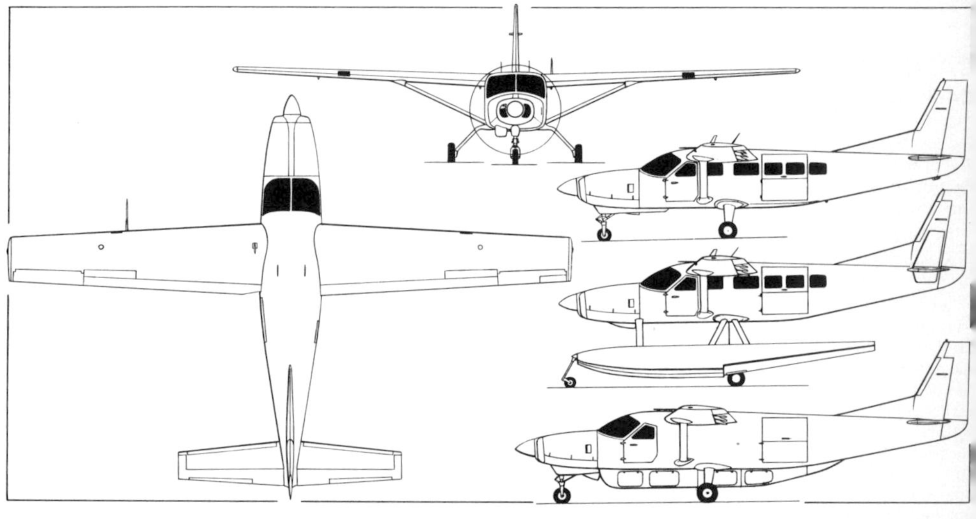

Cessna Model 208 Caravan I landplane, with additional side views of amphibious version (centre) and 'stretched' Model 208B (bottom) *(Pilot Press)*

Wallace aircraft divisions in Wichita were consolidated as production facilities within the company's Aircraft Division in mid-1984.

In September 1985 an agreement was announced between General Dynamics Corporation and Cessna whereby General Dynamics acquired the company as a wholly owned subsidiary.

Subsidiary companies owned by Cessna are the McCauley Accessory Division of Dayton, Ohio; Fluid Power Division of Hutchinson, Kansas; United Hydraulics Corporation of Hampton, Iowa; Cessna Fluid Power Ltd of Glenrothes, Fife, Scotland; Cessna Finance Corporation and Cessna International Finance Corporation in Wichita. It has a 49 per cent interest in Reims Aviation of France.

By 31 December 1985, the company had produced a total of 176,280 aircraft. During 1985, its sales totalled 878 aircraft, including units delivered by Reims Aviation of France (which see). Total employment within the company stood at 8,300 in June 1985.

The company's announced range of production aircraft for 1986 was reduced to seven types: the Caravan I and II, Conquest I and II, and three models of the Citation business jet. Restoration of piston engined models to the production line is not anticipated before the last quarter of 1987.

CESSNA MODEL 152

A total of 7,449 standard Model 152s and Model 152 Aerobats had been built by 31 December 1985, including 589 built by Reims Aviation in France. Manufacture of the Aerobat has ended. Production of the standard Model 152 has been suspended. Descriptions of both can be found in the 1984-85 *Jane's*.

CESSNA SKYHAWK

The Skyhawk is certificated for operation as a floatplane, and can be fitted with skis. A version designated F 172 is produced in France by Reims Aviation.

A total of 35,643 commercial aircraft in the Model 172/Skyhawk series had been built by 31 December 1985, including 2,129 F 172s built in France. In addition, 864 were built during 1966-1983 as T-41A, T-41B, T-41C and T-41D Mescalero military basic trainers.

Production of the Skyhawk has been suspended. A description can be found in the 1985-86 *Jane's*.

CESSNA CUTLASS RG

The Cutlass RG combined the airframe of the Model 172 Skyhawk with the retractable landing gear developed for the Skylane RG.

A total of 1,158 Cutlass RGs had been sold by 31 December 1985. Production has been suspended. A description can be found in the 1985-86 *Jane's*.

CESSNA SKYLANE

A total of 19,773 Model 182/Skylanes of various models had been built by 31 December 1985, including 169 F 182s built by Reims Aviation. Production of the Model 182/Skylane has been suspended. A description appeared in the 1985-86 edition.

CESSNA SKYLANE RG and TURBO SKYLANE RG

Production of these retractable landing gear versions of the Skylane has been suspended.

By 31 December 1985 a total of 2,091 Skylane RGs had been built, including 73 assembled by Reims Aviation in France as Reims 182 Skylane RGs. A description can be found in the 1985-86 *Jane's*.

CESSNA MODEL 185 SKYWAGON

The prototype of the Model 185 Skywagon flew for the first time in July 1960 and the first production model was completed in March 1961.

A total of 4,356 Model 185 Skywagons, including 497 military U-17A/B/Cs, had been built by 31 December 1985.

Skywagon production has been suspended. A full description and illustration can be found in the 1985-86 *Jane's*.

CESSNA AG TRUCK and AG HUSKY

Production of both of these agricultural aircraft was suspended in 1985, and neither was listed for reintroduction in 1986. By 31 December 1985, sales of the Ag Truck totalled 1,949, and 386 examples of the Ag Husky had been delivered. Abbreviated descriptions of both models can be found in the 1985-86 *Jane's*, with a full description of the Ag Truck in the 1984-85 edition.

CESSNA STATIONAIR 6 and TURBO STATIONAIR 6

US Air Force designation: U-26A (Turbo Stationair)

Cessna first renamed the former U206 Skywagon and TU206 Turbo Skywagon as the Stationair and Turbo Stationair respectively. In 1978 a further name change to Stationair 6 and Turbo Stationair 6 highlighted the six-seat capacity of these cargo/utility aircraft. Production of the U206G and TU206G models has been suspended. Full descriptions of both can be found in the 1985-86 *Jane's*.

A total of 7,556 Model 206 Skywagons and Stationairs had been built by 31 December 1985, including 643 de luxe Super Skylanes of similar basic design.

CESSNA MODEL 208 CARAVAN I/U-27A

First flown on 9 December 1982, the engineering prototype of the Caravan I (N208LP) bore little resemblance to any previous Cessna design. The aircraft was claimed by the company to be the first all-new single-engined turboprop general aviation aircraft, and was intended to supplement or replace the thousands of de Havilland Canada Beavers and Otters, and Cessna 180s, 185s and 206s operated throughout the world in a variety of utility roles.

The Caravan I's basic ability to fly fast with a heavy load, to get into and out of unprepared airstrips, and to offer economy and reliability with minimum maintenance, can be extended by the addition of weather radar, air-conditioning, and oxygen systems. Other packages of optional equipment enable the Caravan I to perform aerial firefighting, photographic, agricultural spraying, ambulance/hearse, border patrol, parachuting and supply dropping, surveillance, and a variety of government utility duties, on wheels, floats and skis.

The first production Caravan I was rolled out in August 1984. FAA certification was obtained on 23 October, in landplane configuration, with full production beginning in 1985. FAA certification of an amphibian version was obtained in March 1986, by which time Cessna had delivered 70 Caravan Is to customers in Africa, Australia, Europe, New Zealand, South America and the United States. The first production Caravan I amphibian was delivered to the Royal Canadian Mounted Police for use in remote areas of the Province of Quebec. The RCMP plans to acquire a second Caravan I by the Summer of 1987 and a third in 1988.

In December 1983 Federal Express Corporation of Memphis, Tennessee, placed an order for 30 **Model 208A** Caravan IAs, and has subsequently ordered a total of 109, with options on a further 90. By March 1986 a total of 32 was in service with the carrier, which reported a despatch reliability rate of 99·8 per cent on a fleet average of 2,000 flying hours per month. The Federal Express Model 208As differ from the standard aircraft in having a King avionics installation, no cabin windows or starboard side rear door, more freight tiedowns, an additional cargo net, an under-fuselage cargo pannier constructed from composites materials, a 15·2 cm (6 in) vertical extension to the fin/rudder, realigned exhaust outlet to keep exhaust gases clear of the pannier, and a max T-O weight of 3,629 kg (8,000 lb).

In the Spring of 1985 Cessna released brief details of a military derivative of the Caravan with the factory designation **U-27A**. This is similar to the civil model, but with increased ramp, T-O and landing weights, and is intended for troop transport, medevac, cargo, VIP and forward air control roles. A demonstrator (N9514F) was exhibited at the US Army Aviation Association of America convention in April 1986, and began a tour of US Army installations immediately afterwards. It was being evaluated for possible lease or purchase for air ambulance duties and/or use as an airborne control station for RPVs. Two U-27As have reportedly been delivered to the Liberian Army. The U-27A has the 2·38 m^3 (84 cu ft) cargo pannier of the Model 208A, and can be fitted with six underwing attachment points for a variety of stores, including drop tanks.

On 3 March 1986 the prototype (N9767F) of a 'stretched' version of the Caravan I made its first flight. This aircraft, known as the **Model 208B** and developed at the request of Federal Express Corporation, has a 1,587 kg (3,500 lb) payload and 12·7 m^3 (450 cu ft) of cargo space, including belly cargo pod. Certification was expected in October 1986. Seventy of the Caravan Is on order for Federal Express will be 'stretched' versions, which have a 1·22 m (4 ft 0 in) increase in fuselage length achieved by plug inserts fore and aft of the wing centre-section.

The name Caravan II applies to an unrelated twin-turboprop business and utility transport aircraft, developed jointly by Cessna and Reims Aviation of France and described under the latter company's entry. The following description applies to Cessna's single-engined Model 208 Caravan I:

TYPE: Single-engined turboprop utility aircraft.

WINGS: Braced high-wing monoplane, with constant chord inner panels and tapered outer panels. Wing section NACA 23017.424 at root, NACA 23012 at tip. Dihedral 3° from roots. Incidence 2° 37′ at root, −0° 36′ at tip. Fail-safe two-spar structure. Single streamline section bracing strut each side. Electrically actuated wide span single-slotted flaps occupy more than 70 per cent of wing trailing-edge, and extend to 30° setting for low landing speeds. Ailerons operate in conjunction with slot-lip spoilers for positive roll control. Aileron trim standard.

FUSELAGE: Conventional semi-monocoque structure.

TAIL UNIT: Cantilever structure, with long dorsal fin. All control surfaces horn balanced. Large trim tab in starboard elevator. Rudder trim standard.

LANDING GEAR: Non-retractable tricycle type, with single wheel on each unit. Tubular spring cantilever main units; oil-damped spring nosewheel unit. Mainwheel tyres size 6·50-10; nosewheel 6·50-8. Oversize tyres, mainwheels 8·50-10, nosewheel 22 × 8·00-8, optional. Hydraulically actuated single-disc brake on each mainwheel. Certificated in floatplane and amphibian versions, with floats by Wipline, and with ski landing gear.

POWER PLANT: One Pratt & Whitney Canada PT6A-114 turboprop engine, flat rated at 447 kW (600 shp) to 3,800 m (12,500 ft), and driving a Hartzell three-blade constant-speed reversible-pitch and feathering composites propeller type HC-B3MN3/M10083 with spinner. Integral fuel tanks in wings, total capacity 1,268 litres (335 US gallons), of which 1,257 litres (332 US gallons) are usable.

ACCOMMODATION: Pilot and up to nine passengers or 1,360 kg (3,000 lb) of cargo. Maximum seating capacity with FAR Pt 23 waiver is 14. Cabin has a flat floor with Brownline cargo track attachments for a combination of two- and three-abreast seating, with an aisle between the seats. Forward hinged door for pilot, with direct vision window, on each side of forward fuselage. Airstair door for passengers at rear of cabin on starboard side. Cabin is heated and ventilated. Optional air-conditioning. Two-section horizontally split cargo door at rear of cabin on port side, flush with floor at bottom and with square corners. Upper portion hinges upward, lower portion forward 180°. In a cargo role cabin will accommodate typically two D-size cargo containers or up to ten 208 litre (55 US gallon) drums.

SYSTEMS: Electrical system is powered by 28V 200A starter/generator and 24V 45Ah lead-acid battery (24V 40Ah nickel-cadmium battery optional). Standby electrical system, with 95A alternator, optional. Hydraulic system for brakes only. Oxygen system, capacity 3·31 m^3 (116·95 cu ft), optional. Vacuum system standard. Cabin air-conditioning system optional on c/n 208-00030 onwards. De-icing system, comprising electric propeller de-icing boots, pneumatic wing, wing strut and tail surface boots, electric heated windscreen panel, heated pitot/static probe, ice detector light and standby electrical system, all optional.

AVIONICS AND EQUIPMENT: Standard avionics include Sperry Series 300 nav/com, ADF, 400 transponder and audio console/intercom. Optional avionics include Sperry Series 400, with autopilot and area navigation system, King Silver Crown Basic and IFR avionics packages and Bendix RDS-82 colour weather radar, pod mounted on starboard wing leading-edge. Standard equipment includes sensitive altimeter, electric clock, magnetic compass, attitude and directional gyros, true airspeed indicator, turn and bank indicator, vertical speed indicator, ammeter/voltmeter, fuel flow indicator, ITT indicator, oil pressure and temperature indicator, windscreen defrost, ground service plug receptacle, variable intensity instrument post lighting, map light, overhead courtesy lights (3) and overhead floodlights (pilot and co-pilot), approach plate holder, cargo tiedowns, internal corrosion proofing, vinyl floor covering, emergency locator beacon, partial plumbing for oxygen system, adjustable fore/aft/vertical/reclining pilot's seat with seatbelt and dual inertia reel shoulder restraints, tinted windows, control surface bonding straps, heated pitot and stall warning systems, retractable crew steps (port side), tiedowns and towbar. Optional equipment includes co-pilot's and passenger seats, stowable, folding utility seats, digital clock, fuel totaliser, turn co-ordinator, flight hour recorder, fire extinguisher, dual controls, co-pilot flight instruments, floatplane kit (on c/n 208-00030 onwards), hoisting rings (for floatplane), inboard fuel filling provisions (included in floatplane kit), ice detection light, courtesy lights on wing leading-edge, passenger reading lights, omniflash beacon, rudder gust lock, retractable crew step for starboard side, oversized tyres, electric trim system, oil quick drain valve and fan driven ventilation system.

DIMENSIONS, EXTERNAL (Model 208):
Wing span 15·88 m (52 ft 1 in)
Wing chord: at root 1·98 m (6 ft 6 in)
at tip 1·22 m (4 ft 0 in)
Wing aspect ratio 9·61
Length overall 11·46 m (37 ft 7 in)
Height overall: landplane 4·32 m (14 ft 2 in)
amphibian (on land) 5·33 m (17 ft 6 in)
Tailplane span 6·25 m (20 ft 6 in)
Wheel track: landplane 3·56 m (11 ft 8 in)
amphibian 3·25 m (10 ft 8 in)
Wheelbase: landplane 3·54 m (11 ft 7½ in)
amphibian 4·44 m (14 ft 7 in)
Propeller diameter 2·54 m (8 ft 4 in)
Airstair door: Height 1·27 m (4 ft 2 in)
Width 0·61 m (2 ft 0 in)
Cargo door: Height 1·27 m (4 ft 2 in)
Width 1·24 m (4 ft 1 in)

DIMENSIONS, INTERNAL (Model 208):
Cabin: Length, excl baggage area 4·57 m (15 ft 0 in)
Max width 1·57 m (5 ft 2 in)
Max height 1·30 m (4 ft 3 in)
Volume 9·67 m^3 (341·4 cu ft)

AREAS:
Wings, gross 25·96 m^2 (279·4 sq ft)
Vertical tail surfaces (incl dorsal fin) 3·57 m^2 (38·41 sq ft)
Horizontal tail surfaces 6·51 m^2 (70·04 sq ft)

WEIGHTS AND LOADINGS (Civil Model 208. L: landplane; F: floatplane; A: amphibian):
Weight empty: L 1,724 kg (3,800 lb)
F 2,020 kg (4,454 lb)
A 2,177 kg (4,799 lb)
Max baggage (all) 147 kg (325 lb)
Max fuel (all) 1,009 kg (2,224 lb)
Max ramp weight: L 3,327 kg (7,335 lb)
F, A 3,463 kg (7,635 lb)
Max T-O and landing weight, and max zero-fuel weight:
L 3,311 kg (7,300 lb)
F, A 3,447 kg (7,600 lb)
Max wing loading: L 127·4 kg/m^2 (26·1 lb/sq ft)
F, A 132·8 kg/m^2 (27·2 lb/sq ft)
Max power loading: L 7·41 kg/kW (12·2 lb/shp)
F, A 7·71 kg/kW (12·7 lb/shp)

WEIGHTS (U-27A: L, F and A as above):
Weight empty, standard:
L 1,769 kg (3,900 lb)
F 2,020 kg (4,454 lb)
A 2,177 kg (4,799 lb)
Max ramp weight: L 3,645 kg (8,035 lb)
F, A 3,463 kg (7,635 lb)
Max T-O weight: L 3,629 kg (8,000 lb)
F, A 3,447 kg (7,600 lb)
Max landing weight: L 3,538 kg (7,800 lb)
F, A 3,311 kg (7,300 lb)

PERFORMANCE (Civil Model 208. L: landplane; F: floatplane; A: amphibian):
Max operating speed (all) 175 knots (325 km/h; 202 mph) IAS
Max cruising speed at 3,050 m (10,000 ft):
L 184 knots (341 km/h; 212 mph)
F 159 knots (295 km/h; 183 mph)
A 153 knots (283 km/h; 176 mph)
Stalling speed, power off:
L, flaps up 73 knots (135 km/h; 84 mph) CAS
L, flaps down 60 knots (111 km/h; 69 mph) CAS
F, A, landing configuration 58 knots (107 km/h; 67 mph) CAS
Max rate of climb at S/L: L 370 m (1,215 ft)/min
F 306 m (1,004 ft)/min
A 290 m (952 ft)/min
Service ceiling: L 8,410 m (27,600 ft)
F 7,285 m (23,900 ft)
A 7,010 m (23,000 ft)
Max operating altitude (all) 9,145 m (30,000 ft)
T-O run: L 296 m (970 ft)
T-O run, water: F 468 m (1,535 ft)
A 469 m (1,540 ft)
T-O to 15 m (50 ft): L 507 m (1,665 ft)
T-O to 15 m (50 ft), water: F 843 m (2,765 ft)
A 859 m (2,820 ft)
Landing from 15 m (50 ft): L 472 m (1,550 ft)
Landing run: L 197 m (645 ft)
Range with max fuel, at max cruise power, allowances for start, taxi and 45 min reserves:
L at 3,050 m (10,000 ft) 970 nm (1,797 km; 1,117 miles)
L at 6,100 m (20,000 ft) 1,275 nm (2,362 km; 1,468 miles)
F at 3,050 m (10,000 ft), 30 min reserves 898 nm (1,664 km; 1,034 miles
A at 3,050 m (10,000 ft), 30 min reserves 868 nm (1,608 km; 999 miles)
Range with max fuel at max range power, allowances as above:
L at 3,050 m (10,000 ft) 1,115 nm (2,066 km; 1,284 miles)
L at 6,100 nm (20,000 ft) 1,370 nm (2,539 km; 1,578 miles
g limits +3·8/−1·52

PERFORMANCE (U-27A: L, F and A as above):
Max cruising speed at 3,050 m (10,000 ft):
L 182 knots (337 km/h; 209 mph)
F 158 knots (293 km/h; 182 mph)
A 153 knots (283 km/h; 176 mph)
Stalling speed in landing configuration:
L, F, A 61 knots (113 km/h; 71 mph)
Max rate of climb at S/L: L 314 m (1,030 ft)/min
F 288 m (944 ft)/min
A 271 m (889 ft)/min
Service ceiling: L 7,410 m (24,300 ft)
F 7,285 m (23,900 ft)
A 7,010 m (23,000 ft)
T-O run at S/L: L 365 m (1,195 ft)
T-O run at S/L, water: F 575 m (1,886 ft)
A 588 m (1,927 ft)
T-O to 15 m (50 ft) at S/L: L 662 m (2,170 ft)
T-O to 15 m (50 ft) at S/L, water: F 989 m (3,243 ft)
A 1,019 m (3,341 ft)
Landing from 15 m (50 ft) at S/L, without propeller reversal: L 496 m (1,625 ft)
Landing run at S/L, without propeller reversal:
L 218 m (715 ft)
Range at 3,050 m (10,000 ft) at max cruise power, allowances for T-O climb, cruise, descent, and 45 min reserves:
L 950 nm (1,760 km; 1,094 miles)
F 898 nm (1,664 km; 1,034 miles)
A 868 nm (1,608 km; 1,000 miles)

CESSNA CENTURION, TURBO CENTURION and PRESSURISED CENTURION

A total of 8,397 Model 210/Centurions, plus an additional 843 Pressurised Centurions, had been delivered by 31 December 1985. Production of all Models of the Centurion has been suspended. Full descriptions can be found in the 1985-86 *Jane's*.

CESSNA MODEL T303 CRUSADER

Production of this six-seat, turbocharged twin-engined aircraft has been suspended. A total of 295 T303 Crusaders had been delivered by 31 December 1985. The aircraft was fully described and illustrated in the 1985-86 *Jane's*.

CESSNA MODEL 402C

Production of the Model 402C Utiliner and Model 402C Businessliner has been suspended. A total of 1,535 Model 402s had been delivered by 31 December 1985. Full descriptions and illustrations can be found in the 1985-86 *Jane's*.

REIMS-CESSNA MODEL F 406/CARAVAN II

Details of this joint programme for a twin-turboprop business/utility transport can be found under the Reims Aviation entry in the French section.

CESSNA MODEL 414A CHANCELLOR

Production of the pressurised Model 414A Chancellor has been suspended. By 31 December 1985 Cessna had delivered 542 examples of this aircraft, a full description of which appeared in the 1985-86 *Jane's*.

Cessna Model 208A Caravan IA of Federal Express (left) with prototype of the stretched Model 208B

CESSNA MODEL 421 GOLDEN EAGLE

The prototype of this six/eight-seat pressurised twin-engined business aircraft flew for the first time on 14 October 1965. FAA type approval was received on 1 May 1967 and deliveries began in the same month.

Two developed versions were produced subsequently as the 421B Golden Eagle and 421B Executive Commuter, remaining in production until replaced by the Model 421C Golden Eagle in 1976.

A total of 1,901 Model 421s had been delivered by 31 December 1985. Production was suspended during that year. A full description and illustration can be found in the 1985-86 *Jane's*.

CESSNA MODEL 425 CONQUEST I

Known as the Corsair until late 1982, the Conquest I is a twin-turboprop business aircraft based on the airframe of the Model 421 Golden Eagle (last described in the 1985-86 *Jane's*). Design began on 1 November 1977, and a prototype flew for the first time on 12 September 1978; construction of a pre-production example was started during 1979. FAA certification was gained by mid-1980. Initial deliveries of production aircraft were made in November 1980, and 132 Corsairs were delivered.

Aircraft c/n 119 introduced new avionics options that include the Sperry Series 1000 R/Nav, Collins PN-101 or Sperry RD-44 HSI, and Sperry AA-300 radio altimeter. Compressor wash rings are installed as standard to simplify engine cleaning, and a number of new optional cabin accessories, furnishings and interior trims are available. All Corsair/Conquest I owners are able to participate in the company's CesCom computerised maintenance programme. A total of 214 Corsairs and Conquest Is had been delivered by 31 December 1985.

Cessna Conquest I six/eight-seat twin-turboprop pressurised transport

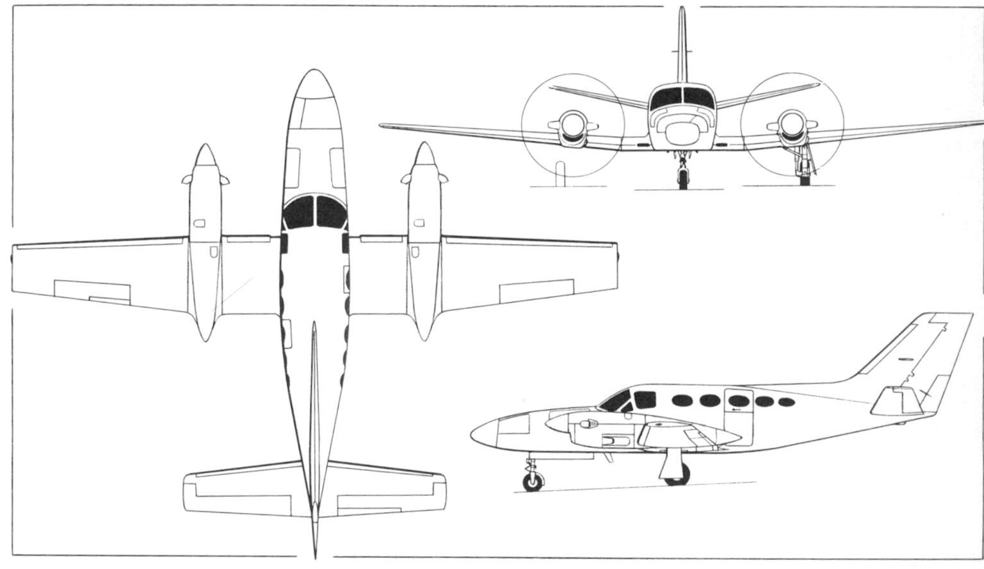

Cessna Conquest I (two Pratt & Whitney Canada PT6A-112 turboprop engines) (*Pilot Press*)

TYPE: Six/eight-seat pressurised light transport.

WINGS: Cantilever low-wing monoplane. Wing section NACA 23018-63 (modified) at root, NACA 23015 (modified) at centreline of engine nacelles, NACA 23009-63 (modified) at tip. Dihedral 5° on outer panels. Incidence 2° 30′ at root, −0° 30′ at tip. All-metal two-spar structure of light alloy, with stamped ribs and surface skins reinforced with spanwise stringers. Outer wing panels of bonded construction. All-metal ailerons and electrically operated trailing-edge split flaps. Trim tab in port aileron. Optional pneumatic de-icing of wing leading-edges.

FUSELAGE: Conventional all-metal semi-monocoque structure, with fail-safe construction in the pressurised section.

TAIL UNIT: Conventional all-metal cantilever structure, with sweptback vertical surfaces. Tailplane has dihedral of 12°. Trim tab in starboard elevator, with dual heavy duty actuator. Trim tab in rudder. Optional pneumatic de-icing of fin and tailplane leading-edges.

LANDING GEAR: Hydraulically retractable tricycle type with single wheel on each unit, main units retracting inward, nosewheel aft. Oleo-pneumatic shock absorbers, with main units of articulated (trailing link) type. Steerable nosewheel. All wheels with tubed tyres, mainwheel tyres size 6·50-10, 10-ply rating, pressure 5·17 bars (75 lb/sq in), nosewheel tyre size 6·00-6, 6-ply rating, pressure 2·76 bars (40 lb/sq in). Hydraulic disc brakes. Parking brake.

POWER PLANT: Two Pratt & Whitney Canada PT6A-112 turboprop engines, flat rated at 335·5 kW (450 shp), each driving a Hartzell Type 9910438-1 or McCauley Type 9910535-1 wide-chord three-blade constant-speed fully-feathering and reversible-pitch metal propeller. Propellers autofeather when engines are at rest. Fuel contained in integral tanks in outer wing panels, nacelle cells, and inboard collector tanks, with combined capacity of 1,411 litres (372·8 US gallons), of which 1,385 litres (366 US gallons) are usable. Refuelling point above each engine nacelle. Oil capacity 17·4 litres (4·6 US gallons). Engine inlet ducts have a separator mechanism to prevent ingestion of water. Propeller de-icing and synchrophaser standard. Engine fire detection system standard.

ACCOMMODATION: Two seats side by side in pilot's compartment, with dual controls. Optional curtain, or solid divider with curtain, to separate pilot's compartment from main cabin. Standard seating provides for four passengers, but optional arrangements have the front passenger seats facing aft and forward-facing seventh and eighth seats. Optional equipment includes storage drawers, refreshment centre, tables, toilet, radio telephone, stereo system, and aft cabin divider. Door is of two-piece type, with built-in airstairs in bottom portion, on port side of cabin at rear. Plug type emergency escape hatch overwing on starboard side of cabin. Foul weather windows on each side of fuselage for pilot and co-pilot. Baggage accommodated in nose with external doors, capacity 272 kg (600 lb), and in rear of cabin area, capacity 227 kg (500 lb). Total baggage capacity 499 kg (1,100 lb). Accommodation is pressurised, heated and air-conditioned. Windscreen defroster standard. Electrically heated windscreen and alcohol windscreen anti-icing optional.

SYSTEMS: Freon air-conditioning system of 17,500 BTU capacity, plus engine bleed air and electric boost heating. Pressurisation system with max differential of 0·35 bars (5·0 lb/sq in) provides a 3,050 m (10,000 ft) cabin altitude to 8,075 m (26,500 ft), or 3,625 m (11,900 ft) cabin altitude to 9,145 m (30,000 ft). Electrical system includes a 28V 250A starter/generator on each engine and a 39Ah nickel-cadmium battery. Hydraulic system, pressure 120 bars (1,750 lb/sq in), for operation of landing gear. Separate hydraulic system for brakes. Vacuum system for blind-flying instrumentation and optional wing and tail unit de-icing. Oxygen system of 0·31 m³ (11·0 cu ft) capacity standard; a 3·25 m³ (114·9 cu ft) capacity system is optional. Engine fire detection system standard, extinguishing system optional.

AVIONICS AND EQUIPMENT: Standard avionics include a basic avionics kit comprising audio panel, cabin and cockpit speakers, combination microphone/headset for pilot, hand held microphone, and an avionics cooling system; Sperry Series 1000 avionics including dual coms, navs and glideslope receivers, ADF, DME, glideslope, marker beacon receiver, RMI, transponder, Series 400 encoding altimeter, 1000A autopilot with PN-101 indicator and C-14 compass system. An alternative factory installed avionics package of Collins Proline II equipment is available. Optional Sperry or Collins avionics to complement the above systems are available, and other options include Sperry flight directors, colour or monochromatic weather radar by Bendix, Collins and Sperry R/Nav systems, and GNS-500A VLF/Omega. Standard equipment includes dual sensitive altimeters (port encoding), electric clock, artificial horizons (port and starboard), directional gyro (starboard only), outside air temperature gauge, turn and bank indicator, dual rate of climb indicators, fuel flow indicators, instrument panel glareshield, sun visors, instrument post lights, map light, emergency floodlight, dual controls, control lock, audible stall warning system, fore and aft adjustable and tilting pilot and co-pilot seats with seat belts and shoulder harnesses, map and storage pockets, four adjustable and reclining passenger seats with seat belts, armrests and headrests, cabin differential pressure gauge, cabin rate of climb indicator, adjustable air-conditioning and ventilator outlets, annunciator panel lights, circuit breaker lights, individual reading lights, entrance door courtesy light, double pane windows, window curtains, cabin fire extinguisher, internal corrosion proofing, soundproofing, cargo tiedown rings, baggage straps, emergency locator transmitter, dual landing lights, taxi and navigation lights, high intensity strobe lights, full flow oil filters, quick drain fuel valves, static discharge wicks, ground power socket, heated pitot and stall warning transmitter, jack pads, nosewheel fender, towbar and all-over paint scheme. Optional equipment includes fifth and sixth passenger seats, digital clock, angle of attack and instantaneous rate of climb indicators, co-pilot's turn and bank indicator, flight hour recorder, inertia reel shoulder harnesses for pilot and co-pilot, rudder gust lock, curtain or rigid flight deck dividers, 'Fasten seat belts—no smoking' sign, a variety of cabin furnishings including drawers, refreshment centres, tables and toilets, 'total flood' cabin fire extinguisher, tinted inner window panes, courtesy light timer, fuselage ice protection plates, ice detection lights, nose baggage compartment light, and heated static source.

DIMENSIONS, EXTERNAL:

Wing span	13·45 m (44 ft 1½ in)
Wing chord: at root	1·77 m (5 ft 9¾ in)
at tip	1·05 m (3 ft 5½ in)
Wing aspect ratio	8·65
Length overall	10·93 m (35 ft 10¼ in)
Height overall	3·84 m (12 ft 7¼ in)
Tailplane span	5·82 m (19 ft 1 in)
Wheel track	5·30 m (17 ft 4½ in)
Wheelbase	3·20 m (10 ft 6 in)
Propeller diameter: Hartzell	2·37 m (7 ft 9¼ in)
McCauley	2·36 m (7 ft 9 in)
Passenger door: Height	1·30 m (4 ft 3 in)
Width	0·64 m (2 ft 1 in)
Height to sill	1·21 m (3 ft 11½ in)
Emergency exit (stbd, overwing)	
Height	0·69 m (2 ft 3 in)
Width	0·52 m (1 ft 8½ in)

Nose baggage doors (each):
Max height 0·41 m (1 ft 4 in)
Width 0·86 m (2 ft 9¾ in)

DIMENSIONS, INTERNAL:
Cabin: Length 4·83 m (15 ft 9¾ in)
Max width 1·40 m (4 ft 7 in)
Max height 1·29 m (4 ft 3 in)
Volume 6·39 m³ (225·6 cu ft)
Nose avionics/baggage compartment volume 0·95 m³ (33·4 cu ft)
Rear cabin baggage volume 0·87 m³ (30·6 cu ft)

AREAS:
Wings, gross 20·90 m² (224·98 sq ft)
Ailerons (total) 1·32 m² (14·16 sq ft)
Trailing-edge flaps (total) 2·14 m² (23·06 sq ft)
Fin 2·06 m² (22·20 sq ft)
Rudder (incl tab) 1·78 m² (19·15 sq ft)
Tailplane 3·84 m² (41·35 sq ft)
Elevators (total, incl tab) 1·99 m² (21·44 sq ft)

WEIGHTS AND LOADINGS:
Weight empty, equipped 2,242 kg (4,944 lb)
Max fuel weight 1,112 kg (2,452 lb)
Max T-O weight 3,901 kg (8,600 lb)
Max ramp weight 3,935 kg (8,675 lb)
Max zero-fuel weight 3,175 kg (7,000 lb)
Max landing weight 3,629 kg (8,000 lb)
Max wing loading 186·7 kg/m² (38·23 lb/sq ft)
Max power loading 5·81 kg/kW (9·56 lb/shp)

PERFORMANCE (at max T-O weight, ISA, except where indicated):
Never-exceed speed Mach 0·52 (230 knots; 426 km/h; 265 mph) IAS
Max cruising speed at 5,485 m (18,000 ft) at AUW of 3,175 kg (7,000 lb) 264 knots (489 km/h; 304 mph)
Cruising speed at 9,145 m (30,000 ft), mid-cruise weight 250 knots (463 km/h; 288 mph)
Econ cruising speed at 9,145 m (30,000 ft), mid-cruise weight 210 knots (389 km/h; 242 mph)
Stalling speed, engines idling:
flaps and landing gear up 88 knots (163 km/h; 102 mph) CAS
flaps and landing gear down 84 knots (156 km/h; 97 mph) CAS
Min single-engined control speed (VMC) 92 knots (170 km/h; 106 mph) IAS
Max rate of climb at S/L 567 m (1,861 ft)/min
Rate of climb at S/L, one engine out 109 m (357 ft)/min
Service ceiling 9,144 m (30,000 ft)
Service ceiling, one engine out 5,240 m (17,200 ft)
T-O run 661 m (2,170 ft)
T-O to 15 m (50 ft) 759 m (2,490 ft)
Landing from 15 m (50 ft) 655 m (2,150 ft)
Landing run 291 m (955 ft)
Range with max fuel at max cruising power, allowances for start, taxi, T-O, climb to cruise altitude, descent, and 45 min reserves at max cruise power:
at 6,100 m (20,000 ft) 1,012 nm (1,874 km; 1,165 miles)
at 9,145 m (30,000 ft) 1,387 nm (2,569 km; 1,596 miles)
Range with max fuel at max range power, allowances as above, and 45 min reserves at max range power:
at 6,100 m (20,000 ft) 1,339 nm (2,480 km; 1,541 miles)
at 9,145 m (30,000 ft) 1,576 nm (2,919 km; 1,814 miles)

CESSNA MODELS 441 and 435 CONQUEST II

Cessna announced on 15 November 1974 that it was developing the twin-turboprop **Model 441** to slot into the market gap between contemporary twin piston engined aircraft and turbofan powered business aircraft. Marketed initially as the Conquest, and as Conquest II from 1983, this aircraft is powered by Garrett TPE331-8-403S turboprop engines, which were developed specially to meet the high-altitude high-speed requirements set for it by Cessna. Its high performance stems in part from use of a high aspect ratio bonded wing, and from the high strength trailing link landing gear.

The prototype of the Conquest/Conquest II flew for the first time on 26 August 1975 and 345 had been delivered by 31 December 1985.

In the Spring of 1986 Cessna was test flying a Conquest II powered by Pratt & Whitney Canada PT6A turboprop engines and known as the **Model 435**. No further details have been released.

Production aircraft from c/n 116 have as standard an automatic engine torque and temperature limiting system, propeller synchrophaser, fuselage ice protection plates, pneumatic actuator for cabin upper door, new low-pressure fuel boost pumps, and fuel pressure switch. From and including c/n 173, the certificated altitude was increased to 10,670 m (35,000 ft); quick-donning pilot and co-pilot oxygen masks were introduced, and additional options include Collins radios with electronic display, a dual inverter installation, Bendix RDR 160 colour radar display, and underseat storage drawers. From c/n 195 the original Hartzell propellers were replaced by McCauley equivalents that offer a weight saving of 5·2 kg (11·5 lb) each.

In addition to benefiting from the company's CesCom computerised maintenance programme, customers now receive a warranty for the Conquest II's Garrett engines, covering them over a period of 3,000 h or 50 months.

Cessna Conquest II (two Garrett TPE331-8-403S turboprop engines)

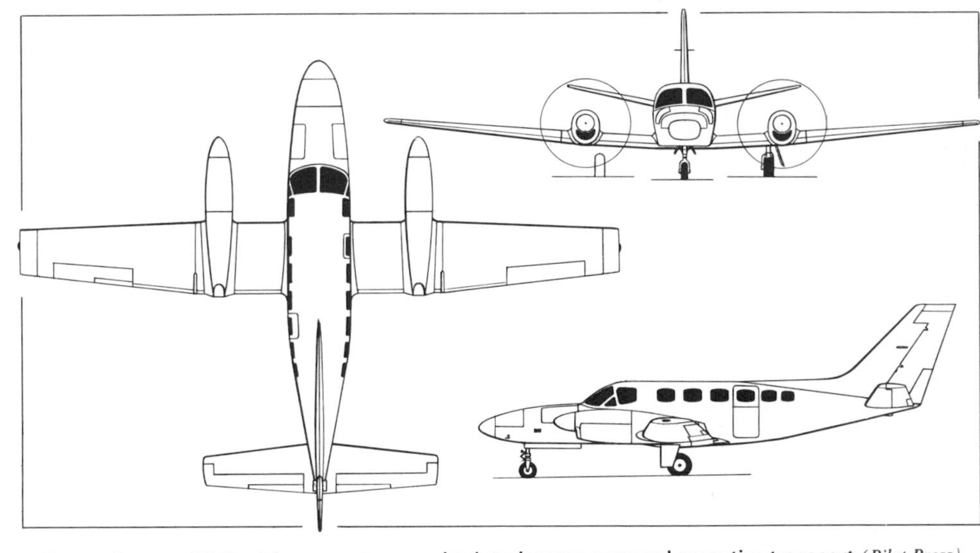

Cessna Conquest II five/eleven-seat pressurised, turboprop powered executive transport *(Pilot Press)*

TYPE: Five/eleven-seat pressurised executive transport.

WINGS: Cantilever low-wing monoplane. Wing section NACA 23018 at root, NACA 23019 at tip. Dihedral 3° 30′ on wing centre-section, 4° 55′ on outer panels. Incidence 2° at root, −1° at construction tip. All-metal three-spar centre-section structure to meet FAR 23 fail-safe requirements: two-spar structure for outer wing panels. Hydraulically operated Fowler trailing-edge flaps of light alloy construction. Plain ailerons of light alloy construction. Trim tab in port aileron. Pneumatic de-icing system optional.

FUSELAGE: All-metal semi-monocoque structure of light alloy.

TAIL UNIT: Cantilever structure with sweptback vertical surfaces. Dihedral 12° on horizontal surfaces. Large tab in each elevator and rudder.

LANDING GEAR: Hydraulically retractable tricycle type with single wheel on each unit. Main units retract inward into wing, nosewheel rearward. Emergency extension by means of a 138 bar (2,000 lb/sq in) rechargeable nitrogen bottle. Cessna oleo-pneumatic shock absorbers. All legs of articulated (trailing link) type. Cleveland mainwheels with tubeless tyres size 22 × 7·75-10, pressure 6·55 bars (95 lb/sq in). Cleveland nosewheel with tubed tyre size 6·00-6, pressure 3·45 bars (50 lb/sq in). Cleveland single-disc hydraulic brakes. Parking brake.

POWER PLANT: Two Garrett TPE331-8-403S turboprop engines, each flat rated at 474 kW (635·5 shp) to 4,875 m (16,000 ft). Hartzell Type HC-B3TN-5E/T10178B-11 constant-speed fully-feathering and reversible-pitch three-blade propellers up to and including airframe c/n 194; McCauley 3GFR34C60T/93JA3 propellers subsequently Total fuel capacity 1,823 litres (481·5 US gallons), of which 1,798 litres (475 US gallons) are usable. Refuelling point on upper surface of each wing. Oil capacity 14·2 litres (3·75 US gallons).

ACCOMMODATION: Seats for four to ten persons, and pilot, in pressurised and air-conditioned cabin. Various optional seating arrangements. Six rectangular windows on each side. Door aft of wing on port side, with upward hinged top portion and downward hinged lower portion with integral airstairs. Emergency exit over wing on starboard side. Baggage door on each side of nose. Max baggage capacity 680 kg (1,500 lb). Optional items include aft cabin divider, refreshment centre, toilet, writing tables and stereo system.

SYSTEMS: Pressurisation system max differential 0·43 bars (6·3 lb/sq in). Freon air-conditioning systems of 8,000 BTU or 16,000 BTU capacity optional. Hydraulic system for operation of flaps and landing gear, pressure 120·7 bars (1,750 lb/sq in). Separate hydraulic system for brakes. Emergency extension of landing gear by means of 138 bar (2,000 lb/sq in) rechargeable gas bottle. Electrical power supplied by two 28V 200A starter/generators; two 24V 22Ah nickel-cadmium batteries housed in nose compartment. Electronic fuel control system. Oxygen bottle, capacity 0·31 m³ (11·0 cu ft) standard; 0·62 or 3·25 m³ (22·0 or 114·9 cu ft) systems optional.

AVIONICS AND EQUIPMENT: Generally similar to those detailed for the Conquest I, except that the Series 1000 autopilot is replaced by the Series 1000 IFCS. There is also a wider range of optional cabin furnishings.

DIMENSIONS, EXTERNAL:
Wing span over tip lights 15·04 m (49 ft 4 in)
Wing chord: at root 1·78 m (5 ft 10 in)
at tip 1·23 m (4 ft 0¼ in)
Wing aspect ratio 9·5
Length overall 11·89 m (39 ft 0¼ in)
Height overall 4·01 m (13 ft 1¾ in)
Tailplane span 5·81 m (19 ft 1 in)
Wheel track 4·28 m (14 ft 0½ in)
Wheelbase 3·81 m (12 ft 5⅞ in)
Propeller diameter 2·29 m (7 ft 6 in)
Cabin door (port, rear): Height 1·30 m (4 ft 3 in)
Width 0·64 m (2 ft 1 in)
Emergency exit (stbd, fwd):
Height 0·67 m (2 ft 2½ in)
Width 0·58 m (1 ft 10¾ in)
Nose baggage doors (each):
Max height 0·41 m (1 ft 4 in)
Width 0·86 m (2 ft 9¾ in)

DIMENSIONS, INTERNAL:
Cabin: Length 5·71 m (18 ft 9 in)
Max width 1·41 m (4 ft 7½ in)
Max height 1·29 m (4 ft 3 in)

AREAS:
Wings, gross 23·56 m² (253·6 sq ft)
Ailerons (total) 1·37 m² (14·74 sq ft)
Trailing-edge flaps (total) 3·99 m² (42·99 sq ft)
Fin 2·54 m² (27·33 sq ft)
Rudder (incl tab) 1·50 m² (16·15 sq ft)

Tailplane 4·21 m² (45·31 sq ft)
Elevators (incl tabs) 1·82 m² (19·57 sq ft)

WEIGHTS AND LOADINGS:
Weight empty, approx 2,631 kg (5,801 lb)
Max usable fuel 1,444 kg (3,183 lb)
Max ramp weight 4,502 kg (9,925 lb)
Max T-O weight 4,468 kg (9,850 lb)
Max landing weight 4,246 kg (9,360 lb)
Max zero-fuel weight 3,855 kg (8,500 lb)
Max wing loading 189·6 kg/m² (38·8 lb/sq ft)
Max power loading 4·79 kg/kW (7·88 lb/shp)

PERFORMANCE (at max T-O weight, ISA, unless otherwise indicated, except speeds are those at mid-cruise weight of 3,788 kg; 8,350 lb):
Never-exceed speed
Mach 0·55 (245 knots; 454 km/h; 282 mph) IAS
Max level speed at 4,875 m (16,000 ft)
295 knots (547 km/h; 340 mph)
Max cruising speed at 7,315 m (24,000 ft)
293 knots (543 km/h; 337 mph)
Econ cruising speed at 10,670 m (35,000 ft)
259 knots (480 km/h; 298 mph)
Econ cruising speed at 7,620 m (25,000 ft)
246 knots (456 km/h; 283 mph)
Stalling speed, gear and flaps up, engines idling
90 knots (167 km/h; 104 mph) CAS
Stalling speed, gear and flaps down, engines idling
76 knots (141 km/h; 88 mph) CAS
Stalling speed, gear and flaps down, power off, at max landing weight 75 knots (139 km/h; 87 mph) CAS
Min single-engined control speed (VMC)
91 knots (169 km/h; 105 mph) IAS
Max rate of climb at S/L 742 m (2,435 ft)/min
Rate of climb at S/L, one engine out
218 m (715 ft)/min
Service ceiling above 10,670 m (35,000 ft)
Service ceiling, one engine out 6,515 m (21,380 ft)
Max certificated operating altitude
10,670 m (35,000 ft)
T-O run 544 m (1,785 ft)
T-O to 15 m (50 ft) 751 m (2,465 ft)
Landing from 15 m (50 ft) at max landing weight
572 m (1,875 ft)
Landing run 334 m (1,095 ft)
Range at max T-O weight with 1,444 kg (3,183 lb) fuel, at max cruising power, allowances for engine start, taxi, T-O, climb, descent and 45 min reserves at max cruise power:
at 7,620 m (25,000 ft)
1,571 nm (2,909 km; 1,807 miles)
at 10,060 m (33,000 ft)
2,063 nm (3,820 km; 2,374 miles)
at 10,670 m (35,000 ft)
2,193 nm (4,064 km; 2,525 miles)
Range at max T-O weight and at max range power, allowances as above:
at 7,620 m (25,000 ft)
1,816 nm (3,363 km; 2,090 miles)
at 10,060 m (33,000 ft)
2,212 nm (4,096 km; 2,545 miles)
at 10,670 m (35,000 ft)
2,291 nm (4,245 km; 2,638 miles)

CESSNA MODEL 550 CITATION II

Announced on 14 September 1976, the Citation II introduced a fuselage lengthened by 1·14 m (3 ft 9 in) compared with the Citation I, an increased span high aspect ratio wing, increased fuel and baggage capacity, and Pratt & Whitney Canada JT15D-4 turbofan engines. The prototype (N550CC) flew for the first time on 31 January 1977, and certification to FAR Pt 25 Transport Category requirements was received in late March 1978 for two-pilot operation. The Model 551 Citation II/SP was subsequently introduced for single-pilot operation, with up to 10 passengers, at a max T-O weight of 5,670 kg (12,500 lb), conforming to FAR Pt 23 requirements.

Production of the Citation II was phased out during 1984 in favour of the improved Citation S/II (which see), at which time 504 Citation IIs had been delivered. At the National Business Aircraft Association convention at New Orleans in September 1985, Cessna announced that it would resume production of the Citation II, and first deliveries are due in the first quarter of 1987.

TYPE: Eight/twelve-seat twin-turbofan executive transport.

WINGS: Cantilever low-wing monoplane without sweepback. Wing section at c/l NACA 23014 (modified), at wing station 247·95 NACA 23012. Incidence 2° 30′ at c/l, −0° 30′ at wing station 247·95. Dihedral 4°. All-metal fail-safe structure with two primary spars, an auxiliary spar, three fuselage attachment points, and conventional ribs and stringers. Manually operated ailerons, with manual trim on port aileron. Electrically operated single-slotted trailing-edge flaps. Hydraulically operated aerodynamic speed brakes. Wing leading-edge forward of each engine is electrically anti-iced. Pneumatic de-icing boots on outer leading-edges.

FUSELAGE: All-metal pressurised structure of circular section. Fail-safe design, providing multiple load paths.

TAIL UNIT: Cantilever all-metal structure. Horizontal surfaces have dihedral of 9°. Large dorsal fin and smaller ventral fin. Manually operated control surfaces. Electric elevator trim with manual override; manual rudder trim.

LANDING GEAR: Hydraulically retractable tricycle type with single wheel on each unit. Main units retract inward into the wing, nose gear forward into fuselage nose. Free-fall and pneumatic emergency extension systems. Goodyear mainwheels with tyres size 22·0 × 8-10, 10-ply rating, pressure 6·90 bars (100 lb/sq in). Steerable nosewheel with Goodyear wheel and tyre size 18·0 × 4·4, 10-ply rating, pressure 8·27 bars (120 lb/sq in). Goodyear hydraulic brakes. Parking brake and pneumatic emergency brake system. Anti-skid system optional.

POWER PLANT: Two Pratt & Whitney Canada JT15D-4 turbofan engines, each rated at 11·12 kN (2,500 lb st) for take-off, mounted in pod on each side of rear fuselage. Integral fuel tanks in wings, with usable capacity of 2,808 litres (742 US gallons).

ACCOMMODATION: Crew of two on separate flight deck, on fully adjustable seats, with seat belts and inertia reel shoulder harness, and sun visors. Fully carpeted main cabin equipped with seats for six to ten passengers, with toilet in six/eight-seat versions. Main baggage area at rear of cabin. Second baggage area in nose. Total baggage capacity 522 kg (1,150 lb). Cabin is pressurised, heated and air-conditioned. Individual reading lights and air inlets for each passenger. Dropout constant-flow oxygen system for emergency use. Plug type door with integral airstair at front on port side and one emergency exit on starboard side. Doors on each side of nose baggage compartment. Tinted windows, each with curtains. Pilot's storm window, birdproof windscreen with de-fog system, anti-icing, standby alcohol anti-icing and bleed air rain removal system.

SYSTEMS: Pressurisation system supplied with engine bleed air, max pressure differential 0·59 bars (8·5 lb/sq in), maintaining a sea level cabin altitude to 6,720 m (22,040 ft), or a 2,440 m (8,000 ft) cabin altitude to 12,495 m (41,000 ft). Hydraulic system, pressure 103·5 bars (1,500 lb/sq in), with two pumps to operate landing gear and speed brakes. Separate hydraulic system for wheel brakes. Electrical system supplied by two 28V 400A DC starter/generators, with two 350VA inverters and 24V 40Ah nickel-cadmium battery. Oxygen system of 0·62 m³ (22 cu ft) capacity includes two crew demand masks and five dropout constant flow masks for passengers. High capacity oxygen system optional. Engine fire detection and extinguishing systems.

DIMENSIONS, EXTERNAL:
Wing span 15·76 m (51 ft 8½ in)
Wing aspect ratio 8·28
Length overall 14·39 m (47 ft 2½ in)
Height overall 4·57 m (15 ft 0 in)
Wheel track 5·36 m (17 ft 7 in)
Wheelbase 5·55 m (18 ft 2½ in)

DIMENSIONS, INTERNAL:
Cabin: Length, front to rear bulkhead
6·37 m (20 ft 10¾ in)
Max height 1·46 m (4 ft 9½ in)
Baggage capacity 1·84 m³ (65 cu ft)

AREAS:
Wings, gross 30·00 m² (322·9 sq ft)
Horizontal tail surfaces (total, incl tab)
6·56 m² (70·6 sq ft)
Vertical tail surfaces (total) 4·73 m² (50·9 sq ft)

WEIGHTS:
Weight empty, equipped 3,306 kg (7,289 lb)
Max fuel weight 2,272 kg (5,009 lb)
Max T-O weight 6,033 kg (13,300 lb)
Max ramp weight 6,123 kg (13,500 lb)
Max zero-fuel weight: standard 4,309 kg (9,500 lb)
optional 4,990 kg (11,000 lb)
Max landing weight 5,760 kg (12,700 lb)

PERFORMANCE (at max T-O weight, ISA, except where indicated):
Max operating speed:
S/L to 4,265 m (14,000 ft)
262 knots (486 km/h; 302 mph) IAS
4,265 m (14,000 ft) to 8,530 m (28,000 ft)
277 knots (513 km/h; 319 mph) IAS
Cruising speed at average cruise weight of 4,990 kg (11,000 lb) at 7,620 m (25,000 ft)
385 knots (713 km/h; 443 mph)
Stalling speed at max landing weight
82 knots (152 km/h; 95 mph) CAS
Max rate of climb at S/L 1,027 m (3,370 ft)/min
Rate of climb at S/L, one engine out
322 m (1,055 ft)/min
Max certificated altitude 13,105 m (43,000 ft)
Service ceiling, one engine out 7,680 m (25,200 ft)
T-O to 15 m (50 ft) 727 m (2,385 ft)
T-O balanced field length (FAR Pt 25) 912 m (2,990 ft)
FAR Pt 25 landing runway length at max landing weight
692 m (2,270 ft)
Range with max fuel, crew of two and six passengers, allowances for T-O, climb, cruise at 13,105 m (43,000 ft), descent, and 45 min reserves
1,657 nm (3,069 km; 1,907 miles)

OPERATIONAL NOISE LEVELS (FAR Pt 36):
T-O 80·1 EPNdB
Approach 90·5 EPNdB
Sideline 86·7 EPNdB

CESSNA MODEL S550 CITATION S/II

US Navy designation: T-47A

Cessna announced on 4 October 1983 first details of the Citation S/II, a new version of the Citation II. The improvements were introduced on the production line from aircraft c/n 506, delivered in the late Summer of 1984. They include a new wing aerofoil section, utilising Citation III supercritical technology, to reduce high-speed drag while retaining the Citation II's slow-speed handling and short-field capability; a modified wing/fuselage fairing to improve localised airflow; an extended wing inboard leading-edge, increasing wing area/lift and providing greater fuel capacity; modified engine pylon contours to reduce drag; sealed aileron/speed brake gaps, and faired flap coves, to reduce drag and improve lift; hydraulically actuated Fowler flaps of graphite composite construction, in two panels on each wing, which extend further inboard to provide additional lift/drag; ailerons of graphite composite construction with geared trim tabs to improve roll access response; a TKS glycol anti-icing system for the wing leading-edges; and a new -4B version of the Citation II's Pratt & Whitney Canada JT15D turbofan engines, which provides greater thrust at high altitudes. Tail unit anti-icing systems are no longer required.

Internal refinements include an increase in tailcone baggage volume to 0·79 m³ (28·0 cu ft); a headroom increase of 12·7 cm (5 in) in the totally private toilet area; soft-touch headliners that reduce sound levels; Citation III style seats with shoulder harness, lateral tracking for more head and elbow room, and built-in life jacket storage; and redesigned sidewall air ducts which improve cabin insulation and heating and also provide a better than ten per cent increase in aisle width. New options include a vanity unit for the toilet, refreshment centres of composite construction, a wide door for use in cargo, air ambulance and other special applications, and Sperry EFIS.

The first production configuration Citation S/II made its first flight on 14 February 1984; FAA certification, with exemption for single-pilot operation, was granted in July 1984. A total of 76 Citation S/IIs had been delivered by 31 December 1985.

In late 1985 Cessna delivered its first Citation S/II

Cessna Citation S/II eight/ten-seat executive jet

ambulance aircraft to the Province of Manitoba, Canada. The aircraft can accommodate single or double stretchers, up to four medical attendants and large quantities of medical oxygen. Two specially-equipped Citation S/IIs have also been delivered to the Chinese government for use by the Airborne Remote Sensing Centre of the Chinese Academy of Sciences. They are operated by the Flight Test Research Institute in Xian.

In May 1983, the US Navy awarded Cessna a $159·4 million contract for 15 Citation S/IIs for use in its Undergraduate Naval Flight Officer Training Systems Upgrade (UNFO/TSU) programme. These aircraft, known as the **Model 552** and designated **T-47A**, are replacing T-39Ds used previously to train personnel in use of air-to-air, air-to-surface, intercept and other radar equipment, as part of a five-year programme, plus a three-year option, covering provision of the aircraft, simulators, maintenance and pilot services. The T-47As differ from standard Citation S/IIs in having JT15D-5 turbofans and a shorter wing span, to increase rate of climb and make possible a speed of Mach 0·733 at 12,200 m (40,000 ft). Emerson supplies the nose mounted APQ-159 radar. The crew normally comprises a civilian pilot, Navy instructor and three students. The first T-47A made its first flight on 15 February 1984 and received FAA certification on 21 November 1984. Delivery was completed in the Summer of 1985.

The following description applies to the current production Model S550, except where indicated:

TYPE: Eight/ten-seat twin-turbofan executive transport.

WINGS: Cantilever low-wing monoplane without sweepback. Incidence 2° 30′ at c/l, −0° 30′ at wing station 247·95. Dihedral 4°. All-metal fail-safe structure with two primary spars, an auxiliary spar, three fuselage attachment points, and conventional ribs and stringers. Manually operated ailerons, of graphite composite construction, each with geared trim tab. Hydraulically operated trailing-edge Fowler flaps of graphite composite construction. Hydraulically operated aerodynamic speed brakes. Glycol anti-icing of leading-edges.

FUSELAGE: All-metal pressurised structure of circular section. Fail-safe design, providing multiple load paths.

TAIL UNIT: Cantilever all-metal structure. Horizontal surfaces have dihedral of 9°. Dorsal fin. Manually operated control surfaces. Electric elevator trim with manual override; manual rudder trim.

LANDING GEAR: Hydraulically retractable tricycle type with single wheel on each unit. Main units retract inward into the wing, nose gear forward into fuselage nose. Free-fall and pneumatic emergency extension systems. Goodyear mainwheels with tyres size 22·0 × 8-10, 12-ply rating, pressure 8·27 bars (120 lb/sq in). Steerable nosewheel with Goodyear wheel and tyre size 18·0 × 4·4, 10-ply rating, pressure 8·27 bars (120 lb/sq in). Goodyear hydraulic brakes. Parking brake and pneumatic emergency brake system. Anti-skid system optional.

POWER PLANT: Two Pratt & Whitney Canada JT15D-4B turbofans each rated at 11·12 kN (2,500 lb st) for take-off, mounted in a pod each side of rear fuselage. Integral fuel tanks in wings, with combined usable capacity of 3,263 litres (862 US gallons).

ACCOMMODATION: Crew of two on separate flight deck, on fully adjustable seats, with seat belts and inertia reel shoulder harness, and sun visors. Seating for six to eight passengers in main cabin. Standard interior configuration provides for six passenger seats, two forward and four aft facing, each with headrest, seat belt and diagonal inertia reel harness; flushing toilet aft; tracked refreshment centre; forward cabin divider with privacy curtain, aft cabin divider with sliding doors. Passenger service units containing an oxygen mask, air vent and reading light for each passenger. Three separate baggage areas, one in nose section, externally accessible, one in aft cabin area, and one in tailcone area, with a combined capacity of up to 658 kg (1,450 lb).

SYSTEMS: Pressurisation system supplied with engine bleed air, max pressure differential 0·61 bars (8·8 lb/sq in), maintaining a sea level cabin altitude to 6,962 m (22,842 ft), or a 2,440 m (8,000 ft) cabin altitude to 13,105 m (43,000 ft). Hydraulic system, pressure 103·5 bars (1,500 lb/sq in), with two pumps to operate landing gear and speed brakes. Pressurised reservoir. Separate hydraulic system for wheel brakes. Electrical system supplied by two 28V 300A engine driven DC starter/generators, with two 350VA inverters and 24V 40Ah nickel-cadmium battery. Oxygen system of 0·62 m³ (22 cu ft) capacity includes two crew demand masks and five dropout constant flow masks for passengers. High capacity oxygen system optional. Engine fire detection and extinguishing systems.

AVIONICS AND EQUIPMENT: Standard avionics package comprises Sperry SPZ-500 integrated flight director/autopilot system, with single-cue command bars, Sperry C-14D compass system, Sperry RD-450 (starboard) HSI, dual Collins VHF-22A com transceivers, dual Collins VIR-32 nav receivers with VOR/LOC, glideslope and marker beacon receivers, dual Collins RMI-30, Collins DME-42 with 339F-12 indicator, TDR-90 transponder, Collins ADF-60, and Sperry Primus 300SL colour weather radar. Optional advanced avionics and instrumentation are available according to customer choice, and include Bendix Series III integrated EFIS, nav/com and radar systems.

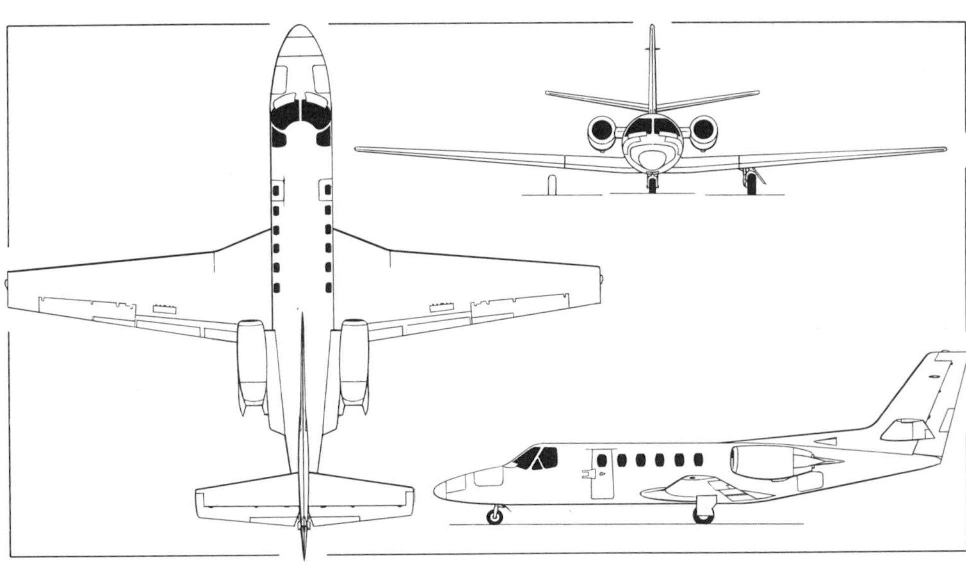

Cessna Citation S/II (Pratt & Whitney Canada JT15D-4B turbofan engines) *(Pilot Press)*

Cessna T-47A, a US Navy training version of the Citation S/II

DIMENSIONS, EXTERNAL:

Wing span over lights: S/II	15·90 m (52 ft 2½ in)
T-47A	14·18 m (46 ft 6 in)
Wing chord (mean): S/II	2·06 m (6 ft 9 in)
Wing aspect ratio: S/II	7·8
Length overall: S/II	14·39 m (47 ft 2½ in)
T-47A	14·60 m (47 ft 10¾ in)
Height overall: S/II	4·57 m (15 ft 0 in)
T-47A	4·51 m (14 ft 9¾ in)
Wheel track	5·36 m (17 ft 7 in)
Wheelbase	5·55 m (18 ft 2½ in)
Tailplane span: S/II	5·79 m (19 ft 0 in)
Cabin door (S/II, optional): Height	1·14 m (3 ft 9 in)
Width	0·89 m (2 ft 11 in)

DIMENSIONS, INTERNAL (S/II):

Cabin:	
Length, front to rear bulkhead	6·37 m (20 ft 10¾ in)
Max height	1·45 m (4 ft 9½ in)
Max width	1·49 m (4 ft 10¾ in)
Baggage capacity (total)	2·27 m³ (80 cu ft)

AREAS (S/II):

Wings, gross	31·83 m² (342·6 sq ft)
Horizontal tail surfaces (total)	6·48 m² (69·8 sq ft)
Vertical tail surfaces (total)	4·73 m² (50·9 sq ft)

WEIGHTS AND LOADINGS:

Weight empty, equipped: S/II	3,630 kg (8,002 lb)
T-47A	4,098 kg (9,035 lb)
Max baggage weight (S/II): internal	272 kg (600 lb)
external	385 kg (850 lb)
Max ramp weight: S/II	6,940 kg (15,300 lb)
Max fuel weight: S/II	2,640 kg (5,820 lb)
Max T-O weight: S/II	6,849 kg (15,100 lb)
T-47A	6,804 kg (15,000 lb)
Max landing weight: S/II	6,350 kg (14,400 lb)
Max zero-fuel weight: S/II	4,990 kg (11,200 lb)
Max wing loading	215·17 kg/m² (44·07 lb/sq ft
Max power loading	1·42 kg/kN (3·02 lb/lb st)

PERFORMANCE (S/II at max T-O weight, except where indicated):

Max operating speed:

S/L to 2,440 m (8,000 ft)
261 knots (483 km/h; 300 mph) IAS

2,440 m (8,000 ft) to 8,935 m (29,315 ft)
276 knots (511 km/h; 318 mph)

above 8,935 m (29,315 ft) Mach 0·721

Cruising speed at mid-cruise weight of 5,443 kg (12,000 lb) at 10,660 m (35,000 ft)
403 knots (746 km/h; 463 mph)

Stalling speed at max landing weight
81 knots (150 km/h; 94 mph)

Max rate of climb at S/L 926 m (3,040 ft)/min

Rate of climb at S/L, one engine out
262 m (860 ft)/min

Max operating altitude 13,105 m (43,000 ft)

T-O balanced field length (FAR Pt 25)
1,045 m (3,430 ft)

FAR 25 landing runway length at max landing weight
930 m (3,050 ft)

Range with six passengers, two crew and baggage
1,800 nm (3,336 km; 2,073 miles)

Range with max fuel 1,998 nm (3,701 km; 2,300 miles)

OPERATIONAL NOISE LEVELS (FAR Pt 36):

T-O	78·0 EPNdB
Approach	91·0 EPNdB
Sideline	90·4 EPNdB

CESSNA MODEL 560

Cessna is reported to be developing a new version of the Citation, designated Model 560, to fill a marketing slot between the Citations S/II and III. Powered by two Pratt & Whitney Canada JT15D-5 turbofan engines, it has a fuselage some 0·61 m (2 ft) longer than that of the Citation S/II. The prototype is expected to fly for the first time in 1987 and to receive FAA certification in 1988.

CESSNA MODEL 650 CITATION III

The Citation III represented Cessna's entry into the high-speed medium-size business jet market. First flight of the first prototype (N650CC) was made on 30 May 1979. The second prototype flew for the first time on 2 May 1980, and FAA certification under FAR Pt 25 Transport Category requirements was gained on 30 April 1982. Flight test experience allowed the maximum operating speed to be increased to Mach 0·83. A maximum speed of Mach 0·90 was demonstrated successfully in a dive.

The first production Citation III was delivered to the Citation Marketing Division in December 1982. It was used as a demonstrator, together with the second and third production aircraft, prior to the start of delivery to customers in Spring 1983. The 100th Citation III was delivered in March 1986 to the Martin Marietta Corporation.

TYPE: Twin-turbofan 8/11-seat long-range executive transport.

WINGS: Cantilever low-wing monoplane. NASA-developed supercritical section. Dihedral 3°. Sweepback at quarter-chord 25°. Conventional two-spar fail-safe structure of light alloy, utilising bonded and riveted construction and built in three sections. Electrically actuated trailing-edge flaps, in three sections on each wing, are of Kevlar and graphite composite construction. Four hydraulically actuated spoilers on the upper surface of each wing, immediately forward of the flaps. The two centre spoilers on each wing can be operated as airbrakes in flight. All eight spoilers can be used for emergency descent, and for lift dumping after touchdown. Hydraulically powered ailerons, with manual reversion, are complemented by the outboard spoiler panel on each wing, which provides additional roll authority after approx 3° of aileron deflection. Stall strips and a stall fence are mounted at approx semi-span of each outer wing panel. Anti-icing of wing leading-edges by engine bleed air.

FUSELAGE: Conventional semi-monocoque light alloy structure of circular cross-section. Fail-safe in pressurised area.

TAIL UNIT: Cantilever T tail structure of light alloy, with swept horizontal and vertical surfaces. Variable incidence tailplane has 3° anhedral. Electric anti-icing of tailplane leading-edges. Fin leading-edge is not anti-iced. Rudder incorporates a boost system to minimise yaw in asymmetric thrust conditions.

LANDING GEAR: Hydraulically retractable tricycle type. Main units retract inward into the undersurface of the wing centre-section, nosewheel forward and upward into the nose. Main units of trailing link type, each with twin wheels; nose unit has a single wheel. Oleo-pneumatic shock absorber in each unit. Hydraulically powered nosewheel steering, with an accumulator to provide steering after a loss of normal hydraulic power. Emergency landing gear extension by manual release and free-fall to locked position; pneumatic blowdown system for backup. Mainwheel tyres size 22·0 × 5·75, 10-ply rating, pressure 10·20 bars (148 lb/sq in). Nosewheel tyre size 18·0 × 4·4, 10-ply rating, pressure 8·62 bars (125 lb/sq in). Fully modulated hydraulically powered anti-skid brake system. In the event of hydraulic system failure, an electrically driven standby pump provides pressure for the brakes. Emergency pneumatic brake system. Parking brake.

POWER PLANT: Two Garrett TFE731-3B-100S turbofan engines, each rated at 16·24 kN (3,650 lb st) for take-off, mounted in pod on each side of rear fuselage. Hydraulically operated Rohr target type thrust reversers standard. Two independent fuel systems, with integral tanks in each wing; usable capacity 4,183 litres (1,105 US gallons). Additional fuel cell behind rear fuselage bulkhead. Single-point pressure refuelling on starboard side of fuselage, to rear of wing trailing-edge. Gravity refuelling point on upper surface of each wing. A boost pump in the port wing fills the fuselage tank when pressure refuelling is not available. Engine intake anti-icing system.

ACCOMMODATION: Crew of two on separate flight deck, and up to nine passengers. Standard interior has six individual seats, with toilet at rear of cabin. The fuselage nose incorporates a radome, high resolution radar, avionics bay and a storage compartment for crew baggage. Electrically heated baggage compartment in rear fuselage with external door on port side. Airstair door forward of wing on port side. Overwing emergency escape hatch on starboard side. Cabin is pressurised, heated and air-conditioned. Windscreen anti-icing by engine bleed air, with alcohol spray backup for port side of the windscreen. Windscreen defogging by warm air, and rain removal by engine bleed air and a mechanically actuated airflow deflector.

SYSTEMS: Environmental control system, with separate control of flight deck and cabin conditions. Direct engine bleed pressurisation system, with nominal pressure differential of 0·64 bars (9·3 lb/sq in), provides 2,440 m (8,000 ft) cabin environment to max certificated altitude and can maintain a sea level cabin environment to approx 7,620 m (25,000 ft). Electrical system includes two 28V 400A DC starter/generators, two 200/115V 5kW three-phase engine driven alternators, two 115V 400Hz solid state static inverters, two 24V 22Ah nickel-cadmium batteries and an external power socket in the tailcone. Hydraulic system of 207 bars (3,000 lb/sq in) powered by two engine driven pressure compensated pumps for operation of spoilers, brakes, landing gear, nosewheel steering and thrust reversers. Hydraulic reservoir with integral reserve and an electrically driven hydraulic pump to provide emergency power. Oxygen system of 1·39 m³ (49 cu ft) capacity with automatic dropout constant-flow oxygen mask for each passenger and a quick-donning pressure demand mask for each crew member. Engine fire detection and extinguishing system.

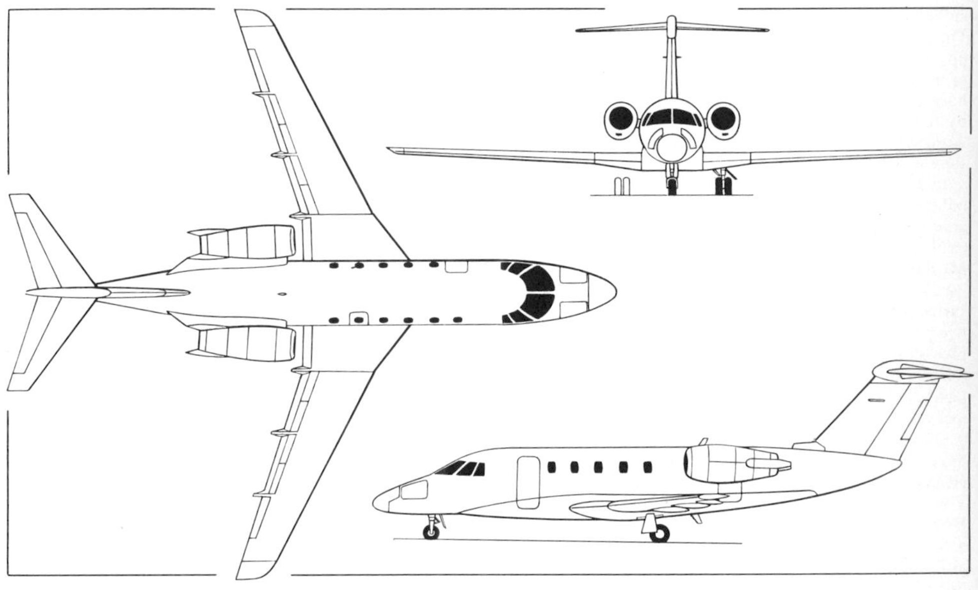

Cessna Citation III (two Garrett TFE731 turbofan engines) *(Pilot Press)*

AVIONICS AND EQUIPMENT: Standard avionics include a Sperry SPZ-650 integrated flight director/autopilot system with AD650A ADI, RD650A HSI and C-14D compass system; Sperry GH-14 ADI and RD-450 HSI with C-14D compass system for co-pilot; AA-300 radio altimeter; dual Collins VHF-22A 720-channel com transceivers, dual VIR-32 nav receivers which include VOR, localiser, glideslope and marker beacon receivers, dual RMI-30, DME-42 DME, TDR-90 transponder; Sperry Primus 300SL colour weather radar; Collins ADF-60 ADF; JET standby attitude gyro; Teledyne angle of attack system; air data computer; dual Avtech audio amplifiers; and Telex microphones, headsets and speakers. A wide range of optional avionics is available including Bendix Series III integrated EFIS, nav/com and radar system. Standard equipment includes dual altimeters, Mach/airspeed indicators, angle of attack indicator, digital clock, instantaneous rate of climb indicators, outside air temperature gauge, crew seats with vertical, fore, aft and recline adjustments, seat belts, shoulder harnesses and inertia reels, six individual passenger seats, three each forward and aft facing with vertical, fore and aft adjustment, lateral tracking and recline adjustments, seat belts and shoulder harnesses, sun visors, flight deck divider with curtain, map case, openable storm windows, electroluminescent and edge-lit instrument panels, stall warning system, cockpit and cabin fire extinguishers, indirect cabin lighting, cabin aisle lights, door courtesy lights, 'Fasten seat belt—No smoking' signs, refreshment centre, cup holders, ashtrays, executive table, aft cabin divider with curtain, emergency exit signs, internal corrosion proofing, emergency battery pack, emergency portable cabin oxygen, navigation and recognition lights, dual landing and taxi lights, dual anti-collision strobe lights, red flashing beacon, dual wing ice lights, lightning protection, static discharge wicks and tiedown provisions.

DIMENSIONS, EXTERNAL:	
Wing span	16·31 m (53 ft 6 in)
Wing mean aerodynamic chord	2·08 m (6 ft 9¾ in)
Wing aspect ratio	8·94
Length overall	16·90 m (55 ft 5½ in)
Height overall	5·12 m (16 ft 9½ in)
Tailplane span	5·60 m (18 ft 4½ in)
Wheel track	2·84 m (9 ft 4 in)
Wheelbase	6·50 m (21 ft 4 in)
Cabin door: Width	0·61 m (2 ft 0 in)
Height	1·37 m (4 ft 6 in)
DIMENSIONS, INTERNAL:	
Cabin:	
Length, front to rear bulkhead	7·01 m (23 ft 0 in)
Length, aft of cockpit divider	5·66 m (18 ft 7 in)
Max width	1·73 m (5 ft 8 in)
Max height	1·78 m (5 ft 10 in)
Baggage capacity (aft)	1·88 m³ (66·4 cu ft)
Crew baggage compartment (nose)	0·17 m³ (6 cu ft)
AREAS:	
Wings, gross	29·00 m² (312 sq ft)
Horizontal tail surfaces (total)	6·26 m² (67·4 sq ft)
Vertical tail surfaces (total)	6·04 m² (65·0 sq ft)
WEIGHTS:	
Weight empty, standard	5,357 kg (11,811 lb)
Max fuel weight	3,349 kg (7,384 lb)
Max T-O weight	9,979 kg (22,000 lb)
Max ramp weight	10,070 kg (22,200 lb)

Cessna Citation III eight/eleven-seat executive transport *(Peter R. March)*

Max landing weight 9,072 kg (20,000 lb)
Max zero-fuel weight 6,940 kg (15,300 lb)
PERFORMANCE (at max T-O weight, ISA, except where indicated):
Max operating speed:
S/L to 2,440 m (8,000 ft) 305 knots (565 km/h; 351 mph) IAS
at 11,132 m (36,524 ft) 278 knots (515 km/h; 320 mph) IAS
above 11,132 m (36,524 ft) Mach 0·851
Max cruising speed at 10,670 m (35,000 ft) and 7,257 kg (16,000 lb) cruise weight 472 knots (874 km/h; 543 mph)
Stalling speed, flaps and wheels down, at max landing weight 97 knots (515 km/h; 112 mph) CAS
Max rate of climb at S/L 1,127 m (3,700 ft)/min
Rate of climb at S/L, one engine out 245 m (805 ft)/min
Time to 13,100 m (43,000 ft) 33 min
Certificated ceiling 15,545 m (51,000 ft)
Ceiling, one engine out 7,165 m (23,500 ft)
FAR Pt 25 T-O field length at S/L 1,581 m (5,186 ft)
FAR Pt 25 landing runway length at max landing weight 884 m (2,900 ft)
Range, with allowances for T-O, climb, descent and 45 min reserves:
2 crew, 6 passengers 2,525 nm (4,679 km; 2,907 miles)
g limits +3·2/−1
OPERATIONAL NOISE LEVELS (FAR Pt 36):
T-O 74·0 EPNdB
Approach 85·0 EPNdB
Sideline 81·0 EPNdB

CHAMPION

CHAMPION AIRCRAFT COMPANY INC

PO Drawer K, Tomball, Texas 77375
Telephone: (713) 370 8080
WORKS: David Wayne Hooks Memorial Airport, 20803 Stuebner-Airline Road, Houston, Texas

In August 1982 B & B Aviation acquired, by purchase of Champion Aircraft Corporation of Osceola, Wisconsin, the rights to manufacture and market the Citabria, Decathlon and Scout light aircraft produced formerly by Bellanca Aircraft Corporation (see 1979-80 *Jane's*). The company was subsequently renamed Champion Aircraft Company Inc, and also held the type certificates for many earlier Aeronca and Champion light aircraft. In addition to providing spares and product support for these types, the company restarted production of the three most recent Champion models.

By April 1985 two production aircraft (one Citabria 150S and a Scout) had been delivered. However, Champion Aircraft was reported to have ceased operation later that year, and its assets were stated to be offered for sale by an investment company that had acquired them.

Full details of the Citabria, Decathlon and Scout can be found in the 1985-86 *Jane's*.

CHRISTEN

CHRISTEN INDUSTRIES INC

AIRCRAFT MANUFACTURING DIVISION
PO Box 547, Afton, Wyoming 83110
Telephone: (307) 886 3151
PRESIDENT AND GENERAL MANAGER: E. H. Andersen Jr

In November 1983 Christen Industries, whose Eagle biplanes are described in the Homebuilts section, acquired the former Pitts Aerobatics company, together with manufacturing and marketing rights to the Pitts Special series of aerobatic biplanes designed by Mr Curtis Pitts. The former Pitts Aerobatics facility at Afton, Wyoming, has been retained as the corporate headquarters of Christen Industries, where manufacture, assembly and testing of the aircraft take place. The company's research and development centre is at Hollister, California.

CHRISTEN A-1 HUSKY

Work began in November 1985 on the design of a new utility aircraft designated A-1 Husky, which Christen Industries believes will be suitable for a range of duties such as bush flying, border patrol, fish and wildlife protection and pipeline inspection. Although it is externally similar in appearance to the Piper Super Cub, the Husky is an entirely new design created with computer-aided design (CAD) techniques. The prototype (N6070H) was being flight tested in the Summer of 1986, with FAA certification anticipated in time for deliveries to begin in March 1987. Christen Industries expects to produce some 25 Huskys annually at its Afton, Wyoming factory.

TYPE: Two-seat light cabin monoplane.

WINGS: Braced high-wing monoplane, with steel tube V bracing struts each side. Wing section modified Clark Y. Aluminium spars and ribs, aluminium sheet leading-edge with Dacron covering overall. Drooped Plane Booster wingtips. Slotted flaps and symmetrical section ailerons of light alloy construction with metal skin. No tabs.

FUSELAGE: Welded full-depth truss structure of 4130 steel tubing, metal skinned to rear of cabin area, the remainder Dacron covered.

TAIL UNIT: Wire- and strut-braced structure of welded steel tubes and channels, covered with Dacron. Fixed incidence tailplane. Trim tab in each elevator.

LANDING GEAR: Non-retractable tailwheel type. Two faired side Vs and half-axles hinged to bottom of fuselage, with internal (under front seat) bungee cord shock absorption. Cleveland mainwheels, tyres size 8·00-6. Oversize 'tundra' tyres optional. Cleveland mainwheel brakes. Steerable leaf-spring tailwheel. Skis and floats optional.

POWER PLANT: One 134 kW (180 hp) Avco Lycoming O-360-C1G flat-four engine, driving a Hartzell two-blade constant-speed metal propeller with spinner. Fuel contained in two metal tanks, one in each wing, total capacity 204 litres (54 US gallons). Fuel filler point in upper surface of each wing, near root.

ACCOMMODATION: Enclosed cabin seating two in tandem, with dual controls. Downward-hinged door on starboard side, with upward-hinged window above. Skylight window in roof.

DIMENSIONS, EXTERNAL:
Wing span 10·73 m (35 ft 2½ in)
Length overall 6·88 m (22 ft 7 in)
Height overall 2·01 m (6 ft 7 in)
Propeller diameter 1·93 m (6 ft 4 in)
AREAS:
Wings, gross 16·72 m² (180·0 sq ft)
Ailerons (total) 1·43 m² (15·4 sq ft)
Trailing-edge flaps (total) 2·09 m² (22·5 sq ft)
Fin 0·43 m² (4·66 sq ft)
Rudder 0·62 m² (6·76 sq ft)
Tailplane 1·48 m² (15·9 sq ft)
Elevators, incl tabs 1·31 m² (14·1 sq ft)
WEIGHTS AND LOADINGS:
Weight empty 522 kg (1,150 lb)
Max T-O weight 816 kg (1,800 lb)
Max wing loading 48·8 kg/m² (10·0 lb/sq ft)
Max power loading 7·45 kg/kW (10·0 lb/hp)
PERFORMANCE:
Cruising speed, 75% power 113 knots (209 km/h; 130 mph)
Stalling speed, flaps down 37 knots (68 km/h; 42 mph)
T-O run 76 m (250 ft)
Landing run, full flap 107 m (350 ft)

Prototype Christen A-1 Husky two-seat light cabin monoplane

PITTS SPECIAL S-1 SERIES

The original single-seat Pitts Special was designed in 1943-44. Construction of a prototype began in 1944 and it flew in September of that year. One of the most successful early models was *Little Stinker,* powered by a 67 kW (90 hp) Continental engine, and built by Mr Pitts in 1947 for Miss Betty Skelton, then an internationally known aerobatic display pilot. *Black Beauty*, built by Pitts for Miss Caro Bailey, was of similar design, but powered by a 93 kW (125 hp) Avco Lycoming O-290-D engine.

Since then even more powerful engines have been installed in Pitts Specials built by both the designer and other people, and those versions of the single-seat Special for which drawings are available are designed to take an Avco Lycoming engine of up to 134 kW (180 hp), as noted in the Sport Aircraft section.

Current versions of the S-1 are as follows:

S-1D. Intended for homebuilders only, with plans available. Generally similar to the S-1S, with original Pitts M-6 non-symmetrical aerofoil section.

S-1S. Production aircraft, FAA type certificated. Available also in kit form, parts, materials and components being produced under an FAA Approved Production Certificate.

S-1T. Advanced version of the S-1 series, available as a production aircraft and in kit form. Described separately.

Details of some of the major successes achieved by US pilots of Pitts Specials in national and international aerobatic competitions, since 1966, were given in the 1972-73 and later *Jane's*.

The details which follow apply to the S-1S factory built aircraft with 134 kW (180 hp) engine, but engines of 74·5-134 kW (100-180 hp) can be fitted to the S-1 Special.

TYPE: Single-seat sporting biplane.

WINGS: Braced biplane type, with single faired interplane strut each side and N type cabane struts. Dual streamline flying and landing wires. Wing section M6. Thickness/chord ratio 12%. Dihedral 0° on upper wing, 3° on lower wings. Incidence 1° 30′ on upper wing, 0° on lower wings. Sweepback at quarter-chord 6° 40′ on upper wing only. Wooden structure, with fabric covering. Frise ailerons on both upper and lower wings, of similar construction to wings. No flaps or tabs.

FUSELAGE: Welded steel tube structure, fabric covered.

TAIL UNIT: Wire braced steel tube structure, fabric covered. Fixed incidence tailplane. Trim tab in each elevator.

LANDING GEAR: Non-retractable tailwheel type. Rubber cord shock absorption. Cleveland mainwheels with 6-ply tyres, size 5·00-5, pressure 2·07 bars (30 lb/sq in). Cleveland hydraulic disc brakes. Steerable tailwheel. Glassfibre fairings on mainwheels.

POWER PLANT: One 134 kW (180 hp) Avco Lycoming IO-360-B4A flat-four engine, driving a Sensenich

Production version of the basic single-seat Christen Pitts Special S-1S

76EM8-O-56/62 two-blade fixed-pitch metal propeller with spinner. Fuel tank aft of firewall, capacity 75 litres (20 US gallons). Refuelling point on upper surface of fuselage, forward of windscreen. Oil capacity 7·5 litres (2 US gallons). Inverted fuel and oil systems standard.

ACCOMMODATION: Single seat in open cockpit. Canopy optional.

DIMENSIONS, EXTERNAL:
- Wing span, upper — 5·28 m (17 ft 4 in)
- Wing chord (constant, both) — 0·91 m (3 ft 0 in)
- Wing aspect ratio — 5·77
- Length overall — 4·71 m (15 ft 5½ in)
- Height overall — 1·92 m (6 ft 3½ in)
- Tailplane span — 1·98 m (6 ft 6 in)
- Propeller diameter — 1·93 m (6 ft 4 in)

AREA:
- Wings, gross — 9·15 m² (98·5 sq ft)

WEIGHTS AND LOADING:
- Weight empty — 326 kg (720 lb)
- Max T-O weight — 521 kg (1,150 lb)
- Max power loading — 3·89 kg/kW (6·38 lb/hp)

PERFORMANCE (at max T-O weight):
- Never-exceed speed — 176 knots (326 km/h; 203 mph)
- Max level speed at S/L — 153 knots (283 km/h; 176 mph)
- Max cruising speed at S/L — 122 knots (227 km/h; 141 mph)
- Stalling speed — 54 knots (100 km/h; 62 mph)
- Max rate of climb at S/L — 792 m (2,600 ft)/min
- Service ceiling — 6,795 m (22,300 ft)
- T-O to 15 m (50 ft) — 331 m (1,085 ft)
- Range with max fuel, no reserves — 273 nm (507 km; 315 miles)

PITTS S-1T SPECIAL

Production of this advanced version of the S-1 series began in early 1981, and it is available as a factory built aircraft or in kit form for amateur construction. Generally similar to other versions of the S-1, it has symmetrical ailerons and wing sections, and the wings have been moved forward 11·5 cm (4½ in) to compensate for the installation of a more powerful engine. This is a a 149 kW (200 hp) Avco Lycoming AEIO-360-A1E flat-four engine driving a Hartzell two-blade constant-speed propeller with spinner. FAA type certification was gained in the Autumn of 1982.

DIMENSIONS, EXTERNAL: As for S-1 except:
- Length overall — 4·72 m (15 ft 6 in)
- Height overall — 1·91 m (6 ft 3 in)

WEIGHTS AND LOADINGS:
- Weight empty — 376 kg (830 lb)
- Max T-O weight — 522 kg (1,150 lb)
- Max wing loading — 57·05 kg/m² (11·68 lb/sq ft)
- Max power loading — 3·50 kg/kW (5·75 lb/hp)

PERFORMANCE (at max T-O weight):
- Never-exceed speed — 176 knots (326 km/h; 203 mph)
- Max level speed at S/L — 161 knots (298 km/h; 185 mph)
- Max cruising speed at S/L — 152 knots (282 km/h; 175 mph)
- Stalling speed — 56 knots (103 km/h; 64 mph)
- Max rate of climb at S/L — 853 m (2,800 ft)/min
- Range with max fuel, 55% power, 30 min reserves — 268 nm (497 km; 309 miles)
- *g* limits — +9/−4·5

PITTS S-2A SPECIAL

First flown in 1967, the S-2A is a two-seat version of the Pitts Special. It is similar to the single-seat S-1 in basic configuration and construction, but is slightly larger overall, with no attempt at commonality of components. The increased size and power, coupled with aerodynamic changes, give the two-seater improved aerobatic and landing characteristics, and make it extremely stable in rough air conditions. Control responses are better than on the S-1. The ailerons are symmetrical and aerodynamically balanced for higher rate of roll at low speeds, and full vertical rolls can be made with ease. The different wing sections used on the S-2A are also symmetrical, providing inverted performance equal to conventional flight and facilitating outside loops.

The S-2A is FAA type certificated in the Normal and Aerobatic categories. It is a production aeroplane, and kits (but not plans) for the homebuilder are available. The homebuilt variant is known as the **S-2A-E**.

TYPE: Two-seat aerobatic biplane.

WINGS: Braced biplane type, with single faired interplane strut each side and N type cabane. Wing section NACA 6400 series on upper wing, 00 series on lower wings. Two-spar wooden (spruce) structure with fabric covering. Aerodynamically balanced ailerons on both upper and lower wings. No flaps or tabs.

FUSELAGE: Welded 4130 steel tube structure with wooden stringers, covered with Dacron fabric except for aluminium top decking and side panels.

Christen Pitts two-seat Model S-2B, capable of unlimited aerobatics with both seats occupied

TAIL UNIT: Wire braced welded 4130 steel tube structure. Fixed surfaces metal covered, control surfaces fabric covered. Trim tab in each elevator.

LANDING GEAR: Non-retractable tailwheel type. Rubber cord shock absorption. Steerable tailwheel. Fairings on mainwheels.

POWER PLANT: One 149 kW (200 hp) Avco Lycoming IO-360-A1A flat-four engine, driving a Hartzell type HC-C2YK-4/C7666A-2 two-blade constant-speed metal propeller with spinner. Fuel tank in fuselage, immediately aft of firewall, capacity 90·5 litres (24 US gallons). Refuelling point on fuselage upper surface forward of front windscreen. Oil capacity 7·5 litres (2 US gallons). Inverted fuel and oil systems standard.

ACCOMMODATION: Two seats in tandem cockpits with dual controls. Rear cockpit can be enclosed by a transparent canopy if required, and an extended one-piece canopy to cover both cockpits is also available. Space for 9 kg (20 lb) baggage aft of rear cockpit when flown in non-aerobatic category.

SYSTEM: Electrical system powered by 12V 40A alternator and non-spill 12V battery.

DIMENSIONS, EXTERNAL:
- Wing span: upper — 6·10 m (20 ft 0 in)
- lower — 5·79 m (19 ft 0 in)
- Wing chord (constant, both) — 1·02 m (3 ft 4 in)
- Length overall — 5·41 m (17 ft 9 in)
- Height overall — 1·94 m (6 ft 4½ in)

AREA:
- Wings, gross — 11·6 m² (125·0 sq ft)

WEIGHTS AND LOADINGS (A: Aerobatic; B: Normal category):
- Weight empty: A, B — 453 kg (1,000 lb)
- Max T-O weight: A — 680 kg (1,500 lb)
- B — 714 kg (1,575 lb)
- Max wing loading: A — 58·6 kg/m² (12·0 lb/sq ft)
- B — 61·5 kg/m² (12·6 lb/sq ft)
- Max power loading: A — 4·56 kg/kW (7·5 lb/hp)
- B — 5·33 kg/kW (7·87 lb/hp)

PERFORMANCE (at max T-O wight. A: Aerobatic; B: Normal category):
- Never-exceed speed: A, B — 176 knots (326 km/h; 203 mph)
- Max level speed at S/L: A, B — 136 knots (253 km/h; 157 mph)
- Max cruising speed at S/L: A, B — 132 knots (245 km/h; 152 mph)
- Stalling speed: A — 51 knots (94 km/h; 58 mph)
- B — 52 knots (95 km/h; 59 mph)
- Max rate of climb at S/L: A — 579 m (1,900 ft)/min
- B — 549 m (1,800 ft)/min
- Service ceiling: A — 6,125 m (20,100 ft)
- B — 4,875 m (16,000 ft)
- T-O to 15 m (50 ft): A — 351 m (1,150 ft)
- Range with max fuel: A — 297 nm (552 km; 343 miles)
- *g* limits — +9/−4·5

PITTS MODEL S-2B

This two-seater differs from the S-2A in having a 194 kW (260 hp) Avco Lycoming AEIO-540-D4A5 flat-six engine, and is intended to be capable of unlimited aerobatics carrying two persons. The heavier power plant necessitated moving the wings and landing gear forward about 15 cm (6 in), and has made possible more room in the front cockpit. Fuel capacity is increased to 110 litres (29 US gallons), and oil capacity to 11·35 litres (3 US gallons).

The prototype S-2B was completed during September 1982. Its capability was demonstrated shortly afterwards when Clint McHenry, carrying a passenger, took first place in the Advanced Category at the US Nationals held at Sherman, Texas.

The S-2B was awarded FAA type certification in the Spring of 1983, in the Aerobatic category, under FAR Pt 23.

DIMENSIONS, EXTERNAL: As for Model S-2A except:
- Length overall — 5·71 m (18 ft 9 in)
- Height overall — 2·01 m (6 ft 7½ in)

WEIGHTS AND LOADINGS:
- Weight empty — 522 kg (1,150 lb)
- Max T-O weight — 737 kg (1,625 lb)
- Max wing loading — 63·55 kg/m² (13·0 lb/sq ft)
- Max power loading — 3·80 kg/kW (6·25 lb/hp)

PERFORMANCE (at max T-O weight):
- Never-exceed speed — 182 knots (338 km/h; 210 mph)
- Max cruising speed — 152 knots (282 km/h; 175 mph)
- Stalling speed — 52 knots (97 km/h; 60 mph)
- Max rate of climb at S/L — 823 m (2,700 ft)/min
- Service ceiling — 6,400 m (21,000 ft)
- Range with max fuel, 55% power, 30 min reserves — 277 nm (513 km; 319 miles)

PITTS MODEL S-2S

Production of this single-seat version of the S-2A began in late 1978. It has a forward fuselage shortened by 0·36 m (1 ft 2 in) to accommodate a 194 kW (260 hp) Avco Lycoming AEIO-540-D4A5 flat-six engine, driving a McCauley Type 1A/200 two-blade fixed-pitch metal propeller with spinner. It also differs from the S-2A by having a maximum fuel capacity of 132·5 litres (35 US gallons) and an oil capacity of 11·4 litres (3 US gallons). The first flight of the prototype was made on 9 December 1977; full type certification was gained in June 1981. The Model S-2S is available either as a factory built aircraft, or in kit form for amateur construction as the **S-2S-E**.

DIMENSIONS, EXTERNAL: As for Model S-2A except:
- Length overall — 5·28 m (17 ft 4 in)
- Height overall — 2·02 m (6 ft 7½ in)

WEIGHTS AND LOADINGS:
- Weight empty — 499 kg (1,100 lb)
- Max T-O weight — 680 kg (1,500 lb)
- Max wing loading — 58·6 kg/m² (12·0 lb/sq ft)
- Max power loading — 3·51 kg/kW (5·77 lb/hp)

PERFORMANCE (at max T-O weight):
- Never-exceed speed — 176 knots (326 km/h; 203 mph)
- Max level speed at S/L — 162 knots (301 km/h; 187 mph)
- Max cruising speed at S/L — 152 knots (282 km/h; 175 mph)
- Stalling speed — 51 knots (94 km/h; 58 mph)
- Max rate of climb at S/L — 853 m (2,800 ft)/min
- *g* limits — +9/−4·5

CLASSIC

CLASSIC AIRCRAFT CORPORATION

Capital City Airport, Lansing, Michigan 48906
Telephone: (517) 321 7500
Telex: 229 430

PRESIDENT: Richard S. Kettles
GENERAL MANAGER: Robert N. Edelstein
PRODUCTION MANAGER: Sylvester Heller
ENGINEERING MANAGER: Donald P. Zurfluh
SALES MANAGER: Donald C. Kettles

CLASSIC WACO CLASSIC F-5

In March 1984 Classic Aircraft Corporation began construction of a prototype Waco Classic F-5 biplane, based on the original Waco YMF-5 and built under the same FAA type certificate. The prototype (N1935B) made its first flight on 20 November 1985 and was expected to be granted FAA certification in March 1986.

Although externally similar to the earlier Waco YMF-5, the Waco Classic F-5 incorporates modern constructional techniques, tolerances and materials. Classic Aircraft anticipates an initial production rate of one aircraft per month. By March 1986 the company held orders for seven F-5s.

TYPE: Three-seat sporting biplane.

WINGS: Braced biplane, with N type interplane struts, wire bracing and N type cabane struts. Streamline section stainless steel landing and flying wires. Wing section Clark Y. 2° dihedral on upper and lower wings. 0° incidence on upper and lower wings. No sweepback. All-wood structure, with Dacron covering. Ailerons on upper and lower wings of all-aluminium construction with chordwise external stiffening. No flaps or tabs.

FUSELAGE: Welded steel tube with internal oiling for corrosion protection. Wooden bulkheads, with overall Dacron covering.

TAIL UNIT: Braced welded-steel tube structure with Dacron covering. Tailplane incidence manually adjustable from cockpit via screwjack actuator. Ground adjustable trim tab on rudder.

LANDING GEAR: Non-retractable tailwheel type. Shock absorption by oil and spring shock struts. Steerable tailwheel. Cleveland 30-67F hydraulic brakes on mainwheels only. Cleveland 40-101A mainwheels, tyre size 7·50-10; Cleveland 40-199A tailwheel, tyre size 3·50-4. Mainwheel fairings standard.

POWER PLANT: One 182·7 kW (245 hp) Jacobs R-755-B2 aircooled radial engine (remanufactured), driving a two-blade fixed-pitch wooden propeller. Engine enclosed with streamline aluminium 'bump' cowling. Fuel contained in two aluminium tanks in upper wing centre-section, total capacity 182 litres (48 US gallons). Refuelling point for each tank in upper wing surface. Auxiliary tanks, capacity 45 litres (12 US gallons) each, optional in either or both inboard upper wing panels. Standard oil capacity 15 litres (4 US gallons); with auxiliary fuel tanks 19 litres (5 US gallons).

ACCOMMODATION: Three seats in tandem open cockpits, two side by side in front position, single seat at rear. Dual controls, seat belts with shoulder harness, and pilot's adjustable seat, standard. Front baggage compartment, capacity 11·3 kg (25 lb); rear baggage compartment, volume 0·2 m³ (7·5 cu ft), capacity 34 kg (75 lb).

SYSTEMS: 24V electrical system with battery, alternator and starter for electrical supply to navigation, strobe and rear cockpit lights. Hydraulic system for brakes only.

AVIONICS AND EQUIPMENT: Emergency locator transmitter standard. Avionics to customer's choice, including King and Narco nav/com, ADF, DME, transponder and encoding altimeter; Foster, II Morrow and Narco Loran-C systems; 3M Stormscope WX-8 and WX-10A; King KCS 55A slaved compass system with KN 72 VOR/LOC converter; Sigtronics SPA-400 intercom; TR-720 hand held transceiver, Avionics West EC-200 stereo AM/FM cassette and Astrotech digital clock. Toe brakes standard in rear cockpit. Compass, airspeed indicator, turn and bank indicator, rate of climb indicator, sensitive altimeter and clock standard in rear cockpit. Rear cockpit windscreen, front and rear cockpit covers, and three-colour paint scheme with choice of two designs, also standard. Optional equipment includes exhaust gas temperature gauge, carburettor temperature gauge, *g* meter, vacuum- or electrically-driven gyro system, Hobbs meter, outside air temperature gauge, instrument post lighting, ground service plug, heated pitot, landing and taxi lights, front and rear cockpit heaters, deluxe interior with carpet, leather sidewalls and interior trim, and front cockpit windscreen.

Prototype Classic Waco Classic F-5 re-creation of the Waco YMF-5 three-seat biplane

DIMENSIONS, EXTERNAL:

Wing span: upper	9·14 m (30 ft 0 in)
lower	8·18 m (26 ft 10 in)
Wing chord at root	1·45 m (4 ft 9 in)
Wing aspect ratio	4·35
Length overall	7·10 m (23 ft 3⅜ in)
Height overall	2·57 m (8 ft 5⅜ in)
Tailplane span	3·19 m (10 ft 5½ in)
Wheelbase	1·95 m (6 ft 5 in)
Propeller diameter	2·44 m (8 ft 0 in)
Propeller ground clearance	0·28 m (11 in)

AREAS:

Wings, gross	21·69 m² (233·5 sq ft)
Ailerons (total)	2·07 m² (22·3 sq ft)
Fin	0·70 m² (7·5 sq ft)
Rudder, incl tab	0·88 m² (9·5 sq ft)
Tailplane	1·31 m² (14·1 sq ft)
Elevators (total)	1·59 m² (17·1 sq ft)

WEIGHTS AND LOADINGS:

Basic weight empty	816 kg (1,800 lb)
Max payload	317 kg (700 lb)
Max fuel weight	136 kg (300 lb)
Max T-O and landing weight	1,134 kg (2,500 lb)
Max wing loading	52·26 kg/m² (10·71 lb/sq ft)
Max power loading	6·21 kg/kW (10·20 lb/hp)

PERFORMANCE (at max T-O weight except where indicated):

Never-exceed speed	186 knots (344 km/h; 214 mph)
Max level speed at S/L	117 knots (217 km/h; 135 mph)
Max cruising speed at S/L	104 knots (193 km/h; 120 mph)
Econ cruising speed at 2,440 m (8,000 ft)	95 knots (177 km/h; 110 mph)
Stalling speed, power off	48 knots (88 km/h; 55 mph)
Max rate of climb at S/L	396 m (1,300 ft)/min
T-O run	61 m (200 ft)
Range, standard fuel, 30 min reserves	286 nm (531 km; 330 miles)

COLEMILL

COLEMILL ENTERPRISES INC

PO Box 60627, Cornelia Fort Air Park, Nashville, Tennessee 37206
Telephone: (615) 226 4256
Telex: 555 197
PRESIDENT: William Colbert

Colemill specialises in performance improvement conversions of light single- and twin-engined aircraft.

COLEMILL PANTHER NAVAJO

Colemill's conversion of the Navajo or Navajo C/R involves more than a new engine installation. In addition to the power plant change, there are redesigned nacelles, additional continuous running fuel pumps, a digital fuel totaliser, heavy duty brakes, and wingtip mounted landing lights. Conversion normally takes 10-14 days. Colemill has also developed 'Zip-Tip' winglets for Panther Navajo and Chieftain conversions. The winglets improve stability in the lower-speed flight zone, down to stalling speed, and also provide cruising speed increases of 4-9 knots (8-16 km/h; 5-10 mph) at altitudes between 3,960 and 7,620 m (13,000 and 25,000 ft), at engine power settings between 45% and 65% of maximum power. This version is, therefore, able to match the cruising speed of the standard Panther Navajo (without winglets) at power settings which offer greater fuel economy.

Following the award of a Supplemental Type Certificate in Summer 1982, operators of Panther conversions of Navajo and Chieftain aircraft can specify winglets from new or as retrofit modifications, replacing the normal extended wingtips of the conversion. They increase wing span to 13·16 m (43 ft 2 in) and wing area by 0·56 m² (6 sq ft).

The basic description of the Navajo, which can be found under the Piper entry in the 1982-83 *Jane's*, applies also to the Panther Navajo, except as follows:

WINGS: As for Piper Navajo except for new wingtips with marked under camber, which increase wing span and area; or alternative choice of winglets, as described in opening paragraph.

LANDING GEAR: As for Piper Navajo except for the introduction of Cleveland four-spot heavy duty disc brakes.

POWER PLANT: Two 261 kW (350 hp) Avco Lycoming TIO-540-J2BD turbocharged engines, each driving a Hartzell four-blade constant-speed fully-feathering metal propeller with 'Q' tips. Pressurised magnetos, Woodward propeller governors, synchrophasers and unfeathering accumulators standard. Fuel system as for basic Navajo, except for the addition of continuous running electrically operated fuel pumps.

EQUIPMENT: Generally as for standard Navajo, but existing fuel flow gauges are replaced by a Shadin Digiflow fuel management computer giving digital readout of fuel remaining/fuel consumed. Supplemental wingtip landing lights can be operated independently of the standard nosewheel mounted landing light, prior to lowering of landing gear.

DIMENSIONS, EXTERNAL: As for Piper Navajo except:

Wing span	13·00 m (42 ft 8 in)

LOADING: As for Piper Navajo except:

Max power loading	5·65 kg/kW (9·3 lb/hp)

PERFORMANCE (at max T-O weight):

Max level speed	269 knots (498 km/h; 309 mph)
Max cruising speed, 75% power at optimum altitude	248 knots (459 km/h; 285 mph)
Cruising speed, 65% power:	
at 7,315 m (24,000 ft)	235 knots (435 km/h; 270 mph)
at 3,660 m (12,000 ft)	206 knots (381 km/h; 237 mph)
Max rate of climb at S/L	610 m (2,000 ft)/min
Rate of climb at S/L, one engine out	122 m (400 ft)/min
Short-field T-O run	229 m (750 ft)
T-O to 15 m (50 ft)	458 m (1,500 ft)
Landing from 15 m (50 ft)	427 m (1,400 ft)

COLEMILL PANTHER II

Colemill's Panther II conversion is based on the Piper Chieftain and includes the installation of new 261 kW (350 hp) Avco Lycoming TIO-540-J2BD and LTIO-540-J2BD turbocharged engines, each driving a Hartzell four-blade constant-speed fully-feathering metal propeller with 'Q' tips. A digital fuel management computer, Woodward propeller governors and synchrophaser, and Cleveland four-spot heavy duty brakes, are also standard. 'Zip-Tip' winglets are optional.

COLEMILL EXECUTIVE 600

The Executive 600 is a Cessna 310, of Model F to Q series, or Cessna 320 (up to and including Model 320C), re-engined by Colemill with two 224 kW (300 hp) Continental IO-520-E flat-six engines, each driving a McCauley three-blade propeller. Dimensions are unchanged; empty weight is increased by about 14 kg (30 lb); other data are as follows:

WEIGHT:

Max T-O weight: 310	2,358 kg (5,200 lb)
320	2,404 kg (5,300 lb)

PERFORMANCE (at max T-O weight):

Max cruising speed (75% power):	
310	205 knots (379 km/h; 236 mph)
320	202 knots (374 km/h; 232 mph)
Cruising speed (65% power):	
310	195 knots (361 km/h; 224 mph)
320	192 knots (355 km/h; 221 mph)
Stalling speed, wheels and flaps down:	
310, 320	64 knots (119 km/h; 74 mph)
Max rate of climb at S/L: 310	762 m (2,500 ft)/min
320	777 m (2,550 ft)/min
Service ceiling: 310, 320	5,940 m (19,500 ft)
T-O to 15 m (50 ft): 310, 320	518 m (1,700 ft)
Landing from 15 m (50 ft): 310, 320	unchanged
Range with max fuel, 45 min reserves:	
310	1,050 nm (1,944 km; 1,208 miles)
320	1,060 nm (1,963 km; 1,220 miles)

COLEMILL PRESIDENT 600

The President 600 is a Beechcraft B55 Baron re-engined by Colemill with two 224 kW (300 hp) Continental IO-520-E flat-six engines, each driving a three-blade propeller. Some 250 President 600 conversions have been delivered.

Dimensions are unchanged; empty weight is increased by about 14 kg (30 lb); other data are as follows:

WEIGHT:
Max T-O weight 2,313 kg (5,100 lb)

PERFORMANCE (at max T-O weight):
Max cruising speed (75% power) 203 knots (376 km/h; 233 mph)
Cruising speed (65% power) 193 knots (357 km/h; 222 mph)
Stalling speed, wheels and flaps down 66 knots (123 km/h; 76 mph)
Max rate of climb at S/L 823 m (2,700 ft)/min
Service ceiling 5,940 m (19,500 ft)
T-O to 15 m (50 ft) 497 m (1,631 ft)
Landing from 15 m (50 ft) unchanged
Range with max fuel, 45 min reserves 1,050 nm (1,944 km; 1,208 miles)

COLEMILL FOXSTAR BARON

The Foxstar is a Beechcraft Baron Model 55 or 58 re-engined with two 224 kW (300 hp) Teledyne Continental IO-550C engines with heavy duty crankcases, each driving a Hartzell Sabre Blade four-blade Q-tip propeller. Other modifications include the installation of Woodward propeller governors and synchrophase system, Shadin Digiflow fuel computer, Zip-Tip winglets, and 60A alternators. The Foxstar conversion is FAA STC approved for all Model C55, D55, E55 and Model 58 Barons, and offers improvements in rate of climb, cruising speed, engine-out performance, and cabin noise and vibration levels.

WEIGHT:
Max T-O weight 2,449 kg (5,400 lb)

PERFORMANCE (at max T-O weight):
Max cruising speed, 75% power 205 knots (380 km/h; 236 mph)
Cruising speed, 65% power 200 knots (371 km/h; 230 mph)
Stalling speed, landing gear and flaps down 74 knots (137 km/h; 85 mph)

Colemill's Panther II conversion with winglets

Max rate of climb at S/L 561 m (1,840 ft)/min
Service ceiling 6,400 m (21,000 ft)
T-O to 15 m (50 ft) 610 m (2,000 ft)
Landing from 15 m (50 ft) 734 m (2,410 ft)
Range with max fuel, 45 min reserves 1,131 nm (2,096 km; 1,302 miles)

COLEMILL STARFIRE BONANZA

The Starfire is a Beechcraft Bonanza re-engined with a 224 kW (300 hp) Teledyne Continental IO-550B engine, driving a Hartzell Sabre Blade four-blade Q-tip propeller. Other modifications include the installation of a Woodward propeller governor, Shadin Digiflow fuel computer/totaliser, Zip-Tip winglets, and a 60A alternator. The Starfire conversion has received FAA STC approval for all Beechcraft Model C33A, E33A, F33A, S35, V35A, V35B and A36 Bonanzas. The conversion offers improvements in rate of climb, cruising speed and cabin noise and vibration levels.

PERFORMANCE:
Cruising speed 176 knots (326 km/h; 203 mph)
Max rate of climb at S/L 369 m (1,210 ft)/min
T-O run 296 m (971 ft)
T-O to 15 m (50 ft) 583 m (1,912 ft)

COMPOSITE

COMPOSITE AIRCRAFT CORPORATION

523 Ridgeview Drive, Florence, Kentucky 41042
Telephone: (606) 371 7247

PRESIDENT: Gerald P. Dietrick
CHIEF ENGINEER: George A. Alther

Details of this company's Composite/Windecker Eagle four-seat light aircraft may be found in the 1985-86 edition of *Jane's*. Finance for production was still being sought in early 1986.

DEE HOWARD

THE DEE HOWARD COMPANY

International Airport, PO Box 17300, San Antonio, Texas 78217
Telephone: (512) 828 1341
Telex: 767380
VICE-PRESIDENT, MARKETING: E. Judson Brandreth Jr

DEE HOWARD XR LEARJET

The Dee Howard Company has developed an overall performance improvement system that is suitable for retrofit on all Model 24 Learjets which have General Electric CJ610-6 or -8A turbojet engines.

The improvements incorporated in the XR Learjet include the provision of a new centre-section glove which reduces drag, improves spanwise lift, and accommodates an additional 245 kg (540 lb) of fuel; a new engine pylon/nacelle configuration that eliminates adverse flow pressure characteristics and channel flow Mach problems, and also improves engine bay cooling; the addition of a small span flow limiter and stall turbulator, at the junction of the inboard and outboard leading-edge on each wing, which produces stall buffet and improves overall stall performance; the introduction of a new leading-edge profile to optimise cruise drag and low-speed stall characteristics; improved ailerons, trailing-edge flaps, outer wing panels, and new tip tank fin cuffs to improve cruise performance; introduction of a new engine exhaust nozzle that improves specific fuel consumption; and installation of a Teledyne angle of attack system. A new Sperry SPZ-500 LR autopilot is to be optional.

Conversion of a suitable Model 24 to XR Learjet configuration provides an extra 400 nm (741 km; 460 miles) of range at a constant cruising speed of Mach 0·78, plus an increase of 680 kg (1,500 lb) in maximum take-off weight, and increased payload.

DEE HOWARD (GATES) LEARJET 25G

Announced on 23 September 1980, this version of the Learjet 25 represented the first product of a co-operative agreement between Gates Learjet and The Dee Howard Company. It is similar in design to the Dee Howard XR Learjet, and has a range more than 20 per cent better than that of other Model 25s. The drag reducing modifications to produce this increased range capability include a thicker inboard section glove on each wing, changing the wing planform at the root and carrying additional fuel; a cambered tip tank fin and tip tank strake; the addition of a second small fence on each wing; introduction of a new wing leading-edge stall strip; and of a considerably changed engine nacelle pylon configuration. Internally, a new flap pre-select system has been added as standard equipment.

In other respects the description of the Learjet 25D (see Gates Learjet Corporation entry) applies also to the 25G, except as follows:

AVIONICS AND EQUIPMENT: Standard avionics as for Learjet 25D, supplemented by J.E.T. FC-110 autopilot with dual yaw damper, IDC barometric altimeter (co-pilot), J.E.T. PS-835D emergency battery and AI-804 attitude gyro, and dual Teledyne IVSI. Standard equipment includes Woodward engine synchroniser, LearAvia engine synchroscope, annunciator light package, and flap pre-select. Sperry Primus 300SL colour weather radar instead of Bendix radar. J.E.T. 104B directional gyros.

DIMENSIONS, INTERNAL: As for Learjet 25D except:
Cabin, between pressure bulkheads:
Length 6·38 m (20 ft 11 in)

AREA:
Wings, gross 22·93 m² (246·8 sq ft)

WEIGHTS AND LOADINGS:
Weight empty, equipped 3,742 kg (8,250 lb)
Max fuel weight 2,991 kg (6,594 lb)
Max T-O weight 7,393 kg (16,300 lb)
Max ramp weight 7,620 kg (16,800 lb)
Max landing weight 6,214 kg (13,700 lb)
Max wing loading 322·5 kg/m² (66·05 lb/sq ft)
Max power loading 282·18 kg/kN (2·76 lb/lb st)

PERFORMANCE (estimated at S/L, ISA):
Cruising speed at 12,500 m (41,000 ft) 464 knots (860 km/h; 534 mph)
T-O balanced field length, FAR Pt 25, at max T-O weight 1,491 m (4,893 ft)
Landing distance, FAR Pt 91, at max landing weight 831 m (2,728 ft)
Max range, crew of two and four passengers, allowances for taxi, T-O, climb, cruise at long-range power, descent and 45 min reserves 1,800 nm (3,335 km; 2,073 miles)

DEE HOWARD BAC 111-400

In February 1986 The Dee Howard Company signed agreements with Rolls-Royce and British Aerospace which will lead to certification of the 50·01 kN (11,243 lb st) Rolls-Royce Tay turbofan engine in BAC One-Eleven Series 400 corporate aircraft. All prototype modification and flight test work will be completed at the company's San Antonio facility, with FAA certification anticipated in December 1987. The replacement of the One-Eleven's Spey 511 engines with the Tay power plant is expected to provide the aircraft with an NBAA IFR range of more than 3,200 nm (5,930 km; 3,685 miles) and to offer a reduction in balanced field length requirements of as much as 30 per cent under 'hot and high' conditions. The modification will include new engine nacelles and Dee Howard-developed thrust reversers, and will enable the aircraft to meet FAR Pt 36 Stage 3 noise requirements. At the time of its agreement with the engine and airframe manufacturers, the company held one order for the conversion, which will be available to corporate operators of the BAC One-Eleven Srs 400. After completion of the first three aircraft, the conversion is expected to take 90 days.

Gates Learjet 25G increased-range conversion of an earlier Learjet 25

DE VORE

DE VORE AVIATION CORPORATION

Verilite Aircraft Co Inc, 6104B Kircher Boulevard NE, Albuquerque, New Mexico 87109
Telephone: (505) 345 8713
Telex: 660436

PRESIDENT: Gilbert De Vore
VICE-PRESIDENT: Arnold Robinson

Founded in 1954, De Vore Aviation specialised initially in consultancy and contract engineering services for aircraft manufacturers. In 1969 the company acquired manufacturing rights to the PK range of seaplane and amphibian floats, and was appointed exclusive supplier of Aerojet General aircraft standby rocket engines (formerly known as JATO). In 1970 De Vore developed its Tel-Tail aircraft vertical tail floodlighting system, and in 1976 began development of a single-box airport visual approach aid, the pulsed light approach slope indicator (PLASI) which has been FAA and US Air Force approved for fixed- and rotating-wing aircraft.

DE VORE MODEL 100 SUNBIRD

In October 1983 De Vore announced its entry into light aircraft manufacturing with a new two-seat design based on the former British designed Ben-Air Sparrowhawk (described in the Addenda of the 1982-83 *Jane's*), for which design and manufacturing rights had been acquired.

The design goal for the De Vore 'Affordable Airplane', initially named Sundancer in a public participation naming contest, and later renamed Sunbird, was to produce a light aeroplane to sell for under $20,000 in 1983 values. The first flight of the prototype, initially planned for September 1984, was delayed while initial funding was sought for the project. This was achieved in the Spring of 1985, and the first flight was scheduled to take place in September 1986, with FAA certification anticipated at the end of 1987. The aircraft will be manufactured in a new 6,503 m² (70,000 sq ft) factory at Double Eagle II Airport, Albuquerque, which is due to be completed in late 1987. Production plans are for some 125 aircraft in the first full year of production, rising to approximately 1,000 aircraft per year by the fifth year of production.

TYPE: Two-seat single-engined light aircraft.

WINGS: Strut braced high-wing monoplane. Wing section NACA 64_1212 Mod B inboard, with extended drooped leading-edge from 52% semi-span outboard. Dihedral 2°. Incidence 2°. No sweepback. Single bracing strut on each side. Structure of foam core sandwich with pre-preg glassfibre faces. Plain flaps and ailerons of same construction as wings. Ailerons have internal spring trim.

FUSELAGE: Aluminium keel and bulkheads, with skins of pre-preg glassfibre/foam core sandwich.

TAIL UNIT: Cantilever structure of pre-preg glassfibre/foam core sandwich. Adjustable horizontal tail surfaces with elevators.

LANDING GEAR: Non-retractable tricycle type. Rubber doughnut suspension on nosewheel leg; aluminium spring struts on main units. Tyre size (all) 5·00-5; pressure 2·14 bars (31·0 lb/sq in). Brakes on mainwheels. Wheel fairings optional.

Full scale mockup of the De Vore Model 100 Sunbird

POWER PLANT: One 46·2 kW (62 hp) Emdair CF-077A two-cylinder four-stroke engine, driving a two-blade fixed-pitch pusher propeller. Single fuel tank in fuselage, capacity 49 litres (13 US gallons).

ACCOMMODATION: Two seats, side by side, in fully enclosed cabin. Canopy slides forward for access. Baggage area behind seats, capacity 22·7 kg (50 lb). Ram air ventilation; cabin heat from exhaust system heat exchanger.

SYSTEMS: Generator/battery electrical system for engine starting, minimum avionics and navigation lights.

AVIONICS: One nav/com with VOR standard.

DIMENSIONS, EXTERNAL:
- Wing span: 9·75 m (32 ft 0 in)
- Wing chord: at root: 1·24 m (4 ft 1¼ in)
- at tip: 1·31 m (4 ft 3¾ in)
- Wing aspect ratio: 7·61
- Length overall: 7·28 m (23 ft 10¾ in)
- Height overall: 2·49 m (8 ft 2 in)
- Tailplane span: 3·28 m (10 ft 9 in)
- Wheel track: 2·15 m (7 ft 0½ in)
- Wheelbase: 2·38 m (7 ft 9¾ in)
- Propeller diameter: 1·73 m (5 ft 8 in)
- Passenger door: Height: 0·86 m (2 ft 10 in)
- Width: 1·11 m (3 ft 8 in)
- Height to sill: 0·68 m (2 ft 3 in)

DIMENSIONS, INTERNAL:
- Cabin: Length: 1·73 m (5 ft 8 in)
- Max width: 1·01 m (3 ft 4 in)
- Max height: 1·14 m (3 ft 9 in)
- Floor area: 1·58 m² (17·0 sq ft)
- Volume: approx 1·42 m³ (50·0 cu ft)

AREAS:
- Wings, gross: 12·49 m² (134·5 sq ft)
- Ailerons (total): 1·03 m² (11·06 sq ft)
- Trailing-edge flaps (total): 1·94 m² (20·9 sq ft)
- Fin: 0·69 m² (7·45 sq ft)
- Rudder: 0·47 m² (5·06 sq ft)
- Tailplane: 1·71 m² (18·4 sq ft)
- Elevators: 0·99 m² (10·7 sq ft)

WEIGHTS AND LOADING:
- Weight empty: 256 kg (565 lb)
- Max T-O weight: 476 kg (1,050 lb)
- Max power loading: 10·3 kg/kW (16·93 lb/hp)

PERFORMANCE:
- Never-exceed speed at S/L: 132 knots (245 km/h; 152 mph)
- Max level speed at S/L: 111 knots (206 km/h; 128 mph)
- Max cruising speed (75% power) at S/L: 100 knots (185 km/h; 115 mph)
- Stalling speed: flaps up: 44 knots (81 km/h; 51 mph)
- flaps down: 38 knots (70 km/h; 44 mph)
- Max rate of climb at S/L: 230 m (755 ft)/min
- T-O run: 302 m (990 ft)
- T-O to 15 m (50 ft): 385 m (1,265 ft)
- Landing run from 15 m (50 ft): 283 m (930 ft)
- Range with max fuel and max payload: 403 nm (747 km; 464 miles)

ECTOR

ECTOR AIRCRAFT COMPANY INC

414 East Hillmont Road, Odessa, Texas 79762
Telephone: (915) 362 1841

PRESIDENT: Timothy H. Parker
CHIEF TEST PILOT: Stephen H. Parker
CHIEF OF PRODUCTION: Bob York
OFFICE MANAGER: Patsy May

ECTOR MOUNTAINEER

For a number of years the Ector Aircraft Company has produced civil versions of the Cessna L-19 Bird Dog (last described in the 1964-65 *Jane's*). Generally similar to the original L-19, Ector's aircraft are rebuilt completely from new off the shelf or serviceable components. The entire airframe is corrosion proofed with zinc chromate before assembly; mounting brackets for floats are built into the basic airframe; and all four side windows can be opened in flight. The rear seat is removable to permit the carriage of cargo.

Production of the more powerful Super Mountaineer model has ceased. A description may be found in the 1985-86 *Jane's*.

By 1 January 1986 a total of 41 Mountaineers had been produced for service with various organisations as glider tugs, for patrol and general purpose duties, and for use as sporting aircraft.

TYPE: Two-seat (optional three-seat) cabin monoplane.

WINGS: Braced high-wing monoplane. Single streamline-section bracing strut each side. Wing section NACA 2412. Dihedral 2° 8'. Incidence 1° 30' at root, −1° 30' at tip. All-metal single-spar structure, with metal skin. Frise all-metal ailerons. Fowler all-metal trailing-edge flaps. No tabs.

FUSELAGE: Conventional all-metal semi-monocoque structure.

TAIL UNIT: Cantilever all-metal structure. Trim tab in elevator. Small auxiliary fins attached to tailplane tips of floatplane version.

LANDING GEAR: Non-retractable tailwheel type. Cantilever spring steel main legs. Goodyear mainwheels with tyres size 6·00-6. Scott steerable tailwheel. Single-disc hydraulic brakes. Floats, skis and tandem wheel rough terrain landing gear optional.

Ector Mountaineer, a civil version of the Cessna L-19 Bird Dog

POWER PLANT: One 159 kW (213 hp) Teledyne Continental O-470-11 flat-four engine, driving a two-blade fixed-pitch metal propeller. One fuel tank in each wing root, total capacity 151 litres (40 US gallons). Refuelling points on wing upper surface. Oil capacity 9·4 litres (2·5 US gallons).

ACCOMMODATION: Normally two seats in tandem in enclosed cabin with 360° field of view. Door on starboard side. All four cabin side windows can be opened fully. Six skylights in roof. Space for baggage behind rear seat. With rear seat removed, 0·85 m³ (30 cu ft) of space is available for freight. Optional conversion to provide three seats. Cabin heated and ventilated.

SYSTEMS: Hydraulic system for brakes only. 12V electrical system.

AVIONICS AND EQUIPMENT: Radio equipment available to customer's requirements. Navigation and landing lights, heated pitot, stall warning indicator, Hobbs hour meter and Whelen three-light strobe system standard. External power socket and wing racks optional.

Dimensions, external:
- Wing span: 10·97 m (36 ft 0 in)
- Wing chord: at root: 1·63 m (5 ft 4 in)
- at tip: 1·09 m (3 ft 7 in)
- Wing aspect ratio: 7·35
- Length overall: 7·86 m (25 ft 9½ in)
- Height overall: 2·29 m (7 ft 6 in)
- Tailplane span: 3·21 m (10 ft 6½ in)
- Propeller diameter: 2·29 m (7 ft 6 in)
- Propeller ground clearance: 0·23 m (9 in)
- Door: Height: 0·64 m (2 ft 1 in)
- Width: 0·81 m (2 ft 8 in)
- Height to sill: 1·12 m (3 ft 8 in)

Weights:
- Weight empty, equipped: 658 kg (1,450 lb)
- Max T-O weight: 1,043 kg (2,300 lb)

Performance (at max T-O weight):
- Max level speed at S/L: 87 knots (161 km/h; 100 mph) IAS
- Max rate of climb at S/L: 366 m (1,200 ft)/min
- Service ceiling: 6,980 m (22,900 ft)
- T-O run: 122 m (400 ft)
- Landing run: 98 m (320 ft)
- Range with max fuel, no reserves: 651 nm (1,207 km; 750 miles)

ENSTROM

THE ENSTROM HELICOPTER CORPORATION

PO Box 277, Twin County Airport, Menominee, Michigan 49858
Telephone: (906) 863 9971
Telex: 263451
President: George B. Rahman
Vice-President, Sales and Service: Paul L. Shultz

The history of Enstrom, since the company was founded in 1959, has been outlined in previous editions of *Jane's*. Ownership passed to Bravo Investments BV of the Netherlands in January 1980. In September 1984 Enstrom was acquired by a group of American investors headed by Mr Dean Kamen of New Hampshire.

A total of more than 807 Enstrom helicopters had been built by 1 January 1986.

ENSTROM MODELS F-28 and 280

Details of the basic Model F-28A and the Model 280 Shark can be found in the 1978-79 *Jane's*. They were replaced by turbocharged versions of both models, under the designations F-28C and 280C respectively. These received FAA certification on 8 December 1975 and were last described in the 1984-85 *Jane's*. Production of these models ceased in November 1981. They were succeeded by the Models F-28F, 280F Shark (described in 1985-86 *Jane's* and now out of production), and the Model 280FX.

F-28F Falcon. Basic version, which received FAA certification in January 1981.

Model 280FX. Developed version of the Model 280F Shark, which began flight testing in December 1983 and received FAA certification under CAR Pt 6 on 14 January 1985. The Model 280FX features completely faired landing skid legs, a redesigned air inlet system, redesigned horizontal and vertical tail surfaces incorporating endplate fins on the horizontal stabiliser, covered tail rotor shaft, and a tail rotor guard. New seats including lumbar support and energy-absorbing foam have been installed. Main and tail rotor gearboxes contain chip detectors. Standard equipment on the Model 280FX includes II Morrow Apollo 611 Loran C; King KY 197 com radio with intercom; KT 76A transponder; headsets; graphic engine monitor; annunciator warning panel for low rotor rpm, overboost, clutch not fully engaged, low fuel pressure and chip detection; and custom seating. Range can be increased to 339 nm (627 km; 390 miles) by installing an internal auxiliary tank. Claimed to remain stable if flown 'feet-off' at 87 knots (161 km/h; 100 mph).

An Enstrom wet or dry dispersal agricultural kit is available for fitment to the F-28F. It comprises two side-mounted hoppers with large quick-fill openings, and spraybooms with a normal span of 9·04 m (29 ft 8 in), but extendable to 11·07 m (36 ft 4 in). A manually operated clutch provides positive control of the centrifugal pump, which has a liquid capacity of 227 litres (60 US gallons)/min. Dry discharge rate is variable from 0 to 272 kg (600 lb)/min. Weight of the entire quickly removable dispersal system is 48 kg (105 lb). Hopper capacity is 340 litres (90 US gallons) of liquid or 0·5 m³ (17·4 cu ft) of dry chemicals.

Type: Three-seat light helicopter.

Rotor System: Fully articulated metal three-blade main rotor. Blades are of bonded light alloy construction, each attached to hub by retention pin and drag link. Blade section NACA 0013·5. Two-blade teetering tail rotor, with blades of bonded light alloy construction. Tail rotor on port side. Blades do not fold.

Rotor Drive: Poly V-belt drive system. Right angle drive reduction gearbox. Main rotor/engine rpm ratio 1 : 7·154; tail rotor/engine rpm ratio 1 : 1·156.

Fuselage: Glassfibre and light alloy cab structure, with welded steel tube centre-section. Semi-monocoque aluminium tailcone structure.

Tail Unit: Both models have horizontal stabiliser forward of tail rotor, with endplate fins.

Landing Gear: Skids carried on Enstrom oleo-pneumatic shock absorbers. Air Cruiser inflatable floats available optionally.

Power Plant: One 168 kW (225 hp) Avco Lycoming HIO-360-F1AD flat-four engine with Rotomaster 3BT5EE10J2 turbocharger. Two fuel tanks, each of 79·5 litres (21 US gallons). Total standard fuel capacity 159 litres (42 US gallons). Auxiliary tank, capacity 49 litres (13 US gallons), can be installed in the baggage compartment. Oil capacity 9·5 litres (2·5 US gallons).

Accommodation: Pilot and two passengers, side by side on bench seat; centre place removable. Fully transparent removable door on each side of cabin. Baggage space aft of engine compartment, capacity 49 kg (108 lb), with external access door. Cabin heated and ventilated.

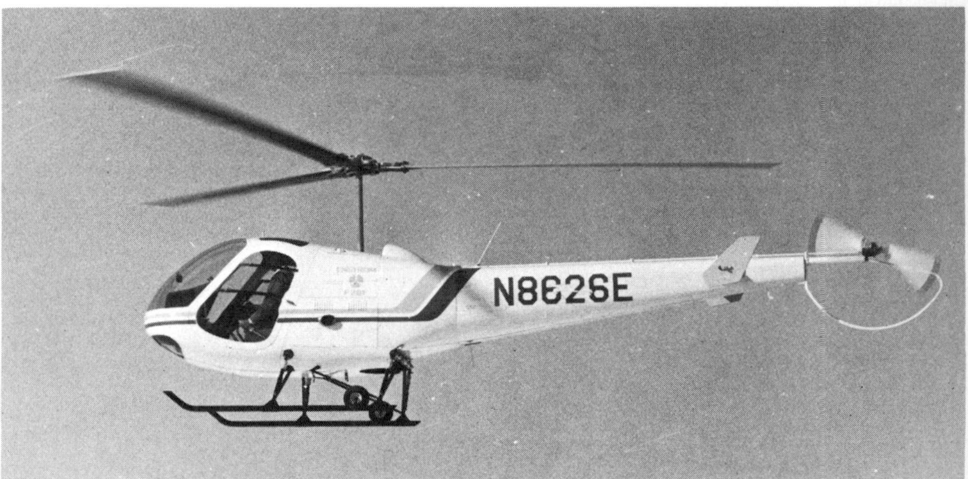

Enstrom F-28F Falcon, current basic version of the F-28 helicopter

Enstrom Model 280FX three-seat light helicopter

Systems: Electrical power provided by 12V 70A engine driven alternator; 24V 100A system optional.

Avionics and Equipment: Nav/com to customer's requirements. Cargo hook, floats, spraygear and litters optional.

Dimensions, external (A: F-28F; B: 280FX):
- Main rotor diameter: 9·75 m (32 ft 0 in)
- Tail rotor diameter: 1·42 m (4 ft 8 in)
- Distance between rotor centres: 5·56 m (18 ft 3 in)
- Main rotor blade chord: 0·24 m (9½ in)
- Length overall, rotors stationary:
  - A: 8·94 m (29 ft 4 in)
  - B: 8·43 m (27 ft 8 in)
- Height to top of rotor head: 2·79 m (9 ft 2 in)
- Skid track: 2·24 m (7 ft 4 in)
- Cabin doors (each): Height: 1·04 m (3 ft 5 in)
- Width: 0·84 m (2 ft 9 in)
- Height to sill: 0·64 m (2 ft 1 in)
- Baggage door: Height: 0·55 m (1 ft 9½ in)
- Width: 0·39 m (1 ft 3½ in)
- Height to sill: 0·86 m (2 ft 10 in)

Dimensions, internal:
- Cabin: Max width: F-28F: 1·47 m (4 ft 10 in)
- 280FX: 1·50 m (4 ft 11 in)
- Baggage compartment volume: F-28F: 0·20 m³ (7 cu ft)
- 280FX: 0·18 m³ (6·3 cu ft)

Areas:
- Main rotor disc: 74·69 m² (804 sq ft)
- Tail rotor disc: 1·66 m² (17·88 sq ft)

Weights and Loadings (A: F-28F Normal category; B: 280FX):
- Weight empty, equipped: A: 680 kg (1,500 lb)
- B: 712 kg (1,570 lb)
- Max T-O weight: A, B: 1,179 kg (2,600 lb)
- Max disc loading: A, B: 15·77 kg/m² (3·23 lb/sq ft)
- Max power loading: A: 7·02 kg/kW (11·55 lb/hp)
- B: 7·71 kg/kW (12·68 lb/hp)

Performance (at AUW of 1,066 kg; 2,350 lb except where indicated):
- Max level speed, S/L to 915 m (3,000 ft):
  - F-28F: 97 knots (180 km/h; 112 mph) IAS
  - 280FX: more than 104 knots (193 km/h; 120 mph) IAS
- Max cruising speed:
  - F-28F: 97 knots (180 km/h; 112 mph)
  - 280FX: 102 knots (188 km/h; 117 mph)
- Econ cruising speed:
  - F-28F: 83 knots (154 km/h; 96 mph)
  - 280FX: 96 knots (177 km/h; 110 mph)
- Max rate of climb at S/L: 442 m (1,450 ft)/min
- Certificated operating ceiling: 3,660 m (12,000 ft)
- Hovering ceiling: IGE: 4,025 m (13,200 ft)
  - IGE at AUW of 1,179 kg (2,600 lb): 2,345 m (7,700 ft)
  - OGE: 2,650 m (8,700 ft)
- Max range, standard fuel, no reserves:
  - F-28F: 228 nm (423 km; 263 miles)
  - 280FX: 260 nm (483 km; 300 miles)
- Max endurance: 280FX: 3 h 30 min

EVERGREEN

EVERGREEN AIR CENTER INC (Subsidiary of Evergreen International Aviation Inc)

Pinal Air Park, Marana, Arizona 85238
Telephone: (602) 622 3671
Telex: 165575
President: Timothy Wahlberg
Vice-President, Engineering and Maintenance:
Paul Strand

Evergreen Air Center undertakes maintenance, modification, repair and overhaul of commercial and military fixed-wing aircraft and helicopters. Recent work has included the conversion of three Lockheed P2V-5 Neptune maritime patrol aircraft into water bombers for operation by Evergreen Air Tankers, an associate company.

EVERGREEN P2V-5 TANKER CONVERSION

One of the P2V-5 Neptunes modified by Evergreen Air Center for operation in a water bombing role is shown in the accompanying illustration. No details are available except that it can carry up to 11,355 litres (3,000 US gallons) of fire retardant in the tank which extends below its former weapons bay. The normal load is 9,460 litres (2,500 US gallons).

The P2V-5 (P-2E) was last described in the 1963-64 *Jane's*.

Evergreen conversion of a Lockheed P2V-5 Neptune for firefighting operations *(Neil A. Macdougall)*

EXCALIBUR

EXCALIBUR AVIATION COMPANY

8337 Mission Road, San Antonio, Texas 78214
Telephone: (512) 927 6201
President: Michael M. Davis

Excalibur Aviation continues to produce its improved versions of the Beechcraft Queen Air. These modified aircraft, named Queenaire 800 and Queenaire 8800, continue to be completed at the rate of one per month, notably for operators in South America. In addition to this continuing programme, Excalibur Aviation is currently modifying military U-8F (Beech Queen Air 65) aircraft for the US National Guard Bureau, Washington, DC. The conversions provide improved reliability, speed and range, together with reduced operating costs.

By early 1986 Excalibur Aviation had completed a total of 137 Queenaire conversions, including 51 for the US Army. Some 13 Beech Model 50 Twin-Bonanzas have also been modified by the company.

EXCALIBUR QUEENAIRE 800 and 8800

The Excalibur modification of Queen Air 65s and 80s includes installation of two 298 kW (400 hp) Avco Lycoming IO-720-A1B eight-cylinder engines, each driving a Hartzell three-blade constant-speed and fully-feathering metal propeller with spinner; new engine mountings; new exhaust system; new low drag engine nacelles; new (or zero-time overhauled and certificated) accessories; and Excalibur fully enclosed wheel well doors. Modifications of the Beechcraft Queen Air 65, A65 and 80 of all serial numbers are designated Queenaire 800; similar modifications to the Queen Air A80 and B80 of all serial numbers have the designation Queenaire 8800.

Weights (A: Queenaire 800; B: Queenaire 8800):
Weight empty, equipped (average):
A 2,449 kg (5,400 lb)
B 2,631 kg (5,800 lb)
Max T-O weight: A 3,628 kg (8,000 lb)
B 3,991 kg (8,800 lb)
Max landing weight: A 3,447 kg (7,600 lb)

An Excalibur Queenaire 800 conversion of a Beech U-8F for the Missouri Army National Guard

B 3,792 kg (8,360 lb)
Performance (at max T-O weight):
Cruising speed, 75% power:
A, B at 2,530 m (8,300 ft) 201 knots (372 km/h; 231 mph)
Cruising speed, 65% power:
A, B at 3,050 m (10,000 ft) 195 knots (362 km/h; 225 mph)
Cruising speed, 45% power at 3,050 m (10,000 ft):
A, B 172 knots (319 km/h; 198 mph)
Stalling speed, gear and flaps up:
A 80 knots (148 km/h; 92 mph)
B 86 knots (160 km/h; 99 mph)
Stalling speed, gear and flaps down:
A 68 knots (126 km/h; 78 mph)
B 70 knots (129 km/h; 80 mph)
Max rate of climb at S/L: A 468 m (1,535 ft)/min
B 454 m (1,490 ft)/min
Rate of climb at S/L, one engine out:
A 110 m (360 ft)/min
B 76 m (250 ft)/min
Service ceiling: A 6,005 m (19,700 ft)
B 5,700 m (18,700 ft)
Service ceiling, one engine out:
A 3,595 m (11,800 ft)
B 3,110 m (10,200 ft)
T-O to 15 m (50 ft): A 520 m (1,706 ft)
B 625 m (2,050 ft)
Landing from 15 m (50 ft): A 663 m (2,176 ft)
B 747 m (2,450 ft)
Range with max fuel at 3,050 m (10,000 ft), with 113·5 litres (30 US gallons) reserves:
A 1,322 nm (2,451 km; 1,523 miles)
B 1,547 nm (2,867 km; 1,782 miles)

FAIRCHILD INDUSTRIES

FAIRCHILD INDUSTRIES INC

Washington Dulles International Airport, 300 West Service Road, PO Box 10803, Chantilly, Virginia 22021-9998
Telephone: (703) 478 5800
Chairman of the Board, President and Chief Executive Officer: Emanuel Fthenakis
Executive Vice-President and Chief Financial Officer: James R. Wilson
Senior Vice-Presidents:
Charles B. Husick (Commercial Aviation)
John J. McDonnell (General Counsel)
Philip Schneider (Communications and Electronics)
John W. Townsend (Planning and Operations)
Rodney L. Woodworth (Commercial and Industrial)
Vice-Presidents:
James P. Allen (Controller)
Hal W. Howes (Government Relations)
James D. Jackson (Secretary)
John W. Sandford (President, Fairchild Republic Company)
James M. Schell (Treasurer)
Thomas F. Spoehr (President, Fairchild Aerospace Products)
Robert J. Terry (Tax Counsel)
Thomas Turner (Corporate Marketing)

AEROSPACE:

Fairchild Aircraft Corporation
See pages 403-405 of this section

Fairchild Republic Company
See following entry

Fairchild Aerospace Products Division
Culver City, California 90230
President: Tom Spoehr

Fairchild Control Systems Company
Manhattan Beach, California 90266

Fairchild Industries is an aerospace, electronics, commercial/industrial products and communications company with business interests in civil and military aircraft, aerospace fasteners, aircraft subsystems, spacecraft and space subsystems, avionics systems, tooling for the plastics industry, and domestic satellite communications systems.

FAIRCHILD REPUBLIC COMPANY

Conklin Street, Farmingdale, Long Island, New York 11735
Telephone: (516) 531 2464
Telex: 96-7735
President: John W. Sandford
Manager, Public Relations: George Thune

Founded on 17 February 1931, as the Seversky Aircraft Company, Republic operated as Republic Aviation Corporation from 1939 until September 1965, when it became a division of Fairchild Hiller Corporation, now Fairchild Industries Inc.

Its work during 1986 has included development and manufacture of the T-46 trainer, support of the A-10 Thunderbolt II aircraft, production of structural components for the Boeing 747 airliner, tail fins and rudders for the Grumman F-14 Tomcat, main landing gear fairings and doors for the Lockheed C-5B Galaxy, and manned spacecraft subassemblies and subsystems. It is currently subcontractor to Saab-Scania of Sweden on the Saab SF 340 transport aircraft (see Swedish section).

FAIRCHILD REPUBLIC THUNDERBOLT II

USAF designation: A-10A

Fairchild Republic built two YA-10A prototypes for evaluation under the US Air Force's A-X close support aircraft programme, and the first of these flew for the first time on 10 May 1972. The first of six A-10A DT and E aircraft flew on 15 February 1975. Details of these early A-10As can be found in the 1977-78 *Jane's*.

The first flight by a production A-10A Thunderbolt II (75-00258) was made on 21 October 1975. Purchase of 739 for the USAF was planned (including the six DT and E aircraft); but funding was terminated in 1983 after 713 production A-10s had been ordered. Delivery of these was completed on 20 March 1984, and units with which they serve were listed in the 1984-85 *Jane's*.

A full structural description of the A-10 can be found in the 1983-84 and earlier editions of *Jane's*. The following details supplement or update the abbreviated entry in the 1985-86 edition:

ARMAMENT: Typical combat load for an A-10A operating in Germany comprises a General Electric GAU-8/A Avenger 30 mm seven-barrel cannon with full ammunition, four Maverick air-to-surface missiles, Pave Penny pod, ALQ-119 pod and max internal fuel. Provision is to be added for the carriage of AIM-9 air-to-air missiles.

WEIGHTS AND LOADINGS:

Operating weight empty	11,612 kg (25,600 lb)
*Basic design weight, equipped	14,729 kg (32,472 lb)
**Forward airstrip weight	15,155 kg (33,412 lb)
Max external ordnance	7,258 kg (16,000 lb)
Max external ordnance with full internal fuel	6,214 kg (13,700 lb)
Max T-O weight	22,680 kg (50,000 lb)
Max wing loading	482·4 kg/m² (98·81 lb/sq ft)
Max power loading	281·39 kg/kN (2·76 lb/lb st)
Thrust/weight ratio	0·4

**incl six 500 lb bombs, 750 rds of ammunition, and 1,134 kg (2,500 lb) of fuel*

***with four Mk 82 bombs, 750 rds of ammunition, and 2,041 kg (4,500 lb) of fuel*

Fairchild Republic A-10A Thunderbolt II single-seat close support aircraft *(Dave Kindred)*

FAIRCHILD REPUBLIC NEXT GENERATION TRAINER

USAF designation: T-46A

On 2 July 1982, it was announced that Fairchild Republic Company had been selected to develop a next generation trainer (NGT) to replace the Cessna T-37 in US Air Force service. The award of an initial $104 million contract climaxed five years of design and development, during which Fairchild had completed a full scale mockup which was used for a tour of USAF bases, and had acquired a 62 per cent scale manned flight demonstrator to accumulate data for incorporation in the submission. Details of the scale version of the NGT can be found in Fairchild's entry in the 1982-83 *Jane's*.

The fixed-price incentive contract awarded to Fairchild for the NGT, later designated T-46A, covered the design, development, construction and testing of two prototypes; the supply of two static test examples; and an option for 54 production T-46As, representing an initial increment of a planned procurement of 650 aircraft for delivery into 1992. Garrett received an initial contract valued at $121·2 million, covering the supply of 29 TFE76-4A (F109-GA-100) engines, with an option on an additional 119. Funding for the first 10 production aircraft, and for long-lead materials for the following 33 aircraft, was approved in 1984, but in March 1986 the USAF announced termination of its planned T-46A programme in favour of alternatives which include re-engining and extensive modification of the existing Cessna T-37 fleet.

The first full scale development aircraft (84-492) was rolled out at Fairchild Republic's Farmingdale, New York, facility on 11 February 1985 and made its first flight from Edwards AFB, California, on 15 October. The second (84-493) was flown from Fairchild Republic's Republic Airport, Long Island, headquarters on 29 July 1986, at which time some 178 hours of flight testing had been completed on the T-46A. Work on the initial batch of ten production aircraft was continuing in the late Summer of 1986, and the US Air Force is expected to accept these irrespective of what solution to its future training needs is decided upon. The first of them was expected to fly before the end of 1986.

TYPE: Two-seat military primary trainer.

WINGS: Cantilever shoulder-wing monoplane, with basic fail-safe light alloy structure. Wing section NASA LS(1). Thickness/chord ratio 14% at mean aerodynamic chord. Anhedral 2° 30′. Incidence 2° at root, −1° 17′ at tip. Sweepback at quarter-chord 3° 30′ 22″. Conventional two-spar wing box with stiffened skins. Kevlar wingtips. Aerodynamically and statically balanced, manually operated ailerons of Kevlar and Nomex honeycomb composite construction. Douglas type hydraulically actuated trailing-edge flaps, with single pivot, of similar construction to ailerons. Spring tab in each aileron; trim tab on starboard wing between aileron and flap.

FUSELAGE: Semi-monocoque fail-safe structure of light alloy, except for Kevlar upper nose skin.

TAIL UNIT: Cantilever fixed incidence tailplane with elevators, endplate fins and rudders of light alloy. Tailplane and fin box of two-spar construction with stiffened skins. Electrically actuated trim tab in starboard side of manually operated elevator. The two rudders are controlled by a single hydraulic servo-actuator which is integrated to include the functions of authority limiting, automatic manual reversion, pedal feel, stability augmentation and trim.

LANDING GEAR: Hydraulically retractable tricycle type by Dowty Equipment of Canada Ltd. Main units retract inward and forward, nose unit forward. Oleo-pneumatic shock absorber in each unit. Goodyear mainwheels and Type VII tyres size 18 × 4·4; Goodyear steerable nosewheel and tyre Type VII size 16 × 4·4. Goodyear hydraulic brakes.

POWER PLANT: Two 5·92 kN (1,330 lb st) Garrett F109-GA-100 (TFE76-4A) turbofan engines, mounted within nacelles beneath the wing roots. One Goodyear bladder fuel cell in fuselage between wing carry-through frames, with capacity of 757 litres (200 US gallons). Single-point refuelling on port side of fuselage above baggage compartment. Air intake ducts, of superformed light alloy, incorporate hot air de-icing of duct lips. Two airbrakes, one in outer surface of each engine nacelle, deflect airstream down and away from nacelles.

ACCOMMODATION: Two persons side by side on Weber ACES II ejection seats, in pressurised and air-conditioned cockpit beneath canopy that opens upward and rearward. Dual controls standard. Baggage space in fuselage, behind cockpit; access from port side of fuselage, forward of engine nacelle. Windscreen de-icing.

SYSTEMS: AiResearch air-conditioning and pressurisation systems. Dual hydraulic system at 207 bars (3,000 lb/sq in) pressure, for actuation of landing gear, nosewheel steering, rudder, trailing-edge flaps and airbrakes. DC electrical system includes two 300A engine driven generators.

AVIONICS: Accommodated in nose bay and in fuselage aft of baggage compartment. Will include AN/ARN-118 Tacan, AN/ARN-127 VOR/ILS/marker beacon receiver, APX-100(V) IFF, AN/ARC-164 UHF/AM, AN/ARC-186(V) VHF/AM and AN/AIC-18 intercom.

DIMENSIONS, EXTERNAL:

Wing span, overall	11·77 m (38 ft 7½ in)
Wing chord (theoretical): at c/l	1·74 m (5 ft 8½ in)
at tip	0·88 m (2 ft 10½ in)
Wing aspect ratio (theoretical)	9·0
Length overall	8·99 m (29 ft 6 in)
Height overall	3·04 m (9 ft 11¾ in)
Tailplane span	3·86 m (12 ft 8 in)
Wheel track	2·26 m (7 ft 5 in)
Wheelbase	3·20 m (10 ft 6 in)
Baggage door: Height	0·71 m (2 ft 4 in)
Width	0·76 m (2 ft 6 in)
Height to sill	0·66 m (2 ft 2 in)

AREAS:

Wings, gross	15·40 m² (165·74 sq ft)
Ailerons (total)	1·18 m² (12·66 sq ft)
Trailing-edge flaps (total)	1·20 m² (12·89 sq ft)
Vertical tail surfaces (total)	2·79 m² (29·99 sq ft)
Horizontal tail surfaces (total, incl tab)	3·43 m² (36·94 sq ft)

WEIGHTS AND LOADINGS:

Weight empty	2,540 kg (5,600 lb)
Max fuel weight	556 kg (1,226 lb)
Max T-O weight	3,314 kg (7,307 lb)
Max ramp weight	3,356 kg (7,398 lb)
Max zero-fuel weight	2,799 kg (6,172 lb)
Max landing weight	3,322 kg (7,324 lb)
Max wing loading	215·2 kg/m² (44·08 lb/sq ft)
Max power loading	279·9 kg/kN (2·75 lb/lb st)

PERFORMANCE (estimated at AUW of 3,215 kg; 7,088 lb):

Max level speed at 9,145 m (30,000 ft)	391 knots (725 km/h; 450 mph)
Max cruising speed at 9,145 m (30,000 ft)	372 knots (689 km/h; 428 mph)

First full scale development Fairchild Republic T-46A trainer

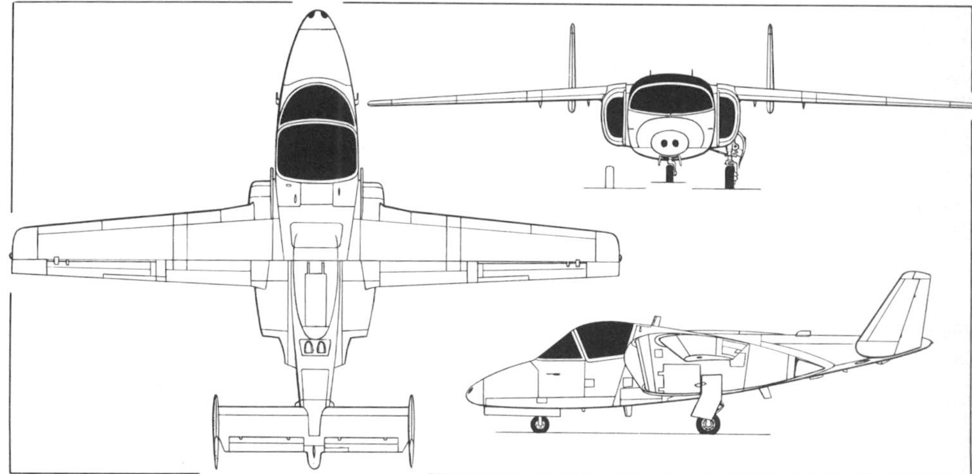

Fairchild Republic T-46A two-seat primary trainer *(Pilot Press)*

Econ cruising speed at 13,100 m (43,000 ft) 301 knots (558 km/h; 347 mph)
Stalling speed, power off:
flaps up 87 knots (161 km/h; 100 mph)
flaps down 82 knots (152 km/h; 94 mph)
Max rate of climb at S/L 1,181 m (3,874 ft)/min
Rate of climb at S/L, one engine out 227 m (746 ft)/min
Service ceiling 13,950 m (45,760 ft)
T-O run 457 m (1,500 ft)
T-O to 15 m (50 ft) 687 m (2,254 ft)
Landing from 15 m (50 ft) 640 m (2,100 ft)
Ferry range with max fuel 1,085 nm (2,011 km; 1,249 miles)

FAIRCHILD REPUBLIC AT-46A and OA-46A

Fairchild Republic announced in 1983 that it is offering on the international market a derivative of the T-46A basic pilot trainer. Designated **AT-46A**, Fairchild claims that this aircraft will provide a full spectrum of pilot training, including basic, gunnery and attack training profiles. It will also perform forward air control and light attack duties, in which form it would be designated **OA-46A**. Generally similar to the T-46A (which see), the AT-46A has in addition an optical sight and stores management system, and is being offered with four underwing hardpoints to accommodate a variety of training stores. The inboard pylons can each accommodate a 7·62 mm gun pod, 0·50 in gun pod, a 250 lb or 500 lb bomb, practice bombs, or a jettisonable fuel tank; the outboard pylons can each carry a pod containing seven 2·75 in rockets, a 250 lb bomb or practice bombs. Maximum store load on each inboard station is 317 kg (700 lb), and 136 kg (300 lb) on each outboard station.

WEIGHTS (A: primary training; B: gunnery training; C: light attack training):
Weapon payload: B 414 kg (914 lb)
C 589 kg (1,299 lb)
Max T-O weight: A 3,432 kg (7,567 lb)
B 3,847 kg (8,481 lb)
C 4,021 kg (8,866 lb)

PERFORMANCE:
Max level speed: A 381 knots (706 km/h; 439 mph)
Max cruising speed at S/L:
A 318 knots (589 km/h; 366 mph)
B 295 knots (547 km/h; 340 mph)
C 303 knots (561 km/h; 349 mph)
Max cruising speed at 4,575 m (15,000 ft):
A 344 knots (637 km/h; 396 mph)
B 316 knots (586 km/h; 364 mph)
C 325 knots (602 km/h; 374 mph)
Rate of climb at S/L, one engine out:
A 207 m (681 ft)/min
B 143 m (471 ft)/min
C 132 m (433 ft)/min
Service ceiling: A 13,600 m (44,620 ft)
T-O run: A 492 m (1,613 ft)
B 608 m (1,996 ft)
C 678 m (2,226 ft)
Landing run: A 367 m (1,205 ft)
Ferry range, internal fuel only:
A 979 nm (1,814 km; 1,127 miles)
g limits: A +6·7
B +6·0
C +5·7
Max sustained *g* at S/L: A +4·19
B +3·95
C +3·39
Max sustained *g* at 4,575 m (15,000 ft): A +3·14
B +2·59
C +2·54

FAIRCHILD AIRCRAFT CORPORATION (Subsidiary of Fairchild Industries)

PO Box 32486, San Antonio, Texas 78284
Telephone: (512) 824 9421
Telex: 767-315
PRESIDENT: Thomas J. Smith
SENIOR VICE-PRESIDENT:
Rodger T. Munt (Marketing)
VICE-PRESIDENTS:
P. D. Bartles (Operations)
A. Bruce Chuber (International Sales)
John P. Herbots (Finance)
Earl E. Morton (Domestic Airline Sales)

Fairchild Aircraft and its predecessors, recorded in previous issues of *Jane's*, have been engaged in manufacture of the Merlin series of twin-turboprop pressurised executive transport aircraft and the Metro airliner since 1966. The 600th Fairchild turboprop aircraft, a Metro III, was delivered on 27 December 1984.

FAIRCHILD MODEL SA227-AC METRO III and EXPEDITER

Swedish Air Force designation: TP88
US military designation: C-26A

The **Metro III** is a 19/20-passenger all-weather pressurised, air-conditioned airliner, certificated under the FAA's Special Federal Air Regulations 41 and 41B, which provide for compliance with ICAO Annex 8 specifications for operation at a gross weight in excess of 5,670 kg (12,500 lb). The standard Metro III is certificated for operation at a max T-O weight of 6,577 kg (14,500 lb), providing a useful load increase of 672 kg (1,482 lb) compared with the Metro II which it superseded. The optional high gross weight version of the Metro III has a max T-O weight of 7,257 kg (16,000 lb). The changes incorporated in the Metro III include a 3·05 m (10 ft 0 in) increase in wing span; more powerful engines, each driving a slow-turning four-blade McCauley propeller; new main landing gear doors, to improve take-off and landing performance and provide better access for maintenance; new streamline nacelle cowlings, with quick-action latches and hinged at the rear to improve engine access; improved handling characteristics; and new fire prevention and containment features, with all inflammable fluid pipework isolated physically from all electric current-carrying components and wiring. The Metro III is certificated for flight into known icing conditions, and has lightning strike protection which the company claims is equal to that in the latest generation of commercial jet transports.

One Metro III has been delivered to the Swedish Air Force for use as a VIP transport, and is known in Swedish service as the **TP88**. The US military designation **C-26A** has been allocated, although no order on behalf of the US services had been announced by Autumn 1986.

Recent orders for Metro IIIs included three aircraft for Wings West Airlines for operation on American Eagle services.

An all-cargo version, known as the **Expediter**, is available, with cabin air-conditioning ducts repositioned to increase cargo space, reinforced cabin floor, cargo nets and guards, and a reduced empty weight which permits a max cargo payload of more than 2,268 kg (5,000 lb). First operator of the Expediter was SAT-AIR, on behalf of United Parcel Service. In April 1985 the first of ten Expediter Is was delivered to the US small package carrier DHL Worldwide Courier Express. This version has structurally reinforced landing gear and main spar to permit an increase in max T-O weight to 7,257 kg (16,000 lb).

TYPE: Twin-turboprop 19/20-passenger commuter airliner.

WINGS: Cantilever low-wing monoplane. Wing section NACA 65_2A215 at root, NACA 64_2A415 at tip. Dihedral 5°. Incidence 1° at root, −2° 30′ at tip. Sweepback at quarter-chord 0° 54′. All-metal two-spar fail-safe structure of aluminium alloy, constructed in one piece. The main spar beams have laminated caps and these, in the centre-section, have titanium laminations. Hydraulically operated double-slotted trailing-edge flaps. Manually controlled trim tab in each aileron. Goodrich pneumatic de-icing boots on wing leading-edges, with automatic bleed air cycling system.

FUSELAGE: All-metal cylindrical semi-monocoque fail-safe structure of 2024 aluminium alloy, flush riveted throughout. All but the nose section is pressurised. Glassfibre honeycomb nosecap can accommodate a 0·46 m (18 in) weather radar antenna.

TAIL UNIT: Cantilever all-metal structure with sweptback surfaces and dorsal fin. Small ventral fin. Electrically adjustable variable incidence tailplane. Manually controlled rudder trim. Goodrich pneumatic de-icing boots on tailplane leading-edges, with automatic bleed air cycling system.

LANDING GEAR: Retractable tricycle type with twin wheels on each unit. Hydraulic retraction, with dual actuators on each unit. All wheels retract forward, main gear into engine nacelles, nosewheels into fuselage. Ozone Aircraft Systems oleo-pneumatic shock absorber struts. Nosewheel steerable. Free-fall emergency extension system, with backup of hand operated hydraulic pump. Goodrich mainwheels with low-pressure tubeless tyres, size 18 × 5·50, type VII. Jay-Em nosewheels and Goodyear low-pressure tubeless tyres, size 16 × 4·40, type VII. Goodrich self-adjusting hydraulically operated disc brakes and anti-skid system.

POWER PLANT: Two 745·5 kW (1,000 shp) dry/820 kW (1,100 shp) wet Garrett TPE331-11U-611G turboprop engines with continuous alcohol-water injection system, each driving a McCauley C652 four-blade constant-speed fully-feathering reversible-pitch metal propeller with spinner. Automatic propeller synchrophasing, and full Beta control reversing, standard. In-flight windmill start capability. Integral fuel tank in each wing, each with a usable capacity of 1,226 litres (324 US gallons). Total usable fuel capacity 2,452 litres (648 US gallons). Refuelling point on each outer wing panel. Automatic fuel heating. Oil capacity 15·1 litres (4 US gallons). Engine inlet de-icing by bleed air. Electric oil cooler inlet anti-icing. Electric propeller de-icing. Flush mounted fuel vents. Single-point rapid defuelling provisions. Negative torque sensing, single red line/autostart, automatic engine temperature limiting, and engine fire extinguishing systems.

ACCOMMODATION: Crew of two on flight deck, each with four-way adjustable seat with folding armrests and shoulder harness, separated from passeger/cargo area by partial bulkhead on port side and armrest height curtain on starboard side. Dual controls standard. Bulkhead between cabin and flight deck optional. Standard accommodation for 19-20 passengers seated two abreast, on each side of centre aisle. 'No smoking' and 'Fasten seat

Fairchild Metro III 19/20-passenger airliners of SunAire of California and Nurnberger Flugdienst of West Germany with, nearest camera, an Expediter I of DHL Worldwide Courier Express

belt' signs. Stowing fold-up seats for rapid conversion to cargo or mixed passenger/cargo configuration. Movable bulkhead between passenger and cargo sections. Snap-in carpeting. Self-stowing aisle filler. Tiedown fittings for cargo at 0·76 m (30 in) spacing. Integral-step passenger door on port side of fuselage, immediately aft of flight deck. Large cargo loading door on port side of fuselage at rear of cabin, hinged at top. Three window emergency exits, one on the port, two on the starboard side. Forward baggage/avionics compartment in nose, capacity 363 kg (800 lb). Pressurised rear cargo compartment, capacity 385 kg (850 lb). Cabin air-conditioned and pressurised. Electric windscreen de-icing. Two-speed windscreen wipers.

SYSTEMS: Garrett automatic cabin pressure control system: max differential 0·48 bars (7·0 lb/sq in), providing a sea level cabin altitude to 5,120 m (16,800 ft). Engine bleed air heating, dual air cycle cooling system, with automatic temperature control. Air blower system for on-ground ventilation. Independent hydraulic system for brakes. Dual engine driven hydraulic pumps, using fire resistant MIL-H-83282 hydraulic fluid, provide 138 bars (2,000 lb/sq in) to operate flaps, landing gear actuators and nosewheel steering. Hydraulic system flow rates 30·3 litres (8 US gallons)/min at idle power, both engines; 46·7 litres (12·34 US gallons)/min at T-O and climb power. Air/oil reservoir, pressure 2·27 bars (33 lb/sq in). Electrical system supplied by two 300A 28V DC starter/generators. Fail-safe system with overload and overvoltage protection. Redundant circuits for essential systems. Two 350VA solid state inverters supply 115V and 26V AC. Two 24V 25Ah nickel-cadmium batteries for main services. Engine fire detection system and fire extinguishing system standard. Wing overheat detection system. Oxygen system of 1·39 m³ (49 cu ft) capacity with flush outlets at each seat; system with capacity of 3·26 m³ (115 cu ft) optional. Stall avoidance system comprising angle indicator, visual and aural warning.

AVIONICS AND EQUIPMENT: Two flight deck and four cabin speakers standard; provisions for installation of remotely mounted or panel mounted avionics, customer furnished weather radar and autopilot. Standard equipment includes pilot and co-pilot foot warmers; edge lit consoles, pedestal and switch panels; integrally lit instruments; annunciator panel with 48 indicators; internally operated control locks, individual reading lights and air vents for each passenger; heated pitot; heated static sources; baggage compartment, cargo compartment, entrance, map and instrument panel, ice inspection, retractable landing, navigation, rotating beacon and taxi lights; automatic engine start cycle; external power socket; and static wicks.

DIMENSIONS, EXTERNAL:
Wing span 17·37 m (57 ft 0 in)
Wing mean aerodynamic chord 1·84 m (6 ft 0·33 in)
Wing aspect ratio 10·5
Length overall 18·09 m (59 ft 4¼ in)
Height overall 5·08 m (16 ft 8 in)
Tailplane span 4·86 m (15 ft 11½ in)
Wheel track 4·57 m (15 ft 0 in)
Wheelbase 5·83 m (19 ft 1½ in)
Propeller diameter 2·69 m (8 ft 10 in)
Passenger door (fwd): Height 1·35 m (4 ft 5 in)
Width 0·64 m (2 ft 1 in)
Cargo door (rear): Height 1·30 m (4 ft 3¼ in)
Width 1·35 m (4 ft 5 in)
Height to sill 1·30 m (4 ft 3¼ in)
Forward baggage doors (two, each):
Height 0·64 m (2 ft 1 in)
Width 0·46 m (1 ft 6 in)

Fairchild Metro IIIA, an advanced version of the Metro III with PT6A-45R turboprop engines

Emergency exits (three, each):
Height 0·71 m (2 ft 4 in)
Width 0·51 m (1 ft 8 in)

DIMENSIONS, INTERNAL:
Cabin, excl flight deck and rear cargo compartment:
Length 7·75 m (25 ft 5 in)
Max width 1·57 m (5 ft 2 in)
Max height (aisle) 1·45 m (4 ft 9 in)
Floor area 13·01 m² (140 sq ft)
Volume 13·88 m³ (490 cu ft)
Rear cargo compartment (pressurised):
Length 2·34 m (7 ft 8 in)
Max width 1·57 m (5 ft 2 in)
Max height 1·32 m (4 ft 4 in)
Volume 3·85 m³ (136 cu ft)
Nose cargo compartment (unpressurised):
Length 1·75 m (5 ft 9 in)
Volume 1·27 m³ (45 cu ft)

AREAS:
Wings, gross 28·71 m² (309 sq ft)
Ailerons (total) 1·31 m² (14·12 sq ft)
Trailing-edge flaps (total) 3·78 m² (40·66 sq ft)
Fin, incl dorsal fin 3·40 m² (36·62 sq ft)
Rudder, incl tab 1·80 m² (19·38 sq ft)
Tailplane 5·08 m² (54·70 sq ft)
Elevators 1·98 m² (21·27 sq ft)

WEIGHTS AND LOADINGS:
Operating weight empty 3,963 kg (8,737 lb)
Max fuel weight 1,969 kg (4,342 lb)
Max T-O weight 6,577 kg (14,500 lb)
Max ramp weight 6,622 kg (14,600 lb)
Max zero-fuel weight 5,670 kg (12,500 lb)
Max landing weight 6,350 kg (14,000 lb)
Max wing loading 230·7 kg/m² (47·25 lb/sq ft)
Max power loading 4·01 kg/kW (6·59 lb/shp)

PERFORMANCE (at max T-O weight, ISA, except where indicated):
Design diving speed
311 knots (576 km/h; 358 mph) CAS
Max operating speed
248 knots (459 km/h; 285 mph) CAS
Max operating Mach No. 0·52
Max cruising speed at mid-cruise weight of 5,670 kg (12,500 lb):
at 4,575 m (15,000 ft)
278 knots (515 km/h; 320 mph)
at 6,100 m (20,000 ft)
273 knots (506 km/h; 314 mph)
at 7,620 m (25,000 ft)
263 knots (487 km/h; 303 mph)
Min single-engine control speed (VMC)
87 knots (161 km/h; 100 mph) IAS
Stalling speed:
flaps and wheels up
98 knots (182 km/h; 113 mph) IAS
flaps and wheels down
87 knots (161 km/h; 100 mph) IAS
Max rate of climb at S/L 722 m (2,370 ft)/min
Rate of climb at S/L, one engine out
210 m (690 ft)/min
Service ceiling 8,380 m (27,500 ft)
Service ceiling, one engine out 4,330 m (14,200 ft)
T-O to 15 m (50 ft), dry power 991 m (3,250 ft)
Landing from 15 m (50 ft) 747 m (2,450 ft)
Range with max standard fuel, two crew, 19 passengers and baggage, 45 min reserves
869 nm (1,610 km; 1,001 miles)

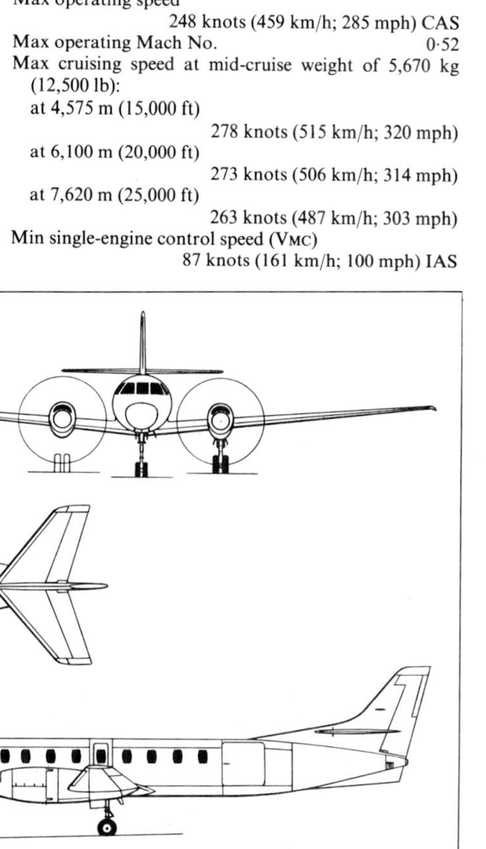

Fairchild Metro III commuter airliner (two Garrett TPE331 turboprop engines) *(Pilot Press)*

FAIRCHILD SPECIAL MISSION AIRCRAFT

Fairchild offers a variety of aircraft, designed specifically for special mission applications, some 34 examples of which have been delivered. Variations based on the Metro III include models for maritime patrol, anti-submarine warfare, flight navigation systems inspection, photo reconnaissance, electronic intelligence, airborne early warning and airborne critical care missions. The maritime patrol variant has a 360° scan Litton AN/APS-504(V) or (V)5, or AIL AN/APS-128D, radar in an underbelly blister fairing, an Omega nav system linked to hand held cameras, and two bulged observation windows, staggered one on each side of the rear fuselage. The ASW version carries sonobuoys and a sonobuoy signal processor, an OTP indicator, and MAD tailboom. Optional equipment for both versions includes a searchlight, IR linescanner, low light level TV, FLIR, sidelooking TV, Doppler radar, droppable liferafts and survival kits, and two 288 litre (76 US gallon) underwing auxiliary fuel tanks. At a max T-O weight of 7,257 kg (16,000 lb), and with underwing tanks, the surveillance versions can complete a 10 hour mission over a radius of 1,050 nm (1,946 km; 1,209 miles) from base, at a height of 7,620 m (25,000 ft) with 45 min fuel reserves.

FAIRCHILD METRO IIIA

This version of the Metro III has Pratt & Whitney Canada engines, for operators who wish to standardise on a common family of P&WC power plants throughout a multi-type fleet of aircraft. The first Metro IIIA was flown for the first time on 31 December 1981.

The general description of the Metro III applies also to the Metro IIIA, except as follows:

POWER PLANT: Two Pratt & Whitney Canada PT6A-45R turboprop engines, each flat rated at 820 kW (1,100 shp). Fuel system as for Metro III.

PERFORMANCE (provisional, at max T-O weight except where indicated):
Cruising speed, max landing weight at 3,050 m (10,000 ft) 279 knots (517 km/h; 321 mph)
Max rate of climb at S/L 689 m (2,260 ft)/min
Rate of climb at S/L, one engine out
250 m (820 ft)/min
Service ceiling 8,100 m (26,600 ft)
Service ceiling, one engine out 5,030 m (16,500 ft)
T-O to 15 m (50 ft) 956 m (3,135 ft)
Landing from 15 m (50 ft) at max landing weight
828 m (2,715 ft)
Range with max payload, max cruising power at 7,620 m (25,000 ft) 663 nm (1,228 km; 763 miles)

FAIRCHILD MERLIN 300 (SA227 TT/41)

This aircraft series originated with the Merlin III, which received FAA certification on 27 July 1970, and was described in the 1974-75 *Jane's*. The later Merlin IIIA was described in the 1977-78 edition, the Merlin IIIB in the 1980-81 edition, and the Merlin IIIC in the 1983-84 edition.

Production of the Merlin IIIC ended in late 1982. It was superseded by a modified version, known then as the Fairchild 300, of which development began in April 1983.

Deliveries of the Merlin 300 began in the Winter of 1984-85, and totalled 10 by early 1986. The power plant is unchanged, the emphasis being primarily on aerodynamic and control system improvements for increased performance and enhanced handling, notably in roll. External changes include the introduction of 0·76 m (2 ft 6 in) winglets and reshaped ailerons. Internally, the control system utilises larger cables and pulleys, requiring much reduced travel of the yoke for roll control.

TYPE: Eight/ten-passenger twin-turboprop executive transport.

WINGS: Generally as for Metro III, but without the increase in wing span, and with winglets and reshaped ailerons.

FUSELAGE: All-metal cylindrical semi-monocoque fail-safe structure of 2024 aluminium alloy, flush riveted throughout. Glassfibre honeycomb nosecap will accommodate a 0·46 m (18 in) weather radar antenna.

TAIL UNIT: As for Metro III.

LANDING GEAR: As for Metro III, except for new power braking and anti-skid systems.

POWER PLANT: Two 671 kW (900 shp) Garrett TPE331-10U-513G turboprop engines, each driving a Dowty Type R.321 four-blade fully-feathering and reversible-pitch metal propeller with synchrophaser. Continuous alcohol/water injection system optional. Fuel system, engine inlet de-icing, and other power plant systems generally as for Metro III.

ACCOMMODATION: Crew of two on flight deck, each on four-way adjustable seat with shoulder harness; dual controls standard. Bulkhead with sliding door divides flight deck from cabin. Accommodation for eight to ten passengers with seats disposed on each side of a central aisle. Rapid relocation of seats and couches is made possible by continuous tracks recessed into floor, permitting layout to be varied according to mission. Passenger door at rear of cabin on port side, with integral airstair. Emergency exit on starboard side of cabin. Sliding door at rear end of cabin to separate it from the entrance vestibule. Baggage space in vestibule to accommodate 136 kg (300 lb); baggage and avionics in unpressurised nose compartment, capacity 272 kg (600 lb). Accommodation pressurised, air-conditioned and ventilated. Electrically heated windscreen. Two-speed windscreen wipers.

SYSTEMS: Generally as for Metro III, except that oxygen system has a capacity of 0·62 m³ (22 cu ft).

AVIONICS AND EQUIPMENT: Optional avionics, and standard and optional equipment, are generally as for Metro III, with the addition of a Collins EHSI-74 electronic horizontal situation indicator.

DIMENSIONS, EXTERNAL:

Wing span	16·60 m (47 ft 10¾ in)
Wing mean aerodynamic chord	1·94 m (6 ft 4½ in)
Wing aspect ratio	7·71
Length overall	12·85 m (42 ft 2 in)
Height overall	5·13 m (16 ft 10 in)
Tailplane span	4·86 m (15 ft 11½ in)
Wheel track	4·57 m (15 ft 0 in)
Wheelbase	3·23 m (10 ft 7 in)
Propeller diameter	2·69 m (8 ft 10 in)
Passenger door (port, rear): Height	1·35 m (4 ft 5 in)
Width	0·64 m (2 ft 1 in)

DIMENSIONS, INTERNAL:

Cabin, excl flight deck and rear compartment:	
Length	3·23 m (10 ft 7 in)
Max width	1·57 m (5 ft 2 in)
Max height	1·45 m (4 ft 9 in)
Volume	9·09 m³ (321 cu ft)
Rear baggage compartment (pressurised):	
Volume	2·12 m³ (75 cu ft)
Nose baggage/avionics compartment (unpressurised):	
Volume	1·27 m³ (45 cu ft)

AREAS: As for Metro III, except:

Wings, gross	25·78 m² (277·50 sq ft)

WEIGHTS AND LOADINGS:

Weight empty, equipped	3,833 kg (8,450 lb)
Fuel load	1,969 kg (4,342 lb)
Max T-O and landing weight	6,001 kg (13,230 lb)
Max ramp weight	6,046 kg (13,330 lb)
Max zero-fuel weight	5,670 kg (12,500 lb)
Max wing loading	232·8 kg/m² (47·68 lb/sq ft)
Max power loading	4·47 kg/kW (7·35 lb/shp)

PERFORMANCE (at max T-O weight, ISA, except where indicated):

Never-exceed speed	265 knots (490 km/h; 305 mph) CAS
Max operating Mach No.	0·63
Max cruising speed, at mid-cruise weight of 5,670 kg (12,500 lb):	
at 3,050 m (10,000 ft)	296 knots (548 km/h; 340 mph)
at 6,100 m (20,000 ft)	300 knots (555 km/h; 345 mph)
at 7,620 m (25,000 ft)	289 knots (535 km/h; 332 mph)
at 9,140 m (30,000 ft)	283 knots (524 km/h; 325 mph)
Min single-engine control speed (VMC)	109 knots (202 km/h; 125 mph) IAS
Stalling speed:	
flaps and wheels up	104 knots (193 km/h; 120 mph)
flaps and wheels down	91 knots (169 km/h; 105 mph)
Max rate of climb at S/L	792 m (2,600 ft)/min
Rate of climb at S/L, one engine out	228 m (750 ft)/min
Service ceiling	9,450 m (31,000 ft)
Service ceiling, one engine out	4,815 m (15,800 ft)
T-O to 15 m (50 ft)	890 m (2,920 ft)
Landing from 15 m (50 ft)	855 m (2,805 ft)
Range with max fuel, allowances for start, T-O, climb and descent plus 45 min reserves:	
at long range cruise power at 8,535 m (28,000 ft)	2,312 nm (4,284 km; 2,662 miles)
at max cruise power at 4,575 m (15,000 ft)	1,795 nm (3,326 km; 2,067 miles)

Fairchild Merlin 300 twin-turboprop business aircraft

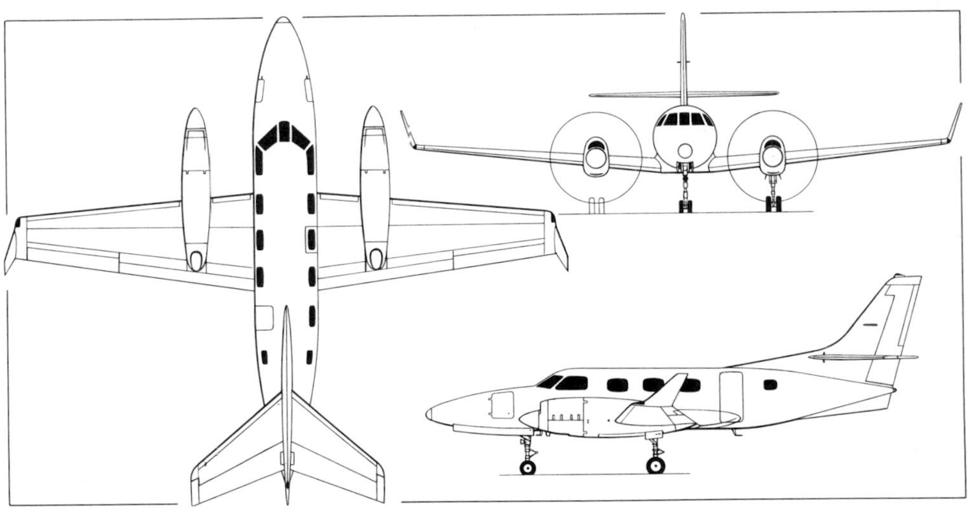
Fairchild Merlin 300 eight/ten-passenger executive transport aircraft *(Pilot Press)*

FAIRCHILD MERLIN IV C (SA227-AT)

The Merlin IV C is a corporate version of the Metro III commuter airliner, differing primarily in its internal configuration. It has reclining passenger seats, couches, and a more luxurious standard of interior furniture, decor and lighting. The refreshment and entertainment centre includes a large buffet cabinet with beverage and food storage and preparation facilities, television and stereo equipment. At the rear of the cabin, separated by a bulkhead and hinged door, are a toilet and baggage compartment.

The Merlin IV C is certificated under the FAA's SFAR Pt 41B and ICAO Annex 8 specifications, and has a T-O and landing weight of 6,577 kg (14,500 lb). Its large cabin volume, and the availability of movable bulkheads and interchangeable cabin furnishings, makes it easily convertible to meet a company's airlift requirements in virtually any arrangement of passengers and/or cargo.

The description and specification of the Metro III apply also to the Merlin IV C, except as follows:

TYPE: Eleven/fourteen-passenger corporate transport.

WEIGHTS AND LOADINGS: As Metro III, except:

Weight empty, equipped	4,318 kg (9,520 lb)

PERFORMANCE (at max T-O weight, ISA, except where indicated):

Max cruising speed, at mid-cruise weight of 5,670 kg (12,500 lb):	
at 3,050-4,575 m (10,000-15,000 ft)	283 knots (524 km/h; 326 mph)
at 6,100 m (20,000 ft)	281 knots (521 km/h; 323 mph)
at 7,620 m (25,000 ft)	273 knots (506 km/h; 314 mph)
Max rate of climb at S/L	750 m (2,460 ft)/min
Rate of climb at S/L, one engine out	207 m (680 ft)/min
Range with max standard fuel, max cruise power at 7,925 m (26,000 ft), 45 min reserves:	
eight occupants	1,653 nm (3,063 km; 1,903 miles)
thirteen occupants	974 nm (1,805 km; 1,121 miles)
Ferry range, conditions and allowances as above, but with two flight crew only	2,117 nm (3,923 km; 2,438 miles)

FLIGHT DYNAMICS — *see Sport Aircraft section*

FRAKES

FRAKES AVIATION

Route 3, PO Box 229-B, Cleburne Airport, Cleburne, Texas 76031

Telephone: (817) 645 9136
Telex: 75-8390

DIRECTORS:
J. Fred Frakes
Joseph Frakes

FRAKES KING AIR CONVERSION

This company, whose Turbo-Mallard conversion of the Grumman G-73 Mallard amphibian was described in the 1975-76 *Jane's*, has developed an engine nacelle and inlet system modification for the Beech Model 90 King Air series of turboprop business aircraft. Frakes claims that the modification, which is available on all Model 90-F90 King Airs, offers lower drag, increased ram air recovery, enhanced take-off, climb and altitude performance, and a 13-26 knot (24-48 km/h; 15-30 mph) increase in cruising speed, depending on model.

FRAKES TURBO-ALBATROSS

Frakes Aviation has developed a turboprop conversion of the Grumman HU-16 Albatross amphibian in which the aircraft's 1,100 kW (1,475 hp) Wright R-1820 radial engines will be replaced with either four Pratt & Whitney Canada PT6A or two Pratt & Whitney Canada PW120 turboprop engines. Work on a prototype Turbo-Albatross conversion was expected to begin during 1986.

GATES LEARJET

GATES LEARJET CORPORATION

Tucson International Airport, PO Box 11186, Tucson, Arizona 85734
Telephone: (602) 746 5100
Telex: 666453

WICHITA PLANT: Mid-Continent Airport, PO Box 7707, Wichita, Kansas 67277
Telephone: (316) 946 2000
Telex: 417441

CHAIRMAN OF THE BOARD: Charles C. Gates
PRESIDENT AND CHIEF EXECUTIVE OFFICER: James B. Taylor
EXECUTIVE VICE-PRESIDENT AND CHIEF OPERATING OFFICER: Donald J. O'Mara
TREASURER AND CHIEF FINANCIAL OFFICER: M. K. Lowry
CORPORATE CONTROLLER AND ASSISTANT TREASURER: D. H. Coley
CORPORATE VICE-PRESIDENTS:
William R. Edgar (Government Relations)
William G. Robinson (Public Affairs)
PRESIDENT, COMBS GATES DENVER: Robert Anderson
PRESIDENT, AIRCRAFT SERVICES CORPORATION: Dale B. Norton
PRESIDENT, J.E.T. INC: Alfred J. Brizzolara
VICE-PRESIDENTS:
Michael I Berger (Resale Marketing)
Donald J. Grommesh (Engineering)
Ralph Lloyd (Marketing Services)
Edward R. Miller (Human Resources)
Richard M. Mooney (Aerospace)
Robert C. Williams (General Sales Manager)
DIRECTOR, CORPORATE PUBLIC RELATIONS: John V. Alexander

Subsidiary Companies:

Gates Learjet Aircraft Services Corporation (GLASCO)
PO Box 7707, Wichita, Kansas 67277
Jet Electronics & Technology, Inc (J.E.T.)
5353 52nd Street, Grand Rapids, Michigan 49508
Combs-Gates Denver, Inc
Stapleton International Airport, Denver, Colorado
Combs-Gates Bradley, Inc
Bradley International Airport, Windsor Locks, Connecticut
Combs-Gates Florida, Inc
Ft Lauderdale/Hollywood International Airport, Ft Lauderdale, Florida
Combs-Gates Indianapolis, Inc
Indianapolis International Airport, Indianapolis, Indiana
Combs-Gates Palm Springs, Inc
Palm Springs Municipal Airport, Palm Springs, California
Combs-Gates Arapahoe
Centennial Airport, Englewood, Colorado

Founded in 1960 by the late William P. Lear Sr, this company was known originally as the Swiss American Aviation Corporation, which was formed to manufacture a high-speed twin-jet executive aircraft known as the Learjet 23 (formerly SAAC-23). Most of the tooling for production of this aircraft was completed in Europe and then, in 1962, all company activities were relocated at Wichita, Kansas; shortly afterwards the company became known as Lear Jet Corporation. In 1967 all of Mr Lear's interests in the company (approximately 60 per cent) were acquired by The Gates Rubber Company of Denver, Colorado, and in January 1970 the company name was changed to Gates Learjet Corporation.

On 28 October 1975 Gates Learjet announced improved 'Century III' models of its Learjet 24, 25 and 35/36, then in production, incorporating a cambered wing and other changes to reduce stall and approach speeds and balanced field length. Century III improvements, details of which can be found in the 1981-82 *Jane's*, became available as a factory retrofit modification for earlier Learjet 24, 25, 35 and 36 models.

Since 1 July 1979, all newly delivered Learjets have also embodied a 'Softflite' handling package to improve stall characteristics. Available for retrospective fit on earlier aircraft, this comprises a full chord shallow fence on each wing, small devices on the inboard leading-edge, and two rows of boundary layer energisers forward of each aileron, to energise the airflow and delay the onset of compressibility. Vortex generators are removed; the stick shaker/pusher is retained but unlikely to be required.

A Softflite I performance kit has since been developed, and has been FAA certificated for all early model Learjet 20 series aircraft with the so-called straight-wing or standard wing configuration, including the original Model 23. The modification incorporates a unique treatment of the wing leading-edge in place of conventional stall strips, and includes the full chord wing fences and boundary layer energisers that form part of the original Softflite package. Designed to improve low-speed performance and handling qualities, the Softflite I modification greatly enhances the aerodynamic stall characteristics of those early 20 series aircraft not equipped with Century III and original Softflite systems improvements.

In June and September 1977 Gates Learjet announced a family of advanced models, with wings of increased span fitted with supercritical winglets. Designated Learjet 28/29 and Learjet 55, these subsequently joined the earlier models in production; but manufacture of the Learjet 28/29 was suspended in 1982.

On 23 September 1980, Gates Learjet and The Dee Howard Company (which see) announced jointly the intention to co-operate on several aircraft development projects. The first of these involved the extended-range Learjet Model 25G, incorporating improvements similar to those of the Dee Howard XR Learjet. These modifications are available from The Dee Howard Company as a retrofit for existing aircraft.

In July 1984 Gates Learjet announced the formation of an Aerospace Division, with headquarters at the company's Wichita manufacturing facility, which will concentrate on high technology developments for the defence and space industries. Projects already assigned to the Aerospace Division include the manufacture of major subassemblies for the intertank structure of the external fuel tank for the Space Shuttle Orbiter vehicle. Work on the $14 million contract, awarded by Martin Marietta's Michoud Division, will be undertaken at the company's Wichita, Kansas, facility, with delivery of the first intertank assemblies scheduled for February 1987 and continuing thereafter over a three-year period.

Manufacture of the Gates Learjet executive/utility transports described in this entry is handled by the company's Aircraft Division at Tucson. In early 1986 the company announced that it was withdrawing from the Gates/Piaggio GP-180 Avanti twin-turboprop business aircraft programme, which it had undertaken jointly with Rinaldo Piaggio SpA of Italy. The Italian manufacturer is continuing with development of the aircraft.

The total number of Learjets of all models delivered exceeded 1,500 by early 1986.

In early 1986 employees engaged in aircraft and aerospace manufacturing by Gates Learjet totalled 1,780. Total employment, company wide, was 2,691.

GATES LEARJET 25D

First flown on 12 August 1966 as the Learjet 25, the current Model 25D accommodates eight passengers and a crew of two. FAA certification in the air transport category (FAR Pt 25) was obtained on 10 October 1967 and the initial delivery was made in November 1967. British CAA certification was received on 26 June 1974.

The basic model, the Century III Learjet 25D, incorporates the Softflite handling package (see introductory notes). In addition, 8° flap settings for take-off are approved for this version, improving the high altitude/hot day take-off performance. Factory installed thrust reversers for the General Electric CJ610-8A turbojet engines are optional. The TBO of these engines, in the Learjet 25D installation, is 5,000 hours. Gates Learjet delivered four Model 25Ds in 1985.

TYPE: Twin-jet light executive transport.

WINGS: Cantilever low-wing monoplane. Wing section NACA 64A 109 with modified leading-edge. Dihedral 2° 30'. Incidence 1°. Sweepback 13° at quarter-chord. All-metal eight-spar structure with milled alloy skins. Manually operated, aerodynamically balanced all-metal ailerons. The Softlite handling package consists of two rows of boundary layer energisers forward of each aileron, full-chord fences, and stall strips on the wing leading-edges. Hydraulically actuated all-metal single-slotted flaps. Hydraulically actuated all-metal spoilers ahead of flaps. Electrically operated trim tab in port aileron. Balance tab in each aileron. Anti-icing by engine bleed air ducted into leading-edges.

FUSELAGE: All-metal flush riveted semi-monocoque fail-safe structure.

TAIL UNIT: Cantilever all-metal sweptback structure, with electrically actuated variable incidence T tailplane and small ventral fin. Conventional manually operated control surfaces. Electrically operated trim tab in rudder. Electrically heated de-icing of tailplane leading-edges.

LANDING GEAR: Retractable tricycle type, with twin wheels on each main unit and single steerable nosewheel. Hydraulic actuation, with backup pneumatic extension. Oleo-pneumatic shock absorbers. Mainwheels fitted with Goodyear 18 × 5·50 10-ply tyres, pressure 7·93 bars (115 lb/sq in). Nosewheel fitted with Goodyear Dual Chine tyre size 18 × 4·40 10-ply rating, pressure 7·24 bars (105 lb/sq in). Goodyear multiple-disc hydraulic brakes. Pneumatic emergency braking system. Parking brakes. Fully modulated anti-skid system.

Small section of wing leading-edge, showing unique treatment introduced by Gates Learjet Softflite I performance kit

POWER PLANT: Two General Electric CJ610-8A turbojet engines, each rated at 13·1 kN (2,950 lb st), pod-mounted on sides of fuselage aft of wings. Fuel in integral wing and wingtip tanks, and a bladder cell in the fuselage; total capacity 3,445 litres (910 US gallons). Oil capacity 3·75 litres (1 US gallon) per engine. Engine inlet anti-icing by bleed air.

ACCOMMODATION: Two seats side by side on flight deck, with dual controls. Up to eight passengers in cabin, with one on inward facing bench seat on starboard side at front, then four on swivel seats which face fore and aft for take-off and landing, with centre aisle, and three on forward facing couch. Toilet and stowage space under front inward facing seat, which can be screened from remainder of cabin by curtain. Two refreshment cabinets, and two folding tables. Plexiglas divider between flight deck and cabin. Baggage compartment aft of cabin. With back of rear bench seat folded down, baggage compartment and rear of cabin can be used to carry cargo or stretchers. In full cargo version, the rearward facing armchair seats are also removed. Two-piece door, with upward hinged portion and downward hinged portion with integral steps, on port side of cabin at front. Emergency exit on starboard side. Cargo door optional. Windscreen anti-icing by engine bleed air with liquid methyl alcohol backup.

SYSTEMS: Air-conditioning by freon R12 vapour cycle system, supplemented by ram air heat exchanger during pressurised flight. Cabin pressurisation by engine bleed air, max differential 0·65 bars (9·4 lb/sq in). Electrical system powered by dual 400A 30V DC starter/generators with AC power supplied from dual 1,000 VA solid state inverters. Dual 24V 37Ah lead-acid batteries; nickel-cadmium batteries optional. Emergency battery pack standard. Dual engine driven hydraulic pumps, each capable of maintaining full system pressure of 103·5 bars (1,500 lb/sq in). Hydraulic system maximum flow rate 18·9 litres (5 US gallons) per min. Cylindrical reservoir pressurised to 1·38 bars (20 lb/sq in). Auxiliary electrically driven hydraulic pump. Pneumatic system at pressure of 124-207 bars (1,800-3,000 lb/sq in) for emergency extension of landing gear and operation of wheel brakes. Engine fire detection and extinguishing system. Oxygen system for emergency use has crew demand masks and passenger dropout masks. Alcohol anti-icing system for radome.

AVIONICS AND EQUIPMENT: Standard avionics, by Collins, include FIS-84/EHSI-74 pilot's flight director; Collins/J.E.T. PN-101/RAI-302 co-pilot's flight indicator; dual VHF-22A com; dual VIR-32 nav; ADF-60; DME-42 with IND-42A indicator; dual TDR-90 transponders; dual Allen 3137 RMIs; Sperry Primus 300SL colour radar; dual J.E.T. VG-206D vertical gyros; dual J.E.T. 104B directional gyros; IDC electric encoding altimeter with altitude alerter and static defect correction module (pilot's side); IDC barometric altimeter for co-pilot; dual

Learjet 25D, the basic model of the Gates Learjet range

Teledyne IVSIs; dual marker beacon indicators; dual Avtech audio systems; J.E.T. FC-110 with dual yaw damper; J.E.T. PS-835D emergency battery and AI-804 attitude gyro; eight day wind-up clock (pilot) and Davtron 877 clock (co-pilot); Woodward engine synchroniser and LearAvia engine synchroscope. Standard equipment includes birdproof windscreen; control locks; depressurisation warning lights; engine fire warning lights; Mach warning; stall warning device; heated pitot tubes and static ports; ice detector; fire axe; cabin fire extinguisher; baggage compartment, cabin dome, courtesy, instrument panel flood, reading, anti-collision, landing, navigation, taxi, and strobe lights; and lightning protection system.

DIMENSIONS, EXTERNAL:

Span over tip tanks	10·84 m (35 ft 7 in)
Wing chord: at root	2·74 m (9 ft 0 in)
at tip	1·40 m (4 ft 7 in)
Wing aspect ratio	5·01
Length overall	14·50 m (47 ft 7 in)
Length of fuselage	13·82 m (45 ft 4 in)
Height overall	3·73 m (12 ft 3 in)
Tailplane span	4·47 m (14 ft 8 in)
Wheel track (c/l shock absorbers)	2·51 m (8 ft 3 in)
Wheelbase	5·84 m (19 ft 2 in)
Cabin door: Height	1·57 m (5 ft 2 in)
Standard width	0·61 m (2 ft 0 in)
Optional width	0·91 m (3 ft 0 in)
Emergency exit: Height	0·71 m (2 ft 4 in)
Width	0·48 m (1 ft 7 in)

DIMENSIONS, INTERNAL:

Cabin, between pressure bulkheads:	
Length	6·38 m (20 ft 11 in)
Max width	1·50 m (4 ft 11 in)
Max height	1·32 m (4 ft 4 in)
Volume, incl baggage compartment	8·47 m³ (299·0 cu ft)
Baggage compartment	1·13 m³ (40·0 cu ft)

AREAS:

Wings, gross	21·53 m² (231·77 sq ft)
Ailerons (total)	1·08 m² (11·70 sq ft)
Trailing-edge flaps (total)	3·42 m² (36·85 sq ft)
Spoilers	0·66 m² (7·05 sq ft)
Fin	3·47 m² (37·37 sq ft)
Rudder, incl tab	0·67 m² (7·18 sq ft)
Tailplane	5·02 m² (54·00 sq ft)
Elevators	1·31 m² (14·13 sq ft)

WEIGHTS AND LOADINGS:

Weight empty, equipped	3,606 kg (7,950 lb)
Max fuel weight	2,766 kg (6,098 lb)
Max T-O weight	6,804 kg (15,000 lb)
Max ramp weight	7,030 kg (15,500 lb)
Max landing weight	6,033 kg (13,300 lb)
Max wing loading	15·9 kg/m² (64·7 lb/sq ft)
Max power loading	259·7 kg/kN (2·54 lb/lb st)

PERFORMANCE (at max T-O weight, ISA, unless stated otherwise):

Never-exceed speed	Mach 0·81
Max operating speed at 7,620 m (25,000 ft)	475 knots (880 km/h; 547 mph)
Max cruising speed, mid-cruise weight, at 14,325 m (47,000 ft)	451 knots (835 km/h; 519 mph)
Econ cruising speed, mid-cruise weight, at 14,325 m (47,000 ft)	428 knots (793 km/h; 493 mph)
Stalling speed, engines idling, at max landing weight: wheels and flaps up	113 knots (209 km/h; 130 mph) IAS
wheels and flaps down	97 knots (180 km/h; 112 mph) IAS
Max rate of climb at S/L	2,080 m (6,830 ft)/min
Rate of climb at S/L, one engine out	582 m (1,910 ft)/min
Service ceiling	15,545 m (51,000 ft)
Service ceiling, one engine out	7,165 m (23,500 ft)
Min ground turning radius	11·43 m (37 ft 6 in)
T-O balanced field length, FAR Pt 25	1,200 m (3,937 ft)
Landing distance, FAR Pt 25, at max landing weight	859 m (2,817 ft)
Range with 4 passengers, max fuel and 45 min reserves	1,430 nm (2,650 km; 1,647 miles)

OPERATIONAL NOISE LEVELS (FAR Pt 36):

T-O	90·9 EPNdB
Approach	103·7 EPNdB
Sideline	95·2 EPNdB

GATES LEARJET 25G

Announced on 23 September 1980, this version of the Learjet 25 represented the first product of the co-operative agreement between Gates Learjet and The Dee Howard Company. It is identical in design to the Dee Howard XR Learjet (which see), and involves modification of a new 'green' Learjet 25D by The Dee Howard Company prior to completion by Gates Learjet; it has a range more than 20 per cent better than that of standard Model 25Ds. Features include an inboard-section glove on each wing, carrying additional fuel; a new nacelle pylon configuration that improves cruise performance; a wingtip tank fin cuff of new design; pressure tuned wing leading-edges; and a new span flow limiter. Range capability is enhanced further by resulting drag reduction. Gates Learjet delivered four Model 25Gs in 1985.

Apart from these aerodynamic improvements, the description of the Learjet 25D applies also to the Learjet 25G, except as follows:

AVIONICS AND EQUIPMENT: Standard avionics as for Learjet 25D, but with flap pre-select.

AREA:

Wings, gross	22·93 m² (246·8 sq ft)

WEIGHTS AND LOADINGS:

Weight empty, equipped	3,742 kg (8,250 lb)
Max fuel weight	2,991 kg (6,594 lb)
Max T-O weight	7,393 kg (16,300 lb)
Max ramp weight	7,620 kg (16,800 lb)
Max landing weight	6,214 kg (13,700 lb)
Max wing loading	322·5 kg/m² (66·05 lb/sq ft)
Max power loading	282·18 kg/kN (2·76 lb/lb st)

PERFORMANCE (estimated at S/L, ISA):

Cruising speed at 12,500 m (41,000 ft)	464 knots (860 km/h; 534 mph)
T-O balanced field length, FAR Pt 25, at max T-O weight	1,491 m (4,893 ft)
Landing distance (FAR Pt 91, at max landing weight)	831 m (2,728 ft)
Max range, crew of two and four passengers, allowances for taxi, T-O, climb, cruise at long-range power, descent and 45 min reserves	1,800 nm (3,335 km; 2,073 miles)

GATES LEARJET 35A and 36A

US Air Force designation: C-21A
Japan MSDF designation: U-36A

Although generally similar in basic configuration to the Learjet 25, the Learjet 35 and 36 are slightly larger in size and powered by turbofan engines. A prototype (known originally as the Learjet Model 26) made its first flight with Garrett TFE731-2 engines on 4 January 1973. The production 35 and 36, announced in May 1973, are almost identical, differing in fuel capacity and accommodation. FAA certification was awarded in July 1974, and customer deliveries began later that year. French and UK certification were gained during 1979.

Century III improvements, the 'Softflite' handling package (see introductory notes) and engine synchronisers are standard for both models; options include a higher max T-O weight of 8,300 kg (18,300 lb). Improvements introduced in the Autumn of 1983 include a J.E.T. FC-530 autopilot with digital mode selection and analog computation for servo control, Rosemount pitot static system, altitude pre-select, daylight readable controller, integrated flight director, 12½° half-bank capability and full-time yaw damper. Also introduced was the T/R-4000 thrust reverser system developed by Gates Learjet in cooperation with The Dee Howard Company. The T/R-4000 has a hydraulic accumulator permitting operation even if the aircraft hydraulic system fails, single-engine deployment capability, quick removal hot section, a locking arrangement preventing deployment at high thrust settings, reverse thrust availability within two seconds after touchdown, throttle retard system, and lower engine (N_1) speed at equivalent reverser thrust. The T/R-4000 is optional on new Learjet 35A/36As, and is available for retrofit to all Century III 30-series Learjets.

At the 1985 National Business Aircraft Association Convention in New Orleans, Gates Learjet introduced a new 'special class' interior for the Model 35A offering increased leg and headroom. Four passengers can be accommodated in club seating on Erda seats which recline and have an electrically actuated inboard, fore and aft tracking facility. A centre console between the rear pair of seats contains stereo headsets and an in-flight telephone. Solid doors fore and aft of the lavatory area, electronic control of the adjustable washbasin cabinet, and 0·61 m (2 ft 0 in) wide fold-out conference/dining tables, are also featured in the new cabin configuration.

Gates Learjet has developed an all-digital flight deck for

Gates Learjet 25G (top) with standard Model 25 below

the Model 35A in which autopilot and flight data are presented on colour CRT screens. A mockup of the installation displayed at the NBAA Convention featured a Collins Pro Line II avionics fit including dual FIS-84 flight integration systems with EHSI-74 electronic horizontal situation indicators, WXR-350 weather radar, ADS-82 air data computer, dual AHS-85 attitude and heading reference systems, APS-85 digital autopilot with glareshield controller, and a new DB audio system. The all-digital flight deck was expected to be available on new production Model 35As from mid-1986.

In addition to the commercial Model 35A/36A, Gates Learjet also offers specialised mission aircraft for a wide range of civilian and paramilitary applications, including aerial survey, photography, reconnaissance (**RC-35A**) with LOROP cameras, SLAR and camera pods, weapons simulation, maritime patrol (described separately), target towing, airways calibration, electronic warfare training simulation and standoff ECM/ESM platform (**EC-35A**), and utility duties (**UC-35A**). Special Missions Learjets are operating in 20 countries, including Argentina, Australia, Brazil, Chile and Sweden. Recent customers have included the People's Republic of China, which took delivery of two Learjet 36As each equipped with geological survey equipment, including Goodyear SLAR in an underbelly pack, in June 1984 and three Model 35As in 1985; the Finnish Defence Forces, which received three Model 35As equipped for sea patrol, reconnaissance, medevac and target towing; and the Japan Maritime Self-Defence Force, which ordered two Learjet 36As for target towing, anti-ship sea skimming missile simulation and ECM duties under the designation **U-36A**. To meet the Japan Defence Agency's mission profile for the aircraft, Gates Learjet introduced longer and increased diameter wingtip tanks to accommodate the HWQ-1T missile seeker simulator and ALQ-6 jammer; an underbelly fairing for long range ocean surveillance radar; an ALE-43 chaff dispenser; an ARS-1-L high speed tow sleeve with scoring; a new two-piece windscreen with electric demisting system for increased speed during low level missions; expanded underwing stores capability; and increases in max T-O and landing weights to accommodate mission equipment. The first U-36A was delivered to the

One of 80 Gates Learjet C-21As leased to US Air Force for operational support missions

JMSDF in November 1985, with the second scheduled for delivery in the Autumn of 1986.

On 19 September 1983 Gates Learjet received a $175·4 million contract for the lease and logistic support of 80 Model 35As, designated **C-21A**, to the US Air Force for its Operational Support Aircraft (OSA) programme. The contract, for an initial five-year lease, with a three-year extension option, and purchase option, was the US Air Force's first major leasing agreement for an 'off the shelf' business jet. The C-21As are replacing North American/Rockwell CT-39 Sabreliners in the Military Airlift Command inventory on high-priority and time-sensitive cargo delivery, pilot proficiency training, passenger airlift and other operational support missions, including medical evacuation. The first C-21A (84-0063) was rolled out at Gates Learjet's Tucson, Arizona, factory on 13 March 1984, and was subsequently delivered to MAC at Scott AFB, Illinois. Deliveries were completed in October 1985. The C-21As are to be based throughout the USA and in Japan and the Federal Republic of Germany. By January 1986 USAF C-21As had accumulated more than 55,000 flight hours, with an average 'mission capable' rate of 96 per cent.

In September 1984 Gates Learjet announced certification of the Marquardt MTR-101 aerial target launch and recovery tow reel for use aboard Learjet aircraft. A Model 35A equipped with the MTR-101 system and the Hayes Universal Tow Target System was displayed at the 1984 Farnborough Air Show.

The description of the Learjet 25D applies also to the Learjet 35A and 36A, except in the following details:

Type: Twin-turbofan light executive transport.

Wings: As for Learjet 25D, except span increased.

Fuselage: As for Learjet 25D, except length increased.

Power Plant: Two Garrett TFE731-2-2B turbofan engines, each rated at 15·6 kN (3,500 lb st), pod-mounted on sides of rear fuselage. Fuel in integral wing and wingtip tanks and a fuselage tank, with a combined usable capacity (Learjet 35A) of 3,524 litres (931 US gallons). Learjet 36A has a larger fuselage tank, giving a combined usable total of 4,201 litres (1,110 US gallons). Refuelling point on upper surface of each wingtip tank. Fuel jettison system. Engine nacelle leading-edges anti-iced by engine bleed air.

Accommodation: Crew of two on flight deck, with dual controls. Up to eight passengers in Learjet 35A; one on inward facing bench seat on starboard side at front, then two pairs of swivel seats which face fore and aft for take-off and landing, with centre aisle, and three on forward facing couch at rear of cabin. Alternative 'mid-cabin' arrangement, available optionally, places a refreshment area in the middle of the cabin, accessible from fore and aft club seating areas, each for four passengers. Learjet 36A can accommodate up to six passengers, one pair of swivel seats being removed. Toilet and stowage space under front inward facing seat which can be screened from remainder of cabin. Refreshment cabinet opposite this seat, aft of passenger door. Baggage compartment with capacity of 226 kg (500 lb) aft of cabin. Two-piece clamshell door at forward end of cabin on port side, with integral steps built into lower half. Emergency exit on starboard side of cabin. Birdproof windscreens.

Systems: Environmental control system comprises cabin pressurisation, ventilation, heating and cooling. Heating and pressurisation by engine bleed air, with a max pressure differential of 0·65 bars (9·4 lb/sq in), maintaining a cabin altitude of 1,980 m (6,500 ft) to an actual altitude of 13,715 m (45,000 ft). Freon R12 vapour cycle cooling system supplemented by a ram-air heat exchanger. Flight control system includes dual yaw dampers, dual stick pushers, dual stick shakers and Mach trim. Anti-icing system includes distribution of engine bleed air for wing, tailplane and engine nacelle leading-edges and windscreen; electrical heating of pitot heads, stall warning vanes and static ports; and alcohol spray on windscreen and nose radome. Hydraulic system supplied by two engine driven pumps, each pump capable of maintaining alone the full system pressure of 103·5 bars (1,500 lb/sq in), for operation of landing gear, brakes, flaps and spoilers. Hydraulic system maximum flow rate 15 litres (4 US gallons) per min. Cylindrical reservoir pressurised to 1·38 bars (20 lb/sq in). Electrically driven hydraulic pump for emergency operation of all hydraulic services. Pneumatic system of 124 to 207 bars (1,800 to 3,000 lb/sq in) pressure for emergency extension of landing gear and operation of brakes. Electrical system powered by two 30V 400A brushless generators, two 1kVA solid state inverters to provide AC power, and two 24V 37Ah lead-acid batteries. Oxygen system for emergency use, with crew demand masks and drop-out masks for each passenger.

Avionics: Standard avionics, by Collins, include FIS-84/EHSI-74 flight director integrated with J.E.T. FC-530 FCS and dual yaw dampers (pilot's side); Collins/J.E.T. PN-101/RAI-302 co-pilot's flight indicator; dual Collins VHF-22A com transceivers; dual VIR-32 nav receivers; ADF-60; dual DME-42 with IND-42C indicators; dual Allen 3137 RMIs; dual Collins TDR-90 transponders; Collins ALT-55B radio altimeter with DRI-55 indicator; Sperry Primus 300SL colour weather radar; dual J.E.T. VG-206D vertical gyros; dual J.E.T. DN-104B directional gyros; J.E.T. PS-835D and AI-804 emergency battery and attitude gyro; IDC electric encoding altimeter with altitude alerter and IDC air data unit (pilot's side); IDC barometric altimeter (co-pilot); dual Teledyne IVSIs; dual marker beacon indicators; dual Avtech audio systems; eight-day wind-up clock (pilot's side); Davtron 877 clock (co-pilot); nacelle heat annunciator; N_1 reminder; avionics master switch; chip detector and flap pre-select.

Special missions Gates Learjet Model 35A with drop hatch, LOROP camera windows, air turbine target reeling packs, surveillance radar and ESM system

Equipment: Standard equipment includes dual angle of attack indicators, dual battery temperature gauges, engine synchronisation meter, cabin differential pressure gauge, cabin rate of climb indicator, interstage and turbine temperature gauges, turbine and fan speed gauges, wing temperature indicator, alternate static source, dual battery overheat warning, depressurisation warning, engine fire warning lights, Mach warning system, dual stall warning system, fire axe, cabin fire extinguisher, flotation jackets for crew and passengers, sound-proofing; baggage compartment, courtesy, instrument panel, flood, map, and reading lights; dual anti-collision, landing, navigation, recognition, strobe, and taxi lights; dual engine fire extinguishing systems with 'systems armed' and fire warning lights, engine synchronisation system, control lock, external power socket, and lightning protection system.

Dimensions, external:

Wing span over tip tanks	12·04 m (39 ft 6 in)
Wing chord: at root	2·74 m (9 ft 0 in)
at tip	1·55 m (5 ft 1 in)
Wing aspect ratio	5·74
Length overall	14·83 m (48 ft 8 in)
Height overall	3·73 m (12 ft 3 in)
Tailplane span	4·47 m (14 ft 8 in)
Wheel track	2·51 m (8 ft 3 in)
Wheelbase	6·15 m (20 ft 2 in)
Passenger door:	
Standard: Height	1·57 m (5 ft 2 in)
Width	0·61 m (2 ft 0 in)
Optional: Height	1·57 m (5 ft 2 in)
Width	0·91 m (3 ft 0 in)
Emergency exit: Height	0·71 m (2 ft 4 in)
Width	0·48 m (1 ft 7 in)

Dimensions, internal (A: Learjet 35A; B: Learjet 36A):

Cabin: Length, incl flight deck:	
A	6·63 m (21 ft 9 in)
B	5·77 m (18 ft 11 in)
Max width	1·50 m (4 ft 11 in)
Max height	1·32 m (4 ft 4 in)
Volume, incl flight deck: A	9·12 m³ (322 cu ft)
B	7·25 m³ (256 cu ft)
Baggage compartment: A	1·13 m³ (40 cu ft)
B	0·76 m³ (27 cu ft)

Area:

Wings, gross	23·53 m² (253·3 sq ft)

Weights and Loadings (A: Learjet 35A; B: Learjet 36A):

Weight empty, equipped: A	4,342 kg (9,571 lb)
B	4,341 kg (9,570 lb)
Max payload: A, B	1,361 kg (3,000 lb)
Max T-O weight: A (basic)	7,711 kg (17,000 lb)
A (optional), B	8,300 kg (18,300 lb)
Max ramp weight: A (basic)	7,824 kg (17,250 lb)
B	8,391 kg (18,500 lb)
Max landing weight: A, B	6,940 kg (15,300 lb)
Max wing loading: A (basic)	327·6 kg/m² (67·1 lb/sq ft)
B	347·1 kg/m² (71·1 lb/sq ft)
Max power loading:	
A (basic)	247·1 kg/kN (2·43 lb/lb st)
B	261·7 kg/kN (2·57 lb/lb st)

Performance (at max T-O weight, except where indicated; A: Learjet 35A at 7,711 kg; 17,000 lb; B: Learjet 36A):

Never-exceed speed: A, B	Mach 0·83
Max level speed at 7,620 m (25,000 ft):	
A, B	471 knots (872 km/h; 542 mph)
Max cruising speed, mid-cruise weight, at 12,500 m (41,000 ft): A, B	460 knots (852 km/h; 529 mph)
Econ cruising speed, mid-cruise weight, at 13,700 m (45,000 ft): A, B	418 knots (774 km/h; 481 mph)
Stalling speed, wheels and flaps down, engines idling:	
A, B	96 knots (178 km/h; 111 mph) IAS
Max rate of climb at S/L: A	1,451 m (4,760 ft)/min
B	1,322 m (4,339 ft)/min
Rate of climb at S/L, one engine out:	
A	448 m (1,470 ft)/min
B	389 m (1,276 ft)/min
Service ceiling: A, B	13,715 m (45,000 ft)
Service ceiling, one engine out: A	7,710 m (25,300 ft)
B	7,165 m (23,500 ft)
T-O balanced field length, FAR Pt 25:	
A at 7,711 kg (17,000 lb)	1,287 m (4,224 ft)
A, B at 8,300 kg (18,300 lb)	1,515 m (4,972 ft)
Landing distance, FAR Pt 25, at max landing weight:	
A, B	937 m (3,075 ft)
Range with 4 passengers, max fuel and 45 min reserves:	
A	2,289 nm (4,239 km; 2,634 miles)
B	2,708 nm (5,015 km; 3,116 miles)

Operational Noise Levels (FAR Pt 36):

T-O: A	83·7 EPNdB
B	83·9 EPNdB
Approach: A	91·4 EPNdB
Sideline: A	86·9 EPNdB
B	87·8 EPNdB

GATES LEARJET SPECIAL-MISSIONS/ SEA PATROL VERSION

A prototype of this special-missions version of the Learjet, equipped for sea patrol duties, was exhibited at the 1979 Paris Air Show, before making a worldwide demonstration tour. This aircraft (N80SM) is a modified Learjet 35A, with a slightly larger cabin than the equally suitable 36A, enabling more observers to be carried during demonstrations. It is designated **PC-35A** by Gates Learjet.

Equipment available for the Sea Patrol version of the special-missions Learjet includes Litton AN/APS-504(V)3 sea surveillance radar, with 360° sweep from the underbelly radome and digital CFAR clutter suppression; low light level TV with video tape and scan conversion; forward-looking infra-red sensors; Daedalus DS-1210 multi-spectral infra-red and ultra-violet line scanner with tape data storage and hard copy printer; mini-computers for data processing, with tape input/output and graphic display capability; ASW sonobuoy drop and detection equipment; radar monitoring equipment (ESM); a hard-point under each wing with an Alkan 165B ejector for survival equipment, flares or up to 453 kg (1,000 lb) of other stores; drop hatch for rescue gear; high-intensity searchlight; reconnaissance, mapping or LOROP cameras; HF, VHF and UHF homers; GNS-1000 VLF Omega navigation system; side-looking airborne radar; Bendix RDR 1300B weather radar; and hand held cameras with position information printout.

Items fitted to the demonstrator make it suitable for location and detection of surface vessels, identification of targets, determination of target activities, and storage of permanent video tape and photographic records of target image, with position, time and date. Its performance ranges from a dash capability of nearly 485 knots (900 km/h; 560 mph) to manoeuvring speeds below 110 knots (200 km/h; 125 mph).

Gates Learjet has delivered three special-missions Learjet 35As to the Finnish Air Force, equipped for a variety of operations, including aerial mapping, air ambulance, air pollution control, oblique photography, rescue, and sea patrol. Primary role is target towing for the Air Force's BAe Hawk combat trainers.

PERFORMANCE (Learjet 36A):
Operating speed:
at 11,275-12,500 m (37,000-41,000 ft) 415 knots (769 km/h; 478 mph)
at 4,575-7,620 m (15,000-25,000 ft) 319 knots (590 km/h; 367 mph)
S/L to 610 m (2,000 ft) 250 knots (463 km/h; 288 mph)
Rate of climb at S/L 1,380 m (4,525 ft)/min
Range:
at high altitude 2,249 nm (4,168 km; 2,590 miles)
at medium altitude 1,617 nm (2,996 km; 1,862 miles)
at low altitude 1,060 nm (1,964 km; 1,220 miles)

GATES LEARJET 55

Gates Learjet announced at the Paris Air Show in June 1977 the company's decision to develop the first two of a new series of wide-body business aircraft known as the Longhorn 50 series; the name Longhorn was dropped subsequently. Stemming from exhaustive engineering and marketing studies, the new aircraft were intended to supplement the earlier range of Learjets, providing a wide-body 'stand-up' cabin, and having accommodation for a maximum of ten passengers in the Model 55, and eight passengers in the Model 56. Subsequently, a decision was made to terminate development of the Model 56 and to proceed instead with longer-range developments of the Learjet 55. As a result, three versions were available in 1986:

Learjet 55. Basic version, as described in detail.

Learjet 55ER. Extended range version, with an additional fuel tank of 163 kg (359 lb) capacity in the tailcone baggage compartment. This tank is available for retrofit on standard 55s already delivered.

Learjet 55LR. Long-range version; as 55ER, plus an additional fuel tank of 298 kg (658 lb) capacity between the standard fuselage tank and rear cabin baggage compartment. Typical seating for seven passengers and two crew. Retrofit of existing 55s to this standard to be available.

The first of two Learjet 55 prototypes (N551GL) flew for the first time on 19 April 1979; the second prototype (N552GL) flew on 15 November 1979. The first production example flew on 11 August 1980, and the second on 3 February 1981. Certification under FAR Pt 25 was received on 18 March 1981. The initial customer delivery was made on 30 April 1981, and 119 Model 55s had been delivered by the end of 1985, in which year 11 Model 55s were delivered.

The long range Learjet Model 55LR received FAA certification in May 1983. During the 1983 Paris Air Show a Learjet Model 55LR established six world speed records, by flying from Los Angeles to Paris in 12 h 37 min and returning in 14 h 16 min, with one refuelling stop each way. On 7 July 1983 a Model 55 established seven new time-to-climb and altitude records for its class, reaching 15,000 m (49,212 ft) in 19 min 25s, and achieving a maximum sustained altitude of 16,093 m (52,798 ft).

In July 1983 Gates Learjet received FAA certification of its Phase 1 performance improvement package for Model 55s, which includes replacement of the original leading-edge stall strips with new strips each containing five small inverted triangular wedges approx 1·5 mm (1/16 in) thick, plus installation of seven individually mounted triangles at a location on the leading-edge forward of the ailerons; installation of automatic ground spoilers; and the addition of automatic performance reserve (APR) to the Garrett TFE731-3A-2B turbofan engines, which automatically provides an additional 0·80 kN (180 lb) of thrust from one engine if thrust from the other engine drops by five per cent or more. Phase 1 improvements are incorporated in all Learjet 55s manufactured after 1 July 1983, and are available as a retrofit package for earlier production aircraft. A Garrett energy management system (GEMS) is available optionally as an extension of APR.

A further performance improvement package, Phase 1A, was introduced on the production line in the Spring of 1984. This package features high-energy brakes with 13 per cent greater brake capacity and up to 50 per cent increased brake life claimed; new wheels; longer axles, and modified landing gear doors, fairings and actuators. The doors and fairings are manufactured from graphite/epoxy and Kevlar/epoxy, respectively. Phase 1A, certificated in February 1984, is also available as a retrofit to earlier Model 55s, with Phase 1 as a prerequisite. The package offers substantial increases in the Learjet 55's high-altitude, hot-day performance. Other improvements to the Learjet 55, introduced from c/n 55-107, include an optional 9,752 kg (21,500 lb) max T-O weight and 8,165 kg (18,000 lb) max landing weight, which, combined with Phase 1 and 1A performance improvement packages, have earned the latest models the marketing title '55 Plus'.

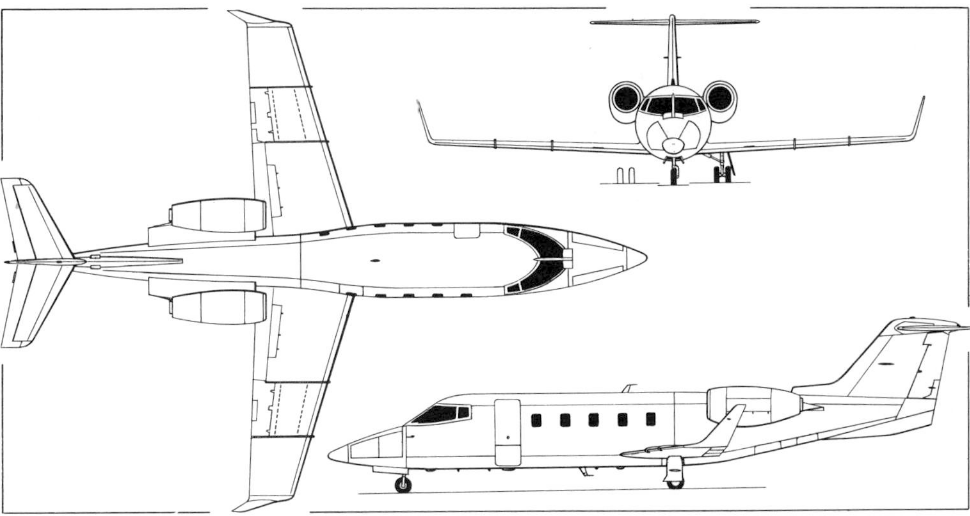

Three-view drawing *(Pilot Press)* **and photograph of the Gates Learjet 55 executive transport**

In March 1985 Gates Learjet received FAA approval for a ten-passenger main cabin configuration (limited to eight passengers in the initial certification). The increase in cabin seating capacity applies to all currently manufactured Model 55s. The 'special class' interior described under the Model 35A is also available for the Learjet 55, in which it provides club seating for four passengers, with a fifth side-facing seat aft of the forward coat closet. A full-width enclosed rear lavatory is installed.

An all-digital flight deck was expected to become available on the Model 55 in mid-1986. Featuring Collins Pro Line II avionics, the installation includes a five-tube EFIS-85 electronic flight instrumentation system, WXR-350 colour weather radar, dual ADS-82 air data computers, dual AHS-85 attitude and heading reference systems, and an APS-85 dual digital autopilot with J.E.T. glareshield autopilot controller.

The Learjet 55 is certificated in and operating from eleven nations, comprising Australia, Austria, Brazil, Canada, France, West Germany, Saudi Arabia, Spain, Switzerland, the United States and Venezuela.

TYPE: Twin-turbofan light executive transport.

WINGS: Cantilever low-wing monoplane. Sweepback 13° at quarter-chord. All-metal multi-spar structure with cavity milled wing skins. Wing upper surface skin tapers in thickness from wing root to wingtip to save weight. The design incorporates an advanced cambered leading-edge, the 'Softflite' handling package (see introductory notes to company entry) and supercritical winglets. Manually operated ailerons. Electrically operated trim tab in port aileron. Hydraulically operated all-metal single-slotted trailing-edge flaps. Hydraulically operated all-metal spoilers mounted on wing upper surface just forward of flaps. Anti-icing by engine bleed air ducted into leading-edges.

FUSELAGE: All-metal flush riveted semi-monocoque fail-safe structure.

TAIL UNIT: Cantilever all-metal sweptback structure, with electrically actuated variable incidence T tailplane. Small ventral fin. Electrically heated de-icing of tailplane leading-edge.

LANDING GEAR: Hydraulically retractable tricycle type, with twin wheels on each main unit and single steerable nosewheel. Mainwheel tyres size 17·5 × 5·75-8, 12 ply, pressure 12·4 bars (180 lb/sq in); nosewheel tyre size 18·0 × 4·4, 10 ply, pressure 7·24 bars (105 lb/sq in). High pressure pneumatic system for emergency extension. Oleo-pneumatic shock absorbers. Chined nosewheel tyre. High energy hydraulic braking system, with pneumatic backup. Fully modulated anti-skid units.

POWER PLANT: Two Garrett TFE731-3A-2B turbofan engines, each rated at 16·46 kN (3,700 lb st), plus 0·80 kN (180 lb st) automatic power reserve, pod-mounted on sides of fuselage aft of wing. Fuel in integral wing tanks and a fuselage bladder tank, with a combined capacity of 3,789 litres (1,001 US gallons) in standard Model 55. Additional fuel capacity of extended-range versions detailed in model listings. Refuelling point on upper surface of each outer wing. Single-point refuelling optional. Engine nacelle leading-edges and fan hubs anti-iced by engine bleed air.

ACCOMMODATION: Crew of two on flight deck, with dual controls. Seating for four to eight passengers in differing interior layouts. Two folding tables. Carpeted floor. Galley refreshment cabinet. Toilet. Baggage space at rear of cabin, and in fuselage nose and tailcone of basic Model 55. Tailcone baggage space reduced on long range versions, but 55LR has baggage area at front of cabin. Two-piece clamshell door at forward end of cabin on port side, with integral steps built into the lower section. Emergency exit/baggage door on starboard side of cabin.

SYSTEMS: Environmental control system comprises cabin pressurisation, ventilation, heating and cooling. Heating and pressurisation are provided by engine bleed air, with a maximum pressure differential of 0·65 bars (9·4 lb/sq in), maintaining a cabin altitude of 2,440 m (8,000 ft) to an actual altitude of 15,545 m (51,000 ft). Freon vapour-cycle cooling system, supplemented by a ram-air system. Anti-icing system includes distribution of engine bleed air to wing leading-edges, engine nacelle leading-edges and fan hubs, and pilot and co-pilot windscreens; electric anti-icing of tailplane leading-edge, pitot heads, stall warning vanes and static ports; and alcohol anti-icing of windscreens. Hydraulic system supplied by two engine driven variable-volume constant-pressure pumps, one on each engine, each capable of maintaining alone the full system pressure of 103·5 bars (1,500 lb/sq in) for operation of landing gear, brakes, flaps and spoilers. Hydraulic system maximum flow rate 15 litres (4 US gallons) per min.

Cylindrical reservoir pressurised to 1·38 bars (20 lb/sq in). Electrically driven hydraulic pump for emergency operation of all hydraulic services. Pneumatic system of 124 to 207 bars (1,800 to 3,000 lb/sq in) pressure for emergency extension of landing gear and operation of brakes. Electrical system powered by two 28V 400A engine driven brushless generators, either of which is capable of maintaining adequate DC power to operate all electrical services; two 1kVA solid state inverters to provide AC power; and two 24V 37Ah lead-acid batteries. Oxygen system of 1·08 m³ (38 cu ft) capacity, with crew demand masks; dropout mask for each passenger, which is presented automatically if cabin altitude exceeds 4,265 m (14,000 ft).

AVIONICS: Standard avionics, by Collins, include items as listed for Models 35A/36A except that FIS-85 flight director integrated with J.E.T. FC-550 FCS with altitude pre-select and dual yaw dampers (pilot); FIS-85 flight director (co-pilot) and Primus 400SL colour weather radar are standard. Options include Sperry ED600 EFIS with Primus 800 weather radar and Data Nav III; Global GNS 1000; Collins 85-2A EFIS; King KHF 95 HF radio and Wulfsberg Flitefone V.

EQUIPMENT: Standard equipment includes sun visors, fire extinguisher and map lights on flight deck. Divider between flight deck and cabin. Cabin equipment includes two folding tables, galley refreshment cabinet, window shades, fire extinguisher and axe, soundproofing and insulation, carpeted floor; a lighting control panel and aisle, entrance step and indirect cabin lights.

DIMENSIONS, EXTERNAL:
Wing span 13·34 m (43 ft 9 in)
Wing chord: at root 2·74 m (9 ft 0 in)
at tip 1·07 m (3 ft 6 in)
Wing aspect ratio 6·72
Length overall 16·79 m (55 ft 1 in)
Length of fuselage 15·93 m (52 ft 3 in)
Height overall 4·47 m (14 ft 8 in)
Tailplane span 4·47 m (14 ft 8 in)
Wheel track 2·51 m (8 ft 3 in)
Wheelbase 7·01 m (23 ft 0 in)
Cabin door: Height 1·70 m (5 ft 7 in)
Width 0·61 m (2 ft 0 in)

DIMENSIONS, INTERNAL:
Cabin: Length between pressure bulkheads:
55, 55ER 6·71 m (22 ft 0 in)
55LR 6·30 m (20 ft 8 in)
Length, cockpit/cabin divider to rear pressure bulkhead:
55, 55ER 5·08 m (16 ft 8 in)
55LR 4·67 m (15 ft 4 in)
Max width 1·80 m (5 ft 11 in)
Max height 1·74 m (5 ft 8½ in)
Volume, incl flight deck:
55, 55ER 13·37 m³ (472 cu ft)
55LR 12·88 m³ (455 cu ft)
Baggage capacity, total: 55 1·69 m³ (60 cu ft)
55ER 1·43 m³ (50·5 cu ft)
55LR 1·88 m³ (66·5 cu ft)

AREAS:
Wings, gross 24·57 m² (264·5 sq ft)
Ailerons (total) 1·09 m² (11·70 sq ft)
Trailing-edge flaps (total) 3·42 m² (36·85 sq ft)
Winglets (total) 1·11 m² (12·00 sq ft)
Spoilers (total) 0·65 m² (7·05 sq ft)
Fin 4·67 m² (50·29 sq ft)
Rudder 0·99 m² (10·65 sq ft)
Tailplane 5·02 m² (54·00 sq ft)
Elevators (total) 1·31 m² (14·13 sq ft)

WEIGHTS AND LOADINGS:
Weight empty: 55 5,502 kg (12,130 lb)
55ER 5,531 kg (12,194 lb)
55LR 5,582 kg (12,306 lb)
Max fuel weight: 55 3,042 kg (6,707 lb)
55ER 3,197 kg (7,049 lb)
55LR 3,496 kg (7,707 lb)
Max T-O weight: 55, normal 8,845 kg (19,500 lb)
55, optional, 55ER, 55LR 9,752 kg (21,500 lb)
Max zero-fuel weight:
all versions 6,804 kg (15,000 lb)
Max landing weight:
all versions 8,165 kg (18,000 lb)
Max wing loading:
55, normal 359·8 kg/m² (73·7 lb/sq ft)
55, optional, 55ER, 55LR
387·7 kg/m² (79·4 lb/sq ft)
Max power loading:
55, normal 268·7 kg/kN (2·64 lb/lb st)
55, optional, 55ER, 55LR
289·3 kg/kN (2·84 lb/lb st)

PERFORMANCE (at max T-O weight except where indicated):
Never-exceed speed:
below 2,440 m (8,000 ft)
300 knots (555 km/h; 345 mph) IAS
2,440 m (8,000 ft) to 11,275 m (37,000 ft)
350 knots (648 km/h; 403 mph) IAS
11,275 m (37,000 ft) to 13,715 m (45,000 ft)
Mach 0·81 to Mach 0·79
above 13,715 m (45,000 ft) Mach 0·79
Max level speed at 9,150 m (30,000 ft):
55 477 knots (884 km/h; 549 mph)
Max cruising speed at 12,500 m (41,000 ft):
all versions 455 knots (843 km/h; 524 mph)
Econ cruising speed at 14,325 m (47,000 ft):
55 419 knots (776 km/h; 482 mph)
Approach speed:
55 133 knots (246 km/h; 153 mph) IAS
Stalling speed, flaps down, engines idling:
55 103 knots (191 km/h; 119 mph) IAS
Max rate of climb at S/L:
55, normal max T-O weight 1,390 m (4,560 ft)/min
55, optional max T-O weight 1,274 m (4,180 ft)/min
Max rate of climb at S/L, one engine out:
55, normal max T-O weight 436 m (1,430 ft)/min
55, optional max T-O weight 378 m (1,240 ft)/min
Max certificated ceiling:
all versions 15,545 m (51,000 ft)
T-O balanced field length, FAR Pt 25:
55, normal max T-O weight 1,384 m (4,540 ft)
55, optional max T-O weight, and other versions
1,707 m (5,600 ft)
Landing distance, FAR Pt 91 at max landing weight:
all versions 1,006 m (3,300 ft)
Range with crew of two, allowances for taxi, T-O, climb, cruise at long-range power, descent and 45 min reserves:
55, four passengers, normal max T-O weight
2,149 nm (3,982 km; 2,474 miles)
55, four passengers, optional max T-O weight
2,296 nm (4,252 km; 2,642 miles)
55ER, four passengers
2,406 nm (4,459 km; 2,770 miles)
55LR, four passengers
2,608 nm (4,833 km; 3,003 miles)

OPERATIONAL NOISE LEVELS (FAR Pt 36):
T-O: 55, normal max T-O weight 84·2 EPNdB
55, optional max T-O weight 86·3 EPNdB
Approach: 55, normal max T-O weight 91·0 EPNdB
Sideline: 55, normal max T-O weight 90·9 EPNdB
55, optional max T-O weight 90·7 EPNdB

GENERAL DYNAMICS

GENERAL DYNAMICS CORPORATION

Pierre Laclede Center, St Louis, Missouri 63105
Telephone: (314) 889 8200
CHAIRMAN AND CHIEF EXECUTIVE OFFICER: Stanley C. Pace
PRESIDENT: Oliver C. Boileau
EXECUTIVE VICE-PRESIDENTS:
Richard E. Adams (Aerospace)
Lester Crown (Chairman, Material Service Corporation)
Standley H. Hoch (Finance)
James R. Mellor (Marine, Business Systems and Corporate Planning)
Russell W. Meyer Jr (Chairman, Cessna Aircraft Company)
George A. Sawyer (Land Systems and International)
VICE-PRESIDENTS:
Melville R. Barlow (General Manager, Electronics Division)
Leonard F. Buchanan (Advanced Engineering and Business Development)
James J. Cunnane (Controller)
Robert H. Duesenberg (General Counsel)
B. Edward Ewing (Operations and Production Engineering)
Otto J. Glasser (Government Relations)
Gary S. Grimes (General Manager, Quincy Shipbuilding)
Alan M. Lovelace (General Manager, Space Systems Division)
John P. Maguire (Secretary)
John E. McSweeny (General Manager, Convair Division)
Arch H. Rambeau (Human Resources)
Herbert F. Rogers (General Manager, Fort Worth Division)
Sterling V. Starr (General Manager, Pomona Division)
Fritz G. Tovar (General Manager, Electric Boat)
Robert W. Truxell (General Manager, Land Systems)
Wayne Wells (Treasurer)
Frederick S. Wood (Contracts and Pricing)

Convair Division:
PO Box 85357, San Diego, California 92138
Telephone: (619) 573 8000
VICE-PRESIDENTS:
R. F. Beuligmann (Research and Engineering)
C. D. Bohle (Finance and Controller)
A. B. Daddi (Industrial Relations)
M. C. Keel (Cruise Missile Programmes)
B. J. Kuchta (Chief Engineer, Cruise Missiles)
K. S. Lake (Operations)
John E. McSweeny (General Manager)
R. N. Molina (Quality Assurance)
E. M. Squires (Cruise Missile Product Line)
J. W. Vega (Advanced Programmes)
A. J. Veitch (Contracts and Estimating)

Fort Worth Division:
PO Box 748, Fort Worth, Texas 76101
Telephone: (817) 777 2000
VICE-PRESIDENTS:
Charles A. Anderson (Research and Engineering)
W. D. Buntin (F-16 Engineering)
F. A. Curtis Jr (F-16 Deputy Director, Plans, Controls and Contracts)
G. L. Davis (F-111 Programmes)
N. E. Day (Material)
W. C. Dietz (Programme Director, Special Projects)
Dain M. Hancock (F-16 International Programmes)
E. Earl Hatchett (Finance)
J. R. Jones (Turkey Joint Venture)
D. Randall Kent (Director, ATF)
Rolf Krueger (Logistics and Support)
J. P. Lamers (Advanced Derivatives)
Herbert F. Rogers (General Manager)
D. B. Scheideman (Contracts and Estimating)
David J. Talley (Quality Assurance)
Theodore S. Webb Jr (F-16 Programmes)
D. J. Wheaton (Marketing)
Charles N. White (Production)
D. S. Zimmer (Industrial Relations)

General Dynamics conducts its US aerospace activities at four divisions: Convair Division, with operations at San Diego, California; Fort Worth Division, with operations at Fort Worth, Texas; Pomona Division, with headquarters at Pomona, California; and Electronics Division, with headquarters in San Diego. Convair Division is responsible for the design, development and production of offensive missile systems, aircraft structures, and systems for space exploration. Current programmes include production of the Tomahawk sea-launched cruise missile for the US Navy, and the ground-launched version for the US Air Force. Fort Worth Division is engaged in the design, development and production of military aircraft and avionics. Pomona Division is engaged in the development and production of tactical missile and gun systems. Electronics Division is involved in new technology to support the development and production of advanced electronics systems. Major programmes include automatic test equipment for high performance aircraft, sophisticated navigation positioning systems, tactical data and command control systems, and range measuring systems.

Fort Worth is currently responsible for production of the F-16 Fighting Falcon multi-role fighter; spares, support and modification/update for the F-111 fighter-bomber; and various ground based radar systems. Convair Division is responsible for production of a major portion of the fuselage for the McDonnell Douglas KC-10A Extender tanker/cargo aircraft, the mid-fuselage section of the Space Shuttle Orbiter vehicle, the Atlas-Centaur launch vehicle used to boost unmanned spacecraft and satellites, and cruise missiles. Convair is also developing a wide-body version of the Centaur that will be used to launch satellites from the Space Shuttle Orbiter.

Convair Division also retains detailed tooling for high usage spares for the Convair-Liner 240/340/440 series of piston-engined transports, and continues to manufacture components for these types.

On 3 March 1985 General Dynamics acquired the Cessna Aicraft Company of Wichita, Kansas (see separate entry in this section).

GENERAL DYNAMICS F-16 FIGHTING FALCON

The F-16 had its origin in the US Air Force's Lightweight Fighter (LWF) prototype programme, in 1972. The history of this programme and a description of the YF-16 prototypes can be found in the 1978-79 and 1977-78 editions of *Jane's* respectively.

The first of two YF-16 prototypes (72-01567) made its official first flight on 2 February 1974 and obtained a level speed of Mach 2 at 12,200 m (40,000 ft) on 11 March 1974. The second YF-16 (72-01568) flew for the first time on 9 May 1974. During subsequent weapon trials, this aircraft extended the planned operational capability of the design by launching successfully both Sparrow and Sky Flash missiles. In 1978, one of the prototypes, fitted with a Thomson-CSF Atlis II (Automatic Tracking and Laser Illumination System) pod, became the first single-seat fighter to hit ground targets with GBU-10 and GBU-16 laser guided bombs without assistance from air/ground locators.

On 13 January 1975 the Secretary of the US Air Force announced that the F-16 had been selected for full scale engineering development. The original YF-16 requirement for an air superiority day fighter was expanded, to give equal emphasis to the air-to-surface role, including provision of radar and all-weather navigation capabilities. The manufacture of eight pre-production aircraft, comprising six single-seat **F-16As** and two two-seat **F-16Bs**, began in July 1975. The first development F-16A made its first flight on 8 December 1976, and the first F-16B on 8 August 1977. The last of the eight development aircraft was the second two-seater, which made its first flight in June 1978. Meanwhile, the US Air Force had indicated its intention to procure a total of 1,388 F-16s, including 204 two-seaters, to replace F-4s in the active force and to modernise the Air Reserve forces. This has since been increased to a planned total of 2,795, of which 1,859 had been contracted and 1,000 delivered by July 1986, with production continuing at a rate of 150 a year, increasing to 180 a year from 1987, with a proposal under consideration to increase this to 216 a year in 1989.

The first production F-16A (78-0001) flew for the first time on 7 August 1978. The first to enter service was delivered to the US Air Force's 388th Tactical Fighter Wing at Hill AFB, Utah, on 6 January 1979; and the F-16 achieved combat-ready status in October 1980, with the 4th Tactical Fighter Squadron of the 388th TFW. In that year the name Fighting Falcon was adopted. By 1983 the type was serving also with the 56th Tactical Training Wing at MacDill AFB, Florida; the 58th TTW at Luke AFB, Arizona; the 363rd TFW at Shaw AFB, South Carolina; the 474th TFW at Nellis AFB, Nevada; the 8th TFW at Kunsan AB, South Korea (PACAF); the 50th TFW at Hahn AB, West Germany (USAFE); and the 401st TFW at Torrejon AB, Spain (USAFE). F-16s also equip the US Air Force's Thunderbird Air Demonstration Squadron.

In February 1982, the US Air Force announced that both the Air National Guard and Air Force Reserve would fly F-16s. First to receive the aircraft was South Carolina ANG's 169th TFG, in 1983. The 466th TFS of the AFR received its first F-16s on 28 January 1984, at Hill AFB, Utah.

On 7 June 1975 a joint announcement by the four NATO countries of Belgium, Denmark, the Netherlands and Norway confirmed their selection of the F-16 to replace F-104s in current service. The initial order was for 348 aircraft (Belgium 116, Denmark 58, the Netherlands 102 and Norway 72), of which 58 were to be two-seaters. Under co-production agreements, final assembly lines for these aircraft were established in Belgium and the Netherlands. About 30 European companies are producing F-16 components, avionics and equipment.

The first F-16 for Europe was delivered to the Belgian Air Force on 26 January 1979. The Royal Netherlands Air Force received its first two F-16s on 6 June 1979, and initial deliveries to the air forces of Norway and Denmark were made respectively on 25 and 28 January 1980. First operational NATO F-16 unit (from 1 January 1981) was No. 349 Squadron of the Belgian Air Force, at Beauvechain. The first Dutch squadron (No. 322) became operational on the F-16 at Leeuwarden on 1 May 1981.

Non-NATO operators include Israel, which has acquired 75 (including eight two-seaters); Egypt (40); Pakistan (40); and Venezuela (24); South Korea began to equip with 36 in 1986, as the first step towards an eventual planned force of 156 F-16s. The Netherlands has ordered 54 more F-16s, and other follow-up orders have been announced by Belgium (44), Denmark (12), the Netherlands (a third batch totalling 57), Israel (75, with plans for 30 more) and Egypt (40, with plans for 36 more). Turkey will have 160, of which deliveries will begin in 1987; Greece has ordered 40, with deliveries beginning in 1988; Thailand has ordered eight F-16As and four F-16Bs. Singapore and Indonesia have each ordered eight F-16A/Bs.

Deliveries from Fort Worth totalled 1,178 by July 1986, with a further 394 delivered from European production.

First combat use of the F-16 was by the Israeli Air Force, which used eight aircraft to destroy Iraq's Osirak nuclear reactor on 7 June 1981, with a top cover of six F-15s.

F-16s of the Pakistan Air Force can carry Thomson-CSF Atlis laser target designation pods.

In early 1986 the F-16 fleet worldwide had surpassed a total of one million flight hours, of which 734,000 had been flown by the USAF, 247,000 by foreign operators, and 19,000 by pre-production aircraft and during testing.

In February 1980, the US Air Force implemented a Multinational Staged Improvement Programme (MSIP) for the F-16, to assure the aircraft's capability to accept future systems under development by the Air Force. As a first stage, aircraft delivered since November 1981 have built-in structural and wiring provisions, and system architecture, that expand the single-seat F-16's multi-role flexibility to perform precision strike, night attack, and beyond-visual-range interception missions. Advanced cockpit displays and controls have been introduced subsequently, and an improved fire control radar will enable F-16s to launch AIM-120A AMRAAM air-to-air missiles at multiple targets in rapid succession. The enhancement programme will also qualify the F-16 for the US Air Force's LANTIRN nav/attack system and ALQ-165 ASPJ jamming system, currently under development.

First flight by an MSIP-configured F-16 was made on 14 December 1982. Designations of production versions are **F-16C** (single-seat) and **F-16D** (two-seat). Externally, the only feature distinguishing the F-16C from an F-16A is a slightly expanded tail fin root fairing to house ASPJ when it becomes available. Internal changes introduced from the first production F-16C include a Westinghouse APG-68 radar, offering greater range and resolution and expanded modes of operation by comparison with the earlier APG-66; an advanced cockpit with up-front controls, multi-function displays, GEC Avionics wide-angle HUD and Fairchild mission data transfer equipment; increased capacity electrical systems; improved computers with solid state cartridge system for loading mission data; and structural changes for increased T-O weight and manoeuvring limits, and MIL-STD-1760 weapon interfaces to provide compatibility with advanced systems, including AMRAAM, LANTIRN and the Litton AN/ALR-74(V) radar threat warning receiver.

The first F-16C for the US Air Force (83-118) was delivered on 19 July 1984; the first F-16D was delivered in September; first operational unit to equip with these models was the 33rd TFS at Shaw AFB, South Carolina. The second batch of 75 aircraft ordered by Israel will be F-16Cs and F-16Ds, as will the aircraft on order for Greece, Korea, Turkey and the second batch for Egypt. Production of the F-16A for the USAF phased cut at Fort Worth in March 1985, but this version is still available for other countries.

Under the USAF's Alternate Engine Program, confirmed in early 1984, future F-16s will be produced with both Pratt & Whitney F100-PW-220 and General Electric F110-GE-100 engines. General Electric is manufacturing 120 F110s under FY 1985 contracts. All Turkish and Israeli F-16C/Ds will have engines of this type, while the South Korean aircraft will have Pratt & Whitney engines.

The USAF and NATO operators are co-operating in an operational capabilities upgrade (OCU) to modernise and expand the capabilities of F-16A/Bs for use of the next generation of air-to-air and air-to-ground weapons systems. Changes will be made to existing F-16A/B radar systems and software, and the aircraft's fire control computer and central interface unit will be improved. The modifications will permit later installation of more modern systems such as the GPS/Navstar satellite navigation system. A data transfer unit and combined altitude radar altimeter will be installed. The OCU programme will be applicable to Block 10 and Block 15 F-16A/Bs, totalling some 1,100 aircraft.

Development of the F-16 is continuing. A series of 55 initial operational test and evaluation flights for the LANTIRN system was successfully completed by the USAF in November 1984, using three F-16s and three LANTIRN pods, averaging two sorties a day against various tactical targets on simulated ordnance drops. Initial operational test and deployment of LANTIRN began in mid-January 1986 on an F-16 from McChord AFB, Washington. Delivery of the first of 700 navigation pods is scheduled for April 1987. A production decision on the targeting pod was expected during 1986.

In mid-1987, flight testing of an infra-red system known as Falcon Eye FLIR is scheduled to begin. This utilises a helmet mounted display and head-steered FLIR sensor forward of the F-16's windscreen. Claimed advantages are night vision without need for an external pod; 24 hour capability for low-altitude high-speed navigation; off-boresight detection and recognition of tank size targets; and multi-role night attack capability by conventional weapons and AIM-9L Sidewinder missiles.

Vehicle Systems Development Corporation of Upland, California, has developed the FloTrak auxiliary ground

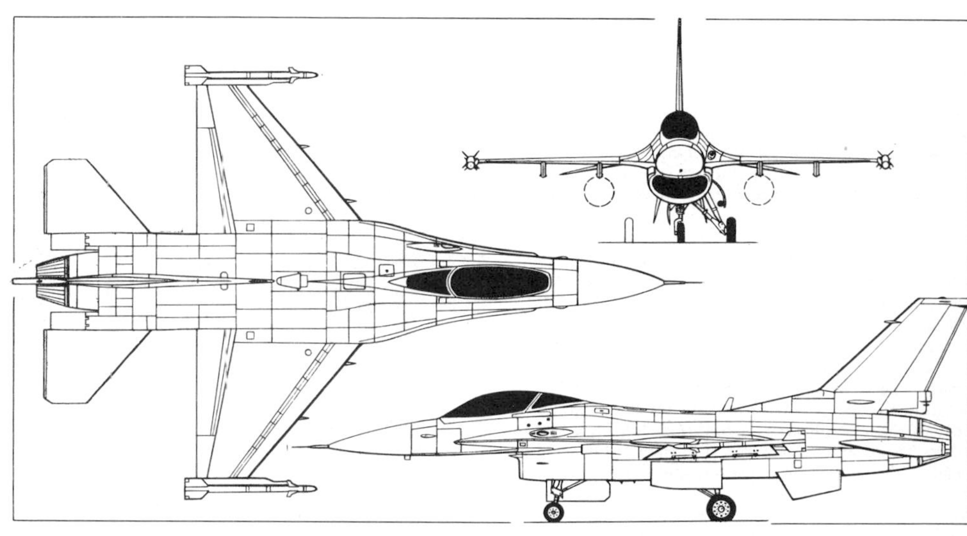

Three-view drawing of General Dynamics F-16C Fighting Falcon *(Pilot Press)*

General Dynamics F-16C Fighting Falcon of the Egyptian Air Force

General Dynamics F-16D two-seat fighter/trainer of the Republic of Korea Air Force

mobility system for the F-16. It consists of an inexpensive plastics track assembly which fits temporarily over the aircraft's tyres, reducing ground pressure by a factor of 3·5, from 19·58 bars (284 lb/sq in) to 5·45 bars (79 lb/sq in). The FloTrak system permits ground towing or taxying over grass, low-strength soils and bomb damaged surfaces, increasing ground mobility and protecting the aircraft's tyres from post-attack debris and rubble. Further development of the system is being undertaken with General Electrics' Plastics Group.

In January 1985 the US Navy selected the **F-16N** as the winner of its supersonic adversary aircraft (SAA) competition. The initial $154·7 million contract is for 14 aircraft, with planned procurement of 26. Deliveries are due to begin in April 1987 at the rate of two per month.

The F-16N is essentially similar to the F-16C, with minor structural modifications involving the substitution of titanium for aluminium in the lower wing fittings and cold working the lower wing skin holes to meet the increased frequency of *g* loadings in the adversary role. The F-16N will be powered by the General Electric F110-GE-100 engine. Other changes from the standard F-16C are: APG-66 multi-mode radar instead of the APG-68; ALR-99 radar warning receiver instead of the ALR-74; and a second ARC-164 UHF radio. No provision will be made for the airborne self-protection jammer (ASPJ), global positioning system (GPS), M61A1 20 mm gun, and alternative mission equipment such as external fuel tanks, pylons, and underwing missile launchers. The aircraft will have wingtip launchers for practice AIM-9 missiles and ACMI AIS pods.

Preliminary plans are for four of the aircraft to be two-seaters, similar to the F-16D. A designation has not been chosen for the two-seat version. The F-16N will be capable of simulating the high performance estimated for the Soviet MiG-29 and Su-27. Growth capability includes external fuel tanks, APG-68, A-A IFF, ECM, improved thrust engine, and in-flight performance tailoring.

In September 1984 General Dynamics was awarded a $62 million USAF contract to develop a reconnaissance variant of the two-seat F-16D, designated **F-16R**, as a potential replacement for the McDonnell Douglas RF-4C in the USAF inventory. Initial effort was directed at simulation evaluation of tasking and co-ordination requirements of a two-man reconnaissance crew in a high-threat, low-altitude, high-speed, night/under-the-weather environment, and began in September 1985, with full mission evaluations starting in December. These were supplemented by a flight demonstration to evaluate a General Dynamics-developed reconnaissance pod for the F-16, incorporating a video camera system to provide display images for the aircraft's crew and high-resolution near-real-time transmission to end users. Some night/all-weather equipment was used, but flight tests were limited to daylight only during the first phase. A second period was scheduled to start in February 1986 to evaluate electro-optical sensors and full near-real-time operations.

F-16s have been operational as tactical reconnaissance aircraft with one European NATO air force since 1983. The aircraft has demonstrated compatibility with four European built reconnaissance pods, including that used on the Tornado. The General Dynamics pod, shown in an accompanying illustration, is 4·40 m (14 ft 5 in) long, weighs 454-567 kg (1,000-1,250 lb) and has a design load factor of 9*g*. Equipment includes wide-angle and long-range cameras, an infra-red linescanner, extendable data link, and video management system. Production deliveries of as many as 410 semi-conformal reconnaissance pods for the USAF could begin in FY 1991, for use on modified F-16D aircraft.

In June 1985 General Dynamics proposed to the USAF a **Specially Configured F-16C** optimised for air defence and selected air-to-ground missions. This aircraft would be offered with a guaranteed hourly maintenance cost and would be configured to enable either General Electric F110-GE-100 or Pratt & Whitney F100-PW-220 engines, or growth variants, to be installed. General Dynamics has proposed the delivery of 216 Specially Configured F-16s, in addition to 504 multi-role F-16C/Ds, over a four-year procurement period commencing in October 1987 and continuing at five aircraft per month.

The Specially Configured F-16C would retain the F-16C's advanced core avionics, advanced cockpit and subsystems, combined with the F-16A's APG-66 radar, and the LN-39 inertial navigation system modified to provide rapid alignment to enable the aircraft to be airborne in less than one minute from a scramble alert.

Other research and development subjects being investigated for the F-16 include artificial intelligence, modular avionics architecture, VHSIC, various weapons, sensors and cockpit displays, secure/anti-jam communications and data links, advanced navigation systems, chemical and electromagnetic pulse hardening, signature reduction and vulnerability reduction. A Falcon Century programme has been instituted to monitor and evaluate developments and to maintain a master plan for F-16 developments into the next century.

The **F-16XL** is described separately. The following description applies to the F-16C and F-16D, as indicated:

TYPE: Single-seat lightweight air combat fighter (F-16C) and two-seat fighter/trainer (F-16D).

F-16R test aircraft equipped with General Dynamics reconnaissance pod

WINGS: Cantilever mid-wing monoplane, of blended wing/body design and cropped delta planform. The blended wing/body concept is achieved by flaring the wing/body intersection, thus not only providing lift from the body at high angles of attack but also giving less wetted area and increased internal fuel volume. In addition, thickening of the wing root gives a more rigid structure, with a weight saving of some 113 kg (250 lb). Basic wing is of NACA 64A-204 section, with 40° sweepback on leading-edges. Structure is mainly of aluminium alloy, with 11 spars, 5 ribs and single upper and lower skins, and is attached to fuselage by machined aluminium fittings. Leading-edge manoeuvring flaps are programmed automatically as a function of Mach number and angle of attack. The increased wing camber maintains effective lift coefficients at high angles of attack. These flaps are one-piece bonded aluminium honeycomb sandwich structures, actuated by a Garrett drive system using rotary actuators. The trailing-edges carry large flaperons (flaps/ailerons), which are interchangeable left with right and are actuated by National Water Lift integrated servo-actuators. The maximum rate of flaperon movement is 52°/s.

FUSELAGE: Semi-monocoque all-metal structure of frames and longerons, built in three main modules: forward (to just aft of cockpit), centre and aft. Nose radome built by Brunswick Corporation. Highly swept vortex control strakes along the fuselage forebody increase lift and improve directional stability at high angles of attack.

TAIL UNIT: Cantilever structure with sweptback surfaces. Fin is multi-spar multi-rib aluminium structure with graphite epoxy skins, aluminium tip and glassfibre dorsal fin and root fairing. Extension of root fairing houses Loral Rapport ECM equipment in Belgian F-16A and F-16Bs, a brake parachute in aircraft for Norway and Venezuela (and, in due course, in the F-16Cs for Turkey). Interchangeable all-moving tailplane halves, constructed of graphite epoxy composite laminate skins mechanically attached to a corrugated aluminium substructure. Each tailplane half has an aluminium pivot shaft, and a removable full depth bonded honeycomb leading-edge. Ventral fins are bonded aluminium honeycomb core with aluminium skins. Split speed-brake inboard of rear portion of each horizontal tail surface to each side of nozzle, each deflecting 60° from the closed position. National Water Lift servo-actuators for rudder and tailplane.

LANDING GEAR: Menasco hydraulically retractable type, nose unit retracting aft and main units forward into fuselage. Nosewheel is located aft of intake, to reduce the risk of foreign objects being thrown into the engine during ground operation, and rotates 90° during retraction to lie horizontally under engine air intake duct. Oleo-pneumatic struts in all units. Goodyear mainwheels and brakes; Goodrich mainwheel tyres, size 25·5 × 8-14, pressure 14·48-15·17 bars (210-220 lb/sq in) at T-O weights less than 11,340 kg (25,000 lb). Steerable nosewheel with Goodrich tyre, size 18 × 5·5-8, pressure 14·82-15·51 bars (215-225 lb/sq in) at T-O weights less than 11,340 kg (25,000 lb). All but two main unit components interchangeable. Brake by wire system on main gear, with Goodyear anti-skid units. Runway arrester hook under rear fuselage.

POWER PLANT: One Pratt & Whitney F100-PW-200 turbofan engine, rated at approx 111·2 kN (25,000 lb st) with afterburning, mounted within the rear fuselage. (General Electric F110-GE-100 and Pratt & Whitney F100-PW-220 to be alternative standard engines in future production aircraft.) Fixed geometry intake, with boundary layer splitter plate, beneath fuselage. Standard fuel contained in wing and five seal-bonded fuselage cells which function as two tanks; internal fuel weight is 3,162 kg (6,972 lb) in F-16C, and approx 17 per cent less in F-16D. In-flight refuelling receptacle in top of centre-fuselage, aft of cockpit. Auxiliary fuel can be carried in drop tanks on underwing and under-fuselage hardpoints.

ACCOMMODATION: Pilot only in F-16C in air-conditioned cockpit. McDonnell Douglas ACES II zero/zero ejection seat. Transparent bubble canopy made of polycarbonate advanced plastics material. The windscreen and forward canopy are an integral unit without a forward bow frame, and are separated from the aft canopy by a simple support structure which serves also as the breakpoint where the forward section pivots upward and aft to give access to the cockpit. A redundant safety lock feature prevents canopy loss. Windscreen/canopy design provides 360° all-round view, 195° fore and aft, 40° down over the side, and 15° down over the nose. To enable the pilot to sustain high *g* forces, and for pilot comfort, the seat is inclined 30° aft and the heel line is raised. In normal operation the canopy is pivoted upward and aft by electrical power; the pilot is also able to unlatch the canopy manually and open it with a backup handcrank. Emergency jettison is provided by explosive unlatching devices and two rockets. A limited displacement, force sensing control stick is provided on the right hand console, with a suitable armrest, to provide precise control inputs during combat manoeuvres. The F-16D has two cockpits in tandem, equipped with all controls, displays, instruments, avionics and life support systems required to perform both training and combat missions. The layout of the F-16D second station is essentially the same as that of the F-16C, and is fully systems-operational. A single-enclosure polycarbonate transparency, made in two pieces and spliced aft of the forward seat with a metal bow frame and lateral support member, provides outstanding view from both cockpits.

SYSTEMS: Hamilton Standard regenerative 12kW bootstrap air cycle environmental control system, using engine bleed air, for pressurisation and cooling. Two separate and independent hydraulic systems supply power for operation of the primary flight control surfaces and the utility functions. System pressure (each) 207 bars (3,000 lb/sq in), rated at 161 litres (42·5 US gallons)/min. Bootstrap type reservoirs, rated at 5·79 bars (84 lb/sq in). Electrical system powered by engine driven Westinghouse 60kVA and Lear Siegler 10kVA generators and ground control units, with Sundstrand constant speed drive. Four dedicated, sealed cell batteries provide transient electrical power protection for the fly by wire flight control system. Application of the control configured vehicle (CCV) principle of relaxed static stability produces a significant reduction in trim drag, especially at high load factors and supersonic speeds. The aircraft centre of gravity is allowed to move aft, reducing both the tail drag and the change in drag on the wing due to changes in lift required to balance the download on the tail. Relaxed static stability imposes a requirement for a highly reliable, full-time-operating, stability augmentation system, including reliable electronic, electrical and hydraulic provisions. The signal paths in this quad-redundant system are used to control the aircraft, replacing the usual mechanical linkages. Direct electrical control is employed from pilot controls to surface actuators. An onboard Sundstrand/Solar jet fuel starter is provided for engine self-start capability. Hamilton Standard turbine compressor, and Sundstrand accessory drive gearbox. Simmonds fuel measuring system. Garrett emergency power unit automatically drives a standby generator and pump to provide uninterrupted electrical and hydraulic power for control in the event of the engine or primary power systems becoming inoperative.

AVIONICS AND EQUIPMENT: Westinghouse APG-68 pulse-Doppler range and angle track radar, with planar array in nose. Forward avionics bay, immediately forward of cockpit, contains radar, air data equipment, inertial navigation system, flight control computer, and space and structural provisions for radar altimeter. Rear avionics bay contains Collins AN/ARN-108 ILS, Tacan and IFF, with space for future equipment. A Dalmo Victor ALR-69 radar warning system is installed. Communications equipment includes Magnavox AN/ARC-164 UHF transceiver; provisions for a Magnavox KY-58 secure voice system; Collins AN/ARC-186 VHF AM/FM transceiver; government furnished AN/AIC-18/25 intercom; and Novatronics interference blanker. Sperry Flight Systems central air data computer. Litton LN-39 inertial navigation system; Collins AN/ARN-108 ILS; Collins AN/ARN-118 Tacan; Teledyne Electronics AN/APX-101 air-to-ground IFF transponder with a government furnished IFF control; government furnished National Security Agency KIT-1A/TSEC cryptographic equipment; Lear Siegler stick force sensors; GEC Avionics wide-angle electronic head-up display; horizontal situation indicator; Teledyne Avionics angle of attack transmitter; Gull Airborne angle of attack indicator; Clifton Precision attitude director indicator; Delco fire control computer; Photo-Sonics gun camera; Kaiser radar electro-optical display. Landing/taxying light on each main landing gear strut. Essential structure and wiring provisions are built into the airframe to allow for easy incorporation of future avionics systems under development for the F-16 by the US Air Force.

ARMAMENT: General Electric M61A1 20 mm multi-barrel cannon in the port side wing/body fairing, equipped with a General Electric ammunition handling system and a 'snapshoot' gunsight (part of the head-up display system) and 515 rounds of ammunition. There is a mounting for an air-to-air missile at each wingtip, one underfuselage centreline hardpoint, and six underwing hardpoints for additional stores. For manoeuvring flight at 5·5*g* the underfuselage station is stressed for a load of up to 1,000 kg (2,200 lb), the two inboard underwing stations for 2,041 kg (4,500 lb) each, the two centre underwing stations for 1,587 kg (3,500 lb) each, the two outboard underwing stations for 318 kg (700 lb) each, and the two wingtip stations for 193 kg (425 lb) each. For manoeuvring flight at 9*g* the underfuselage station is stressed for a load of up to 544 kg (1,200 lb), the two inboard underwing stations for 1,134 kg (2,500 lb) each, the two centre underwing stations for 907 kg (2,000 lb) each, the two outboard underwing stations for 204 kg (450 lb) each, and the two wingtip stations for 193 kg (425 lb) each. There are mounting provisions on each side of the inlet shoulder for the specific carriage of sensor pods (electro-optical, FLIR, etc); each of these stations is stressed for 408 kg (900 lb) at 5·5*g*, and 250 kg (550 lb) at 9*g*. Typical stores loads can include two wingtip mounted AIM-9J/L Sidewinders, with up to four more on the outer underwing stations; Sargent-Fletcher 1,400 litre (370 US gallon; 308 Imp gallon) drop tanks on the inboard underwing stations; a 1,136 litre (300 US gallon; 250 Imp gallon) drop tank on the underfuselage station; a Martin Marietta Pave Penny laser tracker pod along the starboard side of the nacelle; and single or cluster bombs, air-to-surface missiles, or flare pods, on the four inner underwing stations. Stores can be launched from Aircraft Hydro-Forming MAU-12C/A bomb ejector racks, Hughes LAU-88 launchers, or Orgen triple or multiple ejector racks. Westinghouse AN/ALQ-119 and AN/ALQ-131 ECM (jammer) pods can be carried on the centreline and two underwing stations. ALE-47 internal pyrotechnic/chaff dispensers have been specified. Current capabilities include air-to-air combat with gun and Sidewinder missiles; and air-to-ground attack with gun, rockets, conventional bombs, special weapons, laser guided and electro-optical weapons. Specific structure and wiring provisions, and system architecture, are built in to ensure the capability to accept future sensor and weapon systems, including electro-optical and FLIR pods, and advanced beyond-visual-range missiles. Weapons already launched successfully from F-16s, in addition to Sidewinders and AMRAAM, include radar guided Sparrow and Sky Flash air-to-air missiles, and TV guided Maverick air-to-surface missiles. F-16s of the Belgian Air Force carry Matra Magic air-to-air missiles and Norwegian Air Force aircraft carry Penguin anti-shipping missiles. F-16s can be equipped with a variety of reconnaissance pods and the Thomson-CSF Atlis laser designator pod.

DIMENSIONS, EXTERNAL (F-16A, B, C, D):

Wing span over missile launchers	9·45 m (31 ft 0 in)
Wing span over missiles	10·01 m (32 ft 10 in)
Wing aspect ratio	3·0
Length overall	15·01 m (49 ft 3 in)
Height overall	5·09 m (16 ft 8½ in)
Tailplane span	5·59 m (18 ft 4 in)
Wheel track	2·36 m (7 ft 9 in)
Wheelbase	4·00 m (13 ft 1·44 in)

AREAS (F-16A, B, C, D):

Wings, gross	27·87 m² (300·0 sq ft)
Flaperons (total)	5·82 m² (62·64 sq ft)
Leading-edge flaps (total)	6·82 m² (73·42 sq ft)
Vertical tail surfaces (total)	5·09 m² (54·75 sq ft)
Rudder	1·08 m² (11·65 sq ft)
Horizontal tail surfaces (total)	5·92 m² (63·70 sq ft)

WEIGHTS AND LOADINGS:

Weight empty: F-16A	7,364 kg (16,234 lb)
F-16B	7,655 kg (16,876 lb)
F-16C	7,618 kg (16,794 lb)
F-16D	7,896 kg (17,408 lb)
Internal fuel load: F-16A, C	3,162 kg (6,972 lb)
F-16B, D	2,624 kg (5,785 lb)
Max external load: all models	5,443 kg (12,000 lb)
Structural design gross weight (9*g*) with full internal fuel:	
F-16A, B	11,113 kg (24,500 lb)
F-16C, D	11,839 kg (26,100 lb)
Max T-O weight:	
air-to-air, no external tanks:	
F-16A	11,094 kg (24,459 lb)
F-16B	10,849 kg (23,918 lb)
F-16C	11,372 kg (25,071 lb)
F-16D	11,114 kg (24,502 lb)
with external load:	
F-16A, B	16,057 kg (35,400 lb)
F-16C, D	17,010 kg (37,500 lb)
Wing loading:	
at 9,979 kg (22,000 lb) AUW	356 kg/m² (73 lb/sq ft)
at 14,968 kg (33,000 lb) AUW	537 kg/m² (110 lb/sq ft)
Thrust/weight ratio ('clean')	1·1 to 1

PERFORMANCE (F-16A):

Max level speed at 12,200 m (40,000 ft)	above Mach 2·0
Service ceiling	more than 15,240 m (50,000 ft)
Radius of action	more than 500 nm (925 km; 575 miles)
Ferry range, with drop tanks	more than 2,100 nm (3,890 km; 2,415 miles)
Max symmetrical design load factor with full internal fuel, all models	+9

GENERAL DYNAMICS F-16/79

This aircraft is essentially an F-16 tactical fighter powered by a General Electric J79-GE-119 afterburning turbojet engine. It was produced in response to US government authorisation of an FX programme, to develop aircraft for export to nations in which a first-line US fighter might not be required. The F-16/79 meets the FX requirements of being primarily an air defence fighter, while retaining the F-16's multi-role systems capability. It was initiated as a company funded programme by General Dynamics, which leased back from the US Air Force the second F-16B development aircraft (75-0752) for conversion, testing and certification as the F-16/79 export fighter. The first flight was accomplished on 29 October 1980, and company certification flight testing was completed on 19 December 1980.

In January 1985 flight testing began of a British Aerospace Terprom navigation system installed in an F-16/79. Terprom (terrain profile matching) consists of a radar altimeter, INS, and a computer which stores a digital map loaded on pre-programmed tapes. The system takes initial position locating data from the INS (or from a Doppler system with attitude and heading referencing, or an air data system providing airspeed, magnetic heading and barometric pressure information), and compares terrain features recorded by the radar altimeter with digital map data stored in the computer memory to establish exact aircraft position.

Replacement of the 111·2 kN (25,000 lb st) F100-PW-200 by the 80·1 kN (18,000 lb st) J79-GE-119 offers a considerable reduction in aircraft cost. The basic air combat effectiveness of the F-16 is retained, with an increase of some 817 kg (1,800 lb) in the aircraft's empty weight. Changes include internal modification of the engine air intake, to reduce airflow and increase pressure recovery, and lengthening of the rear fuselage fairing, increasing the length of the fuselage (but not overall length) by 0·45 m (1 ft 5½ in). Two versions are available: the single-seat F-16/79A and two-seat F-16/79B.

WEIGHTS:

Weight empty: A	8,088 kg (17,832 lb)
B	8,362 kg (18,436 lb)
Internal fuel load: A	3,162 kg (6,972 lb)
B	2,624 kg (5,785 lb)
Max external load	4,309 kg (9,500 lb)
Max T-O weight (no external load):	
A	11,805 kg (26,025 lb)
B	11,542 kg (25,446 lb)
Max T-O weight: A, B	16,057 kg (35,400 lb)

GENERAL DYNAMICS AFTI/F-16

On 10 July 1982 the General Dynamics AFTI/F-16 made a successful 1 h 14 min first flight from Carswell AFB, Texas. Its development had begun in December 1978, when the US Air Force selected the F-16 as a testbed with which to explore new fighter aircraft technologies under the Advanced Fighter Technology Integration (AFTI) programme, directed by Air Force Systems Command's Flight Dynamics Laboratory (FDL) at Wright-Patterson AFB, Ohio. General Dynamics was awarded a $34·3 million prime contract, under which it modified an F-16A (A-6) returned to the company by the US Air Force on 6 March 1980.

This programme, which is expected to influence the design of future US high-performance combat aircraft, is managed by an AFTI/F-16 Advanced Development Program Office at FDL. Participants include the Naval Air Development Center, which is giving funding and technical support; the Naval Air Test Center, which provided a test pilot for AFTI/F-16 simulations and Phase I of the test programme; the Air Force Armament Laboratory, which is funding and sponsoring the standard avionics integrated fusing (SAIF) development programme to be flight tested during Phase II; NASA's Dryden Flight Research Center at Edwards AFB, California, providing manpower and facilities for flight test operations; and the Air Force Flight Test Center, also at Edwards, which is the USAF organisation responsible for Phases I and II of AFTI/F-16 testing. A Joint Flight Test Organization (JFTO), drawing upon personnel from the above participants, as well as General Dynamics, is carrying out the flight test programme at Edwards AFB and Nellis AFB, Nevada.

New capabilities promised by the AFTI/F-16 originate from early control configured vehicle (CCV) programmes. These sought to develop an unstable high-performance aircraft that would be extremely manoeuvrable, relying upon fly by wire controls and airborne computers to ensure that the aircraft would have optimum handling qualities at all times and under all conditions. More specifically, the AFTI/F-16 programme was preceded by the CCV/YF-16, an F-16 prototype with analog fly by wire control system, modified externally by the addition of two foreplanes and first flown with these foreplanes operative on 24 March 1976. Details of the CCV/YF-16 programme can be found in the 1977-78 *Jane's*.

The concept of the AFTI/F-16 has been growing from that time, with designers aware that the introduction of digital computers would provide far greater overall control capability than was possible with the analog system in the CCV/YF-16. Flight test equipment is housed in a new dorsal fairing which extends from behind the cockpit, and into the rear end of which the vertical tail surfaces are blended. The aircraft also has two foreplanes (canards), similar to those of the CCV/YF-16, mounted on the underside of the engine inlet duct. Its first flight represented the culmination of three years of development and testing, including 1,360 h of wind tunnel tests and comprehensive static testing, of which details can be found in the 1982-83 *Jane's*.

Simulations of the automated manoeuvring attack system (AMAS) are continuing, to evaluate the engineering design and allow pilots to practise critical flight manoeuvres. FDL's LAMARS (large amplitude multi-mode aerospace research simulator) facility is checking out the digital flight control laws of the AFTI/F-16, permitting detailed human factors studies and investigation of AMAS.

The AFTI/F-16 will be the first operationally equipped fighter aircraft to demonstrate the new flight techniques made possible by such an advanced configuration. It will be

General Dynamics F-16/79, armed with wingtip Sidewinder air-to-air missiles

General Dynamics AFTI/F-16 technology testbed aircraft, now fitted with FLIR sensor/tracker

able to turn by sliding sideways without banking and with weapons firing. Such an ability translated to a production fighter would mean that, if a pilot saw a target in his one o'clock position, he would simply command the aircraft to turn towards it and deliver its weapons in less time than it takes a conventional aircraft to bank, turn and fire. The AFTI/F-16 has six flight modes that cannot be duplicated by any current operational aircraft. Known as 'decoupled' or six-degree-of-freedom flight modes, each motion is separated (or decoupled) from the other, usual, motions of a flight manoeuvre. The pilot of a conventional aircraft wishing to turn to starboard must roll into a bank, pull back on the control column to bring the aircraft's nose round and then roll out of the bank. In the AFTI/F-16 he merely depresses the rudder pedals for the aircraft to move to starboard in a wings level turn without any roll.

Evaluation of the six different types of decoupled motion, first tested in the CCV/YF-16 but mechanised differently, is an important part of AFTI/F-16 flight tests. In the longitudinal, or vertical, flight path the motions are direct lift, pitch axis pointing and vertical translation. The pilot commands these longitudinal motions by means of a twist grip on the port throttle; control surfaces affected are the trailing-edge flaps and the all-moving horizontal tail surfaces. Lateral, or sideways, decoupled motions are direct side force, yaw axis pointing and lateral translation. These lateral motions are controlled by the pilot's rudder pedals, which activate three control surfaces: the flaperons (flaps/ailerons), rudder and fuselage mounted twin vertical foreplanes. The pilot can fly conventional manoeuvres as well as the decoupled flight paths, using the standard side stick controller (starboard) and rudder pedals to command coupled flight modes.

However, the AFTI/F-16 coupled flight control system is itself unique. Whereas most aircraft are designed for one specific primary mission, with any diversion from it likely to compromise performance, flight characteristics or weapon effectiveness, the AFTI/F-16 flight control laws were designed to operate well during four missions: normal (take-off, cruising flight, refuelling, formation and landing), air-to-air gunnery, air-to-surface gunnery, and air-to-surface bombing. The pilot can select any one of these four missions on his head-up display (HUD) control panel. Such selection implements instantly the desired control laws and also causes the HUD, fire control computer, stores management system, multi-purpose displays (MPD) and radar to be configured to support that particular flight mode. Any of the standard or decoupled modes can be selected in flight at any time, with the single exception that when the landing gear is down the control laws are configured automatically to the standard, coupled mode.

The flight control hardware (DFCS) comprises three BDX 930 digital computers, each manipulating some 500,000 operations per second and storing in their large memories many task tailored control laws that can be recalled at will by the pilot. Use of digital (rather than analog) computers offers far greater flexibility, and new tasks can be added to the DFCS merely by writing new software programmes. The use of three computers provides reliability and flight safety, since each works in an asynchronous mode and the three are timed to begin any electrical task milliseconds apart. When the calculations are completed the computers compare their output, so ensuring that the correct solution is transmitted to the appropriate control surface(s). Each computer has a basic analog backup system, which means that should all three fail the pilot could still control the aircraft to effect a safe landing.

The DFCS and AMAS are linked to provide the pilot with a range of attack profiles unknown in conventional fighters. He could, as explained earlier, fire weapons while slipping sideways, without banking or flying over the target. Via AMAS, the pilot can decide how much authority to pass to the system. In a fully automated mode AMAS would allow him to sit as little more than an observer. Studies completed by mid-1982 suggested that the AFTI/F-16 could have a bombing accuracy equal to that of the F-16A but with a significant increase in pilot survivability. In an air-to-air mode AFTI/F-16 is expected to attack better from all angles and maintain a higher kill rate than conventional fighters using standard combat manoeuvres. For very precise target acquisition and tracking, AMAS uses a FLIR sensor/tracker pod developed by Westinghouse, mounted at the aircraft's starboard wingroot leading-edge. The FLIR and the aircraft's improved APG-66 radar serve as sensors for AMAS, and the pod contains also a laser system for target ranging (air to-surface) and acquisition (air-to-air). This laser is identical to the type used in Pave Spike pods for daylight target designation. The FLIR sensor can be slewed by the pilot, slaved to another sensor, or is capable of initiating its own target search.

The AFTI/F-16 pilot is intended to wear a helmet mounted sight, enabling him to 'acquire' a target by simply looking towards it and centering the crosshairs of the sight on the target. Each crosshair has a minute light at its tip, and when a light comes on it indicates target direction to the pilot. As soon as he has the target in the centre of the crosshairs all four lights illuminate, and he has merely to depress a button on his side stick controller for the FLIR or radar sensor to slew automatically to align with the target and lock on.

AMAS is integrated with a Delco D^3 high-speed digital fire control computer. This will calculate 'aiming error', or the difference between where the target is and where the AFTI/F-16's weapon is pointed. That data is then transmitted to the DFCS, which immediately activates the aircraft's control surfaces so that it manoeuvres to correct the aiming error. A roll stabilised radar altimeter is linked with AMAS for greater safety during air-to-surface operations. Six antennae, radially configured about the fuselage, provide a 360° roll altitude sensing capability during high *g* manoeuvres at heights down to 61 m (200 ft). The altimeter is integrated with a low-altitude autopilot, which frees the pilot from the need to devote his full attention to terrain avoidance.

A new automated device that will be tested by the AFTI/F-16 as a component of AMAS is a standardised avionics integrated fusing (SAIF) system developed by the Air Force Armament Laboratory. SAIF is a system for setting automatically the fusing parameters in dispenser bombs immediately before their release from the aircraft. Conventional fuses are set before the aircraft takes off on a sortie, which means that the pilot must manoeuvre the aircraft to the preset condition for each bomb release. With SAIF, the fuse will be set immediately before release of the dispenser pod.

The cockpit includes two multi-purpose display (MPD) units, each with 20 electronic pushbuttons, which provide the pilot with alphanumerics (from two programmable display generators) and sensor video (from FLIR and radar) separately or in combination. The pushbuttons provide an interface between the pilot and the DFCS, allowing him to tailor the flight control laws; to change or add flight features, such as drag modulation; and select different control options. They can, additionally, provide an interface with other aircraft systems, and be used to monitor malfunctions that might develop in the DFCS.

A specially developed GEC Avionics HUD with a wide field of view is installed in the cockpit. It incorporates special optics to provide an instantaneous field of view of 15° by 20°, compared with only 9° by 13° for the standard F-16A HUD. It displays in alphanumerics critical flight reference information, weapon aiming and fire control data. The conventional side stick controller on the starboard side of the cockpit has been modified to provide additional switching functions: engage/disengage control of the independent backup flight control system, decoupled flight control modes, and the AMAS. Additional hands-on control is provided for the MPDs, helmet-mounted sight and weapon delivery modes. The twist grip throttle (port) provdes manual control of pitch pointing, vertical translation, and direct lift. Other capabilities, including manual slewing of the FLIR/radar in the direction of the target, are accomplished by using existing throttle switches.

Because the flight manoeuvres of the AFTI/F-16 can result in side forces as high as 2*g*, shoulder restraint pads have been attached to the aircraft bulkhead to provide some measure of support for comfort, while keeping the pilot's head where he can read the HUD. Flight testing will demonstrate whether this system is adequate.

Another advanced technology to be tested during the flight programme is known as Interactive Avionics. Voice warning, relayed via the pilot's headset, will gain his immediate attention: instead of a caution light, which he

General Dynamics F-16XL advanced technology development of the F-16 Fighting Falcon

could miss while watching an enemy target, a voice will give audible warning of an impending or actual emergency covering 34 different situations. Similarly, voice command will allow the pilot to initiate functions normally controlled by manual switches, without taking his hands from the flight controls. The existing UHF radio switch in the throttle will be used to activate the voice command system.

Pilots involved in the AFTI/F-16 programme will each have a personalised voice cassette of how they pronounce the command words. Before take-off, a pilot will load his cassette of voice patterns into a data transfer module for transmission to the voice command computer, which will store them as individual word templates. Each template then serves as the master for the voice recognising system. Explained simply, this means that, before executing a voice command by the pilot, the voice processor must match the pilot's command with the prerecorded template word. Speaking through his normal microphone and listening through his headset, the pilot can use the established voice command vocabulary to specify tasks. Reaction to his spoken order will be printed on the MPDs, confirming that the commanded task has been completed.

Flight testing of the AFTI/F-16 is centred at NASA's Dryden Flight Research Center at Edwards AFB. Phase I tests, involving 118 flights during the first year, were concerned primarily with the DFCS which, essentially, controls the flight path of the aircraft. Other technologies of particular interest during Phase I were the new features in the cockpit, and the pilot's ability to use them efficiently for weapon delivery. Phase II testing, which began in August 1984, calls for 150 flights during and is intended to assess and validate the AMAS hardware.

In late April 1985 the USAF began flight testing the Westinghouse sensor/tracker system. This provides precise target information enabling the aircraft's fire control computer to direct the flight control system to the correct position to deliver weapons against a specific target. Testing of the system continued into the Summer of 1986, and included flight demonstration of automated head-on aerial gunnery and automated low altitude delivery of conventional bombs at an altitude of 61 m (200 ft), with the pilot releasing bombs during a horizontal 5*g* turn. The FLIR/laser system has been integrated with the AFTI/F-16's flight and fire control systems by means of a software update. Flight verification of closed-loop operation of the AMAS will include testing the use of a helmet mounted sight for cueing target sensors; the advanced, triplex digital flight control system; standard avionics integrated fusing to enable the fire control system to automatically fuse weapons just prior to release; a colour digital map display with auto-navigation features; a voice system for pilot control of subsystems and feedback responses; and other cockpit display technologies.

The information generated by this overall programme is to be made available generally to the US aircraft industry for application to the design of future fighter aircraft.

GENERAL DYNAMICS F-16XL

Under the designation F-16XL, General Dynamics undertook company funded development of an advanced version of the F-16 that would incorporate new aerodynamic and systems technologies. The company received support from the US Air Force, which leased to it two F-16A full scale development airframes, Pratt & Whitney F100-PW-200 turbofan engines and one new F-16B forward fuselage. Flight testing was centred at Edwards AFB, California, under contract to the US Air Force. First flight, by the single-seat F-16XL prototype, was made on 3 July 1982. The second, two-seat, prototype, first flown on 29 October 1982, was powered by a General Electric F110-GE-100 engine. By 15 February 1985 the two demonstration aircraft had logged 774 flying hours in 661 flights. By that date the single-seater had flown 351 times, the two-seater 301 times.

As can be seen in the accompanying illustration, the F-16XL has a composites skinned 'cranked arrow' wing, with 50°/70° compound leading-edge sweep. The basic F-16 fuselage was lengthened by 1·42 m (4 ft 8 in), the additional volume being used to increase the internal fuel capacity by 85 per cent, and to provide extra space for avionics and sensors. The long chord of the cranked-arrow wing allowed tandem semi-conformal weapons carriage. Bomb ejectors were mounted directly to the wing structure to take advantage of the more stable underwing airflow. The F-16XL could carry four AMRAAM missiles, semi-submerged under the wing at the fuselage intersection, and one AIM-9 missile on each wingtip.

The better cruise efficiency, increased internal fuel capacity and lower weapon carriage drag resulted in a 48 per cent increase in combat radius on internal fuel only and an 87 per cent increase with external fuel tanks, as compared to the current operational F-16. In addition to the improved mission capabilities with all weapon loads, and higher military power (non-afterburner) penetration speeds, the F-16XL's manoeuvring capabilities (angle of attack, airspeed and attitude) were the same in either air-to-air or air-to-surface configuration. The aircraft demonstrated the ability to roll while maintaining a 30° angle of attack at 90 knots (167 km/h; 104 mph) while loaded with twelve 500 lb bombs.

On 24 February 1984 the Department of Defense announced its choice of the McDonnell Douglas F-15E, rather than the F-16XL, as the US Air Force's dual-role air defence/ground attack fighter. At the same time it announced that it planned to continue development of the single-seat F-16XL derivative, now designated **F-16F**, to provide greater combat effectiveness and survivability against F-16-type targets. In November 1985, however, the USAF announced termination of the development programme. In early 1986 the two F-16XL prototypes were in flyable storage at General Dynamics' Fort Worth facility. A more detailed account of the F-16XL programme can be found in the 1985-86 *Jane's*.

GREAT LAKES

GREAT LAKES AIRCRAFT COMPANY INC

Box 1038, Claremont, New Hampshire 03743
Telephone: (603) 542 4520
President and Production Manager: John LaBelle
Vice-President, Flight Operations and Marketing: Bruce L. Moore

Production of the Great Lakes Sport Trainer was revived in 1974 in Wichita, Kansas, and in 1978 moved to Eastman, Georgia, where manufacture was suspended in 1982. In 1984, under new ownership, Great Lakes Aircraft Company Inc was re-established in Claremont, New Hampshire. The manufacturing facility was to be expanded by April 1986 to a total of 4,273 m² (46,000 sq ft). Scheduled production in the new plant was expected to reach two aircraft per month.

GREAT LAKES SPORT TRAINER MODEL 2T-1A-2

The Great Lakes Sport Trainer was produced with Cirrus and Menasco engines by the original Great Lakes Company, founded on 2 January 1929.

Certification of the Model 2T-1A-1 with 104 kW (140 hp) Avco Lycoming engine was obtained in May 1973, and delivery of production aircraft began in October 1973, but manufacture of this version (described in the 1977-78 *Jane's*) has ended. Current production model is the 2T-1A-2 with 134 kW (180 hp) engine, constant-speed propeller, inverted fuel and oil systems, ailerons on both upper and lower wings, and with manifold pressure and fuel flow gauges as standard. Approved aerobatic manoeuvres are spins, chandelles, lazy eights, loops, barrel rolls, primary rolls, point rolls, slow rolls, snap rolls, Cuban 8s, hammerhead turns, Immelmann turns and 'split S'.

Type: Two-seat sporting biplane.

Wings: Braced biplane, with N-type interplane struts, wire bracing and N type centre-section support struts. Dual streamline-section landing and flying wires. Wing section M-12. No dihedral on upper wing, 2° on lower wings. Sweepback on upper wing 9° 13′. Composite structure, with Douglas fir spars, metal ribs and overall Dacron covering with polyurethane paint finish. Ailerons on upper and lower wings. No flaps or tabs.

Fuselage: Welded chrome-molybdenum steel tube. Warren girder structure, with fabric covering.

Tail Unit: Wire braced aluminium tube structure with formed aluminium ribs, fabric covered. Tailplane incidence manually adjustable from both cockpits. No controllable tabs.

Landing Gear: Non-retractable type, with steerable Scott tailwheel. Divided main legs with spring-oleo shock absorbers standard. Mainwheels size 6·00-6 with Cleveland hydraulic disc brakes. Parking brake. Size 7·00-6 tyres optional. Leg and wheel fairings standard.

Power Plant: One 134 kW (180 hp) Avco Lycoming AEIO-360-B1G6 flat-four engine, driving a Hartzell HC-C2YK-4F/FC7666A-2 two-blade constant-speed metal propeller with spinner. Fully inverted fuel system with 98·5 litre (26 US gallon) centre-section tank in upper wing, and 5·3 litre (1·4 US gallon) inverted header tank. Refuelling point in upper wing surface. Fully inverted oil system, capacity 7·5 litres (2 US gallons).

The first Great Lakes 2T-1A-2 aerobatic biplane built by the relocated company

Accommodation: Two seats in tandem in open cockpits. Rear cockpit sliding bubble canopy optional. Dual controls, with adjustable rudder pedals, standard. Compass, airspeed indicator, altimeter, tachometer, manifold pressure/fuel flow gauge, oil temperature and oil pressure gauges standard in rear cockpit, optional for front cockpit. Cockpit heating optional. Baggage compartment aft of rear cockpit, capacity 18 kg (40 lb), standard.

Systems: Engine-driven 35A alternator and sealed 12V storage battery for electrical supply to navigation lights, two rotating beacons, and rear cockpit instrument lights, standard. Hydraulic system for brakes only.

Avionics and Equipment: Emergency locator transmitter standard. King KX 155 nav/com with KI 208 VOR or KI 209 VOR/GS, KT 76A transponder with or without KE 127 attitude encoder, and voice-activated intercom, optional. Other optional avionics include Apollo Loran C. Standard equipment includes map case, seat belts and shoulder harness, cockpit lights, navigation lights, two omni-flash beacons, and a choice of four paint trims. Optional equipment includes full IFR gyro panel, VSI, CHT gauge, EGT and OAT gauges for rear cockpit, *g* meters for both cockpits, glider towing hook, cockpit covers, David Clark helmet mounted headsets, and custom paint schemes.

Dimensions, external:
- Wing span — 8·13 m (26 ft 8 in)
- Length overall — 6·45 m (21 ft 2 in)
- Height overall — 2·34 m (7 ft 8 in)
- Wheel track — 1·78 m (5 ft 10 in)

Areas:
- Wings, gross — 17·43 m² (187·6 sq ft)
- Ailerons (total) — 2·70 m² (29·10 sq ft)
- Fin — 0·55 m² (5·87 sq ft)
- Rudder — 0·63 m² (6·81 sq ft)
- Tailplane — 1·43 m² (15·44 sq ft)
- Elevators — 0·99 m² (10·68 sq ft)

Weights and Loadings:
- Weight empty — 558 kg (1,230 lb)
- Max payload with full fuel — 380 kg (838 lb)
- Max T-O and landing weight — 816 kg (1,800 lb)
- Max wing loading — 47·0 kg/m² (9·63 lb/sq ft)
- Max power loading — 6·09 kg/m² (10·0 lb/sq ft)

Performance (at max T-O weight):
- Never-exceed speed — 133 knots (246 km/h; 153 mph) IAS
- Max level speed:
  - at S/L — 114 knots (210 km/h; 131 mph)
  - at 3,050 m (10,000 ft) — 108 knots (201 km/h; 125 mph)
- Max cruising speed — 102 knots (190 km/h; 118 mph)
- Approach speed — 65 knots (121 km/h; 75 mph)
- Stalling speed — 50 knots (92 km/h; 57 mph)
- Max rate of climb at S/L — 350 m (1,150 ft)/min
- Service ceiling — 5,180 m (17,000 ft)
- T-O run — 145 m (475 ft)
- T-O to, and landing from, 15 m (50 ft) — 252 m (825 ft)
- Landing run — 122 m (400 ft)
- Range with max fuel, no reserves — 260 nm (482 km; 300 miles)
- Endurance with max fuel (75% power) — 2 h 51 min
- *g* limits — +5·4/−4

GRUMMAN

GRUMMAN CORPORATION

1111 Stewart Avenue, Bethpage, New York 11714
Telephone: (516) 575 0574
Telex: 961430

Chairman of the Board and Chief Executive Officer:
John C. Bierwirth
President and Chief Operating Officer:
John O'Brien
Vice-Chairmen of the Board:
Willard R. Bischoff (Technology)
Robert G. Freese (Finance and Treasurer)
Don F. Huebner (Development)
Senior Vice-Presidents:
George E. R. Kinnear II (Washington Operations)
Robert J. Myers (Data Systems)
Vice-Presidents:
Robert W. Bradshaw (Secretary)
George L. Brown
Natale P. Busi (Controller)
John J. Carroll (Community Affairs)
Dean G. Cassell (Product Integrity and Environmental Protection)
Howard J. Dunn Jr (Audit)
Thomas L. Genovese (General Counsel)
Weyman B. Jones (Public Affairs)
Rolf J. Larson
Raymond Nightingale (Assistant to the President)
Richard Scheuing (Corporate Research)
David Walsh (Marketing)

The Grumman Aircraft Engineering Corporation was incorporated on 6 December 1929. Important changes in the corporate structure of the company were announced in 1969, resulting in the formation of Grumman Corporation, a small holding company, with Grumman Aerospace Corporation, Grumman Allied Industries Inc and Grumman Data Systems Corporation. In February 1985 Grumman Corporation announced the creation of nine operating divisions, each matched to a specific market: Aerostructures; Aircraft Systems; Data Systems; Electronics Systems; Melbourne Systems; Space Systems; St Augustine; Technical Services and Vehicle & Marine. In addition, a Corporate Services Division provides legal, purchasing, contracts and other common services to all the operating divisions.

Divisional Presidents:
Alexander D. Alexandrovich (Space Systems)
Renso L. Caporali (Aircraft Systems)
Fred W. Haise Jr (Technical Services)
Thomas J. McGrath (Aerostructures)
Robert A. Nafis (Electronic Systems)
Robert J. Myers (Data Systems)
Ronald B. Peterson (Vehicle & Marine)
Albert Verderosa (Melbourne Systems)
Joseph J. Walter (St Augustine)

GRUMMAN AIRCRAFT SYSTEMS DIVISION

President: Renso L. Caporali
Senior Vice-Presidents:
Willard R. Bischoff (Technical Operations)
Peter B. Oram (Aircraft Programmes)
Carl A. Paladino (Finance)
Philip S. Vassallo (Product Operations)
Vice-Presidents:
James E. Bourne (Business Operations)
John S. Christiansen (Field Operations)
Michael V. Ciminera (Advanced Systems)
Daniel T. Collins (A-6 Programme)
Thomas J. Doyle (Mohawk Programme)
Harvey S. Fromer (C-2A Programme)
Herbert R. Grossman (Bethpage Operations)
Thomas J. Kane Jr (Business Development)
Joseph P. Kingfield (Quality and Safety Operations)
Henry C. Kline (Integrated Logistics Support)
Vernon S. Kramer (EF-111 Programme)
Thomas J. Lahey (Milledgeville Operations)
Robert C. Miller (Advanced Concepts)
Daniel J. O'Neill (EA-6B Programme)
James E. Philbin (E-2C Programme)
James C. Reed (CASS Programme)
Norman Reinertsen (Operations Analysis)
William C. Trillo (Calverton Operations)
Robert E. Watkins (Stuart Operations)
Robert M. Watson (F-14 Programme)

Current aircraft products of Grumman Corporation include versions of the A-6 Intruder, C-2A Greyhound, EA-6B Prowler, E-2C Hawkeye and F-14 Tomcat for the US Navy, and a tactical jamming version of the General Dynamics F-111, designated EF-111A, for the US Air Force. In mid-1983, Grumman was selected to develop and build the composite graphite-epoxy wings and vertical tail for the prototype and early production models of Israel's new Lavi fighter. A contract to manufacture 270 shipsets of engine nacelles and thrust reversers for the Tay turbofans of Gulfstream IV and Fokker 100 transport aircraft was received in February 1984. An initial contract covering design and manufacture of the complete tail sections of the Bell/Boeing Vertol V-22 Osprey advanced vertical lift aircraft (see Bell entry) was received in August 1984.

Latest Grumman product is a small forward swept wing (FSW) technology demonstrator designated X-29A, built under contract from the US Defense Advanced Research Projects Agency.

Aircraft delivered during 1985 comprised 24 F-14s, 8 E-2Cs, 6 EA-6Bs and 8 A-6Es.

Grumman/Resorts International commuter conversion of the Albatross military amphibian

GRUMMAN/RESORTS INTERNATIONAL G-111 ALBATROSS

By January 1984, Grumman had completed prototype conversion of a UF-2 Albatross amphibian to G-111 configuration and had delivered twelve 'production' aircraft to Resorts International, the originator of the redesign.

The first stage of work on each Albatross conversion involves the inspection and replacement of parts to produce the equivalent of a zero-time airframe, followed by modernisation of the flight deck, and the provision of two additional passenger cabin doors and a 28-seat interior. At the same time, the 1,100 kW (1,475 hp) Wright R-1820-982C9HE3 engines are removed and overhauled, and new fire detection and autofeathering systems installed. The resulting aircraft meets FAR Pt 36 noise level standards.

During inspection of the first airframe to be modified, Grumman found that a rear spar capstrip of 7075-T6 light alloy had suffered deterioration, and it was replaced by a titanium capstrip. Subsequent conversions have all four centre-section capstrips replaced by titanium to give the airframe an unlimited service life. Other modifications include conversion of the port main passenger door and the starboard emergency hatch to open outward, and the lower portion of the main door now incorporates a drop-down ladder.

Twenty-eight non-reclinable seats are provided at 81 cm (32 in) pitch, with facilities for a flight attendant, and there is a toilet at the rear of the cabin. New lightweight solid state avionics include two Collins VHF-20A com, two VIR-30 nav, ADF-30 ADF, and RCA WeatherScout 2 radar. Equipment removed included the autopilot, JATO and drop fuel tank provisions.

The prototype conversion, of a UF-2 Albatross, flew for the first time on 13 February 1979, and FAA certification was received on 29 April 1980.

Of the initial aircraft acquired by Resorts International, its commuter carrier, Chalks International, has five, and another was sold to Pelita Air Service of Indonesia. Grumman purchased 57 HU-16As and Bs for civil conversion, and believes that there is a potential market for conversions of approximately 200 Albatross aircraft which remain in worldwide use. A water bomber version, and a version with Garrett TPE331-15 turboprop engines and Dowty Rotol four-blade propellers, are under consideration.

Details of the HU-16 Albatross last appeared in the 1964-65 *Jane's*, and apply generally to this conversion, except as noted.

Dimensions, external:
Wing span 29·46 m (96 ft 8 in)
Length overall 18·67 m (61 ft 3 in)
Height overall 7·87 m (25 ft 10 in)
Dimensions, internal:
Cabin: Length 7·95 m (26 ft 1 in)
Max height 1·88 m (6 ft 2 in)
Max width 2·26 m (7 ft 5 in)
Floor area 13·47 m² (145 sq ft)
Baggage compartment 7·93 m³ (280 cu ft)
Area:
Wings, gross 96·15 m² (1,035 sq ft)
Weights and Loadings:
Operating weight empty 10,659 kg (23,500 lb)
Max fuel load 2,920 kg (6,438 lb)
Max T-O weight:
land 13,970 kg (30,800 lb)
water 14,129 kg (31,150 lb)
Max landing weight:
land 13,226 kg (29,160 lb)
water 14,129 kg (31,150 lb)
Max wing loading 146·9 kg/m² (30 lb/sq ft)
Max power loading 14·15 kg/kW (10·5 lb/hp)
Performance (at max T-O weight, ISA at S/L except where indicated):
Never-exceed speed 229 knots (424 km/h; 263 mph) IAS
Normal operating speed 206 knots (382 km/h; 237 mph) IAS
Stalling speed, flaps and landing gear down, power off 72 knots (134 km/h; 83 mph) IAS
Max rate of climb, METO power 381 m (1,250 ft)/min
Max operating altitude 2,440 m (8,000 ft)
T-O to 15 m (50 ft): land 1,341 m (4,400 ft)
water 1,349 m (4,425 ft)
Landing from 15 m (50 ft): land 924 m (3,030 ft)
water 966 m (3,170 ft)
Accelerate/stop distance: land 1,825 m (5,990 ft)
water 1,832 m (6,010 ft)
Range at 1,525 m (5,000 ft), cruising speed of 162 knots (300 km/h; 186 mph) TAS, crew of 3 + 28 passengers, 45 min reserves:
land 273 nm (506 km; 314 miles)
water 405 nm (750 km; 466 miles)
Max ferry range, height and speed as above, no reserves:
land, water 1,480 nm (2,742 km; 1,704 miles)

GRUMMAN HAWKEYE

US Navy designations: E-2B, E-2C and TE-2C

The E-2 Hawkeye was developed as a carrier borne early warning aircraft, but is suitable also for land based

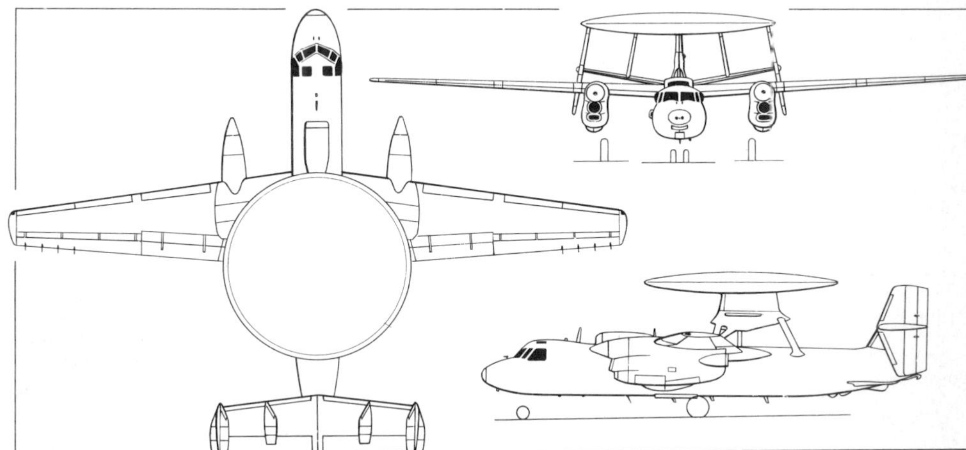

Grumman E-2C Hawkeye twin-turboprop airborne early warning aircraft *(Pilot Press)*

operations. The first of three prototypes flew for the first time on 21 October 1960; these were followed by 56 E-2As, all operational examples of which had been updated to E-2B standard by the end of 1971. Details of these versions have appeared in earlier editions of *Jane's*.

The first of two E-2C prototypes flew on 20 January 1971. Production began in mid-1971 and the first flight of a production aircraft was made on 23 September 1972. Orders from the US Navy for this version now cover 128 aircraft; 101 of these had been delivered by the beginning of 1986, and it is planned for production to continue at the rate of six per year until the early 1990s. Four E-2Cs were supplied to Israel in 1981; Japan accepted four each in 1982 and 1984. Egypt accepted one aircraft in September 1985 and will have four more by Spring 1987. The government of Singapore has taken delivery of two aircraft and was to accept two more by the end of 1986.

The E-2C entered service, with airborne early warning squadron VAW-123 at NAS Norfolk, Va, in November 1973, and went to sea on board the USS *Saratoga* in late 1974. Sixteen other squadrons, including two naval reserve squadrons, have since received E-2C aircraft, and two **TE-2C** training aircraft are also in service.

The Hawkeye can maintain patrol on naval task force defence perimeters in all weathers, at an operating height of about 9,150 m (30,000 ft), and can detect and assess any threat from approaching enemy aircraft over ranges approaching 260 nm (480 km; 300 miles). An AN/APS-138 radar system replaced the original AN/APS-125 in new production E-2Cs in 1983. A retrofit programme is in progress for all previously delivered aircraft. The system includes a new total radiation aperture control antenna (TRAC-A) to reduce sidelobes and offset increased jamming threats. The radar is capable of detecting airborne targets anywhere in a three million cubic mile surveillance envelope while simultaneously monitoring maritime traffic. Long-range detection, automatic target track initiation and high-speed processing combine to enable each E-2C to track, automatically and simultaneously, more than 600 targets and to control more than 40 airborne intercepts. A Randtron Systems AN/APA-171 antenna system is housed in a 7·32 m (24 ft) diameter saucer-shaped rotodome, mounted above the rear fuselage of the aircraft, which revolves in flight at 6 rpm. The Yagi type radar arrays within the rotodome are interfaced to the onboard avionic systems, providing radar sum and difference signals plus IFF.

The AN/APS-138 search radar can detect targets as small as a cruise missile at ranges in excess of 145 nm (268 km; 167 miles). It also monitors movement of enemy ships and land vehicles. The AN/ALR-73 passive detection system (PDS) alerts operators to the presence of electronic emitters at distances up to twice the detection range of the radar system, thus expanding significantly the surveillance capability of the E-2C. Functions of these and other key elements of the E-2C's avionics systems were described more fully in the 1979-80 *Jane's*.

The US Navy has awarded Grumman a $14 million contract to flight test conformal microprocessor controlled phased array radar antennae installed in the wing leading-edges, fuselage and horizontal tail surfaces of an E-2C. The passive array will be evaluated as an advanced anti-jamming ECM system. Tests were scheduled to begin in 1986 and to last three years. Associated equipment will be provided by the General Electric Co. The conformal radar is a potential candidate for the US Navy's future Airborne Multi-Sensor (AMSS) requirement.

E-2Cs are used to monitor air traffic in the Florida skies surrounding Cape Canaveral during Space Shuttle launches and to direct US Coast Guard and US Customs fixed-wing and helicopter crews in many successful interceptions of drug smuggling aircraft. They are also used to direct Israeli fighters engaged in combat missions in the Middle East.

The following details apply to the E-2C Hawkeye:

TYPE: Airborne early warning aircraft.

WINGS: Cantilever high-wing monoplane of all-metal construction. Centre-section is a structural box consisting of three beams, ribs and machined skins. Hinged leading-edge is non-structural and provides access to flying and engine controls. The outer panels fold rearward about skewed-axis hinge fittings mounted on the rear beams, to stow parallel with the rear fuselage on each side. Folding is done through a double acting hydraulic cylinder. Trailing-edges of outer panels and part of centre-section consist of long span ailerons and hydraulically actuated Fowler flaps. When flaps are lowered, ailerons are drooped automatically. All control surfaces are power operated and incorporate devices to produce artificial feel forces. Automatic flight control system (AFCS) can be assigned sole control of the system hydraulic actuators, or AFCS signals can be superimposed on the pilot's mechanical inputs for stability augmentation. Pneumatically inflated rubber de-icing boots on leading-edges.

FUSELAGE: Conventional all-metal semi-monocoque structure.

TAIL UNIT: Cantilever structure, with four fins and three double-hinged rudders. Tailplane dihedral 11°. Portions of tail unit made of glassfibre to reduce radar reflection. Power control and artificial feel systems as for ailerons. Pneumatically inflated rubber de-icing boots on all leading-edges.

LANDING GEAR: Hydraulically retractable tricycle type. Pneumatic emergency extension. Steerable nosewheel unit retracts rearward. Mainwheels retract forward, and rotate to lie flat in bottom of nacelles. Twin wheels on nose unit only. Oleo-pneumatic shock absorbers. Mainwheel tyres size 36 × 11 Type VII 24-ply, pressure 17·9 bars (260 lb/sq in) on ship, 14·5 bars (210 lb/sq in) ashore. Hydraulic brakes. Hydraulically operated retractable tailskid. A-frame arrester hook under tail.

POWER PLANT: Two 3,661 kW (4,910 ehp) Allison T56-A-425 turboprop engines, driving Hamilton Standard type 54460-1 four-blade fully-feathering reversible-pitch constant-speed propellers. These have foam filled blades which have a steel spar and glassfibre shell. Spinners and blades incorporate electric anti-icing. E-2C under flight test in 1986 with T56-A-427 engines, expected to offer a 24 per cent power increase and lower fuel consumption.

ACCOMMODATION: Normal crew of five on flight deck and in ATDS compartment in main cabin, consisting of pilot, co-pilot, combat information centre officer, air control officer and radar operator. Downward hinged door, with built-in steps, on port side of centre-fuselage.

AVIONICS: Randtron AN/APA-171 rotodome (radar and IFF antennae), General Electric AN/APS-138 advanced radar processing system (ARPS) with overland/overwater detection capability (APS-139 in new-build aircraft from 1988, with APS-145 scheduled for introduction in 1990 and eventual retrofit in all E-2Cs), RT-988/A IFF interrogator with Hazeltine OL-76/AP IFF detector processor, Litton AN/ALR-73 passive detection system, Hazeltine AN/APA-172 control indicator group, Litton OL-77/ASQ computer programmer (L-304), ARC-158 UHF data link, ARQ-34 HF data link, ASM-440 in-flight performance monitor, Collins ARC-51A UHF com, AIC-14A intercom, Litton AN/ASN-92 (LN-15C) CAINS carrier aircraft inertial navigation system, Conrac Corporation CP-1085/AS air data computer, APN-153 (V) Doppler, ASN-50 heading and attitude reference system, ARN-52 (V) Tacan, Collins ARA-50 UHF ADF, ASW-25B ACLS and Honeywell APN-171 (V) radar altimeter.

DIMENSIONS, EXTERNAL:

Wing span	24·56 m (80 ft 7 in)
Width, wings folded	8·94 m (29 ft 4 in)
Length overall	17·54 m (57 ft 6¾ in)
Height overall	5·58 m (18 ft 3¾ in)
Diameter of rotodome	7·32 m (24 ft 0 in)
Tailplane span	7·99 m (26 ft 2½ in)
Wheel track	5·93 m (19 ft 5¾ in)
Wheelbase	7·06 m (23 ft 2 in)
Propeller diameter	4·11 m (13 ft 6 in)

AREAS:

Wings, gross	65·03 m² (700 sq ft)
Ailerons (total)	5·76 m² (62·00 sq ft)
Trailing-edge flaps (total)	11·03 m² (118·75 sq ft)
Fin, incl rudder and tab:	
outboard (total)	10·25 m² (110·36 sq ft)
inboard (total)	4·76 m² (51·26 sq ft)
Tailplane	11·62 m² (125·07 sq ft)
Elevators (total)	3·72 m² (40·06 sq ft)

WEIGHTS:

Weight empty	17,265 kg (38,063 lb)
Max fuel (internal, usable)	5,624 kg (12,400 lb)
Max T-O weight	23,556 kg (51,933 lb)

PERFORMANCE (at max T-O weight):

Max level speed	323 knots (598 km/h; 372 mph)
Max cruising speed	311 knots (576 km/h; 358 mph)
Cruising speed (ferry)	268 knots (496 km/h; 308 mph)
Approach speed	103 knots (191 km/h; 119 mph)
Stalling speed (landing configuration)	74 knots (138 km/h; 86 mph)
Service ceiling	9,390 m (30,800 ft)
Min T-O run	610 m (2,000 ft)
T-O to 15 m (50 ft)	793 m (2,600 ft)
Min landing run	439 m (1,440 ft)
Ferry range	1,394 nm (2,583 km; 1,605 miles)
Time on station, 175 nm (320 km; 200 miles) from base	3-4 h
Endurance with max fuel	6 h 6 min

GRUMMAN C-2A GREYHOUND

Grumman announced on 8 February 1982 the receipt of a $30 million advance procurement contract to begin work on 39 additional C-2A carrier on-board delivery (COD) aircraft for the US Navy. This enabled the company to order long lead time items before signing a multi-year production contract in early 1983, valued at $678 million. The first of the new-production C-2As was rolled out on 16 January 1985 and made its first flight on 4 February. It was retained by Grumman for carrier suitability and flight dynamic tests which were completed successfully in mid-1985. The second C-2A was used to check avionics integration and electromagnetic compatibility in a test programme completed in September 1985. The contract calls for eight aircraft in each of the years 1985-88 and seven in 1989 to complete the procurement. Deliveries to the US Navy began in May 1985. The first five new procurement C-2As are serving the Mediterranean Fleet from Sigonella, Sicily. A second squadron was to become operational in 1986 at Cubi Point in the Philippines.

The original C-2A Greyhound, of which 12 are still in service of the 19 delivered during the 1960s, was derived from the E-2A Hawkeye, and was designed specifically to deliver cargo to air groups deployed on US Navy carriers. It was compatible with elevators and hangar decks on CVS-10 and CVA-19 carriers, was catapult launchable using nose-tow gear, and could make arrested landings. Many components of the C-2A and E-2A were common, including the complete turboprop power plants, and the Greyhound had similar all-weather capability to the Hawkeye. Newly manufactured Greyhounds retain the same relationship to new-production E-2C Hawkeyes, and have uprated engines and avionics, improved anti-corrosion protection, and increased passenger comfort. They also introduced a new APU to reduce the need for ground support equipment and

Grumman E-2C Hawkeye early warning and control aircraft of the Republic of Singapore Air Force

First Grumman C-2A Greyhound carrier on-board delivery (COD) transport of second series

provide self-sufficiency for operation at remote locations.

The description which follows is applicable to the new production C-2A based on the E-2C version of the Hawkeye:

TYPE: Twin-turboprop carrier on-board delivery (COD) transport.

WINGS: Chord at root 3·96 m (13 ft 0 in), at tip 1·32 m (4 ft 4 in). Incidence 4° at root, 1° at tip.

FUSELAGE: Conventional semi-monocoque light alloy structure. Cargo door, with integral ramp, forms undersurface of rear fuselage.

TAIL UNIT: Basically as for E-2C, but without tailplane dihedral.

LANDING GEAR: Basically as for E-2C, but with stronger nose gear (adapted from that of A-6A Intruder) to cater for higher AUW. Each nosewheel fitted with 20 × 5·5 Type VII 12-ply tyre. Mainwheel tyre pressure 13·8 bars (200 lb/sq in) on ship, 11·4 bars (165 lb/sq in) ashore.

POWER PLANT: Two 3,661 kW (4,910 ehp) Allison T56-A-425 turboprop engines, each driving a Hamilton Standard Type 54460-1 four-blade fully-feathering reversible-pitch constant-speed propeller with spinner. Two fuel tanks, total capacity 6,905 litres (1,824 US gallons), occupy entire wing centre-section between the beams and the centreline and wing-fold ribs. Fuelling point on inboard side of starboard nacelle. For long-range ferrying, fuel tanks can be supplemented by six 920 litre (243 US gallon) tanks in main cabin. Oil capacity (usable) 23·5 litres (6·2 US gallons). Available, but not specified for US Navy C-2As, is the capability for mounting a flight refuelling probe above the front fuselage.

ACCOMMODATION: Pilot and co-pilot side by side on flight deck, with dual controls. Third crew member is load-master. Lavatory and baggage space aft of flight deck. High-strength cargo compartment floor (1,465 kg/m²; 300 lb/sq ft) incorporates flush tracks for attaching tiedown fittings. Cargo door has integral ramp with detachable treadways. Provision for remotely controlled cargo handling winch. Alternative payloads include 28 passengers or 12 litters and attendants. Door at front of cabin on port side. Although not required for US Navy C-2As, compartment can be adapted to accept Military Airlift Command 463L material handling and support system, with choice of either three 2·74 × 2·24 m (108 × 88 in) master pallets or five 2·24 × 1·37 m (88 × 54 in) modular pallets.

SYSTEMS: Air-conditioning system max pressure differential 0·45 bars (6·5 lb/sq in). Two independent hydraulic systems, pressure 207 bars (3,000 lb/sq in). Flight system has two pumps, each rated at 28·4 litres (7·5 US gallons) per min, with an air/oil separated reservoir, capacity 5 litres (1·31 US gallons). The combined system has two pumps, each rated at 94·6 litres (25 US gallons) per min, with an air/oil separated reservoir, capacity 12·6 litres (3·34 US gallons). Both systems supply control actuators. One system is also responsible for actuating wing fold system, cargo door, steering damper, arrester hook, brakes, landing gear, windscreen wipers, flaps and auxiliary generator. Liquid oxygen breathing system, with two 10 litre (2·6 US gallon) converters, plus portable unit for cargo or personnel attendant. Primary electrical system supplied by two independent 115/200V 400Hz three-phase engine driven generators, each rated at 60kVA. 28V DC secondary subsystem supplied by two independent transformer-rectifiers. Gas turbine APU drives a 10kVA generator through an auxiliary hydraulic pump for ground operation, and also allows ground starting of the turboprop engines without external equipment. In flight, the 10kVA generator functions as an emergency generator.

AVIONICS: HF, VHF, UHF com; Omega, Doppler radar, AHRS, dual VOR, UHF ADF, LF ADF and weather radar.

DIMENSIONS, EXTERNAL: As for E-2C except:

Length overall	17·32 m (56 ft 10 in)
Height overall	4·84 m (15 ft 10½ in)

DIMENSIONS, INTERNAL:

Cabin: Volume	54·4 m³ (1,920 cu ft)
Cargo compartment: Length	8·38 m (27 ft 6 in)
Max width	2·24 m (7 ft 4 in)
Max height	1·65 m (5 ft 5 in)

AREAS: As for E-2C

WEIGHTS:

Weight empty	16,486 kg (36,346 lb)
Internal fuel weight	5,625 kg (12,400 lb)
Max payload: carrier operation	4,536 kg (10,000 lb)
land operation	6,804 kg (15,000 lb)
Max T-O weight	24,654 kg (54,354 lb)

PERFORMANCE (at max T-O weight):

Max level speed	310 knots (574 km/h; 357 mph)
Max cruising speed	260 knots (482 km/h; 299 mph)
Max rate of climb at S/L	796 m (2,610 ft)/min
Service ceiling, ferry mission	10,210 m (33,500 ft)
Min T-O run	665 m (2,180 ft)
T-O to 15 m (50 ft)	932 m (3,060 ft)
Landing from 15 m (50 ft)	691 m (2,266 ft)
Min landing run	435 m (1,428 ft)
Range with 4,536 kg (10,000 lb) freight	over 1,040 nm (1,930 km; 1,200 miles)
Max range, ferry mission	1,560 nm (2,891 km; 1,796 miles)

GRUMMAN INTRUDER

US Navy designations: A-6, EA-6 and KA-6

The basic A-6A (originally A2F-1) Intruder was conceived as a carrier-borne low-level attack bomber equipped specifically to deliver nuclear or conventional weapons on targets completely obscured by weather or darkness. Of well over 600 A-6s built, in successive versions, approximately 350 currently equip operational US Navy and Marine Corps squadrons, and three readiness training squadrons. All older A-6s have been converted to the A-6E/TRAM configuration or into KA-6D tankers. The latest **KA-6D** configuration deletes all weapons systems capability. Grumman's St Augustine Division has been awarded a $190 million contract to convert four A-6Es to KA-6D configuration and to update 49 existing KA-6Ds to the latest standard, which includes provision for the carriage of five 1,514 litre (400 US gallon) drop tanks. The first two of these A-6E conversions had been delivered by late 1984.

Competition for the original A-6 contract was conducted from May to December 1957, Grumman's contender being selected on 31 December 1957. Seven variants of the basic design have been built, of which the A-6A, A-6B and A-6C (described in 1978-79 *Jane's*) are no longer operational. Current operational versions include the EA-6A (27 built) and KA-6D (78 converted from A-6A, and seven from A-6E, of which 68 are still in operation), details of which can be found in the 1980-81 *Jane's*. The following versions are still in production:

EA-6B Prowler. Advanced electronics development of the EA-6A, described separately.

A-6E Intruder. First produced as an advanced conversion of the A-6A with multi-mode radar and an IBM computer similar to that first tested in the EA-6B. First flight of an A-6E was made on 10 November 1970. First squadron deployment was made in September 1972, and the A-6E was approved officially for service use in December 1972. It was planned to acquire a total of 318 A-6Es. Procurement of new airframes is continuing beyond original termination date, with a total of 346 in service in 1985. Current Intruders are to **A-6E/TRAM** (target recognition and attack multisensor) standard, the first example of which flew in October 1974. Delivery of fully provisioned TRAM aircraft began on 14 December 1978, and the first carrier deployment was completed successfully in May 1980. All older A-6Es are due to be converted to TRAM standard by 1988.

Under plans made in early 1981, 50 A-6Es were equipped to carry McDonnell Douglas Harpoon anti-shipping missiles (four per aircraft). Harpoon-capable A-6Es began to be deployed during 1981, and all subsequent new production and converted aircraft are equipped to carry this missile.

Intruder training is carried out using Grumman TC-4C (modified Gulfstream I) aircraft, eight of which are in US Navy/US Marine Corps service. Grumman updated these aircraft to A-6E/TRAM standard during 1978-80.

A-6F Intruder. Under a contract awarded in July 1984, Grumman has initiated a major update programme for the Intruder, which was originally known as the A-6E Upgrade but is now designated A-6F. Norden Systems has been chosen to develop a new 15GHz band multi-mode radar to replace the A-6E's AN/APQ-148. The new radar will feature increased range for target recognition, acquisition and tracking with standoff weapon capability; inverse synthetic aperture radar capability for long-range ship classification; an air-to-air mode for use with Sidewinder or AMRAAM air-to-air self defence missiles; and improved reliability and maintainability. To accommodate the increased information available from the radar, the A-6F will have five multi-function display units in a redesigned cockpit. The pilot will have vertical and horizontal situation displays; the bombardier/navigator will have forward looking infra-red (FLIR), radar and weapons management displays. The MFDs, two AYK-14 tactical computers, ASW-27 two-way data link and signal data recording and maintenance aid system and Kaiser Electronics HUD, which replaces the A-6E's optical sight, will be common with those of the F-14D Tomcat.

Other additions and improvements to be incorporated in the A-6F include an ALR-67 radar warning system; Collins ARC-182 airborne radio communication system; Litton ASN-130 inertial navigation system; ALQ-165 airborne self-protection jammer; replacement of the APN-153 Doppler radar with a global positioning system; improved tactical software; standard common air data computer; FLIR autotracker for automatic target lock-on and tracking; improved bomb racks; and extension of the data bus for weapons pylons to accommodate Maverick, Harpoon and HARM missiles.

General Electric has been selected to provide a 48·07 kN (10,807 lb st) non-afterburning version of its F404 turbofan, designated F404-GE-400D, for the A-6F, which will also have an auxiliary power unit, aircraft mounted accessory drive, revised fuel system with self-sealing armoured fuel lines, fire detecting stations throughout the airframe, and void-filling foam between the outer shell of the airframe and

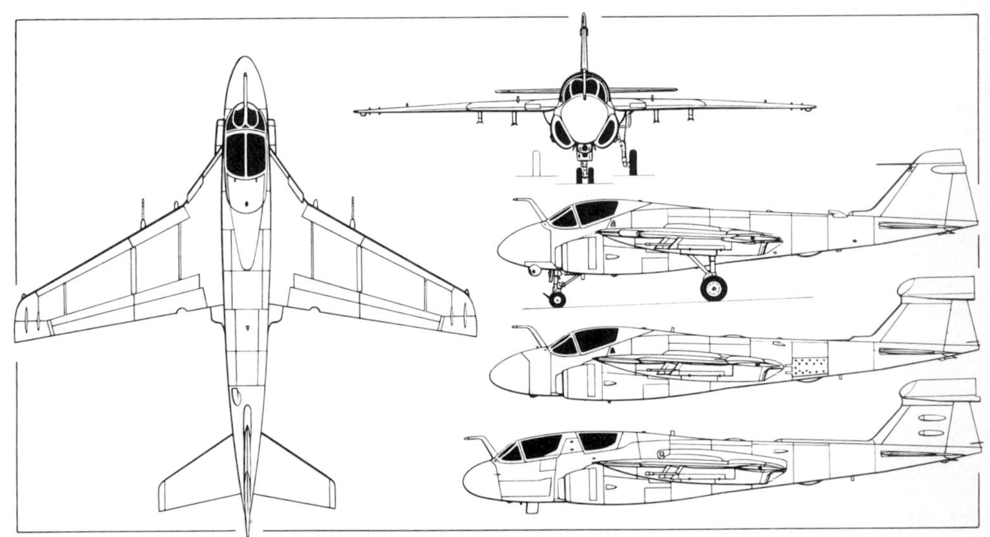

Grumman A-6E/TRAM, with additional side views of EA-6A (centre) and EA-6B (bottom) *(Pilot Press)*

the fuel tanks. Total internal fuel capacity, in three fuselage and four wing tanks, will be 7,228 kg (15,936 lb).

Design work on the A-6F began in July 1984, and construction of a prototype was started during 1985. The programme calls for five development prototypes, the first of which is expected to fly in May 1987, followed by the remaining aircraft in July, September and November 1987 and January 1988. Production deliveries are scheduled to begin in 1989. The US Navy requirement for A-6Fs totals 150 aircraft up to 1995.

Boeing Military Airplane Company has a contract to develop and manufacture new aluminium/composite wings for the A-6E, to overcome fatigue problems believed to result from operation at heavier weights and higher load factors than were envisaged when the aircraft was designed. Flight trials, starting in 1987, are expected to lead to production of the new wings for all existing and future A-6s, and to provide an 8,800-hour service life.

The following description applies to the A-6E:

TYPE: Two-seat carrier-based bomber for close air support, interdiction and deep strike missions.

WINGS: Cantilever mid-wing monoplane, with 25° sweepback at quarter-chord. All-metal structure. Hydraulically operated almost full span leading-edge slats and trailing-edge single-slotted, tracked, area-increasing flaps, with inset spoilers (flaperons) of same span as flaps forward of trailing-edge flaps. Trailing-edge of each wingtip, outboard of flap, splits to form speed-brakes which project above and below wing when extended. Two short fences above each wing. Outer panels fold upward and inward.

FUSELAGE: Conventional all-metal semi-monocoque structure. Bottom is recessed between engines to carry semi-exposed store.

TAIL UNIT: Cantilever all-metal structure. All-moving tailplane, without separate elevators. Electronic antenna in rear part of fin, immediately above rudder.

LANDING GEAR: Hydraulically retractable tricycle type. Twin-wheel nose unit retracts rearward. Single-wheel main units retract forward and inward into air intake fairings. A-frame arrester hook under rear fuselage.

POWER PLANT: Two 41·4 kN (9,300 lb st) Pratt & Whitney J52-P-8B turbojet engines. Max internal fuel capacity 8,873 litres (2,344 US gallons). Provision for up to five external fuel tanks under wing and centreline stations, each of 1,135 litres (300 US gallons) or 1,514 litres (400 US gallons) capacity. Removable flight refuelling probe projects upward immediately forward of windscreen.

ACCOMMODATION: Crew of two on Martin-Baker GRU7 ejection seats, which can be reclined to reduce fatigue during low-level operations. Bombardier/navigator slightly behind and below pilot to starboard. Hydraulically operated rearward sliding canopy.

SYSTEMS: Garrett environmental control system for cockpit and avionics bay. Dual hydraulic systems for operation of flight controls, leading-edge and trailing-edge flaps, wingtip speed-brakes, landing gear brakes and cockpit canopy, each rated at 119·4 litres (31·5 US gallons) per min, with air/oil separated reservoir, pressurised at 2·76 bars (40 lb/sq in). One electrically driven hydraulic pump provides restricted flight capability by supplying the tailplane and rudder actuators only, each rated at 11·4 litres (3 US gallons) per min, with internally pressurised reservoir, pressurised at 1·08 bars (15·7 lb/sq in). Electrical system powered by two Garrett constant speed drive units that combine engine starting and electric power generation, each delivering 30kVA. A Garrett ram air turbine, mounted so that it can be projected into the airstream above the port wing root, provides in-flight emergency electric power for essential equipment.

AVIONICS AND EQUIPMENT: Development of A-6E began with substitution of a single simultaneous multi-mode nav/attack radar, developed by Norden division of UTC, for the two earlier radar systems in A-6A. Following concept of EA-6B, IBM Corporation and Fairchild Camera and Instrument Corporation supplied a new nav/attack computer system and interfacing data converter. Conrac Corporation armament control unit. RCA video tape recorder for post-strike assessment of attacks. Norden AN/APQ-148 multi-mode radar provides simultaneous ground mapping; identification, tracking, and rangefinding of fixed or moving targets; and terrain clearance or terrain following manoeuvres. It can detect, locate and track radar beacons used by forward air controllers when providing close support for ground forces; and has mechanical scanning in azimuth, with a specially developed avionics system for simultaneous vertical scanning. During 1981-83, it was updated by an improved AMTI (airborne moving target indication) to enhance its ability to detect moving targets. Cockpit displays for pilot and bombardier/navigator; terrain data presented on vertical display indicator ahead of pilot. IBM AN/ASQ-133 solid state digital computer is coupled to A-6E's radar, inertial and Doppler navigational equipment, communications and AFCS. As mission data is measured in flight by onboard aerodynamic and electronic sensors, computer compares data with programmed information, computes differences, and provides corrective data to alter parameters of mission. Fairchild Camera and Instrument Corporation signal data converter accepts analog input data from up to 60 sensors, converting data to a digital output that is fed into nav/attack system computer. Conrac armament control unit (ACU) provides all inputs and outputs necessary to select and release weapons. Master arming switch has a 'practice' position that allows ACU to be cycled up to point of firing command. Kaiser AN/AVA-1 multi-mode display serves as a primary flight aid for navigation, approach, landing and weapons delivery. Basic vertical display indicator (VDI) is a 0·20 m (8 in) CRT which shows a synthetic landscape, sky and electronically generated command flight path that move to simulate the motion of these features as they would be seen by pilot through windscreen. Symbols are superimposed to augment basic attitude data, and for attack a second set of superimposed information provides a target symbol, steering symbol, and release and pull-up markers. A solid state radar data scan converter can provide on the same display an apparent real-world perspective of terrain, ten shades of grey defining terrain elevation at ten different segmented contour intervals up to 8·7 nm (16 km; 10 miles) ahead of aircraft. This makes it possible for pilot to fly in either terrain following or terrain avoidance mode at low altitude. Flight path and attack symbols can be superimposed over terrain elevation data on VDI, enabling pilot to attack while avoiding or following terrain in target area. Kaiser micromesh filter prevents 'washout' of data displayed on VDI in sunlight. Naval pilots use VDI as a primary flight instrument, for precise steering in navigation, weapons cues, progress, and status information during attack. For carrier landing, unit is used as a flight director and, linked to the APQ-148 radar, presents steering information, allowing pilot to select descent angle for final approach. Aircraft fitted with TRAM package have, in addition, an undernose precision-stabilised turret, with a sensor package containing both infrared and laser equipment; INS updated with Litton AN/ASN-92 CAINS; new communications-navigation-identification (CNI) system; and automatic carrier landing capability. Sensor package is integrated with multi-mode radar, providing capability to detect, identify and attack a wide range of targets (as well as view the terrain) under adverse weather conditions, and with improved accuracy, using either conventional or laser guided weapons. Bombardier/navigator operates TRAM system by first acquiring target on his radar screen. He then switches to FLIR (forward looking infra-red) system, using an optical zoom to enlarge target's image. After identifying and selecting his targets, bombardier uses a laser designator to mark target with a laser spot, on which his own laser guided weapons, or those from another aircraft, will home. Using TRAM's laser spot detector, A-6E can also acquire a target being illuminated from another aircraft, or designated by a forward air controller on the ground. Under a contract awarded in Spring 1985, Northrop will deliver in October 1986 the first preproduction examples of an infra-red video automatic tracking (IRVAT) system that will computerise and automate the tracking portion of the TRAM system.

Grumman A-6E/TRAM of US Navy Squadron VA-176

ARMAMENT: Five weapon attachment points, each with a 1,633 kg (3,600 lb) capacity (max external stores load 8,165 kg; 18,000 lb). Typical weapon loads are twenty-eight 500 lb bombs in clusters of six, or three 2,000 lb general purpose bombs plus two 1,135 litre (300 US gallon) drop tanks. AIM-9 Sidewinder missiles can be carried for air-to-air use. Harpoon missile capability added to weapons complement of A-6E/TRAM. The HARM missile has been test flown on the A-6E, with operational introduction planned for early 1986. More recently, flight and firing tests have been carried out with the AGM-123A Skipper II, also on an A-6E.

DIMENSIONS, EXTERNAL:
- Wing span — 16·15 m (53 ft 0 in)
- Wing mean aerodynamic chord — 3·32 m (10 ft 10¾ in)
- Width, wings folded — 7·72 m (25 ft 4 in)
- Length overall — 16·69 m (54 ft 9 in)
- Height overall — 4·93 m (16 ft 2 in)
- Tailplane span — 6·21 m (20 ft 4½ in)
- Wheel track — 3·32 m (10 ft 10½ in)
- Wheelbase — 5·24 m (17 ft 2¼ in)

AREAS:
- Wings, gross — 49·1 m² (528·9 sq ft)
- Flaperons (total) — 3·81 m² (41·0 sq ft)
- Trailing-edge flaps (total) — 9·66 m² (104·0 sq ft)
- Leading-edge slats (total) — 4·63 m² (49·8 sq ft)
- Tailplane — 10·87 m² (117·00 sq ft)
- Fin — 5·85 m² (62·93 sq ft)
- Rudder — 1·52 m² (16·32 sq ft)

WEIGHTS AND LOADING:
- Weight empty — 12,132 kg (26,746 lb)
- Fuel load: internal — 7,230 kg (15,939 lb)
- external (five tanks) — 4,558 kg (10,050 lb)
- Max external load — 8,165 kg (18,000 lb)
- Max T-O weight:
  - catapult — 26,580 kg (58,600 lb)
  - field — 27,397 kg (60,400 lb)
- Max zero-stores weight — 20,166 kg (44,460 lb)
- Max landing weight:
  - carrier — 16,329 kg (36,000 lb)
  - field — 20,411 kg (45,000 lb)
- Max wing loading — 557· kg/m² (114·2 lb/sq ft)

PERFORMANCE (no stores, except where stated):
- Never-exceed speed — 700 knots (1,297 km/h; 806 mph)
- Max level speed at S/L — 560 knots (1,037 km/h; 644 mph)
- Cruising speed at optimum altitude — 412 knots (763 km/h; 474 mph)
- Approach speed — 110 knots (204 km/h; 127 mph)
- Stalling speed:
  - flaps up — 142 knots (264 km/h; 164 mph)
  - flaps down — 98 knots (182 km/h; 113 mph)
- Max rate of climb at S/L — 2,323 m (7,620 ft)/min
- Rate of climb at S/L, one engine out — 646 m (2,120 ft)/min
- Service ceiling — 12,925 m (42,400 ft)
- Service ceiling, one engine out — 6,400 m (21,000 ft)
- Min T-O run — 1,185 m (3,890 ft)
- T-O to 15 m (50 ft) — 1,390 m (4,560 ft)
- Landing from 15 m (50 ft) — 774 m (2,540 ft)
- Min landing run — 521 m (1,710 ft)
- Combat range with max external fuel, tanks jettisoned when empty — 2,818 nm (5,222 km; 3,245 miles)
- Range with max military load — 878 nm (1,627 km; 1,011 miles)
- Ferry range, tanks retained — 2,380 nm (4,410 km; 2,740 miles)

GRUMMAN EA-6B PROWLER

The EA-6B is an advanced electronics development of the EA-6A for which Grumman received a prototype design and development contract in the Autumn of 1966. Except for a 1·37 m (4 ft 6 in) longer nose section and large fin pod, the external configuration of this version is the same as that of the basic A-6.

The longer nose section provides accommodation for a total crew of four, the two additional crewmen being necessary to operate the more advanced ECM equipment. This comprises high-powered electronic jammers and modern computer-directed receivers, which provided the US Navy with its first aircraft designed and built specifically for tactical electronic warfare. The prototype EA-6B flew for the first time on 25 May 1968.

Deliveries of production aircraft began in January 1971 and are continuing at a rate of eight per year in 1984, six per year in 1985, 12 per year in 1986, returning to six per year thereafter until 1991.

An ICAP (increased capability) version of the EA-6B, with substantially increased jamming efficiency, is now standard, and the first 21 production EA-6Bs were modified by Grumman to ICAP configuration. Modifications include an expanded onboard tactical jamming system with eight frequency bands, reduced response time, and a new multi-format display. In addition, an automatic carrier landing system (ACLS) to permit carrier recovery in zero-zero weather, a new defensive electronic countermeasures system (DECM) and new communications-navigation-identification (CNI) equipment are installed. The prototype of a more advanced ICAP-2 version, with further improved

Grumman EA-6B Prowler ICAP-2 tactical jamming aircraft

jamming capability, made its first flight on 24 June 1980. Each of the five pods carried under the EA-6B's wings and fuselage originally generated signals within a single frequency band. An ICAP-2 exciter in each pod generates signals in any one of seven frequency bands, and each pod can jam in two different bands simultaneously. ICAP-2 attained IOC in 1984, on new aircraft and by retrofit. To follow this, an ADVCAP (advanced capability) programme was initiated in 1983, when Litton Industries' Amecom Division received a contract to develop a new receiver/processor group for the EA-6B's tactical jamming system. Delivery of the first of six systems for flight testing is scheduled for 1987, with production envisaged to start in 1991.

Ten US Navy squadrons (VAQ-129, 130, 131, 132, 133, 134, 135, 136, 137 and 138) were equipped with the Prowler by mid-1977. The first detachment of US Marine Corps Prowler squadron VMAQ-2 began training on the EA-6B in September 1977 at NAS Whidbey Island, Washington, and the detachment deployed in late 1978. Two additional detachments have since completed training, and at least one is deployed at all times.

The description of the standard A-6E Intruder applies also to the EA-6B, except as follows:

TYPE: Four-seat carrier- or land-based advanced ECM aircraft.

WINGS: As for A-6E, but reinforced to cater for increased gross weight, fatigue life and 5·5*g* load factor.

FUSELAGE: As for A-6E, but reinforcement of underfuselage structure in areas of arrester hook and landing gear attachments, and lengthened by 1·37 m (4 ft 6 in).

TAIL UNIT: As for A-6E, except for provision of a large fin-tip pod to house ECM equipment.

LANDING GEAR: As for A-6E, except for reinforcement of attachments, A-frame arrester hook, and upgrading of structure to cater for increased gross weight.

POWER PLANT: Two Pratt & Whitney J52-P-408 turbojet engines, each rated at 49·8 kN (11,200 lb st).

ACCOMMODATION: Crew of four under two separate upward opening canopies. Martin-Baker GRUEA 7 ejection seats for flight crew. The two additional crewmen are ECM Officers to operate the ALQ-99 equipment from the rear cockpit. Either ECMO can independently detect, assign, adjust and monitor the jammers. The ECMO in the starboard front seat is responsible for communications, navigation, defensive ECM and chaff dispensing.

SYSTEMS: Generally as for A-6E.

AVIONICS: Eaton Corpn (AIL Division) AN/ALQ-99F tactical jamming system, in five integrally powered pods, with a total of 10 jamming transmitters. Each pod covers one of seven frequency bands. Sensitive surveillance receivers in the fin-tip pod for long-range detection of radars; emitter information is fed to a central digital computer (AYK-14 in ICAP-2 aircraft) that processes the signals for display and recording. Detection, identification, direction-finding and jammer-set-on sequence can be performed automatically or with manual assistance from crew.

ARMAMENT: Originally unarmed, but currently being equipped to carry Texas Instruments AGM-88A HARM anti-radar missiles underwing.

DIMENSIONS, EXTERNAL: As for A-6E, except:
- Width, wings folded: 7·87 m (25 ft 10 in)
- Length overall: 18·24 m (59 ft 10 in)
- Height overall: 4·95 m (16 ft 3 in)
- Wheelbase: 5·23 m (17 ft 2 in)

WEIGHTS AND LOADING:
- Weight empty: 14,588 kg (32,162 lb)
- Internal fuel load: 6,995 kg (15,422 lb)
- Max external fuel load: 4,547 kg (10,025 lb)
- T-O weight from carrier in standoff jamming configuration (5 ECM pods): 24,703 kg (54,461 lb)
- T-O weight from field in ferry range configuration (max internal and external fuel): 27,492 kg (60,610 lb)
- Max T-O weight, catapult or field: 29,483 kg (65,000 lb)
- Max zero-fuel weight: 17,708 kg (39,039 lb)
- Max landing weight, carrier or field: 20,638 kg (45,500 lb)
- Max wing loading: 600·5 kg/m² (123 lb/sq ft)

PERFORMANCE (A: no stores; B: 5 ECM pods):
- Never-exceed speed 710 knots (1,315 km/h; 817 mph)
- Max level speed at S/L:
  - A: 566 knots (1,048 km/h; 651 mph)
  - B: 530 knots (982 km/h; 610 mph)
- Cruising speed at optimum altitude:
  - A, B: 418 knots (774 km/h; 481 mph)
- Stalling speed, flaps up, max power:
  - A: 124 knots (230 km/h; 143 mph)
- Stalling speed, flaps down, max power:
  - A: 84 knots (156 km/h; 97 mph)
- Max rate of climb at S/L: A: 3,932 m (12,900 ft)/min
  - B: 3,057 m (10,030 ft)/min
- Rate of climb at S/L, one engine out:
  - A: 1,189 m (3,900 ft)/min
- Service ceiling: A: 12,550 m (41,200 ft)
  - B: 11,580 m (38,000 ft)
- Service ceiling, one engine out:
  - A: 8,930 m (29,300 ft)
- T-O run: B: 814 m (2,670 ft)
- T-O to 15 m (50 ft): A: 869 m (2,850 ft)
  - B: 1,065 m (3,495 ft)
- Landing from 15 m (50 ft): A: 823 m (2,700 ft)
- Landing run: A: 579 m (1,900 ft)
  - B: 655 m (2,150 ft)
- Combat range with max external fuel, tanks jettisoned when empty: 2,085 nm (3,861 km; 2,399 miles)
- Range with max external load, 5% reserves plus 20 min at S/L: B: 955 nm (1,769 km; 1,099 miles)
- Ferry range with max external fuel, tanks retained: 1,756 nm (3,254 km; 2,022 miles)

GRUMMAN TOMCAT

USN designation: F-14

Grumman announced on 15 January 1969 that it had been selected as winner of the design competition for a carrier-based fighter for the US Navy. Known as the VFX during the competitive phase of the programme, this aircraft was later designated F-14. First flight of the F-14A Tomcat prototype took place on 21 December 1970. It was lost in a non-fatal accident, and flight testing was resumed on 24 May 1971 with the second aircraft.

Under initial contracts, Grumman built for the US Navy 12 research and development aircraft. The planned programme was intended to provide 497 Navy Tomcats, including the 12 development aircraft. This total is now to be increased considerably, extending Tomcat production into the 1990s.

Carrier trials started in June 1972, and initial deployment with the fleet began in October 1972, the first two operational squadrons being VF-1 and VF-2. A total of 531 F-14As, including the 12 R&D aircraft, had been delivered to the US Navy by 1 March 1986. By the end of 1986 the US Navy was scheduled to have 26 Tomcat squadrons, including two reserve and two training squadrons, operating from 12 aircraft carriers and the Naval Air Stations at Miramar, California, and Oceana, Virginia. In addition, the Iranian Air Force took delivery of 80 F-14As in 1976-78. These aircraft retained the Phoenix weapon system, but had slightly different ECM equipment from US Navy Tomcats.

Since 1979, Northrop Corporation has been manufacturing television camera sets (TCSs) for installation on F-14s. The TCS is a closed-circuit TV system, offering both wide-angle (acquisition) and telescopic (identification) fields of view. Mounted beneath the nose of the F-14, the TCS automatically searches for, acquires and locks on to distant targets, displaying them on monitors for the pilot and flight officer. By allowing early identification of targets, the system permits crews to make combat decisions earlier than was possible previously. A total of 341 TCS systems had been ordered by March 1985.

Between July and September 1981 a short flight test programme (29 flights by Grumman followed by five US Navy flights) was undertaken with an F-14 (the seventh development aircraft, originally the prototype F-14B) refitted with General Electric F110-GE-400 derivative fighter engines in place of then-standard Pratt & Whitney TF30-P-412As. F-14As delivered at the rate of 24 a year from FY 1983 to FY 1985 have improved TF30-P-414A engines.

In July 1984 Grumman was awarded an $863·8 million fixed price contract for an F-14 update programme which provides for development of the **F-14A(Plus)** with F110-GE-400 engines but otherwise unchanged, and for the **F-14D** with F110-GE-400, digital avionics and a new radar. Grumman is prime contractor for the engine and avionics upgrades, with General Electric and Hughes Aircraft as subcontractors. The F110-GE-400 selected for the F-14A(Plus) and F-14D has 82 per cent parts commonality with the F110-GE-100 engine for the USAF's F-15s and F-16s. A 1·27 m (4 ft 2 in) plug will be inserted in the afterburner section to match the engine to F-14 inlet position and airframe contours, and only secondary structure will require modification to accept the new engine.

The F-14D upgrade modifies some 60 per cent of the F-14A's analog avionics, providing new weapons management, navigation, displays and control functions, with digital bus integration of the Litton ALR-67 threat warning and recognition system, Westinghouse/ITT ALQ-165 airborne self protection jammer (ASPJ), joint tactical information distribution system (JTIDS), infra-red search and track sensor (IRST) and television camera set (TCS), with emphasis on hardware and software commonality with F/A-18 and A-6F programmes. A new radar, designated APG-71, is being developed. It is based on the AN/AWG-9 radar, improved ECCM capability and incorporating monopulse angle tracking, digital scan control, target identification and raid assessment. The APG-71 will feature non-co-operative target identification and be able to counter sophisticated ECM by means of a low-sidelobe antenna and sidelobe blanking guard channel, frequency agility, and a new high-speed digital signal processor based on elements of the USAF's multi-stage improvement programme (MSIP) of the F-15's APG-70 radar. Provision will also be made for integration of the AMRAAM missile. The F-14D will be equipped with Martin-Baker Navy Aircrew Common Ejection Seats (NACES).

Grumman's full scale development programme will involve five aircraft, including an F-14B prototype which was due to fly with definitive F110-GE-400 engines in mid-1986 as part of the F-14A(Plus) programme. The remaining development aircraft are expected to fly at one-month intervals from early 1987. Three will be used for avionics and radar development, in conjunction with a TA-3B Skywarrior aircraft. One will be completed to full F-14D standard and will join that programme after serving on the F-14A(Plus) development programme. The development schedule includes 25 months of US Navy evaluations. Production is due to switch from F-14A to F-14A(Plus) with the FY 1986 aircraft. A total of 38 F-14A (Plus) aircraft

Grumman F-14A Tomcat of US Navy Squadron VF-1 from USS *Kitty Hawk*

will be delivered, commencing in November 1987, before the first of some 300 F-14Ds is delivered in March 1990.

The F110-GE-400 powered F-14A(Plus) and F-14D are expected to show significant performance benefits resulting from the engine's 30 per cent increase in afterburning and non-afterburning thrust over the Pratt & Whitney TF30-P-414A engine. Specific excess energy is increased by 20 per cent, afterburning specific fuel consumption is reduced by 30 per cent, and deck launch intercept radius and combat air patrol time on station are expected to be increased by 60 and 35 per cent respectively, as a result of lower fuel burns and the F110 engined Tomcat's ability to be launched without use of afterburner.

The following description applies to the current operational F-14A:

Type: Two-seat carrier based multi-role fighter.

Wings: Variable-geometry mid-wing monoplane, with 20° of leading-edge sweep in the fully forward position and 68° when fully swept. Oversweep position of 75° for carrier stowage. Wing position is programmed automatically for optimum performance throughout the flight regime, but manual override is provided. A short movable wing outer panel, needing only a comparatively light pivot structure, results from the wide fuselage and fixed centre-section 'glove', with pivot points 2·72 m (8 ft 11 in) from the centreline of the airframe. The inboard wing sections, adjacent to the fuselage, arc upward slightly to minimise cross-sectional area and wave drag, and consist basically of a one-piece electron beam-welded titanium assembly, 6·70 m (22 ft) in span, made from Ti-6Al-4V titanium alloy. Small canard surfaces, known as glove vanes, swing out from the leading-edge of the fixed portion of the wing, to a maximum of 15° in relation to the leading-edge, as Mach number is increased. Spoilers on upper surfaces of wing. Stabilisation in pitch, provided by the canard surfaces, leaves the differential tailplane free to perform its primary control function. Trailing-edge flaps extend over almost entire span. Leading-edge slats.

Fuselage: All-metal semi-monocoque structure, with machined frames, main longerons of titanium, and light alloy stressed skin. The centre-fuselage section is a simple, fuel-carrying box structure; forward fuselage section comprises cockpit and upward hinged nose giving access to radar. The aft section has a tapered aerofoil shape to minimise drag, with a fuel dump pipe projecting from the rear. Speed brakes located on the upper and lower surfaces, between the bases of the vertical tail fins. Rear fuselage and vertical tail surfaces manufactured by Fairchild Republic.

Tail Unit: Twin vertical fins, mounted at the rear of each engine nacelle. Fins and rudders of light alloy honeycomb sandwich. Outward canted ventral fin under each nacelle. The all-flying multi-spar horizontal surfaces have skins of boron epoxy composite material and honeycomb trailing-edges.

Landing Gear: Retractable tricycle type. Twin-wheel nose unit and single-wheel main units retract forward, main units inward into bottom of engine air intake trunks. Original beryllium brakes were replaced with Goodyear lightweight carbon brakes from Spring 1981. Arrester hook under rear fuselage, housed in small ventral fairing. Nose-tow catapult attachment on nose unit.

Engine Intakes: Straight two-dimensional external compression inlets. A double-hinged ramp extends down from the top of each intake, and these are programmed to provide the correct airflow to the engines automatically under all flight conditions. Each intake is canted slightly away from the fuselage, from which it is separated by some 0·25 m (10 in) to allow sufficient clearance for the turbulent fuselage boundary layer to pass between fuselage and intake without causing turbulence within the intake. Engine inlet ducts and aft nacelle structures are manufactured by Rohr Corporation. The inlet duct, constructed largely of aluminium alloy honeycomb, is about 4·27 m (14 ft) long; the aft nacelle structure, of bonded aluminium alloy honeycomb and conventional aluminium alloy sheet, is about 4·88 m (16 ft) in length.

Power Plant: Early aircraft have two Pratt & Whitney TF30-P-412A turbofan engines of 93 kN (20,900 lb st) with afterburning, mounted in ducts which open to provide 180° access for ease of maintenance. Current production aircraft have TF30-P-414As of the same rating. Garrett ATS200-50 air turbine starter. Integral fuel tanks in outer wings, each with capacity of 1,117 litres (295 US gallons); between engines in rear fuselage, with capacity of 2,453 litres (648 US gallons); and forward of wing carry-through structure, capacity 2,616 litres (691 US gallons); plus two feeder tanks with combined capacity of 1,726 litres (456 US gallons). Total internal fuel capacity 9,029 litres (2,385 US gallons). An external auxiliary fuel tank can be carried beneath each intake trunk, each containing 1,011 litres (267 US gallons). Retractable flight refuelling probe on starboard side of fuselage near front cockpit.

Accommodation: Pilot and naval flight officer seated in tandem on Martin-Baker GRU7A rocket assisted zero/zero ejection seats, under a one-piece bubble canopy, hinged at the rear and offering all-round view. Martin-Baker NACES seats on F-14D.

Avionics: Hughes AN/AWG-9 weapons control system, with ability to detect airborne targets at ranges of more than 65-170 nm (120-315 km; 75-195 miles) according to their size, and ability to track 24 enemy targets and attack six of them simultaneously at varied altitudes and distances. AN/AWG-15 fire control set; CP-1066/A central air data computer; CP-1050/A computer signal data converter; AN/ASW-27B digital data link; AN/APX-76(V) IFF interrogator; AN/APX-72 IFF transponder; AN/ASA-79 multiple display indicator group; Kaiser Aerospace AN/AVG-12 vertical and head-up display system. AN/ARC-51 and AN/ARC-159 UHF com; AN/ARR-69 UHF auxiliary receiver; KY-28 cryptographic system; LS-460/B intercom; AN/ASN-92(V) INS; A/A24G39 AHRS; AN/APN-154 beacon augmentor; AN/APN-194(V) radar altimeter; ARA-63A receiver-decoder; AN/ARN-84 micro Tacan; AN/ARA-50 UHF ADF; AN/APR-27/50 radar receiver; AN/APR-25/45 radar warning set. TV optical unit in undernose pod.

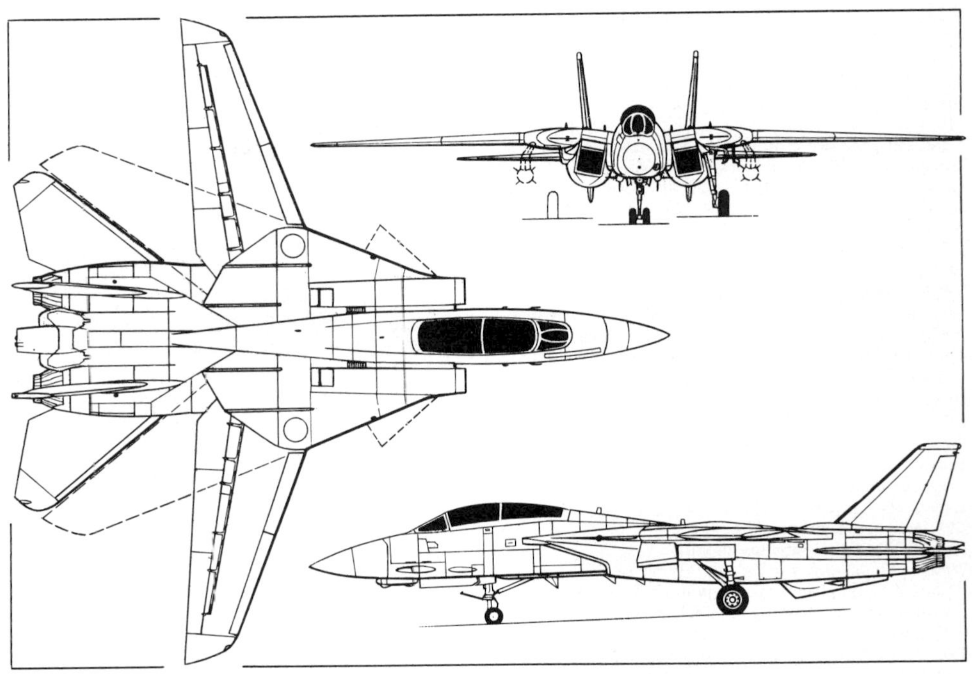

Grumman F-14A Tomcat carrier based multi-mission fighter *(Pilot Press)*

Armament and Operational Equipment: One General Electric M61A-1 Vulcan 20 mm gun mounted in the port side of forward fuselage, with 675 rounds of ammunition. Four Sparrow air-to-air missiles mounted partially submerged in the underfuselage, or four Phoenix missiles carried on special pallets which attach to the bottom of the fuselage. Two wing pylons, one under each fixed wing section, can carry four Sidewinder missiles or two additional Sparrow or Phoenix missiles with two Sidewinders. Various combinations of missiles and bombs to a max external weapon load of 6,577 kg (14,500 lb). ECM equipment includes Goodyear AN/ALE-29 and AN/ALE-39 chaff and flare dispensers, with integral jammers. Small undernose pod for Sanders AN/ALQ-100/126 deception jamming system, relocated under camera package of aircraft with Northrop TCS. During 1980-81, a total of 49 F-14s were allocated to carry TARPS (tactical air reconnaissance pod system), containing a KS-87B frame camera, KA-99 low altitude panoramic camera, and AN/AAD-5 infra-red reconnaissance equipment, on underbelly attachment.

Dimensions, external:

Wing span: unswept	19·54 m (64 ft 1½ in)
swept	11·65 m (38 ft 2½ in)
overswept	10·15 m (33 ft 3½ in)
Wing aspect ratio	7·28
Length overall	19·10 m (62 ft 8 in)
Height overall	4·88 m (16 ft 0 in)
Tailplane span	9·97 m (32 ft 8½ in)
Distance between fin tips	3·25 m (10 ft 8 in)
Wheel track	5·00 m (16 ft 5 in)
Wheelbase	7·02 m (23 ft 0½ in)

Areas:

Wings, gross	52·49 m² (565·0 sq ft)
Horizontal tail surfaces (total)	13·01 m² (140·0 sq ft)
Vertical tail surfaces (total)	10·96 m² (118·0 sq ft)

Weights (P-414A engines):

Weight empty	18,191 kg (40,104 lb)
Fuel (usable): internal	7,348 kg (16,200 lb)
external	1,724 kg (3,800 lb)
T-O weight, clean	26,632 kg (58,715 lb)
T-O weight with 4 Sparrow	27,086 kg (59,714 lb)
T-O weight with 6 Phoenix	32,098 kg (70,764 lb)
Max T-O weight	33,724 kg (74,349 lb)
Design landing weight	23,510 kg (51,830 lb)

Performance:

Max speed at height	Mach 2·34 (1,342 knots; 2,485 km/h; 1,544 mph)
Max speed at low level	Mach 1·2 (792 knots; 1,468 km/h; 912 mph)
Max cruising speed	400-550 knots (741-1,019 km/h; 460-633 mph)
*Carrier approach speed	134 knots (248 km/h; 154 mph)
*Stalling speed	115 knots (213 km/h; 132 mph)
Max rate of climb at S/L	over 9,140 m (30,000 ft)/min
Service ceiling	above 15,240 m (50,000 ft)
Min T-O distance	427 m (1,400 ft)
Min landing distance	884 m (2,900 ft)
Max range with external fuel	approx 1,735 nm (3,220 km; 2,000 miles)

* *carrier landing design gross weight*

GRUMMAN (GENERAL DYNAMICS) RAVEN

US Air Force designation: EF-111A

The programme to convert General Dynamics F-111As into EF-111A electronic warfare aircraft, and to evaluate their ability to provide ECM jamming coverage for air attack forces, was initiated in 1972-73.

Three basic modes of deployment are foreseen for the EF-111A: standoff, penetration, and close air support. In the standoff role, jamming aircraft would operate within their own airspace, at the FEBA (forward edge of the battle area). Out of range of the enemy's ground based weapons, orbiting EF-111As would use their jamming systems to screen the routes of friendly strike aircraft. In the penetration role, the EF-111As would accompany strike aircraft to high-priority targets, their Mach 2 capability making them ideal escort aircraft for such a task. The close air support requirement calls for EF-111A escorts to neutralise anti-air radars while the strike force delivers its attack on enemy armour.

Primary electronic warfare equipment comprises the AN/ALQ-99E tactical jamming system, an improved version of the AN/ALQ-99 system carried by the US Navy's Grumman EA-6B Prowler. The ALQ-99E's jamming transmitters are mounted in the weapons bay, with their antennae covered by a narrow 4·9 m (16 ft) long canoe-shape radome. The fin-tip pod, similar in shape to that of the EA-6B, houses the receiver and antennae. Total weight of the new equipment is about 2,720 kg (3 US tons).

Claimed to be the world's most powerful airborne ECM system, the ALQ-99E's frequency coverage, reliability, and effective use of available jamming power enable the EF-111A to penetrate the world's densest known electronic defences. Its electronic systems can be converted quickly to counter new threats as they develop, and, even if multiple hostile radars switch to a variety of frequencies, the EF-111A's broad range of jamming capabilities can handle them immediately. The electronic warfare officer (EWO) handles a tactical workload previously requiring (as in the EA-6B) several operators; for example, pre-flight programming of the computer with known radars frees the operator to concentrate on new and more urgent threat radars.

Design study contracts were awarded to General Dynamics and Grumman by the US Air Force in 1974, and in January 1975 it was announced that Grumman had been awarded an $85·9 million contract to convert two existing F-111As to EF-111A prototype configuration. A partially modified F-111A, fitted with the weapons bay radome only, was flown for the first time on 15 December 1975. The first flight of a fully aerodynamic prototype (66-049), with fin-tip pod and underbelly radome, was made from Grumman's Calverton, NY, facility on 10 March 1977; the complete system was flown for the first time on 17 May 1977, on the second prototype (66-041). USAF tests verified various mission operational concepts, flight formations, and the jammer's electromagnetic compatibility with other strike aircraft. (These latter tests dispelled an earlier concern that the friendly strike force, as well as enemy threats, might be jammed by the powerful signals emanating from the EF-111A.)

Including the two prototypes, which were subsequently brought up to full production standard, the US Air Force funded the conversion of 42 F-111As (of 86 still operational at the beginning of 1983) to EF-111A standard, to equip two squadrons, all of which have been delivered. The first EF-111A delivered to TAC for operational use was 66-049, in November 1981. The 390th Electronic Combat Squadron became operational on EF-111As in December 1983. In February 1984 the first EF-111A for USAFE arrived at RAF Upper Heyford, Oxfordshire, UK, assigned to the 42nd ECS of the 20th Tactical Fighter Wing.

Upgrading of the EF-111A's tactical jamming systems is being undertaken, to provide improved capability against EW radar, GCI and surface-to-air missile acquisition. When completed the update will have cost about $200 million.

The description of the F-111A in the 1976-77 *Jane's* applies also to the EF-111A, except for the following additional or amended details:

TYPE: ECM tactical jamming aircraft.

WINGS: As detailed for F-111A. Wing section NACA 64A210.68 (modified) at pivot point, NACA 64A209.80, with modified leading-edge, at tip. Dihedral, at 16° sweep, 1°. Incidence, at 16° sweep, 1° at root, −3° at tip.

TAIL UNIT: Fin (built under subcontract by Canadair) reinforced to support 454 kg (1,000 lb) fin-tip antenna pod.

POWER PLANT: Two Pratt & Whitney TF30-P-3 turbofan engines, each rated at 82·3 kN (18,500 lb st) with afterburning. Fuel tanks in wings and fuselage, total capacity 18,919 litres (4,998 US gallons). Oil capacity 30·3 litres (8 US gallons).

ENGINE INTAKES: External compression type with variable diameter double cone spike which expands from 8° 30′ to 26° for supersonic compression. The spike translates independently of the second cone position for more efficient air spillage at low supersonic speeds. Porous spike bleed is distributed over the spike shoulder for compression surface boundary layer control at high Mach numbers. An automatic air inlet control manufactured by Hamilton Standard Division of United Aircraft Corporation controls spike and cone movement as functions of engine duct and underwing glove Mach numbers.

ACCOMMODATION: Crew of two (pilot and electronic warfare officer) side by side in air-conditioned and pressurised cockpit. Portion of canopy over each seat is hinged on aircraft centreline and opens upward. Zero-speed, zero-altitude (including underwater) emergency escape module.

SYSTEMS: Bendix AC electrical system, with Sundstrand 90kVA integrated drive generators (instead of 60kVA in F-111A). Improved air cycle cooling system for avionics; liquid cooling system, with ram air heat exchanger, added.

AVIONICS AND EQUIPMENT: AN/ARC-112 HF com transceiver; Magnavox AN/ARC-164 UHF com transceiver; AN/AIC-25 intercom; AN/AJQ-20A INS; Collins AN/ARN-118 Tacan; Honeywell AN/APN-167 radar altimeter; Collins AN/ARA-50 UHF/DF; AN/ARN-58 ILS; IBM (Federal Systems Division) 4 Pi digital computer; Texas Instruments AN/APQ-110 terrain following radar; AN/APQ-160 attack radar; AN/APX-64 IFF/SIF; Eaton Corpn (AIL Division) AN/ALQ-99E tactical jamming system; Sanders AN/ALQ-137(V)4 ECM self-protection system (SPS); AN/ALR-62(V)4 terminal threat warning system (TTWS); AN/ALR-23 radar countermeasures receiver system (CMRS); AN/ALE-28 electronic countermeasures dispenser system (CMDS). All tactical jamming functions are managed by the EWO who can, through computer management, handle a tactical electronic warfare workload which previously required several operators and more equipment. In addition, the automated system of the EF-111A has exceptional capability for locating, identifying, and assigning jammers to, enemy emitters over a wide range of frequencies. The AN/ALQ-99E jamming system comprises ten transmitters (Raytheon high-band, AEL low-band), five Raytheon exciters, numerous receivers, computers, display systems, and one Raytheon RF calibrator, per aircraft.

Grumman modified EF-111A Ravens of the 390th Electronic Combat Squadron, Mountain Home AFB, Idaho

ARMAMENT: None.

DIMENSIONS, EXTERNAL:

Wing span: spread	19·20 m (63 ft 0 in)
fully swept	9·74 m (31 ft 11·4 in)
Wing mean aerodynamic chord	2·76 m (9 ft 0 in)
Wing aspect ratio (16° sweep)	7·56
Length overall	23·16 m (76 ft 0 in)
Height overall	6·10 m (20 ft 0 in)
Wheel track	3·19 m (10 ft 0·4 in)
Wheelbase	7·44 m (24 ft 4·8 in)

AREA:

Wings, gross (16° sweep)	48·77 m² (525 sq ft)

WEIGHTS:

Weight empty	25,072 kg (55,275 lb)
Max internal fuel	14,738 kg (32,493 lb)
Design T-O weight	33,000 kg (72,750 lb)
Combat T-O weight	31,751 kg (70,000 lb)
Max T-O weight	40,346 kg (88,948 lb)
Max landing weight	37,421 kg (82,500 lb)

PERFORMANCE (estimated for typical mission, at max T-O weight except where indicated. A: basic standoff; B: penetration; C: close air support):

Max level speed:	
A, B, C	1,227 knots (2,272 km/h; 1,412 mph)
Max combat speed at combat weight:	
A, B, C	1,196 knots (2,216 km/h; 1,377 mph)
Average speed, outbound:	
A, C	446 knots (826 km/h; 514 mph)
B	512 knots (949 km/h; 590 mph)
Average speed over combat area:	
A	321 knots (595 km/h; 370 mph)
B	507 knots (940 km/h; 584 mph)
C	462 knots (856 km/h; 532 mph)
Average speed, inbound:	
A, C	432 knots (800 km/h; 497 mph)
B	502 knots (930 km/h; 578 mph)
Stalling speed, power off:	
A, B, C	143 knots (264 km/h; 164 mph)
Rate of climb at S/L, intermediate power:	
A, B, C	1,006 m (3,300 ft)/min
Rate of climb at S/L, one engine out, with afterburning:	
A, B, C	1,021 m (3,350 ft)/min
Service ceiling with afterburning, at combat weight:	
A, B, C	13,715 m (45,000 ft)
T-O run: A, B, C	1,349 m (4,425 ft)
T-O to 15 m (50 ft): A, B, C	1,775 m (5,825 ft)
Landing from 15 m (50 ft) at weight of 26,968 kg (59,455 lb): A, B, C	945 m (3,100 ft)
Landing run at weight of 26,968 kg (59,455 lb):	
A, B, C	602 m (1,975 ft)
Combat radius, with reserves:	
A	200 nm (370 km; 230 miles)
B	807 nm (1,495 km; 929 miles)
C	623 nm (1,155 km; 717 miles)
Ferry range	2,000 nm (3,706 km; 2,303 miles)
Endurance without refuelling	more than 4 h

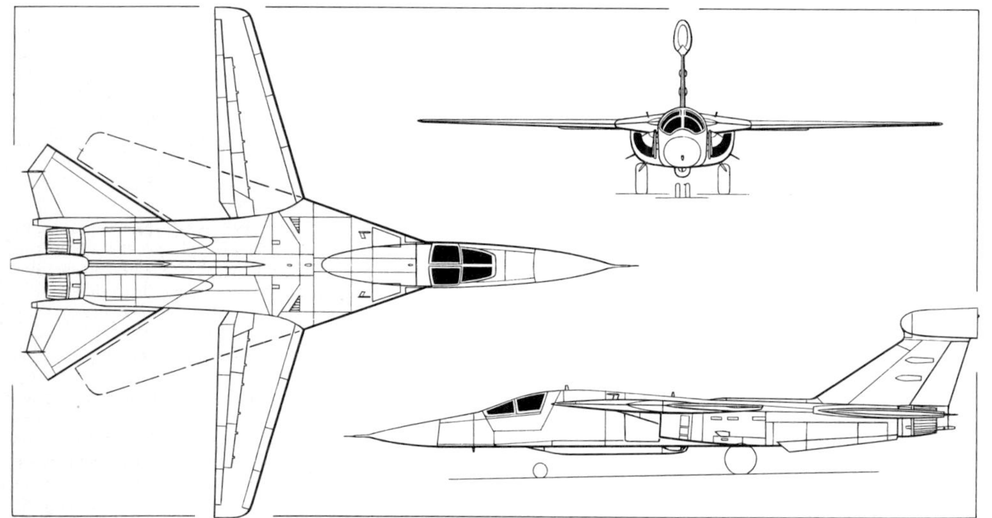

Grumman (General Dynamics) EF-111A Raven electronic warfare aircraft *(Pilot Press)*

GRUMMAN MODEL 712 FORWARD SWEPT WING DEMONSTRATOR

US Air Force designation: X-29A

Grumman has been exploring for some time the benefits offered by a forward swept wing (FSW) design, and conducted a series of wind tunnel test programmes that were funded by the Defense Advanced Research Projects Agency. Monitored by the US Air Force, these programmes verified the aerodynamic benefits of such a design. As a result, it was announced on 22 December 1981 that Grumman had been awarded an $80 million contract to build two single-seat FSW demonstrator aircraft that would be designated X-29A. Basic design had started in January 1981 and, following award of the contract, construction of the airframes began in January 1982. The No. 2 aircraft was used for the formal rollout ceremony on 27 August 1984. On the following day the No. 1 X-29A started taxi trials.

On 14 December 1984 the X-29A made its first flight from NASA's Ames-Dryden Flight Research Center at Edwards AFB, California. With landing gear down, it reached a maximum altitude of 4,575 m (15,000 ft) and a maximum airspeed of 235 knots (435 km/h; 271 mph). Grumman's planned four-flight evaluation of the X-29A was completed successfully in early March 1985 and included checks of handling characteristics, systems operations and structural integrity. On 12 March 1985 the aircraft was delivered to USAF Aeronautical Systems Division, which handed it over to NASA, and it made its first flight with a NASA pilot in command on 2 April. By February 1986 the X-29A had made 39 flights, totalling 47 flight hours and had attained a maximum speed of Mach 1·2, a maximum loading of 5·3*g* and a maximum 20° angle of attack.

Funding has been approved for preparation of the No. 2 aircraft for high angle of attack testing by the US Air Force. Work began on design modifications and installation of flight test instrumentation in January 1986. The aircraft is expected to fly for the first time in July 1987 and to enter a test programme which will include some 45-60 flights. NASA anticipates a flying rate of two flights per week when both X-29As are operational.

Grumman's FSW design offers the promise of a new generation of tactical aircraft that will be smaller, lighter in weight, less costly, but more efficient than contemporary fighters. The concept is not new, as the aerodynamic advantages of forward wing sweep were recognised during the second World War. They include improved manoeuvrability, with virtually spin-proof characteristics, better low-speed handling, and reduced stalling speeds. In addition, such aircraft have the advantage of lower drag across the entire operational envelope, particularly at speeds approaching Mach 1, which will permit the use of a less powerful engine. However, the achievement of a suitable structure to reap these benefits was found to be impracticable at the state of the art prevailing in the 1940s.

With an FSW aircraft of conventional construction, when aerodynamic stresses flex the wing in flight, this increases the angle of attack (and hence the lift) of the outer wing sections. This, in turn, increases the air loads and causes further deformation of the wings; higher speeds will raise these forces until they eventually exceed the strength of the wing structure. To compensate for this divergence problem, FSWs of metal construction had to be stiffened to the point where a weight penalty was incurred, negating any aerodynamic benefit. Grumman appreciated that the advent of advanced composite materials offered a solution. Exceptionally strong and light in weight, an FSW of graphite composite material can be tailored to eliminate twisting when the wing bends.

The single-seat X-29As have a thin supercritical wing of metal/composite construction, with a variable camber trailing-edge that changes the shape of the wing to match flight conditions, and a close-coupled foreplane to reduce supersonic trim drag. A standard Northrop F-5A forward fuselage and nose landing gear, and many off-the-shelf components such as F-16 main landing gear and control surface actuators, were utilised to reduce costs. Flight control is by triplex redundant fly by wire, and the aircraft is designed to be highly (35 per cent) unstable longitudinally. Sufficient flexibility is being built into the programme to allow for the flight testing of other advanced concepts relating to cockpits, two-dimensional exhaust nozzles, weapons carriage, and techniques to reduce further the take-off and landing speed of FSW aircraft.

TYPE: FSW demonstrator aircraft.

WINGS: Cantilever low/mid-wing monoplane. Supercritical wing section. Thickness/chord ratio at root 6·2%, at tip 4·9%. No dihedral. Incidence −6° at WS 20 to +0·8° at WS 163·22. Forward sweep at quarter-chord 33° 44'. Safe-life construction, with substructure of aluminium alloy and titanium, and graphite epoxy composite skins. Full span dual hinged camber-changing trailing-edge flaps/ailerons ('flaperons'), with four National Water Lift integrated servo actuators in each wing. A wing strake extends aft from the trailing-edge at each wing root, each strake with a trailing-edge flap which has its own Moog integrated servo actuator to augment foreplanes for pitch control. No wing de-icing system.

FOREPLANES: All-moving (30° up, 60° down) canard surfaces of conventional aluminium alloy construction, one on each side of the centre-fuselage, outboard of engine inlet ducts. Operated by National Water Lift servo actuators for primary pitch control. No anti-icing system.

FUSELAGE: Semi-monocoque fail-safe structure of aluminium alloy, incorporating pressurised cockpit section.

TAIL UNIT: Sweptback fin and rudder only, of aluminium alloy construction. Rudder operated by National Water Lift integrated servo actuator. No anti-icing system.

LANDING GEAR: Hydraulically retractable tricycle type, all three units retracting forward. Menasco oleo-pneumatic shock absorber in each unit. Goodrich wheels and tyres. Nosewheel tyre size 18 × 6-8, pressure 10·35 bars (150 lb/sq in); mainwheel tyres each 24 × 5·5, pressure 17·25 bars (250 lb/sq in). Goodrich hydraulic carbon disc brakes, aircooled; Goodyear anti-skid units.

POWER PLANT: One General Electric F404-GE-400 afterburning turbofan in the 71·2 kN (16,000 lb st) class. Two bladder fuel cells within the fuselage, and integral tank in each wing strake, giving total capacity of 1,804 kg (3,978 lb) of JP5 fuel. No flight refuelling capability.

ACCOMMODATION: Pilot only, on Martin-Baker GRQ7A ejection seat, beneath upward opening canopy hinged at rear edge. Accommodation air-conditioned and pressurised.

SYSTEMS: AiResearch bootstrap air cycle air-conditioning and pressurisation system, providing cockpit pressure differential of 0·34 bars (5 lb/sq in). Dual engine driven Abex hydraulic pumps for two independent systems, each 207 bars (3,000 lb/sq in) for operation of flight control actuators, landing gear and utility systems. Electrical system includes Westinghouse 40kVA engine driven generator and Lear Siegler 5kVA emergency generator, 500VA converter, two transformer-rectifiers, 20Ah storage battery, and external power socket. Liquid oxygen system with converter. AiResearch emergency power unit, operated by engine bleed air and/or hydrazine fuel, to drive the Lear Siegler emergency generator and a Vickers hydraulic pump of 83 litres (22 US gallons)/min output. Systron-Donner engine fire detection and extinguishing system.

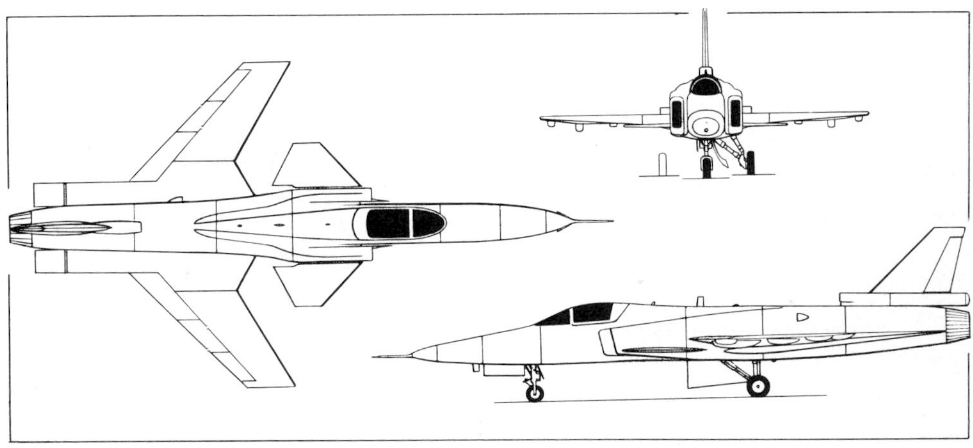

Grumman X-29A FSW demonstrator (General Electric F404-GE-400 turbofan) *(Pilot Press)*

Grumman X-29A FSW (forward swept wing) technology demonstrator

Grumman modified TA-4PTM Skyhawk trainer of the Royal Malaysian Air Force

AVIONICS: Include Litton LR-80 attitude and heading reference system and other navigation equipment, Magnavox AN/ARC-164 UHF com, and Teledyne RT-1063B/APX-101V IFF/SIF. Honeywell triple redundant digital flight control system.

DIMENSIONS, EXTERNAL:

Wing span	8·29 m (27 ft 2½ in)
Wing chord: at root	2·96 m (9 ft 8½ in)
at tip	1·19 m (3 ft 11 in)
Wing aspect ratio	4
Foreplane span	4·15 m (13 ft 7½ in)
Length overall, incl nose probe	16·44 m (53 ft 11¼ in)
Length of fuselage	14·66 m (48 ft 1 in)
Height overall	4·36 m (14 ft 3½ in)
Wheel track	2·30 m (7 ft 6½ in)
Wheelbase	5·48 m (17 ft 11¾ in)

AREAS (exposed):

Wings	17·54 m² (188·84 sq ft)
Foreplane	3·34 m² (35·96 sq ft)
Vertical tail surfaces (total)	3·02 m² (32·51 sq ft)

WEIGHTS:

Weight empty	6,260 kg (13,800 lb)
Max fuel weight	1,804 kg (3,978 lb)
Max T-O weight	8,074 kg (17,800 lb)

PERFORMANCE:

No details received up to June 1986, but max level speed approx Mach 1·6

GRUMMAN/McDONNELL DOUGLAS A-4PTM SKYHAWK

Under a $12 million contract awarded in 1982 Grumman's St Augustine Division has remanufactured a total of 40 McDonnell Douglas A-4 Skyhawk aircraft for the Royal Malaysian Air Force. The Skyhawks, 34 single-seat A-4PTM (Peculiar to Malaysia) and six two-seat TA-4PTM, received new wiring, updated avionics, two additional wing stores stations and refurbished engines. The TA-4PTMs were created by Grumman by a 0·71 m (2 ft 4 in) fuselage 'stretch' to accommodate tandem cockpits and dual controls. Delivery of the aircraft to the RMAF, with which they equip two squadrons based at Kuantan, was completed in February 1986.

GRUMMAN TURBO TRACKER

Grumman has proposed a turboprop modification of its S-2 Tracker anti-submarine warfare aircraft which would involve replacing the S-2's 1,141 kW (1,530 hp) Curtiss-Wright R-1820-82 piston engines with 1,230 kW (1,650 shp) Garrett TPE331-1-AW turboprops. The Turbo Tracker would have a 270 knot (500 km/h; 311 mph) maximum speed at 1,525 m (5,000 ft), a 500 kg (1,102 lb) increase in payload, and improvements in cruising speed, T-O and landing distances and engine TBO. Grumman sees existing operators of piston engined Trackers such as Argentina, Brazil, Peru, South Korea, Taiwan, Turkey and Venezuela as potential customers for the aircraft.

Grumman/McDonnell Douglas A-4PTM remanufactured Skyhawk for Royal Malaysian Air Force

GULFSTREAM AEROSPACE

GULFSTREAM AEROSPACE CORPORATION (Subsidiary of Chrysler Corporation)

PO Box 2206, Savannah, Georgia 31402
Telephone: (912) 964 3000
Telex: 804 705 Gulfjet Sav

CHAIRMAN, PRESIDENT AND CHIEF EXECUTIVE OFFICER:
Allen E. Paulson

EXECUTIVE VICE-PRESIDENT AND CHIEF OPERATING OFFICER: Albert H. Glenn

SENIOR VICE-PRESIDENTS:
James L. Bradbury (Administration)
Charles N. Coppi
E. Brown Pinkston (Government Affairs and Military Marketing)

VICE-PRESIDENTS:
Joseph E. Anckner (International Sales)
Robert Buckley (Manufacturing)
Robert H. Cooper (Used Aircraft Marketing)
Herbert B. Franck (Domestic Marketing and Administration)
Richard Krajec (Treasurer)
John McCarthy (Material)
Allyn P. Robinson (Service and Product Support)
Robert K. Smyth (Flight Operations and Quality Control)
Charles A. Struve (Finance)

SECRETARY AND GENERAL COUNSEL: John P. Innes II

CORPORATE COMMUNICATIONS DIRECTOR:
Alvin F. Balaban

In late June 1985 the Chrysler Corporation announced that it was to acquire Gulfstream Aerospace Corporation for some $637 million. The takeover was completed on 16 August 1985.

Gulfstream Aerospace is currently producing the Gulfstream IV. It had 4,000 personnel in August 1986.

In March 1986 Gulfstream Aerospace acquired a 9,290 m² (100,000 sq ft) aircraft completion facility at Long Beach International Airport, California, which had been operated formerly by AiResearch Aviation. This facility will expand the company's ability to outfit and complete Gulfstream IVs for customer delivery, and will include a product support centre.

GULFSTREAM AEROSPACE GULFSTREAM II-B

Gulfstream modified a total of 40 Gulfstream IIs to II-B configuration, by retrofitting them with Gulfstream III wings. The programme has now been completed. Details can be found in the 1985-86 *Jane's*. The following data update the specification published in that edition:

DIMENSIONS, EXTERNAL:
Length overall — 24·97 m (81 ft 11 in)

WEIGHTS:
Basic operating weight empty — 17,304 kg (38,150 lb)
Max payload — 2,653 kg (5,850 lb)
Payload with max fuel — 1,701 kg (3,750 lb)

PERFORMANCE:
Cruising Mach number at max power at 12,160 m 39,900 ft), AUW of 24,947 kg (55,000 lb) — 0·85
Stalling speed at max landing weight, flaps down — 103 knots (191 km/h; 119 mph)
Max rate of climb at S/L — 1,300 m (4,270 ft)/min
Rate of climb at S/L, one engine out — 448 m (1,470 ft)/min
FAA T-O distance — 1,555 m (5,100 ft)
FAA landing distance — 975 m (3,200 ft)

Range with 8 passengers and baggage, NBAA IFR reserves — 3,640 nm (6,745 km; 4,190 miles)
Range with NBAA VFR reserves — 4,060 nm (7,524 km; 4,675 miles)

GULFSTREAM AEROSPACE GULFSTREAM III

USAF designation: C-20

The prototype Gulfstream III (N901G) made its first flight on 2 December 1979. FAA certification was received on 22 September 1980. A total of 206 had been built when production ended in late 1986.

Customers include the Italian Air Force, which took delivery of a single aircraft in September 1985 for use by the 31° Stormo Presidential Flight. In February 1986 Gulfstream business jets were in government service in 30 countries worldwide.

The United States Air Force announced on 7 June 1983 that it had awarded Gulfstream Aerospace a firm fixed-price contract covering the lease of standard off-the-shelf Gulfstream III transports, with accommodation for five crew and 14 passengers, as replacements for Lockheed C-140 aircraft under the Air Force Special Air Missions task (C-SAM). The contract covered the lease of three aircraft during fiscal years 1983 and 1984. These aircraft, designated **C-20A**, have since been purchased outright and are based at Ramstein AB, West Germany.

In January 1986 the United States Air Force awarded Gulfstream Aerospace a $142·5 million contract for the purchase of eight additional Gulfstream IIIs, of which delivery is expected to be completed by mid-1987. One aircraft will be configured as a C-20A; the remaining seven, outfitted with an advanced mission communications system and revised interior layout, are designated **C-20B**. These aircraft will serve with the 89th Military Airlift Wing at Andrews AFB, Maryland.

The following abbreviated description refers to the standard Gulfstream III transport. A full description can be found in the 1985-86 *Jane's*.

TYPE: Twin-turbofan executive transport.

POWER PLANT: Two Rolls-Royce Spey Mk 511-8 turbofan engines, each 50·7 kN (11,400 lb st), pod-mounted on sides of rear fuselage. Rohr target type thrust reverser forms aft part of each nacelle when in stowed position. All fuel in integral tanks in wings, with total capacity of 15,868 litres (4,192 US gallons).

ACCOMMODATION: Crew of two or three. Standard seating for 19 passengers in pressurised and air-conditioned cabin. Large baggage compartment at rear of cabin, capacity 907 kg (2,000 lb). Integral airstair door at front of cabin on port side. Electrically heated wraparound windscreen.

AVIONICS AND EQUIPMENT: Standard avionics include three Collins VHF com; two Collins VIR-31B VHF nav; two Collins ADF-60A; two Collins transponders; two Collins DME-40; cockpit voice recorders, Sperry SPZ-800 automatic flight guidance and control system; and Collins WXR-250A, or WXR-300; Bendix RDR-1200; or RCA Primus 40 WXD, or Primus 400 weather radar. Collins and Sperry electronic flight instrument systems available optionally. Bendix Series III integrated avionics system also certificated.

DIMENSIONS, EXTERNAL:
Wing span over winglets — 23·72 m (77 ft 10 in)
Wing aspect ratio — 6·0
Wing chord at root (fuselage centreline) — 5·94 m (19 ft 5⅞ in)
Winglet height — 1·63 m (5 ft 4¼ in)
Length overall — 25·32 m (83 ft 1 in)
Fuselage length — 22·66 m (74 ft 4 in)
Height overall — 7·43 m (24 ft 4½ in)
Tailplane span — 8·23 m (27 ft 0 in)
Wheel track — 4·17 m (13 ft 8 in)
Wheelbase — 10·72 m (35 ft 2 in)
Passenger door (fwd, port):
  Height — 1·57 m (5 ft 2 in)
  Width — 0·91 m (3 ft 0 in)
Baggage door (aft): Height — 0·90 m (2 ft 11¾ in)
  Width — 0·72 m (2 ft 4½ in)
Emergency exits (four; two overwing each side):
  Height — 0·48 m (1 ft 7 in)
  Width — 0·66 m (2 ft 2 in)

DIMENSIONS, INTERNAL:
Cabin: Length — 12·60 m (41 ft 4 in)
  Width — 2·24 m (7 ft 4 in)
  Height — 1·85 m (6 ft 1 in)
  Floor area — 20·14 m² (216·8 sq ft)

Gulfstream Aerospace C-20A for the US Air Force

Volume	42·53 m³ (1,502 cu ft)
Aft baggage compartment volume	4·44 m³ (157 cu ft)

WEIGHTS:

Manufacturer's weight empty	14,515 kg (32,000 lb)
Typical operating weight empty	17,236 kg (38,000 lb)
Max fuel load	12,836 kg (28,300 lb)
Typical payload	726 kg (1,600 lb)
Max T-O weight	31,615 kg (69,700 lb)
Max ramp weight	31,842 kg (70,200 lb)
Max zero-fuel weight	19,958 kg (44,000 lb)
Max landing weight	26,535 kg (58,500 lb)

PERFORMANCE:

Max cruising speed
Mach 0·85 (488 knots; 903 km/h; 561 mph)
Long-range cruising speed
Mach 0·77 (442 knots; 818 km/h; 508 mph)
Approach speed at max landing weight
133 knots (246 km/h; 153 mph)
Stalling speed at max landing weight
103 knots (191 km/h; 119 mph)
Max rate of climb at S/L 1,300 m (4,270 ft)/min
Rate of climb at S/L, one engine out
448 m (1,470 ft)/min
Max operating altitude 13,720 m (45,000 ft)
FAA balanced T-O field length 1,554 m (5,100 ft)
FAA landing distance 975 m (3,200 ft)
NBAA range, with 8 passengers and baggage:
IFR reserves 3,650 nm (6,760 km; 4,200 miles)
VFR reserves 4,070 nm (7,542 km; 4,686 miles)

OPERATIONAL NOISE LEVELS (FAR Pt 36):

T-O	91 EPNdB
Approach	97 EPNdB
Sideline	103 EPNdB

GULFSTREAM AEROSPACE GULFSTREAM III (SPECIAL MISSIONS VERSIONS)

Experience with specially equipped Gulfstream IIIs supplied to the Royal Danish Air Force for fishing patrol duties (see 1985-86 *Jane's*) led Gulfstream Aerospace to announce in September 1983 development of a dedicated **SRA-1** (Surveillance and Reconnaissance Aircraft). The prototype SRA-1 (N47449) was first flown on 14 August 1984, following a rollout ceremony at Savannah, Georgia. As rolled out, the SRA-1 prototype featured wingtip mounted antenna pods, but these were subsequently replaced by standard Gulfstream III winglets which will be fitted on all production aircraft unless customer specifications dictate otherwise. The SRA-1 can be supplied with fully integrated or stand-alone systems, according to customer requirements, for electronic surveillance, command control, stand-off high altitude reconnaissance, maritime patrol and surface surveillance, and anti-submarine warfare missions, or combinations of those roles. In addition, the aircraft can be reconfigured rapidly for VIP transportation, as a personnel/administrative transport with 18 passengers plus one attendant, for medical evacuation with 15 litter patients and two medical staff, or as a freight transport for up to 3,220 kg (7,100 lb) of priority cargo.

In electronic surveillance configuration the SRA-1 is equipped with a 20MHz to 1200MHz communications intercept system; a 0·5GHz to 40GHz electronic support measures (ESM) system; and VHF/UHF/HF communications for C³ functions; permitting accurate detection, location, analysis and classification of electronic signals. Operational capabilities include computer data bases to provide automatic signal analysis. A typical electronic surveillance mission for the SRA-1 with a crew of ten would have a gross weight of 31,743 kg (69,981 lb), providing a long-range patrol endurance of 8·8 hours and a range of 3,565 nm (6,607 km; 4,105 miles) with 1,361 kg (3,000 lb) fuel reserves (ISA, zero wind). For a high altitude loiter mission at the same gross weight and reserves, the SRA-1 could remain airborne for 9·6 hours, with a range of 3,257 nm (6,036 km; 3,750 miles)

In the maritime patrol role the SRA-1 is equipped with high definition, all-weather, real-time search radar in a hinged nosecone; a forward looking infra-red system (FLIR); ESM system; and stowage and manual launch systems for survival/rescue equipment, marine markers and flares. With a crew of five, mission gross weight of 30,810 kg (67,924 lb), and a fuel reserve of 1,361 kg (3,000 lb), ISA, zero wind, the SRA-1 has a mission endurance of 9·2 hours and a range of 3,017 nm (5,591 km; 3,474 miles) at a 9,140 m (30,000 ft) patrol altitude. For SAR missions, at a gross weight of 31,842 kg (70,200 lb) including a 1,032 kg (2,276 lb) retained payload, the SRA-1 can operate within a 1,000 nm (1,853 km; 1,151 mile) radius of action and fly an 8-hour mission.

In reconnaissance configuration the SRA-1 is equipped with real-time, all-weather moving target indicator SLAR; long-range oblique photographic cameras, which may include electro-optical capability; and an ESM system. With a crew of seven the aircraft has a loiter endurance of 9·7 hours at altitudes above 7,620 m (25,000 ft).

For anti-submarine warfare missions the SRA-1 can be equipped with a high definition maritime surveillance radar with periscope/snort detection; FLIR; a boom mounted magnetic anomaly detector (MAD) extending from the rear fuselage beneath the fin/rudder; ESM; acoustic processing equipment; sonobuoys; and automated data recording for post-flight mission analysis. Weapons on underwing hardpoints can include a wide variety of air-to-surface and anti-shipping missiles and torpedoes.

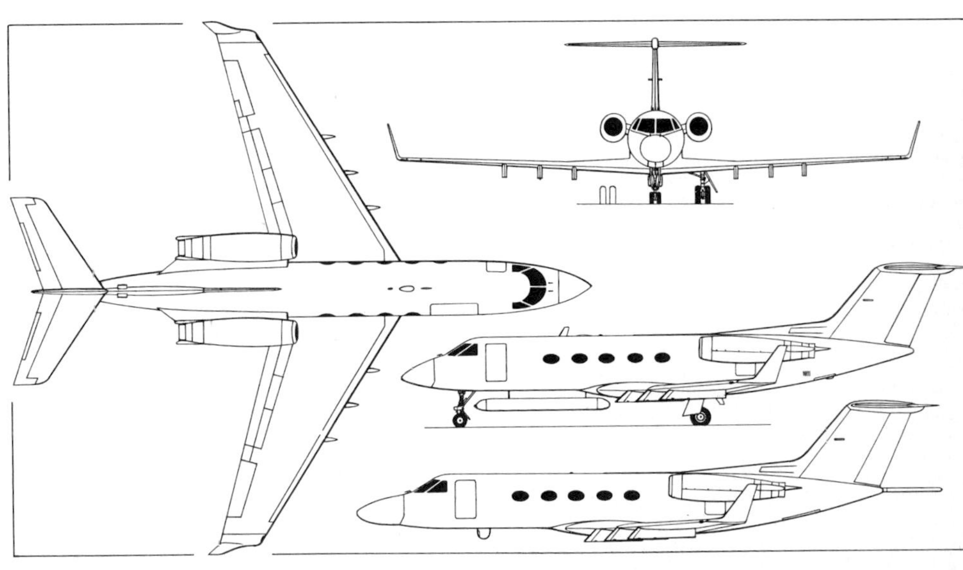
Gulfstream Aerospace SRA-1 SLAR version, with added side elevation (bottom) of ASW version *(Pilot Press)*

Gulfstream Aerospace Gulfstream III of the Egyptian Air Force *(R. Kunert)*

WEIGHTS: As for Gulfstream III except:

Manufacturer's weight empty 14,834 kg (32,703 lb)
Basic weight empty (excl mission equipment)
16,408 kg (36,173 lb)
Max payload (cargo) 3,220 kg (7,100 lb)

PERFORMANCE: As for Gulfstream III except:

NBAA range at Mach 0·77 with with crew of three and 725 kg (1,600 lb) payload:
IFR reserves 3,500 nm (6,486 km; 4,030 miles)
VFR reserves 3,940 nm (7,302 km; 4,537 miles)

GULFSTREAM AEROSPACE GULFSTREAM IV

Gulfstream Aerospace Corporation has developed an improved version of the Gulfstream III which is designated G1159C Gulfstream IV. Its design was initiated in March 1983, and construction of four (three for an 850-hour flight test programme, and one static test airframe) production prototypes began in 1985. Rollout of the first aircraft (N404GA) occurred on 11 September 1985, with a first flight following on 19 September. The second prototype made its first flight on 11 June 1986, at which time the company held orders for 94 Gulfstream IVs. A third test aircraft was expected to fly during August 1986. Initial FAA certification was scheduled for September 1986, with deliveries of ten 'green' production aircraft anticipated by the end of the year. Production of Gulfstream IVs is expected to rise to four per month by the end of 1987, during which year deliveries of 43 are anticipated.

Generally similar to the Gulfstream III, this new version differs primarily in having a structurally redesigned wing, incorporating 30 per cent fewer parts and offering a weight saving of 395 kg (870 lb) with provision for 453 kg (1,000 lb) more internal fuel capacity; a tailplane of increased span; a fuselage lengthened by 1·37 m (4 ft 6 in); a sixth window on each side of the cabin; rudder, ailerons and spoilers made of carbonfibre; new Rolls-Royce RB183-03 Tay Mk 610-8 turbofan engines; and a flight deck incorporating advanced CRT displays and digital avionics.

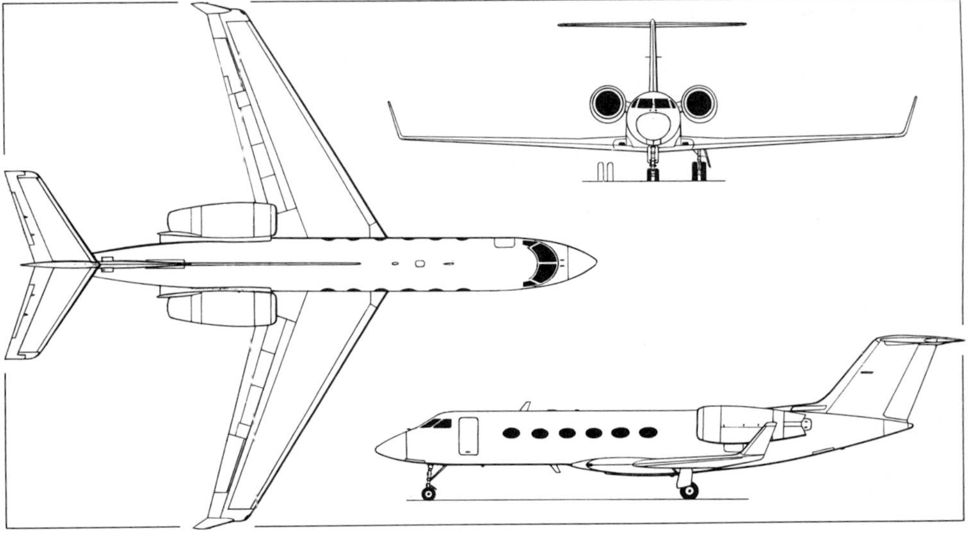
Gulfstream Aerospace Gulfstream IV twin-turbofan executive transport *(Pilot Press)*

Gulfstream Aerospace has extended the SRA-1 concept (see previous entry) to the Gulfstream IV under the designation **SRA-4**. The SRA-4 will be able to perform the same range of missions as the SRA-1, but with an 18 per cent increase in maximum range, 11 per cent increase in endurance and 12 per cent increase in interior equipment volume. The aircraft will be offered in surveillance/reconnaissance, anti-submarine warfare, maritime patrol, medical evacuation, administrative transport and priority cargo variants.

The following details refer to the standard executive transport:

TYPE: Twin-turbofan executive transport.

WINGS: Cantilever low-wing monoplane of light alloy construction, with carbonfibre ailerons and spoilers. Advanced sonic rooftop wing section. Thickness/chord ratio of 10% at wing station 50 and 8·6% at wing station 414. Dihedral 3°. Incidence 3° 30′ at root, −2° at tip. Sweepback at quarter-chord 27° 40′. NASA (Whitcomb) winglets. Plain ailerons, hydraulically powered with manual reversion. Single-slotted Fowler trailing-edge flaps. Three spoilers on upper surface of each wing at 12% chord, immediately forward of trailing-edge flaps, operated differentially to complement ailerons for roll control and collectively to serve as airbrakes. Trim tab in port aileron. Anti-icing of leading-edges by engine bleed air.

FUSELAGE: Conventional semi-monocoque fail-safe pressurised structure of light alloy, with carbonfibre in cabin floor and flight deck areas.

TAIL UNIT: Cantilever T tail of light alloy, except for rudder and some tailplane components of carbonfibre. Swept horizontal and vertical surfaces. Trim tab in rudder and each elevator. Hydraulically powered controls with manual reversion.

LANDING GEAR: Retractable tricycle type with twin wheels on each unit. Main units retract inward, steerable nose unit forward. Mainwheel tyres size 34 × 9·25-16, pressure 12·07 bars (175 lb/sq in). Nosewheel tyres size 21 × 7·25-10, pressure 7·9 bars (115 lb/sq in). Goodyear aircooled carbon brakes, with Goodyear fully modulating anti-skid units. Goodyear digital electronic brake-by-wire system. Dowty electronic steer-by-wire system.

POWER PLANT: Two Rolls-Royce Tay Mk 610-8 turbofan engines, each flat rated at 55·24 kN (12,420 lb st) to ISA +20°C. Target type thrust reversers. Fuel in two integral wing tanks, with total capacity of 16,428 litres (4,340 US gallons). Single pressure fuelling point in leading-edge of starboard wing.

ACCOMMODATION: Crew of two or three. Standard seating for 14 to 19 passengers in pressurised and air-conditioned cabin. Galley, toilet and large baggage compartment, capacity 907 kg (2,000 lb), at rear of cabin. Integral airstair door at front of cabin on port side. Baggage compartment door on port side. Electrically heated wraparound windscreen. Six cabin windows on each side.

SYSTEMS: Cabin pressurisation system max differential 0·65 bars (9·45 lb/sq in). Air-conditioning system. Two independent hydraulic systems, each 207 bars (3,000 lb/sq in). Maximum flow rate 83·3 litres (22 US gallons)/min. Two bootstrap type hydraulic reservoirs, pressurised to 4·14 bars (60 lb/sq in). Garrett GTCP36-100 APU in tail compartment, flight rated to 10,670 m (35,000 ft). Electrical system includes two 36kVA alternators with two solid state 30kVA converters to provide 23kVA 115/200V 400Hz AC power and 250A of regulated 28V DC power; two 24V 40Ah nickel-cadmium storage batteries and external power socket.

AVIONICS AND EQUIPMENT: Standard items include a Sperry fully integrated digital flight management system with six 20·3 cm × 20·3 cm (8 in × 8 in) colour CRT displays, two each for primary flight instruments, navigation and engine instrument and crew alerting systems (EICAS); dual fail-operational flight guidance systems including auto throttles; dual air data systems; dual flight management systems with vertical and lateral navigation and performance management, and digital colour radar. System integration is accomplished through a Sperry avionics standard communications bus (ASCB). Other factory-installed avionics include dual VHF/HF com; dual VOR/LOC/GS and markers; dual DME; dual ADF; dual radio altimeters; dual transponders; dual cockpit audio; dual flight guidance and performance computers; dual laser INS; dual ILS receivers with Cat III capability; attitude/heading reference system; and cockpit voice recorder. The system is designed to provide growth potential for interface with MLS, GPS and VLF Omega in future developments.

DIMENSIONS, EXTERNAL:

Wing span over winglets	23·72 m (77 ft 10 in)
Wing chord:	
at root (fuselage centreline	5·94 m (19 ft 5⅞ in)
at tip	1·85 m (6 ft 0¾ in)
Wing aspect ratio	6·0
Length overall	26·70 m (87 ft 7 in)
Fuselage length	24·03 m (78 ft 10 in)
Fuselage: Max diameter	2·39 m (7 ft 10 in)
Height overall	7·42 m (24 ft 4 in)
Tailplane span	9·75 m (32 ft 0 in)
Wheel track	4·17 m (13 ft 8 in)
Wheelbase	11·61 m (38 ft 1¼ in)
Passenger door (fwd, port):	
Height	1·57 m (5 ft 2 in)
Width	0·91 m (3 ft 0 in)
Baggage door (rear):	
Height	0·72 m (2 ft 4½ in)
Width	0·91 m (2 ft 11¾ in)

DIMENSIONS, INTERNAL:

Cabin:	
Length, incl galley, toilet and baggage compartment	13·74 m (45 ft 1 in)
Max width	2·24 m (7 ft 4 in)
Max height	1·85 m (6 ft 1 in)
Floor area	21·8 m² (235 sq ft)
Volume	47·77 m³ (1,687 cu ft)
Cabin volume	42·96 m³ (1,517 cu ft)
Passenger area volume	30·55 m³ (1,079 cu ft)
Flight deck volume	3·51 m³ (124 cu ft)
Rear baggage compartment volume	4·81 m³ (170 cu ft)

AREAS: As for Gulfstream III except:

Wings, gross	88·29 m² (950·39 sq ft)
Horizontal tail surfaces (total)	14·10 m² (151·72 sq ft)

WEIGHTS AND LOADINGS:

Manufacturer's weight empty	15,150 kg (33,400 lb)
Typical operating weight empty	17,826 kg (39,300 lb)
Max payload	2,132 kg (4,700 lb)
Max fuel weight	13,290 kg (29,300 lb)
Max T-O weight	31,615 kg (69,700 lb)
Max ramp weight	31,842 kg (70,200 lb)
Max zero-fuel weight	19,958 kg (44,000 lb)
Max landing weight	26,535 kg (58,500 lb)
Max wing loading	358·1 kg/m² (73·34 lb/sq ft)
Max power loading	286·0 kg/kN (2·8 lb/lb st)

PERFORMANCE (at max T-O weight, ISA, except where indicated):

Max operating speed	340 knots (629 km/h; 391 mph) CAS *or* Mach 0·88
Max cruising speed at 10,670 m (35,000 ft)	501 knots (928 km/h; 577 mph)
Normal cruising speed at 13,715 m (45,000 ft)	Mach 0·80 (459 knots; 850 km/h; 528 mph)
Stalling speed at max landing weight:	
clean	120 knots (222 km/h; 138 mph)
wheels and flaps down	101 knots (187 km/h; 117 mph)
Approach speed at max landing weight	131 knots (243 km/h; 151 mph)
Max rate of climb at S/L	1,240 m (4,070 ft)/min
Rate of climb at S/L, one engine out	330 m (1,080 ft)/min
Max operating altitude	13,715 m (45,000 ft)
Runway LCN	33
FAA balanced T-O field length at S/L	1,554 m (5,100 ft)
Landing from 15 m (50 ft)	975 m (3,200 ft)
Range with max payload, normal cruising speed and NBAA IFR reserves	3,640 nm (6,745 km; 4,191 miles)
Range with max fuel, eight passengers, at Mach 0·80 and with NBAA IFR reserves	4,300 nm (7,969 km; 4,952 miles)

OPERATIONAL NOISE LEVELS (FAR Pt 36):

T-O	77·7 EPNdB
Approach	90·7 EPNdB
Sideline	92·0 EPNdB

GULFSTREAM AEROSPACE GULFSTREAM IV-B

In March 1985 Gulfstream Aerospace announced details of a proposed airliner version of the Gulfstream IV designated **Gulfstream IV-B**. This aircraft, the configuration of which was prompted by enquiries from two US airline operators, would have a fuselage 5·64 m (18 ft 6 in) longer than that of the Gulfstream IV, achieved by the insertion of plugs forward and aft of the wing centre-section, but would retain its engines, wings, tail surfaces and systems. The Gulfstream IV-B would offer accommodation for 24 passengers in first class seating, plus four crew. The aircraft would have an empty weight of 16,465 kg (36,300 lb), max T-O weight 35,516 kg (78,300 lb), max fuel weight 13,290 kg (29,300 lb), cabin volume 58·3 m³ (2,060 cu ft), baggage compartment volume 4·81 m³ (170 cu ft), and a maximum range with IFR reserves of 3,800 nm (7,042 km; 4,376 miles). A corporate airliner version, and an all-cargo **Gulfstream Cargoliner** variant with a 6,804 kg (15,000 lb) payload capacity, 63·1 m³ (2,230 cu ft) of cargo space and a maximum range of 3,000 nm (5,560 km; 3,454 miles), have also been proposed. In Summer 1986 no decision had been made on development of the Gulfstream IV-B. Gulfstream Aerospace has said that certification could be achieved some 24 months after a launch order.

Gulfstream IV during its first flight on 19 September 1985

GULFSTREAM AEROSPACE CORPORATION, OKLAHOMA OPERATIONS

Wiley Post Airport, Box 22500, Oklahoma City, Oklahoma 73123
Telephone: (405) 789 5000
Telex: 747193
PRESIDENT: Allen E. Paulson
SENIOR VICE-PRESIDENT AND CHIEF OPERATING OFFICER:
Bill M. Humes
VICE-PRESIDENT:
Clifford M. Shirley (Marketing)
DIVISION EXECUTIVES:
Ed Crist (Director, Information Systems)
Sherman Dobbs (Director, Material)
Kenneth L. Hale (Director, Engineering)
Richard Hazlin (Manager, Product Support)
William McGinnis (Director, Manufacturing)
A. Wayne Radko (Controller)
William Ziegler (Director, Personnel)

Gulfstream Aerospace's Oklahoma facility, used formerly for the production of the Gulfstream Commander Jetprop series of turboprop business aircraft, now manufactures components and subassemblies for Gulfstream's jet aircraft.

HAWK

HAWK INTERNATIONAL

57430 Aviation Drive, Yucca Valley, California 92284
Telephone: (619) 365 1831
PRESIDENT: Ernest Hawk

Hawk International (formerly the Aircraft Division of Hawk Industries until 1984), specialises in equipment for oil and water well drilling and fencing. As a result of difficulties in transporting its products, the company's President initiated in July 1977 the design of a freight carrying aircraft that might overcome both the slowness of road transport and the high cost and loading/unloading difficulties of conventional aircraft. He named his project GafHawk 125, signifying general aviation freighter. It is intended to be certificated initially at a gross weight of 5,670 kg (12,500 lb) under FAR Pt 23, although it would be capable of operating at a max T-O weight of 6,577 kg (14,500 lb). Larger and smaller developed versions of the GafHawk 125 are under consideration.

HAWK GAFHAWK 125

Features considered of prime importance in design of the GafHawk included STOL capability for operation into and from small unprepared strips, a turboprop power plant for economic operation, a square-section fuselage for maximum utilisation of internal capacity, undertail loading of bulk cargo at truckbed height, and a single engine for economy, ease of certification and single-pilot operation.

The GafHawk concept was tested initially in the form of a small scale flying testbed known as the MiniHawk, which consisted of an extensively rebuilt Piper Tri-Pacer light aircraft. This made its first flight in 1978, and was described and illustrated in the 1980-81 *Jane's*.

The GafHawk 125 prototype (N101GH) was flown for the first time on 19 August 1982, powered by an 893 kW (1,198 shp) Pratt & Whitney Canada PT6A-45R turboprop engine. In early 1986 negotiations were under way for the establishment of an offshore production facility.

TYPE: Single-engined turboprop freighter.

WINGS: Strut braced high-wing monoplane, with dual steel alloy struts enclosed in an aluminium fairing to provide redundancy, plus short dual auxiliary struts on each side. Wing section NASA GAW-1, modified by use of a leading-edge cuff. Thickness/chord ratio 17%. No dihedral. Constant chord fail-safe structure of light alloy, comprising a leading-edge tubular spar, a box spar, a second tubular spar aft of the box, a total of 78 one-piece ribs, and light alloy skins. Electrically actuated full span trailing-edge flaps of similar construction. Half span spoiler/aileron ('rolleron') hinged to top surface within slot between wing and flap in outer half of each wing, operating differentially through a range of 60° up and 10° down. Rolleron trimming by bungee.

FUSELAGE: Basic rectangular structure of welded square-section chrome-molybdenum steel tubing, covered with non-structural corrugated Alclad light alloy skins. These are attached to the hermetically sealed square tubing by clips, to facilitate the replacement of damaged sections.

TAIL UNIT: Cantilever structure of light alloy. Construction similar to that of wings, but with only fore and aft tubular spars in fin and tailplane. Horn balanced rudder and one-piece elevator. Dorsal fin. Rudder and elevator have servo tabs and electrically actuated trim tabs.

LANDING GEAR: Non-retractable tricycle type, with single wheel on nosewheel and dual wheels on main units. All units have shock absorption by rubber elastomer in compression. Goodyear tyres and wheels of the same size on each unit, with tubed tyres size 8·50-10. For 'bush' operations single main wheel, size 15·00-12, available optionally. Goodyear hydraulic disc brakes. Parking brake.

POWER PLANT: One Pratt & Whitney Canada PT6A-65B/R turboprop engine, with a max continuous rating of 875 kW (1,173 shp), driving a Hartzell five-blade reversible-pitch constant-speed metal propeller with spinner. Fuel tank, made of transparent glassfibre and with a capacity of 1,363 litres (360 US gallons), mounted above forward fuselage, directly over the wing, and providing gravity feed to engine. Refuelling point on upper surface of tank. Two aluminium fuel tanks, with a combined capacity of 3,785 litres (1,000 US gallons), can be installed in the main cargo hold for long ferry flights. Oil capacity 11·5 litres (3 US gallons). Engine air intake incorporates an ice ramp and a foreign particle reducer. Electrically heated de-icing boots for propeller and engine air intake.

ACCOMMODATION: Pilot and co-pilot on flight deck. Dual controls and full blind-flying instrumentation for both pilots standard. Door to flight deck on each side of fuselage; communicating door between flight deck and cargo hold in forward bulkhead. Cabin door on each side, aft of wing. Electrically actuated upward/inward-opening main cargo door, in undersurface of upswept rear fuselage, can be opened in flight. Heavy duty corrugated light alloy floor in cargo hold, with cargo tiedowns along walls at each fuselage gusset frame, and tailgate for loading. Main cabin volume augmented by usable space under flight deck, accommodating pipes and timber up to 6·1 m (20 ft) in length with rear loading door closed. Accommodation heated and ventilated.

SYSTEMS: Electrical system powered by 28V 250A Lear Siegler starter/generator and 28V storage battery. Hydraulic system for brakes only. Vacuum system. De-icing system optional.

AVIONICS AND EQUIPMENT: Standard avionics include King Gold Crown series dual com; dual nav with dual ILS, plus an HSI on the pilot's panel; ADF; DME; radar altimeter; transponder; switching panel; and VOR/localiser-coupled Century II-B autopilot. Standard equipment includes dual blind-flying instrumentation, incl turn co-ordinator and rate of climb indicator; dual airspeed indicators; dual altimeters, one with encoding; eight-day clock; outside air temperature gauge; adjustable pilot/co-pilot seats with armrests; control locks; annunciator panel; cabin, compass, instrument post, landing, navigation, taxi and wingtip strobe lights; two rotating beacons; and heated pitot.

DIMENSIONS, EXTERNAL:
Wing span — 21·79 m (71 ft 6 in)
Wing chord (constant) — 2·11 m (6 ft 11 in)
Wing aspect ratio — 10·4
Length overall — 14·30 m (46 ft 11 in)
Height overall — 5·49 m (18 ft 0 in)
Tailplane span — 7·01 m (23 ft 0 in)
Wheel track (c/l outer tyres) — 3·38 m (11 ft 1 in)
Wheelbase — 4·39 m (14 ft 5 in)
Propeller diameter — 2·74 m (9 ft 0 in)
Rear ramp/door: Length — 1·78 m (5 ft 10 in)
Width — 1·96 m (6 ft 5 in)

DIMENSIONS, INTERNAL:
Cabin: Length at floor level, excl flight deck — 4·72 m (15 ft 6 in)
Max width — 2·03 m (6 ft 8 in)
Max height — 2·13 m (7 ft 0 in)
Volume — 20·22 m³ (714 cu ft)

AREA:
Wings, gross — 45·8 m² (493 sq ft)

WEIGHTS AND LOADINGS (estimated):
Weight empty — 3,085 kg (6,800 lb)
Max design T-O weight — 6,577 kg (14,500 lb)
Max wing loading — 143·6 kg/m² (29·4 lb/sq ft)
Max power loading — 7·52 kg/kW (12·36 lb/shp)

PERFORMANCE (prototype, at max design T-O weight):
Max cruising speed at 3,050 m (10,000 ft) — 120 knots (222 km/h; 138 mph)
Econ cruising speed (55% power) at 3,050 m (10,000 ft) — 110 knots (204 km/h; 127 mph)
Stalling speed, flaps down, power on — 47 knots (87 km/h; 54 mph)
Max rate of climb at S/L — 280 m (920 ft)/min
Service ceiling — 5,485 m (18,000 ft)
T-O run — 287 m (940 ft)
T-O to 15 m (50 ft) — 506 m (1,660 ft)
Landing from 15 m (50 ft) — 436 m (1,430 ft)
Landing run — 201 m (660 ft)
Range with max fuel — 716 nm (1,326 km; 824 miles)

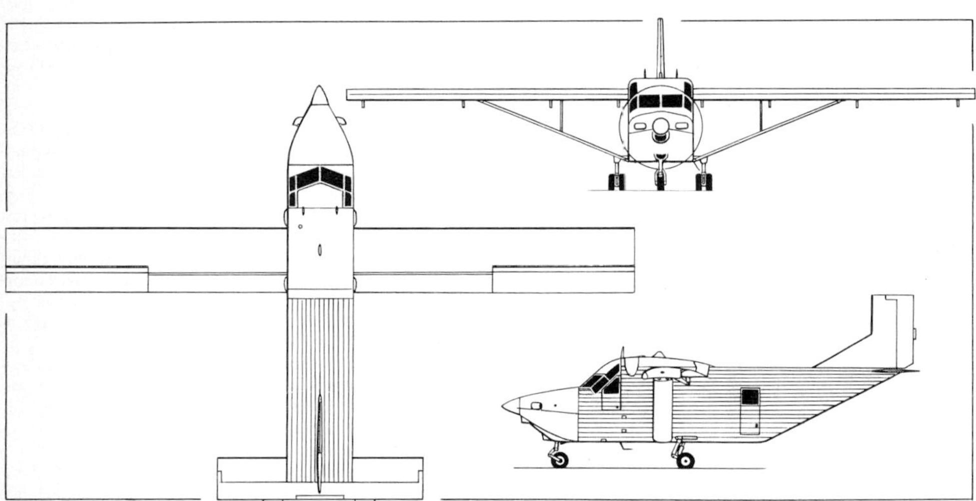

Drawing *(Pilot Press)* **and photograph of Hawk GafHawk 125 (P&WC PT6A-45R turboprop engine)**

HAYES

HAYES INTERNATIONAL CORPORATION (Dothan Division)

PO Box 929, Dothan-Houston County Airport, Dothan, Alabama 36302-0929
Telephone: (205) 983 4571
Telex: 782123

Vice-President and Division Manager:
George A. Lindholm

Hayes International's Dothan Division was appointed by British Aerospace to undertake conversion of the BAe 146 Series 200 (see UK section) to all-cargo configuration. Hayes designed, manufactured and installed a port-side upward opening door (3·30 m; 10 ft 10 in wide by 1·98 m; 6 ft 6 in deep) in the rear fuselage, forward of the rear passenger door; undertook the necessary structural strengthening; and installed interior furnishings and cargo handling equipment.

The converted aircraft is operable in either all-cargo or passenger/cargo combi configuration. It will be marketed by BAe, but Hayes will be responsible for obtaining the FAA supplemental type certificate.

HELIO

HELIO AIRCRAFT LTD

PO Box 604, Highway 126, Pittsburg, Kansas 66762
Telephone: (316) 231 0200
President: James E. Cox

This company acquired from Helio Precision Products in 1976 the tooling, production rights and type certification for all models of the Helio Courier and other Helio STOL designs. Details of these aircraft can be found under the Helio Aircraft Company entry in the 1976-77 and earlier editions of *Jane's*. In mid-1984 Helio was acquired by Aerospace Technology Industries.

HELIO COURIER 700 and 800

Helio Aircraft Ltd is producing the six-seat **Courier 800**. This is a version of the earlier Super Courier Model H-295 in which the 220 kW (295 hp) power plant of the H-295 is replaced by a 298 kW (400 hp) Avco Lycoming IO-720-A1B flat-eight fuel-injected engine. First flight in this form was made on 24 March 1983, and initial deliveries were made during late 1983. The Courier 800 retains, with modified tips, the familiar Helio STOL wing, embodying slotted trailing-edge flaps over 74 per cent of the span, ailerons and spoilers for roll control, and leading-edge slats which extend at high angles of attack and in slow flight. It is available in standard form with tailwheel landing gear, but tricycle wheeled gear, skis or Edo amphibious floats are available optionally.

The company also manufactures the **Courier 700**, which is generally similar to the Courier 800 but has a 261 kW (350 hp) Avco Lycoming TIO-540-J2B turbocharged and fuel-injected flat-six engine. It is available with the same landing gear options as the Courier 800.

Helio Courier Model 800 six-seat STOL transport

HELIO MODEL 21A RAT'LER

Helio displayed a prototype of this low-wing agricultural aircraft at the Agricultural Aviation Convention in Las Vegas, Nevada in December 1984. Designated Model 21A Rat'ler, the aircraft (N4405S) combines the wing, tail unit and 298 kW (400 hp) Avco Lycoming IO-720-A1B engine of the Helio Courier 800 with a new fuselage which incorporates a 1,514 litre (400 US gallon) chemical hopper and a raised single-seat cockpit. Other features include glassfibre wingtips designed to reduce vortices, a new wing carry-through structure, and landing gear legs of composites materials.

Helio Model 21A Rat'ler agricultural aircraft *(Howard Levy)*

HELIO STALLION

There are plans to put back into production the eight/ten-seat utility STOL aircraft which the former Helio Aircraft Company marketed as the Stallion Model H-550A. In 1985 Helio was reported to be working on a number of turbine engined prototypes, one of which was a floatplane.

HILLER — *see Rogerson*

HUGHES — *see McDonnell Douglas*

HYNES

HYNES HELICOPTER (Division of Hynes Aviation Industries Inc)

PO Box 697, Frederick, Oklahoma 73542
Telephone: (405) 335 7511
President: Michael K. Hynes
Vice-President:
Kevin P. Hynes (Technical Services)
Chief Engineer: Humayun Kabir

This company was formed on 1 January 1975 (initially as Brantly-Hynes Helicopter Inc) to replace Brantly Operators Inc, which had acquired all rights in Brantly helicopters in late 1970. Its President, Mr M. K. Hynes, acquired also ownership of the type certificates for the Brantly B-2, B-2A, B-2B and Model 305.

Hynes has put the two-seat H-2 (formerly B-2B) back into production, and announced in 1984 an instrument trainer version, designated **H-2-I**. Approximately 400 B-2B/H-2s have been delivered; Hynes expected to produce four model H-2s in 1986. The former Model 305 will return to production as the Hynes H-5.

Remotely piloted versions of the H-2 and H-5 are now available, as described in the RPVs and Targets section.

HYNES H-2

Type: Two-seat light helicopter.

Rotor System: Three-blade main rotor. Articulated inboard flapping hinges offset 0·07 m (2·67 in) from hub, and coincident flap and lag hinges offset 1·31 m (4 ft 3¾ in) from rotor head. Symmetrical blade section with 29% thickness/chord ratio on inboard portion; NACA 0012 section outboard of hinge. Blades are semi-rigid at hub and fully articulated at inboard/outboard junction (40 per cent blade span) to eliminate ground resonance. Inboard portion of each blade is built around a steel spar, outboard portion has an extruded aluminium leading-edge spar and polyurethane core; aluminium skin is bonded to core and riveted to spar. Blades are attached to head by flapping links; they do not fold, but can be quickly separated at inboard/outboard junction for easy storage. A rotor brake is standard equipment. Two-blade all-metal anti-torque tail rotor.

Rotor Drive: Through automatic centrifugal clutch and planetary reduction gears. Bevel gear take-off from main transmission with flexible coupling via intermediate and upper gearboxes to tail rotor driveshaft. Main rotor/engine rpm ratio 1 : 6·0. Tail rotor/engine rpm ratio 1 : 1.

Fuselage: Stressed skin all-metal structure with conical tail section and small fixed horizontal stabilisers. Tail rotor on swept-up boom extension.

Landing Gear: Alternative skid, wheel or float gear. Skid type has small retractable wheels for ground handling, fixed tailskid and four shock absorbers with rubber in compression. Inflatable pontoons, which attach to standard skids, are available to permit operation from water. Alternative non-retractable tricycle landing gear has oleo-pneumatic shock absorbers in all units, with single wheels on main units and twin castoring nosewheels. Goodyear tyres size 10 × 3½, pressure 2·07 bars (30 lb/sq in), on mainwheels; tyre pressure 1·93 bars (28 lb/sq in) on nosewheels. Goodyear mainwheel brakes.

Power Plant: One 134 kW (180 hp) Avco Lycoming IVO-360-A1A flat-four engine, mounted vertically, with dual fan cooling system. Rubber bag type fuel tank under engine, capacity 117 litres (31 US gallons). Refuelling point on port side of fuselage. Oil capacity 5·7 litres (1·5 US gallons).

Accommodation: Totally enclosed circular section cabin for two persons seated side by side. Forward hinged door on each side. Dual controls, cabin heater and demisting fan standard. Compartment for 22·7 kg (50 lb) baggage in forward end of tail section.

Avionics and Equipment: Provision for all standard nav/com radios. Blind-flying instrumentation available as an option, but the Model B-2B is not certificated for instrument flight. Twin landing lights in nose.

Dimensions, external:

Main rotor diameter	7·24 m (23 ft 9 in)
Main rotor blade chord: inboard	0·225 m (8·85 in)
outboard	0·203 m (8·0 in)
Tail rotor diameter	1·30 m (4 ft 3 in)

Brantly-Hynes Model B-2B in Hynes H-2 configuration *(Brian M. Service)*

Length overall, rotors turning	8·53 m (28 ft 0 in)
Length of fuselage	6·62 m (21 ft 9 in)
Height overall	2·06 m (6 ft 9 in)
Skid track	1·73 m (5 ft 8¼ in)
Passenger doors (each): Height	0·79 m (2 ft 7 in)
Width	0·86 m (2 ft 9¾ in)
Baggage compartment door:	
Mean height	0·25 m (9¾ in)
Length	0·55 m (1 ft 9¾ in)

Dimensions, internal:

Cabin: Length	1·83 m (6 ft 0 in)
Max width	1·19 m (3 ft 11 in)
Max height	0·99 m (3 ft 3 in)
Floor area	2·60 m² (28·0 sq ft)
Volume	2·78 m³ (98·0 cu ft)
Baggage compartment	0·17 m³ (6·0 cu ft)

Areas:

Main rotor blades (each)	0·69 m² (7·42 sq ft)
Main rotor disc	41·16 m² (443 sq ft)
Tail rotor disc	1·32 m² (14·19 sq ft)

Weights and Loadings:

Weight empty: with skids	463 kg (1,020 lb)
with floats	481 kg (1,060 lb)
Max T-O weight	757 kg (1,670 lb)
Max disc loading	18·40 kg/m² (3·77 lb/sq ft)
Max power loading	5·65 kg/kW (9·27 lb/hp)

Performance (at max T-O weight):

Max level speed at S/L	87 knots (161 km/h; 100 mph)
Max cruising speed (75% power)	78 knots (145 km/h; 90 mph)
Max rate of climb at S/L	580 m (1,900 ft)/min
Service ceiling	3,290 m (10,800 ft)
Hovering ceiling IGE	2,040 m (6,700 ft)
Range with max fuel, with reserves	217 nm (400 km; 250 miles)

HYNES H-5

The H-5 (originally Brantly Model 305) is a five-seat helicopter of similar configuration to the H-2, but larger in every respect. The Model 305 prototype flew for the first time in January 1964, and FAA type approval was received on 29 July 1965. The following description applies to the certificated passenger carrying version:

Type: Five-seat light helicopter.

Rotor System and Drive: As described for H-2, except rotor/engine rpm ratio 1 : 6·6.

Fuselage and Tail Unit: As described for H-2.

Landing Gear: Choice of skid, wheel or float gear. Skid type has four oleo struts, two on each side, and small retractable ground handling wheels. The wheel gear has single mainwheels and twin nosewheels, all with oleo-pneumatic shock absorbers. Goodyear mainwheels and tyres size 6·00-6, pressure 2·07 bars (30 lb/sq in); Goodyear nosewheels and tyres size 5·00-5, pressure 1·93 bars (28 lb/sq in). Goodyear single-disc hydraulic brakes on mainwheels.

Power Plant: One 227·4 kW (305 hp) Avco Lycoming IVO-540-B1A flat-six engine, mounted vertically, with dual cooling fans. One rubber fuel cell under engine, capacity 163 litres (43 US gallons). Refuelling point in port side of fuselage. Oil capacity 9·5 litres (2·5 US gallons).

Accommodation: Two individual seats side by side, with dual controls. Rear bench seat for three persons. Door on each side. Rear compartment for 113 kg (250 lb) of baggage, with downward hinged door on starboard side.

Avionics and Equipment: King or Narco radio, to customer's specification. Blind-flying instrumentation is available, but helicopter is not certificated for instrument flight.

Dimensions, external:

Main rotor diameter	8·74 m (28 ft 8 in)
Main rotor blade chord (constant)	0·254 m (10 in)
Tail rotor diameter	1·30 m (4 ft 3 in)
Length overall, rotors turning	10·03 m (32 ft 11 in)
Length of fuselage	7·44 m (24 ft 5 in)
Height overall	2·44 m (6 ft 0⅛ in)
Wheel track	2·10 m (6 ft 10¾ in)
Wheelbase	2·15 m (7 ft 0½ in)
Passenger doors (each): Height	0·82 m (2 ft 8⅛ in)
Width	1·02 m (3 ft 3⅞ in)
Baggage compartment door:	
Mean height	0·30 m (1 ft 0¼ in)
Width	0·69 m (2 ft 3 in)

Dimensions, internal:

Cabin: Length	2·30 m (7 ft 6½ in)
Max width	1·39 m (4 ft 6¾ in)
Max height	1·22 m (4 ft 0½ in)
Baggage compartment	0·47 m³ (16·7 cu ft)

Areas:

Main rotor blades (each)	0·09 m² (11·79 sq ft)
Tail rotor blades (each)	0·05 m² (0·50 sq ft)
Main rotor disc	59·96 m² (645·4 sq ft)
Tail rotor disc	1·32 m² (14·19 sq ft)

Weights and Loadings:

Weight empty	816 kg (1,800 lb)
Max T-O and landing weight	1,315 kg (2,900 lb)
Max zero-fuel weight	1,224 kg (2,700 lb)
Max disc loading	21·92 kg/m² (4·49 lb/sq ft)
Max power loading	5·78 kg/kW (9·51 lb/hp)

Performance (at max T-O weight):

Max level speed at S/L	104 knots (193 km/h; 120 mph)
Max cruising speed at S/L	96 knots (177 km/h; 110 mph)
Max rate of climb at S/L	297 m (975 ft)/min
Service ceiling	3,660 m (12,000 ft)
Hovering ceiling IGE	1,245 m (4,080 ft)
Range with max fuel and max payload, 15 min reserves	191 nm (354 km; 220 miles)

Brantly-Hynes Model 305, returning to production as the Hynes H-5

IAC

INTERNATIONAL AEROMARINE CORPORATION

475 Silverlake Road, Sanford, Florida 32771

President: Joseph W. Gurnow

Vice-President, Engineering: David B. Thurston

International Aeromarine Corporation, which is partly owned by Thurston Aeromarine Corporation, has been formed to develop and gain certification of the TA16 Seafire, the latest in a series of light amphibians designed by Mr David B. Thurston.

IAC TA16 SEAFIRE

Following design and development of the TA16 Trojan amphibian, of which 45 are under construction by Canadian and US homebuilders, Mr Thurston decided to market a production version. This has been named Seafire to distinguish it from the homebuilt version. The Seafire prototype (N16SA), completed in March 1982, was structurally designed and statically tested to the requirements of FAR Pt 23, Amendment 24. It flew for the first time on 10 December 1982 and IAC expected to complete its certification by the end of 1986.

Type: Four-seat light amphibian.

Prototype IAC TA16 Seafire four-seat amphibian *(Howard Levy)*

WINGS: Cantilever shoulder-wing monoplane. Wing section NACA 64_2A215. Dihedral 3°. Incidence 4°. Constant chord wings with no sweepback. All-metal structure. All-metal ailerons of Thurston design, each with ground adjustable trim tab. Single-slotted all-metal trailing-edge flaps. Small fixed stabilising float beneath each wing at approximately two-thirds span.

HULL: All-metal hull of planing type with single step. Retractable water rudder.

TAIL UNIT: Cantilever all-metal T tail. Bungee trim system for elevators.

LANDING GEAR: Hydraulically retractable tricycle type. Main units retract inward; steerable nosewheel retracts forward to close opening in hull, which needs no closure doors. IAC oleo-pneumatic shock absorbers. Parker-Hannifin aluminium alloy wheels, all three size 6·00-6, with tyre size 17·5 × 6·30, 6-ply rating. Tyre pressures: mainwheels 2·76 bars (40 lb/sq in), nosewheel 2·07 bars (30 lb/sq in). Parker-Hannifin dual-pad disc brakes. Parking brake. Wheel landing gear designed to meet Canadian DoT snow-ski load conditions.

POWER PLANT: One 186 kW (250 hp) Avco Lycoming O-540-A4D5 flat-six engine, pylon mounted and braced from the upper surface of the hull directly over the wing, driving a Hartzell two-blade constant-speed metal tractor propeller with spinner. Fuel tank in leading-edge of each wing, with combined capacity of 340 litres (90 US gallons). Refuelling point on upper surface of each wing. Oil capacity 11·5 litres (3 US gallons). Engine air intake incorporates filter and automatic inlet door which opens if main duct becomes blocked by ice or debris.

ACCOMMODATION: Pilot and three passengers in pairs in enclosed cabin, with two-section rearward sliding canopy. Forward section slides aft over rear canopy, and both may then be rotated to either side of hull, or removed, to facilitate loading/unloading of bulky items. All glass tinted. Adjustable seats with belts and shoulder harness. Dual controls and toe brakes. Cabin carpeted. Space for baggage or freight at rear of cabin. Accommodation is heated and ventilated.

SYSTEMS: Electrical system powered by 24V 70A engine driven alternator; 24V 37Ah battery. Electrically driven hydraulic pump provides system pressure of 69 bars (1,000 lb/sq in) for actuation of landing gear. Oxygen system optional.

AVIONICS AND EQUIPMENT: Standard Narco avionics include Nav 122 with localiser, glideslope and marker beacon receiver; Nav 121, ADF 141, CP-135, dual Com 120 and AT-150 transponder. Optional nav/com systems to customer's requirements. Blind-flying instrumentation and emergency locator transmitter standard. Dual IFR instrumentation optional. Standard equipment includes instrument panel, cabin interior, landing and taxi lights; Whelen nav/strobe lights; external power socket; control locks; baggage tiedown straps.

DIMENSIONS, EXTERNAL:

Wing span	11·28 m (37 ft 0 in)
Wing chord, constant	1·52 m (5 ft 0 in)
Wing aspect ratio	7·5
Length overall	8·28 m (27 ft 2 in)
Length of hull	7·42 m (24 ft 4 in)
Height overall	3·28 m (10 ft 9 in)
Tailplane span	3·05 m (10 ft 0 in)
Wheel track	4·01 m (13 ft 2 in)
Wheelbase	3·28 m (10 ft 9 in)
Propeller diameter	2·03 m (6 ft 8 in)

DIMENSIONS, INTERNAL:

Cabin: Length	2·13 m (7 ft 0 in)
Max width	1·01 m (3 ft 4 in)
Max height	1·22 m (4 ft 0 in)
Floor area	1·86 m² (20·0 sq ft)
Volume	2·26 m³ (80·0 cu ft)

AREAS:

Wings, gross	17·00 m² (183·0 sq ft)
Ailerons (total)	1·11 m² (12·0 sq ft)
Trailing-edge flaps (total)	2·51 m² (27·0 sq ft)
Fin	2·34 m² (25·2 sq ft)
Dorsal fin	0·12 m² (1·30 sq ft)
Rudder	0·67 m² (7·2 sq ft)
Tailplane	1·95 m² (21·0 sq ft)
Elevators	1·45 m² (15·6 sq ft)

WEIGHTS AND LOADINGS:

Weight empty, equipped	885 kg (1,950 lb)
Max fuel weight	245 kg (540 lb)
Max T-O and landing weight	1,451 kg (3,200 lb)
Max wing loading	85·44 kg/m² (17·5 lb/sq ft)
Max power loading	7·80 kg/kW (12·8 lb/hp)

PERFORMANCE (at max T-O weight):

Never-exceed speed	160 knots (298 km/h; 185 mph) IAS
Max level speed at 2,135 m (7,000 ft)	152 knots (281 km/h; 175 mph) IAS
Max cruising speed, 75% power at 2,135 m (7,000 ft)	139 knots (257 km/h; 160 mph)
Econ cruising speed, 67% power at 2,135 m (7,000 ft)	135 knots (249 km/h; 155 mph)
Stalling speed, engine idling: flaps up	63 knots (117 km/h; 73 mph)
flaps down	52 knots (97 km/h; 60 mph)
Max rate of climb at S/L	323 m (1,060 ft)/min
Service ceiling	5,485 m (18,000 ft)
T-O run: land	198 m (650 ft)
water	259 m (850 ft)
T-O to 15 m (50 ft): land	305 m (1,000 ft)
water	366 m (1,200 ft)
Landing from 15 m (50 ft): land or water	366 m (1,200 ft)
Range with max fuel	868 nm (1,609 km; 1,000 miles)

IAC

INTERNATIONAL AVIATION CORPORATION

22500 SW 288th Street, Homestead, Florida 33030
Telephone: (305) 248 0222
PRESIDENT: Ronald L. Hauck

On 5 June 1982 IAC acquired a licence to produce the Pilatus Britten-Norman Trislander three-engined feederline transport aircraft in the USA, under the name Tri-Commutair (see 1984-85 *Jane's*). Full licence production and worldwide marketing rights were subject to successful completion of an initial batch of 12 aircraft assembled from British built kits. By Spring 1986, however, only about three of these had been completed.

JAVELIN

JAVELIN AIRCRAFT COMPANY INC

1980 Easy Street, Wichita, Kansas 67230
Telephone: (316) 733 1011

Javelin Aircraft Company, which specialises in the design and manufacture of aircraft special fuel systems, has designed a modification to increase the fuel capacity of early production WSK-PZL Mielec M-18 Dromader agricultural aircraft. These Dromaders (see Polish section) have a fuel capacity of 400 litres (106 US gallons) in integral tanks in the wings; later production aircraft have a fuel system with a total capacity of 719 litres (190 US gallons).

WSK-PZL Mielec sold 14 of the early production M-18s to a Canadian company, and it was these aircraft for which the modification was designed. It involves opening up the top surface of each wing, outboard of the standard integral tank, the removal of three ribs, and the installation of a new metal tank that incorporates internal ribs to replace those that were removed. This provides a total fuel capacity of 848 litres (224 US gallons), considerably increasing the endurance of these Canadian operated aircraft, which serve in a water bombing role. The modification is available to other operators, and by early 1984, the last date for which information has been received, Javelin had modified 30 PZL Mielec M-18s.

Other fuel system conversions developed by Javelin include glassfibre slipper tanks, each of 189 litres (50 US gallons) usable capacity, for Rockwell Commander Models 680V, 680W, 681, 690, 690A and 690B; a 68 litre (18 US gallon) auxiliary fuel system for Cessna 170 and 180 aircraft; and, more recently, an improved 94·5 litre (25 US gallon) auxiliary system for Cessna Models 182N, 182P and 182Q. More than 3,000 Javelin Cessna auxiliary fuel systems have been installed.

Other current work by Javelin includes the construction of stainless steel shielding tanks for nuclear power plants and development of new liquid cooled engines for aircraft use (see Engines section).

JETCRAFT

JETCRAFT USA

500 East Highway 146, Las Vegas, Nevada 89124
Telephone: (702) 361 1200
PRESIDENT: John E. Morgan
CHIEF ENGINEER: Floyd Snow

The original JetCraft company was formed in 1967, with plans to develop a 17-seat commuter airliner and a six-seat executive jet, known as the MJ-II, based on the de Havilland Vampire T.11 jet trainer. Work on the MJ-II was started in England and at Las Vegas, Nevada, in 1968, but was terminated in the mid-1970s when the company went out of business. Details of these activities can be found in the 1969-70 *Jane's*.

JetCraft USA has announced plans to develop a family of business jets, again using airframe parts based on those of the Vampire, but of new manufacture.

JETCRAFT EXECUTIVE MARK I

Initial model in the new JetCraft range is a six/seven-passenger business jet called Executive Mark I. Certification was anticipated in July 1987 under FAR Pt 23. It has a new metal fuselage, with a conventional enclosed pressurised cabin forward of the wing main spar, and new fins and rudders mated to the Vampire's wings and tailbooms. The power plant is a General Electric CF700-2D2 turbofan, rated at 20·02 kN (4,500 lb st) at T-O. Standard fuel capacity is 1,745 litres (461 US gallons), of which 1,703 litres (450 US gallons) are usable. Total fuel capacity with external fuel tanks is 2,653 litres (701 US gallons).

DIMENSIONS, EXTERNAL:

Wing span	11·58 m (38 ft 0 in)
Length overall	12·50 m (41 ft 0 in)
Height overall	2·59 m (8 ft 6 in)

AREAS:

Wings, gross	19·32 m² (208·0 sq ft)

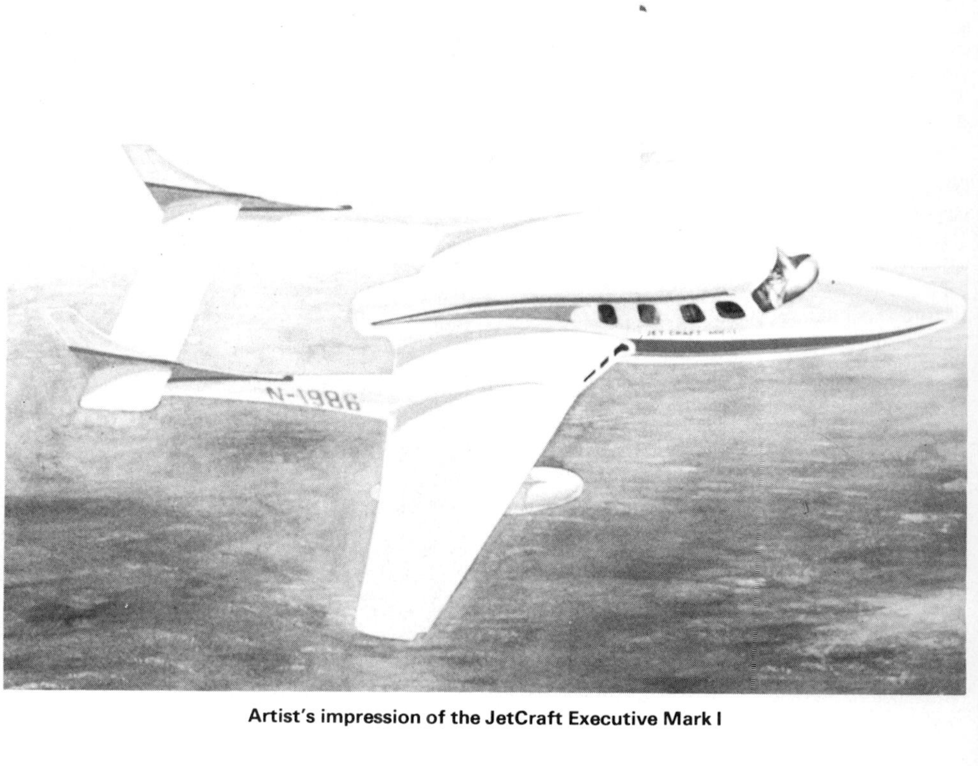

Artist's impression of the JetCraft Executive Mark I

Horizontal tail surfaces (total) 5·20 m² (56·0 sq ft)
WEIGHTS (estimated):
Weight empty 2,449 kg (5,400 lb)
Max T-O and landing weight with external fuel 5,624 kg (12,400 lb)
PERFORMANCE (estimated):
Max operating speed 360 knots (667 km/h; 414 mph) IAS *or* Mach 0·82
Max cruising speed 340 knots (630 km/h; 391 mph)
Stalling speed:
landing gear and flaps up 80 knots (148 km/h; 92 mph)
landing gear and flaps down 70 knots (130 km/h; 81 mph)
Max rate of climb at S/L 1,890 m (6,200 ft)/min
T-O run at S/L, ISA 366 m (1,200 ft)
Max certificated operating ceiling 12,500 m (41,000 ft)
Range with external fuel 3,220 nm (5,967 km; 3,708 miles)

JETCRAFT MARK II JET CRUISER

This six-passenger executive aircraft is generally similar to the Executive Mark I, but is projected with either a Pratt & Whitney Canada PT6A-65AR or Garrett TPE331-14 turboprop engine in a 'pusher' installation in the same location as the Mark I's turbofan. Estimated range is 3,300 nm (6,115 km; 3,800 miles), with a max cruising speed of 373 knots (692 km/h; 430 mph).

JETCRAFT MARK III WHISPER JET

Generally similar in configuration to the Mark I and Mark II aircraft, the Mark III is offered as a ten-seater, with larger cabin (53 cm; 21 in longer and 20 cm; 8 in wider) and a side by side pair of 11·12 kN (2,500 lb st) Pratt & Whitney Canada JT15D-4 turbofans. Estimated range is 1,823 nm (3,379 km; 2,100 miles), with a max cruising speed of 460 knots (853 km/h; 530 mph).

KAMAN

KAMAN AEROSPACE CORPORATION (a subsidiary of Kaman Corporation)

Old Windsor Road, PO Box No. 2, Bloomfield, Connecticut 06002
Telephone: (203) 242 4461
PRESIDENT AND CHIEF EXECUTIVE: Walter R. Kozlow
VICE-PRESIDENTS:
James V. Agonis (Contracts)
Dr Roger A. Massey (Engineering)
John R. Peloso (Finance)
Jay W. Pershing (Materiel)
Dr J. D. G. Rather (Space Science and Energy)
Patrick L. Renehan (Washington Operations)
Dr W. Foster Rich (Advanced Technology)
Donald W. Robinson (Planning and Marketing)
ASST VICE-PRESIDENT, NAVY LIAISON: Owen F. Polleys

The original Kaman Aircraft Corporation was founded in 1945 by Mr Charles H. Kaman, who continues as President and Chairman of the Board of Kaman Corporation. Its initial programme was to develop and test a novel servo-flap control system for helicopter rotors, and the Kaman K-125 of 1947 was the first in a series of 'synchropter' designs with intermeshing contra-rotating rotors and the servo-flap control system. The later H-2 Seasprite naval helicopter utilises the servo-flap control system on a single main rotor.

Current research and development programmes at Kaman Aerospace programmes under the sponsorship of the US Army, US Air Force, US Navy and NASA include work in advanced design of helicopter rotor systems, blades and rotor control concepts, component fatigue life determination, and structural dynamic analysis and testing.

Kaman Aerospace is engaged in several programmes as a subcontractor to aircraft and space prime contractors, involving metal and composite construction. These include design, tooling and fabrication of components such as wing slats, flaps, spoilers, rudders, elevators, doors, engine thrust reversers and acoustic products, and helicopter rotor blades. Military and commercial aircraft programmes in which Kaman participates include the Grumman A-6 and F-14, Rockwell B-1B, Lockheed C-5B, Bell/Boeing Vertol V-22, Boeing 767, Sikorsky CH-53, UH-60 and SH-60 helicopters, the NASA Space Shuttle Orbiter (for which the company provides baffle systems for the external fuel tank), and the TF39 and JT8 engines. Kaman also supplies spare parts for various aircraft types to the US military.

Kaman designed, and since mid-1977 has been producing, all-composite rotor blades for Bell AH-1 HueyCobras in service with the US Army and several other countries. Improved performance, life and operational features have been demonstrated. Kaman is also a supplier of helicopter drone kits to the US Army for use in defence programmes.

Kaman Aerospace is part of Kaman Corporation's Diversified Technologies Group. Kaman Sciences Corporation is engaged in high technology applied research in space systems, C³I nuclear and non-nuclear effects, computer systems, engineering, and natural resources. Kaman Instrumentation Corporation specialises in high precision instrumentation technology including neutron generators, displacement measuring systems, extreme environment transducers, and RF transmission lines. Kamatics Corporation designs and manufactures speciality products including high performance self-lubricating bearings and specialised mechanical drive couplings. Electromagnetic Launch Research Corporation, which joined the group in 1985, specialises in advanced electromagnetic energy and pulsed power research. AirKaman of Jacksonville, Florida, provides airline services, charters, flight training and manufacturing facilities.

KAMAN SEASPRITE

US Navy designations: HH-2 and SH-2

The prototype Seasprite flew for the first time on 2 July 1959, and many versions (described in previous editions of *Jane's*) were produced subsequently for the US Navy. Production of the SH-2F version was restarted in 1981.

From 1967, all of the original UH-2A/B Seasprites were converted progressively to UH-2C twin-engined configuration, with two 932 kW (1,250 shp) General Electric T58-GE-8B turboshaft engines in place of the former single T58. They have since undergone further modification, under the US Navy's Mk I LAMPS (Light Airborne Multi-Purpose System) programme, to provide helicopters for ASW (anti-submarine warfare), ASST (anti-ship surveillance and targeting), SAR (search and rescue), and utility operations. All but two of the US Navy's SH-2s have been upgraded to SH-2F standard.

The following versions were in service in January 1986:

HH-2D. One aircraft, without LAMPS modifications, assigned to oceanography work.

NHH-2D. One aircraft assigned to special test programmes.

SH-2F. Deliveries of this developed Mk I LAMPS version began in May 1973 and the first unit became operational with squadron HSL-33, deployed to the Pacific, on 11 September 1973. Eighty-eight SH-2Fs were delivered, and 16 earlier SH-2Ds were uprated to SH-2F configuration, in a programme that was completed in 1982. Seventy-nine earlier production SH-2Fs remained in US Navy service in January 1986. Eighteen new production SH-2Fs were ordered in the FY 1982 defence budget, and 18 more in FY 1983, of which 33 had been delivered by January 1986. Six more were authorised in FY 1984, six in FY 1985, six in FY 1986, and six requested in FY 1987.

Features of the SH-2F include increased strength landing gear; a shortened wheelbase by relocation of the tailwheel; and T58-GE-8F engines. Recent improvements have been made to the LN-66HP radar, tactical navigation system, ESM, sonobuoy system, data link and other avionics equipment. Current SH-2F enhancement programmes include the development of composite main rotor blades and the installation of new fuel efficient T700-GE-401 engines. Evaluation of a **YSH-2G** prototype fitted with these engines was completed in 1985. The US Navy is considering retrofitting the entire SH-2F inventory with T700-GE-401s.

A maximum gross weight of 6,123 kg (13,500 lb) has been authorised, effective on deliveries made from October 1985. This is 318 kg (700 lb) more than the previous standard SH-2F (1984-85 *Jane's*), and can be utilised as increased payload, or in the form of additional fuel in larger auxiliary tanks to provide extended range and endurance. US Navy tests have proved the SH-2 suitable for dipping sonar operations, air-to-surface missile firing, and equipment with various guns and rockets. The US Navy is evaluating enhanced mission equipment for the SH-2F which includes FLIR, TacNav data transfer, improved ESM, a Global Positioning System, acoustic datalink, acoustic processor with multi-function display, dipping sonar and provision for two Mk 50 torpedoes. Export models of the Seasprite are offered with dipping sonar, acoustic processor, mission computer, additional fuel, and search radar compatible with the semi-active radar seeker of missiles like Sea Skua and Penguin.

Operational deployment of HSL LAMPS Mk I squadrons began on 7 December 1971. By January 1986 more than 460,000 flight hours had been accumulated by LAMPS SH-2D/F detachments deployed on successive long cruises, primarily in the Mediterranean and Pacific, on the following ship classes: FFG-7, DD-963, DDG-993, CG-47, FFG-1, FF-1052, FF-1040, CG-26, CGN-35, CGN-38 and BB-61. The 80+ ships of the DD-963, DDG-993, CG-47 and FFG-7 classes are designed to operate with two LAMPS helicopters and the 72 ships of the other classes with one LAMPS helicopter per ship. Formation of Naval Air Reserve HSL squadrons began in 1984, and at least 24 SH-2Fs will be transferred to Reserve units as new production aircraft are delivered. Active and Reserve LAMPS Mk I SH-2Fs are scheduled to remain operational, alongside LAMPS Mk III (SH-60B), into the next century.

The following details apply to the uprated production version of the SH-2F effective from October 1985 deliveries:

TYPE: Naval anti-submarine warfare and anti-ship surveillance and targeting helicopter, with secondary capability for search and rescue, observation and utility missions.

ROTOR SYSTEM: Four-blade main and tail rotors. Kaman '101' main rotor utilises titanium hub and retention assemblies. Blades of aluminium and glassfibre construction, with servo-flap controls; composite blades effective from 1987 deliveries. Blades folded manually. Main rotor rpm 298.

FUSELAGE AND TAIL UNIT: All-metal semi-monocoque structure, with flotation hull housing main fuel tanks. Nose split on centreline, to fold rearward on each side to reduce stowage space required. Fixed horizontal stabiliser on tail rotor pylon.

LANDING GEAR: Tailwheel type, with forward retracting twin mainwheels and non-retractable tailwheel. Liquid spring shock absorbers in main-gear legs; oleo-pneumatic shock absorber in tailwheel unit, which is fully castoring for taxying but locked fore and aft for T-O and landing. Mainwheels have 8-ply tubeless tyres size 17·5 × 6·25-11, pressure 17·25 bars (250 lb/sq in); tailwheel 10-ply tubeless tyre size 10·00-5, pressure 11·04 bars (160 lb/sq in).

POWER PLANT: Two 1,007 kW (1,350 shp) General Electric T58-GE-8F turboshaft engines, one on each side of rotor pylon structure. Basic fuel capacity of 1,802 litres (476 US gallons), including up to two external auxiliary tanks with a combined capacity of 757 litres (200 US gallons). Ship-to-air helicopter in-flight refuelling (HIFR).

Kaman SH-2F Mk I LAMPS ASW helicopters of US Navy Squadron HSL-35

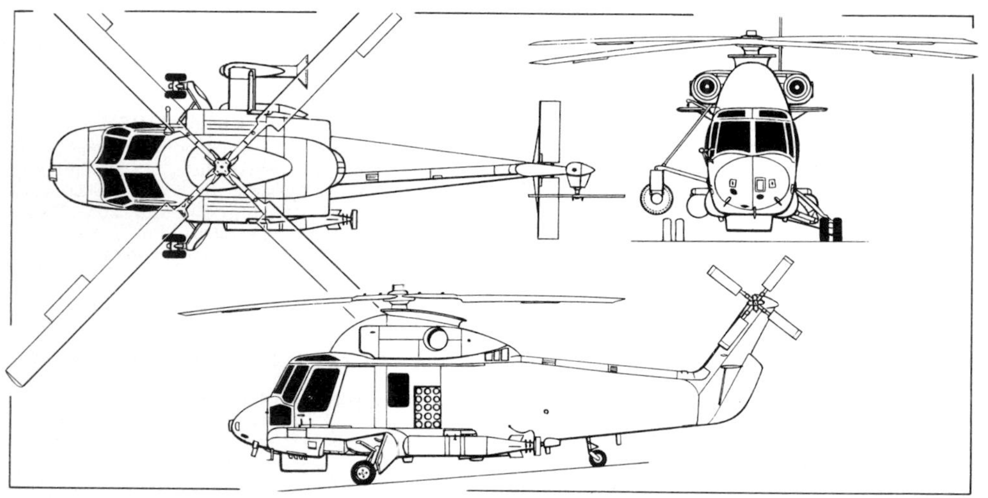

Kaman SH-2F Seasprite Mk I Light Airborne Multi-Purpose System (LAMPS) helicopter *(Pilot Press)*

Accommodation: Crew of three, consisting of pilot, co-pilot/tactical co-ordinator, and sensor operator. One passenger or litter patient with LAMPS equipment installed; four passengers or two litters with sonobuoy launcher removed. Provision for transportation of internal or external cargo.

Avionics, Armament and Operational Equipment: LAMPS Mk I mission equipment includes Canadian Marconi LN-66HP surveillance radar; General Instruments AN/ALR-66 electronic support measures (ESM); Teledyne Systems AN/ASN-123C tactical navigation system; dual Collins AN/ARC-159(V)1 UHF com radios; Texas Instruments AN/ASQ-81(V)2 magnetic anomaly detector; AN/ARR-75 sonobuoy receiver; AN/ASA-26B sonobuoy recorder and AN/AKT-22(V)6 sonobuoy data link; 15 DIFAR and DICASS sonobuoys; eight Mk 25 marine smoke markers; one or two Mk 46 torpedoes; cargo hook for external loads, capacity 1,814 kg (4,000 lb); and externally mounted rescue hoist, capacity 272 kg (600 lb).

Dimensions, external:
Main rotor diameter 13·41 m (44 ft 0 in)
Main rotor blade chord 0·55 m (1 ft 9·6 in)
Tail rotor diameter 2·45 m (8 ft 0½ in)
Tail rotor blade chord 0·236 m (9·3 in)
Length of fuselage, excl tail rotor 12·35 m (40 ft 6 in)
Length overall (rotors turning) 16·03 m (52 ft 7 in)
Length overall, nose and blades folded 11·68 m (38 ft 4 in)
Height overall (rotors turning) 4·72 m (15 ft 6 in)
Height (blades folded) 4·14 m (13 ft 7 in)
Width overall, incl MAD 3·74 m (12 ft 3 in)
Stabiliser span 2·97 m (9 ft 9 in)
Wheel track (outer wheels) 3·30 m (10 ft 10 in)
Wheelbase 5·11 m (16 ft 9 in)
Tail rotor ground clearance 2·13 m (7 ft 0 in)

Weights:
Weight empty 3,193 kg (7,040 lb)
Max T-O weight 6,123 kg (13,500 lb)

Performance (at max T-O weight, except where indicated):
Max level speed at S/L 130 knots (241 km/h; 150 mph)
Normal cruising speed 120 knots (222 km/h; 138 mph)
Max rate of climb at S/L 744 m (2,440 ft)/min
Service ceiling 6,860 m (22,500 ft)
Hovering ceiling IGE 5,670 m (18,600 ft)
Hovering ceiling OGE 4,695 m (15,400 ft)
Personnel transfer radius, 10% reserves 180 nm (333 km; 207 miles)
Ferry range with max fuel, 10% reserves 375 nm (695 km; 431 miles)
Time on station (10% reserves):
ASW at 35 nm (65 km; 40 miles) from base, 1 torpedo 1 h 50 min
ASW as above, 2 torpedoes 1 h 10 min
ASW at 70 nm (130 km; 80 miles) from base, 1 torpedo 1 h 5 min
ASST at 70 nm (130 km; 80 miles) from base 2 h 20 min
SAR at 70 nm (130 km; 80 miles) from base 2 h 5 min

KING'S

THE KING'S ENGINEERING FELLOWSHIP

Municipal Airport, Orange City, Iowa 51041
Telephone: (712) 737 4444
President: Carl A. Mortenson

New aircraft at the EAA's 1985 Oshkosh Convention included a light twin-engined transport known as the Angel, developed for and by The King's Engineering Fellowship, through donations. It was designed by Carl Mortenson, who designed and built an earlier light twin named Evangel, for similar missionary work, in the 1960s (see 1974-75 and earlier editions of *Jane's*). Eight Evangels were built, of which seven were still serving with missionaries in Alaska, Colombia, Micronesia and Peru in 1986.

KING'S MODEL 44 ANGEL

The King's Angel is a twin-engined light transport intended specifically for missionary aviation duties. Design goals included low manufacturing costs, STOL capability, suitability for rough and soft field operation, sturdiness, easy maintenance and repair in the field, and the ability to accommodate bulky cargo.

Its designer, Carl Mortenson, began construction of the prototype at his home but, because of its size, had to move operations to the Municipal Airport at Orange City. The design phase involved more than 11,000 manhours of work on over 1,000 drawings, and the prototype (N44KE) was built on production tooling. It flew for the first time in January 1984, and had logged some 120 flying hours by August 1985. During the test programme, the engines had been raised above the wing on pylons; outboard 'trimmerons' had been added for improved single-engine control (roll control being normally by means of spoilers); and three-blade Q-tip propellers had replaced an earlier type, to reduce engine noise. Later development included replacing the engines immediately on top of the wings, in longer nacelles, to increase cruising speed by an estimated 13 knots (24 km/h; 15 mph).

After FAA certification, it is planned to put the Angel into production, at a possible rate of one every three months, for missionary and other uses.

Type: Twin-engined light utility transport.

Wings: Cantilever low-mid wing monoplane. Wing section modified NACA 23018-23010 with modified leading-edge; thickness/chord ratio of 18% at root, 10% at tip. All-metal riveted structure, with built-up aluminium alloy capstrip spars and 19 die formed ribs each side. Near full span Fowler flaps, with 37° max deflection. Spoilers for roll control, supplemented by outboard 'trimmerons'.

Prototype King's Angel light twin for missionary aviation duties *(Howard Levy)*

Fuselage: Conventional aluminium alloy riveted semi-monocoque structure.

Tail Unit: Cantilever aluminium alloy riveted structure, with sweptback vertical surfaces and long dorsal fin. Full height trim tab in rudder.

Landing Gear: Retractable tricycle type. Electro-hydraulic retraction, mainwheels inward into wingroots, nosewheel rearward. Tyre size: mainwheels 8·50-10, nosewheel 8·50-6. Cleveland brakes.

Power Plant: Two 224 kW (300 hp) Avco Lycoming IO-540-M flat-six engines, mounted on top of the inboard wings and each driving a Hartzell three-blade constant-speed feathering Q-tip pusher propeller. Total fuel capacity 852 litres (225 US gallons). Oil capacity 22·7 litres (6 US gallons).

Accommodation: Enclosed cabin seating up to eight persons, including pilot. Six seats aft of flight deck can be removed for carrying cargo, including four 208 litre (55 US gallons) drums. Four large windows and one smaller circular window on each side of cabin. Horizontally divided 'clamshell' door on port side at front of cabin; emergency exit on starboard side.

Avionics and Equipment: Blind-flying instrumentation standard. King avionics optional.

Dimensions, external:
Wing span 12·19 m (40 ft 0 in)
Wing chord at root 2·29 m (7 ft 6 in)
Length overall 10·13 m (33 ft 3 in)
Height overall 3·51 m (11 ft 6 in)
Wheel track 3·96 m (13 ft 0 in)
Wheelbase 4·57 m (15 ft 0 in)

Weights:
Weight empty 1,701 kg (3,750 lb)
Max T-O weight 2,631 kg (5,800 lb)

Performance:
Cruising speed, 65% power at 3,050 m (10,000 ft) 174 knots (322 km/h; 200 mph)
Landing speed 57 knots (105 km/h; 65 mph)
Service ceiling 5,790 m (19,000 ft)
Service ceiling, one engine out 2,135 m (7,000 ft)
T-O run 183 m (600 ft)
T-O to 15 m (50 ft) 366 m (1,200 ft)
Landing from 15 m (50 ft) 335 m (1,100 ft)
Landing run 183 m (600 ft)
Range with max fuel 1,390 nm (2,575 km; 1,600 miles)
Endurance with 8 occupants 4 h
Endurance with max fuel and 4 occupants 8 h

LAKE

LAKE AIRCRAFT INC

Laconia Airport, Laconia, New Hampshire 03246
Telephone: (603) 524 5868
Telex: 94-3554 Lake Air Lana
President: Armand E. Rivard
Executive Vice-President: Gordon Collins
Vice-President, International: Haig Hagopian

LAKE LA4-200 AMPHIBIAN

Design of the original C-1 Skimmer was started in August 1946. Construction of the prototype began in January 1947 and it flew for the first time in May 1948. From it were developed the improved C-2 Skimmer IV and the Lake LA-4, LA-4A, LA-4P, LA-4S and LA-4T, as described in previous editions of *Jane's*. The further improved LA4-200 received FAA certification in 1970, and is now manufactured in two versions, as follows:

LA4-200 EP. Standard version, as described in detail, which introduced an extended propeller (EP) shaft, 13 cm (5 in) longer, to increase propeller efficiency and reduce cabin noise; a new version of the Avco Lycoming IO-360 engine, the IO-360-A1B6, which is dynamically balanced for smoother operation; an aerodynamically improved engine nacelle, which reduces drag and noise; wing trailing-edge fillets at intersection of wing root and fuselage, to improve low-speed stability and protect the propeller from water spray erosion; hull hydro boosters for improved on-water operation; reinforcement of stabilisation floats and hull station 97 bulkhead; improved cockpit canopy; new instrument panel glareshield; new fresh air vents; additional corrosion proofing; and a new polyurethane paint finish.

LA4-200 EPR. Identical to above, but with reversible-pitch constant-speed propeller, which allows the aircraft to taxi in reverse during such on-water operations as docking or mooring.

By early 1986 a total of 1,156 LA4s had been manufactured.

TYPE: Single-engined four-seat amphibian.

WINGS: Cantilever shoulder-wing monoplane with tapered wing panels attached directly to sides of hull. Wing section NACA 4415 at root, NACA 4409 at tip. Dihedral 5° 30′. Incidence 3° 15′. Structure consists of duralumin leading- and trailing-edge torsion boxes separated by a single duralumin main spar. All-metal ailerons and hydraulically operated slotted flaps over 80 per cent of span. Ground adjustable trim tabs on ailerons. Wing balancer floats are light alloy monocoque structures.

HULL: Single-step all-metal structure, with double-sealed boat hull. Alodined and zinc chromated inside and out against corrosion, with polyurethane paint exterior finish.

TAIL UNIT: Cantilever all-metal structure. Outboard elevator section separate from inboard section and actuated hydraulically for trimming. Retractable water rudder in base of aerodynamic rudder.

LANDING GEAR: Hydraulically retractable tricycle type. Consolidated oleo-pneumatic shock absorbers in main gear, which retracts inward into wings. Nosewheel, with long-stroke oleo, retracts forward. Gerdes mainwheels with Goodyear tyres, size 6·00-6, pressure 2·41 bars (35 lb/sq in). Gerdes nosewheel with Goodyear tyre size 5·00-5, pressure 1·38 bars (20 lb/sq in). Gerdes disc brakes. Parking brake. Nosewheel is free to swivel 30° each side.

POWER PLANT: One 149 kW (200 hp) Avco Lycoming IO-360-A1B6 flat-four engine, mounted on pylon above hull and driving a Hartzell two-blade constant-speed metal pusher propeller. Rajay turbocharger, reversible-pitch and Q-tip propeller, optional. US Rubber DL10 fuel tank in hull, capacity 151 litres (40 US gallons). Refuelling point above hull. Auxiliary fuel in stabilising floats, 28·4 litres (7·5 US gallons) each, optional. Max usable fuel capacity with optional tanks 204 litres (54 US gallons). Oil capacity 7·5 litres (2 US gallons).

ACCOMMODATION: Enclosed cabin seating pilot and three passengers. Front and rear seats removable. Front seats have inertia reel shoulder harness as standard. Dual controls standard; dual brakes for co-pilot optional. Entry through two forward-hinged windscreen sections. Upward hinged gull wing cargo door standard. Baggage compartment, capacity 90·5 kg (200 lb), aft of cabin. Dual windscreen defroster system.

SYSTEMS: Vacuum system for flight instruments. Hydraulic system, pressure 86·2 bars (1,250 lb/sq in), for flaps, horizontal trim and landing gear actuation; handpump provided for emergency operation. Engine driven 12V 60A alternator and 12V 30Ah battery. Janitrol 30,000 BTU heater optional.

AVIONICS AND EQUIPMENT: Basic avionics installation includes com and nav antennae, cabin speaker, microphone and circuit breakers. An extensive range of avionics by Collins, King and Narco, and autopilots by Brittain and Edo-Aire Mitchell, are available to customers' requirements. Standard equipment includes full blind-flying instrumentation, electric clock, manifold pressure gauge, outside air temperature gauge, recording tachometer, fuel pressure and quantity indicators, oil pressure and temperature indicators, cylinder head temperature gauge, ammeter, stall warning device, control locks, carpeted floor, four fresh air vents, tinted glass for all windows, dual windscreen defrosters, inertia reel shoulder harness on fron seats, shoulder restraint on rear seats, map pocket on front seats, baggage tiedown straps, landing and taxi lights, navigation lights, strobe light, heated pitot, fuselage nose bumper, paddle, cleat, line, full flow oil filter, quick fuel drains, and inboard and outboard tiedown rings. Optional equipment includes hour meter, true airspeed indicator, shoulder harness for rear seats, alternate static source, manual/automatic bilge pump, cabin fire extinguisher, and external metallic paint finish.

DIMENSIONS, EXTERNAL:
- Wing span: 11·58 m (38 ft 0 in)
- Wing chord, mean: 1·35 m (4 ft 5·1 in)
- Wing aspect ratio: 8·67
- Length overall: 7·59 m (24 ft 11 in)
- Height overall: 2·84 m (9 ft 4 in)
- Tailplane span: 3·05 m (10 ft 0 in)
- Wheel track: 3·40 m (11 ft 2 in)

Two Lake LA4-200 Amphibians emerging from the water

- Wheelbase: 2·69 m (8 ft 10 in)
- Propeller diameter: 1·88 m (6 ft 2 in)

DIMENSIONS, INTERNAL:
- Cabin: Length: 1·57 m (5 ft 2 in)
  - Max width: 1·05 m (3 ft 5½ in)
  - Max height: 1·32 m (3 ft 11½ in)
  - Floor area: approx 1·53 m² (16·5 sq ft)
  - Volume: approx 1·70 m³ (60·0 cu ft)
- Baggage hold: 0·24 m³ (8·5 cu ft)

AREAS:
- Wings, gross: 15·8 m² (170 sq ft)
- Ailerons (total): 1·16 m² (12·5 sq ft)
- Trailing-edge flaps (total): 2·28 m² (24·5 sq ft)
- Fin: 1·25 m² (13· sq ft)
- Rudder: 0·79 m² (8·5 sq ft)
- Tailplane: 1·45 m² (15·6 sq ft)
- Elevators: 0·78 m² (8·4 sq ft)

WEIGHTS AND LOADINGS:
- Weight empty, equipped: 753 kg (1,660 lb)
- Max T-O and landing weight: 1,220 kg (2,690 lb)
- Max wing loading: 74·2 kg/m² (15·2 lb/sq ft)
- Max power loading: 8·19 kg/kW (13·45 lb/hp)

PERFORMANCE (at max T-O weight. A: EP/EPR; B: EP/EPR with turbocharger):
- Max level speed at S/L:
  - A: 134 knots (248 km/h; 154 mph) IAS
- Max cruising speed: 75% power at 2,440 m (8,000 ft):
  - A: 130 knots (241 km/h; 150 mph)
  - 75% power at 6,100 m (20,000 ft):
  - B: 143 knots (265 km/h; 164 mph)
- Stalling speed:
  - A, B, flaps and landing gear up: 53 knots (98 km/h; 61 mph)
  - A, B, flaps and landing gear down: 39 knots (73 km/h; 45 mph)
- Max rate of climb at S/L: A: 299 m (980 ft)/min
- Rate of climb at 2,440 m (8,000 ft):
  - B: 244 m (800 ft)/min
- Service ceiling: A: 3,810 m (12,500 ft)
- Max operating altitude: B: 6,100 m (20,000 ft)
- T-O run: on land: A: 183 m (600 ft)
  - on water: A: 335 m (1,100 ft)
- Landing run on land: A: 145 m (475 ft)
- Alighting run on water: A: 183 m (600 ft)
- Range with max fuel, at normal cruising speed, with reserves: A: 564 nm (1,046 km; 650 miles)
- Max range with max fuel, with reserves:
  - A: 716 nm (1,327 km; 825 miles)
- Endurance (75% power):
  - A at 2,440 m (8,000 ft): 5 h 36 min
  - B at 6,100 m (20,000 ft): 5 h 12 min

LAKE LA-250 RENEGADE

The Renegade is basically a development of the LA4-200 with lengthened fuselage, providing six-seat accommodation, and has a more powerful engine, together with tail surfaces of greater area. It was designed for STOL capability and is able to make high-speed step turns on water. FAA certification was received in August 1983. Lake Aircraft delivered 17 Renegades during 1985.

The description of the LA4-200 applies also to the LA-250, except as follows:

TYPE: Single-engined six-seat amphibian.

HULL: Generally as for LA4-200, but lengthened by 1·05 m (3 ft 5 in). Deeper V hull bottom and added hull strakes for improved water handling.

TAIL UNIT: Cantilever all-metal structure, with swept fin and rudder and dorsal fillet. High-set tailplane. Outboard portion of elevator on port side is actuated hydraulically and independently as large trim tab. Fin is notched at tailplane position to permit elevator movement. Small retractable water rudder in base of rudder.

LANDING GEAR: As for LA4-200, except wheelbase increased by 0·43 m (1 ft 5 in), and oleo extension increased to provide greater ground clearance.

POWER PLANT: One 186 kW (250 hp) Avco Lycoming IO-540-C4B5 flat-six engine, driving a Hartzell three-blade constant-speed Q-tip metal pusher propeller. Turbocharged TIO-540 engine optional. Standard usable fuel capacity 204 litres (54 US gallons); optional usable capacity of 340 litres (90 US gallons).

Lake LA-250 Renegade, showing cargo door location

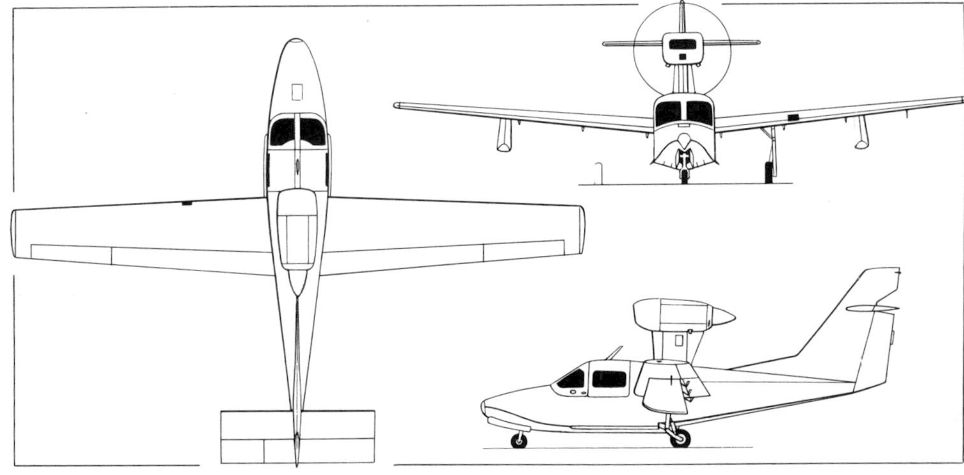

Lake Renegade six-seat amphibian *(Pilot Press)*

ACCOMMODATION: As for LA4-200, but lengthened cabin provides seating for a pilot and five passengers, with increased baggage capacity. Gull wing cargo door standard.

DIMENSIONS, EXTERNAL:

Wing span	11·68 m (38 ft 4 in)
Length overall	8·64 m (28 ft 4 in)
Height overall	3·05 m (10 ft 0 in)
Wheelbase	3·13 m (10 ft 3 in)
Propeller diameter	1·93 m (6 ft 4 in)

DIMENSION, INTERNAL:

Cabin: Length	2·03 m (6 ft 8 in)

WEIGHTS AND LOADINGS:

Weight empty, equipped	839 kg (1,850 lb)
Max T-O and landing weight	1,383 kg (3,050 lb)
Max wing loading	87·6 kg/m² (17·94 lb/sq ft)
Max power loading	7·42 kg/kW (12·2 lb/hp)

PERFORMANCE (at max T-O weight, S/L, ISA):

Never-exceed speed	148 knots (274 km/h; 170 mph)
Max level speed at 1,980 m (6,500 ft)	139 knots (258 km/h; 160 mph)
Max cruising speed, 75% power at 1,980 m (6,500 ft)	132 knots (245 km/h; 152 mph)
Stalling speed, power off: landing gear and flaps up	53 knots (99 km/h; 61 mph) IAS
landing gear and flaps down	48 knots (89 km/h; 56 mph) IAS
Max rate of climb at S/L	274 m (900 ft)/min
Service ceiling	4,480 m (14,700 ft)
T-O run: on land	268 m (880 ft)
on water	381 m (1,250 ft)
Range with max fuel, 30 min reserves	900 nm (1,668 km; 1,036 miles)

LAKE SEAWOLF

The Seawolf, introduced in early 1985, is a military/maritime surveillance variant of the LA-250 Renegade, with an Alkan 6091 rack under each wing to carry a variety of external stores including bombs of up to 200 lb size, rocket launchers, cartridge launchers and machine-gun pods. The weapons boresight position is constant and repeatable even after store removal and re-installation. In addition, the Seawolf can carry and release wing mounted rescue pods designed for use at sea or over land, with contents suitable for desert, Arctic and sea survival. Sea search and rescue pods are equipped with a liferaft, rations, homing and signalling devices; while desert pods have tent, rations, water, and other necessary equipment for survival and rescue.

A variety of radar systems is available, with the antenna mounted at the forward face of the engine pod, between the cooling inlets. The systems offer colour weather detection, a range of 240 nm (445 km; 276 miles), and three search modes: Search 1, employing sea clutter rejection circuitry to assist in detecting small boats down to a minimum range of 275 m (900 ft); Search 2, designed for precision surface mapping where high target resolution is important; and Search 3, which offers normal surface mapping for such tasks as the detection and tracking of oil slicks.

Interface units are available to provide a moving map display, waypoint designation, checklists, beacon navigation and multiple indicators. Provision has also been made for the installation of Loran or Omega navigation equipment.

Lake Seawolf maritime patrol amphibian with underwing SAR pods

Lake Aircraft claims that the Seawolf can fulfil a variety of paramilitary roles, including patrol and reconnaissance, search and rescue, special missions, liaison and logistics support, anti-smuggling duties, fish and wildlife protection, pollution control, law enforcement, and medevac duties. In medevac configuration the cabin can accommodate two litter patients and an attendant, as well as emergency medical equipment, once the passenger seats have been removed.

The prototype Seawolf (N1401G), which made its public debut at the 1985 Paris Air Show, retained the standard 12V electrical system of the civil Renegade; production versions will have a 28V system.

Typical mission profiles for the Seawolf are:

Maritime patrol, with standard fuel and two gun pods; pilot only; take-off weight 1,485 kg (3,274 lb), 70 min fuel reserves; radius of action 100 nm (185 km; 115 miles); outbound leg flown at 120 knots (222 km/h; 138 mph) at 1,830 m (6,000 ft), with 6 h 30 min on station at 450 m (1,500 ft), returning to base at 120 knots at 2,440 m (8,000 ft).

Single strike mission, with standard fuel, and bombs or rockets; pilot only; take-off weight 1,517 kg (3,344 lb), 70 min fuel reserves; flying outbound to target 400 nm (740 km; 460 miles) from base at 120 knots at 6,000 ft, with ten min over target, returning to base at 125 knots (231 km/h; 144 mph) at 3,050 m (10,000 ft).

Multiple strike mission, with standard fuel and rockets; two crew; take-off weight 1,568 kg (3,457 lb), 1 h 50 min fuel reserves; flying to initial target 200 nm (370 km; 230 miles) distant at 6,000 ft, ten min over target, continuing to second target 150 nm (278 km; 172 miles) beyond, ten min over target, returning to base at 10,000 ft.

Search and rescue mission, with external fuel and two SAR packs; pilot only; take-off weight 1,568 kg (3,457 lb), 1 h 50 min fuel reserves; to search locality 250 nm (463 km; 287 miles) from base at 6,000 ft, time on station 8 hours, returning to base at 120 knots at 10,000 ft.

Photo reconnaissance mission, with standard fuel and two reconnaissance pods; two crew; take-off weight 1,430 kg (3,152 lb), 1 h 30 min fuel reserves; flying at 120 knots to three locations at 50 nm (93 km; 57 mile) intervals from base, one hour loiter over each at 1,500 ft, returning 150 nm to base at 120 knots at 6,000 ft.

Ferry flight, with external fuel; two crew; take-off weight 1,563 kg (3,445 lb), 1 h 50 min fuel reserves; range 1,500 nm (2,775 km; 1,726 miles) at 120 knots; endurance 12 h 30 min.

The description of the Renegade applies also to the Seawolf, except as follows:

TYPE: Single-engined multi-role amphibian.

HULL: Interior LPS preservative spray optional.

POWER PLANT: Standard fuel capacity 333 litres (88 US gallons); optional capacity, with external tanks, 568 litres (150 US gallons).

ACCOMMODATION: Enclosed cabin capable of seating up to six persons. All seats except pilot's removable, with a variety of optional internal configurations according to mission. Entry through two forward-hinged windscreen sections. Upward hinged gull wing cargo door standard.

ARMAMENT: Standard 14 in NATO stores mounts on underwing hardpoints, one inboard and one outboard of each wing balancer float, can accommodate a variety of stores, including external fuel tanks, parachute flares, SAR pods, ECM pods, gun pods, reconnaissance pods, rocket launchers, photo-reconnaissance pods, cartridge throwers, flare dispensers, hazardous material containers, practice and general purpose bombs. Inboard stores points can each carry up to 100 kg (220 lb), outboard points can each carry up to 35 kg (77 lb).

DIMENSIONS AND AREAS:
As for Renegade

WEIGHTS:

Weight empty	998 kg (2,200 lb)
*Max ramp and T-O weight	1,565 kg (3,450 lb)
Max landing weight, on land	1,383 kg (3,050 lb)

PERFORMANCE:
As for Renegade, except:

Cruising speed, 55% power	110 knots (204 km/h; 127 mph)
Landing distance, land and water	230 m (755 ft)
Range with standard fuel at 120 knots (222 km/h; 138 mph), with 38 litres (10 US gallons) fuel reserves	876 nm (1,622 km; 1,008 miles)
Range with external tanks at 120 knots (222 km/h; 138 mph), with 38 litres (10 US gallons) fuel reserves	1,500 nm (2,780 km; 1,727 miles)
Endurance: with standard fuel	8 h 30 min
with external tanks	14 h 30 min

**181 kg (400 lb) must be underwing stores*

LAS

LOCKHEED AIRCRAFT SERVICE COMPANY (Component of Lockheed Corporation)

PO Box 33, Ontario International Airport, Ontario, California 91761

Telephone: (714) 988 2411

PRESIDENT: G. H. Smith

VICE-PRESIDENTS:
B. H. Menke (International Programmes)
D. J. Lange (Finance)
D. E. Gore (Administration)
D. R. Watson (Operations)
P. S. Norton (New Business Development)

DIRECTOR OF PUBLIC RELATIONS: John R. Dailey

Lockheed Aeromod Center Inc
PRESIDENT: Charles T. Humann

Lockheed Support Systems Inc
PRESIDENT: Kenneth E. Miller

Lockheed Aircraft Service Company, a component of the Lockheed Aeronautical Systems Group, is claimed to be the world's largest independent aircraft maintenance and modification company. It has designed and installed major modifications, including cargo conversions and specialised interiors, for such aircraft as the Boeing KC-135 and 707; Douglas DC-8; and Lockheed C-130, C-141, L-188 Electra, L-1011 and P-3.

In 1974 LAS began delivery of its Model 280 maintenance recorder, which records 50 h of flight data on an easily accessible cassette. In 1982 it began work on a US Air Force contract to install Model 209 digital flight data recorders, and cockpit voice recorders, on 275 C-141 StarLifters and more than 700 C-130 Hercules aircraft. Also in 1982 the company began deliveries of the Model 209F flight data recorder. This offers a one-third increase in MTBF (mean time between failures; 8,000 instead of 6,000 h) by comparison with the earlier Model 209E.

LOCKHEED C-130 and L-1011 CONVERSIONS

LAS specialises in complex aircraft modifications of all types. During 1981 it completed the modification of a C-130H to airborne emergency hospital configuration for the Royal Saudi Air Force (illustration in 1982-83 *Jane's*). Patients enter via a ramp at the rear of the aircraft, into a reception area; this is followed by three compartments comprising an examination room, operating theatre and intensive care unit. Externally, the C-130H hospital aircraft can be identified by the retractable loop aerial for its communications systems, above the fuselage, and non-standard underwing auxiliary fuel tanks. Each of these tanks contains a rear compartment housing an APU able to provide essential ground power for up to 72 hours, including the operation of medical equipment, environmental systems such as air-conditioning and heating, lighting, and communications.

A second C-130 was modified to an even more advanced standard as an airborne emergency hospital in 1983. Instead of the examination room of the first aircraft, it has a four-bed critical care unit. More extensive X-ray equipment is installed. The centre of the rear compartment can be converted to carry 16 additional litter patients, or 18 ambulatory patients in seats.

By the Spring of 1986, Saudi Arabia had a total of ten C-130 type aircraft employed in its nationwide rapid-response aeromedical service. The three latest aircraft, modified by LAS, are L-100-30HS stretched 'hospital ships'.

In late 1985 LAS was awarded a US Air Force contract to update the Special Operations Forces' AC-130H gunships with new navigation and fire control systems.

In a programme that was completed in 1981, LAS modified the first nine L-1011-500 TriStars to incorporate an active flight control system. Under a programme completed during 1982, six L-1011-500 aircraft were equipped with a digital autopilot system. Modification of L-1011-500 aircraft to meet individual airline specifications was continuing in 1985.

LOCKHEED P-3A CONVERSIONS

A P-3A Orion was modified by LAS in 1984 for use by the US Customs Service, to interdict ships and aircraft smuggling illegal drugs into the USA. The original Texas Instruments nose radar is replaced by a Hughes APG-63 radar and infra-red detection system, for all-weather day/night operations. Three more P-3As have since been modified for the US Customs Service by an operating division of LAS, the Lockheed Aeromod Center Inc (LACI) at Greenville, South Carolina, using kits produced by LAS. In addition to the APG-63 radar, these aircraft have new inertial navigation systems and multi-frequency communications radios compatible with US Customs and Coast Guard ground stations, as well as civilian law enforcement agencies.

LAS was also responsible for modifying the P-3 (AEW&C) to carry its rotodome above the rear fuselage.

In the Summer of 1984, LAS received from the US Navy first-year funding of $11·4 million in a five-year programme to convert up to 30 P-3A ASW aircraft to CP-3A cargo/passenger transport configuration. The converted aircraft will be known by the acronym ABSA (advanced base support aircraft). The first-year contract covers structural and avionics design, and manufacture of a prototype conversion kit. Installation and testing of the kit in a prototype aircraft will be funded in the second year, together with manufacture of nine additional kits. Some items will be supplied by Pacific Aerospace Corporation of New Zealand. The production kits will be installed in the third year by Lockheed Aeromod Center.

LOCKHEED

LOCKHEED CORPORATION

Head Office: Burbank, California 91520
Telephone: (213) 847 6121

Chairman of the Board and Chief Executive Officer:
Lawrence O. Kitchen

President and Chief Operating Officer:
Robert A. Fukrman

Corporate Executive Vice-President, and Chief Financial and Administrative Officer:
Vincent N. Marafino

Group Presidents:
John Brizendine (Aeronautical Systems)
Lawrence A. Smith (Marine Systems)
Richard W. Taylor (Information Systems)
Daniel M. Tellep (Missiles, Space and Electronics Systems)

Senior Vice-President:
Robert H. Wertheim (Science and Engineering)

Corporate Vice-Presidents:
Louis J. Barnard (Human Resources)
H. T. Bowling (Corporate Development)
Clayton H. Chisum (Information and Administrative Services)
Richard K. Cook (Washington Area)
H. David Crowther (Corporate Communications)
Dale H. Daniels (Operations)
Charles de Bedts (Marketing)
Robert C. Johnson (Contracts and Pricing)
Walter B. LaBerge (Science and Technology)
Robert H. Northcutt (Controller)
James J. Ryan (Secretary and Assistant General Counsel)
Joseph G. Twomey (General Counsel)
Anthony G. Van Schaick (Treasurer)

Corporate Officers:
David B. Bowman (Asst Secretary)
A. Gene Otsea (Asst Treasurer)

Aeronautical Systems Group

President: John Brizendine
Lockheed-California Company (see following entry)
Lockheed-Georgia Company (follows Lockheed-California entry)
Lockheed Advanced Aeronautics Company, Valencia, California 91355 (President: Ben R. Rich)
Lockheed Aircraft Service Company (see under LAS heading)
Lockheed Air Terminal Inc, Burbank, California 91510 (President: Viggo M. Butler)

The early history of this company was outlined briefly in previous editions of *Jane's*. In September 1977 the former Lockheed Aircraft Corporation was renamed Lockheed Corporation, to reflect the company's diversified activities.

On 4 April 1983 Lockheed introduced a new corporate structure under which its operating companies and subsidiaries are grouped into four sectors according to their products and marketing.

Lockheed's aircraft production is handled primarily by Lockheed-California Company, Lockheed-Georgia Company and Lockheed Aircraft Service Company (see LAS entry). Its missile and space activities are centred at Lockheed Missiles and Space Company (see the RPVs & Targets section of this edition). Current products of the Lockheed-California and Lockheed-Georgia companies are described hereafter under the individual company headings. By the end of 1982, Lockheed had built a total of approximately 37,000 aircraft. No later total has been notified.

Early in 1984 Lockheed formed a new company, Lockheed Advanced Aeronautics Company (LAAC), based at the Kelly Johnson Research and Development Center, Rye Canyon, California. LAAC is responsible for the design, manufacture and testing of all new Lockheed prototypes, and for aeronautical research and testing on behalf of all Lockheed companies in the Aeronautical Systems Group. Among early projects for LAAC are proposals for the Advanced Tactical Fighter (ATF) and an advanced airlifter. The new company will employ some 4,000 staff by 1987, half based at Rye Canyon, the remainder at Burbank and Marietta. A restructured 'Skunk Works' will eventually become part of LAAC.

Lockheed Air Terminal Inc (LAT), a wholly owned subsidiary, operates and maintains the Hollywood-Burbank Airport, which belongs to the cities of Burbank, Glendale and Pasadena, and provides fuelling and related services at 25 other locations in 11 states, the territory of Guam, and Panama. Lockheed Aircraft Service Co designs and manufactures products for the aerospace industry, and carries out aviation maintenance, modification and management services in the USA and other nations. Much of its work outside the USA is done under subcontract for Lockheed Aircraft International AG, a separate subsidiary.

At the end of December 1985, Lockheed Corporation's total facilities covered more than 2,322,575 m² (25,000,000 sq ft), and it had approximately 87,800 employees in 25 US states and on worldwide company assignments.

LOCKHEED-CALIFORNIA COMPANY (CALAC)

Burbank, California 91520
President: R. Richard Heppe
Executive Vice-President: E. Lloyd Graham
Vice-President and General Manager, Advanced Development Projects: Ben R. Rich

Lockheed-California (Calac) is responsible for production of the P-3 Orion land based anti-submarine warfare aircraft, TR-1 high-altitude tactical surveillance and reconnaissance aircraft and components for Lockheed-Georgia's C-5B. It is engaged in several important research and development programmes, of which few details are yet available. One of them, covered in part by a $4·7 million USAF contract received in Spring 1986, is a four-year four-phase programme involving integrated vehicle and propulsion system concepts applicable to future supersonic cruise aircraft.

LOCKHEED F-19 and XST

In the so-called 'Skunk Works' at Burbank, Lockheed-California has built, under a DARPA-funded contract from the USAF's Flight Dynamics Laboratory, a number of examples of a single-seat fighter/reconnaissance aircraft, of which primary features are low radar, infra-red and optical signatures.

A proof of concept/demonstrator aircraft, known as **XST** (Experimental Stealth Technology), is believed to have made its first flight in 1977. The XST was reportedly a very small aircraft, powered by two 11·12-12·46 kN (2,500-2,800 lb st) General Electric CJ610 turbojet engines. Between five and seven XSTs are believed to have been built, and two at least are thought to have crashed.

An operational derivative made its first flight during 1982 and was designed to offer minimal radar, infra-red, acoustic and visual signatures. General configuration is of blended wing/fuselage design, with anhedralled foreplanes on blended fuselage chines. Two canted fins on each side of the engine exhaust outlets assist IR shielding. A special paint finish also reduces both IR and radar signatures. There are no electromagnetic emissions from the aircraft during its mission.

The aircraft is said to be powered by two General Electric F404-GE-400 turbofans, each rated at 48·0 kN (10,800 lb st) without afterburner. Its size is believed to be similar to that of the F/A-18 Hornet, with folding wings to permit air transportation by C-5 Galaxy. It is said to make little or no exhaust noise, even at close range. US Air Force designation is believed to be F-19, and the official acronym for its assignment has been reported as CSIRS (covert survivable in-weather reconnaissance-strike). In early 1986 reports were received that the 'F-19' was in series production and that operational aircraft had been deployed outside the United States to bases which included one in the United Kingdom. The operating unit for the aircraft is believed to be the 4450th Tactical Test Group, based at Nellis AFB, Nevada.

The following data are estimated and highly provisional:

Dimensions, external:
Wing span 9·65 m (31 ft 8 in)
Width, wings folded 5·0 m (16 ft 5 in)
Length overall 18·0 m (59 ft 0 in)
Height overall 4·0 m (13 ft 1½ in)

Weights:
Weight empty 10,000 kg (22,050 lb)
Max T-O weight 15,000 kg (33,070 lb)

Performance:
Max cruising speed at S/L 560 knots (1,038 km/h; 645 mph)
Combat radius 300-400 nm (556-741 km; 345-460 miles)

LOCKHEED ATF

In July 1985 Lockheed announced the formation of a development team for the company's submission for the USAF Advanced Tactical Fighter (ATF) programme. Lockheed-California's Advanced Development Projects organisation will form the nucleus of the project. Lockheed says that its ATF proposal will make use of advanced composites and metallic structures, advanced avionics, armament, propulsion and flight control systems integrated into a highly automated crew station to achieve major improvements in beyond-visual-range and close-in combat performance. Other design goals include low cost, high reliability and ease of maintenance, with short take-off and landing permitting operation from minimally supported forward battle area bases.

LOCKHEED ER-2 and TR-1

The configuration of the TR-1 is basically that of a powered sailplane, which explains its unusual 'bicycle' landing gear, combined with underwing balancer units which provide stability during take-off and are then jettisoned. Range can, when necessary, be extended by shutting

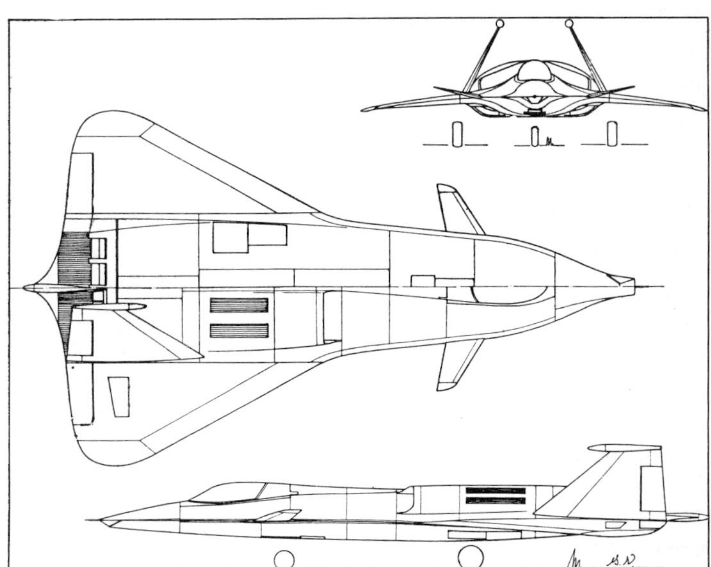

These conjectural drawings of the Lockheed F-19, by Hideo Maki, are reproduced by courtesy of *AiReview*, Tokyo

off the engine and gliding. Because of its configuration the TR-1 requires unusually precise handling during take-off and landing—particularly the latter, since there is an extremely small margin between approach speed and stalling speed. After touchdown, the aircraft comes to rest on one of the down-turned wingtips, which serve as skids.

There are three versions of the TR-1 series, as follows:

TR-1A. Single-seat tactical reconnaissance version, described by the Department of Defense as being "equipped with a variety of electronic sensors to provide continuously available, day or night, high-altitude all-weather standoff surveillance of the battle area in direct support of the US and Allied ground and air forces during peace, crises, and war situations". Tooling for the earlier U-2 had been kept in store at the USAF-owned Plant 42 at Palmdale California, and the FY 1979 defence budget included $10·2 million to reopen the production line in FY 1980. The TR-1A has the same basic airframe as the U-2R (described in 1983-84 *Jane's*), with a J75-P-13B engine, but with the significant addition of an advanced synthetic aperture radar system (ASARS) in the form of a UPD-X side-looking airborne radar (SLAR) and modern electronic countermeasures (ECM). The TR-1A is intended primarily for use in Europe, where its SLAR provides the capability to 'see' approximately 30 nm (55 km; 35 miles) into hostile territory without the need to overfly an actual or potential battle area. The first TR-1A (80-1066) flew for the first time on 1 August 1981. Deliveries began in September 1981, initially to Beale AFB, California.

TR-1B. Two-seat training version of TR-1A. Second cockpit in tandem, above and behind standard cockpit. First TR-1B (80-1064) delivered to Beale AFB in March 1983; second delivered in May 1983.

ER-2. Basically similar to TR-1A but modified for use by NASA as an Earth resources research aircraft. Delivered to Ames Research Center in June 1981. Described under NASA entry in 1982-83 *Jane's*.

Construction of the ER-2 and the first two TR-1As was funded by $42·4 million provided in the FY 1980 budget, the contract for the aircraft being received by Lockheed on 16 November 1979. A further 16 aircraft were ordered under the FY 1981-84 budgets, three more in FY 1985 and four in FY 1986, leaving three to be funded in FY 1987 to complete the planned inventory of 26 TR-1As for the USAF, plus the two TR-1Bs. Some TR-1As are expected to be allocated to the precision location strike system (PLSS) role, following a period of highly successful flight testing. Using a triangulation team of three TR-1As, PLSS will locate enemy defence emitters in near real time and all weathers, to permit attack from standoff ranges by ground or airborne weapon systems. TR-1As allocated to the PLSS mission have a more bulbous slab-sided nose.

Another TR-1A variant reported in 1984 has a large aerofoil-shape structure (radome?) mounted above its fuselage (see accompanying illustration).

In early 1985 Lockheed began flight testing composites structure speed brakes and elevators on a USAF TR-1A, and was reported to be considering testing a composites tailplane and fin on the aircraft. The company has also tested fibre optic cables in place of wiring bundles on the TR-1A.

Fourteen TR-1s are being stationed at RAF Alconbury, Cambridgeshire, England with the USAF's 95th Reconnaissance Squadron, 17th Tactical Reconnaissance Wing. A detachment of this aircraft has been housed at RAF Wethersfield. Although operating in Europe, they remain under the jurisdiction of Strategic Air Command, and not USAFE. The first of these TR-1s was flown to Alconbury during February 1983, and all 14 are scheduled for delivery by early 1987.

The following description applies to the TR-1A except where indicated:

TYPE: High-altitude reconnaissance and research aircraft.

WINGS: Cantilever mid-wing monoplane, with special Lockheed wing section, and wingtip fittings which serve as skids during landing. All-metal structure. Hydraulically actuated trailing-edge flaps (four segments on each wing, two inboard and two outboard of each underwing pod) occupy approx 70 per cent of each wing. Small tubular fuel vent fairing between each outermost flap segment and aileron, projecting slightly aft of the trailing-edge. Two small hydraulically actuated plate type roll/lift spoilers on each wing, forward of outboard flap segments. Trim tab in each aileron. All primary flight controls manually operated, with high-density internal mass balance. Manually extended retractable stall strip in leading-edge of each wing to assist pilot in settling aircraft on runway.

FUSELAGE: All-metal semi-monocoque structure of circular cross-section, with thin-gauge skin. Fineness ratio approx 10:1. Hydraulically actuated forward opening door type airbrake on each side of fuselage aft of wings, used mainly as a landing aid. Payload carrying nose sections and mission bay hatches interchangeable.

TAIL UNIT: Cantilever all-metal structure. Hydraulically variable tailplane incidence, achieved by pivoting entire tail assembly around point at base of fin leading-edge. Balanced rudder and elevators. Trim tab in each elevator.

LANDING GEAR: Retractable bicycle type, with twin mainwheels and twin 8 in diameter steerable tailwheels in tandem, each unit retracting forward into fuselage. Balancer units under outer wings, each with twin small wheels, are jettisoned on take-off. Mainwheel tyre pressure 20·7 bars (300 lb/sq in). Tailwheels and underwing wheels have solid tyres. Brakes on mainwheels. Braking parachute in container under rudder. Provision for an arrester hook (TR-1 has foldable outerwing panels and can be operated from aircraft carriers without any change in aircraft structure or operating weights).

POWER PLANT: One 75·6 kN (17,000 lb st) Pratt & Whitney J75-P-13B turbojet engine. All fuel in inboard and outboard main tanks filling each wing except for tip, each with overwing gravity refuelling point. Normal internal fuel capacity approx 4,448 litres (1,175 US gallons).

ACCOMMODATION: Pilot only, on ejection seat. Side-hinged transparent canopy, protected internally against ultraviolet radiation. Accommodation is air-conditioned and pressurised. Rearview periscope on most aircraft (positions vary). Food warmer, with spaceflight type tubes of food. Second (instructor's) cockpit above and behind standard cockpit in TR-1B.

SYSTEMS: Single hydraulic system, pressure 207 bars (3,000 lb/sq in). Electrical system utilises single AC/DC engine driven generator, with backup AC alternator driven from hydraulic system. Liquid oxygen system for pilot.

AVIONICS AND EQUIPMENT: Typical standard avionics include HF, UHF and VHF com, INS, Tacan, ILS, autopilot, ADF, air data computer, compass, and (for night flying) astro-compass. Equipment includes one vertical and two lateral cameras for training flights, or side-looking airborne radar and T-35 tracking camera for operational missions. Main avionics and equipment compartments are in detachable modular nose section, in a 'Q' bay aft of the cockpit (replaced by second cockpit in TR-1B), and in two large pods mounted underwing at approx one-third span. Each pod is approx 8·23 m (27 ft) long; has a volume of about 2·55 m³ (90 cu ft), and weighs about 544 kg (1,200 lb) complete with sensors and/or equipment. There is a smaller 'E' bay between the 'Q' bay and mainwheel bay; additional small areas in the bottom of the rear fuselage and in the tailcone can also be used to house mission equipment.

Close-up photograph of Lockheed TR-1A shows clearly the shape of the starboard sensor pod

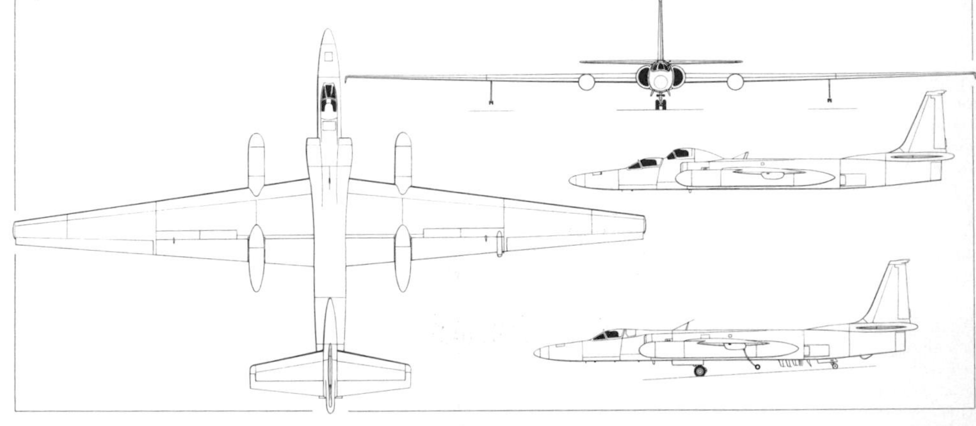

Lockheed TR-1A high-altitude reconnaissance and research aircraft, with additional side elevation (centre) of TR-1B *(Pilot Press)*

Lockheed TR-1A with unidentified equipment mounted on fuselage pylon, possibly for AEW&C evaluation

TR-1B two-seat training version of the TR-1A tactical reconnaissance aircraft, for USAF

The prototype Update III P-3C Orion photographed during test and evaluation by the US Navy

DIMENSIONS, EXTERNAL:
- Wing span: 31·39 m (103 ft 0 in)
- Wing aspect ratio: approx 10·6
- Length overall: 19·20 m (63 ft 0 in)
- Height overall: 4·88 m (16 ft 0 in)

AREA:
- Wings, gross: approx 92·9 m² (1,000 sq ft)

WEIGHTS:
- Weight empty, excl power plant and equipment pods: under 4,535 kg (10,000 lb)
- Max T-O weight: 18,144 kg (40,000 lb)

PERFORMANCE:
- Max cruising speed at normal operational height of 21,650 m (70,000 ft): more than 373 knots (692 km/h; 430 mph)
- Operational ceiling: 27,430 m (90,000 ft)
- Min ground turning radius: 68·6 m (225 ft)
- Max range: more than 2,605 nm (4,830 km; 3,000 miles)
- Max endurance: 12 h
- *g* limit: +2·5

LOCKHEED MODEL 185/285 ORION

US Navy designation: P-3
CAF designation: CP-140 Aurora

In 1958 Lockheed won a US Navy competition for an 'off-the-shelf' ASW aircraft with a developed version of its Electra four-turboprop commercial transport. An aerodynamic prototype flew for the first time on 19 August 1958. A second aircraft, designated YP-3A (formerly YP3V-1), with full avionics, flew on 25 November 1959.

Details of the P-3A initial production version (157 built) and WP-3A can be found in the 1978-79 *Jane's*. The P-3B (144 built) and EP-3B were last described in the 1983-84 edition. Other versions, including special conversions, are as follows:

P-3B (Portugal). In late 1985 the Portuguese Air Force ordered six P-3Bs. These aircraft, formerly operated by the Royal Australian Air Force, will receive major systems updates to improve their ASW effectiveness. Following completion of a prototype by Lockheed in 1988, the remaining aircraft will be modified by Oficinas Gerais de Material Aeronáutico (OGMA) in Portugal (which see).

P-3C. Advanced version with the A-NEW system of sensors and control equipment, built around a Univac digital computer that integrates all ASW information and permits retrieval, display and transmission of tactical data in order to eliminate routine log keeping functions. This increases crew effectiveness by allowing them sufficient time to consider all tactical data and devise the best action to resolve problems. First flight of this version was made on 18 September 1968 and the P-3C entered service in 1969. A total of 279 of this version had been delivered to the US Navy by 1 April 1986, out of a planned force of 316. Nine aircraft have been funded in FY 1986, with a total of 33 requested in FYs 1987-1990.

Aircraft delivered from January 1975 were to **P-3C Update** standard, with new avionics and electronics software developed to enhance their effectiveness. Equipment includes a magnetic drum that gives a sevenfold increase in computer memory capacity, a new versatile computer language, Omega navigation system, improved acoustic processing sensitivity, a tactical display for two of the sensor stations, and an improved magnetic tape transport. A prototype with this equipment was handed over to the US Navy on 29 April 1974.

Lockheed P-3 with large unidentified container beneath fuselage, possibly for SLAR

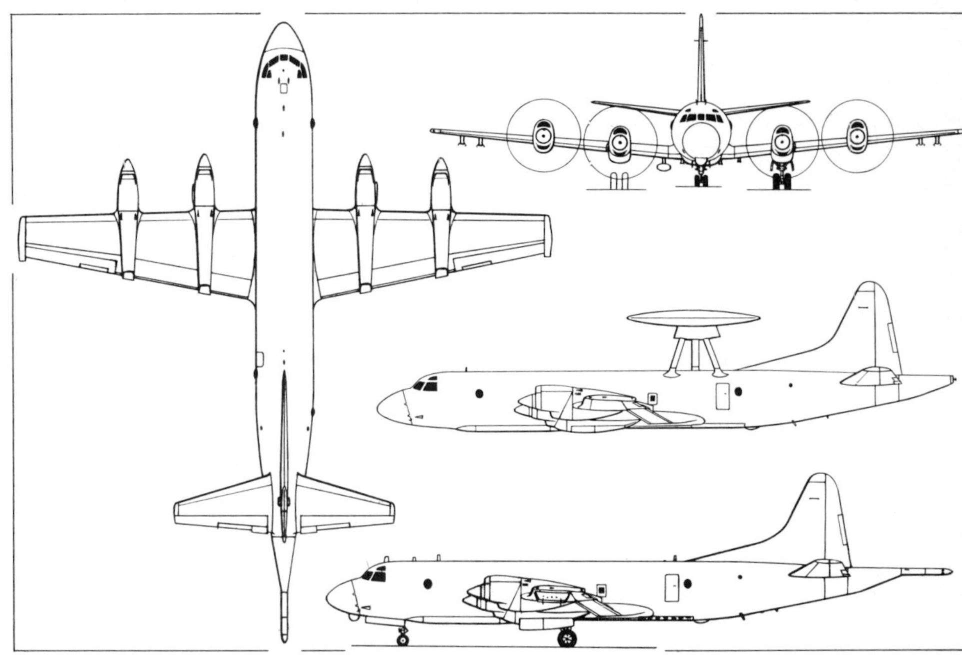

Lockheed P-3C Orion four-turboprop anti-submarine aircraft, with added side elevation (centre) of AEW&C version *(Pilot Press)*

The US Navy and Lockheed began in 1976 a further P-3C avionics improvement programme known as **Update II**. This added an infra-red detection system (IRDS) and a sonobuoy reference system (SRS). The Harpoon missile and control system are included in Update II, which was incorporated into production aircraft from August 1977. The first Update II P-3C was delivered to the Naval Air Development Center in the same month. Ten Update II P-3Cs were delivered to the Royal Australian Air Force in 1978-79 for service with No. 10 Squadron. The RAAF ordered ten more in mid-1982, the last of which was delivered in May 1986. The Royal Netherlands Navy ordered 13 Update II P-3Cs, the first of which was delivered in November 1981. Japan has ordered 75 of a planned 100, of which four were assembled and the remainder are being licence built in Japan by Kawasaki (which see), following delivery of three US built aircraft during 1981. Eighteen had been delivered by Kawasaki by the beginning of 1986.

Update III, of which development began in February 1978, involves mainly ASW avionics, including a new IBM Proteus acoustic processor to analyse signals picked up from the sea, a new sonobuoy receiver which replaces DIFAR (directional acoustic frequency analysis and recording), an improved APU, and environmental controls to cater for increased heat from the avionics and to improve crew comfort further. A prototype Update III P-3C was delivered to the US Navy for test and evaluation in August 1983. Production deliveries began in May 1984. The first delivery of P-3C Update IIIs to a US Navy reserve patrol squadron is scheduled for FY 1988.

Update IV will have improved processing capabilities and a new family of acoustic sensors designed to counter the 'quieting' trend of the Soviet submarine force. Aerodynamic trials of a P-3C equipped with an Eaton AIL Division AN/ALR-77 tactical electronic support measures (ESM) system have been conducted by Lockheed and were expected to be followed by technical and operational evaluation at the Naval Air Test Center, Patuxent River, Maryland, in late 1986. The AN/ALR-77 system, which will form part of Update IV, comprises four wingtip quadrants providing 360° coverage with 36 interferometer antennae, each sub-band being covered by a triplet of antennae.

Two of the eight international records for turboprop aircraft set up in a P-3C by Cdr Donald H. Lilienthal, in early 1971, had not been beaten by mid-1986. They were a speed of 434·97 knots (806·10 km/h; 500·89 mph) over a 15/25 km course; and a time-to-height record, to 12,000 m in 19 min 42·24 s.

P-3D. Proposed new variant, for which requests for proposals were expected in Summer 1986, with contract award tentatively proposed for Spring 1987. Aircraft will be powered by a version of the Allison 501-M80C turboshaft engine adopted for the Bell/Boeing Vertol V-22A Osprey tilt-rotor aircraft. The US Navy is seeking competitive bids for 125 P-3Ds, to be acquired from 1989-94. In mid-1986 Boeing, Lockheed, McDonnell Douglas and Rockwell were reported to be discussing competitive procurement plans, while Lockheed and the US Navy were discussing ownership of the P-3 design and data.

EP-3E. Ten P-3As and two EP-3Bs were converted to EP-3E configuration to replace Lockheed EC-121s in service with VQ-1 and VQ-2 squadrons. Identified by large canoe shape radars on upper and lower surfaces of fuselage and ventral radome forward of wing. EP-3E electronics suites are believed to comprise GTE-Sylvania AN/ALR-60 communications, interception and analysis sytem; Raytheon AN/ALQ-76 noise jamming pod; Loral AN/ALQ-78 automatic ESM system; Magnavox AN/ALQ-108 IFF jammer; Sanders AN/ALR-132 infra-red jammer; ARGO Systems AN/ALR-52 instantaneous frequency measuring equipment; Texas Instruments AN/APS-115 frequency agile search radar; Hughes AN/AAR-37 infra-red detector; Loral AN/ASA-66 tactical display; Cardion AN/ASA-69 scan converter; and Sperry Univac AN/ASQ-114 computer.

P-3F. Six aircraft, similar to the US Navy's P-3Cs, for the Iranian Air Force. Used initially for long-range surface surveillance and subsequently also for ASW missions. Delivery completed in January 1975.

CP-140 Aurora. Version for Canadian Armed Forces (18 built). Described in detail in 1981-82 *Jane's*.

P-3 (AEW&C). Airborne early warning and control (AEW&C) variant. Prototype (N91LC), converted from ex-Royal Australian Air Force P-3B, made first flight on 14 June 1984, fitted with a 7·32 m (24 ft) diameter Randtron APA-171 rotodome above rear fuselage. General Electric AN/APS-138 radar (as on Grumman E-2C Hawkeye) and a 1553A communications and data handling system were to be fitted in 1985 after aerodynamic, performance and loading trials has been completed. Lockheed claims a 14 h endurance for the P-3 (AEW&C). Possible customers for the aircraft include Australia, Canada, Japan and the US Navy. Deliveries could begin 28 months after receipt of sufficient orders to make production viable. A similar AEW package is being proposed for the C-130.

Lockheed has proposed the P-3 (AEW&C) to the Royal Air Force as an alternative to the BAe Nimrod AEW Mk 3. The RAF variant would be offered with AN/APS-145 radar as an alternative to the AN/APS-138, and could be powered by the GE38 Modern Technology Engine (MTE) projected by General Electric and Rolls-Royce. It would have in-flight refuelling capability.

By 1 April 1986 Lockheed-California had delivered 601 P-3s of all versions, and held firm orders totalling 624 at that date. The following data refer to the P-3C, but are generally applicable to other versions, except for the details noted:

Aerodynamic prototype of P-3 (AEW&C) airborne early warning and control version of the Orion

Lockheed EP-3E of US Navy squadron VQ-1 landing at Atsugi, Japan, in May 1985 (*Katsumi Hinata*)

Type: Four-turboprop ASW aircraft.

Wings: Cantilever low-wing monoplane. Wing section NACA 0014 (modified) at root, NACA 0012 (modified) at tip. Dihedral 6°. Incidence 3° at root, 0° 30′ at tip. Fail-safe box beam structure of extruded integrally stiffened aluminium alloy. Lockheed-Fowler trailing-edge flaps. Hydraulically boosted aluminium ailerons. Anti-icing by engine bleed air ducted into leading-edges.

Fuselage: Conventional aluminium alloy semi-monocoque fail-safe structure.

Tail Unit: Cantilever aluminium alloy structure with dihedral tailplane and dorsal fin. Fixed incidence tailplane. Hydraulically boosted rudder and elevators. Leading-edges of fin and tailplane have electric anti-icing system.

Landing Gear: Hydraulically retractable tricycle type, with twin wheels on each unit. All units retract forward, mainwheels into inner engine nacelles. Oleo-pneumatic shock absorbers. Mainwheels have size 40-14 type VII 26-ply tubeless tyres, pressures 7·58-12·41 bars (110-180 lb/sq in) at 36,287 kg (80,000 lb) T-O weight; 12·41 bars (180 lb/sq in) at 57,606 kg (127,000 lb) T-O weight; 13·10 bars (190 lb/sq in) at 61,235 kg (135,000 lb) max normal T-O weight. Nosewheels have size 28-7·7 type VII tubeless tyres, pressure 10·34 bars (150 lb/sq in). Hydraulic brakes. No anti-skid units.

Power Plant: Four 3,661 kW (4,910 ehp) Allison T56-A-14 turboprop engines, each driving a Hamilton Standard 54H60 four-blade constant-speed propeller. Fuel in one tank in fuselage and four wing integral tanks, with total usable capacity of 34,826 litres (9,200 US gallons). Four overwing gravity fuelling points and central pressure refuelling point. Oil capacity (min usable) 111 litres (29·4 US gallons) in four tanks. Electrically de-iced propeller spinners.

Accommodation: Normal ten-man crew. Flight deck has wide-vision windows, and circular windows for observers are provided fore and aft in the main cabin, each bulged to give 180° view. Main cabin is fitted out as a five-man tactical compartment containing advanced electronic, magnetic and sonic detection equipment, an all-electric galley and large crew rest area.

Systems: Air-conditioning and pressurisation system supplied by two engine driven compressors. Pressure differential 0·37 bars (5·4 lb/sq in). Hydraulic system, pressure 207 bars (3,000 lb/sq in), for flaps, control surface boosters, landing gear actuation, brakes and bomb bay doors. Three hydraulic pumps, each rated at 8 US gallons per minute at 0-2,200 lb/sq in, 6 US gallons per minute at 2,975 lb/sq in. Class one non-separated air/oil reservoir, Type B pressurised. Electrical system utilises three 60kVA generators for 120/208V 400Hz AC supply. 24V DC supply. Integral APU with 60kVA generator for ground air-conditioning, electrical supply and engine starting.

Avionics and Equipment: The ASQ-114 general purpose digital computer is the heart of the P-3C system. Together with the AYA-8 data processing equipment and computer controlled display systems, it permits rapid analysis and utilisation of electronic, magnetic and sonic data. Nav/com system comprises two LTN-72 inertial navigation systems; AN/APN-227 Doppler; ARN-81 Loran A and C; AN/ARN-118 Tacan; two VIR-31A VOR/LOC/GS/MB receivers; ARN-83 LF-ADF; ARA-50 UHF direction finder; AJN-15 flight director indicator for tactical directions; HSI for long-range flight directions; glideslope indicator; on-top position indicator; two ARC-161 HF transceivers; two ARC-143 UHF transceivers; ARC-101 VHF receiver/transmitter; AGC-6 teletype and high-speed printer; HF and UHF secure communication units; ACQ-5 data link communication set and AIC-22 interphone set; APX-72 IFF transponder and APX-76 SIF interrogator. Electronic computer controlled display equipment includes ASA-70 tactical display; ASA-66 pilot's display; ASA-70 radar display and two auxiliary readout (computer stored data) displays. ASW equipment includes two ARR-72 sonar receivers; two AQA-7 DIFAR (directional acoustic frequency analysis and recording) sonobuoy indicator sets; hyperbolic fix unit; acoustic source signal generator; time code generator and AQH-4(V) sonar tape recorder; ASQ-81 magnetic anomaly detector; ASA-64 submarine anomaly detector; ASA-65 magnetic compensator; ALQ-78 electronic countermeasures set; APS-115 radar set (360° coverage); ASA-69 radar scan converter; KA-74 forward computer assisted camera; KB-18A automatic strike assessment camera with horizon-to-horizon coverage; RO-308 bathythermograph recorder. Additional equipment includes APN-194 radar altimeter; two APQ-107 radar altimeter warning systems; A/A24G-9 true airspeed computer and ASW-31 automatic flight control system. P-3Cs delivered from 1975 have the avionics/electronics package updated by addition of an extra 393K memory drum and fourth logic unit, Omega navigation, new magnetic tape transport, and an ASA-66 tactical display for the sonar operators. To accommodate the new systems a new operational software computer programme was written in CMS-2 language. GEC Avionics AQS-901 acoustic signal processing and display system in RAAF P-3Cs. AN/ALR-77 passive radar detection system (ESM), to be housed in wingtip pods, is under development by Eaton Corpn (AIL Division), and will also provide targeting data for the aircraft's Harpoon missiles. Testing of the system by Lockheed was due to begin in 1985, following the award of a $4 million contract which included structural and aerodynamic testing of redesigned wingtips. Wing span was to be increased by some 0·81 m (2 ft 8 in) to accommodate ESM antennae and receivers. The AN/ALR-77 equipped P-3C was due to be delivered to the US Navy in November 1985 for functional tests of the system.

ARMAMENT: Bomb bay, 2·03 m wide, 0·88 m deep and 3·91 m long (80 in × 34·5 in × 154 in), forward of wing, can accommodate a 2,000 lb Mk 25/39/55/56 mine, three 1,000 lb Mk 36/52 mines, three Mk 57 depth bombs, eight Mk 54 depth bombs, eight Mk 43/44/46 torpedoes or a combination of two Mk 101 nuclear depth bombs and four Mk 43/44/46 torpedoes. Ten underwing pylons for stores: two under centre-section each side can carry torpedoes or 2,000 lb mines; three under outer wing each side can carry respectively (inboard to outboard) a torpedo or 2,000 lb mine (or searchlight on starboard wing), a torpedo or 1,000 lb mine or rockets singly or in pods; a torpedo or 500 lb mine or rockets singly or in pods. Torpedoes can be carried underwing only for ferrying; mines can be carried and released. Search stores, such as sonobuoys and sound signals, are launched from inside cabin area in the P-3A/B. In the P-3C sonobuoys are loaded and launched externally and internally. Max total weapon load includes six 2,000 lb mines under wings and a 3,290 kg (7,252 lb) internal load made up of two Mk 101 depth bombs, four Mk 44 torpedoes, pyrotechnic pistol and 12 signals, 87 sonobuoys, 100 Mk 50 underwater sound signals (P-3A/B), 18 Mk 3A marine markers (P-3A/B), 42 Mk 7 marine markers, two B.T. buoys, and two Mk 5 parachute flares. Sonobuoys are ejected from P-3C aircraft with explosive cartridge actuating devices (CAD), eliminating the need for a pneumatic system. Australian P-3Cs use BARRA sonobuoys.

DIMENSIONS, EXTERNAL:
Wing span 30·37 m (99 ft 8 in)
Wing chord: at root 5·77 m (18 ft 11 in)
at tip 2·31 m (7 ft 7 in)
Wing aspect ratio 7·5
Length overall 35·61 m (116 ft 10 in)
Height overall 10·27 m (33 ft 8½ in)
Fuselage diameter 3·45 m (11 ft 4 in)
Tailplane span 13·06 m (42 ft 10 in)
Wheel track (c/l shock absorbers) 9·50 m (31 ft 2 in)
Wheelbase 9·07 m (29 ft 9 in)
Propeller diameter 4·11 m (13 ft 6 in)
Cabin door: Height 1·83 m (6 ft 0 in)
Width 0·69 m (2 ft 3 in)

DIMENSIONS, INTERNAL:
Cabin, excl flight deck and electrical load centre:
Length 21·06 m (69 ft 1 in)
Max width 3·30 m (10 ft 10 in)
Max height 2·29 m (7 ft 6 in)
Floor area 61·13 m² (658 sq ft)
Volume 120·6 m³ (4,260 cu ft)

AREAS:
Wings, gross 120·77 m² (1,300 sq ft)
Ailerons (total) 8·36 m² (90 sq ft)
Trailing-edge flaps (total) 19·32 m² (208 sq ft)
Fin, incl dorsal fin 10·78 m² (116 sq ft)
Rudder, incl tab 5·57 m² (60 sq ft)
Tailplane 22·39 m² (241 sq ft)
Elevators, incl tabs 7·53 m² (81 sq ft)

WEIGHTS (P-3B/C):
Weight empty 27,890 kg (61,491 lb)
Max fuel weight 28,350 kg (62,500 lb)
Max expendable load 9,071 kg (20,000 lb)
Max normal T-O weight 61,235 kg (135,000 lb)
Max permissible weight 64,410 kg (142,000 lb)
Design zero-fuel weight 35,017 kg (77,200 lb)
Max landing weight 47,119 kg (103,880 lb)

PERFORMANCE (P-3B/C, at max T-O weight, except where indicated otherwise):
Max level speed at 4,575 m (15,000 ft) at AUW of 47,625 kg (105,000 lb) 411 knots (761 km/h; 473 mph)
Econ cruising speed at 7,620 m (25,000 ft) at AUW of 49,895 kg (110,000 lb) 328 knots (608 km/h; 378 mph)
Patrol speed at 457 m (1,500 ft) at AUW of 49,895 kg (110,000 lb) 206 knots (381 km/h; 237 mph)
Stalling speed: flaps up 133 knots (248 km/h; 154 mph)
flaps down 112 knots (208 km/h; 129 mph)
Max rate of climb at 457 m (1,500 ft) 594 m (1,950 ft)/min
Service ceiling 8,625 m (28,300 ft)
Service ceiling, one engine out 5,790 m (19,000 ft)
T-O run 1,290 m (4,240 ft)
T-O to 15 m (50 ft) 1,673 m (5,490 ft)
Landing from 15 m (50 ft) at design landing weight 845 m (2,770 ft)
Mission radius (3 h on station at 457 m; 1,500 ft) 1,346 nm (2,494 km; 1,550 miles)
Max mission radius (no time on station) at 61,235 kg (135,000 lb) 2,070 nm (3,835 km; 2,383 miles)

Lockheed S-3B Viking with Harpoon missiles, and updated avionics and weapon systems

LOCKHEED PRC-105

Lockheed-California has offered to the People's Republic of China a 105-seat airliner derivative of the P-3 Orion, which itself was developed from the commercial L-188 Electra. The aircraft, designated PRC-105, would feature a fuselage stretch of 1·93 m (6 ft 4 in) and an increase in wing span of 1·52 m (5 ft 0 in) over the P-3, and would be manufactured in China. Lockheed foresees a market for up to 500 such aircraft by the year 2015.

LOCKHEED VIKING

US Navy designation: S-3

Production of 187 **S-3As** (see 1978-79 *Jane's*) for the US Navy ended in mid-1978. All tooling was then placed in storage at Burbank pending a US Navy decision on further orders, and in early 1980 demonstrator versions of the **US-3A** (COD) and **KS-3A** (tanker) were evaluated by the Navy. In 1982 three of the earlier production S-3As were modified to US-3A configuration. The sole KS-3A was also converted to US-3A configuration in late 1983.

As an alternative to the KS-3A dedicated tanker configuration, tests of an S-3A with a 'buddy' refuelling pack under its port wing were conducted in 1984. This technique, which transfers fuel from the tanker's standard internal tanks, and an external tank under the starboard wing, without affecting its multi-mission capability, may be adopted for operational use.

Lockheed announced on 18 August 1981 the receipt of a full scale engineering development contract, from the US Naval Air Systems Command, for an improved avionics system for S-3A Vikings currently in service with the US Navy. With initial funding of $14·5 million, it follows a contract awarded by the Navy in 1980, under which Lockheed-California developed the specifications for an S-3A weapons system improvement programme (WSIP).

Aircraft modified under the WSIP are redesignated **S-3B**. Improvements include increased acoustic processing capacity, expanded electronic support measure capability, better radar processing, a new sonobuoy telemetry receiver system, and provisions for the Harpoon missile. It is anticipated that a total of 160 S-3As could be retrofitted under the programme. Two FSED (full scale engineering development) S-3As were modified initially, the first of which (159742) was redelivered to Palmdale and began flight testing on 13 September 1984. A second aircraft joined the programme in February 1985, and the flight test schedule was completed in August 1985, with redelivery to the US Navy in October. Following a three-month technical evaluation by the Naval Air Test Center at Patuxent River NAS, Maryland, the two S-3Bs were scheduled to undertake a six-month operational evaluation beginning in March 1986.

Two prototype kits to convert S-3As to S-3B production standard have been ordered, and on 28 April 1986 the US Navy contracted Lockheed to supply a first production series of 22 modification kits, together with spares, support equipment and integrated logistics support. Valued at $170·5 million, the contract calls for delivery of the two prototype kits in late 1987, followed by production deliveries at the rate of two per month, commencing January 1988. Modification of S-3As to S-3B standard will be undertaken at Cecil Field NAS, Florida. To equip a projected 15-carrier fleet, Lockheed has also submitted proposals for follow-on production of 82 or 103 new S-3Bs.

AVIONICS, ARMAMENT AND OPERATIONAL EQUIPMENT (S-3B): AYS-1 Proteus acoustic signal processor; modified Sanders AN/OL-320/AYS data processing memory group integrated with IBM AN/UYS-1; updated Sperry Univac AYK-10A(V) air data computer, interfaced with Harpoon air-to-surface missile and other new systems; improved electronic support measures (ESM); Hazeltine AN/ARR-78 sonobuoy receiver system; Precision Echo AN/AQH-7 analog tape recorder, Cubic AN/ARS-2 sonobuoy reference system; Texas Instruments AN/APS-137(V)1 radar, incorporating inverse synthetic aperture radar (ISAR) techniques; modified Goodyear AN/ALE-39 chaff/flare dispensing system; IBM AN/ALR-76 ESM; and provision for carrying McDonnell Douglas Harpoon standoff air-to-surface missiles, and for future advanced navigation and communications systems including Global Positioning System and Joint Tactical Information Distribution System.

LOCKHEED L-1011 (MODEL 385) TRISTAR

Details of the early history of the L-1011 TriStar can be found in previous editions of *Jane's*. The 250th and last production aircraft was rolled out on 19 August 1983. The first aircraft was retained by Lockheed until July 1986, when it was sold to Aviation Sales Company of Miami, Florida, for disassembly and disposal as spares for in-service TriStars. Delivery of the other 249 was completed in 1985.

Lockheed-California is developing a series of modification kits by which Delta Air Lines will uprate six of its TriStars to a new **L-1011-250** extended range configuration. The kits increase total fuel capacity of each aircraft from 71,668 kg (158,000 lb) to 96,905 kg (213,640 lb), to provide a 2,000 nm increase in range to 5,085 nm (9,415 km; 5,850 miles) with 280 passengers and baggage. Key structural sections of the wings, fuselage and landing gear are strengthened to cater for an 18 per cent increase in max T-O weight to 231,330 kg (510,000 lb). Currently installed engines will be replaced by higher thrust Rolls-Royce RB211-524B4 turbofans under separately negotiated arrangements.

Delivery of these kits to Delta, in Atlanta, Georgia, began in 1986 and was to be completed within one year for planned certification in May 1987. The Dash 250 modification is available for approximately 150 other TriStars produced after design changes were implemented to improve the CG envelope (from c/n 1052 onwards). The L-1011-500 version already incorporates the Dash 250 elements.

Details of the L-1011 tanker/freighter conversion for the Royal Air Force can be found under the Marshall of Cambridge entry in the UK section of this edition.

A full description of the TriStar can be found in the 1983-84 and earlier editions of *Jane's*.

LOCKHEED-GEORGIA COMPANY (GELAC)

86 South Cobb Drive, Marietta, Georgia 30063

PRESIDENT: Kenneth W. Cannestra

The main building occupied by Lockheed-Georgia (Gelac) at Marietta is one of the world's largest aircraft production plants under a single roof. Aircraft in current production on its assembly lines are the C-5B Galaxy heavy logistics transport, the C-130 Hercules turboprop transport and its commercial counterpart, the L-100. A major modification programme is under way on USAF C-5A Galaxy transports.

Lockheed-Georgia had approximately 18,700 employees at the beginning of 1986, and had delivered 2,733 aircraft by that time.

LOCKHEED MODEL 382 HERCULES

US Air Force designations: C-130, AC-130, DC-130, EC-130, HC-130, JC-130, MC-130, RC-130 and WC-130

US Navy designations: C-130, DC-130, EC-130 and LC-130

US Marine Corps designation: KC-130

US Coast Guard designation: HC-130

Canadian Armed Forces designation: CC-130

RAF designations: Hercules C. Mk 1, W. Mk 2 and C. Mk 3

Export designations: C-130H, C-130H-30, KC-130H and C-130H-MP

The C-130 was designed to a specification issued by the US Air Force Tactical Air Command in 1951. Lockheed was awarded its first production contract for the C-130A in September 1952, and 461 C-130As and C-130Bs were manufactured. Details of these basic versions and of many variants for special duties can be found in previous editions of *Jane's*. Later military versions of the C-130 are as follows:

C-130E Total number built was 488, not as stated in 1985-86 edition.

C-130H. Similar to earlier Hercules models except for updated avionics, improved wing and more powerful engines: T56-A-15 turboprops rated at 3,661 kW (4,910 ehp) for take-off, but limited to 3,362 kW (4,508 ehp). Deliveries to USAF began in April 1975. In service with many other air forces. In early 1986 total orders for the C-130H stood at 141 aircraft for the USAF and US Coast Guard and 329 for export, including orders placed by Taiwan for 12 aircraft for delivery commencing in late 1986 and an additional eight aircraft for the Japan Air Self-Defence Force.

C-130H-MP. Maritime patrol, search and rescue version, based on C-130H. Max T-O weight 70,310 kg (155,000 lb). Max payload 18,630 kg (41,074 lb). Four 3,362 kW (4,508 ehp) T56-A-15 engines. Standard and optional equipment includes sea search radar, scanner seats with observation windows, computerised INS/Omega navigation system, crew rest and lavatory/galley slide-in module, flare launcher, loudspeaker system, rescue kit airdrop platform, side looking airborne radar, passive microwave imager, low light TV, infra-red scanner, camera with data annotation, and ramp equipment pallet which includes a station for an observer. Search time at an altitude of 1,525 m (5,000 ft) is 2 h 30 min at a radius of 1,800 nm (3,333 km; 2,070 miles); 16 h 50 min at radius of 200 nm (370 km; 230 miles). One aircraft delivered to the Indonesian Air Force, and three to the Royal Malaysian Air Force.

C-130H-30. 'Stretched' version, with structural changes similar to those of RAF Hercules C.Mk 3 (see C-130K paragraph). Seven delivered to the Algerian Air Force, one to the Cameroun Air Force, one to the Dubai Air Wing, seven to the Indonesian Air Force, three to the Nigerian Air Force, one to Saudi Arabia and one to the Royal Thai Air Force. Two of the Nigerian aircraft are convertible into 90-passenger transports, by inserting 15-seat pallets into the cargo hold. Conversion takes less than one hour.

EC-130H 'Compass Call'. Operated by 41st Electronic Combat Squadron of the 552nd AWACW from Davis-Monthan AFB, Arizona and the 66th Electronic Combat Wing at Sembach, West Germany. Works with ground mobile C^3CM systems to jam enemy command control and communications systems.

HC-130H. Extended range version for Aerospace Rescue and Recovery Service of the US Air Force for aerial recovery of personnel or equipment and other duties; total of 43 delivered, of which the first one flew on 8 December 1964. The US Coast Guard subsequently ordered 24. Details in 1979-80 *Jane's*. Four modified as **JHC-130H** with added equipment for aerial recovery of re-entering space capsules. One modified to **DC-130H** for drone control duties.

KC-130H. Probe-drogue tanker version, very similar to the KC-130R. Exported to Argentina (2), Brazil (2), Israel (2), Morocco (2), Saudi Arabia (8) and Spain (5).

MC-130H. Combat Talon II version of C-130H, modified by USAF for special tactical missions including day/night infiltration and exfiltration, resupply of Special Operations ground forces, psychological warfare missions, aerial reconnaissance, and airdropping and surface-to-air retrieval of personnel. Crew of 9-11. Deeper nose radome, carrying Fulton STAR retrieval yoke of type fitted to HC-130H. Other equipment includes terrain following radar, precision ground mapping, inertial navigation system, automatic computed air release point, high-speed low-level aerial delivery and container release systems, ground acquisition receiver/interrogator, secure voice UHF/VHF/FM radios, retractable FLIR pod, angle of attack probe and ALQ-8 ECM pod under port wing, plus in-flight refuelling capability. Six funded in FY 1983-86, with five more requested in FY 1987. By 1992 the USAF MC-130H inventory is expected to total 21 aircraft, supplementing earlier MC-130Es.

C-130K. This is basically a C-130H, modified to meet requirements of the Royal Air Force. Much of the avionics and instrumentation is of UK manufacture. Sixty-six

Lockheed C-130H Hercules transport of the Tunisian Air Force

Lockheed C-130H-30 of United Arab Emirates Air Force

Lockheed EC-130H 'Compass Call' electronic warfare aircraft, identified by fuselage side blisters and undertail antennae

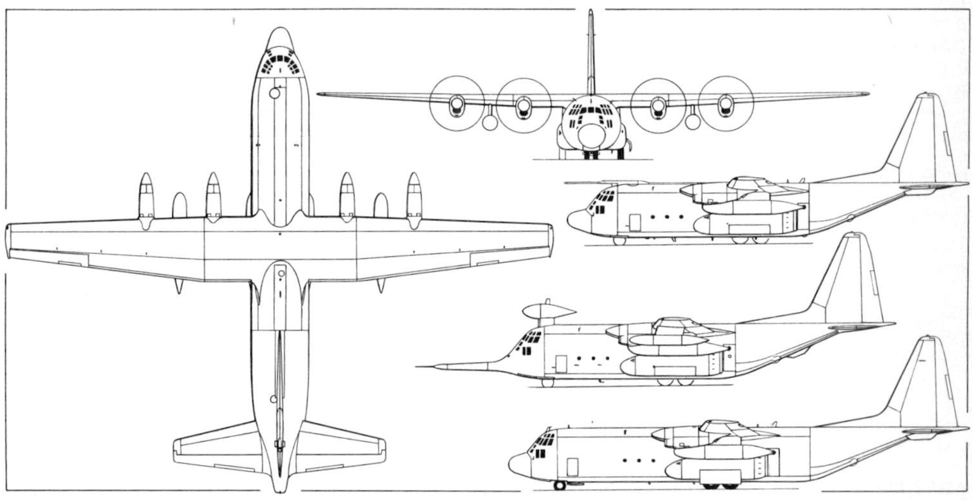

Lockheed C-130H-30 'stretched' Hercules with upper side view of C-130K (RAF C. Mk 1) and centre side view of W. Mk 2 *(Pilot Press)*

delivered as **Hercules C. Mk 1**, of which the first flew on 19 October 1966. One modified by Marshall of Cambridge (Engineering) Ltd in the UK for use by the RAF Meteorological Research Flight, under the designation **Hercules W. Mk 2**. Thirty of the others have been lengthened by 4·57 m (15 ft 0 in) (2·54 m; 8 ft 4 in plug forward of wing, 2·03 m; 6 ft 8 in aft of wing), equivalent to commercial L-100-30 standard. This increases payload capacity to seven cargo pallets instead of five, or four Land-Rovers and four trailers (instead of 3 + 2), or 128 troops instead of 92, or 92 fully equipped paratroops instead of 64, or 97 stretcher patients instead of 74. The first aircraft was modified at Lockheed-Georgia in 1979; the remaining 29 were lengthened by Marshall of Cambridge (see UK section). After modification, these aircraft are redesignated **Hercules C. Mk 3**.

HC-130N. Search and rescue version of the C-130H for recovery of aircrew and retrieval of space capsules after re-entry, using advanced direction finding equipment. Fifteen delivered to US Air Force.

HC-130P. Version of the C-130H, modified to have capability of refuelling helicopters in flight and for mid-air retrieval of parachute-borne payloads. Twenty built for USAF Aerospace Rescue and Recovery Service. Details in 1979-80 *Jane's*.

EC-130Q. Similar to earlier EC-130G, but with improved equipment and crew accommodation, for US Navy command communications (Tacamo) duties. Described as "the only airborne, survivable, communications link with submarine forces, providing HF and VLF SIMOP (simultaneous operations) capability in a collocated environment". Eighteen built.

KC-130R. Probe-drogue tanker version of C-130H: 14 for US Marine Corps. Changes from earlier KC-130F (1975-76 *Jane's*) include engines of 3,362 kW (4,508 ehp), increased T-O and landing weights, pylon mounted fuel tanks to provide additional 10,296 litres (2,720 US gallons) of fuel, and removable 13,627 litre (3,600 US gallon) fuel tank in cargo compartment. All fuel can be used by tanker for extended range. Single-point fuelling of installed and removable tanks via normal filler in wheel well. Operating weight empty 36,279 kg (79,981 lb). Max T-O weight 75,433 kg (166,301 lb). Able to offload up to 23,587 kg (52,000 lb) of fuel, equivalent to 30,283 litres (8,000 US gallons), at mission radius of 1,000 nm (1,850 km; 1,150 miles).

LC-130R. Basically a C-130H with wheel-ski gear for US Navy Squadron VXE-6. Six converted, for service in the Antarctic. Four acquired by USAF Reserve, for use in the Antarctic. Details in 1979-80 *Jane's*.

KC-130T. Tanker for US Marine Corps (Reserve). Similar to KC-130R but with updated avionics, including 'state of the art' INS, Omega and Tacan, a new autopilot and flight director, and solid state search radar. KC-130Ts delivered in late 1984 featured Bendix AN/APS-133 colour radar, flush mounted antennae and orthopaedically designed crew seats. Able to refuel helicopters as well as fighters. Delivery of four to Marine Aerial Refueler Transport Squadron 234 (VMGR-234) of Marine Air Control Group 48 at NAS Glenview, Illinois, began on 23 October 1983. Six additional KC-130Ts on order.

C-130 AEW. Described separately

Commercial versions of the Hercules are described separately.

The C-130 is able to deliver single loads of up to 11,340 kg (25,000 lb) by the ground proximity extraction method. This involves making a flypast 1·2-1·5 m (4-5 ft) above the ground with the rear loading ramp open. The aircraft trails a hook which is attached by cable to the palletised cargo. The hook engages a steel cable on the ground and the cargo is extracted from the aircraft and brought to a stop on the ground in about 30 m (100 ft) by an energy absorption system manufactured by All American Engineering of Wilmington, Delaware. An alternative extraction technique known as LAPES (low altitude parachute extraction system) involves deploying a 6·70 m (22 ft) ribbon parachute to drag the pallet from the cabin. Loads of up to 22,680 kg (50,000 lb) have been delivered by this method.

By January 1986 firm orders for all versions of the Hercules totalled 1,804 for 57 nations. This total comprised 1,115 C-130s for the US services, 582 for foreign military operators, and 107 commercial Hercules. Production continued at the rate of three aircraft a month in 1986, following delivery of 32 aircraft in 1985.

The following details refer specifically to the international C-130H, except where indicated otherwise:

Type: Medium/long-range combat transport.

Wings: Cantilever high-wing monoplane. Wing section NACA 64A318 at root, NACA 64A412 at tip. Dihedral 2° 30′. Incidence 3° at root, 0° at tip. Sweepback at quarter-chord 0°. All-metal two-spar stressed skin structure, with integrally stiffened tapered machined skin panels up to 14·63 m (48 ft 0 in) long. Conventional aluminium alloy ailerons have tandem-piston hydraulic boost, operated by either of two independent hydraulic systems. Lockheed-Fowler aluminium alloy trailing-edge flaps. Trim tab in each aileron. Leading-edges anti-iced by engine bleed air.

Fuselage: Semi-monocoque structure of aluminium and magnesium alloys.

Tail Unit: Cantilever all-metal stressed skin structure. Fixed incidence tailplane, with Kevlar afterbody strake on undersurface at each side, close to fuselage. Trim tab in each elevator and rudder. Elevator tabs use AC electrical power as primary source and DC as emergency source. Control surfaces have tandem-piston hydraulic boost. Hot air anti-icing of tailplane leading-edge, by engine bleed air.

Landing Gear: Hydraulically retractable tricycle type. Each main unit has two wheels in tandem, retracting into fairings built on to the sides of the fuselage. Nose unit has twin wheels and is steerable through 60° each side of centre. Oleo shock absorbers. Mainwheel tyres size 56 × 20-20, pressure 6·62 bars (96 lb/sq in). Nosewheel tyres size 39 × 13-16, pressure 4·14 bars (60 lb/sq in). Goodyear aircooled multiple disc hydraulic brakes with anti-skid units. Retractable combination wheel-skis available.

Power Plant: Four 3,362 kW (4,508 ehp) Allison T56-A-15 turboprop engines, each driving a Hamilton Standard type 54H60 four-blade constant-speed fully-feathering reversible-pitch propeller. Fuel in six integral tanks in wings, with total capacity of 26,344 litres (6,960 US gallons) and two optional underwing pylon tanks, each with capacity of 5,146 litres (1,360 US gallons). Total fuel capacity 36,636 litres (9,680 US gallons). Single pressure refuelling point in starboard wheel well. Overwing gravity fuelling. Oil capacity 182 litres (48 US gallons).

Accommodation: Crew of four on flight deck, comprising pilot, co-pilot, navigator and systems manager. Provision for fifth man to supervise loading. Sleeping quarters for relief crew, and galley. Flight deck and main cabin pressurised and air-conditioned. Standard complements for C-130H are as follows: troops (max) 92, paratroops (max) 64, litters 74 and 2 attendants. Corresponding figures for C-130H-30 are 128 troops, 92 paratroops, and 97 litters. As a cargo carrier, loads can include heavy equipment such as a 12,080 kg (26,640 lb) type F.6 refuelling trailer or a 155 mm howitzer and its high-speed tractor, or up to five 463L pallets of freight (seven in C-130H-30). Hydraulically operated main loading door and ramp at rear of cabin. Paratroop door on each side aft of landing gear fairing. Two emergency exit doors standard; two additional doors optional on C-130H-30.

Systems: Air-conditioning and pressurisation system max pressure differential 0·52 bars (7·5 lb/sq in). Three independent hydraulic systems, utility and booster systems operating at a pressure of 207 bars (3,000 lb/sq in), rated at 65·1 litres (17·2 US gallons)/min for utility and booster systems, 30·3 litres (8·0 US gallons)/min for auxiliary system. Reservoirs are unpressurised. Auxiliary system has handpump for emergencies. Electrical system supplied by four 40kVA AC alternators, plus one 40kVA auxiliary alternator driven by APU in port main landing gear fairing. Four transformer-rectifiers for DC power. Current production aircraft incorporate systems and component design changes for increased reliability. There are differences between the installed components for US government and export versions.

Avionics: Dual 628T-2A HF com, dual 618M-3A VHF com, AN/ARC-164 UHF com, AN/AIC-13 PA system, AN/AIC-18 intercom, dual 621A-6A ATC transponders, DF-301E UHF nav, dual 51RV-4B VHF nav, CMA 771 Omega nav, LTN-72 INS, dual DF-206 ADF, 51Z-4 marker beacon receiver, dual 860E-5 DME, AL-101 radio altimeter, RDR-1F weather radar, dual C-12 compass systems, Mk II GPWS, AP-105V autopilot, and dual FD-109 flight directors

Dimensions, external:
Wing span 40·41 m (132 ft 7 in)
Wing chord: at root 4·88 m (16 ft 0 in)
mean 4·16 m (13 ft 8½ in)
Wing aspect ratio 10·09
Length overall:
all except HC-130H and C-130H-30 29·79 m (97 ft 9 in)
C-130H-30 34·37 m (112 ft 9 in)
Height overall 11·66 m (38 ft 3 in)
Tailplane span 16·05 m (52 ft 8 in)
Wheel track 4·35 m (14 ft 3 in)
Wheelbase 9·77 m (32 ft 0¾ in)
Propeller diameter 4·11 m (13 ft 6 in)
Main cargo door (rear of cabin):
Height 2·77 m (9 ft 1 in)
Width 3·05 m (10 ft 0 in)
Height to sill 1·03 m (3 ft 5 in)
Paratroop doors (each): Height 1·83 m (6 ft 0 in)
Width 0·91 m (3 ft 0 in)
Height to sill 1·03 m (3 ft 5 in)
Emergency exits (each): Height 1·22 m (4 ft 0 in)
Width 0·71 m (2 ft 4 in)

Dimensions, internal:
Cabin, excl flight deck:
Length without ramp:
C-130H 12·22 m (40 ft 1¼ in)
C-130H-30 16·79 m (55 ft 1¼ in)
Length with ramp: C-130H 15·73 m (51 ft 8½ in)
C-130H-30 20·33 m (66 ft 8½ in)
Max width 3·3 m (10 ft 3 in)
Max height 2·81 m (9 ft 2¾ in)
Floor area, excl ramp: C-130H 39·5 m² (425 sq ft)
Volume, incl ramp: C-130H 127·4 m³ (4,500 cu ft)
C-130H-30 165·5 m³ (5,845 cu ft)

Areas:
Wings, gross 162·12 m² (1,745 sq ft)
Ailerons (total) 10·22 m² (110 sq ft)
Trailing-edge flaps (total) 31·77 m² (342 sq ft)
Fin 20·90 m² (225 sq ft)
Rudder, incl tab 6·97 m² (75 sq ft)
Tailplane 35·40 m² (381 sq ft)
Elevators, incl tabs 14·40 m² (155 sq ft)

Weights and Loadings:
Operating weight empty:
C-130H 34,686 kg (76,469 lb)
C-130H-30 36,397 kg (80,242 lb)
Max fuel weight: internal 20,520 kg (45,240 lb)
external 8,020 kg (17,680 lb)
Max payload: C-130H 19,356 kg (42,673 lb)
C-130H-30 17,645 kg (38,900 lb)
Max normal T-O weight 70,310 kg (155,000 lb)
Max overload T-O weight 79,380 kg (175,000 lb)
Max normal landing weight 70,310 kg (155,000 lb)
Max overload landing weight 79,380 kg (175,000 lb)
Max zero-fuel weight, 2·5*g* 54,040 kg (119,142 lb)
Max wing loading 434·5 kg/m² (89 lb/sq ft)
Max power loading 5·23 kg/kW (8·6 lb/ehp)

Performance (C-130H at max T-O weight, unless indicated otherwise):
Max cruising speed 325 knots (602 km/h; 374 mph)
Econ cruising speed 300 knots (556 km/h; 345 mph)
Stalling speed 100 knots (185 km/h; 115 mph)
Max rate of climb at S/L 579 m (1,900 ft)/min
Service ceiling at 58,970 kg (130,000 lb) AUW 10,060 m (33,000 ft)
Service ceiling, one engine out, at 58,970 kg (130,000 lb) AUW 8,075 m (26,500 ft)
Min ground turning radius 19·2 m (63 ft)
Runway LCN at 70,310 kg (155,000 lb) AUW:
asphalt 37
concrete 42
T-O run 1,091 m (3,580 ft)
T-O to 15 m (50 ft) 1,573 m (5,160 ft)
Landing from 15 m (50 ft) at 45,360 kg (100,000 lb) AUW 731 m (2,400 ft)
Landing from 15 m (50 ft) at 58,967 kg (130,000 lb) AUW 838 m (2,750 ft)
Landing run at 58,967 kg (130,000 lb) AUW 518 m (1,700 ft)
Range with max payload, with 5% reserves and allowance for 30 min at S/L 2,046 nm (3,791 km; 2,356 miles)
Range with max fuel, incl external tanks, 7,081 kg (15,611 lb) payload, reserves of 5% initial fuel plus 30 min at S/L 4,250 nm (7,876 km; 4,894 miles)

LOCKHEED L-100 SERIES COMMERCIAL HERCULES

Details of initial versions of the commercial Hercules have appeared in previous editions of *Jane's*; current models are as follows:

L-100-20 (Model 382E). Certificated on 4 October 1968, this 'stretched' version of the Hercules has a 2·54 m (100 in) fuselage extension. A 1·52 m (60 in) fuselage plug is inserted aft of the forward crew door and a 1·02 m (40 in) plug aft of the paratroop doors. Allison 501-D22A engines. Operators/owners in January 1986 were Cargolux Airlines (1), Gabon Air Force (1), Peruvian Air Force (5), Philippine Air Force (4), Safair Freighters (1), St. Lucia Airways (1), Southern Air Transport (2), TAAG Angola Airlines (2), Transamerica Airlines (1), Lockheed-Georgia Company (1).

L-100-30 (Model 382G). Generally similar to the L-100-20, but with the fuselage extended a further 2·03 m (80 in). Early models did not have aft personnel doors which are now standatrd. Saturn Airways (now Transamerica Airlines) was the first operator of this model, in December 1970. Operators/owners in 1986 were Air Algérie (3), Air Botswana (2), Bolivian Air Transport (1), Dubai Air Force (1), Ecuadorean Air Force (1), Gabon Air Force (3), Indonesian Air Force (1), Kuwait Air Force (4), LADE (Argentina) (1), MarkAir Airlines (3), Northwest Territorial Airways (1), Pelita Air Service (6), Petroleos Mexicanos (Pemex) (1), Safair Freighters (7), Saudi Arabia (5), SCIBE Airlift (1), SFAIR-France (2), Southern Air Transport (4), Transamerica Airlines (12), Uganda Air Cargo (1), United Trade International (1) and Zaïre Cargo (1).

Lockheed-Georgia announced on 5 October 1983 that it had applied to the FAA for a supplemental type certificate to enable the civil L-100-30 to carry up to 100 passengers. All C-130 and L-100 aircraft delivered from April 1984 have 0·61 m × 1·22 m (24 in × 48 in) emergency exit doors as standard equipment. Purchasers of the L-100-30 will have the option of buying stretch fuselage plugs equipped with additional exits on each side of the fuselage. Together with the current rear personnel doors, this will provide the necessary six exits for the proposed 100-seat commercial passenger/cargo convertible version. Other changes required for certification include increased liferaft installations, a new oxygen system and a public address system. Already available is a seven-pallet kit containing airliner type seating plus a galley-lavatory pallet. In the certificated 100-passenger configuration, seating and galley-lavatory could be built into the aircraft or installed on pallets to the customer's choice.

Lockheed has developed an airborne hospital version of the L-100-30, designated **L-100-30HS**. Three of this variant have been delivered to Saudi Arabia after modification by Lockheed Aircraft Service Company, with operating theatres and intensive care, advanced anaesthesia and X-ray facilities. Electrical generators and air conditioners contained in underwing pods enable the aircraft to function as remote emergency hospitals for up to 72 hours without external support.

A total of 105 commercial Hercules (all versions) had been delivered by January 1986. Details given for the C-130H apply also to the L-100-20 and L-100-30, except as follows:

TYPE: Medium/long-range transport.

LANDING GEAR: As for C-130H, except mainwheel tyre pressure 3·24-7·38 bars (47-107 lb/sq in) and nosewheel tyre pressure 4·14 bars (60 lb/sq in).

POWER PLANT: Four 3,490 kW (4,680 ehp) Allison 501-D22A turboprop engines.

DIMENSIONS, EXTERNAL:
- Length overall: L-100-20 — 32·33 m (106 ft 1 in)
  - L-100-30 — 34·37 m (112 ft 9 in)
- Wheelbase: L-100-20 — 11·30 m (37 ft 1 in)
  - L-100-30 — 12·32 m (40 ft 5 in)
- Crew door (integral steps):
  - Height — 1·14 m (3 ft 9 in)
  - Width — 0·76 m (2 ft 6 in)
  - Height to sill — 1·04 m (3 ft 5 in)

DIMENSIONS, INTERNAL:
- Cabin, excl flight deck:
  - Length: L-100-20 — 15·04 m (49 ft 4 in)
    - L-100-30, excl ramp — 17·07 m (56 ft 0 in)
    - L-100-30, incl ramp — 19·93 m (65 ft 4¾ in)
  - Max height — 2·74 m (9 ft 0 in)
- Floor area, excl ramp:
  - L-100-20 — 46·36 m² (499 sq ft)
  - L-100-30 — 52·30 m² (563 sq ft)
- Floor area, ramp — 9·57 m² (103 sq ft)
- Volume, incl ramp:
  - L-100-20 — 150·28 m³ (5,307 cu ft)
  - L-100-30 — 171·5 m³ (6,057 cu ft)

WEIGHTS AND LOADINGS:
- Operating weight empty:
  - L-100-20 — 34,301 kg (75,621 lb)
  - L-100-30 — 35,235 kg (77,680 lb)
- Max payload: L-100-20 — 20,942 kg (46,169 lb)
  - L-100-30 — 23,183 kg (51,110 lb)
- Max ramp weight — 70,670 kg (155,800 lb)
- Max T-O weight — 70,308 kg (155,000 lb)
- Max landing weight:
  - L-100-20 — 58,970 kg (130,000 lb)
  - L-100-30 — 61,235 kg (135,000 lb)
- Max zero-fuel weight:
  - L-100-20 — 55,240 kg (121,790 lb)
  - L-100-30 — 58,420 kg (128,790 lb)
- Max fuel weight (both) — 29,418 kg (64,856 lb)
- Max wing loading — 433·5 kg/m² (88·8 lb/sq ft)
- Max power loading — 5·23 kg/kW (8·6 lb/ehp)

PERFORMANCE (at max T-O weight except where indicated):
- Max cruising speed at 6,100 m (20,000 ft) at 54,430 kg (120,000 lb) AUW:
  - L-100-20 — 308 knots (571 km/h; 355 mph)
  - L-100-30 — 315 knots (583 km/h; 363 mph)
- Landing speed:
  - L-100-20 — 126 knots (233 km/h; 145 mph)
  - L-100-30 — 124 knots (230 km/h; 143 mph)
- Max rate of climb at S/L — 518 m (1,700 ft)/min
- Min ground turning radius: L-100-20 — 26·8 m (88 ft)
  - L-100-30 — 27·5 m (90 ft)
- Runway LCN: asphalt — 37
  - concrete — 42
- FAR T-O field length — 1,890 m (6,200 ft)
- FAR landing field length, at max landing weight:
  - L-100-20 — 1,450 m (4,760 ft)
  - L-100-30 — 1,478 m (4,850 ft)
- Range with max payload, 45 min reserves:
  - L-100-20 — 1,926 nm (3,569 km; 2,218 miles)
  - L-100-30 — 1,363 nm (2,526 km; 1,569 miles)
- Range with zero payload, 45 min reserves:
  - L-100-20 — 5,260 nm (9,748 km; 6,057 miles)
  - L-100-30 — 4,979 nm (9,227 km; 5,733 miles)

OPERATIONAL NOISE LEVELS (FAR Pt 36):
- T-O — 97·8 EPNdB
- Approach — 98·8 EPNdB
- Sideline — 92·3 EPNdB

LOCKHEED HTTB

On 19 June 1984, Lockheed-Georgia flew for the first time a high technology testbed (HTTB) conversion of a commercial model L-100-20 Hercules, developed to provide a platform for evaluating new technologies in an airborne environment. Funded through Lockheed-Georgia's internal research and development budget, and supported by some 45 participating vendor companies, the HTTB is being used to conduct STOL flight research, in the development of avionics subsystems, and as a vehicle in which to develop high lift systems, advanced flight controls, cockpit displays, navigation, guidance and enroute survivability systems for future tactical airlift aircraft.

Lockheed-Georgia's all-black high technology testbed (HTTB) Hercules, a converted L-100-20

Externally apparent features of the HTTB include the addition of a long dorsal fin, similar extensions known as 'horsals' (horizontal dorsals) forward of each tailplane root, and an electrically isolated sensor boom of composite materials forward of each wingtip. Initial flight tests in 1984 established the aircraft's baseline performance and flying qualities. Then, during the first of several planned modification programmes, the HTTB was fitted with a 1,000-channel data gathering, analysis and display system known as LADS (Lockheed airborne data system). This permanent system enables engineers to run tests and evaluate data in real time aboard the aircraft. Initially, some 200 channels of data are being used. In addition to LADS, the HTTB carries in its cargo compartment a 10 m (33 ft) long mobile data centre van equipped with TV and telemetry links so that data can be analysed on the ground at remote test sites.

Early HTTB test flights also verified a new electronics mission pod known as SAMSON (Special Avionics Mission Strap-On Now). This uses a Hercules external wing fuel tank, containing its own generator, to house an easily attachable special avionics package, providing the basic C-130 with special mission capability without physical modification of the airframe. Lockheed believes that the SAMSON facility will offer worldwide C-130 operators a viable low-cost electronics mission capability.

Planned modifications to the HTTB which were scheduled for completion by July 1986 include the installation of fully-powered flight controls, fast-acting double-slotted trailing-edge flaps, drooped high camber fixed wing leading-edges, hydraulically actuated spoilers for roll control, extended-chord ailerons and rudder with servo tab, and a new landing gear which will permit sink rates up to 4·48 m (14·7 ft)/s at a landing weight of 58,967 kg (130,000 lb). Wind tunnel testing of a one-tenth scale model of the modified aircraft has indicated that the planned external modifications could offer an increase in lift of up to 25 per cent. STOL experiments with the HTTB were expected to begin in the Summer of 1986. Target STOL performance includes a landing from 15 m (50 ft) in 457 m (1,500 ft) at a landing weight of 63,500 kg (140,000 lb). Landing speed is expected to be about 80 knots (148 km/h; 92 mph).

The HTTB will be modified in January 1987 to incorporate a number of systems improvements, including an onboard command guidance system with laser rangefinder, FLIR and a computer-generated head-up display which will be able to guide the pilot through the final approach and landing phases of flight to fully automatic touchdown without the normal level-off and flare, thus reducing landing distance. Night vision goggles, a cockpit management system, mission computers, weather/mapping radar, conformal phased-array low-sidelobe antennae, and an underwing pod housing FLIR and LLTV sensors will also be evaluated.

Lockheed has been contracted by NASA to design and build a C-130 wing centre-section from composites materials, and hopes to obtain a contract to install and flight test the composites wing on the HTTB testbed aircraft by 1988. In addition to industry research programmes, the HTTB is being offered to university faculties and graduate students who will have opportunities to place experiments aboard the aircraft and to take part in the flight testing of their equipment.

The HTTB, which made its public debut at the 1985 Paris Air Show, set new FAI Class N time-to-height records on 5 March 1985. Taking off at a gross weight of 44,724 kg (98,600 lb), using only 427 m (1,400 ft) of runway, the aircraft climbed to 3,000 m in 3 min 59·4 s; to 6,000 m in 9 min 19·75 s; and to 9,000 m in 18 min 33·72 s.

LOCKHEED C-130 AEW

Lockheed-Georgia announced at the 1985 Paris Air Show a proposed airborne early warning system version of the C-130 Hercules with a GEC Avionics APY 920 radar installation in nose and tail fairings similar to those of the BAe Nimrod AEW.Mk 3. The C-130 AEW could be based on current production C-130H models or on conversions of earlier variants already in service.

Combining the proven airframe of the C-130 with the APY 920 surveillance radar will, Lockheed-Georgia claims, provide an effective long-endurance AEW aircraft with a time on station of 8-12 hours on a typical mission. The AEW information can be combined with other data and intelligence to provide either a stand-alone command and control capability with an extended radius of action, or can be downlinked to a ground- or ship-based air defence headquarters.

Flying at an altitude of 8,230 m (27,000 ft), the C-130 AEW could provide 360° surveillance coverage to the 200 nm (370 km; 230 mile) radar horizon and beyond. Aircraft performance compared with the standard C-130 is little affected, since the drag penalty of the nose and tail radomes is only about 5 per cent. T-O and landing field requirements are unchanged, and the aircraft's in-flight refuelling capability (tanker or receiver) is retained. The Lockheed/GEC Avionics programme provides for the modified airframe to be built and flight tested by Lockheed-Georgia; GEC Avionics would develop, build and test the radar and mission avionics systems, which would then be installed and flight tested by Marshall of Cambridge.

The radar installation would be contained in lightweight modular units (some of which are being tested in the HTTB), installed in the Hercules cargo hold. The forward pallet would contain the radar equipment, including computers and signal processing equipment. The self-contained second module, extensively insulated against sound and vibration, would accommodate up to six AEW control stations in the centre-fuselage area, with growth potential space for additional airborne missions such as Elint, radar data fusion, and track correlation. Communications equipment would be housed in a third pallet, installed in the rear of the hold.

Lockheed-Georgia has said that a production programme for the C-130 AEW could be launched with orders for ten aircraft, which is approximately 10 per cent of the

Artist's impression of proposed Lockheed C-130 AEW with GEC Avionics APY 920 radar

estimated potential worldwide market among existing and new C-130 operators.

DIMENSIONS, EXTERNAL: As for standard C-130 except:

Length overall	35·48 m (116 ft 4¾ in)
Forward radome:	
Length	3·93 m (12 ft 10½ in)
Max width	3·09 m (10 ft 1¾ in)
Max depth	2·42 m (7 ft 11¼ in)
Ground clearance	0·41 m (1 ft 4¼ in)
Rear radome:	
Length	4·17 m (13 ft 8 in)
Max width	3·09 m (10 ft 1¾ in)
Max depth	2·48 m (8 ft 1¾ in)
Ground clearance	2·97 m (9 ft 8¾ in)

WEIGHT (estimated):

Basic aircraft weight	34,473 kg (76,000 lb)
AEW conversion	10,659 kg (23,500 lb)
*Mission fuel	16,103 kg (35,500 lb)
Mission T-O weight	61,235 kg (135,000 lb)

PERFORMANCE: Similar to standard C-130 except:

Ferry range	4,000 nm (7,413 km; 4,606 miles)
Max mission time on station	13 h

**Max capacity 28,123 kg (62,000 lb); tanker giveaway with AEW on board, more than 11,340 kg (25,000 lb)*

LOCKHEED GALAXY

USAF designation: C-5

In early 1978 Lockheed received a USAF contract to manufacture two new sets of wings for the **C-5A**, of a design intended to increase service life to 30,000 h. Apart from the moving surfaces, these wings are of virtually new design, using 7175-T73511 aluminium alloy for greater strength and increased resistance to corrosion. One set was for ground testing, and one for flight trials, which were completed successfully on a prototype installation during 1980, the converted C-5A being redelivered to the USAF in early 1981. The remaining 76 Galaxies in operational service with the USAF are currently being fitted with the new wings in a modification programme scheduled for completion in mid-1987.

The 433rd MAW at Kelly AFB, Texas, became the first AFRES unit to receive the C-5A when the first of 16 aircraft was delivered in December 1984. C-5As will also be transferred to the Air National Guard's 105th MAG, based at Stewart Airport, New York.

On 17 December 1984 a C-5A set a new international record for the greatest payload, a total of 111,462 kg (245,731 lb), lifted to a height of 2,000 m. This flight also set a new US national record for the greatest recorded weight of aircraft flown, the C-5A taking off at a gross weight of 417,685 kg (920,836 lb). Another US national record, for heaviest aircraft landing weight of 397,693 kg (876,762 lb), was established by a C-5A on 16 January 1985.

Full structural and specification details of the C-5A can be found in the 1975-76 *Jane's*. An abbreviated entry appeared in the 1978-79 edition.

In the Summer of 1982, Congress approved a Lockheed proposal to manufacture a C-5N (N : new) version of the Galaxy, to meet an urgent US Air Force requirement for additional heavy airlift capacity. A total of 50 of these transports is requested, under the service designation **C-5B**. Funding has been approved for 29 aircraft, with 21 more requested in FY 1987.

The aircraft internal arrangements and external aerodynamic configuration are the same as those of the C-5A, but the new version will include all of the changes, improvements and modifications incorporated in its predecessor during 12 years of service with the US Air Force.

The first C-5B was rolled out on 12 July, and made its first flight from Dobbins AFB on 10 September 1985 at the start of a 66 hour production flight evaluation programme leading to first delivery to the USAF's 443rd Military Airlift Wing at Altus AFB, Oklahoma, on 8 January 1986. Eight C-5Bs were expected to enter service during 1986. Final delivery is scheduled for February 1989.

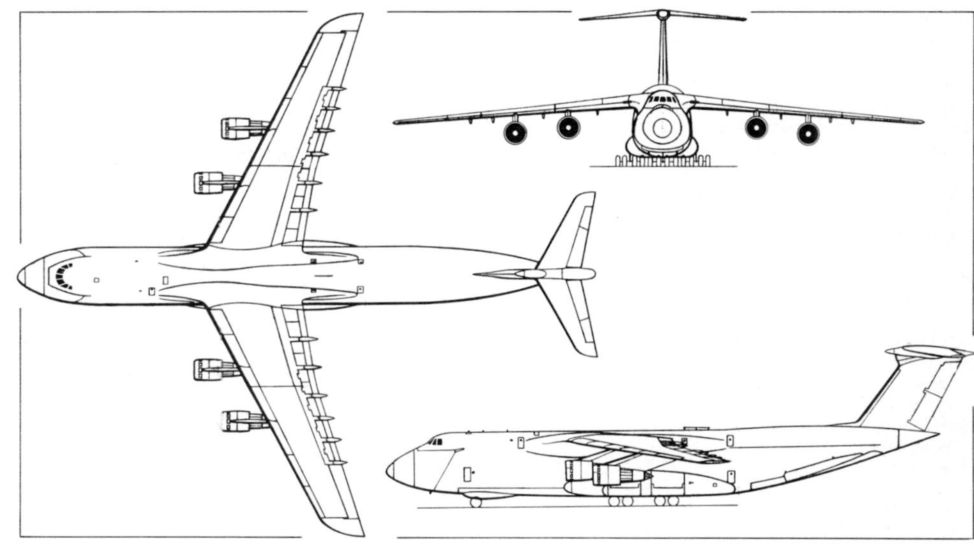

Lockheed C-5B Galaxy heavy logistics transport aircraft *(Pilot Press)*

The following description applies to the C-5B:

TYPE: Heavy logistics transport aircraft.

WINGS: Cantilever high-wing monoplane. Wing section NACA 0012 (mod) at 20 per cent span, NACA 0011 (mod) at 43·7 per cent and 70 per cent span. Anhedral 5° 30′ at quarter-chord. Incidence 3° 30′ at root. Sweepback at quarter-chord 25°. Conventional fail-safe box structure of built-up spars and machined aluminium alloy extruded skin panels. Statically balanced aluminium alloy ailerons. Modified Fowler aluminium alloy trailing-edge flaps. Simple hinged aluminium alloy spoilers forward of flaps. No trim tabs. Sealed inboard slats and slotted outboard slats on leading-edges. Ailerons and spoilers operated by hydraulic servo actuators. Trailing-edge flaps and leading-edge slats actuated by ball screw-jack and torque tube system. Leading-edge slats and slat tracks, leading-edge ribs, and ailerons, are built under subcontract by Canadair Ltd.

FUSELAGE: Conventional semi-monocoque fail-safe structure of 7049-T73, 7050-T736, 7075-T73 and 7475 aluminium alloys.

TAIL UNIT: Cantilever all-metal T tail. All surfaces swept; anhedral on tailplane. All components are single-cell box structures with integrally stiffened aluminium alloy skin panels. Variable incidence tailplane. Elevators in four sections; rudder in two sections. No trim tabs. Rudder and elevators operated through hydraulic servo actuators. Tailplane actuated through hydraulically powered screwjack. No anti-icing equipment.

LANDING GEAR: Retractable tricycle type. Nose unit retracted rearward by hydraulically driven ballscrews. Main units rotated through 90° and retracted inward via hydraulically driven gearbox. Single nose shock absorber and four main gear shock absorbers are of Bendix oleo-pneumatic dual-chamber type. Four wheels on nose unit. Four main units (two in tandem on each side) each comprise a 'triangular footprint' six-wheel bogie made up of a pair of wheels forward of the shock absorber and two pairs aft. All 28 tyres size 49 × 17-20 type VII 26-ply. Tyre pressures: nosewheels 9·45 bars (137 lb/sq in), mainwheels 7·65 bars (111 lb/sq in) with in-flight deflation capability. Goodrich wheels, tyres and carbon disc brakes. Hydro-Aire fully modulating anti-skid units. Ground manoeuvrability enhanced by castoring rear main units.

POWER PLANT: Four General Electric TF39-GE-1C turbofan engines, each rated at 191·2 kN (43,000 lb st). Twelve integral fuel tanks in wings, between front and rear spars, comprising two outboard main tanks (each 13,874 litres; 3,665 US gallons), two inboard main tanks (each 14,755 litres; 3,898 US gallons), two outboard auxiliary tanks (each 18,034 litres; 4,764 US gallons), two inboard auxiliary tanks (each 18,401 litres; 4,861 US gallons); two outboard extended range tanks (each 15,865 litres; 4,191 US gallons), and two inboard extended range tanks (each 15,883 litres; 4,196 US gallons). Total capacity 193,624 litres (51,150 US gallons). Two refuelling points each side, in forward part of main landing gear pods. Flight refuelling capability, via inlet in upper forward fuselage, over flight engineer's station (compatible with KC-135 and KC-10 tankers). Oil capacity 138 litres (36·4 US gallons).

ACCOMMODATION: Standard crew of five, consisting of pilot, co-pilot, flight engineer and two loadmasters, with rest area for 15 people (relief crew, couriers, etc) at front of upper deck. Basic version has seats for 75 troops on rear part of upper deck, aft of wing box. Provision for carrying 270 troops on lower deck, but aircraft will be employed primarily as freighter. Typical loads include two M1 Abrams tanks or sixteen ¾ ton lorries; or one M1 and two Bradley armoured fighting vehicles; or six AH-64A Apache attack helicopters; or 10 Pershing misiles with tow and launch vehicles; or 36 standard 463L load pallets. 'Visor' type upward hinged nose, and loading ramp, permit straight-in loading into front of hold, under flight deck. Rear straight-in loading via ramp which forms undersurface of rear fuselage. Side panels of rear fuselage, by ramp, hinge outward to improve access on ground but do not need to open for airdrop operations in view of width of ramp. Ramp and associated side panels built under subcontract by Canadair Ltd. Provision for aerial delivery system (ADS) kits for paratroops or cargo. Two passengerdoors, one each on port and starboard sides at rear end of lower deck. One crew door on port side at forward end of lower deck. Five evacuation slides and four 25-person liferafts, all supplied by Garrett Air Cruisers. Entire accommodation pressurised and air-conditioned.

First Lockheed C-5B Galaxy for the USAF arriving at Altus AFB, Oklahoma

SYSTEMS: Electronically controlled air-conditioning and pressurisation systems: pressure differential 0·57 bars (8·2 lb/sq in). Four separate hydraulic systems, pressure 207 bars (3,000 lb/sq in) each, supply flying control and utility systems, with power supplied by two identical variable volume, constant pressure pumps on each engine, each rated at 227 litres (60 US gallons)/min. Each system contains an unpressurised hydraulic reservoir. Electrical system includes four 60/80 kVA AC engine driven generators. Two APUs provide auxiliary pneumatic and electrical power. Ground hydraulic power is supplied by two air turbine motors.

AVIONICS AND EQUIPMENT: Communications and navigation equipment to military requirements. Bendix colour weather radar. Three Delco inertial navigation units with triple-mix capabilities. Special equipment includes updated electronic malfunction detection, analysis and recoding subsystem (MADAR II) which scans and analyses more than 800 test points.

DIMENSIONS, EXTERNAL:
- Wing span: 67·88 m (222 ft 8½ in)
- Wing chord: at root: 13·85 m (45 ft 5¼ in)
  - at tip: 4·67 m (15 ft 4 in)
- Wing aspect ratio: 7·75
- Length overall: 75·54 m (247 ft 10 in)
- Length of fuselage: 70·29 m (230 ft 7¼ in)
- Height overall: 19·85 m (65 ft 1½ in)
- Tailplane span: 20·94 m (68 ft 8½ in)
- Wheel track (between outer wheels): 11·42 m (37 ft 5½ in)
- Wheelbase (c/l main gear to c/l nose gear): 22·22 m (72 ft 11 in)
- Crew door (lower deck):
  - Height: 1·80 m (5 ft 11 in)
  - Width: 1·02 m (3 ft 4 in)
  - Height to sill: 3·94 m (12 ft 11 in)
- Passenger door (lower deck):
  - Height: 1·83 m (6 ft 0 in)
  - Width: 0·91 m (3 ft 0 in)
  - Height to sill: 3·56 m (11 ft 8 in)
- Aft loading opening (ramp lowered):
  - Max height: 3·93 m (12 ft 10¾ in)
  - Max width: 5·79 m (19 ft 0 in)
- Aft straight-in loading:
  - Max height: 2·90 m (9 ft 6 in)
  - Max width: 5·79 m (19 ft 0 in)
- Forward loading opening (ramp lowered or straight-in):
  - Max height: 4·11 m (13 ft 6 in)
  - Max width: 5·79 m (19 ft 0 in)
- Height to floor (kneeled):
  - forward: 1·34 m (4 ft 4¾ in)
  - rear: 1·45 m (4 ft 9 in)

DIMENSIONS, INTERNAL:
- Cabins, excl flight deck:
- Length:
  - upper deck, forward: 11·99 m (39 ft 4 in)
  - upper deck, rear: 18·20 m (59 ft 8½ in)
  - lower deck, without ramps: 36·91 m (121 ft 1 in)
  - lower deck, with ramps: 44·09 m (144 ft 8 in)
- Max width:
  - upper deck, forward: 4·20 m (13 ft 9½ in)
  - upper deck, rear: 3·96 m (13 ft 0 in)
  - lower deck: 5·79 m (19 ft 0 in)
- Max height:
  - upper deck: 2·29 m (7 ft 6 in)
  - lower deck: 4·11 m (13 ft 6 in)
- Floor area:
  - upper deck, forward: 50·17 m² (540 sq ft)
  - upper deck, rear: 72·10 m² (776·1 sq ft)
  - lower deck, without ramp: 213·76 m² (2,300·9 sq ft)
- Volume:
  - upper deck, forward: 56·91 m³ (2,010 cu ft)
  - upper deck, rear: 170·46 m³ (6,020 cu ft)
  - lower deck: 985·29 m³ (34,795 cu ft)

AREAS:
- Wings, gross: 576·0 m² (6,200 sq ft)
- Ailerons (total): 23·49 m² (252·8 sq ft)
- Trailing-edge flaps (total): 92·13 m² (991·7 sq ft)
- Leading-edge slats (total): 60·25 m² (648·5 sq ft)
- Spoilers (total): 40·01 m² (430·7 sq ft)
- Fin: 89·29 m² (961·1 sq ft)
- Rudder: 21·06 m² (226·7 sq ft)
- Tailplane: 89·73 m² (965·8 sq ft)
- Elevators: 24·03 m² (258·7 sq ft)

WEIGHTS AND LOADINGS (for 2·25*g*):
- Operating weight empty, equipped: 169,643 kg (374,000 lb)
- Max payload: 118,388 kg (261,000 lb)
- Max fuel weight: 150,815 kg (332,500 lb)
- Max T-O weight: 379,657 kg (837,000 lb)
- Max zero-fuel weight: 288,030 kg (635,000 lb)
- *Max landing weight: 288,415 kg (635,850 lb)
- Max wing loading: 659 kg/m² (135·48 lb/sq ft)
- Max power loading: 496·4 kg/kN (4·88 lb/lb st)

**at 2·7 m (9 ft)/s descent rate*

PERFORMANCE (estimated at max T-O weight, except where indicated):
- Never-exceed speed: 402 knots (745 km/h; 463 mph) CAS or Mach 0·875
- Max level speed at 7,620 m (25,000 ft): 496 knots (919 km/h; 571 mph)
- Max cruising speed at 7,620 m (25,000 ft): 480-490 knots (888-908 km/h; 552-564 mph)
- Econ cruising speed at 7,620 m (25,000 ft): 450 knots (833 km/h; 518 mph)
- Stalling speed at max landing weight, 40° flap, power off: 104 knots (193 km/h; 120 mph)
- Max rate of climb at S/L: 525 m (1,725 ft)/min
- Service ceiling at AUW of 278,960 kg (615,000 lb): 10,895 m (35,750 ft)
- Min ground turning radius: 50·90 m (167 ft 0 in)
- Runway LCN: asphalt: 69
  - concrete: 44
- T-O run at S/L, ISA: 2,530 m (8,300 ft)
- T-O to 15 m (50 ft) at S/L, ISA: 2,987 m (9,800 ft)
- Landing from 15 m (50 ft), max landing weight at S/L, ISA: 1,164 m (3,820 ft)
- Landing run, max landing weight at S/L, ISA: 725 m (2,380 ft)
- Range with max payload, ISA, fuel reserves 5% of initial fuel plus 30 min loiter at S/L: 2,982 nm (5,526 km; 3,434 miles)
- Range with max fuel, ISA, reserves as above: 5,618 nm (10,411 km; 6,469 miles)

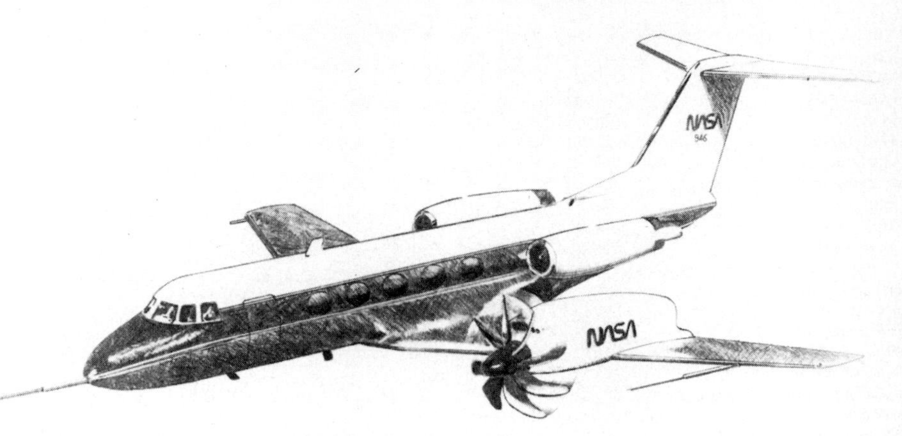

Artist's impression of Lockheed-Georgia/NASA Gulfstream XPT experimental propfan testbed aircraft

LOCKHEED-GEORGIA/NASA PROPFAN

Lockheed-Georgia has been awarded a $59 million contract by NASA to test a fuel-saving advanced propeller (propfan) system. The Propfan Test Assessment (PTA) programme contract covers design, construction and ground testing of the system. A flight test option covers airborne tests of the propfan at speeds up to Mach 0·8 and altitudes up to 10,670 m (35,000 ft). The PTA contract, which is managed by NASA's Lewis Research Center in Cleveland, Ohio, calls for Lockheed to design and build a new nacelle to house an Allison 570-M78 turboshaft engine, and to verify the structural integrity of the propfan propeller and determine its acoustic characteristics. The propfan system, which features eight thin profile blades with highly swept tips, will first be evaluated in outdoor static tests, which were due to begin in May 1986. It will subsequently be mounted on one wing of a Gulfstream II business jet known as the Gulfstream XPT (Experimental Propfan Testbed) which, together with a fuselage section, will undergo acoustic testing in the low speed wind tunnel at NASA's Ames Research Center, commencing in October 1986.

For the flight test phase, scheduled to begin in May 1987, the propfan system will be installed on the port wing of a Gulfstream II. Lockheed's partners in the PTA programme are Allison Gas Turbine (power plant); Gulfstream Aerospace (testbed vehicle); Hamilton Standard (propfan system); Lockheed-California (acoustics) and Rohr Industries (propulsion drive system).

LTV

LTV AEROSPACE AND DEFENSE COMPANY (Subsidiary of The LTV Corporation)

PO Box 225003, Dallas, Texas 75265-5003
Telephone: (214) 979 7711

PRESIDENT AND CHIEF EXECUTIVE OFFICER:
Robert L. Kirk

SENIOR VICE-PRESIDENT:
J. J. Welch Jr (Programme Development)

VICE-PRESIDENTS:
K. R. Chapman (Planning)
R. B. Corlett (Human Resources)
H. W. Fish (International)
D. R. Hagler (General Counsel)
J. E. Hawley (Finance)
Eric Fritz von Marbod (Middle East and Europe)

Vought Aero Products Division
9314 West Jefferson, PO Box 225907, Dallas, Texas 75265

PRESIDENT: Billie M. Smith

SENIOR VICE-PRESIDENTS:
J. J. Ryan (Operations)
Robert J. Patton (Business Development Operations)

VICE-PRESIDENTS:
L. J. Cherry (Marketing)
D. G. Dimos (Finance)
S. C. Laden (Quality)
A. D. Marchant (Materiel)
F. W. Randall Jr (Aircraft Programmes)
William A. Stockstill (Manufacturing Operations)
R. W. Stoner (Engineering and Operations Development)
A. C. Thacker (Manufacturing Development and Support)
Gordon L. Williams (Advanced Development Projects)

DIRECTOR, PUBLIC RELATIONS AND ADVERTISING: Beal Box

Vought Missiles and Advanced Programs Division
PO Box 650003, Dallas, Texas 75265-0003

PRESIDENT: Robert N. Parker

SENIOR VICE-PRESIDENTS:
F. W. Fenter (Advanced Programmes, Technology and Marketing)
Philip C. Gregory (Engineering)

VICE-PRESIDENTS:
P. W. Hare Jr (Anti-Satellite Weapon)
James P. Laughlin (Engineering)
H. LeColst (General Manager, Camden, Arkansas, Operations)
C. H. McKinley (Hypervelocity Missile Systems)
W. J. McMillan (Finance)
A. Yee (General Manager, MLRS Division)

DIRECTOR, PUBLIC RELATIONS AND ADVERTISING:
T. L. Wilson

The former Chance Vought Aircraft Inc, founded in 1917 and a leading producer of aircraft for the US Navy throughout its history, became the Chance Vought Corporation on 31 December 1960. On 31 August 1961, Chance Vought Corporation merged with Ling-Temco Electronics Inc, to form a combined company known as Ling-Temco-Vought Inc (now The LTV Corporation).

What is now known as LTV Aerospace and Defense Company (formerly Vought Corporation) took over responsibility for all LTV's aircraft and space activities, aerospace support and training equipment from 1 January 1976. On 4 April 1984 it was reorganised into the Vought Missiles and Advanced Programs Division and Vought Aero Products Division which, together with AM General Division of Detroit, Michigan, and Sierra Research Division of Buffalo, New York, are responsible for all business and product lines.

Current aerospace products include McDonnell Douglas KC-10 tailplanes and elevators, Lockheed C-130 control surfaces, Boeing 747 tail assemblies, complete tailplane assemblies for the Boeing Model 767, complete tail units for the Boeing 757, including rear fuselage sections, and rear intermediate and rear fuselage sections of the Rockwell B-1B long-range multi-role bomber.

The company also has in production the Scout launch vehicle for NASA; components for manned and unmanned space vehicles; advanced missile, guidance, control and environmental systems; and advanced thermal protection systems.

Vought was selected in April 1980 as prime contractor for the Multiple Launch Rocket System (MLRS) for the US

Army and NATO allies. It is also continuing development of vehicles embodying integral rocket/ramjet propulsion, as part of the US Navy's Supersonic Tactical Missile programme.

In October 1985 LTV's Sierra Research Division was awarded a $34 million US Air Force contract for two airborne platform/telemetry relay systems to be installed on two de Havilland Canada Dash 8 aircraft which will operate as part of the Gulf Range Instrumentation System based at Tyndall AFB, Florida. The installation will include a large electronically steerable phased-array antenna mounted on the lower starboard fuselage side of the aircraft, an eight-channel UHF voice communication relay system, and an AN/APS-128D pulse compression radar for sea surveillance. The first Dash 8 for modification was delivered to LTV on 30 April 1986. (See also de Havilland Canada entry.)

VOUGHT CORSAIR II

US military designation: A-7

An initial contract to develop and build three A-7As was awarded by the US Navy on 19 March 1964; first flight was made on 27 September 1965. Several versions of the A-7 were developed subsequently as Corsair IIs, for the US Navy, the US Air Force, the Hellenic Air Force and the Portuguese Air Force. Details of the A-7A, A-7B, A-7C, A-7D and A-7E can be found in the 1983-84, 1979-80 and earlier editions of *Jane's*.

Orders for all versions totalled 1,545 new-build aircraft when production ended in 1983. The most recent versions of the Corsair II are:

TA-7C. Designation of 60 A-7Bs and A-7Cs converted into tandem two-seat trainers, with operational capability; first example flew on 17 December 1976. Described in previous editions of *Jane's*. Re-delivery began on 22 January 1985 of 49 aircraft upgraded with Allison TF41 engines, new Stencel ejection seats, automatic manoeuvring flaps and an engine monitoring system. Delivery of these was scheduled for completion in September 1986. Six other aircraft are fitted with forward looking infra-red and electronic warfare equipment and are designated **EA-7L**. The US Marine Corps is testing a new night vision system in a TA-7C, which combines the use of the pilot's night goggles with a high resolution, fixed field of view FLIR sensor to project daylight visual capability in darkness. The system is expected to cost $1 million for retrofit to each aircraft already equipped with an inertial navigation system.

A-7H. Land based version of A-7E, retaining the folding wings but without in-flight refuelling capability. First A-7H flew for the first time on 6 May 1975. Total of 60 delivered to three squadrons of the Hellenic Air Force.

TA-7H. Two-seat version for the Hellenic Air Force, with an Allison TF41-A-400 engine. Configuration similar to TA-7C, but no in-flight refuelling capability. Five delivered between July and September 1980.

A-7K. Two-seat version of the US Air Force's A-7D, with fuselage lengthened by 0·86 m (2 ft 10 in), and powered by 64·5 kN (14,500 lb st) Allison TF41-A-1 engine. Total of 31 delivered to US Air National Guard. Basically trainers, these aircraft retain combat capability. Two ANG Corsair II squadrons are being equipped with low-altitude night attack (LANA) capability under an $86·8 million contract awarded by the Air Force's Oklahoma City Air Logistics Center. LTV is retrofitting 44 A-7D and four two-seat A-7Ks with forward looking infra-red (FLIR) and automatic terrain following (ATF) equipment to provide round-the-clock capability. Vought has also tested an augmented wing flap that enables an A-7D or A-7K pilot to reduce landing speed, improve handling characteristics on the approach, and substantially reduce landing roll. The flap, which is 127 mm (5 in) wide, is mounted on the existing wing flap trailing-edge and is intended for retrofit to Air National Guard A-7s. It is expected to be helpful to ANG pilots operating from the short runways and in the varying climatic conditions that they might encounter in Rapid Deployment Force roles. The flap has also been offered to the US Navy.

A-7P. Designation of refurbished A-7As for Esquadra 302 (Grupo 52) of Portuguese Air Force at Mantijo, with TF30-P-408 engines and a mixture of A-7D and A-7E-standard avionics. Initial flight 20 July 1981. Deliveries of initial 19 completed September 1982. A further 30, including six two-seaters, were ordered in 1983; deliveries of these began on 5 October 1984. These aircraft can carry a Northrop AN/ALQ-171(V) electronic countermeasures pod to defeat surface and airborne radar controlled terminal threat systems.

A full structural description can be found in the 1983-84 and previous editions of *Jane's*; a shorter description of the A-7E appeared in the 1985-86 edition.

VOUGHT CORSAIR UPDATE PROGRAMMES

Current activity is centred on a series of update programmes for the Corsair II, which include the **International Corsair II**. This is based on an A-7B airframe that is stripped, fitted with new avionics and communications equipment, overhauled engine, new wiring, and provision for night attack and the latest ordnance, providing, LTV claims, a low-cost multi-mission tactical fighter at one-third of the acquisition costs of new aircraft.

LTV has proposed a modernised supersonic **A-7 Strikefighter** to the USAF as an interim solution for its Close Air Support/Battlefield Air Interdiction (CAS/BAI) requirement. At least 337 A-7Ds and A-7Ks from the Air National Guard would each be retrofitted with an F100-PW-200 or -220 or General Electric F110 afterburning engine; augmented flaps; wing-root strakes; a new-technology wing trailing-edge flap structure; upgraded avionics which could include LANTIRN, provision for Maverick and AIM-9 Sidewinder missile operation and automatic terrain following; all new wiring; and an improved air-conditioning system. LTV says that the A-7 Strikefighter would offer twice the thrust of existing A-7s, with 16 per cent greater speed (Mach 1·12 with afterburner), a 45 per cent decrease in take-off roll and 30 per cent in landing roll, and would provide greater agility and survivability while operating with minimal support in forward battle areas.

Also under consideration by LTV is the **International Corsair III**, based on an A-7B airframe with a 119·6 kN (26,900 lb st) General Electric F110-GE-100 afterburning engine. Structural changes to accommodate the new engine are said by LTV to be less extensive that those required to produce the two-seat variants of the A-7, and involve the addition of a 0·75 m (2 ft 5½ in) constant section to the fuselage mid-section, and a 19 cm (7½ in) addition to the rear fuselage. The fuel system is modified to provide the required flow rates for afterburning operation, and fuel capacity is increased by 651 litres (172 US gallons) to retain the A-7's range and endurance. Other modifications proposed for the International Corsair III include a new digital multi-role avionics suite providing all-weather day and night bombing capability; provision for Texas Instruments FLIR, active and passive ECM systems, GEC Avionics HUD, APQ-126 radar, armour protection and self-sealing fuel tanks; and automatic manoeuvring flaps.

ARMAMENT (International Corsair II): Two internally mounted Mk 12 20 mm cannon, with 680 rounds of ammunition. Six underwing and two fuselage weapon stations, as on A-7E, capable of carrying all USN, USAF, and NATO munitions (max external load more than 6,805 kg; 15,000 lb). Weapon carriers include BRU-10A, MER-7, and TER-7 bomb racks; LAU-3 and LAU-32 wing mounted rocket launchers; LAU-7 fuselage mounted missile launchers; and pods containing 20 or 30 mm guns, ECM, chaff, or auxiliary fuel. Provision also to carry 'buddy' air-to-air refuelling pods.

WEIGHTS (International Corsair II):
Weight empty 9,496 kg (20,935 lb)
Max T-O weight 19,050 kg (42,000 lb)

TYPICAL MISSION PERFORMANCE (International Corsair II at T-O weight of 16,805 kg; 37,050 lb with six Mk 82 bombs and 500 rds of 20 mm ammunition):
Max level speed at S/L 645 knots (1,195 km/h; 743 mph)
Time to 9,145 m (30,000 ft) 1·6 min
T-O run 488 m (1,600 ft)

Vought A-7P Corsair II of the Portuguese Air Force, with underwing AN/ALQ-171(V) ECM pod

Artist's impression of the proposed A-7 Strikefighter supersonic conversion of A-7D/K aircraft

LOCK HAVEN

LOCK HAVEN RE-MAN CENTER

345 Proctor Street, Lock Haven, Pennsylvania 17745
Telephone: (717) 748 0810

PRESIDENT AND GENERAL MANAGER: Arnold H. Andresen

This company was established in the Spring of 1985 by former Piper Aircraft Corporation marketing executive Arnold H. Andresen and William T. Piper Jr, former President of Piper and son of the company's founder. Lock Haven Re-Man has occupied a 1,022 m² (11,000 sq ft) site in the former Piper factory at Lock Haven, where it has begun remanufacturing certain piston-engined Piper aircraft built between the late 1960s and mid-1970s. Initial work included the remanufacturing of a Piper Aztec, a Navajo and two Chieftains to customer order, but the company plans also to buy in stocks of airframes which will be dismantled, inspected, cleaned, reassembled, repainted and equipped with zero-hour engines prior to resale. Lock Haven Re-Man expects to expand its manufacturing facility to 4,645 m² (50,000 sq ft) and its workforce to 30 people within two years. Remanufacturing will be concentrated on the Piper Warrior, Cherokee Six, Aztec and Navajo series. Typical remanufacturing times are one month for a single-engined light aircraft, and nearly three months for a cabin class piston twin such as the Piper Chieftain.

MACHEN

MACHEN INC

South 3608 Davison Boulevard, Spokane, Washington 99204
Telephone: (509) 838 5326

EXECUTIVE VICE-PRESIDENT, MARKETING: James Christy

Machen's current products in 1986 were the Superstar 650 and 680. The Turbo 350 Bonanza and Laser Jet programmes, described in the 1985-86 *Jane's*, are no longer active.

MACHEN SUPERSTAR 650

Under the name Superstar 650, Machen Inc has developed a conversion of the Piper (Ted Smith) Aerostar 600, 601, 601P and 602P which provides new turbochargers, controllers, fuel pumps, fuel injection servos, and improved pressurisation components, as well as uprating each of the Avco Lycoming TIO-540-S1A5 engines to 242 kW (325 hp). Performance improvements include a better twin- and single-engine rate of climb, a higher single-engine service ceiling, and reduced take-off distance and noise levels. By February 1986 a total of 65 Superstar 650 conversions had been completed.

Machen also markets and installs an FAA approved aerodynamic modification kit (SB 73-1) for the standard Aerostar 600 series and Superstar 650, which restores the unrestricted use of flaps and the original centre of gravity limits, following limitations imposed on the 600 series by the FAA in 1983. The kit comprises aileron and rudder hinge gap seals, a strake on the forward fuselage, leading-edge stall strips, and vortex generators on the lower wing surface and on the fin.

The Aerostar 600 was described fully under the Piper entry in the 1982-83 *Jane's*, the 601 and 601P in the 1981-82 *Jane's*, and the 602P in the 1984-85 edition. The descriptions of these aircraft apply also to the Superstar 650, except as noted in this entry.

PERFORMANCE: As for appropriate Aerostar model except:
Cruising speed, average cruise weight at 7,620 m (25,000 ft): 75% power — 240 knots (445 km/h; 276 mph)
65% power — 226 knots (419 km/h; 260 mph)
Min single-engine control speed (VMC) — 79 knots (146 km/h; 91 mph)
Max rate of climb at S/L — 596 m (1,955 ft)/min
Rate of climb at S/L, one engine out — 123 m (402 ft)/min
Service ceiling, one engine out — 4,575 m (15,000 ft)
T-O to 15 m (50 ft) — 604 m (1,980 ft)

Machen Superstar 650 conversion of the Piper Aerostar 601P

MACHEN SUPERSTAR 680

Machen Inc has been producing since 1980 a further conversion of the Piper (Ted Smith) Aerostar 601P, known as the Superstar 680, to provide improved performance. The major element of this modification is the addition of induction air intercoolers to the Superstar 650 model. Four-blade Hartzell propellers are optional.

The description of the Aerostar 601P under the Piper entry in the 1981-82 *Jane's* applies also to the Machen Superstar 680 modification, except as noted. Changed full-conversion weight and performance figures include:

WEIGHTS:
Weight empty, equipped — 1,863 kg (4,106 lb)
Max ramp weight — 2,812 kg (6,200 lb)
Max T-O weight — 2,812 kg (6,200 lb)
Max landing weight — 2,721 kg (6,000 lb)

PERFORMANCE (at max T-O weight except where indicated):
Max cruising speed at 7,620 m (25,000 ft) — 265 knots (491 km/h; 305 mph)
Cruising speed, average cruise weight at 7,620 m (25,000 ft): 75% power — 250 knots (463 km/h; 288 mph)
65% power — 242 knots (448 km/h; 279 mph)
55% power — 232 knots (430 km/h; 267 mph)
Min single-engine control speed (VMC) — 79 knots (146 km/h; 91 mph)
Max rate of climb at S/L — 596 m (1,955 ft)/min
Rate of climb at S/L, one engine out — 122 m (402 ft)/min
Service ceiling — 7,620 m (25,000 ft)
Service ceiling, one engine out — 7,010 m (23,000 ft)
T-O to 15 m (50 ft) — 603 m (1,980 ft)
Range, standard fuel, 45 min reserves — 1,137 nm (2,107 km; 1,309 miles)
Range, auxiliary fuel — 1,441 nm (2,670 km; 1,659 miles)

MAI

MITSUBISHI AIRCRAFT INTERNATIONAL INC (Subsidiary of Mitsubishi Heavy Industries Ltd)

This wholly owned subsidiary of Mitsubishi Heavy Industries Ltd of Japan (which see) was established at San Angelo, Texas, in 1965. Following the sale of all production and marketing rights to the Mitsubishi Diamond II business jet (described under the Beechcraft Beechjet entry in this section), and sale of the existing inventory of MU-2 **Marquise** and **Solitaire** turboprop business aircraft and **Diamond IA** business jets, MAI ceased all operations in the United States and closed its San Angelo factory and Dallas marketing centre.

Deliveries of MU-2 Marquise and Solitaire turboprops totalled 171 and 111 respectively when production ceased in March 1986. By December 1985 a total of 89 Diamond Is and IAs had been delivered, with MAI then holding an inventory of 17 unsold Diamond IAs. Product support for these out of production models is being undertaken by Beech Aircraft Corporation.

Descriptions of the Marquise, Solitaire and Diamond IA can be found in the 1985-86 edition of *Jane's*.

MARSH

MARSH AVIATION COMPANY

5060 East Falcon Drive, Mesa, Arizona 85205
Telephone: (602) 832 3770
Telex: 165 028

VICE-PRESIDENT: William G. Walker Jr

MARSH S2R-T TURBO THRUSH

Marsh Aviation Company has converted the piston engined Rockwell Thrush Commander to turbine power by the installation of a Garrett TPE331-1-101 turboprop engine. Derated to 447 kW (600 shp) for this conversion, the full 580 kW (778 shp) output of the TPE331 is available in emergency. This engine drives a Hartzell constant-speed fully-feathering and reversible-pitch propeller. Single cycle air-conditioning and cockpit heating are provided by engine bleed air, and the agricultural spraypump is also operated by bleed air. The empty weight of the Turbo Thrush is 227 kg (500 lb) less than that of the standard Thrush Commander, providing increased payload capability and improved speed and performance. For agricultural operators working in remote areas the TPE331 installation has the advantage that ordinary automotive diesel fuel can be used if jet fuel is not available.

Standard fuel capacity of the Turbo Thrush is 401 litres (106 US gallons). Standard hopper capacity is 1·50 m³ (53 cu ft) or 1,514 litres (400 US gallons). A larger hopper is available optionally, capacity 1·89 m³ (66·8 cu ft) or 1,892·5 litres (500 US gallons).

Following more than 600 h of flight by two prototypes, an FAA Supplemental Type Certificate was issued and the first production conversion was handed over in September 1976. Turbo Thrush deliveries totalled 75 by February 1985, the majority for operators in Africa, Europe, Mexico, the Middle East and the USA. No further examples had been completed by early 1986.

Details of the Rockwell Thrush Commander can be found in the 1977-78 *Jane's*.

Marsh Turbo Thrush conversion of the Rockwell International Thrush Commander *(Howard Levy)*

DIMENSIONS, EXTERNAL: As for Thrush Commander except:
Length overall — 9·27 m (30 ft 5 in)

WEIGHTS AND LOADINGS: As for Thrush Commander except:
Weight empty — 1,633 kg (3,600 lb)
Max T-O weight: Normal category — 2,721 kg (6,000 lb)
Restricted category — 3,538 kg (7,800 lb)

Typical operating weight (CAR Pt 8)
4,173 kg (9,200 lb)

PERFORMANCE (at 2,721 kg; 6,000 lb T-O weight except where indicated):

Never-exceed speed	138 knots (256 km/h; 159 mph) IAS
Max level speed at 4,420 m (14,500 ft)	178 knots (330 km/h; 205 mph)
Econ cruising speed at 4,420 m (14,500 ft)	139 knots (257 km/h; 160 mph)
Cruising speed, 50% power	127 knots (235 km/h; 146 mph)
Working speed, 50% power	108 knots (201 km/h; 125 mph)
Stalling speed, flaps up	42 knots (77 km/h; 48 mph)
Stalling speed, flaps down	38 knots (71 km/h; 44 mph)
Max rate of climb at S/L	915 m (3,000 ft)/min
Service ceiling	7,620 m (25,000 ft)
T-O run	183 m (600 ft)
Landing run	91 m (300 ft)
Range with max payload	278 nm (515 km; 320 miles)
Ferry range at 60% power	521 nm (966 km; 600 miles)

MARSH G-164 C-T TURBO CAT

Marsh Aviation developed this turbine engine conversion for the Grumman/Gulfstream Aerospace/Schweizer G-164 Super Ag-Cat C by replacing the original piston engine with a 580 kW (778 shp) Garrett TPE331-1-101 turboprop, derated to 447 kW (600 shp).

Certification was gained in 1980, and six Turbo Cats (one A, four Bs and a C) had been completed by 1981. No more have been built since, although the aircraft remains available. Details of the Schweizer Super Ag-Cat C can be found in the 1981-82 *Jane's*, and of the Turbo Cat in the 1984-85 edition.

MARSH/BEECHCRAFT T-34 TURBO MENTOR

A description of Marsh Aviation's turboprop conversion of the Beechcraft T-34A/B Mentor two-seat primary trainer appeared in the 1983-84 *Jane's*. In early 1986 a second prototype was under construction. This aircraft will be powered by a 626 kW (840 shp) Garrett TPE331-6 engine, and will have increased fuel capacity and four underwing stores stations. It was expected to fly in late 1986.

MARSH/GRUMMAN S-2 TURBO CONVERSION

Marsh Aviation has developed a turbine engine conversion for the Grumman S-2 Tracker anti-submarine aircraft. It consists of a number of aerodynamic refinements for drag reduction, and replacement of the S-2's Wright R-1820 piston engines with 1,277 kW (1,712 shp) Garrett TPE331-14 turboprops, each driving a Hartzell five-blade reversible-pitch propeller. The S-2 Turbo is expected to have a cruising speed 60 knots (111 km/h; 69 mph) faster than the standard S-2, with a 50 per cent reduction in fuel consumption at high cruising speed. Take-off and landing runs are reduced by 30 per cent and single-engine rate of climb at max T-O weight increased by 229 m (750 ft)/min. The first Marsh S-2 Turbo, for the California Forestry Department, was expected to fly in early 1986, with production scheduled to begin in the Summer. Marketing is being directed initially at the aerial firefighting industry.

Marsh's Garrett turboprop conversion of Beechcraft T-34A Mentor nearing completion *(Howard Levy)*

Artist's impression of Marsh S-2 Turbo conversion of the S-2 Tracker

MAULE

MAULE AIR INC

Route 5, Box 319, Moultrie, Georgia 31768
Telephone: (912) 985 2045
Telex: 804613 MAULE MOUL
PRESIDENT: Belford D. Maule
VICE-PRESIDENT: Mrs B. D. (June) Maule (Treasurer)
SALES MANAGER: Dan Spader

This company succeeds Maule Aircraft Corporation, which was formed to manufacture the Maule M-4 four-seat light aircraft, production of which ended in 1975. The former company transferred to new facilities in Moultrie, Georgia, in September 1968, and applied for protection under Chapter 11 of US bankruptcy laws in late 1984, when Maule Air Inc was formed to continue production of the uprated M-5 Lunar Rocket and M-7 Super Rocket. The Lunar Rocket has since been discontinued, but five versions of the Super Rocket and new Star Rocket are currently available.

MAULE STAR ROCKET and SUPER ROCKET

Models of the Star Rocket and Super Rocket available in 1986 are as follows:

MX-7 Star Rocket. Certificated on 9 November 1984, the Star Rocket combines the shorter span wing of the former M-5 series with the glassfibre wingtips, increased fuel capacity, ailerons and five-position flaps of the M-7, and the fuselage of the M-6 (1983-84 *Jane's*). It is available as the **MX-7-180** with 134 kW (180 hp) Avco Lycoming O-360-C1F, or as the **MX-7-235** with 175 kW (235 hp) Avco Lycoming O-540-J1A5D or IO-540-W1A5D engine.

M-7-235 Super Rocket. This 1984 replacement for the earlier four-seat M-6-235 is a five-seater with a three-place rear bench. Wing span and weights are increased. Power plant is a 175 kW (235 hp) Avco Lycoming O-540-J1A5D or fuel injected IO-540-W1A5D flat-six engine, driving a Hartzell constant-speed metal propeller. It is available as a landplane or on Edo 797-2500 amphibious floats or Edo 2440B standard floats.

Maule M-7-235 Super Rocket with Edo 797-2500 amphibious landing gear *(Howard Levy)*

Production of all versions totals more than 1,200.

TYPE: Four-seat or five-seat STOL light aircraft.

WINGS: Braced high-wing monoplane. Streamline section V bracing strut each side. USA 35B (modified) wing section. Dihedral 1°. Incidence 0° 30′. All-metal two-spar structure with metal covering and glassfibre tips. All-metal ailerons and flaps. Ailerons linked with rudder tab, so that aircraft can be controlled in flight by using only the control wheel in the cockpit. Cambered wingtips standard.

FUSELAGE: Welded 4130 steel tube structure. Covered with glassfibre, except for metal doors and aluminium skin around cabin.

TAIL UNIT: Braced steel tube structure with glassfibre covering. Trim tab in port elevator. Servo tab in rudder linked to aileron movement. Starboard rudder trim via spring to starboard rudder pedal. Underfin on floatplane and amphibious versions.

LANDING GEAR: Non-retractable tailwheel type. Maule oleo-pneumatic shock absorbers in main units. Maule steerable tailwheel. Cleveland mainwheels with Goodyear or McCreary tyres size 17 × 6·00-6, pressure 1·79 bars (26 lb/sq in). Tailwheel tyre size 8 × 3·50-4, pressure 1·03-1·38 bars (15-20 lb/sq in). Cleveland hydraulic disc brakes. Parking brake. Oversize tyres, size 20 × 8·50-6 (pressure 1·24 bars; 18 lb/sq in), and fairings aft of mainwheels optional. Provisions for fitting optional Edo Model 248B2440 floats or Edo Model 797-2500 amphibious floats, Pee Kay Model 2300 or Aqua Model 2400 floats, or Federal Model C2200H or C3000H or Fli-Lite 3000 Mk IIIA skis.

POWER PLANT: One flat-four or flat-six engine, driving a Hartzell constant-speed propeller, as detailed in model listings. Two fuel tanks in wings with total usable capacity of 151 litres (40 US gallons). Optional auxiliary fuel tanks in outer wings, to provide total capacity of 265 litres (70 US gallons). Refuelling points on wing upper surface. Oil capacity 7·5 litres (2 US gallons) on all models except Super Rocket with O-540-J1A5D engine which has 9·5 litres (2·5 US gallons).

ACCOMMODATION: Pilot and three passengers in Star Rocket, four in Super Rocket, on two front bucket seats and rear bench seat, or optional quickly removed rear sling seat. One door on port side of fuselage, hinged at front edge and opening forward. Three doors on starboard side of fuselage, the forward and centre doors hinged at the front edge, the rear baggage door hinged at the rear edge. The centre and rear doors can be opened together to provide an opening 1·30 m (4 ft 3 in) wide to facilitate loading of bulky cargo. Accommodation heated and ventilated. Windscreen defroster standard. Tinted windscreen optional.

SYSTEMS: Hydraulic system for brakes only. Electrical system powered by 60A engine driven alternator. 28V electrical system optional.

AVIONICS AND EQUIPMENT: A wide range of Collins Micro Line, King, Genave and Narco communication and navigation equipment is available to customer's requirements. Standard equipment includes cylinder head temperature gauge, clock, stall warning device, instrument and cabin dome lights, cabin steps, cargo tiedown rings, navigation lights and port landing lights. Optional equipment includes blind-flying instrumentation, autopilot, wing levelling system, turn co-ordinator, rate of climb indicator, exhaust gas temperature gauge, angle of attack indicator, encoding altimeter, economy mixture control and Sorensen agricultural spraygear.

DIMENSIONS, EXTERNAL (A, Star Rocket; C, Super Rocket):
- Wing span: A — 9·40 m (30 ft 10 in)
  - C — 10·11 m (33 ft 2 in)
- Wing chord, constant: A, C — 1·60 m (5 ft 3 in)
- Wing aspect ratio: A — 6·02
  - C — 6·55
- Length overall: A, C — 6·93 m (22 ft 9 in)
- Height overall: A, C — 1·93 m (6 ft 4 in)
- Tailplane span: A, C — 3·28 m (10 ft 9 in)
- Wheel track: A, C — 1·83 m (6 ft 0 in)
- Wheelbase: A, C — 4·82 m (15 ft 10 in)
- Cabin doors: A, C (fwd, each):
  - Height — 0·84 m (2 ft 9 in)
  - Width — 0·76 m (2 ft 6 in)
  - Height to sill — 0·94 m (3 ft 1 in)
- Cabin door: A, C (centre, stbd):
  - Height — 0·75 m (2 ft 5½ in)
  - Width — 0·69 m (2 ft 3 in)
  - Height to sill — 0·76 m (2 ft 6 in)
- Baggage door: A, C (rear, stbd):
  - Height — 0·58 m (1 ft 11 in)
  - Width — 0·56 m (1 ft 10 in)
  - Height to sill — 0·61 m (2 ft 0 in)

AREAS (A, Star Rocket; C, Super Rocket):
- Wings, gross: A — 14·67 m² (157·9 sq ft)
  - C — 15·60 m² (168·0 sq ft)
- Ailerons (total): A — 1·19 m² (12·8 sq ft)
  - C — 1·07 m² (11·56 sq ft)
- Trailing-edge flaps (total): A — 1·75 m² (18·8 sq ft)
  - C — 2·32 m² (25·0 sq ft)
- Fin: A, C — 1·22 m² (13·14 sq ft)
- Rudder, incl tab: A, C — 0·54 m² (5·83 sq ft)
- Tailplane: A, C — 1·32 m² (14·2 sq ft)
- Elevators, incl tab: A, C — 1·58 m² (17·0 sq ft)

WEIGHTS AND LOADINGS (A: MX-7-180 Star Rocket; B, MX-7-235 Star Rocket; C, Super Rocket):
- Weight empty: A — 613 kg (1,350 lb)
  - B, C — 681 kg (1,500 lb)
- Max baggage: A, B, C — 45 kg (100 lb)
- Max cargo: A, B, C — 317 kg (700 lb)
- Max T-O and landing weight:
  - A, B, C — 1,134 kg (2,500 lb)
- Max wing loading: A, B — 77·3 kg/m² (15·8 lb/sq ft)
  - C — 72·7 kg/m² (14·9 lb/sq ft)
- Max power loading: A — 8·46 kg/kW (13·89 lb/hp)
  - B, C — 6·48 kg/kW (10·64 lb/hp)

PERFORMANCE (at max T-O weight except where stated, landplane versions, as identified under Weights and Loadings):
- Max cruising speed at optimum altitude:
  - A — 126 knots (233 km/h; 145 mph)
  - B, C — 139 knots (257 km/h; 160 mph)
- Stalling speed, flaps down, pilot only:
  - A, B — 35 knots (65 km/h; 40 mph)
  - C — 31 knots (57 km/h; 35 mph)
- Max rate of climb at S/L: A — 366 m (1,200 ft)/min
  - B, C — 610 m (2,000 ft)/min
- Service ceiling: A — 4,575 m (15,000 ft)
  - B, C — 6,100 m (20,000 ft)
- T-O and landing run, pilot only: A — 61 m (200 ft)
  - B (O-540) — 46 m (150 ft)
  - B (IO-540), C — 38 m (125 ft)
- T-O to, and landing from, 15 m (50 ft):
  - A, B, C — 183 m (600 ft)
- Range with max standard fuel:
  - A — 558 nm (1,035 km; 643 miles)
  - B (O-540) — 434 nm (804 km; 500 miles)
  - B (IO-540), C — 478 nm (885 km; 550 miles)
- Range with max fuel: A — 881 nm (1,633 km; 1,015 miles)
  - B (O-540) — 746 nm (1,384 km; 860 miles)
  - B (IO-540) — 846 nm (1,567 km; 974 miles)
  - C (O-540) — 608 nm (1,126 km; 700 miles)
  - C (IO-540) — 651 nm (1,207 km; 750 miles)

MBB

MBB HELICOPTER CORPORATION (Subsidiary of Messerschmitt-Bölkow-Blohm GmbH)

900 Airport Road, PO Box 2349, West Chester, Pennsylvania 19380
Telephone: (215) 431 4150
Telex: 173102
PRESIDENT AND CHIEF EXECUTIVE OFFICER: C. W. Moore
SENIOR VICE-PRESIDENT, MARKETING: Andreas Aastad
EXECUTIVE VICE-PRESIDENT AND GENERAL MANAGER: David Smith

Messerschmitt-Bölkow-Blohm of West Germany (which see) established this subsidiary company in the USA, in early 1979, to take over marketing and product support of the company's family of twin-turbine helicopters in the United States, Central America and Mexico.

In 1983 the company opened the MBB North American Service Center, a 3,252 m² (35,000 sq ft) building housing spares, mechanic and pilot training, and helicopter assembly and modification facilities, and a 2,787 m² (30,000 sq ft) administration building. The MBB complex is located on a 17 hectare (42 acre) site adjacent to the Brandywine Airport, West Chester, Pennsylvania.

MBB Helicopter Corporation markets and supports the entire range of MBB helicopters, to which it has given the names **Twin Jet** (BO 105 CBS), **Lift Ship** (BO 105 LS), and **Space Ship** (BK 117).

MCDONNELL DOUGLAS

MCDONNELL DOUGLAS CORPORATION

Box 516, St Louis, Missouri 63166
Telephone: (314) 232 0232
Telex: 44-857

CORPORATE OFFICE

CHAIRMAN OF THE BOARD OF DIRECTORS, AND CHIEF EXECUTIVE OFFICER: Sanford N. McDonnell

PRESIDENT: John F. McDonnell

CORPORATE STAFF:
- David C. Arnold (Corporate Vice-President, Productivity)
- Jerry G. Brown (Corporate Vice-President, Finance)
- John W. Chase (Corporate Treasurer)
- Walter E. Diggs Jr (Corporate Secretary)
- Robert L. Harmon (Corporate Vice-President, Civic Affairs)
- Robert H. Hood Jr (Corporate Vice-President, Aerospace Business Development)
- James H. MacDonald (Corporate Vice-President, Human Resources)
- Gerald J. Meyer (Corporate Vice-President, Communications)
- John T. Sant (Corporate Vice-President and General Counsel)
- Ralph R. Zoellner (Corporate Vice-President, Europe)

CORPORATE DIRECTOR, PUBLIC RELATIONS:
John L. Cooke

Aerospace Group

CORPORATE VICE-PRESIDENTS AND AEROSPACE GROUP EXECUTIVES:
- Robert L. Johnson
- Robert C. Little

GROUP STAFF:
- Denver D. Clark (Corporate Vice-President, Eastern Region)
- Kenneth Francis (Vice-President, Aerospace Engineering and Operations)
- James S. McDonnell III (Corporate Vice-President, Aerospace Marketing)

Information Systems Group

CHAIRMAN: Robert A. Fischer

CORPORATE VICE-PRESIDENTS AND ISG EXECUTIVE BOARD:
- Jeremy J. Causley
- Gary E. Liebl

McDonnell Douglas Corporation was formed on 28 April 1967, by the merger of the former Douglas Aircraft Company Inc and the McDonnell company. It encompasses both of the original companies and their subsidiaries, and the former Hughes Helicopters Inc, which became a subsidiary in 1984.

At the end of June 1986 McDonnell Douglas employed 103,028 people, worldwide. Total office, engineering, laboratory and manufacturing floor area was 2,862,241 m² (30,808,924 sq ft).

Major operating components of McDonnell Douglas Corporation Aerospace Group are as follows:

McDonnell Aircraft Company
Follows this entry

Douglas Aircraft Company
Follows McDonnell Aircraft Co entry

McDonnell Douglas Helicopter Company
Follows Douglas Aircraft Co entry

McDonnell Douglas Astronautics Company
See Air-launched Missiles section

MCDONNELL AIRCRAFT COMPANY (A Division of McDonnell Douglas Corporation)

Box 516, St Louis, Missouri 63166
Telephone: (314) 232 0232

PRESIDENT: William S. Ross

EXECUTIVE VICE-PRESIDENTS:
- Irving L. Burrows
- John D. Wolf

SENIOR VICE-PRESIDENT: Alvin L. Boyd

VICE-PRESIDENTS:
- Robert C. Bartz (Material)
- John J. Burns (General Manager, Advanced Tactical Fighter)
- John Capellupo (General Manager, F/A-18)
- John W. Gouy (Fiscal Management)
- Thomas M. Gunn (Marketing)
- Herman W. Hamm (Engineering)
- Edwin A. Harper (Programme Manager, AV-8)
- Paul T. Homsher (Product Support)
- Edward B. Kuhlmann (Quality Assurance and Facilities Management)
- Alexander Marshall (International Marketing)
- Virgil Marti (Ombudsman)
- Roger H. Mathews (Avionics)
- Herbert Perlmutter (Operations)
- James C. Restelli (Contracts and Pricing)
- Herschel Sams (Engineering Technology)
- John H. Schulz (Manufacturing)
- Lawrence A. Smith (Advanced Design Engineering)
- Donald D. Snyder (Aircraft Engineering)
- James L. Spehr (General Manager, F-15)
- Darrell F. Waters (Human Resources)
- Gregg J. Zeisler (Controller)

DIRECTOR, EXTERNAL RELATIONS: Timothy J. Beecher

Development and production at St Louis continues to be concentrated on versions of the F-15 Eagle air superiority fighter, AV-8B Harrier II and F/A-18 Hornet naval strike fighter.

MCDONNELL DOUGLAS F-4 PHANTOM II

To reduce injuries to aircrew of F-4s, and loss of aircraft, due to bird strikes during low-level missions, McDonnell Douglas and Goodyear Aerospace have developed an improved, one-piece, bird-resistant windscreen. The first two F-4Es fitted retrospectively with the new windscreen were delivered to the Missouri Air National Guard in 1985 for a one-year test and evaluation programme. Made from

McDonnell Douglas F-4E Phantom II with new Goodyear Aerospace wrapround windscreen

two layers of polycarbonate between two layers of acrylic plastics, the 2·5 cm (1 in) thick windscreen is designed to withstand impact by a 1·8 kg (4 lb) bird at an aircraft speed of 500 knots (925 km/h; 575 mph). Elimination of the former windscreen frame also improves the pilot's field of view.

MCDONNELL DOUGLAS F-15 EAGLE

The US Air Force requested development funding for a new air superiority fighter in 1965, and in due course design proposals were sought from three airframe manufacturers: Fairchild Hiller Corporation, McDonnell Douglas Corporation, and North American Rockwell Corporation. On 23 December 1969 it was announced that McDonnell Douglas had been selected as airframe prime contractor. The resulting contract called for the design and manufacture of 20 aircraft for development testing, these to comprise 18 single-seat **F-15As** and two TF-15A two-seat trainers. First flight of the F-15A was made on 27 July 1972, and the first flight of a two-seat TF-15A trainer (redesignated subsequently **F-15B**) on 7 July 1973.

A production go-ahead for the first 30 operational aircraft (FY 1973 funds) was announced on 1 March 1973. The FY 1974 Defense Procurement Bill authorised production of 62 aircraft, and subsequent Procurement Bills authorised production of a further 622 aircraft through FY 1982. Under the multi-year plans proposed in early 1983, eventual procurement for the US Air Force is expected to total 1,266, excluding the 20 development aircraft, by the early 1990s. An F-15B (the 21st Eagle built) was the first Eagle delivered to the US Air Force, on 14 November 1974. Structural weight of the F-15B is approx 363 kg (800 lb) more than that of the F-15A. Production of the F-15A and B totalled 361 and 58 respectively.

Eagles produced since June 1979 are to **F-15C** and **F-15D** standard, which provides for 6,103 kg (13,455 lb) of internal fuel, and the ability to carry two low-drag conformal fuel tanks (CFT) developed specially for the F-15 by McDonnell Aircraft Company. Each CFT contains approximately 3,228 litres (114 cu ft) of usable volume, which can accommodate 2,211 kg (4,875 lb) of JP-4 fuel. It attaches to the side of either the port or starboard engine air intake trunk (being made in handed pairs), is designed to the same load factors as the basic aircraft, and can be removed in 15 minutes. CFTs could be configured to accommodate avionics such as reconnaissance sensors, radar detection and jamming equipment, a laser designator, low light level TV system, and reconnaissance cameras, in addition to fuel. All external stores stations remain available with the CFTs in use, and McDonnell Douglas has developed for the F-15 a new weapon attachment system which can extend the operating radius with large external loads by up to 40 per cent. Known as tangential carriage, it involves the installation of rows of stub pylons on the lower corner and bottom of each of the CFTs. Up to twelve 1,000 lb class or four 2,000 lb class weapons can be carried on these pylons, instead of on the normal multiple racks which cause more drag and occupy external fuel stations, so limiting the aircraft's range. AIM-7F missiles can also be attached directly to the CFTs.

Evaluation of the tangential carriage concept was undertaken by the US Air Force at Edwards AFB, California, between 18 and 31 August 1983, using the first-built F-15C. In-service F-15Cs and F-15Ds will be able to employ tangential carriage CFTs after completion of the multi-staged improvement programme (MSIP) described in a later paragraph.

The first F-15C (78-468) flew for the first time on 26 February 1979, and the first F-15D on 19 June of that year. Since 1980 the APG-63 radar of F-15C/D aircraft has been equipped with a Hughes Aircraft programmable signal processor, which enables changes to be incorporated in the radar earlier and more cheaply. An updated radar data processor increases memory capability from 24K to 96K. These added features enable the radar to operate in a high-resolution raid assessment mode which can identify clustered targets individually. F-15C and F-15D aircraft delivered prior to the availability of the programmable signal processor and expanded computer will be retrofitted to bring them up to standard. Minor changes have been made to tyres, wheels and brakes to allow for an increased maximum T-O weight, which can be as high as 30,845 kg (68,000 lb) with full internal fuel, CFTs and external tanks. Landing gear and fuel system changes have added about 272 kg (600 lb) to the aircraft's dry weight.

An overload warning system is now being delivered in F-15C/D aircraft which permits the pilot to manoeuvre safely to 9*g* throughout most of the flight envelope at flight design gross weights. It will be retrofitted to all F-15s delivered earlier.

In February 1983 the US Air Force awarded McDonnell Aircraft Co an $86·7 million contract for an initial F-15 multi-staged improvement programme (MSIP). This covers introduction of a Hughes APG-70 radar with memory increase to 1,000K and trebled processing speed; upgrading the aircraft's central computer to store four times as much data and process it three times as quickly; and replacing the current cockpit control panel for the armament control system by a single multi-purpose Sperry colour video screen. Linked to a computer, the Dynamics Control armament control system will be programmable, allowing for the addition of future weapons such as advanced versions of the AIM-7 and AIM-9 and AMRAAM. Other MSIP improvements include a tactical electronic system consisting of a Northrop Enhanced ALQ-135 internal countermeasures system, Loral ALR-56C radar warning receiver, Tracor ALE-45 chaff dispenser, and Magnavox electronic warfare warning system. A further $274·4 million contract was received in December 1983. Flight testing of the new system began in December 1984. The first production F-15C built under MSIP was unveiled at McDonnell Douglas' St Louis plant on 20 June 1985.

By December 1985 a total of 917 Eagles had been delivered, including 794 to the USAF. Active USAF units included the 57th FWW at Nellis AFB, Nevada, the 405th TTW at Luke AFB, Arizona, the 1st TFW at Langley AFB, Virginia, the 36th TFW at Bitburg AB, West Germany, the 49th TFW at Holloman AFB, New Mexico, the 33rd TFW at Eglin AFB, Florida, the 18th TFW at Kadena AB, Okinawa, and the 32nd Tactical Fighter Squadron based at Soesterberg in the Netherlands. The 48th Fighter Interceptor Squadron at Langley AFB, Virginia, was the first US air defence squadron to receive the Eagle. The 21st TFW at Elmendorf AFB, Alaskan Air Command, in support of air defence, converted to F-15s and became operational during 1982; deliveries to the 318th FIS at McChord AFB, Washington, began in June 1983, and to the 5th FIS at Minot, North Dakota, in June 1985. The 57th FIS at Keflavik, Iceland, began re-equipping with F-15s in July 1985.

On 15 September 1985 an F-15 from the 6512th TS at Edwards AFB, operating from Vandenburg AFB, California, carried out the successful destruction of an orbiting satellite (Solwind P78-1) with an air launched LTV anti-satellite (ASAT) weapon. F-15s of the 48th FIS at Langley AFB, Virginia, and 318th FIS at McChord AFB, Washington, are expected to operate in anti-satellite roles as part of ADTAC if the ASAT programme leads to operational deployment of such a weapon.

Equipment of Air National Guard units with F-15A and F-15B aircraft began on 29 June 1985 with the 122nd TFS, at New Orleans, Louisiana, and was to be followed by delivery of F-15As and F-15Bs to the 116th TFW, 159th TFG, Georgia ANG, at Dobbins AFB in 1986.

The F-15 has also been selected by the US Air Force for assignment to the Central Command Rapid Deployment Force. To ensure optimum effectiveness for the aircraft allocated to this mission, the US Air Force has procured 325 sets of conformal fuel tanks and 150 BRU-26A/A six-station multiple bomb racks.

Export deliveries include 51 Eagles for Israel and 62 for Saudi Arabia. The JASDF is purchasing 88 **F-15Js** and 12 **F-15DJs**, of which 86 F-15Js are being licence built in Japan, with Mitsubishi as the prime contractor. The first of the 14 US built aircraft was handed over on 15 July 1980, and the first two were flown to Japan in March 1981.

McDonnell Douglas has developed an air-to-ground attack version of the Eagle, known as the **F-15E** dual role fighter; this is described separately. Also described separately is an advanced STOL version of the Eagle which McDonnell Douglas will develop and flight test for the US Air Force.

The following description applies to the standard F-15C:

TYPE: Single-seat twin-turbofan air superiority fighter, with secondary attack role.

WINGS: Cantilever shoulder-wing monoplane. Wing uses NACA 64A aerofoil section with varying thickness/chord ratios, ranging from 6·6% at the root to 3% at the tip. Leading-edges modified with conical camber. Anhedral 1°. Incidence 0°. Sweepback at quarter-chord 38° 42′. Fail-safe structure, comprising a torque box with integrally stiffened machined skins and conventionally machined ribs, of light alloy and titanium. Leading- and trailing-edges are of conventional light alloy rib/skin construction, and wingtips of aluminium honeycomb. Plain ailerons and plain trailing-edge flaps of aluminium honeycomb. No spoilers or trim tabs. Powered controls, hydraulically operated by National Water Lift actuators. No anti-icing system.

McDonnell Douglas F-15A Eagles of the USAF's 318th Fighter Interceptor Squadron

FUSELAGE: All-metal semi-monocoque structure. Speedbrake on upper centre-fuselage, constructed of graphite/epoxy, aluminium honeycomb and titanium.

TAIL UNIT: Cantilever structure with twin fins and rudders. All-moving horizontal tail surfaces outboard of fins, with extended chord on outer leading-edges. Rudder servo actuators by Ronson Hydraulic Units Corporation. Actuators for horizontal surfaces by National Water Lift Company. Boost and pitch compensator for control stick by Moog Inc, Controls Division.

LANDING GEAR: Hydraulically retractable tricycle type, with single wheel on each unit. All units retract forward. Nose and main units by Cleveland Pneumatic Tool Company, each incorporating an oleo-pneumatic shock absorber. Nosewheel and tyre by Goodyear, size 22 × 6·6-10, pressure 17·93 bars (260 lb/sq in). Mainwheels by Bendix, with Goodyear tyres size 34·5 × 9·75-18, pressure 23·44 bars (340 lb/sq in). Bendix carbon heat-sink brakes. Wheel braking skid control system by Hydro-Aire Division of Crane Company.

POWER PLANT: Two Pratt & Whitney F100-PW-100 turbofan engines, each rated at approx 106·0 kN (23,830 lb st) with afterburning for take-off. Internal fuel in eight Goodyear fuselage tanks, total capacity 7,836 litres (2,070 US gallons). Fuel gauge system by Simmonds Precision Products Inc. Optional conformal fuel tanks attached to side of engine air intakes, beneath wing, each containing 2,839 litres (750 US gallons). Provision for up to three additional 2,309 litre (610 US gallon) external fuel tanks. Max total internal and external fuel capacity 20,441 litres (5,400 US gallons).

ENGINE INTAKES: Straight two-dimensional external compression inlets, on each side of the fuselage. Air inlet controllers by Hamilton Standard. Air inlet actuators by National Water Lift Company.

ACCOMMODATION: Pilot only, on ACES II ejection seat developed by McDonnell Douglas. Stretched acrylic canopy and windscreen. Windscreen anti-icing valve by Dynasciences Corporation.

SYSTEMS: Garrett air-conditioning system. Three independent hydraulic systems (each 207 bars; 3,000 lb/sq in) powered by Abex engine driven pumps; modular hydraulic packages by Hydraulic Research and Manufacturing Company. Lear Siegler generating system for electrical power, with Sundstrand 40/50kVA generator constant speed drive units and Electro Development Corpn transformer-rectifiers. The oxygen system includes a liquid oxygen indicator by Simmonds Precision Products Inc. Garrett APU for engine starting, and for the provision of electrical or hydraulic power on the ground independently of the main engines.

AVIONICS: General Electric automatic analog flight control system standard. Hughes Aircraft APG-63 X-band pulse-Doppler radar (being upgraded to APG-70 by MSIP modification) provides long-range detection and tracking of small high-speed targets operating at all altitudes down to treetop level, and feeds accurate tracking information to the airborne central computer to ensure effective launch of the aircraft's missiles or the firing of its internal gun. For close-in dogfights, the radar acquires the target automatically and the steering/weapon system information is displayed on a head-up display. IBM is subcontractor for the central computer, and McDonnell Douglas Electronics Company for the head-up display. This latter unit projects all essential flight information in the form of symbols on to a combining glass positioned above the instrument panel at pilot's eye level. The display presents the pilot with all the information required to intercept and destroy an enemy aircraft without need for him to remove his eyes from the target. The display also provides navigation and other steering control information under all flight conditions. A transponder for the IFF system, developed by Teledyne Electronics Company, informs ground stations and other suitably equipped aircraft that the F-15 is a friendly aircraft. It also supplies data on the F-15's range, azimuth, altitude and identification to air traffic controllers. The F-15 carries a Hazeltine AN/APX-76 interrogator receiver-transmitter, to inform the pilot if an aircraft seen visually or on radar is friendly. A reply evaluator for the IFF system, which operates with the AN/APX-76, was developed by Litton Systems Inc. A Sperry Flight Systems vertical situation display set, using a cathode ray tube to present radar, electro-optical identification and attitude director indicator formats to the pilot, permits inputs received from the aircraft's sensors and the central computer to be visible to the pilot under any light conditions. Sperry also developed the air data computer for the F-15, as well as an attitude and heading reference set to provide information on the aircraft's pitch, roll and magnetic heading that is fed to cockpit displays. This latter unit also serves as a backup to the Litton inertial navigation set which provides the basic navigation data and is the aircraft's primary attitude reference, enabling the F-15 to navigate anywhere in the world. In addition to giving the aircraft's position at all times, the inertial navigation system provides pitch, roll, heading, acceleration and speed information.

Other specialised equipment for flight control, navigation and communications includes a Collins micro-miniaturised Tacan system; Collins horizontal situation indicator to present aircraft navigation information on a symbolic pictorial display; Collins ADF and ILS receivers; Magnavox UHF transceiver and UHF auxiliary transceiver. The communications sets have cryptographic capability. Dorne and Margolin glideslope localiser antenna, and Teledyne Avionics angle of attack sensors. Northrop (Defense Systems Division) Enhanced AN/ALQ-135(V) internal countermeasures set provides automatic jamming of enemy radar signals; Loral ALR-56C radar warning systems; and Magnavox electronic warfare warning set; and Tracor AN/ALE-45 chaff dispenser.

EQUIPMENT: Bendix tachometer, fuel and oil indicators; Plessey feel trim actuators.

ARMAMENT: Provision for carriage and launch of a variety of air-to-air weapons over short and medium ranges, including four AIM-9L/M Sidewinders, four AIM-7F/M Sparrows or eight AMRAAM, and a 20 mm M61A1 six-barrel gun with 940 rounds of ammunition. General Electric lead-computing gyro. To keep the pilot informed of the status of his weapons and provide for their management, an armament control set has been developed by Dynamic Controls Corporation. Three air-to-surface weapon stations (five if configured with conformal fuel tanks) allow for the carriage of up to 10,705 kg (23,600 lb) of bombs, rockets or additional ECM equipment.

DIMENSIONS, EXTERNAL:
- Wing span: 13·05 m (42 ft 9¾ in)
- Length overall: 19·43 m (63 ft 9 in)
- Height overall: 5·63 m (18 ft 5½ in)
- Tailplane span: 8·61 m (28 ft 3 in)
- Wheel track: 2·75 m (9 ft 0¼ in)
- Wheelbase: 5·42 m (17 ft 9½ in)

AREAS:
- Wings, gross: 56·5 m² (608 sq ft)
- Ailerons (total): 2·46 m² (26·48 sq ft)
- Flaps (total): 3·33 m² (35·84 sq ft)
- Fins (total): 9·78 m² (105·28 sq ft)
- Rudders (total): 1·85 m² (19·94 sq ft)
- Tailplanes (total): 10·34 m² (111·36 sq ft)

WEIGHTS:
- Weight empty, equipped (no fuel, ammunition, pylons or external stores): 12,973 kg (28,600 lb)
- Max fuel load: internal: 6,103 kg (13,455 lb)
  - CFTs (2, total): 4,422·5 kg (9,750 lb)
  - auxiliary tanks (3, total): 5,395·5 kg (11,895 lb)
  - max internal and external: 15,921 kg (35,100 lb)
- T-O weight (interceptor, full internal fuel and 4 Sparrows): 20,244 kg (44,630 lb)
- T-O weight (incl three 2,309 litre; 610 US gallon drop tanks): 26,521 kg (58,470 lb)
- Max T-O weight: with CFTs: 30,845 kg (68,000 lb)

PERFORMANCE:
- Max level speed: more than Mach 2·5 (800 knots; 1,482 km/h; 921 mph CAS)
- Approach speed: 125 knots (232 km/h; 144 mph) CAS
- T-O run (interceptor): 274 m (900 ft)
- Landing run (interceptor), without braking parachute: 1,067 m (3,500 ft)
- Service ceiling: 18,300 m (60,000 ft)
- Ferry range: with external tanks, without CFTs: more than 2,500 nm (4,631 km; 2,878 miles)
  - with CFTs: 3,100 nm (5,745 km; 3,570 miles)
- Max endurance:
  - with in-flight refuelling: 15 h 0 min
  - unrefuelled, with CFTs: 5 h 15 min
- Design g limits: +9/−3

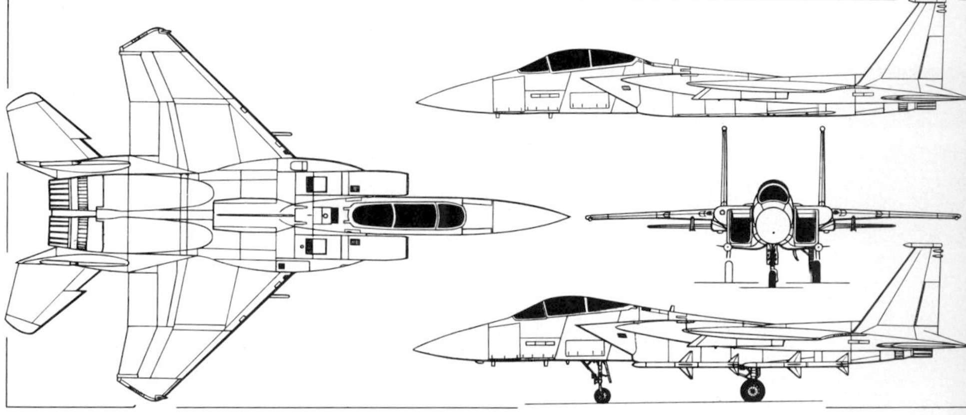

McDonnell Douglas F-15C Eagle single-seat air superiority fighter, with additional side view (top) of two-seat F-15B *(Pilot Press)*

Prototype McDonnell Douglas F-15C fitted with conformal fuel tanks and with a LANTIRN navigational pod under its port engine air intake

MCDONNELL DOUGLAS F-15E EAGLE

The F-15E is a two-seat dual role version of the Eagle capable of performing long-range, deep interdiction, high ordnance payload air-to-ground missions by day or night, and in adverse weather, while retaining its proven air-to-air capabilities. The prototype, known initially as the Strike Eagle, was developed with industry funds as a modification of a two-seat F-15B (71-291). The rear cockpit was upgraded with four multi-purpose CRT displays for radar weapon selection, and monitoring of enemy tracking systems. Production F-15Es will also have front cockpit modifications that will include redesigned controls, a wide field of view head-up display, and three CRTs providing multi-purpose displays for improved navigation, weapons delivery and systems operation, including moving map displays, weapons options, precision radar mapping, and terrain following.

For tactical target missions at night and in all-weather conditions, the F-15E will have advanced radar and infra-red systems. A new high resolution Hughes APG-70 radar, wide-field forward looking infra-red (FLIR) and LANTIRN nav/attack pod will ensure target detection/identification and improve the accuracy of weapons delivery. Successful integration of these systems was demonstrated during 1982 in flight tests at Edwards AFB, California, and Eglin AFB, Florida, resulting in accurate 'blind' weapons delivery.

To accommodate the new avionics, internal fuel capacity has been reduced slightly, to 7,643 litres (2,019 US gallons), by reducing the capacity of one fuselage tank, but for increased payload/range capability the F-15E can utilise standard F-15 conformal fuel tanks with a full complement of bombs carried on integral, tangential bomb racks. The conformal tanks add 5,678 litres (1,500 US gallons) of fuel for increased range, and can be used in conjunction with up to three 2,309 litre (610 US gallon) external fuel tanks. In addition to carrying a variety of guided and unguided bombs and other air-to-ground weapons, the F-15E will retain its air superiority performance and weapons (AIM-7

Artist's impression of F-15E Eagle in dual role configuration, with twelve 500 lb bombs carried tangentially on CFTs, twin LANTIRN pods, and Sidewinder missiles

Sparrow, AIM-9 Sidewinder and AIM-120 AMRAAM). Built-in flexibility will allow for growth and increased variety in weapons carriage.

A digital, triple redundant Lear Siegler flight control system will be installed in the F-15E, permitting coupled automatic terrain following, and a Honeywell ring laser gyro inertial navigation system will provide quick reaction alignment and improved navigational accuracy. A new engine bay under development by McDonnell Douglas will enable the F-15E to be powered by either General Electric F110 or Pratt & Whitney F100 engines. The engine bay structure consists of large titanium sections manufactured with superplastic forming and diffusion bonding processes, and will permit future installation of growth versions of these engines, providing a total of up to 266·9 kN (60,000 lb st) in the aircraft's two-engine installation. An F-15 powered by Pratt & Whitney's improved F100-PW-220 engine was delivered to the 33rd TFW at Eglin AFB, Florida, in August 1986 for in-service evaluation.

US Air Force and McDonnell Douglas pilots began flight testing product improvements for the F-15E on four Eagles, including an F-15C, an F-15D and the prototype Strike Eagle, at Edwards AFB in November 1982. The programme was completed successfully on schedule on 30 April 1983, after more than 200 flights. During the tests, an F-15 took off for the first time at a gross weight of 34,019 kg (75,000 lb), ie 3,175 kg (7,000 lb) more than the standard max T-O weight of the F-15C with conformal fuel tanks. On this occasion, the aircraft was equipped with two CFTs, three other external tanks, and eight 500 lb Mk 82 bombs. In the overall programme 16 different stores loads configurations were tested, including the carriage of 2,000 lb Mk 84 bombs and BDU-38 and CBU-58 weapons, delivered by both visual and radar means.

After evaluating the potential of the dual role Eagle against that of the General Dynamics F-16XL, the USAF announced on 24 February 1984 that it had selected the F-15E for development. Design work began in April 1984 under an initial increment of a $359·4 million fixed-price incentive contract. Construction of the first of three F-15E prototypes began in July 1985. First flight of this prototype was scheduled for December 1986, with the first production aircraft expected to fly a year later. The US Air Force plans to produce 392 dual role Eagles. IOC is expected in late 1988.

The description of the F-15C applies also to the F-15E except:

Type: Two-seat dual role attack/air superiority fighter.

Fuselage: Upper rear fuselage, rear fuselage keel structure, main landing gear doors and some rear fuselage fairings incorporate superplastic-formed/diffusion bonded (SPF/DB) titanium structure, providing additional engine bay volume to permit compatibility with alternative engines.

Landing Gear: As for F-15C, but with Bendix wheels and Michelin tyres on all units. Nosewheel tyre size 22 × 7·75-9, mainwheel tyres size 36 × 11-18; tyre pressure 21·03 bars (305 lb/sq in) on all units. Bendix five-rotor carbon disc brakes.

Accommodation: Two crew, pilot and weapon systems officer, in tandem on McDonnell Douglas ACES II ejection seats. Single-piece, upward-hinged canopy.

Armament: 20 mm M61A1 six-barrel gun in starboard wing root, with 940 rds. General Electric lead computing gyro. Provision on underwing (one per wing) and centreline pylons for air-to-air and air-to-ground weapons and external fuel tanks. Wing pylons use standard rail and ejection launchers for AIM-9 Sidewinder and AIM-120 AMRAAM air-to-air missiles; AIM-7 Sparrow and AIM-120 AMRAAM can be carried on launchers on centreline station or on tangential stores carriers on conformal fuel tanks (maximum total load four each AIM-7 or AIM-9, up to eight AIM-120). Single or triple rail launchers for AGM-65 Maverick air-to-ground missiles can be fitted to wing stations only. Tangential carriage on CFTs provides for up to six bomb racks on each tank, with provision for triple ejector racks on wing and centreline stations. The F-15E can carry a wide variety and quantity of guided and unguided air-to-ground weapons, including Mk 20 Rockeye (26), Mk 82 (26), Mk 83 (15), Mk 84 (seven), BSU-49 (26), BSU-50 (seven), GBU-8 (five), GBU-10 (seven), GBU-12 (15), GBU-15 (two), GBU-22 (15), GBU-24 (five), CBU-52 (25), CBU-58 (25), CBU-71 (25), CBU-87 (25), CBU-89 (25), CBU-90 (25), CBU-92 (25), CBU-93 (25) bombs; LAU-3A rockets (nine), SUU-20 training weapons (five), A/A-37 U-33 tow target (one), B-57 and B-61 series nuclear weapons (five), and AGM-65 Maverick (six). An AXQ-14 data link pod is used in conjunction with the GBU-15; LANTIRN pod illumination is used to designate targets for the GBU-12, -22 and -24 laser guided bombs.

Weights:

Basic operating weight empty	14,379 kg (31,700 lb)
Max weapon load	10,659 kg (23,500 lb)
Max fuel weight: internal	5,952 kg (13,123 lb)
external (2 CFTs and 3 610 USG drop tanks)	9,818 kg (21,645 lb)
Max T-O weight	36,741 kg (81,000 lb)
Max zero-fuel weight	28,440 kg (62,700 lb)
Max landing weight:	
unrestricted	20,094 kg (44,300 lb)
at reduced sink rates	36,741 kg (81,000 lb)

MCDONNELL DOUGLAS F-15 STOL DEMONSTRATOR

In October 1984 McDonnell Douglas was awarded a $117·8 million cost-sharing contract to develop and flight test for the US Air Force Wright Aeronautical Laboratories an advanced technology version of the F-15 with short take-off and landing (STOL) and new manoeuvring capabilities. The programme will investigate four specific technologies: two-dimensional (2-D) thrust vectoring/reversing jet nozzles; integrated flight/propulsion control; rough/soft field STOL landing gear; and advanced pilot/vehicle interfaces.

McDonnell Douglas is modifying its No. 1 F-15B flight test aircraft for the programme, designated Agile Eagle. Controllable foreplanes, adapted from the tailplanes of the F/A-18A Hornet, will be installed above the F-15B's engine air intake trunks, forward of the wings. Mounted at a dihedral angle of 20°, the foreplanes will operate symmetrically or asymmetrically to provide pitch and roll moments, and will be used as stability maintaining surfaces rather than for primary flight control. They will permit the F-15's maximum allowable load factor to be increased from 7·33*g* to 9*g* without additional structural strengthening. Rectangular, two-dimensional vectoring nozzles manufactured from carbonfibre will be installed at the rear of the aircraft's F100 engines, replacing the F-15B's standard afterburner ducts. The nozzles will vector engine thrust by up to 20° upwards or downwards from the longitudinal axis to enhance take-off performance and flight manoeuvring. Thrust reverser vanes in the nozzles will be flight-deployable for rapid deceleration in addition to their short-landing-roll function.

A digital fly by wire system will integrate with the flight control system all functions of foreplanes, flaperons, horizontal tail surfaces and vectoring nozzles to provide high precision control of the aircraft's flight path for landing approach. Structurally reinforced landing gear will permit 3·66 m (12 ft)/s landing impact loads.

The STOL/manoeuvring demonstrator is expected to incorporate use of new aluminium-lithium alloys, and an F-15 with major wing skin panels of this material, made by Alcan Ltd (UK), began flight testing in the Summer of 1986. The new skins are 5 per cent stronger and 9 per cent lighter than the conventional aluminium parts they replace. Aluminium accounts for about 2,948 kg (6,500 lb), or 51 per cent, of the current F-15's empty weight.

Performance parameters specified for the F-15 STOL demonstrator include take-off and landing runs of 457 m (1,500 ft) on a 15 m (50 ft) wide, hard, wet, rough surface runway, at night and in adverse weather, with fuel, gun, ammunition and a 2,721 kg (6,000 lb) external payload. McDonnell Douglas is said to be aiming for take-off and landing runs of 305 m (1,000 ft) and 381 m (1,250 ft) respectively. A 6 to 7 per cent increase in manoeuvring performance over the standard F-15 is anticipated, with a 4,536 kg (10,000 lb) increase in payload when operating from a 457 m (1,500 ft) runway, a 27 per cent reduction in take-off run, 13 per cent improvement in cruise range, 24 per cent better roll rate and up to 100 per cent improvement in pitch rate.

The F-15 STOL demonstrator is scheduled to make its first flight in March 1988. The initial test programme will include some 150 hours of flight testing. Major subcontractors in the programme are Pratt & Whitney, General Electric's Flight Control Division, and the National Water Lift Division of Pneumo Corporation.

MCDONNELL DOUGLAS/BAe AV-8B HARRIER II

Details of the AV-8B Harrier II can be found in the International section.

MCDONNELL DOUGLAS F/A-18A HORNET

Canadian AF designations: CF-18A/B

Spanish Air Force designations: C.15 and CE.15

In the Spring of 1974 the US Department of Defense accepted a proposal from the US Navy to study a low-cost lightweight multi-mission fighter, then identified as the VFAX. In August of that year Congress terminated the VFAX concept, directing instead that the Navy should investigate versions of the General Dynamics YF-16 and Northrop YF-17 lightweight fighter prototypes then under evaluation for the USAF.

McDonnell Douglas concluded that Northrop's contender could be redesigned at minimum cost to meet the Navy's requirements. It then teamed with Northrop to propose a derivative of the YF-17 to meet the Navy's requirement, with McDonnell Douglas as the prime contractor. Identified as the Navy Air Combat Fighter (NACF), this received the name Hornet when selected for further development. Two single-seat versions were proposed originally, of which the F-18A was intended for fighter duties and the A-18 for attack missions. Except for a small amount of operational equipment and missile armament, the two proved so similar that the single designation F/A-18A now covers both configurations. On 8 April 1985 McDonnell Douglas Corporation and Northrop Corporation announced settlement of litigation between them concerning production and sale of F-18 aircraft and technology. Under the terms of the agreement McDonnell Douglas is prime contractor for all existing and future versions of the aircraft, and Northrop is principal subcontractor. The following versions have been announced:

Artist's impression of the advanced technology STOL version of the F-15 Eagle

F/A-18A. Single-seat escort fighter/interdictor to replace F-4, armed with fuselage mounted Sparrows; also a single-seat attack aircraft to replace A-4 and A-7, with FLIR and a laser tracker, which are being developed as part of the Hornet programme, replacing the Sparrow missiles.

F/A-18B. Tandem two-seat version of F/A-18A for training, with combat capability, formerly known as TF/A-18A. Fuel capacity reduced by under 6 per cent.

F/A-18C and F/A-18D. Single- and two-seat aircraft purchased from FY 1986 onwards. Similar to F/A-18A/B, but with provision for carriage of AMRAAM weapons, IR Maverick missiles and airborne self-protection jammers, reconnaissance equipment, new 'air common escape system' ejection seats, improved mission computer, and a flight incident recording and monitoring system. First flight (F/A-18C) Summer 1986; deliveries scheduled to begin in October 1987. F/A-18C/Ds delivered from October 1989 will, in addition, carry equipment for all-weather night attack missions, including a FLIR navigation pod, new HUD and pilot's night vision goggles.

F/A-18(R). The US Navy began evaluation of a simple reconnaissance conversion of the standard F/A-18A in the Autumn of 1982. This involves removal of the gun from the aircraft's nose, and its replacement by a twin-sensor package with two windows in a slightly bulged underfairing. Sensors can include a Fairchild-Weston KA-99 low/medium-altitude panoramic camera and/or Honeywell AAD-5 IR linescan. Additional sensors, including a low altitude camera, are being studied. The F/A-18(R) can be converted overnight to the fighter/attack configuration within the operational squadron. Flight testing of the first F/A-18 fitted with reconnaissance equipment began on 15 August 1984.

CF-18A. Version for Canadian Armed Forces, which plan to purchase 138, including 40 **CF-18B** two-seaters. Selection announced on 10 April 1980. First example made its initial flight on 29 July 1982. Deliveries began with CAF901 and CAF902 on 25 October 1982 and are scheduled to continue at the rate of two per month until 1988. By 1 March 1986 a total of 77 CF-18s had been delivered. First CAF unit was No. 410 Squadron, based at CFB Cold Lake, Alberta, followed by No. 425 at Bagotville, Quebec, and Nos. 439, 409 and 421 Squadrons of No. 1 Canadian Air Group at Sollingen, West Germany. CF-18s are replacing CF-101s, CF-104s and CF-5s. By comparison with US Navy version, CF-18 has different ILS and added spotlight on port side of fuselage for night identification of other aircraft in flight.

Australian F/A-18A/B. Versions for the Royal Australian Air Force. The intention to procure 75 Hornets was announced on 20 October 1981. Two of the RAAF F/A-18Bs were manufactured by McDonnell Douglas, and delivered by air from NAS Lemoore, California, to RAAF Williamtown, near Sydney, on 17 May 1985. The first F/A-18B assembled in Australia by Government Aircraft Factories at Avalon, near Melbourne, made its first flight on 26 February 1985 and was handed over to the RAAF's No. 2 operational conversion unit in the following month. The first Australian manufactured aircraft (F/A-18B A21-104) made its first flight on 3 June 1985. The RAAF's F/A-18s (57 single-seat F/A-18As and 18 two-seat F/A-18Bs) will replace Dassault Mirage III-Os. Three operational squadrons will be formed, with deliveries scheduled for completion in 1990.

EF-18. Version for Spanish Air Force, which has ordered 72 for delivery from 1986, with an option for 12 more. Contract signed in May 1983. First aircraft rolled out 22 November 1985 and due for delivery to Spain with three others in Summer 1986, with IOC anticipated in 1987. In Spanish Air Force service, aircraft will be designated **C.15** (single-seat) and **CE.15** (two-seat).

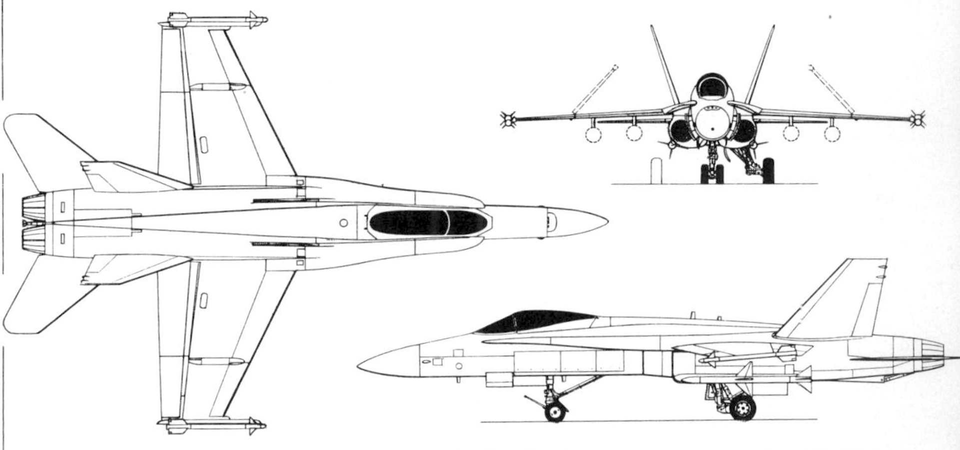

McDonnell Douglas F/A-18A Hornet (two General Electric F404-GE-400 turbofan engines) *(Pilot Press)*

On 22 January 1976 it was announced that full scale development had been initiated by the US Navy, with initial funding of /16 million. Total cost of the development programme included the production of 11 F-18s for the flight test programme. A total of 1,377 Hornets, including the 11 development aircraft, is planned for construction into the 1990s, for the US Navy and Marine Corps. More than 150 of those built will be two-seat trainers. Deliveries of all versions totalled 375 by March 1986, including 287 F/A-18As and F/A-18Bs to the US Navy; the overall total had passed 400 by September 1986.

The first Hornet (160775) made its first flight on 18 November 1978; the second flew on 12 March 1979, and all 11 development aircraft were flying by March 1980, including two TF/A-18A two-seat combat-capable trainers. The first batch of nine production Hornets was authorised in FY 1979, followed by 25 in FY 1980, 60 in FY 1981, 63 in FY 1982, 84 each year from FY 1983 to FY 1987, and 96 per year from FY 1988. In the fourth quarter of 1979, a Hornet became the first modern jet aircraft to complete initial sea trials within one year of its first flight, and the first production aircraft was delivered to the US Navy for operational evaluation in May 1980.

The first development squadron (VFA-125) was formed at NAS Lemoore, California, in November 1980. Operational evaluation and Navy BIS (Bureau of Inspection and Survey) trials began in early 1982. Fleet training began in mid-1982 and the Hornet officially entered operational service on 7 January 1983, with Marine Fighter/Attack Squadron 314 at MCAS El Toro, California, and later with VMFA-531 and VMFA-323. On 1 February 1985 the first Atlantic Fleet F/A-18A operational squadrons began forming at Cecil Field NAS, Florida, after training at NAS Lemoore, California. Also in February, two F/A-18A squadrons, VFA-113 'Stingers' and VFA-25 'Fist of the Fleet' embarked in the aircraft carrier USS *Constellation* for the aircraft's first extended deployment at sea.

In mid-1986 the following US Marine Corps and US Navy squadrons were operational with F/A-18As: VMFA-115 'Silver Eagles' at MCAS Beaufort, South Carolina; VMFA-314 'Black Knights', VMFA-323 'Death Rattlers' and VMFA-531 'Gray Ghosts', all at MCAS El Toro, California; VFA-106 'Gladiators', VFA-131 'Wildcats', VFA-132 'Privateers'. VFA-136 'Knight Hawks' and VFA-137 'Kestrels' with Atlantic Fleet, Cecil Field NAS, Florida; and VFA-25 'Fist of the Fleet', VFA-113 'Stingers', VFA-125 'Rough Raiders', VFA-192 'Golden Dragons', VFA-195 'Dambusters' and VFA-303 'Golden Hawks' with Pacific Fleet, Lemoore NAS, California.

In February 1986 the F/A-18A was selected to replace the US Navy Blue Angels Flight Demonstration Squadron's A-4F Skyhawks from 1987. Eleven early production aircraft, not suitable for shipboard operation, have been fitted with smoke-generating systems and special seat harnesses. The Blue Angels will begin training on the F/A-18A at El Centro NAS, California, in January 1987.

By early 1986 US Marine Corps and US Navy F/A-18As and F/A-18Bs had completed some 150,000 flight hours.

McDonnell Douglas is prime contractor for the Hornet, with the centre of activities at St Louis, Missouri. Northrop builds the centre and rear fuselage, which is delivered totally assembled to McDonnell Douglas. Assembly is completed at St Louis. Details of a projected multi-role land-based version, designated F/A-18L, can be found in the 1985-86 *Jane's*.

The following information applies specifically to the single-seat US Navy F/A-18A:

TYPE: Single-seat naval strike fighter.

WINGS: Cantilever mid-wing monoplane. Moderate sweep multi-spar structure, primarily of light alloy and graphite/epoxy. Boundary layer control achieved by wing root slots. Full span leading-edge manoeuvring flaps have a maximum extension angle of 30°. Single-slotted trailing-edge flaps, actuated by Bertea hydraulic cylinders, deploy to a maximum of 45°. Ailerons, with Hydraulic Research actuators, can be drooped to 45°, providing the advantages of full span flaps for low approach speeds. Leading- and trailing-edge flaps are computer programmed to deflect for optimum lift and drag in both manoeuvring and cruise conditions, and ailerons and flaps are also deflected differentially for roll. Wing root leading-edge extensions (LEX) permit flight at angles of attack exceeding 60°. Wings fold, by means of AiResearch mechanical drive, at the inboard end of each aileron.

FUSELAGE: Semi-monocoque basic structure, primarily of light alloy, with graphite/epoxy used for access doors/panels. Titanium firewall between engines. Airbrake in upper surface of fuselage between tail fins. Pressurised cockpit section of fail-safe construction.

TAIL UNIT: Cantilever structure with swept vertical and horizontal surfaces. Twin outward-canted fins and rudders, mounted forward of all-moving horizontal surfaces (stabilators), which are actuated collectively and differentially by National Water Lift servo-cylinder hydraulic units for pitch and roll control.

LANDING GEAR: Retractable tricycle type, with twin-wheel nose and single-wheel main units. Nose unit retracts forward, mainwheels rearward, turning 90° to stow horizontally inside the lower surface of the engine air ducts. Bendix wheels and brakes. osewheel tyres size 22 × 6·6-10, 20 ply, pressure 24·13 bars (350 lb/sq in) for carrier operations, 10·34 bars (150 lb/sq in) for land operations. Mainwheel tyres size 30 × 11·5-14·5, 24 ply, pressure 24·13 bars (350 lb/sq in) for carrier operations, 13·79 bars (200 lb/sq in) for land operations. Ozone nosewheel steering unit. Nose unit towbar for catapult launch. Arrester hook, for carrier landings, under rear fuselage.

POWER PLANT: Two General Electric F404-GE-400 low bypass turbofan engines, each producing approx 71·2 kN (16,000 lb thrust). Self-sealing fuel tanks and fuel lines; foam in wing tanks and fuselage voids. Internal fuel load approx 4,990 kg (11,000 lb); provision for up to three 1,249 litre (330 US gallon) external tanks, increasing total fuel capacity to more than 7,983 kg (17,600 lb). Flight refuelling probe retracts into upper starboard side of nose. Simmonds fuel gauging system. Fixed ramp air intakes.

ACCOMMODATION: Pilot only in F/A-18A, on Martin-Baker US10S ejection seat in pressurised, heated and air-conditioned cockpit. Martin-Baker Navy Aircrew Common

McDonnell Douglas F/A-18A strike fighters of US Navy Squadron VFA-113 'Stingers'

Ejection Seat (NACES) selected for future installation. Upward opening separate windscreen and canopy, hinged individually.

SYSTEMS: Two completely separate hydraulic systems at 207 bars (3,000 lb/sq in). Max flow rate 212 litres (56 US gallons)/min. Bootstrap type reservoir, pressure 5·86 bars (85 lb/sq in). Quadruplex digital fly by wire flight control system, with direct electrical backup to all surfaces, and direct mechanical backup to stabilators. Garrett air-conditioning system. General Electric electrical power system. Oxygen system. Fire detection and extinguishing systems.

AVIONICS AND EQUIPMENT: Include an automatic carrier landing system (ACLS) for all-weather carrier operations; a Hughes Aircraft AN/APG-65 multi-mode digital air-to-air and air-to-ground tracking radar, with air-to-air modes which include velocity search (VS), range while search (RWS), track while scan (TWS), which can track ten targets and display eight to the pilot, and raid assessment mode (RAM). Itek ALR-67 radar warning receiver; General Electric quadruple-redundant flight control system; two AYK-14 digital computers; Litton AN/ASN-130A inertial navigation system; two Kaiser multi-function CRTs, central Ferranti/Bendix CRT and head-up display; Conrac communications system control; Normalair-Garrett digital data recorder for Bendix maintenance recording system; Smiths standby altimeter; and Kearflex standby airspeed indicator, standby vertical speed indicator, and cockpit pressure altimeter. Garrett APU for engine starting and ground pneumatic, electric and hydraulic power.

ARMAMENT: Nine external weapon stations with a combined capacity of 7,710 kg (17,000 lb) of mixed ordnance at high *g*. These comprise two wingtip stations for AIM-9 Sidewinder air-to-air missiles; two outboard wing stations for an assortment of air-to-ground or air-to-air weapons, including AIM-7 Sparrows and AIM-9 Sidewinders; two inboard wing stations for external fuel tanks or air-to-ground weapons; two nacelle fuselage stations for Sparrows or Martin Marietta AN/ASQ-173 laser spot tracker/strike camera (LST/SCAM) and Ford AN/AAS-38 FLIR pods; and a centreline fuselage station for external fuel or weapons. An M61 20 mm six-barrel gun, with 570 rounds, is mounted in the nose and has a McDonnell Douglas director gunsight, with a conventional sight as backup.

DIMENSIONS, EXTERNAL:

Wing span	11·43 m (37 ft 6 in)
Wing span over missiles	12·31 m (40 ft 4¾ in)
Wing chord: at root	4·04 m (13 ft 3 in)
at tip	1·68 m (5 ft 6 in)
Wing aspect ratio	3·5
Width, wings folded	8·38 m (27 ft 6 in)
Length overall	17·07 m (56 ft 0 in)
Height overall	4·66 m (15 ft 3½ in)
Tailplane span	6·58 m (21 ft 7¼ in)
Wheel track	3·11 m (10 ft 2½ in)

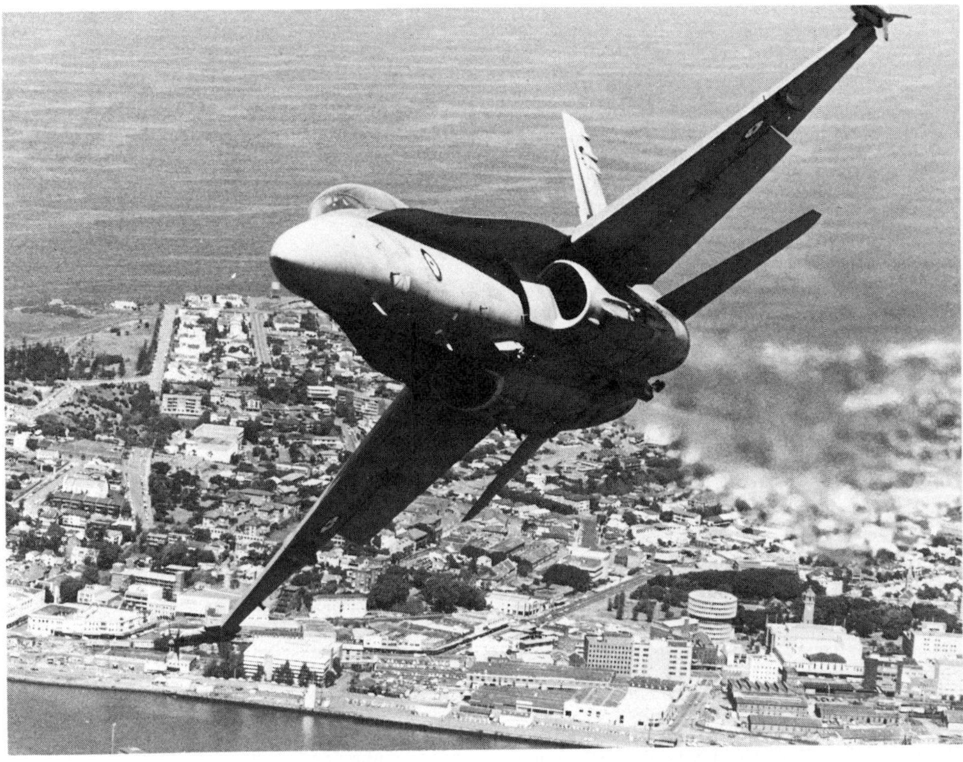

McDonnell Douglas F/A-18B of the Royal Australian Air Force *(The Age, Melbourne)*

Wheelbase	5·42 m (17 ft 9½ in)
AREAS:	
Wings, gross	37·16 m² (400·0 sq ft)
Ailerons, total	2·27 m² (24·4 sq ft)
Leading-edge flaps, total	4·50 m² (48·4 sq ft)
Trailing-edge flaps, total	5·75 m² (61·9 sq ft)
Fins, total	9·68 m² (104·2 sq ft)
Rudders, total	1·45 m² (15·6 sq ft)
Tailplanes, total	8·18 m² (88·1 sq ft)
WEIGHTS:	
Weight empty	10,455 kg (23,050 lb)
Max fuel weight: internal	4,926 kg (10,860 lb)
external	3,053 kg (6,732 lb)
Fighter mission T-O weight	16,651 kg (36,710 lb)
Attack mission T-O weight	22,328 kg (49,224 lb)
PERFORMANCE:	
Max level speed	more than Mach 1·8
Max speed, intermediate power	more than Mach 1·0
Approach speed	134 knots (248 km/h; 154 mph)
Combat ceiling	approx 15,240 m (50,000 ft)
T-O run	less than 427 m (1,400 ft)
Combat radius, fighter mission	more than 400 nm (740 km; 460 miles)
Combat radius, attack mission	575 nm (1,065 km; 662 miles)
Ferry range, unrefuelled	more than 2,000 nm (3,706 km; 2,303 miles)

MCDONNELL DOUGLAS/NORTHROP ATF

McDonnell Douglas and Northrop have signed a teaming agreement covering their individual proposals for the US Air Force's Advanced Tactical Fighter. Submission of formal proposals began on 28 July 1986, and selection of one or more winners was anticipated before the end of the year. If either McDonnell Douglas or Northrop is chosen by USAF, the winning company will be prime contractor for all phases of the programme and the other will be principal subcontractor.

DOUGLAS AIRCRAFT COMPANY (Division of McDonnell Douglas Corporation)

HEADQUARTERS: 3855 Lakewood Boulevard, Long Beach, California 90846
Telephone: (213) 593 5511
PRESIDENT: James E. Worsham
EXECUTIVE VICE-PRESIDENT: William T. Gross
SENIOR VICE-PRESIDENT:
Edward Curtis (Fiscal Management)
VICE-PRESIDENTS:
Robert L. Clepper (General Manager, C-17 Programme)
David A. Conlon (Asst to the President)
John E. Crosthwait (General Manager, T45TS Programme and Special Products)
James H. Douez (Manufacturing)
Eugene F. Dubil (Ombudsman)
Louis F. Harrington (General Manager, Advanced Products)
Glenn L. Hickerson (Commercial Marketing, International)
N. Douglas Ingebretsen (Human Resources)
Robert C. P. Jackson (Plans)
Robert H. Kinder (Government Programme Development)
Ray J. Kleinberg (Controller)
Richard M. Randall (Contracts and Pricing)
Thomas M. Ryan Jr (Product Support)
Roger D. Schaufele (Engineering)
Kim Still (Commercial Marketing, The Americas)
CHIEF COUNSEL: John H. Carroll
DIRECTOR, MEDIA RELATIONS: Donald N. Hanson

The Douglas Aircraft Company operates plants at Long Beach and Torrance, California. The DC (Douglas Commercial) series of designations which had identified the company's civil design ever since the DC-1 of 1933 was superseded in 1983 by a new system using the McDonnell Douglas initials MD. First to bear an MD designation was the Super 80 series of DC-9 derivatives, now known as the MD-80. Existing DC-8, DC-9 and DC-10 designations were unchanged.

MCDONNELL DOUGLAS DC-8 SUPER 71, 72 and 73

A reference to DC-8 aircraft re-engined with CFM56 turbofan engines may be found under the Cammacorp entry in this section.

MCDONNELL DOUGLAS MD-80

Known previously as the Super 80, the MD-80 was developed from the DC-9 specifically to meet the needs of operators on short/medium-range routes who require an aircraft of increased capacity. The basic design has been modified to offer improved economy in operation, reduced fuel consumption, and far quieter engines.

The wings are increased in span by the insertion of wing root plugs and by a 0·61 m (2 ft 0 in) extension on each tip, giving a gross area 28 per cent greater than that of the DC-9 Srs 50. The fuselage is extended by insertion of a 3·86 m (12 ft 8 in) plug forward of the wing, and a 0·48 m (1 ft 7 in) segment aft of the wing. The cabin has 'wide look' decor, with large enclosed overhead baggage compartments, acoustic ceiling and soft fluorescent lighting. Standard fuel capacity is increased by 5,754 litres (1,520 US gallons) as a result of the larger wing.

Systems improvements in the MD-80 series include a new digital electronics integrated flight guidance and control system; a 'dial a flap' system to permit more accurate selection of flap angle for optimum take-off and landing performance; flow-through cooling of the aircraft's avionics compartment; a larger capacity APU; a new recirculating system for ventilation air; and an advanced digital fuel quantity gauging system.

The MD-80 is intended to remain competitive by means of a definitive and thorough product improvement programme. A performance management system (PMS) similar to that already certificated for the DC-10 (which see) became standard on all new MD-80s delivered from April 1983. Other improvements include aerodynamic refinements in some areas; increased use of composites, such as a Kevlar wing/fuselage fillet that became standard during 1983; and cockpit and avionics changes, including advanced attitude and heading reference systems. Sperry Corporation of Phoenix, Arizona, received a contract from Douglas Aircraft Company to develop an EFIS system for the MD-80 series. The system is offered as an optional replacement for electro-mechanical primary flight instrument displays, together with flat plate displays and flight management systems. First deliveries are anticipated during 1987.

The first aircraft in the Super 80/MD-80 series made its initial flight on 18 October 1979; second and third prototypes (N1002G and N1002W) flew on 6 December 1979 and 29 February 1980 respectively. FAA certification was granted on 26 August 1980, and on 12 September the first production aircraft was delivered to Swissair, which had placed an order for 15 in October 1977. On 29 October 1985 the MD-80 fleet completed five years of service with 30 airlines, averaging 175,000 passengers daily. On 4 June 1986 McDonnell Douglas delivered its 300th MD-80 series airliner, an MD-83 for Alaska Airlines. Available models are as follows:

MD-81. Basic version, powered by two Pratt & Whitney JT8D-209 turbofan engines. Emergency thrust reserve becomes available automatically in an engine-out situation. Refanned with a larger diameter single-stage fan, this version of the JT8D engine has a bypass ratio of 1·78, by comparison with 1·00 of earlier versions, resulting in a lower specific fuel consumption and reduced noise emission. In addition, sound suppression materials applied to the inlet, fan duct and tailpipe duct of each nacelle, plus a cold/hot-stream exhaust mixer, reduce engine noise to levels below the requirements of FAR Pt 36 Stage 3, and also satisfy the more stringent requirements of ICAO Chapter 3 established for new aircraft designs. Entered service, with Swissair, on 5 October 1980.

MD-82. Announced on 16 April 1979, with Pratt & Whitney JT8D-217 turbofan engines. Regarded as being particularly suitable for operation from 'hot and high' airports. The higher thrust available makes possible an increased payload and range when operating from standard airports. At an airport such as Denver, Colorado, which is 1,525 m (5,000 ft) above sea level, the MD-82 is able to take off with 155 passengers and their baggage, and have a nonstop range of approximately 1,300 nm (2,409 km; 1,497 miles). First flown on 8 January 1981, and certificated on 30 July 1981 at a max T-O weight of 66,680 kg (147,000 lb), it entered commercial service in August 1981. Otherwise generally similar to MD-81, with same fuel capacity and max landing weight. A second version, with JT8D-217A engines and higher max T-O weight of 67,812 kg (149,500 lb), was certificated in mid-1982, and became available from Autumn 1982. Range with max payload is 2,000 nm (3,700 km; 2,300 miles). On 12 April 1985 agreement was reached with the government of the People's Republic of China for the sale of 26 MD-82s, of which 25 will be partially assembled in the United States and shipped to China for final completion by the Shanghai Aviation Industrial Corporation (SAIC). The sole US assembled aircraft arrived in China on 30 September 1985. First subassemblies were delivered to SAIC in January 1986. The contract, which includes options for 15 additional MD-82s, will continue into 1991. The first SAIC assembled aircraft is expected to be completed in the Spring of 1987.

MD-83. This longer-range version of the MD-80, powered by Pratt & Whitney JT8D-219 engines, was announced on 31 January 1983. At a maximum take-off weight of 72,575 kg (160,000 lb), carrying 155 passengers and baggage, it has a normal range of 2,501 nm (4,635 km; 2,880 miles). The 93·4 kN (21,000 lb st) JT8D-219 engines have a 2 per cent improvement in fuel consumption by comparison with current -217A turbofan engines; greater fuel capacity is provided by the introduction of two fuel tanks in the cargo compartment, each of 2,195 litres (580 US gallons), giving a maximum capacity of 26,498 litres (7,000 US gallons).

The MD-83 flew for the first time on 17 December 1984. FAA certification was received in 1985, with service entry with launch customers Alaska Airlines and Finnair taking place in early 1986. On 14 November 1985 Finnair's first MD-83 made the longest nonstop flight ever recorded by an MD-80 variant, flying from Montreal to Helsinki, a distance of 3,404 nm (6,308 km; 3,920 miles) in 7 h 26 min. In December 1984 McDonnell Douglas Corporation and GPA Group Ltd of Shannon, Eire, formed a joint venture company, Irish Aerospace Limited, to acquire 24 MD-83s for subsequent operating leases to airlines. Six aircraft will be delivered per year in 1986 and 1987, the remaining 12 being delivered from 1988 to 1990 as market conditions dictate. First leases are to Frontier Airlines (four) and BWIA (one), beginning in April 1986.

MD-87. Announced on 3 January 1985, the MD-87 is a short-fuselage variant of the MD-80, with accommodation for 130 single class passengers or 109 passengers in mixed class configuration. Standard power plant will be two Pratt & Whitney JT8D-217C engines, each rated at 89 kN (20,000 lb st) at take-off, offering a 2 per cent improvement in fuel consumption over current -217A engines. Other engines in the JT8D-200 series may be ordered for the MD-87. Standard fuel capacity is 17,748 kg (39,128 lb). Two optional 2,195 litre (580 US gallon) auxiliary tanks increase total capacity to 21,273 kg (46,900 lb). The MD-87 will incorporate McDonnell Douglas' MD-80 series cruise performance improvement package, which includes a fillet fairing between fuselage and engine pylons, a fairing on the auxiliary power unit, improved sealing on the horizontal tail surfaces, low drag flap hinge fairings, and an extended low drag tailcone.

Assembly of the first aircraft began in April 1986, with a first flight scheduled for December. Certification is expected in September 1987, followed by deliveries late in the year, with eight aircraft for Finnair, four for Austrian Airlines, four for Toa Domestic Airlines and ten for SAS.

MD-88. Announced on 23 January 1986, the MD-88 will be powered by Pratt & Whitney JT8D-219 engines and feature EFIS cockpit displays, a flight management system, an onboard windshear detection system and increased use of composites materials in the airframe. A new interior design will provide accommodation for 142 passengers (14 first class and 128 coach class) in five-abreast seating, with wider aisle and redesigned overhead storage bins. First flight is scheduled for the second quarter of 1987, with deliveries commencing to launch customer Delta Air Lines, which has ordered 80, in the last quarter of the year.

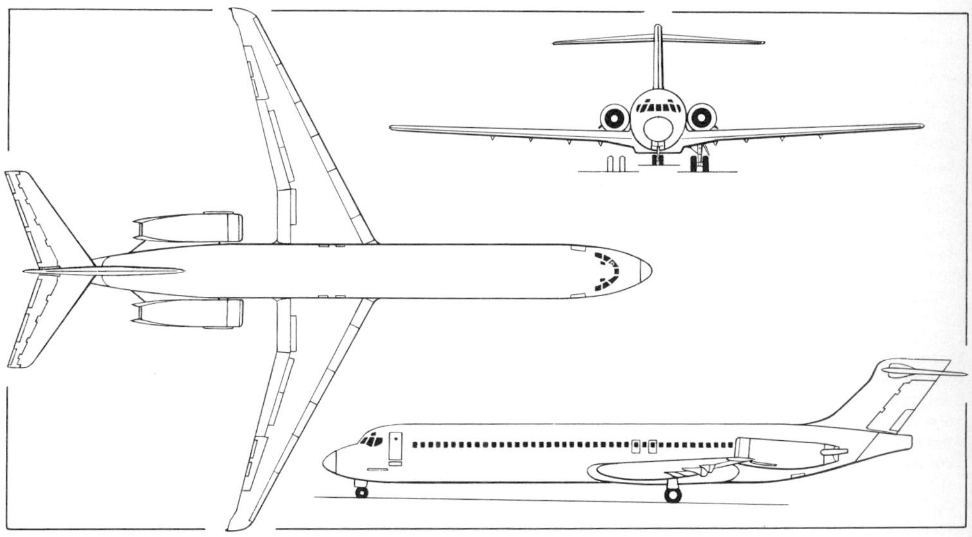

McDonnell Douglas MD-87, a short-fuselage variant of the MD-80 series of twin-turbofan transports *(Pilot Press)*

MD-80 Executive Jets. McDonnell Douglas offers corporate and executive variants of the MD-83 and MD-87. In typical corporate configurations seating 20 passengers the MD-83 offers a maximum range of 4,100 nm (7,598 km; 4,721 miles), while the MD-87 has a maximum range of 4,500 nm (8,339 km; 5,182 miles), each being equipped with auxiliary fuel tanks.

By 1 August 1986 orders and options for the MD-80 series totalled 756, of which 311 had been delivered.

The following description applies specifically to the MD-81, and generally also to the other models, except where indicated:

Type: Twin-turbofan short/medium-range airliner.

Wings: Cantilever low-wing monoplane. Mean thickness/chord ratio 11·0%. Dihedral 3°. Incidence 1° 15'. Sweepback at quarter-chord 24° 30'. All-metal construction, with two spars and spanwise stringers riveted to skin. Glassfibre trailing-edges on wings, ailerons and flaps. Manually controlled aileron on each wing. Wing mounted speed brakes. Full span leading-edge slats. Hydraulically actuated double-slotted trailing-edge flaps over 67 per cent of semi-span. Single boundary layer fence (vortillon) under each wing. Three spoilers per wing; two outboard segments act as flight and ground spoilers, inboard segment is ground spoiler only. Detachable wingtips. Thermal anti-icing of leading-edges.

Fuselage: All-metal semi-monocoque fail-safe structure of heat treated light alloy. Majority of cabin floor constructed of balsa or Nomex core composite. Engine pylons built by Calcor, fuselage panels by Aeritalia.

Tail Unit: Cantilever all-metal structure with electrically actuated variable incidence T tailplane. Manually controlled elevators with control tabs. Hydraulically controlled rudder with manual override. Glassfibre trailing-edges on control surfaces.

Landing Gear: Retractable tricycle type of Cleveland Pneumatic manufacture, with steerabe nosewheels. Hydraulic retraction, nose unit forward, main units inward. Twin Goodyear wheels and tyres on each unit. Mainwheel tyres size 44·5 × 16·5-20, pressure 11·38 bars (165 lb/sq in). Nosewheel tyres size 26 × 6·6-14, pressure 10·34 bars (150 lb/sq in). Goodyear disc brakes. Hydro-Aire Mk IIIA anti-skid units. Douglas ram air brake cooling.

Power Plant: Two Pratt & Whitney JT8D-209 turbofan engines in MD-81, pod mounted one each side of rear fuselage, and each rated at 82·3 kN (18,500 lb st), with emergency thrust reserve of 3·3 kN (750 lb st). MD-82 has JT8D-217s, each rated at 89 kN (20,000 lb st), with emergency thrust reserve of 3·78 kN (850 lb st), or -217As of similar rating. Standard fuel capacity (both models) 21,876 litres (5,779 US gallons). MD-83 has JT8D-219 engines of 93·4 kN (21,000 lb st) and extra 4,390 litres (1,160 US gallons) of fuel in cargo compartment tanks. MD-87 has JT8D-217B engines of 89 kN (20,000 lb st), with an emergency thrust reserve of 3·78 kN (850 lb st). Pressure refuelling point in starboard wing leading-edge. Overwing gravity refuelling points.

Accommodation: Crew of two and observer on flight deck, plus cabin attendants. Seating arrangements are optional to meet specific airline requirements. Maximum optional seating capacity is for 172 passengers. Fully pressurised and air-conditioned. One toilet forward on port side, two at rear of cabin. Provisions for galley at both forward and rear ends of cabin. Passenger door at front of cabin on port side, with built-in electrically operated airstairs, and rear hydraulically operated ventral stairway, are standard. Servicing and emergency exit doors at starboard forward end and port rear end of cabin. Three cargo doors for underfloor holds on starboard side. Overwing emergency exits, two each side.

Systems: Garrett dual air cycle air-conditioning and pressurisation system utilising engine bleed air, max differential 0·54 bars (7·77 lb/sq in). Two separate 207 bar (3,000 lb/sq in) hydraulic systems for operation of spoilers, flaps, slats, rudder, landing gear, nosewheel steering, brakes, rotated thrust reversers and ventral stairway. Maximum flow rate 30·3 litres (8 US gallons)/min. Airless bootstrap type reservoirs, output pressure 2·07 bars (30 lb/sq in). Pneumatic system, for air-conditioning/pressurisation, engine starting and ice protection, utilises 8th or 13th stage engine bleed air and/or APU. Electrical system includes three 40kVA 120/208V three-phase 400Hz alternators, two engine driven, one driven by APU. Oxygen system of diluter demand type for crew on flight deck; continuous flow chemical canister

McDonnell Douglas MD-83 in the insignia of BWIA International/Trinidad and Tobago Airways

Artist's impression of McDonnell Douglas MD-88 in the colours of launch customer Delta Air Lines

type with automatic mask presentation for cabin passengers. Anti-icing of wing and engine inlets, and de-icing of tailplane, by engine bleed air. Electric de-icing of windscreen. APU provides pneumatic and electrical power on ground, and electrical power in flight.

AVIONICS AND EQUIPMENT: All-digital avionics, including dual Sperry integrated flight systems; Sperry Cat IIIA autoland; autopilot and stability augmentation system; performance management system; speed command with digital full-time autothrottles; thrust rating indicator system; dual Honeywell air data systems; automatic reserve thrust; ADF system; and colour weather radar display. Sundstrand head-up display optional.

DIMENSIONS, EXTERNAL (all versions, except as indicated):

Wing span	32·87 m (107 ft 10 in)
Wing chord: at root	7·05 m (23 ft 1½ in)
at tip	1·10 m (3 ft 7½ in)
Wing aspect ratio	9·62
Length overall: except MD-87	45·06 m (147 ft 10 in)
MD-87	39·75 m (130 ft 5 in)
Length of fuselage:	
except MD-87	41·30 m (135 ft 6 in)
MD-87	36·30 m (119 ft 1 in)
Height overall: except MD-87	9·04 m (29 ft 8 in)
MD-87	9·30 m (30 ft 6 in)
Tailplane span	12·24 m (40 ft 2 in)
Wheel track	5·08 m (16 ft 8 in)
Wheelbase: except MD-87	22·07 m (72 ft 5 in)
MD-87	19·18 m (62 ft 11 in)
Passenger door (port, fwd):	
Height	1·83 m (6 ft 0 in)
Width	0·86 m (2 ft 10 in)
Height to sill	2·24 m (7 ft 4 in)
Servicing door (stbd, fwd): Height	1·22 m (4 ft 0 in)
Width	0·69 m (2 ft 3 in)
Height to sill	2·24 m (7 ft 4 in)
Servicing door (port, rear): Height	1·52 m (5 ft 0 in)
Width	0·69 m (2 ft 3 in)
Height to sill	2·67 m (8 ft 9 in)
Freight and baggage hold doors:	
Height	1·27 m (4 ft 2 in)
Width	1·35 m (4 ft 5 in)
Height to sill: fwd	1·17 m (3 ft 10 in)
centre	1·30 m (4 ft 3 in)
rear	1·52 m (5 ft 0 in)
Rear cargo door (MD-87): Height	1·27 m (4 ft 2 in)
Width	0·91 m (3 ft 0 in)
Emergency exits (overwing, port and stbd):	
Height	0·91 m (3 ft 0 in)
Width	0·51 m (1 ft 8 in)

DIMENSIONS, INTERNAL:

Cabin, excl flight deck, incl toilets:	
Length	30·78 m (101 ft 0 in)
Max width	3·07 m (10 ft 1 in)
Max height	2·06 m (6 ft 9 in)
Floor area	89·65 m² (965 sq ft)
Volume	191·9 m³ (6,778 cu ft)
Freight holds (underfloor, MD-81/82):	
fwd	13·14 m³ (464 cu ft)
centre	9·80 m³ (346 cu ft)
rear	12·54 m³ (443 cu ft)
Freight holds (underfloor, MD-83):	
total	29·1 m³ (1,028 cu ft)

AREAS:

Wings, gross	118 m² (1,270 sq ft)
Ailerons (total)	3·53 m² (38·0 sq ft)
Fin, excl dorsal fin	9·51 m² (102·4 sq ft)
Rudder	6·07 m² (65·3 sq ft)
Tailplane	29·17 m² (314·0 sq ft)

WEIGHTS AND LOADINGS (A: MD-81; B: MD-82; C: MD-83, D: MD-87):

Operating weight empty: A	35,571 kg (78,421 lb)
B	35,629 kg (78,549 lb)
C	36,543 kg (80,563 lb)
D standard fuel	33,183 kg (73,157 lb)
D optional fuel	33,851 kg (74,629 lb)
Fuel load:	
A, B, D standard	17,748 kg (39,128 lb)
C, D optional	21,273 kg (46,900 lb)
Max payload (weight limited): A	17,952 kg (39,579 lb)
B	19,709 kg (43,451 lb)
C	18,795 kg (41,437 lb)
D standard	17,619 kg (38,843 lb)
D optional	16,951 kg (37,371 lb)
Max T-O weight: A, D standard	63,503 kg (140,000 lb)
B, D optional	67,812 kg (149,500 lb)
C	72,575 kg (160,000 lb)
Max zero-fuel weight: A	53,524 kg (118,000 lb)
B, C	55,338 kg (122,000 lb)
D	50,802 kg (112,000 lb)
Max landing weight:	
A, D standard	58,060 kg (128,000 lb)
B, D optional	58,967 kg (130,000 lb)
C	63,276 kg (139,500 lb)
Max wing loading:	
A, D standard	534·6 kg/m² (109·5 lb/sq ft)
B, D optional	574·7 kg/m² (117·7 lb/sq ft)
C	615·0 kg/m² (126·0 lb/sq ft)
Max power loading: A	385·8 kg/kN (3·78 lb/lb st)
B, D optional	381·0 kg/kN (3·74 lb/lb st)
C	388·5 kg/kN (3·81 lb/lb st)
D standard	356·8 kg/kN (3·50 lb/lb st)

PERFORMANCE (at max T-O weight except where indicated):

Max level speed (all)	500 knots (925 km/h; 575 mph)
Max cruising speed (all)	Mach 0·80
Normal cruising speed (all)	Mach 0·76
FAA T-O field length: A	2,210 m (7,250 ft)
B	2,271 m (7,450 ft)
C	2,553 m (8,375 ft)
D	1,859 m (6,100 ft)
FAA landing field length, at max landing weight:	
A	1,478 m (4,850 ft)
B	1,500 m (4,920 ft)
C	2,585 m (5,200 ft)
D	1,430 m (4,690 ft)
Range with max fuel:	
D standard	2,980 nm (5,522 km; 3,431 miles)
D optional	3,650 nm (6,764 km; 4,203 miles)
Range (A, B, C with 155 passengers, domestic reserves; D with 130 passengers, domestic reserves):	
A	1,563 nm (2,896 km; 1,800 miles)
B	2,049 nm (3,798 km; 2,360 miles)
C	2,501 nm (4,635 km; 2,880 miles)
D standard	2,372 nm (4,395 km; 2,731 miles)
D optional	2,829 nm (5,243 km; 3,258 miles)

OPERATIONAL NOISE LEVELS (FAR Pt 36):

T-O: A, B, C	90·4 EPNdB
D estimated	88·7 EPNdB
Sideline: A, B, C	94·6 EPNdB
D estimated	92·8 EPNdB
Approach: A, B, C	93·3 EPNdB
D estimated	93·3 EPNdB

MCDONNELL DOUGLAS PROPFAN PROGRAMME

McDonnell Douglas, Aeritalia (Gruppo IRI Finmeccanica) of Italy, Saab-Scania of Sweden and Shanghai Aviation Industrial Corporation of China are co-operating on the development of propfan technology as the basis for a range of derivative and new short-to-medium-range airliners, the first of which is designated **MD-91X**. The aircraft will be powered by an ultra high bypass (UHB) power plant driving highly contoured counter-rotating multi-blade fans. The General Electric Company and the Allison Gas Turbine Division of General Motors are developing demonstrator UHB engines which will begin flight tests on an MD-80 aircraft during 1987. Design studies indicate that on an average length short-haul flight an MD-80 size airliner with UHB propulsion could burn some 25 to 35 per cent less fuel than an advanced turbofan aircraft, and as much as 50 per cent less than current turbofan airliners. The MD-91X is planned as an MD-80 derivative seating 100-140 passengers. Projected max T-O weight is 46,266 kg (102,000 lb), with a 1,500 nm (2,779 km; 1,727 mile) range at a cruising speed of Mach 0·78. Certification and first deliveries could be achieved by 1991. An **MD-92X** derivative could seat up to 160 passengers.

The **MD-94X** is a projected propfan airliner of entirely new design in the 160 to 180 passenger class. In addition to UHB engines, the aircraft would feature laminar and turbulent boundary layer control, very high aspect ratio supercritical wings, flight-critical active stability augmentation, all-electric secondary power systems, digital control systems, fly by wire and fly by light technologies, and cockpit sidestick controllers. Certification could be achieved by 1994.

Artist's impression of McDonnell Douglas ultra high bypass (UHB) propfan derivative of MD-80 series

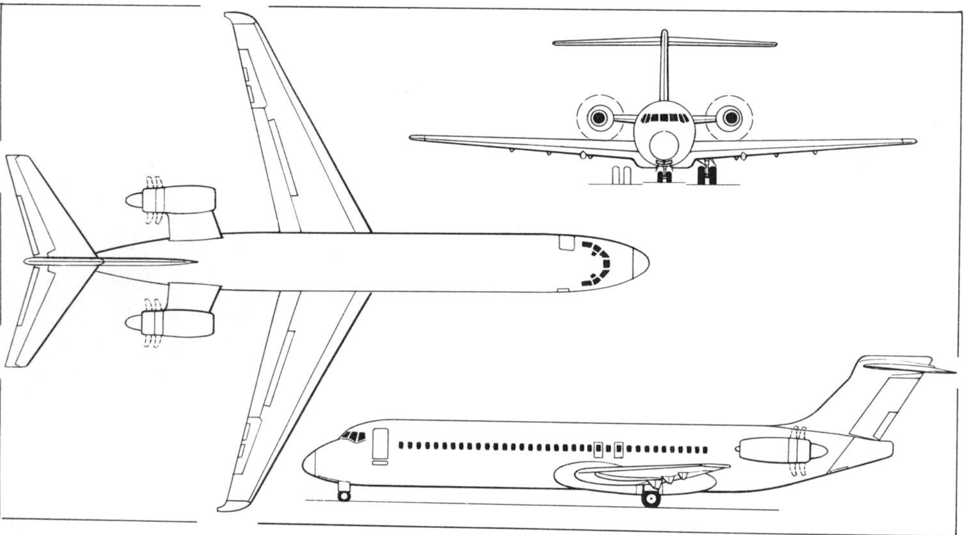

McDonnell Douglas MD-91X, under development as a four-nation programme *(Pilot Press)*

McDonnell Douglas also proposes a UHB retrofit programme for the MD-80 series. Timing of such a programme would depend on development of the MD-91X. The company predicts that an **MD-80 Retrofit** would offer a 41 per cent reduction in fuel burn over a 500 nm (926 km; 575 mile) flight at Mach 0·78 with 142 passengers against an MD-82 flying the same route. Estimated operating weight empty is 38,562 kg (85,015 lb), max T-O weight 62,142 kg (137,000 lb).

MCDONNELL DOUGLAS DC-10

The DC-10 was developed by McDonnell Douglas as an all-purpose commercial transport able to operate economically over ranges from 260 nm to 5,730 nm (480 to 10,620 km; 300 to 6,600 miles), according to Series, and able to carry 270 mixed class passengers, or a maximum of 380 passengers in an all-economy configuration.

There are five basic civil production versions, as follows:

Series 10. Initial version at 185,970 kg (410,000 lb) max T-O weight, powered by three General Electric CF6-6D or -6D1 turbofan engines, each rated at 178 kN (40,000 lb st) or 182·4 kN (41,000 lb st) respectively. Intended for service on domestic routes of 260-3,125 nm (480-5,795 km; 300-3,600 miles). First ordered, by American Airlines, on 19 February 1968. First flight 29 August 1970. Type certificated by FAA on 29 July 1971. First scheduled passenger flight 5 August 1971, by American Airlines. Subsequent version at 206,385 kg (455,000 lb) max T-O weight, and with added centre-wing fuel for ranges of up to 3,652 nm (6,768 km; 4,205 miles) with international reserves.

Series 15. Basically as Series 10, but with max T-O weight of 206,385 kg (455,000 lb), and General Electric CF6-50C2F engines, each rated at 207 kN (46,500 lb st). Range increased to 3,700 nm (6,850 km; 4,258 miles). Two each ordered by Aeroméxico and Mexicana in Summer 1979, for delivery in 1981. Three more ordered subsequently by Mexicana. First flight 8 January 1981. Certificated on 12 June 1981, with deliveries beginning shortly afterwards.

Series 30. Extended range version for intercontinental operations, powered by three General Electric CF6-50A or -50C turbofan engines, each rated at 218 kN (49,000 lb st) or 227 kN (51,000 lb st) respectively. Initial deliveries at 251,745 kg (555,000 lb) max T-O weight, with range of up to 5,150 nm (9,544 km; 5,930 miles). Later versions have CF6-50C1 or C2 engines rated at 233·5 kN (52,500 lb st), or C2B engines rated at 236 kN (53,000 lb st) and max T-O weight of up to 263,085 kg (580,000 lb). Increased fuel capacity. Wing span increased by 3·05 m (10 ft 0 in). Landing gear supplemented by additional dual-wheel bogie unit, mounted on the fuselage centreline between the four-wheel bogie main units. First flight 21 June 1972. FAA certification granted 21 November 1972, simultaneously with first deliveries of production aircraft to KLM and Swissair.

Series 30ER. Developed version of Series 30, with range extended still further by installing a 5,807 litre (1,534 US gallon) auxiliary fuel tank in rear of cargo compartment, giving total capacity of 144,224 litres (38,100 US gallons) and increasing range by up to 200 nm (370 km; 230 miles). More powerful (240·2 kN; 54,000 lb st) CF6-50C2B engines; max T-O weight 263,085 kg (580,000 lb); max range 5,730 nm (10,620 km; 6,600 miles). First order (for two) placed by Swissair in July 1980, plus kits to convert two of its existing DC-10s to Srs 30ER configuration. A larger tank containing 12,556 litres (3,317 US gallons) of fuel is available. First installation was on a Finnair aircraft. Finnair's DC-10 Series 30ERs operate nonstop transpolar flights between Helsinki and Tokyo, a distance of 5,966 nm (11,056 km; 6,870 miles). Thai Airways International announced an order for two DC-10 Series 30ERs on 1 September 1986.

Series 40. Extended range version for intercontinental operations, powered by three Pratt & Whitney turbofan engines. Twenty-two early models, built for Northwest Orient Airlines, had JT9D-20 turbofans, each rated at 220 kN (49,400 lb st) with water injection. First flight of Series 40 (known originally as Series 20) was on 28 February 1972; FAA certification received 20 October 1972. Later versions, built for Japan Air Lines, equipped with JT9D-59A turbofans, each rated at 236 kN (53,000 lb st). First flight of a Series 40 with this latter power plant was on 25 July 1975.

In early 1983, FAA certification was received for a Delco Electronics performance management system (PMS), for installation on the DC-10, which is able to provide fuel savings of 1-3 per cent. The PMS is coupled through the autopilot and autothrottle systems to control automatically the aircraft's pitch and thrust to obtain maximum fuel efficiency during climb, cruise and descent. First PMS-equipped DC-10 to enter service, in March 1983, was a Series 40 aircraft of Japan Air Lines. PMS is being evaluated by the USAF for its KC-10As, and McDonnell Douglas has certificated a similar system for the MD-80 series.

In mid-1986 a DC-10 of Federal Express Corporation was being used to evaluate a new McDonnell Douglas aileron position sensor system using laser pulses and advanced fibre optics to transmit data. Installed for a two-year test programme, it is expected to be a forerunner for sensing systems that could come into use on transport aircraft in the early 1990s.

There are DC-10 convertible and cargo versions designated **Series 30CF** and **30F**, both of which are described separately. On 19 December 1977 the USAF announced selection of the DC-10 Srs 30CF as its Advanced Tanker/Cargo Aircraft (ATCA), and this version also is described separately (see entry for **KC-10A Extender**).

DC-10 subassemblies and components are brought together at Long Beach for final assembly. Certain major subassemblies are produced at other divisions of McDonnell Douglas; Convair Division of General Dynamics Corporation at San Diego, California, is subcontractor for the fuselage, being responsible for five sections totalling 39·01 m (128 ft).

By 1 July 1986, McDonnell Douglas had received firm orders for 379 commercial DC-10s, of which 372 had been delivered.

TYPE: Three-turbofan commercial transport.

WINGS: Cantilever low-wing monoplane of all-metal fail-safe construction. Several different wing sections of Douglas design are used between wing root and tip. Thickness/chord ratio varies from slightly more than 12·2% at root to less than 8·4% at tip. Dihedral 5° 14·4′ inboard, 3° 1·8′ outboard. Incidence ranges from positive at wing root to negative at tip. Sweepback at quarter-chord 35°. All-metal inboard and outboard ailerons, the former used conventionally, the latter only when the leading-edge slats are extended. Double-slotted all-metal trailing-edge flaps mounted on external hinges, with an inboard and outboard flap panel on each wing. Five all-metal spoiler panels on each wing, at the rear edge of the fixed wing structure, forward of the flaps. All spoilers operate in unison as lateral control, speed brake and ground spoilers. Full span three-position all-metal leading-edge slats. Ailerons are powered by Bertea hydraulic actuators, spoilers by Parker-Hannifin hydraulic actuators. Each aileron is powered by either of two hydraulic systems; each spoiler is powered by a single system. All leading-edge slat segments outboard of the engines are anti-iced with engine bleed air.

FUSELAGE: Aluminium alloy semi-monocoque fail-safe structure of circular cross-section. Except for auxiliary areas the entire fuselage is pressurised.

TAIL UNIT: Cantilever all-metal structure standard. Variable incidence tailplane, actuated by Vickers hydraulic motors. Longitudinal and directional controls are fully powered and comprise inboard and outboard elevators, each segment powered by a Bertea tandem actuator; upper and lower rudder each powered by a Bertea actuator. Rudder standby power supplied by two Abex transfer motor pumps. Lighter-weight fin, constructed of graphite composite materials, tested in 1981-82 under NASA contract. Twelve DC-10s in current service have upper rudder segments made of graphite epoxy.

LANDING GEAR (Srs 10): Hydraulically retractable tricycle type, with gravity free-fall for emergency extension. Nosewheel unit retracts forward, Menasco main units inward into fuselage. Twin-wheel steerable nose unit. Main gear comprises two four-wheel bogies. Oleo-pneumatic shock absorbers in all units. Goodyear nosewheels and tyres size 37 × 14-14, pressure 11·03 bars (160 lb/sq in). Goodyear mainwheels and tyres size 52 × 20·5-23, pressure 11·72 bars (170 lb/sq in). Goodyear disc brakes and anti-skid system, with individual wheel control.

LANDING GEAR (Srs 30 and 40): These versions have an additional dual-wheel main unit mounted on the fuselage centreline between the four-wheel bogie units, and this retracts forward. Goodyear nosewheels and tyres size 40 × 15·5-16, pressure 12·41 bars (180 lb/sq in). Four-wheel bogie main units and centreline unit have Goodyear wheels and tyres size 52 × 20·5-23. The former have a pressure of 11·38 bars (165 lb/sq in), the latter 9·65 bars (140 lb/sq in). Otherwise as Srs 10.

POWER PLANT: Three turbofan engines (details under Series descriptions), two of which are mounted on underwing pylons, the third above the rear fuselage at the base of the fin. All engines are fitted with thrust reversers for ground operation. Engine air inlets have load carrying acoustically treated panels for noise attenuation, and each engine fan case and fan exhaust is similarly treated. Three integral wing fuel tanks in Series 10 and 15, with a total capacity of approximately 82,142 litres (21,700 US gallons). Four standard pressure refuelling adapters, two in each wing outboard of the engine pylons. Series 30 and 40 aircraft have four integral wing fuel tanks and an auxiliary tank in the wing centre-section with a connected structural compartment fitted with a bladder cell, giving increased total capacity of approximately 138,165 litres (36,500 US gallons). Additional fuel (approx 18,473 litres; 4,880 US gallons) can be added in existing tanks in Series 10 and 15. Lower cargo hold in Series 30 and 40 can be used to carry an optional long-range tank of either 5,807 litres (1,534 US gallons) or 12,556 litres (3,317 US gallons). Oil capacity, Series 10 and 30: 34·1 litres (9 usable US gallons); Series 40: 56·8 litres (15 usable US gallons).

ACCOMMODATION: Crew of three (pilot, first officer, flight engineer), with seating for two observers, plus cabin attendants. Standard seating for 255 or 270 in mixed class versions, with a maximum of 380 passengers in an economy class arrangement. Two aisles run the length of the cabin, which is separated into sections by cloakroom dividers. In the first class section, with three pairs of reclining seats abreast, the aisles are 0·78 m (2 ft 7 in) wide. In the coach class section, four pairs of seats, with a table between the centre pairs, also have two aisles, these being 0·51 m (1 ft 8 in) wide. One pair of seats is exchanged for a three-seat unit in the nine-abreast high-density layout. Up to nine lavatories located throughout the passenger cabin. Cloakrooms of standard and elevating type distributed throughout the cabin. Cabin windows, 0·28 × 0·41 m (11 in × 16 in), are spaced at 0·51 m (20 in) centres. Overhead stowage modules, fully enclosed and providing stowage for passengers' personal effects, are located on the sidewalls and extend the full length of the cabin. Optional centreline overhead baggage racks available. Eight passenger doors, four on each side, open by sliding inward and upward into the above-ceiling area. Containerised or bulk cargo compartments located immediately forward and aft of the wing, with outward opening doors on the starboard side. A bulk cargo compartment is located in the lower rear section of the fuselage, with its door on the port side. Entire accommodation is fully air-conditioned, with five separate control zones for the standard below-floor galley configuration. Series 30 and 40 aircraft have an optional main cabin galley to replace the lower galley, and in this configuration there are four separate control zones for the air-conditioning. The lower deck galley is provided with five to eight high-temperature ovens, and with refrigerators, storage space for linen, china and other accessories. Serving carts are taken to cabin level by two electric elevators, to a buffet service centre, from where stewardesses serve passengers. To permit quick turn-round at terminals, without interference to passenger movement in the main cabin, the kitchen is provisioned through the cargo doors at ground level.

SYSTEMS: Three parallel continuously operating and completely separate hydraulic systems supply the fully powered flight controls and wheel brakes. Normally, one of the systems supplies power for landing gear actuation. Two reversible motor pumps, each sized to deliver power from one of the other two systems for standby operation of landing gear, can also power any other hydraulically operated unit. Each hydraulic system is powered by two identical engine driven pumps, capable of delivering a total of 265 litres (70 US gallons)/min at 207 bars (3,000 lb/sq in) at take-off. All three hydraulic systems are applied to each primary control axis in a manner which ensures maximum control effectiveness in the event of single or dual hydraulic system failures. A Garrett TSCP-700-4 APU provides ground electrical and pneumatic power, including main engine starting, and auxiliary electrical power in flight.

AVIONICS AND EQUIPMENT: A dual fail-operative landing system is installed to meet Category IIIA weather minima. Digital air data computer meeting ARINC 576 requirements on Srs 10. Triple inertial navigation system meeting ARINC 561 requirements on Srs 30 and 40, with optional dual area navigation system capability.

DIMENSIONS, EXTERNAL:
Wing span: Series 10, 15 — 47·35 m (155 ft 4 in)
Series 30, 40 — 50·40 m (165 ft 4½ in)
Wing chord: at root — 10·71 m (35 ft 1¾ in)
at tip: Series 10 — 3·21 m (10 ft 6½ in)
Series 30, 40 — 2·73 m (8 ft 11½ in)
Wing aspect ratio: Series 10 — 6·8
Series 30, 40 — 7·5
Length overall: Series 10 — 55·30 m (181 ft 5 in)
Series 15, 30, 40 — 55·50 m (182 ft 1 in)
Length of fuselage — 51·97 m (170 ft 6 in)
Height overall — 17·70 m (58 ft 1 in)
Tailplane span — 21·69 m (71 ft 2 in)
Wheel track — 10·67 m (35 ft 0 in)
Wheelbase: Series 10, 40 — 22·07 m (72 ft 5 in)
Series 30 — 22·05 m (72 ft 4 in)

DIMENSIONS, INTERNAL:
Cabin: Length, from rear bulkhead of flight deck to rear cabin bulkhead — approx 41·45 m (136 ft 0 in)
Max width — 5·72 m (18 ft 9 in)
Height (basic) — 2·41 m (7 ft 11 in)
Series 10, 30, 40 in lower-galley configuration:
Forward baggage and/or freight hold (forward of wing):
Containerised volume — 27·2 m³ (960 cu ft)
Bulk volume — 37·9 m³ (1,339 cu ft)
Centre baggage and/or freight hold (aft of wing):
Containerised volume — 36·2 m³ (1,280 cu ft)
Bulk volume — 43·9 m³ (1,552 cu ft)
Rear hold:
Bulk volume — 22·8 m³ (805 cu ft)
Series 30, 40 in upper-galley configuration:
Forward baggage and/or freight hold (forward of wing):
Containerised volume — 72·5 m³ (2,560 cu ft)
Bulk volume — 86·2 m³ (3,045 cu ft)
Centre baggage and/or freight hold (aft of wing):
Containerised volume — 45·3 m³ (1,600 cu ft)
Bulk volume — 54·8 m³ (1,935 cu ft)
Rear hold:
Bulk volume — 14·4 m³ (510 cu ft)

AREAS:
Wings, gross: Series 10 — 358·7 m² (3,861 sq ft)
Series 30, 40 — 367·7 m² (3,958 sq ft)
Ailerons: inboard (total) — 7·68 m² (82·7 sq ft)
outboard (total) — 9·76 m² (105·1 sq ft)
Trailing-edge flaps (total) — 62·1 m² (668·2 sq ft)
Leading-edge slats (total):
Series 10 — 42·05 m² (452·6 sq ft)
Series 30, 40 — 43·84 m² (471·9 sq ft)
Spoilers (total) — 12·73 m² (137·0 sq ft)
Fin — 45·92 m² (494·29 sq ft)
Rudders (total) — 10·29 m² (110·71 sq ft)
Tailplane — 96·6 m² (1,040·2 sq ft)
Elevators (total) — 27·7 m² (298·1 sq ft)

WEIGHTS AND LOADINGS:
Basic weight empty:
Series 10 — 111,086 kg (244,903 lb)
Series 15 — 111,832 kg (246,547 lb)
Series 30 — 121,198 kg (267,197 lb)
Series 40 — 122,951 kg (271,062 lb)
Max payload: Series 10 — 44,678 kg (98,500 lb)
Series 30 — 48,330 kg (106,550 lb)
Series 40 — 46,243 kg (101,950 lb)
Max fuel weight:
Series 10, 15: standard — 66,138 kg (145,810 lb)
optional — 80,971 kg (178,510 lb)
Series 30, 40: standard — 111,387 kg (245,566 lb)
auxiliary tank installed — 116,049 kg (255,844 lb)
large auxiliary tank installed — 121,467 kg (267,790 lb)
Max T-O weight:
Series 10, 15 — 206,385 kg (455,000 lb)
Series 30 — 259,450-263,085 kg (572,000-580,000 lb)
Series 40 (-20 engines) — 251,745 kg (555,000 lb)
Series 40 (-59A engines) — 259,450 kg (572,000 lb)
Max ramp weight:
Series 10 — 207,745 kg (458,000 lb)
Series 30 — 260,815 kg (575,000 lb)
Series 40 (-20 engines) — 253,105 kg (558,000 lb)
Series 40 (-59A engines) — 260,815 kg (575,000 lb)
Max zero-fuel weight:
Series 10 — 151,953 kg (335,000 lb)
Series 30, 40 — 166,922 kg (368,000 lb)
Max landing weight:
Series 10, 15 — 164,880 kg (363,500 lb)
Series 30, 40 — 182,798 kg (403,000 lb)
Max wing loading:
Series 10, 15 — 575·4 kg/m² (117·8 lb/sq ft)
Series 30 — 705·6 kg/m² (144·5 lb/sq ft)
Series 40 (-20 engines) — 684·6 kg/m² (140·2 lb/sq ft)
Series 40 (-59A engines) — 705·6 kg/m² (144·5 lb/sq ft)

PERFORMANCE (at max T-O weight except where indicated):
Never-exceed speed — Mach 0·95
Max level speed at 7,620 m (25,000 ft) — Mach 0·88 (530 knots; 982 km/h; 610 mph)
Max cruising speed at 9,145 m (30,000 ft):
Series 10 (-6D engines) — 499 knots (925 km/h; 575 mph)
Series 10 (-6D1 engines) — 501 knots (928 km/h; 577 mph)
Series 30 — 490 knots (908 km/h; 564 mph)
Series 40 (-20 engines) — 489 knots (906 km/h; 563 mph)
Series 40 (-59A engines) — 498 knots (922 km/h; 573 mph)
Normal cruising speed, all versions — Mach 0·82
T-O speed (V_2):
Series 10 (-6D engines) — 181 knots (335 km/h; 208 mph)
Series 10 (-6D1 engines) — 175 knots (325 km/h; 202 mph)
Series 30 (-50C engines) — 189 knots (351 km/h; 218 mph)
Series 40 (-20 engines) — 187 knots (346 km/h; 215 mph)
Series 40 (-59A engines) — 178 knots (330 km/h; 205 mph)
Landing speed (with full load of passengers and baggage):
Series 10 — 128 knots (238 km/h; 148 mph)
Series 15 — 129 knots (240 km/h; 149 mph)
Series 30, 40 — 138 knots (256 km/h; 159 mph)
Max rate of climb at S/L:
Series 10 (-6D engines) — 817 m (2,680 ft)/min
Series 10 (-6D1 engines) — 838 m (2,750 ft)/min
Series 30 — 884 m (2,900 ft)/min
Series 40 (-20 engines) — 829 m (2,720 ft)/min
Series 40 (-59A engines) — 762 m (2,500 ft)/min
Service ceiling:
Series 10 (-6D engines) at 192,775 kg (425,000 lb) AUW — 10,605 m (34,800 ft)
Series 10 (-6D1 engines) at 192,775 kg (425,000 lb) AUW — 10,730 m (35,200 ft)
Series 30 at 249,475 kg (550,000 lb) AUW — 10,180 m (33,400 ft)
Series 40 (-20 engines) at 242,670 kg (535,000 lb) AUW — 9,660 m (31,700 ft)
Series 40 (-59A engines) — 9,965 m (32,700 ft)
En-route climb altitude, one engine out:
Series 10 at 195,045 kg (430,000 lb) AUW — 4,145 m (13,600 ft)
Series 30 at 251,744 kg (555,000 lb) AUW — 4,360 m (14,300 ft)
Series 40 (-20 engines) at 247,205 kg (545,000 lb) AUW — 3,565 m (11,700 ft)
Series 40 (-59A engines) at 254,010 kg (560,000 lb) AUW — 5,135 m (16,850 ft)
FAA T-O field length:
Series 10 (-6D1 engines) — 3,200 m (10,500 ft)
Series 15 (-50C2F engines) — 2,285 m (7,500 ft)
Series 30 (-50C2 engines) — 3,170 m (10,400 ft)
Series 40 (-59A engines) — 3,135 m (10,280 ft)
FAA landing field length:
Series 10 — 1,585 m (5,200 ft)
Series 15 — 1,600 m (5,250 ft)
Series 30, 40 — 1,630 m (5,350 ft)
Range with max fuel, no payload:
Series 10 — 5,514 nm (10,220 km; 6,350 miles)
Series 15 — 5,466 nm (10,130 km; 6,295 miles)
Series 30 — 6,504 nm (12,055 km; 7,490 miles)
Series 40 — 6,305 nm (11,685 km; 7,260 miles)
Range with max payload at max zero-fuel weight:
Series 10 — 2,350 nm (4,355 km; 2,706 miles)
Series 30 — 4,000 nm (7,413 km; 4,606 miles)
Series 40 (-20 engines) — 3,500 nm (6,485 km; 4,030 miles)
Series 40 (-59A engines) — 4,050 nm (7,505 km; 4,663 miles)

MCDONNELL DOUGLAS DC-10 SERIES 30CF

The Series 30CF is a convertible freighter version of the McDonnell Douglas DC-10 transport. Generally similar to the basic DC-10 Series 30 and 40, it is designed for easy conversion to either passenger or cargo configuration. Its payload can consist of 380 passengers and baggage or 64,860 kg (143,000 lb) of cargo over full intercontinental range; or up to 70,626 kg (155,700 lb) of cargo on domestic transcontinental routes.

The first Series 30CF was powered by three General Electric CF6-50A turbofans. It flew for the first time on 28 February 1973 and initial deliveries were made to Trans International Airlines and Overseas National Airways on 19 April 1973 and 21 April 1973 respectively. In May and June 1977, Overseas National Airways took delivery of two of the later DC-10 Srs 30CFs, powered by General Electric CF6-50C1 engines rated at 233·5 kN (52,500 lb st).

In the passenger configuration, interior layout is generally similar to that of the DC-10, but the Series 30CF was designed to permit overnight conversion to an all-cargo configuration. This entails removal of seats, overhead baggage racks, forward food service centre, cloakrooms

McDonnell Douglas DC-10 Series 30 in the insignia of Brazilian carrier Varig *(Martin Fricke)*

and carpeting from the main cabin, and installation of freight loading tracks and rollers, a cargo tiedown system and restraint nets. Coffee service fixtures and lavatories in the rear cabin may also be removed but are retained normally for regular cargo flights.

The cargo loading system for the Series 30CF is based on that in use in the DC-8 Super Sixty Series freighters. A two-channel network of roller conveyors, adjustable guide rails and pallet restraint fittings is installed in the seat tracks in the cabin floor by use of simple stud and locking pin devices. A 2·59 m high × 3·56 m wide (8 ft 6 in × 11 ft 8 in) cargo door in the side of the fuselage swings upward and allows easy loading of bulky freight.

A total of 30 standard 2·24 m × 2·74 m (7 ft 4 in × 9 ft) cargo pallets, or 22 larger pallets measuring 2·24 m × 3·18 m (7 ft 4 in × 10 ft 5 in) or 2·44 m × 3·05 m (8 ft × 10 ft), can be accommodated in the main cabin. The Series 30CF with upstairs galleys also has 132·2 m³ (4,670 cu ft) of cargo space in the two lower cargo compartments for bulk freight, or for 26 half-size containers, or for five full-size pallets and 16 half-size containers.

A DC-10 Series 30CF delivered to Sabena Belgian World Airlines in 1973 is certificated for carrying combination loads of freight and passengers in the main cabin. Thirty-five CF models had been delivered by 1 April 1985.

While weight and performance figures are generally similar to those of the DC-10 Series 30, the differing figures which follow should be noted for the Series 30CF:

WEIGHTS:

Weight empty	108,385 kg (238,948 lb)
Max T-O weight	267,620 kg (590,000 lb)
Max landing weight	190,962 kg (421,000 lb)

PERFORMANCE:

Landing speed at max landing weight
149 knots (275 km/h; 171 mph)

FAA T-O field length at max T-O weight
3,170 m (10,400 ft)

FAA landing field length at max landing weight
1,868 m (6,130 ft)

Max range with max cargo
3,581 nm (6,637 km; 4,124 miles)

MCDONNELL DOUGLAS DC-10 SERIES 30F

The Series 30F is an all-freighter version of the DC-10. Generally similar to the Series 30CF, it does not incorporate those features which permit conversion to passenger configuration. Its payload capability is 80,282 kg (176,992 lb) of cargo over intercontinental range. The Series 30F is powered by CF6-50C2 engines. Nine DC-10 Series 30Fs are on order for Federal Express. The first was delivered on 24 January 1986. Deliveries will continue into 1988.

The main deck cargo compartment can accommodate 23 standard 2·24 m × 3·18 m (7 ft 4 in × 10 ft 5 in) cargo pallets, or 51 1·57 m × 2·24 m (5 ft 2 in × 7 ft 4 in) demi containers, or 30 pallets measuring 2·24 m × 2·74 m (7 ft 4 in × 9 ft). Below deck forward and centre cargo compartments can accommodate a further 117·8 m³ (4,160 cu ft) of bulk freight using 13 full-width containers, or 116·3 m³ (4,108 cu ft) using 26 half-width containers. The rear below-deck compartment provides a further 14·4 m³ (510 cu ft) of cargo volume.

While the weight and performance figures are generally similar to those of the DC-10 Series 30CF, the differing figures which follow should be noted for the Series 30F:

WEIGHTS:

Weight empty	106,505 kg (234,800 lb)
Max T-O weight	263,085 kg (580,000 lb)
Max landing weight	197,765 kg (436,000 lb)

PERFORMANCE:

Landing speed at max landing weight
152 knots (282 km/h; 175 mph)

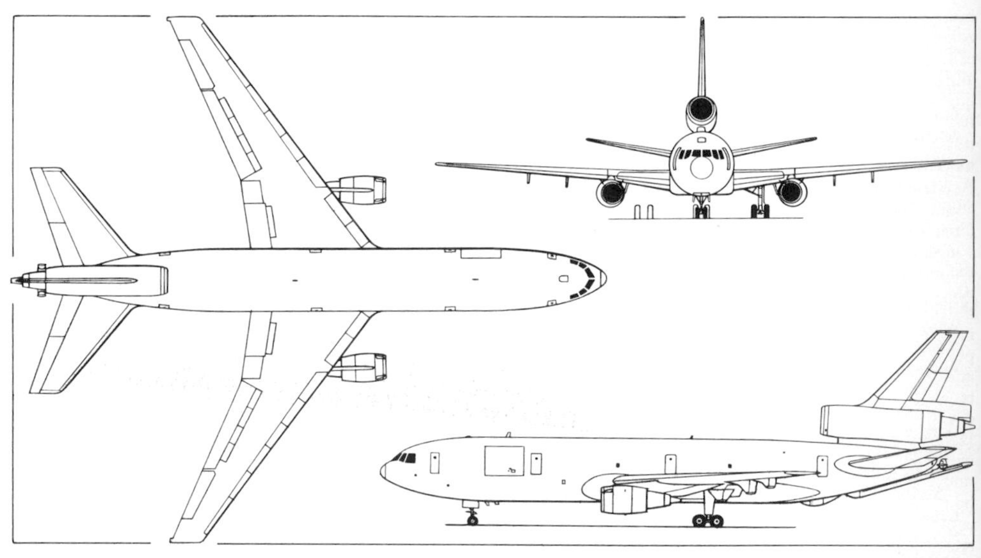

McDonnell Douglas KC-10A Extender advanced tanker/cargo aircraft for the US Air Force *(Pilot Press)*

FAA T-O field length at max T-O weight
3,292 m (10,800 ft)

FAA landing field length at max landing weight
1,926 m (6,320 ft)

Max range with max cargo
3,281 nm (6,080 km; 3,778 miles)

MCDONNELL DOUGLAS EXTENDER

US Air Force designation: KC-10A

The US Air Force announced on 19 December 1977 that, following evaluation of the Boeing 747 and McDonnell Douglas DC-10 to meet its requirement for an advanced tanker/cargo aircraft (ATCA), the DC-10 ATCA was selected to fulfil this role. Subsequently, the aircraft was designated KC-10A and named Extender.

The force of KC-10As greatly enhances the ability of the Air Force to deploy combat aircraft, men and supplies on a global scale. This point was emphasised in a USAF submission to Congress in which the spokesman commented that 40 Boeing KC-135 tankers and a number of cargo aircraft would be needed to fuel an F-4 fighter wing and carry its personnel and equipment from the USA to the Middle East. Just 17 of the proposed KC-10As could fulfil the same task, more economically and efficiently. USAF Military Airlift Command's (MAC) need for support by such aircraft was highlighted during the 1973 Arab-Israeli war, when many countries denied landing rights to MAC aircraft. From these circumstances came the decision to develop an ATCA to support the strategic airlift fleet, under the operational control of the USAF Strategic Air Command.

The initial $28 million contract awarded to McDonnell Douglas covered the funding for initial production planning, engineering and tooling. A second $429,000 contract was for initial planning of a logistics support programme covering the entire KC-10A military tanker fleet.

On 20 November 1978, the Air Force authorised McDonnell Douglas to begin production of the KC-10A. This FY 1979 contract called for an expenditure of $148 million by the Air Force, for the acquisition of two KC-10As, and in payment of the balance of the non-recurring engineering costs. In addition, under a separate $15·6 million contract, McDonnell Douglas was authorised to purchase the initial spare parts and support equipment for the KC-10A system. Four additional KC-10As were ordered by the Air Force in November 1979, under the FY 1980 budget, six were ordered in February 1981 under the FY 1981 budget, and four were ordered in January 1982 under the FY 1982 budget.

In December 1982, the Air Force entered into a multi-year contract with McDonnell Douglas for the purchase of 44 more KC-10s during the fiscal years 1983 to 1987 (4 in 1983, 8 in 1984, 11 in 1985, 12 in 1985 and 9 in 1987). This contract allows suppliers, as well as the Douglas Aircraft Company, to produce equipment and parts in economical quantities. However, the US Congress must still authorise funds each year.

The first KC-10A (serial number 79-0433) made its first flight on 12 July 1980. The first to enter service (serial number 79-0434) was delivered on 17 March 1981 to Barksdale AFB, Louisiana, for operation by SAC, and the second on 30 July 1981. On 23 June 1986 McDonnell Douglas delivered the 45th KC-10A to the USAF. The aircraft are assigned to the US Air Force's 9th Air Refueling Squadron at March AFB, California, 32nd ARS at Barksdale AFB, Louisiana, and 911th ARS at Seymour Johnson AFB, North Carolina. The Air Force Reserve's 77th ARS (Associate) at Seymour Johnson, the 78th ARS (Associate) at Barksdale and the 79th ARS (Associate) at March share the aircraft with the active duty squadrons at their respective bases. By Summer 1986 USAF KC-10As had completed more than 78,000 flight hours, with a 99·6 per cent mission completion success rate.

The modifications necessary to convert the DC-10-30CF to KC-10A configuration include the installation of fuel cells in the lower fuselage compartment; provision of a boom operator station, an aerial refuelling boom, a refuelling receptacle, an improved cargo handling system, and some military avionics systems. Various seating layouts are available in the forward area to permit the transport of a fighter squadron's essential support personnel. Seven bladder fuel cells are installed in the lower fuselage compartments, three forward and four aft of the wing, mounted within framework that restrains and supports the cells. These contain a total of 53,446 kg (117,829 lb) of fuel, equivalent to approx 68,610 litres (18,125 US gallons), and

KC-10A Extender three-turbofan military tanker/transport aircraft, in 'European One' camouflage scheme

are interconnected with the aircraft's basic fuel system, comprising 108,062 kg (238,236 lb). All can be used for extended range, or fuel from the lower deck cells and the aircraft's basic fuel system can be used for in-flight refuelling. The KC-10A is able to deliver 90,718 kg (200,000 lb) of fuel to a receiver 1,910 nm (3,540 km; 2,200 miles) from its home base, and return to base. In February 1985 a KC-10A made a nonstop, unrefuelled flight from Riyadh, Saudi Arabia, to March AFB, covering the 7,800 nm (14,455 km; 8,982 miles) in 17·8 hours and consuming 139,253 kg (307,000 lb) of fuel.

The aerial refuelling operator's station, with access from the upper main deck, is sited in the lower rear fuselage and can accommodate the boom operator, an instructor and an observer, although only the boom operator is needed for a refuelling mission. The station has a rear window and a periscope observation system to give a wide field of view, and is pressurised and air-conditioned. The advanced aerial refuelling boom, which is the production version of a boom developed and tested in prototype form by McDonnell Douglas, provides greater capability than the type installed in the KC-135; in particular, it has a greater transfer flow rate, being rated at 5,678 litres (1,500 US gallons)/min. The boom operator 'flies' it by means of a digital fly by wire control system supplied by Sperry Flight Systems. A hose/reel unit for probe and drogue refuelling is also installed, so that the KC-10A can service US Navy, US Marine Corps and NATO aircraft, as well as older types of fighter still serving with Reserve and ANG units.

The provision of a refuelling receptacle, above the flight deck of the KC-10A, allows greater flexibility on long-range cargo or refuelling operations, extending the range beyond the nominal 6,000 nm (11,112 km; 6,905 miles) with a 45,400 kg (100,000 lb) payload. The improved cargo handling system, by comparison with the basic DC-10-30CF, includes an increased floor area covered by omni-directional rollers, power rollers, and a portable winch to move cargo fore and aft.

Changes to the avionics are concerned chiefly with the deletion of equipment intended specifically for commercial operations, and the addition of UHF and secure com systems, Tacan, IFF, beacon transponder and a radar beacon mode. In addition to its tanker/transport role, the KC-10A can also act as a pathfinder for the aircraft it is refuelling, by providing supplementary navigation and communications services during long-range deployments.

The description of the DC-10 Series 30CF applies to the KC-10A, except as follows:

TYPE: Military flight refuelling/cargo aircraft.

WINGS, FUSELAGE, TAIL UNIT: As for DC-10-30CF, except for omission of most upper deck cabin windows and lower deck cargo doors.

LANDING GEAR: As for DC-10-30CF, except Goodyear nosewheels and tyres size 40 × 15·5-16, pressure 13·10 bars (190 lb/sq in). Four-wheel bogie main units and centreline unit have Goodyear wheels and tyres size 52 × 20·5-23. The former have a pressure of 13·79 bars (200 lb/sq in), the latter 10·69 bars (155 lb/sq in). Goodyear disc brakes and anti-skid system, with individual wheel control.

POWER PLANT: Three 233·53 kN (52,500 lb st) General Electric CF6-50C2 turbofan engines. Basic aircraft fuel system comprises three integral main wing fuel tanks, and an integral auxiliary tank in the wing centre-section with a connected structural compartment fitted with a bladder cell, giving a total capacity of approximately 132,331 litres (34,958 US gallons). Oil capacity 34·1 litres (9 US gallons).

ACCOMMODATION: Three crew on flight deck. Various seating arrangements for a limited number of essential support personnel at forward end of main cabin. Aerial refuelling station, with accommodation and large observation windows for boom operator, instructor and a student observer at aft end of lower fuselage compartment. Five passenger doors on main deck. A 2·59 m × 3·56 m (8 ft 6 in × 11 ft 8 in) cargo door on the port side of the fuselage permits loading of standard USAF 463L pallets, bulk cargo or wheeled vehicles. Maximum capacity for 25 pallets with access from both sides of the compartment, or 27 pallets with a single aisle on the starboard side.

SYSTEMS: As for DC-10-30CF.

AVIONICS AND EQUIPMENT: Include some additional military avionics, comprising navigation, comunication, Tacan, IFF transponder, and modified commercial weather radar. Seven Goodyear Aerospace rubberised fabric fuel cells mounted in the lower fuselage compartments, with combined capacity of 53,446 kg (117,829 lb) fuel, equivalent to approx 68,610 litres (18,125 US gallons), which are interconnected into the aircraft's basic fuel system. Flight refuelling boom mounted under rear fuselage, plus hose/reel unit for probe and drogue refuelling (24·4 m; 80 ft long hose and 66 cm; 26 in diameter drogue). Director lights to guide receiver. Flight refuelling receptacle mounted on fuselage upper surface above flight deck.

DIMENSIONS, EXTERNAL: As for DC-10-30CF except:

Length overall	55·35 m (181 ft 7 in)
Height overall	17·70 m (58 ft 1 in)
Wheel track	10·57 m (34 ft 8 in)

AREAS: As for DC-10-30CF

Artist's impression of proposed McDonnell Douglas MD-11

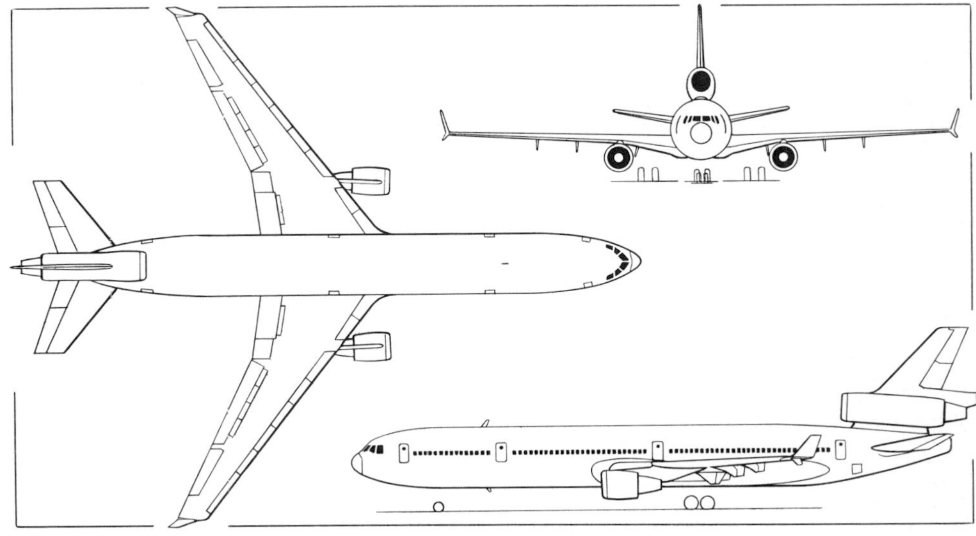

McDonnell Douglas MD-11, designed as an advanced higher-capacity successor to the DC-10 *(Pilot Press)*

WEIGHTS AND LOADING:

Operating weight empty:	
tanker	109,328 kg (241,027 lb)
cargo	110,945 kg (244,591 lb)
Fuel at T-O: tanker	158,291 kg (348,973 lb)
Design fuel capacity	161,508 kg (356,065 lb)
Max cargo payload	76,843 kg (169,409 lb)
Design max T-O weight	267,620 kg (590,000 lb)
Max wing loading	727·8 kg/m² (149·06 lb/sq ft)

PERFORMANCE:

Critical field length	3,124 m (10,250 ft)
Max range with max cargo	3,797 nm (7,032 km; 4,370 miles)
Max ferry range, unrefuelled	9,993 nm (18,507 km; 11,500 miles)

MCDONNELL DOUGLAS MD-11

First details of the MD-11, a proposed advanced, medium/long range successor to the DC-10, were revealed at the 1985 Paris Air Show. The aircraft, which is derived from the DC-10, will feature a fuselage some 5·67 m (18 ft 7 in) longer than the DC-10 Series 30, aerodynamic improvements including upper and lower, outward inclined winglets, and an advanced horizontal tail design with cambered aerofoil, reduced sweepback and integral 'trim tank' with a fuel capacity of 7,571 litres (2,000 US gallons), an advanced two-man all-digital flight deck, and restyled passenger interior. Power plant will be either three General Electric CF6-80C2 or three Pratt & Whitney 4000 turbofans, providing a 10 per cent improvement in range over the DC-10 Series 30, with increased passenger capacity and a 13 to 18 per cent reduction in seat/mile costs.

Three versions of the aircraft are proposed. The basic **MD-11** will accommodate up to 405 single class passengers, 321 passengers in first class and economy configuration, and 276 in typical three-class arrangement, with a maximum range of 6,800 nm (12,600 km; 7,830 miles). In a 'combi' configuration the MD-11 would provide three-class accommodation for 176 passengers and cargo space for six pallets. As an all-freight transport the aircraft would provide capacity for 81,646 kg (180,000 lb) of payload.

McDonnell Douglas is also considering an extended-range **MD-11ER** which would combine the new engines, cockpit and aerodynamics of the MD-11 with a DC-10 sized fuselage accommodating 276 first and economy class passengers, with a maximum range of 7,500 nm (13,905 km; 8,640 miles) and provision for further range increases with auxiliary fuel tanks in the rear fuselage. An **MD-11 Advanced**, with a 12·37 m (40 ft 7 in) fuselage 'stretch', accommodation for 380 first and economy class passengers, and a maximum range of 7,380 nm (13,680 km; 8,500 miles), is being studied for possible introduction in the mid-1990s. A launch decision for the MD-11 was expected in 1986, with a first flight in the last quarter of 1988 and certification in late 1989.

McDONNELL DOUGLAS C-17A

The US Air Force announced on 29 August 1981 that McDonnell Douglas had been selected as prime contractor to develop a new C-17A long-range cargo aircraft, following evaluation of three designs entered for its C-X competition.

The C-X programme is for a long-range, heavy lift air-refuellable cargo transport, intended primarily to provide inter-theatre airlift of outsize loads, including tanks and infantry fighting vehicles, directly into airfields in potential conflict areas. Design requirements therefore include outstanding STOL performance.

The C-X is, however, only one ingredient of an Air Force airlift improvement plan that also includes enhancement of current aircraft capabilities, and expanded cargo-carrying capability for the Civil Reserve Air Fleet. Selection of the McDonnell Douglas C-17A did not, therefore, represent at that stage an Air Force commitment to build, since USAF was still evaluating alternative ways of overcoming the present shortfall in airlift capability. These alternatives included purchase of an additional batch of Lockheed C-5 Galaxies (which see) and/or off-the-shelf commercial transport aircraft.

In January 1982 the Air Force stated that it did not plan full scale development and production of the C-17A at that time. However, on 26 July 1982 McDonnell Douglas announced the award of a $31·6 million Air Force contract for a 'modestly paced' research and development programme, to include such C-17A technologies as would also benefit other airlift programmes, and preserving the option to proceed to full scale engineering development of the C-17A if eventually deemed appropriate. The technologies to be investigated include flaps on a swept supercritical wing, winglets tailored to supercritical wing design, and an engine fan and redirected flow thrust reverser.

On 31 December 1985 the US Air Force awarded the company a $3,387 million fixed price full scale development contract for the C-17A, which will include construction of one flying prototype and two structural test aircraft. Construction of the first C-17A is to begin in 1987, with a first flight scheduled for 1990 and the FSD phase continuing until July 1992. The USAF plans to acquire 210 aircraft by 1999, at a unit cost of $178 million. Major subassemblies will be produced at a new plant now under construction at Salt Lake City, Utah.

The McDonnell Douglas C-17A, making use of technology developed for its earlier YC-15 advanced medium STOL transport prototypes (see 1979-80 *Jane's*), will be able to airlift outsize combat equipment which at present can be carried only by the Lockheed C-5A Galaxy, and offer a short field performance currently provided only by the C-130 Hercules. It will be able to operate from runways only 915 m (3000 ft) long and 18·3 m (60 ft) wide; on the ground, it will be able to execute a 180° turn in only 25 m (82 ft); and a fully loaded aircraft, using thrust reversal, will be able to reverse up a one in 50 gradient.

TYPE: Long-range heavy lift cargo transport.

AIRFRAME: General survivability features include ample provisions for crew and troop shielding; redundant load paths, to minimise the effects of battle damage; facility for critical line-replaceable units (LRUs) to be replaced in flight, and for all LRUs to be replaced without removing other equipment.

WINGS: Cantilever high-wing monoplane, of supercritical section with 25° sweepback. NASA type winglet at each tip, also of supercritical section. Full span leading-edge slats. Externally blown flap system, developed from that used on McDonnell Douglas YC-15, to reduce final approach and landing speeds by directing engine efflux over single-hinged, double-slotted Fowler trailing-edge flaps to provide extra lift. Flaps extend over approx two-thirds of each trailing-edge.

FUSELAGE: Conventional semi-monocoque structure, upswept at rear. Rear-loading ramp/door in underside of rear fuselage. Twin strakes under extreme rear of fuselage.

TAIL UNIT: Cantilever T tail. Sweptback fin, with small dorsal fin; inset rudder, in upper and lower segments. Sweptback tailplane, with elevators.

LANDING GEAR: Hydraulically retractable tricycle type, with free-fall emergency extension. Twin-wheel nose unit and six-wheel main units, designed for sink rate of 5·03 m (16·5 ft)/s and suitable for operation from paved runways or unpaved strips. Cleveland mainwheel units, each consisting of two legs in tandem with three wheels on each leg, retract into fairings on lower fuselage sides; nose unit is forward retracting.

POWER PLANT: Four 164·6 kN (37,000 lb st) Pratt & Whitney PW2037 turbofan engines, pylon-mounted in individual underwing pods and each fitted with a directed-flow thrust reverser deployable both in flight and on the ground. Provision for in-flight refuelling.

ACCOMMODATION: Normal flight crew of pilot and co-pilot, side by side on flight deck, plus a loadmaster. Provision for additional crew members if required for special missions. Access to flight deck via downward opening airstair door on port side of lower forward fuselage. Bunks for crew immediately aft of flight deck area: crew comfort station at forward end of cargo hold. Main cargo hold able to accommodate Army wheeled vehicles, including five-ton expandable vans in two side by side rows, or Jeeps in triple rows, or up to three AH-64A Apache attack helicopters, with straight-in loading via hydraulically actuated rear loading ramp which forms underside of rear fuselage when retracted. Alternatively, aircraft can be equipped as a troop transport, with rows of stowable tip-up seats along the centreline and each side wall, or with litters for medical evacuation mission. Airdrop capability includes single platforms of up to 24,945 kg (55,000 lb), or up to 102 paratroops. The C-17A will be the only aircraft able to airdrop outsize firepower such as the US Army's new infantry fighting vehicle (three of which comprise one deployment load); it will also be able to carry the M1 main battle tank in combination with other vehicles. The cargo handling system includes rails for airdrops and rails/rollers for normal cargo handling. Each row of rails/rollers can be converted quickly by a single loadmaster from one configuration to the other. Cargo tiedown rings, each with a 11,340 kg (25,000 lb) load restraint capability, are installed throughout the cargo area floor. Twelve quick-erecting litter stanchions, each supporting four litters, permanently installed. Main access to cargo hold is via rear loading ramp, which is itself capable of supporting 18,145 kg (40,000 lb) of cargo. Undersurface of rear fuselage aft of ramp is formed by door which moves upward inside fuselage to facilitate loading and unloading. Paratroop door at rear on each side, and two overwater emergency exits overhead, aft of the paratroop doors, and two overhead forward of the wing box.

SYSTEMS: Include fully redundant flight control and hydraulic systems; independent fuel feed systems; electrical system; APU (in tailcone) operable in flight; explosion protection system; and fire suppression system. All phases of cargo operation and configuration change capable of being handled by one loadmaster.

AVIONICS AND EQUIPMENT: Sperry Corporation electronic flight control system, and dual air data computers, with advanced digital avionics and four full-colour multi-function displays (MFDs), two GEC Avionics full flight regime head-up displays, plus integrated mission and communications keyboards (MCKs) and displays (MCDs). Primary flight data presented on HUD and a selectable mode for the MFD. Horizontal navigation situation computer-generated flight plan and weather radar overlay selectable on MFD. Station keeping (SKE), engine and flight control configuration data available on MFDs. All frequency tuning for nav/com accomplished from glareshield control panel. MCD has frequency and channel pre-storage facility and provides for flight plan entry manually or by pre-programmed cassette, permitting insertion of in-flight planning changes without disturbing ongoing navigation. All MCD information for flight and navigation monitoring is presented on the HUD and MFDs. Teledyne Controls warning and caution system. Master warning caution annunciator provides automatic monitoring of all main systems and provides visual alerts on glareshields, aural and voice alerts on intercom. Cargo hold equipment includes integral rails and roller conveyors, in floor (incl ramp); sidewall rails; tiedown rings of 11,340 kg (25,000 lb) rating, spaced at 61 cm (24 in) intervals; cargo winch and retrieval winch; and Oxford type tow/release for cargo platforms. Other equipment suppliers include Delco Electronics (mission computer and electronic control system), Hamilton Standard (aircraft and propulsion data management computer), Honeywell (automatic test equipment, and support equipment data acquisition and control system), LTV (Sierra Research Division) (station keeping equipment), and Telephonic Corporation (radio management system).

DIMENSIONS, EXTERNAL:
- Wing span: 50·29 m (165 ft 0 in)
- Length overall: 53·39 m (175 ft 2 in)
- Height overall: 16·79 m (55 ft 1 in)

DIMENSIONS, INTERNAL:
- Cargo compartment:
  - Length, incl 5·99 m (19 ft 8 in) rear loading ramp: 26·82 m (88 ft 0 in)
  - Max width: 5·49 m (18 ft 0 in)
  - Height under wing: 3·76 m (12 ft 4 in)
  - Max height: 4·11 m (13 ft 6 in)
  - Volume: 592 m³ (20,900 cu ft)

AREA:
- Wings, gross: 353 m² (3,800 sq ft)

WEIGHTS:
- Operating weight empty: 117,480 kg (259,000 lb)
- Typical payload:
  - inter-theatre logistics mission (2·5*g* load factor): 58,605 kg (129,200 lb)
  - heavy logistics mission (2·25*g* load factor): 71,895 kg (158,500 lb)
- Max payload (2·25*g* load factor): 78,110 kg (172,200 lb)
- Max T-O weight: 258,547 kg (570,000 lb)

PERFORMANCE (estimated):
- Normal cruising speed at high altitude: Mach 0·77
- Max cruising speed at low altitude: 350 knots (648 km/h; 403 mph) CAS
- Airdrop speed at S/L: 115-250 knots (213-463 km/h; 132-288 mph) CAS
- Airdrop speed at 7,620 m (25,000 ft): 130-250 knots (241-463 km/h; 150-288 mph) CAS
- Approach speed with max payload: 115 knots (213 km/h; 132 mph) CAS
- Min ground turning radius:
  - three-point turn: 25 m (82 ft)
  - 180° turn: 34·74 m (114 ft)
  - wingtip/tailplane clearance: 72·24 m (237 ft)
- Runway LCN (paved surface): better than 40
- T-O field length with max payload: 2,320 m (7,600 ft)
- Landing field length with max payload, using thrust reversal: 823 m (2,700 ft)
- Radius, T-O with 39,055 kg (86,100 lb) payload in 975 m (3,200 ft), land in 760 m (2,500 ft), T-O with similar payload in 885 m (2,900 ft) and land in 730 m (2,400 ft), all at load factor of 3*g*, no in-flight refuelling: 500 nm (925 km; 575 miles)
- Radius, T-O with 63,865 kg (140,800 lb) payload in 2,320 m (7,600 ft) at load factor of 2·25*g*, land in 915 m (3,000 ft), T-O with zero payload (load factor of 3*g*) in 730 m (2,400 ft) and land in 610 m (2,000 ft), no in-flight refuelling: 1,900 nm (3,520 km; 2,190 miles)
- Range with payloads indicated, with no in-flight refuelling:
  - 78,110 kg (172,200 lb), T-O in 2,320 m (7,600 ft), land in 915 m (3,000 ft), load factor of 2·25*g*: 2,400 nm (4,445 km; 2,765 miles)
  - 71,895 kg (158,500 lb), T-O in 2,320 m (7,600 ft), land in 885 m (2,900 ft), load factor of 2·25*g*: 2,700 nm (5,000 km; 3,110 miles)
  - 58,605 kg (129,200 lb), T-O in 1,830 m (6,000 ft), land in 795 m (2,600 ft), load factor of 2·5*g*: 2,800 nm (5,190 km; 3,225 miles)
  - self-ferry (zero payload), T-O in 1,100 m (3,600 ft), land in 610 m (2,000 ft), load factor of 2·5*g*: 5,000 nm (9,265 km; 5,755 miles)

MCDONNELL DOUGLAS/BAe T45TS

US Navy designation: T-45 Goshawk

Details of the T-45 can be found under the McDonnell Douglas/BAe entry in the International section.

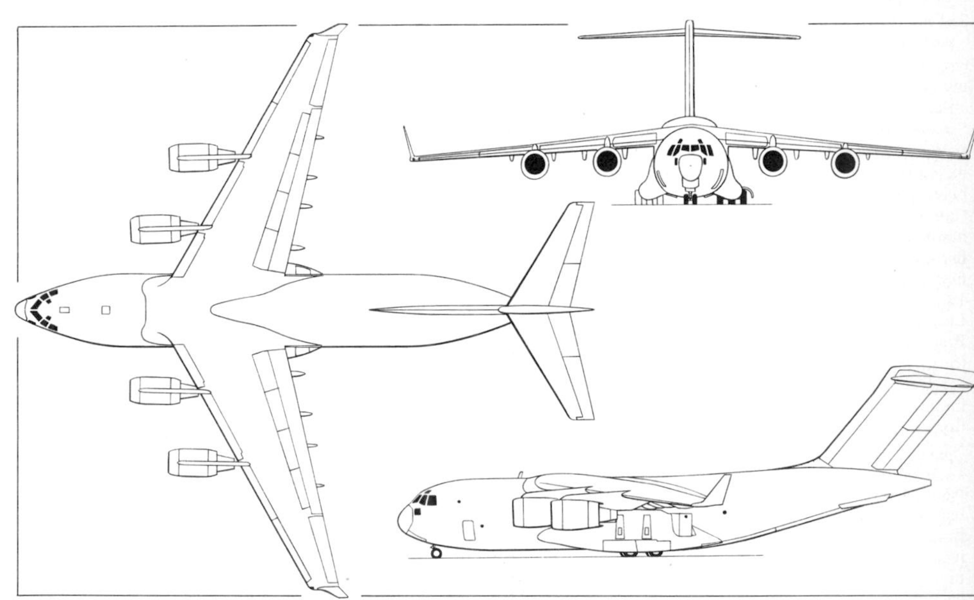

McDonnel Douglas C-17A long-range heavy lift cargo transport *(Pilot Press)*

MCDONNELL DOUGLAS

MCDONNELL DOUGLAS HELICOPTER COMPANY (Subsidiary of McDonnell Douglas Corporation)

5000 East McDowell Road, Mesa, Arizona 85205
Telephone: (602) 891 3000
Telex: 3711268 MD HC E
OTHER WORKS: Culver City, California 90230
Telephone: (213) 305 5000
Telex: 182436 Hu Heli C Culv

CHAIRMAN: Robert C. Little

PRESIDENT AND CHIEF EXECUTIVE OFFICER:
William P. Brown

EXECUTIVE VICE-PRESIDENTS:
Allen C. Haggerty (Engineering and Operations)
Norman B. Hirsh (Programme Management)

VICE-PRESIDENTS:
Dean C. Borgman (Research and Engineering)
David R. Deffenbaugh (Materiel)
Daniel J. DeLany (Project 87)
John C. Dendy (Light Helicopter Programmes)
Stuart D. Dodge (AH-64 Programmes)
Charles J. Gallagher (Product Assurance and Flight Operations)
Paul K. Henney (Operations)
Donald J. Homan (Fiscal Management)
Gerson M. Jacobson (California Manufacturing Center)
Jerome J. Sullivan (Product Support)
VeLoy J. Varner (Marketing)

Martin J. Whalen (Administration)
ASST TO PRESIDENT, GOVERNMENT AFFAIRS:
J. Stanley Kimmit
CHIEF COUNSEL: Peter T. Fagan
DIRECTOR, ARIZONA MANUFACTURING: James J. Schwalm
DIRECTOR, ORDNANCE PROGRAMMES: Reinhardt A. Ryden
DIRECTOR, LHX PROGRAMMES: William R. McDonnell

On 6 January 1984, Hughes Helicopters Inc, with more than 7,000 employees in California and Arizona, became a subsidiary of the McDonnell Douglas Corporation; on 27 August 1985 the company name was changed to McDonnell Douglas Helicopter Company. At that time, more than 4,000 of the 6,400 helicopters that it had produced were still in operation by civil and military operators in nearly 100 countries worldwide, with production of a series of advanced models continuing. Research activities included work on composites rotor blades, hubs and tailbooms, metal insulation and IR suppression systems, the US Army's LHX programme, and Chain Gun ordnance systems for air and ground applications. The company was also designing and fabricating a crashworthy all-composites helicopter fuselage, based on the shape of its MD 500E.

In July 1981 Mesa, Arizona, was selected as the site for the company's AH-64A production and flight test facility. This now comprises a 52,955 m² (570,000 sq ft) Apache assembly, flight test and delivery centre, to which has been added a further 123,980 m² (1,334,500 sq ft) complex of office, engineering and other buildings completed in 1986. In mid-1986 Mesa became the new official headquarters of the company, with a workforce due to total 5,000 by the end of 1986 and 7,000 by 1990. The Arizona plant has a production capacity of 73 helicopters per month, although the combined production rate of MD 500/Apaches will be about 20 per month when the expansion programme is completed in 1987. An 83,613 m² (900,000 sq ft) fabrication and ordnance centre is being developed at Culver City. When completed in 1998, the California facility will provide nearly 92,903 m² (1 million sq ft) of manufacturing, assembly and office space.

Licence manufacture of the Hughes Model 300C is undertaken by Schweizer Aircraft Corporation in Elmira, New York (which see). Other foreign licensees are RACA in Argentina (500D and 500E civil variants); Kawasaki in Japan (500D civil and military variants); Korean Air in the Republic of Korea (500D and 500E civil and military, excluding TOW variants); and BredaNardi in Italy (300C, 500D, 500E and 530F civil variants).

MCDONNELL DOUGLAS MD 500/530 (CIVIL VERSIONS)

The MD 500, which entered full scale production in November 1968, originated as a civil development of the OH-6A Cayuse military helicopter last described in the 1977-78 *Jane's*. From it have since been developed several military export versions; these are described separately.

Civil versions of the MD 500 are as follows:

MD 500. Initial basic production version, with Allison 250-C18A turboshaft engine.

MD 500C. Similar to MD 500, but with Allison 250-C20 engine and improved 'hot and high' performance. Licence manufacture was also undertaken by RACA (Argentina) and Kawasaki (Japan).

MD 500D. Announced in February 1975, the 500D is similar in size and general appearance to the MD 500C. It differs in having a derated Allison 250-C20B engine; a five-blade main rotor; and a T tail, which gives greater flight stability in both high and low speed regimes, as well as better handling characteristics in abnormal manoeuvres. First flight of the prototype took place in August 1974, and the first flight of a production aircraft was made on 9 October 1975. Now replaced on US production line by MD 500E. Licence manufacture continues by RACA (Argentina), BredaNardi (Italy), Kawasaki (Japan) and Korean Air (South Korea).

MD 500E. Longer and more streamlined nose, providing increased legroom for front seat occupants, which replaced the MD 500D as the basic production version. It retains the 500D's Allison 250-C20B engine. Rear seat passengers have 12 per cent more headroom, additional legroom and, as a result of lowering the bulkhead between front and rear seats, a 50 per cent improvement in forward view. First flown on 28 January 1982, the MD 500E (N5294A) incorporates improvements that include a new auxiliary fuel tank; better soundproofing around the transmission and cooling fan, longer main rotor blade abrasion strips, new endplate fins, new 'T' grouping of flight instruments, and an improved heating system. A four-blade tail rotor, a fore-and-aft litter kit, and an air-conditioning system are optional. Deliveries began in December 1982, following FAA certification in the preceding month. By early 1985 a total of 140 had been delivered, including specially equipped models for law enforcement delivered to Police Departments in Oklahoma City, Puerto Rico, St Louis, Tampa, and with 25 law enforcement agencies in the State of California. Eleven MD 500 series helicopters operating with the US Border Patrol from San Diego, California, to Brownsville, Texas, were credited with assisting in the apprehension of 74,000 illegal aliens during FY 1985. Typically, law enforcement MD 500Es are equipped with a 30 million candlepower SX-16 Nightsun searchlight, siren, emergency services communications systems and a rescue net. A four-blade 'Quiet Knight' tail rotor has also been developed to reduce the helicopters' noise level from the ground. Also delivered by early 1985 were eight MD 500Es for the US Army Aviation Systems Command at St Louis.

MD 530F Lifter. Derived from the MD 500D, this version is intended for operation at high altitudes or high temperatures. It has the fuselage configuration of the 500E and a derated 485 kW (650 shp) Allison 250-C30 turboshaft engine which fits into the same engine compartment as the 250-C20B. FAA approval to increase the T-O rating from 280 kW (375 shp) to 317 kW (425 shp) was granted on 11 July 1985. To provide additional lift capability, the main rotor has a 0·3 m (1 ft) increase in diameter, and diameter of the tail rotor is increased by 5 cm (2 in). A cargo hook kit is available, capable of lifting an external load of up to 907 kg (2,000 lb). First flight was made on 22 October 1982; FAA certification was granted on 29 July 1983 and the first customer aircraft was delivered to Rogers Helicopters Inc on 20 January 1984. Recent deliveries include 26 for the Republic of Iraq, for use in training, transportation and agricultural roles.

On 30 August 1984, an MD 530F piloted by Steve Hanvey set two time-to-height records in FAI Class E1b by climbing to 3,000 m in 3 min 15 s, and to 6,000 m in 6 min 34 s.

The following details apply to the current MD 500E and 530F:

TYPE: Turbine powered civil light helicopter.

ROTOR SYSTEM: Five-blade fully articulated main rotor, with blades attached to laminated strap retention system by means of quick-disconnect pins for folding. Each blade consists of an extruded aluminium spar hot-bonded to one-piece wraparound aluminium skin. Trim tab outboard on each blade. Main rotor blades can be folded. Two-blade tail rotor, each blade comprising a swaged steel tube spar and metal skin covering. Four-blade 'quiet' tail rotor, and main rotor brake, optional.

ROTOR DRIVE: Three sets of bevel gears, three driveshafts and one overrunning clutch. Main rotor/engine rpm ratio 1 : 12·594. Tail rotor/engine rpm ratio 1 : 1·956.

FUSELAGE: Aluminium semi-monocoque structure of pod and boom type. Clamshell doors at rear of pod give access to engine and accessories.

TAIL UNIT: T tail with horizontal stabiliser at tip of narrow chord sweptback fin; small auxiliary fin at tip of tailplane on each side; narrow chord sweptback ventral fin with integral tailskid to protect tail rotor in tail-down attitude near ground.

LANDING GEAR: Tubular skids carried on Hughes oleo-pneumatic shock absorbers. Utility floats, snow skis and emergency inflatable floats optional.

POWER PLANT: MD 500E is powered by a 313 kW (420 shp) Allison 250-C20B turboshaft engine, which is derated to 280 kW (375 shp) for T-O and has a max continuous rating of 261 kW (350 shp). MD 530F has a 485 kW (650 shp) Allison 250-C30 turboshaft engine, derated to 317 kW (425 shp) for take-off and 261 kW (350 shp) max continuous. Two interconnected bladder fuel tanks with combined usable capacity of 240 litres (63·4 US gallons). Self-sealing fuel tank optional. Refuelling point on starboard side of fuselage. Auxiliary fuel system, with 79·5 litre (21 US gallon) internal tank, available optionally. Oil capacity 5·7 litres (1·5 US gallons).

ACCOMMODATION: Forward bench seat for pilot and two passengers, with two or four passengers, or two litter patients and one medical attendant, in rear portion of cabin. Low-back front seats and individual rear seats, with fabric or leather upholstery, optional. Baggage space, capacity 0·31 m³ (11 cu ft), under and behind rear seat in five-seat form. Clear space for 1·19 m³ (42 cu ft) of cargo or baggage with only three front seats in place. Two doors on each side. Interior soundproofing optional.

SYSTEM: Aero Engineering Corporation air-conditioning system or Fargo pod mounted air-conditioner optional. Electrical system in 500D includes a 150A engine driven generator and a nickel-cadmium battery.

AVIONICS AND EQUIPMENT (500E): Optional avionics include dual King KY 195 com, KX 175 nav/com, KR 85 ADF, and KT 76 transponder; dual Collins VHF-251 com, VHF-251/351 nav/com, IND-350 nav indicator, ADF-650 ADF, and TDR-950 transponder; intercom system, headsets, microphones; and public address system. Standard equipment includes outside air temperature gauge, 8-day clock, engine hour meter, five sets inertia reel shoulder harness, cargo tiedown fittings, fire extinguisher, first aid kit, passenger steps, ground handling wheels, external power socket, landing light, skid-tip position light, anti-collision strobe lights, navigation lights, cockpit utility light, aft cabin light, and instrument lights. Optional equipment includes shatterproof glass, heating/demisting system, radios and intercom, attitude and directional gyros, rate of climb indicator, nylon mesh seats, inertia reels and shoulder harnesses for pilot and co-pilot, dual controls, cargo hook, cargo racks, underfuselage cargo pod, fire extinguisher, heated pitot tube, extended landing gear, blade storage rack, litter kit, emergency inflatable floats, inflated utility floats, and first aid kit. FAA supplemental certification has been received for installing a 30 million candlepower Spectrolab SX-16 Nightsun searchlight.

DIMENSIONS, EXTERNAL:
Main rotor diameter: 500E — 8·03 m (26 ft 4 in)
530F — 8·33 m (27 ft 4 in)
Main rotor blade chord — 0·171 m (6¾ in)
Tail rotor diameter: 500E — 1·40 m (4 ft 7 in)
530F — 1·45 m (4 ft 9 in)
Distance between rotor centres:
500E — 4·67 m (15 ft 4 in)
530F — 4·88 m (16 ft 0in)
Length overall, rotors turning:
500E — 9·40 m (30 ft 10 in)
530F — 9·78 m (32 ft 1 in)
Length of fuselage — 7·29 m (23 ft 11 in)
Height to top of rotor head (standard skids)
500E — 2·67 m (8 ft 9 in)
530F — 2·62 m (8 ft 7 in)
Tailplane span — 1·65 m (5 ft 5 in)
Skid track (standard) — 1·96 m (6 ft 5 in)
Cabin doors (each): Height — 1·13 m (3 ft 8½ in)
Max width — 0·76 m (2 ft 6 in)
Height to sill: 500E — 0·79 m (2 ft 7 in)
530F — 0·76 m (2 ft 6 in)
Cargo compartment doors (each):
Height — 1·12 m (3 ft 8¼ in)
Width — 0·88 m (2 ft 10½ in)
Height to sill: 500E — 0·71 m (2 ft 4 in)
530F — 0·66 m (2 ft 2 in)

DIMENSIONS, INTERNAL:
Cabin: Length — 2·44 m (8 ft 0 in)
Max width — 1·31 m (4 ft 3½ in)
Max height — 1·52 m (5 ft 0 in)

AREAS:
Main rotor blades (each): 500E — 0·690 m² (7·43 sq ft)
530F — 0·71 m² (7·69 sq ft)
Tail rotor blades (each): 500E — 0·095 m² (1·02 sq ft)
530F — 0·098 m² (1·05 sq ft)

McDonnell Douglas MD 500E of Orange County Sheriff-Coroner's Air Support Bureau, California

Main rotor disc: 500E 50·89 m² (547·81 sq ft)
530F 54·58 m² (587·50 sq ft)
Tail rotor disc: 500E 1·53 m² (16·50 sq ft)
530F 1·65 m² (17·72 sq ft)
Fin 0·56 m² (6·05 sq ft)
Horizontal stabiliser 0·76 m² (8·18 sq ft)

WEIGHTS AND LOADINGS:
Weight empty: 500E 654 kg (1,441 lb)
530F 709 kg (1,564 lb)
Max normal T-O weight: 500E 1,361 kg (3,000 lb)
530F 1,406 kg (3,100 lb)
Max overload T-O weight:
500E, 530F 1,610 kg (3,550 lb)
Max gross weight, external load:
530F 1,701 kg (3,750 lb)
Max normal disc loading:
500E 26·76 kg/m² (5·48 lb/sq ft)
530F 25·78 kg/m² (5·28 lb/sq ft)
Max normal power loading:
500E 4·35 kg/kW (7·14 lb/shp)
530F 2·90 kg/kW (4·77 lb/shp)

PERFORMANCE (A, 500E; B, 530F, at max normal T-O weight):
Never-exceed speed at S/L:
A, B 152 knots (282 km/h; 175 mph)
Max cruising speed at S/L:
A 139 knots (258 km/h; 160 mph)
Max cruising speed at 1,525 m (5,000 ft):
A 134 knots (248 km/h; 154 mph)
B 135 knots (250 km/h; 155 mph)
Max cruising speed from S/L to 1,525 m (5,000 ft):
B 135 knots (250 km/h; 155 mph)
Econ cruising speed at S/L:
A 129 knots (238 km/h; 148 mph)
B 130 knots (241 km/h; 150 mph)
Econ cruising speed at 1,525 m (5,000 ft):
A 119 knots (220 km/h; 137 mph)
B 123 knots (229 km/h; 142 mph)
Max rate of climb at S/L: A 572 m (1,875 ft)/min
B 640 m (2,100 ft)/min
Vertical rate of climb at S/L: A 277 m (910 ft)/min
B 427 m (1,400 ft)/min
Service ceiling: A 4,360 m (14,300 ft)
B more than 5,485 m (18,000 ft)
Hovering ceiling IGE: ISA: A 2,590 m (8,500 ft)
B 4,328 m (14,200 ft)
ISA + 20°C: A 1,830 m (6,000 ft)
B 3,660 m (12,000 ft)
Hovering ceiling OGE: ISA: A 1,860 m (6,100 ft)
B 3,660 m (12,000 ft)
ISA + 20°C: A 945 m (3,100 ft)
B 2,985 m (9,800 ft)
Range, 2 min warm-up, standard fuel, no reserves:
A at S/L 255 nm (473 km; 294 miles)
B at S/L 212 nm (395 km; 245 miles)
A at 1,525 m (5,000 ft) 278 nm (515 km; 320 miles)
B at 1,525 m (5,000 ft) 239 nm (443 km; 275 miles)

MCDONNELL DOUGLAS MODEL 500/530 DEFENDER

Military versions of the MD 500/530, of which more than 1,000 are in use worldwide, are as follows:

Model 500M. Initial uprated version of OH-6A, developed from civil MD 500. Described in 1983-84 *Jane's*.

Model 500MD Defender. Multi-role military version. Airframe and engine as civil MD 500D, from which it differs in having self-sealing fuel cells, engine inlet particle separator, optional armour protection, 'Black Hole' infra-red suppressor, and provisions for the carriage and deployment of a variety of weapons, including TOW missiles. Its diverse capabilities include training, command and control, scout, light attack, ASW, troop lift and logistical support duties. It can carry up to seven people, including the pilot; or, in ambulance configuration, two stretcher patients with attendants in addition to a flight crew of two. Licence assembly manufacture also undertaken by Korean Air in Republic of Korea.

The versions available in 1986 were as follows:

500MD Scout Defender. Basic military version, able to carry a variety of alternative weapons, including fourteen 2·75 in rockets and either a 7·62 mm Minigun with 2,000 rounds of ammunition, a 40 mm grenade launcher, or a 7·62 mm EX-34 Chain Gun machine-gun with 2,000 rounds of ammunition. Operators include Kenyan Army (15) and Republic of Korea Air Force (144).

500MD/TOW Defender. Anti-tank version armed with four TOW air-to-ground missiles. The TOW installation comprises four weapon pods, mounted two each side on a tubular mount carried through the lower aft fuselage, a stabilised telescopic sight mounted on the port side of the nose, sight control and armrest for the gunner, and a steering indicator for the pilot. In service with air forces of Israel (30), Kenya (15) and Republic of Korea (50). Available also in **500MD/MMS-TOW** version, with Hughes Aircraft mast mounted sight.

500MD/ASW Defender. Version for anti-submarine warfare and surface search missions, with two crew, search radar on nose, AN/ASQ-81 towed MAD, smoke marker launchers, hauldown gear, emergency 'popout' floats and armament of two Mk 44 or Mk 46 homing torpedoes. Max T-O weight 1,610 kg (3,550 lb). Can remain on station for 1 h 48 min when operated at a typical ASW mission radius of 22-87 nm (40-160 km; 25-100 miles) from ship or shore base. Using its radar, 500MD/ASW could locate enemy destroyers and gunboats up to 150 nm (275 km; 172 miles) from its base ship during a two-hour patrol. Twelve delivered to Taiwanese Navy.

500MD Defender II. Multi-mission version, introduced in Summer of 1980; none ordered up to early 1985. Five-blade main rotor standard; four-blade 'quiet' tail rotor optional: this turns at a rate 25 per cent slower than the standard two-blade rotor and is reported to be 47 per cent quieter in operation. Other options include Hughes Aircraft mast mounted sight (MMS), two twin-round pods for four TOW anti-tank missiles, 'Black Hole' infra-red suppression system, pod containing two Stinger or other air-to-air missiles, pilot's FLIR night vision system, AN/APR-39 (V-1) equipment to give warning that the helicopter is being tracked by hostile radar-directed weapon systems, self-sealing fuel tanks, auxiliary fuel tanks, and an advanced avionics/mission equipment package. The MMS uses a video link to TV displays for the crew, and includes laser rangefinder. Use of the MMS enables the Defender II to hover virtually out of sight behind trees or natural terrain, while the crew surveys the battlefield over extended ranges.

Standard lightweight avionics equipment (SLAE) as developed for the OH-6A has been adapted for the 500MD with minimal changes. This equipment comprises AN/ARC-164 UHF/AM, AN/ARC-115 UHF/AM, AN/ARC-114 VHF/FM, ARN-89 ADF, APX-72 IFF transponder, AN/ASN-43 directional gyro, ID-1351 heading and bearing indicator, and C-6533/ARC intercom.

500MG Defender. As 530MG, but with 313 kW (420 shp) Allison 250-C20B turboshaft engine and MD 500E rotor system. In July 1985 a **Paramilitary MG Defender** version was introduced which is intended as a low cost helicopter suitable for use by police, border patrol, rescue, narcotics control and internal security authorities. It is offered in both 500E and 530F configurations. In February 1986 McDonnell Douglas Helicopter completed delivery of six 500MG Defenders to the Colombian Air Force, which also received two commercial MD 500Es to serve as trainers.

Nightfox. Introduced in January 1986 as low cost helicopter for night surveillance and military operations. Equipment includes FLIR thermal imaging and night vision goggles, with weapons as for 530MG. Available in both 500MG and 530MG configurations.

530MG Defender. In late 1982 Hughes Helicopters began development of the 530MG Defender, based on the airframe and power plant of the commercial MD 530F Lifter. In consultation with experienced helicopter combat pilots, the company developed what is claimed to be the most advanced military helicopter crew station in the world, with the basic philosophy of reducing the two-man crew workload by relieving them of critical decisions and time-consuming aircraft management tasks. The integrated crew station developed for the 530MG makes use of recent developments in control and display systems technology to provide a compact multi-function display which enhances cockpit field of view and enables hands-on control of the helicopter at all times, with all weapons delivery, communications management, and flight control conducted via the collective and cyclic sticks. It reflects many of the technologies expected to be standard for the US Army's LHX advanced helicopter series.

Design of the Model 530MG was finalised between September and November 1983. The first demonstration aircraft (N530MG) made its first flight on 4 May 1984, and its first public appearance at the Farnborough Air Show in September of that year. Power plant rating was initially as for the MD 530F, but is now derated to 317 kW (425 shp) for take-off. A 79·5 litre (21 US gallon) internal auxiliary fuel tank is optional.

The 530MG Defender is designed primarily for point attack and anti-armour missions, but equally suitable for scout, day and night surveillance, utility, cargo lift, and light attack duties. A programme is under way to develop an over-the-horizon capability for naval applications.

Equipment includes Racal Avionics RAMS 3000 integrated control and display system for all-weather and NOE flight, designed to operate with a MIL-STD-1553B interface and comprising a processor interface unit (PIU), a control display unit (CDU), and a data transfer device (DTD) linked by a dual 1553B databus. A multi-function display incorporates a high resolution monochrome CRT with alpha-numeric and symbolic data overlay capability. The CDU incorporates a monochrome CRT with line keys and keyboard and can be used to conduct all normal flight planning, navigational, frequency selection, and subsystem management functions by use of dedicated keys on the CDU keyboard. Data are transferred to the DTD from a ground loader unit via an RS-232C serial data link which is placed in a cockpit receptacle for update transfer to the data base of the PIU. Other equipment includes Astronautics Corpn autopilot; Decca Doppler navigation system integrated with Racal Doppler velocity sensor; Ferranti FIN 1110 AHRS; twin Collins VHF/UHF AM/FM radios;

McDonnell Douglas 500MD/TOW Defender of the Israeli Air Force during nap-of-the-earth exercises

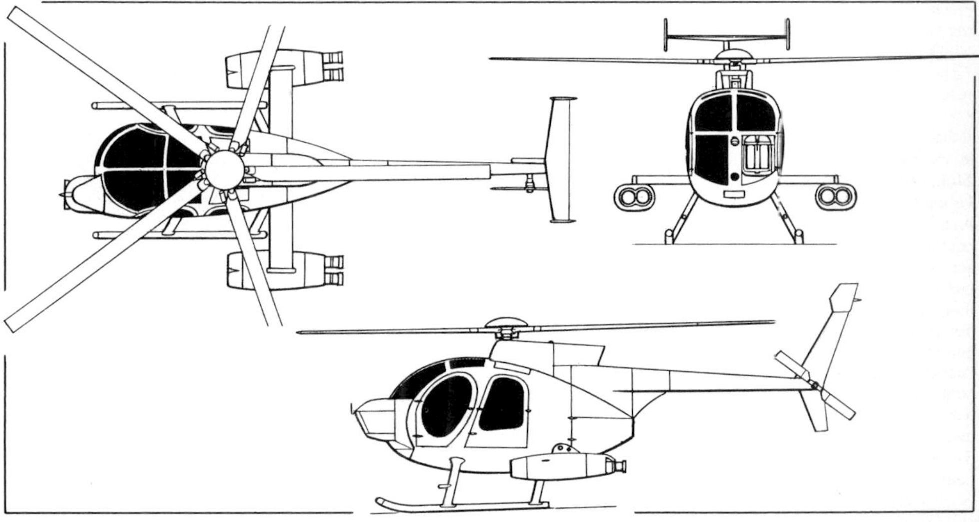
McDonnell Douglas 500MD Defender with TOW missile launchers *(Pilot Press)*

King HF radio, ADF/VOR, radar altimeter and transponder; Telephonics intercom; and SFENA attitude indicator. Optional avionics include Hughes Aircraft TOW mast mounted sight system, FLIR, radar warning receiver, IFF, GPWS and laser rangefinder.

Standard 14 in NATO racks are provided for external stores. Weapons qualified or tested by 1986 included TOW anti-armour missiles, FN pods containing two 7·62 mm or one 0·50 in machine-gun, and 2·75 in rockets in 7-tube or 12-tube launchers. Additional weapons are planned to include four General Dynamics Stinger air-to-air missiles and a 7·62 mm McDonnell Douglas Chain Gun automatic machine-gun. Chaff and infra-red decoy flares can be carried, with automatic chaff ejection on threat detection facility. Both cyclic sticks have triggers for gun or rocket firing; the co-pilot/gunner's visual image display has two handgrips for TOW/FLIR operation.

DIMENSIONS, EXTERNAL (A, 500MD/TOW; B, 530MG):
As for 500E/530F except:

Length of fuselage: A	7·62 m (25 ft 0 in)
B	7·29 m (23 ft 11 in)
Height to top of rotor head:	
A	2·64 m (8 ft 8 in)
B	2·62 m (8 ft 7 in)
B with MMS	3·41 m (11 ft 2½ in)
Height over tail (endplate fins):	
A, B	2·71 m (8 ft 10¾ in)
Width over skids: A	1·95 m (6 ft 4¾ in)
B	1·96 m (6 ft 5 in)
Width over TOW pods: A	3·23 m (10 ft 7¼ in)
Tailskid ground clearance: A	0·67 m (2 ft 2½ in)
B	0·41 m (1 ft 4 in)

WEIGHTS:

Weight empty, equipped: A	896 kg (1,976 lb)
Max T-O weight: A	1,361 kg (3,000 lb)
B, normal	1,406 kg (3,100 lb)
B, max overload	1,610 kg (3,550 lb)

PERFORMANCE (at max normal T-O weight, ISA, except where indicated):

Never-exceed speed at S/L:	
A	130 knots (241 km/h; 150 mph)
Max cruising speed at S/L:	
A, B	119 knots (221 km/h; 137 mph)
Max cruising speed at 1,525 m (5,000 ft):	
A	115 knots (213 km/h; 132 mph)
B	122 knots (226 km/h; 140 mph)
Max rate of climb at S/L:	
A, ISA	503 m (1,650 ft)/min
B, up to ISA + 20°C	631 m (2,070 ft)/min
Vertical rate of climb at S/L:	
B, ISA	606 m (1,990 ft)/min
B, ISA + 20°C	558 m (1,830 ft)/min
Service ceiling: A	4,205 m (13,800 ft)
B	over 4,880 m (16,000 ft)
Hovering ceiling IGE: A, ISA	2,315 m (7,600 ft)
B, ISA	5,060 m (16,600 ft)
A, ISA + 20°C	1,525 m (5,000 ft)
B, ISA + 20°C	4,270 m (14,000 ft)
A, 35°C	1,100 m (3,600 ft)
B, 35°C	2,680 m (8,800 ft)
Hovering ceiling OGE: A, ISA	1,770 m (5,800 ft)
B, ISA	4,300 m (14,100 ft)
A, ISA + 20°C	915 m (3,000 ft)
B, ISA + 20°C	3,475 m (11,400 ft)
A, 35°C	640 m (2,100 ft)
B, 35°C	2,135 m (7,000 ft)
Range with standard fuel, 2 min warmup, no reserves:	
A at S/L	210 nm (389 km; 242 miles)
B at S/L	180 nm (333 km; 207 miles)
A at 1,525 m (5,000 ft)	231 nm (428 km; 266 miles)
B at 1,525 m (5,000 ft)	203 nm (376 km; 233 miles)
Endurance with standard fuel, 2 min warmup, no reserves: A at S/L	2 h 34 min
B at S/L	2 h 6 min
A at 1,525 m (5,000 ft)	2 h 47 min
B at 1,525 m (5,000 ft)	2 h 18 min

MCDONNELL DOUGLAS NOTAR HELICOPTER

On 20 May 1981 Hughes Helicopters announced that, following the award in September 1980 of a $2·2 million 24-month contract by the US Army Applied Technology Laboratory and the Defense Advanced Research Projects Agency, the company had designed and was to build a prototype no-tail-rotor (NOTAR) helicopter. During 1981 an Army OH-6A helicopter was modified to serve as the NOTAR prototype (12917), and this was flown for the first time on 17 December 1981. Details of the programme can be found in the 1982-83 *Jane's*. During 1985 the NOTAR prototype was extensively modified, with a new forward fuselage similar in profile to that of the MD 500E, a 313 kW (420 shp) Allison 250-C20B turboshaft engine, a new fan with composite blades of smaller diameter and greater chord than the original metal bladed fan, and a second air circulation slot on the tailboom. Flight testing of the helicopter resumed on 12 March 1986. Commercial versions of the NOTAR helicopter are under consideration and a system of this kind is being considered also for the US Army's LHX requirement.

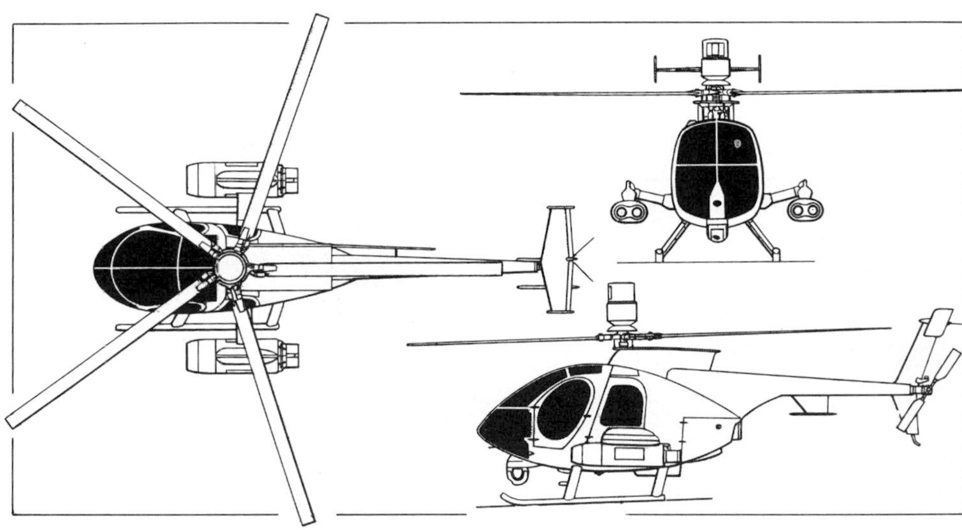

McDonnell Douglas 530MG Defender, with TOW missiles and mast mounted sight *(Pilot Press)*

McDonnell Douglas 530MG Defender with Hughes Aircraft mast mounted sight

McDonnell Douglas 530MG Nightfox helicopter with FLIR thermal imaging system and twin EX-34 Chain Gun installation

McDonnell Douglas NOTAR helicopter in latest configuration

MCDONNELL DOUGLAS APACHE

US Army designation: AH-64A

The Hughes Model 77 was designed to meet the US Army's requirement for an advanced attack helicopter (AAH) capable of undertaking a full day/night/adverse weather anti-armour mission, and of fighting, surviving and 'living with' troops in a front-line environment. Two YAH-64 flight test prototypes were built for competitive evaluation against Bell's YAH-63, and these made their initial flights on 30 September and 22 November 1975 respectively. A ground test vehicle was also completed. The original contract covered, in addition, development of the M230 Chain Gun helicopter weapon for installation in the prototypes. In February 1976 Rockwell's Hellfire missile was chosen to replace the Hughes TOW as the primary anti-tank weapon. By January 1985, YAH-64 prototypes had fired more than 75 Hellfire missiles, nearly 5,600 2·75 in rockets, and more than 65,000 rounds of 30 mm ammunition.

Selection of the YAH-64 was announced on 10 December 1976. Details of the prototype and full scale engineering development programmes can be found in the 1984-85 and earlier editions of *Jane's*. The name Apache was adopted for the AH-64 in late 1981.

Teledyne Ryan is responsible for building the AH-64 fuselage, wings, engine nacelles, avionics bays, canopy and tail unit. A key subsystem is the Martin Marietta target acquisition and designation sight/pilot's night vision sensor (TADS/PNVS), for which an initial production contract (for 13 systems) was awarded on 30 April 1982; the first production TADS/PNVS was delivered in July 1983.

Self-deployment capability was demonstrated on 4 April 1985, when the 14th production Apache, with four 871 litre (230 US gallon) external fuel tanks, made a 1,020 nm (1,891 km; 1,175 mile) nonstop flight from Mesa to Santa Barbara, landing with 30 minutes' fuel remaining. Such ferry range permits deployment from the USA to Europe via a northern Atlantic route, with stops at Goose Bay, Frobisher Bay, Søndrestrøm, Reykjavik and Prestwick. If the required deployment is farther than ferry range the Apache can be carried in C-141B StarLifter and C-5 Galaxy transports (two and six Apaches respectively). Loading trials have also been conducted with a mockup of the McDonnell Douglas C-17A, which could accommodate up to three Apaches.

On 26 March 1982, the Defense Systems Acquisition Review Council gave approval for the production programme to be initiated. This resulted, on 15 April 1982, in a Lot 1 production contract for 11 Apaches, the first of which was delivered on 26 January 1984. The US Army's original requirement for 472 AH-64As was subsequently raised to 536, then cut to 446, increased again to 515 in late 1982 and to 675 in 1984. This is being achieved by procurement of 11 in FY 1982, 48 in FY 1983, 112 in FY 1984, 138 in FY 1985, 144 each in FY 1986 and FY 1987, and 78 in FY 1988, with deliveries scheduled for completion in April 1990. On 25 June 1986 the 100th production Apache was delivered, by which time production had reached 12 per month. On 30 January 1985 the first Apache for the US Army's Training and Doctrine Command (TRADOC) was delivered to the Army Transportation and Logistics School (ATALS) at Fort Eustis, Virginia. Later that month an Apache was delivered to the Army Aviation School at Fort Rucker, Alabama, where all maintenance and maintenance test pilot courses are to be conducted.

Initial operational capability with 1/6 Cav, 6th Air Cavalry Combat Brigade, at Fort Hood, Texas, was expected during 1986, following delivery of four AH-64As to Hood Army Airfield in February. The 6th Cavalry Brigade's 7th Squadron, 17th Cavalry, was to be the first unit to undergo the 90-day Apache Unit Training Programme at Fort Hood, commencing in April 1986.

In January 1986 AH-64As completed 10,000 flight hours in Army service, in addition to 5,000 hours logged by the prototypes during test and development flying.

In 1987 the North Carolina Army National Guard's 28th Aviation Battalion will receive 18 Apaches, becoming the first Guard or Reserve unit to operate the type. The NCARNG's Apaches will be based at a new Army Aviation support facility at Raleigh-Durham Airport.

McDonnell Douglas Helicopter Company has received contracts from the US Army Aviation Applied Directorate to develop an advanced composite main rotor hub and fibre-reinforced thermoplastic secondary structures for the AH-64A, and to develop artificial intelligence applications for fault isolation and diagnosis of the helicopter's systems. A production AH-64A will be used for a five-year vibration analysis study funded by NASA's Langley Research Center.

Two navalised versions of the Apache have been projected, and are described separately. The following description applies to the standard production AH-64A for the US Army:

Type: Twin-engined attack helicopter.

Rotor System: Four-blade fully articulated main rotor and four-blade tail rotor; all blades manufactured by Tool Research and Engineering Corpn (Composite Structures Division). Main rotor blades are of high-camber aerofoil section and broad chord, with sweptback tips, and can be folded or removed for air transportation. Each blade has five stainless steel spars lined with structural glassfibre tubes, a laminated stainless steel skin and a composite rear section, bonded together. Blades are attached to hub by a laminated strap retention system similar to that of the OH-6A, and are fitted with elastomeric lead/lag dampers and offset flapping hinges. Tail rotor comprises two pairs of blades, mounted on port side of pylon/fin support structure at optimum quiet setting of approx 55°/125° to each other. Main and tail rotor blades de-iced by Sierracin Corpn heater blankets. Main rotor driveshaft rotates within a fixed, hollow outer shaft, permitting removal of main transmission without dismantling main rotor system. This results in improved drive system reliability, as flight loads are transmitted to airframe via static mast instead of through main transmission. Entire system is capable of flight in negative *g* conditions.

Rotor Drive: Litton (Precision Gear Division) main transmission and engine nose gearbox; transmission to tail rotor via Aircraft Gear Corpn grease-lubricated intermediate and tail rotor gearboxes, with Bendix driveshafts and couplings. AirResearch cooling fan for tail rotor gearbox. Main transmission designed to operate for one hour after loss of oil; gearboxes can tolerate ballistic damage and continue to operate for up to one hour without failure. Selected dynamic components constructed of 7049 aluminium and electro-slag remelt (ESR) steel; critical parts of transmission (eg, bearings) have ESR collars for protection against hits by 12·7 mm ammunition. Rotor/engine rpm ratios approx 1 : 72·4 for main rotor, approx 1 : 14·9 for tail rotor.

Wings: Cantilever mid-mounted wings of low aspect ratio, built by Teledyne Ryan Aeronautical and located aft of the cockpit. Wings are removable, and attach to sides of fuselage for transport and storage. Two hardpoints beneath each wing for the carriage of mixed ordnance or ferry tanks.

Fuselage: Conventional semi-monocoque aluminium structure, built by Teledyne Ryan Aeronautical. Designed to survive hits by 12·7 mm and 23 mm ammunition.

Tail Unit: Bolted pylon structure, built by Teledyne Ryan Aeronautical, with tail rotor mounted on port side. Low-mounted all-moving tailplane, with Simmonds actuators and Hamilton Standard control electronics.

Landing Gear: Menasco trailing arm type, with single mainwheels and fully castoring, self-centering and lockable tailwheel. Mainwheel tyres size 8·50-10, tailwheel tyre size 5·00-4. Hydraulic brakes on main units. Main gear is non-retractable, but legs fold rearward to reduce overall height for storage and transportation. Energy absorbing main and tail gears are designed for normal descent rates of up to 3·05 m (10 ft)/s and heavy landings at up to 12·8 m (42 ft)/s. Take-offs and landings can be made at structural design gross weight on terrain slopes of up to 12° (head-on) and 10° (side-on).

Power Plant: Two 1,265 kW (1,696 shp) General Electric T700-GE-701 turboshaft engines, derated for normal operations to provide reserve power for combat emergencies, and with automatic one engine out rating of 1,285 kW (1,723 shp). Engines mounted one on each side of fuselage, above wings, with key components armour-protected. Upper cowlings let down to serve as maintenance platforms. Two crash resistant fuel cells in fuselage, combined capacity 1,422 litres (376 US gallons; 313 Imp gallons).

Accommodation: Crew of two in tandem: co-pilot/gunner in front, pilot behind on 48 cm (19 in) elevated seat. Crew seats, by Simula Inc, are of lightweight Kevlar. Teledyne Ryan canopy, with PPG transparencies and transparent acrylic blast barrier between cockpits, is designed to provide optimum field of view. Crew stations are protected by Ceradyne Inc lightweight boron armour shields in cockpit floor and sides, and between cockpits, offering protection against 23 mm high explosive and armour piercing rounds. Sierracin electric heating of windscreen. Seats and structure designed to give crew a 95 per cent chance of surviving ground impacts of up to 12·8 m (42 ft)/s.

Systems: Garrett totally integrated pneumatic system includes a shaft driven compressor, air turbine starters, pneumatic valves, temperature control unit and environmental control unit. Parker Bertea dual hydraulic systems, operating at 207 bars (3,000 lb/sq in), with actuators ballistically tolerant to 12·7 mm direct hits. Redundant flight control system for both rotors. In the event of a dual hydraulic system failure, the system adjusts to Sperry Flight Systems secondary fly by wire control. Bendix electrical power system, with two 35kVA fully redundant engine driven AC generators, two 300A transformer-rectifiers, and URDC standby DC battery. Garrett GTP 36-55(H) 93 kW (125 shp) APU for engine starting and maintenance checking.

Avionics and Equipment: Main avionics bays are adjacent to co-pilot/gunner's position, in large fairings on sides of fuselage. Tempest Enhanced C-10414 secure UHF, VHF,

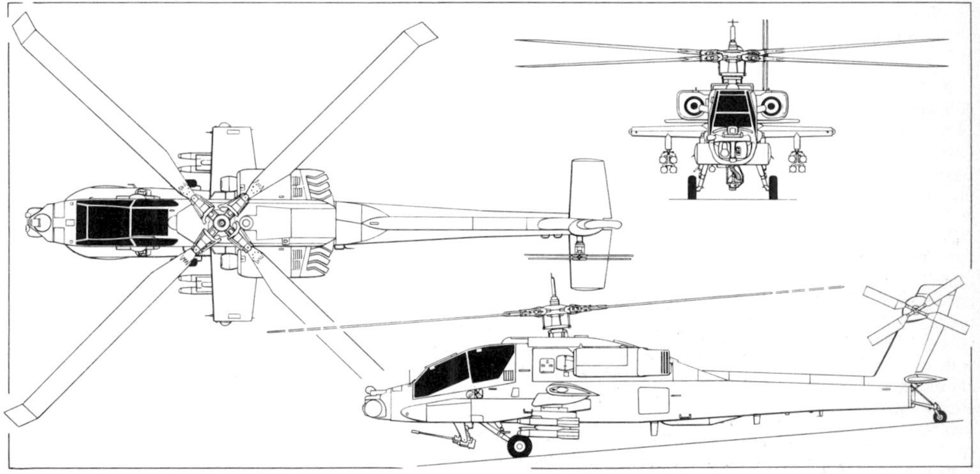
McDonnell Douglas AH-64A Apache tandem two-seat advanced attack helicopter *(Pilot Press)*

AM and FM com. Singer-Kearfott AN/ASN-128 lightweight Doppler navigation system, with Litton LR-80 (AN/ASN-143) strapdown attitude and heading reference system (AHRS). Doppler system, with AHRS, permits nap-of-the-earth navigation and provides for storing target locations. Avionics fit includes an ADF and an IFF transponder with secure encoding. Sperry Flight Systems digital automatic stabilisation equipment (DASE). Aircraft survivability equipment (ASE) consists of an Aerospace Avionics passive radar warning receiver, a Sanders infra-red jammer, chaff dispensers, and a radar jammer. Other avionics include Astronautics Corpn HSI, video display unit, and remote magnetic indicator, and Pacer Systems omnidirectional air data system. A Sperry Flight Systems all-raster symbology generator processes TV data from IR and other sensors, superimposes symbology, and distributes the combination to CRT and helmet mounted displays in the aircraft. 'Black Hole' IR suppression system protects aircraft from heat-seeking missiles: this eliminates an engine bay cooling fan, by operating from engine exhaust gas through ejector nozzles to lower the gas plume and metal temperatures. BITE fault detection/location system.

Armament and Operational Equipment: Armament consists of a McDonnell Douglas M230 Chain Gun 30 mm automatic cannon, located between the mainwheel legs in an underfuselage mounting with Lear Siegler electronic controls. Normal rate of fire is 625 rds/min of Honeywell TP (target practice), HE or HEDP (high explosive dual purpose) ammunition, which is interoperable with NATO Aden/DEFA 30 mm ammunition. Max ammunition load is 1,200 rds. Gun mounting is designed to collapse into fuselage between pilots in the event of a crash landing. Four underwing hardpoints, with Aircraft Hydro-Forming pylons and ejector units, on which can be carried up to sixteen Rockwell Hellfire anti-tank missiles; or up to seventy-six 2·75 in FFAR (folding fin aerial rockets) in their launchers; or a combination of Hellfires and FFAR. Hellfire remote electronics by Rockwell; Bendix aerial rocket control system; multiplex (MUX) system units by Sperry Flight Systems. Co-pilot/gunner (CPG) has primary responsibility for firing gun and missiles, but pilot can override his controls to fire gun or launch missiles. Martin Marietta target acquisition and designation sight and pilot's night vision sensor (TADS/PNVS) comprises two independently functioning systems mounted on the nose. The TADS consists of a rotating turret (± 120° in azimuth, +30/−60° in elevation) that houses the sensor subsystems, an optical relay tube in the CPG's cockpit, three electronic units in the avionics bay, and cockpit-mounted controls and displays. It is used principally for target search, detection and laser designation, with the CPG as primary operator (though it can also provide backup night vision to the pilot in the event of a PNVS failure). Once acquired by the TADS, targets can be tracked manually or automatically for autonomous attack with gun, rockets or Hellfire missiles. The TADS daylight sensor consists of a TV camera with narrow (0·9°) and wide angle (4·0°) fields of view; direct view optics (4° narrow and 18° wide angle); a laser spot tracker; and a International Laser Systems laser rangefinder/designator. The night sensor, in the starboard half of the turret, incorporates a FLIR sight with narrow, medium and wide angle (3·1, 10·1 and 50·0°) fields of view. The PNVS consists of a FLIR sensor (30° × 40° field of view) in a rotating turret (± 90° in azimuth, +20/−45° in elevation) mounted above the TADS; an electronics unit in the avionics bay; and the pilot's display and controls. It provides the pilot with thermal imaging that permits nap-of-the-earth flight to, from and within the battle area at night or in adverse daytime weather, at altitudes low enough to avoid detection by the enemy. PNVS imagery is displayed on a single monocle in front of one of the pilot's eyes; flight information such as airspeed, altitude and heading is superimposed on this imagery to simplify the piloting task. The monocle is a part of the Honeywell Avionics integrated helmet and display sighting system (IHADSS) worn by both crew members.

Mockup of wingtip Sidewinder missile installation for proposed USMC version of Apache

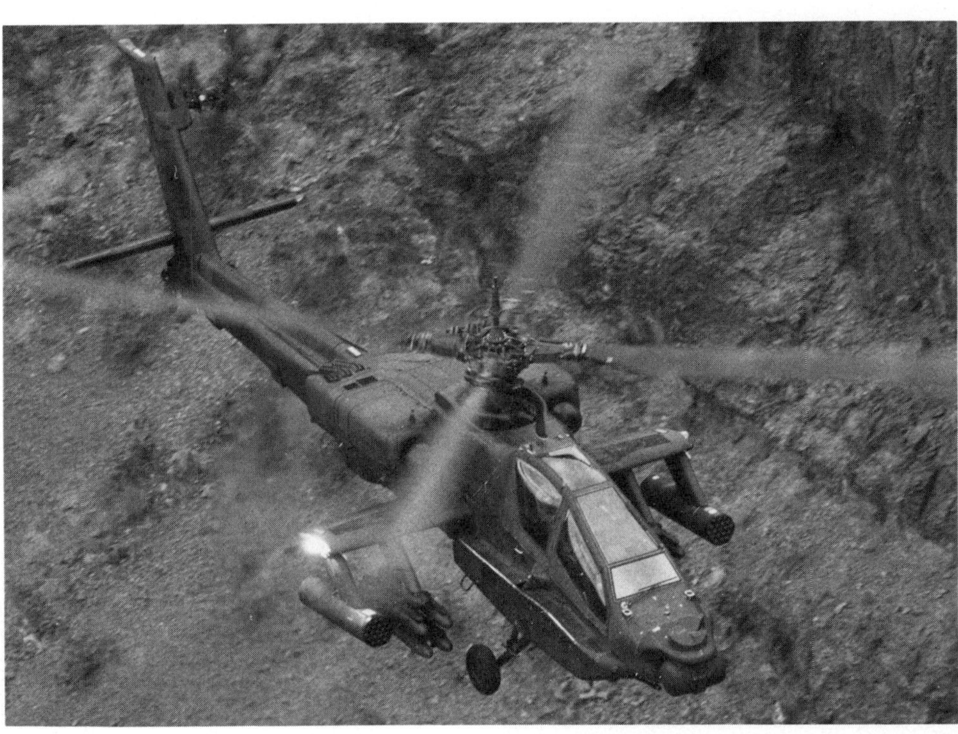

McDonnell Douglas AH-64A Apache armed with Hellfire missiles and FFAR launchers

AH-64 demonstrator for LHX technology, with advanced digital flight control system

Dimensions, external:
- Main rotor diameter 14·63 m (48 ft 0 in)
- Main rotor blade chord 0·53 m (1 ft 9 in)
- Tail rotor diameter 2·79 m (9 ft 2 in)
- Length overall: tail rotor turning 14·68 m (48 ft 2 in)
  - both rotors turning 17·76 m (58 ft 3⅛ in)
- Wing span 5·23 m (17 ft 2 in)
- Height: over tail fin 3·52 m (11 ft 6½ in)
  - over tail rotor 4·30 m (14 ft 1¼ in)
  - to top of rotor head 3·84 m (12 ft 7 in)
  - overall (top of air data sensor) 4·66 m (15 ft 3½ in)
- Distance between c/l of pylons:
  - inboard pair 3·20 m (10 ft 6 in)
  - outboard pair 4·72 m (15 ft 6 in)
- Tailplane span 3·40 m (11 ft 2 in)
- Wheel track 2·03 m (6 ft 8 in)
- Wheelbase 10·59 m (34 ft 9 in)

Areas:
- Main rotor disc 168·11 m² (1,809·5 sq ft)
- Tail rotor disc 6·13 m² (66·0 sq ft)

Weights:
- Weight empty 4,881 kg (10,760 lb)
- Max internal fuel weight 1,157 kg (2,550 lb)
- Max external stores weight 771 kg (1,700 lb)
- Structural design gross weight 6,650 kg (14,650 lb)
- Primary mission gross weight 6,552 kg (14,445 lb)
- Max T-O weight 9,525 kg (21,000 lb)

General Performance (at 6,552 kg; 14,445 lb AUW, ISA except where indicated):
- Never-exceed speed 197 knots (365 km/h; 227 mph)
- Max level and max cruising speed 160 knots (296 km/h; 184 mph)
- Max vertical rate of climb at S/L 762 m (2,500 ft)/min
- Service ceiling 6,400 m (21,000 ft)
- Service ceiling, one engine out 3,290 m (10,800 ft)
- Hovering ceiling: IGE 4,570 m (15,000 ft)
  - OGE 3,505 m (11,500 ft)
- Max range, internal fuel 260 nm (482 km; 300 miles)
- Ferry range, max internal and external fuel, still air 918 nm (1,701 km; 1,057 miles)
- Endurance at 1,220 m (4,000 ft) at 35°C 1 h 50 min
- Max endurance, internal fuel 3 h 9 min
- *g* limits at low altitude and airspeeds up to 164 knots (304 km/h; 189 mph) +3·5/−0·5

Weights for Typical Mission Performance (A: anti-armour at 1,220 m/4,000 ft and 35°C, 4 Hellfire and 320 rds of 30 mm ammunition; B: as A, but with 1,200 rds; C: as A, but with 6 Hellfire and 540 rds; D: anti-armour at 610 m/2,000 ft and 21°C, 8 Hellfire and 1,200 rds; E: air cover at 1,220 m/4,000 ft and 35°C, 4 Hellfire and 1,200 rds; F: as E but at 610 m/2,000 ft and 21°C, 4 Hellfire, 19 rockets, 1,200 rds; G: escort at 1,220 m/4,000 ft and 35°C, 19 rockets and 1,200 rds; H: escort at 610 m/2,000 ft and 21°C, 38 rockets and 1,200 rds):

Mission fuel:
- A 727 kg (1,602 lb)
- G 741 kg (1,633 lb)
- E 745 kg (1,643 lb)
- C 902 kg (1,989 lb)
- B 1,029 kg (2,269 lb)
- D 1,063 kg (2,344 lb)
- H 1,077 kg (2,374 lb)
- F 1,086 kg (2,394 lb)

Mission gross weight:
- A 6,552 kg (14,445 lb)
- E 6,874 kg (15,154 lb)
- G 6,932 kg (15,282 lb)
- B, C 7,158 kg (15, 780 lb)
- D 7,728 kg (17,038 lb)
- F 7,813 kg (17,225 lb)
- H 7,867 kg (17,343 lb)

Typical Mission Performance (A-H as above);

Cruising speed at intermediate rated power:
- C 147 knots (272 km/h; 169 mph)
- D 148 knots (274 km/h; 170 mph)
- F 150 knots (278 km/h; 173 mph)
- B 151 knots (280 km/h; 174 mph)
- E, H 153 knots (283 km/h; 176 mph)
- A 154 knots (285 km/h; 177 mph)
- G 155 knots (287 km/h; 178 mph)

Max vertical rate of climb at intermediate rated power:
- B, C 137 m (450 ft)/min
- H 238 m (780 ft)/min
- F, G 262 m (860 ft)/min

E	293 m (960 ft)/min
D	301 m (990 ft)/min
A	448 m (1,470 ft)/min
Mission endurance: A, E, G	1 h 50 min
C	1 h 17 min
D, F, H	2 h 30 min
B	2 h 40 min

MCDONNELL DOUGLAS APACHE (NAVALISED VERSIONS)

Under a company initiated programme, McDonnell Douglas is considering modification of an Apache prototype to demonstrate to the US Marine Corps and US Navy the potential of navalised versions of the helicopter. Two variants are proposed. Both would be powered by naval standard T700-GE-401 engines and have additional airframe corrosion proofing, Doppler INS, electromagnetic radiation shielding, upgraded brakes, more tiedown points, floating base maintenance provisions, and an automatic hydraulic/mechanical main rotor blade folding system using a new hub design which permits 45° movements of the blades to align with the fuselage for shipboard storage.

The proposed US Marine Corps variant, which could be ready for initial production deliveries by 1988, would retain the target acquisition/detection, pilot night vision and Hellfire missile systems of the AH-64A, but not the 30 mm Chain Gun, which is not seen as a suitable weapon for the air-to-air role. Marines Apaches would also be equipped to fire TOW missiles, 2·75 in and 5 in Zuni unguided rockets and AIM-9L Sidewinder missiles, the latter mounted singly on stub wingtip launching rails.

For the US Navy McDonnell Douglas proposes a 'Sea Apache' which would also retain the TADS/PNVS, and would be fitted with a surface search and target acquisition radar, with either a mast mounted radome or a ventral radome in place of the 30 mm Chain Gun. Missions foreseen for the Sea Apache include anti-shipping strike, over the horizon targeting (OTHT) and combat air patrol/escort. In an anti-shipping role the helicopter would carry up to four Harpoon, Penguin or equivalent missiles. For CAP missions up to six AIM-9Ls and 1,200 rounds of 30 mm (or correspondingly more rounds of smaller calibre, higher velocity) ammunition could be carried. The Sea Apache would have a folding tail section to meet US Navy deck parking requirements, necessitating relocation of the tailwheel some 1·8-2·4 m (6-8 ft) forward of its location on the AH-64A. An underfuselage hardpoint at the centre of gravity position would be equipped with a haul-down system to enhance rough weather operational capability from frigate-class ships.

MCDONNEL DOUGLAS/BELL LHX

In October 1983 the US Army Applied Technology Laboratory awarded Hughes Helicopters two research and development contracts valued at nearly $2 million for work on the LHX programme for a family of light scout/attack and utility helicopters which will replace Bell UH-1, AH-1 and OH-58, and Hughes OH-6A helicopters in the US Army inventory. The contracts were for a two-year preliminary study to determine the best technical approach to an LHX production programme and a one-year study for the application of the company's energy absorbing retractable landing gear to LHX utility helicopters.

Five industry teams are competing for the LHX development and production contracts. The development contract is expected to be awarded in October 1987, and the programme could involve more than 5,000 production helicopters. On 9 April 1986 McDonnell Douglas Helicopter announced that it was joining with Bell Helicopter Textron (which see) to develop its LHX submission. Other partners in the project are Honeywell Inc, Hughes Aircraft Company, Sperry Corporation and Texas Instruments Inc. One proposal is depicted in an accompanying illustration, and features McDonnell Douglas Helicopter's NOTAR system. This system is likely to be utilised only if speeds higher than 200 knots (370 km/h; 230 mph) are not required. McDonnell Douglas is also developing an integrated, automated ARTI one-man cockpit (the so-called 'glass cockpit') for the LHX. It has adapted the front cockpit of an AH-64 (82-8258) with a fly-by-wire digital flight control system and flew this helicopter for the first time on 12 October 1985. The rear cockpit remains standard, for a safety pilot

In early 1985 McDonnell Douglas began ground tests of an MD 500E helicopter equipped with a hingeless and bearingless main rotor with composite blades of graphite and Kevlar 29 as part of its LHX technology advanced rotor programme. Flight testing commenced in April 1985 at the company's Mesa, Arizona, facility. McDonnell Douglas is also building an all-composites rotor hub for the AH-64A as part of the LHX programme. This is expected to fly in 1988.

Allison and Garrett have jointly entered the ATE-109 turboshaft for the US Army's competition for an LHX power plant. The only other known entry is the T800 free power turbine unit proposed jointly by Avco Lycoming and Pratt & Whitney. Both engines are in the 895 kW (1,200 shp) class.

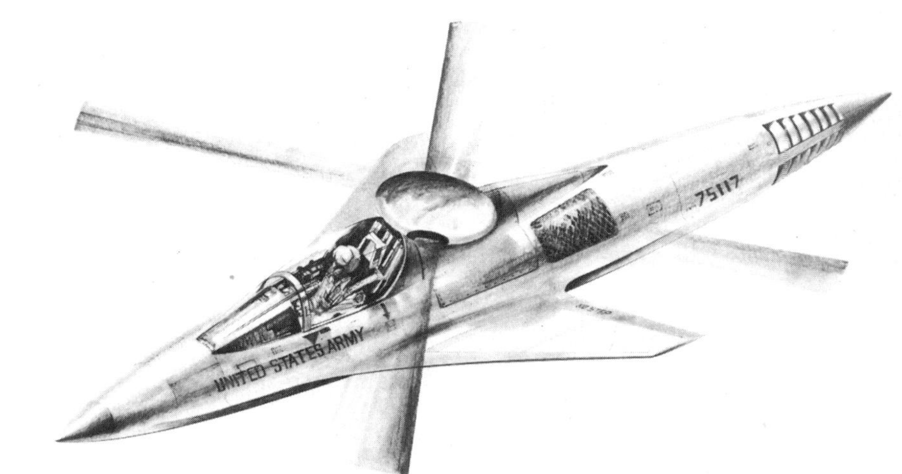

One of several McDonnell Douglas Helicopter Company configurations for the US Army LHX programme

MELEX

MELEX USA

1200 Front Street, Suite 101, Raleigh, North Carolina 27609
Telephone: (919) 828 7645
Telex: 579326 MELEX UF
VICE-PRESIDENT: George Lundy

This company, a subsidiary of Pezetel (PZL) of Poland (which see), is responsible for operational support of some 120 PZL Mielec M-18 Dromader agricultural aircraft operating in the western hemisphere, of which about half were operating in the United States and 15 in Canada by early 1986.

MELEX T45 TURBINE DROMADER

Melex USA, in co-operation with Turbines Inc of Terre Haute, Indiana, has developed a turboprop conversion of the M-18, based on the 895 kW (1,200 shp) Pratt & Whitney Canada PT6A-45AG engine and known as the T45 Turbine Dromader. The prototype (N2856G) flew for the first time on 17 August 1985, and FAA type approval was expected in early 1986. An annual conversion rate of three to four aircraft is anticipated, for the US market alone.

The conversion, which reduces the Dromader's empty weight by about 363 kg (800 lb), provides an increase in normal operating speed of some 20 knots (37 km/h; 23 mph) and a 10 per cent decrease in take-off distance at max T-O weight. Improvements have also been made to the hydraulic and electrical systems.

Prototype Melex T45 Turbine Dromader conversion with Pratt & Whitney Canada PT6A-45AG engine

MELEX DROMADER AMPHIBIAN

Melex USA is also developing an amphibious version of the Dromader which would be able to replenish its tanks for firefighting by collecting water via scoops in its floats while taxying. It was hoped to fly a prototype by late 1986, with certification and customer deliveries beginning in 1987.

MID-CONTINENT

MID-CONTINENT AIRCRAFT CORPORATION

Drawer L, Hayti, Missouri 63851
Telephone: (314) 359 0500
Telex: 447183
PRESIDENT: Richard Reade

MID-CONTINENT KING CAT

Mid-Continent Aircraft Corporation, an operator and distributor of Schweizer (Grumman) Ag-Cats, has obtained an FAA Supplemental Type Certificate for an aircraft known as the King Cat. This is an Ag-Cat re-engined with an 895 kW (1,200 hp) Wright R-1820-202A radial engine, driving a three-blade metal propeller. The engineering work for the STC was carried out by Serv-Aero Engineering Inc (which see). The King Cat has since been certificated in Canada.

Based on the airframe of the Super Ag-Cat C, which has a hopper accommodating 1,893 litres (500 US gallons) of spray or 1,814 kg (4,000 lb) of dry chemicals, the King Cat offers improved high-altitude/high-temperature performance. It is available as a conversion of a Super Ag-Cat C, or a kit is obtainable for installation by the customer or his maintenance organisation. Options which are available include upper wing installation height increase of 20·3 cm (8 in), Serv-O ailerons, increased fuel capacity of 431·5 litres (114 US gallons), Collins cockpit air-conditioning and a 1,893 litre (500 US gallon) water bombing system for fire control.

By 1 January 1986 Mid-Continent had completed 20 King Cat conversions. Examples are in service in the United States, Canada and South Africa.

WEIGHTS AND LOADINGS:

Weight empty, basic	2,184 kg (4,816 lb)
Weight empty: spray equipped	2,257 kg (4,976 lb)
dust equipped	2,225 kg (4,906 lb)
Max T-O weight: FAR 23	2,857 kg (6,300 lb)
CAM 8	3,855 kg (8,500 lb)
Max wing loading:	
FAR 23	78·5 kg/m² (16·07 lb/sq ft)
CAM 8	105·9 kg/m² (21·68 lb/sq ft)
Max power loading:	
FAR 23	3·19 kg/kW (5·25 lb/hp)
CAM 8	4·31 kg/kW (7·08 lb/hp)

PERFORMANCE:

Ferry speed 117 knots (217 km/h; 135 mph)
Typical working speed 87-113 knots (161-209 km/h; 100-130 mph)
Stalling speed, power off, at AUW of 2,857 kg (6,300 lb) 60 knots (111 km/h; 69 mph) CAS
T-O run with 907 kg (2,000 lb) hopper load 293 m (960 ft)
T-O to 15 m (50 ft) with 907 kg (2,000 lb) hopper load 427 m (1,400 ft)
Landing from 15 m (50 ft) at weight of 2,257 kg (4,976 lb) 363 m (1,190 ft)
Landing run at weight of 2,257 kg (4,976 lb) 179 m (588 ft)

Mid-Continent King Cat, a Wright engined conversion of a Super Ag-Cat C

MITSUBISHI — *see MAI*

MOLLER

MOLLER INTERNATIONAL

1222 Research Park Drive, Davis, California 95616
PRESIDENT: Paul S. Moller

Since 1960 Moller International has undertaken research and development projects in aerodynamics, noise suppression and vehicle design, leading to the construction and testing of a number of experimental VTOL aircraft which are said to combine the best features of helicopters and fixed-wing aircraft. A prototype, known originally as the Discojet and later designated **Model XM-4**, is of 'flying saucer' configuration with a two-piece glassfibre airframe. Accommodation is provided for two occupants in a centrally mounted cockpit, around which are mounted eight 37·3 kW (50 hp) Wankel rotary engines driving fan-blade 'thrust modules' which provide lift for hovering flight and thrust for forward flight.

A developed production version known as the **Model 440E Commuter** will seat four occupants, and is illustrated in the accompanying artist's impression. Work on the 440E prototype had been slowed down in 1986 due to increased interest in unmanned versions, but a limited number of Model 440Es is expected to be delivered in 1987. Projected variants include a side by side two-seat **Model 220E** powered by six 74·6 kW (100 hp) rotary engines, giving a maximum speed of 208 knots (386 km/h; 240 mph); and the **Model 660E**, a six-passenger executive/military vehicle powered by an unspecified augmented turbofan engine giving a maximum speed of 339 knots (627 km/h; 390 mph).

MOLLER 440E COMMUTER

(all data provisional)

POWER PLANT: Eight 74·6 kW (100 hp) rotary engines driving 'thrust modules'. Maximum fuel capacity 227 litres (60 US gallons).

DIMENSIONS, EXTERNAL:

Length overall	3·87 m (12 ft 8½ in)
Width overall	5·00 m (16 ft 4¾ in)
Height overall	1·40 m (4 ft 7¼ in)

WEIGHTS:

Weight empty	472 kg (1,040 lb)
Max payload	431 kg (950 lb)
Max T-O weight	1,009 kg (2,225 lb)

PERFORMANCE:

Max level speed 213 knots (394 km/h; 245 mph)
Cruising speed at 45% power 165 knots (306 km/h; 190 mph)
Rate of climb at 65% power 1,432 m (4,700 ft)/min
Hovering ceiling 3,505 m (11,500 ft)
Service ceiling 5,790 m (19,000 ft)
Max range, 20 min reserves 356 nm (660 km; 410 miles)

Prototype Moller XM-4 experimental VTOL craft. Normally a bubble canopy is fitted

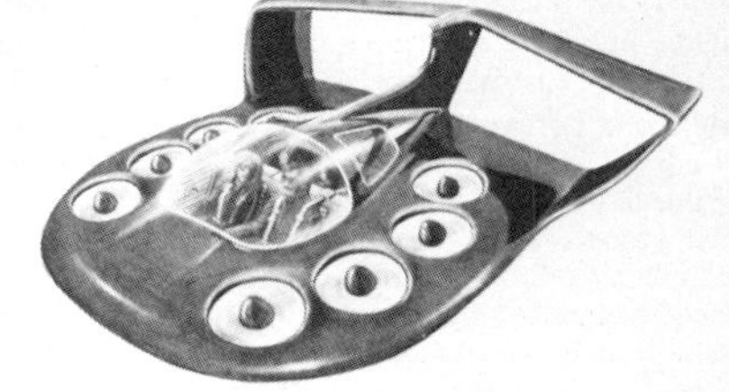

Artist's impression of Moller Model 440E Commuter

MONARCH

MONARCH AVIATION INC

PO Box 520756, Miami, Florida 33152
Telephone: (305) 526 5105
Telex: 51-8767
CHIEF EXECUTIVE OFFICER: Rolando F. Sablon

Monarch Aviation developed all-cargo conversions for the Boeing 727, McDonnell Douglas DC-8 and Lockheed L-1011 TriStar aircraft, and by June 1985 had completed more than 50 conversions and modifications to these airliners.

Details of the Boeing 727-100/-200 conversions were given in the 1985-86 *Jane's*. No new information was received for 1986 publication.

MOONEY

MOONEY AIRCRAFT CORPORATION

PO Box 72, Kerrville, Texas 78028
Telephone: (512) 896 6000
CHAIRMAN: Armand Rivard
VICE-PRESIDENT, MARKETING: Paul Kelly

The original Mooney Aircraft Inc was formed in June 1948, in Wichita, Kansas, from where the single-seat Model M-18 Mooney Mite was produced until 1952. The company transferred to Kerrville, Texas, in 1953 and completed a merger with Alon Inc of McPherson, Kansas, in October 1967. Subsequently, in late 1969, Butler Aviation International acquired 100 per cent stock ownership of Mooney Aircraft, the company name being changed to Aerostar Aircraft Corporation on 1 July 1970. Production of Aerostar aircraft was suspended in early 1972. On 4 October 1973 came news that the Republic Steel Corporation of Cleveland, Ohio, had assumed control of the company, once again named Mooney Aircraft. When Republic merged with LTV Corporation in 1984, ownership of Mooney was taken over by a number of private investors under the title of Mooney Holding Corporation.

In the Spring of 1985 it was announced that M Alexandre Couvelaire, President of the Paris based Euralair/Avialair jet charter and fixed base operator, and M Michel Seydoux, President of MSC, had jointly acquired 70 per cent of Mooney Aircraft, and that Lake Aircraft (which see) had acquired the remaining 30 per cent.

MOONEY 201LM

The original Mooney 201 first flew in June 1976 and received FAA certification in September 1976. The 1986 model, known as the Mooney 201LM Lean Machine, dispenses with all equipment that is not essential while retaining full IFR capability, including an autopilot.

TYPE: Four-seat cabin monoplane.

WINGS: Cantilever low-wing monoplane. Wing section NACA 63_2-215 at root, NACA 64_1-412 at tip. Dihedral 5° 30'. Incidence 2° 30' at root, 1° at tip. Sweepforward 2° 29'. Light alloy structure with flush riveted stretch formed wraparound skins. Full span main spar; rear spar terminates at mid-span of flaps. Sealed-gap differentially operated light alloy ailerons. Electrically operated single-slotted light alloy flaps over 70 per cent of trailing-edge. Vacuum operated, electrically controlled speedbrake optional, in upper surface of each wing at quarter span/two-thirds chord. No tabs.

FUSELAGE: Composite all-metal structure. Cabin section is of welded 4130 chrome molybdenum steel tube with light alloy covering. Rear section is of semi-monocoque construction, with light alloy bulkheads and skin and extruded light alloy stringers.

TAIL UNIT: Cantilever light alloy structure, with variable incidence tailplane. All surfaces covered with wrap-around metal skin.

LANDING GEAR: Electrically retractable levered suspension tricycle type. Nosewheel retracts rearward, main units inward into wings. Rubber disc shock absorbers in main units. Cleveland mainwheels, size 6·00-6, and steerable nosewheel, size 5·00-5. Tyre pressure: mainwheels 2·07 bars (30 lb/sq in), nosewheel 3·38 bars (49 lb/sq in). Cleveland hydraulic single-disc brakes on mainwheels. Parking brakes.

POWER PLANT: One 149 kW (200 hp) Avco Lycoming IO-360-A3B6D flat-four engine, driving a McCauley two-blade constant-speed metal propeller. Q-tip propeller and propeller anti-icing optional. Two integral fuel tanks in wings, with combined usable capacity of 242 litres (64 US gallons). Refuelling points in wing upper surface. Oil capacity 7·5 litres (2 US gallons).

ACCOMMODATION: Cabin accommodates four persons in pairs on individual seats with reclining backs. Fully adjustable seats with lumbar support and luxury fabric or leather trim optional. Dual controls standard. Standard rudder pedals optionally removable to allow more legroom for passenger. Overhead ventilation system. Cabin heating and cooling system, with adjustable outlets and illuminated control. One-piece wraparound windscreen. Tinted Plexiglas windows. Starboard front seat and rear seats removable for freight stowage. Single door on starboard side. Compartment for 54 kg (120 lb) baggage behind cabin, with access from cabin or through door on starboard side. Windscreen defrosting system standard.

SYSTEMS: Hydraulic system for brakes only. Electrical system includes 60A alternator, 12V 35Ah battery, voltage regulator and warning light, together with protective circuit breakers. Standby generator and vacuum system optional. Oxygen system optional.

AVIONICS AND EQUIPMENT: An extensive range of optional avionics by Century, King, Narco and S-Tec, including KAP 100, 150 and Century 31 autopilots, RCA WeatherScout weather radar, 3M Stormscope, and Foster LNS616 Loran C, is available to customer's requirements. Standard equipment includes sensitive altimeter, instrument panel glareshield, sun visors, shoulder harness, annunciator panel with low fuel warning, cabin lights, landing light, navigation lights, taxi light, full flow oil filter, quick oil drain, zinc chromate anti-corrosion treatment, and streamlined propeller spinner. An optional operational package includes blind-flying instrumentation, electric clock, exhaust gas temperature gauge, outside air temperature gauge, turn co-ordinator, microphone jacks, radio master switch, emergency locator transmitter, alternate static source, heated pitot, three light strobe system, com and nav antennae, and cabin speaker. Other optional equipment includes speed-brakes, encoding altimeter, true airspeed indicator, hour meter, de luxe control wheel with map light and microphone button, dual brakes, headrests, all-leather interior furnishing, fuel management system, AM/FM cassette stereo system, cabin fire extinguisher, wingtip recognition lights, pulsating nose mounted landing light, rotating beacon and external power socket.

DIMENSIONS, EXTERNAL:

Wing span	11·00 m (36 ft 1 in)
Wing chord, mean	1·50 m (4 ft 11¼ in)
Wing aspect ratio	7·45
Length overall	7·52 m (24 ft 8 in)
Height overall	2·54 m (8 ft 4 in)
Wheel track	2·76 m (9 ft 0¾ in)
Wheelbase	1·82 m (5 ft 11½ in)
Propeller diameter	1·88 m (6 ft 2 in)
Propeller ground clearance	0·24 m (9½ in)

DIMENSIONS, INTERNAL:

Cabin: Length	2·90 m (9 ft 6 in)
Max width	1·10 m (3 ft 7½ in)
Max height	1·13 m (3 ft 8½ in)
Baggage compartment	0·48 m³ (17 cu ft)

AREA:

Wings, gross	16·24 m² (174·8 sq ft)

WEIGHTS AND LOADINGS:

Weight empty	758 kg (1,671 lb)
Max T-O and landing weight	1,243 kg (2,740 lb)
Max wing loading	76·5 kg/m² (15·67 lb/sq ft)
Max power loading	8·34 kg/kW (13·7 lb/hp)

PERFORMANCE (at max T-O weight):

Never-exceed speed	196 knots (364 km/h; 226 mph)
Max level speed at S/L	175 knots (325 km/h; 202 mph)
Max cruising speed, 75% power at 2,470 m (8,100 ft)	169 knots (314 km/h; 195 mph)
Econ cruising speed, 55% power at 2,470 m (8,100 ft)	145 knots (269 km/h; 167 mph)
Stalling speed:	
flaps up	63 knots (117 km/h; 73 mph) IAS
flaps down	55 knots (102 km/h; 64 mph) IAS
Max rate of climb at S/L	314 m (1,030 ft)/min
Service ceiling	5,730 m (18,800 ft)
T-O to 15 m (50 ft)	463 m (1,517 ft)
Landing from 15 m (50 ft)	491 m (1,610 ft)
Landing run	235 m (770 ft)
Range, 75% power, no reserves	974 nm (1,804 km; 1,121 miles)

MOONEY 205

Introduced in mid-1986, the Mooney 205 is developed from the Mooney 201, but embodies aerodynamic refinements to improve performance, notably in terms of max cruising speed and rate of climb. New landing gear doors fully enclose the main legs and wheels when retracted. The engine cooling flaps have been enlarged and are controlled electrically. A new 28V electrical system gives increased power for cold-weather engine starting and optional avionics. Three new preselected flap positions permit initial extension to 15° at a speed of 132 knots (244 km/h; 152 mph) instead of the former 115 knots (213 km/h; 132 mph). New wingtips incorporate faired navigation and strobe lights. Trailing-edge position lights are standard; high intensity forward facing 'recognition' lights are optional.

The Mooney 205 has an Avco Lycoming IO-360-A3B6D engine, like the 201LM, but can be distinguished externally by its rounded cabin windows and changed paint scheme. Production of the Mooney 205, which received FAA certification on 9 June 1986, was expected to reach 13 per month by September 1986. The aircraft is expected to replace the Mooney 201LM.

DIMENSIONS AND AREAS:
As for Mooney 201LM

WEIGHT:

Max T-O weight	1,243 kg (2,740 lb)

PERFORMANCE (at max T-O weight):

Max level speed	178 knots (330 km/h; 205 mph)
Max cruising speed, 75% power at 2,440 m (8,000 ft)	171 knots (317 km/h; 197 mph)
Stalling speed:	
wheels and flaps up	61 knots (113 km/h; 70 mph) IAS
wheels and flaps down	54 knots (100 km/h; 62 mph) IAS
Max rate of climb at S/L	323 m (1,060 ft)/min
Service ceiling	5,670 m (18,600 ft)
Endurance at max cruising speed	5 h 2 min

MOONEY 252TSE

Mooney introduced the Model 252TSE (Turbo Special Edition) in late 1985 as a replacement for the Turbo Mooney 231, described in the 1985-86 *Jane's*. Externally similar to the Model 231, the Mooney 252TSE differs in having a 156·6 kW (210 hp) Continental TSIO-360-MB-1 engine with Garrett AiResearch TE04 turbocharger with automatic wastegate operation, an intercooler, electric cowl flap, NACA duct for induction air, a 28V electrical system and new landing gear doors which fully enclose the main legs and wheels when retracted. Principal external difference is the rounded cabin window design.

TYPE: Four-seat cabin monoplane.

WINGS: Cantilever low-wing monoplane. Wing section NACA 63_2-215 at root, NCA 64_1-412 at tip. Dihedral 5° 30′. Incidence 2° 30′ at root, 1° at tip. No sweepback, except on wing root leading-edges. Conventional tapered all-metal two-spar structure of light alloy. Horn balanced plain ailerons and electrically actuated trailing-edge flaps of light alloy construction. No tabs.

FUSELAGE AND TAIL UNIT: As for 201LM.

LANDING GEAR: Electrically retractable tricycle type. Steerable nosewheel retracts rearward, main units inward into wings. All wheels faired by doors when retracted. Shock absorption of nosewheel and mainwheel units by Lord rubber discs. Cleveland wheels, with mainwheel tyres size 6·00-6 (6-ply), pressure 2·90 bars (42 lb/sq in). Nosewheel tyre size 5·00-5 (6-ply), pressure 3·38 bars (49 lb/sq in). Cleveland hydraulic brakes. Parking brake.

POWER PLANT: One 156·5 kW (210 hp) Continental TSIO-360-MB-1 flat-six turbocharged engine, driving a McCauley constant-speed metal propeller. Goodrich propeller de-icing optional. Two integral fuel tanks in inner wings, with combined capacity of 297·5 litres (78·6 US gallons), of which 286 litres (75·6 US gallons) are usable. Refuelling points in upper surface of the inboard section of each wing. Oil capacity 7·5 litres (2 US gallons).

ACCOMMODATION: Cabin accommodates four persons in pairs on individual seats. Front seats fully adjustable, with lumbar support. Dual controls standard. Forward hinged door on starboard side. Baggage space aft of rear seat, accessible from cabin and via baggage door on starboard side. Accommodation heated and ventilated.

SYSTEMS: Hydraulic system for brakes only. 28V DC electrical system powered by a 70A engine driven alternator. Dual 70A alternators optional. 28V 20Ah battery. Electric standby vacuum system standard. Oxygen system standard.

AVIONICS AND EQUIPMENT: Avionics options include King 7-A IFR package comprising dual nav/coms, VOR, DME, R/Nav, ADF, and encoding transponder. King KFC 150 integrated flight control system with altitude preselect, S-TEC yaw damper and 3M Stormscope optional. White instrument panel and control wheels optional. Precise Flight speedbrakes optional. Electric propeller de-icing optional.

DIMENSIONS, EXTERNAL AND INTERNAL:
As Mooney 201LM, except:

Length overall	7·75 m (25 ft 5 in)
Height overall	2·51 m (8 ft 3 in)
Tailplane span	3·58 m (11 ft 9 in)
Cabin door (stbd, over wing):	
Height	1·13 m (3 ft 8½in)
Width	0·74 m (2 ft 5 in)
Baggage door (stbd, aft):	
Height	0·52 m (1 ft 8½ in)
Width	0·43 m (1 ft 5 in)
Height to sill	1·17 m (3 ft 10 in)

AREAS:

Wings, gross	16·24 m² (174·8 sq ft)
Ailerons (total)	1·06 m² (11·4 sq ft)
Trailing-edge flaps (total)	1·66 m² (17·9 sq ft)
Fin	0·71 m² (7·7 sq ft)
Rudder	0·52 m² (5·6 sq ft)
Tailplane	1·99 m² (21·42 sq ft)
Elevators	1·21 m² (13·0 sq ft)

WEIGHTS AND LOADINGS:

Weight empty	825 kg (1,820 lb)
Max baggage	54 kg (120 lb)
Max ramp, T-O and landing weight	1,315 kg (2,900 lb)
Max wing loading	80·97 kg/m² (16·6 lb/sq ft)
Max power loading	8·4 kg/kW (13·8 lb/hp)

PERFORMANCE (at max T-O weight):

Max level speed	219 knots (406 km/h; 252 mph)
Max cruising speed, 78% power at 8,230 m (27,000 ft)	200 knots (371 km/h; 230 mph)
Econ cruising speed, 55% power at 7,010 m (23,000 ft)	170 knots (315 km/h; 196 mph)
Stalling speed:	
landing gear and flaps up	61 knots (113 km/h; 71 mph)
landing gear and flaps down	59 knots (110 km/h; 68 mph)
Max rate of climb at S/L	329 m (1,080 ft)/min
Certificated ceiling	8,535 m (28,000 ft)
T-O to 15 m (50 ft)	655 m (2,150 ft)

MOONEY MT20 (TX-1) MILITARY TRAINER

Details of this two-seat primary and military trainer development of the Mooney Turbo 231 may be found in the 1985-86 *Jane's*.

MOONEY 301

Details of this six-seat pressurised light aircraft may be found in the 1985-86 *Jane's*.

MTC

MOSHIER TECHNOLOGIES CORPORATION

599 Fairchild Drive, Mountain View, California 94043
Telephone: (415) 969 9433
CHIEF EXECUTIVE OFFICER: Michael W. Moshier
VICE-PRESIDENT, SPECIAL PROJECTS: Thomas M. Clarke

Moshier Technologies Corporation (MTC) was formed in early 1986 to continue the work of its predecessor, Moshier Technologies, in the development of a small, practical VTOL aircraft. The results of an earlier feasibility study indicated that such an aircraft could be built successfully using many existing off-the-shelf components and technologies.

Design goals established by MTC included a mechanically simple propulsion system, with no moving parts except for those of an advanced turbine engine; a compact airframe with small ground footprint; low acoustic and infra-red signatures; reliability and ease of operation; and multi-fuel capability. A family of such aircraft, collectively known as Aurora, will each incorporate the same generic fluidic propulsion system. The initial variant, known as the Aurora Model 400-M, is being developed for military roles such as personnel transport, reconnaissance, surveillance, rescue, VIP/courier, scout/attack (SCAT) and offensive/defensive duties. MTC proposes to submit the Aurora 400-M as a candidate for the US Army's LHX requirement.

Two- and four-seat commercial derivatives of the aircraft are planned, designated Model 200-C and Model 400-C respectively. MTC foresees these aircraft serving in the business aviation and paramilitary roles such as VIP transport, charter, courier, ambulance/medevac, surveillance, law enforcement, and forest, border and customs patrol duties.

A generic version of the aircraft's fluidic propulsion system has been tested successfully at NASA's Ames facility, and a version matched to the prototype engine of the Aurora 400-M was being developed in the Summer of 1986. After testing of this at the Aeronautical Research Laboratories of Stanford University in Palo Alto, California, MTC will begin construction of the prototype Model 400-M. Once successful hover and low-speed flight trials have been completed, the company will seek joint-venture partners for large scale production.

AURORA MODEL 400-M and MODEL 400-C

The following data, should be regarded as provisional:

TYPE: One- to four-seat VTOL utility aircraft.

AIRFRAME: Semi-monocoque glassfibre and carbonfibre laminated structure over skeletal metal frame.

WINGS: Cantilever main wings at rear of airframe, with sweepback and slight anhedral. Outward-canted winglet at each tip. Cantilever canard surfaces, forward swept and with slight anhedral.

LANDING GEAR: Retractable tricycle type with skids.

POWER PLANT: One turbofan engine of unspecified type rated at 8·01 kN (1,800 lb st). Fluidic amplification propulsion system, nominal ratio 1·8:1, nominal entrainment ratio 20:1, with no moving parts, claimed low dynamic pressure and exhaust temperature, and substantial noise attenuation. Fuel capacity 227 litres (60 US gallons).

ACCOMMODATION: One to four seats in enclosed cabin with upward opening 'gull wing' doors.

SYSTEMS: Fly by wire and fly by light three-axis control system, with second level redundancy.

DIMENSIONS, EXTERNAL:

Wing span	5·79 m (19 ft 0 in)
Length overall	5·03 m (16 ft 6 in)
Width of fuselage	1·22 m (4 ft 0 in)
Height (without skids)	1·52 m (5 ft 0 in)

WEIGHTS AND LOADING:

Weight empty	497 kg (1,095 lb)
Max T-O weight	964 kg (2,125 lb)
Max wing loading	85·5 kg/m² (17·5 lb/sq ft)

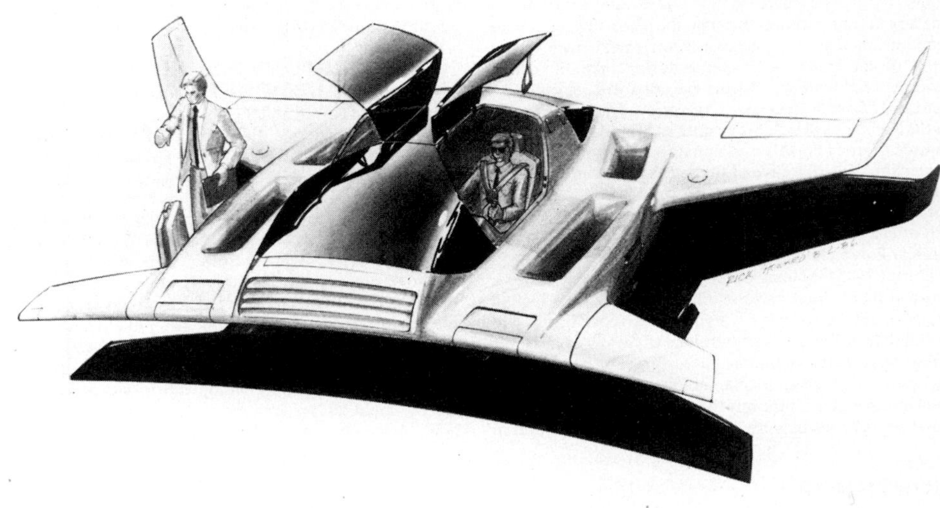

Artist's impression of Moshier Technologies Corporation Aurora Model 400-C VTOL aircraft

PERFORMANCE (estimated, S/L, ISA):

Max level speed	above 195 knots (362 km/h; 225 mph)
Cruising speed, 25% power	195 knots (362 km/h; 225 mph)
Hover ceiling	2,285 m (7,500 ft)

Range, standard flight profile of 3% engine operation in ground idle, 5% in VTOL/hover/translation, 92% in cruising flight more than 347 nm (644 km; 400 miles)

NASA

NATIONAL AERONAUTICS AND SPACE ADMINISTRATION

400 Mayland Avenue SW, Washington, DC 20546

Telephone: (202) 755 2320

PUBLIC AFFAIRS OFFICER: Debra J. Rahn

NASA has several research programmes involving the use of specially equipped or modified aircraft. Details of some of these follow:

NASA AILERON-RUDDER INTERCONNECT PROGRAMME

NASA has modified the basic analog flight control system of a Grumman F-14 Tomcat to demonstrate an aileron-rudder interconnect (ARI), which is designed to co-ordinate turns, prevent wing rock and resist spins under high angle of attack flight conditions. Early configurations were successfully flight tested, but displayed loss of roll power at high angles of attack. In June 1985 NASA resumed flight testing with a new 'cross control' feature which allows the pilot to roll the aircraft in the opposite direction to lateral control stick input, but in the direction of rudder pedal input. This gives the F-14 the roll power needed for tactical manoeuvring at high angles of attack. A 21-flight test programme conducted by NASA, Grumman and US Navy pilots was completed on 9 August 1985. The US Navy is evaluating the ARI programme for possible modifications to its F-14 fleet.

NASA F-14 AIRFLOW EXPERIMENTS

NASA's Ames-Dryden Flight Research Facility is conducting a series of flight tests using a Grumman F-14 Tomcat equipped with a laminar flow wing glove designed by Boeing Commercial Airplane Company. The glove, constructed from a glassfibre/foam composite, is expected to smooth the airflow over the wing and lead to more efficient flight at subsonic and transonic speeds. Measuring devices are embedded in the gloves during manufacture, enabling researchers to record information at varying angles of wing sweep from 20 to 35°. The modified F-14A (NASA 834) flew for the first time on 25 February 1986. The first phase of the programme, comprising some 15-20 flights, uses a glove on the aircraft's port wing that simulates the F-14A's aerofoil to record baseline data for comparison with the second phase of 35-40 flights using a glove designed for flight at Mach 0·7-0·8. A similar wing glove has been tested on a McDonnell Douglas F-15.

NASA ADVANCED TRANSPORT OPERATING SYSTEMS RESEARCH VEHICLE

The Advanced Transport Operating Systems (ATOPS) programme, formerly the Terminal Configured Vehicle programme, conducts research to develop and evaluate aircraft and flight management technology to improve efficiency, capacity and safety in transport aircraft operations. The objective and programme elements were listed in the 1982-83 and earlier editions of *Jane's*.

Test vehicle for the programme is a Boeing 737-100 with a second (rear) flight deck and an array of computers and monitors installed in the passenger cabin. The aircraft is designed to be flown from the forward flight deck with the conventional controls, and from the rear flight deck using a fly by wire digital computer system. From the rear flight deck, the aircraft can be flown with advanced electronic displays and pilot selectable automatic navigation, guidance and control systems. Safety is assured through monitoring, and by takeover capability of the forward flight deck crew. A series of development and demonstration activities is being conducted to develop practical systems and to solicit and encourage acceptance by flight crews and the airlines. A Sperry Corporation colour EFIS display was due to be installed in the Boeing 737-100 in September 1985, replacing monochrome displays. The EFIS includes eight cockpit display units with software to drive attitude, navigation, engine and system displays, and to permit the creation of new display formats or modification of existing ones.

F-106B STORM HAZARDS TESTS

NASA's Langley Research Center is using a Convair F-106B to penetrate storm cloud areas as part of a study into the effects of lightning strikes on aircraft. The Storm Hazards F-106B began storm cell penetrations in 1980, when only ten lightning strikes were recorded. In 1983 the aircraft was struck 250 times. Rates of current rise approaching 100 billion amperes per second have been recorded by sensors in the F-106B's nose boom, and the data are providing NASA with criteria for future lightning strike protection on commercial aircraft, particularly in regard to the effects on composites materials and electronic flight control systems. The F-106B also collects data for research studies on turbulence, wind shear, and heavy rain effects.

GENERAL AVIATION STALL/SPIN FLIGHT RESEARCH

Flight experiments conducted by NASA Langley have shown that a discontinuous wing leading-edge design can provide a large increase in outer wing panel stall angle of attack and a significant improvement in spin resistance without significantly affecting performance or utility. The discontinuous wing leading-edge was first tested in 1978 on a modified AA-1 Yankee, followed by tests on a modified Beech C23 Sundowner, and has most recently been applied to a modified Piper PA-28R Arrow. Prior to wing leading-edge modification, these aircraft would spin over 90 per cent of the times that pro-spin controls were applied. With the modification, the aircraft are highly spin resistant, spinning only 5 per cent of the times that pro-spin controls are applied, and then only with power on and abused loading and aggravated control inputs. The NASA stall/spin research Piper Arrow is fully instrumented for flight test and is equipped with a spin recovery parachute system, quick release door, and a pyrotechnic system that will cleanly cut a door-sized opening in the port side of the fuselage beside the pilot. The outboard half of the leading-edge of each wing incorporates a discontinuous drooped leading-edge of NASA design. Cameras mounted at the wingtips and inside the cabin record airflow over the tufted wings.

Current research effort is on the development of analytical techniques for predicting stall and spin characteristics and on establishing reliable design methods. Future research will be directed at designs for twin-engined aircraft and the extension of single-engine prediction methods to analyse separated airflow on three-dimensional wings, automatic spin prevention systems, and the effects of advanced aerofoil designs on stall and spin resistance.

JETSTAR LAMINAR FLOW CONTROL

NASA is testing a concept of removing the layer of air molecules next to an aircraft's wing surface to increase the flight efficiency of transport aircraft. A Lockheed JetStar has been fitted with laminar flow control systems on the leading-edge of each wing, encased in metallic aerofoil gloves. The system installed on the aircraft's port wing was designed by Lockheed-Georgia and consists of a sandwich of Nomex honeycomb core and graphite epoxy face sheets, covered by a thin sheet of titanium, run the length of the section. Air is drawn through them via 27 spanwise slots within the wing and into the fuselage. A test section on the JetStar's right wing was manufactured by the Douglas Aircraft Company, and has 800 electron beam drilled microscopic holes per square inch of wing surface. Both systems have means of keeping the wing surfaces clean and

NASA's modified Piper PA-28R Arrow with discontinuous wing leading-edge modification

free from ice or impacted insects. The Lockheed system pumps a propylene glycol methyl ether (PGME) and water mixture to the surface through the slots. The Douglas concept employs a retractable insect shield deployed in front of the leading-edge panel during take-off, climb, descent and landing. When extended the shield also increases lift, and when not in use is stored in the underside of the leading-edge box. Spray nozzles behind the shield can be used to spray PGME/water mixture for additional insect protection. The objective of the JetStar flight programme, which is a co-operative effort between NASA's Langley, Virginia and Ames/Dryden Research Facilities, is to establish a technology base for future industry exploitation of laminar flow technology.

During 1985 the laminar flow control JetStar undertook a series of flights from bases in different parts of the United States to test the systems in varying climatic conditions and to simulate airline service conditions as closely as possible. These tests were continuing in early 1986. The aircraft carries a Knollenberg probe, mounted on the top of the fuselage, to measure precisely the number and size of ice and water particles encountered in flight. For ice prevention in winter conditions, glycol is forced through the porous metal section of the starboard wing leading-edge shield section, in addition to the PGME/water mix.

NASA/US NAVY F-8 OBLIQUE-WING DEMONSTRATOR

In late 1984 NASA and the US Navy signed an agreement to flight test an oblique wing variable-sweep demonstrator aircraft, based on NASA's LTV F-8 Crusader digital fly by wire research aircraft. The oblique wing concept was first tested on NASA's AD-1 subsonic experimental aircraft in 1979. The second phase of the programme covers a 12 month period of preliminary design of the F-8's oblique wing, its pivot and flight control software, and the first work by two or more contractors was scheduled to begin in mid-1985. On 13 November 1985 NASA awarded a contract for preliminary design of the oblique wing to Rockwell International's North American Aircraft Operations Division. Subsequent contracts will cover construction and ground testing of the oblique wing demonstrator, with an initial one year, 40-flight test programme expected to begin in January 1989.

The oblique wing F-8 is expected to be capable of speeds up to at least Mach 1·4 with a maximum wing sweep of 60-65°. The first year's flight test programme will be aimed at expanding the flight envelope of the oblique wing configuration, demonstrating its transonic and supersonic capabilities, with some emphasis on high altitude cruise and manoeuvring capabilities, and adapting the modular software of the F-8's digital flight computers to accommodate the characteristics of the oblique wing. Potential applications for future US Navy aircraft include the use of oblique wings on carrier based air defence aircraft, on which the straight-wing configuration could be used for take-off, landing and loiter, and the oblique position for high speed interception of hostile targets.

The NASA/US Navy agreement followed a nine-month feasibility study by Rockwell International. Among benefits highlighted by the Rockwell study for shipboard applications of the oblique wing are a 12-15 per cent weight saving over conventional variable geometry aircraft, and a substantial reduction in deck space required for storage aboard aircraft carriers, because the wing can be pivoted until it is almost aligned with the fuselage.

NORTHROP

NORTHROP CORPORATION

1840 Century Park East, Los Angeles, California 90067
Telephone: (213) 553 6262
Telex: 192893

CHAIRMAN OF THE BOARD AND CHIEF EXECUTIVE OFFICER:
Thomas V. Jones

PRESIDENT AND CHIEF OPERATING OFFICER:
Frank W. Lynch

SENIOR VICE-PRESIDENTS:
Stanley Ebner (Government Relations)
William M. Elliott (General Counsel)
Welko E. Gasich (Executive Vice-President, Programmes)
C. Robert Gates (International)
Donald A. Hicks (Marketing and Technology)
Roy P. Jackson (Operations)
Kent Kresa (Technology Development and Planning)
William G. McGagh (Finance)
John J. Richardson (Human Resources)
Wallace C. Solberg (Operations)

GROUP AND DIVISION VICE-PRESIDENTS:
David N. Ferguson (Electronics Systems Group)
Joseph T. Gallagher (Aircraft)
Gene W. Hauser (Electronics)
L. Bruce James (Ventura)
Fred J. Manzella (Aircraft Services)
John R. Moore (Electro-Mechanical)
John Patierno (Advanced Systems)
Robert Schlenzig (Defense Systems)
Joseph Yamron (Precision Products)

SUBSIDIARY PRESIDENTS:
J. William Jenkins (Northrop Services Inc)
W. J. Shaddix (Northrop Worldwide Aircraft Services Inc)
Jaime Oaxaca (Wilcox Electric Inc)

OTHER VICE-PRESIDENTS:
James H. Ahmann (Military Requirements Analysis)
C. H. Bernstein (Asst to Chief Executive Officer for Analysis)
Louis C. Breckenridge (Central Regional Office)
Albert E. Brewster (Legislative Affairs)
John B. Campbell (Controller)
Ralph D. Crosby Jr (Washington Office)
Les Daly (Public Affairs)
H. W. Deffebach (International Programmes)
James A. Dorsey (Senior Corporate Executive, Pacific Far East)
William A. Fifer (Senior Corporate Executive, Middle East)
Donald D. Foulds (Countertrade)
George J. Friedman (Engineering and Long-Range Planning)
Robert E. Grovert (Senior Corporate Executive, Europe)
W. Richard Howard (Information Resource Management)
H. L. Janssen (Human Resources Planning and Development)
Joe C. Jones (Asst to Chief Executive Officer for Aeronautical Systems)
J. Gaston Kent Jr (Materiel, Facilities and Services)
Milton Kuska (F-5 Programmes and Aircraft Division Marketing)
Stephen J. Lukasik (Technology)
James C. Roche (Analysis Centre)
Stephen R. Smith (Manager, F-20 Programme)
Robert B. Watts Jr (Asst General Counsel)
Dr Max Weiss (Manager, Northrop Research and Technology Center)

CORPORATE TREASURER: Richard B. Lohrer

VICE-PRESIDENT AND CORPORATE SECRETARY:
Sheila M. Gibbons

EXECUTIVE ASST TO CHAIRMAN AND CHIEF EXECUTIVE OFFICER: D. D. Berry

DIRECTOR OF PUBLIC AFFAIRS—EUROPE, MIDDLE EAST AND AFRICA: J. K. Corfield

DIRECTOR, PUBLIC INFORMATION: A. W. Cantafio

This company was formed in 1939 by John K. Northrop and others to undertake the design and manufacture of military aircraft. Although continuing its activities in the design, development and production of aircraft, missiles and target drone systems, Northrop has broadened its scope of operation to include electronics, space technology, communications, support services and commercial products. To reflect this changing character of its business, the company changed its name from Northrop Aircraft Inc to Northrop Corporation in 1959. Since January 1982, its operations have been handled by an Aircraft Group, an Electronics Systems Group, and a Services Group, comprising three, five, and three related divisions/operating subsidiaries respectively.

Aircraft Group consists of four divisions and a wholly-owned subsidiary. The Aircraft Division is responsible for the design and manufacture of fighter aircraft and the manufacture of commercial aircraft major assemblies. Advanced Systems Division manages a number of aerospace programmes and is prime contractor to the USAF for research and development of the Advanced Technology Bomber. Ventura Division activities are described in the RPVs and Targets section. Aircraft Services Division provides technical and support services, as does subsidiary Northrop Worldwide Aircraft Services Inc, of Lawton, Oklahoma. Electronics Systems Group comprises an Electronics Division; Electro-Mechanical Division, which handles advanced missile programmes, electro-optical systems for target identification and target designation; Defense Systems Division, designer and manufacturer of electronics countermeasures systems, including the internal countermeasures set (ICS) for the US Air Force's F-15 Eagle; Precision Products Division; and Wilcox Electric Inc of Kansas City, Missouri. Services Group comprises an Aircraft Services Division; Northrop Services Inc, which provides technical support to NASA at Johnson Space Center in Houston, Texas, the Environmental Protection Agency, the National Institute of Health and the National Cancer Institute; and Northrop Worldwide Aircraft Services, Inc, of Lawton, Oklahoma.

Northrop had 48,000 employees in mid-1986.

NORTHROP CORPORATION AIRCRAFT GROUP

1840 Century Park East, Los Angeles, California 90067
Telephone: (213) 553 6262

GROUP VICE-PRESIDENT: Kent Kresa

VICE-PRESIDENT, BUSINESS OPERATIONS: Richard S. Taylor

VICE-PRESIDENT, INTERNATIONAL BUSINESS OPERATIONS:
L. Duke Golden

VICE-PRESIDENT, ADVANCED TACTICAL SYSTEMS:
Delbert H. Jacobs

DIRECTOR, BUSINESS DEVELOPMENT PLANNING AND ANALYSIS: Gregory W. Jordan

DIRECTOR, ADMINISTRATION: Haven C. Brown

GROUP COUNSEL: Robert B. Watts Jr

Aircraft Division:

One Northrop Avenue, Hawthorne, California 90250
Telephone: (213) 970 2000

VICE-PRESIDENT AND GENERAL MANAGER:
Joseph T. Gallagher

VICE-PRESIDENTS:
Brian Boyer (Manager, Central Manufacturing)
Thomas T. Burger (F/A-18 Programme Manager)
David J. Deering (Integrated Logistics Support)
M. Elkin (Materiel and Offset)
Walter E. Fellers (Chief Designer)
Jack E. Gibilisco (Manufacturing Operations)
Robert A. Graham (Marketing)
J. Michael Hateley (Human Resources & Administration)
Milton Kuska (F-5 Programmes and Division Marketing)
Ed G. Linhart (Central Manufacturing)
M. W. Moberly (Contracts & Pricing)
Lewis A. Nelson (Manager, F-5 and T-38 programmes)
Thomas R. Rooney (Engineering and Advanced Development)
Robert W. Slusser (Information Resources)
Carl Swartz (Division Counsel)
R. S. Taylor (Finance)
S. E. Weeks (Quality Assurance)
Ron Wyatt (Manager, Military Production F/A-18 and F-5 programmes)

Current production at Northrop's Aircraft Division, which has more than 15,500 employees, is centred on the F-5E Tiger II fighter, F-5F two-seat fighter/trainer, RF-5E TigerEye reconnaissance version, F-20 Tigershark fighter, F/A-18A Hornet multi-mission fighter, and major Boeing 747 subcontract work, which includes manufacture of the main fuselage section, the extra-large side loading cargo door, passenger doors and the stretched upper deck of the 747-300.

Northrop is principal subcontractor for the McDonnell Douglas F/A-18A Hornet multi-mission fighter (which see). The company has design and production responsibility for the centre and rear fuselage and the twin vertical tails, including internal systems such as fuel, the environmental control system and auxiliary power system. The 500th shipset of these components was delivered in June 1986. Planned production exceeds 1,660 aircraft, including US Navy, US Marine Corps, Australian, Canadian and Spanish orders.

Northrop has been selected as prime contractor to proceed with research and development of US Air Force advanced technology bomber (ATB) concepts. Key members of the team include Boeing, LTV and General Electric Company Aircraft Engine Group. Details of the programme are classified.

The company is also engaged in research projects involving advanced simulators and composite materials, and is teamed with McDonnell Douglas Corporation in proposals for the USAF's advanced tactical fighter (ATF) programme.

The Aircraft Services Division is working with the Royal Saudi Air Force to provide support for RSAF technical resources, and also provides contracted maintenance and technical training programmes to international military and commercial operators.

NORTHROP TIGER II

USAF designations: F-5E and F-5F

The F-5E was selected in November 1970 by the US government as the winner of a competition to determine the single-seat International Fightr Aircraft (IFA) which was to succeed Northrop's F-5A. The two-seat F-5F was developed subsequently.

The F-5E design places particular emphasis on manoeuvrability by the incorporation of auto-manoeuvring flaps. Full span leading-edge flaps work in conjunction with conventional trailing-edge flaps, and are operated automatically in response to airspeed and angle of attack. The flaps may also be pilot controlled to full down and full up positions. Wing loading is maintained at approximately the same value as on the F-5A, as the result of an increase in area due principally to the widened fuselage, which also increases wing span. The tapered wing leading-edge extension, between the inboard leading-edge and fuselage, was refined to increase the wing area and maximise the lift coefficient of the wing.

The F-5E incorporates other features developed for the Canadian, Dutch and Norwegian F-5s, including two-position nosewheel gear, which increases wing angle of attack on the ground by 3° 22′. In conjunction with the more powerful engines, this improves F-5E take-off performance by some 30 per cent compared with earlier F-5s.

The first F-5E made its first flight on 11 August 1972. USAF Tactical Air Command, with assistance from Air Training Command, was assigned responsibility for training pilots and technicians of user countries. First deliveries, to the US Air Force's 425th Tactical Fighter Squadron, were made in the Spring of 1973, and deliveries to foreign countries began in early 1974. In addition to their use as tactical fighters, F-5Es are operated by the US Air Force, US Navy and US Marine Corps in the 'aggressor' role, to simulate enemy aircraft at major air combat training schools in the USA, England and the Philippines.

In March 1985 the USAF announced plans to upgrade its fleet of 74 F-5Es and F-5Fs. The programme will include new Emerson AN/APQ-159(V)5 radar in the F-5Es and AN/APQ-159(V)6 in F-5Fs, replacing the current APQ-153 radar. The new radars will double detection range and incorporate off-boresight target acquisition and track-while-scan. A new radar warning receiver and radar jammer will also be installed. Northrop will modify the control column grips on the USAF's 70 F-5Es to standardise them with those on the F-5F, and will transfer radar control switches from panel mounts to the control column hand grip.

By January 1986 there were firm commitments for 1,160 F-5Es and 237 F-5Fs, and production was continuing at the rate of three a month. Customers for the F-5E and F-5F have included Bahrain, Brazil, Chile, Ecuador, Ethiopia, Indonesia, Iran, Jordan, Kenya, South Korea, Malaysia, Mexico, Morocco, Philippines, Saudi Arabia, Singapore, Sudan, Switzerland, Taiwan, Thailand, Tunisia, USA and North Yemen.

Current production versions of the Tiger II are as follows:

F-5E. Standard production version, to which the detailed description applies. In production also, under licence, by AIDC in Taiwan and by KA in Korea (which see). Assembly of F-5Es and F-5Fs by the Swiss Federal Aircraft Factory was completed in March 1985. The current Northrop production version has handling quality improvements resulting from installation of a shark-nose radome, automatic leading-edge and trailing-edge manoeuvring flaps, and a larger leading-edge extension.

To extend the range of armament options, certification has been completed for a centreline mounted General Electric 30 mm gun pod firing GAU-8 ammunition.

The F-5Es for seven customer countries have a Litton LN-33 inertial navigation system, capable of accuracy exceeding 1·5 nm (2·7 km; 1·7 miles) CEP per flight hour, which provides attitude reference, range and bearing to preset destinations, as well as true ground track steering. The system is self aligning in 10 min in the gyro compass mode, and can be aligned in 3 min to a stored heading.

F-5F. Tandem two-seat version of F-5E, with fuselage lengthened by 1·22 m (4 ft 0 in). Fire control system and one M39 cannon retained, enabling aircraft to be used for both training and combat duties. First flight was made on 25 September 1974. Two F-5Fs completed flight test and qualification in early 1976. Deliveries began in the Summer of 1976.

RF-5E TigerEye. Reconnaissance version, described separately.

The following details refer to the F-5E, but are generally applicable to the F-5F also, except for details noted under model listings:

TYPE: Single-seat light tactical fighter.

WINGS: Cantilever low-wing monoplane. Wing section NACA 65A004·8 (modified). No dihedral. No incidence. Sweepback at quarter-chord 24°. Multi-spar light alloy structure with heavy plate machined skins. Hydraulically powered sealed-gap ailerons at approximately mid span. Electrically operated light alloy single-slotted trailing-edge flaps inboard of ailerons. Electrically operated leading-edge flaps. No de-icing system.

FUSELAGE: Light alloy semi-monocoque basic structure, with steel, magnesium and titanium used in certain areas. Two hydraulically actuated airbrakes of magnesium alloy, mounted on underside of fuselage forward of mainwheel wells. Rear avionics bay and cockpit pressurised; fail-safe structure in pressurised sections.

TAIL UNIT: Cantilever all-metal structure, with hydraulically powered rudder and one-piece all-moving tailplane. Tailplane incidence varied by hydraulic actuators. No trim tabs. Dual hydraulic actuators of Northrop design for control of rudder and tailplane.

LANDING GEAR: Hydraulically retractable tricycle type, main units retracting inward into fuselage, nosewheel forward. Oleo-pneumatic shock absorbers of Northrop design in all units. Two-position extending nose unit increases static angle of attack by 3° 22′ to reduce T-O distance, and is shortened automatically during the retraction cycle. Gravity operated emergency extension. Mainwheels and tyres size 24 × 8·00-13, pressure 14·48 bars (210 lb/sq in). Steerable nose unit with wheel and tyre size 18 × 6·50-8, pressure 8·27 bars (120 lb/sq in). All-metal multiple-disc brakes of Northrop design.

POWER PLANT: Two General Electric J85-GE-21B turbojet engines, each rated at 22·24 kN (5,000 lb st) with afterburning. Two independent fuel systems, one for each engine. Fuel for starboard engine supplied from two rubber impregnated nylon fabric bladder cells, comprising a centre fuselage cell of 803 litre (212 US gallon) capacity, and a rear fuselage cell of 640 litre (169 US gallon) capacity. Port engine supplied from a forward fuselage cell of 1,120 litre (296 US gallon) capacity. Total internal fuel capacity 2,563 litres (677 US gallons) in F-5E, 2,555 litres (675 US gallons) in F-5F. No fuel is carried in the wings. Fuel crossfeed system allows fuel from either or both cell systems to be fed to either or both engines. Auxiliary jettisonable fuel tanks of 568 or 1,041 litres (150 or 275 US gallons) can be carried on the fuselage centreline pylon and the inboard underwing pylons. Single refuelling point on lower fuselage for fuselage fuel cell and external tank installation. Oil capacity 4·5 litres (1·2 US gallons) per engine.

Northrop F-5E (nearest camera) and two-seat F-5F

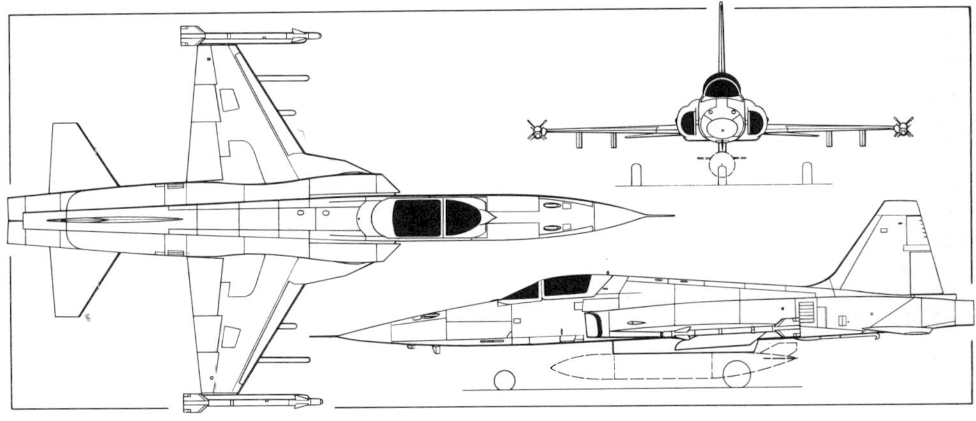

Northrop F-5E Tiger II single-seat twin-jet tactical fighter aircraft *(Pilot Press)*

ENGINE INTAKES: Intakes are supplemented with auxiliary air inlet doors for use during T-O and low-speed flight, to improve compressor face pressure recovery and to decrease distortion. Each door consists of a set of six pivot mounted louvres in removable panels on each side of the fuselage. The doors are actuated by the pilot at T-O, and controlled automatically in flight by Mach sensor switches, and are maintained in the open position at airspeeds below Mach 0·35-0·4.

ACCOMMODATION: Pilot only, in pressurised, heated and air-conditioned cockpit, on rocket powered ejection seat. Upward opening canopy, hinged at rear.

SYSTEMS: Cockpit and rear avionics bay pressurised, heated and air-conditioned by engine bleed air, max pressure differential 0·34 bars (5 lb/sq in). Hydraulic power supplied by two independent systems at a pressure of 207 bars (3,000 lb/sq in), maximum flow rate 32·9 litres (8·7 US gallons) per minute, with non-separated type reservoirs, engine bleed air pressurised at 1·10 bars (16·0 lb/sq in). Flight control system provides power solely for operation of primary flight control surfaces. Utility system provides hydraulic backup power for primary flight control surfaces and operating power for the landing gear, landing gear doors, airbrakes, wheel brakes, nosewheel steering, gun bay purge doors, gun gas deflectors and stability augmentation system. Electrical power supplied by two 13/15kVA 115/200V three-phase 320-480Hz non-paralleled engine driven alternators. Each alternator has the capacity to accept full aircraft power load via an automatic transfer function. 250VA 115V 400Hz single-phase solid state static inverter provides secondary AC source for engine starting. Two 33A 26-32V transformer-rectifiers and a 24V 13Ah nickel-cadmium battery provide DC power. Liquid oxygen system with capacity of 5 litres.

AVIONICS AND EQUIPMENT (F-5E): AN/ARC-164 UHF command radio, 7,000-channel with 25kHz spacing. Emerson Electric AN/APQ-159 lightweight micro-miniature pulse radar for air-to-air search for target detection with range and angle tracking; target information, at a range of up to 20 nm (37 km; 23 miles), is displayed on a 0·13 m (5 in) DVST (direct view storage tube) in cockpit. AN/ASG-31 lead computing optical sight; AN/ARA-50 UHF ADF; AN/AIC-25 intercom; AN/APX-101 IFF; AN/ARN-118 Tacan; attitude and heading reference system; angle of attack system; and central air data computer. Full blind-flying instrumentation. Optional avionics include Litton LN-33 inertial navigation system; AN/ARN-108 instrument landing system; CPU-129/A flight director computer; VHF; VOR/ILS with DME; LF ADF; CRT with scan converter for radar or electro-optical weapon (AGM-65 Maverick); AN/ALE-40 countermeasures dispenser system; and Itek AN/ALR-46 digital or analog radar warning receiver.

AVIONICS AND EQUIPMENT (F-5F): As detailed for F-5E. Optional equipment includes the Northrop AN/AVQ-27 laser target designation set.

ARMAMENT (F-5E): Two AIM-9 Sidewinder missiles on wingtip launchers. Two M39A2 20 mm cannon in fuselage nose, with 280 rds/gun. Up to 3,175 kg (7,000 lb) of mixed ordnance can be carried on one underfuselage and four underwing stations, including M129 leaflet bombs; up to nine Mk 82 GP and Snakeye 500 lb bombs; Mk 36 destructors; Mk 84 2,000 lb bomb; Matra Durandal air-to-surface missiles; LAU-68 (7) 2·75 in rockets; LAU-3 (19) 2·75 in rockets; CBU-24, -49, -52 or -58 cluster bomb units; SUU-20 bomb and rocket packs; SUU-25 flare dispensers; TDU-10 tow targets (Dart); and RMU-10 reel (Dart). Lead computing optical gunsight uses inputs from airborne radar for air-to-air missiles and cannon, and provides a roll stabilised manually depressible reticle aiming reference for air-to-ground delivery. A 'snapshoot' capability is included for attack on violently manoeuvring and fleeting targets. The gunsight incorporates also a detachable 16 mm reticle camera with 15 m (50 ft) film magazine. Optional ordnance capability includes the AGM-65 Maverick; centreline multiple ejector rack; and laser guided bombs.

ARMAMENT (F-5F): Two AIM-9 Sidewinder missiles on wingtip launchers. One M39 20 mm cannon in port side of nose with 140 rounds. Underfuselage and underwing stores as detailed for the F-5E.

DIMENSIONS, EXTERNAL:

Wing span	8·13 m (26 ft 8 in)
Wing span over missiles	8·53 m (27 ft 11⅞ in)

Wing chord: at root 3·57 m (11 ft 8⅝ in)
at tip 0·68 m (2 ft 2⅞ in)
Wing aspect ratio 3·88
Length overall (incl nose probe):
F-5E 14·45 m (47 ft 4¾ in)
F-5F 15·65 m (51 ft 4 in)
Height overall: F-5E 4·07 m (13 ft 4¼ in)
F-5F 4·13 m (13 ft 2 in)
Tailplane span 4·31 m (14 ft 1½ in)
Wheel track 3·80 m (12 ft 5½ in)
Wheelbase: F-5E 5·17 m (16 ft 11½ in)
F-5F 6·52 m (21 ft 1½ in)

AREAS:
Wings, basic 17·3 m² (186·0 sq ft)
Ailerons (total) 0·86 m² (9·24 sq ft)
Trailing-edge flaps (total) 1·95 m² (21·0 sq ft)
Leading-edge flaps (total) 1·14 m² (12·3 sq ft)
Fin 3·85 m² (41·42 sq ft)
Rudder 0·57 m² (6·10 sq ft)
Tailplane 5·48 m² (59·0 sq ft)

WEIGHTS AND LOADINGS:
Weight empty: F-5E 4,410 kg (9,723 lb)
F-5F 4,797 kg (10,576 lb)
Max internal fuel weight: F-5E 1,996 kg (4,400 lb)
F-5F 1,991 kg (4,390 lb)
Max external fuel weight:
F-5E/F-5F 2,415 kg (5,324 lb)
Max T-O weight: F-5E 11,214 kg (24,722 lb)
F-5F 11,409 kg (25,152 lb)
Max landing weight: F-5F 11,406 kg (25,147 lb)
Max zero-fuel weight: F-5E 7,953 kg (17,534 lb)
Max wing loading: F-5E 649·4 kg/m² (133 lb/sq ft)
Max power loading: F-5E 251·6 kg/kN (2·5 lb/lb st)

PERFORMANCE (F-5E at combat weight of 6,055 kg; 13,350 lb, F-5F at combat weight of 6,375 kg; 14,055 lb, unless stated otherwise):
Never-exceed speed
710 knots (1,314 km/h; 817 mph) EAS
Max level speed at 10,975 m (36,000 ft):
F-5E Mach 1·64
F-5F Mach 1·56
Max cruising speed:
F-5E at 10,975 m (36,000 ft) Mach 0·98
Econ cruising speed Mach 0·80
Stalling speed, flaps down, power off:
F-5E 124 knots (230 km/h; 143 mph)
F-5F 136 knots (253 km/h; 157 mph)
Max rate of climb at S/L:
F-5E 10,516 m (34,500 ft)/min
F-5F 10,030 m (32,900 ft)/min
Service ceiling: F-5E 15,790 m (51,800 ft)
F-5F 15,485 m (50,800 ft)
Service ceiling, one engine out:
F-5E over 12,495 m (41,000 ft)
F-5F 12,285 m (40,300 ft)
T-O run:
F-5E at 7,053 kg (15,550 lb) 610 m (2,000 ft)
F-5F at 7,371 kg (16,250 lb) 701 m (2,300 ft)
T-O run at max T-O weight:
F-5E 1,737 m (5,700 ft)
F-5F 1,829 m (6,000 ft)
T-O to 15 m (50 ft):
F-5E at 7,053 kg (15,550 lb) 884 m (2,900 ft)
F-5F at 7,371 kg (16,250 lb) 975 m (3,200 ft)
Landing from 15 m (50 ft):
F-5E at 5,230 kg (11,530 lb), without brake-chute
1,417 m (4,650 ft)
F-5F at 5,554 kg (12,245 lb), without brake-chute
1,524 m (5,000 ft)
Landing run with brake-chute:
F-5E at 5,230 kg (11,530 lb) 762 m (2,500 ft)
F-5F at 5,554 kg (12,245 lb) 792 m (2,600 ft)
Combat radius, F-5E:
with max fuel, two Sidewinder missiles, reserves for 20 min max endurance at S/L and 5 min combat with max afterburning power at 4,575 m (15,000 ft)
570 nm (1,056 km; 656 miles)
with 2,358 kg (5,200 lb) ordnance load, two Sidewinder missiles, max fuel, allowances as above and 5 min combat at military power at S/L, lo-lo-lo mission
120 nm (222 km; 138 miles)
with max fuel, two Sidewinder missiles and two 530 lb bombs, allowances as above and 5 min combat at military power at S/L, hi-lo-hi mission
480 nm (890 km; 553 miles)
Combat radius, F-5F:
with max internal fuel, and allowances comprising 2 min at normal thrust, 1 min at max thrust, 5 min max thrust for combat at 4,575 m (15,000 ft), 20 min loiter at S/L, plus reserve of 5% of initial fuel
520 nm (964 km; 599 miles)
with max fuel, two Sidewinder missiles and two 530 lb bombs, allowances as above, and 5 min combat at military power at S/L, hi-lo-hi mission
450 nm (834 km; 518 miles)
Range, F-5E:
with max fuel and reserves for 20 min max endurance at S/L:
tanks retained 1,340 nm (2,483 km; 1,543 miles)
tanks dropped 1,545 nm (2,863 km; 1,779 miles)

RF-5E TigerEye, showing undernose windows for the installation of cameras and infra-red equipment

Range, F-5F:
ferry range with max fuel, allowances comprising 5 min at normal thrust, 1 min at max thrust, 20 min loiter at S/L, plus reserve of 5% of initial fuel:
crew of two 1,270 nm (2,353 km; 1,462 miles)

NORTHROP RF-5E TIGEREYE

In March 1978, Northrop announced receipt of US government approval for a company funded development and flight demonstration programme of an RF-5E having a modified forward fuselage with quick-change capabilities to accommodate a wide variety of reconnaissance equipment. Both day and night photo missions were demonstrated during the subsequent test programme. Modification of a production F-5E made possible the first flight of the RF-5E prototype in January 1979, and this aircraft made its international debut at the 1979 Paris Air Show. The first production RF-5E, one of two delivered to the Royal Malaysian Air Force in 1983, made its first flight on 15 December 1982. Saudi Arabia has ordered ten, the first two of which were due for delivery in 1985.

Basically similar to the F-5E Tiger II, the RF-5E TigerEye differs by having a modified forward fuselage, and specialised equipment to enable it to fulfil a highly efficient reconnaissance role. The modified forward fuselage extends the overall length by 0·20 m (8 in), and provides 0·74 m³ (26 cu ft) of space to accommodate reconnaissance equipment. To allow maximum flexibility for differing reconnaissance roles, Northrop decided to group the various combinations of proposed cameras/sensors on portable pallets, any one of which could be loaded easily and quickly into this forward fuselage compartment. In addition to the selected pallet, a KS-87D1 oblique frame camera is mounted in a forward nose compartment and provided with lenses of 6 in and 12 in focal length.

Two pallets have been developed to date for the RF-5E, the first comprising a KA-95B medium altitude panoramic camera, KA-56E low altitude panoramc camera, and an RS-710E infra-red linescanner. Pallet 2 also has the KA-56E panoramic camera, with a KA-93B6 panoramic camera with a 145° scan angle for heights of 3,050-15,240 m (10,000-50,000 ft). Pallet 3, in development, is configured for long range oblique photo (LOROP) missions, and carries a single KS-147A LOROP camera of 66 in focal length. Other configurations are being studied, including pallets with mapping cameras, electro-optical, infra-red and elint equipment. Forward looking (FLIR) or downward looking infra-red linescanners, sideways looking airborne radar (SLAR), and sideways looking airborne multi-mode radar (SLAMMR) are also potentially usable in the RF-5E. The video viewfinder system has future growth possibilities for low-light operations and data links to another aircraft or to ground stations for real-time viewing.

The pilot has available advanced nav/com systems to complement the reconnaissance equipment, plus a video viewfinder system which enables him to view the terrain below the aircraft on a cathode ray tube display in the cockpit. Using this system, the pilot can monitor and correct his line of flight during mapping runs, and can also update the INS when passing over recognisable terrain features. In addition, there is a photographic sensor control system (PSCS) which handles many operations automatically.

The RF-5E TigerEye retains the external stores stations of the F-5E, permitting the carriage of up to three external fuel tanks (each 1,041 litres; 275 US gallons) for maximum range performance. It has essentially the same weights, performance and armament capabilities as the F-5E tactical fighter, and on all missions is able to carry one M39 20 mm gun with 280 rounds, plus two AIM-9 Sidewinder missiles.

PERFORMANCE: As for F-5E except:
Mission radius (A, with one drop tank and two AIM-9s; B, with three drop tanks and two AIM-9s):
low altitude throughout:
A 245 nm (454 km; 282 miles)
B 350 nm (648 km; 403 miles)
hi-lo-hi: A 390 nm (723 km; 449 miles)
B 530 nm (982 km; 610 miles)
hi-lo-lo-hi: A 345 nm (639 km; 397 miles)
B 485 nm (898 km; 558 miles)
high altitude throughout:
A 475 nm (830 km; 547 miles)
B 595 nm (1,102 km; 685 miles)

NORTHROP F-20 TIGERSHARK

This tactical fighter (originally designated F-5G) evolved from Northrop studies which showed that a more advanced version of the F-5 with a single 80·0 kN (18,000 lb st) class General Electric F404-GE-100 turbofan engine would result in a combat aircraft with excellent performance at reasonable cost. With an empty weight increase of only 21 per cent compared with the F-5E, the Tigershark has an 80 per cent increase in engine thrust and offers significant performance improvements.

In January 1980, Northrop decided to begin construction and development of the Tigershark. The first aircraft, with analog avionics, an F-5E style canopy and a 71·2 kN (16,000 lb st) engine, made its first flight on 30 August 1982 and by early September 1984 had logged 580 flights before it was lost on 10 October 1984. The second Tigershark, which flew for the first time on 26 August 1983 and was lost on 14 May 1985 due to loss of pilot consciousness, had production standard digital avionics and an enlarged canopy with improved field of view. A third Tigershark joined the flight programme on 12 May 1984 and work began on a fourth aircraft in late 1984. This Tigershark, scheduled to join the flight test programme in early 1987, was to be equipped with the full F-20 avionics system and to serve also as a flight test loads vehicle. Among improvements planned for the fourth aircraft are a larger antenna for the AN/APG-67(V) radar which should provide a 33 per cent increase in detection range in the look-up mode at a range of 50 nm (92 km; 57 miles) against head-on, closing targets; an increase in internal fuel capacity to the planned production standard of 2,290 kg (5,050 lb); and redesigned leading-edge and trailing-edge flaps, driven at two points instead of a single point. They should also be faster acting and offer continuous automatic setting at optional positions not available on the first three aircraft. The building of a fifth prototype was under consideration in early 1986. In 1983 the USAF Systems Command became involved in the F-20 programme, enabling the aircraft to be sold abroad through the foreign military sales (FMS) operation.

The Tigershark has met or bettered all planned performance, reliability and maintainability objectives. During its test programme the aircraft has exceeded Mach 2; manoeuvred at a 9*g* load factor; recorded a 97 per cent mission reliability rate; and demonstrated a scramble time of less than one minute from strip alert, airborne and with all systems operating. The F-20's Honeywell ring laser gyro inertial navigation system has achieved a mean accuracy of 0·8 nm/h, and bomb aiming accuracies in the order of 9·1 m (30 ft) have been recorded in weapons delivery trials.

The F-20 has also successfully fired the AIM-7F Sparrow, AIM-9 Sidewinder and Maverick missiles, 2·75 in folding fin rockets and ammunition from a 30 mm gun pod;

dropped Mk 82 bombs; completed eight consecutive air-to-ground bombing missions in a single day and 12 mock combat missions against simulated enemy intruders in another 12-hour period; demonstrated its AN/APG-67(V) multi-mode radar in all air-to-air modes; and demonstrated both the visual continuously computed impact point (CCIP) mode and the automatic continuously computed release points (CCRP) mode of the air-to-ground weapons delivery system. An F-20 has also been test flown with an operational mission computer programmed in the new US Department of Defense standard defence computer language Ada (MIL-STD-1815A) during demonstration tests at Edwards AFB, California. By September 1986 the F-20 had accumulated over 1,500 flights.

TYPE: Single-seat tactical fighter.

WINGS: Cantilever low-wing monoplane. Wing section NACA 65A004·8 (modified). No dihedral or incidence. Sweepback at quarter-chord 25°. Tapered leading-edge extensions, between the inboard leading-edge and fuselage, are increased in size and refined compared with F-5 series, in conjunction with engine inlet duct redesign. This change to the leading-edge extensions, coupled with increased chord and full span leading-edge flaps, results in effective combat wing loading (50 per cent fuel) of 261 kg/m² (53·5 lb/sq ft) at maximum lift, by employing new aerodynamics technology in the area of vortex induced lift. Strengthening of the wing by increasing the skin thickness of inboard sections has permitted a combat manoeuvre load factor of 9*g*.

FUSELAGE: Light alloy semi-monocoque basic structure, with localised use of steel and titanium. Two hydraulically actuated variable-position airbrakes on underside of fuselage forward of mainwheel wells. Nose design appears slightly flattened and rounded in planform (shark nose) to enhance directional stability at high angles of attack. Area ruling in the mid fuselage section is not required because of the higher thrust available. The rear fuselage cross section is tailored for minimum base drag.

TAIL UNIT: Cantilever all-metal structure. New hydraulically actuated variable incidence tailplane with an exposed area of 3·99 m² (42·9 sq ft). The closed loop digital pitch control augmentation system (PCAS) is designed to facilitate a further-aft CG for reduced trim drag. The tailplane is constructed of full depth aluminium honeycomb with graphite/epoxy composite skins, spar and ribs. The fin has been tailored to improve afterbody flow. The fin is a multi-cell box structure with honeycomb leading-/trailing-edge sections and graphite/epoxy composite, which contains a fuel vent/expansion tank. A ram air inlet is incorporated at the base of the fin to cool the ECS bleed line, accessory gearbox oil, and 40kVA alternator.

LANDING GEAR: Hydraulically retractable tricycle type, with heavy duty Goodyear wheels and anti-skid carbon brakes for weight reduction and increased service life. The nosewheel unit has an extension feature to enhance take-off performance.

POWER PLANT: One 80 kN (18,000 lb st) General Electric F404-GE-100 afterburning turbofan engine installed in the rear fuselage, with fuel control redundancy for single-engine application. Internal fuel system, usable capacity 2,290 kg (5,050 lb), with integral and bladder tanks. Provision for three 1,250 litre (330 US gallon) external tanks.

ENGINE INTAKES: Inlets extended forward, and designed to accommodate the increased boundary layer thickness generated by Mach 2 aircraft. Internal ducting is sized to accommodate planned growth versions of the F404 engine.

ACCOMMODATION: Pilot only, on Stencel SIIIS-3-F-20 zero/zero ejection seat. Larger canopy, with 40 per cent more transparency area than F-5E, plus a low-profile headrest design, considerably extend all-round field of view.

SYSTEMS: Hamilton Standard air-conditioning and demisting systems. Hydraulic system incorporates Ronson actuators, and is pressurised at 207 bars (3,000 lb/sq in). System maximum flow rate is 39·7 litres (10·5 US gallons)/min at 179 bars (2,600 lb/sq in). Reservoir capacity 6·62 litres (1·75 US gallons), engine bleed air pressurised, with variable delivery hydraulic pump. Electrical system utilises Westinghouse 40kVA primary and 5kVA emergency generators and Avtech transformer-rectifiers. Hydro-mechanical/electro-mechanical flight control system with Hamilton Standard electronic dual-channel digital pitch, roll and yaw control augmentation, with mechanical reversion. An OBOGS oxygen system is installed.

AVIONICS: Production Tigershark would have digital avionics, including General Electric AN/APG-67(V) lookup/lookdown coherent multi-mode radar, with advanced digital signal processing; Honeywell ring laser gyro INS and Teledyne Systems solid state digital mission computer; GEC raster head-up display; Raychem multiplex data bus system to MIL-STD-1553B standard; Bendix digital display and control subsystem; and optional AN/ALR-46 radar warning receiver; AN/ALE-40 chaff/flare countermeasures dispenser system; and Northrop AN/ALQ-171(V) conformal countermeasures system.

ARMAMENT AND OPERATIONAL EQUIPMENT: Two 20 mm M39 cannon, with 225 rds/gun, in upper forward fuselage. Centreline, four underwing and two wingtip stations for external stores. Centreline and four underwing pylons can accommodate more than 4,080 kg (9,000 lb) of external weapons or fuel. Typical loads include General Electric GPU-5/A 30 mm gun pod; six Sidewinder air-to-air or four Maverick air-to-surface missiles; nine Mk 82 bombs or four laser guided bombs.

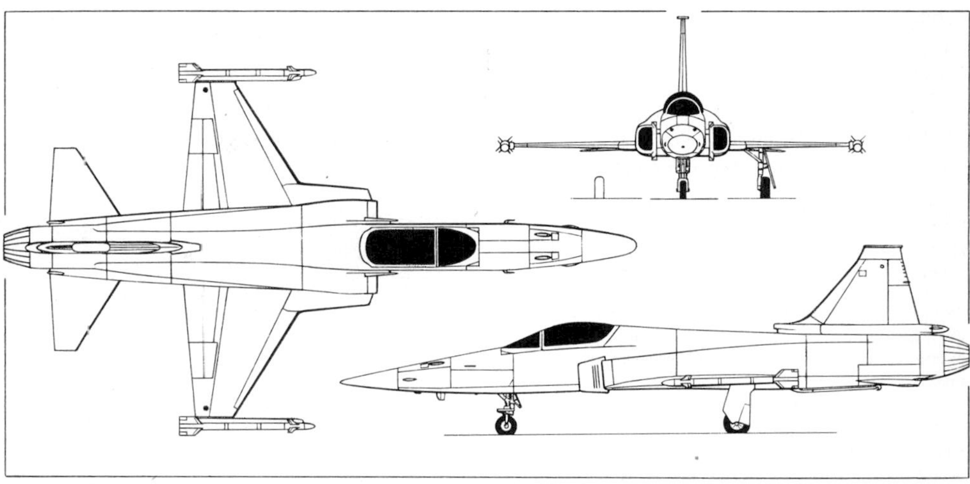

Northrop F-20 Tigershark tactical fighter (General Electric F404-GE-100 turbofan engine) *(Pilot Press)*

Northrop F-20 Tigershark single-seat tactical fighter

DIMENSIONS, EXTERNAL:
- Wing span: without missiles — 8·13 m (26 ft 8 in)
- over missiles — 8·53 m (27 ft 11⅞ in)
- Length overall, excl probe — 14·42 m (47 ft 3¾ in)
- Height overall — 4·22 m (13 ft 10¼ in)
- Tailplane span — 4·72 m (15 ft 6 in)
- Wheel track — 3·80 m (12 ft 5½ in)
- Wheelbase — 5·30 m (17 ft 4½ in)

AREA:
- Wings, gross reference — 18·60 m² (200·0 sq ft)

WEIGHTS (estimated):
- Weight empty — 5,965 kg (13,150 lb)
- Max fuel (usable): internal — 2,290 kg (5,050 lb)
- external — 2,919 kg (6,435 lb)
- Max external stores — more than 4,080 kg (9,000 lb)
- Combat T-O weight, 50 per cent fuel, 2 AIM-9 missiles — 7,264 kg (16,015 lb)
- T-O weight 'clean', max internal fuel, 2 AIM-9 missiles — 8,409 kg (18,540 lb)
- Max T-O weight — 12,700 kg (28,000 lb)
- Combat thrust/weight ratio — 1·12

PERFORMANCE (at 'clean' T-O weight with 2 Sidewinder wingtip missiles except where indicated):
- Max level speed at 13,100 m (43,000 ft) — above Mach 2
- Max rate of climb at S/L — 16,398 m (53,800 ft)/min
- Time to 12,200 m (40,000 ft) — 2 min 18 s
- Combat ceiling at Mach 1·4 — 16,765 m (55,000 ft)
- Service ceiling — 17,315 m (56,800 ft)
- Sustained turn rate at Mach 0·8 at 4,575 m (15,000 ft) — 13·1°/s
- T-O run (S/L, ISA) — 450 m (1,475 ft)
- T-O run at max T-O weight — 1,082 m (3,550 ft)
- Landing run (S/L, ISA) — 655 m (2,150 ft)
- Combat radius with max internal fuel and two 1,249 litre (330 US gallon) external tanks, two Sidewinder missiles, five Mk 82 bombs, 5 min combat at S/L military power, 20 min fuel reserves at S/L, hi-lo-hi mission — 550 nm (1,019 km; 633 miles)
- Combat radius with max internal fuel and three 1,249 litre (330 US gallon) external tanks, two Sidewinder missiles, 2 h 18 min on patrol, 20 min fuel reserves at S/L, combat air patrol mission — 825 nm (1,529 km; 950 miles)
- Ferry range with max internal and external fuel, tanks retained — 1,880 nm (3,984 km; 2,165 miles)
- *g* limit — +9

NORTHROP ATB

During October 1981, it was reported that contracts totalling $7,300 million had been awarded to Northrop, to develop and build prototypes of an advanced technology ('stealth') bomber (ATB) to take over the B-1B's penetration role during the final years of this century. No details are available officially, except that Northrop, as prime contractor, is being assisted by Boeing Aerospace, LTV (Vought) and General Electric Engine Group. However, the ATB has a flying-wing configuration, is expected to be smaller than the B-1B, and is reported to be scheduled to make its first flight in November 1987. Indications in mid-1986 were that the ATB would have four (F101?) engines, and a gross weight in the region of 158,760-170,100 kg (350,000-375,000 lb). In early 1986 Northrop's Advanced Systems Division at Pico Rivera, California, had completed a full scale engineering mockup of the ATB, which was generally similar in shape to the Northrop YB-49 'flying wing' jet bomber. A scaled proof of concept vehicle is believed to have been flying since 1982. Subject to satisfactory flight testing, the USAF plans to acquire 132 ATBs in a $36,600 million programme.

OMAC

OMAC INC

PO Box 3530, Albany, Georgia 31708
Telephone: (912) 436 2425
CHIEF EXECUTIVE OFFICER: Charles V. Mihaylo
SALES MANAGER: Kurt Jensen

OMAC was founded in Reno, Nevada, to develop and market a low cost high performance and economical six/eight-seat turboprop powered business aircraft of canard configuration, known as the Laser 300 (originally OMAC I). Production will be undertaken by Ayres Corporation.

On 30 January 1985 OMAC began operations at a 19,138 m² (206,000 sq ft) headquarters at Albany Municipal Airport, Georgia, where the Ayres factory is also located. Transfer of all engineering, production and flight testing operations from Reno, Nevada, had been completed by that time.

OMAC LASER 300

The Laser 300 prototype flew for the first time on 11 December 1981, but the certification programme was delayed by a ground accident in the Spring of 1982 in which the foreplane was damaged. While this was being repaired, other modifications were made to the original configuration, as detailed in earlier editions of *Jane's*. The modified prototype made its second flight on 18 June 1982, but the test programme was further affected on 22 July, when it suffered damage on landing from its third test flight, after failure of a landing gear locking pin.

A second prototype (N81PH) was flown for the first time on 19 February 1983, becoming an experimental testbed for further modification and design changes. Among these was replacement of the original Avco Lycoming LTP 101-700A-1A turboprop engine with a similarly rated Garrett TPE331-9 in 1984, and the addition of larger winglets. The production design was 'frozen' in April 1985 with further changes which included reconfigured over-cabin fuel tanks/strakes, modified nose contours, enlarged circular cabin cross-section, forward and rear baggage compartments, and adoption of a P&WC PT6A-135A power plant. A new prototype, due to fly in early 1987 embodies these changes and will be used in the FAA certification programme. Certification under FAR Pt 23 is now scheduled for late 1987, at which time production aircraft are expected to be available.

The following description applies to the third prototype:

TYPE: Lightweight business aircraft.

WINGS: Cantilever high-wing monoplane, with 10° sweepback and constant chord. Wing section NACA 64_1-212 (Mod B). Dihedral 1° 30'. Conventional two-spar structure of light alloy, with H section extruded front spar. Leading-edge flaps on outer wing panels. Hydraulically operated half span trailing-edge plain flaps. Half span rod actuated ailerons. Trim tab in port aileron. Winglets fitted at wingtips extend above and below wing. Each lower segment incorporates rudder with outward movement only.

FUSELAGE: Conventional light alloy semi-monocoque pressurised structure. Dorsal and ventral fins.

FOREPLANE: Cantilever monoplane of constant chord. Wing section NACA 64_1-215 (Mod B). Incidence 3°. Conventional two-spar light alloy structure. Both spars of extruded H section. Full span elevator each side. Trim tab in each elevator, electrically and manually actuated, and spring-interlocked with flaps for automatic trimming.

LANDING GEAR: Hydraulically retractable tricycle type. Steerable nosewheel retracts forward. Hydraulic shock absorption. Main units have tubular spring steel legs. Nosewheel tyre size 6·00-6. Mainwheels have heavy duty tyres size 17·5-6·25 × 6. Heavy duty brakes.

POWER PLANT: One Pratt & Whitney Canada PT6A-135A turboprop engine, flat rated at 559 kW (750 shp) and driving a Hartzell three-blade reversible-pitch metal pusher propeller, with 'Q' tips and Beta control. Fuel in integral tanks in strakes along top of cabin, and in rear-fuselage main feed tank, with combined capacity of 1,136 litres (300 US gallons).

ACCOMMODATION: Standard seating for two pilots and five passengers, with dual controls standard. Two forward facing seats for pilot and co-pilot/passenger, with four individual reclining seats; club seating arrangement with executive work-table; or optional two seats with a three-seat bench on port side of cabin. Seats track mounted to permit easy conversion for passenger/cargo use. Baggage compartments forward and aft of cabin seats, with space at rear for toilet with privacy curtain. Airstair door on port side. Emergency exit on starboard side.

SYSTEMS: Air-conditioning and pressurisation system with max cabin pressure differential 0·38 bars (5·5 lb/sq in). Hydraulic system with electrically powered pump for operation of flaps, landing gear, brakes and steerable nosewheel. Electrical system. Oxygen backup system.

AVIONICS AND EQUIPMENT: King avionics will be offered as standard factory fit. Standard equipment includes true airspeed indicator, full co-pilot instrumentation, instrument lights, stall warning device, pitot and stall warning heating systems, alternate static source, courtesy lights, navigation lights, strobe lights, dual landing and taxi lights, and external power socket.

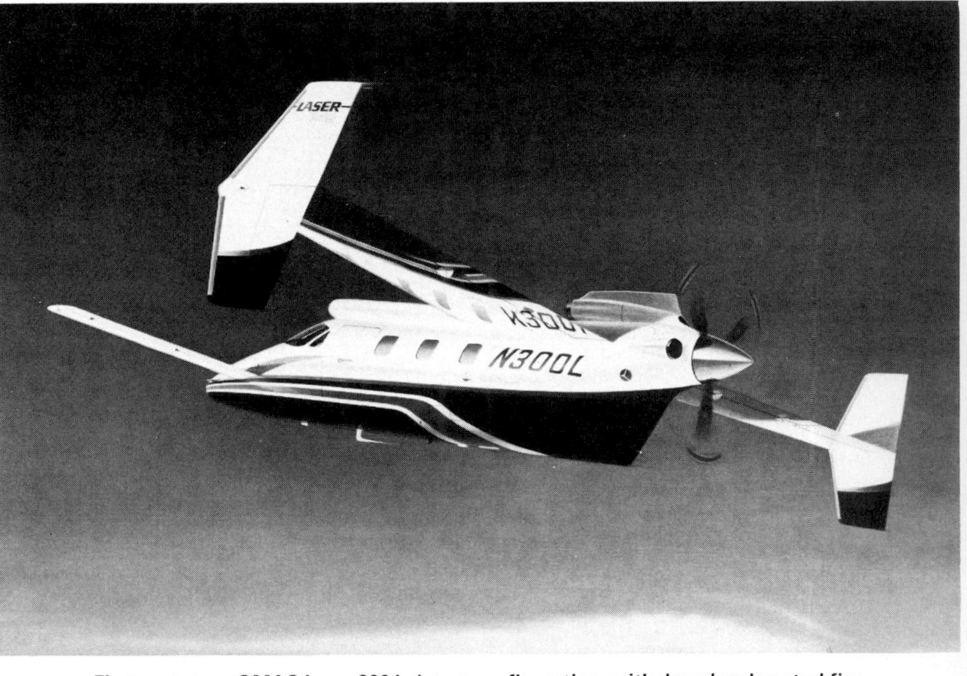

First prototype OMAC Laser 300 in latest configuration, with dorsal and ventral fins

DIMENSIONS, EXTERNAL:
- Wing span: 12·65 m (41 ft 6 in)
- Foreplane span: 5·23 m (17 ft 2 in)
- Length overall: 9·02 m (29 ft 7 in)
- Height overall: 3·00 m (9 ft 10 in)
- Propeller diameter: 2·69 m (8 ft 10 in)

DIMENSIONS, INTERNAL:
- Cabin: Length, excl flight deck: 3·18 m (10 ft 5¼ in)
  - Max height: 1·52 m (5 ft 0 in)
  - Max width: 1·53 m (5 ft 0½ in)
  - Volume: 6·94 m³ (245 cu ft)
- Baggage compartment volume (total): 2·18 m³ (77 cu ft)

AREAS:
- Wings, gross: 21·37 m² (230·0 sq ft)
- Foreplane: 6·50 m² (70·0 sq ft)

WEIGHTS:
- Weight empty: 1,723 kg (3,800 lb)
- Max fuel weight: 907 kg (2,000 lb)
- Max baggage: 236 kg (520 lb)
- Max T-O and landing weight: 2,903 kg (6,400 lb)

PERFORMANCE (estimated at max T-O weight):
- Max cruising speed at 7,620 m (25,000 ft): 252 knots (467 km/h; 290 mph)
- Econ cruising speed: 200 knots (370 km/h; 230 mph)
- Stalling speed: 61 knots (113 km/h; 71 mph)
- Max rate of climb at S/L: 610 m (2,000 ft)/min
- Certification ceiling: 7,620 m (25,000 ft)
- T-O to 15 m (50 ft): 518 m (1,700 ft)
- Landing from 15 m (50 ft): 488 m (1,600 ft)
- Range:
  - with max payload: 1,400 nm (2,594 km; 1,612 miles)
  - with max fuel: 1,880 nm (3,484 km; 2,165 miles)

OMNI

OMNI TITAN CORPORATION

11300 Rockville Pike, Rockville, Maryland 20852
Telephone: (301) 468 0912
Telex: 89-8460
PRESIDENT: Brian Byers

OMNI TURBO TITAN

Omni Titan Corporation has developed a turboprop conversion of the Cessna Model 404 Titan in which the aircraft's 280 kW (375 hp) Continental GTSIO-520-M piston engines are replaced by two Pratt & Whitney Canada PT6A-34 turboprops, each flat rated at 484·7 kW (650 shp). Prototype conversion and certification testing was undertaken by Mr Earl Schafer of Schafer Aircraft, Clifton, Texas (which see). The prototype Omni Turbo Titan (N404GB) made its first flight on 9 June 1984 and its public debut at the National Business Aircraft Association convention in Atlanta, Georgia, the following October. FAA certification was granted on 9 May 1985.

The Omni Turbo Titan conversion uses all off-the-shelf parts to facilitate worldwide spares support. All engine systems have quick-disconnects at the firewall to reduce engine removal time, and the cowlings are of two-part design for ease of access for routine maintenance. The Turbo Titan is configured for 'quick-change' operation as a two-crew, 12-passenger commuter airliner or as a single-crew, all-cargo aircraft with a payload of 1,465 kg (3,230 lb) and 10·76 m³ (380 cu ft) of cabin cargo space, plus an additional 2·12 m³ (75 cu ft) in nose and wing lockers. A maritime surveillance/patrol variant has also been proposed which could accommodate a surface search radar such as the Bendix RDR-1500, together with a suitable FLIR or IR scanning system. On a typical sea patrol mission the Turbo Titan could reach a patrol station 200 nm (370 km; 230 miles) from base in 52 min, remain on station for 5 h 39 min at a speed of 112 knots (207 km/h; 129 mph) at 457 m (1,500 ft), and return to base with one hour's fuel reserves.

Omni Turbo Titan prototype *(Mike Jerram)*

A technical description of the standard Cessna Model 404 Titan may be found in the 1982-83 *Jane's*. The following data refer to the Omni Turbo Titan in commuter airliner configuration. Production deliveries were scheduled to begin in June 1985, at an increased max T-O weight of 4,286 kg (9,450 lb), but no confirmation of this has been received.

WEIGHTS:
- Weight empty: 2,250 kg (4,960 lb)

Basic operating weight 2,404 kg (5,300 lb)
Max fuel weight 1,053 kg (2,322 lb)
Max T-O weight 3,833 kg (8,450 lb)
Max zero-fuel weight 3,674 kg (8,100 lb)
PERFORMANCE (at max T-O weight of 3,833 kg; 8,450 lb):
Max cruising speed at 3,050 m (10,000 ft), ISA 242 knots (449 km/h; 279 mph)
Econ cruising speed at 3,050 m (10,000 ft), ISA 201 knots (372 km/h; 231 mph)
Max rate of climb at S/L 731 m (2,400 ft)/min
Rate of climb at S/L, one engine out 305 m (1,000 ft)/min
Service ceiling 9,450 m (31,000 ft)
Service ceiling, one engine out 6,100 m (20,000 ft)
T-O run 366 m (1,200 ft)
T-O to 15 m (50 ft) 518 m (1,700 ft)
Landing from 15 m (50 ft) 579 m (1,900 ft)
Range with 12 passengers, IFR reserves 559 nm (1,306 km; 644 miles)
Range at normal cruising speed, 3,050 m (10,000 ft), IFR reserves 865 nm (1,603 km; 996 miles)
VFR ferry range, 225 knots (417 km/h; 259 mph) at 5,485 m (18,000 ft), no reserves 1,241 nm (2,300 km; 1,429 miles)

O'NEILL

O'NEILL AIRPLANE COMPANY

791 Livingston Street, Carlyle, Illinois 62231
Telephone: (618) 594 2681
PRESIDENT: Terrence O'Neill

O'NEILL MODEL J MAGNUM

Mr Terrence O'Neill began design work on the Magnum (then known as 'Jake') in 1971, after he had conducted a market survey among charter pilots in Alaska. As first envisaged the aircraft was to have been a straightforward redesign of the Waco Aristo Craft II, with which Mr O'Neill had been involved; but as the project evolved an entirely new design was created. First ground trials of the Magnum began in 1980, but it was not until 1982 that a full flight test programme began after a redesign of the landing gear to its present configuration. The Magnum incorporates a number of novel design features, including a dual nosewheel landing gear arrangement and a jettisonable main fuel tank as a safety precaution in the event of an emergency landing. Since April 1985 modifications have been made to raise the top of the fuselage for increased cabin headroom, and a sideways opening swing tail incorporated.

TYPE: Eight-seat, single-engined high-wing utility monoplane.

WINGS: Strut braced high-wing monoplane. Section NACA 4415. Dihedral 1°. Incidence 3° at root. Sweepforward 3°. 2024-T3 aluminium skinning. Electrically actuated full span flaps, designed to act as dive brakes at a terminal velocity of 161 knots (298 km/h; 185 mph), of aluminium/foam/epoxy construction. Vented full span spoilerons, of similar construction, for roll control. Main wing mounts and bracing strut attachment fittings have a common hingeline, enabling wings to be folded alongside fuselage.

FUSELAGE: Flat sided 4130-N chrome molybdenum steel tube structure with 2024-T3 aluminium skinning.

TAIL UNIT: Cantilever structure. All-moving slatted horizontal tail surface with trimmable anti-servo tab and small 'finlets' near tips. Vertical tail surface has forward canted hinge axis.

LANDING GEAR: Non-retractable, dual nosewheel type. Mainwheels size 600 × 6, pressure 2·34 bars (34 lb/sq in), nosewheels 15 × 600-6, pressure 1·93 bars (28 lb/sq in). Hydraulic oleo strut suspension, Cleveland disc brakes on mainwheels, nosewheels steerable. Wheel fairings on all four wheels. Conventional tailwheel, tricycle and float landing gears optional.

POWER PLANT: One 261 kW (350 hp) Jacobs R-755-S turbocharged radial engine, driving a three-blade constant speed Hartzell B3P20 metal propeller with spinner. Fuel capacity 212 litres (56 US gallons), contained in single tank mounted beneath the forward cabin; 341 litre (90 US gallon) tank optional. Single fuelling point at bottom of port side cabin door. Tank has quick disconnect feature enabling it to be jettisoned in flight via a hand lever on the cabin floor, near the rudder pedals, in an emergency. Oil capacity 19 litres (5 US gallons). Engine cowling is divided vertically and mounted on spherical rod-ends to permit 180° opening for easy engine access.

ACCOMMODATION: Standard seating for pilot and seven passengers, in 2, 3, 3 seating plan, in heated cabin. Seats are quick-removable for cargo carrying. Cabin floor has cargo tiedown points. One cabin door, forward hinged, on each side of cabin. Rear fuselage swing tail, hinged on starboard side, optional. Toilet optional.

AVIONICS AND EQUIPMENT: Avionics fit to customer choice. O'Neill 'Wing to Wind' visual angle of attack indicator mounted on port wing with calibrated air angle vane.

DIMENSIONS, EXTERNAL:
Wing span 9·22 m (30 ft 3 in)
Wing chord at root 1·63 m (5 ft 4 in)
Wing aspect ratio 5·7
Length overall 7·32 m (24 ft 0 in)
Max width, wings folded approx 2·74 m (9 ft 0 in)
Height overall 2·92 m (9 ft 7 in)
Tailplane span 2·44 m (8 ft 0 in)
Wheel track (c/l of shock struts) 2·13 m (7 ft 0 in)
Wheelbase 1·80 m (5 ft 10¾ in)
Propeller diameter (prototype) 2·26 m (7 ft 5 in)

DIMENSIONS, INTERNAL:
Cabin: Length 3·96 m (13 ft 0 in)
Width 1·24 m (4 ft 1 in)
Height 1·27 m (4 ft 2 in)

AREAS:
Wings, gross 14·80 m² (159·3 sq ft)
Trailing-edge flaps (total) 2·90 m² (31·2 sq ft)
Spoilerons (total) 0·93 m² (10·0 sq ft)
Horizontal tail surfaces (excl slats) 1·86 m² (20·0 sq ft)
Vertical tail surface 1·49 m² (16·0 sq ft)

WEIGHTS AND LOADINGS:
Weight empty 930 kg (2,050 lb)
Max T-O and landing weight 1,724 kg (3,800 lb)
Max wing loading 116·49 kg/m² (23·85 lb/sq ft)
Max power loading 6·61 kg/kW (10·86 lb/hp)

PERFORMANCE (provisional, pending completion of flight tests, at gross weight of 1,179 kg; 2,600 lb):
Never-exceed speed 161 knots (298 km/h; 185 mph) IAS
Max cruising speed:
at S/L 122 knots (225 km/h; 140 mph)
at 5,485 m (18,000 ft) 174 knots (322 km/h; 200 mph)
Min ground turning radius 4·27 m (14 ft 0 in)
Range with max standard fuel, 45 min reserves 347 nm (644 km; 400 miles)
Range with optional 341 litre (90 US gallon) fuel tank, 45 min reserves 608 nm (1,127 km; 700 miles)

Prototype O'Neill Magnum eight-seat utility monoplane in its current form, with deeper cabin and swing-tail rear fuselage

ORLANDO

ORLANDO HELICOPTER AIRWAYS INC

PO Box 2802, Orlando, Florida 32802
Telephone: (305) 841 3480 and (305) 323 1756
Telex: 56 4400
PRESIDENT: Fred P. Clark
VICE-PRESIDENT OF SALES: Troy E. Simmons

Orlando Helicopter Airways Inc was founded at Sanford, Florida in 1964, since when the company has been engaged in the remanufacture, sale and operation of Sikorsky helicopters. The company has large stocks of parts and components for Sikorsky S-52, S-55/H-19 and S-58/H-34 helicopters and owns the FAA type certificates for all models of the H-19 series and the H-34. Rotorparts, Inc, an affiliate company, claims the world's largest stocks of Sikorsky S-55 parts, and supplies components for S-55, S-58, S-61 and S-62 helicopters to many overseas governments. Total sales of Sikorsky helicopters remanufactured by Orlando Helicopter Airways exceed 100. Future plans include conversions of later models such as the S-61, S-62 and S-64 series as they are declared surplus by military forces; turbine engine conversions of piston engined helicopters; and experimentation with alternative fuels such as gasoline/alcohol and propane gas in helicopters for agricultural operation.

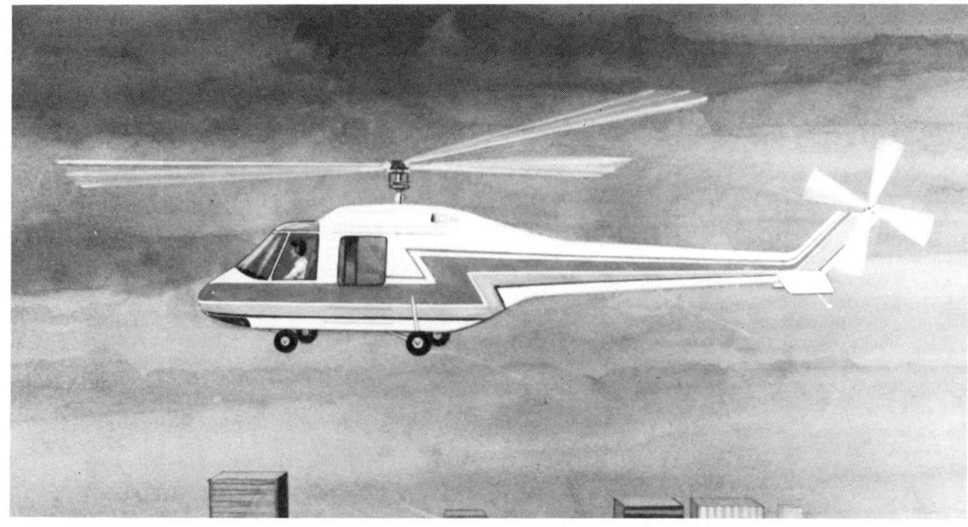

Artist's impression of Orlando OHA-S-52T Clipper turbine conversion of Sikorsky S-52 four-seat helicopter

On 27 October 1985 an agreement was signed with the Guangzhou Machinery Tool Company, and Bates Associates of Hong Kong, for the production of Orlando OHA-S-55 Bearcat helicopters in China. A new company, Guangzhou Orlando Helicopters, will initially assemble US manufactured parts, leading to production of components in China. The 20-year joint venture includes the establishment and operation of helicopter passenger services in China, and will also offer rotor blade overhaul and repair facilities for Far East operators. Future plans include the assembly of larger helicopter types in China. Orlando Helicopter Airways and Bates Associates have also formed Orlando Helicopter Far East Ltd to handle export marketing of helicopters manufactured in China.

ORLANDO/SIKORSKY S-52

Orlando Helicopter Airways offers a four-seat civilian conversion of the S-52 which includes dual controls, night lighting, VHF transceiver and FAA certification. In 1983 the company, in conjunction with Kaylor Energy Products Inc of Menlo Park, California converted an S-52 to electric power. The proof-of-concept machine has been extensively modified for the installation of four electric motors linked by a common shaft to the main transmission. A battery pack of twelve 72V lead-acid batteries is mounted forward of the motors and provides approximately ten minutes' power from a full charge. The power produced by the electric motors is in the order of 183 kW (245 hp). Ground trials began in late 1983. The next phases of the test programme will include use of silver zinc batteries to extend flight time to 30 minutes, and replacement of batteries with an 'instantly rechargeable' lithium hydroxide power system. In the final test phase the four electric motors will be replaced with a single motor. Orlando Helicopter Airways points out a number of advantages to electric powered helicopters, including low noise levels, lack of exhaust emissions, no infra-red signature from the motor, and simplicity of the power system.

A four-seat turbine engined conversion of the S-52, powered by a 313 kW (420 shp) Allison 250-C20B turboshaft engine, is known as the Orlando **OHA-S-52T Clipper**.

ORLANDO/SIKORSKY S-55/H-19

Several remanufactured models of Sikorsky S-55/H-19 series helicopters are offered by Orlando Helicopter Airways:

Vistaplane. Passenger/air ambulance version seating eight passengers in standard version or 11 passengers in high density configuration. For ambulance work up to six litters and two attendants can be accommodated. Cabin floor viewing window optional.

Heli-Camper. VIP model with sleeping facilities for four passengers in fully carpeted and soundproofed cabin; hot and cold water; refrigerator; two-burner stove; shower and wash basin; toilet; air-conditioning. Other standard features include colour television and AM/FM stereo radio and tape deck, roll-up awning, tinted windows, bar and storage cabinets, dual flight controls, full night lighting and dual landing lights, interphone communication system, King 360-channel VHF transceiver and VOR, King transponder, and emergency locator transmitter. Options include an electro-mechanical cargo sling, hydraulic hoist, amphibious floats, rotating spot light, and King KT-96 radio telephone. The Heli-Camper has a stripped and remanufactured airframe, new instruments, new or overhauled dynamic components including main and tail rotor blades, and an overhauled 596 kW (800 hp) Wright Cyclone R-1300-3D piston engine. Fuel capacity 715 litres (189 US gallons); max T-O weight 3,266 kg (7,200 lb); cruising speed 78 knots (145 km; 90 mph); range 304 nm (563 km; 350 miles).

OHA-S-55 Bearcat. Designed for Orlando-developed combination spray and dry dispensing systems for quick conversion from liquid chemicals to dry fertilisers or seeds. Glassfibre chemical tank, capacity 946 litres (250 US gallons) standard. System also allows dry material to be carried internally rather than in underslung bucket. Also adaptable for firefighting. Orlando Helicopter Airways has obtained FAA approval for S-55 operators using Pratt & Whitney R-1340 engines under FAR Parts 91 (Standard), 137 (Agricultural) and 133 (External Load) to use motor fuel in their helicopters, and all Orlando-modified S-55s with R-1340 engines include this approval. Kysor cockpit air-conditioning system optional.

Heavy Lift. External load model for logging, construction and fire-fighting operations, with 1,361 kg (3,000 lb) useful load.

As noted in the Chinese section of this edition, an **OHA-S-55T Challenger** version, with a 522 kW (700 shp) Avco Lycoming LTS 101-700A-3 turboshaft engine, is, together with the standard OHA-S-55, the subject of a co-production agreement with the People's Republic of China, where it will be known as the **Panda**. A proposed **OHA-S-55T Phoenix** variant will feature single- or twin-turbine engines mounted on the transmission deck, and a new streamlined nose section.

ORLANDO/SIKORSKY S-58/H-34

Five remanufactured models of Sikorsky S-58/H-34 series helicopters are offered. The **Agricultural** and **Heavy Lift** versions have a 1,137 kW (1,525 hp) Wright Cyclone R-1820-84 piston engine and are similarly equipped to equivalent versions of the Orlando S-55/H-19.

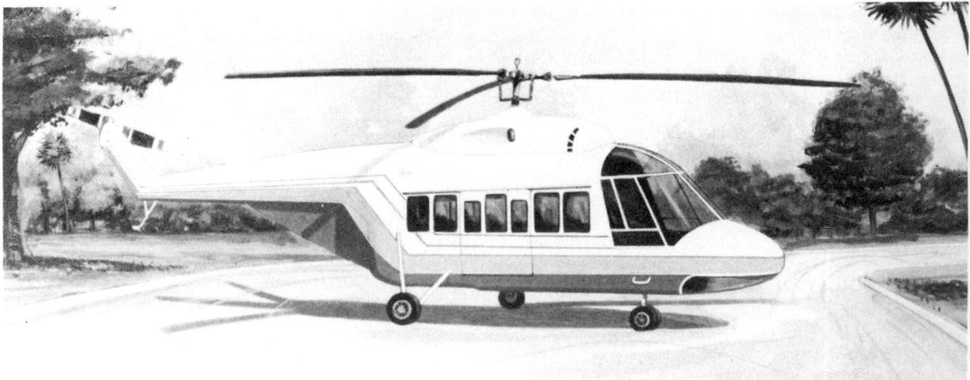

Artist's impression of Orlando OHA-S-55T Phoenix single- or twin-turbine helicopter

Orlando Helicopter Airways OHA-S-55 Bearcat agricultural helicopter

Orlando Helicopter Airways S-58T Orlando Airliner

Heli-Camper. Similarly equipped to S-55 Heli-Camper, but with additional standard features: 8·73 m² (94 sq ft) living area with sculptured carpeting, entertainment centre, separate bar, sleeping accommodation for six passengers, full-size four-burner stove and 0·11 m³ (3·9 cu ft) refrigerator, 3,500W generator, super soundproofing, tinted glass and wraparound windscreen. 1,137 kW (1,525 hp) Wright Cyclone R-1820-84 radial piston engine. Fuel capacity 992 litres (262 US gallons); max T-O weight 5,670 kg (12,500 lb); cruising speed 96 knots (177 km/h; 110 mph); range 304 nm (563 km; 350 miles).

Orlando Airliner. High density version of the Sikorsky S-58T twin-turbine helicopter (see California Helicopters entry in this section). Standard equipment includes dual flight controls; toe brakes; hydraulic rotor brake; two independent servo control systems; cabin, cockpit, instrument, position, night and landing lights; rotating beacon; 24V battery, 1,071 litre (283 US gallon) fuel system; 2,268 kg (5,000 lb) capacity cargo sling; new paintwork; an extended passenger cabin; 18 additional cabin windows (for a total of 22); 18 airline-standard seats (15 forward facing and three rearward facing, standard or lightweight); Flightex soundproofing; tinted cabin windows; and ram air scoop for cabin cooling. Options available for the Orlando Airliner include a 272 kg (600 lb) capacity rescue hoist; pop-out emergency floats; 568 litre (150 US gallon) capacity external auxiliary fuel tank; stereo system; toilet; air-conditioning; one-piece windshield; and customer choice of avionics. By early 1984 Orlando Helicopter Airways had delivered ten Orlando Airliners, including two for New York Helicopter Airways. The Orlando Airliner has a useful load of over 2,268 kg (5,000 lb), maximum speed at S/L of 120 knots (222 km/h; 138 mph), hovering ceiling OGE of 2 440 m (8,000 ft), and range, with auxiliary fuel and 20 min reserves, of 373 nm (692 km; 430 miles).

Flying Armoured Personnel Carrier. Military version of S-58T with extended passenger cabin and 18 opening cabin windows. The entire lower fuselage below the line of the cabin windows is protected with Kevlar soft armour plating. Fuel system similarly armoured, and incorporates self-sealing tanks. Pilot and co-pilot side windows are made from Lexan bullet resistant material, with 6·35 mm (¼ in) 'boiler plate' wing panels for added crew protection, and soft Kevlar armour around and under seats and in engine compartment. Two additional doors, each 0·56 m × 1·17 m (22 in × 46 in) on port side of fuselage, supplementing main cabin sliding door on starboard side. Provision for mounting heavy weapons at door and window stations, and for carrying external stores.

A new version of the Orlando S-58 is under development, and is designated **OHA-S-58T Viking**. It will be offered with a choice of Avco Lycoming LTS-101 or Pratt & Whitney Canada PT6 turbine engines in twin or triple installations. The engines will be mounted on the transmission deck and the Viking will have a redesigned streamlined nose.

PHALANX

PHALANX ORGANIZATION INC

2600 E Wardlow Road, Long Beach, California 90807
Telephone: (213) 595 0701
Telex: 5106003438 PHALANX LGB
CHAIRMAN AND CHIEF EXECUTIVE OFFICER:
William F. Moody Jr
PRESIDENT AND CHIEF OPERATING OFFICER:
William Jamieson

PHALANX MP-18 DRAGON

The general appearance of this unorthodox combat aircraft is shown in an accompanying illustration. Power plant comprises two 20·02 kN (4,500 lb st) Garrett TFE731-5A turbofans, or two 24·02 kN (5,400 lb st) General Electric GE38-F1 turbofans. The Phalanx Organization describes the MP-18 as "a pure VTOL blended wing, double-delta with canard, composite aircraft", having two pairs of 3-D vectoring nozzles with decoupled controls, standard avionics, stealth characteristics and the ability to perform a number of military duties, from strike to anti-helicopter gunship, reconnaissance and high-speed executive officers' transport. Change of role is effected in the field by means of a variety of modules, pods and three alternative afterbody shells.

The MP-18 is the basis for a range of Dragon aircraft which is planned to include the MP-27, MP-36, MP-54 and MP-72, the suffix in each case denoting wing span in feet. Phalanx claims to have identified at least 40 specific military roles and 30 commercial roles for the Dragon series. The MP-9 is a proposed remotely piloted vehicle variant.

In the Spring of 1986 a full-size 'plug' had been completed for the MP-18, from which moulds were to be created for the aircraft's Kevlar/Nomex composite airframe components. Work was progressing on the construction of 12 non-flying prototypes, six for structural testing and six for demonstrating the Dragon's various configurations. A first flight is tentatively scheduled for early 1987.

The following provisional specification refers specifically to the MP-18 version:

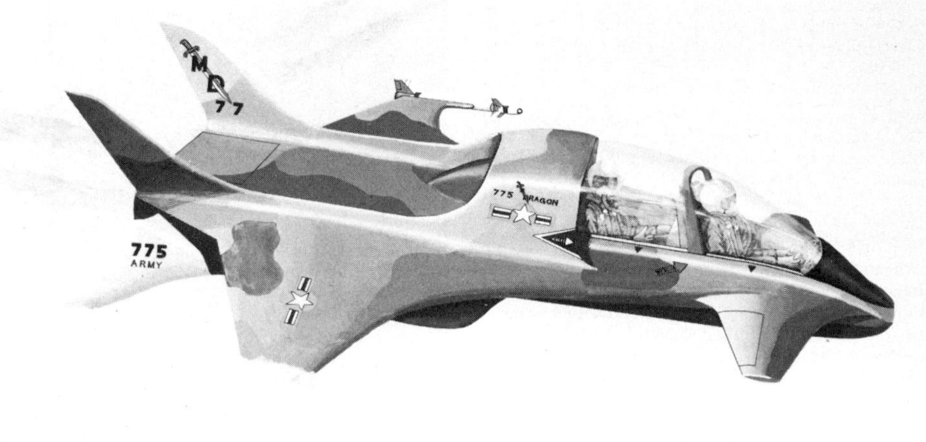

Artist's impression of basic two-seat combat version of Phalanx MP-18 Dragon

DIMENSIONS, EXTERNAL:
Wing span 5·49 m (18 ft 0 in)
Wing span, folded for transport 3·20 m (10 ft 6 in)
Wing aspect ratio 1·8
Foreplane span 2·74 m (9 ft 0 in)
Length overall 7·09 m (23 ft 3 in)
Height overall 1·83 m (6 ft 0 in)
DIMENSIONS, INTERNAL:
Basic two-seat cabin: Length 2·13 m (7 ft 0 in)
Max width 1·06 m (3 ft 6 in)
Nominal height 1·22 m (4 ft 0 in)
AREAS:
Wings, gross 16·72 m² (180·0 sq ft)
Foreplanes, gross 2·09 m² (22·5 sq ft)
WEIGHTS:
Basic weight empty 2,295 kg (5,060 lb)
Max internal fuel 816 kg (1,800 lb)
Max weapons 816 kg (1,800 lb)
Max T-O weight 3,946 kg (8,700 lb)
PERFORMANCE (estimated):
Max level speed Mach 0·96
Max rate of climb at S/L over 7,620 m (25,000 ft)/min
Service ceiling over 18,300 m (60,000 ft)
Field length (land) 12·20 m (40 ft) square
Normal range
1,735-2,085 nm (3,215-3,860 km; 2,000-2,400 miles)
Ferry range
3,910-4,345 nm (7,240-8,045 km; 4,500-5,000 miles)

PIA

PITTSBURGH INSTITUTE OF AERONAUTICS

Box 10897, Pittsburgh, Pennsylvania 15236
Telephone; (412) 462 9011
PRESIDENT: Ivan D. Livi

PIA MODIFIED GRUMMAN OV-1A MOHAWK

To enhance the versatility of its Mohawk aircraft, used for testing engines and avionics, electrical and hydraulic systems, this aviation technician school has installed two Westinghouse J34 turbojet engines in underwing pods. The turbojets occupy the outer wing stations used formerly for external fuel tanks, and supplement the aircraft's normal Avco Lycoming T53 turboprops. The new mountings are designed to facilitate engine changes, and the Mohawk can be operated with either the turbojets or turboprops in use.

PIPER

PIPER AIRCRAFT CORPORATION (Subsidiary of Lear Siegler Inc)

One Piper Drive, PO Box 1328, Vero Beach, Florida 32960
Telephone: (305) 567 4361
Telex: 6815522
PRESIDENT: Frank G. Manning
SENIOR VICE-PRESIDENTS:
Alfred J. Koontz Jr (Finance)
Vincent J. Montuoro (Manufacturing)
VICE-PRESIDENTS:
Ronald L. Barkman (Human Resources)
Marion J. Dees Jr (Engineering)
C. Raymond Johnson (International Sales)
Harvey O. Nay (Product Engineering)
V. Donald Tierney (Assoc General Counsel)
CONTROLLER: William D. Polk
MANAGER, PRESS RELATIONS: Joseph Ponte Jr

Effective 1 March 1984, Piper Aircraft became a subsidiary of Lear Siegler Inc. The manufacturing and R&D facilities at Lock Haven, Pennsylvania, and sheet metal plant at Piper, Pennsylvania, were closed during the second half of 1984. The last of 76,992 aircraft to be manufactured at Lock Haven, a Piper Mojave, left the plant in August 1984. In January 1985 Piper announced the phasing out of the Lakeland, Florida, manufacturing facility, and this was completed by October 1985. All Piper manufacturing activities are now concentrated at Vero Beach, where ground was broken on 1 March 1985 for a new 12,077 m² (130,000 sq ft) plant to accommodate production of the Cheyenne IIIA and 400LS turboprop aircraft which had formerly been built at Lakeland.

In 1971, 1974 and 1977 respectively, Piper announced agreements with Chincul SA (which see) for the manufacture of a broad range of Piper products in Argentina; with EMBRAER (which see) for the development, production and marketing of Piper aircraft in Brazil; and with PZL Mielec (which see) of Poland, which produces a modified version of the Piper Seneca II light twin-engined aircraft, known as the M-20 Mewa, in that country.

PIPER (PA-28-161) WARRIOR II

Design of the Warrior began in June 1972, an important feature being replacement of the earlier constant chord wings of the Cherokee series by a longer span wing with tapered outer panels. As a result of its introduction the Warrior, which at that time had essentially the same 112 kW (150 hp) engine as the discontinued Cherokee Cruiser, was certificated at a maximum T-O weight 79 kg (175 lb) greater. First flight of a prototype was made on 17 October 1972, and FAA certification of the original Model PA-28-151 was granted on 9 August 1973.

The current PA-28-161 Warrior II version, first flown on 27 August 1976, has a 119 kW (160 hp) engine which operates on 100 octane low-lead fuel. The 1986 version offers a basic optional equipment package, **Executive**, comprising: blind-flying instrumentation with 3 in gyros; clock; outside air temperature gauge; exhaust gas temperature gauge; rate of climb and true airspeed indicators; instrument panel white backlighting; overhead red spotlight; cabin dome, avionics dimming, navigation, landing and taxi lights; rotating beacon; assist strap at door; aircraft step; engine primer system; engine driven and electric vacuum pump with vacuum gauge; quick oil drain; wheel fairings; towbar; pilot's vertically adjustable seat, sun visors, alternate static source, heated pitot, emergency locator transmitter, strobe lights, external power socket, and 35Ah battery.

In addition, five optional avionics groups are available for factory installation in the Warrior II.

A total of 2,834 Warriors had been sold by 1 January 1986. Later sales include 12 for the Royal Jordanian Air Academy and 19 for British Aerospace Flying College.

TYPE: Four-seat cabin monoplane.

WINGS: Cantilever low-wing monoplane. Wing section NACA 65²-415 on inboard panels; outboard leading-edge incorporates modification No. 5 of NACA TN 2228. Dihedral 7°. Incidence 2° at root, −1° at tip. Sweepback at quarter-chord 5°. Light alloy single-spar structure with glassfibre wingtips. Plain ailerons of light alloy construction. Four-position manually actuated trailing-edge flaps of light alloy with ribbed skins.

FUSELAGE: Light alloy semi-monocoque structure with glassfibre nose cowl and tailcone.

TAIL UNIT: Cantilever structure of light alloy, except for glassfibre tips on fin and tailplane. Fin and rudder have ribbed light alloy skins. One-piece all-moving tailplane, with combined anti-servo and trim tab. Rudder trimmable, but no trim tab in rudder.

LANDING GEAR: Non-retractable tricycle type. Steerable nosewheel. Piper oleo-pneumatic shock absorbers; single

Piper Warrior II four-seat light cabin monoplane

wheel on each unit. Cleveland wheels with 4-ply tyres size 6·00-6 on main units, pressure 1·65 bars (24 lb/sq in). Cleveland nosewheel and 4-ply tyre size 5·00-5, pressure 1·65 bars (24 lb/sq in). Cleveland disc brakes. Parking brake. Glassfibre wheel fairings optional.

POWER PLANT: One 119 kW (160 hp) Avco Lycoming O-320-D3G flat-four engine, driving a Sensenich two-blade fixed-pitch metal propeller type 74DM6-0-60 with spinner. Fuel in two wing tanks, with total capacity of 189 litres (50 US gallons), of which 181·5 litres (48 US gallons) are usable. Refuelling point on upper surface of each wing. Oil capacity 7·5 litres (2 US gallons).

ACCOMMODATION: Four persons in pairs in enclosed cabin. Individual adjustable front seats with seat belts and shoulder harnesses; bench type rear seat with seat belts. Dual controls and brakes standard. Large door on starboard side. Baggage compartment at rear of cabin, with volume of 0·68 m³ (24 cu ft) and capacity of 91 kg (200 lb). External baggage door on starboard side. Heating, ventilation and windscreen defrosting standard.

SYSTEMS: Hydraulic system for brakes only. Electrical system powered by 14V 60A engine driven alternator. 12V 25Ah battery standard, 12V 35Ah battery optional (standard with Executive equipment package). Dual vacuum system for optional blind-flying instrumentation is available, complete with vacuum gauge, regulator, filter, and annunciator light. Piper Aire air-conditioning system optional.

AVIONICS AND EQUIPMENT: Nav/coms, ADF, autopilot, glideslope and marker beacon receivers, and transponders, by Century Flight Systems, Collins, King and Narco are available in five optional groups, together with an extensive range of other optional avionics. Standard equipment includes recording tachometer, sensitive altimeter, inertial reel shoulder harnesses for all seats, armrests, map pockets, pilot's storm window, stall warning device, carpeted floor, soundproofing, automatic emergency locator transmitter, provisions for air-conditioning, full flow oil filter, tiedown rings and fuel tank quick drains. Optional equipment, in addition to that listed under Executive package, includes encoding altimeter, digital clock, approach plate holder, engine hour recorder, pilot and co-pilot's vertically adjustable seats, pilot and co-pilot headrests, cabin fire extinguisher, improved soundproofing, cup holders, floor and/or overhead ventilation with booster fan, stainless steel control cables, tinted windows, carburettor ice detection system, lockable fuel tank caps, external power receptacle, zinc chromate paint for aluminium parts and polyurethane paint for exterior finish.

DIMENSIONS, EXTERNAL:
- Wing span: 10·67 m (35 ft 0 in)
- Wing chord: at root: 1·60 m (5 ft 3 in)
- at tip: 1·07 m (3 ft 6¼ in)
- Wing aspect ratio: 7·24
- Length overall: 7·25 m (23 ft 9½ in)
- Height overall: 2·22 m (7 ft 3½ in)
- Tailplane span: 3·96 m (12 ft 11¾ in)
- Wheel track: 3·05 m (10 ft 0 in)
- Wheelbase: 2·03 m (6 ft 8 in)
- Propeller diameter: 1·88 m (6 ft 2 in)
- Propeller ground clearance: 0·21 m (8¼ in)
- Cabin door: Height: 0·89 m (2 ft 11 in)
- Width: 0·91 m (3 ft 0 in)
- Baggage door: Height: 0·51 m (1 ft 8 in)
- Max width: 0·56 m (1 ft 10 in)
- Height to sill: 0·71 m (2 ft 4 in)

DIMENSIONS, INTERNAL:
- Cabin: Length (instrument panel to rear bulkhead): 2·46 m (8 ft 1 in)
- Max width: 1·05 m (3 ft 5½ in)
- Max height: 1·24 m (4 ft 1 in)
- Floor area: 2·28 m² (24·5 sq ft)
- Volume (incl baggage area): 3·00 m³ (106·0 cu ft)

AREAS:
- Wings, gross: 15·8 m² (170 sq ft)
- Ailerons (total): 1·23 m² (13·2 sq ft)
- Trailing-edge flaps (total): 1·36 m² (14·6 sq ft)
- Fin: 0·69 m² (7·4 sq ft)
- Rudder: 0·38 m² (4·1 sq ft)
- Tailplane, incl tab: 2·46 m² (26·5 sq ft)

WEIGHTS AND LOADINGS:
- Weight empty, standard: 613 kg (1,352 lb)
- Max T-O and landing weight: 1,106 kg (2,440 lb)
- Max ramp weight: 1,110 kg (2,447 lb)
- Max wing loading: 70·06 kg/m² (14·35 lb/sq ft)
- Max power loading: 9·33 kg/kW (15·25 lb/hp)

PERFORMANCE (at max T-O weight):
- Never-exceed speed: 153 knots (282 km/h; 176 mph)
- *Max level speed at S/L: 127 knots (235 km/h; 146 mph)
- *Best power cruising speed:
  - 75% power at 2,745 m (9,000 ft): 126 knots (233 km/h; 145 mph)
  - 65% power at 3,810 m (12,500 ft): 118 knots (219 km/h; 136 mph)
  - 55% power at 3,810 m (12,500 ft): 107 knots (198 km/h; 123 mph)
- *Best econ cruising speed:
  - 75% power at 2,745 m (9,000 ft): 122 knots (225 km/h; 140 mph)
  - 65% power at 3,810 m (12,500 ft): 116 knots (215 km/h; 134 mph)
  - 55% power at 3,810 m (12,500 ft): 105 knots (195 km/h; 121 mph)
- Stalling speed:
  - flaps up: 56 knots (104 km/h; 65 mph) CAS
  - flaps down: 50 knots (93 km/h; 58 mph) CAS
- Max rate of climb at S/L: 196 m (644 ft)/min
- Service ceiling: 3,355 m (11,000 ft)
- T-O run: 320 m (1,050 ft)
- T-O to 15 m (50 ft): 503 m (1,650 ft)
- Landing from 15 m (50 ft): 354 m (1,160 ft)
- Landing run: 191 m (625 ft)
- *Range with max fuel with allowances for taxi, T-O, climb, and descent, and 45 min reserves at max range power:
  - at best power settings:
    - 75% power at 2,745 m (9,000 ft): 525 nm (972 km; 604 miles)
    - 65% power at 3,810 m (12,500 ft): 553 nm (1,025 km; 637 miles)
    - 55% power at 3,810 m (12,500 ft): 565 nm (1,047 km; 651 miles)
  - at best econ power settings:
    - 75% power at 2,745 m (9,000 ft): 590 nm (1,092 km; 679 miles)
    - 65% power at 3,810 m (12,500 ft): 633 nm (1,173 km; 729 miles)
    - 55% power at 3,810 m (12,500 ft): 640 nm (1,186 km; 737 miles)

Piper Archer II, which has the tapered wings introduced on the Warrior

* *With optional wheel fairings*

PIPER (PA-28-181) ARCHER II

On 9 October 1972 Piper introduced the Cherokee Challenger as successor to the Cherokee 180. In 1974 this was superseded by the Cherokee Archer, with the same basic airframe and power plant, but with many additional equipment and avionics options. In 1976 this aircraft was redesignated PA-28-181 Cherokee Archer II, and in 1978 introduced the tapered wings of the Warrior II.

The Archer II can be fitted with the generally similar optional Executive equipment package, as well as the five optional avionics packages, which are available for the Warrior II. The 1986 model of the Archer II introduced as standard equipment a basic lighting package comprising instrument panel white backlighting, overhead red lighting, cabin dome and radio lights, landing, taxi, navigation and wingtip strobe lights, entrance step, automatic emergency locator transmitter and wheel fairings. The **Executive** package is as for the Warrior II, with deletion of towbar and engine primer system; adding 52·2 kg (115·1 lb) to aircraft basic weight.

A total of 9,714 Cherokee 180s and PA-28-181 Archer IIs had been sold by 1 January 1986. Subsequent sales include a second batch of four for primary flying training of future flight crew of Saudi Arabian Airlines.

TYPE: Four-seat cabin monoplane.

WINGS: Cantilever low-wing monoplane. Wing section NACA 65²-415 on inboard panels; outboard leading-edge has modification No. 5 of NACA TN 2228. Dihedral 7°. Incidence 2° at root, −1° at tip. Sweepback at quarter-chord 5°. Light alloy single-spar structure with glassfibre wingtips. Plain ailerons of light alloy construction. Trailing-edge flaps constructed of light alloy with ribbed skins.

FUSELAGE: Aluminium alloy semi-monocoque structure. Glassfibre engine cowling.

TAIL UNIT: Cantilever structure of aluminium alloy, except for glassfibre tips on fin and tailplane. Fin and rudder have corrugated metal skin. One-piece all-moving horizontal surface with combined anti-servo and trim tab. Trim tab in rudder.

LANDING GEAR: Non-retractable tricycle type. Steerable nosewheel. Piper oleo-pneumatic shock absorbers. Cleveland wheels and Schenuit tyres, size 6·00-6, 4-ply rating, on all three wheels. Mainwheel tyre pressure 1·65 bars (24 lb/sq in), nosewheel 1·24 bars (18 lb/sq in). Cleveland high capacity disc brakes. Parking brake. Wheel speed fairings optional.

POWER PLANT: One 134 kW (180 hp) Avco Lycoming O-360-A4M flat-four engine, driving a Sensenich two-blade fixed-pitch metal propeller with spinner. Fuel in two tanks in wing leading-edges, with total capacity of 189 litres (50 US gallons), of which 181·5 litres (48 US gallons) are usable. Oil capacity 7·5 litres (2 US gallons).

ACCOMMODATION: Four persons in pairs in enclosed cabin. Individual adjustable front seats, with dual controls; individual rear seats. Large door on starboard side. Baggage compartment at rear of cabin, with volume of 0·74 m³ (26 cu ft) and capacity of 90 kg (200 lb); door on starboard side. Hatshelf. Rear seats removable to provide 1·25 m³ (44 cu ft) cargo space. Accommodation heated and ventilated. Windscreen defrosting.

SYSTEMS: Optional Piper Aire air-conditioning system. Electrical system includes 14V 60A alternator and 12V 25Ah battery. 35Ah battery otional (standard with Executive equipment package). Hydraulic system for brakes only. Vacuum system optional

AVIONICS AND EQUIPMENT: As for Warrior II, except that sun visors and towbar are standard. An exhaust gas temperature gauge is optional for the Executive version.

DIMENSIONS, EXTERNAL AND INTERNAL:
- As for Warrior II, except:
- Tailplane span: 3·92 m (12 ft 10½ in)
- Wheelbase: 2·00 m (6 ft 7 in)
- Propeller diameter: 1·93 m (6 ft 4 in)

AREAS: As for Warrior II

WEIGHTS AND LOADINGS:
- Weight empty, equipped (standard): 657 kg (1,449 lb)
- Max T-O and landing weight: 1,156 kg (2,550 lb)
- Max ramp weight: 1,160 kg (2,558 lb)
- Max wing loading: 73·2 kg/m² (15·0 lb/sq ft)
- Max power loading: 8·63 kg/kW (14·17 lb/hp)

PERFORMANCE (at max T-O weight):
- Never-exceed speed: 148 knots (275 km/h; 171 mph) CAS
- *Max level speed at S/L: 129 knots (239 km/h; 148 mph)
- *Best power cruising speed:
  - 75% power at 2,440 m (8,000 ft): 129 knots (239 km/h; 148 mph)
  - 65% power at 3,660 m (12,000 ft): 125 knots (231 km/h; 144 mph)
  - 55% power at 3,810 m (12,500 ft): 111 knots (206 km/h; 128 mph)
- *Best econ cruising speed:
  - 75% power at 2,440 m (8,000 ft): 126 knots (233 km/h; 145 mph)
  - 65% power at 3,660 m (12,000 ft): 122 knots (225 km/h; 140 mph)
  - 55% power at 3,810 m (12,500 ft): 107 knots (198 km/h; 123 mph)
- Stalling speed:
  - flaps up: 59 knots (109 km/h; 68 mph) CAS
  - flaps down: 53 knots (98 km/h; 61 mph) CAS
- Max rate of climb at S/L: 224 m (735 ft)/min
- Service ceiling: 4,160 m (13,650 ft)
- Absolute ceiling: 4,800 m (15,750 ft)
- T-O run: 265 m (870 ft)
- T-O to 15 m (50 ft): 506 m (1,660 ft)
- Landing from 15 m (50 ft): 424 m (1,390 ft)

Landing run 282 m (925 ft)
*Range with max fuel, allowances for taxi, T-O, climb and descent, and 45 min reserves at max range power:
at best power settings:
75% power at 2,440 m (8,000 ft) 520 nm (963 km; 599 miles)
65% power at 3,660 m (12,000 ft) 565 nm (1,047 km; 650 miles)
55% power at 3,810 m (12,500 ft) 580 nm (1,075 km; 668 miles)
at best econ power settings:
75% power at 2,440 m (8,000 ft) 600 nm (1,112 km; 691 miles)
65% power at 3,660 m (12,000 ft) 645 nm (1,196 km; 743 miles)
55% power at 3,810 m (12,500 ft) 670 nm (1,242 km; 772 miles)
With optional wheel fairings

PIPER (PA-28RT-201T) TURBO ARROW IV

The Piper Arrow derived from the Cherokee Arrow II, which was generally similar to the Cherokee Archer II but had a retractable landing gear, more powerful engine, and the untapered wings of the 1975 PA-28-180 Archer. In 1977, Piper updated this model by fitting long span tapered wings identical with those of the Archer II, but with increased fuel capacity, giving improved performance. The 1978 version of this aircraft was named Arrow III, the prototype of which flew for the first time on 16 September 1975, followed by the first production aircraft on 7 January 1977. Piper designation was PA-28R-201. The Turbo Arrow III differed by having a turbocharged engine, mounted in a streamline cowling, and the first production example of this version flew on 1 December 1976.

In 1979 Piper introduced an improved model with an all-moving T tailplane, but production of the Arrow IV with normally aspirated Avco Lycoming IO-360-C1C6 engine ended in 1982. The Turbo Arrow IV, which remains available, embodies the improvements detailed for the Archer II. A total of 870 Turbo Arrow IVs had been sold by 1 January 1986.

The 1986 Turbo Arrow IV introduced as standard an engine driven vacuum pump system; standby electric vacuum pump; advanced instrument panel including gyro horizon, directional gyro, turn rate indicator, rate of climb indicator, outside air temperature gauge and electric clock; heated pitot head; automatic emergency locator beacon; wingtip strobe lights; and a basic lighting package comprising instrument panel white backlighting and red overhead lighting, cabin dome light, navigation, taxi and landing lights and avionics dimming.

An optional **Executive** package comprises deluxe interior with four headrests and window curtains; tinted windscreen and side windows; overhead vent system and vent fan; true airspeed indicator; alternate static source; pilot's and co-pilot's vertically adjustable seats; crew cup holders; 'Quietized' cabin soundproofing; external power receptacle; cigarette lighter; 35Ah battery; and wingtip recognition lights, adding 27·3 kg (60·2 lb) to aircraft basic weight. Other optional equipment includes a three-blade propeller; polished spinner (with three-blade propeller only); cold weather starting kit; engine hour recorder; digital clock; control wheel approach plate holder; lockable fuel caps; and zinc chromate protective finish.

In addition to the above equipment, six avionics packages are available optionally for the Turbo Arrow IV.

The description of the Archer II applies also to the Turbo Arrow IV, except for the following details:

Piper Dakota, a four-seat aircraft with non-retractable landing gear

TAIL UNIT: Cantilever T tail of light alloy construction. All-moving tailplane with trim tab. Rudder trim.

LANDING GEAR: Tricycle type, retracted hydraulically with an electrically operated pump supplying the hydraulic pressure. In addition to the usual 'gear up' warning horn and red light, an automatic extension system drops the landing gear automatically if power is reduced and airspeed drops below 91 knots (169 km/h; 105 mph). The sensing system consists of a small probe mounted on the port side of the fuselage. Being located in the propeller slipstream, it can differentiate between a climb with power on and an approach to land with power reduced. A free-fall emergency extension system is also fitted. An 'anti-retraction' system guards against premature retraction of the landing gear below an airspeed of 74 knots (137 km/h; 85 mph) at take-off, or accidental retraction on the ground. There is also a manual override lever by which the pilot can hold the landing gear retracted as airspeed falls below 91 knots (169 km/h; 105 mph). Main units retract inward into wings, nose unit rearward. All units fitted with oleo-pneumatic shock absorbers. Mainwheels and tyres size 6·00-6, 6-ply rating, pressure 2·07 bars (30 lb/sq in). Nosewheel and tyre size 5·00-5, 4-ply rating, pressure 1·86 bars (27 lb/sq in). High capacity dual hydraulic disc brakes and parking brake.

POWER PLANT: One 149 kW (200 hp) Continental TSIO-360-FB flat-six turbocharged engine, driving a Hartzell two-blade constant-speed metal propeller with spinner. A three-blade propeller is optional, but essential if optional built-in oxygen system is installed. Fuel tanks in wing leading-edges with total capacity of 291 litres (77 US gallons), of which 273 litres (72 US gallons) are usable. Oil capacity 7·5 litres (2 US gallons).

SYSTEMS: Generally as for Archer II and Warrior II, plus electro-hydraulic system for landing gear actuation. An oxygen system of 1·37 m³ (48·3 cu ft) capacity is available optionally.

AVIONICS AND EQUIPMENT: Optional avionics and standard equipment generally as detailed for Warrior II, plus cylinder head temperature gauge, exhaust gas temperature gauge, 65A electric generator, dual range electric auxiliary fuel pump as standard equipment. Optional equipment as listed in Executive paragraph and for Archer II and Warrior II, plus cold weather start kit.

DIMENSIONS, EXTERNAL:
Wing span 10·80 m (35 ft 5 in)
Wing chord: at root 1·60 m (5 ft 3 in)
at tip 1·07 m (3 ft 6¼ in)
Length overall 8·33 m (27 ft 3¾ in)
Height overall 2·52 m (8 ft 3¼ in)
Tailplane span 3·30 m (10 ft 10 in)
Wheel track 3·19 m (10 ft 5½ in)
Wheelbase 2·39 m (7 ft 10¼ in)
Propeller diameter 1·93 m (6 ft 4 in)
Cabin door (stbd): Width 0·91 m (3 ft 0 in)
Height 0·89 m (2 ft 11 in)
Baggage door (stbd): Width 0·56 m (1 ft 10 in)
Height 0·51 m (1 ft 8 in)

DIMENSIONS, INTERNAL:
Cabin:
Length, panel to rear bulkhead 2·46 m (8 ft 1 in)
Max width 1·05 m (3 ft 5½ in)
Max height 1·24 m (4 ft 1 in)
Volume (incl baggage area) 3·00 m³ (106 cu ft)

AREA:
Wings, gross 15·79 m² (170 sq ft)

WEIGHTS AND LOADINGS:
Weight empty 786 kg (1,732 lb)
Max T-O weight 1,315 kg (2,900 lb)
Max ramp weight 1,321 kg (2,912 lb)
Max wing loading 83·29 kg/m² (17·06 lb/sq ft)
Max power loading 8·83 kg/kW (14·5 lb/hp)

PERFORMANCE (at max T-O weight):
Never-exceed speed 186 knots (344 km/h; 214 mph) CAS
Max level speed at 4,265 m (14,000 ft) 178 knots (330 km/h; 205 mph)
Best power cruising speed at optimum altitude:
75% power 172 knots (319 km/h; 198 mph)
65% power 167 knots (309 km/h; 192 mph)
55% power 157 knots (291 km/h; 181 mph)
Best econ cruising speed at optimum altitude:
75% power 168 knots (311 km/h; 193 mph)
65% power 164 knots (304 km/h; 189 mph)
55% power 153 knots (284 km/h; 176 mph)
Stalling speed:
flaps up 63 knots (117 km/h; 72 mph) CAS
flaps down 58 knots (108 km/h; 67 mph) CAS
Max rate of climb at S/L 287 m (940 ft)/min
Max approved operating altitude 6,100 m (20,000 ft)
T-O run 338 m (1,110 ft)
T-O to 15 m (50 ft) 494 m (1,620 ft)
Landing from 15 m (50 ft) 475 m (1,560 ft)
Landing run 197 m (645 ft)
Range with max fuel, allowances for taxi, T-O, climb and descent, and 45 min reserves at max range power:
at best power settings:
75% power 695 nm (1,287 km; 800 miles)
65% power 725 nm (1,343 km; 835 miles)
55% power 775 nm (1,435 km; 892 miles)
at best econ power settings:
75% power 790 nm (1,465 km; 910 miles)
65% power 830 nm (1,539 km; 956 miles)
55% power 900 nm (1,667 km; 1,036 miles)

Piper Turbo Arrow IV retractable gear four-seat cabin monoplane with T tail

PIPER (PA-28-236) DAKOTA

Piper introduced in 1978 an addition to the Warrior, Archer, Arrow line known as the PA-28-236 Dakota, which differs primarily by having a 175 kW (235 hp) Avco Lycoming engine to provide increased performance, and increased capacity fuel tanks to cater for this power plant.

The 1986 version of the Dakota introduced the same standard items as listed for the Turbo Arrow IV, plus high performance wheel fairings. An **Executive** package as detailed for the Arrow IV is also available, and adds 26·9 kg (59·3 lb) to aircraft basic weight. A range of Collins, King and Narco avionics packages is also available optionally.

Licence assembly of the Dakota was undertaken by the Chilean aircraft industry (ENAER, which see); a total of 27 was completed. Piper sales of the PA-28-236 Dakota totalled 705 at 1 January 1986.

The description of the Archer II applies also to the Dakota, except as follows:

Power Plant: One 175 kW (235 hp) Avco Lycoming O-540-J3A5D flat-six engine, driving a Hartzell two-blade constant-speed metal propeller with spinner. Two integral fuel tanks in each wing, with a total capacity of 291·5 litres (77 US gallons), of which 272·5 litres (72 US gallons) are usable. Refuelling points on upper surface of each wing. Oil capacity 11·5 litres (3 US gallons).

Avionics and Equipment: As for the Turbo Arrow IV, six optional factory installed avionics packages are available, as well as a wide range of other avionics equipment to customer's requirements. Optional equipment includes items provided in the Executive package, plus engine hour recorder, digital clock, carburettor ice detector, approach plate holder, cabin fire extinguisher, rotating beacon, external power receptacle, polished propeller spinner, Piper Aire air-conditioning, stainless steel control cables, lockable fuel tank caps, heavy duty tyres and brakes, and zinc chromate treatment of aluminium parts.

Dimensions, external and internal: As for Archer II except:
- Length overall 7·54 m (24 ft 8¾ in)
- Height overall 2·18 m (7 ft 2 in)
- Wheelbase 1·98 m (6 ft 6 in)

Weights and Loadings:
- Weight empty 758 kg (1,672 lb)
- Max T-O weight 1,361 kg (3,000 lb)
- Max ramp weight 1,365 kg (3,011 lb)
- Max wing loading 85·93 kg/m² (17·6 lb/sq ft)
- Max power loading 7·78 kg/kW (12·8 lb/hp)

Performance (at max T-O weight):
- Max level speed at S/L 148 knots (274 km/h; 170 mph)
- Best power cruising speed at optimum altitude:
  - 75% power 144 knots (267 km/h; 166 mph)
  - 65% power 139 knots (257 km/h; 160 mph)
  - 55% power 130 knots (241 km/h; 150 mph)
- Best econ cruising speed at optimum altitude:
  - 75% power 139 knots (258 km/h; 160 mph)
  - 65% power 134 knots (248 km/h; 154 mph)
  - 55% power 126 knots (234 km/h; 145 mph)
- Stalling speed:
  - flaps up 63 knots (117 km/h; 73 mph) CAS
  - flaps down 56 knots (104 km/h; 65 mph) CAS
- Max rate of climb at S/L 338 m (1,110 ft)/min
- Service ceiling 5,335 m (17,500 ft)
- Absolute ceiling 5,945 m (19,500 ft)
- T-O run 270 m (886 ft)
- T-O to 15 m (50 ft) 371 m (1,216 ft)
- Landing from 15 m (50 ft):
  - standard brakes 526 m (1,725 ft)
  - heavy duty brakes 466 m (1,530 ft)
- Landing run: standard brakes 252 m (825 ft)
  - heavy duty brakes 195 m (640 ft)
- Range with max fuel, allowances for taxi, T-O, climb, cruise, descent, and 45 min reserves at max range power:
  - at best power settings at optimum altitude:
    - 75% power 650 nm (1,205 km; 748 miles)
    - 65% power 710 nm (1,315 km; 817 miles)
    - 55% power 750 nm (1,390 km; 863 miles)
  - at best econ power settings at optimum altitude:
    - 75% power 720 nm (1,334 km; 829 miles)
    - 65% power 770 nm (1,427 km; 886 miles)
    - 55% power 810 nm (1,501 km; 933 miles)

PIPER (PA-32-301) SARATOGA

On 17 December 1979, Piper announced that it had begun production of a new family of six-seat single-engined aircraft known as Saratogas, to replace the PA-32 SIX 300 and T tail Lance series (all described in 1979-80 *Jane's*). All Saratogas have a common airframe, with a conventional low-mounted tailplane and a semi-tapered wing of longer span than the wing of the aircraft they supersede.

Three versions of the Saratoga are available:

PA-32-301 Saratoga. Basic version, as described in detail.

PA-32R-301 Saratoga SP. Retractable landing gear version of the Saratoga, described separately.

PA-32R-301T Turbo Saratoga SP. Turbocharged version of the Saratoga SP, described separately.

These aircraft are available with nine optional factory installed avionics packages.

The 1986 versions of the Saratoga introduced as standard equipment blind-flying instrumentation with 3 in attitude and directional gyros; electric clock; outside air temperature gauge; pictorial turn rate, rate of climb and airspeed indicators; basic lighting package which comprises avionics dimming, instrument panel white backlighting and overhead red lighting; waterfall switch panel light; cabin dome, map and reading lights; landing/taxi and navigation lights; rotating beacon; wing strobe lights; entrance step; wheel fairings; engine driven and electric standby vacuum systems with vacuum gauge, regulator, filter and warning lights; 35Ah battery; and automatic emergency locator beacon.

An optional **Executive** package includes a deluxe lounge interior with club seating, headrests for all seats, window curtains, refreshment console and fold-down armrests for fifth and sixth seats; tinted windscreen and side windows; pilot's and co-pilot's vertically adjustable seats; ventilation fan; wingtip recognition lights; 'Quietized' cabin soundproofing; true airspeed indicator; cigarette lighter; 35Ah battery; external power receptacle with weather-tight cap; crew cupholders; courtesy light package comprising automatic forward compartment light, cabin entrance door light and rear cabin entrance door light; heavy duty brakes and tyres on main landing gear; and heavy duty tyre on 6 inch nosewheel. The package adds 33·1 kg (73·1 lb) to basic aircraft weight.

At 1 January 1986, sales of Saratoga models totalled 329.

Type: Six-seat cabin monoplane.

Wings: Cantilever low-wing monoplane. Light alloy single-spar structure with glassfibre wingtips. Plain ailerons of light alloy construction. Electrically operated trailing-edge flaps of light alloy construction with ribbed skins.

Fuselage: Conventional semi-monocoque structure of light alloy. Glassfibre engine cowling.

Tail Unit: Cantilever structure of light alloy, except for glassfibre tips on fin and tailplane. Fin and rudder have ribbed metal skins. One-piece all-moving horizontal surface with combined anti-servo and trim tab. Trimmable rudder.

Landing Gear: Non-retractable tricycle type. Steerable nosewheel. Piper oleo-pneumatic shock absorbers. Single wheel on each unit. Mainwheel tyres size 6·00-6, 8-ply rating, pressure 3·79 bars (55 lb/sq in). Nosewheel tyre size 5·00-5, 6-ply rating, pressure 2·41 bars (35 lb/sq in). Nosewheel tyre size 6·00-6 optional. High capacity disc brakes. Parking brake. Wheel fairings optional. Heavy duty brakes and tyres optional.

Power Plant: One 224 kW (300 hp) Avco Lycoming IO-540-K1G5 flat-six engine, driving a Hartzell two-blade constant-speed metal propeller with spinner. Three-blade propeller optional. Polished spinner optional (three-blade propeller only). Two fuel tanks in each wing with combined capacity of 405 litres (107 US gallons), of which 386 litres (102 US gallons) are usable. Refuelling points on wing upper surface. Oil capacity 11·5 litres (3 US gallons).

Accommodation: Enclosed cabin, seating six people in pairs. Dual controls and toe brakes standard. Two forward hinged doors, one on starboard side forward, overwing; one on port side at rear end of cabin. Space for 45 kg (100 lb) baggage at rear of cabin, with external baggage/utility door on port side. Additional baggage space, capacity 45 kg (100 lb), between engine fireproof bulkhead and instrument panel, with external door on starboard side. Pilot's storm window. Sun visors. Accommodation heated and ventilated. Windscreen defroster standard.

Systems: Piper Aire air-conditioning, vacuum and oxygen systems optional, including a built-in oxygen system of 1·81 m³ (64·0 cu ft) capacity. Hydraulic system for brakes only. Electrical system includes a 14V 60A engine driven alternator, and 12V 25Ah battery. 35Ah battery optional (standard with Executive package).

Avionics and Equipment: A wide range of avionics is available to customer's requirements, including weather radar with internal wing mounted antenna. Standard equipment includes recording tachometer, sensitive altimeter, dual cylinder head temperature and exhaust gas temperature gauges, fore and aft adjustable pilot and co-pilot seats with shoulder and safety belts, armrests, map pockets, glove compartment, soundproofing, stall warning device, provisions for emergency locator transmitter, alternator failure and low oil pressure warning lights, full flow oil filter, fuel quick drains, oil quick drain, jack pads, stowable towbar, and tiedown rings. Optional equipment includes items detailed in Executive package, plus digital clock; encoding altimeter; engine hour recorder; cabin fire extinguisher; stainless steel control cables; and zinc chromate treatment of aluminium parts.

Dimensions, external:
- Wing span 11·02 m (36 ft 2 in)
- Length overall: Saratoga 8·44 m (27 ft 8½ in)
  - Turbo Saratoga 8·59 m (28 ft 2 in)
- Height overall 2·49 m (8 ft 2 in)
- Tailplane span 3·94 m (12 ft 11 in)
- Wheel track 3·23 m (10 ft 7 in)
- Wheelbase 2·36 m (7 ft 9 in)
- Cabin door (fwd, stbd): Height 0·89 m (2 ft 11 in)
  - Width 0·91 m (3 ft 0 in)
- Cabin door (rear, port): Height 0·72 m (2 ft 4½ in)
  - Width 0·71 m (2 ft 4 in)
- Baggage door (fwd): Height 0·41 m (1 ft 4 in)
  - Width 0·56 m (1 ft 10 in)
- Baggage/utility door (rear): Height 0·52 m (1 ft 8½ in)
  - Width 0·66 m (2 ft 2 in)

Dimensions, internal:
- Cabin: Length (instrument panel to rear bulkhead) 3·15 m (10 ft 4¼ in)
  - Max width 1·24 m (4 ft 1 in)
  - Max height 1·07 m (3 ft 6 in)
  - Volume (incl rear baggage area) 5·53 m³ (195·3 cu ft)
- Baggage compartment volume:
  - forward 0·20 m³ (7·0 cu ft)
  - rear 0·49 m³ (17·3 cu ft)

Area:
- Wings, gross 16·55 m² (178·3 sq ft)

Weights and Loadings:
- Weight empty 906 kg (1,998 lb)
- Max T-O weight 1,633 kg (3,600 lb)
- Max ramp weight 1,640 kg (3,615 lb)
- Max wing loading 98·6 kg/m² (20·2 lb/sq ft)
- Max power loading 7·30 kg/kW (12·0 lb/hp)

Performance (at max T-O weight except where indicated):
- Max level speed at optimum altitude 152 knots (282 km/h; 175 mph)
- Best power cruising speed at optimum altitude:
  - at 75% power 150 knots (278 km/h; 173 mph)
  - at 65% power 146 knots (270 km/h; 168 mph)
  - at 55% power 136 knots (252 km/h; 156 mph)
- Best econ cruising speed at optimum altitude:
  - at 75% power 148 knots (274 km/h; 170 mph)
  - at 65% power 144 knots (267 km/h; 166 mph)
  - at 55% power 133 knots (246 km/h; 153 mph)
- Stalling speed:
  - flaps up 66 knots (122 km/h; 76 mph) CAS
  - flaps down 60 knots (111 km/h; 69 mph) CAS
- Max rate of climb at S/L 302 m (990 ft)/min
- Service ceiling 4,875 m (16,000 ft)
- T-O run: 2-blade propeller 361 m (1,183 ft)
  - 3-blade propeller 309 m (1,013 ft)
- T-O to 15 m (50 ft): 2-blade propeller 536 m (1,759 ft)
  - 3-blade propeller 479 m (1,573 ft)
- Landing from 15 m (50 ft):
  - standard brakes 491 m (1,612 ft)
  - heavy duty brakes 466 m (1,530 ft)
- Landing run: standard brakes 223 m (732 ft)
  - heavy duty brakes 198 m (650 ft)
- Range with max fuel, allowances for taxi, T-O, climb, descent, and 45 min reserves at max range power:
  - best power settings at optimum altitude:
    - 75% power 745 nm (1,381 km; 858 miles)
    - 65% power 805 nm (1,492 km; 927 miles)
    - 55% power 849 nm (1,573 km; 978 miles)
  - best econ power settings at optimum altitude:
    - 75% power 823 nm (1,525 km; 948 miles)
    - 65% power 911 nm (1,688 km; 1,049 miles)
    - 55% power 960 nm (1,778 km; 1,105 miles)

Piper PA-32-301 Saratoga six-seat cabin monoplane

PIPER (PA-32R-301) SARATOGA SP

This is a retractable landing gear model of the Saratoga, of which two versions were introduced in 1980:

PA-32R-301 Saratoga SP. Basic version, similar to the PA-32-301 Saratoga but with retractable landing gear and new options as described.

PA-32R-301T Turbo Saratoga SP. As Saratoga SP, but power plant comprises one 224 kW (300 hp) Avco Lycoming TIO-540-S1AD flat-six turbocharged engine, driving a Hartzell two-blade constant-speed metal propeller. (Three-blade propeller optional.) Additional standard equipment for Turbo Saratoga SP includes cylinder head and exhaust gas temperature gauges, engine overboost warning light and manually controlled cowl flaps. Options available for this version include electric propeller and windscreen de-icing, pneumatic wing and tail surface de-icing, and a built-in oxygen system.

Both models are available with nine optional factory installed avionics packages, including a King flight director. The 1986 versions of the Saratoga SP and Turbo Saratoga SP introduced as standard those items listed for the Saratoga, with the exception of wheel fairings and rotating beacon.

An optional **Executive** package, similar to that listed for the Saratoga, is available for both models, and adds 33·1 kg (73·1 lb) to basic aircraft weight.

At 1 January 1986 sales of the Saratoga SP and Turbo Saratoga SP totalled 382 and 378 respectively.

The description of the Saratoga applies also to the retractable landing gear versions, except as follows:

WINGS, TAIL UNIT: Pneumatic de-icing system for wing and tail unit leading-edges is available optionally for the Turbo Saratoga SP.

LANDING GEAR: Hydraulically retractable tricycle type with single wheel on each unit. Main units retract inward, nosewheel aft. Integrated automatic system which extends the landing gear at 102 knots (189 km/h; 17 mph), unless overridden by pilot. Emergency free-fall extension system. Piper oleo-pneumatic shock absorbers. Steerable nosewheel. Mainwheels and tyres size 6·00-6, 8-ply rating, pressure 2·62 bars (38 lb/sq in). Nosewheel and tyre size 5·00-5, 6-ply rating, pressure 2·41 bars (35 lb/sq in). High capacity hydraulic disc brakes. Parking brake. Heavy duty tyres and brakes optional.

POWER PLANT: As for Saratoga except as detailed for Turbo Saratoga SP. Propeller de-icing optional for Turbo Saratoga SP.

ACCOMMODATION: As for Saratoga, but inertia reel safety harnesses standard for all forward facing seats, and pilot's electrically heated windscreen plate optional for Turbo Saratoga SP.

SYSTEMS: As for Saratoga, but electrically driven hydraulic pump for landing gear actuation; built-in oxygen system of 1·81 m³ (64 cu ft) capacity and 95A alternator available optionally for Turbo Saratoga SP.

AVIONICS AND EQUIPMENT: Generally as listed for Saratoga, with amendments as noted in this entry, plus optional wing ice inspection light for Turbo Saratoga SP.

DIMENSIONS, EXTERNAL: As for Saratoga, except:
- Length overall: Saratoga SP 8·45 m (27 ft 8½ in)
  - Turbo Saratoga SP 8·69 m (28 ft 6 in)
- Height overall 2·59 m (8 ft 6 in)
- Wheel track 3·39 m (11 ft 1½ in)
- Wheelbase 2·43 m (7 ft 11½ in)

WEIGHTS AND LOADINGS (A: Saratoga SP; B: Turbo Saratoga SP): As for Saratoga, except:
- Weight empty: A 926 kg (2,041 lb)
  - B 961 kg (2,119 lb)

PERFORMANCE (at max T-O weight, except where indicated. A: Saratoga SP/two-blade propeller; B: Turbo Saratoga SP/two-blade propeller; C: Saratoga SP/three-blade propeller; D: Turbo Saratoga SP/three-blade propeller):
- Max level speed at optimum altitude:
  - A 164 knots (304 km/h; 189 mph)
  - B 191 knots (354 km/h; 220 mph)
  - D 195 knots (361 km/h; 225 mph)
- Best power cruising speed at optimum altitude:
  - at 75% power: A 159 knots (295 km/h; 183 mph)
  - B 177 knots (328 km/h; 204 mph)
  - at 65% power: A 153 knots (283 km/h; 176 mph)
  - B 166 knots (307 km/h; 191 mph)
  - at 55% power: A 144 knots (267 km/h; 166 mph)
  - B 152 knots (282 km/h; 175 mph)
- Best econ cruising speed at optimum altitude:
  - at 75% power: A 157 knots (291 km/h; 181 mph)
  - B 171 knots (317 km/h; 197 mph)
  - at 65% power: A 151 knots (280 km/h; 174 mph)
  - B 160 knots (296 km/h; 184 mph)
  - at 55% power: A 141 knots (261 km/h; 162 mph)
  - B 145 knots (269 km/h; 167 mph)
- Stalling speed, flaps up:
  - A 65 knots (121 km/h; 75 mph) CAS
  - B 63 knots (118 km/h; 73 mph) CAS
- Stalling speed, flaps down:
  - A 59 knots (110 km/h; 68 mph) CAS
  - B 60 knots (111 km/h; 69 mph) CAS
- Max rate of climb at S/L: A 308 m (1,010 ft)/min
  - B 341 m (1,120 ft)/min
- Service ceiling: A 5,090 m (16,700 ft)
  - *B 6,100 m (20,000 ft)
- Absolute ceiling: A 5,595 m (18,350 ft)
  - *B 6,100 m (20,000 ft)
- T-O run, and T-O to 15 m (50 ft): as for Saratoga and Turbo Saratoga
- Landing from 15 m (50 ft), and landing run: as for Saratoga and Turbo Saratoga
- Range with max fuel, allowances for taxi, T-O, climb, descent, and 45 min reserves at max range power:
  - Best power settings at optimum altitude:
    - 75% power: A 784 nm (1,453 km; 903 miles)
    - B 730 nm (1,353 km; 840 miles)
    - 65% power: A 828 nm (1,533 km; 953 miles)
    - B 790 nm (1,465 km; 910 miles)
    - 55% power: A 869 nm (1,611 km; 1,001 miles)
    - B 843 nm (1,562 km; 971 miles)
  - Best econ power settings at optimum altitude:
    - 75% power: A 865 nm (1,603 km; 996 miles)
    - B 844 nm (1,564 km; 972 miles)
    - 65% power: A 937 nm (1,736 km; 1,079 miles)
    - B 920 nm (1,704 km; 1,059 miles)
    - 55% power: A 983 nm (1,822 km; 1,132 miles)
    - B 950 nm (1,760 km; 1,094 miles)

**Max certificated altitude*

Piper PA-32R-301T Turbo Saratoga SP

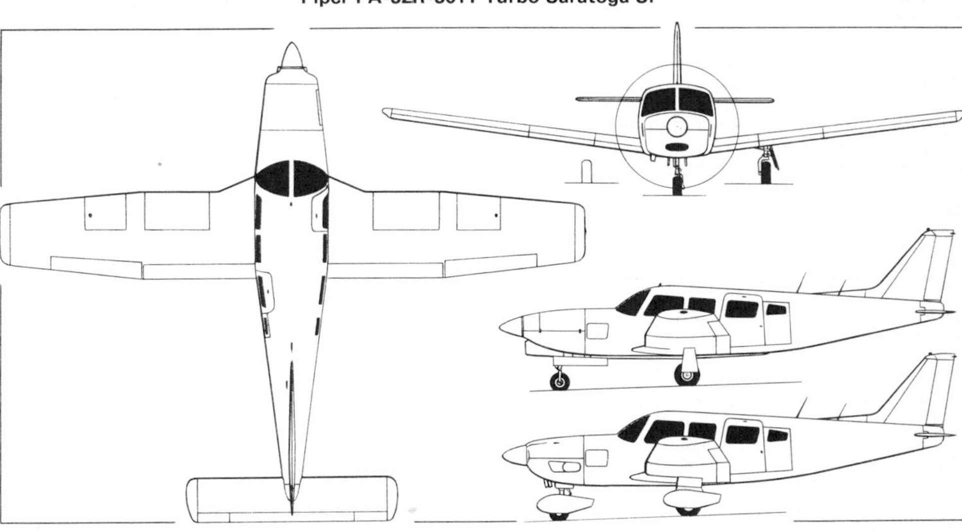

Piper PA-32R-301T Turbo Saratoga SP, with additional side view (bottom right) of PA-32-301 Saratoga *(Pilot Press)*

PIPER (PA-31-350) CHIEFTAIN

Announced on 11 September 1972, the PA-31-350 Chieftain is a lengthened version of the discontinued Navajo C/R, with the fuselage extended by 0·61 m (2 ft 0 in) and with 261 kW (350 hp) counter-rotating turbocharged engines.

The main cabin floor is designed to carry heavy concentrated loads of up to 976 kg/m² (200 lb/sq ft) and, in addition to the 6·14 m³ (217 cu ft) of cargo space in the main cabin, 91 kg (200 lb) of cargo or baggage can be carried in the forward nose compartment, and 68 kg (150 lb) in the rear of each engine nacelle.

Two optional interior groups of equipment are available, depending upon the proposed use of the aircraft:

Standard Interior Group. Six adjustable seats. Pilot and co-pilot seats adjust fore, aft, vertically and tilt, have headrests, folding armrests and under-seat oxygen mask storage. Passenger seats in club arrangement with headrests, folding armrests, seat belts, and magazine storage pockets on each seat back. Inertia reel safety harnesses standard on all forward-facing seats. 'No smoking/Fasten seat belt' sign. Pull-curtain cockpit divider. Choice of eleven interior colour schemes.

Commuter Interior Group. Ten forward facing seats. Eight adjustable and reclining passenger seats with oxygen mask stowage and magazine storage as above. 'No smoking/Fasten seat belt' sign. Pull-curtain cockpit divider. Choice of nine interior colour schemes. Adds 39·5 kg (87 lb) to basic empty weight.

Two optional equipment groups are available for the Chieftain, as follows:

Co-pilot Flight Instrument Group. Includes blind-flying instrumentation with 3 in attitude and directional gyros, clock, rate of climb indicator, sensitive altimeter, true airspeed indicator, heated pitot, alternate static source, and individual rheostat controlled lighting. Group available with electric or vacuum gyros; adding 5·6 kg (12·4 lb) or 5·9 kg (12·9 lb) respectively.

De-icing Group. Pneumatic de-icing boot installation for wing and tail unit leading-edges; electric propeller de-icing; ice inspection light; heated lift detector; fuselage ice protection shields; and electric windscreen de-icing and windscreen wiper port side; adding 28·4 kg (62·7 lb).

Re-certification for flight into known icing conditions, to newer, more stringent standards, applies to aircraft equipped with the optional De-icing Group.

A total of 1,825 Chieftains had been sold by 1 January 1986.

TYPE: Six/ten-seat passenger transport.

WINGS: Cantilever low-wing monoplane. Wing section NACA 63_2415 at root, NACA 63_1212 at tip. 1° aerodynamic twist. 2° 30′ geometric twist. All-metal structure, with heavy stepped down main spar, front and rear spars, lateral stringers, ribs and stressed skin. Wings spliced on centreline with heavy steel plates. Flush riveted forward of main spar. Wing root leading-edge extended forward between nacelle and fuselage. Glassfibre wingtips. Balanced ailerons interconnected with rudder. Trim tab in starboard aileron. Electrically operated flaps. Pneumatic de-icing boots optional.

FUSELAGE: All-metal semi-monocoque structure.

TAIL UNIT: Cantilever all-metal structure, with sweptback vertical surfaces. Trim tabs in rudder and starboard elevator. Elevator horn anti-icing boots standard. Optional pneumatic de-icing boots.

LANDING GEAR: Hydraulically actuated retractable tricycle type, with single wheel on each unit. Manual hydraulic emergency extension. Mainwheels and tyres size 6·50-10, eight-ply rating, pressure 4·14 bars (60 lb/sq in). Steerable nosewheel and tyre size 6·00-6, six-ply rating, pressure 2·90 bars (42 lb/sq in). Toe controlled hydraulic disc brakes. Heavy duty brakes and toe operated brakes for co-pilot optional. Parking brake. Mainwheel doors close when gear is fully extended.

POWER PLANT: Two 261 kW (350 hp) Avco Lycoming flat-six turbocharged counter-rotating engines, one TIO-540-J2BD and one LTIO-540-J2BD, each driving a Hartzell three-blade constant-speed fully-feathering metal propeller. Four rubber fuel cells in wings; inboard cells each contain 212 litres (56 US gallons), outboard cells each 151·5 litres (40 US gallons). Total standard fuel capacity 727 litres (192 US gallons), of which 689 litres (182 US gallons) are usable. Optional fuel tank in each nacelle, reducing baggage capacity, to provide total usable capacity of 893 litres (236 US gallons). Oil capacity 22·7 litres (6 US gallons).

ACCOMMODATION: Pilot and co-pilot on individually adjustable and reclining seats. Dual controls standard. Interior seating and equipment as detailed in optional interior groups. Cabin heated by thermostatically controlled Janitrol 50,000 BTU combustion heater. Piper Aire 16,000 BTU air-conditioning system optional. Baggage/cargo compartments in nose and rear fuselage, capacity of each 91 kg (200 lb), and in the rear of each engine nacelle, each 68 kg (150 lb) when optional fuel tanks are not installed, or 22·7 kg (50 lb) in each when tanks are installed.

SYSTEMS: Hydraulic system utilises two engine driven pumps, 24V electrical system supplied by two engine driven 28V 70A alternators and 24V 17Ah battery; 25Ah battery optional. External power socket standard. Oxygen system of 3·23 m³ (114 cu ft) capacity optional.

AVIONICS AND EQUIPMENT: A full IFR avionics package, including flight control system, is standard on 1985 Chieftains. In addition, there is a wide range of alternative options by Aeronetics, Bendix, Collins, Century Flight Systems, King, Piper, SunAir, United, and Wulfsburg. These include encoding altimeter, HF transceiver, radar altimeter, radio altimeter, radio telephone, R/Nav, V/Nav, and weather radar. Standard equipment includes pilot's blind-flying instrumentation; clock; dual exhaust gas temperature gauges; flight hour recorder; dual manifold pressure gauges; outside air temperature gauge; rate of climb indicator; sensitive altimeter; true airspeed indicator; fully adjustable pilot and co-pilot seats with shoulder safety belts and inertia reels; headrests; folding armrests; alternate static source; heated pitot; alternator and pneumatic failure, low fuel, door ajar, and heater overheat warning lights; stall warning device; corrosion proofing; cabin dome, courtesy, instrument panel, map, reading, landing, navigation, strobe and taxi lights; external power socket; tiedown rings; and stowable towbar. Optional equipment includes items covered by the operational groups as detailed, plus a wide range of cabin equipment including pilot's door, storage cabinets and drawers, tables, shoulder safety belts and inertia reels for passenger seats, fore and aft cabin dividers, auxiliary cabin heater, cabin fire extinguisher, cabin chimes, tinted windows, Thermos unit and refreshment centre, emergency locator transmitter, ground and in-flight recognition lights, lockable fuel caps, and fuselage ice protection shields. Also available optionally is a cargo kit which includes cargo barrier, tiedown rings and net, eight seat track tiedown rings, four-track cargo rollers, two strap/tiedown pouches, and cargo kit provisions.

DIMENSIONS, EXTERNAL:

Wing span	12·40 m (40 ft 8 in)
Length overall	10·55 m (34 ft 7½ in)
Height overall	3·96 m (13 ft 0 in)
Tailplane span	5·52 m (18 ft 1½ in)
Wheel track	4·19 m (13 ft 9 in)
Wheelbase	3·24 m (10 ft 7½ in)
Propeller diameter	2·03 m (6 ft 8 in)
Distance between propeller centres	3·35 m (11 ft 0 in)
Cabin door (port, rear): Height	1·14 m (3 ft 9 in)
Width	0·70 m (2 ft 3½ in)
Utility door (port, rear): Height	1·14 m (3 ft 9 in)
Width	0·43 m (1 ft 5 in)
Baggage door (port, fwd): Height	0·64 m (2 ft 1 in)
Width	0·71 m (2 ft 4 in)

DIMENSIONS, INTERNAL:

Cabin: Length	3·84 m (12 ft 7 in)
Baggage/cargo compartments:	
Engine nacelles (each)	0·37 m³ (13·25 cu ft)
Engine nacelles (each) with optional fuel	0·17 m³ (6·0 cu ft)

WEIGHTS AND LOADINGS:

Weight empty (standard)	1,915 kg (4,221 lb)
Max T-O and landing weight	3,175 kg (7,000 lb)
Max ramp weight	3,196 kg (7,045 lb)
Max wing loading	149·4 kg/m² (30·6 lb/sq ft)
Max power loading	6·08 kg/kW (10·0 lb/hp)

PERFORMANCE (at max T-O weight, except where indicated):

Max level speed at average cruise weight	231 knots (428 km/h; 266 mph)
Cruising speed at average cruise weight:	
75% power at 6,100 m (20,000 ft)	221 knots (409 km/h; 254 mph)
75% power at 3,660 m (12,000 ft)	205 knots (380 km/h; 236 mph)
65% power at 6,100 m (20,000 ft)	210 knots (389 km/h; 242 mph)
65% power at 3,660 m (12,000 ft)	191 knots (354 km/h; 220 mph)
55% power at 4,575 m (15,000 ft)	177 knots (328 km/h; 204 mph)
55% power at 3,660 m (12,000 ft)	173 knots (320 km/h; 199 mph)
Minimum single-engine control speed (VMC)	78 knots (144 km/h; 90 mph)
Stalling speed: flaps up	80 knots (148 km/h; 92 mph)
flaps down	74 knots (137 km/h; 85 mph)
Max rate of climb at S/L	341 m (1,120 ft)/min
Rate of climb at S/L, one engine out	70 m (230 ft)/min
Max certificated altitude	7,315 m (24,000 ft)
Service ceiling, one engine out	4,175 m (13,700 ft)
T-O run	411 m (1,350 ft)
T-O to 15 m (50 ft)	765 m (2,510 ft)
Landing from 15 m (50 ft)	573 m (1,880 ft)
Landing run	319 m (1,045 ft)

Range, with allowances for start, taxi, T-O, climb, and 45 min reserves at long-range cruise power; A with max standard fuel, B with max optional fuel:

75% power at 6,100 m (20,000 ft):	
A	885 nm (1,640 km; 1,019 miles)
B	1,210 nm (2,240 km; 1,392 miles)
75% power at 3,660 m (12,000 ft):	
A	855 nm (1,585 km; 985 miles)
B	1,100 nm (2,038 km; 1,266 miles)
65% power at 6,100 m (20,000 ft):	
A	925 nm (1,714 km; 1,065 miles)
B	1,260 nm (2,333 km; 1,450 miles)
65% power at 3,660 m (12,000 ft):	
A	900 nm (1,667 km; 1,036 miles)
B	1,225 nm (2,268 km; 1,409 miles)
55% power at 4,575 m (15,000 ft):	
A	950 nm (1,761 km; 1,094 miles)
B	1,290 nm (2,389 km; 1,484 miles)
55% power at 3,660 m (12,000 ft):	
A	950 nm (1,761 km; 1,094 miles)
B	1,290 nm (2,389 km; 1,484 miles)

Piper Chieftain six/ten-seat executive/commuter/cargo aircraft

PIPER (PA-31P-350) MOJAVE

Announced by Piper on 20 November 1982, the Mojave is a piston engined counterpart of the turboprop Cheyenne II, of much the same size but with wings of slightly increased span and no tip tanks. It is pressurised, and its direct drive counter-rotating and turbocharged Avco Lycoming engines are similar to those which power the PA-31-350 Chieftain. A prototype is believed to have flown for the first time in late 1979. Certification was gained on 9 June 1983. At 1 January 1986 a total of 50 Mojaves had been delivered.

TYPE: Seven-seat pressurised light transport.

WINGS: Cantilever low-wing monoplane. Dihedral 5° from roots. Wing root leading-edge extended forward between nacelle and fuselage on each side. Electrically actuated flaps. Trim tab in starboard aileron.

FUSELAGE: Semi-monocoque structure, primarily of light alloy, with fail-safe structure in the pressurised section.

TAIL UNIT: Conventional tail unit, with swept vertical surfaces and an extended dorsal fin blended into the upper surface of the fuselage. Horn balanced control surfaces. Trim tab in rudder and starboard elevator.

LANDING GEAR: Retractable tricycle type with single wheel on each unit; main units retract inward into wing roots, nosewheel rearward. Mainwheels and tyres size 6·50-10, eight-ply rating. Steerable nosewheel size 6·00-6 with tyre size 17·5 × 6-25-6, 10-ply rating. Oleo-pneumatic shock absorber in each unit. Hydraulic disc brakes on mainwheels. Parking brake.

POWER PLANT: Two 261 kW (350 hp) Avco Lycoming flat-six turbocharged counter-rotating engines, one TIO-540-V2AD and one LTIO-540-V2AD, each driving a Hartzell three-blade constant-speed and fully-feathering propeller with spinner. Fuel system usable capacity 900 litres (238 US gallons). Oil capacity 24·6 litres (6·5 US gallons).

ACCOMMODATION: Pilot, co-pilot and five passengers, or pilot and six passengers, in pressurised cabin. Four contoured reclining seats for passengers in facing pairs, with side facing seat at rear on starboard side. Foldaway writing tables, a hot/cold refreshment centre, and stereo system, optional. Door with built-in airstair behind wing on port side. Baggage space in nose, wing lockers and rear cabin, with combined capacity of 308 kg (680 lb).

SYSTEM: Pressurisation system with max differential of 0·35 bars (5·0 lb/sq in), to provide a cabin altitude of 2,775 m (9,100 ft) to a height of 7,620 m (25,000 ft).

AVIONICS: Wide range of avionics, including colour weather radar, available from manufacturers that include Bendix, Collins, King and Sperry. Full IFR equipment and autopilot included in basic price.

DIMENSIONS, EXTERNAL:

Wing span	13·56 m (44 ft 6 in)
Length overall	10·52 m (34 ft 6 in)
Height overall	3·96 m (13 ft 0 in)
Tailplane span	5·52 m (18 ft 1½ in)
Wheel track	4·19 m (13 ft 9 in)
Wheelbase	2·64 m (8 ft 8 in)
Propeller diameter	2·03 m (6 ft 8 in)

Piper PA-31P-350 Mojave seven-seat pressurised light transport

Distance between propeller centres 3·86 m (12 ft 8 in)
Passenger door (port, rear):
Height 1·17 m (3 ft 10 in)
Width 0·71 m (2 ft 4 in)
Baggage door (port, nose):
Height 0·53 m (1 ft 9 in)
Width 0·66 m (2 ft 2 in)
Nacelle locker doors (each):
Length 1·02 m (3 ft 4 in)
Width 0·51 m (1 ft 8 in)

DIMENSIONS, INTERNAL:
Cabin: Length, instrument panel to rear bulkhead 4·41 m (14 ft 5¾ in)
Max width 1·27 m (4 ft 2 in)
Max height 1·31 m (4 ft 3½ in)
Baggage compartment volume:
Nose 0·64 m³ (22·5 cu ft)
Nacelle lockers (total) 0·51 m³ (18 cu ft)
Rear cabin 0·62 m³ (22 cu ft)

AREA:
Wings, gross 22·02 m² (237·0 sq ft)

WEIGHTS AND LOADINGS:
Weight empty, standard 2,297 kg (5,064 lb)
Max T-O weight 3,266 kg (7,200 lb)
Max ramp weight 3,286 kg (7,245 lb)
Max zero-fuel weight 3,039 kg (6,700 lb)
Max landing weight 3,175 kg (7,000 lb)
Max wing loading 148·3 kg/m² (30·38 lb/sq ft)
Max power loading 6·26 kg/kW (10·29 lb/hp)

PERFORMANCE (at max T-O weight, S/L, ISA, except where indicated):
Max level speed at mid cruise weight 242 knots (447 km/h; 278 mph)
Cruising speed (mid cruise weight at optimum altitude):
75% power 235 knots (435 km/h; 270 mph)
65% power 221 knots (409 km/h; 254 mph)
60% power 195 knots (361 km/h; 224 mph)
Stalling speed:
flaps up 78 knots (145 km/h; 90 mph)
flaps down 72 knots (134 km/h; 83 mph)
Max rate of climb at S/L 372 m (1,220 ft)/min
Rate of climb at S/L, one engine out 78 m (255 ft)/min
Service ceiling 9,265 m (30,400 ft)
Service ceiling, one engine out 4,360 m (14,300 ft)
T-O run 495 m (1,625 ft)
T-O to 15 m (50 ft) 753 m (2,469 ft)
Landing from 15 m (50 ft) 700 m (2,300 ft)
Landing run 424 m (1,390 ft)
Range with max fuel at optimum altitude with allowances for engine starting, taxi, T-O, climb, and 45 min reserves at max range power:
75% power 1,113 nm (2,061 km; 1,280 miles)
65% power 1,143 nm (2,116 km; 1,315 miles)
60% power 1,221 nm (2,261 km; 1,405 miles)

PIPER (PA-31T-1) CHEYENNE IA

Introduced in 1978, the original Cheyenne I was a low cost version of the established Cheyenne PA-31T, which was redesignated Cheyenne II. FAA certification was received on 23 March 1978, and deliveries began at the end of April 1978. By 1 January 1984 a total of 197 Cheyenne Is had been sold, and the aircraft had been superseded by the improved Cheyenne IA.

Piper received FAA certification for the Cheyenne IA in May 1983. It differs from the earlier model in having new engine cowlings, a 4·4 per cent increase in engine power at altitude, and redesigned exhaust stubs, enabling max cruising speed to be increased. The flight deck is improved by lowering the glareshield and redesigning the overhead switch panel; a new interior layout maximises cabin space, with increased seat travel to provide more legroom, and the nose baggage compartment is redesigned to accommodate large, bulky items. By 1 January 1986 a total of 13 Cheyenne IAs had been sold.

The Cheyenne IA is available with Standard and Executive interior options and two operational group options as follows:

Standard. Six individual seats in pairs, with headrests and armrests. Pilot/co-pilot seats four-way adjustable with shoulder harness and inertia reels; third and fourth cabin seats aft-facing; and all cabin seats with seat belts; window curtains and wall to wall carpet. Rear cabin divider with clothes bar and baggage security net. Forward cabin divider curtain. 'No smoking/Fasten seat belt' sign. Oxygen outlets and masks at each seat position. Options available include a cabin instrumentation panel comprising digital readouts of altitude, outside air temperature, time, and true airspeed; pneumatic door extender; forward cabin combination unit; storage cabinets; folding tables; aft cabin combination unit, which includes side-facing seventh seat/toilet; seventh and eighth seats; tinted cabin windows; cabin fire extinguisher; stereo system; and all-leather seat covering.

Executive. Six individual seats, comprising two crew seats and four reclining chairs in the Standard arrangement. Other standard equipment as described, plus forward cabin combination unit which includes cabin dividers and curtain, electrically heated Thermos unit, cup dispenser, storage for ice, beverages and manuals; two folding tables; pneumatic door extender and aft cabin combination unit which includes side facing seventh seat/toilet, cabin divider with mirror, privacy curtain, refreshment centre; AC power outlet for electric razor; and baggage security net. Options are the same as for the Standard interior, unless included in the Executive package. Adds 55·3 kg (121·9 lb) to basic empty weight.

Piper PA-31T-1 Cheyenne IA twin-turboprop business aircraft

De-icing Group. Pneumatic de-icing boots for wing and tail unit leading-edges, and wing ice inspection light; adding 10·1 kg (22·3 lb) to basic empty weight.

Co-pilot Flight Group. Airspeed and rate of climb indicator, altimeter, electric turn rate indicator, attitude and directional gyros, clock, heated pitot, static system with alternate source, co-pilot's toe brakes and windscreen wiper; adding 8·7 kg (19·2 lb) to basic empty weight.

TYPE: Six/eight-seat cabin monoplane.

WINGS: Cantilever low-wing monoplane. Wing section NACA 63^2A415 at root, NACA 63^1A212 at tip. Dihedral 5°. Incidence 1° 30′ at root, − 1° at tip. Sweepback 0° at 30 per cent chord. Three-spar structure of 2024ST light alloy. Balanced ailerons and single-slotted trailing-edge flaps of 2024ST light alloy. Trim tab in starboard aileron. Pneumatic de-icing boots on wing leading-edges optional.

FUSELAGE: Semi-monocoque structure of 2024ST light alloy, with fail-safe structure in the pressurised areas.

TAIL UNIT: Cantilever structure of 2024ST light alloy with sweptback vertical surfaces. Fixed incidence tailplane. Trim tabs in elevators and rudder. Pneumatic de-icing of fin and tailplane leading-edges optional.

LANDING GEAR: Hydraulically retractable tricycle type with single wheel on each unit, main units retracting inward and nosewheel aft. Nosewheel safety mirror. Piper oleo-pneumatic shock absorbers. Cleveland Type 40-106 mainwheels, with 6·50 × 10 10-ply tyres, pressure 5·52 bars (80 lb/sq in). Cleveland Type 40-120A steerable nosewheel, with 17·5 × 6·25 10-ply rating tyre. Cleveland Type 30-106 brakes. Parking brake.

POWER PLANT: Two 373 kW (500 shp) Pratt & Whitney Canada PT6A-11 turboprop engines, each driving a Hartzell Type HC-BTN-3B three-blade constant-speed reversible-pitch and fully-feathering metal propeller with spinner. Each wing has three interconnected fuel cells and a tip tank, giving a total capacity of 1,385 litres (366 US gallons). NACA type anti-icing non-siphoning fuel tank vents, incorporating flame arresters. Refuelling points on top of engine nacelles and on upper surface of each tip tank. Oil capacity 24·6 litres (6·5 US gallons).

ACCOMMODATION: Pilot and co-pilot on two individual adjustable seats. Dual controls standard. Pilot's storm window. Heated windscreen. Windscreen wiper standard for pilot, optional for co-pilot. Cabin seating for four to six passengers on individual seats. Door with built-in airstair on port side, which has seven locking pins and inflatable pressurisation seal. Dual pane windows. Emergency exit window on starboard side. Cabin heated and air-conditioned. Forward and aft cabin dividers. A wide range of options for cabin includes folding tables, beverage dispensers, pneumatic door extender, storage cabinets and tinted windows. Baggage compartments in nose, capacity 136 kg (300 lb), and rear of cabin, capacity 91 kg (200 lb). External door to nose compartment.

SYSTEMS: Air-conditioning and pressurisation, with pressure differential of 0·38 bars (5·5 lb/sq in). Freon type air-conditioner of 23,000 BTU capacity. Janitrol combustion heater of 35,000 BTU capacity with automatic windscreen defroster. Hydraulic system supplied by dual engine driven pumps for landing gear retraction and brakes. Pneumatic system and vacuum system provided by engine bleed air. Electrical system supplied by two 28V 200A starter/generators and 24V 43Ah nickel-cadmium battery. External power socket standard. Oxygen system of 0·62 m³ (22 cu ft) capacity. De-icing system comprises electric anti-icing boots for air intakes, heated pitot and electric propeller de-icing. Fire detection system with six sensors; engine fire extinguishing system optional.

AVIONICS: A full IFR avionics package, including flight control system (autopilot) is standard on current Cheyenne IAs. Options include alternatives to or duplication of this equipment, plus altitude alerter, encoding altimeter, radar altimeter, radio altimeter, radio telephone, global navigation system, and HF transceivers by various manufacturers.

EQUIPMENT: Installed standard equipment is extensive, and optional items include co-pilot's flight instrument group, digital clock, toe brakes, and windscreen wiper; cargo door, emergency locator transmitter, wing and tail pneumatic de-icing boots, lockable fuel caps, engine fire extinguisher system, engine wash rings, fuselage ice protection plates, ice inspection lights and propeller synchrophaser.

DIMENSIONS, EXTERNAL:
Wing span 12·40 m (40 ft 8 in)
Wing chord: at root 2·61 m (8 ft 6¾ in)
at tip 0·97 m (3 ft 2 in)
Wing aspect ratio 7·37
Length overall 10·57 m (34 ft 8 in)
Height overall 3·89 m (12 ft 9 in)
Tailplane span 6·05 m (19 ft 10 in)
Wheel track 4·19 m (13 ft 9 in)
Wheelbase 2·64 m (8 ft 8 in)
Propeller diameter 2·36 m (7 ft 9 in)
Distance between propeller centres 3·85 m (12 ft 7½ in)
Propeller ground clearance 0·27 m (10½ in)
Passenger door (port, rear):
Height 1·17 m (3 ft 10 in)
Width 0·71 m (2 ft 4 in)
Height to sill 0·97 m (3 ft 2 in)
Baggage door (port, fwd): Height 0·53 m (1 ft 9 in)
Width 0·53 m (1 ft 9 in)
Height to sill 1·10 m (3 ft 7½ in)
Emergency exit (stbd, fwd):
Height 0·64 m (2 ft 1 in)
Width 0·48 m (1 ft 7 in)

DIMENSIONS, INTERNAL:
Cabin: Length, excl flight deck 2·57 m (8 ft 5 in)
Max width 1·27 m (4 ft 2 in)
Max height 1·31 m (4 ft 3½ in)
Floor area 4·37 m² (47 sq ft)

AREAS:
Wings, gross 21·3 m² (229 sq ft)
Ailerons (total) 1·21 m² (13 sq ft)
Trailing-edge flaps (total) 3·12 m² (33·6 sq ft)
Fin 1·37 m² (14·72 sq ft)
Rudder, incl tab 1·20 m² (12·88 sq ft)
Tailplane 3·92 m² (42·2 sq ft)
Elevators, incl tab 2·63 m² (28·3 sq ft)

WEIGHTS AND LOADINGS:
Weight empty 2,315 kg (5,104 lb)
Max T-O and landing weight 3,946 kg (8,700 lb)
Max ramp weight 3,969 kg (8,750 lb)
Max zero-fuel weight 3,266 kg (7,200 lb)
Max wing loading 185·5 kg/m² (38·0 lb/sq ft)
Max power loading 5·30 kg/kW (8·7 lb/shp)

PERFORMANCE (at max T-O weight):
Cruising speed, max cruise power, average cruise weight of 3,400 kg (7,500 lb), at:
3,660 m (12,000 ft) 255 knots (473 km/h; 294 mph)
4,875 m (16,000 ft) 261 knots (484 km/h; 301 mph)
6,100 m (20,000 ft) 257 knots (476 km/h; 296 mph)
7,620 m (25,000 ft) 247 knots (458 km/h; 284 mph)
Minimum single-engine control speed (VMC) 85 knots (157 km/h; 98 mph)
Stalling speed, wheels and flaps up, engines idling 84 knots (156 km/h; 97 mph) IAS
Stalling speed, wheels and flaps down, engines idling 72 knots (133 km/h; 83 mph) IAS
Rotation speed 89 knots (167 km/h; 104 mph)
Approach speed 102 knots (189 km/h; 117 mph) IAS
Max rate of climb at S/L 533 m (1,750 ft)/min
Rate of climb at S/L, one engine out 134 m (440 ft)/min

Service ceiling 8,595 m (28,200 ft)
Service ceiling, one engine out 4,190 m (13,750 ft)
T-O run 436 m (1,429 ft)
T-O to 15 m (50 ft) 745 m (2,444 ft)
Landing from 15 m (50 ft) 690 m (2,263 ft)
Landing from 15 m (50 ft) with propeller reversal 507 m (1,663 ft)
Landing run 484 m (1,589 ft)
Landing run with propeller reversal 281 m (921 ft)
Accelerate/stop distance 1,016 m (3,334 ft)
Range with allowances for start, taxi, T-O, climb, descent, and 45 min reserves at max range cruising power:
max cruising power at:
3,660 m (12,000 ft) 955 nm (1,769 km; 1,099 miles)
4,875 m (16,000 ft) 1,010 nm (1,871 km; 1,163 miles)
6,100 m (20,000 ft) 1,090 nm (2,020 km; 1,255 miles)
7,620 m (25,000 ft) 1,205 nm (2,233 km; 1,387 miles)
max range power at:
3,660 m (12,000 ft) 1,030 nm (1,908 km; 1,186 miles)
4,875 m (16,000ft) 1,130 nm (2,094 km; 1,301 miles)
6,100 m (20,000 ft) 1,205 nm (2,233 km; 1,387 miles)
7,620 m (25,000 ft) 1,285 nm (2,381 km; 1,479 miles)

PIPER (PA-31T-2) CHEYENNE IIXL

On 17 October 1980, Piper announced a fourth member of the Cheyenne family of turboprop business aircraft. Known as the PA-31T-2 Cheyenne IIXL, it is a version of the Cheyenne II (see 1983-84 *Jane's*), with the fuselage lengthened by 0·61 m (2 ft 0 in) to increase cabin volume by 16 per cent and so provide more comfortable accommodation for passengers and crew. In addition, it has Pratt & Whitney Canada PT6A-135 turboprop engines, each rated at 559 kW (750 shp), but flat rated at only 462 kW (620 shp) in this installaton, and driving large diameter three-blade propellers at 1,900 rpm. This results in low noise levels, both internally and externally. By comparison with the Cheyenne II, the IIXL has a max T-O weight more than 180 kg (400 lb) greater. It uses the same type of environmental control unit as the Cheyenne IIIA for cabin heating and air-conditioning, and has interior equipment options similar to those of the IIIA.

FAA certification was received in February 1981, and the first six Cheyenne IIXLs were delivered to Piper sales centres on 2 June 1981. A total of 76 had been delivered by 1 January 1986.

The Cheyenne IIXL can carry an underbelly cargo pod, capable of accommodating 136 kg (300 lb) of freight, including golf bags, skis and bulky luggage. The pod is made of Kevlar and glassfibre, weighs 34 kg (75 lb) and is equipped with two side doors, each measuring 0·88 m × 0·25 m (2 ft 10½ in × 10 in). It can be installed in 30 min. Effect on performance is negligible, involving a 7 per cent reduction in twin-engine rate of climb and 3 per cent reduction in cruising speed at max cruise power.

A full IFR avionics package, including autopilot/flight director and weather radar, plus full icing protection, is standard on the current Cheyenne IIXL.

The description of the Cheyenne IA applies also to the Cheyenne IIXL, except as follows:

FUSELAGE: As for Cheyenne IA, except lengthened by 0·61 m (2 ft 0 in).

POWER PLANT: Two 559 kW (750 shp) Pratt & Whitney Canada PT6A-135 turboprop engines, each flat rated at 462 kW (620 shp) and driving a Hartzell HC-BTN-3B three-blade reversible-pitch constant-speed and fully-feathering metal propeller with spinner. Each wing has three interconnected fuel cells and a tip tank, giving total fuel capacity of 1,416 litres (374 US gallons), of which 1,385 litres (366 US gallons) are usable. Refuelling points in engine nacelles and on upper surface of each tip tank.

Piper PA-31T-2 Cheyenne IIXL, a version of the Cheyenne II with lengthened fuselage

Piper Cheyenne IIIA six/eleven-seat turboprop business aircraft

NACA type anti-icing non-siphoning fuel tank vents with flame arresters. Oil capacity 24·6 litres (6·5 US gallons). Electrically heated air intake anti-icing boot, air intake ice deflection and air bypass doors. Electric propeller de-icing.

DIMENSIONS, EXTERNAL: As for Cheyenne IA except:
Length overall 11·18 m (36 ft 8 in)

DIMENSIONS, INTERNAL:
Cabin: Length, excl flight deck 3·83 m (12 ft 7 in)
Max width 1·27 m (4 ft 2 in)
Max height 1·31 m (4 ft 3½ in)
Forward baggage compartment 0·45 m³ (16 cu ft)
Cargo pod (optional):
Internal length 2·97 m (9 ft 9 in)
Internal width 0·55 m (1 ft 10 in)
Internal depth 0·29 m (11½ in)
Volume 0·47 m³ (16·6 cu ft)

WEIGHTS AND LOADINGS:
Weight empty, standard 2,488 kg (5,486 lb)
Max T-O weight 4,297 kg (9,474 lb)
Max ramp weight 4,327 kg (9,540 lb)
Max landing weight 4,082 kg (9,000 lb)
Max zero-fuel weight 3,447 kg (7,600 lb)
Max wing loading 202·0 kg/m² (41·37 lb/sq ft)
Max power loading 4·65 kg/kW (7·64 lb/shp)

PERFORMANCE (at max T-O weight without cargo pod, except where indicated):
Cruising speed, max cruise power, at average cruise weight of 3,720 kg (8,200 lb):
at 3,960 m (13,000 ft) 275 knots (510 km/h; 317 mph)
at 4,875 m (16,000 ft) 273 knots (506 km/h; 314 mph)
at 6,100 m (20,000 ft) 270 knots (500 km/h; 311 mph)
at 8,840 m (29,000 ft) 255 knots (473 km/h; 294 mph)
Minimum single-engine control speed (V_{MC}) 91 knots (169 km/h; 105 mph)
Stalling speed, engines idling:
flaps and landing gear up 86 knots (160 km/h; 99 mph) IAS
flaps and landing gear down 77 knots (143 km/h; 89 mph) IAS
Rotation speed 101 knots (187 km/h; 116 mph) IAS
Approach speed 104 knots (193 km/h; 120 mph)
Max rate of climb at S/L 533 m (1,750 ft)/min
Rate of climb at S/L, one engine out 143 m (470 ft)/min
Service ceiling 9,875 m (32,400 ft)
Service ceiling, one engine out 4,540 m (14,900 ft)
T-O run 622 m (2,042 ft)
T-O to 15 m (50 ft) 896 m (2,940 ft)
Landing from 15 m (50 ft) 745 m (2,446 ft)
Landing from 15 m (50 ft), with propeller reversal 540 m (1,773 ft)
Landing run 479 m (1,571 ft)
Landing run, with propeller reversal 329 m (1,080 ft)
Accelerate/stop distance 1,276 m (4,186 ft)
Range with max fuel at max cruise power, allowances for start, taxi, T-O, climb, descent, and 45 min reserves at max range power, ISA:
at 3,660 m (12,000 ft) 775 nm (1,435 km; 892 miles)
at 4,875 m (16,000 ft) 856 nm (1,586 km; 986 miles)
at 6,100 m (20,000 ft) 945 nm (1,751 km; 1,088 miles)
at 8,840 m (29,000 ft) 1,175 nm (2,177 km; 1,353 miles)
Range with max fuel at max range power, allowances as above:
at 3,660 m (12,000 ft) 945 nm (1,751 km; 1,088 miles)
at 4,875 m (16,000 ft) 1,075 nm (1,992 km; 1,238 miles)
at 6,100 m (20,000 ft) 1,144 nm (2,121 km; 1,318 miles)
at 8,840 m (29,000 ft) 1,280 nm (2,372 km; 1,474 miles)

PIPER (PA-42) CHEYENNE IIIA

Announced on 26 September 1977, the **Cheyenne III** differed from the I and II by having increased wing span, a lengthened fuselage, a T tail and more powerful PT6A-41 engines. The production prototype flew for the first time on 18 May 1979; FAA certification was gained in early 1980, and deliveries of production aircraft began on 30 June 1980. A total of 88 had been delivered before the Cheyenne III was superseded by the **Cheyenne IIIA**.

Piper received FAA certification for the Cheyenne IIIA in March 1983. It differs principally in having PT6A-61 turboprop engines, flat rated at 537 kW (720 shp), and offers performance improvements which include increased max cruising speed and higher certificated ceiling. Other features include improvements to the interior layout, air-conditioning and electrical systems. Twenty-six had been delivered by 1 January 1986.

A Cheyenne IIIA, equipped with special sensors, was delivered to the US Drug Enforcement Administration on 15 February 1984 for use on a variety of surveillance and identification missions by day and night, and in March 1985 an order for a further eight Cheyenne IIIA Customs High Endurance Tracker (CHET) aircraft was announced by Piper. These aircraft, equipped with infra-red sensors and long-range radars, were delivered at one month intervals commencing in late September 1985. The US Customs Service has options on a further eight Cheyenne IIIAs.

In December 1984 Lufthansa German Airlines ordered three Cheyenne IIIAs, with an option on a fourth, for delivery commencing in the Spring of 1987. The aircraft, which will be equipped with Collins EFIS in flight decks configured to resemble those of Lufthansa's Airbus A310 jet transports, will be used for pilot training.

On 9-10 May 1984 a standard Cheyenne IIIA set a speed record between Boston, Massachusetts, and Paris, flying the 2,995 nm (5,546 km; 3,446 miles) in 10 h 27 min 35 s, at an average 286·3 knots (530·2 km/h; 329·4 mph), with one stop, at Gander, Newfoundland. On 29-30 August 1984 the same aircraft set five more records between Washington and Gander; Gander and London (Luton), England; Washington to London; New York to Gander; and New York to London; covering the overall 3,175 nm (5,880 km; 3,653 mile) great circle route in 10 h 26 min, at an average speed of 304·13 knots (563·59 km/h; 350·20 mph).

The Cheyenne IIIA is available with Standard and Executive interior options, and Co-pilot Flight Groups, as detailed for the Cheyenne IA. A full IFR avionics package, including autopilot/flight director and weather radar, plus full icing protection, is standard equipment on the current Cheyenne IIIA, to which the following description applies:

TYPE: Six/eleven-seat corporate and commuter airline transport.

WINGS: Cantilever low-wing monoplane. Wing section NACA 63_2A415, modified, at root, NACA 63_1A212 at tip. Dihedral 5°. Incidence 1° 30′. No sweepback. Three-spar safe-life structure of light alloy. Ailerons and trailing-edge flaps as for Cheyenne IA. Goodrich pneumatic de-icing boots for wing leading-edges are standard.

FUSELAGE: Conventional semi-monocoque safe-life structure of light alloy.

TAIL UNIT: Cantilever T tail of light alloy construction, with sweptback vertical surfaces. Fixed incidence tailplane. Elevators and rudder of light alloy. Servo tab in rudder; anti-servo tab in elevator. Goodrich de-icing equipment standard for leading-edges of tailplane and fin.

LANDING GEAR: Hydraulically retractable tricycle type with single wheel on each unit. Main units retract inward, nosewheel aft. Pneumatic blow-down system for emergency landing gear extension, with manually operated hydraulic system as backup. Piper oleo-pneumatic shock absorbers. Cleveland mainwheels with tyres size 6·50-10 12-ply Type III, pressure 6·90 bars (100 lb/sq in). Cleveland steerable nosewheel with tyre size 17·5 × 6·25, 10-ply rating Type III, pressure 4·83 bars (70 lb/sq in). Goodrich hydraulically operated disc brakes. Parking brake.

POWER PLANT: Two Pratt & Whitney Canada PT6A-61 turboprop engines, each flat rated at 537 kW (720 shp) and driving a Hartzell three-blade constant-speed feathering and reversible-pitch metal propeller with Q-tips. Automatic propeller feathering system and synchrophaser optional. Each wing has four interconnected fuel cells and a tip tank, with a combined total capacity of 2,158 litres (570 US gallons), of which 2,120 litres (560 US gallons) are usable. NACA type anti-icing and non-siphoning fuel vents incorporating flame arresters. Refuelling points on upper surface of each tip tank and engine nacelle. Oil capacity 24·6 litres (6·5 US gallons). Electric intake anti-icing and propeller de-icing.

ACCOMMODATION: Pilot and co-pilot on four-way adjustable seats with armrests, headrests, shoulder safety belts with inertia reels, and stowage for oxygen mask beneath seats. To be certificated for single pilot operation. Dual controls standard. Pilot's storm window. Cabin seats up to nine passengers, but standard interior includes six reclining and adjustable passenger seats with armrests, headrests, and magazine storage on seat back. Four optional executive interiors available, plus a wide range of options for cabin furnishing. Door with built-in airstair on port side, with seven locking pins and inflatable pressurisation seal. Emergency exit window on starboard side. Baggage compartments in nose and rear of cabin, each with capacity of 136 kg (300 lb), and in each engine nacelle, with a capacity of 45 kg (100 lb), giving a maximum total baggage capacity of 363 kg (800 lb). Accommodation is pressurised, heated and air-conditioned. Pilot's windscreen heated; provisions for heating co-pilot windscreen. Pilot and co-pilot windscreen wipers standard.

SYSTEMS: Garrett pressurisation system with max differential of 0·43 bars (6·3 lb/sq in), maintaining a cabin altitude of 3,050 m (10,000 ft) to a height of 10,060 m (33,000 ft). Environmental control system, combining the functions of heater, air-conditioner and dehumidifier. Hydraulic system supplied by dual engine driven pumps. Pneumatic system and vacuum system supplied by engine bleed air. Electrical system includes two 28V 250A engine driven generators and 24V 43Ah storage battery. Oxygen system of 0·62 m³ (22 cu ft) capacity with ten outlets. De-icing system includes pneumatic wing and tailplane de-icing boots, electric anti-icing of engine air intakes, heated pitots, electric propeller de-icing, and windscreen heating.

AVIONICS AND EQUIPMENT: Generally as for Cheyenne IA, including King 300 and Collins AP-106 autopilot/flight directors. Extensive standard installed equipment includes 'No smoking-Fasten seat belt' sign; carpeted floor; tinted cabin windows; pull-down window shades; curtain between flight deck and cabin; oxygen system with individual masks in storage compartments; indirect fluorescent lighting, individual reading lights, and courtesy lights. Optional equipment includes cabin chimes; stereo system; cabin instrument cluster giving digital readouts of altitude, outside air temperature, time, and true airspeed; cabin fire extinguisher; emergency locator transmitter; and engine fire extinguishing systems.

DIMENSIONS, EXTERNAL:

Wing span over tip tanks	14·53 m (47 ft 8 in)
Wing chord: at root	3·12 m (10 ft 3 in)
at tip	0·97 m (3 ft 2 in)
Wing aspect ratio	7·82
Length overall	13·23 m (43 ft 4¾ in)
Height overall	4·50 m (14 ft 9 in)
Tailplane span	6·65 m (21 ft 10 in)
Wheel track	5·72 m (18 ft 9 in)
Wheelbase	3·23 m (10 ft 7¼ in)
Propeller diameter	2·41 m (7 ft 11 in)
Distance between propeller centres	5·38 m (17 ft 8 in)
Passenger door: Height	1·16 m (3 ft 10 in)
Width	0·73 m (2 ft 5 in)
Nose baggage doors:	
Fwd: height	0·30 m (1 ft 0 in)
width	0·61 m (2 ft 0 in)
Rear: height	0·51 m (1 ft 8 in)
width	0·66 m (2 ft 2 in)
Utility door (aft): Height	0·76 m (2 ft 6 in)
Width	0·47 m (1 ft 6½ in)

DIMENSIONS, INTERNAL:

Cabin (incl flight deck and rear baggage area):	
Length	6·99 m (22 ft 11 in)
Max width	1·30 m (4 ft 3 in)
Max height	1·32 m (4 ft 4 in)
Volume	approx 9·91 m³ (350 cu ft)
Nose baggage compartment	0·46 m³ (16·25 cu ft)
Rear baggage compartment	0·88 m³ (31 cu ft)
Nacelle baggage locker (two, each)	0·16 m³ (5·6 cu ft)

AREAS:

Wings, gross	27·22 m² (293 sq ft)
Ailerons (total)	1·25 m² (13·5 sq ft)
Trailing-edge flaps (total)	3·98 m² (42·8 sq ft)
Fin	2·17 m² (23·36 sq ft)
Rudder, incl tab	1·88 m² (20·2 sq ft)
Tailplane	3·48 m² (37·5 sq ft)
Elevators, incl tab	2·26 m² (24·3 sq ft)

WEIGHTS AND LOADINGS:

Basic weight empty	3,101 kg (6,837 lb)
Max T-O weight	5,080 kg (11,200 lb)
Max ramp weight	5,119 kg (11,285 lb)
Max zero-fuel weight	4,241 kg (9,350 lb)
Max landing weight	4,685 kg (10,330 lb)
Max wing loading	186·6 kg/m² (38·22 lb/sq ft)
Max power loading	4·73 kg/kW (7·78 lb/shp)

PERFORMANCE (at max T-O weight except where indicated):

Max level speed at average cruise weight of 4,218 kg (9,300 lb)	314 knots (582 km/h; 362 mph)
Cruising speed at max cruise power, at average cruise weight of 4,127 kg (9,100 lb):	
at 6,700 m (22,000 ft)	305 knots (565 km/h; 351 mph)
at 7,620 m (25,000 ft)	302 knots (560 km/h; 348 mph)
at 9,145 m (30,000 ft)	293 knots (543 km/h; 337 mph)
at 10,670 m (35,000 ft)	282 knots (523 km/h; 325 mph)
Minimum single-engine control speed (VMC)	91 knots (169 km/h; 105 mph)
Stalling speed, engine idling:	
flaps and gear up	102 knots (189 km/h; 118 mph) IAS
flaps and gear down	89 knots (165 km/h; 103 mph) IAS
Rotation speed	95 knots (176 km/h; 110 mph) IAS
Approach speed	111 knots (206 km/h; 128 mph) IAS
Max rate of climb at S/L	725 m (2,380 ft)/min
Rate of climb at S/L, one engine out	191 m (625 ft)/min
Service ceiling	10,925 m (35,840 ft)
Service ceiling, one engine out	7,070 m (23,200 ft)
T-O run	447 m (1,465 ft)
T-O to 15 m (50 ft)	695 m (2,280 ft)
Landing from 15 m (50 ft)	928 m (3,043 ft)
Landing from 15 m (50 ft) with propeller reversal	788 m (2,586 ft)
Landing run	583 m (1,914 ft)
Landing run with propeller reversal	444 m (1,457 ft)
Accelerate/stop distance	1,025 m (3,363 ft)
Range with max fuel, allowances for taxi, T-O, climb, descent, 45 min reserves at max range power:	
max cruising power at:	
6,700 m (22,000 ft)	1,372 nm (2,542 km; 1,580 miles)
7,620 m (25,000 ft)	1,510 nm (2,798 km; 1,739 miles)
9,460 m (31,000 ft)	1,840 nm (3,409 km; 2,118 miles)
10,670 m (35,000 ft)	2,055 nm (3,808 km; 2,366 miles)
max range power at:	
6,700 m (22,000 ft)	1,803 nm (3,341 km; 2,076 miles)
7,620 m (25,000 ft)	1,945 nm (3,604 km; 2,240 miles)
9,460 m (31,000 ft)	2,170 nm (4,021 km; 2,499 miles)
10,670 m (35,000 ft)	2,270 nm (4,207 km; 2,614 miles)

PIPER CHEYENNE 400 LS

Announced in September 1982, this eight-seat business aircraft (known initially as the Cheyenne IV) combines the basic airframe structure, components and systems of the Cheyenne IIIA with a new power plant, updated electrical system and other changes to ensure optimum performance and economy of operation. The prototype Cheyenne 400 LS (N400PT) flew for the first time on 23 February 1983, followed by a second prototype on 23 June. FAA certification was obtained on 13 July 1984, and deliveries began with an aircraft handed over to the Garrett Turbine Engine Company on 26 July. At 1 January 1986 a total of 29 Cheyenne 400 LSs had been delivered.

The '400' in the designation marks the claim that this is the only corporate turboprop aircraft capable of achieving 400 mph; the 'LS' indicates Piper's link with Lear Siegler.

On 8 February 1985 a Piper Cheyenne 400 LS set two Class C1e world records on a flight from Miami, Florida, to New York City, which was completed in 2 h 51 min, at an average speed of 330·43 knots (612·36 km/h; 380·5 mph),

Piper Cheyenne 400 LS, powered by Garrett TPE331-14A/14B turboprop engines

continuing to Boston, Massachusetts, which was reached in 3 h 24 min 33 s, at an average speed of 319·58 knots (592·24 km/h; 368 mph). Another Cheyenne 400 LS, piloted by Brigadier General (USAF Retd) Charles E. 'Chuck' Yeager, established five world records on 16 April 1985, climbing to an altitude of 3,000 m (9,845 ft) in 1 min 47·7 s; to 6,000 m (19,675 ft) in 3 min 42·3 s; to 9,000 m (29,525 ft) in 6 min 34 s; to 12,000 m (39,375 ft) in 11 min 8·4 s; and flying from San Francisco, California, to New York City in 6 h 39 min 28 s, at an average speed of 302·86 knots (561·26 km/h; 348·75 mph). On 28 May 1985 General Yeager established a further record on a flight from Washington, DC, to Paris which was completed in 10 h 19 min 15 s at an average speed of 322·974 knots (598·53 km/h; 371·91 mph).

TYPE: Twin-turboprop eight-seat light business transport.

WINGS: Cantilever low-wing monoplane, basically similar to those of Cheyenne IIIA, adapted for new power plant and flush riveted throughout. Area inboard of each wheel well strengthened and modified to accept new main landing gear. Outer panels modified to incorporate integral fuel tanks and to carry wingtip tanks to supplement fuel capacity and provide endplate aerodynamic benefits.

FUSELAGE: Basically as for Cheyenne IIIA, but strengthened to cater for increased pressurisation and to embody new multi-ply stretched acrylic cabin windows. Flush riveted throughout.

TAIL UNIT: As for Cheyenne IIIA, with minor modifications to cater for higher speeds. Flush riveted throughout.

LANDING GEAR: Hydraulically retractable tricycle type, with single wheel on each unit. Main units retract inward into wings, nosewheel rearward. Redesigned by comparison with Cheyenne IIIA, for improved ground attitude and increased landing weight. Mainwheels and tyres size 6·50-10, 12-ply rating, pressure 7·58 bars (110 lb/sq in). Steerable nosewheel, size 6·00-6, with 17·5 × 6·25-6 tyre, 10-ply rating, pressure 5·52 bars (80 lb/sq in). Hydraulically actuated dual disc brakes, with multiple brake pads, on each mainwheel.

POWER PLANT: Two 1,226·5 kW (1,645 shp) Garrett TPE331-14A/14B counter-rotating turboprop engines, each flat rated at 746 kW (1,000 shp) and driving a Dowty Rotol ARA-D constant-speed reversible-pitch advanced technology propeller with four carbonfibre/epoxy blades. Blade design and construction incorporates protection from both erosion and lightning strike. The installation of each engine includes new mountings, a new nacelle enclosing the exhaust system, new inlet incorporating bleed air anti-icing, and an exhaust system which discharges the efflux over the wing. Propeller synchrophaser standard. Fuel in integral tanks in outer wings and wingtip tanks. The engines have automatic negative torque control, automatic start sequencing, and use a micro-computer system to record in-flight performance data for engine trend monitoring.

ACCOMMODATION: Crew of two side by side on separate flight deck. Standard cabin has two rearward facing seats at front. Flat floor and table between these seats and two pairs of forward facing seats, with dropped aisle between each pair. Toilet, with solid divider and door, and walk-in baggage area, capacity 136 kg (300 lb), at rear of cabin. Alternative cabin layouts available. Airstair door at rear of cabin on port side. Optional cargo door immediately aft of this, to provide unobstructed wide opening. Double glazed windows. Emergency exit over wing on starboard side. Nose baggage compartment, capacity 136 kg (300 lb), large enough to accommodate skis and golf bags, with two doors on port side.

SYSTEMS: Environmental control system utilises engine bleed air from both engines for heating, cooling and pressurisation. Max pressure differential 0·51 bars (7·5 lb/sq in). Independent emergency bleed air pressurisation system. Completely new electrical system includes two engine driven generators and two batteries. Automatic dropout oxygen masks.

AVIONICS AND EQUIPMENT: A full IFR avionics package, including autopilot/flight director and weather radar, plus full icing protection, is standard equipment. Complete optional system by Collins includes pilot's electronic ADI and electric HSI; multi-function display for radar and nav as well as system functions; co-pilot's mechanical ADI and electronic HSI; digital air data system, FCS 65 flight control system with latest technology digital autopilot; and a complete line of com, nav, radar and long range nav systems. Similar system by Bendix is in form of a five-tube electronic display comprising pilot and co-pilot electronic ADI and electronic HSI; multi-function radar display; electronic engine instrument and crew alerting options; digital air data system; digital autopilot flight control system; and complete line of com, short and long range nav and radar systems.

DIMENSIONS, EXTERNAL: As for Cheyenne IIIA, except:
- Height overall: 5·00 m (16 ft 5 in)
- Propeller diameter: 2·69 m (8 ft 10 in)

DIMENSIONS, INTERNAL: As for Cheyenne IIIA, except:
- Cabin: Max height: 1·42 m (4 ft 8 in)
- Baggage compartment volume:
  - nose: 0·48 m³ (17·0 cu ft)
  - rear: 0·88 m³ (31·0 cu ft)

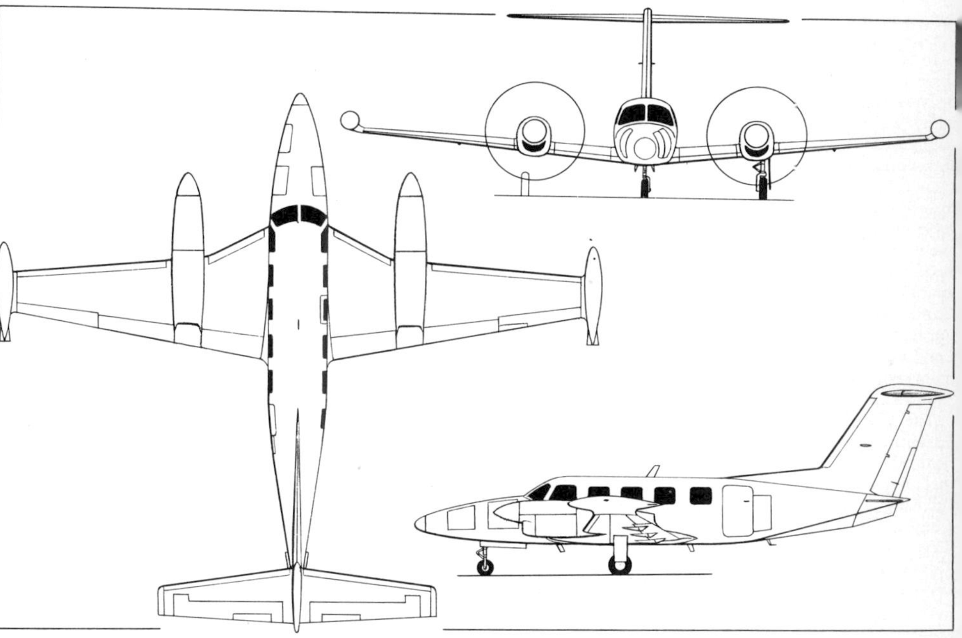

Piper Cheyenne 400 LS twin-turboprop eight-seat business transport *(Pilot Press)*

AREAS: As for Cheyenne IIIA, except:
- Fin: 2·68 m² (28·81 sq ft)
- Rudder, incl tab: 1·60 m² (17·25 sq ft)
- Elevators, incl tabs: 2·26 m² (24·30 sq ft)

WEIGHTS:
- Weight empty, standard: 3,431 kg (7,565 lb)
- Max usable fuel: 1,732 kg (3,819 lb)
- Max T-O weight: 5,466 kg (12,050 lb)
- Max ramp weight: 5,504 kg (12,135 lb)
- Max landing weight: 5,035 kg (11,100 lb)
- Max zero-fuel weight: 4,536 kg (10,000 lb)

PERFORMANCE (at max T-O weight except where indicated):
- Max operating speed: Mach 0·62 (246 knots; 455 km/h; 283 mph EAS)
- Cruising speed at max cruise power at AUW of 4,536 kg (10,000 lb):
  - at 7,315 m (24,000 ft): 351 knots (650 km/h; 404 mph)
  - at 8,850 m (29,000 ft): 346 knots (641 km/h; 398 mph)
  - at 10,670 m (35,000 ft): 334 knots (620 km/h; 385 mph)
  - at 12,500 m (41,000 ft): 294 knots (544 km/h; 338 mph)
- Minimum single-engine control speed (VMC): 99 knots (183 km/h; 114 mph)
- Stalling speed, engines idling:
  - flaps and landing gear up: 93 knots (172 km/h; 107 mph) IAS
  - flaps and landing gear down: 84 knots (156 km/h; 97 mph) IAS
- Max rate of climb at S/L: 988 m (3,242 ft)/min
- Rate of climb at S/L, one engine out: 304 m (997 ft)/min
- Service ceiling: above 12,500 m (41,000 ft)
- Service ceiling, one engine out: 8,745 m (28,700 ft)
- T-O to 15 m (50 ft): 709 m (2,325 ft)
- Landing from 15 m (50 ft) at max landing weight:
  - without reverse thrust: 706 m (2,317 ft)
  - with reverse thrust: 621 m (2,038 ft)
- Accelerate/stop distance: 969 m (3,180 ft)
- Range at max cruise power at 10,670 m (35,000 ft), with allowances for start, taxi, T-O, climb, descent and 45 min reserve at max range power:
  - with 8 passengers: 1,243 nm (2,304 km; 1,432 miles)
  - with 2 passengers: 1,821 nm (3,375 km; 2,097 miles)
- Max range, at max range power at 12,500 m (41,000 ft), allowances as above:
  - with 8 passengers: 1,431 nm (2,652 km; 1,648 miles)
  - with 2 passengers: 2,176 nm (4,033 km; 2,506 miles)

PIPER (PA-34-220T) SENECA III

On 23 September 1971, Piper announced a twin-engined light aircraft which had the company designation PA-34 and, following Piper tradition, the Indian name Seneca. Built at Piper's Vero Beach, Florida, factory, the aircraft was redesignated Seneca II from 1975. On 15 February 1981 Piper introduced an improved PA-34-220T Seneca III, with more powerful engines.

The Seneca III has counter-rotating (C/R) engine and propeller installations. The retractable landing gear is operated by an electro-hydraulic system and includes an emergency extension system which allows the wheels to free fall into the down and locked position. A dual-vane stall warning system provides warning by horn well in advance of the stall in either clean or gear/flaps-down configuration.

The 1985 Seneca III versions introduced as standard an instrument package which includes blind-flying instrumentation with 3 in attitude and directional gyros, electric clock, outside air temperature gauge, pictorial turn rate indicator, rate of climb indicator, airspeed indicator, and dual engine driven pneumatic pumps; a lighting package which includes instrument panel white lighting and overhead red lighting, avionics dimming, cabin dome, map, reading, landing, navigation, taxi, and wing strobe lights; heated pitot; and automatic emergency locator beacon.

Optional equipment groups available for the Seneca III are as follows:

Executive. Comprising deluxe lounge interior with

Piper Seneca III, powered by two Continental TSIO-360-KB turbocharged counter-rotating engines

headrests for all seats, window curtains, assist strap, club seating, refreshment console and fold-down armrest; tinted windscreen and side windows; pilot's and co-pilot's vertically adjustable seats; ventilation fan; wingtip recognition lights; 'Quietized' cabin soundproofing; true airspeed indicator; external power receptacle; crew cup holders; courtesy lighting package including forward baggage compartment light, cabin entrance door light and rear cabin entrance door light; heavy duty brakes and tyres for main landing gear and heavy duty tyre on six inch nosewheel; and towbar, adding 33·1 kg (73·1 lb) to basic aircraft weight.

De-icing Group. Comprising pneumatic de-icing boots for wing and tail unit leadng-edges, electric propeller de-icing, luminous outside air temperature gauge, ice inspection light, electric windscreen de-icing plate for pilot, heated pitot head and two heated lift detectors; adding 22·6 kg (49·9 lb) to basic empty weight.

It was announced on 3 January 1977 that Piper had signed an agreement with Pezetel, the Polish foreign trade organisation, enabling PZL Mielec (which see) to assemble, manufacture and distribute theSeneca in Eastern Europe. These aircraft (several hundred are involved in the agreement) are powered by 164 kW (220 hp) PZL-Franklin engines and are named **M-20 Mewa** (Gull).

At 1 January 1986 a total of 4,259 Senecas had been delivered: 918 Seneca Is, 2,602 Seneca IIs and 739 Seneca IIIs. Subsequent sales include six Seneca IIIs for the Royal Jordanian Air Academy and six for the BAe Flying College.

Type: Six-seat twin-engined light aircraft.

Wings: Cantilever low-wing monoplane. Dihedral 7°. Single-spar wings, Frise ailerons, and wide span electrically operated slotted flaps, of light alloy construction. Glassfibre wingtips. Pneumatic de-icing boots for leading-edges optional.

Fuselage: Light alloy semi-monocoque structure.

Tail Unit: Cantilever structure of light alloy. One-piece all-moving horizontal surface with combined anti-balance and trim tab. Anti-servo tab in rudder. Pneumatic de-icing boots for fin and tailplane leading-edges optional.

Landing Gear: Hydraulically retractable tricycle type. Main units retract inward, nose unit forward. Oleo-pneumatic shock absorbers. Steerable nosewheel. Emergency free-fall extension system. Mainwheels and tyres size 6·00-6, 8-ply rating, pressure 3·79 bars (55 lb/sq in); nosewheel and tyre size 6·00-6, 6-ply rating, pressure 2·76 bars (40 lb/sq in). Nosewheel safety mirror. High capacity disc brakes. Parking brake. Heavy duty tyres and brakes optional.

Power Plant: One 164 kW (220 hp) Continental TSIO-360-KB and one 164 kW (220 hp) Continental LTSIO-360-KB flat-six turbocharged counter-rotating engines, each driving a Hartzell two-blade constant-speed fully-feathering metal propeller with spinner. Three-blade propellers, propeller de-icing, automatic unfeathering and propeller synchrophasers optional. Fuel in two tanks in wings, with a total capacity of 371 litres (98 US gallons) of which 352 litres (93 US gallons) are usable. Optional 57 litre (15 US gallon) auxiliary tank in each wing to provide a max capacity of 485 litres (128 US gallons) of which 466 litres (123 US gallons) are usable. Oil capacity 7·5 litres (2 US gallons). Glassfibre engine cowlings.

Accommodation: Enclosed cabin, seating six people in pairs on individual seats with 0·25 m (10 in) centre aisle. Dual controls standard. Pilot's storm window. Two forward hinged doors, one on starboard side at front, the other on port side at rear. Large optional door adjacent to rear cabin door provides an extra-wide opening for loading bulky items. Passenger seats removable easily to provide different seating/baggage/cargo combinations. Space for 45 kg (100 lb) baggage at rear of cabin, and for 45 kg (100 lb) in nose compartment with external access door on port side. Cabin heated and ventilated. Windscreen defrosters standard. Electrically de-iced windscreen for pilot, and ice inspection light, optional.

Systems: Electro-hydraulic system for landing gear actuation. Electrical system powered by two 14V 65A alternators. 12V 35Ah battery. Oxygen system with six outlets, or built-in oxygen system of 1·81 m³ (64 cu ft), optional. Dual engine driven pneumatic pumps for flight instruments optional. Piper Aire air-conditioning system of 14,500 BTU capacity optional. Janitrol 45,000 BTU combustion heater standard.

Avionics and Equipment: Four optional factory installed packages of avionics are available, these including nav/coms, ADF, autopilot, DME, glideslope and marker beacon receivers, and transponder, by Collins, King and Piper. Options include alternative to or duplication of the above equipment, plus autopilot/flight director systems, encoding altimeter, HF transceiver, R/Nav, radio altimeter, and weather radar, by manufacturers which include the above, plus 3M, Bendix, King, Narco, SunAir and United. Standard equipment includes dual cylinder head and exhaust gas temperature gauges, dual manifold pressure gauges, dual electric tachometers, sensitive altimeter and alternate static source. Pilot's and co-pilot's seats are fore and aft adjustable and reclining, and have inertia reel shoulder and safety belts and armrests; pilot's storm window, sun visors, stall warning device, provisions for emergency locator transmitter, carpeted floor, soundproofing, fuel tank quick drains, jack pads, and tiedown rings. Items in operational groups are available optionally, plus co-pilot's blind-flying instrumentation, encoding altimeter, digital clock, cabin heater, hour recorder, cabin fire extinguisher, vertically adjustable seats for pilot and co-pilot, inertia reel shoulder belt systems for crew and passenger seats, headrests, window curtains, tables, refreshment console, tinted windows, ventilation fan, stainless steel control cables, in-flight recognition lights, towbar, and zinc chromate finish for aluminium parts.

Dimensions, external:
- Wing span: 11·85 m (38 ft 10¾ in)
- Wing chord, constant: 1·60 m (5 ft 3 in)
- Length overall: 8·72 m (28 ft 7½ in)
- Height overall: 3·02 m (9 ft 10¾ in)
- Tailplane span: 4·14 m (13 ft 6¾ in)
- Wheel track: 3·38 m (11 ft 1¼ in)
- Wheelbase: 2·13 m (7 ft 0 in)
- Propeller diameter: 1·93 m (6 ft 4 in)
- Distance between propeller centres: 3·80 m (12 ft 5½ in)
- Cabin door (stbd, fwd): Height: 0·89 m (2 ft 11 in)
  - Width: 0·91 m (3 ft 0 in)
- Cabin door (port, rear): Height: 0·72 m (2 ft 4½ in)
  - Width: 0·71 m (2 ft 4 in)
- Baggage door (stbd, rear): Height: 0·52 m (1 ft 8½ in)
  - Width: 0·66 m (2 ft 2 in)
- Baggage door (port, fwd): Height: 0·53 m (1 ft 9 in)
  - Width: 0·61 m (2 ft 0 in)

Dimensions, internal:
- Cabin (incl flight deck): Length: 3·17 m (10 ft 5 in)
  - Max width: 1·24 m (4 ft 1 in)
  - Max height: 1·07 m (3 ft 6 in)
  - Volume: 5·53 m³ (195·3 cu ft)
- Forward baggage compartment: 0·43 m³ (15·3 cu ft)
- Rear baggage compartment: 0·49 m³ (17·3 cu ft)

Areas:
- Wings, gross: 19·39 m² (208·7 sq ft)
- Ailerons, incl tab (total): 1·17 m² (12·60 sq ft)
- Trailing-edge flaps (total): 1·94 m² (20·84 sq ft)
- Fin: 1·14 m² (12·32 sq ft)
- Rudder, incl tab: 0·71 m² (7·62 sq ft)
- Horizontal tail surfaces (total): 3·60 m² (38·74 sq ft)

Weights and Loadings:
- Weight empty, standard: 1,310 kg (2,888 lb)
- Max usable fuel weight:
  - standard: 253 kg (558 lb)
  - optional: 385 kg (738 lb)
- Max T-O weight: 2,154 kg (4,750 lb)
- Max ramp weight: 2,165 kg (4,773 lb)
- Max zero-fuel weight: 2,027 kg (4,470 lb)
- Max landing weight: 2,047 kg (4,513 lb)
- Max wing loading: 111·1 kg/m² (22·76 lb/sq ft)
- Max power loading: 6·57 kg/kW (10·8 lb/hp)

Performance (at max T-O weight except where indicated):
- Max level speed at optimum altitude, mid cruise weight: 196 knots (363 km/h; 226 mph)
- Cruising speed at optimum altitude, mid cruise weight:
  - 75% power: 193 knots (357 km/h; 222 mph)
  - 65% power: 191 knots (354 km/h; 220 mph)
  - 55% power: 180 knots (333 km/h; 207 mph)
  - 45% power: 168 knots (311 km/h; 193 mph)
- Cruising speed at 3,050 m (10,000 ft), mid cruise weight:
  - 75% power: 179 knots (332 km/h; 206 mph)
  - 65% power: 175 knots (324 km/h; 202 mph)
  - 55% power: 159 knots (295 km/h; 183 mph)
  - 45% power: 143 knots (265 km/h; 165 mph)
- Minimum single-engine control speed (VMC): 65 knots (120 km/h; 75 mph)
- Stalling speed: flaps and landing gear up: 66 knots (122 km/h; 76 mph) CAS
  - flaps and landing gear down: 62 knots (115 km/h; 72 mph) CAS
- Max rate of climb at S/L: 427 m (1,400 ft)/min
- Rate of climb at S/L, one engine out: 73 m (240 ft)/min
- Max certificated ceiling: 7,620 m (25,000 ft)
- Service ceiling, one engine out: 3,750 m (12,300 ft)
- T-O run: 280 m (920 ft)
- T-O to 15 m (50 ft): 369 m (1,210 ft)
- Landing from 15 m (50 ft):
  - standard brakes: 658 m (2,160 ft)
  - heavy duty brakes: 603 m (1,978 ft)
- Landing run: standard brakes: 427 m (1,400 ft)
  - heavy duty brakes: 371 m (1,218 ft)
- Accelerate/stop distance:
  - standard brakes: 732 m (2,400 ft)
  - heavy duty brakes: 636 m (2,088 ft)
- Range with standard fuel, allowances for taxi, T-O, climb, descent, and 45 min reserves at max range power:
  - at optimum altitude:
    - 75% power: 463 nm (858 km; 533 miles)
    - 65% power: 550 nm (1,018 km; 633 miles)
    - 55% power: 630 nm (1,166 km; 725 miles)
    - 45% power: 670 nm (1,240 km; 771 miles)
  - at 3,050 m (10,000 ft):
    - 75% power: 450 nm (833 km; 517 miles)
    - 65% power: 535 nm (990 km; 615 miles)
    - 55% power: 610 nm (1,129 km; 702 miles)
    - 45% power: 632 nm (1,170 km; 727 miles)
- Range with max optional fuel, allowances as above:
  - at optimum altitude:
    - 75% power: 665 nm (1,232 km; 765 miles)
    - 65% power: 785 nm (1,454 km; 904 miles)
    - 55% power: 920 nm (1,705 km; 1,059 miles)
    - 45% power: 990 nm (1,834 km; 1,140 miles)
  - at 3,050 m (10,000 ft):
    - 75% power: 640 nm (1,186 km; 737 miles)
    - 65% power: 758 nm (1,405 km; 873 miles)
    - 55% power: 860 nm (1,593 km; 990 miles)
    - 45% power: 903 nm (1,673 km; 1,040 miles)

PIPER (PA-46-310P) MALIBU

Piper announced on 20 November 1982 a new six-seat cabin monoplane, the PA-46-310P Malibu, which the company claims to be the world's first cabin class, pressurised, piston powered single-engined aircraft. The almost circular section fuselage of the Malibu has practically no taper over the length of the cabin, providing each passenger with an equal level of comfort. The engineering and pre-production prototypes had completed more than 400 and almost 60 flight hours respectively at the time of the company's announcement, and during this period these aircraft met or exceeded all design performance goals. FAA certification was received in September 1983. Production deliveries began in November 1983, and by 1 January 1986 a total of 212 aircraft had been delivered. The 200th production Malibu was delivered to All-State Belting Co of Des Moines, Iowa, on 26 November 1985.

In May 1984 a Malibu set two world records by flying from Tampa, Florida, to Gander, Newfoundland, in 8 h 27 min at an average speed of 213·36 knots (395·15 km/h; 245·53 mph); and then from Gander to Munich, Germany, in 12 h 53 min 55 s at a speed of 197·80 knots (366·32 km/h; 227·62 mph). On 7 December 1984 a Malibu set a world record by flying from Oakland, California, to Honolulu, Hawaii, in 12 h 1 min at an average speed of 173·864 knots (322·194 km/h; 200·2 mph) and on 17 December the same aircraft established another world record on a flight from Honolulu to Sydney, Australia, in 24 h 49 min 22 s, at an average speed of 177·76 knots (329·43 km/h; 204·7 mph).

An optional **Executive** group equipment package comprises executive writing table; forward refreshment centre; cabin stereo system; true airspeed indicator; polished propeller spinner; external power receptacle; lockable fuel caps; and vinyl floor runner, and adds 20·4 kg (45·0 lb) to basic aircraft weight.

In early 1986 it was reported that Piper was believed to be considering development of turboprop, unpressurised and twin-engined variants of the Malibu.

Type: Six-seat all-metal cabin monoplane.

Wings: Cantilever low-wing monoplane of high aspect ratio. Dihedral 4°. Conventional ailerons and hydraulically actuated trailing-edge flaps. Pneumatic de-icing boots on leading-edges optional.

Fuselage: Semi-monocoque structure, primarily of light alloy, with fail-safe construction in the pressurised area.

Tail Unit: Conventional tail unit, with swept vertical surfaces and an extended dorsal fin blended into the upper surface of the rear fuselage. Horn balanced control surfaces. Trim tab in elevator. Pneumatic de-icing boots on leading-edges optional.

Landing Gear: Hydraulically retractable tricycle type with single wheel on each unit; main units retract inward into wing roots, nosewheel rearward, rotating 90° to lie flat under baggage compartment. Oleo-pneumatic shock absorber in each unit. Hydraulic brakes on mainwheels. Parking brake.

Power Plant: One 231 kW (310 hp) Continental TSIO-520-BE flat-six turbocharged engine, driving a Hartzell two-blade constant-speed propeller with spinner. Fuel system capacity 462 litres (122 US gallons), of which 454 litres (120 US gallons) are usable. Oil capacity 7·5 litres (2 US gallons).

Accommodation: Pilot and five passengers in pressurised, heated and ventilated cabin. Centre and rear contoured reclining seats in facing pairs. Foldaway writing table. Airstair door immediately to rear of wing trailing-edge on port side. Overwing emergency exit on starboard side. Unpressurised baggage compartment in nose, and pressurised space at rear of cabin, each with capacity of 45 kg (100 lb). Heated windscreen optional.

Systems: Pressurisation system with max differential of 0·38 bars (5·5 lb/sq in), to provide a cabin altitude of 2,440 m (8,000 ft) to a height of 7,620 m (25,000 ft). Hydraulic system pressure 107 bars (1,550 lb/sq in). One engine driven vacuum pump standard; second pump optional. Standard electrical system has one 60A alternator; second 60A alternator optional. 24V 15Ah battery. Full icing protection is optional, with pneumatic de-icing boots on wing and tail surfaces, electrically heated propeller, pilot's electrically heated anti-ice windscreen plate, wing ice inspection light, heated pitot head, heated lift detector, and dual alternators and vacuum pumps. Approval for flight into known icing conditions was obtained in July 1984.

Avionics and Equipment: Standard King avionics comprise dual nav/coms; VOR/LOC and glideslope; HSI;

ADF; DME; transponder; automatic flight control system and automatic emergency locator beacon. Options include alternatives to or duplication of the above equipment, plus R/Nav; yaw damper; RMI; Texas Instruments and Foster Loran systems; Sperry WeatherScout I colour weather radar; 3M Stormscope; SunAir ASB-100A HF transceiver; and Wulfsberg Flitefone. Standard equipment includes airspeed indicator; magnetic compass; Piper pictorial turn rate indicator; rate of climb indicator; altimeter; eight-day clock; 3 in artificial horizon; electric 3 in pictorial navigation indicator; luminous outside air temperature gauge; heated pitot; ammeter; annunciator panel; electric tachometer; fuel quantity gauge; manifold pressure/fuel flow gauge; oil temperature gauge; oil pressure gauge; cylinder head temperature gauge; turbine inlet temperature gauge; engine hour meter; alternate static source; dual control wheels with elevator trim switch on pilot's wheel; and pilot's and co-pilot's toe brakes. Pilot's and co-pilot's seats are vertically and fore/aft adjusting and have inertia reel shoulder harnesses and safety belts; armrests for all six seats; ashtrays; map holders; pilot's storm window; emergency exit; sun visors; passenger club seating with inertia reel shoulder harnesses and seatbelts on forward facing seats; window curtains; cigar lighter; super soundproofing; fuel tank quick drains; fuel sampler; jack pads and towbar standard. Optional equipment includes ground clearance energy saver system supplying battery power to one com and audio system; panel-mounted digital clock; co-pilot's flight instruments; oxygen system; relief tube; hand held fire extinguisher; stainless steel control cables; and Irish weave or all-leather seats.

Dimensions, external:
- Wing span: 13·11 m (43 ft 0 in)
- Length overall: 8·66 m (28 ft 4¾ in)
- Height overall: 3·44 m (11 ft 3½ in)
- Tailplane span: 4·42 m (14 ft 6 in)
- Wheel track: 3·75 m (12 ft 3½ in)
- Wheelbase: 2·44 m (8 ft 0 in)
- Propeller diameter: 2·03 m (6 ft 8 in)
- Passenger door (port, rear):
  - Height: 1·17 m (3 ft 10 in)
  - Width: 0·61 m (2 ft 0 in)
- Baggage door (port, nose):
  - Height: 0·58 m (1 ft 11 in)
  - Width: 0·48 m (1 ft 7 in)

Dimensions, internal:
- Cabin: Length, instrument panel to rear pressure bulkhead: 3·76 m (12 ft 4 in)
  - Max width: 1·26 m (4 ft 1½ in)
  - Max height: 1·19 m (3 ft 11 in)
- Baggage compartment volume:
  - nose: 0·40 m³ (14 cu ft)
  - rear cabin: 0·57 m³ (20 cu ft)

Area:
- Wings, gross: 16·26 m² (175·0 sq ft)

Weights and Loadings:
- Weight empty, standard: 1,068 kg (2,354 lb)
- Max usable fuel weight: 326 kg (720 lb)
- Max T-O weight: 1,860 kg (4,100 lb)
- Max ramp weight: 1,868 kg (4,118 lb)
- Max wing loading: 114·25 kg/m² (23·4 lb/sq ft)
- Max power loading: 8·05 kg/kW (13·23 lb/hp)

Performance (at max T-O weight, S/L, ISA, except where indicated):
- Max level speed at mid cruise weight: 234 knots (434 km/h; 269 mph)
- Cruising speed at mid cruise weight at optimum altitude:
  - 75% power: 215 knots (398 km/h; 248 mph)
  - 65% power: 205 knots (380 km/h; 236 mph)
  - 55% power: 196 knots (363 km/h; 226 mph)
- Stalling speed:
  - flaps up: 68 knots (126 km/h; 79 mph) CAS
  - flaps down: 58 knots (108 km/h; 67 mph) CAS
- Max rate of climb at S/L: 348 m (1,143 ft)/min
- Service ceiling: 7,620 m (25,000 ft)
- T-O run: 439 m (1,440 ft)
- T-O to 15 m (50 ft): 617 m (2,025 ft)
- Landing from 15 m (50 ft): 463 m (1,520 ft)
- Landing run: 195 m (640 ft)
- Range with max fuel at optimum altitude with allowances for taxi, T-O, climb and descent, and 45 min reserves at max range power:
  - 75% power: 1,330 nm (2,464 km; 1,531 miles)
  - 65% power: 1,420 nm (2,631 km; 1,635 miles)
  - 55% power: 1,555 nm (2,881 km; 1,790 miles)

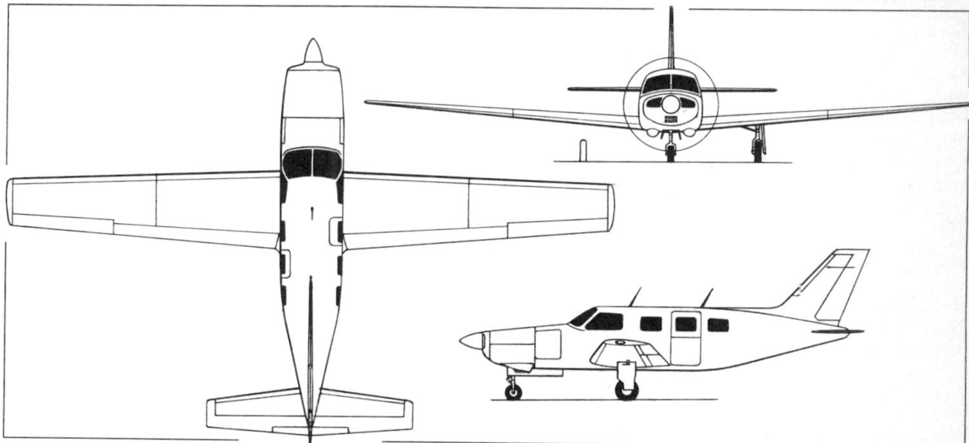

Photograph and three-view drawing *(Pilot Press)* **of the PA-46-310P Malibu, claimed by Piper to be the first cabin class, pressurised, piston powered single-engined aircraft**

AIRLINE DIVISION

The Piper T-1020 and T-1040 commuter airliners, last described in the 1985-86 edition of *Jane's*, are no longer in production, although support continues from the company's Vero Beach base. Production totals were: T-1020, a total of 22 aircraft; T-1040, a total of 23 aircraft.

PROP-JETS

PROP-JETS INC

San Antonio International Airport, 8905 Wetmore Road, San Antonio, Texas 78216
Telephone: (512) 828 0800
Chairman: Peter Paul Luce
President: Paul Whetstone

PROP-JETS INTERCEPTOR 400A

In early 1986 Prop-Jets Inc was seeking a buyer for its **Interceptor 400A** four-seat turboprop light aircraft project, including the prototype, type certificate, tooling and spares. A description of the Interceptor 400A appeared in the 1985-86 edition of *Jane's*.

RAISBECK

RAISBECK ENGINEERING INC

7675 Perimeter Road South, Boeing Field International, Seattle, Washington 98108
Telephone: (206) 763 2000

Chief Executive Officer: James D. Raisbeck
Vice-President, Marketing: John McCarthy
Regional Vice-Presidents, Sales:
James Michael McEniry
Robert P. Steinbach

Raisbeck Engineering Inc continues the work of its founder and Chief Executive Officer, James D. Raisbeck, of developing, certificating, and marketing to the general aviation community advanced technology systems aimed at increasing aircraft performance, productivity and safety. Since leaving The Boeing Company in 1969, he has been responsible for more than 100 certification programmes while Chairman of the Board of Robertson Aircraft Corporation (1969-73) and during development of the Raisbeck Group's Mark II and Mark IV Systems for Lear Jet aircraft and Mark V System (including the first US Transport Category jet application of the NASA supercritical wing) for the Sabreliner 65 as well as for existing Sabreliner 60s and 75As.

Current products of Raisbeck Engineering are described below. Additional programmes, in the study and design stages, include the Mark X which would give the Boeing 727-100 a range of some 5,000 nm (9,260 km; 5,750 miles) with NBAA IFR reserves.

RAISBECK MARK VI SYSTEM

In April 1982, Raisbeck Engineering formed a joint venture with Morrison-Knudsen's Western Aircraft Maintenance Inc of Boise, Idaho, to develop its Mark VI System for the Beechcraft Super King Air 200 series. The partnership with Western Aircraft Maintenance Inc was terminated in December 1985, but the Mark VI System continues to be marketed by Raisbeck Engineering Inc.

Improvements embodied by the Mark VI System include new inboard wing leading-edges of composite material which increase speed and intercooler efficiency through advanced aerodynamics; Goodrich flush wing de-icing boots made practicable by recessing the new inboard leading-edges; flap and aileron seals; extended rear underwing fairings of composite material on engine nacelles to reduce drag; wheel doors which enclose completely the oversize tyres on those Super King Air 200s fitted with high flotation landing gear; low drag windscreen wipers; a flexible stainless steel coupling between exhaust stack and inlet; flush automatic nose vane door which increases air-conditioning efficiency when open and reduces drag by closing when not needed; vanes which direct inlet air up to the compressor with full supercharging effect; and twin ventral strakes under the rear fuselage, instead of the single standard ventral fin, to improve airflow and increase stability and speed.

The Raisbeck Mark VI system received British CAA certification in the Spring of 1986.

HARTZELL/RAISBECK QUIET TURBOFAN PROPELLER SYSTEM

In February 1985 Raisbeck certificated four-blade propeller conversion for the Super King Air 200, known as the Raisbeck Quiet Prop, which it claims will result in considerably reduced flight deck and cabin noise, shorter take-off and landing runs and a rate of climb of 1,102 m (3,616 ft)/min instead of 898 m (2,945 ft)/min for the Mark VI equipped Super King Air with the usual three-blade propellers. The conversion utilises new advanced technology lightweight 2·39 m (7 ft 10 in) diameter 'turbofan' propellers developed by Hartzell, and includes new timers, slip rings and a B.F. Goodrich hot propeller de-icing system. First flight of the propeller took place on a Mark VI-equipped Beechcraft Super King Air B200 on 25 June 1984. By May 1986 more than 100 Quiet Prop systems had been delivered, and production was running at 8-10 per month. By mid-1986 Raisbeck had developed a Quiet Prop installation for the de Havilland Canada DHC-6-300 Twin Otter and expected to begin deliveries of the system for Beechcraft King Air 90 series aircraft in the Autumn of that year. Tests were continuing on various models of the Piper Cheyenne.

RAISBECK MARK VII SYSTEM

Raisbeck's Mark VII System for all versions of the Beechcraft King Air 90 has been broken down into a series of 12 kits which are being certificated individually. The first kit, comprising fully enclosed main landing gear speed doors, was certificated in June 1983; production deliveries began immediately afterwards. Their effect is to decrease time to climb by 14 per cent and add 6 knots (11 km/h; 7 mph) to the cruising speed of the aircraft at 7,315 m (24,000 ft).

The second kit, certificated in September 1983, introduced new area ruled wing lockers, aft of the engine nacelles. These have a combined volume of 0·45 m³ (16 cu ft), with a capacity of 317 kg (700 lb), and will accommodate outsize items such as six pairs of 2·2 m (7 ft 2½ in) skis, while at the same time decreasing drag and increasing cruising speed. They can be installed on Beechcraft King Air, Super King Air and Model 99 aircraft. Deliveries began in April 1986.

The remaining ten kits will include, rear fuselage ventral strakes, increased efficiency intakes, advanced technology four-blade propellers for the King Air 90 series, and a TKS full span ice protection system, replacing the current de-icing boots and associated with wing leading-edge aerodynamic improvements.

Beechcraft Super King Air 200 embodying Raisbeck Mark VI System

Altitude	T-O weight	Ambient conditions	Torque increase	True airspeed increase
5,485 m (18,000 ft)	4,990 kg (11,000 lb)	ISA	29·45 kg-m (213 ft-lb)	27 knots (50 km/h; 31 mph)
9,450 m (31,000 ft)	4,990 kg (11,000 lb)	ISA	16·73 kg-m (121 ft-lb)	31 knots (57 km/h; 36 mph)

Typical Raisbeck Mark VI incremental performance gains

Altitude	T-O weight	Ambient conditions	Ice doors stowed	Ice doors deployed
S/L to 9,450 m (31,000 ft)	5,443 kg (12,000 lb)	ISA	8 minutes less	22 minutes less

Typical Raisbeck Mark VI reductions in time to climb

RAISBECK RAM AIR RECOVERY SYSTEM

Raisbeck Engineering Inc has developed a Ram Air Recovery System (RARS) for Beechcraft Super King Air 200 aircraft which provides improvements in cruising speeds and rates of climb. RARS comprises the installation of a more complete sealing of the engine nacelle air inlet section, a new fixed turning vane, the addition of a 'Coanda effect' curved surface on the rear portion of the movable inertial separator vane, and a new highly porous ice shedder screen. Deliveries of RARS equipped aircraft began on 15 June 1986. The system is approved by Pratt & Whitney Canada, which manufactures the Super King Air 200's engines, and has received FAA certification.

RAM

RAM AIRCRAFT CORPORATION

Waco-Madison Cooper Airport, PO Box 5219, Waco, Texas 76708-0219
Telephone: (817) 752 8381
Telex: 910 894 5248

PRESIDENT:
Jack M. Riley Jr (Administration/Engineering)
VICE-PRESIDENT: Mrs Toni Riley
INTERNATIONAL SALES: Jay Kelly
PROJECT ENGINEER: Phillip Crawford
SALES MANAGER: David Seesing

RAM Aircraft Corporation specialises in the modification of selected single-and twin-engined general aviation aircraft to provide increased performance and efficiency. This is achieved by the installation of engines of greater horsepower, driving propellers of advanced design. With the exception of engines installed in Cessna 172s and Piper PA-28-140 and PA-28-151, all are remanufactured by RAM to a standard that gives a full TBO warranty. All of the resulting modifications have been FAA approved by the award of a supplemental type certificate (STC). Export STC modification kits are available, and these can include either new engines or RAM-remanufactured 100% balanced versions of the Continental TSIO-520 engine in N, NB, VB, E, EB, B, BB, C, H, M and R models and GTSIO-520-L and N. The company offers also an aircraft refurbishing service at its Waco works, including repainting, maintenance, engine remanufacture and the incorporation of STC approved modifications.

Any performance figures not listed in this entry may be considered to be the same as specified by Cessna Aircraft Company, Beech Aircraft Corporation or Piper Aircraft Corporation for their standard production versions of the aircraft.

RAM/CESSNA 172

RAM modifications of the Cessna 172, models D-N, involves the installation of a factory-new 119 kW (160 hp) Avco Lycoming O-320-D2G flat-four engine and, in the case of aircraft manufactured prior to 1968, a new McCauley 1C160/CTM7557 propeller, which is available optionally for later models. On Cessna 172 models D-F a new cowling is also installed. Other options include the installation of four new engine shock mounts, a red rubber baffle seal kit, new air filter, new oil quick drain fitting, oil filter adapter kit and oil filter, RAM super soundproofing and three-colour polyurethane external paint finish. After modification, performance is equivalent to that of the 1980 Cessna 172.

RAM/PIPER PA-28-140/PA-28-151

RAM modification of these two Piper models involves the installation of a factory-new 119 kW (160 hp) Avco Lycoming O-320-D3G flat-four engine. Options are the same as for the RAM/Cessna 172.

PERFORMANCE (A: PA-28-140; B: PA-28-151):
Cruising speed: A — 113 knots (209 km/h; 130 mph)
B — 117 knots (217 km/h; 135 mph)
Max rate of climb at S/L: A — 198 m (650 ft)/min
B — 216 m (710 ft)/min

RAM/CESSNA T206/210

RAM modification of these two Cessna models covers replacement of the 212 kW (285 hp) Continental TSIO-520-C/H flat-six engine in early production aircraft by a 231 kW (310 hp) TSIO-520-M/R. This RAM-remanufactured engine provides performance generally the same as that of later model Cessna production aircraft powered by a 231 kW (310 hp) engine. A Hartzell Q-tip propeller or wide chord McCauley propeller can be included in the modification. Aircraft equipped with latest technology Q-tip propellers offer an increase of 4·3 knots (8 km/h; 5 mph) in cruising speed. Cessna engine baffle seals are replaced by RAM seals of high temperature glassfibre reinforced red silicone rubber material; Alcor direct reading exhaust gas temperature gauge; Slick 6220 pressurised magnetos and RAM super soundproofing are installed. Hoskins CFS-1000 and FT101 computerised fuel management systems are optional, installed in conjunction with the Cessna combination MP/FF gauge. Riley or Turbo Plus intercooler installation optional. For 1966 and later T206s, and 1972 and later T210s, a dual vacuum pump package is available.

PERFORMANCE (A: T206; B: T210):
Cruising speed, 75% power at 6,705 m (22,000 ft):
A — 169 knots (314 km/h; 195 mph)
B — 213 knots (394 km/h; 245 mph)
Max rate of climb at S/L: A, B — 375 m (1,230 ft)/min

RAM/CESSNA T310/320D-F

In this modification the 212 kW (285 hp) Continental TSIO-520-B flat-six engines can be replaced by 224 kW (300 hp) TSIO-520-E, 231 kW (310 hp) TSIO-520-N, or 242 kW (325 hp) TSIO-520-NBR RAM-remanufactured engines. With 231 kW (310 hp) or 242 kW (325 hp) engines the modified aircraft are known as Super T310s or Super T320s. Either separately or in conjunction with this modification, RAM can install aerial mapping/photo reconnaissance dual camera ports, the STC approved installation being suitable for cameras as large as the Wild RC10 and Zeiss RMKA 15/23. The power plant modification includes installation of RAM baffle seals, Silver Fueltron computerised fuel flow system, Alcor direct reading exhaust gas temperature gauge and updated exhaust system. Hartzell Q-tip propellers are standard with -NBR engines and optional for -E and -N engines. Pressurised magnetos are standard with all engines.

PERFORMANCE (A: 224 kW; 300 hp, B: 231 kW; 310 hp, C: 242 kW; 325 hp engines, at max T-O weight of 2,572 kg; 5,670 lb):
Cruising speed, 75% power at 5,485 m (18,000 ft):
A — 213 knots (394 km/h; 245 mph)
B — 230 knots (426 km/h; 265 mph)
C — 235 knots (434 km/h; 270 mph)
Max rate of climb at S/L: A — 640 m (2,100 ft)/min
B — 762 m (2,500 ft)/min
C — 915 m (3,000 ft)/min
Rate of climb at S/L, one engine out:
A — 137 m (450 ft)/min
B — 152 m (500 ft)/min
C — 183 m (600 ft)/min

RAM/CESSNA 340/340A

RAM's modification of the Cessna 340/340A replaces 212 kW (285 hp) Continental TSIO-520-K or 231 kW (310 hp) TSIO-520-N engines by RAM-remanufactured 231 kW (310 hp) TSIO-520-Ns or 242 kW (325 hp) TSIO-520-NBRs respectively, and includes standard and optional items as for Cessna T310/320, including new Hartzell Q-tip propellers, and engine nacelle cooling air exit baffles. In 242 kW (325 hp) form the modified aircraft is known as the Super 340 or Super 340A. The baffles enhance engine cooling, reduce cabin noise and vibration, and reduce tail vibration and fatigue.

PERFORMANCE (A: 231 kW; 310 hp engines with Q-tip propellers. B: 242 kW; 325 hp engines, at max T-O weight of 2,853 kg; 6,290 lb):
Cruising speed, 75% power at 6,100 m (20,000 ft):
A, B — 225 knots (417 km/h; 259 mph)
Max rate of climb at S/L: A — 564 m (1,850 ft)/min
B — 655 m (2,150 ft)/min
Rate of climb at S/L, one engine out:
A — 105 m (345 ft)/min
B — 114 m (375 ft)/min
Time to 5,485 m (18,000 ft): A — 20 min
B — 17 min
Acceleration to 87 knots (161 km/h; 100 mph):
A — 20 s
B — 16 s

RAM/CESSNA 401/402A/402B/402C

In this modification RAM installs remanufactured 224 kW (300 hp) Continental TSIO-520-E or 242 kW (325 hp) TSIO-520-VB engines in Cessna 401 and 402A-C aircraft. Optional equipment includes Slick 6220 pressurised magnetos, a red silicone rubber baffle seal kit, Alcor 46158 exhaust gas temperature gauge and combustion analyser, Silver Fueltron fuel flow management system, Woodward propeller synchrophaser, RAM super soundproofing, Cleveland heavy duty brakes, polished and balanced propellers and three-colour polyurethane external paint finish.

RAM/CESSNA 414

In this modification RAM replaces the 231 kW (310 hp) Continental TSIO-520-J engines installed in Cessna 414s built between 1970 and 1976 by 231 kW (310 hp) TSIO-520-Ns or (in Super 414) 242 kW (325 hp) TSIO-520-NBRs. The installation includes the same standard items as for the Cessna T310/320, but the Hartzell Q-tip propellers are available only for modifications with the 242 kW (325 hp) engines, with which they are standard.

PERFORMANCE (A: 231 kW; 310 hp. B: 242 kW; 325 hp engines, at max T-O weight of 2,953 kg; 6,510 lb):
- Cruising speed, 75% power at 6,100 m (20,000 ft):
  - A: 210 knots (389 km/h; 241 mph)
  - B: 215 knots (398 km/h; 247 mph)
- Max rate of climb at S/L: A: 533 m (1,750 ft)/min
  - B: 610 m (2,000 ft)/min
- Rate of climb at S/L, one engine out:
  - A: 88 m (290 ft)/min
  - B: 104 m (340 ft)/min
- Time to 5,485 m (18,000 ft): A: 20 min
  - B: 18 min
- Acceleration to 87 knots (161 km/h; 100 mph):
  - A: 22 s
  - B: 19 s

RAM/CESSNA 414A and 414AW

RAM's modification of the Cessna 414A replaces the standard 231 kW (310 hp) Continental TSIO-520-J engines by remanufactured TSIO-520-N/NBs of the same horsepower, or (in the Super 414A and AW) by 242 kW (325 hp) TSIO-520-NBRs, with Hartzell Q-tip propellers and standard items as for the Cessna T310/320. FAA approval of a version of this aircraft fitted with 0·89 m (2 ft 11 in) high winglets at each wingtip was received on 1 March 1983. By March 1985 more than 45 modified aircraft had been delivered and modification kits were being prepared for customers in Australia and Europe. The RAM/Cessna 414A operates at a gross weight increase of 153 kg (337 lb). Wingleted RAM/Cessna 414As are designated **414AW**.

WEIGHTS (A: without winglets, B: with winglets; both with 242 kW; 325 hp engines):
- Max T-O weight: A: 3,062 kg (6,750 lb)
  - B: 3,215 kg (7,087 lb)

PERFORMANCE (at max T-O weight):
- Cruising speed, 75% power at 6,100 m (20,000 ft):
  - A, B: 215 knots (398 km/h; 247 mph)
- Max rate of climb at S/L: A: 503 m (1,650 ft)/min
  - B: 478 m (1,570 ft)/min
- Rate of climb at S/L, one engine out:
  - A: 104 m (340 ft)/min
  - B: 98 m (320 ft)/min
- Time to 5,485 m (18,000 ft): A, B: 18 min
- Acceleration to 87 knots (161 km/h; 100 mph):
  - A: 21 s

RAM/CESSNA 421C and 421CW

RAM's modification of the Cessna 421B and 421C Golden Eagle series replaces the standard engine cooling baffles, exhaust risers, slip joints and magnetos with a 'RAM Reliability Package' which includes new red silicone rubber/glassfibre cooling baffle seal material, remanufactured exhaust system and slip joints, and Bendix S6RN-1250 pressurised magnetos. Also included are a Silver Fueltron computerised fuel management system and Alcor direct reading exhaust gas temperature system. An optional package includes RAM or TCM factory remanufactured GTSIO-520-L/N engines, propellers and accessories. In November 1984 RAM received FAA approval for the installation of 0·89 m (2 ft 11 in) winglets to Cessna 421C aircraft up to factory serial number 0799. The first converted aircraft, known as the **RAM/Cessna 421CW**, was delivered in October 1984, and by February 1985 four conversions had been completed, with a planned production rate of two aircraft per month.

First production RAM conversion of a Cessna 421C with winglets, known as RAM/Cessna 421CW

The winglet installation for the Cessna 421C involves removal of the standard 0·46 m (1 ft 6 in) wingtip and replacement with a wing extension and winglet assembly each of which measures 0·93 m (3 ft 0½ in) to the base of the winglet. This adds a total of 0·94 m (3 ft 1 in) to the standard Cessna 421C's wing span. The RAM winglet is constructed from bidirectional carbon graphite cloth impregnated with epoxy resins, with an outer layer which includes interwoven aluminium cloth for electrical conductivity and lighting protection. Existing landing lights, position lights and wingtip strobe lights are installed in the new wingtip/winglet assembly. The RAM/Cessna 421CW Supplemental Type Certificate includes certification for flight into known icing conditions.

A description of the Cessna 421C may be found in the 1985-86 *Jane's*.

DIMENSIONS, EXTERNAL (421CW): As for Cessna 421C except:
- Basic wing span: 13·47 m (44 ft 2½ in)
- Span, winglet tip to winglet tip: 13·83 m (45 ft 4½ in)
- Wing aspect ratio (basic): 8·64
- Effective wing aspect ratio, including winglets: 9·74
- Winglet cant angle: 10°
- Winglet toe-out angle: 2°

AREA (421CW):
- Wings, gross (basic): 21·0 m² (226·0 sq ft)

WEIGHTS AND LOADINGS (421CW):
- Max T-O weight: 3,429 kg (7,560 lb)
- Max zero fuel weight: 2,963 kg (6,533 lb)
- Max wing loading: 163·3 kg/m² (33·45 lb/sq ft)
- Max power loading: 6·12 kg/kW (10·06 lb/hp)

PERFORMANCE (421CW):
- Cruising speed at 75% power at 6,100 m (20,000 ft): 228 knots (422 km/h; 262 mph)
- Cruising speed at 65% power at 6,100 m (20,000 ft): 223 knots (413 km/h; 257 mph)
- Max rate of climb, one engine out at 1,525 m (5,000 ft), ISA: 91 m (300 ft)/min
- Time to 7,315 m (24,000 ft): 24 min

RAM/BEECH BARON 58

This modification installs 231 kW (310 hp) Continental TSIO-520-L/LB or 242 kW (325 hp) TSIO-520-WB engines in Beech Baron Models 58P and 58TC. Optional items include Silver Fueltron electronic fuel flow system, Alcor exhaust gas temperature gauge and combustion analyser, Airborne dry vacuum pumps, Woodward Type II synchrophase system with Woodward propeller governors, red silicone rubber baffle seals, Teflon fuel and oil hoses, Cleveland brakes and wheels. RAM super soundproofing, polished and balanced propellers, and three-colour polyurethane external paint finish.

PERFORMANCE (Baron 58P. A: 231 kW; 310 hp, B: 242 kW; 325 hp):
- Cruising speed, 75% power at 6,100 m (20,000 ft):
  - A: 202 knots (374 km/h; 233 mph)
  - B: 210 knots (389 km/h; 242 mph)
- Max rate of climb at S/L: A: 449 m (1,475 ft)/min
  - B: 457 m (1,500 ft)/min
- Rate of climb at S/L, one engine out:
  - A: 62 m (204 ft)/min
  - B: 82 m (270 ft)/min

RANKIN

RANKIN AIRCRAFT

Rankin Airport, Route 3, Maryville, Missouri 64468
Telephone: (816) 582 3791
PRESIDENT: Joe Rankin

RANKIN COLLEGIATE

Mr Joe Rankin has acquired the type certificate and manufacturing drawings for the former Porterfield CP-65 Collegiate two-seat light aeroplane, more than 400 of which were manufactured prior to the Second World War. A number of modifications have been made to update the design, which is now known as the Rankin Collegiate.

TYPE: Two-seat high-wing cabin monoplane.

WINGS: Strut braced high-wing monoplane, with two parallel bracing struts each side. Incidence 3° 23′. Dihedral 2°. No sweep. Two-spar structure of spruce and plywood, with Ceconite covering. Plain ailerons.

FUSELAGE: Main frame of 4130 welded steel tube, Ceconite covered.

TAIL UNIT: Wire braced welded steel tube structure, Ceconite covered.

LANDING GEAR: Non-retractable tailwheel type. Side Vs and half axles, with rubber shock absorption. Floats and skis optional.

POWER PLANT: One 48·5 kW (65 hp) Continental A65 flat-four engine, driving a two-blade fixed-pitch propeller. Fuel tank capacity 51 litres (13·5 US gallons).

ACCOMMODATION: Two seats in tandem in enclosed cabin with one-piece Plexiglas windscreen. Cabin heated.

DIMENSIONS, EXTERNAL:
- Wing span: 10·59 m (34 ft 9 in)
- Wing chord (constant): 1·52 m (5 ft 0 in)
- Length overall: 6·80 m (22 ft 4 in)
- Height overall: 2·13 m (7 ft 0 in)

AREA:
- Wings, gross: 15·68 m² (168·8 sq ft)

WEIGHTS AND LOADINGS:
- Weight empty: 331 kg (730 lb)
- Baggage: 18 kg (40 lb)
- Max T-O weight: 544 kg (1,200 lb)
- Max wing loading: 34·7 kg/m² (7·10 lb/sq ft)
- Max power loading: 11·23 kg/kW (18·46 lb/hp)

PERFORMANCE:
- Max level speed: 119 knots (222 km/h; 138 mph)
- Cruising speed: 79 knots (148 km/h; 92 mph)
- Landing speed: 34 knots (64 km/h; 40 mph)
- Max rate of climb at S/L: 145 m (475 ft)/min
- Service ceiling: 3,960 m (13,000 ft)
- T-O run: 133 m (437 ft)
- Landing run: 113 m (370 ft)
- Range, with reserves: 199 nm (370 km; 230 miles)

First production Rankin Collegiate two-seat light aircraft

RILEY

RILEY INTERNATIONAL CORPORATION

2206 Palomar Airport Road, Suite B-2, Carlsbad, California 92008
Telephone: (619) 438 9089
Telex: 140414
PRESIDENT: Jack M. Riley

This new company was formed by Mr Jack Riley to continue marketing his well-known conversions of commercially produced light aircraft. Those currently available are described in this entry. Details of the Riley Rocket 340, Riley Turbine 404, Riley Rocket Power 414 and Riley-Modified Corsair may be found in the 1983-84 *Jane's*. The former Riley Turbine P-210 conversion is now listed under the Advanced Aircraft Corporation entry in this section. The former Riley Turbine Eagle 421 appears as the Regent 1500 in the same entry.

RILEY SUPER P-210

In 1983 Riley announced development of the Super P-210 conversion of the Cessna Model 210 Pressurised Centurion. This conversion involves the installation of a Riley intercooler system for the standard 231 kW (310 hp) turbocharged Continental TSIO-520-AF engine. Riley claims that the induction air intercooler with flush NACA duct in the cowling reduces induction air temperatures by up to 45 per cent, greatly improving engine efficiency. The Riley Super P-210 received an FAA supplemental type certificate in late 1984. The Riley induction air intercooler modification has also received FAA approval for the Cessna Turbo Centurion.

PERFORMANCE:
Cruising speed:
at 5,485 m (18,000 ft) 210 knots (389 km/h; 242 mph)
at 7,000 m (23,000 ft) 217 knots (402 km/h; 250 mph)
Max rate of climb at S/L 305 m (1,000 ft)/min
Time to 7,000 m (23,000 ft) 23 min
Service ceiling 7,000 m (23,000 ft)

RILEY SUPER 310

The Super 310 (formal designation R310 Super) represents a similar conversion to that of the Super 340, the existing power plants in the Cessna 310/320 being replaced by 231 kW (310 hp) Continental TSIO-520-Ns with intercoolers. The conversion is FAA approved for the Cessna 310I to 310R, 320B to 320F and T310P to T310R. Installation of the complete kit requires 12 working days.

A description of the Cessna Model 310 appears under the Cessna entry in the 1981-82 *Jane's*. It applies also to the Riley Super 310, except as follows:

POWER PLANT: As described for Riley Super 340, except installed engines are TSIO-520-Ns instead of TSIO-520-Js.

WEIGHTS AND LOADINGS: As for the appropriate Cessna 310/320 model except as follows:
Weight empty increased by 10 kg (22 lb)
Max payload reduced by 10 kg (22 lb)
Max power loading 5·11 kg/kW (8·4 lb/hp)

PERFORMANCE (at max T-O weight):
Max cruising speed, 75% power:
at 7,315 m (24,000 ft) 261 knots (483 km/h; 300 mph)
at 5,485 m (18,000 ft) 243 knots (451 km/h; 280 mph)
at 4,265 m (14,000 ft) 234 knots (435 km/h; 270 mph)
Max rate of climb at S/L 792 m (2,600 ft)/min
Rate of climb at S/L, one engine out 158 m (520 ft)/min
Service ceiling 10,670 m (35,000 ft)
Service ceiling, one engine out 7,620 m (25,000 ft)
T-O to 15 m (50 ft) 503 m (1,650 ft)
Landing from 15 m (50 ft) 546 m (1,790 ft)
Range with max fuel, max cruising speed at 7,315 m (24,000 ft), 30 min reserves 1,042 nm (1,931 km; 1,200 miles)
Range with max fuel, econ cruising speed at optimum altitude, 30 min reserves 1,737 nm (3,218 km; 2,000 miles)

RILEY SUPER 340

The Riley Super 340 (formal designation R340 Super) differs from the standard Cessna 340 primarily through replacement of the latter's TSIO-520-K engines by TSIO-520-Js. The most important change associated with this new engine installation is the addition of an intercooler which allows a higher power output and also improves specific fuel consumption, critical altitude, engine life and reliability.

The prototype Super 340 received FAA certification in June 1974. The standard Cessna 340A for 1976 was updated in a manner similar to that of the Riley Super 340. Consequently, only Cessna 340 aircraft constructed from 1972 until the last of the 1975 models were completed are suitable for this conversion, which is completed by Riley engineers in five working days.

A description of the Cessna Model 340A appears under the Cessna entry in the 1984-85 *Jane's*. It applies also to the Riley Super 340, except as follows:

POWER PLANT: Two 231 kW (310 hp) Continental TSIO-520-J flat-six turbocharged and intercooled engines, each driving a McCauley three-blade propeller. Engine installation upgraded from Cessna 340 to Cessna 414 configuration. Fuel system as for Cessna 340. Optional aft nacelle fuel tanks, each of 75·7 litres (20 US gallons), provide max optional fuel capacity of 920 litres (243 US gallons) when used in conjunction with the Cessna optional 768 litre (203 US gallon) system.

WEIGHTS AND LOADINGS:
Weight empty 1,754 kg (3,868 lb)
Max payload 904 kg (1,993 lb)
Max T-O weight 2,710 kg (5,975 lb)
Max wing loading 158·6 kg/m² (32·47 lb/sq ft)
Max power loading 5·87 kg/kW (9·64 lb/hp)

PERFORMANCE (at max T-O weight):
Max level speed at 7,315 m (24,000 ft) 252 knots (467 km/h; 290 mph)
Max cruising speed, 75% power:
at 7,315 m (24,000 ft) 234 knots (435 km/h; 270 mph)
at 5,485 m (18,000 ft) 226 knots (418 km/h; 260 mph)
at 4,265 m (14,000 ft) 217 knots (402 km/h; 250 mph)
Econ cruising speed at 7,315 m (24,000 ft) 208 knots (386 km/h; 240 mph)
Max rate of climb at S/L 549 m (1,800 ft)/min
Cruise rate of climb at max cruising power 305 m (1,000 ft)/min
Rate of climb at S/L, one engine out 107 m (350 ft)/min
Service ceiling 9,755 m (32,000 ft)
Service ceiling, one engine out 4,875 m (16,000 ft)
T-O run 457 m (1,500 ft)
T-O to 15 m (50 ft) 594 m (1,950 ft)
Landing from 15 m (50 ft) 561 m (1,840 ft)
Landing run 233 m (765 ft)
Range with max fuel, max cruising speed at 7,315 m (24,000 ft), 30 min reserves 1,042 nm (1,931 km; 1,200 miles)
Range with max fuel, econ cruising speed at 7,315 m (24,000 ft), 30 min reserves 1,737 nm (3,218 km; 2,000 miles)

RILEY TURBINE ROCKET 421

This Riley conversion of the pressurised Cessna 421 involves installation of Avco Lycoming LTP 101-700 turboprop engines, each rated normally at 522 ekW (700 ehp), but flat rated in this application at approximately 70 er cent of normal T-O power. Both the Cessna Model 421B and 421C are suitable for this conversion, under the formal designations of R421BL and R421CL respectively. First flight of a Turbine Rocket 421 was made on 10 January 1978, followed by the first production conversion on 4 June 1978. The R421BL was certificated in June 1981.

The description of the Cessna 421C Golden Eagle which appeared under the Cessna entry in the 1985-86 *Jane's* applies also to the Riley Turbine Rocket 421, except that the landing gear is equipped with Cleveland 199-76 heavy duty brakes; each engine drives a Hartzell propeller with Q-tips and Beta propeller reversal; and optional wing fuel tanks are available to add 363 litres (96 US gallons) to the max total capacity.

WEIGHT AND LOADINGS:
Max T-O weight 3,470 kg (7,650 lb)
Max wing loading 173·7 kg/m² (35·58 lb/sq ft)
Max power loading 4·75 kg/kW (7·81 lb/ehp)

PERFORMANCE (at T-O weight of 3,453 kg; 7,612 lb, ISA):
Max cruising speed at 8,230 m (27,000 ft) 270 knots (500 km/h; 311 mph)
Max rate of climb at S/L 1,067 m (3,500 ft)/min
Rate of climb at S/L, one engine out 224 m (735 ft)/min
Service ceiling over 9,145 m (30,000 ft)
Service ceiling, one engine out 6,400 m (21,000 ft)
Min landing field length 686 m (2,250 ft)
Landing run with propeller reversal 152 m (500 ft)
Range with max fuel, IFR reserves 1,300 nm (2,407 km; 1,496 miles)

ROBINSON

ROBINSON HELICOPTER COMPANY INC

24747 Crenshaw Boulevard, Torrance, California 90505
Telephone: (213) 539 0508
Telex: 18-2554
PRESIDENT: Franklin D. Robinson
VICE-PRESIDENT: D. E. Broman
VICE-PRESIDENT, MARKETING: Barbara L. Krauss

Robinson Helicopter Company was formed to design and manufacture a lightweight helicopter which could be competitive in price with current two/four-seat fixed-wing light aircraft. The design of this aircraft, the Robinson R22, began in June 1973 with emphasis on efficiency, low noise emission and minimum maintenance. The first prototype flew for the first time on 28 August 1975, and the second was completed in early 1977. Both were employed in the programme which led to FAA certification on 16 March 1979, and deliveries of production R22s began in October 1979. United Kingdom CAA certification was gained in June 1981.

FAA certification of the improved R22 Alpha was received in October 1983, permitting a 31·75 kg (70 lb) increase in gross weight, to allow development of the R22 for police work and for IFR training. The 500th R22 was delivered to UK distributors Sloane Helicopters in Summer 1985, at which time the aircraft were operating in 25 countries. The further improved R22 Beta model was announced on 5 August 1985.

Three standard R22s operated by Ranger Helicopters set five Class E1a records in Canada on 11-12 May 1982. A speed of 95 knots (176 km/h; 109 mph) was achieved over both 3 km and 25 km courses. Average speed over a 100 km course was 92·233 knots (170·817 km/h; 106·140 mph). Distance records were set by flights of 142·340 nm (263·615 km; 163·802 miles) over a straight course, and 140·655 nm (260·494 km; 161·863 miles) in a closed circuit.

The Robinson R22 Beta, announced in August 1985

ROBINSON MODEL R22 BETA and MARINER

Current standard version of the Robinson helicopter, from c/n 501 onwards, is the **R22 Beta**. It has been available also with floats, as the **R22 Mariner**, since 1985.

TYPE: Two-seat lightweight helicopter.

ROTOR SYSTEM: Two-blade semi-articulated main rotor, with a tri-hinged underslung rotor head to reduce blade flexing, rotor vibration and control force feedback and an elastic teeter hinge stop to prevent blade/boom contact when starting or stopping the rotor in high winds. Main rotor blade section NACA 63-015 (modified). Rigid in plane, and free to flap, these blades are of bonded all-metal construction, with a stainless steel spar and leading-edge, light alloy skin and light alloy honeycomb core. One fixed trim tab on main rotor blades. The two-blade tail rotor, mounted on the port side, is of light alloy bonded construction. Rotor brake optional.

ROTOR DRIVE: V belt drive with sprag type overrunning clutch. The main and tail gearboxes each utilise spiral bevel gears. Maintenance-free flexible couplings of proprietary manufacture are used in both the main and tail rotor drive systems. Main rotor/engine rpm ratio 1:5. Tail rotor/engine rpm ratio 1·28:1.

FUSELAGE: Welded steel tube and light alloy primary structure for cabin, rotor pylon and engine mounting, with full monocoque tailcone. Cabin skins of light alloy and glassfibre.

TAIL UNIT: Cruciform light alloy structure with fixed horizontal stabiliser and vertical fin. Small spring skid (small float on Mariner version) beneath lower half of fin to give protection in a tail-down landing.

LANDING GEAR: Welded steel tube and light alloy skid landing gear, with energy absorbing crosstubes. Twin float/skid gear on Mariner.

POWER PLANT: One 119 kW (160 hp) Avco Lycoming O-320-B2C flat-four engine (derated to 97·5 kW; 131 hp for T-O), mounted in the lower rear section of the main fuselage, and partially exposed to improve cooling and simplify maintenance. Light alloy main fuel tank in upper rear section of the fuselage on port side, usable capacity 72·5 litres (19·2 US gallons). Optional auxiliary fuel tank, capacity 39·75 litres (10·5 US gallons), available from 1985 on new R22 Alphas and Betas only. Oil capacity 5·7 litres (1·5 US gallons).

ACCOMMODATION: Two seats side by side in enclosed cabin, with inertia reel shoulder harness. Cyclic control stick mounted between seats, with dual grips on yoke so that aircraft can be flown from either seat. Conventional dual collective and throttle controls mounted at the port side of each seat. Cyclic control pivots to either side to simplify entry and exit. Curved two-panel windscreen. Removable door, with window, on each side. Police version has observation doors with bubble windows, which are also available as options on other models. Baggage space beneath each seat. Cabin heated and ventilated.

SYSTEM: Electrical system, powered by 12V DC alternator, includes navigation, panel and map lights, dual landing lights, anti-collision light and battery. Second battery optional.

AVIONICS AND EQUIPMENT: A King KY 197 com transceiver is standard; optional avionics include a KN 53 nav receiver, Morrow Apollo I Loran-C, KT 76A transponder and KR 87 ADF. Standard equipment includes rate of climb indicator, sensitive altimeter, quartz clock, hour meter, low rotor rpm warning horn, temperature and chip warning lights for main gearbox and chip warning light for tail gearbox, high-capacity oil cooler, rotor brake, windscreen cover, rotor blade tiedowns, soundproofing, fire extinguisher, and ground handling wheels. Optional equipment includes Hamilton vertical compass, artificial horizon, directional gyro, cabin heater/demister, engine primer, removable port side controls and windscreen covers.

Float equipped Robinson R22 Mariner

Police version standard equipment as above plus: dual com control panel, Wulfsberg Flitefone 40 VHF or UHF radio, removable port side controls, 70A alternator and fire extinguisher. Police version optional equipment: searchlight with dual lamps, PA speaker and siren, second Wulfsberg Flitefone 40 VHF or UHF radio and King KT 76A transponder.

IFR trainer standard avionics and equipment: AIM 500 DVF artificial horizon, King KEA 129 encoding altimeter, Astronautics DC turn co-ordinator, King KCS 55A HSI, King KR 87 ADF, King KX 165 nav/com digital display radio, King KT 76A transponder, King KR 22 marker beacon receiver, and Astro Tech LC-2 digital clock. Standard equipment is the same as for basic Alpha. IFR trainer optional avionics: second Naco Nav 121 VOR, or King KN 63 DME.

DIMENSIONS, EXTERNAL:
- Main rotor diameter: 7·67 m (25 ft 2 in)
- Tail rotor diameter: 1·07 m (3 ft 6 in)
- Main rotor blade chord: 0·18 m (7·2 in)
- Distance between rotor centres: 4·39 m (14 ft 5 in)
- Length overall (rotors turning): 8·76 m (28 ft 9 in)
- Length of fuselage: 6·30 m (20 ft 8 in)
- Fuselage: Max width: 1·12 m (3 ft 8 in)
- Height overall: 2·67 m (8 ft 9 in)
- Skid track: 1·93 m (6 ft 4 in)

DIMENSION, INTERNAL:
- Cabin: Max width: 1·12 m (3 ft 8 in)

AREAS:
- Main rotor blades (each): 0·70 m² (7·55 sq ft)
- Tail rotor blades (each): 0·037 m² (0·40 sq ft)
- Main rotor disc: 46·21 m² (497·4 sq ft)
- Tail rotor disc: 0·89 m² (9·63 sq ft)
- Fin: 0·21 m² (2·28 sq ft)
- Stabiliser: 0·14 m² (1·53 sq ft)

WEIGHTS AND LOADINGS:
- Weight empty (without auxiliary fuel tank) 374 kg (824 lb)
- Fuel weight: standard: 52 kg (115 lb)
- auxiliary: 28·6 kg (63 lb)
- Max T-O and landing weight: 621 kg (1,370 lb)
- Max zero-fuel weight: 569 kg (1,255 lb)
- Max disc loading: 13·43 kg/m² (2·75 lb/sq ft)
- Max power loading: 5·22 kg/kW (8·56 lb/hp)

PERFORMANCE (at max T-O weight):
- Never-exceed speed: 102 knots (190 km/h; 118 mph)
- Max level speed: 97 knots (180 km/h; 112 mph)
- Cruising speed, 75% power at 2,440 m (8,000 ft): 96 knots (177 km/h; 110 mph)
- Econ cruising speed: 82 knots (153 km/h; 95 mph)
- Max rate of climb at S/L: 366 m (1,200 ft)/min
- Rate of climb at 1,525 m (5,000 ft): 323 m (1,060 ft)/min
- Service ceiling: 4,265 m (14,000 ft)
- Hovering ceiling IGE: 2,125 m (6,970 ft)
- Range with auxiliary fuel and max payload, no reserves: 319 nm (592 km; 368 miles)
- Endurance at 65% power, auxiliary fuel, no reserves: 3 h 20 min

ROCKWELL INTERNATIONAL

ROCKWELL INTERNATIONAL CORPORATION

600 Grant Street, Pittsburgh, Pennsylvania 15219

Telephone: (412) 565 2000

CHAIRMAN OF THE BOARD AND CHIEF EXECUTIVE OFFICER:
Robert Anderson

PRESIDENT AND CHIEF OPERATING OFFICER:
Donald R. Beall

EXECUTIVE VICE-PRESIDENT: Martin D. Walker

CORPORATE VICE-PRESIDENTS:
- Kent M. Black (President, Commercial Electronics)
- Robert L. Cattoi (Senior V-P, Research and Engineering)
- Robert A. dePalma (Senior Vice-President, Finance and Planning and Chief Financial Officer)
- J. A. Earley (Corporate Development)
- Richard W. Foxen (Senior V-P, International)
- Charles H. Harff (Senior V-P, General Counsel and Secretary)
- Bastian J. Hello (Senior V-P, Government Relations)
- Sam F. Iacobellis (President, North American Aircraft Operations and B-1B Programme Manager)
- George W. Jeffs (President, North American Space Operations)
- Edward A. Loeser (Senior V-P, Operations)
- Samuel Petok (Senior V-P, Communications)
- Arthur P. Ronan (President, Automotive Operations)
- John J. Roscia (Senior V-P, Asst to Chairman and Chief Executive Officer)
- Charles R. Vennel (Human Resources)
- Donald J. Yockey (President, Defense Electronics Operations)

North American Aviation Inc, incorporated in Delaware in 1928 and a manufacturer of aircraft of various kinds from 1934, and Rockwell-Standard Corporation of Pittsburgh, Pennsylvania, a manufacturer of automotive components and builder of the Aero Commander line of civilian aircraft, merged on 22 September 1967 to form North American Rockwell Corporation.

During 1973 the Corporation adopted its present name, Rockwell International, to reflect its expanding international business. The corporation applies advanced technology to a wide range of products in its four major businesses: **Aerospace**, which is engaged in the research, development and manufacture of military aircraft, manned and unmanned space systems and rocket engines, advanced space-based surveillance systems and high energy laser and other directed energy programmes; **Automotive**, which develops, manufactures and markets components for heavy and medium duty trucks, buses, trailers and heavy duty off-road vehicles, light trucks and cars; **Electronics**, engaged in research, development, manufacture and marketing of a broad range of defence and commercial electronics systems and products for precision guidance and control, tactical weapons command, control, communications and intelligence, precision navigation, avionics, telecommunications and semiconductor applications; and **General Industries**, which develops, manufactures and markets high speed printing presses and related graphic arts equipment, flow control and measurement equipment, components for energy markets including oil, utility, gas and nuclear industries, and industrial sewing machines.

NORTH AMERICAN AIRCRAFT OPERATIONS

100 North Sepulveda Boulevard, El Segundo, California 90245

Telephone: (213) 647 1000

PRESIDENT AND PROGRAMME MANAGER B-1B:
Sam F. Iacobellis

VICE-PRESIDENT, COMMERCIAL AIRCRAFT PROGRAMMES:
James J. Edwards

Palmdale Facility:
2825 East Avenue P, Palmdale, California 93550
Telephone: (805) 273 6000
VICE-PRESIDENT AND GENERAL MANAGER: C. W. Bright

Columbus Facility:
4300 East Fifth Avenue, Columbus, Ohio 43216
Telephone: (614) 239 3344
VICE-PRESIDENT AND GENERAL MANAGER: A. H. Smith

Tulsa Facility:
2000 North Memorial Drive, Tulsa, Oklahoma 74115
Telephone: (918) 835 3111
VICE-PRESIDENT AND GENERAL MANAGER:
William P. Swiech

ROCKWELL INTERNATIONAL BRONCO

US military designation: OV-10

The development history of the Bronco and a detailed structural description can be found in the 1978-79 and earlier editions of *Jane's*; the OV-10A (271 built), OV-10B and B(Z) (6 and 12), OV-10C (40), OV-10E (16) and OV-10F (16) were summarised in the 1982-83 edition. Deliveries of the most recent version, designated OV-10D, were completed in 1980.

In the Spring of 1985 it was reported that the government of South Korea had set aside $240 million in its defence budget for the acquisition of 24 OV-10Ds equipped with 20 mm gun turrets, FLIR systems and laser rangefinder/target designators. If confirmed, the OV-10 production line would be reopened to manufacture the aircraft.

OV-10D. Designation of 17 US Marine Corps OV-10As converted for Night Observation Surveillance (NOS) role. In addition to NOS systems and the basic OV-10A fuselage stores and external fuel capability, the OV-10D NOS has uprated engines, and wing pylons for additional weapons (or external fuel tanks when extended radius/loiter time is required). A Texas Instruments AN/AAS-37 FLIR sensor and laser target designator is installed in a rotating ball turret in the nose. This can be linked to a turret mounted General Electric M97 20 mm cannon, installed beneath the fuselage, in lieu of normal operation with standard OV-10A armament sponsons and centreline station. Equipment includes optional APR-39 radar homing and warning system, ALE-39 chaff/flare dispensers and IR-suppressant engine exhaust system.

The following abbreviated description applies to the OV-10D, except where indicated:

TYPE: Two-seat multi-purpose counter-insurgency and night surveillance aircraft.

POWER PLANT: Two 775·5 kW (1,040 ehp) Garrett T76-G-420/421 turboprop engines, each driving a Hamilton Standard three-blade constant-speed reversible-pitch fully-feathering metal propeller with glassfibre blades. Five self-sealing bladder fuel tanks in wings, with combined capacity of 954 litres (252 US gallons). Gravity refuelling point above each tank on wing upper surface. Provision for carrying one 568 litre (150 US gallon) drop tank on underfuselage pylon, and one 378 litre (100 US gallon) drop tank on each wing pylon. Oil capacity 11·5 litres (3 US gallons).

ACCOMMODATION: Crew of two in tandem, on LW-3B zero/zero ejection seats, under canopy with two large upward opening transparent door panels on each side. Dual controls optional. Cargo compartment aft of rear seat, with rear loading door at end of fuselage pod. Rear seat removable to provide increased space for additional personnel or up to 1,452 kg (3,200 lb) of freight.

SYSTEMS AND AVIONICS: As detailed in 1981-82 *Jane's*.

ARMAMENT: Four weapon attachment points, each with capacity of 272 kg (600 lb), under short sponsons extending from bottom of fuselage on each side, under wings. Fifth attachment point, capacity 544 kg (1,200 lb) under centre-fuselage. Two 7·62 mm M60C machine-guns, each with 500 rounds of ammunition, carried in each sponson. USMC OV-10A has provision also for carrying one AIM-9D Sidewinder missile under each wing. Stores which can be carried on the underfuselage and sponson stations include Mk 81, 82 and 83 GP bombs, Mk 81 and 82 GP (Snakeye) bombs; Mk 77 Mod 2 and Mod 4 fire bombs; LAU-3/A, LAU-10/A, LAU-32/A, LAU-59/A, LAU-60/A, LAU-61/A, LAU-68/A and LAU-69/A rocket packages; SUU-11A/A (7·62 mm Minigun), Mk 4 Mod 0 (20 mm), and GPU-2/A (20 mm) gun pods; SUU-40/A and SUU-44/A with Mk 24 and Mk 45 flares; Mk 12 Mod 0 (Podeye) smoke tank; Mk 86A/A37B-3 MBR with Mk 76 and Mk 106 practice bombs; CBU-55/B cluster bomb. Max weapon load on fuselage stations 1,633 kg (3,600 lb). OV-10D has, in addition, wing pylons with stores capacity of 272 kg (600 lb) each, which can carry CBU-55/B cluster bombs; 250 lb laser guided bombs; LAU-10/A, LAU-68/A and LAU-69/A rocket packages; SUU-40/A and SUU-44/A with Mk 24 and Mk 45 flares. In lieu of sponsons and fuselage centreline load, the OV-10D can carry a General Electric M97 20 mm gun turret, with 1,500 rds, on centreline station hardpoint.

DIMENSIONS, EXTERNAL:

Wing span	12·19 m (40 ft 0 in)
Length overall	13·41 m (44 ft 0 in)
Height overall	4·62 m (15 ft 2 in)
Tailplane span	4·45 m (14 ft 7 in)
Wheel track	4·52 m (14 ft 10 in)
Wheelbase	3·56 m (11 ft 8 in)
Propeller diameter	2·59 m (8 ft 6 in)
Rear loading door: Height	0·99 m (3 ft 3 in)
Width	0·76 m (2 ft 6 in)

Rockwell International OV-10D, with production configuration Night Observation Surveillance (NOS) equipment

AREA:

Wings, gross	27·03 m² (291·0 sq ft)

WEIGHTS AND LOADING:

Weight empty	3,127 kg (6,893 lb)
Normal T-O weight	4,494 kg (9,908 lb)
Overload T-O weight	6,552 kg (14,444 lb)
Max wing loading	242·4 kg/m² (49·6 lb/sq ft)

PERFORMANCE (OV-10D, at weights stated):

Max level speed at S/L, without weapons	250 knots (463 km/h; 288 mph)
Max rate of climb at S/L at normal T-O weight	920 m (3,020 ft)/min
Rate of climb at S/L, one engine out, without weapons	168 m (550 ft)/min
Service ceiling at normal T-O weight	9,150 m (30,000 ft)
Service ceiling, one engine out, without weapons	3,810 m (12,500 ft)
T-O run at normal T-O weight	226 m (740 ft)
T-O to 15 m (50 ft): at normal T-O weight	341 m (1,120 ft)
at max T-O weight	853 m (2,800 ft)
Landing from 15 m (50 ft) at normal T-O weight	372 m (1,220 ft)
Landing run: at normal T-O weight	226 m (740 ft)
at max T-O weight	381 m (1,250 ft)
Combat radius with max weapon load, no loiter	198 nm (367 km; 228 miles)
Ferry range with auxiliary fuel	1,200 nm (2,224 km; 1,382 miles)

ROCKWELL INTERNATIONAL B-1B

The early history of the B-1 bomber has been recorded in the 1982-83 and earlier editions of *Jane's*. The decision to order 100 derivative B-1Bs for the US Air Force was announced by President Reagan in October 1981.

On 20 January 1982 Rockwell signed two contracts. The first was a $1,317 million full scale development contract which required the company to finalise the B-1B design, modify two of the original B-1 prototypes (the second and fourth) and carry out a further flight test programme; the second was an $886 million production contract, which covered construction of the first B-1B and procurement of long-lead items for early production lots. Under this programme the first aircraft to fly, on 23 March 1983, was the modified No. 2 prototype, which was used to evaluate many of the new features and for stability and control, flutter and weapons systems tests until it was lost on 29 August 1984. Now contributing to B-1B development is the No. 4 prototype, which incorporates the remainder of the B-1B improvements and is being used for verification testing of the defensive and offensive avionics systems. The first production B-1B, scheduled originally to fly during March 1985, was five months ahead of schedule in the Summer of 1984 and flew for the first time on 18 October 1984. The next seven production aircraft were ordered under the FY 1983 defence budget, followed by 10 more in FY 1984, 34 in FY 1985 and the remaining 48 requested in FY 1986 budget proposals. Initial delivery, of the second production aircraft (first flown 4 May 1985), to the 96th Bomb Wing at Dyess AFB, Texas, took place on 7 July 1985 and this base was expected to achieve IOC (with 15 of its scheduled 29 aircraft) in 1986. Deliveries will then continue at a rate of approximately four aircraft per month to the 28th Bomb Wing at Ellsworth AFB, South Dakota (35 aircraft), the 319th Bomb Wing at Grand Forks AFB, North Dakota (17 aircraft), and the 384th Bomb Wing at McConnell AFB, Kansas (17 aircraft). Each base will also deploy supporting tankers. Deliveries will be completed in 1988, with two B-1Bs (c/n 1 and 9) allocated for test and development flying.

Operational B-1Bs are able to carry, in three weapons bays, varying combinations of nuclear air-to-ground missiles, conventional or nuclear free-fall bombs, and auxiliary fuel. Using electronic jamming equipment, infra-red countermeasures, radar location and warning systems, other advanced avionics and 'low observable' technology to defeat hostile defensive systems, the B-1B will be able to penetrate present and predicted sophisticated enemy defences well into the 1990s and to operate within less heavily defended areas into the next century. It will also be suitable for deployment in a variety of roles now flown by the Boeing B-52, including anti-submarine patrol or maritime surveillance at long ranges, and aerial minelaying.

Outwardly the B-1B is generally similar to the B-1 prototype No. 4, but has structural strengthening for operation at a gross weight that is increased from 179,170 kg (395,000 lb) to 216,365 kg (477,000 lb). Major airframe improvements include a strengthened landing gear; a movable bulkhead in the forward weapons bay to allow for the carriage of a wide range of different sized weapons, including the ALCM which will be incorporated from the ninth production airframe onwards, and retrofitted to earlier aircraft; optional weapons bay fuel tanks to give extended range; and external stores stations beneath the fuselage to accommodate additional fuel or weapons. The

Rockwell International B-1B strategic bomber in low level flight with wings fully swept

variable engine inlets of the original B-1 are replaced by fixed inlets, and new engine nacelles and simplified overwing fairings have been introduced. These modifications are designed to provide optimum performance for the new high-subsonic low altitude penetration role. The new bomber retains the variable geometry wing of the B-1, its unswept setting allowing rapid take-off from a base threatened by imminent attack, or operation from shorter runways and less sophisticated airfields; the fully swept position is used in supersonic flight and for the primary role of high-subsonic low level penetration. It also retains the crew ejection seats which, in the fourth B-1, replaced the crew escape capsule of the first three prototypes.

It is, however, the high technology avionics that make the major difference between the original B-1 and the B-1B. Although externally similar to the B-1, the B-1B incorporates technological advances that reduce considerably its radar observability and increase its ability to penetrate hostile airspace. The B-1B has a low radar cross-section, and through the application of 'low observable' technology has a radar signature only one per cent that of a B-52. It uses advanced radar and navigation equipment in the category of that developed for the latest generation of fighter aircraft, such as the General Dynamics F-16, as well as avionics technology from both the B-52's offensive system and that of the original B-1. Thus, offensive avionics of the B-1B include advanced forward-looking and terrain following radars, an extremely accurate inertial navigation system, a link to the Air Force Satellite Communications (AFSATCOM) system, and a strategic Doppler radar altimeter. The defensive avionics are built around the AN/ALQ-161 ECM system, with extended frequency coverage, and include tail warning radar and expendable decoys such as chaff and flares. Much of this defensive and offensive avionics equipment has already been flight tested successfully in the B-1 prototypes.

The structure of the B-1B is made principally of aluminium alloys and titanium, and is hardened to withstand nuclear blast and overpressure. More than 60 per cent of the structure and equipment is subcontracted, with some 3,000 subcontractors and suppliers being involved in the programme in addition to AIL/Eaton (defensive avionics), Boeing (offensive avionics) and General Electric (power plant). Principal subcontractors include: Aeronca (engine shrouds); AiResearch (central air data computer and weapons bay door drive); Avco (wings); Bendix (vertical scale flight instrumentation); Brunswick (radomes); Chemtronics (augmentor case and ducts); Cleveland Pneumatic (main landing gear); Crane Hydro-Aire (anti-skid subsystem); Garrett Turbine Engine Co (secondary power system); General Electric, Binghampton (engine thrust control); General Electric, Wilmington (engine instruments); B. F. Goodrich (tyres); Goodyear, Akron (wheels and brakes); Goodyear, Litchfield Park (windows); Hamilton Standard (environmental control systems); Harris (electrical multiplex); Heath (tail warning radome); Hughes Treitler (heat exchangers); IBM (computer control unit and memory); Inco Alloys (MAC-54 alloy); Kaman (engine access doors, rudder and horizontal actuator fairing); Kelsey-Hayes (flap/slat actuator subsystem and rotary launcher drive; Kuras-Alterman (ECM); MAL Tool (stage 2 fan blades); Martin Marietta (horizontal and vertical stabilisers and structural mode control vanes); Menasco (nose landing gear shock strut); Northrop (jamming transmitters); Parker Hannifin (fuel injector and augmentor); Raytheon (phased array antenna); Sanders (electrical display unit); Sierracin (aft crew windows and windscreens); Simmonds Precision (fuel centre of gravity management system); SEDCO (RF antennae); Singer Kearfott (flight instrument signal converter and multiplex interface module); Sperry, Albuquerque (automatic flight control and gyro stabilisation); Sperry, Phoenix (vertical situation displays); Sperry-Vickers (emergency electrical power system and primary hydraulic pumps); SSP Products (engine bleed air ducts); Sterer Engineering (steering and damping subsystem); Sundstrand (constant speed drive, engine bleed air controls, rudder controls and wing sweep system); Swedlow (windscreens); Systron Donner (flight control inertial subsystems); Telephonics (central integrated test system); TRW (fuel pumps); UNC Tech Products (fan stator case); United Aircraft Products (precooler/heat exchangers); Vicars (fuel pumps); Vought Aero Products (aft and intermediate aft fuselage); Weber Aircraft (ejection seats); Western Gear Corp (engine accessory gearboxes); Westinghouse Electric (generator and controls); Woodville Polymer (wing fairing seal system); Woodward Governor (main engine control); and Wyman Gordon (stage 2 HPT disc).

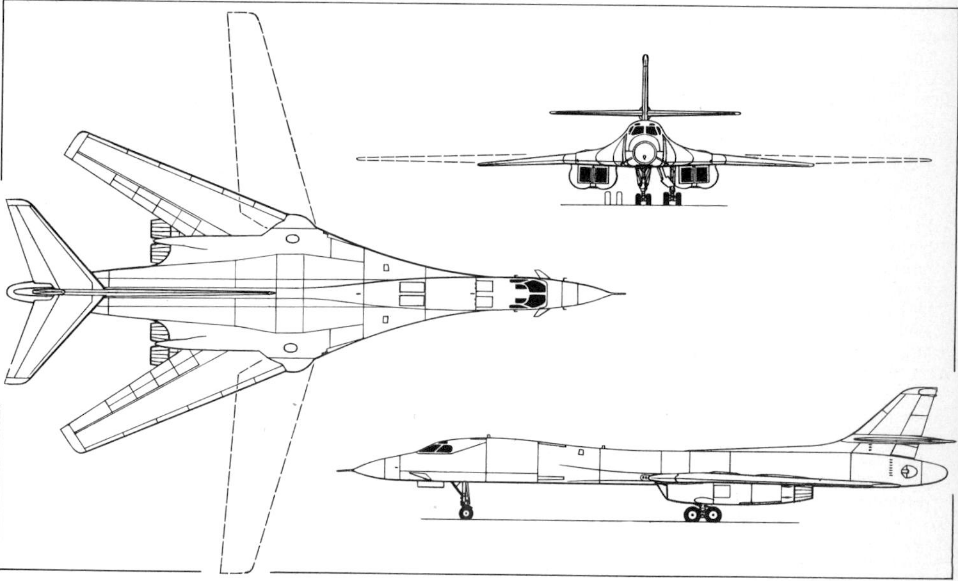
Rockwell International B-1B long-range multi-role strategic bomber *(Pilot Press)*

TYPE: Long-range multi-role strategic bomber.

WINGS: Cantilever low-wing fail-safe blended wing/body structure, with variable geometry on outer panels. The wing carry-through structure, which is sealed as an integral fuel tank, is mainly of diffusion bonded 6AL-4V titanium. The wing pivot mechanism is of the same material, with a pin made from a single 6AL-4V forging on each side, in spherical steel bearings, above and below which are integrally stiffened double cover plates of machined titanium. Wing sweep is actuated by screwjacks, driven by four hydraulic motors; it can be powered by any two of the aircraft's four hydraulic systems, asymmetric movement being prevented by a torque shaft between the two screwjacks. Sweep actuators are covered by a leading-edge 'knuckle' fairing which prevents a gap from opening when the outer panels are swept back. Aft of the wing pivot on each side are overwing fairings which blend the wing trailing-edges and engine nacelles. Each of the outer wing panels, which have 15° of leading-edge sweep when fully forward and 67° 30′ when fully swept, is a conventional two-spar aluminium alloy torsion box structure, with machined spars, ribs, and one-piece integrally stiffened top and bottom skin panels. Wingtips, wing/body fairings, and some outer wing skin panels, are of GRP. Full span seven-segment leading-edge slats on each outer panel can be drooped 20° for take-off and landing. Six-segment single-slotted trailing-edge flaps on each outer panel, with maximum downward deflection of 40°. There are no ailerons; instead, lateral control is provided by four-segment airbrake/spoilers on each outer wing, forward of the outer four flap segments, with a maximum upward deflection of 70°. All control surfaces are operated electro-hydraulically by rods, cables, pulleys and bellcrank levers, except for the two outboard spoilers on each wing which are controlled by a fly by wire system.

FUSELAGE: Conventional area ruled fail-safe stressed-skin structure of closely spaced frames and longerons, built mainly of 2025 and 7075 aluminium alloys. Built in five main sections comprising forward, forward intermediate, wing carry-through, rear intermediate and rear fuselage, the last two of these being manufactured by LTV (Vought Aero Products Division). Titanium used for engine bays and firewalls, tail support structure, rear fuselage skins and other high load or high heat areas. Dorsal spine of steel/boron filled titanium sandwich construction. Nose radome of polyimide quartz; dielectric panels of GRP. Small sweptback movable vane of composite material, with 30° anhedral, on each side of nose, actuated by structural mode control system (SMCS) accelerometers in the fuselage. These sense lateral and vertical motion of the forward fuselage in turbulent conditions and compensate for it by relaying electrical signals to move the vanes, providing both yaw and pitch damping.

TAIL UNIT: Cantilever fail-safe structure with sweepback on all surfaces. Fin is a conventional titanium and aluminium alloy torsion box structure, secured to the rear fuselage by a double shear attachment, bolts on the tailplane spindle, a vertical shear pin in the tailplane spindle fitting, and a shear-bolt joint on the front beam of the box. Aluminium alloy rudder is in three sections, all of which have 25° of travel each side. Two-section all-moving tailplane is operated collectively for control in pitch (between 10° up and 25° down) and differentially (± 20°) for roll, the two halves moving independently on the steel spindle. Rudder and tailplane actuated hydraulically, with fly by wire backup system for use in the event of a mechanical system failure.

LANDING GEAR: Hydraulically retractable tricycle type. Each main unit, which retracts inward and rearward, has two pairs of wheels in tandem. Steerable nose unit has twin wheels and retracts forward. Oleo-pneumatic shock absorber in each unit. Goodyear wheels and carbon brakes. Goodrich tyres. Mainwheel diameter 60 cm (23½ in), tyre size 46 × 16-325, 30-ply rating, pressure 15·2-19·0 bars (220-275 lb/sq in). Nosewheel diameter 41 cm (16 in), tyre size 35 × 11·5-16, 22-ply rating, pressure 14·5 bars (210 lb/sq in).

POWER PLANT: Four General Electric F101-GE-102 augmented turbofan engines, each rated in 133·4 kN (30,000 lb st) class, mounted in pairs beneath the fixed centre-section of the wing, close to the CG, to provide optimum stability in low-altitude turbulence conditions. Fixed geometry inlets. Integral fuel tanks in the fuselage and outer wings; provision for auxiliary fuel tanks to be carried in the two forward weapons bays and beneath the fuselage. Fuel capacity increased considerably over that of the original B-1. A Simmonds Precision fuel management system maintains CG trim automatically as fuel is consumed. Receptacle in upper nose section, forward of windscreen, for in-flight refuelling; aircraft is compatible with KC-10 and KC-135 tankers.

ACCOMMODATION: Four-man operational crew comprising pilot, co-pilot and two systems operators (defensive and offensive) on Weber ACES II ejection seats in a pressurised crew compartment. Crew access is via a downward opening door and retractable ladder under the fuselage, aft of the nosewheel unit.

SYSTEMS: All systems and subsystems are either fail-operative or fail-safe, to ensure that no single system failure prevents accomplishment of the primary mission, and that no second failure in the same system prevents a safe return to base. Hamilton Standard air-conditioning and pressurisation systems. Four independent hydraulic systems, each 276 bars (4,000 lb/sq in) pressure, for actuation of wing sweep, control surfaces, landing gear

Rockwell International B-1B dropping an inert B-83 nuclear free-fall bomb

and weapons bay doors. Hydraulic system maximum flow rate 238·5 litres (63 US gallons) per minute each. Gas/oil reservoirs, pressurised to approximately 11·03 bars (160 lb/sq in). No pneumatic system. Main electrical system has three 115kVA integrated engine driven constant-speed generators, supplying 230/400V three-phase AC power at 400Hz through four main buses. A Harris Corporation self testing electrical multiplex system (EMUX), using mini-computers, controls the B-1B major subsystems: it collects and conditions signals at remote terminals and transmits them from point to point over a common data bus and also supervises all signal data, using a centralised controller/processor. Requiring only two two-wire cables for its operations, EMUX is designed to control such functions as electrical power distribution to subsystems and avionics equipment, engine instruments, environmental control system, fuel system, landing gear, lights and weapons system operations. Apart from the inherent advantages of such a system, its use results in considerable savings in terms of both volume and weight. Two Garrett APUs provide self-start capability for operation from advance airfields and drive an emergency generator to power the essential bus. Quadruplex automatic flight control system (AFCS) controls flight path, roll attitude, altitude, airspeed, autothrottle and terrain following. Flight director panel has heading hold, navigation and automatic approach modes. Central air data computer; gyro stabilisation system; stability control augmentation system; and structural mode control subsystem (SMCS). Engine fire extinguishing system.

AVIONICS: The B-1B uses radar and navigation equipment technology developed for the latest generation of fighter aircraft such as the F-16, as well as avionics technology from the B-52 bomber's updated offensive avionics system. Standard GFE (government furnished equipment) includes communications, IFF, ILS, intercom, some navigation equipment, Honeywell ASN-131 SPN/GEANS radar altimeter (similar to that in B-52) and altimeter indicator, rescue beacon and transponder. Boeing Military Airplane Company is responsible for the B-1B's offensive avionics system (OAS). This includes a Singer Kearfott high accuracy inertial navigation system (developed from that used in the F-16); a Teledyne Ryan AN/APN-218 Doppler velocity sensor, comprising a single antenna/receiver/transmitter unit; Westinghouse AN/APQ-164 multi-mode offensive radar system (ORS), derived from the AN/APG-66 in the F-16, which includes a low-observable phased-array antenna to provide low altitude terrain following and precise navigational functions; IBM avionics control units (ACUs), including two for terrain following based on those used in the B-52 plus a mass storage device (MSD), using AP-101C computers initially (1750As later) to provide programme instructions for navigation, weapons delivery, bomb damage assessment, defensive system computation, and central integrated test; Sperry Flight Systems offensive display sets, similar to those in the B-52, comprising three multi-function displays (two at the offensive systems operator's station and one for the defensive systems operator), an electronics display unit, and a video recorder similar to that used in the B-52; Sanders Associates electronic CRT display units, modified from those developed for the original B-1, to allow the defensive systems operator to analyse threat situations and assign appropriate counter-measures; and Sundstrand data transfer units (similar to those in the B-52) to gather and store mission and flight data.

The defensive avionics system, which is the responsibility of Eaton Corporation's AIL Division, is based on that company's AN/ALQ-161 system, which comprises an AN/ALQ-161A radio frequency surveillance/ECM system (RFS/ECMS), tail warning function (TWF), AN/ASQ-184 defensive management system and an expendable countermeasures system, totalling 108 separate elements. Developed to support the original B-1 over a broad spectrum of missions, including deep solo penetration of hostile airspace, the system was extensively flight tested over a two-year period and a number of additions have extended both the frequency coverage and the repertoire of electronic jamming techniques of the original design. The current AN/ALQ-161 will enable the B-1B to penetrate present and predicted enemy defences well into the 1990s. The system is controlled by a network of digital computers which can be reprogrammed easily; in addition, all electronic systems boxes 'plug in' to a dedicated data bus network, enabling the system to be upgraded continuously to adapt to future threats until well into the next century. To protect the B-1B, the system must counter a very dense environment of signals from increasingly sophisticated hostile radar networks. These radars, if not effectively jammed, would vector fighter aircraft to, or guide missiles and anti-aircraft gunfire against, the B-1B. A single AN/ALQ-161 system contains and controls a large number of Northrop (Defense Systems Divsion) jamming transmitters and Raytheon phased-array antennae. In addition to the jamming hardware, a sophisticated control system, managed by a network of special digital computers, is employed. This network can control the jamming chains so rapidly that each can jam signals from many radars simultaneously. The numerous jamming chains are deployed around the periphery of the B-1B to jam signals in any frequency band coming from any direction. Integrated with the jamming control subsystem is an equally sophisticated network of separate receiving antennae, receivers and processors which act as the 'ears' of the system. By means of this receiving subsystem new signals can be picked up, identified and then jammed, with optimised jamming techniques, in a fraction of a second. One of the advantages of having the receiving function completely integrated with the jamming function, which was unique to the AN/ALQ-161 when it was first designed, is that it allows the receiving system to detect new signals and continue to monitor old signals while jamming in the same frequency band. A special subsystem allows this to be accomplished by monitoring the output of the jamming transmitters and adjusting the receivers continuously. All main systems computers on the B-1B, including the AN/ALQ-161's main computer, are identical, and communicate over a time multiplexing military standard data bus designated 1553. Via this bus, the AN/ALQ-161 cmmunicates with a set of controls and displays used by the defensive systems operator. It also uses this bus to send status reports to a central integrated test system (CITS), which records all in-flight failures and battle damage for later diagnosis and repair. Within the AN/ALQ-161 itself there is also a local status monitoring network called SEAT (status evaluation and test), which reports to CITS and allows the system automatically to route electronic signals around failed components and maintain full jamming response against the highest priority threat signals. Exclusive of cabling, displays and controls, the current AN/ALQ-161 system weighs approximately 2,360 kg (5,200 lb) and consumes about 120 kW of power in 'all-out' jamming mode. Other defensive equipment of the B-1B includes expendable decoys such as chaff and flares.

Lockheed C-141 testbed for B-1B ECM

ARMAMENT: Three internal weapons bays, comprising 9·53 m (31 ft 3 in) double bay forward of the wing carry-through structure and a single 4·57 m (15 ft) long bay aft, with hydraulically actuated doors. Forward bay incorporates a movable bulkhead permitting the accommodation of a wide variety of weapons, of various sizes, and mixed loads. Internal capacity in a nuclear role for up to eight AGM-86B air-launched cruise missiles (ALCMs), twenty-four AGM-69 short range attack missiles (SRAMs), twelve B-28 or twenty-four B-61 or B-83 free fall nuclear bombs; or, in a non-nuclear role, for up to eighty-four 500 lb Mk 82 or twenty-four 2,000 lb Mk 84 bombs. Eight external stores stations beneath the fuselage, on which can be carried an additional fourteen ALCMs or SRAMs, eight B-28s, fourteen B-43/B-61/B-83s, fourteen Mk 84s, or forty-four Mk 82s. Provision for carrying auxiliary fuel tank(s) in weapons bay.

DIMENSIONS, EXTERNAL:
- Wing span: fully spread — 41·67 m (136 ft 8½ in)
- fully swept — 23·84 m (78 ft 2½ in)
- Length overall — 44·81 m (147 ft 0 in)
- Height overall — 10·36 m (34 ft 0 in)
- Tailplane span — 13·67 m (44 ft 10 in)
- Wheel track (c/l of shock absorbers) — 4·42 m (14 ft 6 in)
- Wheelbase — 17·53 m (57 ft 6 in)

AREA:
- Wings, gross — approx 181·2 m² (1,950 sq ft)

WEIGHTS AND LOADING:
- Weight empty, equipped — 87,090 kg (192,000 lb)
- Max weapons load:
  - internal — 34,019 kg (75,000 lb)
  - external — 26,762 kg (59,000 lb)
- Max fuel load — 88,450 kg (195,000 lb)
- Typical conventional weapon load — 29,030 kg (64,000 lb)
- Max T-O weight — 216,365 kg (477,000 lb)
- Max wing loading — approx 1,194 kg/m² (244·6 lb/sq ft)

PERFORMANCE (design):
- Max level speed — approx Mach 1·25
- Low-level penetration speed at approx 61 m (200 ft) — more than 521 knots (965 km/h; 600 mph)
- Max unrefuelled range — approx 6,475 nm (12,000 km; 7,455 miles)

NORTH AMERICAN SPACE OPERATIONS

2230 East Imperial Highway, El Segundo, California 90245
Telephone: (213) 647 5000
PRESIDENT: George W. Jeffs

Satellite Systems Division

2600 Westminster Boulevard, Seal Beach, California 90740-7644
Telephone: (213) 594 3311
PRESIDENT: Glynn S. Lunney

Rocketdyne Division

6633 Canoga Avenue, Canoga Park, California 91304
Telephone: (818) 710 6300
PRESIDENT: Richard Schwartz

Space Transportation Systems Division

12214 Lakewood Boulevard, Downey, California 90241
Telephone: (213) 922 2111
PRESIDENT: Rocco A. Petrone

The Space Transportation Systems Division is responsible for Rockwell International Corporation's engineering design and development, fabrication and assembly, and test and evaluation of both manned and unmanned space systems.

Under contract to NASA, the Rockwell group designed, built and tested the four Shuttle spacecraft (Orbiters) named *Columbia, Challenger, Discovery* and *Atlantis.*

Rockwell's space group, with its major facilities in Downey and Palmdale, California, has contractual support units based in NASA Centers at the Johnson Space Center, Texas, the Kennedy Space Center, Florida, the Marshall Space Flight Center, Alabama, and the National Space Technology Laboratories, Mississippi.

Shuttle Operations Company

600 Gemini Avenue, Houston, Texas 77058
Telephone: (713) 282 3000
PRESIDENT: Robert G. Minor

Rockwell's Shuttle Operations Company performs mission support operations for Johnson Space Center under a contract which consolidated work previously performed by 16 different contractors. Its tasks include project management, maintenance and operations of Mission Control Center-Houston, Shuttle Mission Simulator,

Shuttle Avionics Integration Laboratory, Software Production Facility and the Central Computing Facility; sustaining engineering, flight preparation production, and direct mission operations, testing and support for Space Shuttle operations at the Johnson Space Center. The Rockwell team includes Bendix Field Engineering Corporation, System Development Corporation, Omniplan Corporation, RMS Technologies Incorporated, and System Management American Corporation.

Space Station Systems Division

12214 Lakewood Boulevard, Downey, California 90241
Telephone: (213) 922 2111
PRESIDENT: Seymour Z. Rubenstein

Rockwell's Space Station Systems Division was awarded a $27 million contract by NASA on 15 April 1985 for definition and preliminary design of elements of a permanently manned Space Station to be operational in low-Earth orbit by the mid-1990s. Following the completion of the 21-month contract in 1987 NASA plans to enter into the final design and development of the Space Station, including definition and preliminary design of the structural framework; interface between the Space Station and the Space Shuttle; mechanisms such as the Remote Manipulator Systems; attitude control, thermal control; communications; tracking; data management systems; plans for equipping a module with sleeping quarters, wardroom and galley; and plans for extravehicular activity (EVA).

SPACE TRANSPORTATION SYSTEM

The NASA Space Shuttle is the world's first reusable space transportation system, and will be the keystone of America's space programme for the remainder of this century.

The Shuttle system includes the Rockwell International Shuttle spacecraft (see next entry), capable of carrying up to 29,484 kg (65,000 lb) of cargo into Earth orbit; an external propellant tank and two solid propellant rocket boosters. Other prime contractors are Martin Marietta for the external tank, and Thiokol for the boosters. In operation, the Shuttle is launched vertically, with all engines firing. At an altitude of about 43 km (27 miles), the booster stages separate and descend into the sea by parachute, for recovery. The Shuttle spacecraft continues under its own power, and jettisons its large external propellant tank just before attaining orbit.

In space, the Shuttle spacecraft manoeuvres by means of the two orbit manoeuvring engines. The reaction control engines are used for minor course corrections and adjustments of altitude. Its main tasks are to place satellites into orbit, retrieve satellites from orbit, and repair and service satellites in orbit. It can also be used to put propulsive stages and satellites into precise low Earth orbit, for subsequent transfer to synchronous orbit or to an 'escape' mission into space. It can be used for short duration scientific and applications missions, as an orbiting research laboratory or reconnaissance vehicle, for space rescue, as a tanker for space refuelling, and for support of orbiting space stations.

On some flights a pressurised Spacelab, developed by ten European countries under the leadership of the European Space Agency, is carried in the payload bay. Spacelab is the means by which man-associated experiments can be performed in the payload bay. It includes a pressurised enclosure housing support equipment (to make it habitable) as well as the experimental equipment. When sensors require direct exposure to the space environment, a pallet is used in association with the pressurised enclosure. On other types of mission, a pallet may be used alone, with control of the instruments being exercised from the Shuttle spacecraft cabin or even from the ground. The Spacelabs are designed around a basic seven-day mission.

On conclusion of its mission, the Shuttle spacecraft flies back into the atmosphere towards its land base, protected by a form of heat shielding which is designed to survive 100 missions, unlike ablative heatshields. Once through the re-entry phase, the Shuttle spacecraft is able to glide up to 950 nm (1,760 km; 1,100 miles) to its base, steered by aerodynamic controls.

Special equipment developed for use on the Space Shuttle includes a new type of spacesuit and a rescue system known as a Personal Rescue Enclosure. This consists of a 0·86 m 34 in) diameter ball which contains its own short term simplified life support and communication systems. The ball has three layers (urethane, Kevlar and an outside thermal protective layer) and a small viewing port of tough Lexan.

Essential details of missions flown in 1981-85 can be found in previous editions of *Jane's*.

Details of the boosters and the external tank are as follows:

BOOSTERS (STS-8 and subsequent missions): Two Thiokol solid propellant rocket boosters (each 14,679 kN; 3,300,000 lb st for lift-off) are attached one on each side of the external propellant tank. Current steel skinned boosters each weigh 586,051 kg (1,292,000 lb) at launch. In 1986 the steel skinned boosters will be replaced by boosters with filament wound casings, each weighing 571,082 kg (1,259,000 lb) at launch. The booster cases are designed for 20 re-uses.

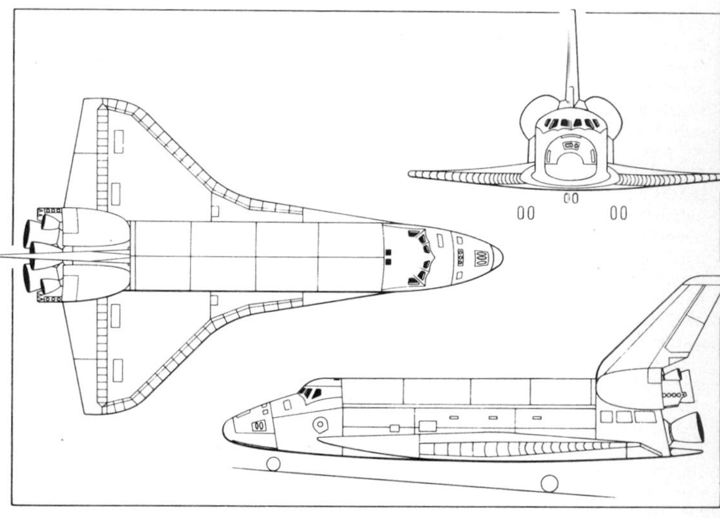

NASA/Rockwell International Shuttle spacecraft
(Michael A. Badrocke)

EXTERNAL PROPELLANT TANK: Contains the main propellants for the Orbiter. It is of aluminium alloy semi-monocoque construction, with a 25 mm (1 in) thick foam external insulation. In the forward end of the tank is a 559 m³ (19,786 cu ft) tank holding 617,774 kg (1,361,936 lb) of liquid oxygen; in the rear end is a 1,514 m³ (53,518 cu ft) tank holding 103,257 kg (227,641 lb) of liquid hydrogen. Total propellant weight 721,031 kg (1,589,577 lb). Between propellant tanks is an unpressurised inter-tank which houses instrumentation and electrical components. Current missions use a lightweight tank weighing 750,980 kg (1,655,600 lb) when filled.

Basic dimensions and weights of the complete Space Transportation System are as follows:

DIMENSIONS, EXTERNAL:

Length overall	56·14 m (184 ft 2·4 in)
Length of external tank	47·00 m (154 ft 2·4 in)
Length of boosters	45·46 m (149 ft 2·0 in)
Height overall	23·35 m (76 ft 7·2 in)

WEIGHTS:

Shuttle system complete (typical)	2,042,576 kg (4,503,033 lb)
Shuttle spacecraft (empty)	67,876 kg (149,642 lb)
External tank (full)	750,980 kg (1,655,600 lb)
Boosters (2), each	586,051 kg (1,292,000 lb)

THRUST:

Total, at lift-off	34,360 kN (7,725,000 lb)
Shuttle main engines (3), each	1,668 kN (375,000 lb)
Boosters (2), each	14,678 kN (3,300,000 lb)

PERFORMANCE:

Payload:

in 185 km (115 mile) orbit, due east	29,485 kg (65,000 lb)
in 500 km (310 mile) orbit, 55° inclination	11,340 kg (25,000 lb)
in 185 km (115 mile) polar orbit	14,515 kg (32,000 lb)

ROCKWELL INTERNATIONAL SHUTTLE SPACECRAFT

The Shuttle spacecraft, primary component of NASA's Space Transportation System, lifts off from Earth like a rocket, operates in orbit as a spacecraft, and returns to land in a manner similar to that of a conventional aeroplane.

Shuttle spacecraft *Columbia* (OV-102) made the first successful, 36-orbit, test flight in April 1981, manned by astronauts John Young (commander) and Capt Robert Crippen (pilot), and has since completed six more successful orbital missions. After STS-5, the Orbiter was modified at Kennedy Space Center, to enable it to carry Spacelab and to accommodate a six-man crew to fly the spacecraft and conduct experiments. After STS-9, *Columbia* returned to Rockwell's Palmdale facility for major modifications, including the installation of operational systems, and returned to service in early 1986.

Challenger (OV-099), the second Earth orbital flight spacecraft, made its first flight on 4 April 1983. It became the first operational spacecraft, with all onboard systems qualified to operate for a minimum of 100 missions without major overhaul. *Challenger* was destroyed in a post-launch explosion during mission 51L on 28 January 1986. *Discovery* (OV-103) made its first flight on 30 August 1984. *Atlantis* (OV-104) was launched for the first time on 3 October 1985, on military mission 51J. *Discovery* and *Atlantis* are approximately 453 kg (1,000 lb) lighter than *Challenger* was, due primarily to replacement of the majority of the low-temperature insulation tiles used on earlier Orbiters by thermal protection blankets. In August 1986 President Reagan ordered a new Shuttle spacecraft to replace *Challenger*. The programme is expected to resume in 1988.

TYPE: Reusable space transportation vehicle.

WINGS: Cantilever low-wing monoplane, of ogival planform. Wing section NACA 0010 (modified). Sweepback 81° on inner leading-edges, 45° on outer leading-edges. Dihedral 3° 30′ on trailing-edges. The main wing assembly, for which Grumman is responsible, is primarily a conventional aluminium alloy structure made up of a corrugated spar web, truss ribs, and riveted skin/stringer and honeycomb skins. Wing has a very blunt leading-edge and is more than 1·52 m (5 ft) thick at the thickest point. Two-segment hydraulically actuated elevons on each trailing-edge, for pitch and roll control, are of aluminium honeycomb construction with a titanium rubbing strip on each of their leading-edges. Hinged panels on the wing upper surface, of titanium and Inconel sandwich, are used to seal the wing/elevon gap; these are the only areas of the wing not covered by the thermal protection system.

FUSELAGE: Conventional semi-monocoque aluminium alloy structure, built in three main portions. Forward fuselage contains the crew module, three forward electronics bays, forward reaction control system and nosewheel unit. The mid fuselage portion is an 18·28 m (60 ft) long section of primary load carrying structure, built by General Dynamics (Convair), and includes the wing carry-through structure. Upper half of the mid fuselage consists of structural payload bay doors, hinged along the side and meeting at the top centreline. These doors are of graphite epoxy bonded honeycomb sandwich construction, with a Nomex core. The forward 9·14 m (30 ft) of each door incorporates Vought radiator panels that are deployed in orbit. Fixed radiator panels are attached to the remaining inner surface on the front of each aft door. The rear of the aft doors can be fitted with fixed radiator panels if required by a specific mission. The rear fuselage interfaces with the removable orbital manoeuvring system (OMS)/ reaction control system (RCS) pods, the wing rear spar, the vertical tail assembly, the body flap, the external tank rear supports, the main propulsion system, the launch umbilical panel, the three rear electronics bays, and other discrete system equipment. A bulkhead heatshield at the rear of the vehicle protects the main engine systems. A large body flap at the rear fuselage protects the main engine nozzles during re-entry, and is actuated hydraulically to serve also as a trimming surface.

TAIL UNIT: Vertical surfaces only, built by Fairchild Republic, of wedge section with 45° sweepback on fin leading-edge. Fin is a conventional aluminium alloy structure. The rudder/speed brake assembly has an aluminium honeycomb skin and is divided into upper and lower sections. Each of these is also split longitudinally and actuated individually to serve as both rudder and speed brake, operated by a Sundstrand hydraulic rotary actuator. The Inconel honeycomb seal over these is the only part of the vertical tail not covered by the thermal protection system. Mission requirements call for a locked rudder/speed brake during boost, orbit and re-entry. The speed brake control is provided from approx Mach 10 to Mach 5; from Mach 5 to landing the rudder and speed brake controls are combined as required. Primary system control is automatic, with manual override.

THERMAL PROTECTION SYSTEM: The thermal protection system (TPS) consists of materials applied externally to maintain the airframe outer skins within an acceptable temperature limit of 176°C (350°F) during re-entry. The TPS materials are designed to perform a minimum of 100 missions, in which temperatures will range from −156°C (−250°F) in space to re-entry temperatures of nearly 1,648°C (3,000°F) on the wing leading-edge and fuselage nose. Coated Nomex felt reusable surface insulation (FRSI) is used where temperatures are less than 371°C (700°F), on the upper portion of the payload bay doors, mid and rear fuselage sides, upper wing, and part of the orbital manoeuvring system (OMS) pods. On OV-102 *Columbia*, low-temperature reusable surface insulation

(LRSI) tiles are used where temperatures go below 648°C (1,200°F) and above 371°C (700°F) nominal. These areas are the lower portion of payload bay doors; forward fuselage; parts of the mid and rear fuselage; upper wing; vertical tail and a portion of the OMS pods. These tiles have a white surface coating, which provides better thermal characteristics in orbit. On OV-099 *Challenger*, some of the LRSI tiles on the OMS pods were replaced with a composite blanket, advanced, flexible, reusable surface insulation (AFRSI), a quilted fabric blanket that is easier to produce, more durable, easier to install and lighter. On *Discovery* and *Atlantis*, AFRSI replaces the majority of the LRSI tiles. High-temperature reusable surface insulation (HRSI) tiles are used where temperatures are below 1,260°C (2,300°F) and above 648°C (1,200°F). The areas are the forward fuselage, lower mid fuselage, lower wing, selected areas of the vertical tail, a portion of the OMS pods, and around the forward fuselage windows. The HRSI has two different densities: one weighs 4 kg/m³ (9 lb/cu ft) and is used in all areas except around the nose and main landing gear doors, nose cap interface, wing leading-edge, reinforced carbon-carbon/HRSI interface, external tank umbilical doors, vent doors, and fin leading-edge. These areas use HRSI tiles with a density of 9·9 kg/m³ (22 lb/cu ft) and have a black surface coating for entry emittance. When the higher density HRSI tiles have been expended, fibrous refractory insulation (FRCI) tiles will be used instead. The FRCI-12 tiles have a density of 5·4 kg/m³ (12 lb/cu ft), and improved strength, durability and resistance to cracking.

LANDING GEAR: Retractable tricycle type, with twin wheels and Menasco oleo-pneumatic shock absorbers on each unit. Hydraulic release, with a pyrotechnic backup for deployment in flight. Landing gear cannot be retracted in flight, after release. Nose unit is retracted forward into fuselage and main units forward into wings before launch. Nose unit is steerable; main units are fitted with Goodrich brakes and Hydro-Aire anti-skid units. All units have Goodrich wheels and tyres. Landing gear is designed to facilitate safe landing at speeds of up to 225 knots (415 km/h; 258 mph). The main gear tyres are rated at 20,410 kg (45,000 lb) and the brakes at 240 × 10⁶ ft-lb.

MAIN PROPULSION: Three Rocketdyne SSME (Space Shuttle Main Engines) high-pressure liquid oxygen/liquid hydrogen engines, each rated at 1,668 kN (375,000 lb st) at sea level and 2,091 kN (470,000 lb thrust) in vacuum at 100 per cent; 1,752 kN (393,800 lb) at sea level and 2,174 kN (488,800 lb) vacuum at 104 per cent; 1,856 kN (417,300 lb) at sea level and 2,283 kN (513,250 lb) vacuum at 109 per cent. The engines can be throttled over a range of 65 to 109 per cent of their rated power level. Each engine is designed for 7½ h of operation, with 55 starts.

ORBIT MANOEUVRING ENGINES: Two Aerojet Liquid Rocket Company (ALRC) bipropellant liquid rocket engines, running on monomethylhydrazine (MMH) and nitrogen tetroxide (N_2O_4), are used for the Orbiter's orbit manoeuvring subsystem (OMS). These engines are housed in pods, one on each side of the Orbiter's rear fuselage. The OMS engines, for which a usable total of 10,830 kg (23,876 lb) of propellant is carried, are used to position the spacecraft in orbit; each develops 26·7 kN (6,000 lb thrust) in space.

REACTION CONTROL ENGINES: The reaction control subsystem (RCS) utilises 38 Marquardt R-40A bipropellant liquid rocket engines (each 3·87 kN; 870 lb vacuum thrust) and six Marquardt R-1E bipropellant liquid rocket vernier thrusters (each 0·11 kN; 24 lb vacuum thrust). Fourteen of the R-40A engines are on the nose and 24 on the aft end, 12 in each OMS/RCS pod; there are two of the R-1E verniers on the nose and two in each aft pod. Propellants are the same as for the OMS engines; 1,096 kg (2,418 lb) is carried in the RCS tanks, and there is provision for crossfeed between the aft OMS and aft RCS tanks.

CREW COMPARTMENT: Self-contained crew module has a fuselage side hatch for access, a hatch into the airlock from the mid section, and a hatch from the airlock into the payload bay. It is divided into three levels, the upper (flight deck) level having side by side seating for two flight crewmen with dual controls. Behind them are seats for one or two mission specialists. On the middle deck provisions are made for three more seats, bunks and a galley, dependent upon particular flight requirements, hygiene section, airlock, three electronics bays, and payload bay access. For rescue missions, seats for three more persons can be fitted in place of the bunks. The lower deck contains environmental control equipment and crew equipment storage.

PAYLOAD BAY: In centre of fuselage, 18·29 m (60 ft) long and 4·57 m (15 ft) in diameter. Retractable manipulator arm on left hand side if required for a particular flight (with provision for a second one on the right), for deploying and retrieving payloads. Complete closed circuit TV system by RCA Astro-Electronics includes a colour camera in the crew compartment and several black and white and or colour cameras in the cargo bay and on the manipulator arm. These facilitate payload handling and provide TV coverage for engineers and the general public on Earth.

SYSTEMS: Environmental control and life support system, made up of four subsystems: atmosphere revitalisation subsystem (ARS), to control atmospheric environment for occupants and thermal environment for electronics; food, water and waste subsystem (FWW), to provide hygiene, and other life support functions; active thermal control subsystem (ATCS), to maintain subsystems and components within specified temperature limits and to provide, via payload door radiator panels, active heat rejection to protect payloads; and an airlock support subsystem. Three redundant hydraulic systems, each of 207 bars (3,000 lb/sq in), supply actuators for the elevons, body flap, rudder/speed brake, and power to actuate main engine thrust vector controls, landing gear, brakes and steering. Electrical power subsystem (EPS) consists, functionally, of a fuel cell power plant (FCP) subsystem, and a power reactant storage and distribution (PRSD) subsystem. There are three FCPs, each providing power at 27·5V to 32·5V DC over a power range of 2-12kW and each connected to one of the three main DC buses; these supply the primary in-flight electrical power used by the Shuttle, generated through the chemical combination and conversion of cryogenic oxygen and hydrogen. In the PRSD subsystem, the cryogenic oxygen and hydrogen tanks are defined as a tank set. The tank sets installed are dependent upon specific flight requirements; up to five sets can be accommodated. Westinghouse remote power control system and master timing unit. Honeywell four channel fly by wire electrical flight control subsystem for operation of all control surfaces and main engine controls. APU subsystem consists of three Sundstrand independent APUs (each 100·7 kW; 135 shp), deriving their energy from the decomposition of hydrazine (N_2H_4).

AVIONICS AND EQUIPMENT: Fully fail-operational/fail-safe guidance, navigation and control system, including three Singer-Kearfott KT-70/SKN-2600 type inertial measuring units; triplex Ku-band microwave scan beam landing system, by the AIL Division of Eaton Corpn; head-up displays (HUD); three Northrop rate gyro assemblies; three Hoffman L-band Tacan; three Bendix accelerometer assemblies; two Honeywell C-band radar altimeters; four AiResearch air data transducers; three Lear Siegler attitude director indicators; two Collins horizontal situation indicators; two Sperry alpha/Mach indicators two Bendix altitude/vertical velocity indicators; two Bendix surface position indicators; two Sperry barometric altimeters; and two Sperry ATC transponders. Communications and tracking equipment includes one (optionally two) Ku-band rendezvous radar/satellite com on starboard side of cargo bay; two Ball star trackers; two 100W Watkins-Johnson S-band TWT amplifiers; two P-band UHF for EVA/ATC com; Conrac S-band FM for Orbiter/ground and Orbiter/payload com; and Ku-band radio for Orbiter/ground com and Ku band for rendezvous. Central data processing is by means of five IBM Advanced System/4 Pi Model AP-101 digital computers and two mass memory units. Four of the computers are interconnected to process guidance, navigation and control inputs and to relay commands to FBW flight control systems; the fifth is provided for independent backup and systems management.

DIMENSIONS, EXTERNAL:
- Wing span: 23·79 m (78 ft 0·68 in)
- Wing aspect ratio: 2·265
- Wing mean aerodynamic chord: 12·06 m (39 ft 6·81 in)
- Length: 37·19 m (122 ft 0·2 in)
- Height: 17·25 m (56 ft 7 in)

DIMENSIONS, INTERNAL:
- Payload bay: Length: 18·29 m (60 ft 0 in)
  - Diameter: 4·57 m (15 ft 0 in)
- Crew module: Volume: 74·33 m³ (2,625 cu ft)

AREAS:
- Wings, gross: 249·91 m² (2,690 sq ft)
- Elevons (total): 38·38 m² (413·14 sq ft)
- Rudder/speed brake: 9·09 m² (97·84 sq ft)
- Vertical tail surfaces (total): 38·39 m² (413·25 sq ft)
- Body flap: 12·61 m² (135·75 sq ft)

WEIGHTS:
- Weight dry: *Columbia*: 70,606 kg (155,661 lb)
- Design landing weight with payload: 14,515 kg (32,000 lb) 96,162 kg (212,000 lb)

PERFORMANCE:
- Orbital speed: approx 15,285 knots (28,325 km/h; 17,600 mph)
- Nominal touchdown speed (unpowered): 180 knots (334 km/h; 208 mph) EAS

ROGERSON

ROGERSON HILLER CORPORATION (Subsidiary of Rogerson Aircraft Corporation)

William R. Fairchild International Airport, Port Angeles, Washington 98362

PRESIDENT: Gerald J. Tobias

Telephone: (206) 452 6891

Telex: RHC 15 2488

Fax: (206) 457 5426

MARKETING: V. Milner, Vice-President, 2201 Alton Avenue, Irvine, California 92714

This company was formed in January 1973, as Hiller Aviation Inc, to acquire from Fairchild Industries the design rights, production tooling and spares of the Hiller 12E series of light helicopters. Initially, it provided product support for helicopters of this type in worldwide service, before restarting production of piston engined and turbine powered versions in three-seat and four-seat configurations. The five-seat FH-1100 was added to the company's products following the purchase of all rights from Fairchild Industries in 1980.

In April 1984, Hiller Aviation became a wholly owned subsidiary of Rogerson Aircraft Corporation, which manufactures aircraft control system parts, fuel tanks, composite materials and components for the aerospace industry. It was renamed Hiller Helicopters, resuming deliveries of the UH-12E and redesignated RH-1100 in July 1984, and has since been renamed Rogerson Hiller Corporation.

In November 1985 Rogerson Hiller occupied a new 13,006 m² (140,000 sq ft) manufacturing facility at William R. Fairchild International Airport, Port Angeles, Washington. In September 1985 the company acquired L.O.M. Corporation, manufacturer of helicopter rotor blades, and renamed the company Aerobond. Production of rotor blades will be undertaken at the Port Angeles factory.

Prototype of the RH-1100M Hornet military version of the RH-1100 *(Brian M. Service)*

HILLER RH-1100

The original FH-1100 was a refined development of the OH-5A helicopter which the former Hiller Aircraft Company designed for the US Army's LOH (Light Observation Helicopter) competition. A total of 246 FH-1100s had been built when production ended in 1974.

The current, improved, RH-1100 production version has

a more powerful engine and main rotor blades of 76 mm (3 in) greater chord, together with a larger diameter tail rotor and a new drive coupling between the engine and the main rotor transmission, to allow operation at a higher gross weight and increased maximum speed.

In early 1985 Hiller announced a multi-mission military variant of the helicopter, designated **RH-1100M Hornet**, the prototype of which made its debut at the 1985 Paris Air Show. The RH-1100M can carry interchangeable weapons systems including two 2·75 in folding fin rocket pods, 7·62 mm machine-guns, 0·50 calibre machine-guns and four TOW missiles. The RH-1100M has provision for an autopilot, forward looking infra-red anti-missile warning systems, air-to-air missile system capability, and chin or roof mounted sight. Hiller believes the RH-1100M's primary markets would be in South America, Africa and parts of Asia. Production deliveries could begin about 18 months after receipt of initial orders. Annual sales of civil and military variants of the RH-1100 are expected to total 30-40 within four years.

The following description applies to the standard civil RH-1100, except where indicated:

TYPE: Five-seat utility helicopter.

ROTOR SYSTEM: Two-blade semi-rigid main rotor of all-metal construction. Blade section NACA 63_2015. Each blade attached to rotor head by single main retention bolt and drag link. Droop stops standard. The main rotor blades each have a rolled stainless steel leading-edge spar bonded to an aluminium trailing section with a honeycomb core. Two-blade tail rotor of stainless steel and honeycomb construction. Main rotor blades fold. Rotor brake optional. Electrically controlled trim system.

ROTOR DRIVE: Mechanical drive through single-stage bevel and two-stage planetary main transmission, with intermediate and tail rotor gearboxes. Main rotor/engine rpm ratio 1:16·30. Tail rotor/engine rpm ratio 1:2·47.

FUSELAGE: Aluminium alloy semi-monocoque structure of pod and boom type.

TAIL UNIT: Vertical fin, and fixed horizontal surface, both of aluminium alloy and honeycomb construction. Tubular guard to protect rotor in tail-down landing.

LANDING GEAR: Skid type with torsion tube suspension, with choice of standard or extended support struts. Extended struts necessary if optional inflatable float installation is required. Ground handling wheels standard.

POWER PLANT: One 313 kW (420 shp) Allison 250-C20B turboshaft engine, derated to 204 kW (274 shp). Single bladder fuel tank in bottom of centre-fuselage with usable capacity of 259 litres (68·5 US gallons). Refuelling point on starboard side of rear fuselage. Oil capacity 2·6 litres (0·7 US gallons).

ACCOMMODATION: Pilot and co-pilot side by side with three passengers to rear, or pilot and four passengers. Four forward hinged doors, two on each side of cabin, with removable centre door post for cargo loading. Dual internal stretcher kit optional. Baggage compartment to rear of cabin, capacity 0·30 m³ (10·5 cu ft). Accommodation ventilated. Cabin heater and windscreen defroster optional.

SYSTEMS: Hydraulic system for cyclic and collective pitch controls. Electrical system includes a 28V 60A DC starter/generator and nickel-cadmium battery.

AVIONICS: A range of nav/com systems is available to customer's requirements.

EQUIPMENT: Standard equipment includes clock, engine hour meter, outside air temperature gauge, fuel filter warning system, night lighting system including two rotating beacons, edge-lit instrument panel, seatbelts, shoulder harness on front seats, sliding rear windows, tinted windows, hardpoint for optional external cargo hook, external power socket, and choice of exterior paint scheme and interior trim. Optional equipment includes stability augmentation system, dual controls, rear seat shoulder harness, cabin fire extinguisher, first aid kit, strobe lights, engine auto relight, reverse scoop intake, heated pitot, loudspeaker/siren, quick-release cargo hook, cargo racks, ambulance kit, dual litter kit, searchlight and Simplex agricultural spraygear.

DIMENSIONS, EXTERNAL:

Main rotor diameter	10·80 m (35 ft 5 in)
Tail rotor diameter	1·83 m (6 ft 0 in)
Distance between rotor centres	6·29 m (20 ft 7½ in)
Main rotor blade chord	0·33 m (13 in)
Length overall, rotors turning	12·57 m (41 ft 3 in)
Length of fuselage	9·08 m (29 ft 9½ in)
Width, rotors folded	1·32 m (4 ft 4 in)
Height overall	2·83 m (9 ft 3½ in)
Skid track	2·20 m (7 ft 2¾ in)

AREAS:

Main rotor disc	91·0 m² (979 sq ft)
Tail rotor disc	2·63 m² (28·3 sq ft)

WEIGHTS (A: RH-1100, B: RH-1100M):

Weight empty: A	687 kg (1,515 lb)
B (TOW)	1,048 kg (2,310 lb)
B (Scout)	726 kg (1,600 lb)
Max payload: A	462 kg (1,020 lb)
Max standard fuel weight: A, B	200·5 kg (442 lb)
Max T-O weight: A	1,292 kg (2,850 lb)
B	1,406 kg (3,100 lb)

PERFORMANCE (at max T-O weight, A and B as above):

Max level speed at S/L:	
A, B	110 knots (204 km/h; 127 mph)
Max cruising speed at 1,525 m (5,000 ft):	
A	110 knots (204 km/h; 127 mph)
Econ cruising speed: A	106 knots (196 km/h; 122 mph)
Max rate of climb at S/L	488 m (1,600 ft)/min
Vertical rate of climb at S/L: A	244 m (800 ft)/min
Service ceiling: A	5,275 m (17,300 ft)
Hovering ceiling: IGE: A	5,180 m (17,000 ft)
OGE: A	3,660 m (12,000 ft)
Range at 1,525 m (5,000 ft) with max fuel, no reserves:	
A	340 nm (629 km; 391 miles)
B (Scout)	534 nm (990 km; 615 miles)
Max endurance at 1,525 m (5,000 ft), no reserves:	
A	3 h 24 min
B	5 h 0 min

HILLER UH-12E HAULER

Rogerson Hiller has resumed delivery of the basic model UH-12E light helicopter. The UH-12E4, UH-12ET and UH-12E4T versions described in the 1985-86 *Jane's* are no longer available.

Customers for the UH-12E include the government of India, to which deliveries of Haulers equipped for agricultural work began in May 1986.

TYPE: Three-seat utility helicopter.

ROTOR SYSTEM: Two-blade main rotor mounted universally on driveshaft, with small servo rotor; the latter is connected directly to the pilot's cyclic control stick, through a universally mounted transfer bearing and simple linkage. Movement of the control stick introduces positive or negative pitch changes to the servo rotor paddles. The resulting aerodynamic forces tilt the rotor head and produce cyclic pitch changes to the rotor blades. Main rotor blades are of bonded stainless steel, with aluminium honeycomb core, and wedge tips. Thickness/chord ratio 12%. Blades are interchangeable individually and are bolted to forks which are retained at the rotor head by tension-torsion bars. Blades do not fold. Rotor brake optional. Two-blade tail rotor of light alloy construction, mounted on port side of tailboom.

ROTOR DRIVE: Mechanical drive through two-stage planetary main transmission. Bevel gear drive to auxiliaries. Tail rotor gearbox (and fan gearbox on piston engined versions). Separate transmission oil system. Main rotor/engine rpm ratio 1 : 8·66. Tail rotor/engine rpm ratio 1 : 1·44.

FUSELAGE: Light alloy fully stressed semi-monocoque platform structure supporting the non-stressed cabin enclosure, engine mounting and landing gear. Tailboom of beaded light alloy sheet with no internal stiffeners.

TAIL UNIT: Horizontal stabiliser on starboard side of tailboom of three-seat versions, with steel tube spar, light alloy ribs and skin. Incidence ground-adjustable. Inverted V stabilising surfaces forward of tail rotor on four-seat versions.

LANDING GEAR: Wide track light alloy tube skids carried on spring steel cross members. Optional extended legs. Ground handling wheels standard. Optional 'zip-on' pontoons can be attached above the skids to permit water or land operations, but require extended landing gear.

POWER PLANT: One 253·5 kW (340 hp) Avco Lycoming VO-540-C2A flat-six engine, installed vertically and derated to 227·5 kW (305 hp). Engine muffler optional. Single bladder fuel cell, capacity 174 litres (46 US gallons), mounted in lower portion of rear fuselage, beneath engine. Two optional auxiliary fuel tanks, mounted in fuselage on each side of engine; capacity 76 litres (20 US gallons) each. Oil capacity 12·5 litres (3·3 US gallons).

ACCOMMODATION: Three persons side by side on bench seat. Seat belts for all occupants; provision for shoulder harness. Dual controls optional. Forward-hinged door on each side, with sliding window. Baggage compartment immediately aft of engine. Heater/defroster optional.

SYSTEM: Electrical system includes a 72A alternator, nickel-cadmium battery, and battery temperature monitor.

AVIONICS AND EQUIPMENT: A range of optional avionics is available. Standard equipment includes engine hour meter, edge-lit instrument panel, outside air temperature gauge, eight-day clock, electrically controlled trim system, tinted glazing, cargo hook hardpoint, external power socket, and polyurethane paint finish. Optional equipment includes Mason cyclic control grip, fire extinguisher, first aid kit, night lighting equipment including two rotating beacons, strobe lights, 454 kg (1,000 lb) capacity quick-release cargo hook, twin heavy duty cargo racks, agricultural spray equipment, loudspeaker/siren, searchlight, and tropical doors. Agricultural equipment includes Simplex Model 3300 system with 9·75 m (32 ft) folding spraybooms and two glassfibre tanks, with total capacity of 416 litres (110 US gallons) or 530 litres (140 US gallons), designed for quick change to dry system; or Simplex Model 4500 system with single tank, capacity 530 litres (140 US gallons) and folding booms.

DIMENSIONS, EXTERNAL:

Main rotor diameter	10·80 m (35 ft 5 in)
Main rotor blade chord (constant)	0·33 m (1 ft 1 in)
Servo rotor diameter	3·05 m (10 ft 0 in)
Tail rotor diameter	1·68 m (5 ft 6 in)
Distance between rotor centres	6·17 m (20 ft 3 in)
Length overall, rotors turning	12·41 m (40 ft 8½ in)
Length of fuselage	8·69 m (28 ft 6 in)
Height to top of rotor head	3·08 m (10 ft 1¼ in)
Skid track	2·29 m (7 ft 6 in)
Cabin doors (standard, each):	
Height	1·13 m (3 ft 8½ in)
Max width	0·81 m (2 ft 8 in)
Height to sill	0·58 m (1 ft 11 in)

DIMENSIONS, INTERNAL:

Cabin: Length	1·52 m (5 ft 0 in)
Max width	1·50 m (4 ft 11 in)
Max height	1·35 m (4 ft 5 in)
Floor area	1·16 m² (12·5 sq ft)

AREAS:

Tail rotor blades (each)	0·094 m² (1·01 sq ft)
Main rotor disc	91·97 m² (990 sq ft)
Tail rotor disc	2·57 m² (27·7 sq ft)

WEIGHTS AND LOADINGS:

Weight empty	798 kg (1,759 lb)
Max T-O weight	1,406 kg (3,100 lb)
Max disc loading	15·28 kg/m² (3·13 lb/sq ft)
Max power loading	6·18 kg/kW (10·16 lb/hp)

PERFORMANCE (at max T-O weight, except where indicated):

Never-exceed and max level speed
83 knots (154 km/h; 96 mph)

New production Hiller UH-12E with Simplex cropspraying system *(Howard Levy)*

Cruising speed 78 knots (145 km/h; 90 mph)
Max rate of climb at S/L 393 m (1,290 ft)/min
Vertical rate of climb at S/L 225 m (740 ft)/min
Service ceiling:
at AUW of 1,270 kg (2,800 lb) 4,570 m (15,000 ft)
at max T-O weight 2,255 m (7,400 ft)
Hovering ceiling IGE:
at AUW of 1,270 kg (2,800 lb) 3,170 m (10,400 ft)
at max T-O weight 2,315 m (7,600 ft)
Hovering ceiling OGE:
at AUW of 1,270 kg (2,800 lb) 2,070 m (6,800 ft)
at max T-O weight 1,155 m (3,800 ft)
Range, 30 min reserves:
standard fuel 150 nm (278 km; 173 miles)
auxiliary fuel 316 nm (585 km; 364 miles)
Endurance with auxiliary fuel, 30 min reserves 4 h 1 min

R/STOL

R/STOL SYSTEMS

Raleigh-Durham Airport, Raleigh, North Carolina 27611

In early 1985 R/STOL Systems acquired the assets of the former Robertson Aircraft Corporation, including some 100 supplemental type certificates for STOL and performance modifications to 40 aircraft types, as detailed in this entry. Robertson had voluntarily ceased operations in mid-1984.

Robertson Aircraft Corporation had been formed by the late Mr James L. Robertson, who had long been a pioneer in the development of STOL aircraft, having been responsible for the Skycraft Skyshark, Wren 460 and STOL modifications to the IMCO CallAir A-9 and B-1. It designed, built and certificated a series of Hi-Lift advanced technology safety and performance systems for standard single- and twin-engined Beech, Cessna and Piper aircraft.

During 1980, Robertson entered into an agreement with Astec Corporation to manufacture and install Astec's Eagle modification to Cessna Citation jet aircraft. In October 1981, it acquired Astec's STCs for the Eagle modification to the Cessna Citation 500, 501 and Citation I, as well as the company's manufacturing facilities.

Robertson also acquired Astec's engineering data and technical staff for two other business jet modification programmes. The first of these covers the installation of higher thrust Pratt & Whitney Canada JT15D-4 engines in an Eagle conversion called the Century V Eagle, for which certification was gained during March 1982. Astec's second (TF25) programme covered the installation of JT15D-5 engines in Learjet 25s.

A new canard-like wingroot airflow energiser was certificated on the Cessna 414A in early 1980. The R/STOL Hi-Lift system for this aircraft includes also Fowler trailing-edge flaps of improved aerofoil section and with longer tracks. A similar programme has adapted the above system for installation on the Cessna 402C and 421C. The wingroot airflow energiser consists of a flat plate 102 mm (4 in) wide which is attached to the fuselage skin forward of each wing. With a length of 0·38 m (1 ft 3 in), each energiser is mounted directly ahead of the wing leading-edge and in line with the wing chord. The addition of this device reduces stalling speed by 6 knots (11 km/h; 7 mph) with flaps up, and by 7 knots (13 km/h; 8 mph) with the flaps extended.

Research contracts with Kansas University and NASA were completed in 1974, covering the design of an Advanced Technology Light Twin (ATLIT). A standard Piper Seneca fuselage was fitted with an experimental wing that had a new aerofoil section and 30 per cent chord full span Fowler flaps. There were no ailerons, and roll control was achieved by the use of upper surface spoilers. Construction of the aircraft was completed by Piper Aircraft Corporation and the first flight was recorded in late 1974.

Following completion of the ATLIT research programme, Robertson embarked on a project to develop spoilers and full span flaps suitable for retrofit on the standard Piper Seneca I. FAA certification of the resulting system represented the first approval of spoilers for use on general aviation aircraft manufactured in the USA (see full description under this entry). This spoiler/full span flap system has since been certificated for Beech Bonanza V35 and A36 series aircraft, and for the Piper PA-32-300 Cherokee SIX and Seneca II.

R/STOL Systems holds an FAA Supplemental Type Certificate covering the installation of RCA WeatherScout I radar inside the leading-edge of the starboard wing of a number of aircraft including the Cessna 182, 206F, T206F, TU206G, U206G and 210 series. The truncated 13 × 30 cm (5 × 12 in) antenna is housed inside a leading-edge cutaway, with the receiver/transmitter built integrally at the back of the antenna. The wing structure is reinforced around the cutaway. A reinforced epoxy/glassfibre radome encloses the opening. Total system weight is 10·5 kg (23·1 lb). WeatherScout I is basically a weather radar, but provides limited ground mapping capability.

R/STOL Systems conversion of the Piper Seneca II features full span trailing-edge flaps, with wing upper surface spoilers for roll control

Beechcraft A36 Bonanza as certificated with R/STOL Hi-Lift system, including full span flaps

R/STOL / BEECH, R/STOL / CESSNA and R/STOL / PIPER SAFETY and PERFORMANCE CONVERSIONS

Continuous improvement has been made on R/STOL's line of Hi-Lift systems for Beech, Cessna and Piper single-engined and smaller twin-engined aircraft. The R/STOL modification, first applied to a Cessna 182, comprises full span wing leading-edge and trailing-edge high-lift systems which greatly reduce the take-off and landing distances normally required by such aircraft.

The existing ailerons are used as an integral part of the full span trailing-edge flap system. When the conventional inboard flaps are lowered for take-off or landing, the ailerons droop with them, virtually doubling the wing lift at low speeds. The ailerons retain their differential operation for roll control when drooped.

In addition, the wing is fitted with a full span distributed-camber leading-edge to provide an optimum spanwise lift distribution for maximum cruise efficiency. The cambered leading-edge also reduces the aerofoil leading-edge pressure peak at high angles of attack, to impart maximum resistance to stall and to provide highly responsive manoeuvrability at low airspeeds. Some types of Cessna single-engined aircraft built since 1972 include this R/STOL leading-edge as a standard production feature.

The full span flap system, in combination with R/STOL's conical cambered wingtips, dorsal and ventral fins, belly mounted vortex generators, and flap/elevator automatic trim system, is applied to various models to offer increased performance.

To improve controllability at low speeds, stall fences are provided between flaps and ailerons, and to complete the Hi-Lift modification the aileron gap is sealed with a strip of aluminium sheet or rubberised canvas These modifications permit safe STOL landings and take-offs by even novice pilots, and cruising speed and range are increased by 2-4 per cent.

Maximum gross weight increases have accompanied the certification of R/STOL modifications of twin-engined aircraft such as the Cessna Super Skymaster and Piper Twin Comanche. This is due primarily to their increased climb performance and slower take-off and landing speeds.

Development of a Hi-Lift system for the Cessna 400 series of twin-engined business aircraft entailed complete redesign of the wings from the rear spar aft to allow installation of

R/STOL VERSIONS OF BEECH MODELS

	Weight empty equipped kg (lb)	Weight gross kg (lb)	Max level speed knots (km/h; mph)	Max cruising speed knots (km/h; mph)	Stalling speed, wheels and flaps down knots (km/h; mph)	Max rate of climb at S/L m (ft)/min	Service ceiling m (ft)	T-O run m (ft)	T-O to 15 m (50 ft) m (ft)	Landing from 15 m (50 ft) m (ft)	Landing run m (ft)	Max range** nm (km; miles)
V35B Bonanza	987 (2,176)	1,542 (3,400)	181 (335; 208)	176 (325; 202)	53 (98; 61)	343 (1,125)	5,443 (17,858)	B 239 (785)	B 420 (1,377)	B 279 (914)	B 146 (478)	875 (1,620; 1,007)
A36 Bonanza	1,009 (2,225)	1,633 (3,600)	177 (327; 204)	169 (313; 194)	54 (100; 62)	309 (1,015)	4,876 (16,000)	276 (904)	485 (1,590)	305 (1,000)	168 (550)	833 (1,543; 958)

B: R/STOL Normal operation. **With optional long-range tanks fitted.

100 per cent Fowler flaps and flap actuated drooping ailerons. This system, in combination with R/STOL's automatic pitch trim system and double hinged rudder, led to FAA certificated decreases in take-off and landing field lengths of approximately 40 per cent.

In 1974, the FAA certificated the Robertson equipped Piper Seneca I, with wing upper surface spoilers for roll control, full span slotted flaps, cambered wingtips and an anti-servo rudder tab. These modifications allow shorter take-off and landing distances; minimum control speed is reduced by 16 per cent, the best rate of climb speed is lowered by 19 per cent, single-engine service ceiling is raised by 213 m (700 ft) and roll response is increased greatly at all speeds and configurations. A similar modification of the Seneca II was certificated during 1976.

More recent activities have entailed fitting full span trailing-edge flaps and spoilers for roll control on a Piper Cherokee SIX; and developing a high differential aileron droop Hi-Lift system for high performance single-engined aircraft, such as the Cessna Model P210 Pressurised Centurion. In this application a new and improved control mechanism droops both ailerons symmetrically to 15° when the trailing-edge flaps are extended to 20° for take-off. For roll control the ailerons travel up and down in high ratio differential: thus, with the control wheel fully to starboard, the starboard aileron moves up 42° to act as a spoiler (27° up from its normal faired position); at the same time the port aileron is deflected downward an additional 12° to a total of 27°. Ailerons are also drooped symmetrically by 15° when the trailing-edge flaps are extended to 30° for approach and landing.

Benefits from this advanced Hi-Lift system include a greatly reduced adverse yaw tendency in turns, and a high roll rate for more precise control when flaps are down and speed low. Control wheel forces are significantly less than with unmodified aircraft, due to a tailoring of aerodynamic forces on the up-moving aileron and a crossover cable which minimises friction in the control runs

Four stall strips, two on each wing, retain the desirable stall characteristics common to all R/STOL Hi-Lift systems. For aircraft fitted with wing leading-edge de-icing boots, rubber strips are cemented to the rubber boots; when these are not fitted, aluminium stall strips are riveted to the wing leading-edge. A strip 130 mm (5 in) long, close to the wing-root, initiates an early warning signal that the aircraft is approaching the stall. A longer strip, mounted further outboard and lower than the first, initiates the stall of the inboard and centre wing sections, while the outboard section and the wingtip are still unaffected by stall conditions. When the aircraft stalls it noses forward and down, under the complete control of ailerons which remain unstalled and effective for roll control.

The R/STOL integrated high-lift and safety systems have been designed for easy field maintenance. They are designed to be applicable to almost the entire range of Cessna and Piper aircraft, and the Beechcraft Bonanza.

Full details of the basic Cessna and Piper airframes are given under the appropriate company headings in this and earlier editions of *Jane's*, and apply also to the R/STOL versions, except for the added Hi-Lift systems as described. Weights and performance details of the entire range of Hi-Lift modifications are given in the accompanying tables. The conversions can be fitted as a retrospective modification to any of the models listed, irrespective of year.

R/STOL/Cessna T210, showing clearly the high differential aileron droop Hi-Lift system

R/STOL/Cessna Century V Eagle, a Citation 500 conversion with advanced wing aerofoil section and JT15D-4 turbofan engines

R/STOL/CESSNA EAGLE, EAGLE SP, LONGWING and CENTURY V EAGLE

The R/STOL **Eagle** (formerly Astec Eagle) conversion entails modifications to the wing contours of the Cessna Citation 500 and Citation I twin-turbofan executive transport aircraft.

Changes to the basic Citation 500 wing include use of an advanced technology aerofoil section of increased thickness and length over the inboard portion of the wing; wingtip extensions of 0·51 m (1 ft 8 in); and the addition of cove seals to the trailing-edge flaps. The thickened wing and the wingtip extensions contain an additional 392 kg (865 lb) of fuel, accounting for about 75 per cent of the approximate 600 nm (1,112 km; 691 mile) increase in range over the basic Citation 500. The remainder of the increase is due to improved aerodynamic efficiency of the Eagle wing.

The R/STOL **Eagle SP** conversion introduces identical modifications to the Citation 501, which is certificated under FAR Pt 23 and approved for single-pilot operation.

The **Longwing** conversion was introduced in 1983 and uses the Eagle wingtip extensions on Citation 500 aircraft, but does not include the wingroot modifications. The conversion increases fuel capacity (by approximately 54 kg; 120 lb on aircraft c/n 001-213) and provides a 10 per cent increase in range. Rate of climb is also improved, and approach speeds reduced.

The **Century V Eagle** designation applies to the R/STOL Eagle with its JT15D-1 or -1A power plant replaced by more powerful JT15D-4 engines, each of 11·12 kN (2,500 lb st). The production rate for Eagle conversions has been set at eight per year.

The description of the Citation I under Cessna's entry in this section applies also to the Eagle, except as follows:

WINGS: Thickness/chord ratio of inboard portions increased from 14% to 19%, and supercritical technology incorporated to improve wing/fuselage airflow. Span increased by comparison with Citation 500, by addition of wingtip extensions.

POWER PLANT: As for Citation 500, except increased fuel capacity provided in the thicker wing centre-section and wingtip extensions.

DIMENSIONS, EXTERNAL:
- Wing span: 14·35 m (47 ft 0½ in)
- Wing chord: at root: 2·95 m (9 ft 8⅛ in)
  - at tip: 0·93 m (3 ft 0½ in)
- Wing aspect ratio: 7·92
- Length overall: 13·26 m (43 ft 6 in)
- Height overall: 4·36 m (14 ft 3¾ in)
- Wheel track: 3·84 m (12 ft 7⅛ in)
- Wheelbase: 4·78 m (15 ft 8¼ in)

WEIGHTS (A: JT15D-1; B: JT15D-1A; C: JT15D-4 power plant):
- Weight empty: A, B: 2,971 kg (6,550 lb)
  - C: 3,016 kg (6,650 lb)
- Max fuel weight: A, B, C: 2,045 kg (4,510 lb)
- Max T-O weight: A, B, C: 5,670 kg (12,500 lb)
- Max zero-fuel weight: A, B, C: 4,309 kg (9,500 lb)
- Max landing weight: A, B, C: 5,148 kg (11,350 lb)

PERFORMANCE (at max T-O weight except where indicated):
- Max cruising speed, AUW of 4,309 kg (9,500 lb), at 10,670 m (35,000 ft):
  - A: 341 knots (631 km/h; 392 mph)
  - B: 357 knots (661 km/h; 411 mph)
  - C: 386 knots (715 km/h; 444 mph)
- Cruising speed, AUW of 4,309 kg (9,500 lb), at 12,500 m (41,000 ft): A: 317 knots (587 km/h; 365 mph)
  - B: 336 knots (623 km/h; 387 mph)
  - C: 375 knots (695 km/h; 432 mph)
- Stalling speed at max landing weight:
  - A, B, C: 78 knots (145 km/h; 90 mph)
- Max certificated altitude: A: 10,670 m (35,000 ft)
  - B: 12,500 m (41,000 ft)
  - C: 13,105 m (43,000 ft)
- Balanced T-O field length: A, B: 907 m (2,975 ft)
  - C: 762 m (2,500 ft)
- FAA landing field length at max landing weight:
  - A, B, C: 722 m (2,370 ft)
- Max range, with 227 kg (500 lb) fuel reserves:
  - A: 1,800 nm (3,336 km; 2,073 miles)
  - C: 1,900 nm (3,521 km; 2,188 miles)

R/STOL VERSIONS OF CESSNA MODELS

	Weight empty equipped kg (lb)	Weight gross kg (lb)	Max level speed knots (km/h; mph)	Max cruising speed knots (km/h; mph)	Stalling speed, wheels and flaps down knots (km/h; mph)	Max rate of climb at S/L m (ft)/min	Single-engine rate of climb at S/L m (ft)/min	Service ceiling m (ft)	T-O run m (ft)	T-O to 15 m (50 ft) m (ft)	Landing from 15 m (50 ft) m (ft)	Landing run m (ft)	Max range** nm (km; miles)	Min control speed knots (km/h; mph)
Model 150 and Commuter	449 (990)	725 (1,600)	110 (204; 127)	105 (195; 121)	26 (48·3; 30)	213 (700)		3,930 (12,900)	A 129 (422) B 161 (527)	A 248 (815) B 273 (895)	A 193 (632) B 230 (755)	A 90 (295) B 106 (348)	790 (1,464; 910)	
Model 172 and Skyhawk†	572 (1,263)	1,043 (2,300)	126 (233; 145)	118 (219; 136)	28 (51·5; 32)	206 (675)		4,150 (13,600)	A 140 (460) B 175 (575)	A 274 (900) B 302 (990)	A 223 (730) B 267 (875)	A 92 (302) B 109 (356)	738 (1,367; 850)	

A, B, **, †, see notes at end of Cessna table.

CESSNA MODELS—continued

	Weight empty equipped kg (lb)	Weight gross kg (lb)	Max level speed knots (km/h; mph)	Max cruising speed knots (km/h; mph)	Stalling speed, wheels and flaps down knots (km/h; mph)	Max rate of climb at S/L m (ft)/min	Single-engine rate of climb at S/L m (ft)/min	Service ceiling m (ft)	T-O run m (ft)	T-O to 15 m (50 ft) m (ft)	Landing from 15 m (50 ft) m (ft)	Landing run m (ft)	Max range** nm (km; miles)	Min control speed knots (km/h; mph)
Model 172 and Skyhawk floatplane*	646 (1,425)	1,007 (2,220)	97 (180; 112)	94 (174; 108)	28 (51·5; 32)	191 (625)		3,765 (12,350)	A 256 (840) B 320 (1,050)	A 405 (1,330) B 451 (1,480)	A 267 (875) B 296 (970)	A 145 (475) B 171 (560)	477 (885; 550)	
Model 180 Skywagon†	707 (1,560)	1,270 (2,800)	152 (282; 175)	144 (267; 166)	32·2 (60; 37)	364 (1,195)		6,215 (20,400)	A 110 (360) B 137 (450)	A 216 (710) B 239 (785)	A 207 (680) B 254 (835)	A 88 (290) B 104 (342)	1,098 (2,035; 1,265)	
Model 180 Skywagon floatplane	850 (1,875)	1,338 (2,950)	142 (264; 164)	133 (246; 153)	32·2 (60; 37)	332 (1,090)		5,425 (17,800)	A 245 (805) B 307 (1,006)	A 369 (1,210) B 402 (1,320)	A 254 (832) B 308 (1,010)	A 145 (475) B 171 (560)	1,063 (1,971; 1,225)	
Model 182 and Skylane†	725 (1,599)	1,338 (2,950)	150 (278; 173)	143 (266; 165)	33 (62; 38)	288 (945)		5,610 (18,400)	A 131 (430) B 164 (537)	A 248 (815) B 270 (885)	A 237 (777) B 280 (920)	A 99 (325) B 117 (384)	1,050 (1,947; 1,210)	
Model 182 RG	800 (1,764)	1,412 (3,112)	187 (347; 215)	173 (321; 199)	42 (80; 48)	317 (1,040)		6,100 (20,000)	A 133 (435)	A 248 (815)	A 237 (777)	A 119 (389)	1,030 (1,909; 1,186)	
Model 185 Skywagon†	721 (1,590)	1,519 (3,350)	159 (295; 183)	149 (277; 172)	34 (63; 39)	320 (1,050)		5,440 (17,850)	A 114 (375) B 143 (469)	A 233 (763) B 265 (870)	A 230 (755) B 271 (890)	A 95 (310) B 111 (365)	972 (1,802; 1,120)	
Model 185 Skywagon floatplane	866 (1,910)	1,505 (3,320)	149 (277; 172)	140 (259; 161)	34 (63; 39)	311 (1,020)		5,210 (17,100)	A 182 (596) B 227 (745)	A 332 (1,090) B 364 (1,195)	A 265 (870) B 326 (1,070)	A 146 (480) B 173 (566)	903 (1,673; 1,040)	
Model 188 Ag Wagon 230	836 (1,844)	1,723 (3,800)	124 (230; 143)	116 (214; 133)	38·5 (71; 44)	245 (805)		4,330 (14,200)	A 207 (680) B 259 (850)	A 338 (1,110) B 431 (1,420)	A 186 (610) B 256 (840)	A 94 (308) B 111 (363)	303 (563; 350)	
Model A188 Ag Wagon 300†	843 (1,859)	1,814 (4,000)	135 (251; 156)	127 (235; 146)	40 (74; 46)	302 (990)		4,905 (16,100)	A 183 (600) B 229 (750)	A 293 (960) B 381 (1,250)	A 186 (610) B 256 (840)	A 94 (308) B 111 (363)	390 (724; 450)	
Model 206 Stationair 6†	785 (1,732)	1,633 (3,600)	155 (288; 179)	148 (274; 170)	36 (66; 41)	296 (970)		4,695 (15,400)	A 147 (482) B 184 (603)	A 302 (990) B 352 (1,155)	A 226 (740) B 270 (885)	A 92 (301) B 108 (355)	916 (1,697; 1,055)	
Model 206 Stationair 6 floatplane	943 (2,080)	1,587 (3,500)	144 (267; 166)	136 (253; 157)	36 (66; 41)	276 (905)		4,450 (14,600)	A 248 (815) B 311 (1,019)	A 454 (1,490) B 486 (1,595)	A 280 (917) B 343 (1,125)	A 148 (485) B 174 (572)	833 (1,544; 960)	
Model T206 Turbo Stationair 6	831 (1,832)	1,633 (3,600)	178 (330; 205)	163 (303; 188)	36 (66; 41)	322 (1,055)		8,260 (27,100)	A 148 (485) B 185 (606)	A 303 (995) B 358 (1,175)	A 226 (740) B 270 (885)	A 92 (301) B 108 (355)	963 (1,786; 1,110)	
Model T206 Turbo Stationair 6 floatplane	979 (2,160)	1,633 (3,600)	164 (304; 189)	148 (274; 170)	36 (66; 41)	311 (1,020)		7,650 (25,100)	A 241 (790) B 301 (987)	A 442 (1,450) B 475 (1,560)	A 283 (928) B 344 (1,130)	A 151 (495) B 178 (584)	911 (1,690; 1,050)	
Model 207 Skywagon and Stationair 7	862 (1,902)	1,723 (3,800)	150 (278; 173)	142 (264; 164)	38·5 (71; 44)	262 (860)		4,205 (13,800)	A 155 (510) B 194 (637)	A 332 (1,090) B 390 (1,280)	A 244 (800) B 298 (975)	A 97 (318) B 114 (375)	829 (1,536; 955)	
Model T207 Turbo Skywagon and Turbo Stationair 7	908 (2,002)	1,723 (3,800)	168 (312; 194)	156 (290; 180)	38·5 (71; 44)	277 (910)		7,650 (25,100)	A 155 (510) B 194 (537)	A 332 (1,090) B 390 (1,280)	A 244 (800) B 298 (975)	A 97 (318) B 114 (375)	812 (1,504; 935)	
Model 210 Centurion II	953 (2,102)	1,723 (3,800)	178 (330; 205)	167 (309; 192)	38·5 (71; 44)	274 (900)		4,905 (16,100)	A 155 (510) B 194 (637)	A 326 (1,070) B 376 (1,232)	A 239 (783) B 293 (960)	A 93 (305) B 110 (360)	1,137 (2,108; 1,310)	
Model T210 Turbo Centurion II	998 (2,202)	1,723 (3,800)	204 (378; 235)	192 (356; 221)	38·5 (71; 44)	293 (960)		9,020 (29,600)	A 160 (525) B 200 (656)	A 328 (1,075) B 401 (1,318)	A 239 (783) B 293 (960)	A 93 (305) B 110 (360)	1,133 (2,100; 1,305)	
Model P210 Pressurised Turbo Centurion II	1,008 (2,222)	1,723 (3,800)	204 (378; 235)	192 (356; 221)	49 (91; 57)	293 (960)		9,020 (29,600)	200 (656)	401 (1,318)	293 (960)	110 (360)	1,133 (2,100; 1,305)	
Model P210 Pressurised Centurion	1,064 (2,345)	1,822 (4,016)	206 (381; 237)	††	55 (102; 63)	283 (930)		7,010 (23,000)	366 (1,200)	607 (1,990)	271 (890)	424 (1,390)	925 (1,714; 1,065)	
Model 310R	1,701 (3,750)	2,495 (5,500)	237 (439; 273)	223 (414; 257)	64 (119; 74)	518 (1,700)	119 (390)	8,350 (27,400)	B 290 (950)	B 448 (1,470)	B 355 (1,165)	B 219 (720)	1,242 (2,301; 1,430)	69 (129; 80) CAS

A, B, *, **, †, ††, see notes at end of Cessna table.

CESSNA MODELS—continued

	Weight empty equipped kg (lb)	Weight gross kg (lb)	Max level speed knots (km/h; mph)	Max cruising speed knots (km/h; mph)	Stalling speed, wheels and flaps down knots (km/h; mph)	Max rate of climb at S/L m (ft)/min	Single-engine rate of climb at S/L m (ft)/min	Service ceiling m (ft)	T-O run m (ft)	T-O to 15 m (50 ft) m (ft)	Landing from 15 m (50 ft) m (ft)	Landing run m (ft)	Max range** nm (km; miles)	Min control speed knots (km/h; mph)
Model 337 Super Skymaster	1,196 (2,638)	2,100 (4,630)	177 (328; 204)	168 (312; 194)	39 (72·5; 45)	369 (1,210)	99 (325)	6,125 (20,100)	A 130 (428) B 163 (535)	A 265 (870) B 322 (1,055)	A 273 (895) B 323 (1,060)	A 105 (343) B 123 (405)	†† ††	
Model T337 Turbo Super Skymaster	1,289 (2,843)	2,131 (4,700)	204 (378; 235)	200 (370; 230)	40 (74; 46)	353 (1,160)	93 (305)	9,265 (30,400)	A 136 (445) B 169 (556)	A 280 (920) B 332 (1,088)	A 273 (895) B 323 (1,060)	A 107 (352) B 126 (415)	†† ††	
Model T337 Pressurised Super Skymaster	1,315 (2,900)	2,132 (4,700)	217 (402; 250)	208 (385; 239)	40 (74; 46)	353 (1,160)	126 (415)	6,100 (20,000)	A 126 (413) B 157 (516)	A 280 (920) B 332 (1,088)	A 273 (895) B 323 (1,060)	A 107 (352) B 126 (415)	†† ††	
Model 340	1,878 (4,140)	2,717 (5,990)	242 (447; 278)	228 (421; 262)	61 (114; 71)	503 (1,650)	96 (315)	9,085 (29,800)					1,372 (2,542; 1,580)	75 (140; 87) CAS
Model 401/402	1,673 (3,690)	2,858 (6,300)	226 (420; 261)	208 (386; 240)	65·5 (121; 75)	491 (1,610)	69 (225)	7,980 (26,180)	A 240 (786) B 300 (983)	A 378 (1,240) B 472 (1,550)	A 354 (1,160) B 442 (1,450)	A 155 (510) B 183 (600)	†† ††	72 (134; 83) 72 (134; 83)
Model 402C	1,849 (4,076)	3,107 (6,850)	††	††	65 (121; 75)	442 (1,450)	91 (300)	9,145 (30,000)	329 (1,080)	533 (1,750)	427 (1,400)	259 (850)	1,220 (2,261; 1,405)	74 (137; 85)
Model 414	1,872 (4,126)	2,880 (6,350)	††	††	67 (124; 77)	457 (1,500)	61 (200)	7,925 (26,000)	A 278 (912) B 347 (1,140)	A 381 (1,250) B 465 (1,525)	A 340 (1,115) B 425 (1,395)	A 183 (600) B 276 (905)	†† ††	72 (134; 83) 72 (134; 83)
Model 414A	1,975 (4,354)	3,062 (6,750)	††	††	65 (121; 75)	480 (1,575)	88 (290)	9,145 (30,000)	329 (1,080)	533 (1,750)	405 (1,330)	238 (780)	1,300 (2,409; 1,497)	73 (135; 84)
Model 421A	1,932 (4,260)	3,102 (6,840)	240 (444; 276)	224 (414; 258)	69 (128; 79)	512 (1,680)	88 (290)	8,230 (27,000)	A 307 (1,008) B 384 (1,260)	A 443 (1,452) B 553 (1,815)	A 419 (1,375) B 524 (1,720)	A 208 (683) B 245 (804)	1,488 (2,756; 1,713) ††	83 (153; 95) 83 (153; 95)
Model 421B	2,011 (4,435)	3,379 (7,450)	245 (454; 282)	230 (426; 265)	71 (132; 82)	564 (1,850)	93 (305)	9,450 (31,000)	A 313 (1,028) B 365 (1,196)	A 428 (1,403) B 535 (1,754)	A 427 (1,400) B 534 (1,752)	A 134 (440) B 158 (517)	1,490 (2,762; 1,716) ††	78 (145; 90) 78 (145; 90)
Model 421C	2,173 (4,790)	3,379 (7,450)	256 (475; 295)	240 (444; 276)	71 (132; 82)	591 (1,940)	107 (350)	9,200 (30,200)	B 396 (1,300)	B 558 (1,830)	B 518 (1,700)	B 317 (1,040)	1,487 (2,755; 1,712)	77 (143; 89) CAS

A: R/STOL STOL operation. B: R/STOL normal operation. *Available also with engines of increased horsepower.
**With optional long-range tanks fitted, if available.
†Leading-edge already installed by Cessna on current models. ††No change from standard aircraft.

R/STOL VERSIONS OF PIPER MODELS

	Weight empty equipped kg (lb)	Weight gross kg (lb)	Max level speed knots (km/h; mph)	Max cruising speed knots (km/h; mph)	Stalling speed, wheels and flaps down knots (km/h; mph)	Max rate of climb at S/L m (ft)/min	Single-engine rate of climb at S/L m (ft)/min	Service ceiling m (ft)	T-O run m (ft)	T-O to 15 m (50 ft) m (ft)	Landing from 15 m (50 ft) m (ft)	Landing run m (ft)	Max range** nm (km; miles)	Min control speed knots (km/h; mph)
PA-28-140 Cherokee	558 (1,232)	975 (2,150)	126 (223; 145)	120 (222; 138)	29 (53·2; 33)	206 (675)		4,480 (14,700)	A 171 (560) B 189 (620)	A 354 (1,160) B 404 (1,325)	A 192 (630) B 221 (725)	A 94 (310) B 110 (360)	†† ††	
PA-28-160 Cherokee	576 (1,270)	997 (2,200)	128 (237; 147)	121 (224; 139)	31 (56·5; 35)	216 (710)		4,970 (16,300)	A 152 (500) B 177 (580)	A 341 (1,120) B 390 (1,280)	A 204 (670) B 226 (740)	A 104 (340) B 114 (375)	†† ††	
PA-28-180 Cherokee	638 (1,406)	1,111 (2,450)	129 (238; 148)	122 (227; 141)	36 (66; 41)	221 (725)		4,313 (14,510)	A 165 (540) B 186 (610)	A 351 (1,150) B 399 (1,310)	A 238 (780) B 262 (860)	A 131 (430) B 146 (480)	596 (1,104; 686) ††	
PA-28R-180 Cherokee Arrow II	611 (1,349)	1,134 (2,500)	149 (275; 171)	142 (262; 163)	35 (64·5; 40)	270 (885)		4,695 (15,400)	A 171 (560) B 195 (640)	A 347 (1,140) B 396 (1,300)	A 259 (850) B 299 (980)	A 145 (475) B 168 (550)	911 (1,690; 1,050)	
PA-28R-200 Cherokee Arrow II	693 (1,528)	1,202 (2,650)	152 (282; 175)	143 (266; 165)	37 (69; 43)	274 (900)		4,570 (15,000)	A 175 (575) B 198 (650)	A 344 (1,130) B 393 (1,290)	A 283 (930) B 319 (1,045)	A 168 (550) B 187 (615)	782 (1,448; 900)	
PA-28-235 Cherokee 235	712 (1,570)	1,361 (3,000)	140 (259; 161)	132 (245; 152)	39 (72; 45)	244 (800)		3,660 (12,000)	A 168 (550) B 191 (625)	A 265 (870) B 302 (990)	A 274 (900) B 312 (1,025)	A 149 (490) B 171 (560)	926 (1,716; 1,066)	

A: R/STOL STOL operation. B: R/STOL normal operation.
**With optional long-range tanks fitted, if available. ††No change from standard aircraft.

PIPER MODELS—continued

	Weight empty equipped kg (lb)	Weight gross kg (lb)	Max level speed knots (km/h; mph)	Max cruising speed knots (km/h; mph)	Stalling speed, wheels and flaps down knots (km/h; mph)	Max rate of climb at S/L m (ft)/min	Single-engine rate of climb at S/L m (ft)/min	Service ceiling m (ft)	T-O run m (ft)	T-O to 15 m (50 ft) m (ft)	Landing from 15 m (50 ft) m (ft)	Landing run m (ft)	Max range** nm (km; miles)	Min control speed knots (km/h; mph)
PA-32-260 Cherokee SIX	783 (1,726)	1,542 (3,400)	144 (267; 166)	137 (254; 158)	38 (71; 44)	259 (850)		4,420 (14,500)	A 180 (590) B 238 (780)	A 317 (1,040) B 341 (1,120)	A 247 (810) B 267 (875)	A 155 (510) B 171 (560)	964 (1,786; 1,110)	
PA-32-300 Cherokee SIX	825 (1,819)	1,542 (3,400)	151 (280; 174)	146 (270; 168)	38 (71; 44)	320 (1,050)		4,955 (16,250)	A 171 (560) B 226 (740)	A 299 (980) B 320 (1,050)	A 247 (810) B 267 (875)	A 158 (520) B 168 (550)	921 (1,706; 1,060)	
PA-24-180 Comanche	694 (1,530)	1,157 (2,550)	149 (277; 172)	143 (266; 165)	35 (64; 40)	293 (960)		5,850 (19,200)	A 183 (600) B 302 (990)	A 324 (1,065) B475 (1,560)	A 262 (860) B 326 (1,070)	A 128 (420) B 149 (490)	868 (1,609; 1,000)	
PA-24-250 Comanche	776 (1,710)	1,315 (2,900)	168 (311; 193)	161 (298; 185)	35·5 (66; 41)	427 (1,400)		6,310 (20,700)	A 187 (615) B 290 (950)	A 296 (970) B 389 (1,275)	A 256 (840) B 347 (1,140)	A 140 (460) B 213 (700)	1,537 (2,848; 1,770)	
PA-24-260 Comanche	812 (1,792)	1,451 (3,200)	174 (322; 200)	164 (304; 189)	36 (66; 41)	410 (1,345)		6,355 (20,850)	A 200 (655) B 302 (990)	A 338 (1,110) B 401 (1,315)	A 268 (880) B 360 (1,180)	A 152 (500) B 226 (740)	1,137 (2,108; 1,310)	
PA-24-260 Turbo Comanche	821 (1,810)	1,451 (3,200)	213 (394; 245)	201 (372; 231)	36 (66; 41)	410 (1,345)		7,620 (25,000)	A 200 (655) B 302 (990)	A 338 (1,110) B 401 (1,315)	A 268 (880) B 360 (1,180)	A 152 (500) B 226 (740)	1,306 (2,422; 1,505)	
PA-24-400 Comanche	966 (2,130)	1,633 (3,600)	196 (364; 226)	189 (351; 218)	39 (72; 45)	506 (1,660)		6,155 (20,200)	A 126 (415) B 168 (550)	A 233 (765) B 271 (890)	A 303 (995) B 379 (1,245)	A 184 (605) B 216 (710)	1,568 (2,905; 1,805)	
PA-30 Twin Comanche*	1,022 (2,253)	1,724 (3,800)	158 (293; 182)	153 (283; 176)	45 (84; 52)	427 (1,400)	79 (260)	6,100 (20,000)	B 206 (675)	B 341 (1,120)	B 355 (1,165)	B 186 (610)	1,481 (2,744; 1,705)	69 (129; 80)
PA-30 Turbo Twin Comanche*	1,088 (2,399)	1,724 (3,800)	213 (394; 245)	197 (365; 227)	45 (84; 52)	427 (1,400)	69 (225)	7,620 (25,000)	B 206 (675)	B 341 (1,120)	B 355 (1,165)	B 186 (610)	1,528 (2,832; 1,760)	69 (129; 80)
PA-39 Twin Comanche C/R*	1,022 (2,253)	1,724 (3,800)	181 (336; 209)	174 (322; 200)	45 (84; 52)	445 (1,460)	79 (260)	6,100 (20,000)	B 206 (675)	B 320 (1,050)	B 355 (1,165)	B 186 (610)	1,468 (2,720; 1,690)	65 (121; 75)
PA-39 Turbo Twin Comanche C/R*	1,088 (2,399)	1,724 (3,800)	212 (393; 244)	197 (365; 227)	45 (84; 52)	427 (1,400)	69 (225)	7,620 (25,000)	B 158 (520)	B 323 (1,060)	B 355 (1,165)	B 189 (620)	1,515 (2,808; 1,745)	65 (121; 75)
PA-23-235 Aztec	1,241 (2,735)	2,177 (4,800)	182 (338; 210)	175 (325; 202)	40 (74; 46)	465 (1,525)	62 (205)	5,515 (18,100)	B 210 (690)	B 331 (1,085)	B 381 (1,250)	B 195 (640)	1,090 (2,020; 1,255)	54 (98; 62)
PA-E23-250 Aztec	1,339 (2,953)	2,266 (4,995)	197 (365; 227)	191 (354; 220)	41 (76; 47)	509 (1,670)	99 (325)	6,615 (21,700)	B 190 (625)	B 315 (1,035)	B 395 (1,295)	B 203 (665)	1,112 (2,060; 1,80)	56 (103; 64)
PA-23-250 Aztec	1,326 (2,925)	2,359 (5,200)	188 (348; 216)	179 (332; 206)	45·5 (84; 52)	491 (1,610)	85 (280)	6,035 (19,800)	B 195 (640)	B 323 (1,060)	B 395 (1,295)	B 203 (665)	916 (1,697; 1,055)	56 (105; 65)
PA-23-250 Turbo Aztec	1,397 (3,080)	2,359 (5,200)	222 (412; 256)	182 (388; 210)	43 (79; 49)	372 (1,220)	64 (210)	9,145 (30,000)	B 195 (640)	B 323 (1,060)	B 395 (1,295)	B 203 (665)	1,050 (1,947; 1,210)	56 (105; 65)
PA-34 Seneca I	1,160 (2,557)	1,905 (4,200)	170 (315; 196)	162 (300; 187)	58 (106; 66)	414 (1,360)	57 (190)	5,730 (18,800)	B 195 (640)	B 320 (1,050)	B 381 (1,250)	B 196 (645)	743 (1,378; 856)	57 (106; 65)
PA-34 Seneca II	1,280 (2,823)	2,073 (4,570)	195 (361; 225)	190 (352; 219)	66 (122; 76)	421 (1,380)	67 (220)	7,620 (25,000)	B 198 (650)	B 332 (1,090)	B 573 (1,880)	B 213 (700)	882 (1,633; 1,015)†	57 (106; 65)

A: R/STOL STOL operation. B: R/STOL normal operation.
**With optional long-range tanks fitted, if available. †1,192 (2,207; 1,371) with optional long-range tanks.

SABRELINER

SABRELINER CORPORATION

6161 Aviation Drive, St Louis, Missouri 63134
Telephone: (314) 731 2260
Telex: 44-7227
OTHER WORKS: Perryville Municipal Airport, Missouri; Long Beach, California
CHAIRMAN OF THE BOARD AND CHIEF EXECUTIVE OFFICER: F. Holmes Lamoreux
PRESIDENT AND CHIEF OPERATING OFFICER: Walter C. Herter
VICE-PRESIDENTS:
Mark T. Bond (Operations, Perryville)
Ralph R. Congiu (Finance and Treasurer)
Thomas J. Crowell (Market Development)
Richard D. Denison (Aircraft Sales)
C. Robert Espy (Sales Programmes)
Bob D. Hanks (Engineering)
Paul C. Hans (Strategic Development)
Jerry L. Leath (Administration)
Allen R. McMahan (Technical Projects and Fleet Support)
Kevin L. Marsh (Material and Logistics)
Susan H. Seabury (Secretary)
ASSISTANT SECRETARY: Gail B. Johnson

Sabreliner Corporation was formed in July 1983 as a subsidiary of the New York merchant banking company Wolsey & Co, following the latter's purchase of the Sabreliner Division of Rockwell International Corporation.

The main activities of Sabreliner Corporation are to provide product support for Sabreliner models currently in service, a total of about 600 aircraft. The company also offers a modification programme for Sabreliner Model 40 and Model 60 aircraft which involves the installation of extended life Pratt & Whitney JT12 engines, Collins EFIS displays, interior and exterior refurbishing and zero-timed engines. In early 1985 Sabreliner Corporation was awarded a logistics support contract for US Navy Grumman TC-4C aircraft based at Whidbey Island, Washington; Oceana, Virginia; and Cherry Point, North Carolina.

SABRE SUPER SEARCHER

In September 1986 Sabreliner Corporation and MEL, a division of the Philips Electronics group, announced plans for a low cost maritime reconnaissance, command and control, search and rescue and radar trainer variant of the Sabreliner, to be equipped with MEL's Super Searcher advanced airborne radar system. A former US Navy T-39D is being converted, for March 1987 completion, as a demonstrator for this version.

SABRELINER MODEL 85

In early 1984 Sabreliner Corporation announced plans to develop a new model, the Sabreliner Model 85. It will employ a new supercritical wing design based on that of the Sabreliner 65 and incorporating winglets: a modified Sabreliner 75 fuselage with a 0·91 m (3 ft 0 in) plug forward of the cabin area and a 0·61 m (2 ft 0 in) plug aft of the pressure bulkhead door to extend the cabin area; a wide entrance door with flat threshold; increased vertical fin area and a new cockpit with Collins EFIS display and new curved windscreen design for improved cockpit view. The Sabreliner 85 will have two 20·02 kN (4,500 lb st) Garrett TFE731-5A turbofan engines with thrust reversers, increased fuel capacity, and an auxiliary power unit certificated for in-flight operation.

Preliminary design work was completed in June 1985, when further development was temporarily suspended until plans for joint venture funding could be finalised.

TYPE: Four/ten-passenger twin-turbofan business aircraft.

DIMENSIONS, EXTERNAL:
Wing span (across winglet tips) 17·17 m (56 ft 4 in)
Wing mean aerodynamic chord 2·75 m (9 ft 0½ in)

Wing aspect ratio 7·15
Length overall 16·36 m (53 ft 8¼ in)
Height overall 5·63 m (18 ft 5½ in)
Tailplane span 5·91 m (19 ft 4½ in)
Wheel track 2·59 m (8 ft 6 in)
Cabin door: Height 1·50 m (4 ft 11 in)
Width 0·91 m (3 ft 0 in)

AREAS:
Wings, gross 38·74 m² (417·0 sq ft)
Ailerons, total excl balance area 1·79 m² (19·30 sq ft)
Trailing-edge flaps, total 4·35 m² (46·80 sq ft)
Winglets (total) 0·97 m² (10·40 sq ft)
Vertical tail surfaces, total 4·49 m² (48·35 sq ft)
Rudder, excl balance area 1·04 m² (11·16 sq ft)
Horizontal tail surfaces, total 8·44 m² (90·90 sq ft)
Elevators, total excl balance area 1·67 m² (17·93 sq ft)

WEIGHTS AND LOADINGS:
Basic operating weight empty 7,212 kg (15,900 lb)
Max fuel weight 5,262 kg (11,600 lb)
Max T-O weight 13,517 kg (29,800 lb)
Max landing weight 12,927 kg (28,500 lb)
Max zero-fuel weight 8,573 kg (18,900 lb)
Max wing loading 339·52 kg/m² (69·54 lb/sq ft)
Max power loading 328·52 kg/kN (3·22 lb/lb st)

PERFORMANCE (estimated, with six passengers, VFR reserves, T-O weight of 12,700 kg; 28,000 lb):
Max operating speed Mach 0·83
Max cruising speed 481 knots (891 km/h; 554 mph)
Normal cruising speed 443 knots (821 km/h; 510 mph)
Long-range cruising speed 416 knots (771 km/h; 479 mph)
FAA balanced field length 1,128 m (3,700 ft)
Landing run 701 m (2,300 ft)
Range:
at max cruising speed 2,250 nm (4,170 km; 2,591 miles)
at normal cruising speed 2,930 nm (5,430 km; 3,374 miles)
at long-range cruising speed 3,500 nm (6,486 km; 4,030 miles)

Artist's impression of Sabreliner Model 85 business jet

SCENIC

SCENIC AIRLINES INC

241 E Reno Avenue, Las Vegas, Nevada 89119-1198
Telephone: (702) 739 5611
CHAIRMAN AND CHIEF EXECUTIVE OFFICER: John R. Seibold
VICE-PRESIDENT, ENGINEERING: Richard Thomas
DIRECTOR, MARKETING AND SALES: Rick L. Nord

SCENIC (DE HAVILLAND CANADA) VISTALINER

Scenic Airlines, which operates sightseeing flights in the Grand Canyon, is converting eight of its DHC-6 Twin Otter transports to Vistaliner configuration. This replaces the original cabin windows with new and larger windows, each 61 cm (2 ft) high × 46 cm (1 ft 6 in) wide, and a single 61 cm (2 ft) high × 81 cm (2 ft 8 in) wide panoramic window on each side. Engineering and modification were undertaken by R. W. Martin Inc, of Palomar, California. The supplementary type certificate is held by Scenic Airlines.

Scenic Airlines' 19-passenger Vistaliner conversion of DHC-6 Twin Otter

SCHAFER

SCHAFER AIRCRAFT MODIFICATIONS INC

PO Box 547, Clifton Municipal Airport, Clifton, Texas 76634
Telephone: (817) 675 8333
Telex: 795902 SCHAFER CFTO
PRESIDENT: Earl Schafer
EXECUTIVE VICE-PRESIDENT AND MARKETING: R. B. Stevens

Mr Earl Schafer established this company during 1977. Initially, work was concentrated on the design and manufacture of auxiliary fuel tanks and the embodiment of modifications in Cessna business aircraft of the 300 and 400 series. Since 1979 the company has been working on a range of aircraft modification programmes of its own concept, of which brief details follow:

SCHAFER COMANCHERO

Under this designation, Schafer markets a conversion of the Piper Pressurised Navajo with 559 kW (750 shp) Pratt & Whitney Canada PT6A-135 turboprops, flat rated at 462 kW (620 shp), replacing the standard 317 kW (425 hp) Avco Lycoming TIGO-541-E1A piston engines. This increases the useful load by 345 kg (760 lb) and offers a considerably longer max range. Max fuel capacity is increased to 1,363 litres (360 US gallons). The company received an FAA STC for the Comanchero in January 1981. A dual camera port installation for high altitude aerial photography is available optionally. Seven Pressurised Navajo conversions had been completed by early 1986.

SECA, a subsidiary of Aérospatiale of France, has been appointed sole modification and service centre for Schafer Comanchero modifications for Europe, the Middle East and Africa.

WEIGHTS AND LOADINGS:
Weight empty 2,177 kg (4,800 lb)
Max baggage weight 218 kg (480 lb)
Max T-O weight 3,538 kg (7,800 lb)
Max wing loading 176·9 kg/km² (36·24 lb/sq ft)
Max power loading 4·07 kg/kW (6·7 lb/shp)

PERFORMANCE: As for Pressurised Navajo except:
Max cruising speed at 6,100 m (20,000 ft) 282 knots (522 km/h; 325 mph)
Max rate of climb at S/L 1,067 m (3,500 ft)/min
Rate of climb at S/L, one engine out 250 m (820 ft)/min
Service ceiling more than 11,280 m (37,000 ft)
Service ceiling, one engine out 6,860 m (22,500 ft)
T-O to 15 m (50 ft) 533 m (1,750 ft)
Landing from 15 m (50 ft) 564 m (1,850 ft)
Max range at 8,840 m (29,000 ft), 45 min reserves 1,530 nm (2,835 km; 1,761 miles)

SCHAFER COMANCHERO 500

Under the above designation, Schafer Aircraft completed a prototype conversion of the Piper Chieftain which, basically, replaced the standard piston engines with turboprops of greater power. Design of the conversion originated in mid-1980, and the prototype Comanchero 500 began its flight testing in late August 1981. Schafer Aircraft expected that the most likely market for the conversion would be among commuter operators, and has received many orders for conversions of customer-supplied aircraft, the work taking approximately two months.

In early 1984 Schafer contracted with EMBRAER of

Schafer Commanchero 500 conversion of Piper Chieftain

Brazil for the licence manufacture of 50 Commanchero 500Bs in Brazil, where the aircraft is known as the Neiva NE-821 Carajá. Two modification kits were supplied by Schafer, the remainder are being manufactured locally by Neiva Industria Aeronáutica SA. The first Carajá produced by Neiva, using an EMB-820 airframe, flew for the first time on 9 March 1984. By early 1985 orders had been received for ten Carajás, of which four had been delivered.

Conversion of the Chieftain to **Comanchero 500B** standard involves replacement of its 261 kW (350 hp) Avco Lycoming TIO-540-J2BD piston engines by two 533 ekW (715 ehp) Pratt & Whitney Canada PT6A-27 turboprop engines, each flat rated at 431 ekW (578 ehp). Optionally, customers can select **Commanchero 500A** standard, with lower cost 410 kW (550 shp) PT6A-20s installed, if they do not require the hot day/high altitude performance offered by the flat rated PT6A-27s. In addition to installation of the turboprop engines, the conversion adds a 132 litre (35 US gallon) supplementary fuel tank in each engine nacelle, increase max T-O weight to 3,629 kg (8,000 lb), and includes as standard an inspection of airframe and replacement, if necessary, of such items as control surface and system bearings and bushings, landing gear bushings, and hydraulic components. Options include special interiors, avionics to customers' requirements, a detachable underfuselage cargo pod with capacity of 0·44 m³ (15·5 cu ft), and 341 litre (90 US gallon) supplementary nacelle tanks in lieu of the standard installation. By early 1986 a total of 15 Commanchero 500 conversions had been completed.

PERFORMANCE (A, Comanchero 500A; B, Comanchero 500B):
- Max cruising speed:
  - A, B at 3,660 m (12,000 ft): 240 knots (445 km/h; 276 mph)
- Max rate of climb at S/L: A: 853 m (2,800 ft)/min
  - B: 732 m (2,400 ft)/min
- Rate of climb at S/L, one engine out:
  - A, B: 259 m (850 ft)/min
- Service ceiling: A: 8,840 m (29,000 ft)
- Service ceiling, one engine out:
  - A, B: 4,725 m (15,500 ft)
- T-O to 15 m (50 ft): A: 759 m (2,490 ft)
- Landing from 15 m (50 ft): A: 724 m (2,375 ft)
- Range with pilot and ten passengers, 13·6 kg (30 lb) baggage allowance per passenger, and 45 min reserves, with standard fuel:
  - A, B: 500 nm (926 km; 575 miles)
- Range with pilot and 181 kg (400 lb) payload:
  - B: 1,300 nm (2,410 km; 1,500 miles)

SCHAFER COMANCHERO 750

Under this designation, Schafer Aircraft Modifications gained an STC during May 1981 for a re-engined Piper Cheyenne II. This modification involves replacement of the standard 462 ekW (620 ehp) Pratt & Whitney Canada PT6A-28 turboprops by PT6A-135 turboprops, which are flat rated at 559 kW (750 shp). A dual camera port installation for high altitude aerial photography is available optionally. By early 1986, two Comanchero 750 conversions had been completed.

Schafer performance figures for the Comanchero 750 conversion are as follows:
- Max cruising speed at 7,620 m (25,000 ft): 278 knots (515 km/h; 320 mph)
- Max rate of climb at S/L: 869 m (2,850 ft)/min
- Rate of climb at S/L, one engine out: 198 m (650 ft)/min
- Max range, econ cruising power at 8,840 m (29,000 ft): 1,630 nm (3,020 km; 1,877 miles)

SCHAPEL

SCHAPEL AIRCRAFT COMPANY

PO Box 60039, Reno, Nevada 89506
Telephone: (702) 972 8937
PRESIDENT: Rodney E. Schapel

Details of a variety of aircraft projects by Schapel Aircraft Company have appeared in previous editions of *Jane's*. The company's latest projects are described below.

SCHAPEL SA-882 FLYING WING

The Schapel SA-882 is a proof of concept research aircraft built to investigate the aerodynamics, control and flying characteristics of tail-less configurations for the proposed S-185 lightweight attack aircraft programme. Design was started in January 1984 and construction of a prototype (N882SA) was completed in November 1984, when ground testing began. The first flight was anticipated in April 1985, since when no further information has been received.

TYPE: Single-seat tail-less research aircraft.

WINGS: Cantilever 'flying wing' type, with sweepback. Aerofoil is Schapel designed, varying in thickness from 18% at centreline to 9% at tip. Dihedral 1° 30′, with non-linear washout. Construction is single-piece, moulded from advanced composites materials. Control surfaces on trailing-edges of each wing from approximately mid span to tip, comprising inboard independently-operated drag rudders, elevators in mid section and ailerons outboard, with some elevator/aileron mixing. Rudders are cable operated, elevators and ailerons pushrod operated.

LANDING GEAR: Fixed tricycle type. Oleo-pneumatic struts on main gear legs; coil spring with oil damping on nose leg. Nosewheel castors and is equipped with shimmy dampers. Brakes on mainwheels; differential braking for ground steering.

POWER PLANT: One 134 kW (180 hp) Mazda liquid-cooled two-chamber rotary engine, turbocharged and fuel injected, driving a three-blade epoxy-Kevlar ground adjustable pusher propeller with spinner via 2·04:1 reduction gearing and a 1·02 m (3 ft 4 in) driveshaft. Fuel capacity 216 litres (57 US gallons).

ACCOMMODATION: Single seat for pilot under one-piece bubble canopy.

SYSTEMS: 12V electrical system. Electrically driven vacuum pump for gyro instruments vacuum system.

DIMENSIONS, EXTERNAL:
- Wing span: 10·36 m (34 ft 0 in)
- Wing aspect ratio: 7·23
- Propeller diameter: 1·32 m (4 ft 4 in)

AREA:
- Wings, gross: 14·86 m² (160·0 sq ft)

WEIGHTS:
- Weight empty: 622 kg (1,372 lb)
- Max T-O weight: 900 kg (1,984 lb)

PERFORMANCE (estimated):
- Max level speed:
  - at 6,100 m (20,000 ft): 222 knots (412 km/h; 256 mph)
  - at S/L: 204 knots (378 km/h; 235 mph)
- Cruising speed at 6,100 m (20,000 ft): 167 knots (309 km/h; 192 mph)
- Stalling speed at S/L: 58 knots (108 km/h; 67 mph)
- Max rate of climb at S/L: 459 m (1,505 ft)/min
- T-O to 15 m (50 ft): 428 m (1,405 ft)
- Landing from 15 m (50 ft): 558 m (1,832 ft)
- Max range at cruising speed: 1,137 nm (2,108 km; 1,310 miles)
- Max endurance: 5 h 18 min

SCHAPEL S-185

Designed as a cost-effective, lightweight single-seat attack aircraft, suitable for pilots with minimum training, the Schapel S-185 is a proposed development of the SA-882 research aircraft. The S-185 would be powered by a single Williams International FJ44 turbofan engine, rated at 6·67 kN (1,500 lb st), and would have a retractable tricycle landing gear permitting operation from relatively short unprepared runway surfaces. Construction is basically similar to that of the SA-882.

In early 1985 efforts were under way to develop market interest in the aircraft prior to construction of a prototype.

DIMENSIONS, EXTERNAL:
- Wing span: 8·89 m (29 ft 2 in)
- Wing aspect ratio: 5·71
- Length overall: 4·88 m (16 ft 0 in)
- Height overall: 1·71 m (5 ft 7¼ in)

AREA:
- Wings, gross: 13·84 m² (149·0 sq ft)

WEIGHTS AND LOADINGS (estimated):
- Weight empty: 748 kg (1,650 lb)
- Max T-O weight: 1,905 kg (4,200 lb)
- Max fuel weight: 544 kg (1,200 lb)
- Max external load: 522 kg (1,150 lb)
- Max wing loading: 137·7 kg/m² (28·2 lb/sq ft)
- Max power loading: 285·61 kg/kN (2·80 lb/lb st)

PERFORMANCE (estimated):
- Max level speed: 357 knots (661 km/h; 411 mph)
- Econ cruising speed: 223 knots (413 km/h; 257 mph)
- Stalling speed: 82 knots (152 km/h; 95 mph)
- Max rate of climb at S/L: 987 m (3,239 ft)/min
- Service ceiling: 10,670 m (35,000 ft)
- T-O run to 15 m (50 ft): 610 m (2,001 ft)
- Landing from 15 m (50 ft): 938 m (3,077 ft)
- Max range: 1,220 nm (2,261 km; 1,405 miles)
- Max endurance: 5 h 48 min

Schapel SA-882 Flying Wing tail-less research aircraft

SCHWEIZER

SCHWEIZER AIRCRAFT CORPORATION

164 Airport Road, PO Box 147, Elmira, New York 14902
Telephone: (607) 739 3821
Telex: 932459 Schweizer Bigf

PRESIDENT: W. Stuart Schweizer

VICE-PRESIDENTS:
Paul Hardy Schweizer
Leslie E. Schweizer (Chief Engineer)

DESIGN ENGINEER AND PUBLICATIONS MANAGER:
James E. Daum

SALES MANAGER, AG-CAT: T. C. Kosier

HELICOPTER MARKETING DIRECTOR: Larry A. Brooks

Schweizer Aircraft Corporation was established in 1939 to design and manufacture sailplanes. Its current sailplane products are described in the appropriate section of this edition.

From mid-1957 until 1979 Schweizer also produced the Grumman (later Gulfstream American) Ag-Cat agricultural aircraft under subcontract. In January 1981 it purchased all rights to the Ag-Cat design, and deliveries of Schweizer Super-B Ag-Cats began in October 1981, since supplemented by a new turboprop version. All marketing and support for the Ag-Cat is undertaken from the Elmira facility.

It was announced on 13 July 1983 that Schweizer was to take over, under licence, sole US manufacture of the Hughes Model 300 series light helicopter, which had been in production by Hughes Helicopters since the late 1950s. Schweizer provides product support for Model 300s already in service, including the TH-55A military training version. Production tooling was shipped to Schweizer during the Summer of 1983, and the first Elmira built Model 300 was completed in June 1984.

Schweizer is well known also as an aircraft subcontractor and is engaged currently in work for Beech, Bell Helicopter, Boeing, Sikorsky and other companies. It is engaged in contractual design and prototyping, and in projects to develop heavy lift vehicles, aerial applicators for pheromones, centrifuges, and spatial disorientation trainers.

SCHWEIZER AG-CAT SUPER-B and AG-CAT TURBINE

The prototype of the original Ag-Cat agricultural biplane flew for the first time on 27 May 1957. First deliveries were made in 1959 and 2,455 Ag-Cats (1,730 G-164A, 659 G-164B, 44 G-164C and 22 G-164D) were built by Schweizer under subcontract. Schweizer resumed production in October 1981 with two versions of an improved G-164B known as the Ag-Cat Super-B. It has also developed a turboprop powered version known as the Ag-Cat Super-B Turbine. Details of current models are as follows:

Ag-Cat Super-B/600 (G-164B). This is the basic Schweizer Ag-Cat, with a 447·5 kW (600 hp) Pratt & Whitney R-1340 nine-cylinder radial aircooled engine, driving a Pacific Propeller Type 12D40/AG100 two-blade constant-speed metal propeller. Improvements incorporated in the Super-B include a hopper with 40 per cent greater capacity (1·51 m³; 53·5 cu ft) than that of earlier models, a 0·97 m (3 ft 2 in) wide stainless steel gatebox and bottom loader valve as standard equipment, plus numerous equipment and airframe improvements. In particular, the upper

Schweizer Ag-Cat Super-B/600 agricultural aircraft

wing has been raised 20 cm (8 in) to improve the pilot's view, and increase load carrying capability, operating speed and climb performance.

Ag-Cat 450B (G-164B). This alternative version of the Super-B is generally similar to the basic model, but is powered instead by a 335·5 kW (450 hp) Pratt & Whitney R-985 nine-cylinder radial aircooled engine. Usable fuel capacity is 242 litres (64 US gallons). The 450B has a 1·23 m³ (43·5 cu ft) hopper, capacity 1,230 litres (325 US gallons). It is available only to special order.

Ag-Cat Super B Turbine (G-164B). Generally similar to the basic Ag-Cat Super-B, but powered by a Pratt & Whitney Canada PT6A turboprop engine. Alternative power plants available for this version are the 373 kW (500 shp) PT6A-11AG, 507 kW (680 shp) PT6A-15AG, and 559 kW (750 shp) PT6A-34AG.

The following description applies generally to all three production models, except where indicated:

TYPE: Single-seat agricultural biplane.

WINGS: Single-bay staggered biplane. NACA 4412 (modified) wing section. Dihedral 3°. Incidence 6°. Aluminium alloy (6061-T6) two-spar structure with 6061-T6 skins on entire top surface, around leading-edge and back to front spar on undersurface. Remainder of undersurface fabric covered. Each D leading-edge is made of five separate sections to facilitate replacement if damaged. Glassfibre wingtips. N type interplane struts. Ailerons of light alloy construction, with fabric covering, on all four wings. Ground adjustable tab on port aileron of lower wings. No flaps.

FUSELAGE: Welded 4130 chrome-molybdenum steel tube structure, covered with duralumin sheet. Removable side panels. 40*g* cockpit.

TAIL UNIT: Welded 4130 chrome-molybdenum steel tube structure, covered with fabric and wire braced. Cable deflector wire from tip of fin to top of cockpit canopy. Controllable trim tab in port elevator. Ground adjustable tabs on rudder and starboard elevator.

LANDING GEAR: Non-retractable tailwheel type. Cantilever spring steel legs. Cleveland wheels with tyres size 8·50-10 6-ply, pressure 2·42 bars (35 lb/sq in). Steerable tailwheel with tyre size 12·4-4·5, pressure 3·45 bars (50 lb/sq in). Cleveland heavy duty aircooled hydraulic disc brakes. Parking brake.

POWER PLANT: One Pratt & Whitney nine-cylinder aircooled radial engine with Pacific Propeller constant-speed propeller, or Pratt & Whitney Canada PT6A turboprop engine, as detailed in model listings. Fuel tanks in upper wing with combined usable capacity of 302 litres (80 US gallons). Single-point refuelling on upper surface of upper wing centre-section. Oil capacity 32·2 litres (8·5 US gallons).

ACCOMMODATION: Single seat in enclosed cockpit. Reinforced fairing aft of canopy for turnover protection. Canopy side panels open outward and down, canopy top upward and to starboard, to provide access. Baggage compartment. Cockpit pressurised against dust ingress and ventilated by ram air. Safety padded instrument panel. Air-conditioning by J.B. Systems optional.

SYSTEMS: Hydraulic system for brakes only. Optional electrical system with 24V alternator, navigation lights and/or strobe lights, external power socket, and electric engine starter.

EQUIPMENT: Radio optional. Standard equipment includes control column lock, instrument glareshield, seat belt and shoulder harness, tinted windscreen, stall warning light, refuelling steps and assist handles, tiedown rings, and urethane paint external yellow finish.

AGRICULTURAL EQUIPMENT: Forward of cockpit, over CG, is a 1·51 m³ (53·5 cu ft) glassfibre hopper, capacity 1,514 litres (400 US gallons), for agricultural chemicals (dry or liquid) with distributor beneath fuselage. Low-volume, ULV or high-volume spray system, with leading- or trailing-edge booms. Emergency dump system for hopper load; can be used also for water bomber operations.

DIMENSIONS EXTERNAL (A: Super-B/600; B: Super-B Turbine G-164B; C: 450B):

Wing span	12·93 m (42 ft 5 in)
Wing chord (constant)	1·47 m (4 ft 10 in)
Wing aspect ratio: upper wing	8·74
biplane, effective mean	5·46
Length overall: A	7·47 m (24 ft 6 in)
B	8·38 m (27 ft 6 in)
C	7·37 m (24 ft 2 in)
Height overall: A, C	3·51 m (11 ft 6 in)
B	3·68 m (12 ft 1 in)
Tailplane span	3·96 m (13 ft 0 in)
Wheel track	2·44 m (8 ft 0 in)
Wheelbase	5·59 m (18 ft 4 in)
Propeller diameter (max)	2·74 m (9 ft 0 in)
Propeller ground clearance	0·27 m (10·8 in)

AREAS:

Wings, gross	36·42 m² (392 sq ft)
Ailerons (total)	2·93 m² (31·5 sq ft)
Fin	1·67 m² (17·97 sq ft)
Rudder	1·12 m² (12·0 sq ft)
Tailplane	2·12 m² (22·8 sq ft)
Elevators	2·06 m² (22·2 sq ft)

WEIGHTS AND LOADINGS:

Weight empty equipped, spray and duster versions:	
A	1,656 kg (3,650 lb)
B	1,429 kg (3,150 lb)
C	1,508 kg (3,325 lb)
Certificated AUW	2,358 kg (5,200 lb)
Max T-O weight (CAM.8)	3,184 kg (7,020 lb)
Max wing loading	87·42 kg/m² (17·91 lb/sq ft)
Max power loading: A	7·12 kg/kW (11·71 lb/hp)
B	5·70-8·54 kg/kW (9·36-14·04 lb/shp)
C	9·49 kg/kW (15·6 lb/hp)

PERFORMANCE (A: Super-B/600; B: Super-B Turbine G-164B with PT6A-15AG engine; C: 450B):

Working speed: A, C	100 knots (185 km/h; 115 mph)
B	113 knots (209 km/h; 130 mph)
T-O to 15 m (50 ft) at 2,358 kg (5,200 lb) certificated AUW: A	320 m (1,050 ft)
B	274 m (900 ft)
C	396 m (1,300 ft)
Design *g* loadings, all versions	+4·2/−1

SCHWEIZER (HUGHES) MODEL 300C

The early history of this helicopter can be found under the Hughes Helicopters entry in previous editions of *Jane's*, and a detailed description of the basic Model 300 was published in the 1976-77 edition. By July 1983, when Hughes announced transfer of production to Schweizer, it had built more than 2,800 of all versions, including the TH-55A Osage for the US Army.

The current Model 300C is a developed version, with improvements to allow a 45 per cent increase in payload. The prototype made its first flight in August 1969, followed by the first Hughes production model in December 1969. FAA certification was received in May 1970. The first Model 300C from Schweizer production flew in June 1984 and was delivered to the Baltimore Police on 29 June. In late 1985 the US Army awarded Schweizer a $4·9 million contract for the supply of 30 Model 300Cs and spare parts. Delivery of 24 TH-300C training versions to the Royal Thai Army began in March 1986 and was scheduled for completion in November. The Model 300C is manufactured also in Italy, by BredaNardi (which see).

The specially equipped 300C available for police patrol has as standard equipment safety mesh seats with inertia reel shoulder harness, ballistic glassfibre armour beneath each seat, a high power public address/siren system, a high intensity controllable searchlight system, an integrated communications system based on the King KY 195 VHF transceiver, a heavy duty 28V 100A electrical system, cabin heater, night lights with strobe beacons, cabin utility light, external power socket, fire extinguisher, first aid kit and mapcase.

TYPE: Three-seat light utility helicopter.

ROTOR SYSTEM: Fully articulated metal three-blade main rotor. Fully interchangeable blades of bonded construction, with constant section extruded aluminium spar, wraparound skin and a trailing-edge section. Blade section NACA 0015. Tracking tabs on blades at three-quarters radius. Elastomeric dampers. Electric cyclic trim. Two-blade teetering tail rotor, each blade comprising a steel tube spar with glassfibre skin. Limited blade folding. No rotor brake.

ROTOR DRIVE: Combination V-belt/pulley and reduction gear drive system. Main rotor and tail rotor gearbox have spiral bevel right-angle drive. Main rotor/engine rpm ratio 1 : 6·8. Tail rotor/engine rpm ratio 1·97 : 1·03.

FUSELAGE: Welded steel tube centre structure, with light alloy, stainless steel and Plexiglas cabin and one-piece light alloy tube tailboom.

TAIL UNIT: Horizontal and vertical fixed stabilising surfaces, made of light alloy ribs and skins.

LANDING GEAR: Skids carried on oleo-pneumatic shock absorbers. Replaceable skid shoes. Two cast magnesium ground handling wheels with 0·25 m (10 in) balloon tyres, pressure 4·14-5·17 bars (60-75 lb/sq in). Available optionally on floats made of polyurethane coated nylon fabric, 4·70 m (15 ft 5 in) long and with a total installed weight of 27·2 kg (60 lb).

POWER PLANT: One 168 kW (225 hp) Avco Lycoming HIO-360-D1A flat-four engine, derated to 142 kW (190 hp), mounted horizontally below seats. Aluminium fuel tank, capacity 103·5 litres (30 US gallons) mounted externally aft of cockpit. Crash resistant fuel tank optional. Provision for aluminium auxiliary fuel tank, capacity 72 litres (19 US gallons), mounted opposite standard tank. Oil capacity 9·5 litres (2·5 US gallons).

ACCOMMODATION: Three persons side by side on sculptured and cushioned bench seat, with shoulder harness, in Plexiglas enclosed cabin. Carpet and tinted canopy standard. Forward hinged, removable door on each side. Dual controls optional. Baggage capacity 45 kg (100 lb). Exhaust muff, or gasoline, heating and ventilation kits available.

SYSTEMS: Standard electrical system includes 24V 70A alternator, 24V battery, starter and external power socket.

Schweizer Model 300C helicopter

AVIONICS AND EQUIPMENT: Optional avionics include Collins VHF-253 or King KY-196 com transceiver and headsets, and ADF650A or KR-86 ADFs, TDR 950 or KT-76A transponders. Standard equipment includes mapcase, first aid kit, fire extinguisher, engine hour meter, and main rotor blade tiedown kit. Optional equipment includes amphibious floats, litter kits, cargo racks with combined capacity of 91 kg (200 lb), external load sling of 408 kg (900 lb) capacity, Simplex Model 5200 agricultural spray or dry powder dispersal kits, Sky Night law enforcement package; instrument training package; throttle governor; 72 litre (19 US gallon) auxiliary fuel tank, night flying kit, dual controls, all-weather cover, heavy duty skid plates, single or dual exhaust mufflers, door lock, dual oil coolers, tinted glass for cabin windows, gasoline or exhaust manifold cabin heating.

DIMENSIONS, EXTERNAL:
Main rotor diameter 8·18 m (26 ft 10 in)
Main rotor blade chord 0·171 m (6¾ in)
Tail rotor diameter 1·30 m (4 ft 3 in)
Distance between rotor centres 4·66 m (15 ft 3½ in)
Length overall, rotor blades fore and aft 9·40 m (30 ft 10 in)
Height over rotor head 2·66 m (8 ft 8⅝ in)
Width, rotor partially folded 2·44 m (8 ft 0 in)
Height to top of cabin 2·19 m (7 ft 2 in)
Cabin width 1·30 m (4 ft 3 in)
Skid track 1·99 m (6 ft 6½ in)
Length of skids 2·51 m (8 ft 3 in)
Passenger doors (each): Height 1·09 m (3 ft 7 in)
Width 0·97 m (3 ft 2 in)
Height to sill 0·91 m (3 ft 0 in)

AREAS:
Main rotor blades (each) 0·70 m² (7·55 sq ft)
Tail rotor blades (each) 0·08 m² (0·86 sq ft)
Main rotor disc 52·5 m² (565·5 sq ft)
Tail rotor disc 1·32 m² (14·2 sq ft)
Fin 0·23 m² (2·5 sq ft)
Horizontal stabiliser 0·246 m² (2·65 sq ft)

WEIGHTS AND LOADING:
Weight empty 474 kg (1,046 lb)
Max T-O weight: Normal category 930 kg (2,050 lb)
external load 975 kg (2,150 lb)
Max disc loading 17·67 kg/m² (3·62 lb/sq ft)

PERFORMANCE (at max Normal T-O weight, ISA):
Never-exceed speed at S/L 91 knots (169 km/h; 105 mph)
Max cruising speed 82 knots (153 km/h; 95 mph)
Speed for max range, at 1,220 m (4,000 ft) 67 knots (124 km/h; 77 mph)
Max rate of climb at S/L 229 m (750 ft)/min
Service ceiling 3,110 m (10,200 ft)
Hovering ceiling: IGE 1,800 m (5,900 ft)
OGE 840 m (2,750 ft)
Range at 1,220 m (4,000 ft), 2 min warm-up, max fuel, no reserves 194 nm (360 km; 224 miles)
Max endurance at S/L 3 h 24 min

SCI

SCALED COMPOSITES INC (Subsidiary of Beech Aircraft Corporation)

Hangar 78, Mojave Airport, Mojave, California 93501
Telephone: (805) 824 4541

PRESIDENT: Elbert L. Rutan
VICE-PRESIDENT AND GENERAL MANAGER:
Herbert A. Iversen

Scaled Composites Inc was acquired by Beech Aircraft Corporation in June 1985, for operation as a wholly owned subsidiary. It had been established by Mr 'Burt' Rutan who continues as President of SCI, to provide an independent research and development organisation that could hire its services to individuals or companies requiring assistance with advanced aeronautical concepts. Aircraft to which it contributed were the NASA AD-1 oblique-wing research aircraft, for which detail design was carried out by Mr Rutan (see 1981-82 *Jane's*); the Fairchild/Ames 62% scale NGT, for which Mr Rutan completed the detail scaling from Fairchild's NGT lofting drawings (see 1982-83 *Jane's*); the M115-6·85 SCAT 1 85% scale demonstrator of the Beech Model 2000 Starship 1 (see Beech Aircraft Corporation in this section); a prototype canard microlight aircraft of composites construction for Lotus in Great Britain (see Sport Aircraft section); and the Model 120-9E proof-of-concept Predator 480 agricultural aircraft described under the ATAC entry in the 1985-86 *Jane's*.

SCI's 2,787 m² (30,000 sq ft) facility at Mojave Airport, which is literally next door to Rutan Aircraft Factory, is well equipped for the construction of one or two prototypes of a particular design concept, and facilities include a large hangar, instrumentation and flight test departments, plus a small machine shop. Future programmes are expected to involve commercial and military projects of a proprietary or classified nature. In early 1986 a new 1,858 m² (20,000 sq ft) composites fabrication facility was being added to the existing plant.

Work in progress in early 1986 included the construction of a composites structure proof of concept test vehicle for a proposed Beechcraft cabin class twin-piston engined pusher business aircraft, and a proposed pressurised single-engined Beechcraft based on the earlier Rutan Design No. 81 (see Beech Aircraft entry in this section).

SEAPLANES INC — *see Turbotech*

SIKORSKY

SIKORSKY AIRCRAFT, DIVISION OF UNITED TECHNOLOGIES CORPORATION

North Main Street, Stratford, Connecticut 06601
Telephone: (203) 386 4000
Telex: 96 4372

OTHER WORKS: Fort Rucker, Alabama; Tallassee, Alabama; Troy, Alabama; South Avenue, Bridgeport, Connecticut; Shelton, Connecticut; Sikorsky Memorial Airport, Stratford, Connecticut; and Development Flight Test Center, West Palm Beach, Florida

PRESIDENT AND CHIEF EXECUTIVE OFFICER: Robert Zincone
EXECUTIVE VICE-PRESIDENT: Eugene Buckley
SENIOR VICE-PRESIDENT:
Ray D. Leoni (Engineering and Advanced Programmes)
VICE-PRESIDENTS:
Robert H. Barlow (H-60 Navy Product Line)
J. Colin Green (Planning and Services)
R. Clark Harris (International Business Development and Strategic Business Planning)
H. Stephen Harvey (Finance)
Joseph M. Hayes (Contracts and Counsel)
Regina M. Hitchery (Human Resources)
Columbus O. Iselin (Europe and Mideast)
John A. Kerns (International Business)
John T. Lewis (Overhaul/Repair and Spares)
Kenneth C. Mard (Worldwide Customer Service)
William E. McClure (Electronic Systems Integration)
William Minter (H-60 Army and Air Force Product Lines)
Robert R. Moore (Materiel)
Mackie D. Mott (Commercial Marketing)
Allan K. Poole Jr (Government Product Support)
Gary F. Rast (Government Business Development)
James J. Satterwhite (Aircraft Engineering)
Albert J. Schwabenbauer (Manufacturing)
Edwin Simon (Communications)
Edmond R. Vianney (Product Integrity)
DIRECTOR OF COMMUNICATIONS: Robert Stangarone
MANAGER OF PUBLIC RELATIONS: Martin H. Moore
MEDIA RELATIONS MANAGER, MILITARY PROGRAMMES:
Fred C. Lash

Founded on 5 March 1923 by the late Igor I. Sikorsky as the Sikorsky Aero Engineering Corporation, this company has been a division of United Technologies since 1929. It became involved in helicopter production in the 1940s, since which time it has produced more than 6,000 rotating-wing aircraft.

Sikorsky's company headquarters and main plant are at Stratford, Connecticut, with a secondary facility nearby at Bridgeport. Development flight test, commercial service and training centres are at West Palm Beach, Florida, where UTC subsidiary Pratt & Whitney has its military engine operation. Sikorsky's laboratories, test stands and data processing facilities are located at Stratford. Employment at all Sikorsky facilities totalled more than 14,000 in 1984, making the company the largest helicopter manufacturer outside the Soviet Union. In 1984 its sales exceeded $1,500 million for the first time.

Current production is centred on the UH-60A Black Hawk and its derivatives, the CH-53E Super Stallion heavy lift helicopter and its derivatives, and the S-76 series. The company's main research programmes concern the XH-59A Advancing Blade Concept (ABC) helicopter; the US Army's Advanced Composite Airframe Program (ACAP) to develop, build and evaluate a helicopter fuselage made entirely of composite materials; the US Army's Advanced Rotorcraft Technology Integration (ARTI) programme; and the DARPA/NASA X-Wing Rotor Systems Research Aircraft (RSRA) programme.

On 3 June 1983 Sikorsky signed a memorandum of understanding to bid jointly for development of the US Army's LHX helicopter.

Sikorsky licensees include Westland of Great Britain, Agusta of Italy, Aérospatiale of France, MBB in West Germany, Mitsubishi of Japan, and Pratt & Whitney Canada Ltd. In the Summer of 1983 Sikorsky and Brazilian manufacturer EMBRAER signed an agreement for the transfer of technology involved in the design and manufacture of components made from composites materials, which could lead to joint development of a new generation helicopter by the two companies within the next five years. In June 1984 Sikorsky and Construcciones Aeronauticas SA (CASA) signed a memorandum of understanding to establish a long term helicopter industrial co-operation programme in Spain. CASA builds tail rotor pylon, tailcone and stabiliser components for the H-60 and S-70 helicopters, and will also have responsibility for final assembly and test flying of helicopters supplied to Spain, which has ordered six S-70Bs for delivery in 1987-88. The first CASA manufactured S-70 components were delivered to Sikorsky in early January 1986. A similar memorandum of agreement was signed between Sikorsky and Short Brothers of Belfast, Northern Ireland, in September 1984. Under this, Shorts was able to enter a special version of the S-70A Black Hawk to meet the AST 404 requirement of the UK Ministry of Defence, as a first step in establishing a joint industrial co-operation programme in the UK.

In September 1984 the Sikorsky S-70B was selected by the Royal Australian Navy as winner of its Role-Adaptable Weapons System competition. Earlier, Sikorsky had signed a number of contracts with Australian manufacturers for helicopter components. In July 1985 the Australian Department of Defence awarded Sikorsky a $158·8 million contract for initial production of eight RAWS S-70Bs for the

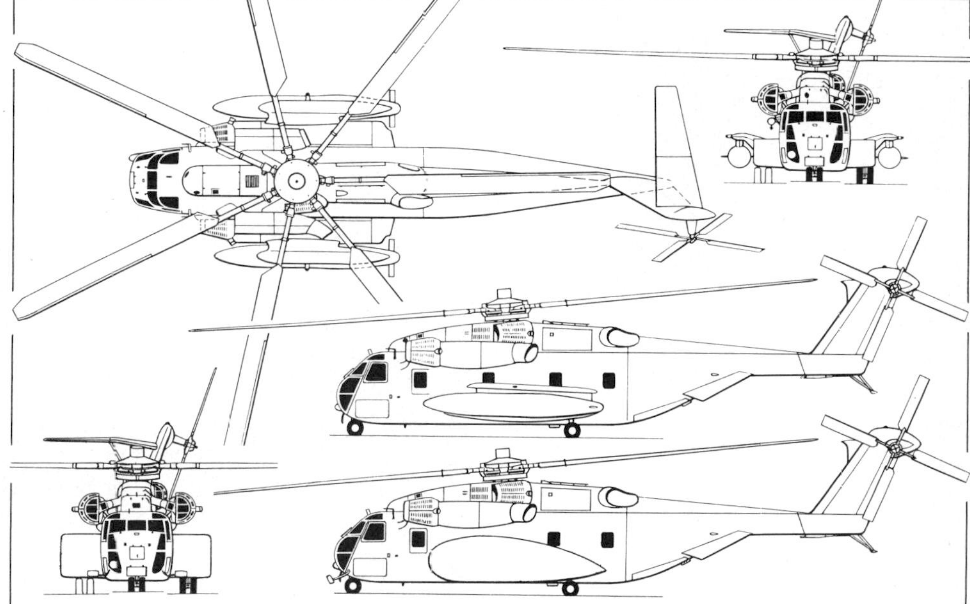

Sikorsky CH-53E Super Stallion, with lower side view and lower front view of MH-53E Sea Dragon *(Pilot Press)*. **See page 516 for details of S-80 export versions**

Royal Australian Navy and in May 1986 an order was placed for 14 S-70As for the Royal Australian Air Force and an additional eight RAWS S-70Bs for the RAN. In 1984, Sikorsky had received contracts from the Cessna Aircraft Company and Rinaldo Piaggio SpA for the manufacture of composites components, and won a US Army contract for helicopter maintenance at Fort Rucker, Alabama. A subsidiary, Sikorsky Support Services Inc, will perform this work.

On 12 February 1986 shareholders of Westland PLC (see United Kingdom section) approved a joint Sikorsky/Fiat plan involving financial and technical support and minor equity participation in the British company. Under the terms of the agreement Westland will be licensed to manufacture the S-70 series of helicopters.

SIKORSKY S-61/SH-3 SEA KING

Manufacture of the S-61 series by Sikorsky has ended, but various military and commercial models remain in production by Agusta in Italy, Mitsubishi in Japan, and Westland in the UK, under whose entries they are described or listed.

SIKORSKY H-53

US Navy designations: CH-53E Super Stallion and MH-53E Sea Dragon

The CH-53E Super Stallion is a major development of the US Marine Corps' CH-53D Stallion twin-engined heavy duty transport helicopter, last described in the 1978-79 *Jane's*. The longer fuselage of the CH-53E, its different rotor system, three engines, uprated transmission and doubled lift capability make it the largest and most powerful helicopter yet put into production outside the Soviet Union.

Sikorsky MH-53E Sea Dragon airborne mine countermeasures helicopter towing a magnetic-influence minesweeping hydrofoil vehicle

Research and development of a growth version of the CH-53 began in 1971. Two years later, Sikorsky received US Navy funding to proceed with Phase I of the CH-53E development programme, which provided for the construction of two prototypes, flight testing and preliminary evaluation. The first prototype YCH-53E flew for the first time on 1 March 1974. Although it was lost in an accident, performance data satisfied the Navy and Phase II, the engineering development programme, began in May 1975. The first production prototype flew on 8 December 1975, and the second in March 1976. In 1978, a total of 20 CH-53Es was approved for production, and the first delivery to the US Marine Corps took place on 16 June 1981. By the beginning of 1985, Sikorsky had firm contracts for 93 CH-53Es, and requirements are expected to exceed 300 aircraft into the next century. The production rate in mid-1984 was two aircraft a month, and 94 CH-53Es had been delivered to the US Marine Corps and Navy by March 1986. A multi-year procurement contract provides for delivery of 4 CH-53Es in FY 1986, 10 in FY 1987, 6 in FY 1988, and 7 in FY 1989. The first European based Super Stallion squadron was formed at Sigonella, Sicily, in the Summer of 1983.

The US Marine Corps operates the CH-53E in an amphibious assault role, carrying up to 55 fully armed troops, for transport of heavy equipment and armament, and for retrieval of disabled aircraft. The US Navy uses it for vertical onboard delivery (VOD), transport duties, and removal of damaged aircraft from aircraft carriers. Operational use, in the Mediterranean area, began in Summer 1983. By April 1986 the US Navy and US Marine Corps fleet of CH-53Es had completed more than 63,000 flight hours.

Future developments planned by Sikorsky for the CH-53E include an all-composites rotor head with new main rotor blades in which the titanium spar will be replaced with carbonfibre. The new blades will have tips incorporating 35° sweep and 16° anhedral. The in-flight blade inspection system will be eliminated. Sikorsky claims a four per cent increase in hover performance with the new blade tips, equating to a 1,361 kg (3,000 lb) increase in useful load for the CH-53E. Other planned improvements include all-composites tail rotor blades, which are now flying on the MH-53E, electric main blade folding, uprated General Electric T64-418 power plants, Omega navigation system, ground proximity warning system, flight crew night vision system, and improvements to the internal cargo handling system. Exhaust infra-red suppressors, missile alerting system, chaff/flare decoy ejectors, a nitrogen fuel inerting system and the ability to refill the hydraulic system from the cargo hold will also be incorporated. The modified CH-53Es might also be equipped with air-to-air missiles for self defence. Initial firing trials with an AIM-9 Sidewinder missile have been conducted at the Naval Air Test Center, NAS Patuxent River, Maryland.

In 1982, Sikorsky received $39 million to develop the **MH-53E Sea Dragon**, an airborne mine countermeasures (AMCM) version of the Super Stallion. The early history of this helicopter was described in detail in the 1982-83 *Jane's*. It has enlarged sponsons to carry nearly 3,785 litres (1,000 US gallons) more fuel, improved hydraulic and electrical systems, and minefield, navigational and AFC systems, including automatic tow couplers and automatic approach to/depart from hover features to enhance its AMCM capabilities. During 1982 a prototype, converted from one of the production prototype CH-53Es, completed a test programme, including a 20 h flight. The first pre-production MH-53E made its initial flight on 1 September 1983. In the Spring of 1986 the MH-53E was undergoing operational evaluation trials with US Navy squadron MH-12 at NAS Norfolk, Virginia and had completed some 100 flight hours with the unit, including the towing of all AMCM equipment and aerial refuelling trials. The first of more than 57 required by the US Navy was delivered on 26 June 1986. A multi-year procurement contract provides for delivery of 10 MH-53Es in FY 1986, 4 in FY 1987, 8 in FY 1988, and 7 in FY 1989. In addition, Japan authorised funding for two MH-53E type minesweeping helicopters in 1986. Empty weight of the MH-53E is 16,482 kg (36,336 lb).

The following details refer to the CH-53E, but are generally applicable also to the MH-53E, except for the changes listed in the previous paragraph:

TYPE: Triple-turbine heavy duty multi-purpose helicopter.

ROTOR SYSTEM AND TRANSMISSION: Fully articulated seven-blade main rotor. Blade twist 14°. Each blade has a

Sikorsky CH-53E Super Stallion heavy-lift helicopter of the US Marine Corps with flight refuelling nose-probe retracted

titanium spar, Nomex honeycomb core and glassfibre epoxy composite skin. Sikorsky blade inspection method (BIM) embodied, utilising pressurised spar. Titanium and steel main rotor head. Hydraulic power folding system for main rotor blades. Four-blade aluminium tail rotor mounted on pylon canted 20° to port. Main gearbox is mounted in blister above main cabin and is rated at 10,067 kW (13,500 shp) for T-O. Rotor brake standard.

FUSELAGE: Watertight semi-monocoque primary structure of light alloy, steel and titanium. Separate cockpit section of glassfibre/epoxy composite. Extensive use of Kevlar for rotor/transmission blister and engine cowlings. Tail rotor pylon folds hydraulically to starboard side. Fuselage stressed to withstand crash force of 20*g* vertically and 10*g* laterally.

TAIL SURFACE: Strut braced stabiliser of gull-wing type on starboard side of inclined tail rotor pylon. Stabiliser and pylon made of Kevlar.

LANDING GEAR: Retractable tricycle type, with twin wheels on each unit. Main units retract into rear of sponsons on each side of fuselage. Fully castoring nosewheels.

POWER PLANT: Three General Electric T64-GE-416 turboshaft engines, each with a max rating of 3,266 kW (4,380 shp) for 10 min, intermediate rating of 3,091 kW (4,145 shp) for 30 min and max continuous power rating of 2,756 kW (3,696 shp). Self-sealing bladder fuel cell in forward part of each sponson, each with capacity of 1,192 litres (315 US gallons). Additional two-cell unit, with capacity of 1,465 litres (387 US gallons) brings total standard internal capacity to 3,849 litres (1,017 US gallons). (Total internal capacity of MH-53E is 12,113 litres; 3,200 US gallons.) Optional drop tank outboard of each sponson, total capacity 4,921 litres (1,300 US gallons). Forward extendable probe for in-flight refuelling. Alternatively, aircraft can refuel by hoisting hose from surface vessel while hovering.

ACCOMMODATION: Crew of three. Main cabin will accommodate up to 55 troops on folding canvas seats along walls and in centre of cabin. Door on forward starboard side of main cabin. Hydraulically operated rear loading ramp. Typical freight loads include seven standard 102 × 122 cm (3 ft 4 in × 4 ft) pallets. Single-point central hook for slung cargo, capacity 16,330 kg (36,000 lb).

SYSTEMS: Hydraulic system, with four pumps, for collective, cyclic pitch, roll, yaw and feel augmentation flight control servo mechanisms; engine starters; landing gear actuation; cargo winches; loading ramp; and blade and tail pylon folding. System pressure 207 bars (3,000 lb/sq in), except for engine starter system which is rated at 276 bars (4,000 lb/sq in). (Separate hydraulic system in MH-53E to power AMCM equipment.) Electrical system includes three 115V 400Hz 40-60kVA AC alternators, and two 28V 200A transformer-rectifiers for DC power. Solar APU.

AVIONICS: Hamilton Standard automatic flight control system, using two digital onboard computers and a four-axis autopilot.

DIMENSIONS, EXTERNAL:

Main rotor diameter	24·08 m (79 ft 0 in)
Main rotor blade chord	0·76 m (2 ft 6 in)
Tail rotor diameter	6·10 m (20 ft 0 in)
Length overall, rotors turning	30·19 m (99 ft 0½ in)
Length, rotor and tail pylon folded	18·44 m (60 ft 6 in)
Length of fuselage	22·35 m (73 ft 4 in)
Width of fuselage	2·69 m (8 ft 10 in)
Width, rotor and tail pylon folded	8·66 m (28 ft 5 in)
Height to top of main rotor head	5·32 m (17 ft 5½ in)
Height overall, tail rotor turning	8·66 m (28 ft 5 in)
Height, rotor and tail pylon folded	5·66 m (18 ft 7 in)
Wheel track (c/l of shock struts)	3·96 m (13 ft 0 in)
Wheelbase	8·31 m (27 ft 3 in)

DIMENSIONS, INTERNAL:

Cabin:	
Length (rear ramp/door hinge to fwd bulkhead)	9·14 m (30 ft 0 in)
Max width	2·29 m (7 ft 6 in)
Max height	1·98 m (6 ft 6 in)

AREAS:

Main rotor disc	455·38 m² (4,901·7 sq ft)
Tail rotor disc	29·19 m² (314·2 sq ft)

WEIGHTS:

Weight empty	15,071 kg (33,226 lb)
Internal payload (100 nm; 185 km; 115 miles radius)	13,607 kg (30,000 lb)
External payload (50 nm; 92·5 km; 57·5 miles radius)	14,515 kg (32,000 lb)
Max external payload	16,330 kg (36,000 lb)
Max T-O weight:	
internal payload	31,640 kg (69,750 lb)
external payload	33,340 kg (73,500 lb)

PERFORMANCE (ISA, at T-O weight of 25,400 kg; 56,000 lb):

Max level speed at S/L	170 knots (315 km/h; 196 mph)
Cruising speed at S/L	150 knots (278 km/h; 173 mph)
Max rate of climb at S/L	762 m (2,500 ft)/min
Service ceiling at max continuous power	5,640 m (18,500 ft)
Hovering ceiling at max power:	
IGE	3,520 m (11,550 ft)
OGE	2,895 m (9,500 ft)
Self-ferry range, unrefuelled, at optimum cruise condition for best range	1,120 nm (2,075 km; 1,290 miles)

SIKORSKY S-70

US Army designations: UH-60A and EH-60A Black Hawk
US Air Force designation: HH-60 Night Hawk
US Marine Corps designation: VH-60A

A detailed account of the development and early history of the S-70/UH-60A can be found in the 1982-83 and earlier editions of *Jane's*. The helicopter was designed to meet the US Army's Utility Tactical Transport Aircraft System (UTTAS) requirement for an aircraft capable of carrying all the elements of an 11-man infantry squad, to replace the UH-1 Iroquois. The first of three Sikorsky YUH-60A prototypes flew for the first time on 17 October 1974. After fly-off evaluation against prototypes of a Boeing Vertol competitor, the Sikorsky design was declared the winner on 23 December 1976, and was named Black Hawk.

Although designed primarily to carry 11 fully equipped troops plus a crew of three, the **UH-60A** has a large cabin which enables it to be used without modification for medical evacuation, reconnaissance, command and control purposes or troop resupply. For external lift missions its cargo hook has a capacity of up to 3,630 kg (8,000 lb). Design is compact, so that the helicopter itself can be airlifted over long ranges. One can be carried in a C-130 Hercules, two in a C-141 StarLifter and six in a C-5 Galaxy, using Sikorsky developed air transportability kits.

The initial US Army contract covered production of 15 UH-60As, with a fixed price option for 368 additional aircraft over a three-year period. By the end of 1981 the total number funded was 342. Then, in April 1982, the Army awarded Sikorsky a contract covering purchase of 294 Black Hawks in a three-year period at a cost of $950 million. Deliveries by the end of FY 1984 were thus scheduled to total 636, and follow-on contracts are expected to take the UH-60A production total to 1,107, with a possible increase to 1,715 by the 1990s. The first production UH-60A flew in October 1978. By 31 January 1986 a total of more than 700 UH-60As and EH-60As had been delivered to the US Army. whose fleet had then accumulated over 385,000 flight hours.

In October 1984 Sikorsky received a second multi-year contract covering FYs 1985-87 for 288 more UH-60As (later raised to 294), bringing the total contracted to 930. By the end of February 1985 UH-60A deliveries totalled 624. The helicopter is deployed with the 101st Airborne Division (Air Assault) at Fort Campbell, Kentucky; 82nd Airborne Division at Fort Bragg, North Carolina; Ninth Infantry Division at Fort Lewis, Washington; 24th Infantry Division at Fort Stewart, Georgia, and with US Army forces in Hawaii, Korea, Panama and West Germany.

The US Air Force also has 11 UH-60As, of which ten were delivered to the 55th Aerospace Rescue and Recovery Squadron at Eglin AFB, Florida, in 1982-83 as an interim remedy for a shortfall in rescue helicopters. Under a programme entitled Credible Hawk the USAF has contracted Sikorsky to modify these UH-60As to incorporate an aerial refuelling probe, auxiliary fuel tank and a fuel management panel. The other is being used for prototype development of the HH-60A Night Hawk (which see).

Sikorsky received an $11·4 million contract in February 1981 for a 24 month programme to develop an external stores support system (ESSS) for the UH-60A. This system consists of a combination of fixed provisions built into the airframe and four removable external pylons from which fuel tanks and a variety of weapons can be suspended. Able to carry more than 2,268 kg (5,000 lb) on each side of the helicopter, the ESSS can accommodate two 870 litre (230

Sikorsky UH-60A Black Hawk with 16 Hellfire missiles on ESSS pylons

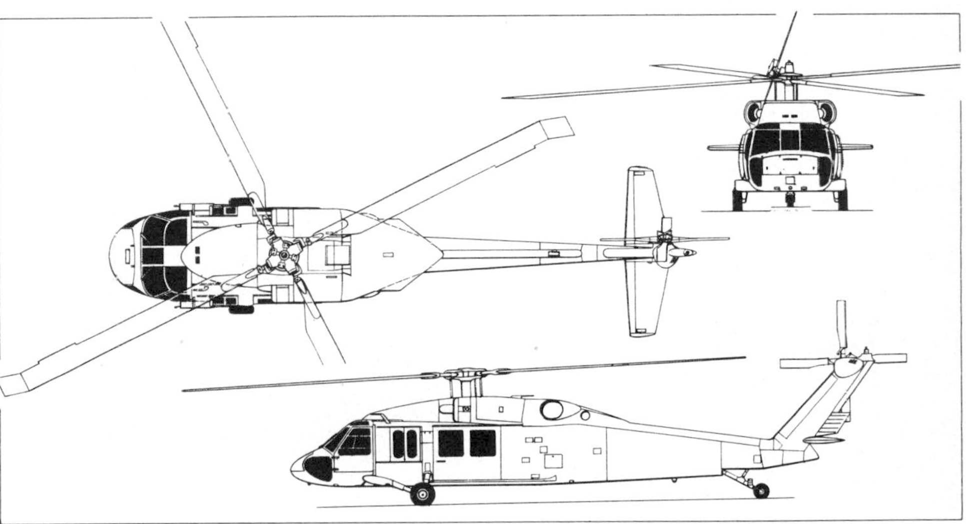

Sikorsky UH-60A Black Hawk combat assault helicopter *(Pilot Press)*

US gallon) fuel tanks outboard, and two 1,703 litre (450 US gallon) tanks inboard. This allows the UH-60A to self deploy 1,200 nm (2,220 km; 1,380 miles) without refuelling. The ESSS also enables the Black Hawk to perform additional roles by carrying Hellfire anti-armour missiles, gun or M56 mine dispensing pods, ECM packs, rockets and motorcycles. Firing demonstrations of the Hellfire were conducted in May 1982.

Delivery of 395 ESSS removable kits on order for the US Army was scheduled to begin in January 1986. Hardpoints for the ESSS have been incorporated on new production UH-60As from c/n 431 onward.

A prototype hover infra-red suppressor system (HIRSS) has successfully completed development and operational testing, and a contract for HIRSS production has been awarded to Sikorsky. The HIRSS cools the engine exhaust so that it no longer presents a target for heat-seeking missiles. The system does not require the helicopter to be in forward motion for effectiveness, as earlier IR suppressing systems did. In early 1986 Hellfire missile qualification testing with the UH-60A was proceeding at Eglin AFB, Florida. Exterior and interior lighting systems compatible with night vision goggles have been developed, and have been incorporated on production UH-60As from November 1985. Also under test on a UH-60A in 1986 was a Honeywell Volcano mine dispensing system which allows a minefield to be laid from the air in less than two minutes.

In February 1985 Sikorsky began a 10-hour initial flight test programme of a UH-60A with a composite structure rear fuselage, under funding from the USAF Systems Command's Aeronautical Systems Division. The composite rear fuselage (CRF) is expected to show advantages over conventional structures which include weight saving, improved damage tolerance and greatly reduced numbers of detail parts and fasteners. If evaluation proves successful, the CRF could be incorporated on production Black Hawks.

Following the initial flight test programme, which included measurement of vibration and loads at up to 2·5*g*, the CRF UH-60A (c/n 352) was to enter a two-year service evaluation at Fort Rucker, Alabama, to demonstrate the improved reliability and maintainability of the composite structure in an operational environment. A second CRF, fitted to the prototype YUH-60A ground test airframe, is undergoing evaluation in Sikorsky's static test facility, to the equivalent of 150 per cent of maximum flight loads. The CRF section replaces most of the Black Hawk structure from a station to the rear of the main rotor mast to the junction with the rear semi-monocoque. Weighing 181 kg (399 lb), the CRF is 10·2 per cent lighter in weight than the sheet metal section it could replace, and would cost 38 per cent less.

Eight medical evacuation kits for installation in Black Hawks were delivered to the US Army in 1981, two of the kits equipping aircraft delivered to the 326th Medical Battalion, Fort Campbell, Kentucky. This Battalion will eventually have 12 medevac equipped aircraft which, in addition to being used for training in military medevac missions, will also be available to provide medical evacuation assistance to civil authorities in parts of Indiana, Illinois, Kentucky and Tennessee.

A usage monitor, which measures certain rotor loadings, is being installed on 30 UH-60As to enable the US Army and Sikorsky to determine optimum replacement times for dynamic components.

The basic design of the UH-60A has proved suitable for a number of derivatives, as follows:

EH-60A. In October 1980, Sikorsky received a US Army contract to prepare a YEH-60A prototype for the installation of 816 kg (1,800 lb) of Quick Fix IIB electronic countermeasures equipment designed to intercept, monitor and jam enemy battlefield communications. Prime contractor for the AN/ALQ-151 ECM kit was Electronic Systems Laboratories, a subsidiary of TRW. The equipment includes four dipole antennae mounted beneath the fuselage together with a deployable whip antenna, and a data bank in the cabin. The YEH-60A flew for the first time on 24 September 1981. In October 1984 Tracor Aerospace Group was awarded a $51 million contract for the conversion of 40 UH-60As to EH-60A ECM/ESM configuration. Tracor will undertake production, integration and installation of the ECM/ESM systems, and will modify and flight test the converted helicopters. The first production EH-60A was completed in late 1985. Plans envisage a total procurement of 80 EH-60As as an element of the US Army's special electronics mission aircraft (SEMA) programme. Sikorsky plans to deliver two airframes per month, totalling 77 helicopters by November 1988.

Prototype Sikorsky HH-60A Night Hawk combat rescue helicopter for the USAF

HH-60A Night Hawk. Combat rescue version for US Air Force, to perform unescorted day/night missions at treetop level over a radius of 250 nm (463 km; 287 miles) from a friendly base, without flight refuelling. Replaces originally proposed HH-60D all-weather version and reduced capability HH-60E, which were cancelled in 1984. Prototype, modified from a UH-60A, flew for the first time on 4 February 1984. Equipment installed initially included a rescue hoist, internal and external auxiliary fuel tanks for a max capacity of 3,545 litres (936·7 US gallons), an air-to-air refuelling probe, additional avionics, and cabin fittings for the installation of rescue equipment. Flight tests were to resume at Edwards AFB, California, in August 1985, following the installation of the aircraft's mission avionics. The Federal Systems Division of IBM has responsibility for design, development, integration and testing of the avionics subsystem. Mission-related equipment includes forward-looking infra-red (FLIR), multi-function cockpit CRT displays, a MIL-STD-1553B multiplex digital data bus, a moving map display, clear and secure UHF/VHF/HF, secure intercom, radio navaids, IFF and beacons. Nav is based on Canadian Marconi Doppler radar, Litton INS, and provisions for future use of the Global Positioning System. Position of survivor's radio signal will be fixed by UHF ADF. Pilot and co-pilot will have night vision goggles. Defensive equipment will include APR-39 radar warning receiver, CM flare/chaff dispenser, and provisions for ALQ-144 infra-red jammer and 7·62 mm machine-guns. Accommodation for crew of two and ten passengers, or four litters and three seated persons. The US Air Force hoped to order 90 fully equipped production HH-60As, with first deliveries in 1988. However, no funding for the HH-60A programme was included in initial FY 1987 budget requests. Engines of production HH-60As will be uprated (1,260 kW; 1,690 shp) T700-GE-401s, while the transmission, rotor brake, approach/hover coupler and rescue hoist will be Seahawk components.

VH-60A. The US Marine Corps requested funding in the FY 1986 defence budget for nine VH-60As to replace Bell VH-1Ns of the Executive Flight Detachment of Marine Helicopter Squadron One.

EH-60B. Variant of UH-60A for US Army's SOTAS (stand-off target acquisition system) programme. First flight was made on 6 February 1981 (see 1981-82 *Jane's*); but the SOTAS programme was halted in September 1981.

UH-60B. Proposed new variant of UH-60A for US Army, under development in mid-1986. Major design improvements proposed include an advanced composites main rotor system with increased blade area and high efficiency aerofoils and tips; improved durability gearbox as used on SH-60B; strengthened flight controls; advanced cockpit with CRT displays and integrated avionics; improved forward view from cockpit; wire strike protection; self defence systems including General Dynamics ATAS missiles; enhanced safety systems, and uprated engines, for which the General Electric T700-GE-701C and Rolls-Royce Turboméca RTM 322-01 are candidates. Predicted max T-O weight is 10,750 kg (23,700 lb). If adopted, deliveries of US Army UH-60Bs could begin by November 1990.

SH-60B Seahawk. US Navy ASW/ASST helicopter, described separately.

SH-60F. US Navy 'CV-Helo' version to replace SH-3H Sea King. See Seahawk entry.

S-70A. Designation of tactical utility version of the US Army's UH-60A Black Hawk which is in production for the export market. Two **S-70A-5s** have been delivered to the air force of the Philippines. On 1 May 1986 the Australian Defence Ministry announced an initial order for 14 **S-70A-9s** to replace Bell UH-1s with the Royal Australian Air Force. Deliveries will commence in September 1987. The total RAAF requirement for S-70A-9s is expected to number at least 50 aircraft. No 9 Squadron, based at Townsville, Queensland, will be the first RAAF unit to receive the S-70A-9. Assembly and testing will be performed in Australia by Hawker de Havilland.

A version of the S-70A with Rolls-Royce Turboméca RTM 322 turboshaft engines and special avionics was submitted as a candidate for the AST 404 requirement of UK Ministry of Defence, under an agreement between Sikorsky and Short Brothers of Belfast, Northern Ireland.

S-70C. Commercial version, described separately.

The following description applies to the standard UH-60A, except where indicated:

TYPE: Twin-turbine combat assault squad transport.

ROTOR SYSTEM: Four-blade main rotor. Sikorsky SC-1095 blade section, with thickness/chord ratio of 9·5%. Middle section has leading-edge droop and trailing-edge tab to overcome vortex impingement from preceding blade in cruising flight. Blade twist 18°. Blade tips swept back 20°. Each blade consists of a hollow oval titanium spar, Nomex honeycomb core, graphite trailing-edge and root, covered with glassfibre/epoxy, with glassfibre leading-edge counterweight, titanium leading-edge sheath and Kevlar tip. Blades are tolerant to 23 mm gunfire damage, and are pressurised and equipped with gauges providing fail-safe confirmation of blade structural integrity. Electrically heated de-icing mat in leading-edge of each blade of both main and tail rotors. Forged titanium one-piece rotor head with C/R Industries elastomeric bearings which require no lubrication, reducing rotor head maintenance by 60 per cent. Bifilar self-tuning vibration absorber on rotor head. Manual blade folding. Canting of tail rotor (20° to port) increases vertical lift and allows greater CG travel. 'Cross beam' four-blade tail rotor of composite materials, eliminating all rotor head bearings.

ROTOR DRIVE: Conventional transmission system with both turbines driving through freewheeling units to main gearbox. This is of modular construction to simplify maintenance. Transmission can operate for 30 min following total oil loss. Intermediate and tail rotor gearboxes oil lubricated. Main rotor shaft can be lowered for storage or air transport.

FUSELAGE: Conventional semi-monocoque light alloy structure, designed to retain 85 per cent of its passenger and flight deck space in a vertical crash at 11·5 m (38 ft)/s, a lateral crash at 9·1 m (30 ft)/s and a longitudinal crash at 12·2 m (40 ft)/s. It can also withstand a combined force of 20*g* forward and 10*g* downward. Composite materials including glassfibre and Kevlar are used for the cockpit doors, canopy, fairings and engine cowlings. Glassfibre/Nomex floors.

TAIL UNIT: Pylon structure with port-canted tail rotor mounted on starboard side. Tail pylon design permits

Sikorsky YEH-60A communications jamming version of the Black Hawk, with whip antenna retracted under rear fuselage

normal forward flight and roll-on landing if tail rotor is destroyed. Large variable incidence tailplane has a control system which senses airspeed, collective lever position, pitch attitude rate and lateral acceleration. Tailplane is set at about +34° incidence in the hover, and −6° for autorotation. Tailplane moved by dual electric actuators, with manual backup. Tailboom folds (to starboard) immediately forward of tail pylon for transport and storage.

LANDING GEAR: Non-retractable tailwheel type with single wheel on each unit. Energy absorbing main gear with a tailwheel which gives protection for the tail rotor in taxying over rough terrain or during a high-flare landing. Axle assembly and main gear oleo shock absorbers by General Mechatronics. Mainwheel tyres size 26 × 10·00-11, pressure 8·96-9·65 bars (130-140 lb/sq in); tailwheel tyre size 15 × 6·00-6, pressure 6·21-6·55 bars (90-95 lb/sq in).

POWER PLANT: Two 1,151 kW (1,560 shp) General Electric T700-GE-700 turboshaft engines; combined transmission rating 2,109 kW (2,828 shp). (T700-GE-701A engines with max T-O rating of 1,285 kW; 1,723 shp optional in export models.) Two crashworthy, bullet-proof fuel cells, with combined usable capacity of 1,361 litres (359·7 US gallons), aft of cabin. Single-point pressure refuelling; or gravity refuelling via point on each tank. Auxiliary fuel can be carried internally in one of several optional arrangements, or externally by the ESS system.

ACCOMMODATION: Two-man flight deck, with pilot and co-pilot on armour protected seats. A third crew member is stationed in the cabin at the gunner's position. Forward hinged jettisonable door on each side for access to flight deck area. Main cabin open to cockpit to provide good communication with flight crew and forward view for squad commander. Accommodation for 11 fully equipped troops, or 14 in high density configuration. Eight troop seats can be removed and replaced by four litters for medevac missions, or to make room for internal cargo. An optional layout is available to accommodate a maximum of six litter patients. Cabin heated and ventilated. External cargo hook, having a 3,630 kg (8,000 lb) lift capability, enables UH-60A to transport a 105 mm howitzer, its crew of five and 50 rounds of ammunition. Rescue hoist of 272 kg (600 lb) capacity optional. Large rearward sliding door on each side of fuselage for rapid entry and exit. Electric windscreen de-icing. (Executive configured interiors for 7-12 passengers are available for the S-70A.)

SYSTEMS: Solar 67 kW (90 hp) T-62T-40-1 APU; Garrett engine start system. An optional winterisation kit provides a second hydraulic accumulator installed in parallel with the APU hydraulic start accumulator, maintaining engine start capability at low ambient temperatures; Bendix 30/40kVA and 20/30kVA electrical power generators; 17Ah nickel-cadmium battery. Engine fire extinguishing system. Rotor blade de-icing system standard on US Army aircraft, optional for export versions.

AVIONICS: Com equipment comprises E-Systems AN/ARC-186 VHF-FM, GTE Sylvania AN/ARC-115 VHF-AM, Magnavox AN/ARC-164 UHF-AM, Collins AN/ARC-186(V) VHF-AM/FM, Bendix AN/APX-100 IFF transponder, Magnavox TSEC/KT-28 voice security set, and intercom. Nav equipment comprises Emerson AN/ARN-89 ADF, Bendix AN/ARN-123(V)1 VOR/marker beacon/glideslope receiver, Sperry AN/ASN-43 gyro compass, Singer Kearfott AN/ASN-128 Doppler, and Honeywell AN/APN-209(V)2 radar altimeter. E-Systems Melpar/Memcor AN/APR-39(V)1 radar warning receiver and Sanders AN/ALQ-144 infra-red countermeasures set. Hamilton Standard AFCS with digital three-axis autopilot.

ARMAMENT AND OPERATIONAL EQUIPMENT: Provision for one or two side-firing machine-guns in forward area of cabin; Hellfire missiles, rockets, mine dispensers and other stores on ESSS; infra-red jamming flares and Tracor XM130 chaff dispenser.

DIMENSIONS, EXTERNAL:

Main rotor diameter	16·36 m (53 ft 8 in)
Main rotor blade chord	0·53 m (1 ft 8¾ in)
Tail rotor diameter	3·35 m (11 ft 0 in)
Length overall (rotors turning)	19·76 m (64 ft 10 in)
Length, rotors and tail pylon folded	12·60 m (41 ft 4 in)
Length of fuselage:	
UH/HH-60A, excl flight refuelling probe	15·26 m (50 ft 0¾ in)
HH-60A, incl retracted refuelling probe	17·38 m (57 ft 0¼ in)
Fuselage: Max width: UH-60A	2·36 m (7 ft 9 in)
HH-60A with auxiliary tanks	5·46 m (17 ft 11 in)
Max depth	1·75 m (5 ft 9 in)
Height overall, tail rotor turning	5·13 m (16 ft 10 in)
Height to top of rotor head	3·76 m (12 ft 4 in)
Height in air transportable configuration	2·67 m (8 ft 9 in)
Tailplane span	4·38 m (14 ft 4½ in)
Wheel track	2·705 m (8 ft 10½ in)
Wheelbase	8·83 m (28 ft 11¾ in)
Tail rotor ground clearance	1·98 m (6 ft 6 in)
Cabin doors (each): Height	1·37 m (4 ft 6 in)
Width	1·75 m (5 ft 9 in)

DIMENSION, INTERNAL:

Cabin: Volume	10·90 m³ (385 cu ft)

AREAS:

Main rotor blades (each)	4·34 m² (46·70 sq ft)
Tail rotor blades (each)	0·41 m² (4·45 sq ft)
Main rotor disc	210·05 m² (2,261 sq ft)
Tail rotor disc	8·83 m² (95·0 sq ft)
Tailplane	4·18 m² (45·0 sq ft)
Vertical stabiliser	3·00 m² (32·3 sq ft)

WEIGHTS:

Weight empty: UH-60A	4,819 kg (10,624 lb)
HH-60A	5,734 kg (12,642 lb)
Mission T-O weight: UH-60A	7,375 kg (16,260 lb)
HH-60A	9,259 kg (20,413 lb)
Max alternative T-O weight:	
UH-60A	9,185 kg (20,250 lb)
S-70A, HH-60A	9,979 kg (22,000 lb)

PERFORMANCE (at mission T-O weight, except where indicated):

Max level speed at S/L:	
UH-60A	160 knots (296 km/h; 184 mph)
HH-60A	145 knots (268 km/h; 167 mph)
Max level speed at max T-O weight:	
UH-60A	158 knots (293 km/h; 182 mph)
Max cruising speed at 1,220 m (4,000 ft) and 35°C (95°F):	
UH-60A	145 knots (268 km/h; 167 mph)
HH-60A	128 knots (237 km/h; 147 mph)
Single-engine cruising speed at 1,220 m (4,000 ft), and 35°C (95°F):	
UH-60A	105 knots (195 km/h; 121 mph)
Vertical rate of climb at S/L:	
UH-60A	over 137 m (450 ft)/min
HH-60A	203 m (665 ft)/min
Service ceiling: UH-60A	5,790 m (19,000 ft)
Hovering ceiling IGE:	
UH-60A, at 35°C	2,895 m (9,500 ft)
Hovering ceiling OGE:	
UH-60A, ISA	3,170 m (10,400 ft)
UH-60A, at 35°C	1,705 m (5,600 ft)
Range with max internal fuel at max T-O weight, 30 min reserves: UH-60A	324 nm (600 km; 373 miles)
Range with external fuel tanks on ESSS pylons:	
UH-60A, with two 230 US gallon tanks	880 nm (1,630 km; 1,012 miles)
UH-60A, with two 230 US gallon and two 450 US gallon tanks	1,200 nm (2,220 km; 1,380 miles)
Endurance: UH-60A	2 h 18 min
HH-60A with max fuel	4 h 51 min

Sikorsky S-70C commercial derivative of the UH-60 series

SIKORSKY S-70C

The S-70C is a commercial variant of the H-60 helicopter series which can be configured for a range of utility missions including heavy construction, external lift, maritime and environmental survey, mineral exploration, forestry and conservation. The S-70C uses the H-60 airframe, dynamics and systems, but is powered by two General Electric CT7-2C or -2D engines. Options available include a de-icing kit for main and tail rotors, 3,630 kg (8,000 lb) capacity external cargo hook, cabin mounted rescue hoist, aeromedical evacuation kit, and a winterisation kit. The S-70C is certificated under FAR Pt 21.25. Delivery of 24 with undernose radar to the People's Republic of China was completed in December 1985. Fourteen have been ordered by the Chinese Nationalist Air Force, Taiwan.

An S-70C (G-RRTM) is being used by Rolls-Royce in the UK as a flying testbed for the Rolls-Royce Turboméca RTM 322 turboshaft engine.

The Sikorsky S-70C is generally similar to the UH-60A, except as follows:

TYPE: Twin-turbine utility helicopter.

POWER PLANT: Two 1,212 kW (1,625 shp) General Electric CT7-2C or 1,285 kW (1,723 shp) CT7-2D turboshaft engines. Combined transmission rating (continuous) 2,334 kW (3,130 shp). Maximum fuel capacity 1,370 litres (362 US gallons).

ACCOMMODATION: Flight deck crew of two, with provision for 12 passengers in standard cabin configuration and up to 19 passengers in high density layout. Forward hinged door on each side of flight deck for access to cockpit area. Large rearward sliding door on each side of main cabin.

DIMENSIONS, INTERNAL:

Cabin: Length	3·84 m (12 ft 7 in)
Max width	2·34 m (7 ft 8 in)
Max height	1·37 m (4 ft 6 in)
Floor area	8·18 m² (88 sq ft)
Volume	10·96 m³ (387 cu ft)
Baggage compartment volume	0·52 m³ (18·5 cu ft)

WEIGHTS:

Weight empty	4,607 kg (10,158 lb)
Max external load	3,630 kg (8,000 lb)
Max T-O weight	9,185 kg (20,250 lb)

PERFORMANCE:

Never-exceed speed	195 knots (361 km/h; 224 mph)
Econ cruising speed	162 knots (300 km/h; 186 mph)
Max rate of climb at S/L	844 m (2,770 ft)/min
Service ceiling	5,240 m (17,200 ft)
Service ceiling, one engine out	1,525 m (5,000 ft)
Hovering ceiling IGE: ISA	2,650 m (8,700 ft)
ISA + 20°C	1,615 m (5,300 ft)
Hovering ceiling OGE: ISA	1,460 m (4,800 ft)
ISA + 20°C	395 m (1,300 ft)
Range at 135 knots (250 km/h; 155 mph) at 915 m (3,000 ft) with max standard fuel, 30 min reserves	255 nm (473 km; 294 miles)
Range, max fuel, no reserves	297 nm (550 km; 342 miles)

SIKORSKY S-70B

US Navy designations: SH-60B and SH-60F Seahawk

The US Navy's LAMPS (light airborne multi-purpose system) programme was initiated in 1970, when the Kaman SH-2D Seasprite won the contract for the LAMPS Mk I aircraft. The Mk II mission was considered beyond the capabilities of the Seasprite; so this phase of the programme was cancelled and the US Navy turned to planning a Mk III version. In 1974, IBM Federal Systems Division was selected as prime contractor for LAMPS Mk III, reflecting the relative importance of the avionics fit compared with the airframe. Fly-off tests of competitive airframes from Boeing Vertol and Sikorsky were conducted in 1977, each manufacturer submitting a developed version of the aircraft built for the US Army's UTTAS competition. Sikorsky was selected to supply the LAMPS Mk III airframe, and General Electric to supply a navalised version of the T700 engine.

A key factor in the selection of the Sikorsky S-70B airframe was its promise of reduced development costs, due to the high degree of commonality with the Army's UH-60A Black Hawk. The designation **SH-60B** and name Seahawk were allocated to the Navy model, which embodies changes to integrate the mission equipment and to provide shipboard compatibility. These changes include the addition of chin mounted pods for ESM equipment, pylons for two torpedoes or auxiliary fuel tanks, a pylon for MAD equipment on the starboard side, installation of more powerful navalised engines; addition of a sensor operator's station and port side launcher for 25 sonobuoys in the cabin; increased fuel capacity; a rescue hoist; automatic

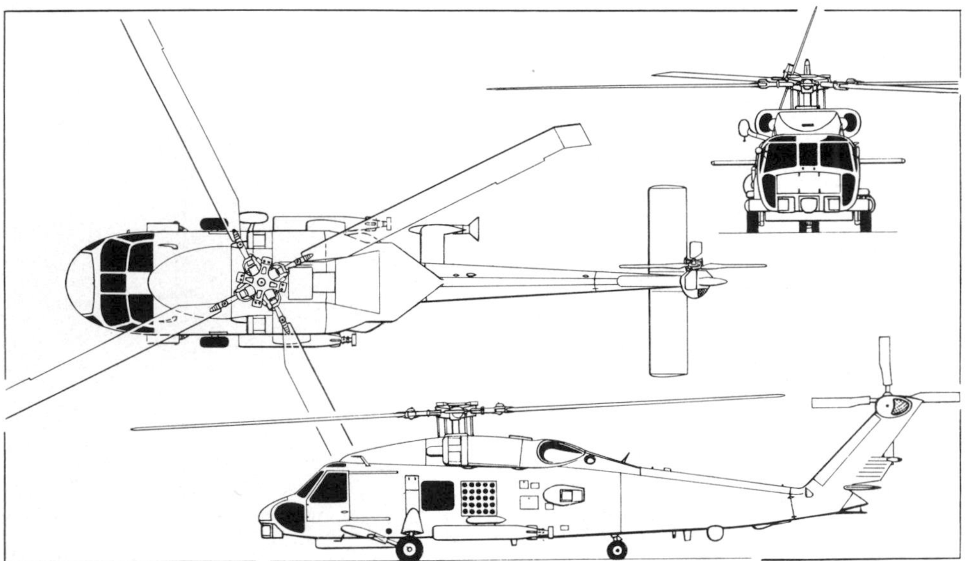

Sikorsky SH-60B Seahawk twin-turbine ASW/ASST helicopter *(Pilot Press)*

First production Sikorsky SH-60B Seahawk, the US Navy's LAMPS Mk III helicopter *(Howard Levy)*

main rotor folding system; main rotor brake; tail pylon folding; modified landing gear; a DAF Indal RAST (recovery assist, secure and traversing) device to haul down the helicopter in rough seas on to a small deck, and stow it in the ship's hangar; a sliding cabin door; hover in-flight refuelling system; and buoyancy features. The pilot's and co-pilot's seats are not armoured.

The first of five prototypes flew on 12 December 1979, and details of subsequent development and operational testing can be found in the 1982-83 *Jane's*. By mid-1982, the prototypes had logged a total of nearly 3,000 flying hours, including extensive shipboard trials. Production of a first batch of 18 SH-60Bs was authorised in FY 1982, followed by 27 more in FY 1983. Total planned requirement by the US Navy is 204 aircraft. The first production Seahawk flew on 11 February 1983, and deliveries to the Navy continue at the rate of two per month, with a total of 62 delivered by February 1986. First USN squadron was HSL-41, at North Island, San Diego, California. Operational deployment began in 1984. Japan has selected the SH-60B to replace the SH-3A/Bs of the JMSDF. Two Sikorsky built Seahawk airframes, designated **XSH-60J**, have been delivered to Mitsubishi at Nagoya for installation of Japanese electronics and mission equipment under a $27 million contract from the Japan Defence Agency's Technical Research and Development Institute. The first of these helicopters is expected to fly in 1987. The SH-60J Seahawk will be built by Mitsubishi, and is scheduled to enter service with the JMSDF in the early 1990s, with replacement of SH-3s completed by the middle of the decade.

On 9 October 1984 the Royal Australian Navy confirmed an initial order for eight Seahawks for its full-spectrum ASW requirement, and ordered a further eight in May 1986. The Seahawks, designated **S-70B-2** RAWS (role adaptable weapon system), will operate from the RAN's 'Adelaide' (FFG-7) class guided missile frigates. Fifteen of the S-70B-2 RAWS will be assembled in Australia by Hawker de Havilland. The RAN helicopters will be equipped with MEL Super Searcher radar and Collins advanced integrated avionics including cockpit controls and displays, navigation receivers and communications transceivers, an airborne target off-hand data link and a tactical data system (TDS). The Spanish Navy has ordered six S-70Bs for 1988 delivery.

US Navy SH-60Bs will be deployed on a total of 106 'Oliver Hazard Perry' class frigates, and 'Spruance' class and Aegis equipped destroyers. They will provide all-weather capability for detection, classification, localisation and interdiction of surface vessels and submarines. Compared with the LAMPS Mk I, range, loiter time and endurance are increased significantly. ASW listening time is increased by 57 min, ASST (anti-ship surveillance and targeting) loiter time by 45 min. The helicopter interfaces with its mother ship via a data link, but can also operate independently. Secondary missions include search and rescue (SAR), vertical replenishment (vertrep), medical evacuation (medevac), fleet support and communications relay.

On 6 March 1985 Sikorsky received a $50·9 million contract for full scale development and production options for a 'CV-Helo' version of the Seahawk designated **SH-60F** and known officially as the CV Inner Zone ASW helicopter. Intended as a replacement for the SH-3H Sea King, this helicopter will operate from aircraft carriers to protect the inner zone of a carrier battle group from submarine attack. The SH-60F will differ from the SH-60B in having all LAMPS Mk III avionics, sensors and pneumatic sonobuoy launcher equipment removed, together with the cargo hook, recovery assist secure and transverse system main probe, tail probe and control panel, although installation provisions will be retained. An integrated ASW mission avionics suite will be installed comprising a MIL-STD-1553B tactical data system with dual Teledyne Systems AN/ASN-123 tactical navigation computers, a tactical data link to other aircraft, a communications control system, and display units for each of the four crew members.

Additional equipment planned for the SH-60F includes an Allied Bendix Oceanics AN/AQS-13F sonar system; internal/external auxiliary fuel system and an additional weapons station on an extended pylon on the left side of the fuselage. Modifications will also include rearrangement of the cabin interior, removal of external sensor fairings, and improvements to the automatic flight control system to permit increased rates of deceleration on automatic approaches in addition to automatic coupled sonar cable angle hover or coupled Doppler hover. Provision will be made for a chaff/sonobuoy launcher system, an attitude/heading referencing system and global positioning system, with future growth potential for a fatigue monitoring system, surface search radar, FLIR, passive ESM, MAD, air-to-surface missile capability and a sonobuoy data link. Secondary missions will include SAR and standby during launch and recovery of the carriers' fixed-wing aircraft to provide a rescue service in case of ditching. The US Navy requirement is for 175 SH-60Fs. The initial contract provides production options for 76 helicopters in five lots. In January 1986 Sikorsky received a contract for the first seven SH-60Fs. By early 1986 some 100 hours of testing had been completed on the helicopter's automatic flight control system installed in an SH-60B. The first SH-60F was expected to fly in late 1986 with production deliveries to the US Navy anticipated during 1988.

In September 1986, the US Navy awarded Sikorsky a contract for an initial production increment of five combat search and rescue/special warfare support (**HCS**) helicopters for the Navy, and two medium range recovery (**MRR**) helicopters for the Coast Guard. The Sikorsky HCS/MRR is a close derivative of the SH-60F. It is expected that 18 will eventually serve with the Navy and 35 with the Coast Guard.

The following description applies to the SH-60B:

TYPE: Twin-turbine ASW/ASST helicopter.

ROTOR SYSTEM: As for UH-60A, except that main rotor blades can be folded by electrical power, and a rotor brake is provided.

AIRFRAME: Identical to UH-60A in construction. Wheelbase is shortened by 46·6 per cent, with twin wheels on tail unit, tyre size 17·5 × 6·00-6. Multiple disc brakes on mainwheels. Landing gear structure is less complex since the SH-60B's vertical impact requirement is 71·5 per cent below that of the UH-60A.

POWER PLANT: Two 1,260 kW (1,690 shp) General Electric T700-GE-401 turboshaft engines. Internal fuel as for UH-60A. Hovering in-flight refuelling capability. Two auxiliary fuel tanks on fuselage pylons optional.

ACCOMMODATION: Pilot and airborne tactical officer/backup pilot in cockpit, sensor operator in specially equipped station in cabin. Dual controls standard. Sliding door with jettisonable window on starboard side. Accommodation is heated, ventilated and air-conditioned.

SYSTEMS: Generally as for UH-60A.

AVIONICS AND EQUIPMENT: Com equipment comprises Collins AN/ARC-159(V)2 UHF and AN/ARC-174(V)2 HF, Hazeltine AN/APX-76A(V) and Bendix AN/APX-100(V)1 IFF transponders, TSEC/KY-75 voice security set, TSEC/KG-45(E-1) com security, Telephonics OK-374/ASC com system control group and Sierra Research AN/ARQ-44 data link and telemetry. Nav equipment comprises Collins AN/ARN-118(V) Tacan, Honeywell AN/APN-194(V) radar altimeter, Teledyne Ryan AN/APN-217 Doppler, and Collins AN/ARA-50 UHF DF. Mission equipment includes Sikorsky sonobuoy launcher, Edmac AN/ARR-75 and R-1651/ARA sonobuoy receiving sets, Texas Instruments AN/ASQ-81(V)2 MAD, Raymond MU-670/ASQ magnetic tape memory unit, Astronautics IO-2177/ASQ altitude indicator, Fairchild AN/ASQ-164 control indicator set and AN/ASQ-165 armament control indicator set, Texas Instruments AN/APS-124 search radar (under front fuselage), IBM AN/UYS-1(V)2 Proteus acoustic processor and CV-3252/A converter display, Control Data AN/AYK-14 (XN-1A) digital computer, and Raytheon AN/ALQ-142 ESM (in chin mounted pods). External cargo hook and rescue hoist standard.

ARMAMENT: Includes two Mk 46 torpedoes.

DIMENSIONS, EXTERNAL: As UH-60A except:

Length overall (rotors and tail pylon folded)	12·47 m (40 ft 11 in)
Width (rotors folded)	3·26 m (10 ft 8½ in)
Height to top of rotor head	3·63 m (11 ft 11 in)
Height overall, tail rotor turning	5·18 m (17 ft 0 in)
Height overall (pylon folded)	4·04 m (13 ft 3¼ in)
Wheel track	2·79 m (9 ft 2 in)
Wheelbase	4·83 m (15 ft 10 in)

AREAS: As UH-60A

WEIGHTS (estimated. A, ASW mission; B, ASST mission; C, Utility role):

Weight empty: A	6,191 kg (13,648 lb)
Mission gross weight: A	9,182 kg (20,244 lb)
B	8,334 kg (18,373 lb)
Max gross weight: C	9,926 kg (21,884 lb)

PERFORMANCE:

Dash speed at 1,525 m (5,000 ft), tropical day
126 knots (234 km/h; 145 mph)

Vertical rate of climb at S/L, 32·2°C (90°F)
213 m (700 ft)/min

Vertical rate of climb at S/L, 32·2°C (90°F), one engine out
137 m (450 ft)/min

SIKORSKY/US ARMY S-75 (ACAP)

On 25 February 1981, it was announced that the US Army's Applied Technology Laboratory had selected Sikorsky as one of two contractors to negotiate a contract for the Army's Advanced Composite Airframe Program (ACAP). The objective was to develop, build and evaluate a helicopter fuselage made entirely of composite materials, in order to achieve a weight saving of 22 per cent, and cost

Sikorsky/US Army S-75 ACAP research helicopter prototype

saving, on production airframes, of 17 per cent, compared with conventional metal airframes, while meeting established military requirements in terms of crashworthiness, ballistics tolerance, reliability, maintainability and reduced radar signature. The S-75 bettered these objectives, with a 23 per cent weight saving and 24 per cent cost saving.

Sikorsky subsequently received a contract worth $17·5 million to build a flying prototype and two ground test airframes under the second phase of ACAP. The resulting aircraft, known as the S-75, has the composite airframe mated to the power plant, transmission and rotor system of a Sikorsky S-76. Subcontractor is Hercules Corporation, which fabricated the tailcone, tail pylon and stabiliser. All other fabrication and final assembly was done by Sikorsky.

First flight of the S-75 was made on 27 July 1984. By March 1985, at the mid-point of its planned 37-hour flight test programme, the S-75 had flown at a max T-O weight of 3,842 kg (8,470 lb), at speeds up to 160 knots (296 km/h; 184 mph), and performed manoeuvres at load factors up to 2·5*g*. The programme continued until April 1985, expanding the flight envelope to include high altitude flight, autorotations, single-engine operation, handling and performance evaluation, vibration surveys and electro-magnetic compatibility trials.

FUSELAGE: Fail-safe composites structure, mostly of graphite and Kevlar materials. Unpressurised.

TAIL UNIT: Graphite/Kevlar structure, similar to S-76, with standard S-76A controls.

LANDING GEAR: Non-retractable tricycle type. Sikorsky-designed high strength pneumatic oleo shock absorption, with inbuilt crashworthiness to MIL-STD-1290. Goodyear wheels and disc brakes, Goodrich tyres, size (all) 15 × 6·00-16, pressure 9·65-10·0 bars (140-145 lb/sq in). Self-centering nosewheel.

ACCOMMODATION: Two crew, plus six combat-equipped soldiers in cabin. One sliding cabin door on each side of cockpit area. Cabin floor has eight tiedown points for cargo.

DIMENSIONS, EXTERNAL:

Main rotor diameter	13·41 m (44 ft 0 in)
Main rotor blade chord	0·39 m (1 ft 3½ in)
Tail rotor diameter	2·44 m (8 ft 0 in)
Distance between rotor centres	8·08 m (26 ft 6 in)
Length overall, rotors turning	16·00 m (52 ft 6 in)
Fuselage: Length	13·31 m (43 ft 8 in)
Max width	2·44 m (8 ft 0 in)
Height to top of rotor head	4·01 m (13 ft 2 in)
Height overall	4·57 m (15 ft 0 in)
Wheel track	2·59 m (8 ft 6 in)
Wheelbase	5·26 m (17 ft 3 in)
Cabin doors: Height	1·12 m (3 ft 8 in)
Width	1·83 m (6 ft 0 in)

DIMENSIONS, INTERNAL:

Cabin: Length	1·78 m (5 ft 10 in)
Max width	1·22 m (4 ft 0 in)
Max height	1·32 m (4 ft 4 in)
Floor area	2·14 m² (23·0 sq ft)
Volume	2·83 m³ (100·0 cu ft)

AREAS: As for S-76

WEIGHTS:

Weight empty	2,912 kg (6,421 lb)
Max T-O weight	3,842 kg (8,470 lb)

PERFORMANCE (at 915 m; 3,000 ft and 35°C; 95°F):

As S-76 except:

Never-exceed speed	160 knots (296 km/h; 184 mph)
Max level speed	142 knots (263 km/h; 164 mph)
Max cruising speed	138 knots (256 km/h; 159 mph)

SIKORSKY S-76 MARK II

Sikorsky Aircraft announced on 19 January 1975 its decision to build a new 12-passenger twin-turbine commercial helicopter, designated S-76, as the first stage of a programme intended to give the company a bigger share of the civil aircraft market. Construction of four prototypes began in May 1976, and the first flight was made, by the No. 2 aircraft (N762SA), on 13 March 1977. Second prototype to fly, in late April 1977, was the No. 3 aircraft, and a further prototype was flown about a month later. FAR Pt 29 certification was received in November 1978 and deliveries began in early 1979.

The S-76 benefits from the design, research and development work carried out on the dynamic system of Sikorsky's UH-60A Black Hawk. The main rotor, for example, is a scaled-down version of that developed for the UH-60A. The helicopter conforms with FAR Pt 29 Category A IFR. By designing and building to this standard, Sikorsky has produced a rugged and reliable civil helicopter, which can be taken 'off the shelf' to satisfy a wide variety of air transport missions. Offshore oil support, corporate executive transport, and general utility operations are regarded as primary markets.

By December 1984 total deliveries had reached 269 aircraft, of which 69 were in corporate use, and total fleet time exceeded 450,000 hours.

All aircraft delivered from 1 March 1982 have been designated **S-76 Mark II** and embody more than 40 standard improvements, including a new cabin ventilation system to provide ample fresh air with no performance penalty; refinements in the major dynamic components; and an increased number of fuselage access panels, these latter features being intended to improve reliability and simplify maintenance. The special type of Allison turboshaft engine now fitted also incorporates refinements, and offers a 5 per cent increase in guaranteed power output. Redesignated Allison 250-C30S (for Sikorsky), the engine has a take-off rating of 485 kW (650 shp). In the light of these improvements, Sikorsky announced on 18 February 1982 that the S-76 Mark II is covered by what the company claims to be the most comprehensive warranty in the industry, extending over two years or 1,000 flight hours. Kits incorporating the Mark II refinements are available to update earlier S-76 aircraft to this standard, most of them without charge.

Between 4-9 February 1982 a new production S-76 Mark II, without special modification, was used to establish 12 records in FAI classes E1d and E1e. These comprise, under E1d, speed over 3 km of 181·037 knots (335·5 km/h; 208·47 mph); speed over 15/25 km of 184·874 knots (342·61 km/h; 212·888 mph); speed over a 100 km closed circuit of 178·728 knots (331·22 km/h; 205·811 mph); climb to 3,000 m in 3 min 11 s; climb to 6,000 m in 8 min 37·3 s; and sustained altitude in level flight of 7,940 m (26,050 ft). The class E1e records comprise a speed over 3 km of 183·725 knots (340·48 km/h; 211·564 mph); speed over 15/25 km of 183·682 knots (340·40 km/h; 211·515 mph); speed over a 100 km closed circuit of (180·599 knots (334·688 km/h; 207·965 mph); speed over a 500 km closed circuit of 186·563 knots (345·74 km/h; 214·833 mph); and speed over a 1,000 km closed circuit of 164·633 knots (305·10 km/h; 189·580 mph). The E1e record over 500 km is also a new class E1 record for all helicopters, held previously, since 1 August 1975, by the Mil A-10 (Mi-24).

On 18 February 1982, Sikorsky also announced the availability of three different quick-change medical kits to convert any version of the S-76 to an ambulance configuration. These include an air medical evacuation system (AMES) kit for operators placing primary emphasis on air ambulance operations, providing maximum intensive care for two patients treated by two attendants; a quick-change single-stretcher kit for use where intensive care transport may be needed quickly on a standby basis; and a kit for the installation of three stretchers, when the S-76 is to be used more specifically as a civil defence or SAR type ambulance.

Allison is developing a new version of the 250-C30 turboshaft which currently powers the S-76 Mark II; designated 250-C34, it will provide a 10 per cent increase in power and was expected to become available in late 1985. A digital computerised fuel control system is being developed by Hamilton Standard to complement this new power plant. When equipped with the 250-C34 the S-76 Mark II will be certificated at a new maximum T-O weight of 4,989 kg (11,000 lb) and have an uprated transmission to handle the increased power.

Optional equipment certificated for the S-76 includes a Sperry SPZS-7000 single-pilot dual-digital automatic flight control system and electronic flight instrument system. Sikorsky has also been developing a composite rotor head and all-composite main rotor blades with graphite-glass-fibre spars for the S-76, together with an ice protection kit weighing 68 kg (150 lb), of which 45 kg (100 lb) is removable during the Summer months.

In the Spring of 1985 Sikorsky began testing an experimental higher harmonic control (HHC) system in an S-76 which has demonstrated a vibration reduction of up to 90 per cent over the standard S-76. In the HHC system, one rod in each of the three channels of the main rotor mechanical control system is replaced with an HHC actuator which drives the corresponding main hydraulic servo mechanism to produce a vibration-cancelling motion of the rotor blades. In a production system the actuators would probably be built into the main servos. The benefits of higher harmonic control include improved crew and passenger comfort, better systems reliability, improved fatigue life, greater stability for weapons aiming and firing, and a potential reduction in weight compared to current generation 'passive' vibration absorbers.

The following versions of the S-76 had been announced by mid-1986:

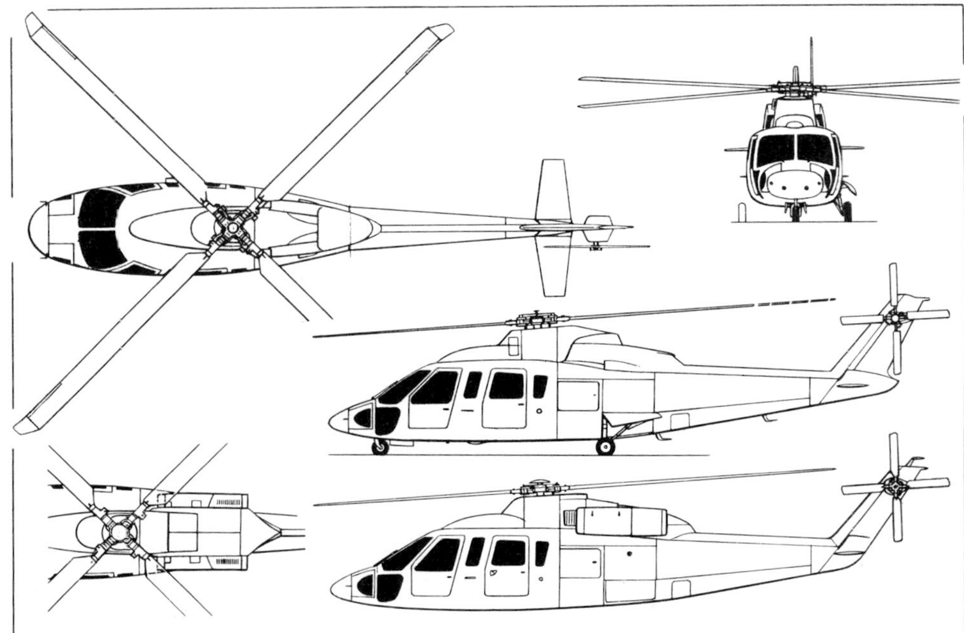

Sikorsky S-76 Mark II eight/twelve-passenger commercial transport helicopter, with lower side view and scrap detail of S-76B *(Pilot Press)*

S-76. Original general purpose all-weather transport, generally as described below for the S-76 Mark II, and covering aircraft delivered prior to 1 March 1982.

S-76 Mark II. Current production version from 1 March 1982, as described in detail.

S-76B. With Pratt & Whitney Canada PT6B-36 power plant; described separately.

S-76 Utility. More basic version of the S-76 Mark II, for a variety of roles. Sliding doors, on each side of the cabin, dual controls, and a cabin floor designed for cargo loadings of up to 976 kg/m² (200 lb/sq ft), are standard. Optional features include non-retractable landing gear with low pressure tyres, to increase rough terrain ground clearance, crash resistant fuel tanks, a similar auxiliary tank of 416 litres (110 US gallons) capacity for installation in the baggage compartment, armoured crew seats, removable troop seats, cargo hook, rescue hoist, engine air particle separators and provisions for stretcher installation. The Philippine Air Force has taken delivery of 17 military S-76 Utility helicopters, of which 12 are **H-76s** configured for COIN, troop/logistic support and medevac duties. Two others are configured for SAR, one with a 12-passenger utility cabin, and two with an 8-passenger cabin.

H-76 Eagle. Military development of the S-76B; described separately.

H-76N. Naval development of the S-76 Utility, described separately.

The following description applies to the S-76 Mark II, except where indicated:

TYPE: Twin-turbine general purpose all-weather helicopter.

ROTOR SYSTEM: Four-blade main rotor, with Sikorsky SC-1095 blade section. Each blade consists of a hollow oval titanium spar, titanium and nickel leading-edge abrasion strips, and glassfibre composite outer covering over Nomex honeycomb core. Blades have swept tips of Kevlar (30° on leading-edges, 10° on trailing-edges). Fully articulated aluminium rotor head, with elastomeric bearings which need no lubrication. Hydraulic lead-lag dampers and bifilar vibration absorbers on rotor head. Cross-beam four-blade tail rotor of composite materials. Rotor brake optional.

ROTOR DRIVE: Conventional transmission system, with both turbines driving through freewheeling units to main gearbox. Intermediate and tail rotor gearboxes are oil lubricated. Max continuous rating of main transmission 969 kW (1,300 shp).

FUSELAGE: Composite structure, comprising glassfibre nose, light alloy honeycomb cabin, semi-monocoque light alloy tailcone and Kevlar doors and fairings.

TAIL UNIT: Pylon structure with tail rotor on port side. All-moving tailplane, which serves also to protect passengers or ground crew from contact with tail rotor.

LANDING GEAR: Hydraulically retractable tricycle type, with single wheel on each unit. Nosewheel retracts rearward, main units inward into rear fuselage; all three units are enclosed by wheel doors when retracted. Mainwheel tyres size 14·5 × 5·5-6, pressure 11·38 bars (165 lb/sq in); nosewheel tyre size 13 × 5·00-4, pressure 9·31 bars (135 lb/sq in). Hydraulic brakes; hydraulic mainwheel parking brake. Non-retractable tricycle gear, with low pressure tyres, optional on Utility version.

POWER PLANT: Two 485 kW (650 shp) Allison 250-C30S turboshaft engines, with max continuous rating of 415 kW (557 shp), mounted above the cabin aft of the main rotor shaft. Standard fuel system has a capacity of 1,064 litres (281 US gallons). Extended range fuel tanks, capacity 401 litres (106 US gallons), optional.

ACCOMMODATION: Pilot and co-pilot plus a maximum of 12 passengers. In this configuration passengers are seated on three four-abreast rows of seats, floor mounted at a pitch of 79 cm (31 in). A number of executive layouts are available, including a four-passenger 'office in the sky' configuration. Executive versions have luxurious interior trim, full carpeting, special soundproofing, radio telephone, and co-ordinated furniture. Dual controls optional. Two large doors on each side of fuselage, hinged at their forward edges; sliding doors are available optionally. Baggage hold aft of cabin, with external access door on each side of the fuselage. Cabin heated and ventilated. Windscreen demisting and dual windscreen wipers. Windscreen heating optional. Optional external cargo hook.

SYSTEMS: Hydraulic system at pressure of 207 bars (3,000 lb/sq in) supplied by two pumps driven from main gearbox. Hydraulic system maximum flow rate 15·9 litres (4·2 US gallons) per minute. Bootstrap reservoir. Pump head pressure 3·45 bars (50 lb/sq in). In VFR configuration, electrical system comprises two 200A DC starter/generators and a 24V 17Ah nickel-cadmium battery. In IFR configuration, system comprises gearbox driven 7·5kVA generator, and a 115V 600VA 400Hz static inverter for AC power. 34Ah battery optional. Engine fire detection and extinguishing system.

AVIONICS AND EQUIPMENT: Standard equipment includes provisions for dual controls; cabin fire extinguishers; cockpit, cabin, instrument, navigation and anti-collision lights; landing light; external power socket; first aid kit; and utility soundproofing. Collins VHF-20 com transceiver and intercom system standard. Optional equipment includes air-conditioning, cargo hook, rescue hoist, emergency flotation gear, engine air particle separators, full IFR instrumentation, litter installation and Hamilton Standard AFCS. Wide range of optional avionics available, according to configuration, including VHF nav receivers, transponder, compass system, weather radar, flight director system, radar altimeter, ADF, DME, VLF nav system and ELT and sonic transmitters.

Sikorsky S-76 Mark II general purpose helicopter in service with the Royal Jordanian Air Force
(Ivo Sturzenegger)

DIMENSIONS, EXTERNAL (A: Mark II; B: Mark II Utility):

Main rotor diameter	13·41 m (44 ft 0 in)
Main rotor blade chord	0·39 m (1 ft 3½ in)
Tail rotor diameter	2·44 m (8 ft 0 in)
Tail rotor blade chord	0·16 m (6½ in)
Length overall, rotors turning	16·00 m (52 ft 6 in)
Fuselage: Length	13·22 m (43 ft 4½ in)
Max width	2·13 m (7 ft 0 in)
Max depth	1·83 m (6 ft 0 in)
Height overall, tail rotor turning:	
A	4·41 m (14 ft 5¾ in)
B	4·52 m (14 ft 9¾ in)
Tailplane span: A	3·05 m (10 ft 0 in)
B	3·15 m (10 ft 4 in)
Wheel track: A	2·44 m (8 ft 0 in)
B	2·54 m (8 ft 4 in)
Wheelbase	5·00 m (16 ft 5 in)
Tail rotor ground clearance	1·97 m (6 ft 5¾ in)

DIMENSIONS, INTERNAL:

Cabin: Length	2·46 m (8 ft 1 in)
Max width	1·93 m (6 ft 4 in)
Max height	1·37 m (4 ft 6 in)
Floor area	4·18 m² (45 sq ft)
Volume	5·78 m³ (204 cu ft)
Baggage compartment volume	1·08 m³ (38 cu ft)

AREAS:

Main rotor disc	141·21 m² (1,520 sq ft)
Tail rotor disc	4·67 m² (50·27 sq ft)
Tailplane	2·00 m² (21·5 sq ft)

WEIGHTS AND LOADING:

Weight empty, standard equipment	2,540 kg (5,600 lb)
Max fuel weight: standard	861 kg (1,898 lb)
auxiliary	325 kg (716 lb)
Max payload	2,132 kg (4,700 lb)
Max external load	1,497 kg (3,300 lb)
Max T-O weight	4,672 kg (10,300 lb)
Max disc loading	33·07 kg/m² (6·77 lb/sq ft)

PERFORMANCE (A: at gross weight of 4,536 kg; 10,000 lb. B: at gross weight of 3,810 kg; 8,400 lb):

Never-exceed speed	155 knots (286 km/h; 178 mph)
Max cruising speed:	
A	145 knots (269 km/h; 167 mph)
B	155 knots (286 km/h; 178 mph)
Cruising speed for max range:	
A	125 knots (232 km/h; 144 mph)
Max rate of climb at S/L	411 m (1,350 ft)/min
Service ceiling: A	4,575 m (15,000 ft)
Service ceiling, one engine out: A	1,890 m (6,200 ft)
B	3,445 m (11,300 ft)
Hovering ceiling IGE: A	1,890 m (6,200 ft)
B	3,415 m (11,200 ft)
Range with 12 passengers, standard fuel, 30 min reserves	404 nm (748 km; 465 miles)
Range with 8 passengers, auxiliary fuel and offshore equipment	600 nm (1,112 km; 691 miles)

SIKORSKY S-76B

The Sikorsky S-76B is a version of the S-76 Mark II with Pratt & Whitney Canada PT6B-36 engines. Installation of the 716 kW (960 shp) turboshaft engines began in October 1983, when a ground test airframe was modified at Sikorsky's West Palm Beach facility for a 200 hour ground test programme which ended on 7 April 1984. A second PT6B-36 powered S-76B (N3123U) began flight testing on 22 June 1984, and was joined by the ground test machine in February 1985 in a test programme which led to FAA certification in late 1985. Sikorsky says that the PT6B-36 engines provide the S-76B with a 48 per cent increase in take-off power, resulting in a 51 per cent increase in useful load under hot and high conditions. With PT6B-36 engines the S-76B's maximum take-off weight is increased by 499 kg (1,100 lb), and the main transmission rating is increased to 1,118 kW (1,500 shp). Other modifications include a 15 per cent reduction in the area of the tail rotor pylon, and reconfigured engine exhaust fairings.

Recent customers for the S-76B include KLM Helicopters, which has ordered four to replace earlier S-76s.

The description of the S-76 Mark II applies also to the S-76B, except as follows:

POWER PLANT: Two 716 kW (960 shp) Pratt & Whitney Canada PT6B-36 turboshaft engines, maximum continuous power rating 649 kW (870 shp). Standard fuel capacity 1,064 litres (281 US gallons); auxiliary tank capacity 208 litres (55 US gallons)

WEIGHTS AND LOADINGS:

Weight empty	2,932 kg (6,465 lb)
Max T-O weight	5,171 kg (11,400 lb)
Max external load	1,497 kg (3,300 lb)
Max disc loading	36·62 kg/m² (7·50 lb/sq ft)
Max power loading	3·61 kg/kW (5·94 lb/shp)

PERFORMANCE (estimated, at max T-O weight):

Never-exceed speed	155 knots (287 km/h; 178 mph)
Max cruising speed	145 knots (269 km/h; 167 mph)
Econ cruising speed	131 knots (243 km/h; 151 mph)
Max rate of climb at S/L	640 m (2,100 ft)/min
Rate of climb at S/L, one engine out	160 m (525 ft)/min
Service ceiling	4,725 m (15,500 ft)
Service ceiling, one engine out	2,440 m (8,000 ft)

Prototype Sikorsky S-76B with 716 kW (960 shp) Pratt & Whitney Canada PT6B-36 turboshaft engines

Hovering ceiling IGE: ISA 2,560 m (8,400 ft)
ISA + 20°C 1,830 m (6,000 ft)
Hovering ceiling OGE: ISA 1,830 m (6,000 ft)
ISA + 20°C 518 m (1,700 ft)
Range with standard fuel, 30 min reserves, 131 knots (243 km/h; 151 mph) at 915 m (3,000 ft) 345 nm (639 km; 397 miles)
Range with max standard fuel, no reserves 385 nm (713 km; 443 miles)
Max range with auxiliary fuel, no reserves 434 nm (804 km; 500 miles)
Endurance, max standard fuel, no reserves 2 h 38 min

SIKORSKY H-76 EAGLE

The Sikorsky H-76 Eagle is a military development of the S-76B. The prototype (N3124G) made its first flight in February 1985 and was introduced at the Paris Air Show in May 1985. It incorporates the optional armoured crew seats, sliding cabin doors and heavy duty floor of that version, and introduces a wide range of optional items that include weapon pylons, an optical sight mounted above the instrument panel, self-sealing high strength fuel tanks, and provisions for door mounted weapons. The main transmission has been upgraded, as have the intermediate and tail rotor gearboxes. The main rotor hub and shaft have been strengthened, chord of the horizontal tail surface increased, dual spars employed in the vertical fin, and tail rotor blade chord increased. Fuselage skin thickness has been increased to withstand the blast of weapons launch. The H-76 can be equipped for troop transport/logistic support, as a gunship, and for roles including airborne assault, air observation post, combat SAR, evacuation, ambulance, and conventional SAR.

The H-76 Eagle can be equipped with either a mast mounted sight (MMS) or roof mounted sight (RMS). Further developments planned for the H-76 include a version armed with air-to-air missiles, of which the helicopter could carry up to 16, although a more likely weapons load would be eight AAMs and two cannon pods; head-up display; laser rangefinder; integrated armament management system; self-protection systems including a radar warning receiver, infra-red jammer and chaff/flare dispensers; high-clearance landing gear; and a Sperry SPZ-7000 automatic flight control system.

The description of the S-76 Mark II applies also to the H-76, except as follows:

Type: Twin-turbine armed utility helicopter.

Rotor System, Rotor Drive, Fuselage, Tail Unit and Landing Gear: Generally as for UH-60A. Strobex rotor blade tracker optional.

Power Plant: As for S-76B, except fuel is contained in two high strength, optionally self-sealing, tanks located below the rear cabin, with a total capacity of 993 litres (262·4 US gallons). Gravity refuelling point on each side of fuselage. Engine ice protection by bleed air anti-icing system. Engine fire detection and extinguishing systems. Engine air particle separator optional.

Accommodation: Pilot and co-pilot, plus varying troop/passenger loads according to role. Armoured pilot seats optional. Ten fully armed troops can be transported, or seven troops when configured as an airborne assault vehicle with multi-purpose pylon system (MPPS) and one 7·62 mm door gun installed. For evacuation use the cabin can be equipped with 12 seats or, in emergency, all seats can be removed and 16 persons can be airlifted sitting on the cabin floor. For SAR use the cabin will accommodate three patients on litters, or six persons lying prone on the floor and on the rear cabin raised deck. The standard medevac layout provides for three litters and a bench seat for two medical attendants.

Systems: Generally as for S-76B, except electrical system has a 17 or optional 34Ah battery.

Avionics and Equipment: Typical avionics include VHF-20A VHF transceiver, AN/ARC-186 VHF-AM/FM com, 719A UHF com, ADF-60A ADF, DF-301E UHF DF, VIR-30A VOR with ILS, glideslope and marker beacon receivers, DME-40 DME, TDR-90 transponder and dual RMI-36 RMI, all by Collins, course deviation indicators, ELT, Andrea A301-61A intercom, cabin speaker system and loudhailer. Typical equipment includes dual controls and instrumentation, stability augmentation system, dual 5 in VGIs, Allen RCA-26 standby self-contained attitude indicator, Collins ALT-50A radio altimeter, soundproofing, 'Fasten seat belt—No smoking' signs, first aid kit, two cabin fire extinguishers, external power socket, provisions for optional emergency flotation system, and provisions for installation of cargo hook with certificated capacity of 1,497 kg (3,300 lb), rescue hoist of 272 kg (600 lb) capacity. Standard lighting includes cockpit, cabin and instrument lights, navigation lights, anti-collision strobe light, and a battery operated self-contained cabin emergency light.

Armament: One 7·62 mm machine-gun can be pintle mounted in each doorway and fired with or without the MPPS system installed. Pintles incorporate field of fire limiters and will accept Fabrique National or Maramount M60D machine-guns. The MPPS can be installed on the cabin floor, providing the capability to carry and deploy pods containing single or twin 7·62 mm machine-guns, 0·50-in machine-guns, 2·75 in and 5 in rocket pods, Mk 66 2·75 in rockets, Oerlikon 68 mm rockets, Hellfire, TOW, Sea Skua and Stinger missiles, and Mk 46 torpedoes. Targeting equipment can include FLIR, Saab-Scania reticle sight, TOW roof sight or TOW mast mounted sight and laser rangefinder.

Dimensions, external and internal, and Areas:
Generally as for S-76B

Weights:
Weight empty 2,545 kg (5,610 lb)
Weight empty, equipped (typical) 3,030 kg (6,680 lb)
Max fuel weight 792 kg (1,745 lb)
Max T-O weight 5,171 kg (11,400 lb)

Performance:
Similar to S-76B, but range highly variable according to loading and mission

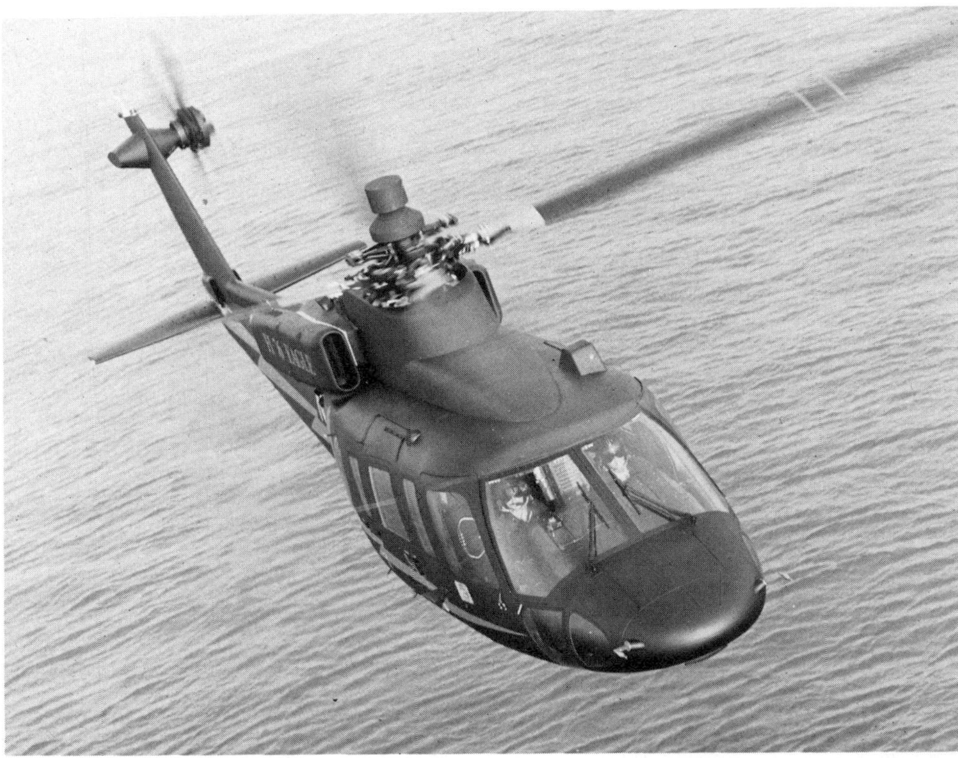

Sikorsky H-76 Eagle military utility helicopter (Pratt & Whitney Canada PT6B-36 turboshaft engines)

SIKORSKY H-76N

In February 1984 Sikorsky announced development of an H-76N naval version of the H-76, designed for anti-ship surveillance and targeting, anti-submarine warfare, surface attack, search and rescue, and utility missions, operating from frigate sized ships. Over-the-horizon targeting (OTHT) and anti-ship (ASV) variants will be available with Ferranti Seaspray 3 and MEL Super Searcher radars in mounted pods. The ASV H-76N will be armed with two British Aerospace Sea Skua air-to-surface missiles. The anti-submarine warfare version will have a dipping sonar, processing suite and two Gould Mark 46 or Marconi Underwater Systems Sting Ray torpedoes. Other developments planned for the naval version of the helicopter include a dual digital AFCS-coupled hover capability, target information data link, a tactical navigation system, hover in-flight refuelling system, roof- or mast-mounted FLIR system, ECM pod, chaff/flare dispensers on the tailboom, strengthened landing gear providing greater ground/deck clearance, folding main rotor blades, and provision for deck securing.

The first H-76N was expected to fly in 1986. It will be offered with a choice of Allison 250-C34S or Pratt & Whitney Canada PT6B-36 engines. Provisional specifications include an estimated empty weight (all versions) of 2,812 kg (6,200 lb) and max T-O weights of 4,473 kg (9,861 lb) for the OTHT variant, 4,968 kg (10,953 lb) for the ASV version and 4,754 kg (10,481 lb) for an H-76N equipped with a 136 kg (300 lb) ECM pod for secondary role jamming. Total fuel capacity for all proposed variants is 999 litres (264 US gallons).

SIKORSKY S-76 SHADOW

Sikorsky has modified an S-76 helicopter to have a new single-pilot cockpit attached to the forward fuselage, to test advanced automated cockpit concepts for the US Army's Advanced Rotorcraft Technology Integration (ARTI) programme. The added cockpit of this Sikorsky Helicopter Advanced Demonstrator of Operator Workload (SHADOW) is designed to have a sidearm controller of the kind first tested in the Summer of 1984 in a modified S-76, and features large window areas which can be partially or totally covered during testing to evaluate cockpit visibility impact on pilot workload and effectiveness. The SHADOW programme is supported by Bendix Flight Systems Division, Hamilton Standard, Kaiser Electronics, Litton Guidance and Control Systems, Northrop Electromechanical Division, Pacer Systems, Rockwell Collins Government Avionics Division, and Singer Kearfott. The single-pilot evaluation cockpit was joined to the forward fuselage of the S-76 SHADOW testbed in April 1985. The SHADOW made its first flight on 24 June 1985, with the single-pilot cockpit unmanned. After an initial 15-hour flight test programme it was due to be fitted with advanced equipment, including fly by wire sidearm control stick, voice interactive system, remote map reader, FLIR, and a programmable symbol generator feeding a head-up display, a visually coupled helmet mounted display, and dual CRT displays with touch-sensitive screens. In early 1986 the SHADOW was scheduled to begin daytime nap of the earth (NOE) navigation and command, control, communication and intelligence (C^3I) systems trials. It will retain its standard flight deck controls in the main cabin, to permit a safety pilot to monitor initial testing.

Artist's impression of Sikorsky H-76N naval helicopter with MEL Super Searcher radar and torpedoes

Sikorsky's partners in the SHADOW programme include Bendix, Kaiser, Litton, Northrop, Pacer Systems, Rockwell Collins, Singer and United Technologies Hamilton Standard division.

SIKORSKY S-72 X-WING PROJECT

Early in 1984 Sikorsky was awarded a contract valued at $77 million to modify one of NASA's two S-72 Rotor Systems Research Aircraft (RSRA: see 1979-80 *Jane's*) into a concept demonstrator for the NASA/Defense Advanced Research Projects Agency (DARPA) X-Wing rotor programme.

As a first step, an S-72 began a 13-flight test programme at NASA's Ames-Dryden Flight Research Facility on 8 May 1984 to prove the aircraft's suitability for flight in a fixed-wing mode. With its main rotor removed and long span wings installed, it expanded its proven performance envelope to 262 knots (485 km/h; 301 mph) and an altitude of 3,050 m (10,000 ft).

Sikorsky has designed the X-wing to replace the conventional rotor on the other S-72 (NASA 741), which was rolled out on 19 August 1986 and was scheduled to fly in this modified form in the Autumn of 1986. The X-wing will enable it to operate in the rotating-wing mode for take-off and hover, and then convert to fixed-wing flight for speeds up to 250 knots (463 km/h; 288 mph). Initial test flights will be conducted with the X-wing locked in the stationary position. The first transitional flights are not expected to take place until 1988 at the earliest.

Compressed air is blown through slots along either edge of the symmetrical aerofoil section of each blade. Separate plenums in the leading- and trailing-edges carry the compressed air to circulation control slots. Rotating-wing flight is made possible by adjusting the flow of air from valves in the pneumodynamic system to the control slots. This provides control of cyclic and collective pitch.

By means of a clutch, the X-wing can be made to stop turning and be locked into its correct fixed-wing position. All airflow from the blades is then ejected from the rearward-facing slots and can be modulated to provide roll control. Two T58-GE-10 turboshaft engines drive the rotor and air compressor. Two TF34-GE-400A turbofans provide propulsion in high-speed flight.

Sikorsky believes that successful trials of the X-wing could lead to development of a wingless demonstrator aircraft which would probably be powered by 'convertible' engines capable of producing combinations of shaft horsepower to drive the rotor system and thrust power for high speed cruising. Such a power plant is currently under development at NASA's Lewis Research Center. An X-wing concept demonstrator using this technology could be flying by 1990, followed by a production standard demonstrator by the year 2000.

CONVENTIONAL FIXED WINGS: Cantilever semi-monocoque type, of all-aluminium two-spar construction. Simple unbalanced ailerons; slotted trailing-edge flaps. All control surfaces are powered, with Sikorsky manufactured actuators.

X-WING: Each X-wing blade is a symmetrical composite sleeve over a supporting I beam of graphite construction. The blades are attached to a lightweight bearingless titanium hub.

FUSELAGE: Semi-monocoque fail-safe structure constructed from aluminium and advanced composites materials.

TAIL UNIT: Cantilever, semi-monocoque tailplane of all-aluminium two-spar construction. Surface is all-moving, with geared elevators and variable incidence control. Swept vertical fin incorporating tail rotor housing, with small horizontal stabiliser in T tail configuration. Ventral extension houses tailplane/elevator mount and tailwheel mounting. All controls powered, with Sikorsky actuators.

LANDING GEAR: Tailwheel type, with retractable main gear units and castoring tailwheel. Mainwheels retract inwards and are actuated hydraulically. Oleo-pneumatic shock absorbers. Goodyear tyres and disc brakes on mainwheels.

POWER PLANT: Two General Electric T58-GE-10 turboshaft engines, each rated at 1,044 kW (1,400 shp), power main rotor and air compressor. Two General Electric TF34-GE-400A engines, each rated at 41·26 kN (9,275 lb st), each mounted in pod at mid-fuselage position, provide propulsion in high-speed flight. Two fuel tanks, one forward with capacity of 1,234 litres (326 US gallons), one aft, capacity 1,306 litres (345 US gallons); total usable capacity 2,476 litres (654 US gallons). Oil capacity (T58 engines) 12·8 litres (3·39 US gallons).

ACCOMMODATION: Crew of two in unpressurised cockpit. Single door on starboard side of forward fuselage. Martin-Baker Mk US10LT crew escape system. Hamilton Standard R-70 air-conditioning system.

SYSTEMS: Pratt & Whitney axial compressor, max pressure 1·38 bars (20 lb/sq in), provides pneumatic pressure for rotor circulation control.

Sikorsky Helicopter Advanced Demonstrator of Operator Workload (SHADOW), based on an S-76

Sikorsky S-72 X-wing rotor systems research aircraft

DIMENSIONS, EXTERNAL:

Main rotor diameter	17·59 m (57 ft 8½ in)
Main rotor blade chord	0·91 m (3 ft 0 in)
Tail rotor diameter	3·24 m (10 ft 7½ in)
Distance between rotor centres	11·89 m (36 ft 11 in)
Wing aspect ratio	5·52
Wing chord: at root	2·93 m (9 ft 7¼ in)
at tip	1·95 m (6 ft 4¾ in)
Length overall, rotors turning	25·17 m (82 ft 7 in)
Fuselage length	21·51 m (70 ft 7 in)
Width, rotors folded	13·75 m (45 ft 1¼ in)
Wheelbase	3·30 m (10 ft 10 in)

AREAS:

Main rotor blades (each)	6·62 m² (71·25 sq ft)
Tail rotor blades (each)	0·38 m² (4·06 sq ft)
Main rotor disc	242·59 m² (2,611·20 sq ft)
Tail rotor disc	8·20 m² (88·30 sq ft)
Ailerons (total)	3·32 m² (35·70 sq ft)
Flaps (total)	5·37 m² (57·80 sq ft)
Fin	6·40 m² (68·86 sq ft)
Rudder	1·92 m² (20·66 sq ft)
Tailplanes: lower	8·20 m² (88·30 sq ft)
upper	1·60 m² (17·2 sq ft)
Elevators (total)	2·46 m² (26·5 sq ft)

WEIGHTS AND LOADINGS:

Max fuel weight	2,041 kg (4,500 lb)
Max T-O and landing weight	15,094 kg (33,276 lb)
Max ramp weight	15,774 kg (34,776 lb)
Max zero-fuel weight	13,733 kg (30,276 lb)
Max disc loading	62·20 kg/m² (12·74 lb/sq ft)
Max power loading	7·23 kg/kW (11·88 lb/shp)

PERFORMANCE (estimated):

Never-exceed speed at S/L	300 knots (556 km/h; 345 mph)
Max level speed at 1,525 m (5,000 ft)	314 knots (582 km/h; 361 mph)
Max cruising speed at 3,050 m (10,000 ft)	285 knots (528 km/h; 328 mph)
Econ cruising speed at 1,525 m (5,000 ft)	200 knots (371 km/h; 230 mph)
Max rate of climb at S/L	867 m (2,850 ft)/min
Service ceiling	3,050 m (10,000 ft)
T-O run	502 m (1,647 ft)
T-O to 15 m (50 ft)	551 m (1,807 ft)
Landing from 15 m (50 ft)	1,154 m (3,787 ft)
Landing run	575 m (1,887 ft)

SIKORSKY S-80

The S-80 is an export version of the USN/USMC CH-53E heavy duty helicopter. It is available in two forms: the **S-80E** is the basic heavy transport helicopter equivalent to the CH-53E; the **S-80M** is the export form of the airborne mine countermeasures MH-53E.

In its simplest configuration, the S-80E has a single-point cargo hook and operates in VFR conditions. Customers can enhance its capability with a variety of optional extras, including troop seats, cabin soundproofing, an internal cargo winch, external hoist of 272 kg (600 lb) capacity, two-point external cargo attachment, automatic blade and tail folding, two 2,460·5 litre (650 US gallon) drop tanks, ground to air and/or in-flight refuelling capability, engine air particle separators, and a wide range of com/nav equipment.

Japan has authorised funding for two S-80Ms, marking the first international sale of the MH-53E variant.

SKYTRADER

SKYTRADER CORPORATION

Richards-Gebaur Air Base, 15900 Kensington, Kansas City, Missouri 64147
Telephone: (816) 322 2811
Telex: 755964 SKYTRADER UD

PRESIDENT, CHAIRMAN AND CHIEF EXECUTIVE OFFICER: John J. Dupont

EXECUTIVE VICE-PRESIDENT, MARKETING: James F. Hudson

VICE-PRESIDENTS:
Ronald P. Barrett (Engineering and Government Programmes)
Major General L. W. Svendsen Jr [USAF, Rtd] (Special Operations Forces Programmes)

In December 1985, Skytrader Corporation announced plans for a manufacturing facility at Richards-Gebaur Air Base near Kansas City. Phase one of the development comprises a 2,044 m² (22,000 sq ft) office/hangar building housing design, engineering and parts manufacturing activities. A second phase will include a 8,631 m² (90,000 sq ft) production building, with a maximum production capacity of eight aircraft per month. Skytrader expects to employ some 300 staff when production of the ST1700 is under way.

In April 1986, Skytrader announced that it had signed agreements with Pilatus Flugzeugwerke of Switzerland giving it rights to assemble from kits and sell non-trainer versions of the Pilatus PC-9 to specific classified markets within the US Department of Defense. Like the military versions of the ST1700, the PC-9 is offered for low intensity conflict missions, counter-insurgency and anti-terrorist operations.

SKYTRADER ST1700 CONESTOGA/ST1700 MD EVADER

Design of a prototype Skytrader 800 was begun in 1972 by Dominion Aircraft Corporation Ltd, a Canadian company with facilities at Renton, Washington. Much of the design work was undertaken by former Boeing Company employees. The first aircraft (N800ST) made its first flight on 21 April 1975, and was last described in the 1979-80 edition of *Jane's*.

The Skytrader 800 was powered by two 298 kW (400 hp) Avco Lycoming IO-720-B1A piston engines. No production was undertaken before Dominion Aircraft ceased trading in 1979, and the project lay dormant until 1983 when Mr John J. Dupont acquired it and formed Skytrader Aircraft (renamed Skytrader Corporation in 1984). In October 1984 first details were announced of the **Skytrader ST1700 Conestoga** which, although based on the earlier Skytrader 800 design, differs in having two Pratt & Whitney Canada PT6A turboprop engines, a T tail, extended and drooped nose ahead of the flight deck for improved lift and field of view, cambered wing and tailplane tips incorporating aerodynamic twist, strengthened main landing gear legs with twin wheels, and overhead cockpit 'eyebrow' windows. The ST1700's cabin is 46 cm (18 in) longer and 10 cm (4 in) wider than that of the Skytrader 800, permitting a variety of quick-change internal configurations.

At the 1985 convention of the Army Aviation Association of America in St Louis, the **Skytrader ST1700 MD** (military derivative) **Evader** was first revealed, and development of this aircraft is now expected to precede production of the commercial ST1700. The Evader has a considerably greater max T-O weight and payload. It will be suitable for a wide variety of military missions, including tactical transport, with accommodation for up to 26 combat-equipped troops, casualty evacuation, cargo carrying and airdropping. A ½463L cargo roller system enables full LAPES, CARP, HARP and HALO airdrop techniques to be employed. There will be four hardpoints under the wings for stores, including external fuel tanks and gun pods, and pylons on the fuselage sides for two Sidewinder self-defence air-to-air missiles. Operations into landing strips 152 m (500 ft) long will be practicable, and a bolt-on fuselage float attaching to the main landing gear structure will permit operation off water. To permit night and 'stealth' missions the ST1700 MD's flight deck will be compatible with night vision goggles. Provision is made for in-flight refuelling capability.

The ST1700 MD Evader is among contenders for a Department of Defense contract for US multi-service light utility aircraft, for which there is an initial requirement for 18 aircraft.

TYPE: Twin-turboprop all-metal STOL commuter airliner and cargo aircraft.

WINGS: High-wing monoplane, with single bracing strut on each side. Constant chord wings, with electrically operated leading-edge slats. Aerofoil section NACA 230-13M. Full span ailerons and flaps on trailing-edge. Trim tab in each aileron. Cambered wingtips.

FUSELAGE: Conventional structure with rectangular cabin section and upswept rear end. Flight deck has large single window on each side forward of crew door and extending from floor height to below instrument panel mounting. Square cabin windows, eight on port side, seven on starboard.

TAIL UNIT: Cantilever T tail, with horizontal surfaces of constant chord. Dorsal fin. Trim tab in rudder.

LANDING GEAR: Non-retractable type. Twin wheels on nose and main legs, with oversize, low pressure tyres.

POWER PLANT: Two 708 kW (950 shp) Pratt & Whitney Canada PT6A-45R turboprop engines, each driving a Hartzell four-blade metal propeller. Internal fuel capacity 1,817 litres (480 US gallons). Provison for up to four 378 litre (100 US gallon) external tanks on underwing hardpoints.

ACCOMMODATION: Crew of two at front of cabin. 'Quick-change' cabin interior provides various internal arrangements including 18-passenger layout with 76 cm (30 in) pitch seating and 41 cm (16 in) aisle width, or all-freight. Access to flight deck via forward hinged door on each side, and to main cabin by airstair door on port side aft of wing. Hydraulically operated rear loading ramp/door, openable in flight for airdropping; double doors on starboard side at rear for oversized items or direct fork-lift loading. Cargo compartment can accept up to six D-type containers, each 1·02 × 1·02 × 1·02 m (40 × 40 × 40 in), or palletised or other cargo. Metric Systems Corporation onboard roller/restraint system for aerial delivery. Nose baggage compartment, capacity 136 kg (300 lb), accessible via upward opening door on port side.

Model of the Skytrader ST1700 MD Evader multi-role STOL aircraft

Prototype Skytrader SCOUT-STOL utility transport

AVIONICS: King Silver Crown system, including KNS-81 R/Nav, Bendix RDS-81 digital four-colour weather radar and King GC-381A radar graphics unit, standard.

DIMENSIONS, EXTERNAL:

Wing span	17·98 m (59 ft 0 in)
Wing chord (constant)	2·03 m (6 ft 8 in)
Length overall	15·85 m (52 ft 0 in)
Height overall	6·10 m (20 ft 0 in)
Fuselage: Max width	1·68 m (5 ft 6 in)
Tailplane span	7·11 m (23 ft 4 in)
Fuselage ground clearance	0·71 m (2 ft 4 in)
Wheel track (c/l of shock struts)	4·27 m (14 ft 0 in)
Rear cargo loading door: Length	2·44 m (8 ft 0 in)
Height from ground to top of cargo compartment	2·44 m (8 ft 0 in)
Double doors (stbd): Height	1·37 m (4 ft 6 in)
Width	1·39 m (4 ft 7 in)
Height to sill	0·91 m (3 ft 0 in)

DIMENSIONS, INTERNAL:

Cabin: Length, excl flight deck and space above ramp/door	7·11 m (23 ft 4 in)
Max width	1·37 m (4 ft 6 in)
Max height	1·65 m (5 ft 5 in)
Cargo volume, incl nose baggage compartment	17·98 m³ (635 cu ft)
Nose baggage compartment	0·69 m³ (24·5 cu ft)

WEIGHTS AND LOADING:

Weight empty: transport	3,810 kg (8,400 lb)
cargo	3,651 kg (8,050 lb)
Max T-O weight	7,710 kg (17,000 lb)
Max power loading	10·89 kg/kW (8·95 lb/shp)

PERFORMANCE (estimated, at max T-O weight except where indicated):

Max cruising speed at S/L	210 knots (389 km/h; 242 mph)
Max cruising speed at 3,050 m (10,000 ft)	190 knots (352 km/h; 219 mph)
Cruising speed, 75% power, at 3,050 m (10,000 ft)	170 knots (315 km/h; 196 mph)
Stalling speed at 7,484 kg (16,500 lb) weight, slats and flaps extended	50 knots (93 km/h; 58 mph)
Min control speed, one engine out	48 knots (89 km/h; 56 mph)
Max rate of climb at S/L	610 m (2,000 ft)/min
Rate of climb at S/L, one engine out	164 m (540 ft)/min
Service ceiling	7,620 m (25,000 ft)
Service ceiling, one engine out	4,875 m (16,000 ft)
T-O run	131 m (430 ft)
T-O to 15 m (50 ft)	257 m (845 ft)
Landing from 15 m (50 ft)	267 m (875 ft)
Landing run	114 m (375 ft)
Range, max internal fuel, 45 min reserves	1,100 nm (2,038 km; 1,266 miles)

SKYTRADER SCOUT-STOL

On 16 May 1986 Skytrader Corporation rolled out its SCOUT-STOL (small combat operations utility transport, short take-off and landing) aircraft, based on the airframe of the earlier Skytrader 800 prototype. This aircraft, which is approximately 85 per cent scale of the Skytrader ST1700 MD Evader, is powered by two 298 kW (400 hp) Avco Lycoming IO-720-B1A piston engines. It will serve as a proof of concept testbed and will also be offered in production form. In mid-1986 plans were in hand for the installation of two 522 kW (700 hp) Thunder Engines TE495-TC700 liquid-cooled V-8 engines, which would offer multi-fuel capability and enhance the aircraft's overall performance.

The SCOUT-STOL is intended as a multi-role aircraft and has a cabin volume of 9·49 m³ (335 cu ft), accommodating up to 16 people. Flight Systems Inc has been contracted to develop a weapons system for the aircraft, permitting the carriage of 2·75 in Hydra rockets, Stinger and Hellfire missiles and 0·50 in calibre machine-gun pods in a gunship role. Deliveries of the SCOUT-STOL could begin six months after receipt of a launch order.

DIMENSIONS, EXTERNAL:

Wing span	16·76 m (55 ft 0 in)
Length overall	12·80 m (42 ft 0 in)

PERFORMANCE:

Stalling speed	39 knots (73 km/h; 45 mph)
T-O and landing run	122 m (400 ft)
Range	2,084 nm (3,862 km; 2,400 miles)

SMITH

MIKE SMITH AERO INC

PO Box 430, Johnson, Kansas 67855
Telephone: (316) 492 6840
President: Michael D. Smith

SMITH XP-99 PROP-JET

Details of the prototype XP-99 Prop-Jet six-seat business aircraft can be found in the 1985-86 edition of *Jane's*. In early 1986 Mr Smith was seeking a buyer for the aircraft after negotiating with several manufacturers and investors to secure funding to proceed with the development programme.

SMITH TRI-TAIL BONANZA

Mike Smith Aero Inc has developed a conventional tail conversion for the Beech V tail Bonanza light aircraft. The modification, which was granted an FAA Supplemental Type Certificate in December 1985 following a first flight in June that year, involves the replacement of the Bonanza's V tail and a 1·83 m (6 ft) section of the rear fuselage with the rear fuselage, tailplane, elevators, fin and rudder from a Beech Model 33 Bonanza, in addition to modifications to the aircraft's control system. The Tri-Tail Bonanza conversion takes some three weeks to complete. The initial production schedule was for one conversion per month during 1986.

Prototype Smith Tri-Tail Bonanza conversion showing unpainted new fuselage and tail surface structure

SMITH BONANZA 400

Mike Smith Aero has developed a conversion of the Beechcraft Model A36 Bonanza in which the aircraft's standard 224 kW (300 hp) Teledyne Continental IO-550-B engine is replaced with a 298 kW (400 hp) Avco Lycoming IO-720 eight-cylinder power plant. The Bonanza 400 is also equipped with wingtip fuel tanks, each with a capacity of 76 litres (20 US gallons), bringing total usable fuel capacity to 431 litres (114 US gallons). A prototype (N1LX) was being evaluated during 1986 prior to a decision to seek FAA certification under a Supplemental Type Certificate. Provisional data include: Weight empty 1,074 kg (2,367 lb); Cruising speed at 3,050 m (10,000 ft) 203 knots (376 km/h; 234 mph); Max rate of climb at S/L in excess of 610 m (2,000 ft)/min.

SOLOY

SOLOY CONVERSIONS LTD

450 Pat Kennedy Way SW, Olympia, Washington 98502
Telephone: (206) 754 7000
Telex: 510 785 0241
President: Joe I. Soloy
Sales Manager: J. T. Koester
Marketing Group Manager: R. K. Furtick

Soloy Conversions has long been known for its turbine engine conversions of Bell 47G and Hiller UH-12E series helicopters. It is now devoting its major effort to expanding production of the Bell 47G conversion, and to work on its Turbine Pac specialised turboprop conversion scheme, development of which is being shared by the Allison Gas Turbine Division of General Motors Corporation. The Turbine Pac can be produced in 16 configurations, ranging from 313 to an eventual 548 kW (420-735 shp).

SOLOY TURBINE PAC CONVERSIONS

The Turbine Pac is a specialised turboprop conversion unit that can be used to update and improve the performance of a variety of fixed-wing aircraft. In its current form it is built around a 313 kW (420 shp) Allison 250-C20S, a 373 kW (500 shp) Allison 250-C28C, or a 485 kW (650 shp) Allison 250-C30 turboshaft engine, with a separate shaft driven 1,800 rpm reduction gearbox to provide the propeller drive. This gearbox is rated at more than 522 kW (700 shp) to allow for future growth versions of the engine.

Flight testing of the Turbine Pac began on 23 November 1981, using a Cessna Model 185 (N5010Y) and an Allison 250-C20 engine. In a programme funded jointly by Soloy, Allison and Hawker Pacific Pty Ltd, a Cessna 185 with a 313 kW (420 shp) 780-1000 Turbine Pac was delivered to Australia in the Spring of 1985 to act as a demonstrator in South-East Asia. A decision to proceed with certification of this conversion is to be made after market response has been evaluated. Subsequent installations have been made and flown in the Robertson/Brico O-2ST utility conversion (see Addenda to 1983-84 *Jane's*); in a Cessna 206 (N638HM) which has a 250-C20S Turbine Pac; and in a Cessna 207 (N21190) which also has a 250-C20S Turbine Pac and made its first flight on 14 January 1984. A second Cessna 207 joined the test programme in Spring 1985, and certification was achieved in early 1986. Soloy certificated the Turbine Pac Cessna 207 at a gross weight of 1,814 kg (4,000 lb). The prototype has demonstrated a cruising speed of 160 knots (297 km/h; 184 mph), a rate of climb at sea level of 518 m (1,700 ft)/min, and a take-off run at max gross weight of less than 175 m (575 ft).

The Soloy Turbine Pac conversion for the Cessna 206 received FAA certification on 22 May 1984 and is in production, with converted aircraft delivered to customers in Australia, Bolivia, Switzerland and the United States. The aircraft is approved for operation on Wipline and PK floats. Under development is an adaptation of the more powerful Allison Series IV turboshaft engine for single- and twin-engined aircraft. Soloy has also completed the experimental installation of a 313 kW (420 shp) Allison 250-B17 Turbine Pac in a Beech Bonanza A36 (N250AT) owned by Allison Gas Turbine Division, which is funding the certification programme for the installation; and the installation of an Allison 250-C30M in an Aérospatiale AStar 350D helicopter, certification of which was granted in early 1986.

The following data refer to the Cessna 206 Turbine Pac conversion:

Cessna Model 206 with Soloy Turbine Pac power plant for a Swiss parachuting club *(Mike Jerram)*

Prototype Soloy Turbine Pac installation in a Cessna 207

Aérospatiale AS 350D AStar helicopter with Allison 250-C30M engine installation by Soloy

POWER PLANT: One 313 kW (420 shp) Soloy Model 763 Turbine Pac/Allison 250-C20S turboprop engine, driving a Hartzell three-blade constant-speed propeller. Fuel capacity 230-348 litres (61-92 US gallons), depending on airframe model. Oil capacity 6·6 litres (7 US quarts).

WEIGHTS:
Weight empty 866 kg (1,910 lb)
Max T-O weight 1,633 kg (3,600 lb)

PERFORMANCE (at max T-O weight):
Never-exceed speed 148 knots (274 km/h; 170 mph) IAS
Max level speed and max cruising speed at 3,050-6,100 m (10,000-20,000 ft) 165 knots (306 km/h; 190 mph)
Econ cruising speed at 6,100 m (20,000 ft) 142 knots (263 km/h; 164 mph)
Stalling speed, flaps down, power off 46 knots (86 km/h; 53 mph) IAS
Max rate of climb at S/L 549 m (1,800 ft)/min
Service ceiling 6,100 m (20,000 ft)
T-O to 15 m (50 ft) at S/L, 20°C (69°F) 335 m (1,100 ft)
Landing from 15 m (50 ft) at S/L, 20°C (69°F) 169 m (553 ft)
Range with 333 litres (88 US gallons) usable fuel, 40% power at 6,100 m (20,000 ft), 30 min reserves 738 nm (1,367 km; 850 miles)

SPITFIRE

SPITFIRE HELICOPTER COMPANY LTD

PO Box 103, Lynnfield, Massachusetts

PRESIDENT: John J. Fetsko

VICE-PRESIDENT, MARKETING: Robert De More

In January 1975 Spitfire Helicopter Company began the design of a lightweight helicopter known as the Spitfire Mark I. Developed from the basic design of the Enstrom F-28A, this has a turbine power plant instead of the Avco Lycoming piston engine of the original aircraft. It was followed by design studies for a number of more advanced helicopters, of which details can be found in the 1984-85 and earlier editions of *Jane's*.

Under a 1978 agreement with Pezetel of Poland, Spitfire received rights to sell in Western markets a modified version, known as the Taurus, of the PZL Swidnik Kania twin-turbine helicopter (see Polish section). There has been no recent news of this agreement, or of Spitfire Helicopters International, which was formed in 1984 in partnership with a Spanish industrial development agency to continue certification and production of Spitfire's designs at a facility near Malaga in Spain.

SUMMIT

SUMMIT AVIATION INC

Summit Airpark, Middletown, Delaware 19709
Telephone: (302) 834 5400
Telex: 83-5499
MILITARY DIRECTOR: Patrick J. Foley

SUMMIT SENTRY O2-337

Summit Aviation developed this version of the Cessna Model T337 for a wide range of military missions. These include forward air control, helicopter escort, light air-to-ground attack, convoy protection, maritime patrol, six-seat personnel carrier, light cargo transport, aerial photography, psychological warfare and airborne discharge. Special configurations are available for VIP transport, medevac and high-altitude missions. In all configurations day or night capability can be provided.

Summit's modifications begin with the purchase of a Model T337, which was described under the Cessna entry in the 1980-81 *Jane's*. Power plant comprises two 168 kW (225 hp) Continental TSIO-360 turbocharged flat-six engines. For orders of fewer than 20 aircraft, Summit rebuilds Cessna T337 airframes to zero-time status. For larger orders the Cessna factory was originally expected to supply new airframes, as required, for Summit to outfit according to customer specification.

With four standard NATO MALL-4A pylons mounted beneath the wings, each able to carry a max load of 159 kg (350 lb), the Summit Sentry can carry weapons which include SUU-11A/A 7·62 mm gun pods; FFV UNI 12·75 mm gun pods; LAU-32A/A, 32B/A, 59A, 68A and 68B/A rocket launchers; CBU-14, SUU/14/A containers and bombs, LUU-1B, 5B, and Mod 6 Mk 3 markers; Mk 24 flares; ADSID; and a combined search radar and speaker system.

Summit O2-337s for the Royal Thai Navy air arm awaiting delivery

Summit supplied six Sentry O2-337s to the Royal Thai Navy air arm in 1980 and a further four in 1983. Other reported operators include the air forces of Haiti, Honduras, Nicaragua and Senegal. According to the *Washington Post* newspaper, at least three were supplied to the Nicaraguan *contras*, via the CIA, under Operation Elephant Herd in 1984.

Available specifications and performance details are as follows:

WEIGHTS:
Weight empty, approx 1,433 kg (3,160 lb)
Max T-O weight 2,359 kg (5,200 lb)
Max landing weight 2,200 kg (4,850 lb)

PERFORMANCE (at max T-O weight):
Max level speed:
at S/L 163 knots (302 km/h; 188 mph)
at 3,050 m (10,000 ft) 179 knots (332 km/h; 206 mph)
Max cruising speed:
at S/L 150 knots (278 km/h; 173 mph)
at 1,525 m (5,000 ft) 155 knots (287 km/h; 178 mph)
at 3,050 m (10,000 ft) 165 knots (306 km/h; 190 mph)
Max rate of climb at S/L 335 m (1,100 ft)/min
Service ceiling 8,690 m (28,500 ft)
T-O run 164 m (538 ft)
Landing run 137 m (449 ft)
Range at 75% power with 560 litres (148 US gallons) usable fuel 955 nm (1,770 km; 1,100 miles)
Max range, long-range cruise power, fuel as above 1,175 nm (2,177 km; 1,353 miles)

SUPER 580

SUPER 580 AIRCRAFT COMPANY

2192 Palomar Airport Road, Carlsbad, California 92008
Telephone: (619) 438 3600
PRESIDENT: Ted Vallas
VICE-PRESIDENT, ENGINEERING AND SALES: James Coleman

This company, a division of Flight Trails Inc, has the licence for a turboprop conversion and remanufacturing programme for the Convair 340/440/580 series of passenger/cargo transports, known as the Super 580, from the Allison Gas Turbine Division of General Motors Corporation.

SUPER 580 AIRCRAFT SUPER 580

The Super 580 conversion employs two Allison 501-D22G turboprop engines, each flat rated at 2,983 kW (4,000 shp), and driving a Hamilton Standard 54H60-77 four-blade, constant-speed feathering and reversing propeller, replacing the Pratt & Whitney R-2800 radial piston engines of the Convair 340/440 or the earlier Allison 501-D13 turboprops of the Convair 580. Compared with the Convair 580, of which some 170 were converted by Convair, the Super 580 is claimed to offer a 2·5 per cent improvement in specific fuel consumption, improved engine-out performance, greater reliability, a 13 per cent increase in range, a 40 per cent increase in hot-day payload capability, cruising speeds up to 325 knots (602 km/h; 374 mph), and a 40 per cent reduction in operating costs.

The Allison 501-D22G engine conversion has been designed as a quick-change nacelle/engine module, manufactured by subcontractor Jay Dee Aircraft Supply Co of Santa Monica, California. Standard fuel capacity is 6,738 litres (1,780 US gallons), with 7,790 litres (2,058 US gallons) and 11,008 litres (2,908 US gallons) available optionally. A Garrett 95.90 auxiliary power unit is installed in the starboard engine nacelle, and a new fire extinguisher system is standard. A tail-mounted APU is available as an option.

The Super 580 remanufacturing programme includes a redesigned flight deck with a King Gold Crown Series 3 avionics package and two Sperry Flight Systems flight directors. A Rockwell Collins flight director system, incorporating an EFIS display and two digital flight directors, is optional. All electrical wiring is replaced, but the aircraft's existing DC electrical system is retained. An AC system may be introduced at a later date, either as standard equipment or as an option. The Super 580's passenger cabin, pressurised at 0·29 bars (4·16 lb/sq in), is configured for 50 passengers in airline seats with 0·91 m (36 in) pitch, and features upgraded soundproofing, lavatory and galley facilities, 0·12 m³ (4·4 cu ft) capacity overhead baggage bins, indirect fluorescent lighting and individual reading lights and air vents.

Three cabin baggage compartments are provided: a 1·44 m³ (50·9 cu ft) forward compartment with a capacity of 227 kg (500 lb); a 5·64 m³ (199·2 cu ft) aft compartment, capacity 816 kg (1,800 lb); and a stowage area for carry-on baggage and garment bags. A 2·20 m³ (77·8 cu ft) belly compartment can accommodate 453 kg (1,000 lb) of cargo.

Piston engined Convair 340/440 aircraft undergoing remanufacture as Super 580s also require modifications to their tail surfaces. A 0·30 m (1 ft 0 in) fin extension and a larger rudder with an additional 1·11 m² (12·0 sq ft) of surface area are added, fin/rudder attachment points strengthened, and horizontal tail surfaces increased in span by 0·51 m (1 ft 8 in) at each tip, with an additional 1·58 m²

Artist's impression of Super 580 Falcon anti-drug surveillance aircraft

(17·0 sq ft) of elevator added. An anti-skid braking system and increased max T-O weight to 26,379 kg (58,156 lb) are available as options.

The first Super 580 conversion was performed by Hamilton Aviation, Tucson, Arizona. First flown after conversion on 21 March 1984, it was configured for quick-change corporate/commuter operations and delivered to The Way International of New Knoxville, Ohio, in June 1984 after receiving FAA approval to CAR 4b by means of a Supplemental Type Certificate. Like Hamilton Aviation's conversion, the first Super 580 Aircraft Company modification, which made its first flight on 20 November 1984, was based on a Convair 580 airframe. The third Super 580, which was being converted in the Spring of 1985, was the first to be based on a piston engined Convair 440. Air Resorts Airlines, which is also a division of Flight Trails Inc, planned to convert three of its Convair 440s to Super 580s during 1985, and will eventually convert all 11 of its aircraft.

The Super 580 Aircraft Company has joined with Westinghouse Electric Corporation in a proposal put before the US Treasury Department for an anti-drug surveillance version of the Super 580. This aircraft, known as the **Super 580 Falcon**, would be equipped with a Westinghouse AN/APG-66S radar mounted on the underside of the fuselage. Super 580 Aircraft is proposing an initial retrofit of 12 Convair 440s for use by the US Drug Enforcement Agency or US Customs Service to patrol southern border areas of the United States. An extension of the programme to 50 aircraft is envisaged. Aerodynamic engineering for the Super 580 Falcon would be performed by General Dynamics' Convair Division. The first conversion could be ready for flight testing in 20 months after go-ahead, with production aircraft available 24 months after contract award. The aircraft would have a cruising speed of 325 knots (602 km/h; 374 mph) and a range of 2,800 nm (5,189 km; 3,224 miles). A typical mission could involve a 200 nm (371 km; 230 mile) positioning leg, a 12 h 30 min loiter and return to base with IFR fuel reserves.

DIMENSIONS, EXTERNAL:
- Wing span: 32·08 m (105 ft 3 in)
- Length overall: 24·84 m (81 ft 6 in)
- Height overall: 8·89 m (29 ft 2 in)

DIMENSIONS, INTERNAL:
- Cabin: Length: 15·75 m (51 ft 8 in)
- Height: 1·98 m (6 ft 6 in)
- Width: 2·69 m (8 ft 10 in)

WEIGHTS:
- Basic operating weight: 14,742 kg (32,500 lb)
- Max fuel weight: 5,421 kg (11,951 lb)
- Max ramp weight: 24,947 kg (55,000 lb)
- Max T-O weight: 24,766 kg (54,600 lb)
- Max landing weight:
  - without anti-skid: 23,587 kg (52,000 lb)
  - with anti-skid: 24,040 kg (53,000 lb)
- Max zero-fuel weight: 21,319 kg (47,000 lb)

PERFORMANCE:
- Never-exceed speed: 349 knots (647 km/h; 402 mph)
- Max cruising speed:
  - at S/L: 280 knots (519 km/h; 322 mph)
  - at 3,050 m (10,000 ft): 310 knots (574 km/h; 357 mph)
- Stalling speed: 75-93 knots (139-173 km/h; 86-107 mph)
- Max rate of climb at S/L: 872 m (2,860 ft)/min
- Rate of climb at S/L, one engine out: 258 m (848 ft)/min
- Service ceiling: 7,620 m (25,000 ft)
- Service ceiling, one engine out: 6,860 m (22,500 ft)
- Range with 18 passengers: 1,920 nm (3,558 km; 2,211 miles)
- Max range, FAR domestic reserves: 2,000 nm (3,706 km; 2,303 miles)

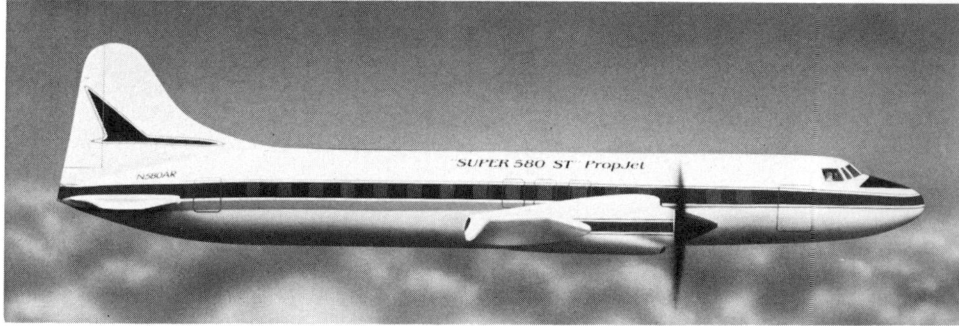

Artist's impression of the Super 580 ST, based on the Convair CV-580 airframe

SUPER 580 AIRCRAFT SUPER 580 ST

In 1984 the Convair Division of General Dynamics Corporation, under subcontract to Allison Division of General Motors, conducted feasibility studies for a 'stretch' of existing Convair 340/440, CV-580 and CV-640 airframes to permit increased payloads of up to 78 passengers or 8,618 kg (19,000 lb) of cargo. Super 580 Aircraft has applied for FAA Supplemental Type Certification for the conversion, to be known as the Super 580 ST (Stretch). Tooling design for the conversion has been completed by San Diego Aircraft Engineering, and a prototype is expected to fly in early 1987, with production aircraft following later that year. Super 580 Aircraft estimates that some 270 Convair airframes are potential candidates for Super 580 ST conversion.

Preliminary data include: length overall 29·18 m (95 ft 9 in); cabin volume 87·7 m³ (3,096 cu ft); cabin floor area 48·1 m² (518 sq ft); cargo capacity nine LD-3 containers or up to seven 2·2 × 2·7 m (88 × 108 in) pallets; passenger baggage capacity, standard 201 kg (444 lb), optional 228 kg (502 lb); empty weight, passenger 16,951 kg (37,370 lb), cargo 14,968 kg (33,000 lb); max T-O weight 27,215 kg (60,000 lb); max landing weight 24,947 kg (55,000 lb); max zero-fuel weight 23,587 kg (52,000 lb).

SWEARINGEN

SWEARINGEN AIRCRAFT CORPORATION

5418 Brewster Drive, San Antonio, Texas 78233
Telephone: (512) 657 2700
PRESIDENT: E. J. Swearingen
VICE-PRESIDENT: C. H. Green
MARKETING MANAGER: Robert H. Thalman

Well known as the designer of the Merlin and Metro twin-turboprop executive transports, Mr 'Ed' J. Swearingen initiated a modification programme to enhance the performance and operating economy of Beechcraft King Air 90 models.

Swearingen Aircraft (formerly Jetcrafters) also manufactures PT6A engine nacelles for Dornier GmbH for the Dornier 128-6, and prototype JT15D nacelles for Pratt & Whitney Canada. Details of Mr Swearingen's latest product, the high performance SX300 two-seat light aircraft, can be found in the Sport Aircraft section.

SWEARINGEN TAURUS MODIFICATION

Any model ofthe Beechcraft King Air 90 series (except the T tail F90) can be improved by incorporation of the Swearingen Taurus modification. This involves replacing the existing engines with Pratt & Whitney Canada PT6A-135 turboprop engines, each flat rated at 522 kW (700 shp); modification of the existing engine nacelles to reduce their height and cross-sectional area; provision of new cowls, engine air inlets, inertial water/ice separators, a new low-profile exhaust system to reduce drag and increase thrust, new oil cooler airflow control system, and a new integral nacelle fuel tank with full lightning strike protection; removal of the existing engine driven cabin supercharger and provision of a new flow control system to provide dual bleed air pressurisation; and the supply of new engine torque indicators.

After embodiment of the Taurus modification, the King Air 90, A90, B90, C90 and E90 are redesignated respectively Taurus 90, A90, B90, C90 and E90. By early 1985 Swearingen had completed 12 Taurus modifications.

Swearingen Taurus modification of a Beechcraft King Air Model 90

Brief details of performance improvements follow:

PERFORMANCE (A: Taurus 90; B: A90; C: B90; D: C90; and E: E90):
- Max cruising speed at optimum altitude:
  - A, B, C, D, E: 278 knots (515 km/h; 320 mph)
- Stalling speed, flaps down:
  - A, B, C, D, E: 69 knots (127 km/h; 79 mph)
- Max rate of climb at S/L: A: 913 m (2,995 ft)/min
  - B: 884 m (2,900 ft)/min
  - C, D: 852 m (2,795 ft)/min
  - E: 814 m (2,670 ft)/min
- Service ceiling: A, B, C, D, E: 11,430 m (37,500 ft)
- T-O to 15 m (50 ft): A, B: 625 m (2,050 ft)
  - C: 533 m (1,750 ft)
  - D: 689 m (2,261 ft)
  - E: 617 m (2,024 ft)
- Landing from 15 m (50 ft): A, B: 716 m (2,350 ft)
  - C, D: 613 m (2,010 ft)
  - E: 643 m (2,110 ft)

TAYLORCRAFT

TAYLORCRAFT AVIATION CORPORATION

PO Box 947, 820 East Bald Eagle Street, Lock Haven, Pennsylvania 17745
PRESIDENT: George A. Ruckle

Taylorcraft Aviation Corporation, which was re-formed on 1 April 1968 primarily to provide product support, also put into production a two-seat trainer/sporting aircraft designated Model F-19 Sportsman 100, based on the well known Taylorcraft Model B of Second World War origin.

In early 1980, the Model F-19 (see 1979-80 *Jane's*) was taken out of production, and the company certificated a higher powered verson designated F-21. This was supplemented by a new Model F-21A for 1983, but the latter model has been discontinued and was replaced by the F-21B during 1985.

On 9 July 1985 the company was acquired by a group of former Piper Aircraft Company employees, and the production facility was moved from its former base at Alliance, Ohio, to the Piper Memorial Airport at Lock Haven, Pennsylvania. The first production aircraft from the new assembly line was rolled out on 9 January 1986.

In early 1986 Taylorcraft Aviation Corporation acquired manufacturing rights for Edo floats, and was negotiating the purchase of type certificates for the Varga Kachina range of two-seat low-wing light aeroplanes (see 1983-84 *Jane's*). The possibility of reintroducing the four-seat Taylorcraft Ranch Wagon, manufactured briefly during the mid-1950s, was also under consideration. In the Spring of 1986 the company had a total of 35 employees.

TAYLORCRAFT MODEL F-21

TYPE: Two-seat trainer/sporting aircraft.

WINGS: Braced high-wing monoplane with V bracing struts each side. Wing section NACA 23012. Dihedral 1°. Composite structure with spruce spars, stamped metal ribs and Dacron covering. Plain wide-span ailerons of similar construction. No flaps. No trim tabs.

FUSELAGE: Welded structure of 4130 steel tube with Dacron covering.

Taylorcraft Model F-21B two-seat trainer/sporting aircraft *(Howard Levy)*

Tail Unit: Wire braced welded steel tube structure with Dacron covering. Trim tab in port elevator.

Landing Gear: Non-retractable tailwheel type. Two side Vs and half-axles. Mainwheels fitted with 6·00-6 4-ply tyres; swivelling tailwheel has tyre of 152 mm (6 in) diameter. Floats and Aero M1500 or M2000 skis optional.

Power Plant: One 88 kW (118 hp) Avco Lycoming O-235-L2C flat-four engine, driving a Sensenich 72CK-O-50 two-blade fixed-pitch metal propeller with spinner. One fuel tank in each wing, with combined capacity of 45·4 litres (12 US gallons), and one fuel tank in fuselage, immediately aft of firewall, with capacity of 45·4 litres (12 US gallons). Total fuel capacity 90·8 litres (24 US gallons). Oil capacity 5·7 litres (1·5 US gallons).

Accommodation: Two seats, with shoulder harnesses, side by side in enclosed cabin. Dual controls standard. Metal door with sliding window each side. Accommodation heated and ventilated.

System: Electrical system powered by 12V 60A engine driven alternator, with 12V storage battery. Wiring provisions for navigation lights. Engine driven vacuum pump when optional blind-flying instrumentation installed.

Equipment: Standard equipment includes recording tachometer, sensitive altimeter, electric oil temperature gauge, oil pressure gauge, ammeter, compass, airspeed indicator, wiring provisions for navigation lights, glove compartment and compartment for radio installation. Optional equipment includes oil cooler, strobe and navigation lights, wheel fairings, emergency locator transmitter, and avionics to customer choice, including full IFR panel with gyros.

Dimensions, external:

Wing span	10·97 m (36 ft 0 in)
Wing chord (constant)	1·60 m (5 ft 3 in)
Length overall	6·74 m (22 ft 1¼ in)
Height overall	1·98 m (6 ft 6 in)
Tailplane span	3·05 m (10 ft 0 in)
Wheel track	1·83 m (6 ft 0 in)
Propeller diameter	1·83 m (6 ft 0 in)

Areas:

Wings, gross	17·07 m² (183·71 sq ft)
Ailerons (total)	1·86 m² (20·0 sq ft)
Fin	0·34 m² (3·7 sq ft)
Rudder	0·59 m² (6·3 sq ft)
Tailplane	1·21 m² (13·0 sq ft)
Elevators, incl tab	0·99 m² (10·66 sq ft)

Weights and Loadings:

Weight empty	435 kg (960 lb)
Max T-O weight	680 kg (1,500 lb)
Max wing loading	39·9 kg/m² (8·17 lb/sq ft)
Max power loading	7·73 kg/kW (12·71 lb/hp)

Performance (at max T-O weight):

Max level speed at S/L	108 knots (201 km/h; 125 mph)
Max cruising speed, 75% power at 2,440 m (8,000 ft)	102-106 knots (190-196 km/h; 118-122 mph)
Stalling speed, power off	38 knots (70 km/h; 43 mph)
Max rate of climb at S/L	267 m (875 ft)/min
Service ceiling	5,485 m (18,000 ft)
T-O run	84 m (275 ft)
T-O to, and landing from, 15 m (50 ft)	107 m (350 ft)
Range with max fuel	347 nm (644 km; 400 miles)

TAYLORCRAFT F-21B

In Spring 1985 Taylorcraft built a prototype of the Model F-21B, and production was reportedly at the rate of one per week in March 1986. The F-21B is similar to the F-21 but with some modifications to the tubular structure to permit an increased max T-O weight and a new fuel system. The 22·7 litre (6 US gallon) tank in each wing is replaced by a 79·5 litre (21 US gallon) tank, and the fuselage tank is deleted, giving a total usable fuel capacity of 159 litres (42 US gallons).

Landing Gear: Tailwheel has pneumatic tyre of 203 mm (8 in) diameter. Scott 203 mm (8 in) diameter tailwheel and Maule P8B-1-2 tundra tailwheel optional. Dual hydraulic toe brakes standard.

Accommodation: Standard equipment includes door locks and window latches, carpeted floor and cargo tiedown straps. Baggage compartment aft of seats, standard capacity 91 kg (200 lb), with extension tube 1·22 m (4 ft) long by 15 cm (6 in) diameter for fishing equipment, and side windows.

Avionics and Equipment: Optional avionics to customer requirements. Standard equipment includes large instrument panel with radio rack in centre, wiring for landing light in port wing, skylight windows, and tiedown rings. Optional equipment includes full blind-flying instrumentation; attitude and directional gyros, electric clock, vacuum system, Whelen wingtip strobe lights and fin strobe light, streamline wheel fairings, Stewart Warner oil cooler installation, and choice of internal and external colour schemes.

Weights and Loadings:

Weight empty	465 kg (1,025 lb)
Max T-O weight	794 kg (1,750 lb)
Max wing loading	46·48 kg/m² (9·52 lb/sq ft)
Max power loading	9·02 kg/kW (14·83 lb/hp)

Performance (at max T-O weight):

Never-exceed speed	128 knots (237 km/h; 147 mph)
Max level speed	108 knots (201 km/h; 125 mph)
Stalling speed, power off	42 knots (78 km/h; 48 mph)
Max rate of climb at S/L	229 m (750 ft)/min
T-O run	107 m (350 ft)
T-O to, and landing from, 15 m (50 ft)	130 m (425 ft)
Landing run	152 m (500 ft)
Range, 75% power with 30 min reserves	636 nm (1,178 km; 732 miles)

g limits:

Normal category, max T-O weight	+3·8/−1·52
Utility category at 626 kg (1,380 lb) AUW	+4·4/−1·76

TAYLORCRAFT F-22 PHOENIX

The Model F-22 made its public debut in prototype form at the 1985 EAA Convention at Oshkosh. A development of the Model F-21B, it differs principally in having manually operated wing flaps which reduce the stalling speed, power off, by 4 knots (8 km/h; 5 mph). Description is as for the Model F-21B except that adjustable bucket seats with storage compartments, and swing-out door windows, are standard, and the tubular structure in the cabin area has been redesigned to facilitate entry and exit. A 91 × 173 cm (36 × 68 in) or 91 × 91 cm (36 × 36 in) skylight window is optional. FAA approval of the F-22 was expected in 1986. The aircraft will be certificated in the Normal and Utility categories, and will be offered with a choice of tailwheel, tricycle, ski or float landing gear.

Weights:

Weight empty	494 kg (1,090 lb)
Baggage capacity	91 kg (200 lb)

Performance (estimated):

Stalling speed, power off, flaps down	38 knots (70 km/h; 43 mph)
T-O run, flaps down	91 m (300 ft)
T-O to, and landing from, 15 m (50 ft)	115 m (375 ft)

Prototype Taylorcraft F-22 Phoenix with tricycle landing gear *(J. M. G. Gradidge)*

THORP

THORP T211 AIRCRAFT INC

Oldman's Airport, Pedrickton, New Jersey 08067
Telephone: (609) 299 3634
Owners: Tom Kurtz, Harry Gehrke and Earl McGuire

THORP T211

This two-seat light aircraft, designed by Mr John Thorp, originated as the T-11 Sky Scooter, which flew for the first time in 1946 with a 48·5 kW (65 hp) engine and was last described in the 1950-51 *Jane's*. Several versions were developed, but plans to market them in kit form did not materialise. Adams Industries subsequently put the type into production as the Thorp T211, with a more powerful engine, for business, recreational and training purposes. The first 14 T211s were assembled from components already in existence.

In 1985, Mr Tom Kurtz, Mr Harry Gehrke and Mr Earl McGuire purchased all rights in the aircraft from Adams Industries, together with tooling and components. Under the new company name, the T211 is again on the market, offered in ready assembled and kit forms.

Thorp T211, offered in ready assembled and kit form by Thorp 211 Aircraft Inc *(Geoffrey P. Jones)*

The details given below appeared in the 1983-84 *Jane's* under the Adams heading. It is not known if the newly offered T211 differs in any major respects, although it has been reported that the company was interested in fitting a two-cylinder engine of 74·5 kW (100 hp) to the T211 to reduce its weight. No confirmation of this has been received.

TYPE: Two-seat cabin monoplane.

WINGS: Cantilever low-wing monoplane. All-metal structure with ribbed skins. Wide span manually operated three-position trailing-edge flaps, and plain ailerons, both with ribbed skins. No trim tabs.

FUSELAGE: All-metal semi-monocoque structure of light alloy.

TAIL UNIT: Cantilever structure of light alloy; elevators, all-moving tailplane and rudder have ribbed skins. Ground adjustable tab on rudder.

LANDING GEAR: Non-retractable tricycle type, with single wheel on each unit. Oleo-pneumatic shock absorber in each unit. All three wheels size 500 × 4. Handbrake and parking brake.

POWER PLANT: One 74·5 kW (100 hp) Continental O-200-A flat-four engine, driving a McCauley two-blade fixed-pitch metal propeller with spinner. Fuel capacity 91 litres (24 US gallons), of which 87 litres (23 US gallons) are usable. Oil capacity 5·7 litres (1·5 US gallons).

ACCOMMODATION: Two seats side by side beneath rearward sliding transparent canopy. Baggage capacity 36 kg (80 lb).

SYSTEM: Electrical system supplied by 12V 20A generator and 12V 25Ah storage battery.

AVIONICS AND EQUIPMENT: Optional avionics package by Collins includes VHF-251 com, VIR-351 nav, IND-350 VOR/LOC receiver/indicator, TDR-950 transponder, noise cancelling microphone and emergency locator transmitter. Optional equipment is as detailed in the Convenience and Operational groups.

DIMENSIONS, EXTERNAL:
- Wing span: 7·62 m (25 ft 0 in)
- Length overall: 5·49 m (18 ft 0 in)
- Height overall: 2·44 m (8 ft 0 in)
- Propeller diameter: 1·70 m (5 ft 7 in)

AREA:
- Wings, gross: 9·75 m² (105·0 sq ft)

WEIGHTS AND LOADINGS:
- Weight empty: 332 kg (733 lb)
- Max T-O and landing weight: 576 kg (1,270 lb)
- Max wing loading: 59·1 kg/m² (12·1 lb/sq ft)
- Max power loading: 7·73 kg/kW (12·7 lb/hp)

PERFORMANCE (at max T-O weight):
- Max level speed at S/L: 137 knots (254 km/h; 158 mph)
- Cruising speed (75% power): 104 knots (193 km/h; 120 mph)
- Stalling speed, flaps down: 34 knots (63 km/h; 39 mph)
- Max rate of climb at S/L: 290 m (950 ft)/min
- Service ceiling: 5,790 m (19,000 ft)
- T-O run: 91 m (300 ft)
- Landing run: 61 m (200 ft)
- Range at 55% power, with max fuel and reserves: 417 nm (772 km; 480 miles)

TURBOTECH

TURBOTECH INC

Pearson Air Park, 1115 E 5th Street, PO Box 61586, Vancouver, Washington 98666
Telephone: (206) 694 6287
PRESIDENT: L. W. Soukup

Turbotech Inc (formerly Seaplanes Inc) is carrying out STOL and/or performance improvements to a variety of lightplanes manufactured by Beech, Cessna, Gulfstream American, Maule, Piper, Stinson and Waco. Performance increases result largely from replacing the original power plant by an engine of increased power. The company has also designed a STOL kit for installation on Cessna 170B, 172, 175, 180, 182, 185, 206 and 210 aircraft. This includes a stall fence, leading-edge cuff and aileron gap seals, which improve take-off and landing performance by approx 7 per cent.

Turbotech Inc conversion of Cessna 185F with 261 kW (350 hp) Avco Lycoming TIO-540-J2BD turbocharged engine

Power plant replacements include removal of the existing engine from Cessna 170, 172 and 175, and Stinson 108 aircraft, and the installation of a 164 kW (220 hp) Franklin flat-six engine and constant-speed propeller. The 186 kW (250 hp) turbocharged Franklin, also with constant-speed propeller, can be installed in the Cessna 172, 175, Stinson 108 and Waco Vela. This power plant is used also for installation in the Maule M-5 Lunar Rocket in lieu of a 157 kW (210 hp) Continental or 164 kW (220 hp) Franklin engine. The 172 kW (230 hp) Continental O-470 is also available for the Stinson 108. Feasibility studies were in progress in 1984 for engine conversions for the Cessna 207, 210 and Cardinal RG.

The 224 kW (300 hp) Avco Lycoming IO-540-K is used for one installation in the Cessna 185, but Turbotech obtained Supplemental Type Certificates during 1982 for two additional engine modifications on this aircraft. These cover the installation of a 261 kW (350 hp) Avco Lycoming TIO-540-J2BD, and the introduction of a Garrett AiResearch turbocharger for the 224 kW (300 hp) Continental IO-520-D of the standard Cessna 185. These conversions give the aircraft full performance to a service ceiling of 7,620 m (25,000 ft) and 7,315 m (24,000 ft) respectively. The Cessna 206 has also been approved with the 261 kW (350 hp) Avco Lycoming TIO-540-J2BD turbocharged engine. A gross weight increase of 93 kg (205 lb) with installation of tip tanks was approved in July 1983.

Recent developments include the installation of a turbocharger on a 224 kW (300 hp) Continental IO-520-D for the Cessna 180, and an add-on turbocharger modification on the Gulfstream American AA-5B Tiger powered by a 134 kW (180 hp) Avco Lycoming O-360-A4K flat-four engine. The **Turbo Tiger** modification includes a high strength stainless exhaust system, retractable cowl flaps, additional oil cooler, Electronics International induction temperature gauge, high pressure fuel pump, and a combined manifold/fuel pressure gauge. The conversion adds 13·6 kg (30 lb) to the aircraft's empty weight. Performance, at max T-O weight, includes a max level speed at 1,070 m (3,500 ft) of 129 knots (240 km/h; 149 mph) IAS; max level speed at 3,050 m (10,000 ft) of 118 knots (219 km/h; 136 mph) IAS; max level speed at 7,620 m (25,000 ft) of 92 knots (170 km/h; 106 mph) IAS; max rate of climb at S/L of 274 m (900 ft)/min; and service ceiling of 7,620 m (25,000 ft).

Performance figures for all other Turbotech conversions that had been certificated by early 1986 are given in the accompanying table.

		Max level speed knots (km/h; mph)	Max cruising speed at 2,135 m (7,000 ft) knots (km/h; mph)	Max rate of climb at S/L m (ft)/min	Service ceiling m (ft)	T-O run m (ft)	Range nm (km; miles)
Cessna 170A/B	A	148 (274; 170)	137 (254; 158)	457 (1,500)	5,485 (18,000)	91 (300)	434 (804; 500)
	F	126 (233; 145)	116 (216; 134)	366 (1,200)	4,265 (14,000)	152 (500)	478 (885; 550)
	G	139 (257; 160)	126 (233; 145)	396 (1,300)	4,875 (16,000)	122 (400)	478 (885; 550)
Cessna 172 land	A	145 (269; 167)	135·5 (251; 156)	427 (1,400)	5,485 (18,000)	91 (300)	521 (966; 600)
Cessna 172 float	A**	126 (233; 145)	118 (217; 135)	335 (1,100)	4,875 (16,000)	320 (1,050)	412 (764; 475)
Cessna 172 land turbo	B	148 (274; 170)*	148 (274; 170)	549 (1,800)	7,620 (25,000)*	84 (275)	521 (966; 600)
Cessna 172 float turbo	B**	135 (249; 155)	135 (249; 155)	457 (1,500)	6,100 (20,000)*	381 (1,250)	412 (764; 475)
Cessna 175	A	145 (269; 167)	135·5 (251; 156)	427 (1,400)	5,485 (18,000)	91 (300)	521 (966; 600)
Cessna 175 turbo	B	148 (274; 170)*	148 (274; 170)	549 (1,800)	7,620 (25,000)	84 (275)	521 (966; 600)
Cessna 180 turbo	J	154 (285; 177)*	165 (306; 190)	366 (1,200)	7,315 (24,000)	244 (800)	551 (1,207; 750)
Cessna 185 land	C	158 (293; 182)	151 (280; 174)	351 (1,150)	5,790 (19,000)	244 (800)	595 (1,287; 800)
Cessna 185 float	C	144 (267; 166)	136 (253; 157)	326 (1,070)	5,180 (17,000)	411 (1,350)	608 (1,126; 700)
Cessna 185 turbo	I	174 (322; 200)	169 (314; 195)§	610 (2,000)	7,620 (25,000)	229 (750)	651 (1,207; 750)
Cessna 185 turbo	J	154 (285; 177)*	165 (306; 190)§§	366 (1,200)	7,315 (24,000)	244 (800)	651 (1,207; 750)
Cessna 206 turbo	I	169 (314; 195)	165 (306; 190)	533 (1,750)	8,230 (27,000)	255 (835)	805 (1,492; 927)
Stinson 108-2/-3	A	139 (257; 160)	131 (243; 151)	488 (1,600)	5,485 (18,000)	91 (300)	521 (966; 600)ϕ
Stinson 108-2/-3 turbo	B	139 (257; 160)*	139 (257; 160)	579 (1,900)	7,620 (25,000)*	84 (275)	521 (966; 600)ϕ
Stinson 108-2/-3	D	139 (257; 160)*	126 (233; 145)	488 (1,600)	5,640 (18,500)	84 (275)	521 (966; 600)ϕ
Stinson 108-2/-3	H	122 (225; 140)	113 (209; 130)	335 (1,100)	4,875 (16,000)	137 (450)	521 (966; 600)ϕ
Beech Bonanza A35-C35 turbo	B	181 (336; 209)	181 (336; 209)	518 (1,700)	6,400 (21,000)*	256 (840)	868 (1,609; 1,000)†
Maule M-4 turbo	B	152 (282; 175)	142 (264; 164)	549 (1,800)	7,620 (25,000)*	84 (275)	564 (1,046; 650)
Maule M-5 turbo	E	149 (277; 172)	156 (290; 180)	411 (1,350)	7,620 (25,000)*	91 (300)	695 (1,287; 800)
Waco Vela turbo	B	169 (314; 195)	161 (298; 185)	442 (1,450)	6,100 (20,000)*	258 (845)	912 (1,690; 1,050)

A 164 kW (220 hp) Franklin 6A-350
B 186 kW (250 hp) Franklin 6AS-350 turbocharged
C 224 kW (300 hp) Avco Lycoming IO-540-K
D 172 kW (230 hp) Continental O-470-K/L/R
E 175 kW (235 hp) Avco Lycoming O-540-J1A5D turbocharged
F 123 kW (165 hp) Franklin 6A4-165-B3
G 134 kW (180 hp) Franklin 6A-335-B
H 134 kW (180 hp) Avco Lycoming O-360
I 261 kW (350 hp) Avco Lycoming TIO-540-J2BD turbocharged
J 224 kW (300 hp) Continental IO-520-D turbocharged
* max certificated speed/altitude
** gross weight increased to 1,134 kg (2,499 lb)
ϕ Stinson 108-2 range 434 nm (804 km; 500 miles)
§ 187 knots (346 km/h; 215 mph) at 6,700 m (22,000 ft)
§§ 178 knots (330 km/h; 205 mph) at 6,700 m (22,000 ft)
† with tip tanks

UNIVAIR

UNIVAIR AIRCRAFT CORPORATION

Route 3, PO Box 59, Aurora, Colorado 80011
Telephone: (303) 364 7661
Telex: 317327
CHAIRMAN OF THE BOARD: Veda Dyer Williams
PRESIDENT: Stephen E. Dyer
VICE-PRESIDENT: Robert M. Williams
MARKETING MANAGER: Michael D. Sellers
SECRETARY: Janice M. Dyer

Univair Aircraft Corporation, founded in 1946, is a company specialising in the manufacture of propellers and components for light aircraft. It holds 19 type certificates and 36 supplemental type certificates, drawings, production tooling and rights to manufacture many post-war 'classic' US light aircraft, including the Ercoupe, Alon, Forney and Mooney M-10 Cadet series; and the Stinson 108 series. Details of these aircraft have appeared in earlier editions of *Jane's,* under their original manufacturers. The company holds 623 parts manufacture approvals (PMAs), covering over 3,000 items for these aircraft. Wing lift struts for fabric wing Cessna 120 and 140 aircraft are but a single example of the parts being manufactured for older designs produced originally by such companies as Aeronca, Cessna, Luscombe, Navion, Piper and Taylorcraft.

Propellers produced by Univair under type certificate include Flottorp wooden fixed-pitch, Flottorp variable-pitch (of Beech-Roby design), Flottorp F1 fixed-pitch and F12 constant-speed metal, Flottorp F200 and Aeromatic 220 automatic propellers.

Univair rebuilt a Piper J3 Cub and re-engined it with a Continental O-200. Certification tests were completed in 1977 and the company was awarded a multiple Supplemental Type Certificate by the FAA for O-200 engine installations in clipped-wing J3 Cubs. Either an Aeromatic automatically adjustable propeller, or a McCauley fixed-pitch metal propeller, can be used with this STC.

In early 1985 Univair acquired Piper Aircraft Corporation's inventory of spare parts for out of production Piper aircraft, including the J-3 Cub, J-4 Cub Coupé, J-5 Cub Cruiser, PA-11 Cub Special, PA-12 Super Cruiser, PA-14 Family Cruiser, PA-15 and PA-17 Vagabond, PA-16 Clipper, PA-20 Pacer and PA-22 Tri Pacer, Caribbean and Colt series.

UNIVAIR STINSON 108-3

In addition to supplying replacement parts for the Stinson 108 series, Univair has developed an engine modification for these aircraft. In May 1983 FAA approval was granted to Univair for replacement of the original 123 kW (165 hp) Franklin engine in the Stinson 108-3 with a 149 kW (200 hp) Avco Lycoming IO-360-A1A, driving a Hartzell constant-speed propeller. The company is also developing a 134 kW (180 hp) Avco Lycoming O-360 installation to replace the 111 kW (150 hp) Franklin engines in Stinson 108, 108-1 and 108-2 models.

The following description applies to the Univair Stinson Model 108-3, with IO-360-A1A engine conversion:

TYPE: Four-seat cabin monoplane.

WINGS: Braced high-wing monoplane, with light alloy V bracing struts each side. Wing section NACA 4412. Dihedral 2° 30'. Incidence 1° 31' at root, 0° 7' at tip. No sweepback. Contant chord two-spar structure of light alloy with fabric covering. Plain ailerons of light alloy and fabric covering, with a fixed slot forward of each aileron. Plain trailing-edge flaps of light alloy stressed skin construction. Ground adjustable tab on each aileron.

Univair Stinson 108 four-seat cabin monoplane with Avco Lycoming IO-360-A1A engine

FUSELAGE: Welded steel tube structure, with fabric covering.

TAIL UNIT: Cantilever all-metal structure of light alloy. Fixed incidence tailplane with horn balanced elevators. Servo tab in port elevator. Horn balanced rudder with servo tab.

LANDING GEAR: Non-retractable tailwheel type. Cantilever main units with spring/hydraulic shock absorbers. Cleveland mainwheels with tyres size 7·00-6, pressure 1·38 bars (20 lb/sq in). Scott 3200 steerable tailwheel, with tyre size 2·80 × 2·50-4, pressure 1·72 bars (25 lb/sq in). Cleveland hydraulic shoe or disc brakes.

POWER PLANT: One 149 kW (200 hp) Avco Lycoming IO-360-A1A flat-four engine, driving a Hartzell two-blade constant-speed metal propeller, type HC-C2YK/7666, with spinner. One fuel tank in each wing; total capacity 189·3 litres (50 US gallons). Refuelling point on inboard upper surface of each wing. Oil capacity 5·66 litres (1·5 US gallons).

ACCOMMODATION: Standard seating for four in two pairs, with rear seats easily removable to accommodate cargo or extra baggage. Door, with window, on each side of cabin. Accommodation heated and ventilated. Space for 45 kg (100 lb) baggage, with external access door.

SYSTEMS: Electrical system powered by 12V DC engine driven alternator, with storage battery.

DIMENSIONS, EXTERNAL:	
Wing span	10·34 m (33 ft 11 in)
Wing chord, constant	1·45 m (4 ft 9 in)
Wing aspect ratio	6·8
Length overall	7·67 m (25 ft 2 in)
Height overall	2·29 m (7 ft 6 in)
Tailplane span	3·40 m (11 ft 2 in)
Wheel track	2·16 m (7 ft 1 in)
Wheelbase	5·66 m (18 ft 7 in)
Propeller diameter	1·93 m (6 ft 4 in)
Propeller ground clearance	0·23 m (9·14 in)
Passenger doors (each): Height	1·22 m (4 ft 0 in)
Width	0·76 m (2 ft 6 in)
Height to sill	0·81 m (2 ft 8 in)
Baggage door: Height	0·61 m (2 ft 0 in)
Width	0·56 m (1 ft 10 in)
Height to sill	0·99 m (3 ft 3 in)
DIMENSIONS, INTERNAL:	
Cabin: Length	1·75 m (5 ft 9 in)
Max width	0·97 m (3 ft 2 in)
Max height	1·42 m (4 ft 8 in)
AREAS:	
Wings, gross	14·4 m² (155 sq ft)
Ailerons (total)	1·675 m² (18·02 sq ft)
Trailing-edge flaps (total)	1·14 m² (12·22 sq ft)
Fin	1·33 m² (14·28 sq ft)
Rudder, incl tab	0·63 m² (6·78 sq ft)
Tailplane	1·36 m² (14·66 sq ft)
Elevators, incl tab	1·60 m² (17·24 sq ft)
WEIGHTS AND LOADINGS:	
Weight empty, equipped	590 kg (1,300 lb)
Max T-O and landing weight	1,088 kg (2,400 lb)
Max wing loading	75·7 kg/m² (15·5 lb/sq ft)
Max power loading	8·12 kg/kW (13·3 lb/hp)
PERFORMANCE (at max T-O weight):	
Never-exceed speed	147 knots (273 km/h; 170 mph)
Max level speed at S/L	132 knots (245 km/h; 152 mph)
Max cruising speed, 75% power at 1,525 m (5,000 ft)	117 knots (217 km/h; 135 mph)
Econ cruising speed at 2,285 m (7,500 ft)	115 knots (212 km/h; 132 mph)
Stalling speed: flaps up	57 knots (105 km/h; 65 mph)
flaps down	53 knots (99 km/h; 61 mph)
Max rate of climb at S/L	305 m (1,000 ft)/min
Service ceiling	5,790 m (19,000 ft)
T-O run	122 m (400 ft)
T-O to 15 m (50 ft)	213 m (700 ft)
Landing from 15 m (50 ft)	198 m (650 ft)
Landing run	91·5 m (300 ft)
Range with max payload, 45 min reserves	412 nm (764 km; 475 miles)

USAC

UNITED STATES AIRCRAFT CORPORATION

3000 North Clybourn Avenue, Burbank, California 91505
Telephone: (818) 843 6076
Telex: 3781862 USAC
PRESIDENT: Stephen J. Snyder
VICE-PRESIDENT: Robert W. Lillibridge

USAC DC-3 TURBO EXPRESS

USAC, which specialises in major structural conversions/modifications to aircraft, and produces turboprop engine quick change packages, has converted a Douglas DC-3 to turboprop power. This has involved much more than a simple replacement of the power plant, for the 935 ekW (1,254 ehp) Pratt & Whitney Canada PT6A-45R engines that have been installed are collectively some 1,588 kg (3,500 lb) lighter than the two radial piston engines that they replace. To maintain the required CG position a 1·02 m (3 ft 4 in) plug has been inserted in the fuselage forward of the wing, providing increased cabin volume for passengers or cargo.

Other changes include strengthening of the engine mounting/wing attachments; the use of Hartzell five-blade propellers; addition of a fairing at the leading-edge of each outer wing panel to improve cruising performance and power-on stall characteristics; and a modified square tipped tailplane to improve longitudinal stability. System changes provide new 300A starter/generators with modern control units, a new electrical system, modified hydraulic system, an updated fire protection system, and updated instrumentation. Fuel capacity has been increased by 3,028 litres (800 US gallons) by the addition of tanks in the outer wing panels.

The prototype USAC Turbo Express conversion of the Douglas DC-3

The first flight of the prototype conversion (N300TX) was made on 28 July 1982. It was anticipated that the best-range cruising speed of the Turbo Express conversion, estimated at 206 knots (381 km/h; 236 mph), would be some 62·5 knots (116 km/h; 72 mph) higher than that of the standard DC-3, carrying a payload increased by some 1,588 kg (3,500 lb) to 5,955 kg (13,128 lb). Fuel consumption is 379 litres (100 US gallons)/h at 165 knots (306 km/h; 190 mph) at 3,050 m (10,000 ft). Stalling speed with 45° flap is 55 knots (102 km/h; 64 mph) IAS.

It was reported in 1984 that Harold's Air Service of Fairbanks, Alaska, had become the first customer for the DC-3 Turbo Express, with an option on a second conversion, following certification on 1 December 1983.

USAF

UNITED STATES AIR FORCE SYSTEMS COMMAND

Aeronautical Systems Division, Wright-Patterson AFB, Dayton, Ohio 45433

ATF Programme Director: Colonel Albert C. Piccirillo

USAF ADVANCED TACTICAL FIGHTER (ATF)

US Air Force designations: YF-22A and YF-23A

The Advanced Tactical Fighter (ATF) represents a United States Air Force requirement for a new air-superiority fighter to replace the McDonnell Douglas F-15 Eagle. The ATF programme also includes development of an advanced technology engine for the aircraft . Concept definition study contracts were awarded in September 1983 to Boeing, General Dynamics, Grumman, Lockheed, McDonnell Douglas, Northrop and Rockwell. These companies submitted their prototype design proposals to the USAF on 28 July 1986.

On 31 October 1986 the USAF announced the selection of Lockheed-California and Northrop to begin the prototype phase of the ATF programme. Under respective designations **YF-22A** and **YF-23A**, each contractor will build two flying prototypes for demonstration and validation purposes, leading to selection of the successful ATF contender in 1991 when the full scale development phase will begin. The prototypes are expected to fly in late 1989. Engines for the ATF will be developed from ground demonstrator power plants which were being readied for testing in late 1986. Pratt & Whitney's prototype engine is designated YF119 and General Electric's YF120. Each of the prototype aircraft will be required to fly with GE and P&W engines.

The USAF has a requirement for up to 750 ATFs, with IOC anticipated in the mid-1990s. The US Navy is also evaluating the ATF as a possible replacement for the Grumman F-14 Tomcat as a fleet air defence interceptor at the end of this century. Up to 550 'navalised' ATFs could be required.

VOLPAR

VOLPAR INC

7701 Woodley Avenue, Van Nuys, California 91406
Telephone: (818) 994 5023
Telex: 651482 VOLPAR B VAN

President and Chief Executive Officer:
Carl G. Hokanson

Vice-Presidents:
Frank V. Nixon (Development)
E. Savva (Operations)

Volpar Inc was formed in 1960 to design, develop and manufacture tricycle landing gear kits for the Beechcraft Model 18.

Volpar next developed and produced kits to convert the Model 18 to turbine power, using the Garrett TPE331 engine. The basic converted aircraft was known as the Turbo 18. Further changes were embodied in a 'stretched' version known as the Turboliner, and in the Turboliner II which gained approval under SFAR 23 for commuter airline operation.

Using nacelles that were developed for the Turbo 18 and Turboliner, Volpar then produced an engine installation marketed under the name Packaged Power which has been fitted to a variety of aircraft including the Beechcraft Model 18, de Havilland Dove, de Havilland Beaver and Grumman Goose. The latest Packaged Power units offer a choice of Garrett TPE331 or Pratt & Whitney Canada PT6A series engines, up to and including the PT6A-65, and have been proposed by Volpar for re-engining Grumman HU-16 Albatross amphibians and Grumman S-2 Tracker anti-submarine aircraft.

Volpar's current activities include systems installations, avionics fitting and customised interior and exterior work on a variety of airline-class aircraft for corporate and commercial operator customers.

VOYAGER

VOYAGER AIRCRAFT INC

Hangar 77, Mojave Airport, California 93501
Telephone: (805) 824 4790

Directors:
Richard G. Rutan
Jeana Yeager

VOYAGER AIRCRAFT VOYAGER

Voyager Aircraft Inc was formed in March 1981 by Richard 'Dick' Rutan, brother of designer Burt Rutan, and Jeana Yeager to build and fly an aircraft designed to make a non-stop, unrefuelled flight around the world. Design work on the aircraft, then known as the Rutan Model 76, was undertaken by Burt Rutan, and construction began at the Rutan Aircraft Factory in the Summer of 1982 in the hands of Bruce Evans, an experienced builder of Rutan's all-composite canard designs. The Voyager (N269VA) was rolled out at Mojave on 2 June 1984 and made a 30-minute first flight on 22 June, piloted by Dick Rutan. A second, three-hour, flight was made on 24 June, and by early July the first long-duration flight, of some eleven hours airborne time, had been completed. In August 1984, on its eleventh flight, with Dick Rutan and Jeana Yeager aboard, Voyager flew from its home base at Mojave, California, to the EAA convention at Oshkosh, Wisconsin, with a single stop at Salina, Kansas.

By July 1986 Voyager had completed 130 hours of test flying in 44 flights. On 10 July the aircraft left Vandenberg AFB, California, to make an unrefuelled five-day flight of 20 laps of a closed circuit course between Santa Barbara and San Francisco. Voyager flew 10,074·4 nm (18,669·8 km; 11,600·9 miles) in 111 hours, returning to Mojave Airport on 15 July. During the flight Voyager averaged a ground speed of 90 knots (167 km/h; 104 mph) and consumed 1,744 litres (460·7 US gallons) of fuel. Gross take-off weight was 2,689 kg (5,929 lb) and landing weight 1,467 kg (3,234 lb).

To meet FAI requirements for certification as an international record, Voyager will have to fly a distance of at least 19,850 nm (36,786 km; 22,858 miles) on its round-the-world flight. Voyager Inc's plans call for a flight of more than 21,711 nm (40,234 km; 25,000 miles), following a southern hemisphere route eastward from the United States, passing the southern tip of Africa, across Australia and Hawaii. Ninety-five per cent of the planned route is over water. The flight is expected to last between 10-12 days, starting and finishing at Edwards Air Force Base in California.

Departure was planned for October 1986. The route will be optimised and updated by Lockheed's Dataplan flight planning system, with weather information provided by the company's Metplan service via a portable onboard terminal. The project is expected to cost a total of $900,000, which is being raised by private donations and commercial sponsorships.

Type: Two-crew, twin-engined centreline thrust long-range aircraft of 'trimaran' configuration.

Wings: Cantilever, high aspect ratio surfaces with solid, oven-cured Magnamite graphite main spars. Skinning from Magnamite graphite sheets over Hexcel paper honeycomb core, with some aramid/glassfibre/epoxy laminate material. Trailing-edge of wing from balsa wood with ColorTex heat-shrunk plastics covering. Small vertical winglet at each tip. Wing section: Roncz 10-80 at root, Roncz 10-82 at tip. Forward canard surface, with slight forward sweep, of similar construction to wings and with small vortex generators on upper surface. Canard section, Roncz 10-46. Ailerons on outer panels of main wing, elevators on forward canard surface. Trim tab on canard.

Fuselage: Structure made from Magnamite graphite/Hexcel honeycomb composite. Two tailbooms of similar construction.

Tail Unit: Single vertical fin mounted on each tailboom. Rudder incorporated in starboard side fin only.

Landing Gear: Retractable tricycle type, tyre size (all) 6·00-6, pressure 10·34 bars (150 lb/sq in). Retraction mechanism is manual and operates independently for each unit. Nosewheel retracted by pulling on D-handle; mainwheels retracted by stainless steel cable with ratcheted pulley, locked by bracket clamped over cable. Manually operated brake on nosewheel only.

Power Plant: Two horizontally opposed piston engines, manufactured by Teledyne Continental, mounted fore and aft of centre fuselage/cabin pod in centreline thrust arrangement, and driving two-blade composite variable-pitch electrically controlled feathering and reversing propellers manufactured by MT Propeller of Straubing, West Germany. Front engine 96·9 kW (130 hp) Teledyne Continental O-240, rear engine 82 kW (110 hp) Teledyne Continental IOL-200. Front engine will be used primarily for take-off and initial high-speed cruise, and will be shut down for much of the record flight attempt. Total fuel capacity 5,636 litres (1,489 US gallons) contained in 17 integral fuel tanks formed by the aircraft's primary structure. Feeder tank forward of cabin area has a sight gauge for contents; all fuel from other tanks pumped selectively via the feeder tank. Tank switching accomplished by two 'eight into one' manual fuel valves. Provision for 'slow overboard' dump of fuel, but no provision for fast fuel dumping.

Accommodation: Centre-section of main fuselage pod contains a cockpit/cabin area with a single pilot's seat on starboard side. Bunk for crew rest and sleep to rear of pilot's position. Two square windows on each side of fuselage adjacent to cockpit. Small bubble canopy in cockpit roof for forward view during take-off and landing. Accommodation is not pressurised.

Avionics and Equipment: A full package of avionics has been supplied by King Radio, including KNS 660 VLF Omega navigation system, KHF 990 long range communications transceiver, KAP 150 autopilot, KX 165 VHF com transceiver, KWX 58 colour digital weather radar with 10 in flat plate phased-array antenna, and a Telonics transponder that will be interrogated by two Argos satellites in Polar orbit for position pinpointing at world flight command post in Washington DC. Portable oxygen concentrator system for use up to 8,535 m (28,000 ft).

Dimensions, external:

Wing span	33·77 m (110 ft 9½ in)
Wing aspect ratio	33·8
Canard span	10·15 m (33 ft 3½ in)
Canard aspect ratio	18·1
Fuselage: Length	7·74 m (25 ft 4¾ in)
Max width	1·00 m (3 ft 3½ in)
Height over tail fins	3·14 m (10 ft 3½ in)
Fuel tank boom length (each)	8·90 m (29 ft 2½ in)

Dimensions, internal:

Cabin: Length	2·29 m (7 ft 6 in)
Width	0·61 m (2 ft 0 in)
Cockpit: Length	1·71 m (5 ft 7 in)
Width	0·55 m (1 ft 9½ in)

Areas:

Wings, gross	33·72 m² (363·0 sq ft)
Canard surfaces (total)	5·67 m² (61·0 sq ft)

Weights:

Structural weight	426 kg (939 lb)
Weight empty	843 kg (1,858 lb)
Weight of fuel	4,052 kg (8,934 lb)
Max T-O weight (world flight)	5,137 kg (11,326 lb)
Landing weight (world flight)	1,032 kg (2,276 lb)

Performance (estimated):

T-O run at max T-O weight	2,743 m (9,000 ft)
Cruising speed (world flight)	70-130 knots (130-241 km/h; 81-150 mph)
Range, max fuel	more than 24,316 nm (45,062 km; 28,000 miles)
Endurance	14 days

Voyager aircraft, built for an unrefuelled round-the-world flight

WILLIAMS

WILLIAMS INTERNATIONAL

2280 West Maple Road, PO Box 200, Walled Lake, Michigan 48088
Telephone: (313) 624 5200
OFFICERS: see Engines section

WILLIAMS V-JET

In order to demonstrate the feasibility of a new generation of lightweight business jets powered by its 8·00 kN (1,800 lb st) FJ44 turbofan engine, Williams International constructed a 1985 mockup of a proposed V-Jet with the aim of stimulating interest among business jet manufacturers and corporate operators. The V-Jet, for which no production plans have been announced, is a three-surface aircraft with forward-swept wings, T tail with sweptback horizontal surfaces, swept fin and unswept canards. The airframe is constructed from composite materials. Two FJ44 turbofan engines are mounted at the rear of the wingroots, with inlets in the forward root areas. Control surfaces are conventional and comprise ailerons, elevators and rudder, with trailing-edge flaps linked to control surfaces on the rear of the forward canard to eliminate trim changes with flap deployment. Projected data for the V-Jet include: wing span 9·75 m (32 ft 0 in); length overall 12·30 m (40 ft 4¼ in); fuselage length 11·76 m (38 ft 7 in); tailplane span 3·50 m (11 ft 6 in); canard span 3·13 m (10 ft 1 in); wheel track 4·95 m (16 ft 3 in); wheelbase 2·64 m (8 ft 8 in); maximum cruising speed Mach 0·84; max rate of climb at S/L 1,539 m (5,050 ft)/min; rate of climb with one engine out 500 m (1,640 ft)/min; maximum range with 45 min reserves 1,520 nm (2,816 km; 1,750 miles); range with two crew, four passengers, at cruising speed of Mach 0·8 at 13,100 m (43,000 ft), 45 min reserves 1,389 nm (2,575 km; 1,600 miles); FAA balanced field length 965 m (3,167 ft).

Williams International believes that a new generation of business jets such as the V-Jet with max T-O weight ranging from 3,175-4,536 kg (7,000-10,000 lb) will have cruise speeds of Mach 0·70-0·85, and will have purchase and operating costs of 50 per cent less than most current business jets.

WILLIAMS X-JET

The Williams X-Jet is a development of the WASP-II (Williams Aerial Systems Platform), described in the 1984-85 *Jane's*. Described as an advanced one-man VTOL system, the craft is powered by a 2·67 kN (600 lb st) Williams International WR19 miniature turbofan engine. The X-Jet can move forward, backward, sideways, hover and rotate on its axis. Maximum speed is approximately 52 knots (96 km/h; 60 mph) and endurance 30 minutes. Williams International envisages military applications for the X-Jet which could include liaison, reconnaissance, mine detection, field communications, courier work and rescue. Civil applications could include law enforcement, firefighting, media coverage, rescue and airborne medical aid.

Mockup of Williams International's projected V-Jet new generation light business jet

Williams International X-Jet one-man VTOL craft

WIPAIRE

WIPAIRE INC

South End Doane Trail, Inver Grove Heights, Minnesota 55075
Telephone: (612) 451 1205
Telex: 297051
PRESIDENT: Robert Wiplinger

WIPAIRE SUPER BEAVER

This company, well known for its range of Wipline floats and amphibious floats for light and utility aircraft, has developed a modification for the de Havilland Canada DHC-2 Beaver. Known as the Wipaire Super Beaver, the conversion is based on surplus US Army and USAF L-20 Beaver airframes, which are completely dismantled, stripped and inspected using dye penetrant tests on all structural attachment points. All nuts, bolts and rod ends are replaced with new items, and old control cables with stainless steel cables. Roof windows are faired over, additional side windows (two per side) added aft of the cabin doors, and a rear cargo hatch installed. The rear cabin area is extended by 0·71 m (2 ft 4 in), and a 0·58 m × 0·35 m (23 in × 14 in) baggage hatch installed. To adjust the aircraft's centre of gravity the battery is moved forward from this area. Heavy soundproofing, tinted windows and articulating Cessna seats are installed in the cabin. All engine accessories for the 335·5 kW (450 hp) Pratt & Whitney R-985 power plant are replaced, and the engine extensively overhauled. A Hartzell three-blade constant-speed metal propeller with spinner replaces the standard two-blade Hamilton Standard unit. Wipaire Model 6000 amphibious floats are available optionally.

Wipaire Inc Super Beaver on amphibious floats

The first Super Beaver was delivered to an Alaskan customer in April 1983. The company anticipates sales of at least six aircraft per year.

WREN

WREN AIRCRAFT INC

Municipal Airport, Route 2, Box 351, Buckeye, Arizona 85326
Telephone: (602) 386 6204
PRESIDENT: Todd Peterson

Production of the Wren 460 by the original Wren Aircraft Corporation, then based at Fort Worth, Texas, came to an end in 1969. Production was resumed by a newly formed Wren Aircraft Inc in February 1982.

WREN 460P

The Wren 460P is a four-seat STOL light aircraft based on the airframe of a Cessna 182. The original prototype flew for the first time in 1963, and FAA certification was received in June 1964. Subsequent versions benefited from improvements made annually by Cessna in the Model 182.

Upgrading to Wren 460P configuration makes no changes to the power or gross weight of the basic Cessna 182 airframe. Four Wren devices provide the aircraft with its slow flying and STOL capabilities, as follows:

1. Full span double-slotted Fowler flaps are installed. The outer panel of the new flaps, on each wing, operates as

both an aileron and a flap in the flaps-extended position. Wing lift coefficient increases from 1·5 to 2·6 as the flaps deflect to their maximum 30° position. A button control on the pilot's control wheel enables the flaps to be retracted instantly on touchdown, for faster braking, without the pilot needing to remove his hands from the wheel or throttle.

2. The basic NACA 2412 wing section nose radius of 2·6 cm (1·01 in) is increased to 3·8 cm (1·50 in) by the use of a sheet metal glove. This postpones wing stalling from the normal 16° angle of attack to 20° and provides a lift coefficient increment of 0·4 independent of flap deflection. The stalling characteristics are extremely docile, with no trace of lateral roll-off.

3. A set of small articulated horizontal control surfaces, known as the ULS (ultra low speed) nose control system, is mounted on the nose of the aircraft, immediately aft of the propeller. These control surfaces, each comprising a stabiliser, elevator and tab, are connected permanently to the conventional elevator control system and work in conjunction with this system. They act in the propeller slipstream to augment pitch control in slow-speed flight. The ULS controls serve to reduce the balancing tail download required to trim out the nose-down pitching moment when the flaps are extended, and this provides an increase in the aircraft's total lift.

4. A set of five feathering drag plates, known as 'Wren's Teeth', is added to each wing upper surface. These drag plates operate on a harmonic linkage with the ailerons and deflect outward through 60° when the aileron is deflected up. This further decreases lift on the downgoing wing and, more importantly, increases drag on the downgoing wing so that the normal adverse aileron yaw is overcome and the aircraft yaws into rather than away from its turn. Positive and immediate roll response to control deflection is achieved down to an indicated airspeed of 31 knots (56 km/h; 35 mph) in ground effect.

The Wren 460 is unusual in its ability to utilise fully its slow flying capability. At 39-52 knots (72-97 km/h; 45-60 mph) only 30 per cent power is required and the aircraft can maintain level flight, in level attitude, with no engine heating or cooling problems. At these speeds, it is even more manoeuvrable than at high cruising speeds.

TYPE: Four-seat STOL light aircraft.

WINGS: Braced high-wing monoplane with single streamline section bracing strut each side. Wing section NACA 2412 (modified) with constant radius leading-edge cuff (fixed droop). Dihedral 1° 44'. Incidence 0° 55' at root, −3° 8' at tip. All-metal structure, Flaps, ailerons and drag plates described in introductory copy.

FUSELAGE, LANDING GEAR: As for standard Cessna 182, except that larger wheels and tyres are fitted. Mainwheels and tyres size 8·00-6, pressure 1·72 bars (25 lb/sq in). Nosewheel and tyre size 6·00-6, pressure 1·45 bars (21 lb/sq in) standard. Nosewheel tyre size 8·00-6 optional, for use on extra rough or extra soft landing areas. Float and ski installations optional.

Wren 460P four-seat STOL light aircraft *(Neil A. Macdougall)*

TAIL UNIT: As for Cessna 182, but with electrically actuated automatic trim system, which adjusts tailplane incidence as flaps are raised and lowered, giving reduced landing and take-off runs.

POWER PLANT: One 172 kW (230 hp) Continental O-470-R flat-six engine, driving a McCauley two-blade constant-speed metal propeller. Hartzell reversible-pitch propeller optional. Standard fuel capacity 303 litres (80 US gallons). Oil capacity 11·4 litres (3 US gallons).

ACCOMMODATION: Four seats in pairs in enclosed cabin, with provision for additional seat for a child. Dual controls optional. Forward hinged door on each side. Three seats removable for freight carrying. Space aft of seats for 54 kg (120 lb) baggage.

SYSTEMS: Air-conditioning system optional. Hydraulic system for brakes. Oxygen system optional. 12V electrical system.

DIMENSIONS, EXTERNAL:

Wing span	10·92 m (35 ft 10 in)
Length overall	8·33 m (27 ft 4 in)
Height overall	2·74 m (9 ft 0 in)
Tailplane span	3·55 m (11 ft 8 in)
ULS surfaces span	2·29 m (7 ft 6 in)
Wheel track	2·74 m (9 ft 0 in)
Wheelbase	1·69 m (5 ft 6½ in)
Propeller diameter: standard	2·08 m (6 ft 10 in)
optional	2·24 m (7 ft 4 in)

DIMENSIONS, INTERNAL:

Cabin: Length	2·74 m (9 ft 0 in)
Max width	1·09 m (3 ft 7 in)
Max height	1·27 m (4 ft 2 in)

AREAS:

Wings, gross	16·30 m² (175·4 sq ft)
Ailerons (total)	1·50 m² (16·1 sq ft)
Trailing-edge flaps, including ailerons (total)	4·25 m² (45·7 sq ft)
Drag plates (total)	0·29 m² (3·1 sq ft)
Fin, incl dorsal fin	1·08 m² (11·6 sq ft)
Rudder	0·65 m² (7·0 sq ft)
Tailplane	1·90 m² (20·4 sq ft)
Elevators	1·46 m² (15·7 sq ft)
ULS surfaces	0·65 m² (7·0 sq ft)

WEIGHTS AND LOADINGS:

Weight empty, equipped	770 kg (1,697 lb)
Max fuel weight	254 kg (560 lb)
Max T-O and landing weight:	
Normal	1,270 kg (2,800 lb)
Restricted category	1,655 kg (3,650 lb)
Max wing loading:	
Normal	77·9 kg/m² (15·96 lb/sq ft)
Max power loading:	
Normal	7·41 kg/kW (12·17 lb/hp)

PERFORMANCE (at max T-O weight):

Max cruising speed at 2,440 m (8,000 ft)	139 knots (257 km/h; 160 mph)
Econ cruising speed at 1,830 m (6,000 ft)	122 knots (225 km/h; 140 mph)
Stalling speed, flaps down, power off	26 knots (47 km/h; 29 mph)
Max rate of climb at S/L	329 m (1,080 ft)/min
Service ceiling	5,850 m (19,200 ft)
T-O and landing run	82 m (270 ft)
T-O to and landing from 15 m (50 ft)	171 m (560 ft)
Landing run, reversible pitch propeller	62 m (205 ft)
Landing from 15 m (50 ft), reversible pitch propeller	138 m (454 ft)
Range with max fuel and max payload	851 nm (1,577 km; 980 miles)

WTA

WTA INC

Lubbock International Airport, Route 3, Box 48A, Lubbock, Texas 79401
Telephone: (806) 765 7242
Telex: 744439
VICE-PRESIDENT: Larry T. Neal

WTA Inc acquired from Piper Aircraft Corporation marketing rights to the PA-18-150 Super Cub and the PA-36 Brave agricultural aircraft, and has renamed the latter as the New Brave in versions with 279 kW (375 hp) and 298 kW (400 hp) engines. Both types are manufactured for WTA by Piper.

WTA (PIPER) PA-18-150 SUPER CUB

The original Piper PA-18 with 67 kW (90 hp) Continental C90-12F engine received FAA Type Approval on 18 November 1949. The PA-18-150, PA-18A-150 agricultural aircraft and PA-18S and PA-18AS seaplanes were all approved on 1 October 1954.

For 1986 the WTA Super Cub is available with three optional equipment groups as follows:

Deluxe group: includes tiedown fittings, parking brakes, control locks, propeller spinner and an electrical system that incorporates a 14V 60A engine driven alternator, 12V 35Ah battery, ammeter, instrument panel light, navigation lights, electric engine starter and a shielded ignition harness.

Basic instrument group: includes air temperature gauge, clock, rate of climb and turn and bank indicators, and venturi tube vacuum system.

Advanced instrument group: as Basic group less venturi tube, plus artificial horizon, directional gyro, vacuum gauge and an engine driven vacuum system.

TYPE: Two-seat light cabin monoplane.

WINGS: Braced high-wing monoplane, with steel tube V bracing struts each side. Wing section USA 35B. Thickness/chord ratio 12%. Dihedral 1°. No incidence at mean aerodynamic chord. Total washout of 3° 18'. Aluminium spars and ribs, aluminium sheet leading-edge and aileron false spar, wingtip bow of ash, with Dacron covering overall and fire resistant Duraclad plastic finish. Plain ailerons and trailing-edge flaps of light alloy construction.

FUSELAGE: Rectangular welded steel tube structure covered with Dacron. Fire resistant Duraclad plastic finish. Metal bottom skin panels optional.

TAIL UNIT: Wire braced structure of welded steel tubes and channels, covered with Dacron. Fire resistant Duraclad plastic finish. Tailplane incidence variable for trimming. Balanced rudder and elevators.

LANDING GEAR: Non-retractable tailwheel type. Two side Vs and half axles hinged to bottom of fuselage. Rubber cord shock absorption. Mainwheel tyres size 6·00-6 four-ply, with 7·00-6 six-ply, or 8·00-6 four-ply, optional. Steerable leaf spring tailwheel. Scott 20 cm (8 in) tailwheel optional. Dual expanding brakes. Parking brake, and Edo or Aqua Model 1900 float installation, optional.

POWER PLANT: One 112 kW (150 hp) Avco Lycoming O-320 flat-four engine, driving a Sensenich two-blade fixed-pitch metal propeller with spinner. Steel tube engine mounting is hinged at firewall, allowing it to be swung to port for access to rear of engine. One 68 litre (18 US gallon) metal fuel tank in each wing. Total fuel capacity 136 litres (36 US gallons), of which 135·5 litres (35·8 US gallons) are usable. Refuelling points on top of wing.

ACCOMMODATION: Enclosed cabin seating two in tandem with dual controls. Adjustable front seat. Rear seat quickly removable for cargo carrying. Inertia reel shoulder harness and seat belts standard for front and rear seats. Heater and adjustable cool air vent. Downward hinged door on starboard side, and upward hinged window above, can be opened in flight. Sliding windows on port side. Baggage compartment aft of rear seat, capacity 22 kg (50 lb).

SYSTEMS: Electrical and vacuum systems optional, as components of factory installed groups listed.

AVIONICS AND EQUIPMENT: Optional avionics include King nav/coms and emergency locator transmitter. Standard equipment includes a recording tachometer, sensitive altimeter, provisions for emergency locator transmitter, stall warning device, seat belts and shoulder safety belts, and engine quick oil drain. Optional equipment includes items listed in factory installed equipment groups, plus electric fuel gauge, cabin fire extinguisher, stainless steel

New production PA-18-150 Super Cub, produced for WTA by Piper, on Edo floats *(Howard Levy)*

control cables, dome light, landing light, strobe light, metallising and polyurethane finish for steel components, and glider tow hook.

DIMENSIONS, EXTERNAL:
- Wing span: 10·76 m (35 ft 3½ in)
- Wing chord (constant): 1·60 m (5 ft 3 in)
- Wing aspect ratio: 7
- Length overall: 6·88 m (22 ft 7 in)
- Height overall: 2·04 m (6 ft 8½ in)
- Tailplane span: 3·20 m (10 ft 6 in)
- Wheel track: 1·84 m (6 ft 0½ in)
- Propeller diameter: 1·88 m (6 ft 2 in)

DIMENSION, INTERNAL:
- Baggage compartment: 0·51 m³ (18 cu ft)

AREAS:
- Wings, gross: 16·58 m² (178·5 sq ft)
- Ailerons (total): 1·75 m² (18·80 sq ft)
- Trailing-edge flaps (total): 1·07 m² (11·50 sq ft)
- Fin: 0·43 m² (4·66 sq ft)
- Rudder: 0·63 m² (6·76 sq ft)
- Tailplane: 1·40 m² (15·10 sq ft)
- Elevators: 1·09 m² (11·70 sq ft)

WEIGHTS AND LOADINGS:
- Weight empty: 429 kg (946 lb)
- Max T-O and landing weight: 794 kg (1,750 lb)
- Max wing loading: 48·8 kg/m² (10·0 lb/sq ft)
- Max power loading: 7·09 kg/kW (11·6 lb/hp)

PERFORMANCE (at max T-O weight):
- Never-exceed speed: 132 knots (246 km/h; 153 mph)
- Max level speed: 113 knots (209 km/h; 130 mph)
- Max cruising speed, 75% power at 1,525 m (5,000 ft): 100 knots (185 km/h; 115 mph)
- Stalling speed, flaps down: 37 knots (69 km/h; 43 mph)
- Max rate of climb at S/L: 293 m (960 ft)/min
- Service ceiling: 5,795 m (19,000 ft)
- Absolute ceiling: 6,495 m (21,300 ft)
- T-O run: 61 m (200 ft)
- T-O to 15 m (50 ft): 153 m (500 ft)
- Landing from 15 m (50 ft): 270 m (885 ft)
- Landing run: 107 m (350 ft)
- Range with max fuel and max payload, 75% power at optimum altitude: 400 nm (741 km; 460 miles)

WTA (PIPER) PA-36 NEW BRAVE

Piper Aircraft Corporation first gave details of the original PA-36 Brave agricultural aircraft on 9 October 1972. With the acquisition of marketing rights for this aircraft, WTA decided to concentrate on versions with 279-298 kW (375-400 hp) engines and renamed them New Braves.

The basic configuration seats the pilot well aft. The long nose is designed to collapse progressively in an emergency. The fuselage is graded in strength to provide high energy absorption and progressive collapse. A sturdy overturn pylon is an integral part of the fuselage structure. The laminated wing spars provide structural redundancy.

The pilot is located in an isolated cockpit capsule which keeps him well clear of main structural members. The floor is 0·30 m (1 ft 0 in) above the lower longerons, and a cockpit width of 0·97 m (3 ft 2 in) allows for substantial deformation of the fuselage structure without hazard to the pilot. The seat is attached to the overturn pylon, and is articulated to allow the pilot's position to change with fuselage deformation. The cockpit capsule is sealed to prevent the ingress of toxic chemicals; and all protrusions, knobs and levers which might cause injury are eliminated. The instrument panel is equipped with a large energy absorbing crash roll.

The cockpit capsule is ventilated via an airscoop in the top of the canopy, which filters the incoming air before discharge through two adjustable diffusers. A heating system is standard, and the inflow of ventilating and/or heated air has the effect of pressurising the cockpit, further discouraging any inflow of toxic fumes or chemicals.

The fuel tanks, located in the wing roots, are filled with reticulated polyurethane foam to serve both as a fire suppressant and as a constant baffle to reduce fuel surge. Fire resistant fuel pipes are wire-reinforced at potential rupture points.

A hopper/tank of 1·08 m³ (38 cu ft) capacity is standard for the New Brave. High, medium or low volume spray systems are available, the first dispensing chemicals at a rate equivalent to 168 litres/hectare (18 US gallons/acre), with a 24·4 m (80 ft) swath width. The standard spray equipment consists of a quickly removable pylon mounted wind driven spraypump, and spraybooms located just aft of the wing trailing-edges. This location reduces drag and allows the pilot to make visual checks of their operation. A new optional dispersal system is also available, comprising a front mounted belt driven hydraulic spray system with stainless steel dropped booms.

All parts of the New Brave's airframe are treated to prevent corrosion damage, with extensive use of polyurethane coating, selection of stainless steel for cables and other moving components in vulnerable areas, and internal oiling of lower truss sections. The design eliminates dust traps and inaccessible areas, and fuselage covering is spaced away from the frame to permit thorough hosing down. To facilitate washing, inspection and maintenance, the side panels are attached by quick release fasteners.

New Brave agricultural aircraft, for which WTA has exclusive marketing rights

Two versions of the New Brave are available:

New Brave 375. Equipped with one 279 kW (375 hp) Avco Lycoming IO-720-D1C flat-eight engine, driving a Hartzell three-blade constant-speed metal propeller with spinner.

New Brave 400. Latest model, with a 298 kW (400 hp) version of the Avco Lycoming IO-720-D1C engine.

The following description applies to both versions of the New Brave:

TYPE: Single-seat agricultural aircraft.

WINGS: Cantilever low-wing monoplane. Wing section NACA 63_3-618. Dihedral 6°. Incidence 2° 30′ at root, 0° 30′ at tip. Conventional two-spar metal structure. Light alloy laminated spars with two-bolt main spar attachment to fuselage structure. Light alloy covering, detachable leading-edges and glassfibre wingtips. Conventional ailerons and trailing-edge flaps. Landing lights in wing leading-edges.

FUSELAGE: Welded chrome-molybdenum steel tube structure. Metal underskin and removable side panels. Glassfibre engine cowling.

TAIL UNIT: Cantilever all-metal structure. Tailplane has glassfibre tips. Tab on rudder and in each elevator. Cable from top of cockpit structure to tip of fin to deflect cables.

LANDING GEAR: Non-retractable tailwheel type. Interchangeable cantilever spring steel main-gear struts, with wire cutters on leading-edges. Cleveland mainwheels type 40-101 with tyres size 8·50-10, 6-ply rating, pressure 1·93-2·21 bars (28-32 lb/sq in). Scott steerable tailwheel type 3450-21 with tyre of 0·25 m (10 in) diameter, pressure 2·41-3·10 bars (35-45 lb/sq in). Cleveland type 30-67B hydraulic brakes. Parking brake.

POWER PLANT: One engine as detailed in model listings. One fuel tank in each wing root. Total fuel capacity for both versions 337 litres (89 US gallons), of which 325·5 litres (86 US gallons) are usable. Refuelling point on upper surface of each wing. Fuel tanks filled with reticulated polyurethane safety foam (Safom). Oil capacity 16 litres (4·25 US gallons).

ACCOMMODATION: Pilot only, on adjustable seat in an isolated cockpit capsule with steel tube overturn structure. Seat, equipped with double shoulder harness and inertia reel, is attached to overturn structure. Wire cutter mounted in centre of windscreen. Combined window and door on each side, hinged at bottom. Cockpit capsule is ventilated and can be heated optionally. Entrance steps optional.

SYSTEMS: Electrical system supplied by 28V 70A alternator with two 12V 25Ah batteries in series. 35Ah capacity batteries optional. Hydraulic system for brakes only.

AVIONICS: Optional factory installed avionics available, as well as a range of transponders.

EQUIPMENT: Hopper/tank of 1·08 m³ (38 cu ft) capacity, for 1,041 litres (275 US gallons) of liquid chemical. Maximum capacity for dry chemicals 998 kg (2,200 lb). Venturi type dry material spreaders of stainless steel available, including a basic design capable of application rates of 5·6 to 224 kg/hectare (5 to 200 lb/acre). Spray system comprises an easily removable wind driven spraypump and 38 mm (1½ in) diameter sprayboom equipped with 60 nozzles. Belt driven hydraulic spray system with stainless steel dropped booms optional. Other optional equipment includes 8-day clock; sensitive altimeter; turn coordinator; emergency locator transmitter; night working light package which includes two 600W cockpit adjustable/retractable working lights, two 450W ground adjustable turning lights, hopper light, and related switching; landing and taxi lights; navigation, instrument panel, rotating beacon, and anti-collision lights; cockpit fire extinguisher; and heater.

DIMENSIONS, EXTERNAL:
- Wing span: 11·82 m (38 ft 9½ in)
- Wing chord: at root: 2·03 m (6 ft 8 in)
- at tip: 1·75 m (5 ft 9 in)
- Wing aspect ratio: 6·66
- Length overall: 8·38 m (27 ft 6 in)
- Height overall: 2·29 m (7 ft 6 in)
- Tailplane span: 4·01 m (13 ft 1¾ in)
- Wheel track: 2·65 m (8 ft 8¾ in)
- Wheelbase: 5·91 m (19 ft 4¾ in)
- Propeller diameter: 2·18 m (7 ft 2 in)
- Propeller ground clearance: 0·23 m (9 in)
- Cockpit doors: Height: 0·76 m (2 ft 6 in)
- Width: 0·71 m (2 ft 4 in)
- Height to sill: 1·57 m (5 ft 2 in)
- Hopper loading door: Length: 1·27 m (4 ft 2 in)
- Width: 0·48 m (1 ft 7 in)

DIMENSIONS, INTERNAL:
- Cockpit: Max width: 0·97 m (3 ft 2 in)
- Max height: 1·32 m (4 ft 4 in)

AREAS:
- Wings, gross: 20·96 m² (225·65 sq ft)
- Ailerons (total): 2·01 m² (21·6 sq ft)
- Trailing-edge flaps (total): 2·32 m² (25·0 sq ft)
- Fin: 0·95 m² (10·2 sq ft)
- Rudder: 0·90 m² (9·7 sq ft)
- Tailplane: 2·11 m² (22·67 sq ft)
- Elevators (incl tabs): 1·92 m² (20·66 sq ft)

WEIGHTS AND LOADINGS (A: Normal category; B: Restricted category):
- Weight empty:
  - no dispersal equipment: 1,118 kg (2,465 lb)
  - sprayer: 1,154 kg (2,544 lb)
  - duster: 1,152 kg (2,540 lb)
- Max T-O weight: A: 1,769 kg (3,900 lb)
  - B: 2,177 kg (4,800 lb)
- Max landing weight: A, B: 1,769 kg (3,900 lb)
- Max wing loading: A: 84·4 kg/m² (17·3 lb/sq ft)
  - B: 103·9 kg/m² (21·3 lb/sq ft)
- Max power loading, New Brave 375:
  - A: 6·33 kg/kW (10·4 lb/hp)
  - B: 7·79 kg/kW (12·8 lb/hp)
- Max power loading, New Brave 400:
  - A: 5·94 kg/kW (9·75 lb/hp)
  - B: 7·31 kg/kW (12·0 lb/hp)

PERFORMANCE (New Brave 375 at Normal category max T-O weight, no dispersal equipment installed):
- Max level speed at optimum altitude: 139 knots (257 km/h; 160 mph)
- Cruising speed, best power mixture:
  - 75% power at 1,705 m (5,600 ft): 129 knots (240 km/h; 149 mph)
  - 65% power at 2,895 m (9,500 ft): 126 knots (233 km/h; 145 mph)
  - 55% power at 4,265 m (14,000 ft): 119 knots (220 km/h; 137 mph)
- Cruising speed, best econ mixture:
  - 75% power at 1,705 m (5,600 ft): 128 knots (236 km/h; 147 mph)
  - 65% power at 2,895 m (9,500 ft): 124 knots (230 km/h; 143 mph)
  - 55% power at 4,265 m (14,000 ft): 117 knots (217 km/h; 135 mph)
- Stalling speed:
  - flaps up: 63 knots (116 km/h; 72 mph) CAS
  - flaps down: 58 knots (106 km/h; 66 mph) CAS
- Max rate of climb at S/L: 320 m (1,051 ft)/min
- T-O run: 218 m (715 ft)
- T-O to 15 m (50 ft): 368 m (1,208 ft)
- Landing from 15 m (50 ft): 564 m (1,850 ft)
- Landing run: 226 m (740 ft)
- Range with max fuel, best econ mixture, with allowances for start, taxi, T-O, climb, descent, and 45 min reserves:
  - 75% power at 1,705 m (5,600 ft): 465 nm (861 km; 535 miles)
  - 65% power at 2,895 m (9,500 ft): 495 nm (917 km; 570 miles)
  - 55% power at 4,265 m (14,000 ft): 525 nm (974 km; 605 miles)

PERFORMANCE (New Brave 375 at Restricted category max T-O weight, except where indicated. A: sprayer; B: duster):
- Max level speed at optimum altitude:
  - A: 123 knots (229 km/h; 142 mph)
  - B: 119 knots (220 km/h; 137 mph)
- Cruising speed, best power mixture at AUW of 1,542 kg (3,400 lb): A: 118 knots (219 km/h; 136 mph)
  - B: 113 knots (209 km/h; 130 mph)
- Max rate of climb at S/L: A: 168 m (550 ft)/min

B 116 m (380 ft)/min
Max rate of climb at S/L at AUW of 1,769 kg (3,900 lb):
A 280 m (920 ft)/min
B 201 m (660 ft)/min
T-O run: A 442 m (1,450 ft)
B 533 m (1,750 ft)
T-O run at AUW of 1,769 kg (3,900 lb):
A 274 m (900 ft)
B 351 m (1,150 ft)
T-O to 15 m (50 ft): A 701 m (2,300 ft)
B 762 m (2,500 ft)
T-O to 15 m (50 ft) at AUW of 1,769 kg (3,900 lb):
A 457 m (1,500 ft)
B 533 m (1,750 ft)
Landing from 15 m (50 ft) at max landing weight:
A, B 439 m (1,440 ft)
Landing run at max landing weight:
A, B 140 m (460 ft)
Range with max fuel, best power mixture, with allowances for start, taxi, T-O, climb, cruise, descent and 45 min reserves at 45% power:
A 392 nm (727 km; 452 miles)
B 372 nm (589 km; 428 miles)

YUGOSLAVIA

SOKO

SOKO VAZDUHOPLOVNA INDUSTRIJA, RO VAZDUHOPLOVSTVO

79000 Mostar
Telephone: (088) 22-121, 33-831, 35-244, 35-541, 37-943, 55-120
Telex: 46-180 YU SOKOMO
GENERAL MANAGER: Dipl Ing Milenko Pjescić
DIRECTOR, AIRCRAFT PRODUCTION: Dipl Ing B. Rogonja
DIRECTOR, HELICOPTER PRODUCTION: Dipl Ing F. Dizdarević
DIRECTOR, RESEARCH AND DEVELOPMENT: Dipl Ing M. Zadro
DIRECTOR, COMMERCIAL: Dipl Oec N. Djurica
INTERNATIONAL SALES MANAGER: Dipl Ing S. Gosto

Founded in 1951, this company manufactures aircraft of its own design and is participating, with Romania, in developing and producing the Orao/IAR-93 strike aircraft described under the SOKO/CNIAR heading in the International section. Details of its SL-40 Liska motor glider can be found in the Sailplanes section.

SOKO also continues to build under licence the Aérospatiale SA 342L Gazelle helicopter, on behalf of the Yugoslav government.

SOKO G-4 SUPER GALEB (SEAGULL)

This light strike and training aircraft was designed to replace the earlier G2-A Galeb and Lockheed T-33 in basic and advanced training units of the Yugoslav Air Force. As can be seen in the accompanying illustrations, the G-4 Super Galeb is a completely new design, inheriting little but its name and role from the original Galeb. It is, however, powered by a higher rated version of the latter's Rolls-Royce Viper turbojet.

The first of two Super Galeb prototypes flew for the first time on 17 July 1978. The second was flown on 18 December 1979, followed by the first of several pre-production aircraft on 17 December 1980. The production Super Galeb, for which the Yugoslav Air Force has placed a substantial order, differs from the pre-production model in having an all-moving tailplane with considerable anhedral, instead of the original conventional horizontal tail surfaces with elevators and no anhedral. The Super Galeb demonstrated at the Paris Air Show in May 1983 was a standard production aircraft of the kind already serving with the Air Force at that time.

TYPE: Two-seat basic trainer and light strike aircraft.

WINGS: Cantilever low-wing monoplane. No dihedral. Sweepback at quarter-chord 22°; leading-edge sweep increased near wing roots. One-piece two-spar all-metal structure, with integrally machined skin panels inboard and chemically milled skin towards wingtips. Shallow boundary layer fence on upper surface of each wing, forward of inboard end of aileron. Wings attached to fuselage at six points. Entire trailing-edge made up of conventional all-metal sealed ailerons and flaps. Ailerons actuated by hydraulic servo jacks, with artificial feel, flaps by electrically controlled hydraulic actuators. No slats or tabs.

SOKO G-4 Super Galeb jet training and light attack aircraft

FUSELAGE: All-metal semi-monocoque structure, with air intake trunk blended into each side. Rear portion, complete with tail surfaces, detachable for access to engine. Door type airbrake under rear fuselage. Landing light in nose, forward of large equipment bay.

TAIL UNIT: Conventional cantilever all-metal structure, with all surfaces sweptback. All-moving horizontal surfaces have 10° anhedral, and are actuated by hydraulic servo jacks, with artificial feel. Mechanically actuated rudder. Dorsal fin. Ground adjustable tab on rudder. Two ventral strakes under jetpipe.

LANDING GEAR: Hydraulically retractable tricycle type, with single wheel on each unit. Nosewheel retracts forward, main units inward into wings. Oleo-pneumatic shock absorber in each leg. Hydraulically steerable nose unit. Trailing link main units. Mainwheels fitted with Dunlop tyres size 615 × 225-10, pressure 4·4 bars (64 lb/sq in), and hydraulic brakes. Nosewheel has Dunlop tyre size 6·50-5·5 TC, pressure 3·0 bars (43·5 lb/sq in). Brake parachute container at base of rudder. Provision for attaching two assisted take-off rockets under centre-fuselage.

POWER PLANT: One Rolls-Royce Viper Mk 632 turbojet engine, rated at 17·8 kN (4,000 lb st). Fuel in three flexible bag tanks in centre-fuselage and an integral tank between the spars of each inner wing. Total internal fuel capacity 1,720 litres (378·5 Imp gallons). Provision for two underwing auxiliary tanks, on inboard pylons, total capacity 625 litres (137·5 Imp gallons). Max fuel capacity 2,345 litres (516 Imp gallons). Gravity refuelling system standard.

ACCOMMODATION: Crew of two in tandem on Martin-Baker zero height/90 knot Mk J8 or zero/zero Mk J10 ejection seats, with ejection through the individual sideways hinged (to starboard) canopy over each seat. Rear seat raised by 25 cm (10 in) to give occupant forward view over front seat occupant. Cockpit pressurised and air-conditioned.

SYSTEMS: Engine compressor bleed air used for pressurisation, air-conditioning, anti-*g* suit and windscreen anti-icing systems, and to pressurise fuel tanks. Duplicated high pressure hydraulic system for flying control servos, flap and airbrake actuators, landing gear retraction and extension, wheel brakes and nosewheel steering. Electrical system supplied by 9kW 28V DC generator, with nickel-cadmium battery for ground/emergency power and self contained engine starting. Two static inverters, total output 600VA, provide 115V 400Hz AC power. Gaseous oxygen system adequate for two crew for 2 h 30 min.

AVIONICS AND EQUIPMENT: Dual controls and full blind-flying instrumentation in each cockpit. Standard nav/com equipment comprises EAS type ER4.671D or VHF RC E163 Kondor VHF com radio, GEC Avionics AD 370B or Iskra VARK-1 radio compass, Collins VIR-30 VOR/ILS, Iskra 75R4 VOR marker beacon receiver, Collins DME 40 and TRT AHV-6 radio altimeter. Optional UHF and V/UHF com, gyro platform and other equipment to customer's specification.

ARMAMENT AND OPERATIONAL EQUIPMENT: Removable ventral gun pod containing 23 mm GSh-23L twin-barrel rapid fire cannon with 200 rds. Two attachments under each wing, with capacity of 350 kg inboard and 250 kg outboard. In addition to standard high explosive bombs and napalm pods, typical Yugoslav stores include S-8-16 cluster bombs, each with eight 16 kg fragmentation munitions; KPT-150 expendable containers, each with up to 40 anti-personnel or 54 anti-tank bomblets; L-57-16MD pods, each with sixteen 57 mm rockets; L-128-04 pods, each with four 128 mm rockets; adaptors for twin 5 in HVAR rockets, single 57 mm VRZ-57 training rockets; SN-3-050 triple carriers for 50 kg bombs; and auxiliary fuel tanks on the inboard attachments. Ferranti D282 gyro gunsight standard. Other types of fire control system optional. A photo reconnaissance/infra-red line-scan pod and night illumination system was under development in early 1985.

DIMENSIONS, EXTERNAL:
Wing span 9·88 m (32 ft 5 in)
Wing aspect ratio 5·01
Length overall 11·86 m (38 ft 11 in)
Height overall 4·28 m (14 ft 0½ in)
Tailplane span 3·97 m (13 ft 0¼ in)
Wheel track 3·49 m (11 ft 5½ in)
Wheelbase 4·15 m (13 ft 7½ in)

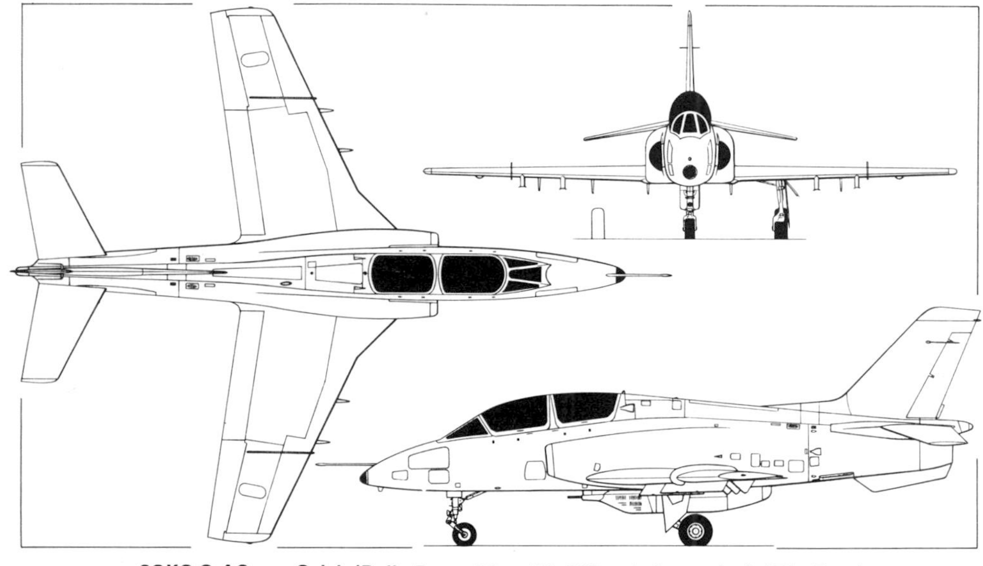

SOKO G-4 Super Galeb (Rolls-Royce Viper Mk 632 turbojet engine) *(Pilot Press)*

AREAS:

Wings, gross	19·5 m² (209·9 sq ft)
Ailerons (total)	1·358 m² (14·62 sq ft)
Trailing-edge flaps (total)	3·340 m² (35·95 sq ft)
Airbrake	0·438 m² (4·71 sq ft)
Fin	3·130 m² (33·69 sq ft)
Rudder	0·689 m² (7·42 sq ft)
Horizontal tail surfaces	4·669 m² (50·26 sq ft)

WEIGHTS:

Weight empty, equipped	3,250 kg (7,165 lb)
T-O weight, training mission	4,760 kg (10,495 lb)
T-O weight, normal combat mission, with 1,350 kg (2,975 lb) of weapons	6,110 kg (13,470 lb)
Max T-O weight, combat overload	6,330 kg (13,955 lb)

PERFORMANCE (at AUW of 4,760 kg; 10,495 lb, except where indicated):

Never-exceed speed	Mach 0·85
Max level speed at 6,000 m (19,680 ft)	491 knots (910 km/h; 565 mph)
Landing speed	89 knots (165 km/h; 103 mph)
Max rate of climb at S/L	1,800 m (5,905 ft)/min
Time to 8,000 m (26,240 ft)	6 min
Absolute ceiling	15,000 m (49,200 ft)
T-O run	600 m (1,970 ft)
T-O to 15 m (50 ft)	950 m (3,120 ft)
Landing from 15 m (50 ft) at landing weight of 3,800 kg (8,375 lb)	750 m (2,460 ft)
Landing run at above landing weight	550 m (1,805 ft)
Combat radius, lo-lo-lo, at AUW of 5,190 kg (11,442 lb), with gun pack and two L-57-16MD rocket packs	162 nm (300 km; 186 miles)
g limits	+8/−4·2

UTVA

UTVA—SOUR METALNE INDUSTRIJE, RO FABRIKA AVIONA

Utve Zlatokrile br 9, 26 000 Pancevo
Telephone: (013) 44755 and (13) 46183
Telex: 131 16
GENERAL MANAGER: Dipl Ing Tesić Milivoje
MANAGER OF AIRCRAFT DEVELOPMENT: Dipl Ing Stamatov Petar
MANAGER FOR TECHNICAL MATTERS: Dipl Ing Soso Milan

UTVA-75

The UTVA-75 is a side by side two-seat training, glider towing and utility lightplane, which was projected, designed and built in partnership by UTVA-Pancevo, Prva Petoletka-Trstenik, Vazduhoplovnotehnicki Institut and Institut Masinskog Fakulteta of Belgrade. Design was started in 1974, to the requirements of FAR Pt 23 (Utility category). Construction of two prototypes was undertaken in 1975; the first of these flew for the first time on 19 May 1976 and the second on 18 December 1976. Series production began immediately and is continuing. More than 100 UTVA-75s have been delivered to civilian flying clubs, others to the Yugoslav Air Force.

TYPE: Two-seat light aircraft.

WINGS: Cantilever low-wing monoplane, with short span centre-section and two constant chord outer panels. Wing section NACA 65²415. Dihedral 0° on centre-section, 6° on outer panels. Conventional all-metal two-spar structure. Ailerons and flaps, with fluted skin, along entire trailing-edge of outer panels, except for tips. Flettner trim tab on each aileron.

FUSELAGE: Conventional all-metal semi-monocoque structure.

TAIL UNIT: Cantilever all-metal structure, with sweptback vertical surfaces. Fluted skin on fin and rudder. Elevator horn balanced. Controllable tab on elevator; ground adjustable tab on rudder.

LANDING GEAR: Non-retractable tricycle type, with single wheel on each unit, and small tail bumper. Prva Petoletka-Trstenik oleo-pneumatic shock absorbers. Dunlop tyres, size 6·00-6 on mainwheels, 5·00-5 on nosewheel. Prva Petoletka-Trstenik hydraulic brakes.

POWER PLANT: One 134 kW (180 hp) Avco Lycoming IO-360-B1F flat-four engine, driving a Hartzell HC-C2YK-1BF/F7666A two-blade variable-pitch metal propeller. Two integral fuel tanks in wings, total capacity 160 litres (35 Imp gallons). Provision for carrying two 100 litre (22 Imp gallon) drop tanks under wings, raising max total capacity to 360 litres (79 Imp gallons). Oil capacity 10 litres (2·2 Imp gallons).

ACCOMMODATION: Two seats side by side in enclosed cabin, with large upward opening jettisonable canopy door over each seat, hinged on centreline. Dual stick type controls standard. Cabin heated and ventilated.

SYSTEMS: Dual hydraulic systems for brakes. 14V DC electrical system, with 35Ah battery, navigation lights, rotating beacon and landing lights as standard equipment.

AVIONICS AND EQUIPMENT: King KY 195B radio optional. Standard equipment includes radio compass.

ARMAMENT AND MILITARY EQUIPMENT: Two fittings for light weapon loads underwing on military UTVA-75s. Each can carry a bomb, 100 kg (220 lb) cargo container, two-round rocket launcher or machine-gun pod.

DIMENSIONS, EXTERNAL:

Wing span	9·73 m (31 ft 11 in)
Wing chord (constant)	1·55 m (5 ft 1 in)
Length overall	7·11 m (23 ft 4 in)
Height overall	3·15 m (10 ft 4 in)
Tailplane span	3·80 m (12 ft 5½ in)
Wheel track	2·58 m (8 ft 5½ in)
Wheelbase	1·99 m (6 ft 6¼ in)
Propeller diameter	1·93 m (6 ft 4 in)
Propeller ground clearance	0·295 m (11¾ in)

AREAS:

Wings, gross	14·63 m² (157·5 sq ft)
Ailerons (total)	1·38 m² (14·85 sq ft)
Flaps (total)	1·61 m² (17·33 sq ft)
Horizontal tail surfaces (total)	3·34 m² (35·95 sq ft)

WEIGHTS:

Weight empty, equipped	685 kg (1,510 lb)
Max crew/military load/baggage	210 kg (463 lb)
Max fuel: standard	103 kg (227 lb)
with drop tanks	256 kg (564 lb)
Max T-O weight	960 kg (2,116 lb)

UTVA-75 training and utility aircraft (Avco Lycoming IO-360-B1F engine)

PERFORMANCE (at max T-O weight):

Max level speed	116 knots (215 km/h; 133 mph)
Max cruising speed	100 knots (185 km/h; 115 mph)
Econ cruising speed	89 knots (165 km/h; 102 mph)
Stalling speed, engine idling:	
flaps up	52 knots (95 km/h; 59 mph)
25° flap	45 knots (82 km/h; 51 mph)
Max rate of climb at S/L	270 m (885 ft)/min
Service ceiling	4,000 m (13,125 ft)
T-O run	125 m (410 ft)
T-O to 15 m (50 ft)	250 m (820 ft)
Landing from 15 m (50 ft)	340 m (1,115 ft)
Landing run	100 m (328 ft)
Range with max standard fuel	432 nm (800 km; 497 miles)
Range with drop tanks, no reserves	1,080 nm (2,000 km; 1,242 miles)
g limits	+6/−3

UTVA-75A

The UTVA-75A is a four-seat version of the UTVA-75 for training, glider towing and utility operations. Design and construction were started in 1984 in partnership by UTVA-Pancevo, Prva Petoletka-Trstenik, Vazduhoplovnotehnicki Institut and Institut Masinskog Fakulteta of Belgrade, to the requirements of FAR Pt 23 (Normal category). The prototype UTVA-75A flew for the first time in 1986. Series production began immediately afterwards, in parallel with continued manufacture of the two-seat UTVA-75. Deliveries are expected to begin in 1987.

TYPE: Four-seat light utility and training aircraft.

WINGS, FUSELAGE, TAIL UNIT, LANDING GEAR, POWER PLANT AND SYSTEMS: As for UTVA-75.

ACCOMMODATION: Four seats in pairs in enclosed cabin, with large upward opening jettisonable canopy door over each fore and aft pair of seats, hinged on centreline. Dual stick type controls standard. Cabin heated and ventilated.

AVIONICS AND EQUIPMENT: King equipment standard, including dual KY 197 720-channel VHF com transceivers; KR 87 digitally tuned ADF with integral electronic flight timer and pushbutton elapsed timer; panel mounted R/Nav system comprising a KNS 81 200-channel nav, 40-channel glideslope indicator and 9-waypoint digital R/Nav computer, combined with a KI 525A pictorial nav indicator; KI 229 RMI; KN 53 200-channel VHF nav with integral 40-channel glideslope indicator and KI 525A indicator; KN 62A 200-channel DME with digital distance, ground speed and time-to-station; KT 79 all solid state digital transponder featuring cross-check readout of encoded altitude and automatic VFR code selection; and KMA 24 audio control console with integral marker beacon receiver.

ARMAMENT: None.

DIMENSIONS, EXTERNAL, and AREAS: As for UTVA-75

WEIGHTS:

Weight empty, equipped	700 kg (1,544 lb)
Max payload	310 kg (683 lb)
Max fuel: standard	103 kg (227 lb)
with drop tanks	256 kg (564 lb)
Max T-O weight	1,163 kg (2,564 lb)

UTVA-75 with underwing pylons for light weapon loads

PERFORMANCE (at max T-O weight):

Max level speed	113 knots (210 km/h; 130 mph)
Max cruising speed	97 knots (180 km/h; 112 mph)
Econ cruising speed	86 knots (160 km/h; 99 mph)
Stalling speed, engine idling:	
flaps up	57 knots (105 km/h; 65 mph)
25° flap	49 knots (90 km/h; 56 mph)
Max rate of climb at S/L	264 m (866 ft)/min
Service ceiling	4,000 m (13,125 ft)
T-O run	200 m (656 ft)
T-O to 15 m (50 ft)	400 m (1,312 ft)
Landing from 15 m (50 ft)	340 m (1,115 ft)
Landing run	180 m (590 ft)
Range with max standard fuel	432 nm (800 km; 497 miles)
Range with drop tanks, no reserves	1,080 nm (2,000 km; 1,242 miles)
g limits	+3·8/−2·2

UTVA LASTA (SWALLOW)

First shown publicly in model form at the 1985 Paris Air Show, the Lasta was designed by the Vazduhoplovno Tehnicki Institut at Zarkovo, near Belgrade, as a primary trainer for the Yugoslav Air Force, to the requirements of FAR Pt 23. Although similar in configuration and purpose to the French Epsilon, and with the same power plant, it is a larger and heavier aircraft. Pupil pilots are intended to progress from the Lasta directly to the SOKO G-4 Super Galeb jet basic trainer, and the cockpits of the two aircraft are fundamentally similar. The Lasta is intended to be suitable for basic, aerobatic, navigation, instrument and night flying training, for basic training in gunnery, rocket firing and bombing, for formation flying and combat manoeuvres.

Manufacture of the Lasta is being undertaken by Fabrika Aviona UTVA at Pancevo. The first of two prototypes flew for the first time in 1985. Tooling was being prepared at that time for a pre-series of ten production Lastas.

TYPE: Tandem two-seat primary trainer and light attack aircraft.

WINGS: Cantilever low-wing monoplane of conventional light alloy two-spar stressed-skin construction. Dihedral from roots. Ailerons and flaps over full span. Trim tab in inboard trailing-edge of each aileron.

FUSELAGE: Conventional light alloy semi-monocoque structure.

TAIL UNIT: Cantilever light alloy stressed-skin structure. Fixed incidence tailplane. Horn balanced rudder. Long dorsal fin and shallow ventral fin. Trim tab in rudder and starboard elevator.

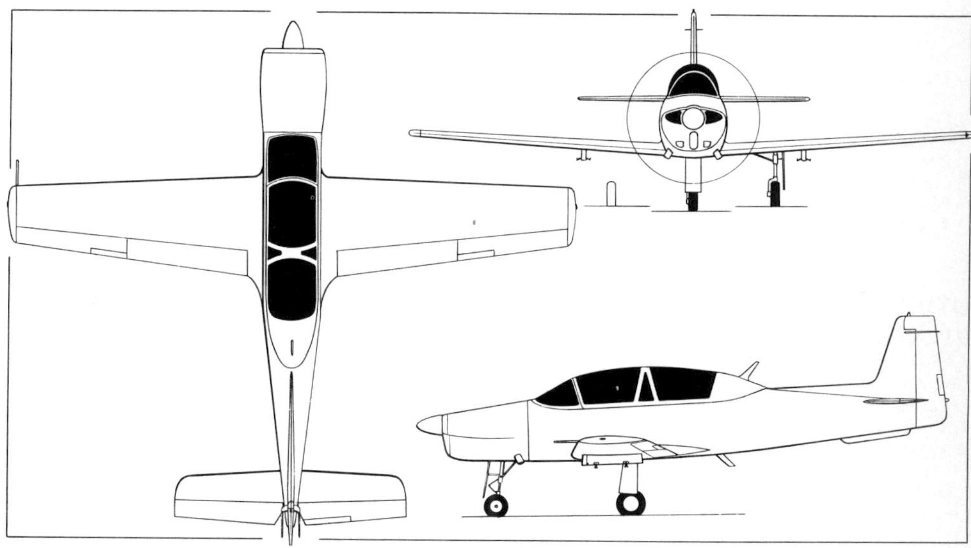

UTVA Lasta (Avco Lycoming AEIO-540-L1B5D engine) *(Pilot Press)*

LANDING GEAR: Hydraulically retractable tricycle type of Prva Petoletka-Trstenik design and manufacture, with single wheel on each unit. Nosewheel retracts rearward, main units inward. Oleo-pneumatic shock absorbers. Nosewheel steerable to 30° each way, via rudder pedals. Dunlop tyres: size 6·00-6 (8PR), pressure 3·8 bars (55 lb/sq in), on mainwheels; size 5·00-5 (8PR), pressure 4·2 bars (61 lb/sq in), on nosewheel. Hydraulic disc brakes.

POWER PLANT: One 224 kW (300 hp) Avco Lycoming AEIO-540-Z1B5D flat-six engine, driving a Hoffmann HO-V-123K-V three-blade constant-speed propeller with spinner. Integral fuel tanks in wings.

ACCOMMODATION: Two seats in tandem, with raised rear seat. Separate canopy over each seat, sideways hinged to starboard.

SYSTEMS: Hydraulic, electrical and oxygen systems standard. Full night lighting.

AVIONICS: Standard equipment will include VHF, VOR, ILS and DME.

ARMAMENT: Two underwing hardpoints for bombs, rocket packs and pods containing twin machine-guns, with total external load of up to 400 kg (882 lb).

DIMENSIONS, EXTERNAL:

Wing span	8·34 m (27 ft 4½ in)
Wing aspect ratio	6·32
Length overall	8·04 m (26 ft 4½ in)
Height overall	4·45 m (14 ft 7¼ in)

AREA:

Wings, gross	11·0 m² (118·4 sq ft)

WEIGHTS:

Weight empty, equipped	1,060 kg (2,337 lb)
Max T-O weight	1,630 kg (3,593 lb)

PERFORMANCE (estimated, at max T-O weight):

Never-exceed speed	302 knots (560 km/h; 348 mph)
Max level speed at S/L	186 knots (345 km/h; 214 mph)
Max rate of climb at S/L	540 m (1,770 ft)/min
T-O run	320 m (1,050 ft)
Landing run	310 m (1,017 ft)

NOTES

(Please note this page is blank for production reasons)

NOTES

(Please note this page is blank for production reasons)

NOTES

(Please note this page is blank for production reasons)

NOTES

(Please note this page is blank for production reasons)

NOTES

(Please note this page is blank for production reasons)

NOTES

(Please note this page is blank for production reasons)

SPORT AIRCRAFT

(incorporating Homebuilt, Microlight and Racing aircraft)

AUSTRALIA

BEDSON

GORDON BEDSON AND ASSOCIATES

PO Box 6, Bundarra, NSW 2359
Telephone: (067) 238212

BEDSON RESURGAM

The Resurgam was designed originally in 1948 for a JAP motorcycle engine. Revised and updated, the aircraft has been offered in plans and kit forms for homebuilding. A Resurgam won the speed event in the 1982 London-Paris microlight race.

TYPE: Single-seat microlight.

AIRFRAME: Conventional high-wing monoplane. Aluminium and wood fuselage. Spruce and plywood wing spars with wood/foam composite ribs. Glassfibre covered leading-edges. Wings, of NACA 4415 section, are strut braced, and de-rig for road transportation. Three-axis control (rudder, elevators, and ailerons or spoilers).

LANDING GEAR: Tricycle type, wheel diameter 11 in. Wood/glassfibre suspension on mainwheels. Nosewheel steerable.

POWER PLANT (typical): One 22·4 kW (30 hp) König SC430 engine, driving a three-blade pusher propeller; 17·9 kW (24 hp) Skylark II engine optional. Total fuel capacity 18 litres (4 Imp gallons).

ACCOMMODATION: Pilot only, in partially enclosed cockpit.

DIMENSIONS, EXTERNAL:

Wing span	8·50 m (27 ft 10½ in)
Wing aspect ratio	7
Length overall	5·64 m (18 ft 6 in)
Propeller diameter	0·99 m (3 ft 3 in)

AREA:

Wings, gross	10·68 m² (115·0 sq ft)

WEIGHTS AND LOADINGS:

Weight empty	99 kg (218 lb)
Max T-O weight	181 kg (399 lb)
Max wing loading	16·95 kg/m² (3·47 lb/sq ft)
Max power loading	8·08 kg/kW (13·3 lb/hp)

PERFORMANCE:

Cruising speed	48 knots (89 km/h; 55 mph)
Stalling speed	27 knots (50 km/h; 31 mph)

BLUE MAX

BLUE MAX ULTRALIGHT

PO Box 42, Nagambie, Victoria 3608
Telephone: (058) 561622
OWNER: Werner Bekker

BLUE MAX ULTRALIGHT BLUE MAX

This single-seat microlight is available in ready to fly form, and three had been sold by January 1986. It is a conventional braced microlight, the engine of which can be switched off during flight, for gliding, and restarted electrically, although it cannot be termed a motor glider.

TYPE: Single-seat microlight aircraft.

AIRFRAME: Strut and wire braced high-wing monoplane. Mainframe and boom constructed of aluminium alloy, with optional glassfibre cockpit pod. Double surfaced wings, with glassfibre ribs, leading-edges and tips, Ceconite covered. Stainless steel cables. No kingpost. Three-axis control (ailerons, all-moving tailplane and horn balanced rudder). Triangular dorsal and ventral fins. Rigging time 15 min.

LANDING GEAR: Non-retractable tailwheel type. Mainwheel tyre size 13 × 5-6. Steel leaf spring main legs. Castoring 4 in diameter tailwheel.

POWER PLANT: One 33·6 kW (45 hp) Rotax 447 two-cylinder two-stroke engine, with reduction gear to a two-blade wooden propeller. Optional 21 kW (28 hp) König 570 engine. Fuel capacity 41 litres (9 Imp gallons).

ACCOMMODATION: Pilot only, in open position. Optional cockpit pod with windscreen.

DIMENSIONS, EXTERNAL: Not quoted

WEIGHTS AND LOADINGS:

Weight empty	115 kg (254 lb)
Max pilot weight	95 kg (210 lb)
Max T-O weight	239 kg (527 lb)
Max wing loading	22·0 kg/m² (4·5 lb/sq ft)
Max power loading (45 hp)	7·11 kg/kW (11·71 lb/hp)

PERFORMANCE (König engine):

Never-exceed speed	85 knots (157 km/h; 97 mph)
Max level and cruising speed	54 knots (100 km/h; 62 mph)
Max rate of climb at S/L	122 m (400 ft)/min
Service ceiling	1,220-1,525 m (4,000-5,000 ft)
T-O run	91 m (300 ft)
Landing run	76 m (250 ft)
Range with max fuel	250 nm (463 km; 287 miles)
Endurance	2 h 45 min

CORBY

JOHN C. CORBY

34 Coronet Court, North Rocks, Sydney, NSW 2151

Mr Corby, a consultant aeronautical engineer, designed and is marketing plans for a single-seat wooden light aircraft known as the Starlet. By early 1986 more than 20 Starlets had been completed, with approximately 50 more under construction in Australia, New Zealand and the USA.

CORBY CJ-1 STARLET

The first Starlet (VH-ULV) was built by members of the Latrobe Valley division of the Australian Ultra Light Aircraft Association. Details of this aircraft were given in the 1974-75 *Jane's*. Another (VH-WDJ), flown by Mr Peter Furlong and powered by a 36·5 kW (49 hp) Ardem XI engine, won an Australian aerobatic championship in 1973.

The Starlet illustrated (VH-MIW) was built in Australia by Mr Laurie Wincen and Mr John Atkinson. Powered by a 56 kW (76 hp) Revmaster 2,100 cc engine, it has a maximum level speed of 145 knots (269 km/h; 167 mph). In 1984 Mr Corby fitted a 45 kW (60 hp) HAPI 1,835 cc modified motorcar engine to his prototype.

The following description applies to the standard Starlet, built to current plans:

TYPE: Single-seat homebuilt aircraft.

AIRFRAME: Cantilever low-wing monoplane of wooden construction. Wing section NACA 43012A. Dihedral 6°. Incidence 2° 30′ at root, − 1° at tip. Laminated main spar of solid spruce, subspars of spruce, built-up girder ribs and D shape nose section. Plywood covering from leading-edge to main spar, remainder fabric covered. Provision for dismantling into two equal halves. Ailerons of spruce with birch plywood covering. Spruce fuselage structure with plywood covering. Cantilever wooden tail unit, with plywood covered fixed incidence tailplane and fin, and fabric covered rudder and elevators.

LANDING GEAR: Non-retractable tailwheel type standard. Separate spring steel leaf type shock absorbing main legs, attached directly to fuselage via a solid spruce/ash beam which also serves as the wing leading-edge attachment member. Wheels, tyres and brakes of customer's choice, subject to mainwheels of 3½ in min diameter (typically, 4·00-4 tyres and Olympic go-kart hubs). Sturmey Archer cycle drum/shoe brakes may be used. Leaf spring tailskid, or tailwheel at customer's option. Wheel fairings optional.

POWER PLANT: Any suitable engine of up to 56 kW (75 hp) and 72 kg (160 lb) weight, driving a two-blade propeller, including a 37·25 kW (50 hp) Volkswagen 1600 cc converted motorcar engine. Fuel tank, capacity 36-43 litres (8·9-5 Imp gallons), aft of engine firewall. Oil capacity 2·25 kg (5 lb).

ACCOMMODATION: Single seat. Sliding canopy optional. Baggage locker behind seat.

DIMENSIONS, EXTERNAL:

Wing span	5·64 m (18 ft 6 in)
Wing chord at root	1·32 m (4 ft 4 in)
Length overall	4·50 m (14 ft 9 in)
Height overall	1·47 m (4 ft 10 in)
Tailplane span	1·98 m (6 ft 6 in)
Wheel track	1·37 m (4 ft 6 in)
Propeller diameter	1·37 m (4 ft 6 in)

AREA:

Wings, gross	6·36 m² (68·5 sq ft)

WEIGHTS AND LOADING:

Weight empty	183-212 kg (405-467 lb)
Max T-O weight (semi-aerobatic)	295 kg (650 lb)
Max T-O weight	322 kg (710 lb)
Max wing loading	50·6 kg/m² (10·36 lb/sq ft)

PERFORMANCE (A: prototype with 36·5 kW; 49 hp engine at 295 kg; 650 lb AUW, B: with 56 kW; 75 hp VW engine at max T-O weight):

Never-exceed speed:	
A	138 knots (255 km/h; 159 mph) IAS
Max level speed: A	117 knots (217 km/h; 135 mph)
B	145 knots (269 km/h; 167 mph)
Max cruising speed:	
A	107 knots (198 km/h; 123 mph)
B	125 knots (232 km/h; 144 mph)
Stalling speed, power off:	
A, B	42 knots (79 km/h; 49 mph)
Typical rate of climb at S/L:	
A	213-259 m (700-850 ft)/min
B	320 m (1,050 ft)/min
Service ceiling: A	4,420 m (14,500 ft)
T-O to, and landing from, 15 m (50 ft):	
A	305-335 m (1,000-1,100 ft)
Range with max fuel: B	231 nm (428 km; 266 miles)
g limits: A, B	±4·5

EASTWOOD

EASTWOOD AIRCRAFT PTY LTD (Division of SOUTH COAST AIR CENTRE PTY LTD)

PO Box 295, Aldinga Airport, Aldinga, South Australia 5173
Telephone: (085) 56 5404 or (08) 382 3457
MANAGER: Geoff Eastwood

EASTWOOD TYRO Mk II

Design of the Tyro was begun by Mr Geoff Eastwood in 1980, after four years of research and development. Construction of the first prototype started in March 1981 and the first flight was achieved in December that year. A second prototype followed and kit production was initiated in June 1982. The current Tyro Mk II version uses a Rotax 277 engine, which superseded the original 37·3 kW (50 hp) 440 cc Fuji Robin engine of the Tyro Mk I. The Rotax 447 engine specified initially for the Mk II is now offered as an option.

By February 1986 a total of five ready-assembled Tyro Mk IIs had been delivered, together with fourteen kits (of 15 ordered) and 72 sets of plans. All component parts are available to those constructing the aircraft from plans. The first kit-built aircraft flew in August 1982 and the first plans-built in December of that year. The exact number flying is unknown. Kits are offered with and without the engine. South Coast Air Centre also offers a teaching facility to pilots of ultralight aircraft. The Tyro's strong construction and bungee rubber suspension allow it to operate off very short grass airstrips and it is said to be ideally suited to rural work, such as cattle spotting, in addition to normal recreational use. Assembly for flight takes 10 minutes.

A two-seat version of the Tyro Mk II is under construction, and was expected to fly towards the end of 1986.

TYPE: Single-seat microlight aircraft; conforms to ANO 95-10.

AIRFRAME: Strut braced high-wing monoplane. Light alloy structure, with pressed wing ribs and stressed skin leading-edges, bolted and pop riveted together. Dacron double surface covering on wing and tail surfaces. Wing section NACA 4418. Dihedral 0° 45′. Incidence 4°. Three-axis control (rudder, all-moving tailplane and ailerons) with stainless steel cables. Primary fuselage boom of light alloy construction.

LANDING GEAR: Non-retractable tailwheel type, with bungee rubber suspension. Mainwheels size 12 × 3·5 in;

Blue Max single-seat microlight

Corby Starlet built by Mr Laurie Wincen and Mr John Atkinson of Cairns, Australia

solid steerable tailwheel size 3 × 1·5 in. Mainwheel tyre pressure 1·31 bars (19 lb/sq in). Floats optional.

Power Plant: One 20 kW (27 hp) Rotax 277 single-cylinder two-stroke engine, with 2·58:1 reduction gear to a Shetler-Canada two-blade wooden propeller. One fuel tank, capacity 20 litres (4·4 Imp gallons). Optional 32 kW (43 hp) Rotax 447 engine.

Accommodation: Single seat in cockpit with nacelle and windscreen.

Dimensions, external:	
Wing span	8·90 m (29 ft 2 in)
Wing chord, constant	1·17 m (3 ft 10 in)
Wing aspect ratio	7·6
Length overall	5·33 m (17 ft 6 in)
Tailplane span	2·29 m (7 ft 6 in)
Propeller diameter:	
with Rotax 277 engine	1·63 m (5 ft 4 in)
with Rotax 447 engine	1·73 m (5 ft 8 in)
Area:	
Wings, gross	10·50 m² (113·0 sq ft)
Weights and Loadings:	
Weight empty	113 kg (250 lb)
Pilot weight range	54·4-91 kg (120-200 lb)
Max T-O weight	218 kg (482 lb)
Max wing loading	20·76 kg/m² (4·26 lb/sq ft)
Max power loading	10·90 kg/kW (17·85 lb/hp)
Performance (Rotax 277 engine, unless stated):	
Never-exceed speed	73 knots (136 km/h; 85 mph)
Max level speed at S/L	69 knots (129 km/h; 80 mph)
Max cruising speed at S/L	56 knots (105 km/h; 65 mph)
Max cruising speed at S/L, Rotax 447 engine	65 knots (121 km/h; 75 mph)
Econ cruising speed at S/L	52 knots (97 km/h; 60 mph)
Econ cruising speed at S/L, Rotax 447 engine	61 knots (113 km/h; 70 mph)
Stalling speed, power off	20 knots (37 km/h; 23 mph)
Max rate of climb at S/L	259 m (850 ft)/min
Max rate of climb at S/L, Rotax 447 engine	427 m (1,400 ft)/min
T-O run	61 m (200 ft)
T-O run, Rotax 447 engine	31 m (100 ft)
Landing run	92 m (300 ft)
Range	130 nm (241 km; 150 miles)
Endurance	2 h 30 min
g limits:	+4/−2 design
	+6/−3 ultimate
Best glide ratio	7

FLIGHT 95

FLIGHT 95

316 Pacific Highway, Lindfield, NSW 2070

Telephone: (02) 5331865

FUN JAVELIN

The Javelin succeeded this company's Mustang design.

Type: Single-seat microlight.

Airframe: High-wing monoplane, with strut bracing. Single surface Dacron covering. Can be dismantled for storage and road transportation.

Landing Gear: Tailwheel type. Spring steel suspension, for operation off unprepared fields.

Power Plant: One 20 kW (27 hp) Rotax 277 single-cylinder two-stroke engine, driving a two-blade propeller. Fuel capacity 9 litres (2 Imp gallons).

Accommodation: Pilot's seat below wing, between mainwheels.

Dimensions, external:	
Wing span	8·50 m (27 ft 10½ in)
Length overall	5·00 m (16 ft 5 in)
Area:	
Wings, gross	12·80 m² (137·8 sq ft)
Weight:	
Weight empty	91 kg (201 lb)
Performance:	
Cruising speed	50 knots (93 km/h; 58 mph)
Stalling speed	17 knots (32 km/h; 20 mph)

FREE FLIGHT

FREE FLIGHT AVIATION PTY LTD

FREE FLIGHT HORNET S10

The prototype Hornet S10 was designed by Mr David Betteridge and made its first flight in early 1979. This aircraft, described briefly in the 1980-81 *Jane's*, had an open cockpit and was built of aluminium and plywood.

The modified S10, known formerly as the Hornet 130S, has an enclosed cockpit and lighter-weight airframe, and is available in ready to fly and kit forms. The wings can be folded back alongside the fuselage, to facilitate storage and trailering. Free Flight signed an agreement with a French company, Ameca, for development of a two-seat derivative of the Hornet S10. Preliminary design work was completed by early 1984, when it was reported that a prototype was not likely to be constructed in the immediate future. No more recent news has been received.

The following details refer to the standard single-seat Hornet S10:

Type: Single-seat homebuilt aircraft; conforms to ANO 95-22.

Airframe: Cantilever low-wing monoplane, of sweptback tail-less configuration, built mainly of light alloy and GRP. Wings have 15° sweepback, 5° dihedral on outer panels, an all-moving rudder at each tip, and are foldable. Two-segment elevon on each trailing-edge for pitch and roll control, outer segments operating differentially as ailerons, inner segments collectively as elevators; ground adjustable tab on each outer segment. Pod type fuselage. Ducted fan to rear of fuselage pod, providing induced airflow to augment lift at low speeds.

Landing Gear: Non-retractable tailwheel type. Main units each carried on single main strut and side V.

Power Plant: Standard power plant is 22 kW (30 hp) 430 cc König three-cylinder two-stroke aircooled radial engine, driving a three-blade ducted-fan pusher propeller. Electric starter, ignition system, silencer and fuel injection are standard. Airframe can accept various engines from 18·5-26 kW (25-35 hp), as well as the Lock Laird 0-500-2 two-cylinder four-stroke of 27 kW (36 hp).

Accommodation: Single seat under semi-enclosed framed canopy which hinges sideways to starboard, with upper half of fuselage, to provide access to cockpit.

Dimensions, external:	
Wing span	7·92 m (26 ft 0 in)
Wing aspect ratio	5·2
Width, wings folded	2·29 m (7 ft 6 in)
Length overall	3·05 m (10 ft 0 in)
Length, wings folded	4·57 m (15 ft 0 in)
Height overall	1·68 m (5 ft 6 in)
Wheel track	1·83 m (6 ft 0 in)
Propeller diameter	0·61 m (2 ft 0 in)
Area:	
Wings, gross	12·08 m² (130·0 sq ft)
Weights and Loadings:	
Weight empty	136 kg (300 lb)
Max T-O weight	295 kg (650 lb)
Wing loading	24·4 kg/m² (5·0 lb/sq ft)
Power loading, standard engine	13·41 kg/kW (21·67 lb/hp)
Performance (at max T-O weight):	
Max cruising speed	85 knots (157 km/h; 98 mph)
Econ cruising speed	78 knots (144 km/h; 89 mph)
Stalling speed	30 knots (56 km/h; 35 mph)
Max rate of climb at S/L	152 m (500 ft)/min
T-O run	61 m (200 ft)
Landing run	107 m (350 ft)
g limit	+6·5 ultimate
Best glide ratio	15

KIMBERLEY

GARETH J. KIMBERLEY

255 Woniora Road, Blakehurst, NSW 2221

Telephone: Sydney (02) 546 4143

KIMBERLEY SKY-RIDER

Design of the Sky-Rider started in early 1977 and construction of a prototype began on 3 October 1977. First flight was achieved on 5 November 1978. Plans are available to amateur constructors, and 171 sets had been sold in 17 countries (mainly Australia and the USA) by February 1986. Five are known to have flown.

Type: Single-seat microlight aircraft; conforms to ANO 95-10 and FAR Pt 103.

Airframe: Wire braced high-wing monoplane. Dihedral 2°. Incidence 4°, with 3° washout. Structure of tubular aluminium alloy, with single surface Dacron covering on wings, double on flaps, ailerons and tail surfaces. Stainless steel cables. Kingpost, pre-formed battens and adjustable camber standard. Three-axis control by ailerons, all-moving tailplane and rudder; flaps also fitted. Can be dismantled for transportation on the roof of a car and for storage.

Landing Gear: Tailwheel type, with spring leg suspension. Mainwheels size 13 × 4 in; pressure 1·24 bars (18 lb/sq in). Castoring solid rubber tailwheel, size 4 × 0·875 in. Mainwheel brakes. Floats and skis optional, as is ballistic recovery parachute.

Power Plant: Typically, one 13·5 kW (18 hp) Fuji Robin 250 cc single-cylinder two-stroke engine, with 2:1 reduction drive to a two-blade wooden fixed-pitch propeller. Fuel tank capacity 6·8 litres (1·5 Imp gallons). Has also been flown with McCulloch MC-101, Sachs 250 and two-cylinder inline Fuji Robin 440 engines; other optional power plants include Cuyuna 430, Rotax and KFM engines. Other propeller sizes optional.

Accommodation: Pilot only in fully open position.

Eastwood Tyro Mk II single-seat microlight

Free Flight Hornet 130S single-seat light aircraft, now known as the S10
(Howard Levy)

Laser Aerobatics Akro Model Z homebuilt aircraft

Kimberley Sky-Rider single-seat microlight

DIMENSIONS, EXTERNAL:

Wing span	9·86 m (32 ft 4 in)
Wing chord: at root	1·52 m (5 ft 0 in)
at tip	1·22 m (4 ft 0 in)
Wing aspect ratio	7·3
Length overall	5·94 m (19 ft 6 in)
Height overall	2·39 m (7 ft 10 in)
Tailplane span	3·15 m (10 ft 4 in)
Wheel track	1·63 m (5 ft 4 in)
Wheelbase	4·04 m (13 ft 3 in)
Propeller diameter	1·37 m (4 ft 6 in)

AREA:

Wings, gross	13·38 m² (144·0 sq ft)

WEIGHTS AND LOADINGS (with Fuji Robin 250 engine):

Weight empty	95 kg (210 lb)
Max pilot weight	91 kg (200 lb)
Max T-O weight	181·5 kg (400 lb)
Max wing loading	13·57 kg/m² (2·78 lb/sq ft)
Max power loading	13·44 kg/kW (22·22 lb/hp)

PERFORMANCE (with Fuji Robin 250 cc engine):

Never-exceed speed	56 knots (104 km/h; 65 mph)
Max level speed	43 knots (80 km/h; 50 mph)
Max cruising speed	39 knots (72 km/h; 45 mph)
Econ cruising speed	35 knots (64 km/h; 40 mph)
Stalling speed:	
flaps up	22 knots (41 km/h; 25 mph)
flaps down, engine idling	18 knots (32 km/h; 20 mph)
Stalling speed IGE	16 knots (29 km/h; 18 mph)
Max rate of climb at S/L	91 m (300 ft)/min
Max permitted flying height (in Australia)	152 m (500 ft)
T-O run	75 m (246 ft)
Landing run	50 m (164 ft)
Range with max fuel	35 nm (64 km; 40 miles)
Endurance with max fuel	1 h
g limits	+2/−0 normal
	+4·5/−1·5 ultimate
	(not stressed for aerobatics)

LASER

LASER AEROBATICS

16 Hillcrest Road, Glen Iris, Victoria 3146

Telephone: (03) 252046

CHIEF ENGINEER: David J. Pilkington, BE, MSc

LASER AEROBATICS AKRO MODEL Z

The Laser Aerobatics Akro Model Z has its ancestry in the American Stephens Akro, and some drawings of the Stephens design were used to gain approval for the Akro Model Z from the Australian Department of Transport (now Department of Aviation) on 2 March 1982. However, apart from a general similarity of configuration, the style of wing attachment, the aileron layout and similar main landing gear legs, the two aircraft are different designs.

Plans for the Laser Aerobatics Akro Model Z are available, and three examples are known to have flown in Australia. Others were being built in Australia (three), the UK (one), continental Europe and the USA in early 1986. Mr Pilkington believes that construction should be undertaken only by experienced builders.

TYPE: Single-seat aerobatic and sporting homebuilt monoplane.

AIRFRAME: Cantilever mid-wing monoplane. Wing section NACA 21012, modified at root by increased main spar depth. Thickness/chord ratio 13·5% at root, 12% at tip. No dihedral, incidence or sweepback. Two spruce spars, plywood ribs with spruce capstrips and stiffeners, covered with plywood skin stiffened by stringers. Wide span horn balanced ailerons, with steel tube spar and wooden ribs, fabric covered. Conventional welded steel tube fuselage, covered with aluminium sheet forward of cockpit and fabric aft. Braced welded steel tube tail unit, fabric covered, comprising fin, horn balanced rudder, tailplane and elevators. Each elevator fitted with trim/balance tab.

LANDING GEAR: Non-retractable tailwheel type. Cantilever spring aluminium main legs. Streamline fairings for mainwheels.

POWER PLANT: One 149 kW (200 hp) Avco Lycoming IO-360 flat-four engine, driving a two-blade Sensenich fixed-pitch or Hoffmann constant-speed propeller with spinner. Fuel tank in fuselage, aft of firewall, capacity 91 litres (24 US gallons).

ACCOMMODATION: Single seat under jettisonable side-hinged one-piece canopy.

DIMENSIONS, EXTERNAL:

Wing span	7·42 m (24 ft 4 in)
Wing chord: at root	1·60 m (5 ft 3 in)
at tip	0·76 m (2 ft 6 in)
Wing aspect ratio	6·04
Length overall	6·20 m (20 ft 4 in)
Tailplane span	2·46 m (8 ft 1 in)
Propeller diameter	1·93 m (6 ft 4 in)

AREA:

Wings, gross	9·10 m² (98·0 sq ft)

WEIGHTS AND LOADINGS:

Weight empty	413 kg (910 lb)
Baggage: turtledeck	13·6 kg (30 lb)
wing roots (total)	9 kg (20 lb)
Max T-O weight: aerobatic	498 kg (1,098 lb)
normal	589 kg (1,298 lb)
Max wing loading	64·72 kg/m² (13·24 lb/sq ft)
Max power loading	3·95 kg/kW (6·49 lb/hp)

PERFORMANCE:

Never-exceed speed	204 knots (378 km/h; 235 mph) CAS
Max level speed at S/L	175 knots (324 km/h; 202 mph)
Stalling speed	56 knots (104 km/h; 65 mph) CAS
Max rate of climb at S/L	915 m (3,000 ft)/min
T-O to 15 m (50 ft)	305 m (1,000 ft)
Landing from 15 m (50 ft)	457 m (1,500 ft)
Range with max fuel, no reserves	300 nm (556 km; 345 miles)

LGT

LIGETI AERO-NAUTICAL PTY LTD

PO Box 362, North Balwyn, Victoria 3104

Telephone: (03) 859 66 00

MANAGING DIRECTOR: Charles K. Ligeti, MSc

Mr Charles K. Ligeti began design studies for a high-performance ultralight aircraft of radical new design in Czechoslovakia in 1976. Construction of a prototype was delayed by legal problems and unavailability of materials. It was started in May 1983, in Australia, after extensive testing of the concept in quarter-scale radio controlled and free flight model forms. The prototype flew for the first time on 25 April 1985, piloted by Mr Ligeti, who reported subsequently that it fulfilled or exceeded all expectations. Plans, prefabricated parts and kits were expected to be made available at a later date.

LGT STRATOS

The LGT Stratos was conceived by Mr Ligeti to combine the efficiency of a canard, the large wing area and small span of a tandem wing configuration, and the strength of an externally braced biplane. It has a sweptback foreplane joined with the high-mounted mainplane at the tips by vertical split rudders. This gives increased wing stiffness, better pilot protection, and reductions in both weight and induced drag.

Because of the small size of the LGT Stratos, it can be transported fully assembled on a trailer behind a car, and kept in an average family garage, eliminating assembly and dismantling. Its aerodynamically clean configuration makes it suitable for soaring.

TYPE: Single-seat microlight aircraft; conforms to ANO 95-10.

AIRFRAME: All-composites structure of Kevlar and glassfibre skins over shaped rigid foam, with carbonfibre spars. Three-axis control. Pitch control by elevator on foreplane; roll control by ailerons on foreplane and mainplane. Wingtip split rudders provide yaw control when used differentially and act as airbrakes when used collectively. Flaps on mainplane. Integral dual-charge ballistic parachute recovery system in fuselage behind pilot.

LANDING GEAR: Non-retractable type, with two mainwheels in tandem and two balancer wheels at wingtips. Steerable front wheel, size 2·80-4, with spring shock absorption and integral rudder. Rear wheel, size 3·50 × 4·10-4, with coil spring shock absorber and drum brake.

ACCOMMODATION: Pilot only, on semi-supine seat, under fully enclosed blown Plexiglas tinted canopy which opens forward by gas strut.

POWER PLANT: One 18 kW (24 hp) König 430 cc three-cylinder two-stroke engine, mounted beneath mainplane and driving directly a three- or six-blade ground-adjustable pusher ducted fan. König 570 SD engine optional. Seat fuel tank, filled with expanded aluminium foil for safety reasons. Standard fuel capacity 22 litres (4·8 Imp gallons).

DIMENSIONS, EXTERNAL:

Wing span	5·31 m (17 ft 5 in)
Length overall	2·44 m (8 ft 0 in)
Height overall	0·90 m (2 ft 11½ in)
Fan diameter	0·65 m (2 ft 1½ in)

AREA:

Wings, gross	7·10 m² (76·4 sq ft)

WEIGHTS AND LOADINGS:

Weight empty	75 kg (166 lb)
Pilot weight range	55-83 kg (121-183 lb)
Max T-O weight	178 kg (392 lb)
Max wing loading	25·07 kg/m² (5·13 lb/sq ft)
Max power loading	9·94 kg/kW (16·33 lb/hp)

PERFORMANCE:

Never-exceed speed	145 knots (270 km/h; 167 mph)
Max level speed	108 knots (200 km/h; 124 mph)
Max cruising speed	97 knots (180 km/h; 112 mph)
Econ cruising speed	92 knots (170 km/h; 105 mph)
Stalling speed: power on	32 knots (58 km/h; 36 mph)
power off	33 knots (61 km/h; 38 mph)
Max rate of climb at S/L	228 m (748 ft)/min
Service ceiling	4,500 m (14,760 ft)
T-O run	100 m (328 ft)
Landing run	75 m (246 ft)
Range with max standard fuel	259 nm (480 km; 298 miles)
Endurance with max standard fuel	4 h 10 min
g limits	+9/−6
Best glide ratio	20

SEABIRD

SEABIRD AVIATION PTY LTD

172 Esplanade, Point Vernon, Queensland 4655
Telephone: (071) 28 1598
Telex: MAMEX AA49648
PRODUCTION MANAGER: P. D. Adams

Seabird Aviation currently markets the single seat SB-1 Rouseabout Mk 5 and a two-seat derivative known as the SB-1 Bushranger. A third aircraft, the SB-3, is under development. This is of very different configuration to the SB-1 and SB-2, being a tractor low-wing monoplane intended for agricultural spraying and other utility applications.

SEABIRD SB-1 ROUSEABOUT Mk 5

The design of this single-seat microlight was assisted during the initial stages by Gordon Bedson, designer of the Resurgam. Construction of the initial prototype began in 1983, and this flew for the first time in November that year. Building to pre-production standard started in 1984, bringing the total number of prototype/pre-production Rouseabouts completed to four. The Rouseabout Mk 5 is the production standard version, of which manufacture for sale began in 1986. By February that year ten had been ordered.

TYPE Single-seat microlight: conforms to FAR Pt 23.

AIRFRAME: Strut braced high-wing monoplane. Wing section NASA GAW-2. Thickness/chord ratio 13%. Dihedral 1° 30′. Incidence 2° 30′. No sweepback. Composite construction, mainly of PVC foam, glassfibre and Kevlar, with carbonfibre spar caps. Dacron covering aft of wing main spar and on control surfaces. Single boom from cockpit pod supports conventional tail unit. Three-axis control (rear full-span ailerons, rudder and wide-chord elevators).

LANDING GEAR: Non-retractable tailwheel type standard (fourth prototype/pre-production aircraft has non-retractable nosewheel gear). Cantilever spring legs. Twin float gear optional.

POWER PLANT: One 22·4 kW (30 hp) König 570 two-stroke four-cylinder radial engine mounted aft of the wing, with 2·5:1 reduction gear to König two-blade wooden fixed-pitch pusher propeller. One fuel tank, capacity 22 litres (5 Imp gallons).

ACCOMMODATION: Single seat in enclosed cockpit. Baggage area aft of seat, capacity 5 kg (11 lb).

DIMENSIONS, EXTERNAL:

Wing span	approx 8·99 m (29 ft 6 in)
Wing chord, constant	1·22 m (4 ft 0 in)
Tailplane span	2·29 m (7 ft 6 in)
Wheelbase	1·52 m (5 ft 0 in)
Propeller diameter	1·52 m (5 ft 0 in)

AREA:

Wings, gross	10·96 m² (118·0 sq ft)

WEIGHTS AND LOADINGS:

Weight empty	136 kg (300 lb)
Pilot weight range	63·5-95 kg (140-210 lb)
Max T-O weight	245 kg (540 lb)
Max wing loading	22·35 kg/m² (4·57 lb/sq ft)
Max power loading	10·94 kg/kW (18·00 lb/hp)

PERFORMANCE:

Never-exceed speed	82 knots (152 km/h; 94 mph)
Max level speed at 1,525 m (5,000 ft)	72 knots (133 km/h; 83 mph)
Max cruising speed at 1,525 m (5,000 ft), 75% power	64 knots (119 km/h; 74 mph)
Econ cruising speed, 65% power	57 knots (106 km/h; 66 mph)
Stalling speed	26 knots (48 km/h; 30 mph)
Max rate of climb at S/L	183 m (600 ft)/min
T-O run	46 m (150 ft)
Landing run	76 m (250 ft)
Range, at 65% power	130 nm (241 km; 150 miles)

SEABIRD SB-2 BUSHRANGER

The SB-2 Bushranger is basically an enlarged and more powerful two-seat derivative of the SB-1 Rouseabout. Design started in 1985 and construction of a prototype began the same year. By February 1986 two production aircraft had been ordered.

Details of the SB-2 Bushranger where they vary from the single-seat Rouseabout follow:

TYPE: Two-seat training and utility microlight: conforms to FAR Pt 23.

AIRFRAME: Similar to Rouseabout but with NLF(1)-0215F wing section and 15% thickness/chord ratio. Wider cockpit pod with extra side windows. Longer tailboom.

LANDING GEAR: Similar to Rouseabout but with larger wheels and reconfigured spring legs. Brakes fitted to mainwheels. Floats and skis optional.

POWER PLANT: One 37·3 kW (50 hp) König 930 two-stroke four-cylinder radial engine, with 2:1 reduction gear to a two-blade wooden fixed-pitch pusher propeller. Two fuel tanks, total capacity 54·5 litres (12 Imp gallons).

ACCOMMODATION: Two seats in enclosed cockpit.

DIMENSIONS, EXTERNAL:

Wing span	approx 10·29 m (33 ft 9 in)
Wing chord, constant	1·37 m (4 ft 6 in)
Length overall	6·71 m (22 ft 0 in)
Width, wings folded	2·44 m (8 ft 0 in)
Tailplane span	2·74 m (9 ft 0 in)
Propeller diameter	1·73 m (5 ft 8 in)

AREA:

Wings, gross	14·12 m² (152·0 sq ft)

WEIGHTS AND LOADINGS:

Weight empty	236 kg (520 lb)
Pilot weight range	63·5-95 kg (140-210 lb)
Max T-O weight	476 kg (1,050 lb)
Max wing loading	33·7 kg/m² (6·9 lb/sq ft)
Max power loading	12·76 kg/kW (21·00 lb/hp)

PERFORMANCE:

Never-exceed speed	98 knots (181 km/h; 112 mph)
Max level speed	86 knots (159 km/h; 99 mph)
Max cruising speed, 75% power	75 knots (139 km/h; 86 mph)
Cruising speed, 65% power	65 knots (120 km/h; 75 mph)
Stalling speed	32 knots (60 km/h; 37 mph)
Max rate of climb at S/L	183 m (600 ft)/min
T-O run	76 m (250 ft)
Landing run	46 m (150 ft)
Range, 65% power	200 nm (370 km; 230 miles)

SEABIRD SB-3

The SB-3, designed also to FAR Pt 23 regulations, differs from the SB-1 and SB-2 in many respects, although it uses similar methods of composite construction. Despite having a strut braced low-mounted location, with pronounced dihedral, the wings are of the same type as those used by the SB-2. The tail fin and rudder are also common to both aircraft, and the SB-3 uses a similar König 930 engine, driving a tractor propeller. The cockpit of the SB-3 is open, and the mainwheels of the tailwheel type landing gear are carried on side Vs and half-axles.

The SB-3 has been designed to carry ultra low volume spray equipment with rotary atomisers, with the spraybooms suspended under the wings. The capacity of the spray tank is 91 litres (20 Imp gallons). It can also be used for other purposes. No details relating to dimensions, weights or performance have been received but it is known that work on a prototype had started by February 1986.

SMITH

ALLAN C. SMITH DEVELOPMENTS PTY LTD

16 Loyalty Road, North Rocks, NSW 2151
Telephone: 630 0211

SMITH FSRW-1

The FSRW-1 amphibian project was begun by Mr Allan C. Smith in 1974, with the assistance of two lecturers from Sydney University. Much of the aircraft's subsequent detail design, construction and development were undertaken by Mr Kim White.

The prototype FSRW-1 (VH-XWS) made its first flight from land on 16 March 1983, followed by its first take-off from water on 2 December that year. Considerable development work followed these early flights, mainly to improve performance, stability, control, and water operation. One result has been replacement of the original all-moving tailplane with a conventional fixed tailplane and elevators, mounted higher on the fin for improved water clearance. Development and refinement of the prototype continue, and plans and kits of component parts for construction of the FSRW-1 by amateur builders may eventually become available.

TYPE: Two-seat homebuilt amphibian.

AIRFRAME: Cantilever high-wing monoplane, made in one piece and removable for transport. Wing section NACA 65_3418. No anhedral or dihedral. Incidence 1° 36′. Glassfibre epoxy structure; spar booms made from unidirectional glassfibre rovings; sandwich skins, with PVC foam core between glass cloth, made in female moulds. Single-slotted flaps and Frise ailerons of similar construction to wings. Flying-boat hull of similar construction to wings. Conventional tail unit, comprising fin and rudder and fixed tailplane with conventional elevators; construction as for wings. Trim tab on each elevator. Water rudder under rear of fuselage.

LANDING GEAR: Fitted with non-retractable nosewheel type for testing from land; removable for water operation. Cleveland wheels, each with tyre size 330 × 125-127. Cleveland brakes. Designed for retractable type. Glassfibre spring legs on main and nose units. Stabilising floats of glassfibre construction, pylon mounted under wingtips, for water operation.

POWER PLANT: One 97 kW (130 hp) Rolls-Royce Continental O-240-A flat-four engine, buried in the fuselage and driving two Hawker de Havilland wooden fixed-pitch tractor propellers carried on V pylons behind and above wings via Flexidyne coupling, shaft and Poly-V belts. Air intakes on fuselage sides, beneath wings, for crankshaft driven cooling fan. Two integral fuel tanks in wings, total capacity 80 litres (21 US gallons). Refuelling points in wing upper surfaces. Oil capacity 5 litres (1·32 US gallons).

ACCOMMODATION: Two seats side by side under side hinged (to starboard) canopy.

SYSTEM: Electrical system, with alternator and battery.

AVIONICS: VHF com.

DIMENSIONS, EXTERNAL:

Wing span	9·97 m (32 ft 8½ in)
Wing chord, constant	1·22 m (4 ft 0 in)
Wing aspect ratio	8·2
Length overall	7·12 m (23 ft 4¼ in)
Height overall	2·38 m (7 ft 9¾ in)
Tailplane span	3·96 m (13 ft 0 in)
Wheel track	2·80 m (9 ft 2¼ in)
Wheelbase	2·70 m (8 ft 10¼ in)
Propeller diameter	1·50 m (4 ft 11 in)
Propeller ground clearance	1·30 m (4 ft 3 in)
Distance between propeller centres	1·80 m (5 ft 11 in)

AREA:

Wings, gross	12·10 m² (130·24 sq ft)

WEIGHTS AND LOADINGS:

Weight empty	670 kg (1,477 lb)
Max fuel weight	55 kg (121 lb)
Max T-O and landing weight	907 kg (2,000 lb)

LGT Stratos single-seat pusher microlight

Fourth prototype/pre-production Seabird SB-1 Rouseabout with tricycle landing gear and original semi-enclosed cockpit

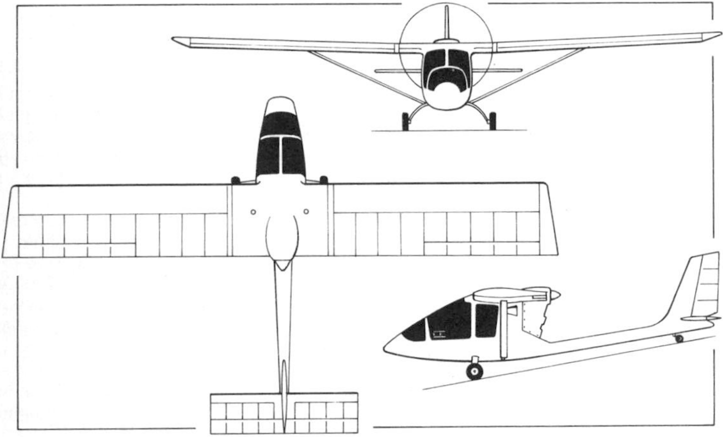

Seabird SB-2 Bushranger two-seat training and utility microlight

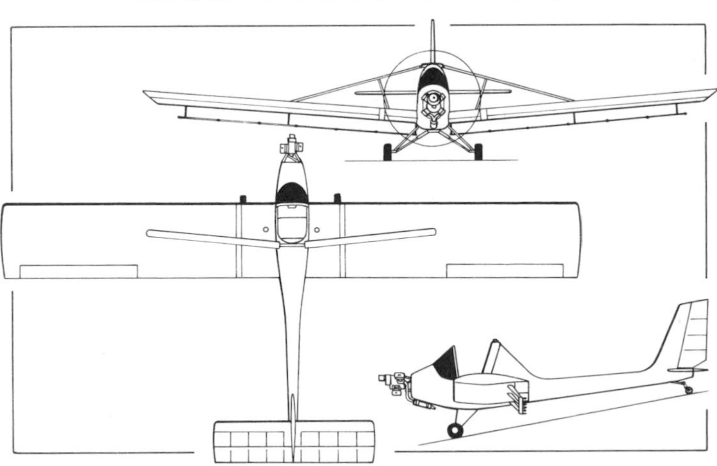

Seabird SB-3 in sprayer configuration

First prototype/pre-production Seabird SB-1 Rouseabout with float landing gear and original semi-enclosed cockpit

Smith FSRW-1 prototype, with raised and fixed tailplane

SV 11B Farmate single-seat microlight

SV 14 two-seat microlight

Max wing loading 74·96 kg/m² (15·36 lb/sq ft)
Max power loading 9·35 kg/kW (15·38 lb/hp)

PERFORMANCE:
Never-exceed speed 142 knots (263 km/h; 163 mph)
Max level speed at S/L 105 knots (195 km/h; 121 mph)
Max and econ cruising speed 100 knots (185 km/h; 115 mph)
Stalling speed 50 knots (93 km/h; 58 mph)
Max rate of climb at S/L 152 m (500 ft)/min
Range with max fuel, 45 min reserves 200 nm (370 km; 230 miles)

SV

SV AIRCRAFT PTY LTD

PO Box 85, Nagambie, Victoria 3608
Telephone: (057) 942711
DIRECTOR: Glenn Lyon

SV 11B FARMATE

Ten Farmates had been built and nine sold by mid-1985, all in ready to fly form.

TYPE: Single-seat microlight aircraft.

AIRFRAME: Strut braced high-wing monoplane. Single bracing strut each side. Pod and boom fuselage, with V tail surfaces. Aluminium alloy structure, with glassfibre skin overall, double surfaced over 19 per cent of wings. Three-axis control, with flaperons and ruddervators.

LANDING GEAR: Non-retractable tailwheel type, with cantilever glassfibre spring main legs. Mainwheels size 12 × 4 in; steerable tailwheel size 2½ × 1 in. Mainwheel brakes and wheel fairings optional.

POWER PLANT: One 20 kW (27 hp) Rotax 277 single-cylinder two-stroke engine, with 2·25:1 reduction gear to a two-blade wooden pusher propeller. Fuel capacity 25 litres (5·5 Imp gallons).

ACCOMMODATION: Pilot only, on supine seat in fully enclosed and highly glazed cockpit.

DIMENSIONS, EXTERNAL:
Wing span 8·00 m (26 ft 3 in)
Wing aspect ratio 8
Length overall 5·30 m (17 ft 4¾ in)
Height overall 1·30 m (4 ft 3¼ in)
Propeller diameter 1·22 m (4 ft 0 in)

AREA:
Wings, gross 8·0 m² (86·1 sq ft)

WEIGHTS AND LOADINGS:
Weight empty 150 kg (331 lb)

Pilot weight range 75-95 kg (165-209 lb)
Max T-O weight 265 kg (584 lb)
Max wing loading 33·13 kg/m² (6·78 lb/sq ft)
Max power loading 12·62 kg/kW (20·85 lb/hp)

PERFORMANCE:
Never-exceed speed 105 knots (194 km/h; 120 mph)
Max level and max cruising speed 80 knots (148 km/h; 92 mph)
Econ cruising speed 60 knots (111 km/h; 69 mph)
Stalling speed:
power on 30 knots (56 km/h; 35 mph)
power off 32 knots (60 km/h; 37 mph)
Max rate of climb at S/L 152 m (500 ft)/min
Service ceiling 3,050 m (10,000 ft)
T-O run 122 m (400 ft)
Landing run 183 m (600 ft)
Range with max fuel 180 nm (333 km; 207 miles)
Endurance with max fuel 3 h
g limits +6/−4

SV 14

A single prototype of this aircraft had been completed by mid-1985.

TYPE: Two-seat microlight aircraft.

AIRFRAME: Strut braced high-wing monoplane. Single bracing strut each side. Pod and boom fuselage, with V tail surfaces and small ventral fin. Aluminium alloy structure, with glassfibre skin overall, double surfaced over 19 per cent of wings. Three-axis control, with flaperons and ruddervators.

LANDING GEAR: Non-retractable tricycle type, with cantilever spring steel legs. Mainwheel size 12 × 5 in; steerable nosewheel size 10 × 4 in. Nosewheel brake and wheel fairings fitted.

POWER PLANT: One 31·3 kW (42 hp) Rotax 447 two-cylinder two-stroke engine, with 2·25:1 reduction gear to a two-blade wooden propeller. Fuel capacity 40 litres (8·8 Imp gallons).

ACCOMMODATION: Pilot only in fully enclosed cockpit.

DIMENSIONS, EXTERNAL:
Wing span 11·40 m (37 ft 5 in)
Wing aspect ratio 11·8
Length overall 5·90 m (19 ft 4¼ in)
Height overall 2·20 m (7 ft 2¾ in)
Propeller diameter 1·37 m (4 ft 6 in)

AREA:
Wings, gross 11·0 m² (118·4 sq ft)

WEIGHTS AND LOADINGS:
Weight empty 213 kg (470 lb)
Pilot weight range 50-80 kg (110-176 lb)
Max T-O weight 400 kg (882 lb)
Max wing loading 36·36 kg/m² (7·45 lb/sq ft)
Max power loading 12·78 kg/kW (21·0 lb/hp)

PERFORMANCE:
Never-exceed speed 80 knots (148 km/h; 92 mph)
Max cruising speed 60 knots (111 km/h; 69 mph)
Econ cruising speed 50 knots (92 km/h; 57 mph)
Stalling speed:
power on 29 knots (54 km/h; 34 mph)
power off 30 knots (56 km/h; 35 mph)
Max rate of climb at S/L 152 m (500 ft)/min
Service ceiling 3,050 m (10,000 ft)
T-O run 183 m (600 ft)
Landing run 244 m (800 ft)
Range with max fuel 200 nm (370 km; 230 miles)
Endurance with max fuel 3 h
g limits +5/−4

THRUSTER

THRUSTER AIRCRAFT (AUSTRALIA) PTY LTD

458 The Boulevarde, Kirrawee, NSW 2232

Telephone: (02) 542 1990

Telex: AA 73953

MANAGER: K. D. Belton

THRUSTER AIRCRAFT THRUSTER and GEMINI

The current single-seat Thruster utility microlight and similar two-seat Gemini (known in Europe as the Thruster TST) incorporate a unique wing design which allows each wing to 'rack' and fold inside the double surface skins for ease of transportation and rapid rigging. Sales of the ready-to-fly Thruster '85 model, the latest version for which figures were made available, totalled 200 aircraft by May 1985. The European main distributor of the Thruster and Gemini is Thruster Aircraft (UK) Ltd, Barton, Bolventor, Launceston, Cornwall PL15 7TZ (*telephone:* 05 6686 514).

TYPE: Single-seat (Thruster) and two-seat (Gemini) microlight aircraft; conform to ANO 95-25 or ANO 95-55 and BCAR section S.

AIRFRAME: Strut braced high-wing monoplane. Mainframe constructed of anodised aluminium alloy. Cockpit pod with polycarbonate windscreen. Double surfaced Dacron covered wings and conventional tail unit. Stainless steel cables. No kingpost. Three-axis control (full span ailerons, elevators and rudder); Gemini has additional flaps. Options include additional instruments, custom wing fittings, high performance 7·92 m (26 ft) span Sports Wing, and agricultural spray equipment. Rigging time about 30 min.

LANDING GEAR: Non-retractable tailwheel type, with steerable tailwheel. Spring steel suspension. No brakes. Optional floats and skis; conversion from land to float gear and vice-versa takes 15 min.

POWER PLANT: One 30 kW (40 hp) Rotax 447 two-cylinder two-stroke engine, with 2·58:1 reduction gear to two-blade wooden propeller. Optional 37·3 kW (50 hp) Rotax 503 engine recommended with float landing gear. Fuel tank capacity 25 litres (5·5 Imp gallons).

ACCOMMODATION: Thruster: Pilot only, in open cockpit. Gemini: Pilot and passenger side by side in open cockpit.

DIMENSIONS, EXTERNAL (both):
Wing span 9·60 m (31 ft 6 in)
Length overall 5·33 m (17 ft 6 in)
Height overall 1·90 m (6 ft 2¾ in)
Propeller diameter 1·70 m (5 ft 7 in)

AREA (both):
Wings, gross 15·00 m² (161·5 sq ft)

WEIGHTS AND LOADINGS (A: Thruster, B: Gemini):
Weight empty: A 135 kg (297 lb)
B 150 kg (330 lb)
Pilot weight range: A 55-90 kg (121-198 lb)
B 65-180 kg (143-397 lb)
Max T-O weight: A 245 kg (540 lb)
B 400 kg (882 lb)
Max wing loading: A 16·33 kg/m² (3·34 lb/sq ft)
B 26·67 kg/m² (5·46 lb/sq ft)
Max power loading: A 8·22 kg/kW (13·5 lb/hp)
B 13·42 kg/kW (22·05 lb/hp)

PERFORMANCE (A: Thruster, B: Gemini):
Never-exceed speed:
A 100 knots (185 km/h; 115 mph)
B 80 knots (148 km/h; 92 mph)
Max level speed: A 80 knots (148 km/h; 92 mph)
B 68 knots (126 km/h; 78 mph)
Max cruising speed: A 70 knots (130 km/h; 81 mph)
B 65 knots (120 km/h; 75 mph)
Econ cruising speed:
A, B 52 knots (96 km/h; 60 mph)
Stalling speed:
power on, A 30 knots (56 km/h; 35 mph)
power on, B 32 knots (60 km/h; 37 mph)
power off, A 32 knots (60 km/h; 37 mph)
power off, B 35 knots (65 km/h; 41 mph)
Max rate of climb at S/L: A 300 m (985 ft)/min
B 250 m (820 ft)/min
T-O run: A 30 m (98 ft)
B 45 m (147 ft)
Landing run: A 30 m (98 ft)
B 50 m (164 ft)
Range with max fuel: A, B 156 nm (289 km; 179 miles)
Endurance, 50% power: A, B 3 h
g limits: A, B +6/−3

ULTRALIGHT

ULTRALIGHT AIRCRAFT INDUSTRIES (AUST) PTY LTD

The Ultralight Aircraft Industries Bunyip single-seat microlight aircraft is no longer in production. Full details and an illustration can be found in the 1985-86 *Jane's*.

WAACO

WEST AUSTRALIAN AIRCRAFT COMPANY

15 Lynwood Avenue, Ringwood East, Victoria 3135
Telephone: (03) 879 4747
MANAGING DIRECTOR: Max Kremke

WAACO STAGGERBIPE Mk 1

The Waaco Staggerbipe is a single-seat, single-engined air recreational vehicle with negative-stagger biplane wings. Design, development, tooling and building of a prototype took Mr Max Kremke three years, with construction beginning in 1983 and the first flight in November 1985.

The Staggerbipe was conceived to fit midway between the conventional microlight and heavier and more sophisticated homebuilt aircraft, combining an empty weight of less than 150 kg (331 lb) with the configuration and controls of a conventional homebuilt. The empty weight of the prototype, with a Volkswagen engine, exceeds this figure, but lighter engines can be fitted. Only this one Staggerbipe has been built to date, but kits, without an engine and instruments, will be made available after test flying has been completed.

TYPE: Single-seat ARV.

AIRFRAME: Negative stagger biplane with single bracing strut each side and N type interplane struts. Wing section NACA 4412. Dihedral 2°. Incidence 3°. No sweepback. Constructed of aluminium alloy and foam/glassfibre. Wings only Dacron fabric covered. Glassfibre nose cowling. Three-axis control, with horn balanced rudder and elevators; ailerons on lower wings only. Trim tab on elevators. Airframe rigging time 10-15 min. Options include recovery parachute.

LANDING GEAR: Non-retractable tailwheel type. Spring steel main legs, with 11·5 × 5 in mainwheel tyres; pressure 1·72 bars (25 lb/sq in). Tailwheel 4 × 1·5 in. Mainwheel brakes. Mainwheel fairings, floats and skis optional.

POWER PLANT: One 30 kW (40 hp) Volkswagen 1,280 cc modified motorcar engine, driving a WAACO 54/33 two-blade wooden fixed-pitch propeller. Optional lighter engine. Glassfibre fuel tank, capacity 30 litres (6·5 Imp gallons). Oil capacity 2·2 litres (0·5 Imp gallon).

ACCOMMODATION: Pilot only, in semo-supine position in enclosed cabin. Window/door panels can be removed for semi-open cockpit. Baggage space aft of seat, capacity 5 kg (11 lb).

DIMENSIONS, EXTERNAL:
Wing span: upper 6·10 m (20 ft 0¼ in)
lower 5·48 m (17 ft 11¾ in)
Wing chord, constant 0·90 m (2 ft 11½ in)
Wing aspect ratio 6·43
Length overall 4·40 m (14 ft 5¼ in)
Height overall 1·60 m (5 ft 3 in)
Tailplane span 1·80 m (5 ft 11 in)
Wheel track 1·50 m (4 ft 11 in)
Wheelbase 3·60 m (11 ft 9¾ in)
Propeller diameter 1·36 m (4 ft 6 in)

AREA:
Wings, gross 10·6 m² (114·1 sq ft)

WEIGHTS AND LOADINGS (Volkswagen engine):
Weight empty 161 kg (355 lb)
Pilot weight range 70-100 kg (155-220 lb)
Max T-O weight 300 kg (661 lb)
Max wing loading 28·3 kg/m² (5·79 lb/sq ft)
Max power loading 10·07 kg/kW (16·53 lb/hp)

PERFORMANCE:
Never-exceed speed 120 knots (222 km/h; 138 mph)
Max level speed 81 knots (150 km/h; 93 mph)
Max cruising speed 70 knots (130 km/h; 81 mph)
Econ cruising speed 60 knots (111 km/h; 69 mph)
Stalling speed:
power on 28 knots (52 km/h; 33 mph)
power off 32 knots (60 km/h; 37 mph)
Max rate of climb at S/L 244 m (800 ft)/min
Service ceiling 4,200 m (13,780 ft)
T-O run 50-60 m (165-197 ft)
T-O to and landing from 15 m (50 ft) 150-200 m (492-656 ft)
Landing run 60-100 m (197-328 ft)
Range 215 nm (400 km; 248 miles)
Endurance, with 30 min reserves 3 h
g limits +9·6/−6

WINTON

SCOTT WINTON

88 Elizabeth Street, Granville, NSW 2147

WINTON SAPHIRE

The Saphire, which first flew in early 1983, is a single-seat, single-engined microlight of conventional high-wing design. It was intended to be marketed in ready to fly form, but no recent news of its status has been received. Further details of this aircraft can be found in the 1985-86 *Jane's*.

Thruster Gemini/TST two-seat microlight *(Brian M. Service)*

Waaco Staggerbipe Mk 1

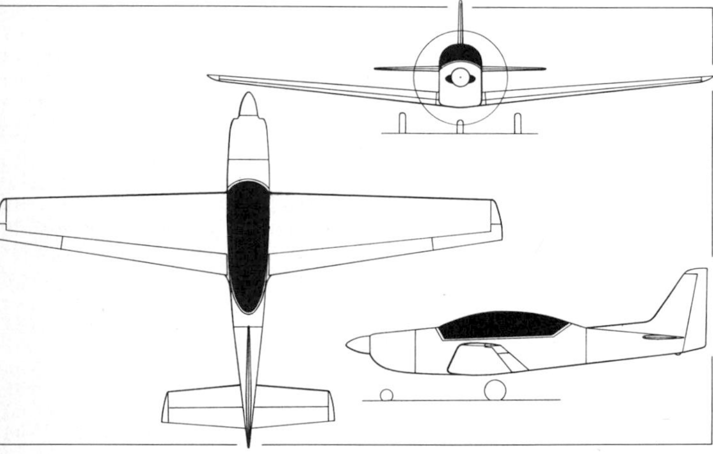
MIM Esqualo II *(Pilot Press)*

Single-seat prototype of the Airtech Canada Skylark

WINTON

WINTON AIRCRAFT

23 Forwells Road, Coomera, Queensland 4210
Telephone: (075) 532027
PROPRIETOR: Colin Winton

This company marketed two single-seat microlight aircraft, the Grasshopper and the Cricket, both designed by Mr Colin Winton. Details, and a photograph of the Grasshopper, can be found in the 1982-83 *Jane's*. A subsequent aircraft was the **Jackeroo**, completed originally with composite wings and an 18 kW (24 hp) 432 cc engine. This may be related to the Jackeroo marketed by Australian Aerolite.

Mr Winton's latest known design is the **Sportsman**, a single-seat mid-wing design with glassfibre fuselage pod, channel-section aluminium tailboom and tricycle landing gear. It is believed that the Sportsman is offered in kit or ready to fly form, though no news as to present status has been received. The power plant is a 1,400 cc VW unit driving a 1·37 m (4 ft 6 in) diameter pusher propeller. Wing span is 7·60 m (24 ft 11¼ in), length overall 4·60 m (15 ft 1 in), wing area 10·70 m² (115·2 sq ft) and empty weight 150 kg (331 lb). The Sportsman cruises at 70 knots (130 km/h; 81 mph) and has a stalling speed of 30 knots (56 km/h; 35 mph).

BRAZIL

MIM

MAURICIO IMPELIZIERI P. MOURA

Av Portugal 2834, 31540, Belo Horizonte
Telephone: 441 0096

Mr Mauricio Impelizieri P. Moura designed and built a two/three-seat sporting aircraft which he named Esqualo-180 (PP-ZIM). This first flew on 6 February 1981. No plans or kits of component parts were made available. Full details of this aircraft, and an illustration, appeared in the 1983-84 *Jane's*.

Mr Moura is currently working on a new two-seat sporting aircraft which he has named the Esqualo II. It is designed to be as inexpensive as an ultralight aircraft imported to Brazil, with many components coming from non-aviation sources. Design began in September 1983 and construction of the prototype started in January 1985.

MIM ESQUALO II

TYPE: Tandem two-seat homebuilt sporting aircraft.

AIRFRAME: Cantilever low-wing monoplane. NACA series 6 laminar flow wing section. Thickness/chord ratio 15% at root; 12% at tip. Dihedral 6° from roots. No incidence or sweepback. Foam and wood composite spar, with glassfibre skins. Balanced ailerons and flaps, the former working as flaperons, of similar composite construction. Composite semi-monocoque fuselage, using wooden longerons and glassfibre/foam/glassfibre sandwich skins. Conventional cantilever tail unit, with slightly sweptback vertical surfaces. Horn balanced rudder. No trim tabs. Dorsal fin. Construction similar to that of wings.

LANDING GEAR: Manually retractable tricycle type. Mainwheels retract inward into wing roots, nosewheel rearward. Mainwheel tyres size 5·00-5, pressure 1·72 bars (25 lb/sq in); nosewheel tyre size 10 × 3·50-4, pressure 1·52 bars (22 lb/sq in). Shock absorbers on main units; spring nosewheel leg. Disc brakes.

POWER PLANT: One 104·5 kW (140 hp) turbocharged Volkswagen Passat 2,000 cc converted motorcar engine with belt reduction drive, driving a two-blade fixed-pitch propeller. One PVC fuel tank in each wing; total capacity 100 litres (22 Imp gallons) of alcohol fuel. Refuelling point in upper surface of each wing. Oil capacity 4 litres (0·9 Imp gallon).

ACCOMMODATION: Two seats in tandem beneath sideways hinged transparent canopy.

SYSTEM: 12V electrical system. Hydraulic system for landing gear retraction.

DIMENSIONS, EXTERNAL:

Wing span	7·75 m (25 ft 5 in)
Wing chord: at root	1·30 m (4 ft 3¼ in)
at tip	0·65 m (2 ft 1½ in)
Wing aspect ratio	8
Length overall	5·88 m (19 ft 3½ in)
Height overall	2·18 m (7 ft 1¾ in)
Tailplane span	2·79 m (9 ft 2 in)
Wheel track	1·90 m (6 ft 2¾ in)
Wheelbase	1·80 m (5 ft 11 in)

AREA:

Wings, gross	7·50 m² (80·73 sq ft)

WEIGHTS AND LOADINGS (estimated):

Weight empty	420 kg (926 lb)
Max T-O weight	710 kg (1,565 lb)
Max wing loading	94·7 kg/m² (19·39 lb/sq ft)
Max power loading	6·79 kg/kW (11·18 lb/hp)

PERFORMANCE (estimated at max T-O weight):

Never-exceed speed	232 knots (430 km/h; 267 mph)
Max cruising speed	167 knots (310 km/h; 193 mph)
Econ cruising speed	159 knots (295 km/h; 183 mph)
Stalling speed, flaps and landing gear down	49 knots (90 km/h; 56 mph)
Max rate of climb at S/L	305 m (1,000 ft)/min

CANADA

AIRTECH

AIRTECH CANADA

PO Box 415, Peterborough Municipal Airport, Peterborough, Ontario K9J 6Z3
Telephone: (705) 743 9483
Telex: 06 962912

AIRTECH CANADA SKYLARK

Following three years of development and three changes of design, wind tunnel testing and flying a quarter-scale radio controlled model, Airtech Canada began marketing in kit form a single-seat microlight known as the Skylark. The prototype flew for the first time on 12 October 1984 and the company then expected 30 Skylarks to be flying by November 1985. Construction of a Skylark is said to take between 100 and 200 working hours. A side by side two-seat training version, known as the **Skylark II** and with a wider cockpit fairing and revised tailplane, was due to make its initial flight in Spring 1985. No recent news regarding the status of the Skylark and Skylark II has been received.

The forward-swept wing and underwing cockpit of the Skylark is claimed to give an excellent view in all flight attitudes; the weight of the pilot has minimal effect on the CG; the spanwise lift distribution inhibits stalling of the wingtips, prevents spinning, and indicates an approaching stall by buffeting the tail surfaces. The following data refer to the single-seat Skylark:

TYPE: Single-seat microlight aircraft; conforms to FAR Part 23.

AIRFRAME: Strut braced high-wing monoplane, with wings,

engine, tail unit and cockpit supported by square-section beam. Forward swept detachable wings of constant chord and thickness except for tapered outer panels. NASA wing section. Airframe of aluminium alloy sheet, extrusions and angles (including stamped ribs), with Teflon bellcrank bearings, aluminium pushrods with spherical couplings, and glassfibre cockpit fairing. Wings and tail surfaces Ceconite 7600 fabric covered. Tailplane can be folded up against fin. Adhesive bonding and blind and solid rivets. Three-axis control (ailerons, elevators and horn balanced rudder).

LANDING GEAR: Non-retractable tricycle type, with three similar size wheels, plus tailskid. Toe operated brakes. Floats and skis optional.

POWER PLANT: One 21 kW (28 hp) König four-cylinder two-stroke radial engine, with 2·8:1 cog/belt reduction drive to a three-blade ground adjustable propeller. Fuel tank capacity 19 litres (5 US gallons). Electric starting.

ACCOMMODATION: Pilot only, in open cockpit with nacelle and moulded windscreen.

DIMENSIONS, EXTERNAL:

Wing span	10·97 m (36 ft 0 in)
Length overall	5·49 m (18 ft 0 in)
Propeller diameter	1·83 m (6 ft 0 in)

AREA:

Wings, gross	16·54 m² (178·0 sq ft)

WEIGHTS AND LOADINGS:

Weight empty	129 kg (284 lb)
Max T-O weight	244 kg (539 lb)
Max wing loading	14·78 kg/m² (3·03 lb/sq ft)
Max power loading	11·67 kg/kW (19·25 lb/hp)

PERFORMANCE:

Never-exceed speed	60 knots (111 km/h; 69 mph)
Max level speed	51 knots (95 km/h; 59 mph)
Normal cruising speed	43 knots (80 km/h; 50 mph)
Max rate of climb at S/L	186 m (610 ft)/min
T-O run	18 m (60 ft)
Landing run	under 18 m (60 ft)
Design g limits	+5/−2·5
Min rate of sink, power off	119 m (390 ft)/min

BIRDMAN

BIRDMAN ENTERPRISES LTD

Box 609, 702-12 Avenue, Nisku, Alberta T0C 2G0
Telephone: (403) 955 7878
Telex: 037 2459

GENERAL MANAGER: Barry Metcalfe
CHIEF ENGINEER AND DESIGNER: Wladimir Talanczuk

Birdman Enterprises formerly produced the Atlas single-seat microlight described and illustrated in the 1983-84 *Jane's*. Current products are the single-seat WT-11 Chinook and the tandem two-seat Chinook 2S.

In 1986 Birdman was expected to release information on an ultralight aircraft designed specifically for agricultural spraying. This aircraft, which has been partially funded by the Canada Regional Industrial Expansion organisation, was started in August 1985. Prototype testing was scheduled to be completed by Spring 1986, with initial production by June-July of that year.

A report in the *China Daily* newspaper on 9 November 1985 stated that China had signed a ten-year agreement with this company to construct 5,000 aircraft for global distribution. Said to represent China's largest-ever aircraft export agreement, the programme is being undertaken by the Beijing Chang Feng Corporation, which was established in July 1984 in response to the government's wishes to convert part of its military industry to civilian use, to speed the nation's modernisation programme.

BIRDMAN WT-11 CHINOOK

Designed in 1982 and first flown on 12 December that year, the Chinook utilises a wing aerofoil section by Prof David Marsden of the University of Alberta. Production began in March 1983 and the aircraft is offered in kit form. Several hundred single-seat WT-11 Chinooks have been produced in two versions: the **WT-11-277** with a Rotax 277 engine and the **WT-11-377** with a 26·8 kW (36 hp) Rotax 377 engine. It is reported that an experienced constructor can assemble a Chinook in 40-60 working hours; an inexperienced constructor requires approximately 100 working hours.

The Chinook does not spin and is said to have gentle stall characteristics. It won the Reserve Grand Champion award at the EAA's Oshkosh '83 meeting, and Reserve Grand Champion at Oshkosh '84. In August 1983 test pilot Mr Dennis Maland flew a standard Chinook with a 20 kW (27 hp) engine to an altitude of 5,640 m (18,500 ft), and in November 1984 Mr Jack Hughes flew a Chinook across Australia, from Orange, NSW, to Perth, a distance of 2,050 nm (3,800 km; 2,360 miles), in 49 flying hours over an elapsed time of 14 days.

TYPE: Single-seat microlight aircraft; conforms to FAI and FAR Pt 103 requirements.

AIRFRAME: Strut braced high-wing monoplane, with three-axis control (ailerons, elevator and rudder), plus flaps, and conventional tail unit. Marsden UA 80/1 wing section, designed for low speed/high lift use, with a lift coefficient of 2·0. Fixed metal tabs on rudder and elevator. Wings are detachable for transportation and storage. Main frame of aluminium alloy tube, plate and sheet, with steel tube bracing struts and landing gear. Dacron covered wings (double surface over 75-80 per cent of area) and tail surfaces. Stainless steel cables. No kingpost. Airframe rigging time 15 min. Optional spray equipment.

LANDING GEAR: Non-retractable tailwheel type, with 16 in diameter mainwheels and 5 in diameter steerable tailwheel. Bungee shock absorption on all three wheels. Optional mainwheel brakes, wheel fairings, floats and skis.

POWER PLANT: WT-11-277: one 20 kW (27 hp) Rotax 277 single-cylinder two-stroke engine standard, with 2·185:1 reduction gear drive to a Shetler two-blade wooden pusher propeller. WT-11-377: one 26·8 kW (36 hp) Rotax 377 engine with 2·58:1 reduction. Standard fuel tank capacity 22·7 litres (6 US gallons). Optional 9·5 or 15 litre (2·5 or 4 US gallon) tank in each wing.

ACCOMMODATION: Pilot only, in enclosed cabin.

DIMENSIONS, EXTERNAL (A: WT-11-277, B: WT-11-377):

Wing span: A, B	10·67 m (35 ft 0 in)
Wing aspect ratio: A, B	8·75
Length overall: A, B	5·34 m (17 ft 6 in)
Height overall: A, B	1·78 m (5 ft 10 in)
Propeller diameter: A	1·37 m (4 ft 6 in)
B	1·52 m (5 ft 0 in)

AREA (A and B as above):

Wings, gross: A, B	13·01 m² (140·0 sq ft)

WEIGHTS AND LOADINGS (A and B as above):

Weight empty: A	113 kg (250 lb)
B	122 kg (270 lb)
Pilot weight range: A	50-113 kg (110-250 lb)
Max T-O weight: A	283 kg (625 lb)
B	285 kg (628 lb)
Max wing loading: A	21·97 kg/m² (4·46 lb/sq ft)
B	21·92 kg/m² (4·49 lb/sq ft)
Max power loading: A	14·15 kg/kW (23·15 lb/hp)
B	10·63 kg/kW (17·44 lb/hp)

PERFORMANCE (at max T-O weight, A and B as above):

Never-exceed speed:	
A, B	73 knots (136 km/h; 85 mph)
Max level speed at S/L:	
A	52 knots (97 km/h; 60 mph)
B	57 knots (106 km/h; 66 mph)
Max cruising speed: A	48 knots (89 km/h; 55 mph)
Econ cruising speed: A	43 knots (80 km/h; 50 mph)
B	48 knots (89 km/h; 55 mph)
Stalling speed:	
A, power on	22 knots (41 km/h; 25 mph) IAS
A, power off	25 knots (45 km/h; 28 mph) IAS
B	26 knots (49 km/h; 30 mph) IAS
Max rate of climb at S/L: A	213 m (700 ft)/min
B	274 m (900 ft)/min
Service ceiling: A, B	4,575 m (15,000 ft)
T-O run: A	31-62 m (100-200 ft)
B	31-46 m (100-150 ft)
T-O to 15 m (50 ft): A	62-91 m (200-300 ft)
B	62-76 m (200-250 ft)
Landing run: A, B	31-62 m (100-200 ft)
Range at cruising speed, 65% power:	
A	130-173 nm (241-321 km; 150-200 miles)
B	86-130 nm (161-241 km; 100-150 miles)
Endurance with standard fuel: A	4 h 24 min
g limits: A	+6/−3
B	+5·8/−2·9
Best glide ratio: A, B	10
Min rate of sink at 28 knots (51 km/h; 32 mph):	
A	99 m (325 ft)/min
Min rate of sink at 30 knots (56 km/h; 35 mph):	
B	107 m (350 ft)/min

BIRDMAN CHINOOK 2S

First flown by test pilot Mr Dennis Maland on 15 October 1983, the Chinook 2S is a tandem two-seat version of the standard single-seat Chinook for flight training, sport flying and light transport use. Structurally similar to the single-seater, the Chinook 2S has a greater wing span, 12·7 cm (5 in) longer cabin with more side glazing, external fuel tanks as standard, a more powerful engine, and a strengthened structure. Dual controls are standard and a door is provided for each occupant. Float and ski landing gears remain options.

The general airframe description of the single-seat Chinook applies also to the Chinook 2S, except as noted above. Assembly time is 60-80 and 120-130 working hours for the experienced and inexperienced constructor respectively.

POWER PLANT: One 30 kW (40 hp) Rotax 447 or 35 kW (47 hp) Rotax 503 engine, with 2·58:1 reduction gear drive. Fuel tank capacity 30 litres (8 US gallons).

DIMENSIONS, EXTERNAL: (A: with 447 engine; B: with 503 engine):

Wing span: A, B	11·28 m (37 ft 0 in)
Wing aspect ratio: A, B	9·25
Length overall: A, B	5·34 m (17 ft 6 in)
Height overall: A, B	1·78 m (5 ft 10 in)
Propeller diameter: A	1·52 m (5 ft 0 in)
B	1·63 m (5 ft 4 in)

AREA:

Wings, gross: A, B	13·75 m² (148·0 sq ft)

WEIGHTS AND LOADINGS (A and B as above):

Weight empty: A	150·5 kg (332·5 lb)
B	154 kg (340 lb)
Pilot weight range: A	50-113 kg (110-250 lb)
Max T-O weight: A	345 kg (760·5 lb)
B	348 kg (768 lb)
Max wing loading: A	25·1 kg/m² (5·1 lb/sq ft)
B	25·3 kg/m² (5·2 lb/sq ft)
Max power loading: A	11·5 kg/kW (19·0 lb/hp)
B	9·94 kg/kW (16·34 lb/hp)

PERFORMANCE (A and B as above):

Never-exceed speed:	
A, B	73 knots (136 km/h; 85 mph)
Max level speed: A	59 knots (109 km/h; 68 mph)
B	62 knots (116 km/h; 72 mph)
Max cruising speed:	
A, B	52 knots (97 km/h; 60 mph)
Econ cruising speed	48 knots (89 km/h; 55 mph)
Stalling speed:	
A, power on	28 knots (52 km/h; 32 mph)
A, B, power off	33 knots (62 km/h; 38 mph)
Max rate of climb at S/L: A	183 m (600 ft)/min
B	213 m (700 ft)/min
Service ceiling: A, B	4,575 m (15,000 ft)
T-O run: A, B	61-76 m (200-250 ft)
T-O to 15 m (50 ft): A, B	91-122 m (300-400 ft)
Landing run: A, B	46-76 m (150-250 ft)
Range at cruising speed, 65% power:	
A, B	130 nm (241 km; 150 miles)
Endurance: A	1 h 30 min
Design g limits: A, B	+3·9/−2
Best glide ratio: A, B	11
Min rate of sink at 39 knots (72 km/h; 45 mph):	
A, B	110 m (360 ft)/min

CANAERO DYNAMICS

CANAERO DYNAMICS AIRCRAFT INC

1780 Albion Road No. 4, Rexdale, Ontario M9V 1C1

Telephone: (416) 741 8288

GENERAL MANAGER: Lorry Smith

CANAERO DYNAMICS TOUCAN T-IV

The Toucan resembles an ARV version of the Cessna Skymaster 'push and pull' twin, with one Rotax 277 engine mounted in the nose and another at the rear of the fuselage pod. It has full single engine flight capability.

Design of the Toucan started in January 1983, and construction of a prototype began in the following April. This flew for the first time in September 1983. Construction of pre-production aircraft began in July 1985 and the first production Toucan flew in January 1986. The four prototype/pre-production aircraft have been followed by an initial batch of twelve production Toucans, completed by June 1986. A second batch of 25 was scheduled to be finished by November that year.

TYPE: Two-seat ARV, suited to recreational flying, pilot training, agricultural spraying, surveillance work and aerial photography.

AIRFRAME: Strut braced high-wing monoplane. D-cell rigid wing of aluminium alloy, with UV resistant double surface skins and glassfibre wingtips. Dihedral 1° 30′. Incidence 4°. Stainless steel cables. Three-axis control (full-span flaperons, twin rudders and elevator). Semi-monocoque fuselage of welded 4130 chrome-molybdenum steel, with twin tailbooms. Recovery parachute standard. Optional instruments.

LANDING GEAR: Non-retractable tricycle type, with independently sprung steel legs and mainwheel brakes. Rough terrain wheels of larger diameter and floats optional. Wheel fairings fitted.

POWER PLANT: Two 20 kW (27 hp) Rotax 277 single-cylinder two-stroke engines fitted in 'push and pull' configuration, with 2·58:1 reduction gear to two-blade wooden propellers (one tractor and one pusher). One fuel tank, capacity 23 litres (5 Imp gallons). Optional 68 litre (15 Imp gallon) auxiliary tank. Optional 26·8 kW (36 hp) Rotax 377 engine.

ACCOMMODATION: Two seats in tandem in fully enclosed and heated cabin.

DIMENSIONS, EXTERNAL:

Wing span	11·74 m (38 ft 6 in)
Wing chord: at root	1·80 m (5 ft 11 in)
at tip	1·04 m (3 ft 5 in)
Wing aspect ratio	8·235
Length overall	5·79 m (19 ft 0 in)
Height overall	2·85 m (9 ft 4 in)

Birdman Enterprises Chinook 2S with ski landing gear

Birdman Enterprises WT-11 Chinook *(Neil A. Macdougall)*

Canaero Dynamics Toucan 'push and pull' twin-engined ARV

Circa Reproductions Nieuport 11 scale replica microlight *(Howard Levy)*

Tailplane span 1·83 m (6 ft 0 in)
Wheel track 1·52 m (5 ft 0 in)
Wheelbase 1·52 m (5 ft 0 in)
Propeller diameter 1·52 m (5 ft 0 in)

AREA:
Wings, gross 16·91 m² (182·0 sq ft)

WEIGHTS AND LOADINGS:
Weight empty 178 kg (393 lb)
Crew weight range 55-102 kg (120-225 lb)
Max T-O weight 408 kg (900 lb)
Max wing loading 24·17 kg/m² (4·95 lb/sq ft)
Max power loading 10·20 kg/kW (16·67 lb/hp)

PERFORMANCE (at max T-O weight except where indicated):
Never-exceed speed 78 knots (144 km/h; 90 mph)
Max level speed at 610 m (2,000 ft) 65 knots (121 km/h; 75 mph)
Max cruising speed at 610 m (2,000 ft) 56 knots (105 km/h; 65 mph)
Econ cruising speed at 610 m (2,000 ft) 48 knots (88 km/h; 55 mph)
Stalling speed, flaps up, engine idling, pilot only 21 knots (39 km/h; 24 mph)
Max rate of climb at S/L, 75 kg (165 lb) pilot only 350 m (1,150 ft)/min
Service ceiling 3,050 m (10,000 ft)
T-O run 31 m (100 ft)
T-O to 15 m (50 ft) 61 m (200 ft)
Landing from 15 m (50 ft) 76 m (250 ft)
Landing run 38 m (125 ft)
Range with max payload 130 nm (241 km; 150 miles)
Range with max standard fuel 147 nm (273 km; 170 miles)
g limits +6/−3

CIRCA

CIRCA REPRODUCTIONS

8027 Argyll Road, Edmonton, Alberta T6C 4A9

Telephone: (403) 474 3948

DESIGNER/PROPRIETOR: Graham R. Lee

Circa Reproductions was founded by Mr Graham Lee to develop and market plans of a ⅞th scale reproduction of the First World War Nieuport 11 Bébé fighter. Alternatively the homebuilder can complete the aircraft as a Nieuport 16, 17, 24, 24*bis* or 27, the 17 onwards having a greater wing area of about 11·6 m² (125 sq ft), or as a German Siemens-Schuckert D.I.

The Nieuport 11 is capable of meeting both Canadian and US ultralight regulations, though the company prefers that it be built as an Experimental category aircraft with a weight that makes it a homebuilt. The Nieuports 16-27 can also be built to satisfy all but US ultralight regulations, and even US requirements could be met by sacrificing replica detail to give an empty weight of 126·5 kg (279 lb) with an 11·5 kg (25 lb) parachute. Another reproduction from Circa is a ⅞th scale Sopwith Triplane, which was expected to be completed in 1986.

One further Circa Reproductions project currently underway is the Pole Cat, a full-size reproduction of the Pietenpol Sky Scout. Using the same materials and methods of construction as the Nieuport, this single-seat Rotax 503 engined aircraft has a different wing area from the Sky Scout to comply with Canadian ultralight regulations but its weight will put it into the Experimental category in the USA. The prototype was expected to be finished by July 1986, with plans to be made available in 1987.

CIRCA REPRODUCTIONS NIEUPORT 11

The prototype Nieuport 11 reproduction took four months to design and build, first flying on 25 July 1984. Plans, including drawings for a wooden replica Lewis gun, are available to amateur constructors, and by February 1986 a total of 175 sets had been sold to customers in Austria, Australia, Belgium, Brazil, Canada, France, Italy, Japan, New Zealand and the USA. It was anticipated that five US and one Australian Nieuport 11s would be flying by May 1986. At least three of these have been fitted with Volkswagen engines and are covered under the Experimental category regulations. Three of the six have been completed as German Siemens-Schuckert D.Is instead of as French Nieuports, using in each case a four-post cabane structure in place of the usual three-point Nieuport wing attachment. Prefabricated engine cowlings are also available. Estimated building time is 600 working hours.

TYPE: Single-seat replica microlight; conforms to FAR Pt 103 (in some variants) and Canadian regulations.

AIRFRAME: Braced single-bay biplane, with slight dihedral on lower wings and slight sweepback. Basically rectangular section fuselage with rounded turtledecking. Conventional tail unit. Tubular aluminium alloy structure, pop riveted and bolted, with duralumin gussets and covered with Ceconite (double surface on wings). Stainless steel cables; vinyl-coated optional. Three-axis control (ailerons, elevators and rudder). Rigging time with inspection 2 h 30 min.

LANDING GEAR: Non-retractable tailskid type, with bungee suspension. Mainwheel diameter 24 in. No brakes. Skis optional.

POWER PLANT: One 22·4 kW (30 hp) Cuyuna ULII-02 engine, with 2·9:1 or 3:1 reduction drive to a two-blade wooden propeller. Optional engines of 18·6-30 kW (25-40 hp). Fuel capacity in prototype 48 litres (10·5 Imp gallons): choice of this or 19 litre (5 US gallon) tank, according to regulation requirements, for plans-built aircraft.

ACCOMMODATION: Pilot only in open cockpit.

DIMENSIONS, EXTERNAL:
Wing span 6·55 m (21 ft 6 in)
Wing aspect ratio 6·14
Length overall 4·98 m (16 ft 4 in)
Height overall 2·29 m (7 ft 6 in)
Propeller diameter 1·83 m (6 ft 0 in)

AREA:
Wings, gross 10·59 m² (114·0 sq ft)

WEIGHTS AND LOADINGS:
Weight empty 115 kg (254 lb)
Max pilot weight 88·5 kg (195 lb)
Max T-O weight 249 kg (550 lb)
Max wing loading 23·53 kg/m² (4·82 lb/sq ft)
Max power loading 11·12 kg/kW (18·33 lb/hp)

PERFORMANCE:
Never-exceed speed 104 knots (193 km/h; 120 mph)
Max level speed with 18·6 kW (25 hp) engine 67 knots (124 km/h; 77 mph) IAS
Max cruising speed 43-56 knots (80-105 km/h; 50-65 mph)
Econ cruising speed 43 knots (80 km/h; 50 mph)
Stalling speed: power on 22 knots (41 km/h; 25 mph)
power off (estimated) 24-25 knots (44-45 km/h; 27-28 mph)
Max rate of climb at S/L (estimated, with 26·8 kW; 36 hp engine) 152 m (500 ft)/min
T-O run 107 m (350 ft)
Landing run 61 m (200 ft)

Range with max fuel
more than 173 nm (322 km; 200 miles)
Endurance with max fuel 4 h 45 min
g limits +4·5/−3·5

CIRCA REPRODUCTIONS SOPWITH TRIPLANE

A prototype of the Circa Reproductions ⅞th scale Sopwith Triplane was to be completed in Summer 1986. Plans to allow amateur construction will become available in 1987, together with a prefabricated engine cowling.

TYPE: Single-seat replica microlight; conforms to Canadian microlight regulations and Experimental aircraft category.

AIRFRAME AND LANDING GEAR: Braced single-bay triplane, with slight dihedral on all wings. Structural materials, control and landing gear (with ski gear option) as for Nieuport 11 replica.

POWER PLANT: Prototype has one 30 kW (40 hp) Volkswagen modified motorcar engine, with 2·4:1 V belt reduction drive to a two-blade wooden propeller. The prototype will be fitted later with a toothed belt reduction system. Max fuel capacity estimated at 45·5 litres (10 Imp gallons).

DIMENSIONS, EXTERNAL:
Wing span 7·06 m (23 ft 2 in)
Wing aspect ratio 8·1
Length overall 5·03 m (16 ft 6 in)
Height overall 2·82 m (9 ft 3 in)
Propeller diameter 1·83-2·01 m (6 ft-6 ft 7 in)
AREA:
Wings, gross 18·30 m² (197·0 sq ft)
WEIGHT:
Weight empty 147 kg (325 lb)
PERFORMANCE:
No data received

ELMWOOD

ELMWOOD AVIATION

RR 4 Elmwood Drive, Belleville, Ontario K8N 4Z4
Telephone: (613) 967 1853

Mr Ronald Basil Mason has been active in the design and construction of light aircraft for many years. In April 1978 he began the design of a two-seat light aircraft known as the CA-05 Christavia Mk I, based on the configuration of aircraft like the Piper Cub and using a new computer designed wing section. His latest aircraft is the four-seat CH-8 Christavia Mk 4.

ELMWOOD CA-05 CHRISTAVIA Mk I

The Christavia Mk I is constructed from easily obtainable materials. The fuselage structure is fabricated from industrial mild steel and the wings are of spruce. The cabin has a large usable area, which can be modified to accommodate freight if required. It is stressed for normal aerobatics, and is said to display good stalling and spinning characteristics.

Construction of the prototype Christavia Mk I (C-GENC) began in June 1980 and this aircraft made its first flight on 3 October 1981. By early 1984 it had accumulated about 500 flying hours, meeting the designer's requirements of short take-off and landing distances, low fuel consumption from a low-powered engine, and low stalling speed, but with a good cruising speed and rate of climb. Maintenance is said to be simple.

Elmwood Aviation is offering plans for construction of the Christavia Mk I, and considers the aircraft suitable for the type of flying carried out by professional organisations like Missionary Aviation Fellowship. By January 1986, more than 200 Christavia Mk Is were under construction in many parts of the world and a large number were flying. Those under construction include several for the mission field.

TYPE: Two-seat homebuilt cabin monoplane.

AIRFRAME: High-wing monoplane, with V bracing struts each side. Computer designed wing section. Dihedral 1° 30′. Incidence 1°. No sweepback. Conventional two-spar structure of Sitka spruce standard, with truss ribs and Dacron covering. Aluminium can be used to fabricate spars and ribs. Balanced Frise ailerons of wooden construction with Dacron covering. No flaps. Flat sided truss fuselage structure of welded 4130 and 1025 steel tube, Dacron covered. Wire-braced tail unit of steel tube, with mild steel plate ribs, Dacron covered. Shim washers used to adjust tailplane incidence. Trim tab on elevators.

LANDING GEAR: Non-retractable tailwheel type. Rubber cord shock absorption. Mainwheels and tyres size 6·00-6. Goodyear or similar hydraulic disc brakes. Steerable tailwheel. Wheel fairings and shock cord covers optional. Float or ski landing gear optional.

POWER PLANT: Prototype has a 48·5 kW (65 hp) Continental A65 flat-four engine, driving a two-blade fixed-pitch propeller. Engines of 37·25 to 112 kW (50 to 150 hp) can be fitted. Spinner optional. Main fuel tank, capacity 57 litres (15 US gallons), in fuselage aft of firewall; auxiliary tank, capacity 23 litres (6 US gallons), in each wing. Refuelling points in nose cowling and wings. Oil capacity 3·8 litres (1 US gallon).

ACCOMMODATION: Two seats in tandem. Door on starboard side. Heated and ventilated. Baggage space behind rear seat, capacity 9 kg (20 lb) at max T-O weight, 34 kg (75 lb) at 499 kg (1,100 lb) AUW. Passenger seat can be removed for freight carrying.

SYSTEM: 12V electrical system standard.

AVIONICS: 360-channel com/nav transceiver and VOR/ADF on prototype. Provision for IFR instrumentation.

DIMENSIONS, EXTERNAL:
Wing span 9·91 m (32 ft 6 in)
Wing chord, constant 1·37 m (4 ft 6 in)
Wing aspect ratio 7·22
Length overall 6·30 m (20 ft 8 in)
Length of fuselage 4·95 m (16 ft 3 in)
Height overall 2·13 m (7 ft 0 in)
Tailplane span 2·74 m (9 ft 0 in)
Wheel track 1·83 m (6 ft 0 in)
Wheelbase 4·47 m (14 ft 8 in)
Propeller diameter 1·83 m (6 ft 0 in)
AREA:
Wings, gross 13·59 m² (146·25 sq ft)
WEIGHTS AND LOADINGS (48·5 kW; 65 hp engine, 57 litres; 15 US gallons fuel):
Weight empty 338 kg (745 lb)
Max T-O weight 590 kg (1,300 lb)
Max wing loading 43·41 kg/m² (8·89 lb/sq ft)
Max power loading 12·16 kg/kW (20·00 lb/hp)
PERFORMANCE (at max T-O weight, engine and fuel as above):
Never-exceed speed 117 knots (217 km/h; 135 mph)
Max level speed at S/L
104 knots (193 km/h; 120 mph)
Cruising speed at 610 m (2,000 ft):
75% power 91 knots (169 km/h; 105 mph)
65% power 87 knots (161 km/h; 100 mph)
45% power 74 knots (137 km/h; 85 mph)
Stalling speed: power off 37 knots (68 km/h; 42 mph)
power on 31 knots (57 km/h; 35 mph)
Rate of climb at S/L 259 m (850 ft)/min
Service ceiling 3,960 m (13,000 ft)
T-O run 107 m (350 ft)
T-O to 15 m (50 ft) 168 m (550 ft)
Landing from 15 m (50 ft) 198 m (650 ft)
Range with standard fuel:
75% power 273 nm (507 km; 315 miles)
65% power 304 nm (563 km; 350 miles)
45% power 382 nm (708 km; 440 miles)
g limits +4·5/−2·8

ELMWOOD CH-8 CHRISTAVIA Mk 4

Design of this four-seat development of the Christavia Mk I started in August 1984; the prototype made its first flight on 3 January 1986, and by 27 January had accumulated 50 flying hours. Plans and an information kit were expected to be made available by April 1986.

TYPE: Four-seat homebuilt cabin monoplane.

AIRFRAME: Similar to Christavia Mk I except as follows: Incidence 3°. Flaps fitted. Ground adjustable tab on rudder.

LANDING GEAR: Non-retractable tailwheel type. Cantilever spring steel main legs, with mainwheels size 6·00-6 and tyre pressure 1·65 bars (24 lb/sq in). Fully swivelling solid tailwheel. Mainwheel brakes. Floats and skis optional.

POWER PLANT: One 100·7-134 kW (135-180 hp) Avco Lycoming flat-four engine, or converted motorcar engine, driving a fixed or variable pitch two-blade propeller. Fuel capacity 136·4 litres (36 US gallons). Refuelling point in wing. Oil capacity 6 litres (1·6 US gallons).

ACCOMMODATION: Four seats in fully enclosed cabin. Door on each side. Heated and ventilated. Baggage space behind rear seats; capacity 45·4 kg (100 lb).

SYSTEMS: Hydraulic system for brakes. Electrical system with alternator.

AVIONICS: VOR/ADF optional.

DIMENSIONS, EXTERNAL:
Wing span 10·67 m (35 ft 0 in)
Wing chord, constant 1·52 m (5 ft 0 in)
Wing aspect ratio 7
Length overall 7·01 m (23 ft 0 in)
Height overall 1·98 m (6 ft 6 in)
Tailplane span 3·05 m (10 ft 0 in)
Wheel track 1·83 m (6 ft 0 in)
Wheelbase 3·66 m (12 ft 0 in)
Propeller diameter 1·78 m (5 ft 10 in)
AREA:
Wings, gross 16·26 m² (175·0 sq ft)
WEIGHTS AND LOADINGS (112 kW; 150 hp engine):
Weight empty 522 kg (1,150 lb)
Max T-O weight 1,043 kg (2,300 lb)
Max wing loading 64·1 kg/m² (13·1 lb/sq ft)
Max power loading 9·31 kg/kW (15·33 lb/hp)
PERFORMANCE:
Never-exceed speed 130 knots (241 km/h; 150 mph)
Max level speed at 610 m (2,000 ft)
111 knots (206 km/h; 128 mph)
Max cruising speed at 610 m (2,000 ft), 75% power
104 knots (193 km/h; 120 mph)
Econ cruising speed, 65% power
102 knots (188 km/h; 117 mph)
Stalling speed: flaps up 35 knots (65 km/h; 40 mph)
12° flap 31 knots (57 km/h 35 mph)
Max rate of climb at S/L 244 m (800 ft)/min
Service ceiling 5,485 m (18,000 ft)
T-O run 91 m (300 ft)
T-O to 15 m (50 ft) 152 m (500 ft)
Landing from 15 m (50 ft) 182 m (600 ft)
Landing run 152 m (500 ft)
Range with max fuel 548 nm (1,017 km; 632 miles)

FLETCHER

DANIEL & RICHARD FLETCHER

Apt 3112, 30 Exeter Road, Ajax, Ontario L1S 2J6
Telephone: (416) 683 0261

FLETCHER BUSHBIRD

Mr D. W. and Mr D. R. Fletcher designed a practical sport/bushplane known as the Bushbird. This has been fully described and illustrated in the 1985-86 and previous editions of *Jane's*. Plans are not available to amateur constructors.

The Bushbird, though designed as a four-seater, is flown under a Department of Transport permit that, under Canadian amateur-built regulations, limits maximum take-off weight to 900 kg (1,985 lb) and two-seat configuration. Should these regulations change, and the Bushbird be modified (including perhaps the installation of a more powerful 134 kW; 180 hp engine), new data will be included in the appropriate edition of *Jane's*.

JONES

MASON JONES

JONES D.2

An accompanying illustration shows a small single-seat sporting biplane, designated D.2 (C-GQNR), which was displayed at the 1985 EAA meeting in Oshkosh, Wisconsin, by Mr Mason Jones from Canada. No details are yet known.

McASCO

McASCO AIRCRAFT DIVISION

4623 Fortune Road SE, Calgary, Alberta
Telephone: (403) 272 3658

MANAGER: Kaye McLeod
DESIGN CONSULTANT: Stan McLeod

Known formerly as, successively, Squaircraft, K & S Aircraft Supply, K & S Aircraft, and Macfam, the McAsco Aircraft Division continues to offer to amateur constructors plans for its SA 102·5 Cavalier (more than 4,000 sets sold) and SA 105 Super Cavalier with retractable landing gear (more than 300 sets sold). In 1985 McAsco also reinstated the SA 103 and SA 104 Cavaliers, which are simplified versions of the SA 105. Each of the SA 103/104/105 models is available in **BCD** (bubble canopy with hinged door on each side) and **BSC** (bubble sliding canopy) forms. BCD and BSC aircraft retain the original windscreen, but have the turtledeck aft of the seats lowered, giving improved rearward view and necessitating revision of the tail fin curve. Other aircraft of which McAsco markets plans include the

Homebuilt example of the Elmwood Aviation CA-05 Christavia Mk I

Elmwood Aviation CH-8 Christavia Mk 4 four-seat homebuilt cabin monoplane

McAsco SA 102·5 Cavalier built by Ms Lindy Mueller of St Louis, Missouri

D.2 sporting biplane built by Mr Mason Jones *(J. M. G. Gradidge)*

McAsco SA 105 Super Cavalier with non-standard fixed tailwheel landing gear and modified canopy *(J. M. G. Gradidge)*

Jungster I and Jungster II, designed by Mr Rim Kaminskas.

A new aircraft, known as the SA 106 Lady Bug, is being designed and a prototype constructed. It will be offered to amateur constructors in plan and possibly kit forms.

McASCO SA 102·5 CAVALIER

TYPE: Two-seat or '2+2' homebuilt aircraft.

AIRFRAME: Cantilever low-wing monoplane. Wing section NACA 23015 at root, NACA 23012 at tip. Dihedral 6°. Incidence 3° 30′ at root, washed out to 1° at tip. No sweepback at quarter-chord. Single wooden box spar, plywood leading-edge, and auxiliary rear spar. Diagonal I section drag spar between front and rear spar in each wing. Entire centre-section is plywood covered and contoured to serve as cabin seat. Outer panels covered with Dacron and finished with a polyurethane compound. Single-slotted Frise ailerons of spruce and plywood. Cable operated split flaps of spruce and birch ply. Optional three-piece wing and electric actuation of flaps. Truss fuselage structure, with four longerons, of spruce and birch plywood construction. Cockpit canopy frame and doors of moulded glassfibre; rear part of top decking fabric covered. Cantilever tail unit of all-wood construction, with sweptback vertical surfaces, Dacron covered. Fixed incidence tailplane. Elevators operated by pushrods. Trim tab in starboard elevator.

LANDING GEAR: Non-retractable tricycle type. All units have spring steel legs of McAsco design. Wheel size 5·00-5, tyre pressure 2·75 bars (40 lb/sq in), on all units. For rough-field operation, 6·00-6 mainwheels with low-profile tyres are optional. Expanding shoe brakes, operated hydraulically by dual toe controls. Glassfibre wheel fairings. Alternative 680 kg (1,500 lb) capacity float or ski landing gear optional.

POWER PLANT: Wide choice of four-cylinder engines available, including 63·5, 67 or 74·5 kW (85, 90 or 100 hp) Continental, 93-97 kW (125-130 hp) Franklin Sport 4A, 80·5 or 86 kW (108 or 115 hp) Avco Lycoming O-235, or 93 or 101 kW (125 or 135 hp) Avco Lycoming O-290. Choice of wood or metal, fixed-pitch or variable-pitch propellers, with diameters from 1·68 m (5 ft 6 in) to 1·83 m (6 ft 0 in). Whichever engine is used, an extension shaft 7·6 to 12·7 cm (3 to 5 in) long is fitted between the propeller and the crankshaft, permitting the use of more streamlined cowling panels and a reduction in the compression of airflow between the propeller and engine. All fuel in permanent wingtip tanks, each with capacity of 75 litres (20 US gallons). Oil capacity 5·7-6·8 litres (1·5-1·8 US gallons), according to engine fitted.

ACCOMMODATION: Side by side seating for pilot and one adult passenger, with optional rear jump-seat for two small children in what would normally be the baggage area. Without this rear seat, up to 56 kg (125 lb) of baggage can be carried, depending upon engine and equipment installations. Forward opening door on each side of heated and ventilated cabin.

AVIONICS AND EQUIPMENT: Standard nav/com equipment, including one or two VHF sets. ADF and transponder optional.

DIMENSIONS, EXTERNAL:

Wing span over tip tanks	8·33 m (27 ft 4 in)
Width, outer wing panels folded	3·63 m (11 ft 11 in)
Wing aspect ratio	6·25
Length overall	6·71 m (22 ft 0 in)
Height overall	2·23 m (7 ft 4 in)
Wheelbase	1·37 m (4 ft 6 in)
Propeller diameter	see under 'Power Plant'

AREA:

Wings, gross	10·87 m² (117·0 sq ft)

WEIGHTS AND LOADINGS:

Basic operating weight empty	408 kg (900 lb)
Max T-O weight	680 kg (1,500 lb)
Max wing loading	62·6 kg/m² (12·8 lb/sq ft)
Power loading (63·5 kW; 85 hp engine)	10·73 kg/kW (17·6 lb/hp)

PERFORMANCE (at max T-O weight, 93 kW; 125 hp Avco Lycoming engine):

Never-exceed speed	199 knots (370 km/h; 230 mph)
Max level speed at 2,135 m (7,000 ft)	160 knots (297 km/h; 185 mph)
Max cruising speed	143 knots (265 km/h; 165 mph)
Econ cruising speed	134 knots (249 km/h; 155 mph)
Stalling speed:	
flaps up	44 knots (81 km/h; 50 mph) IAS
flaps down	35 knots (65 km/h; 40 mph) IAS
Max rate of climb at S/L	over 518 m (1,700 ft)/min
Service ceiling	4,875 m (16,000 ft)
T-O run	107 m (350 ft)
T-O to 15 m (50 ft)	305 m (1,000 ft)
Landing from 15 m (50 ft)	396 m (1,300 ft)
Landing run	183 m (600 ft)
Max range, no reserves	720 nm (1,335 km; 830 miles)

McASCO SA 103 CAVALIER

This aircraft combines a simplified version of the SA 105 airframe with a non-retractable tailwheel type landing gear. It provides a roomier cabin than the SA 102·5, for improved passenger comfort and increased baggage space, and allows use of the many engines in the 93-134 kW (125-180 hp) category that are available, including the Javelin listed under the SA 105 entry. It can be built in BCD or BSC form (see introductory notes).

McASCO SA 104 CAVALIER

The SA 104 differs from the SA 103 in having a non-retractable tricycle landing gear similar to that of the SA 102·5 Cavalier.

McASCO SA 105 SUPER CAVALIER

Although similar in general configuration to the SA 102·5, the SA 105 is an entirely new design, with only the ailerons and wingtip tanks interchangeable between the two types. Overall dimensions are slightly greater, offering improved comfort and more baggage space; and a retractable tricycle landing gear is standard.

First example to fly was N17HJ, built by Mr Hank Q. Johnson of Memphis, Tennessee (see 1984-85 *Jane's*). The example illustrated this year differs from plans in having a non-retractable tailwheel landing gear and modified canopy.

The following description applies to the standard SA 105 built to McAsco plans:

TYPE: Two-seat homebuilt aircraft.

AIRFRAME: Cantilever low-wing monoplane. Wing section NACA 23015 at root, NACA 23010 at tip. Dihedral at chord line 6° from roots. Washout 2° 30′ between ribs 0 and 5. All-wood structure of Sitka spruce spars, fir/mahogany marine ply ribs, and leading-edge skin of Finnish birch plywood. Fabric covering aft of main spar, except for plywood walkways at roots, and tips. Ailerons of similar construction to wings. Split type mechanically actuated (electric or hydraulic actuation optional) flap system has been developed, effectively changing the wing aerofoil section from 230 series to 23 (sailplane) series. These flaps operate at 15°, 30° and 45°, and can be set at negative angles of up to 12° for cruising flight to increase cruising speed. Glassfibre canted wingtip tanks, which have similar effect to winglets, and increase wing area, aspect ratio and lift. Truss fuselage structure, with four longerons, of Sitka spruce and Finnish birch plywood.

Cockpit roof, side window/door frames and engine cowling of glassfibre. Rear fuselage and rear part of top decking fabric covered. Cantilever tail unit of all-wood construction, with sweptback vertical surfaces. Fin and tailplane plywood covered; control surfaces fabric covered. Trim tab in starboard elevator.

LANDING GEAR: Retractable tricycle type, with mechanical (optionally electric or hydraulic) actuation. Main units retract inward into wing roots, nosewheel rearward. Spring steel legs. All three wheels size 5·00-5. Brakes on mainwheels, toe operated from port seat.

POWER PLANT: One Avco Lycoming, Franklin, Javelin Ford or similar engine, with propeller extension shaft. Recommended are 112-119 kW (150-160 hp) Avco Lycoming O-320/IO-320, driving a variable-pitch or constant-speed propeller. Min recommended power plant is 93 kW (125 hp) Franklin 4A-235 or Avco Lycoming O-290/O-290-D2/O-290-G driving a fixed-pitch propeller. Max recommended is the Javelin Aircraft Company's Ford Model 230, representing a Ford Windsor V6 motorcar engine conversion, or a 149 kW (200 hp) Avco Lycoming O-360/IO-360. Total fuel capacity of wingtip tanks 127 litres (28 Imp gallons). Optional sump tanks (with engines over 112 kW; 150 hp) raise total capacity to 152·75 litres (33·6 Imp gallons).

ACCOMMODATION: Two seats side by side in enclosed cabin. Dual controls. Forward hinged window/door on each side in standard form. Available also in **BCD** or **BSC** form with bubble canopy (see introductory notes). Baggage space aft of seats, capacity up to 172 kg (379 lb).

DIMENSIONS, EXTERNAL:
- Wing span over tip tanks: 8·42 m (27 ft 7⅜ in)
- Length overall (nominal): 7·25 m (23 ft 9½ in)
- Wheel track: 2·58 m (8 ft 5½ in)
- Wheelbase: 1·33 m (4 ft 4¼ in)
- Propeller diameter: 1·83 m (6 ft 0 in)

AREA:
- Wings, gross: 11·00 m² (118·5 sq ft)

WEIGHTS AND LOADINGS:
- Weight empty: 431-454 kg (950-1,000 lb)
- Max T-O weight (dependent on engine): up to 885 kg (1,950 lb)
- Max wing loading: 80·5 kg/m² (16·5 lb/sq ft)
- Max power loading, with 119 kW (160 hp) engine: 7·44 kg/kW (12·19 lb/hp)

PERFORMANCE (estimated at AUW of 816 kg; 1,800 lb. A: 93 kW; 125 hp, B: 112 kW; 150 hp, C: 134 kW; 180 hp):
- Never-exceed speed: 200 knots (370 km/h; 230 mph)
- Cruising speed:
  - A: 143-148 knots (265-273 km/h; 165-170 mph)
  - B: 152-156 knots (281-289 km/h; 175-180 mph)
  - C: 165-174 knots (305-322 km/h; 190-200 mph)
- Stalling speed:
  - flaps up: 52-61 knots (97-105 km/h; 60-65 mph) IAS
  - 15° flap: 48-52 knots (89-97 km/h; 55-60 mph) IAS
- Max rate of climb at S/L:
  - A: 183-213 m (600-700 ft)/min
  - B: 274-305 m (900-1,000 ft)/min
  - C: 365-488 m (1,200-1,600 ft)/min
- T-O run: A: 274 m (900 ft)
  - B: 244 m (800 ft)
  - C: 183 m (600 ft)

McASCO SA 106 LADY BUG

McAsco is currently working on a new two-seat sporting monoplane known as the SA 106 Lady Bug. By 15 March 1985 design work was 70 per cent complete, and construction of the first prototype had begun.

The SA 106 is planned in four basic versions: the wooden **SA 106W**, the **SA 106ST** with a steel tube fuselage and metal or wooden wings, the **SA 106SM** constructed entirely of sheet metal, and the all-composites **SA 106Comp**. Plans, and possibly kits of component parts, will be made available to amateur constructors.

The following details refer to the SA 106W first prototype:

TYPE: Tandem two-seat homebuilt sporting aircraft.

AIRFRAME: Cantilever mid-wing monoplane. Wing section NACA 4412. Aluminium alloy tubular main and rear spars, plywood ribs and skins, the whole covered with synthetic fabric and painted. Wings removable, using six bolts that are accessible in cockpit area. Wooden truss fuselage structure, with plywood and fabric covering. Cantilever wooden tail unit.

LANDING GEAR: Non-retractable tricycle type, all units with spring steel legs of McAsco design for initial testing. Convertible to tailwheel configuration, as SA 106W-TD, by removing nose gear, moving main legs forward and installing tailwheel. Fittings for either or both landing gear configurations may be installed during construction.

POWER PLANT: One HAPI, Continental or similar engine in the 48·5-74·5 kW (65-100 hp) range. Fuel in wing spars, capacity 76 litres (20 US gallons).

ACCOMMODATION: Two seats in tandem.

DIMENSIONS, EXTERNAL:
- Wing span: 7·92 m (26 ft 0 in)
- Wing chord: 1·55 m (5 ft 1 in)
- Length overall: 5·79-6·10 m (19-20 ft)

WEIGHTS (approx):
- Weight empty: 272 kg (600 lb)
- Max T-O weight: 544 kg (1,200 lb)

McASCO JUNGSTER I

Design of this aircraft was started in the USA by Mr Rim Kaminskas, as the RK-1, in April 1959. The primary design requirements were to duplicate as closely as possible the performance and flight characteristics of the Bücker Jungmeister. The prototype, described in the 1972-73 *Jane's*, flew for the first time in October 1962. Sets of plans have been available to amateur constructors for many years, with several hundred sets sold.

TYPE: Single-seat homebuilt sporting aircraft.

AIRFRAME: Braced biplane, with two parallel interplane struts each side and N struts supporting centre-section each side. Wing section NACA 4413. Dihedral 1° 30′ on top wing, 3° 30′ on lower wings. Incidence 0° to 30′ on top wing, 30′ to 1° on lower wings on prototype. Examples built with 0° incidence on lower wings. Sweepback 11° on outer panels at quarter-chord. Two-spar structure of Sitka spruce and birch plywood, fabric covered. Wooden Frise ailerons. No flaps or tabs. Spruce truss fuselage structure, fabric covered at rear and plywood covered at front, except for engine cowling which is of aluminium sheet. Braced wooden tail unit structure of spruce and birch ply. Fixed surfaces plywood covered; rudder and elevators fabric covered. No tabs.

LANDING GEAR: Non-retractable tailwheel type. Welded steel tube main gear, with rubber cord shock absorption. Goodyear mainwheel tyres size 5·00-5, pressure 1·72 bars (25 lb/sq in). Goodyear disc brakes.

POWER PLANT: One horizontally opposed aircooled engine, driving a two-blade propeller with spinner. Wide choice of engines available, including 63·4-74·5 kW (85-100 hp) Continental C85, C90 or O-200; 93-97 kW (125-130 hp) Franklin Sport 4, 4A or 4B; 80·5-86 kW (108-115 hp) Avco Lycoming O-235-C or -C1; 93-100·6 kW (125-135 hp) Avco Lycoming O-290-D or -D2; 104·5-112 kW (140-150 hp) Avco Lycoming O-320; or European engines in the same weight/power class. Fuel tank in fuselage aft of firewall, capacity 62 litres (16·5 US gallons); optional 26 litre (7 US gallon) tank in upper wing centre-section, increasing total capacity to 88 litres (23·5 US gallons). Oil capacity 5·75 litres (1·5 US gallons).

ACCOMMODATION: Single seat in open cockpit.

DIMENSIONS, EXTERNAL (prototype):
- Wing span: 5·08 m (16 ft 8 in)
- Wing chord, constant (both): 0·81 m (2 ft 8 in)
- Wing aspect ratio: 6·25
- Length overall: 4·88 m (16 ft 0 in)
- Tailplane span: 2·03 m (6 ft 8 in)
- Propeller diameter: 1·73 m (5 ft 8 in)

AREA:
- Wings, gross: 7·43 m² (80·0 sq ft)

WEIGHTS AND LOADING:
- Weight empty: 275 kg (606 lb)
- T-O weight, aerobatic: 385 kg (850 lb)
- Max T-O weight: 455 kg (1,000 lb)
- Max wing loading: 61·2 kg/m² (12·50 lb/sq ft)

PERFORMANCE (prototype, at max T-O weight, Avco Lycoming O-235 engine):
- Max level speed at S/L: 109 knots (201 km/h; 125 mph) IAS
- Max cruising speed at S/L: 103 knots (192 km/h; 119 mph)
- Stalling speed: 45 knots (84 km/h; 52 mph) IAS
- Max rate of climb at S/L: 455 m (1,500 ft)/min
- Service ceiling: 3,960 m (13,000 ft)
- T-O run: 91 m (300 ft)
- Landing run: 152 m (500 ft)
- Range with max fuel (incl centre-section tank): 260 nm (482 km; 300 miles)
- *g* limits: +9/−6

McASCO JUNGSTER II

Design of the Jungster II was started by Mr Kaminskas as the RK-2 in 1962 and this prototype flew for the first time in March 1966. Plans of this aircraft are also available for purchase from McAsco.

TYPE: Single-seat homebuilt sporting aircraft.

AIRFRAME: Strut braced parasol monoplane. Wing section NACA 2412. No dihedral. Incidence 1°. Sweepback at quarter-chord 15° on outer panels. All-wood spruce structure, covered with plywood and fabric. Frise ailerons. No flaps or tabs. Spruce fuselage structure, fabric covered. Wire braced spruce tail unit. Fixed surfaces covered with birch plywood; control surfaces fabric covered. Fixed incidence tailplane. No tabs.

LANDING GEAR: Non-retractable tailwheel type. Rubber shock absorbers, adapted from truck engine mountings. Mainwheels size 5·00-5. Hydraulic brakes.

POWER PLANT (prototype): One 134 kW (180 hp) Avco Lycoming O-360 flat-six engine, driving a two-blade fixed-pitch propeller. Fuel tank forward of cockpit, capacity 75 litres (20 US gallons). Oil capacity 5·5 litres (0·75 US gallon). Other engines available optionally include those listed under Jungster I description, plus 119 kW (160 hp) Avco Lycoming O-320 and 134 kW (180 hp) Avco Lycoming O-360.

ACCOMMODATION: Single seat in open cockpit.

DIMENSIONS, EXTERNAL:
- Wing span: 6·81 m (22 ft 4 in)
- Wing chord at root: 1·27 m (4 ft 2 in)
- Length overall (tail up): 5·16 m (16 ft 11 in)
- Height to top of wings (tail up): 2·06 m (6 ft 9 in)
- Tailplane span: 2·36 m (7 ft 9 in)
- Wheel track: 1·52 m (5 ft 0 in)
- Propeller diameter: 1·68 m (5 ft 6 in)

AREA:
- Wings, gross: 7·80 m² (84·0 sq ft)

WEIGHTS AND LOADINGS (original 134 kW; 180 hp version):
- Weight empty: 335 kg (739 lb)
- Max T-O weight: 517 kg (1,139 lb)
- Max wing loading: 66·3 kg/m² (13·56 lb/sq ft)
- Max power loading: 3·86 kg/kW (6·33 lb/hp)

PERFORMANCE: (original 134 kW; 180 hp version, at max T-O weight):
- Never-exceed speed: 156 knots (290 km/h; 180 mph) IAS
- Max level speed at S/L: 139 knots (257 km/h; 160 mph)
- Max cruising speed up to 3,050 m (10,000 ft): 135 knots (249 km/h; 155 mph)
- Stalling speed: 48 knots (89 km/h; 55 mph) IAS
- Max rate of climb at S/L: 1,065 m (3,500 ft)/min

REPLICA PLANS

REPLICA PLANS

Replica Plans is no longer trading from the address given in the 1985-86 *Jane's*. No details of a new address or the present status of the company have been received. In view of the large number of S.E.5A replicas being constructed, full information is retained.

REPLICA PLANS S.E.5A REPLICA

The S.E.5A replica was designed to be an easy to build and inexpensive 85 per cent scale representation of the famous first World War fighter, although exact reproduction was waived in favour of making the aircraft simple to construct, using modern and readily available materials.

Design and construction of the first prototype began in 1969, and it flew for the first time in 1970. The prototypes were designed for Continental engines ranging from 48·5 to 74·5 kW (65-100 hp), but larger engines can be installed to the individual homebuilder's preference. More than 300 sets of plans had been sold by early 1986.

TYPE: Single-seat homebuilt sporting biplane.

AIRFRAME: Braced biplane wings of Clark CYH section. Dihedral 3°. Incidence 3°. Ailerons on lower wings only. Centre-section of upper wing houses a small tank which can be used as an auxiliary fuel tank or smoke tank, or can be left out at building stage. The centre-section is carried on four spruce cabane struts and is braced with stainless steel cables and turnbuckles. Spruce interplane struts, with 4130 steel end fittings. Stainless steel flying, landing and incidence wires. Wing ribs of mahogany plywood, with capstrips; spruce spars. From the front spar forward, the leading-edge is covered with glassfibre or aluminium. Wings are fabric covered. Ply skinned fuselage box structure, with fabric covered turtledeck and aluminium forward top decking. Dummy Vickers machine-gun in housing on port side of fuselage, and gunsights on decking forward of windscreen. Tail unit built on spruce spars, with structure generally similar to that of wings. Pushrod operated elevators. Cable operated rudder, with a horn for tailwheel steering.

LANDING GEAR: Non-retractable tailwheel type. Bungee cord shock absorption. Converted motorcycle wheels on main units, size 3·25-16. Size 6·00-2 tailwheel. Mechanical brakes.

POWER PLANT: Various engines can be installed. Performance figures quoted are for aircraft with 63·5 kW (85 hp) Continental C85 flat-four engine, driving a two-blade fixed-pitch wooden propeller. Fuel capacity 72 litres (19 US gallons). Oil capacity 3·8 litres (1 US gallon).

ACCOMMODATION: Single seat in open cockpit.

DIMENSIONS, EXTERNAL:
- Wing span: 6·96 m (22 ft 10 in)
- Wing chord, constant: 1·27 m (4 ft 2 in)
- Height overall: 2·18 m (7 ft 2 in)
- Wheel track: 1·52 m (5 ft 0 in)
- Propeller diameter: 1·83 m (6 ft 0 in)

AREA:
- Wings, gross: 13·01 m² (140·0 sq ft)

WEIGHTS AND LOADINGS:
- Weight empty: 358 kg (790 lb)
- Max T-O weight: 499 kg (1,100 lb)
- Max wing loading: 38·36 kg/m² (7·86 lb/sq ft)
- Max power loading: 7·86 kg/kW (12·94 lb/hp)

PERFORMANCE:
- Max level speed at S/L: 78 knots (145 km/h; 90 mph)
- Max cruising speed: 74 knots (137 km/h; 85 mph)
- Stalling speed: 31 knots (57 km/h; 35 mph)
- Max rate of climb at S/L: 152 m (500 ft)/min

McAsco marketed Jungster I biplane and Jungster II monoplane

McAsco marketed Jungster I built by Mr Dave Clark of Renton, Washington

Replica Plans S.E.5A, built by Mr Ismall Cruz of Kirkland, Washington, and finished in colours and markings of 25th Pursuit Squadron, American Expeditionary Force *(Peter M. Bowers)*

Say Mini-Jumbo homebuilt light aircraft

Seawind International Seawind 2000 amphibian

SAY

MAXWELL A. SAY

RR4, Shelburne, Ontario L0N 1S0

SAY MINI-JUMBO

Mr Maxwell Say began the design of his Mini-Jumbo cabin monoplane (C-GBZF) in 1976 and started constructing it in the following year. It flew for the first time on 19 April 1983 and is believed to be a one-off.

Type: Two-seat homebuilt cabin monoplane.

Airframe: Strut braced high wing monoplane. Wing section GAW-1. Thickness/chord ratio 17%. Dihedral 1° 30′. Incidence 1° 30′. Composite wings constructed of wood, foam, Dynel and epoxy, with ailerons and flaps. Conventional fuselage of steel tube construction, fabric covered. Strut braced tail unit with steel tube structure, comprising fin and rudder, and mid-mounted tailplane with horn balanced elevators and tab. Tailplane ground adjustable.

Landing Gear: Non-retractable tailwheel type, with car type springs and truck rubber shock absorption. Mainwheel tyres size 8·00-4, pressure 1·03 bars (15 lb/sq in). Scot 3200 nosewheel; tyre pressure 2·76 bars (40 lb/sq in). Mainwheel brakes.

Power Plant: One 80·5-85·75 kW (108-115 hp) Avco Lycoming O-235 flat-four engine, driving a McCauley two-blade metal propeller. Two fuel tanks, total capacity 145 litres (32 Imp gallons). Refuelling point in top of wing. Oil capacity 7 litres (1·5 Imp gallons).

Accommodation: Two persons in fully enclosed cabin. Baggage capacity 45 kg (100 lb).

System: Electrical system, using battery, for engine starting and flap actuation.

Dimensions, external:

Wing span	10·36 m (34 ft 0 in)
Wing chord, constant	1·22 m (4 ft 0 in)
Wing aspect ratio	7·5
Length overall	6·71 m (22 ft 0 in)
Height overall	2·03 m (6 ft 8 in)
Tailplane span	3·20 m (10 ft 6 in)
Wheel track	1·83 m (6 ft 0 in)
Wheelbase	4·57 m (15 ft 0 in)
Propeller diameter	1·80 m (5 ft 11 in)

Area:

Wings, gross	13·0 m² (140·0 sq ft)

Weights and Loading:

Weight empty	578 kg (1,275 lb)
Max T-O weight	875 kg (1,930 lb)
Max wing loading	67·33 kg/m² (13·79 lb/sq ft)

Performance (at max T-O weight):

Max level speed at 915 m (3,000 ft)	100 knots (185 km/h; 115 mph)
Max cruising speed at 915 m (3,000 ft)	78 knots (145 km/h; 90 mph)
Stalling speed:	
flaps down, engine idling	31 knots (57 km/h; 35 mph)
flaps up	51 knots (94 km/h; 58 mph)
Max rate of climb at S/L	183 m (600 ft)/min
T-O run	152 m (500 ft)
Landing run	107 m (350 ft)

SEAWIND

SEAWIND INTERNATIONAL INC

PO Box 878, Haliburton, Ontario K0M 1S0

Telephone: (705) 457 1438

President: Leonard R. Creelman

SEAWIND INTERNATIONAL SEAWIND 2000

Seawind International was formed to develop and market in kit form a four-seat all-composite amphibian of advanced configuration, the production version of which is known as the Seawind 2000. Each kit will include all components and materials necessary to build the aircraft, except for the engine, propeller, instruments, battery and upholstery. Except for the canopy, which is one-piece Plexiglas, the airframe is constructed entirely of parts premoulded by Seawind International, under strict quality control, using glassfibre, vinylester resin and PVC foam. Where possible, components are supplied as complete subassemblies One such item is the wing, which is delivered with the wingtip floats pre-moulded in place, and incorporates fuel tanks formed by coating sections between ribs with fuel resistant resin.

Other pre-moulded components include the hull, tail fin and engine support, nose top decking, aileron skins, flap skins, rudder, tailplane and elevator skins, engine cowling and propeller spinner. Construction of the Seawind 2000 from a kit takes about 1,000 working hours.

The production prototype Seawind (C-GFNL) flew for the first time on 23 August 1982. All flight testing has been completed after about 100 flying hours, and the minimum performance requirements of FAR Pt 23 regulations for certificated aircraft were exceeded by a substantial margin. By early 1986, approximately 55 kits had been ordered; production moulds had been completed and assembly from the first production kit had started.

Type: Four-seat light homebuilt amphibian.

Airframe: Cantilever shoulder-wing monoplane. Wing section NLF(1)-0215F. Thickness/chord ratio 15%. Dihedral 3°. Incidence 3° 30′. No sweepback. Built-up glassfibre reinforced plastics (GRP) wing spar and PVC foam ribs, covered with GRP skins. Ailerons, plain flaps and wingtip floats all of GRP/PVC foam construction. Single-step flying-boat hull built of GRP/PVC foam. Cantilever tail unit of GRP, with sweptback fin and rudder. Tailplane and aerodynamically balanced elevator high mounted at rear of platform which extends forward from fin to carry power plant.

Landing Gear: Hydraulically retractable tricycle type,

with 6·00-6 mainwheels and 5·00-5 castoring nosewheel. Cantilever glassfibre spring main legs. Nosewheel has shock absorber. Hydraulic brakes.

Power Plant: One 149 kW (200 hp) Avco Lycoming IO-360-C1C flat-four engine, driving a Hartzell two-blade constant-speed metal propeller with spinner. Two integral fuel cells in wings; total capacity 302 litres (80 US gallons). Refuelling points in top of wings. Oil capacity 7·6 litres (2 US gallons).

Accommodation: Four persons, the rear two on a 1·32 m (4 ft 4 in) wide bench seat. Dual stick controls. Large transparent canopy hinged to open fully to either side. Baggage space behind rear seat.

Systems: Hydraulic system for landing gear and flaps, with electric pump and manual backup. Electrical system, with alternator and 12V 60A battery, for engine starting and avionics.

Dimensions, external:

Wing span	10·67 m (35 ft 0 in)
Wing chord, constant	1·37 m (4 ft 6 in)
Wing aspect ratio	7·8
Length overall	8·23 m (27 ft 0 in)
Height overall	2·90 m (9 ft 6 in)
Tailplane span	3·35 m (11 ft 0 in)
Wheel track	2·19 m (7 ft 2½ in)
Propeller diameter	1·93 m (6 ft 4 in)

Area:

Wings, gross	14·59 m² (157·0 sq ft)

Weights and Loadings:

Weight empty	771 kg (1,700 lb)
Max T-O weight	1,270 kg (2,800 lb)
Max wing loading	87·0 kg/m² (17·83 lb/sq ft)
Max power loading	8·52 kg/kW (14·00 lb/hp)

Performance:

Max level speed at S/L	161 knots (298 km/h; 185 mph)
Max cruising speed at 2,440 m (8,000 ft)	156 knots (290 km/h; 180 mph)
Econ cruising speed	143 knots (266 km/h; 165 mph)
Stalling speed:	
flaps up	52 knots (97 km/h; 60 mph)
flaps and landing gear down	48 knots (89 km/h; 55 mph)
Max rate of climb at S/L	366 m (1,200 ft)/min
Service ceiling	5,180 m (17,000 ft)
T-O run: land	198 m (650 ft)
water	396 m (1,300 ft)
Landing run	366 m (1,200 ft)
Range with max standard fuel	1,042 nm (1,931 km; 1,200 miles)

SKY KING
SKY KING INTERNATIONAL

419 Wellsley Street East, Toronto, Ontario M4X 1H5

President: Richard Spence

The current status of Sky King International is unknown. Full details and an illustration of its Vector 610 and 627 can be found in the 1985-86 *Jane's*.

SKYSEEKER
SKYSEEKER AIRCRAFT CORPORATION

The address and telephone number given in the 1985-86 *Jane's* for the Skyseeker Aircraft Corporation are no longer valid. Details of the Skyseeker Mk III microlight can be found in that edition.

SPECTRUM
SPECTRUM AIRCRAFT INC

No. 3-9531 192nd Street, Surrey, British Columbia V3T 4W2

Telephone: (604) 888 2055

Sales and Marketing Manager: Allan K. Hunkin

The Spectrum Beaver RX-28 and the initial Beaver RX-500 have been joined by a Rotax 503 engined version of the latter named Floater and by the similarly powered RX-550SP (Special Purpose) for commercial applications. Also marketed are tricycle and amphibious versions of the RX-35, which are similar in most respects to the RX-28 but use the 26 kW (35 hp) Rotax 377 engine as standard.

SPECTRUM BEAVER RX-28

Sold in kit and ready-assembled form, the Beaver RX-28 is a high-wing monoplane microlight designed for rough-field operation. By February 1986 a total of at least 250 kits and ready-assembled RX-28s had been sold.

Type: Single-seat microlight aircraft; conforms to FAR Pt 103 and Canadian regulations.

Airframe: Braced high-wing monoplane, with 5° sweepback. Aluminium alloy anodised structure with Dacron covering (double surface on wings), Mylar reinforced leading-edges. Stainless steel bracing wires. Three-axis control (rudder, elevator and ailerons). Glassfibre cockpit fairing and Lexan windscreen standard. Four-point harness standard. Options include fully enclosed cockpit fairing and parachute recovery system. Rigging time 25 min.

Landing Gear: Non-retractable tricycle type with shock absorption and small tailwheel to protect rudder. All three mainwheels of 12 in diameter. Mainwheel brakes standard. Optional independent brakes, streamline wheel fairings, ski and float gear.

Power Plant: One 20 kW (27 hp) Rotax 277 single-cylinder two-stroke engine standard, with 2·58:1 reduction drive to a two-blade wooden pusher propeller; 26 kW (35 hp) Rotax optional. Fuel capacity 19 litres (5 US gallons) standard.

Accommodation: Pilot only, in open cockpit with fairing and windscreen.

Dimensions, external:

Wing span	9·45 m (31 ft 0 in)
Wing aspect ratio	6·54
Length overall	5·38 m (17 ft 8 in)
Height overall	1·73 m (5 ft 8 in)
Propeller diameter	1·52 m (5 ft 0 in)

Area:

Wings, gross	13·75 m² (148·0 sq ft)

Weights and Loadings:

Weight empty	115 kg (253 lb)
Pilot weight range	59-109 kg (130-240 lb)
Max T-O weight	252 kg (556 lb)
Max wing loading	18·3 kg/m² (3·76 lb/sq ft)
Max power loading	12·6 kg/kW (20·6 lb/hp)

Performance (with 79 kg; 175 lb pilot):

Never-exceed speed	61 knots (112 km/h; 70 mph)
Max level speed	50 knots (93 km/h; 58 mph)
Cruising speed	42 knots (77 km/h; 48 mph)
Econ cruising speed	35 knots (64 km/h; 40 mph)
Stalling speed	21 knots (39 km/h; 24 mph)
Max rate of climb at S/L	213 m (700 ft)/min
Service ceiling	3,660 m (12,000 ft)
T-O run	28 m (90 ft)
Landing run	34 m (110 ft)
Range with max fuel	87 nm (161 km; 100 miles)
Endurance	2 h 5 min
g limits	+7·5/−3 ultimate
Best glide ratio	8
Min rate of sink, power off	115 m (375 ft)/min

SPECTRUM BEAVER RX-35 and RX-35 FLOATER

The latest models in the Spectrum Beaver range are the RX-35 and RX-35 Floater, which are available in kit and ready assembled forms. More than 250 had been sold by February 1986. The **RX-35** is the standard tricycle landing gear model, while the **Floater** has amphibious landing gear (instead of the standard land gear) and a choice of engines. Both the RX-35 and the Floater are structurally similar to the RX-28, but the Rotax 377 is the standard power plant. Details, where they differ from the RX-28, are as follows:

Type: Single-seat microlight aircraft; conforms to Canadian regulations.

Airframe: As for RX-28. Rigging time for Floater is 35 min.

Landing Gear: As for RX-28, but with steerable nosewheel. RX-35 Floater has unsprung landing gear, and both models have independent brakes as option to standard mainwheel brakes. Optional amphibious landing gear on Floater

Power Plant: One 26 kW (35 hp) Rotax 377 engine, with 2·58:1 gear reduction to a two-blade wooden pusher propeller. Floater has option of 33·5 kW (45 hp) Rotax 447 engine. Fuel capacity 19 litres (5 US gallons) standard; one optional auxiliary fuel tank, capacity 38 litres (10 US gallons).

Accommodation: Pilot only, in open cockpit with fairing and windscreen.

Dimensions, external:

Wing span	9·45 m (31 ft 0 in)
Wing aspect ratio	6·54
Length overall	5·38 m (17 ft 8 in)
Height overall: RX-35	1·73 m (5 ft 8 in)
Floater	1·85 m (6 ft 1 in)
Propeller diameter	1·63 m (5 ft 4 in)

Area:

Wings, gross	13·75 m² (148·0 sq ft)

Weights and Loadings (A: RX-35, B: Floater):

Weight empty: A	121·5 kg (268 lb)
B	149 kg (328 lb)
Pilot weight range: A	59-118 kg (130-260 lb)
B	59-102 kg (130-225 lb)
Max T-O weight: A	244 kg (539 lb)
B	265 kg (585 lb)
Max wing loading:	
A	17·75 kg/m² (3·64 lb/sq ft)
B	19·3 kg/m² (3·95 lb/sq ft)
Max power loading:	
A	9·38 kg/kW (15·40 lb/hp)
B	10·19 kg/kW (16·71 lb/hp)

Performance (A: RX-35, B: Floater):

Never-exceed speed:	
A, B	61 knots (112 km/h; 70 mph)
Max level speed: A	56 knots (103 km/h; 64 mph)
B	52 knots (97 km/h; 60 mph)
Max cruising speed: A	48 knots (88 km/h; 55 mph)
B	44 knots (82 km/h; 51 mph)
Econ cruising speed:	
A, B	36 knots (68 km/h; 42 mph)
Stalling speed:	
A, power on	22 knots (41 km/h; 25 mph)
B, power on	26 knots (47 km/h; 29 mph)
A, power off	25 knots (45 km/h; 28 mph)
B, power off	22 knots (41 km/h; 25 mph)
Max rate of climb at S/L: A	335 m (1,100 ft)/min
B	119 m (390 ft)/min
Service ceiling: A	3,960 m (13,000 ft)
B	3,660 m (12,000 ft)
T-O run: A	18 m (60 ft)
B	46 m (150 ft)
Landing run: A	35 m (115 ft)
B	31 m (100 ft)
Range with max standard fuel:	
A	78 nm (145 km; 90 miles)
B	69 nm (128 km; 80 miles)
Endurance	2 h
g limits: A	+7·3/−2·9
B	+6·75/−3
Best glide ratio: A, B	8

SPECTRUM BEAVER RX-550 SERIES

The Beaver RX-550 was introduced in November 1983 as a tandem-seat training version of the RX-28. The airframe is structurally similar to that of the single-seat model, but with full dual controls. Rear (instructor's) controls have a mechanical advantage enabling the instructor to override a student's control inputs if necessary.

The initial RX-550 now forms only one of three models in the range, having been joined by the RX-550 Floater and the RX-550SP (Special Purpose). By early 1986 RX-550SPs were being flown in at least seven countries for varied commercial applications, which included herd counting and anti-poaching duties at an African wildlife game reserve and the location of mineral deposits in the Sudan using electronic survey equipment. Stated possible uses for the RX-550SP also include agricultural spraying, cargo handling, air ambulance, and police and military work.

The three models of RX-550 differ as follows:

RX-550. Standard version with 33·5 kW (45 hp) Rotax 447 engine.

RX-550 Floater. Rotax 503 engine of 35·8 kW (48 hp). Heavier empty and max T-O weights and higher performance.

RX-550SP. Similar to Floater but with max payload of 227 kg (500 lb) and useful load of 204 kg (450 lb) for commercial applications. New 34 litre (9 US gallon) seat tank standard to allow 4 h endurance and range of 182 nm (338 km; 210 miles). Heavier suspension using Spectrum's shock absorber landing gear system. Options include agricultural spraygear, and various types of cargo and baggage compartments. Can be flown as a two-seater or with the cargo/baggage compartments in place of the rear seat.

By February 1986 more than 250 RX-550 series aircraft had been sold. Details, where they differ from the RX-28, are as follows:

Type: Two-seat (or single-seat for RX-550SP with commercial payload) microlight aircraft; conform to Canadian microlight regulations.

Airframe: As for RX-28.

Landing Gear: As for RX-28, but with castoring nosewheel and tailwheel for ease of ground handling. Mainwheel diameter 14 in.

Power Plant: RX-550: One 33·5 kW (45 hp) Rotax 447 engine, with 2·58:1 reduction drive to two-blade wooden pusher propeller. RX-550 Floater: One 35·8 kW (48 hp) Rotax 503 engine, with 2·58:1 reduction drive to two- or three-blade wooden or composite propeller. RX-550SP: as for Floater. RX-550 has Rotax 503 option. Fuel capacity 19 litres (5 US gallons) standard on all models except RX-550SP, which has 34 litre (9 US gallon) seat

Spectrum Beaver RX-35 *(Geoffrey P. Jones)*

Spectrum Beaver RX-550SP

Two-seat version of Sylvaire Bushmaster *(J. M. G. Gradidge)*

Spectrum Beaver RX-550 Floater with float landing gear

tank. RX-550 and Floater have optional 38 litre (10 US gallon) long range tanks.

Accommodation: Two seats in tandem; but RX-550SP is normally flown with pilot only (see model paragraphs).

Dimensions, external:

Wing span	10·67 m (35 ft 0 in)
Wing aspect ratio	7·2
Length overall	6·30 m (20 ft 8 in)
Height overall	2·03 m (6 ft 8 in)
Propeller diameter (45 hp)	1·63 m (5 ft 4 in)

Area:

Wings, gross	15·79 m² (170·0 sq ft)

Weights and Loadings (A: RX-550, B: Floater, C: RX-550SP):

Weight empty: A	149 kg (329 lb)
B	192 kg (423 lb)
C	174·5 kg (385 lb)
Max pilot and passenger weights (each):	
A, C	102 kg (225 lb)
B	91 kg (200 lb)
Max T-O weight: A	398 kg (877 lb)
B, C	410 kg (905 lb)
Max wing loadings: A	25·2 kg/m² (5·16 lb/sq ft)
B, C	26·0 kg/m² (5·32 lb/sq ft)
Max power loadings: A	11·88 kg/kW (19·49 lb/hp)
B, C	11·45 kg/kW (18·85 lb/hp)

Performance (A: RX-550, B: Floater, C: RX-550SP):

Never-exceed speed: A	61 knots (112 km/h; 70 mph)
B, C	69 knots (128 km/h; 80 mph)
Max level speed: A	52 knots (97 km/h; 60 mph)
B	61 knots (113 km/h; 70 mph)
C	65 knots (121 km/h; 75 mph)
Max cruising speed: A	48 knots (89 km/h; 55 mph)
B	47 knots (87 km/h; 54 mph)
C	56 knots (105 km/h; 65 mph)
Econ cruising speed: A	42 knots (79 km/h; 49 mph)
B	40 knots (74 km/h; 46 mph)
C	46 knots (85 km/h; 53 mph)
Stalling speed: A	24 knots (44 km/h; 27 mph)
B	27 knots (50 km/h; 31 mph)
C	28 knots (52 km/h; 32 mph)
Max rate of climb at S/L: A	183 m (600 ft)/min
B	213 m (700 ft)/min
C	244 m (800 ft)/min
Service ceiling: A	3,200 m (10,500 ft)
B	3,355 m (11,000 ft)
C	3,660 m (12,000 ft)
T-O run: A, C	54 m (175 ft)
B	84 m (275 ft)
Landing run: A	70 m (230 ft)
B	61 m (200 ft)
C	73 m (240 ft)
Range with max standard fuel:	
A	69 nm (128 km; 80 miles)
B	61 nm (112 km; 70 miles)
C with seat tank	182 nm (338 km; 210 miles)
g limits: A, B, C	+6·75/−3
Best glide ratio: A	7
B	6·5
C	7·5

SUN FUN

SUN FUN ULTRALIGHT AVIATION

6964 152 Street, Surrey, British Columbia V3S 3L5
Telephone: (604) 594 3919

In Summer 1986, Sun Fun Ultralight Aviation was flight testing a prototype staggerwing biplane known as the Kestrel Hawk, which conforms with Canadian ultralight regulations despite its all-metal structure. After more than 20 hours of testing it was described as being "very responsive, very docile, with twice the roll rate and better control than conventional ultralights".

SUN FUN KESTREL HAWK

Type: Two-seat ultralight aircraft.

Airframe: Strut and wire braced back-staggered biplane. All-metal aluminium alloy stressed skin construction, except for Poly-Fiber fabric covering over rear portions of wings and tail unit. Aileron over nearly full span of each lower wing. Pod and boom fuselage. Sweptback fin and rudder; non-swept tailplane and elevators.

Landing Gear: Monowheel under centre-fuselage, tailwheel, and a small balancer wheel under each wing in line with I type interplane struts.

Power Plant: One 37 kW (50 hp) Rotax 503 engine, pylon mounted above and behind top wing, and driving a two-blade pusher propeller.

Accommodation: Two persons in tandem in enclosed cockpit, under large sideways hinged blister canopy.

Dimensions, external:

Wing span	7·62 m (25 ft 0 in)
Length overall	7·32 m (24 ft 0 in)

Weight:

Weight empty	185 kg (408 lb)

Performance ((preliminary):

Cruising speed	70-78 knots (128-145 km/h; 80-90 mph)
Best glide ratio	10

SYLVAIRE

SYLVAIRE MANUFACTURING LTD

PO Box 569, Sylvan Lake, Alberta T0M 1Z0
Telephone: (403) 887 4100
President: Brian Heslin

This company markets the Bushmaster light aircraft, in single-seat and two-seat versions, with Rotax engines of various sizes, in ready to fly and kit forms. The aircraft was designed by Dr David J. Marsden, PEng., of the Department of Mechanical Engineering, University of Alberta, whose work as a designer of high-performance sailplanes has been recorded annually in *Jane's* for a number of years.

SYLVAIRE BUSHMASTER

Although designed as an ultralight aircraft, the Bushmaster is larger than a Cessna 152, has full dual controls in its side by side two-seat form, and is intended to have a service life of 10 to 15 years. It is used widely for crop spraying and commercial carrying duties, as well as recreation and sport, and can be equipped for ambulance, air survey and other professional duties.

The two-seat version uses the same wings and tail unit as the single-seater, so that the flying characteristics of the two models are as nearly as possible identical. Construction from kits requires only assembly, with all composite parts pre-formed and critical holes pre-drilled, allowing completion in 150 to 200 hours.

Type: Single-seat or two-seat light aircraft.

Airframe: Strut braced high-wing monoplane of constant chord, with two parallel streamline section struts each side and short jury struts. Dihedral 2°. Two-spar construction, exclusively of composites, with D cell leading-edge and internal steel cable bracing. Overall covering of Ceconite aircraft grade fabric, finished with Endura plastic paint. Wings easily removable (15 min) for transportation and storage. Full span ailerons with mechanical linkages. No flaps or tabs. Riveted fuselage structure of aluminium alloy tube and channel section, covered with Ceconite fabric and finished with Endura plastic paint. Composites pilot enclosure, with complete double aluminium tube roll cage and aluminium alloy belly pan; sides, bottom and firewall of high density foam sandwich, strengthened with Kevlar. Reinforced glassfibre engine cowling. Conventional wire braced tail unit, similar in construction to fuselage. No tabs. Easily removed and set up in field.

LANDING GEAR: Non-retractable tailwheel type. Mainwheels carried on faired side Vs and bungee-sprung half-axles of 4130 steel tube. Steerable tailwheel. Options include oversize tyres, skis, floats and glassfibre wheel fairings.

POWER PLANT: One 20 kW (27 hp) Rotax 277 or 29·4 kW (39·4 hp) 447 engine with 2·58:1 geared reduction drive to two-blade fixed-pitch propeller in single-seater; Rotax 447 or 34-38 kW (45·6-51 hp) 503 (single or dual carburettor), with similar reduction gear, in two-seater. Fuel capacity 19 litres (5 US gallons) in single-seater; 38 litres (10 US gallons) in two-seater.

ACCOMMODATION: Single upholstered glassfibre seat, or two seats side by side with dual controls, in fully enclosed cabin. Large wrapround Lexan windscreen. Reinforced Lexan door on each side. Heating optional.

EQUIPMENT: Options include agricultural spraygear. Two-seat Bushmaster can be equipped as air ambulance.

DIMENSIONS, EXTERNAL:

Wing span: single-seat	10·58 m (34 ft 8½ in)
two-seat	10·97 m (36 ft 0 in)
Wing aspect ratio: single-seat	7·72
two-seat	8

AREA:

Wings, gross: single-seat	14·49 m² (156·0 sq ft)
two-seat	15·05 m² (162·0 sq ft)

WEIGHTS AND LOADINGS (A: single-seater with Rotax 277, B: single-seater with Rotax 447, C: two-seater with Rotax 447, D: two-seater with Rotax 503):

Weight empty: A	129 kg (283 lb)
B	136 kg (300 lb)
C, D	177 kg (390 lb)
Design max T-O weight: A	272 kg (600 lb)
B, C, D	408 kg (900 lb)
Max wing loading: A	18·8 kg/m² (3·85 lb/sq ft)
B	28·2 kg/m² (5·77 lb/sq ft)
C, D	27·1 kg/m² (5·56 lb/sq ft)
Max power loading: A	13·60 kg/kW (22·22 lb/hp)
B, C	13·88 kg/kW (22·84 lb/hp)
D, with Rotax 503	12·00 kg/kW (19·74 lb/hp)

PERFORMANCE (at max design T-O weight):

Max level speed: A	61 knots (114 km/h; 71 mph)
B, D	69 knots (128 km/h; 80 mph)
C	65 knots (120 km/h; 75 mph)
Cruising speed: A	56 knots (104 km/h; 65 mph)
B, D	63 knots (117 km/h; 73 mph)
C	58 knots (108 km/h; 67 mph)
Stalling speed, power on:	
A, B	18 knots (32 km/h; 20 mph)
C, D	26 knots (49 km/h; 30 mph)
Stalling speed, power off:	
A, B	21 knots (39 km/h; 24 mph)
C, D	31 knots (57 km/h; 35 mph)
Max rate of climb at S/L:	
A, B, C	122 m (400 ft)/min
D	213 m (700 ft)/min
T-O and landing run: A, B	46 m (150 ft)
C, D	76 m (250 ft)

TESORI

TESORI AIRCRAFT LTD

7219-104 Street, Edmonton, Alberta T6E 4B8

Telephone: (403) 439 7878

Telex: 037-2036

MANAGER: John Cameron

TESORI AIRCRAFT PONY

Tesori Aircraft is thought to have sets of plans available for its Pony microlight, which was intended to be produced also in ready assembled form.

TYPE: Single-seat microlight; conforms to FAR Pt 103.

AIRFRAME: Strut braced high-wing monoplane. Dihedral wings with metal spars and ribs and metal leading-edges, double surface Dacron covered. Duralumin monocoque fuselage with conical boom aft of enclosed cabin. King-post standard. Stainless steel cables. Three-axis control (ailerons, elevators and rudder). Options include parachute.

LANDING GEAR: Non-retractable tailwheel type, with 8 × 3·5 in mainwheels and 3 × 3 in tailwheel. Sprung leg suspension. Optional skis.

POWER PLANT: One 19·4 kW (26 hp) KFM engine, driving two-blade wooden propeller. Fuel tank capacity 23 litres (5 Imp gallons).

ACCOMMODATION: Pilot only, in cabin.

DIMENSIONS, EXTERNAL:

Wing span	9·14 m (30 ft 0 in)
Wing aspect ratio	6·25
Length overall	5·49 m (18 ft 0 in)
Height overall	1·52 m (5 ft 0 in)
Propeller diameter	1·73 m (5 ft 8 in)

AREA:

Wings, gross	13·38 m² (144·0 sq ft)

WEIGHTS AND LOADINGS:

Weight empty (unpainted)	113 kg (250 lb)
Pilot weight range	68-86 kg (150-190 lb)
Max T-O weight	199 kg (440 lb)
Max wing loading	14·94 kg/m² (3·06 lb/sq ft)
Max power loading	10·26 kg/kW (16·92 lb/hp)

PERFORMANCE:

Never-exceed speed	82 knots (153 km/h; 95 mph)
Max level speed	56 knots (105 km/h; 65 mph)
Max and econ cruising speed	52 knots (97 km/h; 60 mph)
Stalling speed	21 knots (39 km/h; 24 mph)
Max rate of climb at S/L	183 m (600 ft)/min
Service ceiling	3,660 m (12,000 ft)
T-O run	61 m (200 ft)
Landing run	55 m (180 ft)
Range with max fuel	130 nm (241 km; 150 miles)
Endurance	2 h 10 min
g limits	+6/−4

THOR

THOR AIR

457 Fenmar Drive, Weston, Ontario M9L 2R6

Telephone: (416) 745 4657

Telex: 065-27383

GENERAL MANAGER: Guenter Weber

THOR AIR THOR T-1

The Thor T-1 made its flying debut at Sun 'n' Fun 1984. Three versions have been offered: the single-seat **T-1** (to which the following description applies) and **T-1A**, with 31·3 kW (42 hp) Rotax 447 engine, and the two-seat **T-2**, with 35 kW (47 hp) Rotax 503 engine. By the Spring of 1986 at least 115 kits had been ordered. A 'military version' of the T-2 was known to be under development.

TYPE: Single-seat microlight aircraft.

AIRFRAME: Strut braced high-wing monoplane of aluminium tube and Dacron. Wings have 34° sweepback. Cruciform tail unit, plus wingtip rudders.

LANDING GEAR: Non-retractable tailwheel type, with steerable tailwheel. Ski and float gear optional.

POWER PLANT: One 20 kW (27 hp) Rotax 277 engine standard, with 2:1 reduction drive to a two-blade wooden tractor propeller; 29·8 kW (40 hp) Rotax optional on T-1A. Fuel tank capacity 19 litres (5 US gallons).

ACCOMMODATION: Pilot only, in open cockpit. Pilot enclosure optional.

DIMENSIONS, EXTERNAL:

Wing span	9·83 m (32 ft 3 in)
Length overall	4·19 m (13 ft 9 in)
Height overall	2·36 m (7 ft 9 in)
Propeller diameter	1·27 m (4 ft 2 in)

AREA:

Wings, gross	15·51 m² (167·0 sq ft)

WEIGHTS AND LOADINGS:

Weight empty	108 kg (238 lb)
Max T-O weight	227 kg (500 lb)
Max wing loading	14·60 kg/m² (2·99 lb/sq ft)
Max power loading	10·81 kg/kW (17·86 lb/hp)

PERFORMANCE:

Never-exceed speed	65 knots (120 km/h; 75 mph)
Max level speed	55 knots (101 km/h; 65 mph)
Max cruising speed	48 knots (89 km/h; 55 mph)
Stalling speed	19 knots (36 km/h; 22 mph)
Max rate of climb at S/L	213 m (700 ft)/min
Service ceiling	3,050 m (10,000 ft)
g limits	+6/−4
Best glide ratio	9

THOR AIR JUNO

The Juno is basically an update of the Thor T-1, though it is a side by side two-seater using the low powered Rotax 277 engine as standard power plant. Eighty Junos had been built by February 1985, of which 60 had then been sold. More recent figures have not been made available. It is available in kit and ready assembled forms.

TYPE: Two-seat microlight aircraft; conforms to FAR Pt 103 and Canadian Transport regulations.

AIRFRAME: Strut braced high-wing monoplane, with aluminium alloy mainframe and double thickness Dacron on fuselage sides, dihedral wings (double surface) and tail unit. Wings have marked sweepback. Stainless steel cables. Three-axis control (ailerons, elevators and rudder). Windscreen standard; fully enclosed cockpit optional. Options include ballistic parachute and instrument pack. Rigging time 45 min.

LANDING GEAR: Non-retractable tailwheel type, with steerable tailwheel. Mainwheels size 14½ × 4 in; tailwheel size 4 × 1½ in. No brakes. Bungee suspension. Options include skis and floats.

POWER PLANT: One 20 kW (27 hp) Rotax 277 engine, with 2·58:1 reduction drive to two-blade wooden propeller. Optional 31·3 kW (42 hp) Rotax 447 engine. Fuel tank capacity 20 litres (4·4 Imp gallons).

ACCOMMODATION: Pilot and passenger side by side in partially or fully enclosed cockpit.

DIMENSIONS, EXTERNAL:

Wing span	9·86 m (32 ft 4 in)
Wing aspect ratio	6·3
Length overall	4·45 m (14 ft 7 in)
Height overall	1·93 m (6 ft 4 in)
Propeller diameter	1·52 m (5 ft 0 in)

AREA:

Wings, gross	15·51 m² (167·0 sq ft)

WEIGHTS AND LOADINGS:

Weight empty	129 kg (284 lb)
Pilot weight range	45·5-113 kg (100-250 lb)
Max T-O weight	256 kg (564 lb)
Max wing loading	16·50 kg/m² (3·38 lb/sq ft)
Max power loading	12·80 kg/kW (20·88 lb/hp)

PERFORMANCE:

Never-exceed speed	61 knots (112 km/h; 70 mph)
Max level speed	52 knots (97 km/h; 60 mph)
Max cruising speed	43 knots (80 km/h; 50 mph)
Econ cruising speed	35 knots (64 km/h; 40 mph)
Stalling speed: power on	18 knots (33 km/h; 20 mph)
power off	19 knots (36 km/h; 22 mph)
Max rate of climb at S/L	213 m (700 ft)/min
Service ceiling	3,050 m (10,000 ft)
T-O run	23 m (75 ft)
Landing run	15 m (50 ft)
Range with max fuel	130 nm (241 km; 150 miles)
Endurance	3 h
g limits	+6/−3

ULTIMATE

ULTIMATE AIRCRAFT (Division of Ultimate Aerobatics Ltd)

Guelph Airpark, Guelph, Ontario N1H 6H8

Telephone: (519) 836 8622

PRESIDENT: Gordon Price

This company is a division of Ultimate Aerobatics Ltd which markets kits to modify Pitts S-1 Specials and is also currently designing the two-seat SMT (Super Manoeuvrability Trainer) for sale as a ready assembled and kit aircraft.

Both Ultimate Aerobatics and Ultimate Aircraft have as President Mr Gordon Price, a former RCAF fighter pilot who is currently a DC-9 captain with Air Canada and an aerobatic pilot.

ULTIMATE AIRCRAFT TEN SERIES ALBERTAN

Ultimate Aircraft is offering sets of plans, kits and ready assembled examples of three closely related single-seat biplanes. Each aircraft can be built from a series of 14 separate kits of component parts, themselves offered in alternative 'material', 'assembly' and 'subassembly' forms with differing levels of pre-delivery completion. The kits do not include the engine, instruments, accessories, wheels and brakes.

The basic model of the Albertan series is the **Ten Dash One Hundred** (or 10-100), designed to be an affordable sporting biplane with a 74·5 or 134 kW (100 or 180 hp) engine. Power plants between these ratings can be installed at the customer's option, with changes to the engine mounting, weight and balance. First of the three models to fly, the 10-100 was conceived in March 1985 and flew for the first time in prototype form on 6 October 1985. By 16 March 1986, this aircraft had accumulated 70 flying hours.

The **Ten Dash Two Hundred** (or 10-200) was designed as a modern competition aerobatic aircraft, utilising a 149 kW (200 hp) engine (reports also suggest a 164 kW; 220 hp option) with Ellison throttle body injector and a constant-speed Hoffmann or MT composite propeller.

The final model in the range is the **Ten Dash Three**

Tesori Aircraft Pony prototype

Ultimate Aircraft Ten Dash One Hundred Albertan homebuilt aerobatic aircraft *(Howard Levy)*

Thor Air Thor T-1 *(J. M. G. Gradidge)*

Thor Air Juno two-seat microlight

Hundred (or 10-300), a state of the art competition aircraft, with longer-span wings, incorporating full-span symmetrical ailerons; a longer fuselage; and a 261 kW (350 hp) Avco Lycoming engine (reports suggest the possibility of a 276 kW; 370 hp engine as an option). The company hopes to have a prototype of this model at the 1987 Paris Air Show.

All models have macro-flap control (5° flap with 30° elevator) for improved pitching rates, lower stalling speeds and clean low-speed pull-offs; symmetrical wing section and full span ailerons; sweepback on both upper and lower wings; an aerobatic fuel tank, with header tank inside; Wittman style main landing gear; and a low profile canopy.

By Summer 1986, Ultimate Aircraft had sold the prototype 10-100 and shipped 19 complete Albertan kits.

The following details refer to the prototype Ten Dash One Hundred with a 74·5 kW (100 hp) engine, unless stated otherwise. In this form, it is reported to loop from level flight, and perform two vertical rolls from an entry speed of 139 knots (257 km/h; 160 mph).

Type: Single-seat homebuilt sporting and aerobatic biplane.

Airframe: Braced single-bay biplane, with single welded interplane strut each side. Six cabane struts, arranged as inverted Vs. Wings (no dihedral/anhedral; 7° sweepback) have sitka spruce spars, jig-built ribs with birch plywood gussets and ¼ in square capstrips (epoxy glued together), and are Ceconite covered. Upper and lower ailerons of 2024-T3 and 6061-T6 aluminium alloy. Welded 4130 steel tube fuselage structure, with sitka spruce stringers, aluminium alloy skinned to rear of cockpit, Ceconite thereafter. Aluminium alloy turtledeck. Glassfibre nose cowlings. Conventional braced tail unit of 4130 steel tubing, Ceconite covered.

Landing Gear: Non-retractable tailwheel type, with cantilever spring steel main legs. Cleveland 5·00-5 wheels and tyres, with hydraulic brakes. Haigh lockable tailwheel.

Power Plant: One 74·5 kW (100 hp) Avco Lycoming flat-four engine, driving a two-blade propeller with large spinner. Optionally, one 134 kW (180 hp) engine. One aluminium aerobatic fuel tank, filled with Explosafe, capacity 83 litres (22 US gallons). Optional 57 litre (15 US gallon) strap-on centre-section tank.

Accommodation: Pilot only, in enclosed cockpit, under an 'F-84 type' Plexiglas canopy. Digital cockpit display in 10-200 and 10-300.

Avionics: 10-300 will have R/Nav and DME.

Dimensions, external:

Wing span: 10-100, 10-200	4·83 m (15 ft 10 in)
10-300	5·49 m (18 ft 0 in)
Wing chord, constant	0·91 m (3 ft 0 in)
Wing aspect ratio: 10-100, 10-200	5·33
Length overall: 10-100	5·33 m (17 ft 6 in)
10-200	5·49 m (18 ft 0 in)
10-300	6·40 m (21 ft 0 in)
Height overall	1·68 m (5 ft 6 in)
Tailplane span	2·08 m (6 ft 10 in)
Wheel track	1·78 m (5 ft 10 in)
Wheelbase	3·58 m (11 ft 9 in)

Area:

Wings, gross: 10-100, 10-200	8·92 m² (96·0 sq ft)

Weights and Loadings (10-100):

Weight empty	315 kg (695 lb)
Max T-O weight	567 kg (1,250 lb)
Max wing loading	63·5 kg/m² (13·0 lb/sq ft)
Max power loading	7·61 kg/kW (12·50 lb/hp)

Performance (10-100):

Max level speed	182 knots (337 km/h; 210 mph)
Cruising speed, 75% power	104 knots (193 km/h; 120 mph) IAS
Stalling speed: power off	46 knots (86 km/h; 53 mph)
power on	44 knots (81 km/h; 50 mph)
Max rate of climb at S/L	350 m (1,150 ft)/min
T-O run	180 m (590 ft)
Landing run	155 m (510 ft)
Range, 75% power	434 nm (804 km; 500 miles)
Best glide ratio	6·6
g limits	±8 operating

ULTRAFLIGHT

ULTRAFLIGHT SALES LTD

PO Box 370, Port Colborne, Ontario L3K 1B7
Telephone: (416) 735 8352
Telex: 061-5497
General Manager: Mrs Linda M. Kramer

ULTRAFLIGHT LAZAIR

The Lazair was designed by Mr Dale C. Kramer in 1978, making its first flight in November 1978. It is available in kit form for amateur construction or ready assembled. Sales were well in excess of 1,000 by January 1986.

The following description applies to the modified version introduced in the Spring of 1983, in which major changes include a wider-track main landing gear and twin tailwheels instead of the former non-steerable nosewheel. A convertible fully removable cockpit enclosure is available as an option. The Lazair is offered in three versions: **Series III** is the standard aircraft and is also available in **Series IIIEC** (enclosed cockpit) form with an enclosure of glassfibre reinforced plastic and a Lexan windscreen; **SS Surveillance Special** with two 17 kW (23 hp) KFM 107E engines, increased wing area, radios, lights, public address equipment for police duties and electric starting, also available in EC form; and the **Elite**, which is similar to the SS but, being intended for the recreational microlight pilot who requires a high performance aircraft, is powered by two 15 kW (20 hp) JPX PUL 425 engines. An EC version is available. The Lazair SS is in operation with the Monterey Park Police Department in California.

The Lazair SS is too heavy to be operated in the USA under ultralight regulations, the SS/EC cannot be operated in the USA or Canada under ultralight regulations, and the Elite EC is also too heavy for the US ultralight regulations.

The following data apply to the Lazair Series III, unless stated otherwise:

Type: Single-seat microlight aircraft.

Airframe: Braced high-wing monoplane, with inverted V tail unit. Wings have aluminium alloy D section leading-edge, with foam plastics ribs and upswept wingtips. Wings and tail surfaces are Tedlar covered. Three-axis control by ailerons and 'ruddervators'.

Landing Gear: Non-retractable tailwheel type, with 400 × 8 mainwheels, mainwheel speed fairings and twin castoring tailwheels. Toe operated mainwheel disc brakes. Twin-float and ski gear optional.

Power Plant: Two 7 kW (9·5 hp) 185 cc Rotax single-cylinder two-stroke engines, each with direct drive to a two-blade carbonfibre tractor propeller. Fuel tank capacity 19 litres (5 US gallons).

Accommodation: Pilot only, in open position or in enclosed cockpit.

Dimensions, external:

Wing span	11·07 m (36 ft 4 in)
Wing aspect ratio	9·3
Length overall: standard	4·27 m (14 ft 0 in)
EC versions	4·88 m (16 ft 0 in)
Height overall	1·93 m (6 ft 4 in)
Wheel track (mainwheels)	1·17 m (3 ft 10 in)
Propeller diameter:	
Series III/IIIEC	0·71 m (2 ft 4 in)
SS and SS/EC, and Elite/Elite EC	0·86 m (2 ft 10 in)

Areas:

Wings, gross: Series III	13·19 m² (142·0 sq ft)
SS and SS/EC	14·31 m² (154·0 sq ft)

Weights and Loadings (A: Series III; B: Series IIIEC, C: SS, D: SS/EC, E: Elite, F: Elite EC):

Weight empty: A	100 kg (220 lb)
B	115 kg (253 lb)
C	142 kg (314 lb)
D	156 kg (344 lb)
E	115 kg (254 lb)

F 130 kg (287 lb)
Max pilot weight: A 113·5 kg (250 lb)
Max T-O weight: A 208 kg (460 lb)
Max wing loading: A 15·77 kg/m² (3·24 lb/sq ft)
Max power loading: A 14·85 kg/kW (24·2 lb/hp)

PERFORMANCE (with 77 kg; 170 lb pilot, types as above):
Never-exceed speed:
A, B 54 knots (100 km/h; 62 mph)
C, D 65 knots (120 km/h; 75 mph)
E, F 61 knots (112 km/h; 70 mph)
Max level speed: A, B 53 knots (98 km/h; 61 mph)
C 65 knots (121 km/h; 75 mph)
D 69 knots (129 km/h; 80 mph)
E 54 knots (100 km/h; 62 mph)
F 58 knots (108 km/h; 67 mph)
Max cruising speed: A 35 knots (64 km/h; 40 mph)
B 43 knots (80 km/h; 50 mph)
C, F 52 knots (97 km/h; 60 mph)
D 56 knots (105 km/h; 65 mph)
E 48 knots (89 km/h; 55 mph)
Stalling speed: A 21 knots (39 km/h; 24 mph)
Max rate of climb at S/L: A, B 114 m (375 ft)/min
C, E 213 m (700 ft)/min
D, F 198 m (650 ft)/min
T-O run: A 37 m (120 ft)
B 41 m (135 ft)
C 26 m (85 ft)
D 34 m (110 ft)
E 18 m (60 ft)
F 23 m (75 ft)
Range with max fuel:
A more than 139 nm (257 km; 160 miles)
Endurance with max fuel: A 4 h
g limits: A +4/−1·3
B, C, D +4/−2
E +6·6/−2·8
F +6/−2·5
Best glide ratio at 19 knots (35 km/h; 22 mph):
A 13
Min rate of sink, power off:
A 70 m (230 ft)/min

ULTRAFLIGHT LAZAIR II

First flown on 10 November 1981, the Lazair II is a side by side two-seat version of the Lazair, intended primarily for training, with dual controls. The first Lazair II was registered in Canada in January 1984. A number of production aircraft are now flying. These aircraft are powered by JPX PUL 425 engines. KFM 107E engines of 17 kW (23 hp) each, with electric starting, are available as an option, with which the aircraft is known as the **Lazair II EL**.

The following data apply to the Lazair II, unless stated otherwise:

TYPE: Two-seat microlight aircraft.

POWER PLANT: Two 15 kW (20 hp) JPX PUL 425 two-cylinder two-stroke engines, each with direct drive to a two-blade wooden propeller. Fuel tank capacity 19 litres (5 US gallons).

ACCOMMODATION: Two seats side by side in open position. Dual controls.

DIMENSIONS, EXTERNAL:
Wing span 11·58 m (38 ft 0 in)
Length overall 4·27 m (14 ft 0 in)
Height overall 1·93 m (6 ft 4 in)
Propeller diameter 0·86 m (2 ft 10 in)

AREA:
Wings, gross 14·03 m² (151·0 sq ft)

WEIGHTS AND LOADINGS (A: Lazair II, B: Lazair II EL):
Weight empty: A 130 kg (287 lb)
B 150 kg (330 lb)
Max T-O weight: A 329 kg (725 lb)
Max wing loading: A 23·44 kg/m² (4·8 lb/sq ft)
Max power loading: A 7·34 kg/kW (12·08 lb/hp)

PERFORMANCE (A: Lazair II, B: Lazair II EL; 77 kg; 170 lb pilot):
Never-exceed speed:
A, B 47 knots (88 km/h; 55 mph)
Max level speed: A 47 knots (88 km/h; 55 mph)
Cruising speed: A 35 knots (64 km/h; 40 mph)
B 39 knots (72 km/h; 45 mph)
Stalling speed: A 22 knots (41 km/h; 25 mph)
Max rate of climb at S/L: A 110 m (360 ft)/min
B 137 m (450 ft)/min
T-O run: A 91 m (300 ft)
B 76 m (250 ft)
g limits: A, B +4/−2

ULTRAVIA

ULTRAVIA AERO INC

795 L'Assomption, Repentigny (Montreal), Quebec J6A 5H5
Telephone: (514) 585 6132
Telex: 05 268897
VICE-PRESIDENT: Mrs Lorraine Chauvin

ULTRAVIA LE PELICAN and LONGNOSE PELICAN

Designed by M Jean-René Lepage, Le Pelican flew for the first time in May 1982 and is produced in plan, kit and parts form for amateur construction, or ready to fly. More powerful models, the Super Pelican and LongNose Pelican, were introduced in the Autumn of 1983 and in 1984 respectively. The LongNose Pelican is structurally identical to Le Pelican and the following description is applicable to both models unless otherwise specified:

TYPE: Single-seat microlight aircraft, designed to FAR Pt 23 standards; conforms to FAR Pt 103 and TCAR Section 101.

AIRFRAME: Braced high-wing monoplane, built of aircraft grade aluminium alloy, with D-cell wing leading-edge, composite foam/aluminium wing ribs, one-piece glassfibre engine cowling, and Dacron covering. Full three-axis control by differential ailerons, elevators and rudder. Wings and horizontal tail detachable for transportation and storage.

LANDING GEAR: Non-retractable tailwheel type. Spring steel main legs. Mainwheels size 4·8 × 8; steerable tailwheel of 5 in diameter. Brakes, floats and skis optional.

POWER PLANT: Original Le Pelican has one 15·7 kW (21 hp) Briggs and Stratton 42CL four-stroke flat-twin engine, with direct drive to a two-blade wooden propeller. LongNose has one 20 kW (27 hp) Rotax 277 two-stroke engine with 2·6:1 reduction drive to a two-blade wooden propeller. Removable (portable) fuel tank behind pilot's seat, capacity 19 litres (5 US gallons).

ACCOMMODATION: Single seat in semi-enclosed cabin (open at sides) standard; cabin doors optional.

DIMENSIONS, EXTERNAL:
Wing span 10·67 m (35 ft 0 in)
Wing aspect ratio 9
Length overall 4·57 m (15 ft 0 in)
Height overall 1·98 m (6 ft 6 in)
Propeller diameter: Le Pelican 1·22 m (4 ft 0 in)
LongNose 1·83 m (6 ft 0 in)

AREA:
Wings, gross 12·63 m² (136·0 sq ft)

WEIGHTS AND LOADINGS:
Weight empty 113 kg (250 lb)
Pilot weight range 45-113 kg (100-250 lb)
Max T-O weight 238 kg (525 lb)
Max wing loading 19·0 kg/m² (3·9 lb/sq ft)
Max power loading:
Le Pelican 15·16 kg/kW (25·0 lb/hp)
LongNose 11·33 kg/kW (18·75 lb/hp)

PERFORMANCE (with 79 kg; 175 lb pilot):
Never-exceed speed 78 knots (145 km/h; 90 mph)
Max level speed 56 knots (105 km/h; 65 mph)
Max cruising speed 48 knots (88 km/h; 55 mph)
Econ cruising speed 43 knots (80 km/h; 50 mph)
Stalling speed:
power on 21 knots (39 km/h; 24 mph)
power off 24 knots (45 km/h; 27·5 mph)
Max rate of climb at S/L:
Le Pelican 152 m (500 ft)/min
LongNose 274 m (900 ft)/min
Service ceiling 4,575 m (15,000 ft)
T-O and landing run (typical) 30 m (100 ft)
Range with max fuel:
Le Pelican 217 nm (402 km; 250 miles)
LongNose 130 nm (241 km; 150 miles)
Endurance with max fuel: Le Pelican 5 h
LongNose 3 h
g limits +4/−2 normal
+6/−3 ultimate
Best glide ratio 12
Min rate of sink, power off 76 m (250 ft)/min

ULTRAVIA SUPER PELICAN

The Super Pelican is externally and structurally identical to the original Le Pelican and the LongNose Pelican. Specifications, where different from LongNose Pelican, are as follows:

POWER PLANT: One 26 kW (35 hp) Global four-stroke flat-twin engine, with larger diameter propeller.

DIMENSIONS, EXTERNAL:
Propeller diameter 1·47 m (4 ft 10 in)

LOADING:
Max power loading 9·15 kg/kW (15 lb/hp)

PERFORMANCE (with 79 kg; 175 lb pilot):
Max level speed 65 knots (121 km/h; 75 mph)
Max cruising speed 61 knots (113 km/h; 70 mph)
Econ cruising speed 56 knots (105 km/h; 65 mph)
Max rate of climb at S/L 290 m (950 ft)/min
T-O run (typical) 15 m (50 ft)
Endurance with max fuel 4 h

ULTRAVIA PELICAN CLUB

The two-seat Pelican Club is available in two forms, as a microlight conforming to Canadian regulations and as an Experimental category homebuilt.

Design of the Pelican Club began in 1983 and construction of the prototype started in the following year. This flew for the first time in Spring 1985. Kits became available in Summer 1985; 25 kits had been delivered by April 1986, from which twelve aircraft had been completed.

TYPE: Two-seat recreational aircraft: conforms to ANO 95-22 and FAR Pt 103 in microlight form and to Experimental regulations in homebuilt form.

AIRFRAME: Strut braced high-wing monoplane. Wing section NACA 6315. Vacuum moulded composite monocoque fuselage of glassfibre/epoxy/Clark foam construction; aluminium alloy wings and conventional braced tail unit, with double surface Dacron covering. Ailerons and flaps are covered with fabric on microlight model, with aluminium alloy on homebuilt version. Three-axis control (ailerons, elevators and horn-balanced rudder).

LANDING GEAR: Non-retractable tailwheel type. Spring steel main legs, with glassfibre fairings. Mainwheels size 6·00-6. Steerable tailwheel. Optional brakes. Floats and skis optional. Tricycle gear being developed as an option.

POWER PLANT: Microlight model: One 30 kW (40 hp) Rotax 447 two-cylinder two-stroke engine, with 2·58:1 reduction drive to a two-blade wooden propeller with spinner. Experimental model: One 38·8 kW (52 hp) Rotax 503 two-cylinder two-stroke engine, with 2·58:1 reduction gearbox to a two-blade wooden propeller with spinner. Fuel capacity 38 litres (10 US gallons).

ACCOMMODATION: Two seats side by side in fully enclosed cabin, with removable door on each side. Dual controls. Experimental version has baggage space aft of seats, capacity 22·7 kg (50 lb). Heating and bubble doors optional.

SYSTEM: Optional electric starting.

DIMENSIONS, EXTERNAL:
Wing span: Microlight 10·67 m (35 ft 0 in)
Experimental 10·06 m (33 ft 0 in)
Wing aspect ratio: Microlight 7·9
Length overall 5·94 m (19 ft 6 in)
Height overall 2·54 m (8 ft 4 in)
Tailplane span 2·90 m (9 ft 6 in)
Wheelbase 1·83 m (6 ft 0 in)
Propeller diameter:
Microlight 1·52 m (5 ft 0 in)
Experimental 1·73 m (5 ft 8 in)

AREAS: (A: Microlight, B: Experimental):
Wings, gross: A 14·49 m² (156·0 sq ft)
B 13·47 m² (145·0 sq ft)

WEIGHTS AND LOADINGS (A: Microlight, B: Experimental):
Weight empty: A 170 kg (375 lb)
B 181 kg (400 lb)
Crew weight range: A 45·5-181 kg (100-400 lb)
B 45·5-204 kg (100-450 lb)
Max T-O weight: A 374 kg (825 lb)
B 431 kg (950 lb)
Max wing loading: A 25·83 kg/m² (5·29 lb/sq ft)
B 32·0 kg/m² (6·55 lb/sq ft)
Max power loading: A 14·37 kg/kW (20·63 lb/hp)
B 11·11 kg/kW (18·27 lb/hp)

PERFORMANCE (A and B as above):
Never-exceed speed: A 87 knots (161 km/h; 100 mph)
B 112 knots (209 km/h; 130 mph)
Max level speed: A 74 knots (137 km/h; 85 mph)
B 96 knots (177 km/h; 110 mph)
Max cruising speed: A 65 knots (121 km/h; 75 mph)
B 82 knots (153 km/h; 95 mph)
Econ cruising speed: A 61 knots (113 km/h; 70 mph)
B 75 knots (138 km/h; 86 mph)
Stalling speed:
A, power on 22 knots (41 km/h; 25 mph) IAS
B, power off 32 knots (58 km/h; 36 mph)
Max rate of climb at S/L:
A, at AUW of 340 kg (750 lb) 175 m (580 ft)/min
B 549 m (1,800 ft)/min
Service ceiling:
A, at AUW of 340 kg (750 lb) 3,960 m (13,000 ft)
B 3,960-4,575 m (13,000-15,000 ft)
T-O run: A 46 m (150 ft)
B 31-76 m (100-250 ft)
T-O to 15 m (50 ft): B 152 m (500 ft)
Landing run (without brakes): A 61 m (200 ft)
Range with max fuel: A, B 260 nm (483 km; 300 miles)
Endurance with max fuel: A 6 h
g limits: A +4/−2

VENTURE

VENTURE FLIGHT DESIGN INC

20 Bryson Drive, Richmond Hill, Ontario L4C 6E3
Telephone: (416) 889 5434
PRESIDENT: Brian Eggleston

Details of the Venture Flight Design S1 Solarwind microlight, and an illustration, appeared in the 1985-86 *Jane's*. It has not flown during the past year, but may be retrofitted with a more powerful engine eventually.

Two-seat Lazair II with JPX PUL 425 engines

Lazair Series III microlight with optional cockpit enclosure *(Howard Levy)*

Ultravia Pelican Club homebuilt aircraft *(Howard Levy)*

Ultravia LongNose Pelican

Ultravia Pelican Club with float landing gear

Prototype Western PGK-1 Hirondelle two-seat light aircraft

WESTERN

WESTERN AIRCRAFT SUPPLIES

623 Markerville Road NE, Calgary, Alberta T2E 5X1
Telephone: (403) 276 3087
DIRECTOR: Jean J. Peters

In addition to marketing materials for amateur aircraft constructors, Western Aircraft Supplies has developed an aircraft known as the PGK-1 Hirondelle. Plans and wood kits are available to amateur constructors, as well as preformed engine cowlings, windscreens and fuel tanks. Five sets of plans and five kits were sold in 1985.

WESTERN PGK-1 HIRONDELLE

Design of the PGK-1 Hirondelle began in 1969 and construction of a prototype (C-GWYL) started in July 1970. First flight occurred on 27 June 1976. It is said to be suited for cross-country and recreational flying, and simple enough for first-time constructors to build. All fabric covering is glued in place, rather than stitched.

TYPE: Two-seat homebuilt aircraft.

AIRFRAME: Cantilever low-wing monoplane of constant chord. Wing section NACA 23012. Dihedral 4° from roots. Incidence 4° at root, 2° at tip. No sweepback. Wooden box spar and plank type auxiliary rear spar. Plywood ribs. Dacron covered, with dope and polyurethane finish. Ailerons of wood and fabric construction. No flaps or tabs. Conventional fuselage of spruce bulkheads and spruce longerons, plywood covered to rear of cabin, with outer covering of Dacron. Cabin constructed of wood formers with polystyrene foam infill and glassfibre top. Rounded corners of turtledeck formed from foam and glassfibre. Rear fuselage Dacron covered, with dope and polyurethane finish. Cantilever tail structure of capped spars and plywood ribs, all plywood covered and with outer covering of Dacron. Tab in starboard elevator.

LANDING GEAR: Non-retractable tailwheel type. Tapered spring steel main struts; 5·00-5 tyres on mainwheels. Industrial Dynamics brakes. Cessna 150 mainwheel fairings.

POWER PLANT: One 86 kW (115 hp) Avco Lycoming O-235-C1B flat-four engine, driving a Warnke three-blade ground adjustable propeller. Two glassfibre fuel tanks in leading-edges of wings, each 54·5 litres (12 Imp gallons) capacity. Oil capacity 5·7 litres (1·25 Imp gallons).

ACCOMMODATION: Two seats side by side in enclosed cabin. Dual controls and heater standard.

SYSTEM: Electrical system includes 12V 20A generator for lights, radio and fuel pump.

AVIONICS: Genave Alpha 200B radio and VOR.

DIMENSIONS, EXTERNAL:
- Wing span: 7·92 m (26 ft 0 in)
- Wing chord, constant: 1·40 m (4 ft 7 in)
- Wing aspect ratio: 5·7
- Length overall: 6·27 m (20 ft 7 in)
- Height overall: 2·29 m (7 ft 6 in)
- Wheel track: 2·03 m (6 ft 8 in)
- Wheelbase: 4·39 m (14 ft 5 in)
- Propeller diameter: 1·68 m (5 ft 6 in)

AREA:
- Wings, gross: 10·96 m² (118·0 sq ft)

WEIGHTS AND LOADINGS:
- Weight empty, equipped: 428 kg (944 lb)
- Max T-O weight: 669 kg (1,475 lb)
- Max wing loading: 61·0 kg/m² (12·5 lb/sq ft)
- Max power loading: 7·78 kg/kW (12·83 lb/hp)

PERFORMANCE (at max T-O weight):
- Never-exceed speed: 160 knots (297 km/h; 185 mph)
- Max level speed: 123 knots (228 km/h; 142 mph)
- Max cruising speed: 117 knots (217 km/h; 135 mph)
- Stalling speed: 53 knots (97 km/h; 60 mph)
- Max rate of climb at S/L: over 305 m (1,000 ft)/min
- Service ceiling: 3,840 m (12,600 ft)
- T-O run: approx 228 m (750 ft)
- Endurance, with 45 min reserves: 3 h 36 min

ZENAIR

ZENAIR LTD

King Road, Nobleton, Ontario L0G 1N0
Telephone: (416) 859 4556
PRESIDENT AND DESIGNER: Christophe Heintz

M Heintz, a professional aeronautical engineer, participated in the design of several of the aircraft produced by Avions Pierre Robin. While in France, he also designed and built the prototype of a two-seat light aircraft named the Zénith, intended for amateur construction. More than 200 Zéniths are now flying, and others are under construction, including single-seat and three-seat models, as described in this entry. In addition, Mr Heintz' Zenair company developed the four-seat Zénith-CH 400 for factory production (see main Aircraft section of the 1985-86 *Jane's*).

In 1974 the Zénith-CH 200 was granted the National Association of Sport Aircraft Designers (NASAD, USA) 'seal of quality' No. 108. In 1979 the Mono Z-CH 100 and Tri-Z CH 300 were granted NASAD 'seals of quality' Nos. 115 and 116 respectively; the Mono Z-CH 100, Zénith-CH 200 and CH 250, and Tri-Z CH 300 were granted NASAD kit 'seals of quality' Nos. 301, 302 and 303 respectively.

Zenair Ltd has fifteen full-time employees. Subsidiary manufacturing and distributing companies are Zenair Atlanta Inc (Georgia, USA), Zenair Seattle Inc (Washington, USA), Zenair California (Escondido, California) and Agricopteros (Cali, Colombia). Zenair itself markets plans, component parts and kits for the Colomban MC 12 Cricri (Cricket) twin-engined lightplane, described in the French section, and has sold approximately 100 kits, each complete with two 11·2 kW (15 hp) PUL 212 engines. The company also offers a range of microlight aircraft under the collective name of Zipper.

ZENAIR MONO Z-CH 100

The single-seat Mono Z-CH 100 is of generally similar all-metal construction to the two-seat Zénith, but is slightly smaller overall and is designed to be powered by engines in the 33·5 to 74·5 kW (45 to 100 hp) range. A forward sliding canopy and float kit are not available optionally on this model. The prototype (C-GNYM), which has a Volkswagen engine, made its first flight on 8 May 1975.

Construction drawings and manual, materials, parts and complete kits to build the Mono Zénith are available from Zenair, and at least 130 sets had been sold by early 1986. Building time is estimated at under 600 working hours.

TYPE: Single-seat homebuilt aircraft.

AIRFRAME: Cantilever low-wing monoplane. Wing section GAW-1 (modified). Thickness/chord ratio 15%. Dihedral 6°. Incidence 7° 30′. Single-spar aluminium alloy structure, with aluminium alloy skin, blind riveted. Aluminium alloy piano hinged ailerons. Wings easily removable. Conventional aluminium alloy stressed skin fuselage of basically rectangular section, with rounded top-decking. Single-spar tail unit structures, with ribs and skins of aluminium. Rectangular one-piece all-moving tailplane, with automatic and controllable trim tab.

LANDING GEAR: Non-retractable tricycle type, with rubber block shock absorbers. Tailwheel gear optional. All three Cleveland wheels and tyres size 5·00-5. Hydraulically actuated disc brakes.

POWER PLANT: One 41 kW (55 hp) 1,700 cc converted Volkswagen motorcar engine in prototype, driving a Zenair wooden propeller. Engines from 33·5 kW (45 hp) 1,600 cc Volkswagen to 74·5 kW (100 hp) Continental O-200 optional. Fuel tank in fuselage, capacity 55 litres (12 Imp gallons).

ACCOMMODATION: Single seat under Plexiglas canopy. Baggage compartment aft of seat, capacity 11·3 kg (25 lb).

DIMENSIONS, EXTERNAL:
Wing span 6·71 m (22 ft 0 in)
Wing chord, constant 1·27 m (4 ft 2 in)
Wing aspect ratio 5·28
Length overall 5·94 m (19 ft 6 in)
Height overall 1·98 m (6 ft 6 in)
Tailplane span 2·26 m (7 ft 5 in)
Wheel track 2·13 m (7 ft 0 in)
Wheelbase 1·17 m (3 ft 10 in)
Propeller diameter 1·47 m (4 ft 10 in)

AREA:
Wings, gross 8·50 m² (91·5 sq ft)

WEIGHTS AND LOADINGS (A: 33·5 kW; 45 hp, B: 48·5 kW; 65 hp, C: 74·5 kW; 100 hp engine):
Weight empty: A 263 kg (580 lb)
B 286 kg (630 lb)
C 295 kg (650 lb)
Max T-O weight: A 413 kg (910 lb)
B 435 kg (960 lb)
C 444 kg (980 lb)
Max wing loading: A 48·6 kg/m² (9·95 lb/sq ft)
B 51·2 kg/m² (10·49 lb/sq ft)
C 52·3 kg/m² (10·71 lb/sq ft)
Max power loading: A 12·33 kg/kW (20·22 lb/hp)
B 8·97 kg/kW (14·77 lb/hp)
C 5·96 kg/kW (9·80 lb/hp)

PERFORMANCE (A, B and C as above):
Max level speed; A 103 knots (190 km/h; 118 mph)
B 109 knots (200 km/h; 125 mph)
C 130 knots (240 km/h; 150 mph)
Cruising speed (75% power):
A 91 knots (170 km/h; 105 mph)
B 95 knots (177 km/h; 110 mph)
C 118 knots (218 km/h; 135 mph)
Stalling speed: A 41 knots (76 km/h; 47 mph)
B, C 42 knots (77 km/h; 48 mph)
Max rate of climb at S/L: A 200 m (610 ft)/min
B 250 m (820 ft)/min
C 490 m (1,500 ft)/min
Service ceiling: A 3,050 m (10,000 ft)
B over 3,660 m (12,000 ft)
T-O and landing run: A 229 m (750 ft)
B 168 m (550 ft)
T-O to 15 m (50 ft): A 427 m (1,400 ft)
B 305 m (1,000 ft)
Range with 55 litres (12 Imp gallons) fuel:
A 365 nm (676 km; 420 miles)
B 350 nm (645 km; 400 miles)
C 304 nm (563 km; 350 miles)
g limits ±9 ultimate

ZENAIR ACRO-ZÉNITH CH 150

Developed from the Mono Z-CH 100, the design of this initial version of the Acro-Zénith began in 1979 and the prototype made its first flight on 19 May 1980. The aircraft is intended for aerobatic training and competition flying, with engines of 74·5-134 kW (100-180 hp) and fuel and oil systems equipped for inverted flight. Kits, complete except for engine and tyres, are available to amateur constructors, and by March 1986 twenty-five had been delivered, of which twelve have been completed. All of the more critical parts, such as wing spars and ribs, are premanufactured.

TYPE: Single-seat homebuilt aircraft.

AIRFRAME: Cantilever low-wing monoplane. Wing section NACA 0015. Dihedral 6°. Airframe of duralumin construction, with semi-monocoque fuselage and conventional ailerons, rudder and all-moving tailplane with trim tab.

LANDING GEAR: Non-retractable tailwheel type, with spring mainwheel legs. Mainwheel tyres size 5·00-5, pressure 1·38 bars (20 lb/sq in). Solid tailwheel. Brakes. Skis optional.

POWER PLANT: One 112 kW (150 hp) Avco Lycoming O-320 flat-four engine standard, driving a Zenair two-blade wooden propeller. Fuel tank capacity 55 litres (12 Imp gallons). Can be increased to 136 litres (30 Imp gallons) by use of ferry tank. Fuel and oil systems equipped for inverted flight. Engines of 74·5-134 kW (100-180 hp) can be fitted.

ACCOMMODATION: Pilot only, in enclosed cockpit, under bubble canopy. Baggage capacity 20 kg (44 lb). Cockpit long enough to allow room for parachute. Heated and ventilated.

SYSTEM: Electrical system as required.

AVIONICS: Radio and other equipment as required.

DIMENSIONS, EXTERNAL:
Wing span 6·15 m (20 ft 2 in)
Wing chord, constant 1·27 m (4 ft 2 in)
Wing aspect ratio 4·85
Length overall 6·17 m (20 ft 3 in)
Height overall 1·52 m (5 ft 0 in)
Tailplane span 2·26 m (7 ft 5 in)
Wheel track 1·47 m (4 ft 10 in)
Wheelbase 4·27 m (14 ft 0 in)
Propeller diameter 1·78 m (5 ft 10 in)

AREA:
Wings, gross 7·83 m² (84·3 sq ft)

WEIGHTS AND LOADINGS (A: 86 kW; 115 hp O-235, B: 112 kW; 150 hp O-320, C: 134 kW; 180 hp IO-360 engine. Wooden propeller and ferry tank fitted. No electrics):
Weight empty: A 327 kg (720 lb)
B 331 kg (730 lb)
C 345 kg (760 lb)
Typical aerobatic T-O weight: A 435 kg (960 lb)
B 440 kg (970 lb)
C 454 kg (1,000 lb)
Max T-O weight: B 522 kg (1,150 lb)
Max wing loading: B 66·6 kg/m² (13·64 lb/sq ft)
Max power loading: B 4·66 kg/kW (7·67 lb/hp)

PERFORMANCE (A, B and C as above):
Never-exceed speed:
B 208 knots (386 km/h; 240 mph)
Max level speed at S/L:
B 156 knots (290 km/h; 180 mph)
Max cruising speed at 915 m (3,000 ft):
A 130 knots (241 km/h; 150 mph)
B 139 knots (257 km/h; 160 mph)
C 149 knots (277 km/h; 172 mph)
Econ cruising speed at 915 m (3,000 ft):
B 126 knots (233 km/h; 145 mph)
Stalling speed: A 47 knots (87 km/h; 54 mph)
B 48 knots (89 km/h; 55 mph)
C 49 knots (90 km/h; 56 mph)
Max rate of climb at S/L: A 427 m (1,400 ft)/min
B 670 m (2,200 ft)/min
C 792 m (2,600 ft)/min
Service ceiling: A over 3,660 m (12,000 ft)
B, C over 4,875 m (16,000 ft)
T-O run: B 213 m (700 ft)
T-O to 15 m (50 ft): B 396 m (1,300 ft)
Landing from 15 m (50 ft): B 396 m (1,300 ft)
Landing run: B 183 m (600 ft)
Range with standard fuel:
B 260 nm (483 km; 300 miles)
Range at 55% power, with ferry fuel:
A 807 nm (1,496 km; 930 miles)
B 660 nm (1,223 km; 760 miles)
C 608 nm (1,126 km; 700 miles)
Endurance: B 2 h
g limits ±12 ultimate

ZENAIR SUPER ACRO-ZÉNITH CH 180

The first Super Acro-Zénith CH 180 (C-GZEN) was an unlimited aerobatic aircraft, powered by a 171·5 kW (230 hp) Avco Lycoming IO-360 engine. It differed from the Acro-Zénith CH 150 in several respects, apart from engine, the most obvious external changes being a revised tail unit and wings without dihedral. The front fuel tank capacity is 45·5 litres (10 Imp gallons) and the rear, with header, 77 litres (17 Imp gallons).

The CH 180 is marketed exclusively by Aerovol of 2689A Sandalwood Drive, Ottawa, Ontario K1V 7P4. Eight kits had been delivered by March 1986, of which two had been completed. Construction time is 800 working hours. Engines of up to 149 kW (200 hp) can be fitted.

DIMENSIONS, EXTERNAL:
Wing span 6·15 m (20 ft 2 in)
Length overall 6·17 m (20 ft 3 in)
Height overall 1·65 m (5 ft 5 in)

AREA:
Wings, gross 7·90 m² (85·0 sq ft)

WEIGHTS AND LOADINGS:
Weight empty 363 kg (800 lb)
Max T-O weight 521 kg (1,150 lb)
Max wing loading 66·1 kg/m² (13·53 lb/sq ft)
Max power loading (200 hp) 3·50 kg/kW (5·75 lb/hp)

PERFORMANCE (149 kW; 200 hp engine):
Never-exceed speed 226 knots (418 km/h; 260 mph)
Cruising speed (75% power)
165 knots (305 km/h; 190 mph)
Stalling speed 42 knots (77 km/h; 48 mph)
Max rate of climb at S/L 915 m (3,000 ft)/min
Max rate of roll 270°/s
Range with max fuel, 55% power (123 litres; 27 Imp gallons of fuel) 565 nm (1,046 km; 650 miles)
g limits: ±8 normal
±12 ultimate

ZENAIR ZÉNITH-CH 200

Work on the Zénith-CH 200 began in October 1968. The prototype, registered F-WPZY (later C-FEYC), flew for the first time on 22 March 1970 and was granted French CNRA (homebuilt experimental aircraft) certification. In October 1970 the original wing of NACA 64A315 (modified) section was replaced by one offering improved low-speed characteristics.

Sets of plans and a constructional manual for the Zénith-CH 200 are available to amateur builders, as follows:

French manual with metric measurements from D. Triques, 23 Ave Edouard Belin, Fontaine d'Ouche, F21 Dijon, France.

English manual and drawings to US standards, with Imperial and metric measurements, from Zenair, which offers materials, parts and complete kits for all current Heintz designs. Zenair also designs and manufactures wooden propellers for engines of up to 134 kW (180 hp).

The Zénith-CH 200 is approved by the Australian DCA and the New Zealand airworthiness authorities. Several kits have been exported to these countries, as well as to 40 other countries, including Belgium, Botswana, Colombia, Iceland, Ireland, New Guinea, Norway, South Africa, Spain, Sweden, Switzerland and the UK. By March 1986 a total of 282 kits and 800 sets of plans for the CH 200 and generally similar CH 250 (which see) had been sold; 120 kits had been assembled and 28 aircraft built from plans.

The following description applies to the standard Zénith-CH 200:

TYPE: Two-seat homebuilt aircraft.

AIRFRAME: Cantilever low-wing monoplane. Constant chord wings, of NACA 64A515 (modified) section, are optionally detachable. Dihedral 6° from roots. Single-spar aluminium alloy structure, with blind riveted aluminium alloy skin. Hoerner wingtips. Aluminium alloy piano hinged ailerons and electrically actuated plain flaps on trailing-edge. Conventional aluminium alloy stressed skin fuselage, of basically rectangular section with rounded top decking. Glassfibre engine cowling and fairings. Rectangular one-piece all-moving tailplane, with combined trim and anti-servo tabs. Plans show rudder only, with slight sweepback. Conventional fin and rudder can be fitted if desired. Tailplane and rudder are both single-spar structures with ribs and skin of aluminium alloy. Removable wings available optionally.

LANDING GEAR: Non-retractable tricycle type (tailwheel gear optional), with three identical legs. Rubber block shock absorbers. Steerable nosewheel. All three Cleveland wheels and tyres size 6·00-6. Hydraulically actuated disc brakes on main units. Streamline glassfibre fairings over all three wheels and legs. Float kits and skis are optional.

POWER PLANT: Design suitable for engines from 63·5 kW (85 hp) to 119 kW (160 hp), depending upon economy,

Zenair Mono Z-CH 100 (41 kW; 55 hp Volkswagen engine)

Zenair Acro-Zénith CH 150 single-seat aerobatic and competition aircraft (112 kW; 150 hp Avco Lycoming O-320)

Super Acro-Zénith CH 180 unlimited aerobatic aircraft *(Neil A. Macdougall)*

Zenair Zénith-CH 250M used in Colombia as a fully aerobatic military trainer

Zenair Zénith-CH 200 with float landing gear

cross country flying or aerobatic priority. Fuel tank in fuselage, aft of seats, capacity 90 litres (20 Imp gallons). Optional fuel tanks in wing leading-edges, total capacity 72·5 litres (16 Imp gallons). Refuelling point aft of canopy on port side.

ACCOMMODATION: Side by side seating for pilot and one passenger under sideways opening (to starboard) Plexiglas canopy. Forward sliding canopy optional. Dual controls, with single control column located centrally between seats. Space for 35 kg (77 lb) of baggage aft of seats. Cabin heated and ventilated.

SYSTEMS: 12V battery and generator provide power for engine starting, fuel pump and flap actuation. VHF radio.

DIMENSIONS, EXTERNAL:

Wing span	7·00 m (22 ft 11¾ in)
Wing chord, constant	1·40 m (4 ft 7 in)
Wing aspect ratio	5
Length overall	6·25 m (20 ft 6 in)
Height overall	2·11 m (6 ft 11 in)
Tailplane span	2·30 m (7 ft 6½ in)
Wheel track	2·25 m (7 ft 4½ in)
Wheelbase	1·42 m (4 ft 8 in)
Propeller diameter	1·83 m (6 ft 0 in)

AREA:

Wings, gross	9·80 m² (105·9 sq ft)

WEIGHTS AND LOADINGS (A: 74·5 kW; 100 hp engine, B: 93 kW; 125 hp engine, C: 112 kW; 150 hp engine):

Weight empty: A	408 kg (900 lb)
B	422 kg (930 lb)
C	440 kg (970 lb)
Max T-O weight: A	658 kg (1,450 lb)
B, C	680 kg (1,500 lb)
Max wing loading: A	66·8 kg/m² (13·69 lb/sq ft)
B, C	69·1 kg/m² (14·16 lb/sq ft)
Max power loading: A	8·83 kg/kW (14·50 lb/hp)
B	7·31 kg/kW (12·00 lb/hp)
C	6·07 kg/kW (10·00 lb/hp)

PERFORMANCE (at max T-O weight. A/B/C as above):

Max level speed at S/L:	
A	128 knots (237 km/h; 147 mph)
B	131 knots (243 km/h; 151 mph)
C	145 knots (269 km/h; 167 mph)
Cruising speed (75% power) at S/L:	
A	113 knots (209 km/h; 130 mph)
B	122 knots (227 km/h; 141 mph)
C	132 knots (245 km/h; 152 mph)
Stalling speed, flaps down:	
A	45 knots (84 km/h; 52 mph)
B	47 knots (87 km/h; 54 mph)
C	46 knots (85 km/h; 53 mph)
Max rate of climb at S/L: A	244 m (800 ft)/min
B	335 m (1,100 ft)/min
C	518 m (1,700 ft)/min
Service ceiling: A	4,600 m (15,100 ft)
C	over 4,875 m (16,000 ft)
T-O and landing run: A, B	244 m (800 ft)
C	183 m (600 ft)
T-O to 15 m (50 ft): A	457 m (1,500 ft)
B	427 m (1,400 ft)
C	305 m (1,000 ft)
Range with max fuel:	
A	451 nm (837 km; 520 miles)
B	391 nm (724 km; 450 miles)
C	347 nm (643 km; 400 miles)
g limit	+9 ultimate

ZENAIR ZÉNITH-CH 250

The Zénith-CH 250 is a de luxe version of the Zénith-CH 200 with two 65 litre (14 Imp gallon) fuel tanks in the wings and a 0·71 m³ (25 cu ft) baggage area. A forward sliding canopy and rear windows similar to those of the Tri-Z CH 300 are fitted. Recommended engines are in the 86-119 kW (115-160 hp) range. A tailwheel type or float landing gear can be fitted as alternatives to the standard tricycle type. The number of kits and plans sold to construct the CH 250, and the number flying, are included in the totals for the CH 200 (which see).

WEIGHTS AND LOADINGS (A: 93 kW; 125 hp engine, B: 112 kW; 150 hp engine):

Weight empty: A	431 kg (950 lb)
B	449 kg (990 lb)
Max T-O weight: A	703 kg (1,550 lb)
B	730 kg (1,610 lb)
Max wing loading: A	71·5 kg/m² (14·64 lb/sq ft)
B	74·2 kg/m² (15·20 lb/sq ft)
Max power loading: A	7·56 kg/kW (12·40 lb/hp)
B	6·52 kg/kW (10·73 lb/hp)

PERFORMANCE (A and B as above):

Max level speed: A	130 knots (241 km/h; 150 mph)
B	144 knots (267 km/h; 166 mph)
Cruising speed (75% power):	
A	122 knots (225 km/h; 140 mph)
B	130 knots (241 km/h; 150 mph)
Stalling speed: A	46 knots (86 km/h; 53 mph)
B	45 knots (84 km/h; 52 mph)
Max rate of climb at S/L: A	305 m (1,000 ft)/min
B	518 m (1,700 ft)/min
T-O and landing run: A	259 m (850 ft)
B	198 m (650 ft)
T-O to 15 m (50 ft): A	457 m (1,500 ft)
B	344 m (1,130 ft)
Range with standard fuel:	
A	521 nm (965 km; 600 miles)
B	469 nm (869 km; 540 miles)

ZENAIR TRI-Z CH 300

The three-seat Tri-Z CH 300 is a 'stretched' version of the two-seat CH 200, with a longer fuselage and enlarged cabin, to provide room for a rear bench seat able to carry a third adult, two children or 95 kg (210 lb) of baggage. It has a greater wing span and larger tailplane; a fin and rudder assembly is standard. The ailerons are aerodynamically balanced, and electrically actuated slotted flaps are fitted. Recommended power is in the 93-134 kW (125-180 hp) range. Fuel is carried in two 65 litre (14 Imp gallon) tanks, one in each wing leading-edge. Extra fuel can be carried in similar tanks installed in the outer wing sections. A forward sliding canopy is standard.

The prototype (C-GQTR), built by Harold Allsop of Toronto and powered by a 112 kW (150 hp) Avco Lycoming O-320 engine, made its first flight on 9 July 1977.

Sets of plans and a constructional manual for the Tri-Z CH 300 are available to amateur builders (782 had been sold by March 1986), as are materials, prefabricated component parts and complete kits (320 sold by March 1986). At that time, 105 kit built and 42 plans built Tri-Zs had been completed. Construction from kits takes 1,000 working hours on average.

A Tri-Z CH 300 (C-GOVK) was built by Robin 'Red' Morris, Gerry Boudreau and Doug Holtby in a little over six months, including modifications to the fuel system to provide 773 litres (170 Imp gallons) of fuel in two fuselage and six wing tanks. Max T-O weight of this aircraft is 1,134 kg (2,500 lb), with a 134 kW (180 hp) Avco Lycoming O-360-2F engine and full IFR equipment. It was flown non-stop by 'Red' Morris from Vancouver International Airport to Halifax International Airport between 1 July and 2 July 1978, covering approximately 2,397 nm (4,440 km; 2,759 miles) in a flying time of 22 h 44 min. This set FAI Class C1c records between Vancouver and North Bay (103·831 knots; 192·295 km/h; 119·487 mph); Vancouver and Winnipeg (109·977 knots; 203·678 km/h; 126·560 mph); and Vancouver and Halifax (105·344 knots; 195·097 km/h; 121·228 mph).

DIMENSIONS, EXTERNAL:
- Wing span: 8·10 m (26 ft 6¾ in)
- Wing chord, constant: 1·48 m (4 ft 10½ in)
- Wing aspect ratio: 5·48
- Length overall: 6·85 m (22 ft 5¾ in)
- Height overall: 2·08 m (6 ft 10 in)
- Tailplane span: 2·60 m (8 ft 6¼ in)
- Wheel track: 2·25 m (7 ft 4½ in)
- Wheelbase: 1·45 m (4 ft 9 in)

AREA:
- Wings, gross: 12·00 m² (129·2 sq ft)

WEIGHTS AND LOADINGS (A: 93 kW; 125 hp engine, B: 112 kW; 150 hp engine, C: 134 kW; 180 hp engine):
- Weight empty: A 476 kg (1,050 lb); B 498 kg (1,100 lb); C 517 kg (1,140 lb)
- Max T-O weight: A 816 kg (1,800 lb); B, C 840 kg (1,850 lb)
- Max wing loading: A 68·0 kg/m² (13·93 lb/sq ft); B, C 69·9 kg/m² (14·32 lb/sq ft)
- Max power loading: A 8·77 kg/kW (14·40 lb/hp); B 7·50 kg/kW (12·33 lb/hp); C 6·27 kg/kW (10·28 lb/hp)

PERFORMANCE (A, B and C as above):
- Max level speed: A 130 knots (241 km/h; 150 mph); B 139 knots (257 km/h; 160 mph); C 148 knots (274 km/h; 170 mph)
- Cruising speed (75% power): A 117 knots (217 km/h; 135 mph); B 126 knots (233 km/h; 145 mph); C 133 knots (246 km/h; 153 mph)
- Econ cruising speed: A 109 knots (201 km/h; 125 mph); B 117 knots (217 km/h; 135 mph); C 124 knots (230 km/h; 143 mph)
- Stalling speed, flaps down: A 45 knots (82 km/h; 51 mph); B, C 46 knots (86 km/h; 53 mph)
- Max rate of climb at S/L: A 244 m (800 ft)/min; B 335 m (1,100 ft)/min; C 427 m (1,400 ft)/min
- T-O and landing run: B 244 m (800 ft); C 198 m (650 ft)
- T-O to 15 m (50 ft): B 427 m (1,400 ft); C 335 m (1,100 ft)
- Range (75% power): A 521 nm (965 km; 600 miles); B 460 nm (853 km; 530 miles); C 417 nm (772 km; 480 miles)
- g limits: ±5·7 ultimate

ZENAIR ZODIAC CH 600

Design of the CH 60, from which the CH 600 was derived, began in December 1983 and construction of the prototype started in January 1984. The first flight was achieved in June 1984. Plans and a kit of component parts (45 per cent premanufactured) for the improved CH 600 are available to amateur builders, and by March 1986 a total of 154 sets of drawings and 62 kits had been delivered. Construction from a kit takes about 400 working hours.

Designed for the first time builder and less experienced pilot, the CH 600 has dual controls, a choice of a tricycle or tailwheel type landing gear, and good handling characteristics. The kit includes the airframe, landing gear, controls, canopy, a new 48·5 kW (65 hp) Volkswagen modified motorcar engine, and instruments.

The following data refer to the CH 600:

TYPE: Two-seat homebuilt aircraft.

AIRFRAME: Cantilever low-wing monoplane of aluminium alloy stressed skin construction. Wing section NACA 65018. Dihedral 6°. Incidence 8°. Single spar structure. Outer wing panels removable. Full span elastically hinged ailerons. Conventional fuselage of basically rectangular section, with rounded top-decking. Rectangular single spar tailplane and elevator assembly, with anti-servo trim tab. No fixed fin. Sweptback rudder.

LANDING GEAR: Non-retractable tricycle or tailwheel type, with bungee shock absorption. All three wheels of 16 in diameter. Brakes fitted. Wheel fairings optional (increase cruising speed by 6 per cent). Skis and floats optional.

POWER PLANT: One 48·5 kW (65 hp) JPX modified Volkswagen 1,875 cc motorcar engine, driving a Zenair 60 × 38 two-blade fixed-pitch propeller with spinner. Optional 37·3 kW (50 hp) VW engine without electric starting or 52 kW (70 hp) VW engine. One fuel tank in fuselage, capacity 60 litres (16 US gallons). Refuelling point in top of fuselage.

ACCOMMODATION: Pilot and passenger side by side under sideways opening (to both sides) Plexiglas canopy. Dual controls. Baggage space behind seats. Heated and ventilated.

SYSTEM: Electric starting.

AVIONICS: Equipment level to builder's choice.

DIMENSIONS, EXTERNAL:
- Wing span: 8·20 m (26 ft 10¾ in)
- Wing chord, constant (excl fillet): 1·48 m (4 ft 10¼ in)
- Wing aspect ratio: 5·5
- Length overall: 5·65 m (18 ft 6½ in)
- Width, outer wings removed: 2·29 m (7 ft 6 in)
- Height overall: 1·90 m (6 ft 2¾ in)
- Tailplane span: 2·20 m (7 ft 2¾ in)
- Wheel track: 1·16 m (3 ft 9½ in)
- Wheelbase: 1·92 m (6 ft 3½ in)
- Propeller diameter: 1·52 m (5 ft 0 in)

DIMENSIONS, INTERNAL:
- Cabin: Length 1·25 m (4 ft 1¼ in)
  - Max width: standard 1·00 m (3 ft 3½ in); optional 1·12 m (3 ft 8 in)
  - Max height 1·05 m (3 ft 5¼ in)

AREA:
- Wings, gross: 12·1 m² (130·2 sq ft)

WEIGHTS AND LOADINGS:
- Weight empty, equipped: 268 kg (590 lb)
- Max fuel weight: 50 kg (110 lb)
- Max T-O weight: 476 kg (1,050 lb)
- Max wing loading: 39·35 kg/m² (8·06 lb/sq ft)
- Max power loading: 9·81 kg/kW (16·15 lb/hp)

PERFORMANCE (at max T-O weight):
- Never-exceed speed: 121 knots (225 km/h; 140 mph)
- Max level speed at S/L: 100 knots (185 km/h; 115 mph)
- Max cruising speed: 91 knots (169 km/h; 105 mph)
- Econ cruising speed: 87 knots (161 km/h; 100 mph)
- Stalling speed: 39 knots (71 km/h; 44 mph)
- Max rate of climb at S/L: 219 m (720 ft)/min
- Service ceiling: 3,050 m (10,000 ft)
- T-O run: 183 m (600 ft)
- T-O to 15 m (50 ft): 380 m (1,247 ft)
- Landing from 15 m (50 ft): 380 m (1,247 ft)
- Landing run: 200 m (656 ft)
- Range with max fuel, 75% power: 364 nm (676 km; 420 miles)
- Endurance: 4 h
- g limits: ±6·9

ZENAIR SUPER ZODIAC

Development of this aircraft has been postponed. Brief details can be found in the 1985-86 *Jane's*.

ZENAIR STOL CH 701

This latest Experimental category aircraft from Zenair was flown for the first time in Summer 1986. Unlike the other aircraft in the range, the CH 701 is a strut braced high-wing cabin monoplane, capable of being completed with a tricycle or tailwheel type landing gear, and with floats, amphibious and ski gears as options. Power is provided by a 37·3 kW (50 hp) Rotax 503 engine in the prototype, but options are the INAV/Lotus 4-50 and KFM 112 engines. To achieve STOL performance, full span leading-edge flaps are fitted to the near constant chord wings. Conventional three-axis control is provided by full span auxiliary-aerofoil ailerons, elevators fitted to the constant chord rectangular tailplane and a large slightly sweptback rudder. The main-wheel legs are cantilever spring type.

DIMENSIONS, EXTERNAL:
- Wing span: 8·23 m (27 ft 0 in)
- Length overall: 5·49 m (18 ft 0 in)
- Propeller diameter: 1·73 m (5 ft 8 in)

AREA:
- Wings, gross: 11·33 m² (122·0 sq ft)

WEIGHTS AND LOADINGS:
- Weight empty: 195 kg (430 lb)
- Max T-O weight: 399 kg (880 lb)
- Max wing loading: 35·2 kg/m² (7·21 lb/sq ft)
- Max power loading: 10·70 kg/kW (17·60 lb/hp)

PERFORMANCE (at max T-O weight):
- Never-exceed speed: 104 knots (193 km/h; 120 mph)
- Max level speed at S/L: 74 knots (137 km/h; 85 mph)
- Normal cruising speed: 65 knots (121 km/h; 75 mph)
- Max rate of climb at S/L: 244 m (800 ft)/min
- T-O run: 37 m (120 ft)
- Landing run: 28 m (90 ft)
- g limits: ±6

ZENAIR ZIPPER

In addition to his Zénith series of homebuilt aircraft, M Heintz produces a family of microlight aircraft under the collective name of Zipper. The basic model won the 'Best New Design' award at the 1984 Sun 'n Fun meeting at Lakeland, Florida, and is offered only in factory built form. More than 100 have been built.

TYPE: Single-seat microlight aircraft; conforms to FAR Pt 103-7.

AIRFRAME: Mainframe of 6061-T6 aluminium alloy with welded steel joints and solid riveting. Strut braced monoplane wings, with D leading-edge section, of aluminium/foam construction, with double surface Dacron covering. Can be folded in 5 min for road towing or storage. Three-axis control (all-metal ailerons, elevator and rudder).

LANDING GEAR: Tricycle type, with steerable nosewheel. Wheel size 10 in standard (optional 16 in); glassfibre spring suspension. Float and ski gear, and amphibious wheel/floats, optional.

POWER PLANT: One 19·4 kW (26 hp) JPX PUL 425 two-cylinder flat-twin, with direct drive to a two-blade wooden propeller. Fuel tank capacity 19 litres (5 US gallons) standard; auxiliary tank available optionally.

ACCOMMODATION: Pilot only, in open position. Fully enclosed fairing optional.

DIMENSIONS, EXTERNAL:
- Wing span: 8·53 m (28 ft 0 in)
- Wing aspect ratio: 5·6
- Length overall: 4·42 m (14 ft 6 in)
- Height overall: 1·68 m (5 ft 6 in)
- Propeller diameter: 1·07 m (3 ft 6 in)

AREA:
- Wings, gross: 13·29 m² (143·0 sq ft)

WEIGHTS AND LOADINGS:
- Weight empty: 100 kg (220 lb)
- Pilot weight range: 59-100 kg (130-220 lb)
- Max T-O weight: 200 kg (440 lb)
- Max wing loading: 15·34 kg/m² (3·14 lb/sq ft)
- Max power loading: 10·31 kg/kW (16·92 lb/hp)

PERFORMANCE:
- Never-exceed speed: 47 knots (88 km/h; 55 mph)
- Max level speed: 39 knots (72 km/h; 45 mph)
- Recommended cruising speed: 30 knots (56 km/h; 35 mph)
- Stalling speed: 16 knots (29 km/h; 18 mph)
- Max rate of climb at S/L: 122 m (400 ft)/min
- Service ceiling: above 3,660 m (12,000 ft)
- T-O run: 30 m (100 ft)
- Landing run: 24 m (80 ft)
- Range with max fuel: 87 nm (161 km; 100 miles)
- Endurance with max fuel: 3 h
- g limits: +6/−3
- Best glide ratio: 8
- Min rate of sink, power off: 61 m (200 ft)/min

ZENAIR ZIPPER RX

The Zipper RX is a single-seat microlight, similar to the lighter basic Zipper but recommended for use with Zenair 550 floats. Skis and the other non-standard items remain optional on this model.

Details, where they differ from the Zipper, are as follows:

TYPE: Single-seat microlight aircraft; conforms to FAR Pt 103.

LANDING GEAR: Recommended for use with Zenair 550 floats.

POWER PLANT: One 20 kW (27 hp) Rotax 277 engine, with direct drive to a two-blade wooden propeller. Fuel tank capacity 19 litres (5 US gallons).

WEIGHTS AND LOADINGS:
- Weight empty: 109 kg (240 lb)
- Max T-O weight: 218 kg (480 lb)
- Max wing loading: 16·33 kg/m² (3·36 lb/sq ft)
- Max power loading: 4·75 kg/kW (7·78 lb/hp)

PERFORMANCE:
- Never-exceed speed: 47 knots (88 km/h; 55 mph)
- Max level speed: 42 knots (77 km/h; 48 mph)
- Recommended cruising speed: 30 knots (56 km/h; 35 mph)
- Max rate of climb at S/L: 168 m (550 ft)/min
- T-O run: 25 m (80 ft)
- Landing run: 25 m (80 ft)
- g limits: +6/−3

ZENAIR AG ZIPPER

In 1984 Zenair test flew a modified Zipper fitted with a second PUL 425 engine, a 36·4 litre (8 Imp gallon) chemical tank and a Micro Ag spray system. The project was begun partly in response to interest from developing countries in an inexpensive cropspraying aircraft that could be flown by quickly trained ultralight aircraft pilots. Zenair believes that sales prospects for the AG Zipper are extremely promising, and has signed a joint marketing agreement with the International Aircraft Corporation of N. 34 West 28341 Toglers Wood Road, Pewaukee, Wisconsin 53072, USA, to promote the AG Zipper version. By February 1986 a total of at least 28 had been sold.

The AG Zipper represents a compromise between the Zipper and Zipper II, for maximum payload and performance. It can also be used for recreational flying. Details, where they differ from the single-engined Zipper, are as follows:

TYPE: Twin-engined, single-seat agricultural microlight aircraft; conforms to FAR Pt 103, Canadian Department of Transport and NASAD.

LANDING GEAR: Wheel size 11 in standard for all wheels; optional 16 in wheels. Optional Zenair 750 aluminium floats, skis, or amphibious wheel/float gear.

POWER PLANT: Two 16·4 kW (22 hp) JPX PUL 425 two-cylinder engines, with direct drive to two two-blade wooden propellers. Fuel tank capacity 19 litres (5 US gallons); auxiliary 19 litre (5 US gallon) tank optional.

ACCOMMODATION: Provision for passenger instead of agricultural equipment. Optional windscreen or fully enclosed cockpit fairing.

Zenair Tri-Z CH 300 with tricycle landing gear

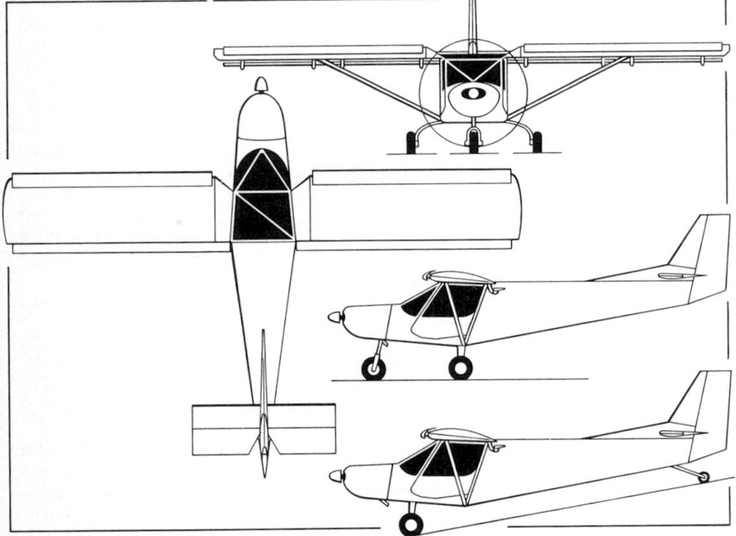

Zenair STOL CH 701 cabin monoplane, showing alternative tricycle and tailwheel landing gear *(Jane's/Mike Keep)*

Zenair Zipper II two-seat instructional and recreational microlight aircraft *(Brian M. Service)*

Zenair Zodiac CH 600 with a nosewheel landing gear

Prototype Zenair STOL CH 701 *(J. M. G. Gradidge)*

Zenair AG Zipper engaged in cropspraying operations

Zenair Zipper single-seat microlight aircraft

AREA:
- Wings, gross: 13·75 m² (148·0 sq ft)

WEIGHTS AND LOADINGS:
- Weight empty: 118 kg (260 lb)
- Useful load: 140 kg (310 lb)
- Max T-O weight: 272 kg (600 lb)
- Max wing loading: 19·78 kg/m² (4·05 lb/sq ft)
- Max power loading: 8·29 kg/kW (13·64 lb/hp)

PERFORMANCE:
- Never-exceed speed: 47 knots (88 km/h; 55 mph)
- Max level speed: 45 knots (84 km/h; 52 mph)
- Recommended cruising speed: 30 knots (56 km/h; 35 mph)
- Max rate of climb at S/L, at 218 kg (480 lb) AUW: 213 m (700 ft)/min
- T-O run: 22 m (70 ft)
- Landing run: 28 m (90 ft)
- *g* limits: +6/−3

ZENAIR ZIPPER II

The Zipper II is a side by side two-seat microlight with twin engines, intended for instructional and recreational flying. Like the AG Zipper, the Zipper II is powered by PUL 425 engines. Options include an auxiliary fuel tank.

Details, where they differ from the Zipper, are as follows:

TYPE: Twin-engined, two-seat microlight; conforms to FAR Pt 103, Canadian Department of Transport and NASAD.

AIRFRAME: Wider fuselage box structure to accommodate two seats side by side. Options as for Zipper.

POWER PLANT: Two 16·4 kW (22 hp) JPX PUL 425 two-cylinder engines, each with direct drive to a wooden two-blade propeller. Fuel tank capacity 19 litres (5 US gallons); auxiliary 19 litre (5 US gallon) tank optional.

DIMENSION, EXTERNAL:
- Wing span: 8·99 m (29 ft 6 in)

AREA:
- Wings, gross: 13·75 m² (148·0 sq ft)

WEIGHTS AND LOADINGS:
- Weight empty: 122 kg (270 lb)
- Useful load: 181 kg (400 lb)
- Max T-O weight: 317 kg (700 lb)
- Max wing loading: 23·08 kg/m² (4·73 lb/sq ft)
- Max power loading: 9·66 kg/kW (15·91 lb/hp)

PERFORMANCE:
- Never-exceed speed: 47 knots (88 km/h; 55 mph)
- Max level speed: 42 knots (77 km/h; 48 mph)
- Recommended cruising speed: 30 knots (56 km/h; 35 mph)
- Max rate of climb at S/L: 140 m (460 ft)/min
- T-O run: 28 m (90 ft)
- Landing run: 31 m (100 ft)
- *g* limits: +5/−2·5

CHINA
(PEOPLE'S REPUBLIC)

BIAA
BEIJING INSTITUTE OF AERONAUTICS & ASTRONAUTICS

1 Sueyuan Road, Beijing

BIAA MIFENG (HONEYBEE)

The **Mifeng-1**, described and illustrated in the 1982-83 *Jane's*, was a single-seat microlight aircraft with a Rogallo type wing, strut-mounted well above the main airframe structure. It was designed and built at the Beijing Aeronautics Institute, and was intended to be powered by a 22·4 kW (30 hp) piston engine. However, its first flight, on 6 June 1979, was as a pilotless, radio controlled aircraft, powered by an 11·2 kW (15 hp) engine, driving a tractor propeller.

The piloted **Mifeng-2** (see photograph) utilises essentially the same fuselage and tailboom, but has rectangular planform semi-rigid wings, with dihedral, conventional tail surfaces, two-axis (rudder and elevators) control, and a pusher engine installation.

A photograph has been received in 1986 of the tandem two-seat **Mifeng-3** biplane, designed by Institute lecturer Hu Jizhong. This machine, which made its first flight on 21 August 1983, is intended for agricultural operations and aerial photography. It is powered by a 22·4 kW (30 hp) two-cylinder aircooled engine, driving a 1·30 m (4 ft 3¼ in) diameter propeller. The main differences compared with the Mifeng-2 are a lengthened fuselage pod and additional short-span lower wings with N interplane struts.

The following data apply to the Mifeng-2:

Dimensions, external:
- Wing span: 10·00 m (32 ft 9¾ in)
- Wing aspect ratio: 6·67
- Length overall: 5·00 m (16 ft 5 in)
- Height overall: 2·70 m (8 ft 10¼ in)
- Wheel track: 1·40 m (4 ft 7¼ in)

Area:
- Wings, gross: 15·00 m² (161·5 sq ft)

Weight:
- Weight empty: 210 kg (463 lb)

Performance:
- Max level speed: 35 knots (65 km/h; 40 mph)
- Max cruising speed: 27 knots (50 km/h; 31 mph)
- T-O run: 45 m (148 ft)
- Landing run: 30 m (99 ft)

HUABEI
HUABEI MACHINERY FACTORY

Shijiazhuang, Hebei Province

The Huabei (formerly Hongxing) Machinery Factory has developed several microlight aircraft, of which details follow:

HUABEI QINGTING 5 series (DRAGONFLY 5)

First flown in late 1983, the **Qingting 5** is powered by a 22·4 kW (30 hp) piston engine driving a two-blade pusher propeller, and carries 9 kg (19·8 lb) of fuel. Configuration is that of a 'powered trike'. The wire braced, constant chord, fabric covered (single surface) semi-rigid wings have raked wingtips and a kingpost, and display marked dihedral. Conventional tail surfaces are fitted to the open tubular mainframe structure, and the tricycle landing gear comprises three wheels of similar size, with a skid to protect the tail. Accommodation for the pilot is open.

The side by side two-seat **Qingting 5A** is generally similar to the Qingting 5, with unchanged power plant; the tandem two-seat **Qingting 5B**, built in 1985, uses a 33·6 kW (45 hp) engine.

Type: Single- and two-seat microlight.

Dimensions, external (A: Qingting 5, B: Qingting 5A, C: Qingting 5B):
- Wing span: A, B: 10·55 m (34 ft 7½ in)
  - C: 10·62 m (34 ft 10 in)
- Wing chord, constant: A: 1·52 m (5 ft 0 in)
- Length overall: A, B: 5·36 m (17 ft 7 in)
  - C: 5·77 m (18 ft 11¼ in)
- Height overall: A, B: 2·83 m (9 ft 3½ in)
  - C: 2·70 m (8 ft 10¼ in)
- Wheel track: A: 1·65 m (5 ft 5 in)
- Tailplane span: A: 2·80 m (9 ft 2¼ in)
- Propeller diameter: A: 1·32 m (4 ft 4 in)

Areas (A, B and C as above):
- Wings, gross: A, B, C: 15·10 m² (162·5 sq ft)

Weights and Loadings (A, B and C as above):
- Weight empty: A, B: 123 kg (271 lb)
  - C: 150 kg (330 lb)
- Max T-O weight: A, B: 241 kg (531 lb)
- Max wing loading: A, B: 15·96 kg/m² (3·27 lb/sq ft)
- Max power loading: A, B: 10·76 kg/kW (17·70 lb/hp)

Performance (A, B and C as above):
- Max level speed: A: 47 knots (88 km/h; 54 mph)
  - C: 54 knots (100 km/h; 62 mph)
- Normal cruising speed: B: 32 knots (60 km/h; 37 mph)
  - C: 35 knots (65 km/h; 40 mph)
- Max rate of climb at S/L: A, B: 204 m (669 ft)/min
  - C: 192 m (630 ft)/min
- T-O run (grass): A, B: 27 m (89 ft)
  - C: 39 m (128 ft)
- Landing run: A, B: 33 m (108 ft)
  - C: 44 m (144 ft)
- Range: B: 63 nm (117 km; 72·5 miles)
  - C: 64 nm (120 km; 74·5 miles)

HUABEI QINGTING 6 (DRAGONFLY 6)

In 1985 Huabei developed the Qingting 6, a new single-seat homebuilt of more refined design than the Qingting 5 series of microlights. As can be seen from the accompanying illustration, it is a strut braced low-wing monoplane, with a fuselage pod and twin booms supporting the twin fins and rudders. It has three-axis control (ailerons, rudders and elevator on the T tailplane), and the mainwheels of the non-retractable tricycle landing gear are carried on cantilever spring legs with wheel fairings. The structure is said to be all-metal. Power is provided by a 59·7 kW (80 hp) Revmaster engine, pylon mounted aft of the pilot's open cockpit and driving a two-blade pusher propeller with spinner.

Dimensions, external:
- Wing span: 9·802 m (32 ft 2 in)
- Length overall: 6·676 m (21 ft 10¾ in)
- Height overall: 1·74 m (5 ft 8½ in)

Area:
- Wings, gross: 11·52 m² (124·0 sq ft)

Weights and Loadings:
- Weight empty: 253 kg (558 lb)
- Max T-O weight: 500 kg (1,102 lb)
- Max wing loading: 43·4 kg/m² (8·89 lb/sq ft)
- Max power loading: 8·38 kg/kW (13·78 lb/hp)

Performance:
- Max level speed: 70 knots (130 km/h; 81 mph)
- Normal cruising speed: 49 knots (90 km/h; 56 mph)
- Max rate of climb at S/L: 128 m (420 ft)/min
- Service ceiling: 3,500 m (11,480 ft)
- T-O run: 107 m (351 ft)
- Landing run: 87 m (285 ft)
- Range: 72 nm (134 km; 83 miles)

JINZHOU
JINZHOU MICROLIGHT HELICOPTER COMPANY

Jinzhou, Liaoning Province

Managing Director/Designer: Dong Dawei

This private company has designed a single-seat microlight helicopter known as the **Yunhe No. 1**, said to have a range of approx 162 nm (300 km; 186 miles). No other details were known at the time of going to press.

NAI
NANJING AERONAUTICAL INSTITUTE

29 Yudaojei Street, Nanjing, Jiangsu Province
Telephone: 41191, 46443
Telex: 34155 NAINJ CN
President: Prof Yu Chenye

NAI AD-100 TRAVELLER

The AD-100 Traveller is a new all-composites single-seat canard microlight aircraft of advanced configuration, designed by NAI in co-operation with Adaso Inc of the USA. The airframe is constructed of glassfibre honeycomb sandwich.

As can be gleaned from the illustration, the rear mounted wings (with endplate fins and rudders) and the constant-chord canard have no dihedral or anhedral, although the wings are slightly sweptback. The Traveller has three-axis control (inset ailerons, elevators on canard, and rudders); and non-retractable tricycle landing gear. Power is provided by a rear mounted 20 kW (27 hp) Rotax 277 single-cylinder two-stroke engine, driving a two-blade pusher propeller.

Type: Single-seat microlight aircraft.

Dimension, external:
- Length overall: 5·021 m (16 ft 5¾ in)

Area:
- Wings, gross: 10·63 m² (114·4 sq ft)

Weight:
- Weight empty: 126 kg (278 lb)

Performance:
- Level speed: 40-46 knots (75-85 km/h; 47-53 mph)
- Service ceiling: 3,400 m (11,150 ft)
- T-O run: 60 m (197 ft)
- Range: 162-189 nm (300-350 km; 186-217 miles)

CZECHOSLOVAKIA

VERNER
VLADA VERNER

VERNER W-02

Mr Verner, an aircraft engineer, designed a small single-seat light aircraft named W-01 Broucek (Beetle) which was last described and illustrated in the 1971-72 *Jane's*. In mid-1985 he was working on a new type, the W-02, with a tail-first configuration similar to that of the Rutan Long-EZ. All available details follow:

Airframe: Cantilever tail-first monoplane, without anhedral or dihedral. Wing section NASA GAW-1. Sweepback 25°. Approx half-span inset ailerons. Sweptback fins at wingtips, with small inset rudders. Constant-chord unswept foreplane with raked tips, carrying near full-span constant-chord elevators. No anhedral or dihedral. Outer wing panels attached to wingroot extensions which carry forward to point immediately aft of foreplanes. Streamline fuselage pod, with long canopy.

Landing Gear: Tricycle type, comprising retractable nosewheel and non-retractable mainwheels carried on cantilever spring legs, with wheel fairings.

Power Plant: One Avia M 332 four-cylinder inverted inline aircooled engine, rated at 104 kW (140 hp) and driving a V-410D pusher propeller.

Accommodation: Probably pilot and passenger in tandem.

Dimensions, external:
- Wing span: 7·00 m (22 ft 11½ in)
- Foreplane span: 4·00 m (13 ft 1½ in)
- Wing aspect ratio: 7·42
- Length overall: 4·60 m (15 ft 1 in)

Areas:
- Wings, gross: 6·60 m² (71·04 sq ft)
- Foreplane, gross: 1·60 m² (17·22 sq ft)

Weights and Loadings:
- Weight empty: 400 kg (882 lb)
- Max T-O weight: 600 kg (1,323 lb)
- Max wing loading: 90·9 kg/m² (18·62 lb/sq ft)
- Max power loading: 5·77 kg/kW (9·45 lb/hp)

Performance (estimated):
- Max level speed: 162 knots (300 km/h; 186 mph)
- Max cruising speed: 135 knots (250 km/h; 155 mph)
- Min flying speed: 54 knots (100 km/h; 62 mph)
- Max rate of climb at S/L: 540 m (1,770 ft)/min
- T-O to 15 m (50 ft): 480 m (1,575 ft)

BIAA Mifeng-2 microlight aircraft *(Aerospace Knowledge)*

Huabei Qingting 5 single-seat microlight *(Andrew Li)*

BIAA Mifeng-3 microlight biplane *(Andrew Li)*

Huabei Qingting 6 homebuilt aircraft *(Andrew Li)*

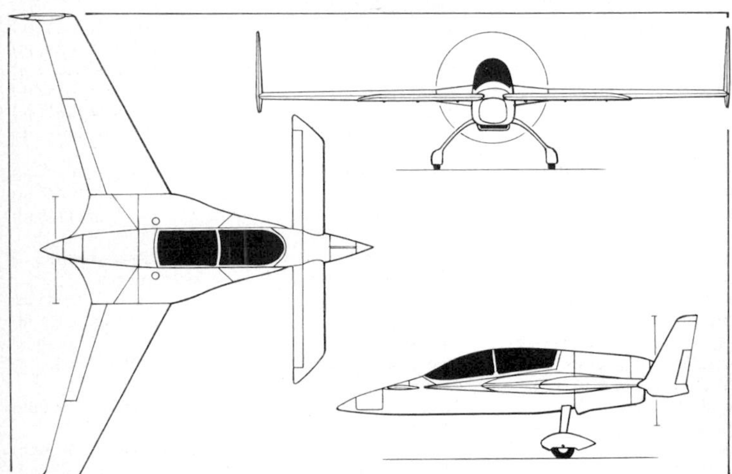
Verner W-02 homebuilt aircraft *(Michael A. Badrocke)*

NAI AD-100 Traveller single-seat microlight

FINLAND

TERVAMÄKI

JUKKA TERVAMÄKI

Harmaapaadentie 12A, 00930 Helsinki 93

Mr Tervamäki first became interested in autogyros in 1956. In 1959 he worked briefly for the Bensen Aircraft Corporation in the USA. He obtained a Diploma in Aeronautical Engineering at the Helsinki Institute of Technology in 1963, and served later in the helicopter section of the Finnish Air Force. He was for two years project manager and chief designer of the PIK-19 Muhinu glider-towing aircraft. In 1974 he modified a Schleicher ASK 14 powered sailplane to make it capable of taxying on large airports; and designed the engine installation for the JT-6 prototype powered sailplane, now built in France as the Siren PIK-20E2F (see Sailplanes section).

Autogyros designed by Mr Tervamäki were completed in 1958 (JT-1), 1965 (JT-2), 1968 (Tervamäki-Eerola ATE-3) and 1972 (JT-5). In January 1984 Mr Tervamäki's latest autogyro flew for the first time as the MT-7. Built and flown by Sig Vittorio Magni, this is described under VPM in the Italian part of this section.

TERVAMÄKI JT-5

The JT-5 is a development of the ATE-3, the major visible differences being the use of a triple tail assembly, to improve static and dynamic stability; a fully enclosed cockpit; improved, low-drag fuselage contours; and extensive use of plastics materials in the basic structure and main components. Other features include an upward directed exhaust, to reduce engine noise, and a simplified carburettor installation and heating system of Tervamäki design.

The prototype JT-5 (OH-XYS) was flown for the first time on 7 January 1973. It was later sold, together with production rights, tools and moulds, to Sig Vittorio Magni of Italy. In 1979 plans, component parts, materials and complete kits of the Magni-Tervamäki MT-5 were made available to amateur constructors by VPM (see Italy). By early 1986 Mr Tervamäki had sold at least 30 sets of plans for the JT-5. The latest to be completed (OH-XRK) is shown in an accompanying photograph. Begun in 1975 by Mr M. Martikainen, it remained incomplete for about ten years before being purchased and completed by Veikko and Matti Silvennoinen of Jyväskylä in central Finland. The first flight was made in September 1985, and by February 1986 this JT-5 had logged about 40 flying hours. Powered by a 52 kW (70 hp) Limbach 2,000 cc engine, it has the open cockpit/windscreen arrangement of the prototype JT-5. Due to fly in 1986 was another JT-5, built by Mr Arvo Taupila whose earlier hybrid ATE-3/JT-5 was illustrated in the 1985-86 *Jane's*.

The following details apply to the standard JT-5:

TYPE: Single-seat homebuilt autogyro.

ROTOR SYSTEM: Two-blade semi-rigid rotor of glassfibre reinforced epoxy resin, with polyurethane plastics foam core. Blades, of constant chord and NACA 8-H-12 section, are each attached to hub by two bolts. A lead bar in each blade leading-edge forms the chordwise balance weight. Rotor mast of streamlined SAE 4130 steel tubing. Rotor head is of a compact offset-gimbal type with centrifugal teeter stops and rotor brake installed. There are two spiral springs for trim adjustment, which is effected via the control stick twist grip handle. Normal rotor rpm is 400, maximum 600. Designed for the JT-5, but not yet fitted, is a modified Cierva type inclined drag hinge which would allow the blades to move to zero pitch when prerotation torque is applied, permitting an increase of 100 rpm in pre-spin speed and, consequently, a shorter take-off.

ROTOR DRIVE: Rotor spin-up by V belt, clutch, 90° gearbox, sliding universal shaft and inertia operated Bendix drive. Overall reduction ratio 8. Rotor spin-up of 300 rpm can be achieved.

AIRFRAME: Basic structure of welded 4130 steel tubing with a glassfibre/RFB honeycomb sandwich cockpit. (RFB or 'Tubus' core material is constructed of cellulose acetate tubes.) All internal cockpit structures of glassfibre reinforced epoxy resin. One-piece aluminium engine cowling. Central main fin and rudder, of glassfibre reinforced epoxy resin, with rigid PVC foam ribs and Courtauld carbonfibre stiffeners. Horizontal tail and auxiliary endplate fins of glassfibre sandwich construction with honeycomb core. Tail assembly attached to fuselage by a single streamlined steel tube. Small tailwheel beneath base of fin.

LANDING GEAR: Non-retractable tricycle type. Main gear legs consist of 4 × 4 cm (1·6 × 1·6 in) glassfibre reinforced epoxy resin springs, encased in streamline fairings of the same material. Cables inside these fairings to main gear drum brakes. Mainwheel tyres size 300 × 100. Compression rubber shock absorption in nose gear. Nosewheel tyre size 260 × 80. Nosewheel steerable by rudder pedals.

POWER PLANT: One 56 kW (75 hp) 1·7 litre Volkswagen engine, converted for autogyro use by Limbach Motorenbau. No oil cooler, generator or electric starter. Two-blade pusher propeller, of glassfibre reinforced epoxy. Glassfibre fuel tank, integrally built into fuselage aft of pilot's seat, capacity 50 litres (11 Imp gallons).

ACCOMMODATION: Single seat under sideways opening Plexiglas canopy. Instrument panel cover and pilot's seat back (the latter also forming a firewall to the engine compartment) open together with the canopy.

DIMENSIONS, EXTERNAL:
- Rotor diameter 7·00 m (22 ft 11½ in)
- Rotor blade chord (constant, each) 0·18 m (7·1 in)
- Length of fuselage 3·50 m (11 ft 5¾ in)
- Height overall 2·00 m (6 ft 6¾ in)
- Wheel track 1·70 m (5 ft 7 in)
- Propeller diameter 1·20 m (3 ft 11¼ in)

AREAS:
- Rotor blades (each) 0·63 m² (6·78 sq ft)
- Rotor disc 38·50 m² (414·4 sq ft)

WEIGHTS:
- Weight empty, equipped 167 kg (368 lb)
- Max T-O weight 290 kg (639 lb)

PERFORMANCE (at max T-O weight):
- Never-exceed speed 97 knots (180 km/h; 111 mph)
- Max level speed at S/L 92 knots (170 km/h; 106 mph)
- Max cruising speed at S/L 81 knots (150 km/h; 93 mph)
- Econ cruising speed 70 knots (130 km/h; 81 mph)
- Min level speed 19 knots (35 km/h; 22 mph)
- Max rate of climb at S/L 180 m (590 ft)/min
- Service ceiling 4,000 m (13,125 ft)
- T-O run 70 m (230 ft)
- T-O to 15 m (50 ft) 120 m (394 ft)
- Landing from 15 m (50 ft) 50 m (165 ft)
- Landing run 5 m (16 ft)
- Range with max fuel, no reserves 189 nm (350 km; 217 miles)

FRANCE

AÉRO DELTA

AÉRO DELTA SERVICE

19 rue Gabriel Péri, 28000 Chartres
Telephone: (37) 21 14 44
DIRECTOR: Francis Tempier

AÉRO DELTA HELIOS

The Helios is a two-seat 'powered trike' unit for attachment to suitable hang gliders. Power plant is a 33·5 kW (45 hp) Hirth 2701R 493 cc engine, driving a two-blade pusher propeller; fuel tank capacity is 23 litres (5 Imp gallons). Production of the Helios began in early 1983. Float and ski gear are available as options.

WEIGHTS:
- Weight empty 140 kg (308 lb)
- Max T-O weight 335 kg (738 lb)

PERFORMANCE:
- Never-exceed speed 38 knots (70 km/h; 44 mph)
- Max level speed 35 knots (64 km/h; 40 mph)
- Cruising speed 27 knots (50 km/h; 31 mph)
- Stalling speed 17 knots (30 km/h; 19 mph)
- Service ceiling 3,000 m (9,840 ft)
- Max rate of climb at S/L 152 m (500 ft)/min
- Best glide ratio 6

AÉRODIS

AÉRODIS SARL

Aéroport Troyes Barberey, 10600 La Chapelle St Luc
Telephone: (25) 74 15 20
Telex: 840291F

US distributor:
Aerodis America Inc, Hooks Airport No 8, 20221 Stuebner-Airline, Spring, Texas 77379
Telephone: (713) 783 7708

Aircraft exhibited at the 1979 Paris Air Show under the auspices of the RSA (Réseau du Sport de l'Air) included the original G-801 prototype of the four-seat all-plastics Orion, designed and built by M Jean Grinvalds. The Orion project had first attracted attention at the 1977 RSA meeting at Brienne-le-Château, where a radio controlled scale model was demonstrated. Design had begun on 1 January 1975, enabling construction of the full-scale Orion prototype (F-PYKF) to be started in July 1976. It flew for the first time on 2 June 1981, and 55 sets of plans of the G-801 were sold in France and Europe in 1982. More than 30 G-801s are under construction.

A prototype of the developed G-802 Orion (F-WZLX) was displayed at the 1983 Paris Air Show and flew for the first time on 4 November 1983. Plans and kits of this version are marketed in France and Europe by Aérodis SARL. Compared with the G-801, the G-802 has a larger cabin, a ventral fin of increased area, improved wing/fuselage fairings, and a three-blade ground adjustable propeller instead of the earlier four-blade fixed-pitch wooden propeller. In March 1983 M Grinvalds signed a contract with an American distributor covering the sale of 510 G-802 kits over a four-year period. The first of these were delivered in mid-February 1984 to Aérodis America, and the first Orion to be assembled in the USA flew for the first time in August 1984. Each kit is supplied complete except for engine, instruments, avionics, wheels and brakes, and interior fittings.

M Grinvalds was killed in a flying accident in 1985, but the Orion programme is continuing.

GRINVALDS G-802 ORION

The following description applies to the standard kit version of the G-802. One airframe has been fitted experimentally with a 119 kW (160 hp) French/Swedish PRV (Peugeot, Renault, Volvo) engine and was exhibited in this form at the 1985 Paris Air Show. It was expected to fly later that year.

TYPE: Four-seat all-plastics homebuilt touring and business aircraft.

AIRFRAME: Cantilever low-wing monoplane, built in one piece tip to tip, and installed in housing moulded into undersurface of fuselage. Wing section NACA 43015 at root, NACA 43012 at tip. Dihedral 4° 30′. Incidence 2° 30′ at root. Composite structure of glassfibre reinforced locally with Kevlar and carbonfibre. Aileron and slotted flap along entire trailing-edge of each wing, of similar construction to wings. Flaps electrically actuated. No tabs. Composite fuselage of glassfibre/epoxy resin, Kevlar and graphite reinforced, with integral tail fin and wing-root stubs and fillets. Cantilever T tail, with fixed tailplane, horn balanced elevator and inset rudder of similar construction to wings. Fixed ventral fin. Tab in elevator.

LANDING GEAR: Retractable tricycle type, with single wheel on each unit. Electric retraction, nosewheel forward, main units inward under fuselage. Manual emergency actuation. Main gear fully enclosed when retracted, by doors attached to legs. All three legs of cantilever plastics blade type. Mainwheel tyres size 355 × 155, pressure 2·45 bars (35·5 lb/sq in); nosewheel tyre size 330 × 130, pressure 1·75 bars (25·5 lb/sq in). Hydraulic disc brakes on mainwheels. Tailskid under ventral fin to protect propeller in tail-down attitude.

POWER PLANT: One 134 kW (180 hp) Avco Lycoming IO-360 flat-four engine in first Orion, mounted inside rear fuselage and driving a tail-mounted three-blade ground adjustable propeller, with spinner, by means of Aerocar shafting. Suited to engines of 112-149 kW (150-200 hp). Access to engine via large door on each side, over wing trailing-edge. Cooling air enters via two underbelly scoops; hot air and exhaust gases ejected through ducts on each side of rear fuselage. Two fuel tanks in wings, with total capacity of 220 litres (58 US gallons). Long range tanks available when flown with pilot and one passenger only, capacity 400 litres (106 US gallons), or pilot only 490 litres (129 US gallons). Refuelling points in wings. Oil capacity 7·5 litres (2·0 US gallons).

ACCOMMODATION: Four persons, in pairs, in enclosed cabin. Upward opening window/door on each side, forward of wing. Baggage space in nose, capacity 30 kg (66 lb). Dual controls.

SYSTEM: Electrical system, powered by battery and alternator, to actuate flaps and landing gear.

DIMENSIONS, EXTERNAL:
- Wing span 9·00 m (29 ft 6½ in)
- Wing chord: at root 1·50 m (4 ft 11 in)
  - at tip 1·00 m (3 ft 3¼ in)
- Wing aspect ratio 7·2
- Length overall 6·85 m (22 ft 5½ in)
- Height overall 2·50 m (8 ft 2½ in)
- Tailplane span 3·00 m (9 ft 10¼ in)
- Wheel track 2·65 m (8 ft 8¼ in)
- Wheelbase 2·60 m (8 ft 6½ in)
- Propeller diameter 1·50 m (4 ft 11 in)

DIMENSIONS, INTERNAL:
- Cabin: Length 2·45 m (8 ft 0½ in)
  - Max height 0·92 m (3 ft 0¼ in)
  - Max width 1·12 m (3 ft 8 in)

AREA:
- Wings, gross 11·22 m² (120·8 sq ft)

WEIGHTS AND LOADINGS (134 kW; 180 hp engine):
- Weight empty, equipped 610 kg (1,345 lb)
- Max T-O weight 1,050 kg (2,315 lb)
- Max wing loading 93·5 kg/m² (19·16 lb/sq ft)
- Max power loading 7·84 kg/kW (12·86 lb/hp)

PERFORMANCE (134 kW; 180 hp engine):
- Never-exceed speed 221 knots (410 km/h; 255 mph)
- Max level speed at 2,440 m (8,000 ft) 178 knots (330 km/h; 205 mph)
- Max cruising speed at S/L (75% power) 162 knots (300 km/h; 186 mph)
- Econ cruising speed at 2,440 m (8,000 ft) 135 knots (250 km/h; 155 mph)
- Stalling speed: flaps up 54 knots (100 km/h; 63 mph)
  - 20° flap 49 knots (90 km/h; 56 mph)
- Max rate of climb at S/L 270 m (885 ft)/min
- Service ceiling 4,500 m (14,775 ft)
- T-O to 15 m (50 ft) 600 m (1,970 ft)
- Landing from 15 m (50 ft) 490 m (1,610 ft)
- Landing run 200 m (655 ft)
- Range at cruising speed, standard fuel 809 nm (1,500 km; 932 miles)
- Max range with long range fuel tanks (65% power) 1,618 nm (3,000 km; 1,864 miles)
- Ferry range with 490 litres (129 US gallons) fuel, pilot only (65% power) 1,983 nm (3,675 km; 2,283 miles)

AÉROKART

SOCIÉTÉ AÉROKART

9 rue d'Austerlitz, 69004 Lyon
Telephone: (7) 828 07 26

WORKS: RN7, Plateau de Louze, 3815 Roussillon
Telephone: (74) 29 59 51

DIRECTORS:
B. Charpenel
R. Feltrin

AÉROKART 4315

Developed from the two-seat prototype A-Kart 30, the Aérokart 3315 first flew in the Summer of 1982. A single-seat high-wing braced monoplane, it entered production in November of that year. A more powerful version is known as the Aérokart 4315, and is described below:

TYPE: Single-seat microlight aircraft.

AIRFRAME: High-wing monoplane. Aluminium alloy frame with double surface covering, wire braced, kingpost standard. Three-axis control (rudder, elevator and ailerons).

LANDING GEAR: Tricycle type, with steerable nosewheel and bungee suspension on mainwheels. No brakes. Nosewheel diameter 26 cm; mainwheels 40 cm.

POWER PLANT: One 32 kW (43 hp) Hirth 2701R-03 engine, mounted inverted with 2·5:1 reduction drive to two-blade pusher propeller. Standard fuel capacity 20 litres (4·4 Imp gallons); 10 litres (2·2 Imp gallons) in reserve tank.

ACCOMMODATION: Pilot only.

DIMENSIONS, EXTERNAL:
- Wing span 10·50 m (34 ft 5½ in)
- Wing aspect ratio 7·35

Tervamäki JT-5 recently completed by Veikko and Matti Silvennoinen of Jyväskylä, Finland

The first Grinvalds G-802 Orion all-plastics homebuilt aircraft

Aile Patrilor 3 two-seat microlight *(J. M. G. Gradidge)*

Aile PX-2000 single-seat microlight *(J. M. G. Gradidge)*

Propeller diameter	1·40 m (4 ft 7 in)
AREA:	
Wings, gross	15·00 m² (161·5 sq ft)
WEIGHTS AND LOADINGS:	
Weight empty	126 kg (278 lb)
Max T-O weight	225 kg (496 lb)
Max wing loading	15·0 kg/m² (3·07 lb/sq ft)
Max power loading	7·02 kg/kW (11·5 lb/hp)
PERFORMANCE (85 kg; 187 lb pilot):	
Never-exceed speed	64 knots (120 km/h; 74 mph)
Max level speed	57 knots (105 km/h; 65 mph)
Max cruising speed	48 knots (90 km/h; 56 mph)
Econ cruising speed	43 knots (80 km/h; 50 mph)
Stalling speed	19 knots (35 km/h; 22 mph)
Max rate of climb at S/L	180 m (590 ft)/min
Service ceiling	3,050 m (10,000 ft)
T-O run	50 m (164 ft)
Landing run	25 m (82 ft)
Range with max fuel	162 nm (300 km; 186 miles)
g limits	+5·5/−2·5 design
Best glide ratio	8
Min rate of sink, power off	132 m (433 ft)/min

AÉROKART 4320

TYPE: Two-seat microlight aircraft.

AIRFRAME: Essentially similar to Aérokart 4315, but with strut bracing in place of wires and kingpost, and increased wing area.

POWER PLANT: One 32 kW (43 hp) Hirth 2701R-03 493 cc engine, with 2·5:1 reduction drive to a two-blade pusher propeller. Fuel tank capacity 20 litres (4·4 Imp gallons) standard, 30 litres (6·6 Imp gallons) optional. Electric start standard.

ACCOMMODATION: Pilot and passenger.

DIMENSIONS, EXTERNAL:	
Wing span	10·50 m (34 ft 5½ in)
Wing aspect ratio	5·5
Length overall	5·80 m (19 ft 0¼ in)
Height overall	2·94 m (9 ft 7¾ in)
AREA:	
Wings, gross	20·00 m² (215·3 sq ft)
WEIGHTS AND LOADINGS:	
Weight empty	146 kg (322 lb)
Max T-O weight	320 kg (705 lb)
Max wing loading	16·0 kg/m² (3·28 lb/sq ft)
Max power loading	9·98 kg/kW (16·4 lb/hp)
PERFORMANCE: As for 4315 except:	
Max cruising speed	43 knots (80 km/h; 50 mph)
Econ cruising speed	35 knots (65 km/h; 40 mph)
Max rate of climb at S/L	138 m (453 ft)/min
T-O run	70 m (230 ft)
Landing run	30 m (99 ft)
Best glide ratio at 35 knots (65 km/h; 40 mph)	7

AÉROPLUM

AÉROPLUM

9 rue de l'Eglise, Janves

AÉROPLUM INTERMEZZO

The Intermezzo two-seat microlight was designed by M Alain Erval. The prototype, powered by an 18·5 kW (25 hp) Hiro liquid-cooled engine, made its first flight on 14 August 1982. A description of the production model can be found in the 1985-86 *Jane's*. No more recent details have been received.

AGRI-PLANE

LA CULTURE DE L'AN 2000 SA

Groupe Roland Périnet et Cie, Route de Poitiers, 86110 Mirebeau

AGRI-PLANE CONDOR 2090

The Agri-Plane 2000 prototype of this crop spraying microlight was displayed at the 1981 Paris Air Show. Full details of the production model, of which there has been no recent news, can be found in the 1985-86 and previous editions of *Jane's*.

AILE

AIR INDUSTRIE LOISIR ENGINEERING SA

Z.I.-49960 Chatelais
Telephone: (41) 61 01 34

DIRECTORS:
François de Candé
André Gabry

AILE PATRILOR 3

Designed by M Patrick Lemonnier, the Patrilor 3 is a dual control rigid-wing two-seater. The aircraft first flew in May 1982 and entered production the following November. An enclosed cockpit, and ski or float landing gear, are optional.

TYPE: Two-seat microlight aircraft.

AIRFRAME: Aluminium alloy frame with double surface covering. Cable bracing; kingpost standard. Three-axis control (rudder, elevator and ailerons). Polycarbonate cockpit fairing and dual controls optional. A version with flaps, known as the Patrilor 3bis, is believed to be offered, and a cropspraying variant, the Agrilor.

LANDING GEAR: Tricycle type, without suspension or brakes.

POWER PLANT: One 32 kW (43 hp) Hirth 2701R 493 cc engine, driving a two-blade tractor propeller; 39·5 kW (53 hp) Robin EC44 2PM engine optional. Fuel tank capacity 33 litres (7·25 Imp gallons).

ACCOMMODATION: Two seats, side by side, in open or semi-enclosed position.

DIMENSIONS, EXTERNAL:	
Wing span	11·75 m (38 ft 6½ in)
Wing aspect ratio	6·39
Length overall	5·90 m (19 ft 4¼ in)
Height overall	2·45 m (8 ft 0½ in)
Propeller diameter	1·42 m (4 ft 8 in)
AREA:	
Wings, gross	21·60 m² (232·5 sq ft)
WEIGHTS AND LOADINGS:	
Weight empty	145 kg (320 lb)
Max T-O weight	320 kg (705 lb)
Max wing loading	14·8 kg/m² (3·04 lb/sq ft)
Max power loading	10·00 kg/kW (16·40 lb/hp)
PERFORMANCE:	
Never-exceed speed	59 knots (110 km/h; 68 mph)
Max level speed	48 knots (90 km/h; 56 mph)
Cruising speed	40 knots (75 km/h; 47 mph)
Stalling speed	19 knots (35 km/h; 22 mph)
Max rate of climb at S/L	150 m (492 ft)/min
Service ceiling	3,000 m (9,840 ft)
T-O and landing run	35 m (115 ft)

Typical range 108 nm (200 km; 124 miles)
g limits +4·5/−3·8 ultimate
Best glide ratio 8
Min rate of sink, power off 180 m (590 ft)/min

AILE PX-2000

Design studies for the PX-2000 began in December 1982, with the prototype's first flight following on 3 April 1983. The aircraft was introduced at the 1983 Paris Air Show.

TYPE: Single-seat microlight aircraft.

AIRFRAME AND LANDING GEAR: Essentially similar to the Patrilor 3, but with rubber suspension on nosewheel and spring suspension on mainwheels. Brakes optional on mainwheels. Glassfibre cockpit fairing, windscreen and glassfibre wheel fairings standard.

POWER PLANT: One 39·5 kW (53 hp) Robin EC44 2PM, with 2·5:1 reduction drive to a two-blade tractor propeller. Robin EC34 PM engine optional. Fuel tank capacity 30 litres (6·6 Imp gallons).

DIMENSIONS, EXTERNAL:
Wing span 9·10 m (29 ft 10¼ in)
Wing aspect ratio 6·57
Length overall 5·30 m (17 ft 4¾ in)
Height overall 2·40 m (7 ft 10½ in)
Propeller diameter 1·65 m (5 ft 5 in)

AREA:
Wings, gross 12·60 m² (135·6 sq ft)

WEIGHTS AND LOADINGS:
Weight empty 140 kg (308 lb)
Max T-O weight 260 kg (573 lb)
Max wing loading 20·6 kg/m² (4·23 lb/sq ft)
Max power loading 6·58 kg/kW (10·81 lb/hp)

PERFORMANCE (prototype, with 77 kg; 170 lb pilot):
Never-exceed speed 91 knots (170 km/h; 105 mph)
Max level speed 75 knots (140 km/h; 87 mph)
Max cruising speed 70 knots (130 km/h; 81 mph)
Stalling speed 19 knots (35 km/h; 22 mph)
Max rate of climb at S/L 306 m (1,004 ft)/min
Service ceiling 3,050 m (10,000 ft)
T-O run 35 m (115 ft)
Landing run 40 m (131 ft)
Range at cruising speed 189 nm (350 km; 217 miles)
g limits +6/−4 ultimate
Best glide ratio 10
Min rate of sink, power off 120 m (394 ft)/min

ALBARDE

ALBARDE RUTY

This aircraft, shown in an accompanying illustration, was displayed at the RSA's 1986 convention at Brienne. It is a tandem two-seater, with wings and tail unit strongly reminiscent of the familiar Jodel configuration. No details were available in August 1986.

ASL

CLUB D'AVIONS SUPERS LÉGERS DU CHER

A group of nine persons, of whom six are instructors at colleges of technical training, formed this club in order to collaborate on design and construction of an inexpensive rigid-wing two-seat ultralight aircraft. A biplane configuration was chosen, to ensure that the wings would be short enough to stow in a trailer when the aircraft is dismantled for towing behind a family car. To provide the best possible all-round view for the occupants, the cockpit was positioned forward of the wings, with a pusher engine under the trailing-edge of the upper wings. Work started in 1983, and the aircraft was displayed at the RSA's 1986 rally at Brienne.

ASL 18

TYPE: Two-seat ultralight biplane.

AIRFRAME: Strut braced biplane of all-wood construction, with Dacron covering on wings and tail control surfaces. Constant chord single-spar wings, without ailerons. Upper wings are fixed on inverted V cabane and single bracing strut each side, with single interplane strut each side, all of light alloy tubing. Lower wings are pivoted for roll control. Wing section NACA 23009. Dihedral 4°. Plywood covered forward of spar. Balsa wingtips. Basically rectangular fuselage, with eight frames, four longerons and plywood covering. Removable top decking between wings for access to controls. Glassfibre nose fairing. Strut braced tailplane mounted on top of short fin, both plywood covered. Elevator and large horn balanced rudder have plywood leading-edge and Dacron covering overall.

LANDING GEAR: Non-retractable tricycle type. Non-steerable nosewheel carried in light alloy fork. Mainwheels carried on arched cantilever legs of light alloy/spruce sandwich. Go-kart tyres, and brakes of powered bicycle type. Small tail bumper.

POWER PLANT: One 1,600 cc converted Volkswagen motorcar engine, carried on welded steel tube mounting and driving a homebuilt two-blade wooden pusher propeller. Plastics fuel tank behind port seat.

ACCOMMODATION: Two staggered side by side seats of plywood/balsa sandwich in open cockpit with windscreen. Dual controls.

DIMENSIONS, EXTERNAL:
Wing span, both 7·86 m (25 ft 9½ in)
Wing chord, constant 1·20 m (3 ft 11¼ in)
Wing aspect ratio 6·55
Length overall 6·24 m (20 ft 5¾ in)
Tailplane span 2·61 m (8 ft 6¾ in)
Propeller diameter 1·30 m (4 ft 3¼ in)

AREA:
Wings, gross 17·56 m² (189·0 sq ft)

WEIGHTS:
Weight empty 175 kg (386 lb)
Max T-O weight 365 kg (805 lb)

PERFORMANCE (estimated):
Max level speed 67 knots (125 km/h; 78 mph)
Stalling speed 25 knots (45 km/h; 28 mph)
Max rate of climb at S/L 144 m (472 ft)/min
g limits +7/−3

AVIASUD

AVIASUD ENGINEERING SA

Zone Industrielle de la Palud, 83600 Fréjus
Telephone: (33) 94 53 94 00
Telex: 461 172F AVIASUD
GENERAL MANAGER: François Goethals
TECHNICAL MANAGER: Bernard d'Otreppe

AVIASUD SIROCCO

Design of the Sirocco began in 1982, when construction of a prototype also started. The first flight was achieved in July 1982. Production began in January 1983. By January 1986 a total of 144 of these aircraft had been built. The Sirocco is distributed in many countries, including Australia, South Africa and the USA.

In September 1984, Patrice Franceschi, a French journalist, began the first round-the-world flight by microlight using a Sirocco. M Franceschi had flown over 30,000 km, from Paris to Thailand, via Dakar, Recife and Los Angeles, by February 1986.

A two-seat version of the Sirocco was being studied but no recent news of this has been received.

TYPE: Single-seat microlight aircraft; conforms to FAR Pt 103.

AIRFRAME: Wire braced high-wing monoplane, with constant chord sweptback rigid wings using MacCready TK 7315 (modified) aerofoil section. Thickness/chord ratio 15%. Dihedral 1°. Incidence 4°. Sweepback at quarter-chord 10°. Aluminium wing structure, with composites front spar and double surface Dacron covering. Stainless steel cables and kingpost standard. Wings are foldable. Pod and boom fuselage of moulded glassfibre and polyester, with epoxy resin. Three-axis control (rudder, all-moving tailplane and spoilers). Conventional glassfibre tail unit, with foam ribs. Anti-tab and trim tab on tailplane.

LANDING GEAR: Non-retractable tricycle type, comprising mainwheels on self-sprung glassfibre cantilever legs and steerable nosewheel. Wheel size 330 × 100 mm. Tyre pressure 1·08 bars (16 lb/sq in). Mainwheel brakes, wheel fairings, floats and skis optional. Nosewheel brake standard.

POWER PLANT: One 26 kW (35 hp) Rotax 377, 17 kW (23 hp) König 430RD, 22·4 kW (30 hp) KFM 107ER or 19·4 kW (26 hp) JPX PUL 425 engine, with 2·58:1 reduction gear to a Halter two-blade wooden pusher propeller. Electric start standard. Fuel capacity 20 litres (4·4 Imp gallons) standard, 40 litres (8·8 Imp gallons) optional.

ACCOMMODATION: Pilot only, in semi-enclosed or fully enclosed cockpit. Baggage space aft of seat, capacity 30 kg (66 lb).

AVIONICS: Radio and VOR optional.

DIMENSIONS, EXTERNAL:
Wing span 10·12 m (33 ft 2½ in)
Wing chord, constant 1·35 m (4 ft 5¼ in)
Wing aspect ratio 7·42
Length overall 5·85 m (19 ft 2¼ in)
Height overall 2·80 m (9 ft 2¼ in)
Tailplane span 2·20 m (7 ft 2½ in)
Wheel track 1·75 m (5 ft 9 in)
Wheelbase 1·40 m (4 ft 7 in)
Propeller (Rotax engine) 1·45 m (4 ft 9 in)

AREA:
Wings, gross 13·80 m² (148·5 sq ft)

WEIGHTS AND LOADINGS:
Weight empty 114-130 kg (251-286 lb)
Pilot weight range 55-120 kg (121-264 lb)
Max T-O weight 250 kg (551 lb)
Max wing loading 18·11 kg/m² (3·71 lb/sq ft)
Max power loading 9·62 kg/kW (15·74 lb/hp)

PERFORMANCE:
Never-exceed speed 64 knots (120 km/h; 74 mph)
Max level speed 62 knots (115 km/h; 71 mph)
Max cruising speed 54 knots (100 km/h; 62 mph)
Econ cruising speed 43 knots (80 km/h; 50 mph)
Stalling speed, engine idling 21 knots (40 km/h; 25 mph)
Max rate of climb at S/L 300 m (985 ft)/min
Service ceiling 6,500 m (21,325 ft)
T-O run 35 m (115 ft)
T-O to 15 m (50 ft) 90 m (295 ft)
Landing from 15 m (50 ft) 150 m (492 ft)
Landing run 30-50 m (98-164 ft)
Range with max standard fuel 162 nm (300 km; 186 miles)
Range with max fuel 270 nm (500 km; 310 miles)
Endurance with max standard fuel 4 h
g limits +6·7/−3·6

AVIASUD MISTRAL

The Mistral two-seat microlight is designed for recreational flying but is also suited to professional activities currently performed by high-cost conventional aeroplanes and helicopters, such as pilot training, aerial photography, TV and surveillance, banner towing, and cropspraying. A biplane configuration was selected to keep the wing span small for easy transportation, give good roll control, ensure an optimum weight/strength ratio, enable the all-moving lower wings to function as full-span ailerons, and provide all-round visibility with the cockpit positioned ahead of the wings. The side by side seating arrangement places the crew at the centre of gravity.

Design began in January 1984 and construction of a prototype started the following September. The first flight was achieved in June 1985. Production of ready assembled aircraft began in February 1986, by which time 21 had been ordered. Studies are being made into the possibility of supplying kits to the US market.

TYPE: Two-seat microlight and ARV aircraft; designed to FAR Pt 23.

AIRFRAME: Braced biplane, with constant chord single spar wings. Wing section NACA 23012. Dihedral 3°. Incidence 4°. Sweepforward 7°. Duralumin wing spars and wooden ribs, double surface covered. Glassfibre/carbonfibre/epoxy and polyester semi-monocoque fuselage. Conventional tail unit of similar construction to wings. Streamline interplane and cabane struts. Three-axis control (all-moving lower wings, all-moving mass balanced tailplane and mass balanced rudder). Anti-tab on lower wings and trim/anti-tab on elevator. Optional recovery parachute.

LANDING GEAR: Non-retractable tricycle type; mainwheels with brakes on glassfibre sprung legs. Nosewheel on leg with telescopic shock absorption. Mainwheels size 360 × 100 mm; nosewheel 330 × 100 mm. Mainwheel tyre pressure 1·47 bars (21 lb/sq in); nosewheel tyre pressure 0·98 bars (14 lb/sq in). Optional floats and skis.

POWER PLANT: One 47 kW (63 hp) Rotax 532 two-cylinder two-stroke engine, with 2·58:1 reduction gear to a ULX two-blade wooden propeller or three-blade adjustable pitch glassfibre propeller. One fuel tank, capacity 68 litres (15 Imp gallons).

ACCOMMODATION: Semi-enclosed side by side seating for pilot and passenger; enclosed cockpit will become future option. Baggage space under seats, capacity 20 kg (44 lb). Optional heating.

SYSTEM: 12V electrical system for instruments.

AVIONICS: Radio and VOR optional.

DIMENSIONS, EXTERNAL:
Wing span 9·40 m (30 ft 10 in)
Wing chord, constant 0·85 m (2 ft 9½ in)
Wing aspect ratio 6·68
Length overall 5·90 m (19 ft 4 in)
Height overall 2·20 m (7 ft 2½ in)
Tailplane span 2·70 m (8 ft 10¼ in)
Wheel track 1·75 m (5 ft 9 in)
Wheelbase 1·45 m (4 ft 9 in)
Propeller diameter 1·70 m (5 ft 7 in)

AREA:
Wings, gross 17·90 m² (192·7 sq ft)

WEIGHTS AND LOADINGS:
Weight empty 174 kg (383 lb)
Max T-O weight 400 kg (882 lb)
Max wing loading 22·3 kg/m² (4·58 lb/sq ft)
Max power loading 8·51 kg/kW (14·00 lb/hp)

PERFORMANCE (at max T-O weight):
Never-exceed speed 94 knots (175 km/h; 108 mph)
Max level speed at S/L 81 knots (150 km/h; 93 mph)

Albarde Ruty tandem two-seat homebuilt monoplane *(J. M. G. Gradidge)*

ASL 18 two-seat ultralight biplane *(Geoffrey P. Jones)*

Aviasud Sirocco single-seat microlight aircraft

Aviasud Mistral two-seat microlight biplane *(Alain Guillou)*

Barbero RB 60, a highly modified Auster J/1 Autocrat *(J. M. G. Gradidge)*

Single-seat Bardou Choucas I trike module, attached to a typical hang glider wing

Max cruising speed	73 knots (135 km/h; 84 mph)
Econ cruising speed	54 knots (100 km/h; 62 mph)
Stalling speed:	
power on	30 knots (55 km/h; 34·5 mph)
power off	33 knots (60 km/h; 38 mph)
Max rate of climb at S/L	240 m (785 ft)/min
Service ceiling	4,000 m (13,125 ft)
T-O run	80 m (262 ft)
T-O to 15 m (50 ft)	180 m (590 ft)
Landing from 15 m (50 ft)	200 m (656 ft)
Landing run	80 m (262 ft)
Range	270 nm (500 km; 310 miles)
Endurance	8 h
g limits	+4/−2 design
	+6/−3 ultimate

BARBERO

BARBERO RB 60

Among new types seen at the 1986 RSA convention at Brienne was the Barbero RB 60 (F-PPZG). As will be evident from the accompanying illustration, this is a highly modified Auster J/1 Autocrat (last described in the 1955-56 *Jane's*), with an Avco Lycoming engine, clipped wings and a revised tail unit. No other details are known.

BARDOU

ROBERT BARDOU

Bugard, 65320 Trie-sur-Baïse
Telephone: (62) 35 54 50

BARDOU CHOUCAS (JACKDAW)

The Choucas is a seat/fuselage/landing gear module which can be used in combination with several different power plants and various proprietary hang glider wings. It is made of laminated glassfibre and epoxy, reinforced with Kevlar and carbonfibre.

The Choucas I is a single-seater; the Choucas II is a tandem-seating two-place version. Both versions entered production but no recent news has been received. The module, equipped with tricycle landing gear with steerable nosewheel, weighs 40 kg (88 lb) and has a 25 litre (5·5 Imp gallon) fuel tank. Floats, skis and auxiliary fuel tank are available for current versions. A ducted fan powered version is reported to be under development.

BOUDEAU

MICHEL BOUDEAU

Résidence du Parc de St Maur F, 75 avenue St André de Novigens, 34000 Montpellier

BOUDEAU MB.10

M Boudeau has designed and built a half-scale representation of a Second World War Spitfire fighter. Registered F-PEMB, it flew for the first time on 8 June 1985 and is shown in an accompanying illustration. Construction is of wood and fabric, and the MB.10 is powered by a 78 kW (105 hp) Continental flat-four engine. All available details follow:

PERFORMANCE:
- Max level speed: 124 knots (230 km/h; 143 mph)
- Max cruising speed: 113 knots (210 km/h; 130 mph)
- Stalling speed: 60 knots (110 km/h; 69 mph)
- Range with max fuel: 432 nm (800 km; 497 miles)

BREDELET AND GROS

Til Châtel

BREDELET AND GROS BG-1

Seen at the RSA meeting at Birrfeld, Switzerland, in August 1985, the BG-1 is a four-seat all-metal cantilever high-wing monoplane (F-PYOL) built by MM Bredelet and Gros. It flew for the first time on 4 September 1982. Features include a 97 kW (130 hp) Rolls-Royce Continental engine, laminated plastics mainwheel legs, and full-length Perspex doors for optimum sideways field of view.

DIMENSIONS, EXTERNAL:
- Wing span: 8·54 m (28 ft 0¼ in)
- Length overall: 7·00 m (22 ft 11½ in)

WEIGHTS AND LOADING:
- Weight empty: 450 kg (992 lb)
- Max T-O weight: 750 kg (1,653 lb)
- Max power loading: 7·73 kg/kW (12·72 lb/hp)

PERFORMANCE:
- Max level speed: 113 knots (210 km/h; 130 mph)
- Cruising speed: 94 knots (175 km/h; 109 mph)
- Stalling speed: 46 knots (85 km/h; 53 mph)
- Max rate of climb at S/L: 600 m (1,970 ft)/min
- Service ceiling: 5,600 m (18,375 ft)
- Range with max fuel: 432 nm (800 km; 497 miles)

BRIFFAUD

GEORGES BRIFFAUD

32 rue Pierre Curie, 78000 Versailles

On the basis of ten years' experience in aviation, M Georges Briffaud began the design and construction of a small single-seat light aircraft of the Mignet tandem-wing type in 1974. After 5,000 hours of work, the prototype (F-WYOJ), known as the G.B. 10 Pou-Push, was flown for the first time on 23 June 1983 by M Desmots. Subsequent testing was taken over by the designer's son, M Michel Briffaud, and certification (CNRA) was obtained in July 1984. By April 1986 the Pou-Push (now F-PYOJ) had completed 50 flying hours, with only the addition of reduction gear to the power plant, substitution of a larger propeller, and replacement of the original friction brake on the nosewheel with a drum brake.

BRIFFAUD G.B. 10 POU-PUSH

TYPE: Single-seat tandem-wing homebuilt aircraft.

AIRFRAME: Forward wing comprises two strut braced semi-span structures which can be varied independently in incidence for roll control and collectively for pitch control. NACA 25000 series wing section. Slight dihedral from roots. Each half-span is made up of a main box spar with spruce booms and okoumé plywood webs, forming a D leading-edge torsion box with plywood skin; spruce trellis ribs; an auxiliary rear spar; and overall fabric covering. Trim tab in inboard trailing-edge of each half-span. Rear wing, of similar section and construction, is fixed, except for a wide-span central flap which deflects only upward to increase rate of descent. All-wood box fuselage of okoumé plywood over spruce frames and longerons. Lower surface fabric covered. Top decking and nosecone of composites. Triangular endplate fin at each tip of rear wing, with independent horn balanced rudder that deflects only outward and is returned to a neutral position by a spring. Fins and rudders are of wood with fabric covering.

LANDING GEAR: Non-retractable tricycle type, with single wheel on each unit. One-piece cantilever arch structure of composites carries mainwheels, with sprung wire bracing. Duralumin nosewheel fork is carried on a composites spring. Drum brake on steerable nosewheel. Wire guard under rear fuselage to protect propeller and rudders in taildown attitude.

POWER PLANT: One 22 kW (30 hp) Hirth 276R aircooled two-cylinder inline two-stroke engine, with 1·79:1 oil-bath reduction gear to a two-blade wooden fixed-pitch pusher propeller. A 25·4 kW (34 hp) DAF flat-twin modified motorcar engine may be fitted at a later date. Fuel comprises petroleum/oil (3·5%) mixture in composites tank on CG, capacity 38 litres (8·35 Imp gallons).

ACCOMMODATION: Single seat in enclosed cockpit, under one-piece removable transparent canopy. Control by conventional stick and rudder pedals.

SYSTEM: Electrical system includes 12V generator on engine for starting, and 12V 14A battery inside removable nosecone.

DIMENSIONS, EXTERNAL:
- Wing span: front: 7·20 m (23 ft 7½ in)
  - rear: 5·50 m (18 ft 0½ in)
- Length overall: 4·37 m (14 ft 4 in)
- Height overall: 1·52 m (5 ft 0 in)
- Propeller diameter: 1·20 m (3 ft 11¼ in)

AREA:
- Wings, gross: 13·75 m² (148·0 sq ft)

WEIGHTS AND LOADINGS:
- Weight empty: 175 kg (386 lb)
- Max T-O weight: 285 kg (628 lb)
- Max wing loading: 20·72 kg/m² (4·24 lb/sq ft)
- Max power loading: 12·95 kg/kW (20·93 lb/hp)

PERFORMANCE:
- Cruising speed: 59 knots (110 km/h; 68 mph)
- Stalling speed: 30 knots (55 km/h; 34 mph)
- Rate of climb at S/L with 77 kg (170 lb) pilot: 138 m (453 ft)/min
- Range with max fuel: 216 nm (400 km; 248 miles)

CENTRAIR

SA CENTRAIR

Aérodrome Le Blanc, BP 44, 36300 Le Blanc
Telephone: (54) 37 07 96
Telex: 750 272 F

In addition to its manufacture of powered fixed-wing aircraft and sailplanes, described in the appropriate sections of this edition, Centrair is marketing a microlight named the Parafan, which can be flown after as little as one hour's instruction.

CENTRAIR PARAFAN

Development of the Parafan was started in November 1984. Five prototypes were built and tested over a six-month period before the aircraft was considered ready for production. It offers pendulum stability in flight, can be landed safely power-off and, although the wing is not intended to be detachable (to prevent incorrect attachment), the Parafan can be transported on a small trailer or on the roof of a family car.

TYPE: Single-seat parawing microlight aircraft.

AIRFRAME: Conventional aluminium alloy trike unit, suspended under a NASA type ram air sports parachute wing by two clusters of steering cables. These are attached to the control column which, apart from a throttle, is the only flying control needed by the pilot. The nosewheel is steerable on the ground by means of the same control column.

POWER PLANT: One 20 kW (27 hp) Rotax 277 single-cylinder two-stroke engine, driving through reduction gear a composites four-blade pusher propeller mounted inside a guard-ring. Dual silencer standard.

AREA:
- Parawing: 37·0 m² (398·0 sq ft)

WEIGHT:
- Max T-O weight, excl pilot: 84 kg (185 lb)

PERFORMANCE:
- Manoeuvring speed: 19 knots (35 km/h; 22 mph)
- T-O run: 20-30 m (65-98 ft)
- Landing run: 0-20 m (0-65 ft)

CHASLE

YVES CHASLE

11 Lohsst-Concorde, 65310 Odof

CHASLE YC-100 HIRONDELLE

The YC-12 Tourbillon and LMC-1 Sprintair light aircraft, designed by M Chasle for amateur construction, were described in *Jane's* in the 1970s. His latest design, the YC-100 single-seat microlight, first flown on 1 May 1985, was demonstrated at the 1985 RSA meeting at Brienne and is shown in an accompanying illustration. It is a strut braced high-wing monoplane of fabric covered wooden construction, with open-sided cabin, powered by an 18 kW (24 hp) König engine driving a pusher propeller. Some non-stressed components, such as the nose of the fuselage, are made of composites. Three-axis control is fitted.

DIMENSIONS, EXTERNAL:
- Wing span: 8·20 m (26 ft 11 in)
- Length overall: 5·50 m (18 ft 0½ in)

WEIGHTS:
- Weight empty: 110 kg (243 lb)
- Max T-O weight: 210 kg (463 lb)

PERFORMANCE:
- Max level speed: 70 knots (130 km/h; 80 mph)
- Cruising speed: 54 knots (100 km/h; 62 mph)
- Stalling speed: 25 knots (45 km/h; 28 mph)
- Max rate of climb at S/L: 150 m (490 ft)/min

CMV

CONSTRUCTION MACHINES VOLANTES

2 *bis* avenue Montesquleu, 91200 Athis-Mons
Telephone: (6) 048 51 22
PROPRIETOR: Antoine Modica

The CMV Eclair microlights, last described and illustrated in the 1985-86 *Jane's*, have been superseded by the Ninja range. While of basically similar appearance, the Ninjas have strengthened and modified airframes and use Air Creation Alpha 20 Plus or other wings, including those of the Quartz series of 16-20 m² (172·2-215·3 sq ft) area.

CMV NINJA SERIES

The Ninja series comprises three basic models: the single-seat **Ninja Monoplace**, the tandem two-seat **Ninja Bi-Place** and the **Ninja Agri** agricultural sprayer. Each is based upon a foldable tetrahedral trike unit of AU4G anodised tubing, with rear axle suspension, nosewheel brake, and with optional equipment including a ballistic parachute and skis.

The single-seater uses the Alpha 17 wing as standard, although other wings are available. It is offered with a 20 kW (27 hp) Rotax 277 or Robin EC25 engine, and a plastic 11 litre (2·4 Imp gallon) fuel tank. A 'heavy' variant with a 24 kW (32 hp) engine allows the carriage of light freight.

The two-seat Ninja has features of the Monoplace plus propeller braking and tandem seats for the crew. With the Alpha 20 Plus wing as standard, it is offered with a 37·3 kW (50 hp) Robin EC44PM, 30·5 kW (41 hp) Rotax 447, 38 kW (51 hp) Rotax 462, 33·6 kW (45 hp) Rotax 503 or Citroen Visa engine and a 24 litre (5·3 Imp gallon) fuel tank. The Ninja Agri is similar to the Bi-Place but is fitted with a 23 m² (247·6 sq ft) ADAC wing and either a 16 nozzle sprayboom and pump, Micronair electrical spraygear, or dust spreader for its intended agricultural role. It has a swath width of 10 m (33 ft). A kit allows the Agri to be converted into the two-seat configuration as required.

CMV offers the Ninjas ready assembled, as kits for amateur construction, or in component form. The company also offers training facilities. The following details refer to the standard two-seater with a 40% double surface Alpha 20 Plus wing and EC44PM engine, unless stated otherwise:

DIMENSIONS, EXTERNAL:
- Wing span: 10·0 m (32 ft 10 in)
- Nose angle: 122°

AREA:
- Wings, gross: 19·8 m² (213·125 sq ft)

WEIGHTS:
- Weight empty: 162 kg (357 lb)
- Weight empty (Agri): 157 kg (346 lb)
- Max T-O weight: 320 kg (705 lb)

PERFORMANCE:
- Never-exceed speed: 59 knots (110 km/h; 68 mph)
- Max level speed: 46 knots (85 km/h; 53 mph)
- Cruising speed: 35 knots (65 km/h; 40 mph)
- Stalling speed: 22 knots (40 km/h; 25 mph)
- Max rate of climb at S/L: 180 m (590 ft)/min
- *g* limits: +6/−3

Boudeau MB.10 half-scale Spitfire representation *(Geoffrey P. Jones)*

Bredelet and Gros BG-1 four-seat monoplane *(Roland Eichenberger)*

Briffaud G.B. 10 Pou-Push tandem-wing aircraft

Centrair Parafan single-seat parawing microlight *(Geoffrey P. Jones)*

Prototype Chasle YC-100 Hirondelle microlight *(Geoffrey P. Jones)*

CMV Ninja Bi-Place two-seat microlight aircraft

CMV Ninja Monoplace single-seat microlight aircraft

CMV Ninja Agri agricultural microlight aircraft

COLOMBAN

MICHEL COLOMBAN

37bis rue Lakanal, 92500 Rueil-Malmaison
Telephone: 47 51 88 76

Formerly with the Morane and Potez companies, and now an aerodynamicist with Aérospatiale, M Colomban designed and built a very small and unique twin-engined lightplane named the Cricri. Its construction required some 1,200 hours of work and cost about 35,000 francs (1985 prices), including the engines.

Plans and a manual for building the latest MC 15 version of the Cricri are available to amateur constructors from M Colomban. They are in the French and English languages with European-standard metric dimensions.

News has been received of a further aircraft being designed and built by M Colomban. The only details yet available are that it is a two-seater and is expected to be economical to operate.

COLOMBAN MC 15 CRICRI

The MC 10 prototype of the Cricri was powered by two Rowena 6507J single-cylinder two-stroke engines of 137 cc, each giving 6·7 kW (9 hp) and weighing 6·5 kg (14·3 lb). It was claimed to be the smallest twin-engined aeroplane then flying, and the only one able to lift a useful load equivalent to 170 per cent of its own empty weight. Special constructional features permitted assembly or dismantling in only five minutes. Its light weight and small size made it particularly easy to transport on a trailer towed by car and to store in a garage or shed.

The Cricri was flown for the first time on 19 July 1973 by Robert Buisson, a 68-year-old pilot who had already logged 12,000 flying hours. A number of design refinements were made later that year, after which testing was resumed. Within fifteen days the Cricri had logged a total of 13 trouble-free flying hours, including rolls, reversements, 'split S' manoeuvres and inverted flight, made possible by its Tillotson diaphragm carburettor. Flight tests at up to 135 knots (250 km/h; 155 mph) confirmed that no special piloting skills were needed to fly the aircraft.

In particular, the Cricri handled like a single-engined design. This resulted from the fact that the two small engines were mounted close together, and from the carefully conceived shape of the cockpit canopy which deflected the propeller slipstream over the tail surfaces in such a way that the failure of one engine would produce no dangerous handling problems. If one engine of the prototype was throttled back fiercely, with hands and feet off the controls, it was said to do no more than begin a gentle turn.

Construction of a number of improved and re-engined Cricris was undertaken by friends of M Colomban, and the first of these to be completed (No. 4, built by M Gérard Constant of Dreux) was exhibited in the static park at the 1977 Paris Salon. This aircraft, powered by two 125 cc McCulloch MC-101 single-cylinder two-stroke engines (each 8·9 kW; 12 hp), flew for the first time in July 1978 and performed entirely satisfactorily. Take-off was achieved in 80 m (263 ft), in a time of 7 s, in zero wind, followed by a stabilised climb at a rate of 360 m (1,180 ft)/min. On the other hand, the MC-101 engines were clearly too sophisticated for this application. So, although they proved generally satisfactory, they were superseded by Valmet SM 160J engines on both M Constant's Cricri and on the version shown on the plans then available to amateur constructors. With Valmet engines the Cricri was designated MC 12. However, Valmet engines became unavailable. As a result, a specially modified version of the JPX PUL 425 was developed for the Cricri, known as the JPX PUL 212. With engines of this type, the Cricri is designated MC 15.

A second amateur built Cricri (No. 14, F-PYIJ) was flown in 1980, by father and son Jacques and Robert Laurent of Rennes. This was one of two MC 12s that appeared at the 1981 EAA Fly-in at Oshkosh, where it received a Designer's Award. Six MC 12s have flown in France, the latest built by M J. M. Monleau (No. 7), M Jacques Nuville (No. 8) and M Antoine Herault (No. 6). Official publication of Cricri plans was in April 1981 and by early 1986 more than 420 sets had been sold to amateur builders in France and neighbouring countries. The first aircraft built to these plans flew in 1983, and by February 1986 a total of 36 Cricris had been flown in France. Between 120 and 150 others were known to be under construction at that time.

Spinning trials with M Monleau's aircraft have suggested that the Cricri is difficult to put into a spin. After seven quite rapid turns, it will come out in half to three-quarters of a turn without requiring any action by the pilot. This aircraft has also achieved a measured speed of 159 knots (295 km/h; 183 mph) in a dive.

TYPE: Single-seat light homebuilt aircraft.

AIRFRAME: Cantilever low-wing monoplane of constant chord. Laminar-flow aerofoil derived from a Wortmann section. Thickness/chord ratio 21·7%. Dihedral 4° from roots. Incidence 1° at root, −30' at tip. No sweep. Single-spar light alloy box wing structure. Spar comprises a web riveted to 2024 light alloy angle-section booms. Inboard end of spar in each wing is of 'forked tongue' form, like that of many sailplanes, to permit rapid assembly and dismantling of wings (2 minutes). Closely spaced Klégécel ribs are bonded fore and aft of the spar. Skin consists of a single sheet of 2017 light alloy, bonded to structure under pressure after its leading edge has been formed. No rear spar. Wing box is closed at root by a riveted metal rib. Entire trailing-edge is occupied by two-section external flaps of the kind fitted to many wartime Junkers aircraft, operating collectively as high-lift devices and differentially as ailerons. Flaps are spar-less, consisting of a metal monocoque structure, with four metal ribs per section (at each tip and each pivot point), filled with Klégécel over the entire span and over 20 per cent of the chord. Flaps are each actuated via a ball-joint at the root. No controls pass through the wing box. Simple metal box fuselage structure of 2017 sheet made in two parts to reduce space required for manufacture. Fuselage structure stiffened by Klégécel stringers, bonded in place. Frames of 2017 light alloy riveted in position in line with the attachments for the wings, landing gear, tail unit and engine mountings. Cantilever T type tail unit, with sweptback vertical surfaces and all-moving constant-chord horizontal surface. Construction similar to that of wings. No tabs. Tailplane actuated by control rods, rudder by cables. Tailplane provided with artificial loading by bungee cord.

LANDING GEAR: Non-retractable tricycle type. Nosewheel fitted with bungee shock absorption and linked to rudder bar for steering. Each mainwheel carried on cantilever leg of glassfibre/epoxy laminations. Mainwheel tyres size 210 × 70, pressure 1·80 bars (28 lb/sq in). Nosewheel tyre size 200 × 50, pressure 0·80 bars (11 6 lb/sq in). Small diameter motorcycle drum brakes. Provision for fairings on all three wheels.

POWER PLANT: Two JPX PUL 212 single-cylinder two-stroke engines, each rated at 11 kW (15 hp) at 6,000 rpm. Yamaha inlet valves. Tillotson diaphragm carburettors for all-attitude flight. Each engine drives a two-blade propeller of composite glassfibre-epoxy construction. Plastics fuel tank in fuselage, capacity 23 litres (5 Imp gallons). Auxiliary tank in fuselage under consideration in 1985.

ACCOMMODATION: Single seat under large transparent canopy, hinged to open sideways to starboard. Ventilation through port in side of fuselage. No heating.

DIMENSIONS, EXTERNAL:

Wing span	4·90 m (16 ft 0¾ in)
Wing chord: incl flap (constant)	0·63 m (2 ft 0¾ in)
excl flap (constant)	0·48 m (1 ft 6¾ in)
Wing aspect ratio	7·75
Length overall	3·91 m (12 ft 10 in)
Height overall	1·20 m (3 ft 11¼ in)
Tailplane span	1·55 m (5 ft 1 in)
Wheel track	1·10 m (3 ft 7¼ in)
Wheelbase	1·15 m (3 ft 9¼ in)
Propeller diameter	0·695 m (2 ft 3½ in)
Distance between propeller centres	0·95 m (3 ft 1½ in)

DIMENSIONS, INTERNAL:

Cabin: Length	1·30 m (4 ft 3¼ in)
Max width	0·55 m (1 ft 9½ in)
Max height	0·82 m (2 ft 8¼ in)

AREA:

Wings, gross	3·10 m² (33·4 sq ft)

WEIGHTS AND LOADINGS:

Weight empty	80 kg (176 lb)
Max T-O and landing weight	170 kg (375 lb)
Max wing loading	54·84 kg/m² (11·23 lb/sq ft)
Max power loading	7·73 kg/kW (12·50 lb/hp)

PERFORMANCE (MC 15 at max T-O weight):

Max speed measured in dive	159 knots (295 km/h; 183 mph)
Max level speed	119 knots (220 km/h; 137 mph)
Max cruising speed (75% power)	108 knots (200 km/h; 124 mph)
Stalling speed: flaps down	39 knots (72 km/h; 45 mph)
flaps up	50 knots (93 km/h; 58 mph)
Max rate of climb at S/L	390 m (1,280 ft)/min
Rate of climb at S/L, one engine out	90 m (295 ft)/min
Service ceiling	5,000 m (16,400 ft)
T-O run	100 m (330 ft)
T-O to 15 m (50 ft)	300 m (985 ft)
Landing from 15 m (50 ft)	350 m (1,150 ft)
Landing run	150 m (495 ft)
Range with max fuel	215 nm (400 km; 248 miles)
g limits	+9/−4·5 ultimate
Best glide ratio, engines off and T-O configuration, at 60 knots (110 km/h; 69 mph)	11

CONTROT

CONTROT POU

Among the many recently built light aircraft of Mignet Pou du Ciel tandem-wing configuration exhibited at the RSA's 1986 convention at Brienne was the very small single-seat Controt Pou, shown in an accompanying illustration. The only detail available in August 1986 was that it is powered by a 24 kW (32 hp) DAF 44 engine. The familiar Mignet control system is retained, with an all-moving pivoted forward wing and large rudder, without a fixed fin.

COSMOS

COSMOS SARL

Rue du Stade, 21121 Fontaine-les-Dijon
Telephone: (80) 57 47 47
Telex: 530 035 LAMOUETTE

DIRECTORS:
Guy Renaud
Gérard Thévenot

Cosmos SARL was founded by M Gérard Thévenot, a European hang glider champion noted for his La Mouette range of hang glider wings (which see). Cosmos produces three types of trike unit matched to La Mouette wings: the Dragster single-seat, Bidulm two-seat units and Cosmagri crop-sprayer. Many hundreds have been sold.

COSMOS DRAGSTER 25

TYPE: Single-seat microlight aircraft, with flexible wings.

AIRFRAME: Aluminium alloy tube with double surface Dacron wings and stainless steel bracing cables. Weight shift control. Optional streamline nose fairing.

LANDING GEAR: Tricycle type, with all three wheels size 300 × 120. Nosewheel braking.

POWER PLANT: One 18·6 kW (25 hp) 250 cc Fuji Robin EC25PS two-stroke engine, with 2·4:1 reduction drive to a two-blade pusher propeller; 24 kW (32 hp) 340 cc EC34PM engine optional. Standard fuel capacity 12 litres (2·6 Imp gallons).

ACCOMMODATION: Pilot only, in open position.

DIMENSIONS, EXTERNAL:

Wing span	10·10 m (33 ft 1½ in)
Wing aspect ratio	6·8
Leading-edge length	6·20 m (20 ft 4 in)
Length overall	6·20 m (20 ft 4 in)
Nose angle	119°
Propeller diameter	1·37 m (4 ft 6 in)

AREA:

Wings, gross	16·00 m² (172·2 sq ft)

WEIGHTS AND LOADINGS:

Weight empty	85 kg (187 lb)
Pilot weight range	50-100 kg (110-220 lb)
Max T-O weight	195 kg (430 lb)
Max wing loading	12·2 kg/m² (2·50 lb/sq ft)
Max power loading	10·46 kg/kW (17·2 lb/hp)

PERFORMANCE:

Never-exceed speed	40 knots (75 km/h; 46 mph)
Max cruising speed	32 knots (60 km/h; 37 mph)
Stalling speed, power off	17 knots (30 km/h; 19 mph)
Max rate of climb at S/L	150 m (490 ft)/min
Service ceiling	2,500 m (8,200 ft)
T-O run	30 m (98 ft)
Landing run	40 m (131 ft)
Range with max fuel	81 nm (150 km; 93 miles)
Endurance with max fuel	2 h 30 min
g limits	+6/−3

COSMOS DRAGSTER 34

Essentially similar to the Dragster 25, except as follows:

LANDING GEAR: As for Dragster 25 except Dragster 34 III FC model has sprung suspension on all three units.

POWER PLANT: One 24 kW (32 hp) Fuji Robin EC34PM, with 2·4:1 reduction drive to a three-blade wooden propeller. Fuel tank capacity 33 litres (7·3 Imp gallons).

DIMENSIONS, EXTERNAL:

Wing aspect ratio	5·3
Leading-edge length	5·80 m (19 ft 0½ in)
Propeller diameter	1·40 m (4 ft 7 in)

AREA:

Wings, gross	19·00 m² (204·5 sq ft)

WEIGHTS AND LOADINGS:

Weight empty	95 kg (209 lb)
Max T-O weight	230 kg (507 lb)
Max wing loading	12·1 kg/m² (2·48 lb/sq ft)
Max power loading	9 64 kg/kW (15·84 lb/hp)

PERFORMANCE:

Max rate of climb at S/L	210 m (690 ft)/min
Service ceiling	3,500 m (11,475 ft)
Range with max fuel	162 nm (300 km; 186 miles)
Endurance with max fuel	5 h

Colomban MC 15 Cricris at Rennes in 1985

Controt Pou single-seat tandem-wing biplane *(J. M. G. Gradidge)*

Cosmos Cosmagri cropspraying microlight

Cosmos Dragster 34 III FC trike unit

Cosmos Dragster 25 single-seat trike unit

Cosmos Bidulm 44 with streamline nose fairing

COSMOS BIDULM 44

TYPE: Two-seat microlight aircraft, with flexible wings.

POWER PLANT: One 37 kW (50 hp) Fuji Robin 440 cc two-cylinder two-stroke engine. Fuel tank capacity 10 litres (2·2 Imp gallons).

DIMENSIONS, EXTERNAL:	
Wing span	10·60 m (34 ft 9¼ in)
Wing aspect ratio	5·9
Length (trike only)	2·40 m (7 ft 10½ in)
Height overall	2·45 m (8 ft 0½ in)
AREA:	
Wings, gross	19·00 m² (204·5 sq ft)
WEIGHTS AND LOADING:	
Weight empty	125 kg (275 lb)
Max T-O weight	283 kg (624 lb)
Max wing loading	14·89 kg/m² (3·05 lb/sq ft)
PERFORMANCE:	
Max level speed	46 knots (85 km/h; 53 mph)
Cruising speed	32 knots (60 km/h; 37 mph)
Best glide ratio	7

COSMOS COSMAGRI

As the name implies, this flexible wing, two-seat weight-shift microlight is designed specifically for agricultural cropspraying. Available in kit form or ready to fly, it has a main frame of duralumin, with double surface Dacron wings and stainless steel bracing cables. Tricycle landing gear; bungee shock absorption. Wheel size (all) 400 × 100 mm. Nosewheel braking. Floats, skis and towing system optional.

POWER PLANT: One 38·8 kW (52 hp) Rotax 503 engine, with 2·4:1 reduction drive to a two-blade wooden pusher propeller; 44·75 kW (60 hp) Arrow flat-twin engine available optionally. Standard fuel capacity 20 litres (4·4 Imp gallons).

DIMENSIONS, EXTERNAL:	
Wing span	10·50 m (34 ft 5½ in)
Wing aspect ratio	5·0
Leading-edge length	6·40 m (21 ft 0 in)
Keel length	2·20 m (7 ft 2½ in)
Height overall	3·80 m (12 ft 5½ in)
Propeller diameter	1·60 m (5 ft 3 in)
AREA:	
Wings, gross	22·00 m² (236·8 sq ft)
WEIGHTS AND LOADINGS:	
Weight empty	145 kg (320 lb)
Pilot weight range	50-110 kg (110-242 lb)
Max T-O weight	360 kg (794 lb)
Max wing loading	16·36 kg/m² (3·35 lb/sq ft)
Max power loading	9·11 kg/kW (14·97 lb/hp)
PERFORMANCE:	
Max level speed	43 knots (80 km/h; 50 mph)
Max cruising speed	38 knots (70 km/h; 43 mph)
Stalling speed	20 knots (37 km/h; 23 mph)
Max rate of climb at S/L	240 m (785 ft)/min
Range with max fuel	75·5 nm (140 km; 87 miles)
g limits	+6/−3
Best glide ratio	6
Min rate of sink	90 m (295 ft)/min

COUPÉ-AVIATION

COUPÉ-AVIATION

La Trute, Azay-sur-Cher, 37270 Montlouis sur Loire

Telephone: (47) 50 41 84

M Jacques Coupé designed and built a two-seat lightplane designated JC-01 (F-PXKV), which was flown for the first time on 16 March 1976. Plans are available to amateur constructors, together with plans of the more powerful JC-2 which flew for the first time in 1981.

COUPÉ-AVIATION JC-01

The accompanying photograph of the JC-01 shows it as originally flown. It has since been fitted with a sweptback fin and rudder. Further JC-01s are being built, some powered by modified Volkswagen motorcar engines of 1,600 or 1,700 cc.

TYPE: Two-seat homebuilt sporting aircraft.

AIRFRAME: Cantilever low-wing monoplane of constant chord. Conventional single-spar structure of wood, with lightweight lattice ribs and fabric covering. Leading-edge fixed slot. Slotted ailerons of similar construction to wings. Lattice fuselage of wood, with wood and fabric covering. Wooden fin (integral with fuselage), rudder and elevators fabric covered. Fixed incidence tailplane has plywood skin. Manually operated trim tab in elevator.

LANDING GEAR: Non-retractable tailwheel type. Shock absorption of main units by rubber in compression, and of tailwheel by coil spring. Mainwheel tyres size 420 × 150. Cable operated caliper brakes.

POWER PLANT: One 48·5 kW (65 hp) Continental A65-8F flat-four engine, driving a two-blade fixed-pitch wooden propeller with spinner. Fuel tank forward of cockpit, capacity 60 litres (13 Imp gallons).

ACCOMMODATION: Two seats side by side, beneath rearward sliding transparent canopy. Dual controls. Accommodation is heated and ventilated.

DIMENSIONS, EXTERNAL:
Wing span 8·35 m (27 ft 4¾ in)
Wing aspect ratio 5·95
Length overall 6·40 m (21 ft 0 in)

AREA:
Wings, gross 11·69 m² (125·83 sq ft)

WEIGHTS AND LOADINGS:
Weight empty 330 kg (728 lb)
Max T-O weight 580 kg (1,279 lb)
Max wing loading 49·6 kg/m² (10·16 lb/sq ft)
Max power loading 11·96 kg/kW (19·68 lb/hp)

PERFORMANCE (as originally flown, at max T-O weight):
Max level speed 108 knots (200 km/h; 124 mph)
Max cruising speed 81 knots (150 km/h; 93 mph)
Econ cruising speed 76 knots (140 km/h; 87 mph)
T-O speed 27 knots (50 km/h; 31 mph)
Approach speed 37-44 knots (70-80 km/h; 43-50 mph)
Stalling speed 25 knots (45 km/h; 28 mph)
T-O run 90 m (295 ft)

COUPÉ-AVIATION JC-2

The JC-2 is generally similar to the JC-01 but has a more powerful engine and tricycle landing gear. Construction of the prototype (F-WYJI/F-PYJI) was started in September 1976, and it flew for the first time in May 1981. By early 1986, about six JC-2s were under construction by amateurs, with 74·5 kW (100 hp) engines. It is intended to market the JC-2 in kit form.

TYPE: Two-seat homebuilt aircraft.

AIRFRAME: Cantilever low-wing monoplane of constant chord, built in one piece. Wing section NACA 23012. Dihedral 0° on centre-section, 5° on outer panels. Incidence 4° at root. Main box spar has spruce booms and plywood webs. I type rear spar has spruce booms and plywood web, reinforced to carry slotted ailerons and slotted flaps. Ribs of similar construction. Plywood leading-edge with fixed slot. Wings, ailerons and flaps covered with Dacron overall. Conventional truss fuselage of wood, with three main frames; forward portion covered with plywood. Fabric covering overall. Conventional cantilever wood tail unit, with slightly sweptback vertical surfaces. Fixed surfaces plywood covered; control surfaces fabric covered. Trim tab on elevator.

LANDING GEAR: Non-retractable tricycle type, with single wheel on each unit. Swivelling nosewheel, size 330 × 130, with oleo-pneumatic shock absorber. Mainwheels size 420 × 150, with mechanical brakes and oleo-pneumatic shock absorption.

POWER PLANT: One 67 kW (90 hp) Continental flat-four engine in prototype, driving a two-blade fixed-pitch wooden propeller. Fuel tank, capacity 90 litres (19·75 Imp gallons), in fuselage aft of firewall.

ACCOMMODATION: Two glassfibre seats side by side under large rearward sliding transparent canopy. Baggage space, capacity 20 kg (44 lb), aft of seats. Cabin ventilated and heated.

EQUIPMENT: Almost to IFR standards.

DIMENSIONS, EXTERNAL:
Wing span 8·35 m (27 ft 4¾ in)
Wing aspect ratio 5·95
Length overall 6·40 m (21 ft 0 in)

AREA:
Wings, gross 11·70 m² (126·0 sq ft)

WEIGHTS AND LOADINGS:
Weight empty 500 kg (1,103 lb)
Max T-O weight 750 kg (1,653 lb)
Max wing loading 64·1 kg/m² (13·12 lb/sq ft)
Max power loading 11·19 kg/kW (18·37 lb/hp)

PERFORMANCE (with 67 kW; 90 hp engine):
Max level speed 108 knots (200 km/h; 124 mph)
Max cruising speed 97 knots (180 km/h; 112 mph)
Econ cruising speed 86 knots (160 km/h; 99 mph)
Approach speed 54 knots (100 km/h; 62 mph)
Stalling speed: flaps up 27 knots (50 km/h; 31 mph)
flaps down 24 knots (45 km/h; 28 mph)

COUPÉ-AVIATION JC-3

The JC-3 differs from the JC-01 primarily in having a sweptback fin and a 51 kW (68 hp) Volkswagen 1,700 cc converted motorcar engine. It is believed that two examples were under construction by amateurs in early 1985 but no recent news has been received.

CROSES

EMILIEN CROSES

63 route de Davayé (Aérodrome), 71000 Charnay les Macon

Telephone: (85) 38 07 31

Since M Emilien Croses began work as a designer/constructor in 1947, he has been responsible for nine different prototypes, all of which have been certfiicated. Addition of the initial 'B' in the designation of some of these reflects assistance given to M Croses by M R. Bujon, a specialist metal worker. Other assistance has been given by MM J. Mottez with stressing and aerodynamics; Alain Croses with aerodynamic studies; and Yves Croses, an engineer specialising in applications of high strength plastics and glassfibre.

CROSES EAC-3 POUPLUME

As in the familiar Mignet designs, the Pouplume single-seat tandem-wing biplane has a fixed rear wing and a pivoted forward wing which dispenses with the need for ailerons and elevators. A conventional rudder is fitted, with a large tailwheel built into its lower edge.

Construction is conventional, with spruce wing structure and a square-section spruce fuselage covered with okoumé ply. The main landing gear consists of Vespa scooter wheels carried on a wooden cross-member.

The power unit in the prototype (EAC-3-01) is a 7·8 kW (10·5 hp) Moto 232 cc two-stroke motorcycle engine, with chain reduction drive to the propeller shaft. The reduction ratio is 3·5 : 1, giving a propeller speed of 1,300 rpm. Fuel capacity is 10 litres (2·2 Imp gallons).

The EAC-3-01 Pouplume took 600 h to build and flew for the first time in June 1961. It was followed, in 1967, by a second prototype (EAC-3-02), with a 20 cm (8 in) longer fuselage. M Croses is offering sets of plans to other constructors, and at least 12 Pouplumes had flown by early 1986. The one shown in the accompanying illustration was built in France by an amateur constructor.

A version known as the **Pouplume Sport** differs in having a 1,500 cc Volkswagen engine and reduced span of 6·40 m (21 ft 0 in). About 55 Pouplume Sports are thought to be under construction.

The following data apply to the standard Moto-powered Pouplume:

DIMENSIONS, EXTERNAL:
Wing span: forward wing 7·80 m (25 ft 7 in)
rear wing 7·00 m (23 ft 0 in)
Length overall 4·70 m (15 ft 3 in)
Height overall 1·80 m (5 ft 11 in)

AREA:
Wings, gross 16·02 m² (172·2 sq ft)

WEIGHTS AND LOADINGS:
Weight empty 110-140 kg (243-310 lb)
Max T-O weight 220-260 kg (485-573 lb)
Max wing loading, at 260 kg AUW 16·23 kg/m² (3·3 lb/sq ft)
Max power loading, at 260 kg AUW and with 7·8 kW engine 33·33 kg/kW (54·57 lb/hp)

PERFORMANCE (A: 7·8 kW; 10·5 hp engine, B: 13·4 kW; 18 hp engine):
Max level speed: A 38 knots (70 km/h; 43 mph)
B 65 knots (120 km/h; 75 mph)
Econ cruising speed: A 27 knots (50 km/h; 31 mph)
B 38 knots (70 km/h; 43 mph)
T-O speed: A 14 knots (25 km/h; 16 mph)
Landing speed: A 10 knots (18 km/h; 11 mph)
T-O run: A 60 m (200 ft)
B 40 m (131 ft)
Landing run: A 24 m (80 ft)
Fuel consumption: A 4·5 litres (1 Imp gallon)/h

CROSES EC-6 CRIQUET (LOCUST)

This design by Emilien Croses is a development of his earlier EC-1-02 prototype and is a side by side two-seater based on the familiar Mignet tandem-wing formula. Construction of the prototype was started in March 1964 and the EC-6-01 flew for the first time on 6 July 1965.

Plans of the wooden version of the Criquet, of which details follow, are available to amateur constructors. At least seven examples were flying by early 1986, with about 60 more under construction.

An all-plastics version, known as the LC-10, was described briefly in the 1977-78 *Jane's*. Plans of this are not available.

TYPE: Two-seat tandem-wing homebuilt aircraft.

AIRFRAME: Forward wing built in one piece and pivoted on two streamlined supports, giving variable incidence between −2° and +12°. Fixed rear (lower) wing. Wing section NACA 23012 (modified). Each wing has a two-spar wooden structure, with plywood leading-edge, overall fabric covering and some components of glassfibre. Ailerons optional. Spruce fuselage, covered with plywood. Glassfibre engine cowling. Plywood covered spruce fin and rudder. No tailplane or elevators.

LANDING GEAR: Non-retractable tailwheel type. Mainwheels, size 420 × 150, carried on single cantilever arch structure made from ash wood on a forme and covered with glassfibre. Tailwheel, same size, semi-enclosed in bottom of rudder.

POWER PLANT: One 67 kW (90 hp) Continental flat-four engine, driving a modified SIPA two-blade propeller. Fuel capacity originally 60 litres (13 Imp gallons); planned to be increased to 90 litres (20 Imp gallons).

ACCOMMODATION: Two seats side by side in enclosed cabin. Door on starboard side. Constructors can utilise either the special Mignet type of control system or a conventional system with ailerons and rudder bar.

DIMENSIONS, EXTERNAL:
Wing span: forward wing 7·80 m (25 ft 7 in)
rear wing 7·00 m (22 ft 11½ in)
Wing chord (constant, each) 1·20 m (3 ft 11¼ in)
Length overall 4·65 m (15 ft 3 in)

AREA:
Wings, gross 16·02 m² (172·2 sq ft)

WEIGHTS AND LOADINGS:
Weight empty 290 kg (639 lb)
Max T-O weight 550 kg (1,213 lb)
Max wing loading 34·33 kg/m² (7·03 lb/sq ft)
Max power loading 8·21 kg/kW (13·48 lb/hp)

PERFORMANCE (officially certificated, at max T-O weight):
Max level speed at S/L 115 knots (213 km/h; 132 mph)
Max cruising speed 92 knots (170 km/h; 106 mph)
Econ cruising speed 86 knots (160 km/h; 99 mph)
Min flying speed 22 knots (40 km/h; 25 mph)
Will not stall
T-O time (max) 6 s
Time to 2,000 m (6,560 ft) 6 min 14 s

CROSES EC-8 TOURISME

This three-seat touring aircraft is generally similar to the standard wooden Criquet but can have an 'all-terrain' landing gear comprising two tandem pairs of mainwheels. At least two EC-8s are flying, that illustrated (F-PTXC) having conventional single mainwheel units.

CROSES B-EC-9 PARAS-CARGO

Unique in being a cargo transport for construction and operation by amateurs, the B-EC-9 employs the same Mignet tandem-wing configuration and simple wood construction as earlier Croses designs. Like them, it can be built with conventional three-axis controls or the special two-control system devised by Henri Mignet, with large 'tab' control surfaces on the trailing-edge of the rear wing.

The Paras-Cargo was designed to be offered to amateur constructors and clubs in the form of both plans and kits of components, but only the prototype is known to have been completed. Details and an illustration can be found in the 1984-85 *Jane's*.

CROSES

YVES CROSES

35 Avenue de Saxe, 69006, Lyon

CROSES AIRPLUME

M Yves Croses has used the tandem wing Mignet principle for the Airplume. It is a two-seat aircraft, the prototype of which made its first flight on 5 October 1983. The power plant is a 26 kW (35 hp) Cuyuna engine driving a two-blade tractor propeller. Limbach or Rectimo engines are options. Fuel capacity is 100 litres (22 Imp gallons). The Airplume's composite structure is constructed of glassfibre reinforced polyester and carbonfibre. Tandem open cockpits are provided for two people, each weighing up to 75 kg (165 lb). Two- or three-axis control is available, and rigging time is about 30 min. A total of 26 kits had been sold in the first year of availability, plus two ready assembled Airplumes. No recent news has been received.

DIMENSIONS, EXTERNAL:
Wing span 7·90 m (25 ft 11 in)
Length overall 5·20 m (17 ft 0¾ in)
Height overall 1·80 m (5 ft 11 in)

AREA:
Wings, gross 19·00 m² (204·5 sq ft)

WEIGHTS AND LOADINGS:
Weight empty 174 kg (383 lb)
Max T-O weight 324 kg (714 lb)
Max wing loading 17·05 kg/m² (3·49 lb/sq ft)
Max power loading 12·46 kg/kW (20·40 lb/hp)

PERFORMANCE (Cuyuna engine, and two 75 kg; 165 lb occupants, except where stated):
Never-exceed speed 81 knots (150 km/h; 93 mph)
Max level speed 70 knots (130 km/h; 81 mph)
Econ cruising speed 54 knots (100 km/h; 62 mph)
Max rate of climb at S/L:
solo 300 m (985 ft)/min
dual 180 m (590 ft)/min
Endurance 2 h 30 min

Coupé-Aviation JC-01 two-seat lightplane

Coupé-Aviation JC-2 with more powerful engine and tricycle landing gear

Croses EAC-3 Pouplume light aircraft (Moto engine)

Croses EC-6 Criquet *(Geoffrey P. Jones)*

Croses EC-8 Tourisme built by M Jacques Langlois *(Geoffrey P. Jones)*

Croses Airplume two-seat tandem wing aircraft *(Geoffrey P. Jones)*

Le Solitaire, a single-seat light aircraft built by M R. Cuvelier *(Geoffrey P. Jones)*

Cuvelier/Lacroix Autoplan 2L12 tandem-wing biplane *(Geoffrey P. Jones)*

CUVELIER

ROLAND CUVELIER

Villers en Argonne

M Cuvelier has designed and built a number of light aircraft, of which two are shown in accompanying illustrations.

CUVELIER LE SOLITAIRE

The general appearance of this single-seat homebuilt monoplane is shown in the illustration of the prototype, taken at Brienne. Although 95 per cent complete in 1985, it will not be finished and flown until M Cuvelier has ended his work on the Lacroix 2L12 and LNB 11.

CUVELIER/LACROIX 2L12 and LNB 11

An accompanying illustration, taken at Brienne in July 1986, shows M Cuvelier's modernised reproduction of the Autoplan 2L12 single-seat tandem-wing biplane that was designed in France by the late Léon Lacroix in the years immediately after the Second World War. Work on it was started in the Summer of 1984. When complete, M Cuvelier intends to build a two-seat Lacroix/Nazaris/Bourdin Autoplan LNB 11.

TYPE: Single-seat tandem-wing homebuilt aircraft.

AIRFRAME: Cantilever tandem-wing biplane of Autoplan type, with fixed forward wing, carrying full-span ailerons, and all-moving rear wings. Large trimming surface at root of port rear wing. Conventional fuselage, fin and rudder. Construction entirely of wood (Oregon pine and birch plywood), with fabric covering on outer wings, aft of leading-edge D spar, and rudder. Wings are conventional two-spar constant-chord structures.

LANDING GEAR: Non-retractable tailwheel type. Cantilever arch mainwheel legs, with wheel fairings.

POWER PLANT: One 19·4 kW (26 hp) Citroën Visa converted motorcar engine, with direct drive to a two-blade fixed-pitch wooden propeller, with large spinner.

ACCOMMODATION: Pilot only, in open cockpit.

DIMENSIONS, EXTERNAL:

Wing span: forward	6·20 m (20 ft 4 in)
rear	4·40 m (14 ft 5¼ in)
Length overall	3·30 m (10 ft 10 in)

AREA:

Wings, total, gross	9·00 m² (96·875 sq ft)

WEIGHT:

Weight empty	about 120 kg (265 lb)

DANIS

AILE VOLANTE B. DANIS

71 rue Roger François, 94700 Maisons Alfort
Telephone: (1) 4368 22 37

DIRECTORS:
Bernard Danis
Jean-Pierre Danis

Based on his company's Sabre and Mercure one-man and two-man hang gliders, M Danis offers various trike units to convert these gliders into microlight aircraft. Current production microlights are the Faucheux, Mercure/Tempête 20, Mercure/Sabre S21 and Mercure/Sabre S23.

DANIS FAUCHEUX

First flown in October 1981, the Faucheux combines the Danis trike unit with a Tempête 17 hang glider wing.

TYPE: Single-seat flexwing microlight aircraft.

AIRFRAME: Aluminium alloy trike unit. Dacron covering, double surface over 60 per cent of wing area. Reinforced Mylar leading-edge. Stainless steel cable bracing; kingpost standard. Weight shift control.

LANDING GEAR: Tricycle type, with brake on steerable nosewheel. Mainwheel diameter 40 cm; nosewheel diameter 26 cm.

POWER PLANT: One 15 kW (20 hp) Solo 335 or 13·8 kW (18·5 hp) Robin EC25PS engine, with 2·8:1 reduction drive to a two-blade propeller. Fuel capacity 10 litres (2·2 Imp gallons) in main tank, 23 litres (5·1 Imp gallons) in reserve.

ACCOMMODATION: Pilot only, in open position.

DIMENSIONS, EXTERNAL:
- Wing span: 10·00 m (32 ft 9¾ in)
- Wing aspect ratio: 5·9
- Height overall: 3·12 m (10 ft 2¾ in)
- Propeller diameter: 1·37 m (4 ft 6 in)

AREA:
- Wings, gross: 16·80 m² (180·8 sq ft)

WEIGHTS AND LOADINGS:
- Weight empty: 71 kg (156·5 lb)
- Max T-O weight: 180 kg (397 lb)
- Max wing loading: 10·7 kg/m² (2·19 lb/sq ft)
- Max power loading: 12·08 kg/kW (19·85 lb/hp)

PERFORMANCE:
- Never-exceed speed: 53 knots (100 km/h; 62 mph)
- Max level speed: 46 knots (85 km/h; 53 mph)
- Max cruising speed: 30 knots (55 km/h; 34 mph)
- Stalling speed: 17 knots (30 km/h; 19 mph)
- Max rate of climb at S/L: 120 m (394 ft)/min
- Service ceiling: 2,000 m (6,560 ft)
- T-O run: 20 m (66 ft)
- Landing run: 15 m (50 ft)
- Typical range: 65 nm (120 km; 74 miles)
- *g* limits: +3·5/−2·3
- Min rate of sink: 66 m (216 ft)/min
- Best glide ratio: 8

DANIS MERCURE

TYPE: Tandem two-seat microlight aircraft, with flexible wings.

AIRFRAME AND LANDING GEAR: Similar to Faucheux, but offered with three wing/power plant combinations. Tempête 20 with 80 per cent double surface covering; Sabre S21 with 45 per cent double surface; and Sabre S23 with 30 per cent double surface.

POWER PLANT: Tempête 20: one 32 kW (43 hp) modified Cuyuna 430RR engine. Sabre S21: one 34·3 kW (46 hp) Hirth 2701R engine. Sabre S23: one 31·3 kW (42 hp) Hirth 276R engine. Reduction gear drive to two-blade pusher propeller. Fuel capacities as for Faucheux.

The following specifications apply to the Mercure/Tempête 20:

DIMENSIONS, EXTERNAL:
- Wing span: 10·40 m (34 ft 1½ in)
- Wing aspect ratio: 5·5
- Length overall: 4·00 m (13 ft 1½ in)
- Height overall: 2·91 m (9 ft 6½ in)
- Propeller diameter: 1·40 m (4 ft 7 in)

AREA:
- Wings, gross: 19·80 m² (213·1 sq ft)

WEIGHTS AND LOADINGS:
- Weight empty: 120 kg (264·5 lb)
- Max T-O weight: 290 kg (639 lb)
- Max wing loading: 14·6 kg/m² (2·99 lb/sq ft)
- Max power loading: 9·04 kg/kW (14·86 lb/hp)

PERFORMANCE:
- Never-exceed speed: 70 knots (130 km/h; 80 mph)
- Max level speed: 59 knots (110 km/h; 68 mph)
- Max cruising speed: 40 knots (75 km/h; 47 mph)
- Stalling speed: 19 knots (35 km/h; 22 mph)
- Max rate of climb at S/L: 150 m (492 ft)/min
- Service ceiling: 3,000 m (9,840 ft)
- T-O and landing run: 20 m (66 ft)
- Typical range: 81 nm (150 km; 93 miles)
- *g* limits: +3·5/−2·3
- Best glide ratio: 8·5

DELEMONTEZ-DESJARDINS

DELEMONTEZ-DESJARDINS D-01 IBIS

This three-seat light aircraft (F-PZIK), built by M Desjardins and first flown on 12 June 1985, is basically a Jodel D.11 derivative with non-retractable tricycle landing gear. Construction is conventional, of wood and fabric, and the Ibis is powered by a 74·5 kW (100 hp) Avco Lycoming flat-four engine, driving a two-blade fixed-pitch wooden propeller.

DIMENSIONS, EXTERNAL:
- Wing span: 8·22 m (26 ft 11¾ in)
- Length overall: 6·20 m (20 ft 4 in)

WEIGHTS AND LOADING:
- Weight empty: 395 kg (871 lb)
- Max T-O weight: 617 kg (1,360 lb)
- Max power loading: 8·28 kg/kW (13·60 lb/hp)

PERFORMANCE:
- Max level speed: 105 knots (195 km/h; 121 mph)
- Cruising speed: 92 knots (170 km/h; 105 mph)
- Min flying speed: 43 knots (80 km/h; 50 mph)
- Max rate of climb at S/L: 180 m (590 ft)/min

DOHET

RAYMOND DOHET

5 rue des Grands Agustins, 75006 Paris
Telephone: (1) 46 33 15 79

DOHET ARTHUR

Raymond Dohet built a series of single-seat trike type microlights using the 'monopole' wing suspension system. His Dohet III design, which he entered in the 1982 London-Paris microlight race, has been developed into a commercial product named Arthur. It is intended primarily for use with the Véliplane Centaure or Danis Sabre 23 hang glider wings, although M Dohet has flown the Arthur with a smaller Alpha wing to achieve higher speeds. M Dohet's trike units are characterised by their extremely robust construction. By early 1986 seven had been built. Plans are available.

TYPE: Single- or two-seat flexible-wing microlight; conforms to FAI and French national standards.

AIRFRAME: Duralumin and steel tube frame. Single surface Dacron covered wing; stainless steel bracing. Kingpost standard. Weight shift control.

LANDING GEAR: Tricycle type with all three wheels size 400 × 30. Steerable nosewheel. Rubber suspension on all units.

POWER PLANT: One 22·4 kW (30 hp) Citroën 650 cc converted automobile engine, with direct drive to a two-blade wooden pusher propeller. Citroën 1300 or VW1600 engines optional, as is a ducted twelve-blade plastics fan. Fuel tank capacity 23 litres (5 Imp gallons).

ACCOMMODATION: Pilot only in open position.

DIMENSIONS, EXTERNAL:
- Wing span: 10·00 m (32 ft 9¾ in)
- Propeller diameter: 1·20 m (3 ft 11¼ in)

AREAS:
- Wings, gross: standard: 23·0 m² (247·6 sq ft)
- Alpha: 20·0 m² (215·3 sq ft)

WEIGHTS AND LOADINGS:
- Weight empty: 150 or 175 kg (331 or 386 lb)
- Pilot weight range: 60-120 kg (132-265 lb)
- Max T-O weight: 325 kg (716 lb)
- Max wing loading:
  - standard: 14·13 kg/m² (2·89 lb/sq ft)
  - Alpha: 16·25 kg/m² (3·32 lb/sq ft)
- Max power loading: 14·51 kg/kW (23·87 lb/hp)

PERFORMANCE:
- Max level speed: 43 knots (80 km/h; 50 mph)
- Max cruising speed:
  - propeller: 35 knots (65 km/h; 40 mph)
  - fan, Alpha wing: 40 knots (75 km/h; 47 mph)
- Econ cruising speed: 30 knots (55 km/h; 34 mph)
- T-O run: 50 m (164 ft)
- Landing run: 30 m (98 ft)
- Range with max fuel: 135 nm (250 km; 155 miles)
- Endurance with max fuel: 4 h

DURUBLE

ROLAND DURUBLE

40 rue de Paradis, Les Essarts, 76530 Grand-Couronne
Telephone: (35) 32 20 63

M Roland Duruble, with MM Guy Chanut and Legrand, of Rouen, designed and built a two-seat all-metal light aircraft named the Edelweiss RD-02, which flew for the first time on 7 July 1962. Plans of the similar Edelweiss RD-02A are available to amateur constructors, together with plans of an enlarged version, known as the Edelweiss RD-03.

DURUBLE EDELWEISS RD-02A

The Edelweiss RD-02A is an improved and higher-powered version of the original RD-02, details of which appeared in the 1972-73 *Jane's*. Designed in the Utility category, it is similar in many respects to the RD-03 and uses the same wings and tail surfaces. The fuselage, while remaining a conventional semi-monocoque structure, is shorter and accommodates only two persons side by side. The first RD-02A to fly, on 1 December 1984, was built by Mr Ken Taylor of Vancouver, Canada.

Many of the details given for the RD-03 apply also to the RD-02A. The following data reflect some of the differences:

TYPE: Two-seat homebuilt aircraft.

POWER PLANT: One 74·5 kW (100 hp) Continental O-200-A flat-four engine. Two fuel tanks in wings, total capacity 100 litres (22 Imp gallons).

DIMENSIONS, EXTERNAL:
- Wing span: 8·82 m (28 ft 11¼ in)
- Length overall: 6·45 m (21 ft 7¼ in)

WEIGHTS AND LOADINGS:
- Weight empty, equipped: 455 kg (1,003 lb)
- Max T-O weight: 715 kg (1,576 lb)
- Max wing loading: 62·8 kg/m² (12·86 lb/sq ft)
- Max power loading: 9·60 kg/kW (15·76 lb/hp)

PERFORMANCE:
- Never-exceed speed: 170 knots (316 km/h; 196 mph)
- Max level speed at S/L: 132 knots (245 km/h; 152 mph)
- Max cruising speed (75% power): 120 knots (223 km/h; 138 mph)
- Econ cruising speed (65% power): 115 knots (213 km/h; 132 mph)
- Stalling speed: flaps up: 54 knots (100 km/h; 63 mph)
  - flaps down: 51 knots (93 km/h; 58 mph)
- Service ceiling: 4,500 m (14,775 ft)
- T-O to 15 m (50 ft): 450 m (1,475 ft)
- Landing from 15 m (50 ft): 500 m (1,640 ft)
- Range with max fuel, 30 min reserves:
  - at max cruising speed: 453 nm (840 km; 521 miles)
  - at econ cruising speed: 518 nm (960 km; 596 miles)

DURUBLE RD-03 EDELWEISS 150

The RD-03 Edelweiss 150 is designed to FAR 23 standards. It can be flown under the Utility category in two-seat form or, with seating for a pilot and three passengers (total weight 308 kg; 680 lb), in Normal category.

Plans of the RD-03 have been available since the Autumn of 1970. Nine Edelweiss 150s are known to be under construction in France, three in Belgium, eleven in Canada and the USA, and one in Spain. The first RD-03 (F-WYIT), constructed mainly by M Serge Gastan but with the assistance of M Duruble, made its first flight in early 1982 and is shown in an accompanying illustration. This is a special aircraft, with complete IFR instrumentation, VOR and other equipment for night flying. It also has a special 'plastic like' paint finish and has demonstrated a higher performance than the standard RD-03, including a max level speed of 154 knots (285 km/h; 177 mph); cruising speed at S/L (75% power) of 139 knots (257 km/h; 160 mph); and cruising speed (65% power) of 133 knots (247 km/h; 153 mph).

TYPE: Two/four-seat homebuilt aircraft.

AIRFRAME: Cantilever low-wing monoplane. Duralumin airframe. Wing section NACA 23000 series. Thickness/chord ratio 18% at root, 12% at tip. Dihedral 6° 5′ from roots. Incidence 3° at root, 0° at tip. No wing sweepback. Single-spar wing structure, with slotted trailing-edge flaps and slotted ailerons. No trim tabs. Conventional semi-monocoque fuselage. Cantilever tail unit, with sweptback vertical surfaces. Fixed incidence tailplane. Trim tab in each elevator, one actuated by flap linkage and the other manually.

LANDING GEAR: Retractable tricycle type. Hydraulic retraction, nosewheel rearward, main units inward into wings. Duruble hydro-air shock absorbers in all three units. Mainwheel tyres size 355 × 150, nosewheel tyre size 330 × 130. Pressure (all tyres) 1·24 bars (18 lb/sq in). Hydraulic disc brakes.

POWER PLANT: One 112 kW (150 hp) Avco Lycoming flat-four engine. Fuel capacity 180 litres (39·6 Imp gallons), fully usable in Normal category.

ACCOMMODATION: Seats for two, three or four persons in fully enclosed cabin.

SYSTEM: Hydraulic system, pressure 69 bars (1,000 lb/sq in), for flap and landing gear actuation.

AVIONICS AND EQUIPMENT: Radio optional. Blind-flying instrumentation not fitted.

DIMENSIONS, EXTERNAL:
- Wing span: 8·82 m (28 ft 11¼ in)
- Wing chord: at root: 1·70 m (5 ft 7 in)
  - at tip: 0·85 m (2 ft 10 in)
- Wing aspect ratio: 6·95
- Length overall: 6·88 m (22 ft 7 in)
- Height overall: 2·35 m (7 ft 8½ in)
- Tailplane span: 3·05 m (10 ft 0 in)

AREA:
- Wings, gross: 11·39 m² (122·6 sq ft)

WEIGHTS AND LOADINGS:
- Weight empty, equipped (VFR): 510 kg (1,124 lb)
- Max T-O and landing weight:
  - Utility: 840 kg (1,852 lb)
  - Normal: 1,010 kg (2,227 lb)
- Max wing loading: Utility: 73·75 kg/m² (15·10 lb/sq ft)
  - Normal: 88·67 kg/m² (18·16 lb/sq ft)
- Max power loading: Utility: 7·50 kg/kW (12·35 lb/hp)
  - Normal: 9·02 kg/kW (14·85 lb/hp)

Danis Mercure with Tempête 20 wing

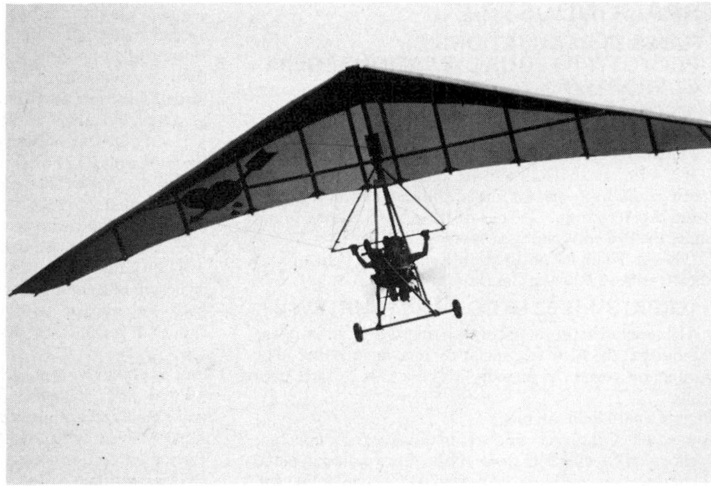
Danis Faucheux single-seat trike unit

Delemontez-Desjardins D-01 Ibis three-seat light aircraft *(Geoffrey P. Jones)*

Raymond Dohet's Arthur trike unit

Egrette Sophie two-seat microlight aircraft *(Geoffrey P. Jones)*

Duruble RD-03 Edelweiss two/four-seat light aircraft built by M Serge Gastan

PERFORMANCE (at max T-O weight, as specified):

Never-exceed speed:	
Utility	170 knots (316 km/h; 196 mph)
Normal	182 knots (339 km/h; 210 mph)
Max level speed at S/L:	
Utility	148 knots (275 km/h; 171 mph)
Normal	146 knots (270 km/h; 168 mph)
Max cruising speed at S/L (75% power):	
Utility	135 knots (250 km/h; 155 mph)
Normal	133 knots (246 km/h; 153 mph)
Econ cruising speed at S/L:	
Utility	128 knots (238 km/h; 148 mph)
Normal	126 knots (234 km/h; 145 mph)
Stalling speed, flaps up:	
Utility	59 knots (108 km/h; 67 mph)
Normal	62 knots (115 km/h; 72 mph)
Stalling speed, flaps down:	
Utility	54 knots (100 km/h; 63 mph)
Normal	57 knots (105 km/h; 66 mph)
Max rate of climb at S/L:	
Utility	354 m (1,160 ft)/min
Normal	300 m (985 ft)/min
Service ceiling: Utility	5,030 m (16,500 ft)
Normal	4,575 m (15,000 ft)
T-O to 15 m (50 ft): Utility	450 m (1,475 ft)
Normal	510 m (1,675 ft)
Landing from 15 m (50 ft): Utility	500 m (1,640 ft)
Normal	515 m (1,690 ft)
Range with max fuel, 30 min reserves, at max cruising speed: Utility	512 nm (950 km; 590 miles)
Normal	593 nm (1,100 km; 685 miles)

EGRETTE

ASSOCIATION EGRETTE

12 allée des Marronniers, Sillery, 51500 Rilly-la-Montagne

EGRETTE SOPHIE

Association Egrette was formed by a group of ten friends to build a two-seat ultralight aircraft named Sophie. This achievement earned for them the Barret de Nazaris cup, presented by *Pilote Privé* magazine, at the 1984 RSA rally at Brienne.

TYPE: Side by side two-seat microlight aircraft.

AIRFRAME: Strut-braced high-wing monoplane of constant chord. Airframe basically of AU4G light alloy, with Dacron covering. Wing section NACA 23012. Three-axis control (full-span auxiliary-aerofoil ailerons, elevators and rudder). Pod and boom fuselage with conventional cantilever tail unit.

LANDING GEAR: Non-retractable tricycle type, with cantilever main legs.

POWER PLANT: One 32 kW (43 hp) Hirth HL2701 493 cc two-stroke engine, driving a two-blade pusher propeller.

ACCOMMODATION: Two seats side by side in fully enclosed cabin.

DIMENSIONS, EXTERNAL:	
Wing span	10·20 m (33 ft 5½ in)
Wing aspect ratio	5·88
Length overall	6·30 m (20 ft 8 in)
AREA:	
Wings, gross	17·70 m² (190·5 sq ft)
WEIGHTS AND LOADINGS:	
Weight empty	174 kg (383 lb)
Max T-O weight	375 kg (827 lb)
Max wing loading	21·19 kg/m² (4·34 lb/sq ft)
Max power loading	11·72 kg/kW (19·23 lb/hp)
PERFORMANCE:	
Max level speed	65 knots (120 km/h; 75 mph)
Cruising speed	54 knots (100 km/h; 62 mph)
Stalling speed	25 knots (45 km/h; 28 mph)
Max rate of climb at S/L (estimated)	150 m (495 ft)/min
Endurance	4 h

ERPALS INDUSTRIE

ETUDES ET REALISATIONS DE PROTOTYPES POUR L'AVIATION LÉGÈRE ET SPORTIVE

13 rue Chaudot, 89300 Joigny
Telephone: (16) 86 62 43 88

Erpals manufactures the Piel C.P. 320 Emeraude, C.P.324 Emeraude Club and (to order) the Diamant, for sale in ready-to-fly and kit forms, at its factory on Auxerre-Branches Aérodrome. Details of these types can be found under the Piel entry in this section of *Jane's*.

It has also built the prototype of a single-seat light aircraft known as the J.H.03 Le Courlis.

ERPALS J.H.03 LE COURLIS (CURLEW)

The single-seat prototype of this canard light aircraft was exhibited at the RSA meeting at Brienne in July 1985. The production version is intended to be a side by side two-seater.

TYPE: Canard light aircraft.

AIRFRAME: Cantilever mid-set mainplanes of constant chord, with dihedral from roots. Conventional metal construction, with spars of riveted AU4G light alloy, and light alloy ribs, skin and internal diagonal bracing. Leading-edges on prototype consist of blocks of high density shaped foam, separated by AU4G nose ribs and covered with several laminations of glassfibre. On subsequent aircraft leading-edges will be moulded from special lightweight high density composites. All-metal slotted ailerons, and small four-position trailing-edge flaps at wingroots, of AU4G light alloy. Flaps at 25° up setting function as airbrakes. All control surfaces rod actuated. No tabs. Cantilever tapered foreplane surfaces, without dihedral, mid-set on front fuselage at lower level than mainplanes. Forward sweep at roots. Construction similar to that of mainplanes. Inset all-metal elevators, rod actuated. No tabs. Pod and boom fuselage of ovoid cross-section. Prototype has wooden girder structure in pod, with wood frames and composite skin, and a wooden tailboom. Subsequent aircraft will have all-metal structure of light alloy tubing and riveted skins. Swept-back fin, integral with tailboom, and horn balanced rudder of metal construction. Rudder rod actuated. No tab.

LANDING GEAR: Non-retractable tricycle type. Mainwheels of 320 mm diameter, carried on cantilever legs of laminated carbonfibre plastics and fitted with JPX disc brakes. Steerable nosewheel, actuated by rudder pedals, carried on double acting mechanical shock strut. Wheel fairings optional.

POWER PLANT: One 37 kW (50 hp) JPX conversion of 1,600 cc Volkswagen motorcar engine in prototype, on anti-vibration mounting and with exhaust silencing. Three-blade pusher propeller, with spinner. Two-seat production version will have 48 kW (65 hp) JPX Volkswagen engine. One fuel tank, capacity 18 litres (4 Imp gallons) between power plant and cabin; one in leading-edge of each mainplane root. Total fuel capacity 58 litres (12·75 Imp gallons).

ACCOMMODATION: Pilot only in prototype, under sideways hinged canopy. Two seats side by side in subsequent aircraft. Adjustable seat. Dual controls in two-seater.

DIMENSIONS, EXTERNAL:

Wing span	9·16 m (30 ft 0¾ in)
Foreplane span	4·68 m (15 ft 4¼ in)
Wing chord (constant)	0·825 m (2 ft 8½ in)
Length overall	5·88 m (19 ft 3½ in)
Height overall	1·85 m (6 ft 1 in)
Wheel track	1·43 m (4 ft 8½ in)
Wheelbase	1·59 m (5 ft 2½ in)
Propeller diameter	1·22 m (4 ft 0 in)

WEIGHTS: Not available

PERFORMANCE (estimated):

Never-exceed speed	189 knots (350 km/h; 217 mph)
Max level speed	162 knots (300 km/h; 186 mph)
Cruising speed	135 knots (250 km/h; 155 mph)
Stalling speed	33 knots (61 km/h; 38 mph)
Max rate of climb at S/L	324 m (1,063 ft)/min
T-O run	170 m (558 ft)
Landing run	250 m (820 ft)
Range with max fuel	648 nm (1,200 km; 745 miles)

FÉRÉ

RENÉ FÉRÉ

Vievigne, 21310 Mirebeau s/Beze

M René Féré has designed and built a small single-seat light aircraft designated F.3 (F-PYJF), which flew for the first time in March 1981. Details of this aircraft, of which plans are available to other constructors, follow.

M Féré is currently working on a new side by side two-seat aircraft known as the Féré F.4. No details of this are available at present, except that it is derived from the F.3 and will have a 1,600 cc Volkswagen engine.

FÉRÉ F.3

TYPE: Single-seat homebuilt sporting monoplane.

AIRFRAME: Cantilever low-wing monoplane, built in one piece. Wing section NACA 23013. Dihedral 5° 48′ on outer panels only. Incidence 3° 30′ at tips. All-wood structure with single box spar. Leading-edge covered with okoumé plywood; fabric covering overall. Plain ailerons of wood with fabric covering. No flaps. Wing attached to fuselage by five bolts. Plywood covered wooden fuselage of basically square section, with rounded top decking. Polyester engine cowling. Conventional cantilever wooden tail unit. Fixed surfaces plywood covered; rudder and elevators fabric covered. Controllable trim tab in port elevator. Ground adjustable tab on rudder.

LANDING GEAR: Non-retractable tailwheel type. Cantilever main legs with rubber block shock absorption. Mainwheels size 350 × 8, fitted with drum brakes. Tailwheel carried on leaf spring and steerable with rudder.

POWER PLANT: One 30 kW (40 hp) converted 1,200 cc Volkswagen engine, with Zenith carburettor and Bendix magneto, driving an EVRA D9-28 two-blade fixed-pitch wooden propeller. Fuel tank, capacity 29 litres (6·4 Imp gallons), forward of cockpit. Provision for auxiliary tank, capacity 16 litres (3·5 Imp gallons), in baggage space.

ACCOMMODATION: Single seat under sideways-hinged tinted one-piece canopy. Baggage space behind seat.

DIMENSIONS, EXTERNAL:

Wing span	6·90 m (22 ft 7¾ in)
Wing aspect ratio	5·65
Length overall	5·20 m (17 ft 0¾ in)

AREA:

Wings, gross	8·42 m² (90·63 sq ft)

WEIGHTS AND LOADINGS:

Weight empty	200 kg (441 lb)
Max T-O weight	316 kg (696 lb)
Max wing loading	37·53 kg/m² (7·69 lb/sq ft)
Max power loading	10·53 kg/kW (17·40 lb/hp)

PERFORMANCE:

Max level speed	105 knots (195 km/h; 121 mph)
Max cruising speed	92 knots (170 km/h; 106 mph)
Stalling speed	37 knots (68 km/h; 42 mph)
Max rate of climb at S/L	270 m (885 ft)/min
Service ceiling	4,000 m (13,125 ft)
Range with standard fuel	243 nm (450 km; 280 miles)

FEUGRAY

G. FEUGRAY

Two different types of high-performance monoplane designed by M G. Feugray took part in the World Aerobatic Championships held in the UK in August 1986. Only the following brief details were available when this edition of *Jane's* closed for press:

FEUGRAY ASA 200

This single-seat aerobatic monoplane (F-WYGN), similar in configuration to the well-known Mudry CAP 21, has a 171·5 kW (230 hp) Avco Lycoming flat-four engine.

WEIGHT:

Weight empty	450 kg (992 lb)

PERFORMANCE:

Never-exceed speed	194 knots (360 km/h; 223 mph)
g limits	+8/−6

FEUGRAY TR 260

Similar in general configuration to the Laser/Akro series of single-seat aerobatic aircraft, the TR 260 (F-WTXK) was completed in early 1985 at St André de l'Eule, France. It is a cantilever mid-wing monoplane, with conventional unswept cantilever tail surfaces and non-retractable tailwheel type landing gear. Power plant is a 246 kW (330 hp) Avco Lycoming engine. Fuel capacity is 190 litres (41·8 Imp gallons).

WEIGHTS:

Weight empty	620 kg (1,367 lb)
Max T-O weight	850 kg (1,874 lb)

PERFORMANCE:

Never-exceed speed	243 knots (450 km/h; 280 mph)
Max level speed	216 knots (400 km/h; 248 mph)
Stalling speed	49 knots (90 km/h; 56 mph)
T-O run	150 m (492 ft)
Landing run	450 m (1,476 ft)
Range with max fuel	540 nm (1,000 km; 621 miles)
g limits	±10

FRANCE AEROLIGHTS

FRANCE AEROLIGHTS SA

Aérodrome de Libourne, Les Artigues-de-Lussac, 33570 Lussac
Telephone: (57) 84 73 22
Telex: 570 598 F
DIRECTOR: Bruno Ziegler

France Aerolights was originally established to market American manufactured microlights in France. The company's initial products were the **First One** and **First Two** single- and two-seat machines. These are essentially simple tube and Dacron microlights with strut braced high wings, three-axis controls and tricycle undercarriages. An agricultural version of the First design, with spraybooms, is known as the **Agri First**. The same basic aircraft without spraybooms and with two extra seats is known as the **Enduro**. The more sophisticated Mach 01 and Mach 20 were introduced in May 1983.

FRANCE AEROLIGHTS MACH 01 and MACH 20

The **Mach 01** and **Mach 20** are respectively single- and two-seat versions of the same aircraft, the general appearance of which is shown in an accompanying photograph. The prototype for the Mach series made its first flight in October 1982. The Mach 01 was introduced publicly at the 1983 Paris Air Show.

TYPE: One/two-seat microlight aircraft.

AIRFRAME: Conventional high-wing monoplane. Duralumin welded tube fuselage with glass/carbonfibre composite cockpit 'pod'. Duralumin wing spars with aluminium ribs, Dacron covering. V strut bracing. Three-axis control (rudder, elevator and ailerons). GAP-C1 aerofoil section.

LANDING GEAR: Tricycle type, with tailskid. Glassfibre or spring steel main suspension. Mainwheels diameter 35 cm; nosewheel 26 cm. Brakes on mainwheels. Wheel fairings and float gear optional.

POWER PLANT: One Hirth 2701R 493 cc two-cylinder two-stroke engine (36 kW; 48 hp in Mach 01, 39 kW; 52 hp in Mach 20), with 2·5 reduction drive to a two-blade pusher propeller. Fuel tank capacity (both versions) 20 litres (4·4 Imp gallons).

ACCOMMODATION: Pilot only (Mach 01), or pilot and passenger (Mach 20), in enclosed cockpit.

DIMENSIONS, EXTERNAL:

Wing span: 01	9·80 m (32 ft 1¾ in)
20	10·80 m (35 ft 5¼ in)
Wing aspect ratio: 01	6·53
20	7·20
Length overall (both)	6·20 m (20 ft 4 in)
Height overall (both)	2·20 m (7 ft 2½ in)
Propeller diameter (both)	1·20 m (3 ft 11¼ in)

AREAS:

Wings, gross: 01	14·70 m² (158·2 sq ft)
20	16·20 m² (174·4 sq ft)

WEIGHTS AND LOADINGS:

Weight empty: 01	120 kg (264 lb)
20	150 kg (331 lb)
Max T-O weight: 01	220 kg (485 lb)
20	326 kg (718 lb)
Max wing loading: 01	14·97 kg/m² (3·07 lb/sq ft)
20	20·12 kg/m² (4·12 lb/sq ft)
Max power loading: 01	6·15 kg/kW (10·1 lb/hp)
20	8·40 kg/kW (13·8 lb/hp)

PERFORMANCE:

Never-exceed speed (both)	75 knots (140 km/h; 87 mph)
Max level speed at S/L (both)	70 knots (130 km/h; 81 mph)
Max cruising speed (both)	62 knots (115 km/h; 71 mph)
Econ cruising speed (both)	46 knots (85 km/h; 53 mph)
Stalling speed (both)	22 knots (40 km/h; 25 mph)
Max rate of climb at S/L: 01	270 m (886 ft)/min
20	180 m (590 ft)/min
Service ceiling (both)	3,000 m (9,840 ft)
T-O run (both)	50 m (164 ft)
Landing run (both)	25 m (82 ft)
Max range at econ cruising speed (both)	135 nm (250 km; 155 miles)
g limits (both)	+6/−3
Best glide ratio at 35 knots (65 km/h; 40 mph) (both)	10
Min rate of sink at 35 knots (65 km/h; 40 mph) (both)	120 m (394 ft)/min

Féré F.3 single-seat all-wood light aircraft *(Geoffrey P. Jones)*

Single-seat prototype of the Erpals J.H.03 Le Courlis *(Geoffrey P. Jones)*

Feugray ASA 200 single-seat aerobatic monoplane *(Austin J. Brown)*

Feugray TR 260 single-seat aerobatic aircraft *(Austin J. Brown)*

France Aerolights single-seat Mach 01 *(Brian M. Service)*

Gatard AG 02 Poussin No. 12, built by M J. P. Marie *(Austin J. Brown)*

Partially completed prototype Gardan GY-120, without all of its fuselage structure and minus Dacron covering *(J. M. G. Gradidge)*

GARDAN

AVIONS YVES GARDAN

580 rue Hélène Boucher, Zone Industrielle, 78530 Buc

Telephone: (3) 956 28 82

GARDAN GY-120

The latest aircraft built by this well known French lightplane designer is the GY-120 tandem two-seat microlight, with a 30-37·25 kW (40-50 hp) Hirth, Robin or similar engine. The prototype flew for the first time on 27 April 1984.

TYPE: Two-seat microlight aircraft.

AIRFRAME: Aluminium alloy airframe with Dacron covering. Gardan high-lift aerofoil section. Cable bracing, kingpost standard. Three-axis controls (rudder, elevator and ailerons). Half span flaps.

LANDING GEAR: Non-retractable tailwheel type. Mainwheel diameter 40 cm; steerable tailwheel, diameter 13 cm. Mainwheel brakes optional. Rubber mainwheel shock absorption; coil spring tailwheel suspension.

POWER PLANT (prototype): One 30 kW (40 hp) Hirth 270R-03E engine, with 2·7:1 reduction drive to a two-blade tractor propeller. Production aircraft will be offered with optional Robin EC44, JPX or Rotax 503 power plants. Fuel capacity 30 litres (6·6 Imp gallons).

DIMENSIONS, EXTERNAL:

Wing span	10·00 m (32 ft 9¾ in)
Wing aspect ratio	5·7
Length overall	5·85 m (19 ft 2¼ in)
Height overall	2·50 m (8 ft 2½ in)
Propeller diameter	1·50 m (4 ft 11 in)

AREA:

Wings, gross	17·50 m^2 (188·4 sq ft)

WEIGHTS AND LOADINGS:

Weight empty	175 kg (386 lb)
Max T-O weight	350 kg (772 lb)
Max wing loading	20·0 kg/m^2 (4·10 lb/sq ft)
Max power loading (prototype)	11·74 kg/kW (19·29 lb/hp)

PERFORMANCE (estimated):

Never-exceed speed	75 knots (140 km/h; 87 mph)
Max level speed at S/L	65 knots (120 km/h; 75 mph)
Max cruising speed	59 knots (110 km/h; 68 mph)
Max rate of climb at S/L	150 m (490 ft)/min
Service ceiling	3,000 m (9,840 ft)
T-O run	40 m (131 ft)
Landing run	30 m (98 ft)
Range with max fuel, no reserves	162-189 nm (300-350 km; 186-217 miles)
g limits	+6·6/−3·3 ultimate
Best glide ratio	10

GATARD

AVIONS A. GATARD

Villa la Devallée, 17130 Montendre s/Royan

Telephone: (46) 49 42 76

M Albert Gatard has developed a control system for aeroplanes which involves the use of a variable incidence lifting tailplane of large area, and has built a series of aircraft, including the Alouette, Poussin and Pigeon, incorporating his ideas. Plans of the Poussin are available to amateur constructors. The Alouette and Pigeon have been described in previous editions of *Jane's*.

Instead of altering the wing angle of attack to increase lift on these aircraft, the pilot lowers full-span slotted aileron/flaps and adjusts the tailplane to maintain pitching equilibrium. In consequence, the aircraft climb with the fuselage datum at no more than 4° to the horizontal, which preserves a good forward view and low body drag.

GATARD STATOPLAN AG 02 POUSSIN (CHICK)

M Gatard built two prototypes of the Poussin, and the detailed description applies to the second of these, which introduced a number of design improvements, in its original form. Flight tests revealed excellent aerobatic qualities and the power plant is modified to permit up to 20 s of inverted flying.

This prototype was extensively flight tested at the Centre d'Essais en Vol at Istres, and the performance figures quoted are those which were obtained during the tests. As a result of recommendations by the CEV, a 27 kW (36 hp) Rectimo (modified Volkswagen VW 1200) engine is suggested as the most suitable power plant for use by amateur constructors of the Poussin. The second prototype was re-engined with a 1,200 cc Volkswagen, by M Mathevet of Mollard-Chateauneuf (Loirs), on behalf of M Gatard. Installation of this engine was expected to improve the CG position and make possible a max speed of approx 92 knots (170 km/h; 106 mph), a max cruising speed of approx 83 knots (155 km/h; 96 mph) and a rate of climb at S/L of 210 m (690 ft)/min.

Many Poussins are being built by amateur constructors, and several have been completed and flown, including one (F-PYBS) with a non-standard tricycle landing gear. One of the latest to fly is shown in an accompanying illustration.

The plans were refined during 1978-79, and the version of the Poussin since offered for amateur construction is designated **AG 02Sp**. The wingtips are more rounded, with inset ailerons. The wing structure has been modified to permit an increased max T-O weight of 305 kg (672 lb); and the landing gear has been refined to give an increase of about 5 per cent in cruising speed.

The following details apply to the AG 02 Poussins now flying:

TYPE: Single-seat homebuilt monoplane.

AIRFRAME: Cantilever low-wing monoplane. Wooden airframe structure, plywood covered. Single-spar wings of NACA 23012 section. Dihedral 4°. Incidence 3° 30′ at root, 2° at tip. Full-span slotted aileron/flaps, each in two sections which are moved together but at different angles (inboard sections up to 35°, outboard up to 20°) to give the effect of increased aerodynamic twist of the complete wing/aileron/flap assemblies. Aileron/flaps are linked with the variable incidence tailplane. Perforated airbrake, under fuselage, operates automatically when the main aileron/flaps are lowered at large angles, as during landing. Braced tail unit, with variable incidence all-moving tailplane of NACA 2309 section. Endplates fitted to tailplane to increase vertical fin area and effective tailplane span. No elevators. Rudder trim tab actuated by lateral movement of control column, permitting full control by means of the control column alone in normal flight.

LANDING GEAR: Non-retractable tailwheel type. Cantilever levered suspension main units with rubber band shock absorption. Modified Dunlop brakes. Steerable tailwheel.

POWER PLANT: One 18 kW (24 hp) modified Volkswagen flat-four engine, driving a Gatard two-blade fixed-pitch wooden propeller. Provision for fitting any alternative engine of up to 30 kW (40 hp) weighing between 50 and 60 kg (110-132 lb). Fuel tank aft of firewall, capacity 30 litres (6·6 Imp gallons). Oil capacity 2 litres (0·45 Imp gallons).

ACCOMMODATION: Single seat under large rearward sliding transparent canopy. Baggage space aft of seat. Two map pockets.

DIMENSIONS, EXTERNAL:
- Wing span: 6·40 m (21 ft 0 in)
- Wing chord, constant: 1·00 m (3 ft 3¼ in)
- Length overall: 4·53 m (14 ft 10½ in)
- Height overall: 1·50 m (4 ft 11 in)
- Wheel track: 1·50 m (4 ft 11 in)
- Wheelbase: 3·20 m (10 ft 6 in)

AREA:
- Wings, gross: 6·15 m² (66·2 sq ft)

WEIGHTS AND LOADINGS:
- Weight empty: 170 kg (375 lb)
- Max T-O weight: 280 kg (617 lb)
- Max wing loading: 45·5 kg/m² (9·33 lb/sq ft)
- Max power loading: 15·56 kg/kW (25·71 lb/hp)

PERFORMANCE (at max T-O weight):
- Never-exceed speed: 116 knots (216 km/h; 134 mph)
- Max cruising speed: 77 knots (144 km/h; 89 mph)
- Max speed for aerobatics: 69 knots (130 km/h; 80 mph)
- Stalling speed: 35 knots (65 km/h; 41 mph)
- Max rate of climb at S/L: 132 m (435 ft)/min
- T-O run: 190 m (625 ft)
- T-O to 15 m (50 ft): 435 m (1,425 ft)
- Landing from 15 m (50 ft): 320 m (1,050 ft)
- Landing run: 200 m (655 ft)

HUMBERT

HUMBERT MOTO DU CIEL

First seen at the 1985 RSA rally at Brienne, the Moto du Ciel is a tandem two-seat ultralight 'look-alike' of the well known Breezy Model RLU-1 homebuilt, last described in the 1982-83 *Jane's*. Few details are available, except that the prototype, illustrated on the next page, has a 1,600 cc Volkswagen engine, driving a pusher propeller. It flew for the first time in March 1985.

DIMENSIONS, EXTERNAL:
- Wing span: 11·30 m (37 ft 1 in)
- Length overall: 6·50 m (21 ft 4 in)

WEIGHTS:
- Weight empty: 173 kg (382 lb)
- Max T-O weight: 393 kg (866 lb)

PERFORMANCE:
- Max level speed: 59 knots (110 km/h; 68 mph)
- Min flying speed: 27 knots (50 km/h; 31 mph)
- Max rate of climb at S/L: 180 m (590 ft)/min
- Range with max fuel: 378 nm (700 km; 435 miles)

JODEL

AVIONS JODEL SA

HEAD OFFICE: 36 Route de Seurre, 21200 Beaune
DESIGN OFFICE: 21-Darois
PRESIDENT-DIRECTOR GENERAL: J. Delemontez

The Société des Avions Jodel was formed in March 1946, by MM Jean Delemontez and the late Edouard Joly, with the former acting as business and technical manager and the latter as test pilot.

Its first activities were concerned with the repair of gliders and light aircraft of the Service d'Aviation Légère et Sportive, on behalf of the State. Simultaneously, the company designed and built the D.9 Bébé Jodel single-seat light monoplane, which made its first flight in January 1948. This aeroplane, which is certificated with various power plants, proved ideal for amateur construction and can be built in as little as 500 man-hours.

As the result of official tests with the D.9, the French authorities placed an order for the development and construction of two prototypes of a two-seat model, the D.11 fitted with a 33·6 kW (45 hp) Salmson, and the D.111 with a 56 kW (75 hp) Minié engine. Subsequent developments of the D.11 include the D.112 and D.119, which have a 48·5 kW (65 hp) and 67 kW (90 hp) Continental engine respectively. These designs also have been built, both commercially and by amateurs, and more than 5,000 aircraft of Jodel design have flown throughout the world.

Avions Jodel now devotes its activities mainly to designing advanced developments of its established types and to acting as a consultant to those building and developing its designs.

JODEL D.9 BÉBÉ SERIES

TYPE: Single-seat homebuilt monoplane.

AIRFRAME: Cantilever low-wing monoplane. Single-spar one-piece wing with wide-span centre-section of constant chord and thickness and two tapering outer portions set at a coarse dihedral angle (14°). Spar and ribs of spruce and plywood, with fabric covering. Ailerons similar in construction. Rectangular section fuselage of spruce and plywood. Cantilever tail unit also of spruce and plywood, with plywood covering on tailplane and fabric covered rudder and elevators. No fin.

LANDING GEAR: Non-retractable cantilever main legs with rubber in compression springing. Leaf spring tailskid or tailwheel. Cable brakes.

POWER PLANT: One modified Volkswagen flat-four engine is standard, but other engines of 18·6 to 48·5 kW (25 to 65 hp) may be fitted. Fuel tank in fuselage, capacity 25 litres (5·5 Imp gallons).

ACCOMMODATION: Single seat in open cockpit. Enclosed cockpit optional.

DIMENSIONS, EXTERNAL:
- Wing span: 7·00 m (22 ft 11 in)
- Wing chord (centre-section, constant): 1·40 m (4 ft 7 in)
- Wing aspect ratio: 5·45
- Length overall: 5·45 m (17 ft 10½ in)

AREA:
- Wings, gross: 9·0 m² (96·8 sq ft)

WEIGHTS AND LOADINGS:
- Weight empty: 190 kg (420 lb)
- Max T-O weight: 320 kg (705 lb)
- Max wing loading: 35·56 kg/m² (7·28 lb/sq ft)
- Max power loading (18·6 kW): 17·20 kg/kW (28·20 lb/hp)

PERFORMANCE (30 kW; 40 hp engine, at max T-O weight):
- Max level speed at S/L: 87 knots (160 km/h; 100 mph)
- Cruising speed: 74 knots (137 km/h; 85 mph)
- Stalling speed: 35 knots (65 km/h; 40 mph)
- Max rate of climb at S/L: 180 m (590 ft)/min
- T-O run: 110 m (360 ft)
- Landing run: 100 m (330 ft)
- Range with max fuel: 217 nm (400 km; 250 miles)

JODEL D.11 and D.119

The original D.11, with 33·6 kW (45 hp) Salmson engine, was the basic model in the series of Jodel two-seaters for amateur and commercial production. The version for amateur construction with 67 kW (90 hp) Continental engine is designated D.119.

A typical D.11 was built over an eight-year period by Wayne Nelson, an aeronautical engineer of Bountiful, Utah. The wing is of wood, covered with Dacron, the fuselage and tail unit of wood covered with glassfibre. Changes from the standard design include a fixed fin forward of the rudder, and cantilever spring main landing gear legs. This D.11 spans 8·23 m (27 ft 0 in), has an empty weight of 340 kg (750 lb) and loaded weight of 562 kg (1,240 lb), and is powered by a 48·5 kW (65 hp) Continental A65-8 flat-four engine. Performance is as follows:

PERFORMANCE:
- Max level speed at S/L: 93 knots (173 km/h; 108 mph)
- Cruising speed: 86 knots (161 km/h; 100 mph)
- Landing speed: 35 knots (65 km/h; 40 mph)
- Max rate of climb at S/L: 152 m (500 ft)/min
- Service ceiling: 4,875 m (16,000 ft)
- T-O run: 152 m (500 ft)
- Landing run: 244 m (800 ft)
- Range with max fuel: 260 nm (482 km; 300 miles)

JODEL D.112 CLUB and D.113

The D.112 is a two-seat dual-control version of the D.9. Except for increased overall dimensions, a wider fuselage and enclosed side by side cockpit, the D.112 conforms in layout and structure to the D.9, but is fitted normally with a 48·5 kW (65 hp) Continental flat-four engine. Fuel capacity is 60 litres (13 Imp gallons).

The version built in Sweden as the D.113 differs from the D.112 in several minor respects.

DIMENSIONS, EXTERNAL:
- Wing span: 8·20 m (26 ft 10 in)
- Length overall: 6·36 m (20 ft 10 in)
- Dihedral on outer wings: 19°

AREA:
- Wings, gross: 12·72 m² (136·9 sq ft)

WEIGHTS AND LOADINGS:
- Weight empty: 270 kg (600 lb)
- Max T-O weight: 520 kg (1,145 lb)
- Max wing loading: 40·88 kg/m² (8·37 lb/sq ft)
- Max power loading: 10·72 kg/kW (17·62 lb/hp)

PERFORMANCE (at max T-O weight):
- Max level speed at S/L: 102 knots (190 km/h; 118 mph)
- Max cruising speed: 92 knots (170 km/h; 105 mph)
- Econ cruising speed: 81 knots (150 km/h; 93 mph)
- Stalling speed: 38 knots (70 km/h; 43 mph)
- Max rate of climb at S/L: 193 m (632 ft)/min
- T-O run: 137 m (450 ft)
- Landing run: 120 m (395 ft)
- Range with max fuel: 323 nm (600 km; 373 miles)

JODEL D.18

The 1981-82 *Jane's* contained details of the Delemontez-Cauchy DC-1 low-cost two-seat amateur-built light aircraft. No plans of this are available, but M Delemontez is producing plans of a slightly modified version, known as the Jodel D.18, with a different wing section, revised ailerons, all-moving tailplane and other changes. Installation of a 1,700 cc Volkswagen engine, instead of the usual Continental, has resulted in a more streamlined cowling and improved performance. Fuel capacity is 60 litres (13·2 Imp gallons) in two tanks.

The prototype D.18 (F-PYQM), built by Ateliers Amateur de Montauban, was exhibited at the 1985 RSA rally at Brienne.

DIMENSIONS, EXTERNAL:
- Wing span: 7·50 m (24 ft 7¼ in)
- Length overall: 5·70 m (18 ft 8½ in)

AREA:
- Wings, gross: 10·0 m² (107·6 sq ft)

WEIGHTS AND LOADING:
- Weight empty: 240 kg (530 lb)
- Max T-O weight: 450 kg (992 lb)
- Max wing loading: 45·0 kg/m² (9·22 lb/sq ft)

PERFORMANCE:
- Max level speed: 135 knots (250 km/h; 155 mph)
- Cruising speed: 92 knots (170 km/h; 105 mph)
- Stalling speed: 39 knots (72 km/h; 45 mph)
- Max rate of climb at S/L: 180 m (590 ft)/min
- T-O to 15 m (50 ft): 260 m (853 ft)
- Landing from 15 m (50 ft): 450 m (1,477 ft)
- Endurance: 5 h

JUNQUA/ANDREAZZA

ROGER JUNQUA and JEAN-YVES ANDREAZZA

36 impasse d'Agen, 33800 Bordeaux
Telephone: (33) 56 91 81 17

In 1980, M Roger Junqua began the design of a tandem two-seat canard light aircraft known as the RJ-02 Volucelle. Construction of the prototype (F-WJQA) was started in the Spring of 1983 by M Jean-Yves Andreazza, assisted by M Junqua's son, Jean-Claude. This aircraft was expected to fly for the first time in May 1986.

JUNQUA/ANDREAZZA RJ-02 VOLUCELLE

TYPE: Tandem two-seat homebuilt canard aircraft.

AIRFRAME: Cantilever shoulder-mounted wings, with large winglets and inset rudders, at rear of fuselage. All-wood, Styrodur foam filled constant chord wings, with ailerons and high-lift flaps. Foreplanes at nose, of similar construction, fitted with elevators. Conventional wooden truss fuselage, plywood covered.

LANDING GEAR: Non-retractable tricycle type, with single wheel on each unit. Mainwheels carried on one-piece cantilever arch structure of Croses type. Autocycle

Humbert Moto du Ciel two-seat microlight *(Geoffrey P. Jones)*

Jodel D.9 Bébé built by Mr Orville Bondarenko of Smooth Rock Falls, Ontario, Canada *(Neil A. Macdougall)*

Version of Jodel D.9 with tricycle landing gear, photographed at 1986 RSA convention at Brienne *(J. M. G. Gradidge)*

Jodel D.112 Club two-seat homebuilt aircraft *(Geoffrey P. Jones)*

Prototype Jodel D.18 with 1,700 cc Volkswagen engine *(Stuart MacConnacher)*

Jurca M.J.2D Tempête built by M Francis Sire *(Gil Rivet)*

Junqua/Andreazza RJ-02 Volucelle two-seat canard homebuilt aircraft

brakes with aluminium discs on mainwheels, controlled by bicycle brake lever on control column.

Power Plant: One 38 kW (51 hp) Volkswagen 1,600 cc modified motorcar engine, driving a two-blade fixed-pitch wooden pusher propeller. Two fuel tanks, total capacity 56 litres (12·3 Imp gallons). Refuelling points in top of wings. Oil capacity 4 litres (0·9 Imp gallons).

Accommodation: Two seats in tandem, with dual controls, under one-piece transparent canopy. Optional heating. Baggage space to rear of seats, accessible from inside cockpit, capacity 20 kg (44 lb).

System: 12V 10A electrical system.

Avionics: 720 channel VHF radio. Optional NDB or VOR.

Dimensions, external:
- Wing span 6·00 m (19 ft 8¼ in)
- Length overall 4·50 m (14 ft 9 in)
- Height overall 1·60 m (5 ft 3 in)
- Propeller diameter 1·30 m (4 ft 3¼ in)

Weights and Loading:
- Weight empty 230 kg (507 lb)
- Max T-O weight 420 kg (926 lb)
- Max power loading 11·05 kg/kW (18·16 lb/hp)

Performance (estimated):
- Never-exceed speed 140 knots (259 km/h; 161 mph)
- Max level speed 130 knots (241 km/h; 150 mph)
- Max cruising speed 110 knots (204 km/h; 126 mph)
- Econ cruising speed 97 knots (180 km/h; 112 mph)
- Stalling speed, flaps down 46 knots (86 km/h; 53 mph)
- Max rate of climb at S/L 240 m (785 ft)/min
- Range with max fuel and max payload 380 nm (704 km; 437 miles)

JUNQUA RJ-03 IBIS

Construction of the prototype of a 'production' version of the Volucelle, known as the RJ-03 Ibis, was well underway in April 1986. The Ibis differs from the Volucelle in having a larger fuselage to accommodate two persons up to 1·90 m (6 ft 3 in) tall. It is powered by a 1,600 cc VW engine, is equipped with an electrical system, heater, VHF and NDB, and will have a range of 485 nm (900 km; 559 miles) with VFR reserves.

JURCA

MARCEL JURCA

2 rue des Champs Philippe, 92250 La Garenne-Colombes

Telephone: 242 9633

M Marcel Jurca, an ex-military pilot and hydraulics engineer, designed a series of high-performance light aircraft of which plans have been supplied to other constructors on a purely amateur basis.

A prototype of his first design, the M.J.1, was built but did not fly. To gain experience, M Jurca next built a two-seat Jodel light aircraft, with the help of members of the Aéro Club of Courbevoie, and this flew for the first time in 1954.

The same team then built a prototype of M Jurca's second design, the M.J.2 Tempête single-seat light aircraft, incorporating many Jodel components. It proved so successful that sets of plans were offered to amateur constructors and many Tempêtes are now flying or under assembly throughout the world.

M Jurca developed from the Tempête the two-seat M.J.5 Sirocco and the M.J.51 Sperocco, and has produced a further series of designs by scaling down the basic airframes of Second World War fighters to two-thirds or three-quarters of the original size. The latest Jurca designs include the M.J.100, a 224 kW (300 hp) full-size representation of a Supermarine Spitfire, a full-size Messerschmitt Bf 109, and the M.J.52 Zéphyr. Plans for the M.J.100 and M.J.52 became available in the Spring of 1985.

For builders in North America, Australia and New Zealand, Jurca plans are available from Mr Ken Heit, 1733 Kansas, Flint, Michigan 48506, USA (telephone [313] 232 5395). Ets Degouy Aviation, 1 Allée du Faubourg, 60100 Creil, France (telephone 4 471 4117) intends to manufacture kits and individual component parts for all Jurca aircraft, including the M.J.100 Spit.

JURCA M.J.2 and M.J.22 TEMPÊTE

The prototype M.J.2 Tempête was flown for the first time, by its designer, on 27 June 1956. At least 45 Tempêtes are now flying, with about 20 more under construction, in France, Denmark, Luxembourg, Portugal, the UK, the United States and Canada, all amateur built.

The type of engine fitted to a particular aircraft is indicated by a suffix letter in its designation. Suffix letters are A for the 48·5 kW (65 hp) Continental A65, B for the 56 kW (75 hp) Continental A75, C for the 63·5 kW (85 hp) Continental C85, D for the 67 kW (90 hp) Continental C90-8/C90-14F, E for the 74·5 kW (100 hp) Continental O-200-A, F for the 78·5 kW (105 hp) Potez 4 E-20, G for the 86 kW (115 hp) Potez 4 E-30, H for the 78·5-86 kW (105-115 hp) Avco Lycoming O-235, I for the 93 kW (125 hp) Avco Lycoming O-290-G, K for the 101-104 kW (135-140 hp) Avco Lycoming O-290-D2, N for the 112 kW (150 hp) Avco Lycoming or Continental, P for the 119 kW (160 hp) Avco Lycoming or Continental, and R for the 134 kW (180 hp) Avco Lycoming or Continental. The standard version is the M.J.2A. The M.J.2D cruises at 105 knots (195 km/h; 121 mph) and climbs to 1,000 m (3,280 ft) in 3 minutes. It can also perform aerobatics without loss of height.

Construction of the prototype of a version known as the **M.J.22**, with a 112 kW (150 hp) engine and strengthened airframe, was begun in the Rouen area of France by M Yves Chopart. This aircraft was finally completed and flown by the former Siravia Ltd, a company which went on to construct eighteen more. A further M.J.22 is under construction in Germany.

The Tempête is basically a single-seat aircraft, but the 112 and 134 kW (150 and 180 hp) versions have provision for carrying behind the pilot on cross-country flights a second person weighing not more than 55 kg (121 lb). This is not permitted by the DGAC in France; but a two-seater has flown in the USA, built by Mr Don Kerkhof of Mankato, Minnesota. The suffix 'A' is added to the aircraft designation in two-seat configuration.

The following details apply generally to all basic single-seat M.J.2 models:

TYPE: Single-seat homebuilt monoplane.

AIRFRAME: Cantilever low-wing monoplane. NACA 23012 wing section. Wing incidence varies according to engine power: the 48·5 kW (65 hp) version has an incidence of 4° at root, 2° at tip. No dihedral. All-wood one-piece single-spar wing structure with fabric covering. Fabric covered wooden ailerons. All-wood fuselage of basic rectangular section, plywood covered. Mostly wooden cantilever tail unit, with tailplane and fin plywood covered, elevators and rudder fabric covered. Trim tab on starboard elevator.

LANDING GEAR: Non-retractable tailwheel type. Jodel D.112 cantilever legs with rubber in compression springing. Jodel D.112 mainwheels and Dunlop 420 × 150 tyres. Jodel D.112 tailskid or tailwheel.

POWER PLANT: One 48·5 kW (65 hp) Continental A65 flat-four engine, driving a Ratier two-blade wooden propeller with ground adjustable pitch. Provision for fitting 56, 63·5, 67, or 74·5 kW (75, 85, 90 or 100 hp) Continental, 78·5 or 86 kW (105 or 115 hp) Potez or 93 kW (125 hp) Avco Lycoming engine. Jodel engine mounting and cowling. Jodel fuel tank, capacity 60 litres (13·2 Imp gallons), aft of firewall in fuselage.

ACCOMMODATION: Single seat under long rearward-sliding transparent canopy.

DIMENSIONS, EXTERNAL:
- Wing span: 6·00 m (19 ft 8 in)
- Wing chord (basic): 1·40 m (4 ft 7 in)
- Wing aspect ratio: 4·5
- Length overall: 5·855 m (19 ft 2½ in)
- Height overall: 2·40 m (7 ft 10 in)
- Tailplane span: 2·50 m (8 ft 2 in)
- Wheel track: 2·30 m (7 ft 6½ in)

AREA:
- Wings, gross: 7·98 m² (85·9 sq ft)

WEIGHTS AND LOADINGS (48·5 kW; 65 hp engine):
- Weight empty: 90 kg (639 lb)
- Max T-O weight: 430 kg (950 lb)
- Max wing loading: 53·9 kg/m² (11·04 lb/sq ft)
- Max power loading: 8·87 kg/kW (14·62 lb/hp)

PERFORMANCE (48·5 kW; 65 hp engine):
- Max level speed: 104 knots (193 km/h; 120 mph)
- Cruising speed: 89 knots (165 km/h; 102 mph)
- Landing speed: 44 knots (80 km/h; 50 mph)
- Max rate of climb at S/L: 170 m (555 ft)/min
- Service ceiling: 3,500 m (11,500 ft)
- T-O run: 250 m (820 ft)
- Endurance: 3 h 20 min

JURCA M.J.3H DART

The M.J.3H Dart is a single-seat all-wood monoplane, with the fuselage of the M.J.2 Tempête and the wings of the M.J.5 Sirocco. The one and only prototype, built by Mr Denis Jacobs of Dayton, Ohio, made its first flight in 1977. Full details and an illustration of the Dart can be found in the 1983-84 *Jane's*.

JURCA M.J.5 SIROCCO

The M.J.5 Sirocco is a tandem two-seat monoplane, developed from the M.J.2 Tempête as a potential club training and touring aircraft. It is fully aerobatic when flown as a two-seater.

The longer-span wings have an extended leading-edge inboard of the fence on each side and a completely new tip shape. A sweptback fin and rudder are standard.

The prototype M.J.5 flew for the first time on 3 August 1962, powered by a 78·5 kW (105 hp) Potez 4 E-20 engine. It was fitted originally with a non-retractable landing gear, but retractable landing gear and a 119·5 kW (160 hp) Avco Lycoming O-320 engine were fitted in 1966, followed by a 134 kW (180 hp) Avco Lycoming engine later. Its fuel capacity is 116 litres (25·5 Imp gallons).

By mid-February 1967, five more Siroccos were flying, one of them factory-built at Nancy. This aircraft, powered by a 74·5 kW (100 hp) Continental engine, completed tests at Istres in January 1969. The French government then concluded an agreement with Constructions Aéronautiques Lorraines, François et Cie of Nancy, which built an airframe for static tests, in March 1971. These were required in view of the fact that the Sirocco is regarded as a basic trainer suitable for amateur construction; and it was awarded subsequently a certificate of airworthiness in the Utility category. Supplementary tests were conducted at the CEV with another Sirocco, powered by a 100·5 kW (135 hp) Avco Lycoming O-320 engine.

A full C of A, covering Aerobatic requirements and unlimited spinning, is applicable only when a power plant of 112 kW (150 hp) minimum rating is installed.

The version of the Sirocco for amateur construction is generally similar to the factory built version, with optional retractable landing gear. This can include a retractable tailwheel, which is now shown as an alternative on the plans. Slotted ailerons are also optional, and can be retrofitted to Siroccos already completed.

At least 41 Siroccos are reported to be flying or under construction by amateurs in France, Canada, West Germany, Switzerland, England and the USA, with various engines.

The type of engine fitted to a particular aircraft is indicated by a suffix letter in its designation. Suffix letters are A for the 67 kW (90 hp) Continental C90-8 or -14F, B for the 74·5 kW (100 hp) Continental O-200-A, C for the 78·5 kW (105 hp) Potez 4 E-20, D for the 86 kW (115 hp) Potez 4 E-30, E for the 78·5 kW (105 hp) Hirth, F for the 93 kW (125 hp) Avco Lycoming, G for the 100·5 kW (135 hp) Regnier, H for the 119·5 kW (160 hp) Avco Lycoming, K for the 134 kW (180 hp) Avco Lycoming and L for the 149 kW (200 hp) Avco Lycoming. Addition of the numeral 1 indicates a non-retractable landing gear and the numeral 2 indicates a retractable landing gear. Thus, the designation of the original prototype in its current form is M.J.5K2. The example built at Nancy for certification has a 74·5 kW (100 hp) Continental engine and so is designated M.J.5B1.

Two examples of the M.J.5K, flying in Vichy and Montelimar, France, are each fitted with a 134 kW (180 hp) Avco Lycoming engine and Christen fuel system for inverted flight. Work on two M.J.5L Siroccos, with 149 kW (200 hp) Avco Lycoming engines, was started in 1975, in the USA and France, for use in international aerobatic championships. One of these, an M.J.5L2, was built by Mr John Tumilowicz of Wading River, New York State. First flown in August 1982, it has a rate of climb at S/L of 565 m (1,850 ft)/min.

A Sirocco with 86 kW (115 hp) Avco Lycoming O-235-C2B engine and 1·85 m (6 ft 0¾ in) diameter propeller was constructed by Luftsportgruppe Liebherr-Aero-Technik (LAT) in West Germany. This has a modified rudder of reduced height and greater chord, and a jettisonable, sideways-hinged cockpit canopy, and was intended for certification for aerobatic flying. The details which follow apply to this aircraft, but are generally typical of all versions:

DIMENSIONS, EXTERNAL:
- Wing span: 7·00 m (23 ft 0 in)
- Wing aspect ratio: 4·9
- Length overall: 6·15 m (20 ft 2 in)
- Height overall, tail up:
  - standard model: 2·80 m (9 ft 2¼ in)
  - LAT version: 2·60 m (8 ft 6¼ in)
- Tailplane span: 3·24 m (10 ft 7½ in)
- Wheel track: 2·80 m (9 ft 2¼ in)

AREA:
- Wings, gross: 10·00 m² (107·64 sq ft)

WEIGHTS AND LOADINGS:
- Weight empty: 430 kg (947 lb)
- Max T-O weight: 680 kg (1,499 lb)
- Max wing loading: 68·0 kg/m² (13·93 lb/sq ft)
- Max power loading (90 hp): 10·15 kg/kW (16·66 lb/hp)

PERFORMANCE (at max T-O weight):
- Max level speed: 127 knots (235 km/h; 146 mph)
- Cruising speed: 116 knots (215 km/h; 134 mph)
- Stalling speed: 44 knots (80 km/h; 50 mph)
- Time to 1,000 m (3,280 ft): 4 min
- Service ceiling: 5,000 m (16,400 ft)
- T-O run: 250 m (820 ft)
- Landing run: 200 m (655 ft)
- Endurance: 4 h 20 min

JURCA M.J.5 SIROCCO (SPORT WING)

A special version of the Sirocco, with 86 kW (115 hp) engine and increased span, has been developed for the New Zealand and Australian market. The wing of this aircraft, known as a 'Sport' wing, embodies one additional rib and inter-rib bay each side. The modification is available in the English language set of Sirocco plans.

JURCA M.J.51 SPEROCCO

Using knowledge gained from flight experience with the M.J.5 and the Canadian prototype M.J.7, M Jurca developed, with the assistance of M J. Lecarme, a design incorporating features of each aircraft. It is known as the M.J.51 Sperocco, the name being a contraction of 'Special Sirocco', and is intended for high performance aerobatic and competition flying. Like other Jurca designs, the M.J.51 is suitable for amateur construction.

The wings, of Habib 64000 748 laminar flow profile, are essentially those of the M.J.7 Gnatsum. They are without dihedral, and the angle of incidence varies according to the rating of the engine that is installed, as in the Tempête. The fuselage is of completely new design, with a basically triangular cross-section, but is of similar construction to that of the M.J.5. The tail unit consists of M.J.7 horizontal surfaces with a shorter and wider-chord fin and rudder. Landing gear is of the M.J.5 type and is fully retractable.

Any horizontally opposed engine of 112-179 kW (150-240 hp) may be installed. Fuel is contained in two wing tanks, each of 55 litres (12 Imp gallons) capacity, and one fuselage tank of 45 or 100 litres (10 or 22 Imp gallons) capacity.

The M.J.51 seats two persons in tandem under a one-piece sliding canopy, the rear seat being 10 cm (3·9 in) higher than the front seat.

The first M.J.51, powered by a 149 kW (200 hp) Avco Lycoming AIO-360 engine, is being constructed by M Serge Brillant at Melun and was nearing completion in 1985.

DIMENSIONS, EXTERNAL:
- Wing span: 7·623 m (25 ft 0 in)
- Length overall: 7·24 m (23 ft 9 in)

AREA:
- Wings, gross: 11·00 m² (118·4 sq ft)

WEIGHT AND LOADINGS:
- Max T-O weight: 730 kg (1,653 lb)
- Max wing loading: 66·36 kg/m² (13·59 lb/sq ft)
- Max power loading (200 hp): 4·90 kg/kW (8·27 lb/hp)

PERFORMANCE (estimated, with 112 kW; 150 hp Lycoming engine):
- Max level speed: 149 knots (275 km/h; 171 mph)
- Max cruising speed (75% power): 135 knots (250 km/h; 155 mph)
- Stalling speed: 49 knots (90 km/h; 56 mph)
- Time to 1,000 m (3,280 ft): 1 min 30 s

JURCA M.J.52 ZÉPHYR

The M.J.52 Zéphyr is a very light two-seat monoplane, based on the M.J.5 Sirocco but using a converted Volkswagen motorcar engine or Continental flat-four engine in the 30-48·5 kW (40-65 hp) range. It has been designed to conform to FAR Pt 23 Utility category requirements, yet to be simple to construct in a garage or similar building and inexpensive in terms of materials and working hours.

The fuselage is a simple box structure of plywood, fabric covered. The low-mounted cantilever wings are conventional structures, intended to utilise prefabricated wooden spars and ribs of constant section. Fuel tanks are carried at the wingtips, each with a capacity of 25 kg (55 lb). Flaps and wing folding are optional. Landing gear can be fixed or retractable, with laminated or telescopic tubular legs.

The M.J.52 is a slightly staggered side by side two-seater, with a central control column to allow the aircraft to be flown from either seat. The canopy is ideally moulded in one piece, but can be made as a framed structure if facilities for moulding are not available to the builder.

Plans of the M.J.52 have been available since Spring 1985.

TYPE: Two-seat light monoplane.

DIMENSIONS, EXTERNAL:
- Wing span: 9·06 m (29 ft 8¾ in)
- Length overall: 6·28 m (20 ft 7¼ in)

AREA:
- Wings, gross: 13·50 m² (145·3 sq ft)

WEIGHTS AND LOADINGS:
- Weight empty: 333 kg (734 lb)
- Max T-O weight: 517 kg (1,140 lb)
- Max wing loading: 38·3 kg/m² (7·84 lb/sq ft)
- Max power loading (50 hp): 13·86 kg/kW (22·80 lb/hp)

PERFORMANCE (37·3 kW; 50 hp engine):
- Max level speed: 59 knots (110 km/h; 68 mph)
- Stalling speed: 22 knots (40 km/h; 25 mph)
- Endurance: 5 h
- *g* limits: +8/−4 ultimate

JURCA M.J.7 and M.J.77 GNATSUM

The Gnatsum is a scale replica, for amateur construction, of the North American P-51 Mustang single-seat fighter of the Second World War. Its name 'Gnatsum' is 'Mustang' reversed.

Initially, M Jurca designed the wings, fuselage, tail surfaces and manually retractable landing gear. The engine installation was deliberately not designed, to permit constructors to utilise any of the suitable Avco Lycoming, Continental, Ranger or other power plants that are available.

During construction of the M.J.7 prototype in Canada (see below), a number of modifications and improvements were made to the basic design. These were embodied in the

Jurca M.J.5M2 Sirocco (164 kW; 220 hp engine) built by Mr Chuck Johnson of Edmonton, Alberta, Canada

Jurca M.J.7 Gnatsums built in Canada by Capt Wayne Foster and Mr Jack Baptiste

Jurca M.J.8 1-Nine-OH built by Mr Ronald Kitchen of Carson City, Nevada

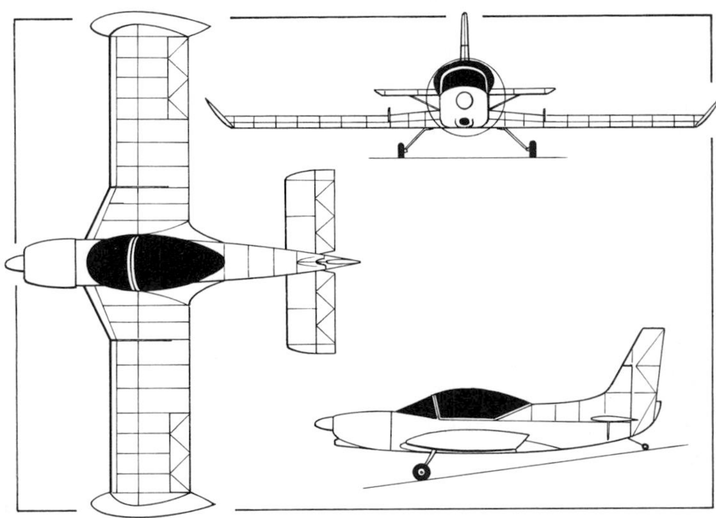

Jurca M.J.52 Zéphyr two-seat light aircraft *(Michael A. Badrocke)*

Jurca M.J.12 Pee-40 under construction by Mr Russell J. Moynagh of Santa Ana, California

Jurca M.J.10 Spit built by Mr Don McMurtrie of Bartlesville, Oklahoma

drawings, which are available from M Jurca in two forms, as follows:

M.J.7. To two-thirds scale. Prototype (CF-XZI, now N51HR) built in the works of Falconar Aircraft Ltd on the Industrial Airport, Edmonton, Alberta, Canada, and first flown on 31 July 1969. Granted DoT type approval by early 1970. Described under the 'SAL' entry in the Canadian section of the 1973-74 *Jane's*. The second M.J.7 built in Canada was the one with a 149 kW (200 hp) Ranger engine constructed by Captain W. T. Foster, to which data given at the end of this entry apply. Two other Gnatsums were flown in 1977, under the SAL designation, built by Mr Bill Slater and Mr Ross Grady of the USA. By early 1986 at least 12 M.J.7s were flying in the USA. Plastics fuselage shells for the M.J.7 are available from Boeve Brothers of Holland, Michigan, USA.

M.J.77. To three-quarters scale. Examples under construction, or completed, by Mr Bob Aughton in Michigan, M Glorieux of Pau, M Riazola of Egletons and M Semenadisse of Hyères, near Toulon, France.

Unlike previous small-scale replicas of the Mustang, the Gnatsum is scaled down precisely. Use of an inline engine, such as the 134 kW (180 hp) or 149 kW (200 hp) Ranger, permits the fuselage cowling lines to follow closely those of the original. Alternative installation of a 149 kW (200 hp) Avco Lycoming flat-four aircooled engine requires fairing blisters over the cylinders.

M Jurca's plans provide for alternative plywood covered semi-monocoque fuselage construction, a wooden box structure covered with two plastics shells, a structure of metal tubing covered with two plastics shells or aluminium sheet, or the tubular structure covered with polyurethane foam and glassfibre.

The M.J.77 built by M Semenadisse, for which specification data are quoted, is of all-wood construction with a 186 kW (250 hp) Potez 4 D-32 inline engine, driving a Hartzell three-blade constant-speed propeller. It flew for the first time on 25 January 1983.

DIMENSIONS, EXTERNAL (A: Capt Foster's M.J.7, B: M Semenadisse's M.J.77):
Wing span: A 7·52 m (24 ft 8¼ in)
B 8·50 m (27 ft 10½ in)
Length overall: A 6·55 m (21 ft 6 in)
B 7·40 m (24 ft 3¼ in)
AREA:
Wings, gross: A 10·41 m² (112·0 sq ft)
B 13·40 m² (144·2 sq ft)
WEIGHTS AND LOADINGS (A and B as above):
Weight empty: A 673 kg (1,485 lb)
B 1,035 kg (2,281 lb)
Max T-O weight: A 850 kg (1,875 lb)
B 1,300 kg (2,866 lb)
Max wing loading: A 81·65 kg/m² (16·72 lb/sq ft)
B 97·0 kg/m² (19·87 lb/sq ft)
Max power loading: A 5·70 kg/kW (9·38 lb/hp)
B 6·99 kg/kW (11·46 lb/hp)
PERFORMANCE (A: Capt Foster's M.J.7, B: M Semenadisse's M.J.77 with two 80 kg; 176 lb occupants):
Never-exceed speed:
B 215 knots (400 km/h; 248 mph)
Max level speed: A 190 knots (351 km/h; 218 mph)
B 167 knots (310 km/h; 193 mph)
Cruising speed:
A at 2,135 m (7,000 ft) 175 knots (325 km/h; 202 mph)
B at 2,400 rpm 151 knots (280 km/h; 174 mph)
B at 2,000 rpm 124 knots (230 km/h; 143 mph)
Take-off speed:
A, flaps up 70-75 knots (131-139 km/h; 81-87 mph)
B 60 knots (110 km/h; 69 mph)
Landing speed:
A, flaps up 65-70 knots (121-130 km/h; 75-81 mph)
A, flaps down 63 knots (117 km/h; 73 mph)
B 49 knots (90 km/h; 56 mph)
Stalling speed:
A, flaps down 57 knots (106 km/h; 66 mph)
B, clean 54 knots (100 km/h; 62 mph)
B, landing configuration 46 knots (85 km/h; 53 mph)
Max rate of climb at S/L: A 305 m (1,000 ft)/min
B 366 m (1,200 ft)/min
T-O run: A 457 m (1,500 ft)
B 300 m (985 ft)
Landing run: A 610-762 m (2,000-2,500 ft)

JURCA M.J.7S SOLO

Intended as a single-seat advanced trainer, the M.J.7S Solo is basically similiar to the M.J.7 Gnatsum but does not retain the underbelly scoop which the latter inherited from the original P-51 Mustang design. A prototype is under construction by M Duhamel of Strasbourg, with a 134 kW (180 hp) Avco Lycoming AIO-360 flat-four engine, but progress is slow.

The wing section of the M.J.7S is quoted as Habib 64-000 748-MJ7-104.

DIMENSIONS, EXTERNAL:
Wing span 7·523 m (24 ft 8½ in)
Length overall, tail up 6·664 m (21 ft 10 in)
Tailplane span 3·00 m (9 ft 10 in)
AREA:
Wings, gross 10·80 m² (116·2 sq ft)

JURCA M.J.8 and M.J.80 1-NINE-OH

The M.J.8 is a single-seat sporting aircraft which has been designed by M Jurca by scaling down to three-quarters of the original dimensions the airframe of the Focke-Wulf Fw 190A fighter. Its general appearance is shown in the accompanying illustration.

The prototype, built by Mr Ronald Kitchen of Carson City, Nevada, flew for the first time on 30 March 1975. A second example was built by Mr J. Kiska of Norwalk, Connecticut; and Mr Evan Wolfe of California initiated construction of an enlarged M.J.8, in an attempt to produce a full-size 'Fw 190'. This has been designated **M.J.80**. Work has begun on the first M.J.8s to be constructed in the UK and Germany, the former by Mr Bellhouse. A French M.J.8 is being built by M Eveille of Bordeaux.

Mr Kitchen's M.J.8 now has a 231 kW (310 hp) Avco Lycoming engine, and the design is suitable for the alternative use of any horizontally opposed or radial engine in the 119-231 kW (160-310 hp) range. The landing gear is retractable.

DIMENSIONS, EXTERNAL (M.J.8):
Wing span 7·87 m (25 ft 10 in)
Wing chord: at root 1·70 m (5 ft 7 in)
at tip 0·90 m (2 ft 11½ in)
Length overall 6·63 m (21 ft 9 in)
Tailplane span 2·84 m (9 ft 4 in)
AREA:
Wings, gross 10·20 m² (109·8 sq ft)
WEIGHTS AND LOADINGS (M.J.8 with 119·5 kW; 160 hp engine):
Weight empty 400 kg (880 lb)
Max T-O weight 626 kg (1,380 lb)
Max wing loading 61·4 kg/m² (12·57 lb/sq ft)
Max power loading 5·24 kg/kW (8·63 lb/hp)
PERFORMANCE (M.J.8, estimated, with 119·5 kW; 160 hp engine):
Max level speed at S/L 139 knots (257 km/h; 160 mph)
Max cruising speed 124 knots (230 km/h; 143 mph)
Stalling speed 49 knots (90 km/h; 56 mph)
Max rate of climb at S/L 503 m (1,650 ft)/min

JURCA M.J.9 ONE-OH-NINE

A prototype three-quarter scale Messerschmitt Bf 109 fighter of the Second World War is being constructed by Mr Werner Hohn of Carson City, Nevada. This has been designated M.J.9. A second example is being built by Mr Heyser of Tustin, California.

JURCA M.J.10 SPIT

The M.J.10 is a single-seat, three-quarter scale representation of the Supermarine Spitfire which can also be modified as a two-seater. It is suitable for any horizontally opposed or inline engine of 119-231 kW (160-310 hp), although some slight variations from the Spitfire's contours are necessary in the former case. Construction is entirely of wood, except for the glassfibre engine cowling and fabric covering on the control surfaces. The single-spar wing is similar in construction to that of the Sirocco. The manually operated retractable landing gear is fitted with helicoidal spring shock absorbers.

The basic plans adopted the Spitfire Mk IX as the standard M.J.10 version, but alternative detail plans are available for representing both Merlin and Griffon engined models, including the Mks VC and XIV, and for clipped, standard or extended span wings.

The first M.J.10 to fly was built by Mr Don McMurtrie of Bartlesville, Oklahoma, USA. Powered by a 224 kW (300 hp) modified Jaguar V12 motorcar engine, it first flew in 1982 but was involved in an accident after 12 flying hours when the direct-driven fuel pump failed in flight. Other M.J.10s include one built by Mr Ray Forbes of California.

DIMENSIONS, EXTERNAL:
Wing span:
standard 8·40 m (27 ft 6¾ in)
clipped 7·46 m (24 ft 5½ in)
Length overall 7·125 m (23 ft 4½ in)
AREA:
Wings, gross 12·60 m² (135·6 sq ft)
WEIGHTS AND LOADINGS (119·5 kW; 160 hp engine):
Weight empty 658 kg (1,450 lb)
Max T-O weight 907 kg (2,000 lb)
Max wing loading 72·0 kg/m² (14·74 lb/sq ft)
Max power loading 7·59 kg/kW (12·50 lb/hp)
PERFORMANCE (estimated, with 119·5 kW; 160 hp engine):
Max level speed at S/L 139 knots (257 km/h; 160 mph)
Cruising speed 124 knots (230 km/h; 143 mph)
Stalling speed 49 knots (90 km/h; 56 mph)
Max rate of climb at S/L 503 m (1,650 ft)/min
T-O run 200 m (660 ft)

JURCA M.J.100

Plans have been available since the Spring of 1985 for a full-size representation of the Supermarine Spitfire. Known as the M.J.100, it is of wooden construction and uses a 186 kW (250 hp) engine. Kits of component parts to build the M.J.100 are being made available from Ets Degouy Aviation (see introductory notes).

JURCA M.J.12 PEE-40

The M.J.12 is a three-quarter scale representation of the Curtiss P-40 single-seat fighter of the Second World War. It spans 8·524 m (27 ft 11½ in) and has an overall length (tail up) of 7·62 m (25 ft 0 in).

Three M.J.12s were begun in North America, one by Mr Ron Kitchen of Carson City, Nevada, who built the prototype M.J.8, another by Mr Russell J. Moynagh of Santa Ana, California, and the third by Captain Wayne Foster in Canada, who previously built an M.J.7.

LANDRAY

GILBERT LANDRAY

28 rue Remonteur, 91560 Crosne
Telephone: (6) 948 1019

M Landray has designed and built a series of light aircraft of Mignet tandem-wing configuration. Reference to the GL01, GL02 and GL03, with illustrations, can be found in the 1982-83 *Jane's*. His latest product, the GL06, was demonstrated at the 1986 RSA rally at Brienne.

LANDRAY GL06

Few details of this side by side two-seat tandem-wing light aircraft were available in August 1986, but its general configuration can be seen in an accompanying illustration. Construction is of wood, with fabric covering. The power plant is a 1,600 cc converted Volkswagen motorcar engine, with nominal rating of 34·3 kW (46 hp), and driving a two-blade wooden fixed-pitch propeller. Control is by the classic Mignet formula, with pivoted forward wing and rudder. The mainwheels of the tailwheel landing gear are carried on side Vs and half axles, with shock absorbers incorporated in the Vs. Access to the open cockpit is facilitated by hingeing the large windscreen.

LANOT

LANOT AVIATION

Zone Industrielle de Lons, Avenue Gay Lussac, BP 111 Lons, 64143 Billere Cédex
Telephone: (59) 62 52 27

LANOT AVIATION AQUITAIN

TYPE: Side by side two-seat microlight aircraft.

AIRFRAME: Strut braced high-wing monoplane, with constant chord wings which have no leading-edge camber and, like the conventional tail unit, are double surfaced. Dihedral 3°. Three-axis control (ailerons, elevators and rudder). Entire structure of composite materials. Wings and tail unit removable. Rigging time 20 min.

LANDING GEAR: Non-retractable tricycle type. Faired and steerable nosewheel. Mainwheels, with brakes, carried on cantilever spring legs of carbonfibre.

POWER PLANT: Two 18·6 kW (25 hp) KFM 107ER engines, with 2:1 belt reduction to two two-blade pusher propellers.

ACCOMMODATION: Pilot and passenger side by side in semi-enclosed cockpit. Side panels optional, to enclose cockpit fully. Dual controls.

DIMENSIONS, EXTERNAL:
Wing span 11·85 m (38 ft 10½ in)
Length overall 5·50 m (18 ft 0½ in)
Height overall 3·00 m (9 ft 10 in)
AREA:
Wings, gross 20·0 m² (215·3 sq ft)
WEIGHTS AND LOADINGS:
Weight empty 175 kg (386 lb)
Max T-O weight 400 kg (882 lb)
Max wing loading 20·0 kg/m² (4·10 lb/sq ft)
Max power loading 10·75 kg/kW (17·64 lb/hp)
PERFORMANCE:
Never-exceed speed 67 knots (125 km/h; 77 mph)
Max level speed 59 knots (110 km/h; 68 mph)
Max cruising speed 46 knots (85 km/h; 53 mph)
Econ cruising speed 35 knots (65 km/h; 40 mph)
Stalling speed 22 knots (40 km/h; 25 mph)
Max rate of climb at S/L 240 m (785 ft)/min
Range 151 nm (280 km; 174 miles)
g limits +6/−4
Min rate of sink at 27 knots (50 km/h; 31 mph), power off 60 m (197 ft)/min

LATÉCOÈRE

SOCIÉTÉ INDUSTRIELLE D'AVIATION LATÉCOÈRE SA

S.I.L.A.T., 135 rue de Périole, 31079 Toulouse Cédex
PARIS OFFICE: 79 avenue Marceau, 75116 Paris
Telephone: (1) 720 01 05
Telex: 613712F
PRESIDENT: P. G. Latécoère

LATÉCOÈRE 225

At the 1983 Paris Air Show Société Industrielle d'Aviation Latécoère SA announced the development of the Latécoère 225 microlight amphibian, designed by Nono Hersen. The aircraft is of canard configuration with an all-composite structure and sweptback main wings. The fuselage has an enclosed cockpit, with a hull bottom surface. Movable foreplane is mounted on a tubular boom projecting from top of fuselage. A tailwheel landing gear is fitted, the mainwheel fairings serving as sponsons for off-water flying when the mainwheels are in the retracted position. Mainwheels have disc brakes; tailwheel is steerable. The prototype was originally powered by an 18 kW (24 hp) JPX PUL 425 engine driving a pusher propeller; replaced in 1985 by a KFM 107 engine. Total fuel capacity 23 litres (5 Imp gallons). Three-axis control.

The prototype (F-WZLM) made its first flight on 18 July 1984.

DIMENSIONS, EXTERNAL:
Wing span 8·03 m (26 ft 4 in)
Length overall 4·95 m (16 ft 3 in)
AREAS:
Wings, gross 11·85 m² (127·6 sq ft)
Foreplane 1·85 m² (19·91 sq ft)
WEIGHTS AND LOADING:
Weight empty 127 kg (280 lb)
Max T-O weight 250 kg (551 lb)
Max power loading 13·89 kg/kW (22·96 lb/hp)
PERFORMANCE:
Max level speed at S/L 65 knots (120 km/h; 75 mph)
Min flying speed 25 knots (45 km/h; 28 mph)
T-O distance: grass 80 m (262 ft)
water 150 m (492 ft)

LEDERLIN

FRANÇOIS LEDERLIN

2 rue Charles Peguy, 38000 Grenoble

M Lederlin, an architect, designed and built a two-seat light aeroplane based on the familiar Mignet 'Pou-du-Ciel' formula. Although derived from the Mignet HM-380 and designated 380-L, it retains little of the original except for the wing section. First flight was made on 14 September 1965, a restricted C of A being granted in the following month.

Plans of the 380-L, annotated in English and with both English and metric measurements, are available to amateur constructors, and several examples are under construction or already flying.

LEDERLIN 380-L

TYPE: Two-seat light homebuilt aircraft.

AIRFRAME: Tandem-wing biplane. Wing section 3·40-13. Dihedral 3° 30′ on outer sections only (both wings). Incidence variable from 0° to 12° (forward wing). Incidence of rear wing 6°. No sweepback. Each wing is made in two parts, bolted together at the centreline. Construction is conventional, with wooden box spar and trellis ribs, plywood leading-edge and overall fabric covering. The variable incidence front wing is pivoted on the cabane structure by balljoints and on the bracing struts (one each side) by cardan joints. No ailerons or flaps. Long-span tab on trailing-edge of rear wing, controllable in flight. Welded steel tube fuselage, covered with light alloy to front of cabin and with fabric on rear fuselage, over light spruce formers. Tail unit comprises fin and rudder, of spruce and ply with fabric covering. Ground adjustable tab in rudder.

LANDING GEAR: Non-retractable tailwheel type. Cantilever main legs consist of conical spring steel rods, inclined rearward. Fournier mainwheels and tyres, size 380 × 150, with mechanical brakes. Large tailwheel, carried on telescopic leg with spring shock absorber, can be steered by the rudder controls through a linkage engaged by the pilot.

POWER PLANT: One 67 kW (90 hp) Continental C90-14F flat-four engine, driving a McCauley two-blade fixed-pitch metal propeller. Single fuel tank, capacity 85 litres (18·75 Imp gallons). Oil capacity 4·5 litres (1 Imp gallon).

ACCOMMODATION: Two seats side by side in enclosed cabin.

Landray GL06 two-seat tandem-wing lightplane *(J. M. G. Gradidge)*

Lanot Aviation Aquitain *(Brian M. Service)*

Lederlin 380-L two-seat light aircraft (Continental C90-14F engine) *(Peter J. Bish)*

Lendepergt LP-1 Sibylle four-seat amphibian *(J. M. G. Gradidge)*

The unorthodox Latécoère 225 microlight amphibian *(James Gilbert)*

Forward-hinged door on each side. Controls comprise a rudder bar for directional control and a stick, suspended from the roof of the cabin and free laterally, to control the incidence of the forward wing. A further lever, suspended from the roof, controls the tab on the rear wing. Baggage space aft of seats.

DIMENSIONS, EXTERNAL:

Wing span: forward	7·92 m (26 ft 0 in)
rear	6·00 m (19 ft 8¼ in)
Wing chord (constant, each)	1·30 m (4 ft 3¼ in)
Length overall	4·77 m (15 ft 7¾ in)
Height overall	2·08 m (6 ft 10 in)
Wheel track	2·05 m (6 ft 8¾ in)
Wheelbase	3·10 m (10 ft 2 in)
Propeller diameter	1·83 m (6 ft 0 in)
Doors (each): Height	0·90 m (2 ft 11½ in)
Width	0·75 m (2 ft 5½ in)
Height to sill	0·50 m (1 ft 7½ in)

DIMENSIONS, INTERNAL:

Cabin: Max width	1·07 m (3 ft 6 in)
Max height	1·03 m (3 ft 4 in)
Baggage space	0·20 m³ (7 cu ft)

AREAS:

Wings, gross: forward	9·92 m² (106·8 sq ft)
rear	7·43 m² (80·0 sq ft)

WEIGHTS AND LOADINGS:

Weight empty	360 kg (794 lb)
Max T-O weight	600 kg (1,323 lb)
Max wing loading	34·58 kg/m² (7·08 lb/sq ft)
Max power loading	8·96 kg/kW (14·70 lb/hp)

PERFORMANCE (at max T-O weight):

Never-exceed speed	126 knots (233 km/h; 145 mph)
Max level speed at 305 m (1,000 ft)	109 knots (201 km/h; 125 mph)
Max cruising speed	97 knots (180 km/h; 112 mph)
Econ cruising speed at 610 m (2,000 ft)	87 knots (161 km/h; 100 mph)
Stalling speed, power off	26 knots (49 km/h; 30 mph)
Max rate of climb at S/L	275 m (900 ft)/min
Service ceiling	over 3,660 m (12,000 ft)
T-O run	122 m (400 ft)
Landing run	153 m (500 ft)
Range at econ cruising speed	477 nm (885 km; 550 miles)

LEFEBVRE

ROBERT LEFEBVRE

The late M Lefebvre built and flew a small single-seat racing aircraft named the Busard, assisted by pupils of the A. Camus technical school at Rouen. Basis of the design was the MP.204 prototype racer with 56 kW (75 hp) Minié engine, designed by Max Plan and first flown on 5 June 1952. By comparison with the MP.204, the Busard was lightened, and simplified for construction by amateurs. At least fifteen sets of plans to build the aircraft were sold.

Full details of the Busard and an illustration can be found in the 1985-86 *Jane's*.

LENDEPERGT

Telephone: (16 1 43) 65 61 36

LENDEPERGT LP-1 SIBYLLE

The prototype of this four-seat amphibian (F-PYQS) was shown at the RSA's 1986 rally at Brienne. As can be seen in an accompanying illustration, it resembles closely the two-seat Osprey which is marketed in the USA by Mr George Pereira (see Osprey Aircraft in US section), but embodies much original design. Few details were available in August 1986, except that the LP-1 has a 119 kW (160 hp) Avco Lycoming flat-four engine, driving a two-blade fixed-pitch pusher propeller. First flight was made in July 1986.

DIMENSIONS, EXTERNAL:

Wing span	9·40 m (30 ft 10 in)
Length overall	6·60 m (21 ft 8 in)

WEIGHTS:

Weight empty	600 kg (1,323 lb)
Max T-O weight	1,000 kg (2,205 lb)

PERFORMANCE (estimated):

Max level speed	151 knots (280 km/h; 174 mph)
Cruising speed	135 knots (250 km/h; 155 mph)
Stalling speed	49 knots (90 km/h; 56 mph)
Max rate of climb at S/L	240 m (787 ft)/min
Service ceiling	5,000 m (16,400 ft)
Range with max fuel	1,080 nm (2,000 km; 1,240 miles)

LESAGE

CHRISTIAN LESAGE

Clamart

Among aircraft flown by French competitors at the 1986 World Aerobatic Championships in the UK was the Lesage DL260 (F-WYSP) which resembles closely the well-known Mudry CAP 21. All available details follow:

LESAGE DL260

TYPE: Single-seat aerobatic monoplane.

POWER PLANT: One 194 kW (260 hp) Avco Lycoming AEIO-540 flat-six engine, driving a two-blade propeller. Standard fuel capacity 50 litres (11 Imp gallons). Long range tank increases total capacity to 100 litres (22 Imp gallons).

WEIGHTS:

Weight empty	540 kg (1,190 lb)
Max T-O weight	650 kg (1,433 lb)

PERFORMANCE:

Never-exceed speed	216 knots (400 km/h; 248 mph)
Max cruising speed	189 knots (350 km/h; 217 mph)
Stalling speed	54 knots (100 km/h; 62 mph)
T-O run	150 m (492 ft)
Landing run	400 m (1,313 ft)
Range with max fuel	270 nm (500 km; 310 miles)
g limits	±10

LUCANT

MOTO LUCANT

Among exhibits at the 1986 RSA convention at Brienne was the prototype of a two-seat monoplane with ducted fan engine, built by M Anton Lucant. All available details follow:

MOTO LUCANT MONOPLANE

The prototype of this tandem two-seat light aircraft is shown in an accompanying illustration. It is powered by a 47 kW (63 hp) Rotax 532 two-cylinder two-stroke engine, driving a seven-blade ducted fan mounted behind the fuselage pod.

DIMENSIONS, EXTERNAL:

Wing span	11·00 m (36 ft 1 in)
Length overall	6·20 m (20 ft 4 in)

WEIGHT:

Max T-O weight	420 kg (926 lb)

PERFORMANCE:

Max level speed	87 knots (162 km/h; 100 mph)
Stalling speed	20 knots (37 km/h; 23 mph)

LUCAS

EMILE LUCAS

Corbonod, 01420 Seyssel
Telephone: (50) 59 27 54

M Emile Lucas markets plans of three versions of his L5 light aircraft, with seats for two to four persons. He has also designed a motor glider, designated L6-7, which is described in the Sailplanes section of this edition.

LUCAS L5

M Emile Lucas built a two/three-seat light aircraft designated Lucas L5. Design began in 1969, and construction of the prototype was undertaken in the designer's living room. First flight was made on 13 August 1976. Plans are available to other amateur builders, and 36 more L5s were known to be flying or under construction by early 1986, some with non-retractable and others with retractable landing gear. The first L5 built to plans, by M Germain Labyt, flew in August 1980.

There are now three basic versions of the L5, as follows:

L5. Initial two/three-seat model, similar to prototype, to which detailed description applies.

L5 200. Airframe generally similar to L5, but with three seats as standard. Prototype (F-WJOB, now F-PJOB) built by M J. Dandec, Général Engineer of the French Navy in Nantes, flew for the first time on 1 October 1984 with a 70 kW (94 hp) Rolls-Royce Continental O-200-E engine, driving a two-blade fixed-pitch propeller. Alternative power plants include Avco Lycoming O-320. One fuel tank in fuselage, capacity 73 litres (16 Imp gallons) and one in each wing, capacity 25 litres (5·5 Imp gallons). Total capacity 123 litres (27 Imp gallons). Accommodation for three persons and no baggage, or two persons and 65 kg (143 lb) baggage. Prototype has non-retractable tricycle type landing gear, Jolliet ER 360 VHF radio and Narco VOR.

L5 360. As basic L5, but with four seats in pairs. Prototype (F-WZRQ), built by M Devicq of Le Havre, flew for the first time on 14 March 1984 with a 134 kW (180 hp) Avco Lycoming O-360 engine, driving a two-blade fixed-pitch propeller. One fuel tank in fuselage, capacity 80 litres (17·6 Imp gallons) and two in wings, each 50 litres (11 Imp gallons). Accommodation for four without baggage or three with 30 kg (66 lb) baggage. Prototype has mechanically retractable tailwheel type landing gear, Narco VHF radio and VOR.

The following details apply to the basic L5 but the airframe description is generally applicable to all versions:

TYPE: Two/three-seat homebuilt monoplane.

AIRFRAME: Cantilever low-wing monoplane. All-metal airframe of AU2G and AU4G light alloy, including metal ailerons and two-position flaps. Wing section NACA 23015(mod). Dihedral 3°. Incidence 3°. No sweepback. Wing chord sharply reduced at each wingtip by curved trailing-edge. Leading-edge of each wing extended forward at root to house main landing gear leg when retractable landing gear is fitted. No tabs. Conventional fuselage, and cantilever tail unit with constant chord tailplane and horn balanced one-piece elevator. Swept-back fin and horn balanced rudder. No tabs.

LANDING GEAR: Non-retractable tricycle or mechanically retractable tailwheel type, both having been fitted to prototype during development. Rubber shock absorption. Wheel size 420 × 150 on nose and main units. Hydraulic brakes.

POWER PLANT: Prototype had one 85·75 kW (115 hp) Avco Lycoming O-235 flat-four engine, driving an EVRA two-blade fixed-pitch propeller with spinner. Basic L5s built to plans can have an engine of between 93 and 134 kW (125-180 hp). One fuel tank standard in fuselage. Total fuel capacity 75 or 115 litres (16·5 or 25·3 Imp gallons) in L5; see model listings for other versions.

ACCOMMODATION: Two seats side by side under transparent canopy. Provision for third seat when using engine of more than 85·75 kW (115 hp). Baggage capacity 30 kg (66 lb).

AVIONICS: Jolliet ER400 VHF radio.

DIMENSIONS, EXTERNAL:

Wing span	9·20 m (30 ft 2¼ in)
Wing aspect ratio	7·2
Length overall	6·30 m (20 ft 8 in)
Height overall	2·10 m (6 ft 10¾ in)
Propeller diameter	1·70 m (5 ft 7 in)

AREA:

Wings, gross	11·90 m² (128·1 sq ft)

WEIGHTS AND LOADINGS (A: prototype, B: L5 200 with O-200 engine, C: L5 360):

Weight empty, equipped: A	505 kg (1,113 lb)
B	470 kg (1,036 lb)
C	540 kg (1,190 lb)
Max T-O weight: A	746 kg (1,644 lb)
B	720 kg (1,587 lb)
C	906 kg (1,997 lb)
Max wing loading: A	62·7 kg/m² (12·84 lb/sq ft)
B	60·5 kg/m² (12·39 lb/sq ft)
C	76·1 kg/m² (15·59 lb/sq ft)
Max power loading: A	8·70 kg/kW (14·30 lb/hp)
B	10·29 kg/kW (16·88 lb/hp)
C	6·76 kg/kW (11·09 lb/hp)

PERFORMANCE (A: prototype, B: L5 200 with O-200 engine, C: L5 360):

Never-exceed speed:	
A, B	161 knots (300 km/h; 186 mph)
C	172 knots (320 km/h; 199 mph)
Max level speed:	
A, with retractable landing gear	146 knots (270 km/h; 168 mph)
A, with fixed gear	127 knots (235 km/h; 146 mph)
B	116 knots (215 km/h; 133 mph)
C	170 knots (315 km/h; 196 mph)
Max cruising speed:	
A, with retractable landing gear	138 knots (255 km/h; 158 mph)
A, with fixed gear	108 knots (200 km/h; 124 mph)
B	100 knots (185 km/h; 115 mph)
C	135 knots (250 km/h; 155 mph)
Econ cruising speed:	
A, with retractable landing gear	116 knots (215 km/h; 134 mph)
A, with fixed gear	97 knots (180 km/h; 112 mph)
B	92 knots (170 km/h; 106 mph)
C	124 knots (230 km/h; 143 mph)
Max rate of climb at S/L: A	300 m (985 ft)/min
B	260 m (855 ft)/min
T-O to 15 m (50 ft): A	280 m (920 ft)
B	500 m (1,640 ft)
Landing from 15 m (50 ft): A	380 m (1,245 ft)
Range with max fuel:	
A	539 nm (1,000 km; 621 miles)
B, two occupants, 15 min reserves	499 nm (925 km; 575 miles)
C, 30 min reserves	539 nm (1,000 km; 621 miles)

MAVIC

SOCIÉTÉ MAVIC

01990 Saint Triviersur Moignans
Telex: 310090

Mavic manufactures parts, kits and/or completed examples of the French Croses Airplume and Tisserand Hydroplum II (which see), and of the US Avid Flyer.

MIGNET

SOCIÉTÉ D'EXPLOITATION DES AÉRONEFS HENRI MIGNET

Logis des Pierrières, Saint-Romain de Benêt, 17600 Saujon
Telephone: (46) 02 26 00
DIRECTOR: Alain Mignet

AVIONS MIGNET HM-1000 BALERIT

The Balerit represents a microlight adaptation of the well-known Mignet Pou du Ciel (Flying Flea) tandem-wing configuration, in which the aircraft is controlled by means of the pivoted forward wing and a rudder, with no conventional roll control surfaces. It flew for the first time on 9 April 1984.

Design of the HM-1000 Balerit began in 1982 and construction of pre-production aircraft started in July 1985. The first pre-production Balerit flew on 21 November that year, and series production began in early 1986.

TYPE: Side by side two-seat microlight aircraft.

AIRFRAME: Tandem-wing biplane, primarily of AU4G (2017A) and AG4MC (5086) light alloy construction, but with carbonfibre rudder. Each wing built in three sections that fold and stack for transportation. Dihedral 2° 48′ on outer panels. The variable incidence front wing is pivoted on the open fuselage structure by a balljoint and on the bracing struts by cardan joints. No ailerons or flaps. Wings double surface skinned. Two-axis control (front wing and horn balanced rudder). No fin. Optional extras include a glassfibre cockpit fairing and windscreen.

LANDING GEAR: Non-retractable tricycle type, with bungee suspension. All three wheels size 400 × 8. Optional mudguards, floats and skis.

POWER PLANT: One 34·3 kW (46 hp) Rotax 503 two-cylinder two-stroke engine, with belt drive to a Mignet two- or three-blade wooden pusher propeller. Fuel capacity 24 litres (5·3 Imp gallons). Optional twin-carburettor Rotax 503-2V engine.

ACCOMMODATION: Two seats side by side in open position.

DIMENSIONS, EXTERNAL:

Wing span: front	7·30 m (23 ft 11½ in)
rear	5·50 m (18 ft 0½ in)
Wing chord, constant: front	1·50 m (4 ft 11 in)
rear	1·20 m (3 ft 11¼ in)
Length overall	5·00 m (16 ft 5 in)
Height overall	1·88 m (6 ft 2 in)
Wheelbase	1·90 m (6 ft 2¾ in)
Propeller diameter	1·48 m (4 ft 10¼ in)

AREA:

Wings, gross (total)	17·55 m² (189·0 sq ft)

WEIGHTS AND LOADINGS:

Weight empty	175 kg (386 lb)
Max T-O weight	374 kg (824 lb)
Max wing loading	21·3 kg/m² (4·36 lb/sq ft)
Max power loading	10·90 kg/kW (17·91 lb/hp)

PERFORMANCE (at max T-O weight):

Never-exceed speed	48 knots (90 km/h; 56 mph)
Min flying speed	22 knots (40 km/h; 25 mph)
Max rate of climb at S/L	180 m (590 ft)/min
T-O run	45 m (148 ft)
Landing run	25 m (82 ft)
g limits	+7/−5

Lesage DL260 single-seat competitive aerobatic aircraft *(Austin J. Brown)*

Moto Lucant two-seat ducted-fan monoplane *(Geoffrey P. Jones)*

Lucas L5 with retractable tailwheel landing gear, owned by M Pliez of Evreux

Lucas L5 200 with non-retractable tricycle landing gear *(Geoffrey P. Jones)*

Lucas L5 360 constructed by M Devicq

Nicollier HN 433 Menestrel *(Austin J. Brown)*

Avions Mignet HM-1000 Balerit two-seat microlight

NICOLLIER

AVIONS H. NICOLLIER

13 rue de Verdun, 25000 Besançon
Telephone: (81) 53 57 01

M Nicollier, who began flying sailplanes and powered aircraft when he was 16 years old, has designed four light aircraft. Plans of three have been made available to other constructors.

NICOLLIER HN 433 MENESTREL

The prototype of this single-seat aircraft (F-WKXO) flew for the first time on 25 November 1962 and continues in use. Plans are available, and Menestrels are currently under construction, or already being flown, by amateurs in several countries. Completed wing spars and kits of materials are available from the Siravia company, of Pons. Moulded canopies, cowlings and wheel fairings are available from Avions H. Nicollier.

Type: Single-seat homebuilt aircraft.

Airframe: Cantilever low-wing monoplane. Constant chord on inner half of each wing; semi-elliptical outer panels. All-wood single-spar structure, with plywood covering on leading-edge and inboard 25 per cent of each wing. Dacron fabric covered overall. Plain wooden ailerons, Dacron fabric covered. No flaps or tabs. Conventional wooden truss fuselage of basic rectangular section, with curved top decking. Plywood covered, except for sides of rear fuselage and top decking. Dacron fabric covering overall. Cantilever wood tail unit. Fin and tailplane plywood covered; rudder and elevators Dacron fabric covered. No tabs.

Landing Gear: Cantilever main units, with Vespa motor scooter wheels, and tailskid.

Power Plant: One 22 kW (30 hp) converted Volkswagen 1,300 cc motorcar engine, with aluminium pistons and dual ignition, in prototype. Suited to Rectimo-VW engines of 22-37·3 kW (30-50 hp). Two-blade fixed-pitch propeller.

Accommodation: Single seat in enclosed cockpit.

Dimensions, external:

Wing span	7·00 m (22 ft 11½ in)
Wing aspect ratio	6·0
Length overall	5·30 m (17 ft 4½ in)
Height overall	1·48 m (4 ft 10¼ in)

Area:

Wings, gross	8·20 m² (88·26 sq ft)

Weights and Loadings:

Weight empty	201 kg (443 lb)
Weight empty, with battery and radio	209 kg (461 lb)
Max T-O weight	330 kg (727 lb)
Max wing loading	40·2 kg/m² (8·24 lb/sq ft)
Max power loading	15·00 kg/kW (24·23 lb/hp)

Performance (A: prototype, B: with 29 kW; 39 hp 1,200 cc engine, C: with 1,500 cc engine, at max T-O weight):

Never-exceed speed:	
B, C	135 knots (250 km/h; 155 mph)
Max level speed at S/L:	
A	92 knots (170 km/h; 105 mph)
B	100 knots (185 km/h; 115 mph)
C	108 knots (200 km/h; 124 mph)
Max cruising speed: A	81 knots (150 km/h; 93 mph)
B	86 knots (160 km/h; 99 mph)
C	97 knots (180 km/h; 112 mph)
Econ cruising speed: A	78 knots (145 km/h; 90 mph)

Stalling speed:
A, power off 35 knots (65 km/h; 41 mph)
B, C, engine idling 26 knots (48 km/h; 30 mph)
B, C, power on 22 knots (40 km/h; 25 mph)
Approach speed:
B, C 38-43 knots (70-80 km/h; 43-50 mph)
Max rate of climb at S/L: A, B 180 m (590 ft)/min
C 258 m (845 ft)/min
Service ceiling: B 3,800 m (12,475 ft)
T-O run: B 120 m (394 ft)
C 100 m (328 ft)
Max range:
A, with 20 min reserves
229 nm (425 km; 264 miles)
B, C 278 nm (515 km; 320 miles)
g limits −4·4/−2·2

NICOLLIER HN 434 SUPER-MENESTREL

A completely redesigned version of the Menestrel has been developed as the HN 434 Super-Menestrel, plans of which are available to amateur constructors. It has improved performance by virtue of using a more powerful 1,500 cc or 1,600 cc Volkswagen modified motorcar engine, and fuel capacity is increased. Pilot comfort is improved. The Super-Menestrel is also simpler to construct. About fifteen Super-Menestrels were under construction in France in early 1986, and at least two have flown.

NICOLLIER HN 600 WEEK-END

The HN 600 Week-end is a single-seat light aircraft, designed for economical construction and operation by amateurs. The structure is simple, of wood and fabric, with some components of Klégécel foam. Plans became available in 1981. A number of major components, such as the wing spar, ribs, cowlings and canopy, were to be made available in completed form from the Siravia company, of Pons.

The general appearance of the Week-end is shown in an accompanying three-view drawing. Recommended power plant is a converted Volkswagen 1,500 cc motorcar engine of 22-37 kW (30-50 hp).

DIMENSIONS, EXTERNAL:
Wing span 7·00 m (22 ft 11½ in)
Length overall 5·25 m (17 ft 2¾ in)
AREA:
Wings, gross 3·20 m² (88·26 sq ft)
WEIGHTS AND LOADING:
Weight empty 185 kg (408 lb)
Max T-O weight 310 kg (683 lb)
Max wing loading 37·8 kg/m² (7·74 lb/sq ft)
PERFORMANCE (estimated, at max T-O weight):
Max level speed 108 knots (200 km/h; 124 mph)
Max cruising speed 92 knots (170 km/h; 106 mph)
Stalling speed 33 knots (60 km/h; 38 mph)
Max rate of climb at S/L 210 m (688 ft)/min
Range with max fuel at 86 knots (160 km/h; 99 mph)
345 nm (640 km; 397 miles)

NOIN

ETS NOIN AÉRONAUTIQUES

RN 85, Châteauvieux, 05130 Tallard
Telephone: (92) 54 15 04

This company markets, in kit form and ready to fly, a single-seat self-launching ultralight glider known as Sirius.

NOIN SIRIUS

TYPE: Single-seat self-launching glider.

AIRFRAME: Strut braced high-wing monoplane, with single aerofoil type bracing strut each side. Single-spar wooden wings, with plywood D type leading-edge torsion box and Dacron covering overall. Airbrakes and ailerons. Semi-monocoque fuselage of pod and boom type, made of glassfibre reinforced with carbonfibre. Cruciform tail unit comprises fixed incidence tailplane, elevators, large horn balanced rudder and triangular ventral fin. Rigging time 10 min.

LANDING GEAR: Two non-retractable wheels in tandem, semi-enclosed in base of fuselage pod. Small skid at bottom of tail fin. Wingtips embody landing skids.

POWER PLANT: One 13·4 kW (18 hp) JPX 425 two-stroke engine mounted as pusher at rear of fuselage pod; restartable in flight. Two-blade wooden propeller. Under consideration as alternative is KFM 107 engine of 18·6 or 22·4 kW (25 or 30 hp). Fuel capacity 5 to 10 litres (1·1-2·2 Imp gallons).

ACCOMMODATION: Single seat in cockpit with full Lexan canopy or windscreen.

AVIONICS: Radio optional.

DIMENSIONS, EXTERNAL:
Wing span 11·18 m (36 ft 8¼ in)
Wing aspect ratio 10·76
Length overall 5·90 m (19 ft 4¼ in)
Propeller diameter 0·95 m (3 ft 1½ in)
AREAS:
Wings, gross 11·61 m² (125·0 sq ft)
Wings, gross, plus lift-struts 14·50 m² (156·0 sq ft)
WEIGHT:
Weight empty 125 kg (276 lb)
PERFORMANCE, POWERED:
Never-exceed speed 65 knots (120 km/h; 75 mph)
Max level speed 48 knots (90 km/h; 56 mph)
Stalling speed 27 knots (49 km/h; 31 mph)
Max rate of climb at S/L 90 m (295 ft)/min
T-O run 100 m (328 ft)
Landing run 50 m (164 ft)
Endurance with max fuel 1 h 50 min
PERFORMANCE, UNPOWERED:
Best glide ratio at 40 knots (75 km/h; 47 mph) 20
Min rate of sink 0·85 m (2·8 ft)/s
g limits −4·4/−2·2 normal
+6·6/−3·3 ultimate

PENA

LOUIS PENA

Dax

PENA CAPENA

Two examples of this single-seat aerobatic aircraft were observed during the Summer of 1986. One, registered F-WZTC, was built by M Louis Pena at Dax, first flown on 24 July 1984, and seen at the 1986 World Aerobatic Championships in the UK. Capena 02 (F-PYTQ), built by M F. Sire for M Michel Cala, was displayed at the RSA rally at Brienne. The general appearance of this latter aircraft is shown in an accompanying illustration. Available details of F-WZTC follow:

TYPE: Single-seat aircraft for competitive aerobatics.

POWER PLANT: One Avco Lycoming AEIO-360 flat-four engine, driving a two-blade propeller with spinner. Basic fuel capacity 40 litres (8·8 Imp gallons), increased to 85 litres (18·7 Imp gallons) for cross-country flights.

WEIGHTS:
Weight empty 440 kg (970 lb)
Max T-O weight 550 kg (1,212 lb)
PERFORMANCE:
Never-exceed speed 200 knots (372 km/h; 231 mph)
Max cruising speed 175 knots (325 km/h; 202 mph)
Stalling speed 43 knots (80 km/h; 50 mph)
Max rate of climb at S/L 960 m (3,150 ft)/min
T-O run 100 m (328 ft)
Landing run 600 m (1,968 ft)
Max range with full fuel 324 nm (600 km; 372 miles)
g limits +10/−7

PIEL

AVIONS CLAUDE PIEL

Le Mas de Darnetz, 19300 Egletons
Telephone: (16 55) 93 09 79
PROPRIETOR: Mme Claude Piel

The late M Claude Piel designed several light aircraft, including the Emeraude, Super Diamant and Beryl, of which sets of plans are available to amateur constructors. In addition, Avions Claude Piel granted licence rights for their manufacture by several commercial concerns (see 1977-78 *Jane's* and the Erpals company in this section of the current edition). M Piel's final design was the C.P. 150 Onyx.

The authorised distributor for plans of Piel designs available to amateur constructors is:

D. Trivisonno, 10426 Parc Georges Blvd, Montreal, Quebec H1H 4Y3, Canada.

PIEL EMERAUDE and SUPER EMERAUDE

There have been several factory-built versions of the Emeraude and Super Emeraude. In addition, the designs continue to be available for amateur construction; by early 1986 some 420 sets of plans had been sold in France and others by Mr Trivisonno of Canada. Current versions are as follows:

C.P.301. With 67 kW (90 hp) Continental engine.

C.P.304. With 63·4 kW (85 hp) Continental C85-12F engine and wing flaps.

C.P.305. With 86 kW (115 hp) Avco Lycoming engine.

C.P.308. With 56 kW (75 hp) Continental engine.

C.P.320. With Super Emeraude wings and 74·5 kW (100 hp) Continental engine. Available also in ready-to-fly and kit forms from Erpals, with alternative tailwheel or tricycle landing gear.

C.P.320A. As C.P.320, but with sweptback fin.

C.P.321. As C.P.320, with 78·5 kW (105 hp) Potez engine.

C.P.323A. With 112 kW (150 hp) Avco Lycoming engine and sweptback fin. **C.P.323AB** has tricycle landing gear.

C.P.324 Emeraude Club. With 56 kW (75 hp) JPX 2100 engine. Available in ready-to-fly and kit forms from Erpals, with optional tailwheel or tricycle landing gear.

In addition, Mr Jason Petroelje of Holland, Michigan, brought to the 1979 EAA Fly-in an Emeraude (N78JP) with retractable tailwheel type landing gear. Another Emeraude with retractable landing gear was built by Mr Roger G. Hight of Ohio. Known as the Smaragd X, it is powered by a 74·5 kW (100 hp) Continental O-200 engine. This aircraft, which gained the 'Outstanding Workmanship' award at the 1981 Oshkosh Fly-in, was illustrated in the 1984-85 *Jane's*. It flew for the first time on 17 June 1981.

The Emeraude is one of the types approved by the Popular Flying Association for amateur construction in the United Kingdom.

The following details refer to the basic C.P.301 Emeraude and C.P.320 Super Emeraude, but are generally applicable to all versions:

TYPE: Two-seat light monoplane.

AIRFRAME: Cantilever low-wing monoplane. All-wood airframe, fabric covered except for wooden skins on tailplane. NACA 23012 wing section. Dihedral 5° 40′. Incidence 4° 10′. Inner half of each wing is rectangular in plan, outer half semi-elliptical, with a single spar. Slotted ailerons and flaps. Conventional box section fuselage with domed top decking. Cantilever tail unit; fin integral with fuselage. One-piece tailplane. Trim tab on starboard elevator.

LANDING GEAR: Non-retractable tailwheel type. Cantilever main legs have rubber in compression springing. Hydraulic brakes.

POWER PLANT (C.P.301): One 67 kW (90 hp) Continental C90-12F flat-four engine. Two-blade fixed-pitch wooden propeller. Fuel tank in fuselage, behind fireproof bulkhead, capacity 80 litres (17·6 Imp gallons). Provision for auxiliary tank, capacity 40 litres (8·8 Imp gallons).

POWER PLANT (C.P.320): One 74·5 kW (100 hp) Continental O-200 flat-four engine, driving a two-blade fixed-pitch wooden propeller. Fuel as for C.P.301.

ACCOMMODATION: Enclosed cockpit seating two side by side with dual controls. Sides of canopy hinge forward for access and exit. Heating and ventilation.

DIMENSIONS, EXTERNAL:
Wing span 8·04 m (26 ft 4½ in)
Wing chord: at root 1·50 m (4 ft 11 in)
at tip 0·55 m (1 ft 9½ in)
Wing aspect ratio 5·95
Length overall: C.P.301 6·30 m (20 ft 8 in)
C.P.320 6·45 m (21 ft 2 in)
Height overall: C.P.301 1·85 m (6 ft 0¾ in)
C.P.320 1·90 m (6 ft 2¾ in)
Wheel track 2·05 m (6 ft 8¾ in)
Propeller diameter: C.P.301 1·80 m (5 ft 11 in)
C.P.320 1·78 m (5 ft 10 in)
AREA:
Wings, gross 10·85 m² (116·7 sq ft)
WEIGHTS AND LOADINGS:
Weight empty: C.P.301 380 kg (838 lb)
C.P.320 410 kg (903 lb)
Max T-O weight: C.P.301 650 kg (1,433 lb)
C.P.320 700 kg (1,543 lb)
Max wing loading: C.P.301 59·9 kg/m² (12·27 lb/sq ft)
C.P.320 64·5 kg/m² (13·21 lb/sq ft)
Max power loading: C.P.301 9·70 kg/kW (15·92 lb/hp)
C.P.320 9·40 kg/kW (15·43 lb/hp)
PERFORMANCE (at max T-O weight):
Never-exceed speed:
C.P.301 118 knots (220 km/h; 136 mph)
C.P.320 149 knots (277 km/h; 172 mph)
Max level speed:
C.P.301 110 knots (205 km/h; 127 mph)
C.P.320 124 knots (230 km/h; 143 mph)
Max cruising speed (75% power) at 1,200 m (3,940 ft):
C.P.301 108 knots (200 km/h; 124 mph)
C.P.320 119 knots (220 km/h; 137 mph)
Econ cruising speed (65% power) at 1,200 m (3,940 ft):
C.P.301 101 knots (187 km/h; 116 mph)
C.P.320 110 knots (205 km/h; 127 mph)
Approach speed, flaps down:
C.P.301, C.P.320 65 knots (120 km/h; 75 mph)
Stalling speed, flaps up:
C.P.301 51 knots (92 km/h; 58 mph)
C.P.320 53 knots (97 km/h; 61 mph)
Stalling speed, flaps down:
C.P.301 46 knots (85 km/h; 53 mph)
C.P.320 49 knots (90 km/h; 56 mph)
Max rate of climb at S/L:
C.P.301 168 m (551 ft)/min
C.P.320 240 m (787 ft)/min
Service ceiling: C.P.301 4,000 m (13,125 ft)
C.P.320 4,300 m (14,100 ft)

Nicollier HN 434 Super-Menestrel

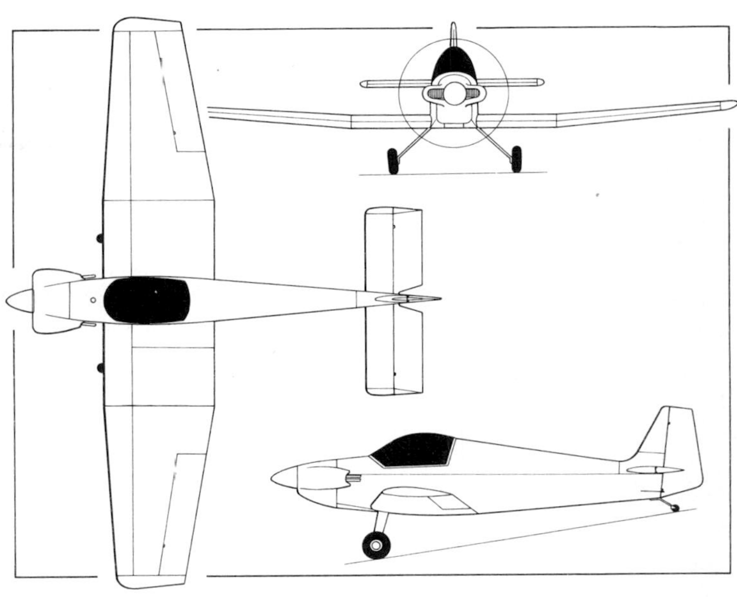
Nicollier HN 600 Week-end (Volkswagen 1,500 cc motorcar engine) *(Michael A. Badrocke)*

Noin Sirius self-launching ultralight glider *(J. M. G. Gradidge)*

Piel C.P.301A Emeraude constructed in Germany *(Geoffrey P. Jones)*

Pena Capena single-seat aerobatic aircraft *(J. M. G. Gradidge)*

Piel C.P.1320 built by M A. Kieger *(Geoffrey P. Jones)*

T-O run: C.P.301	250 m (820 ft)
C.P.320	230 m (755 ft)
T-O to 15 m (50 ft): C.P.301	440 m (1,443 ft)
C.P.320	400 m (1,312 ft)
Landing from 15 m (50 ft): C.P.301	475 m (1,558 ft)
C.P.320	490 m (1,608 ft)
Landing run: C.P.301	250 m (820 ft)
C.P.320	260 m (853 ft)
Range at econ cruising speed:	
C.P.301, C.P.320	538 nm (1,000 km; 620 miles)

PIEL C.P.1320

Design of this aircraft was started in January 1977, to combine the general characteristics of the Super Emeraude with the Super Diamant's three-seat cabin and fuel tanks in the wings. It can be fitted with engines of 112 kW (150 hp) to 149 kW (200 hp) and the prototype C.P.1320 (F-PYIE), built by Mr Lascoutounas of Blanquefort, near Bordeaux, has a 119·5 kW (160 hp) Avco Lycoming and non-standard tricycle landing gear (see Addenda to 1981-82 *Jane's*). By early 1986, at least forty sets of plans had been sold to amateur constructors in France, and others by Mr Trivisonno of Canada (see introductory notes); several C.P.1320s are under construction, and a small number are flying.

Type: Three-seat homebuilt monoplane.

Airframe: Cantilever low-wing monoplane of wooden construction. NACA 23012 wing section. Dihedral 3°. Incidence 2°. Slotted ailerons and slotted flaps. Conventional semi-monocoque fuselage. Cantilever tail unit, with sweptback fin and long dorsal fin integral with fuselage. Constant chord tailplane and elevator. Tab in elevator.

Landing Gear: Tailwheel type. Main units retract inward. Electrical retraction. Non-retractable tailwheel. Drum brakes on mainwheels.

Power Plant: Prototype has one 119 kW (160 hp) Avco Lycoming flat-four engine, driving a two-blade EVRA fixed-pitch wooden propeller. Single fuel tank in fuselage, capacity 70 litres (15·4 Imp gallons), and two fuel tanks in wings with total capacity of 70 litres (15·4 Imp gallons). Max fuel capacity 140 litres (30·8 Imp gallons).

Accommodation: Three seats, under rearward sliding transparent canopy.

Dimensions, external:	
Wing span	7·90 m (25 ft 11 in)
Wing chord: at root	1·64 m (5 ft 4½ in)
at tip	1·14 m (3 ft 9 in)
Wing aspect ratio	5·62
Length overall	6·60 m (21 ft 8 in)
Height overall	1·80 m (5 ft 11 in)
Tailplane span	2·50 m (8 ft 2½ in)
Wheel track	2·20 m (7 ft 2½ in)
Propeller diameter	1·80 m (5 ft 11 in)
Area:	
Wings, gross	11·10 m² (119·48 sq ft)
Weights and Loadings:	
Weight empty	470 kg (1,036 lb)
Max T-O weight	800 kg (1,764 lb)
Max wing loading	72·1 kg/m² (14·77 lb/sq ft)
Max power loading	6·69 kg/kW (11·03 lb/hp)
Performance:	
Never-exceed speed	183 knots (340 km/h; 211 mph)
Max level speed	162 knots (300 km/h; 186 mph)
Max cruising speed (75% power)	145 knots (270 km/h; 167 mph)
Econ cruising speed (65% power)	132 knots (245 km/h; 152 mph)
Approach speed, flaps down	70 knots (130 km/h; 81 mph)
Stalling speed: flaps up	54 knots (100 km/h; 62 mph)
flaps down	52 knots (95 km/h; 59 mph)
Max rate of climb at S/L	600 m (1,968 ft)/min
Service ceiling	5,000 m (16,400 ft)
T-O run	200 m (657 ft)
T-O to 15 m (50 ft)	420 m (1,378 ft)
Landing from 15 m (50 ft)	600 m (1,968 ft)
Landing run	300 m (984 ft)
Range with max fuel (65% power)	593 nm (1,100 km; 683 miles)
g limits: normal	+5/−2·5
aerobatic (two occupants, max T-O weight 720 kg; 1,585 lb)	+6/−3

PIEL SUPER DIAMANT

The Super Diamant is essentially a three/four-seat version of the Emeraude. It is fully certificated for commercial production and is manufactured to order by Erpals (which see) for sale in ready to fly and kit forms, with optional tailwheel or tricycle landing gear. The Super Diamant is available also in plan form for construction by amateurs. Current versions are as follows:

C.P.604. Prototype (F-PMEC) flown in Summer of 1964, with a 108 kW (145 hp) Continental engine. Current version has swept vertical tail surfaces.

C.P.605. Much-modified four-seat ('2 + 2') version, with 112 kW (150 hp) Avco Lycoming O-320-E2A engine. Fully certificated for commercial production, as well as for amateur construction. Details in 1973-74 *Jane's*.

C.P.605B. Version of C.P.605 with retractable tricycle landing gear.

By early 1986 a total of at least 49 sets of Super Diamant

plans had been sold in France, and others by Mr Trivisonno of Canada (see introductory notes).

TYPE: Three/four-seat light homebuilt monoplane.

AIRFRAME: Cantilever low-wing monoplane. All-wood airframe, fabric covered except for fixed tail surfaces which are plywood covered. Single-spar wings made in one piece. Wing section NACA 23012. Dihedral 5° 40′. Incidence 4° 10′. Slotted ailerons and slotted flaps. Conventional fuselage of basic rectangular section and cantilever tail unit, with sweptback fin and rudder. Ground adjustable tab on each elevator.

LANDING GEAR (C.P.604): Non-retractable tailwheel type. Mainwheels size 420 × 150. Hydraulic brakes. Wheel fairings. Steerable tailwheel, size 155 × 50.

LANDING GEAR (C.P.605B): Retractable tricycle type. Mainwheels retract inward. All three wheels and tyres size 400 × 100.

POWER PLANT: One flat-four engine (typically 119 kW; 160 hp Avco Lycoming IO-320-B1A or O-360-D1C), driving a two-blade fixed-pitch wooden propeller. Fuel tank in fuselage, capacity 85 litres (18·7 Imp gallons). Provision for additional tankage to give total capacity of 160 litres (35 Imp gallons). Oil capacity 4 litres (0·9 Imp gallons).

ACCOMMODATION: Three or four seats ('2 + 2') in enclosed cabin under large rearward-sliding transparent canopy.

DIMENSIONS, EXTERNAL (C.P.605B):
Wing span 9·20 m (30 ft 2¼ in)
Wing chord at root 1·50 m (4 ft 11 in)
Wing aspect ratio 6·4
Length overall 7·00 m (22 ft 11¾ in)
Height overall 2·00 m (6 ft 6¾ in)
Wheel track 3·00 m (9 ft 10 in)
Propeller diameter 1·80 m (5 ft 11 in)

AREA:
Wings, gross 13·30 m^2 (143·2 sq ft)

WEIGHTS AND LOADINGS (C.P.605B):
Weight empty 520 kg (1,146 lb)
Max T-O weight 850 kg (1,873 lb)
Max wing loading 63·9 kg/m^2 (13·09 lb/sq ft)
Max power loading 7·11 kg/kW (11·71 lb/hp)

PERFORMANCE (C.P.605B, at max T-O weight):
Never-exceed speed 151 knots (280 km/h; 174 mph)
Max level speed 141 knots (260 km/h; 162 mph)
Max cruising speed (75% power) at 1,200 m (3,940 ft) 132 knots (245 km/h; 152 mph)
Econ cruising speed (65% power) at 1,200 m (3,940 ft) 124 knots (230 km/h; 143 mph)
Approach speed, flaps down 68 knots (125 km/h; 78 mph)
Stalling speed: flaps up 49 knots (90 km/h; 56 mph)
flaps down 45 knots (82 km/h; 51 mph)
Max rate of climb at S/L 330 m (1,082 ft)/min
Service ceiling 5,000 m (16,400 ft)
T-O run 160 m (525 ft)
T-O to 15 m (50 ft) 380 m (1,247 ft)
Landing from 15 m (50 ft) 600 m (1,969 ft)
Landing run 270 m (886 ft)
Range at econ cruising speed 620 nm (1,150 km; 714 miles)

PIEL C.P.70, C.P.750 and C.P.751 BERYL

The prototype **C.P.70 Beryl** was displayed publicly for the first time in August 1965. It combines the wing of the C.P.30 Emeraude, virtually unchanged, with a fuselage containing two seats in tandem, and non-retractable tricycle landing gear. It is powered by a 48·5 kW (65 hp) Continental engine. Plans of this version are not available from Mr Trivisonno of Canada.

Intended for aerobatic flying, the **C.P.750 Beryl** is also similar in general appearance to the Emeraude but has a longer, steel tube fuselage seating two persons in tandem, slightly reduced span, non-retractable tailwheel type landing gear, 112 kW (150 hp) Avco Lycoming engine and other changes. The C.P.750 has been built principally by amateur constructors in Canada.

A further variant is the **C.P.751**, shown in an accompanying illustration. This aircraft (F-PYHM) was built by M Daniel Poulet and made its first flight at Les Mureaux on 2 March 1980. It introduced several new design features and has a 134 kW (180 hp) Avco Lycoming O-360-A engine. Although this is the only C.P. 751 flying in France at present, several are under construction or flying in Canada and the USA.

By early 1986 a total of at least 27 sets of plans for all versions of the Beryl had been sold in France, and others by Mr Trivisonno of Canada (see introductory notes).

TYPE: Two-seat homebuilt aerobatic monoplane.

AIRFRAME: Cantilever low-wing monoplane. Wing section NACA 23012. Dihedral 5° 40′. Incidence 4° 10′. All-wood single-spar wings, made in one piece, with fabric covering. Slotted ailerons and slotted flaps of wood construction with fabric covering. Fabric covered fuselage of wood (C.P.70) or welded steel tube (C.P.750). Cantilever wood tail unit; fixed surfaces plywood covered, control surfaces fabric covered. Ground adjustable tab on each elevator.

LANDING GEAR (C.P.70): Non-retractable tricycle type.

LANDING GEAR (C.P.750): Non-retractable tailwheel type. Mainwheels size 420 × 150, pressure 1·65 bars (24 lb/sq in). Hydraulic brakes. Wheel fairings. Steerable tailwheel.

POWER PLANT (C.P.70): One 48·5 kW (65 hp) Continental C65-8F flat-four engine, driving a two-blade wooden propeller. Fuel tank in fuselage, capacity 70 litres (15·4 Imp gallons).

POWER PLANT (C.P.750): One 112 kW (150 hp) Avco Lycoming O-320-E2A flat-four engine, driving an EVRA two-blade fixed-pitch wooden propeller. Fuel tank in fuselage, capacity 70 litres (15·4 Imp gallons), with provision for two auxiliary tanks in wings to give total capacity of 140 litres (30·75 Imp gallons). Oil capacity 5 litres (1·0 Imp gallon).

ACCOMMODATION: Two seats in tandem under rearward sliding transparent canopy. Rear seat of C.P.70 is wide enough to accommodate one adult and a child, or two children.

DIMENSIONS, EXTERNAL:
Wing span: C.P.70 8·25 m (27 ft 0¾ in)
C.P.750 8·04 m (26 ft 4½ in)
Wing chord at root 1·50 m (4 ft 11 in)
Wing aspect ratio: C.P.70 5·95
C.P.750 5·85
Length overall: C.P.70 6·45 m (21 ft 2 in)
C.P.750 6·90 m (22 ft 7¾ in)
Height overall: C.P.70 1·60 m (5 ft 3 in)
C.P.750 2·10 m (6 ft 10¾ in)
Wheel track: C.P.70 2·00 m (6 ft 6¾ in)
C.P.750 2·40 m (7 ft 10½ in)
Propeller diameter 1·80 m (5 ft 11 in)

AREAS:
Wings, gross: C.P.70 10·85 m^2 (116·8 sq ft)
C.P.750 11·00 m^2 (118·4 sq ft)

WEIGHTS AND LOADINGS:
Weight empty: C.P.70 320 kg (705 lb)
C.P.750 480 kg (1,058 lb)
Max T-O weight: C.P.70 540 kg (1,190 lb)
C.P.750 760 kg (1,675 lb)
Max wing loading: C.P. 70 49·8 kg/m^2 (10·2 lb/sq ft)
C.P. 750 69·1 kg/m^2 (14·15 lb/sq ft)
Max power loading: C.P.70 11·13 kg/kW (18·31 lb/hp)
C.P.750 6·79 kg/kW (11·17 lb/hp)

PERFORMANCE (at max T-O weight):
Never-exceed speed:
C.P.70 118 knots (220 km/h; 136 mph)
C.P.750 183 knots (340 km/h; 211 mph)
Max level speed:
C.P.70 95 knots (175 km/h; 109 mph)
C.P.750 151 knots (280 km/h; 174 mph)
Max cruising speed (75% power) at 1,200 m (3,940 ft):
C.P.70 84 knots (156 km/h; 97 mph)
C.P.750 143 knots (265 km/h; 165 mph)
Econ cruising speed (65% power) at 1,200 m (3,940 ft):
C.P.70 78 knots (145 km/h; 90 mph)
C.P.750 135 knots (250 km/h; 155 mph)
Approach speed, flaps down:
C.P.70 54 knots (100 km/h; 63 mph)
C.P.750 70 knots (130 km/h; 81 mph)
Stalling speed, flaps up:
C.P.70 41 knots (75 km/h; 47 mph)
C.P.750 54 knots (100 km/h; 63 mph)
Stalling speed, flaps down:
C.P.70 39 knots (70 km/h; 44 mph)
C.P.750 52 knots (95 km/h; 59 mph)
Max rate of climb at S/L:
C.P.70 120 m (394 ft)/min
C.P.750 390 m (1,280 ft)/min
Service ceiling: C.P.70 3,000 m (9,850 ft)
C.P.750 5,200 m (17,060 ft)
T-O run: C.P.70 280 m (919 ft)
C.P.750 190 m (623 ft)
T-O to 15 m (50 ft): C.P.70 420 m (1,378 ft)
C.P.750 350 m (1,148 ft)
Landing from 15 m (50 ft): C.P.70 280 m (919 ft)
C.P.750 520 m (1,706 ft)
Landing run: C.P.70 140 m (459 ft)
C.P.750 280 m (919 ft)
Range at econ cruising speed:
C.P.70 323 nm (600 km; 372 miles)
C.P.750 593 nm (1,100 km; 683 miles)

PIEL C.P.80

The C.P.80 was designed as a single-seat racing aircraft for amateur construction. The basic version is made of wood, as described; but M Calvel of l'Hospitalet du Larzac adapted the design to enable his C.P.80 Zef to be constructed of laminated plastics. This was the first C.P.80 to fly, followed in July 1974 by the C.P.80 Racer No. 01 (F-PVQF) built by M Claude Piel.

A total of at least 81 sets of plans had been sold in France by early 1986, plus those distributed by Mr Trivisonno of Canada (see introductory notes). Twelve C.P.80s are known to be flying.

TYPE: Single-seat homebuilt racing aircraft.

AIRFRAME: Cantilever low-wing monoplane. Wing section NACA 23012. Dihedral 3°. Incidence 2° (constant). No sweep at quarter-chord. Conventional single-spar wood structure, plywood covered and with polyester plastics tips. Ailerons mass balanced and cable actuated. No flaps or tabs. Conventional plywood covered wooden fuselage of basic rectangular section, with four longerons, nine frames and domed rear decking. Polyester plastics engine cowling. Steel tube engine mounting attached to fireproof bulkhead. Cantilever plywood covered all-wood tail unit, with vertical surfaces swept back at 50° on leading-edge. All-moving constant chord horizontal surfaces, with centrally positioned anti-balance and trim tab, and with mass balance arm projecting forward inside fuselage. Horn balanced rudder. Control surfaces cable operated.

LANDING GEAR: Non-retractable tailwheel type. Mainwheels carried on cantilever spring legs of treated AU4SG alloy. Steerable tailwheel carried on steel spring. Hydraulic brakes on mainwheels. At least one aircraft (F-PYFY) has been built with retractable main landing gear.

POWER PLANT: One 67 kW (90 hp) Continental C90-8F flat-four engine, driving through a short extension shaft a two-blade fixed-pitch wooden propeller. Provision for other engines, including 48·5 kW (65 hp) Continental. Fuel tank of AG-3 alloy, capacity 40 litres (8·8 Imp gallons) aft of firewall, with refuelling point in top-decking.

ACCOMMODATION: Pilot only, in enclosed cockpit, under sideways hinged transparent canopy.

DIMENSIONS, EXTERNAL:
Wing span 6·00 m (19 ft 8¼ in)
Wing chord: at aircraft centreline 1·35 m (4 ft 5¼ in)
at tip 0·90 m (2 ft 11½ in)
Wing aspect ratio 5·8
Length overall 5·30 m (17 ft 4¾ in)
Height overall 1·70 m (5 ft 7 in)
Tailplane span 1·58 m (5 ft 2¼ in)
Wheel track 1·60 m (5 ft 3 in)
Wheelbase 3·50 m (11 ft 5¾ in)
Propeller diameter 1·52 m (5 ft 0 in)

AREA:
Wings, gross 6·20 m^2 (66·7 sq ft)

WEIGHTS AND LOADINGS (67 kW; 90 hp engine):
Weight empty 260 kg (573 lb)
Max T-O weight 380 kg (837 lb)
Max wing loading 61·3 kg/m^2 (12·56 lb/sq ft)
Max power loading 5·67 kg/kW (9·30 lb/hp)

PERFORMANCE (estimated, with 67 kW; 90 hp engine, at max T-O weight):
Never-exceed speed 205 knots (380 km/h; 236 mph)
Max level speed 167 knots (310 km/h; 193 mph)
Max cruising speed (75% power) at 1,200 m (3,940 ft) 151 knots (280 km/h; 174 mph)
Econ cruising speed (65% power) at 1,200 m (3,940 ft) 130 knots (240 km/h; 149 mph)
Approach speed 70 knots (130 km/h; 81 mph)
Stalling speed 52 knots (95 km/h; 59 mph)
Max rate of climb at S/L 720 m (2,360 ft)/min
Service ceiling 6,000 m (19,685 ft)
T-O run 200 m (656 ft)
T-O to 15 m (50 ft) 400 m (1,312 ft)
Landing from 15 m (50 ft) 360 m (1,181 ft)
Landing run 200 m (656 ft)
Range at econ cruising speed 243 nm (450 km; 280 miles)
g limits +8/−6

PIEL C.P.90 PINOCCHIO

The C.P.90 Pinocchio is essentially a smaller, single-seat development of the basic Emeraude, intended for aerobatic and general sporting flying. Its design was started in 1965, and about eight sets of plans have been sold in France; they are not currently available from Mr Trivisonno of Canada.

AIRFRAME: Cantilever low-wing monoplane, of similar general planform to Emeraude. All-wood airframe, fabric covered. Wing section NACA 23012. Dihedral 5° 40′. Incidence 3°. Slotted ailerons, no flaps. Fuselage of basic rectangular cross-section, with domed decking. Cantilever tail unit, similar to that of Emeraude. Trim tab in elevator.

LANDING GEAR: Non-retractable tailwheel type. Streamline leg and wheel fairing on each main unit. Spring in compression shock absorbers. Mainwheel tyres size 380 × 150. Hydraulic brakes.

POWER PLANT: One 74·5 kW (100 hp) Continental O-200 flat-four engine, driving a two-blade wooden propeller. Single fuel tank, capacity 60 litres (13·2 Imp gallons).

ACCOMMODATION: Single seat under fully transparent rearward sliding canopy; Pinocchio II illustrated has canopy missing, prior to first flight.

AVIONICS: VHF/VOR transceiver

DIMENSIONS, EXTERNAL:
Wing span 7·20 m (23 ft 7½ in)
Wing chord: at root 1·50 m (4 ft 11 in)
at tip 0·545 m (1 ft 9½ in)
Wing aspect ratio 5·4
Length overall 6·00 m (19 ft 8¼ in)
Height overall 1·80 m (5 ft 11 in)
Tailplane span 2·60 m (4 ft 1½ in)
Wheel track 1·60 m (5 ft 3 in)
Propeller diameter 1·80 m (5 ft 11 in)

AREA:
Wings, gross 9·65 m^2 (103·9 sq ft)

WEIGHTS AND LOADINGS:
Weight empty 335 kg (738 lb)
Max T-O weight 500 kg (1,102 lb)
Max wing loading 51·8 kg/m^2 (10·61 lb/sq ft)
Max power loading 6·71 kg/kW (11·02 lb/hp)

PERFORMANCE (estimated, at max T-O weight):
Never-exceed speed 171 knots (320 km/h; 198 mph)

Piel C.P.605B Super Diamant with retractable landing gear *(Geoffrey P. Jones)*

Piel C.P.751 Beryl built by M Daniel Poulet *(Geoffrey P. Jones)*

Almost complete Piel C.P.90 Pinocchio II constructed by M Pradurous, in November 1985

Piel C.P.80 single-seat racing aircraft

Pottier P.50R Bouvreuil built in Switzerland by M Sugnaux *(Wolfgang Wagner)*

Piel C.P.150 Onyx with glassfibre fuselage built by M Jean-Claude Piel *(Geoffrey P. Jones)*

Max level speed	141 knots (260 km/h; 162 mph)
Max cruising speed (75% power) at 1,200 m (3,940 ft)	132 knots (245 km/h; 152 mph)
Econ cruising speed (65% power) at 1,200 m (3,940 ft)	124 knots (230 km/h; 143 mph)
Approach speed	59 knots (110 km/h; 68 mph)
Stalling speed	41 knots (75 km/h; 47 mph)
Max rate of climb at S/L	480 m (1,575 ft)/min
Service ceiling	6,000 m (19,685 ft)
T-O run	180 m (590 ft)
T-O to, and landing from, 15 m (50 ft)	300 m (985 ft)
Landing run	160 m (525 ft)
Range at econ cruising speed	296 nm (550 km; 341 miles)

PIEL C.P.150 ONYX

Last aircraft designed by the late M Claude Piel, the prototype C.P.150 Onyx was exhibited at the 1983 Paris Air Show, and is shown in an accompanying illustration. Plans are currently available only from Mme Piel, in France; sets have been sold to customers in France, Belgium, the Netherlands and the UK. At least 110 Onyx were under construction at that time; four had flown by December 1985 and four more were expected to fly by Spring 1986.

One of the latest examples (No. 48), built by M Piel's son Jean-Claude and shown in an accompanying illustration, has a glassfibre fuselage of more streamlined form. It flew for the first time in December 1985.

TYPE: Single-seat microlight aircraft.

AIRFRAME: Tandem wings. Rear-mounted (lower) tapered cantilever main wings with fins and rudders at tips. Ailerons fitted near tips. No dihedral. Simple structure comprising spar, box-type leading-edge and Klégécel ribs, Tergal fabric covered. Can be stowed against fuselage sides for transportation and trailering. Forward wing built in one piece and pivoted on two streamlined supports, giving variable incidence. Two forward wing control rods, and four pivot points. Elevator fitted in centre-section of forward wing. Same construction as rear wings. Can be carried longitudinally for transportation and trailering. Tapering rectangular-section wooden fuselage with three frames, plywood covered. Alternative glassfibre structure being utilised by some builders. Fin and rudder attached to tip of each rear-mounted wing, with wooden spars and Klégécel ribs, Tergal fabric covered.

LANDING GEAR: Non-retractable tricycle type. Mainwheels carried on forks constructed from AU4G, supported on cantilever legs splayed from fuselage sides. Streamline fairings over upper portion of wheels optional. Nosewheel carried on steel spring leg, with optional streamline fairing.

POWER PLANT: One 8·8 kW (12 hp) Solo engine, mounted above rear wings and driving a pusher propeller.

ACCOMMODATION: Pilot only, in open cockpit.

DIMENSIONS, EXTERNAL:

Wing span	7·30 m (23 ft 11½ in)
Length overall	3·53 m (11 ft 7 in)

AREAS:

Wings, gross: rear wing	9·10 m² (97·95 sq ft)
front wing	3·70 m² (39·83 sq ft)

WEIGHTS AND LOADINGS:

Weight empty	70 kg (154 lb)
Max T-O weight	180 kg (397 lb)
Max wing loading	14·06 kg/m² (2·88 lb/sq ft)
Max power loading	20·45 kg/kW (33·08 lb/hp)

PERFORMANCE (unpowered):

Best glide ratio	16

POTTIER

JEAN POTTIER

4 rue de Poissy, 78130 les Mureaux
Telephone: 099 13-85

In addition to the light aircraft and sailplanes that he designed jointly with M Robert Jacquet, during his period as technical director at Société CARMAM, M Pottier is responsible for the purely amateur projects of which details follow. Another of M Pottier's designs is the Kit Club 14-34, of which details can be found in the Sailplanes section of this edition.

POTTIER P.50 BOUVREUIL (BULLFINCH)

Designed by M Jean Pottier, the Bouvreuil is a single-seat racing monoplane, intended for construction by amateurs. Construction is entirely of wood, except for the plastics engine cowling and mainwheel fairings.

The Bouvreuil can be fitted with a variety of engines in the

48·5-86 kW (65-115 hp) category. It has also been designed from the start to have either a non-retractable (P.50) or retractable (P.50R) landing gear.

The first Bouvreuil to be completed was number 04, built in Switzerland by M Sugnaux of Billens, which flew for the first time on 27 July 1979 and was displayed at the 1979 RSA meeting at Brienne in France. This aircraft (HB-YBF) has a 74·5 kW (100 hp) Continental O-200 engine, slotted flaps and electrically retractable tailwheel type landing gear. It differs from plans in having extended and cambered wing-tips, and two underwing attachments for camera pods or external fuel tanks. Equipment includes VHF radio and VOR. Number 04 has a wing span of 6·48 m (21 ft 3 in), wing area of 7·5 m² (80·7 sq ft), length of 5·25 m (17 ft 2¾ in), height of 1·70 m (5 ft 7 in), empty weight of 360 kg (794 lb) and max T-O weight of 450 kg (992 lb). Its max rate of climb at S/L is 360 m (1,180 ft)/min.

The French built 02 has a 48·5 kW (65 hp) Continental engine and non-retractable landing gear. By early 1986 about four other Bouvreuils were under construction, and the latest P.50 to fly was built in Luxembourg.

TYPE: Single-seat homebuilt racing monoplane.

AIRFRAME: Cantilever low-wing monoplane. All-wood airframe. Wing section NACA 23015 at root, NACA 23012 at tip. Dihedral from roots. Full span ailerons and flaps. No tabs. Semi-monocoque fuselage, with plastics engine cowling. Cantilever tail unit, with swept vertical surfaces. Trim tab in each elevator.

LANDING GEAR: Alternative retractable or non-retractable tailwheel type. Wheel fairings standard on non-retractable mainwheels. Steerable tailwheel. Independent mainwheel brakes.

POWER PLANT: Standard power plant is a 67 kW (90 hp) Continental C90 flat-four engine, driving a two-blade fixed-pitch propeller with spinner. Other engines of 48·5 to 86 kW (65-115 hp) are optional. Fuel capacity 60 litres (13 Imp gallons) for racing, 100 litres (22 Imp gallons) for touring. Provision for carrying one removable auxiliary fuel tank under each wing.

ACCOMMODATION: Single seat in enclosed cabin, under large rearward-sliding transparent canopy.

DIMENSIONS, EXTERNAL:
- Wing span: 6·20 m (20 ft 4 in)
- Wing aspect ratio: 5·10
- Length overall: 5·65 m (18 ft 6½ in)

AREA:
- Wings, gross: 7·50 m² (80·7 sq ft)

WEIGHTS AND LOADINGS (67 kW; 90 hp engine):
- Weight empty: 270 kg (595 lb)
- Max T-O weight: 400 kg (882 lb)
- Max wing loading: 53·33 kg/m² (10·92 lb/sq ft)
- Max power loading: 5·97 kg/kW (9·80 lb/hp)

PERFORMANCE (estimated, with 67 kW; 90 hp engine and non-retractable landing gear):
- Max level speed: 167 knots (310 km/h; 192 mph)
- Max cruising speed (75% power): 151 knots (280 km/h; 174 mph)
- Stalling speed: 44 knots (80 km/h; 50 mph)
- *g* limits: ±10

POTTIER P.70S

This small sporting aircraft is derived from the P.70B, designed by M Pottier and built by M Alain Besneux (see 1976-77 *Jane's*). Design of the P.70S was started in January 1974; by 1985 about seventeen were flying, with others under construction. The first P.70S to fly, in 1977, was No. 23 (F-PYEF), powered by a 30 kW (40 hp) Volkswagen 1,500 cc engine and embodying some design changes, including a tailwheel type landing gear (illustrated in 1978-79 *Jane's*).

The following details apply to the standard P.70S:

TYPE: Single-seat homebuilt sporting aircraft.

AIRFRAME: Cantilever mid-wing monoplane. All-metal airframe of 2024 alloy. Wing section NACA 4415. No dihedral. Incidence 2°. No sweep. Constant chord wings, with I beam main spar and channel section rear spar. Entire trailing-edge of each wing formed by aileron hinged to upper surface and plain flap hinged to bottom surface. No tabs. Fuselage built up on five frames. Cantilever tail unit, with sweptback vertical surfaces. Minimal fixed fin. No tabs.

LANDING GEAR: Non-retractable tricycle type. Cantilever main legs.

POWER PLANT: One 30-44·7 kW (40-60 hp) Volkswagen converted motorcar engine, driving a two-blade fixed-pitch propeller. Single fuel tank in fuselage, aft of firewall, capacity 40 litres (8·75 Imp gallons).

ACCOMMODATION: Pilot only, in enclosed cockpit.

DIMENSIONS, EXTERNAL:
- Wing span: 5·85 m (19 ft 2¼ in)
- Wing chord, constant: 1·25 m (4 ft 1¼ in)
- Wing aspect ratio: 4·8
- Length overall: 5·15 m (16 ft 10¾ in)
- Height overall: 1·60 m (5 ft 3 in)
- Tailplane span: 2·10 m (6 ft 10¾ in)
- Wheel track: 1·20 m (3 ft 11¼ in)
- Propeller diameter: 1·30 m (4 ft 3¼ in)

AREA:
- Wings, gross: 7·20 m² (77·5 sq ft)

WEIGHTS AND LOADINGS:
- Weight empty, equipped: 215 kg (474 lb)
- Max T-O and landing weight: 325 kg (716 lb)
- Max wing loading: 45·1 kg/m² (9·24 lb/sq ft)
- Max power loading (40 hp): 10·83 kg/kW (17·90 lb/hp)

PERFORMANCE (A: standard P.70S with 30 kW; 40 hp engine, B: 44·7 kW; 60 hp engine, at max T-O weight except where indicated):
- Never-exceed speed at S/L:
  - A, B: 129 knots (240 km/h; 149 mph)
- Max level speed at S/L:
  - A: 97 knots (180 km/h; 112 mph)
  - B: 116 knots (215 km/h; 133 mph)
  - No. 23: 110 knots (205 km/h; 127 mph)
- Max cruising speed at S/L:
  - A: 89 knots (165 km/h; 103 mph)
  - B: 108 knots (200 km/h; 124 mph)
  - No. 23: 100 knots (185 km/h; 115 mph)
- Econ cruising speed at S/L:
  - A: 65 knots (120 km/h; 75 mph)
- Stalling speed, flaps down:
  - A, B: 38 knots (70 km/h; 44 mph)
- Max rate of climb at S/L: A: 150 m (490 ft)/min
  - B: 330 m (1,080 ft)/min
- Service ceiling: A: 4,500 m (14,775 ft)
- T-O run: A: 350 m (1,150 ft)
  - B: 200 m (657 ft)
- Range: A, B: 215 nm (400 km; 248 miles)
- *g* limit: A, B: +9 ultimate

POTTIER P.80S

The Pottier P.80S is a small single-seat sporting aircraft derived from the P.70S. Overall dimensions, structures, weights and performance are unchanged, but the P.80S is a low-wing monoplane and has a restyled cockpit hood. The prototype is powered by a 30 kW (40 hp) Rectimo 4 AR 1200 engine, itself a derivative of the Volkswagen motorcar engine, but engines of 30-44·7 kW (40-60 hp) can be fitted. Fuel capacity is 50 litres (11 Imp gallons).

Design of the P.80S began in January 1977 and construction of the prototype (F-PYEB) started in June 1977 at the Paris Air Show. Rollout was achieved at the Show on 12 June. By 1986 about twenty had flown, with others under construction by amateur builders.

POTTIER P.100TS and P.110TS

The P.100TS and P.110TS are small high-wing monoplanes of generally similar configuration, accommodating two and three persons respectively. The first example of the P.100TS (F-WYJC) flew for the first time on 16 October 1980. It has an NACA 4415 wing section and a 74·5 kW (100 hp) Continental engine; subsequent examples could be fitted with Avco Lycoming or Continental engines of 48·5-93 kW (65-125 hp), the P.110TS with Avco Lycoming or Continental engines of 67-112 kW (90-150 hp). Fuel capacity of each aircraft is 90 litres (19·8 Imp gallons). Plans are not available to amateur builders.

TYPE: Two-seat (P.100TS) and three-seat (P.110TS) homebuilt monoplanes.

DIMENSIONS, EXTERNAL (A: P.100TS, B: P.110TS):
- Wing span: A: 6·85 m (22 ft 5¾ in)
  - B: 7·70 m (25 ft 3 in)
- Wing chord, constant: 1·35 m (4 ft 5¼ in)
- Wing aspect ratio: A: 5·2
  - B: 5·9
- Length overall: A: 6·50 m (21 ft 4 in)
  - B: 7·00 m (23 ft 0 in)
- Height overall: A: 2·20 m (7 ft 2½ in)
  - B: 2·25 m (7 ft 4½ in)
- Wheel track: A, B: 1·70 m (5 ft 7 in)

AREAS:
- Wings, gross: A: 9·25 m² (99·56 sq ft)
  - B: 10·00 m² (107·64 sq ft)

WEIGHTS AND LOADINGS (A: P.100TS with 74·5 kW; 100 hp engine, B: P.110TS with 112 kW; 150 hp engine):
- Weight empty: A: 435 kg (959 lb)
- Max baggage: A: 33 kg (72·7 lb)
  - B: 46 kg (101·4 lb)
- Max T-O weight: A: 680 kg (1,500 lb)
  - B: 700 kg (1,543 lb)
- Max wing loading: A: 73·5 kg/m² (15·06 lb/sq ft)
  - B: 70·0 kg/m² (14·34 lb/sq ft)
- Max power loading: A: 9·13 kg/kW (15·00 lb/hp)
  - B: 6·25 kg/kW (10·29 lb/hp)

PERFORMANCE (estimated, A: P.100TS with 93 kW; 125 hp engine, B: P.110TS with 112 kW; 150 hp engine):
- Max level speed:
  - A: 135 knots (250 km/h; 155 mph)
  - B: 143 knots (265 km/h; 165 mph)
- Max cruising speed:
  - A: 127 knots (235 km/h; 146 mph)
  - B: 135 knots (250 km/h; 155 mph)
- Stalling speed: A, B: 44 knots (80 km/h; 50 mph)
- Max rate of climb at S/L: A: 372 m (1,220 ft)/min
  - B: 390 m (1,280 ft)/min
- T-O run: A, B: 230 m (755 ft)
- Range with max fuel:
  - A, B: 351 nm (650 km; 404 miles)
- Endurance, with 45 min reserves: A: 3 h 30 min
  - B: 3 h
- *g* limit: A, B: +5·7 ultimate

POTTIER P.105TS

The Pottier P.105TS is, as its designation suggests, a hybrid of the P.100TS and P.110TS. Power is provided by an Avco Lycoming or Continental engine of 48·5-104·5 kW (65-140 hp). Two P.105TS aircraft are known to be under construction; plans are not available to amateur constructors.

TYPE: Two-seat homebuilt monoplane.

DIMENSIONS, EXTERNAL:
- Wing span: 7·70 m (25 ft 3 in)
- Wing chord, constant: 1·35 m (4 ft 5¼ in)
- Wing aspect ratio: 5·9
- Length overall: 6·50 m (21 ft 4 in)
- Height overall: 2·20 m (7 ft 2½ in)
- Wheel track: 1·70 m (5 ft 7 in)

AREA:
- Wings, gross: 10·00 m² (107·64 sq ft)

WEIGHTS AND LOADINGS:
- Weight empty: 350 kg (772 lb)
- Max T-O weight: 600 kg (1,323 lb)
- Max wing loading: 60·0 kg/m² (12·29 lb/sq ft)
- Max power loading (65 hp): 12·37 kg/kW (20·35 lb/hp)

PERFORMANCE (A: 48·5 kW; 65 hp engine, B: 104·5 kW; 140 hp engine):
- Max level speed: A: 95 knots (175 km/h; 109 mph)
  - B: 135 knots (250 km/h; 155 mph)
- Max cruising speed:
  - A: 86 knots (160 km/h; 99 mph)
  - B: 129 knots (240 km/h; 149 mph)
- Stalling speed: 41 knots (75 km/h; 47 mph)
- Rate of climb at S/L: A: 144 m (472 ft)/min
  - B: 396 m (1,300 ft)/min
- T-O run: A: 320 m (1,050 ft)
  - B: 180 m (590 ft)
- Range with max fuel:
  - A, B: 351 nm (650 km; 404 miles)
- *g* limit: +5·7 ultimate

POTTIER P.170S

The P.170S is a tandem two-seat version of the P.70S. It is of all-metal (AU4G) construction and has a retractable tricycle landing gear. Power is provided by a 37·3-52 kW (50-70 hp) Volkswagen modified motorcar engine. Plans are available to amateur constructors; by 1986 at least two P.170Ss were flying, with others under construction.

TYPE: Two-seat homebuilt sporting aircraft.

DIMENSIONS, EXTERNAL:
- Wing span: 5·95 m (19 ft 6¼ in)
- Wing chord, constant: 1·25 m (4 ft 1¼ in)
- Wing aspect ratio: 4·8
- Length overall: 5·70 m (18 ft 8½ in)
- Height overall: 1·65 m (5 ft 5 in)
- Wheel track: 1·20 m (3 ft 11¼ in)

AREA:
- Wings, gross: 7·40 m² (79·65 sq ft)

WEIGHTS AND LOADINGS:
- Weight empty: 230 kg (507 lb)
- Max T-O weight: 445 kg (981 lb)
- Max wing loading: 60·1 kg/m² (12·31 lb/sq ft)
- Max power loading (50 hp): 11·93 kg/kW (19·62 lb/hp)

PERFORMANCE (A: 37·3 kW; 50 hp engine, B: 52 kW; 70 hp engine):
- Max level speed: A: 95 knots (175 km/h; 109 mph)
  - B: 108 knots (200 km/h; 124 mph)
- Max cruising speed:
  - A: 84 knots (155 km/h; 96 mph)
  - B: 102 knots (190 km/h; 118 mph)
- Stalling speed: A, B: 41 knots (75 km/h; 47 mph)
- Max rate of climb at S/L: A: 150 m (490 ft)/min
  - B: 300 m (980 ft)/min
- T-O run: A: 380 m (1,250 ft)
  - B: 220 m (722 ft)
- Landing from 15 m (50 ft): A, B: 350 m (1,150 ft)
- Range with standard 50 litres (11 Imp gallons) of fuel, 45 min reserves: A, B: 215 nm (400 km; 248 miles)
- *g* limit: A, B: +6·6 ultimate

POTTIER P.180S

The P.180S is a side by side two-seat version of the P.80S. It is of all-metal (AU4G) construction and has a non-retractable tricycle landing gear. Power is provided by a 41-67 kW (55-90 hp) Volkswagen modified motorcar engine. Plans are available to amateur constructors. By 1986 about thirteen were flying, with many more under construction by amateur builders.

TYPE: Two-seat sporting aircraft.

DIMENSIONS, EXTERNAL:
- Wing span: 6·50 m (21 ft 4 in)
- Wing chord, constant: 1·25 m (4 ft 1¼ in)
- Wing aspect ratio: 5·3
- Length overall: 5·35 m (17 ft 6½ in)
- Height overall: 1·70 m (5 ft 7 in)
- Wheel track: 1·65 m (5 ft 5 in)

AREA:
- Wings, gross: 7·80 m² (83·96 sq ft)

WEIGHTS AND LOADINGS:
- Weight empty: 240 kg (529 lb)
- Max T-O weight: 470 kg (1,036 lb)
- Max wing loading: 60·2 kg/m² (12·34 lb/sq ft)
- Max power loading (55 hp): 11·46 kg/kW (18·84 lb/hp)

PERFORMANCE (estimated, A: 41 kW; 55 hp engine, B: 67 kW; 90 hp engine):
- Max level speed: A: 97 knots (180 km/h; 112 mph)

Pottier P.70S with standard tricycle landing gear *(M. J. Hooks)*

Pottier P.80S single-seat homebuilt sporting monoplane *(Wolfgang Wagner)*

First Pottier P.100TS (74·5 kW; 100 hp Continental engine) *(Geoffrey P. Jones)*

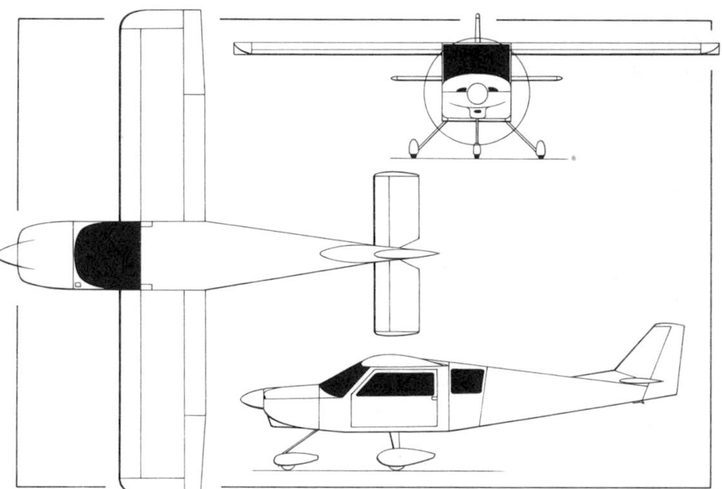

Pottier P.110TS three-seat homebuilt aircraft *(Michael A. Badrocke)*

Pottier P.170S, a tandem two-seat version of the P.70S *(Stuart MacConnacher)*

Pottier P.180S two-seat version of the P.80S *(Stuart MacConnacher)*

Proust/Sigur Lespace homebuilt helicopter, with main rotor missing *(Geoffrey P. Jones)*

Prevot two-seat microlight prototype *(Geoffrey P. Jones)*

B 124 knots (230 km/h; 143 mph)
Max cruising speed:
A 89 knots (165 km/h; 102 mph)
B 119 knots (220 km/h; 137 mph)
Stalling speed 41 knots (75 km/h; 47 mph)
Max rate of climb at S/L: A 168 m (550 ft)/min
B 330 m (1,080 ft)/min
T-O run: A 330 m (1,080 ft)
B 200 m (656 ft)
Landing from 15 m (50 ft) 350 m (1,150 ft)
Range 270 nm (500 km; 310 miles)
g limit +5·7 ultimate

PREVOT

PREVOT ULM

An ultralight seen for the first time at Brienne in July 1985 was the two-seat pod and boom high-wing monoplane built by M R. Prevot and shown in an accompanying illustration. First flown in June 1985, it has a Hirth engine, driving a pusher propeller. No further details are known.

DIMENSIONS, EXTERNAL:
Wing span 8·36 m (27 ft 5¼ in)
Length overall 6·00 m (19 ft 8¼ in)
WEIGHTS:
Weight empty 175 kg (386 lb)
Max T-O weight 325 kg (716 lb)
PERFORMANCE:
Max level speed 81 knots (150 km/h; 93 mph)
Cruising speed 54 knots (100 km/h; 62 mph)
Min flying speed 27 knots (50 km/h; 31 mph)
Max rate of climb at S/L 120 m (393 ft)/min

PROUST/SIGUR

CHRISTIAN PROUST

PROUST/SIGUR LESPACE

Little is known of this homebuilt helicopter (F-WYQC), except that it was designed and built by M Christian Proust and M Sigur and that it is powered by a 99 kW (133 hp) RotorWay RW 133 watercooled flat-four engine. As can be gleaned from the accompanying illustration, the Lespace is of conventional layout, with a single main rotor (missing in photograph), tail-mounted two-blade anti-torque rotor, small horizontal stabilising surfaces, and a ventral fin with skid.

QUAISSARD

G. QUAISSARD

4 rue Boileau, 01000 Bourg en Bresse

QUAISSARD GQ-01 MONOGAST

M G. Quaissard designed and built a small single-seat monoplane known as the Monogast. Design began in November 1979 and the one-off aircraft flew for the first time on 15 November 1984.

TYPE: Single-seat homebuilt cabin monoplane.

AIRFRAME: Strut braced high-wing monoplane of wooden construction with fabric covering; conventional in layout and control.

LANDING GEAR: Non-retractable tailwheel type, with mainwheels carried on two faired side Vs and half axles (with bungee shock absorption). Mainwheel tyre pressure 1·47 bars (21 lb/sq in). Mainwheel brakes.

POWER PLANT: One 35 kW (47 hp) Volkswagen 1,600 cc modified motorcar engine, driving a two-blade wooden propeller. Fuel tank capacity 35 litres (7·7 Imp gallons). Oil capacity 2 litres (0·44 Imp gallon).

ACCOMMODATION: Pilot only, in fully enclosed cabin with door on starboard side.

AVIONICS: VHF TR720 radio.

DIMENSIONS, EXTERNAL:
- Wing span: 7·33 m (24 ft 0½ in)
- Length overall: 5·58 m (18 ft 3¾ in)
- Propeller diameter: 1·38 m (4 ft 6½ in)

AREA:
- Wings, gross: 8·00 m² (86·1 sq ft)

WEIGHTS AND LOADINGS:
- Weight empty: 192 kg (423 lb)
- Max T-O weight: 304 kg (670 lb)
- Max wing loading: 38·0 kg/m² (7·78 lb/sq ft)
- Max power loading: 8·69 kg/kW (14·26 lb/hp)

PERFORMANCE:
- Never-exceed speed: 91 knots (170 km/h; 105 mph)
- Max level speed: 86 knots (160 km/h; 99 mph)
- Max cruising speed: 78 knots (145 km/h; 90 mph)
- Econ cruising speed: 65 knots (120 km/h; 75 mph)
- Stalling speed: 33 knots (60 km/h; 38 mph)
- Max rate of climb at S/L: 198 m (650 ft)/min
- T-O run to 15 m (50 ft): 360 m (1,180 ft)
- Landing from 15 m (50 ft): 355 m (1,165 ft)
- Range with max standard fuel: 280 nm (520 km; 323 miles)

SOYER/BARRITAULT

CLAUDE SOYER and JEAN BARRITAULT

Claude Soyer: BP 19, 49160 Longue-Jumelles
Jean Barritault: 10 rue G. Clémençeau, 49150 Baugé

SOYER/BARRITAULT SB1 ANTARÈS

The SB1 Antarès is a roomy two-seat training aircraft, designed by M Claude Soyer, and developed and built by him in partnership with M Jean Barritault over a period of eight and a half years. Stress calculations were entrusted largely to M Christian Briand, a DGAC test pilot, who also piloted the SB1 on its first test flight on 24 May 1984.

When plans eventually become available they will show an airframe of more simple design, a three-seat cabin with two side by side front seats and a rear bench, a non-retractable tricycle type landing gear, and 89·5 kW (120 hp) engine. The following description applies to the prototype (F-WSBI):

TYPE: Tandem two-seat homebuilt touring aircraft.

AIRFRAME: Cantilever low-wing monoplane of constant chord, with dihedral from roots. Wing section NACA 4417. Dihedral 4°. Incidence 2°. No twist or sweep. Wooden wings, made in one piece, with two spruce spars, ribs, stiffeners, a plywood leading-edge with alternate wood and Klégécel nose ribs, and plywood skin over the inter-spar box, covered overall with Dacron. Slotted flaps and ailerons of wood, with Dacron covering, over full span except at wingtips. Flaps actuated electrically. Ailerons fully balanced. No tabs. Large polyester fairings over wing/fuselage junctions. Conventional fuselage of four spruce longerons, firewall and two main bulkheads to carry the wings, main landing gear and rear seat, with okoumé plywood skin and overall Dacron covering. Engine cowling is split on centreline, with each half rearward hinged to provide complete access to engine. A special air intake and filter for the carburettor is attached to the starboard cowling and opens with it. Conventional cantilever tail unit, with sweptback vertical surfaces. Fixed surfaces plywood covered; control surfaces Dacron covered. Controllable trim tab in port elevator.

LANDING GEAR: Retractable tricycle type. Mainwheels retract inward into wings, under fuselage, and are fully enclosed when up. Oleo-pneumatic shock absorbers in main units. Steerable, non-retractable tailwheel carried on steel leaf spring. Brakes on mainwheels.

POWER PLANT: One 119 kW (160 hp) Avco Lycoming O-320-D2A flat-four engine, driving a two-blade metal propeller. Fuel tanks in wings, total capacity 300 litres (66 Imp gallons).

ACCOMMODATION: Two seats in tandem under large sideways-hinged (to starboard) transparent canopy. Front seat on port side of cabin; rear seat staggered to starboard side, with baggage space opposite.

AVIONICS: Com/nav radio, ADF and transponder.

DIMENSIONS, EXTERNAL:
- Wing span: 9·88 m (32 ft 5 in)
- Wing chord, constant: 1·235 m (4 ft 0¾ in)
- Wing aspect ratio: 8·0
- Length overall: 7·20 m (23 ft 7½ in)
- Height overall: 1·90 m (6 ft 3 in)
- Tailplane span: 3·30 m (10 ft 10 in)
- Wheel track: 2·16 m (7 ft 1 in)

DIMENSIONS, INTERNAL:
- Cabin: Width: 0·85 m (2 ft 9½ in)
- Max height: 0·93 m (3 ft 0½ in)

AREA:
- Wings, gross: 12·20 m² (131·3 sq ft)

WEIGHTS AND LOADINGS:
- Weight empty: 642 kg (1,415 lb)
- Fuel weight: 216 kg (476 lb)
- Max T-O weight: 1,012 kg (2,231 lb)
- Max wing loading: 82·95 kg/m² (16·99 lb/sq ft)
- Max power loading: 8·50 kg/kW (13·94 lb/hp)

PERFORMANCE:
- Never-exceed speed: 178 knots (330 km/h; 205 mph)
- Cruising speed: 135 knots (250 km/h; 155 mph)
- Range with max fuel, 45 min reserves: 1,215 nm (2,250 km; 1,398 miles)

STERN

RENÉ STERN

10 rue du Château, 57730 Folschviller

STERN ST 80 BALADE

M René Stern and M Staudt designed and built a small single-seat light aircraft known as the ST 80 Balade. Design began in 1978 and construction of the aircraft followed in 1980. The ST 80 flew for the first time on 17 July 1983. At the 1983 European Air meeting at Brienne, it was awarded a prize for the best design and construction. It has undergone testing at the official French CEV flight test centre at Istres, whose report is available.

Plans are available to amateur builders, together with kits containing major component parts.

TYPE: Single-seat homebuilt aircraft.

AIRFRAME: Cantilever low-wing monoplane. All-wood airframe with fabric covering, except for fuselage which has wooden skins. Wing section NACA 43015 at root, NACA 43012 at tip. Dihedral 6°. Incidence 5°. Wings fold upward for transportation. Ailerons. No flaps. Conventional fuselage of basic rectangular section. Cantilever tail unit, comprising angular fin and rudder, tailplane and elevators.

LANDING GEAR: Non-retractable tricycle type. Cantilever AU4G spring steel legs. Mainwheel diameter 33 cm; nosewheel diameter 26 cm. Brakes fitted.

POWER PLANT: One 45 kW (60 hp) Limbach 1,700 cc engine in prototype, driving a two-blade fixed-pitch propeller. Alternative Volkswagen modified motorcar engine in 1,600 cc to 2,000 cc range. Fuel capacity 32 litres (7 Imp gallons).

ACCOMMODATION: Single seat below sideways hinged (to starboard) transparent canopy.

AVIONICS: ER5 Jolliet radio.

DIMENSIONS, EXTERNAL:
- Wing span: 6·40 m (21 ft 0 in)
- Wing chord: at root: 1·25 m (4 ft 1¼ in)
- at tip: 0·80 m (2 ft 7½ in)
- Length overall: 4·90 m (16 ft 0¾ in)
- Propeller diameter: 1·40 m (4 ft 7 in)

AREA:
- Wings, gross: 7·0 m² (75·35 sq ft)

WEIGHTS AND LOADINGS:
- Weight empty: 230 kg (507 lb)
- Max T-O weight: 340 kg (750 lb)
- Max wing loading: 48·57 kg/m² (9·95 lb/sq ft)
- Max power loading: 7·56 kg/kW (12·50 lb/hp)

PERFORMANCE:
- Never-exceed speed: 135 knots (250 km/h; 155 mph)
- Max level speed: 97-108 knots (180-200 km/h; 112-124 mph)
- Max cruising speed: 86 knots (160 km/h; 99 mph)
- Stalling speed: 44 knots (80 km/h; 50 mph)
- Max rate of climb at S/L: 240 m (785 ft)/min

TISSERAND

CLAUDE TISSERAND

Fior di Linu, Pietranera, 20200 Bastia, Corsica
Telephone: (95) 31 67 67

M Claude Tisserand has designed and built two light amphibians of generally similar layout, except for wing arrangements and accommodation. Both the single-seat Hydroplum and the side by side two-seat Hydroplum II are said to conform with Experimental category and microlight (ULM) regulations. Plans of the Hydroplum are already available.

TISSERAND HYDROPLUM

Design of this single-seat amphibian began in 1983, when construction of the prototype also started. It made its first flight in September that year and an example was displayed at the 1985 Paris Air Show.

TYPE: Single-seat amphibian.

AIRFRAME: Strut braced high-wing monoplane, with mid-span stabilising floats. Airframe of plywood construction. Wing section NACA 2415. Dihedral 3°. Incidence 3°. Three-axis control (spoilers, elevators and rudder), with water rudder attached to heel of hull. Single step monocoque hull, with boom supporting the conventional tail unit.

LANDING GEAR: Retractable taildragger type, with 30 cm diameter mainwheels attached to side Vs and spring struts which raise above waterline when retracted. Heel of hull appears to act as tailskid. No brakes.

POWER PLANT: One 30 kW (40 hp) Hirth 440 cc two-cylinder in-line two-stroke engine, with 2·3:1 reduction gear to a two-blade wooden pusher propeller of Tisserand manufacture. Fuel tank capacity 40 litres (8·8 Imp gallons).

ACCOMMODATION: Pilot only, in open cockpit with small windscreen.

DIMENSIONS, EXTERNAL:
- Wing span: 9·25 m (30 ft 4¼ in)
- Wing chord, constant: 1·40 m (4 ft 7 in)
- Wing aspect ratio: 6·6
- Length overall: 5·90 m (19 ft 4¼ in)
- Height overall: 1·40 m (4 ft 7 in)
- Tailplane span: 2·40 m (7 ft 10½ in)
- Wheel track: 1·60 m (5 ft 3 in)
- Propeller diameter: 1·40 m (4 ft 7 in)

AREA:
- Wings, gross: 13·00 m² (139·93 sq ft)

WEIGHTS AND LOADINGS:
- Weight empty: 145 kg (319 lb)
- Pilot weight range: 60-90 kg (133-198 lb)
- Max T-O weight: 260 kg (573 lb)
- Max wing loading: 20·0 kg/m² (4·10 lb/sq ft)
- Max power loading: 8·67 kg/kW (14·33 lb/hp)

PERFORMANCE (at max T-O weight):
- Never-exceed speed: 70 knots (130 km/h; 80 mph)
- Max level speed: 59 knots (110 km/h; 68 mph)
- Max cruising speed: 49 knots (90 km/h; 56 mph)
- Econ cruising speed: 43 knots (80 km/h; 50 mph)
- Stalling speed: 30 knots (55 km/h; 34 mph)
- Max rate of climb at S/L: 300 m (985 ft)/min
- T-O run: on land: 80 m (262 ft)
- on water: 100 m (328 ft)
- Landing run: on land: 80 m (262 ft)
- on water: 50 m (164 ft)
- Range with max standard fuel: 145 nm (270 km; 167 miles)

TISSERAND HYDROPLUM II

The Hydroplum II is basically a side by side two-seat development of the Hydroplum, but in layout is best described as a sesquiplane with enclosed accommodation for the pilot and passenger. Despite having upper and lower wings, total wing area remains the same as for the Hydroplum.

Design and construction of the prototype began in 1985, and the first flight was scheduled provisionally for June 1986. No confirmation of this has been received. The Hydroplum II will be made available in kit form, requiring approximately 500 working hours to assemble.

TYPE: Side by side two-seat amphibian.

AIRFRAME: Strut braced sesquiplane, with V interplane struts in addition to upper wing bracing struts. Stabilising floats built into lower wingtips. Airframe of duralumin and glassfibre construction, probably with carbon reinforcement. Wing section NACA 2412. Dihedral 3°. Incidence 3°. Three-axis control (ailerons on upper wings, elevators and rudder). Moulded monocoque single step hull with water rudder at heel. Boom supports wire-braced conventional tail unit.

LANDING GEAR: Retractable tricycle type. Mainwheels, diameter 30 cm, with oleo-pneumatic shock absorbers,

Quaissard GQ-01 Monogast single-seat homebuilt cabin monoplane

Stern ST 80 single-seat homebuilt aircraft *(Geoffrey P. Jones)*

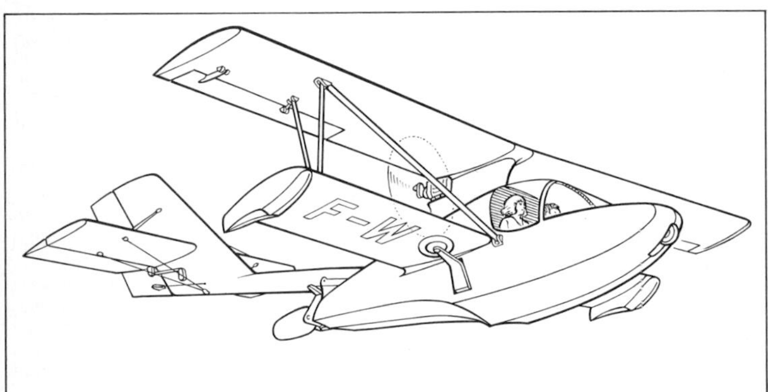
Artist's impression of the Tisserand Hydroplum II amphibian *(Jane's/Mike Keep)*

The SB1 Antarès designed and built in Baugé, France, by M Claude Soyer and M Jean Barritault

Hydroplum amphibian, designed by M Claude Tisserand

retracting into undersurface of lower wingroots; nosewheel, diameter 25 cm, retracting into nose of hull.

POWER PLANT: One 48·5 kW (65 hp) Rotax 532 two-cylinder two-stroke engine, with 2·6:1 reduction gear to a two-blade wooden pusher propeller. Fuel tank capacity 30 litres (6·6 Imp gallons).

ACCOMMODATION: Pilot and passenger side by side in enclosed cockpit, under transparent canopy. Optionally, cockpit can be semi-enclosed.

DIMENSIONS, EXTERNAL:
- Wing span: upper — 8·40 m (27 ft 6¾ in)
- Wing chord: upper, constant — 1·00 m (3 ft 3½ in)
- Wing aspect ratio — 8·4
- Length overall — 5·90 m (19 ft 4¼ in)
- Height overall — 1·90 m (6 ft 2¾ in)
- Tailplane span — 2·80 m (9 ft 2¼ in)
- Wheel track — 1·80 m (5 ft 11 in)
- Propeller diameter — 1·60 m (5 ft 3 in)

AREA:
- Wings, gross — 13·00 m² (139·93 sq ft)

WEIGHTS AND LOADINGS:
- Weight empty — 175 kg (386 lb)
- Max T-O weight — 360 kg (793 lb)
- Max wing loading — 27·7 kg/m² (5·67 lb/sq ft)
- Max power loading — 7·42 kg/kW (12·20 lb/hp)

PERFORMANCE (at max T-O weight):
- Never-exceed speed — 86 knots (160 km/h; 99 mph)
- Max level speed — 73 knots (135 km/h; 84 mph)
- Max cruising speed — 65 knots (120 km/h; 75 mph)
- Econ cruising speed — 54 knots (100 km/h; 62 mph)
- Stalling speed — 35 knots (65 km/h; 41 mph)
- Max rate of climb at S/L — 240 m (785 ft)/min
- T-O run: on land — 120 m (394 ft)
- on sea — 150 m (492 ft)
- Landing run: on land — 120 m (394 ft)
- on sea — 80 m (262 ft)

ULM PYRÉNÉES

ULM PYRÉNÉES

65200 Orignac
Telephone: (62) 95 20 83
DIRECTOR: Marcel Peres

This company produces four trike units for attachment to standard hang gliders: the single-seat **Sport**, **Super-Sport** and **Challenger**, and the two-seat, twin-engined **Royal**.

ULM PYRÉNÉES SPORT and SUPER-SPORT

The Sport is offered with two engine ratings. The standard Sport has a 10·4 kW (14 hp) Solo engine with direct drive to a two-blade wooden pusher propeller. The Super-Sport has a 14 kW (19 hp) Solo engine with direct drive. Fuel capacity for both versions is 5 litres (1·1 Imp gallons).

TYPE: Single-seat weight shift microlights with flexible wings.

AIRFRAME AND LANDING GEAR: Duralumin tube frame, single surface Dacron covered wing with stainless steel bracing. Tricycle landing gear, with 260 × 85 (Sport) or 300 × 100 (Super-Sport) wheels.

ACCOMMODATION: Pilot only, in open position.

AREA:
- Wings, gross (both) — 16·00 m² (172·2 sq ft)

WEIGHTS (A: Sport, B: Super-Sport):
- Weight empty: A — 56 kg (123 lb)
- B — 64 kg (141 lb)
- Max pilot weight: A — 85 kg (187 lb)
- B — 110 kg (242 lb)

PERFORMANCE:
- Never-exceed speed (both) — 37 knots (70 km/h; 43 mph)
- Stalling speed (both) — 21 knots (38 km/h; 24 mph)
- Max rate of climb at S/L: A — 90 m (295 ft)/min
- B — 150 m (492 ft)/min
- Min rate of sink, power off: A — 90 m (295 ft)/min
- B — 132 m (433 ft)/min

ULM PYRÉNÉES CHALLENGER

The Challenger single-seat microlight is powered by a 20 kW (27 hp) Rotax 277 engine with reduction drive to a two-blade wooden pusher propeller. Total fuel capacity is 10 litres (2·2 Imp gallons). Description is similar to that of the Sport/Super-Sport, except for an empty weight of 76 kg (168 lb), max pilot weight 120 kg (264 lb), stalling speed of 22 knots (40 km/h; 25 mph), max rate of climb at S/L of 192 m (630 ft)/min, and min rate of sink of 180 m (590 ft)/min.

ULM PYRÉNÉES ROYAL

The Royal is a two-seat weight-shift microlight, powered by two 14 kW (19 hp) Solo engines each with reduction drive to a two-blade wooden pusher propeller. It has a wing area of 21 m² (226 sq ft) and an empty weight of 92 kg (203 lb); max weight for pilot plus passenger is 210 kg (463 lb). Never-exceed speed is 43 knots (80 km/h; 50 mph), stalling speed 25 knots (45 km/h; 28 mph), max rate of climb at S/L 132 m (433 ft)/min, and min rate of sink 120 m (394 ft)/min.

VAN LITH

JEAN VAN LITH

During the past year Mr Van Lith has refurbished his Van Lith VI two/three-seat high-wing monoplane, last described and illustrated in the 1960-61 *Jane's*. His eighth aircraft, a single-seat low-wing monoplane (F-PYOV), was exhibited at the 1986 RSA rally at Brienne and is described below. Under construction is a small high-wing monoplane, the Van Lith IX.

VAN LITH VIII

TYPE: Single-seat homebuilt monoplane.

AIRFRAME: Conventional low-wing monoplane of wooden construction, covered entirely with plywood. Wings are built in three parts: a centre-section, 2·48 m (8 ft 1¾ in) wide, without dihedral, and two dihedral outer panels with large elliptical tips. Slotted trailing-edge flaps on centre-section. Ailerons over full constant-chord span of outer wings. Basically rectangular fuselage, with domed top decking, partially glazed aft of canopy. Cantilever tail unit with horn balanced rudder; trim tab in starboard elevator.

LANDING GEAR: Non-retractable type with steerable Scott tailwheel. Mainwheels size 380 × 150, with cable brakes. Tailwheel size 155 × 50.

POWER PLANT: One 41 kW (55 hp) Hirth F 20B-A1 two-cylinder inline two-stroke engine, driving a two-blade wooden propeller through a toothed belt type reduction gear, ratio 2:1. Main glassfibre fuel tank aft of firewall; second tank behind pilot's seat.

ACCOMMODATION: Pilot only, under one-piece canopy.

SYSTEM: Electrical system, with alternator, starter and 12V 20Ah battery.

DIMENSIONS, EXTERNAL:

Wing span	7·50 m (24 ft 7¼ in)
Wing chord, constant	1·25 m (4 ft 1¼ in)
Length overall	6·12 m (20 ft 1 in)
Height overall	2·20 m (7 ft 2¾ in)

AREA:

Wings, gross	9·00 m² (96·875 sq ft)

WEIGHTS AND LOADINGS:

Weight empty	210 kg (463 lb)
Max T-O weight	350 kg (772 lb)
Max wing loading	38·9 kg/m² (7·96 lb/sq ft)
Max power loading	8·54 kg/kW (14·04 lb/hp)

PERFORMANCE:

Design cruising speed	75 knots (140 km/h; 87 mph)

ZENITH-AVIATION

ZENITH-AVIATION

19 rue Lavoisier, 92002 Nanterre Cédex
Telephone: (1) 47 25 90 22
Telex: 610166 F
CHAIRMAN AND GENERAL MANAGER:
Stanislas Durand
TECHNICAL MANAGER: Jacques Courant
WORKS: Boulevard Sagnat, BP 3, 42230 Roche-la-Molière
Telephone: (77) 90 06 11
Telex: 330139 F
WORKS MANAGER: Roger Granjon

Zenith-Aviation is a subsidiary of the Matra group company Solex, and has a workforce of some 250 people. In September 1983 it acquired from Aéronautic 2000 (see 1984-85 *Jane's*) a full licence to build, market and support the latter's Baroudeur microlight aircraft at its 2,000 m² (21,528 sq ft) factory in Roche-la-Molière.

ZENITH-AVIATION (AÉRONAUTIC 2000) BAROUDEUR

The Baroudeur first flew in September 1981 and was subsequently developed in both single- and two-seat versions, of which only the two-seater remains current. The prototype two-seat Baroudeur flew for the first time in 1982. A military version was shown publicly at the Paris Air Show in June 1983, as an anti-tank aircraft capable of carrying two or four rocket launchers mounted on outriggers located above the mainwheels. The first four aircraft were delivered to the French Army in November 1983, to airborne units at Toulouse, Bayonne and Nancy for evaluation and tactical trials as military microlights, given the Barboudeur's capability to be folded and parachuted into a combat zone or carried by a light vehicle.

Following Zenith-Aviation's involvement with the Baroudeur, the aircraft's capabilities were expanded and the 1986 series includes versions for recreational, training, agricultural and military purposes. Flight testing of the Farming Baroudeur began on 10 May 1984, with trials showing the aircraft to be easy to handle, even at low speed, while carrying a 38 nozzle sprayboom and a 100 litre (22 Imp gallon) chemical tank for a 12 m (39 ft) swath width. On 29 June 1984 trials began of a Baroudeur fitted with multi-track and thermographic cameras, for remote detection tests at the INRA agricultural research institute at Crignon.

On the initiative of Zenith-Aviation, Aéronautic 2000 and the manufacturer of rocket launchers, Luchaire, rocket firing trials with the military Baroudeur began in December 1984 at the Centre d'Essais en Vol (CEV) flight test centre at Cazaux. Fitted with two 89 mm rocket launchers under each wing (each fitted with inert or smoke bomb warheads), a safety stand to prevent ground firing, an electronic-spot bombsight, trigger joystick, a selection and safety box enabling a single rocket or two symmetrical rockets to be fired, and special anti-induction safety relays, the first launches were made at altitudes of 10 m (33 ft) and 300 m (985 ft) against a target 800 m (2,625 ft) distant. On 13 February 1985 a second series of launches took place, from an altitude of 300 m (985 ft) at a target 800 m (2,625 ft) away. The first rocket impacted 10 metres (33 ft) from the target but the second and third scored direct hits from the two-seat Baroudeur, despite a wind speed of 15 knots at sea level and 45 knots at 500 m altitude.

In June 1984, Air Chief Marshal Disbach Sing of the Indian Air Force evaluated the two-seat Baroudeur at Persan-Beaumont, with a view to using it for training at military bases in India. In the same month, Indian Major-General Narendra Sing began separate trials to assess the Baroudeur's suitability for sport flying purposes at Indian flying clubs.

The following details apply to the current two-seat version of the Baroudeur, in recreational and training form, unless stated otherwise. Zenith had completed 150 factory built Baroudeurs by February 1986; a kit version was due to become available in 1985, but no confirmation of this has been received.

TYPE: Two-seat microlight aircraft.

AIRFRAME: High-wing monoplane, with constant chord wings and conventional tail surfaces. Duralumin main frame. Wing section TK7315. Thickness/chord ratio 12°. Dihedral 2°. Incidence 4°. Double surface fabric covered wings and control surfaces. Stainless steel cables. Kingpost fitted. Three-axis control (ailerons, elevators and rudder). Options include dashboard with turn-and-bank indicator, airspeed indicator, variometer, revolution counter, radio, recovery parachute and agricultural spraygear.

LANDING GEAR: Non-retractable tricycle type, with all-terrain capability. Tyre pressure (all) 1·5 bars (22 lb/sq in). Optional mainwheel brakes. Shock absorbers. Optional floats, skis and wheel fairings.

POWER PLANT: One 38 kW (51 hp) Rotax 462 two-cylinder two-stroke or 37·3 kW (50 hp) Fuji Robin two-stroke engine, driving a two-blade wooden propeller via reduction gearing. Standard fuel tank capacity 20 litres (4·4 Imp gallons); 40 litre (8·8 Imp gallon) tank optional.

ACCOMMODATION: Two seats side by side in open cockpit. Dual controls. Optional polyester and canvas cockpit fairings and wraparound windscreen, or new streamline fully-transparent semi-enclosed fairing.

ARMAMENT: Four or six launchers for 89 mm rockets can be carried underwing on military version.

DIMENSIONS, EXTERNAL:

Wing span	10·90 m (35 ft 9¼ in)
Wing chord: at root	1·50 m (4 ft 11 in)
at tip	1·40 m (4 ft 7 in)
Wing aspect ratio	7·5
Length overall	5·60 m (18 ft 4½ in)
Height overall	2·40 m (7 ft 10½ in)
Tailplane span	2·50 m (8 ft 2½ in)
Wheel track	1·50 m (4 ft 11 in)
Wheelbase	1·68 m (5 ft 6¼ in)
Propeller diameter	1·60 m (5 ft 3 in)

AREA:

Wings, gross	17·00 m² (182·99 sq ft)

WEIGHTS AND LOADINGS:

Weight empty	175 kg (385 lb)
Max T-O weight	385 kg (849 lb)
Max wing loading	22·35 kg/m² (4·58 lb/sq ft)
Max power loading (51 hp)	10·00 kg/kW (16·43 lb/hp)

PERFORMANCE (at max T-O weight):

Never-exceed speed	59 knots (110 km/h; 68 mph)
Max level speed at S/L	54 knots (100 km/h; 62 mph)
Max cruising speed	48 knots (90 km/h; 56 mph)
Econ cruising speed	38 knots (70 km/h; 43 mph)
Stalling speed	25 knots (45 km/h; 28 mph)
Max rate of climb at S/L	180 m (590 ft)/min
Service ceiling	3,000 m (9,840 ft)
T-O run	50 m (164 ft)
T-O to 15 m (50 ft)	400 m (1,312 ft)
Landing from 15 m (50 ft)	200 m (656 ft)
Landing run	40 m (132 ft)
Range: standard fuel	54 nm (100 km; 62 miles)
40 litre tank	151 nm (280 km; 174 miles)
Endurance: standard fuel	2 h
40 litre tank	3 h
Best glide ratio	8
Min rate of sink	108 m (354 ft)/min

GERMANY
(FEDERAL REPUBLIC)

AFG

ALLGÄUER UL-FLUGZEUGBAU GmbH

Schillerstrasse 35, 8942 Ottobeuren

AFG KOLIBRI

The general appearance of this single-seat mid-wing monoplane microlight can be seen in an accompanying illustration. The structure is of GfK sandwich, with a pod and boom fuselage, constant chord wings, V tail surfaces, three-axis control (ailerons and ruddervators), non-retractable nosewheel and sprung mainwheel, with brake, and small underwing balancer wheels. The König or Hirth power plant is pylon mounted behind the open cockpit and drives a three-blade pusher propeller. The double-surface wings have a Wortmann FX-63-137 section. Fuel capacity is 20 litres (4·4 Imp gallons). No other details are known, apart from the brief dimensional and performance data that follow.

DIMENSIONS, EXTERNAL:

Wing span	10·40 m (34 ft 1½ in)
Length overall	5·50 m (18 ft 0½ in)

PERFORMANCE:

Cruising speed	48 knots (90 km/h; 56 mph)
Climbing speed	29 knots (55 km/h; 34 mph)

AKAFLIEG MÜNCHEN

FLUGTECHNISCHE FORSCHUNGSGRUPPE an der TECHNISCHEN UNIVERSITÄT MÜNCHEN

Arcisstrasse 21, Postfach 202420, 8000 München 2
Telephone: 089 28 61 11
DIRECTOR: Andre Schülke
DESIGN MANAGER: Peter Hirt

AKAFLIEG MÜNCHEN Mü 30 SCHLACRO

Akaflieg München is the flying academy which produced the Mü 28 aerobatic sailplane, described in the Sailplanes section of the 1985-86 *Jane's*. Its latest design is the Mü 30, a tandem two-seat aerobatic monoplane suitable also for glider towing, hence its name Schlacro (schlepp = towing, acro = aerobatic).

Intended to be an affordable compromise between the varied demands of the two applications (although low-speed flying capability suits both the requirements of glider towing and the necessity for tight loops during aerobatics), the design phase has been concluded and construction of a prototype started in Spring 1985.

The one-piece symmetrical wing is constructed of CfK, GfK and aramid composites, and is fitted with flaps that can be extended 0° to 60° according to whether minimum speed, a steep approach or other considerations are paramount. The conventional tubular steel fuselage (GfK, aramid and aluminium covered) and the composites tail unit were, however, designed to optimise aerobatics. Power is provided by a 156 kW (210 hp) Porsche PFM 3200 engine, driving a Hoffmann HO-V-123 three-blade propeller with large spinner. A non-retractable tailwheel landing gear is fitted, with cantilever spring mainwheel legs and mainwheel fairings. Fuel capacity is 148 litres (32·5 Imp gallons), in two integral wing tanks.

TYPE: Two-seat aerobatic and glider-towing monoplane.

DIMENSIONS, EXTERNAL:

Wing span	8·70 m (28 ft 6½ in)
Wing aspect ratio	6·41
Length overall (flying attitude)	7·30 m (23 ft 11½ in)
Height overall	2·20 m (7 ft 2½ in)
Tailplane span	3·30 m (10 ft 10 in)
Propeller diameter	2·00 m (6 ft 6¾ in)

AREA:

Wings, gross	11·80 m² (127·0 sq ft)

Van Lith VIII single-seat homebuilt monoplane *(J. M. G. Gradidge)*

Zenith Baroudeur carrying two underwing rocket launchers during military trials

Model of the Akaflieg München Mü 30 Schlacro aerobatic and glider towing aircraft

Zenith Baroudeur with new fully transparent streamline cockpit fairing *(Geoffrey P. Jones)*

AFG Kolibri single-seat microlight monoplane

Albatros AN-22 Twin side by side two-seat microlight aircraft designed by the late Albert Neukom *(Geoffrey P. Jones)*

Weights and Loadings (estimated):

Weight empty	565 kg (1,245 lb)
T-O weight for glider towing	700 kg (1,543 lb)
Max T-O weight	850 kg (1,874 lb)
Max wing loading	72·0 kg/m² (14·7 lb/sq ft)
Max power loading	5·45 kg/kW (8·92 lb/hp)

Performance (estimated, at max T-O weight except where indicated):

Max level speed	162 knots (300 km/h; 186 mph)
Cruising speed, 75% power	146 knots (270 km/h; 168 mph)
Max rate of climb at S/L	540 m (1,770 ft)/min
Rate of climb at S/L, at T-O weight of 700 kg (1,543 lb):	
with 15 metre Class sailplane	420 m (1,378 ft)/min
with 2-seat aerobatic sailplane	300 m (984 ft)/min
T-O to 15 m (50 ft)	270 m (886 ft)
Landing from 15 m (50 ft)	310 m (1,017 ft)
g limits	±8

ALBATROS

ALBATROS ULTRA FLIGHT GmbH

Eysseneckstrasse 19, 6000 Frankfurt am Main 1

Telephone: (069) 72 0451

Telex: 41 89465

The late Albert Neukom (see entry in Switzerland subsection) designed the AN-22 for production in Germany, where Point Aviation was given exclusive manufacturing and marketing rights. The first of two prototypes made its first flight in March 1983. In May 1983 Mr Neukom also completed the prototype of a two-seater version, the **AN-22 Twin**.

More recently, the AN-22 has been taken over by Albatros Ultra Flight GmbH and some modifications have been made to the airframe. The most significant change has been to the wing, which is now considerably smaller in span but with a greater chord. It is not known whether the AN-22 is available at present for purchase. This applies also to the former Howatherm Milan, which has been taken over by Albatros and was last described and illustrated in the 1985-86 *Jane's*.

ALBATROS AN-22

Type: Single-seat microlight aircraft.

Airframe: Conventional high-wing monoplane. Aluminium tube fuselage frame; cockpit pod optional. Double surface wing, strut braced. Three-axis control (rudder, elevator and ailerons).

Landing Gear: Tricycle type, with rubber suspension on mainwheels. Nosewheel steering. Mainwheel diameter 30 cm; nosewheel 26 cm. Mainwheel brakes.

Power Plant: One 16·4 kW (22 hp) König SC430 three-cylinder engine, with 1·3:1 V belt reduction drive to two-blade pusher propeller mounted coaxially with tail support boom. Propeller blades fold for power-off flight. Fuel capacity 20 litres (4·4 Imp gallons).

Accommodation: Pilot only in open position.

Dimensions, external:

Wing span	9·00 m (29 ft 6½ in)
Wing chord: at root	1·48 m (4 ft 10¼ in)
at tip	1·38 m (4 ft 6½ in)
Wing aspect ratio	8·5
Length overall	5·70 m (18 ft 8½ in)
Height overall	1·30 m (4 ft 3 in)

Area:

Wings, gross	13·5 m² (145·3 sq ft)

Weights and Loadings:

Weight empty	130 kg (287 lb)
Max T-O weight	239 kg (527 lb)
Max wing loading	17·7 kg/m² (3·63 lb/sq ft)
Max power loading	14·57 kg/kW (23·95 lb/hp)

Performance:

Never-exceed speed	59 knots (110 km/h; 68 mph)
Max level speed	49 knots (90 km/h; 56 mph)
Max cruising speed	38 knots (70 km/h; 43 mph)
Stalling speed	25 knots (45 km/h; 28 mph)
Max rate of climb at S/L	120 m (395 ft)/min
T-O distance	80 m (262 ft)
Landing distance	45 m (148 ft)
Range at cruising speed	118 nm (220 km; 136 miles)
g limits	+6/−3 ultimate
Min rate of sink	84 m (275 ft)/min

BINDER

BINDER AVIATIK GmbH

Flugplatz Donaueschingen-Villingen, 7710 Donaueschingen
Telephone: 0771 3078/9
Telex: 7 92 889 AVIAT D
MANAGER: Heinz Westphal

BINDER BA83 MISTRAL II

The Mistral was designed and developed for Binder Aviatik GmbH by Ikarusflug Bodensee; the first of three prototypes flew on 30 September 1983. It is being manufactured in co-operation between the two companies and production began in 1985.

TYPE: Single-seat microlight aircraft, conforming to West German national standards.

AIRFRAME: Conventional high-wing monoplane. Main frame of aluminium alloy tubing. Double surfaced wings, with aluminium alloy front and rear spars and glassfibre reinforced leading-edges, Dacron covered. Dihedral 2°. Double surfaced tail unit. Vinyl coated stainless steel cable bracing; kingpost standard. Three-axis control (rudder, elevator and full span ailerons).

LANDING GEAR: Tricycle type, with nosewheel steering and braking. Bungee suspension. Wheel sizes: main 300 × 100 mm; nose 260 × 85 mm.

POWER PLANT: One 21 kW (28 hp) König SD 570 four-cylinder radial engine, with 1·75:1 or 1·5:1 belt reduction to a two-blade wooden pusher propeller. Electric starting. Fuel capacity 20 litres (4·4 Imp gallons).

ACCOMMODATION: Pilot only in open position.

DIMENSIONS, EXTERNAL:
- Wing span: 9·40 m (30 ft 10 in)
- Wing aspect ratio: 6·35
- Length overall: 5·88 m (19 ft 3½ in)
- Height overall: 2·60 m (8 ft 6¼ in)
- Propeller diameter: 1·30 m (4 ft 3 in)

AREA:
- Wings, gross: 13·90 m² (149·6 sq ft)

WEIGHTS AND LOADINGS:
- Weight empty: 114 kg (251 lb)
- Pilot weight range: 70-117 kg (154-258 lb)
- Max T-O weight: 231 kg (509 lb)
- Max wing loading: 16·6 kg/m² (3·40 lb/sq ft)
- Max power loading: 11·06 kg/kW (18·18 lb/hp)

PERFORMANCE:
- Never-exceed speed: 59 knots (110 km/h; 68 mph)
- Max level and max cruising speed: 46 knots (85 km/h; 53 mph)
- Econ cruising speed: 32 knots (60 km/h; 37 mph)
- Stalling speed:
  - power on: 24·5 knots (45 km/h; 28 mph)
  - power off: 25 knots (46 km/h; 29 mph)
- Max rate of climb at S/L: 90 m (295 ft)/min
- T-O run: 70 m (230 ft)
- Landing run: 50 m (164 ft)
- Range with max fuel: 102 nm (190 km; 118 miles)
- Endurance with max fuel: 2 h 12 min
- *g* limits: +6/−3
- Best glide ratio: 9
- Min rate of sink, power off: 96 m (315 ft)/min

BOROWSKI

LTB-BOROWSKI

Ob der Au 12 (Flugplatz Winzeln-Schramberg), 7239 Fluom-Winzeln 1
Telephone: 07402 1674; (Works) 07422 53644
DIRECTOR: Falk Borowski

BOROWSKI AN-20K PICCOLO

The Piccolo is a modified and slightly larger version of the Neukom AN-20B (see Swiss part of this section), a prototype of which underwent certification trials to JAR 22 in 1985. It was hoped to begin series production by the end of that year, but no recent news has been received. The production version has a larger area wing.

TYPE: Single-seat microlight motor glider.

AIRFRAME AND LANDING GEAR: Generally as described for Neukom AN-20B.

POWER PLANT: One 18·6 kW (25 hp) KFM 107ER two-cylinder two-stroke engine, with 2·1:1 reduction drive to a three-blade pusher propeller. Electric starting and in-flight restarting. Fuel capacity 22 litres (4·8 Imp gallons).

DIMENSIONS, EXTERNAL (A: prototype, B: production version):
- Wing span: A: 12·60 m (41 ft 4 in)
  - B: 13·30 m (43 ft 7½ in)
- Wing aspect ratio: A: 15·72
  - B: 16·62
- Length overall: A, B: 6·30 m (20 ft 8 in)

AREAS:
- Wings, gross: A: 10·10 m² (108·7 sq ft)
  - B: 10·64 m² (114·5 sq ft)

WEIGHTS AND LOADINGS:
- Weight empty: A: 160 kg (353 lb)
  - B: 165 kg (364 lb)
- Max T-O weight: A: 260 kg (573 lb)
  - B: 285 kg (628 lb)
- Max wing loading: A: 25·74 kg/m² (5·27 lb/sq ft)
  - B: 26·78 kg/m² (5·48 lb/sq ft)

PERFORMANCE (A at max T-O weight; estimates for B are identical):
- Never-exceed speed: 91 knots (170 km/h; 105 mph)
- Max cruising speed: 67 knots (125 km/h; 78 mph)
- Econ cruising speed: 59 knots (110 km/h; 68 mph)
- Stalling speed: 30 knots (54 km/h; 34 mph)
- Max rate of climb at S/L: 120 m (394 ft)/min
- Best glide ratio: 20
- Min rate of sink: 57 m (187 ft)/min

DJURIC

VLADIMIR DJURIC

Königstrasse 92, 7031 Ehningen
Telephone: 07034 4971

Herr Djuric has built a two-seat light helicopter, known as the Lala 1. Design began in 1977 and construction of the prototype started in 1980. It first flew in 1984, after it had been exhibited at an OUV meeting in Germany. As of January 1986 the Lala 1 had not been certificated under Experimental regulations.

DJURIC LALA 1

TYPE: Two-seat homebuilt helicopter.

ROTOR SYSTEM AND DRIVE: Two-blade rigid main rotor of duralumin and Styrodur construction, and two-blade tail rotor. Steel drive shafts.

AIRFRAME: Welded steel tube mainframe, with metal skins around cockpit and engine bay, and open truss structure aft.

LANDING GEAR: Non-retractable tricycle type. All three wheels size 4 × 8. Tyre pressure 1·5 bars (22 lb/sq in). Sprung mainwheel legs. No brakes.

POWER PLANT: One 85·75 kW (115 hp) NSU Wankel Ro 80 428 cc converted motorcar engine. Fuel tank capacity 40 litres (8·75 Imp gallons). Oil capacity 3 litres (0·66 Imp gallon).

ACCOMMODATION: Pilot and passenger side by side in a fully enclosed cabin, with a fully glazed and forward hinged door on each side.

SYSTEM: 12V electrical system with generator and 35Ah battery.

DIMENSIONS, EXTERNAL:
- Main rotor diameter: 7·60 m (24 ft 11¼ in)
- Length overall: 8·60 m (28 ft 2½ in)
- Height overall: 2·80 m (9 ft 2¼ in)
- Wheel track: 1·72 m (5 ft 7¾ in)
- Wheelbase: 1·60 m (5 ft 3 in)

WEIGHTS:
- Weight empty: 375 kg (827 lb)
- Max T-O weight: 500 kg (1,102 lb)

PERFORMANCE (estimated):
- Never-exceed speed: 102 knots (190 km/h; 118 mph)
- Range: 242 nm (450 km; 279 miles)

FIREBIRD

FIREBIRD SCHWEIGER & JEHLE

Hitzleriederstrasse 15 (Postfach 38), 8959 Seeg/Allgäu
Telephone: 08364 412 1078
Telex: 541412
MANAGER: Eberhardt Jehle

Firebird Leichtflugzeugbau GmbH ceased trading in September 1984. Firebird Schweiger & Jehle is now producing a range of Firebird microlight aircraft from the same address. The following aircraft were in production in 1984, when the last report was received from the company.

FIREBIRD M1

First flown in 1978, the Firebird M1 has a manually deployed parachute recovery system, by means of which the aircraft and pilot can be lowered safely to the ground in an emergency. A two-seat training version is designated **T1**.

TYPE: Single-seat microlight aircraft.

AIRFRAME: Sweptwing monoplane configuration, with two-axis control by wingtip rudders, frontal elevator and weight shift. Two moulded carbonfibre struts on each side brace the wings to an aluminium tube pyramid structure underneath them which serves also as mount for the engine, pilot's sling seat, and landing gear. Wing has an FM-4-81 section and is covered with Dacron, held in place by ten aluminium battens on each side. Entire airframe can be dismantled for transportation and storage.

LANDING GEAR: Tricycle type, with all wheels of similar size.

POWER PLANT: One 14·8 kW (19·9 hp) 210 cc Solo 335 two-stroke, 19·4 kW (26 hp) three-cylinder König or 23 kW (31 hp) four-cylinder König engine, with reduction drive to a two-blade (optionally three-blade) pusher propeller. Fuel tank capacity 10 litres (2·2 Imp gallons).

ACCOMMODATION: Pilot only in open position.

DIMENSIONS, EXTERNAL:
- Wing span: 10·00 m (32 ft 9¾ in)
- Wing aspect ratio: 6·7
- Length overall: 6·66 m (21 ft 10¼ in)
- Wheel track: 1·50 m (4 ft 11 in)
- Propeller diameter:
  - two-blade (König): 1·07 m (3 ft 6 in)
  - two-blade (Solo): 1·37 m (4 ft 6 in)
  - three-blade (König): 1·20 m (3 ft 11¼ in)

AREA:
- Wings, gross: 15·00 m² (161·5 sq ft)

WEIGHTS AND LOADINGS:
- Weight empty: 98 kg (216 lb)
- Max T-O weight: 190 kg (419 lb)
- Max wing loading: 12·66 kg/m² (2·59 lb/sq ft)
- Max power loading: 10·55 kg/kW (17·3 lb/hp)

PERFORMANCE:
- Never-exceed speed: 43 knots (80 km/h; 50 mph)
- Cruising speed: 32 knots (60 km/h; 37 mph)
- Stalling speed: 19 knots (35 km/h; 22 mph)
- Rate of climb at S/L at 165 kg (363 lb) AUW: 120 m (394 ft)/min
- T-O and landing run: 30 m (99 ft)
- Range with max fuel: 81 nm (150 km; 93 miles)
- Endurance with max fuel: 2 h
- *g* limits: +4/−2
- Min rate of sink, power off: 108 m (354 ft)/min

FIREBIRD TRICX

The TriCX is Firebird's latest known microlight design; it is illustrated in an accompanying photograph.

TYPE: Single-seat microlight aircraft; three-axis control system.

POWER PLANT: One 15 kW (20 hp) Solo UL 2335 engine, driving a three-blade pusher propeller. Fuel tank capacity 20 litres (4·4 Imp gallons).

DIMENSIONS, EXTERNAL:
- Wing span: 11·15 m (36 ft 7 in)
- Wing aspect ratio: 7·31

AREA:
- Wings, gross: 17·00 m² (183·0 sq ft)

WEIGHTS AND LOADINGS:
- Weight empty: 82 kg (181 lb)
- Max T-O weight: 170 kg (375 lb)
- Max wing loading: 10·0 kg/m² (2·05 lb/sq ft)
- Max power loading: 11·33 kg/kW (18·6 lb/hp)

PERFORMANCE:
- Never-exceed speed: 43 knots (80 km/h; 50 mph)
- Cruising speed: 35 knots (65 km/h; 40 mph)
- Stalling speed: 19 knots (35 km/h; 22 mph)
- Max rate of climb at S/L: 120 m (394 ft)/min
- T-O and landing run: 30 m (99 ft)
- Endurance with max fuel: 2 h
- *g* limits: +6/−3

HFL

HFL-FLUGZEUGBAU GmbH

In der Marsch 3, 2120 Lüneburg
Telephone: (04131) 3 64 88
TECHNICAL MANAGER: Dipl Ing Konrad Herz

HFL STRATOS

The 1984-85 *Jane's* included a novel microlight known as the HFL-UL, on which the constant chord monoplane wings had detachable outer panels, which could be mounted alternatively at the base of the chassis to convert the aircraft into a biplane. One prototype was built. This aircraft had strut braced wings and a conventional tail unit.

In 1985 the first flight took place of the 'production' model of the HFL-UL, known as the Stratos. This differs from the prototype mainly in having cantilever wings and a new twin-boom tail unit with twin rudders and an elevator. The illustration in the 1985-86 *Jane's* showed the Stratos as a biplane. The description applies to this Stratos, which conforms to West German national microlight standards and is available in ready assembled form.

For the more enthusiastic microlight pilot, HFL now also offers a non-convertible monoplane version of the Stratos, with a smaller fuselage that can be totally enclosed by fabric. This version offers cleaner aerodynamics and a best glide ratio of 23.

Binder BA83 Mistral II with cockpit fairing

Prototype of the Borowski AN-20K Piccolo *(Peter F. Selinger)*

Djuric Lala 1 two-seat homebuilt helicopter *(Wolfgang Wagner)*

Firebird M1 sweptwing microlight aircraft *(J. M. G. Gradidge)*

HFL Stratos convertible monoplane/biplane, in monoplane configuration

Firebird TriCX *(Wolfgang Wagner)*

TYPE: Single-seat microlight monoplane/biplane.

AIRFRAME: Cantilever high-wing monoplane or biplane. Aluminium alloy tubing fuselage frame; carbon-Kevlar tubes supporting tail surfaces. Carbonfibre/GfK wing structure, of Wortmann FX-63-137 aerofoil section. Polyester fabric covering. Stainless steel cables. Windscreen standard. Three-axis control (twin rudders, adjoining elevator, and ailerons). Rigging time 20 min.

LANDING GEAR: Non-retractable tricycle type, with steerable nosewheel incorporating brake. Nosewheel size 200 × 80. Bungee suspension.

POWER PLANT: One 21 kW (28 hp) König SD 570 four-cylinder two-stroke engine, with reduction drive to two-blade adjustable-pitch wooden propeller. Fuel tank capacity 20 litres (4·4 Imp gallons).

ACCOMMODATION: Pilot only in open cockpit.

DIMENSIONS, EXTERNAL (A: monoplane, B: biplane):

Wing span: A	13·60 m (44 ft 7½ in)
B	7·40 m (24 ft 3¼ in)
Wing aspect ratio: A	12·3
Length overall: A, B	6·40 m (21 ft 0 in)
Height overall: A, B	2·20 m (7 ft 2½ in)
Propeller diameter: A, B	1·50 m (4 ft 11 in)

AREAS:

Wings, gross: A	15·00 m² (161·5 sq ft)
B	16·00 m² (172·2 sq ft)

WEIGHTS AND LOADINGS:

Weight empty: A, B	150 kg (331 lb)
Pilot weight range	60-100 kg (132-220 lb)
Max T-O weight: A, B	265 kg (584 lb)
Max wing loading: A, B	17·7 kg/m² (3·63 lb/sq ft)
Max power loading: A, B	12·62 kg/kW (20·86 lb/hp)

PERFORMANCE (estimated for both versions except where indicated):

Never-exceed speed	70 knots (130 km/h; 80 mph)
Max level speed	49 knots (90 km/h; 56 mph)
Max cruising speed	43 knots (80 km/h; 50 mph)
Econ cruising speed	38 knots (70 km/h; 43 mph)
Stalling speed:	
power on	22 knots (40 km/h; 25 mph)
power off	25 knots (45 km/h; 28 mph)
Max rate of climb at S/L	150 m (490 ft)/min
Service ceiling	3,000 m (9,850 ft)
T-O run	100 m (328 ft)
Landing run	50 m (164 ft)
Range with max fuel	135 nm (250 km; 155 miles)
Endurance with max fuel	3 h
g limits	+6/−4
Best glide ratio (monoplane)	20

HOFFMANN

WOLF HOFFMANN FLUGZEUGBAU KG

Sportflugplatz, 8870 Günzburg
Telephone: 0 82 21/14 17
Telex: 531 625 HOFBG D
WORKS: Hoffmann Aircraft GmbH, PO Box 100, A-1214 Vienna, Austria
Telephone: 0222 253 691
Telex: 112 820 HAC

Hoffmann has had international success with its H-36 Dimona motor glider, of which 170 had been delivered by February 1986. This aircraft, and the H-38 Observer which is not yet in production, are described in the Sailplanes section of this edition.

Only three examples of the H-39 Diana microlight had been produced by February 1986, when production was to special order only. The original König engine has been superseded by a 20 kW (27 hp) Rotax 277 single-cylinder engine driving a three-blade pusher propeller, though the following data refer to the König engined model.

HOFFMANN H-39 DIANA

The Diana, shown in an accompanying photograph, is a three-axis microlight of advanced aerodynamic design and is constructed primarily of carbonfibre and Kevlar epoxy. It has high-mounted wings of Wortmann FX-63-137 aerofoil section, braced by a V strut each side. No other bracing. It is thought unlikely that the two-seat variant of Diana is available, as mentioned in the 1985-86 *Jane's*.

TYPE: Single-seat microlight aircraft.

LANDING GEAR: Non-retractable tricycle type, with steerable nosewheel incorporating brake.

POWER PLANT: One 21 kW (28 hp) König SD570 four-cylinder radial engine, with direct drive to two-blade pusher propeller. Electric start. Fuel capacity 20 litres (4·4 Imp gallons).

ACCOMMODATION: Pilot only in open cockpit. Plexiglas canopy available as option.

DIMENSIONS, EXTERNAL:
- Wing span: 10·00 m (32 ft 9¾ in)
- Wing aspect ratio: 8·0
- Length overall: 5·60 m (18 ft 4½ in)
- Height overall: 5·60 m (18 ft 4½ in)
- Propeller diameter: 1·07 m (3 ft 6 in)

AREA:
- Wings, gross: 12·50 m² (134·5 sq ft)

WEIGHTS AND LOADINGS:
- Weight empty: 120 kg (265 lb)
- Max T-O weight: 240 kg (530 lb)
- Max wing loading: 19·2 kg/m² (3·93 lb/sq ft)
- Max power loading: 11·43 kg/kW (18·9 lb/hp)

PERFORMANCE:
- Never-exceed speed: 73 knots (135 km/h; 84 mph)
- Cruising speed: 54 knots (100 km/h; 62 mph)
- Stalling speed: 22 knots (40 km/h; 25 mph)
- Service ceiling: 4,400 m (14,435 ft)
- T-O run: 20 m (66 ft)
- Landing run: 30 m (99 ft)
- Range with max fuel: 162 nm (300 km; 186 miles)
- Endurance with max fuel: 3 h
- *g* limits: +6/−3 ultimate

HOWATHERM

HOWATHERM GmbH & Co KG

Postfach 301146, 6589 Brücken
Telephone: 06782 861
Telex: 426248

HOWATHERM MILAN

The Howatherm Milan first flew in March 1983 and was introduced publicly at the Aero 83 Salon at Friedrichshafen. Two prototypes are known to have flown. More recently, the Milan has been taken over by Joachim Krenz of Albatros Ultra Flight GmbH (which see), but no information has been received regarding production. A detailed description of the Milan appeared in the 1985-86 *Jane's*, together with an illustration.

IKARUS

IKARUS DEUTSCHLAND COMCO GmbH

Tannenweg 20, 7031 Aidlingen
Telephone: 07034 4081

IKARUS-COMCO SHERPA I

The Sherpa I was designed by Hans Gigax (see Switzerland subsection) and made its first flight in May 1982. Production of the aircraft has been licensed to Ikarus-Comco in West Germany. Orders for several hundred Sherpa Is have been received.

TYPE: Single-seat microlight aircraft.

AIRFRAME: Aluminium tube framework. Wings double surface covered and cable braced. Kingpost standard. Cruciform tail surfaces. Three-axis controls (rudder, elevator and ailerons).

LANDING GEAR: Tricycle type, with steerable nosewheel. Brake optional.

POWER PLANT: One 16·4 kW (22 hp) Hirth 263R engine, with 1·8:1 reduction drive to a two-blade tractor propeller. Fuel capacity 26 litres (5·7 Imp gallons).

ACCOMMODATION: Pilot only in open position.

DIMENSIONS, EXTERNAL:
- Wing span: 10·50 m (34 ft 5½ in)
- Wing aspect ratio: 7
- Length overall: 4·95 m (16 ft 3 in)
- Height overall: 2·82 m (9 ft 3 in)
- Propeller diameter: 1·40 m (4 ft 7 in)

AREA:
- Wings, gross: 15·70 m² (169 sq ft)

WEIGHTS AND LOADINGS:
- Weight empty: 100 kg (220 lb)
- Max T-O weight: 215 kg (474 lb)
- Max wing loading: 13·69 kg/m² (2·80 lb/sq ft)
- Max power loading: 13·11 kg/kW (21·5 lb/hp)

PERFORMANCE:
- Never-exceed speed: 59 knots (110 km/h; 68 mph)
- Max level speed: 48 knots (90 km/h; 56 mph)
- Max cruising speed: 43 knots (80 km/h; 50 mph)
- Stalling speed: 22 knots (40 km/h; 25 mph)
- Max rate of climb at S/L: 91 m (300 ft)/min
- T-O run: 60 m (197 ft)
- Landing run: 40 m (131 ft)
- Range with max fuel: 81 nm (150 km; 93 miles)
- *g* limits: +6/−3 ultimate
- Best glide ratio: 7
- Min rate of sink, power off: 122 m (400 ft)/min

IKARUS-COMCO SHERPA II

The Sherpa II is a more powerful two-seat version of the Sherpa I, which entered production in the Summer of 1983. Description as for Sherpa I except as follows:

POWER PLANT: One 31·3 kW (42 hp) Hirth 276R engine with 1·8:1 reduction drive to a two-blade, 1·60 m (5 ft 3 in) diameter tractor propeller.

WEIGHTS AND LOADINGS:
- Weight empty: 115 kg (253 lb)
- Max T-O weight: 300 kg (661 lb)
- Max wing loading: 19·1 kg/m² (3·91 lb/sq ft)
- Max power loading: 9·58 kg/kW (15·75 lb/hp)

PERFORMANCE:
- Max level speed: 43 knots (80 km/h; 50 mph)
- Max cruising speed: 38 knots (70 km/h; 43 mph)
- Stalling speed: 23 knots (42 km/h; 26 mph)
- Max rate of climb at S/L: 122 m (400 ft)/min
- T-O run: 45 m (148 ft)
- Landing run: 35 m (115 ft)

IKARUS-COMCO FOX-D

This Swiss Gigax-designed microlight is a single-seater, which first flew in December 1982. It has an aluminium alloy frame with partially enclosed cockpit pod. Cable bracing with kingpost standard. Three-axis control (rudder, elevators and ailerons). Tricycle landing gear; wheel diameter 30 cm.

POWER PLANT: One 16·4 kW (22 hp) Hirth 383 cc engine with belt reduction drive (1·5:1) to a two-blade wooden tractor propeller. Fuel capacity 13 litres (2·8 Imp gallons). Provision for auxiliary tank.

DIMENSIONS, EXTERNAL:
- Wing span: 10·00 m (32 ft 9¾ in)
- Wing aspect ratio: 7·58
- Length overall: 4·75 m (15 ft 7 in)
- Height overall: 2·65 m (8 ft 8¼ in)
- Propeller diameter: 1·40 m (4 ft 7 in)

AREA:
- Wings, gross: 13·20 m² (142·0 sq ft)

WEIGHTS AND LOADINGS:
- Weight empty: 100 kg (221 lb)
- Max T-O weight: 215 kg (474 lb)
- Max wing loading: 16·29 kg/m² (3·34 lb/sq ft)
- Max power loading: 13·11 kg/kW (21·55 lb/hp)

PERFORMANCE:
- Never-exceed speed: 56 knots (105 km/h; 65 mph)
- Max cruising speed: 40 knots (75 km/h; 47 mph)
- Stalling speed: 23 knots (42 km/h; 26 mph)
- Max rate of climb at S/L: 120 m (395 ft)/min
- T-O and landing run on grass: 30-40 m (98-131 ft)
- Range with max fuel: approx 108 nm (200 km; 124 miles)
- Best glide ratio: 8
- *g* limits: +6/−3 ultimate

MBB

MESSERSCHMITT-BÖLKOW-BLOHM GmbH

Postfach 801109, Ottobrunn bei München, 8000 München 80
Telephone: (089) 60 00 0
Telex: ZENTRALE 5 287-0 MBB D

MBB FK6

The FK6 was built as a private project by workers at MBB's Speyer factory under the guidance of Herr Otto Funk, who also acted as test pilot when the aircraft (D-MBBI) made its first flight in early 1985.

TYPE: Single-seat microlight aircraft.

AIRFRAME: High-wing monoplane, braced by single strut on each side. Wings have a Wortmann FX-62-K-153 section, a light alloy spar, light alloy ribs at root and tip, the remaining ribs of Conticell, and are covered with light alloy skin (forward) and fabric (rear). Ailerons and plain flaps have a light alloy box spar, ribs and fabric covering. Forward fuselage consists of a GfK shell over a steel tube frame, and is attached to an aluminium alloy tailboom which supports the 'butterfly' tail unit. Fixed tail surfaces and 'ruddervators' have light alloy frames, with metal and fabric covering respectively. Ailerons and flaps are interconnected.

LANDING GEAR: Non-retractable tailwheel type, with mainwheels on cantilever glassfibre spring legs, and small tailwheel steerable with rudder.

POWER PLANT: One 16·2 kW (22 hp) Göbler-Hirth 263-A-03E engine, driving a two-blade pusher propeller. Electric starting.

ACCOMMODATION: Pilot only, in open cockpit with windscreen.

AVIONICS: Dittel FSG 50 VHF radio.

DIMENSIONS, EXTERNAL:
- Wing span: 11·00 m (36 ft 1 in)
- Wing aspect ratio: 9·45
- Length overall: 5·41 m (17 ft 9 in)
- Wheel track: 1·42 m (4 ft 8 in)

AREA:
- Wings, gross: 12·8 m² (137·8 sq ft)

WEIGHTS AND LOADINGS:
- Weight empty: 150 kg (331 lb)
- Max T-O weight: 250 kg (551 lb)
- Max wing loading: 19·5 kg/m² (3·99 lb/sq ft)
- Max power loading: 15·43 kg/kW (25·39 lb/hp)

PERFORMANCE:
- Max level speed: 81 knots (150 km/h; 93 mph)
- Cruising speed: 65 knots (120 km/h; 75 mph)
- T-O and landing run: 70 m (230 ft)
- Range at cruising speed, with 25 litres (5·5 Imp gallons) of fuel: 404 nm (750 km; 466 miles)

REUTER

DIPL-ING ADOLF K. REUTER

Am Grassenberg 6, 3550 Marburg/Lahn
Telephone: 06421 65209

REUTER ARCO

Dipl-Ing Adolf K. Reuter designed and built the prototype of a single-seat strut-braced monoplane microlight known as the ARCO. Basic structure is of metal tubing, with Styrodur plastics ribs of NACA 4412 section in the rigid wing. Three-axis control (ailerons, elevator and rudder) is fitted; the non-retractable tricycle landing gear is supplemented by a small tailwheel. The fully enclosed cockpit has a canopy which hinges upward and back for access. Power plant is a 17 kW (23 hp) König three-cylinder engine, driving a pusher propeller, with two fuel tanks in the wing centre-section.

DIMENSIONS, EXTERNAL:
- Wing span: 10·00 m (32 ft 9¾ in)
- Wing chord, constant: 1·505 m (4 ft 11¼ in)
- Length overall: 6·00 m (19 ft 8¼ in)
- Height overall: 2·61 m (8 ft 6¾ in)
- Elevator span: 2·50 m (8 ft 2½ in)
- Wheelbase: 2·15 m (7 ft 0¾ in)

AREA:
- Wings, gross: 15·20 m² (163·6 sq ft)

WEIGHTS AND LOADINGS:
- Weight empty: 149 kg (329 lb)
- Max T-O weight: 300 kg (661 lb)
- Max wing loading: 19·74 kg/m² (4·04 lb/sq ft)
- Max power loading: 17·65 kg/kW (28·74 lb/hp)

PERFORMANCE:
- Max level speed: 65 knots (120 km/h; 75 mph)
- Max cruising speed (75% power): 48 knots (90 km/h; 56 mph)
- Stalling speed: 24 knots (45 km/h; 28 mph)
- Max rate of climb at S/L: 120 m (393 ft)/min
- T-O and landing run: 50 m (164 ft)
- Range with max fuel: 172 nm (320 km; 198 miles)
- Best glide ratio: 12

Hoffmann H-39 Diana

Ikarus-Comco Fox-D single-seat microlight *(Wolfgang Wagner)*

Ikarus-Comco Sherpa I

MBB FK6 single-seat microlight aircraft

Reuter ARCO single-seat microlight monoplane

Temple-Wing TE-F3A

TEMPLE

PROF DIPL-ING BERNHARD E. R. J. DE TEMPLE
Am Pfingstborn 23, 6501 Heidesheim/Rhein
Telephone: 06 132 58566

TEMPLE-WING TE-F3A

Development of the TE-F3A powered hang glider resulted from encouraging tests with the unpowered TE-F1 (1980-81 *Jane's*) and TE-F2 (1981-82 edition), and the powered TE-F3 prototype (1984-85 edition).

The TE-F3A is unusual in being powered by four small engines, intended to exploit the principles of 'motor-mass' control. Flight control is achieved solely via the inverted V tail unit, since the addition of wing ailerons is said to produce overcontrol, with resulting difficulties in flight.

The TE-F3 prototype flew for the first time on 3 November 1982 but was damaged during tests in September 1983. Flight trials resumed on 24 September and were followed by the first flight of the TE-F3A on 7 September 1984. Plans to build the TE-F3A, plus prefabricated engine kits, are available, and several sets have been sold. The following data apply to the TE-F3A:

TYPE: Single-seat four-engined microlight.

AIRFRAME: Wire braced high-wing monoplane, with main frame constructed of aluminium alloy and duralumin. Kingpost fitted. Stainless steel cables. Wings consist of pre-stressed sheets of foam plastics, secured by three thin strips on each sheet. Tail surfaces of GfK reinforced foam plastics, with GfK reinforced Styrodur rudders. Two-axis control via tail surfaces, with similar flight characteristics to a three-axis system.

LANDING GEAR: Tailwheel type.

POWER PLANT: Four 4 kW (5·4 hp) engines, each with direct drive to a two-blade wooden pusher propeller.

ACCOMMODATION: Pilot only in open position.

DIMENSIONS, EXTERNAL:

Wing span	10·30 m (33 ft 9½ in)
Wing chord, constant	1·50 m (4 ft 11 in)
Length overall	4·70 m (15 ft 5 in)
Height overall	3·08 m (10 ft 1¼ in)

AREA:

Wings, gross	15·45 m² (166·3 sq ft)

WEIGHTS:

Weight empty	110 kg (243 lb)
Pilot weight range	75-90 kg (166-198 lb)

PERFORMANCE:

Max level speed	38 knots (70 km/h; 43 mph)
T-O speed	19 knots (35 km/h; 22 mph)

No other data available at present

THALHOFER

LUDWIG THALHOFER
Allmandstrasse 12, 7440 Nürtingen 7
Telephone: 07022 54090

THALHOFER BRONCO

The Bronco is a three-axis control aircraft with a Wortmann FX-63-137 wing section and 2° dihedral; construction is of aluminium alloy, GfK and plastics. Options include a cockpit fairing, a further fairing to reach the wing, and wheel fairings. Production began in mid-1983. More than 100 are thought to have been built. A two-seat version remains under development, with tandem accommodation.

TYPE: Single-seat microlight aircraft.

POWER PLANT: One 20 kW (27 hp) König SC430 three-cylinder radial engine, with 1·8:1 reduction belt to a three-blade pusher propeller. Electric starting. Fuel tank capacity 20 litres (4·4 Imp gallons). Fuel load 14 kg (31 lb).

DIMENSIONS, EXTERNAL:

Wing span	10·10 m (33 ft 1¾ in)
Wing chord, constant	1·20 m (3 ft 11¼ in)
Wing aspect ratio	8·5
Length overall	5·70 m (18 ft 8½ in)
Height overall	2·20 m (7 ft 2½ in)
Wheel track	1·60 m (5 ft 3 in)

Propeller diameter 1·32 m (4 ft 4 in)
AREA:
Wings, gross 12·00 m² (129·2 sq ft)
WEIGHTS AND LOADINGS:
Weight empty 115 kg (253·5 lb)
Max T-O weight 245 kg (540 lb)
Max wing loading 20·42 kg/m² (4·18 lb/sq ft)
Max power loading 12·25 kg/kW (20·00 lb/hp)
PERFORMANCE:
Never-exceed speed 59 knots (110 km/h; 68 mph)
Max level speed 54 knots (100 km/h; 62 mph)
Max cruising speed 49 knots (90 km/h; 56 mph)
Econ cruising speed 40 knots (75 km/h; 47 mph)
Stalling speed 24 knots (43 km/h; 27 mph)
Max rate of climb at S/L 120 m (394 ft)/min
T-O run (on grass) 70 m (230 ft)
T-O to 15 m (50 ft) 170 m (558 ft)
Range with max fuel 70 nm (130 km; 81 miles)
Endurance with max fuel 2 h 30 min
Best glide ratio 12
g limits ±6

THEWA-TECHNICS — *see Marko-Elektronik (Poland)*

ULTRALEICHT

ULTRALEICHT-FLUGGERÄTEBAU GmbH

Twist 9, 4455 Wietmarschen
Telephone: 059 36 64 80
Telex: 98617
DIRECTOR: Helmut Wilden

ULTRALEICHT WILDENTE

TYPE: Single-seat microlight.

AIRFRAME: Conventional high-wing monoplane, with rigid strut braced wings and tail surfaces carried on boom from wing trailing-edge. Wings have light alloy basic structure, with metal covered leading-edge, some structure of PVC hard foam and glassfibre. Full span ailerons. Steel tube fuselage structure, with fabric covering on tailboom. Three-axis control (ailerons, elevators, rudder).

LANDING GEAR: Non-retractable tricycle type, with optional wheel-skis. Mainwheels carried on cantilever glassfibre legs. Steerable nosewheel, with brake. Mainwheel tyre size 260 × 85 mm; pressure 2·2 bars (31 lb/sq in).

POWER PLANT: One 21 kW (28 hp) Göbler-Hirth F 263 two-cylinder two-stroke engine, driving a two-blade pusher propeller. Fuel capacity 20 litres (4·4 Imp gallons).

ACCOMMODATION: Pilot only, in open cockpit.

DIMENSIONS, EXTERNAL:
Wing span 10·50 m (34 ft 5½ in)
Wing chord, constant 1·50 m (4 ft 11 in)
Wing aspect ratio 7·16
Length overall 5·90 m (19 ft 4¼ in)
Height overall 2·75 m (9 ft 0¼ in)
Wheel track 1·55 m (5 ft 1 in)
Propeller diameter 1·35 m (4 ft 5¼ in)
AREA:
Wings, gross 15·4 m² (165·75 sq ft)
WEIGHTS:
Weight empty 115 kg (253 lb)
Max T-O weight 220 kg (485 lb)
PERFORMANCE:
Max level speed 54 knots (100 km/h; 62 mph)
Cruising speed 35 knots (65 km/h; 40 mph)
Stalling speed at max T-O weight 25 knots (45 km/h; 28 mph)
Max rate of climb at S/L at max T-O weight 108 m (354 ft)/min
T-O run 50-70 m (164-230 ft)
Landing run 40-50 m (131-164 ft)
Min rate of sink 96 m (315 ft)/min
Range 140 nm (260 km; 162 miles)
g limits +6/−3 ultimate

ULTRALEICHT WILDENTE 2

This tandem two-seat version of the Wildente has an open steel tube tailboom extending from the bottom of its fuselage structure, and a 28 kW (38 hp) Göbler-Hirth F27 02R engine mounted at the trailing-edge of the wing centre-section. In other respects it is generally similar to the single-seater.

DIMENSIONS, EXTERNAL:
Wing span 11·00 m (36 ft 1 in)
Length overall 7·10 m (23 ft 3½ in)
Height overall 2·50 m (8 ft 2½ in)
AREA:
Wings, gross 16 50 m² (177·6 sq ft)
WEIGHTS:
Weight empty 150 kg (331 lb)
Max T-O weight 350 kg (772 lb)
PERFORMANCE:
Never-exceed speed 54 knots (100 km/h; 62 mph)
Min flying speed 32 knots (60 km/h; 37 mph)
Stalling speed 30 knots (55 km/h; 35 mph)
Max rate of climb at S/L 102 m (335 ft)/min
T-O run 90-100 m (295-328 ft)
Landing run 90 m (295 ft)
Min rate of sink 98 m (320 ft)/min
g limits +4/−2

VOGT

HELMUT VOGT

Mörikestrasse 20, 7982 Baienfurt
Telephone: 0751 46840

VOGT LO-120

The LO-120 is a tandem two-seat dual-control microlight trainer that is covered by the homebuilt Experimental category when larger engines are fitted. Design began in March 1983 and construction of the prototype started in the following June. This flew for the first time on 10 May 1984. Kits of the major component parts are available to amateur builders, and by February 1986 three sets had been delivered. Each kit includes the prefabricated wings, fuselage, landing gear and engine.

TYPE: Tandem two-seat microlight trainer and homebuilt aircraft.

AIRFRAME: Cantilever high-wing monoplane. Single surface wood and glassfibre composite wings of constant chord. Wing section Göttingen G-625. Thickness/chord ratio 20%. No incidence or sweepback. Three-axis control (ailerons, spoilers, and elevators carried on inverted V tail surfaces). Wooden fuselage of very narrow cross-section. Twin booms to carry tail unit attached to wings.

LANDING GEAR: Non-retractable tricycle type, with 300 × 85 mm mainwheels carried on side Vs and half axles with spring suspension. Nosewheel size 265 × 85 mm, with brake.

POWER PLANT: One 27 kW (36 hp) Rotax 337 two-cylinder two-stroke engine standard, with reduction gear to a Mühlbauer two-blade wooden pusher propeller. Two fuel tanks, with total capacity of 32 litres (7 Imp gallons). One refuelling point in each wing. Optional engines are 21 kW (28 hp) Hirth or 16·4 kW (22 hp) Lloyd LS 400.

ACCOMMODATION: Pilot and passenger in tandem in open positions. Dual controls. Optional canopy.

SYSTEM: Battery for engine starting and radio.

AVIONICS: Dittel FSG 60 radio.

DIMENSIONS, EXTERNAL:
Wing span 12·00 m (39 ft 4½ in)
Wing chord, constant 1·50 m (4 ft 11 in)
Wing aspect ratio 8
Length overall 7·00 m (22 ft 11½ in)
Height overall 1·75 m (5 ft 9 in)
Tailplane span 2·00 m (6 ft 6¾ in)
Wheel track 1·50 m (4 ft 11 in)
Wheelbase 1·80 m (5 ft 11 in)
Propeller diameter 1·60 m (5 ft 3 in)
AREA:
Wings, gross 18·00 m² (193·75 sq ft)
WEIGHTS AND LOADINGS:
Weight empty 150 kg (331 lb)
Pilot weight range 60-130 kg (132-286 lb)
Max T-O weight 340 kg (749 lb)
Max wing loading 18·89 kg/m² (3·87 lb/sq ft)
Max power loading 12·59 kg/kW (20·81 lb/hp)
PERFORMANCE (at max T-O weight):
Never-exceed speed 70 knots (130 km/h; 80 mph)
Max cruising speed 49 knots (90 km/h; 56 mph)
Econ cruising speed 38 knots (70 km/h; 43 mph)
Stalling speed 26 knots (48 km/h; 30 mph)
Max rate of climb at S/L 150 m (492 ft)/min
Service ceiling 4,000 m (13,125 ft)
T-O run 60 m (197 ft)
T-O to 15 m (50 ft) 250 m (820 ft)
Landing from 15 m (50 ft) 300 m (984 ft)
Landing run 150 m (492 ft)
Range with max standard fuel 215 nm (400 km; 248 miles)
Range with max payload 188 nm (350 km; 217 miles)

WELLER

ROMAN WELLER

WELLER UW-7

An accompanying illustration shows the UW-7, designed by Herr Roman Weller. It is a single-seat microlight similar in appearance to the pre-First World War Santos-Dumont Demoiselle. It appears to have wire braced, double surface high-mounted wings, a metal tube main frame and conventional tail surfaces. Control is probably three-axis, via ailerons, rudder and triangular elevators. The power plant is of unknown type (two-cylinder) and drives a two-blade wooden propeller. Fuel is carried in a bullet tank above the open wing centre structure. A taildragger landing gear is fitted, comprising two large spoked and sprung mainwheels and a skid attached to the bottom of the tail fin. Accommodation for the pilot is open, with a wicker seat to complete the antique look. No other details are available.

INDONESIA

WIWEKO

WIWEKO SOEPONO

Akasamitra Homebuilt Aircraft Club, PO Box 164, Jakarta 10002

While serving as head of the Indonesian Air Force Design and Construction Branch in 1948, Mr Wiweko Soepono designed and built the WEL-1 (Wiweko Experimental Lightplane). Powered by a 15 kW (20 hp) Harley Davidson motorcycle engine, it had the distinction of being the first powered aircraft designed and built in the Republic of Indonesia. After making its first flight and being displayed in an aviation exhibition, the original WEL-1 was destroyed by a grenade explosion while being transported by rail.

To meet requests from both the Air Force and Armed Forces museums, an exact replica of the WEL-1 was built, under the direction and guidance of Mr Wiweko, by Akasamitra, a homebuilt aircraft club. Another version, with a Revmaster engine, made its first flight on 13 August 1981, and a similar aircraft is displayed at the Armed Forces Museum in Jakarta.

WIWEKO WEL-1

Data on the WEL-1 with a Revmaster engine are as follows:

TYPE: Single-seat homebuilt aircraft.

AIRFRAME: Strut braced parasol monoplane. Wing section NACA 2415. Dihedral 2°. Incidence 3° 48′. Wooden two-spar structure, built in two halves, attached to fuselage by tubular centre-section pylons and braced by parallel lift struts of streamline section steel tubing. Wings and ailerons are fabric covered. No flaps. Welded steel tube fuselage structure, fabric covered. Curved decking aft of cockpit, aluminium covered. Wire braced welded steel tube tail unit structure, fabric covered.

LANDING GEAR: Non-retractable tailwheel type, with divided main legs of tubular steel construction and rubber block shock absorption. Mainwheel tyres size 5·00-5. Fully castoring tailwheel. Cleveland Model 30-9 brakes.

POWER PLANT: One 52 kW (70 hp) Revmaster 2100 D converted Volkswagen motorcar engine, driving a two-blade fixed-pitch wooden propeller. Aluminium fuel tank in fuselage, aft of firewall, capacity 40 litres (8·8 Imp gallons). Refuelling point on upper surface of fuselage, forward of windscreen. Oil capacity 4 litres (0·8 Imp gallons).

ACCOMMODATION: Single seat in open cockpit.

DIMENSIONS, EXTERNAL:
Wing span 9·00 m (29 ft 6 in)
Wing chord, constant 1·45 m (4 ft 9 in)
Length overall 5·05 m (16 ft 7 in)
Height overall 2·40 m (7 ft 10 in)
AREA:
Wings, gross 13·65 m² (146·9 sq ft)
WEIGHTS AND LOADINGS:
Weight empty 300 kg (660 lb)
T-O weight 430 kg (946 lb)
Max wing loading 31·5 kg/m² (6·45 lb/sq ft)
Max power loading 8·27 kg/kW (13·51 lb/hp)
PERFORMANCE:
Max level speed 57 knots (105 km/h; 65 mph)
Cruising speed 55 knots (101 km/h; 63 mph)
Stalling speed 33 knots (61 km/h; 38 mph)
Service ceiling 3,660 m (12,000 ft)

Prototype of the Thalhofer Bronco with cockpit fairings *(Wolfgang Wagner)*

UW-7 microlight, designed by Herr Roman Weller *(Wolfgang Wagner)*

Latest version of the Wiweko WEL-1 with Revmaster engine

Murphy Sprite 2+2 homebuilt light aircraft *(Paul R. Duffy)*

Ultraleicht Wildente single-seat microlight with wheel-skis *(Wolfgang Wagner)*

Two-seat Ultraleicht Wildente 2 microlight *(Wolfgang Wagner)*

Vogt LO-120 tandem two-seat microlight trainer and homebuilt aircraft

IRELAND

MURPHY

A. MURPHY

Weston

MURPHY SPRITE

The Murphy Sprite (EI-BOY) is a 2+2 homebuilt light aircraft which had its origins in the Practavia Sprite, last described in the main UK Aircraft section of the 1981-82 *Jane's*, but embodies considerable redesign. First flown on 18 December 1985, it is shown in an accompanying illustration.

The power plant is a 104 kW (139 hp) Rolls-Royce Continental O-240-E flat-four, driving a two-blade fixed-pitch propeller. Fuel capacity is 191 litres (42 Imp gallons). Available details follow:

WEIGHTS:

Weight empty	486 kg (1,072 lb)
Max T-O weight	748 kg (1,650 lb)

PERFORMANCE:

Max level speed	146 knots (270 km/h; 168 mph)
Stalling speed	51 knots (95 km/h; 59 mph)
Range with max fuel	935 nm (1,730 km; 1,075 miles)

ITALY

ALPAIR

ALPAIR

10059 Susa, Turin
Telephone: (0122) 50177
GENERAL MANAGER: Giuseppe Forno

ALPAIR EXCEL

The Excel is a single-seat powered trike unit that can be attached to a range of hang gliders. Designed by Sig Bianchi, the Excel was put into production in 1984 and fifteen had been sold by mid-1985. A two-seat version, with a Rotax 503 engine, is said to be under development.

TYPE: Single-seat microlight powered trike unit with hang glider wing.

AIRFRAME: Mainframe of Avionol light alloy tubing. Dacron covered flexwing, with weight-shift control. Fuel tank/fin above engine.

LANDING GEAR: Tricycle type with steerable nosewheel. Cantilever mainwheel legs; speed fairings on all wheels.

POWER PLANT: One 30·6 kW (41 hp) Rotax 447 two-cylinder two-stroke engine driving a two-blade pusher propeller. Fuel in fin tank.

ACCOMMODATION: Pilot only in open position.

DIMENSIONS, EXTERNAL:

Length overall	1·70 m (5 ft 7 in)
Height overall	2·30 m (7 ft 6½ in)

WEIGHTS:

Weight empty	115 kg (253 lb)
Max T-O weight	225 kg (496 lb)

PERFORMANCE:

Max level speed	48 knots (89 km/h; 55 mph)
Cruising speed	43 knots (80 km/h; 50 mph)
Stalling speed	17 knots (30 km/h; 19 mph)
Max rate of climb at S/L	270 m (885 ft)/min
T-O and landing run	35 m (115 ft)
Endurance	2 h 30 min
Best glide ratio	8
g limits	+6/−3

AUI

AVIAZIONE ULTRALEGGERA ITALIANA

Via Sempione 9, 28040 Marano Ticino (NO)
Telephone: (0321) 97565/6
Telex: 616332 RIERO I
PRESIDENT: Gabriele Concato
ENGINEERING: Emilio Garatti
MARKETING: Claudio Garatti
PRESS OFFICE: Via Vetulonia 43-12, Rome
Telephone: (06) 7553625

AUI was formed to design and manufacture the first all-Italian ultralight production aircraft, the T7 Leone, which flew for the first time on 15 August 1984. About 100 examples were under construction in 1986, mainly for export. Some reports have suggested the possible construction of the Leone under licence in South Africa by Microlight Flight Systems, but these had not been substantiated at the time of going to press.

AUI T7 LEONE

TYPE: Single-seat microlight monoplane.

AIRFRAME: Wire braced constant chord high-wing monoplane, with kingpost structure. Wings have tubular aluminium alloy spars and Dacron covering. Full span ailerons on wing trailing-edge. Welded chrome molybdenum steel tube fuselage structure, with one-piece light alloy tubular tailboom. Tail unit has wire braced aluminium alloy tube structure, Dacron covered.

LANDING GEAR: Non-retractable tailwheel type, with mainwheel brakes.

POWER PLANT: One 22·4 kW (30 hp) KFM 107ER aircooled flat-twin two-stroke engine, driving a fixed-pitch pusher propeller.

ACCOMMODATION: Pilot only, in open cockpit.

DIMENSIONS, EXTERNAL:

Wing span	9·40 m (30 ft 10 in)
Length overall	6·40 m (21 ft 0 in)
Height overall	2·80 m (9 ft 2¼ in)

AREA:

Wings, gross	13·50 m² (145·3 sq ft)

WEIGHTS AND LOADINGS:

Weight empty	115 kg (254 lb)
Max T-O weight	230 kg (507 lb)
Max wing loading	17·04 kg/m² (3·49 lb/sq ft)
Max power loading	10·27 kg/kW (16·90 lb/hp)

PERFORMANCE:

Max level speed	65 knots (120 km/h; 74 mph)
Cruising speed	51 knots (95 km/h; 59 mph)
Stalling speed	24 knots (43 km/h; 27 mph)
Max rate of climb at S/L	180 m (590 ft)/min
Service ceiling	3,050 m (10,000 ft)
T-O and landing run	35 m (115 ft)
Endurance with max fuel	4 h

CUP

CENTRO ULTRALEGGERI PARTENOPEO

via S. Maria del Pianto 42, Naples
Telephone: (081) 759 00 45
DIRECTOR: Fabrizio Pisani

CUP was formed in 1984, to design and build a three-axis single-seat microlight aircraft known as the F3. The prototype flew for the first time on 25 April 1986.

CUP F3

TYPE: Single-seat microlight aircraft.

AIRFRAME: Cantilever mid-wing monoplane of all-metal construction, except for Dacron covering on wings and tail surfaces. Constant chord wings, built in three sections, with foldable outer panels. Wing section NACA 2415. Two 2024 light alloy wing main spars, and aluminium alloy covered leading-edge. Semi-monocoque fuselage with flat skins, except for fairing aft of cockpit and glassfibre nose fairing. Cantilever tail unit, with sweptback vertical surfaces and one-piece horizontal surface with trim tab. Long dorsal fin. Three-axis control (spoilers, elevator and rudder).

LANDING GEAR: Non-retractable tricycle type, with steerable nosewheel, and mainwheel brakes.

POWER PLANT: One 18·6 kW (25 hp) KFM 107ER two-cylinder two-stroke aircooled engine, mounted above fuselage and driving a two-blade fixed-pitch wooden pusher propeller. Fuel capacity 19 litres (4·2 Imp gallons). Engine has electric starter and can be restarted in flight.

ACCOMMODATION: Pilot only, in open cockpit, with windscreen.

DIMENSIONS, EXTERNAL:

Wing span	9·68 m (31 ft 9 in)
Wing aspect ratio	6·9
Length overall	4·98 m (16 ft 4 in)
Height overall	2·05 m (6 ft 8¾ in)

AREA:

Wings, gross	13·55 m² (145·8 sq ft)

WEIGHTS AND LOADINGS:

Weight empty	115 kg (254 lb)
Max T-O weight	220 kg (485 lb)
Max wing loading	16·24 kg/m² (3·33 lb/sq ft)
Max power loading	11·8 kg/kW (19·4 lb/hp)

PERFORMANCE:

Max level speed	55 knots (102 km/h; 63 mph)
Cruising speed	48 knots (90 km/h; 56 mph)
Stalling speed	24 knots (44 km/h; 28 mph)
Max rate of climb at S/L	180 m (590 ft)/min
Service ceiling	2,000 m (6,560 ft)
T-O and landing run	50 m (164 ft)
Endurance	3 h
Best glide ratio	12
g limits	+3·5/−2

DEDALUS

DEDALUS Srl

Viale Campania 29, 20133 Milan
Telephone: (02) 71 63 41
GENERAL MANAGER: Marco Baggi

DEDALUS POPPY

Sig Marco Baggi designed and built an extremely light aircraft known as the Poppy. Design began in August 1983 and construction of a prototype started one month later. This flew for the first time in May 1984, the same month that construction began of a pre-production aircraft. Production of the Poppy was begun in October 1984 and by 1986 a large number of kits of component parts had been sold. Construction takes approximately 300 working hours.

The following details apply to the current, improved, version of the Poppy, of which ten examples had been completed by mid-1986.

TYPE: Single-seat homebuilt cabin monoplane.

AIRFRAME: Braced high-wing monoplane, with aluminium alloy V bracing struts each side. Entire airframe has geodetic structure of Sitka spruce, with Dacron fabric covering. Wing section Rhode St Genese 34. Thickness/chord ratio 7·5. Dihedral from roots. Constant chord ailerons. No flaps. Wings can be folded against fuselage in 20 minutes for trailering. Rectangular section fuselage, with optional glassfibre engine cowling. Tail unit comprises large fin, rudder and tapering tailplane with one-piece elevator.

LANDING GEAR: Non-retractable tailwheel type. Cantilever spring mainwheel legs. Pirelli mainwheel tyres of 10 in diameter. Drum brakes.

POWER PLANT: One 18·6 kW (25 hp) KFM 107E engine, driving an Aerosviluppi two-blade fixed-pitch propeller. One fuel tank in fuselage, capacity 20 litres (4·4 Imp gallons).

ACCOMMODATION: Single seat in enclosed and heated cabin.

AVIONICS: Radio optional.

DIMENSIONS, EXTERNAL:

Wing span	10·60 m (34 ft 9¼ in)
Wing chord, constant	1·5 m (4 ft 11 in)
Length overall	5·90 m (19 ft 4¼ in)
Height overall	1·90 m (6 ft 2¾ in)
Tailplane span	2·30 m (7 ft 6½ in)
Propeller diameter	1·40 m (4 ft 7 in)

AREA:

Wings, gross	15·00 m² (161·5 sq ft)

WEIGHTS AND LOADINGS:

Weight empty	114 kg (252 lb)
Max T-O weight	210 kg (463 lb)
Max wing loading	14·00 kg/m² (2·87 lb/sq ft)
Max power loading	11·29 kg/kW (18·52 lb/hp)

PERFORMANCE:

Never-exceed speed	64 knots (120 km/h; 74 mph)
Max level speed	54 knots (100 km/h; 62 mph)
Max cruising speed	49 knots (90 km/h; 56 mph)
Econ cruising speed	43 knots (80 km/h; 50 mph)
Stalling speed	22 knots (40 km/h; 25 mph)
Max rate of climb at S/L	183 m (600 ft)/min
Service ceiling	3,050 m (10,000 ft)
T-O to 15 m (50 ft)	50 m (164 ft)
Landing from 15 m (50 ft)	100 m (328 ft)
Range with max fuel	108 nm (200 km; 124 miles)

HOBBYSTICA

HOBBYSTICA AVIO

via Migliara 52/5, 04014 Pontinia (Latina)
Telephone: (0773) 85 01 22
DIRECTOR: Roberto Racogna

HOBBYSTICA AVIO A-2-S BARRACUDA

Five examples of the standard Barracuda, designed by Sig Racogna, had been built by mid-1986. An aerobatic version, with a 30 kW (40 hp) Hirth engine, was under construction at that time.

TYPE: Single-seat microlight aircraft.

AIRFRAME: Wire braced high-wing monoplane. Constant chord wings have two spars of aluminium alloy tubing, aluminium ribs, and are Dacron covered, with conical cambered glassfibre tips and full-span flaperons. Chrome-molybdenum steel tube fuselage with Dacron covering. Conventional tail unit, of similar construction to wings, with sweptback vertical surfaces. Three-axis control (flaperons, elevators and rudder).

LANDING GEAR: Non-retractable tricycle type, with cantilever glassfibre spring main legs and mainwheel fairings. Steerable nosewheel with shock absorber.

POWER PLANT: One 22·4 kW (30 hp) KFM 107 Maxi two-cylinder two-stroke engine, with reduction drive to a two-blade fixed-pitch wooden propeller. Fuel capacity 20 litres (4·4 Imp gallons).

ACCOMMODATION: Pilot only in semi-enclosed cockpit.

DIMENSIONS, EXTERNAL:

Wing span	8·30 m (27 ft 2¾ in)
Wing aspect ratio	5·86
Length overall	5·02 m (16 ft 5¾ in)
Height overall	1·97 m (6 ft 5½ in)

AREA:

Wings, gross	11·75 m² (126·5 sq ft)

WEIGHTS AND LOADINGS:

Weight empty	114 kg (252 lb)
Max T-O weight	240 kg (529 lb)
Max wing loading	20·42 kg/m² (4·18 lb/sq ft)
Max power loading	10·71 kg/kW (17·63 lb/hp)

PERFORMANCE:

Max level speed	75 knots (138 km/h; 86 mph)
Cruising speed	61 knots (113 km/h; 70 mph)
Stalling speed, flaps down	24 knots (43 km/h; 27 mph)
Max rate of climb at S/L	180 m (590 ft)/min
Service ceiling	3,000 m (9,840 ft)
T-O run	70 m (230 ft)
Landing run	50 m (164 ft)
Endurance	3 h
Best glide ratio	12
g limits	+6/−3

Alpair Excel single-seat microlight trike unit *(Aviodata)*

AUI T7 Leone single-seat microlight *(Aviodata)*

CUP F3 single-seat microlight aircraft *(Aviodata)*

Dedalus Poppy single-seat cabin monoplane *(Aviodata)*

Hobbystica Avio A-2-S Barracuda single-seat microlight *(Aviodata)*

Iannotta I-66L San Francesco two-seat cabin monoplane

IANNOTTA

DOTT ING ORLANDO IANNOTTA

Via Eduardo Nicolardi 254, 80131 Naples

Dott Ing Orlando Iannotta has designed and built a two-seat cabin monoplane known as the I-66L San Francesco (I-JANV). This is a derivative of his earlier I-66 San Francesco single-seater (see 1973-74 *Jane's*), of which at least three examples have flown. The I-66L completed its flight test programme in the Autumn of 1981, and is also certificated as a motor glider by the RAI. Plans became available to amateur constructors in late 1983.

IANNOTTA I-66L SAN FRANCESCO

TYPE: Two-seat light cabin monoplane and motor glider.

AIRFRAME: Braced high-wing monoplane, with steel tube V bracing struts each side. Wing section NACA 23012. Dihedral 2°. Incidence 3° 30′. No sweepback. All-wood two-spar structure, with plywood covered leading-edge, the rest fabric covered. Fabric covered wooden ailerons. No flaps. Fabric covered steel tube fuselage structure, with wooden formers, of basically rectangular section. Wire braced tail unit structure of welded steel tube, fabric covered. Tailplane incidence variable in flight for trimming.

LANDING GEAR: Non-retractable tailwheel type. Main units consist of two side Vs and half-axles, hinged to cabane below fuselage. Rubber cord shock absorption. Mainwheel tyres size 5·00-5. Steerable leaf spring tailwheel. Brakes fitted.

POWER PLANT: One 51 kW (68 hp) Limbach SL 1700E engine, with dual ignition and electric starting in flight. Two-blade fixed-pitch wooden propeller of new type replaces original. Fuel tank in each wing; total fuel capacity 70 litres (15·4 Imp gallons).

ACCOMMODATION: Two seats in tandem in enclosed cabin, with dual controls and instrument panels. Forward opening door on starboard side.

AVIONICS: VHF transceiver.

DIMENSIONS, EXTERNAL:

Wing span	9·34 m (30 ft 7¾ in)
Wing chord, constant	1·50 m (4 ft 11 in)
Wing aspect ratio	6·41
Length overall	6·60 m (21 ft 8 in)
Fuselage: Max height	1·05 m (3 ft 5¼ in)
Max width	0·70 m (2 ft 3½ in)
Propeller diameter	1·45 m (4 ft 9 in)

AREA:

Wings, gross	13·61 m² (146·5 sq ft)

WEIGHTS AND LOADINGS:

Weight empty	268 kg (591 lb)
Max T-O weight	462 kg (1,018 lb)
Max wing loading	33·95 kg/m² (6·95 lb/sq ft)
Max power loading	9·06 kg/kW (14·97 lb/hp)

PERFORMANCE, POWERED:

Max level speed	81 knots (150 km/h; 93 mph)
Cruising speed at S/L	70 knots (130 km/h; 81 mph)
Landing speed	35 knots (65 km/h; 41 mph)
Max rate of climb at S/L	210 m (690 ft)/min
Service ceiling	3,800 m (12,470 ft)
Range with max fuel	378 nm (700 km; 435 miles)

PERFORMANCE, UNPOWERED:

Best glide ratio at 50 knots (93 km/h; 58 mph)	14
Min rate of sink at 48 knots (88 km/h; 55 mph)	1·40 m (4·59 ft)/s

ITALZAIR

NIKE AERONAUTICA

via Barberia 14, 40123 Bologna

ITALZAIR

The Italzair is an Italian version of the Canadian Ultraflight Lazair twin-engined single-seat microlight aircraft (which see). No details were known in Summer 1986, but the general appearance of the Italzair can be seen in an accompanying illustration.

PARMESANI

SANDRO PARMESANI

20070 San Martino in Strada (Milan)
Telephone: (0371) 79 70 70

Sig Parmesani has built a number of microlight aircraft. Details of the two latest designs follow:

PARMESANI P.A.8

Three examples of the P.A.8 had been completed by mid-1986.

TYPE: Tandem two-seat microlight aircraft.

AIRFRAME: Strut braced high-wing monoplane with three-axis control (ailerons, elevators and rudder). Wings have chrome-molybdenum steel tube spars and ribs, covered with Dacron. Steel tube fuselage frame, with glassfibre nose fairing and windscreen.

LANDING GEAR: Non-retractable tricycle type, with steerable nosewheel.

POWER PLANT: One 48·5 kW (65 hp) Arrow GT500 two-cylinder two-stroke engine, driving a two-blade wooden pusher propeller. Engine has electric starter and can be restarted in flight.

ACCOMMODATION: Tandem two-seat open cockpit, with dual controls.

DIMENSIONS, EXTERNAL:
- Wing span — 10·00 m (32 ft 9¾ in)
- Wing aspect ratio — 6·67
- Length overall — 5·20 m (17 ft 0¾ in)
- Height overall — 1·75 m (5 ft 9 in)

AREA:
- Wings, gross — 15·00 m² (161·5 sq ft)

WEIGHTS AND LOADINGS:
- Weight empty — 148 kg (326 lb)
- Max T-O weight — 320 kg (705 lb)
- Max wing loading — 21·33 kg/m² (4·37 lb/sq ft)
- Max power loading — 6·60 kg/kW (10·85 lb/hp)

PERFORMANCE:
- Max level speed — 57 knots (105 km/h; 65 mph)
- Cruising speed — 48 knots (90 km/h; 56 mph)
- Stalling speed — 25 knots (45 km/h; 28 mph)
- Max rate of climb at S/L — 180 m (590 ft)/min
- Service ceiling — 3,000 m (9,840 ft)
- T-O run — 50 m (164 ft)
- Landing run — 45 m (148 ft)
- Endurance — 3 h 30 min
- Best glide ratio — 10
- *g* limits — +6/−3

PARMESANI ALEX-I

TYPE: Single-seat microlight aircraft.

AIRFRAME: Strut braced parasol monoplane with three-axis control (ailerons, elevators and rudder). Constant chord wings of Clark Y section. Wing and tail unit spars and ribs, and fuselage structure, of chrome-molybdenum steel tubing with overall Dacron covering. Aluminium alloy engine cowling.

LANDING GEAR: Non-retractable tailwheel type. Mainwheels carried on side Vs and half-axles, hinged to bottom of fuselage, with bungee shock absorption. Steerable tailwheel on leafspring. Expanding brakes on mainwheels.

POWER PLANT: One 22·4 kW (30 hp) KFM 107 Maxi two-cylinder two-stroke engine, with reduction drive to a two-blade wooden propeller.

ACCOMMODATION: Pilot only, in open cockpit, with windscreen.

DIMENSIONS, EXTERNAL:
- Wing span — 9·10 m (29 ft 10¼ in)
- Wing aspect ratio — 6·9
- Length overall — 5·20 m (17 ft 0¾ in)
- Height overall — 1·60 m (5 ft 3 in)

AREA:
- Wings, gross — 12·00 m² (129·2 sq ft)

WEIGHTS AND LOADINGS:
- Weight empty — 115 kg (254 lb)
- Max T-O weight — 220 kg (485 lb)
- Max wing loading — 18·33 kg/m² (3·75 lb/sq ft)
- Max power loading — 9·78 kg/kW (16·17 lb/hp)

PERFORMANCE:
- Max level speed — 54 knots (100 km/h; 62 mph)
- Cruising speed — 48 knots (90 km/h; 56 mph)
- Stalling speed — 18 knots (33 km/h; 21 mph)
- Max rate of climb at S/L — 270 m (885 ft)/min
- Service ceiling — 3,000 m (9,840 ft)
- T-O and landing run — 30 m (99 ft)
- Endurance — 3 h
- Best glide ratio — 12
- *g* limits — +6/−3

POLARIS

POLARIS Srl

via Flaminia 208, 06021 Costacciaro (PG)
Telephone: (075) 917 01 86

POLARIS AIR DINGHY

Designed by Sig Renato 'Sonny' Levi, a well-known designer of racing craft, the Polaris Air Dinghy can be operated as a normal aerofoil boat or, with a hang glider flexwing, such as the Polaris Delta and Gamma (which see), as an ultralight water-based aircraft. More than 600 have been built.

TYPE: Single-seat boat or light aircraft.

AIRFRAME: Fuselage pod, two floats and connecting structure of glassfibre and Kevlar. Standard hang glider flexwing. Control by weight shift.

POWER PLANT: One 22·4 kW (30 hp) KFM 107ER two-cylinder two-stroke engine, driving a fixed-pitch pusher propeller. Fuel capacity 20 litres (4·4 Imp gallons).

DIMENSIONS, EXTERNAL (aircraft):
- Length overall — 3·93 m (12 ft 10¾ in)
- Width over floats — 2·17 m (7 ft 1½ in)
- Height overall — 3·47 m (11 ft 4¾ in)

WEIGHTS (aircraft):
- Weight empty — 105 kg (232 lb)
- Max T-O weight — 250 kg (551 lb)

PERFORMANCE (aircraft):
- Max level speed — 43 knots (80 km/h; 50 mph)
- Cruising speed — 32 knots (60 km/h; 37 mph)
- Stalling speed — 16 knots (30 km/h; 19 mph)
- T-O and landing run — 30 m (99 ft)
- Endurance — 4 h

SIRIO

SIRIO 2 Srl

Via Roma 52, 33050 Seveliano-Bagnaria Arsa
Telephone: (0432) 929128
PRESIDENT AND GENERAL MANAGER: Paolo Pravisani

SIRIO 2 SIRIO

The Sirio is a development of the French Aviasud Sirocco microlight aircraft that flew for the first time in September 1984. It is marketed by CSAM Srl of Via Boscovich 17, 20124 Milan (*telephone* [02] 655 4742). Fifty Sirios were built in 1985 and 100 were expected to be completed in 1986, mainly for export to Middle East and African customers. A tandem two-seat version is under development as the Sirio T.

TYPE: Single-seat microlight aircraft.

AIRFRAME: Strut-braced high-wing monoplane, without the kingpost fitted to the Sirocco. Dacron covered wings with 11° sweepback. Pod and boom fuselage of moulded glassfibre and Kevlar. Braced tail unit. Three-axis control (spoilers, all-moving tailplane and rudder).

LANDING GEAR: Non-retractable tailwheel type, with cantilever spring legs. Brakes fitted.

POWER PLANT: One 18·6 kW (25 hp) KFM107ER two-cylinder two-stroke engine, with reduction drive to a two-blade fixed-pitch pusher propeller.

ACCOMMODATION: Pilot only, in open cockpit with windscreen.

DIMENSIONS, EXTERNAL:
- Wing span — 10·11 m (33 ft 2 in)
- Wing aspect ratio — 7·43
- Length overall — 5·83 m (19 ft 1½ in)
- Height overall — 2·20 m (7 ft 2½ in)

AREA:
- Wings, gross — 13·75 m² (148·0 sq ft)

WEIGHTS AND LOADINGS:
- Weight empty — 114 kg (251 lb)
- Max T-O weight — 224 kg (494 lb)
- Max wing loading — 16·29 kg/m² (3·34 lb/sq ft)
- Max power loading — 12·04 kg/kW (19·76 lb/hp)

PERFORMANCE:
- Max level speed — 54 knots (100 km/h; 62 mph)
- Cruising speed — 46 knots (85 km/h; 53 mph)
- Stalling speed — 22 knots (40 km/h; 25 mph)
- Max rate of climb at S/L — 275 m (900 ft)/min
- T-O run — 30 m (98 ft)
- Landing run — 20 m (66 ft)
- Endurance — 2 h 30 min
- *g* limits — +6/−3

ULTRASPORT

ULTRASPORT SRL

Frazione Montebruno, 10060 Garzigliana (To)
Telephone: (0121) 541384/5
GENERAL MANAGER: Marco Bartolozzi
ENGINEERING: Luigi Accusani
PUBLIC RELATIONS: Frederica Mazzonis

Manufacturing rights to produce the Eagle, Eagle XL, and "any possible variations" were sold to Ultrasport in February 1984 by the Eagle's designer, Mr Romuald Drlik. Rights to manufacture the Eagle were previously held by American Aerolights Inc of the USA (see 1983-84 and earlier *Jane's*). Ultrasport now markets two models of the Eagle, the XL and the 2 PLC. It also has two versions (known as Foxcat) of the American Aircraft Falcon.

ULTRASPORT EAGLE XL

A description of the original US built Eagle can be found under the American Aerolights heading in the 1983-84 *Jane's*, and under Ultrasport in the 1984-85 edition. The XL is essentially a full three-axis version, with roll control spoilers added and a Rotax engine as standard.

TYPE: Single-seat microlight aircraft; conforms to FAR Pt 103.

AIRFRAME: Sweptback flexible-wing monoplane, with non-swept foreplane and elevator; rudders at wingtips. Main frame is of aluminium alloy, carbonfibre and Kevlar, with Dacron covering (double surface on foreplane and part of wing) and vinyl coated stainless steel cables. Kingpost standard. Features include pre-formed battens. Three-axis control by spoilers, foreplane elevator and wingtip rudders. Options include wheel fairings, digital flight instrumentation, and provision for tow launch.

LANDING GEAR: Non-retractable tricycle type. Coil sprung suspension. Steerable nosewheel. All wheels and tyres size 3·00/3·50-5; nosewheel brake standard. Optional floats and skis.

POWER PLANT: One 26 kW (35 hp) Rotax 377 two-stroke engine, with reduction drive to a two-blade pusher propeller. Fuel tank capacity 15 litres (4 US gallons).

ACCOMMODATION: Pilot only, in open position.

DIMENSIONS, EXTERNAL:
- Wing span — 10·67 m (35 ft 0 in)
- Foreplane span — 2·74 m (9 ft 0 in)
- Wing aspect ratio — 7·49
- Foreplane aspect ratio — 4·91
- Length overall — 4·57 m (15 ft 0 in)
- Height overall — 2·74 m (9 ft 0 in)
- Propeller diameter — 1·37 m (4 ft 6 in)

AREA:
- Wings/foreplane, gross — 16·44 m² (177·0 sq ft)

WEIGHTS AND LOADINGS:
- Weight empty — 112·5 kg (248 lb)
- Pilot weight range — 54·5-109 kg (120-240 lb)
- Max T-O weight — 231 kg (510 lb)
- Max wing/foreplane loading — 14·06 kg/m² (2·88 lb/sq ft)
- Max power loading — 8·88 kg/kW (14·57 lb/hp)

PERFORMANCE (with 68 kg; 150 lb pilot):
- Never-exceed speed — 56 knots (104 km/h; 65 mph)
- Max level speed — 43 knots (80 km/h; 50 mph)
- Econ cruising speed — 32 knots (60 km/h; 37 mph)
- Stalling speed — 21 knots (39 km/h; 24 mph)
- Max rate of climb at S/L — 229 m (750 ft)/min
- Service ceiling — 5,335 m (17,500 ft)
- T-O and landing run — 38 m (125 ft)
- Range with max fuel — 78 nm (145 km; 90 miles)
- Endurance with max fuel — 2 h 45 min

Italzair single-seat microlight, a version of the Canadian Ultraflight Lazair *(Aviodata)*

Parmesani P.A.8 two-seat microlight aircraft *(Aviodata)*

Parmesani Alex-I single-seat microlight aircraft *(Aviodata)*

Polaris Air Dinghy water-based ultralight aircraft *(Aviodata)*

Sirio microlight aircraft, marketed by CSAM

Ultrasport Eagle XL single-seat microlight *(Aviodata)*

Ultrasport F2 Foxcat version of the American Aircraft Falcon *(Aviodata)*

F2 Twin Foxcat under development by Ultrasport *(Aviodata)*

g limits	+8/−2·5
Best glide ratio	7
Min rate of sink, power off	91 m (300 ft)/min

ULTRASPORT EAGLE 2 PLC

This two-seat version of the Eagle XL has a more powerful 34·3 kW (46 hp) Rotax 503 engine, and does not conform to FAR Pt 103.

ULTRASPORT F2 FOXCAT

The F2 Foxcat is an Ultrasport version of the American Aircraft Falcon described in the US part of this section. It is powered by a 20 kW (27 hp) Rotax 277 single-cylinder two-stroke engine and, like the Eagle XL, replaces some aluminium alloy in the airframe by Kevlar and carbonfibre. Data are generally similar to those for the American version.

ULTRASPORT F2 TWIN FOXCAT

This is a two-seat derivative of the single-seat Foxcat, powered by a 48·5 kW (65 hp) Arrow GT500 two-stroke flat-twin engine. It was still under development in 1986. Weight empty and max T-O weight are reportedly 170 kg (375 lb) and 400 kg (882 lb) respectively and cruising speed 81 knots (150 km/h; 93 mph).

VPM

VPM SnC

Via per Besnate 10, 21040 Jerago (Va)
Telephone: 0331 217328
WORKS MANAGER: Vittorio Magni

Sig Magni purchased from Mr Jukka Tervamäki of Finland the prototype, and all tooling, moulds and production rights, of the latter's JT-5 single-seat autogyro. In 1979 VPM SnC was established to produce plans, component parts and complete kits for amateur builders of the updated MT5 version of this autogyro. A later autogyro, developed as an enlarged two-seat version of the MT5 and known as the MT7, has since been flown. The exact status of this aircraft is unknown, though an address in Italy has been published in an aviation magazine by a person seeking investors and a market for the MT7.

VPM MT5

The description of the Tervamäki JT-5 in the Finnish section of this edition is generally applicable also to the VPM MT5, the main difference being use of a 1,700 cc Limbach engine to power the MT5. However, the MT5 has slightly greater overall dimensions, resulting in changes to the all-up weight and performance, as follows:

DIMENSIONS, EXTERNAL:
- Rotor diameter: 7·19 m (23 ft 7 in)
- Length of fuselage: 3·61 m (11 ft 10 in)
- Height overall: 1·96 m (6 ft 5 in)

WEIGHTS:
- Weight empty: 167 kg (368 lb)
- Max T-O weight: 300 kg (661 lb)

PERFORMANCE:
- Max level speed: 81 knots (150 km/h; 93 mph)
- Max cruising speed: 70 knots (130 km/h; 81 mph)
- Min level speed: 22 knots (40 km/h; 25 mph)
- Max rate of climb at S/L: 183 m (600 ft)/min
- Service ceiling: 4,000 m (13,125 ft)
- T-O run: 80 m (262 ft)

VPM MT7

The MT7, the design of which was undertaken in early 1980 at the request of Sig Magni, is basically an enlarged two-seat version of the MT5. Design of the airframe, control and rotor systems was entrusted to Mr Jukka Tervamäki of Finland, with VPM concentrating on the engine installation, instrumentation, landing gear and other details. The rotor head and rotor blades are basically enlarged versions of those used on the JT-5. Power plant is a 112 kW (150 hp) Avco Lycoming O-320 flat-four engine. Design emphasis was placed on aerodynamic refinement to give the aircraft the best possible cross-country performance at low power settings.

The prototype MT7 flew for the first time in January 1984. As shown in the accompanying illustration, it is generally similar in configuration to the MT5, the most obvious differences being the twin fin and rudder tail unit, with a forward-swept horizontal surface, and a more streamlined landing gear with wheel fairings.

DIMENSIONS, EXTERNAL:
- Rotor diameter: 8·70 m (28 ft 6½ in)
- Length of fuselage: 4·40 m (14 ft 5¼ in)
- Width overall, excl rotor: 2·10 m (6 ft 10¾ in)
- Height overall: 2·40 m (7 ft 10½ in)

WEIGHTS:
- Weight empty: 290 kg (639 lb)
- Max T-O weight: 480 kg (1,058 lb)

PERFORMANCE (estimated):
- Max level speed: 95 knots (175 km/h; 109 mph)
- Max cruising speed: 81 knots (150 km/h; 93 mph)
- Max rate of climb at S/L: 180 m (590 ft)/min
- Range: 161 nm (300 km; 186 miles)

LUXEMBOURG

WOLFF

ATELIERS PAUL WOLFF

1 Rue des Romains, L-8284 Kehlen
Telephone: Luxembourg 309954

WOLFF FLASH-3

First modern homebuilt aircraft designed and constructed in the Grand Duchy of Luxembourg, the Flash-3 (LX-LPW) is an all-composites three-seater. Design began in July 1983 and construction of the prototype started in December that year. It was exhibited at the 1985 RSA meeting at Brienne in France and was expected to make its first flight in early 1986.

The Flash-3 is being marketed in the form of a series of component kits, with an estimated construction time of 600 to 700 hours. The kits contain all component parts, except for the engine, propeller and instruments. By January 1986, nine kits had been ordered.

TYPE: Three-seat homebuilt aircraft.

AIRFRAME: Cantilever low-wing monoplane. Entire airframe constructed of vinylester and resin composites, partially strengthened with carbonfibre. Wing section NACA 43012_5 at root, 43010 at tip. Dihedral 4° 30′. Incidence 2° 30′ at root, 1° at tip. No sweepback. Main spar laminated inside wings. Ailerons and electrically actuated flaps interconnected. Conventional moulded monocoque fuselage and T tail, with all-moving tailplane, anti-servo tab, fin, and rudder.

LANDING GEAR: Electrically and hydraulically retracted tricycle type, with all three wheels size 5·00-5 (pressure 2·76 bars; 40 lb/sq in). Shock absorbers. Mainwheel hydraulic brakes.

POWER PLANT: One 112 kW (150 hp) Avco Lycoming O-320 flat-four engine, driving a Mühlbauer two-blade metal constant-speed propeller with spinner. Fuel capacity: standard tank 261 litres (69 US gallons); long range tank 541 litres (143 US gallons); long range tank with tip tanks 641 litres (169·3 US gallons). One 119 kW (160 hp) Duncan rotary engine will be fitted to prototype at later date.

ACCOMMODATION: Pilot and two passengers under large rearward sliding canopy. Baggage capacity 120 kg (264 lb).

AVIONICS: IFR instrumentation plus Micrologic ML 6000 Loran C and radio com standard.

DIMENSIONS, EXTERNAL:
- Wing span, over tip tanks: 8·53 m (27 ft 11¾ in)
- Wing chord: at root: 1·50 m (4 ft 11 in)
- at tip: 0·81 m (2 ft 8 in)
- Wing aspect ratio, without tip tanks: 6·9
- Width, wings folded: 2·49 m (8 ft 2 in)
- Length overall: 7·93 m (26 ft 0¼ in)
- Height overall: 2·11 m (6 ft 11 in)
- Tailplane span: 3·00 m (9 ft 10 in)
- Wheel track: 1·50 m (4 ft 11 in)
- Wheelbase: 2·29 m (7 ft 6 in)
- Propeller diameter: 1·93 m (6 ft 4 in)

AREA:
- Wings, gross: 10·00 m² (107·64 sq ft)

WEIGHTS AND LOADINGS:
- Weight empty: 508 kg (1,120 lb)
- Max T-O weight: without tip tanks: 996 kg (2,196 lb)
- with tip tanks: 1,066 kg (2,350 lb)
- Max wing loading: 106·6 kg/m² (21·83 lb/sq ft)
- Max power loading: 9·52 kg/kW (15·67 lb/hp)

PERFORMANCE (at max T-O weight):
- Never-exceed speed: 255 knots (472 km/h; 293 mph)
- Max level speed at S/L: 197 knots (365 km/h; 227 mph)
- Max cruising speed at S/L: 186 knots (345 km/h; 214 mph)
- Econ cruising speed at 3,050 m (10,000 ft): 180 knots (334 km/h; 207 mph)
- Stalling speed, flaps down: 44 knots (81 km/h; 50 mph)
- Max rate of climb at S/L: 366 m (1,200 ft)/min
- Service ceiling: 5,430 m (17,820 ft)
- T-O run: 230 m (755 ft)
- Landing run: 210 m (689 ft)
- Range with standard fuel: 1,776 nm (3,291 km; 2,045 miles)
- Range with max fuel: 3,664 nm (6,791 km; 4,220 miles)

POLAND

JANOWSKI

JAROSLAW JANOWSKI

ul Nowomiejska 2 m 29, 91-061 Lodz

JANOWSKI J-2 POLONEZ

As a follow-up to his well-known J-1B Don Kichot single-seat ultra-light monoplane, Mr Janowski designed in 1971 a smaller aircraft of generally similar configuration which he named J-2 Polonez. The prototype, built by Mr Josef Leniec, was described and illustrated in model form in the 1979-80 *Jane's*. It flew for the first time on 22 August 1977. In 1982, Mr Leniec modified it by replacing the original monowheel main landing gear with a conventional tailwheel gear having two mainwheels carried on a curved cantilever one-piece leg. The following description applies to the prototype Polonez in its current form:

TYPE: Single-seat homebuilt microlight aircraft.

AIRFRAME: Cantilever mid-wing monoplane of all-wood construction. Wing section NACA 23012. Constant-chord single-spar wing structure, with leading-edge plywood covered, rest of wing fabric covered. Fabric covered ailerons. No tabs. Pod and boom fuselage with enclosed cabin faired into nose. Wooden single-boom structure supporting cantilever tail unit, with T tailplane. Fin plywood covered; remainder fabric covered. Sweptback vertical surfaces and constant-chord non-swept horizontal surfaces. Tab in trailing-edge of horizontal surfaces, plus two mass balance arms projecting forward of leading-edge.

LANDING GEAR: Non-retractable tailwheel type.

POWER PLANT: One 22·5 kW (30 hp) Trabant aircooled two-stroke two-cylinder motorcar engine, mounted at top of fuselage aft of cabin and driving a two-blade fixed-pitch wooden pusher propeller. The aircraft may be fitted with any other suitable engine of 18·5-30 kW (25-40 hp).

DIMENSIONS, EXTERNAL:
- Wing span: 7·00 m (23 ft 0 in)
- Wing chord, constant: 1·06 m (3 ft 6 in)
- Wing aspect ratio: 7
- Length overall: 4·84 m (15 ft 10½ in)
- Height overall: 1·35 m (4 ft 5¼ in)
- Tailplane span: 2·00 m (6 ft 6¾ in)
- Propeller diameter: 1·06 m (3 ft 6 in)

AREA:
- Wings, gross: 7·00 m² (75·35 sq ft)

WEIGHTS AND LOADINGS:
- Weight empty: 105 kg (231 lb)
- Normal T-O weight: 235 kg (518 lb)
- Max wing loading: 33·57 kg/m² (6·87 lb/sq ft)
- Max power loading: 10·44 kg/kW (17·27 lb/hp)

PERFORMANCE:
- Max level speed: 86 knots (160 km/h; 99 mph)
- Cruissing speed: 65 knots (120 km/h; 75 mph)
- Stalling speed: 33 knots (60 km/h; 38 mph)
- Max rate of climb at S/L: 180 m (590 ft)/min
- Endurance: 3 h

MARGANSKI

EDWARD MARGANSKI

ul Poprzeczna 21, 43-300 Bielsko-Biala

MARGANSKI DK-3 KASIA

Mr Edward Marganski, an aeronautical engineer and designer of the PZL M-17 two/three-seat twin-boom light aircraft (last described and illustrated in the 1978-79 *Jane's*), has designed and built a very small twin-engined homebuilt aircraft known as the DK-3 Kasia. Construction began in 1981, following tests with a ⅕th scale model, and the full-size aircraft (SP-PEA) flew for the first time on 29 October 1984.

The DK-3 has a GRP structure and was designed to be suited to fast cross-country flights of up to 1,000 km range and for operation from prepared airfields. It fulfils the requirements of FAR 23. A single-engined version has also been designed, using an engine in the 30-44·5 kW (40-60 hp) range. The following details refer to the twin-engined DK-3:

TYPE: Single-seat homebuilt light sporting aircraft.

AIRFRAME: Cantilever low-wing monoplane. Constant chord wings, of section FX-67-170K. Glassfibre structure. Narrow-chord flaps and 'flaperons'. Conventional monocoque fuselage structure of glassfibre/epoxy resin and glassfibre tail unit comprising sweptback integral fin, rudder and all-moving tailplane with servo tabs.

LANDING GEAR: Non-retractable tricycle type. Main units have steel spring legs; nosewheel unit has rubber in compression shock absorption. Mainwheels size 300 × 125; nosewheel 255 × 110.

POWER PLANT: Two 18·6 kW (25 hp) KFM 107E flat-twin engines in cowlings on sides of fuselage nose, each driving a two-blade fixed-pitch wooden propeller with large spinner. Two fuel tanks, with total capacity of 60 litres (13 Imp gallons).

ACCOMMODATION: Single reclining seat under sideways hinged (to starboard) one-piece canopy.

AVIONICS: Provision for radio and VOR/ILS.

DIMENSIONS, EXTERNAL:
- Wing span: 7·10 m (23 ft 3½ in)
- Length overall: 4·45 m (14 ft 7¼ in)
- Height overall: 1·80 m (5 ft 11 in)
- Propeller diameter: 0·87 m (2 ft 10¼ in)

AREA:
- Wings, gross: 3·50 m² (37·67 sq ft)

VPM MT7 two-seat autogyro (Avco Lycoming O-320 engine) *(Aviodata)*

VPM MT5 single-seat autogyro *(Geoffrey P. Jones)*

Wolff Flash-3 three-seat homebuilt aircraft

Janowski J-2 Polonez built by Mr Josef Leniec *(Andrzej Glass)*

Marko-Elektronik/Janowski J-5 composites homebuilt aircraft constructed in West Germany by Herr Heintz Wagenseil *(Geoffrey P. Jones)*

Marganski DK-3 Kasia twin-engined single-seat light aircraft *(A. Proszalek)*

WEIGHTS AND LOADINGS:

Weight empty, equipped	180 kg (397 lb)
Max T-O weight	310 kg (683 lb)
Max wing loading	88·57 kg/m² (18·14 lb/sq ft)
Max power loading	16·67 kg/kW (27·32 lb/hp)

PERFORMANCE:

Max level speed	140 knots (260 km/h; 162 mph)
Max cruising speed	113 knots (210 km/h; 130 mph)
Stalling speed	57 knots (105 km/h; 66 mph)
T-O run	350 m (1,148 ft)
T-O to 15 m (50 ft)	480 m (1,575 ft)
Landing run	250 m (820 ft)
Max range	540 nm (1,000 km; 621 miles)
g limits	+4·5/−1·8

MARKO-ELEKTRONIK

MARKO-ELEKTRONIK COMPANY

Lublinek, Aeroklub Lodzki, 93-469 Lodz

MARKO-ELEKTRONIK/JANOWSKI J-5

The 1984-85 *Jane's* included a description of the J-5 composites light homebuilt monoplane, one of the latest designs from Mr Jaroslaw Janowski. The aircraft branch of the Marko-Elektronik Company was established to offer for export kits of component parts to construct the J-5.

The aircraft is marketed in West Germany by Thewa-technics of Dorfstrasse 77, 8939 Markt Wald (*tel:* 08262 1868). The following description applies to this company's version, known as the Marco-J5:

THEWA-TECHNICS MARCO-J5

Kits to build the Marco-J5 include all major components such as the wings, control surfaces, fuselage shell, fuselage frames and tail surfaces ready for final assembly and to a high standard of surface finish. All fairings and cowlings are premoulded; the landing gear and control system are assembled ready for installation. Instruments and materials for assembly and finishing are available.

TYPE: Single-seat homebuilt aircraft.

AIRFRAME: Cantilever mid-wing monoplane built entirely of glassfibre reinforced plastics. Constant chord single-spar wings, with dihedral from roots and downswept tips housing small balancing wheels. Wortmann wing section. Pod and boom fuselage, with large one-piece canopy. Three-axis control by full-span flaperons on wings and elevators on V tail.

LANDING GEAR: Single retractable mainwheel under fuselage, tailwheel and wingtip balancing wheels; alternative non-retractable tailwheel type with two mainwheels covered by streamline fairings.

POWER PLANT: One 22·4 kW (30 hp) KFM 107ER two-cylinder two-stroke engine, driving a two-blade pusher propeller. Fuel capacity 30 litres (6·6 Imp gallons).

ACCOMMODATION: Pilot only, in enclosed cockpit, with sidestick controls.

DIMENSIONS, EXTERNAL:

Wing span	8·10 m (26 ft 7 in)
Wing aspect ratio	10·1
Length overall	4·70 m (15 ft 5 in)
Height overall	1·40 m (4 ft 7¼ in)

AREA:

Wings, gross	6·50 m² (70·0 sq ft)

WEIGHTS AND LOADINGS:

Weight empty	140 kg (309 lb)
Max T-O weight	250 kg (551 lb)
Max wing loading	38·5 kg/m² (7·87 lb/sq ft)
Max power loading	11·2 kg/kW (18·4 lb/hp)

PERFORMANCE:

Max level speed	113 knots (210 km/h; 130 mph)
Cruising speed	86 knots (160 km/h; 99 mph)
Max rate of climb at S/L	180 m (590 ft)/min
T-O run	180 m (590 ft)
Range with max fuel	378 nm (700 km; 435 miles)
Best glide ratio	21

OSTROWSKI

JERZY OSTROWSKI

OSTROWSKI BIPLANE

Details of the single-seat microlight biplane built by the late Mr Jerzy Ostrowski can be found in the 1985-86 *Jane's*.

SINGAPORE

CANA

CANA AIRCRAFT COMPANY

CKH Building, 50 Playfair Road, 03-02, Singapore 1336
Telephone: 2809725/2809726
Telex: 33872 CANA
DIRECTOR: Wilson Yong

The Cana Aircraft Company is currently offering kits of component parts to allow construction of the Andreasson MFI-9 HB two-seat monoplane. The company may also put the MFI-9 into series production at a later date. Details of the MFI-9 HB can be found under the Andreasson entry in the Swedish section.

SOUTH AFRICA

MFS

MICROLIGHT FLIGHT SYSTEMS PTY LTD

53 Old Main Road, Hillcrest, 3600 Natal
Telephone: (031) 75 3920
MANAGING DIRECTOR: John Young

Having completed manufacture of its single-seat XCR microlight, basically a modified Eagle with a 26 kW (35 hp) Cuyuna 430RR engine and structural changes, MFS currently concentrates on its Shadow tandem two-seater. This aircraft is known as the Shadow Trainer in the USA.

MFS SHADOW

TYPE: Two-seat microlight aircraft; conforms to South African Department of Civil Aviation certification requirements.

AIRFRAME: Conventional high-wing monoplane with cruciform tail surfaces. Main structure of D65S (AA6261) aluminium alloy tubing equivalent to US 6061. Single surface fabric covered. Kingpost standard. Three-axis control (spoilers, rudder and elevators).

LANDING GEAR: Tricycle type, with tempered spring steel legs and large tyres. Steerable nosewheel.

POWER PLANT: One 39·5 kW (53 hp) Rotax 503 two-cylinder two-stroke engine, driving a wooden pusher propeller. Fuel capacity 20 litres (4·4 Imp gallons).

ACCOMMODATION: Two seats in tandem in fully open position.

DIMENSIONS, EXTERNAL:
- Wing span: 9·75 m (32 ft 0 in)
- Wing chord, constant: 1·52 m (5 ft 0 in)
- Wing aspect ratio: 6·4
- Length overall: 5·69 m (18 ft 8 in)
- Height overall: 3·07 m (10 ft 1 in)
- Propeller diameter: 1·35 m (4 ft 5 in)

AREA:
- Wings, gross: 14·86 m² (160·0 sq ft)

WEIGHTS AND LOADINGS:
- Weight empty: 146 kg (321 lb)
- Max T-O weight: 317 kg (700 lb)
- Max wing loading: 21·33 kg/m² (4·38 lb/sq ft)
- Max power loading: 8·02 kg/kW (13·21 lb/hp)

PERFORMANCE:
- Never-exceed speed: 52 knots (96 km/h; 60 mph)
- Cruising speed (79% power): 39 knots (72 km/h; 45 mph)
- Stalling speed: 23 knots (42 km/h; 26 mph)
- Max rate of climb at S/L: 198 m (650 ft)/min
- Service ceiling: 3,660 m (12,000 ft)
- T-O run: 30·5 m (100 ft)
- T-O to 15 m (50 ft): 92 m (300 ft)
- Landing run: 25 m (80 ft)

SWEDEN

ANDREASSON

BJÖRN ANDREASSON

Collins Väg 22B, 23600 Höllviksnäs

Mr Andreasson has designed twelve different types of light aircraft, the first as the BA-1 hang glider of 1932 and including a cargo glider (BA-3), a sailplane (BA-2) and various powered aircraft. Of these, the BA-7 was built in series by AB Malmö Flygindustri as the MFI-9B Trainer/Militrainer and by MBB in West Germany as the BO 208 C Junior (see 1970-71 *Jane's*). Plans of a version designated MFI-9 HB are available, and this is described below. Kits of component parts to allow construction of the MFI-9 HB are currently being produced by Mr Wilson Yong, Cana Aircraft Company, Singapore.

An earlier design, the BA-4 biplane, was modernised by Mr Andreasson for members of the Swedish branch of the Experimental Aircraft Association, and a prototype was built by MFI apprentices as part of their training programme. To distinguish it from the original BA-4, it is designated BA-4B.

Another of Mr Andreasson's designs, the BA-12, is described under the MFI heading in this section.

ANDREASSON BA-4B

The prototype BA-4B, built by MFI apprentices, was of all-metal construction. The design provides for alternative all-wooden wings. Plans for homebuilders are available from Mr Andreasson.

TYPE: Single-seat fully aerobatic homebuilt biplane.

AIRFRAME: Braced biplane type, with a single streamline-section interplane strut each side. A streamline-section bracing strut runs from the bottom fuselage longeron on each side to the top of the interplane strut, and an N cabane structure supports the centre-section. Incidence, upper wing 3°, lower wings 4°. Stagger 20°. Dihedral, upper wing 2°, lower wings 4°. Alternative all-metal or all-wood structure, with solid spars, covered with heavy plywood skin. Pop riveted ailerons, of simplified sheet metal construction, on lower wings only. No flaps. Provision for fitting detachable plastics wingtips. Sheet metal fuselage structure, with external stringers, making extensive use of pop riveting. Turtledeck either sheet metal or reinforced plastics. Cantilever tail unit of pop riveted sheet metal construction.

LANDING GEAR: Non-retractable tailwheel type. Cantilever spring steel main legs. Mainwheels size 5·00-4 or 5·00-5. Hydraulic brakes. Steerable tailwheel carried on leaf spring.

POWER PLANT: Prototype has 74·5 kW (100 hp) Rolls-Royce Continental O-200-A flat-four engine. Provision for other engines, including Volkswagen conversions. Standard fuel tank, capacity 50 litres (11 Imp gallons), forward of cockpit. Provision for carrying external 'bullet' tank of 50 litres (11 Imp gallons) capacity under fuselage.

ACCOMMODATION: Single seat in open cockpit.

AVIONICS AND EQUIPMENT: Provision for battery, VHF radio and IFR instrumentation.

DIMENSIONS, EXTERNAL:
- Wing span: upper: 5·34 m (17 ft 7 in)
  - lower: 5·14 m (16 ft 11 in)
- Wing chord (upper and lower, constant): 0·80 m (2 ft 7½ in)
- Wing aspect ratio (upper and lower): 6
- Length overall: 4·60 m (15 ft 0 in)
- Tailplane span: 2·00 m (6 ft 6¾ in)

AREA:
- Wings, gross: 8·30 m² (89·3 sq ft)

WEIGHT AND LOADINGS:
- Max T-O weight: 375 kg (827 lb)
- Max wing loading: 45·2 kg/m² (9·26 lb/sq ft)
- Max power loading: 5·03 kg/kW (8·27 lb/hp)

PERFORMANCE (prototype, at max T-O weight):
- Max level speed: 122 knots (225 km/h; 140 mph)
- Max cruising speed: 104 knots (193 km/h; 120 mph)
- Min flying speed: 35 knots (64 km/h; 40 mph)
- Max rate of climb at S/L: 610 m (2,000 ft)/min
- T-O and landing run: less than 100 m (330 ft)
- Range with standard fuel: 152 nm (280 km; 175 miles)

ANDREASSON MFI-9 HB

The prototype BA-7 two-seat homebuilt monoplane was designed and built in the United States by Mr Bjorn Andreasson, making its first flight on 10 October 1958. Details of this aircraft can be found in the 1960-61 *Jane's*. By the early 1960s the BA-7 was in quantity production in Sweden, by Malmö Flygindustri, for sale in Scandinavia and certain South American countries, and by Bölkow-Entwicklungen in West Germany. Power was provided by a 74·5 kW (100 hp) Continental O-200-A flat-four engine, which continues to be the recommended power plant for the latest MFI-9 HB version for homebuilding.

Production of the type in Sweden covered the MFI-9 basic version, first flown on 9 August 1962, the MFI-9B Trainer, and its military counterpart, the MFI-9B Militrainer primary training aircraft. German production concentrated on the BO 208C Junior, similar to the MFI-9. Later marketed by MBB, after the formation of this company in 1969, the 200th German Junior was delivered in that year.

Plans for the MFI-9 HB, a redrawn version of the MFI-9 for amateur builders, are currently available from Mr Andreasson. The description and data refer to this version. Kits of component parts are available from the Cana Aircraft Company in Singapore (which see). The MFI-9 HB is fully certificated to FAR Pt 23 in the Utility category at gross weight. It is said to be simple to construct, with no double curvatures to fabricate.

TYPE: Two-seat homebuilt aerobatic light monoplane.

AIRFRAME: Braced shoulder-wing monoplane. Single bracing strut each side. Wing section NACA 23009, modified to have leading-edge droop. Dihedral 1°. Incidence 2°. Sweepforward 3°. All-metal single-spar structure. Wingtips of glassfibre reinforced plastics. All-metal mass balanced ailerons and electrically operated plain flaps. No trim tabs. All-metal box fuselage, with no double curvature. External longerons. Cantilever all-metal tail unit, with sweptback fin and rudder and all-moving tailplane. Anti-servo and trim tab on horizontal surface.

LANDING GEAR: Non-retractable tricycle type. Cantilever tapered steel spring main legs. Steerable nosewheel, with steel springs and hydraulic damping, is operated by the rudder pedals. Wheels size 5·00-5 on nose unit and 5·50-5 on main units. Mainwheel tyre pressure 2·07 bars (30 lb/sq in), nosewheel tyre pressure 1·38 bars (20 lb/sq in). Hydraulic disc brakes and parking brake. Ski and float gears optional.

POWER PLANT: One 74·5 kW (100 hp) Continental O-200-A flat-four engine, driving a two-blade fixed-pitch metal propeller. Other engines of similar weight and power rating can be used. Fuel tank behind cockpit, capacity 80 litres (21 US gallons). Oil capacity 4·7 litres (1·25 US gallons).

ACCOMMODATION: Two seats side by side in enclosed cabin, with dual controls. Rearward hinged canopy serves as door. Heating and ventilation standard. Baggage compartment aft of seats, capacity 20 kg (44 lb). Utility shelf above baggage compartment.

SYSTEM: Electrical system with 30A generator. 12V standby battery.

DIMENSIONS, EXTERNAL:
- Wing span: 7·43 m (24 ft 4½ in)
- Wing chord, constant: 1·22 m (4 ft 0 in)
- Length overall: 5·85 m (19 ft 2¼ in)
- Height overall: 2·00 m (6 ft 6¾ in)
- Tailplane span: 2·84 m (9 ft 3¾ in)
- Wheel track: 2·00 m (6 ft 6¾ in)

AREA:
- Wings, gross: 8·70 m² (93·65 sq ft)

WEIGHTS AND LOADINGS:
- Weight empty: 340 kg (750 lb)
- Max T-O weight: 575 kg (1,267 lb)
- Max wing loading: 66·1 kg/m² (13·54 lb/sq ft)
- Max power loading: 7·72 kg/kW (12·67 lb/hp)

PERFORMANCE:
- Max level speed: 130 knots (240 km/h; 149 mph)
- Max cruising speed: 127 knots (236 km/h; 147 mph)
- Econ cruising speed at S/L: 113 knots (210 km/h; 130 mph)
- Stalling speed, power off: 44 knots (80 km/h; 50 mph)
- Max rate of climb at S/L: 270 m (885 ft)/min
- Service ceiling: 4,500 m (14,775 ft)
- T-O run, grass: 150 m (492 ft)
- Landing run: 130 m (427 ft)
- Range with max payload: 431 nm (800 km; 497 miles)

Andreasson BA-4B single-seat fully aerobatic homebuilt biplane *(R. Kunert)*

MFI-9B built in Sweden by Malmö

Andreasson BA-12 Slandan microlight

Ekström Humlan built by Mr Tommy Nilsson of Björklinge, Sweden

EKSTRÖM

STAFFAN W. EKSTRÖM
Jupitervägen 43, 181 6 Lidingö
Telephone: (08) 766 34 48

EKSTRÖM HUMLAN

Mr Ekström initiated design of this single-seat autogyro in June 1971. Construction of the prototype (SE-HXE) began in April 1972, and it flew for the first time in June 1973. At least 11 Humlans have been completed and flown in Sweden. Three of these (SE-HXA, E and G) had completed their 75 h flight test period by early 1985; the other eight were then still under test and between them had accumulated 234 flying hours. Nineteen more were being built in Sweden at that time.

The prototype was flown initially with the standard tricycle landing gear, as described. It was fitted subsequently with twin floats, each weighing 16 kg (35 lb), as illustrated in the 1978-79 *Jane's*.

The Humlan illustrated was built by Mr Tommy Nilsson of Björklinge and is powered by a 67 kW (90 hp) McCulloch 4318 engine driving a Troyer propeller. Fuel capacity is 35 litres (7·7 Imp gallons). Empty weight and max T-O weight are 135 kg (298 lb) and 297 kg (655 lb) respectively. Max cruising speed at S/L, at max AUW, is 65 knots (120 km/h; 74 mph).

Type: Single-seat homebuilt autogyro.

Rotor System: Single two-blade semi-rigid rotor, attached to hub by a single bolt. Ztan Zee aluminium rotor blades. Blade section NACA 8H-12.

Rotor Drive: Flexible shaft for rotor spin-up only, to 140 rpm, via gearbox and two V belts.

Airframe: Cruciform chassis of 6061-T6 square-section aluminium tube, on which is mounted a pod type nacelle. Conventional single fin and rudder, and fixed tailplane with dihedral, built of 0·4 mm and 0·8 mm aluminium sheet.

Landing Gear: Non-retractable tricycle type, with additional small wheel beneath tail. Rubber shock absorption on tailwheel only. Aluminium or plastics go-kart wheels on main and nose units. Mainwheel tyres size 4·00-4; pressure 0·88 bars (12·8 lb/sq in). Nosewheel is steerable and self-centering, and is fitted with drum brake. Optional glassfibre floats or skis.

Power Plant: One 67 kW (90 hp) McCulloch AF 100-X3 four-cylinder engine, driving a two-blade fixed-pitch pusher propeller, is standard. SE-HXI and L have a 1,700 cc Limbach engine; SE-HXU has a 1,834 cc converted Volkswagen motorcar engine. Fuel tank, capacity 32 litres (7 Imp gallons), behind seat. Fuel is a petrol/oil mixture, with 5% oil.

Accommodation: Single seat in open cockpit. One-piece curved windscreen. Shoulder harness fitted.

Dimensions, external (wheel landing gear):

Rotor diameter	6·80 m (22 ft 3¾ in)
Length overall	3·42 m (11 ft 2¾ in)
Height overall	1·98 m (6 ft 6 in)
Width over mainwheels	1·65 m (5 ft 5 in)
Propeller diameter	1·20 m (3 ft 11¼ in)

Weights (A: wheel landing gear, B: floats):

Weight empty: A	145 kg (320 lb)
B	182 kg (401 lb)
Normal max T-O weight: A	260 kg (573 lb)
B	285 kg (628 lb)
Max T-O weight: A, B	295 kg (650 lb)

Performance (A: wheel landing gear, B: floats, at 260 kg; 573 lb AUW):

Never-exceed speed:	
A, B	97 knots (180 km/h; 111 mph)
Max cruising speed:	
A	81 knots (150 km/h; 93 mph)
B	65 knots (120 km/h; 74 mph)
Econ cruising speed:	
A	65 knots (120 km/h; 74 mph)
B	54-59 knots (100-110 km/h; 62-68 mph)
Max rate of climb at S/L: A	300 m (984 ft)/min
B	180 m (590 ft)/min
T-O run: A	60 m (197 ft)
B	200 m (656 ft)
T-O to 15 m (50 ft): A	100 m (328 ft)
B	400 m (1,312 ft)
Landing from 15 m (50 ft), zero wind:	
A	30 m (98 ft)
Landing run, zero wind: A	5 m (16 ft)
Max range, no reserves:	
A	97 nm (180 km; 112 miles)
B	75 nm (140 km; 87 miles)

MFI

MALMÖ FORSKNINGS & INNOVATIONS AB
(Malmö Research & Development Ltd)
Smedstorpsgatan, S-212 28 Malmö
Telephone: (040) 18 07 05
Telex: 12442 FOTEX S
Technical Manager: Bjorn Andreasson

ANDREASSON BA-12 SLANDAN (DRAGONFLY)

Mr Bjorn Andreasson (see Andreasson in this section) is well known as a designer of light aircraft for amateur construction. The BA-12 Slandan (Dragonfly) is his first microlight design; a prototype was built by students of a college in Malmö and flew in 1984. The Slandan is being handled by MFI (Malmö Forsknings & Innovations) AB and is at present being produced in kit form and as a completed aircraft by the Royal Swedish Aero Club. MFI had itself completed the first five aircraft as demonstrators.

The Slandan is of all-composites construction, using glassfibre, Kevlar and carbonfibre/Derakane, with the pilot seated in a pod fuselage beneath a tubular boom which carries the engine, battery, fuel, wings, and butterfly type tail unit with small ventral fin (replacing the originally designed inverted V tail unit). The wings have a new low-speed aerofoil section developed in Sweden, and are fitted with spar caps made from carbonfibre pultrusions. It was planned to use an 18·6 kW (25 hp) Lotus engine in the aircraft, but this appears to have been dropped in favour of alternative 21 kW (28 hp) König or 26 kW (35 hp) Rotax 447 engines. Fuel tank capacity is 19 litres (5 US gallons).

Dimensions, external:

Wing span	10·00 m (32 ft 9¾ in)
Length overall	5·00 m (16 ft 4¾ in)
Height overall	2·00 m (6 ft 6¾ in)

Weights and Loading:

Weight empty	135 kg (298 lb)
Fuel	20 kg (44 lb)
Max T-O weight	250 kg (551 lb)
Max power loading (König)	11·90 kg/kW (19·68 lb/hp)

Performance:

Max cruising speed	54 knots (100 km/h; 62 mph)
Stalling speed	22 knots (40 km/h; 25 mph)
Max rate of climb at S/L	245 m (805 ft)/min
T-O run	50 m (164 ft)
Range, with König engine	108 nm (200 km; 124 miles)

SWITZERLAND

BERGER

BERGER-HELICOPTER

CH 6515 Gudo TI
Telephone: (092) 64 21 71
DIRECTOR: Hans Berger

Mr Berger built and flew prototypes of two light helicopters, which were last described and illustrated in the 1984-85 *Jane's*. These were the BX-50A single-seater and the BX-110A two-seater. Mr Berger has since designed a new helicopter/convertiplane known as the Giro-Heli BX-111.

BERGER GIRO-HELI BX-111

Mr Berger's new design is the BX-111, a side by side two-seat high-speed convertiplane with coaxial two-blade rotors and a 'pusher' ducted fan at the tail. Work on the BX-111, which is shown in an accompanying illustration, was well advanced in early 1986, with design assistance from a retired former engineer of the Douglas Aircraft Company.

Construction of the BX-111 is of light alloy, including the rotor blades, which have an NACA 23012 aerofoil section and rotate at 500 rpm. For take-off, the 186·4 kW (250 hp) Wankel-Berger turbocharged rotary engine will drive the rotors. At a forward speed of 87 knots (161 km/h; 100 mph) the full power from the engine will be transferred automatically from the rotors to the variable-pitch ducted fan, after which the rotors will autorotate. Speed should thereby be increased to 152 knots (281 km/h; 175 mph). As soon as speed falls below 87 knots (161 km/h; 100 mph), power will be restored to the rotors.

DIMENSIONS, EXTERNAL:
- Rotor diameter (each) 6·20 m (20 ft 4 in)
- Fuselage: Length 6·40 m (21 ft 0 in)
  - Max width 2·20 m (7 ft 2½ in)
  - Height 2·65 m (8 ft 8⅓ in)

AREA:
- Rotor discs (each) 30·19 m² (324·97 sq ft)

WEIGHTS:
- Weight empty 495 kg (1,091 lb)
- Max T-O weight 862 kg (1,900 lb)

PERFORMANCE (estimated):
- Max level speed 152 knots (281 km/h; 175 mph)
- Max rate of climb at S/L 516 m (1,693 ft)/min
- Range with max fuel 241 nm (447 km; 278 miles)

BEZZOLA

GION BEZZOLA

c/o RSA-Switzerland, Route de Payerne 21, CH-1470 Estavayer-le-Lac

BEZZOLA GB-3 VETRO

Mr Gion Bezzola is the President of the RSA-Switzerland, that nation's experimental aircraft association. The 1985-86 *Jane's* carried a photograph on page 932 identified as the latest aircraft designed by Mr Bezzola, the GB-3 Vetro (HB-YCO). It is now known that the twin-engined aircraft illustrated was not the GB-3 Vetro, which was developed from the GB-2 Retro and is illustrated in this edition. No details of the GB-3 Vetro have been received, but by referring to the description of the GB-2 Retro in the 1983-84 *Jane's* it becomes clear that the Vetro is of the same general layout, though refined.

BRÄNDLI

MAX BRÄNDLI

Höheweg 2, CH 2553 Safnern
Telephone: (032) 55 18 28

BRÄNDLI BX-2 CHERRY

Mr Max Brändli and his son have designed and built a two-seat light aircraft known as the BX-2 Cherry. Construction of the prototype (HB-YBX) started in June 1979 and it made its first flight on 24 April 1982. Flight testing to gain certification in the Experimental category from the Swiss Air Ministry took approximately 25 flying hours, and this was awarded on 20 September 1982. By December 1985 the Cherry had accumulated 500 flying hours during 1,000 flights, including many cross-country flights all over Europe and to the polar circle.

Detailed plans for the Cherry became available in the Summer of 1984, written in German. By January 1986, sixty sets of plans had been sold to amateur constructors in Europe and the USA. The canopy and main spar are available in prefabricated form. Since 1983 the Cherry has won eleven awards, perhaps the most significant being the FAI's Henri Mignet Diploma which it received in New Delhi in 1985.

TYPE: Two-seat light aircraft.

AIRFRAME: Cantilever low-wing monoplane. Wing section NACA 747A415. Dihedral 4°. Incidence 3°. Sweepback at quarter-chord 0° 24′. Wing structure includes wooden spar and Styrofoam skin covered with glassfibre. Frise ailerons and flaps of foam and glassfibre construction. Wings fold for transportation and storage. Conventional fuselage, with wooden structure, plywood and glassfibre covered. Conventional tail unit, comprising fin and rudder and all-moving tailplane, of similar construction to wings. Tab on tailplane, which folds for transportation and storage.

LANDING GEAR: Retractable tricycle type. Manual actuation. All wheels remain partially exposed after retraction. Cantilever spring main legs of glassfibre construction. Rubber coil shock absorption for nosewheel. Similar size wheels on each unit, built by Mr Brändli. Each wheel fitted with 12 in diameter Vredestein tyre. Mainwheel tyre pressure 2 bars (29 lb/sq in). Nosewheel tyre pressure 1·7 bars (24·65 lb/sq in). Brändli-built wheel brakes.

POWER PLANT: One 48·5 kW (65 hp) Continental A65 flat-four engine, driving a Brändli-built two-blade fixed-pitch wooden propeller with spinner. Alternative engines include 52 kW (70 hp) Limbach L 2000. One fuel tank in forward fuselage, capacity 72 litres (15·8 Imp gallons). Refuelling point in forward fuselage.

ACCOMMODATION: Two seats side by side under forward sliding canopy. Baggage space behind seats. Ventilated.

SYSTEM: Electrical system includes 7Ah battery and 15W generator.

AVIONICS: Radio and VOR fitted.

DIMENSIONS, EXTERNAL:
- Wing span 7·00 m (22 ft 11½ in)
- Wing chord: at root 1·30 m (4 ft 3 in)
  - at tip 1·00 m (3 ft 3¼ in)
- Wing aspect ratio 5·7
- Length overall 5·23 m (17 ft 2 in)
- Width, wings folded 1·95 m (6 ft 4¾ in)
- Height overall 2·02 m (6 ft 7½ in)
- Tailplane span 2·40 m (7 ft 10½ in)
- Wheel track 1·80 m (5 ft 11 in)
- Wheelbase 1·25 m (7 ft 4½ in)
- Propeller diameter 1·60 m (5 ft 3 in)

AREA:
- Wings, gross 8·50 m² (91·5 sq ft)

WEIGHTS AND LOADINGS (A65 engine):
- Weight empty, equipped 310 kg (683 lb)
- Max payload 190 kg (419 lb)
- Max T-O and landing weight 550 kg (1,212 lb)
- Max wing loading 64·7 kg/m² (13·25 lb/sq ft)
- Max power loading 11·34 kg/kW (18·65 lb/hp)

PERFORMANCE (with A65 engine, at max T-O weight, except where indicated):
- Never-exceed speed 140 knots (260 km/h; 161 mph)
- Max level speed at 915 m (3,000 ft) 121 knots (225 km/h; 140 mph)
- Max cruising speed at 915 m (3,000 ft) 113 knots (210 km/h; 130 mph)
- Stalling speed, flaps down, engine idling, at AUW of 510 kg (1,125 lb) 46 knots (84 km/h; 53 mph)
- Max rate of climb at S/L 180 m (590 ft)/min
- Service ceiling 4,200 m (13,775 ft)
- T-O run 280 m (918 ft)
- T-O to 15 m (50 ft) 530 m (1,739 ft)
- Landing from 15 m (50 ft) 380 m (1,247 ft)
- Landing run 150 m (492 ft)
- Range with max fuel and max payload no reserves 475 nm (880 km; 546 miles)

BRÜGGER

MAX BRÜGGER

CH 1724 Zénauva
Telephone: (037) 33 29 20

Brief details of the Brügger Colibri 1 single-seat light aircraft, which flew for the first time on 30 October 1965, were given in the 1967-68 and 1971-72 *Jane's*.

More recent designs are the Colibri 2 and MB-3. Details and an illustration of the MB-3 can be found in the 1980-81 *Jane's*.

BRÜGGER MB-2 COLIBRI 2

Mr Brügger began design of the Colibri 2 in January 1966. Construction was started a year later, and the prototype flew for the first time on 1 May 1970. Plans are available to amateur constructors, and about 250 Colibri 2s were under construction or flying in Europe by early 1986.

TYPE: Single-seat homebuilt light aircraft.

AIRFRAME: Cantilever low-wing monoplane. Wing section NACA 23012. Dihedral from roots. Two-spar constant chord wings. Wings and ailerons built of spruce with fabric covering. No flaps or tabs. Plywood covered wooden fuselage. Cantilever all-wood tail unit. Rudder only; no fin. All-moving horizontal surfaces, with Flettner type elevators.

LANDING GEAR: Non-retractable tailwheel type, with coil spring shock absorption on main units. Mainwheels size 400 × 100, with streamline fairings. Tailwheel mounted on leaf spring. Mechanically operated disc brakes.

POWER PLANT: One 30 kW (40 hp) 1,600 cc Volkswagen engine (Brügger modification), driving a Brügger two-blade fixed-pitch wooden propeller with plastics coated blades. Fuel in single fuselage tank, capacity 33 litres (7·25 Imp gallons). Oil capacity 2·5 litres (0·55 Imp gallons).

ACCOMMODATION: Single seat under one-piece moulded transparent canopy, with quarterlights to rear.

DIMENSIONS, EXTERNAL:
- Wing span 6·00 m (19 ft 8¼ in)
- Wing chord, constant 1·40 m (4 ft 7 in)
- Length overall 4·80 m (15 ft 9 in)
- Height overall 1·60 m (5 ft 3 in)
- Tailplane span 2·00 m (6 ft 6¾ in)
- Wheel track 1·80 m (5 ft 11 in)
- Propeller diameter 1·38 m (4 ft 6⅓ in)

AREA:
- Wings, gross 8·20 m² (88·25 sq ft)

WEIGHTS AND LOADINGS:
- Weight empty 215 kg (474 lb)
- Max T-O and landing weight 330 kg (727 lb)
- Max wing loading 40·24 kg/m² (8·24 lb/sq ft)
- Max power loading 11·00 kg/kW (18·18 lb/hp)

PERFORMANCE (at max T-O weight):
- Max speed at 1,000 m (3,280 ft) 97 knots (180 km/h; 111 mph)
- Econ cruising speed (70% power) at 1,000 m (3,280 ft) 86 knots (160 km/h; 99 mph)
- Stalling speed 33 knots (60 km/h; 38 mph)
- Max rate of climb at S/L 180 m (590 ft)/min
- Service ceiling 4,500 m (14,760 ft)
- T-O and landing run 200 m (656 ft)
- Range with max fuel 270 nm (500 km; 310 miles)

COLANI

LUIGI COLANI

Flugzeugbau Rolf Müller, CH-5623 Boswil

COLANI PONTRESINA

Long renowned as a protagonist of advanced design, Mr Colani has proposed the Pontresina as an aircraft capable of exceeding the current world speed records for propeller driven aircraft. A mockup was exhibited at the 1985 Friedrichshafen Fair, and is shown in an accompanying illustration.

Few details are available, except that the Pontresina is intended to be powered by a Mazda eight-rotor Wankel type engine, developing 1,044 kW (1,400 hp) and driving two four-blade coaxial contra-rotating propellers of advanced form. An inscription on the side of the fuselage suggested that the airframe is intended to be made primarily of carbonfibre, with a speed of Mach 0·9 as the objective. Control surfaces appear to comprise full-span flaperons on the trailing-edge of the delta wings and a rudder inset in the ventral fin. There is a flush intake for engine cooling air at each side of the dorsal tail fin.

Wrongly identified in the Addenda to the 1985-86 *Jane's,* **this aircraft is the Krebser Twin Baby (HB-YCK). No details are available** *(Roland Eichenberger)*

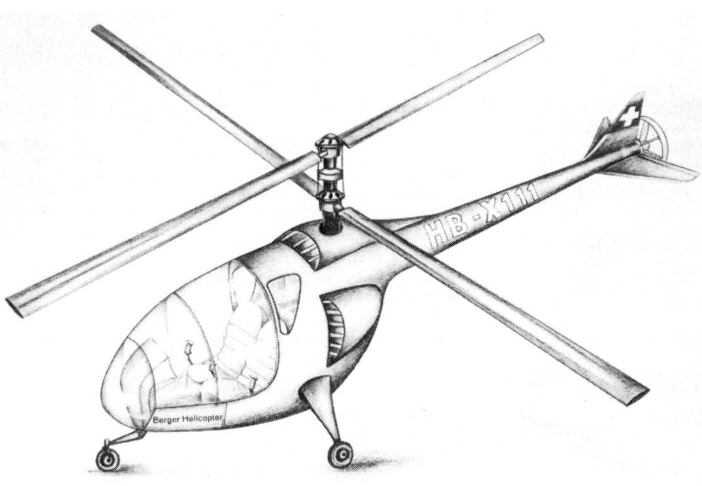

Artist's impression of the Berger BX-111 two-seat homebuilt convertiplane

Brändli BX-2 Cherry two-seat light aircraft *(J. M. G. Gradidge)*

Bezzola GB-3 Vetro homebuilt *(Roland Eichenberger)*

Brügger MB-2 Colibri 2 single-seat light aircraft *(R. Kunert)*

Sky-Patrol version of Sky-Craft AJS 2000 two-seat multi-purpose microlight

Mockup of Colani Pontresina high speed monoplane *(Wolfgang Wagner)*

SKY-CRAFT

SKY-CRAFT SA

MARKETING: SPICE SA, 1 Place du Marché, CH-1260 Nyon
Telephone: (022) 61 65 41
Telex: 27300 SPICE CH
WORKS: 38 Grand-Rue, CH-2732 Reconvilier
Telephone: (032) 91 15 11
Telex: 289367 NOTC CH

SKY-CRAFT AJS 2000

The AJS 2000 is a three-axis microlight claimed to be suitable for a wide variety of working roles as well as for recreational flying, by virtue of a variable wing camber system regulated by the use of interconnected landing and camber flaps, which greatly improves landing characteristics and gives the aircraft exceptional slow-flying performance. It is available in the following versions:

Sky-Farmer. Fully equipped for agricultural/health spraying (LV or ULV), with a 100 litre (22 Imp gallon) tank for chemicals and CIBA-Geigy spraygear. Tank easily replaceable by second seat when not required for spraying operations.

Sky-Hopper. Single-seat sport flying version, with lower powered engine.

Sky-Patrol. Military version, with Kevlar reinforced cockpit module. Applications include aerial surveillance and photography, with provision (at user's option) for weapon carriage.

Sky-Trainer. Dual control two-seater for training, liaison and parachuting.

Sky-Worker. Version able to carry 100 kg (220 lb) of payload, parachutable if required, in place of second seat. Load is located at CG, so that trim is not affected.

TYPE: Single/two-seat multi-purpose microlight.

AIRFRAME: High-wing monoplane, braced on each side by V struts. Typical tubular anti-corrosion mainframe structure (wind tunnel tested), with GRP fuselage pod and double surfaced Dacron covered wings. Conventional tail surfaces have single thickness covering. Standard three-axis control (ailerons, elevators and rudder) exercised by joystick and rudder pedals; integrated landing and camber flaps to enhance landing and slow-flying performance. Basic instrumentation and ballistic parachute standard. Options include additional instruments, VHF radio and cockpit heating system, plus appropriate mission equipment. Rigging time (two persons) 10 min.

LANDING GEAR: Non-retractable tricycle type, with all three wheels of similar size. Nosewheel steerable via rudder pedals. Optional floats and skis.

POWER PLANT: One 21/22·4 kW (28/30 hp) two-stroke engine in Sky-Hopper, or 37·3/38·8 kW (50/52 hp) two-cylinder two-stroke with dynamo starter in two-seat/mixed use versions, driving respectively a two- or three-blade pusher propeller. Fuel tank capacity 20 litres (4·4 Imp gallons) in single-seater, 30 litres (6·6 Imp gallons) in other versions. Provision for 20 litre (4·4 Imp gallon) auxiliary fuel tank.

ACCOMMODATION: Sky-Hopper has pilot's seat only; other versions have, at CG, provision for a second seat or payload/equipment platform.

DIMENSIONS, EXTERNAL (all versions):
Wing span 10·16 m (33 ft 4 in)

Wing aspect ratio 7·65
Length overall 5·95 m (19 ft 6¼ in)
AREA (all versions):
Wings, gross 13·5 m² (145·3 sq ft)
WEIGHTS AND LOADINGS (A: single-seat, no payload; B: mixed use versions):
Weight empty: A 125 kg (275 lb)
B 160 kg (353 lb)
Max T-O weight: A 250 kg (551 lb)
B 390 kg (860 lb)
Max wing loading: A 18·52 kg/m² (3·79 lb/sq ft)
B 28·89 kg/m² (5·92 lb/sq ft)
Max power loading: A 11·18 kg/kW (18·36 lb/hp)
B 10·47 kg/kW (17·20 lb/hp)
PERFORMANCE (A and B as above, except where indicated):
Cruising speed (75% power):
A 40 knots (75 km/h; 47 mph)
B 43 knots (80 km/h; 50 mph)
Cruising speed (55% power):
A 32 knots (60 km/h; 37 mph)
B 38 knots (70 km/h; 43 mph)
T-O speed, flaps up: A 22 knots (40 km/h; 25 mph)
B 27 knots (50 km/h; 31 mph)
T-O speed, flaps down: A 17 knots (30 km/h; 19 mph)
B 22 knots (40 km/h; 25 mph)
Landing speed, flaps up:
A, B 25 knots (45 km/h; 28 mph)
Landing speed, flaps down:
A, B 17 knots (30 km/h; 19 mph)
T-O run at S/L: A 30 m (100 ft)
B 40 m (132 ft)
Landing run: A 25 m (82 ft)
B 40 m (132 ft)
Range (Sky-Patrol):
standard fuel 81 nm (150 km; 93 miles)
auxiliary fuel 162 nm (300 km; 186 miles)
Endurance: A 2 h 20 min
B (except Sky-Patrol) 2 h 0 min
Sky-Patrol (standard fuel) 1 h 30 min
Sky-Patrol (auxiliary fuel) 3 h 0 min

SWISS AEROLIGHT

SWISS AEROLIGHT PRODUCTIONS

CP 22, Pt Lancy 1, 1213 Geneva
Telephone: (022) 93 37 22 and (022) 98 78 29
DIRECTOR: Dominique Loup

SWISS AEROLIGHT FUN FLY

Design of this microlight began in May 1983 and construction of a prototype started in the following month. The first flight took place on 15 September the same year. The Fun Fly is a side by side two-seater of simple construction, enabling one person to rig it for flight in 25 minutes from dismantled (transport) state. It is available in plans, kit, individual component part and ready assembled forms. By February 1986, many sets of plans had been sold and 69 kits/assembled aircraft ordered; at least 15 Fun Flys have flown.

TYPE: Two-seat single-engined microlight.

AIRFRAME: Cantilever high-wing monoplane. Basic open fuselage structure of AC-100 light alloy square-section tube. Wing of constant chord, made in two halves, of thick section and with 1° dihedral and 6° incidence. Plywood D section leading-edge; wooden main spar with ash booms and plywood webs; aluminium alloy tube rear spar; ribs of polystyrene and plywood; Dacron covering. Position of wing variable fore and aft to cater for one or two persons. Ailerons and tail surfaces of aluminium alloy and wood, Dacron covered. Variable incidence tailplane. Three-axis control (ailerons, elevators and rudder).

LANDING GEAR: Tricycle landing gear with all-terrain 40 × 8 cm tyres on mainwheels, 30 cm diameter tyre on nosewheel. Brake on nosewheel. Optional floats and skis.

POWER PLANT: One 39·5 kW (53 hp) Rotax 503 two-cylinder two-stroke engine, driving a two-blade wooden pusher propeller through 3:1 reduction gearing. Provision for alternative power plants weighing not more than 70 kg (154 lb). Two fuel tanks aft of seats, with capacity of 48 litres (10·5 Imp gallons). Provision for two further tanks of same capacity.

ACCOMMODATION: Two persons side by side. Space for carrying baggage or equipment such as tents, skis, a folding bicycle or windsurfing board. Optional extras include seat harness and cockpit fairing.

DIMENSIONS, EXTERNAL:
Wing span 11·20 m (36 ft 9 in)
Wing aspect ratio 7
Wing chord, constant 1·50 m (4 ft 11 in)
Length overall 5·50 m (18 ft 0½ in)
Height overall 2·20 m (7 ft 2½ in)
Propeller diameter 1·55 m (5 ft 1 in)
AREA:
Wings, gross 17·50 m² (188·4 sq ft)
WEIGHTS AND LOADINGS:
Weight empty 175 kg (386 lb)
Max T-O weight 375 kg (826 lb)
Max wing loading 21·4 kg/m² (4·38 lb/sq ft)
Max power loading 9·50 kg/kW (15·58 lb/hp)
PERFORMANCE:
Never-exceed speed 86 knots (160 km/h; 99 mph)
Max level speed 65 knots (120 km/h; 74 mph)
Max cruising speed 57 knots (105 km/h; 65 mph)
Econ cruising speed 43 knots (80 km/h; 50 mph)
Stalling speed 30 knots (55 km/h; 35 mph)
Max rate of climb at S/L 305 m (1,000 ft)/min
T-O and landing run 50 m (164 ft)
Service ceiling 4,500 m (14,775 ft)
Range 215 nm (400 km; 248 miles)
Best glide ratio 15
Min rate of sink 90 m (295 ft)/min
g limits −9·5/−4·5 ultimate

UNION OF SOVIET SOCIALIST REPUBLICS

AEROPRAKT

AEROPRAKT (Youth Design Bureau)

The Aeroprakt was established to design and build light aircraft for sporting use. Having completed seven previous powered and unpowered aircraft, plus a hydrofoil and a hydroplane, work began in 1982 on a light single-seat aeroplane with a Vikhr-30 engine, under the designation A-10. Initial design was by I. Vakhrushev and M. Volynets, and it was decided subsequently to fit a more powerful 30 kW (40 hp) CZ modified motorcycle engine to the prototype, which was completed in the Spring of 1983.

Following initial trials, reduction gear and a larger diameter propeller were fitted, and the aircraft was redesignated A-11M Hamlet. The modified aircraft proved to have substantially improved handling qualities and performance, notably in terms of rate of climb.

AEROPRAKT A-11M HAMLET

The A-11M has a mix of conventional and composite construction. It is likely that the present design, or a derivative, will eventually be put into production.

TYPE: Single-seat aerobatic microlight aircraft.

AIRFRAME: Cantilever low-wing monoplane. Constant chord wings have a glassfibre main spar and expanded foam ribs, covered by two layers of glassfibre. Wing section Wortmann FXS 02-196 (modified). Dihedral 3°. Full-span auxiliary aerofoil flaperons, with carbonfibre spar, foam core and glassfibre skin. Wooden fuselage, with pine longerons and plywood skins. Forward bulkhead of 0·5 mm duralumin with honeycomb infill. Glassfibre engine cowling. Conventional tail unit with swept vertical surfaces, of glassfibre construction except for fabric covering on rudder and rear portion of horizontal surfaces. Three-axis control (flaperons, all-moving tailplane and rudder). Trim tab on port flaperon.

LANDING GEAR: Non-retractable tricycle type. Cantilever spring plastics main legs; oleo-pneumatic shock absorber in steerable nose gear. All tyres size 250 × 110 mm. Wheel fairings.

POWER PLANT: One 30 kW (40 hp) CZ 400 cc single-cylinder modified motorcycle engine, with reduction gear to a two-blade propeller with spinner. Fuel tank capacity 24 litres (5·3 Imp gallons) forward of cockpit.

ACCOMMODATION: Pilot only in enclosed cockpit, beneath forward-hinged Perspex canopy with carbonfibre frame.

DIMENSIONS, EXTERNAL:
Wing span 5·30 m (17 ft 4½ in)
Length overall 4·40 m (14 ft 5¼ in)
AREA:
Wings, gross 3·60 m² (38·75 sq ft)
WEIGHTS AND LOADINGS:
Weight empty 124 kg (273 lb)
Max T-O weight 214 kg (472 lb)
Max wing loading 59·4 kg/m² (12·18 lb/sq ft)
Max power loading 7·13 kg/kW (11·80 lb/hp)
PERFORMANCE:
Max level speed 81 knots (50 km/h; 93 mph)
Cruising speed 54 knots (00 km/h; 62 mph)
Max rate of climb at S/L 46 m (150 ft)/min

AEROPRAKT A-5 GIDRA

Another project from this youth design bureau is the A-5 Gidra, a single-seat high-wing flying-boat powered by a 26 kW (35 hp) Buran engine with pusher propeller. Designed under the leadership of Y. Yakovlev and V. Miroshnik, it has an open cockpit for the pilot. No more is known at the present time.

ANTONOV

ANTONOV SLAVUTITCH M-1

This powered version of the Slavutitch-UT (see Hang Gliders subsection) made its first flight on 1 August 1982. The trike unit has 280 × 85 mm mainwheels and a 200 × 80 mm nosewheel, open pilot seat, instrument panel, and overhead joystick control for wing-warping. Engine is a 17·2 kW (23 hp) Neptun two-cylinder two-stroke, with reduction drive to an AL-9 two-blade pusher propeller. Fuel tank capacity 8 kg (17·6 lb), or approx 10 litres (2·2 Imp gallons).

DIMENSIONS, EXTERNAL:
Wing span 8·80 m (28 ft 10½ in)
Wing aspect ratio 4·45
Length overall 4·40 m (14 ft 5¼ in)
Height overall 3·40 m (11 ft 2 in)
Propeller diameter 0·91 m (3 ft 0 in)
AREA:
Wings, gross 17·40 m² (187·3 sq ft)
WEIGHTS:
Weight empty 74·5 kg (164 lb)
Max pilot weight 87·5 kg (193 lb)
Max T-O weight 170 kg (375 lb)
PERFORMANCE:
Max level speed 35 knots (65 km/h; 40 mph)
Max cruising speed 30 knots (55 km/h; 34 mph)
Stalling speed 22 knots (40 km/h; 25 mph)
Max rate of climb at S/L 360 m (1,181 ft)/min
Service ceiling 500 m (1,640 ft)
Range 16 nm (30 km; 18·5 miles)
Min rate of sink, power off 120 m (393 ft)/min

BYELYI

BYELYI A-6

Little is known of this microlight, which is a strut braced high-wing single-seater powered by a 26 kW (35 hp) Buran engine with pusher propeller. Of probable all-composites construction, it has a pod and boom fuselage, conventional tail unit and tricycle landing gear. Accommodation is open, with a faired instrument panel at the nose.

DIMENSIONS, EXTERNAL:
Wing span 6·90 m (22 ft 8 in)
Length overall 4·50 m (14 ft 9 in)
WEIGHT:
Max T-O weight 198 kg (436 lb)
PERFORMANCE:
Max level speed 97 knots (180 km/h; 112 mph)

DMITRIEV

V. DMITRIEV

Frunze

DMITRIEV Kh-14A

The Kh-14A was the smallest aircraft exhibited at the 1984 SLA meeting, but did not fly at that time. Designed and built by Mr V. Dmitriev, it is powered by a 31·3 kW (42 hp) Chezyet modified motorcycle engine and has an empty weight of 45 kg (99 lb). Wing span, length and wing area are 5·18 m (17 ft), 3·23 m (10 ft 7 in) and 1·90 m² (20·45 sq ft) respectively.

Swiss Aerolight Fun Fly two-seat microlight *(Brian M. Service)*

Aeroprakt A-11M Hamlet single-seat microlight

LAK (Oshkinis) BROK-1M Garnis single-seat microlight

FROLOV

V FROLOV

FROLOV MONOPLANE

Mr V Frolov exhibited an enclosed cockpit high-wing monoplane at the 1984 SLA meeting, powered by a 63·4 kW (85 hp) MT-8 engine. Almost nothing is known of this aircraft, except that it has a max T-O weight of 270 kg (595 lb) and a max level speed of 70 knots (130 km/h; 81 mph).

KOROLYEV

Y. KOROLYEV

Pugachev, near Balakovo

KOROLYEV STIMUL-10

This microlight aircraft was designed by school students at Pugachev under the leadership of Mr Y. Korolyev. The only known details are that it has a 31·3 kW (42 hp) Chezyet modified motorcycle engine, a wing area of 4·30 m² (46·3 sq ft) and a max T-O weight of 160 kg (353 lb).

LAK

LITOVSKAYA AVIATSIONNAYA KONSTRUKTSIYA (Lithuanian Aircraft Construction)

Prenaisk, Litovsk (Lithuania)

OFFICERS: see Sailplanes section

Lithuania has a strong recreational aircraft following, as demonstrated when twenty different aircraft gathered for a meeting near the Neman River. Although only brief details are available of most Lithuanian homebuilt and microlight aircraft, technical competence is viewed as high.

Romas and Bronius Vaineikis have built several aircraft, including the VRB-5 helicopter, VRB-6 tandem-wing aeroplane with 'flaperons', and a powered version of the BRO-11 glider with twin engines. G. Konchus and P. Shakalis from Kaunas have built a microlight biplane; and I. Yakavichus and R. Shekshtial from Vilnius were awarded the first prize at the Neman meeting for their Laumzhirgis, which has interchangeable wings to convert the aircraft from a monoplane to a biplane.

Further rotating-wing aircraft have been built by Y. Valunas from Prenai, whose V-1 incorporates an engine and transmission of his own construction, and electrician E. Zhilius from Taurag. The latter's aircraft has a welded titanium airframe and is powered by a 31·3 kW (42 hp) engine.

The following details relate specifically to the single-engined BROK-1M Garnis, which has reportedly been flown by more than 300 persons.

LAK BROK-1M GARNIS

The BROK-1M is a powered microlight version of the Oshkinis BRO-23KR Garnis primary training glider (see Sailplanes section), with modifications that include a tricycle landing gear with cantilever main units. Designed by Bronius Oshkinis, with the assistance of Cheslovas Kishonas, the aircraft is powered by a 17·2 kW (23 hp) Vikhr air-cooled marine engine, mounted on a tubular pylon above the wing, with direct drive to a pusher propeller. Like the BRO-23KR, it has an open cockpit and can be operated on a central skid or tricycle landing gear.

DIMENSIONS, EXTERNAL:

Wing span	8·2 m (26 ft 11 in)
Length overall	5·1 m (17 ft 1½ in)

AREA:

Wings, gross	10·4 m² (111·9 sq ft)

WEIGHTS AND LOADINGS:

Weight empty	115 kg (253 lb)
Max T-O weight	195 kg (430 lb)
Max wing loading	18·75 kg/m² (3·84 lb/sq ft)
Max power loading	11·34 kg/kW (18·70 lb/hp)

PERFORMANCE:

Max level speed	54 knots (100 km/h; 62 mph)
Stalling speed	27 knots (50 km/h; 31 mph)

SHCHEGLOV

V. SHCHEGLOV

SHCHEGLOV MIKRO-2M

Mr V. Shcheglov has designed and built a low-wing monoplane known as the Mikro-2M, with a 27 kW (36 hp) engine and pusher propeller, and open accommodation for the pilot only. The few known details follow:

DIMENSIONS, EXTERNAL:

Wing span	7·50 m (24 ft 7 in)
Length overall	4·36 m (14 ft 4 in)

WEIGHTS AND LOADING:

Weight empty	127 kg (280 lb)
Max T-O weight	210 kg (463 lb)
Max power loading	7·78 kg/kW (12·86 lb/hp)

UNITED KINGDOM

AEOLUS

AEOLUS AVIATION

DESIGNER: A. K. McGrath

The Aeolus single-seat microlight was designed by Mr Kevin McGrath and flown for the first time in October 1982. It was claimed to be the first British microlight with a fully enclosed fuselage and cockpit. A small series was built. A two-seat variant with side by side accommodation was reportedly under development, but no news of this has been received and the address for the company that appeared in the 1985-86 *Jane's* is no longer current. Full details of the Aeolus can be found in the 1985-86 *Jane's*.

AEROTECH

AEROTECH INTERNATIONAL LTD

Unit 2, Buckingham Road Industrial Estate, Brackley, Northants
Telephone: (0280) 700289
Telex: 946240 CWEASY G
DIRECTORS:
C. A. Taylor
M. J. McBride

The 1985-86 *Jane's* carried details of the MW5 Sorcerer under the heading of its designer, Mr Michael W. J. Whittaker. This microlight is currently marketed by Aerotech International, which is offering it in ready-assembled form. A few MW5 Sorcerers are also under construction from the plans offered previously by Mr Whittaker.

Mr Whittaker has also produced a new aircraft known as the MW6, which is detailed under "Whittaker" in this section.

AEROTECH/WHITTAKER MW5 SORCERER

TYPE: Single-seat microlight aircraft; conforms to FAI/CAA requirements.

AIRFRAME: Strut braced high-wing monoplane. Constant chord rigid wings, of NACA 4412 aerofoil section, with dihedral and 1° washout. Bracing strut on each side. Aluminium alloy spar tubes and drag struts, plywood ribs with spruce capstrips, and fabric covering. Fuselage main frame of aluminium alloy. Bullet nose fairing with windscreen. Three-axis control (ailerons, rudder and elevator), with galvanised steel control cables. Rigging time 20 min.

LANDING GEAR: Tricycle type, with unsprung steerable nosewheel and mainwheels. Wheel/tyre sizes 350 × 4 (nose) and 350 × 6 (main). Brakes, wheel fairings, floats and skis optional.

POWER PLANT: One 26·1 kW (35 hp) Fuji Robin EC34 engine, with reduction drive to a two-blade wooden propeller or one 44·7 kW (60 hp) Fuji Robin EC40 with 2·8:1 reduction drive. Fuel tank capacity 30 litres (6·6 Imp gallons).

ACCOMMODATION: Pilot only, in open position behind nose fairing and windscreen.

AVIONICS: Radio optional.

DIMENSIONS, EXTERNAL:
Wing span 8·53 m (28 ft 0 in)
Wing aspect ratio 5·6
Length overall 5·03 m (16 ft 6 in)
Height overall 2·51 m (8 ft 3 in)
Propeller diameter 1·37 m (4 ft 6 in)

AREA:
Wings, gross 13·01 m² (140·0 sq ft)

WEIGHTS AND LOADINGS (60 hp engine):
Weight empty 140 kg (308 lb)
Pilot weight range 45-90 kg (100-200 lb)
Max T-O weight 265 kg (584 lb)
Max wing loading 20·37 kg/m² (4·17 lb/sq ft)
Max power loading 5·93 kg/kW (9·73 lb/hp)

PERFORMANCE (60 hp engine, at max T-O weight):
Never-exceed speed 87 knots (161 km/h; 100 mph)
Max level speed 60 knots (111 km/h; 69 mph)
Max cruising speed 58 knots (107 km/h; 67 mph)
Econ cruising speed 50 knots (92 km/h; 57 mph)
Stalling speed 28 knots (52 km/h; 33 mph)
Max rate of climb at S/L 427 m (1,400 ft)/min
T-O run 40 m (131 ft)
Landing run 60 m (197 ft)
Range with max fuel 173 nm (320 km; 199 miles)
Endurance with max fuel 1 h 30 min
g limits +4/−2
Best glide ratio 9

CFM

COOK FLYING MACHINES (trading as CFM Metal-Fax Ltd)

Unit 2D, Eastlands Industrial Estate, Leiston, Suffolk IP16 4LL
Telephone: 0728 832353
Telex: 987703 CHACOM G
DIRECTORS:
David G. Cook (Managing)
T. M. Plewman

CFM SHADOW

The prototype Shadow was designed, built and flight tested in 1983 by Mr David Cook. On 4 August 1983 it set an FAI world record of 68·18 knots (126·36 km/h; 78·52 mph) for speed over a 3 km course. This was followed on 3 March 1984 by a distance record of 294·56 nm (545·52 km; 338·97 miles) for a flight from Parham, Suffolk, to St Jude, Cornwall.

Production of the first batch of five Shadows began in January 1984. Nineteen aircraft had been produced by December 1985 and the Shadow is also available in kit form, in four separate stages. Type approval to BCAR CAP482-Section S was gained in May 1985. An optional dual control version received CAA certification in January 1986. A Shadow was fourth overall in the 1985 World Championships at Millau in France, and Shadows took first and second places in the 1985 Norwich Air Race.

ULV cropspraying trials have demonstrated the suitability of the Shadow in this role. A multi-function surveillance fit for photography, video recording, and closed-circuit TV microwave transmission to a command vehicle/station (see ASVEC entry in RPVs and Targets section), is also available.

TYPE: Single/two-seat microlight aircraft; conforms to FAI and UK CAA requirements.

AIRFRAME: Strut braced high-wing monoplane. Aluminium alloy airframe, with cantilever wing, strut supported. Wings have foam/glassfibre ribs with plywood skinning on forward section and double surface polyester covering. Fuselage pod of glassfibre and honeycomb laminates, and aluminium tube tailboom. Twin fins on tailplane; large ventral rudder. Three-axis control (ailerons, elevator and rudder); wing flaps also fitted. Options include an airframe recovery parachute system and a custom-built trailer/hangar.

LANDING GEAR: Non-retractable tricycle type, with glassfibre rod main legs, and 350 × 6 mainwheels with differential brakes; size 300 × 4 castoring nosewheel is bungee sprung. Tailskid under base of rudder. Options include floats.

POWER PLANT: One 30 kW (40 hp) 437 cc Rotax 447 two-cylinder two-stroke engine, with 2·58:1 reduction drive to a two-blade wooden pusher propeller. Standard fuel tank has 23 litre (5 Imp gallon) capacity; optional second tank of 72·7 litres (16 Imp gallons) capacity.

ACCOMMODATION: Pilot and optional second person in tandem in enclosed cockpits, with polycarbonate canopies. Dual controls optional.

DIMENSIONS, EXTERNAL:
Wing span 10·03 m (32 ft 11 in)
Wing aspect ratio 6·58
Length overall 6·40 m (21 ft 0 in)
Height overall 1·73 m (5 ft 8 in)
Propeller diameter 1·30 m (4 ft 3 in)

AREA:
Wings, gross 15·0 m² (162·0 sq ft)

WEIGHTS AND LOADINGS:
Weight empty 150 kg (331 lb)
Pilot weight range 55-90 kg (121-198 lb)
Max passenger/payload weight 90 kg (198 lb)
Max T-O weight 348 kg (767 lb)
Max wing loading 23·2 kg/m² (4·73 lb/sq ft)
Max power loading 11·60 kg/kW (19·18 lb/hp)

PERFORMANCE (at max T-O weight):
Never-exceed speed 93 knots (173 km/h; 108 mph)
Max level speed 82 knots (153 km/h; 95 mph)
Max cruising speed 65 knots (121 km/h; 75 mph)
Econ cruising speed 56 knots (105 km/h; 65 mph)
Min flying speed 33 knots (62 km/h; 38 mph)
Max rate of climb at S/L 213 m (700 ft)/min
Service ceiling (without oxygen) 3,050 m (10,000 ft)
T-O run 90 m (295 ft)
Landing run, with braking 75 m (246 ft)
Range: standard fuel 113 nm (209 km; 130 miles)
with additional tank 521 nm (965 km; 600 miles)
g limits +6/−3 static, ultimate

COATES

J. R. COATES

The Spinney, Breachwood Green, Hitchin, Hertfordshire SG4 8PL

Mr Coates has had a long association with homebuilt aircraft, his Luton Minor with Bristol Cherub III engine (G-AMAW) having been the first British homebuilt completed after the Second World War. This Minor is still owned and flown by Mr Coates. More recently he designed and built a two-seat light aircraft known as the S.A.II Swalesong, which was described fully in the 1975-76 *Jane's*. Drawings to allow amateur construction are not available, but a simplified version, the S.A.III, has been developed and was said to be suitable for homebuilding. No recent news of this aircraft has, however, been received. Full details of the S.A.III Swalesong can be found in the 1985-86 *Jane's*.

FLEXI-FORM

FLEXI-FORM SKYSAILS (Division of Lite Air Industries Ltd)

Brown Street Mill, Macclesfield, Cheshire SK11 6SA
CHIEF EXECUTIVE: M. Hurtley

FLEXI-FORM DUAL STRIKER TRIKE

Flexi-Form produces wings in its Striker range for adoption to trike units produced by other manufacturers and also offers the complete Dual Striker Trike microlight for export. The Striker wing has a 'tailed' sail. Several hundred Striker wings have been built; production of the complete two-seat microlight has been modest by comparison.

The address given may no longer be current.

TYPE: Two-seat microlight aircraft; conforms to FAI/CAA (BCAR Section S). Also available as FAI Class 1 hang glider, without trike unit.

AIRFRAME: Main frame of aluminium alloy and steel, with vinyl coated stainless steel cables. Wing is covered with double thickness Terylene over 60 per cent of the sail area and incorporates an integral horizontal tail for added stability. Standard features include kingpost, ribs, preformed battens, ripstop webbing on trailing-edge, floating keel pocket and adjustable camber. Glassfibre 'fuselage' fairing optional. Control is by wing tilt/weight shift. Optional equipment includes cockpit fairing, steering damper and emergency parachute system.

LANDING GEAR: Tricycle type, with 14 × 3 in mainwheels and tyres. Same size steerable nosewheel, with brake. Rubber in compression suspension.

POWER PLANT (optional): One 35·8 kW (48 hp) 440 cc Fuji Robin engine, with 2·3:1 reduction drive to a two-blade wooden pusher propeller. Fuel tank capacity 26·5 litres (5·8 Imp gallons).

ACCOMMODATION: Pilot and passenger in tandem in fully exposed position except for optional nose fairing.

DIMENSIONS, EXTERNAL:
Wing span 11·35 m (37 ft 3 in)
Wing aspect ratio 6·5
Length overall 4·93 m (16 ft 2 in)
Leading-edge length (hang glider) 6·05 m (19 ft 10 in)
Keel length (hang glider) 3·66 m (12 ft 0 in)
Height overall 3·96 m (13 ft 0 in)
Propeller diameter 1·57 m (5 ft 2 in)

AREA:
Wings, gross 19·88 m² (214·0 sq ft)

WEIGHTS AND LOADINGS:
Weight empty 146 kg (322 lb)
Pilot weight range 55-180 kg (121-397 lb)
Max T-O weight (microlight) 339 kg (747 lb)
Max wing loading 17·04 kg/m² (3·49 lb/sq ft)
Max power loading 9·47 kg/kW (15·57 lb/hp)

PERFORMANCE (at max T-O weight):
Max level speed 48 knots (88 km/h; 55 mph)
Max cruising speed 43 knots (80 km/h; 50 mph)
Econ cruising speed 40 knots (74 km/h; 46 mph)
Stalling speed 25 knots (47 km/h; 29 mph)
T-O to 15 m (50 ft) 180 m (590 ft)
Landing from 15 m (50 ft) 190 m (625 ft)
Range with max fuel 150 nm (278 km; 172 miles)
Endurance with max fuel 4 h
g limits +6/−4 ultimate

FLIGHT RESEARCH

FLIGHT RESEARCH

Rochester House, Ashfield Crescent, Ross-on-Wye, Herefordshire HR9 5PH
Telephone: 0989 67678

FLIGHT RESEARCH NOMAD 425 and NOMAD TRIBE

The Nomad is a powered trike unit for use with a Solar Wings Typhoon S4 (medium) 15·42 m² (166·0 sq ft) hang glider wing. It is unusual in having a prone pilot position and tailwheel (reverse tricycle) landing gear. The power plant for the prototype was a 140 cc Solo engine, with 3·5:1 reduction gear, driving a folding two-blade pusher propeller of 1·30 m (4 ft 3 in) diameter.

The latest pilot-only version is the Nomad 425F, which uses a 19·4 kW (26 hp) JPX PUL 425 engine without reduction gear to the two-blade pusher propeller. It retains

Aerotech/Whittaker MW5 Sorcerer microlight *(Edwin A. Shackleton)*

Flexi-Form Dual Striker Trike microlight

CFM Shadow single/two-seat microlight

Prototype Gardner T-M Scout

control by weight shift and ground steering via the rear wheel.

The Nomad Tribe is similar to the Nomad 425F but uses the 16·72 m² (180·0 sq ft) Solar Wings Typhoon S4 (large) wing to make possible the carriage of a second person. At the time of writing the Nomad Tribe was in prototype stage.

Maximum level speed of the Nomad 425F has been quoted as 44 knots (82 km/h; 51 mph) and range 121 nm (225 km; 140 miles).

FLYLITE

FLYLITE (EAST ANGLIA)

Mattishall Road, East Dereham, Norfolk NR20 3BU
Telephone: 0362 4907

FLYLITE SUPER SCOUT

The single-seat Super Scout is a developed version of the Australian Wheeler Scout microlight (see 1984-85 *Jane's*). Modifications include a glassfibre cockpit pod and the incorporation of an improved wing-warping system for roll control, operated by cables and pushrods. The power plant is a 15·7 kW (21 hp) Fuji Robin EC25PS with 2·2:1 reduction drive to a two-blade 1·22 m (4 ft 0 in) diameter tractor propeller. Fuel capacity 6 litres (1·3 Imp gallons).

DIMENSIONS, EXTERNAL:
- Wing span: 8·77 m (28 ft 9¼ in)
- Wing aspect ratio: 7·6
- Length overall: 5·35 m (17 ft 6½ in)
- Height overall: 1·94 m (6 ft 4½ in)

AREA:
- Wings, gross: 10·10 m² (108·7 sq ft)

WEIGHTS AND LOADINGS:
- Weight empty: 69 kg (152 lb)
- Max T-O weight: 162 kg (357 lb)
- Max wing loading: 16·0 kg/m² (3·28 lb/sq ft)
- Max power loading: 10·32 kg/kW (17·0 lb/hp)

PERFORMANCE:
- Never-exceed speed: 65 knots (120 km/h; 75 mph)
- Max level speed: 39 knots (72 km/h; 45 mph)
- Stalling speed: 19 knots (36 km/h; 22 mph)
- Max rate of climb at S/L: 76 m (250 ft)/min
- T-O run: 60 m (200 ft)
- Landing run: 30 m (100 ft)
- Range with max fuel: 52 nm (96 km; 60 miles)
- *g* limits: ±3 ultimate
- Best glide ratio: 8

GARDNER

DEGA APPLIED TECHNOLOGY

114 Wymondley Road, Hitchen, Hertfordshire SG4 9PX
Telephone: 0462 57474
Telex: 827547 CG BUS G REF DEGA
DIRECTOR: Derek Gardner

GARDNER T-M SCOUT

The Gardner T-M Scout is a single-engined wire braced low aspect ratio biplane, based (at two-thirds scale) on the US Thomas-Morse S-4 series of advanced trainers built in 1916-18. Although classed as a microlight, it is a truly small light aeroplane intended for experienced pilots. Design began in 1980 and construction of a prototype was started in 1981. This flew for the first time in 1985, when the construction of a pre-production aircraft was initiated. After CAA certification has been completed, and flight trials concluded, complete kits of part finished materials will be marketed for home construction, with an assembly time of 150 to 200 hours.

TYPE: Single-seat microlight biplane; conforms to BCAR section S-CAP 482.

AIRFRAME: Conventional biplane wings of grade A spruce, Polish pine and aluminium alloy (ribs); 65% double surface covered with lightweight woven heat-shrunk material, clear doped. Wing thickness/chord ratio 7%. Dihedral 3° on lower wings only. Incidence 6° on upper wings, 3° on lower wings. No sweep. Galvanised steel cables. Fuselage of woven glass laminate bonded with polyester resin. Tail unit structure and covering similar to wings. Three-axis control (wing warping, elevators and rudder) by conventional stick and rudder pedals. Tailplane incidence ground adjustable.

LANDING GEAR: Non-retractable tailskid type. Mainwheels size 20 × 2, pressure 3·1-3·4 bars (45-50 lb/sq in). Bungee suspension. No brakes. Aerofoil surface between mainwheels.

POWER PLANT: One 18 kW (24 hp) König SC 430 three-cylinder aircooled radial two-stroke engine, driving a Gardner two-blade fixed-pitch wooden propeller. 2·2:1 reduction gear being fitted in early 1986. Specially designed exhaust silencer. Fuel capacity 9 litres (2 Imp gallons).

ACCOMMODATION: Pilot only in open cockpit with windscreen. Safety harness standard.

SYSTEM: 12V electrical system.

DIMENSIONS, EXTERNAL:
- Wing span: upper: 5·74 m (18 ft 10 in)
  - lower: 5·16 m (16 ft 11 in)
- Wing chord: upper: 1·09 m (3 ft 7 in)
  - lower: 0·91 m (3 ft 0 in)
- Wing aspect ratio: 5·02
- Length overall: 4·32 m (14 ft 2 in)
- Height overall: 1·80 m (5 ft 11 in)
- Tailplane span: 1·93 m (6 ft 4 in)
- Wheel track: 1·07 m (3 ft 6 in)
- Wheelbase: 3·15 m (10 ft 4 in)
- Propeller diameter: direct drive: 1·37 m (4 ft 6 in)
  - with reduction gear: 1·47 m (4 ft 10 in)

AREA:
- Wings, gross: 10·03 m² (108·0 sq ft)

WEIGHTS AND LOADINGS:
- Weight empty (prototype): 70 kg (154 lb)
- Pilot weight range: 59-90 kg (130-198 lb)
- Max design T-O weight: 204 kg (450 lb)
- Max wing loading: 20·4 kg/m² (4·17 lb/sq ft)
- Max power loading: 11·4 kg/kW (18·75 lb/hp)

PERFORMANCE (at max design T-O weight):
- Never-exceed speed: 64 knots (119 km/h; 74 mph)
- Max level speed: 54 knots (100 km/h; 62 mph)
- Max cruising speed: 45 knots (83 km/h; 52 mph)
- Econ cruising speed: 42 knots (78 km/h; 48 mph)
- Stalling speed, engine idling: 29 knots (54 km/h; 34 mph)
- Max rate of climb at S/L: 122 m (400 ft)/min
- T-O run: 27 m (90 ft)
- T-O to 15 m (50 ft): 223 m (730 ft)
- Landing from 15 m (50 ft): 260 m (850 ft)
- Landing run: 46 m (150 ft)
- Range with max standard fuel: 34 nm (64 km; 40 miles)
- Range with max payload: 27 nm (51 km; 32 miles)
- *g* limits: +6/−3 ultimate

HORNET

HORNET MICROLIGHTS (TEMPLEWARD LTD)

Bankfoot Mills, Wibsey Bank, Bankfoot, Bradford, Yorkshire BD6 3JU
Telephone: 0274 308642
DIRECTOR: R. R. Wolfenden
AERONAUTICAL ENGINEER: R. Pattrick

This company markets a range of 'powered trike' units suitable for fitting to proprietary hang glider wings such as the Gyr, Cutlass (including two-seater), Sabre, Nimrod, Raven and Striker. The resulting microlights are designated as follows:

Hornet Standard. Single-seater, available now with a 20 kW (27 hp) Rotax 277 engine and electric starting. Reduction drive to two-blade wooden pusher propeller. Fuel tank capacity 12 litres (2·6 Imp gallons). Available for export only.

Hornet Executive. Improved single-seater, with 26 kW (35 hp) Rotax 377 engine. Available for export only.

Hornet Dual Trainer Raven. This current microlight has been developed from the Hornet Dual Trainer, which was itself formerly known as the Supreme. The Supreme, the design of which began in late 1981, was fitted with a Cutlass wing and Fuji engine. Construction of the prototype started in early 1982 and this flew for the first time in March of that year. Construction of production aircraft began shortly afterwards, and the first of them flew in July 1982.

Hornet Invader. The original Hornet Invader remains available for export only. The latest modified Hornet Invader was expected to be granted section S airworthiness clearance by Summer 1986. It incorporates the Raven double-surface wing, a Rotax 447 engine, and a redesigned cockpit for improved aerodynamics and pilot comfort.

Optional extras on the above, where not fitted as standard, include magnesium alloy wheels, brakes, chromium plated joints, glassfibre reinforced polyester resin cockpit (single-seaters only), electric engine start, auxiliary fuel tank(s), and ski landing gear.

HORNET EXECUTIVE

DIMENSIONS, EXTERNAL:

Wing span	9·96 m (32 ft 8 in)
Wing aspect ratio	6·47
Length overall	2·44 m (8 ft 0 in)
Height overall	3·23 m (10 ft 7 in)
Propeller diameter	1·37 m (4 ft 6 in)

AREA:

Wings, gross	15·33 m² (165·0 sq ft)

WEIGHT:

Weight empty	81·6 kg (180 lb)

PERFORMANCE:

Stalling speed, power off	16-18 knots (29-33 km/h; 18-20 mph)
T-O run	18 m (60 ft)
Landing run	24 m (80 ft)
Endurance with max fuel	2 h 30 min
Best glide ratio	8

HORNET INVADER

Design of the original Hornet Invader started in September 1982 and construction of a prototype began in the following December. This prototype flew for the first time in February 1983 and the building of pre-production aircraft started in March of that year. Full production began in April 1983, and the first production aircraft flew in the following month.

The Hornet Invader is a two-seater with an enclosed cockpit, independent suspension on all wheels, and ski gear as an option. It is available for export only. An updated version is described separately.

TYPE: Two-seat microlight aircraft.

AIRFRAME: Flexi-Form Striker or Puma Sprint hang glider wing, with typical kingpost and cable bracing. Kingpost extends beneath wing to support a glassfibre and polyester fuselage pod for occupants, power plant and landing gear. The pod is flared at the base to provide fairings over the mainwheels, which are road wheels, permitting the de-rigged aircraft to be towed behind a motorcar. Steering of aircraft is by conventional hang glider A frame crossbar.

LANDING GEAR: Non-retractable tricycle type. Nosewheel is self-centering. Stainless steel axles, taper roller bearings, and independent suspension on all three wheels. Alloy wheels, brakes on mainwheels.

POWER PLANT: One 39·5 kW (53 hp) modified Fuji Robin EC44-2P1 two-cylinder two-stroke engine, mounted at rear of fuselage pod and driving a two-blade pusher propeller via toothed belt drive. Fuel capacity 19·3 litres (4·25 Imp gallons).

ACCOMMODATION: Pilot and passenger side by side in fuselage pod. One-piece single-curvature windscreen forms unbroken contour from nose to rear of cockpit, the sides of which are open.

WEIGHT:

Weight empty	131·5 kg (290 lb)

PERFORMANCE:

Cruising speed	52 knots (96 km/h; 60 mph)

HORNET INVADER (updated)

Developed from the original Hornet Invader, this updated derivative uses a Southdown International Raven double-surface wing and Rotax 447 engine.

TYPE: Two-seat microlight aircraft.

AIRFRAME: Raven hang glider wing of L48 aerofoil section, with 3° anhedral. Kingpost standard. Vinyl-coated stainless steel cable bracing. Wing has 100% double surface skins. Weight shift control. Fuselage structure is triangular spaceframe of aluminium alloy tubing, with Kevlar skin. Recovery parachute optional.

LANDING GEAR: Non-retractable tricycle type. Mainwheels size 16 × 4 in. Nosewheel size 12 × 4 in, with brake. Tyre pressure (all three) 1·03 bars (15 lb/sq in). Rubber bungee suspension. Floats and skis optional.

POWER PLANT: One 30 kW (40 hp) Rotax 447 two-cylinder two-stroke engine, with 2·58:1 reduction gear to a Hornet Microlight two-blade fixed-pitch wooden pusher propeller. Single fuel tank, capacity 25 litres (5·5 Imp gallons).

ACCOMMODATION: Two seats side by side in almost totally enclosed fuselage pod.

EQUIPMENT: Specialist equipment available upon application.

DIMENSIONS, EXTERNAL:

Wing span	10·97 m (36 ft 0 in)
Wing chord: at centre	3·05 m (10 ft 0 in)
at tip	0·41 m (1 ft 4 in)
Wing aspect ratio	8
Length overall	3·05 m (10 ft 0 in)
Height overall	3·30 m (10 ft 10 in)
Wheelbase	1·35 m (4 ft 5 in)
Propeller diameter	1·52 m (5 ft 0 in)

AREA:

Wings, gross	15·0 m² (161·5 sq ft)

WEIGHTS, LOADINGS AND PERFORMANCE:
Not yet available

HORNET DUAL TRAINER RAVEN

This microlight is basically the former Hornet Dual Trainer now fitted with a Southdown International Raven double-surface wing and a Rotax 447 engine.

TYPE: Two-seat microlight aircraft; conforms to BCAR Section S.

AIRFRAME: Raven hang glider wing. Kingpost standard. Vinyl-coated stainless steel cable bracing. Weight shift control. Fuselage structure is triangular spaceframe of aluminium alloy tubing. Recovery parachute optional.

LANDING GEAR: Non-retractable tricycle type. Mainwheels size 16 × 4 in; pressure 1·03 bars (15 lb/sq in). Nosewheel size 12 × 4 in, with brake. Unsprung wheels, with one-piece main axle.

POWER PLANT: One 30 kW (40 hp) Rotax 447 two-cylinder two-stroke engine, with 2·58:1 reduction gear to a Hornet Microlights two-blade fixed-pitch wooden pusher propeller. Single fuel tank, capacity 25 litres (5·5 Imp gallons).

ACCOMMODATION: Two seats side by side in open position. Seat pouch for light accessories.

SYSTEM: Bosch magneto for electrical system.

EQUIPMENT: Specialised equipment available upon application.

DIMENSIONS, EXTERNAL:

Wing span	10·97 m (36 ft 0 in)
Wing chord: at centre	3·05 m (10 ft 0 in)
at tip	0·41 m (1 ft 4 in)
Wing aspect ratio	8
Length overall	3·05 m (10 ft 0 in)
Height overall	3·35 m (11 ft 0 in)
Wheelbase	1·35 m (4 ft 5 in)
Propeller diameter	1·52 m (5 ft 0 in)

AREA:

Wings, gross	15·0 m² (161·5 sq ft)

WEIGHTS AND LOADINGS:

Weight empty	140 kg (308 lb)
Pilot weight range	55-90 kg (122-198 lb)
Max T-O weight	336 kg (740 lb)
Max wing loading	22·4 kg/m² (4·59 lb/sq ft)
Max power loading	11·3 kg/kW (18·5 lb/hp)

PERFORMANCE:

Never-exceed speed	86 knots (161 km/h; 100 mph)
Max level speed	71 knots (132 km/h; 82 mph)
Max cruising speed	65 knots (121 km/h; 75 mph)
Econ cruising speed	54 knots (100 km/h; 62 mph)
Stalling speed at min cockpit weight, engine idling	19 knots (36 km/h; 22 mph)
Max rate of climb at S/L	198 m (650 ft)/min
Service ceiling	3,050 m (10,000 ft)
T-O run	37 m (120 ft)
Landing run	55 m (180 ft)
Range with max fuel	147 nm (273 km; 170 miles)
Endurance with max fuel	3 h

ISAACS

JOHN O. ISAACS

23 Linden Grove, Chandler's Ford, Hampshire SO5 1LE
Telephone: 042 15 60885

Mr Isaacs designed and built a single-seat light aircraft, the airframe of which is basically a ⁷⁄₁₀th scale wooden version of that of the Hawker Fury fighter of the 1930s. Constructional drawings are available to amateur builders. Mr Isaacs has also built the wings for a full-size Fury replica (G-BKBB) produced by Westward Airways of Land's End Aerodrome, Penzance, Cornwall.

He has also designed and built an all-wood scaled-down version of the Supermarine Spitfire single-seat fighter of the Second World War, of which plans are available.

ISAACS FURY II

Design of the Isaacs Fury was started in January 1961 and construction of the aircraft began in April 1961. It flew for the first time on 30 August 1963, powered by a 48·5 kW (65 hp) Walter Mikron engine (see 1965-66 *Jane's*).

In 1966-67 Mr Isaacs modified the Fury prototype to Mk II standard, by restressing the airframe and installing a 93 kW (125 hp) Avco Lycoming engine, and flew the aircraft in this form in the Summer of 1967. The first of its subsequent owners, Mr W. Raper, made further refinements to the aircraft, including the addition of blister fairings over the engine cylinders.

Many Fury plans have been supplied to amateur constructors throughout the world, and 12 Furies were known to have flown by January 1986. The Fury illustrated won the 'best homebuilt' prize at the 1985 PFA Rally.

TYPE: Single-seat homebuilt light biplane.

AIRFRAME: Staggered biplane, with N interplane struts each side and two N strut assemblies supporting centre-section of top wing above fuselage. Conventional wire bracing. Wing section RAF 28. Thickness/chord ratio 9·75%. Dihedral 1° on top wing, 3° 30′ on bottom wings. Incidence 3° 20′ on top wing, 3° 50′ on bottom wings. Spruce 'plank' spars and Warren girder ribs, with fabric covering. Fabric covered spruce ailerons on top wing only. No flaps. Spruce fuselage structure, covered with birch plywood. Strut braced spruce tail unit of 'plank' spars and girder ribs, fabric covered. Ground adjustable tab in port elevator.

LANDING GEAR: Non-retractable type, with tailskid. Cross-axle tied to Vs with rubber cord shock absorption. Mainwheels consist of WM.2 35·5 cm (14 in) rims spoked to home-made hubs. Dunlop tyre, size 3·25-14, pressure approx 2·28 bars (33 lb/sq in). Brakes optional.

POWER PLANT (prototype): One 93 kW (125 hp) Avco Lycoming O-290 flat-four engine. Two-blade fixed-pitch propeller. Fuel tank in fuselage, aft of fireproof bulkhead, capacity 45·5 litres (10 Imp gallons) or 54·5 litres (12 Imp gallons).

ACCOMMODATION: Single seat in open cockpit. Small door above top longeron on port side opens downward. Space for light baggage aft of seat. Radio optional.

DIMENSIONS, EXTERNAL:

Wing span: upper	6·40 m (21 ft 0 in)
lower	5·54 m (18 ft 2 in)
Wing chord (both, constant)	1·07 m (3 ft 6 in)
Wing aspect ratio (upper)	6
Length overall	5·87 m (19 ft 3 in)
Height over tail (flying attitude)	2·16 m (7 ft 1 in)
Tailplane span	2·13 m (7 ft 0 in)
Wheel track	1·27 m (4 ft 2 in)

AREA:

Wings, gross	11·50 m² (123·8 sq ft)

WEIGHTS AND LOADINGS (93 kW; 125 hp Avco Lycoming engine):

Weight empty	322 kg (710 lb)
Max permissible T-O weight	450 kg (1,000 lb)
Max wing loading	39·13 kg/m² (8·08 lb/sq ft)
Max power loading	4·84 kg/kW (8·00 lb/hp)

PERFORMANCE (with uncowled 93 kW; 125 hp engine):

Max level speed	100 knots (185 km/h; 115 mph)
Stalling speed	33 knots (61 km/h; 38 mph)
Max rate of climb at S/L	488 m (1,600 ft)/min
g limit	+9

ISAACS SPITFIRE

Construction of the prototype of Mr Isaacs' ⁶⁄₁₀-scale Spitfire (G-BBJI) began in the Summer of 1969, and it flew for the first time on 5 May 1975. Since sold, it is now based near Oakham, Leicestershire. Plans for the Isaacs Spitfire are available to homebuilders, and twelve sets have been supplied to constructors in various countries; two were known to be under active construction in the UK by January 1986.

TYPE: Single-seat homebuilt sporting aircraft.

AIRFRAME: Cantilever low-wing monoplane of semi-elliptical planform. Wing section NACA 2200 series. Thickness/chord ratio 13·2% at root, 6% at tip. Dihedral 6°. Incidence 2° at root, −30′ at tip. Two-spar wing built in one piece, mainly of spruce, with birch plywood covering, except for ailerons which are fabric covered. Spruce fuselage structure, covered with birch plywood. Cantilever tail unit of plywood covered spruce.

LANDING GEAR: Non-retractable tailwheel type on prototype. Cantilever main legs. Dunlop 5·00-5 tyres, wheels and hydraulic disc brakes.

POWER PLANT: One 74·5 kW (100 hp) Continental O-200

Single-seat Hornet Executive

Hornet Invader microlight with enclosed fuselage pod *(Mike Jerram)*

Hornet Dual Trainer Raven two-seat microlight

Isaacs Fury II single-seat homebuilt biplane *(R. Kunert)*

Mainair Gemini Flash 2

Prototype Isaacs Spitfire single-seat light sporting aircraft *(Geoffrey P. Jones)*

flat-four engine, or alternative engine in same category. Two-blade ground adjustable Ratier metal propeller. Fuel tank in fuselage, aft of fireproof bulkhead, capacity 45·5 litres (10 Imp gallons).

ACCOMMODATION: Single seat under transparent blister canopy. Space for light baggage aft of seat.

DIMENSIONS, EXTERNAL:

Wing span	6·75 m (22 ft 1½ in)
Wing chord at root	1·52 m (5 ft 0 in)
Length overall	5·88 m (19 ft 3 in)
Height overall	1·73 m (5 ft 8 in)
Tailplane span	1·92 m (6 ft 3½ in)
Wheel track	1·80 m (5 ft 11 in)

AREA:

Wings, gross	8·08 m² (87·0 sq ft)

WEIGHTS AND LOADINGS:

Weight empty	366 kg (805 lb)
Max T-O weight	499 kg (1,100 lb)
Max wing loading	61·76 kg/m² (12·64 lb/sq ft)
Max power loading	6·70 kg/kW (11·00 lb/hp)

PERFORMANCE (at max T-O weight):

Max level speed	130 knots (240 km/h; 150 mph)
Cruising speed	116 knots (215 km/h; 134 mph)
Stalling speed, 'clean'	45-47 knots (84-87 km/h; 52-54 mph)
Stalling speed, with optional fuselage airbrake extended	41 knots (76 km/h; 47 mph)
Max rate of climb at S/L	336 m (1,100 ft)/min
g limits	+9/−4·5 factored

MAINAIR

MAINAIR SPORTS LTD

Unit 2, Alma Industrial Estate, Regent Street, Rochdale, Lancashire OL12 0HQ
Telephone: 0706 55134
Telex: 635091 ALBION G attn MAINAIR

DIRECTORS:
John A. Hudson
Peter W. Hudson

POWER MANAGER: Geoffrey Ball

Mainair produces a range of 'powered trike' units to suit flexwing hang gliders, and complete microlight aircraft. The current range comprises the Scorcher, Zipper, Gemini 2 and Gemini Flash 2. By early 1986 at least 340 trike units (all versions) had been produced.

During 1984 the company achieved full CAA approval as an A1 microlight manufacturer and gained type approval for the Gemini/Tri-Flyer Flash and Sprint microlights (see 1985-86 *Jane's*).

MAINAIR GEMINI 2 and GEMINI FLASH 2

These two-seat microlights are much refined versions of the earlier Tri-Flyer; the **Gemini 2** is supplied as a trike unit only, without the flexwing of the **Gemini Flash 2**.

On 26 February 1985, a standard Gemini Flash 2 was flown by Mr Bob Calvert to an altitude shown on his twin altimeters as 6,126/6,218 m (20,100/20,400 ft).

The following details refer to the Gemini Flash 2.

TYPE: Two-seat flexible wing microlight aircraft; conforms to FAI/CAA requirements, and meets BCAR Section S requirements for dual control microlights.

AIRFRAME: Trike unit of 6082-T6 aluminium alloy, with vinyl coated galvanised steel bracing cables. Kingpost standard. Flash extremely taut, highly defined flexible wing, with 76% double surface Dacron covering, and small fin.

LANDING GEAR: Tricycle type, with telescopic side struts and optional gas spring front fork shock absorption. All wheels size 4·00 × 10. Nosewheel steering and braking. Optional wheel fairings and skis.

POWER PLANT: One 29·4 kW (39·4 hp) Rotax 447, 34 kW (45·6 hp) Rotax 503 or 38 kW (51 hp) Rotax 462 two-cylinder two-stroke engine, with reduction drive to a two-blade wooden pusher propeller. Fuel tank capacity 21 litres (4·6 Imp gallons). Optional auxiliary tank of 24 litres (5·2 Imp gallons) capacity.

ACCOMMODATION: Two seats in open cockpit in glassfibre pod. Can be supplied without cockpit pod for export only.

DIMENSIONS, EXTERNAL:

Wing span	10·6 m (34 ft 9½ in)
Wing aspect ratio	7·147
Length overall	3·46 m (11 ft 4¼ in)
Height overall	3·83 m (12 ft 6¾ in)
Width over wheel fairings	1·68 m (5 ft 6 in)
Wheelbase	1·88 m (6 ft 2 in)
Propeller diameter	1·575 m (5 ft 2 in)

AREA:

Wings, gross	15·57 m² (167·6 sq ft)

Weights and Loadings:
- Weight empty (447 engine) 146 kg (322 lb)
- Total crew weight range 70-180 kg (154-397 lb)
- Max T-O weight 344 kg (758 lb)
- Max wing loading 22·09 kg/m² (4·52 lb/sq ft)
- Max power loading 10·24 kg/kW (16·84 lb/hp)

Performance:
- Never-exceed speed 77 knots (143 km/h; 89 mph)
- Cruising speed 43 knots (80 km/h; 50 mph)
- Econ cruising speed 42 knots (78 km/h; 48 mph)
- Stalling speed: power on 25 knots (47 km/h; 29 mph)
- power off 24 knots (45 km/h; 28 mph)
- Max rate of climb at S/L: solo 300 m (985 ft)/min
- dual 150 m (492 ft)/min
- Service ceiling 3,050 m (10,000 ft)
- T-O to 15 m (50 ft) 180 m (591 ft)
- Landing from 15 m (50 ft) 150 m (492 ft)
- Range with standard fuel 69 nm (128 km; 80 miles)
- Endurance 2 h
- g limits +6/−4 ultimate
- Best glide ratio 9
- Min rate of sink, power off 137 m (450 ft)/min

MAINAIR SCORCHER

Said to be suited to the pilot wishing for high performance or competition, the Scorcher is Mainair's highest powered single-seat microlight. It is also available as a trike unit only, and the flexwing can be purchased separately.

The general descriptions of the airframe and landing gear given under the Gemini Flash 2 entry apply also to the Scorcher, except that the Scorcher wing is 83% double surface.

Type: Single-seat microlight aircraft.

Power Plant: One 29·4 kW (39·4 hp) Rotax 447 two-cylinder two-stroke engine, driving a two-blade pusher propeller via reduction gear. Fuel capacity 24 litres (5·2 Imp gallons) standard; optional 20 litre (4·4 Imp gallon) auxiliary tank.

Accommodation: Pilot only, in open position, in glassfibre cockpit pod.

Dimensions, external:
- Wing span 9·20 m (30 ft 2 in)
- Wing aspect ratio 6·79
- Length overall 2·88 m (9 ft 5½ in)
- Height overall 3·60 m (11 ft 10 in)
- Width over wheel fairings 1·56 m (5 ft 1½ in)
- Wheelbase 1·81 m (5 ft 11¼ in)
- Propeller diameter 1·575 m (5 ft 2 in)

Area:
- Wings, gross 12·6 m² (135·6 sq ft)

Weights:
- Weight empty 122 kg (269 lb)
- Max pilot weight 90 kg (198 lb)

Performance:
- Never-exceed speed 78 knots (145 km/h; 90 mph)
- Cruising speed 43 knots (80 km/h; 50 mph)
- Stalling speed 24 knots (45 km/h; 28 mph)
- Max rate of climb at S/L 250 m (820 ft)/min
- g limits +6/−4 ultimate

MAINAIR ZIPPER

Available from mid-1986, the Zipper microlight is a single-seater conforming to BCAR Section S requirements. Power is provided by a 20 kW (27 hp) Rotax 277 single-cylinder two-stroke engine. No other details were available at the time of writing.

MICROFLIGHT

MICROFLIGHT AIRCRAFT LTD

Hangar 6, Shobdon Airfield, Herefordshire HR6 9NR
Telephone: (056 881) 8864

Directors:
Michael Campbell-Jones (Design)
John Hollings (Managing)

MICROFLIGHT SPECTRUM

The Spectrum is a development of Mr Michael Campbell-Jones' Ladybird, described in the 1983-84 *Jane's*. By late January 1986 the prototypes had accumulated 160 flying hours. Once CAA approval has been gained, the Spectrum will be made available in ready assembled form.

Type: Single-seat microlight aircraft; conforms to FAI/CAA requirements.

Airframe: Strut braced high-wing monoplane. Wing section NACA 4412 modified. No anhedral or dihedral. Incidence 5°. Sweepback at quarter-chord 6°. Aluminium alloy airframe, with double surfaced glassfibre and carbonfibre composite wing and conventional tail surfaces. Glassfibre and carbonfibre fuselage pod with open cockpit and windscreen. Stainless steel cables. Three-axis control (ailerons, elevators and rudder). Optional parachute. Rigging time 20 min.

Landing Gear: Non-retractable tricycle type with steerable nosewheel. All wheels 12 × 4 in, tyre pressure 1·72 bars (25 lb/sq in). Nosewheel brake. Spring leg suspension. Floats optional.

Power Plant: One 30 kW (40 hp) Rotax 447 two-cylinder two-stroke engine, with 2·5:1 reduction gear to a two-blade wooden propeller. Fuel tank capacity 22·7 litres (5 Imp gallons).

Accommodation: Pilot only, in open cockpit.

System: 12V electrical system.

Dimensions, external:
- Wing span 12·00 m (39 ft 4½ in)
- Wing chord: at root 1·56 m (5 ft 1½ in)
- at tip 1·00 m (3 ft 3½ in)
- Wing aspect ratio 9·6
- Length overall 5·00 m (16 ft 5 in)
- Height overall 2·10 m (6 ft 10¾ in)
- Tailplane span 3·00 m (9 ft 10 in)
- Wheel track 1·45 m (4 ft 9 in)
- Wheelbase 1·75 m (5 ft 9 in)
- Propeller diameter 1·57 m (5 ft 2 in)

Area:
- Wings, gross 15·0 m² (161·5 sq ft)

Weights and Loadings:
- Weight empty 150 kg (330 lb)
- Pilot weight range 50-180 kg (110-396 lb)
- Max T-O weight 330 kg (727 lb)
- Max wing loading 22·0 kg/m² (4·5 lb/sq ft)
- Max power loading 11·00 kg/kW (18·18 lb/hp)

Performance:
- Never-exceed speed 90 knots (166 km/h; 103 mph)
- Max level speed 60 knots (111 km/h; 69 mph)
- Max cruising speed 50 knots (93 km/h; 58 mph)
- Econ cruising speed 42 knots (78 km/h; 48 mph)
- Stalling speed, power on 25 knots (47 km/h; 29 mph)
- Max rate of climb at S/L 244 m (800 ft)/min
- Service ceiling 3,660 m (12,000 ft)
- T-O run 65 m (213 ft)
- T-O to 15 m (50 ft) 92 m (302 ft)
- Landing run 50 m (164 ft)
- Landing from 15 m (50 ft) 77 m (253 ft)
- Range 105 nm (194 km; 121 miles)
- g limits +6/−4

MIDLAND

MIDLAND ULTRALIGHTS LTD

Kilworth Marina, North Kilworth, Lutterworth, Leicestershire LE17 6JB
Telephone: 0858 880484

This company is manufacturing the French Aviasud Sirocco (which see) to BCAR Section S standard, under the designation **Sirocco 377 GB**. Several modifications have been made to conform with British regulations, including the use of heavier cables and a stronger nosewheel mounting, and a reduction in engine noise level. Max T-O weight and max level speed are 240 kg (529 lb) and 60 knots (111 km/h; 69 mph) respectively.

NIPPER

NIPPER KITS AND COMPONENTS LTD

Foxley, Blackness Lane, Keston, Kent BR2 6HL
Telephone: (0689) 58351

Directors:
D. P. L. Antill (Chairman)
A. F. Ayles
A. S. Pearcey

Complete worldwide rights for the Nipper aircraft were purchased from Belgium in 1966, and it was marketed by Nipper Aircraft Ltd as a ready to fly lightplane and in the form of several stages of kits for amateur construction.

Nipper Aircraft Ltd went into receivership in May 1971. Prior to this Mr D. P. L. Antill, its Managing Director, acquired all rights in the Nipper, and on 20 October 1971 formed a new company, Nipper Kits and Components Ltd, to supply spares for existing aircraft and to encourage and support amateur construction of the Nipper. Plans, kits of component parts and an advisory service for amateur constructors continue to be available, and an average of twelve sets of plans is sold each year. A further two kits were sold during 1985. Of four Nippers known to be under construction, two were expected to fly for the first time in 1986.

NIPPER Mk IIIb

The Nipper Mk IIIb is normally powered by a 1,600 cc Rollason Ardem engine, but constructors may increase engine capacity to 1,835 cc (subject to PFA approval), to improve performance. An alternative power plant is the award-winning PFA-approved Barry Smith aerobatic engine.

Compared with the earlier Mk III and IIIA, this version has a wider instrument panel to accept additional instruments to the owner's choice, and a new canopy of increased length and width to provide extra room inside the cockpit. It can be fitted with wingtip fuel tanks which almost double the standard fuel capacity. With these tanks fitted, but empty, the Mk IIIb remains aerobatic. Flutter tests were completed satisfactorily at speeds up to 156 knots (290 km/h; 180 mph).

Type: Single-seat homebuilt light monoplane.

Airframe: Cantilever mid-wing monoplane. Modified NACA 43012A wing section. Dihedral 5° 30′. Incidence 2°. All-wood one-piece single-spar structure, with plywood covered leading-edge and overall fabric covering. Wooden ailerons with fabric covering. No flaps. Portion of port wing root trailing-edge is made of light alloy and hinged, with built-in footrest, so that it can be folded down to assist access to cockpit. Wing is quickly removable, to permit aircraft to be towed behind a motorcar. Welded steel tube fuselage structure. Underfuselage fairing of glassfibre. Rear fuselage fabric covered. Braced tailplane and elevators of wood construction. No fin. Rudder of steel tube construction with fabric covering.

Landing Gear: Non-retractable tricycle type. Nieman transverse rubber ring shock absorbers. Steerable nosewheel. Continental tyres, size 4·00-4, pressure 1·79 bars (26 lb/sq in). Disc brakes.

Power Plant: One 41 kW (55 hp) Rollason Ardem XI flat-four engine standard, driving a two-blade fixed-pitch wooden propeller with glassfibre spinner. Alternatively, Nipper recommends the fuel-injected 48·5 kW (65 hp) Barry Smith aerobatic engine of 1,834 cc, with fuel and oil systems for inverted flight, direct drive to Bendix dual aircraft magneto, and screened harness and spark plugs. Mk IIIb has downward facing stainless steel exhaust pipes for increased life and reduced noise level in cockpit. Fuel tank between engine and cockpit, capacity 34 litres (7·5 Imp gallons). Provision for two 16·5 litre (3·6 Imp gallon) wingtip fuel tanks. Oil capacity 3·5 litres (0·77 Imp gallons).

Accommodation: Single seat under blown Perspex canopy which hinges sideways to starboard. Small baggage space aft of seat.

Avionics: Standard radio is now the battery operated 720-channel Walter Dittel FSG 50 or, optionally, an FSG 60M with 4-channel memory, installed in port wing root or instrument panel.

Dimensions, external:
- Wing span: without tip tanks 6·00 m (19 ft 8 in)
- with tip tanks 6·25 m (20 ft 6 in)
- Wing chord: at c/l 1·40 m (4 ft 7¼ in)
- at tip 1·10 m (3 ft 7¼ in)
- Wing aspect ratio 4·8
- Length overall 4·56 m (15 ft 0 in)
- Height overall 1·91 m (6 ft 3 in)
- Tailplane span 2·14 m (7 ft 0 in)
- Wheel track 1·40 m (4 ft 7 in)
- Wheelbase 1·13 m (3 ft 8 in)

Area:
- Wings, gross 7·50 m² (80·70 sq ft)

Weights and Loadings (Ardem engine):
- Weight empty 210 kg (465 lb)
- Max T-O weight: Aerobatic 310 kg (685 lb)
- Normal 340 kg (750 lb)
- Max wing loading 45·33 kg/m² (9·29 lb/sq ft)
- Max power loading 8·29 kg/kW (13·64 lb/hp)

Performance (Ardem engine, at max T-O weight):
- Never-exceed speed 126 knots (235 km/h; 146 mph)
- Max level speed at S/L:
- without tip tanks 93 knots (173 km/h; 107 mph)
- with tip tanks 83 knots (155 km/h; 96 mph)
- Max cruising speed (75% power) at S/L:
- without tip tanks 81 knots (150 km/h; 93 mph)
- Econ cruising speed at S/L 78 knots (145 km/h; 90 mph)
- Stalling speed, power off 33 knots (61 km/h; 38 mph)
- Max rate of climb at S/L 198 m (650 ft)/min
- Service ceiling 3,660 m (12,000 ft)
- T-O run 85 m (280 ft)
- T-O to 15 m (50 ft) 338 m (1,110 ft)
- Landing from 15 m (50 ft) 457 m (1,500 ft)
- Landing run 110 m (360 ft)
- Range with max internal fuel, 30 min reserves 173 nm (320 km; 200 miles)
- Range with tip tanks 390 nm (720 km; 450 miles)
- g limits +6/−3

Microflight Aircraft Spectrum with floats

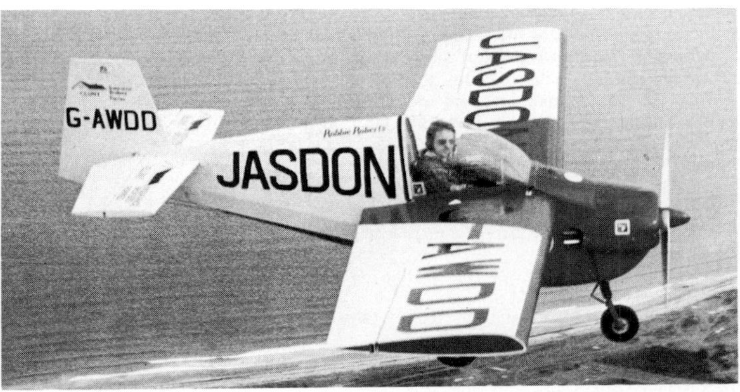

Nipper Mk IIIb single-seat light aircraft *(Tim Griffith)*

Pegasus Forger T.503

Noble Hardman Aviation Snowbird two-seat cabin monoplane

NOBLE HARDMAN

NOBLE HARDMAN AVIATION LTD

Pembidural House, Pandy, Abergavenny, Gwent NP7 8EA
Telephone: 0873 890367
Telex: 437269
MANAGING DIRECTOR: D. L. Hardman

NOBLE HARDMAN AVIATION SNOWBIRD

On 4 January 1983 the design began of a side by side two-seat cabin microlight known as the Snowbird. Construction of a prototype started on 10 June that year and this aircraft flew for the first time on 2 September 1984. Meanwhile, a pre-production Snowbird had been started on 17 January. The Snowbird is available for purchase, presumably with the intended Lotus four-cylinder engine which was to supersede the Arrow G500 used on the prototype/pre-production aircraft. No confirmation of this, however, has been received.

The following details refer to the Arrow powered prototype:

TYPE: Two-seat cabin microlight aircraft; conforms to FAI/CAA requirements.

AIRFRAME: Strut braced high-wing monoplane, with slight dihedral and 7° incidence on wings. Conventional structure, with aluminium and steel tubular fuselage and tail unit, Dacron covered; composite wings with main and rear spars, glassfibre reinforced plastics ribs and aluminium alloy D section leading-edge, Dacron covered. Ground adjustable tab on rudder. Three-axis control (ailerons, elevators and rudder). Trailing-edge flaps.

LANDING GEAR: Non-retractable tricycle type, with sprung main legs and shock absorber on nose unit. All wheels of similar size. Drum brakes on mainwheels.

POWER PLANT: One 44·7 kW (60 hp) Arrow G500 two-stroke engine, with direct drive to a two-blade fixed-pitch propeller with spinner. Fuel tank capacity 27 litres (6 Imp gallons).

ACCOMMODATION: Two seats side by side in enclosed cabin. Door on each side.

DIMENSIONS, EXTERNAL:	
Wing span	9·70 m (31 ft 10 in)
Wing chord, constant	1·60 m (5 ft 3 in)
Wing aspect ratio	6·23
Length overall	6·80 m (22 ft 3¾ in)
Height overall	2·40 m (7 ft 10½ in)
Tailplane span	2·40 m (7 ft 10½ in)
AREA:	
Wings, gross	15·1 m² (162·5 sq ft)
WEIGHTS AND LOADINGS:	
Max payload	173 kg (381 lb)
Max T-O weight	350 kg (771 lb)
Max wing loading	23·2 kg/m² (4·74 lb/sq ft)
Max power loading	7·83 kg/kW (12·85 lb/hp)
PERFORMANCE:	
Never-exceed speed	78 knots (144 km/h; 90 mph)
Max level speed	56 knots (105 km/h; 65 mph)
Max cruising speed	52 knots (97 km/h; 60 mph)
Econ cruising speed	39 knots (72 km/h; 45 mph)
Max rate of climb at S/L	366 m (1,200 ft)/min
Range	243 nm (450 km; 280 miles)

PEGASUS

PEGASUS TRANSPORT SYSTEMS LTD

PO Box 29, Marlborough, Wiltshire SN8 1PF
Telephone: 0672 53504
DIRECTORS:
Frederick Hogarth (Chairman)
Dr Peter Palmer
Murray Rose
Graham Slater

CAA-approved manufacturing subsidiary:
Solar Wings Ltd, 56 George Lane, Marlborough, Wiltshire SN8 4DA
Telephone: 0672 54414
Telex: 449703
DIRECTORS:
S. M. G. Rose (Managing)
D. S. Raymond
G. J. Slater
M. S. Southall

Current microlights in production include the Rotax engined Pegasus tandem tourers available with XL or Flash wings, the Robin engined Pegasus Tug, and the Solo engined Pegasus Photon single-seater. Development continues of the Pegasus Forger as a military trainer, and the Pegasus Dragoon, an ATGW carrier. Other development work includes the Pegasus Minimum System which allows a small power unit to be strapped onto the pilot of a standard Solar Typhoon free-flight wing, and a new amphibious float system for the Rotax engined trikes.

Two projects expected to be completed during 1986 were the introduction of a Rotax 462 engine in the Pegasus two-seat trainer/tourers, capable of meeting the stringent noise regulations of West Germany, and a new high-performance wing intended to replace the Flash for competition flying. On the systems side, Pegasus will be marketing the SkyEye video reconnaissance equipment with a modified two-seat aircraft, designed for the management and security of landed estates.

In the 1985 UK national competitions, the Pegasus XL and Pegasus Flash won the league championship; and Britain's team in the World Microlight Championship used three Pegasus aircraft. On the free-flight side, the Solar Typhoon won both national leagues, and three were used by the British team which won the World Hang Gliding Championships.

PEGASUS FORGER T.503

TYPE: Two-seat flexwing microlight military trainer.

AIRFRAME: Mainframe is triangulated structure of aluminium alloy tube, supporting Dacron single surface Rogallo type wing with kingpost and stainless steel cable bracing. Control by weight shift; features include floating crossbar.

LANDING GEAR: Tricycle type, with quasi-leafspring suspension and 16 in wheel on each unit; steerable nosewheel.

POWER PLANT: One 30 kW (40 hp) Fuji Robin EC44 432 cc two-cylinder two-stroke engine, mounted behind seat with toothed belt 2·6:1 reduction drive to two-blade mahogany pusher propeller. Fuel in two, four or six 4·5 litre (1 Imp gallon) tanks above engine. Electric starting optional.

ACCOMMODATION: Two seats side by side in open position. Dual controls.

DIMENSIONS, EXTERNAL:	
Wing span	10·46 m (34 ft 4 in)
Wing aspect ratio	6·04
Length overall	3·05 m (10 ft 0 in)
Height overall	3·66 m (12 ft 0 in)
Propeller diameter	1·52 m (5 ft 0 in)
AREA:	
Wings, gross	18·12 m² (195·0 sq ft)
WEIGHTS AND LOADINGS:	
Weight empty	145 kg (320 lb)
Pilot weight range	45-159 kg (100-350 lb)
Max T-O weight	308 kg (680 lb)
Max wing loading	17·04 kg/m² (3·49 lb/sq ft)
Max power loading	10·27 kg/kW (17·00 lb/hp)
PERFORMANCE:	
Never-exceed speed	58 knots (107 km/h; 66 mph)
Max level speed	56 knots (105 km/h; 65 mph)
Max cruising speed	45 knots (83 km/h; 52 mph)
Stalling speed	22 knots (41 km/h; 25 mph)
Max rate of climb at S/L:	
single-seat	229 m (750 ft)/min
two-seat	70 m (230 ft)/min
g limits	+6/−4

PEGASUS FLASH

The Pegasus Flash is a high-performance dual-purpose tourer/trainer, of which 32 had been built by mid-1986. It first flew in the Summer of 1985, and the first production aircraft was delivered four months later, after proving itself to be the fastest flexwing aircraft in the world during the World Microlight Championships.

TYPE: Two-seat flexwing microlight aircraft; conforms to FAI/CAA and BCAR Section S requirements.

AIRFRAME: Trike unit is designed to be compatible with range of Pegasus flexwings. Mainframe is monopole structure of HT 30 TF aluminium tubes, with tandem seats suspended in seat frame. Control in pitch and roll provided by normal weight-shift control frame. Structure of wing similar to that of fifth generation free-flight wings, having floating crossboom and using 75 per cent double surface disciplined by battens on both surfaces.

LANDING GEAR: As for Pegasus Panther XL.

POWER PLANT: One 29·4 kW (39·4 hp) Rotax 447 two-cylinder two-stroke engine, with 2·58:1 reduction gear driving a two-blade mahogany pusher propeller. Fuel capacity either 24 or 45 litres (5·2 or 10 Imp gallons).

DIMENSIONS, EXTERNAL:
- Wing span: 10·67 m (35 ft 0 in)
- Wing aspect ratio: 7·0
- Propeller diameter: 1·57 m (5 ft 2 in)

AREA:
- Wings, gross: 15·61 m² (168·0 sq ft)

WEIGHTS AND LOADINGS:
- Weight empty: 145·5 kg (321 lb)
- Crew weight range: 55-180 kg (121-396 lb)
- Max suspended load: 293 kg (646 lb)
- Max T-O weight: 344 kg (758 lb)
- Max wing loading: 22·02 kg/m² (4·51 lb/sq ft)
- Max power loading: 11·70 kg/kW (19·24 lb/hp)

PERFORMANCE:
- Never-exceed speed: 77 knots (142 km/h; 88 mph)
- Max cruising speed: 69 knots (127 km/h; 79 mph)
- Econ cruising speed: 43 knots (79 km/h; 50 mph)
- Stalling speed at max AUW: 25 knots (46 km/h; 29 mph)
- Max rate of climb at S/L: solo 327 m (1,075 ft)/min
  - dual 180 m (590 ft)/min
- g limits: +6/−4 tested at max AUW; +4/−2 recommended

PEGASUS PANTHER XL

The Panther XL is a dual purpose tourer/trainer, a Pegasus version of the former Ultra Sports Panther, of which over 100 were built. Its XL wing is a development of the Typhoon series of championship flex-wings. It first flew in the autumn of 1984 and the first production aircraft was delivered six months later.

TYPE: Two-seat single-engined flex-wing microlight aircraft; conforms to FAI/CAA definitions and built to BCAR Section S standards.

AIRFRAME: Trike unit in basic form is simple load-carrying module designed to be compatible with a range of Pegasus flex-wings. Frame is a monopole structure of aluminium tubes. Control in pitch and roll by normal weight-shift control-frame. Structure of wing similar to that of fifth generation free-flight wings, having floating crossboom and 55 per cent double-surface covering disciplined by battens on both surfaces.

LANDING GEAR: Wire braced tricycle type. Rear wheels fitted to stub axles; main axle is wire braced aluminium strut. Nosewheel steering incorporates trailing-link spring suspension.

POWER PLANT: One 30 kW (40 hp) Fuji Robin 432 cc two-cylinder two-stroke engine, with 2·6:1 toothed-belt reduction drive to two-blade wooden pusher propeller. Fuel tank capacity 22 litres (4·8 Imp gallons).

ACCOMMODATION: Tandem seats, suspended in seat frame. Cockpit fairing with small windscreen.

DIMENSIONS, EXTERNAL:
- Wing span: 10·36 m (34 ft 0 in)
- Wing aspect ratio: 6·15
- Propeller diameter: 1·52 m (5 ft 0 in)

AREA:
- Wings, gross: 17·47 m² (188·0 sq ft)

WEIGHTS AND LOADINGS:
- Weight empty: 148 kg (326 lb)
- Max suspended load: 301 kg (663 lb)
- Total crew weight range: 55-190 kg (121-419 lb)
- Max T-O weight: 350 kg (771 lb)
- Max wing loading: 20·03 kg/m² (4·10 lb/sq ft)
- Max power loading: 11·67 kg/kW (19·28 lb/hp)

PERFORMANCE:
- Never-exceed speed: 58 knots (107 km/h; 66 mph)
- Cruising speed: 45 knots (83 km/h; 52 mph)
- Stalling speed: 24 knots (45 km/h; 28 mph)
- Max rate of climb at S/L: dual 117 m (385 ft)/min
- g limits: +6/−4 tested at max AUW; +4/−2 recommended

PEGASUS XL

The Pegasus XL is identical to the Panther XL except for having a Rotax engine. It flew for the first time in Autumn 1984 and the first production aircraft was delivered five months later. By early 1986, 54 had been built.

AIRFRAME: As Panther XL.

POWER PLANT: One 30 kW (40 hp) Rotax 447 two-cylinder two-stroke engine, with 2·58:1 reduction drive to two-blade wooden pusher propeller. Fuel tank capacity 24 litres (5·2 Imp gallons) standard or 45 litres (10 Imp gallons) optional.

DIMENSIONS AND WING AREA: As for Panther XL.

WEIGHTS AND LOADINGS: As for Panther XL except:
- Weight empty: 145 kg (320 lb)

PERFORMANCE: As for Panther XL except:
- Max cruising speed: 52 knots (96 km/h; 60 mph)
- Econ cruising speed: 39 knots (72 km/h; 45 mph)
- Max rate of climb at S/L:
  - solo: 305 m (1,000 ft)/min
  - dual: 122 m (400 ft)/min

PEGASUS TUG

The Pegasus Tug is a dedicated flex-wing glider tug suitable also for towing advertising banners. Its XLT wing is a development of the XL but its performance is matched to that of the Solar Typhoon and is thus compatible with most fifth generation hang-gliders. In accordance with the modular aerodyne principles on which Pegasus marketing policies are based, the Tug's trike may be flown with the standard XL instead of the XLT, and used then as a twin-seat tourer/trainer. The prototype first flew in early 1985, and the first production aircraft was sold seven months later.

The description of the Pegasus XL applies also to the Tug, except as follows:

TYPE: Two-seat flexwing microlight; conforms to FAI/CAA definitions and built to BCAR Section S standards.

POWER PLANT: One 34·3 kW (46 hp) Rotax 503 two-cylinder two-stroke engine, with 2·58:1 toothed-belt reduction drive to two-blade wooden pusher propeller. Fuel capacity as for Pegasus Panther XL.

ACCOMMODATION: As Tug, should be flown solo. May be flown as two-seat tourer/trainer.

DIMENSIONS: As for Pegasus XL except:
- Wing span: 11·28 m (37 ft 0 in)
- Wing aspect ratio: 6·58

AREA:
- Wings, gross: 18·95 m² (204·0 sq ft)

WEIGHTS AND LOADINGS:
- Weight empty: 150 kg (330 lb)
- Total crew weight range: 55-130 kg (121-286 lb)
- Max suspended load: 280 kg (617 lb)
- Max T-O weight: 350 kg (771 lb)
- Max wing loading: 18·47 kg/m² (3·78 lb/sq ft)
- Max power loading: 10·20 kg/kW (16·76 lb/hp)

PERFORMANCE:
- Never-exceed speed: 50 knots (92 km/h; 57 mph)
- Max cruising speed: 48 knots (88 km/h; 55 mph)
- Econ cruising speed: 39 knots (72 km/h; 45 mph)
- Stalling speed: 21 knots (39 km/h; 25 mph)
- Max rate of climb at S/L:
  - solo: 335 m (1,100 ft)/min
  - towing: 152 m (500 ft)/min
- g limits: +6/−4 tested at max AUW; +4/−2 recommended

PEGASUS PHOTON

The Pegasus Photon is a lightweight single-seat tourer designed to meet the civilian market requirement for a low-cost microlight capable of soaring engine-off, and a military market requirement for an easily concealed exfiltration vehicle. It first flew in December 1985; the first production aircraft was delivered four months later. Fourteen had been built by early 1986.

TYPE: Single-seat flexwing microlight; conforms to FAI/CAA definitions and built to BCAR Section S standards.

AIRFRAME: As for Panther XL, except wing is 75 per cent double surface, disciplined by battens on both surfaces.

LANDING GEAR: As for Pegasus Panther XL.

POWER PLANT: One 10·4 kW (14 hp) Solo 210 single-cylinder two-stroke engine. Fuel tank capacity 10 litres (2·2 Imp gallons).

DIMENSIONS, EXTERNAL:
- Wing span: 9·75 m (32 ft 0 in)
- Wing aspect ratio: 7·3
- Propeller diameter: 1·42 m (4 ft 8 in)

AREA:
- Wings, gross: 13·47 m² (145·0 sq ft)

WEIGHTS AND LOADINGS:
- Weight empty: 69·5 kg (153 lb)
- Max pilot weight: 90 kg (198 lb)
- Max suspended load: 137 kg (302 lb)
- Max T-O weight: 159·5 kg (351 lb)
- Max wing loading: 11·82 kg/m² (2·42 lb/sq ft)
- Max power loading: 15·34 kg/kW (25·00 lb/hp)

PERFORMANCE:
- Never-exceed speed: 56 knots (104 km/h; 64 mph)
- Max cruising speed: 52 knots (96 km/h; 60 mph)
- Econ cruising speed: 35 knots (64 km/h; 40 mph)
- Stalling speed at max AUW: 17 knots (32 km/h; 20 mph)
- Max rate of climb at S/L: 137 m (450 ft)/min
- g limits: +6/−4 tested at max AUW; +4/−2 recommended

PEGASUS DRAGOON

The Pegasus Dragoon is basically a military high-performance single-seat anti-tank guided weapon carrier, designed to move quickly onto the axes of armoured thrusts. It is derived from the Pegasus tourer/trainers, but has a reinforced landing gear for rough field operations. Dragoons would operate in pairs, one carrying (in addition to the pilot's personal weapon and kit) the Milan Post and night sight plus two munitions, the second carrying (in addition to personal weapon and kit) four munitions. Fully loaded, the Dragoon has an endurance of 3 hours. It has automatic map-reading navigation equipment with Doppler or air data input, and its pilot can use night vision goggles. The first production Dragoons are planned for the Spring of 1987.

TYPE: Single-seat military flexwing aircraft.

AIRFRAME: Trike unit is designed to be compatible with range of Pegasus flexwings. Main frame is monopole structure of HT 30 TF aluminium tubes. Solo seating suspended in frame in such a way as to allow fast conversion into tandem twin seating. Control in pitch and roll provided by normal weight-shift control frame. Structure of wing similar to that of fifth generation free-flight wings, having floating crossboom and using extensive double surface, disciplined by battens above and below.

LANDING GEAR: Wire braced tricycle type. Rear wheels fitted to stub axles, reinforced with independent suspension; main axle is wire braced aluminium strut. Nosewheel steering incorporates trailing link spring suspension.

POWER PLANT: One 29·4 kW (39·4 hp) Rotax 447 two-cylinder two-stroke engine, with 2·58:1 reduction gear driving a two-blade wooden pusher propeller. Fuel capacity either 24 or 45 litres (5·2 or 10 Imp gallons).

WEIGHT:
- Max payload: 100 kg (220 lb)

PFA

THE POPULAR FLYING ASSOCIATION

Terminal Building, Shoreham Airport, Shoreham-by-Sea, West Sussex BN4 5FF

Telephone: 079 17 61616

VICE-CHAIRMAN AND CHIEF EXECUTIVE: F. I. V. Walker

The PFA markets plans of the Luton L.A.4a Minor, Currie Wot and Druine Turbulent. Other types of which plans are still in demand from the Association include the Isaacs Fury, Evans VP-1 and VP-2, and Pazmany PL-4, described under their designers' names in this section of *Jane's*.

CURRIE WOT

This aircraft was designed by Mr J. R. Currie in 1937, since when examples have been built and flown with a variety of engines (see 1985-86 and previous editions of *Jane's*). The Currie Wot has also formed the basis for several scale replica aircraft, including S.E.5As and Hawker Furies.

The following details refer to aircraft built to standard plans, as obtainable from the PFA. An average of five sets of plans for the Currie Wot is sold each year.

TYPE: Single-seat fully aerobatic homebuilt biplane.

AIRFRAME: Braced biplane wings, with two parallel interplane struts each side and N centre-section support struts. Wing section Clark Y. Dihedral (both wings) 3°. No incidence. Conventional spruce and plywood structure, with fabric covering. Fabric covered ailerons on lower wings only. No flaps. Fuselage of plywood box construction, with overall fabric covering. Cantilever tail unit of spruce and plywood, with fabric covering. Fixed incidence tailplane. Adjustable tab on rudder. Trim tab in port elevator.

LANDING GEAR: Non-retractable two-wheel type. Rubber cord shock absorption. Mainwheels fitted with Dunlop tyres, size 400 × 8, pressure 1·24 bars (18 lb/sq in). No brakes.

POWER PLANT: One Volkswagen 1,600 cc modified motor-car engine is often installed, driving a two-blade fixed-pitch wooden propeller. Alternative engines up to 74·5 kW (100 hp) can include a 48·5 kW (65 hp) Walter Mikron III four-cylinder inverted inline, or 67 kW (90 hp) Continental C90 flat-four engine. Fuel tank aft of firewall, capacity 54·5 litres (12 Imp gallons). Oil capacity 7 litres (1·5 Imp gallons).

ACCOMMODATION: Single seat in open cockpit.

DIMENSIONS, EXTERNAL:
- Wing span (both): 6·73 m (22 ft 1 in)
- Wing chord (both), constant: 1·07 m (3 ft 6 in)
- Wing aspect ratio: 6·3
- Length overall: 5·58 m (18 ft 3½ in)
- Height overall: 2·06 m (6 ft 9 in)
- Wheel track: 1·38 m (4 ft 6½ in)

AREA:
- Wings, gross: 13·0 m² (140·0 sq ft)

WEIGHTS AND LOADING:
- Weight empty: 250 kg (550 lb)
- Max T-O weight: 408 kg (900 lb)
- Max wing loading: 31·4 kg/m² (6·43 lb/sq ft)

PERFORMANCE (at max T-O weight):
- Never-exceed speed: 112 knots (209 km/h; 130 mph)
- Max level speed at 610 m (2,000 ft): 83 knots (153 km/h; 95 mph)
- Max cruising speed at 610 m (2,000 ft): 78 knots (145 km/h; 90 mph)
- Econ cruising speed at 610 m (2,000 ft): 69 knots (129 km/h; 80 mph)
- Stalling speed: 35 knots (65 km/h; 40 mph)

Pegasus XL microlight aircraft

Pegasus Photon lightweight single-seat microlight

Pegasus Dragoon, armed with four Milan anti-tank missiles, and with a Milan Post mounted on the mainframe wing support structure

Pegasus Panther XL microlight aircraft

Druine D31 Turbulents

Currie Wot built as a scale representation of a Royal Aircraft Factory S.E.5A fighter of the First World War *(R. Kunert)*

Max rate of climb at S/L	183 m (600 ft)/min
Range with max fuel	208 nm (385 km; 240 miles)

DRUINE D31 TURBULENT

The following data apply to the D31 Turbulent as factory-built in the UK for many years by Rollason Aircraft and Engines Ltd. Rollason's version was generally similar to the standard Druine design. Main differences were that it had wheels of slightly greater size and a tailskid instead of a tailwheel, although a tailwheel was available optionally.

The fitting of optional wheel fairings and a sliding canopy increased speed by about 7 knots (13 km/h; 8 mph).

Plans for the Turbulent are available to amateur constructors, from the PFA, and an average of four or five sets is sold each year.

TYPE: Single-seat homebuilt monoplane.

AIRFRAME: Cantilever low-wing monoplane. Wing section NACA 23012. Dihedral 4°. Incidence 3° 40′. All-wood two-spar structure, covered with fabric. Built-in leading-edge slot on outer 45% of half-span. Wooden slotted ailerons with fabric covering. No flaps or tabs. Conventional rectangular four-longeron wood fuselage structure with domed decking, plywood covered. Cantilever wooden tail unit structure. Fixed surfaces plywood covered, movable surfaces fabric covered. No tabs.

LANDING GEAR: Non-retractable tailwheel type (optional tailskid). Compression-spring shock absorbers. Dunlop or Goodyear mainwheels and tyres, size 14 × 3, pressure 1·95 bars (28 lb/sq in). Vespa mechanical brakes. Wheel fairings, taxying and parking brakes optional. Skis or floats may be fitted as alternative to wheels.

POWER PLANT: One 33·5 kW (45 hp) Rollason Ardem 4CO2 Mk IV or 41 kW (55 hp) Ardem Mk V flat-four engine, driving a two-blade fixed-pitch wooden propeller. Fuel tank in fuselage forward of cockpit, capacity 39 litres (8·5 Imp gallons). Oil capacity 2·25 litres (0·5 Imp gallons).

ACCOMMODATION: Pilot only, in open cockpit (sliding canopy optional). Baggage locker aft of seat, capacity 11·5 kg (25 lb).

AVIONICS: Provision for lightweight radio.

DIMENSIONS, EXTERNAL:

Wing span	6·58 m (21 ft 7 in)
Wing chord, constant	1·90 m (3 ft 11 in)
Wing aspect ratio	5·4
Length overall	5·33 m (17 ft 6 in)
Height overall	1·52 m (5 ft 0 in)
Tailplane span	1·98 m (6 ft 6 in)
Wheel track	1·73 m (5 ft 8 in)
Wheel/tailskid base	3·81 m (12 ft 6 in)

AREA:

Wings, gross	7·20 m² (77·5 sq ft)

WEIGHTS AND LOADING:

Weight empty	179 kg (395 lb)
Max T-O weight	281 kg (620 lb)
Max wing loading	39·03 kg/m² (8·00 lb/sq ft)

PERFORMANCE (with 33·5 kW; 45 hp engine, at max T-O weight):

Never-exceed speed	108 knots (202 km/h; 125 mph)
Max level speed	95 knots (176 km/h; 109 mph)
Max cruising speed	87 knots (161 km/h; 100 mph)
Econ cruising speed	76 knots (141 km/h; 87 mph)
Stalling speed	39 knots (71 km/h; 44 mph)
Max rate of climb at S/L	137 m (450 ft)/min
Service ceiling	2,740 m (9,000 ft)
T-O run from grass	95 m (310 ft)
T-O to 15 m (50 ft) from grass	125 m (410 ft)
Landing from 15 m (50 ft) on grass	98 m (320 ft)
Landing run on grass	52 m (170 ft)
Range with max fuel, normal allowances	217 nm (400 km; 250 miles)

LUTON L.A.4a MINOR

The first Luton Minor flew in 1936 and proved entirely suitable for construction and operation by amateur builders and pilots. Examples were built pre-war in England and other parts of the world.

In 1960, the design was modernised and restressed completely to the latest British Airworthiness Requirements, allowing for a power increase to 41 kW (55 hp) and a maximum flying weight of 340 kg (750 lb).

Minors are under construction in many parts of the world, and a considerable number of amateur built examples have been completed and flown successfully since mid-1962. At least one of them, built in Australia by R. A. Pearman and H. Nash, obtained a full Certificate of Airworthiness. An average of eight sets of plans is sold each year by the PFA.

The following description applies to the aircraft in the form previously marketed by Phoenix, except where indicated. The 1983-84 edition of *Jane's* quoted performance figures for a Minor powered by a 27·5 kW (37 hp) Aeronca-JAP J.99 engine.

TYPE: Single-seat homebuilt monoplane.

AIRFRAME: Strut braced parasol monoplane. Wing section RAF 48. No dihedral. Wooden two-spar structure in two halves, attached to the fuselage by tubular centre-section pylons and braced by parallel lift struts of streamline-section steel tubing. Wings removable for ground transport and storage. Leading-edge and tips plywood covered, remainder fabric covered. Plain ailerons of wood construction, fabric covered, hinged directly from rear spar. No flaps. Rectangular all-wood fuselage structure. Sides and bottom plywood covered. Curved decking aft of cockpit fabric covered. Cantilever all-wood tail unit structure, fabric covered. Aerodynamically balanced rudder.

LANDING GEAR: Non-retractable tailwheel type with divided main legs of tubular steel construction. Rubber disc shock absorbers. Brakes and wheel fairings optional. Fully castoring tailwheel.

POWER PLANT: One 1,600 cc Volkswagen modified motor-car engine is usually installed, driving a two-blade fixed-pitch wooden propeller. Fuel tank forward of cockpit, capacity 29·5 litres (6·5 Imp gallons). Provision for additional tanks in wings.

ACCOMMODATION: Single seat in open cockpit. Coupé top optional. Baggage space aft of seat.

DIMENSIONS, EXTERNAL:

Wing span	7·62 m (25 ft 0 in)
Wing chord, constant	1·60 m (5 ft 3 in)
Wing aspect ratio	5
Length overall	6·32 m (20 ft 9 in)
Height overall	2·29 m (7 ft 6 in)

AREA:

Wings, gross	11·6 m² (125·0 sq ft)

WEIGHTS AND LOADING:

Weight empty	177 kg (390 lb)
Max T-O weight	340 kg (750 lb)
Max wing loading	29·3 kg/m² (6·0 lb/sq ft)

PERFORMANCE (Volkswagen 1,600 cc engine, at normal T-O weight):

Max level speed at 457 m (1,500 ft)	65 knots (120 km/h; 75 mph)
Normal cruising speed	60 knots (111 km/h; 69 mph)
Stalling speed	25 knots (45 km/h; 28 mph)
Max rate of climb at S/L	107 m (350 ft)/min
T-O run	92 m (300 ft)
Landing run	36·5 m (120 ft)
Range:	
with standard fuel	155 nm (290 km; 180 miles)
with auxiliary tanks	340 nm (645 km; 400 miles)

SOUTHDOWN

SOUTHDOWN AÉROSTRUCTURE

Lasham Airfield, Alton, Hampshire GU34 5SR
Telephone: 025 683 359
DIRECTOR: Ken Fripp

SOUTHDOWN PIPISTRELLE 2B (BAT)

The Pipistrelle was designed in France in mid-1981 by M Robert Jacquet, who formed the Aérostructure company to manufacture this aircraft. Flight testing of the 2A prototype was completed by the end of that year, and production of the Pipistrelle 2B started during the first half of 1982. A total of 20 Pipistrelles was built in France.

Production rights were acquired by the newly established Southdown Aérostructure in Great Britain. Modifications have been made to comply with British Civil Airworthiness Requirements, and CAA approval was expected in 1985. The latest model, conforming to UK regulations, is known as the **Pipistrelle 2C**.

The following details refer to the Pipistrelle 2B:

TYPE: Single-seat microlight aircraft; conforms to FAI, CAA and French national requirements.

AIRFRAME: Braced high-wing monoplane with pod and boom fuselage. Constant chord wings, of Wortmann section, have a leading-edge/main spar structure of glassfibre, forming an integral fuel tank and extending to 36 per cent chord. Aft of this are the glassfibre/epoxy resin ribs, and a subspar supporting duralumin ailerons. Spoilers forward of, and linked to, ailerons. Entire wing covered in Aerolene. Single bracing strut each side. Glassfibre fuselage, moulded in two halves, with tubular tailboom supporting a V tail of similar construction to wings. Three-axis control by ailerons and 'ruddervators'. Control surfaces operated by sealed-bearing pushrods. Aircraft can be dismantled in 10 min, by two persons, for transportation and storage.

LANDING GEAR: Non-retractable tailwheel type, with cantilever glassfibre legs and Motobécane tyres, size 2·75 × 10, on main units. No brakes. Steerable tailwheel, with tyre size 200 × 50.

POWER PLANT: One 22·4 kW (30 hp) JPX PUL 505 two-cylinder piston engine, mounted aft of cockpit and wing with direct drive to a two-blade wooden pusher propeller. Manual starting. Integral fuel tank in wing leading-edge, capacity 30 litres (6·6 Imp gallons).

ACCOMMODATION: Pilot only, in open cockpit.

DIMENSIONS, EXTERNAL:

Wing span	11·20 m (36 ft 9 in)
Wing aspect ratio	9·3
Length overall	5·00 m (16 ft 5 in)
Height overall	1·80 m (5 ft 11 in)
Propeller diameter	0·95 m (3 ft 1½ in)

AREA:

Wings, gross	13·50 m² (145·3 sq ft)

WEIGHTS AND LOADINGS:

Weight empty	130 kg (287 lb)
Pilot weight range	55-90 kg (122-198 lb)
Max T-O weight	250 kg (551 lb)
Max wing loading	18·52 kg/m² (3·79 lb/sq ft)
Max power loading	11·16 kg/kW (18·37 lb/hp)

PERFORMANCE:

Never-exceed speed	70 knots (130 km/h; 81 mph)
Max cruising speed	54 knots (100 km/h; 62 mph)
Econ cruising speed	46 knots (85 km/h; 53 mph)
Stalling speed, power off	23 knots (42 km/h; 26 mph)
Max rate of climb at S/L	180 m (590 ft)/min
Service ceiling	3,000 m (9,840 ft)
T-O run	30-40 m (98-132 ft)
Landing run	30 m (98 ft)
Range with max fuel	162 nm (300 km; 186 miles)
Endurance	3 h
g limits	+4/−2
Best glide ratio	14

TAYLOR

T. TAYLOR

79 Springwater Road, Leigh-on-Sea, Essex SS9 5BW
Telephone: (0702) 521484

The late Mr John F. Taylor, AMIED, an amateur constructor, designed and built the prototype of a single-seat light sporting monoplane, designated J.T.1. Construction took about 14 months, and it flew for the first time on 4 July 1959.

A second design by Mr Taylor, the J.T.2 Titch, was awarded second prize in the Midget Racer Design Competition organised by Mr Norman Jones of the Rollason company in 1964. A prototype was built and flown successfully, but crashed on 16 May 1967, killing its designer.

The designer's son, Mr T. Taylor, is continuing to market plans of both aircraft to amateur constructors.

TAYLOR J.T.1 MONOPLANE

Plans of the Taylor monoplane have been sold to amateur constructors in the United Kingdom and about 30 other countries in all parts of the world. Ninety-three J.T.1s are known to have flown in Australia, Canada, New Zealand, South Africa, the UK and USA.

Aircraft currently flying or under construction are fitted with a variety of engines, including the 30 kW (40 hp) Aeronca E 113, 48·5 kW (65 hp) Continental A65, 48·5 kW (65 hp) Avco Lycoming, 53·7 kW (72 hp) two-stroke McCulloch and the modified Volkswagen series. Aircraft with the 48·5 kW (65 hp) engines have a 10 cm (4 in) longer nose and 25 cm (10 in) longer rear fuselage to maintain the correct CG position.

One accompanying illustration shows a J.T.1 that was originally completed (as CF-YCB) in 1966, but was refurbished by its current owner, Mr Robert A. Finch. Powered by a Volkswagen engine and now known as the Spitfire Kitten Mark I, it has a max T-O weight of 294 kg (649 lb), a max level speed of 108 knots (201 km/h; 125 mph) and range of 217 nm (402 km; 250 miles). Mr Finch is reportedly planning to produce wood kits of the modified aircraft. It was said to be the first foreign-built homebuilt aircraft to be FAA certificated in the USA.

The following details apply to the standard J.T.1 built to current plans:

TYPE: Single-seat fully aerobatic homebuilt monoplane.

AIRFRAME: Cantilever low-wing monoplane. Wing section RAF 48. Constant chord. Dihedral on outer panels 4°. Incidence 3°. Wooden two-spar structure, comprising centre-section and outer panels. Plywood and fabric covering. Differential ailerons. Split trailing-edge flaps. No tabs. Conventional plywood covered wood fuselage, with four main longerons and curved formers. Centre-section integral with fuselage. Cantilever fin and fixed incidence tailplane are plywood covered wood structures. Elevators and rudder are fabric covered wood structures.

LANDING GEAR: Non-retractable two-wheel type. Cantilever main legs, with coil spring shock absorption. Size 5 × 4 (305 mm; 12 in) mainwheels, tyre pressure 1·65 bars (24 lb/sq in). Leaf spring tailskid with steerable skid-pad. One example, built by Mr R. Ladd in the USA (see 1972-73 *Jane's*), has manually actuated inward-retracting main gear.

POWER PLANT: One 30 kW (40 hp) Volkswagen 1,500 cc modified motorcar engine, driving a two-blade propeller. Fuel tank aft of firewall, capacity 32 litres (7 Imp gallons).

ACCOMMODATION: Single seat under transparent Perspex canopy. Aerobatic harness. Small locker aft of seat.

DIMENSIONS, EXTERNAL:

Wing span	6·40 m (21 ft 0 in)
Wing aspect ratio	6
Length overall	4·57 m (15 ft 0 in)
Height over tail	1·47 m (4 ft 10 in)
Tailplane span	1·98 m (6 ft 6 in)
Wheel track	1·52 m (5 ft 0 in)

AREA:

Wings, gross	7·06 m² (76·0 sq ft)

WEIGHTS AND LOADINGS:

Weight empty	195 kg (430 lb)
Max T-O weight	299 kg (660 lb)
Max wing loading	42·4 kg/m² (8·68 lb/sq ft)
Max power loading	9·97 kg/kW (16·50 lb/hp)

PERFORMANCE:

Never-exceed speed	113 knots (209 km/h; 130 mph)
Max level speed at S/L	100 knots (185 km/h; 115 mph)
Econ cruising speed	87 knots (161 km/h; 100 mph)
Never-exceed speed with flaps down	56 knots (105 km/h; 65 mph)
Stalling speed: flaps up	40 knots (75 km/h; 46 mph)
flaps down	33 knots (62 km/h; 38 mph)
Max rate of climb at S/L	305 m (1,000 ft)/min
Range	252 nm (466 km; 290 miles)
g limits	±9

TAYLOR J.T.2 TITCH

Construction of the prototype Titch was started in February 1965 and it flew for the first time on 22 January 1967.

Thirty Titches are known to have been completed from plans, and flown in France, New Zealand, South Africa, Switzerland, the UK, USA and Zimbabwe. These are powered by engines ranging from 33·6 kW (45 hp) Volkswagen 1,600 cc modified motorcar engines to 78·3 kW (105 hp) Avco Lycomings. Plans for monoplanes and Titches have also been supplied to amateur constructors in Alaska, Argentina, Brazil, Denmark, Finland, Iceland, Ireland, Italy, Japan, Kenya, Mexico, Spain and Sweden.

The following description refers to the prototype:

TYPE: Single-seat homebuilt monoplane.

AIRFRAME: Cantilever low-wing monoplane. Taylor-modified NACA 23012 wing section. Dihedral 5° on top surface. Incidence 3°. Spruce structure with main box spar and 'plank' auxiliary spar. Plywood and fabric covering. Plain manually operated ply covered flaps over half-span and fabric covered differential ailerons. All-wood fuselage, with four main longerons, four secondary longerons and double-curvature ply covering. Aluminium cockpit side panels. All-wood tail unit structure, with fixed incidence tailplane. Fixed surfaces plywood covered, control surfaces fabric covered.

LANDING GEAR: Non-retractable tailwheel type. Steerable tailwheel. Chrome-vanadium compression coil-spring shock absorbers. Wheels of constructor's manufacture with 4-ply tyres size 5·00-4 and drum brakes.

POWER PLANT: One 63·5 kW (85 hp) Continental C85 flat-four engine, driving a Hegy wooden two-blade scimitar propeller. Glassfibre fuel tank between firewall and instrument panel, capacity 45·5 litres (10 Imp gallons). (1,834 cc VW engined version has 32 litre; 7 Imp gallon fuel tank.)

ACCOMMODATION: Single seat, with aerobatic harness, under bubble canopy hinged along starboard side.

DIMENSIONS, EXTERNAL:

Wing span	5·72 m (18 ft 9 in)
Wing chord: at root	1·37 m (4 ft 6 in)
at tip	0·91 m (3 ft 0 in)
Wing aspect ratio	5·14
Length overall	5·05 m (16 ft 7 in)
Height overall	1·42 m (4 ft 8 in)
Tailplane span	1·98 m (6 ft 6 in)
Wheel track	1·52 m (5 ft 0 in)
Propeller diameter	1·52 m (5 ft 0 in)

AREA:

Wings, gross	6·32 m² (68·0 sq ft)

WEIGHTS AND LOADINGS (A: 63·5 kW; 85 hp Continental engine, B: 44·7 kW; 60 hp Volkswagen 1,834 cc engine):

Weight empty: A	227 kg (500 lb)
B	218 kg (480 lb)
Max T-O weight: A	345 kg (760 lb)
B	335 kg (740 lb)
Max wing loading: A	54·59 kg/m² (11·18 lb/sq ft)
B	53·01 kg/m² (10·88 lb/sq ft)
Max power loading: A	5·43 kg/kW (8·94 lb/hp)
B	7·49 kg/kW (12·33 lb/hp)

PERFORMANCE (A and B as above, at max T-O weight except where indicated):

Never-exceed speed	195 knots (362 km/h; 225 mph)
Max level speed: A	174 knots (322 km/h; 200 mph)
B	113 knots (209 km/h; 130 mph)
Normal cruising speed:	
A	135 knots (250 km/h; 155 mph)
B	100 knots (185 km/h; 115 mph)
Econ cruising speed: A	95 knots (177 km/h; 110 mph)
B	89 knots (166 km/h; 103 mph)
Best approach speed	65 knots (121 km/h; 75 mph)
Stalling speed, flaps up:	
A	51 knots (94 km/h; 58 mph)
B	46 knots (86 km/h; 53 mph)
Stalling speed, flaps down:	
A	44 knots (81 km/h; 50 mph)
B	40 knots (74 km/h; 46 mph)
T-O speed	54 knots (100 km/h; 62 mph)
Touchdown speed	48 knots (89 km/h; 55 mph)
Max rate of climb at S/L	488 m (1,600 ft)/min
Range	330 nm (611 km; 380 miles)
g limits	±9

Luton L.A.4a Minor light monoplane

Southdown Aérostructure Pipistrelle *(Mike Jerram)*

Taylor J.T.1 monoplane built in Finland by Jouko Lehikoinen (1,500 cc Volkswagen engine)

Modified Taylor J.T.1 monoplane, known by its present owner as the Spitfire Kitten Mark I *(Howard Levy)*

Twin-engined prototype of the Tirith Firebird, showing shrouded propellers

Taylor J.T.2 Titch built and flown in Switzerland *(Martin Fricke)*

TIRITH

TIRITH MICROPLANE LTD

77 Alston Drive, Bradwell Abbey, Milton Keynes MK13 9HG
Telephone: 0908 311544
Telex: 826813 AQUATC G
CHAIRMAN AND CHIEF EXECUTIVE: B. P. Hogan, MA
DIRECTORS:
L. M. Hogan
E. J. McIntyre-Brown
R. D. McIntyre-Brown
W. A. Pyatt
M. G. Wright

Tirith currently has two three-axis control microlights in its range and has reportedly taken over the rights to the US Birdman RB-1 (formerly TL-1) designed by the late Emmett Tally. Little information regarding modifications and updates to be incorporated into the Birdman design was available at the time of writing, though it is believed that composites will be incorporated into the airframe in areas where wood was used previously. The Tirith version will be known as the Ultra 1.

TIRITH FIREBIRD FB-1

The first Firebird prototype, which flew in October 1982, was a single-engined single-seater. It was found to be underpowered, and was cannibalised to build a second, twin-engined prototype. This version was developed into the standard single-seat model.

Unusual in having a ducted installation for its two pusher propellers, the Firebird was designed by Prof D. Howe and Mr J. H. Webb of the College of Aeronautics, Cranfield. Production of the single-seater is not yet under way.

TYPE: Single-seat microlight aircraft; conforms to FAI/CAA requirements, and to CAP 482 Section S.

AIRFRAME: Strut braced high-wing monoplane, built of aluminium alloy and rigid composite materials (glassfibre, epoxy and foam plastics). Constant chord wings, fuselage pod, composite tailboom, and conventional tail surfaces. Full three-axis controls (ailerons, elevator and rudder), actuated by pushrods. Half span flaps.

LANDING GEAR: Non-retractable tricycle type, with 10 in diameter wheel on each unit. Mainwheels carried on self-sprung glassfibre composite cantilever legs; steerable nosewheel with brake.

POWER PLANT: Two 16·5 kW (22 hp) 432 cc NGL WAM 432 two-cylinder two-stroke engines, mounted side by side behind pilot's seat, each with direct drive to a two-blade wooden pusher propeller turning inside a wide chord annular shroud. Single fuel tank, capacity 36·5 litres (8 Imp gallons).

ACCOMMODATION: Pilot only, in open sided cockpit, with one-piece wraparound windscreen.

DIMENSIONS, EXTERNAL:
Wing span 9·03 m (29 ft 7½ in)
Wing aspect ratio 5·61
Length overall 5·61 m (18 ft 5 in)
Height overall 2·74 m (9 ft 0 in)
Propeller diameter 0·84 m (2 ft 9 in)
AREA:
Wings, gross 14·52 m² (156·3 sq ft)
WEIGHTS AND LOADINGS:
Weight empty 140 kg (308 lb)
Pilot weight range 55-90 kg (121-198 lb)
Max T-O weight 250 kg (551 lb)
Max wing loading 17·2 kg/m² (3·52 lb/sq ft)
Max power loading 7·62 kg/kW (12·53 lb/hp)
PERFORMANCE (at max T-O weight):
Never-exceed speed 73 knots (135 km/h; 84 mph)
Max level speed 52 knots (96 km/h; 60 mph)
Max cruising speed 48 knots (88 km/h; 55 mph)
Stalling speed 23 knots (42 km/h; 26 mph)
Max rate of climb at S/L 260 m (850 ft)/min
T-O to, and landing from, 15 m (50 ft) 92 m (300 ft)
Endurance with max fuel, with reserves 2 h
g limits +6/−3

TIRITH FIREBIRD FB-2

The Firebird FB-2 is a two-seat development of the FB-1, with side by side seating. Airframe is structurally similar, but with a fully enclosed cabin. The prototype has been completed. It is expected to have a performance broadly comparable with that of the FB-1. Details as for the FB-1 except:

DIMENSIONS, EXTERNAL:
Wing span 9·59 m (31 ft 5½ in)
Wing aspect ratio 5·96
AREA:
Wings, gross 15·43 m² (166·1 sq ft)
WEIGHTS AND LOADINGS:
Weight empty 150 kg (331 lb)
Pilot weight range 55-90 kg (121-198 lb)
Max T-O weight 350 kg (771 lb)
Max wing loading 22·7 kg/m² (4·65 lb/sq ft)
Max power loading 10·67 kg/kW (17·52 lb/hp)

WESTWIND

WESTWIND CORPORATION LTD

29 Hillcrest Avenue, Edgware, Middlesex HA8 8NZ
Telephone: (01) 958 8539
DIRECTOR: Joe Sudwarts

WESTWIND PHOENIX SG-1

The Phoenix SG-1 was designed and built by Mr Bruce Giddings while he was with Soleair Aviation (1983-84 *Jane's*). Westwind Corporation acquired all rights to the aircraft in September 1983, and the first production standard machine made its first flight in November 1983. The Phoenix SG-1 is intended primarily as a 'working' microlight for cropspraying, observation and bush transport, especially in Third World countries. A small number of Phoenix SG-1s has been built.

TYPE: Two-seat canard microlight; conforms to BCAR Section S requirements.

AIRFRAME: Main structure of aluminium alloy, with GRP fuselage pod. Sweptback (18°) wing surfaces, strut and stainless steel cable braced, with glassfibre/foam winglets. Foreplane is a non-lifting, de-stabilising pitch control surface. Three-axis control (tip rudders, foreplane and spoilers).

LANDING GEAR: Non-retractable tricycle type, with bungee suspension. Mainwheels size 4 × 6; steerable nosewheel size 3·50 × 6. Brakes on mainwheels. Floats and amphibious float gear optional.

POWER PLANT (prototype): One 37·3 kW (50 hp) Fuji Robin EC44-2PM engine, with reduction drive to a two-blade wooden pusher propeller. Trials are being conducted with 37·3 kW (50 hp) and 60 kW (80 hp) watercooled engines. Standard fuel capacity 32 litres (7 Imp gallons) in two integral tanks in fuselage fairing.

ACCOMMODATION: Two seats in open cockpit, with windscreen.

EQUIPMENT: Cropspraying equipment optional.

DIMENSIONS, EXTERNAL:
Wing span 10·97 m (36 ft 0 in)
Wing aspect ratio 6·5
Length overall 4·62 m (15 ft 2 in)
Height overall 2·90 m (9 ft 6 in)
Propeller diameter 1·57 m (5 ft 2 in)

AREA:
Wings, gross 18·58 m² (200·0 sq ft)

WEIGHTS AND LOADINGS:
Design weight empty 150 kg (330 lb)
Max T-O weight 397 kg (875 lb)
Max wing loading 21·39 kg/m² (4·38 lb/sq ft)
Max power loading (50 hp) 10·66 kg/kW (17·50 lb/hp)

PERFORMANCE:
Never-exceed speed 87 knots (161 km/h; 100 mph)
Max level and max cruising speed 65 knots (120 km/h; 75 mph)
Econ cruising speed 56 knots (104 km/h; 65 mph)
Stalling speed:
power on 28 knots (52 km/h; 32 mph)
power off 31 knots (57 km/h; 35 mph)
Max rate of climb at S/L:
with pilot only 366 m (1,200 ft)/min
at max T-O weight 183 m (600 ft)/min
T-O run 61 m (200 ft)
Landing run 46 m (150 ft)
Range with max fuel 113 nm (209 km; 130 miles)
Endurance with max fuel, 10 min reserves 2 h
g limits +6/−2·5 ultimate

WHITTAKER

MICHAEL W. J. WHITTAKER

Dawlish Cottage, Pincots Lane, Wickwar, Wooton-under-Edge, Gloucestershire GL12 8NY
Telephone: Wickwar (045 424) 598

Mr Michael Whittaker's MW5 Sorcerer is currently being marketed by Aerotech International (which see). His latest design is the MW6, a tandem two-seater that fulfils both microlight and homebuilt regulations.

WHITTAKER MW6

Design of this two-seat aircraft began in 1985, when construction of the single prototype was started. This flew for the first time in May 1986. It is not known whether the MW6 will become available to amateur builders.

The MW6 follows the basic layout of the earlier MW5 Sorcerer, but does not have the streamline nose fairing of that type.

TYPE: Two-seat homebuilt and microlight aircraft.

AIRFRAME: Strut braced high-wing monoplane. Constant chord rigid wings, of NACA 4412 section, with 1° dihedral and 1° 30′ incidence. Bracing strut on each side. Aluminium alloy spar, wooden ribs, double surface fabric covered. Fuselage mainframe of aluminium alloy tubes, bolted together. Three-axis control (ailerons, rudder and all-moving tailplane), with fixed tab on tailplane.

LANDING GEAR: Non-retractable tricycle type, with unsprung nosewheel and mainwheels carried on spring legs. Mainwheels size 6·00-6, pressure 1·73 bars (25 lb/sq in); nosewheel size 4·00-4, pressure 1·38 bars (20 lb/sq in). No brakes.

POWER PLANT: One 37·3 kW (50 hp) Fuji Robin EC44PM 432 cc two-cylinder two-stroke engine, with 2·6:1 reduction gear to a Newton two-blade wooden propeller. Fuel capacity 18 litres (4 Imp gallons). Optional 34 kW (45·6 hp) Rotax 503 two-cylinder two-stroke engine.

ACCOMMODATION: Pilot and passenger in tandem in open position.

DIMENSIONS, EXTERNAL:
Wing span 9·75 m (32 ft 0 in)
Wing chord, constant 1·52 m (5 ft 0 in)
Wing aspect ratio 6·4
Length overall 5·33 m (17 ft 6 in)
Height overall 2·59 m (8 ft 6 in)
Tailplane span 2·74 m (9 ft 0 in)
Wheel track 1·52 m (5 ft 0 in)
Wheelbase 1·22 m (4 ft 0 in)
Propeller diameter 1·57 m (5 ft 2 in)

AREA:
Wings, gross 14·86 m² (160·0 sq ft)

WEIGHTS AND LOADINGS:
Weight empty 150 kg (330 lb)
Crew weight range 46-181 kg (100-400 lb)
Max T-O weight 340 kg (750 lb)
Max wing loading 22·9 kg/m² (4·69 lb/sq ft)
Max power loading 9·12 kg/kW (15·00 lb/hp)

PERFORMANCE:
Never-exceed speed 65 knots (120 km/h; 74 mph)
Max level speed 55 knots (102 km/h; 63 mph)
Max cruising speed 50 knots (93 km/h; 58 mph)
Econ cruising speed 45 knots (83 km/h; 52 mph)
Stalling speed, power off 28 knots (52 km/h; 33 mph)
Max rate of climb at S/L: solo 290 m (950 ft)/min
dual 152 m (500 ft)/min
Service ceiling 3,050 m (10,000 ft)
T-O run 61 m (200 ft)
Landing run 55 m (180 ft)
Range with max standard fuel 78 nm (144 km; 90 miles)

WORLD WIDE

WORLD WIDE RACING SERVICES

281 Hithermoor Road, Stanwell Moor, Staines, Middlesex TW19 6AZ
Telephone: Colnbrook 2019
Telex: 849234

World Wide Racing Services announced in early 1984 that it would manufacture in Britain the Canadian Ultravia Le Pelican (which see), powered by a 26 kW (35 hp) Global 1,039 cc two-cylinder four-stroke engine. The UK version will be known as the Super Pelican. Several modifications to the airframe are expected, including strengthening of the landing gear and the addition of wing drag struts.

UNITED STATES OF AMERICA

ABERNATHY

BOB ABERNATHY

Brooks, Georgia

Among aircraft available to the US team at the 1986 World Aerobatic Championships was an aircraft of the Stephens Akro/Laser type built by Mr Bob Abernathy and known as the Streaker (NILM).

ABERNATHY STREAKER

The general appearance of this small single-seat aerobatic competition aircraft is shown in an accompanying illustration. Few details are available except that it flew for the first time in 1983 and was piloted by Linda Meyers in Summer 1986.

POWER PLANT: One 149 kW (200 hp) Avco Lycoming AEIO-360-A1D flat-six engine, driving a two-blade propeller. Fuel capacity 68 litres (18 US gallons) standard, 136 litres (36 US gallons) with auxiliary tank.

WEIGHTS:
Weight empty 468 kg (1,031 lb)
Max T-O weight 590 kg (1,300 lb)

PERFORMANCE:
Never-exceed speed 208 knots (386 km/h; 240 mph)
Max cruising speed 165 knots (306 km/h; 190 mph)
Stalling speed 54 knots (100 km/h; 62 mph)
T-O run 153 m (500 ft)
Landing run 244 m (800 ft)
Range with auxiliary tank 700 nm (1,295 km; 805 miles)
g limits ±9

ACEY DEUCY

ACEY DEUCY SPORT AIRCRAFT INC

4 Donald Drive, Middletown, Rhode Island 02840
Telephone: (401) 846 6757
PRESIDENT: John C. Powell

John Powell, formerly a Commander in the US Navy, designed and built a two-seat parasol monoplane known as the P-70 Acey Deucy, of which plans are available to amateur constructors from Acey Deucy Sport Aircraft. Design of the aircraft was started in 1966; construction began during 1968, and it flew for the first time on 20 June 1970. It has since accumulated about 600 hours flying time.

A total of 498 sets of plans for the Acey Deucy had been sold by early 1986, when about 20 were flying. The first aircraft built from plans flew in 1972.

One Acey Deucy, powered by a 74·5 kW (100 hp) Continental O-200 engine and with a twin float landing gear, was built by Mr Richard Layton of Acton, Massachusetts, and Mr Herbert Talbot of Tequesta, Florida. An illustration of this Acey Deucy can be found in the 1985-86 *Jane's*. An Acey Deucy fitted with a sliding canopy over the cockpits was illustrated in the 1982-83 edition.

Mr Powell has modified his prototype Acey Deucy to biplane configuration, referring to it as the Acey Deucy Mk II Biplane. Details and an illustration of this can be found in the 1984-85 *Jane's*.

POWELL P-70 ACEY DEUCY

TYPE: Two-seat homebuilt monoplane.

AIRFRAME: Braced parasol monoplane with steel tube V bracing struts on each side, auxiliary bracing struts and N centre-section struts. Wing section NACA 4412. Dihedral 1° on outer panels. Incidence 2°. No sweepback. Wings have wood spars and ribs, and Frise ailerons of wood, all fabric covered. No flaps or trim tabs. Welded 4130 steel tube fuselage, with wood stringers, and wire braced tail unit with U channel ribs, all fabric covered. Tailplane incidence adjustable by screwjack at leading-edge. Trim tab on port elevator.

LANDING GEAR: Non-retractable tailwheel type. Two side Vs and half axles hinged to fuselage structure. Shock absorption by springs in compression. Goodyear mainwheels and tyres size 8·00-4 or 6·00-6, pressure 0·83 bars (12 lb/sq in). Motor scooter caliper brakes. At least one Acey Deucy is flying as a seaplane, with floats of 750 kg (1,650 lb) displacement.

POWER PLANT: Designer recommends use of Continental engines from 48·5-67 kW (65 to 90 hp), although at least one Acey Deucy has a 74·5 kW (100 hp) Continental (see introductory copy) and another has an Avco Lycoming O-290-D. Prototype has one 48·5 kW (65 hp) Continental A65 flat-four engine, driving a McCauley two-blade fixed-pitch metal propeller. One fuel tank in fuselage, immediately aft of firewall, capacity 53 litres (14 US gallons). Refuelling point on top of fuselage, forward of front cockpit. Oil capacity 3·75 litres (1 US gallon).

ACCOMMODATION: Two persons in tandem, in open cockpits with windscreens. Sliding canopy optional. Small door by front cockpit on starboard side. Baggage space, with 11·3 kg (25 lb) capacity.

Westwind Phoenix SG-1 canard microlight

Whittaker MW6 two-seat aircraft *(Edwin A. Shackleton)*

Powell P-70 Acey Deucy monoplanes built by Dr Dale E. Turner of Punta Gorda, Florida, and Mr Chandler Sarles of Arcadia, Florida

Abernathy Streaker aerobatic competition aircraft *(Austin J. Brown)*

Acro Sport I built by students of Mosley High School in Panama City, Florida, under the leadership of Mr Frank Smith

DIMENSIONS, EXTERNAL:	
Wing span	9·91 m (32 ft 6 in)
Wing chord, constant	1·52 m (5 ft 0 in)
Wing aspect ratio	6·5
Length overall	6·32 m (20 ft 9 in)
Height overall	2·06 m (6 ft 9 in)
Tailplane span	2·59 m (8 ft 6 in)
Wheel track	1·83 m (6 ft 0 in)
Propeller diameter	1·88 m (6 ft 2 in)
AREA:	
Wings, gross	14·4 m² (155·0 sq ft)

WEIGHTS AND LOADINGS (prototype):	
Weight empty	340 kg (750 lb)
Max T-O weight	578 kg (1,275 lb)
Max wing loading	40·2 kg/m² (8·23 lb/sq ft)
Max power loading	11·92 kg/kW (19·62 lb/hp)

PERFORMANCE (prototype):	
Never-exceed speed	117 knots (217 km/h; 135 mph)
Max level speed at S/L	90 knots (167 km/h; 104 mph)
Max cruising speed at S/L	82 knots (153 km/h; 95 mph)
Econ cruising speed at S/L	69 knots (129 km/h; 80 mph)
Stalling speed, engine idling	26 knots (49 km/h; 30 mph)
Max rate of climb at S/L	190 m (625 ft)/min
Service ceiling (approx)	over 2,745 m (9,000 ft)
T-O and landing run	76 m (250 ft)
T-O to 15 m (50 ft)	approx 213 m (700 ft)
Landing from 15 m (50 ft)	274 m (900 ft)
Range, with 30 min reserves	217 nm (402 km; 250 miles)

ACRO SPORT

ACRO SPORT INC

PO Box 462, Hales Corners, Wisconsin 53130
Telephone: (414) 529 2609
PRESIDENT: LaFonda Jean Kinnaman

Acro Sport Inc currently sells plans of the single-seat Acro Sport I biplane, the Super Acro Sport, the Volkswagen-engined Pober Pixie parasol monoplane, the two-seat Acro Sport II biplane, the Cougar Model 1 cross-country high-wing monoplane and the Corben Jr Ace/Super Ace types. The Acro Sport I, Super Acro Sport, Acro Sport II and Pober Pixie were all designed by Mr Paul H. Poberezny, President of the entirely separate Experimental Aircraft Association.

ACRO SPORT I

The Acro Sport I was designed by Mr Paul Poberezny specifically for construction by school students as a pupils' project. First flight of the prototype (N1AC) was made on 11 January 1972, only 352 days after its design was started. Plans and construction manuals are available to homebuilders, and about 12,000 sets had been sold by early 1986. More than fifty Acro Sport Is were flying by then.

The following details apply to the prototype:

TYPE: Single-seat aerobatic homebuilt biplane.

AIRFRAME: Braced single-bay biplane wings, with single streamline-section interplane strut each side. N centre-section struts. Double streamline-section flying and landing wires. Wing section Munk M-6. Dihedral: upper 0°, lower 2°. Incidence (both) 1° 30′. Conventional two-spar structure, with spruce spars and ribs, single wire drag and anti-drag truss, fabric covered. Glassfibre wingtips. Ailerons, on all four wings, of wood construction with fabric covering. No flaps. Cutout in trailing-edge of upper wing. Fuselage structure of welded steel tube, with wooden stringers, fabric covered. Glassfibre nose cowl and light alloy engine cowlings. Wire braced welded steel tube tail unit, with fabric covering. Controllable trim tab on port side of elevator; servo tab on starboard side.

LANDING GEAR: Non-retractable tailwheel type, modified from Piper J-3 components. Two side Vs and half axles. Rubber bungee shock absorption. Mainwheel tyres size 5·00-5, pressure 1·86-1·93 bars (27-28 lb/sq in). Cleveland or Goodyear hydraulic brakes. Glassfibre wheel fairings. Steerable tailwheel. Parking brake.

POWER PLANT: Prototype has a 134 kW (180 hp) Avco Lycoming engine, driving a Sensenich two-blade fixed-pitch metal propeller with spinner. Basic power plant is a 74·5 kW (100 hp) Continental O-200 flat-four engine. Single fuel tank immediately aft of firewall, capacity 104 litres (20 US gallons). Refuelling point on upper surface of fuselage. Small smoke oil tank, capacity 19 litres (5 US gallons), forward of instrument panel, could also be used for fuel.

ACCOMMODATION: Single seat in open cockpit, which is large enough to accommodate a pilot 1·95 m (6 ft 5 in) tall and weighing 115 kg (250 lb). Baggage space behind headrest, capacity 16 kg (35 lb).

DIMENSIONS, EXTERNAL:	
Wing span: upper	5·97 m (19 ft 7 in)
lower	5·82 m (19 ft 1 in)
Wing chord (both), constant	0·91 m (3 ft 0 in)
Wing aspect ratio, upper	6·6

Length overall 5·33 m (17 ft 6 in)
Height overall 1·83 m (6 ft 0 in)
Tailplane span 2·16 m (7 ft 1 in)
Wheel track 1·78 m (5 ft 10 in)
Propeller diameter 1·93 m (6 ft 4 in)

AREA:
Wings, gross 10·73 m² (115·5 sq ft)

WEIGHTS AND LOADINGS:
Weight empty, equipped 335 kg (739 lb)
Max T-O and landing weight 534 kg (1,178 lb)
Max wing loading 49·77 kg/m² (10·20 lb/sq ft)
Max power loading (prototype) 3·99 kg/kW (6·54 lb/hp)

PERFORMANCE (at max T-O weight):
Never-exceed speed 156 knots (289 km/h; 180 mph)
Max level speed 132 knots (245 km/h; 152 mph)
Max cruising speed 113 knots (209 km/h; 130 mph)
Econ cruising speed 91 knots (169 km/h; 105 mph)
Stalling speed 44 knots (81 km/h; 50 mph)
Max rate of climb at S/L 1,066 m (3,500 ft)/min
T-O run 46 m (150 ft)
T-O to 15 m (50 ft) 107 m (350 ft)
Landing from 15 m (50 ft) 267 m (875 ft)
Landing run 244 m (800 ft)
Range with max fuel 304 nm (563 km; 350 miles)

SUPER ACRO SPORT

The design of this modified version of the Acro Sport I was started in January 1971. Construction began in the following year and the first flight of the prototype Super Acro Sport was made on 21 March 1973. Modifications include use of an IO-360 engine and a wing section modified from the Munk M-6 on the original Acro Sport to NACA 23012. They were made to improve aerobatic performance in inverted or outside aerobatic manoeuvres. The aircraft is intended for unlimited International Class aerobatic competition at world championship level.

The differences by comparison with the standard Acro Sport I are covered in a supplement to the basic plans available from Acro Sport Inc. The description of the Acro Sport I applies also to the Super Acro Sport, except as follows:

TYPE: Single-seat advanced homebuilt aerobatic biplane.

AIRFRAME: Wings as for Acro Sport I, except section NACA 23012. Tail unit as for Acro Sport I, except for controllable trim tab on starboard side of elevator, servo tab on port side.

LANDING GEAR: As Acro Sport I, except Cleveland hydraulic brakes. Steerable tailwheel has a solid tyre.

POWER PLANT: Prototype has a 149 kW (200 hp) Avco Lycoming IO-360-A2A flat-four engine, driving a Sensenich two-blade fixed-pitch metal propeller type 76EM8-0-60 with spinner. Fuel system and capacity as for Acro Sport I. Oil capacity 7·5 litres (2 US gallons).

DIMENSIONS, EXTERNAL: As for Acro Sport I, except:
Length overall 5·30 m (17 ft 4½ in)

WEIGHTS AND LOADINGS:
Weight empty 401 kg (884 lb)
Max T-O weight 612 kg (1,350 lb)
Max wing loading 57·0 kg/m² (11·7 lb/sq ft)
Max power loading 4·11 kg/kW (6·75 lb/hp)

PERFORMANCE (at max T-O weight):
Never-exceed speed 156 knots (289 km/h; 180 mph)
Max level speed at S/L 135 knots (251 km/h; 156 mph)
Max cruising speed 117 knots (217 km/h; 135 mph)
Stalling speed 44 knots (81 km/h; 50 mph)
Max rate of climb at S/L 1,128 m (3,700 ft)/min
Service ceiling 4,575 m (15,000 ft)
T-O run 38 m (125 ft)
T-O to 15 m (50 ft) 91 m (300 ft)
Landing from 15 m (50 ft) 274 m (900 ft)
Landing run 244 m (800 ft)
Range with max fuel 260 nm (482 km; 300 miles)

ACRO SPORT II

The Acro Sport II is a two-seat aerobatic biplane derived from the Acro Sport I, by Mr Paul Poberezny, for the pilot with only a low number of flying hours to his credit. Design began in 1976 and construction started in 1977. The first flight was achieved on 9 July 1978. Plans are available to the homebuilder and more than 1,000 sets had been sold by early 1986. More than 30 Acro Sport IIs were flying at that time.

TYPE: Two-seat homebuilt aerobatic biplane.

AIRFRAME: As for Acro Sport I.

LANDING GEAR: As for Acro Sport I, except for mainwheel tyres size 6·00-6; pressure unchanged.

POWER PLANT: Prototype has one 134 kW (180 hp) Avco Lycoming O-360-A4B engine, driving a Sensenich two-blade fixed-pitch metal propeller with spinner. Can be powered by engines of 74·5-149 kW (100-200 hp). Fuel capacity 98·4 litres (26 US gallons).

ACCOMMODATION: Two seats in tandem cockpits. Baggage space, capacity 13·6 kg (30 lb).

DIMENSIONS, EXTERNAL:
Wing span: upper 6·60 m (21 ft 8 in)
lower 6·32 m (20 ft 9 in)
Wing chord, constant 1·09 m (3 ft 7 in)
Length overall 5·75 m (18 ft 10¼ in)
Height overall 2·03 m (6 ft 7¾ in)
Wheel track 1·85 m (6 ft 0¾ in)

AREA:
Wings, gross 14·12 m² (152·0 sq ft)

WEIGHTS AND LOADINGS:
Weight empty 397 kg (875 lb)
Max T-O weight 689 kg (1,520 lb)
Max wing loading 48·8 kg/m² (10·0 lb/sq ft)
Max power loading (prototype) 5·14 kg/kW (8·44 lb/hp)

PERFORMANCE (prototype):
Max cruising speed 107 knots (198 km/h; 123 mph)
Stalling speed 46 knots (86 km/h; 53 mph)
Max rate of climb at S/L 457 m (1,500 ft)/min
T-O run 91 m (300 ft)
g limits +6·5/−4·5

POBER P-9 PIXIE

Design and construction of this lightweight sporting aircraft began simultaneously in January 1974, and the first flight was made in July 1974. The aircraft was seen to be similar to the Heath Parasol, but with a completely different fuselage to accommodate larger pilots, and powered by a converted Volkswagen motorcar engine. It made its public debut at the 1974 EAA Fly-in at Oshkosh, Wisconsin. Soon afterwards, the prototype was re-engined with a Limbach-VW engine, and a special pressure cowl was fitted to improve cooling and increase the cruising speed. Several of the dozen Pixies currently flying use the 48·5 kW (65 hp) Continental engine. The prototype has flown experimentally on 100% alcohol fuel.

Plans are available to amateur constructors, and more than 900 sets had been sold by early 1986. Acro Sport Inc is also developing a two-seat bi-wing parasol aircraft as a follow-on to the Pixie.

TYPE: Single-seat lightweight homebuilt sporting aircraft.

AIRFRAME: Braced parasol monoplane. Two streamline-section struts and wire bracing each side. Wing section Clark Y. Dihedral 2°. Incidence 2°. Conventional wooden wing structure utilising spruce spars, mahogany plywood and fabric covering. Full-span Frise ailerons. No flaps. No trim tabs. Welded fuselage structure of 4130 chrome molybdenum steel tubing with wood formers and fabric covering. Wire braced tail unit of welded 4130 chrome molybdenum steel tubing, fabric covered. Fixed incidence tailplane. No trim tabs.

LANDING GEAR: Non-retractable tailwheel type. Side Vs with half-axles carry mainwheels. Shock absorption by rubber bungee. Mainwheel tyres size 5·00-5, pressure 2·07 bars (30 lb/sq in). Tailwheel tyre of solid type. Cleveland brakes. Glassfibre fairings over mainwheels. The 1983-84 *Jane's* illustrated a Pixie with a ski landing gear.

POWER PLANT: One 44·5 kW (60 hp) Limbach SL 1700 EA flat-four engine, driving a Sensenich two-blade propeller. Equally suited to INAV Volkswagen engine conversions. Fuel tank in wing centre-section, capacity 46·6 litres (12·3 US gallons). Refuelling point in wing upper surface. Oil capacity 2·84 litres (0·75 US gallons).

ACCOMMODATION: Single seat in open cockpit. Door on starboard side. Baggage capacity 9 kg (20 lb).

DIMENSIONS, EXTERNAL:
Wing span 9·09 m (29 ft 10 in)
Wing chord, constant 1·37 m (4 ft 6 in)
Length overall 5·26 m (17 ft 3 in)
Height overall 1·88 m (6 ft 2 in)
Wheel track 1·60 m (5 ft 3 in)
Propeller diameter 1·35 m (4 ft 5 in)

AREA:
Wings, gross 12·47 m² (134·25 sq ft)

WEIGHTS AND LOADINGS:
Weight empty 246 kg (543 lb)
Max T-O weight 408 kg (900 lb)
Max wing loading 32·7 kg/m² (6·70 lb/sq ft)
Max power loading 9·17 kg/kW (15·00 lb/hp)

PERFORMANCE (at max T-O weight):
Never-exceed speed 113 knots (209 km/h; 130 mph)
Max level speed at S/L 89 knots (166 km/h; 103 mph)
Max cruising speed 72 knots (134 km/h; 83 mph)
Stalling speed 26 knots (49 km/h; 30 mph)
Max rate of climb at S/L 213 m (700 ft)/min
Service ceiling 3,810 m (12,500 ft)
T-O and landing run 91 m (300 ft)
T-O to 15 m (50 ft) 305 m (1,000 ft)
Landing from 15 m (50 ft) 152 m (500 ft)
Range with max fuel 251 nm (466 km; 290 miles)

COUGAR MODEL 1

The Cougar was designed by Mr Robert E. Nesmith, an early EAA member who wanted to encourage aviation among teenage boys and those people who felt they had been left out of flying due to the high cost of production aircraft. Construction of the prototype began in 1957, and the original fuselage was increased in size several times to accommodate taller pilots. At the July 1962 EAA Convention at Rockford, Illinois, Leonard and Rita Eaves' Cougar with folding wings for easy home storage won third place in the design contest. More than 100 Cougars have been built; the plans are now marketed by Acro Sport Inc.

TYPE: Two-seat high-wing homebuilt sporting aircraft.

AIRFRAME: Two-spar wooden wings with single streamlined strut to front spar on each side. Wings covered with ¹/₁₆ in plywood top and bottom. Dihedral 1°. Incidence 1°. Wing section modified NACA 4900-series. Ailerons of 4130 steel tubing with aluminium trailing-edges and 100% static balance. No flaps. Cutout on leading-edge of wing root for increased visibility. Welded steel tube fuselage structure with fabric covering. Glassfibre nose cowling and light alloy engine cowlings. Cantilever welded steel tube tail unit with fabric covering.

LANDING GEAR: Non-retractable tailwheel type, with tapered rod spring main legs. Mainwheel tyres size 5·00-5, pressure 1·86-1·93 bars (27-28 lb/sq in). Glassfibre wheel fairings. Steerable tailwheel.

POWER PLANT: Suitable engines range from 48·5 to 93·2 kW (65-125 hp), including the Continental C-65, C-85 and O-200; and Avco Lycoming O-235 and O-290. Single fuel tank immediately aft of firewall, capacity 11·4 kg (25 lb).

ACCOMMODATION: Two seats side by side in enclosed cockpit, large enough to accommodate persons 1·93 m (6 ft 4 in) tall. Baggage space behind pilot and passenger, capacity 27 kg (60 lb).

DIMENSIONS, EXTERNAL:
Wing span 6·25 m (20 ft 6 in)
Wing chord, constant 1·22 m (4 ft 0 in)
Wing aspect ratio 5·125
Length overall 5·77 m (18 ft 11 in)
Height overall 1·68 m (5 ft 6 in)
Tailplane span 1·88 m (6 ft 2 in)
Propeller diameter 1·63 m (5 ft 4 in)

AREA:
Wings, gross 7·62 m² (82·0 sq ft)

WEIGHTS AND LOADING:
Weight empty: standard 283 kg (624 lb)
with folding wings 312 kg (689 lb)
Max T-O weight 567 kg (1,250 lb)
Max wing loading 74·4 kg/m² (15·24 lb/sq ft)

PERFORMANCE (at max T-O weight):
Never-exceed speed 169 knots (313 km/h; 195 mph)
Max level speed 152 knots (281 km/h; 175 mph)
Max cruising speed 143 knots (265 km/h; 165 mph)
Econ cruising speed 104 knots (193 km/h; 120 mph)
Stalling speed 46 knots (86 km/h; 53 mph)
Max rate of climb at S/L 396 m (1,300 ft)/min
T-O run 152 m (500 ft)
T-O to 15 m (50 ft) 244 m (800 ft)
Landing from 15 m (50 ft) 214 m (700 ft)
Landing run 183 m (600 ft)
Range with max fuel 521 nm (965 km; 600 miles)

CORBEN JR ACE

The Corben Jr Ace was designed by Mr O. G. Corben in the 1920s as a follow-on to his Baby Ace. Rights to the Corben Jr Ace (and Super Ace) have been acquired by Acro Sport Inc. Several aircraft have been built to the Jr Ace plans, to which the following details apply:

TYPE: Two-seat homebuilt monoplane.

AIRFRAME: Braced parasol-wing monoplane, with two spars and internal drag/anti-drag wires. Wing section Clark Y. Dihedral 2°. Incidence 2°. Ailerons have wooden spars and ribs. Fuselage structure of welded steel tube and wooden stringers, fabric covered. Light alloy engine cowling. Wire braced tail unit, with fabric-covered steel tube structure.

LANDING GEAR: Non-retractable tailwheel type, with two side Vs and half-axles. Heavy duty shock absorbers. Mainwheels size 20 × 4 in.

POWER PLANT: One 33·6 kW (45 hp) Szekely, Aeromarine AR-350, Continental D65 or similar engine, driving a two-blade propeller. Fuel tank aft of firewall, capacity 38 litres (10 US gallons).

ACCOMMODATION: Two seats side by side in open or, optionally, enclosed cockpit. Baggage space aft of cockpit.

DIMENSIONS, EXTERNAL:
Wing span 10·35 m (33 ft 11½ in)
Wing chord, constant 1·52 m (5 ft 0 in)
Wing aspect ratio 6·9
Length overall 5·73 m (18 ft 9½ in)
Height overall 2·29 m (7 ft 6 in)
Tailplane span 2·44 m (8 ft 0 in)
Wheel track 1·70 m (5 ft 7 in)
Propeller diameter 1·93 m (6 ft 4 in)

AREA:
Wings, gross 15·61 m² (168·0 sq ft)

WEIGHTS AND LOADING:
Weight empty 255 kg (563 lb)
Max T-O weight 442 kg (975 lb)
Max wing loading 28·3 kg/m² (5·80 lb/sq ft)

PERFORMANCE (at max T-O weight):
Never-exceed speed 104 knots (193 km/h; 120 mph)
Max level speed at S/L 74 knots (137 km/h; 85 mph)
Max cruising speed 65 knots (121 km/h; 75 mph)
Econ cruising speed 61 knots (113 km/h; 70 mph)
Stalling speed 31 knots (57 km/h; 35 mph)
Max rate of climb at S/L 152 m (500 ft)/min
Service ceiling over 3,960 m (13,000 ft)
T-O run 46 m (150 ft)
T-O to 15 m (50 ft) 69 m (225 ft)
Landing from 15 m (50 ft) 61 m (200 ft)
Landing run 46 m (150 ft)
Range with max fuel 173 nm (322 km; 200 miles)

Acro Sport II aerobatic biplane built by Mr Jack Elenbaas of Holland, Michigan, with non-standard rounded wingtips, spring steel landing gear legs and a Plexiglas canopy over both cockpits

Super Acro Sport in knife-edge flight *(Dick Stouffer)*

Acro Sport Pober P-9 Pixie built by Mr Jose Barcellos of Porto Alegre, Brazil, and first flown in 1985

Corben Jr Ace built by Mr Wilton Weser of DesPlaines, Illinois

Cougar Model 1 built by Mr Charles Goodrich of Detroit, Michigan

Two-seat Advanced Aviation King Cobra *(Brian M. Service)*

ADVANCED AVIATION

ADVANCED AVIATION INC

323 North Ivey Lane, PO Box 16716, Orlando, Florida 32861

Telephone: (305) 298 2920

MARKETING MANAGER: Angel Matos

Current products available from Advanced Aviation include the Cobra microlight in various forms, the King Cobra and the HighCraft Buccaneer single-seat microlight amphibian. Advanced Aviation is also producing and marketing a land-based derivative of the single-seat Buccaneer, known as the Carrera, and a two-seat version designated Buccaneer II.

ADVANCED AVIATION COBRA

Single-seat aircraft of the Cobra series are similar in design and construction to Advanced Aviation's earlier Huski/Coyote series (see 1983-84 *Jane's*), but each model is slightly more compact and offers an improved performance. The prototype flew for the first time in 1982.

The current standard model is the **B377 Cobra B**, which qualifies under both microlight and Experimental regulations. The basically similar **B447 Cobra VIP**, which first flew in 1984, has disc brakes and a cushioned seat as standard, and is powered by the higher rated Rotax 447 engine, putting it in the Experimental category. The Rotax 532LC-engined **B532 AG Cobra**, which also flew for the first time in 1984, is equipped for cropspraying. More than 300 Cobra kits have been sold.

The following details refer to the Cobra B, unless stated otherwise, but are generally applicable to the other models in the Cobra series, except for differences noted above:

TYPE: Single-seat microlight; conforms to FAR Pt 103. Cobra VIP and AG Cobra conform to FAA Experimental category as homebuilt aircraft.

AIRFRAME: Wire braced high-wing monoplane with 1° 30′ dihedral. Aluminium alloy structure throughout, with double surface wing covering. Vinyl-coated stainless steel cables. Kingpost standard. Three-axis control (ailerons, elevators and rudder.) Options include adjustable trim tab on elevator, nose cowling, and recovery parachute, plus lights and instruments for Cobra VIP and radio for AG Cobra.

LANDING GEAR: Tricycle type, with all three wheels size 4 × 4 in. (AG Cobra has 6 × 4 in wheels.) Spring leg suspension. Brakes optional. (Mainwheel brakes standard on Cobra VIP and AG Cobra.) Floats and skis optional.

POWER PLANT: One 26 kW (35 hp) Rotax 377 two-cylinder two-stroke engine, with reduction gear to a two-blade wooden pusher propeller. (Cobra VIP has 30 kW; 40 hp Rotax 447 two-cylinder engine and AG Cobra uses a 48·5 kW; 65 hp Rotax 532LC liquid cooled two-cylinder engine with 2·58:1 reduction gear. Optional Rotax 532LC engine for Cobra VIP.) All models have 19 litre (5 US gallon) fuel tank.

ACCOMMODATION: Pilot only, in open position.

DIMENSIONS, EXTERNAL:

Wing span	10·57 m (34 ft 8 in)
Length overall	5·46 m (17 ft 10¾ in)
Height overall	2·51 m (8 ft 3 in)
Tailplane span	2·74 m (9 ft 0 in)
Wheel track	1·55 m (5 ft 1 in)
Propeller diameter: Cobra B	1·52 m (5 ft 0 in)
Cobra VIP and AG Cobra	1·73 m (5 ft 8 in)

AREA:

Wings, gross	13·56 m² (146·0 sq ft)

WEIGHTS AND LOADINGS (A: Cobra B, B: Cobra VIP, C: AG Cobra):

Weight empty: A	114 kg (252 lb)
B	147 kg (325 lb)
C	166 kg (365 lb)
Pilot weight range: A	50-102 kg (110-225 lb)
B	63·5-134 kg (140-295 lb)
C	50-113 kg (110-250 lb)
Max T-O weight: A	238 kg (525 lb)
B	319 kg (705 lb)
C	351 kg (775 lb)
Max wing loading: A	17·5 kg/m² (3·59 lb/sq ft)
B	23·6 kg/m² (4·83 lb/sq ft)
C	25·9 kg/m² (5·31 lb/sq ft)

Max power loading: A 9·15 kg/kW (15·00 lb/hp)
B 10·63 kg/kW (17·63 lb/hp)
C 7·24 kg/kW (11·92 lb/hp)

PERFORMANCE (A: Cobra B, B: Cobra VIP, C: AG Cobra):
Never-exceed speed:
A, B, C 65 knots (120 km/h; 75 mph)
Max level speed: A 55 knots (101 km/h; 63 mph)
B, C 59 knots (109 km/h; 68 mph)
Max cruising speed: A 52 knots (97 km/h; 60 mph)
B, C 55 knots (101 km/h; 63 mph)
Econ cruising speed:
A, C 39 knots (72 km/h; 45 mph)
B 42 knots (77 km/h; 48 mph)
Stalling speed: A 21 knots (39 km/h; 24 mph)
B, engine idling 22 knots (41 km/h; 25 mph)
C 28 knots (52 km/h; 32 mph)
Max rate of climb at S/L: A 229 m (750 ft)/min
B 366 m (1,200 ft)/min
C 168 m (550 ft)/min
Service ceiling: A 4,575 m (15,000 ft)
B, C 3,660 m (12,000 ft)
T-O run: A 30 m (100 ft)
B 23 m (75 ft)
C 107 m (350 ft)
T-O to 15 m (50 ft): A 84 m (275 ft)
B 76 m (250 ft)
C 152 m (500 ft)
Landing from 15 m (50 ft): A 76 m (250 ft)
B 107 m (350 ft)
C 152 m (500 ft)
Landing run: A 46 m (150 ft)
B 76 m (250 ft)
C 107 m (350 ft)
Range: A 78 nm (145 km; 90 miles)
B 83 nm (154 km; 96 miles)
C 52 nm (96 km; 60 miles)
Endurance: A, B 2 h
C 1 h 30 min

ADVANCED AVIATION B532 KING COBRA B

This two-seat version of the Cobra is powered normally by a 48·5 kW (65 hp) Rotax 532 engine, with optional engines of 32 kW (43 hp), 34·3 kW (46 hp) and 37·3 kW (50 hp). It flew for the first time in 1983 and is similar in construction to the single-seat Cobras. Like the Cobra VIP and AG Cobra, its weight puts it outside microlight regulations, but it qualifies as an FAA homebuilt aircraft.

The King Cobra uses the standard Cobra series wing, and overall dimensions remain the same, but the landing gear wheels/tyres are size 6 × 4 in. Options are similar to those of the single-seaters.

TYPE: Two-seat homebuilt aircraft; conforms to FAA Experimental category.

WEIGHTS AND LOADINGS:
Weight empty 147 kg (325 lb)
Crew weight range 50-190 kg (110-420 lb)
Max T-O weight 351 kg (775 lb)
Max wing loading 25·9 kg/m² (5·31 lb/sq ft)
Max power loading 7·24 kg/kW (11·92 lb/hp)

PERFORMANCE:
Never-exceed speed 65 knots (120 km/h; 75 mph)
Max level speed 59 knots (109 km/h; 68 mph)
Max cruising speed 55 knots (101 km/h; 63 mph)
Econ cruising speed 43 knots (80 km/h; 50 mph)
Stalling speed 27 knots (50 km/h; 31 mph)
Max rate of climb at S/L 198 m (650 ft)/min
Service ceiling 3,660 m (12,000 ft)
T-O and landing run 76 m (250 ft)
T-O to, and landing from, 15 m (50 ft) 152 m (500 ft)
Range 65 nm (120 km; 75 miles)
Endurance 1 h 30 min

ADVANCED AVIATION (HIGHCRAFT) BUCCANEER

The Buccaneer, which entered production in the Spring of 1983, is a somewhat unusual microlight: it is produced in bolt-together kit form primarily as an amphibious flying-boat, but can be built as a landplane for later upgrade to amphibian. Construction time is quoted as 50 hours, rigging time as 25 minutes.

Advanced Aviation is responsible for production and marketing of the Buccaneer. The following details refer to the **Model XA/350** amphibian, with the latest Rotax 377 engine as standard power plant:

TYPE: Single-seat amphibious microlight aircraft; conforms to FAR Pt 103.

AIRFRAME: Wire braced high-wing monoplane, with conventional tail unit. Aluminium alloy structure, double surface Dacron covered, except for glassfibre two-step hull and stabilising floats. Vinyl-coated stainless steel cables. Kingpost standard. Three-axis control (ailerons, elevators and rudder). Optional adjustable trim tab on elevator. Optional instruments and recovery parachute.

LANDING GEAR: Retractable tailwheel type for amphibious operations. Spring leg suspension. Skis optional.

POWER PLANT: One 26 kW (35 hp) Rotax 377 two-cylinder two-stroke engine, with reduction drive to an Ultra Prop four-blade composites ground-adjustable pusher propeller. Fuel tank capacity 17 litres (4·5 US gallons). Optional 20 kW (27 hp) Rotax 277 single-cylinder engine in **Model XA/280** or 30 kW (40 hp) Rotax 447 two-cylinder engine in **Model XA/430**.

ACCOMMODATION: Pilot only in semi-enclosed cabin.

DIMENSIONS, EXTERNAL (all models):
Wing span 10·21 m (33 ft 6 in)
Wing aspect ratio 6·93
Length overall: landplane 5·33 m (17 ft 6 in)
amphibian 5·84 m (19 ft 2 in)
Height overall 2·26 m (7 ft 4¾ in)
Tailplane span 2·44 m (8 ft 0 in)
Wheel track 1·40 m (4 ft 7 in)
Wheelbase 3·66 m (12 ft 0 in)
Propeller diameter 1·52 m (5 ft 0 in)

AREA (all models):
Wings, gross 15·05 m² (162·0 sq ft)

WEIGHTS AND LOADINGS (XA/350):
Weight empty 144 kg (318 lb)
Pilot weight range 50-113 kg (110-250 lb)
Max T-O weight 272 kg (600 lb)
Max wing loading 18·1 kg/m² (3·7 lb/sq ft)
Max power loading 10·46 kg/kW (17·14 lb/hp)

PERFORMANCE (XA/350 with 77 kg; 170 lb pilot):
Never-exceed speed 65 knots (120 km/h; 75 mph)
Max level speed at S/L 55 knots (101 km/h; 63 mph)
Max cruising speed at S/L 48 knots (89 km/h; 55 mph)
Econ cruising speed at S/L 39 knots (72 km/h; 45 mph)
Stalling speed at S/L 21 knots (39 km/h; 24 mph)
Max rate of climb at S/L 229 m (750 ft)/min
Service ceiling 3,960 m (13,000 ft)
T-O run: on land 38 m (125 ft)
on water 49 m (160 ft)
T-O to 15 m (50 ft): on land 96 m (315 ft)
from water 107 m (350 ft)
Landing from 15 m (50 ft): on land 137 m (450 ft)
Range 87 nm (161 km; 100 miles)
Endurance 2 h 15 min
g limits +5/−3·5
Best glide ratio 8

ADVANCED AVIATION (HIGHCRAFT) CARRERA

One of two new prototypes taken to the 1986 Sun 'n Fun meeting by Advanced Aviation was the single-seat Carrera (Racer), a land-based-only derivative of the Buccaneer with a non-retractable landing gear and elongated nose. It is proposed with three engine options and varying wing spans, the 20 kW (27 hp) Rotax 277 option falling under microlight regulations, the model with a 26 kW (35 hp) Rotax 377 coming under both microlight and Experimental categories, and the 30 kW (40 hp) Rotax 447 model being classified as an Experimental category type. All have 2·58:1 reduction gear, and fuel capacity of 15 litres (4 US gallons). Construction time is reportedly 50 hours and rigging time 25 minutes.

The following details are preliminary:

DIMENSIONS, EXTERNAL (A: Rotax 277, B: Rotax 377, C: Rotax 447):
Wing span: A, B 10·52 m (34 ft 6 in)
C 9·33 m (30 ft 7¼ in)
Length overall: A, B, C 6·19 m (20 ft 3½ in)
Height overall: A, B, C 1·83 m (6 ft 0 in)
Propeller diameter: A, B, C 1·63 m (5 ft 4 in)

AREA:
Wings, gross: A, B 12·45 m² (134·0 sq ft)

WEIGHTS AND LOADINGS (A, B, C as above):
Weight empty: A 114 kg (252 lb)
B 122 kg (270 lb)
C 129 kg (285 lb)
Max pilot weight: A 102 kg (225 lb)
B 113 kg (250 lb)
C 118 kg (260 lb)
Max T-O weight: A 238 kg (525 lb)
B 249 kg (550 lb)
C 272 kg (600 lb)
Max wing loading: A 17·6 kg/m² (3·60 lb/sq ft)
B 18·4 kg/m² (3·77 lb/sq ft)
C 22·8 kg/m² (4·67 lb/sq ft)
Max power loading: A 11·90 kg/kW (19·44 lb/hp)
B 9·58 kg/kW (15·71 lb/hp)
C 9·07 kg/kW (15·00 lb/hp)

PERFORMANCE (A, B, C as above):
Never-exceed speed:
A, B, C 73 knots (136 km/h; 85 mph)
Max level speed: A 52 knots (96 km/h; 60 mph)
B 55 knots (101 km/h; 63 mph)
C 65 knots (121 km/h; 75 mph)
Cruising speed: A 43 knots (80 km/h; 50 mph)
B 48 knots (89 km/h; 55 mph)
C 52 knots (97 km/h; 60 mph)
Max rate of climb at S/L: A 168 m (550 ft)/min
B 213 m (700 ft)/min
C 259 m (850 ft)/min
Service ceiling: A 3,965 m (13,000 ft)
B 4,570 m (15,000 ft)
C 4,265 m (14,000 ft)
T-O run: A, C 38 m (125 ft)
B 30 m (100 ft)
Landing run: A, B 38 m (125 ft)
C 46 m (150 ft)

ADVANCED AVIATION (HIGHCRAFT) XA/650 BUCCANEER II

This side by side two-seat derivative of the Buccaneer amphibian flew for the first time on 14 March 1986. It retains the general configuration and construction of the single-seater but has increased wing chord, larger ailerons and tail surfaces, is longer, and uses larger diameter tubing in its structure. The landing gear is retracted via a cockpit lever instead of manually. Power plant is a 48·5 kW (65 hp) Rotax 532 two-cylinder two-stroke engine, with 2·58:1 reduction gear. Fuel capacity is 45 litres (12 US gallons).

The Buccaneer II was trailered to the 1986 Sun 'n Fun meeting after completing only 5 flying hours, and the data below are preliminary. Kits will be made available, complete except for instruments.

DIMENSIONS, EXTERNAL:
Wing span 10·21 m (33 ft 6 in)
Length overall 6·65 m (21 ft 9½ in)
Height overall 2·13 m (7 ft 0 in)
Propeller diameter 1·73 m (5 ft 8 in)

AREA:
Wings, gross 15·89 m² (171·0 sq ft)

WEIGHTS AND LOADINGS:
Weight empty 236 kg (520 lb)
Max crew weight 195 kg (430 lb)
Max T-O weight 465 kg (1,025 lb)
Max wing loading 29·3 kg/m² (6·00 lb/sq ft)
Max power loading 9·59 kg/kW (15·8 lb/hp)

PERFORMANCE (preliminary, crew weight 154 kg; 340 lb):
Never-exceed speed 74 knots (136 km/h; 85 mph)
Max level speed at S/L 65 knots (120 km/h; 75 mph)
Max cruising speed at S/L 54 knots (100 km/h; 62 mph)
Econ cruising speed at S/L 50 knots (92 km/h; 57 mph)
Stalling speed: power off 29 knots (53 km/h; 33 mph)
Max rate of climb at S/L 167 m (550 ft)/min
T-O run: on land or water 77 m (250 ft)

ADVANCED COMPOSITE

ADVANCED COMPOSITE TECHNOLOGY

PRESIDENT: Mark A. Calder

Advanced Composite Technology appears to have been established by Mr Mark Calder to market plans and kits of the Wren microlight, which was developed under the company name of Wren Aircraft Inc. No details regarding any changes to the aircraft have been received, and no current address is known.

ADVANCED COMPOSITE TECHNOLOGY WREN

The Wren is a kit- or plans-built strut braced high-wing cabin monoplane, two prototypes of which were built in the Winter of 1982-83, one of them for static testing. Several more Wrens have since been built.

TYPE: Single-seat microlight aircraft; conforms to FAR Pt 103.

AIRFRAME: Built mainly of glassfibre, Kevlar and carbon-fibre, with a foam plastics core and Dacron covered, the Wren also utilises various kinds of wood and plywood. A reinforced fuselage centre-section of tubing serves also as roll cage, and is intended to survive rollover loads of up to 13*g*. Windscreen standard, enclosed cabin optional. Three-axis control (rudder, elevator and ailerons).

LANDING GEAR: Non-retractable tailskid type, with two side Vs and half axles. Mainwheels size 6·00-6. Brakes, floats and skis optional.

POWER PLANT: One 28·3 kW (38 hp) Kawasaki 440A two-cylinder two-stroke engine standard, with 2·25:1 belt reduction to 58 × 24 two-blade wooden propeller. Rotax 277 engine optional. Fuel capacity 17·4 litres (4·6 US gallons) in a single tank within the engine cowling. Auxiliary fuel tank optional.

DIMENSIONS, EXTERNAL:
Wing span 10·97 m (36 ft 0 in)
Wing aspect ratio 8·1
Length overall 5·49 m (18 ft 0 in)
Height overall 1·73 m (5 ft 8 in)
Propeller diameter 1·45 m (4 ft 9 in)

AREA:
Wings, gross 14·86 m² (160·0 sq ft)

WEIGHTS AND LOADINGS:
Weight empty 109 kg (241 lb)
Pilot weight range 41-91 kg (90-200 lb)
Max T-O weight 258 kg (570 lb)
Max wing loading 7·38 kg/m² (3·56 lb/sq ft)
Max power loading 9·13 kg/kW (15·00 lb/hp)

PERFORMANCE (at max T-O weight, Kawasaki engine):
Never-exceed speed 82 knots (152 km/h; 95 mph)
Max level speed 52 knots (97 km/h; 60 mph)

HighCraft Buccaneer microlight amphibian, marketed by Advanced Aviation *(Howard Levy)*

Carrera prototype, developed from the HighCraft Buccaneer and marketed by Advanced Aviation *(Howard Levy)*

The first kit built Wren microlight, constructed by Mr John Doerfler of Page, Arizona *(Howard Levy)*

HighCraft Buccaneer II two-seat homebuilt amphibian, marketed by Advanced Aviation *(Howard Levy)*

Aerocar Sooper-Coot Model A amphibian

Econ cruising speed	43 knots (80 km/h; 50 mph)
Stalling speed:	
power on	15 knots (28 km/h; 17 mph)
power off	20 knots (37 km/h; 23 mph)
Max rate of climb at S/L	335 m (1,100 ft)/min
Service ceiling	4,265 m (14,000 ft)
T-O run	30 m (100 ft)
Landing run	76 m (250 ft)
Range with max fuel	156 nm (289 km; 180 miles)
g limits	+6·2/−3·2
Best glide ratio	11
Min rate of sink, power off	76 m (250 ft)/min

AEROCAR

AEROCAR INC

PO Box 1171, Longview, Washington 98632
Telephone: (206) 423 8260

President and General Manager: Moulton B. Taylor

In February 1948 Aerocar Inc began developing a flying automobile designed by Mr M. B. Taylor. The prototype Aerocar, with an Avco Lycoming O-290 engine, was completed in October 1949. It was followed by a pre-production Aerocar Model I, with an Avco Lycoming O-320 engine, and this was used for tests which led to FAA airworthiness certification of the Aerocar on 13 December 1956. Four additional Model I Aerocars were completed subsequently for demonstration tours of the United States and for sale to customers, and were followed by the prototype of a refined Model III Aerocar. Details of the development and history of these roadable aircraft can be found in the 1979-80 and earlier editions of *Jane's*.

Aerocar Inc, which is basically a three-person operation, decided that legislation and economics inhibited further development of the Aerocar, and has since devoted most of its activity to other projects, notably the single-seat Mini-Imp, which embodies features of the Aerocar and is suitable for amateur construction. The later Micro-Imp is built mainly of glassfibre reinforced paper known as TPG (Taylor Paper Glass), for which other applications are being found.

In 1966 Aerocar built the prototype of a light flying-boat for a private customer. It was followed by two further aircraft, named Coot, on similar lines but fitted with tricycle landing gear for amphibious operation. Several hundred sets of plans for this aircraft, now known as the Sooper-Coot, have been sold to amateur constructors.

Development of the four-seat Imp by Aerocar, as recorded in the 1984-85 and previous editions of *Jane's*, is no longer taking place. In 1984, following a stroke suffered by Mr Taylor, the complete Imp programme was sold to Mr Michael Brown of Dayton, Ohio, who also took over the prototype then under construction in St Louis. Details can be found under the separate 'Brown' entry in this section. Similarly, the Perigee programme now appears under the name of its new owner, Mr Jerry Holcomb.

AEROCAR SOOPER-COOT MODEL A

The prototype of this aircraft flew for the first time in February 1971. It logged approximately 100 hours powered by an 89·5 kW (120 hp) Franklin 225 engine, driving a Sensenich fixed-pitch metal propeller. This was subsequently replaced by a 134 kW (180 hp) Franklin 335 engine, driving a Hartzell constant-speed metal propeller, and the aircraft has been flown extensively since 1972 with this more powerful engine.

The 'float-wing' configuration of the Sooper-Coot permits rough-water operation and, since the close proximity of the wings to the water forms a 'pressure wedge', unusually low take-off and landing speeds are possible without recourse to flaps or other lift enhancing devices.

The structure is basically of wood, but the tailboom and tail unit can be of steel tube and fabric, wood monocoque or all-metal construction. The rearward-folding wings, of NACA 4415 section, can be folded by one person. The fabric covered ailerons are of metal construction and statically balanced. There are no tip floats. Construction of the hull, which has only seven bulkheads, is straightforward, without the complication of wheel well doors. Tailplane and elevators also fold and the elevators have trim tabs. All control surfaces are statically balanced. The tricycle landing gear is manually retractable into the wings, but an alternative powered retraction system is shown on the plans.

Recommended power plant for the Sooper-Coot is a Franklin flat-six engine of either 134 or 164 kW (180 or 220 hp). However, many builders of the Sooper-Coot are fitting a 157 kW (210 hp) Continental IO-360. To minimise expenditure, others are fitting Avco Lycoming O-320 and O-320-B engines of 119 kW (160 hp). These are reported to be satisfactory if only a limited weight of optional equipment is installed in the aircraft. However, a constant-speed propeller has proved essential to maintain reasonable performance with the O-320/320-B. Maximum fuel capacity is 189 litres (50 US gallons).

Certain component parts (including the glassfibre engine cowls, glassfibre hull shell, foredeck, instrument panel, tail fairings, engine cooling fan blades and spring steel main landing gear legs), and plans, are available to amateur constructors. The company also maintains a list of recommended suppliers of welded assemblies and machined components. Many hundreds of Sooper-Coots were under construction in 1986, and more than 130 are known to be flying in the USA and other countries.

Dimensions, external:

Wing span	10·97 m (36 ft 0 in)
Wing chord, constant	1·52 m (5 ft 0 in)
Length overall	6·10 to 6·71 m (20 ft 0 in to 22 ft 0 in)

Height overall 2·44 m (8 ft 0 in)
Width folded 2·44 m (8 ft 0 in)
Tailplane span 3·05 m (10 ft 0 in)

AREA:
Wings, gross 16·72 m² (180·0 sq ft)

WEIGHTS AND LOADINGS:
Weight empty 499 kg (1,100 lb)
Max T-O weight 884 kg (1,950 lb)
Max wing loading 52·88 kg/m² (10·83 lb/sq ft)
Max power loading (180 hp) 6·60 kg/kW (10·83 lb/hp)

PERFORMANCE (134 kW; 180 hp engine, at max T-O weight):
Never-exceed speed 120 knots (223 km/h; 139 mph)
Max cruising speed 113 knots (209 km/h; 130 mph)
Econ cruising speed at 50% power 95 knots (177 km/h; 110 mph)
Max rate of climb at S/L 381 m (1,250 ft)/min
T-O run (land) 61 m (200 ft)
T-O (water) 6-8 s

AEROCAR MINI-IMP

The Mini-Imp is a single-seat version of the Aerocar Imp, to which it is generally similar (see 'Brown' entry in this section). The basic structure is all metal and is assembled with bolts and pop-rivets, thereby eliminating the need for welding skill. It is claimed that only a bench drill, sander and bandsaw are needed for home construction of the Mini-Imp, in addition to the usual hand tools and a pop-riveter. Average time taken for construction is 1,500 working hours.

The Mini-Imp prototype was powered by a 51 kW (68 hp) Limbach 1,900 cc flat-four engine driving a wooden propeller, and was retrofitted with a folding wing which permits the builder to construct the aircraft in small areas, and is a standard feature on the plans. These have been available since 1978, together with parts kits. More than 250 amateur-built Mini-Imps are being constructed, and at least ten are flying. Recommended power plant is the turbocharged Revmaster 2100D, driving a St Croix mechanically controllable propeller with Kevlar blades; but individual builders are fitting a variety of engines, including the 74·5 kW (100 hp) Continental O-200, 86 kW (115 hp) Avco Lycoming O-235, and two-cylinder 44·5 kW (60 hp) Franklin.

The description of the Imp applies also to the Mini-Imp, except as follows:

TYPE: Single-seat homebuilt sporting aircraft.

AIRFRAME: As for Imp. Wing pivots 90° to a fore and aft position for towing by motorcar.

POWER PLANT: Recommended engine is the turbocharged Revmaster 2100D, driving a St Croix controllable propeller via the standard extended driveshaft incorporating a Flexidyne dry fluid coupling. Alternative engines in the 44·5-74·5 kW (60-100 hp) range may be installed. Fuel tank in wing centre-section, capacity 45·4 litres (12 US gallons), plus tip tanks, each of 34 litres (9 US gallons) capacity. Refuelling point on wing upper surface.

ACCOMMODATION: Single semi-reclining moulded glassfibre bucket seat beneath sideways-opening (to port) transparent canopy. Seat folds forward to provide access to space for baggage.

DIMENSIONS, EXTERNAL:
Wing span 7·77 m (25 ft 6 in)
Wing chord, constant 0·91 m (3 ft 0 in)
Length overall 4·88 m (16 ft 0 in)
Height over fuselage 1·24 m (4 ft 1 in)
Height over propeller 1·89 m (6 ft 2½ in)
Tailplane span 1·98 m (6 ft 6 in)
Propeller diameter 1·45 m (4 ft 9 in)

WEIGHTS AND LOADING:
Weight empty 236 kg (520 lb)
Max T-O weight 362 kg (800 lb)
Max power loading (Limbach) 7·10 kg/kW (11·76 lb/hp)

PERFORMANCE (Limbach engine except where indicated):
Never-exceed speed 260 knots (482 km/h; 300 mph)
Max cruising speed at S/L 130 knots (241 km/h; 150 mph)
Max cruising speed (Revmaster engine, estimated) over 173 knots (322 km/h; 200 mph)
Stalling speed 44 knots (81 km/h; 50 mph)
Max rate of climb at S/L 366 m (1,200 ft)/min
T-O run 183 m (600 ft)
Range over 434 nm (804 km; 500 miles)
g limits ±9

AEROCAR MICRO-IMP

The Micro-Imp is of similar configuration to the Mini-Imp, but is constructed primarily of glassfibre reinforced paper known as TPG (Taylor Paper Glass). Static testing showed this to be far stronger than originally estimated, resulting in the redesign of many components to reduce weight. As an example, a main wing spar of TPG, weighing only 6 kg (13 lb), was static tested satisfactorily at a load of 589·5 kg (1,300 lb). Metal inlays are used throughout the TPG construction to accommodate compressive loadings.

Design of the Micro-Imp was started in August 1978. Construction of the prototype (N9HT), with a 13·4 kW (18 hp) 600 cc Citroën 2CV engine, began in December 1978, and this aircraft made its first flight during the Summer of 1981. Subsequent adoption of an Aerocar-designed ground-adjustable propeller improved performance. Further improvement followed installation of an Aerocar-developed controllable-pitch propeller weighing only 4 kg (9 lb), but performance was still considered inadequate. In 1983 the Citroën engine was converted to 800 cc and fitted with lighter (magnesium) components, in the hope of increasing its power to 22·4 kW (30 hp). It still proved incapable of giving much more than 15 kW (20 hp), with the result that Aerocar is looking into the possibility of using a two-stroke engine in the Micro-Imp.

Drawings to allow amateur constructors to build the Micro-Imp are almost complete, but the programme has been delayed pending the availability of a suitable engine. The aircraft is designed to be constructed in a single-car garage, using a minimum of special tools and equipment. No welding is required.

TYPE: Single-seat homebuilt sporting aircraft.

AIRFRAME: Cantilever high-wing monoplane with structure made almost entirely of TPG. This comprises paper core covered with glassfibre in a matrix of polyester resin, covered overall with ripstop Dacron. Metal inlays built into TPG. Wing section NASA GA(PC)-1. Thickness/chord ratio 15%. No anhedral or dihedral. Incidence 3°. Full-span constant chord 'flaperons' of similar construction to wings. 'Flaperons' droop for flap function, and can be set in slight 'up' position for efficient cruise. Wings removable by one person. Non-structural and removable fuselage nosecone of moulded glassfibre. Inverted V tail unit. Anhedral 35°. Variable incidence tailplane surfaces.

LANDING GEAR: Manually retractable tricycle type. Main units retract vertically. Cantilever spring steel tube main legs. Three plastics wheels, diameter 10 in. Tyres size 3·00-4, pressure 3·45 bars (50 lb/sq in). Aerocar mechanical brakes.

POWER PLANT: One modified Citroën 2CV motorcar engine (see introductory notes), driving a tail-mounted Aerocar two-blade controllable metal pusher propeller via Flexidyne dry fluid coupling. One fuel tank aft of seat, capacity 26·5 litres (7 US gallons). Refuelling point on top of fuselage. NASA flush air intake ducts, plus cooling fan. A turbocharging system will become available at a later date.

ACCOMMODATION: Single semi-reclining seat under sideways-hinged (to port) transparent canopy. Baggage space above engine.

AVIONICS: Radair 10A 10-channel radio, operated by nickel-cadmium battery.

DIMENSIONS, EXTERNAL:
Wing span 8·23 m (27 ft 0 in)
Wing chord, constant 0·91 m (3 ft 0 in)
Wing aspect ratio 9
Length overall 4·57 m (15 ft 0 in)
Max width of fuselage 0·69 m (2 ft 3 in)
Height overall 1·22 m (4 ft 0 in)
Tailplane span 2·13 m (7 ft 0 in)
Wheel track 1·22 m (4 ft 0 in)
Wheelbase 1·37 m (4 ft 6 in)
Propeller diameter 1·07 m (3 ft 6 in)

WEIGHTS AND LOADING:
Weight empty 113 kg (250 lb)
Max T-O weight 238 kg (525 lb)
Max power loading (20 hp) 15·87 kg/kW (26·25 lb/hp)

PERFORMANCE (estimated):
Never-exceed speed 120 knots (223 km/h; 139 mph)
Max level speed 104 knots (193 km/h; 120 mph)
Max cruising speed 95 knots (175 km/h; 109 mph)
Econ cruising speed 87 knots (161 km/h; 100 mph)
Stalling speed 42 knots (78 km/h; 48 mph)
Max rate of climb at S/L 152 m (500 ft)/min
Service ceiling 3,050 m (10,000 ft)
T-O run 152 m (500 ft)
T-O to 15 m (50 ft) 290 m (950 ft)
Landing from 15 m (50 ft) 274 m (900 ft)
Landing run 122 m (400 ft)

TAYLOR BULLET 2100

Following the success of the TPG method of construction for the Micro-Imp, Aerocar designed a two-seat counterpart also utilising TPG. It is known as the Taylor Bullet 2100, because of its similarity in configuration to the Gallaudet Bullet of 1912, which achieved a remarkable performance for its time, including a maximum speed of 87 knots (161 km/h; 100 mph). The prototype Bullet 2100, built by Mr Molt Taylor and Mr Jerry Holcomb, began its taxying tests in February 1985 and was shown at Oshkosh that year. By late January 1986 it had accumulated about 40 flying hours. Plans to allow amateur construction of the Bullet 2100 were made available during Winter 1985, together with some difficult to fabricate component parts such as the landing gear, driveshaft unit, welded components, wheels and brakes.

TYPE: Side by side two-seat homebuilt aircraft.

AIRFRAME: Cantilever shoulder-wing monoplane. Wing section GA(PC)-1. Forward sweep 5°. Warren truss type wing structure using laminated paper ribs and basic spar webs (TPG), with aluminium inlays for spar caps which taper in thickness well out into wing panels until caps are formed of wood inlays for outer 0·9 m (3 ft) of each panel. Wooden rib caps. Wing leading-edges covered with moulded glassfibre skins. Overall Dacron wing covering, finished with synthetic resin enamel. Warren truss full span 'flaperons' (with 'up' position capability for effective drag reduction in cruising flight). Y tail surfaces, with TPG spars and ribs (with aluminium inlays on spars where compressive loading occurs) and glassfibre skins, covered overall with Dacron and finished with synthetic resin enamel, as are tailboom and main fuselage. 'Horizontal' tail is trimmable. Wings fold backward beside fuselage for storage and trailering. Nosecone removable for engine maintenance. Baggage compartment is large enough for full set of golf clubs, plus trolley or other items, and is loaded via door on starboard side of fuselage under wing.

LANDING GEAR: Tailwheel type, with electric retraction (manual backup) of mainwheels only. Size 11·4 × 5 mainwheels on cantilever legs. Steerable tailwheel at base of ventral fin. Toe operated hydraulic brakes.

POWER PLANT: One 52·2 kW (70 hp) Revmaster 2100D with dual solid state ignition (modified Volkswagen motorcar engine) in nose of prototype, driving a manually controllable reversible-pitch Kevlar pusher propeller via a 'Flexidyne' dry fluid shaft system. Design suited to other engines, including 74·5 kW (100 hp) Revmaster, Continental O-200 or Avco Lycoming O-235. Two glassfibre fuel tanks above baggage compartment, refuelled from single point in tailcone, with total capacity of 83 litres (22 US gallons). Oil capacity 3·8 litres (1 US gallon).

ACCOMMODATION: Pilot and passenger side by side in enclosed cockpit, under canopy. Cockpit heating standard.

SYSTEM: Electrical system with 12V alternator and two 12V batteries, for engine starting, landing gear actuation, lights and avionics.

AVIONICS: Prototype has 720-channel transceiver, transponder, Loran C, two-channel interphone.

DIMENSIONS, EXTERNAL:
Wing span 10·36 m (34 ft 0 in)
Wing chord, constant portion 1·22 m (4 ft 0 in)
Wing aspect ratio 8·5
Width, wings folded 2·44 m (8 ft 0 in)
Length overall 5·72 m (18 ft 9 in)
Length, wings folded 7·01 m (23 ft 0 in)
Height overall 1·83 m (6 ft 0 in)
Tailplane span 2·44 m (8 ft 0 in)
Wheel track 2·03 m (6 ft 8 in)
Propeller diameter 1·42 m (4 ft 8 in)

AREA:
Wings, gross 12·63 m² (136·0 sq ft)

WEIGHTS AND LOADINGS:
Weight empty 453 kg (1,000 lb)
Max baggage 35 kg (78 lb)
Max T-O weight 748 kg (1,650 lb)
Max wing loading 59·22 kg/m² (12·13 lb/sq ft)
Max power loading 14·33 kg/kW (23·57 lb/hp)

PERFORMANCE (at max T-O weight):
Max level speed at S/L 130 knots (241 km/h; 150 mph)
Max cruising speed 122 knots (225 km/h; 140 mph)
Stalling speed, flaperons down 39 knots (73 km/h; 45 mph)
Max rate of climb at S/L 260 m (850 ft)/min
T-O run 152 m (500 ft)
Landing run 122 m (400 ft)
Range with max fuel 434 nm (805 km; 500 miles)
g limits +4 normal
+6 ultimate

AERO COMPOSITES

AERO COMPOSITES INC

1201 4th Street, PO Box 246, Fulton, Illinois 61252
Telephone: (815) 589 3308
PRESIDENT: Craig D. Huizenga
VICE-PRESIDENT: Karen Huizenga

AERO COMPOSITES SEA HAWKER

The all-composites amphibious Sea Hawker was designed by Mr Garry LeGare, well known for his contribution to the Quickie Q2 project. The strutless biplane performed three flight demonstrations on both land and water at the EAA's 1985 convention in Oshkosh, Wisconsin, marking its Oshkosh debut. The demonstrator aircraft, which is the second company-built prototype, is prepared to production standard and utilises a 112 kW (150 hp) Avco Lycoming O-320 engine, driving a three-blade wooden fixed-pitch propeller. By January 1986, this aircraft had accumulated over 400 flying hours.

Aerocar Mini-Imp single-seat sporting monoplane

Aerocar Micro-Imp (Citroën 2CV engine)

Aero Composites Sea Hawker with landing gear down

Taylor Bullet 2100 with nosecone removed

Aero Composites Sea Hawker amphibious biplane *(Debby LeGare)*

Aero Dynamics Sparrow Hawk Mk II two-seat light aircraft *(Arnold F. Swanberg)*

The Sea Hawker's amphibious rough-field landing gear permits landings on water, asphalt, grass, snow, mud, and rough fields. Use of high impact Kevlar and carbonfibre throughout the aircraft provides framework rigidity to withstand hard rough-field landings. The glassfibre covered rubbing strips strategically placed on the hull allow a safe gear-up emergency landing on hard surfaces.

Under the original owners, Aero Gare, design of the Sea Hawker began in 1981. Construction of the first prototype started in February 1982 and this flew for the first time in the following July. The building of other prototypes began in January 1983. Kits to allow amateur construction of the amphibian became available in 1983. The Sea Hawker was marketed subsequently by Leg-Air Corporation. In December 1985, this company was purchased by Aero Composites to locate manufacturing centrally in the USA and to maintain reasonable production costs. The principals of Aero Composites, Craig and Karen Huizenga, are manufacturing and marketing Sea Hawker kits, which can be purchased in several different ways, enabling builders to spread the cost over a longer period.

The Sea Hawker comprises 22 premoulded components, including the hull, upper fuselage with Plexiglas canopy preinstalled, wing skins with spars and leading-edge caps, engine cowling, tail sections, pylons, and optional Kevlar spinner. Kits include all raw materials, and all welded or machined parts are cadmium plated to resist corrosion. A detailed construction manual (designed for the first time builder) accompanies each kit.

By January 1986, a total of 200 kits and 250 sets of plans had been sold; four Sea Hawkers had flown, including the first two customer-built examples. Construction takes between 1,000 and 1,500 working hours.

TYPE: Two-seat all-composites homebuilt amphibian.

AIRFRAME: Cantilever biplane, with 5° dihedral on all wings. Incidence 3° 30′. NASA wing section. Composite construction of glassfibre and carbonfibre, with spar caps moulded into skins. Constant chord full-span slotted ailerons on lower wings deflect with slotted flaps on upper wings for take-off and landing. Single-step hull of Kevlar, glassfibre and carbonfibre, with integral fin. Tail unit comprises sweptback large-area fin and rudder, mid-mounted tailplane and balanced elevators. Water rudder under fin.

LANDING GEAR: Retractable tricycle type, with single nosewheel and two wheels on each main unit with shock absorbers. Main units carried under lower wings, with fairings which form stabilising floats when retracted. Mainwheels and tyres size 4·00-5 (pressure 1·24 bars; 18 lb/sq in). Castoring nosewheel retracts forward, with fairing forming underside of nose when retracted. Electric/hydraulic retraction. Hydraulic brakes on mainwheels.

POWER PLANT: Engine choice from 74·5 to 119 kW (100-160 hp). The plans built prototype has a 112 kW (150 hp) Avco Lycoming O-320. Two- or three-blade wooden fixed-pitch pusher propeller. Two fuel tanks, in centre-section of upper and lower wings, each with 132·5 litre (35 US gallon) capacity. (With 74·5-93 kW; 100-125 hp engine, one tank only.) Oil capacity 7·5 litres (2 US gallons).

ACCOMMODATION: Two seats side by side under rearward hinged one-piece canopy. Instrument panel attached to canopy and raised clear of cockpit area when canopy opened. Baggage area behind seats and small compartments under floor and seats.

SYSTEMS: Hydraulic system for landing gear. 12V DC electrical system.

DIMENSIONS, EXTERNAL:
- Wing span: 7·32 m (24 ft 0 in)
- Length overall: 6·40 m (21 ft 0 in)
- Height overall: 2·06 m (6 ft 9 in)
- Tailplane span: 2·59 m (8 ft 6 in)
- Wheel track: 2·51 m (8 ft 3 in)
- Wheelbase: 2·39 m (7 ft 10 in)
- Propeller diameter: 1·63 m (5 ft 4 in)

DIMENSIONS, INTERNAL:
- Cockpit: Max width: 1·12 m (3 ft 8 in)
- Baggage space: 0·85 m³ (30 cu ft)

AREA:
- Wings, gross: 10·96 m² (118·0 sq ft)

WEIGHTS AND LOADINGS (112 kW; 150 hp engine, unless stated otherwise):
- Weight empty: 386 kg (850 lb)
- Max T-O weight: 726 kg (1,600 lb)
- Max wing loading: 66·2 kg/m² (13·56 lb/sq ft)
- Max power loading (160 hp): 6·10 kg/kW (10·00 lb/hp)

PERFORMANCE (A: 74·5 kW; 100 hp engine, B: 119 kW; 160 hp engine, unless stated otherwise):
- Never-exceed speed:
  - B: 147 knots (273 km/h; 170 mph)
- Max level and cruising speed at S/L:
  - B: 139 knots (257 km/h; 160 mph)
- Cruising speed: A: 100 knots (185 km/h; 115 mph)
- Econ cruising speed:
  - B: 129 knots (238 km/h; 148 mph)
- Stalling speed, flaps down:
  - A: 33 knots (60 km/h; 37 mph)
  - B: 37 knots (68 km/h; 42 mph)
- Max rate of climb at S/L: A: 183 m (600 ft)/min
  - B: 335 m (1,100 ft)/min
- Service ceiling: A: 3,950 m (13,000 ft)
  - B: 5,475 m (18,000 ft)
- T-O and landing run: A: 183 m (600 ft)
  - B: 153 m (500 ft)
- T-O to 15 m (50 ft): B: 213 m (700 ft)
- Landing from 15 m (50 ft): B: 244 m (800 ft)
- Range with max fuel, 45 min reserves (150 hp engine): 1,042 nm (1,931 km; 1,200 miles)
- *g* limits: +5/−3

AERO DYNAMICS

AERO DYNAMICS LTD

19131 59th Drive NE, Arlington Airport, Arlington, Washington 98223
Telephone: (206) 435 8550

AERO DYNAMICS SPARROW HAWK Mk II

Aero Dynamics has built and flown a two-seat light sporting aircraft known as the Sparrow Hawk Mk II. Designed using computer technology, it integrated conventional aluminium construction with advanced composites. composites.

Four separate kits are available to construct the Sparrow Hawk Mk II: a composites kit including the fuselage and canopy; boom and centre wing kit; outer wing kit; and the optional finishing kit with Rotax 532 engine, propeller, spinner, battery, upholstery package and basic instruments. Further options include wheel fairings, HAPI Magnum, and cabin heating.

TYPE: Side by side two-seat homebuilt cabin monoplane.

AIRFRAME: Cantilever mid-wing monoplane. Wing dihedral 3°. Aluminium alloy (2024-T6) wing ribs and spar, and 7075-T6 leading-edge, covered with Stits Poly-Fiber or, optionally, aluminium alloy. Similarly constructed ailerons. Outer wing panels detachable for trailering or storage. All-composites fuselage of Kevlar/foam sandwich construction. Twin tailbooms of Kevlar, with carbonfibre reinforcement. Twin fins and horn balanced rudders, latter of foam wrapped with Kevlar. Constant chord tailplane, between fins, with 2024-T4 ribs and 7075-T6 leading-edge, covered with Stits Poly-Fiber, or optionally, aluminium. Anti-servo tab on tailplane.

LANDING GEAR: Non-retractable tricycle type, with aluminium alloy (2024-T6) anodised legs and rubber shock absorbers. Nosewheel steerable. Cleveland 5 in diameter mainwheels, with Cleveland brakes.

POWER PLANT: One 47 kW (63 hp) Rotax 532 two-cylinder two-stroke engine, driving a two-blade pusher propeller with large spinner, via reduction gear. Fuel capacity 60 litres (16 US gallons).

ACCOMMODATION: Two persons side by side under large forward hinged canopy. Baggage capacity 65 cm³ (4 cu ft).

DIMENSIONS, EXTERNAL:

Wing span	10·49 m (34 ft 5 in)
Wing chord, constant	1·27 m (4 ft 2 in)
Wing aspect ratio	8·27
Length overall	5·44 m (17 ft 10 in)
Height overall	2·11 m (6 ft 11 in)
Wheel track	2·26 m (7 ft 5 in)
Wheelbase	2·15 m (7 ft 0½ in)

AREA:

Wings, gross	13·29 m² (143·0 sq ft)

WEIGHTS AND LOADINGS:

Weight empty	227 kg (500 lb)
Max T-O weight	454 kg (1,000 lb)
Max wing loading	34·14 kg/m² (6·99 lb/sq ft)
Max power loading	9·66 kg/kW (15·87 lb/hp)

PERFORMANCE (first prototype):

Never-exceed speed	108 knots (201 km/h; 125 mph)
*Max level speed	91-104 knots (169-193 km/h; 105-120 mph)
*Cruising speed	82-96 knots (153-177 km/h; 95-110 mph)
Stalling speed	32 knots (58 km/h; 36 mph)
Max rate of climb at S/L: dual	229 m (750 ft)/min
solo	274 m (900 ft)/min
Service ceiling	3,660 m (12,000 ft)
T-O run	76 m (250 ft)
Landing run	91 m (300 ft)
Range with max fuel	312 nm (579 km; 360 miles)
g limits	+6/−4

* *Depending on propeller options*

AERO INNOVATIONS

AERO INNOVATIONS INC

Route 1, Box 1175, Pipe Creek, Texas 78063
Telephone: (512) 535 4334
GENERAL MANAGER: Norris E. Warner

AERO INNOVATIONS FIESTA

Aero Innovations designed and built the prototype of a single-seat cabin microlight, known as the Fiesta. Kits and ready assembled aircraft are available; in 1985 the prototype and manufacturing rights were offered for sale.

TYPE: Single-seat cabin microlight; conforms to FAR Pt 103.

AIRFRAME: Strut braced high-wing monoplane. Computer refined wing aerofoil and fuselage structures. Wings of rigid PVC/foam core sandwich, double surface Dacron covered on 18 per cent of wing area. Rectangular section fuselage and conventional tail unit structures of Dacron covered chrome molybdenum steel. Three-axis control (ailerons, elevators and rudder). Flaps fitted. Rigging time 20 min.

LANDING GEAR: Tailwheel type, with 480/400 × 8 GRP mainwheels, with brakes, and solid plastics steerable tailwheel of 4 in diameter. Glassfibre legs on all three units.

POWER PLANT: One 20 kW (27 hp) Rotax 277 engine, with 2·58:1 reduction drive to a two-blade wooden propeller. Fuel tank capacity 19 litres (5 US gallons).

ACCOMMODATION: Pilot only, in enclosed cabin.

DIMENSIONS, EXTERNAL:

Wing span	9·14 m (30 ft 0 in)
Wing aspect ratio	7·5
Length overall	5·03 m (16 ft 6 in)
Height overall	1·68 m (5 ft 6 in)
Propeller diameter	1·52 m (5 ft 0 in)

AREA:

Wings, gross	10·87 m² (117·0 sq ft)

WEIGHTS AND LOADINGS:

Weight empty	113 kg (250 lb)
Pilot weight range	41-104 kg (90-230 lb)
Max T-O weight	231 kg (510 lb)
Wing loading, at 204 kg (450 lb) AUW	18·8 kg/m² (3·85 lb/sq ft)
Power loading, at 204 kg (450 lb) AUW	10·15 kg/kW (16·67 lb/hp)

PERFORMANCE:

Never-exceed speed	61 knots (112 km/h; 70 mph)
Max level speed	55 knots (101 km/h; 63 mph)
Max cruising speed	48 knots (89 km/h; 55 mph)
Econ cruising speed	43 knots (80 km/h; 50 mph)
Stalling speed: power on	18 knots (33 km/h; 20 mph)
power off	24 knots (44 km/h; 27 mph)
Max rate of climb at S/L	183 m (600 ft)/min
Service ceiling	4,115 m (13,500 ft)
T-O run	38 m (125 ft)
Landing run	46 m (150 ft)
Range with max fuel	147 nm (273 km; 170 miles)
Endurance	4 h
g limits at 204 kg (450 lb) AUW	+4/−2

AERO MIRAGE

AERO MIRAGE INC

3009 NE 20th Way, Gainesville, Florida 32609
Telephone: (904) 377 4146

AERO MIRAGE TC-2

The design team at Aero Mirage, headed by Mr Ken Fickett, has designed and built from composite materials the prototype of a two-seat monoplane known as the Mirage TC-2. Intended to be an affordable high-performance commuter, it first flew on 16 May 1983 and is now available in staged kit form to amateur builders. It uses I section wing and tailplane spars of glassfibre reinforced plastics with foam core webs. The remainder of the airframe is constructed of Kevlar, Klégécel, S-glass and vinylester resin.

The following details refer to the prototype, unless stated otherwise:

TYPE: Two-seat homebuilt aircraft.

AIRFRAME: Cantilever low-wing monoplane. Wing section NACA 64415. Main and secondary spars and wing centre-section bonded to the fuselage. Composite construction as detailed in introduction. Simple flaps, with maximum deflection of 40°. Wings removable for storage and transportation. Fuselage pre-moulded from Kevlar and Klégécel. Composite tail unit, with sweptback fin, narrow chord rudder and all-moving tailplane with trim tab.

LANDING GEAR: Electro-hydraulic retractable tricycle type. Cleveland mainwheels, size 5·00-5, with brakes and Lamb tyres size 11 × 4·00-5. Brock nosewheel size 2·50-4.

POWER PLANT: One 74·5 kW (100 hp) Continental O-200-A flat-four engine, driving a Prince Aircraft Co 'P' tip two-blade wooden propeller. Other engines recommended as suitable up to 74·5 kW (100 hp), though both an Avco Lycoming O-235 and O-290 are being fitted to Mirages. Standard fuel capacity 95 litres (25 US gallons), in integral wing tanks; capacity with auxiliary tanks 144 litres (38 US gallons).

ACCOMMODATION: Two semi-reclined seats side by side under front hinged canopy, with tinted Plexiglas. Baggage capacity 18 kg (40 lb).

DIMENSIONS, EXTERNAL:

Wing span	6·40 m (21 ft 0 in)
Wing chord, constant	0·91 m (3 ft 0 in)
Wing aspect ratio	6·9
Length overall	5·05 m (16 ft 7 in)
Height overall	1·78 m (5 ft 10 in)
Width, wings removed	2·14 m (7 ft 0 in)
Propeller diameter	1·57 m (5 ft 2 in)

DIMENSION, INTERNAL:

Cockpit width	1·12 m (3 ft 8 in)

AREA:

Wings, gross	5·95 m² (64·0 sq ft)

WEIGHTS AND LOADINGS (A: prototype, B: with 48·5 kW; 65 hp engine, C: with 63·4 kW; 85 hp engine):

Weight empty: A	290 kg (640 lb)
B	238 kg (525 lb)
C	272 kg (600 lb)
Max T-O weight: A	517 kg (1,140 lb)
B	431 kg (950 lb)
C	476 kg (1,050 lb)
Max wing loading: A	86·9 kg/m² (17·8 lb/sq ft)
B	72·4 kg/m² (14·8 lb/sq ft)
C	80·1 kg/m² (16·4 lb/sq ft)
Max power loading: A	6·94 kg/kW (11·40 lb/hp)
B	8·89 kg/kW (14·62 lb/hp)
C	7·51 kg/kW (12·35 lb/hp)

PERFORMANCE (A: prototype, B: with 48·5 kW; 65 hp engine, C: with 63·4 kW; 85 hp engine):

Design never-exceed speed:	
A	225 knots (416 km/h; 259 mph)
Max level speed at S/L:	
A	181 knots (335 km/h; 208 mph)
B	157 knots (291 km/h; 181 mph)
C	168 knots (311 km/h; 193 mph)
Design cruising speed:	
A	172 knots (319 km/h; 198 mph)
Cruising speed, 75% power, at S/L:	
A	165 knots (306 km/h; 190 mph)
B	142 knots (264 km/h; 164 mph)
C	155 knots (288 km/h; 179 mph)
Stalling speed:	
A, flaps down	50 knots (92 km/h; 57 mph)
A, flaps up	55 knots (102 km/h; 63 mph)
Landing run	137 m (450 ft)
g limits: A at max T-O weight	±5
A at 431 kg (950 lb)	±6

AEROSPORT

AEROSPORT LTD

Box 278, Holly Springs, North Carolina 27540
Telephone: (919) 552 6375
PRESIDENT: E. B. Trent

The current Aerosport Ltd was formed in 1983. Since that time, it has marketed plans and component parts of four light aircraft designed for construction by amateurs. Details follow of the Scamp A, which is the only aircraft currently available. The former Aerosport Quail is now described under the 'D 2' heading.

AEROSPORT SCAMP A

The prototype of the single-seat all-metal Scamp A flew for the first time on 21 August 1973. It was intended primarily for operation from grass strips, and tricycle landing gear was chosen as being more rational for a generation of amateur pilots who had received their initial flight training on aircraft equipped with landing gear of this configuration. Stressed to +6*g* and −3*g*, the Scamp A can be used for limited aerobatics; and emphasis has been placed on simple construction techniques to make it an easy project for the homebuilder.

Plans and parts, except for the engine, are available to amateur constructors and have been approved by the National Association of Sport Aircraft Designers (NASAD). A total of 905 sets of plans had been sold by early 1986. Forty-two Scamps were flying, and 18 more were then under construction, including four in the UK. Those flying include examples built in New Zealand, Sweden and the UK.

Some examples of an agricultural version, known as Scamp B, were assembled in South America from Aerosport component parts and marketed commercially (see under Colombia in main Aircraft section of the 1984-85 *Jane's*).

TYPE: Single-seat homebuilt aircraft.

AIRFRAME: Braced biplane wings, with V interplane struts each side. Wing section NACA 23012. Flying and landing wires of streamline section. Single 2 in by 5 in extruded section of 6061-T6 light alloy forms a pylon to support the centre-section of the upper wing. Dihedral 3° on lower wings only. All-metal two-spar structures of light alloy. Plain ailerons of light alloy construction, with piano hinge at upper surface, on upper wing only. No flaps. No trim tabs. Semi-monocoque all-metal fuselage of light alloy. Braced T tail of light alloy construction. Single bracing strut on each side. Fixed incidence tailplane. Ground adjustable trim tab on rudder.

LANDING GEAR: Non-retractable tricycle type. Cantilever spring main-gear struts of light alloy. Wheel fairing on each unit optional.

POWER PLANT: Prototype has one 44·5 kW (60 hp) 1,834 cc Volkswagen modified motorcar engine with single ignition. Design suitable for Volkswagen engines of up to 2,100 cc, driving a 56-38 two-blade fixed-pitch wooden propeller, though Aerosport recommends 1,834 cc as optimum in terms of overall performance, fuel consumption, engine life and reliability. Fuel tank in fuselage nose, aft of firewall, capacity 30·5 litres (8 US gallons). Refuelling point on fuselage upper surface, forward of windscreen.

ACCOMMODATION: Single seat in open cockpit.

DIMENSIONS, EXTERNAL:

Wing span	5·33 m (17 ft 6 in)
Wing chord, constant	0·91 m (3 ft 0 in)
Length overall	4·27 m (14 ft 0 in)
Height overall	1·69 m (5 ft 6½ in)
Wheel track	1·52 m (5 ft 0 in)
Wheelbase	1·17 m (3 ft 10 in)
Propeller diameter	1·42 m (4 ft 8 in)

AREA:

Wings, gross	9·75 m² (105·0 sq ft)

Aerosport Scamp A built in the UK

Aero Innovations Fiesta microlight *(Don Downie)*

Aero Mirage TC-2 all-composites lightplane

Air Command 447 Commander microlight gyroplane *(Howard Levy)*

Aerotique Parasol microlight aircraft *(Howard Levy)*

Weights and Loadings:

Weight empty	236-249 kg (520-550 lb)
Max T-O weight	348-362 kg (768-798 lb)
Max wing loading	37·1 kg/m² (7·6 lb/sq ft)
Max power loading	8·13 kg/kW (13·30 lb/hp)

Performance (1,834 cc engine):

Never-exceed speed	108 knots (201 km/h; 125 mph)
Max level speed	91 knots (169 km/h; 105 mph)
Cruising speed	78 knots (145 km/h; 90 mph)
Max manoeuvring speed	72 knots (134 km/h; 83 mph)
Stalling speed	39 knots (73 km/h; 45 mph)
Service ceiling (estimated)	3,660 m (12,000 ft)
T-O run	122 m (400 ft)
Landing run	122 m (400 ft)
Range at cruising speed	108 nm (201 km; 125 miles)

AEROTECH

AEROTECH DYNAMICS CORPORATION

Route 1, Box 125, Lawtey, Florida 32058
Telephone: (904) 964 6741

This company acquired in 1984 the design rights to the Aerostat 340, originally produced by Aerolight Flight Development Inc (see 1983-84 *Jane's*). Its **Wind Rider** is believed to be a modified version of the Aerostat 340. A two-seat version with a 43·3 kW (58 hp) Kawasaki 440 or a 36 kW (48 hp) Rotax 503 engine, known as the **Wind Rider II**, is also believed to be available. Both are conventional three-axis control high-wing monoplanes, with kingpost, cable bracing, aluminium alloy airframe and tricycle landing gear. The two-seat Wind Rider II has a wing span and wing area of 11·89 m (39 ft) and 18·12 m² (195 sq ft) respectively, a max T-O weight of 317 kg (700 lb) and max level speed of 39 knots (72 km/h; 45 mph).

AEROTIQUE

AEROTIQUE AVIATION INC

The address for Aerotique Aviation Inc given in the 1985-86 *Jane's* appears no longer to be current. The exact status of the company is unknown, though it is thought that Mr Bob Cowan purchased the full rights in the aircraft from the former company president, Mr Richard Kohm.

AEROTIQUE PARASOL

This single-seat three-axis microlight, a replica of the Heath Parasol, was first flown in prototype form by Yesteryear Aviation, from whom Aerotique acquired manufacturing rights in September 1983. Production was launched in Spring 1984 and was expected to be running at about ten per month by July, but it is believed that this was not attained. The Aerotique version has Ceconite covered wings with aluminium ribs, instead of the Stits fabric covered wooden ribs of the prototype, and a 20 kW (27 hp) Rotax 277 engine instead of the 26·1 kW (35 hp) Cuyuna ULII-02. It was made available in ready to fly form only.

Type: Single-seat microlight aircraft; conforms to FAR Pt 103 (FAR Pt 23 certification applied for).

Airframe: Strut supported parasol monoplane of conventional lightplane configuration and conventional three-axis control surfaces. Construction of steel tube, aluminium, wood and fabric. Fully covered airframe, with open cockpit.

Landing Gear: Taildragger type, with twin mainwheels and a tailskid. Bungee mainwheel suspension.

Power Plant: One 20 kW (27 hp) Rotax 277 engine, with 2:1 reduction drive to a two-blade wooden tractor propeller. Fuel capacity 18·5 litres (4·9 US gallons).

Dimensions, external:

Wing span	9·75 m (32 ft 0 in)
Wing aspect ratio	7·31
Length overall	5·33 m (17 ft 6 in)
Height overall	1·88 m (6 ft 2 in)
Propeller diameter	1·47 m (4 ft 10 in)

Area:

Wings, gross	13·38 m² (144·0 sq ft)

Weights and Loadings:

Weight empty	114 kg (251 lb)
Max T-O weight	236 kg (520 lb)
Max wing loading	17·62 kg/m² (3·61 lb/sq ft)
Max power loading	11·30 kg/kW (18·57 lb/hp)

Performance (prototype with 35 hp Cuyuna engine):

Never-exceed speed	67 knots (125 km/h; 78 mph)
Max level speed	55 knots (101 km/h; 63 mph)
Max cruising speed	52 knots (97 km/h; 60 mph)
Stalling speed	21 knots (39 km/h; 24 mph)
Max rate of climb at S/L	213 m (700 ft)/min
g limits	+6/−2·5
Best glide ratio	12

AIR COMMAND

AIR COMMAND MANUFACTURING INC

Liberty Landing Airport, Route 3, Box 197A, Liberty, Missouri 64068

Telephone: (816) 781 9313

President: Dennis Fetters

AIR COMMAND 447 COMMANDER

The 447 Commander was claimed to be the world's first production microlight gyroplane. It meets the microlight aircraft regulations, but the airframe was designed to accept the 38·8 kW (52 hp) Rotax 503 or 47·7 kW (64 hp) Rotax 532, and a full cockpit enclosure, without modifications.

The 447 Commander is available as a ready assembled aircraft or as a kit that can be assembled quickly, using just six hand tools. Approximately 200 single-seat Commanders have been sold, mostly to customers in the USA, but also in Australia, Israel, Japan, Korea and Venezuela.

Type: Single-seat microlight gyroplane; conforms to FAR Pt 103 with Rotax 447 and 503 engine, and to FAI/CAA regulations with Rotax 532.

Airframe: Aluminium alloy structure, finished in black

polyethylene enamel with silver dipped anodised trim. Rotor has two McCutchen SkyWheel laminar flow blades, of carbonfibre and glassfibre composite construction with 6061-T6 aluminium leading-edge spar and aerofoil hub. Three-axis control. Large rudder. Options include Wunderlich rotor spin-up and rotor brake. Can be trailered; folds to pass through standard home doorway, with rotor removed. Rigging time 10 min.

LANDING GEAR: Tricycle type plus tailwheel, with 12½ × 4 in mainwheels and 8½ × 3 in steerable nosewheel. Hagger hydraulic mainwheel disc brakes. Shock absorption. Optional floats, skis and mainwheel fairings.

POWER PLANT: One 30 kW (40 hp) Rotax 447 two-cylinder two-stroke engine, with 2·58:1 reduction drive to a four- or five-blade composite pusher propeller. Optional 38·8 kW (52 hp) Rotax 503 or 47·7 kW (64 hp) Rotax 532 two-cylinder two-stroke engine. Seat fuel tank, capacity 19 litres (5 US gallons). One 34 litre (9 US gallon) auxiliary tank optional.

ACCOMMODATION: Pilot in open position. Provision for passenger.

DIMENSIONS, EXTERNAL:
Rotor diameter — 7·01 m (23 ft 0 in)
Rotor blade chord — 0·20 m (8 in)
Length overall — 3·25 m (10 ft 8 in)
Height overall — 2·13 m (7 ft 0 in)
Max width — 1·70 m (5 ft 7 in)
Propeller diameter — 1·80 m (5 ft 11 in)

AREA:
Rotor disc — 38·6 m² (415·5 sq ft)

WEIGHTS:
Weight empty — 107 kg (235 lb)
Pilot weight range — 55-136 kg (120-300 lb)
Max T-O weight — 388 kg (856 lb)

PERFORMANCE (Rotax 447 engine):
Never-exceed speed — 130 knots (241 km/h; 150 mph)
Max level and cruising speed — 55 knots (101 km/h; 63 mph)
Econ cruising speed — 39 knots (72 km/h; 45 mph)
Min flying speed — 5-7 knots (10-13 km/h; 6-8 mph)
Max rate of climb at S/L — over 305 m (1,000 ft)/min
Service ceiling — 4,575 m (15,000 ft)
T-O run — 30 m (100 ft)
Range with standard fuel — 87 nm (161 km; 100 miles)
Endurance — 2 h
g limit — +9
Best glide ratio — 6

AIR COMMAND 532 COMMANDER ELITE

The 532 Commander Elite became available in kit form in Spring 1985. It is similar to the 447 Commander but uses the 47·7 kW (64 hp) Rotax 532 two-cylinder two-stroke engine as standard with a five-blade propeller. It conforms to the FAA Experimental homebuilt requirements, and as such the kit is less than 50 per cent completed.

The only known weight and performance data are as follows:

WEIGHT:
Useful load — over 136 kg (300 lb)

PERFORMANCE:
Max level and cruising speed — 96 knots (177 km/h; 110 mph)
Econ cruising speed — 56 knots (105 km/h; 65 mph)
Max rate of climb at S/L — 366 m (1,200 ft)/min

AIR COMMAND 532 COMMANDER TWO-SEATER

By means of a conversion kit, a standard 532 Commander Elite can be modified into a two-seater under homebuilt regulations. Fitting a second control stick makes it suitable for training purposes. A rotor of 7·01 m (23 ft) or 7·62 m (25 ft) diameter can be employed. Further details were not available at the time of writing.

AIRCRAFT DESIGNS

AIRCRAFT DESIGNS INC

11082 Bel Aire Court, Cupertino, California 95014
Telephone: (408) 255 2194
PRESIDENT: Martin Hollmann

Mr Hollmann has designed two gyroplanes, of which plans, materials and component parts are available to amateur constructors.

HOLLMANN HA-2M SPORTSTER

Design of this gyroplane began in June 1969, and construction of the first prototype was started in December 1972. The first flight of the prototype was made in October 1974; test flying was completed by January 1976. The same year the prototype won a 'Best Original Design' award at the EAA Oshkosh meeting and an 'Outstanding New Design' award at the PRA Fly-in at Rockford.

The Sportster utilises a mechanical pre-rotator which engages the engine, via a clutch, to pre-spin the rotor to 230 rpm prior to take-off. This allows the aircraft to take off after a very short run, and is expected to permit jump starts after brief further development. A rotor brake is utilised to slow the rotor after landing and to stop the blades for taxying. A tension spring is adjusted from within the cockpit to trim the control stick in pitch.

By early 1986 more than 65 Sportsters were under construction in the USA, Canada, New Zealand and Sweden. Most of these are powered by an Avco Lycoming O-320 engine, rated at 112 kW (150 hp); but Mr Bob Grayson, who lives at a height of 1,980 m (6,500 ft) in Montana, selected a 119 kW (160 hp) Avco Lycoming engine and larger rotor blades than standard. At least 12 Sportsters are flying.

TYPE: Two-seat homebuilt gyroplane.

ROTOR SYSTEM: Two-blade rotor of NACA 8-H-12 section. Solidity ratio 0·035. Pre-cone angle 2°. Blade pitch +2½°. Metal blades, each made up of a 2024-T8511 leading-edge extrusion, aluminium formed ribs and Alclad skin, riveted and bonded together. Rotor rpm 380.

AIRFRAME: Square-tube 6061-T6 aluminium fuselage structure, bolted together. Aluminium skin. Glassfibre fairings. Two mast tubes. Large rear window for 360° view. Twin fins and balanced rudders carried on short tailbooms; aluminium structure, with 2024-T3 Alclad skins pop riveted in place. Glassfibre tips. Fixed horizontal surface between fins.

LANDING GEAR: Non-retractable tricycle type, with single wheel on each unit. Two small tailwheels. Mainwheel tyres size 18 × 6, pressure 1·8 bars (26 lb/sq in). Nosewheel tyre of 0·25 m (10 in) diameter, pressure 1·8 bars (26 lb/sq in). Mechanical drum brake on nosewheel.

POWER PLANT: One 97 kW (130 hp) Franklin Sport 4B flat-four engine, driving a Troyer 6635 pusher propeller, on prototype. One fuel tank of 45·4 litres (12 US gallons) capacity, with refuelling point inside cockpit. Oil capacity 5·7 litres (1·5 US gallons). Most other aircraft fitted with an Avco Lycoming O-320 engine, rated at 112 kW (150 hp), driving a Troyer 6648 propeller.

ACCOMMODATION: Two seats side by side in cabin with open sides.

SYSTEMS: Standard aircraft instruments and Narco Mk IV radio in prototype. 12V battery. Rotor pre-rotation system to spin rotor to 230 rpm.

DIMENSIONS, EXTERNAL:
Rotor diameter — 8·53 m (28 ft 0 in)
Rotor blade chord, constant — 0·23 m (9 in)
Length overall — 3·66 m (12 ft 0 in)
Height to top of rotor head — 2·34 m (7 ft 8 in)
Tailplane span — 1·17 m (3 ft 10 in)
Wheel track — 2·06 m (6 ft 9 in)
Wheelbase — 1·42 m (4 ft 8 in)
Propeller diameter — 1·68 m (5 ft 6 in)

DIMENSIONS, INTERNAL:
Cabin: Max width — 0·914 m (3 ft 0 in)
Max height — 1·45 m (4 ft 9 in)

WEIGHTS (A: prototype, B: 112 kW; 150 hp engine):
Weight empty, equipped: A — 281 kg (620 lb)
Max T-O and landing weight: A — 476 kg (1,050 lb)
B — 500 kg (1,100 lb)

PERFORMANCE (A: prototype, B: 112 kW; 150 hp engine):
Never-exceed speed at S/L:
A — 78 knots (145 km/h; 90 mph)
Max cruising speed at S/L:
A — 65 knots (121 km/h; 75 mph)
Econ cruising speed at S/L:
A — 52 knots (97 km/h; 60 mph)
Stalling speed: A — 25 knots (45 km/h; 28 mph)
Max rate of climb at S/L: A — 213 m (700 ft)/min
B — 274 m (900 ft)/min
Service ceiling — 2,440 m (8,000 ft)
T-O run — 107 m (350 ft)
Landing run — 0-6 m (0-20 ft)
Range: with max fuel — 78 nm (145 km; 90 miles)
with max payload — 61 nm (112 km; 70 miles)

HOLLMANN BUMBLE BEE

Mr Martin Hollmann began constructional work on the Bumble Bee microlight gyroplane in March 1983. The prototype flew in January 1984. Since then a number of refinements have been made to the aircraft. These have included the adoption of a Rotax 447 engine in place of the original Kawasaki, driving a larger diameter propeller, and the use of a mechanical pre-rotator which engages the engine (via a clutch) to pre-spin the rotor to a maximum of 300 rpm prior to take-off.

The Bumble Bee is available in bolt together kit form or can be built from plans, using prefabricated component parts. By February 1986 at least nine Bumble Bees had been sold. Development of the Bumble Bee continues, and a retrofit cockpit enclosure is being fabricated for sale to owners of new and already flying aircraft. As planned, this will also enclose the engine, allowing the cockpit to be heated.

TYPE: Single-seat, single-engined microlight gyroplane; conforms to FAR Pt 103.

AIRFRAME: Fuselage structure of 6061-T6 square aluminium tubing, with glassfibre/foam sandwich cruciform tail surfaces. Fixed horizontal tailplane. Two-blade rotor of NACA 8-H-12 section, with 2024-T8511 aluminium alloy leading-edges and glassfibre/foam/epoxy trailing-edges, finished with Imron polyurethane enamel. Rotor pre-spin and lock available. Rigging time 10 min.

LANDING GEAR: Tricycle type, with shock absorption by bungee cord. Mainwheel diameter 16 in; steerable nosewheel, diameter 8 in. Nosewheel brake.

POWER PLANT: One 30 kW (40 hp) Rotax 447 two-cylinder two-stroke engine, driving a two-blade wooden pusher propeller. Fuel capacity 19 litres (5 US gallons). Starter equipment optional.

ACCOMMODATION: Pilot only, in open position, with Lexan windscreen pop riveted to instrument console.

AVIONICS: Radio optional.

DIMENSIONS, EXTERNAL:
Rotor diameter — 7·01 m (23 ft 0 in)
Rotor blade chord — 18 cm (7 in)
Length overall — 3·35 m (11 ft 0 in)
Height overall — 2·29 m (7 ft 6 in)
Wheel track — 2·22 m (7 ft 3½ in)
Propeller diameter — 1·52 m (5 ft 0 in)

AREA:
Rotor disc — 38·55 m² (415·0 sq ft)

WEIGHTS AND LOADINGS:
Weight empty — 102 kg (225 lb)
Pilot weight range — 68-113 kg (150-250 lb)
Max T-O weight — 227 kg (500 lb)
Max disc loading — 5·86 kg/m² (1·20 lb/sq ft)
Max power loading — 7·57 kg/kW (12·50 lb/hp)

PERFORMANCE:
Never-exceed speed — 69 knots (129 km/h; 80 mph)
Max level speed — 56 knots (103 km/h; 64 mph)
Econ cruising speed — 35 knots (64 km/h; 40 mph)
Min flying speed — 4·5 knots (8 km/h; 5 mph)
Max rate of climb at S/L — 366 m (1,200 ft)/min
Service ceiling — 3,660 m (12,000 ft)
T-O run, without rotor pre-spin — 76 m (250 ft)
with rotor pre-spin — 30 m (100 ft)
Range with max fuel — 56 nm (105 km; 65 miles)
Endurance — 1 h
g limits — +3·5/−1

AIRCRAFT DEVELOPMENT

AIRCRAFT DEVELOPMENT INC

1326, N. Westlink Blvd, Wichita, Kansas 67212
Telephone: (316) 722 7736
PRESIDENT: Richard Jimenez

AIRCRAFT DEVELOPMENT EZ-1

Design work on the EZ-1 began in 1978. The prototype made its first flight on 31 July 1983 and introduced the Scotch-A-Frame bonding technique, using adhesive tape and aluminium clad glassfibre. In 1984 Aircraft Development marketed a Scotch-A-Frame kit, allowing customers to build a small section of an EZ-1 surface using the new technique. Several hundred of these kits have been sold, some to overseas purchasers. As a result, requests for information on the EZ-1 have included foreign interest in purchasing manufacturing rights, while two US microlight manufacturers have incorporated the constructional method and materials into portions of their own aircraft designs.

TYPE: Single-seat microlight aircraft; conforms to FAR Pt 103 requirements.

AIRFRAME: Conventional low-wing monoplane. Aluminium alloy fuselage structure. Wing and tail surface spars from foam/glassfibre/graphite sandwich with aluminium skinning using self-adhesive 'Scotch-A-Frame' bonding technique over 85 per cent of the structure. Three-axis control (rudder, elevator and ailerons), plus wing flaps.

LANDING GEAR: Tricycle type, with glassfibre main-gear legs. Castoring nosewheel; brakes on mainwheels. Wheel size (all) 10·6 × 3·50.

POWER PLANT: One 15 kW (20 hp) Zenoah G25B-1 engine, with 2:1 reduction drive to a two-blade wooden pusher propeller. One 18·6 kW (25 hp) engine (type unknown) planned for later production. Total fuel capacity 16·3 litres (4·3 US gallons).

ACCOMMODATION: Pilot only, in open position.

DIMENSIONS, EXTERNAL:
Wing span — 9·45 m (31 ft 0 in)
Wing aspect ratio — 7·45
Length overall — 5·33 m (17 ft 6 in)
Height overall — 1·98 m (6 ft 6 in)
Propeller diameter — 1·27 m (4 ft 2 in)

AREA:
Wings, gross — 11·98 m² (129·0 sq ft)

WEIGHTS AND LOADINGS:
Weight empty — 106 kg (234 lb)
Pilot weight range — 45-102 kg (100-225 lb)
Max T-O weight — 229 kg (505 lb)
Max wing loading — 19·1 kg/m² (3·91 lb/sq ft)

Air Command's two-seat conversion of a 532 Commander Elite *(Howard Levy)*

Aircraft Designs (Hollmann) HA-2M Sportster two-seat gyroplane *(J. M. G. Gradidge)*

Aircraft Development EZ-1 prototype

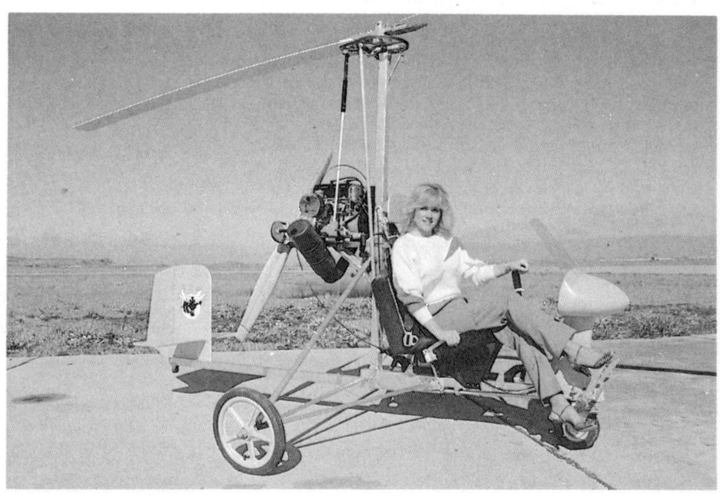

Aircraft Designs (Hollmann) Bumble Bee microlight gyroplane

Alderfer Gyro Chopper II single-seat autogyro *(J. M. G. Gradidge)*

The Airplane Factory Das Ultralighterfighter

Max power loading (20 hp) 15·27 kg/kW (25·25 lb/hp)

PERFORMANCE (at max T-O weight, 20 hp engine):

Never-exceed speed	60 knots (112 km/h; 70 mph)
Max level speed	43 knots (80 km/h; 50 mph)
Max cruising speed	39 knots (72 km/h; 45 mph)
Econ cruising speed	36 knots (67 km/h; 42 mph)
Stalling speed	23 knots (42 km/h; 26 mph)
Max rate of climb at S/L	106 m (348 ft)/min
Service ceiling	2,285 m (7,500 ft)
T-O run	91 m (300 ft)
Landing run	61 m (200 ft)
Range with max fuel	67 nm (124 km; 77 miles)
Endurance with max fuel	1 h 43 min
g limits:	+9/−4·5 design
	+6/−3 ultimate
Best glide ratio	8

AIRPLANE FACTORY

THE AIRPLANE FACTORY INC

PO Box 24035, Dayton, Ohio 45424
Telephone: (513) 849 6533
PRESIDENT: W. Douglas Hoy

DAS ULTRALIGHTERFIGHTER

Das Ultralighterfighter is a microlight replica of the First World War Fokker E.III Eindecker, conforming to FAR Pt 103 standards. The aircraft is supplied in prefabricated kit form.

TYPE: Single-seat, single-engined microlight aircraft.

AIRFRAME: Conventional mid-wing monoplane. Structure of aluminium alloy and chromoly steel. Wings double surface Dacron covered. Stainless steel cable bracing; kingpost standard. Open cockpit, with small windscreen. Three-axis control (rudder, elevator and spoilers). Parachute recovery system and replica machine-gun optional.

LANDING GEAR: Taildragger type, with 20 × 1¼ mainwheels and bungee suspension. Castoring tailskid. Floats optional.

POWER PLANT: One 20 kW (27 hp) Rotax 277 engine, with 2·58:1 reduction drive to two-blade wooden tractor propeller. Fuel tank capacity 16·7 litres (4·4 US gallons).

ACCOMMODATION: Pilot only, in open cockpit.

DIMENSIONS, EXTERNAL:

Wing span	10·97 m (36 ft 0 in)
Wing aspect ratio	8·8
Length overall	6·25 m (20 ft 6 in)
Height overall	2·29 m (7 ft 6 in)
Propeller diameter	1·63 m (5 ft 4 in)

AREA:

Wings, gross	13·66 m² (147·0 sq ft)

WEIGHTS AND LOADINGS:

Weight empty	112 kg (247 lb)
Max pilot weight	102 kg (225 lb)
Max T-O weight	229 kg (505 lb)
Max wing loading	16·80 kg/m² (3·44 lb/sq ft)
Max power loading	11·45 kg/kW (18·70 lb/hp)

PERFORMANCE (with 77 kg; 170 lb pilot):

Never-exceed speed	65 knots (120 km/h; 75 mph)
Max level and max cruising speed	55 knots (101 km/h; 63 mph)
Econ cruising speed	43 knots (80 km/h; 50 mph)
Stalling speed:	
power on	20 knots (37 km/h; 23 mph)
power off	22 knots (40 km/h; 25 mph)
Max rate of climb at S/L	183 m (600 ft)/min
Service ceiling	2,750 m (9,000 ft)
T-O run	30 m (100 ft)
Landing run	46 m (150 ft)
Range with max fuel	130 nm (241 km; 150 miles)
Endurance with max fuel	4 h
g limits	+6/−3

ALDERFER

4278 Shafer Road, Hamilton, Ohio

ALDERFER GYRO CHOPPER II

As can be seen in an accompanying illustration, taken at Oshkosh in 1985, the Gyro Chopper II (N1388Q) is a fairly conventional single-seat autogyro except for its semi-enclosed cabin. It is powered by an engine mounted behind the pilot's seat and driving a two-blade pusher propeller. No details are known.

ALDERFER GYRO CHOPPER III

This tandem two-seat gyroplane (N63EA) was shown at the EAA's 1986 convention at Oshkosh, where it won the award for outstanding new design. It is powered by a 47 kW (63 hp) Rotax 532 two-cylinder liquid-cooled two-stroke engine mounted, with its radiator, forward of what appears to be a RotorWay Scorpion composites cabin enclosure. The engine drives a large three-blade tractor propeller through reduction gearing. Another unusual feature is that the two-blade teetering rotor is carried on a bridge structure well forward of the main mast assembly.

WEIGHTS:

Weight empty	161 kg (355 lb)
Max T-O weight	385 kg (850 lb)

AMERICAN AIR

AMERICAN AIR TECHNOLOGY

1290 Bodega Avenue, Petaluma, California 94952
Telephone: (707) 762 1800
DESIGNER: Craig Catto

AMERICAN AIR TECHNOLOGY SOLO and DUAL

American Air Technology claims to have been the first to introduce a factory assembled all-composites ultralight. Development began in September 1982 and the aircraft, known as the **Solo**, became available on 15 June 1984 during the EAA's third annual Ultralight Convention at Oshkosh. A side by side two-seat version is under development, to be marketed as a kit requiring 150-200 working hours to assemble and known as the **Dual**.

TYPE: Single-seat microlight aircraft (Solo), and two-seat homebuilt aircraft (Dual); Solo conforms to FAR Pt 103.

AIRFRAME: Strut braced high-wing monoplane of conventional aeroplane configuration. Liebeck 1004 wing section. Composites structure of carbonfibre, S-glass, rigid foam and epoxy, with Kevlar skins. Three-axis control (ailerons, elevators and rudder). Ballistic parachute standard. Rigging time 10 min.

LANDING GEAR: Tricycle type. One-piece laminated cantilever mainwheel legs. Production aircraft have steel tube nosewheel leg with solid glassfibre insert. All three wheels of similar size. Steerable nosewheel.

POWER PLANT: One 20 kW (27 hp) Rotax 277 single-cylinder two-stroke engine on steel tube engine mounting in Solo, with helical-gear reduction drive to two-blade wooden propeller. Dual A has one 47·7 kW (64 hp) Rotax 532 two-cylinder two-stroke engine and Dual B one 74·5 kW (100 hp) Continental O-200 flat-four engine.

ACCOMMODATION: Solo has cabin accommodation for the pilot only; Dual accommodates the pilot and passenger side by side.

DIMENSIONS, EXTERNAL (A: Solo, B: Dual A):

Wing span: A	9·14 m (30 ft 0 in)
B	10·52 m (34 ft 6 in)
Length overall: A, B	5·94 m (19 ft 6 in)
Height overall: A, B	2·29 m (7 ft 6 in)
Wheel track: A, B	1·88 m (6 ft 2 in)
Propeller diameter: A	1·52 m (5 ft 0 in)

AREA:

Wings, gross: B	11·89 m² (128·0 sq ft)

WEIGHTS AND LOADINGS:

Weight empty: B	166 kg (365 lb)
Max T-O weight: B	347 kg (765 lb)
Max wing loading: B	29·2 kg/m² (5·98 lb/sq ft)
Max power loading: B	7·27 kg/kW (11·95 lb/hp)

PERFORMANCE (A and B as above):

Never-exceed speed: A	71 knots (132 km/h; 82 mph)
Cruising speed:	
A	35-52 knots (64-97 km/h; 40-60 mph)
B	96 knots (177 km/h; 110 mph)
Stalling speed: A	24 knots (44 km/h; 27 mph)
B	32 knots (58 km/h; 36 mph)
Max rate of climb at S/L:	
A, at 35 knots (64 km/h; 40 mph)	168 m (550 ft)/min
B, at 48 knots (89 km/h; 55 mph)	183 m (600 ft)/min
T-O run: A	28 m (90 ft)
B	61 m (200 ft)
Landing run: A	18 m (60 ft)
B	61 m (200 ft)
Min rate of sink:	
A, at 30 knots (55 km/h; 34 mph)	82 m (270 ft)/min
Best glide ratio:	
A, at 35 knots (64 km/h; 40 mph)	12
B, at 48 knots (89 km/h; 55 mph)	12
g limits: A	+8/−3·5

AMERICAN AIRCRAFT

AMERICAN AIRCRAFT INC

4310 Rankin Lane NE, Albuquerque, New Mexico 87107
Telephone: (505) 344 6366
GENERAL MANAGER: J. Robert Shaw
CONSULTANT: Larry Newman
SALES MANAGER: Emory Ellis

American Aircraft was formed in 1983 by Mr Larry Newman, specifically to produce and market the Falcon microlight. In March 1984 a licence agreement was concluded with Sonaca (Belgium) to manufacture and distribute the Falcon (both models) in Europe, Africa, and continental Asia (except China). Other versions are produced by Ultrasport in Italy (which see). In October 1985, the controlling interest in American Aircraft was purchased by the John A. Carlson Company of San Francisco.

AMERICAN AIRCRAFT FALCON

The prototype of the Falcon was shown and flown at the 1982 EAA Fly-in at Oshkosh, Wisconsin. Release of ready to fly production aircraft began in the Spring of 1983; kits are also available.

Approximately 200 Falcons were flying in early 1986. A kit option is available, as the **Falcon-Z** (FAA Experimental category), for a shorter span version with electric starting, engine fairing, and increased maximum and max cruising speeds of 78 knots (145 km/h; 90 mph) and 69 knots (129 km/h; 80 mph) respectively.

The following description applies to the standard single-seat version:

TYPE: Single-seat microlight aircraft; conforms to FAR Pt 103.

AIRFRAME: Strut braced high-wing monoplane with cantilever foreplane, constructed of aluminium alloy, carbonfibre, glassfibre, Kevlar and foam plastics. Sweptback rigid main wings, with foam ribs and double surface Tedlar covering, are detachable for transportation and storage. No external bracing cables. Low-drag Kevlar/graphite fuselage pod. Three-axis control by ailerons, elevators on foreplane, and twin dependent wingtip rudders. Windscreen, shoulder harness, seat belt, instrumentation and cabin heater standard. Ballistic parachute optional.

LANDING GEAR: Tricycle type, with size 3·00/3·50-5 mainwheels, carried on metal legs. Steerable and retractable nosewheel, with brake. Speed fairings standard on mainwheels.

POWER PLANT: One 20 kW (27 hp) Rotax 277 single-cylinder two-stroke engine, with helical-gear reduction drive to an Orion Propfan three-blade glassfibre pusher propeller. Fuel tank capacity 19 litres (5 US gallons).

ACCOMMODATION: Pilot only in open or, optionally, Lexan fully enclosed cockpit.

DIMENSIONS, EXTERNAL:

Wing span	10·97 m (36 ft 0 in)
Foreplane span	3·71 m (12 ft 2 in)
Wing aspect ratio	7·85
Foreplane aspect ratio	7·40
Length overall	4·34 m (14 ft 3 in)
Height overall	1·70 m (5 ft 7 in)
Wheel track	1·78 m (5 ft 10 in)
Wheelbase	2·13 m (7 ft 0 in)
Propeller diameter	1·37 m (4 ft 6 in)

AREA:

Wings and foreplane, gross	16·26 m² (175·0 sq ft)

WEIGHTS AND LOADINGS:

Weight empty	113 kg (250 lb)
Pilot weight range	50-95 kg (110-210 lb)
Max T-O weight	236 kg (520 lb)
Max wing/foreplane loading	14·50 kg/m² (2·97 lb/sq ft)
Max power loading	12·69 kg/kW (20·80 lb/hp)

PERFORMANCE (with 68 kg; 150 lb pilot):

Never-exceed speed	65 knots (120 km/h; 75 mph)
Max level speed	55 knots (101 km/h; 63 mph)
Max cruising speed	52 knots (97 km/h; 60 mph)
Stalling speed	24 knots (44 km/h; 27 mph)
Max rate of climb at S/L	198 m (650 ft)/min
Service ceiling	4,575 m (15,000 ft)
T-O and landing run	61 m (200 ft)
Range with max fuel	145 nm (269 km; 167 miles)
Endurance with max fuel	2 h 48 min
g limits	+6/−3
Best glide ratio	15
Min rate of sink, power off, at 35 knots (64 km/h; 40 mph)	less than 76 m (250 ft)/min

AMERICAN AIRCRAFT FALCON XP

A prototype of this tandem two-seat version of the Falcon was accepted by the FAA in August 1984 as an experimental homebuilt. It has a 33·6 kW (45 hp) Rotax 503 engine with 57 litres (15 US gallons) of fuel, elongated fuselage pod, mainwheel disc brakes, reduced wing sweep (10° instead of 15°), and sweptback vertical fins above the wingtip rudders. US production began that month, and a substantial number had been sold by early 1986. The first aircraft from Belgian production was expected in about March 1985.

A prototype floatplane variant was being tested in 1985. This has a three-float system (fuselage float and two outriggers at mid span) with built-in retractable wheels, which can be attached in less than 20 minutes.

Data for the standard Falcon XP are as for the single-seater except:

DIMENSIONS, EXTERNAL:

Length overall	5·18 m (17 ft 0 in)

WEIGHTS AND LOADINGS:

Weight empty	227 kg (500 lb)
Max pilot/passenger weight	154 kg (340 lb)
Max T-O weight	approx 431 kg (950 lb)
Max wing/foreplane loading	26·49 kg/m² (5·43 lb/sq ft)
Max power loading	12·85 kg/kW (21·11 lb/hp)

PERFORMANCE (A: one occupant, B: two occupants):

Max level speed: A, B	78 knots (145 km/h; 90 mph)
Max cruising speed:	
A, B	69 knots (129 km/h; 80 mph)
Stalling speed, power on:	
A	35 knots (65 km/h; 40 mph)
B	40 knots (73 km/h; 45 mph)
Max rate of climb at S/L: A	244 m (800 ft)/min
B	152 m (500 ft)/min
Service ceiling: A	4,265 m (14,000 ft)
B	3,200 m (10,500 ft)
T-O run: A	61 m (200 ft)
B	92 m (300 ft)
Landing run: A	76 m (250 ft)
B	122 m (400 ft)
Range at cruising speed with 38 litres (10 US gallons) of fuel:	
A	260 nm (483 km; 300 miles)
B	217 nm (402 km; 250 miles)
Best glide ratio: B	14

AMERICAN MICROFLIGHT

AMERICAN MICROFLIGHT INC

8225 East Montebello, Scottsdale, Arizona 85253
Telephone: (602) 994 4631
PRESIDENT: William G. Sadler

AMERICAN MICROFLIGHT SADLER VAMPIRE

This pusher engined twin-boom microlight aircraft is unusual in being almost entirely of metal construction. It first flew in mid-1982 and gained the 'Grand Champion Design' award at Oshkosh in August of that year. Production of ready to fly aircraft began in February 1983, and was at the rate of about four per month in 1984.

It has been reported that American Microflight intends to produce a more powerful and heavier version for the homebuilt market, capable of 109 knots (201 km/h; 125 mph). Basic differences between the microlight and homebuilt versions include the use of thicker aluminium sheet skins for the latter, which will be able to withstand ±12*g* ultimate loads and attain a maximum rate of climb of about 183 m (600 ft)/min. Full span ailerons will be fitted. No further details were available in early 1986.

Other versions of the Vampire about which little is known are the military SVCIAF (Sadler Vampire Counter Insurgency Attack Fighter) and its two-seat training counterpart.

The following details refer to the microlight version of the Sadler Vampire.

AIRFRAME: Cantilever shoulder-wing monoplane with twin tailbooms and twin fins and rudders. Constant chord wings have an aluminium main spar, NACA 63_3-A21A laminar flow aerofoil section, stamped ribs, flush riveted skin of aluminium sheet, and full span four-position trailing-edge split flaps. Kevlar fuselage pod. Aluminium tailbooms. Tail unit of similar construction to wings. Three-axis control by full span spoilers, elevator and twin rudders. Wings can be folded for transportation and storage. Rigging time 10 min.

LANDING GEAR: Non-retractable tricycle type, with trailing link bungee suspension and size 4·10 × 4 wheel and tyre on each unit. Steerable nosewheel, with brake. Retractable gear optional.

POWER PLANT: One 15 kW (20 hp) KFM 107ER or Solo 210 cc engine standard, with reduction drive to a two-blade

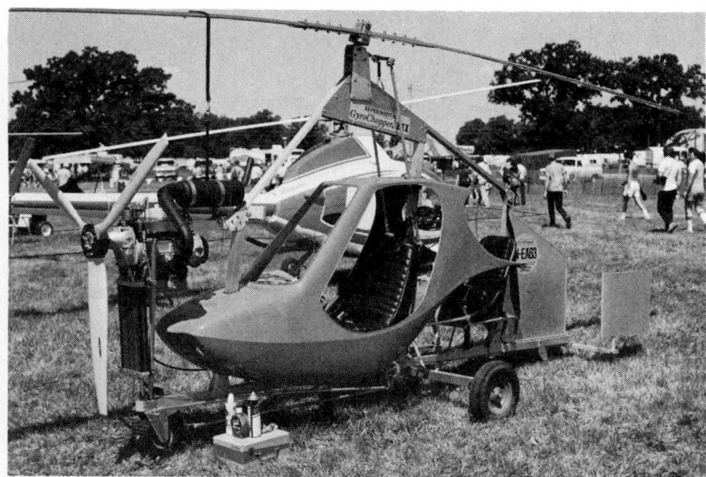

Alderfer Gyro Chopper III two-seat gyroplane *(J. M. G. Gradidge)*

American Microflight Sadler Vampire microlight aircraft *(Howard Levy)*

American Aircraft Falcon single-seat microlight aircraft

Two-seat American Aircraft Falcon XP *Glamorous Glennis* **owned by Brigadier-General 'Chuck' Yeager** *(J. M. G. Gradidge)*

Anderson EA-1 Kingfisher amphibian *(Peter M. Bowers)*

Prototype American Air Technology Solo microlight *(Brian M. Service)*

metal pusher propeller. Fuel capacity 17 litres (4·5 US gallons). Inverted flight fuel system available optionally.

ACCOMMODATION: Pilot only in open cockpit or, optionally, with fully enclosed tinted Lexan canopy.

DIMENSIONS, EXTERNAL:

Wing span	8·53 m (28 ft 0 in)
Wing aspect ratio	7·2
Length overall	5·33 m (17 ft 6 in)
Height overall	1·42 m (4 ft 8 in)
Propeller diameter	1·27 m (4 ft 2 in)

AREA:

Wings, gross	10·78 m² (116·0 sq ft)

WEIGHTS AND LOADINGS (with KFM engine):

Weight empty	113·5 kg (250 lb)
Pilot weight range	54·5-100 kg (120-220 lb)
Max T-O weight	249 kg (550 lb)
Max wing loading	23·14 kg/m² (4·74 lb/sq ft)
Max power loading	16·74 kg/kW (27·50 lb/hp)

PERFORMANCE (with KFM engine):

Never-exceed speed	86 knots (160 km/h; 100 mph)
Max level speed	55 knots (101 km/h; 63 mph)
Max cruising speed	52 knots (97 km/h; 60 mph)
Econ cruising speed	48 knots (89 km/h; 55 mph)
Stalling speed, flaps down	23 knots (42 km/h; 26 mph)
Max rate of climb at S/L	107 m (350 ft)/min
Service ceiling	3,200 m (10,500 ft)
T-O run	107 m (350 ft)
Landing run	61 m (200 ft)
Range with max fuel	260 nm (483 km; 300 miles)
Endurance with max fuel	5 h
g limits	±6

AMERICAN MICROFLIGHT SADLER VAMPIRE TRAINER

This 26 kW (35 hp) Zenoah G50 engined two-seat trainer version of the Vampire was seen for the first time at a recreational aircraft meeting held in Los Angeles in 1984. It is probably still at the prototype stage. No further details are known.

AMERICAN MICROFLIGHT SVCIAF

Reports have appeared of a military derivative of the Vampire for use as a counter insurgency and attack aircraft. Powered by a 48·5 kW (65 hp) engine, and with a bullet resistant Kevlar fuselage pod and thicker Lexan windscreen for pilot protection, it is said to be able to carry up to 136 kg (300 lb) of stores on underwing hardpoints. Drawings show two launch pods for 2·75 in rockets under the wings and two guns built into the wing leading-edges in line with the booms, with ammunition reloading via two wing centre-section panels. The wings of the SVCIAF (Sadler Vampire Counter Insurgency Attack Fighter) fold for transportation, and rigging by one person takes only 5 min in the field. The spoilers of the standard Vampire are replaced by ailerons outboard of conventional four-position flaps. Take-off and landing are practicable from 183 m (600 ft) stretches of road.

A side by side two-seat training version has also been reported.

ANDERSON

EARL ANDERSON

ADDRESS FOR PLANS: Warner Aviation Inc, Thunderhill Aerodrome, Route 4, Box 501, Covington, Louisiana 70433

Telephone: (504) 892 3721

Mr Earl Anderson, a retired Boeing 747 captain, designed and built a light amphibian which he named EA-1 Kingfisher. The first flight was made on 24 April 1969. After a time, Mr Anderson replaced the original 74·5 kW (100 hp) Continental engine by an 86 kW (115 hp) Avco Lycoming O-235-C1, driving a Sensenich M76AM-4-44 propeller. With this power plant the Kingfisher has an empty weight of 495 kg (1,092 lb), a max T-O weight of 725 kg (1,600 lb) and improved performance.

Plans were originally made available to amateur constructors via the Anderson Aircraft Corporation; but all rights to the Kingfisher have been transferred to Captain R. M. Warner. Kingfisher plans cover the increase in weight now applicable to the prototype. The Kingfisher was designed to accept alternative power plants of up to 104 kW (140 hp), but on the basis of experience with the 86 kW (115 hp) Avco Lycoming engine, homebuilders are discouraged from installing more powerful engines than this. However, one constructor fitted a 119 kW (160 hp) Avco Lycoming engine and reportedly has been satisfied with the results. He completed a flight from Washington State to the mountain lakes of Alaska in this aircraft.

By early 1986 well over 200 sets of Kingfisher plans had been sold, and more than 100 aircraft were under construction in the USA, UK, Canada, Mexico, Sweden, West Germany and Panama. Homebuilt Kingfishers are known to be flying in the USA, New Zealand and Australia.

The following details apply to the prototype Kingfisher in its original configuration. Performance figures quoted should be taken as approximate.

ANDERSON EA-1 KINGFISHER

TYPE: Two-seat light homebuilt amphibian.

AIRFRAME: Braced high-wing monoplane with streamline-section V bracing struts each side (standard J3, PA-11 or PA-12 Piper Cub wing). Stabilising floats mounted beneath wings, adjacent to wingtips, are constructed of ¾ in square mahogany stringers, covered with 1/16 in mahogany plywood coated with glassfibre. Conventional flying-boat hull of wooden construction with spruce frames and longerons, covered with 1/16 in and ¼ in mahogany plywood coated with glassfibre. Strut braced tail unit of steel tubing, fabric covered.

LANDING GEAR: Retractable tailwheel type. Each main unit is retracted forward, manually and individually, with spring-loaded assist mechanism. Bungee shock absorption.

POWER PLANT: One 74·5 kW (100 hp) Continental O-200 flat-four engine, driving a fixed-pitch two-blade tractor propeller. Alternatively an Avco Lycoming O-235-C1 of 86 kW (115 hp) or other engine of up to 112 kW (150 hp) can be fitted (see introduction). Single fuel tank in hull, immediately forward of windscreen, capacity 76 litres (20 US gallons). Refuelling point on nose. Oil capacity 5·7 litres (1·5 US gallons).

ACCOMMODATION: Two seats, side by side, in enclosed cabin. Piper Tri-Pacer windscreen. Door on port side.

SYSTEM: 30A alternator for radios, lights and starter.

DIMENSIONS, EXTERNAL:

Wing span	11·00 m (36 ft 1 in)
Length overall	7·16 m (23 ft 6 in)
Height overall	2·44 m (8 ft 0 in)
Wheel track	1·52 m (5 ft 0 in)
Propeller diameter	1·83 m (6 ft 0 in)

WEIGHTS AND LOADING (O-200 engine):

Weight empty	468 kg (1,032 lb)
Max T-O weight	680 kg (1,500 lb)
Max power loading	9·13 kg/kW (15·00 lb/hp)

PERFORMANCE (with O-200 engine, at max T-O weight):

Never-exceed speed	104 knots (193 km/h; 120 mph)
Max level speed	104 knots (193 km/h; 120 mph)
Cruising speed at 305 m (1,000 ft)	74 knots (136 km/h; 85 mph)
Stalling speed	39 knots (73 km/h; 45 mph)
Max rate of climb at S/L	152-183 m (500-600 ft)/min
Service ceiling	3,050 m (10,000 ft)
Range with max fuel	173 nm (322 km; 200 miles)

AUSTIN AEROSPACE

AUSTIN AEROSPACE CORPORATION

Suite 1006, 575 Madison Avenue, New York, NY 10022
Telephone: (212) 605 0436
Telex: 710 992 8979 ADNAN
WORKS: Maryland
CHAIRMAN: Michael Austin

AUSTIN HAWK

The Hawk is optimised for military battlefield support roles and nap-of-the-earth flying. Production and sales by February 1985 totalled 210 aircraft; no more recent figures have been received.

Airborne weapons test fired from the Hawk include the French Luchaire Strim anti-tank rocket, one of which can be carried on each of the aircraft's four underwing attachment points. Two ASP 0·30 in machine-guns can be carried under the inner wings, each capable of firing 1,100 rds/min. Other proposed weapons loads include M60 machine-guns, M203 40 mm grenade launchers, M67 fragmentation grenades, smoke canisters, phosphorus grenades and tear gas. A remotely operated airborne video camera package has also been developed for surveillance missions.

The Hawk has an aluminium structure with twin tail-booms and twin fins, and with double surface Dacron covered wing and tail surfaces. It has two-axis control (ailerons and spoilers) and a tricycle landing gear. Power is provided by a 24 kW (32 hp) engine, driving a wooden two- or three-blade pusher propeller. Fuel tank capacity is 76 litres (20 US gallons). There is provision for a passenger and a cockpit fairing is optional.

DIMENSIONS, EXTERNAL:

Wing span	8·23 m (27 ft 0 in)
Length overall	5·79 m (19 ft 0 in)
Height overall	2·13 m (7 ft 0 in)

WEIGHTS AND LOADING:

Weight empty	147 kg (325 lb)
Max T-O weight	360 kg (795 lb)
Max power loading	15·00 kg/kW (24·84 lb/hp)

PERFORMANCE:

Max level speed	76 knots (140 km/h; 87 mph)
Max cruising speed	65 knots (121 km/h; 75 mph)
Stalling speed	37 knots (68 km/h; 42 mph)
Max rate of climb at S/L	168 m (550 ft)/min
Service ceiling	3,350 m (11,000 ft)
Best glide ratio	17

BAC

BRUTSCHE AIRCRAFT CORPORATION

1800 West 1887 South, Woods Cross, Utah 84087
Telephone: (801) 295 5222
DESIGNER: Neal Brutsche

This company is developing a family of sport aircraft, the first of which, the Freedom 28, was undergoing flight trials in mid-1986. It will be followed by the Freedom 48 single-seat homebuilt version, with a heavier wing and more powerful Rotax 503 engine. Later, the range will be extended to include a two-seat sport/trainer with an engine in the 48·5-60 kW (65-80 hp) bracket and a T-O weight of about 408 kg (900 lb).

BAC FREEDOM 28

Resembling a scaled-down Cessna L-19 Bird Dog, but with more angular tail surfaces, the Freedom 28 is expected to become available in kit form, complete with engine and instruments, in early 1987. Predrilled pilot holes in the components will eliminate the need for jigs, enabling the aircraft to be assembled in an average 200 to 300 hours. The wings fold for trailering and storage.

TYPE: Single-seat microlight aircraft.

AIRFRAME: Strut braced high-wing monoplane, with single streamline section bracing strut each side. Two-spar metal wing structure with interspar torque box at root of each wing. D section leading-edge, with hydroformed ribs, attaches to torque box. Ceconite fabric covering. Aluminium alloy full-span flaperons. Aluminium alloy (2024) semi-monocoque fuselage and conventional unswept tail unit, with fabric covering only on elevators.

LANDING GEAR: Non-retractable tailwheel type, with wire braced main legs carrying wheels with size 6·00-6 low-pressure tyres. Steerable tailwheel. Hydraulic brakes optional.

POWER PLANT: One 20 kW (27 hp) Rotax 277 engine, driving a two-blade wooden propeller through reduction gearing. Fuel capacity 19 litres (5 US gallons).

ACCOMMODATION: Pilot only, in semi-enclosed cockpit. Cabin side windows optional.

SYSTEM: Electrical system optional.

DIMENSIONS, EXTERNAL:

Wing span	8·46 m (27 ft 9 in)
Wing aspect ratio	7·06
Length overall	5·31 m (17 ft 5 in)

AREA:

Wings, gross	10·13 m² (109·0 sq ft)

WEIGHTS AND LOADINGS:

Weight empty	115 kg (254 lb)
Max baggage	18 kg (40 lb)
Max T-O weight	227 kg (500 lb)
Max wing loading	22·4 kg/m² (4·59 lb/sq ft)
Max power loading	11·35 kg/kW (18·52 lb/hp)

PERFORMANCE:

Never-exceed speed	80 knots (148 km/h; 92 mph)
Cruising speed	53 knots (98 km/h; 61 mph)
Max manoeuvring speed	40 knots (74 km/h; 46 mph)
Stalling speed, flaperons down	21 knots (39 km/h; 24 mph)
Max rate of climb at S/L	183 m (600 ft)/min
T-O run	54 m (175 ft)
Landing run	61 m (200 ft)
Endurance	2 h 48 min

BARRACUDA

W. B. BUETHE ENTERPRISES INC

PO Box 486, Cathedral City, California 92234
Telephone: (619) 324 9454
PRESIDENT: Dr William B. Buethe

This company markets plans and kits to build the Barracuda high-performance two-seat light aircraft. Estimated building time for a Barracuda is 1,500 hours.

BARRACUDA

The prototype Barracuda (N19GS) was designed and built by Mr Geoffrey Siers, a former RAF fighter pilot and design engineer with BAC, who emigrated to the USA in 1964. Construction was started in June 1969 and it flew for the first time on 29 June 1975. At the EAA Fly-in at Oshkosh in 1976, the Barracuda won the 'Most Outstanding New Design' award.

The prototype flew originally with a 164 kW (220 hp) Avco Lycoming GO-435-2 engine. This was replaced with a more powerful O-540 engine in 1979.

The second Barracuda to be completed and flown was N78WB, built by Dr Buethe and seen in the accompanying illustration. This flew for the first time on 11 January 1981 and incorporates several minor changes when compared with the original prototype. These include all-welded aluminium fuel tanks, full IFR avionics panel, and a more secure latching mechanism for the canopy.

By early 1986, a total of 535 sets of plans to build the Barracuda had been sold and 13 aircraft were then flying. The description applies to the Barracuda built by Dr Buethe, which was built over a period of 8½ years and had accumulated more than 500 flying hours by early 1986. An estimated six further Barracudas will have been completed by the end of 1986.

TYPE: Two-seat all-wooden homebuilt sporting monoplane.

AIRFRAME: Cantilever low-wing monoplane, made in three pieces: two constant chord outer panels and a centre-section which is integral with the fuselage. Wing section NACA 64_2415. Upper surface of centre-section each side has slight anhedral, but bottom surface has neither anhedral nor dihedral. Dihedral of 5° on outer panels. No incidence. Basic structure of spruce, with mahogany and birch plywood covering. Box section main spar with spruce booms and ply webs; truss type ribs of spruce. Frise ailerons of wood and glassfibre. Electrically actuated wooden plain flap on entire centre-section trailing-edge, extending under fuselage. Conventional spruce fuselage and tail unit, covered with birch plywood stressed skins. Glassfibre tailplane tips. Electrically actuated trim tab in port elevator. Rudder has bungee trim.

LANDING GEAR: Retractable tricycle type. Electro-hydraulic retraction, mainwheels inward, nosewheel rearward; all wheels fully enclosed by doors when retracted. Emergency extension by gravity. Legs made from 4130 steel tubing, with steel coil spring shock absorption. Cleveland wheels, size 5·00-5, with 14 in diameter tyres. Cleveland aircooled brakes.

POWER PLANT: One 186 kW (250 hp) Avco Lycoming IO-540-C4B5 flat-six engine, driving a Hartzell HC-C3YR-1RF three-blade constant-speed propeller. Suitable for engines of 112-224 kW (150-300 hp). Two welded aluminium fuel tanks in centre-section forward of spar, total capacity 166·5 litres (44 US gallons). Provision for two 23 litre (6 US gallon) auxiliary tanks in outboard wing panels. Oil capacity 11·5 litres (3 US gallons).

ACCOMMODATION: Two armchair seats, with thigh support, side by side under upward hinged individual 'gull-wing' canopy doors. Dual controls. Baggage space behind seats. Cabin heated and ventilated.

SYSTEMS: Electric pump supplies hydraulic system. Electrical supply via 12V DC system.

AVIONICS: Full IFR: dual Collins Microline nav/com, Century 2-B autopilot, King DME and Narco AT-6 transponder.

DIMENSIONS, EXTERNAL:

Wing span	7·54 m (24 ft 9 in)
Wing chord: at root	2·11 m (6 ft 11 in)
outer panels, constant	1·45 m (4 ft 9 in)
Length overall	6·55 m (21 ft 6 in)
Wheel track	2·54 m (8 ft 4 in)
Propeller diameter	2·18 m (7 ft 2 in)

DIMENSION, INTERNAL:

Cabin: Max width	1·07 m (3 ft 6 in)

AREA:

Wings, gross	11·15 m² (120·0 sq ft)

WEIGHTS AND LOADINGS:

Weight empty	712 kg (1,570 lb)
Baggage capacity	27 kg (60 lb)
Max T-O weight	1,043 kg (2,300 lb)
Max wing loading	93·5 kg/m² (19·2 lb/sq ft)
Max power loading	5·61 kg/kW (9·20 lb/hp)

PERFORMANCE:

Never-exceed speed	217 knots (402 km/h; 250 mph)
Max level speed at 2,135 m (7,000 ft)	181 knots (335 km/h; 208 mph)
Cruising speed (62% power) at 2,450 m (8,050 ft)	162 knots (300 km/h; 187 mph)
Stalling speed: 'clean'	56 knots (103 km/h; 64 mph)
wheels and flaps down	54 knots (100 km/h; 62 mph)
Max rate of climb at S/L	762 m (2,500 ft)/min
Range at max T-O weight, 65% power, with auxiliary tank, 30 min reserves	800 nm (1,480 km; 920 miles)

Camouflaged Austin Hawk microlights, with and without cockpit fairing

BAC Freedom 28 single-seat microlight aircraft *(J. M. G. Gradidge)*

Barracuda two-seat sporting monoplane, built by Dr W. B. Buethe

Beard Two Easy four-seat homebuilt aircraft *(J. M. G. Gradidge)*

Beachy Breezer single-seat microlight *(J. M. G. Gradidge)*

BEACHNER — *see V-8 Special*

BEACHY

ERNEST BEACHY

Bealer Enterprises Inc, Clarion, Texas

BEACHY BREEZER

The general appearance of this fabric covered single-seat high-wing microlight is shown in an accompanying illustration. It has strut braced rigid wings, conventional three-axis control with full-span flaperons, tailwheel landing gear and an open cockpit. The power plant is a 15 kW (20 hp) Cuyuna single-cylinder two-stroke engine driving a two-blade wooden pusher propeller.

WEIGHTS:

Weight empty	110 kg (241 lb)
Max T-O weight	231 kg (510 lb)

PERFORMANCE:

Cruising speed	48 knots (88 km/h; 55 mph)
Landing speed	17·5 knots (32 km/h; 20 mph)

BEARD

BEARD TWO EASY

This four-seat version of the Long-EZ/Cozy two-seat canards was displayed for the first time at the 1986 Oshkosh Fly-in. Registered N227RB, it has a 134 kW (180 hp) Avco Lycoming O-360 flat-four engine and a max T-O weight of 998 kg (2,000 lb). No other details are known.

BEAUJON

BEAUJON AIRCRAFT CO

PO Box 2121, Ardmore, Oklahoma 73402

PRESIDENT: Henry Beaujon

Mr Beaujon markets plans and a constructor's manual for a range of six microlights known as the Mach ·07, BJ-2, Minimac, Hardnose, Viewmaster and Windward. All are powered by a 22·4 kW (30 hp) Cuyuna engine and are closely similar in dimensions, weights and performance. Basic differences are as follows:

Mach-07. Wing attached directly to main structural member. Underslung seat and tailwheel landing gear. Tractor engine/propeller arrangement. All-metal structure.

Minimac and Hardnose. Similar to Mach ·07 except for tricycle landing gear and no ventral fin. Hardnose has engine in low-mounted position, ahead of pilot.

BJ-2. Similar to Minimac and Hardnose, except for pusher engine/propeller arrangement.

Viewmaster and Windward. Parasol wing, with seat above main structural member. All-wood construction. Pusher engine/propeller arrangement. Redesigned tail unit, with triangular dorsal fin and rudder of different shape. Taildragger landing gear for Windward; single wheel and skids at nose and tail for Viewmaster.

Brief details of the Mach ·07 follow:

BEAUJON MACH ·07

TYPE: Single-seat microlight aircraft.

AIRFRAME: Strut braced high-wing monoplane. Single surface wings. Aluminium alloy tubular airframe. Cruciform tail surfaces. Three-axis control (rudder, elevator and spoilers).

LANDING GEAR: Tailwheel type. Bungee mainwheel suspension. No brakes.

POWER PLANT: One 22·4 kW (30 hp) Cuyuna engine, driving a two-blade tractor propeller. Fuel capacity 9·5 litres (2·5 US gallons).

ACCOMMODATION: Pilot only, in open position.

DIMENSIONS, EXTERNAL:

Wing span	10·06 m (33 ft 0 in)
Wing chord, constant	1·52 m (5 ft 0 in)
Length overall	5·64 m (18 ft 6 in)

AREA:

Wings, gross	15·33 m² (165·0 sq ft)

WEIGHTS AND LOADINGS:

Weight empty	104 kg (230 lb)
Max T-O weight	204 kg (450 lb)
Max wing loading	13·31 kg/m² (2·73 lb/sq ft)
Max power loading	9·13 kg/kW (15·0 lb/hp)

PERFORMANCE:

Max level speed	42 knots (77 km/h; 48 mph)
Max cruising speed	37 knots (69 km/h; 43 mph)
Stalling speed	18 knots (33 km/h; 20 mph)
Max rate of climb at S/L	183 m (600 ft)/min
T-O run	25 m (80 ft)
Landing run	18 m (60 ft)

BELL

F. M. BELL ULTRA LITE AIRCRAFT INC

1020 I-45 North, Willis, Texas 77378

Telephone: (409) 856 5518

PRESIDENT: Frederick M. Bell

F. M. Bell Ultra Lite Aircraft offers kits to assemble four aircraft, namely the single-seat Spitfire I microlight, the side by side two-seat Experimental category Spitfire II, the aerobatic Sonic Spitfire and the Clipper. The Sonic Spitfire, for which separate details were not received, is almost certainly a Spitfire I especially built for aerobatics. It has full span ailerons, clipped wings for increased manoeuvrability and quick response, double sleeved spars, diagonals, cage rails, uprights, extra struts, double hinge points and dual rudder cables.

F. M. BELL ULTRA LITE AIRCRAFT SPITFIRE I

The Spitfire I is the standard single-seat Spitfire, of which at least 300 kits and ready assembled aircraft have been sold. It is the only version offered in ready to fly form as an alternative to kit form. Options include armament for a military role.

TYPE: Single-seat microlight aircraft; conforms to FAR Pt 103.

AIRFRAME: Braced high-wing monoplane, with aerofoil section bracing struts. Main frame of aluminium alloy, with vinyl coated stainless steel cables. Wings and conventional tail unit double surfaced with Dacron.

Three-axis control (ailerons, elevators and rudder), with flaps. Rigging time 30 min.

LANDING GEAR: Non-retractable tricycle type, with all three wheels size 3·50-10. Steerable nosewheel. Glassfibre wheel fairings. Optional mainwheel brakes, floats and skis.

POWER PLANT: One 30 kW (40 hp) Rotax 447 two-cylinder two-stroke engine, with 2·58:1 reduction gear to a two-blade wooden propeller. Options are Rotax 377 and Rotax 503. Some aircraft are fitted with Kawasaki 440 engines. Fuel tank capacity 19 litres (5 US gallons).

ACCOMMODATION: Pilot only, in open position. Glassfibre cockpit fairing.

DIMENSIONS, EXTERNAL:

Wing span	9·14 m (30 ft 0 in)
Length overall	5·44 m (17 ft 10 in)
Height overall	2·29 m (7 ft 6 in)
Propeller diameter	1·73 m (5 ft 8 in)

AREA:

Wings, gross	14·12 m² (152·0 sq ft)

WEIGHTS AND LOADINGS:

Weight empty	113 kg (250 lb)
Pilot weight range	46-136 kg (100-300 lb)
Max T-O weight	249 kg (550 lb)
Max wing loading	17·63 kg/m² (3·61 lb/sq ft)
Max power loading	8·30 kg/kW (13·75 lb/hp)

PERFORMANCE:

Never-exceed speed	74 knots (136 km/h; 85 mph)
Max level speed	55 knots (101 km/h; 63 mph)
Max cruising speed	48 knots (89 km/h; 55 mph)
Econ cruising speed	43 knots (80 km/h; 50 mph)
Stalling speed: power on	17 knots (31 km/h; 19 mph)
power off	19 knots (36 km/h; 22 mph)
Max rate of climb at S/L	259 m (850 ft)/min
Service ceiling	3,810 m (12,500 ft)
T-O run	30 m (100 ft)
Landing run	54 m (175 ft)
Range with max fuel	104 nm (193 km; 120 miles)
Endurance	2 h 15 min
g limits	+6/−4
Min rate of sink, power off	137 m (450 ft)/min

F. M. BELL ULTRA LITE AIRCRAFT SPITFIRE II

The Spitfire II is basically a side by side two-seat version of the Spitfire I, though its heavier weight puts it into the Experimental category for homebuilt aircraft. It uses the more powerful Rotax 503 engine with dual carburettor. At least 100 Spitfire II kits have been sold. Options include armament for military use.

Details, where they differ from the Spitfire I, are as follows:

TYPE: Two-seat homebuilt aircraft; conforms to FAI/CAA Experimental aircraft category.

AIRFRAME: Wider cockpit fairing and windscreen. Inverted V struts forward of windscreen instead of Spitfire I's single strut. Agricultural cropspraying equipment optional.

LANDING GEAR: 4·50-6 mainwheels and 4·50-4 steerable nosewheel.

POWER PLANT: One 35·8 kW (48 hp) Rotax 503 engine, with 2·58:1 gear reduction to a two-blade wooden propeller. Alternative 37·3 kW (50 hp) liquid-cooled Rotax engine.

ACCOMMODATION: Two persons side by side in open cockpit.

WEIGHTS AND LOADINGS:

Weight empty	150 kg (330 lb)
Max T-O weight	385 kg (850 lb)
Max wing loading	23·4 kg/m² (4·8 lb/sq ft)
Max power loading	10·75 kg/kW (17·71 lb/hp)

PERFORMANCE:

Never-exceed speed	87 knots (161 km/h; 100 mph)
Max level speed	74 knots (137 km/h; 85 mph)
Max cruising speed	61 knots (113 km/h; 70 mph)
Econ cruising speed	52 knots (97 km/h; 60 mph)
Stalling speed: power on	28 knots (52 km/h; 32 mph)
power off	30 knots (55 km/h; 34 mph)
Max rate of climb at S/L	244 m (800 ft)/min
Service ceiling	3,660 m (12,000 ft)
T-O and landing run	61 m (200 ft)
Range with max fuel	130 nm (241 km; 150 miles)
Endurance	3 h
g limits	+6/−4
Best glide ratio	6
Min rate of sink, power off	152 m (500 ft)/min

F. M. BELL ULTRA LITE AIRCRAFT CLIPPER

The Clipper differs from the other aircraft in the F. M. Bell Ultra Lite Aircraft range in having a more conventional aeroplane configuration. The fuselage is completely Dacron covered and the engine is nose mounted.

Four versions of the Clipper are available, thereby making the aircraft a microlight or Experimental category type according to whether it is in single- or two-seat form. Both seating arrangements are available with tricycle or tailwheel landing gears. Kits to assemble the Clipper are available, and more than 50 have been sold. Options include armament for military use.

The following details refer to the single-seat Clipper; the airframe and power plant are similar for the two-seater:

TYPE: Single-seat microlight aircraft; conforms to FAR Pt 103. (The two-seat Clipper conforms to the Experimental category.)

AIRFRAME: Braced parasol wing monoplane of conventional layout. Main frame of welded chrome molybdenum steel tubing and aluminium alloy, Dacron covered. Wing and tail unit double surface Dacron covered. Stainless steel cables. Open cockpit with small windscreen. Three-axis control (ailerons, elevators and rudder), with flaps. Rigging time 30 min.

LANDING GEAR: Tailwheel or tricycle type. Mainwheels size 4·50-6; steerable tailwheel diameter 5 in. Bungee suspension. Options include floats and skis.

POWER PLANT: One 30 kW (40 hp) Rotax 447 engine, with 2·58:1 gear reduction to a two-blade wooden propeller with spinner. Fuel tank capacity 19 litres (5 US gallons). Auxiliary tank optional, capacity 38 litres (10 US gallons).

ACCOMMODATION: Pilot only, in open cockpit.

DIMENSIONS, EXTERNAL:

Wing span	9·14 m (30 ft 0 in)
Length overall	5·28 m (17 ft 4 in)
Height overall	2·29 m (7 ft 6 in)
Propeller diameter	1·73 m (5 ft 8 in)

AREA:

Wings, gross	14·12 m² (152·0 sq ft)

WEIGHTS AND LOADINGS:

Weight empty	125 kg (275 lb)
Pilot weight range	50-158 kg (110-350 lb)
Max T-O weight	308 kg (680 lb)
Max wing loading	22·0 kg/m² (4·5 lb/sq ft)
Max power loading	10·27 kg/kW (17·00 lb/hp)

PERFORMANCE:

Never-exceed speed	74 knots (136 km/h; 85 mph)
Max level speed	56 knots (105 km/h; 65 mph)
Max cruising speed	52 knots (97 km/h; 60 mph)
Econ cruising speed	48 knots (89 km/h; 55 mph)
Stalling speed: power on	17 knots (31 km/h; 19 mph)
power off	19 knots (36 km/h; 22 mph)
Max rate of climb at S/L	244 m (800 ft)/min
Service ceiling	3,660 m (12,000 ft)
T-O run	30 m (100 ft)
Landing run	46 m (150 ft)
Range with max standard fuel	87 nm (161 km; 100 miles)
Endurance	2 h 20 min
g limits	+6/−4
Best glide ratio	6
Min rate of sink, power off	137 m (450 ft)/min

BENSEN

BENSEN AIRCRAFT CORPORATION

PO Box 31047, Raleigh-Durham Airport, Raleigh, North Carolina 27622

Telephone: (919) 787 4224/0945

PRESIDENT: J. Donald Dean

MANAGER, SALES AND MARKETING: Ronald H. Clarke

The Bensen Aircraft Corporation was formed by Dr Igor B. Bensen, formerly Chief of Research of the Kaman company, to develop a series of lightweight autogyros and rotary-wing gliders suitable for production in kit form for amateur construction as well as in ready to fly condition. More than 100,000 sets of plans to build these aircraft have been sold; the number flown to date is estimated to be more than 10,000.

BENSEN MODEL B-8 GYRO-GLIDER

The Gyro-Glider is a simple unpowered rotor kite which can be towed behind even a small motorcar and has achieved free gliding with the towline released. It is available as a kit of parts for amateur construction. Alternatively, would-be constructors can purchase a set of plans, with building and flying instructions. No pilot's licence is required to fly it in the United States and many thousands of kits and plans have been sold. Capability of conversion into powered form, as the Gyro-Copter (which see), is an inherent feature of the design.

The original Model B-7 Gyro-Glider was described in the 1958-59 *Jane's*. It was followed by the Model B-8, which is offered as either a single-seater or two-seater, the latter version being suitable for use as a pilot trainer.

The Model B-8 consists basically of an inverted square-section tubular aluminium T frame structure of which the forward arm supports the lightweight seat, towing arm, rudder bar and landing gear nosewheel. The rear arm supports a large stabilising fin and rudder, made normally of plywood, but optionally of metal. The main landing gear wheels are carried on a tubular axle near the junction of the T frame. The free-turning two-blade rotor is universally mounted at the top of the T frame and is normally operated directly by a hanging stick control. A floor control column is available as optional equipment. Pedal controls for the rudder are standard.

The Gyro-Glider rotor is made normally of laminated plywood, with a steel spar. Factory-built all-metal rotor blades are available as optional items. Bensen has produced more than 11,000 complete blades for the Gyro-Glider and Gyro-Copter, plus kits for homebuilt construction of another 4,000 blades.

The two-seat trainer version of the Gyro-Glider is fitted with castoring crosswind landing gear and has an extra-wide wheel track. It will maintain level flight down to 16·5 knots (30·5 km/h; 19 mph).

DIMENSIONS, EXTERNAL:

Rotor diameter	6·10 m (20 ft 0 in)
Length of fuselage	3·45 m (11 ft 4 in)
Height overall	1·90 m (6 ft 3 in)

BENSEN MODEL B-8W HYDRO-GLIDER

The basic structure of this floatplane rotor kite is similar to that of the B-8 Gyro-Glider and conversion from one to the other is simple. Main change is that the wheel landing gear is replaced by two floats. The original round floats have been superseded by flat-bottomed pontoons of polyurethane foam covered by glassfibre, which give better planing, with less spray.

The Hydro-Glider is towed by a motorboat.

BENSEN MODEL B-8M and B-8V GYRO-COPTERS and B-8MW HYDRO-COPTER

First flown on 6 December 1955, the Gyro-Copter is a powered autogyro conversion of the Gyro-Glider, designed for home construction from kits or plans. More than 5,000 have been built. When fitted with floats the aircraft is known as a **Hydro-Copter**.

The **B-8M** version of the Gyro-Copter has a more powerful engine than the original B-7M and can be equipped with an optional mechanical rotor drive. By engaging this drive, the rotor can be accelerated to flying speed while the aircraft is stationary. Then, by transferring the power to the pusher propeller, it is possible to take off in only 15 m (50 ft), with the rotor autorotating normally.

Other items available optionally include a 67 kW (90 hp) McCulloch engine instead of the normal 53·5 kW (72 hp) engine and the newly introduced Rotax 532 engine (see entry on B-85), a stronger aluminium bolted-together engine mounting, a larger diameter rotor, an offset gimbal rotor head, a redundant mast consisting of a pair of closely matched alloy tubes instead of the normal square-tube mast, a floor control column instead of the normal overhead type of column, dual ignition, nosewheel arrester, Bensen manufactured pontoons of polyurethane foam covered with glassfibre, and a detachable glassfibre open cabin nacelle for single-seat Gyro-Copters of 1976 or later type (only with redundant mast and aluminium engine mount of new design). All-metal rotor blades and tail surfaces are available as alternatives to the standard wooden components.

The prototype Model B-8M Gyro-Copter flew for the first time on 8 July 1957 and the first production model on 9 October 1957.

The B-8M is roadable, requiring no removal of, or changes in, its equipment for transition from air to ground travel. The rotor is merely stopped in a fore and aft position by a lock. Gyro-Copters have been driven on highways and have negotiated heavy city traffic with ease in a number of public demonstrations in the USA.

The **B-8V**, which flew for the first time in the Autumn of 1967, is basically a standard B-8M, but is powered by a 1,600 or 1,835 cc Volkswagen engine. In unmodified form the VW1600 yields just adequate flight performance at 272 kg (600 lb) gross weight. Since Bensen engineers considered that most Gyro-Copters would not have a gross weight as high as 600 lb, the VW1600 engine justified inclusion as an alternative power plant to the standard McCulloch engine, but the VW1835 is more popular.

Plans and an instruction manual for converting the B-8M to a B-8V, or for mounting a VW engine on a standard B-8 airframe, are available. More than 300 VW conversions are known to have flown in the USA.

TYPE: Single-seat light homebuilt autogyro.

ROTOR SYSTEM: Two-blade rotor of metal construction. Blade section Bensen G3. Teetering hub, with no lag hinges or collective pitch control. A larger-diameter rotor is available as an alternative, produced by replacing the standard 0·64 m (2 ft 1 in) hub plate with one of 0·86 m (2 ft 10 in). (A 1·22 m; 4 ft 0 in hub is available for special projects.) No anti-torque rotor. Rotor speed 400 rpm.

ROTOR DRIVE (optional): A flexible shaft drive is available to spin up the rotor. Alternatively, an auxiliary motor can be added to convert the aircraft to Powergyro standard (see separate entry).

AIRFRAME: Square-section tubular 6061-T6 aluminium fuselage structure. Optional redundant twin rotor mast of alloy tubes. Vertical fin and rudder of ¼ in plywood. Optional all-metal tail surfaces.

LANDING GEAR: Non-retractable tricycle type, with auxiliary tailwheel. No shock absorbers. Steerable nosewheel. General Tire wheels, size 12-4 in. Tyre pressure 0·69 bars (10 lb/sq in). Brake on nosewheel. Optional skis and floats.

POWER PLANT: One 53·5 kW (72 hp) McCulloch Model 4318AX flat-four two-stroke engine (or, optionally, a 67 kW; 90 hp McCulloch 4318GX engine of similar

Bell Ultra Lite Aircraft Spitfire I *(Geoffrey P. Jones)*

Two-seat Bell Ultra Lite Aircraft Spitfire II

Bensen Model B-8MW Hydro-Copter

Bell Ultra Lite Aircraft Clipper in single-seat tailwheel configuration

Bensen Model B-80 registered in the UK *(Peter J. Bish)*

Prototype Bensen Powergyro with continuously powered rotor

weight and dimensions), driving a two-blade fixed-pitch Bensen BA-595 wooden pusher propeller with leading-edges covered with Kevlar and stainless steel. Alternatively, one Volkswagen flat-four four-stroke engine, the most popular version of which is the 54·4 kW (73 hp) Volkswagen 1,835 cc engine, driving a Troyer Model 50-26-65 two-blade fixed-pitch wooden pusher propeller. Fuel tank under pilot's seat, capacity 22·75 litres (6·0 US gallons). Can be fitted with auxiliary tank for ferrying. Optional plastics tank shaped as pilot's seat, replacing standard tank and seat and increasing fuel capacity to 36·5 litres (9·7 US gallons).

ACCOMMODATION: Open seat. Overhead azimuth stick and rudder pedal controls. Optional floor control column. Safety belt. Optional glassfibre open cabin nacelle.

DIMENSIONS, EXTERNAL:
- Rotor diameter: standard — 6·10 m (20 ft 0 in)
- optional — 6·70 m (22 ft 0 in)
- Rotor blade chord — 0·18 m (7 in)
- Length of fuselage — 3·45 m (11 ft 4 in)
- Height overall — 1·90 m (6 ft 3 in)
- Wheel track — 1·52 m (5 ft 0 in)
- Propeller diameter:
  - 53·5 kW (72 hp) McCulloch — 1·22 m (4 ft 0 in)
  - Volkswagen — 1·27 m (4 ft 2 in)

AREAS (standard rotor):
- Rotor blades (each) — 0·54 m² (5·83 sq ft)
- Rotor disc — 29·19 m² (314·2 sq ft)

WEIGHTS (standard rotor):
- Weight empty: B-8M — 112 kg (247 lb)
- B-8V — 158 kg (348 lb)
- Max T-O weight: B-8M — 227 kg (500 lb)
- B-8V — 272 kg (600 lb)

PERFORMANCE (at max T-O weight, with standard rotor):
- Max level speed at S/L:
  - B-8M — 74 knots (137 km/h; 85 mph)
  - B-8V — 52 knots (96 km/h; 60 mph)
- Max cruising speed at S/L:
  - B-8M — 52 knots (96 km/h; 60 mph)
  - B-8V — 43 knots (80 km/h; 50 mph)
- Econ cruising speed:
  - B-8M, B-8V — 39 knots (72 km/h; 45 mph)
- Min speed in level flight:
  - B-8M — 13 knots (24 km/h; 15 mph)
  - B-8V — 18 knots (32 km/h; 20 mph)
- T-O speed at S/L:
  - B-8M — 18 knots (32 km/h; 20 mph)
  - B-8V — 22 knots (40 km/h; 25 mph)
- Landing speed: B-8M — 6 knots (12 km/h; 7 mph)
  - B-8V — 9 knots (16 km/h; 10 mph)
- Max rate of climb at S/L:
  - B-8M — 305 m (1,000 ft)/min
  - B-8V — 198 m (650 ft)/min
- Service ceiling: B-8M — 3,800 m (12,500 ft)
  - B-8V — 2,440 m (8,000 ft)
- T-O run, unpowered rotor, zero wind:
  - B-8M — 92 m (300 ft)
  - B-8V — 122 m (400 ft)
- T-O run, powered rotor, zero wind:
  - B-8M — 15 m (50 ft)
- Landing run in 9 knot (16 km/h; 10 mph) wind:
  - B-8M, B-8V — 0 ft
- Landing run in zero wind: B-8M — 6 m (20 ft)
  - B-8V — 7·5 m (25 ft)
- Normal range: B-8M — 86 nm (160 km; 100 miles)
  - B-8V — 130 nm (241 km; 150 miles)
- Ferry range: B-8M — 260 nm (482 km; 300 miles)
  - B-8V — 345 nm (643 km; 400 miles)
- Endurance: B-8M — 1 h 30 min
  - B-8V — 2 h 15 min

BENSEN MODEL B-80 and B-80D GYRO-COPTER

In an attempt to reduce Gyro-Copter operating costs, and the problems associated with aviation fuel shortages at some airports, Bensen adapted the Gyro-Copter to fly on 100 octane low-lead fuel (100LL Avgas) instead of 110/130 octane aviation fuel. Further development allowed the Gyro-Copter to use Exxon leaded 'high test' motorcar fuel. The test aircraft was designated Model B-80, and was flown with 53·5 kW (72 hp) and 67 kW (90 hp) McCulloch X engines, equipped with new carburettors, propellers and throttle controls to prevent knock and pre-ignition of the lower octane motorcar fuel.

Bensen first marketed the B-80 during 1980 in 'Gold Seal Kit' form, as a kit-only all-metal companion to the B-8M. The kit contained all hardware and instructions to complete the aircraft, including flight check, but no plans. Towards the end of that year, hybrid versions of the B-8M and B-80 were made available, to take advantage of interchangeability of certain components between the two models. By 1981, the dividing line between the B-8M and B-80 had become even less distinct, as customers may now choose which components they wish to build from plans and which from kits. Standard recommended power plant is the 53·5 kW (72 hp) McCulloch Model 4318AX, approved for use with automobile fuel, but other engines are being used successfully, as on the B-8M. A de luxe version of the aircraft is available as the **B-80D**.

BENSEN MODEL B-85 ROTAX GYRO-COPTER

The Model B-85 is basically a standard Gyro-Copter fitted with a Rotax Model 532 two-cylinder two-stroke engine. While the McCulloch engine remains an option for buyers of the powered Gyro-Copter, the Rotax has the advantages of being liquid cooled and muffled for reduced noise levels. It can be started by the pilot from the cockpit, and uses automobile fuel instead of more expensive aviation fuel. The Rotax Model 532 uses lightweight 'gearbelt' pulleys as reduction gear for the propeller.

BENSEN POWERGYRO

Introduced at the 1986 Sun 'n Fun Fly-in, the Powergyro completes the 30-year development cycle of the Gyro-Copter series and will become Bensen's standard kit-built configuration. Based on the standard Model B-8M, it has a separate motor located under the rotor hub which powers the rotor continuously during all stages of flight. This decreases the take-off run and, once airborne, gives the Powergyro greater speed, lift capability and overall performance than the basic Gyro-Copter. Maximum level speed is above 87 knots (161 km/h; 100 mph).

The rotor torque produced by this drive system is not apparent in flight, being balanced by the side force on the rudder, located in the slipstream of the aircraft's pusher propeller. The rotor uses a fixed autorotative pitch. Thus, whether the main engine is on or off, the Powergyro can always glide to a normal power-off landing. The governed rotor drive motor maintains constant rotor speed to ease handling.

Initially, the motor supplied as standard with Powergyro kits, and available for retrofit to existing Gyro-Copters, will give the equivalent of 2 per cent of total engine power. Later, Bensen expects to offer three further motors providing 5, 10 and 20 per cent of total power. The 10 per cent motor will permit vertical 'jump take-off'; the 20 per cent motor will give the Powergyro a hovering capability.

The flexible shaft type of Gyro-Copter pre-rotation drive will continue to be available optionally.

BLACK

FRANK E. BLACK

1681 Yellow Glen Drive, Cincinnati, Ohio 45230

BLACK BLACKBIRD

An accompanying illustration shows the Blackbird autogyro (N71SR) built by Mr Frank E. Black. Few details are known, except that it is of typical gyroplane layout with an engine and two-blade propeller in pusher configuration, a tail fin and large rudder supporting small horizontal surfaces. The tricycle landing gear uses oleo-pneumatic shock absorbers, and a small tailwheel prevents damage to the rudder during take-off and landing. Accommodation is provided for a pilot only, in an open cockpit with windscreen.

BOAC

BARNEY OLDFIELD AIRCRAFT COMPANY

PO Box 228, Needham, Massachusetts 02192

Barney Oldfield Aircraft Co markets plans and material kits for the 'Baby' Lakes, a scaled-down version of the Great Lakes Sport Trainer, the prototype of which was designed and built by Mr Andrew Oldfield, who died during 1970. More than 930 sets of drawings had been sold by early 1986, and many 'Baby' Lakes are under construction. About 100 are known to be flying.

A variant of the 'Baby' Lakes is the 'Super Baby', with a more powerful engine and other modifications. Plans are available and at least 25 sets have been sold. Another variant is the 'Buddy Baby', plans for which were scheduled to be available by Autumn 1986.

Under development are inverted oil and fuel systems for the 'Baby' Lakes, so that it can be used as a low cost aerobatic aircraft.

OLDFIELD 'BABY' LAKES

The 'Baby' Lakes illustrated was built strictly to plans by Mr Ralph D. Crapse of Immokalee, Florida. It is powered by a 74·5 kW (100 hp) Continental engine, has an empty weight of 237 kg (522 lb) and cruises at over 113 knots (209 km/h; 130 mph). The following information applies to the standard plans-built 'Baby' Lakes.

TYPE: Single-seat homebuilt sporting biplane.

AIRFRAME: Braced biplane, with N interplane struts, double landing and flying wires and N centre-section support struts. Wing section modified M6, tapering to USA 27 46 cm (18 in) from tips. Incidence 2° 30′ on top wing, 1° 30′ on bottom wing. Wood structure of spruce spars and Warren truss ribs, with overall fabric covering. Ailerons on lower wings only. No flaps. Welded steel tube fuselage structure, fabric covered. Wire braced welded steel tube tail unit, fabric covered.

LANDING GEAR: Non-retractable tailwheel type. Oleo main legs with size 5·00-4 wheels. Steerable tailwheel. Mainwheel fairings optional.

POWER PLANT: One 63·4 kW (85 hp) Continental flat-four engine, driving a two-blade fixed-pitch propeller. Provision for alternative engines of between 37·25 and 74·5 kW (50 and 100 hp). Fuel tank in front fuselage, capacity 45 litres (12 US gallons).

ACCOMMODATION: Single seat, normally in open cockpit. Cockpit canopy optional.

DIMENSIONS, EXTERNAL:

Wing span: upper	5·08 m (16 ft 8 in)
Wing chord (both wings, constant)	0·91 m (3 ft 0 in)
Length overall	4·19 m (13 ft 9 in)
Height overall	1·37 m (4 ft 6 in)

AREA:

Wings, gross	7·99 m² (86·0 sq ft)

WEIGHTS AND LOADINGS (59·5 kW; 80 hp Continental A80 engine):

Weight empty	215 kg (475 lb)
Max T-O weight	385 kg (850 lb)
Max wing loading	48·2 kg/m² (9·9 lb/sq ft)
Max power loading	6·47 kg/kW (10·63 lb/hp)

PERFORMANCE (A80 engine, at max T-O weight):

Max level speed at S/L	117 knots (217 km/h; 135 mph)
Cruising speed at S/L	102 knots (190 km/h; 118 mph)
Stalling speed	44 knots (81 km/h; 50 mph)
Max rate of climb at S/L	610 m (2,000 ft)/min
Service ceiling	5,200 m (17,000 ft)
T-O run	91 m (300 ft)
Landing run (no brakes)	122 m (400 ft)
Max range	217 nm (400 km; 250 miles)
g limits	±9

OLDFIELD 'SUPER BABY' LAKES

The prototype 'Super Baby' Lakes (N362RB), based on the 'Baby' Lakes but with an 85·75 kW (115 hp) Avco Lycoming O-235 flat-four engine, was built by Mr Ray Ball, Mr Alan Lane and Mr Richard Lane, and flew for the first time in 1976. Following completion of more than 100 flying hours by early 1977, plans were made available to other constructors, with provision for fitting Avco Lycoming engines of 80·5 to 93 kW (108-125 hp). A few other plans-built 'Super Babies' are known to be flying.

The O-235 engine of the prototype drives a 69-54 Met-L-Prop two-blade metal propeller. Other modifications compared with the 'Baby' Lakes include use of a Burtch die spring landing gear, and routed wing spars which allow installation of wing fuel tanks without any appreciable increase in the empty weight by comparison with the wings of a standard 'Baby'. To prevent the possibility of fuel starvation, due to the high acceleration at take-off interrupting forward fuel flow from the main tank, a 0·95 litre (1 US quart) header tank is installed forward of the carburettor. Covering is Dacron, finished with Stits Poly-Fiber and Imeron polyurethane colour.

Take-off distances are reduced by 20-25 per cent compared with the 'Baby'. Other data measured with the prototype 'Super Baby' are as follows:

DIMENSIONS, EXTERNAL:

As for 'Baby' Lakes, except:

Length overall	4·34 m (14 ft 3 in)

WEIGHTS:

Weight empty	218 kg (480 lb)
Max T-O weight	385 kg (850 lb)

PERFORMANCE:

Max level speed	135 knots (249 km/h; 155 mph) IAS
Cruising speed (75% power)	117 knots (217 km/h; 135 mph) IAS
Stalling speed	48 knots (89 km/h; 55 mph) IAS
Max rate of climb at S/L	915 m (3,000 ft)/min
T-O run	69 m (225 ft)
Landing run	130 m (425 ft)
Max range, with wing tanks	260 nm (483 km; 300 miles)

OLDFIELD 'BUDDY BABY' LAKES

The two-seat 'Buddy Baby' utilises standard 'Baby' wings and tail unit. To prevent a significant increase in wing loading, a 41 cm (16 in) upper wing centre-section has been introduced, together with short stub-wings built integrally with the fuselage to increase the lower span by a similar amount.

The fuselage is a completely new design, which has been widened and stretched only enough to permit seating positions for two average-sized (77 kg; 170 lb) people in a configuration much like that of a 'buddy seat' on a motorcycle. Dual throttle and rudder pedals are provided, with a single dual-position joystick. The aircraft is flown solo from the rear seat and dual from the front position.

BOUNSALL

BOUNSALL AIRCRAFT

PO Box 506, Mesquite, Nevada 89024

Telephone: (702) 346 5722

PRESIDENT: Curtiss Bounsall

Mr Eddie Bounsall, the owner of a gold mine (hence the name of his aircraft), began the design of a small strut braced high-wing monoplane known as the Prospector in 1980. The prototype, built by Mr Bounsall and his son Curtiss, flew for the first time in 1982.

The Prospector was designed to be economical to operate, possess STOL performance, be capable of operation from rough and remote mining airstrips, and cope with mountain flying. It is thus well suited to operation by farmers and ranchers, in addition to normal flying operations.

A lighter version is known as the Super Prospector. Details of this aircraft, and the original Prospector, follow:

BOUNSALL PROSPECTOR

Plans to build the Prospector are available to amateur constructors.

TYPE: Single-seat homebuilt bush monoplane.

AIRFRAME: Strut braced high-wing monoplane. Wing section modified Pietenpol. Dihedral approx 1° 30′. Incidence 1° 30′. Mostly wooden structure, with spruce spars, plywood ribs, aluminium alloy trailing-edges and metal fittings, fabric covered. Constant chord ailerons of similar construction to wings. Conventional fuselage structure of welded 4130 steel tubing, fabric covered. Glassfibre engine cowling. All-moving rudder with trailing-edge tab, and all-moving rectangular tailplane with inset trim tab, of similar construction to wings.

LANDING GEAR: Non-retractable tailwheel type. Two side Vs with half-axles hinged to fuselage structure. Shock absorption of main units by spring in compression. Cleveland mainwheels. Tyres size 6·00-6 on mainwheels. Wheel fairings on main units. Hydraulic disc brakes.

POWER PLANT: Prototype has 42 kW (56 hp) HAPI 1,835 cc modified Volkswagen motorcar engine with starter and alternator, driving a Hegy two-blade propeller with spinner. Design suitable for Volkswagen engines of 1,600 cc to 2,150 cc. Fuel capacity 42 litres (11 US gallons).

ACCOMMODATION: Single seat in fully enclosed and well glazed cabin. Door on starboard side. Heated and ventilated. Baggage space aft of seat, capacity 9 kg (20 lb).

SYSTEM: 12V electrical system with alternator and nav lights.

AVIONICS: Radios carried, including CB.

DIMENSIONS, EXTERNAL:

Wing span	8·53 m (28 ft 0 in)
Wing chord, constant	1·32 m (4 ft 4 in)
Length of fuselage	4·78 m (15 ft 8 in)
Height overall	1·84 m (6 ft 0½ in)
Tailplane span	2·24 m (7 ft 4 in)

DIMENSIONS, INTERNAL:

Cabin: Max width	0·71 m (2 ft 4 in)
Max height	0·97 m (3 ft 2½ in)

AREA:

Wings, gross	10·59 m² (114·0 sq ft)

WEIGHTS AND LOADINGS:

Weight empty	248 kg (546 lb)
Max fuel weight	30 kg (66 lb)
Max T-O weight	411 kg (906 lb)

Original Bowers Fly Baby with biplane wings as a Fly Baby 1-B
(Peter M. Bowers)

Oldfield (BOAC) 'Baby' Lakes built by Mr Ralph D. Crapse

Bowers Fly Baby 1-A built by Mr John Thorne of Coupland, Texas
(Peter M. Bowers)

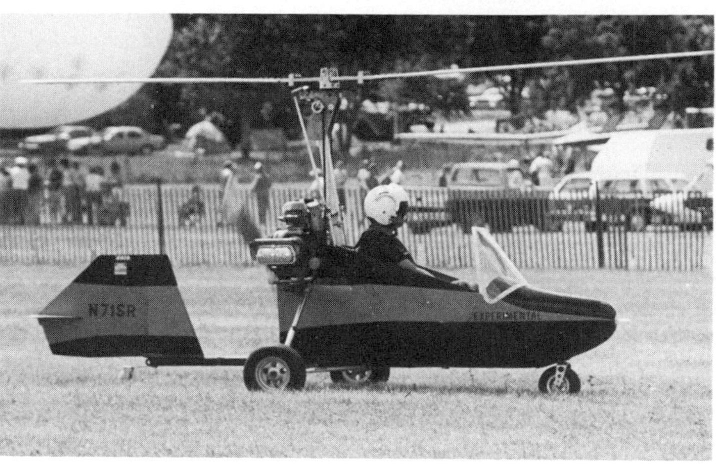

Black Blackbird single-seat homebuilt autogyro *(J. M. G. Gradidge)*

Bounsall Prospector alongside the Bounsall Super Prospector prototype when under construction

Max wing loading 38·8 kg/m² (7·95 lb/sq ft)
Max power loading 9·79 kg/kW (16·18 lb/hp)

PERFORMANCE:
Never-exceed speed 117 knots (217 km/h; 135 mph)
Max level speed at 1,370 m (4,500 ft) 82 knots (153 km/h; 95 mph)
Max cruising speed at 1,370 m (4,500 ft) 74 knots (137 km/h; 85 mph)
Stalling speed, engine idling 39 knots (73 km/h; 45 mph) IAS
Max rate of climb at 1,280 m (4,200 ft) 122 m (400 ft)/min

BOUNSALL SUPER PROSPECTOR

The Super Prospector is a rugged STOL bush and sporting aircraft, based on the original Prospector but lighter in weight. It was designed to be inexpensive to build and operate. Plans and kits of component parts are available to amateur builders.

When compared with the smaller but heavier Prospector, the Super Prospector has a conventional wire braced tail unit comprising a tapering tailplane with rounded horn balanced elevators, a fin and horn balanced rudder; it has no starter or alternator.

TYPE: Single-seat homebuilt bush monoplane.

POWER PLANT: One 44·7 kW (60 hp) Volkswagen 1,835 cc modified motorcar engine, driving a 60 × 30 Hegy two-blade propeller. Fuel capacity 45·4 litres (12 US gallons).

DIMENSIONS, EXTERNAL:
Wing span 9·04 m (29 ft 8 in)
Wing chord, constant 1·31 m (4 ft 3¾ in)
Length overall 5·89 m (19 ft 4 in)

AREA:
Wings, gross 11·22 m² (120·75 sq ft)

WEIGHTS AND LOADINGS:
Weight empty 200 kg (440 lb)
Max T-O weight 363 kg (800 lb)
Max wing loading 32·4 kg/m² (6·63 lb/sq ft)
Max power loading 8·12 kg/kW (13·33 lb/hp)

PERFORMANCE (estimated):
Cruising speed 78 knots (145 km/h; 90 mph)
Stalling speed 32 knots (58 km/h; 36 mph)
Max rate of climb at S/L 183 m (600 ft)/min
Range with max fuel 260 nm (483 km; 300 miles)

BOWERS

PETER M. BOWERS

10458 16th Avenue South, Seattle, Washington 98168

Mr Peter Bowers is a principal source of detailed information on vintage aircraft in the United States, and has provided much of the data for a number of replicas of First World War aircraft now under construction or flying.

Mr Bowers has built a number of aircraft himself. In particular, he designed and constructed prototypes of a single-seat light aircraft known as the Fly Baby, of which plans are available, and which is flying in very large numbers, in both monoplane and biplane forms.

BOWERS FLY BABY 1-A

The prototype Fly Baby monoplane was produced to compete in an Experimental Aircraft Association design contest, organised to encourage the development of a simple, low-cost, easy-to-fly aeroplane that could be built by inexperienced amateurs for recreational flying. It was built in 720 working hours and flew for the first time on 27 July 1960. As only one other aircraft was completed by the specified closing date, the contest was postponed for two years.

When the EAA contest was finally held in the Summer of 1962, Fly Baby was placed first and won a prize of $2,500. Home construction plans of the aircraft are available and a total of 4,200 sets had been sold by early 1986. Construction of well over 700 Fly Babies is known to have been undertaken, of which about 400 have flown, including some based on detailed drawings and instructions published in *Sport Aviation*, journal of the EAA.

The Fly Baby monoplane has been tested as a twin-float seaplane, in which configuration it has a max AUW of 454 kg (1,000 lb) and cruising speed of 84 knots (156 km/h; 97 mph). A version operated on skis was illustrated in the 1980-81 *Jane's*.

During 1968, Mr Bowers designed and built biplane wings for the Fly Baby, which are interchangeable with the monoplane wings. The monoplane version is known as the Fly Baby 1-A, and the biplane as the Fly Baby 1-B (described separately).

Several individual amateur builders amended the plans during 1973 to allow for construction of two-seat versions of the Fly Baby. Although Mr Bowers does not recommend this conversion, he has made some additions to the plans to cater for the conversion, including a 0·97 m (3 ft 2 in) wide fuselage, a 1·52 m (5 ft 0 in) span wing centre-section to support a shock absorbing landing gear similar to that of the Ryan ST/PT-22 of 1934-42, the use of heavier flying wires with swaged fork ends, a raised aft turtledeck to offset the drag of the larger cockpit and a recommendation to use an engine of 63·5 to 80 kW (85 to 107 hp). The outer wing panels are unchanged, giving the two-seat Fly Baby a span of 9·45 m (31 ft 0 in) and wing area of 12·4 m² (133·5 sq ft).

Mr Bowers feels that the use of side by side seating is a great performance handicap to the basic design, and approves the tandem arrangement by Mr Victor F. Meznarsic (see page 545 of 1983-84 *Jane's*). At present, he is developing a 'stretched' tandem two-seater, to be fitted with longer two-bay biplane wings, in a deliberate attempt to resemble a First World War type such as the B.E.2c. This will be a low-performance 'fun flier' on engines up to 74·5 kW (100 hp), and will not be aerobatic.

Because of the shortage of aircraft engines in the 48·5-63·5 kW (65-85 hp) range, Mr Bowers approves reluctantly the use of VW engines of over 1,800 cc.

The following description applies to the original single-seat Fly Baby 1-A:

TYPE: Single-seat light homebuilt monoplane.

AIRFRAME: Wire braced low-wing monoplane. Double ½ in 1 × 19 stainless steel bracing wires. Wing section NACA 4412. Wooden two-spar structure, covered with Dacron fabric and finished with two coats of nitrate dope and one coat of automotive enamel. Wings rotate about a special fitting to fold back alongside the fuselage for towing. Conventional plywood covered wood fuselage of rectangular section. Decking behind cockpit, including pilot's headrest, is removable and can be replaced with higher transparent section matched with a sliding transparent cockpit canopy for enclosed cockpit operation. Wire braced wood tail unit, fabric covered.

LANDING GEAR: Non-retractable tailwheel type. Main landing gear struts of laminated wood, braced by crossed steel wires. Steel tube straight-across axle faired with streamline section steel tube. Ends of axles project beyond wheel hubs to serve as anchor points for wing bracing wires. Shock absorption by low pressure 8·00-4 tyres, carried on Piper Cub wheels, with hydraulic brakes.

POWER PLANT: One 63·5 kW (85 hp) Continental C75 flat-four engine, driving a two-blade fixed-pitch propeller. Fuel tank from Piper J-3 Cub, capacity 60·5 litres (16 US gallons).

ACCOMMODATION: Single seat in open or enclosed cockpit. Baggage in underfuselage 'tank' which can be removed and carried like a suitcase.

DIMENSIONS, EXTERNAL:
- Wing span: 8·53 m (28 ft 0 in)
- Wing chord, constant: 1·37 m (4 ft 6 in)
- Length overall: 5·64 m (18 ft 6 in)
- Height, wings folded: 1·98 m (6 ft 6 in)

WEIGHTS AND LOADING:
- Weight empty: 274 kg (605 lb)
- Max T-O weight: 419 kg (924 lb)
- Max power loading: 6·60 kg/kW (10·87 lb/hp)

PERFORMANCE (at max T-O weight):
- Max level speed at S/L: over 104 knots (193 km/h; 120 mph)
- Cruising speed: 91-96 knots (169-177 km/h; 105-110 mph)
- Landing speed: 39 knots (73 km/h; 45 mph)
- Max rate of climb at S/L: 335 m (1,100 ft)/min
- T-O and landing run: 76 m (250 ft)
- Range with max fuel: 277 nm (515 km; 320 miles)

BOWERS FLY BABY 1-B

During 1968 Mr Bowers designed and built a set of interchangeable biplane wings for the original prototype Fly Baby and with these fitted it flew for the first time on 27 March 1969. Thirteen more biplanes, designated Fly Baby 1-B, have been completed and flown.

The biplane wings have the same aerofoil section and incidence as those of the monoplane version, but the rib webs are made of 1/16 in instead of ⅛ in plywood and the wingtip bows are formed from ½ in aluminium tube instead of laminated wood strips. This lightweight construction limits weight increase to only 21 kg (46 lb) for an increase of 2·79 m² (30 sq ft) in wing area. Span is reduced by 1·83 m (6 ft) and chord by 0·30 m (1 ft). Ailerons are fitted to the lower wings only.

To facilitate entry to the cockpit the upper wing has been located well forward, and in order to bring the centre of lift in line with the original CG, both planes have been given 11° of sweepback. Changeover from monoplane to biplane configuration can be accomplished by two people in approximately one hour.

The biplane is intended to use the same engines as the monoplane, for which Mr Bowers does not recommend anything heavier than the Continental O-200. Since some biplane builders have desired to use the 93 kW (125 hp) Avco Lycoming O-290, a modification has been authorised for the biplane, whereby the wing sweep is decreased by 5° for CG reasons.

TYPE: Single-seat light homebuilt biplane.

AIRFRAME: Forward-stagger single bay biplane with N interplane and centre-section struts. Landing and flying bracing wires. Sweepback 11°. Wooden structure with Dacron covering. Rib webs constructed of 1/16 in plywood, wingtip bows formed of ½ in aluminium tube. Ailerons on lower wings only. Otherwise same as Fly Baby 1-A.

POWER PLANT: One 63·5 kW (85 hp) Continental C85 flat-four engine.

DIMENSIONS, EXTERNAL:
- Wing span: 6·71 m (22 ft 0 in)
- Wing chord, both wings, constant: 1·07 m (3 ft 6 in)
- Height overall: 2·08 m (6 ft 10 in)

AREA:
- Wings, gross: 13·94 m² (150·0 sq ft)

WEIGHTS AND LOADINGS:
- Weight empty: 295 kg (651 lb)
- Max T-O weight: 440 kg (972 lb)
- Max wing loading: 31·64 kg/m² (6·48 lb/sq ft)
- Max power loading: 6·93 kg/kW (11·44 lb/hp)

PERFORMANCE (at max T-O weight):
- Cruising speed: 75 knots (140 km/h; 87 mph)
- Max rate of climb at S/L: 267 m (875 ft)/min

BROCK

KEN BROCK MANUFACTURING INC

11852 Western Avenue, Stanton, California 90680
Telephone: (714) 898 4366

Ken Brock Manufacturing, a division of Santa Ana Metal Stamping, is a company with a factory floor area of 929 m² (10,000 sq ft) at its plant near Los Angeles. It specialises in the fabrication of component parts for a wide range of aircraft, including the Thorp T-18, and manufactures and sells kits of parts for the construction by amateurs of its own KB-2 Freedom Machine and KB-3 gyroplanes and the Avion microlight. Its founder, Mr Ken Brock, has been involved with rotorcraft design, construction and flight testing since 1957, and was the southern California distributor for Bensen Aircraft between 1960 and 1980. As early as 1964 he made a cross-country flight of 391 nm (724 km; 450 miles) in a gyroplane, from El Mirage, California, to Las Vegas, Nevada, and back. This was followed by other notable flights, including in 1971 a transcontinental flight over a distance of 2,952 nm (5,471 km; 3,400 miles) between Long Beach, California, and Kitty Hawk, North Carolina, during a ten-day period.

KEN BROCK KB-2 FREEDOM MACHINE

Design of the KB-2 as an aircraft suitable for construction by amateurs from kits of parts began in 1970; the prototype flew before the end of that year. Manufacture of kits began in 1979, for sale from 1980; several hundred have been sold.

The KB-2 is built from eight kits of parts that are available individually or together. A McCulloch or Volkswagen engine, propeller and associated components, are also available as a kit to complete the KB-2. Construction requires a work area of 3·05 × 3·05 m (10 × 10 ft) and simple hand tools. Assembly of the basic airframe takes approximately 1½ hours. The KB-2 can be assembled ready for testing in unpowered form in one weekend. Instruction to fly the KB-2 is available at the Ken Brock flight training centre.

TYPE: Single-seat light homebuilt autogyro.

ROTOR SYSTEM: Single two-blade semi-rigid rotor, with an aluminium spar and riveted metal skins. Blade section modified Clark Y. Teetering offset-gimbal hub.

AIRFRAME: Inverted T fuselage structure of mainly bolted square section aluminium tubing. Only three welded parts. Fin, rudder and tailplane form tail unit, made of aluminium ribs, spars and skins, riveted together, or alternative wooden construction.

LANDING GEAR: Non-retractable tricycle type, with auxiliary tailwheel. No shock absorbers. Steerable and self-centering nosewheel. Mainwheel tyre size 12 × 3·5-6 in. Nosewheel tyre size 8 × 2·7-4 in. Tyre pressure (all) 1·38 bars (20 lb/sq in). Dual hydraulic brakes optional.

POWER PLANT: One 53·7 kW (72 hp) McCulloch 4318A or Volkswagen modified motorcar engine (max power rating 74·5 kW; 100 hp), driving a two-blade wooden fixed-pitch propeller. Patented seat/fuel tank, capacity 33·7 litres (8·9 US gallons). Oil capacity for Volkswagen engine 3·8 litres (1 US gallon).

ACCOMMODATION: Single seat in exposed position. Floor control column.

DIMENSIONS, EXTERNAL:
- Rotor diameter: 6·70 m (22 ft 0 in)
- Rotor blade chord: 0·18 m (7 in)
- Length of fuselage: 3·43 m (11 ft 3 in)
- Max width: 1·73 m (5 ft 8 in)
- Max height: 2·03 m (6 ft 8 in)
- Propeller diameter: 1·22 m (4 ft 0 in)

AREAS:
- Rotor blades (each): 0·54 m² (5·80 sq ft)
- Rotor disc: 35·32 m² (380·1 sq ft)

WEIGHTS:
- Weight empty: 109 kg (240 lb)
- Max T-O weight: 272 kg (600 lb)

PERFORMANCE (at max T-O weight):
- Never-exceed speed: 87 knots (161 km/h; 100 mph)
- Max level speed: 78 knots (145 km/h; 90 mph)
- Max cruising speed: 65 knots (121 km/h; 75 mph)
- Econ cruising speed: 56 knots (105 km/h; 65 mph)
- T-O speed: 17 knots (32 km/h; 20 mph)
- Max rate of climb at S/L: over 305 m (1,000 ft)/min
- Service ceiling: 3,050 m (10,000 ft)
- T-O run: 61 m (200 ft)
- T-O to 15 m (50 ft): 91 m (300 ft)
- Landing from 15 m (50 ft): 15 m (50 ft)
- Landing run: 3 m (10 ft)
- Range with max fuel: 130 nm (241 km; 150 miles)
- Endurance: 2 h

KEN BROCK KB-3

The KB-3 is a new microlight development of the KB-2, that is available in kit form. It uses a rotor of the same diameter as the heavier aircraft, but the tail unit comprises a rudder only, the mast is 25 cm (1 ft) taller, and a 90° pre-rotator is fitted to the rotor to eliminate the need for a gearbox. A bowed mainwheel axle provides improved ground clearance.

TYPE: Single-seat microlight autogyro.

LANDING GEAR: Non-retractable tricycle type, with auxiliary tailwheel. Bowed mainwheel axle, with 4 in diameter Brock aluminium wheels. Steerable 5 in diameter nosewheel, with hydraulic disc brake. Parking brake.

POWER PLANT: One 47·7 kW (64 hp) Rotax 532 two-stroke engine, with 2·58:1 reduction gear to a two-blade propeller.

DIMENSIONS, EXTERNAL:
- Rotor diameter: 6·70 m (22 ft 0 in)
- Length of fuselage: 3·35 m (11 ft 0 in)
- Width overall, rotor fore and aft: 1·57 m (5 ft 2 in)
- Propeller diameter: 1·52 m (5 ft 0 in)

WEIGHTS:
- Weight empty: 108 kg (237 lb)
- Max T-O weight: 283 kg (625 lb)

PERFORMANCE:
- Cruising speed: 52-56 knots (97-105 km/h; 60-65 mph)
- Max rate of climb at S/L: 213-244 m (700-800 ft)/min
- T-O run: 31-46 m (100-150 ft)
- Landing run: 0-1·5 m (0-5 ft)

KEN BROCK AVION

The Avion was designed by the late Mr Bob Lovejoy, who in the early 1970s was responsible for the highly successful Quicksilver manufactured by Eipper (which see). Mr Ken Brock is continuing development, production and marketing (in kit form) of the aircraft, which complies with FAR Pt 103 and AC 103-7.

TYPE: Single-seat microlight aircraft.

AIRFRAME: Conventional high-wing monoplane. Aluminium alloy airframe, double surface Dacron covered wings and tail surfaces. Strut braced wings, cruciform tail surfaces. No other bracing. Three-axis control (rudder, elevator and ailerons). Rigging time 15-20 min.

LANDING GEAR: Tricycle type, with rubber sprung mainwheel suspension. Mainwheel size 4·10 × 3·50. Steerable nosewheel, size 3·40 × 3·00-5, with brake.

POWER PLANT: One 20 kW (27 hp) Rotax 277 engine, with reduction drive to a two-blade wooden pusher propeller. Total fuel capacity 19 litres (5 US gallons) in patented seat fuel tank.

ACCOMMODATION: Pilot only, in open position. An enclosure is being developed.

DIMENSIONS, EXTERNAL:
- Wing span: 8·84 m (29 ft 0 in)
- Wing aspect ratio: 5·76
- Length overall: 4·72 m (15 ft 6 in)
- Height overall: 2·08 m (6 ft 10 in)
- Propeller diameter: 1·22 m (4 ft 0 in)

AREA:
- Wings, gross: 13·47 m² (145·0 sq ft)

WEIGHTS AND LOADINGS:
- Weight empty: 109 kg (240 lb)
- Pilot weight range: 59-95 kg (130-210 lb)
- Max T-O weight: 227 kg (500 lb)
- Max wing loading: 16·83 kg/m² (3·45 lb/sq ft)
- Max power loading: 10·87 kg/kW (17·86 lb/hp)

PERFORMANCE:
- Never-exceed speed: 69 knots (128 km/h; 80 mph)
- Max level speed: 45 knots (84 km/h; 52 mph)
- Max cruising speed, 75% power: 42 knots (77 km/h; 48 mph)
- Econ cruising speed: 39 knots (72 km/h; 45 mph)
- Stalling speed: power on and power off: 24 knots (44 km/h; 27 mph)
- Max rate of climb at S/L: 213 m (700 ft)/min
- Service ceiling: 3,050 m (10,000 ft)
- T-O run: 55 m (180 ft)
- Landing run: 46 m (150 ft)
- Range with standard fuel: 121 nm (225 km; 140 miles)
- Endurance with standard fuel: more than 4 h
- *g* limits: +6/−4
- Best glide ratio: 7
- Min rate of sink, power off: 152 m (500 ft)/min

Ken Brock KB-2 Freedom Machine

Ken Brock KB-3 microlight development of the KB-2 autogyro *(Howard Levy)*

Ken Brock Avion single-seat three-axis microlight (third prototype)

Brokaw Bullet with Avco Lycoming TIO-541-E engine

BROKAW

BROKAW AVIATION INC

2625 Johnson Point, Leesburg, Florida 32748
Telephone: (904) 787 2329
PRESIDENT: Bergon F. Brokaw, MD, FACFP

BROKAW BULLET

Dr B. F. Brokaw, a former US Navy pilot, and Dr Ernest R. Jones, who has a PhD in aeronautical engineering, combined their talents to design and build a low-wing monoplane which was claimed to be the world's fastest two-seat homebuilt. Dr Brokaw was concerned primarily with overall design and construction, Dr Jones with stress analysis and structural design.

Basic intention was to develop a high-speed all-weather two-seat homebuilt suitable for cross-country flying. Aerobatic potential was of secondary consideration, but the Bullet, which was known originally as the BJ-520, is stressed to ± 6*g* for aerobatics and 9*g* ultimate, with a claimed 20 to 30 per cent safety margin.

Design began in August 1966 and construction of the prototype started six months later. First flight was made on 18 November 1972, and during the Summer of 1973 work was carried out to clean up the airframe to take better advantage of the design potential. This included the provision of wheel-well doors, and reduction of the drag of the engine cooling system, achieved by the use of baffles, ducts and direct ram-air cooling.

Major redesign and modification were undertaken in 1976, and the prototype resumed flying in 1977 as the Bullet. Subsequent refinements include changes to the wing span and section. By early 1985 the Bullet had logged well over 1,000 flying hours and had been flown in all weather conditions, including light ice. Further modifications were undertaken, including the installation of a more powerful engine and changes to the engine cowling, cockpit arrangement and canopy. (For performance and other data relating to the original version, powered by a 212·5 kW; 285 hp Continental TSIO-520-B turbocharged engine, see 1975-76 *Jane's*.)

Dr Brokaw formed Brokaw Aviation Inc to market plans of the Bullet and a construction manual to amateur constructors. Although full kits are not available, it was intended also to supply certain components such as the canopy, cowling and, possibly, bulkheads and ribs, to simplify the task of the homebuilder. More than 20 Bullets are under construction, including two with tailwheel landing gear. One of these is powered by an Avco Lycoming TIO-720 engine; other amateur-built Bullets will have a 410 kW (550 hp) Ranger twelve-cylinder V engine or a 449 kW (602 hp) turbocharged Geschwender V-8.

TYPE: Two-seat homebuilt sporting aircraft.

AIRFRAME Cantilever low-wing monoplane. Laminar flow wing section: NACA 64A412 at root, NACA 64A410 at tip. Dihedral 4° 30′. Incidence 1° at root, 0° at tip. Conventional structure of 2024-T3 light alloy. Ailerons and trailing-edge flaps of light alloy. Semi-monocoque fuselage of light alloy. Cantilever light alloy tail unit. Fixed incidence tailplane. Electrically operated trim tabs in elevators and rudder.

LANDING GEAR: Hydraulically retractable tricycle type. Main and nose units and associated hydraulic system are from a Navion aircraft. Main units retract inward and nosewheel rearward. Single wheel on each main unit, with 15 × 6·00-6 low-profile tyre, pressure 4·48 bars (65 lb/sq in). Nosewheel tyre size 14 × 5·00-4, pressure 3·10 bars (45 lb/sq in). Goodyear hydraulic brakes on mainwheels.

POWER PLANT: One 283 kW (380 hp) Avco Lycoming TIO-541-E flat-six engine, driving a Sensenich three-blade constant-speed metal propeller with spinner. Alternative power plant is 213 kW (285 hp) Teledyne Continental TSIO-520-B flat-six engine, driving a McCauley three-blade constant-speed metal propeller with spinner, or other engine of 223-449 kW (300-602 hp), including the Avco Lycoming IO-720/TIO-720. Four integral wing fuel tanks, with capacity of 363 litres (96 US gallons). Refuelling points at wingtips. Oil capacity 11·3 litres (3 US gallons).

ACCOMMODATION: Two seats in tandem beneath transparent individual canopies. Port half of each canopy hinged near centreline to open upwards. Baggage space, which accommodates 31·8 kg (70 lb), aft of rear seat. Cabin heated and ventilated.

SYSTEMS: Hydraulic system at 103·5 bars (1,500 lb/sq in) for landing gear retraction and brakes. 28V 70A alternator for electrical system. Oxygen system for pilot and passenger, with capacity of 5 hours.

AVIONICS AND EQUIPMENT: Full IFR instrumentation, including DGO 10, DME 70, dual Narco 360-channel transceivers and dual VORs, ADF, transponder, marker beacon and ILS. Landing gear warning lights, navigation lights and external power socket.

DIMENSIONS, EXTERNAL:
- Wing span: 7·44 m (24 ft 4¾ in)
- Wing chord: at root: 1·52 m (5 ft 0 in)
  - at tip: 0·76 m (2 ft 6 in)
- Wing aspect ratio: 6
- Length overall: 6·25 m (20 ft 6 in)
- Height overall: 2·69 m (8 ft 10 in)
- Tailplane span: 2·69 m (8 ft 10 in)
- Wheel track: 2·54 m (8 ft 4 in)
- Wheelbase: 1·80 m (5 ft 11 in)
- Propeller diameter: 1·98 m (6 ft 6 in)

AREA:
- Wings, gross: 8·79 m² (94·59 sq ft)

DIMENSIONS, INTERNAL:
- Cockpit: Length: 2·54 m (8 ft 4 in)
  - Max width: 0·91 m (3 ft 0 in)
  - Max height: 1·37 m (4 ft 6 in)

WEIGHTS AND LOADINGS (TIO-541-E engine):
- Weight empty: 922 kg (2,033 lb)
- Max T-O weight: 1,425 kg (3,142 lb)
- Max wing loading: 162·2 kg/m² (33·22 lb/sq ft)
- Max power loading: 5·04 kg/kW (8·27 lb/hp)

PERFORMANCE (TIO-541-E engine):
- Max level and normal cruising speed (75% power) at 7,315 m (24,000 ft): 303 knots (562 km/h; 349 mph)
- Econ cruising speed (55% power) at 7,315 m (24,000 ft): 255 knots (473 km/h; 294 mph)
- Stalling speed: 'clean': 79 knots (174 km/h; 91 mph)
  - wheels and flaps down: 76 knots (142 km/h; 88 mph)
- Max rate of climb at S/L: 762 m (2,500 ft)/min
- Service ceiling: over 8,535 m (28,000 ft)
- T-O run: 396 m (1,300 ft)
- T-O to 15 m (50 ft): 610 m (2,000 ft)
- Landing from 15 m (50 ft): 853 m (2,800 ft)
- Landing run: 488 m (1,600 ft)
- Range at econ cruising speed, 45 min reserves: 1,600 nm (2,964 km; 1,842 miles)

BROWN

MICHAEL BROWN

c/o Climber Aviation, 2909 Edgemoor Lane, Dayton, Ohio 45439
Telephone: (513) 223 7510

In 1984 the Imp light aircraft programme was purchased from Aerocar Inc by Mr Brown, including the prototype then under construction in St Louis.

BROWN (AEROCAR) IMP

Design of the Imp (an acronym derived from Independently Made Plane) began in January 1972. Many design features of the Aerocar were embodied, including folding wings and a pusher propeller aft of the tail unit. Construction of a two-seat prototype began in August 1972, but non-availability of the Franklin engine which was intended to power the aircraft led to the decision to give priority instead to the single-seat Mini-Imp (which see, in Aerocar entry).

Eventually, it was decided to resume the Imp programme by converting the original prototype to two-plus-two configuration, with the pilot and one passenger seated side by side at the front of the cabin and two folding seats at the rear for children. The aircraft was completed in this form by Mr Brown, powered by a 97 kW (130 hp) Franklin engine, driving a two-blade controllable-pitch propeller. It is shown in this form in the accompanying illustration, which also shows the dorsal fin that was added to supplement the original inverted V tail surfaces. The empty weight of the aircraft was reduced by 7 kg (15 lb) by deleting the road towing capability.

As the next stage in the development programme, Mr Brown intended to fit a four-blade controllable-pitch propeller of reduced diameter. Eventually, the Imp will be tested in the originally planned full four-seat form, with a more powerful engine and increased fuel capacity.

The data that follow refer to the Imp as detailed on current information sheets. Mr Brown intends to offer plans to amateur constructors in due course.

Type: Two-plus-two or four-seat homebuilt aircraft.

Airframe: Cantilever high-wing monoplane. Wing section GA(PC)-1. No dihedral. Incidence 4°. No sweepback. Constant-chord wings, of all-metal construction except for glassfibre leading-edge shell. Wings fold rearward alongside fuselage for storage. All-metal ailerons, each with trim tab. No flaps. Fuselage has all-metal structure, covered with a glassfibre shell forward of the wing and with metal covered rear fuselage. Inverted V tail surfaces, of all-metal construction, with variable incidence tailplane. Dorsal fin can be trimmed on the ground but is fixed in flight.

Landing Gear: Electrically retractable tricycle type, main units retracting outward. Highway type wheels and 6-ply tyres. Tyre pressure 2·76 bars (40 lb/sq in). Rosenhan wheel brakes.

Power Plant: Prototype in two-plus-two configuration currently fitted with one 97 kW (130 hp) Franklin engine, driving a two-blade controllable-pitch pusher propeller, which will be replaced with a four-blade version of smaller diameter. Four-seat Imp will have a 149 kW (200 hp) Avco Lycoming engine. Two-plus-two prototype has one fuel tank of 53 litres (14 US gallons) capacity in each wing root, giving total capacity of 106 litres (28 US gallons). Four-seater will have increased fuel capacity of 170 litres (45 US gallons). Refuelling points in upper surface of wings, inboard of wing fold. Oil capacity 7·5 litres (2 US gallons).

Accommodation: Two seats, side by side, at front of enclosed cabin, with two folding seats at rear of prototype. Large baggage space if rear seats folded against bulkhead. Airstair doors.

System: Electrical system powered by 12V 60A engine driven alternator.

Avionics: Narco Escort 110 radio, Avenger Loran C and Type 50A transponder.

Dimensions, external:
Wing span 8·84 m (29 ft 0 in)
Wing chord, constant 1·22 m (4 ft 0 in)
Wing aspect ratio 7
Width, wings folded 2·13 m (7 ft 0 in)
Length overall 6·71 m (22 ft 0 in)
Height overall (propeller blades horizontal) 1·68 m (5 ft 6 in)
Tailplane span 2·44 m (8 ft 0 in)
Wheel track 1·83 m (6 ft 0 in)
Wheelbase 2·11 m (6 ft 11 in)
Propeller diameter: two-blade 1·83 m (6 ft 0 in)
four-blade 1·52 m (5 ft 0 in)

Dimension, internal:
Cockpit: Max width 1·12 m (3 ft 8 in)

Area:
Wings, gross 10·41 m² (112·0 sq ft)

Weights and Loadings (A: Two-plus-two; B: Four-seat, estimated):
Weight empty: A 519 kg (1,144 lb)
B 567 kg (1,250 lb)
Baggage: A 77 kg (170 lb)
B 91 kg (200 lb)
Design max T-O weight: A 680 kg (1,500 lb)
B 998 kg (2,200 lb)
Max wing loading: A 65·4 kg/m² (13·39 lb/sq ft)
B 95·9 kg/m² (19·64 lb/sq ft)
Max power loading: A 7·01 kg/kW (11·54 lb/hp)
B 6·70 kg/kW (11·00 lb/hp)

Performance (prototype, estimated):
Max level speed 156 knots (290 km/h; 180 mph)
Stalling speed 58 knots (107 km/h; 66 mph)
Max rate of climb at S/L 309 m (1,013 ft)/min

BRYAN

COURTNEY BRYAN

8875 Dog Leg Road, Dayton, Ohio

BRYAN PHOENIX SL

As can be seen in an accompanying illustration, the Phoenix SL (N1007P) is a side by side two-seat homebuilt with a tandem-wing configuration similar to that of the Quickie Q2 and Viking Dragonfly. The cockpit glazing is different, in that it has a separate wrapround windscreen and sideways hinged canopy, with a further large window in the top of the decking above the rear wing. A non-retractable tricycle landing gear is fitted, with cantilever main legs and steerable nosewheel. The power plant is a 74·5 kW (100 hp) Continental O-200 flat-four engine, driving a two-blade wooden propeller. No spinner was fitted at the time of the aircraft's appearance at the 1986 Oshkosh meeting.

Dimension, external:
Wing span 7·78 m (25 ft 6 in)

Weights:
Weight empty 408 kg (900 lb)
Max T-O weight 658 kg (1,450 lb)

BUCK SPORT

BUCK SPORT AIRCRAFT INC

PO Box 868, Columbus, Georgia 31902
Telephone: (404) 689 8884
Proprietor: Harold D. Buck

This company markets kits of component parts and materials, less engine, for a lightweight all-metal single-seat sporting aircraft known as the Mini Coupe. Design originated in June 1968, and the prototype made its first flight in September 1971. Building of the Mini Coupe has been approved also in Australia and Switzerland, where aircraft are being constructed.

BUCK SPORT AIRCRAFT MINI COUPE

At least 180 sets of plans of the Mini Coupe have been sold, and more than 100 examples are known to be flying.

Type: Single-seat homebuilt sporting aircraft.

Airframe: Cantilever low-wing monoplane. Wing section modified Clark Y. Thickness/chord ratio 7%. Incidence 0°. Conventional metal stressed skin structure of constant chord, with endplate or glassfibre wingtips. Plain all-metal ailerons. No flaps. No trim tabs. All-metal semi-monocoque fuselage, with optional high or low turtle-deck to rear of cockpit. Cantilever all-metal tail unit, with twin endplate fins and rudders of constant chord. Fixed incidence tailplane. Manually controlled trim tab in centre of elevator.

Landing Gear: Non-retractable tricycle type. Shock absorption on all units depends on use of oversize tyres. Mainwheel tyres size 14 × 6·00-6, pressure 0·55 bars (8 lb/sq in). Nosewheel tyre size 12 × 6·00-5, pressure 0·34 bars (5 lb/sq in). Azuza drum and band brakes.

Power Plant: One 48·5 kW (65 hp) modified Volkswagen 1,600 cc motorcar engine, driving a Reese-Shores two-blade fixed-pitch wooden propeller. (Two aircraft fitted with 48·5 kW; 65 hp Continental.) One metal fuel tank in fuselage, immediately aft of firewall, capacity 49 litres (13 US gallons). Refuelling point on fuselage upper surface, forward of windscreen.

Accommodation: Single seat in open cockpit standard. Transparent cockpit canopy optional. Baggage compartment aft of headrest, volume 0·085 m³ (3 cu ft).

System: Provision for electrical system, for engine starter and radio.

Dimensions, external:
Wing span: endplates 6·81 m (22 ft 4 in)
glassfibre tips 7·32 m (24 ft 0 in)
Wing chord, constant 1·07 m (3 ft 6 in)
Length overall 4·98 m (16 ft 4 in)
Height overall 1·80 m (5 ft 11 in)
Tailplane span 1·83 m (6 ft 0 in)
Wheel track 1·83 m (6 ft 0 in)
Wheelbase 0·97 m (3 ft 2 in)
Propeller diameter 1·37 m (4 ft 6 in)

Area:
Wings, gross 7·76 m² (83·5 sq ft)

Weights and Loadings (A: with open cockpit and endplate wingtips; B: with enclosed cockpit, glassfibre wingtips, wheel fairings and spinner):
Weight empty: A 224 kg (494 lb)
B 247 kg (545 lb)
Max T-O weight: A 374 kg (825 lb)
B 368 kg (812 lb)
Max wing loading: A 48·2 kg/m² (9·88 lb/sq ft)
B 47·5 kg/m² (9·72 lb/sq ft)
Max power loading: A 7·71 kg/kW (12·69 lb/hp)
B 7·59 kg/kW (12·49 lb/hp)

Performance (at max T-O weight with 1,600 cc engine; A and B as above):
Never-exceed speed:
A 125 knots (231 km/h; 145 mph)
Max level speed at 610 m (2,000 ft):
A 91 knots (169 km/h; 105 mph)
B 113 knots (209 km/h; 130 mph)
Max cruising speed at 610 m (2,000 ft):
A 78 knots (145 km/h; 90 mph)
B 103 knots (191 km/h; 119 mph)
Stalling speed, power off:
A 42 knots (78 km/h; 48 mph)
B 39 knots (73 km/h; 45 mph)
Stalling speed, power on:
A 38 knots (70 km/h; 43 mph)
B 33 knots (61 km/h; 38 mph)
Max rate of climb at S/L: A 213 m (700 ft)/min
B 259 m (850 ft)/min
Service ceiling: A 3,810 m (12,500 ft)
T-O run: A 122 m (400 ft)
B 92 m (300 ft)
T-O to 15 m (50 ft): A 274 m (900 ft)
Landing from 15 m (50 ft): A 274 m (900 ft)
Landing run: A 152 m (500 ft)
B 122 m (400 ft)
Range with max fuel, 20 min reserves:
A, B 260 nm (482 km; 300 miles)

BURKE

BURKE AIRCRAFT

2045 Mars Road, Livermore, California 94550
Telephone: (415) 449 5992
Telex: 176859
Proprietor: Larry P. Burke

Since 1978 Mr Burke has designed several aircraft which are currently operating under FAR Pt 103.7 regulations, and his Burke Aircraft company custom builds aircraft in the microlight and FAA Experimental (homebuilt) categories. Under construction in early 1985 were a 'look-alike' representation of the Messerschmitt Bf 109 Second World War fighter, and a single/two-seat design known as the Ultramental. No more recent news of these has been received. Details of the Ultramental follow.

BURKE ULTRAMENTAL

The Ultramental is so named because, by varying the airframe skin thickness, choice of engine and fuel capacity, it can qualify under either the Ultralight or Experimental category regulations of the FAA. It is unusual in the former category in being almost entirely of metal construction. The first flight had been scheduled for April 1985, but no confirmation of its achievement has been received. Already by then a small number of aircraft had been built and sold. Production aircraft are available in plans, kit and ready to fly forms.

Type: Single-seat or side by side two-seat light aircraft; **Ultramental 1** conforms to FAR Pt 103, heavier **Ultramental 2** to FAA Experimental category requirements.

Airframe: Cantilever low-wing monoplane, with conventional semi-monocoque fuselage and cruciform tail surfaces. Tapered wings have NACA 23015 (root) and NACA 23012 (tip) aerofoil sections, with ailerons and three-position flaps on trailing-edge, and can be folded for transportation and stowage. Wing structure comprises an aluminium tube main spar,with stamped ribs and pop riveted skins of 0·012 in thick aluminium sheet (0·016 to 0·020 in on Ultramental 2). Sweptback fin and rudder, non-swept tailplane and elevators; no tabs.

Landing Gear: Tricycle type (non-retractable on Ultramental 1, retractable on Ultramental 2), with rubber disc suspension and trailing-link main units. Mainwheels and tyres size 5·00-4, nosewheel and tyre 4·00-4. Disc brakes on mainwheels; castoring nosewheel.

Power Plant: One 26·1 kW (35 hp) Cuyuna 430 or 34·3 kW (46 hp) Rotax 503 engine in Ultramental 1, with 2·11:1 reduction drive to a two-blade wooden propeller; 38·8 kW (52 hp) Rotax 503 engine in Ultramental 2. Single in-wing fuel tank in Ultramental 1, capacity 19 litres (5 US gallons); two wing tanks in Ultramental 2, with combined capacity of 57 litres (15 US gallons).

Accommodation: Two seats side by side under fully transparent canopy; or single seat in slimmer fuselage.

Brown (Aerocar) Imp 2+2 prototype (97 kW; 130 hp Franklin engine)

Bryan Phoenix SL two-seat homebuilt aircraft *(J. M. G. Gradidge)*

Bushby/Long MM-1 Midget Mustang built in the USA *(J. M. G. Gradidge)*

Buck Sport Aircraft Mini Coupe with open cockpit and glassfibre wingtips

DIMENSIONS, EXTERNAL (both):
- Wing span: 9·14 m (30 ft 0 in)
- Wing aspect ratio: single-seat: 6·67
  - two-seat: 6·21
- Length overall: 5·49 m (18 ft 0 in)
- Height overall: 2·13 m (7 ft 0 in)
- Propeller diameter: 1·52 m (5 ft 0 in)

AREA (both):
- Wings, gross: single-seat: 12·54 m² (135·0 sq ft)
  - two-seat: 13·47 m² (145·0 sq ft)

WEIGHTS AND LOADINGS (A: Ultramental 1, B: Ultramental 2):
- Weight empty: A (single-seat): 113 kg (250 lb)
  - A (two-seat): 149 kg (328 lb)
  - B (two-seat): 158 kg (350 lb)
- Max T-O weight: A (single-seat): 249 kg (550 lb)
  - A (two-seat): 330 kg (728 lb)
  - B (two-seat): 340 kg (750 lb)
- Max wing loading:
  - A (single-seat): 19·88 kg/m² (4·07 lb/sq ft)
  - A (two-seat): 24·50 kg/m² (5·02 lb/sq ft)
  - B (two-seat): 25·24 kg/m² (5·17 lb/sq ft)
- Max power loading:
  - A (single-seat, 35 hp): 9·56 kg/kW (15·71 lb/hp)
  - A (single-seat, 45 hp): 7·44 kg/kW (12·22 lb/hp)
  - A (two-seat, 35 hp): 12·66 kg/kW (20·80 lb/hp)
  - A (two-seat, 45 hp): 9·85 kg/kW (16·18 lb/hp)
  - B (two-seat, 52 hp): 8·78 kg/kW (14·42 lb/hp)

PERFORMANCE (at max T-O weight except where indicated. A: single-seat microlight/35 hp, B: two-seat microlight/45 hp, C: two-seat homebuilt/52 hp):
- Never-exceed speed:
  - A: 91 knots (169 km/h; 105 mph)
  - B: 73 knots (136 km/h; 85 mph)
  - C: 99 knots (185 km/h; 115 mph)
- Max level speed:
  - A, B: 55 knots (101 km/h; 63 mph)
  - C: 87 knots (161 km/h; 100 mph)
- Max cruising speed: A: 52 knots (96 km/h; 60 mph)
  - C: 78 knots (145 km/h; 90 mph)
- Econ cruising speed: A: 43 knots (80 km/h; 50 mph)
- Stalling speed, power off:
  - A, 20° flap: 24 knots (44 km/h; 27 mph)
  - B: 29 knots (54 km/h; 34 mph)
  - C, flaps up: 35 knots (65 km/h; 40 mph)
- Max rate of climb at S/L:
  - A at AUW of 227 kg (500 lb): 305 m (1,000 ft)/min
- Service ceiling: A: 5,030 m (16,500 ft)
- T-O run:
  - A with 100 kg (220 lb) pilot: 46 m (150 ft)
- Landing run:
  - A (hard runway, full braking): 31 m (100 ft)
- Range at econ cruising speed:
  - A: 108 nm (201 km; 125 miles)
- *g* limits: +5·4/−2·7

BUSHBY

BUSHBY AIRCRAFT INC

674 Route 52, Minooka, Illinois 60447
Telephone: (815) 467 2346

Mr Robert W. Bushby began by building a Midget Mustang single-seat sporting monoplane, using drawings, jigs and certain components produced by the aircraft's designer, the late David Long. He has since produced the aircraft in kit form and also offers sets of plans of the Midget Mustang and a two-seat derivative known as the Mustang II to amateur constructors.

BUSHBY/LONG MM-1 MIDGET MUSTANG

The prototype of the Midget Mustang was completed in 1948 by David Long, then chief engineer of the Piper company. He flew it in the National Air Races that year, and in 1949 was placed fourth in the Continental Trophy Race at Miami.

Two basic versions were developed by Robert Bushby from the original design, as follows:

MM-1-85. Powered by 63·5 kW (85 hp) Continental C85-8FJ or -12 engine. Flew for the first time on 9 September 1959.

MM-1-125. Powered by 101 kW (135 hp) Avco Lycoming O-290-D2 engine. Otherwise similar to MM-1-85. Flew for first time in July 1963. New propeller introduced during 1973 to improve max speed and cruising speed.

Approximately 326 Midget Mustangs had been completed by early 1986, with 1,100 more under construction throughout the world. Several of those now flying have a 112 kW (150 hp) Avco Lycoming O-320 engine, providing a cruising speed of 234 knots (435 km/h; 270 mph) at 2,440 m (8,000 ft). Some have been fitted with retractable main landing gear.

The following details apply to the two basic versions:

TYPE: Single-seat fully aerobatic homebuilt sporting monoplane.

AIRFRAME: Cantilever low-wing monoplane. Wing section NACA 64A212 at root, NACA 64A210 at tip. Dihedral 5°. Incidence 1° 30'. Two-spar flush riveted stressed skin aluminium structure. Aluminium statically balanced ailerons and plain trailing-edge flaps. Aluminium flush riveted stressed skin monocoque fuselage. Cantilever all-metal tail unit. Controllable trim tab in port elevator.

LANDING GEAR: Non-retractable tailwheel type. Cantilever spring steel main legs. Steerable tailwheel. Goodyear wheels and tyres, size 5·00-5, pressure 1·24 bars (18 lb/sq in). Goodyear hydraulic disc brakes.

POWER PLANT (MM-1-85): One 63·5 kW (85 hp) Continental C85-8FJ or -12 flat-four engine, driving a McCauley two-blade metal fixed-pitch propeller. Fuel tank aft of firewall, capacity 57 litres (15 US gallons). Optional integral wing fuel tanks, each with capacity of 57 litres (15 US gallons). Optional wingtip tanks, each with capacity of 13 litres (3·5 US gallons). Oil capacity 3·75 litres (1 US gallon).

POWER PLANT (MM-1-125): One 101 kW (135 hp) Avco Lycoming O-290-D2 flat-four engine, driving a Sensenich two-blade metal fixed-pitch propeller. Fuel tank aft of firewall, capacity 57 litres (15 US gallons). No provision for wingtip tanks. Oil capacity 5·75 litres (1·5 US gallons).

ACCOMMODATION: Single seat in enclosed cabin. Canopy hinged on starboard side. Space for 5·5 kg (12 lb) of baggage aft of seat. Room for back parachute.

AVIONICS AND EQUIPMENT: Radio optional. No provision for blind-flying instrumentation. Electrical system available on MM-1-85 only.

DIMENSIONS, EXTERNAL:
- Wing span: 5·64 m (18 ft 6 in)
- Wing span over tip tanks:
  - MM-1-85: 5·99 m (19 ft 8 in)
- Wing chord: at root: 1·53 m (5 ft 0 in)
  - at tip: 0·76 m (2 ft 6 in)
- Wing aspect ratio: 4
- Length overall: 5·00 m (16 ft 5 in)
- Height overall: 1·37 m (4 ft 6 in)
- Tailplane span: 1·98 m (6 ft 6 in)
- Wheel track: 1·55 m (5 ft 1 in)

DIMENSIONS, INTERNAL:
- Cabin: Max width: 0·56 m (1 ft 10 in)
- Baggage space: 0·057 m³ (2 cu ft)

AREA:
- Wings, gross: 6·32 m² (68·0 sq ft)

WEIGHTS AND LOADINGS:
- Weight empty: MM-1-85: 261 kg (575 lb)
  - MM-1-125: 268 kg (590 lb)
- Max T-O and landing weight:
  - MM-1-85: 397 kg (875 lb)
  - MM-1-125: 408 kg (900 lb)
- Max wing loading:
  - MM-1-85: 62·8 kg/m² (12·87 lb/sq ft)
  - MM-1-125: 64·6 kg/m² (13·24 lb/sq ft)
- Max power loading:
  - MM-1-85: 6·25 kg/kW (10·29 lb/hp)
  - MM-1-125: 4·04 kg/kW (6·67 lb/hp)

PERFORMANCE (at max T-O weight):
- Never-exceed speed: 243 knots (450 km/h; 280 mph)
- Max level speed at S/L:
  - MM-1-85: 165 knots (306 km/h; 190 mph)
  - MM-1-125: 195 knots (362 km/h; 225 mph)
- Max cruising speed at 2,440 m (8,000 ft):
  - MM-1-85: 171 knots (317 km/h; 197 mph)
  - MM-1-125: 187 knots (346 km/h; 215 mph)
- Econ cruising speed:
  - MM-1-85: 129 knots (238 km/h; 148 mph)
  - MM-1-125: 143 knots (265 km/h; 165 mph)
- Stalling speed, flaps down:
  - MM-1-85: 50 knots (92 km/h; 57 mph)
  - MM-1-125: 53 knots (97 km/h; 60 mph)
- Max rate of climb at S/L:
  - MM-1-85: 533 m (1,750 ft)/min
  - MM-1-125: 670 m (2,200 ft)/min

Service ceiling: MM-1-85 over 4,875 m (16,000 ft)
MM-1-125 5,790 m (19,000 ft)
T-O run: MM-1-85 137 m (450 ft)
MM-1-125 122 m (400 ft)
T-O to 15 m (50 ft): MM-1-85 274 m (900 ft)
MM-1-125 213 m (700 ft)
Landing from 15 m (50 ft) 365 m (1,200 ft)
Landing run 152 m (500 ft)
Range with max fuel:
MM-1-85 347 nm (640 km; 400 miles)
MM-1-125 325 nm (603 km; 375 miles)
Range with max fuel and tip tanks:
MM-1-85 651 nm (1,200 km; 750 miles)

BUSHBY M-II MUSTANG II

Design of this side by side two-seat derivative of the Midget Mustang was started in 1963. Construction of a prototype began in 1965 and it flew for the first time on 9 July 1966. During 1968 Mr Bushby designed an alternative non-retractable tricycle landing gear for the Mustang II, and amateur constructors have the option of either configuration. Another option is wing folding, to permit storage in a home garage. About 1,200 Mustang IIs were being built by amateurs in early 1986, at which time 281 had been completed.

The description applies to the de luxe model, which is stressed for +6*g*, and the empty weight quoted includes IFR instrumentation and nav/com equipment. The M-II can also be operated as an aerobatic aircraft in what Bushby Aircraft calls the 'Sport' configuration. This is identical to the de luxe model except that the electrical system, radio, additional IFR instrumentation, soundproofing and upholstery, wheel fairings, and some baggage capacity are deleted. The 'Sport' model has an empty weight of 340 kg (750 lb), T-O weight of 567 kg (1,250 lb) and is stressed for +9*g*.

A Hartzell controllable-pitch propeller has replaced the original fixed-pitch propeller as standard, and the performance figures quoted for the 119 kW (160 hp) engine are obtained with this propeller. The figures quoted for the 93 kW (125 hp) engine are those obtained with the fixed-pitch propeller.

TYPE: Two-seat light homebuilt sporting aircraft.

AIRFRAME: Cantilever low-wing monoplane. Outer wings similar to those of Midget Mustang, attached to new constant chord centre-section of short span. Wing section NACA 64A212 at root, NACA 64A210 at tip. Dihedral 5° on outer wings only. Incidence 1° 30′. Two-spar flush riveted stressed skin aluminium structure. Wing folding optional. Aluminium statically balanced ailerons and plain trailing-edge flaps. No trim tabs. Aluminium flush riveted stressed skin monocoque fuselage. Cantilever all-metal tail unit. Fixed incidence tailplane. Controllable trim tab in starboard elevator.

LANDING GEAR: Standard version has non-retractable tailwheel type. Cantilever spring steel main legs. Goodyear 5·00-5 mainwheels and tyres, pressure 1·38 bars (20 lb/sq in). Goodyear hydraulic disc brakes. Steerable tailwheel. Alternatively, non-retractable tricycle type. Cantilever spring steel main legs. Cleveland or Goodyear mainwheels and tyres size 5·00-5. Non-steerable nosewheel, mounted on oleo-pneumatic shock strut and free to swivel up to 16° either side. Goodyear nosewheel and tyre size 5·00-5. Goodyear or Cleveland hydraulic disc brakes. Wheel fairings optional on either type of landing gear.

POWER PLANT: Normally one 119 kW (160 hp) Avco Lycoming O-320 flat-four engine, driving a Hartzell two-blade controllable-pitch metal propeller. Provision for other engines including a 93 kW (125 hp) Avco Lycoming O-290, driving a two-blade fixed-pitch metal propeller. Fuel tank aft of firewall, capacity 94·6 litres (25 US gallons). Optional integral wing fuel tanks, each with a capacity of 45 litres (12 US gallons). Refuelling point on starboard side of fuselage aft of firewall. Provision for wingtip tanks. Oil capacity 7·5 litres (2 US gallons).

ACCOMMODATION: Two seats side by side, under large rearward sliding transparent canopy. Dual controls. Baggage space aft of seats, capacity 34 kg (75 lb).

SYSTEMS: 12V electrical system, supplied by Delco-Remy 15A generator and Exide 33A battery.

AVIONICS AND EQUIPMENT: Provision for full IFR instrumentation and dual nav/com system.

DIMENSIONS, EXTERNAL:
Wing span 7·37 m (24 ft 2 in)
Width folded 2·44 m (8 ft 0 in)
Wing chord: at root 1·47 m (4 ft 10 in)
at tip 0·79 m (2 ft 7 in)
Wing aspect ratio 5·5
Length overall 5·94 m (19 ft 6 in)
Height overall 1·60 m (5 ft 3 in)
Height folded 1·73 m (5 ft 8 in)
Tailplane span 2·29 m (7 ft 6 in)
Wheel track 2·08 m (6 ft 10 in)
Propeller diameter:
93 kW (125 hp) 1·73 m (5 ft 8 in)
119 kW (160 hp) 1·83 m (6 ft 0 in)

DIMENSIONS, INTERNAL:
Cabin: Max width 1·02 m (3 ft 4 in)
Baggage space 0·16 m³ (5·5 cu ft)

AREA:
Wings, gross 9·02 m² (97·12 sq ft)

WEIGHTS AND LOADINGS:
Weight empty, equipped (N: nosewheel, T: tailwheel landing gear):
N 93 kW (125 hp) engine 413 kg (911 lb)
T 93 kW (125 hp) engine 408 kg (900 lb)
N 119 kW (160 hp) engine 425 kg (938 lb)
T 119 kW (160 hp) engine 420 kg (927 lb)
*Max T-O and landing weight 680 kg (1,500 lb)
*Max wing loading (160 hp) 75·4 kg/m² (15·44 lb/sq ft)
*Max power loading (160 hp) 5·71 kg/kW (9·38 lb/hp)

**Except for countries that restrict max wing loading to 73·2 kg/m² (15 lb/sq ft), where T-O weight of 658 kg (1,450 lb) applies*

PERFORMANCE (with tailwheel, at max T-O weight):
Never-exceed speed:
93 kW (125 hp) 173 knots (322 km/h; 200 mph)
119 kW (160 hp) 211 knots (391 km/h; 243 mph)
Max level speed at S/L:
93 kW (125 hp) 156 knots (290 km/h; 180 mph)
119 kW (160 hp) 200 knots (370 km/h; 230 mph)
Max cruising speed at 2,285 m (7,500 ft):
93 kW (125 hp) 152 knots (282 km/h; 175 mph)
119 kW (160 hp) 181 knots (335 km/h; 208 mph)
Stalling speed, flaps down:
93 kW (125 hp) 47 knots (87 km/h; 54 mph)
119 kW (160 hp) 51 knots (94 km/h; 58 mph)
Stalling speed, flaps up:
93 kW (125 hp) 51 knots (94 km/h; 58 mph)
119 kW (160 hp) 53 knots (96 km/h; 60 mph)
Max rate of climb at S/L:
93 kW (125 hp) 305 m (1,000 ft)/min
119 kW (160 hp) 670 m (2,200 ft)/min
Service ceiling: 93 kW (125 hp) 4,875 m (16,000 ft)
119 kW (160 hp) 6,400 m (21,000 ft)
T-O run: 93 kW (125 hp) 198 m (650 ft)
119 kW (160 hp) 137 m (450 ft)
T-O to 15 m (50 ft):
93 kW (125 hp) 320 m (1,050 ft)
119 kW (160 hp) 198 m (650 ft)
Landing from 15 m (50 ft):
93 kW (125 hp) 290 m (950 ft)
119 kW (160 hp) 259 m (850 ft)
Landing run: 93 kW (125 hp) 215 m (700 ft)
119 kW (160 hp) 168 m (550 ft)
Range with standard fuel (75% power):
93 kW (125 hp) 416 nm (770 km; 480 miles)
119 kW (160 hp) 373 nm (692 km; 430 miles)
Range with optional wingtip tanks:
119 kW (160 hp) 542 nm (1,005 km; 625 miles)

BUTTERWORTH

G. N. BUTTERWORTH

Richmond Airport, Heaton Orchard Road, West Kingston, Rhode Island 02892
Telephone: (401) 789 0384

BUTTERWORTH WESTLAND WHIRLWIND MARK II

Mr G. N. Butterworth designed and built a ⅔-scale representation of a Second World War Westland Whirlwind single-seat fighter. Design began on 20 October 1976, and construction of the prototype started simultaneously. Based on the wings and horizontal tail surfaces of a Grumman American AA-1A Trainer, construction took 900-950 working hours over a nine-month period. First flight was made in July 1977.

Plans are available to amateur constructors, and 15 sets had been sold by early 1986, when three Whirlwind Mark IIs were known to be under construction.

TYPE: Single-seat homebuilt ⅔-scale replica fighter.

AIRFRAME: Cantilever low-wing monoplane, based on those of a Grumman American AA-1A Trainer. Dihedral 2°. Incidence 2°. Aluminium structure, except for outer wing panels which are made of 29 mm (1·125 in) Sitka spruce spars and solid polyurethane foam filling, covered with Dynel and polyester resins. Outer wings removable in 15 minutes to permit road trailering. No flaps or tabs. Conventional all-aluminium semi-monocoque fuselage, with ·02 in skins and ·03 in bulkheads. Cantilever aluminium tail unit. High mounted horizontal surfaces based on those of a Grumman American AA-1A Trainer. Trim tab on starboard elevator.

LANDING GEAR: Hydraulically retractable tailwheel type. Mainwheels retract forward into engine nacelles. Cleveland wheels. Mainwheel tyres size 6·00-6. Tailwheel diameter 4 in. Oleo shock absorbers. Cleveland disc brakes.

POWER PLANT: Two 48·5 kW (65 hp) 1,600 cc Volkswagen modified motorcar engines, each driving a Rand fixed-pitch three-blade propeller. Two fuel tanks, total capacity 76 litres (20 US gallons). Refuelling points in top of glassfibre engine cowlings. Oil capacity (total) 5·5 litres (1·5 US gallons).

ACCOMMODATION: Single seat under rearward sliding transparent canopy. No heating or ventilation.

DIMENSIONS, EXTERNAL:
Wing span 8·53 m (28 ft 0 in)
Wing chord, constant 1·22 m (4 ft 0 in)
Length overall 5·94 m (19 ft 6 in)
Height overall 2·16 m (7 ft 1 in)
Tailplane span 2·49 m (8 ft 2 in)
Wheel track 2·44 m (8 ft 0 in)
Propeller diameter 1·35 m (4 ft 5 in)
Distance between propeller centres 2·13 m (7 ft 0 in)

WEIGHTS AND LOADING:
Weight empty 472 kg (1,042 lb)
Max T-O weight 635 kg (1,400 lb)
Max power loading 6·55 kg/kW (10·77 lb/hp)

PERFORMANCE:
Max level and cruising speed 126 knots (233 km/h; 145 mph)
Econ cruising speed 87 knots (161 km/h; 100 mph)
Stalling speed 56 knots (103 km/h; 64 mph)
Max rate of climb at S/L 229 m (750 ft)/min
Service ceiling 2,440 m (8,000 ft)
T-O run 366 m (1,200 ft)
T-O to 15 m (50 ft) 549 m (1,800 ft)
Landing from 15 m (50 ft) 549 m (1,800 ft)
Landing run 427 m (1,400 ft)
Range with max fuel 608 nm (1,126 km; 700 miles)

CAROTHERS

CHUCK CAROTHERS AIR SHOW

1530 South Street, Lincoln, Nebraska 68502

The 1985-86 *Jane's* included details of the Carothers CAM Special (Carothers Aerobatic Midwing). Regrettably, Mr Chuck Carothers died from injuries sustained in an accident while flying the CAM Special for a television show.

CASCADE

CASCADE ULTRALITES INC

4700 188th Street North-East, Arlington, Washington 98223

Telephone: (206) 435 8614

PRESIDENT: Steven J. Grossruck

CASCADE KASPERWING 1-80

Design of the Kasperwing, originally using a Manta Fledge hang glider as basis, was begun by Mr Grossruck in order to flight test the theories of Mr Witold Kasper regarding what he described as 'vortex lift'. Mr Kasper, formerly an aerodynamicist with the Boeing company, believes that it is possible to develop a wing configuration which, at angles of attack of 30° or more, can induce a spanwise vortex that will produce enough lift to bring about drastic reductions in aircraft stalling speed and rate of sink. Mr Kasper tested his theories on two tailless gliders in the 1960s, and subsequently on a powered glider, proving the concept and demonstrating near-vertical descents and zero-forward-speed landings.

The current Cascade Kasperwing, now bearing little resemblance to the Fledge on which it was based, continues in production.

Four versions are available, as follows:

1-80B. Basic version, without fuselage pod and powered by a 17·2 kW (23 hp) Zenoah 242 cc engine.

1-80BX. As 1-80B, but having as standard a fully enclosed glassfibre pod for the pilot, wheel fairings, 19 litre (5 US gallon) fuel tank, and electric engine starting, any or all of which are optional with the standard 1-80 model. In addition, the BX can be supplied with a more powerful Kawasaki 440 engine. Pilot fairing improves handling characteristics as well as providing protection against the elements.

1-80C. Introduced for 1984. As 1-80BX, but with three-axis control (tip rudders, elevons and spoilers), 20 kW (27 hp) Rotax 277 engine, movable pilot seat for pitch trim, telescopic landing gear shock absorption, and mainwheel brakes.

Mr G. N. Butterworth's ⅔-scale replica of a Westland Whirlwind fighter

Standard Cascade Kasperwing 1-80B

Cassutt Special owned by Mr Thompson of the UK *(R. Kunert)*

Bushby M-II Mustang II with retractable landing gear, built by Mr George Linkis of Hickory Hills, Illinois *(Howard Levy)*

Kasperwing 1-80C, showing its telescopic landing gear units

1-80CR. As 1-80C, but with 35 kW (47 hp) Rotax 503 engine. Does not comply with FAR Pt 103.

TYPE: Single-seat microlight aircraft; all except 1-80CR conform to FAR Pt 103.

AIRFRAME: Aluminium alloy main frame, with vinyl coated stainless steel cables. Kingpost standard. Semi-rigid wing, with ribs, covered in single thickness Dacron. Two-axis control system standard on B/BX (weight shift, reflexed wingtips, and endplate fins and rudders); three-axis control optional on B/BX, standard on C/CR.

LANDING GEAR: Tricycle type, with 11 × 5 wheel and tyre on each unit. Castoring, steerable nosewheel; no brakes on B/BX. Float gear available optionally.

POWER PLANT: One piston engine, as shown under model listings, with reduction drive to a two-blade wooden pusher propeller. Fuel tank capacity 9·5 litres (2·5 US gallons) standard on B; 19 litre (5 US gallon) tank optional on B, standard on BX/C/CR.

ACCOMMODATION: Pilot only, in enclosed pod or in open position (see model details).

DIMENSIONS, EXTERNAL (all versions):

Wing span	10·67 m (35 ft 0 in)
Wing aspect ratio	6·8
Length overall	3·86 m (12 ft 8 in)
Height overall	2·29 m (7 ft 6 in)
Wheel track	1·57 m (5 ft 2 in)
Propeller diameter: B, BX	1·37 m (4 ft 6 in)
C	1·52 m (5 ft 0 in)

AREA (all versions):

Wings, gross	16·72 m² (180·0 sq ft)

WEIGHTS AND LOADINGS:

Weight empty: B	72·5 kg (160 lb)
BX	86 kg (190 lb)
C	111 kg (245 lb)
Pilot weight range: B, BX	59-100 kg (130-220 lb)
C	45-113 kg (100-250 lb)
Max T-O weight: B	172 kg (380 lb)
BX	190·5 kg (420 lb)
C	238 kg (525 lb)
Max wing loading: B	10·30 kg/m² (2·11 lb/sq ft)
BX	11·38 kg/m² (2·33 lb/sq ft)
C	14·23 kg/m² (2·91 lb/sq ft)
Max power loading: B	10·0 kg/kW (16·52 lb/hp)
BX (Zenoah)	11·08 kg/kW (18·26 lb/hp)
C	11·41 kg/kW (18·75 lb/hp)

PERFORMANCE (with 68 kg; 150 lb pilot):

Never-exceed speed:	
B, BX	52 knots (96 km/h; 60 mph)
C	73 knots (136 km/h; 85 mph)
Max level speed: B, BX	48 knots (89 km/h; 55 mph)
C	52 knots (96 km/h; 60 mph)
Max cruising speed: B	39 knots (72 km/h; 45 mph)
BX	43 knots (80 km/h; 50 mph)
C	48 knots (89 km/h; 55 mph)
Econ cruising speed: B	30 knots (56 km/h; 35 mph)
BX, C	39 knots (72 km/h; 45 mph)
Stalling speed (all versions):	
power on	20 knots (36 km/h; 22 mph)
power off	16 knots (29 km/h; 18 mph)
Max rate of climb at S/L:	
B	183-244 m (600-800 ft)/min
BX	183 m (600 ft)/min
C	244 m (800 ft)/min
Service ceiling (all versions)	4,575 m (15,000 ft)
T-O run (all versions)	15-23 m (50-75 ft)
Landing run (all versions)	15 m (50 ft)
Range with standard fuel:	
B	74 nm (137 km; 85 miles)
BX	173 nm (322 km; 200 miles)
C	130 nm (241 km; 150 miles)
Endurance with standard fuel: B	2 h 15 min
BX	5 h
C	3 h 30 min
g limits: B	+7/−4 ultimate
C	+9/−6 ultimate
Best glide ratio: B	10
BX	12
C	9
Min rate of sink, power off:	
B, BX	61 m (200 ft)/min

CASSUTT

While employed as an airline pilot, Capt Tom Cassutt designed and built in 1954 a small single-seat racing monoplane known as the Cassutt Special I (No. 111), in which he won the 1958 National Air Racing Championships. In 1959, he completed a smaller aircraft on the same lines, known as the Cassutt Special II (No. 11). Twenty years later, Cassutt Specials took first, second and third places at the 1979 Cleveland National Air Races, and won the EAA 500 mile efficiency race at Oshkosh in all categories in both 1979 and 1980.

Plans and kits of parts of the original design, and plans of a sporting version of No. 111 with a larger cockpit, were made available to amateur constructors by the National Aeronautics and Manufacturing Co Inc, which was purchased by Mr Stanley E. Whiting and transferred to Independence, Missouri, in 1985. However, this address appears to be no longer current and no information regarding changes has been received. About 2,000 sets of plans have been sold; more than 125 Cassutt Specials are flying, and many others were under construction in early 1986, in Australia, France, West Germany, New Zealand, South Africa, Sweden, the UK and elsewhere.

CASSUTT SPECIAL I

The following description applies to the Cassutt Special I as offered in Racing and Sport versions by the National Aeronautics and Manufacturing Co Inc. The Sport model, for sport flying and aerobatics, is essentially the same as the Racing model, except for having a greater wing span and area, slightly raised seat for the pilot, and alternative open or enclosed cockpit.

TYPE: Single-seat homebuilt racing monoplane.

AIRFRAME: Cantilever mid-wing monoplane. Wing section Cassutt 1107. No incidence or dihedral. All-wood two-spar structure with spruce ribs, solid spars and plywood skin, fabric covered. Ailerons are of welded steel tube construction, fabric covered. No flaps as standard, but a few constructors have added flaps. No tabs. Steel tube fuselage structure, fabric covered. Cantilever steel tube tail unit, with fabric covering. No tabs.

LANDING GEAR: Non-retractable tailwheel type. Wittman cantilever spring steel main legs. Mainwheel tyres size 5·00-5. Wheel fairings standard.

POWER PLANT: One Continental flat-four engine in the 63·5-74·5 kW (85-100 hp) range, driving a two-blade propeller. Fuel capacity 55 litres (14·5 US gallons). Oil capacity 3·8 litres (1 US gallon).

ACCOMMODATION: Single seat in enclosed cockpit.

DIMENSIONS, EXTERNAL (A: Racing, B: Sport):
Wing span: A 4·57 m (15 ft 0 in)
B 5·18 m (17 ft 0 in)
Wing chord (constant): A, B 1·37 m (4 ft 6 in)
Length overall: A, B 4·88 m (16 ft 0 in)
Height overall: A, B 1·22 m (4 ft 0 in)
Tailplane span 1·19 m (3 ft 11 in)
Wheel track 1·37 m (4 ft 6 in)

AREAS:
Wings, gross: A 6·27 m² (67·5 sq ft)
B 7·11 m² (76·5 sq ft)

WEIGHTS AND LOADINGS:
Weight empty: A, B 227 kg (500 lb)
Max T-O weight: A, B 363 kg (800 lb)
Max wing loading: A 57·9 kg/m² (11·85 lb/sq ft)
B 51·1 kg/m² (10·46 lb/sq ft)
Max power loading (85 hp engine):
A, B 5·72 kg/kW (9·41 lb/hp)

PERFORMANCE (63·5 kW; 85 hp engine):
Max level speed:
A, B more than 174 knots (322 km/h; 200 mph)
Max cruising speed:
A, B more than 156 knots (290 km/h; 180 mph)
Landing speed: A 61 knots (113 km/h; 70 mph)
B 52 knots (97 km/h; 60 mph)
Max rate of climb at S/L: A 457 m (1,500 ft)/min
B 914 m (3,000 ft)/min
Range: A, B 425 nm (788 km; 490 miles)
g limit: A, B +6·5

CASSUTT SPECIAL II

TYPE: Single-seat homebuilt racing monoplane.

AIRFRAME: Cantilever mid-wing monoplane. Wing section Cassutt 13106. No incidence or dihedral. All-wood structure. No flaps. Steel tube fuselage structure, fabric covered. Cantilever steel tube tail unit, fabric covered. The prototype (No. 11) has small centre fin and auxiliary fins on the tailplane tips.

LANDING GEAR: Non-retractable tailwheel type. Wittman cantilever spring steel main legs. Mainwheel tyre size 5·00-5. Wheel fairings standard.

POWER PLANT AND ACCOMMODATION: As for Cassutt Special I.

DIMENSIONS, EXTERNAL:
Wing span 4·16 m (13 ft 8 in)
Wing chord, constant 1·47 m (4 ft 10 in)
Wing aspect ratio 2·83
Length overall 4·88 m (16 ft 0 in)
Height overall 1·16 m (3 ft 10 in)
Tailplane span 1·14 m (3 ft 9 in)
Wheel track 0·97 m (3 ft 2 in)

AREA:
Wings, gross 6·13 m² (66·0 sq ft)

WEIGHTS AND LOADINGS:
Weight empty 196 kg (433 lb)
Max T-O weight 363 kg (800 lb)
Max wing loading 59·2 kg/m² (12·12 lb/sq ft)
Max power loading 5·72 kg/kW (9·41 lb/hp)

PERFORMANCE (at max T-O weight):
Max level speed at S/L 204 knots (378 km/h; 235 mph)
Max cruising speed 174 knots (322 km/h; 200 mph)
Stalling speed 54 knots (100 km/h; 62 mph)
Max rate of climb at S/L 915 m (3,000 ft)/min
Endurance with max fuel 3 h

CATTO

CATTO AIRCRAFT

PO Box 474, San Andreas, California 95429

CATTO AIRCRAFT ACRO-X

Catto Aircraft is offering to amateur constructors a complete kit of component parts to assemble the Acro-X single-seat 'X-wing' sporting biplane. Construction is said to take approximately 600 working hours, using the pre-welded and fabricated components supplied.

As can be seen from the accompanying illustration, the Acro-X is of unusual configuration. It has sweptback and tapering rear-mounted biplane wings, the upper wings with dihedral and the lower with anhedral, 'X' wire braced. Ailerons are fitted. The upper and lower wings are connected by vertical tail fin endplates, with inset rudders and semi-enclosed non-retractable mainwheels. A retractable nosewheel is carried beneath the tapered nose, which supports a constant chord foreplane with elevators. Power is provided by a single engine installed in the rear of the fuselage nacelle, driving a two-blade pusher propeller.

The only known details of the Acro-X follow:

DIMENSION, EXTERNAL:
Wing span 4·98 m (16 ft 4 in)

AREA:
Wings, gross 7·06 m² (76·0 sq ft)

WEIGHTS:
Weight empty 181 kg (400 lb)
Max T-O weight 306 kg (675 lb)

PERFORMANCE:
Never-exceed speed 143 knots (265 km/h; 165 mph)
Cruising speed 96 knots (177 km/h; 110 mph)
Stalling speed 41 knots (76 km/h; 47 mph)

CGS

CGS AVIATION INC

345 Eddy Road, Cleveland, Ohio 44108
Telephone: (216) 851 5400
PRESIDENT: Gary Titzel
OWNER AND MARKETING MANAGER: C. Slusarczyk

The original Chuck's Glider Supplies (see earlier editions of *Jane's*) became incorporated in 1979 and split into two companies, of which CGS Aircraft Inc continued to manufacture the Falcon series of hang gliders (1980-81 *Jane's*) until it closed down in 1981.

The second company, CGS Aviation Inc, formerly manufactured power plants for hang gliders and microlights. It now produces a microlight of its own design, known as the Hawk, which is available in various single-seat, two-seat (Hawk II) and agricultural (AG Hawk) models. The Hawk amphibian is believed not yet to be available.

CGS HAWK

The Hawk, first flown in January 1982, is available in NASAD 'Seal of Quality' approved kit form in four versions: the **Hawk B**, which conforms to FAR Pt 103; the more powerful **Hawk A**, which does not; the tandem two-seat **Hawk II**, which is marketed as a homebuilt; and the **AG Hawk** cropsprayer. It won the 'Best New Design' award at the 1982 Oshkosh meeting.

CGS Aviation has arranged with an Italian company, Pietro Certano and Co of 10040 Druento, Torino (*telephone* 39 11 9846 728 and *telex* 211094 CERTAOI), to build the Hawk under licence for distribution in Europe, and also has a major Japanese distributor. The agreement with Israel, as detailed in the 1984-85 *Jane's*, has been terminated.

The Rotax 447 engined and slightly modified AG Hawk has a 60·5 litre (16 US gallon) chemical hopper and a Spray Miser ultra-low volume control droplet applicator. It can spray at a speed of 43-48 knots (80-89 km/h; 50-55 mph), with a swath width of 18·3 m (60 ft).

The following description applies to the Hawk B, except where indicated:

TYPE: Single-seat microlight aircraft; Hawk B conforms to FAR Pt 103-7.

AIRFRAME: Strut braced high-wing monoplane, with 2° dihedral. Incidence 4°. Main frame of aluminium and steel tubing, with Dacron covering. Strut braced wings have aluminium leading- and trailing-edges which serve as spars, and aluminium ribs, double surface Dacron covered. Stainless steel cables. Three-axis control (ailerons, elevators and rudder), with flaps. Agricultural spraytank (60·6 litres; 16 US gallons capacity) on AG Hawk.

LANDING GEAR: Non-retractable tricycle type standard, with steerable nosewheel, 4·50-5 wheels and tyres on all units, and CGS disc brakes. Tailwheel and float gear optional.

POWER PLANT: One 20 kW (27 hp) Rotax 277 in Hawk B, 26·1 kW (35 hp) Rotax 447 in Hawk A, 29·8 kW (40 hp) Rotax 447 in Hawk II and 37·3 kW (50 hp) Rotax 503 in AG Hawk, in each case with reduction drive to a two-blade pusher propeller. Another power plant choice is the 26 kW (35 hp) Kawasaki 440TA two-cylinder engine. Electric start optional. Fuel tank behind pilot's seat, capacity 19 litres (5 US gallons).

ACCOMMODATION: Pilot only, in fully enclosed cockpit, with removable side panels.

DIMENSIONS, EXTERNAL:
Wing span 8·79 m (28 ft 10 in)
Wing aspect ratio 6·16
Length overall: except Hawk II 6·30 m (20 ft 8 in)
Hawk II 6·53 m (21 ft 5 in)
Height overall 2·08 m (6 ft 10 in)
Wheel track 1·83 m (6 ft 0 in)
Wheelbase 2·03 m (6 ft 8 in)
Propeller diameter 1·52 m (5 ft 0 in)

AREA:
Wings, gross 12·54 m² (135·0 sq ft)

WEIGHTS AND LOADINGS:
Weight empty: Hawk A and B 114 kg (251 lb)
Hawk II 149 kg (330 lb)
Max T-O weight: Hawk A and B 250 kg (550 lb)
AG Hawk 295 kg (650 lb)
Hawk II 363 kg (800 lb)
Max wing loading:
Hawk A and B 19·88 kg/m² (4·07 lb/sq ft)
AG Hawk 23·50 kg/m² (4·81 lb/sq ft)
Hawk II 28·92 kg/m² (5·93 lb/sq ft)
Max power loading:
Hawk A 9·56 kg/kW (15·71 lb/hp)
Hawk B 11·95 kg/kW (19·64 lb/hp)
AG Hawk 7·91 kg/kW (13·00 lb/hp)
Hawk II 12·17 kg/kW (20·00 lb/hp)

PERFORMANCE:
Never-exceed speed (all versions) 74 knots (137 km/h; 85 mph)
Max cruising speed:
Hawk A, B and Hawk II 52 knots (97 km/h; 60 mph)
Spraying speed:
AG Hawk 43-48 knots (80-88 km/h; 50-55 mph)
Stalling speed:
Hawk A and B 23 knots (42 km/h; 26 mph)
Hawk II 27 knots (49 km/h; 30 mph)
Max rate of climb at S/L:
Hawk A and B 213 m (700 ft)/min
AG Hawk more than 183 m (600 ft)/min
Hawk II 198 m (650 ft)/min
T-O run at S/L: Hawk A and B 46 m (150 ft)
AG Hawk 91 m (300 ft)
Hawk II 61 m (200 ft)
Landing run at S/L:
Hawk A, B and AG Hawk 46 m (150 ft)
Hawk II 61 m (200 ft)
g limits (all versions) +6/−4
Best glide ratio: Hawk A and B 8·85
Hawk II 8·7

CHRISTEN

CHRISTEN INDUSTRIES INC

PO Box 547, Afton, Wyoming 83110
Telphone: (307) 886 3151
PRESIDENT: Frank L. Christensen
MARKETING DEPARTMENT: Edmond A. Heinbockel

Christen Industries is responsible for the Eagle series of high-performance aerobatic biplanes. The special-purpose single-seat Eagle I, described briefly in previous editions of *Jane's*, is not available to amateur constructors; but the two-seat Eagle II is marketed in the form of 25 parts-kits supplied by Christen Industries. Each kit makes up a separate portion of the aircraft and is supported by a very detailed construction manual. This allows the cost of building the aircraft to be spread over a period of time. Only common hand tools (no power tools) are required in construction, and no previous aircraft experience is thought necessary. Christen believes that a typical homebuilder could complete the aircraft in 1,400 to 1,600 man-hours.

Christen Industries also markets factory built examples of the Pitts Special series of aerobatic biplanes, as described in the main Aircraft section of this edition. Plans of some versions of the Pitts Special are available to amateur constructors, as listed under the separate Pitts entry in this section of *Jane's*.

Since transferring its aircraft manufacturing and administrative facilities to Afton, Wyoming, Christen has devoted its Hollister, California, plant to full-time research and development.

CHRISTEN EAGLE II

Design of the Eagle II began in June 1974. Construction of a prototype started in August 1975 and it flew for the first time in February 1977. Construction of pre-production Eagles began in the same month. Manufacture of kits was initiated by Christen Industries in October 1977. By January 1986 construction of more than 600 Eagle IIs had started and over 250 were known to have been completed by amateur builders.

The Eagle II can be used for advanced aerobatic training and comfortable cross-country flying, as well as competition standard aerobatics. It has a maximum roll rate of 204° a second.

TYPE: Two-seat unlimited class homebuilt aerobatic biplane.

AIRFRAME: Braced biplane with steel tube I-type main interplane struts. Symmetrical sections. Thickness/chord ratio 15%. Dihedral 1° 30′ on lower wings, 0° on upper wing. Incidence 0°. Sweepback at quarter-chord 7° 30′ on upper wing, 0° on lower wings. Wooden spars and ribs; metal leading- and trailing-edges, polyester fabric covered. Conventional ailerons on upper and lower wings, of similar construction to wings. No flaps or tabs. Conventional fuselage structure of welded 4130N steel tubing. Covered with removable light alloy panels from firewall to back of rear seat. Rear fuselage fabric covered. Conventional wire braced tail unit, comprising a tailplane and elevators fitted with boost tabs, and fin and rudder, all of welded steel tube, polyester fabric covered.

LANDING GEAR: Non-retractable tailwheel type. Aluminium spring main legs. Main tyres size 5·00-5, pressure 1·52

The single-seat 'X-wing' Catto Aircraft Acro-X *(J. M. G. Gradidge)*

Christen Industries Eagle II two-seat aerobatic biplane built by Mr T. Wright of Federal Way, Washington *(Peter M. Bowers)*

CGS Aviation Hawk A single-seat aircraft with optional float landing gear

CGS Aviation AG Hawk cropsprayer

Cloud Dancer Jenny ¾ scale representation of a Curtiss JN-4D *(Howard Levy)*

bars (22 lb/sq in). Cleveland hydraulic disc brakes. Streamline wheel fairings.

Power Plant: One 149 kW (200 hp) Avco Lycoming AEIO-360-A1D flat-four engine, driving a Hartzell 81HC-C2YK-4CF/FC7666A-2 constant-speed propeller. One fuel tank in fuselage, capacity 98·4 litres (26 US gallons). Refuelling point in upper fuselage. Oil capacity 7·5 litres (2 US gallons). Fuel system allows unlimited inverted flight.

Accommodation: Two seats in tandem beneath one-piece side-hinged bubble canopy. Heated. Baggage hold in turtledeck, capacity 13·6 kg (30 lb).

Systems: 12V DC battery for starting and radio.

Avionics: Edo-Aire RT-563 or RT-553 radio.

Dimensions, external:

Wing span	6·07 m (19 ft 11 in)
Wing chord, constant	1·02 m (3 ft 4 in)
Length overall	5·64 m (18 ft 6 in)
Height overall	1·98 m (6 ft 6 in)
Tailplane span	2·13 m (7 ft 0 in)
Wheel track	1·83 m (6 ft 0 in)
Wheelbase	3·96 m (13 ft 0 in)
Propeller diameter	1·93 m (6 ft 4 in)

Dimensions, internal:

Cabin: Length	2·13 m (7 ft 0 in)
Max width	0·71 m (2 ft 4 in)
Max height	0·99 m (3 ft 3 in)

Area:

Wings, gross	11·61 m² (125·0 sq ft)

Weights and Loadings:

Weight empty	465 kg (1,025 lb)
Max T-O and landing weight	725 kg (1,600 lb)
Max wing loading	62·5 kg/m² (12·8 lb/sq ft)
Max power loading	4·87 kg/kW (8·00 lb/hp)

Performance:

Never-exceed speed	184 knots (341 km/h; 212 mph)
Max level speed at S/L	160 knots (296 km/h; 184 mph)
Max cruising speed at 1,825 m (6,000 ft)	143 knots (265 km/h; 165 mph)
Econ cruising speed at 1,825 m (6,000 ft)	137 knots (254 km/h; 158 mph)
Stalling speed	51 knots (94 km/h; 58 mph)
Max rate of climb at S/L	645 m (2,120 ft)/min
Service ceiling	5,180 m (17,000 ft)
T-O run	244 m (800 ft)
T-O to 15 m (50 ft)	381 m (1,250 ft)
Landing from 15 m (50 ft)	480 m (1,575 ft)
Range with max fuel and max payload	330 nm (611 km; 380 miles)
g limits	+9/−6

CHUCK's

CHUCK's AIRCRAFT CO

Adkins, Texas

CHUCK's AIRCRAFT AIR CUB

The Air Cub strut braced parasol-wing microlight has been flying for several years and is available as a ready assembled aircraft or in kit form. It has the general layout associated with the Piper Cub, but with an open cockpit. Three-axis control is standard (ailerons, rudder and elevators) and the landing gear is of the tailwheel type.

CLOUD DANCER

CLOUD DANCER AEROPLANE WORKS INC

Hangar 21, Delaware Municipal Airport, Delaware, Ohio 43015

Telephone: (614) 363 5009 and 548 5456

President: Gary Kubina

Business Manager: James Magee

CLOUD DANCER JENNY

The Cloud Dancer Jenny is a three quarters scale representation of the First World War Curtiss JN-4D training biplane. The likeness extends to the provision of two cockpits in tandem (see accompanying photograph), even though the scale version is a single-seater with no provision to carry a passenger. The Jenny is available in ready to fly and kit form.

Type: Single-seat microlight aircraft; conforms to FAR Pt 103.

Airframe: Strut braced biplane. Aluminium alloy and stainless steel airframe, with Dacron covering (double surface on wings). Three-axis control system (spoilers, elevators and rudder).

Landing Gear: Non-retractable tailskid type. Main gear comprises two side Vs and cross axle, with bungee sprung suspension. Mainwheel tyres size 20 × 2·125. No brakes.

Power Plant: One 26 kW (35 hp) Cuyuna ULII-02 two-cylinder two-stroke engine, with 3:1 reduction drive to Ritz two-blade wooden tractor propeller. Three fuel tanks, combined capacity 19 litres (5 US gallons).

Accommodation: Pilot only, in open cockpit with windscreen.

Dimensions, external:

Wing span (upper)	9·64 m (28 ft 4 in)
Wing aspect ratio (upper/lower)	8·71/7·08
Length overall	5·54 m (18 ft 2 in)
Height overall	2·29 m (7 ft 6 in)
Propeller diameter	1·83 m (6 ft 0 in)

Area:

Wings, gross	17·30 m² (186·2 sq ft)

Weights and Loadings:

Weight empty	112·5 kg (248 lb)
Pilot weight range	45-102 kg (100-225 lb)
Max T-O weight	227 kg (500 lb)
Max wing loading	13·13 kg/m² (2·69 lb/sq ft)
Max power loading	8·69 kg/kW (14·29 lb/hp)

Performance:

Never-exceed speed	60 knots (111 km/h; 69 mph)
Max level speed	54 knots (100 km/h; 62 mph)
Max cruising speed	50 knots (93 km/h; 58 mph)
Econ cruising speed	45 knots (83 km/h; 52 mph)
Stalling speed:	19 knots (34 km/h; 21 mph)
Max rate of climb at S/L	305 m (1,000 ft)/min
Service ceiling	3,810 m (12,500 ft)
T-O and landing run	38 m (125 ft)
Range with max fuel	113 nm (209 km; 130 miles)
Endurance with max fuel	2 h 30 min
g limits	+4/−2
Best glide ratio	5·5

CLUTTON-TABENOR

ERIC CLUTTON

Route 4, PO Box 1109C, Edmond, Oklahoma 73034

Mr Clutton resided in Staffordshire, England, before emigrating to the USA in February 1983. His FRED (Flying Runabout Experimental Design) was designed as a powered aircraft that could be flown by any reasonably experienced glider pilot without further training. Other aims were that it should be able to operate from small, rough fields and be roadable.

First flight of the prototype (G-ASZY) was made on 3

November 1963, with a 20 kW (27 hp) 500 cc Triumph 5T motorcycle engine. Details of the considerable subsequent development of this aircraft can be found in the UK section of the 1982-83 *Jane's*. Plans of FRED in its Series 2 form became available to amateur constructors in February 1970. Continued development led subsequently to FRED Series 3, as described in this entry.

CLUTTON-TABENOR FRED SERIES 3

FRED Series 3 first flew with an A65 engine in December 1982, and is now the standard form for plans-built aircraft. It is described by its builder as being virtually unstallable with power on or off. Max nose-up attitude, power on, gives 25-28 knots (46-52 km/h; 29-32 mph) IAS, and turns can be accomplished in this attitude. Rate of climb at max T-O weight is 213 m (700 ft)/min. Wings can be folded by one person unaided, and the tail unit is quickly detachable for easy transportation. Folded and tail-less width of FRED is 1·30 m (4 ft 3 in).

Approximately 300 sets of plans for FRED Series 2 and 3 had been sold by early 1986, when a small number of aircraft were flying, including several in the USA and one in New Zealand. Most are powered by a direct drive 1,600 cc Volkswagen engine.

The following details apply basically to Mr Clutton's FRED Series 3 in its current form:

TYPE: Single-seat homebuilt light aircraft.

AIRFRAME: Wire braced parasol monoplane. Wing section Göttingen 535. Thickness/chord ratio 17·2%. Some dihedral. 1° washout at tips. Spruce and plywood structure, with torsion box leading-edge, auxiliary rear spar and drag spar, fabric covered. Non-differential ailerons. No flaps or trim tabs. Fuselage uses spruce longerons. Plywood covered to rear of cockpit, except for aluminium top decking. Fabric covering on rear fuselage, except for plywood top decking, front portion of which is removable for access to baggage locker. Cantilever tail unit of spruce and plywood. No fixed fin. Tailplane incidence adjustable on ground. Pushrod operated elevators. No tabs.

LANDING GEAR: Non-retractable mainwheels and tailskid. Main units sprung with motorcycle rear suspension springs. Motor scooter or industrial truck wheels. Tyre pressure 1·79 bars (26 lb/sq in). No brakes.

POWER PLANT: One 48·5 kW (65 hp) Continental A65 flat-four engine now standard. Single fuel tank in centre-section, capacity 34 litres (9 US gallons). Provision for second centre-section tank. Oil capacity 3·5 litres (0·9 US gallons).

ACCOMMODATION: Single seat in open cockpit.

DIMENSIONS, EXTERNAL:
- Wing span: 6·86 m (22 ft 6 in)
- Wing chord, constant: 1·52 m (5 ft 0 in)
- Wing aspect ratio: 4·4
- Length overall: 5·18 m (17 ft 0 in)
- Height overall: 1·83 m (6 ft 0 in)
- Tailplane span: 2·13 m (7 ft 0 in)
- Wheel track: 1·22 m (4 ft 0 in)
- Wheelbase: 3·20 m (10 ft 6 in)
- Propeller diameter: 1·83 m (6 ft 0 in)

AREA:
- Wings, gross: 10·22 m² (110·0 sq ft)

WEIGHTS AND LOADINGS:
- Weight empty: 242 kg (533 lb)
- Max T-O weight: 350 kg (773 lb)
- Max wing loading: 34·3 kg/m² (7·03 lb/sq ft)
- Max power loading: 7·22 kg/kW (11·89 lb/hp)

PERFORMANCE (with 1,600 cc Volkswagen modified motor-car engine, at max T-O weight):
- Max cruising speed: 70 knots (130 km/h; 81 mph)
- Econ cruising speed: 55 knots (101 km/h; 63 mph)
- Approach speed: 40-45 knots (74-84 km/h; 46-52 mph)
- Range with max fuel: 173 nm (320 km; 200 miles)

COLLINS

COLLINS AERO

386 Fairville Road RD1, Chadds Ford, Pennsylvania 19317
Telephone: (215) 388 2393

COLLINS AERO W-7 DIPPER

Mr Willard C. Collins has designed, built and flown a side by side two-seat amphibious flying-boat known as the W-7 Dipper. Design began in April 1964 and construction of the single prototype started in the following October. The first flight was achieved on 24 August 1982 and certification in the Experimental category was gained in May 1984.

TYPE: Two-seat homebuilt amphibious flying-boat.

AIRFRAME: Strut-braced high-wing monoplane, using aluminium alloy wings from a Cessna 150, with balancing floats added close to wingtips. Modified Cessna 150 basic fuselage, with instrument panel and windscreen moved forward by 0·91 m (3 ft 0 in) and glassfibre boat hull and nose cowling added for water operations. Basically Cessna 150 tail unit, but with fin of increased height and tailplane raised by 0·46 m (1 ft 6 in). Dorsal fin added.

LANDING GEAR: Retractable tricycle type. 5·00-5 nosewheel retracts upward, 6·00-6 mainwheels upward also but into opening on each side that was formerly the rear window of the Cessna 150. Tyre pressures: mainwheels 1·79 bars (26 lb/sq in), nosewheel 1·38 bars (20 lb/sq in). Retraction is actuated electrically, with a motor for each individual unit, assisted by bungee in the fuselage for main units. Polyurethane in compression shock absorption.

POWER PLANT: One 134 kW (180 hp) Avco Lycoming O-360 flat-four engine, driving a Sensenich two-blade fixed-pitch wooden pusher propeller. Two fuel tanks in wings, capacity 49 litres (13 US gallons) each, and one 49 litre (13 US gallon) fuselage tank. Oil capacity 7·5 litres (2 US gallons).

ACCOMMODATION: Pilot and passenger in enclosed cockpit, under transparent canopy.

SYSTEM: Generator for electrical system.

AVIONICS: Narco nav/com and SRD Loran C.

DIMENSIONS, EXTERNAL:
- Wing span: 10·16 m (33 ft 4 in)
- Length overall: 7·72 m (25 ft 4 in)
- Height overall: 2·84 m (9 ft 4 in)
- Tailplane span: 3·05 m (10 ft 0 in)
- Wheel track: 2·34 m (7 ft 8 in)
- Wheelbase: 2·95 m (9 ft 8 in)
- Propeller diameter: 1·88 m (6 ft 2 in)

AREA:
- Wings, gross: 14·86 m² (160·0 sq ft)

WEIGHTS AND LOADINGS:
- Weight empty, equipped: 481 kg (1,060 lb)
- Max T-O weight: 798 kg (1,760 lb)
- Max wing loading: 53·7 kg/m² (11·00 lb/sq ft)
- Max power loading: 5·96 kg/kW (9·78 lb/hp)

PERFORMANCE:
- Never-exceed speed: 160 knots (296 km/h; 184 mph)
- Max level speed at 2,135 m (7,000 ft): 130 knots (241 km/h; 150 mph)
- Max cruising speed: 120 knots (222 km/h; 138 mph)
- Econ cruising speed: 100 knots (185 km/h; 115 mph)
- Stalling speed: 45 knots (84 km/h; 52 mph)
- Max rate of climb at S/L: 427 m (1,400 ft)/min
- Service ceiling: 5,485 m (18,000 ft)
- T-O run: 122 m (400 ft)
- T-O to 15 m (50 ft): 183 m (600 ft)
- Landing from 15 m (50 ft): 213 m (700 ft)
- Landing run: 152 m (500 ft)
- Range with max fuel: 500 nm (926 km; 575 miles)

COUNTRY AIR

COUNTRY AIR INC

1230 Shepherd Street, Hendersonville, North Carolina 28739
Telephone: (704) 692 7784

COUNTRY AIR J-6 KARATOO

At a sale of the assets of the former Grover Aircraft Corporation, Mr Jesse Anglin purchased rights to the J-6 Karatoo and founded Country Air to market kits to amateur constructors. Mr Anglin was the designer of the Karatoo, having sold the aircraft to Grover.

Reports suggest that the Country Air version of the Karatoo is different from that offered by Grover, with the fuselage lengthened and made marginally wider, the tail unit and turtledeck redesigned, and the wings given a new aerofoil section.

The details below are for the Grover J-6 Karatoo:

TYPE: Side by side two-seat homebuilt aircraft.

AIRFRAME: Strut braced high-wing cabin monoplane. Fabric covered constant chord wings. Conventional fuselage and tail unit.

LANDING GEAR: Non-retractable tailwheel type. Main units comprise two side Vs and half-axles and carry streamline wheel fairings.

POWER PLANT: Powered normally by a 39 kW (52 hp) Rotax 503 two-cylinder engine, driving a two-blade 64 × 38 wooden propeller. A 48·5 kW (65 hp) Volkswagen engine, driving a 54 × 40 propeller, is optional.

DIMENSIONS, EXTERNAL:
- Wing span: 9·91 m (32 ft 6 in)
- Length overall: 6·10 m (20 ft 0 in)
- Height overall: 1·68 m (5 ft 6 in)

AREA:
- Wings, gross: 13·56 m² (146·0 sq ft)

WEIGHTS AND LOADINGS (A: Rotax engine, B: Volkswagen engine):
- Weight empty: A: 172 kg (380 lb)
- B: 195 kg (430 lb)
- Max T-O weight: A, B: 408 kg (900 lb)
- Max wing loading: A, B: 30·1 kg/m² (6·16 lb/sq ft)
- Max power loading: A: 10·46 kg/kW (17·31 lb/hp)
- B: 8·41 kg/kW (13·85 lb/hp)

PERFORMANCE:
- Never-exceed speed: A, B: 113 knots (209 km/h; 130 mph)
- Max level speed: A: 74 knots (137 km/h; 85 mph)
- B: 89 knots (165 km/h; 103 mph)
- Cruising speed: A: 65 knots (120 km/h; 75 mph)
- B: 78 knots (145 km/h; 90 mph)
- Max rate of climb at S/L: A: 228 m (750 ft)/min
- B: 198 m (650 ft)/min
- T-O run: A: 46 m (150 ft)
- B: 61 m (200 ft)
- Best glide ratio: A, B: 10·5

COUNTRY AIR SPACE WALKER

Latest design by Mr Jesse D. Anglin, the Space Walker reproduces the classic configuration of Ryan monoplanes of the late 1930s but is built of modern materials and uses modern engines. The prototype, exhibited at the 1986 Oshkosh meeting, is typical of the amateur built version, with a Continental piston engine of 48·5 kW (65 hp), for which drawings and component parts are available. It is expected to be followed by a ready-to-fly production microlight version with a 48·5 kW (65 hp) Rotax two-cylinder two-stroke engine and reduced empty weight of 186 kg (410 lb).

The following details apply to the homebuilt Space Walker:

TYPE: Single-seat homebuilt aircraft.

AIRFRAME: Cantilever low-wing monoplane, with dihedral from roots. Fabric covered wooden wings are removable without disconnecting control cables or tubes. Welded chrome-molybdenum steel tube fuselage and wire braced tail unit, also fabric covered. Conventional three-axis control. Horn balanced rudder and elevators.

LANDING GEAR: Non-retractable tailwheel type. Mainwheels, with streamline fairings, carried on faired side Vs and half-axles, with bungee shock absorption.

POWER PLANT: One 48·5-63 kW (65-85 hp) Continental flat-four engine, driving a two-blade wooden propeller with spinner. Fuel capacity 38 litres (10 US gallons).

ACCOMMODATION: Single seat in open cockpit with large windscreen.

DIMENSIONS, EXTERNAL:
- Wing span: 7·93 m (26 ft 0 in)
- Wing aspect ratio: 5·78
- Length overall: 5·49 m (18 ft 0 in)
- Height overall: 1·60 m (5 ft 3 in)

AREA:
- Wings, gross: 10·87 m² (117·0 sq ft)

WEIGHTS AND LOADINGS (48·5 kW; 65 hp Continental):
- Weight empty: 245 kg (540 lb)
- Max T-O weight: 385 kg (850 lb)
- Max wing loading: 35·42 kg/m² (7·26 lb/sq ft)
- Max power loading: 7·94 kg/kW (13·08 lb/hp)

PERFORMANCE (48·5 kW; 65 hp Continental):
- Never-exceed speed: 135 knots (249 km/h; 155 mph)
- Max level speed at S/L: 108 knots (201 km/h; 125 mph)
- Cruising speed: 97 knots (180 km/h; 112 mph)
- Stalling speed: power off: 37 knots (68 km/h; 42 mph)
- power on: 33 knots (61 km/h; 38 mph)
- Max rate of climb at S/L: 259 m (850 ft)/min
- *g* limits: +6/−5

Co Z

Co Z DEVELOPMENT CORPORATION

2046 North 63rd Place, Mesa, Arizona 85205

Co Z DEVELOPMENT COZY

The Cozy was conceived as a side by side two-seat development of the Rutan Long-EZ by Mr Nathan D. Puffer. Design began in January 1980 and construction of the prototype started in the following July, with the consent of Burt Rutan. The first flight was achieved on 19 July 1982.

The Cozy was intended originally to be a 'one of a kind'. However, following consultations with the Rutan Aircraft Factory, Mr Puffer received a licence to market the Cozy. For this purpose, the Co Z Development Corporation was established. Plans have been available since December 1983 and approximately 200 sets have been sold. More than 100 Cozys are reportedly under active construction.

The accompanying illustration shows the Cozy built by Uli and Linda Wolters. First flown on 19 June 1985, it was the first plans-built Cozy to be completed and differs from standard by having a 2·5 cm (1 in) increase in wing span, and modifications to the canard and nose gear doors. The cockpit canopy has been arranged to open further. Empty and max T-O weights are 469 kg (1,035 lb) and 748 kg

Clutton-Tabenor FRED Series 2 (1,600 cc Volkswagen engine) *(R Kunert)*

First plans-built Co Z Development Corporation Cozy, built by Uli and Linda Wolters *(Howard Levy)*

Collins Aero W-7 Dipper amphibious flying-boat *(Howard Levy)*

Country Air J-6 Karatoo *(Howard Levy)*

Country Air Space Walker homebuilt monoplane *(J. M. G. Gradidge)*

The single-seat Cvjetkovic CA-61R (Continental A65 engine)

First Cvjetkovic CA-65A, built by students of the Kelowna Secondary School, Kelowna, British Columbia, Canada

(1,650 lb) respectively; maximum speed is 190 knots (352 km/h; 219 mph), cruising speed 170 knots (315 km/h; 196 mph), rate of climb 366 m (1,200 ft)/min, service ceiling 7,010 m (23,000 ft) and range 1,198 nm (2,220 km; 1,380 miles), powered by a 119 kW (160 hp) Avco Lycoming O-320-D2E engine.

The description of the RAF Long-EZ applies also to the Cozy, except in the following details, which refer specifically to the prototype:

TYPE: Two/three-seat homebuilt sporting aircraft.

AIRFRAME: Wider fuselage than Long-EZ to allow side by side seating.

LANDING GEAR: Tricycle type, with fixed main units and manually retractable nosewheel which is carried on a glassfibre strut. Cleveland wheels. Tyres size 5·00-5. Cleveland brakes.

POWER PLANT: One 88 kW (118 hp) Avco Lycoming O-235-L2C flat-four engine, driving a Tift two-blade fixed-pitch wooden pusher propeller.

ACCOMMODATION: Normally two persons side by side under side hinged (to starboard) canopy. Large baggage space to rear of seats, or, alternatively, a third seat. Heated and ventilated.

AVIONICS AND EQUIPMENT: King com/nav, R/Nav, DME, ADF, glideslope and marker beacon receivers, transponder, audio panel and intercom in prototype plus blind-flying instrumentation.

DIMENSIONS, EXTERNAL:

Wing span	7·96 m (26 ft 1¼ in)
Length overall	5·12 m (16 ft 9½ in)
Height overall	2·30 m (7 ft 6½ in)
Propeller diameter	1·60 m (5 ft 3 in)

AREA:

Wings, gross	8·88 m² (95·6 sq ft)

WEIGHTS AND LOADINGS:

Weight empty, basic	386 kg (850 lb)
Max T-O weight	680 kg (1,500 lb)
Max wing loading	76·6 kg/m² (15·7 lb/sq ft)
Max power loading	7·73 kg/kW (12·71 lb/hp)

PERFORMANCE:

Max level speed at S/L	165 knots (306 km/h; 190 mph)
Max cruising speed at 2,440 m (8,000 ft)	156 knots (290 km/h; 180 mph)
Econ cruising speed at 3,660 m (12,000 ft)	124 knots (230 km/h; 143 mph)
Stalling speed	53 knots (97 km/h; 60 mph)
Max rate of climb at S/L	457 m (1,500 ft)/min
Service ceiling	6,100 m (20,000 ft)
T-O run	213 m (700 ft)
T-O to 15 m (50 ft)	396 m (1,300 ft)
Landing from 15 m (50 ft)	518 m (1,700 ft)
Landing run	183 m (600 ft)
Range with max fuel, at 122 knots (225 km/h; 140 mph) at 3,660 m (12,000 ft), with 1½ h reserves	1,563 nm (2,896 km; 1,800 miles)

CUELLAR

JESSE CUELLAR

7171 Spring Grove, San Antonio, Texas 78249

CUELLAR MONOPLANE

Mr Jesse Cuellar has designed and is building the prototype of a single-seat pusher monoplane, with a fully enclosed cockpit, that is very similar in configuration to the former Bede BD-5 (see 1977-78 *Jane's*). To be powered by a 21 kW (28 hp) two-stroke engine and with an airframe of moulded glassfibre and foam sandwich, it will possess some soaring capability. Eventually, the monoplane will be made available as a complete kit.

The few known details follow:

TYPE: Single-seat homebuilt aircraft.

DIMENSIONS, EXTERNAL:

Wing span	6·71 m (22 ft 0 in)
Length overall	3·96 m (13 ft 0 in)

WEIGHT:

Weight empty	approx 102 kg (225 lb)

CVJETKOVIC

ANTON CVJETKOVIC

5324 West 121 Street, Hawthorne, California 90250
Telephone: (213) 644 7931

When living in Yugoslavia, Mr Anton Cvjetkovic designed a single-seat light aeroplane designated CA-51 and powered by a modified Volkswagen engine. A prototype was built by members of Zagreb Aeroclub in 1951, and was followed by five more aircraft of the same type.

After moving to the USA, Mr Cvjetkovic began work, in May 1960, on the design of an improved light aircraft which he designated CA-61. Construction of a prototype was started in February 1961 and it flew for the first time in August 1962. Plans are available to amateur constructors, together with plans of a two-seat all-wood aircraft designated CA-65, and an all-metal version, designated CA-65A.

Several hundred sets of plans of these aircraft have been sold, and completed aircraft are flying in Australia, Canada, South Africa and the USA.

CVJETKOVIC CA-61/-61R MINI ACE

The CA-61 can be built as a single-seat or side by side two-seat light aircraft, with any Continental engine of between 48·5 and 63·5 kW (65 and 85 hp). Alternatively, the single-seater can be fitted with a modified Volkswagen engine. Construction takes less than 1,000 h.

The design was modified during 1973 to allow for installation of retractable landing gear; when constructed in this form the aircraft is designated **CA-61R**.

The following details refer specifically to the single-seat CA-61 prototype:

TYPE: Single-seat homebuilt light aircraft.

AIRFRAME: Cantilever low-wing monoplane. Wing section NACA 4415. Dihedral 3°. No incidence. Structure consists of two spruce spars, each built in one piece, built-up spruce girder ribs and plywood covered leading-edge torsion box, with fabric covering overall. Fabric covered spruce ailerons. No flaps. Conventional wooden fuselage of basic square section, plywood covered. Cantilever wooden tail unit, covered with plywood. Fixed incidence tailplane. Trim tab in elevator.

LANDING GEAR: Non-retractable tailwheel type. Cantilever main legs, with helical spring shock absorption. Goodyear mainwheels and tyres, size 5·00-5 Type III, and Model L5 brakes. Steerable tailwheel.

POWER PLANT: One 48·5 kW (65 hp) Continental A65 flat-four engine, driving a Flottorp 63-55 two-blade fixed-pitch propeller. Fuel in two steel tanks in fuselage, with capacities of 45 litres (12 US gallons) and 19 litres (5 US gallons) respectively. Total fuel capacity 64 litres (17 US gallons). Oil capacity 4·5 litres (1·25 US gallons).

ACCOMMODATION: Single seat in enclosed cockpit.

AVIONICS AND EQUIPMENT: Prototype fitted with Nova Star radio and Omni.

DIMENSIONS, EXTERNAL:

Wing span	8·38 m (27 ft 6 in)
Wing chord, constant	1·40 m (4 ft 7 in)
Wing aspect ratio	6·0
Length overall	5·77 m (18 ft 11 in)
Height overall (in flying position)	2·08 m (6 ft 10 in)
Wheel track: single-seat	2·49 m (8 ft 2 in)
two-seat	2·62 m (8 ft 7 in)

AREA:

Wings, gross	11·75 m² (126·5 sq ft)

WEIGHTS AND LOADINGS:

Weight empty: single-seat	275 kg (606 lb)
two-seat	363 kg (800 lb)
Max T-O weight: single-seat	430 kg (950 lb)
two-seat	590 kg (1,300 lb)
Max wing loading:	
single-seat	36·7 kg/m² (7·51 lb/sq ft)
Max power loading:	
single-seat	12·16 kg/kW (14·62 lb/hp)

PERFORMANCE:

Max level speed at S/L	104 knots (193 km/h; 120 mph)
Normal cruising speed	87 knots (161 km/h; 100 mph)
Min flying speed:	
single-seat	37 knots (68 km/h; 42 mph)
two-seat	44 knots (81 km/h; 50 mph)
Range with max fuel:	
single-seat	369 nm (685 km; 425 miles)
two-seat	321 nm (595 km; 370 miles)

CVJETKOVIC CA-65

Design of this side by side two-seat light aircraft was started in September 1963. Construction of the prototype began in March 1964 and it flew for the first time in July 1965. Plans are available.

The CA-65 closely resembles the CA-61 in general appearance, but has a more powerful engine and retractable landing gear. A folding-wing version was introduced during 1967.

TYPE: Two-seat homebuilt light aircraft.

AIRFRAME: Cantilever low-wing monoplane. Modified NACA 4415 wing section. Dihedral 0° on centre-section, 3° on outer wings. Structure consists of two spruce spars, each built in one piece, and ribs cut mainly from 9·5 mm (3/8 in) thick marine mahogany plywood, completely plywood covered. Fabric covered spruce ailerons. On the folding-wing version, the outer wings fold upward from their junction with the centre-section. Conventional wooden fuselage of basically square section, plywood covered. Manually operated landing flap under fuselage. Cantilever wooden tail unit, with marine mahogany plywood ribs in tailplane and fin. Fixed surfaces covered with plywood. Elevator and rudder fabric covered. Fixed incidence tailplane.

LANDING GEAR: Mechanically retractable tailwheel type. Mainwheels retract inward. Goodyear mainwheels and tyres, size 5·00-5 Type III. Goodyear type L5 brakes. Steerable tailwheel.

POWER PLANT: One 93 kW (125 hp) Avco Lycoming O-290-G flat-four engine, driving a Sensenich 66-68 two-blade fixed-pitch propeller. (Other Avco Lycoming engines of 80·5-112 kW; 108-150 hp can be fitted.) Two aluminium fuel tanks in fuselage, each with capacity of 53 litres (14 US gallons). Total fuel capacity 106 litres (28 US gallons).

ACCOMMODATION: Two seats side by side in enclosed cockpit, with dual controls; although hydraulic brakes can be operated only by the pilot. Forward opening canopy.

SYSTEM: Electrical system standard.

RADIO: Bayside BEI-990 radio fitted in prototype.

DIMENSIONS, EXTERNAL:

Wing span	7·62 m (25 ft 0 in)
Width, wings folded	2·74 m (9 ft 0 in)
Length overall	5·79 m (19 ft 0 in)
Height overall (in flying position)	2·24 m (7 ft 4 in)
Height, wings folded	3·05 m (10 ft 0 in)
Wheel track	2·11 m (6 ft 11 in)
Propeller diameter	1·73 m (5 ft 8 in)

AREA:

Wings, gross	10·03 m² (108·0 sq ft)

WEIGHTS AND LOADINGS:

Weight empty	408 kg (900 lb)
Max T-O weight	680 kg (1,500 lb)
Max wing loading	67·9 kg/m² (13·9 lb/sq ft)
Max power loading	7·31 kg/kW (12·00 lb/hp)

PERFORMANCE (at max T-O weight):

Max level speed	156 knots (290 km/h; 180 mph)
Normal cruising speed	135 knots (249 km/h; 155 mph)
Stalling speed	48 knots (89 km/h; 55 mph)
Max rate of climb at S/L	305 m (1,000 ft)/min
Service ceiling	4,575 m (15,000 ft)
T-O run	137 m (450 ft)
Landing run	183 m (600 ft)
Range with max fuel	434 nm (804 km; 500 miles)
g limits	+9/−6 ultimate

CVJETKOVIC CA-65A

This aircraft is an all-metal version of the wooden CA-65, with swept vertical tail surfaces.

The general description of the CA-65 applies also to the CA-65A, except in the following details:

AIRFRAME: The wing structure consists of a single main spar and an auxiliary wing spar, with aluminium sheet ribs and skin, riveted throughout. The main wing spar cap is made of extruded and bent-up sheet aluminium angles, tapered towards the tip to produce a wing of uniform bending strength. Ribs are formed from 0·025 in aluminium sheet. Wing skin is of 2024-T3 aluminium alloy sheet. All-metal fuselage, with four aluminium angle longerons and built-up frames. Fuselage skin is of 0·025-0·032 in 2024-T3 aluminium alloy sheet. To simplify formation of the curvature on the upper fuselage, the skins are broken up into small sections of flat panels. Cantilever all-metal tail unit, with swept vertical surfaces and dorsal fin. Construction similar to that of the wings.

POWER PLANT: The structure is designed to accommodate an Avco Lycoming engine of 80·5-112 kW (108-150 hp).

DIMENSIONS, EXTERNAL: As for Model CA-65 except:

Wing span	7·75 m (25 ft 5 in)
Length overall	5·99 m (19 ft 8 in)
Height overall	2·29 m (7 ft 6 in)

AREA:

Wings, gross	10·16 m² (109·4 sq ft)

PERFORMANCE (112 kW; 150 hp engine):

Max level speed	151 knots (280 km/h; 174 mph)
Normal cruising speed	130 knots (241 km/h; 150 mph)
Stalling speed	48 knots (89 km/h; 55 mph)
Max rate of climb at S/L	466 m (1,530 ft)/min
Service ceiling	4,570 m (15,000 ft)
T-O run	99 m (325 ft)
Landing run	183 m (600 ft)
Range with max fuel	460 nm (853 km; 530 miles)
g limits	+9/−6 ultimate

D 2

D 2 INC

PO Box 265, Bend, Oregon 97709

PROPRIETOR: Sidney L. Ellis

D 2 Inc has acquired the designs of the Davis DA-2A and DA-5A and the Aerosport Quail. It is remarketing them in plan and kit forms. The DA-5A is to be flight tested with a Volkswagen modified motorcar engine, replacing the 48·5 kW (65 hp) Continental A65 on the prototype. If this installation is successful, the company will market an engine mounting and cowling for those purchasing plans only and wishing to fit the Volkswagen alternative engine.

D 2 (DAVIS) DA-2A

This side by side two-seat light aircraft was flown for the first time on 21 May 1966, after 18 months of spare-time work and an expenditure of $1,600. At the Experimental Aircraft Association's annual Fly-in a few weeks later, it gained the awards for both the most outstanding design and the most popular aircraft. Plans were made available subsequently, and by early 1986 about 120 DA-2As were under construction and approximately 45 were flying. The design has since been taken over by D 2 Inc, which offers both plans and kits of the DA-2A.

The DA-2A is of simple all-metal construction and has an all-moving V tail (included angle 100°). The wings are of constant chord, without flaps. Dihedral is 5°. The non-retractable tricycle landing gear has cantilever spring steel main legs and a steerable nosewheel. Power plant in the prototype is a 48·5 kW (65 hp) Continental A65-8 flat-four engine; but the DA-2A is stressed for engines of up to 74·5 kW (100 hp). Total fuel capacity is 75 litres (20 US gallons) and oil capacity 3·75 litres (1 US gallon).

There is baggage space aft of the side by side seats or, alternatively, a child's seat may be located in this position.

DIMENSIONS, EXTERNAL:

Wing span	5·86 m (19 ft 2¾ in)
Wing chord, constant	1·31 m (4 ft 3½ in)
Wing aspect ratio	4·48
Length overall	5·44 m (17 ft 10¼ in)
Height overall	1·65 m (5 ft 5 in)

DIMENSIONS, INTERNAL:

Cabin: Length	1·49 m (4 ft 6¾ in)
Max width	1·04 m (3 ft 5 in)
Max height	1·14 m (3 ft 8¾ in)

AREA:

Wings, gross	7·66 m² (82·5 sq ft)

WEIGHTS AND LOADINGS (A: A65-8 engine, B: 67 kW; 90 hp Continental engine):

Weight empty: A	277 kg (610 lb)
B	340 kg (750 lb)
Max T-O weight: A	510 kg (1,125 lb)
B	567 kg (1,250 lb)
Max wing loading: A	66·4 kg/m² (13·6 lb/sq ft)
B	74·0 kg/m² (15·15 lb/sq ft)
Max power loading: A	10·52 kg/kW (17·31 lb/hp)
B	8·46 kg/kW (13·89 lb/hp)

PERFORMANCE (A: A65-8 engine, B: 67 kW; 90 hp Continental engine, at max T-O weight):

Max level speed at S/L:	
A	104 knots (193 km/h; 120 mph)
B	121 knots (225 km/h; 140 mph)
Cruising speed: A	100 knots (185 km/h; 115 mph)
B	109 knots (201 km/h; 125 mph)
Landing speed: A	54 knots (100 km/h; 62 mph)
B	61 knots (113 km/h; 70 mph)
Range with max fuel: A	390 nm (725 km; 450 miles)
Range with max fuel, with reserves:	
B	347 nm (644 km; 400 miles)

D 2 (DAVIS) DA-5A

Design of this aircraft began in October 1972, and Mr Davis and his son began construction of the prototype on 4 May 1974. The first flight of the DA-5A was made on 22 July 1974.

Plans of the DA-5A are available to amateur constructors. The following details refer to the initial Continental powered DA-5A:

TYPE: Single-seat homebuilt aircraft.

AIRFRAME: Cantilever low-wing monoplane. Wing section Clark Y. Thickness/chord ratio 12%. Dihedral 5°. Incidence 0°. Light alloy wings with single spar, ribs of 2024-T3 alloy, and stressed skins. Plain ailerons of light alloy construction. No flaps. Light alloy stressed skin fuselage, with four frames and stainless steel firewall. Steel tube overturn structure aft of pilot's seat. All-moving V tail (included angle 100°) with steel tube spar and light alloy ribs and skins. Anti-servo tabs in trailing-edges.

LANDING GEAR: Non-retractable tricycle type. Mainwheel legs of light alloy streamline section mounted rigidly to wing spar. Shock absorption by tyres and rubber grommets. Mainwheel tyres size 14 × 5-4, pressure 1·03 bars (15 lb/sq in). Steerable nosewheel with tyre size 10 × 3-4, pressure 1·03 bars (15 lb/sq in). Rosenhan drum brakes.

POWER PLANT: One 48·5 kW (65 hp) Continental A65 flat-four engine, driving a Hegy type 60-70 two-blade fixed-pitch wooden propeller with spinner. Fuel tank in fuselage, immediately aft of firewall, capacity 64·3 litres (17 US gallons). Refuelling point on fuselage upper surface forward of windscreen. Oil capacity 3·75 litres (1 US gallon).

ACCOMMODATION: Single seat beneath canopy hinged on port side.

DIMENSIONS, EXTERNAL:

Wing span	4·76 m (15 ft 7¼ in)
Wing chord, constant	1·12 m (3 ft 8 in)
Wing aspect ratio	4·26
Length overall	4·80 m (15 ft 9 in)
Height overall	1·35 m (4 ft 5¼ in)
Span over V tail	1·60 m (5 ft 3 in)
Wheel track	1·55 m (5 ft 1 in)
Wheelbase	1·12 m (3 ft 8 in)
Propeller diameter	1·52 m (5 ft 0 in)

DIMENSION, INTERNAL:

Cockpit: Max width	0·53 m (1 ft 9 in)

AREA:

Wings, gross	5·31 m² (57·2 sq ft)

Prototype D'Apuzzo D-201 Sportwing, built by Mr Larry Stangil of Ferndale, Pennsylvania

D 2 (Aerosport) Quail single-seat homebuilt aircraft

D 2 (Davis) DA-5A single-seat homebuilt sporting aircraft

Davis DA-2A side by side two-seat light aircraft *(J. M. G. Gradidge)*

WEIGHTS AND LOADINGS:
Weight empty 208 kg (460 lb)
Max T-O weight 351 kg (775 lb)
Max wing loading 66·2 kg/m² (13·55 lb/sq ft)
Max power loading 7·24 kg/kW (11·92 lb/hp)
PERFORMANCE (at max T-O weight):
Never-exceed speed 147 knots (273 km/h; 170 mph)
Max level speed at S/L 139 knots (257 km/h; 160 mph)
Max cruising speed at S/L 122 knots (225 km/h; 140 mph)
Econ cruising speed at S/L 104 knots (193 km/h; 120 mph)
Stalling speed 52 knots (97 km/h; 60 mph)
Max rate of climb at S/L 244 m (800 ft)/min
Service ceiling 4,420 m (14,500 ft)
T-O run 183 m (600 ft)
T-O to 15 m (50 ft) 259 m (850 ft)
Landing from 15 m (50 ft) 335 m (1,100 ft)
Landing run 183 m (600 ft)
Range with max fuel 390 nm (724 km; 450 miles)

D 2 (AEROSPORT) QUAIL

Design of the Quail by Aerosport Inc began in January 1970, and construction of the prototype was started in July 1971. It flew for the first time in December 1971, with an all-moving tailplane; but the designers incorporated a fixed incidence tailplane with elevators before plans and construction kits were made available to amateur constructors. A total of 398 sets of plans had been sold by 1983. Approximately 18 Quails were then under construction and about ten flying. It was subsequently dropped from the Aerosport range, but is now available from D 2.

TYPE: Single-seat homebuilt cabin monoplane.

AIRFRAME: Cantilever high-wing monoplane. Wing section NACA 23015. All-metal two-spar wings of 2024-T3 and 6061-T6 light alloy. Plain ailerons of light alloy construction. Trailing-edge flaps. Endplates optional. Semi-monocoque all-metal fuselage of 2024-T3 light alloy. Cantilever all-metal tail unit of light alloy, with swept vertical surfaces. Fixed incidence tailplane. Trim tab on rudder and elevator of prototype; optional for later aircraft.

LANDING GEAR: Non-retractable tricycle type. Cantilever spring main gear struts of light alloy. Nosewheel shock absorption by rubber in compression. Mainwheels and tyres size 5·30 × 4·50-6; nosewheel and tyre size 2·80 × 2·50-4. Tyre pressure 1·38 bars (20 lb/sq in). Barrel type wheel brakes. Nosewheel steerable. Optional wheel fairings.

POWER PLANT: One 1,600 cc modified Volkswagen motor-car engine, driving a 54-36 two-blade fixed-pitch wooden propeller. Provision for installation of Volkswagen engines from 1,500 cc to 1,800 cc capacity. Two fuel tanks in wings, and 7·5 litre (2 US gallon) meter tank; total capacity 38 litres (10 US gallons). Refuelling point in top of each wing.

ACCOMMODATION: Single seat in enclosed cabin, which is heated. Door on starboard side is hinged at top and opens upwards. Stowage for 9 kg (20 lb) baggage.

DIMENSIONS, EXTERNAL:
Wing span 7·32 m (24 ft 0 in)
Wing chord, constant 1·07 m (3 ft 6 in)
Wing aspect ratio 6·87
Length overall 4·85 m (15 ft 11 in)
Height overall 1·69 m (5 ft 6½ in)
Tailplane span 1·83 m (6 ft 0 in)
Wheel track 1·52 m (5 ft 0 in)
Wheelbase 1·22 m (4 ft 0 in)
Propeller diameter 1·37 m (4 ft 6 in)
AREA:
Wings, gross 7·8 m² (84·0 sq ft)
WEIGHTS AND LOADING:
Weight empty 242 kg (534 lb)
Normal T-O weight 345 kg (762 lb)
Max T-O weight 359 kg (792 lb)
Max wing loading 46·04 kg/m² (9·43 lb/sq ft)
PERFORMANCE (at max T-O weight):
Max level speed at S/L 113 knots (209 km/h; 130 mph)
Max cruising speed 100 knots (185 km/h; 115 mph)
Econ cruising speed 96 knots (177 km/h 110 mph)
Stalling speed, flaps down 42 knots (78 km/h; 48 mph)
Max rate of climb at S/L 259 m (850 ft)/min
Service ceiling (estimated) 3,660 m (12,000 ft)
T-O run 91 m (300 ft)
Landing run 122 m (400 ft)
Range with max fuel, no reserves 200 nm (370 km; 230 miles)

D'APUZZO

NICHOLAS E. D'APUZZO

1029 Blue Rock Lane, Blue Bell, Pennsylvania 19422
Telephone: (215) 646 4792

Mr D'Apuzzo, who was formerly employed by the Naval Air Development Center, Warminster, Pennsylvania, as a project manager on specialised projects, retired from the Navy Department during 1973. He retains an association with the Navy on a consultant basis.

He has designed several sporting aircraft for amateur construction, among the best known of which are the PJ-260 single-seat aerobatic biplane described under the Parsons-Jocelyn heading in the 1974-75 *Jane's*; and the D-260/D-295 Senior Aero Sport, a two-seat version of the PJ-260 which was described and illustrated in the 1983-84 and previous editions. His latest design for which plans are currently available is the D-201 Sportwing, a more economical aircraft than the Senior Aero Sport which it superseded.

Thirty-two PJ-260s and Senior Aero Sports are known to have been completed by amateur constructors in the USA, with about 33 more under construction.

D'APUZZO D-201 SPORTWING

The D-201 is a completely redesigned development of the PJ-260/D-260 Senior Aero Sport series. Special attention was given to reducing the cost and complexity of building the aircraft, while retaining the safety aspects of the previous models. The aircraft features long span ailerons on the lower wings only, to reduce weight and to simplify construction; the front cockpit was enlarged by 7·6 cm (3 in), without affecting the rear cockpit; and the wing panel structures and tailplane assembly were redesigned. Many preformed parts are available to the homebuilder.

Construction of the prototype D-201 (N34LS) began in January 1977. It received its FAA licence in June 1981. Plans for construction of the D-201 Sportwing by amateur builders are available. The following description, and performance data based on initial testing, apply to the prototype:

TYPE: Two-seat homebuilt sporting biplane.

AIRFRAME: Conventional braced biplane. Wing section NACA M-12 (modified). Dihedral 0° on upper wings; 0° 30′ on lower wings. Incidence 2° on all wings. Sweepback 9° 15′ on upper wings only, outboard of centre-section. Long span ailerons, on lower wings only. N interplane struts and cabane struts. Conventional steel tube fuselage structure, with aluminium alloy panels forward of cockpit and fabric covering aft. Conventional wire braced tail unit. Trim tab in starboard elevator. All control surfaces horn balanced.

LANDING GEAR: Non-retractable tailwheel type. Cantilever spring steel main units. Wheel fairings.

POWER PLANT: One 119 kW (160 hp) Avco Lycoming IO-320-B1A flat-four engine driving a Hartzell constant-speed propeller in prototype. Design suitable for any Avco Lycoming engine from the 93 kW (125 hp) O-235 to the 149 kW (200 hp) O-360.

ACCOMMODATION: Two seats in tandem. Optional canopy over rear cockpit.

SYSTEM: Full electrical system, including generator and starter.

AVIONICS: Radio and intercom.

DIMENSIONS, EXTERNAL:
Wing span: upper 8·23 m (27 ft 0 in)
lower 7·86 m (25 ft 9½ in)
Wing chord, constant 1·17 m (3 ft 10 in)
Length overall, tail up 6·59 m (21 ft 7½ in)
Height overall, tail down 2·34 m (7 ft 8 in)
Elevator span 3·15 m (10 ft 4 in)
Wheel track 2·57 m (8 ft 5 in)
AREA:
Wings, gross 17·14 m² (184·5 sq ft)
WEIGHTS AND LOADINGS:
Weight empty 591 kg (1,303 lb)
Design max T-O weight 862 kg (1,900 lb)
Max wing loading 50·3 kg/m² (10·3 lb/sq ft)
Max power loading 7·24 kg/kW (11·88 lb/hp)
PERFORMANCE (at max T-O weight):
Max level speed at 2,135 m (7,000 ft) 115 knots (212 km/h; 132 mph)
Max cruising speed at 2,135 m (7,000 ft) 106 knots (196 km/h; 122 mph)
Stalling speed 41 knots (76 km/h; 47 mph)
Max rate of climb at S/L 320 m (1,050 ft)/min
T-O run 128 m (420 ft)
T-O to 15 m (50 ft) 229 m (750 ft)
Landing from 15 m (50 ft) 290 m (950 ft)
Landing run 168 m (550 ft)
Range with max fuel 313 nm (579 km; 360 miles)

DAVENPORT

BRAD DAVENPORT

4802 Edison Avenue, Boulder, Colorado

DAVENPORT NUGGET

The Nugget (NX5131) is a single-seat homebuilt aircraft of classical single-bay biplane configuration. It is powered by a 112 kW (150 hp) Avco Lycoming O-320 flat-four engine, contained in an annular cowling with representations of the cylinder head fairings associated with some radial engine installations. The cockpit is fitted with a sliding canopy. The mainwheels, with streamline fairings, are carried on faired side Vs and half-axles with shock absorbers. Control surfaces comprise ailerons on the lower wings, rudder and elevators.

Only other details known are the wing span of 7·01 m (23 ft 0 in) and empty weight of 408 kg (900 lb).

Davenport Nugget homebuilt biplane *(Peter M. Bowers)*

Prototype Davis Wing DX-1 homebuilt aircraft

DAVIS

DAVIS WING LTD

PO Box 1103, Nampa, Idaho 83653-1103
PRESIDENT: Gilbert E. Davis

Mr Gilbert E. Davis has flown the prototype of a small single-seat flying wing design inspired by Northrop research aircraft and bombers of the 1940s. The initial version, described in this entry, will be made available in kit form for amateur construction. Projected follow-ons include a two-seater and a jet powered version.

DAVIS WING DX-1

The prototype Davis Wing (N5531N), known as *Starship Alpha*, was flown for the first time on 10 June 1986, after years of research, design and construction. Construction kits are offered, containing everything needed to complete the basic Davis Wing DX-1 'production' version with the exception of paint and hydraulic fluid.

TYPE: Single-seat homebuilt flying wing aircraft.

AIRFRAME: Sweptback flying wing configuration with small central cockpit pod. Majority of airframe built of pre-moulded composites, including glassfibre, Nomex honeycomb, aramid fibres, graphite fibres and various foams. Other materials include 4130 steel tubing, stainless steel and aluminium alloy. Two-spar wings, with leading-edge fixed slots at tips. Small vertical fin in trailing-edge of each wing extends forward as shallow boundary layer fence almost to leading-edge (not fitted to prototype, which has single ventral fin). Trailing-edge of each wing carries a split flap inboard of fin, an elevon immediately outboard of fin, and split drag rudders plus a trim flap between elevon and tip. Depression of both rudder pedals opens port and starboard drag rudders for operation as air-brakes.

LANDING GEAR: Hydraulically retractable tricycle type, with additional small tailwheel to protect propeller during rotation. Cleveland wheels, size 6·00-6, with standard tyres on main units; size 5·00-5 with 11½ in Lamb tyre on nosewheel. Oleo-pneumatic shock absorbers. Emergency extension system standard.

POWER PLANT: One 48·5 kW (65 hp) Rotax two-cylinder liquid-cooled two-stroke engine installed in rear of cockpit pod and driving a three-blade wooden pusher propeller. Fuel capacity 120 litres (31·7 US gallons) standard, 325 litres (85·8 US gallons) optional.

ACCOMMODATION: Pilot only, under one-piece transparent canopy in enclosed cockpit. Standard equipment includes seat belt and shoulder harness, standard engine instruments and minimum instruments for VFR flight. Options include radio, IFR instruments and cockpit heating. Baggage space more than 0·5 m³ (18 cu ft).

DIMENSIONS, EXTERNAL:
Wing span 12·19 m (40 ft 0 in)
Wing aspect ratio 6·67
Length overall 3·66 m (12 ft 0 in)
Height to top of canopy 1·62 m (5 ft 3½ in)
Wheel track 2·93 m (9 ft 7¼ in)
Propeller diameter 1·53 m (5 ft 0 in)

AREA:
Wings, gross 22·30 m² (240·0 sq ft)

WEIGHTS AND LOADINGS:
Weight empty 256 kg (565 lb)
Normal T-O weight 442 kg (975 lb)
Max T-O weight 590 kg (1,300 lb)
Max wing loading 26·46 kg/m² (5·42 lb/sq ft)
Max power loading 12·2 kg/kW (20·0 lb/hp)

PERFORMANCE:
Max level speed at S/L 130 knots (240 km/h; 150 mph)
Stalling speed 35 knots (67 km/h; 42 mph)
Max rate of climb at S/L 426 m (1,400 ft)/min
Max operating height 7,620 m (25,000 ft)
T-O run: normal T-O weight 40 m (130 ft)
max T-O weight 54 m (175 ft)
Range at 70% power and 116 knots (215 km/h; 133 mph):
normal T-O weight 869 nm (1,609 km; 1,000 miles)
max T-O weight 2,520 nm (4,665 km; 2,900 miles)
Max range at 50% power and 100 knots (185 km/h; 115 mph):
normal T-O weight 1,130 nm (2,090 km; 1,300 miles)
max T-O weight 3,125 nm (5,790 km; 3,600 miles)
g limits, normal T-O weight +4·4/−1·7

DAVIS

LEEON D. DAVIS

PLANS AND PARTS: Joe Gauthier, GFG Enterprises, 9 Kowal Drive, Cromwell, Connecticut 06416
Telephone: (203) 635 4058

Details of the first light aircraft designed by Mr Davis, the DA-1A five-seat high-wing monoplane, can be found in the 1960-61 *Jane's*. He completed subsequently the prototype of a two-seat low-wing monoplane designated DA-2A, of which plans were made available to other builders from Mr Joe Gauthier. The DA-2A has since been acquired by D 2 Inc (which see), along with the Davis DA-5A.

A reference to Mr Davis's DA-6 can be found in the 1983-84 *Jane's*. His latest aircraft is the prototype DA-7, designed for FAA type certification.

DAVIS DA-7

Unlike earlier designs by Leeon Davis, which were for amateur construction, the DA-7 is intended for certification in the proposed Primary Aircraft category and subsequent commercial production in ready-to-fly form. It has the same low-wing monoplane/V tail/tricycle landing gear configuration as its predecessors, and is of conventional light alloy construction. The aim was to use modern concepts and materials in a way that would package the same number of seats, and the same power plant, as those of a Cessna 152 in an aircraft hundreds of pounds lighter in weight and considerably faster. This was seen as the best way of reducing costs for both training and cross-country flying.

The general appearance of the DA-7 can be seen in the accompanying illustration. It is a side by side two-seater, with USA 35B wing section and an 86 kW (115 hp) Avco Lycoming O-235-L2C flat-four engine.

DIMENSIONS, EXTERNAL:
Wing span 6·25 m (20 ft 6 in)
Wing chord, constant 1·33 m (4 ft 4½ in)
Wing aspect ratio 4·69
Length overall 5·84 m (19 ft 2 in)

AREA:
Wings, gross 8·33 m² (89·7 sq ft)

WEIGHTS AND LOADINGS:
Weight empty 327 kg (720 lb)
Max T-O weight 576 kg (1,270 lb)
Max wing loading 69·15 kg/m² (14·16 lb/sq ft)
Max power loading 6·71 kg/kW (11·04 lb/hp)

PERFORMANCE:
Max cruising speed (75% power) 126 knots (233 km/h; 145 mph)
Stalling speed 51 knots (94 km/h; 58 mph)

DEGRAW

RICHARD R. DEGRAW

5820 Squires Road, Jackson, Michigan 49201
Telephone: (517) 536 8493

DEGRAW HUMMINGBIRD

The Hummingbird two-seat homebuilt helicopter (N5275Y) was designed and built by Mr Richard R. DeGraw and made its first untethered flight on 3 November 1984. The first autorotation was completed successfully on 19 December 1985, and a total of 39 h 55 min flying time had been logged by 31 January 1986. Plans of the helicopter are not being made available for amateur construction due to its complicated design. Details of the Hummingbird in its original form, and an illustration, can be found in the 1985-86 *Jane's*. The following changes have been made to the aircraft since that entry was compiled:

ROTOR SYSTEM: Current Rotor Hawk aluminium main rotor blades have a non-symmetrical flat-bottomed section with a thickness/chord ratio of 11% at quarter-chord and 0·21 m (8¼ in) blade chord.

ROTOR DRIVE: Engine/rotor rpm ratio is now 8·0:1.

TAIL UNIT: Now three sweptback all-moving vertical surfaces of arrowhead form, operating as rudders, and a fixed horizontal surface on each side of tailboom (see illustration).

AREAS:
Vertical tail surfaces (total) 1·25 m² (13·5 sq ft)
Horizontal tail surfaces (total) 0·40 m² (4·3 sq ft)

WEIGHT:
Weight empty 508 kg (1,120 lb)

PERFORMANCE: (measured by 31 January 1986):
Speed 70 knots (130 km/h; 80 mph) IAS
Rate of climb at 20°F at 450 m (1,500 ft) 762 m (2,500 ft)/min

DELTA TECHNOLOGY

DELTA TECHNOLOGY

12953 East Garvey Boulevard, Baldwin Park, California 91706
Telephone: (818) 814 1467
PRESIDENT AND CHIEF EXECUTIVE OFFICER:
Walter S. Robinson
VICE-PRESIDENT: Michael Garjian

In the Summer of 1983 Delta Technology acquired all assets of the former Delta Sailplane Corporation, including all design and manufacturing rights, and all parts inventory, of the Nomad and Honcho series of microlight aircraft. In September of that year it moved to a new 2,787 m² (30,000 sq ft) facility at Baldwin Park, California, which has more than three times the manufacturing area of the former factory.

DELTA NOMAD II

Marketed as a kit for homebuilders, the Nomad II is a more powerful version of the DS-26A and B produced by the former Delta Sailplane Corporation (see 1982-83 *Jane's*). The Nomad II is also available with wings and tail surfaces ready assembled.

TYPE: Single-seat microlight aircraft.

AIRFRAME: Strut braced high-wing monoplane. All-aluminium frame, assembled with bolts and pop rivets. Tubular wing spars and fuselage boom. Auxiliary wing box spar, of formed sheet metal, to support ailerons. All flying surfaces covered with doped Ceconite fabric. Full aerodynamic control in all three axes by ailerons, elevators and rudder. Wings and tail detachable for transportation.

A new Davis design, the DA-7, intended for FAA certification *(Howard Levy)*

Current modified tail unit of DeGraw Hummingbird two-seat light helicopter

Denney Kitfox (Rotax 503 engine) with wings folded *(John Wegg)*

Denney Kitfox with Rotax 532LC engine in annular cowling *(Peter M. Bowers)*

Delta Technology Honcho II

POWER PLANT: One 20 kW (27 hp) 269 cc Rotax Model 277 two-cylinder two-stroke engine, with reduction drive to a two-blade pusher propeller. Standard fuel tank capacity 19 litres (5 US gallons).

DIMENSIONS, EXTERNAL:	
Wing span	11·00 m (36 ft 1 in)
Wing aspect ratio	8·84
Length overall	5·75 m (18 ft 10½ in)
Height overall	2·87 m (9 ft 5 in)
Propeller diameter	1·22 m (4 ft 0 in)
AREA:	
Wings, gross	13·69 m² (147·34 sq ft)
WEIGHTS AND LOADINGS:	
Weight empty	97 kg (214 lb)
Max T-O weight	200·5 kg (442 lb)
Max wing loading	14·6 kg/m² (3·0 lb/sq ft)
Max power loading	9·61 kg/kW (15·78 lb/hp)
PERFORMANCE (at max T-O weight):	
Never-exceed speed	56 knots (104 km/h; 65 mph) CAS
Max level speed	49 knots (90 km/h; 56 mph) CAS
Max cruising speed	42 knots (77 km/h; 48 mph) CAS
Stalling speed	20 knots (37 km/h; 23 mph) CAS
Max rate of climb at S/L	201 m (660 ft)/min
Absolute power ceiling	4,575 m (15,000 ft)
T-O run, firm ground	31 m (100 ft)
Range with max fuel	139 nm (257 km; 160 miles)
Endurance with max fuel	4 h 6 min
g limits	+6·67/−2·5
Best glide ratio	15·8
Min rate of sink, power off	55 m (180 ft)/min

DELTA HONCHO II and SUPER-HONCHO

Generally similar to the Nomad, except for a shorter fuselage and shorter span wings, the Honcho II has as standard a tricycle landing gear with 11 in diameter balloon tyres, a steerable nosewheel, and a small tailskid attached to the underfin. It retains the 20 kW (27 hp) engine of the Nomad II. The Super-Honcho is fitted with a 37·3 kW (50 hp) 498 cc Rotax Model 503 and larger diameter propeller. Fuel capacity is unchanged.

DIMENSIONS, EXTERNAL (A: Honcho II, B: Super-Honcho):	
Wing span: A, B	9·80 m (32 ft 2 in)
Wing aspect ratio: A, B	7·88
Length overall: A	5·35 m (17 ft 6½ in)
B	5·46 m (17 ft 11 in)
Height overall: A	2·87 m (9 ft 5 in)
B	3·02 m (9 ft 11 in)
Propeller diameter: A	1·22 m (4 ft 0 in)
B	1·37 m (4 ft 6 in)
AREA:	
Wings, gross: A, B	12·20 m² (131·35 sq ft)
WEIGHTS AND LOADINGS:	
Weight empty: A	108 kg (239 lb)
B	110 kg (243 lb)
Max T-O weight: A	190·5 kg (420 lb)
B	238 kg (525 lb)
Max wing loading: A	15·6 kg/m² (3·19 lb/sq ft)
B	19·5 kg/m² (4·0 lb/sq ft)
Max power loading: A	9·13 kg/kW (15·0 lb/hp)
B	6·39 kg/kW (10·5 lb/hp)
PERFORMANCE (at max T-O weight):	
Never-exceed speed:	
A	60 knots (112 km/h; 70 mph) CAS
B	69 knots (128 km/h; 80 mph) CAS
Max level speed:	
A	50 knots (93 km/h; 58 mph) CAS
B	55 knots (101 km/h; 63 mph) CAS
Max cruising speed:	
A	43 knots (80 km/h; 50 mph) CAS
B	50 knots (93 km/h; 58 mph) CAS
Stalling speed: A	22 knots (41 km/h; 25 mph) CAS
B	24 knots (44 km/h; 27 mph) CAS
Max rate of climb at S/L: A	213 m (700 ft)/min
B	481 m (1,580 ft)/min
Absolute power ceiling: A	3,810 m (12,500 ft)
B	5,335 m (17,500 ft)
T-O run, firm ground: A	29 m (95 ft)
B	18·5 m (60 ft)
Range with max fuel: A	139 nm (257 km; 160 miles)
B	121 nm (225 km; 140 miles)
Endurance with max fuel: A	3 h 36 min
B	2 h 24 min
g limits: A	+6·67/−2·5
B	+6·67/−3·5
Best glide ratio: A	12·6
B	11·4
Min rate of sink, power off: A	62 m (204 ft)/min
B	69 m (228 ft)/min

DENNEY

DENNEY AEROCRAFT COMPANY

6140 Morris Hill Lane, Boise, Idaho 83704
Telephone: (208) 322 1716

DENNEY AEROCRAFT KITFOX

The Kitfox was designed as a two-seat cabin monoplane with exceptional short-field performance. It is conventional in layout and construction, and is marketed in the form of five component kits.

TYPE: Side by side two-seat light homebuilt aircraft.

AIRFRAME: Strut braced high-wing monoplane, with V bracing struts and jury struts each side. Dihedral from roots. Constant chord structure, with spars of aluminium alloy tubing, plywood ribs and drooped glassfibre wingtips, with Stits Poly-Fiber covering overall. Full span auxiliary aerofoil flaperons. Wings fold for trailering and storage. Conventional flat sided steel tube fuselage structure, with Stits Poly-Fiber covering. Conventional strut braced tail unit of steel tube, covered with Stits Poly-Fiber. Tailplane mounted partway up fin.

LANDING GEAR: Non-retractable tailwheel type. Mainwheels, size 20 × 7-8, carried on faired steel tube side Vs and half-axles, with bungee suspension and optional hydraulic disc brakes. Steerable Maule tailwheel, diameter 6 in. Aircraft is towable on mainwheels. Floats and skis optional.

POWER PLANT: One 38·8 kW (52 hp) Rotax 503 two-cylinder two-stroke engine, with 2·58:1 reduction cog-belt drive to two-blade wooden propeller with spinner. Rotax 532LC engine, driving a three-blade propeller, optional. Fuel capacity 37 litres (9·75 US gallons) standard. Two wing tanks optional; total capacity 45 litres (12 US gallons).

ACCOMMODATION: Two seats side by side in enclosed cabin, with door on each side. Dual controls standard. Cargo pod optional.

DIMENSIONS, EXTERNAL:
- Wing span 9·55 m (31 ft 4 in)
- Wing chord, constant 1·07 m (3 ft 6¼ in)
- Wing aspect ratio 7·5
- Width, wings folded 2·39 m (7 ft 10 in)
- Length overall 5·21 m (17 ft 1 in)
- Height overall 1·70 m (5 ft 7 in)
- Propeller diameter 1·73 m (5 ft 8 in)

AREA:
- Wings, gross 11·92 m² (128·3 sq ft)

WEIGHTS AND LOADINGS:
- Weight empty 177 kg (390 lb)
- Pilot weight range 68-113 kg (150-250 lb)
- Max recommended pilot and passenger weight 181 kg (400 lb)
- Max T-O weight 385 kg (850 lb)
- Max wing loading 32·2 kg/m² (6·6 lb/sq ft)
- Max power loading 9·92 kg/kW (16·35 lb/hp)

PERFORMANCE (pilot only, Rotax 503 engine):
- Never-exceed speed 78 knots (145 km/h; 90 mph)
- Max level speed 74 knots (137 km/h; 85 mph)
- Max cruising speed 65 knots (121 km/h; 75 mph)
- Stalling speed:
  - power on 24 knots (44 km/h; 27 mph)
  - power off 26 knots (49 km/h; 30 mph)
- Max rate of climb at S/L 442 m (1,450 ft)/min
- Service ceiling 6,100 m (20,000 ft)
- T-O run 23 m (75 ft)
- Landing run 46 m (150 ft)
- Range with max fuel, 70% power 239 nm (442 km; 275 miles)
- Endurance approx 3 h
- *g* limits +6/−3

DIEHL

DIEHL AERO-NAUTICAL

1855 North Elm, Jenks, Oklahoma 74037
Telephone: (918) 299 4445
PRESIDENT: Dan Diehl

DIEHL XTC HYDROLIGHT

The XTC (indicating both its function as a cross-terrain craft and the 'ecstasy' to be felt by its pilot) is a canard configuration, optionally amphibious, open or closed cockpit single-seater with full three-axis control. Design of the XTC began in December 1981, when construction of the prototype also started. This flew for the first time in March 1982. Production of kits began a year later. The XTC is constructed entirely of pre-moulded composites and is available in kit form only. It may be operated as an ultralight under FAR Pt 103 or as a homebuilt in the Experimental category. By February 1986 23 XTCs were flying from 64 kits delivered. The aircraft is designed for quick assembly; a lightweight road trailer is optional.

TYPE: Single-seat microlight or homebuilt landplane or amphibian.

AIRFRAME: Cantilever mid-mounted rear wing and high-set foreplane, of graphite and epoxy, with double surface Mylar, Tedlar or fabric covering. Thickness/chord ratio 14%. Wing dihedral 5°. Wing incidence 3°. Stabilising floats integral with wingtips. Three-axis control (rudder, foreplane elevators and spoilers). Glassfibre semi-monocoque fuselage. Twin fins and rudders of similar construction to wings. Optional instruments and trailer.

LANDING GEAR: Retractable tricycle type, with all three wheels size 10·6 × 3·5. Mainwheel tyre pressure 2·07 bars (30 lb/sq in); steerable nosewheel, tyre pressure 1·38 bars (20 lb/sq in). Spring mainwheel legs. Mainwheel brakes.

POWER PLANT: One 18·6 kW (25 hp) 294 cc KFM 107ER two-cylinder engine, with 2·2:1 reduction drive to a Prince two-blade wooden pusher propeller, or one 20 kW (27 hp) Rotax 277 single-cylinder engine with 2·5:1 reduction drive, or one 32 kW (43 hp) Rotax 447 two-cylinder engine with 2·0:1 reduction drive. Fuel tank capacity 19 litres (5 US gallons); 38 litres (10 US gallons) optional.

ACCOMMODATION: Pilot only, in enclosed or open cockpit, with capacity for 4·5 kg (10 lb) baggage aft of seat.

SYSTEM: 5A electrical system with alternator on engine.

DIMENSIONS, EXTERNAL:
- Wing span 9·75 m (32 ft 0 in)
- Wing chord: at root 1·52 m (5 ft 0 in)
  - at tip 0·91 m (3 ft 0 in)
- Wing aspect ratio 6·97
- Foreplane span 2·67 m (8 ft 9 in)
- Length overall 4·62 m (15 ft 2 in)
- Height overall 1·45 m (4 ft 9 in)
- Wheel track 1·83 m (6 ft 0 in)
- Wheelbase 3·66 m (12 ft 0 in)
- Propeller diameter 1·32 m (4 ft 4 in)

AREA:
- Wings, gross 13·66 m² (147·0 sq ft)

WEIGHTS AND LOADINGS:
- Weight empty 136 kg (300 lb)
- Pilot weight range 45-90 kg (100-200 lb)
- Max T-O weight 254 kg (560 lb)
- Max wing loading 18·55 kg/m² (3·8 lb/sq ft)
- Max power loading 13·66 kg/kW (22·4 lb/hp)

PERFORMANCE (KFM 107 engine, unless otherwise stated):
- Never-exceed speed 69 knots (129 km/h; 80 mph)
- Max level speed 52 knots (97 km/h; 60 mph)
- Max cruising speed:
  - KFM 107 43 knots (80 km/h; 50 mph)
  - Rotax 277 56 knots (104 km/h; 65 mph)
- Econ cruising speed 39 knots (72 km/h; 45 mph)
- Stalling speed 24 knots (44 km/h; 27 mph)
- Max rate of climb at S/L 152 m (500 ft)/min
- Service ceiling 3,110 m (10,200 ft)
- T-O and landing distance:
  - land and water 61 m (200 ft)
- T-O to, and landing from, 15 m (50 ft) 91 m (300 ft)
- Range with standard fuel 130 nm (241 km; 150 miles)
- Endurance with standard fuel 2 h 30 min
- *g* limits ±4
- Best glide ratio 14

DiMASCIO

DiMASCIO 'P-40'

An accompanying illustration shows a scale reproduction of a Second World War Curtiss P-40 single-seat fighter (N44PD) built by Mr P. DiMascio. No details are available, except that it is based on Bushby Midget Mustang plans, extensively modified. The landing gear is retractable.

DOUBLE EAGLE

DOUBLE EAGLE AIRCRAFT

4928 Eleanor Drive, Charlotte, North Carolina 28208
Telephone: (704) 392 5981 or 392 7013

DOUBLE EAGLE MODEL RF

Mr Eugene Livingston is the owner of Double Eagle Aircraft, and has been in the aircraft repair and development business for more than thirty years. He holds both a commercial pilot's licence and a glider pilot's licence, and over the course of many years has been responsible for constructing twenty-five aircraft in the 'experimental' category, including two aircraft of his own design.

Mr Livingston's latest aircraft is the Double Eagle Model RF, which is offered for construction by amateur builders in a series of kits. Design and construction of the prototype Double Eagle began in 1970 and this flew for the first time in 1979. The Double Eagle is one of the few twin-engined aircraft offered for amateur construction. It was described and illustrated in the 1985-86 and previous editions of *Jane's*.

DRIGGERS

MIKE DRIGGERS

Thomasville, North Carolina

DRIGGERS VERT-X

Mr Mike Driggers was employed formerly by the Bensen Aircraft Corporation, during which time he built a Gyro-Copter. In 1984, after ten months of development and construction, he flew a torque-free bolt-together helicopter of his own design, known initially as the Prop-Copter but now renamed Vert-X. The two 7·5 kW (10 hp) Chrysler West Bend engines were each mounted originally on a strut attached at 90° to the rotor blades. This strut has now been repositioned parallel to the blades, which has greatly reduced stick forces. At the same time, the original wooden propellers were superseded by Kevlar and carbonfibre two-blade propellers. The Vert-X is constructed of 6061-T6 square-section aluminium and has a Bede BD-5 swept fin and rudder. The rotor blades came from a Hughes 269 helicopter. A tricycle landing gear is standard. The prototype carries a small fuel tank of 1·9 litres (0·5 US gallon) capacity above the teetering rotor head for test flying, but an 11·3 litre (3 US gallon) tank will be standard. Mr Driggers expects to make kits available.

TYPE: Single-seat microlight helicopter.

DIMENSIONS, EXTERNAL:
- Rotor diameter 7·92 m (26 ft 0 in)
- Rotor blade chord 0·18 m (7 in)
- Length of fuselage 2·44 m (8 ft 0 in)
- Propeller diameter 0·71 m (2 ft 4 in)

WEIGHTS:
- Weight empty 82 kg (180 lb)
- Max T-O weight 204 kg (450 lb)

PERFORMANCE:
- Design cruising speed 43 knots (80 km/h; 50 mph)
- Max rate of climb at S/L 244 m (800 ft)/min
- Range with 11·3 litre (3 US gallon) fuel tank 43 nm (80 km; 50 miles)
- Endurance with 11·3 litre (3 US gallon) fuel tank 1 h

DURAND

DURAND ASSOCIATES INC

84th and McKinley Road, Omaha, Nebraska 68122
Telephone: (402) 571 7058

DURAND Mk V

Mr William H. Durand, a professional engineer, designed and built a two-seat all-metal biplane known as the Durand Mk V (N100DV). Design began in 1967, construction in 1970, and the first flight was achieved on 28 June 1978. Flight testing showed that the Durand Mk V cannot be stalled.

Plans of the Durand Mk V are available to amateur builders, and 73 sets had been sold by early 1986. Three Durand Mk Vs, other than the prototype, had been completed by that date.

TYPE: Two-seat homebuilt sporting biplane.

AIRFRAME: Negative stagger biplane with wings of constant chord. Wing section NACA 23012. Dihedral 0° upper wing, 2° 30′ lower wings. Incidence 3° both wings. No sweepback. Strut braced light alloy stressed skin structure with spars of box form. Full span flaps on upper and lower wings. Spoilers instead of ailerons, forward of flaps on lower wings only. Semi-monocoque fuselage of 2024-T3 light alloy. Cabin area skinned externally and internally, and insulated for temperature and sound. Cantilever tail unit of light alloy. All-moving tailplane has built-up box spar; fin and rudder have U section spars. Full span combined trim tab and anti-servo tab in tailplane.

LANDING GEAR: Non-retractable tricycle type. Cantilever main legs of reinforced glassfibre. All three wheels of Cleveland manufacture, with tyres size 5·00-5, pressure 2·07 bars (30 lb/sq in). It is intended to design fairings for the mainwheels. Cleveland hydraulic brakes.

POWER PLANT: One 112 kW (150 hp) Avco Lycoming O-320-E2A flat-four engine, driving a Sensenich two-blade fixed-pitch metal propeller with spinner. Fuel tank in forward fuselage, aft of firewall, capacity 93 litres (24·5 US gallons). Two auxiliary wing tanks optional, each 15 litres (4 US gallons), to provide max fuel capacity of 123 litres (32·5 US gallons). Refuelling point for main tank on upper surface of forward fuselage. Oil capacity 7·5 litres (2 US gallons).

ACCOMMODATION: Two seats side by side beneath forward sliding canopy. Full dual controls. Baggage space aft of seats, max capacity 58 kg (128 lb). Windscreen defroster. Cabin heated and ventilated.

SYSTEMS: Hydraulic system for brakes only. Electrical

Diehl XTC Hydrolight *(Ernest Koppe)*

DiMascio 'P-40', based on Midget Mustang plans *(Howard Levy)*

Driggers Vert-X microlight helicopter *(Howard Levy)*

Durand Mk V all-metal two-seat biplane *(Howard Levy)*

Modified Dyke Delta built by Mr Bernie Schaknowski (Avco Lycoming O-360 engine) *(Peter M. Bowers)*

system includes 60A engine driven alternator and 12V storage battery.

AVIONICS: Edo-Aire Mitchell nav/com can be installed optionally. Prototype has full IFR instrumentation, but is intended basically for VFR flying.

DIMENSIONS, EXTERNAL:

Wing span, both	7·47 m (24 ft 6 in)
Wing chord, constant (both)	0·914 m (3 ft 0 in)
Wing aspect ratio, effective biplane	5·1
Length overall	6·17 m (20 ft 3 in)
Height overall	2·03 m (6 ft 8 in)
Tailplane span	2·71 m (8 ft 10½ in)
Wheel track	2·13 m (7 ft 0 in)
Wheelbase	1·83 m (6 ft 0 in)
Propeller diameter	1·83 m (6 ft 0 in)

DIMENSIONS, INTERNAL:

Cabin: Length	2·03 m (6 ft 8 in)
Max width	1·09 m (3 ft 7 in)
Max height	1·22 m (4 ft 0 in)

AREA:

Wings, gross	13·38 m² (144·0 sq ft)

WEIGHTS AND LOADINGS:

Weight empty	549 kg (1,210 lb)
Max T-O weight	834 kg (1,840 lb)
Max wing loading	62·4 kg/m² (12·8 lb/sq ft)
Max power loading	7·45 kg/kW (12·27 lb/hp)

PERFORMANCE (at max T-O weight):

Never-exceed speed	147 knots (272 km/h; 169 mph)
Max cruising speed at 2,285 m (7,500 ft)	117 knots (217 km/h; 135 mph)
Econ cruising speed at 2,285 m (7,500 ft)	109 knots (201 km/h; 125 mph)
Landing speed	48 knots (89 km/h; 55 mph)
Max rate of climb at S/L	366 m (1,200 ft)/min
Absolute ceiling, estimated	4,575 m (15,000 ft)
T-O run	168 m (550 ft)
T-O to 15 m (50 ft)	503 m (1,650 ft)
Landing from 15 m (50 ft)	274 m (900 ft)
Landing run	137 m (450 ft)
Range, no reserves:	
standard fuel	347 nm (644 km; 400 miles)
max optional fuel	451 nm (837 km; 520 miles)

DYKE

DYKE AIRCRAFT

2840 Old Yellow Springs Road, Fairborn, Ohio 45324
Telephone: (513) 878 9832

Mr John W. Dyke was the designer of a small delta-wing aircraft, designated JD-1 Delta, which he built with Mrs Jennie Dyke. This was described in the 1964-65 *Jane's.* Subsequently, Mr Dyke developed the design, and the first flight of the JD-2 Delta was made in July 1966.

DYKE AIRCRAFT JD-2 DELTA

Plans of the JD-2 are available to amateur constructors, and a total of about 360 were thought to be under construction in early 1986, in Australia, Brazil, Canada, France, West Germany, Japan, New Zealand, South Africa, the United Kingdom and the United States. Thirty-five Deltas have been completed and flown.

As a help to the homebuilder, hardware and tubing kits are available.

A feature of the Dyke Delta is that the outer wing panels can be folded flat above the cockpit for easy towing and to allow storage in a single-car garage.

The Dyke Delta illustrated (N78BS) was built by Mr Bernie Schaknowski of Clay, NY. First flown on 1 June 1980, it differs from the standard Dyke Delta by having a lengthened nose, giving an overall length of 6·70 m (22 ft); glassfibre covering on the underfuselage, control surfaces and fin; mass balanced elevons; additional instruments; and other detail refinements. Power plant is a 134 kW (180 hp) Avco Lycoming O-360 flat-four engine. This aircraft won an 'Outstanding Workmanship' award at Oshkosh 1983. A standard Dyke Delta was illustrated in the 1980-81 *Jane's.*

TYPE: Delta-winged sporting homebuilt aircraft.

AIRFRAME: Delta wing of modified NACA 63012 and 66015 section. No dihedral. No incidence. Sweepback of wing centre-section 61°. Sweepback of outer wing panels 31°. Welded 4130 steel tube structure, with stainless steel capstrips to which the laminated glassfibre skins are secured by pop rivets. Aluminium skin optional. Trailing-edge elevons extending from centreline to approximately two-thirds span. Elevons have a basic structure of metal but are Poly-Fiber fabric covered. Trim tab at inboard edge of each elevon. Wing outer panels fold upward and lay above the fuselage so that the JD-2 can be towed on the landing gear. Folding and unfolding can be carried out by one person. Welded steel tube fuselage, with stainless steel capstrips and glassfibre skins, except for undersurface which has 4130 steel tube capstrips and Poly-Fiber fabric covering. Welded steel tube tail unit, with swept fin and rudder, both Poly-Fiber fabric covered. Optional all-moving T tailplane, with steel tube main spar and aluminium skin, for improved low-speed trim when a heavier engine, such as the 149 kW (200 hp) Avco Lycoming, is installed.

LANDING GEAR: Manually retractable tricycle type, all units retracting aft. Shock absorption by torsion bars of 6150 heat-treated steel. Mainwheels have tyres size 14 × 5-6, pressure 3·10 bars (45 lb/sq in). Steerable nosewheel, tyre size 12 × 5-4, pressure 2·07 bars (30 lb/sq in). Firestone hydraulic brakes.

POWER PLANT: Prototype has one 134 kW (180 hp) Avco Lycoming O-360 flat-four engine, driving a McCauley two-blade fixed-pitch propeller with spinner. Constant-speed propeller and 149 kW (200 hp) engine installation optional. Glassfibre fuel tank in fuselage, immediately aft of cabin, capacity 178 litres (47 US gallons), with pilot and two passengers. Fuel capacity reduced to 87 litres (23 US gallons) as a four-seat aircraft. Refuelling point on port side of aft fuselage upper surface. Oil capacity 7·5 litres (2 US gallons).

ACCOMMODATION: Standard accommodation for pilot, on single forward seat, and three passengers on aft bench seat. Access by upward opening canopy, hinged on starboard side. Accommodation is ventilated. Limited space for baggage in starboard wing centre-section.

SYSTEMS: Hydraulic system for brakes only. Vacuum system for instruments. Electrical supply from 12V DC generator; solid state inverter provides 110V AC at 400Hz.

AVIONICS AND EQUIPMENT: Genave Series 200A 200-channel nav and com transceiver, and 720 channel com. Blind-flying instrumentation standard.

DIMENSIONS, EXTERNAL:
Wing span 6·87 m (22 ft 2½ in)
Wing chord at root:
centre-section 4·27 m (14 ft 0 in)
outer panels 2·90 m (9 ft 6 in)
Wing chord at tip 0·51 m (1 ft 8 in)
Wing aspect ratio 2·7
Length overall 5·79 m (19 ft 0 in)
Width, wings folded 2·24 m (7 ft 4 in)
Height overall 1·68 m (5 ft 6 in)
Height overall, wings folded 1·83 m (6 ft 0 in)
Tailplane span (T tail) 0·91 m (3 ft 0 in)
Wheel track 1·97 m (6 ft 5½ in)
Wheelbase 2·13 m (7 ft 0 in)
Propeller diameter 1·88 m (6 ft 2 in)

DIMENSIONS, INTERNAL:
Cabin: Length 1·88 m (6 ft 2 in)
Max width 1·22 m (4 ft 0 in)
Max height 1·02 m (3 ft 4 in)
Floor area 1·67 m² (18 sq ft)
Baggage space 0·17 m³ (6 cu ft)

AREA:
Wings, gross 16·07 m² (173·0 sq ft)

WEIGHTS AND LOADINGS (with 134 kW; 180 hp or 149 kW; 200 hp engine):
Weight empty: basic equipped 481 kg (1,060 lb)
IFR equipped 490 kg (1,080 lb)
Max T-O weight 884 kg (1,950 lb)
Max landing weight 816 kg (1,800 lb)
Max wing loading 55·0 kg/m² (11·3 lb/sq ft)
Max power loading (180 hp) 6·60 kg/kW (10·83 lb/hp)

PERFORMANCE (at max T-O weight with 134 kW; 180 hp engine, except where indicated):
Never-exceed speed 191 knots (354 km/h; 220 mph)
Max level speed at 2,285 m (7,500 ft), constant-speed propeller 174 knots (322 km/h; 200 mph)
Max cruising speed at 2,285 m (7,500 ft), fixed-pitch propeller 156 knots (290 km/h; 180 mph)
Max cruising speed, constant-speed propeller 165 knots (306 km/h; 190 mph)
Max cruising speed, with 149 kW (200 hp) engine and constant-speed propeller 174 knots (322 km/h; 200 mph)
Econ cruising speed at 2,285 m (7,500 ft) 135 knots (249 km/h; 155 mph)
Max rate of climb at S/L 610 m (2,000 ft)/min
Service ceiling 4,420 m (14,500 ft)
Service ceiling, with 149 kW (200 hp) engine 5,485 m (18,000 ft)
T-O run 213 m (700 ft)
T-O to 15 m (50 ft) 549 m (1,800 ft)
Landing from 15 m (50 ft) 549 m (1,800 ft)
Landing run 244-305 m (800-1,000 ft)
Range with max fuel and pilot only, at 66% power 755 nm (1,400 km; 870 miles)
Range with max payload 576 nm (1,067 km; 663 miles)

EARTHSTAR

EARTHSTAR AIRCRAFT INC

Star Route 313, Santa Margarita, California 93453
Telephone: (805) 438 5235

Earthstar Aircraft has acquired the distribution and continued manufacturing rights of the Laughing Gull, Laughing Gull II and Ultra Gull microlight aircraft. In 1985 a larger production facility was constructed, and tooling is being established for an increase in production.

EARTHSTAR LAUGHING GULL and LAUGHING GULL II

The first of five prototype Laughing Gulls flew in 1976 and between them accumulated more than 800 flying hours. The Laughing Gull and its two-seat derivative, the Laughing Gull II were designed with certificated aircraft construction and safety features, and meet FAR Pt 103 requirements for microlights and trainers.

The Laughing Gull is available in ready assembled **LG1** form with a Rotax 277 engine, or can be purchased as an **LG1H** homebuilt kit with engine options of up to 30 kW (40 hp). The **T2** Laughing Gull II is fitted with dual controls as a trainer, and **T2H** homebuilt kits are available with engine options of up to 44·7 kW (60 hp). A cropduster model is also available.

TYPES: Single-seat (Laughing Gull) and two-seat (Laughing Gull II) single-engined microlight and homebuilt aircraft; conform to FAR Pt 103/7 in LG1 and T2 forms and FAA Experimental requirements in LG1H and T2H homebuilt forms.

AIRFRAME: Strut braced high-wing monoplanes, each with welded 4130 chromoly steel tube fuselage structure, fully enclosed cockpit with Lexan windows, tailboom and conventional tail unit. Airframe structure, other than fuselage, of 6061-T6 and 2024-T3 aluminium alloy. Double surface wings, with Dacron/Stits covering. Three-axis control (ailerons, elevators and rudder). Rigging time 10-20 min.

LANDING GEAR: Non-retractable tricycle type, with pultruded glassfibre rod shock absorbing legs. Mainwheel brakes. Steerable nosewheel. Tailwheel landing gear optional.

POWER PLANT: Laughing Gull: standard engine is one 20 kW (27 hp) Rotax 277 single-cylinder two-stroke, with 2·58:1 reduction gear to a pusher propeller. Homebuilt version can have engine of up to 30 kW (40 hp). Fuel tank capacity 19 litres (5 US gallons). Laughing Gull II: standard engine is one 44·7 kW (60 hp) Rotax 532. Homebuilt version can have engine of up to 44·7 kW (60 hp). Fuel capacity 38 litres (10 US gallons).

ACCOMMODATION: Single seat in fully enclosed cockpit (Laughing Gull); two seats in fully-enclosed cockpit, with dual controls (Laughing Gull II). Options include removable cockpit side windows.

DIMENSIONS, EXTERNAL (A: LG1, B: T2H):
Wing span: A 9·14 m (30 ft 0 in)
B 9·75 m (32 ft 0 in)
Length overall: A 5·49 m (18 ft 0 in)
B 5·79 m (19 ft 0 in)
Height overall: A 1·83 m (6 ft 0 in)
B 1·98 m (6 ft 6 in)
Propeller diameter: A 1·52 m (5 ft 0 in)

AREAS (A: LG1, B: T2H):
Wings, gross: A 13·94 m² (150·0 sq ft)
B 14·86 m² (160·0 sq ft)

WEIGHTS AND LOADINGS (A: LG1, B: T2H):
Weight empty: A 113 kg (250 lb)
B over 158 kg (350 lb)
Max T-O weight: A 227 kg (500 lb)
B 363 kg (800 lb)
Max wing loading: A 16·1 kg/m² (3·3 lb/sq ft)
B 24·4 kg/m² (5·0 lb/sq ft)
Max power loading: A 11·35 kg/kW (18·52 lb/hp)
B 8·12 kg/kW (13·33 lb/hp)

PERFORMANCE (A: LG1, B: T2H, unless stated otherwise):
Never-exceed speed:
A 82 knots (153 km/h; 95 mph)
B 104 knots (193 km/h; 120 mph)
Max level speed: A 55 knots (101 km/h; 63 mph)
B 91 knots (169 km/h; 105 mph)
Cruising speed:
A 48-52 knots (89-97 km/h; 55-60 mph)
B 74-78 knots (137-145 km/h; 85-90 mph)
Stalling speed: A 22 knots (41 km/h; 25 mph)
B 28 knots (52 km/h; 32 mph)
Max rate of climb at S/L: A 213 m (700 ft)/min
B 244 m (800 ft)/min
Service ceiling: A, B 4,420 m (14,500 ft)
T-O run: A 30 m (100 ft)
B 55 m (180 ft)
Landing run: A 30 m (100 ft)
B 69 m (225 ft)
Range with max fuel:
A 132 nm (244 km; 152 miles)
g limits: A, B +6/−4
Laughing Gull homebuilt +7/−5
Laughing Gull II +5·5/−3·8
Best glide ratio 12

EARTHSTAR ULTRA GULL

The Ultra Gull is a very different design to the company's Laughing Gull and Laughing Gull II, and has a special arrangement of high lift devices that allows it to be so small that no rigging is necessary before flying (as it is trailered fully assembled). The Ultra Gull has two fixed wings in tandem, the tips of which are connected by twin vertical stabilisers. This arrangement controls the wingtip vortices, giving the aircraft extra stability and better performance.

Three versions of the Ultra Gull are available, those in kit form coming in two phases (welded components or fast build). The basic single-seat Ultra Gull **U1** microlight is marketed in ready to fly form with a 15 kW (20 hp) Solo engine. The Ultra Gull Deluxe (**DU1**) has conventional three-axis control (ailerons, elevators and rudders), a fully enclosed cockpit with Lexan windows, steerable nosewheel and independent mainwheel brakes. In ready to fly form it has a 20 kW (27 hp) Rotax 277 engine with reduction gear. The third model in the range is the Ultra Gull Deluxe Homebuilt **DU1H**. It has the same features as the DU1 but with the ability to have any Rotax engine of 20-44·7 kW (27-60 hp) with reduction gear. This model can cruise at 122 knots (225 km/h; 140 mph).

The following details refer to the Ultra Gull DU1 and DU1H, unless stated otherwise.

TYPES: U1/DU1: Single-seat microlight aircraft. DU1H: Single-seat homebuilt aircraft.

AIRFRAME: All models are tandem wing biplanes, with wingtip stabilisers. Aluminium skinned wings, with tubular spar and foam core. Welded 4130 chromoly steel fuselage. All models have three-axis control (ailerons, elevators and rudders). Rigging time 1 min.

LANDING GEAR: Non-retractable tricycle type, with shock absorption. DU1 and DU1H have steerable nosewheel and independent mainwheel brakes.

POWER PLANT: U1: One 15 kW (20 hp) Solo engine, with 2·12:1 reduction gear to a three-blade pusher propeller. Engines for other models as detailed in introduction, all with 2·58:1 reduction gear. Fuel tank capacity 19 litres (5 US gallons), except 38 litres (10 US gallons) for DU1H.

ACCOMMODATION: Pilot only, in fully enclosed cockpit with Lexan windows.

DIMENSIONS, EXTERNAL (A: DU1, B: DU1H):
Wing span: A 7·32 m (24 ft 0 in)
B 6·10 m (20 ft 0 in)
Length overall: A, B 3·05 m (10 ft 0 in)
Height overall: A, B 1·83 m (6 ft 0 in)
Propeller diameter: A 1·52 m (5 ft 0 in)
B varies
U1 1·22 m (4 ft 0 in)

AREAS (A: DU1, B: DU1H):
Wings, gross: A 11·15 m² (120·0 sq ft)
B 7·43 m² (80·0 sq ft)

WEIGHTS AND LOADINGS (A: DU1, B: DU1H):
Weight empty: A 102 kg (225 lb)
B more than 105 kg (232 lb)
U1 91 kg (200 lb)
Max pilot weight: A, B 100 kg (220 lb)
Max T-O weight: A, B and U1 227 kg (500 lb)
Max wing loading: A 20·36 kg/m² (4·17 lb/sq ft)
B 30·55 kg/m² (6·25 lb/sq ft)
Max power loading: A 11·35 kg/kW (18·52 lb/hp)
B up to 5·08 kg/kW (8·33 lb/hp)

PERFORMANCE (A: DU1, B: DU1H with 44·7 kW; 60 hp engine):
Never-exceed speed:
A 87 knots (161 km/h; 100 mph)
B 134 knots (249 km/h; 155 mph)
Max level speed: A 55 knots (101 km/h; 63 mph)
B 130 knots (241 km/h; 150 mph)
Cruising speed: A 52 knots (97 km/h; 60 mph)
B 122 knots (225 km/h; 140 mph)
Stalling speed: A 24 knots (44 km/h; 27 mph)
B 28 knots (52 km/h; 32 mph)
Max rate of climb at S/L: A 274 m (900 ft)/min
B 472 m (1,550 ft)/min
Service ceiling: A, B 4,420 m (14,500 ft)
T-O run: A 38 m (125 ft)
B 43 m (140 ft)
Landing run: A 43 m (140 ft)
B 40 m (130 ft)
Range with max fuel:
A 145 nm (268 km; 167 miles)
g limits: A, B ±6
Best glide ratio: A 11·5
B 11

EASTERN ULTRALIGHTS

EASTERN ULTRALIGHTS INC

102 Fort Meyers Drive, PO Box 21, Indian Lake Estates, Florida 33855

Eastern Ultralights Inc appeared in the 1984-85 and previous editions of *Jane's* as manufacturer of the single-seat Snoop and Snoop Plus microlights and the side by side two-seat Snoop II. No information regarding the availability of these aircraft has been received since 1983, although it is believed that the Snoop and Snoop II are available in kit form, and that development of the double surface and shorter span Snoop Plus continues. A full description of these aircraft, and an illustration, can be found in the 1984-85 *Jane's*.

EAVES

LEONARD EAVES

Oklahoma City, Oklahoma

The 1968-69 *Jane's* carried details of the Skeeter 1M (N1111V), a side by side two-seat cabin monoplane with fabric covered, square section fuselage, cantilever low wings and conventional tail unit. Designed and built by Mr Leonard Eaves and first flown in 1966, it was followed during the 1970s by the Sting Ray, an unusual reverse delta-winged cabin monoplane of all-metal construction. Details of this aircraft are given below, together with initial

Earthstar Laughing Gull microlight aircraft

Earthstar Ultra Gull in Deluxe form

Eaves Sting Ray all-aerofoil two-seat cabin monoplane *(Howard Levy)*

Ebershoff-Steen Skybolt with a rear cockpit canopy *(Dr Dean Hall)*

Eaves Catfish under construction *(Howard Levy)*

information on Mr Eaves' latest design, the more conventional Catfish.

EAVES STING RAY

As a follow-on aircraft to the Skeeter, Mr Eaves designed an all-aerofoil proof-of-concept monoplane known as the Sting Ray, of which construction started in the early 1970s. It was flown for the first time in the mid-1970s. Differing substantially from the Skeeter, the Sting Ray has reverse delta wings, a T tail and an airframe skinned with metal. Weight and performance figures have not been released by Mr Eaves, although it has been reported that the Sting Ray is in the 272 kg (600 lb) empty weight and 87 knots (161 km/h; 100 mph) class. It is being used as a testbed for Mr Eaves' conversion of a Corvair aircooled motorcar engine. Flying time by early 1986 was reportedly less than two hours.

TYPE: Side by side two-seat homebuilt cabin monoplane.

AIRFRAME: All-metal airframe without wing spars, constructed mainly of welded square and angle tubing with stressed aluminium alloy skins. Drag and anti-drag tubes fitted internally to wings. Wing section NACA 64415 at root and 64412 for outer panels. Short ailerons on trailing-edge of outer panels, replacing original spoilers. T tail, with constant-chord one-piece elevator on fixed tailplane, and small fin and rudder, with dorsal fin.

LANDING GEAR: Tailwheel type, with 6·00-6 mainwheels which are designed to retract mechanically into wing centre-section wells, but are currently locked down. Steel tube mainwheel legs. Steerable tailwheel.

POWER PLANT: One 63·4 kW (85 hp) Corvair modified motorcar engine, with 1·39:1 reduction gear to two-blade propeller. Fuel tank in forward fuselage, capacity 57 litres (15 US gallons).

ACCOMMODATION: Two seats side by side in enclosed cabin. Entrance via port glazed door panel, which is integral with glazed roof panel and hinged on centreline. Baggage space.

DIMENSIONS, EXTERNAL:

Wing span	5·49 m (18 ft 0 in)
Wing chord: at root	4·88 m (16 ft 0 in)
at tip	0·203 m (8 in)
Length overall	5·49 m (18 ft 0 in)
Propeller diameter	1·63 m (5 ft 4 in)

EAVES CATFISH

The Catfish is Mr Eaves' latest design, with construction of the prototype continuing in early 1986. Like the Sting Ray, it is a side by side two-seat cabin monoplane of all-metal construction, with the square-section fuselage contributing to the aerofoil properties of the wings. However, its wings are of conventional cantilever low-mounted type, with 1·22 m (4 ft) detachable constant-chord outer panels connected to tapered centre-section panels. Wing section is NACA 64415. A single main wing spar is used, constructed of welded tubing with wraparound skins. The airframe is covered with metal skins from a B-36 bomber.

The Catfish has a mechanically retractable tailwheel landing gear, the wheel wells for which are left uncovered after retraction to act as air intakes for the watercooled 112-115·6 kW (150-155 hp) General Motors V-6 modified motorcar engine. The metal propeller is carried on an 0·66 m (2 ft 2 in) extension shaft; and the aircraft's 132·5 litres (35 US gallons) of fuel are contained in one 57 litre (15 US gallon) fuselage tank and two tip tanks. The cabin is entered via a starboard side door, and a baggage compartment is provided.

DIMENSIONS, EXTERNAL:

Wing span	7·32 m (24 ft 0 in)
Length overall	5·64 m (18 ft 6 in)
Height overall	1·52 m (5 ft 0 in)
Propeller diameter	1·52 m (5 ft 0 in)

WEIGHT:

Weight empty	420 kg (925 lb)

EBERSHOFF

EBERSHOFF AND COMPANY

Irongate IV, 777 South Wadsworth Boulevard, Suite 206, Lakewood, Colorado 80226
Telephone: (303) 980 8686

Mr David L. Ebershoff designed a modified version of the Steen Skybolt two-seat aerobatic biplane. Simplicity of construction was the primary aim of the redesign, as well as improved aerobatic capability, due largely to a significant increase in engine power and increased rate of roll. Construction of his prototype began in August 1978 and was completed in September 1981.

Plans for the Ebershoff-Steen Skybolt are available to amateur constructors, and by January 1986 a total of at least 4,300 sets had been sold.

EBERSHOFF-STEEN SKYBOLT

TYPE: Two-seat aerobatic homebuilt biplane.

AIRFRAME: Braced biplane with single interplane strut each side. N centre section struts. Streamline section landing and flying wires. Symmetrical wings. Wing sections: upper NACA 63_2A015, lower NACA 0012. Dihedral 0° on upper wing, 0° 30′ on lower wings. Incidence (both) 0° 30′. Sweepback 6° on upper wing only. Wooden two-spar structure, with spruce spars, routed to reduce weight, built-up ribs, and fabric covering. Fabric covered symmetrical ailerons on upper and lower wings. Cutout in centre-section trailing-edge of upper wing. Welded fuselage of 4130 chrome-molybdenum steel tube, with fabric covering. Wire braced welded tail unit of 4130 chrome-molybdenum steel tube, with fabric covering. Adjustable trim tab and dynamic balance in each elevator.

LANDING GEAR: Non-retractable tailwheel type. Two side Vs and half axles hinged to fuselage structure. Shock absorption by rubber bungee. Cleveland magnesium wheels with tyres size 6·00-6. Pressure 1·72 bars (25 lb/sq in). Cleveland hydraulic disc brakes. Rattray glassfibre fairings for mainwheels.

POWER PLANT: One 268·5 kW (360 hp) Avco Lycoming IO-540-K1A5 flat-six engine, driving a Hartzell constant-speed aerobatic propeller. Engine modified by Firewall Forward in Fort Collins, Colorado, with high dome helicopter pistons, milled heads, crankcase etc. Fuselage fuel tank immediately aft of firewall, capacity 110 litres (29 US gallons). Optional tank of 37·8 litres (10 US gallons) capacity is installed in centre-section of upper wing. Total fuel capacity 147·8 litres (39 US gallons). Refuelling points on fuselage upper surface, forward of windscreen, and on top surface of wing. Oil capacity 11·4 litres (3 US gallons).

ACCOMMODATION: Two seats in tandem in open cockpit. Provision for removable canopy over rear cockpits. Baggage space aft of rear seat, capacity 13·6 kg (30 lb).

AVIONICS: Battery-powered Edo-Aire 553RT radio and VOR nav/com transceiver.

DIMENSIONS, EXTERNAL:

Wing span: upper	7·32 m (24 ft 0 in)
lower	7·01 m (23 ft 0 in)
Wing chord, constant (both)	1·07 m (3 ft 6 in)
Length overall	5·79 m (19 ft 0 in)
Height overall	2·13 m (7 ft 0 in)
Propeller diameter	2·13 m (7 ft 0 in)

AREA:

Wings, gross	14·2 m² (152·7 sq ft)

WEIGHTS AND LOADINGS:

Weight empty	612 kg (1,350 lb)
Max T-O weight	907 kg (2,000 lb)
Max wing loading	53·9 kg/m² (13·1 lb/sq ft)
Max power loading	3·38 kg/kW (5·56 lb/hp)

PERFORMANCE (at max T-O weight):

Max level speed	191 knots (354 km/h; 220 mph)
Cruising speed	143 knots (265 km/h; 165 mph)
Landing speed	53 knots (97 km/h; 60 mph)
Max rate of climb at S/L	975 m (3,200 ft)/min
T-O run	134 m (440 ft)
Range with max fuel	325 nm (603 km; 375 miles)
g limits	±12

EICH

JAMES P. EICH

1820 W Grand Avenue, Alhambra, California 91801
Telephone: (818) 289 1983

After gaining considerable experience from flying a Barnett J-3M rotorcraft, Mr Eich designed and built a two-seat gyroplane of which details follow. Design started in 1975 and construction of the prototype began the following year. First flight was achieved in 1977.

Detailed drawings and instructions for building the JE-2 are available from: Tech Man Company, 8525 E Duarte Road, San Gabriel, California 91775. By January 1986 forty sets of plans had been sold.

EICH JE-2 GYROPLANE

The JE-2 prototype (N47143) now has a more powerful C85 engine, in place of the A65 that was installed initially, and rotor blades of marginally increased chord which have reduced the aircraft's speed. At least one other amateur-built JE-2 is flying, in the Netherlands (PH-GYR, with a 71 kW; 95 hp C95 engine).

The following details apply specifically to the prototype:

TYPE: Two-seat light autogyro.

ROTOR SYSTEM: Two-blade aluminium teetering rotor. Six struts forming the rotor pylon pick up the top of the fuselage structure at the corners of the front (passenger's) cockpit.

ROTOR DRIVE: Pre-rotation system only, comprising a Poulan chain saw motor which drives the rotor shaft through a V belt slip-belt 'clutch'.

AIRFRAME: Square section welded girder fuselage of chrome molybdenum steel tubing, covered with Dacron and finished with Stits Poly-dope. Fixed horizontal stabiliser, triangular ventral fin and rudder. Fin is of Dacron, integral with fuselage covering. Stabiliser and rudder are of sheet aluminium, with simple ribs and spars of aluminium tubing.

LANDING GEAR: Non-retractable tricycle type. Spring in compression shock absorption. Mainwheel tyres size 5·00-5, pressure 0·7 bars (10 lb/sq in). Steerable nose-wheel with tyre size 5·00-4, pressure 1·4 bars (20 lb/sq in). Go-kart brakes on mainwheels.

POWER PLANT: One 63·5 kW (85 hp) Continental C85 engine, driving a two-blade Eich wooden fixed-pitch propeller. Optional engines from A65 to O-200. One fuel tank aft of firewall, capacity 64·5 litres (17 US gallons). Oil capacity 3·8 litres (1 US gallon).

ACCOMMODATION: Two seats in tandem in open cockpits, with windscreens. Dual controls.

DIMENSIONS, EXTERNAL:

Main rotor diameter	7·92 m (26 ft 0 in)
Rotor blade chord	0·203 m (8 in)
Length of fuselage	4·27 m (14 ft 0 in)
Height overall	2·59 m (8 ft 6 in)
Wheel track	1·83 m (6 ft 0 in)
Wheelbase	1·65 m (5 ft 5 in)
Propeller diameter	1·78 m (5 ft 10 in)

WEIGHTS:

Weight empty	211 kg (465 lb)
Max T-O weight	417 kg (920 lb)

PERFORMANCE (with current rotor blades):

Never-exceed speed at 915 m (3,000 ft)	82 knots (153 km/h; 95 mph)
Max level speed at 915 m (3,000 ft)	70 knots (129 km/h; 80 mph)
Max cruising speed at 915 m (3 000 ft)	61 knots (113 km/h; 70 mph)
Econ cruising speed at 915 m (3,000 ft)	48 knots (89 km/h; 55 mph)
Min flying speed (no stall)	39 knots (73 km/h; 45 mph)
Max rate of climb at 915 m (3,000 ft)	91·5 m (300 ft)/min
T-O run with pre-rotation	153 m (500 ft)
T-O to 15 m (50 ft)	366 m (1,200 ft)
Landing from 15 m (50 ft)	61 m (200 ft)
Landing run	15 m (50 ft)
Range with max fuel and max payload	156 nm (290 km; 180 miles)

EIPPER

EIPPER INDUSTRIES

PO Box 1572, Temecula, California 92390
Telephone: (714) 676 6886
Telex: 499 0565
PRESIDENT: Lyle Byrum

Eipper's activities continue to concentrate upon the highly successful Quicksilver series of microlight aircraft, the initial versions of which were designed in 1972 by Mr Bob Lovejoy.

EIPPER QUICKSILVER

Production of weight-shift hang glider versions of the Quicksilver, which totalled about 2,000, ended in 1981. Eipper then developed the Quicksilver E powered hang glider (1983-84 *Jane's*), followed by the MX, the MX Super homebuilt version and the two-seat MXII. Further details of these models can be found in the 1984-85 edition. The most recent known variants are:

Quicksilver MXL. Developed three-axis version of MX, introduced in 1983. Smaller wing with rounded tips. Rigid seat. Rudder and full span ailerons linked to foot pedals.

Quicksilver MXL II. Side by side two-seat version of MXL. Wing area increased to 15·42 m² (166 sq ft).

The following data apply to the single-seat MXL:

TYPE: Single-seat microlight aircraft; conforms to both FAR Pt 103 and FAI requirements.

AIRFRAME: High-wing monoplane, with rudder and one-piece elevator supported on U-shaped rear twin booms. Wing dihedral 8°, incidence 2° 30'. Kingpost above centre-section. Framework of anodised aluminium alloy tubing. Stainless steel fittings; vinyl coated stainless steel cables. Dacron covered wings (double surface), elevator and rudder. Stick type controls.

LANDING GEAR: Tricycle type, with single unsprung 11 × 5·60 wheel/tyre on each unit. Non-steerable nosewheel. Mainwheel brakes optional. Wheel fairings, skis, floats and amphibious gear optional.

POWER PLANT: One 26 kW (35 hp) Rotax 337 two-cylinder two-stroke engine, with 2:1 belt reduction to two-blade wooden pusher propeller. Fuel capacity 19 litres (5 US gallons) standard.

ACCOMMODATION: Pilot only, in open position. Nose fairing optional.

DIMENSIONS, EXTERNAL:

Wing span	9·14 m (30 ft 0 in)
Wing aspect ratio	6·0
Length overall	5·51 m (18 ft 1 in)
Height overall	2·95 m (9 ft 8 in)
Propeller diameter	1·32 m (4 ft 4 in)

AREAS:

Wings, gross:	
MXL	13·94 m² (150·0 sq ft)
MXL II	15·42 m² (166·0 sq ft)

WEIGHTS AND LOADINGS:

Weight empty	112 kg (247 lb)
Pilot weight range	54-109 kg (120-240 lb)
Max T-O weight	249 kg (550 lb)
Max wing loading (MXL)	17·92 kg/m² (3·67 lb/sq ft)
Max power loading	9·96 kg/kW (16·4 lb/hp)

PERFORMANCE (with 79·5 kg; 175 lb pilot):

Never-exceed speed	64 knots (119 km/h; 74 mph)
Max level speed	53 knots (98 km/h; 61 mph)
Max cruising speed	47 knots (87 km/h; 54 mph)
Econ cruising speed	36 knots (66 km/h; 41 mph)
Stalling speed, power off	24 knots (44 km/h; 27 mph)
Max rate of climb at S/L	259 m (850 ft)/min
Service ceiling	3,050 m (10,000 ft)
T-O and landing run	23 m (75 ft)
Range with max fuel	99 nm (183 km; 114 miles)
Endurance with max fuel	2 h 43 min
g limits	+6/−3·8
Best glide ratio	7

EIPPER QUICKSILVER GT

The Quicksilver GT, despite its name, is an entirely new aircraft by designer David Cronk, and was introduced in 1984. The initial standard GT280 has a Rotax 277 engine and is available with cable (GT280C) or strut bracing (GT280S) at customer's option. The GT has tapered Dacron-covered wings, with both ailerons and four-position flaps, and meets FAA and PUMA (Powered Ultralight Manufacturers Association) standards. The single-boom fuselage is a two-piece 13 cm (5 in) diameter aluminium tube, supporting conventional cruciform tail surfaces. The spring loaded steerable nosewheel is fitted with a friction brake. A glassfibre nose 'bullet' and windscreen are standard; options include a wraparound fuselage pod or a full cockpit enclosure. Future planned versions include a GT350C (Rotax 377 engine) and kit built (FAA homebuilt) GT400 with a Rotax 477.

The following data apply to the GT280:

POWER PLANT: One 20 kW (27 hp) Rotax 277 engine, with 2·58:1 belt reduction to two-blade wooden pusher propeller. Fuel capacity 19 litres (5 US gallons).

DIMENSIONS, EXTERNAL:

Wing span	9·14 m (30 ft 0 in)
Wing aspect ratio	6·16
Length overall	6·20 m (20 ft 4 in)
Height overall	2·39 m (7 ft 10 in)
Propeller diameter	1·52 m (5 ft 0 in)

AREA:

Wings, gross	13·56 m² (146·0 sq ft)

WEIGHTS AND LOADINGS:

Weight empty, incl parachute:	
GT280C	122·5 kg (270 lb)
GT280S	124 kg (273 lb)
Max T-O weight	236 kg (520 lb)
Max wing loading	17·38 kg/m² (3·56 lb/sq ft)
Max power loading	11·24 kg/kW (18·57 lb/hp)

PERFORMANCE:

Never-exceed speed	64 knots (119 km/h; 74 mph)
Max level speed	50 knots (93 km/h; 58 mph)
Max cruising speed	48 knots (88 km/h; 55 mph)
Stalling speed, flaps down, power off	24 knots (44 km/h; 27 mph)
Max rate of climb at S/L	183 m (600 ft)/min
g limits	+4/−2 design
Best glide ratio	7

EVANS

EVANS AIRCRAFT

PO Box 744, La Jolla, California 92037

Mr W. S. Evans, while employed as a design engineer with the Convair Division of General Dynamics Corporation, set out to design for the novice homebuilder an all-wood aircraft that would be easy to build and safe to fly. He was prepared to sacrifice both appearance and performance to achieve this aim. Two years of spare-time design and a year of construction produced a strut braced low-wing monoplane with an all-moving tail unit, and powered initially by a 30 kW (40 hp) Volkswagen engine. Mr Evans named it the Volksplane but it was subsequently redesignated VP-1.

Mr Evans next developed a two-seat version of the VP-1, known as the VP-2. This is powered by a higher-rated Volkswagen engine, but in other respects has only minor constructional variations from the VP-1.

Plans of both models are available to amateur constructors, and approximately 4,000 sets had been sold by early 1986. Plans for European customers are supplied through the Popular Flying Association (PFA) in the UK (which see). VP-1 and VP-2 aircraft are currently flying in Australia, Belgium, Canada, France, West Germany, Italy, Ireland, Japan, New Zealand, Switzerland, the UK and the USA.

EVANS VP-1

TYPE: Single-seat homebuilt light aircraft.

AIRFRAME: Strut braced low-wing monoplane. Two streamline-section bracing struts on each side. Wing section NACA 4412. Square tips. Dihedral 5°. Conventional wood structure with two rectangular spar beams, internal wooden compression struts and diagonal wire bracing, dispensing with the need for a complicated box spar. Fabric covering. Ailerons of wood construction, fabric covered. No trim tabs. No flaps. Rectangular section all-wood fuselage, consisting essentially of three bulkheads, four longerons and plywood skin. Stressed skin design eliminates the need for diagonal bracing. Glassfibre fairing aft of pilot's seat. No fixed fin. The rudder is constructed of plywood ribs clamped to a 5 cm (2 in) aluminium tube which is mounted vertically through the rear fuselage and pivots in two nylon bushes. Leading- and trailing-edges are of wood and the whole unit is fabric covered. The fabric covered all-moving

Eich JE-2 Gyroplane (Continental C85 engine) with pre-rotation gear fitted

Eipper Quicksilver GT *(Brian M. Service)*

Eipper Quicksilver MXL with optional pilot fairing and wheel fairings

Evans VP-1 single-seat light aircraft, built in the UK with enclosed cockpit *(Geoffrey P. Jones)*

Two-seat Evans VP-2 with non-standard enclosed cockpit *(R. Kunert)*

Evergreen Ultralite Shadow II 503 light aircraft

tailplane is a wooden cantilever structure, comprising ply ribs blocked and glued to a simple constant section box spar. Both rudder and tailplane have anti-servo tabs.

Landing Gear: Non-retractable mainwheels and tailskid. Mainwheels carried on a bent section of heavy gauge 24ST-3 aluminium bar, wire braced by diagonal cables. Shock absorption by low pressure tyres. Mainwheels and tyres size 6·00-6, pressure 0·83 bars (12 lb/sq in). Hydraulic brakes operated by single hand lever.

Power Plant: One 30 kW, 39·5 kW or 44·5 kW (40 hp, 53 hp or 60 hp) modified Volkswagen motorcar engine, driving a Hegy two-blade propeller, with pitch of 0·61 m (24 in) for 30 kW (40 hp) engine, 0·76 m (30 in) for 39·5 kW (53 hp) and 0·91 m (36 in) for 44·5 kW (60 hp). Glassfibre fuel tank aft of firewall and integral with the forward fuselage cowling, capacity 30 litres (8 US gallons). Filling point on top of fuselage, forward of windscreen.

Accommodation: Single seat in open cockpit standard, although enclosed cockpit is commonplace on aircraft built in the UK. No baggage stowage.

Dimensions, external:

Wing span	7·32 m (24 ft 0 in)
Wing chord, constant	1·27 m (4 ft 2 in)
Length overall	5·49 m (18 ft 0 in)
Height overall	1·56 m (5 ft 1½ in)
Tailplane span	2·13 m (7 ft 0 in)
Wheel track	1·50 m (4 ft 11 in)
Propeller diameter	1·37 m (4 ft 6 in)

Area:

Wings, gross	9·29 m² (100·0 sq ft)

Weights and Loadings:

Weight empty	200 kg (440 lb)
Max T-O weight	340 kg (750 lb)
Max wing loading	36·6 kg/m² (7·5 lb/sq ft)
Max power loading (40 hp)	11·33 kg/kW (18·75 lb/hp)

Performance (30 kW; 40 hp engine, at T-O weight of 295 kg; 650 lb):

Never-exceed speed	104 knots (193 km/h; 120 mph)
Cruising speed	65 knots (121 km/h; 75 mph)
Stalling speed	35 knots (65 km/h; 40 mph)
Max rate of climb at S/L	122 m (400 ft)/min
T-O run (average breeze)	137 m (450 ft)
Landing run (average breeze)	61 m (200 ft)

EVANS VP-2

Except for an increase in overall dimensions, two seats side by side, and adoption of a higher rated Volkswagen engine as standard, the basic VP-2 is generally similar to the VP-1.

Type: Two-seat homebuilt light aircraft.

Airframe: Generally similar to VP-1, except for NACA 4415 wing section and increased wing span and chord. Fuselage width increased by 0·305 m (1 ft 0 in). No fin. Increased rudder area. All-moving tailplane of increased span and chord.

Landing Gear: Similar to VP-1. Wheel track increased by 0·23 m (9 in).

Power Plant: One 44·5 kW (60 hp) 1,834 cc or 48·5 kW (65 hp) 2,100 cc modified Volkswagen motorcar engine, driving a two-blade propeller. Glassfibre fuel tank aft of firewall, capacity 53 litres (14 US gallons).

Accommodation: Two seats side by side in open cockpit standard, although enclosed cockpit is commonplace on aircraft built in the UK.

Dimensions, external:

Wing span	8·23 m (27 ft 0 in)
Wing chord, constant	1·47 m (4 ft 10 in)
Length overall	5·87 m (19 ft 3 in)
Tailplane span	2·44 m (8 ft 0 in)
Wheel track	1·73 m (5 ft 8 in)
Propeller diameter	1·52 m (5 ft 0 in)

Area:

Wings, gross	12·08 m² (130·0 sq ft)

Weights and Loadings:

Weight empty	290 kg (640 lb)
Max T-O weight	471 kg (1,040 lb)
Max wing loading	39·06 kg/m² (8·0 lb/sq ft)
Max power loading (60 hp)	10·58 kg/kW (17·33 lb/hp)

Performance (44·5 kW; 60 hp engine, at max T-O weight):

Never-exceed speed	104 knots (193 km/h; 120 mph)
Max level speed	87 knots (161 km/h; 100 mph)
Max cruising speed	65 knots (121 km/h; 75 mph)
Stalling speed	35 knots (65 km/h; 40 mph)
Max rate of climb at S/L:	
pilot only	213 m (700 ft)/min
pilot and passenger	122 m (400 ft)/min

EVERGREEN

EVERGREEN ULTRALITE INC (A Division of First Class Aircraft Inc)

14215 NE 193rd Place, Woodinville, Washington 98072

Telephone: (206) 487 0230

Vice-President: Daniel T. Krpan

EVERGREEN ULTRALITE SHADOW I 377

Type: Single-seat microlight aircraft; conforms to FAR Pt 103.

Airframe: Conventional high-wing monoplane with cruciform tail surfaces. Main structure of aluminium alloy. Wings have 40 per cent double surface Dacron covering, with kingpost and vinyl coated stainless steel cable bracing. Three-axis control (rudder, elevator and spoilers). Optional instruments and parachute recovery system.

LANDING GEAR: Tricycle type, with steerable nosewheel. Brakes and floats optional.

POWER PLANT: One 26 kW (35 hp) Rotax 377 engine, with 2·4:1 reduction drive via Flexidyne clutch mechanism to a three-blade composite material ground-adjustable pusher propeller. Fuel tank capacity 16 litres (4·25 US gallons).

ACCOMMODATION: Pilot only, in open position.

DIMENSIONS, EXTERNAL:

Wing span	9·75 m (32 ft 0 in)
Length overall	4·95 m (16 ft 3 in)
Height overall	3·00 m (9 ft 10 in)
Propeller diameter	1·50 m (4 ft 11 in)

AREA:

Wings, gross	14·86 m² (160·0 sq ft)

WEIGHTS AND LOADINGS:

Weight empty	114 kg (251 lb)
Pilot weight range	45-147 kg (100-325 lb)
Max T-O weight	261 kg (576 lb)
Max wing loading	17·58 kg/m² (3·60 lb/sq ft)
Max power loading	10·44 kg/kW (17·19 lb/hp)

PERFORMANCE:

Never-exceed speed	54 knots (101 km/h; 63 mph)
Max level speed	52 knots (97 km/h; 60 mph)
Max cruising speed	39 knots (72 km/h; 45 mph)
Stalling speed:	
power on	18 knots (32 km/h; 20 mph)
power off	19 knots (36 km/h; 22 mph)
Max rate of climb at S/L	274 m (900 ft)/min
Service ceiling	3,660 m (12,000 ft)
T-O run	26 m (85 ft)
Landing run	23 m (75 ft)
Range with max fuel	82 nm (153 km; 95 miles)
Endurance with max fuel	2 h 15 min
g limits	+4·4/−2·5

EVERGREEN ULTRALITE SHADOW II 503

The Shadow II is a side by side two-seat version of the Shadow I. It is essentially similar, except as follows:

TYPE: Two-seat light aircraft.

POWER PLANT: One 34·3 kW (46 hp) Rotax 503 engine and 19 litre (5 US gallon) fuel tank.

WEIGHTS AND LOADINGS:

Weight empty	141 kg (310 lb)
Max T-O weight	340 kg (750 lb)
Max wing loading	22·56 kg/m² (4·62 lb/sq ft)
Max power loading	8·84 kg/kW (14·51 lb/hp)

PERFORMANCE: As for Shadow I except:

Never-exceed speed	56 knots (104 km/h; 65 mph)
Max cruising speed	43 knots (80 km/h; 50 mph)
Econ cruising speed	41 knots (76 km/h; 47 mph)
Stalling speed	23 knots (42 km/h; 26 mph)
Max rate of climb at S/L	137 m (450 ft)/min
T-O run	52 m (170 ft)
Landing run	40 m (130 ft)

FIRST STRIKE

FIRST STRIKE AVIATION INC

4 Wade Avenue, Piggott, Arkansas 72454
Telephone: (501) 598 5126
PRESIDENT: Bobby Baker
VICE-PRESIDENT: Bruce James
SECRETARY-TREASURER: Kay Baker

FIRST STRIKE BOBCAT and SUPERCAT

Conceived by Mr Bobby Baker, the Bobcat is a microlight of conventional aeroplane configuration. Design began in August 1983 and construction of the prototype started in the following October. The first flight was achieved in May 1984. Kit production was established in April 1985 and by late January 1986 a total of 124 had been sold, in addition to about 500 sets of plans. Kits have been delivered to customers in Australia, Canada, Denmark, Costa Rica, Puerto Rico, Sweden and the USA.

Although suitable for limited use as agricultural and firefighting aircraft, with a few examples to be found on farms, most Bobcats are flown as recreational lightplanes.

The total number of kits delivered (as quoted above) includes examples of the similar but Experimental category Supercat. In addition to its more powerful Rotax 377 two-cylinder engine, it has stronger fuselage and wing construction, 45 kg (100 lb) extra load carrying capacity, a longer airframe life, and performance improvements, including a shorter take-off run and better rate of climb. Supercat kits include an engine with reduction gearbox, quick connect streamline aluminium tubing wing struts, heavy duty tailwheel, and the necessary materials for the wing and fuselage modifications. Estimated building time of a Bobcat/Supercat is 150-200 working hours. Individual component parts are available to builders using plans only.

TYPE: Single-seat microlight (Bobcat) and homebuilt (Supercat) aircraft.

AIRFRAME: Strut-braced low-wing monoplane, with conventional wire braced upward foldable tail unit. Fuselage uses spruce longerons and plywood bulkheads, the wings spruce capped foam ribs with plywood D section leading-edge, all Ceconite 7600 fabric covered. Glassfibre engine cowling. Three-axis control system (ailerons, elevators and rudder). Rigging time 20 min.

LANDING GEAR: Non-retractable tailwheel type, with steerable tailwheel on moulded glassfibre spring. Size 4·80 × 4·00-8 mainwheels, with optional drum brakes, carried on two side Vs and half axles of 4130 steel tubing.

POWER PLANT: Bobcat: one 20 kW (27 hp) Rotax 277 single-cylinder two-stroke engine, with 2·1:1 belt reduction drive to a two-blade wooden propeller with spinner. Supercat: one 26 kW (35 hp) Rotax 377 two-cylinder engine, with 2·58:1 reduction gearbox. Fuel capacity 19 litres (5 US gallons) in Bobcat.

ACCOMMODATION: Single seat in semi-enclosed cabin (upward hinged glassfibre roof panel, forward and rear windscreens, no cockpit side glazing).

DIMENSIONS, EXTERNAL:

Wing span	8·43 m (27 ft 8 in)
Length overall	4·65 m (15 ft 3 in)
Height overall	1·83 m (6 ft 0 in)
Wheel track	1·83 m (6 ft 0 in)
Propeller diameter: Bobcat	1·52 m (5 ft 0 in)
Supercat	1·73 m (5 ft 8 in)

AREA:

Wings, gross	10·41 m² (112·0 sq ft)

WEIGHTS AND LOADINGS (A: Bobcat, B: Supercat):

Weight empty: A	114 kg (251 lb)
B	136 kg (300 lb)
Max T-O weight: A	226 kg (500 lb)
B	283 kg (625 lb)
Max wing loading: A	21·8 kg/m² (4·46 lb/sq ft)
B	27·2 kg/m² (5·58 lb/sq ft)
Max power loading: A	11·30 kg/kW (18·52 lb/hp)
B	10·88 kg/kW (17·86 lb/hp)

PERFORMANCE (A: Bobcat, B Supercat):

Never-exceed speed: A	69 knots (128 km/h; 80 mph)
B	86 knots (161 km/h; 100 mph)
Max level speed: A	55 knots (101 km/h; 63 mph)
B	65 knots (121 km/h; 75 mph)
Max cruising speed:	
A	39-43 knots (72-80 km/h; 45-50 mph)
B	48-52 knots (89-97 km/h; 55-60 mph)
Stalling speed: A	24 knots (44 km/h; 27 mph)
B	28 knots (52 km/h; 32 mph)
Max rate of climb at S/L: A	213 m (700 ft)/min
B	305 m (1,000 ft)/min
T-O run: A	38 m (125 ft)
B	23 m (75 ft)
Landing run: A	61 m (200 ft)
g limits: A	±4
B	+5·5/−4·5

FISHER

FISHER FLYING PRODUCTS INC

Route 2, Box 282S, South Webster, Ohio 45682
Telephone: (614) 778 3185
PRESIDENT: Michael E. Fisher
VICE PRESIDENT, MARKETING: Clifford Rock

All known details of Mr Fisher's Flyer were given in the 1982-83 *Jane's*. The Barnstormer and Boomerang, described in the 1983-84 *Jane's*, were offered in plan form for amateur construction. Mr Fisher's current products are thought to be the FP-101, FP-202 Koala, Super Koala, FP-303, FP-404 and FP-505.

FISHER FP-101

First flown in mid-1982, the FP-101 is marketed in kit form (airframe only, or with 20 kW; 27 hp Rotax 277 engine).

TYPE: Single-seat microlight aircraft; conforms to FAR Pt 103.

AIRFRAME: Braced high-wing monoplane with fully covered fuselage and cruciform tail surfaces. Aluminium tube V bracing struts. Moulded glassfibre engine cowling. Rest of structure of geodetic wood construction, covered with doped Stits Poly-Fiber fabric (double surface on wings). Stainless steel cables. Three-axis control (ailerons, elevators and rudder). Rigging time 15 min.

LANDING GEAR: Non-retractable tailwheel type, with welded legs. Mainwheel size 14 × 4 in, with bungee shock absorption. 3 in steerable tailwheel. Brakes and wheel fairings optional.

POWER PLANT: Engine supplied by manufacturer is a 20 kW (27 hp) Rotax 277 single-cylinder two-stroke, with 2·58:1 geared reduction drive to a two-blade wooden propeller. Electric starting optional. Fuel tank capacity 19 litres (5 US gallons).

ACCOMMODATION: Pilot only, in semi-enclosed cockpit. Lexan windscreen standard; side curtains and manifold heater optional.

DIMENSIONS, EXTERNAL:

Wing span	8·79 m (28 ft 10 in)
Wing aspect ratio	7·17
Length overall	5·03 m (16 ft 6 in)
Height overall	1·73 m (5 ft 8 in)
Propeller diameter	1·52 m (5 ft 0 in)

AREA:

Wings, gross	10·78 m² (116·0 sq ft)

WEIGHTS AND LOADINGS:

Weight empty	112 kg (247 lb)
Pilot weight range	45·5-100 kg (100-220 lb)
Max T-O weight	227 kg (500 lb)
Max wing loading	21·06 kg/m² (4·31 lb/sq ft)
Max power loading (Rotax 277 engine)	11·35 kg/kW (18·52 lb/hp)

PERFORMANCE (Rotax 277 engine):

Never-exceed speed	54 knots (101 km/h; 63 mph)
Max level speed	52 knots (97 km/h; 60 mph)
Max cruising speed	48 knots (88 km/h; 55 mph)
Econ cruising speed	43 knots (80 km/h; 50 mph)
Stalling speed	23 knots (42 km/h; 26 mph)
Max rate of climb at S/L	183 m (600 ft)/min
T-O run	46 m (150 ft)
Landing run	38 m (125 ft)
Range with max fuel	130 nm (241 km; 150 miles)
Endurance with max fuel	3 h
g limits	+4·6/−2·3
Best glide ratio	9

FISHER FP-202 KOALA

The FP-202 Koala is similar to the FP-101, but has rounded tail surfaces, simulating the appearance of a Piper Cub.

A large number of Koala kits have been sold. In addition, the aircraft became available in ready assembled form in May 1985. In this form it has a fully enclosed cabin with removable side windows, detachable wings for towing and storage, and a basic instrument panel. A horn balanced rudder, increased cabin glazing and wing flaps are fitted to all Koalas, which can be completed optionally with a pre-welded chrome-molybdenum steel tube fuselage. Description is otherwise as for FP-101.

DIMENSIONS, EXTERNAL:

Wing span	8·84 m (29 ft 10 in)
Wing aspect ratio	7·42
Length overall	5·41 m (17 ft 9 in)
Height overall	1·70 m (5 ft 7 in)

AREA:

Wings, gross	11·15 m² (120·0 sq ft)

WEIGHTS AND LOADING:

Weight empty	113 kg (250 lb)
Max T-O weight	227 kg (500 lb)
Max wing loading	20·36 kg/m² (4·17 lb/sq ft)

PERFORMANCE:

Never-exceed speed	65 knots (121 km/h; 75 mph)
Max cruising speed	52 knots (97 km/h; 60 mph)
Econ cruising speed	48 knots (89 km/h; 55 mph)
Stalling speed:	
power on	23 knots (42 km/h; 26 mph)
power off	21 knots (39 km/h; 24 mph)
Max rate of climb at S/L	228 m (750 ft)/min
T-O run	46 m (150 ft)
Landing run	38 m (125 ft)
Range with max fuel	143 nm (265 km; 165 miles)
Endurance with max fuel	3 h
g limits	+4·6/−2·3
Best glide ratio	9

FISHER SUPER KOALA

The Super Koala is a two-seat variant of the Koala, with side by side seating, a more powerful Rotax 503 engine, increased dimensions and weights, and higher performance. The prototype flew for the first time in the Spring of 1984 and the company began delivering kits in January 1985. Two types of kit are available: the standard kit that takes approximately 400 working hours to complete and a quick-build kit requiring only 150 working hours due to the factory prefabricated spars, ribs, fuselage sides, tail unit, bulkheads, formers, engine cowling, fuel tank and other items. Like the FP-202, the Super Koala can be fitted optionally with a pre-welded chrome-molybdenum steel tube fuselage.

The description of the FP-101 applies generally to the Super Koala, except as follows:

TYPE: Two-seat microlight aircraft; has training exemption to FAR Pt 103 and conforms to Canadian regulations.

AIRFRAME: As for FP-101, but with side by side seating and dual controls. Increased cabin glazing. Horn balanced rudder and wing flaps. Rigging time 20 min.

POWER PLANT: One 35·8 kW (48 hp) Rotax 503 engine (optionally 47·7 kW; 64 hp Rotax 532), with 2·58:1 geared reduction to two-blade wooden propeller. Fuel tank capacity 19 litres (5 US gallons). Auxiliary tank can be carried, of up to 19 litres (5 US gallons) capacity. Electric starting optional.

First Strike Bobcat cabin microlight

First kit built First Strike Supercat homebuilt cabin monoplane, constructed by Mr John Parker in nine weeks *(Howard Levy)*

Fisher FP-202 Koala

Fisher FP-101 single-seat microlight

Fisher FP-303 low-wing microlight aircraft

Fisher FP-404 Classic single-seat light biplane *(Geoffrey P. Jones)*

DIMENSIONS, EXTERNAL:
- Wing span: 9·45 m (31 ft 0 in)
- Wing aspect ratio: 6·9
- Length overall: 5·51 m (18 ft 1 in)
- Height overall: 1·70 m (5 ft 7 in)
- Propeller diameter: 1·83 m (6 ft 0 in)

AREA:
- Wings, gross: 13·0 m² (140·0 sq ft)

WEIGHTS AND LOADINGS:
- Weight empty: 152 kg (335 lb)
- Pilot weight range: 45·5-163 kg (100-360 lb)
- Max T-O weight: 335 kg (740 lb)
- Max wing loading: 25·8 kg/m² (5·29 lb/sq ft)
- Max power loading: 9·36 kg/kW (15·42 lb/hp)

PERFORMANCE:
- Never-exceed speed: 78 knots (145 km/h; 90 mph)
- Max level speed: 69 knots (129 km/h; 80 mph)
- Max cruising speed: 65 knots (121 km/h; 75 mph)
- Econ cruising speed: 48 knots (88 km/h; 55 mph)
- Stalling speed: power on: 26 knots (49 km/h; 30 mph)
- power off: 28 knots (52 km/h; 32 mph)
- Max rate of climb at S/L: 244 m (800 ft)/min
- T-O and landing run: 61 m (200 ft)
- Range with max standard fuel: 126 nm (233 km; 145 miles)
- Endurance: 2 h
- g limits: +4·6/−2·3
- Best glide ratio: 9
- Min rate of sink at 39 knots (72 km/h; 45 mph): 91 m (300 ft)/min

FISHER FP-303

The FP-303 first flew in January 1984 and was displayed at the Sun 'n Fun meeting in Lakeland, Florida, in the Spring of that year. By February 1985, when the last information was received, a total of 86 FP-303 kits had been sold.

TYPE: Single-seat microlight aircraft; conforms to FAR Pt 103 and FAI/CAA regulations.

AIRFRAME: Braced low-wing monoplane. Fuselage structure of plywood, with geodetic framework aft of open cockpit, Dacron covered. Constant chord strut braced wings are constructed around I beam main spar, capped with solid plywood web, double surface Dacron covered. Three-axis control (ailerons, elevators and rudder), with flaps. Rigging time 5 min.

LANDING GEAR: Non-retractable tailwheel type, with steerable tailwheel. Mainwheel size 14 × 4 in; tailwheel diameter 3 in. Optional brakes on mainwheels.

POWER PLANT: One 20 kW (27 hp) Rotax 277 engine, with 2·58:1 reduction drive to a two-blade wooden propeller. Fuel capacity 9·5 litres (2·5 US gallons). Optional 9·5 litre (2·5 US gallon) auxiliary tank.

ACCOMMODATION: Pilot only, in open cockpit. Optional cockpit enclosure.

DIMENSIONS, EXTERNAL:
- Wing span: 8·43 m (27 ft 8 in)
- Wing aspect ratio: 6·92
- Length overall: 5·03 m (16 ft 6 in)
- Height overall: 1·57 m (5 ft 2 in)
- Propeller diameter: 1·52 m (5 ft 0 in)

AREA:
- Wings, gross: 10·3 m² (111·0 sq ft)

WEIGHTS AND LOADINGS:
- Weight empty: 107 kg (235 lb)
- Pilot weight range: 45·5-95 kg (100-210 lb)
- Max T-O weight: 204 kg (450 lb)
- Max wing loading: 19·8 kg/m² (4·05 lb/sq ft)
- Max power loading: 10·20 kg/kW (16·67 lb/hp)

PERFORMANCE:
- Never-exceed speed: 60 knots (112 km/h; 70 mph)
- Max level speed: 52 knots (97 km/h; 60 mph)
- Max cruising speed: 50 knots (93 km/h; 58 mph)
- Econ cruising speed: 43-48 knots (80-89 km/h; 50-55 mph)
- Stalling speed: power on: 21 knots (39 km/h; 24 mph)
- power off: 23 knots (42 km/h; 26 mph)
- Max rate of climb at S/L: 228 m (750 ft)/min
- Service ceiling: 3,350 m (11,000 ft)
- T-O run: 38 m (125 ft)
- Landing run: 40 m (130 ft)
- Range with max standard fuel: 72 nm (133 km; 83 miles)

Endurance	1 h 30 min
g limits	+4·6/−2·3
Best glide ratio	9
Min rate of sink at 35 knots (64 km/h; 40 mph)	91 m (300 ft)/min

FISHER FP-404 CLASSIC

The FP-404 is a single-seat light biplane, available as a complete or partial kit. The single-bay wooden geodetic wings have tubular N type interplane struts, cabane struts and V struts, the latter attached to the bottom of the wooden geodetic fuselage at the juncture with the side V main legs of the tailwheel type landing gear. The mainwheels can be faired; the tailwheel is steerable. A semi-symmetrical wing section is employed, and three-axis control is standard (full-span ailerons, elevators and rudder). Both the tailplane and fin are strut braced. The pilot's cockpit is open but is provided with a small windscreen. Either a 35·8 kW (48 hp) Rotax 503 or a 47·7 kW (64 hp) Rotax 532 engine can be fitted. Mr John Smith assisted Mr Michael Fisher in the FP-404's design, and the first kits have been delivered to US customers. Rigging time is 20 minutes.

The following details apply to the version with a Rotax 503 engine:

DIMENSIONS, EXTERNAL:	
Wing span	5·49 m (18 ft 0 in)
Length overall	4·42 m (14 ft 6 in)
AREA:	
Wings, gross	11·15 m² (120·0 sq ft)
WEIGHTS AND LOADINGS:	
Weight empty	127 kg (280 lb)
Max T-O weight	245 kg (540 lb)
Max wing loading	21·97 kg/m² (4·50 lb/sq ft)
Max power loading	6·80 kg/kW (11·25 lb/hp)
PERFORMANCE:	
Max cruising speed	70 knots (128 km/h; 80 mph)
Econ cruising speed	52 knots (97 km/h; 60 mph)
Stalling speed	26 knots (49 km/h; 30 mph)
Max rate of climb at S/L	213 m (700 ft)/min
T-O run	38 m (125 ft)
g limits	+6/−3
Best glide ratio	8

FISHER FP-505 SKEETER

The FP-505 single-seat parasol-wing microlight is a derivative of John Smith's Skeeter, modified to employ Fisher components. It uses an FP-101/202 type wing and FP-202 landing gear, with the tail unit and wingtips contoured to Pietenpol style of the 1930s. Like the other aircraft in the Fisher range, the FP-505 airframe is of wooden geodetic construction with fabric covering, with the landing gear and attachment fittings of 6061-T6 aluminium alloy. Kits are available with or without the engine; or the engine can be purchased separately, with reduction gear and propeller. Construction time is estimated at 200-250 hours. Rigging time is 15 minutes.

TYPE: Single-seat microlight aircraft.

POWER PLANT: One 20 kW (27 hp) Rotax 277 single-cylinder two-stroke engine, with 2·58:1 reduction gear to a two-blade propeller. Fuel capacity 19 litres (5 US gallons). Fuel consumption 5·6 litres (1·5 US gallons) of auto fuel per hour.

DIMENSIONS, EXTERNAL:	
Wing span	8·53 m (28 ft 0 in)
Length overall	5·03 m (16 ft 6 in)
AREA:	
Wings, gross	10·41 m² (112·0 sq ft)
WEIGHTS AND LOADINGS:	
Weight empty	111 kg (245 lb)
Max T-O weight	227 kg (500 lb)
Max wing loading	21·78 kg/m² (4·46 lb/sq ft)
Max power loading	11·35 kg/kW (18·52 lb/hp)
PERFORMANCE:	
Cruising speed	48-52 knots (89-97 km/h; 55-60 mph)
Stalling speed	23 knots (42 km/h; 26 mph)
Max rate of climb at S/L	213-244 m (700-800 ft)/min
T-O run	46 m (150 ft)
g limits	+4·6/−2·3

FISHER CULEX

The prototype (N85MF) of this tandem two-seat, twin-engined kit built aircraft was displayed for the first time at Oshkosh 86 and is shown in an accompanying illustration. It is powered by two 59·6 kW (80 hp) Limbach 2000 engines, each driving a Hoffmann two-blade variable-pitch propeller, and has a fuel capacity of 174 litres (46 US gallons). Wing and tail unit are cantilever. The cockpit is enclosed by a blister canopy.

DIMENSIONS, EXTERNAL:	
Wing span	9·40 m (30 ft 10 in)
Wing chord, constant	1·52 m (5 ft 0 in)
Wing aspect ratio	6·17
Length overall	6·20 m (20 ft 4 in)
Height overall	1·93 m (6 ft 4 in)
AREA:	
Wings, gross	14·31 m² (154·0 sq ft)
WEIGHTS AND LOADINGS:	
Weight empty	431 kg (950 lb)
Max T-O weight: aerobatic	680 kg (1,500 lb)
utility	794 kg (1,750 lb)
Max wing loading	55·48 kg/m² (11·36 lb/sq ft)
Max power loading	6·62 kg/kW (10·94 lb/hp)
PERFORMANCE (estimated at utility T-O weight):	
Never-exceed speed	182 knots (338 km/h; 210 mph)
Max level speed	130 knots (241 km/h; 150 mph)
Max cruising speed	113 knots (209 km/h; 130 mph)
Stalling speed	37 knots (68 km/h; 42 mph)
Max rate of climb at S/L	548 m (1,800 ft)/min
Rate of climb at S/L, one engine out	152 m (500 ft)/min
T-O run	92 m (300 ft)
Landing run	76 m (250 ft)
Range with max fuel	677 nm (1,255 km; 780 miles)
g limits	+6·5/−3

FISHERCRAFT

FISHERCRAFT INC

4356 Narrows Road, Perry, Ohio 44081
Telephone: (216) 259 4412
PRESIDENT: Ed Fisher

FISHERCRAFT ZIPPY SPORT

Fishercraft Inc is marketing plans of a single-seat cabin lightplane known as the Zippy Sport, designed by Mr Ed Fisher. Design of the Zippy Sport began in the Spring of 1979 and construction of the first prototype started that Summer. This aircraft (N81ZS) flew for the first time on 9 October 1982 and received FAA certification in the Unlimited Experimental category in January 1983. By then a second prototype was under construction, built from the plans available to amateur constructors, and a third followed. By January 1986 fifty-five sets of plans had been sold and aircraft were under construction in Canada, the UK and USA. Three Zippy Sports have flown, with three more expected to fly in 1986.

The following description applies to the plans-built Zippy Sport:

TYPE: Single-seat homebuilt aircraft.

AIRFRAME: Strut braced high-wing monoplane. Wing section NACA 4412. No dihedral or anhedral. Incidence 1° 30′. Wooden spars and duralumin ribs, fabric covered. V struts each side. Near full span ailerons of aluminium alloy construction. Wings fold for transportation and storage. Rectangular section steel tube fuselage, fabric covered. Conventional cantilever tail unit, also of steel tubing with fabric covering.

LANDING GEAR: Non-retractable tailwheel type. Cantilever aluminium alloy spring main legs. Azusa aluminium go-kart mainwheels, fitted with Carlisle 3·50-5 tyres of 10½ in diameter. Pressure 1·72 bars (25 lb/sq in). Kilian solid rubber castoring tailwheel. Azusa mainwheel drum brakes. ABS plastics wheel fairings.

POWER PLANT: One 22·4 kW (30 hp) Cuyuna 430 RR two-cylinder two-stroke engine, or 1,200 cc Volkswagen modified motorcar engine, or Rotax 447, driving a Culver fixed-pitch two-blade wooden propeller. Direct drive for Volkswagen engine; reduction belt for two-stroke engines. One fuel tank in forward fuselage, capacity 19 litres (5 US gallons). Refuelling point on starboard side of fuselage.

ACCOMMODATION: Pilot only in cabin. Forward hinged door on starboard side of fuselage.

DIMENSIONS, EXTERNAL:	
Wing span	8·03 m (26 ft 4 in)
Wing chord, constant	1·19 m (3 ft 11 in)
Wing aspect ratio	6·7
Length overall	5·44 m (17 ft 10 in)
Width, wings folded	1·83 m (6 ft 0 in)
Height overall	1·52 m (5 ft 0 in)
Tailplane span	1·98 m (6 ft 6 in)
Wheel track	1·17 m (3 ft 10 in)
Wheelbase	3·81 m (12 ft 6 in)
Propeller diameter	1·42-1·52 m (4 ft 8 in-5 ft 0 in)
AREA:	
Wings, gross	9·34 m² (100·5 sq ft)
WEIGHTS AND LOADINGS (A: Cuyuna, B: Volkswagen, C: Rotax engine):	
Weight empty: A	156·5 kg (345 lb)
B	186 kg (410 lb)
C	159 kg (350 lb)
Max T-O weight: A, C	272 kg (600 lb)
B	299 kg (660 lb)
Max wing loading: A, C	29·15 kg/m² (5·97 lb/sq ft)
B	32·08 kg/m² (6·57 lb/sq ft)
Max power loading: A	12·14 kg/kW (20·00 lb/hp)
B	9·72 kg/kW (16·00 lb/hp)
PERFORMANCE:	
Never-exceed speed	121 knots (225 km/h; 140 mph)
Max level speed at 305 m (1,000 ft)	102 knots (190 km/h; 118 mph)
Max cruising speed at 305 m (1,000 ft)	82 knots (153 km/h; 95 mph)
Econ cruising speed at 305 m (1,000 ft)	69 knots (129 km/h; 80 mph)
Stalling speed, power off:	
A	33 knots (62 km/h; 38 mph)
B	36 knots (66 km/h; 41 mph)
Max rate of climb at S/L	229 m (750 ft)/min
Service ceiling	3,050 m (10,000 ft)
T-O run	107 m (350 ft)
T-O to 15 m (50 ft)	182 m (600 ft)
Landing from 15 m (50 ft)	182 m (600 ft)
Landing run	107 m (350 ft)
Range with 1·9 litre (0·5 US gallon) reserve	173 nm (322 km; 200 miles)
g limits	+4·4/−3·1

FLIGHT DYNAMICS

FLIGHT DYNAMICS INC

PO Box 5070, State University Station, Raleigh, North Carolina 27650
Telephone: (919) 781 6198
PRESIDENT: Thomas H. Purcell Jr

FLIGHT DYNAMICS SUPERMARINE S.6 REPLICA

Following trials with a single-seat twin-engined seaplane test vehicle, described in the main US Aircraft section of the 1985-86 *Jane's*, this company has constructed a prototype of what it terms a simulation of the Supermarine S.6 Schneider Trophy seaplane. This first flew in October 1985. The constant chord wings of 10·6 m (33 ft 0 in) span and 13·28 m² (143 sq ft) area are constructed of Klégécel spars with linear glass spar caps, foam ribs and glassfibre/epoxy skin. Aerofoil section is GAW-2.

The fuselage forward of the single-seat open cockpit comprises a frame of aluminium tubing, a stainless steel firewall and a welded steel tube engine mount, with the rear fuselage structure of composite foam and glassfibre reinforced epoxy. The tail unit is also of foam and glassfibre/epoxy. Wing and tail surfaces are wire braced. Control is via a conventional column and rudder pedals, with ailerons, elevators, rudder and trailing-edge flaps which provide preset positions for T-O or cruising flight. Power plant is a 20 kW (27 hp) Rotax 277 engine, driving a two-blade fixed-pitch wooden propeller via an integral gearbox. Provisional performance figures indicate a cruising speed of 43 knots (80 km/h; 50 mph) and a T-O run on water of about 91 m (300 ft) at 22 knots (40 km/h; 25 mph). In production form the aircraft will have rounded wing and tailplane tips, a spinner and false cowlings to simulate more closely the S.6's appearance. A ballistic recovery parachute is carried aft of the cockpit.

Flight Dynamics plans to develop the aircraft into a similar landplane replica of the 1934 Brown Racer *Miss Los Angeles*.

FLSZ

FLIGHT LEVEL SIX-ZERO

PO Box 9980, Colorado Springs, Colorado 80932

FLSZ DER KRICKET DK-1

Flight Level Six-Zero is a company formed by Cyril B. Smith, Donald D. Miller, John W. Dooley and Roy E. Wheeler, to design, build, and market plans of an original biplane designated Der Kricket DK-1. Design emphasis has been to develop a 'good old-fashioned biplane', that would be easy to build, fly and maintain, and economical in operation. Design and construction of the prototype began in 1971, and this aircraft flew for the first time on 19 September 1978. A second prototype flew five days later. Plans to construct the Der Kricket DK-1 are available, consisting of 33 drawings and a constructional manual.

TYPE: Single-seat homebuilt sporting biplane.

AIRFRAME: Braced equal-span biplane, with streamline-section I interplane struts, and N cabane struts, but no flying wires. Aerofoil section NACA 4412. Wings moderately staggered. No dihedral, incidence or sweepback. Each wing is a two-spar structure of light alloy, including pop riveted light alloy skins. Tips of Styrofoam covered with glassfibre. Plain ailerons on lower wings only. No flaps or trim tabs. Basic fuselage structure of bolted and riveted light alloy angle, covered by light alloy skins. Can be built in flat-sided form or with more rounded contours, achieved by adding a single piece of angle each side. Cantilever light alloy tail unit, comprising all-moving fin and all-moving tailplane. Tips of Styrofoam covered with glassfibre. Both surfaces have an anti-servo tab.

Fisher FP-505 Skeeter parasol microlight *(Howard Levy)*

Fisher Culex two-seat twin-engined kit built monoplane *(J. M. G. Gradidge)*

Flight Dynamics Supermarine S.6 replica in prototype form, without the rounded wing and tailplane tips, spinner and false engine cowlings

Fishercraft Zippy Sport

FLSZ Der Kricket DK-1 single-seat sporting biplane

Forsgren LF-1 single-seat homebuilt monoplane *(J. M. G. Gradidge)*

LANDING GEAR: Non-retractable tailwheel type. Main units consist of wire braced light alloy struts. Azusa mainwheels with tyres size 5·00-5. Azusa 8 in diameter tailwheel. Azusa mechanical brakes. Speed fairings on main units.

POWER PLANT: One modified Volkswagen motorcar engine of 37·3-48·5 kW (50-65 hp), driving a Cassidy two-blade fixed-pitch wooden propeller with spinner. Fuel tank in fuselage, aft of firewall, capacity 30·3 litres (8 US gallons). Refuelling point on upper surface of fuselage, just forward of upper wing leading-edge. Oil capacity 3·8 litres (1 US gallon).

ACCOMMODATION: Single seat in open cockpit.

DIMENSIONS, EXTERNAL:

Wing span (both)	4·88 m (16 ft 0 in)
Wing chord, constant (both)	0·91 m (3 ft 0 in)
Wing aspect ratio	5·33
Length overall	4·88 m (16 ft 0 in)
Height overall	1·68 m (5 ft 6 in)
Tailplane span	1·98 m (6 ft 6 in)
Wheel track	1·52 m (5 ft 0 in)
Wheelbase	3·05 m (10 ft 0 in)
Propeller diameter	1·37 m (4 ft 6 in)

AREA:

Wings, gross	8·92 m² (96·0 sq ft)

WEIGHTS AND LOADING:

Weight empty	249 kg (550 lb)
Max T-O weight	354 kg (780 lb)
Max wing loading	39·67 kg/m² (8·125 lb/sq ft)

PERFORMANCE (at max T-O weight):

Never-exceed speed	120 knots (222 km/h; 138 mph)
Max level speed	100 knots (185 km/h; 115 mph)
Max cruising speed	95 knots (177 km/h; 110 mph)
Econ cruising speed	82 knots (153 km/h; 95 mph)
Stalling speed, power off	46 knots (84 km/h; 52 mph)
Max rate of climb at S/L	253 m (830 ft)/min
Service ceiling	3,660 m (12,000 ft)
T-O run	213 m (700 ft)
T-O to 15 m (50 ft)	335 m (1,100 ft)
Landing from 15 m (50 ft)	290 m (950 ft)
Landing run	198 m (650 ft)
Range with max fuel	173 nm (322 km; 200 miles)

FORSGREN

LYLE FORSGREN

1690 Brentwood, Oshkosh, Wisconsin 54904

FORSGREN LF-1

Mr Lyle Forsgren, an engineering manager with Mercury Marine, has designed and built a single-seat light homebuilt aircraft known as the LF-1 (N183LF). Construction took about 600 working hours over a two year period, and it first appeared in public at the 1984 Oshkosh Fly-in where it won the 'Outstanding Design Innovation' award. By Autumn 1985 the LF-1 had accumulated more than 125 flying hours, originally with a tailwheel landing gear but more recently with a tricycle type.

Plans and/or kits to build the LF-1 are not yet available, but may be offered at a future date. A new two-seat aircraft is currently under development by Mr Forsgren.

TYPE: Single-seat light homebuilt aircraft.

AIRFRAME: Cantilever low-wing monoplane of mostly metal construction. Wing section GAW-1/-2 modified. Thickness/chord ratio 15%. Dihedral 4° 30′. Monnett extruded wing spar, with 2024-T3 aluminium alloy ribs, and bonded and pop-riveted aluminium alloy skins. Ailerons and flaps over full span. Conventional flat-sided all-metal fuselage, with four 6061-T6 aluminium tube longerons, bulkhead which forms seatback, and 2024-T3 aluminium alloy skins. Glassfibre canopy frame and engine cowlings. Conventional cantilever tail unit, with constant chord tailplane and statically balanced elevators, fin and rudder.

LANDING GEAR: Non-retractable tricycle type. Cantilever main legs, formed from single piece of 2024-T351 aluminium alloy. Mainwheels size 3·50-4 with brakes, of Gerdes manufacture. Offset (to starboard) swivelling nosewheel leg with shock absorption.

POWER PLANT: One 21 kW (28 hp) Mercury marine 25XD liquid-cooled converted outboard motor, driving a 38 × 22 in two-blade raked-tip wooden propeller made by Ed Sterba, with spinner. Two fuel tanks, with capacities of 11·4 and 19 litres (3 and 5 US gallons).

ACCOMMODATION: Pilot only, under Quickie canopy hinged to starboard. Cockpit heated.

SYSTEM: Electrical system, with 60W alternator and battery.

AVIONICS: Nav/com radio fitted.

DIMENSIONS, EXTERNAL:

Wing span	8·08 m (26 ft 6 in)
Wing chord	0·86 m (2 ft 10 in)
Fuselage length	4·37 m (14 ft 4 in)

AREA:

Wings, gross	6·97 m² (75·0 sq ft)

WEIGHTS AND LOADINGS:

Weight empty	147 kg (325 lb)
Max T-O weight	249 kg (550 lb)
Max wing loading	35·79 kg/m² (7·33 lb/sq ft)
Max power loading	11·86 kg/kW (19·64 lb/hp)

PERFORMANCE:

Max level speed	100 knots (185 km/h; 115 mph)
Cruising speed	91 knots (169 km/h; 105 mph)
Stalling speed	35 knots (65 km/h; 40 mph)
Max rate of climb at S/L	152 m (500 ft)/min

FREEDOM FLIERS

FREEDOM FLIERS INC

PO Box 479, Rowlett, Texas 75088
Telephone: (214) 278 7927
Telex: 203941 ACTD UR
PRESIDENT: Gary C. Vick

In 1977 Mr James (Jack) McCornack designed the original Pterodactyl Pfledge prototype, so named because it was based on the Manta Fledge IIB hang glider. This was followed in 1978 by the Pfledge X, and in the following year by the Pfledge OR (Oshkosh Replica), described under the Pterodactyl heading in the 1982-83 *Jane's*.

Mr McCornack sold manufacturing rights in the Pterodactyl range to Freedom Fliers in early 1984, in order to devote his own time more fully to research, design and development.

FREEDOM FLIERS ASCENDER

Aircraft currently in production are the **Ascender II+** and **Ascender II+2**, both of which are derived from the Pfledge and Ptraveler. Manufacture of the Ascender II ceased in 1984; for details see 1984-85 *Jane's*. The Ascender II+ entered production in mid-1982, followed by the two-seat version later that year.

The following description applies to both the Ascender II+ and the II+2:

TYPE: Single-seat/two-seat microlight aircraft. Ascender II+ when flown with single seat and 5 US gallon fuel tank conforms to FAR Pt 103. Ascender II+2 (and II+ when flown with passenger and/or 10 US gallon fuel tank) must be registered as light aircraft under FAA regulations.

AIRFRAME: Braced monoplane wing, with tubular aluminium leading-edge spar, tubular secondary spar and lightweight light alloy ribs. Sweepback 18°. Dihedral 6°. Dacron double surface covering. Wing braced to light alloy tube 'fuselage' and to kingpost by vinyl coated stainless steel cables. Canard surface covered with Stits fabric. Three-axis control standard, by spoilers, overwing drag rudders and stick operated front elevator.

LANDING GEAR: Tricycle type, with glassfibre suspension on main units, bungee on steerable nose unit. Wheel diameter 20 in (main), 16 in (nose). Wheel brakes optional. Other options include float, amphibious float and ski landing gears.

POWER PLANT: One 26·1 kW (35 hp) Cuyuna ULII-02 two-stroke engine standard, with reduction drive to a two-blade wooden pusher propeller. Optional twin carburettor and tuned exhaust system, enabling engine to deliver 33·6 kW (45 hp). Fuel capacity 19 litres (5 US gallons) on II+, 38 litres (10 US gallons) on II+2. Without passenger, II+2 has a 152 litre (40 US gallon) fuel load option, giving a range of 521 nm (965 km; 600 miles).

ACCOMMODATION: Pilot or pilot and passenger in open position.

DIMENSIONS, EXTERNAL (both models):
- Wing span: 10·06 m (33 ft 0 in)
- Wing aspect ratio: 6·72
- Length overall: 5·08 m (16 ft 8 in)
- Height overall: 2·77 m (9 ft 1 in)
- Propeller diameter: 1·37 m (4 ft 6 in)

AREAS:
- Wings, gross: 15·05 m² (162·0 sq ft)
- Elevator: 1·02 m² (11·0 sq ft)

WEIGHTS AND LOADINGS:
- Weight empty: II+ 107 kg (235 lb)
  - II+2 113 kg (250 lb)
- Pilot weight range:
  - II+ (two persons) and II+2 45·5-136 kg (100-300 lb)
- Max T-O weight: II+ (pilot only) 243 kg (535 lb)
  - II+2 317 kg (700 lb)
- Max wing/foreplane loading:
  - II+ 15·09 kg/m² (3·09 lb/sq ft)
  - II+2 19·73 kg/m² (4·04 lb/sq ft)
- Max power loading:
  - II+ (30 hp) 10·85 kg/kW (17·8 lb/hp)
  - II+ (45 hp) 7·23 kg/kW (11·9 lb/hp)
  - II+2 (30 hp) 14·15 kg/kW (23·3 lb/hp)
  - II+2 (45 hp) 9·43 kg/kW (15·5 lb/hp)

PERFORMANCE (at max T-O weight, 30 hp engine rating):
- Never-exceed speed:
  - both 60 knots (112 km/h; 70 mph)
- Max level speed: both 52 knots (97 km/h; 60 mph)
- Max cruising speed: II+ 39 knots (72 km/h; 45 mph)
  - II+2 48 knots (88 km/h; 55 mph)
- Econ cruising speed: II+ 30 knots (56 km/h; 35 mph)
  - II+2 35 knots (64 km/h; 40 mph)
- Stalling speed: II+ 24 knots (44 km/h; 27 mph)
  - II+2 26 knots (49 km/h; 30 mph)
- Max rate of climb at S/L: II+ 274 m (900 ft)/min
  - II+2 122 m (400 ft)/min
- Service ceiling: II+ 6,100 m (20,000 ft)
  - II+2 3,660 m (12,000 ft)
- T-O run: II+ 28 m (90 ft)
  - II+2 61 m (200 ft)
- Landing run: II+ 18 m (60 ft)
  - II+2 46 m (150 ft)
- Range with max fuel, with reserves:
  - II+ 87 nm (161 km; 100 miles)
  - II+2 130 nm (241 km; 150 miles)
- Endurance with max fuel, with reserves: II+ 3 h
  - II+2 4 h
- Best glide ratio: II+ 8
  - II+2 7·5
- Min rate of sink, power off: II+ 145 m (475 ft)/min
  - II+2 168 m (550 ft)/min

FREEDOM FLIERS BUCKEYE

Designed for smooth, stable flight, this powered parachute is named after a distinctively marked butterfly. Introduced in 1984, the Buckeye is available in kit form and as prefabricated parts. It comprises a powered trike and sports parachute. Altitude and rate of climb are determined by means of throttle setting; attitude is controlled with two hand control columns.

TYPE: Single-seat parawing microlight aircraft.

AIRFRAME: Aluminium alloy frame, on to which is mounted a hammock seat, pusher engine with propeller guard, and tricycle landing gear with steerable nosewheel. Buckeye's wing is a ram air sports parachute, made of nylon and having its steering lines attached to a pair of control columns for directional control. Double propeller guard.

LANDING GEAR: Tricycle type. Mainwheels size 10·6 × 3·5 in; nosewheel 4·8 × 4·0-8 in. Glassfibre spring rod suspension. Skis optional.

POWER PLANT (standard): One 26·1 kW (35 hp) Cuyuna ULII-02 engine with 2:1 belt reduction to a two-blade wooden pusher propeller. Alternative engine is 27·6 kW (37 hp) Rotax 377 with 2·58:1 gear reduction. Three-blade wooden propeller optional. Fuel tank capacity 9·5 litres (2·5 US gallons); auxiliary tank of same capacity optional.

ACCOMMODATION: Pilot only, in open position.

DIMENSIONS, EXTERNAL:
- Parachute span: 10·21 m (33 ft 6 in)
- Parachute aspect ratio: 2·84
- Propeller diameter: 1·45 m (4 ft 9 in)

AREA:
- Parachute, gross: 36·70 m² (395·0 sq ft)

WEIGHTS:
- Weight empty: 81 kg (179 lb)
- Pilot weight range: 38·5-84 kg (85-185 lb)
- Max T-O weight: 172 kg (379 lb)

PERFORMANCE:
- Speed (constant): 22 knots (42 km/h; 26 mph)
- Max rate of climb at S/L: 107 m (350 ft)/min
- Service ceiling: more than 2,135 m (7,000 ft)
- T-O run: 91 m (300 ft)
- Landing run: 30 m (100 ft)
- Range, standard fuel: 43 nm (80 km; 50 miles)
- Endurance, max fuel: 2 h 30 min
- Best glide ratio: 2·5
- Rate of sink, power off: 293 m (960 ft)/min

FREEDOM MASTER

FREEDOM MASTER CORPORATION

450 Hamlin Avenue, Satellite Beach, Florida 32937
Telephone: (305) 773 9270
PRESIDENT: Arthur M. Lueck

FREEDOM MASTER FM-2 AIR SHARK I

Mr Arthur Lueck began design studies for the FM-2 in April 1983, and development and construction work started in early 1984, assisted by his two sons and other colleagues. The prototype (N202FM) made a successful first flight on 5 April 1985, at which time an information pack was available for amateur constructors. Kits of pre-moulded parts became available in November 1985 and the first kit-built FM-2 was expected to fly for the first time in April 1986. Military interest has also been shown in the aircraft.

TYPE: Four-seat homebuilt sporting amphibian.

AIRFRAME: Cantilever mid-wing monoplane, of NASA NLF-0215-F aerofoil section, fitted with trailing-edge Fowler slotted flaps and plain ailerons. Thickness/chord ratio 15%. Dihedral 7°. Incidence 3° at root, 1° at tip. Forward sweep 5° at quarter-chord. Single main spar/auxiliary spar/ribs construction, with spar caps of S-2 glassfibre or Kevlar rovings. All aerofoils are vacuum moulded. Main wing upper shell is a glassfibre/epoxy and foam plastics sandwich, with lower surfaces of high strength Kevlar/epoxy. Control surfaces are of Kevlar/epoxy with a Nomex honeycomb core. Winglet at each wingtip, of glassfibre/epoxy. Single-step hull, of extremely clean aerodynamic shape, with Kevlar/epoxy undersurface and glassfibre/epoxy bulkheads and upper shell. Cantilever tail unit, with sweptback vertical surfaces and high mounted tailplane and elevators. Construction similar to that of wings, including use of Kevlar/epoxy for vacuum moulded elevators and rudder. Tabs on elevator and rudder.

LANDING GEAR: Retractable tricycle type, with single wheel on each unit. Size 15 × 6·00-6·00 mainwheels retract inward, 11 × 4·00-5·00 nosewheel rearward. Tyre pressures: 3·10 bars (45 lb/sq in) for mainwheels, 2·07 bars (30 lb/sq in) for tailwheel. Oleo-pneumatic shock absorbers. Disc brakes on Cleveland mainwheels.

POWER PLANT: One 149 kW (200 hp) Avco Lycoming IO-360C1C flat-four engine, pod mounted on a Kevlar/epoxy pylon above the fuselage and driving a modified Hartzell two-blade metal, constant-speed pusher propeller. Two fuel tanks in wings, with total capacity of 379-530 litres (100-140 US gallons). Oil capacity 7·5 litres (2 US gallons).

ACCOMMODATION: Pilot and passenger side by side in fully enclosed cabin, with seats for two more people in rear of cabin. 'Gull' type window/doors, hinged on centreline and opening upward. Baggage capacity 54 kg (120 lb).

SYSTEMS: Full 12V 60A DC electrical system. Electro hydraulic system for landing gear retraction.

AVIONICS: Options include S-Tec autopilot.

ARMAMENT: Hardpoints for weapons and other stores optional.

DIMENSIONS, EXTERNAL:
- Wing span: 9·96 m (32 ft 8 in)
- Wing chord: at root 1·54 m (5 ft 0½ in)
  - at tip 0·71 m (2 ft 4¼ in)
- Wing aspect ratio: 8·08
- Length overall: 6·93 m (22 ft 9 in)
- Height overall: 2·49 m (8 ft 2 in)
- Tailplane span: 2·95 m (9 ft 8 in)
- Wheel track: 2·74 m (9 ft 0 in)
- Wheelbase: 2·44 m (8 ft 0 in)
- Propeller diameter: 1·83 m (6 ft 0 in)

DIMENSIONS, INTERNAL:
- Cockpit: Width 1·14 m (3 ft 9 in)
  - Height 1·02 m (3 ft 4 in)

AREA:
- Wings, gross: 12·26 m² (132·0 sq ft)

WEIGHTS AND LOADINGS:
- Weight empty: 590 kg (1,300 lb)
- Max T-O weight: 1,179 kg (2,600 lb)
- Max wing loading: 96·2 kg/m² (19·7 lb/sq ft)
- Max power loading: 7·91 kg/kW (13·00 lb/hp)

PERFORMANCE (at max T-O weight, except where stated):
- Never-exceed speed: 182 knots (338 km/h; 210 mph)
- Max level speed at S/L: 173 knots (322 km/h; 200 mph)
- Max cruising speed at 2,285 m (7,500 ft): 182 knots (338 km/h; 210 mph)
- Econ cruising speed at 2,285 m (7,500 ft): 148 knots (274 km/h; 170 mph)
- Stalling speed:
  - clean, power off 58 knots (108 km/h; 67 mph)
  - flaps and landing gear down, power off 48 knots (89 km/h; 55 mph)
- Max rate of climb at S/L, at AUW of 998 kg (2,200 lb): 610 m (2,000 ft)/min
- Service ceiling: 5,485 m (18,000 ft)
- T-O run on land: 335 m (1,100 ft)
- T-O to 15 m (50 ft): from land 472 m (1,550 ft)
  - from water 670 m (2,200 ft)
- Landing from 15 m (50 ft): 472 m (1,550 ft)
- Landing run: 305 m (1,000 ft)
- Range with max payload: 1,389 nm (2,575 km; 1,600 miles)
- Range with max standard fuel: 2,431 nm (4,506 km; 2,800 miles)
- Range with max optional fuel, at econ cruising speed: 3,560 nm (6,598 km; 4,100 miles)
- *g* limits: +10 design, ultimate; +4·6/−3·5 normal

GAA

GOLDEN AGE AIRCRAFT INC

Route 3, PO Box 42, Highway 2933, McKinney, Texas 75069
Telephone: (214) 542 5632
SECRETARY AND TREASURER: Carolyn W. Marks

This company has no connection with the Golden Age Aircraft Company (see 1985-86 *Jane's*), which was formed in Ohio by its former President, Mr Gene Eubanks. It has developed three aircraft. The first is a scale representation of the Ryan STA tandem two-seat primary trainer of the 1930s. The second is another tandem two-seat open-cockpit monoplane derived from the STA and known as the Sport Trainer. Kits to build this aircraft are available, with a fuselage of welded 4130 steel tubing and a 37·3 kW (50 hp) engine, or it can be purchased from GAA in flyaway form. The company's third model is a single-seat high-wing cabin monoplane known as the Monarch, of which no details are available.

Freedom Fliers Ascender II + 2

Freedom Fliers Buckeye parawing microlight *(Howard Levy)*

Ganzer Model 75 Gemini side by side two-seat twin-engined light aircraft

Freedom Master Air Shark I four-seat homebuilt amphibian *(NASA, Kennedy Space Center)*

Goldwing Aerostar lightened to conform with FAR Pt 103 *(Howard Levy)*

GANZER

DAVID W. GANZER

2773 Corona Avenue, Mojave, California 93501
Telephone: (805) 824 2246

GANZER MODEL 75 GEMINI

Mr David W. Ganzer has designed and built a two-seat sporting aircraft named the Gemini. It is of foam and glassfibre construction and has rear-mounted main wings, with winglet surfaces at each tip, and foreplanes. However, unlike aircraft of similar appearance, such as the Rutan VariEze/Long-EZ, the Gemini has two engines, installed in 'push and pull' layout. Design of the Gemini began in August 1980, with the assistance of Mr Burt Rutan, and construction started in March of the following year. The first flight was achieved in June 1982, since when an improved foreplane has been installed.

Sets of plans and kits to construct the Gemini were planned to be marketed to amateur constructors.

TYPE: Two-seat homebuilt sporting aircraft.

AIRFRAME: Cantilever mid-wing monoplane with compound leading-edge sweepback. Wing section Eppler 1230. Thickness/chord ratio 15%. No dihedral or anhedral. Sweepback at quarter-chord 18°. Glassfibre and foam sandwich construction. Tapering ailerons. Swept vertical 'winglet' surfaces at each wingtip, of similar construction to wings, with small inset rudders. Cantilever foreplanes of similar construction to wings. Dihedral 6°. Mostly constant chord. Full span slotted flaps. Bungee trim. Composite fuselage of foam and glassfibre. Engines installed in nose and rear of fuselage.

LANDING GEAR: Tricycle type, with fixed cantilever main units and electro/hydraulically retracting (rearward) nosewheel. Oleo-pneumatic shock absorption for nosewheel. Cleveland 5·00-5 mainwheels fitted with Goodyear tyres size 15 × 6·00-5, pressure 3·10 bars (45 lb/sq in). Nosewheel tyre size 10 × 5·00-4, 254 mm (10 in), pressure 3·45 bars (50 lb/sq in). Cleveland disc brakes. Wheel fairings can be fitted to main units.

POWER PLANT: Two 48·5 kW (65 hp) Volkswagen Type 4 2,000 cc modified motorcar engines, driving two-blade fixed-pitch wooden propellers. Fuel tanks, of composite construction, form strakes that fair the wing roots on each side of the fuselage; total capacity 189 litres (50 US gallons). Oil capacity 3·8 litres (1 US gallon) per engine.

ACCOMMODATION: Two persons side by side under one-piece side-hinged (to starboard) canopy. Baggage area behind seats. Heated.

SYSTEM: 35A alternator on each engine for electrical system.

AVIONICS: Nav/com radio standard.

DIMENSIONS, EXTERNAL:

Wing span	8·41 m (27 ft 7¼ in)
Wing chord: at root	1·09 m (3 ft 6¾ in)
at tip	0·51 m (1 ft 8 in)
Wing aspect ratio	8·6
Foreplane span	4·83 m (15 ft 10 in)
Length overall	5·33 m (17 ft 6 in)
Length of fuselage	4·75 m (15 ft 7 in)
Height overall	2·29 m (7 ft 6 in)
Wheel track	1·52 m (5 ft 0 in)
Wheelbase	1·78 m (5 ft 10 in)
Propeller diameter	1·42 m (4 ft 8 in)

AREA:

Wings and foreplane, gross	10·70 m² (115·14 sq ft)

WEIGHTS AND LOADINGS:

Weight empty, operating	535 kg (1,180 lb)
Max T-O weight	862 kg (1,900 lb)
Max wing loading	80·6 kg/m² (16·5 lb/sq ft)
Max power loading	17·77 kg/kW (29·23 lb/hp)

PERFORMANCE:

Never-exceed speed	173 knots (321 km/h; 200 mph)
Max level speed	161 knots (298 km/h; 185 mph)
Max cruising speed	148 knots (273 km/h; 170 mph)
Econ cruising speed	135 knots (249 km/h; 155 mph)
Stalling speed	52 knots (95 km/h; 59 mph)
Max rate of climb at S/L	275 m (900 ft)/min
Rate of climb at S/L, one engine out	46 m (150 ft)/min
Service ceiling, one engine out	1,830 m (6,000 ft)
T-O run	approx 366 m (1,200 ft)
T-O to 15 m (50 ft)	approx 610 m (2,000 ft)
Landing from 15 m (50 ft)	610 m (2,000 ft)
Landing run	335 m (1,100 ft)
Range:	
with max fuel	1,042 nm (1,931 km; 1,200 miles)
with max payload	695 nm (1,287 km; 800 miles)
g limits	+6/−3

GOLDWING

GOLDWING LTD

PO Box 1123, Amador County Airport, Building No. 3, Jackson, California 95642
Telephone: (209) 223 0384

PRESIDENT: Brian Glenn

VICE-PRESIDENTS:
Brian Jensen
Reklai Salazar

Goldwing Ltd was formed in 1980, initially to produce the Goldwing microlight aircraft designed by Mr Craig Catto of Catto Aircraft Inc. No 1985 or 1986 updates were received, but so far as is known this company continues to produce single-seat versions of the Goldwing.

GOLDWING GOLDWING and AEROSTAR

The Goldwing was designed by Mr Craig Catto in 1978 and flew for the first time in January 1979. It became available in production kit form in 1980. Assembly time is 100 hours or less; the Goldwing can be dismantled for transportation, and can be reassembled for flight in 10 min. The Goldwing is also available as a factory built aircraft. About 1,000 have been sold.

The following versions were in production in 1984-85:

Goldwing ST. Standard kit built version.

Gold Duster. Cropspraying version; described in 1982-83 *Jane's*.

Goldwing II. Two-seat tandem version, supplied as factory built aircraft only.

Aerostar (formerly Goldwing UL). Lighter-weight version of Goldwing ST with reduced performance, to conform to FAR Pt 103. Carbonfibre main spar, more angular fuselage cross-section, wider mainwheel track. Available as factory built aircraft only.

The following description applies generally to all US built single-seat Goldwings, except where a specific version is indicated:

TYPE: Single-seat microlight aircraft; Aerostar conforms to FAR Pt 103.

AIRFRAME: Canard monoplane configuration, with swept-back cantilever main wings and non-swept foreplane. Wings have aluminium alloy/Styrofoam/ glassfibre main spar (carbonfibre spar on Aerostar) and a foam core, with laminated glassfibre skin, and are fitted with ailerons and interconnected outboard overwing spoilers; NASA type winglet, with independently actuated split rudder, at each tip. Rudders can be actuated simultaneously to act as dive brakes. Foreplane is fitted with an elevator. Wedge shaped fuselage nacelle, of foam and glassfibre on an aluminium frame.

LANDING GEAR: Non-retractable tricycle type, with coil spring and damper shock absorption. Mainwheels and tyres size 20 × 2·125 in; brakes optional. Steerable nosewheel. Ski and float gear optional.

POWER PLANT: One 26 kW (35 hp) Cuyuna 430R two-cylinder two-stroke engine in ST, with direct drive to a two-blade pusher propeller; 20 kW (27 hp) Rotax 277 in Aerostar; 37·3 kW (50 hp) Rotax 503 in Goldwing II. Fuel capacity 22 litres (6 US gallons) in ST; 11 litres (3 US gallons) in Aerostar.

ACCOMMODATION: Pilot only, in open cockpit, with semi-reclining seat and windscreen.

DIMENSIONS, EXTERNAL (A: Goldwing ST, B: Aerostar, C: II):

Wing span: A, B	9·14 m (30 ft 0 in)
C	9·75 m (32 ft 0 in)
Length overall (all)	3·66 m (12 ft 0 in)
Height overall (all)	1·52 m (5 ft 0 in)

AREAS:

Wings and foreplane, gross:	
A	13·01 m² (140·0 sq ft)
B	13·75 m² (148·0 sq ft)
C	15·79 m² (170·0 sq ft)

WEIGHTS AND LOADINGS:

Weight empty: A	127 kg (280 lb)
B	115 kg (254 lb)
C	154 kg (340 lb)
Max T-O weight: A, B	245 kg (540 lb)
C	358 kg (790 lb)
Max wing loading: A	18·85 kg/m² (3·86 lb/sq ft)
B	17·82 kg/m² (3·65 lb/sq ft)
C	22·70 kg/m² (4·65 lb/sq ft)
Max power loading: A	9·42 kg/kW (15·43 lb/hp)
B	12·25 kg/kW (20·00 lb/hp)
C	9·60 kg/kW (15·80 lb/hp)

PERFORMANCE:

Never-exceed speed:	
A, B	61 knots (112 km/h; 70 mph)
C	65 knots (120 km/h; 75 mph)
Cruising speed (all)	52 knots (97 km/h; 60 mph)
Stalling speed: A, B	23 knots (42 km/h; 26 mph)
C	28 knots (52 km/h; 32 mph)
Max rate of climb at S/L: A	244 m (800 ft)/min
B	183 m (600 ft)/min
C	152 m (500 ft)/min
T-O run: A	45 m (150 ft)
B	30 m (100 ft)
C	60 m (200 ft)
Landing run: A	60 m (200 ft)
B	45 m (150 ft)
C	76 m (250 ft)
Endurance with max fuel: A, B	3 h
C	1 h 30 min
g limits (all)	+6/−4
Best glide ratio: A, B	16
C	13
Min rate of sink, power off:	
A, B	99 m (325 ft)/min
C	137 m (450 ft)/min

GREENWOOD

GREENWOOD AIRCRAFT INC

PO Box 401, Alexandria, Minnesota 56308
Telephone: (612) 762 2020
PRESIDENT: Marvin H. Greenwood
VICE-PRESIDENT, MARKETING: John Hall

GREENWOOD WITCH

The Witch was designed by Mr Marvin Greenwood. Two prototypes had been built by August 1982, when the aircraft made its first public appearance at Oshkosh, Wisconsin. No information has been received since early 1983, but a modified prototype was exhibited at Sun 'n Fun 1984 and production of ready to fly aircraft was then under way at the rate of one aircraft per week. The Witch is believed to remain available.

TYPE: Single-seat microlight aircraft.

AIRFRAME: Strut braced high-wing monoplane with Dacron covered aluminium wings. All-metal ailerons. Wing outer panels fold up and over centre-section for stowage; entire wing unit can then be swivelled fore and aft for transportation. Main fuselage structure of welded chrome molybdenum steel tube, supporting an all-metal T tail with all-moving tailplane. Full three-axis control system, actuated by pushrods. No flying wires.

LANDING GEAR: Non-retractable tricycle type, with 15 × 5 mainwheels and smaller steerable nosewheel. No brakes.

POWER PLANT: One 16·4 kW (22 hp) Zenoah G25B1 single-cylinder two-stroke engine, with 2·5:1 V belt reduction drive to a Ritz 54 × 27 two-blade wooden pusher propeller. Single fuel tank in wing centre-section, capacity 19 litres (5 US gallons).

ACCOMMODATION: Pilot only, in open position. Pilot fairing and windscreen optional.

DIMENSIONS, EXTERNAL:

Wing span	9·14 m (30 ft 0 in)
Wing aspect ratio	6·0
Length overall	5·54 m (18 ft 2 in)
Height overall	2·13 m (7 ft 0 in)
Propeller diameter	1·37 m (4 ft 6 in)

AREA:

Wings, gross	13·93 m² (150·0 sq ft)

WEIGHTS AND LOADINGS:

Weight empty	112·5 kg (248 lb)
Max T-O weight	224 kg (494 lb)
Max wing loading	16·06 kg/m² (3·29 lb/sq ft)
Max power loading	13·66 kg/kW (22·45 lb/hp)

PERFORMANCE:

Never-exceed speed	78 knots (144 km/h; 90 mph)
Max level speed	55 knots (101 km/h; 63 mph)
Max cruising speed	43 knots (80 km/h; 50 mph)
Stalling speed, power off	23 knots (42 km/h; 26 mph)
Max rate of climb at S/L	152 m (500 ft)/min
T-O run	46 m (150 ft)
Landing run	30 m (100 ft)
g limits	+3·8/−2
Best glide ratio	7·6

GREGA

JOHN W. GREGA

355 Grand Boulevard, Bedford, Ohio 44146

In addition to the standard Aircamper design, of which plans are available from Mr Don Pietenpol (see under 'Pietenpol'), a modernised version has been developed by Mr John Grega. Plans of this are available to homebuilders, and by 1986 about 1,400 sets had been sold.

GN-1 AIRCAMPER

The prototype of this modernised version of the Aircamper two-seat light monoplane flew for the first time in November 1965. It used cut-down Piper J-3 Cub wings and bracing struts, and J-3 Cub landing gear. More recently, further updating of the plans has given builders the choice of wood or steel tube fuselage construction. Other differences compared with the standard Aircamper are as follows:

POWER PLANT: One 48·5 kW (65 hp) Continental A65-8 flat-four engine in prototype, driving a two-blade 72/41 fixed-pitch metal propeller. Other engines of up to 63·5 kW (85 hp) can be installed. Fuel tanks aft of firewall, capacity 45 litres (12 US gallons), and in wing centre-section, capacity 22·5 litres (6 US gallons). Oil capacity 3·75 litres (1 US gallon).

DIMENSIONS, EXTERNAL:

Wing span	8·84 m (29 ft 0 in)
Wing chord, constant	1·52 m (5 ft 0 in)
Wing aspect ratio	6
Length overall	5·51 m (18 ft 1 in)
Height overall	2·06 m (6 ft 9 in)
Tailplane span	2·29 m (7 ft 6 in)
Wheel track	1·60 m (5 ft 3 in)

AREA:

Wings, gross	13·94 m² (150·0 sq ft)

WEIGHT AND LOADINGS:

Max T-O weight	499 kg (1,100 lb)
Max wing loading	35·8 kg/m² (7·33 lb/sq ft)
Max power loading	10·29 kg/kW (16·92 lb/hp)

PERFORMANCE (at max T-O weight):

Max level speed at S/L	100 knots (185 km/h; 115 mph)
Max cruising speed at S/L	78 knots (145 km/h; 90 mph)
Stalling speed	31 knots (56 km/h; 35 mph)
Max rate of climb at S/L	152 m (500 ft)/min
T-O run	122 m (400 ft)
Landing run	76 m (250 ft)
Range with max fuel	347 nm (640 km; 400 miles)

GROVE

GROVE AIRCRAFT COMPANY

8736 Verlane Drive, San Diego, California 92119
Telephone: (619) 562 1268

Grove Aircraft Company, owned by Mr Robert P. Grove, exhibited at the 1985 EAA meeting at Oshkosh the prototype (N84GR) of a two-seat high-performance cross-country aircraft, of all-composites construction, named Whisper. Plans are available to amateur constructors. By February 1986, 26 sets had been sold and two aircraft had already been completed.

GROVE GR-2 WHISPER

Design of the Whisper began in June 1981 and construction of the single prototype started in April 1982. This aircraft made its first flight in May 1985.

TYPE: Two-seat homebuilt cross-country aircraft.

AIRFRAME: Cantilever low-wing monoplane, with 4° dihedral from roots. Tapered planform. Wing section NACA 64212. Incidence 1° 30′. Sweepback 10° at quarter-chord. Hot wire shaped Styrofoam core, around composites main spar, with glassfibre skin. Aileron and slotted flap form almost entire trailing-edge of each semi-span. No tabs. Finely streamlined fuselage of mouldless composites (styrofoam/glassfibre), over spruce longerons. Cantilever tail unit of similar construction to wings. Sweptback vertical surfaces. Fin integral with rear fuselage. Horn balanced rudder and elevators. Spring loaded elevator trim.

LANDING GEAR: Non-retractable tailwheel type. Sweptback cantilever Spring main units, with wheel size 5·00-5 (tyre pressure 2·41 bars; 35 lb/sq in) and brakes. Streamline fairings over mainwheels. Lockable tailwheel.

POWER PLANT: One 119 kW (160 hp) Avco Lycoming IO-320-B1A flat-four engine, driving an Hartzell E2Y two-blade constant-speed metal propeller with spinner. Three fuel tanks, each 57 litres (15 US gallons). Refuelling points in wingtips and fuselage aft of firewall. Oil capacity 7·6 litres (2 US gallons).

ACCOMMODATION: Two seats side by side in enclosed cockpit. Two upward opening canopy/doors, hinged on centreline. Space for 45 kg (100 lb) baggage aft of seats.

SYSTEM: Electrical system with battery and alternator.

DIMENSIONS, EXTERNAL:

Wing span	7·72 m (25 ft 4 in)
Wing chord: at root	1·22 m (4 ft 0 in)
at tip	0·76 m (2 ft 6 in)
Wing aspect ratio	7·9
Length overall	6·48 m (21 ft 3 in)
Height overall	1·53 m (5 ft 0 in)
Tailplane span	2·44 m (8 ft 0 in)
Wheel track	1·68 m (5 ft 6 in)
Wheelbase	5·18 m (17 ft 0 in)
Propeller diameter	1·83 m (6 ft 0 in)

AREA:

Wings, gross	7·53 m² (81·0 sq ft)

WEIGHTS AND LOADINGS:

Weight empty	494 kg (1,088 lb)
Max T-O weight	816 kg (1,800 lb)
Max wing loading	108·5 kg/m² (22·22 lb/sq ft)
Max power loading	6·86 kg/kW (11·25 lb/hp)

PERFORMANCE:

Never-exceed speed	217 knots (402 km/h; 250 mph)
Max level speed at 610 m (2,000 ft)	205 knots (380 km/h; 236 mph)
Max cruising speed at 2,135 m (7,000 ft)	195 knots (362 km/h; 225 mph)
Econ cruising speed at 2,745 m (9,000 ft)	187 knots (346 km/h; 215 mph)
Stalling speed, flaps down (engine idling)	54 knots (100 km/h; 62 mph)
Max rate of climb at S/L	762 m (2,500 ft)/min
Service ceiling	7,620 m (25,000 ft)
T-O run	244 m (800 ft)
T-O to 15 m (50 ft)	305 m (1,000 ft)
Landing from 15 m (50 ft)	579 m (1,900 ft)
Landing run	457 m (1,500 ft)
Range with max fuel and max payload	869 nm (1,609 km; 1,000 miles)

Greenwood Witch microlight *(Brian M. Service)*

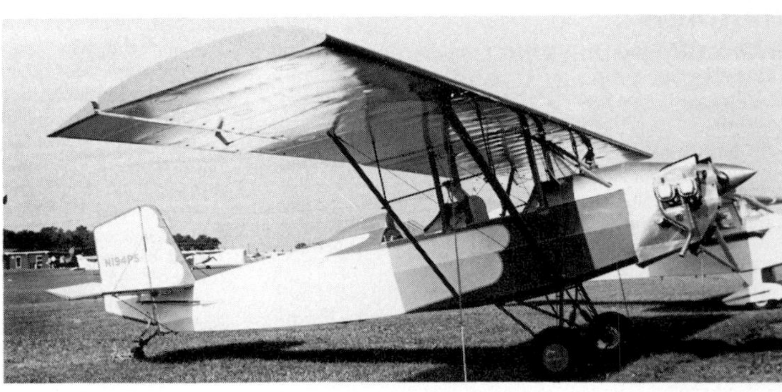

Grega GN-1 Aircamper two-seat light monoplane *(J. M. G. Gradidge)*

Grove GR-2 Whisper high-performance two-seat homebuilt aircraft *(Howard Levy)*

Cygnet SF-2A, designed and built by Captain A. M. Sisler of Bloomington, Minnesota, and marketed by HAPI Engines

Junkers CL-I representation produced from a Snow S-2 agricultural aircraft by Mr Joseph Haigh of Okeechobee, Florida *(Chris Gingell)*

GROVER

GROVER AIRCRAFT CORPORATION

PO Box 647, 824 Locust Street, Hendersonville, North Carolina 28793
Telephone: (704) 697 7958
DESIGNER: Jesse D. Anglin

Grover Aircraft, known initially as Anglin Special Aero Planes Incorporated, produced four designs in the Experimental (homebuilt) and microlight categories. These were the J-3 Kitten, Super Kitten, J-4 Sportster and J-6 Karatoo. The Kitten received the 'Best New Design' award at Sun 'n Fun 84 and the Karatoo won the 'Outstanding New Custom Built Design' award at the 1985 EAA Oshkosh Fly-in. However, Grover Aircraft ceased trading in December 1985. The company's assets were put up for auction in March 1986, and the J-6 Karatoo was purchased by Mr Jesse Anglin, who has established a new company to produce it, named Country Air (which see).

Full details of the Kitten, Super Kitten and Sportster can be found in the 1985-86 *Jane's*, together with illustrations of the Sportster and Kitten.

HAIGH

JOSEPH HAIGH

Okeechobee, Florida

HAIGH ERSATZ JUNKERS CL-I

Mr Joseph Haigh has modified a Snow S-2 agricultural aircraft to represent a German Junkers CL-I fighter-reconnaissance aircraft of the First World War. Modifications include substitution of metal skin for fabric, relocation of the pilot's cockpit to a position in the front fuselage, removal of the chemical hopper, and installation of a second cockpit mounting a dummy machine-gun. The aircraft is powered by a 179 kW (240 hp) Continental radial engine.

DIMENSION, EXTERNAL:
Wing span — 12·19 m (40 ft 0 in)
WEIGHTS:
Weight empty — 952 kg (2,100 lb)
Max T-O weight — 1,574 kg (3,470 lb)
PERFORMANCE:
Cruising speed — 83 knots (154 km/h; 96 mph)

HAPI

HAPI ENGINES INC

Eloy Municipal Airport, RR 1 Box 1000, Eloy, Arizona 85231
Telephone: (602) 466 9244

In October 1983 HAPI Engines acquired the rights to market Captain A. M. Sisler's Cygnet SF-2A. The original prototype, known as the SF-2 Whistler, gained the 'Outstanding Design Contribution' award at the 1973 EAA Fly-in at Oshkosh. Capt Sisler subsequently improved the design as the Cygnet SF-2A, making it easier to build, aerodynamically cleaner, 23 kg (50 lb) lighter and with folding wings so that it could be towed on its own main landing gear. NASAD-approved plans of the Cygnet were made available initially through the Sisler Aircraft Company, and continue to be marketed by HAPI Engines. By early 1985, when the last figures were received, a total of 284 sets of plans had been sold and six Cygnets were flying. HAPI offers also a completely pre-welded airframe kit.

HAPI Engines Incorporated is also dealer for the Viking Dragonfly and quick-assembly 'Snap' Dragonfly.

CYGNET SF-2A

TYPE: Two-seat homebuilt light aircraft.

AIRFRAME: Strut braced shoulder-wing monoplane of all-wood construction, sweptforward 5° from roots. Wing section NACA 3413. Dihedral 3° 30′. Each wing consists of a main spar, light front and rear auxiliary spars, six plywood ribs, some stringers, geodetic upper and lower coverings of spruce strips, and an overall Dacron covering. Fabric covered wooden ailerons, without tabs. No flaps. Wings fold for towing and storage. Conventional welded chrome molybdenum steel tube fuselage and strut braced tail unit, Dacron covered. Trim tab in port elevator. Ground adjustable tab on rudder.

LANDING GEAR: Non-retractable tailwheel type. Two side Vs and half axles of welded steel tube. Bungee shock absorption. Mainwheel tyres size 5·00-5 on prototype; size 6·00-6 tyres or skis optional. Steerable tailwheel. Work has begun to develop floats to allow operation from water.

POWER PLANT: One 44·7 kW (60 hp) 1,834 cc HAPI converted Volkswagen motorcar engine, driving a two-blade propeller. Fuel capacity 57 litres (15 US gallons).

ACCOMMODATION: Two seats side by side in enclosed cockpit. Windscreen made up of two door panels, hinged on centreline. Baggage capacity 23 kg (50 lb).

SYSTEM: Prototype has full electrical system, with 20A alternator and dual electronic ignition. Plans include provision for electric starter.

DIMENSIONS, EXTERNAL:
Wing span — 9·14 m (30 ft 0 in)
Wing chord, constant — 1·27 m (4 ft 2 in)
Wing aspect ratio — 7·1
Length overall — 5·79 m (19 ft 0 in)
Height overall — 1·78 m (5 ft 10 in)
Tailplane span — 2·39 m (7 ft 10 in)
Propeller diameter — 1·47 m (4 ft 10 in)
DIMENSION, INTERNAL:
Cockpit width — 0·99 m (3 ft 3 in)
AREA:
Wings, gross — 11·60 m² (124·8 sq ft)
WEIGHTS AND LOADINGS:
Weight empty — 265 kg (585 lb)
Max T-O weight — 499 kg (1,100 lb)
Max wing loading — 43·0 kg/m² (8·81 lb/sq ft)
Max power loading — 11·16 kg/kW (18·33 lb/hp)
PERFORMANCE (at max T-O weight):
Max level speed — 94 knots (174 km/h; 108 mph)
Cruising speed at 2,440 m (8,000 ft) — 87 knots (161 km/h; 100 mph)
Stalling speed:
power off — 42 knots (78 km/h; 48 mph)
power on — 37 knots (68 km/h; 42 mph)
Max rate of climb at S/L — 177 m (580 ft)/min
T-O to 15 m (50 ft) — 213 m (700 ft)
Landing from 15 m (50 ft) — 168 m (550 ft)
g limit — +4

HARMON

HARMON ENGINEERING COMPANY

PO Box 227, Rt 4, Sherman, Texas 75090
Telephone: (214) 893 2682
PRESIDENT: James B. Harmon

Following an accident to a single-seat sporting aircraft named Der Donnerschlag (The Thunderclap), the lightly damaged airframe was rebuilt as the prototype of a variant named Mister America. Design of the variant was started in November 1974, and it flew for the first time on 31 October 1975.

Plans of Mister America are available. Several more examples are under construction and at least one has flown.

Mr Harmon is currently working on a number of new projects; no details of these were available at the time of going to press.

HARMON 1-2 MISTER AMERICA

TYPE: Single-seat homebuilt sporting aircraft.

AIRFRAME: Wire braced shoulder-wing monoplane. Original wing section, with thickness/chord ratio of 14·5%. Dihedral 1°-2°. Incidence 0°. Wooden structure with fabric covering. Two simple beam spars; built-up ribs. Plain ailerons of similar construction. No flaps. Provision for ground adjustable tabs in ailerons, if required. Dual flying and landing wires each side, landing wires attached to cabane structure at forward end of fuselage, which also forms windscreen support. Welded fuselage and wire braced tail unit of 4130 chrome molybdenum steel tube with fabric covering. Wooden stringer turtledeck, with fabric covering. Aluminium and glassfibre engine cowling. Tailplane incidence ground adjustable. Provision for ground adjustable trim tabs, if required.

LANDING GEAR: Non-retractable tailwheel type. Main units consist of two Vs, attached to fuselage structure, wire braced and with a through axle. Shock absorption by rubber bungee. Cleveland 5·00-5 mainwheels and tyres, pressure 1·03 bars (15 lb/sq in). Aviation Products 4 in steerable tailwheel. Cleveland disc brakes with air cooling. Faired main legs and wheels.

POWER PLANT: One 44·7-48·5 kW (60-65 hp) 1,650 cc Volkswagen modified motorcar engine, driving a two-blade fixed-pitch 54-36 propeller. Fuel tank aft of engine firewall, capacity 34 litres (9 US gallons). Refuelling point forward of windscreen.

ACCOMMODATION: Single seat in open cockpit.

DIMENSIONS, EXTERNAL:

Wing span	5·99 m (19 ft 8 in)
Wing chord, constant	1·22 m (4 ft 0 in)
Wing aspect ratio	4·916
Length overall	4·62 m (15 ft 2 in)
Height overall	1·52 m (5 ft 0 in)
Tailplane span	1·78 m (5 ft 10 in)
Wheel track	1·52 m (5 ft 0 in)
Wheelbase	3·51 m (11 ft 6 in)
Propeller diameter	1·37 m (4 ft 6 in)

DIMENSION, INTERNAL:

Cockpit: Max width	0·52 m (1 ft 8½ in)

AREA:

Wings, gross	7·06 m² (76·0 sq ft)

WEIGHTS AND LOADING:

Weight empty	195 kg (430 lb)
Max T-O weight	295 kg (650 lb)
Max wing loading	41·74 kg/m² (8·55 lb/sq ft)

PERFORMANCE:

Never-exceed speed	143 knots (265 km/h; 165 mph)
Max level speed at S/L	109 knots (201 km/h; 125 mph)
Max cruising speed at S/L	95 knots (177 km/h; 110 mph)
Econ cruising speed at S/L	87 knots (161 km/h; 100 mph)
Stalling speed	42 knots (78 km/h; 48 mph)
Max rate of climb at S/L	244 m (800 ft)/min
Service ceiling	3,660 m (12,000 ft)
T-O run	61 m (200 ft)
T-O to 15 m (50 ft)	122 m (400 ft)
Landing from 15 m (50 ft)	152 m (500 ft)
Landing run	92 m (300 ft)
Range with max fuel	347 nm (643 km; 400 miles)

HATZ

HATZ AIRPLANE SHOP

Route 2, Gleason, Wisconsin 54435
INFORMATION: Dudley Kelly, Rt 4, Versailles, Kentucky 40383
NEWSLETTER: Martin Schmunk, Rt 2, Gleason, Wisconsin 54435

Mr John D. Hatz designed and built the prototype of a two-seat lightweight biplane, designated CB-1, of which plans are available to amateur constructors. Design and construction started in September 1959, and the first flight of the CB-1 was made on 19 April 1968. It was then powered by a 63·5 kW (85 hp) Continental C85-12 engine, but this was replaced subsequently by a 112 kW (150 hp) Avco Lycoming O-320.

The first plans-built CB-1 flew for the first time on 15 June 1975, powered by a Continental O-200 engine. Well over three hundred sets of plans have been sold and 33 CB-1 Biplanes are known to have flown. Since 1984 Weldtech of Benton City, Washington, has offered a pre-welded fuselage and tailfin structure, which incorporates the engine mount fittings, rudder pedal axles, front and rear seat supports and the tailplane rear attachment tubes. It also offers a rib kit for CB-1 horizontal and vertical tail surfaces.

HATZ CB-1 BIPLANE

The following amended details conform with the plans currently marketed by Hatz:

TYPE: Two-seat lightweight homebuilt biplane.

AIRFRAME: Braced single-bay biplane, with N interplane struts each side. N centre-section struts and streamline-section flying and landing wires. Wing section Clark Y. Dihedral 2°, on lower wings only. Incidence (both wings) 0°. Wooden two-spar structure with fabric covering. Cutout in trailing-edge of upper wing. Plain unbalanced ailerons of wood construction, with fabric covering, on upper and lower wings. No flaps. No trim tabs. Fuselage and wire braced tail unit of welded steel tube, with fabric covering. Trim tab in elevator.

LANDING GEAR: Non-retractable tailwheel type. Two side Vs and half-axles hinged to fuselage structure. Steel spring shock absorption. Mainwheels size 6·50-6, with Goodyear tyres, pressure 1·03 bars (15 lb/sq in). Cleveland hydraulic wheel brakes. Glassfibre fairings on mainwheels.

POWER PLANT: One 86 kW (115 hp) Avco Lycoming O-235 flat-four engine, driving a Sensenich two-blade fixed-pitch metal propeller. Single fuel tank in centre-section of upper wing, capacity 68 litres (18 US gallons). Refuelling point on upper surface of upper wing centre-section. Oil capacity 7·5 litres (2 US gallons).

ACCOMMODATION: Two seats in tandem in open cockpits.

SYSTEM: Electrical system, with 12V 12A DC engine driven generator and 12V battery, for engine starting, navigation and instrument lights.

DIMENSIONS, EXTERNAL:

Wing span (both)	7·72 m (25 ft 4 in)
Wing chord, constant (both)	1·27 m (4 ft 2 in)
Wing aspect ratio	6·06
Length overall	5·79 m (19 ft 0 in)
Height overall	2·39 m (7 ft 10 in)
Tailplane span	2·74 m (9 ft 0 in)
Wheel track	1·83 m (6 ft 0 in)
Propeller diameter	1·78 m (5 ft 10 in)

AREA:

Wings, gross	16·54 m² (178·0 sq ft)

WEIGHTS AND LOADINGS:

Weight empty	397 kg (875 lb)
Max T-O weight	726 kg (1,600 lb)
Max wing loading	43·9 kg/m² (8·99 lb/sq ft)
Max power loading	8·44 kg/kW (13·91 lb/hp)

PERFORMANCE (at max T-O weight):

Never-exceed speed	130 knots (241 km/h; 150 mph)
Max cruising speed	78 knots (145 km/h; 90 mph)
Stalling speed	35 knots (65 km/h; 40 mph)
Max rate of climb at S/L	244 m (800 ft)/min
T-O run	approx 122 m (400 ft)
Range with max fuel, 30 min reserves	174 nm (322 km; 200 miles)

HEADBERG

HEADBERG AVIATION INC

265 Needles Trail, Longwood, Florida 32750
Telephone: (305) 788 0471

The Sky Scooter is a light sporting monoplane of which the prototype was designed and built by Mr Ken Flaglor. This aircraft was powered originally by a 13·5 kW (18 hp) Cushman golf-kart engine, with which it made its first flight in June 1967. Performance was marginal; as a result, Mr Flaglor replaced the Cushman with a Volkswagen engine.

In 1979, all design rights in the Sky Scooter were transferred to Headberg Aviation Inc, which increased the number of parts available individually or in kits. More than 450 sets of plans have been sold, and many Sky Scooters are flying. Average time of construction is quoted as 500 hours.

HEADBERG (FLAGLOR) SKY SCOOTER

TYPE: Light homebuilt sporting monoplane.

AIRFRAME: High-wing monoplane, braced by wires attached to fuselage and to kingpost mounted above centre-section. Wing section NACA 23012. Dihedral 2°. Incidence 3°. Two-spar structure with wood drag and anti-drag bracing. Aluminium leading-edge, spruce spars, plywood ribs and wingtips, and wooden trailing-edge, Ceconite covered. Conventional wooden ailerons. No flaps. No trim tabs. Spruce fuselage, plywood covered in the forward cockpit area, Ceconite covered aft. Fuselage of triangular section aft of the wing. Wing centre-section and engine mounting constructed of 4130 steel tube. Spruce and plywood tail unit, with strut bracing. No fixed fin. No trim tabs.

LANDING GEAR: Non-retractable tailwheel type. Cantilever spring steel main units. Steerable tailwheel. Mainwheels of go-kart type, size 4·10 × 3·50-5. Tyre pressure 1·38 bars (20 lb/sq in). Go-kart brakes.

POWER PLANT: One 30 kW (40 hp) Volkswagen 1,500 cc flat-four engine, with Vertex magneto, driving a two-blade Troyer 54-28 propeller. Single fuel tank in fuselage nose, capacity 19 litres (5 US gallons). Refuelling point on top of fuselage forward of windscreen. Oil capacity 2·37 litres (2·5 US quarts).

ACCOMMODATION: Single seat in open cockpit protected by deep windscreen.

DIMENSIONS, EXTERNAL:

Wing span	8·48 m (27 ft 10 in)
Wing chord, constant	1·27 m (4 ft 2 in)
Wing aspect ratio	6·7
Length overall	4·72 m (15 ft 6 in)
Height overall	2·13 m (7 ft 0 in)
Tailplane span	2·18 m (7 ft 2 in)
Wheel track	1·37 m (4 ft 6 in)

AREA:

Wings, gross	10·68 m² (115·0 sq ft)

WEIGHTS AND LOADINGS:

Weight empty	177 kg (390 lb)
Max T-O and landing weight	283 kg (625 lb)
Max wing loading	26 5 kg/m² (5·43 lb/sq ft)
Max power loading	9·43 kg/kW (15·63 lb/hp)

PERFORMANCE:

Max level speed	69 knots (129 km/h; 80 mph)
Max cruising speed	61 knots (112 km/h; 70 mph)
Econ cruising speed	56 knots (105 km/h; 65 mph)
Stalling speed	30 knots (55 km/h; 34 mph)
Max rate of climb at S/L	183 m (600 ft)/min
T-O and landing run	76 m (250 ft)
Range with max fuel, no reserves	152 nm (282 km; 175 miles)

HIGHCRAFT

HIGHCRAFT AERO-MARINE

PO Box 1771, 110 Mingo Trail, Longwood, Florida 32750
Telephone: (305) 339 5744
VICE-PRESIDENT: John Gruener

In 1985 HighCraft Aero-Marine and Advanced Aviation, both of Florida, signed an agreement, under the terms of which the latter company manufactures and markets HighCraft's Buccaneer. In the same year, HighCraft began development of a two-seat version of the Buccaneer, which is also produced and marketed by Advanced Aviation, together with a land-based derivative known as the Carrera. Descriptions of all of these aircraft can be found under the Advanced Aviation entry in this section.

HOLCOMB

JERRY HOLCOMB

1010 NE 122nd Avenue, Vancouver, Washington 98684
Telephone: (206) 892 7732

HOLCOMB PERIGEE

The Perigee was conceived as a single-seat sporting aircraft, utilising the TPG form of construction described under the Aerocar heading in this section. Design began in December 1983. Construction of the prototype, known originally as the Ultra Imp, was started by Mr Holcomb in February 1984, and it flew for the first time in March 1986.

The Perigee is offered for amateur construction in plans form, supported by the availability of component parts. The latter include a premoulded glassfibre nosecone, propeller spinner, wingtips, wing and tailplane skins, wheel fairings, driveshaft assemblies, landing gear components, moulded Plexiglas canopy and pusher propeller. By February 1986, six sets of plans had been sold.

TYPE: Single-seat homebuilt sporting aircraft.

AIRFRAME: Strut-braced shoulder-wing monoplane. Wing

Harmon Mister America sporting aircraft

Hatz CB-1 homebuilt biplane

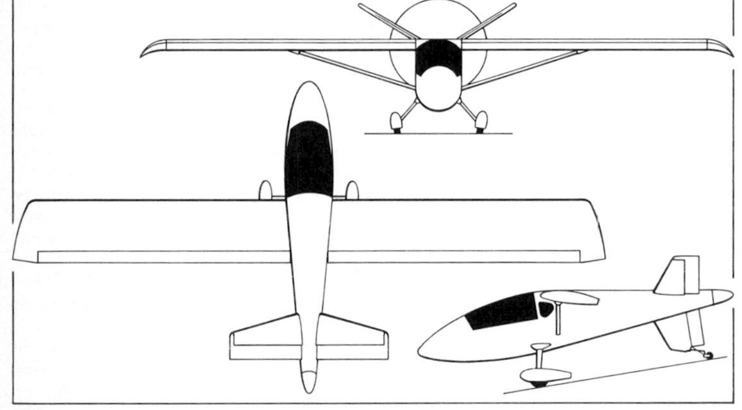

Holcomb Perigee single-seat homebuilt pusher monoplane *(Jane's/Mike Keep)*

Hoskins modified Pitts S-2B *Double Take*, taxying on its inverted landing gear *(Howard Levy)*

Headberg (Flaglor) Sky Scooter light sporting monoplane *(Peter M. Bowers)*

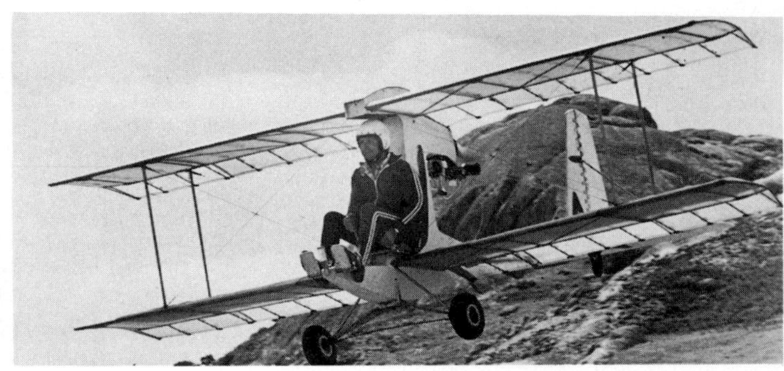

Hovey Whing Ding II built by Mr Lin Bruty of Mt Emu Farm, Australia *(The Herald & Weekly Times, Melbourne)*

section GA(PC)-1 modified. Thickness/chord ratio 16%. Dihedral 0° 30′. Incidence 2°. No sweepback. Composite removable wings of TPG/aluminium alloy/glassfibre construction, with full span constant-chord flaperons. Down-turned wingtips. Streamline semi-monocoque composites fuselage, with spruce longerons, TPG bulkheads, cockpit floor, tailcone and side skins, glassfibre nose, and some aluminium alloy components. Composites Y tail unit, with variable-incidence 'butterfly' tailplane, horn-balanced elevators, and ventral fin with rudder. Tail surfaces have spar of 2024 aluminium alloy/TPG/spruce, with TPG ribs and premoulded glassfibre skins.

Landing Gear: Non-retractable tailwheel type, with 5 × 3·5 in mainwheels (tyre pressure 2·76 bars; 40 lb/sq in) and 3 in diameter steerable solid tailwheel on heat-treated steel spring leg attached to fin. Cantilever mainwheel spring legs of 2024 aluminium alloy. Mainwheel brakes. Optional skis.

Power Plant: One 26 kW (35 hp) Cuyuna 430 two-cylinder two-stroke engine, with 2·1:1 Flexisheave HTD reduction gear and drive shaft to a Taylor Model 1 two-blade variable-pitch pusher propeller of Kevlar composites construction. One fuel tank, capacity 30 litres (8 US gallons). Two optional auxiliary tip tanks with wingtip refuelling points, each 23 litres (6 US gallons) capacity. Optional engines are Rotax 447, 503 and 532.

Accommodation: Pilot only, in enclosed cockpit under Plexiglas canopy. Plexiglas side windows. No internal baggage space.

System: Electrical system with alternator.

Avionics: 720-channel Narco 830 nav/com.

Dimensions, external:

Wing span	8·53 m (28 ft 0 in)
Wing chord, constant	0·91 m (3 ft 0 in)
Wing aspect ratio	9·68
Length overall	4·57 m (15 ft 0 in)
Height overall	1·42 m (4 ft 8 in)
Tailplane span	2·41 m (7 ft 11 in)
Wheel track	1·22 m (4 ft 0 in)
Wheelbase	2·57 m (8 ft 5 in)
Propeller diameter (max)	1·32 m (4 ft 4 in)

Area:

Wings, gross	7·53 m² (81·0 sq ft)

Weights and Loadings:

Weight empty	145 kg (320 lb)
Max design T-O weight	272 kg (600 lb)
Max wing loading	36·18 kg/m² (7·41 lb/sq ft)
Max power loading	10·46 kg/kW (17·14 lb/hp)

Performance (at max T-O weight):

Never-exceed speed	139 knots (257 km/h; 160 mph)
Max level speed at S/L	104 knots (193 km/h; 120 mph)
Max cruising speed	96 knots (177 km/h; 110 mph)
Econ cruising speed	87 knots (161 km/h; 100 mph)
Stalling speed, flaps up (engine idling)	37 knots (68 km/h; 42 mph)
Max rate of climb at S/L	259 m (850 ft)/min
Service ceiling	3,810 m (12,500 ft)
T-O and landing run	91 m (300 ft)
T-O to 15 m (50 ft)	137 m (450 ft)
Landing from 15 m (50 ft)	213 m (700 ft)
Range with max standard fuel	347 nm (643 km; 400 miles)
g limits	+6/−4 design

HOSKINS

CRAIG HOSKINS

Salt Lake City, Utah

HOSKINS UPSIDE-DOWN PITTS S-2B

Mr Craig Hoskins, an airshow aerobatic pilot, has modified his Pitts S-2B biplane to enable it to take off and land upside down on a second landing gear fixed to the upper wings and tail fin. Used as an added attraction during his act, the inverted gear comprises cantilever spring steel mainwheel legs connected to a structure of 2024-T6 heat treated tubing which is itself attached to the additionally strutted and braced wing structure. Standard S-2 wheels, tyres, brakes and fairings are used on the inverted gear. The inverted Haigh tailwheel unit is attached to a strengthened tail structure. The inverted landing gear is reportedly stressed for 4*g*.

HOVEY

ROBERT W. HOVEY

Aircraft Specialties Co, PO Box 1074, Canyon Country, California 91351

Telephone: (805) 252 4054

Mr Hovey has designed and built four very lightweight aircraft, plans of which are available to amateur constructors.

HOVEY WHING DING II (WD-II)

Mr Hovey's objective in designing the Whing Ding was to produce an aircraft which would require minimal construction time and have STOL performance, and which could be dismantled quickly for transportation. First flight was made in February 1971, at which time the Whing Ding II received FAA certification in the Experimental category. A second prototype was completed subsequently.

Over 14,000 sets of plans have been sold and many Whing Dings are under construction or flying.

Type: Single-seat microlight biplane; conforms to FAR Pt 103.

AIRFRAME: Braced single-bay biplane with parallel streamline section interplane struts. Landing and flying wires, the rear flying wires being used to control warping of upper wing. Wooden two-spar non-swept fabric covered wings with ribs and wingtip bows of light alloy tube. Leading-edge faired in with rigid urethane foam. No ailerons, flaps or tabs. Fuselage is a mahogany plywood box with pine stringers, filled with urethane foam. This narrow fuselage provides attachment points for the seat, rudder bar and controls, and sockets for the wing spars. A reinforced extension at the top of the fuselage carries the engine. Aluminium tube tailboom, reinforced by high strength alloy sheet at forward end, bonded with epoxy resin and filled with free-foam urethane. Fabric covered wooden tail surfaces, with strut braced all-moving tailplane. No trim tabs.

LANDING GEAR: Non-retractable tailwheel type. Mainwheels carried on spring type strut of laminated fir covered with a layer of polyester glassfibre. Go-kart mainwheels with 11 in diameter tyres. Tailwheel has solid rubber tyre. Alternative steel tube landing gear available.

POWER PLANT: One 10·5 kW (14 hp) McCulloch MC-101A single-cylinder two-stroke engine, with V belt reduction drive to a two-blade wooden fixed-pitch pusher propeller. Fuel tank capacity 1·9 litres (0·5 US gallons).

ACCOMMODATION: Pilot only, in open position.

DIMENSIONS, EXTERNAL:
Wing span (both) 5·69 m (18 ft 8 in)
Wing aspect ratio 5·9
Length overall 4·27 m (14 ft 0 in)
Height overall 1·68 m (5 ft 6 in)
Propeller diameter 1·22 m (4 ft 0 in)

AREA:
Wings, gross 9·85 m^2 (106·0 sq ft)

WEIGHTS AND LOADINGS:
Weight empty, incl fuel 55·5 kg (123 lb)
Max T-O weight 140 kg (310 lb)
Max wing loading 14·27 kg/m^2 (2·92 lb/sq ft)
Max power loading 13·47 kg/kW (22·14 lb/hp)

PERFORMANCE (at max T-O weight):
Never-exceed speed 52 knots (96 km/h; 60 mph)
Max level speed at S/L 43 knots (80 km/h; 50 mph)
Econ cruising speed at S/L 35 knots (64 km/h; 40 mph)
Stalling speed 23 knots (42 km/h; 26 mph)
Service ceiling 1,220 m (4,000 ft)
T-O run 76 m (250 ft)
Landing run 46 m (150 ft)
Range 17 nm (32 km; 20 miles)

HOVEY BETA BIRD

The Beta Bird (originally Bushwacker) is basically a monoplane version of the Whing Ding II. Design began in June 1977, and construction of the prototype started three months later. It was first flown in April 1979; the 40 h flight test programme to lift FAA test area restrictions was completed on 14 December 1979, and by early 1986 approximately 400 sets of plans had been sold.

TYPE: Single-seat microlight monoplane.

AIRFRAME: Braced high-wing monoplane, with V strut on each side. Wing section Hovey BB-14. Thickness/chord ratio 14%. No dihedral. Incidence 3°. No sweepback. Constant chord structure, with two spruce spars and ribs of single-piece aluminium tubes. Fabric covering. Full span ailerons which can be drooped to a maximum of 16° to reduce take-off and landing runs. No trim tabs. Wings fold aft about a pinjoint in the rear spar. Closed box fuselage of 3·2 mm (⅛ in) mahogany plywood glued to 12·7 mm (½ in) square pine stringers, which is filled with urethane foam to stiffen and stabilise the plywood skin. This narrow fuselage provides attachment points for the seat, rudder bar and controls, wing and engine. Aluminium tube tailboom is reinforced by high strength alloy sheet at the forward end, this being wrapped around the tube and bonded with epoxy resin. The entire tube is filled with free-foam urethane. Wire braced tail unit of aluminium tube, connected with pop riveted gussets and fabric covered. Conventional tailplane with elevators. No trim tabs.

LANDING GEAR: Non-retractable tailwheel type. Mainwheels each carried on steel tube assembly, or spring strut of laminated fir covered with a layer of polyester glassfibre. Go-kart mainwheels with 11 in diameter tyres, pressure 1·38 bars (20 lb/sq in). Steerable tailwheel has solid rubber tyre. Gerdes toe-operated brakes.

POWER PLANT: One 33·5 kW (45 hp) Volkswagen 1,385 cc modified motorcar engine, driving a Hovey two-blade fixed-pitch pusher propeller. Fuel tank within the vertical fuselage extension to which the engine is mounted, capacity 28·4 litres (7·5 US gallons). Oil capacity 3·8 litres (1 US gallon).

ACCOMMODATION: Pilot only, on exposed seat.

SYSTEM: Battery only, as source of electric power for basic instruments and radio.

AVIONICS: Six-channel VHF com radio.

DIMENSIONS, EXTERNAL:
Wing span 7·77 m (25 ft 6 in)
Width, wings folded 2·44 m (8 ft 0 in)
Wing chord, constant 1·07 m (3 ft 6 in)
Wing aspect ratio 7·3
Length overall 5·33 m (17 ft 6 in)
Height overall 1·83 m (6 ft 0 in)
Tailplane span 2·44 m (8 ft 0 in)
Wheelbase 1·52 m (5 ft 0 in)
Propeller diameter 1·37 m (4 ft 6 in)

AREA:
Wings, gross 8·08 m^2 (87·0 sq ft)

WEIGHTS AND LOADINGS:
Weight empty 184 kg (405 lb)
Max fuel weight 20·4 kg (45 lb)
Max T-O weight 295 kg (650 lb)
Max wing loading 36·47 kg/m^2 (7·47 lb/sq ft)
Max power loading 8·81 kg/kW (14·44 lb/hp)

PERFORMANCE (at max T-O weight):
Never-exceed speed 82 knots (153 km/h; 95 mph) IAS
Max level speed at 915 m (3,000 ft) 74 knots (137 km/h; 85 mph)
Max cruising speed at 915 m (3,000 ft) 61 knots (113 km/h; 70 mph)
Econ cruising speed 52 knots (96 km/h; 60 mph)
Stalling speed, flaps down, power on 35 knots (65 km/h; 40 mph)
Max rate of climb at S/L over 122 m (400 ft)/min
T-O and landing run 76 m (250 ft)
T-O to and landing from 15 m (50 ft) 152 m (500 ft)
Range with max fuel, no reserves 113 nm (209 km; 130 miles)

HOVEY DELTA BIRD

First flown in January 1981, the Delta Bird is a tractor biplane, larger than the Whing Ding II, though with minimal structure, and with a more powerful engine. Plans and instructional manuals became available in 1982, and about 600 sets have been sold, as well as many parts, kits and assemblies.

TYPE: Single-seat microlight biplane; conforms to FAR Pt 103.

AIRFRAME: Braced single-bay biplane. Aluminium tube structure, with fabric covering and pop riveted gusset joints. Full span ailerons on upper wings only. No flaps, spoilers or tabs. Simple aluminium tube fuselage, with pop riveted gusset joints. Conventional tail surfaces, of similar construction to wings and fuselage.

LANDING GEAR: Non-retractable tailwheel type, with bungee cord shock absorption on main units and aluminium leaf spring on tailwheel. Tyres size 11·5 × 4·5 in on main units; 5 in diameter solid tailwheel. No brakes.

POWER PLANT: One 22·5 kW (30 hp) Cuyuna 430R two-cylinder two-stroke engine, driving a two-blade fixed-pitch propeller. Single fuel tank in centre of upper wing, capacity 11·4 litres (3 US gallons).

ACCOMMODATION: Pilot only, in open position.

DIMENSIONS, EXTERNAL:
Wing span: upper 7·32 m (24 ft 0 in)
lower 6·15 m (20 ft 2 in)
Wing aspect ratio 6·56
Length overall 4·60 m (15 ft 1 in)
Height overall 1·78 m (5 ft 10 in)
Propeller diameter 1·42 m (4 ft 8 in)

AREA:
Wings, gross 14 86 m^2 (160·0 sq ft)

WEIGHTS AND LOADINGS:
Weight empty 104 kg (230 lb)
Max pilot weight 100 kg (220 lb)
Max T-O weight 209·5 kg (462 lb)
Max wing loading 14·1 kg/m^2 (2·89 lb/sq ft)
Max power loading 9·35 kg/kW (15·40 lb/hp)

PERFORMANCE (at max T-O weight):
Never-exceed speed 69 knots (129 km/h; 80 mph)
Max level speed at S/L 48 knots (88 km/h; 55 mph)
Max cruising speed at S/L 43 knots (80 km/h; 50 mph)
Econ cruising speed at S/L 35 knots (64 km/h; 40 mph)
Stalling speed 24 knots (44 km/h; 27 mph)
Max rate of climb at S/L 122 m (400 ft)/min
Service ceiling 2,440 m (8,000 ft)
T-O and landing run 76 m (250 ft)
Range with max fuel 61 nm (112 km; 70 miles)
g limits +3·5 (+5·25 ultimate)

HOVEY DELTA HAWK and SUPER HAWK

In 1983 Mr Hovey introduced the **Delta Hawk** which has a new power plant and fuselage allied to the wings, tail, landing gear and control system of the Delta Bird. By early 1986 at least 150 sets of plans for this aircraft had been sold. The Delta Hawk is also available in ready to fly form.

The following description applies to the Delta Hawk. The **Super Hawk**, introduced in 1985, has identical dimensions and performance, but has a Rotax engine, pop riveted all-metal fuselage skin, and an empty weight of 113 kg (250 lb).

TYPE: Single-seat, single-engined microlight biplane; conforms to FAR Pt 103 requirements.

AIRFRAME: Aluminium alloy structure. Double surface Dacron covered wings, strut and stainless steel cable braced. Three-axis control (rudder, elevators and full span ailerons).

LANDING GEAR: Non-retractable tailwheel type. Mainwheels size 5 × 3, with hydraulic brakes. Steerable tailwheel.

POWER PLANT: One 28·7 kW (38·5 hp) 440 cc Kawasaki 440 engine, with 2·2:1 reduction drive to a two-blade wooden propeller. Fuel capacity 13·25 litres (3·5 US gallons).

ACCOMMODATION: Pilot only in open cockpit, with windscreen.

DIMENSIONS, EXTERNAL:
Wing span 7·32 m (24 ft 0 in)
Wing aspect ratio 6·9
Length overall 4·75 m (15 ft 7 in)
Height overall 1·83 m (6 ft 0 in)
Propeller diameter 1·52 m (5 ft 0 in)

AREA:
Wings, gross 14·12 m^2 (152·0 sq ft)

WEIGHTS AND LOADINGS:
Weight empty 112 kg (248 lb)
Pilot weight range 54-100 kg (120-220 lb)
Max T-O weight 202 kg (446 lb)
Max wing loading 14·31 kg/m^2 (2·93 lb/sq ft)
Max power loading 7·04 kg/kW (11·58 lb/hp)

PERFORMANCE:
Never-exceed speed 69 knots (128 km/h; 80 mph)
Max level speed 55 knots (101 km/h; 63 mph)
Max cruising speed 52 knots (97 km/h; 60 mph)
Econ cruising speed 43 knots (80 km/h; 50 mph)
Stalling speed 24 knots (44 km/h; 27 mph)
Max rate of climb at S/L 213 m (700 ft)/min
T-O and landing run 61 m (200 ft)
Range with max fuel 65 nm (120 km; 75 miles)
g limits ±6

HUMMEL

HUMMEL AIRCRAFT

509 East Butler Street, Bryan, Ohio 43506
Telephone: (419) 636 3390

HUMMEL AIRCRAFT HUMMEL BIRD

Mr Morry Hummel formed Hummel Aircraft to market plans for his Hummel Bird single-seat light aircraft. As can be seen from the accompanying illustration, the Hummel Bird is a modified Watson Windwagon, with a fully enclosed cockpit, a choice of engines, and tricycle or tailwheel type landing gear. Construction of the prototype began in April 1980 and the first flight was achieved in June 1981. At the 1982 Oshkosh Fly-in, the Hummel Bird received the 'Best Modified Homebuilt' award.

By early 1986 a total of about 250 sets of plans of the Hummel Bird had been sold; these cover the modifications that have to be made to the basic Watson Windwagon plans, which must be purchased first from Gary Watson. Plans for the half Volkswagen engine are also available, and Mr Hummel is a dealer for the alternative Global Machine Tool Corporation engine that can be fitted to the Hummel Bird. Hummel Aircraft also offers several completed components, namely the engine mounting, windscreen and canopy, and hand-hammered wing root fairings. Other component parts can be fabricated upon request.

It was intended to introduce some improvements to the prototype Hummel Bird during the Summer of 1985, including the use of shock absorbers in the landing gear, an engine cowling and wing fuel tanks. The cowling was not completed to schedule, due to an accident involving Mr Hummel, but was expected to be finished by July 1986. Mr Hummel also expected to have produced by then removable wingtip extensions to convert the prototype into a motor glider. With the 0·91 m (3 ft) extensions fitted, the wing area will increase to 6·60 m^2 (71·0 sq ft). Removal of the wing extensions will take 5 minutes.

TYPE: Single-seat homebuilt light aircraft.

AIRFRAME: Cantilever low-wing monoplane. Airframe of pop riveted 2024-T3 aluminium alloy. Wing section Clark Y. Constant chord. Dihedral 5° on outer panels only. Outer wing sections removable for trailering or storage; prototype can be fitted with wingtip extensions to become a motor glider. Removing wings takes 20 min. Conventional ailerons. No flaps. Tab on aileron. Conventional semi-monocoque fuselage. Cantilever tail unit, comprising slightly tapered tailplane with elevators, slightly swept fin and rudder, and dorsal fin. Adjustable spring load on elevators.

LANDING GEAR: Non-retractable tailwheel or tricycle type, employing tubular legs. Ken Rand mainwheels, fitted with 3·50 × 4·00-5 tyres. Shock absorbers introduced during Summer 1985. Ken Rand brakes. Legs fitted with streamlined fairings. Half fairings for mainwheels, protruding rearward.

POWER PLANT: Prototype fitted with half Volkswagen modified motorcar engine built from discarded components, rated at 22·4 kW (30 hp) and driving a Prince Aircraft two-blade propeller. One Volkswagen engine of up to 27·6 kW (37 hp) or a 27·6 kW (37 hp) Global

Hovey Delta Bird

Hovey Super Hawk microlight biplane

Hovey Beta Bird lightweight monoplane (1,385 cc Volkswagen engine)

Hummel Aircraft Hummel Bird, fitted with half of a Volkswagen engine and tailwheel type landing gear

Hummel Bird with Global engine and tricycle landing gear

Hutchinson AG Master homebuilt agricultural aircraft *(J. M. G. Gradidge)*

Machine Tool Corporation engine can be fitted alternatively. Standard fuel capacity 21 litres (5·5 US gallons). Wing tanks introduced during Summer 1985. Oil capacity 1·65 litres (3·5 US pints).

ACCOMMODATION: Single seat under hinged (to starboard) canopy. Heated and ventilated. Baggage space behind seat, max capacity 18 kg (40 lb).

DIMENSIONS, EXTERNAL:

Wing span	5·49 m (18 ft 0 in)
Wing chord, constant	0·97 m (3 ft 2 in)
Wing aspect ratio	6·0
Length overall	4·06 m (13 ft 4 in)
Width, wings removed	1·83 m (6 ft 0 in)
Height overall	1·37 m (4 ft 6 in)
Tailplane span	1·83 m (6 ft 0 in)
Wheel track	1·78 m (5 ft 10 in)
Wheelbase, tailwheel type	2·79 m (9 ft 2 in)
Propeller diameter	1·14 m (3 ft 9 in)

AREA:

Wings, gross	5·02 m² (54·0 sq ft)

WEIGHTS AND LOADINGS (prototype):

Weight empty	122 kg (268 lb)
Max T-O weight	248 kg (548 lb)
Max wing loading	49·6 kg/m² (10·15 lb/sq ft)
Max power loading	11·07 kg/kW (18·27 lb/hp)

PERFORMANCE (22·4 kW; 30 hp half Volkswagen engine):

Never-exceed speed	130 knots (241 km/h; 150 mph)
Max level speed	104 knots (193 km/h; 120 mph)
Normal cruising speed	91 knots (169 km/h; 105 mph)
Econ cruising speed	82 knots (153 km/h; 95 mph)
Stalling speed	39 knots (73 km/h; 45 mph)
Max rate of climb at S/L	213 m (700 ft)/min
T-O run	122 m (400 ft)
T-O to 15 m (50 ft)	580 m (1,900 ft)
Landing from 15 m (50 ft)	457 m (1,500 ft)
Landing run	183 m (600 ft)
Range	260 nm (483 km; 300 miles)

HUTCHINSON

HUTCHINSON AIRCRAFT COMPANY

PO Box 169, Bay St Louis, Mississippi 39520
Telephone: (601) 467 2707 or 467 2743
PRESIDENT AND DESIGNER: Jack Hutchinson

HUTCHINSON AG MASTER

The AG Master single-seat ULV agricultural aircraft is the result of eleven years of research and development, the design criteria including: pilot safety; simplicity of construction, operation and maintenance; and reduction of chemical and operating costs. It can produce a swath width of 13·75 m (45 ft), with an application of 0·9 litre (0·25 US gallon) of chemicals per acre, which (allowing for a ten minute turnaround time) could allow 60 hectares (150 acres) to be sprayed in an hour.

The AG Master is available as a kit under the Experimental category regulations, and reportedly takes about 50 working hours to construct.

TYPE: Single-seat homebuilt agricultural aircraft.

AIRFRAME: Strut-braced low-wing monoplane. Airframe constructed of 4130 chrome molybdenum steel tubing, covered with Surfkote (heat shrunk Mylar and Dacron sandwich material) that is pre-sewn into envelopes. Near full-span ailerons. Conventional strut-braced tail unit.

LANDING GEAR: Non-retractable tailwheel type, with two side Vs and half axles for main gear, which is fitted with 6·00-6 high flotation balloon tyres. Mainwheel disc brakes.

POWER PLANT: One engine of unspecified type, driving a two-blade propeller. One 38 litre (10 US gallon) fuel tank in fuselage, aft of seat. Recoil starter in cockpit.

ACCOMMODATION: Pilot only, in open cockpit with windscreen. Roll-over bar, presumably in aft turtleback. Quickly removable, aerofoil configured Broyhill Aero SprA spraybooms under wings, and removable aerodynamic 76 litre (20 US gallon) chemical hopper under fuselage, between mainwheel legs.

SYSTEM: Electrical system, with 20Ah battery.

DIMENSIONS, EXTERNAL:

Wing span	8·74 m (28 ft 8 in)

Length overall 5·33 m (17 ft 6 in)
Height overall 2·01 m (6 ft 7 in)
AREA:
Wings, gross 13·54 m² (145·7 sq ft)
WEIGHTS AND LOADING:
Weight empty 204 kg (450 lb)
Max T-O weight 454 kg (1,000 lb)
Max wing loading 33·5 kg/m² (6·86 lb/sq ft)
PERFORMANCE (at max T-O weight):
Never-exceed speed, with sprayblooms 70 knots (129 km/h; 80 mph)
T-O speed 35 knots (65 km/h; 40 mph)
Design manoeuvring speed 45 knots (83 km/h; 52 mph)
Min approach speed 40 knots (74 km/h; 46 mph)
Max rate of climb at S/L 91 m (300 ft)/min
T-O run 137 m (450 ft)
T-O to 15 m (50 ft) 244 m (800 ft)
Landing from 15 m (50 ft) 152 m (500 ft)

IAC

INTERNATIONAL AEROMARINE CORPORATION

475 Silverlake Road, Sanford, Florida 32771
PRESIDENT: Joseph W. Gurnow
VICE-PRESIDENT, ENGINEERING: David B. Thurston

IAC TA16 TROJAN

The TA16 Trojan, a four-seat light amphibian designed by Mr David B. Thurston, was conceived originally for the homebuilt market. A production version became the TA16 Seafire. The Trojan and Seafire are identical and thus the details of the Seafire in the main section of this edition apply equally to the Trojan.

An accompanying illustration shows the Trojan built by Mr William M. Johnson of Leland, North Carolina, the first completed Trojan of some 45 said to be under construction in Canada and the USA.

IAC

INTERNATIONAL AIRCRAFT CORPORATION

N34 W28341 Taylors Wood Road, Pewaukee, Wisconsin 53072
Telephone: (414) 691 4452
Telex: 664 559
PRESIDENT: Chip Erwin
VICE-PRESIDENT: Larry Whiting

IAC AG-7 and TR-7

The AG-7 was designed by Mr Chris Heintz specifically as a microlight for agricultural work. It won the 'Best New Design' award at the EAA's Sun 'n Fun fly-in at Lakeland in 1984, and went into production as a factory assembled aircraft.

The AG-7 is a single-seater. It is equipped with a Micro-Ag controlled droplet applicator system and uses vegetable oil as the chemical carrier, instead of water, for greater spread. The chemical hopper has a 38 litre (10 US gallon) capacity and, set to disperse one pint of chemical with an equal amount of vegetable oil per acre, will cover 78·5 hectares (194 acres) per hour. Including turn and refill time, typically 53 per cent of flight time, the average coverage by the AG-7 is 41·6 hectares (103 acres) per hour. Swath width is 10·7 m (35 ft) at a spray speed of 30 knots (56 km/h; 35 mph).

A purpose built two-seat, dual control version of the AG-7 for mainly training purposes is the TR-7, which is structurally similar to, and is powered by the same power plant as, the AG-7. The AG-7, and presumably the TR-7, can also be used for crop seeding, spotting and infra-red photography.

The following description applies to the AG-7 (unless stated otherwise):

TYPE: Single-seat agricultural microlight aircraft.

AIRFRAME: Braced high-wing monoplane, with sail type wing using double surface Dacron for easy folding and transportation. Mainframe of aluminium alloy, with square section boom supporting the engine, wings and conventional tail unit. Stainless steel cables. Three-axis control (ailerons, elevators and rudder). Rigging time 5 min. Options include ballistic parachute and camera mount. Provision for passenger, dual controls and dual engine controls in TR-7 form.

LANDING GEAR: Tricycle type, with all three unsprung wheels size 15 × 4. Steerable nosewheel. Optional skis and floats.

POWER PLANT: Two 16·4 kW (22 hp) JPX PUL 425 engines, with direct drive to two two-blade wooden propellers. Fuel tank capacity 22·7 litres (6 US gallons). Two 22·7 litre (6 US gallon) auxiliary tanks optional.

ACCOMMODATION: Pilot only, in open position. Agricultural equipment fitted as detailed above.

DIMENSIONS, EXTERNAL:
Wing span 8·99 m (29 ft 6 in)
Propeller diameter, each 0·91 m (3 ft 0 in)
AREA:
Wings, gross 13·75 m² (148·0 sq ft)
WEIGHTS AND LOADING:
Weight empty 122 kg (270 lb)
Pilot plus passenger weight range (TR-7) 23-181 kg (50-400 lb)
Max T-O weight 317 kg (700 lb)
Max power loading 9·66 kg/kW (15·91 lb/hp)
PERFORMANCE:
Never-exceed and max level speed 47 knots (88 km/h; 55 mph)
Max cruising speed 35 knots (64 km/h; 40 mph)
Econ cruising speed 30 knots (56 km/h; 35 mph)
Stalling speed 16 knots (29 km/h; 18 mph)
Max rate of climb at S/L 140 m (460 ft)/min
Service ceiling 3,660 m (12,000 ft)
T-O run 27 m (90 ft)
Landing run 30 m (100 ft)
Range with max standard fuel 52 nm (96 km; 60 miles)
Endurance 2 h 30 min
g limits +6/−3

INAV

INAV Ltd
(Subsidiary of Aviation Composites, UK)

220 Regency Court, Suite 101, Wankesha, Wisconsin 53186
Telephone: (414) 784 1561
GENERAL MANAGER: John T. Monnett
PUBLIC RELATIONS: Betty Monnett

This company was formed as Monnett Experimental Aircraft Inc, by Mr John T. Monnett, to market plans and certain components of an original-design Formula V racer known originally as the Monnett II Sonerai. This received the 'Best in Class Formula V Racer' award at the EAA Fly-in at Oshkosh in 1971, as well as an award for its outstanding contribution to low-cost flying. Later, Mr Monnett designed a two-seat version of the Sonerai, with the result that the original single-seat model became known as Sonerai I, the two-seat model as Sonerai II.

In 1985 INAV Ltd (Innovative Aviation) purchased the assets of Monnett Experimental Aircraft and continued to make available the existing range of aircraft. In addition INAV is distributing the Mercury microlight and Lotus Magnum engine, developed in the UK, and in 1986 made available new wingtips for the Sonerai II-LTS. The company is now also offering a materials kit for the Wittman Tailwind, described under the Wittman entry in this section.

Details of the Monerai S homebuilt sailplane, Monerai P with auxiliary engine and Moni motor glider can be found in the Sailplanes section.

INAV SONERAI I

Mr Monnett began design of the Sonerai in September 1970, construction starting two months later. First flight was made in July 1971, with FAA certification in the Experimental category. Plans and certain components are available to amateur constructors, including engine cowlings, clear or tinted Plexiglas cockpit canopy, main landing gear struts, formed aluminium ribs, tapered rod tail spring, fuel tanks, spar kits, instruments, injector carburettor and wheels and brakes. Estimated building time is 800 working hours when a pre-welded fuselage is not used.

Approximately 550 sets of plans have been sold, and more than 400 Sonerai Is are under construction or flying.

TYPE: Single-seat homebuilt Formula V racing aircraft.

AIRFRAME: Cantilever mid-wing monoplane. Folding wings of aluminium alloy construction, with NACA 64212 aerofoil section. No dihedral, incidence or sweepback. Full span aluminium alloy ailerons. No flaps or tabs. Welded chrome molybdenum steel tube fuselage and tail unit, fabric covered except for glassfibre engine cowlings. Tailplane incidence ground adjustable. No trim tabs.

LANDING GEAR: Non-retractable tailwheel type. Cantilever spring main gear of light alloy. Mainwheels and tyres size 5·00-5. Caliper type wheel brakes. Glassfibre fairings on mainwheels.

POWER PLANT: One 44·7 kW (60 hp) Volkswagen 1,600 cc modified motorcar engine, driving a Hegy two-blade propeller with spinner. Alternative Volkswagen engines of up to 2,180 cc may be fitted. Fuel tank in fuselage, immediately aft of firewall, capacity 37·8 litres (10 US gallons). Refuelling point on fuselage upper surface forward of canopy. Oil capacity 2·82 litres (0·75 US gallons).

ACCOMMODATION: Single seat under jettisonable Plexiglas bubble canopy, hinged at the starboard side.

AVIONICS: Battery powered 100-channel com transceiver.

DIMENSIONS, EXTERNAL:
Wing span 5·08 m (16 ft 8 in)
Wing chord, constant 1·37 m (4 ft 6 in)
Length overall 5·08 m (16 ft 8 in)
Height overall 1·52 m (5 ft 0 in)
Tailplane span 1·98 m (6 ft 6 in)
Wheel track 1·22 m (4 ft 0 in)
Propeller diameter 1·27 m (4 ft 2 in)
AREA:
Wings, gross 6·97 m² (75·0 sq ft)
WEIGHTS AND LOADINGS:
Weight empty 199 kg (440 lb)
Max pilot weight 113 kg (250 lb)
Utility max T-O weight 340 kg (750 lb)
Max T-O weight 454 kg (1,000 lb)
Max wing loading 65·1 kg/m² (13·33 lb/sq ft)
Max power loading 10·16 kg/kW (16·67 lb/hp)
PERFORMANCE (at max T-O weight):
Max level speed at S/L 148 knots (273 km/h; 170 mph)
Max cruising speed, 75% power 130 knots (241 km/h; 150 mph)
Econ cruising speed 109 knots (201 km/h; 125 mph)
Stalling speed 35 knots (65 km/h; 40 mph)
Max rate of climb at S/L 305 m (1,000 ft)/min
T-O and landing run 183 m (600 ft)
Range, with reserves 217-260 nm (402-482 km; 250-300 miles)
g limits ±6g

INAV SONERAI II, IIL, II-LT and II-LTS

The success of the Sonerai encouraged Mr Monnett to begin the design and construction of the two-seat **Sonerai II** in December 1972. Generally similar to the Sonerai, it differs by being slightly larger and by having a more powerful Volkswagen engine. The prototype made its first flight in July 1973. Orders had been received for 1,800 sets of plans and at least 1,100 Sonerai IIs were under construction and 500 flying by early 1986. Many components, complete kits for fuselage and wings, and materials, are available to amateur constructors. Estimated building time is 850 working hours.

One variant, first flown in June 1980, is the **Sonerai IIL**, with low-wing instead of mid-wing configuration and 3° of dihedral. The two designs are identical in all other respects. The prototype IIL is powered by a 2,180 cc Aero Vee Volkswagen modified motorcar engine. Another variant of the Sonerai II, first flown in January 1983, is the **Sonerai II-LT**, which is similar to the Sonerai IIL but has a 2,180 cc VW engine as standard, a tricycle landing gear and larger front cockpit for the taller pilot. A retrofit kit has been produced to allow existing Sonerais to be fitted with the tricycle gear. The latest variant is the **Sonerai II-LTS**, which is basically a 'stretched' version of the Sonerai II-LT, first flown in June 1984.

The description of the Sonerai I applies also to Sonerai II, IIL, II-LT and II-LTS except as follows:

TYPE: Two-seat homebuilt high-performance sporting aircraft.

AIRFRAME: Sonerai II wings as for Sonerai, except span increased. Sonerai IIL, II-LT and II-LTS have low-wing configuration. New wingtips available for II-LTS (see illustration). All versions have lengthened fuselage and fixed incidence tailplane of reduced span.

POWER PLANT: One 1,700 cc Volkswagen modified motorcar engine with Monnett conversion, developing 48·5-52·2 kW (65-70 hp) and driving a two-blade ground adjustable wooden propeller. Alternative Volkswagen engines of 1,600 to 2,180 cc may be fitted, and the 2,180 cc version is standard for the Sonerai II-LT and II-LTS. Standard fuel capacity 37·8 litres (10 US gallons) for all versions except Sonerai II-LTS, which has standard capacity of 68 litres (18 US gallons), using turtledeck fuel tank which is optional on other versions. Oil as for Sonerai.

ACCOMMODATION: Two seats in tandem beneath transparent bubble canopy, hinged on starboard side. Dual controls.

AVIONICS: Prototype Sonerai II has alternator powered 100-channel radio.

DIMENSIONS, EXTERNAL: As Sonerai I, except:
Wing span 5·69 m (18 ft 8 in)
Length overall:
all except Sonerai II-LTS 5·74 m (18 ft 10 in)
Sonerai II-LTS 6·20 m (20 ft 4 in)
Tailplane span 1·83 m (6 ft 0 in)
Propeller diameter 1·32-1·37 m (4 ft 4 in to 4 ft 6 in)
AREA:
Wings, gross 7·80 m² (84·0 sq ft)

Sonerai II-LT alongside the component parts available from INAV for construction of the Sonerai II series

Standard mid-wing version of the INAV Sonerai II *(R. Kunert)*

INAV Sonerai II-LTS with prototype examples of the new-style wingtips

International Aircraft Corporation AG-7 with wings folded

INAV/Aviation Composites Mercury two-seat microlight *(J. M. G. Gradidge)*

Mr Bob Iseman's replica of a First World War Fokker D.VII fighter *(Howard Levy)*

IAC TA16 Trojan built by Mr William M. Johnson *(Howard Levy)*

Weights and Loadings (A: Sonerai II, B: IIL, C: II-LT, D: II-LTS):

Weight empty: A, B	227 kg (500 lb)
C	236 kg (520 lb)
D	245 kg (540 lb)
Utility max T-O weight: A, B, C	431 kg (950 lb)
D	458 kg (1,010 lb)
Max T-O weight: A, B, C, D	521 kg (1,150 lb)
Max wing loading:	
A, B, C, D	66·8 kg/m² (13·69 lb/sq ft)
Max power loading, with 70 hp engine:	
A, B, C, D	9·98 kg/kW (16·43 lb/hp)

Performance (A: Sonerai II/IIL with 1,700 cc engine, B: Sonerai II/IIL with 2,180 cc engine, C: Sonerai II-LT with 2,180 cc engine, D: Sonerai II-LTS with 2,180 cc engine):

Max level speed at S/L:	
A	139 knots (257 km/h; 160 mph)
B	152 knots (282 km/h; 175 mph)
C, D	148 knots (274 km/h; 170 mph)
Max cruising speed at S/L, 75% power:	
A	122 knots (225 km/h; 140 mph)
B	135 knots (249 km/h; 155 mph)
C, D	130 knots (241 km/h; 150 mph)
Econ cruising speed at S/L:	
A	113 knots (209 km/h; 130 mph)
Stalling speed: A, B	38 knots (71 km/h; 44 mph)
C	39 knots (73 km/h; 45 mph)
D	44 knots (81 km/h; 50 mph)
Max rate of climb at S/L: A	152 m (500 ft)/min
B, C	244 m (800 ft)/min
D	213 m (700 ft)/min
T-O run, ISA: A	274 m (900 ft)
B, C, D	213 m (700 ft)
Landing run: A	152 m (500 ft)
Range, with reserves:	
A, B, C	304 nm (563 km; 350 miles)
D	521 nm (965 km; 600 miles)
g limits: pilot only, Aerobatic category, A, B, C	±6
pilot only, Aerobatic category, D	+6/−4
max T-O weight, Utility category, A, B, C, D	±4·4

INAV/AVIATION COMPOSITES MERCURY

This side by side two-seat microlight was designed by Burt Rutan, originally for Lotus Cars Ltd of the UK, under whose entry the single-seat prototype was illustrated in the 1985-86 *Jane's*. The production airframe is manufactured by Aviation Composites (Pound Lane, Thatcham, Newbury, Berkshire RG13 9XX, England) and the Mercury is marketed by INAV in the USA.

The Mercury (N86NV) exhibited at Oshkosh in 1986 is shown in an accompanying illustration. It is a sweptwing canard with three-axis control by tip rudders incorporated in the winglets, elevators on the foreplane, and elevons. The mainwheels of the tricycle landing gear are carried on cantilever aluminium alloy spring legs; only the nosewheel is retractable. A small ventral fin serves also to protect the propeller from contact with the ground during rotation. Power plant is a 37·5 kW (50 hp) KFM 112 flat-four engine, mounted aft of the enclosed cockpit. The airframe structure is of glassfibre/foam/graphite/epoxy.

Dimensions, external:	
Wing span	9·75 m (32 ft 0 in)
Length overall	5·54 m (18 ft 2 in)
Area:	
Wings, gross	14·03 m² (151·0 sq ft)
Weight and Loadings:	
Max T-O weight	363 kg (800 lb)
Max wing loading	25·9 kg/m² (5·30 lb/sq ft)
Max power loading	9·73 kg/kW (16·0 lb/hp)
Performance (estimated):	
Max cruising speed	93 knots (172 km/h; 107 mph)
Landing speed	35 knots (65 km/h; 40 mph)
Max rate of climb at S/L	255 m (835 ft)/min
Range with max fuel	378 nm (700 km; 435 miles)

ISEMAN

BOB ISEMAN

Clearwater, Florida

ISEMAN FOKKER D.VII REPLICA

Mr Bob Iseman took 3½ years to research and construct his D.VII fighter replica, which flew for the first time in April 1985. Powered by a 130·5 kW (175 hp) inverted Ranger 6-440C-2 inline engine, it is painted in the markings of Hermann Goering's First World War D.VII.

No further details were available at the time of writing.

JAVELIN

JAVELIN AIRCRAFT COMPANY INC

Municipal Airport, Augusta, Kansas 67010
Telephone: (316) 733 1011
President and Chief Engineer: David D. Blanton

Javelin Aircraft Company Inc was founded on 1 March 1953 to manufacture a low cost automatic pilot for small aircraft; this was followed by equipment manufacture, and aircraft development work. Following restoration of a Curtiss Robin between 1957 and 1961, which won the National Championship award for the best restored antique aircraft in 1961, Javelin sought an Arrow Sport biplane for similar treatment. Unable to find a suitable aircraft, the company began design and development of a new biplane on 1 January 1964. The resulting aircraft (N71DB), named Wichawk, flew for the first time on 24 May 1971.

Javelin Aircraft does not produce assembled Wichawks, but plans, wing ribs and fuel tanks are available to amateur constructors. About 250 Wichawks were under construction in early 1986; at least 14 were already flying. Sets of plans have been sold to amateur constructors in Argentina, Australia, Canada and the USA. The first plans-built Wichawk (N29JC) made its first flight on 2 August 1975 powered by a 168 kW (225 hp) Continental O-470-11 engine. Two other Wichawks are powered by 134 kW (180 hp) Avco Lycoming O-360 engines, one with a Continental E-225-8, and one with a 172 kW (230 hp) Continental O-470-R. The eighth amateur built Wichawk to fly (N75WT), in 1980, was the first three-seater, with a single cockpit aft of the normal side by side two-seat cockpit. Powered by a Continental E-225-4 engine, this aircraft has an empty weight of 679 kg (1,496 lb). The latest Wichawk to fly is a two-seater built in Australia by retired Qantas Boeing 747 captain, Mr Bill Taylor (see accompanying illustration).

In addition, Javelin Aircraft manufactures 190 litre (50·2 US gallon) glassfibre slipper fuel tanks for the Rockwell Commander and Turbo-Commander 680/690 series; constructs 223 litre (59 US gallon) additional wing tanks for early models of the Polish PZL M-18 Dromader agricultural aircraft; is marketing plans for a conversion of the turbocharged or non-turbocharged Ford Pinto motorcar engines, which develop 119 kW (160 hp) and 93 kW (125 hp) respectively and have been flight tested in a 1956 Cessna 172 lightplane; and is flight testing a Ford Windsor V6 in a Cessna 175 and a 1,600 cc Ford Escort engine in a Cessna 150. About 700 sets of engine conversion drawings had been sold by early 1986.

JAVELIN WICHAWK

Type: Two/three-seat homebuilt sporting biplane.

Airframe: Braced single-bay biplane, with streamline section N cabane and interplane struts. Streamline section landing and flying wires. Wing section NACA 23015. 2° dihedral on lower wings only. Incidence 0°. No sweepback. Composite wings, with two wooden spars and 2024-T3 light alloy ribs, fabric covered. Simple sealed ailerons on lower wings only. No flaps. Geared trim tab. Welded fuselage of 4130 chrome molybdenum steel tube with light alloy tubular stringers, fabric covered. Wire braced welded tail unit of 4130 chrome molybdenum steel tube with fabric covering. Fixed incidence tailplane. Trim tab in starboard elevator.

Landing Gear: Non-retractable tailwheel type. Mainwheels carried on side Vs hinged to lower fuselage longerons. Shock absorption by automotive shock struts, similar to those of Piper PA-20, and rubber shock cord. Mainwheels and tyres size 6·00-6. Cleveland toe brakes. Steerable tailwheel.

Power Plant: Prototype has one 134 kW (180 hp) Avco Lycoming O-360 flat-four engine, driving a Sensenich two-blade fixed-pitch propeller type 76EM8-0-56. McCauley propellers optional. Provision for alternative horizontally opposed or radial engines from 112 kW (150 hp) to 224 kW (300 hp), for which Javelin can provide installation drawings. Engines currently being installed, other than those mentioned previously, include the 175 kW (235 hp) Avco Lycoming O-435, 224 kW (300 hp) Avco Lycoming O-540 and 224 kW (300 hp) Continental O-520. Fuel tank of 94·5 litre (25 US gallon) capacity in upper wing centre-section, and one of 56·8 litre (15 US gallon) capacity in fuselage aft of firewall. Refuelling points above tanks. Oil capacity of prototype 7·5 litres (2 US gallons).

Accommodation: Two seats side by side in open cockpit. Provision for tandem two-seat or three-seat configurations. Drawings available for rearward sliding transparent cockpit canopy. Dual controls standard. Baggage compartment aft of seats, capacity 45·4 kg (100 lb). Baggage locker in turtleback, capacity 9 kg (20 lb).

Systems: Electrical system powered by 12V 50A engine driven generator. Hydraulic system for brakes only.

Dimensions, external:

Wing span (upper)	7·32 m (24 ft 0 in)
Wing chord (both, constant)	1·27 m (4 ft 2 in)
Wing aspect ratio	5·76
Length overall	5·87 m (19 ft 3 in)
Height overall	2·18 m (7 ft 2 in)
Tailplane span	2·44 m (8 ft 0 in)
Wheel track	1·87 m (6 ft 1½ in)
Propeller diameter	1·93 m (6 ft 4 in)

Dimensions, internal:

Cockpit: Max width	0·93 m (3 ft 0½ in)
Baggage compartment	0·34 m³ (12 cu ft)

Area:

Wings, gross	17·2 m² (185·0 sq ft)

Weights and Loadings (A: prototype with 134 kW; 180 hp engine, B: three-seat version with six-cylinder engine):

Weight empty: A	582·5 kg (1,284·5 lb)
B	635 kg (1,400 lb)
*Max T-O weight: A	907 kg (2,000 lb)
B	978 kg (2,156 lb)
Max wing loading: A	52·8 kg/m² (10·81 lb/sq ft)
B	56·9 kg/m² (11·65 lb/sq ft)
Max power loading: A	6·77 kg/kW (11·11 lb/hp)

* *Max T-O weight is increased to 998 kg (2,200 lb) with high-powered engines*

Performance (prototype with 134 kW; 180 hp engine):

Never-exceed speed	156 knots (289 km/h; 180 mph)
Max level speed at S/L	121 knots (225 km/h; 140 mph)
Max cruising speed	110 knots (204 km/h; 127 mph)
Landing speed	39 knots (73 km/h; 45 mph)
Stalling speed	50 knots (92 km/h; 57 mph) IAS
Max rate of climb at S/L	518 m (1,700 ft)/min
T-O run	46 m (150 ft)
g limits	+12/−6

KELLY

DUDLEY R. KELLY

Route 4, Versailles, Kentucky 40383
Telephone: (606) 873 5253

Mr Dudley R. Kelly designed a biplane known as the Kelly-D, with the emphasis on improved efficiency and easier and cheaper construction than that of other designs in the same category, with full accommodation for two adults. Design was initiated on 22 May 1977, and the prototype (N24JF), built by Mr Jim Foster, made its first flight on 20 December 1981, after an elapsed construction time of under two years. Plans became available to amateur constructors on 1 January 1983. Several Kelly-Ds are known to be under construction.

Two Kelly-Ds factory built by Rogers Aircraft of Sanford, Florida, were the first to be completed after the prototype. A modified Kelly-D was developed on the basis of experience with these aircraft, to offer greatly improved ground handling and a lower landing speed. It uses a new wing section and has a 0·61 m (2 ft) increase in span. This version is now the only one released for home building and the details refer to it. Pre-welded component parts for the Kelly-D are available.

The prototype of a new single-seat Kelly D-1 was being constructed in early 1986. No details were available in mid-1986, except that it was to be powered by a 30 kW (40 hp) engine.

KELLY-D

Type: Two-seat lightweight homebuilt biplane.

Airframe: Single-bay biplane, with wire braced parallel interplane struts each side. Inverted V centre-section struts and streamline section landing and flying wires. Wing section NACA 4412. Dihedral 3°, on lower wings only. Incidence 2° on both wings. Constant chord, with no sweepback but considerable stagger. Wooden two-spar structure, with fabric covering. Aerodynamically balanced ailerons of wooden construction, fabric covered, on lower wing only. Conventional welded steel tube fuselage and wire braced tail unit, with fabric covering. Fixed incidence tailplane. Trim tab in port elevator.

Landing Gear: Non-retractable tailwheel type. Two side Vs and half-axles hinged to fuselage structure. Shock absorption of main units by steel coil spring on each compression strut. Mainwheel tyres size 6·00-6, pressure 1·24 bars (18 lb/sq in). Tailwheel diameter 6 in. Cleveland hydraulic disc brakes. Fairings over mainwheels.

Power Plant: One 86 kW (115 hp) Avco Lycoming O-235 flat-four engine, driving a Sensenich two-blade fixed-pitch propeller. Flight testing will also be undertaken with a 48·5 kW (65 hp) Continental C65 engine. Fuel tank in fuselage, aft of firewall, with capacity of 91 litres (24 US gallons). Refuelling point on upper surface of fuselage, forward of front cockpit. Oil capacity 5·7 litres (1·5 US gallons).

Accommodation: Two seats in tandem in open cockpits. Baggage space aft of pilot's seat in rear cockpit, capacity 18 kg (40 lb).

Systems: Hydraulic system for brakes only. Electrical system includes starter/generator and 12V storage battery.

Avionics and Equipment: Genave Alpha 200B radio. Navigation lights.

Dimensions, external:

Wing span (both)	8·03 m (26 ft 4 in)
Wing chord, constant (both)	1·27 m (4 ft 2 in)
Wing aspect ratio	5·84
Length overall	5·87 m (19 ft 3 in)
Height overall	2·36 m (7 ft 9 in)
Tailplane span	2·82 m (9 ft 3 in)
Wheel track	1·83 m (6 ft 0 in)
Wheelbase	4·04 m (13 ft 3 in)
Propeller diameter	1·88 m (6 ft 2 in)

Area:

Wings, gross	19·54 m² (210·38 sq ft)

Weights and Loadings:

Basic operating weight empty	431 kg (950 lb)
Max T-O and landing weight	726 kg (1,600 lb)
Max wing loading	37·15 kg/m² (7·61 lb/sq ft)
Max power loading	8·44 kg/kW (13·91 lb/hp)

Performance:

Cruising speed	78 knots (145 km/h; 90 mph)
Stalling speed	39 knots (73 km/h; 45 mph)
Max rate of climb at S/L, pilot only	274 m (900 ft)/min
Range with max fuel, 20 min reserves	243 nm (450 km; 280 miles)

KIMBREL

MICHAEL G. KIMBREL

1333 Garrard Creek Road, Oakville, Washington 98568
Telephone: (206) 273 9203

Mr Michael G. Kimbrel currently offers plans for the construction of one Experimental category and two microlight aircraft of his own design, details of which follow. He also markets plans for the SNS-2 Guppy biplane, described under the Sorrell entry.

KIMBREL DORMOY BATHTUB Mk 1

Mr Kimbrel built a single-seat homebuilt aircraft known as the Bathtub Mk 1, basing it on details of the Dormoy Bathtub of 1924 published in a 1960 aviation magazine. Construction took seven years of part-time work and cost $700. The Bathtub Mk 1 flew for the first time on 29 April 1978. It has since logged more than 100 flying hours without a major problem. Drawings are available to amateur builders and at least 454 sets had been sold by early 1986. Several plans-built Bathtubs have flown.

Type: Single-seat homebuilt monoplane.

Airframe: Strut and wire braced parasol monoplane wings of wooden construction, Dacron covered. Clark Y wing section. No dihedral. Plain ailerons. No flaps. Fuselage consists of Dacron-covered steel tube nacelle, with wire braced steel tubes aft to support a tail unit of similar construction. Braced tailplane, with one-piece elevator, forms T tail on top of triangular fin and rounded rudder.

Landing Gear: Non-retractable tailwheel type. Main units carry 0·51 m (1 ft 8 in) heavy duty bicycle wheels with specially prepared steel hubs and Oilite bronze bearings. Spokes will be fitted eventually with fabric covers.

Power Plant: Prototype has one 30 kW (40 hp) 1,200 cc Volkswagen modified motorcar engine, driving a Hegy 54 × 26 two-blade propeller. Other Bathtubs have flown with 27 kW (36 hp) Volkswagen, 45 kW (60 hp) Franklin and 30 kW (40 hp) Continental engines. Fuel tank capacity 21·5 litres (5·7 US gallons).

Accommodation: Single seat in open cockpit.

Dimensions, external:

Wing span	7·29 m (23 ft 11 in)
Wing chord: inboard	1·07 m (3 ft 6 in)
over ailerons	1·14 m (3 ft 9 in)
Length overall	4·14 m (13 ft 7 in)
Height overall	2·03 m (6 ft 8 in)

Area:

Wings, gross	7·80 m² (84·0 sq ft)

Weights and Loadings (prototype):

Weight empty	137 kg (302 lb)
Max T-O weight	245 kg (540 lb)
Max wing loading	31·4 kg/m² (6·43 lb/sq ft)
Max power loading	8·17 kg/kW (13·50 lb/hp)

Performance (prototype):

Max level speed	56 knots (105 km/h; 65 mph)
Cruising speed	48 knots (88 km/h; 55 mph)
Stalling speed	31 knots (57 km/h; 35 mph)
Max rate of climb at S/L	122 m (400 ft)/min
Absolute ceiling	1,980 m (6,500 ft)
T-O run	152 m (500 ft)
Landing run	91 m (300 ft)
Range with max fuel	87 nm (161 km; 100 miles)

KIMBREL BUTTERFLY

Following on from the Bathtub, Mr Kimbrel designed and built the Butterfly in 1983 for the Aircraft Recreation

Javelin Wichawk built by Mr Bill Taylor of Sydney, Australia *(Qantas)*

The first Kelly-D two-seat biplane built from plans, by Rogers Aircraft of Sanford, Florida

Kimbrel Banty single-seat amateur-built microlight

Kimbrel Butterfly microlight prototype

Kimbrel Dormoy Bathtub Mk 1 (Continental A40 engine) built by Mr Harley Dahler of Nokomis, Illinois

Vehicle competition at Oshkosh. Plans to allow amateur construction became available in 1985. Because building a Butterfly is labour intensive (requiring about 500 working hours), there is no intention to produce ready assembled aircraft.

Type: Single-seat microlight aircraft; conforms to FAR Pt 103.

Airframe: Conventional high-wing monoplane. Fuselage boom consists of 7·6 cm (3 in) diameter aluminium irrigation tube, with aluminium tubing in the cockpit area, bolted and pop riveted. Spruce/plywood wings with aluminium leading-edges, 100 per cent double surface Stits fabric covering. Aerofoil section USA35B (modified). Galvanised steel cable bracing. Kingpost standard. Conventional tail unit. Three-axis control (ailerons, elevator and rudder). Wings fold alongside fuselage for road transportation and storage. Rigging time 10 min.

Landing Gear: Non-retractable two-wheel type, with 16 in mainwheels and skid under tail. Split axle for main units with bungee shock absorption; tennis balls for nose ski shock absorption. No brakes.

Power Plant: One 20 kW (27 hp) Rotax 277 engine, with 2:1 belt reduction drive to a two-blade wooden propeller. Fuel tank capacity 19 litres (5 US gallons).

Accommodation: Pilot only, in partially enclosed 'bathtub' without doors.

Dimensions, external:

Wing span	11·13 m (36 ft 6 in)
Wing aspect ratio	9
Length overall	6·55 m (21 ft 6 in)
Propeller diameter	1·27 m (4 ft 2 in)

Area:

Wings, gross	13·66 m² (147·0 sq ft)

Weights and Loadings:

Weight empty	90 kg (198 lb)
Max pilot weight	93 kg (205 lb)
Max T-O weight	195 kg (430 lb)
Max wing loading	14·3 kg/m² (2·92 lb/sq ft)
Max power loading	9·75 kg/kW (15·93 lb/hp)

Performance:

Never-exceed speed	52 knots (96 km/h; 60 mph)
Max level speed	52 knots (96 km/h; 60 mph)
Cruising speed	39 knots (72 km/h; 45 mph)
Min speed:	
power on	19 knots (36 km/h; 22 mph)
power off	22 knots (41 km/h; 25 mph)
Max rate of climb at S/L	more than 137 m (450 ft)
Service ceiling	more than 2,440 m (8,000 ft)
T-O run	40 m (130 ft)
Landing run	61 m (200 ft)
Range with max standard fuel	78 nm (145 km; 90 miles)
Endurance with standard fuel	2 h 30 min
g limits	+4/−2 design

KIMBREL BANTY

Mr Kimbrel's latest aircraft, the simple low-cost Banty microlight, is offered in plans form only for amateur construction. Building takes an estimated 500 working hours.

Design began in January 1984 and was based partly on the Heath Parasol, although of larger overall dimensions. The prototype flew for the first time on 9 June 1985.

Type: Single-seat non-aerobatic microlight aircraft.

Airframe: Strut and wire braced parasol-wing monoplane. Fabric covered all-wood construction, except for 6061-T6 aluminium alloy tubing for cabane and lift struts. Folding wing uses modified USA35B section. Dihedral 3°. Slight sweepback. Flaps standard. Flat-sided fuselage and conventional tail unit with strut-braced tailplane and cantilever fin. Three-axis control (ailerons, elevators and rudder). Wing folding takes about 4 min.

Landing Gear: Non-retractable tailskid type, with mainwheels carried on 2024-T3 axle. Small nosewheel to prevent damage to propeller.

Power Plant: One 20 kW (27 hp) Rotax 277 single-cylinder two-stroke engine, with 2·5:1 Hegar belt reduction to a Shettler two-blade propeller. Fuel capacity 19 litres (5 US gallons).

Accommodation: Pilot only, in open cockpit with windscreen.

Dimensions, external:

Wing span	9·75 m (32 ft 0 in)
Wing chord, constant	1·27 m (4 ft 2 in)
Width, wings folded	2·41 m (7 ft 11½ in)
Length overall	5·74 m (18 ft 10 in)
Height overall	1·83 m (6 ft 0 in)
Propeller diameter	1·52 m (5 ft 0 in)

Weights and Loading:

Weight empty	108 kg (237 lb)
Pilot weight range	50-102 kg (110-225 lb)
Max T-O weight	227 kg (500 lb)
Max power loading	11·35 kg/kW (18·52 lb/hp)

Performance:

Cruising speed	43 knots (80 km/h; 50 mph)
T-O run, 10° flaps	67 m (220 ft)
g limit	+6

KOLB

KOLB COMPANY INC

RD 3, Box 38, Phoenixville, Pennsylvania 19460
Telephone: (215) 948 4136
President: Homer Kolb

KOLB ULTRASTAR

Designed to succeed the twin-engined Flyer, which was described in the 1983-84 *Jane's* and is now out of production, the single-engined UltraStar appeared in March 1982 and is offered in kit form.

Type: Single-seat microlight aircraft; conforms to FAR Pt 103.

Airframe: High-wing monoplane, with single bracing strut each side. Welded chrome-molybdenum steel cage structure, with aluminium tailboom. Two-spar wings, with double surface Dacron covering. Three-axis control (full span ailerons, elevators and rudder). Wings and horizontal tail foldable for transportation and storage.

LANDING GEAR: Tailwheel type, with 15 × 4 in mainwheels on two side Vs and half axles and 4 in steerable tailwheel. No brakes. Floats and skis optional.

POWER PLANT: One 26 kW (35 hp) Cuyuna ULII-02 two-cylinder two-stroke engine, with poly-V belt reduction system to a two-blade wooden pusher propeller; 26 kW (35 hp) Rotax 377 engine optional. Two fuel tanks, each with capacity of 6·6 litres (1·75 US gallons).

ACCOMMODATION: Pilot only, in open position.

DIMENSIONS, EXTERNAL:

Wing span	8·38 m (27 ft 6 in)
Wing aspect ratio	5·14
Length overall	6·40 m (21 ft 0 in)
Height overall	1·83 m (6 ft 0 in)
Propeller diameter	1·27 m (4 ft 2 in)

AREA:

Wings, gross	13·47 m² (145·0 sq ft)

WEIGHTS AND LOADINGS:

Weight empty	114 kg (252 lb)
Pilot weight range	54·5-106·5 kg (120-235 lb)
Max T-O weight	229 kg (505 lb)
Max wing loading	16·75 kg/m² (3·43 lb/sq ft)
Max power loading	8·81 kg/kW (14·43 lb/hp)

PERFORMANCE (at max T-O weight):

Never-exceed speed	65 knots (120 km/h; 75 mph)
Max level speed	55 knots (101 km/h; 63 mph)
Max cruising speed	43 knots (80 km/h; 50 mph)
Econ cruising speed	39 knots (72 km/h; 45 mph)
Stalling speed, power on	22 knots (41 km/h; 25 mph)
Max rate of climb at S/L	244 m (800 ft)/min
T-O and landing run	31 m (100 ft)
g limits	+4/−2

KOLB TWINSTAR

Introduced at the 1984 Sun 'n Fun meeting in Florida, the TwinStar is a side by side two-seat microlight aircraft, now fitted as standard with the more powerful Rotax 503 engine. It is available in three pre-welded kits, with a glassfibre nose fairing, Lexan windscreen and instruments among the options.

TYPE: Side by side two-seat aircraft: conforms to FAR Pt 103 for microlights and Experimental category for homebuilts.

AIRFRAME: Strut-braced high-wing monoplane, with welded 4130 chrome-molybdenum steel cage structure and aluminium boom supporting conventional tail surfaces. Wings have aluminium tube spar with aluminium ribs, 100 per cent double surface Stits Dacron covered. Wings and horizontal tail surfaces fold for transportation in 10 min. Special Kolb wing section. Thickness/chord ratio 12%. Dihedral 2°. Incidence 4°. No sweepback. No kingpost. Anodised cables. Three-axis control (full span ailerons, elevators with trim tab, and rudder). Options include ballistic recovery parachute, instruments and strobe light. Rigging time 10 min.

LANDING GEAR: Non-retractable tailwheel type. Cantilever solid 7075-T6 tapered spring legs for mainwheels, with 16 × 6 in balloon tyres, pressure 0·69 bars (10 lb/sq in). Steerable tailwheel, diameter 5 in. Mainwheel brakes, floats and skis optional.

POWER PLANT: One 35 kW (47 hp) Rotax 503 two-cylinder two-stroke engine, with 2·58:1 Rotax reduction gearing to a Culver slow turning two-blade wooden pusher propeller. Distance between engine and crew minimises engine noise; gearbox vibration dampened. One fuel tank, capacity 19 litres (5 US gallons).

ACCOMMODATION: Pilot and passenger side by side in open position. Optional glassfibre nose fairing and windscreen. Optional intercom in helmets.

DIMENSIONS, EXTERNAL:

Wing span	9·15 m (30 ft 0 in)
Wing aspect ratio	5·63
Width, wings folded	1·68 m (5 ft 6 in)
Length overall: without fairing	6·38 m (20 ft 11 in)
with fairing	6·96 m (22 ft 10 in)
Height overall	1·73 m (5 ft 8 in)
Tailplane span	2·41 m (7 ft 11 in)
Propeller diameter	1·68 m (5 ft 6 in)

AREA:

Wings, gross	14·86 m² (160·0 sq ft)

WEIGHTS AND LOADINGS:

Weight empty, without fairing	134 kg (295 lb)
Pilot weight range, solo	59-113 kg (130-250 lb)
Max T-O weight	311 kg (685 lb)
Max wing loading	20·9 kg/m² (4·28 lb/sq ft)
Max power loading	8·89 kg/kW (14·57 lb/hp)

PERFORMANCE (at max T-O weight):

Never-exceed speed	65 knots (120 km/h; 75 mph)
Max level speed at 305 m (1,000 ft)	59 knots (109 km/h; 68 mph)
Max cruising speed at 305 m (1,000 ft)	46 knots (85 km/h; 53 mph)
Econ cruising speed at 305 m (1,000 ft)	39 knots (72 km/h; 45 mph)
Stalling speed, power off	25 knots (45 km/h; 28 mph)
Max rate of climb at S/L:	
two crew	259 m (850 ft)/min
solo	457 m (1,500 ft)/min
T-O and landing run, on grass	61 m (200 ft)
g limits	+4/−2

KOLB FIRESTAR

Latest microlight from Kolb is the single-seat FireStar, which has features of the UltraStar and TwinStar but is the first in the range to incorporate a semi-enclosed cockpit rather than the previous open position or optional nose fairing. It uses a low tailboom of TwinStar type and a reduced-span version of the TwinStar's wing. Other changes include a centre-mounted joystick (in place of the usual side stick) and increased fuel capacity. The constructional kit is said to be the most pre-manufactured of any Kolb aircraft, with a completely pre-welded 4130 chrome-molybdenum steel tube fuselage. Optional items include completed wing ribs, balloon tyres and instruments.

TYPE: Single-seat microlight aircraft: conforms to FAR Pt 103·7.

LANDING GEAR: Non-retractable tailwheel type, with standard or optional large balloon mainwheel tyres on 7075-T6 tapered solid spring legs. Steerable tailwheel.

POWER PLANT: One 26 kW (35 hp) Rotax 377 engine with Rotax reduction gearbox, driving a two-blade pusher propeller. Fuel tank capacity 19 litres (5 US gallons).

ACCOMMODATION: Pilot only, in semi-enclosed cockpit with Lexan windscreen.

DIMENSIONS, EXTERNAL:

Wing span	8·36 m (27 ft 5 in)
Width, wings folded	1·42 m (4 ft 8 in)
Length overall	6·17 m (20 ft 3 in)
Height overall	1·73 m (5 ft 8 in)
Propeller diameter	1·68 m (5 ft 6 in)

AREA:

Wings, gross	13·75 m² (148·0 sq ft)

WEIGHTS AND LOADING:

Weight empty	120 kg (264 lb)
Max T-O weight	249 kg (549 lb)
Max power loading	9·58 kg/kW (15·69 lb/hp)

PERFORMANCE:

Never-exceed speed	69 knots (128 km/h; 80 mph)
Max level speed	55 knots (101 km/h; 63 mph)
Max cruising speed	43 knots (80 km/h; 50 mph)
Stalling speed	22 knots (41 km/h; 25 mph)
Max rate of climb at S/L	366 m (1,200 ft)/min
T-O run, on grass	31 m (100 ft)
g limits	+4/−2

LACO

LACO

PO Box 415, Desert Hot Springs, California 92240
Telephone: (619) 329 9354

LACO-125 and LACO-145

Mr Joe Laven designed and built a two-seat light biplane known as the **LACO-125**. Design started in May 1971 and, following construction of two scale models to check the basic configuration, construction of the prototype (N1KN) began in April 1972. First flight was made on 29 May 1977 by Stolp Starduster test pilot Mr Eric Shilling.

This prototype was sold in 1981, and was replaced by a second aircraft, which is designated **LACO-145** as it is powered by a 108 kW (145 hp) Continental C145 engine. Minor changes on this later aircraft include the addition of a trim tab on the elevator, and small internal structural modifications. The engine cowl and exhaust system were redesigned in 1983.

Plans for construction of the LACO-125 and LACO-145 are available to amateur constructors. The following description applies to both aircraft, except where indicated otherwise:

TYPE: Two-seat light homebuilt biplane.

AIRFRAME: Braced single-bay biplane. Wing section NACA 2412. Dihedral 2° and incidence 2° on lower wings only. Conventional structure, with two spruce spars, spruce capstrips, mahogany ribs, aluminium leading- and trailing-edges and chrome molybdenum steel fittings, all fabric covered. N interplane struts; two N struts support centre of upper wing above fuselage. Modified Frise ailerons on lower wings only, of similar construction to wings. No flaps or trim tabs. Welded Warren truss fuselage of chrome molybdenum steel tubing, with mahogany formers and spruce stringers, fabric covered. Conventional braced tail unit of welded chrome molybdenum steel tube, fabric covered. Trim tab optional on LACO-125, and not fitted to prototype. LACO-145 has trim tab on elevator as standard.

LANDING GEAR: Non-retractable tailwheel type, with steerable tailwheel. Polyurethane spring shock absorption of LACO design. Cleveland mainwheels, size 6·00-6. McKay Aero Research MF-7 mainwheel fairings. Cleveland hydraulic brakes.

POWER PLANT: LACO-125: One 93 kW (125 hp) Continental C-125-2 flat-six engine, driving a McCauley 72 × 52 two-blade fixed-pitch propeller. LACO-145: One 108 kW (145 hp) Continental C145 flat-six engine, driving a McCauley 76 × 51 two-blade fixed-pitch propeller. Fuel tank in fuselage, capacity 91 litres (24 US gallons). Oil capacity 7·5 litres (2 US gallons).

ACCOMMODATION: Two seats in tandem in open cockpits. Front cockpit can be covered over for flight as a single-seater.

SYSTEM: Engine driven generator, lights and 30A starting system.

AVIONICS: Genave 100-channel transceiver.

DIMENSIONS, EXTERNAL:

Wing span: upper	6·93 m (22 ft 8¾ in)
lower	6·29 m (20 ft 7½ in)
Wing chord: upper (constant)	1·14 m (3 ft 9 in)
lower (constant)	1·07 m (3 ft 6 in)
Length overall	5·94 m (19 ft 6 in)
Height overall	2·18 m (7 ft 2 in)
Tailplane span	2·64 m (8 ft 8 in)
Wheel track	1·88 m (6 ft 2 in)
Wheelbase	4·47 m (14 ft 8 in)
Propeller diameter: LACO-125	1·83 m (6 ft 0 in)
LACO-145	1·93 m (6 ft 4 in)

AREA:

Wings, gross	13·94 m² (150·0 sq ft)

WEIGHTS AND LOADINGS:

Weight empty	390 kg (860 lb)
Max T-O weight	635 kg (1,400 lb)
Max wing loading	45·6 kg/m² (9·33 lb/sq ft)
Max power loading	6·83 kg/kW (11·20 lb/hp)

PERFORMANCE (A: LACO-125, B: LACO-145):

Never-exceed speed:	
A	139 knots (257 km/h; 160 mph)
B	156 knots (290 km/h; 180 mph)
Max level speed: A	108 knots (200 km/h; 124 mph)
B	113 knots (209 km/h; 130 mph)
Max cruising speed:	
A	98 knots (182 km/h; 113 mph)
B	104 knots (193 km/h; 120 mph)
Stalling speed, power off:	
A	49 knots (90 km/h; 56 mph)
B	48 knots (89 km/h; 55 mph)
Stalling speed, power on:	
A	44 knots (81 km/h; 50 mph)
B	42 knots (78 km/h; 48 mph)
Max rate of climb at S/L: A	274 m (900 ft)/min
B	366 m (1,200 ft)/min
Range with max fuel:	
A	282 nm (523 km; 325 miles)
B	269 nm (499 km; 310 miles)

LANGHURST

LOUIS F. LANGHURST

Route 1, Box 315, Carriere, Mississippi 39426

Telephone: (601) 798 2880

LANGHURST REPLICA JUNKERS Ju 87B-2 'STUKA'

Mr Louis F. Langhurst, a retired design engineer, designed and built a ⁷⁄₁₀th-scale tandem two-seat replica of the German Junkers Ju 87B-2 'Stuka' dive bomber of the Second World War, finished in the personal markings of Major Hans-Ulrich Rudel of III Gruppe, Schlachtgeschwader 2 'Immelmann'. Research and design took two years and construction occupied 8,000 working hours over a six-year period. First flight was made on 19 July 1978. Construction is of steel tubing, with aluminium skinning, using many components of a salvaged Fairchild PT-19. The nose cowling of the prototype is of aluminium, with epoxy glassfibre for compound curved parts; but other constructors can make the cowling entirely of glassfibre, as used for the mainwheel fairings. The control surfaces are identical in form with those of the original, with auxiliary aerofoil ailerons and flaps, but the dive-brakes remain fixed in flight. Power is provided by a 164 kW (220 hp) Avco Lycoming GO-435-B engine, fuelled from a 117 litre (31 US gallon) tank, and driving a three-blade propeller. Other GO-435 series engines can be used by constructors. Mr Langhurst was awarded the 'Replica Fighters of America Annual Award of Excellence' for the aircraft at the 1979 EAA Fly-in.

A designer-builder's guide is available to amateur constructors; more than 100 had been sold worldwide by early 1986. It is known that at least one more Langhurst Ju 87B-2 is currently under construction, in New York State, and this was well advanced by early 1986. The prototype replica is currently on display at the San Diego Aero-Space Museum in California.

Kolb FireStar single-seat microlight *(J. M. G. Gradidge)*

Kolb UltraStar microlight *(Brian M. Service)*

Kolb TwinStar two-seat microlight and homebuilt aircraft

LACO-145 two-seat light biplane

Langhurst 7/10th-scale Ju 87B-2 replica, with the famous Second World War 'Stuka' pilot, Hans-Ulrich Rudel, standing in the cockpit

Leader's International JB-1000 microlight aircraft

Dimensions, external:

Wing span	9·91 m (32 ft 6 in)
Wing aspect ratio	6·45
Length overall	7·32 m (24 ft 0 in)
Height to top of canopy	2·29 m (7 ft 6 in)
Wheel track	2·26 m (7 ft 5 in)

Area:

Wings, gross	15·24 m² (164·0 sq ft)

Weights and Loadings:

Weight empty	762 kg (1,680 lb)
Max T-O weight	1,032 kg (2,275 lb)
Max wing loading	67·7 kg/m² (13·87 lb/sq ft)
Max power loading	6·29 kg/kW (10·34 lb/hp)

Performance:

Max level speed	119 knots (220 km/h; 137 mph)
Cruising speed	102 knots (190 km/h; 118 mph)
Landing speed	54 knots (100 km/h; 62 mph)
Max rate of climb at S/L	over 305 m (1,000 ft)/min

LEADER'S

LEADER'S INTERNATIONAL INC

212 North Mecklenburg Avenue, South Hill, Virginia 23970
Telephone: (804) 447 4919
President: Dr Rolf Brand

LEADER'S INTERNATIONAL JB-1000

The JB-1000 is a microlight aircraft of composite construction which is available in plan, kit and ready assembled forms.

Special features of the JB-1000 include a patented drive system that is concentrically mounted on the upper fuselage boom.

Type: Single-seat microlight aircraft; conforms to FAR Pt 103.

Airframe: Braced high-wing monoplane. Main frame constructed of carbonfibre and Kevlar, with cockpit pod, and upper and lower tailbooms supporting sweptback fin and rudder and tailplane with elevators. Dihedral double surfaced wings of similar composite construction. Stainless steel cables. Three-axis control (ailerons, elevators and rudder), with flaps.

Landing Gear: Non-retractable unsprung taildragger type, with tail resting on fin undersurface on prototypes. Production aircraft have steerable tailwheel. Mainwheel brakes.

Power Plant: One 20 kW (27 hp) Rotax 277 single-cylinder two-stroke engine, with 2·5:1 reduction drive to three-blade composite pusher propeller. Fuel tank capacity 19 litres (5 US gallons).

Accommodation: Pilot only, in semi-enclosed cockpit.

Dimensions, external:

Wing span	9·14 m (30 ft 0 in)
Wing aspect ratio	6
Length overall	6·10 m (20 ft 0 in)
Height overall	1·78 m (5 ft 10 in)
Propeller diameter	1·52 m (5 ft 0 in)

Area:

Wings, gross	13·47 m² (145·0 sq ft)

Weights and Loadings:

Weight empty	113 kg (250 lb)
Pilot weight range	63·5-100 kg (140-220 lb)
Max T-O weight	238 kg (525 lb)
Max wing loading	17·09 kg/m² (3·5 lb/sq ft)
Max power loading	11·90 kg/kW (19·44 lb/hp)

Performance:

Never-exceed speed	65 knots (120 km/h; 75 mph)
Max level speed	52 knots (97 km/h; 60 mph)
Max cruising speed	39 knots (72 km/h; 45 mph)
Econ cruising speed	36 knots (68 km/h; 42 mph)
Stalling speed: power on	22 knots (41 km/h; 25 mph)
power off	24 knots (44 km/h; 27 mph)
Max rate of climb at S/L	122 m (400 ft)/min
Service ceiling	3,660 m (12,000 ft)
T-O run	29 m (95 ft)
Landing run	30 m (100 ft)
g limits	+4/−2
Best glide ratio	8

LEADER'S INTERNATIONAL AM-DS1

In the Autumn of 1985, Leader's International released details of this new single-seat aircraft, similar in configuration to the JB-1000, which it claimed to be the first 'minimum' aircraft designed from the outset for low-cost military use. The single-seat pilot's module of the AM-DS1 is made of Kevlar for resistance to ground fire and crash damage, as well as for low radar signature, and is fully enclosed by a large one-piece transparent canopy. The seat is moulded integrally with the shell of this module. A non-retractable tricycle landing gear is fitted, with shock absorbers built into the mainwheel legs.

Use of a more powerful engine than those in other aircraft of this kind is said to offer a speed range from 26 to 200 knots (48-370 km/h; 30-230 mph), with a maximum useful load of 453 kg (1,000 lb). This could include two machine-guns or rocket pods. Missions that could be performed by the AM-DS1 are thought to include surveillance, infiltration, anti-helicopter combat, liaison and ground support. An RPV version has also been projected.

LEADER'S INTERNATIONAL AM-DSII

Similar in many respects to the AM-DS1, this single-seat light aircraft was exhibited at Oshkosh 86 to test the market for production in kit form. Construction is largely of Kevlar, with non-retractable tailwheel landing gear, auxiliary aerofoil flaperons, and (like the JB-1000) a unique SCAT (system for compact axial thrust) pusher propeller installation. This utilises a six-blade propeller which turns around the tailboom. In the prototype, this is of large diameter slow-turning type; but blades of different form can be fitted as required. The standard plug-in wings can be replaced with longer span wings for soaring. A more powerful engine can be used with the standard wings for aerobatics. The prototype has a 40·25 kW (54 hp) Rotax 503 engine, and a 75 litre (20 US gallon) fuel tank.

DIMENSION, EXTERNAL:
- Wing span: 7·62 m (25 ft 0 in)

AREA:
- Wings, gross: 11·6 m² (125·0 sq ft)

WEIGHTS AND LOADINGS:
- Weight empty: 215 kg (475 lb)
- Max T-O weight: 363 kg (800 lb)
- Max wing loading: 31·3 kg/m² (6·40 lb/sq ft)
- Max power loading: 9·02 kg/kW (14·8 lb/hp)

PERFORMANCE:
- Max level speed: 64 knots (119 km/h; 74 mph)
- Max cruising speed: 56 knots (104 km/h; 65 mph)
- Stalling speed: 29 knots (53 km/h; 33 mph)
- Max rate of climb at S/L: 183 m (600 ft)/min
- T-O and landing run: 76 m (250 ft)

LIGHT AERO

LIGHT AERO INC

PO Box 728, 4823 Aviation Way, Caldwell, Idaho 83606
Telephone: (208) 454 2600
PRESIDENT: Dean Wilson

Light Aero Inc markets in kit form the Avid Flyer landplane (with float option) and the Avid Amphibian flying-boat. The Flyer is offered with standard STOL or 'speed' wings.

LIGHT AERO AVID FLYER

Light Aero offers to amateur constructors FAA approved kits of component parts to build the side by side two-seat Avid Flyer, a fully towable high-wing monoplane that takes from 200 to 400 working hours to assemble. It is available as a single kit, which includes pre-welded structures, assembled wing ribs, the engine, propeller and instruments; or as six separate kits to spread the cost of purchase over a period of time. By early 1986 a total of 200 kits had been sold.

The Avid Flyer features two forms of interchangeable wings, the original high-lift STOL wings with unique near full span auxiliary aerofoil flaperons (which are said to give the aircraft light and responsive control) and shorter span 'speed' wings using a new wing section. With the 'speed' wings fitted, cruising speed is increased to 95 knots (177 km/h; 110 mph) and stalling speed becomes 35 knots (65 km/h; 40 mph) at max T-O weight.

TYPE: Two-seat homebuilt sporting monoplane.

AIRFRAME: High-wing monoplane, with streamline section V bracing struts each side. Slight dihedral. Jig drilled aluminium tube spars and I beam plywood ribs, covered with heat shrunk Dacron. Near full span flaperons hinged at the centre of pressure, of similar construction to wings. Wings can be folded back in less than 5 minutes for storage and towing, with no controls to disconnect. Welded fuselage of 4130 chrome molybdenum tubing, Dacron covered except for nose which has pre-moulded glassfibre cowlings. Fin constructed as integral part of fuselage structure. Rudder, strut braced tailplane and elevators have welded structure of 4130 chrome molybdenum tubing, covered with heat shrunk Dacron.

LANDING GEAR: Non-retractable nosewheel or tailwheel type, with 4130 steel tube side Vs and half-axles. Motorcycle tyres and brakes on mainwheels. Can be towed on mainwheels. Optional oversize wheels and tyres, floats, skis and wheel-skis.

POWER PLANT: One 48·5 kW (65 hp) Rotax 532 two-cylinder engine, driving a two-blade fixed-pitch propeller via 2·58:1 Rotax reduction gear. Fuel capacity 34 litres (9 US gallons).

ACCOMMODATION: Two seats side by side in fully enclosed and heavily glazed cabin. Lexan doors optional. Heater standard. Dual controls; individual toe brakes on port side.

SYSTEM: Electrical system.

DIMENSIONS, EXTERNAL:
- Wing span: STOL wings: 9·11 m (29 ft 10½ in)
  - 'Speed' wings: 7·30 m (23 ft 11½ in)
- Wing chord: excl flaperons: 1·07 m (3 ft 6 in)
  - incl flaperons: 1·30 m (4 ft 3 in)
- Wing aspect ratio: STOL wings: 7·29
  - 'Speed' wings: 5·90
- Width, wings folded: 2·37 m (7 ft 9½ in)
- Length overall: 5·18 m (17 ft 0 in)
- Height overall: 1·70 m (5 ft 7 in)
- Propeller diameter: 1·83 m (6 ft 0 in)

AREA:
- Wings, gross: STOL wings: 11·38 m² (122·5 sq ft)
  - 'Speed' wings: 9·04 m² (97·31 sq ft)

WEIGHTS AND LOADINGS:
- Weight empty:
  - STOL wings: 154-172 kg (340-380 lb)
  - 'Speed' wings: 150-168 kg (330-370 lb)
- Max T-O weight: 385 kg (850 lb)
- Max wing loading:
  - STOL wings: 33·83 kg/m² (6·94 lb/sq ft)
  - 'Speed' wings: 42·59 kg/m² (8·73 lb/sq ft)
- Max power loading: 7·94 kg/kW (13·08 lb/hp)

PERFORMANCE (with STOL wings. A: flown as single-seater at 263 kg; 580 lb AUW, B: two-seater at 385 kg; 850 lb AUW, C: single-seater with floats at 279 kg; 616 lb AUW, D: two-seater with floats at 363 kg; 800 lb AUW—with 'Speed' wings. E: single-seater at 263 kg; 580 lb AUW, F: two-seater at 385 kg; 850 lb AUW):
- Never-exceed speed:
  - A, B, C, D: 78 knots (145 km/h; 90 mph)
  - E, F: 108 knots (201 km/h; 125 mph)
- Max cruising speed:
  - A, B, C, D: 74 knots (137 km/h; 85 mph)
  - E, F: 95 knots (177 km/h; 110 mph)
- Stalling speed: A, C: 22 knots (41 km/h; 25 mph)
  - B: 28 knots (52 km/h; 32 mph)
  - D: 26 knots (49 km/h; 30 mph)
  - E: 29 knots (53 km/h; 33 mph)
  - F: 35 knots (65 km/h; 40 mph)
- Max rate of climb at S/L: A: 686 m (2,250 ft)/min
  - B: 427 m (1,400 ft)/min
  - C: 393 m (1,290 ft)/min
  - D: 233 m (764 ft)/min
  - E: 640 m (2,100 ft)/min
  - F: 419 m (1,375 ft)/min
- Service ceiling: A: 8,535 m (28,000 ft)
  - B: 5,335 m (17,500 ft)
  - C: 5,790 m (19,000 ft)
  - D: 3,660 m (12,000 ft)
  - E: 6,100 m (20,000 ft)
  - F: 4,575 m (15,000 ft)
- T-O run: A: 15 m (50 ft)
  - B: 43 m (140 ft)
  - C: 54 m (176 ft)
  - D: 91 m (297 ft)
  - E: 38 m (125 ft)
  - F: 92 m (300 ft)
- T-O to 15 m (50 ft): A: 46 m (150 ft)
  - B: 104 m (340 ft)
  - E: 76 m (250 ft)
  - F: 152 m (500 ft)
- Landing run: A: 30 m (100 ft)
  - B: 46 m (150 ft)
  - E: 152 m (500 ft)
  - F: 183 m (600 ft)
- Range with max fuel: 260 nm (483 km; 300 miles)
- *g* limits: +3·8 (+5·7 ultimate)

LIGHT AERO AVID AMPHIBIAN

First flown on 12 July 1985, and displayed at Oshkosh 85 in the following month, the three-seat Avid Amphibian (prototype N47AA) is available in kit form for amateur construction. It can be built optionally for land operation only.

TYPE: Three-seat homebuilt amphibian or landplane.

AIRFRAME: High-wing monoplane, with V bracing struts to bottom of fuselage on each side. Original high lift wing section, with 6% camber and 12·5% thickness/chord ratio. Wing structure comprises a 63 mm (2·5 in) diameter 6061-T6 aluminium alloy tube leading-edge spar, a similar rear spar, birch plywood ribs, and aluminium and steel drag tubes, covered with Ceconite. Downward canted wingtips serve as stabilising floats on water. Full span trailing-edge flaperons of auxiliary aerofoil type, of similar construction to wings. Wings fold for trailering and stowage. Single-step flying-boat hull, with structure of 4130 steel tube, covered with glassfibre shells back to step and Ceconite over rear fuselage. Conventional wire braced tail unit of 4130 steel tube covered with Ceconite. Sweptback vertical surfaces. Horizontal surfaces mid-mounted on fin. No tabs.

LANDING GEAR: Mainwheels, with low-pressure tyres, retract into sponson on each side of hull. Steerable tailwheel.

POWER PLANT: One 48·5 kW (65 hp) Rotax 532 two-cylinder engine, at rear of streamlined pylon above wing, driving a two-blade Hendrickson wooden pusher propeller through Rotax 2·58:1 reduction gearing. Engine c/l canted downward 3·5° to direct slipstream towards horizontal tail surfaces. Plastics fuel tank in pylon, capacity 45 litres (12 US gallons).

ACCOMMODATION: Two seats side by side in enclosed cabin, with third seat to rear.

DIMENSIONS, EXTERNAL:
- Wing span: 10·97 m (36 ft 0 in)
- Wing chord:
  - excl flaperons (constant): 1·07 m (3 ft 6 in)
  - incl flaperons (constant): 1·30 m (4 ft 3 in)
- Wing aspect ratio: 8·64
- Width overall, wings folded: 2·59 m (8 ft 6 in)
- Length overall: 5·92 m (19 ft 5 in)
- Length overall, wings folded: 7·45 m (24 ft 5 in)
- Height overall: 1·75 m (5 ft 9 in)
- Propeller diameter: 1·91 m (6 ft 3 in)

AREA:
- Wings, gross: 13·94 m² (150·0 sq ft)

WEIGHTS AND LOADINGS:
- Weight empty: 254 kg (560 lb)
- Max T-O weight: 544 kg (1,200 lb)
- Max wing loading: 39·06 kg/m² (8·00 lb/sq ft)
- Max power loading: 11·22 kg/kW (18·46 lb/hp)

PERFORMANCE (estimated. A: solo at 363 kg; 800 lb AUW, B: at max T-O weight):
- Never-exceed speed: A, B: 69 knots (128 km/h; 80 mph)
- Max cruising speed: A, B: 65 knots (120 km/h; 75 mph)
- Stalling speed: A: 22 knots (41 km/h; 25 mph)
  - B: 29 knots (53 km/h; 33 mph)
- Max rate of climb at S/L: A: 503 m (1,650 ft)/min
  - B: 286 m (940 ft)/min
- Service ceiling: A: 6,285 m (20,625 ft)
  - B: 3,580 m (11,750 ft)
- T-O run: A on land: 31 m (100 ft)
  - A on water: 55 m (180 ft)
  - B on land: 92 m (300 ft)
  - B on water: 230 m (756 ft)
- T-O to 15 m (50 ft):
  - A on land: 77 m (250 ft)
  - B on land: 183 m (600 ft)
- Landing run: A on land: 107 m (350 ft)
  - A on water: 92 m (300 ft)
  - B on land: 183 m (600 ft)
  - B on water: 84 m (275 ft)

LIGHT MINIATURE

LIGHT MINIATURE AIRCRAFT INC

Building 411, Opa-Locka Airport, Opa-Locka, Florida 33054
Telephone: (305) 681 4068
PRESIDENT: Fred F. McCallum

Light Miniature Aircraft's three-quarter scale Piper J-3 Cub replica, the LM-1, was designed to fulfil the requirements of an air recreational vehicle (ARV) in the USA. However, with a 4·5 kg (10 lb) weight reduction it can be classified as an ultralight in many foreign countries. Light Miniature has produced a specific ultralight variant as the LM-1U, the differences being detailed below. The company is also constructing an Experimental category version for the homebuilt market as the **LM-1X**, using a Rotax 377 engine and with increased fuel capacity. This is expected to have an empty weight of 129 kg (285 lb). The detailed descriptions that follow apply specifically to the LM-1 and LM-1U. The general airframe description should apply also to the LM-1X.

Light Miniature has also produced three-quarter scale prototypes of an Aeronca Champ (LM-3) and Taylorcraft (LM-2), both of which will be offered in kit form in the ultralight and Experimental categories. A two-seater is reportedly being developed as the LM-4. The LM-3X three-quarter scale homebuilt version of the Champ was unveiled at the 1985 Sun 'n Fun Meeting.

LIGHT MINIATURE AIRCRAFT LM-1

Mr Fred F. McCallum and Mr Fred Latulip have designed and built a small classic style high-wing monoplane known as the LM-1. This is basically a single-seat three-quarter scale Piper J-3 Cub replica, and is considered to fill the gap for aircraft of conventional layout between ultralights and higher performance homebuilts. Design of the LM-1 began on 30 March 1982, and construction of the prototype started on 15 April that year. The first flight was achieved on 15 July 1983 and certification was gained on 27 July.

Plans for the LM-1 are available, and by late 1985 a total of 140 sets had been sold. Twenty-three LM-1s were then under construction. Estimated building time from plans is 600 working hours. Complete kits, partial kits and component parts for the LM-1 are available from Wicks Aircraft Supply, Highland, Illinois 62249.

TYPE: Single-seat ARV cabin monoplane.

AIRFRAME: Strut braced high-wing monoplane. Wing section NACA 4412 modified. Dihedral 2°. Incidence 0°. Dacron covered wings, with Sitka spruce spar booms, plywood webs and stamped 2024-T3 aluminium ribs. Ailerons of similar construction to wings, with ground adjustable tabs. Wooden fuselage, plywood covered to rear of cabin and overall Dacron covering. Wire braced tail unit, comprising tailplane with elevators, fin and balanced rudder, all of wood with Dacron covering. Ground adjustable tabs on elevators.

Leader's International AM-DSII light aircraft *(J. M. G. Gradidge)*

Prototype three-seat Avid Amphibian

Light Miniature Aircraft LM-1 ARV monoplane *(Howard Levy)*

Light Aero Avid Flyer fitted with optional twin floats

Light Aero Avid Flyer with tailwheel landing gear and optional wheel-skis

Light Miniature Aircraft LM-3X homebuilt aircraft *(Howard Levy)*

Light Miniature Aircraft LM-1U microlight

LANDING GEAR: Non-retractable tailwheel type. Main gear comprises two side Vs and half-axles hinged to fuselage structure. Azusa brakes. Steerable tailwheel.

POWER PLANT: One 22·4 kW (30 hp) Cuyuna 430RR two-cylinder two-stroke engine, driving a two-blade propeller. One fuel tank in fuselage, capacity 21 litres (5·5 US gallons). Refuelling point on engine cowling.

ACCOMMODATION: Pilot only, in fully enclosed cabin. Downward hinged door on starboard side.

DIMENSIONS, EXTERNAL:

Wing span	8·23 m (27 ft 0 in)
Wing chord, constant	1·37 m (4 ft 6 in)
Length overall	5·38 m (17 ft 8 in)
Width, wings folded	2·26 m (7 ft 5 in)
Height overall	1·70 m (5 ft 7 in)
Tailplane span	2·26 m (7 ft 5 in)
Wheel track	1·32 m (4 ft 4 in)
Propeller diameter	1·27 m (4 ft 2 in)

AREA:

Wings, gross	11·29 m² (121·5 sq ft)

WEIGHTS AND LOADINGS:

Weight empty	156 kg (345 lb)
Max T-O and landing weight	272 kg (600 lb)
Max wing loading	24·1 kg/m² (4·94 lb/sq ft)
Max power loading	12·14 kg/kW (20·00 lb/hp)

PERFORMANCE:

Never-exceed speed	65 knots (120 km/h; 75 mph)
Max level speed and max cruising speed at 610 m (2,000 ft)	56 knots (105 km/h; 65 mph)
Econ cruising speed	43 knots (80 km/h; 50 mph)
Stalling speed, engine idling	21 knots (39 km/h; 24 mph)
Max rate of climb at S/L	137 m (450 ft)/min
T-O run	61 m (200 ft)
Landing run	91-107 m (300-350 ft)
Range with 30 min reserves	139 nm (257 km; 160 miles)

LIGHT MINIATURE AIRCRAFT LM-1U

In November 1984 Light Miniature began the design of an ultralight variant of the LM-1, and this became the LM-1U. The construction of a prototype started almost immediately and it flew for the first time on 7 April 1985. By February 1986, five LM-1U kits had been ordered, of which four had been delivered and two assembled.

TYPE: Single-seat microlight cabin monoplane: conforms to FAR Pt 103.

AIRFRAME: As for LM-1, except: wing section Göttingen 387 modified, with thickness/chord ratio of 14·5%; aluminium alloy airframe, except for wooden wing spars and overall Dacron covering. Three-axis control (ailerons, elevators with ground adjustable tab, and rudder). No wing folding. Ballistic parachute optional.

LANDING GEAR: Non-retractable tailwheel type, with 15 × 6·00 Carlisle mainwheel tyres (pressure 0·83 bars; 12 lb/sq in). Brakes fitted to mainwheels. Optional floats.

POWER PLANT: One 20 kW (27 hp) Rotax 277 single-cylinder two-stroke engine, with 2·54:1 reduction gear to a two-blade wooden propeller. One glassfibre fuel tank, capacity 20·5 litres (5·4 US gallons).

ACCOMMODATION: Pilot only, in enclosed cabin. Space aft of seats for up to 11·3 kg (25 lb) of baggage, depending on weight of pilot.

DIMENSIONS, EXTERNAL:

Wing span	9·14 m (30 ft 0 in)
Wing chord, constant	1·22 m (4 ft 0 in)
Length overall	5·44 m (17 ft 10 in)
Height overall	1·70 m (5 ft 7 in)
Tailplane span	2·21 m (7 ft 3 in)
Wheel track	1·42 m (4 ft 8 in)
Wheelbase	4·04 m (13 ft 3 in)
Propeller diameter	1·52 m (5 ft 0 in)

AREA:

Wings, gross	10·87 m² (117·0 sq ft)

WEIGHTS AND LOADINGS:

Weight empty	114 kg (252 lb)
Pilot weight range	62-102 kg (135-225 lb)

Max T-O weight 238 kg (525 lb)
Max wing loading 21·92 kg/m² (4·49 lb/sq ft)
Max power loading 11·90 kg/kW (19·44 lb/hp)

PERFORMANCE:
Never-exceed speed 73 knots (136 km/h; 85 mph)
Max level speed at 305 m (1,000 ft) 61 knots (113 km/h; 70 mph)
Max cruising speed at 305 m (1,000 ft), 80% power 52 knots (97 km/h; 60 mph)
Econ cruising speed at 305 m (1,000 ft) 47 knots (87 km/h; 54 mph)
Stalling speed, engine idling 23 knots (42 km/h; 26 mph)
Max rate of climb at S/L 168 m (550 ft)/min
T-O run 61 m (200 ft)
Landing run 91 m (300 ft)
Range, with 15 min reserves 156 nm (289 km; 180 miles)

LIGHT MINIATURE AIRCRAFT LM-3X

The LM-3X is the Experimental category homebuilt variant of the three-quarter scale Aeronca 7AC Champ replica. It is not an exact scale replica, as the cabin is marginally wider and higher than scale to improve accommodation. Kits to build the LM-3X include the 26 kW (35 hp) Rotax 377 engine. Floats are available as an option.

The airframe description of the LM-1 applies generally to the LM-3X, except that the wing leading-edges are constructed of glassfibre; the fuselage longerons, uprights and cross members are of 6061-T6 aluminium alloy with wooden formers and stringers; the engine cowling is of glassfibre; and the overall skin covering material is Ceconite.

WEIGHT:
Weight empty approx 141 kg (310 lb)

PERFORMANCE:
Cruising speed 56 knots (105 km/h; 65 mph)
Stalling speed 25 knots (45 km/h; 28 mph)
Max rate of climb at S/L 152 m (500 ft)/min
T-O run 76 m (250 ft)
Endurance 4 h
Best glide ratio 9

LITECRAFT

LITECRAFT INC

Route 4, Box 48, Vacherie, Louisiana 70090
Telephone: (504) 265 3075
PRESIDENT: Eugene Borne
MARKETING: Jerry Kitchens

LITECRAFT BEARCAT

First shown publicly at Sun 'n Fun 1984, the Bearcat bears a close external resemblance to the Piper Cub. The original Ultra Classics microlight design (see 1984-85 *Jane's*) has since increased in weight and now falls into the FAA's Experimental category, requiring 51 per cent or more homebuilder participation. Kits and prefabricated parts are available.

Variants of the Bearcat include a biplane, a military version (no details received), and the cropspraying Ag Bearcat (described separately). The following description applies to the standard version:

TYPE: Single-seat homebuilt aircraft; does not conform to FAR Pt 103.

AIRFRAME: Strut braced high-wing monoplane, built of chrome molybdenum steel tube and fully covered with Dacron (double surface on wings), polyester and glassfibre; stainless steel control cables. Three-axis control (ailerons, elevators and rudder). Wings and elevators fold for transportation.

LANDING GEAR: Non-retractable tailwheel type. Bungee sprung mainwheels with wheel fairings and leaf-sprung steerable 5 in diameter tailwheel. Optional brakes, skis and floats.

POWER PLANT: One 31·3 kW (42 hp) Rotax 447 engine with 2·58:1 reduction drive to a two-blade wooden propeller; more powerful Rotax 503 available optionally. Fuel tank capacity 19 litres (5 US gallons).

ACCOMMODATION: Pilot only, in semi-enclosed cabin. Full cockpit enclosure optional.

DIMENSIONS, EXTERNAL:
Wing span 9·21 m (30 ft 2½ in)
Wing aspect ratio 6·1
Length overall 5·69 m (18 ft 8 in)
Height overall 1·83 m (6 ft 0 in)
Propeller diameter 1·73 m (5 ft 8 in)

AREA:
Wings, gross 13·93 m² (150·0 sq ft)

WEIGHTS AND LOADINGS:
Weight empty 125 kg (275 lb)
Max pilot weight 113 kg (250 lb)
Max T-O weight 317 kg (700 lb)
Max wing loading 22·77 kg/m² (4·67 lb/sq ft)
Max power loading 10·14 kg/kW (16·67 lb/hp)

PERFORMANCE (at max T-O weight):
Never-exceed speed 104 knots (193 km/h; 120 mph)
Max level speed 61 knots (112 km/h; 70 mph)
Max cruising speed 43 knots (80 km/h; 50 mph)
Stalling speed: power on 23 knots (42 km/h; 26 mph)
power off 25 knots (46 km/h; 28 mph)
Max rate of climb at S/L 305 m (1,000 ft)/min
g limits +6/−4

LITECRAFT AG BEARCAT

Structural testing has been completed on this cropspraying version of the standard Bearcat. Only slight modification was required to the airframe to accept the Spray Miser Ag system. The standard engine is the 31·3 kW (42 hp) Rotax 447, but the airframe will accept engines rated up to 48·5 kW (65 hp), and these are to be offered as options. Full span trailing-edge 'flaperons' help to reduce T-O run, improve climb rate, and create a downdraught on the spray pattern, thus increasing crop penetration and decreasing wingtip vortex effect on the spray pattern. Standard equipment includes a 12V high volume electric pump capable of flow rates of over 30·3 litres (8 US gallons)/min at 1·38 bars (20 lb/sq in), a 98·4 litre (26 US gallon) glassfibre underbelly chemical tank, and welded aluminium 'wet' booms.

WEIGHTS AND LOADINGS:
Weight empty 127 kg (280 lb)
Max T-O weight 385 kg (850 lb)
Max wing loading 27·65 kg/m² (5·67 lb/sq ft)
Max power loading 12·32 kg/kW (20·24 lb/hp)

PERFORMANCE:
Never-exceed speed 95 knots (177 km/h; 110 mph)
Max level speed 64 knots (119 km/h; 74 mph)
Max cruising speed 59 knots (109 km/h; 68 mph)
Max rate of climb at S/L 366 m (1,200 ft)/min
Service ceiling 6,400 m (21,000 ft)
T-O run 52 m (170 ft)
Landing run 46 m (150 ft)
Range with max fuel 104 nm (193 km; 120 miles)
Endurance with max fuel 2 h

LITE-FLITE

LITE-FLITE INC

27715 Katy Freeway, Houston, 1-10 West Katy, Texas 77450
Telephone: (713) 392 9000

LITE-FLITE AERO-FOX

Lite-Flite is offering a ready assembled single-seat microlight known as the Aero-Fox. Of aluminium alloy construction, Dacron covered, and powered by a 20 kW (27 hp) Rotax 277 single-cylinder two-stroke engine with reduction gear to a two-blade tractor propeller, it is of classic three-axis layout. The strut braced high wing appears to be of constant chord and double surface, with slight dihedral. The conventional tail unit is also strut braced, and the landing gear is of non-retractable tailwheel type. Accommodation, suited to large pilots, is semi-enclosed, with the cockpit fronted by a large windscreen. Rigging time is 20-30 min.

PERFORMANCE:
Max cruising speed over 52 knots (97 km/h; 60 mph)
Econ cruising speed 48 knots (89 km/h; 55 mph)
Stalling speed 19 knots (36 km/h; 22 mph)
Max rate of climb at S/L 244 m (800 ft)/min

LOEHLE

LOEHLE ENTERPRISES

'The Aviation Valley', Shipmans Creek Road, Wartrace, Tennessee 37183
Telephone: (615) 857 3419
PRESIDENT: Michael Loehle

In November 1984 Mr Michael Loehle, then the President of UFM of Kentucky (now known as UFM of Ky Inc), purchased the Ritz Aircraft and Ritz Propeller companies and moved UFM to the Ritz works in Tennessee. A new company, Loehle Aviation Inc, was formed at the same time, and these four companies now operate as divisions of Loehle Enterprises. The Ritz Aircraft company continues to market the late Mr Gerry Ritz's Standard Model A, and kits of the Aeroplane XP are still available from UFM of Ky Inc, both at the Wartrace address above. Mr Loehle's most recent products are The Fun Machine microlight biplane and the 5151 Mustang homebuilt aircraft, both marketed by Loehle Aviation.

RITZ STANDARD MODEL A

TYPE: Single-seat microlight aircraft; conforms to FAR Pt 103.

AIRFRAME: Strut braced parasol wing monoplane with conventional tail surfaces. Two-spar wing has Warren truss wooden beam and rib structure with 'geodetic' cross bracing, and is braced to fuselage by aluminium V struts on each side. Tail unit is of similar construction. Fuselage is 'geodetic' structure, with steel frame and plywood box cockpit/nose section. Fuselage, wings and tail have Dacron covering. Three-axis control (differential ailerons, elevators and rudder); wing position can be adjusted fore and aft to offset CG changes, depending on pilot weight.

LANDING GEAR: Non-retractable tailwheel type, with 4 × 14 mainwheels on laminated plywood legs. Steerable tailwheel size 1·25 × 4. Mainwheel brakes optional.

POWER PLANT: One 16·5 kW (22 hp) Zenoah single-cylinder two-stroke engine, with reduction gear to a Ritz two-blade wooden pusher propeller. Fuel capacity 19 litres (5 US gallons).

ACCOMMODATION: Single seat in open cockpit, with optional windscreen.

DIMENSIONS, EXTERNAL:
Wing span 10·97 m (36 ft 0 in)
Wing aspect ratio 9·26
Length overall 5·49 m (18 ft 0 in)
Height overall 1·68 m (5 ft 6 in)
Wheel track 1·68 m (5 ft 6 in)
Propeller diameter 1·37 m (4 ft 6 in)

AREA:
Wings, gross 13·01 m² (140·0 sq ft)

WEIGHTS AND LOADINGS:
Weight empty 91 kg (200 lb)
Pilot weight range 57-125 kg (125-275 lb)
Max T-O weight 227 kg (500 lb)
Max wing loading 17·43 kg/m² (3·57 lb/sq ft)
Max power loading 13·83 kg/kW (22·73 lb/hp)

PERFORMANCE:
Never-exceed speed 60 knots (112 km/h; 70 mph)
Max level speed 52 knots (97 km/h; 60 mph)
Max cruising speed 48 knots (88 km/h; 55 mph)
Stalling speed:
power on 14 knots (26 km/h; 16 mph)
power off 16 knots (29 km/h; 18 mph)
Max rate of climb at S/L more than 122 m (400 ft)/min
T-O run (concrete) 30 m (100 ft)
Landing run approx 61 m (200 ft)
Range with max fuel 217 nm (402 km; 250 miles)
Endurance with max fuel 5 h
g limits +4·5/−2
Best glide ratio 15

UFM of KY AEROPLANE XP

The original Aeroplane of 1982 was essentially a powered and strengthened version of the UFM Easy Riser swept-wing biplane, to which was added a horizontal tail surface. The 1983 Aeroplane XP introduced conventional cruciform tail surfaces, the former drag rudders aft of the outer wings being deleted; the latest model has a slightly shorter wing span, increased wing area, and a Cuyuna ULII-02 (instead of 430R) engine, driving a Ritz two-blade wooden propeller.

TYPE: Single-seat microlight aircraft.

AIRFRAME: Constant chord sweptwing (15°) biplane, of unequal span, with underslung 'trike' unit and conventional tail surfaces. Construction is of aluminium alloy with double thickness Dacron covering.

LANDING GEAR: Non-retractable tricycle type, with 20 in diameter mainwheels and 16 in diameter steerable nosewheel. Floats optional.

POWER PLANT: One 26 kW (35 hp) Cuyuna ULII-02 two-cylinder two-stroke engine, with 2 1 belt reduction drive to a Ritz two-blade wooden pusher propeller. Fuel tank capacity 19 litres (5 US gallons).

ACCOMMODATION: Pilot only, in open position. Cockpit fairing optional.

DIMENSIONS, EXTERNAL:
Wing span 8·53 m (28 ft 0 in)
Wing aspect ratio 4·5
Length overall 3·51 m (11 ft 6 in)
Height overall 2·34 m (7 ft 8 in)
Propeller diameter 1·37 m (4 ft 6 in)

AREA:
Wings, gross 16·17 m² (174·0 sq ft)

WEIGHTS AND LOADINGS:
Weight empty 111 kg (244 lb)
Max T-O weight 227 kg (500 lb)
Max wing loading 14·01 kg/m² (2·87 lb/sq ft)
Max power loading 6·49 kg/kW (14·29 lb/hp)

PERFORMANCE:
Never-exceed speed 64 knots (119 km/h; 74 mph)
Max level speed 52 knots (97 km/h; 60 mph)
Max cruising speed 43 knots (80 km/h; 50 mph)

Ritz Standard Model A *(Howard Levy)*

Fourth prototype Litecraft Bearcat *(Howard Levy)*

Loehle Aviation The Fun Machine

Loehle Aviation 5151 Mustang homebuilt aircraft *(Howard Levy)*

Prototype LoPresti Sharkfire at Oshkosh 1985, prior to its first flight *(J. M. G. Gradidge)*

Stalling speed — 19 knots (34 km/h; 21 mph)
Max rate of climb at S/L — 305 m (1,000 ft)/min
g limits — +9/−5 ultimate
Best glide ratio — 8

LOEHLE AVIATION THE FUN MACHINE

The first aircraft from the newly formed Loehle Aviation Inc was The Fun Machine, available for purchase as a bolt-together kit. To assist would-be constructors, seminars are held at the factory once a month, with travel concessions against kit purchase.

TYPE: Single-seat microlight; conforms to FAR Pt 103.

AIRFRAME: Equal span braced two-bay biplane, with sweep-back on upper and lower wing surfaces. Structure of aluminium alloy, with double surface Mylar laminated Dacron on wings and boom-carried tail unit. Vinyl coated stainless steel cables. Three-axis control (four spoilerons in wings, elevators, and rudder), with separate control lever for steep descent using lower spoilerons only. Airframe rigging time 50 min.

LANDING GEAR: Non-retractable tricycle type, with glass-fibre rod legs. Mainwheels size 20 × 2·125; nosewheel size 16 × 1·75. Options include floats and skis.

POWER PLANT: One 26 kW (35 hp) Cuyuna ULII-02 two-cylinder two-stroke engine, with 2:1 reduction drive to a Ritz two-blade wooden pusher propeller. Fuel tank capacity 19 litres (5 US gallons).

ACCOMMODATION: Pilot only, in open position. Cockpit fairing optional.

DIMENSIONS, EXTERNAL:
Wing span — 8·53 m (28 ft 0 in)
Wing aspect ratio — 4·5
Length overall — 3·51 m (11 ft 6 in)
Height overall — 2·34 m (7 ft 8 in)
Propeller diameter — 1·37 m (4 ft 6 in)

AREA:
Wings, gross — 16·16 m² (174·0 sq ft)

WEIGHTS AND LOADINGS:
Weight empty — 110 kg (244 lb)
Pilot weight range — 50-113 kg (110-250 lb)
Max T-O weight — 227 kg (500 lb)
Max wing loading — 14·01 kg/m² (2·87 lb/sq ft)
Max power loading — 8·73 kg/kW (14·29 lb/hp)

PERFORMANCE:
Never-exceed speed — 64 knots (119 km/h; 74 mph)
Max level speed — 52 knots (97 km/h; 60 mph)
Max cruising speed — 43 knots (80 km/h; 50 mph)
Econ cruising speed — 39 knots (72 km/h; 45 mph)
Stalling speed: power on — 16 knots (29 km/h; 18 mph)
power off — 19 knots (34 km/h; 21 mph)
Max rate of climb at S/L — 305 m (1,000 ft)/min
Service ceiling — more than 5,485 m (18,000 ft)
T-O and landing run — 31 m (100 ft)
Range with max fuel — 108 nm (201 km; 125 miles)

LOEHLE AVIATION 5151 MUSTANG

Mr Michael Loehle's latest aircraft is an approximate ¾-scale representation of a Second World War P-51 Mustang fighter, which is offered in kit form under Experimental category regulations. Design began in late March 1985, with the three basic aims of low cost, easy handling and a building time of around 350 working hours. The prototype (N202XP) flew for the first time on 30 January 1986 and was still undergoing its 40 hour mandatory flight test period in February that year, when limited kit production had already begun.

A single seater with sliding bubble canopy, the 5151 Mustang is constructed primarily of wood, with both conventional and geodetic structures. The whole assembly is glued together, using T-88 epoxy, and is fabric covered. Power is provided by a 34 kW (46 hp) Rotax 503 two-cylinder engine, with 2·58:1 reduction drive to a Ritz 68 × 32 propeller. Fuel capacity is 19 litres (5 US gallons), with optional 38 or 57 litre (10 or 15 US gallon) tanks available as alternatives. A non-retractable tailwheel type landing gear with telescopic tubular main legs is standard, but retractable gear is available as an option. Other options include brakes and a four-blade propeller.

DIMENSIONS, EXTERNAL:
Wing span — 8·36 m (27 ft 5 in)
Wing chord: at root — 1·98 m (6 ft 6 in)
at tip — 1·22 m (4 ft 0 in)
Length overall — 6·96 m (22 ft 10 in)

AREA:
Wings, gross — 12·54 m² (135·0 sq ft)

WEIGHTS AND LOADINGS:
Weight empty — 180 kg (397 lb)
Max T-O weight — 317 kg (700 lb)
Max wing loading — 25·34 kg/m² (5·19 lb/sq ft)
Max power loading — 9·32 kg/kW (15·35 lb/hp)

PERFORMANCE:
Never-exceed speed — 82 knots (152 km/h; 95 mph)
Cruising speed — 61-65 knots (113-121 km/h; 70-75 mph)
Stalling speed — 24-25 knots (44-45 km/h; 27-28 mph)
Max rate of climb at S/L — 152 m (500 ft)/min
T-O run — 46 m (150 ft)
Landing run — 61 m (200 ft)
Range with standard fuel — 108 nm (201 km; 125 miles)
g limits for wings — +4/−2

LOPRESTI

LOPRESTI BROTHERS AIRCRAFT INC

Box 574-656, Kerrville, Texas 78208
Telephone: (512) 257 3847

LOPRESTI SHARKFIRE

Mr LeRoy P. LoPresti, former President of Mooney Aircraft Corporation, and his sons David, Curt and Jim, have formed LoPresti Brothers Aircraft to develop a new high-performance moulded composite monoplane for the homebuilt market. As can be seen from the accompanying illustration, the tandem two-seat Sharkfire is a cantilever low-wing monoplane of conventional layout. However, it reportedly uses the NASA developed NLF 0215 natural laminar-flow wing section and is powered by a 119 kW (160 hp) Avco Lycoming O-320 engine driving a two-blade wooden propeller with large spinner. Fuel capacity is 129 litres (34 US gallons). The mainwheels retract into wingroot fillets.

DIMENSIONS, EXTERNAL:

Wing span	6·07 m (19 ft 11 in)
Length overall	6·62 m (21 ft 8 in)

AREA:

Wings, gross	5·57 m² (60·0 sq ft)

WEIGHTS AND LOADINGS:

Weight empty	227 kg (500 lb)
Max T-O weight	646 kg (1,424 lb)
Max wing loading	116 kg/m² (23·7 lb/sq ft)
Max power loading	5·43 kg/kW (8·90 lb/hp)

PERFORMANCE (estimated):

Max level speed	217 knots (402 km/h; 250 mph)
Max cruising speed	204 knots (378 km/h; 235 mph)
Max rate of climb at S/L	487 m (1,600 ft)/min
Range with max fuel	800 nm (1,480 km; 920 miles)

MANTA

MANTA PRODUCTS INC

1647 East 14th Street, Oakland, California 94606
Telephone: (415) 536 1500
SECRETARY AND CHIEF PILOT: William J. Armour

MANTA FOXBAT

With a powered 'trike' unit added, the Fledge III/IIIET (see Hang Gliders in 1985-86 *Jane's*) is known as the FoxBat; more than 300 have been built and sold. The FoxBat conforms to FAR Pt 103 regulations for microlight aircraft, and differs from the hang glider in the following respects:

AIRFRAME: As Fledge III, plus 'trike' unit comprising glassfibre sprung landing gear (non-braking 20 × 2·125 mainwheels and steerable 5 × 4·10 nosewheel), open seat for pilot, and power plant.

POWER PLANT: One 30 kW (40 hp) 440 cc Kawasaki two-stroke engine, with reduction drive to a two- or three-blade pusher propeller. Fuel tank capacity 19 litres (5 US gallons).

DIMENSIONS, EXTERNAL: As Fledge III/IIIET plus:

Propeller diameter	0·91 m (3 ft 0 in)

WEIGHTS AND LOADINGS (standard version):

Weight empty	97·5 kg (215 lb)
Pilot weight	45-136 kg (100-300 lb)
Max T-O weight	247 kg (545 lb)
Max wing loading	16·93 kg/m² (3·47 lb/sq ft)
Max power loading	8·29 kg/kW (13·63 lb/hp)

PERFORMANCE (at max T-O weight):

Never-exceed and max level speed	54 knots (101 km/h; 63 mph)
Max cruising speed	48 knots (88 km/h; 55 mph)
Econ cruising speed	35 knots (64 km/h; 40 mph)
Stalling speed	20 knots (37 km/h; 23 mph)
Max rate of climb at S/L	335 m (1,100 ft)/min
Service ceiling	5,490 m (18,000 ft)
T-O and landing run	23 m (75 ft)
Range with max fuel	120 nm (222 km; 138 miles)
Endurance with max fuel	2 h 20 min
g limits	+7·5/−6

MARQUART

ED MARQUART

Flabob Airport, Riverside, California

In 1955 Mr Ed Marquart established Marquart Aircraft Repairs. In the course of the next two years he designed and built his third aircraft, the single-seat MA-3 Maverick (described briefly in 1982-83 *Jane's*). The Maverick was followed by the two-seat MA-5 Charger, plans of which are available to amateur builders.

MARQUART MA-5 CHARGER

The Charger is a two-seat sporting biplane of quite different type to the MA-3 Maverick. Whereas the Maverick has straight wings, the upper wing of the Charger is swept and N cabane struts are used in addition to N interplane struts. The fuselage is of steel tube construction, fabric covered, but does not have Maverick's high turtle-decking. The front cockpit is located well under the trailing-edge of the upper wing, the latter having a cutout to improve all-round view. The tail unit is also changed, making use of a horn balanced rudder and split elevators.

The Charger illustrated was built by Dr Roy Wicker and has been painted to represent a US Navy fighter-bomber of Fighting Six squadron based on the aircraft carrier USS *Saratoga* during the 1930s. Dr Wicker, who previously completed a scale replica of a French Nieuport 24*bis* fighter of the First World War and has also restored aircraft, completed his Charger from plans in 1981. It is powered by a 134 kW (180 hp) Avco Lycoming O-360-A1G6, driving a McCauley CFA-76 × 60 two-blade fixed-pitch propeller. Some modifications to the plans have been incorporated into this Charger, including the use of 6·5-8 Beechcraft Bonanza wheels with Goodyear tyres.

The following brief details apply to Dr Wicker's MA-5 Charger:

TYPE: Two-seat homebuilt sporting biplane.

DIMENSIONS, EXTERNAL:

Wing span	7·32 m (24 ft 0 in)
Length overall	6·71 m (22 ft 0 in)

WEIGHTS AND LOADING:

Weight empty	554 kg (1,222 lb)
Max T-O weight	816 kg (1,800 lb)
Max power loading	6·09 kg/kW (10·00 lb/hp)

PERFORMANCE:

Max level speed	126 knots (233 km/h; 145 mph)
Max cruising speed	117 knots (217 km/h; 135 mph)
Landing speed	48 knots (89 km/h; 55 mph)
Max rate of climb at S/L	366 m (1,200 ft)/min
Service ceiling	3,960 m (13,000 ft)
T-O run	91 m (300 ft)
Landing run	152 m (500 ft)
Range with max fuel	249 nm (462 km; 287 miles)

MATHEWS

LYLE MATHEWS

2141 Shannon Way, Mesa, Arizona 85205

The Petit Breezy high-wing monoplane microlight was described in the 1983-84 *Jane's*. Plans for the single- and two-seat Breezy and Breezy Plus are available from Mr Glen Kindell of 6032 East McKellips Road (Suite 4), Mesa, Arizona 85205. Among Mr Mathews' first microlight designs were the C.C.C., P.U.P. and Mr Easy, all of which are described below. He also markets plans for a family of homebuilt ultralight and light sporting aircraft named J-3 Junior, Parasol Jr, Turnerkraft Biplane, and a new aircraft known as Simple Simon. No details of these have been received.

MATHEWS C.C.C.

The C.C.C. (Cross Country Cruiser) is a single-seat high-wing monoplane microlight aircraft with aluminium alloy tube structure and tricycle landing gear. The airframe is fabric covered. The C.C.C. is available in plan form for homebuilding.

POWER PLANT: Prototype flown with 16·4 kW (22 hp) Lloyd engine. The airframe is designed for any suitable power plant in the 11·2-22·4 kW (15-30 hp) range.

DIMENSIONS, EXTERNAL:

Wing span	10·36 m (34 ft 0 in)
Wing aspect ratio	7·0

AREA:

Wings, gross	15·33 m² (165·0 sq ft)

WEIGHT:

Weight empty	77 kg (169 lb)

PERFORMANCE:

Max level speed	45 knots (84 km/h; 52 mph)
Cruising speed	30 knots (56 km/h; 35 mph)
Stalling speed	19 knots (36 km/h; 22 mph)
Max rate of climb at S/L	107 m (350 ft)/min
T-O run	27 m (90 ft)

MATHEWS P.U.P.

The P.U.P. (Perfect Ultralight Plane) is an unequal span biplane with fully covered wings and conventional tail surfaces, an openwork fuselage of rectangular section aluminium alloy tube, and a 'taildragger' landing gear. Wing spars and ribs, and tail surface framework, are also of aluminium tube; wings and tail are Dacron covered, with extensive use of gussets and pop rivets. Plans are available to amateur constructors.

TYPE: Single-seat microlight aircraft.

POWER PLANT: Prototype flown originally with a 16·5 kW (22 hp) Lloyd engine, driving a two-blade propeller; exchanged in 1983 for a Kawasaki 440 engine.

DIMENSIONS, EXTERNAL:

Wing span (upper)	7·315 m (24 ft 0 in)
Propeller diameter (Kawasaki)	1·37 m (4 ft 6 in)

AREA:

Wings, gross	13·28 m² (143·0 sq ft)

WEIGHTS AND LOADINGS:

Weight empty	112 kg (248 lb)
Max T-O weight	204 kg (450 lb)
Max wing loading	15·38 kg/m² (3·15 lb/sq ft)
Max power loading	12·36 kg/kW (20·45 lb/hp)

PERFORMANCE (estimated with Kawasaki engine):

Cruising speed	35 knots (64 km/h; 40 mph)
Stalling speed	25 knots (46 km/h; 28 mph)
Max rate of climb at S/L	183 m (600 ft)/min

MATHEWS Mr EASY

Mr Mathews displayed a new aircraft at the 1985 Oshkosh meeting. The general appearance of this single-seat biplane microlight can be seen in an accompanying illustration. It is powered by a Rotax 447 two-stroke engine, mounted as a 'pusher' behind the centre-section of the upper wing. Only known details follow:

DIMENSIONS, EXTERNAL:

Wing span	7·32 m (24 ft 0 in)
Length overall	5·18 m (17 ft 0 in)

WEIGHT:

Weight empty	119 kg (261 lb)

MAXAIR

MAXAIR AIRCRAFT CORPORATION

32 Water Street, Glen Rock, Pennsylvania 17327
Telephone: (717) 235 5512 or 2107
Telex: 4996511
PRESIDENT: Dennis Franklin
MANAGER: William Hanson
DIRECTOR OF MARKETING AND SALES: Phillip Lockwood

Maxair has ended production of the Hummer single-seat microlight, described in the 1985-86 *Jane's*, but parts are still available for the estimated 450 Hummers still flying. Production is now concentrated on the expanding Drifter series of microlight and homebuilt aircraft described in this entry.

MAXAIR DRIFTER SERIES

Five models of the Drifter are in current production in kit form, as follows:

DR277. Original single-seat model with Rotax 277 engine, introduced in early 1983 and the only version available also in ready assembled form. Conforms to FAR Pt 103 requirements.

DR503. More powerful single-seater with Rotax 503 engine.

XP503. Tandem two-seat version of DR503. Higher weight makes it an Experimental category homebuilt aircraft.

MU503. Tandem two-seat utility counterpart of XP503, suitable for heavy duty applications such as floatplane operation and agricultural spraying. Strengthened wings and landing gear permit a 245 kg (540 lb) useful load. Rotax 532 engine available optionally.

DR532. New high-performance single-seat version with Rotax 532 engine, shorter wing span and wide-chord full span ailerons for quick roll response. Classed as Experimental category homebuilt aircraft.

TYPE: DR277 and DR503 conform to FAR Pt 103, other models to FAA Experimental requirements.

AIRFRAME: Wire braced high-wing monoplane. Main frame of chrome molybdenum steel and aluminium alloy tube, braced by kingpost and stainless steel cables. Wings and tail surfaces have double surface Dacron covering. Full three-axis control (ailerons, elevators and rudder). Options include dual controls for two-seaters.

LANDING GEAR: Tailwheel type, with self-sprung steel tube legs. Mainwheels size 11 × 5 in; steerable tailwheel, diameter 4 in. Glassfibre wheel fairings available for all models except MU503. Brakes and floats optional.

POWER PLANT: DR277: One 20 kW (27 hp) Rotax 277 single-cylinder two-stroke engine with reduction drive to two-blade wooden pusher propeller. DR503, XP503 and MU503: One 34 kW (46 hp) Rotax 503 two-cylinder engine, with reduction drive to two-blade wooden pusher propeller. MU503 (optional) and DR532: One 47·7 kW (64 hp) Rotax 532 two-cylinder engine, with reduction drive to two-blade wooden pusher propeller. Fuel tank capacity 19 litres (5 US gallons).

ACCOMMODATION: Pilot only (DR277, DR503 and DR532), or two persons in tandem (XP503 and MU503). Open seats standard, but glassfibre nose fairing and windscreen available optionally. Other options include cargo carrier or agricultural spraygear for MU503 only.

DIMENSIONS, EXTERNAL (A: DR277, B: XP503, C: MU503, and D: DR532):

Wing span: A, B, C	9·14 m (30 ft 0 in)
D	7·01 m (23 ft 0 in)
Wing aspect ratio: A, B, C	5·92
D	4·52
Length overall: A, B, C, D	5·79 m (19 ft 0 in)
Height overall: A	2·72 m (8 ft 11 in)
B, C, D	2·77 m (9 ft 1 in)
Propeller diameter: A, B, C, D	1·52 m (5 ft 0 in)

Manta FoxBat Fledge IIIET

Marquart MA-5 Charger built by Dr Roy Wicker *(J. M. G. Gradidge)*

Mathews Mr Easy biplane microlight *(J. M. G. Gradidge)*

Two-seat Maxair Drifter XP503 *(Geoffrey P. Jones)*

Single-seat Maxair Drifter DR277

Maxair Drifter MU503 with cargo container

Maxair Drifter DR532 high-performance single-seater

AREA:
Wings, gross: A, B, C — 14·12 m² (152·0 sq ft)
D — 10·87 m² (117·0 sq ft)

WEIGHTS AND LOADINGS (A, B, C and D as above):
Weight empty: A — 109 kg (240 lb)
B — 152 kg (335 lb)
C — 163 kg (360 lb)
D — 136 kg (300 lb)
Max pilot weight: A — 104 kg (230 lb)
D — 106 kg (235 lb)
Max T-O weight: A — 227 kg (500 lb)
B — 356 kg (785 lb)
C — 408 kg (900 lb)
D — 254 kg (560 lb)
Max wing loading:
A — 16·08 kg/m² (3·29 lb/sq ft)
B — 25·21 kg/m² (5·16 lb/sq ft)
C — 28·90 kg/m² (5·92 lb/sq ft)
D — 23·37 kg/m² (4·79 lb/sq ft)
Max power loading: A — 11·35 kg/kW (18·52 lb/hp)
B — 10·47 kg/kW (17·21 lb/hp)
C — 12·00 kg/kW (19·74 lb/hp)
D — 5·32 kg/kW (8·75 lb/hp)

PERFORMANCE (A and D with 79 kg; 175 lb pilot, B and C with two 79 kg; 175 lb crew):
Never-exceed speed: A — 65 knots (120 km/h; 75 mph)
Max level speed: A — 55 knots (101 km/h; 63 mph)
B, C — 65 knots (120 km/h; 75 mph)
D — 74 knots (137 km/h; 85 mph)
Max cruising speed: A — 48 knots (88 km/h; 55 mph)
Econ cruising speed: A — 35 knots (64 km/h; 40 mph)
Stalling speed: A — 23 knots (42 km/h; 26 mph)
B — 27 knots (50 km/h; 31 mph)
C — 32 knots (58 km/h; 36 mph)
D — 30 knots (55 km/h; 34 mph)
Max rate of climb at S/L: A, B, C — 183 m (600 ft)/min
D — 366 m (1,200 ft)/min
Service ceiling: A — 3,050 m (10,000 ft)
T-O run: A — 46-84 m (150-275 ft)
B, C — 76-107 m (250-350 ft)
D — 79 m (260 ft)
Landing run: A — 54-84 m (175-275 ft)
B, C — 76-107 m (250-350 ft)
D, without brakes — 152 m (500 ft)
Range, 65% power: A — 104 nm (193 km; 120 miles)
B, C, D — 87 nm (161 km; 100 miles)
Endurance with max fuel: A — 2 h 30 min
g limits: A — +6/−3·3
Best glide ratio:
A, at 31 knots (58 km/h; 36 mph) — 8·2
B, C, at 39 knots (72 km/h; 45 mph) — 8·0
D, at 35 knots (64 km/h; 40 mph) — 5·5
Min rate of sink, power off: A — 69 m (225 ft)/min

MEAD

MEAD ENGINEERING COMPANY

1325 Valleyview, Wichita, Kansas 67212

MEAD ADVENTURE

The late Mr George Mead began in April 1977 the design of a small single-seat sporting monoplane named the Adventure. Construction started six months later, and the prototype (N36ME) flew for the first time in October 1978. In early 1981 Mr Mead changed the landing gear from tricycle to tailwheel configuration. At the same time, the original 59·5 kW (80 hp) Continental A80 engine was replaced by a Continental O-200, enclosed in a newly formed cowling with cleaner cylinder head bulges; and the following description refers to the aircraft in this current form, as illustrated. Plans are available to amateur constructors, and by 1986 approximately 100 sets had been sold.

TYPE: Single-seat homebuilt sporting monoplane.

AIRFRAME: Cantilever low-wing monoplane. Aerofoil section NACA 23018 at root, NACA 23012 at tip. Dihedral 4° 30′. Incidence 0° 30′. Sweepback at quarter-chord 1° 18′. Composite structure of glassfibre/epoxy facings over a plastics foam core, and incorporating a built-up box spar extending over 70% of span. Small plain ailerons, inboard of wingtips, of glassfibre/foam sandwich. Wide span single-slotted trailing-edge flaps of similar construction. Separate electrically actuated roll trim surface set in trailing-edge of wing, at starboard wingtip. Composite fuselage and cantilever tail unit, made from sandwich panels with glassfibre/epoxy facings and plastics foam core. Fixed incidence tailplane. Bungee elevator trim. No trim tabs.

LANDING GEAR: Non-retractable tailwheel type fitted currently. Main legs comprise a glassfibre/epoxy spring formed as a one-piece inverted bow. Mainwheel tyres size 3·40 × 3·00-5, pressure 3·79 bars (55 lb/sq in). Rosenhan hydraulic brakes. Speed fairings fitted to mainwheels.

POWER PLANT: One 74·5 kW (100 hp) Continental O-200 flat-four engine, driving a two-blade fixed-pitch propeller with spinner. Other engines can be fitted, including Continentals and Volkswagen conversions from 48·5 kW (65 hp). Two fuselage fuel tanks, one immediately aft of firewall, the other in turtledeck, with combined capacity of 87 litres (23 US gallons). Refuelling points on upper surface of forward and aft fuselage. Oil capacity 3·8 litres (1 US gallon).

ACCOMMODATION: Single seat in enclosed cockpit, beneath sideways opening transparent canopy. Baggage space aft of seat. Accommodation is heated and ventilated.

SYSTEMS: Electrical system has small storage battery. Hydraulic system for brakes only.

DIMENSIONS, EXTERNAL:

Wing span	6·10 m (20 ft 0 in)
Wing chord: at root	0·76 m (2 ft 6 in)
at tip	0·46 m (1 ft 6 in)
Wing aspect ratio	10·0
Length overall	4·80 m (15 ft 9 in)
Height overall	1·37 m (4 ft 6 in)
Tailplane span	2·56 m (8 ft 4¾ in)
Wheel track	0·91 m (3 ft 0 in)
Wheelbase	3·10 m (10 ft 2 in)
Propeller diameter	1·57 m (5 ft 2 in)

AREA:

Wings, gross	3·72 m² (40·0 sq ft)

WEIGHTS AND LOADINGS:

Basic operating weight	222 kg (490 lb)
Max T-O and landing weight	372 kg (820 lb)
Max wing loading	100·1 kg/m² (20·5 lb/sq ft)
Max power loading	4·99 kg/kW (8·20 lb/hp)

PERFORMANCE (A: prototype as originally flown. B: prototype in current form, at max T-O weight):

Never-exceed speed:	
A	183 knots (338 km/h; 210 mph)
B	195 knots (362 km/h; 225 mph)
Max level speed at S/L:	
A	156 knots (290 km/h; 180 mph)
B	188 knots (349 km/h; 217 mph)
Max cruising speed at 2,440 m (8,000 ft):	
A	152 knots (282 km/h; 175 mph)
B	184 knots (341 km/h; 212 mph)
Econ cruising speed at 2,440 m (8,000 ft):	
A	135 knots (249 km/h; 155 mph)
B	163 knots (303 km/h; 188 mph)
Stalling speed, flaps up:	
A	61 knots (113 km/h; 70 mph)
B	66 knots (121 km/h; 75 mph)
Stalling speed, 45° flap, engine idling:	
A	50 knots (92 km/h; 57 mph)
B	55 knots (101 km/h; 62 mph)
Max rate of climb at S/L: A	488 m (1,600 ft)/min
B	670 m (2,200 ft)/min
Service ceiling: A	6,100 m (20,000 ft)
T-O run: A	183 m (600 ft)
T-O to 15 m (50 ft): A	305 m (1,000 ft)
Landing from 15 m (50 ft): A	457 m (1,500 ft)
Landing run: A	244 m (800 ft)
Range with max fuel at econ cruising speed, with reserves: A	695 nm (1,285 km; 800 miles)
B	825 nm (1,529 km; 950 miles)

MEADOWLARK

MEADOWLARK ULTRALIGHT CORPORATION

PO Box 1524, Medford, Oregon 97501
Telephone: (503) 779 8284
PRESIDENT: Jerry Crippen

MEADOWLARK ULTRALIGHT MEADOWLARK MODEL C

The Meadowlark entered production, in ready to fly form, in October 1982. The Model C variant features a new undercarriage suspension system and redesigned tail surfaces for easier stowage.

TYPE: Single-seat microlight aircraft; conforms to FAR Pt 103.

AIRFRAME: Strut braced high-wing monoplane, with conventional tail surfaces. Main frame of aluminium alloy. Wings have a leading-edge D spar, Styrofoam ribs, and double surface transparent Mylar covering; tail surfaces are similar. Three-axis control (ailerons, elevators and rudder).

LANDING GEAR: Tricycle type, with 20 in diameter mainwheels and 16 in diameter steerable nosewheel with brake. Floats optional.

POWER PLANT: One 26 kW (35 hp) Cuyuna ULII-02 two-cylinder two-stroke engine, with reduction drive to a two-blade wooden propeller. Fuel tank capacity 13·2 litres (3·5 US gallons).

ACCOMMODATION: Pilot only, in open position.

DIMENSIONS, EXTERNAL:

Wing span	10·67 m (35 ft 0 in)
Wing aspect ratio	8·51
Length overall	6·05 m (19 ft 10 in)
Height overall	2·01 m (6 ft 7 in)
Propeller diameter	1·37 m (4 ft 6 in)

AREA:

Wings, gross	13·38 m² (144·0 sq ft)

WEIGHTS AND LOADINGS:

Weight empty	113 kg (250 lb)
Max pilot weight	125 kg (275 lb)
Max T-O weight	249 kg (550 lb)
Max wing loading	19·53 kg/m² (4·0 lb/sq ft)
Max power loading	9·58 kg/kW (15·71 lb/hp)

PERFORMANCE (with 82 kg; 180 lb pilot):

Never-exceed speed	56 knots (104 km/h; 65 mph)
Max level speed	48 knots (88 km/h; 55 mph)
Max cruising speed	39 knots (72 km/h; 45 mph)
Stalling speed:	
power on	18 knots (33 km/h; 20 mph)
power off	19 knots (36 km/h; 22 mph)
Max rate of climb at S/L	305 m (1,000 ft)/min
Service ceiling	above 3,050 m (10,000 ft)
T-O run	23 m (75 ft)
Landing run	30 m (100 ft)
Range with max fuel	78 nm (145 km; 90 miles)
Endurance with max fuel	2 h
g limits	+3·1/−1·7

MERGANSER

MERGANSER AIRCRAFT CORPORATION

PO Box 8, Annapolis, Maryland 21404

MERGANSER AIRCRAFT MERGANSER

Mr Peter D. Van Dine, a builder of high performance sailing boats, designed and constructed the prototype of a tandem two-seat amphibious flying-boat known as the Merganser. This first prototype was built of glassfibre and foam and was fitted initially with a 74·5 kW (100 hp) Continental O-200-A engine driving a three-blade fixed-pitch pusher propeller. With this power plant and propeller the aircraft achieved only short, straight and level flights. The Merganser was retrofitted, therefore, with a 48·5 kW (65 hp) Revmaster 2100D converted Volkswagen motorcar engine and a Maloof three-blade constant-speed propeller of slightly greater diameter. This combination gave a reduction in take-off weight of approximately 45·4 kg (100 lb), with no reduction in payload.

The first Merganser was flight tested for 70 hours, during which it became clear that stability and performance could be improved with configuration changes. A quarter-scale radio controlled model of the Merganser in revised configuration was built, and results from testing this were encouraging.

A second redesigned prototype was built to continue the flight test programme. Early flights indicate excellent performance. As can be seen from the accompanying illustration, design changes include a fin and rudder at each wingtip, replacing the mid-span fins and canted winglets of the original prototype. Other changes involve the use of a single skin of moulded graphite fibre (which reduced empty weight dramatically) and a new two-blade carbonfibre propeller, an increase in wing span, adoption of an Eppler wing section, and use of new higher aspect ratio foreplanes positioned forward and lower on the nose of the hull. The Revmaster 2100D engine is uprated.

Kits of premoulded component parts to build the Merganser are available, without engine, propeller or instruments. The aircraft is said not to stall, and can take off from water in six to eight seconds at a test weight of 390 kg (860 lb).

The details below refer to the latest prototype.

TYPE: Two-seat canard amphibious flying-boat.

LANDING GEAR: Retractable tricycle landing gear, with glassfibre legs (not fitted for early flights).

POWER PLANT: One 56 kW (75 hp) Revmaster 2100D modified Volkswagen motorcar engine, driving a two-blade carbonfibre constant-speed pusher propeller. Two fuel tanks in wings, each 26·5 litres (7 US gallons) capacity. Optional total capacity of 76 litres (20 US gallons).

DIMENSIONS, EXTERNAL:

Wing span	5·79 m (19 ft 0 in)
Foreplane span	2·79 m (9 ft 2 in)
Length overall	4·37 m (14 ft 4 in)
Height, landing gear retracted	1·38 m (4 ft 6¼ in)
Propeller diameter	1·45 m (4 ft 9 in)

AREA:

Wings, gross	9·29 m² (100·0 sq ft)

WEIGHTS:

Weight empty: flying-boat	195 kg (430 lb)
amphibian	213 kg (470 lb)
Max T-O weight: flying-boat	431 kg (950 lb)
amphibian	453 kg (1,000 lb)

PERFORMANCE (estimated):

Max level speed	139 knots (257 km/h; 160 mph)
Max cruising speed	130 knots (241 km/h; 150 mph)
Min flying speed	46 knots (84 km/h; 52 mph)
Range: standard fuel	565 nm (1,045 km; 650 miles)
max fuel	808 nm (1,495 km; 930 miles)

MIRA SLOVAK

MIRA SLOVAK AVIATION

PO Box 822, Santa Paula, California 93060

MIRA SLOVAK UR-1

The design began some years ago of an unlimited class single-seat racing aircraft for Mr Mira Slovak. Little is known of the UR-1, beyond the details that follow:

AIRFRAME: Cantilever low-wing monoplane, with conventional three-axis control (ailerons, elevators and rudder). Wing section NACA 64009 modified. Dihedral 5°. Incidence 1°. Sweepback at quarter chord 0·76°.

LANDING GEAR: Retractable tricycle type, with all three wheels of same size (5·00-5).

POWER PLANT: One 1,044 kW (1,400 hp) engine of unspecified type with water injection and twin turbochargers, driving a modified Hartzell five-blade constant-speed propeller. Airscoop under rear fuselage.

ACCOMMODATION: Pilot only, under low bubble canopy, faired into rear decking.

DIMENSION:

Propeller diameter	2·27 m (7 ft 5½ in)

WEIGHTS:

Fuel weight	159 kg (350 lb)
Water weight	125 kg (275 lb)
Max T-O weight	1,361 kg (3,000 lb)

MIRAGE

MIRAGE AIRCRAFT INC

3936 Austin Street, Klamath Falls, Oregon 97603
Telephone: (503) 884 4011
PRESIDENT: Larry Burton

MIRAGE CELERITY

The prototype Celerity two-seat homebuilt aircraft (N5104X) flew for the first time on 18 May 1985 and was displayed at that year's EAA meeting at Oshkosh. Design had begun in 1981 and construction of the prototype had started in the following year.

Mirage Aircraft offers plans to construct the Celerity, with which an inexperienced builder could take more than 3,000 working hours to complete the task. Various kits and upholstery patterns to cut working time are available via Wicks Aircraft Supply. These kits include: ribs and spars; fuselage, tail unit and engine cowling; airframe skin of foam, glassfibre and epoxy resin; metal fittings; Plexiglas canopy, windscreen, side windows and turtledeck; instrument panel; landing gear legs and mounting plates; and the landing gear legs and mounting plates plus all hydraulic and electrical accessories but no wheels or tyres. The tip tanks are also available upon request. Use of the spar and metal fittings kits alone could cut working time by up to one-third. Kits became available in Spring 1986; by February 1986 three sets of plans had been sold.

TYPE: Two-seat homebuilt aircraft.

AIRFRAME: Cantilever low-wing monoplane. Wing section NACA 23015 at root, NACA 23010 at tip. Incidence 1° 30′. Airframe structure of wood, with composite skins of foam, glassfibre and epoxy resin. Wings fitted with ailerons and flaps. Conventional cantilever tail unit, with sweptback fin and rudder. Trim tab on elevators.

LANDING GEAR: Hydraulically retractable tailwheel type. Telescopic tube main legs with coil springs. Mainwheels (with brakes) size 5·00-5; tyre pressure 2·76 bars (40 lb/sq in). 4 in diameter tailwheel.

Mead Adventure in current 'taildragger' form *(J. M. G. Gradidge)*

Second prototype of the Merganser Aircraft Merganser two-seat amphibious flying-boat *(Leroy White)*

Meadowlark Ultralight Meadowlark Model C

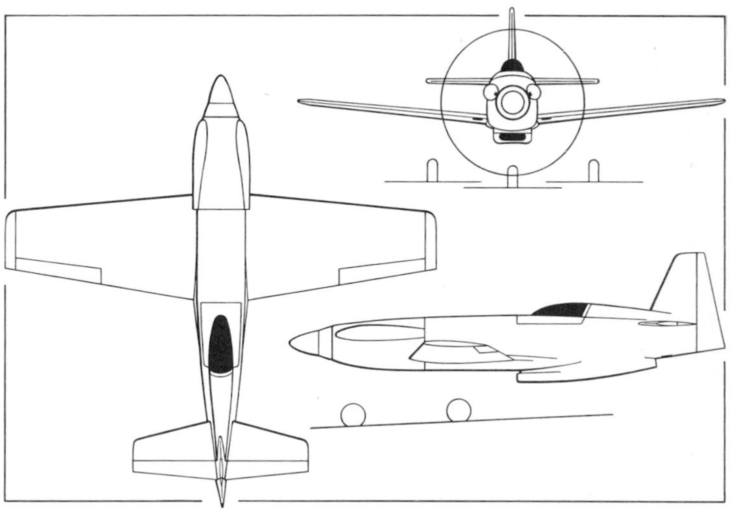

Provisional three-view of Mira Slovak UR-1 racing aircraft *(Jane's/Mike Keep)*

Mirage Celerity two-seat homebuilt aircraft

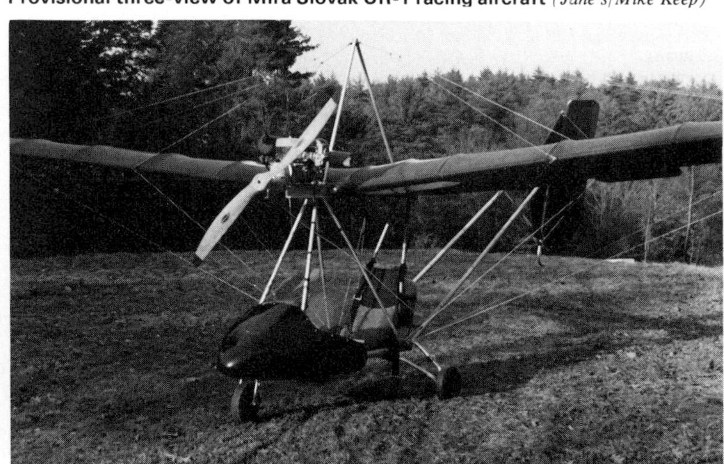

Mirage Aircraft Mirage II in current configuration

POWER PLANT: One 119 kW (160 hp) Avco Lycoming O-320-B1A flat-four engine, driving a Hartzell two-blade constant-speed propeller with large spinner. Two fuel tanks, with total capacity of 114 litres (30 US gallons). Two auxiliary tip tanks, each of 38 litres (10 US gallons) capacity. Oil capacity 7·6 litres (2 US gallons). Optional engines of 74·5-134 kW (100-180 hp).

ACCOMMODATION: Two seats side by side under upward hinged Plexiglas canopy. Baggage capacity 27 kg (60 lb).

SYSTEMS: Hydraulic system for landing gear. 12V 35A electrical system.

AVIONICS: L-Nav 25 Loran C, full IFR and radio optional.

DIMENSIONS, EXTERNAL:

Wing span over tip tanks	7·01 m (23 ft 0 in)
Wing chord: at root	1·52 m (5 ft 0 in)
at tip	0·91 m (3 ft 0 in)
Wing aspect ratio	5·75
Length overall	6·55 m (21 ft 6 in)
Height overall	1·68 m (5 ft 6 in)
Tailplane span	2·13 m (7 ft 0 in)
Wheel track	2·74 m (9 ft 0 in)
Wheelbase	3·68 m (12 ft 1 in)
Propeller diameter	1·93 m (6 ft 4 in)

DIMENSION, INTERNAL:

Cockpit: Max width	1·02 m (3 ft 4 in)

AREA:

Wings, gross	8·36 m² (90·0 sq ft)

WEIGHTS AND LOADINGS:

Weight empty	530 kg (1,169 lb)
Max T-O weight	828 kg (1,825 lb)
Max wing loading	99·02 kg/m² (20·28 lb/sq ft)
Max power loading	6·96 kg/kW (11·41 lb/hp)

PERFORMANCE (at max T-O weight):

Econ cruising speed	165 knots (306 km/h; 190 mph)
Stalling speed	46 knots (86 km/h; 53 mph)
Max rate of climb at S/L	549 m (1,800 ft)/min
T-O run	244 m (800 ft)
T-O to 15 m (50 ft)	274 m (900 ft)
Landing from 15 m (50 ft)	396 m (1,300 ft)
Landing run	305 m (1,000 ft)
Range with max standard fuel	781-868 nm (1,448-1,609 km; 900-1,000 miles)

MIRAGE

MIRAGE AIRCRAFT INC

10 Granaudo Circle, Southwick, Massachusetts 01077
Telephone: (413) 569 3559
PRESIDENT: Gary L. Hoover

This company acquired the design rights to the former Ultralight Flight Mirage microlight aircraft, which it markets in kit form as the Mirage II.

MIRAGE AIRCRAFT MIRAGE II

The Mirage II differs from the original Mirage models in having a tractor instead of pusher engine installation.

TYPE: Single-seat microlight aircraft; conforms to FAR Pt 103.

AIRFRAME: High-wing monoplane, with cruciform tail surfaces and three-axis control ('spoilerons', elevators and rudder). Main frame of aluminium alloy, braced by kingposts and stainless steel cables. Dacron covering for wings (double surface) and tail surfaces. Constant chord wings standard; tapered wings optional. Other options include double spoilers, parachute and instruments.

LANDING GEAR: Tricycle type, with 250 × 5 in shock-dampened wheel on each unit. Steerable nosewheel. No brakes. Optional skis or floats.

POWER PLANT: Standard engine is a 26·1 kW (35 hp) Rotax 377, with reduction drive to a two-blade wooden propeller; Rotax 277, Rotax 447 or Kawasaki 340 engine available optionally. Fuel tank capacity 19 litres (5 US gallons).

ACCOMMODATION: Pilot only, in open cockpit with nose pod and windscreen.

DIMENSIONS, EXTERNAL:

Wing span	9·75 m (32 ft 0 in)
Wing aspect ratio	7·3
Length overall	5·49 m (18 ft 0 in)
Height overall	2·49 m (8 ft 2 in)
Propeller diameter	1·63 m (5 ft 4 in)

AREA:

Wings, gross (standard)	13·1 m² (141·0 sq ft)

WEIGHTS AND LOADINGS:

Weight empty	111·5 kg (246 lb)
Max pilot weight	101·5 kg (224 lb)
Max T-O weight	227 kg (500 lb)
Max wing loading	17·30 kg/m² (3·55 lb/sq ft)

Max power loading (Rotax 377)
8·69 kg/kW (14·28 lb/hp)

PERFORMANCE (Rotax 447 engine):

Never-exceed speed	60 knots (112 km/h; 70 mph)
Max level speed	55 knots (101 km/h; 63 mph)
Max cruising speed	50 knots (93 km/h; 58 mph)
Econ cruising speed	40 knots (74 km/h; 46 mph)
Stalling speed: power on	22 knots (41 km/h; 25 mph)
power off	24 knots (44 km/h; 27 mph)
Max rate of climb at S/L	457 m (1,500 ft)/min
Service ceiling (estimated)	4,575 m (15,000 ft)
T-O run	23 m (75 ft)
Landing run	37 m (120 ft)
Range with max fuel	108 nm (201 km; 125 miles)
Endurance with max fuel	3 h
g limits	+4/−3
Best glide ratio	7·25
Min rate of sink, power off	122 m (400 ft)/min

MITCHELL WING

MITCHELL AEROSPACE COMPANY

1900 S. Newcomb, Porterville, California 93257
Telephone: (209) 781 8100
DIRECTOR: James M. Meade

Mitchell Wing Inc (formerly Mitchell Aircraft Corporation) produces plans and kits for the Mitchell Wing B-10, U-2, P-38 Lightning and a P-38 agricultural derivative known as the AG-38A Terrier. Its latest products are the A-10 Silver Eagle and a two-seat TU-10 Double Eagle version, available in ready to fly forms.

MITCHELL WING B-10

Design of this aircraft originated in 1975, and it flew for the first time in 1976, powered by a 9 kW (12 hp) McCulloch MC-101 engine. There are three powered versions, all of which use the basic hang glider wing:

B-10F. Foot launch powered version, with a tubular frame structure that serves as fuselage, engine mounting, and open cockpit for the pilot. Two mainwheels only, at rear end of fuselage frame.

B-10. Powered version with tricycle landing gear.

SR-10. Proposed military and environmental version of the B-10, described in the 1982-83 *Jane's*.

In 1981 Mitchell introduced a 'podule' (a cross between a hanging pod and a cockpit module), designed specifically for the B-10. The kit, which weighs only 6·8 kg (15 lb), includes pre-moulded glassfibre fairing, windscreen, matching wheel fairings, and nosewheel brake assembly.

Factory built ready to fly B-10s became available in 1982. Approximately 3,000 complete aircraft, kits and plan sets have been sold.

TYPE: Single-seat microlight monoplane; conforms to FAR Pt 103.

AIRFRAME: Tapered parasol monoplane. Wing section NACA 23015. Dihedral 6° on outer wing panels. Sweepback at quarter-chord 12°. Structure of wood and fabric, with D section leading-edge, foam ribs, and wooden web spar. Trailing-edge ribs of built-up truss type, those in centre-section carrying the rear spar for accessory attachment points. Dacron covering, with small section of wing undersurface, immediately above the cockpit, left uncovered to simplify access to seat. Mitchell patented 'stabilators' occupy entire trailing-edge of each outer wing panel, functioning differentially as ailerons and collectively as elevators. Rudders, mounted above each wingtip, operated conventionally for yaw control; can also be actuated differentially as airbrakes for increased descent rates. Outer wing panels fold over centre-section for transportation. Braced fuselage framework of aluminium tube.

LANDING GEAR: B-10F has two mainwheels only; B-10 has non-retractable tricycle type with steerable nosewheel. All wheels of nylon, with tubed tyres size 4·10 × 3·50-4. Nosewheel brake.

POWER PLANT: One 15 kW (20 hp) Honda 250 cc two-stroke engine, driving a two-blade fixed-pitch pusher propeller via a 2·25:1 reduction gear. Fuel tank capacity 5·7 litres (1·5 US gallons); auxiliary tanks optional.

ACCOMMODATION: Pilot only, on sling seat or in optional 'podule'. (Two-seat version available.)

DIMENSIONS, EXTERNAL:

Wing span	10·36 m (34 ft 0 in)
Wing aspect ratio	8·5
Width, wings folded	5·49 m (18 ft 0 in)
Height overall	1·22 m (4 ft 0 in)
Propeller diameter	1·22 m (4 ft 0 in)

AREA:

Wings, gross	12·63 m² (136·0 sq ft)

WEIGHTS AND LOADINGS:

Weight empty	91 kg (200 lb)
Max pilot weight	136 kg (300 lb)
Max T-O weight: standard	238 kg (525 lb)
restricted	329 kg (725 lb)
Max wing loading: standard	18·8 kg/m² (3·8 lb/sq ft)
restricted	26·0 kg/m² (5·3 lb/sq ft)

PERFORMANCE (B-10 at max standard T-O weight):

Max level speed	56 knots (105 km/h; 65 mph)
Max cruising speed at S/L	43 knots (80 km/h; 50 mph)
Econ cruising speed at S/L	31 knots (58 km/h; 36 mph)
Stalling speed	21 knots (39 km/h; 24 mph)
Max rate of climb at S/L	122 m (400 ft)/min
Service ceiling	3,660 m (12,000 ft)
T-O run	61 m (200 ft)
Landing run	30 m (100 ft)
Range with max standard fuel and max payload	35 nm (64 km; 40 miles)
Range with auxiliary fuel	434 nm (805 km; 500 miles)
g limits	±6
Best glide ratio	17

MITCHELL WING U-2 SUPERWING

Mr Don Mitchell designed the U-2 with the aim of developing a microlight superior in controllability, performance, and structure to powered hang gliders. The prototype first flew during 1979. Orders for plans and/or kits total more than 1,500.

TYPE: Single-seat microlight monoplane; does not conform to FAR Pt 103.

AIRFRAME: Wings of production kits are generally similar to those of the B-10, except for a modified Wortmann section of 19% thickness/chord ratio, and combined fin and rudder assemblies at the wingtips, the rear 65 per cent of each being movable. Fuselage structure of chrome-molybdenum steel tube within wing centre-section. Two hardwood runners extend full length of this structure, beneath the pilot's seat, for protection in wheels-up landing.

LANDING GEAR: Manually retractable tricycle type, all units retracting rearward. Optional non-retractable gear. Steerable nosewheel. Nylon wheels with tubed tyres size 4·10 × 3·50-4. Friction brake operating on surface of nosewheel tyre.

POWER PLANT: As described for B-10. Plastics fuel tank mounted within wing has capacity of 5·7 litres (1·5 US gallons). Auxiliary tanks optional.

ACCOMMODATION: Pilot only, on reinforced canvas sling seat beneath one-piece bubble canopy, secured by fore and aft locking pins, and easily removed for entry/exit. Mylar panels in cockpit floor to provide downward view. Cockpit ventilated.

DIMENSIONS, EXTERNAL: As for B-10 except:

Length overall	2·84 m (9 ft 4 in)
Height overall	0·91 m (3 ft 0 in)

WEIGHTS AND LOADING:

Weight empty	136 kg (300 lb)
Max pilot weight	136 kg (300 lb)
Max standard T-O weight	272 kg (600 lb)
Max standard wing loading	21·5 kg/m² (4·4 lb/sq ft)

PERFORMANCE (at max standard T-O weight):

Max level speed at S/L	74 knots (137 km/h; 85 mph)
Max cruising speed at S/L	56 knots (105 km/h; 65 mph)
Stalling speed	26 knots (47 km/h; 29 mph)
Max rate of climb at S/L	152 m (500 ft)/min
Service ceiling	3,660 m (12,000 ft)
T-O run	61 m (200 ft)
Landing run	38 m (125 ft)
Range with max standard fuel and max payload	39 nm (72 km; 45 miles)
Range with auxiliary fuel	434 nm (805 km; 500 miles)
g limits	±10
Best glide ratio	27

MITCHELL WING P-38 LIGHTNING

Mr James Meade's objective in designing the P-38 was to produce a conventionally controlled microlight aircraft, with reasonable performance, which could be assembled by four people in one day. It flew for the first time in late 1980 and became available in plan/kit form in March 1981. Assembly time is quoted as 100 man-hours (from factory supplied kit), or 300 if built from plans.

An **AG-38A Terrier** agricultural version, with a 12V battery, 53 litre (14 US gallon) ULV spraytank, two Beeco Mist sprayheads and an electric spraypump, is also available. This appears to be developed from the original AG-38 Falcon agricultural model, though no confirmation of this has been received. Empty and max T-O weights of this version are 144 kg (317 lb) and 318 kg (700 lb) respectively. The military **AG-38-A War Eagle** is described separately. Many hundreds of P-38s/Terriers/Falcons have been sold.

The following description applies to the standard P-38:

TYPE: Single-seat microlight aircraft; does not conform to FAR Pt 103.

AIRFRAME: Braced monoplane, with twin tailbooms and twin fins and rudders. Main structure of aluminium, with quick-fit ribs and Dacron covered wing and tail surfaces. Wing section NACA 23015. Full span ailerons, set below and behind wings. One-piece elevator aft of tailbooms. Wings can be folded back alongside fuselage for transportation and storage. Options include flight instrumentation and night lights.

LANDING GEAR: Non-retractable tricycle type, with glassfibre rod mainwheel legs, 10 in wheels, and nosewheel drum braking. Options include 20 in wheels for rough field operation, mainwheel fairings, and ski or float gear.

POWER PLANT: One 22 kW (30 hp) 250 cc Cuyuna 430 two-stroke engine, driving a two-blade wooden pusher propeller via a 2·25:1 reduction gear. Fuel tank capacity 5·7 litres (1·5 US gallons). Options include electric engine starting and 15 litre (4 US gallon) auxiliary fuel tank.

ACCOMMODATION: Pilot only, in open cockpit. Cockpit 'podule' optional.

DIMENSIONS, EXTERNAL:

Wing span	8·53 m (28 ft 0 in)
Length overall	5·49 m (18 ft 0 in)
Height overall	1·52 m (5 ft 0 in)

AREA:

Wings, gross	11·52 m² (124·0 sq ft)

WEIGHTS AND LOADINGS:

Weight empty	136 kg (300 lb)
Max pilot weight	136 kg (300 lb)
Max T-O weight: standard	249 kg (550 lb)
restricted	340 kg (750 lb)
Max wing loading: standard	21·6 kg/m² (4·4 lb/sq ft)
restricted	29·5 kg/m² (6·0 lb/sq ft)

PERFORMANCE (at max standard T-O weight):

Max level speed	52 knots (97 km/h; 60 mph)
Max cruising speed	48 knots (88 km/h; 55 mph)
Stalling speed	28 knots (51 km/h; 32 mph)
Max rate of climb at S/L	76-91 m (250-300 ft)/min
T-O run	68 m (225 ft)
Landing run	61 m (200 ft)
Range with max standard fuel	43 nm (80 km; 50 miles)
Range with auxiliary fuel	434 nm (805 km; 500 miles)
g limits	±6

MITCHELL WING AG-38-A WAR EAGLE

The AG-38-A War Eagle is an enlarged military version of the P-38/AG-38 series, with a more powerful engine, increased fuel and provision for a variety of operational equipment. It is available in prefabricated or kit form.

POWER PLANT: One 29·4 kW (39·4 hp) Rotax 447 two-cylinder two-stroke engine, driving a three-blade wooden pusher propeller through 2·2:1 reduction gearing. Standard fuel capacity 24 litres (6·5 US gallons). Optional long-range fuel tank, capacity 151 litres (40 US gallons).

OPERATIONAL EQUIPMENT: Optional items include two M60 machine-gun mounts; four Strem 89 rocket mounts; wind-driven agricultural spraypump with full-span 25 nozzle spray system and 151 litre (40 US gallon) hopper capacity; ballistic parachute; radios; video camera, transmitter and antenna; Kevlar pilot protection and night vision goggles.

DIMENSIONS, EXTERNAL:

Wing span	10·36 m (34 ft 0 in)
Wing chord, constant	1·27 m (4 ft 2 in)
Length overall	5·79 m (19 ft 0 in)
Height overall	2·11 m (6 ft 11 in)
Propeller diameter	1·47 m (4 ft 10 in)

AREA:

Wings, gross	14·86 m² (160·0 sq ft)

WEIGHTS AND LOADINGS:

Weight empty	168 kg (370 lb)
Max pilot weight	104 kg (230 lb)
Max T-O weight: Normal	363 kg (800 lb)
Restricted category	476 kg (1,050 lb)
Max wing loading (Restricted category)	32·03 kg/m² (6·56 lb/sq ft)
Max power loading (Restricted category)	16·19 kg/kW (26·65 lb/hp)

PERFORMANCE (Normal category, 77 kg; 170 lb pilot):

Never-exceed speed	75 knots (139 km/h; 86 mph)
Best cruising speed	60 knots (111 km/h; 69 mph)
Stalling speed, power off	30 knots (56 km/h; 35 mph)
Max rate of climb at S/L	152 m (500 ft)/min
T-O run	61 m (200 ft)
Endurance with max fuel	1 h 40 min

MITCHELL WING A-10 SILVER EAGLE

Based on the B-10, but with significant improvements, the A-10 was designed to conform to all FAA ultralight (microlight) regulations, including FAR Pt 103, and is produced in ready to fly form only. Major difference from the B-10 lies in the use of metal (A for aluminium), rather than wood and fabric, in its construction. A two-seat model is designated **TU-10 Double Eagle**.

TYPE (A-10): Single-seat microlight aircraft; conforms to FAR Pt 103.

AIRFRAME: Configuration generally similar to that of B-10 (which see), with almost identical planform and similar control system. Cantilever wings are of D cell construction, with shear web and upper/lower spar caps, and have an NACA 23015 aerofoil section Wings formed by new process based on honeycomb, using injections of NASA developed SP502 foam. All skins of Alclad aluminium sheet; all fuselage tubing and spar caps of aircraft aluminium; aerodynamic fairings of pre-moulded lightweight glassfibre. Floor mounted control stick actuates pitch and roll control 'stabilators'; rudder pedals provide independent operation of NASA (Whitcomb) winglets at wingtips, which double as drag rudders for directional control. Wings and tip rudders can be folded for transportation and storage, as on B-10.

Mitchell Wing AG-38-A War Eagle with optional armaments

Mitchell Wing A-10 Silver Eagle, with wings folded *(Howard Levy)*

Demonstration of Mitchell Wing AG-38 cropsprayer in China

Mitchell Wing U-2, with non-retractable landing gear

Mooney Mite single-seat light aircraft *(J. M. G. Gradidge)*,

LANDING GEAR: Tricycle type, with independent cantilever torque tube suspension on all three units, steerable nosewheel (with brake), and speed fairings on all three wheels. Floats optional.

POWER PLANT: One 17·2 kW (23 hp) Zenoah 242 cc two-stroke engine in A-10, with 2:1 Manta Poly-V reduction drive to 54 × 24 two-blade wooden pusher propeller; standard fuel capacity 11·4 litres (3 US gallons). TU-10 has a 29·4 kW (39·4 hp) Rotax 447 engine and 22·7 litres (6 US gallons) of fuel.

ACCOMMODATION: Pilot only, in open cockpit with moulded glassfibre fuselage fairing.

DIMENSIONS, EXTERNAL:
- Wing span: A-10 — 10·46 m (34 ft 4 in)
  - TU-10 — 11·38 m (37 ft 4 in)
- Wing aspect ratio: A-10 — 8·67
  - TU-10 — 9·17
- Length overall — 2·59 m (8 ft 6 in)
- Height overall — 1·88 m (6 ft 2 in)

AREAS:
- Wings, gross: A-10 — 12·45 m² (134·0 sq ft)
  - TU-10 — 14·12 m² (152·0 sq ft)

WEIGHTS AND LOADINGS:
- Weight empty: A-10 — 113 kg (250 lb)
  - TU-10 — 151 kg (332 lb)
- Pilot weight range:
  - A-10 — 54·5-129 kg (120-285 lb)
  - TU-10 (two persons) — 54·5-192·5 kg (120-425 lb)
- Max T-O weight: A-10 — 251 kg (553 lb)
- Wing loading: A-10 — 20·16 kg/m² (4·13 lb/sq ft)
  - TU-10 at 306 kg (675 lb) AUW — 21·68 kg/m² (4·44 lb/sq ft)
- Power loading: A-10 — 14·59 kg/kW (24·04 lb/hp)
  - TU-10 at 306 kg (675 lb) AUW — 10·41 kg/kW (17·13 lb/hp)

PERFORMANCE (with full fuel; A-10, prototype with 75 kg; 165 lb pilot, TU-10 estimated with pilot and passenger):
- Max level speed: A-10 — 55 knots (101 km/h; 63 mph)
  - TU-10 — 65 knots (121 km/h; 75 mph)
- Max cruising speed, 75% power:
  - A-10, TU-10 — 50 knots (93 km/h; 58 mph)
- Stalling speed, power off:
  - A-10 — 24 knots (44 km/h; 27 mph)
  - TU-10 — 27 knots (50 km/h; 31 mph)
- Max rate of climb at S/L: A-10 — 195 m (640 ft)/min
  - TU-10 — 152 m (500 ft)/min
- Service ceiling: A-10, TU-10 — 3,660 m (12,000 ft)
- T-O run: A-10 — 69 m (225 ft)
  - TU-10 — 99 m (325 ft)
- Landing run: A-10 — 61 m (200 ft)
  - TU-10 — 91 m (300 ft)
- Range with max fuel, 75% power, no reserves:
  - A-10 — 131 nm (243 km; 151 miles)
  - TU-10 — 150 nm (278 km; 173 miles)
- Endurance, conditions as above: A-10 — 2 h 24 min
  - TU-10 — 2 h 36 min
- *g* limits: A-10 — ±5·5
- Best glide ratio: A-10 — 16
  - TU-10 — 15
- Min rate of sink, power off:
  - A-10 — 73 m (240 ft)/min
  - TU-10 — 85 m (280 ft)/min

MOONEY MITE

MOONEY MITE AIRCRAFT CORPORATION

PO Box 3999, Charlottesville, Virginia 22903

Mooney Mite Aircraft Corporation was formed to market to amateur constructors plans of the Mooney Mite, a version of the Mooney M-18 first designed and built as a production aircraft by Mooney Aircraft Inc.

MOONEY MITE

TYPE: Single-seat homebuilt sporting aircraft.

AIRFRAME: Cantilever low-wing monoplane. Wing section NACA 63215 at root, NACA 64415 at tip. Dihedral 5° 30′ from roots. Incidence 4°. Conventional single-spar structure of wood, with plywood D leading-edge torsion box, and fabric covering aft of the spar. Ailerons and trailing-edge flaps of welded steel tube construction with fabric covering. Forward section of fuselage of welded steel tube with light alloy skins. Rear fuselage of wood monocoque construction with fabric covering. Cantilever welded steel tube tail unit, fabric covered. Tailplane incidence variable by 'Safe-Trim' system that interconnects tail trim with trailing-edge flaps to establish automatically the correct settings for take-off, climb, approach and landing.

LANDING GEAR: Manually retractable tricycle type. Shock absorption of main units by rubber in compression. Nosewheel steerable. Mainwheels of Cleveland, Firestone or Goodyear manufacture, with tyres size 5·00-5. Hydraulic brakes.

POWER PLANT: One 48·5 kW (65 hp) Avco Lycoming O-145-B2 flat-four aircooled engine, driving a Sensenich Type 66CB-54 two-blade fixed-pitch propeller with spinner. Fuel tank in fuselage, capacity 41·5 litres (11 US gallons). Provision for auxiliary tank, capacity 23 litres (6 US gallons). Oil capacity 3·75 litres (1 US gallon).

ACCOMMODATION: Single seat beneath rearward sliding transparent canopy. Space for 18 kg (40 lb) baggage to rear of seat.

SYSTEM: Electric power supplied by wind driven generator mounted on pylon on upper surface of rear fuselage.

DIMENSIONS, EXTERNAL:
- Wing span — 8·19 m (26 ft 10½ in)
- Length overall — 5·37 m (17 ft 7¼ in)
- Height overall — 1·89 m (6 ft 2½ in)
- Tailplane span — 2·54 m (8 ft 4 in)
- Wheel track — 1·55 m (5 ft 1 in)
- Wheelbase — 1·22 m (4 ft 0 in)
- Propeller diameter — 1·60 m (5 ft 3 in)

AREA:
- Wings, gross — 8·83 m² (95·0 sq ft)

WEIGHTS AND LOADINGS:
- Weight empty — 229 kg (505 lb)
- Max T-O weight — 353 kg (780 lb)
- Max wing loading — 40·08 kg/m² (8·21 lb/sq ft)
- Max power loading — 7·28 kg/kW (12·00 lb/hp)

PERFORMANCE (at max T-O weight):
- Max level speed at S/L — 124 knots (230 km/h; 143 mph)
- Econ cruising speed, 50% power at S/L — 99 knots (183 km/h; 114 mph)
- Min controllable speed, power on — 33 knots (62 km/h; 38 mph)
- Landing speed, power off — 39 knots (72 km/h; 45 mph)
- Stalling speed, power off — 38 knots (70 km/h; 43 mph)

Max rate of climb at S/L 332 m (1,090 ft)/min
Service ceiling 5,915 m (19,400 ft)
T-O run 213 m (698 ft)
T-O to 15 m (50 ft) 305 m (1,000 ft)
Landing from 15 m (50 ft) 366 m (1,200 ft)
Landing run 73 m (240 ft)
Range at econ cruising speed, standard fuel 382 nm (708 km; 440 miles)
Range with auxiliary fuel 521 nm (965 km; 600 miles)

MORGAN

MORGAN AIRCRAFT

MORGAN AIRCRAFT BUSHMASTER II

Introduced at the 1985 Sun 'n Fun meeting, the strut braced Bushmaster II is a light side by side two-seat parasol wing monoplane that is available in kit form. It has a metal structure, fabric covered (double skin on wing), with a constant chord wing and conventional wire braced tail unit. Three-axis control (ailerons, elevators and horn balanced rudder) and a 'taildragger' landing gear, with side Vs and bungee sprung half axles for the main units, are standard. Power is provided by a 38 kW (51 hp) Rotax 503 two-cylinder engine, driving a four-blade propeller with spinner. Fuel capacity is 57 litres (15 US gallons). Accommodation for the crew is open.

DIMENSIONS, EXTERNAL:
Wing span 9·14 m (30 ft 0 in)
Length overall 5·37 m (17 ft 8 in)

WEIGHTS:
Weight empty 136 kg (300 lb)
Max T-O weight 295 kg (650 lb)

PERFORMANCE:
Max level speed 78 knots (145 km/h; 90 mph)
Cruising speed 59 knots (109 km/h; 68 mph)
g limits +6/−4

MORRISEY

MORRISEY AIRCRAFT CORPORATION

PO Box 27530, Las Vegas, Nevada 89126
Telephone: (702) 648 1240

Mr Bill Morrisey, a former engineering test pilot and designer of the Varga Kachina light aircraft (originally the Morrisey Nifty), continues to market the Bravo monoplane. In the past year, considerable time was devoted to an attempt to reacquire rights in the Varga Kachina, as a result of which progress on the four-seat Padre version of the Bravo has been slower than intended.

MORRISEY BRAVO OM-1 and PADRE

The unique Bravo OM-1 design allows the builder/owner to select accommodation for a pilot only in an open cockpit, pilot only in an enclosed cockpit, a pilot and passenger in tandem under a long canopy, or the four-seat **Padre** configuration. In open cockpit form the **Bravo I Model OM-1** is known as the **Primary**. Still as a single-seater but with an enclosed cockpit, wheel fairings and several internal additions, the type becomes the **Bravo I Advanced OM-1**. The tandem two-seater is the **Bravo II Model OM-1-2**, which uses the same airframe but has the windscreen and instrument panel moved forward after a portion of the forward fuselage top cowling has been removed. This provides the space to install a front seat and controls. The four-seat Padre 'family' version of the Bravo uses a longer and wider cabin area and wider span wing centre-section, married to the existing rear fuselage, tail unit and outer wings. The control system is also altered.

The decision to proceed with the Bravo followed a visit by Mr Morrisey to the 1980 Oshkosh Fly-in, where he became aware of the trend towards smaller, faster aircraft. Believing that this ignored the potential of a larger aircraft, offering greater comfort, acceptable performance and ability to operate from unprepared fields, Mr Morrisey decided to build One More aeroplane (OM-1). Work on the Bravo began in January 1981, and the prototype (N124BM) in Primary form flew for the first time on 30 June that year. A 40 h test programme was completed to FAA certification standards, and type certification will follow at a later date. Meanwhile, after a year's flying, the aircraft was converted as the prototype Bravo II. The prototype had accumulated more than 700 flying hours by 1 January 1985.

The Bravo series is being made available to amateur constructors in kit form. A comprehensive sales and service support organisation has been established from the new fabrication and subassembly plant in Las Vegas, and a 465 m² (5,000 sq ft) hangar at North Las Vegas Airport which is the flight testing and sales activity facility. The kits include the welded fuselage structure, wing spars and ribs, glassfibre wing leading-edges, and skins for the wings, ailerons and optional flaps. Delivery of kits began in April 1985. Morrisey Aircraft itself is also building three more complete aircraft, including a Bravo I and Bravo II for demonstration and sales purposes. One of them may be fitted with a 149 kW (200 hp) Ford V-6 converted 3,800 cc motorcar engine, as developed by Javelin Aircraft of Wichita. The third completed aircraft will be the four-seat Padre.

The brief details which follow apply to the prototype, completed as a single-seater with open cockpit, unless otherwise stated:

TYPE: Single- or two-seat light homebuilt aircraft.

AIRFRAME: Cantilever low-wing monoplane. Metal wing structure and skins. (Kits provide for glassfibre leading-edges with foam ribs.) Ailerons and optional half-span flaps. Steel tube fuselage, with Dacron covering from rear of the cockpit aft; aluminium covered from rear of cockpit forward. Conventional cantilever tail unit of all-metal construction, with corrugated skins on one-piece elevator and rudder.

LANDING GEAR: Non-retractable tailwheel type. Cantilever tapered steel spring main gear legs. Wheel fairings fitted to main units of OM-1 Advanced and OM-1-2.

POWER PLANT: One 112 kW (150 hp) Avco Lycoming O-320 flat-four engine, driving a two-blade propeller. Other engines of 74·5-149 kW (100-200 hp) optional.

ACCOMMODATION: One person in open cockpit or under sliding canopy, or two persons in tandem under long canopy. Four-seat version projected. Baggage space, capacity 22·7 kg (50 lb).

DIMENSIONS, EXTERNAL:
Wing span: OM-1, OM-1-2 8·08 m (26 ft 6 in)
projected four-seater 9·45 m (31 ft 0 in)
Length overall 6·55 m (21 ft 6 in)
Height overall 2·13 m (7 ft 0 in)
Wheel track 2·24 m (7 ft 4 in)

WEIGHTS AND LOADINGS:
Weight empty 438 kg (965 lb)
Max T-O weight: Normal 771 kg (1,700 lb)
Utility 680 kg (1,500 lb)
Max power loading:
Normal 6·88 kg/kW (11·33 lb/hp)
Utility 6·07 kg/kW (10·00 lb/hp)

PERFORMANCE (Utility weight, 112 kW; 150 hp engine):
Max level speed at S/L 135 knots (249 km/h; 155 mph)
Cruising speed (75% power) 123 knots (229 km/h; 142 mph)
Stalling speed, flaps down 50 knots (92 km/h; 57 mph)
Max rate of climb at S/L 457 m (1,500 ft)/min
Range 434 nm (804 km; 500 miles)

NAC

NATIONAL AIRCRAFT CORPORATION

NATIONAL AIRCRAFT DREAM

The prototype of the Dream single-seat, single-engined microlight aircraft, designed by Mr James Bede and described in the 1985-86 *Jane's*, was not completed, due to cost overrun. National Aircraft Corporation is no longer in business.

NEICO

NEICO AVIATION INC

403 South Ojai Street, Santa Paula, California 93060

Neico Aviation markets kits of component parts to construct the Lancair 200, designed by Mr Lance A. Neibauer. It is a side by side two-seat sporting and cross-country monoplane of all-composite construction, and kits include a completely premoulded airframe with main spars, the retractable tricycle landing gear, and flight control systems. All parts requiring welding are pre-welded.

NEICO AVIATION LANCAIR 200

Design of the Lancair 200 began in January 1981 and construction of the prototype started in January 1983. This flew for the first time in June 1984 at Chino, California. In the following August construction began of a pre-production aircraft, the Lancair having received its certification in the Experimental category from the FAA that July. Production of kits began in May 1985. By January 1986 a total of 60 had been delivered to customers in Australia, Canada, New Zealand and the USA, with production running at 2½ kits each week.

TYPE: Two-seat homebuilt sporting and cross-country monoplane.

AIRFRAME: Cantilever low-wing monoplane. Wing section NLF 0215F. Dihedral 3°. Incidence 2° 30′ at root, 1° at tip. Composite airframe of glassfibre, Nomex honeycomb, Polyimide Rohacell foam and epoxy resin. Conventional ailerons and flaps. Wings fold. Swept tail fin integral with fuselage. Horn balanced rudder. Horn balanced elevators, with trim tab.

LANDING GEAR: Retractable tricycle type, hydraulically actuated. Nosewheel retracts rearward; mainwheels retract inward. Trailing arm and synthetic rubber 'donut' disc shock absorbers. Rosenhan wheel on each unit, with Lamb tyre. Rosenhan brakes.

POWER PLANT: One 74·5 kW (100 hp) Continental O-200 flat-four engine, driving a two-blade fixed-pitch propeller with spinner (Avco Lycoming O-235 being tested in early 1986). Single header and two auxiliary wing fuel tanks, total capacity 106-114 litres (28-30 US gallons). Refuelling points in fuselage and wingtips. Oil capacity 4·7 litres (1·25 US gallons).

ACCOMMODATION: Two seats side by side under forward opening canopy. Heated and ventilated. Baggage hold, capacity 0·23 m³ (8·0 cu ft).

SYSTEMS: Hydraulic system for landing gear. Electrical system.

DIMENSIONS, EXTERNAL:
Wing span 7·16 m (23 ft 6 in)
Wing chord: at root 1·17 m (3 ft 10 in)
at tip 0·72 m (2 ft 4½ in)
Wing aspect ratio 7·27
Length overall 5·99 m (19 ft 8 in)
Width, wings folded 2·54 m (8 ft 4 in)
Height overall 1·85 m (6 ft 1 in)
Tailplane span 1·93 m (6 ft 4 in)
Wheel track 2·31 m (7 ft 7 in)
Wheelbase 1·22 m (4 ft 0 in)
Propeller diameter 1·47-1·52 m (4 ft 10 in-5 ft 0 in)

DIMENSIONS, INTERNAL:
Cabin: Length 1·57 m (5 ft 2 in)
Max width 1·08 m (3 ft 6½ in)
Max height 0·98 m (3 ft 2½ in)

AREA:
Wings, gross 7·06 m² (76·0 sq ft)

WEIGHTS AND LOADINGS:
Weight empty 295 kg (650 lb)
Max T-O weight 578 kg (1,275 lb)
Max wing loading 81·93 kg/m² (16·78 lb/sq ft)
Max power loading 7·76 kg/kW (12·75 lb/hp)

PERFORMANCE:
Never-exceed speed 240 knots (445 km/h; 277 mph)
Max level speed at S/L 185 knots (343 km/h; 213 mph)
Max cruising speed 170 knots (315 km/h; 196 mph)
Econ cruising speed 165 knots (306 km/h; 190 mph)
Stalling speed, engine idling 48 knots (89 km/h; 55 mph)
Max rate of climb at S/L 457 m (1,500 ft)/min
Service ceiling 5,485-6,100 m (18,000-20,000 ft)
T-O and landing run 183 m (600 ft)
Range with max fuel 868 nm (1,609 km; 1,000 miles)

NORTHSTAR

NORTHSTAR LTD

5221 West Montebello No. 15, Glendale, Arizona 85301
Telephone: (602) 931 9462

NORTHSTAR VIKING

The Viking is a sweptwing biplane with pedal controlled tip rudders and a stick controlled canard elevator. Construction is of aluminium alloy with Dacron covering. A tricycle landing gear, with steerable nosewheel, is standard. Mainwheel diameter 20 in; nosewheel 16 in. Nosewheel brake. Float gear is available optionally.

POWER PLANT: One 28·5 kW (38 hp) Kawasaki 440 two-cylinder two-stroke engine, with 2·25:1 reduction drive to

Morrisey Bravo OM-1 in Advanced (top) and two-seat OM-1-2 versions *(OM-1-2 photo: Howard Levy)*

Neico Aviation Lancair 200 two-seat sporting and cross-country light aircraft *(Howard Levy)*

Northstar Viking canard biplane microlight

Nostalgair N2 Mouse *(Howard Levy)*

Nostalgair Questor low-wing monoplane *(J. M. G. Gradidge)*

Nostalgair N3 Pup single-seat microlight aircraft *(Peter M. Bowers)*

a two-blade ground adjustable pitch wooden pusher propeller. Fuel tank capacity 19 litres (5 US gallons).

DIMENSIONS, EXTERNAL:

Wing span	9·75 m (32 ft 0 in)
Propeller diameter	1·52 m (5 ft 0 in)

AREA:

Wings, gross	15·79 m² (170·0 sq ft)

WEIGHTS AND LOADINGS:

Weight empty	110·5 kg (244 lb)
Max pilot weight	102 kg (225 lb)
Max T-O weight	228 kg (502 lb)
Max wing loading	14·4 kg/m² (2·95 lb/sq ft)
Max power loading	8·04 kg/kW (13·2 lb/hp)

PERFORMANCE:

Never-exceed speed	47 knots (88 km/h; 55 mph)
Econ cruising speed	39 knots (72 km/h; 45 mph)
Stalling speed	20 knots (38 km/h; 23 mph)
Max rate of climb at S/L	244 m (800 ft)/min
g limits	+5/−3
Best glide ratio	7

NOSTALGAIR

NOSTALGAIR INC

140 Ashwood Road (PO Box 2049), Hendersonville, North Carolina 28739
Telephone: (704) 692 8566

PRESIDENT: James E. Gill

Nostalgair's first venture into the microlight market was its N3 Pup, a single-seat lightweight representation of the Piper Cub. This was followed by the N2 Mouse in 1985, a microlight representation of the Aeronca C-2. Both are available in kit form, with welded chromoly steel tube fuselage structures, stamped aluminium ribs, completed wooden spars and landing gears. Glassfibre components for the Mouse are pre-formed. Stits Dacron is used to cover the airframes of both aircraft, which are strut braced high-wing monoplanes with conventional tail units (three-axis control via ailerons, elevators and rudder) and tailwheel landing gears. A clipped wing variant of the Pup is the new Super Pup, of which no details have been received.

Nostalgair has extended its range by acquiring the former Omni-Weld Questor from its marketing company, Questor Aircraft.

NOSTALGAIR N2 MOUSE

The Mouse is a microlight representation of the Aeronca C-2, available to home constructors in kit form.

TYPE: Single-seat microlight aircraft.

AIRFRAME: Strut braced high-wing cabin monoplane, as described above. Triangular-section fuselage structure. Options include adjustable carburettor.

LANDING GEAR: Non-retractable taildragger type, with bungee suspension. Optional brakes.

POWER PLANT: One 18·6 kW (25 hp) Global Machine Tools 920 cc two-cylinder four-stroke engine, directly driving a two-blade wooden propeller. Optional 26 kW (35 hp) engine. Fuel tank capacity 17 litres (4·5 US gallons).

ACCOMMODATION: Pilot only, in semi-enclosed cabin. Optional glazed side doors to enclose cabin fully. Optional heating.

DIMENSIONS, EXTERNAL:

Wing span	8·84 m (29 ft 0 in)
Length overall	5·18 m (17 ft 0 in)
Height overall	1·52 m (5 ft 0 in)

AREA:

Wings, gross	12·45 m² (134·0 sq ft)

WEIGHTS AND LOADINGS:

Weight empty	113 kg (250 lb)
Max T-O weight	238 kg (525 lb)
Max wing loading	19·12 kg/m² (3·92 lb/sq ft)
Max power loading	12·80 kg/kW (21·00 lb/hp)

PERFORMANCE:

Never-exceed speed	73 knots (136 km/h; 85 mph)
Max level speed	55 knots (101 km/h; 63 mph)
Max cruising speed	52 knots (97 km/h; 60 mph)
Stalling speed	24 knots (44 km/h; 27 mph)
Max rate of climb at S/L	213 m (700 ft)/min

NOSTALGAIR N3 PUP

Nostalgair's microlight representation of the Piper Cub is the N3 Pup, available in ready to fly, plans or kit form. A total of 125 had been ordered by early 1985 (when the last update was received), of which 51 had been completed.

TYPE: Single-seat microlight aircraft; conforms to FAR Pt 103.

AIRFRAME: Strut braced high-wing cabin monoplane, as described above. Square-section fuselage, with glassfibre engine cowling. Options include ballistic parachute.

LANDING GEAR: Non-retractable tailwheel type, with side Vs and half axles for mainwheels. Bungee sprung mainwheels of 14 in diameter; steerable tailwheel of 4 in diameter. Options include floats, skis and mainwheel brakes.

POWER PLANT: One 18·6 kW (25 hp) Global Machine Tools GMT 7892 920 cc two-cylinder four-stroke engine, directly driving a two-blade wooden propeller. Glassfibre fuel tank, capacity 15·9 litres (4·2 US gallons). Options include adjustable carburettor and 26·1 kW (35 hp) GMT engine.

ACCOMMODATION: Pilot only, in semi-enclosed cabin. Optional cabin side doors, windows and heating.

DIMENSIONS, EXTERNAL:
Wing span 9·14 m (30 ft 0 in)
Wing aspect ratio 7·32
Length overall 5·08 m (16 ft 8 in)
Height overall 1·57 m (5 ft 2 in)
Propeller diameter 1·42 m (4 ft 8 in)

AREA:
Wings, gross 11·43 m² (123·0 sq ft)

WEIGHTS AND LOADINGS:
Weight empty 112 kg (248 lb)
Max T-O weight 242 kg (535 lb)
Max wing loading 21·24 kg/m² (4·35 lb/sq ft)
Max power loading 13·01 kg/kW (21·40 lb/hp)

PERFORMANCE:
Never-exceed speed 82 knots (152 km/h; 95 mph)
Max level speed 55 knots (101 km/h; 63 mph)
Max cruising speed 50 knots (93 km/h; 58 mph)
Stalling speed 22 knots (41 km/h; 25 mph)
Max rate of climb at S/L 198 m (650 ft)/min
Service ceiling 1,525 m (5,000 ft)
T-O run 38 m (125 ft)
Landing run 61 m (200 ft)
Range with max fuel 173 nm (322 km; 200 miles)
Endurance with max fuel 3 h
g limits +6/−3
Best glide ratio 12

NOSTALGAIR QUESTOR

In 1984 Nostalgair acquired the Questor Aircraft manufacturing and distribution company, which continues to produce kits of the Questor at its factory in Fort Worth, Texas. These include pre-welded and pre-formed major items such as spars, mainwheel struts and skins, so that the homebuilder can concentrate mainly on assembly and finish; this takes 200-250 hours.

TYPE: Single-seat homebuilt aircraft.

AIRFRAME: All-aluminium cantilever low-wing monoplane, except for glassfibre engine cowling. Kit assembly requires pop riveting only, all prefabricated parts being pre-welded or riveted by manufacturer. I-spar wings detachable for transportation and storage. Three-axis control (full span flaperons, elevators and rudder). Other options, within basic kit price, include wingtip fairings, spinner and moulded turtleback with headrest.

LANDING GEAR: Non-retractable tricycle type is standard, with mainwheel hydraulic brakes and steerable nosewheel. Tailwheel gear is available optionally. Optional mainwheel fairings.

POWER PLANT: One 28 kW (37·5 hp) Global Machine Tool Co two-cylinder four-stroke engine, driving a two-blade propeller (spinner optional). Fuel tank capacity 38 litres (10 US gallons) of avgas or mogas.

ACCOMMODATION: Pilot only, in fully enclosed cockpit, under a bubble canopy. Options include cockpit side panels with armrest and instrument panel cover.

DIMENSIONS, EXTERNAL:
Wing span: prototype 5·49 m (18 ft 0 in)
optional 8·53 m (28 ft 0 in)
Length overall 4·72 m (15 ft 6 in)
Height overall 1·12 m (3 ft 8 in)

AREA (prototype):
Wings, gross approx 4·92 m² (53·0 sq ft)

WEIGHTS AND LOADINGS (prototype):
Weight empty 122 kg (270 lb)
Max pilot weight 106·5 kg (235 lb)
Max T-O weight 240 kg (530 lb)
Max wing loading approx 48·8 kg/m² (10·0 lb/sq ft)
Max power loading 8·60 kg/kW (14·13 lb/hp)

PERFORMANCE (prototype):
Max cruising speed 104 knots (193 km/h; 120 mph)
Stalling speed 41 knots (76 km/h; 47 mph)
Service ceiling 3,050 m (10,000 ft)
Range with max fuel, incl reserves 521 nm (965 km; 600 miles)
Max endurance more than 5 h
g limits +6/−3 design
Best glide ratio 13

NUWACO

NUWACO AIRCRAFT COMPANY

2978 E Euclid Place, Littleton, Colorado 80121
Telephone: (303) 798 8121 or 799 0633
PRESIDENT: Ernest A. Bode

NUWACO T-10

Mr Ernest A. Bode, who in the past has converted Stearman biplanes for agricultural work and restored antique aircraft for enthusiasts, has formed NuWaco to market kits of a modernised version of the pre-war Waco 10-T taperwing biplane. Development of the T-10 took more than five years, from September 1978 to the first flight on 5 May 1984.

NuWaco offers a kit of component parts to construct the T-10, with all parts requiring welding skill furnished in completed form except for the engine mounting. In addition, the basic kit can be supplemented by further kits at the builder's discretion. By the end of January 1986, NuWaco had received eight orders and deliveries had begun.

TYPE: Three-seat homebuilt replica biplane.

AIRFRAME: Strut and wire braced single-bay biplane. Welded chrome-molybdenum steel tube fuselage and tail unit, and wooden two-spar wings, all fabric covered. Wing section M-6. Thickness/chord ratio 12%. No dihedral. Incidence 1° 30′. Conventional control via ailerons on upper and lower wings, elevators and rudder. Variable incidence wire-braced tailplane.

LANDING GEAR: Non-retractable tailwheel type. Mainwheels size 6·00-8 (tyre pressure 2·62 bars; 38 lb/sq in), with streamline fairings, carried on faired Vs and side struts with shock absorbers. Solid 4 in diameter tailwheel. Hydraulic toe-operated brakes (Cleveland recommended).

POWER PLANT: Suited to engines of 164-336 kW (220-450 hp). Prototype fitted with one 205 kW (275 hp) Jacobs R-755-B2 seven-cylinder radial engine, driving a Hamilton Standard 2B-20 two-blade constant-speed metal propeller (ground adjustable propeller optional). One fuel tank in fuselage, capacity 227 litres (60 US gallons). Two auxiliary fuel tanks optional. Oil capacity 25 litres (6·7 US gallons). Optional engines include Continental W-670, Pratt & Whitney R-985, Wright R-975 or J5, and Jacobs R-755-A2.

ACCOMMODATION: Three seats in two open cockpits, with two passengers forward of pilot. Optional canopy. Baggage space aft of pilot's seat, capacity 18 kg (40 lb).

SYSTEM: Optional electrical system.

DIMENSIONS, EXTERNAL:
Wing span 9·22 m (30 ft 3 in)
Wing chord: at root 1·60 m (5 ft 3 in)
at tip 0·76 m (2 ft 6 in)
Wing aspect ratio 5·76
Length overall 6·96 m (22 ft 10 in)
Height overall 2·69 m (8 ft 10 in)
Tailplane span 3·10 m (10 ft 2 in)
Wheel track 1·93 m (6 ft 4 in)
Wheelbase 3·52 m (11 ft 6½ in)
Propeller diameter: standard 2·74 m (9 ft 0 in)
optional 2·59 m (8 ft 6 in)

AREA:
Wings, gross 21·09 m² (227·0 sq ft)

WEIGHTS AND LOADINGS:
Weight empty 798 kg (1,760 lb)
Max T-O weight 1,179 kg (2,600 lb)
Max wing loading 55·9 kg/m² (11·45 lb/sq ft)
Max power loading, prototype 5·75 kg/kW (9·45 lb/hp)

PERFORMANCE (at max T-O weight):
Never-exceed speed 173 knots (321 km/h; 200 mph)
Max level speed at 2,440 m (8,000 ft) 139 knots (257 km/h; 160 mph)
Max cruising speed at 2,440 m (8,000 ft) 122 knots (225 km/h; 140 mph)
Econ cruising speed at 2,440 m (8,000 ft) 113 knots (209 km/h; 130 mph)
Stalling speed 44 knots (81 km/h; 50 mph)
Service ceiling 6,400 m (21,000 ft)
T-O run 83 m (270 ft)
Landing run 244 m (800 ft)
Range 564 nm (1,046 km; 650 miles)
Endurance with max standard fuel 5 h

OPTERYX

OPTERYX ULTRALIGHT AIRCRAFT

OpteryX Engineering Ltd, 11556 Coal Creek Heights Drive, Golden, Colorado 80403
Telephone: (303) 642 7434
PRESIDENT: Don South
VICE-PRESIDENT: Thomas E. Rogers Jr

OPTERYX III

The OpteryX is custom built to the individual buyer's requirements.

TYPE: Single-seat microlight aircraft, conforming to FAR Pt 103.

AIRFRAME: OpteryX utilises a standard Manta Fledge III wing, complete with tip rudders, mated to a 'powered trike' unit and a stick controlled frontal elevator.

LANDING GEAR: Tricycle type, with 20 in diameter wheel on all three units. Mainwheels carried on glassfibre axle and roller bearings; steerable nosewheel has bungee suspension. Options include mainwheel disc brakes and speed fairings.

POWER PLANT: One 30 kW (40 hp) Cuyuna 430R engine, with 2:1 reduction drive to a two-blade wooden pusher propeller. Two fuel tanks, combined capacity 19 litres (5 US gallons).

ACCOMMODATION: Pilot only, in open position, on manually adjustable rigid seat. Options include windscreen and provision for a passenger.

DIMENSIONS, EXTERNAL:
Wing span 10·49 m (34 ft 5 in)
Length overall 5·03 m (16 ft 6 in)
Height overall 2·95 m (9 ft 8 in)
Propeller diameter 1·32 m (4 ft 4 in)

AREA:
Wings, gross 15·79 m² (170·0 sq ft)

WEIGHTS AND LOADINGS:
Weight empty 112 kg (248 lb)
Pilot weight range 52-120 kg (115-265 lb)
Max T-O weight 321 kg (708 lb)
Max wing loading 20·3 kg/m² (4·16 lb/sq ft)
Max power loading 10·70 kg/kW (17·70 lb/hp)

PERFORMANCE:
Never-exceed speed 52 knots (96 km/h; 60 mph)
Max level speed 50 knots (93 km/h; 58 mph)
Max cruising speed 48 knots (88 km/h; 55 mph)
Econ cruising speed 39 knots (72 km/h; 45 mph)
Stalling speed 24 knots (44 km/h; 27 mph)
Max rate of climb at S/L 305 m (1,000 ft)/min
Service ceiling 7,315 m (24,000 ft)
T-O run 30 m (100 ft)
Landing run 45 m (150 ft)
Range with max fuel more than 173 nm (322 km; 200 miles)
Endurance with max fuel 4 h 30 min
g limits +3·5/−2·5

OPTION AIR

OPTION AIR RENO

PRESIDENT: Carl D. Barlow

OPTION AIR RENO ACAPELLA

Mr Carl D. Barlow formed Option Air Reno to market kits of component parts that can be added to a Bede BD-5 fuselage, canopy, nosewheel, wings and tail-fins (two required) to produce his twin-boom Acapella. Design of the Acapella began in January 1978 and prototype construction started in June the same year. The first flight was achieved on 6 June 1980, and production of kits began in June 1981. The kits included an engine mount, glassfibre cowling, new 2·44 m (8 ft) wing centre-section, tailbooms, tailplane, elevator, main landing gear, many smaller components, and all necessary plans for the conversion.

The address for Option Air Reno that appeared in the 1985-86 *Jane's* is no longer current and no new address has been received. Full details of the Acapella, and an illustration, can be found in that edition.

OSPREY

OSPREY AIRCRAFT

3741 El Ricon Way, Sacramento, California 95864
Telephone: (916) 483 3004

Osprey Aircraft was formed originally to market to amateur constructors plans of the Osprey I aircraft designed and built by Mr George Pereira. This was an unusual project for the homebuilder, being a flying-boat, intended for operation on and from enclosed waters rather than the open sea. The plans drawn up by Mr Pereira included drawings of a special trailer for carriage of the aircraft, which allowed the pilot to launch and recover the Osprey unassisted. Details of this aircraft can be found in the 1974-75 *Jane's*.

OpteryX III single-seat microlight

NuWaco T-10 taperwing three-seat homebuilt biplane

Pereira GP4 prototype two-seat homebuilt cross-country aircraft *(Scott Kemper)*

UK registered Pereira Osprey II two-seat amphibian *(Peter J. Bish)*

Mr Pereira subsequently completed the prototype of a two-seat amphibian version designated Osprey II, as described here. Mr Pereira's latest aircraft, his fourth, is a high performance cross-country landplane known as the GP4.

PEREIRA GP3 OSPREY II

Design and construction of the Osprey II, a two-seat amphibian development of the Osprey I, began in January 1972.

Mr Pereira developed an unusual form of hull construction for this aircraft. When the all-wood fuselage structure had been completed and controls installed, the undersurface was given a deep coating of polyurethane foam. This was then sculptured to the requisite hull form before being covered with several protective layers of glassfibre cloth bonded with resin. The resulting structure is light, but extremely strong, with good shock resisting characteristics.

First flight of the Osprey II from water was made in April 1973, the amphibian becoming airborne in less than 244 m (800 ft), with no tendency to porpoise at any speed. Modifications carried out in early 1974 included lengthening of the cabin by 0·18 m (7 in), and installation of an Avco Lycoming O-320 engine in place of the original Franklin Sport, in a new cowling. Since then the shape of the fin has been changed. Sets of plans, as well as material and component kits, are available to amateur constructors. By early 1986, more than 1,000 sets of plans had been sold to potential builders in 48 countries, and at least 35 Ospreys have flown.

TYPE: Two-seat homebuilt amphibian.

AIRFRAME: Cantilever mid-wing monoplane, of constant chord. Wing section NACA 23012. Dihedral 4° 30′. Incidence 5°. All-wood wings, with single box spar and auxiliary rear spar for aileron attachment. Forward of the main spar the wing is plywood covered to form a rigid 'D' section. Aft of the spar the wing is fabric covered. Conventional ailerons, 100% mass balanced. No flaps. Wingtip stabilising floats of polyurethane foam covered with glassfibre. All-wood hull of longerons and frames covered with 2·5 mm (3/32 in) marine plywood. Hull undersurface contours formed from polyurethane foam, protected by several layers of glassfibre cloth bonded with resin. Cantilever all-wood tail unit, with swept vertical surfaces; tailplane mounted high on fin, which is integral with hull. Incidence of tailplane ground adjustable. Controllable trim tab in starboard elevator. Water rudder, contained within the base of the aerodynamic rudder, is spring loaded in the down position and retracted by cable.

LANDING GEAR: Retractable tricycle type, with single wheel on each unit. Main units retract inward into the wing roots, the wheel wells being covered by doors in the retracted position. Nosewheel retracts forward into the nosecone and is also enclosed by a door. Manual retraction system. Shock absorption by coil springs. Cleveland mainwheels and tyres size 5·00-5. Nosewheel, of industrial type with roller bearings, has a tyre of 10 in diameter. Cleveland hydraulic disc brakes.

POWER PLANT: One 112 kW (150 hp) Avco Lycoming O-320 flat-four engine, mounted on a steel tube pylon structure which is bolted to the wing truss. Fahlin 67 × 53 two-blade wooden pusher propeller. One glassfibre fuel tank standard, mounted beneath the main spar at the wing centre-section, usable capacity 98·4 litres (26 US gallons). Refuelling point on starboard side of hull, just aft of cabin. New wing tanks available to replace fuselage tank, allowing increased baggage area.

ACCOMMODATION: Two seats side by side beneath transparent canopy, which is hinged at rear and swings upward. Dual controls standard; but toe operated wheel brakes on starboard side only. Baggage compartment aft of seats, capacity 41 kg (90 lb). With wing fuel tanks fitted, baggage area is large enough to store scuba diving tanks or camping gear.

SYSTEMS: Hydraulic system for brakes only. Electrical system powered by engine driven generator.

DIMENSIONS, EXTERNAL:

Wing span	7·92 m (26 ft 0 in)
Wing chord, constant	1·52 m (5 ft 0 in)
Wing aspect ratio	5·2
Length overall	6·25 m (20 ft 6 in)
Height overall (wheels down)	1·83 m (6 ft 0 in)
Tailplane span	2·44 m (8 ft 0 in)
Wheel track	2·59 m (8 ft 6 in)
Wheelbase	2·13 m (7 ft 0 in)
Propeller diameter	1·68 m (5 ft 6 in)

AREA:

Wings, gross	12·08 m² (130·0 sq ft)

WEIGHTS AND LOADINGS:

Weight empty	440 kg (970 lb)
Max T-O weight	707 kg (1,560 lb)
Max wing loading	58·6 kg/m² (12·0 lb/sq ft)
Max power loading	6·31 kg/kW (10·40 lb/hp)

PERFORMANCE (at max T-O weight except where indicated):

Never-exceed speed	130 knots (241 km/h; 150 mph)
Max cruising speed at 75% power	113 knots (209 km/h; 130 mph)
Econ cruising speed at 55% power	94 knots (175 km/h; 109 mph)
Stalling speed	53 knots (97 km/h; 60 mph)
Max rate of climb at S/L, with pilot only	365 m (1,200 ft)/min
Rate of climb at S/L	305 m (1,000 ft)/min
T-O run: land	122 m (400 ft)
water	159 m (520 ft)
Range with wing tanks	313 nm (579 km; 360 miles)

PEREIRA GP4

Mr Pereira's latest aircraft is the GP4, the design of which began in 1980, when construction of the prototype started. This aircraft flew for the first time in 1984 and has completed its flight test programme.

Plans to construct the GP4 will be available in late 1986. In addition, pre-welded fittings and a wood kit will be made available to reduce construction time.

TYPE: Two-seat homebuilt cross-country monoplane.

AIRFRAME: Cantilever low-wing monoplane, of wooden construction except for foam and glassfibre used in cowling and fairings. Wing section Laminar 63 series. Thickness/chord ratio 12%. Dihedral 5°. Incidence 2°. One-piece main wing spar. Conventional ailerons. Electrically actuated flaps. Horn balanced elevators and rudder. Electrically actuated trim tab on elevator.

LANDING GEAR: Manually retractable tricycle type, with steerable nosewheel. Coil spring suspension. Mainwheels size 5·00-5; 10 in diameter tailwheel. Hydraulic brakes.

POWER PLANT: One 149 kW (200 hp) Avco Lycoming IO-360 flat-four engine, driving a Hartzell two-blade constant-speed metal propeller with large spinner. Two fuel tanks in wings and one in fuselage, with total capacity of 204 litres (54 US gallons). Oil capacity 7·6 litres (2 US gallons).

ACCOMMODATION: Two seats side by side under transparent canopy. Baggage capacity 34 kg (75 lb).

SYSTEM: 12V electrical system. Full lighting including tip strobes. Hydraulic system for brakes.

AVIONICS: IFR panel, with nav/com, glideslope receiver, VOR, Loran C and transponder, on prototype.

DIMENSIONS, EXTERNAL:

Wing span	7·52 m (24 ft 8 in)
Wing aspect ratio	5·54
Length overall	6·55 m (21 ft 6 in)
Wheel track	2·44 m (8 ft 0 in)
Propeller diameter	1·83 m (6 ft 0 in)

DIMENSION, INTERNAL:

Cabin width	1·02 m (3 ft 4 in)

AREA:

Wings, gross	9·66 m² (104·0 sq ft)

WEIGHTS AND LOADINGS:

Weight empty	566 kg (1,248 lb)
Max T-O weight	900 kg (1,985 lb)
Max wing loading	93·2 kg/m² (19·09 lb/sq ft)
Max power loading	6·04 kg/kW (9·93 lb/hp)

PERFORMANCE (initial tests):

Cruising speed, 75% power	208 knots (386 km/h; 240 mph)
Stalling speed, 'clean'	57 knots (105 km/h; 65 mph)
Max rate of climb at S/L:	
2 crew, 102 litres (27 US gallons) fuel	670 m (2,200 ft)/min
max T-O weight	457 m (1,500 ft)/min
Range: 75% power	955 nm (1,770 km; 1,100 miles)
60% power (195 knots; 362 km/h; 225 mph)	1,085 nm (2,011 km; 1,250 miles)
g limits	+8/−6

PARAPLANE

PARAPLANE CORPORATION

5801 Magnolia Avenue, Pennsauken, New Jersey 08109
Telephone: (609) 663 2234
PRESIDENT: Steve Snyder

PARAPLANE PARAPLANE

The ParaPlane utilises a sport parachute as its 'wing', attached to a 'powered trike' airframe. The aerofoil section parachute can be held open by two ground assistants before ground roll begins, though this is not necessary. It takes about five seconds to deploy as the lifting surface.

Deliveries of the ParaPlane began in April 1984 and more than 600 have reportedly been despatched to customers in 13 countries, including an undisclosed number to all US military services except the US Air Force. Recreational flying is not recommended in winds in excess of 13 knots (24 km/h; 15 mph).

The latest ParaPlanes can be equipped with a new tuned exhaust system, wide-chord propellers and a capacitator discharge ignition, which result in a 15 per cent increase in thrust and a payload increase of 22·5 kg (50 lb). Engine noise level is decreased by 20-30 per cent using this system.

TYPE: Single-seat microlight aircraft.

AIRFRAME: Aircraft's 'wing' is an inherently stable ram air sport parachute, made of nylon and having single-axis control through steering lines attached to foot pedals to provide directional control. The airframe consists of a sturdy T frame of aluminium alloy, similar to that of a Bensen Gyro-Copter; on this is mounted the pilot's rigid seat, the power pack, fuel tank and landing gear. Rigging time approx 15 min.

LANDING GEAR: Tricycle type, with all three wheels of similar size. Mainwheels are fully castoring; nosewheel is steered by foot pedals.

POWER PLANT: Two 11·2 kW (15 hp) Solo 210 cc single-cylinder two-stroke engines, mounted within an aluminium tube cage aft of the pilot and driving, via a multiple belt reduction gear, two two-blade counter-rotating pusher propellers on concentric shafts. Fuel tank capacity 17 litres (4·5 US gallons).

ACCOMMODATION: Pilot only, in open position.

DIMENSIONS, EXTERNAL:
Parachute span 9·30 m (36 ft 6 in)
Parachute chord 3·96 m (13 ft 0 in)
Airframe length 1·73 m (5 ft 8 in)
Airframe height 1·70 m (5 ft 7 in)
Propeller diameter (each) 1·29 m (4 ft 3 in)

AREA:
Parachute 37·16 m² (400·0 sq ft)

WEIGHTS:
Weight empty 69 kg (153 lb)
Max pilot weight 84 kg (185 lb)
Max T-O weight 170 kg (375 lb)

PERFORMANCE:
Max level and cruising speed 22 knots (41 km/h; 26 mph)
Glide speed, engine idling 18 knots (34 km/h; 21 mph)
Max rate of climb 150 m (495 ft)/min
Service ceiling more than 1,525 m (5,000 ft)
T-O run 30-46 m (100-150 ft)
Range 43 nm (80 km; 50 miles)
Endurance 1 h 30 min
Best glide ratio: on one engine 12
power off 3

PARKER

CALVIN Y. PARKER

PO Box 625, Coolidge, Arizona 85228-0625
Telephone: (602) 723 5660

Mr Cal Parker flew in 1969 an improved version of the lightweight all-metal homebuilt aircraft which he had designed and built earlier as Jeanie's Teenie. With completion of the new prototype, the original model became known as Teenie One. Plans for the Jeanie's Teenie were available for three years prior to Teenie Two plans being marketed.

A new two-seat version of the Teenie Two has been completed as the Double Teenie. This is suited to modified Volkswagen and Continental engines, and a 44·7 kW (60 hp) Franklin will also be tested. Other aircraft designed by Mr Parker for which details are not yet available include the Gaviota and Teenie V. Mr Parker has revealed that these employ methods of construction which he developed while working on space programmes in the early 1960s.

PARKER TEENIE TWO

Mr Parker's original aim in starting work on the Teenie series was to build an aircraft specifically to utilise the Volkswagen motorcar engine and, at the same time, to produce an all-metal design that would present few constructional problems to homebuilders with virtually no metal-working experience. This was achieved, and no special tools or jigs are needed beyond a tool to close and form the cadmium plated steel pop rivets that are used for practically all assembly. One gauge of aluminium sheet and one size of light alloy angle section are used for almost all of the structure, except for chromoly steel tube and sheet which are required for construction of the landing gear and control actuation tubes respectively. For simplicity and economy, push/pull tubes are used for all flying controls.

Teenie Two is considerably refined when compared to the original Teenie One, to produce a much 'cleaner' aeroplane. Its structure is stressed for full aerobatics, but the fuel and oil systems are not suitable for inverted flight.

Plans, including details of modifications for the Volkswagen engine, and complete kits of parts, are available to amateur constructors, and approximately 3,600 sets of plans have been sold. Well over 300 Teenie Twos have been built from plans, including several overseas. In June 1979 the Australian DoT gave approval for construction of the Teenie Two in that country.

TYPE: Single-seat homebuilt light aircraft.

AIRFRAME: Cantilever low-wing monoplane. All-metal airframe with light alloy skins. Wing section NACA 4415. Two-spar wings, with detachable outer panels. Light alloy ribs. Plain ailerons. No flaps. Semi-monocoque fuselage, with longerons of light alloy angle and three built-up bulkheads. Cantilever tail unit, with swept vertical surfaces. Small dorsal fin eliminates need for fourth bulkhead by carrying loads from fin leading-edge to centre bulkhead. Conventional rudder and elevators.

LANDING GEAR: Non-retractable tricycle type. Shock absorption provided by springs in compression and rubber hose. All three wheels same size, with tyres size 10·5 × 4·00-4, pressure 1·72 bars (25 lb/sq in). Mechanically actuated wheel brakes.

POWER PLANT: One 31·5 kW (42 hp) 1,600 cc or 30 kW (40 hp) 1,500 cc Volkswagen modified motorcar engine (conversion parts sold by Parker), driving a two-blade fixed-pitch wooden propeller (a computer designed propeller gives optimum performance for take-off, climb and cruise). Standard fuselage fuel tank, immediately aft of firewall, capacity 34 litres (9 US gallons). A 45·5 litre (12 US gallon) fuel tank can be installed instead if the pilot is under 1·83 m (6 ft) tall. Refuelling point on top of fuselage, forward of windscreen. Oil capacity 2·5 litres (0·66 US gallons).

ACCOMMODATION: Single seat in open cockpit. Drawings of optional canopy available; this increases max level speed to 122 knots (225 km/h; 140 mph).

SYSTEM: Prototype now fitted with alternator, starter and battery to power lights and radio, giving an increase in empty weight of 18 kg (40 lb).

DIMENSIONS, EXTERNAL:
Wing span 5·49 m (18 ft 0 in)
Wing chord, constant 1·02 m (3 ft 4 in)
Width, wings detached 1·83 m (6 ft 0 in)
Length overall 3·91 m (12 ft 10 in)

WEIGHTS AND LOADING:
Weight empty 140 kg (310 lb)
Max T-O weight 267 kg (590 lb)
Max power loading 8·48 kg/kW (14·05 lb/hp)

PERFORMANCE (at max T-O weight, 1,600 cc engine):
Max level speed 104 knots (193 km/h; 120 mph)
Max cruising speed (75% power) 95 knots (177 km/h; 110 mph)
Landing speed 44 knots (81 km/h; 50 mph)
Max rate of climb at S/L:
standard propeller 244 m (800 ft)/min
52 × 37 propeller 305 m (1,000 ft)/min
Service ceiling 4,575 m (15,000 ft)
Range 347 nm (643 km; 400 miles)

PAYNE

VERNON W. PAYNE

18 Rancho Drive, Escondido, California 92026

Mr Vernon Payne continues to advertise plans for three models of the single-seat Knight Twister sporting biplane and of the two-seat Knight Twister Co-Ed. However, no new photograph of a completed aircraft or news of plans sales has been received recently.

Details of the last known versions of the Knight Twister can be found in the 1985-86 *Jane's*.

PAZMANY

PAZMANY AIRCRAFT CORPORATION

PO Box 80051, San Diego, California 92138
Telephone: (714) 276 0424

This company was formed by Mr Ladislao Pazmany to develop and market a two-seat light aircraft known as the PL-1 Laminar, which he had designed. Some 5,000 design hours and 4,000 hours of construction went into the prototype PL-1, which was flown for the first time on 23 March 1962. Subsequent editions of *Jane's* recorded the history of the PL-1, of which about 375 sets of plans were sold, leading to construction of many amateur built examples and quantity production in Taiwan for the Chinese Nationalist Air Force.

Pazmany Aircraft Corporation no longer markets plans of the PL-1, of which details can be found in the 1979-80 *Jane's*; instead, plans and instructions for building the improved PL-2 and the lightweight, low cost single-seat PL-4A are available to amateur constructors and many aircraft of these types are being built or already flying.

PAZMANY PL-2

In October 1963, shortly after flight trials of the PL-1 began, Mr Pazmany initiated a complete redesign of the aircraft. The resulting PL-2 is almost identical with the PL-1 in external configuration. Cockpit width is increased by 5 cm (2 in); wing dihedral is increased, and the internal structure is extensively changed, to simplify construction and reduce weight.

Static tests of every major assembly up to ultimate loads had been made by early 1967. The first PL-2 to be completed, by Mr H. Pio of Ramona, California, made its first flight on 4 April 1969, powered by an Avco Lycoming O-290-G engine. The first plans built PL-2 flew in October 1971 and a total of 385 sets of plans had been sold by early 1986. Aircraft built and flown include several examples for evaluation and use by foreign military training centres (see 1977-78 *Jane's*).

TYPE: Two-seat homebuilt aircraft.

AIRFRAME: Cantilever low-wing monoplane. Wing section NACA 63_2615. Dihedral 5°. Incidence −1° 20′. Aluminium alloy single-spar wing structure in one piece, with leading-edge torsion box. Wingtips and fillets of glassfibre. Plain piano-hinged ailerons and flaps of aluminium alloy construction. No trim tabs. Conventional aluminium alloy semi-monocoque fuselage, with flat or single-curvature skins. Glassfibre tailcone and engine cowling. Cantilever aluminium alloy tail unit, with one-piece all-moving tailplane. Glassfibre fin and tailplane tips. Anti-servo tab, which also serves as trim tab, on tailplane.

LANDING GEAR: Non-retractable tricycle type, with all three oleo-pneumatic shock absorbers interchangeable. Goodyear wheels and tyres, size 5·00-5 on all units. Tyre pressure 2·14 bars (31 lb/sq in). Goodyear brakes. Steerable nosewheel.

POWER PLANT: One Avco Lycoming flat-four engine, driving a two-blade metal or wooden propeller. Recommended power plants include the 80·5 kW (108 hp) O-235-C1, 93 kW (125 hp) O-290-G (ground power unit), 101 kW (135 hp) O-290-D2B or 112 kW (150 hp) O-320-A. Some PL-2s are fitted with O-360 engines. Fuel in two glassfibre wingtip tanks, each of 47 litres (12·5 US gallons) capacity. Some PL-2s built with additional integral wing tanks, total capacity 94 litres (25 US gallons).

ACCOMMODATION: Two seats side by side under rearward sliding transparent canopy. Dual controls. Space for 18 kg (40 lb) baggage aft of seats. Heater and airscoops for ventilation.

SYSTEMS: Hydraulic system for brakes. Electrical system with battery and alternator.

AVIONICS: VHF com/nav optional.

DIMENSIONS, EXTERNAL:
Wing span 8·53 m (28 ft 0 in)
Wing chord, constant 1·27 m (4 ft 2 in)
Wing aspect ratio 6·7
Length overall 5·90 m (19 ft 3½ in)
Height overall 2·44 m (8 ft 0 in)
Tailplane span 2·44 m (8 ft 0 in)
Wheel track 2·60 m (8 ft 5½ in)
Wheelbase 1·30 m (4 ft 3 in)

DIMENSIONS, INTERNAL:
Cabin: Length 1·27 m (4 ft 2 in)
Width 1·07 m (3 ft 6 in)
Height 1·02 m (3 ft 4 in)

AREA:
Wings, gross 10·78 m² (116·0 sq ft)

WEIGHTS AND LOADINGS (A with 80·5 kW; 108 hp engine, B with 93 kW; 125 hp, C with 101 kW; 135 hp, D with 112 kW; 150 hp):
Weight empty: A 396 kg (875 lb)
B, C 408 kg (900 lb)
D 409 kg (902 lb)
Max T-O weight: A 642 kg (1,416 lb)
B, C 655 kg (1,445 lb)
D 656 kg (1,447 lb)
Max wing loading: A 59·6 kg/m² (12·21 lb/sq ft)
B, C 60·8 kg/m² (12·46 lb/sq ft)
D 60·9 kg/m² (12·47 lb/sq ft)
Max power loading: A 7·98 kg/kW (13·11 lb/hp)
B 7·04 kg/kW (11·56 lb/hp)
C 6·49 kg/kW (10·70 lb/hp)
D 5·86 kg/kW (9·65 lb/hp)

PERFORMANCE (at max T-O weight):
Max level speed at S/L:
A 120 knots (222 km/h; 138 mph)
B 125 knots (232 km/h; 144 mph)
C 128 knots (238 km/h; 148 mph)
D 133 knots (246 km/h; 153 mph)

Pazmany PL-2 built in Australia by Mr Warwick Greville of Broken Hill, NSW

Pazmany PL-4A built by Mr Roberto Gilli of Pergamino, Argentina

Parker Teenie Two powered by a modified Volkswagen engine

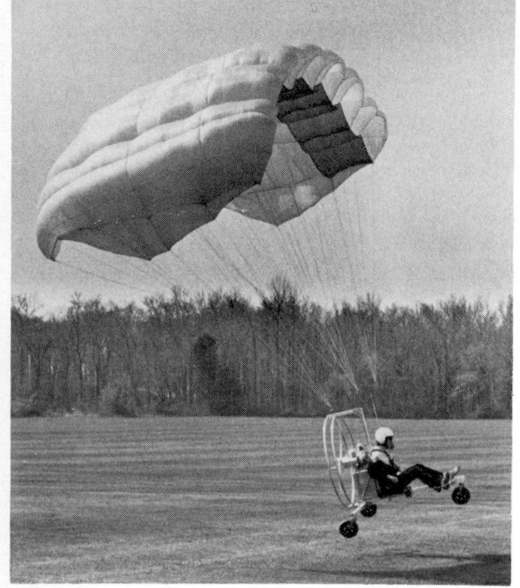

ParaPlane flared for landing *(Howard Levy)*

Phoenix Development & Specialties Phoenix single-seat microlight

Econ cruising speed:
- A: 103 knots (192 km/h; 119 mph)
- B: 111 knots (206 km/h; 128 mph)
- C: 113 knots (209 km/h; 130 mph)
- D: 118 knots (219 km/h; 136 mph)

Stalling speed (flaps down):
- A: 46 knots (84 km/h; 52 mph)
- B, C, D: 47 knots (87 km/h; 54 mph)

Max rate of climb at S/L: A: 390 m (1,280 ft)/min
- B: 457 m (1,500 ft)/min
- C: 488 m (1,600 ft)/min
- D: 518 m (1,700 ft)/min

Range at econ cruising speed:
- A: 427 nm (790 km; 492 miles)
- B: 422 nm (780 km; 486 miles)
- C: 428 nm (792 km; 493 miles)
- D: 330 nm (610 km; 381 miles)

Endurance: 4 h 6 min

PAZMANY PL-4A

This lightweight single-seat low-wing monoplane was designed for easy low cost construction by amateur builders, and to provide a safe aircraft that would be economical in operation. Design began in January 1971 and the prototype flew for the first time on 12 July 1972. Sets of plans, kits of prefabricated components, glassfibre wingtips and fuel tank, and transparent cockpit canopy are available to amateur constructors.

The first plans built PL-4A flew in 1976. By the beginning of 1986 a total of 691 sets of plans had been sold.

TYPE: Single-seat homebuilt sporting aircraft.

AIRFRAME: Cantilever low-wing monoplane. All-metal (aluminium alloy) construction, except for glassfibre cambered wingtips, fairings, engine cowling, spinner, elevator trim kit and fuel tank. Wing section NACA 63_3418. Dihedral 5°. Incidence 3°. No sweepback. Wing structure comprises main spar, Z section rear beam, sheet metal ribs and skins. Wings fold alongside fuselage for towing or storage. Plain piano-hinged ailerons. No flaps. No trim tabs. Semi-monocoque fuselage, with bulkheads built up from bent sheet metal channels and standard extruded angles for longerons, and with sheet metal skins. Cantilever T tail. All-moving tailplane standard, with large anti-servo tab which serves also as a trim tab. Optional fixed tailplane with elevator.

LANDING GEAR: Non-retractable tailwheel type. Spring steel cantilever main legs. Single go-kart wheel on each main unit, with 4·10 × 3·50-6 four-ply tyre, pressure 4·48 bars (65 lb/sq in). Steerable and castoring tailwheel with solid tyre size 5 × 1·5-1·5. Go-kart hydraulic disc brakes by Hurst-Airheart.

POWER PLANT: One 1,600 cc modified Volkswagen motorcar engine with Becar V belt reduction of 2¼ : 1, developing approximately 37·5 kW (50 hp) and driving a two-blade fixed-pitch wooden propeller of Pazmany design, manufactured by Ted Hendricson. Optional Volkswagen engine conversions from Revmaster, Limbach and others, of up to 2,100 cc, or Continental A65 or C80. Glassfibre fuel tank immediately aft of firewall, usable capacity 45 litres (12 US gallons). Refuelling point on upper fuselage forward of windscreen. Oil capacity 2·8 litres (0·75 US gallons).

ACCOMMODATION: Single seat under transparent Plexiglas canopy, hinged on starboard side. Compartment aft of seat for 9 kg (20 lb) baggage. Cabin heated and ventilated.

SYSTEMS: Hydraulic system for brakes only. Electrical system with generator and a 12V 25Ah battery situated in baggage compartment.

AVIONICS: Optional radio.

DIMENSIONS, EXTERNAL:
- Wing span: 8·13 m (26 ft 8 in)
- Wing chord, constant: 1·02 m (3 ft 4 in)
- Wing aspect ratio: 8·0
- Length overall: 5·04 m (16 ft 6½ in)
- Width, wings folded: 2·44 m (8 ft 0 in)
- Height overall: 1·73 m (5 ft 8 in)
- Tailplane span: 2·29 m (7 ft 6 in)
- Wheel track: 2·06 m (6 ft 9 in)
- Wheelbase: 3·56 m (11 ft 8 in)
- Propeller diameter: 1·73 m (5 ft 8 in)

AREA:
- Wings, gross: 8·27 m² (89·0 sq ft)

WEIGHTS AND LOADINGS:
- Weight empty: 262 kg (578 lb)
- Max T-O and landing weight: 385 kg (850 lb)
- Max wing loading: 46·6 kg/m² (9·55 lb/sq ft)
- Max power loading (50 hp): 10·27 kg/kW (17·00 lb/hp)

PERFORMANCE (37·5 kW; 50 hp engine, at max T-O weight):
- Never-exceed speed: 161 knots (299 km/h; 186 mph)
- Max level speed at S/L: 109 knots (201 km/h; 125 mph)
- Max cruising speed at S/L: 85 knots (158 km/h; 98 mph)
- Econ cruising speed at S/L: 78 knots (145 km/h; 90 mph)
- Stalling speed:
  - power on: 40 knots (74 km/h; 46 mph)
  - power off: 42 knots (78 km/h; 48 mph)
- Max rate of climb at S/L: 198 m (650 ft)/min
- Service ceiling: 3,960 m (13,000 ft)
- Min ground turning radius: 3·05 m (10 ft 0 in)
- T-O run: 148 m (486 ft)
- Landing run: 133 m (436 ft)
- Range with max fuel, no allowances: 295 nm (545 km; 340 miles)
- Endurance: 3 h 48 min

PHOENIX

PHOENIX DEVELOPMENT & SPECIALTIES INC

PO Box 271, Westmoreland, Tennessee 37186

Telephone: (615) 644 3324

PRESIDENT: John W. Tucker

PHOENIX DEVELOPMENT & SPECIALTIES PHOENIX

Phoenix Development & Specialties developed a single-seat microlight, of which kits are available. Although listed here as the Phoenix, it has been suggested that the aircraft is now marketed as the Sunbird. No confirmation of this has been received from the company.

TYPE: Single-seat microlight; conforms to FAR Pt 103.

AIRFRAME: Wire braced high-wing monoplane. Mainframe of aluminium alloy, with boom supporting the dihedral wings and conventional tail unit. Wings and tail covered with single surface Dacron. Vinyl coated stainless steel bracing cables. Kingpost and windscreen standard. Three-axis control (spoilers, elevators and rudder). Options include ballistic parachute. Rigging time 20 min.

LANDING GEAR: Tailwheel type. Mainwheels size 1·25 × 20

in; steerable tailwheel size 1 × 4 in. Bungee suspension. No brakes. Optional floats.

Power Plant: One 26 kW (35 hp) Cuyuna ULII-02 two-cylinder two-stroke engine, with 2·25:1 reduction gear to a two-blade wooden propeller. Cuyuna 430 engine optional. Fuel tank capacity 19 litres (5 US gallons).

Accommodation: Pilot only, in open position. Optional glassfibre nose cowling.

Dimensions, external:

Wing span	9·19 m (30 ft 2 in)
Wing aspect ratio	8
Length overall	4·93 m (16 ft 2 in)
Height overall	2·44 m (8 ft 0 in)
Propeller diameter	1·37 m (4 ft 6 in)

Area:

Wings, gross	13·94 m² (150·0 sq ft)

Weights and Loadings:

Weight empty	113 kg (250 lb)
Pilot weight range	57-102 kg (125-225 lb)
Max T-O weight	238 kg (525 lb)
Max wing loading	16·26 kg/m² (3·33 lb/sq ft)
Max power loading	9·15 kg/kW (15·00 lb/hp)

Performance:

Never-exceed speed	54 knots (101 km/h; 63 mph)
Max level speed	48 knots (89 km/h; 55 mph)
Max cruising speed	39 knots (72 km/h; 45 mph)
Econ cruising speed	35 knots (64 km/h; 40 mph)
Stalling speed: power on	18 knots (33 km/h; 20 mph)
power off	20 knots (37 km/h; 23 mph)
Max rate of climb at S/L	152 m (500 ft)/min
Service ceiling	3,050 m (10,000 ft)
T-O run	23 m (75 ft)
Landing run	30 m (100 ft)
Range with max fuel	95 nm (177 km; 110 miles)
Endurance	2 h 10 min
g limits	+4/−3

PIETENPOL

DONALD PIETENPOL

215, 21st Street SE, Rochester, Minnesota 55904

The prototype of Mr Bernard H. Pietenpol's Aircamper two-seat parasol monoplane flew for the first time in 1929, powered by a 30 kW (40 hp) Ford Model A engine. Plans were published in the magazine *Modern Mechanics and Inventions* in the following year and large numbers of Aircampers, with a wide variety of power plants, were built by amateurs, either from the magazine plans or from kits of parts marketed by Mr Pietenpol. Plans continue to be available.

The original Aircamper was of all-wood construction, with fabric covering, but some examples completed recently, or currently being built, have a steel tube fuselage and tail unit.

The accompanying illustration shows an Aircamper in the optional two-seat configuration. A further version, embodying many Piper Cub components, is described under the Grega entry in this section.

PIETENPOL B4 AIRCAMPER

Type: Single-seat homebuilt light aircraft. (Basic design makes provision for second seat.)

Airframe: Parasol monoplane, with two parallel bracing struts each side and centre-section cabane structure. Pietenpol special wing section. Thickness/chord ratio 16·6%. No dihedral. Incidence 2°. Fabric covered two-spar wood structure. Tips may be rounded or square. Plain wooden ailerons with fabric covering. No flaps. Wooden de Havilland truss fuselage of Sitka spruce, covered with birch plywood to back of rear cockpit and fabric on rear fuselage. Wire braced wood and steel tube tail unit, covered with fabric.

Landing Gear: Divided main gear, with spring shock absorption, modified from Piper J-3 Cub gear. Mainwheel tyres size 8·00-4, pressure 1·03 bars (15 lb/sq in). Piper hydraulic brakes. Steerable tailwheel.

Power Plant: One 45 kW (60 hp) Chevrolet Corvair converted motorcar engine, driving a two-blade wooden propeller, fitted currently to Mr Pietenpol's aircraft. Various engines have been fitted in amateur built Aircampers. One fuel tank in wing, capacity 38 litres (10 US gallons); two tanks in fuselage, total capacity 30 litres (8 US gallons). Oil capacity 4·75 litres (1·25 US gallons).

Accommodation: Single seat in open cockpit standard. Second seat optional.

Dimensions, external:

Wing span	8·84 m (29 ft 0 in)
Wing chord, constant	1·52 m (5 ft 0 in)
Wing aspect ratio	6
Propeller diameter	1·52 m (5 ft 0 in)

Area:

Wings, gross	13·47 m² (145·0 sq ft)

Weight

Weight empty	282 kg (622 lb)

Performance:

Max level and never-exceed speed	95 knots (177 km/h; 110 mph)
Max cruising speed	74 knots (137 km/h; 85 mph)
Econ cruising speed	69 knots (129 km/h; 80 mph)
Stalling speed	33 knots (62 km/h; 38 mph)
Max rate of climb at S/L	152 m (500 ft)/min
T-O and landing run	76 m (250 ft)
Range, 30 min reserves	330 nm (611 km; 380 miles)

PINAIRE

PINAIRE ENGINEERING INC

1313 Newton Avenue, Evansville, Indiana 47715
Telephone: (812) 477 9818
President: Lon Pinaire

PINAIRE ULTRA-AIRE and ULTRA-AIRE II

The original single-seat Ultra-Aire was entered in the Aircraft Recreation Vehicle competition in 1983.

In 1985 flight testing of a side by side two-seat version, known as the Ultra-Aire II, was in progress. In most respects this was similar to the single-seater, though larger and powered by a Rotax 447 engine. Neither model will stall. It has been reported that the Ultra-Aire II will not be marketed, but no confirmation of this has been received.

Pinaire offers the Ultra-Aire in kit and ready assembled forms.

Types: Single-seat (Ultra-Aire) and two-seat (Ultra-Aire II) microlight aircraft; conform to FAR Pt 103.

Airframe: Sweptback high-wing monoplane, of aluminium tube and single surface Dacron construction, with end-plate fins and foreplane. Three-axis control (tip rudders, elevators on foreplane, and spoilerons). Kingpost and vinyl coated cable wing bracing. Options include windscreen and cockpit fairing. Rigging time 20 min.

Landing Gear: Tricycle type (nosewheel steerable), with axially-oriented glassfibre mainwheel legs; optional speed fairings on all wheels. Other options include floats and mainwheel brakes.

Power Plant: Ultra-Aire: One 26 kW (35 hp) Cuyuna ULII-02 two-cylinder two-stroke engine, with 1·96:1 reduction drive to a two-blade pusher propeller. Ultra-Aire II: One 30 kW (40 hp) Rotax 447 two-cylinder engine, with 2·58:1 reduction to two-blade wooden pusher propeller. Fuel tank capacity 19 litres (5 US gallons).

Dimensions, external (A: Ultra-Aire, B: Ultra-Aire II):

Wing span: A	7·92 m (26 ft 0 in)
B	9·75 m (32 ft 0 in)
Foreplane span: A	3·05 m (10 ft 0 in)
B	3·66 m (12 ft 0 in)
Length overall: A	4·32 m (14 ft 2 in)
B	4·67 m (15 ft 4 in)
Height overall: A, B	2·11 m (6 ft 11 in)
Propeller diameter: A	1·37 m (4 ft 6 in)
B	1·73 m (5 ft 8 in)

Areas (A: Ultra-Aire, B: Ultra-Aire II):

Wings, gross: A	12·08 m² (130·0 sq ft)
B	14·86 m² (160·0 sq ft)
Foreplane, gross: A	1·86 m² (20·0 sq ft)
B	2·23 m² (24·0 sq ft)

Weights and Loadings (A: Ultra-Aire, B: Ultra-Aire II):

Weight empty: A	109 kg (240 lb)
B	136 kg (300 lb)
Pilot weight range: B	68-181 kg (150-400 lb)
Max T-O weight: A	249 kg (550 lb)
B	340 kg (750 lb)
Max wing loading: A	17·87 kg/m² (3·66 lb/sq ft)
B	20·0 kg/m² (4·1 lb/sq ft)
Max power loading: A	9·58 kg/kW (15·71 lb/hp)
B	11·33 kg/kW (18·75 lb/hp)

Performance (A: Ultra-Aire, B: Ultra-Aire II):

Never-exceed speed: A	65 knots (120 km/h; 75 mph)
B	61 knots (112 km/h; 70 mph)
Max level speed: A	55 knots (101 km/h; 63 mph)
B	52 knots (97 km/h; 60 mph)
Max cruising speed: A, B	35 knots (64 km/h; 40 mph)
Econ cruising speed: B	30 knots (56 km/h; 35 mph)
Max rate of climb at S/L: A	183 m (600 ft)/min
T-O run: B	46 m (150 ft)
Landing run: B	61 m (200 ft)
Endurance: B	1 h 15 min
g limits: A	+6/−4
B	+5/−3
Best glide ratio: A	8

PIONEER

PIONEER INTERNATIONAL AIRCRAFT INC (a subsidiary of Pioneer International Corporation)

According to press reports, Pioneer International Aircraft has ceased trading. Full details of its FlightStar and two-seat DualStar can be found in the 1985-86 *Jane's*.

PITTS

CHRISTEN INDUSTRIES INC

PO Box 547, Afton, Wyoming 83110
Telephone: (307) 886 3151
President: F. L. Christensen

In addition to marketing factory built examples of the single-seat and two-seat Pitts Special biplanes, Christen Industries supplies plans of the S-1S single-seater to amateur constructors in S-1S-EW and S-1D-EW forms. It also markets component kits for various S-1 and S-2 series aircraft. No plans are available separately for the S-2 series or the S-1T.

PITTS SPECIAL

The versions of the single-seat S-1 for which plans are currently available are designated **S-1D-EW** and **S-1S-EW**. Details are generally similar to those given for the factory built S-1S in the main US Aircraft section of this edition, but there are important differences in the two versions. The plans for the S-1S include drawings for four-aileron symmetrical wings. The S-1D has four-aileron wings of M-6 aerofoil section, which are not symmetrical.

The versions of the Pitts Special for which kits are currently available are designated **S-1S-E** (single-seat, 134 kW; 180 hp and fixed-pitch propeller); **S-1T-E** (single-seat, 149 kW; 200 hp and constant-speed propeller); **S-2S-E** (single-seat, 194 kW; 260 hp and constant-speed propeller); **S-2-E** (two-seat, 134 kW; 180 hp and fixed-pitch propeller); and **S-2A-E** (two-seat, 149 kW; 200 hp and constant-speed propeller). Further details of the S-2 Series can be found in the main US Aircraft section of this edition.

POLLIWAGEN

POLLIWAGEN INC

40940 Eleanora Way, PO Box 860, Murrieta, California 92362
Telephone: (714) 677 7877
President: Joseph P. Alvarez

POLLIWAGEN

The Polliwagen is a side by side two-seat sporting aircraft with all-composites structure, stressed for aerobatics and designed for amateur construction. The first of three prototypes flew for the first time in July 1977. Plans are available, together with a wide range of component parts, including a prefabricated fuselage, elevator, spars and wing skins. All fittings are prefabricated and pre-assembled. Landing gear can be retractable or non-retractable. By early 1986 a total of about 1,700 sets of plans had been sold, and more than 400 Polliwagens were known to be under construction and flying, in many countries. A network of dealers has been established in the USA, Canada, Australia and Switzerland.

In addition to the alternative engines listed, Polliwagen is evaluating trial installations of a 59·5 kW (80 hp) Limbach L2000 engine, driving a Hoffmann variable-pitch propeller, and an 89·5 kW (120 hp) Duncan Wankel-type single-rotor engine driving either a fixed-pitch or variable-pitch propeller.

Type: Two-seat homebuilt sporting aircraft.

Airframe: Cantilever low-wing monoplane. Airframe entirely of glassfibre epoxy composite, pre-moulded in female moulds, embodying sailplane technology. NL(S)-0715F wing section. Thickness/chord ratio 15%.

Two-seat Pietenpol Aircamper built in Canada *(Neil A. Macdougall)*

Prototype Pinaire Ultra-Aire II two-seat microlight aircraft

Prototype Poltergeist Sportster (1,600 cc Volkswagen engine)

Polliwagen two-seat light sporting aircraft *(Roland Eichenberger)*

Dihedral 4°. Incidence 1° 30′. No wing sweepback. Ailerons and trailing-edge flaps of similar construction; both have an upward setting of 10° for higher cruising speed. Flaps have a maximum downward setting of 40°, so that they can be used for aerodynamic braking. Electrically actuated trim tab in port aileron. Wingtip tanks increase effective span by reducing drag. Wings removable in under 5 min for trailering. Fuselage comprises basically one bottom and two side D spars, designed in such a way that the cockpit would break outward if subjected to impact loads. Cantilever T tail, with sweepback on all surfaces. Fin integral with fuselage. All-moving horizontal surfaces trimmed by electrically actuated servo.

Landing Gear: Retractable tricycle type standard. Main units retract inward, nosewheel rearward. Non-retractable gear optional. Rosenhan mainwheels and nosewheel, all with tyre size 11·4 × 5. Mainwheel tyre pressure 2·62 bars (38 lb/sq in); nosewheel 1·38 bars (20 lb/sq in). Rosenhan hydraulic disc brakes.

Power Plant: One 56 kW (75 hp) Revmaster 2100 D Turbo, which is a turbocharged Volkswagen engine, driving a Maloof two-blade constant-speed metal propeller. Alternative installation of 74·5 kW (100 hp) Continental O-200, 86 kW (115 hp) Avco Lycoming O-235 and 112 kW (150 hp) Avco Lycoming O-320 engines, each driving a Warnke propeller. Total of more than 132 litres (35 US gallons) of fuel in two wingtip tanks and a gravity feed tank in the fuselage nose. Refuelling point in upper surface of each tip tank.

Accommodation: Two seats side by side under rearward articulating clear or tinted canopy. Accommodation is heated and ventilated. Baggage compartment, capacity 18 kg (40 lb).

Systems: All flying controls actuated through pushrods and bearings. Electrical system includes 20A engine driven alternator and storage battery. Oxygen system of 0·62 m³ (22 cu ft) capacity.

Avionics and Equipment: Dual nav/coms. Provisions for three-axis electric trim adaptable to autopilot. Blind-flying instrumentation optional.

Dimensions, external:
- Wing span over tip tanks: 7·92 m (26 ft 0 in)
- Wing chord, constant: 1·07 m (3 ft 6 in)
- Wing aspect ratio: 7·43
- Length overall: 4·88 m (16 ft 0 in)
- Height overall: 1·70 m (5 ft 7 in)
- Tailplane span: 2·18 m (7 ft 2 in)
- Wheel track: 1·83 m (6 ft 0 in)
- Wheelbase: 1·09 m (3 ft 7 in)
- Propeller diameter: 1·45 m (4 ft 9 in)

Area:
- Wings, gross: 8·36 m² (90·0 sq ft)

Weights and Loadings (A: Revmaster, B: Continental O-200, C: Avco Lycoming O-320 engine):
- Weight empty: A, B: 295 kg (650 lb)
  - C: 340 kg (750 lb)
- Max fuel weight: standard tanks: 54 kg (120 lb)
  - wing tanks: 92·5 kg (204 lb)
- Max T-O weight: A: 567 kg (1,250 lb)
  - B: 612 kg (1,350 lb)
  - C: 680 kg (1,500 lb)
- Max wing loading: A: 67·8 kg/m² (13·89 lb/sq ft)
  - B: 73·2 kg/m² (15·00 lb/sq ft)
  - C: 81·4 kg/m² (16·67 lb/sq ft)
- Max power loading: A: 10·13 kg/kW (16·67 lb/hp)
  - B: 8·21 kg/kW (13·50 lb/hp)
  - C: 6·07 kg/kW (10·00 lb/hp)

Performance (A: turbocharged Revmaster, B: Continental O-200, C: Avco Lycoming O-320 engine, at max T-O weight):
- Never-exceed speed: 217 knots (402 km/h; 250 mph)
- Max level speed:
  - A, B: 174 knots (322 km/h; 200 mph)
  - C: 208 knots (386 km/h; 240 mph)
- Cruising speed (75% power) at S/L:
  - A: 139 knots (257 km/h; 160 mph)
  - B: 165 knots (306 km/h; 190 mph)
  - C: 191 knots (354 km/h; 220 mph)
- Cruising speed (75% power) at 2,600 m (8,500 ft)
  - A: 146 knots (270 km/h; 168 mph)
  - B: 169 knots (314 km/h; 195 mph)
  - C: 200 knots (370 km/h; 230 mph)
- Stalling speed, flaps and landing gear down:
  - A: 45 knots (82 km/h; 51 mph)
  - B: 50 knots (92 km/h; 57 mph)
  - C: 52 knots (97 km/h; 60 mph)
- Max rate of climb at S/L: A: over 213 m (700 ft)/min
  - B: 396 m (1,300 ft)/min
  - C: 457 m (1,500 ft)/min
- T-O run: A: 152 m (500 ft)
  - B: 128 m (420 ft)
  - C: 110 m (360 ft)
- Landing run: A: 152 m (500 ft)
- Range with max fuel (75% power), 45 min reserves:
  - A: 1,320 nm (2,446 km; 1,520 miles)
  - B: 1,155 nm (2,140 km; 1,330 miles)
  - C: 1,042 nm (1,931 km; 1,200 miles)
- g limits at 500 kg (1,100 lb) AUW: +9/−6

POLTERGEIST

POLTERGEIST AIRCRAFT DIVISION

Babee-Saf Inc, PO Box 927, Oconomowoc, Wisconsin 53066

Public Relations: Bruce Hollander

Bruce Hollander, Doc Kauffman and Roger Plate collaborated on the design and construction of a prototype single-seat homebuilt aircraft known as the Poltergeist Sportster (N3944H), which flew for the first time in 1985. The aircraft conforms to Formula V racing specifications, although the usually open cockpit would require a bubble canopy for such use.

Plans and a builder's manual are available to amateur constructors.

POLTERGEIST SPORTSTER

Type: Single-seat homebuilt sporting aircraft.

Airframe: Cantilever mid-wing monoplane of constant chord. Wing section NACA 2309 series. Dihedral 0°. Incidence 1° 30′. Fabric covered wood structure, with one-piece laminated spar and plywood ribs. Full span ailerons of narrow chord. No flaps or tabs. Welded 4130 steel tube fuselage, with fabric covering. Conventional cantilever tail unit of 4130 steel tube, with fabric covering. Variable incidence tailplane. No tabs.

Landing Gear: Non-retractable tailwheel type. Size 5·00-5 mainwheels carried on short cantilever spring steel legs and fitted with streamline fairings. Mainwheel tyre pressure 3·10 bars (45 lb/sq in). Small tailwheel. Brakes on mainwheels.

Power Plant: One 30 kW (40 hp) Volkswagen 1,600 cc converted motorcar engine, with Posa carburettor, Amsoil foam air filter and tuned exhaust system, driving a Rehm-Dousmanwis two-blade wooden propeller with aluminium spinner. One fuel tank, capacity 53 litres (14 US gallons). Entire engine compartment and front fuselage covered with large glassfibre cowling/coaming.

Accommodation: Pilot only, in open cockpit with windscreen. Canopy can be fitted for racing and flying in inclement weather. Baggage space, capacity 6·8 kg (15 lb).

DIMENSIONS, EXTERNAL:
- Wing span: 5·33 m (17 ft 6 in)
- Wing chord, constant: 1·37 m (4 ft 6 in)
- Wing aspect ratio: 4·08
- Length overall: 4·57 m (15 ft 0 in)
- Height overall: 1·37 m (4 ft 6 in)
- Wheel track: 0·91 m (3 ft 0 in)
- Wheelbase: 3·66 m (12 ft 0 in)
- Propeller diameter: 1·22 m (4 ft 0 in)

AREA:
- Wings, gross: 6·97 m² (75·0 sq ft)

WEIGHTS:
- Weight empty: 208 kg (460 lb)
- Pilot weight range: 68-91 kg (150-200 lb)

PERFORMANCE (open cockpit, at max T-O weight):
- Never-exceed and max level speed at S/L: 130 knots (241 km/h; 150 mph)
- Max cruising speed: 126 knots (233 km/h; 145 mph)
- Econ cruising speed: 117 knots (217 km/h; 135 mph)
- Stalling speed: 46 knots (84 km/h; 52 mph)
- T-O and landing run: 275 m (900 ft)
- T-O to 15 m (50 ft): 457 m (1,500 ft)
- Landing from 15 m (50 ft): 488 m (1,600 ft)
- Range with max fuel: 304 nm (563 km; 350 miles)

PRESCOTT

PRESCOTT AERONAUTICAL CORPORATION

1006 West 53rd Street North, PO Box 4590, Wichita, Kansas 67204
Telephone: (316) 832 1400
CHAIRMAN: Linden Blue
PRESIDENT: Tom Prescott
VICE-PRESIDENT, MARKETING: Les Jordan
PUBLIC RELATIONS: Steve Caine

Mr Tom Prescott and Mr Stan Blankenship, graduate aeronautical engineers who held management positions at Gates Learjet Corporation, co-founded Prescott Aeronautical Corporation in late 1983 to manufacture and market kits of component parts for the Prescott Pusher four-seat light aircraft.

Design of the Pusher began in July 1983, and it is claimed to be the first aircraft to be totally designed using CAD/CAM (computer aided design and computer aided manufacturing) techniques. Wind tunnel tests on a one-fifth scale model, at Wichita State University in November 1983, were followed in late January 1984 by flight trials using a one-fifth scale radio controlled model. Construction of the full-size prototype (N41PP) began in June 1984; it made its first public appearance at Oshkosh 85, following its first flight on 9 July 1985.

PRESCOTT PUSHER

Kits to build the Prescott Pusher are sold in three basic and upgrade packages. First is a **basic airframe kit**. Second is a **complete airframe fixed-gear kit**, which includes also mechanical flaps, non-retractable landing gear, control systems and Plexiglas windscreen and canopy. The third standard is a **complete airframe retractable-gear kit**, including hydraulic system and components for retractable landing gear and flaps. Delivery of the first of 33 component kits for the complete aircraft began in November 1985. All kits were expected to be available by September 1986. The complete airframe kits include basic instruments, but not avionics, interior or engine and propeller. Optional instruments, avionics and interior kits will be offered separately.

TYPE: Four-seat homebuilt aircraft.

AIRFRAME: Cantilever low-wing monoplane. Wing section NLF(1)-0215. Dihedral 3°, with cambered glassfibre wingtips housing combined strobe/anti-collision and navigation lights. Incidence 2°. Sweepback at quarter-chord 10° 15′. Wings of aluminium alloy construction, including ailerons and mechanically or hydraulically actuated flaps. Negative 10° cruise/aileron flap setting. Streamlined fuselage of heli-arc welded 4130 square-section steel tubes, covered by non-structural glassfibre shells in two parts plus a nose section. Cantilever T tail of aluminium alloy construction, with swept vertical surfaces and full span balanced elevator. Electrically actuated trim tab in elevator. Dorsal fin and ventral fin.

LANDING GEAR: Retractable (optionally non-retractable) tricycle type, with hydraulic actuation. Main units retract inward, nose unit rearward. All wheels and tyres size 5·00-5. Composite spring shock absorbing main legs, oleo nose leg. Hydraulic mainwheel brakes. Tailskid to protect propeller in taildown attitude.

POWER PLANT: One 134 kW (180 hp) Avco Lycoming O-360-A2A flat-four engine, mounted in rear fuselage and driving a propeller of customer's choice: options include Great American two-blade wooden fixed-pitch, Hoffmann three-blade wood/composite variable-pitch or constant-speed, or Advanced Technology four-blade composite variable-pitch or constant-speed pusher propeller. Prototype fitted with Hoffmann three-blade constant-speed propeller in June 1986, giving improved performance compared with former two-blade fixed-pitch propeller. Optional power plant will be a 156 kW (210 hp) Mazda fuel injected and turbocharged, liquid cooled rotary engine with reduction gear. Two fuel tanks in wing leading-edges, with total capacity of 170 litres (45 US gallons). Optional 57 litre (15 US gallon) auxiliary tank. Oil capacity 7·5 litres (2 US gallons).

ACCOMMODATION: Pilot and three passengers in pairs under transparent canopy, port half of which is hinged on centreline to open upward. Baggage compartment aft of rear seats, with 45·6 kg (100 lb) capacity.

SYSTEMS: Hydraulic system for flaps and landing gear. 24V electrical system. Optional oxygen bottle in baggage compartment.

AVIONICS: Loran C and optional radio kits available.

DIMENSIONS, EXTERNAL:
- Wing span: 8·94 m (29 ft 4 in)
- Wing chord: at root: 1·43 m (4 ft 8½ in)
- at tip: 0·91 m (3 ft 0 in)
- Wing aspect ratio: 7·76
- Length overall: 6·18 m (20 ft 3¼ in)
- Height overall: 2·67 m (8 ft 9 in)
- Tailplane span: 3·35 m (11 ft 0 in)
- Wheel track: 1·61 m (5 ft 3½ in)
- Wheelbase: 2·44 m (8 ft 0 in)
- Propeller diameter (max): 1·57 m (5 ft 2 in)

DIMENSION, INTERNAL:
- Cabin width: 1·07 m (3 ft 6 in)

AREA:
- Wings, gross: 10·29 m² (110·8 sq ft)

WEIGHTS AND LOADINGS:
- Weight empty: 635 kg (1,400 lb)
- Max fuel weight: 150 kg (330 lb)
- Max T-O weight: 1,088 kg (2,400 lb)
- Max wing loading: 105·75 kg/m² (21·66 lb/sq ft)
- Max power loading (180 hp): 8·12 kg/kW (13·33 lb/hp)

PERFORMANCE (O-360 engine and retractable landing gear):
- Never-exceed speed: 206 knots (383 km/h; 238 mph)
- Max level speed at S/L: 184 knots (340 km/h; 212 mph)
- Max cruising speed at S/L: 160 knots (296 km/h; 184 mph)
- Cruising speed at 2,285 m (7,500 ft): 156 knots (290 km/h; 180 mph)
- Stalling speed: flaps up: 63 knots (117 km/h; 73 mph)
- flaps down: 58 knots (108 km/h; 67 mph)
- Max rate of climb at S/L: 290 m (950 ft)/min
- Service ceiling: 5,485 m (18,000 ft)
- T-O to 15 m (50 ft): 526 m (1,725 ft)
- Landing from 15 m (50 ft): 473 m (1,550 ft)
- Range with max standard fuel: 869 nm (1,609 km; 1,000 miles)
- Range with max payload: 738 nm (1,368 km; 850 miles)

PROWLER

PROWLER AVIATION INC

Auto Aviation Development Company, 3641 Soquel Drive, Soquel, California 95073
Telephone: (408) 462 5321
PRESIDENT: George Morse

PROWLER AVIATION PROWLER

In January 1982 Mr George Morse began the design of a two-seat high-performance aircraft named Prowler (N611AA) that was to be reminiscent of the Second World War Supermarine Spitfire fighter. Construction started in December of that year and it achieved its first flight on 17 March 1985. It is believed that Prowler Aviation intends to offer kits to allow amateur construction of the aircraft. These will include the engine, flight and engine instruments, tools and an instruction manual.

TYPE: Two-seat high-performance homebuilt aircraft.

AIRFRAME: Cantilever low-wing monoplane of aluminium alloy construction. Wing section NACA 64A212 at roots, NACA 64A210 at tips. Dihedral 5°. Incidence 2° 30′. Ailerons and flaps. Cantilever tail unit comprising tailplane and elevators with trim tabs, rudder and horn balanced rudder with tab.

LANDING GEAR: Retractable tailwheel type. Mainwheels size 1·5 × 6·00-6; tyre pressure 1·52 bars (22 lb/sq in); tailwheel size 2·80-8, tyre pressure 1·72 bars (25 lb/sq in). Shock absorbers on main legs, which retract inward into wingroots, ahead of radiator ducts. Mainwheel brakes.

POWER PLANT: One 168 kW (225 hp) Auto Aviation modified Oldsmobile F-85 eight-cylinder glycol cooled motorcar engine, driving a McCauley D3A 32C90/82 NC-2 three-blade metal constant-speed propeller with spinner, via 1·67:1 reduction gear. Three fuel tanks, with total capacity of 136 litres (36 US gallons). Two 45 litre (12 US gallon) auxiliary fuel tanks, to give total possible fuel capacity of 227 litres (60 US gallons). Oil capacity 7·5 litres (2 US gallons).

ACCOMMODATION: Two seats in tandem in enclosed cockpit, beneath bubble canopy. Baggage space in rear of cockpit, capacity 16 kg (35 lb).

SYSTEMS: Hydraulic system. 12V DC electrical system.

AVIONICS: King KX155 radio.

DIMENSIONS, EXTERNAL:
- Wing span: 7·72 m (25 ft 4 in)
- Wing chord: at root: 1·73 m (5 ft 8 in)
- at tip: 0·89 m (2 ft 11 in)
- Wing aspect ratio: 6·17
- Length overall: 6·40 m (21 ft 0 in)
- Height overall: 2·21 m (7 ft 3 in)
- Tailplane span: 2·55 m (8 ft 4½ in)
- Wheel track: 2·16 m (7 ft 1 in)
- Wheelbase: 4·45 m (14 ft 7 in)
- Propeller diameter: 1·98 m (6 ft 6 in)

AREA:
- Wings, gross: 9·66 m² (104·0 sq ft)

WEIGHTS AND LOADINGS:
- Weight empty: 618 kg (1,362 lb)
- Max T-O weight: 975 kg (2,150 lb)
- Max wing loading: 100·9 kg/m² (20·67 lb/sq ft)
- Max power loading: 5 80 kg/kW (9·56 lb/hp)

PERFORMANCE (at max T-O weight):
- Never-exceed speed: 217 knots (402 km/h; 250 mph) IAS
- Max level speed at S/L: 191 knots (354 km/h; 220 mph) IAS
- Max cruising speed at 2,135 m (7,000 ft): 174 knots (322 km/h; 200 mph)
- Econ cruising speed at 2,135 m (7,000 ft): 148 knots (274 km/h; 170 mph)
- Stalling speed, flaps up, power off: 48 knots (89 km/h; 55 mph) IAS
- Max rate of climb at S/L: 549 m (1,800 ft)/min
- Service ceiling: 5,180 m (17,000 ft)
- T-O and landing run: 457 m (1,500 ft)
- T-O to 15 m (50 ft): 488 m (1,600 ft)
- Landing from 15 m (50 ft): 610 m (2,000 ft)
- Range with max standard fuel: 1,042 nm (1,931 km; 1,200 miles)
- Range with auxiliary fuel: 1,302 nm (2,414 km; 1,500 miles)

QUAD CITY

QUAD CITY ULTRALIGHT AIRCRAFT CORPORATION

3610 Coaltown Road, Moline, Illinois 61265
Telephone: (309) 764 3515
PRESIDENT: Charles Hamilton

QUAD CITY CHALLENGER and CHALLENGER II

The Challenger was designed to fit between wire braced microlights and the elaborate fully enclosed types, yet be easy and quick to construct from a kit, simple to fly and easily transportable. Challenger prototypes were flown in November and December 1982 and kits became available in late Summer 1983.

With the Rotax 277 or KFM 107 engine installed, the Challenger falls within FAR Pt 103 for microlights. However, the Challenger was designed and engineered to take engines of up to 37·3 kW (50 hp), and can therefore have a 26 kW (35 hp) Rotax 377 or 30 kW (40 hp) Rotax 447 engine fitted, whereby it comes within the FAA's Experimental aircraft regulations for homebuilts. A flying-boat variant of the Challenger was exhibited at the 1984 Sun 'n Fun Fly-in at Lakeland, Florida, but this is thought not to be available for purchase. An illustration appeared in the 1984-85 *Jane's*.

In early 1984 a tandem two-seat version of Challenger appeared in prototype form, as the Challenger II. It differs principally in having a longer fuselage and has the Rotax 447 engine as standard. It was designed as an FAR Pt 103 microlight trainer but has also been approved as a 51 per cent Experimental homebuilt category aircraft.

Quad City Ultralight Aircraft now offers Lexan side doors to fit the Challenger II, with cabin heating ducted from the engine.

The following structural details apply to both the Challenger and Challenger II:

TYPE: Single-seat microlight (Challenger) and two-seat microlight trainer (Challenger II); conform to FAR Pt 103 and FAA Experimental category for homebuilts.

AIRFRAME: Strut braced high-wing monoplane with conventional strut braced tail unit. Main frame constructed from

Prowler Aviation Prowler all-metal two-seat homebuilt aircraft

Two-seat Quad City Challenger II

Single-seat Quad City Challenger *(Hal Adkins)*

Prototype Prescott Pusher four-seat homebuilt aircraft

Quickie Aircraft Corporation Quickie in Swiss markings *(Roland Eichenberger)*

aluminium alloy and chromalloy steel, with zero porosity heat shrinkable Dacron covering fuselage and mainly double surface wings and tail unit. Stainless steel cables. Three-axis control (ailerons, elevators and rudder), with optional 'flaperons'. Options include agricultural spray equipment (for Challenger II only). Rigging time 20 min.

LANDING GEAR: Non-retractable tricycle type. All three wheels size 5 × 11·5 in. Steerable nosewheel. Optional mainwheel brakes. Other options include floats, skis and wheel fairings.

POWER PLANT: Challenger: One 22·4 kW (30 hp) KFM 107ER Maxi two-cylinder or 20 kW (27 hp) Rotax 277 single-cylinder two-stroke engine, with 2·1:1 belt reduction to a two-blade wooden pusher propeller. Optional Rotax 377 and 447 engines. Challenger II: One 30 kW (40 hp) Rotax 447 two-cylinder engine, with 2·1:1 belt reduction to a two-blade wooden pusher propeller. Fuel tank capacity 19 litres (5 US gallons). Optional 19 litre (5 US gallon) auxiliary fuel tank.

ACCOMMODATION: Pilot in open cockpit in Challenger; pilot and passenger in open tandem cockpits in Challenger II. Windscreen standard. Optional side curtains; Lexan doors optional for Challenger II.

DIMENSIONS, EXTERNAL (A: Challenger, B: Challenger II):

Wing span: A, B	9·60 m (31 ft 6 in)
Wing aspect ratio: A	6·89
B	5·67
Length overall: A	5·49 m (18 ft 0 in)
B	6·10 m (20 ft 0 in)
Height overall: A, B	1·83 m (6 ft 0 in)
Propeller diameter: A, B	1·32 m (4 ft 4 in)

AREAS:

Wings, gross: A	13·38 m² (144·0 sq ft)
B	16·26 m² (175·0 sq ft)

WEIGHTS AND LOADINGS (A: Challenger with KFM 107, B: Challenger II):

Weight empty: A	109 kg (240 lb)
B	136 kg (300 lb)
Pilot weight range: B	68-136 kg (150-300 lb)
Max T-O weight: A	227 kg (500 lb)
B	363 kg (800 lb)
Max wing loading: A	17·1 kg/m² (3·5 lb/sq ft)
B	21·0 kg/m² (4·3 lb/sq ft)
Max power loading: A	11·35 kg/kW (16·67 lb/hp)
B	12·05 kg/kW (20·00 lb/hp)

PERFORMANCE (A: Challenger with KFM 107, B: Challenger II):

Never-exceed speed: A	74 knots (136 km/h; 85 mph)
B	78 knots (145 km/h; 90 mph)
Max level speed: A, B	55 knots (101 km/h; 63 mph)
Max cruising speed: A	48 knots (88 km/h; 55 mph)
B	52 knots (97 km/h; 60 mph)
Econ cruising speed: A	43 knots (80 km/h; 50 mph)
B	48 knots (89 km/h; 55 mph)
Stalling speed: A	23 knots (42 km/h; 26 mph)
B	26 knots (49 km/h; 30 mph)
Max rate of climb at S/L: A	213 m (700 ft)/min
B, pilot only	305 m (1,000 ft)/min
B, pilot and passenger	152 m (500 ft)/min
Service ceiling: A, B	3,660 m (12,000 ft)
T-O and landing run: A, B	46 m (150 ft)
Range with max standard fuel:	
A	130 nm (241 km; 150 miles)
B	104 nm (193 km; 120 miles)
Endurance: A	2 h 30 min
B	2 h 10 min
g limits: A, B	+6/−4
Best glide ratio: A, B	10

QUICKIE

QUICKIE AIRCRAFT CORPORATION

Building 68, Mojave Airport, Mojave, California 93501
Telephone: (805) 824 4313

Quickie Aircraft Corporation is a company formed in 1978 by Gene Sheehan and the late Tom Jewett to develop the Quickie aircraft and to sell complete kits, including engine, to amateur constructors who wish to build this type. It later developed a two-seat version known as the Quickie Q2, for which kits have been available since February 1981.

QUICKIE AIRCRAFT CORPORATION QUICKIE

Designed with the assistance of Burt Rutan, the Quickie is a single-seat light aircraft of unusual configuration. Construction of the prototype (N77Q) was started on 13 August 1977, and it was completed in 400 working hours over a three month period. First flight was achieved on 15 November 1977. Subsequently extensive stall/departure/spin testing revealed that the Quickie could not be made to spin.

Complete kits, including engines, have been available since June 1978. Each includes prefabricated cowling, canopy, all machined parts, all welded parts, and some of the tools, in order to reduce building time to 400 man-hours for the inexperienced builder. More than 1,500 single-seat Quickie and two-seat Q2 kits have been delivered, and many completed aircraft have flown.

TYPE: Single-seat homebuilt sporting aircraft of canard configuration.

AIRFRAME: Tapered cantilever shoulder-wing monoplane. Dihedral from roots. Wings have two unidirectional glassfibre spars and shaped low density rigid foam core, covered with glassfibre. Constant chord inboard ailerons. No flaps. Tapered and slightly sweptback cantilever foreplane, mounted low on forward fuselage, with marked anhedral. Construction similar to that of wings. Mainwheel housings attached to tips. Full span tapered elevator/flaps. Semi-monocoque fuselage of banana shape, formed from 25 mm (1 in) thick foam, with glassfibre covering inside and out, and tapering towards rear. Foam/glassfibre sandwich bulkheads. Cantilever sweptback vertical fin and narrow chord rudder of similar construction to wings.

LANDING GEAR: Non-retractable tailwheel type. Mainwheels positioned at tips of foreplane in swept fairings. A kit to provide 50 per cent larger tyres for grass field operation is optional. Steerable tailwheel aft of fuselage.

POWER PLANT: One modified Onan horizontally opposed two-cylinder four-stroke engine, developing originally 13·5 kW (18 hp) at 3,600 rpm and driving a two-blade fixed-pitch wooden propeller. Modifications to cylinder heads and exhaust system allow newly-supplied engines to develop 16·4 kW (22 hp) at 3,800 rpm: a retrofit kit is available to convert 13·5 kW (18 hp) engines to develop this increased output. Fuel capacity 30·3 litres (8 US gallons). Fuel consumption approx 44·2 km/litre (104 miles/US gallon).

ACCOMMODATION: Single seat under one-piece side-hinged canopy. Cockpit suitable for pilot up to 1·98 m (6 ft 6 in) tall and weighing up to 95 kg (210 lb). Max baggage capacity with lighter pilot 13·6 kg (30 lb). With engine developing 16·4 kW (22 hp), a 100 kg (220 lb) pilot, maximum fuel, and 5·4 kg (12 lb) of baggage can be carried.

DIMENSIONS, EXTERNAL:
Wing span 5·08 m (16 ft 8 in)
Foreplane span 4·67 m (15 ft 4 in)
Length overall 5·28 m (17 ft 4 in)

DIMENSIONS, INTERNAL:
Cockpit: Length 1·63 m (5 ft 4 in)
Width 0·56 m (1 ft 10 in)
Height 0·86 m (2 ft 10 in)

AREAS:
Wings, gross 2·52 m² (27·08 sq ft)
Foreplane, gross 2·47 m² (26·57 sq ft)

WEIGHTS AND LOADINGS (A: 13·5 kW; 18 hp engine, B: 16·4 kW; 22 hp engine):
Weight empty: A, B 109 kg (240 lb)
Max T-O weight: A 218 kg (480 lb)
B 236 kg (520 lb)
Max wing loading, gross incl foreplane:
A 43·7 kg/m² (8·95 lb/sq ft)
B 47·3 kg/m² (9·69 lb/sq ft)
Max power loading: A 16·15 kg/kW (26·67 lb/hp)
B 14·39 kg/kW (23·64 lb/hp)

PERFORMANCE:
Max level speed: A 109 knots (202 km/h; 126 mph)
B 122 knots (225 km/h; 140 mph)
Max cruising speed:
A 105 knots (195 km/h; 121 mph)
B 115 knots (214 km/h; 133 mph)
Stalling speed, power off:
A 46 knots (86 km/h; 53 mph)
Stalling speed, power on:
A 43 knots (79 km/h; 49 mph)
Normal rate of climb at S/L: A 130 m (425 ft)/min
B 183 m (600 ft)/min
Max rate of climb at 1,525 m (5,000 ft):
A 110 m (360 ft)/min
B 152 m (500 ft)/min
Service ceiling: A 3,750 m (12,300 ft)
B 4,665 m (15,300 ft)
T-O run: A 201 m (660 ft)
B 137 m (450 ft)
Landing run: A 255 m (835 ft)
B 183 m (600 ft)
Range at normal cruising speed:
A 477 nm (885 km; 550 miles)
B 456 nm (845 km; 525 miles)
Range at econ cruising speed:
A, B 712 nm (1,320 km; 820 miles)

QUICKIE AIRCRAFT CORPORATION QUICKIE Q2

Detail design of a two-seat version of the Quickie began in the Autumn of 1979, and the prototype was built by Garry LeGare, the principal of Leg-Air which is the Canadian distributor for Quickie Aircraft Corporation. This flew for the first time on 1 July 1980, before being transferred to Quickie's Mojave facility for development flying. Generally similar to the standard Quickie configuration, it differs primarily in having a wider fuselage, with a cockpit width of 1·10 m (3 ft 7½ in), to allow for side by side seating; a more powerful Revmaster engine; aerodynamic refinements; and foreplane and vertical tail surfaces of increased area. Following the development of the Quickie Q-200 (described separately) the new section foreplane of this aircraft has become standard on the Q2.

The Q2 is marketed in the form of a kit containing all that is needed to build the aircraft, including the power plant and instruments. The fuselage is supplied as four prefabricated shells to simplify construction, and all components requiring machining or welding are prefabricated. Delivery of kits began on 9 February 1981, and in the single month of August that year 250 Q2s were sold. A composite construction starter kit is available, to test the skills of a would-be amateur builder before he or she undertakes construction of a Q2.

Details of a kit that is available to convert the Q2 to tricycle landing gear configuration can be found under the Tri-Q Development entry in this section.

Ten Q2s have been built under contract from Quickie Aircraft Corporation by the Chinese State Factory at Shanghai, under a scheme to familiarise Chinese personnel with composite materials and construction techniques. The first of these aircraft flew in Summer 1983.

The description of the Quickie applies also to the Quickie Q2, except as follows:

TYPE: Two-seat homebuilt sporting aircraft of canard configuration.

AIRFRAME: Wings and foreplane generally as for Quickie, except some modification of the aerofoil sections, and the incorporation of aerodynamic refinements. Foreplane increased in span and area, with NASA LS(1)-0417 mod section. Fuselage of increased width and length, built up from four prefabricated fuselage shells.

POWER PLANT: One 47·7 kW (64 hp) Revmaster 2100DQ flat-four engine, driving a two-blade fixed-pitch wooden propeller with spinner. Fuel capacity 76 litres (20 US gallons).

ACCOMMODATION: Pilot and passenger side by side in enclosed cockpit. Sideways opening transparent canopy, hinged on starboard side. Dual controls optional. Space for 18 kg (40 lb) baggage aft of seats.

DIMENSIONS, EXTERNAL:
Wing span 5·08 m (16 ft 8 in)
Foreplane span 5·08 m (16 ft 8 in)
Length overall 5·97 m (19 ft 7 in)

AREA:
Wings/foreplane, gross 6·22 m² (67·0 sq ft)

WEIGHTS AND LOADINGS:
Weight empty 215 kg (475 lb)
Max T-O weight 454 kg (1,000 lb)
Max wing loading, gross incl foreplane
72·9 kg/m² (14·93 lb/sq ft)
Max power loading 9·52 kg/kW (15·63 lb/hp)

PERFORMANCE (A: pilot only at 340 kg; 750 lb AUW. B: pilot and passenger at 454 kg; 1,000 lb max T-O weight):
Max level speed: B 156 knots (290 km/h; 180 mph)
Stalling speed: A 53 knots (99 km/h; 61 mph)
B 56 knots (103 km/h; 64 mph)
Max rate of climb at S/L: A 366 m (1,200 ft)/min
B 244 m (800 ft)/min
Service ceiling: A 5,790 m (19,000 ft)
B 4,575 m (15,000 ft)
T-O run: A 110-137 m (360-450 ft)
B 186-198 m (610-650 ft)
Landing run: A 219 m (720 ft)
B 241 m (790 ft)
Range with max fuel at max cruising speed, 45 min reserves: B 592 nm (1,097 km; 682 miles)
Range with max fuel at econ cruising speed, 45 min reserves: B 886 nm (1,641 km; 1,020 miles)

QUICKIE AIRCRAFT CORPORATION QUICKIE Q-200

Introduced in 1983, the Quickie Q-200 differs from the Q2 (which continues in production) in having a 74·5 kW (100 hp) Continental O-200 flat-four engine, giving much increased performance. It also introduced a foreplane of different section (NASA LS(1)-0417 Mod), which is now standard on both versions of the Quickie. This expands the CG range, lowers stalling speed at max T-O weight, reduces rudder sensitivity, inhibits spin tendencies, shortens T-O runs, and eliminates the trim changes required previously when flying in rain.

The general description and specification of the Q2 apply also to the Q-200, except as follows:

DIMENSIONS, EXTERNAL:
Length overall 6·05 m (19 ft 10 in)

WEIGHTS AND LOADINGS:
Weight empty 229 kg (505 lb)
Max T-O weight 499 kg (1,100 lb)
Max wing loading 80·17 kg/m² (16·42 lb/sq ft)
Max power loading 6·70 kg/kW (11·00 lb/hp)

PERFORMANCE:
Max level speed 191 knots (354 km/h; 220 mph)
Max cruising speed (75% power)
180 knots (333 km/h; 207 mph)
Econ cruising speed 104 knots (193 km/h; 120 mph)
Stalling speed: power on 54 knots (100 km/h; 62 mph)
power off 56 knots (103 km/h; 64 mph)
Max rate of climb at S/L at AUW of 408 kg (900 lb)
488 m (1,600 ft)/min
Service ceiling 6,400 m (21,000 ft)
T-O run 186 m (610 ft)
Landing run 290 m (950 ft)

RAF

RUTAN AIRCRAFT FACTORY INC

Jane's has been informed that Rutan Aircraft Factory ceased to market homebuilt aircraft plans on 13 July 1985. No RAF aircraft is now available in plans or kit form, and only a builder support service is functioning to assist those who purchased plans before that date.

Full details of the VariViggen, VariEze and Long-EZ, and brief details of the Defiant, can be found in the 1985-86 and previous editions of *Jane's*.

RAND ROBINSON

RAND ROBINSON ENGINEERING INC

5395 Industrial Drive, Site A, Huntington Beach, California 92649

Telephone: (714) 898 3811

In 1974, the late Mr Kenneth Rand formed Rand Robinson Engineering Inc to market plans for the KR-1 single-seat lightweight sporting aircraft, and of a slightly larger two-seat version, designated KR-2. His last design was the KR-3 light amphibian, described in the 1978-79 *Jane's*.

A new design designated KR-100 has been prepared during the past year, according to Mrs Jeannette Rand. Little information on this is available, except that it is a Continental O-200 powered single-seater for cross-country flights. Construction will be similar to the KR-1 and KR-2 and many prefabricated components will be available to amateur builders.

RAND ROBINSON KR-1

Mr Kenneth Rand began designing the prototype of this single-seat lightweight sporting aircraft in 1969; construction of the prototype was started in 1970 and the first flight was made in February 1972. Plans are available to amateur constructors; many thousands of sets have been sold and at least 200 KR-1s are known to be flying.

The performance figures that are quoted relate generally to the prototype fitted with a 67 kW (90 hp) 2,074 cc Volkswagen engine. Performance figures with the original 27 kW (36 hp) 1,200 cc VW engine can be found in the 1975-76 *Jane's*.

TYPE: Single-seat homebuilt sporting aircraft.

AIRFRAME: Cantilever low-wing monoplane. Wing section RAF 48. Thickness/chord ratio 15%. Dihedral 5°. Incidence 5° at root, 2° at tip. No sweepback. Composite two-spar structure. Front spar of spruce; rear spar built of spruce and plywood. Most ribs formed from polyurethane foam, spaces between ribs being filled with polyurethane foam slab. Structure covered with Dynel reinforced epoxy. Pre-moulded wing skins are available. Outer wing panels removable for storage. Ailerons of polyurethane foam, with Dynel reinforced epoxy covering, over full span of outer panels. Trailing-edge flaps standard. Composite fuselage, lower half of spruce longerons with plywood skin, upper surface of carved Styrofoam covered with Dynel epoxy. Firewall is a plywood, asbestos and stainless steel lamination. Cantilever tail unit, with spruce spars, the remainder of the structure being of carved polyurethane foam, Dynel epoxy covered. Fixed incidence tailplane. Trim tabs in rudder and elevator.

LANDING GEAR: Manually retractable tailwheel type standard; main units retract aft into wing centre-section. Shock absorption by flat spring crossbar to which main units are attached. Mainwheel tyres size 10½ × 4·00-5, pressure 2·07 bars (30 lb/sq in). Steerable tailwheel with solid tyre of 3 in diameter. Manual drum brakes. Optional non-retractable gear with cantilever aluminium alloy leafspring legs, and Cleveland wheels and brakes, or Rosenhan wheels and brakes as used with retractable gear.

POWER PLANT: One Volkswagen modified motorcar engine, driving a Maloof two-blade two-position metal propeller with spinner. Prototype has a Rajay turbocharged 67 kW (90 hp) 2,074 cc VW. Fuel tankage with this engine comprises one tank immediately aft of firewall, capacity 38 litres (10 US gallons), and one 76 litre (20 US gallon) tank in each wing, giving total capacity of 190 litres (50 US gallons). Refuelling point on fuselage upper surface, forward of windscreen. Oil capacity 2·8 litres (0·75 US gallons).

ACCOMMODATION: Pilot only, beneath rearward sliding transparent cockpit canopy. Baggage space aft of seat.

SYSTEM: Electrical power supplied by 20A alternator and 12V 14Ah storage battery. Bosch electric starter.

AVIONICS AND EQUIPMENT: Edo-Aire 720-channel transceiver with 200-channel Auto Omni. Full blind-flying panel.

DIMENSIONS, EXTERNAL:
Wing span 5·18 m (17 ft 0 in)
Wing chord: at root 1·22 m (4 ft 0 in)
at tip 0·91 m (3 ft 0 in)
Wing aspect ratio 4·5
Length overall 3·89 m (12 ft 9 in)
Width, wings removed 1·52 m (5 ft 0 in)
Height overall 1·07 m (3 ft 6 in)
Tailplane span 1·52 m (5 ft 0 in)
Wheel track 1·27 m (4 ft 2 in)
Propeller diameter 1·35 m (4 ft 5 in)

DIMENSIONS, INTERNAL:
Cockpit: Length 1·22 m (4 ft 0 in)
Max width 0·51 m (1 ft 8 in)

Two-seat Quickie Q2 built in the UK *(Air Portraits)*

Rand Robinson KR-2 built in Austria *(Roland Eichenberger)*

Rand Robinson KR-2T, built by Mr Pete Balfour of Kitchener, Ontario, Canada *(Neil A. Macdougall)*

Rand Robinson KR-1 (37·3 kW; 50 hp Volkswagen engine) built in Canada *(J. M. G. Gradidge)*

Max height 0·76 m (2 ft 6 in)
Baggage space 0·11 m^3 (4 cu ft)

AREA:
Wings, gross 5·76 m^2 (62·0 sq ft)

WEIGHTS AND LOADINGS (A: 27 kW; 36 hp, B: 67 kW; 90 hp):
Weight empty, equipped: A 154 kg (340 lb)
B 218 kg (480 lb)
Max T-O and landing weight: A 272 kg (600 lb)
B 408 kg (900 lb)
Max wing loading: A 47·3 kg/m^2 (9·68 lb/sq ft)
B 70·9 kg/m^2 (14·52 lb/sq ft)
Max power loading: A 10·07 kg/kW (16·67 lb/hp)
B 6·09 kg/kW (10·00 lb/hp)

PERFORMANCE (A: 27 kW; 36 hp. B: 67 kW; 90 hp, at max T-O weight):
Never-exceed speed:
A 140 knots (259 km/h; 161 mph)
B 217 knots (402 km/h; 250 mph)
Max level speed at S/L:
A 130 knots (241 km/h; 150 mph)
B 191 knots (354 km/h; 220 mph)
Max cruising speed at 1,525 m (5,000 ft):
A 130 knots (241 km/h; 150 mph)
B 191 knots (354 km/h; 220 mph)
Econ cruising speed at 5,485 m (18,000 ft):
B 217 knots (402 km/h; 250 mph)
Stalling speed: A, B 39 knots (73 km/h; 45 mph)
Max rate of climb at S/L: A 183 m (600 ft)/min
B 457 m (1,500 ft)/min
Service ceiling: A 3,660 m (12,000 ft)
B 9,145 m (30,000 ft)
T-O run: A, B 122 m (400 ft)
T-O to 15 m (50 ft): A, B 244 m (800 ft)
Landing from 15 m (50 ft): A, B 305 m (1,000 ft)
Landing run: A, B 152 m (500 ft)
Range with max fuel:
B 2,600 nm (4,825 km; 3,000 miles)

RAND ROBINSON KR-2

The KR-2 is a slightly larger side by side two-seat version of the KR-1, to which it is generally similar in construction. Design began in 1973 and the prototype flew for the first time in July 1974, with a Rajay turbocharged 2,074 cc Volkswagen engine, driving a Maloof two-position propeller. More than 7,000 sets of plans and a great many kits have been sold; at least 350 KR-2s are known to be flying.

An accompanying illustration shows the Rand Robinson KR-2T, a modified KR-2 with tandem seats under a bubble canopy and non-retractable landing gear. Built by Mr Pete Balfour of Kitchener, Ontario, Canada, it is powered by a 48·5 kW (65 hp) Continental engine.

TYPE: Two-seat homebuilt sporting aircraft.

AIRFRAME: As for KR-1, except wing span increased by 1·12 m (3 ft 8 in), and fuselage dimensions and wheel track increased.

POWER PLANT: Airframe designed to accept Volkswagen modified motorcar engines of 1,600 to 2,200 cc. Great Plains conversion recommended. Fuel tank immediately aft of firewall, capacity 38 litres (10 US gallons). One fuel tank in each wing, capacity 53 litres (14 US gallons). Total fuel capacity 144 litres (38 US gallons). Refuelling point on fuselage upper surface, forward of windscreen.

ACCOMMODATION: Two persons, side by side, beneath transparent cockpit canopy.

AVIONICS AND EQUIPMENT: Provision for wide range of avionics and blind-flying instruments. Prototype has full IFR panel, dual nav/com transceivers, glideslope receiver, three-light marker beacon receiver, and radar transponder with altitude reporting.

DIMENSIONS, EXTERNAL:
Wing span 6·30 m (20 ft 8 in)
Wing chord: at root 1·22 m (4 ft 0 in)
at tip 0·91 m (3 ft 0 in)
Wing aspect ratio 5·5
Length overall 4·42 m (14 ft 6 in)
Height overall 1·07 m (3 ft 6 in)
Tailplane span 1·52 m (5 ft 0 in)
Wheel track 1·52 m (5 ft 0 in)
Propeller diameter 1·32 m (4 ft 4 in)

DIMENSIONS, INTERNAL:
Cockpit: Length 1·22 m (4 ft 0 in)
Max width 0·91 m (3 ft 0 in)
Max height 0·76 m (2 ft 6 in)
Baggage space 0·11 m^3 (4 cu ft)

AREA:
Wings, gross 7·43 m^2 (80·0 sq ft)

WEIGHTS AND LOADINGS (prototype, A: without turbocharger, B: with turbocharger):
Weight empty, equipped: A 200 kg (440 lb)
B, with IFR and electrics 263 kg (580 lb)
Max T-O and landing weight: A 363 kg (800 lb)
B 499 kg (1,100 lb)
Max wing loading: A 48·8 kg/m^2 (10·0 lb/sq ft)
B 67·1 kg/m^2 (13·75 lb/sq ft)

PERFORMANCE (prototype, at max T-O weight. A: without turbocharger, B: with turbocharger):
Never-exceed speed:
A, B 186 knots (346 km/h; 215 mph)
Max level speed at S/L:
A 156 knots (290 km/h; 180 mph)
B 161 knots (298 km/h; 185 mph)
Max cruising speed:
A at 1,525 m (5,000 ft)
156 knots (290 km/h; 180 mph)
B at 5,485 m (18,000 ft)
191 knots (354 km/h; 220 mph)
Econ cruising speed at 3,660 m (12,000 ft):
A 148 knots (274 km/h; 170 mph)
Stalling speed: A 39 knots (73 km/h; 45 mph)
Max rate of climb: A at S/L 244 m (800 ft)/min
B at 5,485 m (18,000 ft) 244 m (800 ft)/min
Service ceiling: A 4,875 m (16,000 ft)
B 7,925 m (26,000 ft)
T-O run: A, B 122 m (400 ft)
T-O to 15 m (50 ft): A, B 244 m (800 ft)
Landing from 15 m (50 ft): A, B 305 m (1,000 ft)
Landing run: A, B 152 m (500 ft)
Range with max fuel:
B 1,735 nm (3,215 km; 2,000 miles)

RANS

RANS COMPANY

1104 East Highway 40 By-Pass, Hays, Kansas 67601
Telephone: (913) 625 6346
PROPRIETOR: Randy Schlitter

RANS S-4 COYOTE

The Coyote is a single-seat microlight or homebuilt aircraft of conventional lightplane appearance. Design began in July 1982 and construction of the prototype started in November of that year. It first flew in March 1983. The construction of components for kits, and ready assembled aircraft under FAR Pt 103, began in November 1983, and the first of these aircraft flew in the following month. By February 1986, a total of 49 kits had been delivered.

TYPE: Single-seat light aircraft; conforms to FAR Pt 103 as a microlight.

AIRFRAME: Braced high-wing cabin monoplane. Wing thickness/chord ratio 15%. Dihedral 1° 30′. Incidence 2°. Fuselage structure of round section aluminium alloy tubing; wings have aluminium alloy tube spars and ribs. Dacron/Ceconite covering over entire airframe, double surface for wings and conventional strut braced tail unit. Variable incidence tailplane. Three-axis control (rudder, elevators and ailerons), with flaps and pitch trim via spring on control column.

LANDING GEAR: Non-retractable tailwheel type standard, with bungee shock absorption. Steerable tailwheel. (Optional tricycle type, with steerable bungee sprung nosewheel.) Size 5·00-6 mainwheels (tyre pressure 2·07 bars; 30 lb/sq in); size 3·50-4 tailwheel (tyre pressure 1·38 bars; 20 lb/sq in). Optional floats and skis, disc brakes and bush tyres.

POWER PLANT: One 30 kW (40 hp) Rotax 447 two-cylinder two-stroke engine, with 2·58:1 reduction drive to a Shettler two-blade wooden propeller. One fuel tank in wing, capacity 19 litres (5 US gallons).

ACCOMMODATION: Pilot only, in semi-enclosed cabin. Optional side doors.

AVIONICS: Optional.

DIMENSIONS, EXTERNAL:

Wing span	8·99 m (29 ft 6 in)
Wing chord, constant	1·30 m (4 ft 3 in)
Wing aspect ratio	6·82
Length overall	5·18 m (17 ft 0 in)
Height overall	1·68 m (5 ft 6 in)
Tailplane span	2·29 m (7 ft 6 in)
Wheel track	1·83 m (6 ft 0 in)
Wheelbase	3·96 m (13 ft 0 in)
Propeller diameter	1·52 m (5 ft 0 in)

AREA:

Wings, gross	11·85 m² (127·5 sq ft)

WEIGHTS AND LOADINGS:

Weight empty	126 kg (278 lb)
Max T-O weight	255 kg (563 lb)
Max wing loading	21·48 kg/m² (4·4 lb/sq ft)
Max power loading	8·50 kg/kW (14·08 lb/hp)

PERFORMANCE:

Never-exceed speed	74 knots (136 km/h; 85 mph)
Max level speed at 610 m (2,000 ft)	67 knots (124 km/h; 77 mph)
Max and econ cruising speed	56 knots (105 km/h; 65 mph)
Stalling speed:	
power on, flaps up	18 knots (33 km/h; 20 mph)
power on, flaps down	13 knots (24 km/h; 15 mph)
power off, flaps up	22 knots (41 km/h; 25 mph)
power off, flaps down	18 knots (33 km/h; 20 mph)
Max rate of climb at S/L	366 m (1,200 ft)/min
Service ceiling	4,265 m (14,000 ft)
T-O run	12 m (40 ft)
T-O to 15 m (50 ft)	91 m (300 ft)
Landing from 15 m (50 ft)	99 m (325 ft)
Landing run	23 m (75 ft)
Range with standard fuel	112 nm (209 km; 130 miles)
Range with max payload	87 nm (161 km; 100 miles)
Best glide ratio	10·1
Min rate of sink, power off	107 m (350 ft)/min

RANS S-7 COURIER

RANS is offering for amateur construction a quick-build kit (150 working hours, approximately) for its new two-seat Courier. Following the general configuration of the Coyote, the Courier is fitted with dual controls and is therefore suited to training in addition to recreational flying and such utility tasks as agricultural spraying.

Design of the Courier by Mr Schlitter, with engineering assistance from Mr Steve Woods of Sport Flight Engineering, began in June 1985. Work on the prototype started simultaneously, and it flew for the first time in October 1985. The production of kits began in December of that year.

TYPE: Two-seat homebuilt aircraft.

AIRFRAME: Strut braced high-wing cabin monoplane. Fuselage and tail structure of welded 4130 steel, and wing structure of aluminium alloy, with all components supplied in finished form, including all welding, machining, moulding and stamping. Wing thickness/chord ratio 15%. Dihedral 1°. Incidence 2°. No sweepback. Half-span ailerons and flaps. Conventional wire braced tail unit, with trim tab on elevator. Wings fold for storage and transportation. Fabric covering overall, with pre-sewn wing envelopes.

LANDING GEAR: Non-retractable tailwheel type, with bungee sprung main legs, comprising side Vs and half axles, and steerable spring steel tailwheel. Mainwheels size 6·50-6; tailwheel size 4·50-4. Bush tyres and brakes standard. Optional floats and skis.

POWER PLANT: One 35 kW (47 hp) Rotax 503 two-cylinder two-stroke engine, with 2·58:1 reduction gear to a Shettler two-blade wooden fixed-pitch propeller.

ACCOMMODATION: Two persons in enclosed cabin, with dual controls. Upward hinged door, 1·52 m (5 ft) wide, on each side of cabin, can be locked open during flight. Baggage space, capacity 0·085 m³ (3 cu ft), with built-in cargo restraint.

DIMENSIONS, EXTERNAL:

Wing span	8·92 m (29 ft 3 in)
Wing chord, constant	1·55 m (5 ft 1 in)
Wing aspect ratio	5·66
Width, wings folded	2·44 m (8 ft 0 in)
Length overall	6·05 m (19 ft 10 in)
Height overall	1·91 m (6 ft 3 in)
Tailplane span	2·44 m (8 ft 0 in)
Wheel track	1·83 m (6 ft 0 in)
Wheelbase	4·88 m (16 ft 0 in)
Propeller diameter	1·73 m (5 ft 8 in)

AREA:

Wings, gross	14·03 m² (151·0 sq ft)

WEIGHTS AND LOADINGS:

Weight empty	168 kg (370 lb)
Max T-O weight	415 kg (915 lb)
Max wing loading	29·6 kg/m² (6·06 lb/sq ft)
Max power loading	11·86 kg/kW (19·47 lb/hp)

PERFORMANCE (at max T-O weight):

Never-exceed speed	104 knots (193 km/h; 120 mph)
Max level speed at 610 m (2,000 ft)	72 knots (134 km/h; 83 mph)
Max cruising speed	63 knots (117 km/h; 73 mph)
Econ cruising speed	52 knots (97 km/h; 60 mph)
Stalling speed:	
power on, flaps up	22 knots (41 km/h; 25 mph)
power on, flaps down	16 knots (29 km/h; 18 mph)
power off, flaps up	31 knots (57 km/h; 35 mph)
power off, flaps down	26 knots (49 km/h; 30 mph)
Max rate of climb at S/L	183 m (600 ft)/min
Service ceiling	4,115 m (13,500 ft)
T-O run	77 m (252 ft)
T-O to 15 m (50 ft)	137 m (448 ft)
Landing from 15 m (50 ft)	122 m (400 ft)
Landing run	93 m (303 ft)
Range with max fuel	299 nm (555 km; 345 miles)
Range with max payload	278 nm (515 km; 320 miles)

R.D.

R.D. AIRCRAFT

PO Box 211, Mayville, New York 14757
Telephone: (716) 753 2111
PRESIDENT: Robert G. Dart
ENGINEER: Emerson W. Stevens

R.D. Aircraft currently offers six aircraft in its line of microlights and homebuilts. These fall into two main series, known as the Skycycle series and the Skycycle Gypsy series, as follows:

R.D. SKYCYCLE and SKYCYCLE II

The Skycycle first flew in early 1982 and is marketed in plans, prefabricated kit, component and ready assembled forms. By March 1986, 23 kits and 27 sets of plans had been sold. A side by side two-seat trainer version with dual controls, known as the **Skycycle II**, was first flown in April 1984. The Skycycle II meets the requirements for two-seat microlight trainers under FAR Pt 103. Available in all the forms of the single-seater, three ready assembled Skycycle IIs and four sets of plans had been sold by March 1986.

TYPES: Single-seat (Skycycle) and two-seat training (Skycycle II) microlight aircraft; conform to FAR Pt 103 requirements.

AIRFRAME: Wire-braced parasol wing monoplane. Main frame and tail surfaces of welded steel tube. Wings have wooden spars, foam/wood ribs and double surface Dacron/Ceconite covering. Wing section: (Skycycle) RAF-6 modified; (Skycycle II) USA-35B. Dihedral (both) 2°. Incidence: (Skycycle) 2°; (Skycycle II) 3° 30′. Galvanised cable bracing. Welded steel kingpost standard. Three-axis control (rudder, elevators and ailerons).

LANDING GEAR: Non-retractable tailwheel type. Mainwheels size 4·10 × 3·5-4, pressure 1·03 bars (15 lb/sq in). Solid steerable tailwheel, size 2·5 × 1·1. Axle-beam suspension. Mainwheel brakes. Optional skis and floats.

POWER PLANT: One 15 kW (20 hp) Snowmobile two-stroke engine (or similar) with 2·25:1 belt reduction drive for Skycycle, and one 26 kW (35 hp) Cuyuna ULII-02 two-cylinder two-stroke engine with 2·4:1 belt reduction drive for Skycycle II, to two-blade wooden propeller. Alternative engines for the Skycycle are 15 kW (20 hp) Zenoah, 16·4 kW (22 hp) Yamaha 246 cc, 15 kW (20 hp) CGS Powerhawk and 18·6 kW (25 hp) KFM 107SR. Optional engines for the Skycycle II are 28·3 kW (38 hp) Kawasaki TA440 and 26 kW (35 hp) Rotax 377. Fuel capacity 19 litres (5 US gallons).

ACCOMMODATION: Pilot only (Skycycle), and pilot and passenger with dual controls (Skycycle II), in open cockpits.

DIMENSIONS, EXTERNAL (A: Skycycle, B: Skycycle II):

Wing span: A	9·65 m (31 ft 8 in)
B	10·77 m (35 ft 4 in)
Wing chord, constant: A, B	1·52 m (5 ft 0 in)
Wing aspect ratio: A	6·55
B	7·3
Length overall: A	5·99 m (19 ft 8 in)
B	6·02 m (19 ft 9 in)
Height overall: A	1·98 m (6 ft 6 in)
B	2·11 m (6 ft 11 in)
Tailplane span: A, B	2·39 m (7 ft 10 in)
Wheel track: A	1·32 m (4 ft 4 in)
B	1·73 m (5 ft 8 in)
Wheelbase: A	4·27 m (14 ft 0 in)
B	4·42 m (14 ft 6 in)
Propeller diameter: A	1·37 m (4 ft 6 in)
B	1·52 m (5 ft 0 in)

AREAS (A: Skycycle, B: Skycycle II):

Wings, gross: A	14·21 m² (153·0 sq ft)
B	15·89 m² (171·0 sq ft)

WEIGHTS AND LOADINGS (A: Skycycle, B: Skycycle II):

Weight empty: A	112·5 kg (248 lb)
B	152 kg (336 lb)
Pilot weight range: A	50-118 kg (110-260 lb)
B	55-154 kg (120-340 lb)
Max T-O weight: A	227 kg (500 lb)
B	326 kg (720 lb)
Max wing loading: A	15·96 kg/m² (3·27 lb/sq ft)
B	20·56 kg/m² (4·21 lb/sq ft)
Max power loading: A	15·22 kg/kW (25·00 lb/hp)
B	12·54 kg/kW (20·57 lb/hp)

PERFORMANCE (A: Skycycle, B: Skycycle II, at max T-O weight except where indicated):

Never-exceed speed:	
A, B	56 knots (104 km/h; 65 mph)
Max level speed: A	48 knots (90 km/h; 56 mph)
B	50 knots (93 km/h; 58 mph)
Max cruising speed: A	48 knots (88 km/h; 55 mph)
B	46 knots (85 km/h; 53 mph)
Econ cruising speed: A	30 knots (56 km/h; 35 mph)
B	36 knots (68 km/h; 42 mph)
Stalling speed:	
A, power on	21 knots (39 km/h; 24 mph)
B, power on	25 knots (47 km/h; 29 mph)
A, power off	24 knots (44 km/h; 27 mph)
B, power off	28 knots (52 km/h; 32 mph)
Max rate of climb at S/L: A	244 m (800 ft)/min
B	260 m (850 ft)/min
Service ceiling: A, B	3,660 m (12,000 ft)
T-O run (68 kg; 150 lb pilot): A	18 m (60 ft)
B (solo)	25 m (80 ft)
Landing run (without brakes): A	30 m (100 ft)
B (solo)	37 m (120 ft)
Range with max fuel: A	174 nm (322 km; 200 miles)
B	147 nm (273 km; 170 miles)
Endurance: A	4 h
B	2 h
g limits: A, B	+3·5/−2

R.D. SKYCYCLE GYPSY SERIES

This series encompasses four individual aircraft. The basic model is the **Skycycle Gipsy** single-seat microlight, conforming to FAR Pt 103 and derived directly from the Skycycle. It uses the same cable braced wings, with incidence increased to 5°, tail unit and rear fuselage. Though the divided main landing gear is of different arrangement, the wheel size remains the same, as do the power plant options, with the addition of the 20 kW (27 hp) Rotax 277. The engine cowling and forward fuselage are improved, and the wing bracing is revised. The prototype Skycycle Gypsy flew for the first time in early 1984, and this model is now available in the form of plans, kits, components and ready assembled aircraft. By March 1986 four kits and seven sets of plans had been sold.

The single-seat **Skycycle Gypsy II** prototype first flew in Summer 1985. It differs from the Skycycle Gypsy only in having its wings braced with tubular aluminium alloy V struts each side, instead of by means of a kingpost.

First flown in September 1985, the **Skycycle Cabin Gypsy** is similar to the Gypsy II but with slightly smaller dimensions, a fully enclosed cabin and standard use of a 20 kW (27 hp) Rotax 277 single-cylinder two-stroke engine with 2·58:1 reduction gearbox and Rotax propeller. By March 1986, two ready assembled aircraft and two sets of plans had been sold.

The fourth aircraft in the series is the **Gypsy Trainer**, the only two-seat model, with an enclosed cabin and a 30 kW (40 hp) Rotax 447 two-cylinder two-stroke engine as the only available power plant (with a 2·58:1 reduction gearbox and a Shettler two-blade wooden propeller). Fuel capacity is increased to 30 litres (8 US gallons). The prototype was scheduled to fly for the first time in Spring 1986.

DIMENSIONS, EXTERNAL (A: Gypsy, B: Gypsy II, C: Cabin Gypsy, D: Gypsy Trainer):

Wing span: A, B	9·65 m (31 ft 8 in)
C	8·97 m (29 ft 5 in)
D	9·35 m (30 ft 8 in)
Wing chord, constant: A, B, C, D	1·52 m (5 ft 0 in)
Wing aspect ratio: A, B	6·55
C	5·97
D	6·19
Length overall: A, B	6·20 m (20 ft 4 in)
C, D	6·17 m (20 ft 3 in)
Height overall: A	2·08 m (6 ft 10 in)
B, C, D	1·80 m (5 ft 11 in)
Tailplane span: A, B, C, D	2·39 m (7 ft 10 in)
Wheel track: A, B, C	1·37 m (4 ft 6 in)
D	1·68 m (5 ft 6 in)
Wheelbase: A, B	4·47 m (14 ft 8 in)
C, D	4·37 m (14 ft 4 in)
Propeller diameter: A, B	1·37 m (4 ft 6 in)
C	1·52 m (5 ft 0 in)
D	1·73 m (5 ft 8 in)

AREAS (A, B, C, D as above):

Wings, gross: A, B	14·21 m² (153·0 sq ft)
C	13·47 m² (145·0 sq ft)
D	14·12 m² (152·0 sq ft)

RANS Coyote without cabin doors

R.D. Aircraft Skycycle Cabin Gypsy microlight aircraft

R.D. Aircraft Skycycle Gypsy II microlight aircraft

RANS S-7 Courier homebuilt aircraft

R.D. Aircraft Skycycle Gypsy microlight with float landing gear

R. D. Aircraft Skycycle II two-seat microlight

R.D. Aircraft Skycycle single-seat microlight

WEIGHTS AND LOADINGS (A, B, C, D as above):

Weight empty: A — 112 kg (246 lb)
B — 111 kg (244 lb)
C — 114 kg (251 lb)
D — 159 kg (350 lb)
Pilot weight range: A, B, C — 50-118 kg (110-260 lb)
D — 55-154 kg (120-340 lb)
Max T-O weight: A, B, C — 227 kg (500 lb)
D — 363 kg (800 lb)
Max wing loading: A, B — 15·97 kg/m² (3·27 lb/sq ft)
C — 16·84 kg/m² (3·45 lb/sq ft)
D — 25·68 kg/m² (5·26 lb/sq ft)
Max power loading: A, B — 15·22 kg/kW (25·00 lb/hp)
C — 11·35 kg/kW (18·52 lb/hp)
D — 12·10 kg/kW (20·00 lb/hp)

PERFORMANCE (A, B, C, D as above):

Never-exceed speed:
A, B, C — 56 knots (104 km/h; 65 mph)
D — 69 knots (128 km/h; 80 mph)
Max level speed: A, B — 49 knots (90 km/h; 56 mph)
C — 55 knots (101 km/h; 63 mph)
D — 61 knots (113 km/h; 70 mph)
Max cruising speed: A, B — 48 knots (88 km/h; 55 mph)
C — 50 knots (93 km/h; 58 mph)
D — 55 knots (101 km/h; 63 mph)
Econ cruising speed:
A, B — 32 knots (60 km/h; 37 mph)
C — 35 knots (64 km/h; 40 mph)
D — 39 knots (72 km/h; 45 mph)
Stalling speed:
A, B, C, power on — 21 knots (39 km/h; 24 mph)
A, power off — 28 knots (52 km/h; 32 mph)
B, C, power off — 24 knots (44 km/h; 27 mph)
D, power off — 31 knots (57 km/h; 35 mph)
Max rate of climb at S/L: A, B, D — 244 m (800 ft)/min
C — 274 m (900 ft)/min
Service ceiling: A, B, D — 3,660 m (12,000 ft)
C — 3,960 m (13,000 ft)
T-O run (68 kg; 150 lb pilot): A, B — 18 m (60 ft)
C — 23 m (75 ft)
D, solo — 37 m (120 ft)
Landing run (without brakes): A, B — 30 m (100 ft)
C — 37 m (120 ft)
D — 46 m (150 ft)
Range with max fuel:
A, B, D — 174 nm (322 km; 200 miles)
C — 156 nm (289 km; 180 miles)
g limits: A, B, C — +3·5/−2
D — +3·8/−1·9

ROBERTS

ROBERTS SPORT AIRCRAFT

PO Box 9217, Yakima, Washington 98909
Telephone: (509) 457 4377

This company has developed an all-composites twin-boom light aircraft known as the Sceptre, in single-seat and side by side two-seat versions. These are available in both ready to fly and component kit form for home construction. The kits contain everything needed to build a Sceptre, including engine, propeller, instruments and interior furnishings.

The first prototype Sceptre I flew initially in November 1983, followed by the second in September 1984. The third aircraft that appeared at Oshkosh '85 was the production prototype.

ROBERTS SCEPTRE I

Components for the Sceptre are manufactured in female moulds from a sandwich material of glassfibre, pre-impregnated with epoxy resin, and Nomex honeycomb core. This ensures accurate aerodynamic shape, glass smooth surface finish and minimal maintenance requirements, combined with high strength to weight ratio.

TYPE: Single-seat homebuilt aircraft.

AIRFRAME: Cantilever mid-wing monoplane of composites construction. Wings built in three sections. Outer wings detach from centre-section for trailering and storage. Box beam spars of pre-impregnated and unidirectional glassfibre, and glassfibre/Nomex honeycomb sandwich skin covering, bonded with aircraft quality structural epoxy. Statically balanced ailerons of glassfibre/Nomex sandwich. No flaps or tabs. Crash resistant fuselage, moulded from glassfibre/Nomex honeycomb, with additional rollover protection built into canopy frame. Firewall between cockpit and engine. Twin tailbooms mounted at extremities of wing centre-section. Twin sweptback fins and rudders and interconnecting tip-mounted tailplane and elevator, of same construction as wings and ailerons. Control surfaces statically balanced. No tabs. Small ventral fin under extremity of each tailboom.

LANDING GEAR: Non-retractable tricycle type, with steerable nosewheel. Mainwheels and nosewheel carried on 4130 steel legs, with heavy duty oleo pneumatic shock absorbers and side Vs on main units. All three tyres 11·4-5. Hydraulic mainwheel brakes. Wheel fairings optional.

POWER PLANT: One 39 kW (52 hp) Rotax 503 aircooled two-stroke engine standard, driving two-blade laminated maple fixed-pitch pusher propeller through 2·6:1 multi-belt reduction drive. Spinner optional. Watercooled 48 kW (65 hp) Rotax engine optional. Integral fuel tanks in wings, total capacity 76 litres (20 US gallons).

ACCOMMODATION: Pilot's seat integral with fuselage structure. Four-point seat belt and shoulder harness standard. Cockpit ventilated. Cockpit heating available with 48 kW (65 hp) engine only.

EQUIPMENT: Standard items include tinted canopy, instrument panel with airspeed indicator, altimeter, tachometer, compass, slip indicator, dual cylinder head temperature gauges, exhaust gas temperature gauge, dual fuel gauges, and electric starter. Optional items include de luxe cockpit interior, increased ventilation, recognition and strobe lights, radio package and custom paint scheme.

DIMENSIONS, EXTERNAL:
Wing span 8·05 m (26 ft 5 in)
Wing chord: at root 1·52 m (5 ft 0 in)
at tip 1·99 m (6 ft 6¼ in)
Length overall 5·92 m (19 ft 5 in)
Height overall 1·50 m (4 ft 11 in)
Tailplane span 2·31 m (7 ft 7 in)
Propeller diameter 1·63 m (5 ft 4 in)

DIMENSION, INTERNAL:
Cockpit: Max width 0·70 m (2 ft 3½ in)

AREA:
Wings, gross 10·36 m² (111·5 sq ft)

WEIGHTS AND LOADINGS:
Weight empty 304 kg (670 lb)
Max T-O weight 474 kg (1,045 lb)
Max wing loading 45·75 kg/m² (9·37 lb/sq ft)
Max power loading 12·15 kg/kW (20·10 lb/hp)

PERFORMANCE (A, 52 hp engine; B, 65 hp engine):
Max level speed at S/L:
A 100 knots (185 km/h; 115 mph)
B 108 knots (199 km/h; 124 mph)
Stalling speed: both 39 knots (73 km/h; 45 mph)
Max rate of climb at S/L: A 198 m (650 ft)/min
B 228 m (750 ft)/min
Service ceiling: both 4,265 m (14,000 ft)
T-O run: A 122 m (400 ft)
B 92 m (300 ft)
T-O to 15 m (50 ft): A 168 m (550 ft)
B 137 m (450 ft)
Landing from 15 m (50 ft): both 198 m (650 ft)
Landing run: both 92 m (300 ft)
g limits +4·4/−1·7

ROBERTS SCEPTRE II

The Sceptre II is generally identical to the Sceptre I, except that the fuselage is widened to accommodate two persons side by side, and a 63·4 kW (85 hp) Limbach engine driving a Hoffmann propeller is standard. First flown in late 1985; production was expected to begin in January 1986, with deliveries from April that year.

DIMENSIONS, EXTERNAL: As for Sceptre I

DIMENSION, INTERNAL:
Cockpit: Max width 1·04 m (3 ft 5 in)

WEIGHTS AND LOADINGS:
Weight empty 363 kg (800 lb)
Max T-O weight 567 kg (1,250 lb)
Max wing loading 54·73 kg/m² (11·21 lb/sq ft)
Max power loading 8·94 kg/kW (14·71 lb/hp)

PERFORMANCE:
Max level speed 108 knots (201 km/h; 125 mph)
Stalling speed 42 knots (77 km/h; 48 mph)
Max rate of climb at S/L 244 m (800 ft)/min
T-O and landing run 122 m (400 ft)
T-O to 15 m (50 ft) 168 m (550 ft)
Landing from 15 m (50 ft) 198 m (650 ft)

ROTEC

ROTEC ENGINEERING INC

PO Box 220, Duncanville, Texas 75138
Telephone: (214) 298 2505
Telex: 288777 ROTEC DCVL
PRESIDENT: William W. Adaska
MARKETING CO-ORDINATOR: James E. Sigsbee

Formerly a helicopter engineer with Bell and Aérospatiale, Mr Adaska formed Rotec in 1975 and has been developing the Rally series of microlight aircraft since 1977. The seven aircraft that make up the Rotec range, available in kit form or ready to fly, are the Rally 2B, two-seat Rally 3, Rally Sport, Rally Champ, the enclosed cabin Panther, the Panther Plus and the Panther 2 Plus. By early 1986 Rotec had delivered more than 6,800 aircraft worldwide. A ballistic parachute recovery system is available on all Rotec models.

ROTEC RALLY 2B

Details of the earlier Rally 2 and Rally Marine can be found in the 1982-83 *Jane's*. The higher powered Rally 2B has a 26 kW (35 hp) Cuyuna engine as standard, and is professionally built for economical and reliable flying.

TYPE: Single-seat microlight aircraft; conforms to FAR Pt 103.

AIRFRAME: Braced high-wing monoplane. Main frame of anodised aluminium tubing, with single thickness Dacron covered wing and tail surfaces. Vinyl coated stainless steel cables. Kingpost standard. Three-axis control (spoilerons, elevators and rudder). Wing endplates optional. Rigid nose structure. Optional features include instrument panel.

LANDING GEAR: Tailwheel type, with 20 in diameter mainwheels and pneumatic tyres and two 5 in castoring tailwheels. No brakes. Optional snow skis and glassfibre floats.

POWER PLANT: One 28·3 kW (38 hp) Rotax 377 two-stroke engine, with new vibration dampened gear drive to a two-blade wooden pusher propeller. This replaces former 26 kW (35 hp) Cuyuna 430 engine as standard. Fuel capacity 13·25 litres (3·5 US gallons) standard.

ACCOMMODATION: Pilot only, in open position, on rigid seat. Optional windscreen and agricultural spray kit.

DIMENSIONS, EXTERNAL:
Wing span 9·45 m (31 ft 0 in)
Wing aspect ratio 6·2
Length overall 5·13 m (16 ft 10 in)
Height overall 3·15 m (10 ft 4 in)
Propeller diameter 1·37 m (4 ft 6 in)

AREA:
Wings, gross 14·40 m² (155·0 sq ft)

WEIGHTS AND LOADING:
Weight empty 98 kg (216 lb)
Max pilot weight 100 kg (220 lb)
Max T-O weight 208 kg (460 lb)
Max wing loading 13·04 kg/m² (2·67 lb/sq ft)

PERFORMANCE (with 79·5 kg; 175 lb pilot, 75% power except where indicated):
Never-exceed speed 43 knots (80 km/h; 50 mph)
Max cruising speed 35 knots (64 km/h; 40 mph)
Stalling speed:
full power 13 knots (25 km/h; 15 mph)
power off 16 knots (29 km/h; 18 mph)
Max rate of climb at S/L 152 m (500 ft)/min
Service ceiling above 3,050 m (10,000 ft)
T-O run, full power 23 m (75 ft)
Landing run 15 m (50 ft)
Range with max fuel 73 nm (135 km; 84 miles)
Endurance with max fuel 2 h 6 min
g limits +3/−1·5
Best glide ratio 7

ROTEC RALLY 3

The Rally 3, introduced in 1981, is a larger, side by side two-seat version of the 2B, to which it is otherwise basically similar except in having a 35·8 kW (48 hp) 497 cc Rotax two-cylinder two-stroke engine with gearbox drive as standard, horn balanced rudder and elevators, and a new patent-pending rough field landing gear with swing arms and optional 4 in 'tundra tyres'. Fuel capacity as for Rally 2B. Dual controls are standard, and wheel, float or ski landing gear can be fitted. A full range of options is available, including a glassfibre cockpit pod and agricultural spraygear. The Rally 3 is also suited to other utility tasks, such as ranching, aerial photography and security surveillance. The US Army purchased the Rally 3 for evaluation in 1983.

DIMENSIONS, EXTERNAL:
Wing span 11·58 m (38 ft 0 in)
Wing aspect ratio 7·6
Length overall 5·28 m (17 ft 4 in)
Height overall 3·25 m (10 ft 8 in)

AREA:
Wings, gross 17·65 m² (190·0 sq ft)

WEIGHTS AND LOADING:
Weight empty 129 kg (285 lb)
Pilot and passenger (max) 195 kg (430 lb)
Wing loading at 283 kg (625 lb) AUW 16·06 kg/m² (3·29 lb/sq ft)

PERFORMANCE (with 159 kg; 350 lb useful load, 75% power, full fuel, except where indicated):
Never-exceed speed 43 knots (80 km/h; 50 mph)
Max cruising speed 35 knots (64 km/h; 40 mph)
Stalling speed:
full power 18 knots (33 km/h; 20 mph)
power off 20 knots (36 km/h; 22 mph)
Max rate of climb at S/L, full power 137 m (450 ft)/min
Service ceiling above 3,050 m (10,000 ft)
T-O run, full power 30 m (100 ft)
Landing run 25 m (80 ft)
Range with max standard fuel 87 nm (161 km; 100 miles)
Endurance with max standard fuel 2 h 30 min
Best glide ratio 7

ROTEC RALLY SPORT

The Rotec Rally Sport was designed to withstand flight manual approved aerobatic manoeuvres, and is the *only* Rally approved for this type of flying. It appeared in 1983. Unauthorised aerobatics in the Rally 2B and Rally 3 can result in structural overload. The Sport combines the proven aspects of these earlier models with an airframe stressed to higher *g* limits, and also incorporates a number of advanced engineering features of its own. A parachute is required during aerobatics, and at least five hours of aerobatic flight time in a certificated aircraft is recommended before attempting aerobatics in the Rally Sport.

As with the other models, a wide range of customer options is available. More than 1,200 Rally Sports had been built by February 1986.

AIRFRAME: Generally similar in construction to Rally 2B, but stressed for higher load factors. Rudder and enlarged elevators are horn balanced as for Rally 3. Glassfibre cockpit pod and wing endplates optional.

POWER PLANT: One 35·8 kW (48 hp) 496 cc Rotax 503 two-cylinder two-stroke engine, with gearbox drive to a two-blade wooden pusher propeller. Fuel tank capacity 13·25 litres (3·5 US gallons).

DIMENSIONS, EXTERNAL:
Wing span 8·23 m (27 ft 0 in)
Wing aspect ratio 5·4
Length overall 5·05 m (16 ft 7 in)
Height overall 3·15 m (10 ft 4 in)
Propeller diameter 1·52 m (5 ft 0 in)

AREA:
Wings, gross 12·54 m² (135·0 sq ft)

WEIGHTS AND LOADINGS:
Weight empty 112 kg (248 lb)
Pilot weight range (incl parachute) 45·5-100 kg (100-220 lb)
Max wing loading 16·1 kg/m² (3·3 lb/sq ft)
Max power loading 5·66 kg/kW (9·3 lb/hp)

PERFORMANCE (with 79·5 kg; 175 lb pilot, 75% power and full fuel, except where indicated):
Never-exceed and max level speed 52 knots (96 km/h; 60 mph)
Max cruising speed 43 knots (80 km/h; 50 mph)
Econ cruising speed 30 knots (56 km/h; 35 mph)
Stalling speed:
full power 18 knots (33 km/h; 20 mph)
power off 20 knots (37 km/h; 23 mph)
Max rate of climb at S/L, full power more than 305 m (1,000 ft)/min
Service ceiling above 3,050 m (10,000 ft)
T-O run, full power 21 m (70 ft)
Landing run 23 m (75 ft)
Range with max fuel 72 nm (133 km; 83 miles)
Endurance with max fuel 1 h 30 min
g limits +6/−3
Min roll rate 150°/s
Best glide ratio 6·8

ROTEC RALLY CHAMP

The Rally Champ is a lower-powered, low-cost version (ready to fly or kit) of the Rally 2B. Options include wing endplates.

AIRFRAME: Similar in construction to Rally 2B. Control cables are constructed of Kevlar.

LANDING GEAR: Tailwheel type, with 20 in diameter mainwheels and 5 in castoring tailwheel. No brakes. Optional skis.

Roberts Sceptre I single-seat homebuilt aircraft *(Howard Levy)*

Rotec Rally 3

Rotec Rally Sport *(Howard Levy)*

Rotec Rally 2B amphibian

Rotec Rally Champ

Rotec Panther microlight, with semi-enclosed cabin

Rotec Sea Panther homebuilt cabin monoplane

POWER PLANT: One 20 kW (27 hp) Rotax 277 two-cylinder two-stroke engine, with gearbox drive to a two-blade wooden pusher propeller. Fuel tank capacity 13·25 litres (3·5 US gallons).

ACCOMMODATION: Pilot only, in open position. Optional cockpit pod.

DIMENSIONS, EXTERNAL:

Wing span	9·45 m (31 ft 0 in)
Wing aspect ratio	6·2
Length overall	5·13 m (16 ft 10 in)
Height overall	3·15 m (10 ft 4 in)
Propeller diameter	1·37 m (4 ft 6 in)

AREA:

Wings, gross	14·40 m² (155·0 sq ft)

WEIGHTS AND LOADING:

Weight empty	92 kg (202 lb)
Pilot weight range	55-91 kg (120-200 lb)
Max T-O weight	192 kg (424 lb)
Max wing loading	13·38 kg/m² (2·74 lb/sq ft)

PERFORMANCE (at 75% power except where indicated, with 79 kg; 175 lb pilot):

Never-exceed speed	43 knots (80 km/h; 50 mph)
Max cruising speed	35 knots (64 km/h; 40 mph)
Econ cruising speed	30 knots (56 km/h; 35 mph)
Stalling speed:	
full power	16 knots (30 km/h; 18 mph)
power off	18 knots (33 km/h; 20 mph)
Max rate of climb at S/L, full power	137 m (450 ft)/min
Service ceiling	3,050 m (10,000 ft)
T-O run, full power	30 m (100 ft)
Landing run, zero wind	15 m (50 ft)
Range with max fuel	74 nm (136 km; 85 miles)
Endurance with max fuel	2 h 20 min
g limits	+3·5/−1·5
Best glide ratio	7·5

ROTEC PANTHER

The Panther was introduced in 1984 as a third generation microlight of cabin type.

AIRFRAME: Strut braced high-wing monoplane. Mainframe of aluminium alloy, with double surface Dacron covered wings and tail surfaces. Stainless steel cables. Single 12·7 cm (5 in) diameter tailboom supporting the tail surfaces. Three-axis control (rudder, elevator and spoilers).

LANDING GEAR: Tailwheel type, with 16 in diameter mainwheels and 5 in steerable tailwheel. Air or spring suspension. Brakes, skis and floats optional.

POWER PLANT: One 20 kW (27 hp) Rotax 277 engine, with gearbox drive to two-blade wooden pusher propeller. Rotax 377 and 447 engines optional. Fuel capacity 19 litres (5 US gallons).

ACCOMMODATION: Pilot only, in semi-enclosed cabin, with Lexan windscreen. Baggage capacity 0·34 m³ (12 cu ft). Optional cabin heating.

DIMENSIONS, EXTERNAL:

Wing span	10·36 m (34 ft 0 in)
Length overall	4·88 m (16 ft 10 in)
Height overall	1·91 m (6 ft 3 in)
Propeller diameter	1·37 m (4 ft 6 in)

AREA:
Wings, gross 13·75 m² (148·0 sq ft)
WEIGHTS AND LOADING:
Weight empty 113 kg (250 lb)
Pilot weight range 45-91 kg (100-200 lb)
Max wing loading 13·7 kg/m² (2·8 lb/sq ft)
PERFORMANCE (with 79 kg; 175 lb pilot, 75% power and full fuel, except where indicated):
Never-exceed speed 53 knots (99 km/h; 62 mph)
Max cruising speed 50 knots (93 km/h; 58 mph)
Stalling speed:
full power 19 knots (36 km/h; 22 mph)
power off 21 knots (39 km/h; 24 mph)
Max rate of climb at S/L, full power 122 m (400 ft)/min
Service ceiling 3,050 m (10,000 ft)
T-O run, full power 37 m (120 ft)
Landing run, zero wind 23 m (75 ft)
Range with max standard fuel 149 nm (277 km; 172 miles)
g limits +4/−1·9
Best glide ratio 9

ROTEC PANTHER PLUS and SEA PANTHER

Rotec's follow-on aircraft to the Panther, the Panther Plus, is not a microlight but is covered by the FAA's Experimental homebuilt category. It is available in ready to fly form or as a kit with more than 50 per cent of the assembly to be completed by the purchaser. Construction takes about 40 hours.

The Panther Plus is said to be suited to military applications, in piloted or drone form. It is known that the company proposed a variant to the USAF as an airborne communications platform, with a multi-blade slow-turning propeller, engine muffler and IR suppression features, radar absorbent paint and composite materials replacing metal tubing in the airframe. Other applications could include observation and target acquisition.

The standard Panther Plus employs many of the features of the Panther, but has a fully enclosed cabin of refined configuration and is powered by a 31·3 kW (42 hp) Rotax 447 two-cylinder two-stroke engine with gearbox drive. Rigging time is about five minutes. A twin-float variant of the Panther Plus is the Sea Panther, with foam core glassfibre floats of 3·45 m (11 ft 4 in) length. The Sea Panther has a maximum speed of 69 knots (129 km/h; 80 mph), a cruising speed of 65 knots (121 km/h; 75 mph), a range of 152 nm (281 km; 175 miles), and a useful load of 152 kg (335 lb).

The description of the Panther applies also to the Panther Plus, except as detailed above and below.

AIRFRAME: As Panther but with fully enclosed cabin.
LANDING GEAR: Mainwheels size 4 × 13 in; tailwheel 2 × 4 in. Mainwheel brakes optional.
DIMENSIONS, EXTERNAL:
Wing span 10·36 m (34 ft 0 in)
Length overall 4·88 m (16 ft 10 in)
Height overall 2·06 m (6 ft 9 in)
Propeller diameter 1·52 m (5 ft 0 in)
AREA:
Wings, gross 13·75 m² (148·0 sq ft)
WEIGHTS AND LOADINGS:
Weight empty 134 kg (295 lb)
Pilot weight range 63·5-111 kg (140-245 lb)
Max T-O weight 286 kg (630 lb)
Baggage capacity 18 kg (40 lb)
Max wing loading 20·8 kg/m² (4·26 lb/sq ft)
Max power loading 9·14 kg/kW (15·00 lb/hp)
PERFORMANCE:
Never-exceed speed 74 knots (136 km/h; 85 mph)
Max level speed 65 knots (121 km/h; 75 mph)
Max cruising speed 61 knots (113 km/h; 70 mph)
Econ cruising speed 52 knots (97 km/h; 60 mph)
Stalling speed:
full power 19 knots (34 km/h; 21 mph)
power off 23 knots (42 km/h; 26 mph)
Max rate of climb at S/L 244 m (800 ft)/min
Service ceiling more than 3,050 m (10,000 ft)
T-O run 28 m (90 ft)
Landing run 23 m (75 ft)
Range with max fuel 152 nm (281 km; 175 miles)
Endurance 2 h 30 min
g limits +3·5/−1·5
Best glide ratio 9·5

ROTEC PANTHER 2 PLUS

The Panther 2 Plus is Rotec's latest aircraft, which is basically a Panther Plus with a lengthened cabin to provide tandem seating for a pilot and passenger. Both pilot and passenger have their own doors. Whilst the Rotax 447 engine remains the standard power plant, options are the 35·8 kW (48 hp) Rotax 503 and a 48·5 kW (65 hp) Rotax. Gearbox drive is standard. An auxiliary 13·25 litre (3·5 US gallon) fuel tank is offered to supplement the standard 19 litre (5 US gallon) tank. Options include floats (**as Sea Panther 2 Plus**), skis, wheel fairings, dual controls, electric starter, cabin heating, executive interior, Loran C navigation equipment, mainwheel brakes and baggage compartment. Agricultural spraying equipment is another recently qualified option of the Panther 2 Plus. Weighing 15·4 kg (34 lb), the equipment has a swath width of 14 m (45 ft) to cover 1·8 hectares (4½ acres) of land per minute. Interest has been shown also in utilisation of the Panther 2 Plus for various military applications, including battlefield surveillance, target acquisition, local reconnaissance and commando deployment. Lightweight systems and weapons can be installed.

Aircraft ordered after 15 September 1985 have full span ailerons, modified wing section and washout, an aerofoil contoured fin and aerodynamically balanced rudder, to improve yaw control, rate of roll and cross-wind landing. From the beginning of 1986 new air adjustable steel shock absorbers became standard to improve rough field capacity. Mylar fabric also became available for wing covering in January 1986.

TYPE: Two-seat cabin monoplane; conforms to FAA Experimental category.
DIMENSIONS, EXTERNAL:
Wing span 10·36 m (34 ft 0 in)
Length overall 5·59 m (18 ft 4 in)
Height overall 2·13 m (7 ft 0 in)
Propeller diameter 1·65 m (5 ft 5 in)
AREA:
Wings, gross 17·09 m² (184·0 sq ft)
WEIGHTS AND LOADINGS:
Weight empty 179 kg (395 lb)
Pilot and passenger weight range (combined) 136-208 kg (300-460 lb)
Max T-O weight 422 kg (930 lb)
Max wing loading 24·7 kg/m² (5·05 lb/sq ft)
Max power loading 11·79 kg/kW (19·37 lb/hp)
PERFORMANCE (standard aircraft, except where indicated):
Never-exceed speed 74 knots (136 km/h; 85 mph)
Max level speed 69 knots (129 km/h; 80 mph)
Max cruising speed 67 knots (125 km/h; 78 mph)
Econ cruising speed 56 knots (105 km/h; 65 mph)
Stalling speed: power on 21 knots (39 km/h; 24 mph)
power off 25 knots (47 km/h; 29 mph)
Max rate of climb at S/L: 2 crew 167 m (550 ft)/min
pilot only more than 274 m (900 ft)/min
Sea Panther 152 m (500 ft)/min
Service ceiling more than 3,050 m (10,000 ft)
T-O run 54 m (175 ft)
T-O run, Sea Panther 106 m (350 ft)
Landing run 38 m (125 ft)
Range with max fuel 173 nm (322 km; 200 miles)
Endurance 2 h 30 min
g limits +3·5/−1·5
Best glide ratio 9

ROTORWAY

ROTORWAY AIRCRAFT INC

7411 W. Galveston, Chandler, Arizona 85224
Telephone: (602) 961 1001

Mr B. J. Schramm formed the Schramm Aircraft Company in 1958, to market, in both ready to fly and prefabricated component form, a single-seat helicopter of his own design, named the Javelin. Details of this aircraft, which flew for the first time in August 1965, can be found in the 1967-68 *Jane's*.

Subsequently, a new company named RotorWay Aircraft Inc was formed to market to amateur constructors plans and kits of components to build Mr Schramm's single-seat Scorpion helicopter, described as a production version of the Javelin (see 1972-73 *Jane's*). After a period this aircraft was superseded by the two-seat Scorpion Too, now known as the Scorpion 133. A completely new two-seat helicopter named the Exec was introduced in 1980.

RotorWay currently offers Exec component kits for construction by amateur builders, the RW-152 engine, and a training programme for the constructor/pilot which covers flight training, operation and theory, and maintenance. New-start Scorpion kits are no longer available.

RotorWay has developed a new rotor blade system, which can be retrofitted to both the Scorpion 133 and Exec. All new Execs have as standard this 'hi-lift blade system' with asymmetrical aerofoil rotor blades. The main benefit is a dramatic improvement in power-off autorotation. Descent rates are reduced by several hundred feet per min over conventional systems. Additionally, due to reduced drag, the helicopter is more efficient with power on.

ROTORWAY EXEC

TYPE: Two-seat homebuilt helicopter.
ROTOR SYSTEM: Asymmetrical section two-blade main rotor. All-metal aluminium alloy blades are attached to aluminium alloy teetering rotor hub by retention straps. Teetering tail rotor, with two blades each comprising a 4130 steel spar and aluminium alloy skin. Swashplate for cyclic pitch control. Cable through rotor shaft to blades for collective pitch control. Optional elastomeric rotor hub.
ROTOR DRIVE: Drive from engine to countershaft via four dual power bands. Drive from countershaft to main rotor shaft via sprocketed triple-row chain. Tail rotor driven by 3 belts in tandem from countershaft. Overrunning clutch employed in countershaft assembly.
AIRFRAME: Basic 4130 steel tube structure for fuselage pod, with removable inspection panels. Monocoque tailboom of aluminium alloy. Small horizontal stabiliser, and a one-piece sweptback dorsal/ventral fin, are mounted on the port side of the tailboom.
LANDING GEAR: Tubular skid type.
POWER PLANT: One 113·3 kW (152 hp) RotorWay RW-152 watercooled flat-four engine, mounted vertically aft of cabin area. Standard fuel capacity 64·4 litres (17 US gallons).
ACCOMMODATION: Two individual seats, side by side in enclosed cabin.
EQUIPMENT: Optional equipment includes dual controls, elastomeric rotor hub, floats and agricultural spraygear.
DIMENSIONS, EXTERNAL:
Main rotor diameter 7·72 m (25 ft 4 in)
Tail rotor diameter 1·27 m (4 ft 2 in)
Length of fuselage 6·55 m (21 ft 6 in)
Height to top of main rotor 2·39 m (7 ft 10 in)
Landing skid track 1·55 m (5 ft 1 in)
WEIGHTS:
Weight empty 376 kg (830 lb)
Max T-O weight 599 kg (1,320 lb)
PERFORMANCE (at max T-O weight):
Max level speed 100 knots (185 km/h; 115 mph)
Normal cruising speed 82 knots (153 km/h; 95 mph)
Max rate of climb at S/L 366 m (1,200 ft)/min
Hovering ceiling, with two persons:
IGE 2,285 m (7,500 ft)
OGE 1,370 m (4,500 ft)
Range with max fuel at optimum cruising power 174 nm (323 km; 201 miles)

SANDS

RON SANDS INC

RD 1, Box 341, Mertztown, Pennsylvania 19539-9611
Telephone: (215) 682 6788

RON SANDS FOKKER Dr. I REPLICA TRIPLANE

Ron Sands Inc has available plans and kits to construct a full-size replica of the Fokker Dr. I First World War fighter. By late January 1986 ten kits and 120 sets of plans had been sold, from which eight kit built and ten plans built aircraft were already flying. The company also offers fully or partially assembled aircraft to special order.

TYPE: Single-seat homebuilt replica triplane.
AIRFRAME: Strut braced single-bay triplane, with I type interplane struts and inverted V cabane struts. Wooden fuselage and welded 4130 steel tube wings and tail unit, fabric covered. Göttingen wing section. No dihedral or anhedral. Incidence 2°. Ailerons on upper wing only. Triangular tailplane with elevators, and rounded rudder, without fin. Adjustable tailplane incidence, via skim washers.
LANDING GEAR: Non-retractable tailskid type; can use 6 in solid tailwheel. Size 710 × 90 mm mainwheel tyres; pressure 2·76 bars (40 lb/sq in). Mainwheels carried on side Vs and aerofoil section cross-axle, with bungee shock absorption.
POWER PLANT: Engines recommended are: one 112-134 kW (150-180 hp) Avco Lycoming O-320/O-360 flat-four; one 108, 123 or 138 kW (145, 165 or 185 hp) Warner seven-cylinder radial; or one 82 or 89·5 kW (110 or 120 hp) LeRhone nine-cylinder radial engine. Each drives a two-blade wooden fixed-pitch propeller. Fuel tank capacity 85 litres (22·5 US gallons). Two optional auxiliary tanks, each of 11·4 litres (3 US gallons). Oil capacity 15 litres (4 US gallons).
ACCOMMODATION: Pilot only, in open cockpit, with windscreen. Baggage space aft of seat, capacity 9 kg (20 lb). Two replica Spandau machine-guns, constructed of aluminium, on decking forward of cockpit.
SYSTEM: Optional electrical system.
DIMENSIONS, EXTERNAL:
Wing span: upper 6·73 m (22 ft 1 in)
centre 6·25 m (20 ft 6 in)
lower 5·77 m (18 ft 11 in)
Wing chord, constant 0·98 m (3 ft 2⅝ in)
Length overall 5·80 m (19 ft 0¼ in)
Height overall 2·87 m (9 ft 5 in)
Tailplane span 2·69 m (8 ft 10 in)
Wheel track 1·70 m (5 ft 7 in)
Wheelbase 4·45 m (14 ft 7 in)

Rotec Panther Plus in military guise

Rotec Panther 2 Plus with agricultural spraybars and pesticide tank and battery mounted outside the cabin

Saunders S-4 research aircraft in flight

Ron Sands Fokker Dr. I Triplane replica (Warner radial engine)

RotorWay Exec two-seat light helicopter

Prototype Saunders Jet Hawk jet-thrust homebuilt aircraft

AREA:

Wings, gross	18·75 m² (201·84 sq ft)

WEIGHTS AND LOADINGS:

Weight empty	544 kg (1,200 lb)
Pilot weight range	50-102 kg (110-225 lb)
Max T-O weight	726 kg (1,600 lb)
Max wing loading	38·7 kg/m² (7·93 lb/sq ft)
Max power loading (165 hp)	5·90 kg/kW (9·70 lb/hp)

PERFORMANCE (at max T-O weight):

Never-exceed speed at 3,050 m (10,000 ft) 139 knots (257 km/h; 160 mph)
Max level speed at 3,050 m (10,000 ft) 104 knots (193 km/h; 120 mph)
Max cruising speed at 3,050 m (10,000 ft) 96 knots (177 km/h; 110 mph)
Econ cruising speed at 3,050 m (10,000 ft) 78 knots (145 km/h; 90 mph)

Stalling speed: power off	31 knots (57 km/h; 35 mph)
Max rate of climb at S/L	549 m (1,800 ft)/min
Service ceiling	4,570 m (15,000 ft)
T-O run	91 m (300 ft)
T-O to 15 m (50 ft)	152 m (500 ft)
Landing from 15 m (50 ft)	122 m (400 ft)
Landing run	61 m (200 ft)
Range	217 nm (402 km; 250 miles)
Endurance	2 h 30 min

SAUNDERS

DON R. SAUNDERS

9913 NE Banton Avenue, Vancouver, Washington 98686
Telephone: (206) 573 3491

SAUNDERS S-4A JET HAWK II

Mr Don R. Saunders designed and built a single-seat research aircraft known as the S-4, to gain data for a projected low-cost jet sporting aircraft suitable for homebuilders. Design began in 1976 and, after thousands of hours spent in design and development, the S-4 flew for the first time on 25 December 1981. Having completed its test programme, the S-4 was dismantled in mid-1982. Work on the follow-on aircraft, known as the Jet Hawk, began thereafter, with emphasis on low cost and simplicity rather than high performance. It is approximately one-third smaller than the original S-4, and will be followed by the generally similar S-4A Jet Hawk II, with improved aerodynamics and higher performance. This represents the version to be offered in plan form to amateur constructors. All three models use a Mazda engine, driving a 0·71 m (2 ft 4 in) diameter fan.

The following details refer to the S-4A Jet Hawk II:

TYPE: Single-seat jet-thrust homebuilt aircraft.

AIRFRAME: Cantilever low-wing monoplane, with slight sweepback. Steel tube airframe, covered with foam and glassfibre. Two-spar wings with mass balanced near full-span horn balanced ailerons. Slender fuselage with pointed nose. Large air inlet on each side, above wing-roots. Cantilever tail unit with sweptback fin and narrow-chord rudder, tailplane and horn balanced elevators.

LANDING GEAR: Retractable tricycle type, with 5·00-5 in tyres on mainwheels that retract to lie flat between front and rear underwing fairings. Size 3·40-5 in tyre on forward retracting nosewheel.

POWER PLANT: One stock Mazda converted motorcar engine, or 224 kW (300 hp) Turbo Mazda, driving a five-blade wide-chord shrouded fan in rear fuselage to produce high velocity jet of air. Engine mounted in centre of fuselage. Pitch of fan blades ground adjustable. Fuel capacity 75 litres (20 US gallons) in tank behind pilot's seat.

ACCOMMODATION: Pilot only, on reclining seat under bubble canopy.

DIMENSIONS, EXTERNAL:

Wing span	7·32 m (24 ft 0 in)
Length overall	5·79 m (19 ft 0 in)

AREA:

Wings, gross	9·10 m² (98·0 sq ft)

WEIGHTS AND LOADINGS (A: with standard Mazda engine, B: with 224 kW; 300 hp Turbo Mazda engine):

Weight empty: A	385 kg (850 lb)
B	399 kg (880 lb)
Max T-O weight: A	567 kg (1,250 lb)
B	590 kg (1,300 lb)
Max wing loading: A	62·5 kg/m² (12·8 lb/sq ft)
B	64·9 kg/m² (13·3 lb/sq ft)
Max power loading: B	2·63 kg/kW (4·33 lb/hp)

PERFORMANCE (estimated):

Max level speed: A	147 knots (273 km/h; 170 mph)
B	217 knots (402 km/h; 250 mph)
Stalling speed: A	48 knots (89 km/h; 55 mph)
B	50 knots (92 km/h; 57 mph)
Max rate of climb at S/L: A	244 m (800 ft)/min
B	732 m (2,400 ft)/min

SEQUOIA

SEQUOIA AIRCRAFT CORPORATION

2000 Tomlynn Street, PO Box 6861, Richmond, Virginia 23230
Telephone: (804) 353 1713
PRESIDENT: Alfred P. Scott

Sequoia Aircraft Corporation was formed by Mr Alfred P. Scott to develop the Sequoia cabin monoplane. Work on this aircraft was begun in July 1975, with all design and engineering by Mr David B. Thurston, a consultant whose other designs have included the Colonial Skimmer (now the Lake Buccaneer), the Teal and Marlin amphibians, and the TA-16 Trojan/Seafire prototype amphibian.

Two variations of the basic Sequoia design are available. The Model 300 Sequoia is a side by side two-seat aircraft, with two aft-facing rear seats optional and a sliding bubble canopy. The Model 302 Kodiak is a four-seat aircraft with an enclosed cabin.

These aircraft have a high degree of commonality of parts. Plans and kits consisting of formed and machined parts have been produced and delivered to amateur constructors who are building the first examples of the aircraft. In early 1986, twenty aircraft were under construction and the company expected one to be flying in 1986. However, Sequoia has indicated that it might stop selling plans alone of the Model 300, concentrating instead on the full kits. At present, the Model 302 Kodiak is not offered as a full kit, as the fuselage has not been prepared in kit form.

In addition to the above, Sequoia Aircraft Corporation has offered both aircraft as military trainers to countries that wish to assemble their own aircraft, using local labour.

In addition, Sequoia is marketing plans and kits for construction of the Italian Falco F.8L light aircraft.

MODEL 300 SEQUOIA

TYPE: Two-seat homebuilt utility and aerobatic monoplane.

AIRFRAME: Cantilever low-wing monoplane. Wing section NACA 64_2A215 at root, NACA 64A210 at tip. Dihedral 3° from roots. Incidence 3° 30′ at root. Washout 2°. Wings have all-metal flush riveted structure with single I-beam spar, 2024-T4 Alclad ribs, 2024-T3 Alclad skin and glassfibre tips. Frise balanced ailerons of aluminium alloy construction with rubber seals. Slotted aluminium alloy flaps. Welded 4130 steel tube fuselage structure, covered entirely with lightweight shell of glassfibre/PVC foam/glassfibre sandwich, attached to tubing with glassfibre and epoxy resin. Conventional cantilever tail unit of flush riveted aluminium alloy construction. Elevators each fitted with trim tab. Rudder trim is bungee system.

LANDING GEAR: Retractable tricycle type. Electro-hydraulic retraction. Oleo-pneumatic shock absorbers.

POWER PLANT: One 224 kW (300 hp) Avco Lycoming TIO-540-S1AD flat-six engine, driving a Hartzell two-blade constant-speed propeller. Other Avco Lycoming engines of 175-224 kW (235-300 hp) may be used. Two integral fuel tanks in wings, with total capacity of 291·5 litres (77 US gallons). Provision for tip tanks of approximately 75 litres (20 US gallons) capacity each; and two underwing attachment points for additional fuel tanks, radar or stores of up to 272 kg (600 lb) combined weight. Refuelling points in wingtips.

ACCOMMODATION: Two seats side by side, beneath sliding Plexiglas canopy. An aft-facing rear seat can be installed to provide a two-plus-two layout. Baggage compartment, capacity 45·4 kg (100 lb).

AVIONICS: A completely flush antenna system is being designed. The nav antennae will be in the glassfibre wingtips and the remainder will be under the fuselage shell.

DIMENSIONS, EXTERNAL:

Wing span	9·14 m (30 ft 0 in)
Wing chord: at root	1·68 m (5 ft 6 in)
at tip	0·91 m (3 ft 0 in)
Wing aspect ratio	6·92
Length overall	7·62 m (25 ft 0 in)
Height overall	2·90 m (9 ft 6 in)
Propeller diameter	2·03 m (6 ft 8 in)

AREA:

Wings, gross	12·08 m² (130·0 sq ft)

WEIGHTS AND LOADINGS:

Weight empty	816 kg (1,800 lb)
Max T-O weight: utility	1,270 kg (2,800 lb)
aerobatic	1,088 kg (2,400 lb)
Max wing loading: utility	105·2 kg/m² (21·54 lb/sq ft)
aerobatic	90·1 kg/m² (18·46 lb/sq ft)
Max power loading:	
utility (300 hp)	5·67 kg/kW (9·33 lb/hp)
aerobatic (300 hp)	4·86 kg/kW (8·00 lb/hp)

PERFORMANCE (estimated):

Never-exceed speed	243 knots (450 km/h; 280 mph)
Max level speed at S/L	195 knots (362 km/h; 225 mph)
Max cruising speed at 2,440 m (8,000 ft)	185 knots (343 km/h; 213 mph)
Stalling speed: 'clean'	75 knots (139 km/h; 86 mph)
flaps and wheels down	60 knots (111 km/h; 69 mph)
Max rate of climb at S/L	664 m (2,180 ft)/min
Service ceiling	7,620 m (25,000 ft)
T-O run	457 m (1,500 ft)
T-O to 15 m (50 ft)	610 m (2,000 ft)
Landing run	548 m (1,800 ft)
Range at max cruising speed, with 45 min reserves	868 nm (1,609 km; 1,000 miles)

SEQUOIA MODEL 302 KODIAK

The Kodiak is a four-seat development of the Model 300 Sequoia, using the same wing assembly, tail unit, landing gear, power plant and mount, engine cowling, firewall, control system, instrument panel and windscreen. Wingtip fuel tanks can be fitted to increase range; gull-wing doors provide access to the enclosed cabin; and the aircraft is designed to be fully aerobatic.

Power plant is in the 186-224 kW (250-300 hp) Avco Lycoming IO-540/TIO-540-S1AD range, driving a Hartzell two-blade constant-speed propeller with a diameter of 2·03 m (6 ft 8 in). Empty weight will be 839 kg (1,850 lb); max T-O weight 1,451 kg (3,200 lb); fuel capacity 341 litres (90 US gallons).

SEQUOIA FALCO F.8L

Sequoia Aircraft markets plans and kits to build the Falco F.8L high-performance low-wing monoplane, designed in Italy by Ing Stelio Frati and first flown on 15 June 1955. The aircraft was last marketed in Italy by Laverda SpA. In its current form, for amateur construction, it incorporates significant improvements, such as increased fuel, a more efficient exhaust system, improved engine induction system, a propeller spinner and engine cowling of improved design, and a new instrument panel and electrical system.

The kits obtainable from Sequoia Aircraft comprise 23 separate packages which can be purchased collectively or, if the constructor wishes to spread the cost, be acquired as necessary. They do not include the engine, propeller, avionics, instruments, tyres and inner tubes. By late January 1986 a total of 422 sets of plans had been sold. Ten homebuilt Falcos had flown by that date. In addition, the Chilean Air Force has shown interest in the Falco as a trainer and has built a single example which flew for the first time in July 1985. This is being used as a demonstrator to attract possible orders for ENAER, the state owned aircraft company (see main Aircraft section).

The first homebuilt Falco, built from plans by Mr Laurence E. Wohlers of Tucson, Arizona, flew for the first time on 14 June 1982. The first Falco built from Sequoia kits (N545SF) was completed by Mr David A. Aronson of Minneapolis, Minnesota, and flew for the first time on 20 July 1984. The Falco built by Mr Karl Hansen in 23 months from plans and kits, powered by the standard 160 hp engine, demonstrated a cruising speed of 191 knots (354 km/h; 220 mph) before installation of the landing gear doors.

TYPE: Two-seat homebuilt monoplane.

AIRFRAME: Cantilever low-wing monoplane, built of aircraft grade Sitka spruce and birch plywood throughout, with exception of optional metal control surfaces and glassfibre wing fillets. Laminar flow NACA $64_2$212·5 wing section at root, NACA $64_2$210 at tip. Thickness/chord ratio 12·5% at root and 10% at tip. Dihedral 5°. Incidence at root 3°. Washout 3°. All-wood one-piece single-spar wings, built integrally with forward portion of fuselage and plywood covered, with overall fabric covering. Frise ailerons and electrically operated plain flaps can be of wood and fabric or all-metal construction. Optional leading-edge modification gives milder stall and slightly reduced cruising speed. Moulded glassfibre wing fillets. Plywood covered semi-monocoque fuselage, with wooden frames and longerons, fabric covered overall. Normally built in two sections, comprising a centre-section integral with the wings, and a tailcone; but can be built in one piece. Cantilever all-wood tailplane and fin integral with rear portion of fuselage. Rudder and elevators can be of wood and fabric or all-metal construction. Controllable trim tab in starboard elevator.

LANDING GEAR: Retractable tricycle type. Manual or optional electrical retraction, with mechanical emergency actuation. Oleo-pneumatic shock absorbers. Single-disc hydraulic brakes. Steerable nosewheel.

POWER PLANT: One 119 kW (160 hp) Avco Lycoming IO-320-B1A flat-four engine, driving a Hartzell constant-speed two-blade propeller with spinner, is standard for kit-built aircraft. Optional engines for which Sequoia offers installation kits are the 112 kW (150 hp) IO-320-A1A and 134 kW (180 hp) IO-360-B1E. Fuel in two metal tanks, capacity 151 litres (40 US gallons). Optional 7·6 litre (2 US gallon) header tank to permit inverted flight.

ACCOMMODATION: Enclosed cabin for two persons side by side. Pacific Scientific 40*g* five-point harness system. Rearward sliding transparent canopy. Dual controls standard. Cabin heated and ventilated. Baggage locker behind seats. Provision for fitting seat for a child of not more than 40 kg (88 lb) weight in baggage space.

SYSTEM: Electrical system of 12V, with either 35Ah Gill or 27Ah Globe battery. Prestolite 60A or 70A alternator. System used for cabin lighting, landing lights, navigation lights, strobes, etc.

AVIONICS: To customer's specification, with provision for IFR avionics. Completely internal antenna system optional.

DIMENSIONS, EXTERNAL:

Wing span	8·00 m (26 ft 3 in)
Wing aspect ratio	6·4
Length overall	6·50 m (21 ft 4 in)
Height overall	2·29 m (7 ft 6 in)

AREA:

Wings, gross	10·00 m² (107·6 sq ft)

WEIGHTS AND LOADINGS (O-320-B3B engine):

Weight empty	550 kg (1,212 lb)
Payload with max fuel	194 kg (428 lb)
Max aerobatic weight	748 kg (1,650 lb)
Max T-O weight	853 kg (1,880 lb)
Max wing loading	85·3 kg/m² (17·47 lb/sq ft)
Max power loading	7·17 kg/kW (11·75 lb/hp)

PERFORMANCE (119 kW; 160 hp engine):

Never-exceed speed	208 knots (386 km/h; 240 mph)
Max level speed at S/L	184 knots (341 km/h; 212 mph)
Cruising speed at 1,830 m (6,000 ft), 75% power	165 knots (306 km/h; 190 mph)
Stalling speed, flaps and wheels down	54 knots (100 km/h; 62 mph)
Max rate of climb at S/L	347 m (1,140 ft)/min
Service ceiling	5,790 m (19,000 ft)
Range at econ cruising speed	868 nm (1,609 km; 1,000 miles)

SILHOUETTE

SILHOUETTE AIRCRAFT INC

848 East Santa Maria Street, Santa Paula Airport, Santa Paula, California 93060
Telephone: (805) 525 4545
Telex: 324463 Task Research

Silhouette Aircraft is a division of Task Research Incorporated, which has itself been involved in the Northrop Tigershark and Lockheed TR-1 programmes, has produced materials for US Army helicopter rotor blades, and manufactured kits for the Rutan Long-EZ, Rutan Defiant and Viking Dragonfly homebuilts. Silhouette Aircraft offers to amateur constructors kits to build the SA-60 Silhouette, a single-seat sport and recreational monoplane that is designed and tested to FAR Pt 23 standards, and is simple and quick to construct, using pre-moulded components. The kit contains all that is necessary to build a Silhouette, including the engine, propeller and instrumentation. Bolt-on wing extensions are also offered to convert the Silhouette into a motor glider; a long-span RPV version has also been envisaged.

SILHOUETTE AIRCRAFT SA-60 SILHOUETTE I

Design of the Silhouette began in April 1984, when construction of a prototype was also started. This flew for the first time on 3 July 1984. In October that year the production of kits began and several Silhouettes built from kits have flown.

TYPE: Single-seat homebuilt sport and recreational monoplane.

AIRFRAME: Cantilever low-wing monoplane. Tapering surfaces with glassfibre spar, pre-cut foam cores, glassfibre skins and pre-moulded wingtips. Half span ailerons of composite construction. Centreline dive brake optional. Basically circular section fuselage of glassfibre and Nomex honeycomb construction, pre-moulded in halves with integral tail fin. Pre-moulded turtledeck, bulkheads, nose bowl, engine cowling covers and wingroot fairings. Conventional tail unit, with constant chord tailplane and elevators, fin and rudder. Tailplane has pre-formed spar. All surfaces of foam and glassfibre construction. Pre-moulded dorsal and ventral fins. Trim tab on elevator optional.

LANDING GEAR: Non-retractable tricycle type, with glassfibre legs and streamline wheel fairings. Cleveland mainwheels, size 5·00-5. Cleveland brakes.

POWER PLANT: One 30 kW (40 hp) Rotax 447 fan cooled two-cylinder engine, driving a 60 × 48 Aerotec fixed-pitch wooden propeller with spinner. Single fuel tank, capacity 38 litres (10 US gallons).

ACCOMMODATION: Single seat under pre-moulded one-piece canopy. Pre-moulded instrument panel.

DIMENSIONS, EXTERNAL:

Wing span: standard	9·75 m (32 ft 0 in)
with optional wing extensions	12·50 m (41 ft 0 in)
Wing aspect ratio: standard	13·47
Length overall	5·87 m (19 ft 3 in)
Height overall	2·03 m (6 ft 8 in)
Tailplane span	2·44 m (8 ft 0 in)
Propeller diameter	1·47 m (4 ft 10 in)

AREA:

Wings, gross: standard	7·06 m² (76·0 sq ft)

WEIGHTS AND LOADING:

Weight empty: standard	223 kg (490 lb)
Max T-O weight	351 kg (775 lb)

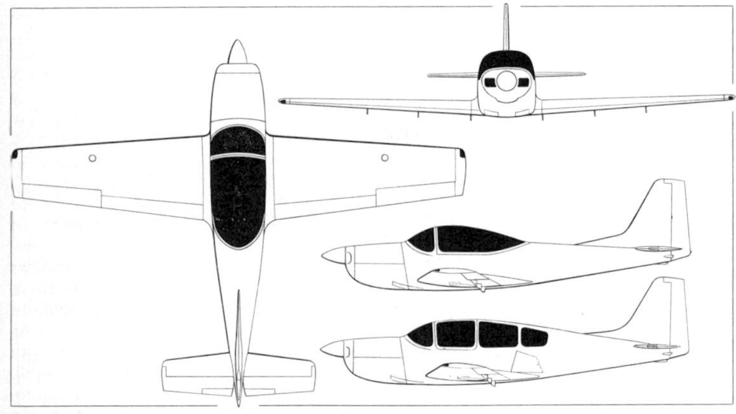

Model 300 Sequoia two-seat utility and aerobatic aircraft, with additional (lower) side view of Model 302 Kodiak *(Pilot Press)*

Long-wing Silhouette Aircraft SA-60 Silhouette I motor glider (foreground) and version with standard wings (rear) *(Howard Levy)*

Falco F.8L built from Sequoia kits, by Mr Jim DeAngelo of Wallingford, Connecticut

Max wing loading	49·8 kg/m² (10·20 lb/sq ft)
PERFORMANCE (standard wings):	
Never-exceed speed	147 knots (273 km/h; 170 mph)
Max level speed	117 knots (217 km/h; 135 mph)
Max cruising speed	104 knots (193 km/h; 120 mph)
Econ cruising speed	96 knots (177 km/h; 110 mph)
Stalling speed	42 knots (77 km/h; 48 mph)
Max rate of climb at S/L	244 m (800 ft)/min
Service ceiling	4,575 m (15,000 ft)
T-O run	244 m (800 ft)
Landing from 15 m (50 ft)	244 m (800 ft)
Landing run	152 m (500 ft)
Range with max fuel	more than 434 nm (804 km; 500 miles)
Best glide ratio	17·5

SIMPSON MIDWEST

SIMPSON MIDWEST ULTRALIGHTS

Route 1, Box 114, Fisk, Missouri 63940
Telephone: (314) 686 3578

SIMPSON LITTLE BI

The Little Bi has been advertised as an ultralight biplane, with conventional three-axis control, available in plans and kit forms for amateur construction. The aircraft's constant chord wings are strut and cable braced. The fuselage structure is of aluminium tubing with glassfibre and Styrofoam. Double surface Dacron covering. The tricycle landing gear has a steerable nosewheel.

The prototype Little Bi was powered by a 14·9 kW (20 hp) Cuyuna 215R engine, but a 20 kW (27 hp) Rotax 277 single-cylinder two-stroke engine is now believed to be standard for amateur built aircraft, driving a two-blade tractor propeller. Fuel capacity 16·3 litres (4·3 US gallons). No updated information for 1986 was received.

DIMENSIONS, EXTERNAL:	
Wing span: upper	7·32 m (24 ft 0 in)
lower	6·10 m (20 ft 0 in)
Length overall	4·57 m (15 ft 0 in)
AREA:	
Wings, gross	16·54 m² (178·0 sq ft)
WEIGHTS AND LOADINGS:	
Weight empty	93 kg (205 lb)
Max T-O weight	204 kg (450 lb)
Max wing loading	12·33 kg/m² (2·53 lb/sq ft)
Max power loading	10·20 kg/kW (16·67 lb/hp)
PERFORMANCE:	
Max level speed	43 knots (80 km/h; 50 mph)
Cruising speed	35 knots (64 km/h; 40 mph)
Stalling speed	18 knots (32 km/h; 20 mph)
T-O run	38 m (125 ft)

SKYHIGH

SKYHIGH ULTRALIGHTS INC

PO Box 64, Langhorne, Pennsylvania 19047

SKYHIGH SKYBABY

The Skybaby was designed as a low cost aircraft, for which plans and prefabricated component parts are available. Several hundred sets of plans have been sold.

TYPE: Single-seat microlight aircraft.

AIRFRAME: High-wing monoplane, with conventional tail surfaces. Constructed of aluminium alloy tube and plywood, with sheet steel and Dacron covering; braced by kingpost and stainless steel cables. Three-axis control system (ailerons, elevators and rudder).

LANDING GEAR: Tailwheel type, with two side Vs and half axles for the main units. Bungee suspension. Steerable tailwheel. No brakes.

POWER PLANT: Any suitable engine of 9-15 kW (12-20 hp), mounted aft of seat/wing support pylon structure with reduction drive to a two-blade pusher propeller. Prototype powered by McCulloch MC-101 engine; options include 15 kW (20 hp) single-cylinder Cuyuna 215. Fuel capacity 11·4 litres (3 US gallons).

ACCOMMODATION: Pilot only, in open cockpit.

DIMENSIONS, EXTERNAL:	
Wing span	9·75 m (32 ft 0 in)
Length overall	5·18 m (17 ft 0 in)
Height overall	1·52 m (5 ft 0 in)
AREA:	
Wings, gross	11·89 m² (128·0 sq ft)
WEIGHTS AND LOADINGS:	
Weight empty	70 kg (155 lb)
Max T-O weight	163 kg (360 lb)
Max wing loading	13·72 kg/m² (2·81 lb/sq ft)
Power loading (20 hp)	10·87 kg/kW (18·00 lb/hp)
PERFORMANCE:	
Never-exceed speed	43 knots (80 km/h; 50 mph)
Max level speed	35 knots (64 km/h; 40 mph)
Max cruising speed	30 knots (56 km/h; 35 mph)
Stalling speed	21 knots (39 km/h; 24 mph)
Max rate of climb at S/L	69 m (225 ft)/min
T-O run	61 m (200 ft)
Landing run	30 m (100 ft)
g limits	+5/−3 ultimate
Best glide ratio	9

SKYLINES

SKYLINES ENTERPRISES

1,100 Madison Lane, Salinas, California 93912
Telephone: (404) 398 3433

Skylines Enterprises is stated to be the world's largest manufacturer of microlight flying equipment. As detailed in the 1984-85 *Jane's*, Skylines Enterprises designed powered trike units, which could be attached to any USHGMA certificated hang glider. From available information it appears that Skylines also markets complete microlights as its Cosmos Dragsters, as detailed below.

SKYLINES COSMOS DRAGSTER 25 and 34

The Dragsters are powered trike units, with steerable nosewheels, attached to Cosmos hang gliders. A 24 kW (32 hp) Fuji Robin 340 cc engine is standard for the Cosmos Dragster 34, with 2·6:1 reduction drive to a two-blade wooden pusher propeller of 1·47 m (4 ft 10 in) diameter; the lower powered 13·4 kW (18 hp) 250 cc Robin engine is available optionally as the Cosmos Dragster 25. Fuel capacity is 9·5 litres (2·5 US gallons) standard; 19 litre (5 US gallon) tank optional. Single- and two-seat Cosmos Dragsters are available.

DIMENSIONS, EXTERNAL:	
Wing span	10·36 m (34 ft 0 in)
Length overall	1·75 m (5 ft 9 in)
Height overall	3·66 m (12 ft 0 in)
AREA:	
Wings, gross	10·96 m² (118·0 sq ft)
WEIGHTS AND LOADINGS (A: Cosmos Dragster 25, B: Cosmos Dragster 34):	
Weight empty: A	74·5 kg (164 lb)
B	84 kg (185 lb)
Useful load: A	123 kg (271 lb)
B	113 kg (250 lb)
Max T-O weight: A, B	204 kg (450 lb)
Max power loading: A	15·22 kg/kW (25·00 lb/hp)
B	8·50 kg/kW (14·06 lb/hp)
PERFORMANCE (A: Cosmos Dragster 25, B: Cosmos Dragster 34):	
Max level speed: A, B	41 knots (75 km/h; 47 mph)
Max cruising speed: A	27 knots (50 km/h; 31 mph)
B	30 knots (55 km/h; 34 mph)
Stalling speed: A, B	20 knots (36 km/h; 22 mph)
Max rate of climb at S/L: A	137 m (450 ft)/min
B	229 m (750 ft)/min
T-O run: A, B	28 m (90 ft)
Landing run: A, B	46 m (150 ft)
g limits: A, B	+6·9/−4 design

SKYOTE

SKYOTE AEROMARINE LTD

PO Box 808, Clark, Colorado 80428
PRESIDENT: O. E. Bartoe Jr

This company was formed to sell sets of plans and component parts for the Skyote aerobatic biplane. Its President is the designer of the aircraft.

SKYOTE AEROMARINE SKYOTE

Construction of the prototype Skyote (N8XX), with a 67 kW (90 hp) Continental C90F engine, began in March 1975 and the first flight of this aircraft took place on 23 April 1976. FAA certification in the Aerobatic category was applied for on 17 February 1977. At that time, components for five other aircraft were being produced. The first of these (N102DB, illustrated) was completed by Mr Duane Burnett of Boulder, and first flew in Summer 1978, powered by a

67 kW (90 hp) Continental C90-8 engine. Plans were made available to amateur constructors, together with wing and other material kits. By early 1986 a total of 60 sets of plans had been sold, but the design was withdrawn from the market temporarily in March 1986 pending resolution of the product liability situation in the USA.

Skyote serial number 001 (N25PB, illustrated in 1983-84 *Jane's*) was completed in July 1981 by Mr O. E. Bartoe. This aircraft is powered by an 88 kW (118 hp) Avco Lycoming O-235-K2A engine, and has a maximum rate of climb of 549 m (1,800 ft)/min.

TYPE: Single-seat homebuilt aerobatic biplane.

AIRFRAME: Braced biplane, with two parallel interplane struts each side and two pairs of centre-section support struts. Wing section NACA (1.8)412. No anhedral or dihedral. Incidence 2°. Sweepback on all wings at quarter-chord 7° 12'. Forward staggered upper wing. All structure of 2024 aluminium, with hydroformed ribs, fabric covered. Plain ailerons on upper and lower wings, torque tube actuated. Truss fuselage structure and wire braced tail unit of welded 4130N chrome molybdenum steel tubing, fabric covered. Ground adjustable tailplane incidence. No tabs.

LANDING GEAR: Non-retractable tailwheel type. Mainwheels carried on side Vs and half-axles. Type 1280HD bungee cord shock absorption. Cleveland mainwheels and tyres size 18 × 6·00-6. Tyre pressure 1·24 bars (18 lb/sq in). Cleveland hydraulically actuated disc brakes.

POWER PLANT: Aircraft used for FAA certification programme has one 88 kW (118 hp) Avco Lycoming O-235-K2A flat-four engine, driving a Sensenich two-blade fixed-pitch propeller. Other engines can be installed, including 67 kW (90 hp) Continental C85 or C90, or 74·5 kW (100 hp) O-200. Fuel tanks in wing centre-section and fuselage, each with capacity of 24·6 litres (6·5 US gallons). Total fuel capacity 49·2 litres (13 US gallons). Refuelling points in top of wing centre-section and top of fuselage. Oil capacity 7·5 litres (2 US gallons).

ACCOMMODATION: Single seat in open cockpit. Baggage compartment behind seat.

DIMENSIONS, EXTERNAL:
- Wing span: 6·10 m (20 ft 0 in)
- Wing chord, constant: 0·97 m (3 ft 2 in)
- Wing aspect ratio: 4·22
- Length overall: 4·95 m (16 ft 3 in)
- Height overall: 2·03 m (6 ft 8 in)
- Tailplane span: 2·03 m (6 ft 8 in)
- Wheel track: 1·22 m (4 ft 0 in)
- Wheelbase: 3·66 m (12 ft 0 in)
- Propeller diameter: 1·88 m (6 ft 2 in)

AREA:
- Wings, gross: 11·43 m² (123·0 sq ft)

WEIGHTS AND LOADINGS (Continental C90-8F engine):
- Weight empty: 269 kg (593 lb)
- Max T-O weight: 406 kg (895 lb)
- Max wing loading: 35·54 kg/m² (7·28 lb/sq ft)
- Max power loading: 6·06 kg/kW (9·94 lb/hp)

PERFORMANCE (Continental C90-8F engine):
- Never-exceed speed: 137 knots (253 km/h; 157 mph)
- Cruising speed: 97 knots (180 km/h; 112 mph)
- Stalling speed: 38 knots (71 km/h; 44 mph)
- Max rate of climb at S/L: 457 m (1,500 ft)/min
- Service ceiling: 5,030 m (16,500 ft)
- Range with max fuel: 180 nm (333 km; 207 miles)

SMITH

WILLIAM M. SMITH

Space 77, 7 Muldoon Road, Anchorage, Alaska 99504

SMITH CHANNEL WING

This aircraft embodies a single-channel version of the twin-channel wing configuration used on experimental aircraft built and flown by Mr W. R. Custer in the 1950s (see CCW-5 in 1954-55 *Jane's*). The concept was claimed at that time to offer STOL and even VTOL capability. Use of oversize tyres on the mainwheels and steerable tailwheel of Mr Smith's aircraft implies that it is intended for 'bush' operations from short, unprepared airstrips where such capability would be of particular value.

Few details of the Smith Channel Wing are known, except that it has a 134 kW (180 hp) Avco Lycoming engine, mounted in the rear of the fuselage pod and driving a propeller that turns inside the wing duct. The constant chord fabric covered wings are each fitted with a flap and large aileron extending over the full span. Tail surfaces, carried on twin booms, comprise small fixed fins and large horn-balanced rudders, and one-piece elevator with tab.

SMYTH

JERRY SMYTH

ADDRESS FOR PLANS: Wicks Aircraft Supply, 410 Pine Street, Highland, Illinois 62249
Telephone: (618) 654 7447

In February 1958 Mr Smyth began the design of a sporting monoplane that would be reasonably easy to construct, easy to fly, stressed to 9*g* for limited aerobatics, of good appearance and offering economic operation. Construction of the prototype began in January 1967. First flight of what Mr Smyth named the Model 'S' Sidewinder was made on 21 February 1969, and this aircraft received the 'Outstanding Design' award at the EAA Fly-in at Rockford, Illinois, in 1969. Plans and parts are available to amateur constructors.

SMYTH MODEL 'S' SIDEWINDER

The following description applies to Mr Smyth's prototype:

TYPE: Two-seat homebuilt sporting monoplane.

AIRFRAME: Cantilever low-wing monoplane. Wing section NACA 64-612 at root, NACA 64-210 at tip. Dihedral 4°. Incidence 1° 30'. No sweepback. All-metal structure comprising a centre-section and two outer wing panels. Built-up main spar of ·04 in 2024-T3 aluminium U-sections, to which flat aluminium capstrips are riveted; secondary spar is of formed sections. Eleven equally spaced ribs in each wing panel are made of ·025 in 6061-T4 aluminium. The wing skin, of ·025 in 2024-T3 aluminium, is in three sections: leading-edge, lower and upper skin, and is flush riveted. Wings filled with epoxy. Simple sealed-gap ailerons of aluminium construction, each attached to secondary spar by piano hinge. No trim tabs or flaps. Welded steel tube fuselage, with aluminium formers and skin. Electrically operated speed brake may be fitted on lower fuselage. Cantilever all-metal tail unit, with swept vertical surfaces. All-moving tailplane with electrically operated anti-servo tab.

LANDING GEAR: Non-retractable tricycle type. Wittman cantilever spring steel main gear. Mainwheels and tyres size 5·00-5, pressure 1·72 bars (25 lb/sq in). Nose unit carries a 10 in diameter wheel and smooth tyre, free castoring and non-steerable, pressure 1·72 bars (25 lb/sq in). Cleveland hydraulic brakes. Glassfibre fairings on all wheels. Aircraft have been completed with retractable landing gear (see 1975-76 *Jane's*) and tailwheel type landing gear (see 1980-81 *Jane's*).

POWER PLANT: Provision for installation of engines from 67-134 kW (90-180 hp). Prototype has a 93 kW (125 hp) Avco Lycoming O-290-G flat-four engine, driving a two-blade fixed-pitch aluminium propeller with spinner. Fuel tank in fuselage, forward of instrument panel, capacity 66·2 litres (17·5 US gallons). Refuelling point on top of fuselage, forward of windscreen. Provision for wingtip tanks. Oil capacity 7·5 litres (2 US gallons).

ACCOMMODATION: Pilot and passenger, side by side under rearward sliding bubble canopy. Compartment for 40·8 kg (90 lb) of baggage aft of seats. Cabin heated and ventilated.

SYSTEMS: Hydraulic system for brakes and, optionally, for operation of aerodynamic speed brake. Engine driven generator provides 35A 12V DC for instruments, lights, electrically operated tailplane tab and optional electrically driven hydraulic pump to operate aerodynamic speed brake.

AVIONICS: Simple 10-channel VHF com transceiver.

DIMENSIONS, EXTERNAL:
- Wing span: 7·57 m (24 ft 10 in)
- Wing chord: at root: 1·52 m (5 ft 0 in)
  - at tip: 0·91 m (3 ft 0 in)
- Wing aspect ratio: 6·85
- Length overall: 5·89 m (19 ft 4 in)
- Height overall: 1·66 m (5 ft 5½ in)
- Tailplane span: 2·33 m (7 ft 7¾ in)
- Wheel track: 1·70 m (5 ft 7 in)
- Wheelbase: 1·30 m (4 ft 3 in)
- Propeller diameter: 1·70 m (5 ft 7 in)

DIMENSIONS, INTERNAL:
- Cabin: Max width: 0·97 m (3 ft 2 in)
- Baggage compartment: 0·25 m³ (9 cu ft)

AREA:
- Wings, gross: 8·92 m² (96·0 sq ft)

WEIGHTS AND LOADINGS:
- Weight empty: 393 kg (867 lb)
- Max T-O and landing weight: 657 kg (1,450 lb)
- Max wing loading: 73·7 kg/m² (15·1 lb/sq ft)
- Max power loading: 7·06 kg/kW (11·60 lb/hp)

PERFORMANCE (at max T-O weight):
- Never-exceed speed: 173 knots (321 km/h; 200 mph)
- Max level speed at 610 m (2,000 ft): 161 knots (298 km/h; 185 mph)
- Max cruising speed, 75% power at 610 m (2,000 ft): 139 knots (257 km/h; 160 mph)
- Stalling speed: 48 knots (89 km/h; 55 mph)
- Max rate of climb at S/L:
  - at 0°C: 366 m (1,200 ft)/min
  - at 24°C: 274 m (900 ft)/min
- Service ceiling: 4,575 m (15,000 ft)
- T-O run: 244 m (800 ft)
- T-O to and landing from 15 m (50 ft): 610 m (2,000 ft)
- Landing run: 457 m (1,500 ft)
- Range with max fuel, no reserves: 369 nm (684 km; 425 miles)

SORRELL

SORRELL AIRCRAFT COMPANY LTD

16525 Tilley Road S, Tenino, Washington 98589
Telephone: (206) 264 2866

Sorrell Aircraft designed and built a small single-seat negative stagger biplane known as the SNS-2 Guppy, which first flew in 1967. The company offers a kit of component parts for its construction, while Mr Michael Kimbrel (see Kimbrel entry) sells plans only. Further details of this aircraft are given here.

Sorrell followed the Guppy with a two-seat aerobatic biplane named the SNS-6 Hiperbipe, with the intention of providing a true HIgh PERformance BIPlanE that would be suitable for construction by amateurs. Flight testing confirmed that the aircraft had an outstanding aerobatic performance and, when demonstrated and displayed at the 1973 EAA Fly-in at Oshkosh, it received the 'Outstanding New Design' award. Kits for the fully developed SNS-7 version are available to amateur constructors.

Sorrell's latest designs are the SNS-8 Hiperlight, Hiperlight EXP and the two-seat SNS-9 Hiperlight EXP II.

SORRELL SNS-2 GUPPY

In 1967 the late Mr Hobie Sorrell flew his SNS-2 Guppy cabin biplane for the first time, powered by a 13·5 kW (18 hp) OMC Cushman Model 200 engine, having begun its design in 1964. This 'back staggered' single-seater was purchased in 1971 by Mr Michael Kimbrel (see Kimbrel entry), who offers sets of drawings to amateur constructors wishing to build an SNS-2 Guppy. It can accommodate tall and heavy pilots even with the Cushman engine, but more powerful engines can be fitted and the prototype has also flown with Citroën, DAF and 24 kW (32 hp) Rotax engines. The Guppy is not aerobatic.

By early 1986 at least six Guppys had flown, powered by 27 kW (36 hp) Volkswagen, 18·6 kW (25 hp) Onan and 24 kW (32 hp) Global engines. Sorrell Aircraft itself offers a Guppy kit of component parts, which includes a 24 kW (32 hp) Rotax 377 engine, propeller and instruments.

TYPE: Single-seat homebuilt cabin biplane.

AIRFRAME: Strut braced single-bay biplane. Modified Grant X wing section. Thickness/chord ratio 10%. Dihedral 1° 30' on upper wing, 3° on lower wings. Incidence 2° on upper wing, 3° on lower wings. Negative stagger 28 cm (11 in). Wide chord welded steel tube I interplane struts and diagonal jury struts from lower wing roots to points approximately ⅔ span of upper wings. Conventional structure of wood, with a single spar, plywood D section leading-edge, balsa ribs with spruce capstrips (or plywood ribs), steel tube wingtips, and aluminium fittings and wing drag member, all covered with Dacron. Full span ailerons on lower wings only, of aluminium tubing with riveted aluminium skins. Wings do not fold. Conventional fuselage of spruce and plywood, covered with Dacron. Steel tube engine mounting. Wire braced conventional tail unit of welded 4130 chrome molybdenum steel tube, Dacron covered.

LANDING GEAR: Non-retractable tailwheel type. Wittman landing gear legs of 6150 spring steel rod. 5 in magnesium go-kart mainwheels fitted with 5·00-5 Beechcraft Bonanza nosewheel tyres. Solid castoring tailwheel, diameter 2¼ in.

POWER PLANT: Prototype has a 13·5 kW (18 hp) OMC Cushman Model 200 engine, driving a two-blade wooden propeller. Other engines of up to 27 kW (36 hp) can be fitted, including Volkswagen modified motorcar engines. Sorrell kit includes 24 kW (32 hp) Rotax 377 engine. Fuel capacity 23 litres (6·5 US gallons).

ACCOMMODATION: Single seat in fully enclosed cabin. Entry via hinged top and forward port side windows. Windscreen frame of steel construction.

DIMENSIONS, EXTERNAL:
- Wing span: 6·48 m (21 ft 3 in)
- Wing chord: basic: 0·91 m (3 ft 0 in)
  - at aileron: 0·94 m (3 ft 1 in)

Skyote Aeromarine Skyote (Continental C90 engine) *(Peter M. Bowers)*

Smith Channel Wing STOL 'bush' aircraft *(Neil A. Macdougall)*

Smyth Sidewinder (Avco Lycoming IO-320 engine) built 20% oversize by Mr G. Walker of Renton, Washington *(Peter M. Bowers)*

Sorrell SNS-7 Hiperbipe two-seat aerobatic biplane *(Peter M. Bowers)*

Sorrell SNS-2 Guppy built to plans

Sorrell SNS-8 Hiperlight *(Peter M. Bowers)*

Length overall — 4·70 m (15 ft 5 in)
Height overall — 1·57 m (5 ft 2 in)
AREA:
Wings, gross — 11·98 m² (129·0 sq ft)
WEIGHTS AND LOADINGS (prototype with Cushman engine):
Weight empty — 159 kg (350 lb)
Max T-O weight — 272 kg (600 lb)
Max wing loading — 22·7 kg/m² (4·65 lb/sq ft)
Max power loading — 20·15 kg/kW (33·33 lb/hp)
PERFORMANCE (prototype with Cushman engine):
Never-exceed speed — 78 knots (144 km/h; 90 mph)
Max level speed — 69 knots (129 km/h; 80 mph)
Cruising speed — 61 knots (113 km/h; 70 mph)
Stalling speed, power off — 26 knots (49 km/h; 30 mph)
Max rate of climb at S/L — 91 m (300 ft)/min
Absolute ceiling — 3,110 m (10,200 ft)
T-O run — 91 m (300 ft)
Landing from 15 m (50 ft) — 91 m (300 ft)
Range — 182 nm (338 km; 210 miles)
g limit — +4 recommended

SORRELL SNS-7 HIPERBIPE

Design of the Hiperbipe began in 1964; construction of the SNS-6 first prototype started in June 1971. This aircraft made its initial flight in March 1973; a second prototype, modified to the SNS-7 standard offered to homebuilders, followed in March 1975. Plans are not sold separately; a basic kit package, containing construction drawings for the aircraft and certain completed components, is available. By early 1986 at least 30 Hiperbipes were flying.

The following details refer to the second prototype:

TYPE: Two-seat homebuilt aerobatic biplane.

AIRFRAME: Braced single-bay biplane, of modified NACA 0012 wing sections. Dihedral 1° 30′ on lower wings only. Incidence 1° 30′ on upper wing, 2° 30′ on lower wings. Sweepback 4° 30′ on lower wings only. Wide chord welded 4130 steel I interplane struts and dual streamline section landing and flying wires. Conventional structure of spruce spars, web ribs and stressed plywood skin, fabric covered overall. Centre-section of upper wing is skinned with transparent plastics to allow improved view for aerobatics. Cambered wingtips. Four full span 'flaperons' of aluminium alloy sheet pop riveted to aluminium torque tubes. No tabs. Fuselage and wire braced tail unit of welded 4130 chrome molybdenum steel tube, fabric covered. Glassfibre engine cowling. Large dorsal fin. Tailplane and inset elevator extend aft of rudder trailing-edge. No tabs.

LANDING GEAR: Non-retractable tailwheel type. Wittman tapered spring steel rod main gear, with single wheel, glassfibre wheel fairing, and leg fairing on each unit. Cleveland 6·00-6 mainwheels, with low profile tyres. Maule 6 in steerable tailwheel. Cleveland hydraulic spot disc brakes.

POWER PLANT: One 134 kW (180 hp) Avco Lycoming IO-360-B1E flat-four engine, driving a Hartzell HC-C2YK-4AF two-blade constant-speed metal propeller with spinner. Fuel tank in fuselage, capacity 147·5 litres (39 US gallons). Christen 801 inverted oil system, capacity 7·5 litres (2 US gallons).

ACCOMMODATION: Two seats side by side in enclosed cabin. Dual controls standard. Forward hinged door on each side. Baggage capacity 36 kg (80 lb). Cabin heated and ventilated.

SYSTEM: Full electrical system, with lights.

AVIONICS AND EQUIPMENT: Narco Com 11A 360-channel radio.

DIMENSIONS, EXTERNAL:
Wing span — 6·96 m (22 ft 10 in)
Wing chord, constant — 1·016 m (3 ft 4 in)
Length overall — 6·35 m (20 ft 10 in)
Height overall — 1·80 m (5 ft 10¾ in)
Tailplane span — 2·87 m (9 ft 5 in)
Wheel track — 2·16 m (7 ft 1 in)
Propeller diameter — 1·93 m (6 ft 4 in)
DIMENSIONS, INTERNAL:
Cabin: Length — 1·40 m (4 ft 7 in)
Max width — 1·07 m (3 ft 6 in)
AREA:
Wings, gross (projected) — 13·9 m² (150·0 sq ft)
WEIGHTS AND LOADINGS:
Weight empty — 561 kg (1,236 lb)
Max T-O weight: Aerobatic — 766 kg (1,690 lb)
Normal — 867 kg (1,911 lb)
Max wing loading:
Aerobatic — 55·0 kg/m² (11·27 lb/sq ft)
Normal — 62·2 kg/m² (12·74 lb/sq ft)
Max power loading:
Aerobatic — 5·72 kg/kW (9·39 lb/hp)
Normal — 6·47 kg/kW (10·62 lb/hp)
PERFORMANCE (at max T-O weight):
Never-exceed speed — 195 knots (362 km/h; 225 mph)
Max level speed at S/L — 149 knots (277 km/h; 172 mph)
Max cruising speed at S/L — 139 knots (257 km/h; 160 mph)
Econ cruising speed — 130 knots (241 km/h; 150 mph)
Stalling speed:
flaperons down — 43 knots (79 km/h; 49 mph)
flaperons up — 51 knots (94 km/h; 58 mph)
Max rate of climb at S/L — 457 m (1,500 ft)/min
Service ceiling, estimated — 6,100 m (20,000 ft)
T-O run — 122 m (400 ft)
Landing run — 181 m (595 ft)
Range — 436 nm (807 km; 502 miles)

SORRELL SNS-8 HIPERLIGHT AND HIPERLIGHT EXP

Generally similar in overall appearance to the larger

Hiperbipe, the Hiperlight is claimed to be capable of limited aerobatics. As initially flown in mid-1983, its maximum level speed at full throttle exceeded that required to conform with FAR Pt 103. However, subsequent tests with a different propeller reduced performance to meet the FAA regulations for ultralight aircraft. More than 15 Hiperlights were flying by January 1985, when the last figures were received. The Hiperlight is available in kit, prefabricated parts or ready to fly form.

The **Hiperlight EXP** is generally similar to the basic version, has a more powerful Rotax 377 engine, basic instrumentation and hydraulic disc brakes as standard and Stits Poly-Fiber airframe covering. The EXP airframe requires only 75-100 working hours to complete.

TYPE: Single-seat microlight biplane; conforms to FAR Pt 103.

AIRFRAME: Strut braced equal span biplane with negative stagger. Wing framework and ribs are of welded aluminium alloy tube, with double surface Dacron covering. Cockpit/centre-fuselage structure of welded chrome-molybdenum steel tube, also Dacron covered. Rear fuselage and conventional tail surfaces of Dacron covered welded aluminium tubing. Full three-axis control system (full span 'flaperons', elevators and rudder). Optional instrument package available for Hiperlight.

LANDING GEAR: Non-retractable tailwheel type, with cantilever spring steel legs and low pressure 6·00-6 tyres; steerable 5 in tailwheel. Brakes on mainwheels. Optional floats and skis.

POWER PLANT: One 20 kW (27 hp) Rotax 277 single-cylinder two-stroke engine (Hiperlight) or 26·8 kW (36 hp) Rotax 377 engine (Hiperlight EXP), with reduction drive to a two-blade wooden tractor propeller. Fuel tank behind pilot, capacity 19 litres (5 US gallons).

ACCOMMODATION: Pilot only, in fully enclosed glazed cabin, with lower door transparencies for additional downward view.

DIMENSIONS, EXTERNAL:
- Wing span — 6·71 m (22 ft 0 in)
- Length overall — 4·72 m (15 ft 6 in)
- Height overall — 1·60 m (5 ft 3 in)
- Propeller diameter — 1·52 m (5 ft 0 in)

AREA:
- Wings, gross — 13·01 m² (140·0 sq ft)

WEIGHTS AND LOADINGS (A, Hiperlight; B, Hiperlight EXP):
- Weight empty: A — 111·5 kg (246 lb)
- B — 136 kg (300 lb)
- Max pilot weight: A — 104 kg (230 lb)
- Max T-O weight: A — 227 kg (500 lb)
- B — 250 kg (550 lb)
- Max wing loading: A — 17·43 kg/m² (3·57 lb/sq ft)
- B — 19·22 kg/m² (3·93 lb/sq ft)
- Max power loading: A — 11·27 kg/kW (18·52 lb/hp)
- B — 8·47 kg/kW (15·28 lb/hp)

PERFORMANCE (A: Hiperlight, B: Hiperlight EXP, with 77 kg; 170 lb pilot):
- Never-exceed speed: A — 82 knots (152 km/h; 95 mph)
- B — 74 knots (136 km/h; 85 mph)
- Max level speed: A — 55 knots (101 km/h; 63 mph)
- Max cruising speed: A — 52 knots (96 km/h; 60 mph)
- B — 65 knots (120 km/h; 75 mph)
- Stalling speed, power off:
  - A — 24 knots (44 km/h; 27 mph)
  - B — 26 knots (48 km/h; 30 mph)
- Max rate of climb at S/L: A — 183 m (600 ft)/min
- B — 305 m (1,000 ft)/min
- Service ceiling: A — 3,660 m (12,000 ft)
- T-O run: A — 46 m (150 ft)
- B — 38 m (125 ft)
- Landing run: A — 53 m (175 ft)
- B — 31 m (100 ft)
- Range with max fuel: A — 174 nm (322 km; 200 miles)
- B — 139 nm (257 km; 160 miles)
- Endurance with max fuel: A — 3 h
- *g* limits at max T-O weight: A — +6/−4
- B — +6/−3
- Best glide ratio: B — 11

SORRELL SNS-9 EXP II

First flown on 22 May 1985, the EXP II (N9EX) is the prototype of the SNS-9 side by side two-seat sport/trainer, with dual controls and basic instrumentation as standard. Like other recent Sorrell designs, it is a small back-staggered biplane. The strut and wire braced wings are made of pop riveted aluminium alloy, covered with Stits Poly-Fiber. The welded steel tube fuselage is also Poly-Fiber covered, with access to the side by side seats via the hinged port side panel of the large Perspex windscreen. The prototype is powered by a 31·3 kW (42 hp) Rotax 447 two-stroke engine with pull cord starting. Standard fuel capacity is 34 litres (9 US gallons). Assembly from pre-welded component kits is said to require 300 hours of work.

The EXP II flew 1,435 nm (2,655 km; 1,650 miles) cross-country from the Sorrell factory at Tenino, Washington, in order to participate in the 1985 EAA meeting at Oshkosh, Wisconsin.

TYPE: Two-seat homebuilt cabin biplane.

DIMENSIONS, EXTERNAL:
- Wing span — 7·11 m (23 ft 4 in)
- Length overall — 5·49 m (18 ft 0 in)
- Height overall — 1·63 m (5 ft 4 in)

AREA:
- Wings, gross — 13·75 m² (148·0 sq ft)

WEIGHTS AND LOADINGS:
- Weight empty — 162 kg (356 lb)
- Max T-O weight — 367 kg (810 lb)
- Max wing loading — 26·7 kg/m² (5·47 lb/sq ft)
- Max power loading — 11·73 kg/kW (19·29 lb/hp)

PERFORMANCE (estimated at max T-O weight):
- Never-exceed speed — 91 knots (169 km/h; 105 mph)
- Max cruising speed — 74 knots (136 km/h; 85 mph)
- Stalling speed — 34 knots (63 km/h; 39 mph)
- Max rate of climb at S/L — 183 m (600 ft)/min
- T-O and landing run on grass — 92 m (300 ft)
- Range with max standard fuel — 221 nm (410 km; 255 miles)
- Best glide ratio — 12
- Min rate of sink, power off — 1·64 m (5·4 ft)/s
- *g* limits — +3·8/−1·9

SPENCER

SPENCER AMPHIBIAN AIR CAR INC

11019-A Glenoaks Boulevard, Pacoima, California 91331
Telephone: (818) 899 1010

Mr P. H. Spencer, who made his first solo flight in a powered aircraft on 15 May 1914, has been associated with the design of several single-engined amphibians, dating back to 1930, when Amphibians Inc of Garden City, Long Island, NY, put the Privateer amphibian into production. This was followed by the Spencer-Larsen, Spencer Air Car S-12, Republic Seabee RC 1, RC 2 and RC 3, and the more recent Canadian Trident TR-1.

All of these designs were variations of Mr Spencer's basic Air Car configuration, on which he was granted a patent on 3 January 1950. This was originally a two-seat amphibian powered by an 82 kW (110 hp) engine, and was developed into a four-seat version, known as the S-12-C. Mr Spencer then completed the design of the more advanced S-12-D, of which plans are available to homebuilders as well as certain glassfibre mouldings and metal assemblies. Since that time development has continued, the installation of a Teledyne Continental Tiara 6-285 engine in the prototype (N111DA) resulting in a change of designation to S-12-E. The wing sweepback was also increased, from 3° to 5°. By January 1986, this aircraft had accumulated 2,000 flying hours, 1,500 of them with the Tiara engine.

The first S-12-E Air Car to be completed from Mr Spencer's plans made its first flight on 1 August 1974. By February 1986 thirteen Air Cars were flying, with two more expected to join them by April, including one built in New Zealand. A further Air Car was expected to fly later in 1986. Eleven of the completed aircraft are S-12-Es with the Tiara engine; one has a 149 kW (200 hp) Avco Lycoming IO-360 and the other a Continental E-185. Mr Spencer does not recommend an engine of less than 194 kW (260 hp) if full performance capability is required.

The sale of plans and kits continues, and Air Cars are being built in several countries, with a variety of power plants ranging from 149 to 224 kW (200 to 300 hp). By February 1986, eighty kits and 192 sets of plans had been sold. Only one plans built Air Car had flown by then, the remainder having been built from kits. Component parts available for purchase are produced at the address quoted, and include all metal parts, wing ribs and spars, and glassfibre components.

The landing gear system was recently redesigned for electrical operation, and the aileron and flap systems have been greatly simplified to reduce installation time by at least 50 per cent.

SPENCER AMPHIBIAN AIR CAR Sr MODEL S-12-E

TYPE: Four-seat homebuilt amphibian.

AIRFRAME: Strut braced high-wing monoplane, with single streamline-section strut each side. Specially designed STOL (modified NACA 4415) wing section. Dihedral 1°. Incidence 3°. Sweepback at quarter-chord 5°. Conventional two-spar wing structure of wood, steel and glassfibre. Frise ailerons of wooden construction, with trim tab. Electrically operated trailing-edge flaps. Glassfibre stabilising float mounted on strut beneath each wing at approximately two-thirds span. Conventional single-stepped hull with wood frames, longerons and skin, sheathed in glassfibre and Kevlar. Welded steel tube structure to provide wing and engine mountings and attachment points for landing gear. Cantilever tail unit, comprising conventional fin and rudder, and all-moving tailplane set approximately midway up fin. Combined anti-servo and trim tab in tailplane. Retractable water rudder in base of aerodynamic rudder.

LANDING GEAR: Electrically retractable tricycle type. Mainwheels retract aft to take up a near-vertical position on each side of the cabin. Nosewheel retracts forward through almost 180° and is partially housed in the nose of the hull, above the waterline, to form a nose fender. Cantilever spring steel main gear. Mainwheels and tyres size 7·00-6. Nosewheel and tyre size 6·00-6. Tyre pressure 2·07 bars (30 lb/sq in) on all wheels. Cleveland hydraulic disc brakes.

POWER PLANT: One 224 kW (300 hp) Teledyne Continental Tiara 6-285 flat-six engine or a similarly rated Avco Lycoming IO-540-K1A5, each with 2:1 reduction to a Hartzell HC-E3YR-7LF three-blade constant-speed reversible-pitch metal pusher propeller. Three fuel tanks, in fuselage and wing stabilising floats, with total capacity of 360 litres (95 US gallons). Oil capacity 8·5 litres (2·25 US gallons).

ACCOMMODATION: Four seats in pairs in enclosed glassfibre cabin. Backs of front seats fold forward to improve access. Rear seats fold back against bulkhead to provide cargo or baggage space. Baggage space in rear fuselage, aft of rear cabin bulkhead. Door on each side of fuselage, hinged at forward edge. Bow door on starboard side, hinged on centreline and opening upward. Dual controls standard. Accommodation heated and ventilated.

SYSTEMS: Hydraulic system for brakes only. Electrical system supplied by 24V 50A engine driven alternator.

AVIONICS AND EQUIPMENT: Complete IFR instrumentation. Bendix 360 nav/com transceiver.

DIMENSIONS, EXTERNAL:
- Wing span — 11·38 m (37 ft 4 in)
- Wing chord, constant — 1·52 m (5 ft 0 in)
- Wing aspect ratio — 7·57
- Length overall — 7·92 m (26 ft 0 in)
- Height overall, landing gear down — 3·58 m (11 ft 9 in)
- Tailplane span — 3·66 m (12 ft 0 in)
- Wheel track — 2·44 m (8 ft 0 in)
- Wheelbase — 3·10 m (10 ft 2 in)
- Propeller diameter — 2·13 m (7 ft 0 in)
- Cabin doors (port and starboard, each):
  - Height — 0·97 m (3 ft 2 in)
  - Width — 1·02 m (3 ft 4 in)
  - Height to sill — 0·86 m (2 ft 10 in)
- Cabin door (bow, starboard):
  - Length — 0·89 m (2 ft 11 in)
  - Width — 0·51 m (1 ft 8 in)

DIMENSIONS, INTERNAL:
- Cabin: Length — 2·59 m (8 ft 6 in)
- Max width — 1·14 m (3 ft 9 in)

AREA:
- Wings, gross — 17·1 m² (184·0 sq ft)

WEIGHTS AND LOADINGS:
- Weight empty — 993 kg (2,190 lb)
- Max T-O weight — 1,451 kg (3,200 lb)
- Max wing loading — 84·9 kg/m² (17·39 lb/sq ft)
- Max power loading — 6·48 kg/kW (10·67 lb/hp)

PERFORMANCE (at max T-O weight):
- Never-exceed speed — 147 knots (273 km/h; 170 mph) IAS
- Max level speed at 2,440 m (8,000 ft) — 135 knots (249 km/h; 155 mph)
- Max cruising speed at 2,440 m (8,000 ft) — 126 knots (233 km/h; 145 mph)
- Econ cruising speed at 3,050 m (10,000 ft) — 109 knots (201 km/h; 125 mph)
- Stalling speed, flaps down, power off — 39 knots (73 km/h; 45 mph)
- Max rate of climb at S/L — 320 m (1,050 ft)/min
- Service ceiling — 4,875 m (16,000 ft)
- T-O run from calm water — 213 m (700 ft)
- T-O to 15 m (50 ft) — 290 m (950 ft)
- Landing from 15 m (50 ft) — 305 m (1,000 ft)
- Landing run — 213 m (700 ft)
- Range, 65% power at 2,315 m (7,600 ft), 20 min reserves — 695 nm (1,285 km; 800 miles)
- Endurance — 7 h

SPIRIT ONE

SPIRIT ONE CORPORATION

PO Box 207, Georgetown, Texas 78626
Telephone: (512) 259 2436

SPIRIT ONE CORPORATION SPIRIT 1

Mr Al Datz has designed and built a very lightweight single-seat cantilever high-wing monoplane for sport flying. As can be seen from the accompanying illustration, it is of unique detail design although conventional in configuration. The entire airframe is covered in glassfibre, and the pusher propeller for the 30 kW (40 hp) Volkswagen modified motorcar engine turns within a narrow-chord shroud. Fuel capacity is 75 litres (20 US gallons). The one-piece elliptical wing has ailerons that travel only upward,

The more powerful Sorrell Hiperlight EXP *(Peter M. Bowers)*

EXP II prototype of the Sorrell SNS-9 sport/trainer *(Peter M. Bowers)*

Sport Flight Sky Pup single-seat microlight aircraft

Spirit One Corporation's unique Spirit 1 very lightweight monoplane *(Howard Levy)*

Squadron Aviation Fokker D.VII

The prototype of the Spencer Amphibian Air Car *(Don Dwiggins)*

and spoilers that can be operated both independently, for aileron turns with no adverse yaw and for improved crosswind handling, and collectively to function as speed brakes and reduce lift after landing and so offer better ground control. Wing section is NASA GAW-1. The fuselage is made of spruce and plywood, wrapped in glassfibre. The normal nosewheel landing gear can be supplemented by retractable floats to make the Spirit 1 suitable for amphibious operations. A motorcycle type 'buddy seat' can be fitted for a lightweight passenger.

The Spirit 1 is said to be simple to construct, requiring fewer working hours than many comparable projects. Plans are available to amateur builders, and it was planned to market kits.

DIMENSIONS, EXTERNAL:

Wing span	7·32 m (24 ft 0 in)
Length overall	4·73 m (15 ft 6 in)
Diameter of ducted fan	1·02 m (3 ft 4 in)

AREA:

Wings, gross	6·69 m² (72·0 sq ft)

WEIGHTS AND LOADINGS:

Weight empty	145 kg (320 lb)
Max T-O weight	340 kg (750 lb)
Max wing loading	50·8 kg/m² (10·4 lb/sq ft)
Max power loading	11·33 kg/kW (18·75 lb/hp)

PERFORMANCE (estimated):

Max level speed	65 knots (120 km/h; 75 mph)
Max cruising speed (70% power)	54 knots (100 km/h; 62 mph)
Stalling speed	25 knots (47 km/h; 29 mph)
T-O run	49 m (160 ft)
Landing run	38 m (125 ft)
Range with max fuel	347 nm (643 km; 400 miles)

SPORT FLIGHT

SPORT FLIGHT ENGINEERING INC

PO Box 2164, Grand Junction, Colorado 81502
Telephone: (303) 245 3899
PRESIDENT: Stephen K. Wood
VICE-PRESIDENT: Dennis Haimerl

SPORT FLIGHT SKY PUP

The Sky Pup is a second generation microlight, incorporating the concepts proven in the development of the earlier Blue Light Special (designed and built in 1980). It is offered in plan form for homebuilding, and is claimed to be simple to build and safe and efficient to fly. Average construction time varies between 350 and 450 working hours. By February 1986, a total of about 2,000 sets of plans had been sold.

TYPE: Single-seat microlight aircraft; conforms to FAR Pt 103.

AIRFRAME: Cantilever high-wing monoplane of wood and foam construction, with Dacron double surface covering on wings. NACA 43018 wing section. Dihedral 6°. Incidence 5°. Wings use wooden spars, hot-wire cut foam ribs, birch plywood D cell leading-edges and wood capstrips. Wings detach from centre-section for storage and transportation. Fuselage employs wooden bulkheads and longerons, and foam sheet panels, fabric covered overall. Conventional tail unit, with variable incidence tailplane. Two-axis control (elevators and rudder).

LANDING GEAR: Non-retractable two-wheel type. Size 20 × 2·125 mainwheels, with wood spring suspension. No brakes. Tailskid under rear fuselage.

POWER PLANT: One 20 kW (27 hp) Rotax 277 single-cylinder two-stroke engine, with integral 2·58:1 reduction gear to a Culver two-blade wooden propeller. Wide variety of other engines in 13·5-20 kW (18-27 hp) class being fitted by homebuilders. Fuel capacity 9·5 litres (2·5 US gallons).

ACCOMMODATION: Pilot only, in open cockpit.

DIMENSIONS, EXTERNAL:

Wing span	9·45 m (31 ft 0 in)
Wing chord, constant	1·27 m (4 ft 2 in)
Wing aspect ratio	7·39
Length overall	4·85 m (15 ft 11 in)
Height overall	1·32 m (4 ft 4 in)
Tailplane span	1·88 m (6 ft 2 in)
Wheel track	1·52 m (5 ft 0 in)
Propeller diameter	1·52 m (5 ft 0 in)

AREA:

Wings, gross	12·08 m² (130·0 sq ft)

WEIGHTS AND LOADINGS:

Weight empty	91 kg (200 lb)
Max pilot weight	86 kg (190 lb)
Max T-O weight	182 kg (400 lb)
Max wing loading	15·04 kg/m² (3·08 lb/sq ft)
Max power loading	9·02 kg/kW (14·81 lb/hp)

PERFORMANCE:

Never-exceed speed	60 knots (111 km/h; 69 mph)
Max level speed	53 knots (98 km/h; 61 mph)
Max cruising speed	49 knots (92 km/h; 57 mph)
Econ cruising speed	45 knots (84 km/h; 52 mph)
Stalling speed	23 knots (42 km/h; 26 mph)
Max rate of climb at S/L	244 m (800 ft)/min
Service ceiling	6,100 m (20,000 ft)
T-O run	46 m (150 ft)
Landing run	76 m (250 ft)
Range with max fuel	104 nm (193 km; 120 miles)
Endurance with max fuel	2 h
g limits	+3·8/−1·9 design +6/−3 ultimate
Best glide ratio	12
Min rate of sink, power off	79 m (260 ft)/min

SQUADRON

SQUADRON AVIATION INC

PO Box 23276, Columbus, Ohio 43226
Telephone: (614) 497 1123
PRESIDENT: W. G. McDermitt

This company markets kits of scale representations of First World War aircraft, including the Fokker D.VII, S.E.5A and Spad S.XIII. Ready to fly versions are also available. These can operate as homebuilt aircraft, or as microlights under FAR Pt 103 if built within regulations. The following description applies to the Fokker D.VII, which is typical of the series. A total of 41 kits had been delivered, and about 35 assembled, by January 1986.

SQUADRON AVIATION FOKKER D.VII

TYPE: Single-seat fighter representation: conforms to FAR Pt 103 microlight regulations.

AIRFRAME: Strut and wire braced biplane. Built of aluminium alloy, with Dacron covering. Stainless steel cables. Wing dihedral 3° 30′. Incidence 1° 30′. Cruciform tail surfaces, incorporating triangular tailplane and fin. Three-axis control (spoilers, elevators and horn balanced rounded rudder).

LANDING GEAR: Non-retractable two-wheel type, with 20 in diameter mainwheels on side Vs and cross-axle, and bungee suspension. Tyre pressure 1·52 bars (22 lb/sq in). Tailskid. Mainwheel brakes. Options include differentially actuated disc brakes and steerable tailwheel.

POWER PLANT: One 26 kW (35 hp) Cuyuna ULII-02 two-cylinder two-stroke engine, with 3:1 reduction drive to an Aerotec two-blade wooden propeller. Fuel tank capacity 19 litres (5 US gallons). Optional Rotax 377 engine.

ACCOMMODATION: Pilot only, in open cockpit with windscreen.

DIMENSIONS, EXTERNAL:

Wing span	7·31 m (24 ft 0 in)
Wing chord, constant	1·07 m (3 ft 6 in)
Length overall	4·88 m (16 ft 0 in)
Height overall	1·93 m (6 ft 4 in)
Tailplane span	2·44 m (8 ft 0 in)
Wheel track	1·22 m (4 ft 0 in)
Wheelbase	3·66 m (12 ft 0 in)
Propeller diameter	1·83 m (6 ft 0 in)

AREA:

Wings, gross	15·61 m² (168·0 sq ft)

WEIGHTS AND LOADINGS:

Weight empty	113 kg (250 lb)
Max pilot weight	102 kg (225 lb)
Max T-O weight	238 kg (525 lb)
Max wing loading	15·25 kg/m² (3·12 lb/sq ft)
Max power loading	9·13 kg/kW (15·00 lb/hp)

PERFORMANCE:

Never-exceed speed	73 knots (136 km/h; 85 mph)
Max level speed	54 knots (101 km/h; 63 mph)
Max and econ cruising speed	45 knots (84 km/h; 52 mph)
Stalling speed	16 knots (29 km/h; 18 mph)
Max rate of climb at S/L	305 m (1,000 ft)/min
Service ceiling	3,810 m (12,500 ft)
T-O run	15 m (50 ft)
T-O to 15 m (50 ft)	31 m (100 ft)
Landing from 15 m (50 ft)	61 m (200 ft)
Landing run	46 m (150 ft)
Range	86·5-173 nm (161-322 km; 100-200 miles)
g limits	+4/−2
Best glide ratio	6·5

STAR FLIGHT

STAR FLIGHT AIRCRAFT

Liberty Landing Airport, Route 3, Box 197, Liberty, Missouri 64066
Telephone: (816) 781 2250
PRESIDENT: Richard Turner

Star Flight's original weight shift Starfire was followed in 1982 by the three-axis Tri-Star and in 1983 by the Super Star, which were both described and illustrated in the 1983-84 *Jane's*. The TX1000, detailed in the 1984-85 *Jane's*, is also out of production. Star Flight's current aircraft are the XC 280, XC 320 and XC 2000. These are basically similar in construction, though the tandem two-seat XC 2000 has larger diameter wing spars and heavier cables.

STAR FLIGHT XC SERIES

The **XC 280 Stiletto**, the basic model of the XC range with a Rotax 377 engine and smallest wing span, was flown at the Sun 'n Fun Fly-in in 1984. With a greater wing area the aircraft becomes the **XC 320**. The **XC 2000** combines the larger wing area of the XC 320 with a more powerful Rotax 447 engine, a heavier airframe and two-seat accommodation. Options for the XC 2000 include cropspraying equipment, when the aircraft is known as the XC 2000 **AgLite** and is flown as a single-seater.

Each aircraft of the XC series is available in plans form, as component parts, or as a kit. The XC 2000 kit is approved by the FAA for amateur built 'Experimental' status.

TYPE: Single- and two-seat microlights; conform to FAR Pt 103.

AIRFRAME: Braced high-wing monoplane. Mainframe of aluminium alloy tubing, with black anodised and black gloss epoxy coating. Single surface Dacron covering on wings and tail unit. Vinyl coated stainless steel cables. Three-axis control (spoilers, elevators and rudder).

LANDING GEAR: Tricycle type, with 4·00-5 mainwheel and nosewheel tyres. Nosewheel steerable. Options include wheel fairings and floats.

POWER PLANT: XC 280 and XC 320: One 24 kW (32 hp) Rotax 377 two-cylinder two-stroke engine, with 2·58 reduction drive to a two-blade wooden pusher propeller; 20 kW (27 hp) Rotax 277 single-cylinder two-stroke engine optional. XC 2000: One 30 kW (40 hp) Rotax 447 two-cylinder two-stroke engine, with 2·58:1 reduction gear to a two-blade wooden pusher propeller. AgLite believed to have four-blade propeller. Fuel tank capacity 19 litres (5 US gallons).

ACCOMMODATION: Pilot, or pilot and passenger, in open position. Glassfibre cockpit pod with windscreen optional, as are dual controls for XC 2000.

DIMENSIONS, EXTERNAL (A: XC 280, B: XC 320, C: XC 2000):

Wing span: A	8·69 m (28 ft 6 in)
B	9·91 m (32 ft 6 in)
Wing aspect ratio: A	6
B	7
Length overall: A, B, C	5·18 m (17 ft 0 in)
Height overall: A, B, C	2·44 m (8 ft 0 in)
Propeller diameter: A, B, C	1·52 m (5 ft 0 in)

AREA (A: XC 280, B: XC 320, C: XC 2000):

Wings, gross: A	13·66 m² (147·0 sq ft)
B, C	15·33 m² (165·0 sq ft)

WEIGHTS AND LOADINGS (A: XC 280, B: XC 320, C: XC 2000):

Weight empty: A	107 kg (235 lb)
B	113 kg (250 lb)
C	143 kg (314 lb)
Pilot weight range:	
A, B	59-113 kg (130-250 lb)
Crew weight range:	
C	59-204 kg (130-450 lb)
Max T-O weight: A, B	227 kg (500 lb)
C	340 kg (750 lb)
Max wing loading: A	15·33 kg/m² (3·14 lb/sq ft)
C	21·04 kg/m² (4·31 lb/sq ft)
Max power loading: A, B	9·46 kg/kW (15·63 lb/hp)
C	11·33 kg/kW (18·75 lb/hp)

PERFORMANCE (A: XC 280, B: XC 320, C: XC 2000):

Never-exceed speed:	
A, C	56 knots (104 km/h; 65 mph)
B	47 knots (88 km/h; 55 mph)
Max level speed: A	42 knots (77 km/h; 48 mph)
B	36 knots (68 km/h; 42 mph)
C	39 knots (72 km/h; 45 mph)
Stalling speed:	
A, power on	20 knots (37 km/h; 23 mph)
B, power on	18 knots (32 km/h; 20 mph)
C, power on	21 knots (39 km/h; 24 mph)
A, power off	23 knots (42 km/h; 26 mph)
B, power off	21 knots (39 km/h; 24 mph)
C, power off	25 knots (45 km/h; 28 mph)
Max rate of climb at S/L: A, C	183 m (600 ft)/min
B	244 m (800 ft)/min
Service ceiling: A, B, C	4,575 m (15,000 ft)
T-O run: A	61 m (200 ft)
B	38 m (125 ft)
C	76 m (250 ft)
Landing run: A, B, C	61 m (200 ft)
Range with max fuel: A	78 nm (145 km; 90 miles)
B	69 nm (128 km; 80 miles)
C	39 nm (72 km; 45 miles)
g limits: A, B, C	+6/−4 ultimate

STAR-LITE

STAR-LITE AIRCRAFT INC

2219 Orange Blossom, San Antonio, Texas 78247
Telephone: (512) 494 9812
PRESIDENT: Mark D. Brown

STAR-LITE AIRCRAFT STAR-LITE SL-1

Mr Mark Brown, a professional aerospace engineer with the Fairchild Aircraft Corporation, has formed Star-Lite Aircraft to market kits of component parts and construction manuals of his Star-Lite SL-1 sporting monoplane. It was designed to be lightweight, through use of vacuum moulded sandwich composite materials, and economical to operate.

Design of the Star-Lite began on 15 January 1980 and construction of the prototype (N88SL) started on 17 February 1982. This aircraft flew for the first time on 17 May 1983, with a 15 kW (20 hp) Zenoah 250 engine. At Oshkosh '83, the Star-Lite won the 'Outstanding New Design' award, and at the same meeting took first place against fifteen other flight tested aircraft in the ARV (Air Recreation Vehicle) design competition organised by *The Western Flyer* magazine and sponsored by Dupont Kevlar Division, the EAA, AOPA and other organisations. By winning the ARV competition for aircraft offering low cost flying, the Star-Lite was awarded the Kevlar Trophy and $3,000.

The Star-Lite is offered to amateur constructors in three separate kits, containing everything needed to build the aircraft, with construction manuals. Each kit contains the more difficult to fabricate component parts in completed form, divided among a fuselage kit; an engine kit which includes a 30 kW (40 hp) Rotax 447 engine, propeller and instruments; and a wing and control surface kit. Construction time averages about 400 working hours. By February 1986 a total of 67 complete kits had been ordered, of which 55 had been delivered. By then five Star-Lites had already been completed.

TYPE: Single-seat homebuilt sporting monoplane

AIRFRAME: Tapered cantilever low-wing monoplane. Wing section NACA 2415. Dihedral 5°. Incidence 3° 30′. No sweepback. Wooden wing structure, with double tapered main spar and tapered rear spar, and pre-impregnated epoxy-glassfibre skins. Long span Frise flaperons of aluminium construction, with spring trim tab. Monocoque fuselage of pre-moulded composite construction, using sandwich of pre-impregnated epoxy-glassfibre with PVC foam core. Integral wing fillets and fin. Conventional cantilever tail unit of composite sandwich construction, comprising sweptback fin, narrow chord rudder, tailplane and elevators with spring trim tab.

LANDING GEAR: Non-retractable tailwheel type. Cantilever composite leaf spring main legs. Size 3·40-5 Azusa mainwheels, tyre pressure 1·72 bars (25 lb/sq in). Wheel fairings optional. Goodyear solid tailwheel of 4 in diameter. Azusa mainwheel brakes.

POWER PLANT: One 30 kW (40 hp) Rotax 447 two-cylinder two-stroke engine, with 2·238:1 reduction gear to a Perry Wood two-blade fixed-pitch wooden propeller with spinner. One fuel tank in fuselage, capacity 30 litres (8 US gallons). Refuelling point in fuselage nose.

ACCOMMODATION: Single seat under side hinged transparent canopy.

SYSTEM: Electrical system with engine driven 14A alternator.

AVIONICS: Optional portable com radio.

DIMENSIONS, EXTERNAL:

Wing span	6·55 m (21 ft 6 in)
Wing chord: at root	1·02 m (3 ft 4 in)
at tip	0·51 m (1 ft 8 in)
Wing aspect ratio	8·1
Length overall	4·98 m (16 ft 4 in)
Height overall	1·22 m (4 ft 0 in)
Tailplane span	2·13 m (7 ft 0 in)
Wheel track	1·27 m (4 ft 2 in)
Wheelbase	2·95 m (9 ft 8 in)
Propeller diameter	1·27 m (4 ft 2 in)

AREA:

Wings, gross	5·30 m² (57·0 sq ft)

WEIGHTS AND LOADINGS:

Weight empty	109 kg (240 lb)
Pilot weight range	41-91 kg (90-200 lb)
Max T-O weight	227 kg (500 lb)
Max wing loading	42·8 kg/m² (8·77 lb/sq ft)
Max power loading	7·57 kg/kW (12·50 lb/hp)

PERFORMANCE:

Never-exceed speed	130 knots (241 km/h; 150 mph)
Max level speed at 915 m (3,000 ft)	121 knots (225 km/h; 140 mph)
Max cruising speed at 915 m (3,000 ft)	104 knots (193 km/h; 120 mph)
Econ cruising speed at 915 m (3,000 ft)	87 knots (161 km/h; 100 mph)
Stalling speed, flaps down, engine idling	37 knots (68 km/h; 42 mph)
Max rate of climb at S/L	366 m (1,200 ft)/min
Service ceiling	more than 4,875 m (16,000 ft)
T-O and landing run	91 m (300 ft)
T-O to 15 m (50 ft)	122 m (400 ft)
Landing from 15 m (50 ft)	244 m (800 ft)
Range	347 nm (643 km; 400 miles)
g limits	+6/−4

STATLER

WILLIAM H. STATLER

9300 Encino Avenue, Northridge, California 91325
Telephone: (213) 886 1854

While employed as an aeronautical engineer with Lockheed, from 1940 to 1972, Mr Statler built at home two Formula One racers now known as *Little Mike* and *Miss Bernardino*. Following his retirement from Lockheed, he began work, in January 1973, on a two-seat homebuilt aircraft capable of limited aerobatic flying. Construction of what became the Firefly started in June 1973. The Firefly was rolled out in May 1976, and the first flight took place

Squadron Aviation Spad S.XIII

Star Flight AgLite agricultural version of the XC 2000, with spraygear

The second Star-Lite SL-1 to fly, built from kits by Mr Mark Brown *(Howard Levy)*

Squadron Aviation S.E.5A

Statler Firefly two-seat homebuilt monoplane *(Don Dwiggins)*

Star Flight XC 280 Stiletto microlight aircraft

Star Flight XC 2000 two-seat microlight aircraft

on 8 October 1976. Plans and a construction manual are available to amateur builders.

STATLER FIREFLY

TYPE: Two-seat homebuilt monoplane.

AIRFRAME: Cantilever low-wing monoplane. Wing section NACA 2412. Dihedral 5°. Incidence 2°. No sweepback. All-metal construction, with aluminium ribs and flush riveted skins. Glassfibre wingtips. All-metal ailerons and electrically actuated plain trailing-edge flaps. Ground adjustable tab on starboard aileron. Wings detachable for transportation. All-metal semi-monocoque fuselage, with flush riveted aluminium skin. Glassfibre engine cowl. Cantilever all-metal tail unit, with swept vertical surfaces. Fixed tailplane set at − 3° incidence. Trim tab on elevator, controllable from either cockpit.

LANDING GEAR: Non-retractable tricycle type. Cantilever spring main units made from a single piece of aluminium. Ercoupe nosewheel, on oleo strut. Mainwheel tyres size 12 × 6·00-6, pressure 1·93 bars (28 lb/sq in). Nosewheel tyre size 10 × 5·00-5, pressure 1·93 bars (28 lb/sq in). Gerdes hydraulic brakes. Glassfibre wheel fairings.

POWER PLANT: One 63·5 kW (85 hp) Continental C85-12F flat-four engine, driving two-blade Wayne's Woodcraft fixed-pitch 62 × 54 propeller. Two interconnected fuel tanks in fuselage, total capacity 68 litres (18 US gallons). Refuelling point on forward tank. (Third Firefly completed, N7FF, has wingtip tanks.) Oil capacity 5·7 litres (1·5 US gallons).

ACCOMMODATION: Two seats in tandem, under GB bubble canopy which is hinged on starboard side. Baggage compartment, capacity 22·6 kg (60 lb), in turtleback aft of rear cockpit.

SYSTEMS: Hydraulic system for brakes. Electrical system includes engine driven generator and 12V 35Ah battery for engine starting, wing flap actuation and instruments.

AVIONICS: Bayside portable transceiver.

DIMENSIONS, EXTERNAL:

Wing span	5·84 m (19 ft 2 in)
Wing chord, constant	1·27 m (4 ft 2 in)
Wing aspect ratio	4·6
Length overall	5·77 m (18 ft 11 in)
Height overall	2·15 m (7 ft 0½ in)
Tailplane span	2·82 m (9 ft 3 in)
Wheel track	1·37 m (4 ft 6 in)
Wheelbase	1·50 m (4 ft 11 in)
Propeller diameter	1·57 m (5 ft 2 in)

AREA:

Wings, gross	7·43 m² (80·0 sq ft)

WEIGHTS AND LOADINGS:
Weight empty 379 kg (835 lb)
Max T-O weight 590 kg (1,300 lb)
Max wing loading 79·3 kg/m² (16·25 lb/sq ft)
Max power loading 9·29 kg/kW (15·29 lb/hp)
PERFORMANCE:
Never-exceed speed 208 knots (386 km/h; 240 mph)
Max cruising speed at S/L 139 knots (257 km/h; 160 mph)
Econ cruising speed at 1,980 m (6,500 ft) 124 knots (230 km/h; 143 mph)
Stalling speed, flaps up 55 knots (102 km/h; 63 mph)
Max rate of climb at S/L 244 m (800 ft)/min
Service ceiling 4,875 m (16,000 ft)
T-O run 283 m (930 ft)
T-O to 15 m (50 ft) 354 m (1,160 ft)
Landing from 15 m (50 ft) 488 m (1,600 ft)
Landing run 152 m (500 ft)
Range with max fuel, no reserves 347 nm (543 km; 400 miles)

STEEN

STEEN AERO LAB INC

15623 De Gaulle Circle, Brighton, Colorado 80601
Telephone: (303) 659 7182

Mr Lamar Steen, an aerospace teacher in a Denver, Colorado, high school, designed a two-seat fully aerobatic biplane named Skybolt which was built as a class project in the school. Simplicity of construction was a primary aim of the design, begun in June 1968. Building began on 19 August 1969, and the first flight was made in October 1970. The Skybolt received an EAA award for 'Best School Project'. Plans are available to amateur constructors, together with fuselage and wing kits; more than 3,500 sets of plans have been sold, and many Skybolts are flying.

STEEN SKYBOLT

The following description applies to the prototype with 134 kW (180 hp) Avco Lycoming engine, built under Mr Steen's supervision:

TYPE: Two-seat homebuilt aerobatic biplane.

AIRFRAME: Braced biplane with single interplane strut each side. N centre-section struts. Streamline section landing and flying wires. Wing sections: upper wing NACA 63_2A015, lower wing NACA 0012. Dihedral 0° on upper wing, 2° 30′ on lower wings. Incidence (both) 1° 30′. Sweepback 6° on upper wing only. Wooden two-spar structures with spruce spars, built-up ribs and fabric covering. Fabric covered Frise ailerons on upper and lower wings. Cutout in centre-section trailing-edge of upper wing. Welded fuselage and wire braced tail unit of 4130 chrome molybdenum steel tube, with fabric covering. Adjustable trim tab in port elevator.

LANDING GEAR: Non-retractable mainwheels and tailwheel. Two side Vs and half axles hinged to fuselage structure. Shock absorption by rubber bungee. Cleveland mainwheels with tyres size 6·00-6, pressure 1·72 bars (25 lb/sq in). Cleveland hydraulic disc brakes. Glassfibre fairings for mainwheels.

POWER PLANT: One 134 kW (180 hp) Avco Lycoming HO-360-B1B flat-four engine, driving a McCauley two-blade fixed-pitch propeller with spinner. Provision for alternative engines of 93-194 kW (125-260 hp). Fuselage fuel tank, immediately aft of firewall, capacity 110 litres (29 US gallons). Optional tank of 37·8 litres (10 US gallons) capacity can be installed in centre-section of upper wing. Total optional fuel capacity 151·2 litres (40 US gallons). Refuelling points on fuselage upper surface, forward of windscreen, and on top surface of upper wing. Oil capacity 7·5 litres (2 US gallons).

ACCOMMODATION: Two seats in open cockpits. Provision for canopy over rear cockpit. Space for 13·6 kg (30 lb) baggage aft of rear seat.

SYSTEM: Hydraulic system for brakes only.

AVIONICS: Battery powered Alpha 200 nav/com transceiver.

DIMENSIONS, EXTERNAL:
Wing span: upper 7·32 m (24 ft 0 in)
lower 7·01 m (23 ft 0 in)
Wing chord, constant (both) 1·07 m (3 ft 6 in)
Length overall 5·79 m (19 ft 0 in)
Height overall 2·13 m (7 ft 0 in)
Propeller diameter 1·88 m (6 ft 2 in)
AREA:
Wings, gross 14·2 m² (152·7 sq ft)
WEIGHTS AND LOADINGS:
Weight empty 490 kg (1,080 lb)
Max T-O weight 748 kg (1,650 lb)
Max wing loading 52·7 kg/m² (10·8 lb/sq ft)
Max power loading 5·58 kg/kW (9·17 lb/hp)
PERFORMANCE (at max T-O weight):
Max level speed 126 knots (233 km/h; 145 mph)
Cruising speed 113 knots (209 km/h; 130 mph)
Landing speed 44 knots (81 km/h; 50 mph)
Max rate of climb at S/L 752 m (2,500 ft)/min
Service ceiling 5,500 m (18,000 ft)
T-O run 122 m (400 ft)
Range with max fuel 390 nm (720 km; 450 miles)
g limits +12/−10

STEWART

JIM D. STEWART

1605 US 1 South S-3E, Jupiter, Florida 33477

STEWART S-51D

Mr Jim D. Stewart, an aeronautical engineer, began design of the S-51D, a 7/10th-scale representation of a North American P-51D Mustang fighter of the Second World War, some twenty years ago. The first example to be completed was an all-metal version, built by Mr Frank Yamrick of Wilkes Barre, Pennsylvania, and first flown in May 1985. It has been followed by an all-wood example, built by Mr Jim Howard of Austin, Texas, with the assistance of Mr Mike Ray of Plant City, Florida. This made its initial flight in December 1985 and is illustrated in an accompanying photograph. The detailed description below also refers to this model, unless stated otherwise.

Kits to allow amateur construction of the all-metal version of the S-51D were expected to be available in Summer 1986, and are complete except for the engine, propeller, gearbox, instruments and avionics.

TYPE: Single- or two-seat 7/10th-scale fighter representation.

AIRFRAME: Cantilever low-wing monoplane of all-wood construction (kit built S-51Ds will be all-metal). Wing section 66-215(216). Built-up one-piece spruce box spar, tapering at tips, with laminated spruce plywood ribs (15 per side) and stringers. Electrically actuated flaps of similar construction to wings, with 40° max deflection. Semi-monocoque fuselage, with spruce bulkheads and longerons, and conventional cantilever tail unit (with rudder tab) of similar construction to wings. All surfaces have plywood skins (double walled on fuselage), covered overall with glassfibre and Imron paint.

LANDING GEAR: Hydraulically retractable tailwheel type. 4130 steel tube mainwheel upper struts and 2 in diameter oleo-pneumatic struts, with forks of 2024-T4 and wheel well doors of aluminium alloy. Mainwheel tyres size 6·00-6. Retractable swivelling and lockable tailwheel, with 4130 steel fork and 3 × 8 in tyre.

POWER PLANT: One 224 kW (300 hp) Chevrolet converted motorcar engine, driving a Hartzell four-blade propeller with Beech A200 spinner, via 2:1 reduction gear. Two wing fuel tanks, each with capacity of 95 litres (25 US gallons).

ACCOMMODATION: Pilot and passenger in tandem, under rearward sliding bubble canopy.

DIMENSIONS, EXTERNAL:
Wing span 7·92 m (26 ft 0 in)
Wing chord: at root 1·83 m (6 ft 0 in)
at tip 0·91 m (3 ft 0 in)
Length overall 6·71 m (22 ft 0 in)
Height overall 1·91 m (6 ft 3 in)
Wheel track 2·44 m (8 ft 0 in)
Propeller diameter 2·16 m (7 ft 1 in)
WEIGHTS AND LOADING:
Weight empty 912 kg (2,010 lb)
Max T-O weight 1,188 kg (2,620 lb)
Max power loading 5·30 kg/kW (8·73 lb/hp)
PERFORMANCE:
Cruising speed 205 knots (380 km/h; 236 mph)
Stalling speed 65 knots (121 km/h; 75 mph)
Max rate of climb at S/L 488 m (1,600 ft)/min
g limits +9/−4

STODDARD-HAMILTON

STODDARD-HAMILTON AIRCRAFT INC

18701 58th Avenue NE, Arlington, Washington 98223
Telephone: (206) 435 8533
PRESIDENT: Theodore Setzer
CHAIRMAN: Thomas S. Hamilton
VICE-PRESIDENT, ENGINEERING: Robert Gavinsky

STODDARD-HAMILTON GLASAIR TD and FT

The **Glasair TD** (taildragger) was originally designated SH-2 (SH-1 applying to a previous tandem two-seater designed by Mr Tom Hamilton). Design began in 1976 and construction of the prototype started in 1978. This aircraft (N88TH) flew in 1979, powered by an 85·75 kW (115 hp) Avco Lycoming O-235 flat-four engine. The second Glasair (N89SH), fitted with a 112 kW (150 hp) Avco Lycoming O-320 engine and higher canopy, was completed in late 1980.

Stoddard-Hamilton offers kits of parts to build the basic **Glasair TD** (non-retractable tailwheel gear), **Glasair FT** (non-retractable tricycle gear, first flown on 26 February 1985) and **Glasair RG** (retractable gear, described separately); these include all items except engine, propeller and instruments. Approximately 750 kits had been sold by late 1985, and production continues at a rate of twenty kits per month, all intended to utilise a 112-134 kW (150-180 hp) Avco Lycoming engine. By late 1985, 700 kits had been delivered and some 120 Glasairs were then flying. On average 1,500 working hours are needed to complete a Glasair.

All versions of the basic Glasair were to be superseded by the Glasair II and III, described separately, from 1 July 1986.

TYPE: Two-seat homebuilt monoplane.

AIRFRAME: Tapered cantilever low-wing monoplane. Wing section NASA LS(I)-0413. Dihedral 3°. Incidence 2° 20′. No sweepback. One-piece wing of glassfibre and foam composite construction standard, with continuous main spar of moulded glassfibre, four ribs per wing and glassfibre skins, coated with gelcoat. Optional detachable wingtip extensions, or 'wet' wingtip extensions containing auxiliary fuel. Ailerons, with trim tab, and flaps of composite construction. Conventional fuselage of composite construction, as for wings, moulded in two half-shells and belly panel, with firewall and only two bulkheads. Conventional cantilever tail unit. Composite construction, as for wings. Fin integral with fuselage. Fixed tab on rudder.

LANDING GEAR: Non-retractable tailwheel type (TD) or non-retractable tricycle type (FT). Tricycle gear retrofittable to existing TDs. McCreary mainwheel tyres size 5·00-5 (pressure 2·41-3·45 bars; 35-50 lb/sq in). Cantilever glassfibre main legs. Mainwheel fairings of glassfibre. Faired tailwheel and leg on TD. Cleveland hydraulic brakes. Dual brake kit optional.

POWER PLANT: Almost any Avco Lycoming O-320 or IO-320 engine of 112 or 119 kW (150 or 160 hp) can be fitted (with the exception of the O-320-H series) or a 134 kW (180 hp) IO-360, driving a two-blade fixed-pitch or constant-speed wooden or metal propeller with spinner. IO-360 is usual engine choice. Integral fuel tank in wing leading-edge and header tank on aft face of firewall. Total fuel capacity 159 litres (42 US gallons). Capacity increased to 208 litres (55 US gallons) when 'wet' extended wingtips installed. Oil capacity 7·5 litres (2 US gallons).

ACCOMMODATION: Two persons side by side in enclosed cabin, with dual controls. Dual gullwing, dual sliding, or port internal sliding/starboard gullwing canopy optional. Baggage capacity 36-45·5 kg (80-100 lb). Heated and ventilated.

AVIONICS: IFR panel can be installed.

DIMENSIONS, EXTERNAL:
Wing span: standard wingtips 7·09 m (23 ft 3 in)
wingtip extensions 8·31 m (27 ft 3 in)
Wing chord: at root 1·30 m (4 ft 3 in)
at tips 0·83 m (2 ft 8½ in)
Wing aspect ratio: standard wingtips 6·16
with wingtip extensions 7·60
Length overall 5·66 m (18 ft 7 in)
Height overall 2·18 m (7 ft 2 in)
Tailplane span 2·67 m (8 ft 9 in)
Wheel track 1·73 m (5 ft 8 in)
Propeller diameter 1·73-1·83 m (5 ft 8 in-6 ft 0 in)
DIMENSION, INTERNAL:
Cabin: Width 0·99 m (3 ft 3 in)
AREAS:
Wings, gross: standard 7·55 m² (81·3 sq ft)
with wingtip extensions 8·51 m² (91·6 sq ft)
WEIGHTS AND LOADINGS (A: TD with 119 kW; 160 hp engine, C: FT with 119 kW; 160 hp engine):
Weight empty: A 420 kg (925 lb)
C 435 kg (960 lb)
Max T-O weight: A 726 kg (1,600 lb)
C 771 kg (1,700 lb)
Max wing loading:
A, standard wingtips 96·1 kg/m² (19·68 lb/sq ft)
C, standard wingtips 102·1 kg/m² (20·91 lb/sq ft)
Max power loading: A 6·10 kg/kW (10·00 lb/hp)
C 6·48 kg/kW (10·63 lb/hp)
PERFORMANCE (A: TD with 119 kW; 160 hp, B: TD with 134 kW; 180 hp, C: FT with 119 kW; 160 hp, D: FT with 134 kW (180 hp) engine, in each case with standard wingtips):
Max level speed at S/L:
A 200 knots (370 km/h; 230 mph)
B 209 knots (388 km/h; 241 mph)
C 196 knots (364 km/h; 226 mph)
D 207 knots (383 km/h; 238 mph)

Steen Skybolt built in the UK by Mr Alexander and Mr Todd *(R. Kunert)*

Stoddard-Hamilton Glasair TD two-seat monoplane, built to production standards (112 kW; 150 hp Avco Lycoming O-320 engine)

Stewart S-51D built by Mr Jim Howard of Austin, Texas *(Howard Levy)*

Prototype Stoddard-Hamilton Glasair III at Oshkosh '86 *(J. M. G Gradidge)*

Stoddard-Hamilton Glasair RG built by Mr Jerry Gruber of Akhart, Indiana, with non-standard winglets and rear cockpit windows *(J. M. G. Gradidge)*

Max cruising speed (75% power at S/L):
- A — 180 knots (335 km/h; 208 mph)
- B — 189 knots (351 km/h; 218 mph)
- C — 177 knots (328 km/h; 204 mph)
- D — 186 knots (344 km/h; 214 mph)

Cruising speed (75% power at 2,440 m; 8,000 ft):
- A — 195 knots (360 km/h; 224 mph)
- B — 202 knots (375 km/h; 233 mph)
- C — 192 knots (356 km/h; 221 mph)
- D — 201 knots (372 km/h; 231 mph)

Econ cruising speed (55% power at 2,440 m; 8,000 ft):
- A — 156 knots (290 km/h; 180 mph)
- B — 164 knots (304 km/h; 189 mph)
- C — 154 knots (285 km/h; 177 mph)
- D — 161 knots (298 km/h; 185 mph)

Stalling speed: pilot only, flaps up:
- A, B, C, D — 55 knots (102 km/h; 63 mph)

pilot only, flaps down:
- A, B, C, D — 51 knots (94 km/h; 58 mph)

max T-O weight, flaps down:
- A, B, C, D — 54 knots (100 km/h; 62 mph)

Max rate of climb at S/L, at max T-O weight:
- A, C — 426 m (1,400 ft)/min
- B, D — 518 m (1,700 ft)/min

Max rate of climb at S/L, pilot only:
- A, C — 701 m (2,300 ft)/min
- B — 838 m (2,750 ft)/min
- D — 823 m (2,700 ft)/min

Service ceiling: A — over 6,100 m (20,000 ft)

T-O run: A — 241 m (790 ft)
- A, pilot only — 119 m (390 ft)
- C — 213 m (700 ft)
- C, pilot only — 116 m (380 ft)

Landing run: A — 168 m (550 ft)
- A, pilot only — 145 m (475 ft)
- C — 162 m (530 ft)
- C, pilot only — 133 m (435 ft)

Range with max standard fuel (55% power):
- A, B, C, D — 868 nm (1,609 km; 1,000 miles)

Range with wingtip tanks:
- A, B, C, D — 1,215 nm (2,253 km; 1,400 miles)

g limits at 726 kg (1,600 lb) AUW — +6/−4 limit, +9/−6 ultimate

STODDARD-HAMILTON GLASAIR RG

The prototype (N87SH) of this version of the Glasair with retractable landing gear was flown for the first time on 13 July 1982, and kits for the Glasair RG became available in Spring 1983. By early 1986 approximately 300 kits had been sold; from 1 July 1986, the model described will be superseded by the Glasair II & III (which see).

The RG illustrated was built by Mr Jerry Gruber of Akhart, Indiana. First flown on 1 March 1985, it has non-standard winglets designed by Mr John Roncz, rear cockpit windows, and is powered by a 119 kW (160 hp) IO-320-B1A engine. It received 'Grand Champion' awards at the 1985 Oshkosh and Sun 'n Fun EAA meetings. Differences in the standard RG by comparison with the fixed gear Glasair are as follows:

LANDING GEAR: Retractable tricycle type; nosewheel retracts rearward, mainwheels inward into wing roots. All units fully enclosed when retracted. Electro-hydraulic actuation. Oleo-pneumatic shock absorber in each unit. Cleveland free-castoring nosewheel size 5·00-5, with smaller Lamb tyre. Cleveland mainwheels with tyres size 5·00-5, pressure about 2·5 bars (35 lb/sq in). Brakes.

POWER PLANT: One 134 kW (180 hp) Avco Lycoming IO-360 flat-four engine, driving a two-blade Hartzell constant-speed metal propeller, is recommended. A 119 kW (160 hp) IO-320 is optional.

SYSTEM: Electrical system standard.

WEIGHTS AND LOADING:
- Weight empty — 499 kg (1,100 lb)
- Max T-O weight — 816 kg (1,800 lb)
- Max power loading — 6·09 kg/kW (10·00 lb/hp)

PERFORMANCE (A: with 134 kW; 180 hp engine, B: with 119 kW; 160 hp engine):

Max level speed: A — 222 knots (412 km/h; 256 mph)
- B — 209 knots (388 km/h; 241 mph)

Max cruising speed (75% power) at S/L:
- A — 197 knots (365 km/h; 227 mph)
- B — 189 knots (351 km/h; 218 mph)

Max cruising speed (75% power) at 2,440 m (8,000 ft):
- A — 210 knots (389 km/h; 242 mph)
- B — 203 knots (377 km/h; 234 mph)

Econ cruising speed (55% power) at 2,440 m (8,000 ft):
- A — 173 knots (320 km/h; 199 mph)
- B — 165 knots (306 km/h; 190 mph)

Stalling speed:
- A and B, pilot only, flaps up — 56 knots (103 km/h; 64 mph)
- A and B, pilot only, flaps down — 52 knots (95 km/h; 59 mph)
- A and B, max T-O weight, flaps down — 55 knots (102 km/h; 63 mph)

Max rate of climb at S/L:
- A, solo — 823 m (2,700 ft)/min
- B, solo — 701 m (2,300 ft)/min
- A, max T-O weight — 518 m (1,700 ft)/min
- B, max T-O weight — 427 m (1,400 ft)/min

T-O run: A — 183 m (600 ft)

Landing run: A — 162 m (530 ft)

Range at econ cruising speed:
- A, B — 999 nm (1,850 km; 1,150 miles)

Range with wingtip tanks:
- A, B — 1,346 nm (2,494 km; 1,550 miles)

g limits: A, B — +6/−4, +9/−6 ultimate

STODDARD-HAMILTON GLASAIR II and III

The Glasair II is under development in TD, FT and RG forms to supersede the basic Glasair series. Powered by the same 160 and 180 hp engines, the Glasair II has been redesigned to provide a slightly larger cabin for increased comfort, and will be supplied in kit form with more preformed/moulded components to cut estimated building time by 550 working hours. Performance will be similar to that of the present Glasairs (which see). The Glasair II RG model will utilise a simpler and less expensive retractable landing gear system than the Glasair RG. Tooling for kit production was nearing completion in early 1986, when construction of a prototype Glasair II had begun. Delivery of kits was scheduled to begin in September 1986.

The Glasair III is a completely new addition to the company's range, designed to offer exceptional performance, constructional simplicity and economical kit price. Like the Glasair II it incorporates new components and constructional techniques, is said to cut working time by 675 hours compared with the present Glasair RG, and will be supplied with all exterior airframe components primed and ready to paint. The Glasair III has a longer and wider fuselage for increased baggage space, payload capacity and comfort. It features a thicker windscreen to improve protection against bird strikes at its higher speeds, and has additional glassfibre laminates, integral longerons, and a lay-up schedule which provides a structurally stronger and torsionally stiffer fuselage. The Glasair III wing is also strengthened, and carries 76 litres (20 US gallons) more fuel than previous models.

The retractable landing gear is furnished with prefabricated main gear support structure boxes, which greatly simplify landing gear installation and jigging. In addition, a stainless steel nose gear box is provided, to simplify installation and increase fire protection. A new hydraulic nose gear shimmy damper, redesigned longer struts to provide the necessary ground clearance, gear uplocks to provide positive gear door closure, and a manual wobble pump for emergency gear extension, are other landing gear features.

A prototype Glasair III was displayed at Oshkosh '86, and kit tooling was nearing completion in early 1986.

The following details refer to the Glasair III only.

POWER PLANT: One 194 or 224 kW (260 or 300 hp) Avco Lycoming engine.

PERFORMANCE (estimated, with 224 kW; 300 hp engine):

Max level speed at S/L	260 knots (483 km/h; 300 mph)
Econ cruising speed at 3,660 m (12,000 ft)	239 knots (443 km/h; 275 mph)
Stalling speed	57 knots (105 km/h; 65 mph)
Max rate of climb at S/L	1,143 m (3,750 ft)/min

STOLP

STOLP STARDUSTER CORPORATION

4301 Twining Flabob Airport, Riverside, California 92509
Telephone: (714) 686 7943
PRESIDENT AND GENERAL MANAGER: William C. Clouse Jr
SECRETARY-TREASURER: Sumiko Hampson

Mr Louis A. Stolp and Mr George M. Adams designed and built a light single-seat sporting biplane known as the Starduster, which flew for the first time in November 1957; and founded Stolp Starduster Corporation to market plans, components and basic materials for the Starduster and subsequent designs. On 1 May 1972 this company was acquired by Jim and Hanako Osborne, who continued to trade under the original name. On 1 May 1981 the company was purchased from the Osbornes by Mr William C. Clouse Jr, now President and General Manager.

Plans of the SA-100 Starduster and SA-700 Acroduster 1 are no longer available; but the company continues to market plans, kits and materials for the two-seat Starduster Too (well over 2,000 sets of plans sold), single-seat Starlet, aerobatic V-Star, and Acroduster Too. A new biplane has flown in prototype form, known as the Super Starduster.

STOLP SA-300 STARDUSTER TOO

The SA-300 Starduster Too is an enlarged two-seat version of the original SA-100 Starduster, and is suitable for engines of 93-194 kW (125-260 hp).

Some Starduster Toos have radial engines instead of the more usual horizontally-opposed aircooled type. Examples illustrated in previous editions of *Jane's* have been fitted with Continental W-670 and Warner Super Scarab engines. The weight and performance figures quoted apply to the Starduster Too registered N2MR, which won the 'Grand Champion' award at the 1977 EAA Fly-in at Oshkosh and was illustrated in the 1979-80 *Jane's*. It has a 149 kW (200 hp) Avco Lycoming HIO-360-A1A horizontally-opposed engine, driving a McCauley constant-speed propeller.

TYPE: Two-seat homebuilt sporting biplane.

AIRFRAME: Biplane wings of unequal span with a single interplane strut each side. Multiple centre-section bracing struts. Streamline section landing and flying wires. Wing section M-6 modified. Dihedral 1° 30′ on lower wings only. Incidence 1° on lower wings only. Sweepback on leading-edge of upper wing 6°. All-wood structure with spruce spars and ribs of 6·5 mm (¼ in) plywood, fabric covered. Ailerons of wooden construction, fabric covered, on both upper and lower wings. No trailing-edge flaps. Welded 4130 steel tube fuselage and tail unit, with fabric covering. Glassfibre turtleback. Wire braced fixed incidence tailplane.

LANDING GEAR: Non-retractable tailwheel type. Rubber cord shock absorption. Wheel fairings on main units. Hydraulic brakes.

POWER PLANT (prototype): One 134 kW (180 hp) Avco Lycoming O-360-A1A flat-four engine, driving a two-blade fixed-pitch propeller with spinner. Fuel tank in fuselage, immediately aft of firewall.

ACCOMMODATION: Two seats in tandem open cockpits.

DIMENSIONS, EXTERNAL:

Wing span: upper	7·32 m (24 ft 0 in)
Wing chord, constant (both)	1·22 m (4 ft 0 in)
Length overall	6·63 m (21 ft 9 in)
Height overall	2·21 m (7 ft 3 in)

WEIGHTS AND LOADING (typical; with 149 kW; 200 hp engine):

Weight empty	517 kg (1,139 lb)
Max T-O weight	907 kg (2,000 lb)
Max power loading	6·09 kg/m² (10·00 lb/sq ft)

PERFORMANCE (typical; with 149 kW; 200 hp engine):

Max level speed	174 knots (322 km/h; 200 mph)
Max cruising speed	133 knots (246 km/h; 153 mph)
Econ cruising speed	100 knots (185 km/h; 115 mph)
Stalling speed	51 knots (94 km/h; 58 mph)
Sustained rate of climb, with pilot only	548 m (1,800 ft)/min

STOLP SA-500 STARLET

The SA-500 Starlet is a single-seat swept parasol monoplane. The wing is of wooden construction with spruce spars, plywood web and capstrip ribs, with Dacron covering. It has a Clark YH section; sweepback is 9° and incidence 3° 30′. The fuselage is of welded 4130 steel tube with Dacron covering, and the tail unit is a braced structure of the same materials. The non-retractable tailwheel type landing gear has cantilever main legs with wheel fairings. Power plant in the prototype consists of a 1,500 cc Volkswagen flat-four engine, driving a two-blade fixed-pitch propeller with spinner. Other engines of 63·5-93 kW (85-125 hp) may be fitted, the 80·5 kW (108 hp) Avco Lycoming being recommended.

Construction of the prototype occupied three months and cost /1,500. First flight was made on 1 June 1969.

The following details refer to the prototype:

DIMENSIONS, EXTERNAL:

Wing span	7·62 m (25 ft 0 in)
Wing chord	0·91 m (3 ft 0 in)
Length overall	5·18 m (17 ft 0 in)
Height overall	2·03 m (6 ft 8 in)

AREA:

Wings, gross	7·71 m² (83·0 sq ft)

WEIGHT AND LOADING:

Max T-O weight	340 kg (750 lb)
Max wing loading	44·1 kg/m² (9·04 lb/sq ft)

PERFORMANCE (at max T-O weight):

Cruising speed	78 knots (145 km/h; 90 mph)
Landing speed	48-52 knots (89-97 km/h; 55-60 mph)

STOLP SA-750 ACRODUSTER TOO

The SA-750 is a two-seat aerobatic biplane generally similar to the Starduster Too. It has symmetrical wings, the upper wing being swept back 6°. The prototype has a 149 kW (200 hp) Avco Lycoming IO-360 engine driving a two-blade constant-speed propeller. The front cockpit is open and has a small windscreen. A bubble canopy for the rear cockpit is faired neatly to the turtledeck.

DIMENSIONS, EXTERNAL:

Wing span: upper	6·53 m (21 ft 5 in)
Length overall	5·64 m (18 ft 6 in)
Height overall	2·08 m (6 ft 10 in)

AREA:

Wings, gross	12·1 m² (130·0 sq ft)

PERFORMANCE (at max T-O weight):

Cruising speed	139 knots (257 km/h; 160 mph)
Stalling speed	61 knots (113 km/h; 70 mph)
Max rate of climb at S/L	701 m (2,300 ft)/min
g limits	±9

STOLP SA-900 V-STAR

To meet the demand for low cost, low horsepower aircraft with aerobatic capability, Stolp has introduced the SA-900 V-Star, which is essentially a biplane version of the single-seat SA-500 Starlet. The wings, of Clark YH section, have N centre-section and I interplane struts. Incidence of the upper wing is 2° 30′ and that of the lower wings 2°. The upper wing is sweptback 6°.

The prototype has a 48·5 kW (65 hp) Continental flat-four engine, driving a two-blade fixed-pitch propeller, but engines of 44·5-93 kW (60-125 hp) may be installed.

DIMENSIONS, EXTERNAL:

Wing span: upper	7·01 m (23 ft 0 in)
Length overall	5·23 m (17 ft 2 in)
Height overall	2·26 m (7 ft 5 in)

AREA:

Wings, gross	13·1 m² (141·0 sq ft)

PERFORMANCE (prototype, at max T-O weight):

Cruising speed	65 knots (121 km/h; 75 mph)
Stalling speed	31 knots (57 km/h; 35 mph)
Max rate of climb at S/L	183 m (600 ft)/min
g limits	±9

STOLP SUPER STARDUSTER

The latest biplane from Stolp Starduster Corporation is the Super Starduster (N191DG), which is the first of a new series of special aerobatic aircraft, built for Mr Dick Green, a pilot with Continental Airlines who competes in unlimited class aerobatic competitions.

Design of the Super Starduster began in May 1981; construction of the prototype started in September of that year, and the first flight was achieved on 1 April 1983. The aircraft features a unique linkage between the ailerons and flaps, allowing the former to serve as flaps (down) with stick back, or flaps (up) with stick forward for outside loops.

TYPE: Single-seat homebuilt aerobatic biplane.

AIRFRAME: Biplane type, with single I interplane strut each side and N centre-section cabane struts. Streamline section landing and flying wires. Osborne A-1 symmetrical wing section (modified). Thickness/chord ratio 9·5%. No anhedral, dihedral or incidence. Sweepback on leading-edge of upper wing 6°. All-wood structure, with spruce spars and birch ribs, Dacron fabric covered. Ailerons of wooden construction, fabric covered, on upper and lower wings, serve also as flaps during normal and inverted flight. Ailerons symmetrical and servo-boosted. Welded steel tube fuselage and wire braced tail unit, the former covered with fabric, aluminium alloy and glassfibre, and the latter with fabric. Ground adjustable servo-boosted trim tabs on rudder and elevator.

LANDING GEAR: Non-retractable tailwheel type. Cleveland mainwheels, size 5·00-5. Lamb 11·4 × 5 mainwheel tyres. Streamline fairings on main units. Cleveland brakes.

POWER PLANT: One 149 kW (200 hp) Avco Lycoming IO-360-A1A flat-four engine, driving a Hartzell aerobatic two-blade constant-speed propeller with large spinner. One fuel tank in fuselage, capacity 113·5 litres (30 US gallons). Refuelling point in top of fuselage. Oil capacity 7·6 litres (2 US gallons).

ACCOMMODATION: Pilot only, under side-hinged (to starboard) one-piece canopy.

SYSTEM: Electrical system powered by 12V 30A Globe gel-cell.

AVIONICS: Terra 720-channel radio.

DIMENSIONS, EXTERNAL:

Wing span	5·94 m (19 ft 6 in)
Wing chord, mean	0·97 m (3 ft 2 in)
Length overall	4·88 m (16 ft 0 in)
Height overall	2·13 m (7 ft 0 in)
Tailplane span	2·44 m (8 ft 0 in)
Wheel track	1·37 m (4 ft 6 in)
Wheelbase	2·74 m (9 ft 0 in)
Propeller diameter	1·88 m (6 ft 2 in)

AREA:

Wings, gross	9·75 m² (105·0 sq ft)

WEIGHTS AND LOADINGS:

Basic operating weight empty	426 kg (940 lb)
Max T-O weight	680 kg (1,500 lb)
Max wing loading	69·7 kg/m² (14·3 lb/sq ft)
Max power loading	4·56 kg/kW (7·50 lb/hp)

PERFORMANCE:

Never-exceed speed	182 knots (338 km/h; 210 mph) IAS
Max level speed at 2,440 m (8,000 ft)	156 knots (289 km/h; 180 mph) IAS
Max cruising speed at 2,440 m (8,000 ft)	139 knots (257 km/h; 160 mph) IAS
Econ cruising speed at 2,440 m (8,000 ft)	122 knots (225 km/h; 140 mph) IAS
Stalling speed, power off	48 knots (89 km/h; 55 mph) IAS
Max rate of climb at S/L	914 m (3,000 ft)/min
Service ceiling	3,810 m (12,500 ft)
T-O run	61 m (200 ft)
T-O to 15 m (50 ft)	213 m (700 ft)
Landing from 15 m (50 ft)	396 m (1,300 ft)
Landing run	335 m (1,100 ft)
Range with max fuel	440 nm (816 km; 507 miles)

STRIPLIN

STRIPLIN AIRCRAFT CORPORATION

PO Box 2001, Lancaster, California 93539
Telephone: (805) 945 2522
PRESIDENT: Kenneth Striplin

Striplin Aircraft Corporation renamed itself Ranger Aviation in March 1983 (see 1983-84 *Jane's*), but had reverted to its former title by mid-1984. The company's Lone Ranger and Sky Ranger are continuing in production in their current Silver Cloud form.

STRIPLIN LONE RANGER SILVER CLOUD and SKY RANGER SILVER CLOUD II

The Silver Cloud is a modified version of the original 1980 Lone Ranger (1983-84 *Jane's*). Principal differences are that the wings have a new NASA aerofoil section and are of composite construction; other weight-saving changes have also been made. The aircraft is classified as a microlight in its **Lone Ranger Silver Cloud** single-seat form; the two-seat **Sky Ranger Silver Cloud II** falls within the FAA's

Stolp SA-750 Acroduster Too built by Mr Lowell Slater (224 kW; 300 hp engine)

Stolp SA-900 V-Star (Avco Lycoming O-290-D2 engine) *(Howard Levy)*

Stolp Starduster Too built by Mr Francis Lundo of Seattle, Washington (134 kW; 180 hp Avco Lycoming engine) *(Peter M. Bowers)*

Stolp Super Starduster special aerobatic biplane built for Mr Dick Green *(Don Dwiggins)*

Stolp SA-500 Starlet built in England by Mr S. S. Miles *(Air Portraits)*

Striplin's side by side two-seat Sky Ranger Silver Cloud II *(Howard Levy)*

Striplin Lone Ranger Silver Cloud *(J. M. G. Gradidge)*

Experimental category and must be registered and flown by a licensed pilot.

Type: Single-seat microlight aircraft (Lone Ranger) or two-seat homebuilt aircraft (Sky Ranger).

Airframe: Cantilever high-wing monoplane, with provision for wing bracing struts. Wings are slightly swept-back (7° on leading-edges) and tapered, and can be folded back alongside fuselage for transportation and storage. Basic load bearing wing box structure formed from I beam main spar and D section leading-edge of wood and glassfibre, with glassfibre and foam ribs and Dacron covering. Leading-edge is of pre-formed foam with glassfibre skin; full span 'flaperons' on trailing-edges, of glassfibre/foam construction. Pod and boom fuselage, the forward portion having base frame of unidirectional glassfibre, impregnated with epoxy resin, with moulded outer shell of glassfibre. At top of pod is U shaped channel, in which is buried a lightweight metal tube to which the wings are bolted and which also supports rear fuselage and tail unit. Tailboom is triangular section glassfibre and foam sandwich structure; tail surfaces of similar construction to wings. Recovery parachute standard on both models.

Landing Gear: Non-retractable tricycle type, with laminated glassfibre legs and steerable nose unit. Tailwheel type, float and ski gear, wheel fairings and oversize wheels available optionally.

Power Plant: Lone Ranger: One 15 kW (20 hp) Cuyuna 215R engine, with 2·2:1 reduction drive to a two-blade propeller. Fuel capacity 19 litres (5 US gallons). Sky Ranger: One 34·3 kW (46 hp) Rotax 503 engine. Fuel capacity 38 litres (10 US gallons).

Accommodation: Pilot only in Lone Ranger; pilot and passenger in Sky Ranger. Cockpit has large windscreen and open sides; removable side panels optional.

Dimensions, external (A: Lone Ranger Silver Cloud, B: Sky Ranger Silver Cloud II):

Wing span: A	9·75 m (32 ft 0 in)
B	10·19 m (33 ft 5 in)
Wing aspect ratio: A	8·53
B	8·79
Length overall (both)	4·88 m (16 ft 0 in)
Height overall: A	2·13 m (7 ft 0 in)
B	2·44 m (8 ft 0 in)
Propeller diameter: A	1·37 m (4 ft 6 in)
B	1·52 m (5 ft 0 in)

Areas:

Wings, gross: A	11·15 m² (120·0 sq ft)
B	11·80 m² (127·0 sq ft)

Weights and Loadings:

Weight empty: A	111 kg (245 lb)
B	159 kg (350 lb)
Max T-O weight: A	227 kg (500 lb)
B	454 kg (1,000 lb)
Max wing loading: A	20·36 kg/m² (4·17 lb/sq ft)
B	38·42 kg/m² (7·87 lb/sq ft)
Max power loading: A	15·07 kg/kW (25·00 lb/hp)
B	13·24 kg/kW (21·74 lb/hp)

Performance:

Never-exceed speed: A	69 knots (128 km/h; 80 mph)
B	86 knots (161 km/h; 100 mph)
Max level speed: A	55 knots (101 km/h; 63 mph)
B	69 knots (129 km/h; 80 mph)
Stalling speed: A	22 knots (41 km/h; 25 mph)
B	26 knots (47 km/h; 29 mph)
Max rate of climb at S/L (both)	183 m (600 ft)/min
T-O run: A	23 m (75 ft)
B	46 m (150 ft)
Landing run: A	23 m (75 ft)
Range with max fuel: A	182 nm (338 km; 210 miles)
B	217 nm (402 km; 250 miles)
g limits: A	+6/−4
Best glide ratio: A	14
B	13

SUMMIT

SUMMIT AIRCRAFT CORPORATION

PO Box 884, Denton, Texas 76201

Telephone: (817) 566 0060

President: Roland Schmitt

SUMMIT AIRCRAFT TRIDENT T-3

Summit Aircraft Corporation's Trident T-3 has a joined wing, comprising two sets of wings arranged to form diamond shapes when viewed from the front and above.

The joined wing was invented and patented by Dr Julian Wolkovitch, President of ACA Industries Inc of California, who flew a joined wing glider in 1974. Since 1979 NASA and the US Navy have supported research into this type of wing, proving it to have several advantages over a conventional wing, including lighter weight and higher stiffness, less induced drag, higher trimmed maximum lift coefficient, plus built-in direct sideforce capability. It is self bracing and offers good crash protection.

A venture capital group later financed the construction of a microlight joined wing aircraft, which became the Trident T-3, with Dr Wolkovitch on the design team. Two prototypes were flown and kits are available. Almost all the materials in the wings and fuselage are composites. The kit includes the engine, and a pre-moulded fuselage and wings, and the Trident is claimed to be the first self powered joined wing aircraft offered for sale to the public.

TYPE: Single-seat microlight aircraft; conforms to FAR Pt 103.

AIRFRAME: Joined wing layout, with sweptback dihedral forward wings meeting anhedral rear wings at juncture with wider chord dihedral outer wing panels with winglets. Mainframe of PVC foam and bi/uni-directional glassfibre. Stainless steel cables. Three-axis control (spoilers, elevators and rudders). Rigging time 15 min.

LANDING GEAR: Tricycle type, with steerable nosewheel. Glassfibre spring legs. Optional floats, skis and wheel fairings.

POWER PLANT: One 22·4 kW (30 hp) KFM 107ER two-cylinder two-stroke engine, with 2·51:1 reduction drive to a two-blade wooden pusher propeller. Fuel tank capacity 18·4 litres (4·85 US gallons).

ACCOMMODATION: Pilot only, in open position, standard. Optional enclosed and heated cabin.

DIMENSIONS, EXTERNAL:
- Wing span — 10·06 m (33 ft 0 in)
- Wing aspect ratio — 6·9
- Length overall — 4·95 m (16 ft 3 in)
- Height overall — 1·93 m (6 ft 4 in)
- Propeller diameter — 1·37 m (4 ft 6 in)

AREA:
- Wings, gross — 13·2 m² (142·0 sq ft)

WEIGHTS AND LOADINGS:
- Weight empty — 115 kg (254 lb)
- Pilot weight range — 55-113 kg (120-250 lb)
- Max T-O weight — 242 kg (534 lb)
- Max wing loading — 18·36 kg/m² (3·76 lb/sq ft)
- Max power loading — 10·80 kg/kW (17·8 lb/hp)

PERFORMANCE:
- Never-exceed speed — 71 knots (132 km/h; 82 mph)
- Max level speed — 55 knots (101 km/h; 63 mph)
- Max cruising speed — 48 knots (89 km/h; 55 mph)
- Econ cruising speed — 39 knots (72 km/h; 45 mph)
- Stalling speed — 21 knots (39 km/h; 24 mph)
- Max rate of climb at S/L — 122 m (400 ft)/min
- Service ceiling — 3,050 m (10,000 ft)
- T-O run — 30 m (100 ft)
- Landing run — 23 m (75 ft)
- Range with max fuel — 143 nm (265 km; 165 miles)
- Endurance — 3 h 30 min
- *g* limits — +4·67/−2·33 design

SUN AEROSPACE

SUN AEROSPACE GROUP INC

PO Box 317, Nappanee, Indiana 46550
Telephone: (219) 773 3220
PRESIDENT: Russell A. McDonald

SUN AEROSPACE SUN RAY 100

Design of the basic single-seat **Sun Ray 100** began in 1982, and construction of a proof of concept prototype started in the following year. This aircraft (N3932K) made its first flight on 4 September 1983, and was being modified in early 1986 as a testbed for the intended homebuilt kit versions.

Available options for the Sun Ray 100 will include a retractable landing gear, and a centre hull attachment to permit operation from water in amphibious form. A two-seat version, with alternative tandem or side by side seating, will also be offered as the **Sun Ray 200**.

The following description applies to the Model 100:

TYPE: Single-seat homebuilt landplane or amphibian.

AIRFRAME: Cantilever monoplane, with foreplane. Wings formed on a foam/Kevlar spar (stiffened with layers of graphite and spruce), with Kevlar D-cell leading-edge, foam ribs wrapped in Kevlar, and aluminium alloy trailing-edge, with Mylar covering on ribbed area. Wing section Roncz 1104 (laminar flow). Inverted gull centre wing, serving as mount for power plant, with no control surfaces; detachable outer wing panels, with marked dihedral. Foam/Kevlar full-span ailerons on outer panels. Twin fins and rudders of foam/Kevlar, at junction of centre wing and outer panels. Removable foam/Kevlar foreplane at nose of fuselage, of Roncz 1104 type section, with full-span elevators of similar construction. Fuselage of Kevlar, braced on inner surface with spruce and Kevlar/foam stiffeners. Rear of cockpit closed by Kevlar bulkhead. Optional foam/glassfibre hull attaches to fuselage for amphibious operations. Sponsons used with hull kit attach to Kevlar/foam/glassfibre rails that are integral with fins and project forward to foreplane.

LANDING GEAR: Non-retractable (optionally retractable) tricycle type with telescopic tube/spring suspension. Wheels size 4·50 × 4·00. Castoring nosewheel; brakes on mainwheels.

POWER PLANT: One 38·8 kW (52 hp) Kawasaki TA440B two-cylinder two-stroke engine, with 1·97:1 reduction drive to a Propeller Engineering three-blade ground adjustable wooden pusher propeller. Fuel capacity 34 litres (9 US gallons) in a single tank behind rear cockpit bulkhead.

ACCOMMODATION: Pilot only in open cockpit standard; canopy optional. Baggage capacity 9 kg (20 lb).

SYSTEM: 12V electrical system.

DIMENSIONS, EXTERNAL:
- Wing span — 9·75 m (32 ft 0 in)
- Length overall — 4·06 m (13 ft 4 in)
- Height overall — 1·83 m (6 ft 0 in)
- Foreplane span — 4·88 m (16 ft 0 in)
- Wheel track — 2·44 m (8 ft 0 in)
- Propeller diameter — 1·37 m (4 ft 6 in)

AREA:
- Wings, gross (incl foreplane) — 13·56 m² (146·0 sq ft)

WEIGHTS AND LOADINGS:
- Weight empty — 181 kg (400 lb)
- Pilot weight range — 46-100 kg (100-220 lb)
- Max T-O weight — 363 kg (800 lb)
- Max wing loading — 26·77 kg/m² (5·48 lb/sq ft)
- Max power loading — 9·36 kg/kW (15·38 lb/hp)

PERFORMANCE:
- Never-exceed speed — 86 knots (161 km/h; 100 mph)
- Max level speed — 78 knots (145 km/h; 90 mph)
- Max cruising speed — 74 knots (137 km/h; 85 mph)
- Econ cruising speed — 69 knots (129 km/h; 80 mph)
- Stalling speed — 35 knots (65 km/h; 40 mph)
- Max rate of climb at S/L — 183 m (600 ft)/min
- Service ceiling — 4,115 m (13,500 ft)
- T-O run — 92 m (300 ft)
- T-O to 15 m (50 ft) — 152 m (500 ft)
- Landing from 15 m (50 ft) — 92 m (300 ft)
- Landing run — 46 m (150 ft)
- Range — 369 nm (684 km; 425 miles)

SWEARINGEN

SWEARINGEN AIRCRAFT CORPORATION

5418 Brewster Place, San Antonio, Texas 78233
Telephone: (512) 657 2700
PRESIDENT: Edward J. Swearingen

SWEARINGEN SX300

Mr Ed Swearingen, internationally renowned designer of many production aircraft, including the Merlin and Metro commuter airliners, has designed and built a small two-seat light aircraft of very high performance, designated SX300. This is his 29th aircraft design, and is approved by the FAA for amateur construction. Design and construction of the prototype at his San Antonio works both started in 1982, and the SX300 made its first flight on 11 July 1984; construction of kits for sale to amateur builders began simultaneously. Seventy-nine separate kits are being offered, consisting of all component parts for the fuselage, wings, tail unit, landing gear, cockpit completion and engine installation respectively, but not the engine, propeller, interior trim or instruments. By mid-1986 a total of 89 complete SX300 kits had been ordered.

TYPE: Two-seat high performance homebuilt aircraft.

AIRFRAME: Cantilever low-wing monoplane. NASA/Dan Somers NLF (1) 0416 wing section. Dihedral 4°. Incidence −1° at root. Sweepback at quarter-chord 0° 45′. Tapered wings of conventional stressed skin aluminium alloy construction, with two aluminium alloy spars. Wingtips of composite material. Conventional ailerons with mechanical servo tabs and large-area hydraulically operated single-slotted flaps, all of aluminium alloy construction. Variable bungee trim in aileron control. Semi-monocoque fuselage of aluminium alloy, with flush riveted skins. Top and forward cowlings, and landing gear well doors, of composite materials. Conventional aluminium alloy tail unit, with stretch-formed leading-edges, comprising sweptback fin, horn balanced rudder, tailplane and elevators. Mechanically actuated trim tab in elevator.

LANDING GEAR: Hydraulically retractable tricycle type. All wheels retract rearward into fuselage and are completely enclosed when up. Oleo-pneumatic shock absorbers. Cleveland aluminium wheels and 5·00-5 tyres on all units. Tyre pressure 3·45 bars (50 lb/sq in). Cleveland hydraulic disc brakes.

POWER PLANT: One 224 kW (300 hp) Avco Lycoming IO-540-L1C5 flat-six engine, driving a Hartzell HC-E3YR-1RF/F8468T-12 three-blade constant-speed metal propeller. Two integral fuel tanks in wings, total capacity 257 litres (68 US gallons). Oil capacity 11·4 litres (3 US gallons). Optional engine is Avco Lycoming IO-540-K series.

ACCOMMODATION: Two seats side by side under forward hinged canopy. Baggage space aft of seats, capacity 32 kg (70 lb). Heating, ram cooling air ventilation, and demisting air.

SYSTEMS: Hydraulic system, pressure 103 bars (1,500 lb/sq in). Electrical system with 70A 14V alternator for avionics, lights and some instruments.

AVIONICS: Optional, including autopilot. Prototype has King radios.

DIMENSIONS, EXTERNAL:
- Wing span — 7·43 m (24 ft 4½ in)
- Wing chord: at root — 1·19 m (3 ft 11 in)
- at tip — 0·60 m (1 ft 11½ in)
- Wing aspect ratio — 8·4
- Length overall — 6·44 m (21 ft 1½ in)
- Height overall — 2·39 m (7 ft 10 in)
- Tailplane span — 2·26 m (7 ft 5 in)
- Wheel track — 1·68 m (5 ft 6 in)
- Wheelbase — 1·30 m (4 ft 3 in)
- Propeller diameter — 1·88 m (6 ft 2 in)

DIMENSIONS, INTERNAL:
- Cabin: Length — 1·27 m (4 ft 2 in)
- Max width — 1·04 m (3 ft 5 in)
- Max height — 0·99 m (3 ft 3 in)

AREA:
- Wings, gross — 6·5 m² (70·77 sq ft)

WEIGHTS AND LOADINGS:
- Weight empty, equipped, less fuel — 725 kg (1,600 lb)
- Max T-O weight — 1,089 kg (2,400 lb)
- Max wing loading — 165·6 kg/m² (33·91 lb/sq ft)
- Max power loading — 4·86 kg/kW (8·00 lb/hp)

PERFORMANCE (estimated at max T-O weight except where indicated):
- Never-exceed speed — 274 knots (507 km/h; 315 mph)
- Max level speed at S/L — 247 knots (459 km/h; 285 mph)
- Max cruising speed (75% power) at 2,745 m (9,000 ft) — 239 knots (442 km/h; 275 mph)
- Econ cruising speed (65% power) at 3,050 m (10,000 ft) — 230 knots (426 km/h; 265 mph)
- Stalling speed: power off and flaps up — 78 knots (145 km/h; 90 mph) CAS
- flaps down, at 839 kg (1,850 lb) AUW — 62 knots (115 km/h; 71 mph) CAS
- Max rate of climb at S/L — 731 m (2,400 ft)/min
- T-O run — approx 335 m (1,100 ft)
- Landing run — approx 610 m (2,000 ft)
- Range, no reserves — 999 nm (1,852 km; 1,151 miles)
- *g* limits — ±6; ±9 ultimate

TACT-AVIA

TACT-AVIA CORPORATION

PO Box 11201, Marina del Rey, California 90291
Telephone: (213) 821 5214

Tact-Avia Corporation has developed over a three year period a seven-eighths scale representation of the German Fokker E.III Eindecker monoplane fighter of 1915-16, which is available for construction by amateur builders in plan or kit forms. It is described by Tact-Avia as an ultralight aircraft, although the company recognises that its weight and performance are too high to allow it to qualify for this category under the FAA's current criteria.

Tact-Avia uses the same basic airframe for its two more recent products, the Morane-Mini and Bristol-Bit, which are scale representations of the First World War Morane-Saulnier Type N and Bristol M.1C.

TACT-AVIA FOKKER-LITE

The Fokker-Lite Eindecker has been developed for recreational flying and is said to be simple and inexpensive to construct. It uses a modern high-lift low-speed wing aerofoil section and is powered by a Fuji Robin engine.

TYPE: Single-seat seven-eighths scale representation of a Fokker E.III.

AIRFRAME: Wire braced mid-wing monoplane of constant chord, except for raked tips. Constructed of aluminium tubing with 'cherry max' rivets; fabric covered. Conventional ailerons. Wings removable for storage and transportation. Wing installation and rigging time is 10 min. Rectangular box fuselage, comprising a forward section fabricated from chrome molybdenum steel tubing and a

Second prototype Summit Aircraft Corporation Trident T-3 'joined wing' microlight aircraft *(Howard Levy)*

Sun Aerospace Group Sun Ray 100 in amphibious form

Tact-Avia Fokker-Lite seven-eighths scale representation of a First World War Fokker E.III Eindecker fighter

Prototype Swearingen SX300 high performance homebuilt aircraft

Tamarind International Commuter IIB, with roomier cabin

Tamarind International Commuter IIA two-seat light helicopter

rear section built from spruce, the whole fabric covered. Conventional wire braced tail unit of similar construction to wings, comprising a circular fin and rudder and a tailplane with large-area elevators.

LANDING GEAR: Non-retractable type with tailskid.

POWER PLANT: One 37·3 kW (50 hp) Fuji Industries Robin EC44PM two-stroke engine, driving a two-blade propeller through 3:1 reduction gearing. Fuel capacity 23 litres (6 US gallons).

ACCOMMODATION: Single seat in open cockpit. Dummy machine-gun ahead of cockpit.

DIMENSIONS, EXTERNAL:
- Wing span: 8·92 m (29 ft 3 in)
- Length overall: 5·64 m (18 ft 6 in)
- Height overall: 2·13 m (7 ft 0 in)
- Propeller diameter: 1·83 m (6 ft 0 in)

WEIGHTS AND LOADING:
- Weight empty: 138 kg (305 lb)
- Max T-O weight: 249 kg (550 lb)
- Max power loading: 6·68 kg/kW (11·00 lb/hp)

PERFORMANCE:
- Max level speed at S/L: 65 knots (121 km/h; 75 mph)
- Cruising speed: 52 knots (97 km/h; 60 mph)
- Stalling speed: 25 knots (45 km/h; 28 mph)
- Max rate of climb at S/L: 183 m (600 ft)/min
- T-O run: 76 m (250 ft)

TAMARIND

TAMARIND INTERNATIONAL LTD

PO Box 459, Olla, Louisiana 71465
Telephone: (318) 495 5183
Telex: 58364 NLN
CHAIRMAN: Leon C. Vial III
PRESIDENT: John A. Mathews
VICE-PRESIDENTS: Dr Robert C. Rice
Raymond B. Tilyou

Details of the early history of the Commuter helicopter programme can be found under the Helicom and International Helicopters entries in the 1983-84 and previous editions of *Jane's*. Tamarind International has been responsible for producing and marketing the current Commuter IB, IIA and IIB models since January 1984, when it purchased International Helicopters and transferred the entire Commuter operation to Olla, Louisiana. It also makes available the roomier cabin assembly of the Commuter IIB for retrofit to the Commuter IIA and older Commuter II, and was producing an ultralight helicopter of a different type when this entry was compiled. No details of this last aircraft are available.

TAMARIND INTERNATIONAL COMMUTER IIA

A description of the original Helicom Commuter Jr Model H-1A single-seat helicopter last appeared in the 1972-73 *Jane's*. The Commuter IIA is a more powerful two-seater, of generally similar configuration but embodying a number of refinements.

TYPE: Two-seat light homebuilt helicopter.

ROTOR SYSTEM: Two-blade main rotor and two-blade tail rotor. Blade section NACA 0012. Main rotor blades each comprise a solid extruded 7075-T6 aluminium leading-edge spar, extending to 30 per cent chord, solid aluminium alloy V section trailing-edge, cast ribs and Alclad skins, epoxy bonded together, with some rivets for added strength. Tail rotor has blades of stainless steel riveted to a short steel spar. All-metal drive system. Conventional main rotor gearbox has specially designed centrifugal clutch, and steel shaft drive to tail rotor gearbox. Main rotor/engine rpm ratio 1:5·5.

AIRFRAME: Basic fuselage truss of welded 4130 chrome molybdenum steel tube. Glassfibre and Plexiglas cabin enclosure. Rear structure not covered. Small horizontal stabiliser and triangular ventral fin, constructed also of welded 4130 chrome molybdenum steel tube. Tailboom detachable.

LANDING GEAR: Steel tube skids, with optional ground handling wheels. Neoprene shock absorption.

POWER PLANT: One 112 kW (150 hp) Avco Lycoming O-320 flat-four engine, with dual ignition, mounted vertically aft of cabin. Two cylindrical fuel tanks of welded stainless steel, one each side of main rotor driveshaft, above engine, with combined capacity of 83 litres (22 US gallons). Cooling fan standard. Oil capacity 6·6 litres (1·75 US gallons).

ACCOMMODATION: Pilot and passenger, side by side on bench seat. Cabin width 1·02 m (3 ft 4 in). Conventional helicopter controls.

DIMENSIONS, EXTERNAL:
- Main rotor diameter: 7·62 m (25 ft 0 in)
- Main rotor blade chord: 0·20 m (8 in)
- Tail rotor diameter: 1·23 m (4 ft 0½ in)
- Length of fuselage: 6·88 m (22 ft 6¾ in)
- Length overall: 8·84 m (29 ft 0 in)
- Width of fuselage: 1·02 m (3 ft 4 in)
- Width over skids: 1·86 m (6 ft 1 in)
- Height overall: 2·52 m (8 ft 3¼ in)

AREA:
- Main rotor disc: 45·6 m² (490·9 sq ft)

WEIGHTS:
- Weight empty: 318 kg (700 lb)
- Max T-O weight: 590 kg (1,300 lb)

PERFORMANCE (at max T-O weight):
- Max level speed: 87 knots (161 km/h; 100 mph)
- Max cruising speed: 78 knots (145 km/h; 90 mph)
- Service ceiling: 3,960 m (13,000 ft)
- Hovering ceiling IGE: 2,135 m (7,000 ft)
- Range with max fuel: 195 nm (362 km; 225 miles)

TAMARIND INTERNATIONAL COMMUTER IIB

Design of this roomier derivative of the Commuter IIA was begun in May 1980 and construction of a prototype started in June of that year. Because changes were confined to the cabin, the first flight was achieved in July 1980. A total of at least 169 Commuter IIBs have been ordered, of which many have flown. Most dimensions are not changed by the rounded glassfibre and Plexiglas cabin enclosure. However, fuel capacity is 76 litres (20 US gallons).

DIMENSIONS, INTERNAL:
- Cabin: Max length: 1·73 m (5 ft 8 in)
  - Max width: 1·17 m (3 ft 10 in)
  - Max height: 1·27 m (4 ft 2 in)

WEIGHTS:
Weight empty 318 kg (700 lb)
Max T-O weight 590 kg (1,300 lb)

PERFORMANCE:
Never-exceed speed 95 knots (177 km/h; 110 mph)
Max level speed at S/L 87 knots (161 km/h; 100 mph)
Max cruising speed at S/L 78 knots (145 km/h; 90 mph)
Econ cruising speed at S/L 68 knots (126 km/h; 78 mph)
Max rate of climb at S/L 350 m (1,150 ft)/min
Vertical rate of climb at S/L 326 m (1,071 ft)/min
Service ceiling 3,350 m (11,000 ft)
Hovering ceiling: IGE 2,440 m (8,000 ft)
OGE 1,830 m (6,000 ft)
Range with max payload 195 nm (362 km; 225 miles)

TAYLOR

TAYLOR AERO INC

5855 State Route 40, Tipp City, Ohio 45371
Telephone: (513) 845 1226
PRESIDENT: Robert H. Taylor

TAYLOR TA-2/3 BIRD

Mr C. Gilbert Taylor, designer of the original Cub lightplane and founder of the former Taylor Aircraft (Taylorcraft) Company, began the design of the Bird in 1960. Construction started in 1968 and, in its original form, the aircraft received in 1976 the EAA's 'Best New Design' award at the Oshkosh Fly-in. Since then, the design has been updated by Mr Taylor and his sons, Bruce and Robert. It now has a T tail and larger wheels for rough-field operations, and in this form has completed its FAA flight requirements.

Test pilot reports indicated outstanding visibility, and crosswind and ground handling capability, as well as docile, 'flat' stall characteristics. Due to a slot arrangement forward of the ailerons, a high-velocity airflow is maintained over the ailerons to provide positive lateral control at all attitudes and exceptionally good low speed flying characteristics.

Plans and additional data are available to homebuilders, who can complete the aircraft in **TA-2** form, with tailwheel landing gear, or **TA-3** form, with tricycle gear. By January 1986, 87 sets of plans had been sold. Construction of ten aircraft is known to have been undertaken, with two completed. Three of those under construction are using the tricycle landing gear option, as TA-3s, and one is to be powered by a Volkswagen modified motorcar engine with direct drive, instead of the standard Subaru engine. Partial assembly kits are also available to amateur builders, covering the fin, rudder, tailplane and elevators. Eight had been sold by January 1986. Difficult to fabricate components, such as the main load-bearing member and pre-formed glassfibre fairings, can also be purchased. Conversion of the widely available Subaru engine requires no machining, and is well within the skill of the average handyman. Engine and propeller reduction drawings are available as a set of separate plans, plus a propeller reduction kit and plans for constructing a clamp-on towbar.

TYPE: Two-seat homebuilt aircraft.

AIRFRAME: Cantilever shoulder-wing monoplane. Wing section NACA 23015. No dihedral. Incidence 3°. Conventional aluminium alloy structure, with rectangular box-type main spar, drawn ribs and pop riveted Alclad T3 skin. Plastics composite root section, which remains attached to fuselage when main wing panels are folded for towing or storage. Endplates at tips, toed in 2° and canted 10° for directional stability. Full span slotted metal ailerons. No flaps or tabs. Main load-bearing member of fuselage comprises a 5·4 m (17 ft 8½ in) long, 150 mm (6 in) diameter 6063-T6 or 6061-T6 aluminium alloy tube, to which are bolted two pylons for the cabin/landing gear/engine/wing group and the tail unit assembly. All fairings, including cabin enclosures, of glassfibre. Cantilever T tail has aluminium alloy spars and ribs, covered with Alclad T-3 skins. Constant chord horizontal surfaces, with statically balanced one-piece elevator and tab.

LANDING GEAR: Non-retractable tailwheel type standard (TA-2). At least three Birds being built with tricycle type (TA-3). Cantilever main units constructed of unidirectional reinforced non-woven glassfibre and epoxy resin. Industrial 8·00-4 mainwheels and toe-operated hydraulic disc brakes. Size 4 × 1·5 in steerable tailwheel, when applicable, carried on spring leg. Mainwheel tyre pressure 1·38 bars (20 lb/sq in). Optional floats and skis.

POWER PLANT: One 53·7 or 84·3 kW (72 or 113 hp) watercooled Subaru 1,600 cc or 1,800 cc converted motorcar engine, driving a two-blade wooden fixed-pitch pusher propeller via a separate bolt-on 2:1 reduction unit with two V belts. Engine requires no basic modifications. Optionally, one Volkswagen modified motorcar engine. Fuel capacity 57 litres (15 US gallons), in two tanks in wingroot leading-edges. Oil capacity 3·8 litres (1 US gallon).

ACCOMMODATION: Two seats in tandem in fully enclosed cabin. Access by sliding forward entire nose fairing and windscreen assembly.

SYSTEMS: Hydraulic system for brakes. Electrical system with 12V battery and 35A alternator.

AVIONICS: Full IFR panel and King KN 155 nav/com radio optional.

DIMENSIONS, EXTERNAL:
Wing span 7·92 m (26 ft 0 in)
Wing chord, constant 1·27 m (4 ft 2 in)
Wing aspect ratio 6·24
Width, wings folded 2·44 m (8 ft 0 in)
Length overall 5·59 m (18 ft 4 in)
Height overall 1·68 m (5 ft 6 in)
Tailplane span 1·83 m (6 ft 0 in)
Wheel track 1·64 m (5 ft 4½ in)
Wheelbase 3·63 m (11 ft 11 in)
Propeller diameter 1·52 m (5 ft 0 in)

AREA:
Wings, gross 10·07 m² (108·42 sq ft)

WEIGHTS AND LOADINGS:
Weight empty 277 kg (610 lb)
Max T-O weight 526 kg (1,160 lb)
Max wing loading 52·2 kg/m² (10·70 lb/sq ft)
Max power loading (72 hp) 9·80 kg/kW (16·11 lb/hp)

PERFORMANCE:
Never-exceed speed 121 knots (225 km/h; 140 mph)
Max level speed 113 knots (209 km/h; 130 mph)
Max cruising speed 91 knots (169 km/h; 105 mph)
Econ cruising speed 82 knots (153 km/h; 95 mph)
Stalling speed 39 knots (73 km/h; 45 mph)
Service ceiling 4,265 m (14,000 ft)
T-O run 137 m (450 ft)
T-O to 15 m (50 ft) 183 m (600 ft)
Landing from 15 m (50 ft) 168 m (550 ft)
Landing run 122 m (400 ft)
Range, with max fuel, no reserves 295 nm (547 km; 340 miles)

T.E.A.M.

TENNESSEE ENGINEERING AND MANUFACTURING INC

State Route 53 and Ivy Bluff Road, Route 1, Box 338C, Bradyville, Tennessee 37026
Telephone: (615) 765 5397
DESIGNER: Wayne Ison
EXECUTIVE VICE-PRESIDENT: Curtis W. Barry

T.E.A.M. MINIMAX

First shown at the 1985 Oshkosh meeting, the miniMAX can be classified as either a microlight or Experimental category homebuilt aircraft. The standard engine is a Rotax 277, but either a Rotax 377 or 447 can be fitted optionally. Design began in August 1984 and construction of the first prototype started in the following October. This flew for the first time in February 1985. In July that year a second miniMAX prototype was flown, this time built from a T.E.A.M. kit.

The miniMAX is available as a kit, minus instruments and paint; alternatively, the airframe or plans can be purchased separately. By early April 1986, fifteen kits had been delivered and ten sets of plans sold.

TYPE: Single-seat microlight and homebuilt aircraft: conforms to FAR Pt 103 (microlight) and Experimental regulations.

AIRFRAME: Strut braced shoulder-wing monoplane. Airframe of wooden Warren truss construction, fabric covered. Wing section NACA 4415. Dihedral 3°. Incidence 4°. Double surface wings. Three-axis control (full-span flaperons, elevator and rudder). Variable incidence tailplane.

LANDING GEAR: Non-retractable tailwheel type, with 4·00-6 mainwheels (tyre pressure 0·69 bars; 10 lb/sq in) and 4 in diameter solid tailwheel. Mainwheels carried on unsprung side Vs and cross axle. Brakes optional.

POWER PLANT: One 20 kW (27 hp) Rotax 277 single-cylinder two-stroke engine, with 2·58:1 reduction gear to a two-blade wooden propeller. Fuel capacity 19 litres (5 US gallons). Optional Rotax 377 and 447 engines.

ACCOMMODATION: Single seat in open cockpit with windscreen. Small baggage area in turtledeck headrest, capacity 2·3 kg (5 lb).

DIMENSIONS, EXTERNAL:
Wing span 7·62 m (25 ft 0 in)
Wing chord, constant 1·37 m (4 ft 6 in)
Wing aspect ratio 5·56
Length overall 4·72 m (15 ft 6 in)
Height overall 1·60 m (5 ft 3 in)
Tailplane span 2·29 m (7 ft 6 in)
Wheel track 1·37 m (4 ft 6 in)
Wheelbase 3·53 m (11 ft 7 in)
Propeller diameter 1·52 m (5 ft 0 in)

AREA:
Wings, gross 10·45 m² (112·5 sq ft)

WEIGHTS AND LOADINGS:
Weight empty 104 kg (230 lb)
Max pilot weight 104 kg (230 lb)
Max T-O weight 208 kg (460 lb)
Max wing loading 19·97 kg/m² (4·09 lb/sq ft)
Max power loading (Rotax 277 engine) 10·40 kg/kW (17·04 lb/hp)

PERFORMANCE:
Never-exceed speed 65 knots (120 km/h; 75 mph)
Max level speed at S/L 52 knots (97 km/h; 60 mph)
Max cruising speed at S/L 48 knots (89 km/h; 55 mph)
Econ cruising speed at S/L 43 knots (80 km/h; 50 mph)
Stalling speed, engine idling:
flaps up 23 knots (42 km/h; 26 mph)
20° flap 19 knots (36 km/h; 22 mph)
Max rate of climb at S/L 244 m (800 ft)/min
Service ceiling 3,050 m (10,000 ft)
T-O run 46 m (150 ft)
Landing run 55 m (180 ft)
Range 95·5 nm (177 km; 110 miles)
Endurance 2 h 30 min
g limits +4·4/−2·2

TERATORN

TERATORN AIRCRAFT INC

1604 South Shore Drive, Clear Lake, Iowa 50428
Telephone: (515) 357 7161
PRESIDENT: Dale Kjellsen

This company was formerly known as Motorized Gliders of Iowa; it is now named after its first microlight aircraft, the Teratorn, which first appeared in Winter 1982. In addition to its Tierra UL and Tierra II, the company introduced in 1986 the Tierra SP, of which no details have been received.

TERATORN TIERRA UL

Introduced in 1983, the Tierra is a full three-axis microlight, the general appearance of which is shown in an accompanying photograph. The Tierra offers a facility to be converted to a two-seater (operated in the US Experimental category), with the centrally positioned single-pilot seat moved sideways to accommodate the second occupant.

Three models are currently offered, using Rotax 277, 377 and 447 engines. In other respects they are almost identical.

TYPE: Single-seat microlight aircraft; conforms to FAR Pt 103.

AIRFRAME: Strut braced high-wing monoplane, of aluminium alloy and Mylar coated Dacron construction, with double surface covering. Open fuselage structure standard. Three-axis control via yoke and pedals (full span ailerons, elevators and rudder). Tailplane incidence ground adjustable.

LANDING GEAR: Non-retractable tailwheel type, with spring leg suspension and steerable tailwheel. Optional floats and skis.

POWER PLANT: Three engine choices: one 20 kW (27 hp) Rotax 277 single-cylinder two-stroke engine, with 2·58:1 reduction gear to an Ultra Prop three-blade fixed-pitch composites pusher propeller and with 19 litres (5 US gallons) fuel capacity; one 26 kW (35 hp) Rotax 377 two-cylinder two-stroke engine, with reduction gear to an Ultra Prop three- or four-blade ground adjustable composites pusher propeller and with 23 litres (6 US gallons) fuel; or one 29·4 kW (39·4 hp) Rotax 447 two-cylinder two-stroke engine, with reduction gear to an Ultra Prop three- or four-blade ground adjustable composites pusher propeller or two-blade fixed-pitch wooden pusher propeller, and with 23 litres (6 US gallons) of fuel.

ACCOMMODATION: Pilot only, in open position. Optional windscreen, semi-enclosed or fully enclosed cockpit.

SYSTEM: Optional electric engine starting.

DIMENSIONS, EXTERNAL:
Wing span 9·45 m (31 ft 0 in)
Wing aspect ratio 6·24
Length overall 5·49 m (18 ft 0 in)
Height overall 1·68 m (5 ft 6 in)
Tailplane span 2·74 m (9 ft 0 in)
Wheelbase 3·81 m (12 ft 6 in)

AREA:
Wings, gross 14·31 m² (154·0 sq ft)

WEIGHTS AND LOADINGS (A: Rotax 277, B: Rotax 377, C: Rotax 447):
Weight empty: A 114 kg (252 lb)
B, C 125 kg (275 lb)

Taylor TA-2 Bird two-seat homebuilt aircraft

T.E.A.M. miniMAX single-seat microlight and homebuilt aircraft

The two-seat Teratorn Tierra II homebuilt aircraft *(Peter M. Bowers)*

Those Flying Machines Pegasus II, with Cuyuna 430 engine *(J. M. G. Gradidge)*

Teratorn Aircraft's single-seat Tierra UL

Pilot weight range: A, B, C	55-113 kg (120-250 lb)
Max T-O weight: A	227 kg (500 lb)
B	238 kg (525 lb)
C	261 kg (575 lb)
Max wing loading: A	15·87 kg/m² (3·25 lb/sq ft)
B	16·65 kg/m² (3·41 lb/sq ft)
C	18·21 kg/m² (3·73 lb/sq ft)
Max power loading: A	11·35 kg/kW (18·52 lb/hp)
B	9·15 kg/kW (15·00 lb/hp)
C	8·88 kg/kW (14·59 lb/hp)

PERFORMANCE (A, B, C as above):

Never-exceed speed:	
A	65 knots (120 km/h; 75 mph)
B, C	69 knots (129 km/h; 80 mph)
Max level speed at 762 m (2,500 ft):	
A	52 knots (97 km/h; 60 mph)
B, C	61 knots (113 km/h; 70 mph)
Max cruising speed at 762 m (2,500 ft):	
A	49 knots (92 km/h; 57 mph)
B, C	56 knots (105 km/h; 65 mph)
Econ cruising speed at 762 m (2,500 ft):	
A	46 knots (85 km/h; 53 mph)
B, C	52 knots (97 km/h; 60 mph)
Stalling speed: A	21 knots (39 km/h; 24 mph)
B, C	25 knots (45 km/h; 28 mph)
Max rate of climb at S/L: A	183 m (600 ft)/min
B	244 m (800 ft)/min
C	274 m (900 ft)/min
Service ceiling: A, B, C	3,050 m (10,000 ft)
T-O run: A	31 m (100 ft)
B, C	23 m (75 ft)
Landing run: A, B, C	46 m (150 ft)
Range with max fuel:	
A, B	104 nm (193 km; 120 miles)
C	86·5 nm (161 km; 100 miles)

TERATORN TIERRA II

This is a two-seat Tierra, with a 48·5 kW (65 hp) Rotax 532 engine, wing flaps, enclosed cabin with rigid Lexan doors, and breakaway steerable tailwheel. Options include floats, skis and agricultural spraying equipment. The latter, introduced in 1985 as an option for the 'workhorse' Tierra II, has been sold to customers in Canada, Mexico and the USA.

Unlike the Tierra ULs, the Tierra II falls under the Experimental category as a homebuilt aircraft, although it is generally similar.

TYPE: Two-seat homebuilt aircraft.

AIRFRAME: As for Tierra ULs, except for in-cabin adjustment of tailplane incidence. Enclosed cabin for crew.

LANDING GEAR: As for Tierra ULs, with hydraulically actuated brakes. Same options.

POWER PLANT: One 48·5 kW (65 hp) Rotax 532 two-cylinder two-stroke engine, with reduction gear to a two-blade fixed-pitch wooden pusher propeller. Fuel capacity 45·4 litres (12 US gallons).

ACCOMMODATION: Pilot and passenger side by side in fully enclosed cabin with rigid Lexan doors.

DIMENSIONS, EXTERNAL:

Wing span	11·20 m (36 ft 9 in)
Wing chord, constant (incl ailerons)	1·55 m (5 ft 1 in)
Length overall	5·69 m (18 ft 8 in)
Height overall	1·85 m (6 ft 1 in)
Tailplane span	5·69 m (8 ft 11 in)
Wheel track	1·60 m (5 ft 3 in)
Wheelbase	3·76 m (12 ft 4 in)
Propeller diameter	1·78 m (5 ft 10 in)

AREA:

Wings, gross	17·65 m² (190·0 sq ft)

WEIGHTS:

No data received, except:

Crew weight range	55-204 kg (120-450 lb)

PERFORMANCE:

Never-exceed speed	73 knots (136 km/h; 85 mph)
Max level speed at 762 m (2,500 ft)	61 knots (113 km/h; 70 mph)
Max cruising speed at 762 m (2,500 ft)	52 knots (97 km/h; 60 mph)
Econ cruising speed at 762 m (2,500 ft)	48 knots (89 km/h; 55 mph)
Stalling speed	27 knots (50 km/h; 31 mph)
Max rate of climb at S/L	183 m (600 ft)/min
Service ceiling	3,050 m (10,000 ft)
T-O run	38 m (125 ft)
T-O to 15 m (50 ft)	122 m (400 ft)
Landing run	54 m (175 ft)
Range with max fuel	208 nm (386 km; 240 miles)

TFM

THOSE FLYING MACHINES (TFM INC)

705 East Gardena Boulevard, Gardena, California 90248
Telephone: (213) 532 2030
PRESIDENT: John Woods

TFM PEGASUS II and PEGASUS SUPRA

The **Pegasus II** and **Pegasus Supra** are generally similar, except that the latter has conventional three-axis control (using spoilerons), 2·4:1 engine reduction drive and other changes. The following details refer to the Pegasus II:

TYPE: Single-seat microlight aircraft; conforms to FAR Pt 103.

AIRFRAME: High-wing monoplane, with frontal elevator. Main frame of anodised aluminium alloy with mostly single surface Dacron covering. Adjustable kingpost and vinyl coated stainless steel cables. Pitch control by canard elevator, yaw control by wingtip rudders.

LANDING GEAR: Tricycle type, with all three wheels/tyres size 10 × 2 in. Glassfibre rear axle. Steerable nosewheel. No brakes. Options include skis and floats.

POWER PLANT: One 26 kW (35 hp) two-cylinder Cuyuna 430R engine, with 2·2:1 reduction belt drive to a two-blade wooden pusher propeller. Fuel tank capacity 16 litres (4·2 US gallons).

ACCOMMODATION: Pilot only, in open position. Optional windscreen.

DIMENSIONS, EXTERNAL:

Wing span	10·72 m (35 ft 2 in)
Wing aspect ratio	6·79
Length overall	4·70 m (15 ft 5 in)
Height overall	2·30 m (9 ft 10 in)

Propeller diameter 1·45 m (4 ft 9 in)
AREA:
Wings, gross 16·91 m² (182·0 sq ft)
WEIGHTS AND LOADINGS:
Weight empty 92 kg (203 lb)
Max T-O weight 228 kg (503 lb)
Max wing loading 13·48 kg/m² (2·76 lb/sq ft)
Max power loading 8·74 kg/kW (14·37 lb/hp)
PERFORMANCE:
Never-exceed speed 55 knots (101 km/h; 63 mph)
Max level speed 48 knots (88 km/h; 55 mph)
Cruising speed 43 knots (80 km/h; 50 mph)
Stalling speed 22 knots (41 km/h; 25 mph)
Max rate of climb at S/L 289 m (950 ft)/min
Service ceiling 4,115 m (13,500 ft)
T-O run 23-30 m (75-100 ft)
Range with max fuel 104 nm (193 km; 120 miles)
Endurance with max fuel 3 h
g limits +6/−2
Best glide ratio 7
Min rate of sink, power off 107 m (350 ft)/min

TFM PEGASUS TITAN

The Titan is a microlight design said to meet FAR Pt 103 and FAA homebuilt specifications. It has a strut braced high wing, fitted with flaps and covered with Ceconite, and an all-composites pod and boom fuselage bearing large conventional tail surfaces and a tricycle landing gear. Power plant is a Kawasaki 340 engine. Few other details are known.

TYPE: Single-seat microlight aircraft.

DIMENSION, EXTERNAL:
Wing span 9·75 m (32 ft 0 in)
AREA:
Wings, gross 11·9 m² (128·0 sq ft)
PERFORMANCE:
Max level speed 55 knots (101 km/h; 63 mph)

THOMPSON

THOMPSON AIRCRAFT

336 Fitzwater Street, Philadelphia, Pennsylvania 19147
Telephone: (215) 925 8942
Telex: 845241

PRESIDENT: Richard R. Thompson

Mr Thompson designed, built, flew and patented the prototype of a unique ultralight aircraft known as the Thompson Boxmoth, which featured rhomboidal wing cells in its original form. A second patent was awarded for his universal propeller assembly, and a third is pending for the landing gear.

Development of the Boxmoth began in October 1968; construction of the prototype began in 1970 and this flew for the first time in November 1975. Patent rights in the Boxmoth are reserved by Mr Thompson, and no production, use or sale of the Boxmoth concept is permitted without authorisation. Licences are available, together with three-view drawings, photos, notes and progress reports of the development and flight testing of the prototype, which has undergone continuous refinement, as recorded annually in *Jane's*.

The Boxmoth is specifically designed for construction by amateur builders, using locally available components, materials and hardware. Its construction requires no welding, machining, sheet metal, woodwork, or conventional fabric or dope. Any high-performance, lightweight snowmobile, motorcycle or outboard engine can be fitted. The wings fold against the main frame for towing behind a car or for storage in a one-car garage.

THOMPSON BOXMOTH B

In 1985 the prototype Boxmoth B had its lower wings shortened from 7·32 m (24 ft) to 6·71 m (22 ft) span and the struts on the wingtips swept forward. Glassfibre main landing gear struts replaced the earlier Lexan polycarbonate plastics struts. The most recent improvements include relocation of the rudder to the rearmost vertical strut and the adoption of a new (Swallow type) elevator with V cutaway to allow the rudder 60° of swing. A 4·5 kg (10 lb) counterbalance on the end of a 3·05 m (10 ft) long 1¼ in aluminium alloy tube, projecting from the centre of the lower wings, offsets the weight shift incurred by moving the rudder aft.

TYPE: Single-seat homebuilt biplane.

AIRFRAME: Strut and wire braced biplane, with woven/laminated polyethylene double surface covering over wings and control surfaces. Airframe of 2 in and 1 in aluminium alloy irrigation piping. Vinyl coated stainless steel cables. Two-axis control (elevators and rudder). Wings fold for storage.

LANDING GEAR: Non-retractable tailwheel type, with braced glassfibre spring main side Vs and cross axle. Mainwheels size 16 × 4; tailwheel size 6 × 2. No brakes.

POWER PLANT: Prototype has one 41 kW (55 hp) 650 cc Hirth R-28 two-cylinder two-stroke engine, driving an Arrow two-blade fixed-pitch wooden propeller via two-strand chain drive 3:1 reduction gearing. One fuel tank, capacity 9·5 litres (2·5 US gallons).

ACCOMMODATION: Underslung PVC seat for pilot, mounted between two bottom longerons. Baggage position in front of pilot, with 4·5 kg (10 lb) capacity.

DIMENSIONS, EXTERNAL:
Wing span, upper 7·32 m (24 ft 0 in)
Wing chord, constant 1·83 m (6 ft 0 in)
Wing aspect ratio: front 4
rear 6
Width, wings accordian folded 1·22 m (4 ft 0 in)
Length overall 7·92 m (26 ft 0 in)
Height overall 3·66 m (12 ft 0 in)
Tailplane span 2·44 m (8 ft 0 in)
Wheel track 1·83 m (6 ft 0 in)
Wheelbase 4·88 m (16 ft 0 in)
Propeller diameter 1·78 m (5 ft 10 in)
AREA:
Wings, gross 42·74 m² (460·0 sq ft)
WEIGHTS AND LOADINGS:
Weight empty 204 kg (450 lb)
Pilot weight range 45·5-79·5 kg (100-175 lb)
Max T-O weight 295 kg (650 lb)
Max wing loading 6·88 kg/m² (1·41 lb/sq ft)
Max power loading 7·20 kg/kW (11·82 lb/hp)
PERFORMANCE (at max T-O weight):
Never-exceed speed 39 knots (72 km/h; 45 mph)
Max level speed at S/L 35 knots (64 km/h; 40 mph)
Max and econ cruising speed 30 knots (56 km/h; 35 mph)
Stalling speed 22 knots (41 km/h; 25 mph)
Max rate of climb at S/L, estimated 152 m (500 ft)/min
Service ceiling, estimated 1,525 m (5,000 ft)
T-O run 92 m (300 ft)
T-O to 15 m (50 ft), estimated 152 m (500 ft)
Landing from 15 m (50 ft), estimated 31 m (100 ft)
Landing run 15 m (50 ft)
Range 8·7 nm (16 km; 10 miles)

THORP

SUNDERLAND AIRCRAFT

5 Griffin Drive, Apalachin, NY 13732

SPORT AIRCRAFT INC

104 E Avenue K4 Unit G, Lancaster, California 93535
Telephone: (805) 949 2312

These two companies now market plans of the Thorp T-18 two-seat all-metal sporting aircraft designed by Mr John W. Thorp. In addition, various component parts to build the aircraft are available from Sport Aircraft Inc.

An earlier Thorp aircraft, the Sky Skooter, is again being offered in ready assembled form and as a kit (see Thorp 211 Aircraft Inc in main Aircraft section).

THORP S-18 (T-18C-W)

The early history and achievements of the Thorp T-18 have been described in the 1985-86 and previous editions of *Jane's* under the entry for Thorp Engineering Company. The version for which plans and components are currently available combines features of the T-18C, with folding wings designed by Mr Luther Sunderland, and the T-18W embodying a wide-body modification also developed by Mr Sunderland. Designated S-18, it is not only easy to transport by road but utilises a new aerofoil section which offers a considerably reduced stalling speed.

Well over 200 T-18s and S-18s have been completed since the first example was flown on 12 May 1964.

TYPE: Two-seat homebuilt sporting aircraft.

AIRFRAME: Cantilever low-wing monoplane of aluminium alloy construction. Wing section LDS-4-212. Dihedral 8° on outer panels only. Two-spar wings which can be folded back on each side of fuselage in 10 min by one person. Normally no flaps, but a flap installation is under design. Conventional semi-monocoque fuselage and cantilever tail unit, the former without double curvature.

LANDING GEAR: Non-retractable tailwheel type. Cantilever main legs. Steerable tailwheel. Mainwheel tyres size 5·00-5.

POWER PLANT: One Avco Lycoming or Continental flat-four engine in 100-134 kW (135-180 hp) category, driving a two-blade constant-speed or fixed-pitch propeller. Fuel tank aft of firewall, capacity 110 litres (29 US gallons). Optional integral tank in wing leading-edge.

ACCOMMODATION: Two seats side by side, with dual controls. Large rearward sliding canopy.

DIMENSIONS, EXTERNAL:
Wing span 6·35 m (20 ft 10 in)
Wing chord, constant 1·27 m (4 ft 2 in)
Wing aspect ratio 5·05
Width, wings folded 2·44 m (8 ft 0 in)
Length overall 5·89 m (19 ft 4 in)
Height overall 1·55 m (5 ft 1 in)
Tailplane span 2·10 m (6 ft 11 in)
Propeller diameter 1·73 m (5 ft 8 in)
DIMENSION, INTERNAL:
Cockpit: Max width 1·02 m (3 ft 4 in)
AREA:
Wings, gross 8·0 m² (86·0 sq ft)
WEIGHTS AND LOADINGS (112 kW; 150 hp Avco Lycoming):
Weight empty 419 kg (923 lb)
Max T-O weight 680 kg (1,500 lb)
Max wing loading 85·16 kg/m² (17·49 lb/sq ft)
Max power loading 6·07 kg/kW (10·0 lb/hp)
PERFORMANCE (112 kW; 150 hp Avco Lycoming):
Max level speed at S/L 159 knots (295 km/h; 183 mph)
Max cruising speed (75% power) at 2,590 m (8,500 ft) 156 knots (290 km/h; 180 mph)
Stalling speed 53 knots (97 km/h; 60 mph)
Max rate of climb at S/L 366 m (1,200 ft)/min
Service ceiling 6,100 m (20,000 ft)
Range with max fuel 460 nm (853 km; 530 miles)

THUNDER WINGS

THUNDER WINGS (a division of Thunder Development Inc)

7326 East Evans Road, Scottsdale, Arizona 85260
VICE-PRESIDENT, MARKETING: David A. Bratset

This company was established by Thunder Development Inc, which was itself formed in 1975 by a group of men who wished to build and fly replicas of Second World War combat aircraft. Their first product was a half-scale representation of the Focke-Wulf Fw 190A, powered by a 74·5 kW (100 hp) Continental O-200 flat-four engine, and using the carved foam and outside glassfibre layup constructional technique.

After careful consideration of the structure, flight characteristics and scale proportions of this small fighter replica, it was decided to adopt an entirely different approach to the programme before marketing kits and plans to other amateur constructors. A basic scale of approximately 80 per cent was selected to permit the installation of more powerful engines without prejudicing the scale proportions and general appearance of the aircraft. It was realised also that this larger scale would offer room for full-size military pilot seats, with provision for seat or back parachutes, instrument panels spacious enough for full gyros and IFR avionics, and systems such as oxygen and remote fire extinguishing.

To ensure availability of a suitable power plant for the representations of inline engined aircraft, Thunder developed from the Jaguar V-12 motorcar engine what it calls the Lightning Merlin. Drawings are available for this conversion, which involves the addition of a reduction gear; future developments may add dual magneto ignition, a fuel injection system and turbocharging. For constructors of radial engined replicas, such as the 80 per cent Fw 190A, the standard Continental W670 seven-cylinder aircraft engine provides an easily obtainable authentic appearance.

Thunder Wings was established as a division of Thunder Development Inc to market plans and kits of the 80 per cent replicas. Initially, these aircraft were designed with laminated spruce wing spars, wooden spars for the fin, tailplane and all control surfaces, and a welded steel tube fuselage. The airframe was then covered with a set of pre-moulded skins that reproduced accurately the shape of the original full-scale fighter. Subsequently, Thunder Wings developed all-composite internal structures to supplement the wood and steel tube, resulting in considerable reduction of structure weight and simplifying construction for the homebuilder. The composite kits became available in 1981. Thunder Wings currently offers the Spitfire and P-40C in either all-composite or wood and steel structural forms; but the Fw 190A is available only in wood and steel form.

The company intended to sell only 100 kits of each replica, and each is offered in three individual component groups (fuselage, wing, and controls and accessories) to spread the purchase cost over a period of time. The kits do not include the Lightning Merlin or Continental power plant.

THUNDER WINGS CURTISS P-40C

TYPE: Eight-tenths scale homebuilt combat aircraft replica.

AIRFRAME: Cantilever low-wing monoplane built in three sections. Wing section NACA 23015. Two-spar structure, with spars and ribs of moulded sandwich composite material. Preformed skins attached by structural bonding. Ailerons, of similar construction, have single spar.

Thompson Boxmoth in 1985 configuration, with aft rudder

Thorp T-18 built by Mr Ford Hendricks of Seattle, Washington *(Peter M. Bowers)*

Thunder Wings scale replica of a Curtiss P-40C

Thunder Wings scale replica of a Focke-Wulf Fw 190A, with wood and steel structure

Thunder Wings eight-tenths scale replica of the Supermarine Spitfire IX

No trailing-edge flaps. No tabs. Semi-monocoque fuselage, incorporating bulkheads, centre-section spars and interior bracing of composite material, covered by preformed half-shells. Conventional cantilever tail unit of similar construction to wings. The tailplane incorporates two spars; elevators, fin and rudder each have a single spar. No tabs.

LANDING GEAR: Hydraulically retractable type with a single wheel on each unit. Main units retract aft and turn through 90° as they are raised to lie flush in the undersurface of the wing. Non-retractable tailwheel.

POWER PLANT: One 224 kW (300 hp) Lightning Merlin V-12 piston engine, driving a three-blade constant-speed propeller with spinner. Radiators in scale position under engine. Fuel contained in integral wing tanks with a standard capacity of 170 litres (45 US gallons). Long-range tanks of 265 litre (70 US gallon) capacity optional.

ACCOMMODATION: Pilot and optional passenger, seated in tandem. Removable rear window cover inserts can be installed when no passenger is carried, to maintain authentic appearance of replica. Rearward sliding cockpit canopy.

SYSTEMS: Electrical system includes engine driven alternator. Hydraulic system for landing gear actuation. Vacuum system for flight instruments. Fire extinguishing and oxygen systems optional.

AVIONICS AND EQUIPMENT: Optional avionics can include 720-channel com transceiver, VOR/ILS, GS and marker beacon receivers, transponder with altitude encoder, digital approach timer, annunciator panel, and associated antennae. Full blind-flying instrumentation optional.

DIMENSIONS, EXTERNAL:
- Wing span: 9·14 m (30 ft 0 in)
- Length overall: 7·62 m (25 ft 0 in)
- Height overall: 3·05 m (10 ft 0 in)

AREA:
- Wings, gross: 14·03 m² (151·0 sq ft)

WEIGHTS AND LOADINGS (composite structure):
- *Weight empty, equipped: 1,064 kg (2,345 lb)
- Max T-O weight: 1,324 kg (2,919 lb)
- Max wing loading: 94·4 kg/m² (19·33 lb/sq ft)
- Max power loading: 5·91 kg/kW (9·73 lb/hp)

**includes all listed optional avionics and equipment*

PERFORMANCE (at max T-O weight, flown solo):
- Cruising speed: 174 knots (322 km/h; 200 mph)
- Range with standard fuel: 434 nm (805 km; 500 miles)
- Range with optional long-range fuel: 651 nm (1,207 km; 750 miles)
- g limits: ±6

THUNDER WINGS FOCKE-WULF Fw 190A

The Fw 190A is offered in wood and steel structural form only.

AIRFRAME: Wings as for P-40C. Welded steel tube fuselage, covered with pre-moulded skins. Tail unit as for P-40C, but with trim tab in rudder and starboard elevator.

LANDING GEAR: As for P-40C, except that main units retract inward.

POWER PLANT: One 179 kW (240 hp) Continental W670 seven-cylinder aircooled radial piston engine, driving a three-blade fixed-pitch wooden propeller with spinner. Fuel capacity 189·25 litres (50 US gallons).

ACCOMMODATION: Pilot only, beneath transparent canopy. Baggage space with capacity of 18 kg (40 lb).

DIMENSIONS, EXTERNAL:
- Wing span: 8·53 m (28 ft 0 in)
- Length overall: 7·01 m (23 ft 0 in)
- Height overall: 2·44 m (8 ft 0 in)

AREA:
- Wings, gross: 12·26 m² (132·0 sq ft)

WEIGHTS AND LOADINGS:
- *Weight empty, equipped: 897 kg (1,978 lb)
- Max T-O weight: 1,168 kg (2,575 lb)
- Max wing loading: 95·25 kg/m² (19·5 lb/sq ft)
- Max power loading: 6·53 kg/kW (10·73 lb/hp)

**Empty weight quoted includes optional avionics, equipment and systems as detailed for P-40C*

PERFORMANCE (at max T-O weight):
- Cruising speed: 161 knots (298 km/h; 185 mph)
- Range: 544 nm (1,009 km; 627 miles)
- g limits: ±6

THUNDER WINGS SUPERMARINE SPITFIRE Mk IX

Details of the Spitfire Mk IX are generally similar to those of the P-40C except as follows:

AIRFRAME: Trim tab in rudder and port elevator.

LANDING GEAR: Main units retract outward.

POWER PLANT: Engine drives a four-blade propeller with spinner. Fuel capacity 246 litres (65 US gallons).

ACCOMMODATION: Pilot only, beneath rearward sliding transparent canopy. Hinged access panel on port side of cockpit. Baggage space with capacity of 13·6 kg (30 lb).

DIMENSIONS, EXTERNAL:
- Wing span: 8·23 m (27 ft 0 in)
- Length overall: 7·01 m (23 ft 0 in)
- Height overall: 2·74 m (9 ft 0 in)

AREA:
- Wings, gross: 11·89 m² (128·0 sq ft)

WEIGHTS AND LOADINGS (composite structure):
- *Weight empty, equipped: 751 kg (1,655 lb)
- Max T-O weight: 1,023 kg (2,255 lb)
- Max wing loading: 86·0 kg/m² (17·6 lb/sq ft)
- Max power loading: 4·57 kg/kW (7·52 lb/hp)

**Empty weight quoted includes optional avionics, equipment and systems as detailed for P-40C*

PERFORMANCE (at max T-O weight):
- Cruising speed: 195 knots (362 km/h; 225 mph)
- Range: 705 nm (1,306 km; 812 miles)
- g limits: ±6

TM

TM AIRCRAFT

Mr W. Terry Miller designed and built a tandem two-seat light monoplane known as the TM-5. Design began in 1974 and construction of the prototype (N1053Y) started two years later. The first flight was achieved in 1980. Plans and some component parts became available, to allow amateur construction, and a few TM-5s are being built in Canada and the USA. However, all such marketing has now ended.

Full details of the TM-5 and an illustration can be found in the 1985-86 *Jane's*.

TOPA

TOPA AIRCRAFT COMPANY

1401 Offshore, Oxnard, California 93033

Telephone: (805) 985 5629

PRESIDENT: Chris Spangenberg

TOPA SCOUT

The Topa Scout was designed as a single-seat ultralight aircraft, with a strong airframe for safety and durability, and full three-axis control. It has a slightly higher wing loading than is common for aircraft of this type, to allow it to fly in gusty wind conditions that would prevent many other types from flying.

The prototype Scout was displayed at Oshkosh 1982 in unfinished condition, but has since been completed and has undergone its flight test programme.

From February 1983, plans and some component parts to construct the Scout have been available for purchase by amateur builders. Components available include the landing gear, engine mount, wing ribs and some sheet metal parts.

TYPE: Single-seat homebuilt sporting aircraft.

AIRFRAME: Strut braced high-wing monoplane. Thickness/chord ratio 15%. Dihedral from roots. Wide span, narrow chord ailerons. Boom type fuselage, with narrow forward section providing attachment points for seat, wings and struts. Wire braced tail unit, carried on boom. Large area fin and horn balanced rudder; mid-mounted tailplane and balanced elevators. Airframe constructed of aluminium alloy (2024-T3), with Stits Poly-Fiber covering on the wings, tail unit and control surfaces.

LANDING GEAR: Non-retractable tailwheel type. Spoked mainwheels, diameter 20 in. Oleo-pneumatic shock absorbers. Tailwheel diameter 4 in. Disc brakes.

POWER PLANT: One 35 kW (47 hp) Rotax engine, carried above wings, driving a two-blade wooden pusher propeller (prototype fitted originally with 22·5 kW; 30 hp Cuyuna engine). Single fuel tank, capacity 28·5 litres (7·5 US gallons).

ACCOMMODATION: Pilot only, on open seat. Optional enclosed cockpit on later model.

DIMENSIONS, EXTERNAL:
- Wing span: 10·52 m (34 ft 6 in)
- Wing aspect ratio: 7
- Length overall: 6·40 m (21 ft 0 in)
- Height overall: 2·13 m (7 ft 0 in)
- Propeller diameter: 1·37 m (4 ft 6 in)

AREA:
- Wings, gross: 14·86 m² (160·0 sq ft)

WEIGHTS AND LOADINGS:
- Weight empty: 195 kg (431 lb)
- Pilot weight range: 68-113 kg (150-250 lb)
- Max T-O weight: 317 kg (700 lb)
- Max wing loading: 21·39 kg/m² (4·38 lb/sq ft)
- Max power loading (47 hp): 9·06 kg/kW (14·89 lb/hp)

PERFORMANCE (estimated):
- Never-exceed speed: 60 knots (112 km/h; 70 mph)
- Max level speed: 52 knots (96 km/h; 60 mph)
- Max cruising speed: 41 knots (76 km/h; 47 mph)
- Econ cruising speed: 39 knots (72 km/h; 45 mph)
- Stalling speed: 29 knots (54 km/h; 33 mph)
- Max rate of climb at S/L: 183 m (600 ft)/min
- T-O run: 76 m (250 ft)
- Range with max fuel: 139 nm (257 km; 160 miles)
- *g* limits: +8·5/−5

TRI Q

TRI Q DEVELOPMENT COMPANY

PO Box 519, Vandalia, Ohio 45377

TRI Q QUICKIE Q2 MODIFICATION

A modification to the Quickie Q2, primarily to provide a tricycle landing gear, is available from Tri Q Development Co. Design by Mr Scott Swing began in January 1985 and construction of a prototype started simultaneously. This aircraft flew for the first time on 13 March that year, and production kits for the modification became available in June 1985. The first Q2 modified from a Tri Q kit flew in July 1985. By January 1986 a total of 68 kits had been delivered, and six modified aircraft were flying. The modification is said to ease ground handling. The main legs of the new tricycle landing gear are canted forward by 25 cm (10 in) and are attached to the seat back bulkhead and a new lower bulkhead; while the forward canted nosewheel unit is attached to the firewall and the rear of the foreplane. All landing gear units in production form are constructed of S-glass and include streamline wheel fairings. Rosenhan wheels size 11·4 × 5 in are used on the main units; the 10 × 4 in nosewheel is a Cessna 180 tailwheel. Mainwheel and nosewheel tyre pressures are 2·76 bars (40 lb/sq in) and 2·07 bars (30 lb/sq in) respectively. Rosenhan toe-operated brakes are fitted.

The change to a tricycle landing gear allows the usual anhedral to be deleted from the foreplane which, like the wings, is increased in span by 0·91 m (3 ft) as a further feature of the modification. As a result, the Tri-Q modified Q2's landing speed is said to be 9 knots (16 km/h; 10 mph) lower than that of the standard Quickie Q2, and rate of climb is claimed to be 46-61 m (150-200 ft)/min greater. The landing run is reduced by the modification; other benefits include improved view for the pilot on the ground and a tighter turning circle. Weight empty is 272 kg (600 lb) and max T-O weight 499 kg (1,100 lb).

TUBE WORKS

TUBE WORKS

6320 Highland Road, Pontiac, Michigan 48054
Telephone: (313) 666 1388

TUBE WORKS PHOENIX

The Phoenix is a single-seat, single engined microlight, conforming to FAR Pt 103. It is available in kit form, which an inexperienced builder should be able to assemble in a single weekend.

AIRFRAME: Wire braced high wing monoplane, with single-surface fabric covered wings and tail unit. Marked dihedral on constant chord wings. Mainframe of satin anodized aluminium alloy tubing. Vinyl-coated stainless steel wires.

LANDING GEAR: Tricycle type, with all three wheels of similar size and fitted with fairings. Tailskid protects rudder.

POWER PLANT: One 20 kW (27 hp) Rotax 277 single-cylinder two-stroke engine, with reduction gear to two-blade pusher propeller. Fuel tank capacity 19 litres (5 US gallons).

ACCOMMODATION: Pilot only, in open position.

DIMENSIONS, EXTERNAL:
- Wing span: 9·75 m (32 ft 0 in)
- Length overall: 5·59 m (18 ft 4 in)
- Height overall: 2·95 m (9 ft 8 in)
- Propeller diameter: 1·52 m (5 ft 0 in)

AREA:
- Wings, gross: 14·86 m² (160·0 sq ft)

WEIGHTS:
- Weight empty: 108 kg (239 lb)
- Payload (with full fuel): 113 kg (250 lb)

PERFORMANCE (with 77 kg; 170 lb pilot):
- Max level speed: 45 knots (83 km/h; 52 mph)
- Stalling speed: 20 knots (37 km/h; 23 mph)
- Max rate of climb at S/L: 244 m (800 ft)/min
- Service ceiling: 3,660 m (12,000 ft)
- T-O run: 20 m (65 ft)
- Landing run, grass: 18 m (60 ft)

TURNER

TURNER AIRCRAFT

5803 Waterview Drive, Arlington, Texas 76016
Telephone: (817) 457 5081
PRESIDENT: E. L. Gene Turner

The 1966-67 *Jane's* contained details of a single-seat sporting aircraft designated T-40, which was designed and built by Mr E. L. Turner and flew for the first time on 3 April 1961. This aircraft was modified by Mr Turner and his son into a prototype of the two-seat T-40A and has since formed the basis of a succession of developed versions of the same general design.

Plans of the T-40, T-40A and Super T-40A are available to homebuilders; many hundreds of sets have been sold.

The latest version of the basic T-40 design is the T-77, utilising the NASA GAW general aviation wing section; spoilers without ailerons for roll control; and aerodynamically operated leading-edge slats.

All existing Turner aircraft have folding wings, for reduced hangar space requirements and for transport by trailer. Approval for construction by amateur builders has been attained in the UK.

In addition to the T-40/T-77 series, Turner has developed a microlight aircraft known as the T-100D Mariah.

TURNER T-77

The T-77 (N115ET) utilises the fuselage of the earlier Turner T-40A and incorporates simplified model aeroplane type construction. The wing has a highly modified and computer-developed version of the NASA GAW general aviation section and incorporates a folding mechanism. A retractable tandem-type landing gear was intended to be fitted; but in order to get the aircraft completed without delay, a non-retractable gear was substituted initially.

The T-77, which is not aerobatic, flew for the first time on 16 July 1981.

TYPE: Two-seat homebuilt sporting aircraft.

AIRFRAME: Cantilever low-wing monoplane. Airframe of all-wood (fir) construction, with mahogany plywood covering. Two-spar wings, of NASA GAW-2 general aviation section. Hoerner low-drag tips. Aerodynamically operated leading-edge slats. Manually operated full span split flaps. Spoilers without supplemental ailerons, in four sections, for roll control, and ground spoilers. Wings fold rearward. Glassfibre engine cowling. Central section of fuselage embodies the wing centre-section structure, landing gear, engine mounting and cockpits. Rear fuselage carries the T tail unit, the horizontal surface of which is of all-flying type with anti-servo tab (serving also as a trim tab). Glassfibre dorsal fin.

LANDING GEAR: Non-retractable tricycle type. Cleveland mainwheels and tyres, size 15 × 6·00-6, pressure 3·10 bars (45 lb/sq in). Cleveland brakes.

POWER PLANT: One 112 kW (150 hp) Avco Lycoming flat-four engine, driving a McCauley two-blade fixed-pitch propeller, type 65/57. Fuel tanks in front fuselage, capacity 95 litres (25 US gallons), and in centre-section, capacity 60 litres (16 US gallons). Oil capacity 3·75 litres (1 US gallon).

ACCOMMODATION: Pilot and passenger side by side under rearward sliding transparent canopy. Space for 22·5 kg (50 lb) baggage aft of seats.

AVIONICS: Prototype has Narco Mark III, Com III, Nav II, transponder, AM/FM radio receiver, CB transceiver, and single-axis autopilot.

DIMENSIONS, EXTERNAL:
- Wing span: 8·53 m (28 ft 0 in)
- Wing chord: 1·08 m (3 ft 6½ in)
- Wing aspect ratio: 9·2
- Length overall: 6·12 m (20 ft 1 in)
- Width, wings folded: 2·39 m (7 ft 10 in)
- Height overall: 1·83 m (6 ft 0 in)
- Tailplane span: 1·96 m (6 ft 5 in)

DIMENSIONS, INTERNAL:
- Cabin: Length: 1·78 m (5 ft 10 in)
- Max width: 1·02 m (3 ft 4 in)

AREA:
- Wings, gross: 9·48 m² (102·0 sq ft)

WEIGHTS AND LOADINGS:
- Weight empty: 376 kg (828 lb)
- Max T-O and landing weight: 748 kg (1,650 lb)
- Max wing loading: 79·0 kg/m² (16·2 lb/sq ft)
- Max power loading: 6·68 kg/kW (11·00 lb/hp)

PERFORMANCE (at max T-O weight):
- Never-exceed speed: 225 knots (418 km/h; 260 mph)
- Max level speed at S/L: 165 knots (306 km/h; 190 mph)
- Max cruising speed at S/L: 152 knots (282 km/h; 175 mph)
- Econ cruising speed at S/L: 122 knots (225 km/h; 140 mph)
- Stalling speed: flaps up: 51 knots (94 km/h; 58 mph)
- flaps down: 41 knots (76 km/h; 47 mph)
- Max rate of climb at S/L: 457 m (1,500 ft)/min
- Estimated service ceiling: 6,400 m (21,000 ft)
- T-O run: 152 m (500 ft)
- T-O to 15 m (50 ft): 305 m (1,000 ft)
- Landing run: 91 m (300 ft)
- Range, max payload, 20 min reserves: 521 nm (965 km; 600 miles)

TURNER T-100D MARIAH

Design of the T-100, which is to FAR Pt 23 (Normal category) requirements, began in 1982, and the prototype was completed within three months, making its public debut at Oshkosh in August of that year. First flight by this aircraft (N116ET) was made on 19 December 1982, the aircraft then having an all-flying horizontal tail similar to that of the T-40. The production prototype T-100B differed in having a redesigned forward fuselage and cabin and other improvements. Kits of the T-100D production version for homebuilders will become available if sufficient demand is established.

TYPE: Single-seat microlight aircraft; conforms to FAR Pt 103.

AIRFRAME: Cantilever high-wing monoplane with foldable wings, central fuselage/engine pod, twin tailbooms, twin fins and rudders. Full three-axis control system (rudders, ailerons and all-moving horizontal tail); wing flaps also fitted. Construction from either wood or composite materials, either from plans/kits or in factory built form. Standard equipment includes shoulder harness, seat belt, energy absorbing seat cushion, airspeed indicator, altimeter, tachometer and EGT gauge.

LANDING GEAR: Non-retractable tricycle type. Steerable nosewheel, with brake. Floats may become available.

POWER PLANT: Prototype powered by a 15 kW (20 hp) Cuyuna 215 single-cylinder two-stroke engine, with 2:1 reduction drive to a three-blade wooden pusher propeller. Production T-100B powered by a KFM 105ER or Ultra engine, permitting improved streamlining of rear end of fuselage/engine pod. Fuel capacity 19 litres (5 US gallons).

ACCOMMODATION: Pilot only, in semi-enclosed cockpit. Windscreen standard. Cockpit side windows optional.

DIMENSIONS, EXTERNAL:
- Wing span: 9·75 m (32 ft 0 in)

Tri Q Development tricycle landing gear on a Quickie Q2

Topa Scout single-seat lightweight sporting aircraft *(Howard Levy)*

Prototype Turner T-77 two-seat homebuilt sporting aircraft

Tube Works Phoenix microlight *(J. M. G. Gradidge)*

Production prototype Turner T-100B Mariah microlight aircraft

Ultra Efficient Products Invader Mk III-B *(Howard Levy)*

Wing aspect ratio	7·24
Width, wings folded	2·44 m (8 ft 0 in)
Length overall	5·18 m (17 ft 0 in)
Height overall	1·70 m (5 ft 7 in)
Propeller diameter	1·07 m (3 ft 6 in)
AREA:	
Wings, gross	13·14 m² (141·4 sq ft)
WEIGHTS AND LOADINGS:	
Weight empty	114 kg (251 lb)
Max pilot weight	100 kg (220 lb)
Max T-O and landing weight	228 kg (504 lb)
Max wing loading	17·38 kg/m² (3·56 lb/sq ft)
Max power loading	15·2 kg/kW (25·2 lb/hp)
PERFORMANCE:	
Never-exceed speed	78 knots (143 km/h; 89 mph)
Max level speed	53 knots (98 km/h; 61 mph)
Max cruising speed	48 knots (89 km/h; 55 mph)
Econ cruising speed	43 knots (80 km/h; 50 mph)
Stalling speed:	
power on	18 knots (34 km/h; 21 mph)
power off	23 knots (44 km/h; 27 mph)
Range with max fuel	125 nm (231 km; 144 miles)
Endurance with max fuel	3 h 25 min
g limits	+5·8/−2·9

ULTRA EFFICIENT PRODUCTS

ULTRA EFFICIENT PRODUCTS INC

1158 Lewis Avenue, Sarasota, Florida 33577

PRESIDENT: Nicholas R. Leichty

This company currently has three microlight aircraft available to amateur constructors, known as the Invader Mk III-B, Penetrater and Demoiselle.

ULTRA EFFICIENT PRODUCTS INVADER Mk III-B

The Invader Mk III made its debut at the 1982 Sun 'n Fun meeting in Florida, when it won the award for the most outstanding aircraft. It is intended for amateur construction. Plans, kits, ready assembled aircraft and some prefabricated parts, are available from Ultra Efficient Products; by early 1986 approximately 500 sets of plans, five kits and three ready assembled aircraft had been sold, with at least 150 under active construction and about 50 flying. The current version is designated Invader Mk III-B.

TYPE: Single-seat microlight aircraft; conforms to FAR Pt 103.

AIRFRAME: Cantilever shoulder-wing monoplane with pod and boom fuselage, V tail surfaces and tricycle landing gear. Constant chord dihedral wings have centre-section box of laminated spruce stringers and birch plywood with foam plastics core; outer panels of plywood and foam plastics. Wing ribs of Styrofoam; covering of Mylar or Dacron, except for plywood leading-edge. Aluminium alloy fuselage pod, built in left and right halves, welded together and Dacron covered; 10 cm (4 in) diameter aluminium tailboom. 'Ruddervators' have aluminium spar tube, Styrofoam ribs, and Mylar or Dacron covering. Three-axis control. Rigging time 15 min.

LANDING GEAR: Non-retractable tricycle type, with steel tube legs and bungee cord shock absorption. All three wheels and tyres normally same size (3·50 × 10 in); smaller nosewheel optional. Steerable nosewheel; brakes optional.

POWER PLANT: One 14·2 kW (19 hp) 277 cc Rotax single-cylinder two-stroke engine, with 2·25:1 reduction drive to two-blade wooden pusher propeller. Fuel tank capacity 19 litres (5 US gallons).

ACCOMMODATION: Pilot only, in open cockpit. Windscreen and enclosed cockpit optional.

DIMENSIONS, EXTERNAL:	
Wing span	9·45 m (31 ft 0 in)
Wing aspect ratio	6·77
Length overall	5·49 m (18 ft 0 in)
Height overall	1·83 m (6 ft 0 in)
Propeller diameter	1·12 m (3 ft 8 in)
AREA:	
Wings, gross	13·19 m² (142·0 sq ft)
WEIGHTS AND LOADINGS:	
Weight empty	102 kg (225 lb)
Pilot weight range	59-91 kg (130-200 lb)
Max T-O weight	204 kg (450 lb)
Max wing loading	15·48 kg/m² (3·17 lb/sq ft)
Max power loading	14·37 kg/kW (23·68 lb/hp)
PERFORMANCE:	
Never-exceed speed	60 knots (112 km/h; 70 mph)
Max level speed	52 knots (97 km/h; 60 mph)
Max cruising speed	43 knots (80 km/h; 50 mph)
Stalling speed	22 knots (41 km/h; 25 mph)
Max rate of climb at S/L	183 m (600 ft)/min
T-O run (grass)	46 m (150 ft)
Landing run (grass)	55 m (180 ft)
g limits (at 165 kg; 365 lb AUW)	±3·5
Best glide ratio: open cockpit	14
enclosed cockpit	16

ULTRA EFFICIENT PRODUCTS PENETRATER

Shown at the 1985 Sun 'n Fun meeting, this new microlight aircraft is being marketed by Ultra Efficient products in kit form (three sub-kits allowing cost to be spread over a longer period), with a reported assembly time of 40 h.

TYPE: Single-seat microlight aircraft.

AIRFRAME: Cantilever low-wing monoplane. Wings (identical to outer wing panels of Invader) use wooden I beam spars, foam ribs with spruce capstrips, plywood covered foam D-cell leading-edge and aluminium trailing-edge, Mylar double surface covered. Ailerons and optional flaps. Fuselage boom of 4 in aluminium alloy tube, supporting V tail with all-moving 'ruddervators' of similar construction to wings, except for aluminium alloy tubular spar. Three-axis control via single control column. Rigging time 15 min.

Landing Gear: Tricycle type, with aluminium legs. All three wheels of similar size.

Power Plant: One 15 kW (20 hp) Zenoah G25B engine, with direct drive or optional 2·24:1 reduction system to a two-blade propeller. Fuel tank capacity 19 litres (5 US gallons).

Accommodation: Pilot only, in prone position, with elbow rests and foot stirrups.

Avionics: Optional.

Dimensions, external:
Wing span 7·32 m (24 ft 0 in)
Wing aspect ratio 5·33
Length overall 4·88 m (16 ft 0 in)
Height overall 1·83 m (6 ft 0 in)
Propeller diameter 1·42 m (4 ft 8 in)

Area:
Wings, gross 10·03 m² (108·0 sq ft)

Weights and Loadings:
Weight empty 79·5 kg (175 lb)
Max T-O weight 181 kg (400 lb)
Max wing loading 18·08 kg/m² (3·70 lb/sq ft)
Max power loading 12·07 kg/kW (20·00 lb/hp)

Performance (at max T-O weight):
Never-exceed speed 69 knots (128 km/h; 80 mph)
Max level speed at S/L 52 knots (97 km/h; 60 mph)
Stalling speed 21 knots (39 km/h; 24 mph)
Max rate of climb at S/L 290 m (950 ft)/min
Service ceiling 2,440 m (8,000 ft)
T-O run 23 m (75 ft)
T-O to 15 m (50 ft) 76 m (250 ft)
Landing run 15 m (50 ft)
Range at cruising speed 217 nm (402 km; 250 miles)
g limits ±6
Best glide ratio 14
Min rate of sink at 35 knots (64 km/h; 40 mph) 76 m (250 ft)/min

ULTRA EFFICIENT PRODUCTS DEMOISELLE

Designed to resemble Alberto Santos-Dumont's famous Demoiselle of 1909-10, this microlight aircraft has its steel tube fuselage structure painted a shade of tan and 'ringed' to give the tubes the appearance of bamboo, from which the original was constructed.

Available in plans form only, supported by some prefabricated component parts, the single-seat Demoiselle is said to take approximately 600 working hours to build. As can be seen from the accompanying illustration, the fabric covered wood and plywood wire braced wings are of constant chord and have marked dihedral. A fabric covered steel tube cruciform tail unit is fitted, all-moving in both axes. Field assembly time is 30 minutes. Power is provided by a 15 kW (20 hp) Zenoah G25B engine, driving a two-blade propeller via a 2·5:1 reduction system; and fuel capacity is 11·4 litres (3 US gallons).

Dimensions, external:
Wing span 8·23 m (27 ft 0 in)
Length overall 6·40 m (21 ft 0 in)
Height overall 2·13 m (7 ft 0 in)
Propeller diameter 1·52 m (5 ft 0 in)

Area:
Wings, gross 13·94 m² (150·0 sq ft)

Weights and Loadings:
Weight empty 111 kg (245 lb)
Max T-O weight 215 kg (475 lb)
Max wing loading 15·46 kg/m² (3·17 lb/sq ft)
Max power loading 14·33 kg/kW (23·75 lb/hp)

Performance (at max T-O weight):
Never-exceed speed 52 knots (96 km/h; 60 mph)
Max level speed at S/L 43 knots (80 km/h; 50 mph)
Stalling speed 21 knots (39 km/h; 24 mph)
Max rate of climb at S/L 152 m (500 ft)/min
Service ceiling 1,220 m (4,000 ft)
T-O run 46 m (150 ft)
T-O to 15 m (50 ft) 107 m (350 ft)
Landing run 31 m (100 ft)
Range at cruising speed 86 nm (161 km; 100 miles)
g limits +4/−3
Best glide ratio at 35 knots (64 km/h; 40 mph) 8
Min rate of sink at 35 knots (64 km/h; 40 mph) 107 m (350 ft)/min

ULTRALIGHT FLIGHT

ULTRALIGHT FLIGHT SALES & DISTRIBUTION

1619 Bellevue Drive, Mt Airy, North Carolina 27030
Telephone: (919) 786 9000
President: Harold Brown

UF has sold the design rights in its Mirage microlight to Mirage Aircraft Inc, under whose heading this aircraft is now described.

ULTRALIGHT FLIGHT PHANTOM

The Phantom was designed in 1982 by Mr John Dempsey as a high performance microlight with full three-axis control. In particular, a thin section wing and full span ailerons provide rapid acceleration and rate of roll, and a pilot fairing provides in-flight comfort and protection. Available in kit form, many hundreds of Phantoms have been built. A two-seat variant, known as the Phantom II, is reportedly under development.

Type: Single-seat microlight aircraft; conforms to FAR Pt 103.

Airframe: High-wing monoplane, with cruciform tail surfaces and three-axis control (full span tapered ailerons, elevators and rudder). Wing has two aluminium spars (leading-edge and main spar), 32 ribs, double surface Dacron covering and kingpost/stainless steel cable bracing. Libek thin-section aerofoil, with double camber. Main frame of aluminium alloy tube, with 10 cm (4 in) diameter tubular tailboom.

Landing Gear: Tricycle type, with steerable nosewheel. All wheels/tyres size 4·10 × 3·50. Wheel brakes, wheel fairings, ski and float gear optional.

Power Plant: One 26 kW (35 hp) Kawasaki TA-440A two-cylinder two-stroke engine, with 1·9:1 V belt reduction to 58 × 22 two-blade wooden propeller. Other engines of up to 48 kW (64 hp) may be fitted. Fuel tank capacity 19 litres (5 US gallons).

Accommodation: Pilot only, in open cockpit, with glassfibre fairing pod and windscreen.

Dimensions, external:
Wing span 8·69 m (28 ft 6 in)
Wing aspect ratio 5·72
Length overall 5·11 m (16 ft 9 in)
Height overall 2·21 m (7 ft 3 in)
Propeller diameter 1·47 m (4 ft 10 in)

Area:
Wings, gross 13·19 m² (142·0 sq ft)

Weights and Loadings:
Weight empty 114 kg (252 lb)
Pilot weight range 41-97 kg (90-215 lb)
Max T-O weight 231 kg (510 lb)
Max wing loading 17·51 kg/m² (3·59 lb/sq ft)
Max power loading 8·88 kg/kW (14·57 lb/hp)

Performance:
Never-exceed speed 86 knots (160 km/h; 100 mph)
Max level speed 54 knots (100 km/h; 62 mph)
Max cruising speed 48 knots (89 km/h; 55 mph)
Econ cruising speed 39 knots (72 km/h; 45 mph)
Stalling speed, power on 23 knots (42 km/h; 26 mph)
Max rate of climb at S/L 244 m (800 ft)/min
Service ceiling 4,420 m (14,500 ft)
T-O run 30·5 m (100 ft)
Landing run 12-46 m (40-150 ft)
Range with max fuel 126 nm (233 km; 145 miles)
Endurance with max fuel 2 h
g limits +6/−4 design
+9·9/−6·6 ultimate
Best glide ratio 7

ULTRA SAIL

ULTRA SAIL INC

58 Davis Street, Locust Valley, New York 11560
Telephone: (516) 676 5210
President: Erwin Rodger

ULTRA SAIL CLOUD DANCER

Designed by Mr Erwin Rodger, the Cloud Dancer was first seen at Oshkosh in 1983 and is now marketed as prefabricated parts or in flyaway form by his Ultra Sail company. Five aircraft had been ordered and three built by early 1986. Construction time is only 16 hours. Although qualified as a microlight, the Cloud Dancer is intended primarily for power-off soaring.

Type: Single-seat microlight aircraft; conforms to FAR Pt 103.

Airframe: Cantilever low-wing monoplane of aluminium alloy pod and boom form. Tubular fuselage boom supports V tail with trim tab, and Kevlar nose fairing with windscreen. Constant chord wings, double surfaced with Dacron. Thickness/chord ratio 12%. Dihedral 6°. Incidence 4°. Pylon structure to support engine pod. Stainless steel control cables. Three-axis control by spoilers and 'ruddervators'. Ballistic parachute optional. Rigging time 8 min.

Landing Gear: Tailwheel type, with steerable tailwheel and glassfibre leaf springs on mainwheels. Mainwheels/tyres size 11 × 4 in; no brakes. Optional oversize tyres and inflatable floats.

Power Plant: One 20 kW (27 hp) Rotax 277 single-cylinder two-stroke engine, with 2·238:1 reduction gearing to a Shettler two-blade wooden pusher propeller. Fuel tank capacity 19 litres (5 US gallons). Electric starting optional.

Accommodation: Pilot only, in open cockpit. Heating and instrumentation optional. Baggage capacity 20-30 kg (45-67 lb) with 170 lb pilot.

Dimensions, external:
Wing span 12·19 m (40 ft 0 in)
Wing chord, constant 1·04 m (3 ft 5 in)
Wing aspect ratio 12·3
Length overall 5·18 m (17 ft 0 in)
Height overall 1·52 m (5 ft 0 in)
Tailplane span 1·52 m (5 ft 0 in)
Wheel track 1·52 m (5 ft 0 in)
Wheelbase 3·66 m (12 ft 0 in)
Propeller diameter 1·22 m (4 ft 0 in)

Area:
Wings, gross 12·08 m² (130·0 sq ft)

Weights and Loadings:
Weight empty 113 kg (250 lb)
Pilot weight range 50-100 kg (110-220 lb)
Max T-O weight 236 kg (520 lb)
Max wing loading 19·52 kg/m² (4·00 lb/sq ft)
Max power loading 11·80 kg/kW (19·26 lb/hp)

Performance:
Never-exceed speed 60 knots (112 km/h; 70 mph)
Max level speed 55 knots (101 km/h; 63 mph)
Max cruising speed 48 knots (88 km/h; 55 mph)
Econ cruising speed 35 knots (64 km/h; 40 mph)
Stalling speed: power on 22 knots (41 km/h; 25 mph)
power off 24 knots (44 km/h; 27 mph)
Max rate of climb at S/L 183 m (600 ft)/min
Service ceiling 5,485 m (18,000 ft)
T-O run 40 m (130 ft)
T-O to, and landing from, 15 m (50 ft) 122 m (400 ft)
Landing run 61 m (200 ft)
Range with max fuel 260 nm (482 km; 300 miles)
Range with max payload 217 nm (402 km; 250 miles)
Max endurance 6 h 30 min
g limits ±4·5
Best glide ratio 15
Min rate of sink, power off 76 m (250 ft)/min

UP

UP SPORTS (ULTRALITE PRODUCTS)

PO Box 659-H, Front Street, Temecula, California 92390
Telephone: (714) 676 5652
Telex: 910 332 1306

UP ARROW P-3

The P-3 is a powered microlight having a twin-boom fuselage, Dacron covered wings and a Tedlar covered tail unit. A prototype was shown at an exhibition in Los Angeles in late 1984, at which time the company was understood to be awaiting new FAA microlight regulations before putting the P-3 into production.

V-8 SPECIAL

Plans and Kits from: Bill Mizell, 5016 North 70th Drive, Glendale, Arizona 85303
Telephone: (602) 846 0435

The late Mr Chris Beachner, who was killed in a flying accident on 7 August 1985, had designed and built a tandem two-seat sporting monoplane known as the V-8 Special. First flown on 22 September 1978, the Special underwent numerous changes over the ensuing years, the most important of which was replacement of the original wood, foam and glassfibre fuselage by a lighter structure of welded steel tubing. Other improvements included modifications to the landing gear, wings and movable control surfaces. Plans to build the Special have been available since 1983.

Following Mr Beachner's death, rights in the V-8 Special were purchased by Mr Bill Mizell, who currently offers plans, kits, engine conversion plans and ready converted V-8 engines. Mr Mizell is also offering plans and kits of the **V-8 Special SXS**, a side by side seating model with optional non-retractable tricycle or tailwheel landing gear, or fully retractable gear. By early 1986 approximately 200

Ultra Efficient Products Penetrater single-seat microlight *(Howard Levy)*

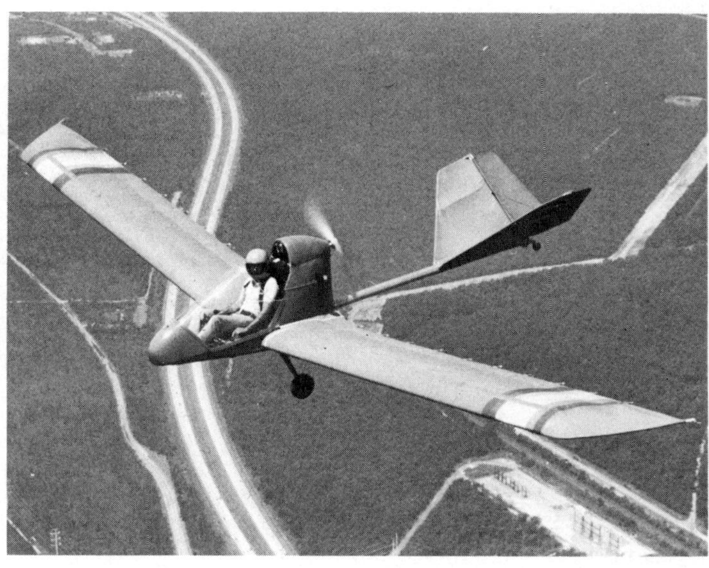

Ultra Sail Cloud Dancer microlight powered glider *(Howard Levy)*

Ultra Efficient Products Demoiselle single-seat microlight *(Howard Levy)*

Ultralight Flight Phantom

Van's RV-3 built by Mr Arlin Pestes of Gresham, Oregon

Tandem two-seat V-8 Special *(Howard Levy)*

sets of plans for the V-8 Special had been sold, together with the first five SXS kits.

V-8 SPECIAL

Type: Tandem two-seat homebuilt sporting aircraft.

Airframe: Cantilever low-wing monoplane. Main and secondary wing spars of glassfibre/epoxy resin. Polyurethane foam and glassfibre/epoxy resin shells. Ailerons, flaps and endplates of similar construction. Welded steel tube fuselage structure, covered with a shell of glassfibre/epoxy over a polyurethane foam core. Cantilever tail unit structure, with glassfibre/epoxy resin spars and solid carved polyurethane foam core covered with glassfibre/epoxy.

Landing Gear: Retractable or non-retractable tailwheel type. Gerdes mainwheels, size 5·00-5. Non-retractable steerable tailwheel. Gerdes brakes on mainwheels.

Power Plant: One 93 kW (125 hp) Beachner modified Buick watercooled motorcar engine, with direct drive or reduction unit to a Warnke two-blade fixed-pitch propeller. Roots type supercharger optional. Two fuel tanks in fuselage, of 79·5 litres (21 US gallons) and 49 litres (13 US gallons) capacity respectively.

Accommodation: Two seats in tandem under rearward sliding modified Monnett Sonerai II bubble canopy. Baggage area aft of rear seat, capacity about 18 kg (40 lb).

Dimensions, external:
- Wing span: 7·32 m (24 ft 0 in)
- Length overall: 5·64 m (18 ft 6 in)
- Propeller diameter: 1·45 m (4 ft 9 in)

Area:
- Wings, gross: 8·92 m² (96·0 sq ft)

Weights and Loadings:
- Weight empty: 381 kg (840 lb)
- Max T-O weight: 588 kg (1,296 lb)
- Max wing loading: 65·9 kg/m² (13·5 lb/sq ft)
- Max power loading: 6·32 kg/kW (10·37 lb/hp)

Performance:
- Max cruising speed: more than 165 knots (305 km/h; 190 mph)
- Cruising speed (50% power): 128 knots (238 km/h; 148 mph) IAS
- Stalling speed:
  - landing gear and flaps up: 56 knots (103 km/h; 64 mph) IAS
  - flaps down: 35 knots (65 km/h; 40 mph)
- Max rate of climb at S/L: 457 m (1,500 ft)/min

VANEK

CHUCK VANEK

7246 North Mohawk, Portland, Oregon 97203

VANEK VANCRAFT

Mr Chuck Vanek won the 'Reserve Grand Champion' award at the 1985 Oshkosh meeting for his Vancraft tandem two-seat autogyro. Powered by a 74·5 kW (100 hp) SCAT modified Volkswagen motorcar engine, driving a two-blade pusher propeller, it uses a small horizontal stabiliser and a fin and rudder of larger area. High performance has been achieved by careful streamlining, with the crew seated in a semi-enclosed cabin with tall windscreen. The wheels of the non-retractable tricycle landing gear are faired, and the two-blade rotor is attached to a faired hub. The rotor blades are reportedly of unique design. No further details are known.

VAN'S

VAN'S AIRCRAFT

PO Box 160, North Plains, Oregon 97133
Telephone: (503) 647 5117

Mr Richard VanGrunsven designed and built a single-seat all-metal sporting aircraft known as Van's RV-3. It was built over a 2½-year period from 1968, and won its designer the 'Best Aerodynamic Detailing' award at the 1972 EAA Fly-in.

After the RV-3's first flight, and subsequent EAA award, Mr VanGrunsven formed Van's Aircraft to market plans to amateur constructors. More than 1,000 sets of plans have been sold, with at least 200 aircraft under construction and over 100 RV-3s flying by early 1986.

Van's Aircraft also offers its RV-4 sporting two-seater and has shown the redesigned prototype of its RV-6.

VAN'S RV-3

Type: Single-seat homebuilt sporting monoplane.

Airframe: Cantilever low-wing monoplane. Airframe of 2024-T3 light alloy. Wing section NACA 23012. Dihedral 3° 30′. Incidence 1°. Constant chord wings, with I beam main spar, light rear spar, pressed ribs and moulded glassfibre tips. Bottom-hinged plain trailing-edge flaps. Frise ailerons. No tabs. Semi-monocoque fuselage, with glassfibre engine cowling. Cantilever tail unit, with glassfibre tips. Trim tab in port elevator.

Landing Gear: Non-retractable tailwheel type. Cantilever tapered steel spring main gear struts, with streamline fairings. Cleveland mainwheels with tyres size 14 × 5·00-5, pressure 1·38 bars (20 lb/sq in). Steerable tailwheel with 6 in diameter tyre. Cleveland brakes. Glassfibre streamline fairings on mainwheels.

POWER PLANT: One 93 kW (125 hp) Avco Lycoming O-290-G (GPU) flat-four engine, driving a Sensenich two-blade fixed-pitch propeller with spinner. Fuel capacity 91 litres (24 US gallons).

ACCOMMODATION: Pilot only, beneath rearward sliding Plexiglas bubble canopy. Baggage space aft of seat, capacity 0·23 m³ (8 cu ft).

DIMENSIONS, EXTERNAL:

Wing span	6·07 m (19 ft 11 in)
Wing chord, constant	1·37 m (4 ft 6 in)
Wing aspect ratio	4·43
Length overall	5·79 m (19 ft 0 in)
Height overall	1·55 m (5 ft 1 in)
Tailplane span	2·13 m (7 ft 0 in)
Wheel track	1·73 m (5 ft 8 in)
Wheelbase	4·29 m (14 ft 1 in)
Propeller diameter	1·73 m (5 ft 8 in)

DIMENSION, INTERNAL:

Cabin: Width	0·64 m (2 ft 1 in)

AREA:

Wings, gross	8·36 m² (90·0 sq ft)

WEIGHTS AND LOADINGS:

Weight empty	315 kg (695 lb)
Max T-O weight	476 kg (1,050 lb)
Max wing loading	57·0 kg/m² (11·67 lb/sq ft)
Max power loading	5·12 kg/kW (8·40 lb/hp)

PERFORMANCE (at max T-O weight):

Never-exceed speed	191 knots (354 km/h; 220 mph)
Max level speed at S/L	169 knots (314 km/h; 195 mph)
Max cruising speed at 2,440 m (8,000 ft)	161 knots (298 km/h; 185 mph)
Econ cruising speed at 3,050 m (10,000 ft)	139 knots (257 km/h; 160 mph)
Stalling speed: flaps up	46 knots (84 km/h; 52 mph)
flaps down	42 knots (78 km/h; 48 mph)
Max rate of climb at S/L	579 m (1,900 ft)/min
Service ceiling	6,400 m (21,000 ft)
T-O run	61 m (200 ft)
Landing run	91 m (300 ft)
Range, no reserves	520 nm (965 km; 600 miles)

VAN'S RV-4

This tandem two-seat sportsplane for homebuilders is similar in external apearance to the RV-3; it is, however, some 20 per cent larger and there is no commonality of airframe components. The design goal was to retain in a two-seat aircraft the overall performance and flight characteristics of the single-seat RV-3. The first flight of the prototype RV-4 (N14RV) was made on 21 August 1979. Plans and kits have been available to homebuilders since the Summer of 1980. By early 1986, a total of at least 1,050 sets of plans had been sold, with about 600 aircraft under construction and 32 RV-4s flying.

TYPE: Two-seat homebuilt sporting monoplane.

AIRFRAME: As for RV-3, except wing section Van's Aircraft 135.

LANDING GEAR: As for RV-3, except mainwheel tyre pressure 1·52 bars (22 lb/sq in).

POWER PLANT: One 112 kW (150 hp) Avco Lycoming O-320-E1F flat-four engine, driving a Cassidy two-blade fixed-pitch wooden propeller with spinner. Fuel capacity 121 litres (32 US gallons).

ACCOMMODATION: Two seats in tandem; pilot seated forward under sideways opening canopy, passenger beneath rearward sliding Plexiglas canopy. Baggage compartments forward of instrument panel and aft of rear seat, total capacity 13·6 kg (30 lb).

DIMENSIONS, EXTERNAL:

Wing span	7·01 m (23 ft 0 in)
Wing chord, constant	1·47 m (4 ft 10 in)
Wing aspect ratio	4·76
Length overall	6·21 m (20 ft 4½ in)
Height overall	1·60 m (5 ft 3 in)
Tailplane span	2·54 m (8 ft 4 in)
Wheel track	1·88 m (6 ft 2 in)
Propeller diameter	1·73 m (5 ft 8 in)

DIMENSIONS, INTERNAL:

Cabin: Max width	0·71 m (2 ft 4 in)
Max height	1·12 m (3 ft 8 in)

AREA:

Wings, gross	10·22 m² (110·0 sq ft)

WEIGHTS AND LOADINGS:

Weight empty	404 kg (890 lb)
Max T-O weight	680 kg (1,500 lb)
Max wing loading	66·6 kg/m² (13·64 lb/sq ft)
Max power loading	6·07 kg/kW (10·00 lb/hp)

PERFORMANCE (at max T-O weight):

Never-exceed speed	182 knots (338 km/h; 210 mph)
Max level speed at S/L	175 knots (323 km/h; 201 mph)
Max cruising speed at 2,440 m (8,000 ft)	162 knots (299 km/h; 186 mph)
Econ cruising speed (55% power at 2,440 m; 8,000 ft)	142 knots (264 km/h; 164 mph)
Stalling speed	47 knots (87 km/h; 54 mph)
Max rate of climb at S/L	503 m (1,650 ft)/min
Service ceiling	5,945 m (19,500 ft)
T-O run	137 m (450 ft)
Landing run	130 m (425 ft)
Range with max fuel (55% power)	695 nm (1,287 km; 800 miles)

VAN'S RV-6

This side by side two-seat light aircraft, a variation of the RV-4, was designed by Mr VanGrunsven at the request of Mr Art Chard of Bronson, Missouri, who completed detail design of the fuselage and built it in 15 months. First flight of the original prototype (N6RV) was made on 26 April 1977. Like the RV-3 and RV-4, it is of all-metal construction, with glassfibre cowlings, wingtips and fairings. The basic wing and tail unit components are the same as those of the RV-4. Power plant is a 119 kW (160 hp) Avco Lycoming O-320 flat-four engine, driving a fixed-pitch propeller.

Construction of a redesigned prototype (N66RV) began in January 1985 and this appeared in public at the June 1986 Merced, California, Fly-in. It is possible that plans and kits of the RV-6 will be marketed.

DIMENSIONS, EXTERNAL:

Wing span	7·32 m (24 ft 0 in)
Wing chord, constant	1·47 m (4 ft 10 in)
Length overall	6·10 m (20 ft 0 in)

WEIGHTS AND LOADING:

Weight empty	454 kg (1,000 lb)
Max T-O weight	680 kg (1,500 lb)
Max power loading	5·71 kg/kW (9·38 lb/hp)

PERFORMANCE:

Max level speed	156 knots (290 km/h; 180 mph)
Max cruising speed	139 knots (257 km/h; 160 mph)
Landing speed	44 knots (81 km/h; 50 mph)
Range with max fuel	417 nm (772 km; 480 miles)

VELOCITY

VELOCITY AIRCRAFT

200 West Airport Drive, Sebastian, Florida 32958

VELOCITY AIRCRAFT VELOCITY

Design of the Velocity 2+2 composites canard monoplane was begun in December 1984 by Mr Dan Maher, a marine engineer and builder of a Rutan Long-EZ. Construction of the prototype, with the assistance of Mr Pete Hoffmann and Mr Neil Hunter, took seven months, entirely by hand lay-up of glassfibre. This aircraft (N401DM) then made its debut at the 1985 Sun 'n Fun meeting.

Velocity Aircraft offers the Velocity in kit form, minus the engine, propeller, instruments and avionics. The glassfibre components in the kit are moulded.

TYPE: Two-plus-two high performance homebuilt aircraft.

AIRFRAME: Cantilever mid-wing monoplane, with foreplanes. Airframe of foam cores, unidirectional/biaxial-triaxial glassfibre and epoxy resin. Rear mounted wings, with sweepback, using modified Eppler aerofoil section. Three Roncz 'vortilons' under leading-edge of each wing. Endplate fins and rudders. Electro-hydraulic speed brake, recessed into bottom of fuselage, and electric roll and pitch trim. Constant chord foreplanes on nose, with near full-span elevators. No dihedral or anhedral. Original foreplane aerofoil section.

LANDING GEAR: Tricycle type, with hydraulically retractable 3·40-5 nosewheel on glassfibre leg and aluminium fork. Cantilever non-retractable glassfibre main legs with removable streamline wheel fairings. Mainwheels and brakes from a Cessna Skymaster.

POWER PLANT: Any Avco Lycoming engine of 112 to 149 kW (150 to 200 hp) or Continental IO-360. Prototype has one 134 kW (180 hp) Avco Lycoming HIO-360 flat-four engine, driving a Ted Henderson two-blade wooden pusher propeller with trailing-edge cuffs, modified Q tips and glassfibre covering. Two 129 litre (34 US gallon) fuel tanks in wings, plus 19 litre (5 US gallon) gravity tank, giving total fuel capacity of 277 litres (73 US gallons).

ACCOMMODATION: Four persons in fully enclosed cabin pod, with port gull-wing door which opens over centre of roof. Front bucket seats; rear bench seat. Small baggage area behind rear seat.

SYSTEMS: Electrical and hydraulic systems standard.

DIMENSIONS, EXTERNAL:

Wing span	8·72 m (28 ft 7½ in)
Foreplane span	4·42 m (14 ft 6 in)
Length overall	5·49 m (18 ft 0 in)
Height overall	2·44 m (8 ft 0 in)
Wheel track	2·03 m (6 ft 8 in)
Wheelbase	2·64 m (8 ft 8 in)
Propeller diameter	1·73 m (5 ft 8 in)

DIMENSIONS, INTERNAL:

Cockpit: Max width	1·08 m (3 ft 6½ in)
Max length	2·06 m (6 ft 9 in)
Max height	1·05 m (3 ft 5½ in)

AREAS:

Wings, gross	8·92 m² (96·0 sq ft)
Foreplane, gross	1·83 m² (19·7 sq ft)

WEIGHTS AND LOADINGS:

Weight empty	499 kg (1,100 lb)
Max T-O weight	1,020 kg (2,250 lb)
Max wing loading	94·88 kg/m² (19·45 lb/sq ft)
Max power loading	7·61 kg/kW (12·50 lb/hp)

PERFORMANCE (prototype, at max T-O weight):

Max cruising speed at 610 m (2,000 ft)	191 knots (354 km/h; 220 mph)
Cruising speed at 2,285 m (7,500 ft)	182 knots (338 km/h; 210 mph)
Max rate of climb at S/L	305 m (1,000 ft)/min
Range with max fuel	1,736 nm (3,218 km; 2,000 miles)

VIKING

VIKING AIRCRAFT LTD

RR No. 1, PO Box 1000V, Eloy, Arizona 85231
Telephone: (602) 466 7538
PRESIDENT: Rex Taylor

VIKING DRAGONFLY

The Dragonfly is a side by side two-seat light aircraft of canard configuration. Its design was started by Mr Robert J. Walters in September 1979, and in the following Winter Mr Walters formed Viking Aircraft to build a prototype for flight testing.

Construction began in January 1980 and the first flight of the prototype Dragonfly was achieved on 16 June the same year. It has since become a NASAD approved aircraft.

Plans to build the Dragonfly became available in 1980, together with a pre-formed engine cowling and canopy. By early 1985 (when the last update was received) about 1,500 sets of plans had been sold, together with 70 kits of prefabricated component parts to construct the Dragonfly, requiring no complex jigging or tooling. In this form the aircraft is known as the 'Snap' Dragonfly. It is estimated that the kits save the builder more than 700 working hours.

In its original configuration, with mainwheels at the tips of the foreplane, the aircraft is now designated **Dragonfly Mark I**. In parallel production, for operation from unprepared strips and narrow taxiways, is the **Dragonfly Mark II**. This has its main landing gear in the form of short cantilever units under the wings, with individual hydraulic toe brakes, and increased foreplane and elevator areas. In 1985, a **Dragonfly Mark III** version, with non-retractable tricycle landing gear, was undergoing flight trials.

More than 50 Dragonfly Mark Is are flying.

TYPE: Two-seat homebuilt sporting aircraft.

AIRFRAME: Tapered cantilever shoulder-wing monoplane of canard configuration. Wing section Eppler 1213. Thickness/chord ratio 15%. 3° dihedral from roots. No incidence or sweepback. Composite structure of styrene foam, glassfibre, carbonfibre and epoxy. Inboard ailerons of composite construction, with spring trim. Tapered cantilever foreplane of GU25 section, mounted low on forward fuselage. Thickness/chord ratio 17%. Anhedral 3° from roots on Dragonfly Mark I; dihedral from roots on Mark II. Incidence − 1°. No sweepback. Construction similar to wings. Mainwheel housings attached to tips on Mark I. Tips turned down on Mark II. Near full span tapered elevators. Two ground adjustable tabs plus spring trim. Semi-monocoque fuselage, formed (not carved) from 12·5 mm (½ in) thick urethane foam, with strips of 18 mm (¾ in) foam bonded along edges to allow large-radius external corners. Fuselage covered with glassfibre inside and out, and tapered towards rear. Cantilever sweptback vertical fin and tapered narrow-chord rudder of similar construction to wings.

LANDING GEAR: Non-retractable tailwheel type on Marks I and II. Non-retractable tricycle type on Mark III. Mainwheels positioned at tips of canard foreplane in swept fairings on Mark I. Mark II has mainwheels carried on non-retracting glassfibre spring legs under wings, with streamline wheel fairings. Shock absorption by flexing of foreplane only on Mark I. Azusa 5 in aluminium mainwheels with 11 × 4·00-5 or 11 × 5·00-5 tyres and hydraulic disc brakes on Marks I and II. Solid 4 in tailwheel tyre on Marks I and II.

POWER PLANT: One 44·5 kW (60 hp) HAPI 1,835 cc modified Volkswagen motorcar engine, driving a Great American Propeller Company 52 × 40 fixed-pitch two-blade wooden propeller; 1,600 cc engine, rated at 33·5 kW (45 hp), optional. Fuel tanks in fuselage, total capacity 56·8 litres (15 US gallons). Refuelling point on fuselage side. Oil capacity 2·8 litres (0·75 US gallon).

ACCOMMODATION: Two seats side by side under one-piece side-hinged canopy. Dual side-stick controls. Baggage space aft of seats. Ventilated.

SYSTEM: 20A alternator. 14Ah battery.

DIMENSIONS, EXTERNAL:

Wing span	6·71 m (22 ft 0 in)
Wing chord: at root	0·71 m (2 ft 4 in)

Original prototype of the Van's RV-6 *(Peter M. Bowers)*

Van's RV-4 built by Mr Larry Berg of Nanoose Bay, British Columbia, Canada

Velocity Aircraft Velocity all-composites four-seat homebuilt aircraft *(Howard Levy)*

Viking Aircraft Dragonfly Mark I *(R Kunert)*

Volmer VJ-22 Sportsman two-seat homebuilt amphibian

Dragonfly Mark II with faired mainwheels under wings

at tip	0·51 m (1 ft 8 in)
Wing aspect ratio	11
Foreplane span: Mk I	6·10 m (20 ft 0 in)
Foreplane chord: Mk I at root	0·91 m (3 ft 0 in)
Mk I at tip	0·56 m (1 ft 10 in)
Length overall	5·79 m (19 ft 0 in)
Height overall: Mk I	1·22 m (4 ft 0 in)
Wheel track: Mk I	6·10 m (20 ft 0 in)
Mk II	2·44 m (8 ft 0 in)
Wheelbase	4·88 m (16 ft 0 in)
Propeller diameter	1·32 m (4 ft 4 in)

DIMENSION, INTERNAL:

Cabin: Width	1·09 m (3 ft 7 in)

AREAS:

Wings, gross	4·51 m² (48·5 sq ft)
Foreplane, gross: Mk I	4·51 m² (48·5 sq ft)
Mk II	4·97 m² (53·5 sq ft)

WEIGHTS AND LOADINGS (Dragonfly Mk I with A: 1,835 cc, B: 1,600 cc engine):

Weight empty: A	274 kg (605 lb)
B	267 kg (590 lb)
Max payload: A	184 kg (405 lb)
Max T-O and landing weight: A	488 kg (1,075 lb)
Max wing loading, gross area incl foreplane:	
A	54·1 kg/m² (11·08 lb/sq ft)
Max power loading: A	10·97 kg/kW (17·92 lb/hp)

PERFORMANCE (Dragonfly Mk I with A: 1,835 cc, B: 1,600 cc engine):

Never-exceed speed:	
A	156 knots (289 km/h; 180 mph)
Max level speed at S/L:	
A	146 knots (270 km/h; 168 mph) IAS
B	137 knots (254 km/h; 158 mph) IAS
Max cruising speed (75% power):	
A	143 knots (266 km/h; 165 mph)
B	135 knots (249 km/h; 155 mph)
Econ cruising speed at 2,285 m (7,500 ft):	
A	121 knots (225 km/h; 140 mph)
Stalling speed, power on:	
A	39 knots (73 km/h; 45 mph) IAS
Max rate of climb at S/L:	
A, pilot only	320 m (1,050 ft)/min
B, pilot only	244 m (800 ft)/min
A, pilot and passenger	259 m (850 ft)/min
B, pilot and passenger	183 m (600 ft)/min
Service ceiling: A	5,640 m (18,500 ft)
B	5,180 m (17,000 ft)
T-O run: A	137 m (450 ft)
B	152 m (500 ft)
T-O to 15 m (50 ft): A	366 m (1,200 ft)
Landing from 15 m (50 ft): A	457 m (1,500 ft)
Landing run: A	213 m (700 ft)
Range with max fuel, 30 min reserves:	
A	434 nm (804 km; 500 miles)
g limits	+4·4/−2
Best glide ratio	14·5

VOLMER

VOLMER AIRCRAFT

Box 5222, Glendale, California 91201
Telephone: (818) 247 8718

Mr Volmer Jensen, well known as a designer of sailplanes and gliders, also designed and built a two-seat homebuilt amphibian named the Sportsman. Details of this aircraft follow, together with entries for the powered versions of the Volmer VJ-23 Swingwing and VJ-24 Sunfun hang gliders.

VOLMER VJ-22 SPORTSMAN

Construction of the prototype Sportsman began in September 1957 and this aircraft flew for the first time on 22 December 1958. It has since logged more than 1,840 flying hours, covering a total distance equivalent to six times around the world.

Plans of the Sportsman are available to amateur constructors. Over 800 sets had been sold by early 1986 and more than 100 Sportsman amphibians are flying. Some have tractor propellers, but this modification is not recommended by Mr Jensen. Two people can assemble or dismantle the Sportsman in 30 minutes when trailered. Take-off from water takes approximately 20 seconds.

The following details refer to Mr Jensen's prototype:

TYPE: Two-seat homebuilt amphibian.

AIRFRAME: Braced high-wing monoplane. Dihedral 1°. Incidence 3°. Wings are standard Aeronca Chief or Champion assemblies with wooden spars, light alloy ribs and fabric covering, and carry stabilising floats under the tips. Plans of specially designed wing, with wooden ribs and spars, available. Streamline V bracing struts each side. Conventional flying-boat hull of spruce construction, covered with mahogany plywood and coated with glassfibre. Strut braced steel tube tail unit, fabric covered.

LANDING GEAR: Retractable tailwheel type. Rubber cord shock absorption. Manual retraction. Cleveland wheels and mechanical brakes. Tyre pressure 1·38 bars (20 lb/sq in). Castoring manually retractable tailwheel with integral water rudder.

POWER PLANT: One 63·5 kW (85 hp) Continental C85, 67 kW (90 hp) or 74·5 kW (100 hp) Continental O-200-B flat-four engine, driving a Sensenich two-blade fixed-pitch pusher propeller. Fuel in a single tank, capacity 76 litres (20 US gallons). Oil capacity 4·25 litres (4·5 US quarts).

ACCOMMODATION: Two seats side by side in enclosed cabin with dual controls.

DIMENSIONS, EXTERNAL:

Wing span	11·12 m (36 ft 6 in)
Wing chord	1·52 m (5 ft 0 in)
Wing aspect ratio	7·2

Length overall 7·32 m (24 ft 0 in)
Height overall 2·44 m (8 ft 0 in)
AREA:
Wings, gross 16·3 m² (175·0 sq ft)
WEIGHTS AND LOADINGS (63·5 kW; 85 hp):
Weight empty 454 kg (1,000 lb)
Max T-O weight 680 kg (1,500 lb)
Max wing loading 41·84 kg/m² (8·57 lb/sq ft)
Max power loading 10·71 kg/kW (17·65 lb/hp)
PERFORMANCE (63·5 kW; 85 hp, at max T-O weight):
Max level speed at S/L 83 knots (153 km/h; 95 mph)
Max cruising speed 74 knots (137 km/h; 85 mph)
Stalling speed 39 knots (72 km/h; 45 mph)
Max rate of climb at S/L 183 m (600 ft)/min
Service ceiling 3,960 m (13,000 ft)
Range with max fuel, no reserves
260 nm (480 km; 300 miles)

VOLMER VJ-23E SWINGWING

Following the success of David Cook in the UK in installing an engine on his VJ-23 Swingwing hang glider (see Hang Gliders subsection), drawings for a **VJ-23E** powered version (fuel capacity 3·75 litres; 1 US gallon) are available from Volmer Aircraft.

AIRFRAME: Cantilever high-wing monoplane, constructed of steel tube, spruce, mahogany and plywood, with double surface Dacron or other fabric covering. Three-axis control (ailerons, elevators and rudder). Cruciform tail unit carried on fuselage boom, with triangular ventral fin and tailplane.

LANDING GEAR: Mainwheels only for ground handling.

POWER PLANT: One small engine carried above wing on pylon structure (see 1981-82 *Jane's* for details of David Cook's installation).

ACCOMMODATION: Pilot only in open hang glider position.

DIMENSIONS, EXTERNAL:
Wing span 9·93 m (32 ft 7 in)
Length overall 5·31 m (17 ft 5 in)
Height overall 1·83 m (6 ft 0 in)
AREA:
Wings, gross 16·63 m² (179·0 sq ft)
WEIGHTS:
Weight empty 54·5 kg (120 lb)
Pilot weight range 45·5-91 kg (100-200 lb)

VOLMER VJ-24W SUNFUN

The VJ-24 hang glider was developed from the VJ-23 Swingwing (which see), from which it differs primarily in having wings and tail of fabric covered aluminium tube instead of wooden spars and ribs; parallel chord instead of tapered planform wings, of increased span with V bracing struts; and a pair of ground handling wheels.

The **VJ-24E** (1983-84 *Jane's*) is a powered version with a 7·5 kW (10 hp) McCulloch go-cart engine driving a pusher propeller, with a total fuel capacity of 3·8 litres (1 US gallon) in a tank beneath the wing.

The **VJ-24W** has an 11·2 kW (15 hp) Yamaha engine driving a tractor propeller, 5·7 litre (1·5 US gallon) fuel tank, two-wheel landing gear, and cockpit pod with windscreen. The most recent developments for the VJ-24W Sunfun include Cessna type spring steel landing gear, a steerable tailwheel, tuned exhaust system, propeller-stopping mechanism for soaring flight, swept fin and rudder, and a more streamlined nosecone. One VJ-24W has been flown on alcohol fuel distilled from coal and apple juice.

In October 1982 NASA began trials with a modified VJ-24W adapted for remotely piloted flight. This aircraft, known as the LRV-2 (Low Reynolds Number Vehicle) was used to investigate the possibility of pilotless aircraft operating for long periods at extremely high altitudes as low-cost 'satellites' for relaying communications signals or monitoring Earth resources.

Plans of all versions of the VJ-24 are available from Volmer Aircraft. Rights to manufacture and market kits for the VJ-24 and VJ-24W are held by Airway Aircraft, PO Box 3025, Glendale, California 91201.

The following details apply to the VJ-24W:

DIMENSIONS, EXTERNAL:
Wing span 11·13 m (36 ft 6 in)
Length overall 5·64 m (18 ft 6 in)
Height overall 1·75 m (5 ft 9 in)
AREA:
Wings, gross 15·14 m² (163·0 sq ft)
WEIGHTS AND LOADINGS:
Weight empty 75 kg (165 lb)
Max T-O weight 156 kg (345 lb)
Max wing loading 10·30 kg/m² (2·12 lb/sq ft)
Max power loading 14·0 kg/kW (23·0 lb/hp)
PERFORMANCE:
Cruising speed 24 knots (45 km/h; 28 mph)
Stalling speed 13 knots (25 km/h; 15 mph)

WAG-AERO

WAG-AERO INC

PO Box 181, 1216 North Road, Lyons, Wisconsin 53148
Telephone: (414) 763 9586
PRESIDENT: Richard H. Wagner

Wag-Aero supplies plans and kits of parts which enable amateur constructors to build modern replicas of the Piper J-3, Vagabond and PA-14 Family Cruiser light aircraft.

WAG-AERO SPORT TRAINER

Wag-Aero plans and kits offer homebuilders the choice of four different modern versions of the famous J-3.

Known as the **Sport Trainer**, the basic two-seat sporting aircraft follows the original design, but benefits by utilising up-to-date constructional techniques. The wing has a wooden main spar and ribs, light alloy leading-edge and fabric covering. The fuselage and tail unit are of welded 4130 chrome molybdenum steel tube with fabric covering. The Sport Trainer can be powered by any flat-four Continental, Franklin or Avco Lycoming engine of between 48·5 and 93 kW (65 and 125 hp).

Also available are the **Acro Trainer**, which differs from the standard version by having a strengthened fuselage, shortened wings (8·23 m; 27 ft), modified lift struts, improved wing fittings and rib spacing, and a new leading-edge; the **Observer**, which is a replica L-4 military liaison aircraft; and the **Super Sport**, with structural modifications to accept engines of up to 112 kW (150 hp), which is suitable for glider towing, bush operations, or for operation as a floatplane.

Design of the Sport Trainer began in 1974 and construction of a prototype started in December of that year. First flight took place on 12 March 1975. By early 1986 more than 1,600 sets of plans for Sport Trainers had been sold.

The following details apply to the standard Sport Trainer:

DIMENSIONS, EXTERNAL:
Wing span 10·73 m (35 ft 2½ in)
Wing chord, constant 1·60 m (5 ft 3 in)
Wing aspect ratio 6·96
Length overall 6·82 m (22 ft 4½ in)
Height overall 2·03 m (6 ft 8 in)
AREA:
Wings, gross 16·58 m² (178·5 sq ft)
WEIGHTS AND LOADINGS:
Weight empty 327 kg (720 lb)
Max T-O weight 635 kg (1,400 lb)
Max wing loading 38·3 kg/m² (7·84 lb/sq ft)
Max power loading (125 hp) 6·83 kg/kW (11·20 lb/hp)
PERFORMANCE (at max T-O weight):
Max level speed at S/L
89 knots (164 km/h; 102 mph)
Cruising speed 82 knots (151 km/h; 94 mph)
Stalling speed 34 knots (63 km/h; 39 mph)
Max rate of climb at S/L 149 m (490 ft)/min
Service ceiling over 3,660 m (12,000 ft)
T-O run 114 m (375 ft)
Range at cruising speed with standard fuel (45·5 litres; 12 US gallons) 191 nm (354 km; 220 miles)
Range with auxiliary fuel (98·5 litres; 26 US gallons)
395 nm (732 km; 455 miles)

WAG-AERO WAG-A-BOND

The name Wag-A-Bond covers two aircraft which can be built by amateur constructors: a replica of the PA-15 Vagabond, known as the **Classic**, and the **Traveler**. The latter is a modified and updated version of the Vagabond with port and starboard doors, overhead skylight window, extended sleeping deck (conversion from aircraft to camper interior taking about two minutes and accommodating two persons), extended baggage area, engine of up to 85·7 kW (115 hp), and provision for a full electrical system.

The prototype Wag-A-Bond was completed by Wag-Aero in May 1978. The following details apply to both versions, unless stated otherwise:

TYPE: Two-seat light homebuilt monoplane.

AIRFRAME: Strut braced high-wing monoplane. Fabric covered all-wood structure of spruce spar and ribs, with mahogany plywood gussets. Fabric covered aluminium ailerons. V bracing struts. Steel drag and anti-drag wires. Welded 4130 steel tube and flat plate fuselage structure, and wire braced steel tube tail unit, all fabric covered.

LANDING GEAR: Non-retractable tailwheel type. Welded steel tube side Vs and half-axles. Bungee shock absorption. Cleveland mainwheels, size 6·00-6, and 7·00-6 tyres, covered by fairings. Cleveland brakes. Skis optional.

POWER PLANT: Traveler can be powered by an Avco Lycoming engine of 80·5-85·7 kW (108-115 hp), driving a two-blade wooden or metal propeller. Classic can be powered by a Continental engine of 48·5-74·5 kW (65-100 hp) driving a similar propeller. Fuel capacity of Traveler 98·5 litres (26 US gallons). Fuel capacity of Classic 45·5 litres (12 US gallons).

ACCOMMODATION: Two persons side by side in enclosed cabin. Baggage area, capacity 27 kg (60 lb) for Traveler, 18 kg (40 lb) for Classic.

SYSTEMS: Traveler has provision for full electrical system.

DIMENSIONS, EXTERNAL:
Wing span 8·32 m (29 ft 3½ in)
Length overall 5·66 m (18 ft 7 in)
Height overall 1·83 m (6 ft 0 in)
AREA:
Wings, gross 13·70 m² (147·5 sq ft)
WEIGHTS AND LOADINGS (A: Traveler, B: Classic):
Weight empty: A 329 kg (725 lb)
B 290 kg (640 lb)
Max T-O weight: A 658 kg (1,450 lb)
B 567 kg (1,250 lb)
Max wing loading: A 48·0 kg/m² (9·83 lb/sq ft)
B 41·4 kg/m² (8·47 lb/sq ft)
Max power loading:
A (115 hp) 7·68 kg/kW (12·61 lb/hp)
B (100 hp) 7·61 kg/kW (12·50 lb/hp)
PERFORMANCE (A: Traveler, B: Classic):
Max level speed: A 118 knots (219 km/h; 136 mph)
B 91 knots (169 km/h; 105 mph)
Cruising speed: A 108 knots (200 km/h; 124 mph)
B 83 knots (153 km/h; 95 mph)
Stalling speed: A, B 39 knots (73 km/h; 45 mph)
Max rate of climb at S/L: A 259 m (850 ft)/min
B 190 m (625 ft)/min

WAG-AERO 2+2 SPORTSMAN

The latest product of Wag-Aero is the 2+2 Sportsman, which is based on the PA-14 Family Cruiser. This aircraft is a true four-seater, with the option of a hinged rear fuselage decking to provide easy access to the baggage and rear seat areas. The rear seat itself can be removed so that cargo or a stretcher can be carried, loaded via the hinged decking.

Plans and material kits are available for the 2+2 Sportsman, the latter with many preformed, pre-bent and finished component parts. A pre-welded fuselage structure is also available. By early 1986 more than 425 sets of plans had been sold.

TYPE: Four-seat light homebuilt monoplane.

AIRFRAME: Strut braced high-wing monoplane. Similar construction to Wag-A-Bond, with glassfibre tips. Alternatively, drawings and materials provided to modify standard PA-12, PA-14 or PA-18 wings. Upper and lower spoilers. Welded 4130 steel tube and flat plate fuselage, fabric covered. Hinged top decking to rear of cabin optional, to provide easy access to baggage area and rear seat.

LANDING GEAR: Similar to Wag-A-Bond.

POWER PLANT: One engine of 93-149 kW (125-200 hp), driving a two-blade propeller. Usable fuel capacity 148 litres (39 US gallons).

ACCOMMODATION: Individual front seats and rear bench seat for total of four persons. Baggage area to rear of bench seat. Rear seat removable for stretcher or cargo carrying.

AVIONICS: Space for full IFR avionics and instrumentation.

DIMENSIONS, EXTERNAL:
Wing span 10·90 m (35 ft 9 in)
Wing chord, constant 1·60 m (5 ft 3 in)
Length overall 7·12 m (23 ft 4½ in)
Height overall 2·02 m (6 ft 7½ in)
AREA:
Wings, gross 16·18 m² (174·12 sq ft)
WEIGHTS AND LOADINGS:
Weight empty 490 kg (1,080 lb)
Max T-O weight 998 kg (2,200 lb)
Max wing loading 61·7 kg/m² (12·63 lb/sq ft)
Max power loading (200 hp) 6·70 kg/kW (11·00 lb/hp)
PERFORMANCE (typical; actual data depend on engine fitted):
Max level speed 112 knots (207 km/h; 129 mph)
Cruising speed 108 knots (200 km/h; 124 mph)
Stalling speed 33 knots (62 km/h; 38 mph)
Max rate of climb at S/L 244 m (800 ft)/min
Service ceiling 4,510 m (14,800 ft)
Range at cruising speed 582 nm (1,078 km; 670 miles)

WAR

WAR AIRCRAFT REPLICAS

348 South Eighth Street, Santa Paula, California 93060
Telephone: (805) 525 8212
PRESIDENT: James McKeehan

War Aircraft Replicas is a company formed to market plans and kits from which amateur constructors can build ½-scale replicas of a series of second World War aircraft. The term '½-scale' is not strictly accurate, but refers to the general overall dimensions of the aircraft. For example, to provide adequate accommodation for the pilot, the cockpit is considerably larger than ½-scale, and the area of the horizontal and vertical tail surfaces has been increased beyond scale to ensure adequate stability.

The basic concept involves the use of a common-design wooden fuselage box and spar structure. The desired contours to duplicate a particular aircraft are obtained by

Mr Volmer Jensen flying a VJ-24W Sunfun microlight aircraft

WAR half-scale replica of the Focke-Wulf Fw 190 *(Geoffrey P. Jones)*

Wag-Aero 2+2 Sportsman with a hinged top decking for easy access to rear cabin area *(Raettig Photo Service)*

Volmer VJ-23E powered version of the Swingwing hang glider

Wag-Aero Observer, a replica of the Piper L-4 *(J. M. G. Gradidge)*

Wag-Aero Wag-A-Bond, a version of the Piper Vagabond suitable for construction by homebuilders *(Raettig Photo Service)*

WAR half-scale replica of the Republic P-47 Thunderbolt built by Mr Gil Hallquist of Mesa, Arizona (80·5 kW; 108 hp Avco Lycoming O-235-C2C engine) *(Howard Levy)*

using carved polyurethane foam, covered with high-strength laminating fabric and epoxy resin to form a lightweight and rigid structure that is stressed to ±6*g*, allowing for aerobatic manoeuvres. By changing fuselage contours, using different engine cowlings and wingtips, and by shape changes to tail unit surfaces, it was considered that a number of different aircraft could be copied with reasonable similarity to the full-scale combat types.

The Focke-Wulf 190 was chosen as the first prototype to be completed, its design starting in July 1973 and construction in February 1974. The first flight of this aircraft was made on 21 August 1974. Many hundreds of sets of plans of the WAR Focke-Wulf 190, Vought F4U Corsair, Republic P-47 Thunderbolt and Hawker Sea Fury had been sold by early 1986. Prototype replicas of the North American P-51D Mustang and Mitsubishi Zero were expected to be completed during 1985, but no confirmation has been received.

The description which follows applies specifically to the Focke-Wulf 190 replica, but is applicable generally to the range of aircraft for which the company is producing plans, components and kits.

WAR AIRCRAFT REPLICAS FOCKE-WULF 190

Type: Half-scale homebuilt combat aircraft replica.

Airframe: Cantilever low-wing monoplane, built in three sections: nominal 2·44 m (8 ft) centre-section, integral with fuselage box, and two nominally 1·83 m (6 ft) outer panels. Wing section NACA 23015 at root, 23012 at tip. Dihedral 5°. Incidence 2°. Washout 2°. Primary structure of wood, with a laminated hollow plywood covered front spar and solid laminated rear spar. Plywood ribs are used at the root, both faces of the centre-section joints and at the tip sections, with intermediate ribs of polyurethane foam. Aerofoil contours built up with carved polyurethane foam, bonded in place. High strength laminating fabric and epoxy resin used for covering and for internal strengthening. Frise ailerons with wooden front spar bonded to a shaped form of urethane foam with fabric/epoxy covering. No flaps. Ground adjustable tab on each aileron. Fuselage of similar general construction to wings, with a standard four-longeron box built from ¾ in fir stringers, ¾ in by ½ in diagonals and cross pieces, ⅟₁₆ in birch plywood covering and a metal faced ⅛ in plywood firewall. Fuselage contoured by carved polyurethane foam with fabric/epoxy covering. Cantilever wooden tail unit, utilising the same construction technique as for the wings. Fixed tailplane with elevators. Ground adjustable trim tab on rudder and each elevator.

Landing Gear: Electrically retractable tailwheel type, with manual emergency retraction system. Mainwheels retract inward into wings. Fixed tailwheel. Spring shock struts on main units. Mainwheels and tyres size 3·50 × 4·10-5. Cleveland hydraulic disc brakes.

Power Plant: One 74·5 kW (100 hp) Continental O-200 flat-four engine or 1,600 cc modified Volkswagen motorcar engine, driving a three-blade fixed-pitch wooden propeller with spinner. Fuel tank in fuselage, immediately aft of firewall, with capacity of 38 litres (10 US gallons). Refuelling point on upper surface of fuselage, forward of windscreen.

Accommodation: Single seat beneath rearward sliding cockpit canopy. Accommodation heated and ventilated.

Systems: Hydraulic system for brakes only. Electrical system powered by 12V engine driven alternator.

Dimensions, external:

Wing span	6·10 m (20 ft 0 in)
Wing chord: at root	1·3 m (4 ft 6 in)
at tip	0·79 m (2 ft 7 in)
Wing aspect ratio	5·7
Length overall	5·05 m (16 ft 7 in)
Height overall	2·13 m (7 ft 0 in)
Tailplane span	2·29 m (7 ft 6 in)
Wheel track	2·03 m (6 ft 8 in)
Wheelbase	3·25 m (10 ft 8 in)
Propeller diameter	1·52 m (5 ft 0 in)

Area:

Wings, gross	6·50 m² (70·0 sq ft)

Weights and Loadings (O-200 engine):

Weight empty	286 kg (630 lb)
Max T-O weight	408 kg (900 lb)
Max wing loading	62·8 kg/m² (12·9 lb/sq ft)
Max power loading	5·48 kg/kW (9·00 lb/hp)

Performance (O-200 engine, at max T-O weight):

Max level speed at 1,065 m (3,500 ft)	169 knots (314 km/h; 195 mph)
Max cruising speed at 1,065 m (3,500 ft)	126 knots (233 km/h; 145 mph)
Econ cruising speed at 1,065 m (3,500 ft)	108 knots (201 km/h; 125 mph)
Stalling speed	48 knots (89 km/h; 55 mph)
Max rate of climb at S/L	305 m (1,000 ft)/min
Service ceiling	3,810 m (12,500 ft)
T-O run	305 m (1,000 ft)

Landing from 15 m (50 ft)	550 m (1,800 ft)
Landing run	366 m (1,200 ft)
Range with max fuel	347 nm (643 km; 400 miles)

WAR AIRCRAFT REPLICAS F4U CORSAIR

The ½-scale F4U Corsair replica shown in an accompanying illustration was built by Mr Richard Schaper of Blue Earth, Minnesota, to War Aircraft Replicas plans. Construction is as described for the WAR Focke-Wulf 190, and the aircraft is powered by a 74·5 kW (100 hp) Continental O-200-A flat-four engine, driving a four-blade propeller.

DIMENSIONS, EXTERNAL:

Wing span	6·10 m (20 ft 0 in)
Wing chord: at root	1·37 m (4 ft 6 in)
at tip	0·86 m (2 ft 10 in)
Length overall	5·03 m (16 ft 6 in)
Height overall	1·52 m (5 ft 0 in)
Wheel track	2·03 m (6 ft 8 in)
Propeller diameter	1·52 m (5 ft 0 in)

WEIGHTS AND LOADING:

Weight empty	418 kg (921 lb)
Max T-O weight	544 kg (1,200 lb)
Max power loading	7·30 kg/kW (12·00 lb/hp)

PERFORMANCE (at max T-O weight):

Max level speed	147 knots (273 km/h; 170 mph)
Max cruising speed	121 knots (225 km/h; 140 mph)
Landing speed	78 knots (145 km/h; 90 mph)
Max rate of climb at S/L	426 m (1,400 ft)/min
T-O run	305 m (1,000 ft)
Landing run	457 m (1,500 ft)
Range with max fuel	347 nm (643 km; 400 miles)

WAR AIRCRAFT REPLICAS P-47 THUNDERBOLT

Construction is as described for the WAR Focke-Wulf 190, and the aircraft is powered by a 52-74·5 kW (70-100 hp) geared Volkswagen or 74·5 kW (100 hp) Continental O-200-A engine, driving a four-blade wooden fixed-pitch or ground adjustable propeller. The P-47 can be built with either a high turtledeck rear fuselage and early type canopy or a bubble canopy.

DIMENSIONS, EXTERNAL:

Wing span	6·10 m (20 ft 0 in)
Wing chord: at root	1·37 m (4 ft 6 in)
at tip	0·76 m (2 ft 6 in)
Length overall	5·18 m (17 ft 0 in)
Wheel track	2·06 m (6 ft 9 in)
Propeller diameter	1·52 m (5 ft 0 in)

WAR AIRCRAFT REPLICAS HAWKER SEA FURY

Construction is as described for the WAR Focke-Wulf 190, and the aircraft is powered by a 74·5 kW (100 hp) Continental O-200-A engine, driving a four-blade propeller. The first replica Sea Fury has been completed by Mr Peter Pykett of Andover, Hampshire, England. First flown on 24 February 1986, it took four years to construct from plans.

DIMENSIONS, EXTERNAL:

Wing span	6·10 m (20 ft 0 in)
Wing chord: at root	1·37 m (4 ft 6 in)
at tip	0·80 m (2 ft 7½ in)
Length overall	5·11 m (16 ft 9 in)
Wheel track	2·06 m (6 ft 9 in)
Propeller diameter	1·52 m (5 ft 0 in)

WAR AIRCRAFT REPLICAS MITSUBISHI A6M5 ZERO (ZEKE 52)

Construction is as described for the WAR Focke-Wulf 190, and power is provided by a 74·5 kW (100 hp) Continental O-200-A engine.

DIMENSIONS, EXTERNAL:

Wing span	6·40 m (21 ft 0 in)
Wing chord: at root	1·37 m (4 ft 6 in)
at tip	0·80 m (2 ft 7½ in)
Length overall	5·03 m (16 ft 6 in)
Wheel track	2·21 m (7 ft 3 in)
Propeller diameter	1·52 m (5 ft 0 in)

WATSON

WATSON WINDWAGON COMPANY

Route 1, Box 51, Newcastle, Texas 76372
Telephone: (817) 862 5615
OWNER: Gary Watson

WATSON GW-1 WINDWAGON

Mr Gary Watson designed and built a diminutive single-seat all-metal monoplane known as the GW-1 Windwagon (N64614). Although this was Mr Watson's first design, he was previously a member of a team that constructed a Parker Teenie Two.

Design of the Windwagon began in 1976 and construction of the prototype took six months; the engine was taken from a derelict Volkswagen 'Beetle', cut in half and reworked. First flight was made on 19 April 1977.

Plans to build the Windwagon are available to amateur builders, and 1,000 sets have been sold (including details for modifying the VW engine). Five hundred plans built Windwagons have been completed. Kits are also available, and by January 1986 about 100 had been sold.

TYPE: Single-seat homebuilt monoplane.

AIRFRAME: Cantilever low-wing monoplane of pop riveted aluminium alloy construction. Wing section Clark Y. Constant chord. Dihedral 5°. Wings built in three 1·83 m (6 ft 0 in) sections, the outer wing sections being removable for trailering. Conventional ailerons. No flaps. Conventional semi-monocoque fuselage. Cantilever tail unit, comprising constant chord tailplane with elevators, slightly swept fin and rudder. No tabs.

LANDING GEAR: Non-retractable tricycle type, employing tubular legs. All three wheels size 3·50-4 (tyre pressure 1·38 bars; 20 lb/sq in). No shock absorbers. Mainwheel hydraulic brakes.

POWER PLANT: One 22·4 kW (30 hp) 900 cc half-Volkswagen modified motorcar engine, driving a Hegy two-blade wooden propeller with spinner (illustration shows the previously used Dick Bohls four-blade propeller). Fuel capacity 15·14 litres (4 US gallons). Oil capacity 1·4 litres (1·5 US quarts).

ACCOMMODATION: Single semi-reclining seat in open cockpit. Large windscreen. Baggage space behind seat, capacity 9 kg (20 lb).

DIMENSIONS, EXTERNAL:

Wing span	5·49 m (18 ft 0 in)
Wing chord, constant	0·91 m (3 ft 0 in)
Length overall	3·96 m (13 ft 0 in)
Height overall	1·07 m (3 ft 6 in)
Wheel track	1·83 m (6 ft 0 in)
Wheelbase	1·22 m (4 ft 0 in)
Propeller diameter: Hegy	1·22 m (4 ft 0 in)
Dick Bohls four-blade	1·02 m (3 ft 4 in)

AREA:

Wings, gross	5·02 m² (54·0 sq ft)

WEIGHTS AND LOADINGS:

Weight empty	124 kg (273 lb)
Max T-O weight	220 kg (485 lb)
Max wing loading	43·84 kg/m² (8·98 lb/sq ft)
Max power loading	9·82 kg/kW (16·17 lb/hp)

PERFORMANCE:

Never-exceed speed	121 knots (225 km/h; 140 mph)
Max level speed	117 knots (217 km/h; 135 mph)
Cruising speed	over 87 knots (161 km/h; 100 mph)
Landing speed	39 knots (73 km/h; 45 mph)
Stalling speed	35 knots (65 km/h; 40 mph)
Max rate of climb at S/L	137 m (450 ft)/min
Service ceiling	3,660 m (12,000 ft)
T-O run	76 m (250 ft)
Landing run	91 m (300 ft)
Range	260 nm (483 km; 300 miles)

WENDT

WENDT AIRCRAFT ENGINEERING

9900 Alto Drive, La Mesa, California 92041
Telephone: (714) 463 8473

Wendt Aircraft Engineering designed and built the prototype of a two-seat sporting monoplane known as the WH-1 Traveler. The design originated on 4 September 1969, and construction of the prototype began on 26 November of the same year. The first flight was made on 15 March 1972. Plans of the Traveler are available to amateur constructors; at least 60 sets have been sold and eight aircraft are known to be under construction or completed.

WENDT WH-1 TRAVELER

TYPE: Two-seat homebuilt sporting aircraft.

AIRFRAME: Cantilever low-wing monoplane. Wing section NACA 64_3A-418. Dihedral 5° 30'. Incidence 2°. No sweepback. Constant chord two-spar structure. Spruce spars, marine plywood ribs, pine leading- and trailing-edges and ³⁄₃₂ in mahogany plywood skin from leading-edge to 37% chord. Aft of main spar, wing is Dacron covered. Plain ailerons, hinged at upper surface, made of spruce with plywood ribs, and Dacron covered. No flaps. Bungee trim on control column. Glassfibre wingtips. Conventional fuselage structure of spruce frames and longerons, plywood formers and tension ties, with steel tube overturn structure in the cockpit section. Fuselage undersurface and sides covered with ⅛ in mahogany plywood. Upper surface Dacron covered. Glassfibre nose cowl. Cantilever wooden tail unit with swept vertical surfaces and all-moving tailplane. Each surface has a spruce spar, spruce and plywood ribs, and a ¹⁄₁₆ in mahogany plywood torsion box. All surfaces Dacron covered. Static balance weights near tips of tailplane leading-edge. Tailplane has a half span trim and anti-balance tab. Tailplane tips of glassfibre.

LANDING GEAR: Non-retractable tricycle type. Cantilever spring steel main gear. Steerable nosewheel has coil spring shock absorption. Cleveland 5·00-5 wheels with Armstrong tyres, pressure 2·07 bars (30 lb/sq in). Cleveland caliper brakes. Glassfibre wheel fairings.

POWER PLANT: Prototype has one 56 kW (75 hp) Continental A75 flat-four engine, driving a McCauley Type 1C90 two-blade fixed-pitch metal propeller with glassfibre spinner. Design is suitable for installation of engines from 48·5-74·5 kW (65 to 100 hp). One aerofoil shape glassfibre fuel tank at each wingtip, capacity 41·5 litres (11 US gallons). Total fuel capacity 83 litres (22 US gallons). Refuelling points on upper surface of each wingtip. Oil capacity 3·8 litres (1 US gallon).

ACCOMMODATION: Pilot and passenger in tandem, beneath canopy which has a large transparent panel each side. Canopy hinged on port side. Dual controls standard. Stowage for 23 kg (50 lb) baggage aft of rear seat.

SYSTEM: Electrical system powered by 30A engine driven alternator. 12V 25Ah storage battery in glassfibre battery box in aft fuselage.

AVIONICS: Prototype has a Narco Escort 110 com transceiver.

DIMENSIONS, EXTERNAL:

Wing span	9·14 m (30 ft 0 in)
Wing chord, constant	1·20 m (3 ft 11¼ in)
Wing aspect ratio	7·63
Length overall	5·94 m (19 ft 6 in)
Height overall	2·08 m (6 ft 10 in)
Tailplane span	2·44 m (8 ft 0 in)
Wheel track	1·93 m (6 ft 4 in)
Wheelbase	1·45 m (4 ft 9 in)
Propeller diameter	1·80 m (5 ft 11 in)

DIMENSION, INTERNAL:

Cabin: Max width	0·71 m (2 ft 4 in)

AREA:

Wings, gross	10·96 m² (118·0 sq ft)

WEIGHTS AND LOADINGS:

Weight empty, equipped	408 kg (900 lb)
Max T-O and landing weight	635 kg (1,400 lb)
Max wing loading	57·9 kg/m² (11·86 lb/sq ft)
Max power loading	11·34 kg/kW (18·67 lb/hp)

PERFORMANCE (at max T-O weight):

Never-exceed speed	142 knots (264 km/h; 164 mph)
Max level speed at 1,220 m (4,000 ft)	114 knots (211 km/h; 131 mph)
Max cruising speed at 1,220 m (4,000 ft)	107 knots (198 km/h; 123 mph)
Econ cruising speed at 1,220 m (4,000 ft)	100 knots (185 km/h; 115 mph)
Stalling speed	50 knots (92 km/h; 57 mph)
Max rate of climb at S/L:	
no passenger	229 m (750 ft)/min
with passenger	152 m (500 ft)/min
Service ceiling	3,960 m (13,000 ft)
T-O run	244 m (800 ft)
Landing run	213 m (700 ft)
Range, no reserves:	
with max fuel	503 nm (933 km; 580 miles)
with max payload	416 nm (772 km; 480 miles)

WESTERN

WESTERN AIRCRAFT CORPORATION

CHAIRMAN: George Hamilton

The address given in the 1985-86 *Jane's* for Western Aircraft Corporation is no longer current. Details and an illustration of the company's Westair 204 can be found in that edition of *Jane's*.

WHATLEY

VASCOE WHATLEY Jr

PO Box 474, Allendale, South Carolina 29810

WHATLEY SPECIAL

Following earlier construction of an Evans VP-1, Mr Vascoe Whatley Jr designed and built a small single-seat biplane known as the Whatley Special (N87VW). Based partly on the Gere Sport, a biplane of the 1930s, it was designed to be light, cheap to operate (hence its original name Econobipe), easy to build and fly, and to use a mainly wooden airframe and a Volkswagen modified motorcar

WAR half-scale replica of a Hawker Sea Fury, built in the UK by Mr Peter Pykett *(Geoffrey P. Jones)*

WAR half-scale replica of the F4U Corsair built by Mr Richard Schaper of Blue Earth, Minnesota (74·5 kW; 100 hp Continental O-200-A engine) *(Howard Levy)*

Wendt WH-1 Traveler two-seat homebuilt aircraft

Watson GW-1 Windwagon (half an 1,800 cc Volkswagen modified motorcar engine), with Dick Bohls four-blade propeller *(J. M. G. Gradidge)*

White Der Jäger D.IX without wheel fairings, built by Mr B. W. Salyer *(J. M. G. Gradidge)*

Whatley Special single-seat light biplane

engine. It flew for the first time on 23 June 1981.

Plans are available to amateur builders, and by early 1986 at least 243 sets had been sold. Whatley Specials are being constructed in Belgium, Canada, Ireland, Mexico, Norway and the USA.

TYPE: Single-seat homebuilt biplane.

AIRFRAME: Braced biplane. Wing section NACA 4412 (modified). Dihedral 2° 30′ on lower wings. No dihedral on upper wing. Incidence on upper wing only. Sweepback on upper wing 7°. N type interplane struts. Cabane struts of 4130 steel tubing. Douglas fir wooden structure, except for okoumé mahogany plywood ribs and some metal components, Dacron covered. Ailerons on lower wings. No flaps. Conventional Dacron covered Douglas fir wooden fuselage, with okoumé plywood side panels from rear of cockpit to engine cowling. Wire braced tailplane and elevators, and large-area fin and rudder. Construction as for wings.

LANDING GEAR: Non-retractable tailwheel type. Main units comprise side Vs and long shock struts of steel tubing and EMT construction. Shock absorbers made of alternating discs of neoprene and aluminium. 5 in go-kart mainwheels. Steerable tailwheel. Drum brakes.

POWER PLANT: One Volkswagen 2,232 cc modified motorcar engine, driving a two-blade fixed-pitch propeller. Two fuel tanks in fuselage, aft of firewall, total capacity 34 litres (9 US gallons).

ACCOMMODATION: Single seat in open cockpit. Baggage space.

DIMENSIONS, EXTERNAL:
- Wing span: upper — 6·22 m (20 ft 5 in)
- lower — 5·82 m (19 ft 1 in)
- Wing chord: upper — 0·91 m (3 ft 0 in)
- lower — 0·76 m (2 ft 6 in)

WEIGHTS:
- Weight empty — 222 kg (490 lb)
- Max T-O weight — 336 kg (740 lb)

PERFORMANCE:
- Cruising speed — 65 knots (121 km/h; 75 mph)

WHITE

E. MARSHALL WHITE

Meadowlark Airport, 5141 Warner Avenue, Huntington Beach, California 92649
Telephone: (714) 846 2409

WHITE WW-1 DER JÄGER D.IX

Mr Marshall White designed an unusual homebuilt aircraft named Der Jäger D.IX, which is reminiscent of several German designs, mainly of First World War vintage. The wings are patterned on those of an Albatros D.Va, with the landing gear fairings of the Focke-Wulf Stösser and tail unit of the Fokker D.VII.

Design and construction of the prototype started simultaneously at the beginning of 1969, as Mr White's fifth homebuilt, and first flight of the prototype was made on 7 September 1969.

Plans and kits of materials, as well as some of the more difficult-to-construct parts in finished form, are available to amateur constructors, and at least 75 Der Jäger D.IXs are under construction. The first completed aircraft to be seen at an EAA Fly-in at Oshkosh, in 1974, was N1007, built by Mr Ray D. Fulwiler of Algoma, Wisconsin, with a 112 kW (150 hp) Avco Lycoming engine.

The following details apply to the prototype in its original form. It has since been re-engined with a 112 kW (150 hp) Avco Lycoming.

TYPE: Single-seat homebuilt biplane.

AIRFRAME: Forward stagger single-bay biplane with N interplane and centre-section struts. Single streamlined lift strut from each side of lower fuselage to attachment point of forward interplane strut on upper wing. No flying or landing wires. Aerofoil section M-6. Incidence 3° upper wing, 2° lower wings. Spruce spars and plywood ribs, fabric covered. Internal steel tube bracing. Ailerons in both top and bottom wings. Scalloped trailing-edge to both wings. Welded 4130 steel tube fuselage and wire braced tail unit, fabric covered. Aluminium engine cowling. Tail unit has sheet metal ribs. Balanced rudder and elevator. Ground adjustable trim tabs in elevator.

LANDING GEAR: Non-retractable tailwheel type. Main legs each consist of an A frame, welded into the fuselage, with tension springs in the centre-fuselage to cushion landing shock. Mainwheels and tyres size 5·00-5. Glassfibre wheel fairings.

POWER PLANT: One 86 kW (115 hp) Avco Lycoming O-235-C1 flat-four engine, driving a McCauley two-blade propeller. Structure suitable for alternative power plants from 1,600 cc Volkswagen up to 112 kW (150 hp). Fuel contained in two tanks, one in upper wing centre-section, capacity 53 litres (14 US gallons), one in fuselage, capacity 38 litres (10 US gallons); total 91 litres (24 US gallons).

ACCOMMODATION: Single seat in open cockpit, with headrest faired into wood or glassfibre fuselage turtleback.

EQUIPMENT: Two dummy machine-guns mounted on top of fuselage, forward of cockpit. Dummy bomb, carried between legs of main landing gear, can be adapted as oil tank for smoke discharge system.

DIMENSIONS, EXTERNAL:
- Wing span: upper — 6·10 m (20 ft 0 in)
- lower — 4·88 m (16 ft 0 in)
- Wing chord: upper at root — 1·07 m (3 ft 6 in)
- upper at tip — 1·22 m (4 ft 0 in)
- lower, constant — 0·91 m (3 ft 0 in)
- Length overall — 5·18 m (17 ft 0 in)
- Tailplane span — 2·44 m (8 ft 0 in)
- Wheel track — 1·52 m (5 ft 0 in)
- Propeller diameter — 1·68 m (5 ft 6 in)

AREA:
- Wings, gross — 10·68 m² (115·0 sq ft)

WEIGHTS AND LOADINGS:
- Weight empty — 242 kg (534 lb)
- Max T-O weight — 403 kg (888 lb)
- Max wing loading — 37·7 kg/m² (7·72 lb/sq ft)
- Max power loading (150 hp) — 3·60 kg/kW (5·92 lb/hp)

PERFORMANCE (at max T-O weight):
- Never-exceed speed — 152 knots (282 km/h; 175 mph)
- Max level speed at 610 m (2,000 ft) — 126 knots (233 km/h; 145 mph)
- Max cruising speed at 610 m (2,000 ft) — 116 knots (214 km/h; 133 mph)
- Stalling speed — 47 knots (87 km/h; 54 mph)
- Max rate of climb at S/L — 732 m (2,400 ft)/min
- T-O run — 46 m (150 ft)

WHITE LIGHTNING

WHITE LIGHTNING AIRCRAFT CORPORATION

PO Drawer 40, Sheldon, South Carolina 29941

WHITE LIGHTNING AIRCRAFT WHITE LIGHTNING

The White Lightning is a new four-seat all-composites homebuilt aircraft, available for amateur construction in kit form (under 1,000 working hours to assemble). It was designed by former Formula 1 racing pilot Mr Nick Jones of Beaufort, South Carolina, beginning in June 1984. Construction of the prototype was mostly the responsibility of his partner, Mr Ray Ward, who took only 600 working hours because of previous Glasair building experience. The first flight was achieved on 8 March 1985, and the prototype was exhibited at that year's Sun 'n Fun meeting. This aircraft differs from the production kit version in having shorter ailerons and a welded steel tube landing gear. The White Lightning is said to be aerobatic with two persons on board at an all-up weight of 839 kg (1,850 lb). The present kit comes complete, except for the engine, propeller, instruments and avionics. It is planned to offer these items later, in the form of optional individual kits, plus long range fuel tanks.

TYPE: Four-seat homebuilt aircraft.

AIRFRAME: Cantilever low-wing monoplane of composites construction. Wing section NACA 602215. Wings have graphite tubular 'wet' main spar, and glassfibre front and rear spars and ribs, all pre-cast in the lower glassfibre skin. Wings are delivered with the glassfibre upper skin in place, leaving the factory moulded glassfibre leading-edge to be attached. Fowler flaps and ailerons. Composites fuselage moulded in upper and lower halves, with cast-in bulkheads and main landing gear support boxes. Conventional cantilever tail unit, with spars and ribs of fin and tailplane pre-cast into one skin of each.

LANDING GEAR: Retractable tricycle type, with electro-hydraulic actuation. Aluminium alloy legs delivered completely assembled. Steerable nosewheel. Mainwheels retract rearward into lower fuselage sides; nosewheel also retracts rearward into pre-assembled wheel well.

POWER PLANT: Prototype has one 156·6 kW (210 hp) Continental IO-360 engine, driving a three-blade composite constant-speed propeller with spinner. Standard fuel capacity 227 litres (60 US gallons), of which 106 litres (28 US gallons) are carried in 'wet' wing main spar and remainder in 'wet' wing area behind front spar.

ACCOMMODATION: Four persons in pairs in enclosed cabin with semi-reclining seats, each with individual upward hinging and glazed glassfibre canopy door. Max baggage capacity 154 kg (340 lb) in 1·70 m³ (60 cu ft) compartment.

DIMENSIONS, EXTERNAL:
- Wing span: 8·43 m (27 ft 8 in)
- Length overall: 7·11 m (23 ft 4 in)
- Height overall: 2·18 m (7 ft 2 in)
- Tailplane span: 2·74 m (9 ft 0 in)
- Wheel track: 1·83 m (6 ft 0 in)
- Propeller diameter: 1·93 m (6 ft 4 in)

DIMENSION, INTERNAL:
- Cabin: Max width: 1·07 m (3 ft 6 in)

AREA:
- Wings, gross: 8·27 m² (89·0 sq ft)

WEIGHTS AND LOADINGS:
- Weight empty: 612 kg (1,350 lb)
- Max T-O weight: 1,088 kg (2,400 lb)
- Max wing loading: 131·7 kg/m² (26·97 lb/sq ft)
- Max power loading: 6·95 kg/kW (11·43 lb/hp)

PERFORMANCE (at max T-O weight):
- Max cruising speed at S/L: over 217 knots (402 km/h; 250 mph)
- Stalling speed: 79 knots (145 km/h; 90 mph)
- Max rate of climb at S/L:
  - Two persons: 671 m (2,200 ft)/min
  - Four persons: 457 m (1,500 ft)/min
- Range with max fuel: 1,303 nm (2,414 km; 1,500 miles)
- *g* limits: +6/−4 aerobatic

WIND DANCER

PO Box 8434, Santa Fe, New Mexico 87504
Telephone: (505) 473 0654

WIND DANCER

Wind Dancer is a proof of concept/styling exercise prototype gyroplane promoted by Mr David Gittens. It was designed and built during the first seven months of 1986, with the assistance of a number of friends and manufacturers, enabling the prototype to be displayed at Oshkosh in August 1986.

TYPE: Single-seat light autogyro.

AIRFRAME: Skywheels two-blade composites rotor carried on a Ken Brock heavy duty rotor head. Basic frame and rotor mast of 4130 steel tubing, with body and tail unit of polyurethane/glassfibre sandwich. Large central rudder not in place when accompanying photograph was taken.

LANDING GEAR: Non-retractable tricycle type, plus small tailwheel.

POWER PLANT: One 89·5 kW (120 hp) Aerotek 655 cc rotary piston engine, mounted aft of cockpit and driving an Ed Sterba 54/56 two-blade wooden propeller. Engine operates on automotive fuel.

ACCOMMODATION: Single seat under tinted one-piece canopy in highly streamlined cockpit pod.

DIMENSIONS, EXTERNAL:
- Rotor diameter: 7·93 m (26 ft 0 in)
- Rotor blade chord: 0·203 m (8 in)
- Length overall, excl rotor: 4·02 m (13 ft 2 in)
- Height overall, excl rotor: 2·29 m (7 ft 6 in)
- Width overall, excl rotor: 2·14 m (7 ft 0 in)

WEIGHTS:
- Weight empty: 191 kg (420 lb)
- Max T-O weight: 340 kg (750 lb)

PERFORMANCE (designed):
- Max level speed: 108 knots (201 km/h; 125 mph)
- Cruising speed: 78 knots (145 km/h; 90 mph)
- T-O speed: 31 knots (56 km/h; 35 mph)
- Min flying speed: 25 knots (45 km/h; 28 mph)
- Max rate of climb at S/L: 366 m (1,200 ft)/min
- Service ceiling: 4,420 m (14,500 ft)
- T-O run: 77 m (250 ft)
- Landing run: 1·50 m (5 ft)
- Range with max fuel: 304 nm (563 km; 350 miles)

WITTMAN

S. J. WITTMAN

7200 SE 85th Lane, Ocala, Florida 32672

Famous as a racing pilot since 1926, Steve Wittman has designed and built a large number of different racing and touring aeroplanes.

Most popular current Wittman design is the W-8 Tailwind side by side two-seat light aeroplane. The prototype was built in 1952-53. Sets of plans and prefabricated components were made available to amateur builders and several hundred Model W-8 Tailwinds are flying, including a number built in foreign countries. Many more are under construction.

WITTMAN O & O SPECIAL

Mr Wittman's latest aircraft is the O & O (Oshkosh to Ocala) Special, a two-seater of similar general layout to the Tailwind. Powered by a 167·8 kW (225 hp) Continental O-470-J engine, it flew for the first time on 17 November 1985. Provisional performance figures include a max level speed of 156 knots (290 km/h; 180 mph) and a stalling speed similar to that of the Tailwind W-8.

WITTMAN TAILWIND MODEL W-8

Some Tailwinds have been built with tricycle landing gear, retractable mainwheels and other design changes. The following data refer to the standard W-8 Tailwind built to Mr Wittman's plans:

TYPE: Two-seat homebuilt cabin monoplane.

AIRFRAME: Braced high-wing monoplane. Wing section is a combination of NACA 4309 (upper surface) and NACA 0006 (lower surface). Thickness/chord ratio 11·5%. No dihedral. Incidence 1°. Wooden structure with plywood and fabric covering. Single bracing strut each side. Ailerons and flaps of steel and stainless steel construction. Steel tube fuselage, fabric covered. Cantilever tail unit of steel and stainless steel. Ground adjustable trim tabs in control surfaces.

LANDING GEAR: Non-retractable tailwheel type. Spring steel cantilever main legs. Goodyear 15 × 5 mainwheels and tyres, pressure 2·21 bars (32 lb/sq in). Goodyear brakes.

POWER PLANT: Normally one 67 kW (90 hp) Continental C90-12F flat-four engine, driving a Sensenich or Flottorp two-blade fixed-pitch wood propeller. Alternative engines are the 63·5 kW (85 hp) Continental C85, 74·5 kW (100 hp) Continental O-200, 86 kW (115 hp) Avco Lycoming O-235 or 104·5 kW (140 hp) Avco Lycoming O-290. One fuel tank of 94·5-132·5 litres (25-35 US gallons) capacity in fuselage. Oil capacity 1·85-2·8 litres (1-1½ US gallons).

ACCOMMODATION: Two seats side by side in enclosed cabin, with door on each side. Space for 27 kg (60 lb) baggage.

DIMENSIONS, EXTERNAL:
- Wing span: 6·86 m (22 ft 6 in)
- Wing chord, constant: 1·22 m (4 ft 0 in)
- Wing aspect ratio: 5·5
- Length overall: 5·87 m (19 ft 3 in)
- Height overall: 1·73 m (5 ft 8 in)
- Tailplane span: 2·03 m (6 ft 8 in)
- Wheel track: 1·65 m (5 ft 5 in)
- Propeller diameter: 1·63 m (5 ft 4 in)

DIMENSIONS, INTERNAL:
- Cabin: Height: 1·00 m (3 ft 3½ in)
  - Max width: 1·02 m (3 ft 4 in)

AREA:
- Wings, gross: 8·36 m² (90·0 sq ft)

WEIGHTS AND LOADINGS (74·5 kW; 100 hp Continental O-200 engine):
- Weight empty: 318 kg (700 lb)
- Max T-O weight: 590 kg (1,300 lb)
- Max wing loading: 70·5 kg/m² (14·44 lb/sq ft)
- Max power loading: 8·81 kg/kW (14·44 lb/hp)

PERFORMANCE (74·5 kW; 100 hp Continental O-200 engine at max T-O weight):
- Never-exceed speed: 160 knots (297 km/h; 185 mph)
- Max level speed at S/L: 143 knots (265 km/h; 165 mph)
- Max cruising speed: 139 knots (257 km/h; 160 mph)
- Econ cruising speed: 113 knots (209 km/h; 130 mph)
- Stalling speed, flaps down: 48 knots (89 km/h; 55 mph)
- Max rate of climb at S/L: 275 m (900 ft)/min
- Service ceiling: more than 4,875 m (16,000 ft)
- T-O run: 245 m (800 ft)
- T-O to 15 m (50 ft): 405 m (1,325 ft)
- Landing from 15 m (50 ft): 350 m (1,150 ft)
- Landing run: 183 m (600 ft)
- Range with max payload at 3,050 m (10,000 ft), no reserves:
  - at 139 knots (257 km/h; 160 mph): 521 nm (965 km; 600 miles)
  - at 122 knots (225 km/h; 140 mph): 607 nm (1,125 km; 700 miles)

WITTMAN TAILWIND MODEL W-10

Recent revisions to the Tailwind plans have produced a new version known as the Model W-10. This is basically a W-8 with a 112 kW (150 hp) Avco Lycoming, 108 kW (145 hp) Continental, or aluminium block Oldsmobile or Buick V-8 engine. Airframe improvements include a new and more efficient wingtip design. Empty and max T-O weights of this version, with Continental O-300 engine, are 381 kg (840 lb) and 646 kg (1,425 lb) respectively, and maximum speed 174 knots (322 km/h; 200 mph). Cruising speed is 139-165 knots (257-306 km/h; 160-190 mph), depending upon the type of engine fitted.

WOLF

DONALD S. WOLF

17 Chestnut Street, Huntington, New York 11743
Telephone: (516) 427 9678

Mr Donald S. Wolf has designed and built a sporting biplane known as the W-11 Boredom Fighter. Styled to represent a single-seat biplane fighter of First World War vintage, although based on no single aircraft, it is said to be fairly simple to construct, using a minimum of special tools. It is capable of accommodating a pilot up to 1·85 m (6 ft 1 in) tall and weighing up to 91 kg (200 lb), is intended primarily for sport flying and is not fully aerobatic. Power plant can vary between 37·5 and 74·5 kW (50-100 hp), but a 48·5 kW (65 hp) Continental A65 engine is recommended.

Design of the Boredom Fighter began in July 1976 and construction of the prototype started in August 1977. The first flight was achieved on 30 August 1979 and by January 1986 the prototype had accumulated a total of 350 flying hours. Plans are available to amateur constructors, and 90 Boredom Fighters were under construction in late 1985 in Australia, Canada, continental Europe, the UK and the USA. Four had flown by that time, confirming the performance data established by the prototype.

WOLF W-11 BOREDOM FIGHTER

TYPE: Single-seat homebuilt biplane.

AIRFRAME: Braced single-bay biplane, with I-type interplane struts and N-type cabane struts. Wing section NACA 4412. Dihedral 1° on all wings. Incidence 0° on upper wing, 1° 30′ on lower wings. No sweepback. Wooden structure, with solid spruce spars and truss ribs, fabric covered. Constant chord ailerons on lower wings, of similar construction to wings. No flaps. Spruce Warren truss fuselage, with mahogany plywood covering in cockpit area; fabric covered rear fuselage. Wire braced spruce tail unit, fabric covered, comprising conventional tailplane and elevators, rounded fin and rudder. Bungee trim on elevators.

LANDING GEAR: Non-retractable tailwheel type. Two side

White Lightning Aircraft White Lightning four-seat homebuilt composites monoplane *(Howard Levy)*

Proof of concept prototype Wind Dancer gyroplane *(J. M. G. Gradidge)*

Wittman Tailwind W-8 two-seat homebuilt aircraft *(R. Kunert)*

Replica Pitts *Samson*, built by Mr Steve Wolf of Athol, Indiana *(Howard Levy)*

Wittman O & O Special *(J. M. G. Gradidge)*

Wolf W-11 Boredom Fighter built by Mr Fred Machado Jr of Camarillo, California *(John Wegg)*

Wittman Tailwind W-10 two-seat light aircraft *(J. M. G. Gradidge)*

Vs and half-axles. Rubber bungee shock absorption. Shinn mainwheels, size 6·00-6, with Goodyear tyres. Wolf tailwheel and tyre. Shinn cable operated brakes.

POWER PLANT: One 48·5 kW (65 hp) Continental A65 engine recommended, driving a Lewis 72 × 43 two-blade fixed-pitch wooden propeller. One fuel tank in fuselage, capacity 56·8 litres (15 US gallons). Refuelling point in top of fuselage. Oil capacity 3·8 litres (1 US gallon).

ACCOMMODATION: Pilot only, in open cockpit. Foot heater. Baggage space aft of seat, capacity 3·6 kg (8 lb).

DIMENSIONS, EXTERNAL:

Wing span, both	6·10 m (20 ft 0 in)
Wing chord, constant	0·76 m (2 ft 6 in)
Wing aspect ratio	8
Length overall	4·79 m (15 ft 8½ in)
Height overall	1·83 m (6 ft 0 in)
Tailplane span	1·93 m (6 ft 4 in)
Wheel track	1·52 m (5 ft 0 in)
Wheelbase	3·66 m (12 ft 0 in)
Propeller diameter	1·83 m (6 ft 0 in)

AREA:

Wings, gross	9·06 m² (97·5 sq ft)

WEIGHTS AND LOADINGS:

Weight empty, equipped	214·5 kg (473 lb)
Max T-O weight	349 kg (770 lb)
Max wing loading	38·6 kg/m² (7·9 lb/sq ft)
Max power loading	7·20 kg/kW (11·85 lb/hp)

PERFORMANCE:

Never-exceed speed	117 knots (217 km/h; 135 mph)
Max level speed at 610 m (2,000 ft)	102 knots (190 km/h; 118 mph)
Max cruising speed at 610 m (2,000 ft)	95 knots (175 km/h; 109 mph)
Econ cruising speed at 610 m (2,000 ft)	87 knots (161 km/h; 100 mph)
Stalling speed, engine idling	37 knots (68 km/h; 42 mph)
Max rate of climb at S/L	366 m (1,200 ft)/min
Service ceiling	approx 4,875 m (16,000 ft)
T-O run on grass	46 m (150 ft)
T-O on grass to 15 m (50 ft)	91 m (300 ft)
Landing on grass from 15 m (50 ft)	122 m (400 ft)
Landing run on grass	91 m (300 ft)
Range with max fuel, 20 min reserves	404 nm (750 km; 466 miles)

WOLF

STEVE WOLF

Athol, Indiana

WOLF (PITTS) SAMSON REPLICA

Mr Steve Wolf flew for the first time on 15 May 1985 a full-size replica of the Curtis Pitts biplane *Samson*, the original of which had been built in the mid-1940s and used by aerobatic pilot Jess Bristow and others for air show work. The replica took two years and three weeks to complete.

Powered by a 336 kW (450 hp) Pratt & Whitney Wasp radial engine, driving a Hamilton-Standard two-blade propeller with spinner, the replica is used normally for air shows, skywriting (using a 68 litre; 18 US gallon smoke/oil tank) and glider towing. On 2 August 1985 it beat the former Class C1b record for time to climb to 3,000 m, set by Miss Svetlana Savitskaya of the Soviet Union in a Yak-50, with a new time of 3 min 59·27 s.

TYPE: Two-seat homebuilt aerobatic biplane replica.

AIRFRAME: Single-bay braced biplane. Wing section NACA

23012. I type interplane struts. Conventional wire braced tail unit.

LANDING GEAR: Non-retractable tailwheel type, with faired mainwheels.

POWER PLANT: As detailed in introduction. Fuel capacity 216 litres (57 US gallons). Oil capacity 23 litres (6 US gallons).

ACCOMMODATION: Pilot and passenger in tandem open cockpits; front cockpit can be covered.

DIMENSIONS, EXTERNAL:

Wing span	7·32 m (24 ft 0 in)
Wing chord, constant	1·27 m (4 ft 2 in)
Length overall	6·25 m (20 ft 6 in)
Propeller diameter	3·05 m (10 ft 0 in)

WEIGHTS AND LOADING:

Weight empty	789 kg (1,740 lb)
Max T-O weight	1,134 kg (2,500 lb)
Max power loading	3·38 kg/kW (5·56 lb/hp)

PERFORMANCE (at max T-O weight):

Cruising speed at 3,660 m (12,000 ft) 169 knots (314 km/h; 195 mph)

Max rate of climb at S/L 1,220 m (4,000 ft)/min

WOOD WING

WOOD WING SPECIALTY

PO Box 1258-KP, Tehachapi, California 93561
Telephone: (805) 822 7850

PLUMB CRACKER JACK

Wood Wing Specialty is offering plans and kits to allow amateur construction of the Cracker Jack, designed by Mr Peter Plumb.

The Cracker Jack is a strut braced high-wing single-seat monoplane of conventional layout, with the pilot accommodated in a semi-enclosed cockpit. The landing gear is of tailwheel type, with the mainwheels carried on side Vs and half axles. Power is provided by a modified DAF motorcar engine. No other details are known.

SAILPLANES

AUSTRALIA

LYNCH

JOHN F. LYNCH

RMB 161, Tocumwal, NSW 2714
Telephone: 058742594

LYNCH (PILATUS) B4M1

Mr Lynch has motorised two examples of the Pilatus B4-PC11A sailplane which, in early 1986, were operating on a Permit to Fly pending full certification under JAR 22 (Normal category). Design began in 1984, and the first conversion was flown initially with a single-cylinder Fuji Robin engine. A Rotax engine was fitted later, but neither installation proved entirely satisfactory, and in February 1985 a change was made to a 17·9 kW (24 hp) König SC 430 three-cylinder two-stroke with 1·75:1 reduction drive to a König two-blade wooden pusher propeller with folding, ground adjustable blades. This installation is non-retractable, being mounted on a pylon aft of the cockpit, and has a 12V motorcycle battery for engine starting and fuel pump drive. Fuel capacity is 20·5 litres (4·5 Imp gallons). The four-cylinder König SD 570 engine can be fitted optionally.

Of originally Swiss design and manufacture, the B4-PC11A was last produced by the Japanese company Nippi, under whose heading a detailed description of the sailplane last appeared in the 1983-84 *Jane's*. Wingtip wheels have been added to Mr Lynch's B4M1 version, and the engine installation was undergoing continuing refinement in early 1986. A streamline pod cowling was being fitted, and the power pod has been tested to withstand a 16*g* impact; in the event of a crash, it is designed to break to one side to avoid contact with the cockpit. The entire installation can be removed in 5 minutes to restore the aircraft to normal sailplane configuration.

DIMENSIONS, EXTERNAL:
- Wing span: 15·00 m (49 ft 2½ in)
- Wing aspect ratio: 16·01
- Length overall: 6·57 m (21 ft 6¾ in)
- Height over tail: 1·57 m (5 ft 2 in)
- Propeller diameter: 1·50 m (4 ft 11 in)

AREA:
- Wings, gross: 14·05 m² (151·2 sq ft)

WEIGHT AND LOADINGS:
- Max T-O weight: 350 kg (771 lb)
- Max wing loading: 24·91 kg/m² (5·10 lb/sq ft)
- Max power loading: 19·55 kg/kW (32·15 lb/hp)

PERFORMANCE (at max T-O weight):
- Never-exceed speed: 130 knots (241 km/h; 149 mph)
- Max level speed: 70 knots (130 km/h; 81 mph)
- Max cruising speed: 60 knots (111 km/h; 69 mph)
- Econ cruising speed: 55 knots (102 km/h; 63 mph)
- Stalling speed: 33 knots (62 km/h; 38 mph)
- Max rate of climb at S/L: 100 m (330 ft)/min
- T-O run: 107 m (350 ft)
- Landing run: 61 m (200 ft)
- Range with max fuel: 270 nm (500 km; 311 miles)
- Best glide ratio: 29-30

TODHUNTER

R. W. TODHUNTER

5 Leemon Street, Condell Park, NSW 2200

Mr Reg Todhunter is developing a very lightweight powered sailplane known as the Blue Wren. He is being assisted by Mr Milton Lalas, a senior aeronautical engineer, Mr Ernest Todhunter, a senior electrical engineer, and Mr Bob Letson, an experienced aircraft welder.

TODHUNTER T-5 BLUE WREN

Basic design and stressing of the Blue Wren was completed by early 1980, and construction began in January of that year. It was designed initially to comply with the Australian Dept of Air Transport ANO Section 95-10 (ie, restricted to a max T-O weight of 181 kg; 400 lb), but was later reworked to increase pilot protection and *g* limits.

The accompanying photograph shows the aircraft before its first flight on 14 July 1984. In August 1984 it competed, but was not flown, in the Sailplane Homebuilders Association design contest in the USA. Although preliminary flights exhibited good handling characteristics, modifications have been made to improve aileron stiffness. Further tests were scheduled for March 1985, but no news has been received since the beginning of that year.

TYPE: Single-seat lightweight powered sailplane.

AIRFRAME: Cantilever tapered high-wing monoplane, with Wortmann FX-05-H-126 wing section. Dihedral 2° 30′. Incidence 2° 30′. Sweepforward 2° 6′ at quarter-chord. Wings are constructed of aluminium alloy, foam and glassfibre, with trailing-edge flap/spoilers and ailerons, and are detachable for transportation and storage. Turned-down wingtips. Pod type fuselage of glassfibre over a steel tube frame. Tapered 2024-T3 aluminium alloy tailboom faired to bottom of pod. Engine, mounted above boom, is faired in behind streamlined cockpit canopy and drives a pusher propeller centred behind wing trailing-edge. Propeller can be stopped in horizontal position to reduce drag in soaring mode. Cantilever fixed incidence T tailplane, with elevator, of plastics foam with glassfibre skin. Elevator has spring trim. Non-retractable semi-recessed unsprung monowheel (tyre size 10 × 3 in), with drum brake; tailskid. Single 40° reclining seat under one-piece single curvature canopy.

POWER PLANT: One 11 kW (15 hp) TS 162 two-stroke flat-twin engine, driving (on prototype) a 0·91 m (3 ft) diameter fixed-pitch wooden pusher propeller via a reduction drive. Single fuselage fuel tank, capacity 7 litres (1·5 Imp gallons).

DIMENSIONS, EXTERNAL:
- Wing span: 11·00 m (36 ft 1 in)
- Wing aspect ratio: 14·96
- Length overall: 5·69 m (18 ft 8 in)
- Height over tail: 1·07 m (3 ft 6¼ in)

AREA:
- Wings, gross: 8·08 m² (87·0 sq ft)

WEIGHTS AND LOADINGS:
- Weight empty: 122 kg (268 lb)
- Max T-O weight: 204 kg (450 lb)
- Max wing loading: 25·24 kg/m² (5·17 lb/sq ft)
- Max power loading: 18·55 kg/kW (30·0 lb/hp)

PERFORMANCE, UNPOWERED (estimated at max T-O weight):
- Best glide ratio at 50 knots (93 km/h; 58 mph): 27
- Min rate of sink at 39 knots (72 km/h; 45 mph): 0·76 m (2·50 ft)/s
- Stalling speed: 35 knots (64 km/h; 40 mph)
- Max speed (smooth air): 95 knots (176 km/h; 109 mph)
- Max speed (rough air): 80 knots (148 km/h; 92 mph)
- *g* limits: +4·67/−2·5

AUSTRIA

BRDITSCHKA

HB-BRDITSCHKA GmbH & Co KG

Postfach 12, Dr Adolf Schärf Strasse 42-46, A-4053 Haid-Ansfelden
Telephone: 07229/88355 or 88283
Telex: 021909
DIRECTOR: Ing Heino Brditschka

This company produces two versions of the HB-23 two-seat motor glider. Design of the original tandem-seat HB-21 began in 1973, and of the side by side HB-23 in 1979. The HB-22 (1983-84 *Jane's*) was a prototype only.

BRDITSCHKA HB-23 HOBBYLINER and SCANLINER

The HB-21, HB-21/2400 and HB-23/2000 versions of this motor glider are no longer in production. Details can be found in the 1985-86 *Jane's*. The following models were in production in 1986:

HB-23/2400 Hobbyliner. Side by side version with T tail, 74·5 kW (100 hp) engine, and increased fuel capacity. In production, with 30 built by February 1986.

HB-23/2400 Scanliner. Observation version of HB-23, with bubble canopy to provide optimum air to ground forward view. In production. Export order for 11 for an unnamed military customer announced in late 1985.

TYPE: Two-seat motor glider.

AIRFRAME: Cantilever high-wing monoplane. Wortmann wing sections: FX-61-184 at root, FX-60-126 at tip. Dihedral 2° on outer panels. Incidence 3°. No sweep. Single main box spar of PhBu 7 (laminated beechwood) and plywood, wooden ribs, and overall plywood covering. All-wood ailerons. Spoilers on upper surface. Main fuselage pod is a welded steel tube latticework truss with glassfibre skin; rear fuselage comprises upper and lower tailbooms, covered in plywood except for triangular cutout in area of propeller rotation. Plywood covered wooden tail unit comprises fin, rudder, fixed incidence T tailplane, and elevators. Trim tab in starboard elevator. Non-retractable tricycle landing gear. Mainwheels have self-sprung cantilever glassfibre legs, size 5·00-5 tyres (pressure 2·5 bars; 36·3 lb/sq in) and independent Tost brakes. Steerable nosewheel, with size 4·00-4 tyre, pressure 3·0 bars (43·5 lb/sq in). Fully enclosed cabin for two persons, on side by side adjustable seats; 0·23 m³ (8·1 cu ft) of baggage space aft of seats. One-piece fixed canopy forward, aft of which are twin window/doors hinged on centreline and opening upward. VFR instrumentation standard, IFR panel optional.

POWER PLANT: One 74·5 kW (100 hp) 2,400 cc Volkswagen G or G/2 modified four-cylinder motorcar engine, mounted aft of cabin with rubber belt drive to a Hoffmann HO-14C/172 130LD two-blade fixed-pitch pusher propeller (variable-pitch propeller optional). Single fuel tank in wing centre-section, capacity 66 litres (14·5 Imp gallons).

DIMENSIONS, EXTERNAL:
- Wing span: Hobbyliner: 16·40 m (53 ft 9¾ in)
  - Scanliner: 16·30 m (53 ft 5¾ in)
- Wing chord: at root: 1·54 m (5 ft 0½ in)
  - at tip: 0·60 m (1 ft 11½ in)
- Wing aspect ratio: Hobbyliner: 14·11
  - Scanliner: 13·93
- Width, outer wing panels removed: 7·15 m (23 ft 5½ in)
- Length overall: 8·15 m (26 ft 9 in)
- Height overall: 2·60 m (8 ft 6½ in)
- Wheelbase: 2·34 m (7 ft 8¼ in)

AREAS:
- Wings, gross: 19·067 m² (205·2 sq ft)
- Ailerons (total): 1·46 m² (15·72 sq ft)
- Spoilers (total): 0·48 m² (5·17 sq ft)
- Fin: 0·977 m² (10·52 sq ft)
- Rudder: 0·62 m² (6·67 sq ft)
- Tailplane: 1·26 m² (13·56 sq ft)
- Elevators, incl tab: 1·044 m² (11·24 sq ft)

WEIGHTS AND LOADINGS:
- Weight empty, equipped:
  - Hobbyliner: 550 kg (1,212 lb)
  - Scanliner: 580 kg (1,278 lb)
- Max T-O weight: Hobbyliner: 750 kg (1,653 lb)
  - Scanliner: 800 kg (1,763 lb)
- Max wing loading:
  - Hobbyliner: 39·33 kg/m² (8·06 lb/sq ft)
  - Scanliner: 41·96 kg/m² (8·60 lb/sq ft)
- Max power loading:
  - Hobbyliner: 10·06 kg/kW (16·53 lb/hp)
  - Scanliner: 10·74 kg/kW (17·64 lb/hp)

PERFORMANCE, UNPOWERED (both versions):
- Best glide ratio at 53 knots (98 km/h; 61 mph): 24-26
- Min rate of sink at 50 knots (92 km/h; 57 mph): 1·20 m (3·94 ft)/s
- Stalling speed: 41 knots (75 km/h; 47 mph)
- Max speed (smooth air): 108 knots (200 km/h; 124 mph)
- Max speed (rough air): 93 knots (173 km/h; 107 mph)
- *g* limits: Hobbyliner: +5·3/−2·65
  - Scanliner (semi-aerobatic, up to T-O weight of 750 kg): +5·3/−3
  - Scanliner (Utility category): +4·4/−3

PERFORMANCE, POWERED (at max T-O weight):
- Never-exceed speed:
  - both versions: 108 knots (200 km/h; 124 mph)
- Max level speed:
  - Hobbyliner: 101 knots (187 km/h; 116 mph)
- Max cruising speed (75% power):
  - both versions: 93 knots (173 km/h; 107 mph)
- Stalling speed:
  - both versions: 41 knots (75 km/h; 47 mph)
- Max rate of climb at S/L:
  - both versions: 270 m (886 ft)/min
- Service ceiling: Hobbyliner: 7,000 m (22,960 ft)
  - Scanliner: 5,000 m (16,400 ft)
- T-O run: Hobbyliner: 200 m (656 ft)
  - Scanliner: 160 m (525 ft)
- Landing run: both versions: 210 m (689 ft)
- Range with max fuel, no reserves:
  - Hobbyliner: 459 nm (850 km; 528 miles)
  - Scanliner: 431 nm (800 km; 497 miles)
- Patrol endurance: Scanliner: up to 6 h

Mr John Lynch's prototype B4M1 self-launching conversion of a Pilatus B4-PC11A sailplane, shown with König SC 430 engine and original non-folding propeller

Todhunter T-5 Blue Wren homebuilt powered sailplane

BRAZIL

IPE

INDÚSTRIA PARANAENSE DE ESTRUTURAS

Caixa Postal 7931, Rua J. Durski 357, 80.000 Curitiba, Paraná State

MANAGER: Eng J. C. Boscardin

IPE KW 1 b 2 QUERO QUERO II

Brazilian Air Force designation: Z-16

Four prototypes of the Quero Quero were built (first flight 1 October 1972), followed by 148 production examples. Series production was halted at that point, but US certification, to make possible exports to that country, was in process in mid-1985. This was still awaited in early 1986. Sales have been made to Brazilian flying clubs, the Brazilian Air Force Academy (16) and private owners.

TYPE: Single-seat training glider.

AIRFRAME: Cantilever high-wing monoplane, with Scheibe Spatz wing section, built of wood and plywood (Brazilian pine). Upper/lower surface spoilers. Non-retractable monowheel and tailwheel. One-piece canopy.

DIMENSIONS, EXTERNAL:
- Wing span: 15·00 m (49 ft 2½ in)
- Wing aspect ratio: 19·23
- Length overall: 6·47 m (21 ft 2¾ in)
- Height overall: 1·34 m (4 ft 4¾ in)

AREA:
- Wings, gross: 11·70 m² (125·9 sq ft)

WEIGHTS AND LOADING:
- Weight empty: 170 kg (374 lb)
- Max T-O weight: 270 kg (595 lb)
- Max wing loading: 21·3 kg/m² (4·36 lb/sq ft)

PERFORMANCE (at max T-O weight):
- Best glide ratio at 39 knots (73 km/h; 45 mph): 28
- Min rate of sink at 33 knots (62 km/h; 39 mph): 0·64 m (2·10 ft)/s
- Stalling speed: 33 knots (60 km/h; 38 mph)
- Max speed (rough and smooth air): 81 knots (150 km/h; 93 mph)
- Max aero-tow speed: 65 knots (120 km/h; 75 mph)
- Max winch-launching speed: not applicable
- *g* limit: +8

IPE KW 1 GB

This is a 15 metre Class version of the Quero Quero, developed for competition use by aerodynamicist Francisco Leme Galvão and constructor J. C. Boscardin, and built of wood and glassfibre. The monowheel is retractable. The GB version has a best glide ratio of 34 and a min rate of sink of 0·64 m (2·10 ft)/s at 38 knots (70 km/h; 43 mph). Two prototypes have been built. By 1 March 1986 the first of these (PP-ZUM) had amassed more than 60 hours' flying; the second (PP-ZUN), incorporating 50 litres (11 Imp gallons) of water ballast, was then about to make its first flight.

IPE 02b NHAPECAN II

Brazilian Air Force designation: TZ-14

The IPE 02 Nhapecan I first prototype (PP-ZQL) flew for the first time on 24 May 1979, and was described and illustrated in the 1983-84 *Jane's*.

The second prototype, known as the IPE 02b Nhapecan II, was considerably redesigned, with different dimensions and a more modern wing section based on the work of the Brazilian engineer Francisco Leme Galvão. As a result, performance was noticeably improved, and certification has been followed by the delivery of 15 to the Brazilian Air Force Academy. Final certification was due in July 1986, and US certification is under way.

TYPE: Tandem two-seat training sailplane.

AIRFRAME: Shoulder-wing monoplane with Galvão BR-JKNA 3511/04 wing section. Ailerons and upper/lower surface spoilers. Wooden wings and tail surfaces; steel tube (4130) fuselage with glassfibre skin. Non-retractable monowheel, in streamline fairing, and tailwheel.

DIMENSIONS, EXTERNAL:
- Wing span: 16·60 m (54 ft 5½ in)
- Wing aspect ratio: 16·02
- Length overall: 8·54 m (28 ft 0¼ in)
- Height over tail: 1·90 m (6 ft 2¾ in)

AREA:
- Wings, gross: 17·20 m² (185·1 sq ft)

WEIGHTS AND LOADING:
- Weight empty: 340 kg (749 lb)
- Max T-O weight: 560 kg (1,234 lb)
- Max wing loading: 32·56 kg/m² (6·67 lb/sq ft)

PERFORMANCE (at max T-O weight):
- Best glide ratio at 48 knots (88 km/h; 55 mph): better than 32
- Min rate of sink at 38 knots (70 km/h; 43 mph):
  - single-seat: 0·65 m (2·13 ft)/s
  - two-seat: 0·75 m (2·46 ft)/s
- Stalling speed: 37 knots (68 km/h; 43 mph)
- Max speed (smooth air): 108 knots (200 km/h; 124 mph)

IPE 03

Construction of a prototype of this side by side two-seat motor glider was still awaiting funding in early 1986. The airframe is intended to be made of wood and plywood, with a glassfibre skin; the wings are designed to be folded back alongside the fuselage for transportation and storage.

General appearance of the IPE 03 can be seen from the accompanying three-view drawing. Leading particulars are as follows:

DIMENSIONS, EXTERNAL:
- Wing span: 16·00 m (52 ft 6 in)
- Wing aspect ratio: 16·00
- Length overall: 7·20 m (23 ft 7½ in)
- Height overall: 2·20 m (7 ft 2¾ in)

AREA:
- Wings, gross: 16·00 m² (172·2 sq ft)

WEIGHTS:
- Weight empty: 350 kg (772 lb)
- Max T-O weight: 600 kg (1,322 lb)

PERFORMANCE (estimated):
- Max level speed: 135 knots (250 km/h; 155 mph)
- Stalling speed: 33 knots (60 km/h; 38 mph)
- Best glide ratio: 30

RIO CLARO

AÉRO CLUBE DE RIO CLARO

Rua Cinco 1152, 13.500 Rio Claro, São Paulo State

The Rio Claro aero club began building, under the direction of Eng Sylvio de Oliveira, two prototypes of an all-wood sporting glider known as the **Araponga**. General appearance can be seen in the accompanying three-view drawing; no recent news of progress has been received.

DIMENSIONS, EXTERNAL:
- Wing span: 12·30 m (40 ft 4¼ in)
- Length overall: 6·80 m (22 ft 3¾ in)

WEIGHTS:
- Weight empty: 150 kg (331 lb)
- Max T-O weight: 240 kg (529 lb)

CHINA

(PEOPLE'S REPUBLIC)

STATE AIRCRAFT FACTORIES

WORKS: see Aircraft section

Sailplane development in China began in 1958, when a number of Polish gliding instructors were invited into the country to train air force cadets. Since that time the Chinese industry has manufactured more than 1,000 gliders of various types. The X prefix in designations stands for Xiangji, the Chinese word for glider.

CHENGDU X-7 JIAN FAN (SWORD POINT)

Built at the Chengdu sailplane factory in Sichuan Province, the X-7 was flown for the first time in October 1966. A total of 130 had been built by the beginning of 1980; present production status is not known.

TYPE: Tandem two-seat basic training glider.

AIRFRAME: High-wing monoplane, braced by single I strut on each side. Wing section Göttingen 535 (modified). Dihedral from roots. Single-spar constant chord wings, comprising a glassfibre/honeycomb/epoxy sandwich torsion box, fabric covered aft of spar. Glassfibre ailerons and upper surface airbrakes. Semi-monocoque glassfibre pod and boom fuselage, moulded in two halves and joined at centreline. Fabric covered glassfibre cruciform tail unit; fin built integrally with fuselage. Non-retractable monowheel, nose-skid and tailskid. Tandem open cockpits, with windscreen.

DIMENSIONS, EXTERNAL:
- Wing span: 13·07 m (42 ft 10½ in)
- Wing aspect ratio: 9·49
- Length overall: 7·06 m (23 ft 2 in)
- Height over tail: 1·60 m (5 ft 3 in)

AREA:
- Wings, gross: 18·00 m² (193·75 sq ft)

WEIGHTS AND LOADING:
- Weight empty: 220 kg (485 lb)
- Max T-O weight: 370 kg (816 lb)
- Max wing loading: 20·55 kg/m² (4·21 lb/sq ft)

Brditschka HB-23/2400 Hobbyliner side by side two-seat motor glider

Brditschka HB-23/2400 Scanliner, showing enlarged bubble canopy

Prototype IPE KW 1 GB (15 metre Class)

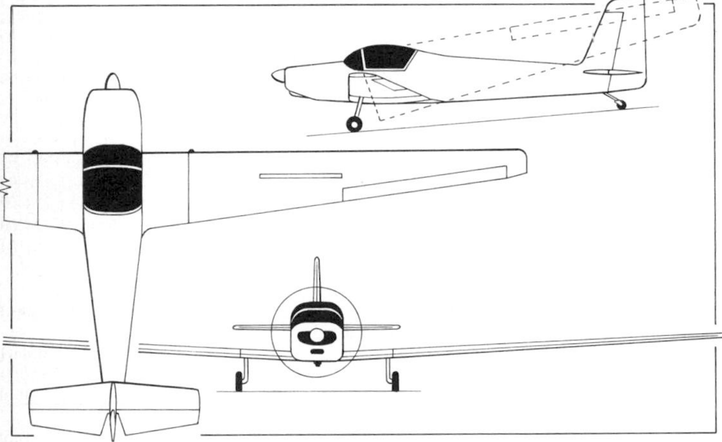
IPE 03 two-seat motor glider *(Michael A. Badrocke)*

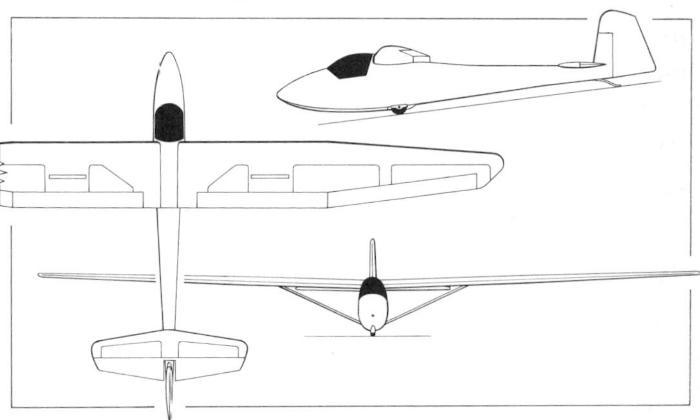
Rio Claro Araponga all-wood sporting glider *(Michael A. Badrocke)*

IPE 02b Nhapecan II two-seat training sailplanes for the Brazilian Air Force Academy

Shenyang X-10 Qian Jin single-seat sailplane

Shenyang X-9 two-seat training glider, with enclosed cockpits *(Charles M. Gyenes)*

Chengdu X-7 Jian Fan two-seat glassfibre training glider *(Charles M. Gyenes)*

PERFORMANCE (at max T-O weight):
- Best glide ratio at 30 knots (55 km/h; 34 mph) 12
- Min rate of sink at 29 knots (53 km/h; 33 mph) 1·40 m (4·59 ft)/s
- Stalling speed 25 knots (45 km/h; 28 mph)
- Max speed (smooth air) 81 knots (150 km/h; 93 mph)
- Max speed (rough air) 54 knots (100 km/h; 62 mph)
- Max winch-launching speed 43 knots (80 km/h; 50 mph)
- *g* limits +4/−2

SHENYANG X-9

Used extensively in the Chinese People's Republic, the X-9 is a tandem two-seat training glider, said to have flying characteristics similar to those of the Schweizer SGS 2-33 (see US section). It is a braced high-wing monoplane, of wood and aluminium construction. Design and first flight took place in 1977, and approx 150 had been built by the Autumn of 1980. The X-9 is reported to still be in production.

DIMENSIONS, EXTERNAL:
- Wing span 14·42 m (47 ft 3¾ in)
- Wing aspect ratio 11·00
- Length overall 7·335 m (24 ft 0¾ in)
- Height over tail 2·32 m (7 ft 7¼ in)

AREA:
- Wings, gross 18·90 m² (203·4 sq ft)

WEIGHTS AND LOADING:
- Weight empty 230 kg (507 lb)
- Max T-O weight 380 kg (837 lb)
- Max wing loading 20·10 kg/m² (4·12 lb/sq ft)

PERFORMANCE (at max T-O weight):
- Best glide ratio at 32 knots (60 km/h; 37 mph) 17
- Min rate of sink at 30 knots (55 km/h; 34 mph) 0·96 m (3·15 ft)/s
- Stalling speed 24 knots (43 km/h; 27 mph)
- Max speed (smooth air) 81 knots (150 km/h; 93 mph)
- Max speed (rough air) 54 knots (100 km/h; 62 mph)
- Max aero-tow speed 65 knots (120 km/h; 75 mph)
- Max winch-launching speed 54 knots (100 km/h; 62 mph)

SHENYANG X-10 QIAN JIN (FORWARD)

This single-seat high performance sailplane is a licence built version of the Polish SZD-8/14 Jaskolka, modernised to utilise both wood and glassfibre construction. It has been built in large numbers, and is probably the most widely used single-seater in China. Production was reportedly continuing in 1985.

DIMENSIONS, EXTERNAL:
- Wing span 16·00 m (52 ft 6 in)
- Wing aspect ratio 18·29
- Length overall 7·625 m (25 ft 0¼ in)
- Height over tail 1·605 m (5 ft 3¼ in)

AREA:
- Wings, gross 14·00 m² (150·7 sq ft)

WEIGHTS AND LOADING:
- Weight empty 264 kg (582 lb)
- Max T-O weight 354 kg (780 lb)
- Max wing loading 25·3 kg/m² (5·18 lb/sq ft)

PERFORMANCE (at max T-O weight):
- Best glide ratio at 38 knots (70 km/h; 43 mph) 26
- Min rate of sink at 37 knots (68 km/h; 42 mph) 0·75 m (2·46 ft)/s
- Stalling speed 33 knots (60 km/h; 38 mph)
- Max speed (smooth air) 135 knots (250 km/h; 155 mph)
- Max speed (rough air) 97 knots (180 km/h; 112 mph)
- Max aero-tow speed 81 knots (150 km/h; 93 mph)
- Max winch-launching speed 59 knots (110 km/h; 68 mph)

CZECHOSLOVAKIA

AEROTECHNIK

AEROTECHNIK

Letiste Kunovice, 68604 Uh. Hradiste
Telephone: Uh. Hradiste 5510 and 5511
Telex: 60380

In addition to the overhaul and re-engining of Zlin 226s and 326s, Aerotechnik is now producing for Czech aeroclubs the L-13SW Vivat, a motor glider version of the Let L-13 Blanik.

AEROTECHNIK L-13SW VIVAT

Design of the L-13SW began in the Summer of 1976, and construction of three prototypes started in the Autumn of the following year. The first of these (OK-068) made its initial flight on 10 May 1978. Aerotechnik is now manufacturing 200 of these aircraft for use by Czech aeroclubs, the first production example being flown for the first time in November 1983. About 30 had been completed by early 1986, in which year Aerotechnik expected to reach full annual output of 20 aircraft.

The Vivat, which features side by side seating instead of the tandem layout of the Blanik sailplane on which it is based, has been optimised for both elementary and advanced training. Authorised manoeuvres include sharp turns and stalls up to 60°, slips, skids, and unlimited spinning.

The following description applies to the initial production version:

TYPE: Side by side two-seat motor glider.

AIRFRAME: Cantilever mid-wing monoplane. NACA wing sections: 63_2A615 at root, 63_2A612 at tip. Dihedral 3°. Incidence 4° at root, 1° at tip. Sweepforward 5° at quarter-chord. All-metal single-spar wings, with light alloy riveted skin and wingtip 'salmons'. Fabric covered light alloy ailerons and slotted area-increasing flaps. DFS type light alloy airbrakes in upper and lower surfaces. Oval section fuselage, forward portion being a welded metal tube structure with glassfibre skin, rear portion a riveted light alloy semi-monocoque. Light alloy fin and fixed incidence tailplane; fabric covered rudder and elevators. Trim tab in each elevator. Horizontal tail surfaces fold upward for transportation. Mechanically semi-retractable rubber sprung monowheel, with size 350 × 135-125 mm tyre (pressure 3·2 bars; 46·4 lb/sq in); non-retractable rubber sprung controllable tailwheel, with size 200 × 50-90 mm tyre (pressure 1·2 bars; 17·4 lb/sq in); and retractable outrigger wheels in wingtip 'salmons'. Moravan NP mechanical brake on monowheel. One-piece Plexiglas bubble canopy, raised upwards and rearwards on struts to permit access to cockpit. Tesla LS 5 VHF com radio and standard VFR instrumentation.

POWER PLANT: One 48·5 kW (65 hp) Aerotechnik (formerly Walter) Mikron III S (A) in-line engine, driving an Aeron Brno V 208 fixed-pitch or Hoffmann HO-V-62R two-blade wooden propeller with spinner. Welded light alloy fuel tank in centre-fuselage, max capacity 50 litres (11 Imp gallons).

DIMENSIONS, EXTERNAL:
- Wing span: 16·705 m (54 ft 9¾ in)
- Wing aspect ratio: 13·81
- Length overall: 8·30 m (27 ft 2¾ in)
- Height overall: 2·30 m (7 ft 6½ in)

AREA:
- Wings, gross: 20·20 m² (217·4 sq ft)

WEIGHTS AND LOADINGS:
- Weight empty, equipped: 463 kg (1,021 lb)
- Max T-O weight: 670 kg (1,477 lb)
- Max wing loading: 33·17 kg/m² (6·79 lb/sq ft)
- Max power loading: 13·8 kg/kW (22·72 lb/hp)

PERFORMANCE, UNPOWERED (at max T-O weight with propeller feathered. A: V 208, B: HO-V-62R):
- Best glide ratio:
  - A at 48 knots (90 km/h; 56 mph): 21
  - B at 53 knots (98 km/h; 61 mph): 24
- Min rate of sink:
  - A at 43 knots (80 km/h; 50 mph): 1·20 m (3·94 ft)/s
  - B at 46 knots (85 km/h; 53 mph): 1·05 m (3·44 ft)/s
- Stalling speed: A, B: 34 knots (62 km/h; 39 mph)
- Max speed (smooth air):
  - A, B: 124 knots (230 km/h; 143 mph)
- Max speed (rough air):
  - A, B: 86 knots (160 km/h; 99 mph)
- *g* limits: A, B: +5·3/−2·6

PERFORMANCE, POWERED (at max T-O weight; A and B as above):
- Max cruising speed:
  - A: 94 knots (175 km/h; 109 mph)
  - B: 100 knots (185 km/h; 115 mph)
- Econ cruising speed: A: 84 knots (155 km/h; 96 mph)
  - B: 86 knots (160 km/h; 99 mph)
- Stalling speed: A, B: 33 knots (60 km/h; 37 mph)
- Max rate of climb at S/L: A: 140 m (460 ft)/min
  - B: 198 m (650 ft)/min
- Service ceiling: A, B: 4,000 m (13,125 ft)
- T-O run: A: 200 m (655 ft)
  - B: 110 m (361 ft)
- T-O to 15 m (50 ft): A: 430 m (1,410 ft)
  - B: 370 m (1,214 ft)
- Landing from 15 m (50 ft): A, B: 370 m (1,214 ft)
- Landing run: A, B: 110 m (361 ft)
- Range (depending on weight of crew):
  - A, B, 30 litres (6·6 Imp gallons) fuel: 205 nm (380 km; 236 miles)
  - A, B, 50 litres (11 Imp gallons) fuel: 345 nm (640 km; 398 miles)

VSO

VYVOJOVÁ SKUPINA ORLICAN

c/o Orlican Národní Podnik, 56537 Chocen
Telephone: Chocen 951411
Telex: 0 196 210
CHIEF DESIGNER: Dipl Ing Jan Janovec

This group was formed by members of the former VSB (1973-74 *Jane's*) and some of the design staff of the Orlican National Works. Its first product is the VSO 10.

VSO 10 GRADIENT

Design of the VSO 10 began in March 1972. Construction of three prototypes (one for structural test and two for flight test) began in 1975, and the first flight took place on 26 October 1976. Series production began in December 1978. By the beginning of 1986 a total of 133 had been delivered to Czechoslovak aeroclubs, including 12 of the VSO 10C Club Class version with non-retractable monowheel.

TYPE: Single-seat Standard and Club Class sailplane.

AIRFRAME: Cantilever shoulder-wing monoplane, with Wortmann wing sections: FX-61-163 at root, FX-60-126 at tip. Dihedral 3°. All-wood single-spar forward-swept wings with glassfibre sandwich skin. All-metal DFS airbrakes on upper surfaces. All-wood slotted ailerons. Glassfibre monocoque front and centre fuselage sections, latter reinforced by steel tube frame. Monocoque rear fuselage of aluminium alloy sheet. Metal T tail with fabric covered elevators and rudder. Fixed incidence tailplane. Retractable rubber sprung monowheel (tyre pressure approx 2·45 bars; 35·5 lb/sq in), with drum brake. Semi-recessed unsprung tailwheel. Detachable cockpit canopy. Provision for 56 litres (12·3 Imp gallons) water ballast.

DIMENSIONS, EXTERNAL:
- Wing span: 15·00 m (49 ft 2½ in)
- Wing aspect ratio: 18·75
- Length overall: 7·00 m (22 ft 11¾ in)
- Height over tail: 1·38 m (4 ft 6¼ in)

AREA:
- Wings, gross: 12·00 m² (129·2 sq ft)

WEIGHTS AND LOADING (both versions):
- Weight empty: 250 kg (551 lb)
- Max T-O weight: 380 kg (837 lb)
- Max wing loading: 31·67 kg/m² (6·49 lb/sq ft)

PERFORMANCE (at max T-O weight):
- Best glide ratio:
  - 10 at 49 knots (90 km/h; 56 mph): 36
  - 10C at 51 knots (95 km/h; 59 mph): 34
- Min rate of sink:
  - 10 at 39 knots (73 km/h; 45 mph): 0·64 m (2·10 ft)/s
  - 10C at 43 knots (79 km/h; 49 mph): 0·72 m (2·36 ft)/s
- Stalling speed: 10: 37 knots (68 km/h; 43 mph)
  - 10C: 38 knots (70 km/h; 44 mph)
- Max speed (smooth air):
  - 10, 10C: 135 knots (250 km/h; 155 mph)
- Max speed (rough air), and max aero-tow speed:
  - 10, 10C: 86 knots (160 km/h; 99 mph)
- Max winch-launching speed:
  - 10, 10C: 65 knots (120 km/h; 75 mph)
- *g* limits: 10, 10C: +5·3/−3·5

FRANCE

AÉROSTRUCTURE

AÉROSTRUCTURE SARL

Zone Industrielle La Lande, rue de Ricodonne, 33450 Saint-Loubès
Telephone: (16 56) 38 91 74
Telex: 550 777 F
PRESIDENT/DIRECTOR GENERAL: Robert Jacquet
COMMERCIAL DIRECTOR: Alain Roux

This company (see also Sport Aircraft section) has built and flown the prototype of a single-seat motor glider known as the Lutin 80. Production had not been launched by early 1986.

In August 1983 Aérostructure SARL purchased from Fournier Aviation (see 1983-84 *Jane's*) production rights to the latter company's RF-10, designed by M René Fournier. Manufacture of the RF-10 is undertaken jointly by Aérostructure (70 per cent) and Marmande Aéronautique (30 per cent).

AÉROSTRUCTURE LUTIN 80

The Lutin 80, known originally as the PLM 80 (Planeur Léger Motorisé), is a single-seat motor glider with a configuration which recalls that of the Polish SZD-45 Ogar of the 1970s. The prototype (F-WAQM) flew for the first time on 3 May 1983. Development was continuing in 1985.

TYPE: Single-seat motor glider.

AIRFRAME: Cantilever mid-wing monoplane, of laminated glassfibre/epoxy resin construction, conforming to category MU of JAR 22. Wortmann FX-66S-196-V1 section wings, with 2° dihedral from roots. 4° sweep-forward at 40 per cent chord. Incidence 1° 30′. Ailerons and upper surface airbrakes. Pod and boom fuselage. Cantilever T tailplane, with elevator. Wings and horizontal tail detachable for transportation and storage. Mechanically retractable JPX monowheel, size 300 × 100, with hydraulic disc brake; semi-recessed 200 mm diameter tailwheel; small strut mounted nylon balancer wheel under each wing at approx one-third span. One-piece moulded cockpit canopy, opening sideways to starboard.

POWER PLANT: One 28·5 kW (38 hp) JPX PAL 640 three-cylinder two-stroke engine, mounted aft of cockpit and driving a three-blade pusher propeller with foldable glassfibre blades. Fuel tank capacity 30 litres (6·6 Imp gallons).

DIMENSIONS, EXTERNAL:
- Wing span: 11·00 m (36 ft 1 in)
- Wing aspect ratio: 18·91
- Length overall: 5·10 m (16 ft 8¾ in)
- Height overall: 1·10 m (3 ft 7¼ in)
- Propeller diameter: 0·94 m (3 ft 1 in)

AREA:
- Wings, gross: 6·40 m² (68·9 sq ft)

WEIGHTS AND LOADINGS:
- Weight empty: 155 kg (342 lb)
- Max T-O weight: 275 kg (606 lb)
- Max wing loading: 42·9 kg/m² (8·79 lb/sq ft)
- Max power loading: 9·71 kg/kW (15·95 lb/hp)

PERFORMANCE, UNPOWERED (estimated):
- Best glide ratio at 51 knots (95 km/h; 59 mph): 32
- Min rate of sink: 0·70 m (2·30 ft)/s
- Stalling speed: 41 knots (75 km/h; 47 mph)
- Max speed (smooth air): 118 knots (220 km/h; 137 mph)
- *g* limits: +5·9/−2·65

PERFORMANCE, POWERED (estimated):
- Never-exceed speed: 140 knots (260 km/h; 161 mph)
- Max level speed: 118 knots (220 km/h; 137 mph)
- Max cruising speed: 108 knots (200 km/h; 124 mph)
- Econ cruising speed: 92 knots (170 km/h; 105 mph)
- Stalling speed: 41 knots (75 km/h; 47 mph)
- Max rate of climb at S/L: 360 m (1,181 ft)/min
- Service ceiling: approx 5,000 m (16,400 ft)
- Range with max fuel: 324 nm (600 km; 373 miles)
- Endurance with max fuel: 4 h

AÉROSTRUCTURE (FOURNIER) RF-10

First flown on 6 March 1981, the RF-10 is generally similar to the Fournier RF-9 (1981-82 *Jane's*) but is of plastics construction and has a carbonfibre main spar. A more powerful engine is fitted, fuel capacity is increased, all control surfaces are balanced, and the main landing gear has larger wheels. Two prototypes were built by Fournier Aviation in 1981, with low-set tailplanes, but a T tail was adopted for the production version, the first of which flew on 10 May 1984.

Aerotechnik L-13SW Vivat, a powered version of the Blanik sailplane

VSO 10 Gradient single-seat high performance sailplane *(Adolf Wilsch)*

Prototype Aérostructure Lutin 80 small single-seat motor glider *(Brian M. Service)*

Aérostructure (Fournier) RF-10 motor glider in production form, with T tail *(J. M. G. Gradidge)*

By the time French certification was granted on 23 October 1984 a total of 11 RF-10s had been completed, and by early 1985 orders from French production totalled 30, of which 13 had been delivered to customers in France, Portugal and the UK. An initial French production run of 40 has been launched, and RF-10s were being completed at a rate of four per month in early 1985, the latest date for which information has been received.

Aeromot de Porto Alegre has a licence to assemble the RF-10 in Brazil, and received one aircraft as a pattern for an eventual total of 100; the Brazilian company will also undertake some partial manufacture.

TYPE: Side by side two-seat training and sporting motor glider.

AIRFRAME: Cantilever low-wing monoplane, of glassfibre construction with a carbonfibre main spar. NACA 64^3-618 section unswept wings, with 3° 30′ dihedral from roots. Ailerons of GRP; light alloy Schempp-Hirth upper surface airbrakes. Wings can be detached from fuselage for transportation; outer portion of each wing can be folded inward for stowage, without disconnecting aileron controls. Semi-monocoque glassfibre fuselage, slightly swept fin and rudder, small dorsal fin, and fixed incidence T tailplane with elevator. Entire tail unit of GRP. Mechanically retractable mainwheels (tyre size 330 × 130), with hydraulic suspension and JPX hydraulic disc brakes; steerable tailwheel with size 210 × 65 tyre. One-piece cockpit canopy opens upward and rearward. Dual controls standard.

POWER PLANT: One 59·5 kW (80 hp) Limbach L 2000 LO I flat-four engine, driving a Hoffmann two-blade three-position variable-pitch propeller. Fuel in two main tanks in wings, combined capacity 90 litres (19·75 Imp gallons). Electric starter and 12V 30A alternator.

DIMENSIONS, EXTERNAL:
- Wing span: 17·47 m (57 ft 3¾ in)
- Wing aspect ratio: 16·32
- Width, wings folded: 9·60 m (31 ft 6 in)
- Length overall: 7·89 m (25 ft 10¾ in)
- Height over tail: 1·93 m (6 ft 4 in)

AREA:
- Wings, gross: 18·70 m^2 (201·3 sq ft)

WEIGHTS AND LOADINGS:
- Weight empty: 560 kg (1,234 lb)
- Max T-O weight: 770 kg (1,697 lb)
- Max wing loading: 41·2 kg/m^2 (8·44 lb/sq ft)
- Max power loading: 12·9 kg/kW (21·22 lb/hp)

PERFORMANCE, UNPOWERED (at max T-O weight):
- Best glide ratio at 54 knots (100 km/h; 62 mph): 30
- Min rate of sink at 49 knots (90 km/h; 56 mph): 0·80 m (2·62 ft)/s
- Stalling speed: 39 knots (72 km/h; 45 mph)
- Max speed (smooth air): 119 knots (220 km/h; 136 mph)
- Max speed (rough air): 97 knots (180 km/h; 112 mph)
- g limits: +5·3/−2·65

PERFORMANCE, POWERED (at max T-O weight):
- Max cruising speed: 102 knots (190 km/h; 118 mph)
- Econ cruising speed: 97 knots (180 km/h; 112 mph)
- Stalling speed: 39 knots (72 km/h; 45 mph)
- Max rate of climb at S/L: 210 m (690 ft)/min
- Service ceiling: 5,000 m (16,400 ft)
- Range with max fuel: 540 nm (1,000 km; 621 miles)

CENTRAIR

SA CENTRAIR

Aérodrome Le Blanc, BP 44, 36300 Le Blanc
Telephone: (54) 37 06 91 and 37 07 96
Telex: 750272 F
PRESIDENT/DIRECTOR GENERAL: Marc Ranjon

Centrair was founded in January 1970 by M Marc Ranjon, an ex-Aéronavale pilot and a flying and gliding instructor. It had an early 1986 workforce of 89 people, with another 21 at its Chauvigny subsidiary, Composites Aéronautiques Avancés (CA2). These two companies specialise in constructions using carbonfibre, glassfibre and Kevlar. Centrair has a covered factory space of 7,000 m^2 (75,347 sq ft), of which 2,000 m^2 (21,528 sq ft) is fully air-conditioned, equipped with a laser cutting table and autoclave. CA2 has 500 m^2 (5,382 sq ft) spread over nine locations. The two companies have their own research and development department, and are major subcontractors for Aérospatiale, Dassault-Breguet, Matra and other French aerospace companies (see main Aircraft section). Centrair also produces four versions of the Schleicher ASW 20 (see German part of this section), as listed in the 1982-83 *Jane's*, and had delivered 140 of these by early 1986.

CENTRAIR 101 and PÉGASE

Of all-French design, the Centrair 101 was available in 1986 in the following versions:

101 Club. Basic version, with non-retractable monowheel, no water ballast and no instrumentation. First flown November 1981, certificated June 1982. Total of 26 delivered by early 1986.

Pégase A. As 101, but with retractable monowheel. Prototype (F-WFRA), first flown on 20 November 1981, was of this version. Certificated June 1982; winglet version first flown May 1982. Total of 240 built by early 1986.

Pégase B. Identical to Pégase A except standard water ballast capacity of 160 litres (35·2 Imp gallons). First flown May 1984. Total of 62 ordered by January 1986, of which eight had been delivered.

Pégase BC. Standard Class version, with new COAP 3 inboard wing profile and small winglets standard. First flown 2 January 1984, winning French and European Championships later that year. Ten built; superseded by Pégase D. Details in 1985-86 *Jane's*.

Pégase C and CC. Versions for Standard Class competition use, with carbonfibre main spar. Prototype only of each (one with winglets, one without); first flight 18 December 1982. Details in 1985-86 *Jane's*.

Pégase D. Definitive competition version, embodying experience gained with Pégase BC. Total of 65 ordered by January 1986; due for certification in March 1986.

TYPE: Single-seat Standard or Club Class sailplane.

AIRFRAME: Cantilever shoulder-wing monoplane, constructed of Conticell sandwich (Klégécel in BC) and epoxy resin, with glassfibre roving spar. Onera wing sections: COAP 1 at root (COAP 3 in BC), COAP 2 at tip. Dihedral 2° 18′. Double plate upper surface airbrakes. Turned-down wingtips. Glassfibre/epoxy resin monocoque fuselage (reinforced with carbonfibre on all except 101). Cantilever T tailplane, with elevator. All control surfaces mass balanced. Retractable (all Pégase variants) or non-retractable (101 Club) unsprung monowheel (size 5·00-5, pressure 3·5 bars; 50·75 lb/sq in), with drum brake (hydraulic disc brake on Pégase B/BC from September 1985); rubber tail bumper, with metal skid or recessed wheel. Nosewheel on 101 Club. Nose or CG towing hook. One-piece cockpit canopy, hinged at front and opening upward. Pégase B and D have two 80 litre (17·6 Imp gallon) leading-edge water ballast tanks as standard.

DIMENSIONS, EXTERNAL (all versions):
- Wing span: 15·00 m (49 ft 2½ in)
- Wing aspect ratio: 21·43

Length overall 6·82 m (22 ft 4½ in)
Height over tail 1·42 m (4 ft 8 in)
AREA:
Wings, gross (all versions) 10·50 m² (113·0 sq ft)
WEIGHTS AND LOADINGS:
Weight empty, equipped:
101, Pégase A, D 251 kg (553 lb)
Pégase B 258 kg (569 lb)
Max T-O weight: 101 380 kg (838 lb)
Pégase A 455 kg (1,003 lb)
Pégase B, D 505 kg (1,113 lb)
Max wing loading: 101 36·2 kg/m² (7·42 lb/sq ft)
Pégase A 43·3 kg/m² (8·87 lb/sq ft)
Pégase B, D 48·1 kg/m² (9·86 lb/sq ft)
PERFORMANCE (at max T-O weight):
Best glide ratio:
101 at 50 knots (92 km/h; 57 mph) 38
Pégase A at 53 knots (98 km/h; 61 mph) 40
Pégase B at 55 knots (102 km/h; 63 mph) 40
Pégase D at 57 knots (105 km/h; 65 mph) 43
Min rate of sink:
101 at 39 knots (72 km/h; 45 mph) 0·65 m (2·13 ft)/s
Pégase A at 43 knots (80 km/h; 50 mph) 0·67 m (2·20 ft)/s
Pégase B at 45 knots (83 km/h; 51 mph) 0·65 m (2·13 ft)/s
Pégase D at 45 knots (83 km/h; 51 mph) 0·63 m (2·07 ft)/s
Max speed (smooth air):
all versions 135 knots (250 km/h; 155 mph)
Max speed (rough air):
all versions 97 knots (180 km/h; 112 mph)
Max aero-tow and max winch-launching speed:
all versions 86 knots (160 km/h; 99 mph)

CENTRAIR 2001 MARIANNE

The Marianne is a tandem two-seat sailplane for training and aerobatics. All structural calculations were made by Dassault-Breguet, and the programme receives financial assistance from the French government. The Marianne was the winner of an FFVV competition, and 250 are expected to be acquired for use by French aero clubs.

First flight by prototype F-WGMA was made on 19 September 1985. Provisional certification was expected in March 1986; full certification was anticipated by the end of 1986, by which time Centrair expected to have delivered 60 production examples.

AIRFRAME: Cantilever shoulder-wing monoplane. Onera laminar flow aerofoil sections: COAP 1 at root, COAP 2 at tip. Laminated wings, of Klégécel/glassfibre/epoxy resin construction with glassfibre roving spar. Dihedral 3°. Ailerons of similar construction. No flaps. Double plate aluminium upper surface airbrakes. Laminated fuselage of Klégécel, glassfibre, carbonfibre and epoxy. Cantilever T tailplane, with elevator; construction of glassfibre and epoxy. Non-retractable 5·00-5 monowheel, tyre pressure 3·5 bars (50·75 lb/sq in), with hydraulic disc brake; non-retractable 3·00-3 nosewheel. Two seats in tandem under separate canopies: front canopy opens forward, rear canopy sideways to starboard. No water ballast. Aero-tow and winch-launching hooks.

DIMENSIONS, EXTERNAL:
Wing span 18·50 m (60 ft 8½ in)
Wing aspect ratio 19·90
Length overall 9·00 m (29 ft 6½ in)
Height over tail 1·55 m (5 ft 1 in)
AREA:
Wings, gross 17·20 m² (185·1 sq ft)
WEIGHTS AND LOADING:
Weight empty 435 kg (959 lb)
Max T-O weight 655 kg (1,444 lb)
Max wing loading 38·08 kg/m² (7·80 lb/sq ft)
PERFORMANCE (at max T-O weight):
Best glide ratio at 51 knots (95 km/h; 59 mph) 40
Min rate of sink at 46 knots (85 km/h; 53 mph) 0·65 m (2·13 ft)/s
Stalling speed 37 knots (67 km/h; 42 mph)
Max speed (smooth air) 135 knots (250 km/h; 155 mph)
Max speed (rough air), and max aero-tow speed 92 knots (170 km/h; 105 mph)
Max winch-launching speed 70 knots (130 km/h; 81 mph)
g limits +4·3/−1·5 ultimate

CENTRAIR 2001M MARIANNE M

By January 1986 Centrair had received 23 orders for this powered version of the Marianne, and hoped to fly a prototype in December 1986. Airframe is identical to the sailplane but has underwing balancer wheels for take-off and landing.

POWER PLANT: One 45 kW (60 hp) Volkswagen engine (JPX modification), driving a two-blade fixed-pitch propeller and mounted in a detachable pod which also accommodates a 15 litre (3·3 Imp gallon) fuel tank.

WEIGHTS AND LOADINGS:
Weight empty, equipped 500 kg (1,102 lb)
Max T-O weight 725 kg (1,598 lb)
Max wing loading 42·15 kg/m² (8·64 lb/sq ft)
Max power loading 16·21 kg/kW (26·64 lb/hp)
PERFORMANCE, POWERED (estimated at max T-O weight):
Max cruising speed 108 knots (200 km/h; 124 mph)
Econ cruising speed 84 knots (155 km/h; 96 mph)
Stalling speed 49 knots (90 km/h; 56 mph)
Best glide ratio at 54 knots (100 km/h; 62 mph) 31
Min rate of sink at 52 knots (96 km/h; 60 mph) 1·00 m (3·28 ft)/s

FOURNIER

AVIONS FOURNIER

DIRECTOR: René Fournier

It was reported in early 1986 that M René Fournier had re-established a company to put his RF-5 motor glider back into series production in the Spring. The two-seat RF-5, last described fully under the Sportavia heading in the 1978-79 *Jane's*, will be powered by a 59 kW (80 hp) Limbach L 2000 engine.

ISSOIRE

ISSOIRE-AVIATION SA (Groupe Siren)

Aérodrome d'Issoire-le-Broc (Puy-de-Dôme), BP No. 7, 63501 Issoire Cédex
Telephone: (73) 89 01 54
Telex: 990 185 F ISSAVIA
PRESIDENT-DIRECTOR GENERAL: Xavier Laguette
TECHNICAL DIRECTOR: Xavier Lauras

This company is one of four forming the Siren group, the others being Siren SA (which see), Aéro Berry and Pelletier Exploitation.

Issoire is responsible for the PIK-20E2F and PIK-30 self-launching sailplanes.

ISSOIRE PIK-20E2F

Details of the PIK-20 sailplane can be found under the Eiri heading in the Finnish sections of the 1979-80 and previous editions of *Jane's*.

The prototype of the PIK-20E powered version flew for the first time on 2 October 1976 and was described in the 1977-78 *Jane's*. The production prototype made its first powered flight on 18 March 1978, and series production began in late 1978. Approx 50 were delivered by Eiri before production in Finland ended in 1980. A description can be found in the 1980-81 *Jane's*.

The French built version has a Rotax 505 (instead of 501) engine and is designated PIK-20E2F. By January 1985 a total of 126 PIK-20s had been delivered, including Eiri production.

As part of a programme to collect airflow data on flight at low Reynolds numbers, NASA's Dryden Research Center is using a PIK-20 as a testbed to develop wing profiles appropriate to high-altitude low-speed flight. Such flight characteristics are of interest to researchers investigating possible designs for high-altitude unmanned aircraft which could serve as long term communications relays, using solar power and beamed microwave energy for electric propulsion.

For initial testing, a hot-wire anemometer and tape recorder are attached to the PIK-20's wing. The recorded sound registers distinct differences as the airflow changes from laminar (a smooth, soft sound) to transitional (a hissing noise) to turbulent (a roar). The pilot, using a cockpit microphone, gives a simultaneous voice record of his flight profile, and the airflow changes are demonstrated visually by coating the wing with dark oil, which forms distinctive patterns as the flow changes. Later testing is expected to include installing experimental aerofoil glove sections on the aircraft's wings.

The following description applies to the standard production PIK-20E2F:

TYPE: Single-seat self-launching 15 metre Class sailplane.

AIRFRAME: Cantilever shoulder-wing monoplane with T tail. Wortmann wing sections: FX-67-K-170 at root, FX-67-K-150 at tip. Dihedral 3°. Sweepback 1° 21·6′. Glassfibre/epoxy/PVC foam sandwich wings. Spars of carbonfibre reinforced epoxy. Schempp-Hirth airbrakes standard. Plain flaps ('flaperons') function as both flaps and ailerons. Provision for 80 litres (17·5 Imp gallons) of water ballast. Glassfibre/epoxy monocoque fuselage, reinforced with ribs and carbonfibre. Optional Tost towing hook. T tail of similar construction to wings. Fixed incidence tailplane, with one-piece elevator. Retractable sprung Tost monowheel with drum brake. Steerable rubber sprung tailwheel. Non-retractable wing-tip wheels. Forward hinged one-piece cockpit canopy.

POWER PLANT: One 32 kW (43 hp) Rotax 505 two-cylinder two-stroke engine, with reduction drive to a Hoffmann two-blade fixed-pitch wooden propeller and retracting manually into fuselage aft of cockpit when not in use. Electric starter. Kevlar fuel tank, capacity 30 litres (6·6 Imp gallons).

DIMENSIONS, EXTERNAL:
Wing span 15·00 m (49 ft 2½ in)
Wing aspect ratio 22·50
Length overall 6·53 m (21 ft 5 in)
Height over tail 1·47 m (4 ft 10 in)
AREA:
Wings, gross 10·00 m² (107·6 sq ft)
WEIGHTS AND LOADINGS:
Weight empty 310 kg (683 lb)
Max water ballast 80 kg (176 lb)
Max T-O weight 470 kg (1,036 lb)
Max wing loading 47·0 kg/m² (9·63 lb/sq ft)
Max power loading 14·62 kg/kW (24·03 lb/hp)
PERFORMANCE, UNPOWERED (at max T-O weight, engine retracted):
Best glide ratio at 63 knots (117 km/h; 73 mph) 41
Min rate of sink at 47 knots (88 km/h; 55 mph) 0·70 m (2·30 ft)/s
Stalling speed 41 knots (75 km/h; 47 mph)
Max speed (smooth air) 154 knots (285 km/h; 177 mph)
Max speed (rough air) 119 knots (220 km/h; 136 mph)
Max aero-tow speed 105 knots (195 km/h; 121 mph)
Max winch-launching speed 67 knots (125 km/h; 78 mph)
PERFORMANCE, POWERED (at max T-O weight except where indicated):
Cruising speed (75% power) at 370 kg (816 lb) AUW 73 knots (135 km/h; 84 mph)
Stalling speed 41 knots (75 km/h; 47 mph)
Max rate of climb at S/L 162 m (531 ft)/min
Service ceiling 5,200 m (17,050 ft)
T-O to 15 m (50 ft) less than 500 m (1,640 ft)
Landing run 300 m (985 ft)
Range with max fuel 156 nm (290 km; 180 miles)

ISSOIRE PIK-30

Construction of this aircraft, which is basically a 17 metre Open Class version of the PIK-20E2F, started in 1983. The prototype first flew in April 1984 followed by a second aircraft, to production standard, in December 1984. French certification was awarded in September 1985. Twenty PIK-30s had been ordered by February 1986, including one for evaluation by the French Air Force and others for customers in France, New Zealand, UK and USA. Production is at the rate of one per month.

The PIK-30 incorporates removable, 1 metre long, glassfibre wingtips, enabling it to qualify also in the FAI 15 m class if desired.

POWER PLANT: As for PIK-20E2F, plus automatic system for vertical positioning of propeller when engine is stopped.

DIMENSIONS, EXTERNAL: As PIK-20E2F except:
Wing span 17·00 m (55 ft 9¼ in)
Wing aspect ratio 27·19
AREA:
Wings, gross 10·63 m² (114·42 sq ft)
WEIGHTS AND LOADINGS:
Weight empty 310 kg (683 lb)
Max T-O weight 460 kg (1,014 lb)
Max wing loading 43·27 kg/m² (8·86 lb/sq ft)
Max power loading 14·38 kg/kW (23·58 lb/hp)
PERFORMANCE, UNPOWERED (at max T-O weight):
Best glide ratio at 59 knots (110 km/h; 68 mph) 45
Min rate of sink at 41 knots (75 km/h; 47 mph) 0·54 m (1·77 ft)/s
Stalling speed 38 knots (70 km/h; 44 mph)
Max speed (smooth air) 151 knots (280 km/h; 174 mph)
Max speed (rough air), and max aero-tow speed 102 knots (190 km/h; 118 mph)
Max winch-launching speed 67 knots (125 km/h; 78 mph)
g limits +5·3/−2·65
PERFORMANCE, POWERED (at max T-O weight):
Max cruising speed 73 knots (135 km/h; 84 mph)
Econ cruising speed 65 knots (120 km/h; 75 mph)
Stalling speed 38 knots (70 km/h; 44 mph)
Max rate of climb at S/L 240 m (785 ft)/min
T-O run 280 m (920 ft)
Landing run 300 m (985 ft)
Range with max fuel 162 nm (300 km; 186 miles)

Centrair Pégase BC single-seat Standard Class sailplane *(Peter F. Selinger)*

Prototype Centrair Marianne two-seat training and aerobatic sailplane

Pottier Kit Club 15-34 prototype homebuilt sailplane

Issoire built PIK-30 self-launching sailplane, with power plant extended

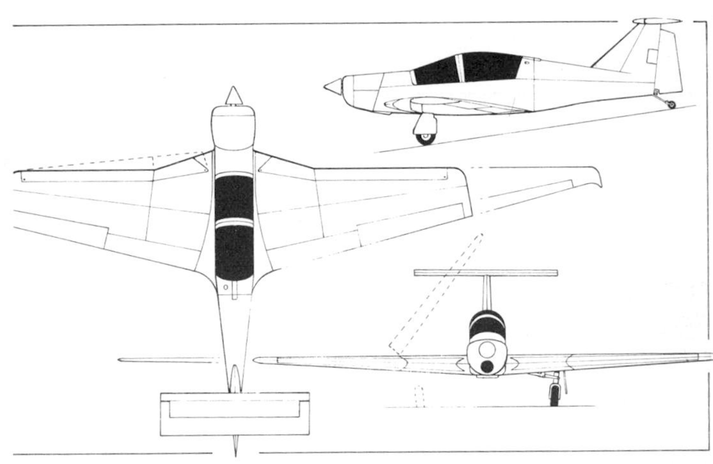
Lucas L6-7 sport aircraft, with extended-wing motor glider version shown in scrap view *(Michael A. Badrocke)*

LUCAS

EMILE LUCAS

Corbonod, 01420 Seyssel
Telephone: (1) 50 59 27 54

LUCAS L6-7

The prototype of this tandem two-seat aircraft was under construction in the Spring of 1986, with first flight now expected in Summer 1987.

The L6-7 is designed as a sporting aircraft in its basic form, capable of conversion to a motor glider by the addition of a 2 m (6 ft 6¾ in) extension panel to each outer wing. Power plant is a 62 kW (83 hp) Limbach flat-four engine, driving a two-blade variable-pitch propeller. Standard fuel capacity is 50 litres (11 Imp gallons), in a fuselage tank aft of the rear cockpit, but this can be increased in the motor glider by a further 260 litres (57·2 Imp gallons) carried in four tanks in the wings.

A description of the L6-7 airframe and accommodation can be found in the Sport Aircraft section; the following details apply to the motor glider version:

DIMENSIONS, EXTERNAL:
Wing span 13·50 m (44 ft 3½ in)
Wing aspect ratio 11·39
AREA:
Wings, gross 16·00 m² (172·2 sq ft)
WEIGHTS AND LOADINGS:
Weight empty 485 kg (1,069 lb)
Normal T-O weight (fuselage fuel only) 690 kg (1,521 lb)
Max T-O weight (fuselage and wing fuel) 905 kg (1,995 lb)
Wing loading:
at normal T-O weight 43·12 kg/m² (8·84 lb/sq ft)
at max T-O weight 56·56 kg/m² (11·59 lb/sq ft)
Power loading:
at normal T-O weight 11·16 kg/kW (18·33 lb/hp)
at max T-O weight 14·63 kg/kW (24·04 lb/hp)
PERFORMANCE (estimated, at normal T-O weight except where indicated):
Max cruising speed 195 knots (361 km/h; 224 mph)
Econ cruising speed 165 knots (306 km/h; 190 mph)
Max rate of climb at S/L 195 m (640 ft)/min
Service ceiling 5,500 m (18,045 ft)
T-O run 360 m (1,181 ft)
Landing run 200 m (656 ft)

POTTIER

AVIONS POTTIER

4 rue de Poissy, 78130 Les Mureaux
Telephone: (3) 099 13 85

POTTIER KIT CLUB 15-34

This is essentially the same sailplane as the CARMAM J.P.15-36A Aiglon (1983-84 *Jane's*), with some constructional simplification to make it suitable for amateur builders. Prototype construction began in November 1975; first flight was made on 6 November 1976.

French certification was received on 15 February 1979. First kits for homebuilders became available in mid-March 1979, and 40 had been built and flown by early 1984, the latest date for which information has been received.

TYPE: Single-seat homebuilt sailplane.

AIRFRAME: Cantilever mid-wing monoplane, with Wortmann wing sections: FX-67-K-170 at root, FX-60-126 at tip. Dihedral 3°. Single-spar spruce wings, with plywood covering and steel tipped wingtip 'salmons'. Plain ailerons, which can be operated differentially or in unison. Schempp-Hirth upper/lower surface airbrakes. Provision for 80 kg (176 lb) of water ballast. Fabric covered wooden fuselage and tail unit, except for glassfibre nosecone; sweptback fin is integral with fuselage. All-moving tailplane, rear part of which is fabric covered. Non-retractable unsprung monowheel, size 330 × 130 mm, with brake; tail bumper. Detachable cockpit canopy.

DIMENSIONS, EXTERNAL:
Wing span 15·00 m (49 ft 2½ in)
Wing aspect ratio 20·45
Length overall 6·25 m (20 ft 6 in)
Height over tail 1·40 m (4 ft 7 in)
AREA:
Wings, gross 11·00 m² (118·4 sq ft)
WEIGHTS AND LOADING:
Weight empty 225 kg (496 lb)
Max T-O weight 420 kg (926 lb)
Max wing loading 39·0 kg/m² (7·99 lb/sq ft)
PERFORMANCE (at max T-O weight):
Best glide ratio at 42 knots (77 km/h; 48 mph) 36
Min rate of sink at 39 knots (72 km/h; 45 mph) 0·63 m (2·07 ft)/s
Stalling speed 34 knots (62 km/h; 39 mph)
Max speed (rough and smooth air), and max aero-tow speed 135 knots (250 km/h; 155 mph)
Max winch-launching speed 65 knots (120 km/h; 75 mph)
g limits +8·3/−4

SIREN

SIREN SA

22-24 Allée des Jachères, Sofilic 431, 94263 Fresnes-Cédex
Telephone: (1) 4668 30 31
Telex: PELT 201090 F

WORKS: 36200 Argenton-sur-Creuse
Telephone: (54) 241447
Telex: 751 417 F

JOINT COMMERCIAL DIRECTOR: Jean-Jacques Dufour

The Siren group was formed in July 1979 by Issoire-Aviation (which see), Siren SA, CARMAM (which has now ceased trading), and Pelletier Exploitation. Aéro Berry is now also a member.

The Siren group is responsible for production and marketing of the PIK-20E2F and PIK-30 powered sailplanes. These are described under the Issoire heading.

STRALPES AÉRO

STRALPES AÉRO SARL

BP 14, Aérodrome RN6, 73190 Challes-les-Eaux
Telephone: (79) 70 49 27
DIRECTOR: Christian Brondel

STRALPES Aéro (Société de Traitement, Réparation, Approvisionnement, Livraison de Pièces En Stratifié) was formed in March 1979, and has a 1,580 m² (17,000 sq ft) factory and a workforce of about 12 people. It is a distributor and maintenance centre for Glaser-Dirks sailplanes, and has developed the ST-11 and other designs of its own. No update of this company's entry was received for 1986.

STRALPES AÉRO ST-11

Objective of the ST-11's designers was to produce a low cost sailplane for club and personal use, with a wing span of less than 15 m and built of composite materials. The prototype (F-WBCB) made its first flight on 29 August 1982. General appearance is shown in the accompanying photograph. An **ST-11M** powered version has also been designed. Orders for five ST-11s and three ST-11Ms were reportedly in hand in early 1985.

TYPE: Single-seat Club Class sailplane.

AIRFRAME: Cantilever mid-wing monoplane, with cruciform tail unit, non-retractable semi-recessed monowheel and tailskid. Wings have a STRALPES Aéro (modified Wortmann) section, with thickness/chord ratio of 15% at root and 12·6% at tip. Carbonfibre main spar, upper surface airbrakes, and glassfibre/epoxy sandwich skin. One-piece cockpit canopy. No water ballast.

POWER PLANT (ST-11M): One 11 kW (15 hp) JPX PUL 212 single-cylinder two-stroke engine, pylon mounted in dorsal pod aft of cockpit and driving a pusher propeller with two foldable blades. Fuel tank capacity 10 litres (2·2 Imp gallons).

DIMENSIONS, EXTERNAL:
Wing span 11·60 m (38 ft 0¾ in)
Wing aspect ratio 20·57
Length overall 5·55 m (18 ft 2½ in)
Height over tail 1·135 m (3 ft 8¾ in)
Propeller diameter (ST-11M) 0·85 m (2 ft 9½ in)

AREA:
Wings, gross 6·54 m² (70·4 sq ft)

WEIGHTS AND LOADINGS:
Weight empty: ST-11 110 kg (243 lb)
ST-11M 120 kg (265 lb)
Max T-O weight: ST-11 230 kg (507 lb)
ST-11M 240 kg (529 lb)
Max wing loading: ST-11 35·17 kg/m² (7·20 lb/sq ft)
ST-11M 36·70 kg/m² (7·51 lb/sq ft)
Max power loading:
ST-11M 21·46 kg/kW (35·27 lb/hp)

PERFORMANCE, UNPOWERED (ST-11 at wing loading of 29 kg/m²; 5·94 lb/sq ft):
Best glide ratio at 54 knots (100 km/h; 62 mph) 35
Min rate of sink at 43 knots (80 km/h; 50 mph) 0·65 m (2·13 ft)/s
Stalling speed 37 knots (68 km/h; 42 mph)
Max speed (rough and smooth air) 124 knots (230 km/h; 143 mph)
Max aero-tow speed 89 knots (165 km/h; 102 mph)
Max winch-launching speed 70 knots (130 km/h; 80 mph)
g limits (JAR 22) +5·3/−2·65

PERFORMANCE, POWERED (ST-11M, estimated at max T-O weight):
Max cruising speed 89 knots (165 km/h; 102 mph)
Econ cruising speed approx 70 knots (130 km/h; 80 mph)
Max rate of climb at S/L 120 m (393 ft)/min
T-O run approx 150 m (495 ft)
Range with max fuel 105 nm (195 km; 121 miles)

STRALPES AÉRO ST-12

Projected tandem two-seat development of ST-11. Details include wing span and area of 16·00 m (52 ft 6 in) and 12·90 m² (138·85 sq ft), max T-O weight of 460 kg (1,014 lb) and best glide ratio of 38. One reported ordered in early 1985.

STRALPES AÉRO ST-14

Projected ultra-lightweight motor glider, with same power plant as ST-11M. Braced parasol monoplane, with single-seat open cockpit. Data include wing span and area of 11·60 m (38 ft 0¾ in) and 11·00 m² (118·4 sq ft), empty weight of 70-90 kg (155-199 lb) and max T-O weight of 180 kg (397 lb). Three reported ordered in early 1985.

GERMANY

(FEDERAL REPUBLIC)

AKAFLIEG BERLIN

AKADEMISCHE FLIEGERGRUPPE BERLIN eV

Technische Universität Berlin, Strasse des 17 Juni 135, 1000 Berlin 12 (Charlottenburg)
Telephone: (030) 314 4995

AKAFLIEG BERLIN B-13

This latest design by Akaflieg Berlin is a side by side two-seat sailplane having a submerged power plant for cross-country flying; it is not self-launching. Its intended general appearance can be seen in the accompanying three-view drawing. Design began in November 1981, and construction started in October 1982. First flight was planned for Spring 1985, but difficulties have reportedly been encountered in matching the wings (from a DG-500) with the wider fuselage of the B-13. Tests were expected in mid-1985 using instead the fuselage of a Streifeneder Falcon.

TYPE: Two-seat Open Class sailplane, with auxiliary power plant.

AIRFRAME: Cantilever mid-wing monoplane. Wortmann FX-73-K-170/22 section from root to tip. No dihedral or incidence. Sweepforward 1° 12′ at quarter-chord. Entire wing, including ailerons, trailing-edge flaps and Schempp-Hirth upper surface airbrakes, of carbonfibre (CfK) construction. Fuselage intended to be built of carbon and aramid (AfK) fibres. Cantilever T tail, with elevator, is of similar construction to wings. Mechanically retractable monowheel, with size 5·50-5 tyre and GfK/AfK shock absorption; semi-recessed tailwheel. Two seats side by side under framed canopy. Provision for water ballast.

POWER PLANT: One 24 kW (32 hp) Rotax 377 two-cylinder two-stroke engine, mounted in nose and driving a five-blade propeller; when not flying under power, blades can be retracted into nosecone. Fuel tank capacity 20 litres (4·4 Imp gallons).

DIMENSIONS, EXTERNAL:
Wing span 22·80 m (74 ft 9¾ in)
Wing aspect ratio 27·36
Length overall 8·30 m (27 ft 2¾ in)
Height over tail 1·85 m (6 ft 1 in)
Propeller diameter 0·85 m (2 ft 9½ in)

AREA:
Wings, gross 19·00 m² (204·5 sq ft)

WEIGHTS AND LOADING:
Weight empty, equipped 464 kg (1,023 lb)
Max T-O weight 684 kg (1,508 lb)
Max wing loading 36·0 kg/m² (7·37 lb/sq ft)

PERFORMANCE (estimated at max T-O weight):
Max speed (smooth air) 135 knots (250 km/h; 155 mph)
Max speed (rough air) 97 knots (180 km/h; 112 mph)
Max winch-launching speed 64 knots (120 km/h; 74 mph)
g limits +5·3/−2·65

AKAFLIEG BRAUNSCHWEIG

AKADEMISCHE FLIEGERGRUPPE BRAUNSCHWEIG eV

Flughafen Akafliegheim, 3300 Braunschweig
Telephone: 0531 3952149

AKAFLIEG BRAUNSCHWEIG SB-13

Construction of the prototype SB-13 began in 1985, and the first flight is planned for 1987.

TYPE: Standard Class sailplane.

AIRFRAME: Cantilever mid-wing 'flying wing' monoplane with Horstmann-Quast HQ-34N aerofoil section at root, HQ-36K at tip. Dihedral 4°. Incidence −1° 48′ at mid span, −0° 48′ at tip. Wings have compound sweepback (15° max, 12° mean, at quarter-chord), are turned up at tips to form winglets/fins and rudders, and are built of carbonfibre (HT and HM) reinforced plastics, with two tanks in each wing for a total of 120 litres (26·4 Imp gallons) of water ballast. Two carbonfibre elevons on each trailing-edge, carbon/metal Schempp-Hirth airbrakes in upper surface. Fuselage is a load-bearing shell of GRP. Size 300 × 100 mm monowheel, tyre pressure 3·2 bars (46 lb/sq in), and 260 × 85 mm nosewheel, tyre pressure 2·6 bars (38 lb/sq in), both fully retractable; brake on monowheel. Single seat under one-piece Plexiglas canopy which opens sideways to starboard.

DIMENSIONS, EXTERNAL:
Wing span 15·00 m (49 ft 2½ in)
Wing aspect ratio 19·07
Length of fuselage 3·60 m (11 ft 9¾ in)
Height over tail 1·96 m (6 ft 5¼ in)

AREA:
Wings, gross 11·80 m² (127·0 sq ft)

WEIGHTS AND LOADING:
Weight empty 220-240 kg (485-529 lb)
Max water ballast 120 kg (264·5 lb)
Max T-O weight 435 kg (959 lb)
Max wing loading 36·86 kg/m² (7·55 lb/sq ft)

PERFORMANCE (estimated at wing loading of 27 kg/m²; 5·53 lb/sq ft):
Stalling speed 37 knots (68 km/h; 43 mph)
Max speed (rough and smooth air) above 113 knots (210 km/h; 130 mph)
Max aero-tow speed 91 knots (170 km/h; 105 mph)
Max winch-launching speed 81 knots (150 km/h; 93 mph)
g limits (JAR 22) +5·3/−2·65

AKAFLIEG DARMSTADT

AKADEMISCHE FLIEGERGRUPPE DARMSTADT eV

Technische Hochschule, Magdalenenstrasse 8, 6100 Darmstadt
Telephone: 06151 24720

The Fliegergruppe of Darmstadt University has been designing, building and flying sailplanes since 1921. Its postwar products have been described in several previous editions of *Jane's*.

AKAFLIEG DARMSTADT D-40

A prototype of this new variable geometry sailplane was due to make its first flight in late 1985. The fuselage is that of a Rolladen-Schneider LS3. The wings have a Wortmann FX-67-VG-170 aerofoil section, 1° 28′ sweepforward at the leading-edge, and are fitted with variable area Fowler type trailing-edge flaps which, when extended, increase wing area by 21 per cent.

TYPE: Single-seat 15 metre Class sailplane.

AIRFRAME: Constructed of glassfibre (GfK), carbonfibre (CfK), aramid fibre (SfK) and balsa wood, as follows: wings of SfK/CfK-balsa sandwich; spar of CfK rovings with GfK-balsa webs; flaps of SfK-balsa sandwich with CfK stringers; tail unit has GfK skin and SfK fittings.

DIMENSIONS, EXTERNAL:
Wing span 15·00 m (49 ft 2½ in)
Wing aspect ratio: flaps in 23·81
flaps out 19·56
Length overall 6·75 m (22 ft 1¾ in)
Height over tail 1·315 m (4 ft 3¾ in)

AREAS:
Wings, gross: flaps in 9·45 m² (101·7 sq ft)
flaps out 11·50 m² (123·8 sq ft)

WEIGHTS AND LOADINGS:
Weight empty (approx) 270 kg (595 lb)
Water ballast 120 kg (264 lb)
Max T-O weight (approx):
without water ballast 330 kg (727 lb)
with water ballast 495 kg (1,091 lb)
Max wing loading, flaps in (approx):
without water ballast 35 kg/m² (7·15 lb/sq ft)
with water ballast 52 kg/m² (10·73 lb/sq ft)
Max wing loading, flaps out (approx):
without water ballast 29 kg/m² (5·87 lb/sq ft)
with water ballast 43 kg/m² (8·81 lb/sq ft)

PERFORMANCE:
No details received

STRALPES Aéro ST-11 prototype Club Class sailplane

Akaflieg Berlin B-13 Open Class sailplane, as originally designed *(Michael A. Badrocke)*

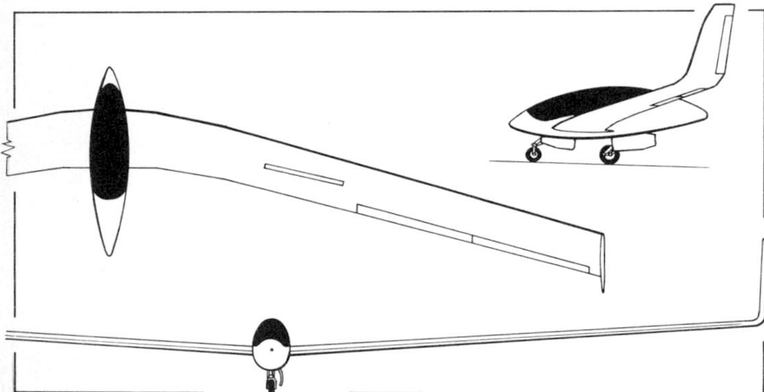

Provisional drawing of the Akaflieg Braunschweig SB-13 *(Michael A. Badrocke)*

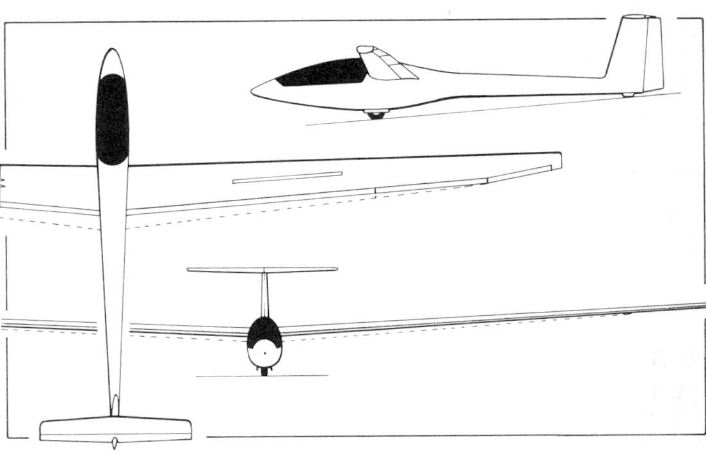

Akaflieg Darmstadt D-40 experimental variable geometry sailplane *(Michael A. Badrocke)*

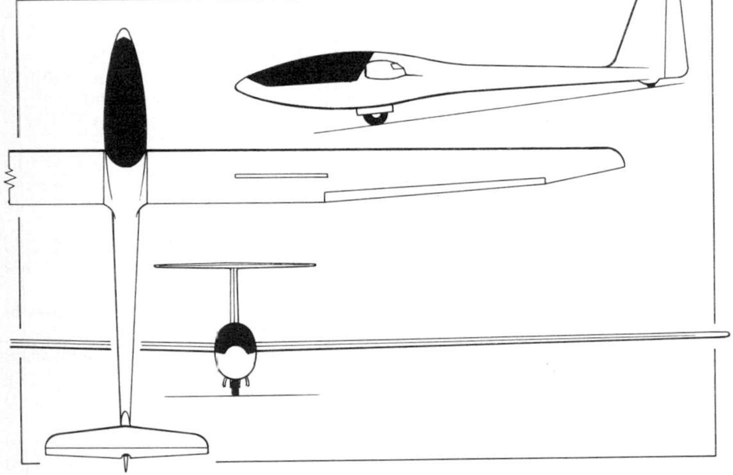

Akaflieg Karlsruhe AK-5 all-plastics Standard Class sailplane *(Michael A. Badrocke)*

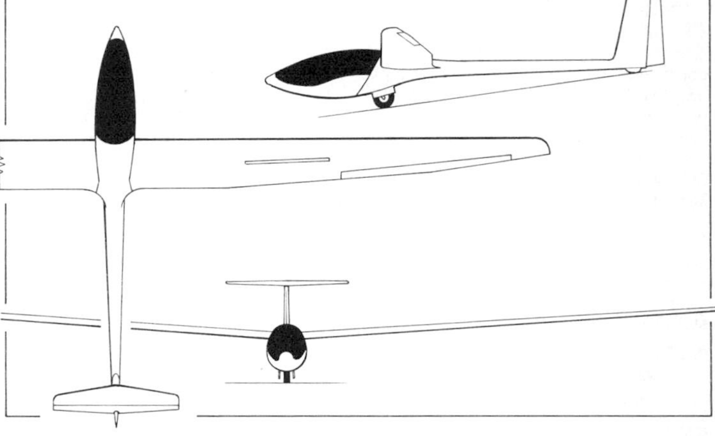

Akaflieg Hannover's latest design, the Standard Class AFH 24 *(Michael A. Badrocke)*

AKAFLIEG HANNOVER

AKADEMISCHE FLIEGERGRUPPE HANNOVER eV

Welfengarten 1, 3000 Hannover 1
Telephone: (0410511) 7626422 or 703032
PUBLIC RELATIONS MANAGER: Norbert Martinkat Jr

AKAFLIEG HANNOVER AFH 24

Features of the AFH 24 single-seat Standard Class sailplane include a forward-sliding nose section for cockpit access instead of a hinged canopy. General configuration has undergone some change during the past year and is now that of a shoulder-wing monoplane, with a minimal diameter rear fuselage supporting a T tail; landing gear comprises a retractable monowheel and tail bumper. The wings, fitted with upper surface spoilers, are essentially those of a Glaser-Dirks DG-300, but have a modified HQ (Horstmann-Quast) aerofoil section. Construction is mainly of GfK, carbon and aramid fibre composites.

Design of the AFH 24 began in October 1982; first flight was planned for 1986.

DIMENSIONS, EXTERNAL:

Wing span	15·00 m (49 ft 2½ in)
Wing aspect ratio	21·84
Fuselage: Max width	0·64 m (2 ft 1¼ in)
Max depth	0·81 m (2 ft 8 in)

AREA:

Wings, gross	10·30 m² (110·9 sq ft)

WEIGHTS AND LOADING:

Weight empty	240 kg (529 lb)
Max T-O weight	500 kg (1,102 lb)
Max wing loading	48·5 kg/m² (9·94 lb/sq ft)

PERFORMANCE (estimated):

Max speed (smooth air)	162 knots (300 km/h; 186 mph)

AKAFLIEG KARLSRUHE

AKADEMISCHE FLIEGERGRUPPE KARLSRUHE eV

Akademische Fliegergruppe an der Universität Karlsruhe eV, Kaiserstrasse 12, 7500 Karlsruhe 1
Telephone: 0721 608 2044
INFORMATION: Roland Minges

AKAFLIEG KARLSRUHE AK-5

Design of this single-seat FAI Standard Class sailplane began in August 1984, with the objective of providing group members with experience in designing and building sailplanes using composite materials. The AK-5 is expected to have a performance comparable with such other German types as the Glaser-Dirks DG-300, Rolladen-Schneider LS4, Schempp-Hirth Discus and Streifeneder Falcon.

General appearance of the AK-5 can be seen in an accompanying three-view drawing.

TYPE: Single-seat Standard Class sailplane.

AIRFRAME: Cantilever mid-wing monoplane with T tailplane and separate elevator. Horstmann-Quast HQ-21 wing section from root to tip. Dihedral 3°. Incidence 1°. Sweepforward approx 0° 18′ at quarter-chord. Entire airframe built of glassfibre composites. Schempp-Hirth airbrakes in upper surface. Tanks in wings for 160 litres (35·2 Imp gallons) of water ballast. Retractable monowheel, with brake; non-retractable tailwheel. Canopy hinged at front, opening upward.

DIMENSIONS, EXTERNAL:

Wing span	15·00 m (49 ft 2½ in)
Wing aspect ratio	21·11
Length overall	6·80 m (22 ft 3¾ in)
Height over tail	1·45 m (4 ft 9 in)

AREA:

Wings, gross	10·656 m² (114·7 sq ft)

WEIGHTS AND LOADING:
Weight empty, equipped 245 kg (540 lb)
Max water ballast 160 kg (353 lb)
Max T-O weight 485 kg (1,069 lb)
Max wing loading 45·51 kg/m² (9·32 lb/sq ft)

PERFORMANCE (estimated at wing loading of 35 kg/m²; 7·17 lb/sq ft):
Best glide ratio at 51 knots (95 km/h; 59 mph) 41
Min rate of sink at 45 knots (84 km/h; 52 mph) 0·60 m (1·97 ft)/s
Stalling speed 38 knots (70 km/h; 44 mph)
Max speed (smooth air) 146 knots (270 km/h; 168 mph)
Max speed (rough air), and max aero-tow speed 105 knots (195 km/h; 121 mph)
Max winch-launching speed 81 knots (150 km/h; 93 mph)
g limits +5·3/−2·65

AKAFLIEG MÜNCHEN

FLUGTECHNISCHE FORSCHUNGSGRUPPE an der TECHNISCHEN UNIVERSITÄT MÜNCHEN

Arcisstrasse 21, Postfach 202420, 8000 München 2
Telephone: 089 28 61 11

DIRECTOR: Andre Schülke
DESIGN MANAGER: Peter Hirt

Akaflieg München's most recent sailplane, the Mü 28, was described and illustrated in the 1984-85 *Jane's*.

München's latest project is the Mü 30 Schlacro glider tug/aerobatic aircraft, details of which can be found in the Sport Aircraft section.

AKAFLIEG STUTTGART

AKADEMISCHE FLIEGERGRUPPE STUTTGART eV

Pfaffenwaldring 35, 7000 Stuttgart 80
Telephone: 0711 685 2443

PRESIDENT: Rainer Diet

AKAFLIEG STUTTGART FS-32

This new single-seat 15 metre Class sailplane is still in the detail design stage, and no date has yet been set for the first flight. General appearance is shown in an accompanying three-view drawing.

Main features of the FS-32 are the Fowler type high lift slotted flaps, which are of Wortmann FX-81-K-144 aerofoil section and in two segments on each wing. With the ailerons, they occupy the entire trailing-edge. The wings are to be constructed of carbonfibre and other composite materials, and will have upper surface airbrakes. The carbon/aramid/glassfibre fuselage is modified from that of a Schempp-Hirth Ventus b, and has an improved version of the Ventus T tail. Landing gear comprises a retractable monowheel and semi-recessed tailwheel. The flapped wings are expected to permit a reduction in stalling speed compared with other 15 m Class sailplanes, and to bring about a considerable improvement in all-round handling and performance.

DIMENSIONS, EXTERNAL:
Wing span 15·00 m (49 ft 2½ in)
Wing aspect ratio 22·64

AREA:
Wings, gross 9·94 m² (107·0 sq ft)

WEIGHT (estimated):
Max T-O weight 250-260 kg (551-573 lb)

PERFORMANCE (estimated):
Best glide ratio at 54 knots (100 km/h; 62 mph) 43
Min rate of sink at 49 knots (90 km/h; 56 mph) 0·60 m (1·97 ft)/s

DOKTOR FIBERGLAS

DOKTOR FIBERGLAS (URSULA HÄNLE)

Postfach 1112, 5438 Westerburg
Telephone: 02663 3420

DIRECTOR: Ursula Hänle

HÄNLE H 101 SALTO

This single-seat Standard and Club Class sailplane was produced originally by the Start + Flug company, which delivered 60 before its closure in the Spring of 1978. The 65th example was under construction in early 1986.

The Salto is based on the Glasflügel Standard Libelle, from which it differs chiefly in having a V tail. It first flew in 1971, and is certificated by the LBA and FAA for both Utility and Aerobatic category flying. In the latter category it is fitted with the standard span (13·30 m; 43 ft 7½ in) wings; in the Utility category it is available either with 13·30 m wings or with detachable tips which extend the span to 15·50 m (50 ft 10¼ in)

TYPE: Single-seat Standard and Club Class sailplane.

AIRFRAME: Cantilever mid-wing monoplane. Wings have Conticell sandwich shell and HH type glassfibre spar caps, and detachable tip extensions (except in Aerobatic category). Dihedral 3° from roots. Glassfibre ailerons and four flush-fitting airbrakes on trailing-edges. Glassfibre monocoque fuselage. Cantilever V tail (included angle 99°), with glassfibre fixed surfaces and glassfibre/honeycomb sandwich balanced 'ruddervators'. Non-retractable semi-recessed monowheel, size 300 × 100 mm, with glassfibre shock absorption and internally expanding brake. Non-retractable semi-recessed tailwheel. Brake parachute attachment standard on all versions. Canopy opens sideways to starboard.

DIMENSIONS, EXTERNAL (A: Aerobatic, U: Utility):
Wing span: A 13·30 m (43 ft 7½ in)
U (optional) 15·50 m (50 ft 10¼ in)
Wing aspect ratio: A 20·62
U (optional) 26·40
Length overall 5·70 m (18 ft 8½ in)
Height over tail 0·80 m (2 ft 7½ in)

AREAS:
Wings, gross: A 8·58 m² (92·4 sq ft)
U (optional) 9·10 m² (98·0 sq ft)

WEIGHTS AND LOADINGS:
Weight empty: A 182 kg (401 lb)
U 187 kg (412 lb)
Max T-O weight: A 280 kg (617 lb)
U 310 kg (683 lb)
Max wing loading: A 32·6 kg/m² (6·68 lb/sq ft)
U (13·3 m) 36·1 kg/m² (7·40 lb/sq ft)
U (15·5 m) 34·0 kg/m² (6·97 lb/sq ft)

PERFORMANCE (at max T-O weight except where indicated):
Best glide ratio at 51 knots (94 km/h; 58 mph):
A 35
U 36
Min rate of sink at 39 knots (72 km/h; 45 mph):
A, U (15·5 m), at AUW of 280 kg (617 lb) 0·70 m (2·30 ft)/s
A, U (15·5 m), at AUW of 250 kg (551 lb) 0·60 m (1·97 ft)/s
U (13·3 m), at AUW of 250 kg (551 lb) 0·55 m (1·80 ft)/s
Stalling speed: A 38 knots (70 km/h; 44 mph)
U 34 knots (62 km/h; 39 mph)
Max speed (rough and smooth air):
A 151 knots (280 km/h; 174 mph)
U 135 knots (250 km/h; 155 mph)
Max aero-tow speed:
A, U 81 knots (150 km/h; 93 mph)
Max winch-launching speed:
A, U 70 knots (130 km/h; 81 mph)
g limits: A +7/−4·9

EEL

ENTWICKLUNG UND ERPROBUNG VON LEICHTFLUGZEUGEN

Anechostrasse 16, 8000 München 82

DIRECTORS: Heiner Neumann
Dieter Reich

ULF-1

The original ULF-1 (Ultra Leicht Flugzeug) was designed by Dieter Reich and built by Heiner Neumann. First flight was made in November 1977, and certification was received in July 1980. Plans (but not kits or materials) became available to amateur constructors, and about 150 sets had been sold by the beginning of 1985, from which more than 30 ULF-1s were then believed to have been completed and flown.

TYPE: One-man rigid-wing foot launched glider.

AIRFRAME: Cantilever high-wing monoplane. Wings have Wortmann FX-63-137 section, and comprise a single spruce spar, plywood nose section, plywood/balsa ribs and fabric covering. Thickness/chord ratio 18% at root, 15% at tip. Fuselage is a fabric covered wooden frame, of triangular cross-section aft of cockpit. Cantilever tail unit, of similar construction to wings. Single sliding seat for pilot, who retracts his legs after foot launch to operate rudder pedals. Landing is made on a nose-skid and glassfibre tube (fishing rod) tailskid. Three-axis aerodynamic control by ailerons, one-piece elevator and rudder. Wings and tail can be removed for transportation and storage.

DIMENSIONS, EXTERNAL:
Wing span 10·40 m (34 ft 1½ in)
Wing aspect ratio 8·07
Length overall 5·55 m (18 ft 2½ in)
Height overall 2·55 m (8 ft 4½ in)

AREA:
Wings, gross 13·40 m² (144·2 sq ft)

WEIGHTS AND LOADING:
Weight of glider 46 kg (101·5 lb)
Pilot weight 60-90 kg (132-198 lb)
Max T-O weight 136 kg (300 lb)
Max wing loading 10·1 kg/m² (2·07 lb/sq ft)

PERFORMANCE:
Best glide ratio at 30 knots (55 km/h; 34 mph) 15
Min rate of sink at 19-22·5 knots (35-40 km/h; 22-25 mph) 0·80 m (2·62 ft)/s
Max speed 38 knots (70 km/h; 43 mph)
Stalling speed 18 knots (32 km/h; 20 mph)
g limits +6/−4

FAG ESSLINGEN

FLUGTECHNISCHE ARBEITSGEMEINSCHAFT AN DER FACHHOCHSCHULE FÜR TECHNIK ESSLINGEN eV

Kanalstrasse 33, 7300 Esslingen/Neckar

FAG ESSLINGEN E 14

Under the leadership of Herr Karl Pfister, students at FAG Esslingen have designed a new, very lightweight Standard Class sailplane designated E 14. General appearance is shown in an accompanying three-view drawing. Wing section is Wortmann FX-63-137, and construction is mainly of carbon and aramid fibre sandwich composites.

DIMENSIONS, EXTERNAL:
Wing span 15·00 m (49 ft 2½ in)
Wing aspect ratio 27·78
Length overall 6·75 m (22 ft 1¾ in)

AREA:
Wings, gross 8·10 m² (87·2 sq ft)

WEIGHTS AND LOADING:
Weight empty 130 kg (287 lb)
Max water ballast 120 kg (264·5 lb)
Max T-O weight 350 kg (772 lb)
Max wing loading 43·21 kg/m² (8·85 lb/sq ft)

PERFORMANCE (estimated):
Best glide ratio approx 45
Max speed (smooth air) 145 knots (270 km/h; 167 mph)

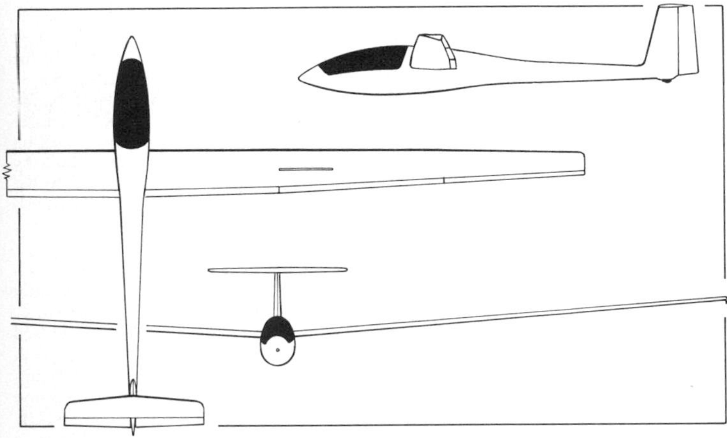

The 15 metre Class Akaflieg Stuttgart FS-32 *(Michael A. Badrocke)*

EEL (Reich & Neumann) ULF-1 foot launched glider

Hänle (Doktor Fiberglas) H 101 Salto *(Peter F. Selinger)*

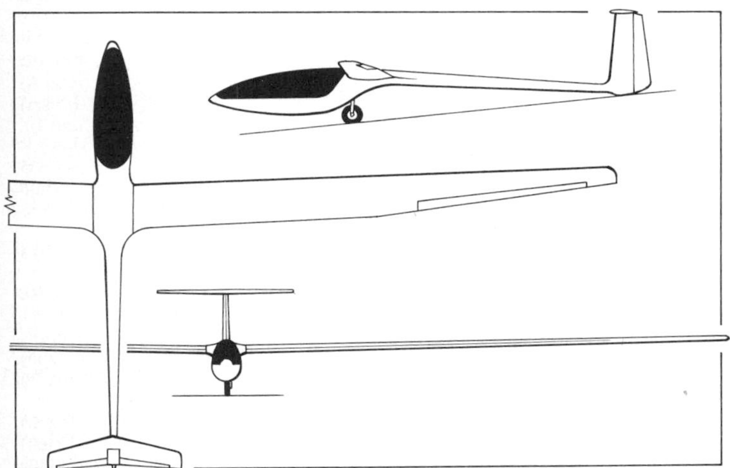

FAG Esslingen E 14 lightweight sailplane *(Michael A. Badrocke)*

Glaser-Dirks DG-400 self-launching sailplane *(Wolfgang Wagner)*

GLASER-DIRKS

GLASER-DIRKS FLUGZEUGBAU GmbH

Im Schollengarten 19-20, Postfach 47, 7520 Bruchsal 4
Telephone: 07257 1071
Telex: 782241 gldg

Directors: Gerhard Glaser and Dipl-Ing Wilhelm Dirks

Glaser-Dirks was formed in 1973; it delivered its 500th aircraft (a DG-400) in 1983. The company designed, and remains the type certificate holder for, the DG-101 and DG-300 sailplanes, now manufactured by Elan in Yugoslavia (which see). Production of the DG-200/202 series ended in 1984. Glaser-Dirks' main current activity concerns production of the DG-400 and, in partnership with Elan, development of the new DG-500.

GLASER-DIRKS DG-400

The DG-400 is a self-launching development of the DG-202 (1984-85 *Jane's*), from which it differs principally in having a slightly deeper rear fuselage to accommodate the power plant when retracted. As with the unpowered versions, the DG-400 has 15 m span wings with add-on tips which increase the span to 17 m. The prototype (D-KOLL) flew for the first time on 1 May 1981. Deliveries began in June 1982; a total of 155 had been built by 1 January 1986, of 200 then on order.

Type: Single-seat self-launching sailplane.

Airframe: Cantilever shoulder-wing monoplane. Wing section Wortmann FX-67-K-170-17 at root, FX-67-K-170 (15 m span) or FX-60-K-126 (17 m span) at tip. Dihedral 3° from roots. Incidence −1°. Carbonfibre roving main spar, wing skin, flaps and ailerons. Schempp-Hirth aluminium airbrakes on upper surfaces. All-glassfibre semi-monocoque fuselage, fin and rudder. Glassfibre/foam sandwich T tailplane, with carbonfibre elevator. Manually retractable monowheel, size 5·00-5, tyre pressure 3·0 bars (43·5 lb/sq in), with Tost drum brake; size 200 × 50 tailwheel, tyre pressure 2·0 bars (29 lb/sq in). One-piece cockpit canopy, hinged at front to open upwards. Water ballast tank in each wing, combined capacity 90 litres (19·8 Imp gallons).

Power Plant: One 32 kW (43 hp) Rotax 505 two-stroke engine, pylon-mounted on fuselage aft of wing trailing-edge and driving a Hoffmann two-blade fixed-pitch propeller. Installation retracts, electrically, rearward into fuselage when not in use. Single fuselage fuel tank standard, capacity 20 litres (4·4 Imp gallons). Optional 15 litre (3·3 Imp gallon) tank in each wing, in lieu of water ballast, raising total fuel capacity to 50 litres (11 Imp gallons).

Dimensions, external:
- Wing span: 15 m — 15·00 m (49 ft 2½ in)
  - 17 m — 17·00 m (55 ft 9¼ in)
- Wing aspect ratio: 15 m — 22·50
  - 17 m — 27·34
- Length overall — 7·00 m (22 ft 11¾ in)
- Height over tail — 1·40 m (4 ft 7 in)
- Propeller diameter — 1·29 m (4 ft 2¾ in)

Areas:
- Wings, gross: 15 m — 10·00 m² (107·6 sq ft)
  - 17 m — 10·57 m² (113·8 sq ft)

Weights and Loadings:
- Weight empty — 305 kg (672 lb)
- Max T-O weight: 15 m — 480 kg (1,058 lb)
  - 17 m — 460 kg (1,014 lb)
- Max wing loading: 15 m — 48·0 kg/m² (9·84 lb/sq ft)
  - 17 m — 43·5 kg/m² (8·91 lb/sq ft)
- Max power loading: 15 m — 14·9 kg/kW (24·6 lb/hp)
  - 17 m — 14·0 kg/kW (23·1 lb/hp)

Performance, unpowered (at max T-O weight):
- Best glide ratio at 59 knots (110 km/h; 68 mph):
  - 15 m — 47
  - 17 m — 45
- Min rate of sink at 43 knots (80 km/h; 50 mph):
  - 15 m — 0·60 m (1·97 ft)/s
  - 17 m — 0·50 m (1·64 ft)/s
- Stalling speed: 15 m — 35 knots (65 km/h; 41 mph)
  - 17 m — 34 knots (63 km/h; 40 mph)
- Max speed (smooth air) — 146 knots (270 km/h; 168 mph)
- Max speed (rough air), and max aero-tow speed — 102 knots (190 km/h; 118 mph)
- Max winch-launching speed — 70 knots (130 km/h; 81 mph)
- *g* limits — +6/−4

Performance, powered (at max T-O weight):
- Max cruising speed — 76 knots (140 km/h; 87 mph)
- Econ cruising speed — 70 knots (130 km/h; 81 mph)
- Stalling speed: 15 m — 35 knots (65 km/h; 41 mph)
  - 17 m — 34 knots (63 km/h; 40 mph)
- Max rate of climb at S/L — 234 m (768 ft)/min
- Service ceiling — 5,000 m (16,400 ft)
- T-O run at 15°C — 170 m (558 ft)
- Landing run — 50 m (164 ft)
- Range with max fuel:
  - level cruise — 215 nm (400 km; 248 miles)
  - 'saw-tooth' cruise/soar — 404 nm (750 km; 466 miles)

GLASER-DIRKS DG-500M

The DG-500 Elan is a new two-seat sailplane designed jointly with Glaser-Dirks' Yugoslav partner Elan, under whose entry further details can be found. The DG-500M, produced by Glaser-Dirks, will serve as first prototype for the series and was due to make its first flight in May or June 1986. This aircraft has 22·0 m (72 ft 2 in) span wings, and a power plant installation similar to that of the DG-400 but uprated to 44·7 kW (60 hp). Glaser-Dirks will be the type certificate holder for all versions of the DG-500, but will act only as a distributor for other versions, for all countries except Yugoslavia.

GROB

BURKHART GROB FLUGZEUGBAU (Subsidiary of Grob-Werke GmbH & Co KG)

Postfach 150, 8948 Mindelheim
DIRECTOR: Dipl-Ing Burkhart Grob

This company built 200 Schempp-Hirth Standard Cirrus under licence between 1972 and 1975. Its workforce of about 160 people currently manufactures light aircraft (see Aircraft section), sailplanes and a motor glider of its own design, of which approximately half are exported. Sailplanes and motor gliders are designed according to JAR 22 European airworthiness requirements. Total works area is 210,000 m² (2,260,420 sq ft), including 10,000 m² (107,640 sq ft) of covered space.

GROB G 102 SERIES III

Representing a further development of the Astir II series (see 1983-84 and earlier editions of *Jane's*), the G 102 has lower wing loading, better take-off and landing characteristics, and a longer cockpit with a more upright seat.

The original Club III version (1984-85 *Jane's*) is no longer produced. The following two versions were available in 1986:

G 102 Club IIIb. Current basic version, with non-retractable monowheel (further aft than on original Club III); nosewheel added. No provision for water ballast. Recent sales include two to the Royal Jordanian Gliding Club.

G 102 Standard III. Standard Class version, having retractable monowheel with drum brake, non-retractable tailwheel, and water ballast tanks.

A total of 1,395 single-seat Astir/G 102 sailplanes had been built by January 1986.

TYPE: Single-seat Standard and Club Class sailplanes.

AIRFRAME: Cantilever mid-wing monoplane with T tail. Eppler E 603 wing section. Wing sweepback 1°. Glassfibre main spar; wings and tail surfaces have glassfibre/epoxy resin sandwich skin. Ailerons are of glassfibre sandwich, with elastic gap seals. Schempp-Hirth upper surface aluminium airbrakes. Glassfibre semi-monocoque fuselage, with towing/launching hook. Carbonfibre reinforced fuselage, fin and canopy frame. Retractable Tost monowheel on Standard III (non-retractable on Club version), tyre pressure 2·5 bars (36·3 lb/sq in), with internally expanding drum brake (disc brake optional on Club IIIb); rubber sprung tailwheel; nosewheel on Club IIIb. Canopy opens sideways to starboard. Provision for 100 kg (220 lb) water ballast in Standard III.

DIMENSIONS, EXTERNAL:
Wing span — 15·00 m (49 ft 2½ in)
Wing aspect ratio — 18·15
Length overall — 6·70 m (21 ft 11¾ in)
Height over tail — 1·26 m (4 ft 1½ in)

AREA:
Wings, gross — 12·40 m² (133·5 sq ft)

WEIGHTS AND LOADINGS (A: Club IIIb, B: Standard III):
Weight empty: A — 248 kg (546 lb)
B — 255 kg (562 lb)
Max T-O weight: A — 380 kg (838 lb)
B — 450 kg (992 lb)
Max wing loading: A — 30·6 kg/m² (6·27 lb/sq ft)
B — 36·3 kg/m² (7·44 lb/sq ft)

PERFORMANCE (at max T-O weight):
Best glide ratio:
A at 49 knots (90 km/h; 56 mph) — 35·5
B at 56 knots (105 km/h; 65 mph) — 38
Min rate of sink:
A at 42 knots (78 km/h; 48 mph) — 0·65 m (2·13 ft)/s
B at 46 knots (85 km/h; 53 mph) — 0·70 m (2·30 ft)/s
Stalling speed — 33 knots (60 km/h; 38 mph)
Max speed (rough and smooth air) — 135 knots (250 km/h; 155 mph)
Max aero-tow speed — 91 knots (170 km/h; 105 mph)
Max winch-launching speed — 65 knots (120 km/h; 75 mph)

GROB G 103 TWIN II

RAF designation: Viking TX. Mk 1

This tandem two-seat sailplane for training and club flying is the successor to the Twin Astir I (291 built: 1979-80 *Jane's*), from which it differs mainly in having lower-mounted wings, a more streamlined fuselage, modified landing gear, improved cockpit layout and reduced weight. First flight was made in late 1979, and FAA certification was granted on 26 March 1982. Production of the Twin II totalled 555 by January 1986, including Acros, and was continuing at a rate of ten each month.

Formal acceptance of the G 103 into service with the Royal Air Force took place on 5 October 1984 at the Air Cadet Central Gliding School, Syerston, Nottinghamshire. A total of 100 Acros was delivered to the RAF. Four Acros were ordered by the Royal Jordanian Gliding Club in early 1986.

TYPE: Tandem two-seat training and club sailplane.

AIRFRAME: Cantilever low/mid-wing monoplane, of similar construction to G 102 Series III. Conventional ailerons; no flaps. Cantilever T tail. Non-retractable nosewheel and monowheel, both semi-recessed; plus tailwheel. Individual canopies, opening sideways to starboard. No water ballast provision.

DIMENSIONS, EXTERNAL:
Wing span — 17·50 m (57 ft 5 in)
Wing aspect ratio — 17·21
Length overall — 8·18 m (26 ft 10 in)
Height over tail — 1·55 m (5 ft 1 in)

AREA:
Wings, gross — 17·80 m² (191·6 sq ft)

WEIGHTS AND LOADING:
Weight empty — 370 kg (815 lb)
Max T-O weight — 580 kg (1,278 lb)
Max wing loading — 32·6 kg/m² (6·68 lb/sq ft)

PERFORMANCE (at max T-O weight except where indicated):
Best glide ratio at 56 knots (105 km/h; 65 mph) — 36
Min rate of sink at 43 knots (80 km/h; 50 mph) — 0·64 m (2·10 ft)/s
Stalling speed (carrying pilot only) — 34 knots (62 km/h; 39 mph)
Max speed (smooth air) — 135 knots (250 km/h; 155 mph)
Max speed (rough air), and max aero-tow speed — 91 knots (170 km/h; 105 mph)
Max winch-launching speed — 65 knots (120 km/h; 75 mph)
g limits: Twin II — +5·3/−2·65
Twin II Acro — +7/−5

GROB G 109B

The prototype G 109 (D-KBGF), with a 56 kW (75 hp) Limbach engine, flew for the first time on 14 March 1980. Series production began in the Summer of 1981, and the G 109 is now certificated in 17 countries, including West Germany and the USA under JAR 22. Production of the initial G 109 version (see 1983-84 *Jane's*) totalled 160.

The G 109B, of which a prototype was flown in March 1983, differs mainly in having modified wings, of greater span, and a more powerful engine. The first production G 109B flew in August 1983, and 222 had been built by January 1986, when the rate of production was eight per month. The Royal Jordanian Gliding Club has ordered two G 109Bs.

TYPE: Side by side two-seat motor glider.

AIRFRAME: Cantilever low-wing monoplane with T tail. Wings of Eppler E 580 section (thickness/chord ratio 16·1%) from root to tip. Dihedral 3°. Incidence 2°. No sweepback. Construction of glassfibre (GfK) and carbonfibre (KfK); ailerons of GfK. Schempp-Hirth airbrakes in upper surface only. No water ballast. Wings are foldable rearward, and have automatic connection and disconnection of aileron controls. Fuselage is a GfK monocoque. Fixed incidence tailplane, with elevator; entire tail unit is of GfK, except for KfK rudder. Non-retractable tailwheel type landing gear. Mainwheels have tyres size 380 × 150 mm, pressure 2·5 bars (36·25 lb/sq in), and are fitted with hydraulic disc brakes and speed fairings; tailwheel tyre size 250 × 85 mm. Side by side seats for pilot and passenger. Centre of canopy consists of two doors, hinged on c/l to open upward. Additional viewing port in each side of fuselage, forward of wing root. Standard instrumentation and radio. Optional equipment includes VOR, ADF, DME, transponder, and electric variometer.

POWER PLANT: One 67 kW (90 hp) Grob 2500 engine, driving a Hoffmann two-blade three-speed variable-pitch wooden propeller with spinner. Fuselage fuel tank, capacity 100 litres (22 Imp gallons).

DIMENSIONS, EXTERNAL:
Wing span — 17·40 m (57 ft 1 in)
Wing aspect ratio — 15·93
Length overall — 8·10 m (26 ft 7 in)
Height over tail — 1·80 m (5 ft 10¾ in)

AREA:
Wings, gross — 19·00 m² (204·5 sq ft)

WEIGHTS AND LOADINGS:
Weight empty, equipped — 620 kg (1,367 lb)
Max T-O weight — 850 kg (1,874 lb)
Max wing loading — 44·7 kg/m² (9·16 lb/sq ft)
Max power loading — 12·69 kg/kW (20·8 lb/hp)

PERFORMANCE, UNPOWERED (at max T-O weight):
Best glide ratio at 62 knots (115 km/h; 71 mph) — 28
Min rate of sink at 57 knots (105 km/h; 65 mph) — 1·10 m (3·61 ft)/s
Stalling speed — 40 knots (73 km/h; 46 mph)
Max speed (rough and smooth air) — 130 knots (240 km/h; 149 mph)
g limits — +5·3/−2·65

PERFORMANCE, POWERED (at max T-O weight):
Never-exceed speed — 130 knots (240 km/h; 149 mph)
Max cruising speed — 111 knots (205 km/h; 127 mph)
Econ cruising speed — 97 knots (180 km/h; 112 mph)
Stalling speed — 40 knots (73 km/h; 46 mph)
Max rate of climb at S/L — 198 m (650 ft)/min
Service ceiling — 6,000 m (19,675 ft)
T-O run — 196 m (645 ft)
Landing run — 200 m (656 ft)
Range at 97 knots (180 km/h; 112 mph) with max fuel — 809 nm (1,500 km; 932 miles)

HOFFMANN

WOLF HOFFMANN FLUGZEUGBAU KG

Sportflugplatz, 8870 Günzburg/Ulm
Telephone: 08221 1417
Telex: 531625 HOFBG D
WORKS: Richard Neutra-Gasse, A-1214 Vienna, Austria
Telephone: (0043) 222 253691
DIRECTOR: Dipl-Ing Wolf D. Hoffmann

HOFFMANN H-36 DIMONA

The prototype of this two-seat motor glider flew for the first time on 9 October 1980, and was followed by two further prototypes. The Dimona was awarded LBA type certification on 30 March 1982, and also has a British C of A. By Spring 1986 a total of nearly 170 had been delivered.

Production now takes place in a new 2,000 m² (21,528 sq ft) factory at Neustadt-Ost airfield near Vienna, Austria. The workforce was expected to increase from 65 in Spring 1986 to 85 by the end of the year.

TYPE: Side by side two-seat motor glider; positive aerobatics permissible.

AIRFRAME: Cantilever low/mid-wing monoplane, constructed of GfK. Wing section Wortmann FX-63-137. Upper surface airbrakes. Wings are attached independently to fuselage by bolts, and can be folded back alongside fuselage for transportation and storage. Fuselage sidewalls and frames are strengthened with extensive GfK rovings. Double shell in cockpit area. Cantilever T tail. Non-retractable tailwheel type landing gear, with 6 in mainwheels and steerable tailwheel. Cantilever GfK mainwheel legs. Fairings on main legs and wheels. Cockpit canopy hinged at rear to open upwards. Baggage space aft of seats.

POWER PLANT: One 59·7 kW (80 hp) Limbach L 2000 EBI engine, driving a Hoffmann HO-V62/160 two-blade three-position propeller. Fuel tank capacity 80 litres (17·5 Imp gallons).

DIMENSIONS, EXTERNAL:
Wing span — 16·00 m (52 ft 6 in)
Wing aspect ratio — 16·84
Length overall — 6·85 m (22 ft 5¾ in)
Height over tail — 1·625 m (5 ft 4 in)
Propeller diameter — 1·60 m (5 ft 3 in)

AREA:
Wings, gross — 15·20 m² (163·6 sq ft)

WEIGHTS AND LOADINGS:
Weight empty — 520 kg (1,146 lb)
Max T-O weight — 770 kg (1,697 lb)
Max wing loading — 50·7 kg/m² (10·38 lb/sq ft)
Max power loading — 12·91 kg/kW (21·21 lb/hp)

PERFORMANCE, UNPOWERED (at max T-O weight):
Best glide ratio at 56 knots (105 km/h; 65 mph) — 27
Min rate of sink at 43 knots (80 km/h; 50 mph) — 0·90 m (2·95 ft)/s
Stalling speed — 39 knots (72 km/h; 45 mph)
Max speed (smooth air) — 148 knots (275 km/h; 171 mph)
Max speed (rough air) — 113 knots (210 km/h; 130 mph)
g limits: — +5·3/−2·65 (permissible) +9·3 (ultimate)

PERFORMANCE, POWERED (at max T-O weight):
Max cruising speed — 97 knots (180 km/h; 112 mph)
Econ cruising speed — 92 knots (170 km/h; 106 mph)
Stalling speed — 39 knots (72 km/h; 45 mph)
Max rate of climb at S/L — 210 m (689 ft)/min
Service ceiling — 6,000 m (19,675 ft)
T-O run — 180 m (590 ft)
Landing run — 150 m (492 ft)
Range with max fuel — 540 nm (1,000 km; 621 miles)

HOFFMANN H-38 OBSERVER

Based on the H-36 Dimona (which see), the Observer differs principally in having a tricycle landing gear and a new front fuselage section with extensive transparency areas that offer a field of view comparable with that of a helicopter. It is offered with either a 59·7 kW (80 hp) or 78·3 kW (105 hp) engine, buried in the fuselage behind the cabin, with the propeller shaft running through the centre of the cabin between the two side by side seats. All-composite airframe construction gives it a low radar signature, and it can be equipped with IFR avionics and aerial cameras. Standard and long-range (LR) versions are available with either engine.

POWER PLANT: One 59·7 kW (80 hp) Limbach L 2000 EBI or 78·3 kW (105 hp) L 2500 EBI engine, driving a two-blade variable-pitch propeller. Fuel capacity 80 litres (17·6 Imp gallons) standard, doubling to 160 litres (35·2 Imp gallons) on LR versions.

DIMENSIONS, EXTERNAL:
Wing span — 16·10 m (52 ft 10 in)

Grob G 102 Club IIIb single-seat sailplane *(Peter F. Selinger)*

Grob G 103 Acro tandem two-seat sailplane *(Brian M. Service)*

Grob G 109B two-seat motor glider

Mockup of the Hoffmann H-38 Observer surveillance and reconnaissance aircraft *(Wolfgang Wagner)*

Schleicher ASK 13, still in production by Jubi at Oerlinghausen *(Peter F. Selinger)*

Hoffmann H-36 Dimona two-seat motor glider *(Peter F. Selinger)*

Wing aspect ratio 16·91
Width, wings folded 2·20 m (7 ft 2½ in)
Length overall 7·25 m (23 ft 9½ in)
Length, wings folded 9·80 m (32 ft 2 in)

AREA:
Wings, gross 15·33 m² (165·0 sq ft)

WEIGHTS:
Weight empty (all versions) 550 kg (1,212 lb)
Max T-O weight:
H-38/2000, H-38/2500 770 kg (1,697 lb)
H-38/2000LR, H-38/2500LR 850 kg (1,874 lb)

PERFORMANCE, POWERED (A: H-38/2000, B: H-38/2000LR, C: H-38/2500, D: H-38/2500LR):
Never-exceed speed (all versions) 148 knots (275 km/h; 170 mph)
Max level speed: A, B 110 knots (205 km/h; 127 mph)
C, D 121 knots (225 km/h; 140 mph)
Cruising speed: A, B 102 knots (190 km/h; 118 mph)
C, D 110 knots (205 km/h; 127 mph)
Stalling speed: A, C 38 knots (70 km/h; 44 mph)
B, D 40 knots (74 km/h; 46 mph)
Max rate of climb at S/L: A 210 m (689 ft)/min
B 180 m (590 ft)/min
C 270 m (886 ft)/min
D 240 m (787 ft)/min
T-O run: A 180 m (590 ft)
B 200 m (656 ft)
C 150 m (492 ft)
D 160 m (525 ft)
Range with max fuel:
A 675 nm (1,250 km; 777 miles)
B 1,350 nm (2,500 km; 1,554 miles)
C 620 nm (1,150 km; 715 miles)
D 1,240 nm (2,300 km; 1,430 miles)
Best glide ratio (all versions) 28

JUBI

JUBI GmbH SPORTFLUGZEUGBAU

Flugplatz 2, 4811 Oerlinghausen
Telephone: 05202 3422

Jubi is currently the sole production source for the Schleicher ASK 13 two-seat sailplane.

JUBI (SCHLEICHER) ASK 13

This tandem-seat sailplane was developed by Schleicher from the K 7, which is in worldwide use by gliding clubs. The prototype first flew in July 1966.

Production by Schleicher has ended, but the ASK 13 is still manufactured, under licence, by Jubi.

TYPE: Tandem two-seat training and high-performance sailplane.

AIRFRAME: Cantilever mid-wing monoplane. Wing section developed from Göttingen 535 and 549. Sweepforward at quarter-chord 6°. Dihedral 5°. Single-spar wooden wings, with fabric covering. Wooden ailerons, with plywood covering; Schempp-Hirth metal airbrakes above and below each wing. Welded steel tube fuselage with spruce formers and fabric main covering. Nose made of glassfibre. Turtledeck aft of canopy is plywood shell. Cantilever wooden tail unit, plywood covered except for fabric covered rear portion of rudder and elevators. Flettner tab in starboard elevator. Non-retractable sprung monowheel, with Tost drum brake; skid in front of wheel; steel tailskid. Canopy opens sideways to starboard.

DIMENSIONS, EXTERNAL:
Wing span 16·00 m (52 ft 6 in)
Wing aspect ratio 14·63
Length overall 8·18 m (26 ft 9½ in)
Height over tail 1·60 m (5 ft 3 in)

AREA:
Wings, gross 17·50 m² (188·4 sq ft)

WEIGHTS AND LOADING:
Weight empty 290 kg (640 lb)
Max T-O weight 480 kg (1,060 lb)
Max wing loading 26·8 kg/m² (5·49 lb/sq ft)

PERFORMANCE (at 470 kg; 1,036 lb T-O weight):
Best glide ratio at 49 knots (90 km/h; 56 mph) 28
Min rate of sink at 38 knots (70 km/h; 43 mph) 0·80 m (2·62 ft)/s
Stalling speed 33 knots (61 km/h; 38 mph)
Max speed (smooth air) 108 knots (200 km/h; 124 mph)
Max speed (rough air), and max aero-tow speed 76 knots (140 km/h; 87 mph)
Max winch-launching speed 54 knots (100 km/h; 62 mph)
g limit (safety factor of 2) +4

KUFFNER

LEICHTFLUGZEUGBAU WERNER KUFFNER

Mühltal 12, 5401 Rhens
Telephone: 02628 3049
PROPRIETOR: Werner Kuffner

KUFFNER WK-1b

Design of this advanced motor glider began with construction of the WK-1 prototype (D-KEWK) in 1979. It made its first flight on 13 July 1984 and was described in the 1984-85 *Jane's*. By September of that year it had accumulated 20 hours' flying in a reduced flight test programme, devoted mainly to validating the propulsion system.

The WK-1b is the intended production version, which differs from the prototype mainly in having the wing span extended from 18·80 m (61 ft 8¼ in) to 22 m (72 ft 2¼ in), with new aerofoil section and the addition of airbrakes. Other changes have been made to the fuselage structure and the propeller.

Features of the WK-1b include placing the engine at the CG, where it drives a 'midships propeller with folding blades, and retractable outrigger wheels, connected to the wing flaps, which give self-launch capability.

In February 1986 Herr Kuffner was awaiting the outcome of an application for local government funding to enable series production to begin.

TYPE: Two-seat motor glider.

AIRFRAME: Cantilever shoulder-wing monoplane. Wortmann wing sections: FX-73-170-K/20 at root, FX-73-170-K/22 at tip. Dihedral 3°. Incidence 0°. Tapered centre-section and tapered outer panels, built of CFRP. Full span trailing-edge flaps. Schempp-Hirth airbrakes in centre-section upper surface. Forward and centre fuselage of aluminium and steel tube respectively, with fibre reinforced composite skin; rear fuselage all-metal. Non-swept cruciform tail surfaces; variable incidence tailplane, with elevators, mounted part-way up fin. Retractable monowheel, protruding slightly when retracted to protect fuselage in event of a belly landing. Semi-recessed tailwheel. Electrically actuated rearward retracting outrigger wheel under each wing. One-piece forward sliding canopy. Side by side seats for two persons.

POWER PLANT: One 44·75 kW (60 hp) 1,000 cc BMW two-cylinder boxer engine, mounted in fuselage aft of cockpit and driving a Kuffner propeller with three rearward folding blades which rotate around rear fuselage. Electronic double ignition and fuel injection. Between engine and propeller is a centrifugal clutch by means of which blades remain folded until engine reaches 1,600 rpm, thereafter beginning to turn and unfold gradually. Fuel tank in each outboard end of wing centre-section, each with capacity of 25 litres (5·5 Imp gallons).

DIMENSIONS, EXTERNAL:
- Wing span: 22·00 m (72 ft 2¼ in)
- Wing aspect ratio: 26·59
- Length overall: 8·00 m (26 ft 3 in)
- Height over tail: 2·10 m (6 ft 10¾ in)
- Propeller diameter: 1·60 m (5 ft 3 in)

AREA:
- Wings, gross: 18·20 m² (195·9 sq ft)

WEIGHTS AND LOADINGS:
- Weight empty: 470 kg (1,036 lb)
- Max T-O weight: 700 kg (1,543 lb)
- Max wing loading: 38·46 kg/m² (7·88 lb/sq ft)
- Max power loading: 14·45 kg/kW (23·74 lb/hp)

PERFORMANCE, UNPOWERED (at max T-O weight except where indicated):
- *Best glide ratio at 55 knots (103 km/h; 64 mph): 42
- *Min rate of sink at 43 knots (80 km/h; 50 mph): 0·65 m (2·13 ft)/s

PERFORMANCE, POWERED (at max T-O weight except where indicated):
- Max level speed: 140 knots (260 km/h; 161 mph)
- Max cruising speed: 108 knots (200 km/h; 124 mph)
- *Stalling speed: 41 knots (75 km/h; 47 mph)
- Max rate of climb at S/L: 180 m (590 ft)/min
- Range with max fuel, no reserves: 540 nm (1,000 km; 621 miles)

**At AUW of 638 kg (1,406 lb)*

ROLLADEN-SCHNEIDER

ROLLADEN-SCHNEIDER FLUGZEUGBAU GmbH

Mühlstrasse 10 (Postfach 1130), 6073 Egelsbach/Hessen
Telephone: 06103 4126
OFFICERS: Walter Schneider and Dipl-Ing Wolf Lemke

Current activities are concerned with continuing manufacture of the LS4 and development of the LS6. Rolladen-Schneider's 1,000th sailplane, an LS4, was completed in 1981.

ROLLADEN-SCHNEIDER LS4

Design of this Standard Class sailplane began in the Winter of 1979/80, and the prototype (D-6680) flew for the first time on 28 March 1980. In the 1983 World Championships at Hobbs, New Mexico, USA, LS4s took 13 of the first 15 places in the Standard Class, including all of the first six places.

The LS4 utilises a modified LS3-a fuselage combined with a new, thin-section wing, mid-mounted on the fuselage. The **LS4-a** is identical except for an additional rubber spring on the monowheel (introduced also on the LS4 from mid-1983), and twin water ballast bag tanks in each wing, increasing the volume to 80-85 litres (17·6-18·7 Imp gallons) per wing.

A total of 550 LS4s and LS4-as had been built by February 1986.

TYPE: Single-seat Standard Class sailplane.

AIRFRAME: Cantilever mid-wing monoplane, of glassfibre/Conticell foam construction. Wings have thickness/chord ratio of 15% at root and 13% at tip (modified Wortmann sections), 3° 30' dihedral, and 0° incidence. Schempp-Hirth upper surface airbrakes. No flaps. Provision for 140 litres (30·8 Imp gallons) water ballast in wings on LS4, 160-170 litres (35·2-37·4 Imp gallons) on LS4-a. Semi-monocoque fuselage. Cantilever T tailplane, with elevator. Entire structure of GfK sandwich. Retractable Tost rubber sprung monowheel, tyre pressure 2·94 bars (43 lb/sq in); tailskid. Tost Kobold brake on mainwheel. Canopy hinged at front to open upward.

DIMENSIONS, EXTERNAL:
- Wing span: 15·00 m (49 ft 2½ in)
- Wing aspect ratio: 21·43
- Length overall: 6·83 m (22 ft 5 in)
- Height over tail: 1·26 m (4 ft 1½ in)

AREA:
- Wings, gross: 10·50 m² (113·0 sq ft)

WEIGHTS AND LOADINGS (A: LS4, B: LS4-a):
- Weight empty: A: 238 kg (525 lb)
  - B: 240 kg (529 lb)
- Max T-O weight: A: 472 kg (1,040 lb)
  - B: 525 kg (1,157 lb)
- Max wing loading: A: 44·9 kg/m² (9·21 lb/sq ft)
  - B: 50·0 kg/m² (10·25 lb/sq ft)

PERFORMANCE (at max T-O weight):
- Best glide ratio at 54 knots (100 km/h; 62 mph): 40·5
- Min rate of sink at 40 knots (75 km/h; 47 mph): 0·60 m (1·97 ft)/s
- Stalling speed: 37 knots (68 km/h; 43 mph)
- Max speed (smooth air):
  - A: 146 knots (270 km/h; 168 mph)
  - B: 151 knots (280 km/h; 174 mph)
- Max speed (rough air) and max aero-tow speed:
  - A: 97 knots (180 km/h; 112 mph)
  - B: 102 knots (190 km/h; 118 mph)
- Max winch-launching speed:
  - A: 70 knots (130 km/h; 81 mph)
  - B: 75 knots (140 km/h; 87 mph)
- *g* limits:
  - at 97 knots (180 km/h; 112 mph): +5·3/−2·65
  - at 146 knots (270 km/h; 168 mph): +4/−1·5

ROLLADEN-SCHNEIDER LS6

The LS6 is a successor to the LS3. Development had been started by the beginning of 1982, and the prototype (D-0662) flew for the first time on 1 December 1983. Series production began in August 1984. LS6s gained first, second and sixth places in the 1985 World Championships, held in Italy.

TYPE: 15 metre Class single-seat sailplane.

AIRFRAME: Cantilever mid-wing monoplane, constructed mainly of PVC foam and glassfibre. Wings have modified Wortmann sections, 4° dihedral, no sweep (forward or back), and carbonfibre spar caps. Ailerons and flaps are of Kevlar, glassfibre and Rohacell foam sandwich. Schempp-Hirth upper surface airbrakes. Water ballast tanks in wings. Glassfibre monocoque fuselage, with integral fin of PVC foam sandwich; Kevlar rudder. Fixed incidence T tailplane with elevator, built of PVC foam sandwich, carbonfibre and glassfibre. Rubber sprung (three element) Tost monowheel, as on LS4 but with new folding-strut retraction mechanism; choice of tailskid or 200 mm tailwheel. Tost Kobold mainwheel brake. One-piece Plexiglas canopy, hinged at front and opening upward; instrument panel opens with canopy.

DIMENSIONS, EXTERNAL:
- Wing span: 15·00 m (49 ft 2½ in)
- Wing aspect ratio: 21·43
- Length overall: 6·65 m (21 ft 9¾ in)
- Height over tail (with tailwheel): 1·30 m (4 ft 3¼ in)

AREA:
- Wings, gross: 10·50 m² (113·0 sq ft)

WEIGHTS AND LOADING:
- Weight empty: 250 kg (551 lb)
- Max water ballast: 180 kg (397 lb)
- Max T-O weight: 525 kg (1,157 lb)
- Max wing loading: 50·0 kg/m² (10·25 lb/sq ft)

PERFORMANCE:
- Best glide ratio: more than 40
- Min rate of sink: less than 0·60 m (1·97 ft)/s
- Max speed (smooth air): 151 knots (280 km/h; 174 mph)
- Stalling speed: 36 knots (65 km/h; 41 mph)

SCHEIBE

SCHEIBE FLUGZEUGBAU GmbH

HEAD OFFICE AND WORKS: August-Pfaltz-Strasse 23, Postfach 1829, 8060 Dachau, near Munich
Telephone: 08131 72083 and 72084
Telex: 05 26 650
MANAGERS: Dipl-Ing Egon Scheibe and Ing Christian Gad

Scheibe Flugzeugbau GmbH was founded at the end of 1951 by Dipl-Ing Scheibe; its first type produced in quantity was the Mü-13E Bergfalke I.

Subsequently, Scheibe has built many new types of sailplane, and since 1957 has been a major producer of motor gliders in the Federal Republic of Germany. Principal production model in 1985-86 continued to be the SF-25C/C-2000 Falke; the SF-25E Super-Falke, SF-28A Tandem-Falke and SF-36 motor gliders, and the SF-34 sailplane, remain available, although production in recent years has been minimal.

Scheibe has built more than 2,000 aircraft of various types, in addition to many kits for home construction by amateurs. Gliders of Scheibe design are built under licence by gliding clubs as well as by foreign companies.

SCHEIBE SF-25C FALKE 86 (FALCON)

The SF-25C is an improved version of the SF-25B Falke, to which it is structurally similar. The primary difference is the use of a more powerful engine, giving an enhanced performance. Type certification was granted in September 1972.

By January 1985 a total of 386 SF-25C Falkes had been built by Scheibe, a further 50 were built under licence by Sportavia in Germany. Scheibe also produced 20 **SF-25C-S**, with Hoffmann feathering propellers, as detailed in earlier editions of *Jane's*.

Current models, known as **SF-25C Falke 86**, have the design improvements listed in the 1977-78 *Jane's*. With optional 59·5 kW (80 hp) Limbach engine, they are known as **SF-25C-2000**. Optional features include an additional exhaust outlet and a slower-turning propeller. With this installation the nominal noise level is reduced to less than 60 dB.

TYPE: Side by side two-seat motor glider, particularly suitable for basic and advanced training.

AIRFRAME: Cantilever low-wing monoplane. Forward swept wooden wings, with airbrakes and aerodynamically balanced ailerons. Fully folding wings optional. Fabric covered welded steel tube fuselage; forward section coated with laminated glassfibre. Wooden tail unit. Non-retractable rubber sprung monowheel with brake and aerodynamic fairing; steerable tailwheel; sprung outrigger stabilising wheel under each wing. Alternative twin-wheel main gear available optionally, with streamline wheel fairings.

POWER PLANT: One 48·5 kW (65 hp) Limbach SL 1700 EA modified Volkswagen engine (59·5 kW; 80 hp L 2000 EA in SF-25C-2000), driving a two-blade propeller. Feathering propeller optional. Electric starter. Fuel in single fuselage tank, capacity 55 litres (12·1 Imp gallons) standard, 80 litres (17·6 Imp gallons) optional.

SYSTEM: 12V electrical system.

DIMENSIONS, EXTERNAL:
- Wing span: 15·30 m (50 ft 2½ in)
- Wing aspect ratio: 12·86
- Length overall: 7·60 m (24 ft 11¼ in)
- Height over tail: 1·85 m (6 ft 0¾ in)

AREA:
- Wings, gross: 18·20 m² (195·9 sq ft)

WEIGHTS AND LOADINGS:
- Weight empty: approx 400 kg (882 lb)
- Max T-O weight: 650 kg (1,433 lb)
- Max wing loading: 35·71 kg/m² (7·32 lb/sq ft)
- Max power loading: C: 13·41 kg/kW (22·05 lb/hp)
  - C-2000: 10·89 kg/kW (17·91 lb/hp)

PERFORMANCE, UNPOWERED (at max T-O weight):
- Best glide ratio: 23-24
- Min rate of sink: approx 1·00 m (3·28 ft)/s

PERFORMANCE, POWERED (at max T-O weight):
- Max level speed: C: 97 knots (180 km/h; 112 mph)
  - C-2000: 102 knots (190 km/h; 118 mph)
- Max cruising speed: C: 86 knots (160 km/h; 99 mph)
  - C-2000: 92 knots (170 km/h; 106 mph)
- Stalling speed (both): 36 knots (65 km/h; 41 mph)
- Max rate of climb at S/L: C: 138 m (453 ft)/min
  - C-2000: 192 m (630 ft)/min
- Service ceiling: C: 5,000 m (16,400 ft)
- T-O run: C: approx 180 m (590 ft)
  - C-2000: approx 100 m (328 ft)
- Landing run: C: 100 m (328 ft)
- Range with max fuel (both): approx 378 nm (700 km; 435 miles)

Kuffner WK-1 prototype for the WK-1b two-seat motor glider

15 m Class Rolladen-Schneider LS6 *(Peter F. Selinger)*

Rolladen-Schneider LS4 Standard Class sailplane *(Peter F. Selinger)*

Scheibe SF-25C-2000 two-seat motor glider *(Peter F. Selinger)*

Retractable monowheel version of the Scheibe SF-36 *(Adolf Wilsch)*

First SF-34 to be completed by Hungarian workers at Scheibe's factory *(Peter F. Selinger)*

Scheibe SF-36 two-seat motor glider with twin-wheel main gear *(Peter F. Selinger)*

SCHEIBE SF-25E SUPER-FALKE

Developed from the SF-25C-S, the Super-Falke has increased wing span and a rubber sprung monowheel; a cabin heater is standard. Production aircraft have a tail-wheel and upper surface Schempp-Hirth airbrakes.

A 48·5 kW (65 hp) Limbach SL 1700 EA I engine is fitted, with a 12V battery and alternator for electric engine starting. Fuel capacity is 45 litres (9·9 Imp gallons).

The Super-Falke was flown for the first time in the Summer of 1974; 60 had been delivered by January 1983, but only three more had been completed by January 1986. Details of the SF-25E can be found in the 1985-86 and earlier editions of *Jane's*.

SCHEIBE SF-28A TANDEM-FALKE

The Tandem-Falke, as its name implies, is a further development of the Falke series of motor gliders in which the two seats are arranged in tandem. Design began in 1970, and the prototype (D-KAFJ) flew for the first time in May 1971, powered by a 33·5 kW (45 hp) Stamo MS 1500 engine. Details of the production version have appeared in the 1985-86 and earlier editions of *Jane's*. Production had totalled 118 by January 1983, but only two more examples have been completed since that time.

SCHEIBE SF-34 DELPHIN (DOLPHIN)

Design of the SF-34 sailplane began in 1978, and it flew for the first time on 28 October that year. Twenty had been completed by the beginning of 1985; one more had been built by January 1986.

TYPE: Tandem two-seat training and sporting sailplane.

AIRFRAME: Cantilever mid-wing monoplane. Wortmann wing sections: FX-61-184 at root, FX-60-126 at tip. Glassfibre roving main spar. Wings and tail unit of GfK honeycomb sandwich; fuselage is a GfK shell. Schempp-Hirth airbrake in upper surface of each wing. Non-retractable semi-exposed monowheel and nosewheel, tyre sizes 5·00-4 and 265 × 85 respectively; tailskid. Tandem seats under frameless one-piece sideways opening flush canopy. Towing hooks under nose and at CG.

DIMENSIONS, EXTERNAL:
- Wing span: 15·80 m (51 ft 10 in)
- Wing aspect ratio: 16·87
- Length overall: 7·50 m (24 ft 7¼ in)
- Height over tail: 1·50 m (4 ft 11 in)

AREA:
- Wings, gross: 14·80 m² (159·3 sq ft)

WEIGHTS AND LOADING:
- Weight empty: 320 kg (705 lb)
- Max T-O weight: 540 kg (1,190 lb)
- Max wing loading: 36·5 kg/m² (7·48 lb/sq ft)

PERFORMANCE (at max T-O weight):
- Best glide ratio at 51 knots (95 km/h; 59 mph): 35
- Min rate of sink at 41 knots (75 km/h; 47 mph): 0·70 m (2·30 ft)/s
- Stalling speed: 36 knots (65 km/h; 41 mph)
- Max speed (rough and smooth air): 135 knots (250 km/h; 155 mph)
- Max aero-tow speed: 88 knots (163 km/h; 101 mph)
- Max winch-launching speed: 67 knots (125 km/h; 78 mph)

SCHEIBE SF-36

A prototype of this two-seat motor glider (D-KOOP) was flown for the first time in the Summer of 1980; production began in January 1981, and five had been completed by January 1983. Only one further example has been built since then.

TYPE: Side by side two-seat motor glider.

AIRFRAME: Cantilever low-wing monoplane of GfK construction, utilising wings and tail unit of SF-34 sailplane. Dihedral 1° 30′. Wings detachable for transportation and storage. Twin-wheel main landing gear similar to that of SF-25C Falke 86, or single mainwheel plus underwing outriggers. Forward sliding cockpit canopy. Baggage space aft of seats.

POWER PLANT: One 59·5 kW (80 hp) Limbach L 2000 EI engine, driving a two-blade fixed-pitch propeller. Feathering propeller optional. Fuel capacity 55 litres (12 Imp gallons).

DIMENSIONS, EXTERNAL:
- Wing span: 16·35 m (53 ft 7¾ in)

Wing aspect ratio 17·14
Length overall 7·18 m (23 ft 6¾ in)
Height over tail 1·50 m (4 ft 11 in)

AREA:
Wings, gross 15·60 m² (167·9 sq ft)

WEIGHTS AND LOADINGS:
Weight empty 500 kg (1,102 lb)
Max T-O weight 715 kg (1,576 lb)
Max wing loading 45·8 kg/m² (9·38 lb/sq ft)
Max power loading 11·98 kg/kW (19·7 lb/hp)

PERFORMANCE, UNPOWERED (at max T-O weight):
Best glide ratio at 51 knots (95 km/h; 59 mph) 29
Min rate of sink at 49 knots (90 km/h; 56 mph) 0·90 m (2·95 ft)/s
Stalling speed 41 knots (75 km/h; 47 mph)
Max speed (rough and smooth air) 113 knots (210 km/h; 130 mph)

PERFORMANCE, POWERED (at max T-O weight):
Max and econ cruising speed 97 knots (180 km/h; 112 mph)
Stalling speed 39 knots (72 km/h; 45 mph)
Max rate of climb at S/L 180 m (590 ft)/min
Service ceiling 6,000 m (19,675 ft)
T-O run 200 m (656 ft)
Landing run 150 m (492 ft)
Endurance 4-5 h

SCHEMPP-HIRTH

SCHEMPP-HIRTH FLUGZEUGBAU GmbH

Krebenstrasse 25, Postfach 143, 7312 Kirchheim-Teck
Telephone: 07021 2441 and 6097
Telex: 7267817 hate
DIRECTOR: Dipl-Ing Klaus Holighaus

Schempp-Hirth specialises in the production of high-performance Open Class and 15 metre Class sailplanes. Dipl-Ing Klaus Holighaus is 100% shareholder.

Production of the Schempp-Hirth Standard Cirrus is undertaken by Jastreb in Yugoslavia (which see).

The 'Oehler system' power plant installation, described under the Ventus heading, is also available for the Janus C and Nimbus 3/24·5.

SCHEMPP-HIRTH NIMBUS 3

The prototype Nimbus 3 (D-2111) flew for the first time on 21 February 1981. Nimbus 3s took the first three places in the Open Class of the 1981 World Championships, first two places in the 1982 European Championships, and eight of the first ten places (including all of the first six) at the 1983 World Championships. At the 1985 World Championships, held in Italy, Nimbus 3s took the first six places.

A **Nimbus 3/24·5** version, with add-on wingtip extensions, is also available; a total of nearly 100 (both versions) had been completed by early 1986. Nimbus 3s fitted with the Oehler power plant system (see Ventus entry) are designated **Nimbus 3T** (for Turbo). The two-seat **Nimbus 3D** is described separately.

TYPE: Single-seat Open Class sailplane.

AIRFRAME: Cantilever mid-wing monoplane. Four-piece (six on 3/24·5), thin section (Wortmann/Holighaus) wings, with 14% thickness/chord ratio, fitted with ailerons, trailing-edge flaps, Schempp-Hirth upper surface airbrakes, and inboard/outboard leading-edge tanks for up to 280 litres (61·5 Imp gallons) of water ballast. Turned-down wingtips. Cantilever T tailplane, with elevators. Forward fuselage is a glassfibre shell; rear fuselage of carbonfibre, reinforced by GfK/foam sandwich webs. Wing shells of carbonfibre/foam sandwich, with carbonfibre spar caps and GfK/foam sandwich shear webs. Carbonfibre/GfK/foam sandwich tailplane, with CF/GfK elevators; CF/foam sandwich fin, with GfK/foam sandwich rudder. Fully retractable monowheel, with shock absorption; tail bumper. One-piece canopy, opening sideways.

DIMENSIONS, EXTERNAL:
Wing span: 3 22·90 m (75 ft 1½ in)
3/24·5 24·50 m (80 ft 4½ in)
Wing aspect ratio: 3 32·17
3/24·5 35·94
Length overall 7·63 m (25 ft 0½ in)
Height over tail 1·55 m (5 ft 1 in)

AREAS:
Wings, gross: 3 16·30 m² (175·45 sq ft)
3/24·5 16·70 m² (179·76 sq ft)

WEIGHTS AND LOADINGS:
Weight empty: 3 392 kg (864 lb)
3/24·5 396 kg (873 lb)
Max T-O weight: 3 750 kg (1,653 lb)
3/24·5 700 kg (1,543 lb)
Max wing loading: 3 46·0 kg/m² (9·43 lb/sq ft)
3/24·5 41·9 kg/m² (8·59 lb/sq ft)

PERFORMANCE (at max T-O weight except where indicated):
Best glide ratio at 51 knots (95 km/h; 59 mph), wing loading of 29 kg/m² (5·94 lb/sq ft):
3 55
3/24·5 58
Min rate of sink at 40 knots (75 km/h; 47 mph):
3 0·44 m (1·44 ft)/s
3/24·5 0·41 m (1·35 ft)/s
Stalling speed: 3 33 knots (60 km/h; 38 mph)
3/24·5 32 knots (59 km/h; 37 mph)
Max speed (smooth air) 146 knots (270 km/h; 168 mph)
Max speed (rough air):
3 108 knots (200 km/h; 124 mph)
3/24·5 102 knots (190 km/h; 118 mph)
Max aero-tow speed 97 knots (180 km/h; 112 mph)
Max winch-launching speed 81 knots (150 km/h; 93 mph)
g limits at design manoeuvring speed +5·3/−2·65

SCHEMPP-HIRTH NIMBUS 3D

A prototype of this Open Class two-seater (D-KCJC) flew for the first time on 2 May 1986. It combines a modified Janus fuselage with the long-span Nimbus 3/24·5 wing and a reinforced main spar, has 2° of forward sweep at the leading-edge, and a small skid in place of the Janus nosewheel. Due to enter production in late 1986, the Nimbus 3D is fitted with a retractable dorsal power plant for self-launch capability.

TYPE: Open Class two-seat self-launching sailplane.

AIRFRAME: Cantilever mid-wing monoplane. Wortmann wing sections: FX-79-K-143/17 at root, FX-77-135/20 at tip. Dihedral 3°. Incidence 1° 30′. Wings, fuselage and tail unit otherwise generally as described for Nimbus 3, except that fuselage is entirely of carbon and aramid fibre, water ballast tanks (each of 84 litres; 18·5 Imp gallons capacity) are in outer wing panels only, and wingtips are not turned down. Retractable unsprung monowheel (tyre size 5·00-5, pressure 4·5 bars; 65 lb/sq in), with brake, plus tailskid. Two seats in tandem, under one-piece canopy which opens sideways to starboard.

POWER PLANT: One 19·4 kW (26 hp) Solo 2350 auxiliary engine, installed in retractable mounting aft of cockpit and driving an OE-FL 5·88/83 propeller with five foldable blades. Fuel in single fuselage tank, capacity 20 litres (4·4 Imp gallons).

DIMENSIONS, EXTERNAL:
Wing span 24·60 m (80 ft 8½ in)
Wing aspect ratio 35·91
Length overall 8·70 m (28 ft 6½ in)
Height over tail 1·39 m (4 ft 6¾ in)
Propeller diameter 0·88 m (2 ft 10¾ in)

AREA:
Wings, gross 16·85 m² (181·4 sq ft)

WEIGHTS AND LOADINGS (A: without/B: with, power plant):
Weight empty: A approx 460 kg (1,014 lb)
B approx 500 kg (1,102 lb)
Max water ballast 168 kg (370 lb)
Max T-O weight: A 750 kg (1,653 lb)
B 800 kg (1,763 lb)
Max wing loading: A 44·51 kg/m² (9·12 lb/sq ft)
B 47·48 kg/m² (9·73 lb/sq ft)
Max power loading: B 41·24 kg/kW (67·83 lb/hp)

PERFORMANCE, UNPOWERED (estimated at max T-O weight):
Best glide ratio at 62 knots (115 km/h; 71 mph) more than 55
Min rate of sink at 43 knots (80 km/h; 50 mph) 0·45 m (1·48 ft)/s
Stalling speed 41 knots (75 km/h; 47 mph)
Max speed (smooth air) 135 knots (250 km/h; 155 mph)
Max speed (rough air) 105 knots (195 km/h; 121 mph)
Max aero-tow speed 97 knots (180 km/h; 112 mph)
Max winch-launching speed 81 knots (150 km/h; 93 mph)
g limits +5·4/−3·4

PERFORMANCE, POWERED (estimated at max T-O weight):
Max cruising speed 67 knots (125 km/h; 78 mph)
Econ cruising speed 49 knots (90 km/h; 56 mph)
Stalling speed 42 knots (78 km/h; 49 mph)
Max rate of climb at S/L 42 m (138 ft)/min
Range with max fuel 135 nm (250 km; 155 miles)

SCHEMPP-HIRTH JANUS

The Janus design was started by Dipl-Ing Holighaus in 1969, and the prototype made its first flight in the Spring of 1974.

Production began in January 1975 with the second, improved aircraft; a **Janus B** version became available in March 1978, with fixed incidence tailplane; the **Janus C** has 20 m span carbonfibre wings and a carbonfibre tailplane. At the end of 1985 Janus C sailplanes held FAI records for distance in a straight line, distance to a fixed goal, out and return distance to a goal, and speed around triangular courses of 100 km and 300 km.

The **Janus CM** powered version of the C, first flown in 1978, has a 45 kW (60 hp) watercooled engine, pylon mounted aft of the cockpit and retracting rearward into the top of the fuselage when not in use. Empty and max T-O weights are 465 kg (1,025 lb) and 700 kg (1,543 lb) respectively. This version holds world records in FAI Class DM-2 for multi-seat motor gliders for out and return distance to a goal, and speed over triangular courses of 300 and 500 km. The **Janus CT** is similar, but has the Oehler system power installation described under the Ventus entry.

By early 1986 production totalled 225 Janus, Janus B, Janus C, Janus CM and Janus CT, including 24 of the CM version.

The following description applies to the standard Janus B, except where indicated:

TYPE: Tandem two-seat high-performance training sailplane.

AIRFRAME: Cantilever mid-wing monoplane. Wortmann wing sections: FX-67-K-170 at root, FX-67-K-15 at tip. Dihedral 4°. Sweepforward 2° on leading-edge. Glassfibre/foam sandwich wings, with glassfibre monocoque ailerons, trailing-edge flaps and Schempp-Hirth upper surface airbrakes. Ailerons and flaps interconnected. Glassfibre fuselage shell, with bonded-in foam bulkheads, on a welded steel tube central frame. Cantilever glassfibre/foam sandwich fixed incidence T tailplane, with elevator. Non-retractable semi-recessed monowheel (diameter 380 mm) and nosewheel. Continental tyres: pressure 2·69 bars (39 lb/sq in) on mainwheel; pressure 0·79 bars (11·5 lb/sq in) on nosewheel. Tost drum brake on mainwheel. Bumper under rear fuselage. Jettisonable tail drag-chute. One-piece canopy opens sideways to starboard. Provision for 200 kg (440 lb) of water ballast.

DIMENSIONS, EXTERNAL:
Wing span: B 18·20 m (59 ft 8½ in)
C 20·00 m (65 ft 7½ in)
Wing aspect ratio: B 19·95
C 22·99
Length overall 8·62 m (28 ft 3¼ in)
Height over tail 1·45 m (4 ft 9 in)

AREAS:
Wings, gross: B 16·60 m² (178·7 sq ft)
C 17·40 m² (187·3 sq ft)

WEIGHTS AND LOADINGS:
Weight empty: B 365 kg (805 lb)
C 355 kg (783 lb)
Max T-O weight: B 620 kg (1,366 lb)
C 700 kg (1,543 lb)
Max wing loading: B 37·0 kg/m² (7·58 lb/sq ft)
C 40·0 kg/m² (8·20 lb/sq ft)

PERFORMANCE (at max T-O weight except where indicated):
Best glide ratio at wing loading of 36·5 kg/m² (7·48 lb/sq ft) and speed of 59 knots (110 km/h; 68 mph):
B 39·5
C 43·5
Min rate of sink at above wing loading and speed of 49 knots (90 km/h; 56 mph):
B 0·70 m (2·30 ft)/s
C 0·60 m (1·97 ft)/s
Stalling speed at above wing loading:
B, C 38 knots (70 km/h; 43 mph)
Max speed (rough and smooth air):
B 118 knots (220 km/h; 136 mph)
C 135 knots (250 km/h; 155 mph)
Max aero-tow speed:
B 91 knots (170 km/h; 105 mph)
C 97 knots (180 km/h; 112 mph)
Max winch-launching speed:
B 65 knots (120 km/h; 75 mph)
C 81 knots (150 km/h; 93 mph)
g limits: B, C +5·3/−2·65

SCHEMPP-HIRTH VENTUS

First flown on 3 May 1980, the Ventus (Latin for wind) features a thin section carbonfibre wing. It is available with a choice of two fuselages, the Ventus b having a slightly larger cockpit for pilots more than 1·75 m (5 ft 9 in) tall.

Ventus sailplanes took third, fourth and seventh places in their class at the 1981 World Championships; first three places in the 1982 European Championships; and six of the first ten places (including first place) in the 1983 World Championships.

In 1982 Schempp-Hirth introduced the **Ventus b/16·6**, with detachable CFRP/GfK wingtip extensions, for Open Class competition.

In 1981, a Ventus was fitted experimentally by Herr Claus Oehler with a 7·5 kW (10 hp) two-cylinder piston engine, driving a small-diameter propeller with five folding blades. Mounted aft of the cockpit and retracting rearward into the upper centre-fuselage, this installation added only 25-35 kg (55-77 lb) to the aircraft's weight. Using a 9 kW (12 hp) or 13·5 kW (18 hp) engine and 15 litre (3·3 Imp gallon) fuel tank, this installation became available in 1982 on the Ventus b/16·6, which is then known as the **Ventus b/T**. Engine and wingtips are readily removable for reversion to 15 metre Class flying.

Ventus production (all versions) totalled 280 by early 1986. The following description applies to the standard Ventus a/b except where indicated:

TYPE: Single-seat 15 metre Class sailplane.

AIRFRAME: Cantilever mid-wing monoplane, with newly developed Wortmann/Holighaus/Althaus thin-section wings of all-carbonfibre construction, including skins. Two-segment ailerons. Schempp-Hirth trailing-edge flaps/airbrakes. Fuselage centre frame of steel tube to carry main wing and landing gear loads. Cantilever fixed incidence T tailplane, with elevator; rudder area increased on Ventus b. Retractable monowheel; tail

Schempp-Hirth Nimbus 3/24·5 venting water ballast *(Peter F. Selinger)*

Prototype Schempp-Hirth Nimbus 3D, first flown in May 1986 *(Peter F. Selinger)*

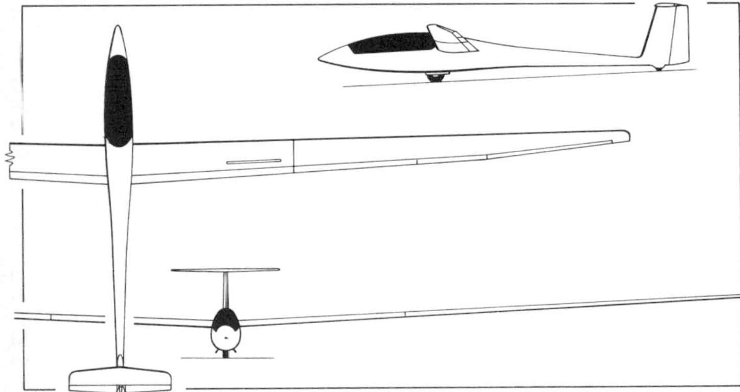

Schempp-Hirth's new Open Class two-seater, the Nimbus 3D *(Michael A. Badrocke)*

Schempp-Hirth Janus C *(Peter F. Selinger)*

Schempp-Hirth Ventus b *(Peter F. Selinger)*

Janus CM, with 45 kW (60 hp) power plant installation *(Peter F. Selinger)*

Schempp-Hirth Discus a Standard Class sailplane *(Peter F. Selinger)*

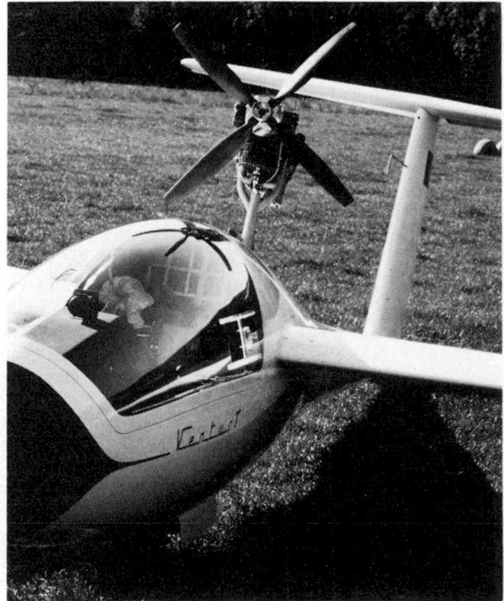

Ventus b/T with Webra engine *(Peter F. Selinger)*

bumper. One-piece cockpit canopy, opening sideways to starboard. Provision for 150 kg (331 lb) of water ballast.

DIMENSIONS, EXTERNAL:
- Wing span: a/b — 15·00 m (49 ft 2½ in)
- b/16·6 — 16·60 m (54 ft 5½ in)
- Wing aspect ratio: a/b — 23·66
- b/16·6 — 27·67
- Length overall (all versions) — 6·35 m (20 ft 10 in)
- Height overall (all versions) — 1·27 m (4 ft 2 in)

AREAS:
- Wings, gross: a/b — 9·51 m² (102·4 sq ft)
- b/16·6 — 9·96 m² (107·2 sq ft)

WEIGHTS AND LOADINGS:
- Weight empty: a/b — 220 kg (485 lb)
- b/16·6 — 223 kg (492 lb)
- Max T-O weight:
  - a/b and b/16·6 — 430 kg (948 lb)
- Max wing loading: a/b — 45·2 kg/m² (9·26 lb/sq ft)
- b/16·6 — 43·2 kg/m² (8·85 lb/sq ft)

PERFORMANCE, UNPOWERED (at max T-O weight except where indicated):
- Best glide ratio at wing loading of 35 kg/m² (7·17 lb/sq ft):
  - a/b at 56 knots (105 km/h; 65 mph) — 44
  - b/16·6 at 48 knots (90 km/h; 56 mph) — 46·5
- Min rate of sink at 41 knots (75 km/h; 47 mph):
  - a/b — 0·58 m (1·90 ft)/s
  - b/16·6 — 0·56 m (1·84 ft)/s
- Stalling speed: a/b — 36 knots (65 km/h; 41 mph)
- b/16·6 — 35 knots (64 km/h; 40 mph)
- Max speed (smooth air, all versions) — 135 knots (250 km/h; 155 mph)
- Max speed (rough air, all versions) — 108 knots (200 km/h; 124 mph)
- Max aero-tow speed (all versions) — 97 knots (180 km/h; 112 mph)
- Max winch-launching speed (all versions) — 81 knots (150 km/h; 93 mph)
- *g* limits at design manoeuvring speed — +5·3/−2·65

PERFORMANCE, POWERED (Ventus b/T):
- Max cruising speed — approx 70 knots (130 km/h; 81 mph)
- Rate of climb (depending upon altitude and ambient temperature) — 38-68 m (125-225 ft)/min
- Range (combining powered climbs and engine-off glides) — more than 108 nm (201 km; 125 miles)

SCHEMPP-HIRTH DISCUS

Nearly 100 production examples of this Standard Class sailplane had been built by early 1986, in two versions. The first prototype, **Discus a** (D-6111), flew for the first time on 21 April 1984 and the second prototype, **Discus b** (D-8111), made its initial flight on 17 May 1984. The Discus a utilises the fuselage and tail unit of the 15 metre Class Ventus a. The Discus b has the longer fuselage of the Ventus b, incorporating a roomier cockpit.

Discus sailplanes of both versions took five of the first six places at the 1985 World Championships held at Rieti, Italy.

TYPE: Single-seat Standard Class sailplane.

AIRFRAME: Cantilever mid-wing monoplane, with 3° dihedral. No details have been released of the wing aerofoil section. Boundary layer control is achieved with lower surface turbulator strips. Kinked, sweptback leading-edges on outer sections. Centre-section is unswept, with constant chord. The wings are of GRP with a carbonfibre main spar, and have inboard and smaller outboard ailerons of GRP (the latter deflecting upward only), plus Schempp-Hirth upper surface airbrakes. Fuselage and tail unit as described for Ventus a/b. Retractable rubber sprung monowheel (tyre size 4·00-4, pressure 4·41 bars; 64 lb/sq in), with drum brake; fixed rubber tailskid. Provision for 184 litres (40·5 Imp gallons) of water ballast.

DIMENSIONS, EXTERNAL:
Wing span (both) 15·00 m (49 ft 2½ in)
Wing aspect ratio (both) 21·27
Length overall: a 6·35 m (20 ft 10 in)
b 6·58 m (21 ft 7 in)
Height over tail (both) 1·27 m (4 ft 2 in)

AREA:
Wings, gross (both) 10·58 m² (113·9 sq ft)

WEIGHTS AND LOADING:
Weight empty: a 228 kg (502 lb)
b 233 kg (514 lb)
Max T-O weight (both) 525 kg (1,157 lb)
Max wing loading (both) 49·62 kg/m² (10·16 lb/sq ft)

PERFORMANCE (both versions, at max T-O weight):
Best glide ratio at 54 knots (100 km/h; 62 mph) 42·2
Min rate of sink at 42 knots (78 km/h; 49 mph) 0·58 m (1·90 ft)/s
Stalling speed 36 knots (66 km/h; 41 mph)
Max speed (smooth air) 135 knots (250 km/h; 155 mph)
Max speed (rough air) 108 knots (200 km/h; 124 mph)
Max aero-tow speed 97 knots (180 km/h; 112 mph)
Max winch-launching speed 81 knots (150 km/h; 93 mph)
g limits +5·3/−2·65

SCHLEICHER

ALEXANDER SCHLEICHER GmbH & Co

HEAD OFFICE AND WORKS: Postfach 60, 6416 Poppenhausen/Wasserkuppe
Telephone: 06658 225

This company is one of the oldest manufacturers of sailplanes in the world. Its founder, Alexander Schleicher, won a contest for training sailplanes in 1927 at the Wasserkuppe. In the same year he built at Poppenhausen a small factory for manufacturing gliders, two of his best known pre-war products being the Rhönbussard and Rhönadler, designed by Hans Jacobs. Since its formation, the Schleicher company has built more than 4,800 wood/metal gliders and over 2,000 FRP sailplanes and motor gliders.

During the Second World War, the factory was engaged in the repair of Baby IIb sailplanes. For a time afterwards it became a furniture factory, but it began producing sailplanes once more in 1951. Those designed by Ing Rudolf Kaiser are prefixed ASK; those with ASW designations are designed by Ing Gerhard Waibel. An ASH prefix indicates the work of Schleicher's youngest designer, Martin Heide. Schleicher also manufactures and markets spare parts, constructional materials, and dust- and weatherproof covers for sailplanes.

SCHLEICHER ASK 13

Production of the ASK 13 by Schleicher, which totalled 603, has ended, but the ASK 13 is still being manufactured, under licence, by Jubi GmbH (which see).

SCHLEICHER ASW 19

This sailplane, which flew for the first time on 23 November 1975, is essentially an improved version of the ASW 15 B (1977-78 *Jane's*), from which it differs in having a T tail unit. Production began in the Spring of 1976, and more than 400 had been built by the beginning of 1986, when production was terminated. This total includes five delivered in 1983 to the UK Air Cadets, by whom they are known as the **Valiant**.

Full details of the Standard and Club Class versions of the ASW 19 can be found in the 1985-86 *Jane's*.

SCHLEICHER ASW 20, 20 B and 20 C

The ASW 20 was designed to take advantage of the March 1975 CIVV regulations for unlimited 15 metre sailplanes, and is fitted with trailing-edge flaps as well as large upper surface spoilers. It has an additional high-drag flap range incorporating a special mechanism to eliminate pitch and airspeed changes when changing flap position.

The prototype ASW 20 made its first flight on 29 January 1977, and approx 495 had been built by Schleicher by the beginning of 1986.

Current production models are designated ASW 20 B and ASW 20 C, the former having a reinforced wing structure enabling it to carry more water ballast in good soaring conditions. Seven ASW 20 B prototypes took part in the 1983 World Championships, taking 2nd, 3rd, 6th and 10th places in the 15 m Class. The B and C models differ from the original ASW 20 in having a modified wing undersurface with lower drag and DFVLR patented 'turbulators' (see ASW 22 entry for description) which smooth out the airflow in the area of the flap hinges. Other improvements include metal foil sealing of the wing control surfaces (optional), automatic elevator connection, disc (instead of drum) brake, and instrument panel hinged to open with the canopy. These modifications also apply to the BL and CL models, described separately.

Recent successes include 3rd, 4th, 5th and 6th places in the 1986 Australian nationals (ASW 20), 3rd place in the 1985 World Championships (ASW 20 B), and 1st and 2nd in the 1986 South African nationals (ASW 20 B). The following details apply to the ASW 20 B and C:

TYPE: Single-seat 15 metre Class sailplane.

AIRFRAME: Cantilever mid-wing monoplane. Wing sections Wortmann FX-63-131-K (modified DFVLR/Horstmann-Quast) at root, Wortmann FX-60-126 at tip. Dihedral 2° 20′. No sweepforward at quarter-chord. Glassfibre roving wing main spar. Wings of GRP/hard foam sandwich, with leading-edge bag tanks for water ballast. Schempp-Hirth metal airbrakes in upper surface. GRP monocoque fuselage. Cantilever T tail and elevator, with new Wortmann aerofoil sections. Five-position trailing-edge wing flaps (travel −12° to +40°). Ailerons are linked with flaps, and are automatically deflected upward when 'flaps down' is selected for landing. All control surfaces are of aramid/GRP, and are partly mass balanced. Retractable sprung monowheel, size 5·00-5, with hydraulic disc brake. Rubber tailskid with wear plate is standard; optional fit of tailskid with polyamid roller, or fixed 210 × 65 mm tailwheel with pneumatic tyre and fairing. One-piece Plexiglas canopy, hinged at front and opening upward, can be jettisoned in emergency. Tost towing hook at CG. Options include oxygen bottle, barograph, battery and headrest.

DIMENSIONS, EXTERNAL:
Wing span 15·00 m (49 ft 2½ in)
Wing aspect ratio 21·43
Length overall 6·82 m (22 ft 4½ in)
Height over tail 1·45 m (4 ft 9 in)

AREA:
Wings, gross 10·50 m² (113·0 sq ft)

WEIGHTS AND LOADINGS:
Weight empty: B 260 kg (573 lb)
C 250 kg (551 lb)
Max water ballast: B 160 kg (352 lb)
C 120 kg (264 lb)
Max T-O weight with water ballast:
B 525 kg (1,157 lb)
C 454 kg (1,001 lb)
Max wing loading: B 50·00 kg/m² (10·25 lb/sq ft)
C 43·24 kg/m² (8·86 lb/sq ft)

PERFORMANCE (at max T-O weight except where indicated):
Best glide ratio:
B (without ballast) at 54 knots (100 km/h; 62 mph) 42·5
B (with ballast) at 65 knots (120 km/h; 75 mph) 43
C (without ballast) at 54 knots (100 km/h; 62 mph) 42
C (with ballast) at 62 knots (115 km/h; 71 mph) 42
Min rate of sink:
B and C (without ballast) at 45 knots (84 km/h; 52 mph) 0·59 m (1·93 ft)/s
C (with ballast) at 52 knots (96 km/h; 60 mph) 0·68 m (2·23 ft)/s
Stalling speed (without ballast):
B, C 35 knots (65 km/h; 41 mph)
Max speed (smooth air):
B 151 knots (280 km/h; 174 mph)
C 143 knots (265 km/h; 165 mph)
Max speed (rough air):
B 103 knots (191 km/h; 118 mph)
C 143 knots (265 km/h; 165 mph)
Max aero-tow speed:
B 103 knots (191 km/h; 118 mph)
C 97 knots (180 km/h; 112 mph)
Max winch-launching speed:
B 70 knots (129 km/h; 80 mph)
C 67 knots (125 km/h; 78 mph)
g limits:
B at 103 knots (191 km/h; 118 mph), C (without ballast) at 94 knots (174 km/h; 108 mph) +5·3/−2·65
B at 151 knots (280 km/h; 174 mph), C (without ballast) at 143 knots (265 km/h; 165 mph) +4/−1·5

SCHLEICHER ASW 20 L, 20 BL and 20 CL

The ASW 20 L (for Lang: long), first flown in May 1977, is a version of the ASW 20 with detachable outer wing panels, increasing the span to 16·59 m (54 ft 5¼ in) for Open Class competition. Production began in late 1978, and approx 245 had been built by the beginning of 1986. Current models are the ASW 20 BL and CL, to which the following data apply:

TYPE: Single-seat Open Class sailplane.

AIRFRAME: Generally as for ASW 20 B and C except for wings, which have detachable span-increasing outer panels. Reduced water ballast in BL, no provision for water ballast in CL.

DIMENSIONS, EXTERNAL: As ASW 20 B and C except:
Wing span 16·59 m (54 ft 5¼ in)
Wing aspect ratio 24·91

AREA:
Wings, gross 11·05 m² (118·9 sq ft)

WEIGHTS AND LOADINGS:
Weight empty: BL 265 kg (584 lb)
CL 255 kg (562 lb)
Max water ballast: BL 50 kg (110 lb)
Max T-O weight: BL 430 kg (948 lb)
CL 380 kg (837 lb)
Max wing loading: BL 38·91 kg/m² (7·97 lb/sq ft)
CL 34·39 kg/m² (7·05 lb/sq ft)

PERFORMANCE (at max T-O weight except where indicated):
Best glide ratio at 48 knots (90 km/h; 56 mph):
BL (without ballast) and CL 45
Min rate of sink at 43 knots (80 km/h; 50 mph):
BL (without ballast) and CL 0·56 m (1·83 ft)/s
Stalling speed:
BL (without ballast) and CL 35 knots (64 km/h; 40 mph)
Max speed (smooth air):
BL, CL 135 knots (250 km/h; 155 mph)
Max speed (rough air):
BL 97 knots (180 km/h; 112 mph)
CL 89 knots (165 km/h; 103 mph)
Max aero-tow speed:
BL 89 knots (165 km/h; 103 mph)
CL 86 knots (160 km/h; 99 mph)
Max winch-launching speed:
BL 70 knots (130 km/h; 80 mph)
CL 65 knots (120 km/h; 75 mph)
g limits:
BL at 97 knots (180 km/h; 112 mph) +5·3/−2·65
CL at 89 knots (165 km/h; 103 mph) +5·3/−2·65

SCHLEICHER ASK 21

Designed by Ing Kaiser, the ASK 21 prototype flew for the first time on 6 February 1979; it received LBA certification on 18 April 1980. Approx 290 had been built by the beginning of 1986, including ten in 1983 for the UK Air Cadets, by whom they are known as the **Vanguard**.

TYPE: Tandem two-seat competition and training sailplane.

AIRFRAME: Cantilever mid-wing monoplane. Two-piece wings, primarily of GfK/foam sandwich construction with GfK roving spar. Wortmann wing sections: FX-S-02-196 from root to inboard of ailerons, FX-60-126 at tip. Dihedral 4°. Sweepforward at quarter-chord 1° 30′. Schempp-Hirth upper surface metal airbrakes. GfK/honeycomb sandwich fuselage. Fixed T tailplane and separate elevator; rudder and elevator partly mass-balanced. Non-retractable semi-recessed nosewheel (size 4·00-4) and rubber sprung monowheel (size 5·00-5), the latter with hydraulic disc brake; steel shod rubber tailskid standard, pneumatic tailwheel (210 × 65 mm) optional. Front and rear canopies hinged at front and rear respectively, both opening upward.

DIMENSIONS, EXTERNAL:
Wing span 17·00 m (55 ft 9¼ in)
Wing aspect ratio 16·10
Length overall 8·35 m (27 ft 4¾ in)
Height over tail 1·55 m (5 ft 1 in)

AREA:
Wings, gross 17·95 m² (193·2 sq ft)

WEIGHTS AND LOADING:
Weight empty 360 kg (794 lb)
Max T-O weight 600 kg (1,323 lb)
Max wing loading 33·4 kg/m² (6·84 lb/sq ft)

PERFORMANCE (carrying pilot only):
Best glide ratio at 46 knots (85 km/h; 53 mph) 34
Min rate of sink at 36 knots (67 km/h; 42 mph) 0·65 m (2·13 ft)/s
Stalling speed 34 knots (62 km/h; 39 mph)
Max speed (smooth air) 151 knots (280 km/h; 174 mph)
Max speed (rough air) 135 knots (250 km/h; 155 mph)
Max aero-tow speed 94 knots (175 km/h; 109 mph)
Max winch-launching speed 70 knots (130 km/h; 81 mph)
g limits at 97 knots (180 km/h; 112 mph) +6·5/−4

SCHLEICHER ASW 22 and 22 B

Extensive use is made of composite materials in the construction of this Open Class sailplane, which has combined flaps/airbrakes similar to those fitted to the ASW 20. A special feature of the wing design is the provision of about 1,000 tubular apertures ('turbulators') in the underside, over 17 m (55 ft 9¼ in) of the span, through which air can be vented to provide a form of boundary layer control and improve performance at the upper end of the speed range.

Design of the ASW 22 began in 1979, and the prototype (D-7122) flew for the first time on 4 July 1981. ASW 22s took seventh and eighth places in the 1983 World Championships of that year, and came first and third in the 1986 Australian nationals. Production ended in July 1985, a total of 39 having been completed, all with 22 m (72 ft 2¼ in) span wings. A description can be found in the 1985-86 *Jane's*.

In January 1986 Schleicher began building a prototype of a new **ASW 22 B** version, with wing span increased from 22 to 25 metres and other improvements including a new HQ17 aerofoil section on the inner wings. This has now replaced the original model in production. The description which follows applies to the ASW 22 B:

TYPE: Single-seat Open Class sailplane.

AIRFRAME: Cantilever mid-wing monoplane. Wing sections DFVLR-HQ17 at root, Delft University DU84-132 V3 at tip. Dihedral 3° 30′. Incidence 5°. Sweepback 0° 48′ on

Schleicher ASW 20 C Open Class sailplane *(Peter F. Selinger)*

Schleicher ASK 21 tandem two-seat sailplane *(Peter F. Selinger)*

Schleicher ASW 22 B 25 metre span Open Class sailplane

Schleicher ASW 20 FP built in France by Centrair *(Peter F. Selinger)*

Schleicher ASW 22 Open Class sailplane

Schleicher ASK 23 training and performance sailplane

outer panels only. Main wing structure of carbonfibre/epoxy (90 per cent) and GfK (10 per cent). Trailing-edge flaps and ailerons are of Kevlar construction. Schempp-Hirth aluminium upper surface airbrakes. Monocoque fuselage of carbon/aramid/glass FRP. Cantilever T tail with carbonfibre/epoxy sandwich tailplane, AfK sandwich fin, and Kevlar sandwich elevator and rudder. Main landing gear is a twin-wheel (size 5·00-5) retractable unit, both with rubber shock absorption and one with Cleveland hydraulic disc brake. Foam rubber tailskid, with wear plate, is standard; non-retractable tailwheel (size 210 × 65 mm) is optional. Tost CG towing hook, covered in flight by landing gear doors. Four 60 litre (13·2 Imp gallon) water ballast tanks in wing leading-edges. One-piece jettisonable canopy, hinged at front to open upward.

DIMENSIONS, EXTERNAL:
- Wing span 25·00 m (82 ft 0¼ in)
- Wing aspect ratio 38·32
- Length overall 8·10 m (26 ft 7 in)
- Height over tail 1·66 m (5 ft 5½ in)

AREA:
- Wings, gross 16·31 m² (175·6 sq ft)

WEIGHTS AND LOADING:
- Weight empty, equipped 450 kg (992 lb)
- Max water ballast 235 kg (518 lb)
- Max T-O weight 750 kg (1,653 lb)
- Max wing loading 45·98 kg/m² (9·42 lb/sq ft)

PERFORMANCE (estimated):
- *Best glide ratio at 51 knots (95 km/h; 59 mph) 60
- *Min rate of sink at 43 knots (80 km/h; 50 mph) 0·41 m (1·35 ft)/s
- *Stalling speed 35 knots (65 km/h; 41 mph)
- Max speed (smooth air) 151 knots (280 km/h; 174 mph)
- Max speed (rough air), and max aero-tow speed 102 knots (190 km/h; 118 mph)
- Max winch-launching speed 75 knots (140 km/h; 87 mph)
- *g* limits +5·3/−2·65

* *without ballast*

SCHLEICHER ASW 22 BE

Three prototypes of this motor glider version of the ASW 22 B are being built, construction having started in November 1985. First flight, by D-KKJP, took place on 22 March 1986.

AIRFRAME: As for ASW 22 B except for changes necessary to accommodate power plant, and two (instead of four) 60 litre (13·2 Imp gallon) water ballast tanks in wings.

POWER PLANT: One 31·6 kW (42·4 hp) Bombardier Rotax 505 engine, driving a two-blade propeller. Fuel in one fuselage and two inboard wing tanks, combined capacity 70 litres (15·4 Imp gallons).

DIMENSIONS, EXTERNAL: As ASW 22 B, plus:
- Propeller diameter 1·58 m (5 ft 2¼ in)

WEIGHTS AND LOADINGS:
- Weight empty, equipped 510 kg (1,124 lb)
- Max water ballast 120 kg (264 lb)
- Max T-O weight 750 kg (1,653 lb)
- Max wing loading 45·98 kg/m² (9·42 lb/sq ft)
- Max power loading 23·73 kg/kW (38·99 lb/hp)

PERFORMANCE, UNPOWERED (estimated): As ASW 22 B, except:
- *Best glide ratio at 59 knots (110 km/h; 68 mph) 60
- *Min rate of sink at 46 knots (85 km/h; 53 mph) 0·46 m (1·51 ft)/s
- *Stalling speed 41 knots (76 km/h; 48 mph)

* *without ballast*

PERFORMANCE, POWERED (estimated):
- Max cruising speed 92 knots (170 km/h; 106 mph)
- Econ cruising speed (alternate climbing/gliding profile) 49 knots (90 km/h; 56 mph)
- Stalling speed 44 knots (80 km/h; 50 mph)
- Max rate of climb at S/L 132 m (433 ft)/min
- T-O run 200 m (656 ft)
- Range with max fuel 431 nm (800 km; 497 miles)

SCHLEICHER AS 22-2

Schleicher built this two-seat version of the ASW 22 originally for record attempts by pilot Erwin Müller. It flew for the first time on 29 September 1984, and was described and illustrated in the 1985-86 *Jane's*. It is currently serving as prototype for the new ASH 25 (which see).

DIMENSIONS, EXTERNAL, AND WING AREA: As in 1985-86 *Jane's*

WEIGHTS AND LOADING:
- Weight empty 440 kg (970 lb)
- Max water ballast 120 kg (264 lb)
- Max T-O weight 750 kg (1,653 lb)
- Max wing loading 48·4 kg/m² (9·91 lb/sq ft)

PERFORMANCE (estimated at max T-O weight):
- Best glide ratio at 56 knots (104 km/h; 65 mph) over 55
- Min rate of sink at 44 knots (82 km/h; 51 mph) 0·46 m (1·51 ft)/s
- Stalling speed (2-seat) 41 knots (76 km/h; 48 mph)
- Max speed (smooth air) 135 knots (250 km/h; 155 mph)

Max speed (rough air), and max aero-tow speed
92 knots (170 km/h; 105 mph)
Max winch-launching speed
70 knots (130 km/h; 80 mph)
g limits +5·94/−3·94

SCHLEICHER ASK 23

Announced in the Spring of 1981, the ASK 23 is essentially a successor to the K 8 as a single-seat training and club glider, but making use of GfK constructional materials. Design began in November 1980; production started in October 1983, and about 55 had been manufactured by the beginning of 1986.

Schleicher is also developing an **ASK 23B**, suitable for cloud flying and aerobatic manoeuvres in accordance with JAR 22 Category U. This will have empty and max T-O weights of 235 kg (518 lb) and 360 kg (793 lb); speeds and other performance data are as for the original ASK 23, to which the following description applies:

TYPE: Single-seat training and performance sailplane.

AIRFRAME: Cantilever shoulder-wing monoplane. Wortmann wing sections: FX-61-168 at root, FX-60-126 at tip. Dihedral 2° 40′. Sweepback 0° 53′ 24″ at quarter-chord. Construction of GfK/foam sandwich, with glassfibre roving main spar and aluminium upper surface airbrakes. GfK honeycomb sandwich fuselage shell. Cantilever T tail, of similar construction to wings, with separate elevator. Landing gear comprises a 260 × 85 mm nosewheel, non-retractable rubber sprung 5·00-5 mainwheel (with Tost drum brake), and rubber sprung tailskid. One-piece forward opening Plexiglas canopy, with emergency jettison. Nose and CG towing hooks standard.

DIMENSIONS, EXTERNAL:
Wing span 15·00 m (49 ft 2½ in)
Wing aspect ratio 17·44
Length overall 7·10 m (23 ft 3½ in)
Height over tail 1·40 m (4 ft 7 in)

AREA:
Wings, gross 12·90 m² (138·8 sq ft)

WEIGHTS AND LOADING:
Weight empty 230 kg (507 lb)
Max T-O weight 380 kg (837 lb)
Max wing loading 29·5 kg/m² (6·04 lb/sq ft)

PERFORMANCE (at 340 kg; 750 lb T-O weight):
Best glide ratio at 43 knots (80 km/h; 50 mph) 33·7
Min rate of sink at 40 knots (74 km/h; 46 mph)
0·62 m (2·03 ft)/s
Stalling speed 33 knots (60 km/h; 38 mph)
Max speed (smooth air) 118 knots (220 km/h; 137 mph)
Max speed (rough air), and max aero-tow speed
80 knots (148 km/h; 92 mph)
Max winch-launching speed
67 knots (125 km/h; 77 mph)
g limits at 80 knots (148 km/h; 92 mph) +5·3/−2·65

SCHLEICHER ASW 24

The ASW 24, the prototype of which was due to fly in 1986, is intended as a successor to the ASW 19. An all-new design, it incorporates a new wing aerofoil section developed by the Department of Aerospace Engineering at Delft University of Technology in the Netherlands.

TYPE: Standard Class sailplane.

AIRFRAME: Cantilever mid-wing monoplane, with Delft University DU84-158 aerofoil section from root to tip. Dihedral 3°. Incidence 4°. Two-piece wing, of glass/aramid fibre and hard foam sandwich construction, with carbonfibre spar caps; ailerons of aramid/foam sandwich. Double-panelled aluminium airbrakes in upper wing surface, with spring loaded FRP cover plates. Fuselage is a carbon/aramid/glass FRP monocoque. Cantilever T tail, with elevator, is of carbon/aramid/glass FRP and hard foam sandwich. Retractable rubber sprung monowheel (tyre size 5·00-5), with hydraulic disc brake, plus tailskid. Canopy hinged at front, opening upward. Wing tanks for 170 litres (37·4 Imp gallons) of water ballast. CG towing hook standard. Options include nose towing hook, tailwheel with 210 × 65 mm pneumatic tyre, oxygen bottle and battery.

DIMENSIONS, EXTERNAL:
Wing span 15·00 m (49 ft 2½ in)
Wing aspect ratio 22·50
Length overall 6·55 m (21 ft 6 in)
Height over tail 1·30 m (4 ft 3¼ in)

AREA:
Wings, gross 10·00 m² (107·6 sq ft)

WEIGHTS AND LOADING:
Weight empty, equipped 225 kg (496 lb)
Max water ballast 170 kg (375 lb)
Max T-O weight 500 kg (1,102 lb)
Max wing loading 50·0 kg/m² (10·24 lb/sq ft)

PERFORMANCE (estimated, at max T-O weight except where indicated):
*Best glide ratio at 57 knots (105 km/h; 65 mph) 43
*Min rate of sink at 43 knots (80 km/h; 50 mph)
0·58 m (1·90 ft)/s
*Stalling speed 38 knots (69 km/h; 43 mph)
Max speed (smooth air) 145 knots (270 km/h; 168 mph)
Max speed (rough air) and max aero-tow speed
110 knots (205 km/h; 127 mph)
Max winch-launching speed
75 knots (140 km/h; 87 mph)
g limits +5·3/−2·65
* *at AUW of 315 kg (694 lb)*

SCHLEICHER ASH 25

Prototype construction of the ASH 25 (D-1025) started in January 1986, a year after design, by Martin Heide, began. The AS 22-2 (which see) has been used as the basis of the design, with some fuselage modifications. First flight was made on 11 May 1986.

TYPE: Open Class tandem two-seat sailplane.

AIRFRAME: Wings and tail unit as for AS 22-2, but two 60 litre (13·2 Imp gallon) water ballast tanks only (in outer panels). Fuselage is a hybrid carbon/aramid FRP monocoque. Retractable rubber sprung monowheel, tyre size 380 × 150 mm, pressure 3·5 bars (51 lb/sq in), with brake; retractable tailwheel, tyre size 210 × 65 mm, pressure 2·5 bars (36 lb/sq in). Canopies similar to those of ASK 21.

DIMENSIONS, EXTERNAL:
Wing span 25·00 m (82 ft 1 in)
Wing aspect ratio 38·32
Length overall 8·97 m (29 ft 5¼ in)
Height over tail 1·66 m (5 ft 5½ in)

AREA:
Wings, gross 16·31 m² (175·6 sq ft)

WEIGHTS AND LOADING:
Weight empty, equipped approx 470 kg (1,036 lb)
Max water ballast 120 kg (264 lb)
Max T-O weight 750 kg (1,653 lb)
Max wing loading 45·98 kg/m² (9·42 lb/sq ft)

PERFORMANCE (estimated, at max T-O weight except where indicated):
*Best glide ratio at 48 knots (90 km/h; 56 mph) 58
*Min rate of sink at 40 knots (75 km/h; 47 mph)
0·40 m (1·31 ft)/s
*Stalling speed 36 knots (65 km/h; 41 mph)
Max speed (smooth air) 151 knots (280 km/h; 174 mph)
Max speed (rough air) and max aero-tow speed
103 knots (190 km/h; 118 mph)
Max winch-launching speed
75 knots (140 km/h; 87 mph)
* *at wing loading of 34 kg/m² (6·97 lb/sq ft)*

SCHLEICHER ASH 25 MB

First flown (D-KOWB) on 28 March 1986, the ASH 25 MB combines the wings of the ASW 22 B/BE with a carbonfibre/balsa sandwich fuselage, an ASW 22 tail unit and the Rotax 505 engine of the ASW 22 BE. Weight empty (equipped) is 501 kg (1,104 lb).

VALENTIN

VALENTIN FLUGZEUGBAU GmbH

Flugplatzstrasse 18 (Postfach 26), 8728 Hassfurt
Telephone: 09521 4730

MANAGING DIRECTOR:
Dipl-Ing Bernard Valentin

SALES MANAGER: Dipl-Ing Rudolf Neumann

HEAD OFFICE AND OTHER WORKS: Germanenstrasse 2 (Postfach 1165), 8901 Königsbrunn
Telephone: (08231) 4033/4

This company is producing the Taifun two-seat motor glider. In July 1981 it took over the former MFB company (see 1981-82 *Jane's*), and became responsible for producing that company's Mistral-C sailplane. Development work and construction of metal components takes place at Königsbrunn; production of GRP components, and final assembly, are undertaken at Hassfurt.

VALENTIN TAIFUN 17E (TYPHOON)

The Taifun motor glider was proposed originally in two versions, the 15 m span Taifun 15E and 17 m span Taifun 17E, as detailed in the 1983-84 and previous editions of *Jane's*. Construction of the first prototype, to Taifun 17E configuration, began in July 1979, and this aircraft (D-KONO) made its first flight on 28 February 1981. A second prototype was used for extended trials and development of the mechanical (instead of the original electrical) undercarriage retraction gear, a shock absorbing engine mounting, and other improvements.

In 1982, due to lack of sufficient interest in the smaller version, it was decided to begin production only of the Taifun 17E. German certification of this version was awarded on 29 April 1983, and series manufacture began in mid-year. About 80 had been built by mid-1986.

A reduced span variant, the **Taifun 12E**, is currently being developed for the lightplane market and is described in the main Aircraft section. The following description applies to the Taifun 17E:

TYPE: Two-seat motor glider.

AIRFRAME: Cantilever low-wing monoplane with T tail. Wortmann FX-67-K-170/17 wing section. Dihedral 3°. Incidence 0° 48′. Sweepforward 0° 38′ 24″ at quarter-chord. Wings and ailerons of glassfibre/foam sandwich, with double T section glassfibre roving main spar booms. All-glassfibre cambered trailing-edge flaps, interconnected with ailerons at 8° setting only. Schempp-Hirth upper surface airbrakes. Wings fold back alongside fuselage for transportation and storage. Fuselage is a stressed skin structure of glassfibre and foam sandwich, reinforced with carbonfibre in the cockpit area. Fixed incidence T tailplane, with horn balanced elevator, of similar construction to wings. Flettner tab in port half of elevator. Mechanically retractable tricycle landing gear, with hydraulically damped pneumatic shock absorbers, Goodyear 5 in mainwheel tyres, pressure 2·5 bars (36 lb/sq in), and Cleveland hydraulic mainwheel disc brakes. Single nosewheel or tailwheel. Cockpit seats two persons side by side under rearward sliding canopy.

POWER PLANT: One 59 kW (80 hp) Limbach L 2000 EB four-cylinder four-stroke engine, driving a Hoffmann HO-V62R/L-160T two-blade variable-pitch feathering propeller. Fuel in two wing tanks, total capacity 90 litres (19·8 Imp gallons).

DIMENSIONS, EXTERNAL:
Wing span 17·00 m (55 ft 9¼ in)
Wing aspect ratio 16·42
Length overall 7·782 m (25 ft 6½ in)
Height over tail 2·48 m (8 ft 1½ in)
Tailplane span 3·30 m (10 ft 10 in)
Wheel track 2·36 m (7 ft 9 in)
Wheelbase 1·75 m (5 ft 9 in)
Propeller diameter 1·60 m (5 ft 3 in)

AREA:
Wings, gross 17·60 m² (189·4 sq ft)

WEIGHTS AND LOADINGS:
Weight empty 600 kg (1,323 lb)
Max T-O weight 820 kg (1,808 lb)
Max wing loading 46·59 kg/m² (9·55 lb/sq ft)
Max power loading 13·75 kg/kW (22·6 lb/hp)

PERFORMANCE, UNPOWERED (at max T-O weight):
Best glide ratio at 57 knots (105 km/h; 65 mph) 30
Min rate of sink at 46 knots (85 km/h; 53 mph)
0·95 m (3·12 ft)/s
Stalling speed 39 knots (72 km/h; 45 mph)
Max speed (smooth air)
132 knots (245 km/h; 152 mph)
Max speed (rough air)
100 knots (185 km/h; 115 mph)
g limits +5·3/−2·65

PERFORMANCE, POWERED (at max T-O weight):
Max cruising speed 111 knots (205 km/h; 127 mph)
Stalling speed 39 knots (72 km/h; 45 mph)
Max rate of climb at S/L 192 m (630 ft)/min
Service ceiling 5,000 m (16,400 ft)
T-O run 270 m (885 ft)
Landing run 200 m (655 ft)
Range with max fuel 675 nm (1,250 km; 777 miles)

VALENTIN TAIFUN 17E-90

This new version of the Taifun 17E was test flown by the DFVLR in 1986. It differs basically in having a 65 kW (87 hp) Limbach L 2400 EB1B engine and Mühlbauer MTV-1-A/L 160-03 two-blade propeller, giving enhanced performance.

WEIGHTS:
Weight empty 610 kg (1,345 lb)
Max T-O weight 850 kg (1,874 lb)

PERFORMANCE: As for Taifun 17E except:
Max level speed 132 knots (245 km/h; 152 mph)
Max cruising speed 119 knots (220 km/h; 137 mph)
T-O run 250 m (820 ft)

VALENTIN MISTRAL-C

The original Mistral was described and illustrated under the Strauber heading in the 1976-77 *Jane's*. The Mistral-C made its first flight on 21 October 1976, and 25 of this model had been completed by the beginning of 1980.

A new Mistral-Flugzeugbau (MFB) production facility was completed in 1980, which from January 1981 continued manufacture of the Mistral-C at the rate of five per month. On 1 July 1981 MFB was taken over by Valentin, to continue production of the Mistral-C; by the beginning of 1985 Valentin had built 70 Mistrals.

TYPE: Single-seat Club Class sailplane.

AIRFRAME: Cantilever shoulder-wing monoplane with T tail. Wortmann wing sections: FX-61-163 at root, FX-60-126 at tip. Dihedral 4° 12′. Sweepforward 1° at quarter-chord. Main wings and tail of GRP/foam/Conticell CC60 sandwich, ailerons of GRP. Schempp-Hirth aluminium airbrakes on upper surfaces. GRP monocoque fuselage, with one-piece sideways hinged canopy. Fixed incidence tailplane, with spring trim. Non-retractable monowheel, tyre pressure 2·5 bars (36·25 lb/sq in), with Tost brake; tailskid.

DIMENSIONS, EXTERNAL:
Wing span 15·00 m (49 ft 2½ in)

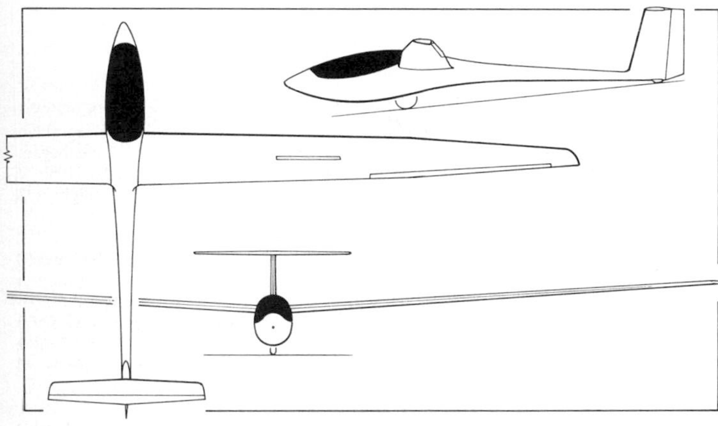

Schleicher ASW 24 Standard Class sailplane *(Michael A. Badrocke)*

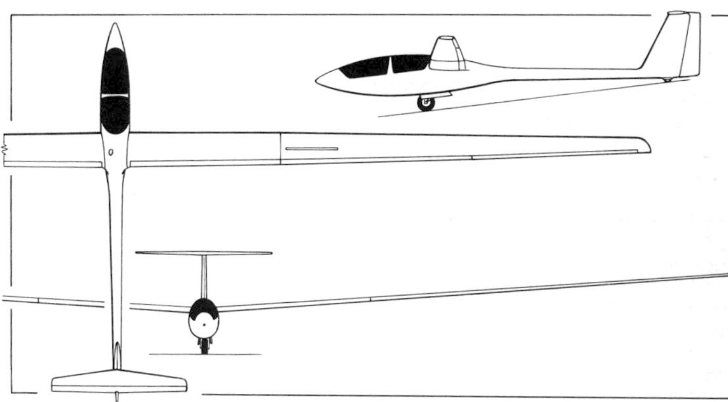

Schleicher ASH 25 Open Class sailplane, developed from the AS 22-2 *(Michael A. Badrocke)*

ASH 25, designed by Schleicher's Martin Heide *(Peter F. Selinger)*

Valentin Taifun 17E two-seat motor glider

Aviatechnika Góbé R-26S two-seat training sailplane *(Peter J. Bish)*

Valentin Mistral-C single-seat Club Class sailplane *(Peter F. Selinger)*

Wing aspect ratio 20·74
Length overall 6·73 m (22 ft 1 in)
Height over tail 1·42 m (4 ft 8 in)
AREA:
Wings, gross 10·85 m² (116·8 sq ft)
WEIGHTS AND LOADING:
Weight empty approx 225 kg (496 lb)
Max T-O weight 350 kg (771 lb)
Max wing loading 32·3 kg/m² (6·62 lb/sq ft)
PERFORMANCE (at max T-O weight except where indicated):
Best glide ratio at 51 knots (95 km/h; 59 mph) 37·5
Min rate of sink at 43 knots (80 km/h; 50 mph) 0·66 m (2·17 ft)/s
Stalling speed at AUW of 295 kg (650 lb) 35 knots (65 km/h; 41 mph)
Max speed (smooth air) 135 knots (250 km/h; 155 mph)
Max speed (rough air) and max aero-tow speed 86 knots (160 km/h; 99 mph)
Max winch-launching speed 70 knots (130 km/h; 81 mph)
g limits:
at 135 knots (250 km/h; 155 mph) +4/−1·5
at 86 knots (160 km/h; 99 mph) (JAR 22) +5·3/−2·65

HUNGARY

AVIATECHNIKA

MANUFACTURER: **XII. sz. AFIT**, Szombathely, H-9700 Zanati u. 4
Telephone: 36 94 11341
SOLE EXPORTER: **Technika Hungarian Foreign Trading Company**, PO Box 125, H-1475 Budapest
Telephone: 338 305 and 340 149
Telex: 225 765

AVIATECHNIKA GÓBÉ R-26S

The first of two R-26 prototypes made its initial flight on 6 May 1961, and 50 of the original version were put into production in the mid-1960s, as last described in the 1965-66 *Jane's*. The Góbé is apparently still in production, and an example was displayed at the Paris Air Show in June 1983. The current version, to which the following details apply, is designated R-26S.

TYPE: Two-seat training sailplane.

AIRFRAME: Cantilever shoulder-wing monoplane. Constant chord wings of Göttingen 549 (modified) section, having 3° dihedral and 1° 30′ of forward sweep. Single-spar wings, with leading-edge torsion box covered by riveted metal skin; fabric covering aft of 35 per cent chord line. Schempp-Hirth perforated metal airbrakes in upper and lower surfaces. Frise type slotted ailerons, of fabric covered metal construction. Metal-frame fuselage, with metal and fabric covering. Conventional fabric covered metal tail surfaces, with tailplane mounted at intersection of fin and dorsal fin. Balanced rudder; ground adjustable tab on port elevator. Non-retractable, partly recessed rubber sprung monowheel, with brake; faired tailskid under rear fuselage. Towing hook/cable release under front fuselage, forward of monowheel. Two seats in tandem under one-piece framed canopy which opens sideways to starboard.

DIMENSIONS, EXTERNAL:
Wing span 14·00 m (45 ft 11¼ in)
Wing aspect ratio 10·89
Length overall 9·00 m (29 ft 6⅓ in)
Height over tail 1·96 m (6 ft 5¼ in)
AREA:
Wings, gross 18·00 m² (193·75 sq ft)
WEIGHTS AND LOADING:
Weight empty 220-240 kg (485-529 lb)
Max T-O weight 440 kg (970 lb)
Max wing loading 24·4 kg/m² (5·00 lb/sq ft)
PERFORMANCE (at max T-O weight):
Best glide ratio at 44 knots (81 km/h; 50 mph) 23·7
Min rate of sink at 44 knots (81 km/h; 50 mph) 0·97 m (3·18 ft)/s
Max speed (smooth air) 113 knots (210 km/h; 130 mph)
Max speed (rough air) 77 knots (143 km/h; 89 mph)
Max aero-tow speed 70 knots (130 km/h; 81 mph)
Max winch-launching speed 59 knots (110 km/h; 68 mph)
g limits +5·3/−2·65

INDIA

CIVIL AVIATION DEPARTMENT

TECHNICAL CENTRE, CIVIL AVIATION DEPARTMENT

Civil Aviation Department, R. K. Puram, New Delhi 110066

WORKS: Technical Centre, opposite Safdarjung Airport, New Delhi 110003

Telephone: 611504

DIRECTOR GENERAL: Air Marshal C. K. S. Raje

DEPUTY DIRECTOR GENERAL: K. B. Ganesan

DIRECTOR (R & D): P. R. Chandrasekhar

The Technical Centre of the Indian Civil Aviation Department undertakes the type certification of aircraft; development of design, airworthiness and operational standards; the study of operational problems; development testing and standardisation of aeronautical materials; laboratory investigation of accidents; fatigue research; and the evaluation of aircraft performance and economics.

Since 1950 the Centre has undertaken the design and development of gliders utilising predominantly indigenous materials. The first of these gliders was flown in November 1950. Since then the Centre has built nine types for use at gliding clubs and centres in India, as listed in previous editions of *Jane's*. Of these, six have been original designs.

The Technical Centre does not undertake quantity production of gliders. Drawings of designs developed at the Centre are supplied to interested organisations with permission to manufacture them in series.

ATS-1 ARDHRA

This two-seat training sailplane was designed by the team responsible earlier for the Mrigasheer, last described in the 1980-81 *Jane's*. The Ardhra prototype (VT-GEJ) made its first flight on 5 March 1979 and was certificated by the Indian DGCA on 2 November of that year.

The Ardhra has been approved for use by the National Cadet Corps, and is now in production at the Kanpur Division of Hindustan Aeronautics Ltd. A second prototype (VT-GEN), flown for the first time on 28 June 1981, was representative of the production version, of which 50 have been ordered by the Indian Air Force. Twenty-seven of these had been completed by 1 March 1985, including 12 fitted with an enlarged canopy (illustration in 1985-86 *Jane's*).

TYPE: Tandem two-seat advanced training sailplane.

AIRFRAME: Cantilever shoulder-wing monoplane. Wortmann FX-61-184 wing section from root to tip. Dihedral 3°. Incidence 3° at root. Sweepforward 3° at leading-edge; 2° washout on outer half of each wing. Plywood covered two-spar wooden wings, plywood covered on leading- and trailing-edges; plain wood ailerons; wood airbrakes in upper and lower wing surfaces. Tail unit of similar construction, but with rear portions of rudder and elevator fabric covered. Horn balanced rudder; mass and horn balanced elevator. Plywood covered tab in starboard elevator. Semi-monocoque wood fuselage, with plywood covering. Nosecone of glassfibre. Non-retractable unsprung monowheel, tyre size 6·00-4. Rubber sprung nose-skid, with replaceable steel shoe, and rubber sprung tailskid.

DIMENSIONS, EXTERNAL:
- Wing span: 16·50 m (54 ft 1½ in)
- Wing aspect ratio: 12·47
- Length overall: 8·61 m (28 ft 3 in)
- Height over tail: 2·464 m (8 ft 1 in)

AREA:
- Wings, gross: 21·83 m² (235·0 sq ft)

WEIGHTS AND LOADING:
- Weight empty: 328 kg (723 lb)
- Max T-O weight: 508 kg (1,120 lb)
- Max wing loading: 23·28 kg/m² (4·77 lb/sq ft)

PERFORMANCE (at max T-O weight):
- Best glide ratio at 47 knots (87 km/h; 54 mph): 26
- Min rate of sink at 39 knots (72 km/h; 45 mph): 0·78 m (2·56 ft)/s
- Stalling speed: 33 knots (61 km/h; 38 mph)
- Max speed (smooth air): 113 knots (210 km/h; 130 mph)
- Max speed (rough air): 69 knots (127 km/h; 79 mph)
- Max aero-tow speed and max winch-launching speed: 59 knots (110 km/h; 68 mph)
- *g* limits: +5·3/−2·65

MG-1

Design of this two-seat motor glider was started in October 1981. First flight was made on 30 May 1983; type certification was awarded in December 1985.

TYPE: Two-seat motor glider.

AIRFRAME: Cantilever low-wing monoplane, with Wortmann FX-61-184 wing section from root to tip. Dihedral 3° 15′ from roots. Incidence 3°. Sweepforward 1° 30′ at quarter-chord; 2° washout on outer half of each wing. Wooden wings (Himalayan spruce and plywood), with fabric covered plain ailerons. No flaps. Spruce and plywood upper and lower surface airbrakes. Fuselage is of welded BST45/CM steel tube, fabric covered except for glassfibre engine cowling. Cantilever non-swept tail unit, with low-set tailplane; construction similar to that of wings. Trim tab in starboard elevator. Non-retractable tailwheel type landing gear, with rubber cord shock absorption. Mainwheel tyres size 6·00-6 Type III, pressure 1·03-1·17 bars (15-17 lb/sq in); steerable tailwheel with 6 × 2·00 solid rubber tyre. HAL mechanically operated internally expanding shoe brakes on mainwheels. Side by side seats for two persons under rearward sliding canopy. Basic flight/engine instrumentation and radio standard.

POWER PLANT: One 74·5 kW (100 hp) Rolls-Royce Continental O-200-A flat-four engine, driving a Hoffmann V62R/170Y two-blade adjustable pitch propeller with spinner. Single metal fuel tank in fuselage, capacity 60 litres (13·2 Imp gallons).

DIMENSIONS, EXTERNAL:
- Wing span: 16 50 m (54 ft 1½ in)
- Wing aspect ratio: 12·47
- Length overall: 8·00 m (26 ft 3 in)
- Height overall (flying attitude): 2·50 m (8 ft 2½ in)
- Tailplane span: 3·00 m (9 ft 10 in)
- Wheel track: 2·00 m (6 ft 6¾ in)
- Propeller diameter: 1·70 m (5 ft 7 in)

AREA:
- Wings, gross: 21·83 m² (235·0 sq ft)

WEIGHTS AND LOADINGS:
- Weight empty, equipped: 560 kg (1,235 lb)
- Max T-O weight: 748 kg (1,650 lb)
- Max wing loading: 34·3 kg/m² (7·02 lb/sq ft)
- Max power loading: 10·04 kg/kW (16·5 lb/hp)

PERFORMANCE, UNPOWERED (at max T-O weight):
- Best glide ratio at 57 knots (105 km/h; 65 mph): 26
- Min rate of sink at 49 knots (90 km/h; 56 mph): 1·00 m (3·28 ft)/s
- Stalling speed: 38 knots (70 km/h; 44 mph)
- Max speed (smooth air): 132 knots (245 km/h; 152 mph)
- Max speed (rough air): 86 knots (160 km/h; 99 mph)
- *g* limits: +5·3/−2·65

PERFORMANCE, POWERED (at max T-O weight):
- Max cruising speed: 103 knots (190 km/h; 118 mph)
- Econ cruising speed, 75% power: 86 knots (160 km/h; 99 mph)
- Stalling speed: 34 knots (62 km/h; 39 mph)
- Max rate of climb at S/L: 180 m (590 ft)/min
- Service ceiling: 4,575 m (15,000 ft)
- T-O run: 170 m (558 ft)
- Landing run: 135 m (443 ft)
- Range with max fuel: 302 nm (560 km; 348 miles)

POLAND

PW

POLITECHNIKA WARSZAWSKA (Warsaw University of Technology)

Research Group for Aircraft Composite Structures Technology, ul. Nowowiejska 22/24, 00-665 Warszawa

Telephone: 21007 965

Telex: 813307 PW PD

DIRECTOR: Dr Roman Switkiewicz

PW-2 GAPA

The PW-2 Gapa is the productionised version of the ULS (Ultralekkiego Szybowca: ultralight sailplane) which flew for the first time on 27 September 1981 and was described and illustrated in the 1984-85 *Jane's*.

Construction of three PW-2 prototypes began in September 1984, and the first flight was made on 25 July 1985. Designed for basic training and recreation, the Gapa can be winch or bungee launched, or tow launched by an aircraft or motorcar. Its light glassfibre structure meets all requirements of JAR 22, and a novel feature are the wing strut fairings, which are hinged and can be pivoted for use as airbrakes.

The PW-2 is available in plans or kit form, as well as ready to fly. Manufacture of 15 production examples was authorised for 1986.

TYPE: Single-seat ultra-lightweight sailplane.

AIRFRAME: Braced high-wing monoplane. Constant chord wings, of NACA 4415 constant section from root to tip. Dihedral 1°. Incidence 3°. No sweep. Single-spar wings, spar and D nose section forming a glassfibre torsion box; fabric covered glassfibre structure aft of spar. Glassfibre ailerons, projecting aft of trailing-edge. No spoilers. Fairing behind each bracing strut pivots to act as airbrake. Keel type fuselage, of glassfibre laminate. Conventional unbraced tail unit, of similar construction to rear portion of wings. Non-retractable rubber sprung monowheel, tyre size 255 × 110 mm, pressure 1·8 bars (26 lb/sq in); no brake. Nose-skid and small tailskid. Single seat in open cockpit with windscreen.

DIMENSIONS, EXTERNAL:
- Wing span: 11·00 m (36 ft 1 in)
- Wing aspect ratio: 9·53
- Length overall: 5·50 m (18 ft 0¾ in)
- Height over tail: 2·45 m (8 ft 0½ in)

AREA:
- Wings, gross: 12·70 m² (136·7 sq ft)

WEIGHTS AND LOADING:
- Weight empty, equipped: 110 kg (243 lb)
- Max T-O weight: 220 kg (485 lb)
- Max wing loading: 17·32 kg/m² (3·55 lb/sq ft)

PERFORMANCE (at max T-O weight):
- Best glide ratio at 37 knots (69 km/h; 43 mph): 16
- Min rate of sink at 31 knots (58 km/h; 36 mph): 1·00 m (3·28 ft)/s
- Stalling speed: 27 knots (50 km/h; 31 mph)
- Max speed (smooth air): 81 knots (150 km/h; 93 mph)
- Max speed (rough air) and max aero-tow speed: 64 knots (120 km/h; 74 mph)
- Max winch-launching speed: 54 knots (100 km/h; 62 mph)
- *g* limits: +5·3/−2·65

PW-3 and PW-4

These are planned as progressive developments of the PW-2, the PW-3 having inset ailerons and an enclosed cabin, increasing the empty weight to 160 kg (353 lb) and the best glide ratio to 18. The PW-4 will be a powered version, with a nose mounted engine and non-retractable tricycle landing gear. Empty weight is estimated at 250 kg (551 lb), max and stalling speeds at 81 knots (150 km/h; 93 mph) and 30 knots (55 km/h; 35 mph) respectively.

The PW-3 is expected to appear in 1986-87, and the PW-4 in the 1988-90 period.

SZD

PRZEDSIEBIORSTWO DOŚWIADCZALNO-PRODUKCYJNE SZYBOWNICTWA (Experimental and Production Concern for Gliders) PZL-BIELSKO

HEAD OFFICE AND WORKS: ul. Cieszyńska 325, 43-300 Bielsko-Biala 1

Telephone: 250 21 to 250 26

Telex: 035-259 PZL PL

DIRECTOR: Ing Jerzy Cieśla

SALES REPRESENTATIVE: Pezetel, 61 Aleja Stanow Zjednoczonych (PO Box 6), 00-991 Warszawa 44

Telephone: 10 80 01

Telex: 813314

The Instytut Szybownictwa (Gliding Institute), formed officially in January 1946 at Bielsko-Biala, has since undergone several changes of name, as detailed in the 1977-78 *Jane's*. The change to the present title took place in July 1975, but the well known designation initials SZD are retained. This organisation is responsible for the design and development of nearly all Polish sailplanes. Production plants are at Bielsko-Biala, Wroclaw and Jezów. Design of a 22/24 m (72 ft 2¼ in/78 ft 9 in) Open Class **Jantar 22/24**, with detachable wingtips, has been completed.

Between 1947 and 1 January 1986 the Polish aircraft industry produced 4,496 gliders of more than 115 different types, and SZD sailplanes have been exported all over the world in substantial numbers.

SZD-42-2 JANTAR 2B (AMBER 2B)

Designed by Dipl-Ing Adam Kurbiel, the SZD-42-2 Open Class sailplane is based on the SZD-42-1. The prototype flew for the first time on 13 March 1978, and 102 Jantar 2Bs had been built by 1 January 1986.

TYPE: Single-seat Open Class sailplane.

AIRFRAME: Cantilever shoulder-wing monoplane. Wortmann wing sections: FX-67K-150 at root, FX-67K-170 at tip. Dihedral 2°. Sweepback 0° at quarter-chord. Single-spar four-part ribless wings with foam filled glassfibre/epoxy resin sandwich skin. Two-part hinged ailerons; top-hinged 'elastic' flaps. Light alloy DFS type airbrakes. All-glassfibre/epoxy resin shell fuselage; centre portion

Indian Civil Aviation Dept ATS-1 Ardhra two-seat training sailplane

First prototype of the Indian Civil Aviation Department MG-1 motor glider

A prototype of the Politechnika Warszawska PW-2 Gapa

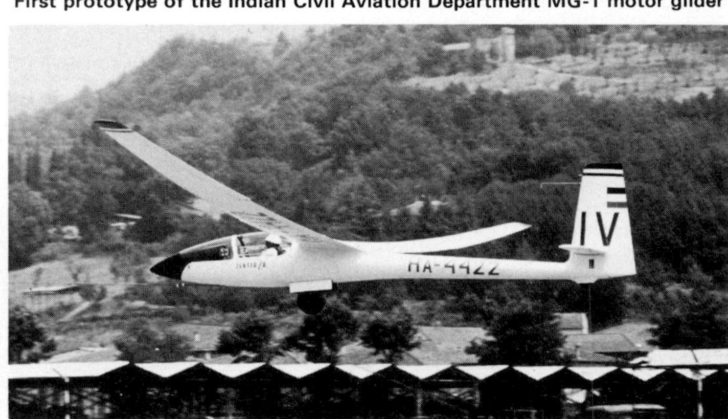

SZD-42-2 Jantar 2B Open Class sailplane *(Peter F. Selinger)*

SZD-48-3 Jantar Standard 3 single-seat sailplane *(Peter F. Selinger)*

SZD-48-3M Brawo, developed from the Jantar Standard 3 *(Peter F. Selinger)*

has a steel tube frame coupling together the wings, fuselage and landing gear. Cantilever cruciform tail unit of glassfibre/epoxy resin. Monowheel, diameter 400 mm, with two rubber shock absorbers and disc brake. Tailwheel diameter 200 mm. Water ballast provision 167 litres (36·7 Imp gallons). Improvements made to elevator spring trim, monowheel retraction system and cockpit comfort. Hinged canopy and provision for CG tow hook.

DIMENSIONS, EXTERNAL:
- Wing span: 20·50 m (67 ft 3 in)
- Wing aspect ratio: 29·49
- Length overall: 7·18 m (23 ft 6¾ in)
- Height over tail: 1·76 m (5 ft 9¼ in)

AREA:
- Wings, gross: 14·25 m² (153·4 sq ft)

WEIGHTS AND LOADING:
- Weight empty: 362 kg (798 lb)
- Max T-O weight:
  - without water ballast: 458 kg (1,010 lb)
  - with water ballast: 649 kg (1,430 lb)
- Max wing loading: 45·6 kg/m² (9·28 lb/sq ft)

PERFORMANCE (at max T-O weight):
- Best glide ratio at 56 knots (103 km/h; 64 mph): 50·3
- Min rate of sink at 44 knots (80 km/h; 50 mph): 0·46 m (1·51 ft)/s
- Stalling speed: 43 knots (79 km/h; 49 mph)
- Max speed (smooth air): 135 knots (250 km/h; 155 mph)
- Max speed (rough air): 108 knots (200 km/h; 124 mph)
- Max aero-tow speed: 76 knots (140 km/h; 87 mph)
- Max winch-launching speed: 62 knots (115 km/h; 71 mph)
- *g* limits: +5·3/−2·65

SZD-48-3 JANTAR STANDARD 3

This Standard Class sailplane is the current version of the SZD-48-1 and SZD-48-2 Jantar Standard 2, which were described in the 1983-84 *Jane's*. Production of these versions, which totalled 313, ended in March 1983.

The prototype SZD-48-3 Jantar Standard 3 was flown for the first time on 9 February 1983, and 160 of this version had been built by 1 January 1986.

TYPE: Single-seat Standard Class sailplane.

AIRFRAME: Cantilever shoulder-wing monoplane, with NN-8 wing section. Dihedral 1° 30′. Single glassfibre roving main spar, with glassfibre/foam/glassfibre moulded skins (no ribs) and plain ailerons. Glassfibre upper/lower surface airbrakes. Glassfibre fuselage, with steel tube central support structure, rear portion stiffened by half-frames and fin ribs. Cantilever T tail of similar construction to wings. Fin integral with fuselage; mass balanced rudder, with upward angled lower edge to avoid damage in tail-down landing. Mass balanced elevator, with spring trim. Retractable unsprung monowheel, tyre size 350 × 135 mm, with disc brake; semi-recessed tailwheel, diameter 200 mm. One-piece canopy, hinged at front and opening upward. Optional CG towing hook on mainwheel fork. Provision for 150 litres (33 Imp gallons) water ballast.

DIMENSIONS, EXTERNAL:
- Wing span: 15·00 m (49 ft 2½ in)
- Wing aspect ratio: 21·11
- Length overall: 6·85 m (22 ft 5¾ in)
- Height over tail: 1·51 m (4 ft 11½ in)

AREA:
- Wings, gross: 10·66 m² (114·7 sq ft)

WEIGHTS AND LOADING:
- Weight empty: 274 kg (604 lb)
- Max T-O weight:
  - without water ballast: 390 kg (860 lb)
  - with water ballast: 540 kg (1,190 lb)
- Max wing loading: 50·7 kg/m² (10·38 lb/sq ft)

PERFORMANCE (at max T-O weight):
- Best glide ratio at 66 knots (123 km/h; 76 mph): 40
- Min rate of sink at 52 knots (97 km/h; 60 mph): 0·77 m (2·53 ft)/s
- Stalling speed: 45 knots (82 km/h; 51 mph)
- Max speed (smooth air): 154 knots (285 km/h; 177 mph)
- Max speed (rough air): 108 knots (200 km/h; 124 mph)
- Max aero-tow speed: 81 knots (150 km/h; 93 mph)
- Max winch-launching speed: 67 knots (125 km/h; 77 mph)
- *g* limits: +5·3/−2·65

SZD-48-3M BRAWO

Designed in 1984 by Stanisław Zientek, the Brawo flew for the first time on 13 April 1985. Three (SP-3333, '34 and '35) were built for Polish Aeroclub use in the 1985 World Championships (Standard Class). The Brawo is a modified version of the Jantar Standard 3, form which it differs in the following respects.

AIRFRAME: Reinforced wings, with 3° dihedral, airbrakes on upper surface only, and water ballast reduced to 130 litres (28·5 Imp gallons), plus a 7 litre (1·5 Imp gallon) water tank in the tail.

DIMENSIONS, EXTERNAL:
- Wing aspect ratio: 20·64
- Length overall: 6·71 m (22 ft 0¼ in)

AREA:
- Wings, gross: 10·90 m² (117·3 sq ft)

WEIGHTS AND LOADING:
- Weight empty: 240 kg (529 lb)
- Max water ballast: 118 kg (260 lb)
- Max T-O weight: 490 kg (1,080 lb)
- Max wing loading: 44·95 kg/m² (9·21 lb/sq ft)

PERFORMANCE (at max T-O weight):
- Best glide ratio at 65 knots (120 km/h; 75 mph): 40
- Stalling speed: 35 knots (64 km/h; 40 mph)
- Max speed (rough air): 97 knots (180 km/h; 112 mph)
- *g* limits: +7·95/−3·97

SZD-50-3 PUCHACZ (EAGLE OWL)

The Puchacz, designed by Dipl-Ing Adam Meus, is a high performance sailplane intended particularly for training and performance flying. It was modified and developed from a prototype, designated SZD-50-1 Dromader, which first flew on 21 December 1976.

A second prototype made its initial flight on 20 December 1977, and the first production SZD-50-2 Puchacz (SP-3151) followed on 13 April 1979. A total of 132 had been built by 1 January 1986, with exports made to Argentina, Austria, Canada, China, Denmark, Finland, East and West Germany, Greece, Sweden, Switzerland, Turkey, the UK and the USSR. The current version of the Puchacz, designated SZD-50-3, has a larger horizontal tail situated 30 cm (11¾ in) higher on the fin, an enlarged rudder, and a fairing over the mainwheel. Inverted flight and extended aerobatic manoeuvres became permissible in 1986.

TYPE: Tandem two-seat high performance training sailplane.

AIRFRAME: Cantilever mid-wing monoplane, mainly of glassfibre sandwich construction. Wortmann wing sections. Plain ailerons. Upper/lower surface airbrakes. Glassfibre fuselage, supported in central portion by two wooden frames, with integral fin. Glassfibre sandwich cruciform tail unit, with fabric covered glassfibre rudder. Non-retractable semi-recessed nosewheel (size 255 × 110 mm) and sprung monowheel (size 350 × 135 mm, with disc brake), and tailskid. One-piece canopy opens sideways.

DIMENSIONS, EXTERNAL:
- Wing span: 16·67 m (54 ft 8¼ in)
- Wing aspect ratio: 15·30
- Length overall: 8·38 m (27 ft 6 in)
- Height over tail: 2·04 m (6 ft 8¼ in)

AREA:
- Wings, gross: 18·16 m² (195·5 sq ft)

WEIGHTS AND LOADING:
- Weight empty: 360 kg (794 lb)
- Max T-O weight: 570 kg (1,256 lb)
- Max wing loading: 31·4 kg/m² (6·43 lb/sq ft)

PERFORMANCE (at max T-O weight):
- Best glide ratio at 46 knots (85 km/h; 53 mph): 30
- Min rate of sink at 40 knots (75 km/h; 47 mph): 0·70 m (2·30 ft)/s
- Stalling speed: 33 knots (60 km/h; 38 mph)
- Max speed (smooth air): 116 knots (215 km/h; 133 mph)
- Max speed (rough air): 86 knots (160 km/h; 99 mph)
- Max aero-tow speed: 81 knots (150 km/h; 93 mph)
- Max winch-launching speed: 59 knots (110 km/h; 68 mph)
- *g* limits: +5·3/−2·65

SZD-51-1 JUNIOR

Designed in 1979 by Dipl-Ing Stanislaw Zientek, and first flown in SZD-51-0 prototype form on 31 December 1980, the Junior is a single-seat Club Class sailplane of GRP construction. Production began at Wroclaw in 1984, and 12 Juniors had been completed by 1 January 1986.

TYPE: Single-seat Club Class sailplane.

AIRFRAME: Cantilever shoulder-wing monoplane, with FX-S02-196 (root) and FX-S02/1-158 (tip) wing sections. Dihedral 3° from roots. Incidence 1° 30′. No sweep. Single glassfibre I section roving main spar, with glassfibre/foam/glassfibre sandwich moulded skins (no ribs). Schempp-Hirth duralumin upper surface airbrakes. Airbrake boxes and airbrakes, and aileron pushrod control system, suspended on main spar. Glassfibre fuselage, with steel tube central support structure; rear portion stiffened by PVC foam half-frames and foam ribs. Fin, which carries VHF aerial, is integral with fuselage; rudder fabric covered. Cantilever T tail unit, of similar construction to wings; elevators have mass balance and spring trim. Non-retractable unsprung monowheel (tyre size 350 × 135 mm), with SZD disc brake; semi-recessed tailwheel, tyre size 200 × 50 mm; auxiliary front skid. Nose and CG towing hooks. One-piece Mecaplex canopy, opening sideways to starboard.

DIMENSIONS, EXTERNAL:
- Wing span: 15·00 m (49 ft 2½ in)
- Wing aspect ratio: 17·98
- Length overall: 6·69 m (21 ft 11½ in)
- Height overall: 1·54 m (5 ft 0⅔ in)

AREA:
- Wings, gross: 12·51 m² (134·7 sq ft)

WEIGHTS AND LOADING:
- Weight empty: 242 kg (533 lb)
- Max T-O weight: 355 kg (783 lb)
- Max wing loading: 28·4 kg/m² (5·81 lb/sq ft)

PERFORMANCE (at wing loading of 26 kg/m²; 5·33 lb/sq ft):
- Best glide ratio at 43 knots (80 km/h; 50 mph): 35
- Min rate of sink at 39 knots (72 km/h; 45 mph): 0·59 m (1·94 ft)/s
- Stalling speed: 33 knots (60 km/h; 38 mph)
- Max speed (smooth air): 119 knots (220 km/h; 137 mph)
- Max speed (rough air): 81 knots (150 km/h; 93 mph)
- Max aero-tow speed: 75 knots (140 km/h; 87 mph)
- Max winch-launching speed: 69 knots (128 km/h; 79 mph)
- *g* limits: +5·3/−2·65

SZD-52 JANTAR 15 and KROKUS

These developments of the well known Jantar family were designed by Adam Kurbiel. All were built in prototype form only (five versions), as listed in the 1984-85 *Jane's*. Brief details of the proposed **SZD-52-4 Krokus** production version can be found in the 1985-86 edition. No further development, or production, has been undertaken.

WSK PZL-KROSNO

WYTWÓRNIA SPRZETU KOMUNIKACYJNEGO PZL-KROSNO (Transport Equipment Manufacturing Centre, Krosno)

38-400 Krosno n. Wislokiem
Telephone: 229 11
Telex: 83263
GENERAL MANAGER: Ing Jan Czerniecki

WSK PZL-Krosno has designed a two-seat training glider intended for widespread use by Polish aeroclubs. Known as the KR-03 Puchatek, it is Krosno's first glider design for more than 20 years.

PZL-KROSNO KR-03 PUCHATEK ('POOH')

Polish aeroclubs (Aeroklub PRL) are suffering a shortage of two-seat sailplanes suitable for basic and advanced training. Only dozens remain of the Bocian, the most popular type for more than 25 years, plus a handful of the earlier Czaplas. Their place was intended to be taken by the SZD-50 Puchacz (which see), but supplies of this aircraft have been slow, due mainly to a reliance on imported composite materials which require hard currency payments and have made the cost of the Puchacz unacceptably high.

In an attempt to remedy this deficiency, PZL-Krosno designed the Puchatek ('Pooh', after A. A. Milne's famous Winnie-the-Pooh) in response to a specification issued in June 1982. This meets Aeroklub PRL requirements in terms of cost, materials and ease of maintenance, as well as providing adequate performance.

Preliminary design work, under the leadership of Eng Jerzy Krawczyk, started in January 1983, and construction of a static test aircraft began in mid-1984. The first flying prototype (SP-P336), using the second airframe, flew for the first time on 1 August 1985. A third Puchatek was under construction at that time, and it was hoped to obtain Polish certification by the end of that year. This was to be followed in 1986 by manufacture of a pre-production quantity for evaluation by Aeroklub PRL, leading to the start of series production in 1987. The head of Aeroklub PRL has said that up to 600 Puchateks may be built to meet present and future requirements. After basic training on the Puchatek, students would graduate to the SZD-51-1 Junior (which see).

TYPE: Tandem two-seat basic training sailplane.

AIRFRAME: Cantilever mid-wing monoplane. Constant chord wings of Wortmann FX-S-2/1-158 section, set at incidence of 5°. Sweepforward 3°. Dihedral 4° from roots. Conventional structure of duralumin main and auxiliary spars and ribs, each wing being attached to fuselage by three bolts. Forward portion of each wing is duralumin skinned, rear portion fabric covered. Two-segment plain ailerons on each wing, of fabric covered metal construction. Ailerons, and upper/lower surface airbrakes at mid span, actuated by pushrods. Fuselage is an all-metal monocoque, reinforced with nine frames but having no longitudinal stiffening. Forward (cockpit) section consists of two riveted halves of PA-2 duralumin sheet; rear section comprises two conical sections of PA-7 duralumin sheet. Conventional T tail surfaces, fin (integral with fuselage) and fixed incidence tailplane being all-metal (PA-2/PA-7), rudder and elevators of fabric covered metal construction. Trim tab in port elevator. Non-retractable 350 × 135 mm sprung monowheel, 140 mm rubber sprung self-centering tailwheel, and rubber sprung ash nose-skid. Tandem seats for instructor (at rear) and pupil. Two-piece canopy, both sections opening sideways to starboard. Dual controls and radio standard.

DIMENSIONS, EXTERNAL:
- Wing span: 16·38 m (53 ft 9 in)
- Wing chord, constant: 1·20 m (3 ft 11¼ in)
- Wing aspect ratio: 13·80
- Length overall: 8·24 m (27 ft 0½ in)
- Height over tail: 1·50 m (4 ft 11 in)

AREA:
- Wings, gross: 19·44 m² (209·25 sq ft)

WEIGHTS AND LOADING:
- Weight empty: 280 kg (617 lb)
- Max T-O weight: 460 kg (1,014 lb)
- Max wing loading: 23·65 kg/m² (4·85 lb/sq ft)

PERFORMANCE:
- Best glide ratio: 24·6
- Min rate of sink: 0·80 m (2·62 ft)/s
- Stalling speed: 32 knots (58·5 km/h; 37 mph)
- Max speed (smooth air): 108 knots (200 km/h; 124 mph)

ROMANIA

ICA

INTREPRINDEREA DE CONSTRUCTII AERONAUTICE (Aeronautical Construction Enterprise)

Str. Aeroportului 1, Casuta Postala 198, 2200 Brasov
Telephone: 16719 and 16722
Telex: 61266
TECHNICAL DIRECTOR: Eng Ion Georgescu

As detailed in the Aircraft section, the current activities of the Romanian aircraft industry are divided between four main centres: IAv Bucuresti, IAv Bacau, IAv Craiova and ICA Brasov. In addition to its work on powered aircraft (which see), the ICA is responsible for all sailplane development and production. The principal Romanian designer of sailplanes was Dipl Ing Iosif Silimon, who died in February 1981. His designs are prefixed with the letters IS. Details of his earlier sailplanes have appeared in many previous editions of *Jane's*.

IS-28B2

This high performance sailplane was developed from the IS-28B (1975-76 *Jane's*), which made its first flight on 26 April 1973, and the IS-28B1 (1976-77 edition). Standard version since 1976, of which more than 360 had been built by early 1985, is the IS-28B2, with Hütter (instead of DFS type) airbrakes and trailing-edge split flaps. Production is continuing, and exports have been made to about 20 countries which include Argentina, Australia, Botswana, Canada, Colombia, France, West Germany, Hungary, India, Norway, the UK and the USA.

TYPE: Tandem two-seat training and aerobatic sailplane.

AIRFRAME: Cantilever shoulder-wing monoplane. Wortmann wing sections: FX-61-163 at root, FX-60-126 at tip. Forward swept all-metal wings, with L section main spar booms and dural web, dural auxiliary spar, and dural ribs. Upper surface Hütter metal airbrakes. Ailerons and split trailing-edge flaps fabric covered. No tabs. All-metal semi-monocoque forward and centre fuselage. Rear fuselage is duralumin monocoque. Cantilever T tail, with moderate tailplane dihedral. Elevator trailing-edges and rudder fabric covered. Trim tab in each elevator. Semi-retractable monowheel with oleo-pneumatic shock absorber and disc brake; non-retractable tailwheel. Canopy opens sideways (to starboard) and can be jettisoned in flight. Dual controls standard. Nose towing hook, with Tost cable release, is standard; CG towing hook optional.

DIMENSIONS, EXTERNAL:
- Wing span: 17·00 m (55 ft 9¼ in)
- Wing aspect ratio: 15·84
- Length overall: 8·45 m (27 ft 8¾ in)
- Height over tail: 1·87 m (6 ft 1½ in)

AREA:
- Wings, gross: 18·24 m² (196·3 sq ft)

WEIGHTS AND LOADINGS:
- Weight empty: 400 kg (882 lb)
- Max T-O weight: single-seat: 520 kg (1,146 lb)
  - two-seat: 590 kg (1,300 lb)
- Max wing loading:
  - single-seat: 28·51 kg/m² (5·84 lb/sq ft)
  - two-seat: 32·34 kg/m² (6·62 lb/sq ft)

PERFORMANCE (at max T-O weight except where indicated):
- Best glide ratio:
  - single-seat at 51 knots (94 km/h; 58 mph): 33
  - two-seat at 54 knots (100 km/h; 62 mph): 33
- Min rate of sink:
  - single-seat at 43 knots (80 km/h; 50 mph): 0·74 m (2·43 ft)/s
  - two-seat at 46 knots (85 km/h; 53 mph): 0·78 m (2·56 ft)/s
- Stalling speed: single-seat: 37 knots (67 km/h; 42 mph)
  - two-seat: 39 knots (72 km/h; 45 mph)
- Max speed (smooth air): 124 knots (230 km/h; 143 mph)
- Max speed (rough air): 91 knots (169 km/h; 105 mph)
- Max aero-tow speed: 76 knots (140 km/h; 87 mph)
- Max winch-launching speed: 59 knots (110 km/h; 68 mph)
- *g* limits: +6·5/−4 (single-seat); +5·3/−2·65 (two-seat)

SZD-50-3 Puchacz two-seat training sailplane

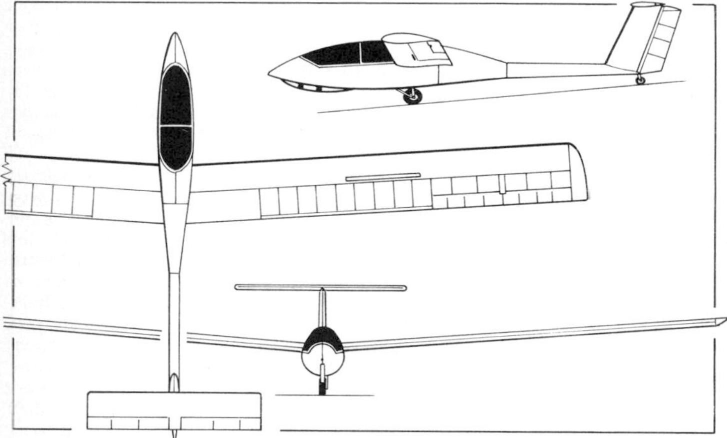
WSK PZL-Krosno KR-03 Puchatek two-seat training sailplane *(Michael A. Badrocke)*

IS-28M2A two-seat motor glider

SZD-51-1 Junior Club Class sailplane

IS-28B2 tandem two-seat high performance training sailplane *(Adolf Wilsch)*

IS-29D2 single-seat sailplane *(Peter F. Selinger)*

IS-28M2A

Two motor glider versions of the IS-28B2 were developed initially, with tandem (IS-28M1) and side by side seating (IS-28M2). The former was described in the 1981-82, the latter in 1984-85 and earlier editions of *Jane's*. The IS-28M1 has since been redesignated IAR-34.

The rear fuselage is essentially the same as that of the IS-28B2, but the powered version is of low-wing configuration and has a redesigned forward fuselage, cockpit canopy and main landing gear.

The prototype (YR-1013) flew for the first time on 26 June 1976, and more than 70 had been built by early 1985, with production continuing. All since c/n 41 are fitted with reinforced wings and are designated IS-28M2A. The aircraft is certificated in Australia, Japan, Norway, Portugal and the UK, and has been supplied to customers in Argentina, Australia, Canada, Denmark, Hungary, India, Israel, Norway, the Philippines, Spain, Sweden, Switzerland, the UK and the USA.

TYPE: Two-seat motor glider.

AIRFRAME: Cantilever low-wing monoplane, of mainly metal construction. Wortmann wing sections: FX-61-163 at root, FX-60-126 at tip. Dihedral 2°. Sweepforward 2° 30′ at quarter-chord. Single-spar wings, with aluminium ribs and skin, fabric covered metal ailerons and (optionally) all-metal split flaps on trailing-edges. Flaps can be set to a negative position. All-metal two-section Hütter airbrakes on upper surfaces. Conventional fuselage, in three parts: metal front portion, built up on two longerons and cross-frames and having glassfibre fairings and engine cowling panels; aluminium alloy monocoque centre portion; and rear portion of aluminium alloy frames and skin. Cantilever aluminium alloy T tail, with dihedral tailplane. Rudder and elevator trailing-edges fabric covered. Trim tab in each elevator. Two retractable mainwheels, with rubber disc shock absorbers and mechanically operated drum brakes, side by side under fuselage centre-section; steerable tailwheel, also with shock absorber. Side by side seats under rearward sliding canopy. Dual controls standard.

POWER PLANT: One 50·7 kW (68 hp) Limbach SL 1700 EI (optionally a 59·5 kW; 80 hp Limbach L 2000 EOI) flat-four engine, driving a Hoffmann HO-V-62R/L160T two-blade adjustable-pitch fully-feathering propeller with spinner. Single fuel tank aft of cockpit, capacity 40 litres (8·8 Imp gallons) standard, 60 litres (13·2 Imp gallons) optional.

DIMENSIONS, EXTERNAL: As IS-28B2 except:
- Length overall — 7·00 m (22 ft 11½ in)
- Height over tail — 2·15 m (7 ft 0¾ in)
- Wheel track — 1·36 m (4 ft 5½ in)

WEIGHTS AND LOADINGS:
- Weight empty — 560 kg (1,234 lb)
- Max T-O weight — 760 kg (1,675 lb)
- Max wing loading — 41·7 kg/m² (8·54 lb/sq ft)
- Max power loading: 68 hp — 14·7 kg/kW (24·1 lb/hp)
- 80 hp — 12·7 kg/kW (20·9 lb/hp)

PERFORMANCE, UNPOWERED (at max T-O weight):
- Best glide ratio at 54 knots (100 km/h; 62 mph) — 27
- Min rate of sink at 43 knots (80 km/h; 50 mph) — 1·20 m (3·94 ft)/s
- Stalling speed, flaps down — 36 knots (66 km/h; 41 mph)
- Max speed (smooth air) — 113 knots (210 km/h; 130 mph)
- Max speed (rough air) — 95 knots (177 km/h; 110 mph)
- g limits — +5·3/−2·65

PERFORMANCE, POWERED (at max T-O weight):
- Never-exceed speed — 113 knots (210 km/h; 130 mph)
- Max level speed:
  - 68 hp — 97 knots (180 km/h; 112 mph)
  - 80 hp — 100 knots (185 km/h; 115 mph)
- Max cruising speed — 92 knots (170 km/h; 106 mph)
- Econ cruising speed — 70 knots (130 km/h; 81 mph)
- Stalling speed — 36 knots (65 km/h; 41 mph)
- Max rate of climb at S/L: 68 hp — 120 m (394 ft)/min
  - 80 hp — 138 m (453 ft)/min
- Service ceiling: 68 hp — 4,700 m (15,420 ft)
  - 80 hp — 5,000 m (16,400 ft)
- T-O run (grass) — 250 m (820 ft)
- T-O to 15 m (50 ft) (grass): 68 hp — 593 m (1,945 ft)
  - 80 hp — 430 m (1,410 ft)
- Landing run — 90 m (295 ft)
- Range with max fuel, no reserves — 243 nm (450 km; 280 miles)
- g limits — +5·3/−2·65

IS-29D2

Descriptions can be found in the 1980-81 and earlier editions of *Jane's* of the IS-29B, D, D3, D4, E, E4, G, and IS-31(E3). None of these versions is now in production. Models current in 1985 were as follows:

IS-29D2. Current Standard Class version, with improved cockpit and controls, Hütter airbrakes, separate tailplane and elevator, and improved rigging system. Certificated in Australia, Canada, West Germany, Hungary, Switzerland, Turkey, the USA and elsewhere. More than 200 built; in production.

IS-29D2 Club. Club Class version of D2, with flaps deleted and non-retractable monowheel. Certification granted. Small number built, including some for Australia; in production.

The following description applies to the IS-29D2, except where indicated:

TYPE: Single-seat Standard Class (Club class) sailplane.

AIRFRAME: Cantilever shoulder-wing monoplane, with T tail. Wortmann wing sections: FX-61-163 at root, FX-61-126 at tip. All-metal wings, with main spar, false rear spar and riveted dural skin. Full span trailing-edge flaps and ailerons, coupled to operate in unison but can be disconnected for separate operation during landing. Hütter airbrake in upper surface of each wing. All-metal semi-monocoque fuselage. Detachable glassfibre nose-cap. Cantilever all-metal T tail, with full span elevator. Retractable sprung monowheel, with brake; non-retractable tailwheel. Canopy hinges sideways to starboard and can be jettisoned in flight.

DIMENSIONS, EXTERNAL:
- Wing span: 15·00 m (49 ft 2½ in)
- Wing aspect ratio: 21·63
- Length overall: 7·30 m (23 ft 11½ in)
- Height over tail: 1·68 m (5 ft 6¼ in)

AREA:
- Wings, gross: 10·40 m² (111·9 sq ft)

WEIGHTS AND LOADING:
- Weight empty: 240 kg (529 lb)
- Max T-O weight: 360 kg (793 lb)
- Max wing loading: 34·62 kg/m² (7·09 lb/sq ft)

PERFORMANCE (at max T-O weight):
- Best glide ratio at 50 knots (93 km/h; 58 mph):
  - D2: 37
  - D2 Club: 36
- Min rate of sink at 42 knots (78 km/h; 48 mph): 0·65 m (2·13 ft)/s
- Stalling speed:
  - D2 (flaps down): 36 knots (65 km/h; 41 mph)
  - D2 Club: 41 knots (75 km/h; 47 mph)
- Max speed (smooth air): 121 knots (225 km/h; 140 mph)
- Max speed (rough air): 93 knots (172 km/h; 107 mph)
- Max aero-tow speed: 76 knots (140 km/h; 87 mph)
- Max winch-launching speed: 70 knots (130 km/h; 81 mph)
- *g* limits: +5·3/−2·65

IS-30

The IS-30, which underwent flight testing in the Spring of 1978, is based on the IS-28B2. Two prototypes were built. Eight production aircraft had been ordered by Spring 1982, and production was continuing in 1985. The modified IS-30A (1984-85 *Jane's*) is not in production.

TYPE: Tandem two-seat sailplane.

AIRFRAME: All-metal cantilever shoulder-wing monoplane. Wortmann wing sections: FX-61-163 at root, FX-60-126 at tip. Dihedral 2°. Incidence 4°. No sweep on leading-edge. Hütter two-plate upper and lower surface metal airbrakes. All-metal ailerons; flaps optional. All-metal semi-monocoque fuselage, generally similar to IS-28B2. All-metal cantilever T tail, with full span elevator. Standard landing gear comprises a non-retractable rubber sprung 5 in Tost monowheel and 210 × 65 mm tailwheel; a semi-retractable 6 in monowheel and 280 × 85 mm nosewheel are available optionally. One-piece canopy opens sideways to starboard, and can be jettisoned in flight. Dual controls standard; fully equipped front and rear instrument panels optional. Nose towing hook, with Tost cable release, standard; CG towing hook optional. No provision for water ballast.

DIMENSIONS, EXTERNAL, AND WING AREA: As IS-28B2 except:
- Height over tail: 2·27 m (7 ft 5½ in)

WEIGHTS AND LOADINGS: As IS-28B2

PERFORMANCE (at max T-O weight): As IS-28B2 except:
- Stalling speed:
  - single-seat: 38 knots (70 km/h; 43 mph)
  - two-seat: 41 knots (75 km/h; 47 mph)
- Max speed (smooth air):
  - single-seat: 135 knots (250 km/h; 155 mph)
  - two-seat: 121 knots (225 km/h; 140 mph)
- Max speed (rough air): 86 knots (160 km/h; 99 mph)
- Max winch-launching speed: 67 knots (125 km/h; 78 mph)

IS-32

First shown publicly at the Paris Air Show in June 1977, the IS-32 tandem two-seat Open Class sailplane was developed from the IS-28B2. Certification is to BCAR Section E.

Three more IS-32s had been built by 1983, and small scale production was continuing in early 1985. Customers to date have been from Australia, the UK and the USA.

TYPE: Tandem two-seat Open Class sailplane.

AIRFRAME: All-metal cantilever shoulder-wing monoplane. Wortmann wing sections: FX-67-K-170 at root, FX-67-K-150 at tip. Dihedral 2° 30′. Incidence 2°. Sweepforward 2° on leading-edge. Hütter two-plate upper and lower surface metal airbrakes. All-metal interconnected flaps and ailerons. All-metal semi-monocoque fuselage, generally similar to IS-28B2 and IS-30. All-metal cantilever T tail, with full span elevator. Mechanically retractable Tost monowheel, size 5·00-5, with Tost double shoe brake and oleo-pneumatic shock absorber; semi-recessed 210 × 65 mm tailwheel. One-piece jettisonable canopy, opening sideways to starboard; tinted canopy optional. Dual controls standard; fully equipped front and rear instrument panels optional. Nose towing hook, with Tost cable release. No provision for water ballast.

DIMENSIONS, EXTERNAL:
- Wing span: 20·00 m (65 ft 7½ in)
- Wing aspect ratio: 27·25
- Length overall: 8·36 m (27 ft 5¼ in)
- Height over tail: 2·27 m (7 ft 5½ in)

AREA:
- Wings, gross: 14·68 m² (158·0 sq ft)

WEIGHTS AND LOADING:
- Weight empty: 400 kg (882 lb)
- Max T-O weight: 590 kg (1,300 lb)
- Max wing loading: 40·2 kg/m² (8·23 lb/sq ft)

PERFORMANCE (at max T-O weight):
- Best glide ratio at 59 knots (110 km/h; 68 mph): 44·5
- Min rate of sink at 49 knots (90 km/h; 56 mph): 0·62 m (2·03 ft)/s
- Stalling speed: 42 knots (78 km/h; 49 mph)
- Max speed (smooth air): 105 knots (195 km/h; 121 mph)
- Max speed (rough air): 87 knots (161 km/h; 100 mph)
- Max aero-tow speed: 76 knots (140 km/h; 87 mph)
- Max winch-launching speed: 59 knots (110 km/h; 68 mph)
- *g* limits: +4/−1·5

IAR-35

The IAR-35 is a single-seat all-metal glider designed to JAR 22 requirements, essentially for aerobatics but also for general purpose use. The wings have a 'flaperon' trailing-edge, for improved manoeuvrability and low landing speed. Design began in 1984, and the prototype (illustrated) made its first flight in May 1986.

TYPE: Single-seat aerobatic sailplane.

AIRFRAME: Cantilever shoulder-wing monoplane, with constant chord non-swept centre-section (NACA 64-015) and tapered outer panels. Dihedral 0° on centre-section, 2° on outer panels. Incidence 1°. Three-spar wing structure, with stiffened skins and ribs, each wing being attached to fuselage by two fittings each side. All-metal statically balanced ailerons (outboard) and flaps (inboard) occupy entire trailing-edge, the flaps operating also as 'flaperons' to supplement the ailerons. Automatic and aerodynamic trim tab in each aileron. All-metal DFS type upper and lower surface airbrakes. Metal endplate, with sprung rubber balancer wheel, at each wingtip. Fuselage has a steel alloy tubular mainframe in cockpit/wing/mainwheel area, with aluminium alloy frames and longerons elsewhere, all being covered with duralumin skin panels. Sweptback fin and statically balanced rudder; fixed incidence, strut braced tailplane with statically balanced elevators. Trim tab in each elevator. Ailerons, flaps, airbrakes and elevators are actuated by pushrods; rudder and elevator tabs are cable actuated. Mechanically retractable 340 × 125 mm monowheel, with brake; semi-recessed, non-retractable 210 × 65 mm tailwheel. Single seat for pilot (adjustable for height and inclination), under one-piece detachable Plexiglas canopy.

DIMENSIONS, EXTERNAL:
- Wing span: 12·00 m (39 ft 4½ in)
- Wing aspect ratio: 13·33
- Length overall: 6·20 m (20 ft 4 in)
- Height over tail: 1·45 m (4 ft 9 in)

AREA:
- Wings, gross: 10·80 m² (116·2 sq ft)

WEIGHTS AND LOADING:
- Weight empty: approx 230 kg (507 lb)
- Max T-O weight: 330 kg (727 lb)
- Max wing loading: 30·55 kg/m² (6·26 lb/sq ft)

PERFORMANCE (estimated):
- Best glide ratio at 51 knots (95 km/h; 59 mph): 28
- Min rate of sink at 43 knots (80 km/h; 50 mph): 0·85 m (2·79 ft)/s
- Stalling speed: flaps up: 38 knots (69 km/h; 43 mph)
  - flaps down: 33 knots (60 km/h; 38 mph)
- Max speed (smooth air): 217 knots (402 km/h; 250 mph)
- Max speed (rough air): 105 knots (194 km/h; 120 mph)
- *g* limits: +8/−7

SWEDEN

RADAB

AB RADAB

PO Box 81054, S-104 81 Stockholm
Telephone: (46) 8 440610
Telex: 124 43 FOTEX S Att WINDEXRADAB
MANAGING DIRECTOR: Harald Unden
CO-DESIGNER: Sven Ridder

RADAB WINDEX 1200

This small single-seat motor glider was designed in 1981 to meet the requirements of JAR 22 (Aerobatic category). Construction of the Windex 1100 prototype (SE-XSD) started in January 1982, and this made its first flight, unpowered, on 15 March 1985. Test flying with a 16·4 kW (22 hp) Limbach engine started in the Summer of 1985, but production aircraft are slightly higher powered with a new engine comprising three chain-saw cylinders in line and offering 18·6 kW (25 hp). The prototype had hot-wire shaped wings of 11·00 m (36 ft 1 in) span, but production kit aircraft, designated Windex 1200, have Nomex honeycomb moulded wings of increased span, though the wing area remains unchanged. The tailplane, originally mounted halfway up the fin, has been raised to a T configuration to simplify rudder geometry and improve elevator efficiency.

The prototype was described and illustrated in the 1985-86 *Jane's*. The following details apply to the 1986 production kit version:

TYPE: Single-seat homebuilt motor glider.

AIRFRAME: Cantilever mid-wing monoplane, with KTH-FFA (Stockholm Royal Institute of Technology) laminar flow wing section having 17% thickness/chord ratio from root to tip. Dihedral 3° 30′ from roots. Incidence 2° 35′ 24″. No sweep. Wings have a single spar of unidirectional glassfibre, with glassfibre/epoxy/Nomex honeycomb sandwich skin, and are detachable for transportation and storage. Bottom-hinged plain flaps/airbrakes, top-hinged balanced ailerons, and downswept winglets at tips, are all of similar construction, as are the fuselage, sweptback fin and rudder, and non-swept T tailplane and elevators. Non-retractable, partially enclosed unsprung monowheel at CG, with 305 mm diameter tyre and band brake. Tailwheel; recessed wheel at base of each winglet.

POWER PLANT: One 18·6 kW (25 hp) three-cylinder air-cooled two-stroke chain-saw engine, with V belt reduction drive to a Radab propeller which has mechanically operated variable pitch and feathering and two Kevlar blades. Engine is mounted halfway up fin, with propeller shaft tilted at 8° to thrust line, lowering resultant thrust vector axis due to slipstream deflection by horizontal tail. Single aluminium fuel tank below wing spar central joint, capacity approx 20 litres (4·4 Imp gallons). Single moulded, reclined bucket seat under two-piece canopy, rear portion of which opens upward. Ballistic parachute optional.

DIMENSIONS, EXTERNAL:
- Wing span: 12·00 m (39 ft 4½ in)
- Wing aspect ratio: 19·43
- Length overall: 5·00 m (16 ft 5 in)
- Height over tail: 1·25 m (4 ft 1¼ in)
- Propeller diameter: 1·00 m (3 ft 3¼ in)

AREA:
- Wings, gross: 7·41 m² (79·8 sq ft)

WEIGHTS AND LOADINGS:
- Weight empty: 120 kg (264 lb)
- Max T-O weight: 250 kg (551 lb)
- Max wing loading: 33·74 kg/m² (6·91 lb/sq ft)
- Max power loading: 13·44 kg/kW (22·05 lb/hp)

PERFORMANCE, UNPOWERED (estimated at max T-O weight):
- *Best glide ratio at 49 knots (90 km/h; 56 mph): 34
- *Min rate of sink at 40 knots (75 km/h; 47 mph): 0·70 m (2·30 ft)/s
- Stalling speed: 32 knots (59 km/h; 37 mph)
- Max speed (smooth air): 170 knots (316 km/h; 196 mph)
- Max speed (rough air): 94 knots (175 km/h; 109 mph)
- *g* limits: +7/−5

* *11·00 m span prototype*

PERFORMANCE, POWERED (estimated at max T-O weight):
- Never-exceed speed: 170 knots (316 km/h; 196 mph)
- Max level speed: 130 knots (240 km/h; 149 mph)
- Max cruising speed: 108 knots (200 km/h; 124 mph)
- Econ cruising speed (30% power): 85 knots (157 km/h; 97 mph)
- Stalling speed, flaps down: 33 knots (60 km/h; 38 mph)
- Max rate of climb at S/L: 240 m (787 ft)/min
- T-O run (grass): 100 m (328 ft)
- Landing run: 80 m (262 ft)
- Range with max fuel, no reserves: 485 nm (900 km; 559 miles)

Danish-registered IS-30 two-seat sailplane *(Adolf Wilsch)*

ICA Brasov IS-32 Open Class sailplane

Prototype of the aerobatic single-seat IAR-35

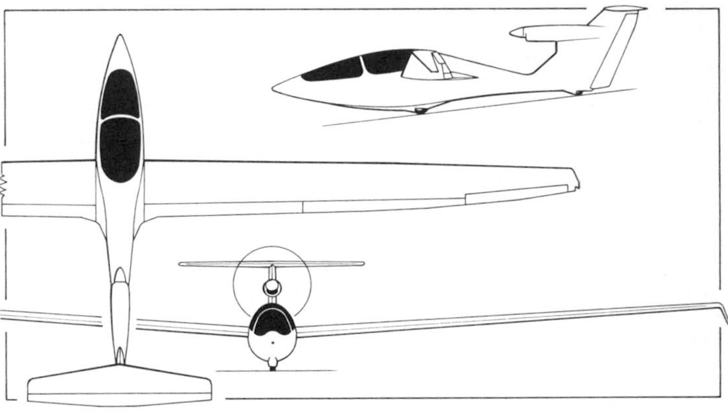

Radab Windex 1200 powered sailplane *(Michael A. Badrocke)*

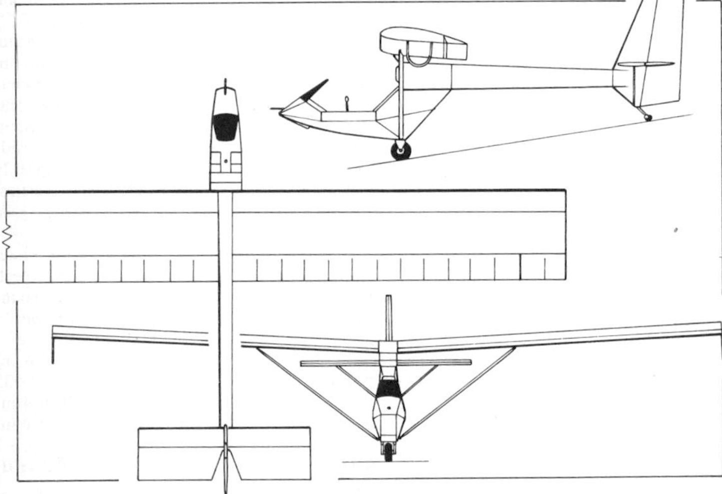

The ANB primary training glider designed by students of the Kuibyshev Aviation Institute *(Michael A. Badrocke)*

Self-launch prototype of the Canard SC sailplane

SWITZERLAND

CANARD

CANARD AVIATION AG
(Division of H. Bucher Leichtmetallbau)

Sagenrainstrasse 5, CH-8636 Wald
Telephone: (055) 952055

CANARD AVIATION CANARD SC

The Canard SC is based on the Canard-2 FL foot launched sailplane designed by Dipl-Ing Hans U. Farner, which was described and illustrated in the 1982-83 and earlier editions of *Jane's*. A prototype of the Canard SC was first flown on 23 July 1983, and made 40 flights, totalling about 20 hours, in its first year. To accelerate the flight test programme, it was given self-launch capability by mounting a 15 kW (11·2 hp) König three-cylinder two-stroke engine, with a foldable propeller, on a pylon between the V struts and main wing.

Flight tests of the powered SC were so successful that after registration of the glider version, planned for Summer 1985, it was intended to obtain certification, to JAR 22, of a powered sailplane variant. This was originally scheduled for Autumn 1985, but development was suspended temporarily in order to concentrate on more important activities. It was due to be resumed in Spring 1986, thereby postponing certification until the end of 1986 at the earliest.

Designated **Canard SCM**, the powered version will have a 11·2-13·4 kW (15-18 hp) three-cylinder two-stroke engine with a special low-noise propeller/exhaust system. It will be possible to convert Canard SC sailplanes into Canard SCMs by installing the power modification kit. After the construction of a small pre-series number, Canard Aviation may consider granting a licence for production.

TYPE: Single-seat sailplane (SC) or motor glider (SCM).

AIRFRAME: 'Parasol monoplane' configuration, with single-spar anhedral main wing at rear supported by V-form pylons which act as both lifting surfaces and 'vertical' fins; fixed incidence foreplane, with elevator. Aerofoil sections: Wortmann FX-63-137 (main wings and V struts), Eppler E 1232 (foreplane), and Clark Y (11·7% thickness/chord ratio) (winglets). Wings have ailerons; trailing-edges of V tail pylons movable to act as spoilers. Construction is of glassfibre, Kevlar and carbonfibre rovings, CIBA XB 3052 epoxy and Rohacell foam plastics. Three-axis control by ailerons, forward elevator, and dependent winglet/rudder at each wingtip. Non-retractable semi-recessed bungee sprung steerable mono-wheel, size 260 × 85 mm, with brake; semi-recessed fixed tailwheel, size 200 × 50 mm. Pre-series aircraft under construction in January 1985 have revised, sideways opening, canopy.

POWER PLANT (SCM): One 15 to 18 kW (11·2 to 13·4 hp) three-cylinder two-stroke radial engine with reduction drive to a two-blade pusher propeller with foldable Kevlar blades. Single fuel tank, capacity 10 litres (2·2 Imp gallons). Entire engine unit (but not fuel tank) can be removed for normal soaring flights.

DIMENSIONS, EXTERNAL:
- Wing span: 13·50 m (44 ft 3½ in)
- Foreplane span: 3·80 m (12 ft 5½ in)
- Wing aspect ratio: 21·19
- Foreplane aspect ratio: 6·02
- Length overall: 4·75 m (15 ft 7 in)
- Height overall: 2·23 m (7 ft 3¾ in)
- Propeller diameter (SC prototype): 1·10 m (3 ft 7¼ in)

AREAS:
- Wings, gross: 8·60 m² (92·57 sq ft)
- Foreplane, gross: 2·40 m² (25·83 sq ft)

WEIGHTS AND LOADINGS:
- Weight empty: SC (without engine): 130 kg (287 lb)
  - SCM: 150 kg (331 lb)
- Max T-O weight: SC: 240 kg (529 lb)
  - SCM: 270 kg (595 lb)
- Max wing/foreplane loading:
  - SC: 21·8 kg/m² (4·46 lb/sq ft)
  - SCM: 24·5 kg/m² (5·02 lb/sq ft)

PERFORMANCE, UNPOWERED (SC, estimated at max T-O weight):
- Best glide ratio at 39 knots (72 km/h; 45 mph): 25-30
- Min rate of sink at 33 knots (62 km/h; 38 mph): 0·60-0·70 m (1·97-2·30 ft)/s
- Max speed (smooth air): 97 knots (180 km/h; 112 mph)
- Max speed (rough air): 68 knots (126 km/h; 78 mph)
- Stalling speed: SC: 28 knots (51 km/h; 32 mph)
  - SCM: 30 knots (55 km/h; 35 mph)

PERFORMANCE, POWERED (SCM, estimated at max T-O weight):
- Max rate of climb at S/L: 90-120 m (295-395 ft)/min
- T-O distance (on concrete): 80-100 m (265-330 ft)

UNION OF SOVIET SOCIALIST REPUBLICS

KAPU

KUIBYSHEV AVIATION INSTITUTE AND PRODUCTION UNIT

KAPU ANB

This single-seat training glider was designed by students of the Kuibyshev Aviation Institute and constructed by workers and engineers of the Kuibyshev Aviation Production Unit. It will be used for the basic instruction and training of students in Youth Gliding Schools of the Defence Community. It was first flown in 1983 at Mt Klementyevo, in the Crimea, by test pilot B. Parfenov.

TYPE: Single-seat primary training glider.

AIRFRAME: Strut braced high-wing monoplane with TsAGI R-III aerofoil section. Cruciform tail configuration, with strut braced tailplane. Constant chord wings with dihedral; full span ailerons. All-metal structure, with fabric (muslin) covered fuselage, wings and tail surfaces. Wing has tubular spar and single bracing struts. Single-piece integral ribs are drop forged, as are the aileron frame and ribs. Wing leading-edge is reinforced with thin duralumin strip. Constant chord tailplane and elevator (with cutaway for rudder clearance) are mounted near base of fin. Tail structure similar to wing. Single-seat open cockpit, with windscreen. Non-retractable mainwheel, castoring tailwheel, and wingtip skids. No brakes.

DIMENSIONS, EXTERNAL:
Wing span approx 9·00 m (29 ft 6½ in)
Wing aspect ratio approx 7·71
Length overall 5·40 m (17 ft 8¾ in)
Height overall approx 1·80 m (5 ft 11 in)

AREA:
Wings, gross 10·50 m² (113·0 sq ft)

WEIGHTS AND LOADING:
Weight empty 75 kg (165 lb)
Max T-O weight 165 kg (364 lb)
Max wing loading 15·71 kg/m² (3·22 lb/sq ft)

PERFORMANCE (at max T-O weight):
Max speed (smooth air) 89 knots (165 km/h; 102 mph)
Stalling speed 30 knots (55 km/h; 35 mph)
Landing speed 19 knots (35 km/h; 22 mph)

LAK

LITOVSKAYA AVIATSIONNAYA KONSTRUKTSIYA (Lithuanian Aircraft Construction)

Prenaisk, Litovsk SSR (Lithuania)
DIRECTOR: Vitautas Pakarskas
DEPUTY DIRECTOR: V. Myakshryunas
CHIEF DESIGNERS:
Boleslavas Karvyalis
Bronius Oshkinis
CHIEF TEST PILOT: Vitautas Shliumba
HEAD OF PRODUCTION: Antanas Paknis

As described in the 1985-86 and earlier editions, this factory originated in 1969 with the initial objective of developing a plastics-construction sailplane. Its first (and the first Soviet) plastics sailplane, designed by Boleslavas Karvyalis, was the BK-7 Lietuva, which was first flown on 8 December 1972 and was described and illustrated in the 1975-76 *Jane's*. This has undergone progressive development, the latest version being the LAK-12.

LAK is now the sole overhaul centre in the USSR for Czechoslovak Blanik sailplanes. Repairs have also been undertaken of German MBB Phoebus and Schleicher ASW 15 plastics sailplanes. A new, larger factory was opened in 1981 to build the BRO-23KR and LAK-14 elementary training gliders.

Production of the Oshkinis BRO-11M (alias LAK-2), last described in the 1984-85 *Jane's*, has probably ended. More recent designs include the LAK-5 motor glider and 15 metre Class LAK-11 sailplane, all known details of which are given in this entry.

LAK-5 NYAMUNAS

The LAK-5 is a side by side two-seat motor glider of national design, of which several prototypes were under construction in 1980. The aircraft, designed by engineer K. Iochas, is named after a river in Lithuania, and is intended primarily for training pilots of sailplanes and powered aircraft for participation in national and international competitions, and for record attempts. Other possible applications include forest fire-spotting patrol, meteorological investigation, and geological reconnaissance.

According to a report in *Skrzydlata Polska* in 1982, the Nyamunas is of GRP construction. The 62 kW (83 hp) engine is mounted aft of the cockpit and drives a two-blade pusher propeller. Little has been heard of the LAK-5 since that time, and its present status is uncertain.

DIMENSIONS, EXTERNAL:
Wing span 20·60 m (67 ft 7 in)
Wing aspect ratio 22·00
Length overall 8·00 m (26 ft 3 in)

AREA:
Wings, gross 19·29 m² (207·6 sq ft)

WEIGHTS AND LOADINGS:
Weight empty 530 kg (1,168 lb)
Max T-O weight 750 kg (1,653 lb)
Max wing loading 38·88 kg/m² (7·97 lb/sq ft)
Max power loading 12·12 kg/kW (19·92 lb/hp)

PERFORMANCE, UNPOWERED:
Best glide ratio 42
Min rate of sink at 43 knots (80 km/h; 50 mph) 0·60 m (1·97 ft)/s

PERFORMANCE, POWERED:
Max level speed 135 knots (250 km/h; 155 mph)
Econ cruising speed 58 knots (107 km/h; 66 mph)
Stalling speed 41 knots (76 km/h; 48 mph)

LAK-11 NIDA

This single-seat 15 metre Class sailplane, named after a tributary of the River Vistula, was designed by Ionas Bankauskas and flew for the first time on 6 July 1982. Aircraft SSSR-006 was illustrated in the October 1985 issue of *Krilya Rodini*, at which time the Nida was stated to have entered series production. The wings have a glasscloth skin with expanded plastics foam infill and, like the glassfibre monocoque fuselage, are reinforced with carbonfibre tape.

DIMENSIONS, EXTERNAL:
Wing span 15·00 m (49 ft 2½ in)
Wing aspect ratio 21·99
Length overall 6·76 m (22 ft 2¼ in)

AREA:
Wings, gross 10·23 m² (110·1 sq ft)

WEIGHTS AND LOADINGS:
Weight empty 220 kg (485 lb)
Max water ballast 160 kg (352 lb)
Max T-O weight: without ballast 330 kg (727 lb)
with ballast 480 kg (1,058 lb)
Max wing loading:
without ballast 32·26 kg/m² (6·61 lb/sq ft)
with ballast 46·92 kg/m² (9·61 lb/sq ft)

PERFORMANCE (A: at 330 kg; 727 lb, B: at 480 kg; 1,058 lb AUW):
Best glide ratio:
A at 49 knots (91 km/h; 57 mph) 40
B at 59 knots (110 km/h; 69 mph) 42
Min rate of sink:
A at 40 knots (73 km/h; 46 mph) 0·56 m (1·84 ft)/s
B at 48 knots (88 km/h; 55 mph) 0·68 m (2·23 ft)/s
Stalling speed: A 36 knots (65 km/h; 41 mph)
B 42 knots (78 km/h; 49 mph)
Max speed (smooth air):
A, B 145 knots (270 km/h; 167 mph)
Max speed (rough air):
A 49 knots (91 km/h; 56 mph)
B 59 knots (110 km/h; 68 mph)
Max aero-tow speed: A 39 knots (73 km/h; 45 mph)
B 47 knots (88 km/h; 54 mph)

LAK-12 LIETUVA (LITHUANIA)

The Lietuva was the first all-plastics sailplane produced in the USSR, and in its latest known form is designated LAK-12. Development began in 1969; details of the BK-7/7A/7V/7S, LAK-9/9M and LAK-10 early versions can be found in the 1982-83 *Jane's*.

The LAK-12 is the sixth and latest production version. Compared with the earlier versions originated by Boleslavas Karvyalis, it was considerably redesigned under the leadership of Kiastutis Gechas. It is intended as a training aircraft for high class glider pilots participating in all-Soviet and international events, and for record attempts. Compared with the LAK-10 it has a more comfortable cockpit, with improved instrument layout, a better positioned control column, and a one-piece canopy. Streamlining of the airframe is enhanced, the wings are lowered to a mid position, the fuselage and horizontal tail surfaces are of completely new design, and construction makes extensive use of composite materials, including carbonfibre for the wing spars and other components.

First flight of the LAK-12 took place on 21 December 1979. Flight testing was completed in 1980, and deliveries of production aircraft began later that year. A total of 100 Lietuvas had been delivered by late 1985, including 70 LAK-12s.

TYPE: Single-seat Open Class sailplane.

AIRFRAME: Cantilever mid-wing monoplane. Wortmann wing sections: FX-67-K-170 from root to junction with outer panels, then tapering to FX-67-K-150 at tip. No wing fillets. Main wing spar is a carbonfibre T beam. Trailing-edge flaps and interconnected ailerons are attached to auxiliary rear spar. Airbrakes on upper surfaces only. Wings, flaps and ailerons have a skin of three-ply glasscloth, with foam plastics infill between each layer; carbonfibre tape is used to reinforce flap construction. Fuselage, and integral fin, are of glassfibre construction, reinforced with carbonfibre tape. Slightly swept fin and rudder, and non-swept low-mounted tailplane and elevators (all of Wortmann FX-71-L-150/25 section), are of similar construction to wings. Rudder and elevators are mass balanced. Retractable monowheel, with mechanical brake and oleo-pneumatic shock absorber; non-retractable shock absorbing tail bumper. One-piece cockpit canopy. Provision for 250 litres (55 Imp gallons) water ballast in wing leading-edge tanks.

DIMENSIONS, EXTERNAL:
Wing span 20·42 m (67 ft 0 in)
Wing aspect ratio 28·50
Length overall 7·23 m (23 ft 8½ in)
Height over tail 1·70 m (5 ft 7 in)

AREA:
Wings, gross 14·63 m² (157·5 sq ft)

WEIGHTS AND LOADING:
Weight empty 340 kg (749 lb)
Max T-O weight:
without water ballast 430 kg (948 lb)
with water ballast 650 kg (1,433 lb)
Max wing loading 44·42 kg/m² (9·10 lb/sq ft)

PERFORMANCE (at max T-O weight except where indicated):
Best glide ratio at 61 knots (113 km/h; 70 mph) 48
Min rate of sink at 46 knots (85 km/h; 53 mph), at 430 kg (948 lb) AUW 0·50 m (1·64 ft)/s
Stalling speed 36 knots (65 km/h; 41 mph)
Max speed (smooth air) 135 knots (250 km/h; 155 mph)
Max aero-tow speed 62 knots (115 km/h; 71 mph)

OSHKINIS BRO-23KR GARNIS (STORK)

Designed in 1981, the BRO-23KR is a single-seat open-cockpit primary training glider, designed to provide a successor to the BRO-11M/LAK-2. Mr Oshkinis was assisted in its design by pilots Ch. Kishonas and K. Rinkyavichus of the Kaunassky hang gliding club. Production is believed to have started in about 1983 or 1984.

AIRFRAME: Strut and steel cable braced high-wing monoplane. Constant chord slotted wings have a GA(W)-1 aerofoil section, 16% thickness/chord ratio, dihedral from roots, full span ailerons and turned-down tips. Ribs and spar are of woven glassfibre, with three-ply glasscloth skin forward of main spar. Spaces between ends of ribs filled with flat plates made of two layers of glasscloth. Trailing fixed portion of wings is cast with epoxy filler, using longitudinal glassfibre, and covered with glasscloth. Entire ribbed surface is then covered with Lavsan film, glued in position and heat-shrunk to fit. Ailerons are of similar construction. Wingtips of textolite. GRP fuselage, including cockpit, is built in two halves. T tail unit is of similar construction to wings. Five rubber blocks provide main landing shock absorption, to which can be fitted a wide GRP snow skid for Winter flying; the same skid with a wheel attached for Summer use; a tricycle undercarriage for 'aeroplane landing' training; or floats for waterborne operation. Self-sprung tail bumper of glassfibre reinforced resin. Aircraft has been tested also with a small nosewheel. Open cockpit, lined with polyurethane and fitted with windscreen and foam plastics reclining seat.

DIMENSIONS, EXTERNAL:
Wing span 8·20 m (26 ft 10¾ in)
Wing aspect ratio 6·47
Length overall 6·40 m (21 ft 0 in)
Height over tail 2·20 m (7 ft 2½ in)

AREA:
Wings, gross 10·40 m² (111·9 sq ft)

WEIGHTS AND LOADING:
Weight empty 83·5 kg (184 lb)
Max T-O weight 158·5 kg (349 lb)
Max wing loading 15·2 kg/m² (3·11 lb/sq ft)

PERFORMANCE:
Best glide ratio 15
Min rate of sink 1·00 m (3·28 ft)/s
Stalling speed 23 knots (42 km/h; 27 mph)
Max speed (smooth air) 54 knots (100 km/h; 62 mph)

LAK-14 STRAZDAS (THRUSH)

Designed by Antanas Paknis, the LAK-14 was developed as a successor to the Oshkinis BRO-11M/LAK-2 (1984-85 *Jane's*), together with the Oshkinis BRO-23KR. Early aircraft retained the wooden wing spars and ribs of the LAK-2; later production LAK-14s were intended to have all-GRP wings.

AIRFRAME: Strut braced high-wing monoplane, with TsAGI R-P aerofoil section, 14% thickness/chord ratio, 5° dihedral, and full span ailerons. Wings of initial production aircraft have wooden spars and ribs (to be replaced by glassfibre reinforced polyester resin units on later aircraft), and a glassfibre skin. Wingtips are covered with glasscloth. Forward fuselage, including cockpit floor, is entirely of three-ply glassfibre with a 5 mm foam infill, except for a wooden nose fairing to which the towing cable is attached. Main load bearing frame aft of this section, to which are attached wings and struts, landing gear, and rear fuselage with integral fin. Tailplane, attached to fuselage main longeron, has foam plastics ribs and a two-ply glasscloth skin.

DIMENSIONS, EXTERNAL:
Wing span 7·34 m (24 ft 1 in)
Wing aspect ratio 5·08
Length overall 5·25 m (17 ft 2¾ in)
Height over tail 2·30 m (7 ft 6½ in)

AREA:
Wings, gross 10·60 m² (114·1 sq ft)

WEIGHTS AND LOADING:
Weight empty 100 kg (220 lb)
Max T-O weight 185 kg (408 lb)
Max wing loading 17·5 kg/m² (3·58 lb/sq ft)

PERFORMANCE:
Best glide ratio at 28 knots (52 km/h; 32 mph) 13
Min rate of sink at 27 knots (50 km/h; 31 mph) 1·10 m (3·61 ft)/s
Max speed (rough and smooth air) 54 knots (100 km/h; 62 mph)
Stalling speed 25 knots (45 km/h; 28 mph)
g limits +4/−2

LAK-5 Nyamunas two-seat motor glider *(Skrzydlata Polska)*

LAK-12 Lietuva Open Class sailplane (reproduced from *Letectvi + Kosmonautika*)

LAK-14 Strazdas, produced to succeed the BRO-11M (reproduced from *Krilya Rodini*)

Oshkinis BRO-23KR primary training glider (reproduced from *Krilya Rodini*)

Lightwing L6FS Mouse experimental lightweight sailplane

INAV Monerai P self-launching 12 metre sailplane

UNITED KINGDOM

LIGHTWING

LIGHTWING RESEARCH

68 Timberleys, Littlehampton, West Sussex BN1 6QB
Telephone: (0903) 722578
DESIGNER/BUILDER: John M. Lee

LIGHTWING L6FS MOUSE

Lightwing has been in existence for ten years, designing and building aircraft for slow-speed flight research. The Mouse was conceived specifically to investigate the suitability of its wing section, configuration and handling qualities for a subsequent foot-launchable sailplane. It is the designer's aim to reintroduce inexpensive glider flying to the UK. Construction of the Mouse prototype started in January 1984, and the first flight took place three months later. It has been found safe and easy to operate with two people, launch being achieved with bungee or car wheel winch. A pre-production prototype was under construction in early 1985, and kits or plans were then expected to be available in 1986. Provision is made to accommodate a power plant.

TYPE: Single-seat lightweight research sailplane.

AIRFRAME: Cantilever high-wing monoplane with cruciform tail unit. Wings have a Göttingen 535 aerofoil section. Dihedral 0° on upper surface. Incidence 3°. No sweep at 30 per cent chord. Hemlock and birch ply wings, with plywood ailerons. No flaps, spoilers or airbrakes. Rectangular box fuselage with plywood bulkheads and longerons. Tail unit comprises plywood box spars with ribs built around. Fabric covered wings, fuselage and tail surfaces. All-moving tailplane. Light ash skid incorporating rubber block shock absorption. Streamlined, open cockpit. No water ballast.

POWER PLANT (optional: not fitted up to early 1985): One 8·6 kW (11·5 hp) Aspira lawn mower engine, driving a Lightwing gull-blade propeller. Engine mounted plastics fuel tank, capacity 1 litre (0·2 Imp gallons).

DIMENSIONS, EXTERNAL:
- Wing span: 10·67 m (35 ft 0 in)
- Wing aspect ratio: 8·01
- Length overall: 6·48 m (21 ft 3 in)
- Height over tail: 1·68 m (5 ft 6 in)
- Propeller diameter: 0·61 m (2 ft 0 in)

AREA:
- Wings, gross: 14·21 m² (153·0 sq ft)

WEIGHTS AND LOADING (without engine):
- Weight empty: 72·5 kg (160 lb)
- Max T-O weight: 163 kg (360 lb)
- Max wing loading: 11·47 kg/m² (2·35 lb/sq ft)

PERFORMANCE, UNPOWERED:
- Best glide ratio at 22 knots (40 km/h; 25 mph): 16
- Min rate of sink: 0·82 m (2·70 ft)/s
- Stalling speed: 13 knots (24 km/h; 15 mph)
- Max speed (smooth air): 52 knots (96 km/h; 60 mph)
- Max speed (rough air): 43 knots (80 km/h; 50 mph)
- Max aero-tow speed and max winch-launching speed: 35 knots (64 km/h; 40 mph)
- g limits: +6/−3

PERFORMANCE, POWERED (estimated):
- Max cruising speed: 26 knots (48 km/h; 30 mph)
- Econ cruising speed: 22 knots (40 km/h; 25 mph)
- Stalling speed: 16 knots (29 km/h; 18 mph)
- T-O run (winch launch): 9 m (30 ft)
- Landing run: 15 m (50 ft)
- Range with max fuel: 260 nm (482 km; 300 miles)

UNITED STATES OF AMERICA

BRYAN

BRYAN AIRCRAFT INC

Williams County Airport, PO Box 488, Bryan, Ohio 43506
Telephone: (419) 636 1340

DIRECTOR: R. E. Schreder

No news of this company's activities has been received since early 1983. Details of its known products at that time can be found in the 1985-86 *Jane's*.

INAV

INAV LTD

895 West 20th Avenue, PO Box 2984, Oshkosh, Wisconsin 54903
Telephone: (414) 426 1212
GENERAL MANAGER: John Monnett

INAV Ltd (Innovative Aviation), a wholly owned subsidiary of the British company Aviation Composites, purchased the assets of Monnett Experimental Aircraft Inc in July 1985. It is continuing to produce the former company's range of aircraft kits and designs.

In addition to the Sonerai powered aircraft (see Sport Aircraft section), INAV produces kits of parts for the Monerai single-seat homebuilt sailplane. By January 1986 a total of 400 Monerai kits had been sold, and more than 100 aircraft had flown. Latest design is the Moni lightweight motor glider.

INAV MONERAI

The **Monerai S**, development of which began in 1976, flew for the first time in March 1978. The kit includes many extruded or preformed components, to permit quick construction with a minimum of equipment or experience. Average construction time is 300 hours.

A 12·00 m (39 ft 4½ in) increased span version, known as the **Monerai Max**, is also available. This has an aspect ratio of 18 and a best glide ratio of 33. Retrofit kits are available to existing Monerai owners.

The **Monerai P** is identical to the S version, but has a small auxiliary engine to permit self-launch and for climb. Assembly time for the Monerai power pod is approximately 15 to 20 hours. The pod kit includes a moulded glassfibre cowl, folding propeller, welded aluminium fuel tank, exhaust system and motor mount. When the engine is started, the blades are deployed by centrifugal force. They retract automatically when the engine is stopped, to reduce drag.

The following details apply to the Monerai S, except where indicated:

TYPE: Single-seat homebuilt sailplane.

AIRFRAME: Cantilever mid-wing monoplane. Wing section Wortmann FX-61-192 (modified). Dihedral 4°. Aluminium main spar of extruded, modified I section; rear spar is an aluminium C channel. Constant chord allows all the aluminium preformed ribs to be identical, and single-piece aluminium skin to wrap around from trailing-edge to trailing-edge. Skin bonded to spars and ribs with Hysol epoxy. Glassfibre wingtips. Aileron and flap skins are preformed and ready for assembly. Fuselage is built up from chrome molybdenum steel tube and is covered by a non-structural premoulded glassfibre shell. A 12·7 cm (5 in) diameter extruded aluminium tube is attached to the frame and extends 3·66 m (12 ft) to the rear where an upright, all-flying, all-aluminium V tail is attached. Non-retractable monowheel, with mechanical brake. Tailskid standard; steerable tailwheel optional. One-piece flush-fitting canopy. No provision for water ballast.

POWER PLANT (Monerai P): One 15 kW (20 hp) 250 cc Zenoah G25B-2 single-cylinder two-stroke engine initially; replaced from 1985 by an 18·5 kW (25 hp) König three-cylinder radial engine with electric starting. Two-blade propeller, with folding blades. Fuel capacity 7·6 litres (2 US gallons).

DIMENSIONS, EXTERNAL:
- Wing span: 10·97 m (36 ft 0 in)
- Wing aspect ratio: 16·60
- Length overall: 5·97 m (19 ft 7 in)
- Height over tail: 1·32 m (4 ft 4 in)

AREA:
- Wings, gross: 7·25 m² (78·0 sq ft)

WEIGHTS AND LOADINGS:
- Weight empty: S: 100 kg (220 lb)
  - P: 122 kg (270 lb)
- Max T-O weight: S: 204 kg (450 lb)
  - P: 227 kg (500 lb)
- Max wing loading: S: 28·11 kg/m² (5·76 lb/sq ft)
  - P: 31·28 kg/m² (6·41 lb/sq ft)
- Max power loading:
  - P (Zenoah): 15·2 kg/kW (25·0 lb/hp)
  - P (König): 12·27 kg/kW (20·0 lb/hp)

PERFORMANCE, UNPOWERED (at max T-O weight):
- Best glide ratio at 52 knots (97 km/h; 60 mph):
  - S: 28
  - P: 22
- Min rate of sink:
  - S at 48 knots (89 km/h; 55 mph): 0·85 m (2·80 ft)/s
  - P at 42 knots (77 km/h; 48 mph): 0·91 m (3·00 ft)/s
- Stalling speed: S: 33 knots (62 km/h; 38 mph)
  - P: 35 knots (65 km/h; 40 mph)
- Max speed (smooth air):
  - S, P: 104 knots (193 km/h; 120 mph)
- Max speed (rough air):
  - S, P: 78 knots (145 km/h; 90 mph)
- Max aero-tow speed: S: 78 knots (145 km/h; 90 mph)
- *g* limits: ±6

PERFORMANCE, POWERED (P at max T-O weight):
- Max cruising speed: 69 knots (129 km/h; 80 mph)
- Econ cruising speed: 52 knots (97 km/h; 60 mph)
- Stalling speed: 33 knots (62 km/h; 38 mph)
- Max rate of climb at S/L: 152 m (500 ft)/min
- T-O and landing run: 91 m (300 ft)
- Endurance: at full throttle: 1 h
  - at cruise power: 2 h
- *g* limits: ±5·2

INAV MONI

The Moni is a single-seat all-metal motor glider for amateur construction. The prototype (N107MX) flew for the first time at the end of July 1981. Deliveries began in July 1982, and 367 kits had been sold by early 1986, from which 75 aircraft had been completed and flown. A version with tricycle landing gear was flown in March 1983, and is available in addition to the standard model. The original 16·4 kW (22 hp) KFM 107 engine has since been replaced by the slightly more powerful KFM 107 Maxi.

TYPE: Single-seat homebuilt motor glider.

AIRFRAME: All-aluminium cantilever low-wing monoplane. Constant chord wings, with dihedral from roots and turned-down tips, can be folded for transportation and storage, and are of conventional spar, rib and bonded skin construction. Slab sided fuselage, of bonded and riveted construction, with rounded top-decking. Cantilever V tail. Three-axis control by 'flaperons' and 'ruddervators'. Non-retractable monowheel and steerable tailwheel standard, each with moulded speed fairing, plus balancer wheel in each wingtip. Tricycle gear and wheel fairings available optionally. One-piece Plexiglas canopy.

POWER PLANT: One 22·4 kW (30 hp) KFM 107 Maxi two-cylinder engine, driving a two-blade propeller with spinner. Fuel capacity 15 litres (4 US gallons) standard, 22·7 litres (6 US gallons) optional. Engine has electric starter and can be restarted in flight.

DIMENSIONS, EXTERNAL:
- Wing span: 8·38 m (27 ft 6 in)
- Wing aspect ratio: 10·08
- Length overall: 4·46 m (14 ft 7½ in)
- Height over tail (tricycle gear version): 1·07 m (3 ft 6 in)
- Propeller diameter: 0·84 m (2 ft 9 in)

AREA:
- Wings, gross: 6·97 m² (75·0 sq ft)

WEIGHTS AND LOADINGS:
- Weight empty: 118 kg (260 lb)
- Max T-O weight: 227 kg (500 lb)
- Max wing loading: 32·5 kg/m² (6·67 lb/sq ft)
- Max power loading: 13·8 kg/kW (22·7 lb/hp)

PERFORMANCE, UNPOWERED (at max T-O weight):
- Best glide ratio at 43 knots (80 km/h; 50 mph): 20
- Min rate of sink at 42 knots (77 km/h; 48 mph): 0·91 m (3·00 ft)/s
- Stalling speed: 33 knots (62 km/h; 38 mph)
- Max speed (smooth air): 104 knots (193 km/h; 120 mph)
- *g* limits: +6/−4

PERFORMANCE, POWERED (at max T-O weight, 16·4 kW; 22 hp engine):
- Max cruising speed (75% power): 96 knots (177 km/h; 110 mph)
- Econ cruising speed: 69 knots (128 km/h; 80 mph)
- Stalling speed: 33 knots (62 km/h; 38 mph)
- Max rate of climb at S/L: 152 m (500 ft)/min
- Service ceiling: 3,810 m (12,500 ft)
- T-O run on grass: 122 m (400 ft)
- Landing run: 152 m (500 ft)
- Range with max fuel: 278 nm (515 km; 320 miles)
- *g* limits: +6/−4

MARSKE

MARSKE AIRCRAFT CORPORATION

130 Crestwood Drive, Michigan City, Indiana 46360
Telephone: (219) 879 7039
PRESIDENT: James J. Marske

MARSKE MONARCH

The Monarch was designed and built by Mr Jim Marske, and made its first flight on 4 July 1974. Plans and kits are available, and 96 sets of drawings had been sold by the beginning of 1985, from which eight Monarchs had been completed.

In 1976 Mr Marske successfully test flew the Monarch prototype in self-launching form, with a 9 kW (12 hp) McCulloch engine installed behind the pilot's seat, driving a 0·635 m (2 ft 1 in) diameter pusher propeller. This did not provide sufficient power, but is expected to be adequate for the Monarch E which is at least 9·1 kg (20 lb) lighter. First flight of the company's own Monarch E was scheduled for May 1985, and it was planned to test fly the 12 hp McCulloch engine in this aircraft.

The earlier Monarch B was described in the 1977-78 *Jane's*; the following description applies to the Monarch C and subsequent versions, including the D (longer span ailerons) and E (revised spoiler location, overhead window and larger rudder).

TYPE: Single-seat ultralight homebuilt glider.

AIRFRAME: Braced high-wing monoplane, with single extruded aluminium strut each side. Wing section NACA 43012A, reflexed at 75 per cent chord. Dihedral 2°. Sweepforward 3° at quarter-chord. Moulded glassfibre D leading-edge, with glassfibre front spar web and booms, corrugated glassfibre web ribs with wooden capstrips, wooden rear spar and trailing-edge, and Dacron covering. Inset transparency in centre of leading-edge on Monarch E. Ailerons (outboard) and elevators (inboard) each have single Sitka spruce spar and foam plastics ribs. Fixed tab on each elevator. All control surfaces Dacron covered. Aluminium spoiler above each wing. Simple minimal beam type fuselage of laminated glassfibre, moulded in two halves and joined at centreline. Forward section supports pilot's seat, with nose fairing over instrument panel; rear section forms integral fin leading-edge. CG tow hook on each side of nose fairing. Fin and rudder, above and below level of wings. Glassfibre leading-edge (fin), wooden trailing-edge (rudder), foam ribs and fabric covering. No horizontal tail surfaces. Reinforced underfuselage landing skid. Single landing wheel, below and slightly behind pilot's open seat. Conventional floor-mounted control column.

DIMENSIONS:
- Wing span: 12·80 m (42 ft 0 in)
- Wing aspect ratio: 9·53
- Length overall: 3·71 m (12 ft 2 in)
- Height over tail: 2·39 m (7 ft 10 in)

AREA:
- Wings, gross: 17·19 m² (185·0 sq ft)

WEIGHTS AND LOADING:
- Weight empty: C, D: 100 kg (220 lb)
- Pilot weight range: 45-104 kg (100-230 lb)
- Max T-O weight: 204 kg (450 lb)
- Max wing loading: 11·72 kg/m² (2·40 lb/sq ft)

PERFORMANCE:
- Best glide ratio at 35 knots (64 km/h; 40 mph): 19
- Min rate of sink at 26 knots (48 km/h; 30 mph): 0·82 m (2·70 ft)/s
- Stalling speed: 21 knots (39 km/h; 24 mph)
- Max speed (smooth air): 61 knots (113 km/h; 70 mph)
- Max speed (rough air), max aero-tow and max winch-launching speed: 43 knots (80 km/h; 50 mph)
- T-O and landing run: 12 m (40 ft) or less
- * *g* limits: +8/−4 ultimate

* *Has been static loaded to +9·6g without failure*

MARSKE PIONEER II

Designed some years ago as a simple, high performance sailplane for amateur construction, the Pioneer I prototype first flew in 1971. From it were developed the initial Pioneer IA, and then the smaller and lighter Pioneer II which made its first flight in July 1972.

The Pioneer II-A featured NACA 23012R/23010R wing sections and short bubble canopy, these being changed in the Pioneer II-B to a longer canopy and NACA 33012R/33010R wing sections which considerably improved low-speed performance. Improvements in the current Pioneer II-C, to which the following description applies, include a further refinement of the wing aerofoil section, closer spacing of the wing nose ribs, a simplified fuselage structure with lighter and more comfortable glassfibre bucket seat, reduction of 51 mm (2 in) in cockpit height and 102 mm (4 in) lower top line to the nose to improve forward view. Like the Monarch, the Pioneer is highly resistant to stalls and spins.

By early 1985 Marske had sold 83 sets of Pioneer drawings, and 16 of these aircraft had been flown.

TYPE: Single-seat homebuilt sailplane.

AIRFRAME: Cantilever mid-wing monoplane. Dihedral 4° 30′. Incidence 6°. Sweepforward 2° at quarter-chord. Modified NACA 33012 wing section. Wings have a single I-section spruce main spar, plywood ribs and D-tube skins; remainder fabric covered. Ailerons and inboard mounted elevators have spruce ribs and spars, with fabric covering. Upper and lower surface spoilers each consist of aluminium plate hinged at forward edge. Short, stubby fuselage has a welded steel tube frame and two-part outer shell of moulded glassfibre/epoxy. Upper half, including top-decking and fin, incorporates all necessary ribs and stiffeners bonded into place; lower half is supplied with all bulkheads bonded in. Rudder is of fabric covered wood construction. Single 30·5 cm (12 in) mainwheel, with drag brake, slightly aft of CG; 2 in castoring tailwheel. Towing hook on each side of fuselage under wing leading-edge, near CG. One-piece removable cockpit canopy.

DIMENSIONS, EXTERNAL:
- Wing span: 12·98 m (42 ft 7 in)
- Wing aspect ratio: 12·59
- Length overall: 3·81 m (12 ft 6 in)
- Height over tail: 1·98 m (6 ft 6 in)

AREA:
- Wings, gross: 13·38 m² (144·0 sq ft)

WEIGHTS AND LOADING:
- Weight empty: 159 kg (380 lb)
- Pilot weight range: 57-104 kg (125-230 lb)
- Max T-O weight: 295 kg (650 lb)
- Max wing loading: 22·0 kg/m² (4·51 lb/sq ft)

PERFORMANCE (at max T-O weight):
- Best glide ratio at 52 knots (97 km/h; 60 mph): 35
- Min rate of sink at 39 knots (72 km/h; 45 mph): 0·70 m (2·30 ft)/s
- Stalling speed: 31 knots (57 km/h; 35 mph)
- Max speed (rough and smooth air): 113 knots (209 km/h; 130 mph)
- Max aero-tow speed: 87 knots (161 km/h; 100 mph)
- Max winch-launching speed: 61 knots (113 km/h; 70 mph)
- *g* limits: +5·3/−2·65

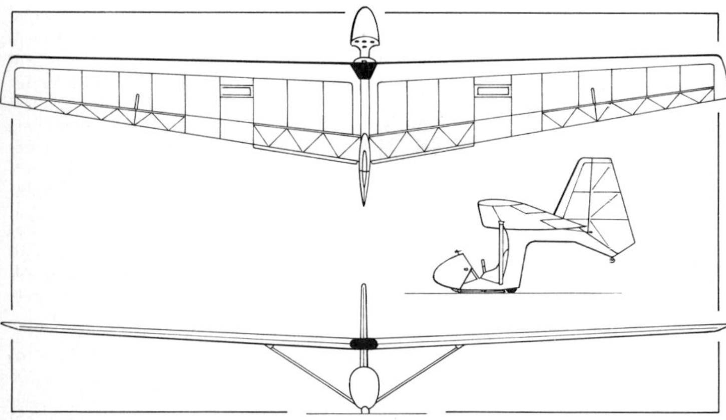

Marske Monarch E single-seat ultralight glider *(Michael A. Badrocke)*

INAV Moni with optional tricycle landing gear

Maupin Woodstock One homebuilt sailplane

Marske Pioneer II-C homebuilt sailplane

Maupin Windrose single-seat homebuilt self-launching sailplane

MAUPIN

JIM MAUPIN

26338 Zephyr, Harbor City, California 90710

MAUPIN WOODSTOCK ONE

The Woodstock One was designed by Mr Jim Maupin and was flown for the first time in early 1970. It has been flight tested to include spins (four turns) and stalls; and has been dived at 110 per cent of its never-exceed speed. Performance and handling are claimed to be easier and better than those of a Schweizer SGS 1-26.

Plans, including an instructional booklet, are available to amateur constructors, and by early 1986 about 400 sets of plans had been sold, in the USA and 20 other countries. Homebuilders' kits are no longer available.

TYPE: Single-seat homebuilt sailplane.

AIRFRAME: Cantilever shoulder-wing monoplane, of Douglas fir and birch construction with some fabric covering. Culver wing sections (thickness/chord ratio 18% at root, 13% at tip). Airbrakes on upper wing surfaces. Non-retractable semi-recessed monowheel. Undernose towing hook. Plans depict both open and enclosed cockpits, and a powered version with a non-retractable pylon mounted power plant aft of the cockpit.

DIMENSIONS, EXTERNAL:
- Wing span: 11·89 m (39 ft 0 in)
- Wing aspect ratio: 14·53
- Length overall: 5·87 m (19 ft 3 in)
- Height over tail: 1·30 m (4 ft 3 in)

AREA:
- Wings, gross: 9·73 m² (104·7 sq ft)

WEIGHTS AND LOADING:
- Weight empty: 106·5 kg (235 lb)
- Max T-O weight: 204 kg (450 lb)
- Max wing loading: 20·9 kg/m² (4·29 lb/sq ft)

PERFORMANCE (at max T-O weight):
- Best glide ratio at 39 knots (72 km/h; 45 mph): 24
- Min rate of sink at 35 knots (64 km/h; 40 mph): 0·79 m (2·60 ft)/s
- Stalling speed: 28 knots (52 km/h; 32 mph)
- Max speed (smooth air): 87 knots (161 km/h; 100 mph)
- Max speed (rough air): 68 knots (125 km/h; 78 mph)
- Max aero-tow speed, and max winch-launching speed: 56 knots (105 km/h; 65 mph)
- *g* limit: +5

MAUPIN WINDROSE

The Windrose self-launching sailplane, first flown in 1983, is now available in plans form, with instruction book. It is intended that the sailplane will later be marketed as a complete kit for homebuilding, or partial kit (eg hardware, moulded fuselage pod). Its general appearance is shown in an accompanying photograph.

A second prototype, with a 30 kW (40 hp) Rotax engine, was being built in early 1986. The following description applies to the lower powered first prototype with a Cuyuna engine:

TYPE: Single-seat self-launching sailplane.

AIRFRAME: Cantilever shoulder-wing monoplane, of pod and boom configuration. Wings each made of five blocks of plastics foam, hot wire cut with rib pattern at each end; each piece is notched top and bottom to take spar cap, and dowel is pushed into foam between spar caps and glued in position. Unidirectional glassfibre spar caps are laid into notches in foam blocks before skinning. Ailerons (interchangeable left/right) on inboard trailing-edges. Delta shaped spoiler on wing centre-section. Basic fuselage formed by two plywood boxes, one forming tailboom, the other extending forward under pilot, joined by two boxed-in plywood slabs. One-piece balanced elevator; one-piece balanced rudder, with small ventral fin. Enclosed cockpit. Towing hook.

POWER PLANT: One 24·6 kW (33 hp) Cuyuna ULII-02 two-cylinder two-stroke engine, driving a pusher propeller. Fuel capacity 19 litres (5 US gallons).

DIMENSIONS, EXTERNAL:
- Wing span: 12·65 m (41 ft 6 in)
- Wing aspect ratio: 17·94
- Length overall: 6·58 m (21 ft 7 in)
- Height overall: 1·68 m (5 ft 6 in)
- Propeller diameter: 0·81 m (2 ft 8 in)

AREA:
- Wings, gross: 8·92 m² (96·0 sq ft)

WEIGHTS AND LOADINGS:
- Weight empty: 232 kg (512 lb)
- Normal T-O weight: 317 kg (700 lb)
- Max T-O weight: 335 kg (740 lb)
- Wing loading:
  - at normal T-O weight: 35·59 kg/m² (7·29 lb/sq ft)
  - at max T-O weight: 37·64 kg/m² (7·71 lb/sq ft)
- Power loading:
  - at normal T-O weight: 12·89 kg/kW (21·2 lb/hp)
  - at max T-O weight: 13·62 kg/kW (22·4 lb/hp)

PERFORMANCE, UNPOWERED (A: at normal T-O weight, B: at max T-O weight, Cuyuna engine):
- Best glide ratio at 45 knots (84 km/h; 52 mph):
  - A, B: 29
- Min rate of sink:
  - A, B at 40 knots (74 km/h; 46 mph): 0·70 m (2·30 ft)/s
- Max speed (smooth air)
  - A: 114 knots (212 km/h; 132 mph)
  - B: 110 knots (204 km/h; 127 mph)
- Max speed (rough air):
  - A: 87 knots (161 km/h; 100 mph)
  - B: 83 knots (154 km/h; 96 mph)
- Manoeuvring speed:
  - A: 76 knots (142 km/h; 88 mph)
  - B: 73 knots (135 km/h; 84 mph)

PERFORMANCE, POWERED (Cuyuna engine):
- Max rate of climb at S/L: 152 m (500 ft)/min
- Ceiling: 3,960 m (13,000 ft)
- T-O run at S/L, ISA: 213 m (700 ft)

MONNETT — *see INAV*

RUTAN

RUTAN AIRCRAFT FACTORY INC

Building 13, Mojave Airport, Mojave, California 93501

Telephone: (805) 824 2645

Rutan Aircraft Factory no longer markets kits or plans of aircraft for amateur construction. Support service is available for those who purchased plans prior to July 1986.

SCHWEIZER

SCHWEIZER AIRCRAFT CORPORATION

PO Box 147, Elmira-Corning Regional Airport, Elmira, New York 14902
Telephone: (607) 739 3821
Telex: 932459
OFFICERS: see Aircraft section

Schweizer Aircraft Corporation has long been the leading American designer and manufacturer of sailplanes. Its current products include the SGS 2-33A, SGS 1-36 Sprite and SGM 2-37.

Schweizer now owns all rights to the (originally Grumman) Ag-Cat series of agricultural aircraft. It is responsible also for current manufacture and support of the Hughes Model 300 helicopter, and undertakes a variety of aircraft subcontract manufacturing. Further details of these activities can be found under the Schweizer heading in the main Aircraft section.

SCHWEIZER SGS 2-33A

The SGS 2-33 was developed to meet the demand for a medium priced two-seat sailplane for training and general family soaring. The prototype was first flown in the Autumn of 1966 and received FAA Type Approval in February 1967. Production began in January 1967, and 85 of the original **2-33** model were built. These were superseded by the current **2-33A** production version, and the **2-33AK** kit version for amateur construction. Sales of the 2-33A and 2-33AK by January 1985 totalled 470 and 20 respectively. No further sales had been recorded by January 1986, but the aircraft continues to be available.

TYPE: Tandem two-seat training sailplane.

AIRFRAME: Strut braced high-wing monoplane. Aluminium alloy structure with metal skin and all-metal ailerons. Upper and lower surface airbrakes fitted. Welded chrome-molybdenum steel tube fuselage. Nose covered with glassfibre, remainder with Ceconite fabric. Steel tube tail unit, covered with Ceconite fabric. Braced tailplane. Non-retractable Cleveland monowheel immediately aft of nose-skid. Rubber block shock absorption for skid. Wingtip wheels. Canopy opens sideways to port.

DIMENSIONS, EXTERNAL:
Wing span 15·54 m (51 ft 0 in)
Wing aspect ratio 11·85
Length overall 7·85 m (25 ft 9 in)
Height over tail 2·83 m (9 ft 3½ in)

AREA:
Wings, gross 20·39 m² (219·48 sq ft)

WEIGHTS AND LOADING:
Weight empty 272 kg (600 lb)
Max T-O weight 472 kg (1,040 lb)
Max wing loading 23·14 kg/m² (4·74 lb/sq ft)

PERFORMANCE (at max T-O weight except where indicated):
Best glide ratio at 45 knots (84 km/h; 52 mph) dual, 39 knots (72 km/h; 45 mph) solo 22·25
Min rate of sink:
dual at 37 knots (68 km/h; 42 mph) 0·95 m (3·10 ft)/s
solo at 33 knots (61 km/h; 38 mph) 0·79 m (2·60 ft)/s
Stalling speed: dual 31 knots (57 km/h; 35 mph)
solo 27 knots (50 km/h; 31 mph)
Max speed (rough and smooth air), and max aero-tow speed 85 knots (158 km/h; 98 mph)
Max winch-launching speed 60 knots (111 km/h; 69 mph)
g limits +4·67/−2·56

SCHWEIZER SGS 1-36 SPRITE

The Sprite was designed to offer modern performance, handling and appearance to up to 99 per cent of the solo glider pilots in the USA and overseas as a personal, school or club sailplane. Although a new design, it utilises some components of the 1-34 and 1-35 in its construction. The Sprite is, however, aimed at a different market from these earlier types, and is intended to be a 'one-design' class, as was the 1-26. The Sprite is also intended to fulfil a worldwide need for a single-seat Club Class sailplane.

Two versions are available:

36903-1. With forward-positioned monowheel, sprung tailwheel, and no nose-skid. One example of this version, used by NASA's Dryden Research Center, was fitted with a pivoting tailplane for flight research into aircraft controllability problems, particularly those involving deep stall situations. This tailplane can be set at approx 60° nose down.

36903-3. With monowheel further aft, unsprung tailwheel, and aluminium nose-skid. This version is recommended for school and club operation, where sturdiness and ease of ground handling are important considerations.

The prototype flew for the first time on 2 August 1979. FAA certification was received in September 1980, and by January 1985 a total of 43 had been sold. No further sales notified since that time, but the aircraft remained available in 1986.

TYPE: Single-seat multi-purpose sailplane.

AIRFRAME: Cantilever mid-wing monoplane, of all-aluminium construction. Wortmann wing sections: FX-61-163 at root, FX-60-126 at tip. Incidence 1° at root, 0° 4′ at tip. Airbrakes in upper and lower wing surfaces. Cantilever T tail, with elevators. Non-retractable semi-recessed 5·00-5 monowheel, with hydraulic brake, and tailwheel; aluminium nose-skid on 36903-3 version. CG towing hook optional. Canopy opens sideways to port.

DIMENSIONS, EXTERNAL:
Wing span 14·07 m (46 ft 2 in)
Wing aspect ratio 15·15
Length overall 6·27 m (20 ft 7 in)
Height over tail 1·45 m (4 ft 9 in)

AREA:
Wings, gross 13·07 m² (140·72 sq ft)

WEIGHTS AND LOADING:
Weight empty 215 kg (475 lb)
Max T-O weight 322 kg (710 lb)
Max wing loading 24·64 kg/m² (5·05 lb/sq ft)

PERFORMANCE (at max T-O weight):
Best glide ratio at 46 knots (85 km/h; 53 mph) 31
Min rate of sink at 36 knots (68 km/h; 42 mph) 0·68 m (2·25 ft)/s
Stalling speed 31 knots (57 km/h; 35 mph)
Max speed (rough and smooth air), and max aero-tow speed 105 knots (195 km/h; 121 mph)
Max winch-launching speed 68 knots (126 km/h; 78 mph)
g limits +5·33/−2·67

SCHWEIZER SGM 2-37

US Air Force designation: TG-7A

First details of this two-seat motor glider were announced in early 1982. The prototype (N36221) flew for the first time on 21 September 1982, and certification was received in the following February. Eight were delivered to the USAF Academy at Colorado Springs for sailplane flight training duties. Modified versions for other roles are being studied.

TYPE: Two-seat motor glider.

AIRFRAME: Cantilever low-wing monoplane, of all-metal construction. Wortmann wing sections: FX-61-163 from root to station 246, FX-60-126 at tip. Dihedral 3° 30′ on outer panels. Incidence 1° at root, 0° at tip. No sweepback. Aluminium airbrake in upper and lower surface of each outer panel. Aluminium alloy top-hinged ailerons; no flaps. Semi-monocoque fuselage of aluminium alloy. Slightly swept fin and rudder; non-swept all-moving tailplane, with anti-servo tab. Non-retractable mainwheels, with cantilever legs, urethane block shock absorbers, Cleveland disc brakes and 14 × 5 × 5 in tyres, pressure 2·41 bars (35 lb/sq in); non-retractable and castoring Scott tailwheel, with 6 × 2 × 3 in solid tyre (USAF aircraft have 5·00-5 mainwheels for operation from hard runways). Two seats side by side under rearward sliding canopy, with dual controls. Baggage compartment aft of seats, max capacity 45 kg (100 lb).

POWER PLANT: One 83 kW (112 hp) Avco Lycoming O-235-L2C flat-four engine, driving a Sensenich 72CK-0-50 two-blade fixed-pitch metal propeller. Optional engines include 112 kW (150 hp) Avco Lycoming O-320-E26 and 134 kW (180 hp) Avco Lycoming O-360-A series, with choice of McCauley fixed-pitch climb propeller for glider towing or Hoffmann HO-V-72 constant-speed feathering propeller for soaring. Single fuel tank in port wing standard, capacity 59 litres (15·5 US gallons), of which 54 litres (14·2 US gallons) are usable. Provision for optional similar tank, in starboard wing, increasing total capacity to 118 litres (31 US gallons).

DIMENSIONS, EXTERNAL:
Wing span 18·14 m (59 ft 6 in)
Wing aspect ratio 18·09
Length overall 8·36 m (27 ft 5 in)
Height over tail 2·37 m (7 ft 9½ in)
Wheel track 2·79 m (9 ft 2 in)
Wheelbase 5·74 m (18 ft 10 in)
Propeller diameter 1·83 m (6 ft 0 in)

DIMENSIONS, INTERNAL:
Cockpit: Max width 1·14 m (3 ft 9 in)
Baggage compartment volume 0·76 m³ (27 cu ft)

AREA:
Wings, gross 18·18 m² (195·71 sq ft)

WEIGHTS AND LOADINGS:
Weight empty 572 kg (1,260 lb)
Max T-O weight 839 kg (1,850 lb)
Max wing loading 46·14 kg/m² (9·45 lb/sq ft)
Max power loading 10·11 kg/kW (16·5 lb/hp)

PERFORMANCE, UNPOWERED (at max T-O weight):
Best glide ratio at 52 knots (97 km/h; 60 mph) 22
Min rate of sink at 49 knots (90 km/h; 56 mph) 1·13 m (3·70 ft)/s
Stalling speed 42 knots (78 km/h; 48 mph)
Max speed (smooth air) 115 knots (214 km/h; 133 mph)
Max speed (rough air) 88 knots (162 km/h; 101 mph)
g limits +5·3/−2·67

PERFORMANCE, POWERED (at max T-O weight):
Max cruising speed at 2,285 m (7,500 ft), 75% power 99 knots (183 km/h; 114 mph)
Econ cruising speed 82 knots (153 km/h; 95 mph)
Stalling speed 42 knots (78 km/h; 48 mph)
Max rate of climb at S/L 328 m (1,075 ft)/min
Service ceiling above 7,315 m (24,000 ft)
T-O run (grass) 152 m (500 ft)
T-O to 15 m (50 ft) (grass) 310 m (1,018 ft)
Landing from 15 m (50 ft) (grass) 386 m (1,266 ft)
Landing run 126 m (412 ft)
Range with standard fuel, 75% power, no reserves 213 nm (396 km; 246 miles)
Range with max optional fuel 520 nm (963 km; 598 miles)
Endurance at 50% power, no reserves 3 h 30 min
g limits +5·3/−2·67

SILHOUETTE

SILHOUETTE AIRCRAFT INC

848 East Santa Maria Street, Santa Paula Airport, Santa Paula, California 93060
Telephone: (805) 525 4545

SILHOUETTE AIRCRAFT SILHOUETTE

As explained in the Sport Aircraft section, the Silhouette is produced in kit form in two versions, the aerobatic sport aircraft being convertible to a Utility category motor glider by the addition of bolt-on wing extensions. These result in the following changes:

TYPE: Single-seat motor glider.

AIRFRAME: As described in Sport Aircraft section, plus bolt-on wing extension panels comprising stub spars, pre-shaped polystyrene cores and materials for glassfibre/epoxy skin. No washout in extensions.

POWER PLANT: Engine and standard fuel capacity details as for sport aircraft version. Motor glider has option for variable-pitch feathering propeller, but no option for larger fuel tank.

DIMENSIONS, EXTERNAL:
Wing span 12·50 m (41 ft 0 in)
Wing chord at tip 0·39 m (1 ft 3½ in)
Wing aspect ratio 19·32

AREA:
Wings, gross 8·08 m² (87·0 sq ft)

WEIGHTS AND LOADING:
Weight empty 231 kg (510 lb)
Max T-O weight 351 kg (775 lb)
Max wing loading 43·5 kg/m² (8·91 lb/sq ft)

PERFORMANCE (motor glider at max T-O weight):
Never-exceed speed 104 knots (193 km/h; 120 mph) IAS
Max cruising speed 87 knots (161 km/h; 100 mph) IAS
Econ cruising speed 57 knots (105 km/h; 65 mph) IAS
Stalling speed:
power on 40 knots (74 km/h; 46 mph) IAS
power off 44 knots (80 km/h; 50 mph) IAS
Max rate of climb at S/L 229 m (750 ft)/min
T-O run 244 m (800 ft)
Landing run 168 m (550 ft)
Endurance at max cruising speed 4 h 6 min
g limits +4·4/−2
Best glide ratio 25

STROJNIK

PROF ALEX STROJNIK

2337 East Manhatton Drive, Tempe, Arizona 85282
Telephone: (602) 838 1832

Mr Strojnik, a Professor of Physics at Arizona State University, has designed a homebuilt motor glider known as the S-2A.

STROJNIK S-2A

The S-2A is a single-seat motor glider, design and construction of which began in September 1977. The S-2 prototype (N8037X) was flown for the first time in November 1980, and plans for the slightly lighter S-2A are now available. A total of 45 sets of plans and partial kits had been sold by March 1985.

TYPE: Single-seat motor glider.

AIRFRAME: Cantilever shoulder-wing monoplane, with Wortmann wing sections. Dihedral 2° on outer panels. Incidence 0°. No sweep. Carbonfibre and aluminium main spar; wing skin, ailerons and trailing-edge flaps of glassfibre. No airbrakes. Pod and boom fuselage; pod has a glassfibre skin and plywood bulkheads, boom is an aluminium tube. Glassfibre tail unit, with elevators on low-set tailplane. Non-retractable unsprung twin mainwheels in tandem, each with tyre size 10 × 3·75 in,

Schweizer SGS 2-33A two-seat general purpose sailplane *(Peter F. Selinger)*

Schweizer SGS 1-36 Sprite training and club sailplane (36903-3 version)

Schweizer TG-7A (SGM 2-37) in service with the US Air Force Academy

Strojnik S-2 prototype for the S-2A homebuilt motor glider

DG-101G Elan Standard Class sailplane *(Peter F. Selinger)*

Elan/Glaser-Dirks DG-300 Elan Standard Class sailplane *(Peter F. Selinger)*

pressure 31·86 bars (56 lb/sq in), with friction brakes. One-piece Plexiglas canopy, opening sideways to starboard. Standard sailplane instrumentation and radio. No provision for water ballast.

POWER PLANT: One 21 kW (28 hp) Kohler K 340-2AX piston engine, mounted aft of cockpit and driving a Farrington two-blade (foldable) fixed-pitch wooden pusher propeller with spinner. Single fuselage fuel tank, capacity 7·5 litres (2 US gallons).

DIMENSIONS, EXTERNAL:
- Wing span: 15·00 m (49 ft 2½ in)
- Wing aspect ratio: 19·07
- Length overall: 6·88 m (22 ft 7 in)
- Height over tail: 1·65 m (5 ft 5 in)
- Propeller diameter: 0·94 m (3 ft 1 in)

AREA:
- Wings, gross: 11·80 m² (127·0 sq ft)

WEIGHTS AND LOADINGS (S-2):
- Weight empty: 280 kg (617 lb)
- Max T-O weight: 444 kg (980 lb)
- Max wing loading: 37·7 kg/m² (7·72 lb/sq ft)
- Max power loading: 21·14 kg/kW (35·0 lb/hp)

PERFORMANCE, UNPOWERED (S-2 at max T-O weight):
- Best glide ratio at 48 knots (88 km/h; 55 mph): 34
- Min rate of sink at 35 knots (64 km/h; 40 mph): 0·67 m (2·20 ft)/s
- Stalling speed, flaps down: 33 knots (62 km/h; 38 mph)
- Max speed (smooth air): 129 knots (240 km/h; 149 mph)
- Max speed (rough air): 87 knots (161 km/h; 100 mph)
- g limits: +5·3/−4·2

PERFORMANCE, POWERED (S-2 at max T-O weight):
- Max cruising speed: 78 knots (145 km/h; 90 mph)
- Econ cruising speed: 43 knots (80 km/h; 50 mph)
- Stalling speed: 33 knots (62 km/h; 38 mph)
- Max rate of climb at S/L: 107 m (350 ft)/min
- T-O run: 610 m (2,000 ft)
- Landing run: 91 m (300 ft)
- Range with max fuel: 87 nm (161 km; 100 miles)

YUGOSLAVIA

ELAN

ELAN TOVARNA ŠPORTNEGAORODJA N.SOL.O

Begunje St 1, 64275 Begunje na Gorenjskem
Telephone: (064) 75 010, 75 218 and 75 560
Telex: 34518
MANAGER, SAILPLANES DIVISION: Dipl Ing Tone Čerin

Formed in 1944 by a group of 10 workers to make skis for Yugoslavia's partisan fighters, Elan is now well known as a manufacturer of sports equipment, glassfibre pleasure and fishing craft, and gliders. Since 1979 it has been associated with Glaser-Dirks of the Federal German Republic (which see), and is now the sole production centre for that company's DG-101 series of Standard Class sailplanes. It is responsible also for production of the jointly designed DG-300 Elan, and is designing and developing the new two-seat DG-500 Elan which was to fly in May 1986.

ELAN (GLASER-DIRKS) DG-101 ELAN

The basic DG-100 was a modified and lighter-weight development of the Akaflieg Darmstadt D-38. By the end of 1978 Glaser-Dirks had completed 105 DG-100s, including 16 DG-100Gs. From early 1979 production was transferred to Elan, which introduced the improved DG-101 models on to the line from c/n E58 in early 1981. By March 1986 Elan had produced 192 of these sailplanes (158 DG-100G/101G and 34 DG-100/101).

Improvements in the 101 models include a one-piece cockpit canopy, roomier cockpit (as in the DG-202), new instrument console, more efficient water ballast valves, and a sprung monowheel.

Three versions are available, as follows:

DG-101 Elan. Standard Class version. All-moving T tailplane, fitted with full span anti-Flettner tab, and provision for 100 kg (220 lb) of water ballast.

DG-101G Elan. As DG-101 Elan, but with conventional fixed incidence tailplane and spring-trim elevator.

DG-101(G) Club Elan. Club version, with non-retractable monowheel, and choice of all-moving or conventional tailplane. No water ballast. Convertible to Standard Class DG-101 Elan.

TYPE: Single-seat Standard or Club Class sailplane.

AIRFRAME: Cantilever shoulder-wing monoplane. Wortmann wing sections: FX-61-184 at centreline, FX-60-126 at tip. Dihedral 3° from roots. Sweepforward 0° 48′ at quarter-chord. Glassfibre roving main spar. Glassfibre/Conticell/foam sandwich wings, ailerons and T tailplane; all glassfibre semi-monocoque fuselage, fin and rudder. Automatic self-connecting elevator on DG-101G Elan. Schempp-Hirth duralumin airbrakes on wing upper surfaces. Water ballast tank in each wing (except on Club Elan), combined capacity 100 kg (220 lb). Manually retractable sprung monowheel (non-retractable on Club version), with Tost drum brake, and tailwheel. Tyre size 361 × 126-127 mm, pressure 2·5 bars (36·25 lb/sq in), on monowheel; tailwheel tyre size 200 × 50-100 mm, pressure 2·0 bars (29 lb/sq in). One-piece cockpit canopy, hinged at nose and opening upward.

DIMENSIONS, EXTERNAL:
- Wing span: 15·00 m (49 ft 2½ in)
- Wing aspect ratio: 20·45
- Length overall: 7·00 m (22 ft 11¾ in)
- Height over tail: 1·40 m (4 ft 7 in)

AREA:
- Wings, gross: 11·00 m² (118·4 sq ft)

WEIGHTS AND LOADINGS (A: DG-101; B: DG-101G; C: DG-101 (G) Club version):
- Weight empty, equipped: A 235 kg (518 lb)
  - B 230 kg (507 lb)
  - C 225 kg (496 lb)
- Max T-O weight:
  - A and B (with water ballast) 418 kg (921 lb)
  - C 385 kg (849 lb)

Max wing loading:
A and B (with water ballast) 38·0 kg/m² (7·78 lb/sq ft)
C 35·0 kg/m² (7·17 lb/sq ft)
PERFORMANCE (at max T-O weight):
Best glide ratio:
A, B, at 57 knots (105 km/h; 65 mph) 39
C at 49 knots (90 km/h; 56 mph) 36
Min rate of sink at 40 knots (74 km/h; 46 mph):
A, B 0·59 m (1·94 ft)/s
C 0·60 m (1·97 ft)/s
Stalling speed: A, B, C 33 knots (60 km/h; 38 mph)
Max speed (rough and smooth air):
A, B, C 140 knots (260 km/h; 161 mph)
Max aero-tow speed:
A, B, C 89 knots (165 km/h; 103 mph)
Max winch-launching speed:
A, B, C 70 knots (130 km/h; 81 mph)
g limit: A, B, C +6·1

ELAN/GLASER-DIRKS DG-300 ELAN

This new Standard Class desgn, first flown on 27 April 1983, is a joint venture by Elan and Glaser-Dirks, and is a developed version of the DG-101G, which it resembles closely. Design began in July 1982, and five pre-series aircraft were built by Elan. One of these obtained seventh place in the Standard Class at the June 1983 World Gliding Championships held at Hobbs, New Mexico, USA. Series production began in December 1983, at which time 110 had been ordered; including the five pre-series examples, Elan had completed 160 DG-300s by March 1986.

Principal differences from the DG-101G include a new low-drag, laminar flow wing section, developed by engineers of the German DFVLR, which incorporates a tubular boundary layer distribution system for optimum lift; larger airbrakes; location of the wings slightly further aft, with an improved wing/fuselage junction; a 20 cm (7·9 in) reduction in fuselage length; improved directional stability, resulting from an improved fin aerofoil section and reduced rudder depth; a 2 cm (0·79 in) wider and more comfortable cockpit; automatically connecting controls; and provision for an auxiliary water ballast tank in the fin.

TYPE: Single-seat Standard Class sailplane.

AIRFRAME: Cantilever shoulder-wing monoplane, with Horstmann-Quast 300 G-D (Mod 2) aerofoil section. Incidence 3°. Sweepforward 0° 30′ at quarter-chord. Glassfibre/Conticell/foam sandwich wings, with Schempp-Hirth duralumin airbrakes in upper surface. All-glassfibre semi-monocoque fuselage. Cantilever T tailplane, with elevator; tail unit construction as described for DG-101G. Landing gear and cockpit canopy as for DG-101G. Standard provision for 130 or 190 litres (28·6 or 41·8 Imp gallons) of water ballast in wings; optional tank in fin has max capacity of 5·5 litres (1·2 Imp gallons).

DIMENSIONS, EXTERNAL:
Wing span 15·00 m (49 ft 2½ in)
Wing aspect ratio 21·91
Length overall 6·80 m (22 ft 3¾ in)
Height over tail 1·40 m (4 ft 7 in)
AREA:
Wings, gross 10·27 m² (110·5 sq ft)
WEIGHTS AND LOADING:
Weight empty 245 kg (540 lb)
Max T-O weight 525 kg (1,157 lb)
Max wing loading 51·1 kg/m² (10·47 lb/sq ft)
PERFORMANCE (at max T-O weight except where indicated):
Best glide ratio:
at wing loading of 32 kg/m² (6·55 lb/sq ft) and speed of 54 knots (100 km/h; 62 mph) 41
at wing loading of 50 kg/m² (10·24 lb/sq ft) and speed of 66 knots (122 km/h; 76 mph) 42
Min rate of sink:
at wing loading of 32 kg/m² (6·55 lb/sq ft) and speed of 39 knots (72 km/h; 45 mph) 0·59 m (1·94 ft)/s
at wing loading of 50 kg/m² (10·24 lb/sq ft) and speed of 48 knots (88 km/h; 55 mph) 0·68 m (2·23 ft)/s
Stalling speed at wing loading of 32 kg/m² (6·55 lb/sq ft) 35 knots (65 km/h; 41 mph)
Max speed (smooth air) 147 knots (270 km/h; 168 mph)
Max speed (rough air), and max aero-tow speed 108 knots (200 km/h; 124 mph)
Max winch-launching speed 70 knots (130 km/h; 80 mph)
g limits: +5·3/−2·65 (at V_A)
+4/−1·5 (at V_{NE})

ELAN DG-500 ELAN

Elan began designing this two-seat sailplane jointly with Glaser-Dirks during the second half of 1981. After an interruption to concentrate on development of the DG-300, the prototype was expected to fly in May 1986.

Four versions are planned. The prototype, designated **DG-500M**, will feature a retractable power plant (developing approx 44·7 kW; 60 hp) in an installation similar to that of the Glaser-Dirks DG-400. Its 22·0 m (72 ft 2 in) span wings will have interconnected flaps and ailerons. Other features will include a retractable monowheel, semi-recessed nosewheel and tailwheel, four-part carbonfibre wings, automatic control connections, and an improved cockpit based on that of the DG-101 Elan but with separate canopies. The basic **DG-500 Elan** glider version will have the same dimensions, but an increased span variant will also be available to satisfy new FAI regulations. The **DG-500 Trainer** will be similar, but with a non-retractable monowheel and 18·00 m (59 ft 1 in) span wings without flaps.

JASTREB

JASTREB FABRIKA AVIONA I JEDRILICA (Jastreb Aircraft and Sailplanes Factory)

ul. Podvrsanska 17 Ziro, 26300 Vrsac
Telephone: (013) 813 639
Telex: 13193 YU JASTREB
DIRECTOR: Teodorović Radovan

Jastreb, known formerly as VTC, is the production centre for two versions of the Standard Cirrus sailplane, designed originally by Schempp-Hirth in West Germany and built subsequently under licence by VTC at Vrsac (see 1981-82 *Jane's*). It also manufactures the VUK-T, designed at the University of Belgrade, and a two-seat motor glider known as the SOLE-77.

Herr Georg Bräuchle of West Germany has acquired the moulds and manufacturing rights for the 15 metre Glasflügel 304 sailplane, and has an agreement with Jastreb to build this sailplane in Yugoslavia at the rate of two to three per month. Apparently this has not yet started.

JASTREB (SCHEMPP-HIRTH) STANDARD CIRRUS 75-VTC

Designed by Dipl-Ing Klaus Holighaus of Schempp-Hirth, this Standard Class version of the Cirrus entered production in Germany in the Summer of 1969, following its first flight in March 1969. By April 1977, when West German production ended, a total of 700 Standard Cirrus had been built, including 200 under licence by Grob Flugzeugbau.

Licence manufacture has been undertaken since January 1979 by VTC (now Jastreb) in Yugoslavia. Production total is not known.

TYPE: Single-seat Standard and Club Class sailplane.

AIRFRAME: Cantilever mid-wing monoplane. Wortmann wing section. Dihedral 3°. Sweepback 1° 18′ at leading-edge. Glassfibre/foam sandwich wings, ailerons and tail surfaces. Schempp-Hirth glassfibre airbrakes on upper surfaces. Glassfibre fuselage shell, stiffened with bonded-in foam rings. All moving T tailplane. Retractable monowheel standard; non-retractable faired monowheel optional. Tost wheel with drum brake and Continental tyre, pressure 3·45 bars (50 lb/sq in). Canopy opens sideways to starboard. Provision for 60 kg (132 lb) of water ballast.

DIMENSIONS, EXTERNAL:
Wing span 15·00 m (49 ft 2½ in)
Wing aspect ratio 22·50
Length overall 6·41 m (21 ft 8½ in)
Height over tail 1·32 m (4 ft 4¾ in)
AREA:
Wings, gross 10·00 m² (107·6 sq ft)
WEIGHTS AND LOADINGS:
Weight empty 220 kg (485 lb)
Max T-O weight:
without water ballast 330 kg (727 lb)
with water ballast 390 kg (860 lb)
Max wing loading:
without water ballast 33·0 kg/m² (6·76 lb/sq ft)
with water ballast 39·0 kg/m² (7·99 lb/sq ft)
PERFORMANCE (at max T-O weight):
Best glide ratio at 49 knots (90 km/h; 56 mph) 38·5
Min rate of sink at 38 knots (70 km/h; 44 mph) 0·57 m (1·87 ft)/s
Stalling speed 34 knots (62 km/h; 39 mph)
Max speed (rough and smooth air) 119 knots (220 km/h; 137 mph)
Max aero-tow speed 81 knots (150 km/h; 93 mph)
Max winch-launching speed 65 knots (120 km/h; 75 mph)
g limit +10

JASTREB STANDARD CIRRUS G/81

The Standard Cirrus G/81 was developed by Jastreb from the Standard Cirrus 75-VTC, and differs from it in the following respects. As with the 75-VTC, Jastreb has not indicated how many have been produced.

AIRFRAME: As 75-VTC except for lack of option for non-retractable monowheel; new canopy, based on that of Schempp-Hirth Mini-Nimbus, opening sideways to starboard; roomier cockpit, able to accommodate a larger pilot; and a variable incidence T tailplane with separate elevator. CG tow hook standard, nose hook optional.

DATA: As for Cirrus 75-VTC

JASTREB VUK-T

The prototype of this single-seat all-plastics sailplane was designed and built at Belgrade University in 1976, and made its first flight in 1977. Production, started by Jastreb in January 1979, totalled 65 by early 1986.

Chief features of the VUK-T are the use of plastics stressed-skin construction and a supercritical wing section. The sailplane is designed to OSTIV airworthiness requirements, and is cleared for cloud flying, aerobatics and spinning.

TYPE: Single-seat advanced training sailplane.

AIRFRAME: Cantilever mid-wing monoplane. NASA GAW-1 supercritical wing section from root to tip, with no twist. Thickness/chord ratio 17%. Dihedral 3°. Glassfibre roving main spar, integral with the upper and lower wing skins, which are of glassfibre/Conticell foam sandwich. Auxiliary rear spar carries the top-hinged plain ailerons. Schempp-Hirth airbrakes in upper surfaces at 50 per cent chord. Fuselage is of glassfibre sandwich construction forward, glassfibre monocoque aft. Cantilever T tailplane, with separate elevator, of similar construction to wings. Retractable sprung monowheel, with brake, and non-retractable tailwheel. Semi-reclining seat under one-piece flush-fitting jettisonable canopy which opens sideways to starboard. No water ballast provision.

DIMENSIONS, EXTERNAL:
Wing span 15·00 m (49 ft 2½ in)
Wing aspect ratio 15·00
Length overall 6·50 m (21 ft 4 in)
Height over tail 1·35 m (4 ft 5¼ in)
AREA:
Wings, gross 15·00 m² (161·5 sq ft)
WEIGHTS AND LOADING:
Weight empty 245 kg (540 lb)
Max T-O weight 355 kg (782 lb)
Max wing loading 23·67 kg/m² (4·85 lb/sq ft)
PERFORMANCE (at max T-O weight):
Best glide ratio at 51 knots (95 km/h; 59 mph) 37·5
Min rate of sink at 42 knots (78 km/h; 49 mph) 0·65 m (2·13 ft)/s
Stalling speed 32 knots (59 km/h; 37 mph)
Max speed (smooth air) 129 knots (240 km/h; 149 mph)
Max speed (rough air) 81 knots (150 km/h; 93 mph)
Max aero-tow speed 70 knots (130 km/h; 80 mph)
Max winch-launching speed 65 knots (120 km/h; 75 mph)
g limits (safety factor 1·5) +5·3/−2·65

JASTREB SOLE-77

The Jastreb SOLE-77 is a side by side two-seat motor glider, built of glassfibre reinforced epoxy resin, for elementary and advanced training; it can also be used for basic aerobatics. Other applications include atmospheric sampling, photogrammetry, and study of air currents. The monowheel is retractable; the tailwheel, linked to the rudder pedals, is fully castoring, and there is a small removable outrigger wheel beneath each wing. The cockpit canopy, which is hinged at the front and opens upward, is jettisonable. The 59·7 kW (80 hp) 2,000 cc Limbach engine drives a two-blade propeller; there is provision for an auxiliary fuel tank. Without this tank, standard fuel load is 50 kg (110 lb).

Production began in 1984; it is not known how many have been built.

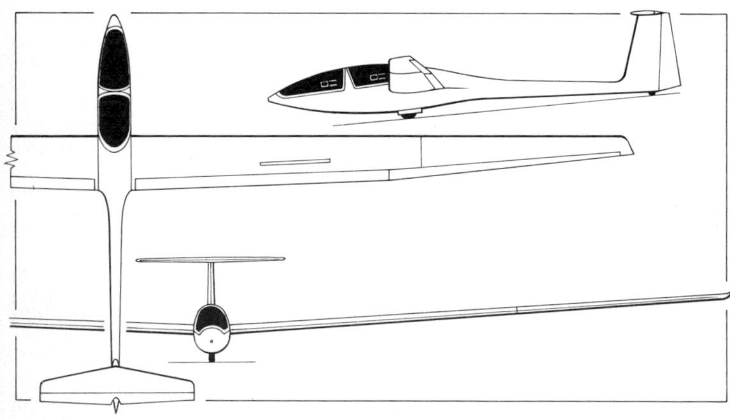

Elan DG-500 Elan tandem two-seat sailplane *(Michael A. Badrocke)*

Jastreb Standard Cirrus G/81, developed from the 75-VTC

Jastreb SOLE-77 two-seat motor glider

Prototype SOKO SL-40 Liska single-seat motor glider

Jastreb VUK-T all-plastics training sailplane

DIMENSIONS, EXTERNAL:
- Wing span: 16·40 m (53 ft 9¾ in)
- Length overall: 7·67 m (25 ft 2 in)

WEIGHTS AND LOADING:
- Weight empty: 500 kg (1,102 lb)
- Max T-O weight: 750 kg (1,653 lb)
- Max power loading: 12·56 kg/kW (20·67 lb/hp)

PERFORMANCE, UNPOWERED (at max T-O weight):
- Best glide ratio: 29
- Max speed (smooth air): 124 knots (230 km/h; 143 mph)

PERFORMANCE, POWERED (at max T-O weight):
- Max cruising speed: 92 knots (170 km/h; 106 mph)
- Stalling speed: 34 knots (63 km/h; 40 mph)
- Max rate of climb at S/L: 186 m (610 ft)/min
- Service ceiling: 4,500 m (14,760 ft)
- T-O to 15 m (50 ft): 350 m (1,148 ft)
- Range with max standard fuel: 378 nm (700 km; 435 miles)
- Endurance with max standard fuel: 5 h

SOKO

SOUR SOKO VAZDUHOPLOVNA INDUSTRIJA

88000 Mostar
Telephone: (088) 22 121
Telex: 46 180 YU SOKOMO

CHAIRMAN AND PRESIDENT: Dipl Ing Milenko Pjescić
VICE-PRESIDENT, RESEARCH AND DEVELOPMENT: Dipl Ing Mladen Zadro

SOKO SL-40 LISKA

Construction of the prototype Liska single-seat motor glider began at the end of 1975, design having started about a year earlier. It flew for the first time on 19 February 1981. The flight test programme is running behind schedule, due to the flight test department's high workload with other projects. Some definitive performance data were established during 1985, and initial test results have tended to confirm other estimated values. Domestic aeroclub and foreign interest in the Liska has been shown.

TYPE: Single-seat motor glider.

AIRFRAME: Cantilever low-wing monoplane. Wortmann wing sections: FX-61-184 at root, FX-61-163 at tip. Dihedral 4° from roots. Incidence 2°. Sweepforward 0° 22′ 48″ at quarter-chord. Single-spar light alloy wings, of stressed skin construction, with light alloy slotted ailerons. Light alloy DFS type spoiler on each wing, inboard of aileron. Light alloy semi-monocoque fuselage. Single-spar stressed skin light alloy tail unit, with swept-back fin and rudder, and non-swept all-moving tailplane. Plain hinged light alloy trim and balance tabs in tailplane. Hydraulically retractable monowheel, retracting forward, is a Moravan-Otrokovice unit taken from a Let L-13 sailplane; it has SOKO rubber in compression shock absorption, and a mechanically actuated brake. Non-retractable steerable tailwheel, with solid rubber tyre. Non-retractable outrigger under each wing. Mainwheel tyre size 350 × 135 × 150 mm, pressure 2·45 bars (35·5 lb/sq in). Cockpit canopy opens sideways to starboard. Compartment behind seat, accessible from cockpit, for 5 kg (11 lb) of baggage. Cockpit is heated and ventilated; 12V 34Ah battery and engine driven alternator provide power for instruments (including standard blind-flying panel) and Dittel FSG-16 VHF com radio. Oxygen system, VOR/LOC and ADF are optional.

POWER PLANT: One 33·5 kW (45 hp) Pieper-Stark Stamo MS 1500/2 piston engine, driving a Hoffmann HO11-137B85L or HO11-150B70L two-blade fixed-pitch propeller. Single metal fuel tank aft of cockpit, capacity 40 litres (8·8 Imp gallons). Refuelling point immediately aft of cockpit on port side. Oil capacity 2·5 litres (0·55 Imp gallons).

DIMENSIONS, EXTERNAL:
- Wing span: 15·00 m (49 ft 2½ in)
- Wing aspect ratio: 14·78
- Length overall: 6·40 m (21 ft 0 in)
- Height over tail: 2·00 m (6 ft 6¾ in)
- Wheel track (outriggers): 6·00 m (19 ft 8¼ in)
- Wheelbase: 4·40 m (14 ft 5¼ in)
- Propeller diameter:
  - HO11-137B85L: 1·37 m (4 ft 6 in)
  - HO11-150B70L: 1·50 m (4 ft 11 in)

AREA:
- Wings, gross: 15·225 m² (163·9 sq ft)

WEIGHTS AND LOADINGS:
- Weight empty: 358 kg (789 lb)
- Max T-O weight: 500 kg (1,102 lb)
- Max wing loading: 32·8 kg/m² (6·72 lb/sq ft)
- Max power loading: 14·9 kg/kW (24·5 lb/hp)

PERFORMANCE, UNPOWERED (at max T-O weight, propeller windmilling):
- Best glide ratio at 57 knots (105 km/h; 65 mph): 22
- Min rate of sink at 53 knots (98 km/h; 61 mph): 1·26 m (4·13 ft)/s
- Stalling speed: 39 knots (72 km/h; 45 mph)
- *g* limits: +5·3/−3·2

PERFORMANCE, POWERED (at max T-O weight):
- *Never-exceed speed: 116 knots (215 km/h; 133 mph)
- *Max level speed at S/L: 94 knots (175 km/h; 109 mph)
- *Econ cruising speed: 57 knots (105 km/h; 65 mph)
- Stalling speed, engine idling, wheels down: 33 knots (61 km/h; 38 mph)
- *Max rate of climb at S/L: 204 m (669 ft)/min
- *Service ceiling: 6,600 m (21,650 ft)
- T-O run: 280 m (919 ft)
- T-O to 15 m (50 ft): 590 m (1,935 ft)
- *Landing run: 126 m (413 ft)
- Range at 500 m (1,640 ft) with max fuel, no reserves: 506 nm (938 km; 582 miles)
- Endurance at 48 knots (90 km/h; 56 mph) with max fuel, no reserves: 9 h 30 min

* *Estimated*

HANG GLIDERS

AUSTRALIA

MOYES

MOYES DELTA GLIDERS PTY LTD

173 Bronte Road, Waverley, Sydney, NSW 2024
Telephone: (02) 387 5114
Telex: INTSY AA 10101 MOYESGLIDE
Fax: 61 2 3874472
DIRECTOR: Steve Moyes

Current production models are the Mars 150, 170 and 190, and the GTR 148, 162, 175 and 210. The GTR is the most recent design, with the GTR 210 designed to fit to trike units.

Moyes gliders for the US market are now built in Australia. However, the Italian company Icaro 2000 srl, of Via Lungalago, 1-21038 Reno de Leggiuno (*telephone* [0332] 647 923; *telex* 326427 PRODEF I; *fax* 39 332 647477), builds Moyes gliders under licence.

MOYES MARS

The Moyes Mars series of hang gliders was introduced in 1983, and well over 350 have been produced. Three versions are currently available: the Mars 150 with a 13·94 m² (150 sq ft) wing area, Mars 170 with a 15·98 m² (172 sq ft) area, and the Mars 190 with an area of 17·65 m² (190 sq ft). The Mars 170, which has USHGMA certification, was designed primarily as a training glider, intended for pilots with no previous experience up to eighteen months of regular flying. It has a sink rate equal to the best performing gliders but should be limited to non-aerobatic manoeuvres. It is certificated for towing and floats are fitted for use over water. It is not capable of spins.

The Mars series have aluminium alloy airframes, each with a single surface Dacron flex-wing, vinyl coated stainless steel cables and reflex bridles. The airframes are stressed to $+6/-4g$. Details of the Mars series are given in the table at the end of this section.

MOYES GTR

The Moyes GTR series of hang gliders are in the Utility class, with their model numbers corresponding directly to the wing areas of the gliders. The GTR 162 is available in VG (variable geometry) form, on which the pilot can control how easy it is to spin, the roll rate, glide speed and rate of sink. The GTR 162 VG has USHGMA certification, which was also being sought in Spring 1986 for the newer and smaller GTR 148.

Each model in the GTR series has glassfibre wingtips, an 85 per cent double surface flex-wing, internal cable supported floating crossbar, stainless steel reflex bridles and aluminium/glassfibre composite battens. The VG model(s) have the Bill Moyes-invented compensator fitted, an automatic in-flight reflex bridle adjuster that harmonises with the variable geometry setting. Therefore the pilot can select variable geometry 'on' or 'off', with the bridle lines matching the sail tension setting. When the VG is 'off', the compensator pulls the kingpost forward; when the VG is 'on', the compensator allows the top front wire to straighten and the kingpost to move aft and relax the reflex bridle lines.

Details of the GTR series are given in the table at the end of this section.

FRANCE

LA MOUETTE

SARL LA MOUETTE

1 rue de la Petite Fin, 21121 Fontaine les Dijon
Telephone: (80) 56 66 47
Telex: 350 053 F
DIRECTOR: J. M. Thevenot

Models currently in production are the Atlas, Profil and Hermes series of hang gliders (see details following and in table at the end of this section). Manufacture of the Azur (1985-86 *Jane's*) has ended.

LA MOUETTE ATLAS

Produced in three models, of which 7,000 had been built by January 1986. All have a 2017A aluminium alloy frame, Dacron sail (double over 40 per cent of area), and cables of vinyl coated stainless steel, and all are stressed to $+6/-4g$. Kingpost standard on all models. Weight shift control. All can be flown prone, seated or supine.

LA MOUETTE PROFIL

In 1982 designer Jean-Louis Darlet developed a system for dividing a hang glider's wing into two sections to enable each 'split' section to flap independently, increasing roll rate and manoeuvrability. La Mouette adopted the Darlet system for its Profil hang glider, which is produced in two models. Airframe is similar to the Atlas/Azur, with Mylar reinforced leading-edges and Zicral alloy battens. La Mouette had built 1,300 Profils by January 1986.

LA MOUETTE HERMES

Hermes takes the place of the Azur in La Mouette's current product range, with new features which include a smoother, more tightly woven sail which is said not to deform with heavy loads or prolonged use. A Dacron leech line, with adjustable tension, is concealed in the trailing-edge seam from keel to tip, and the Hermes wing is certificated with a 'variable geometry' option. La Mouette had built 300 Hermes by January 1986.

GERMANY
(FEDERAL REPUBLIC)

FINSTERWALDER

THOMAS FINSTERWALDER (DRACHENFLUG GmbH)

Pagodenburgstrasse 8, 8000 München 60
Telephone: 811 65 28
CONTACT: A. Decker

FINSTERWALDER TOPFEX

The Topfex, illustrated in an accompanying photograph, first flew in November 1984. A total of 62 had been built by February 1986. It has an aluminium alloy tube airframe, with profiled kingpost and control bar as standard, and the Dacron sail is double surfaced over 75 per cent of the wing area. Other known data are in the table at the end of this section.

FIREBIRD

FIREBIRD SCHWEIGER & JEHLE KG

Postfach 28, Hitzleriederstrasse 15, 8959 Seeg
Telephone: (08364) 8282 1078
MANAGER: Eberhard Jehle

Firebird Leichtflugzeugbau GmbH, which until September 1984 produced Firebird microlights (described in the 1984-85 *Jane's*), is now trading as Firebird Schweiger & Jehle KG.

FIREBIRD WORLD CUP 90-S SCHOOL GLIDER

The World Cup 90-S School Glider, stressed to $+6/-3g$, has the most modest performance of the company's range of hang gliders. It has an aluminium airframe. Set-up time is 5 min. Maximum speed is 29 knots (55 km/h; 34 mph). Other details can be found in the table at the end of this section.

FIREBIRD UNO

Stressed to $+6/-3g$, this intermediate performance glider has a 35 per cent double surface wing. Set-up time is 5 min. Maximum speed is 35 knots (65 km/h; 40 mph). The smaller **Uno Piccolo** was introduced for 1986. Other details can be found in the table at the end of this section.

FIREBIRD QUATTRO

Dimensionally identical to the Uno, and similarly stressed, the Quattro has a 65 per cent double surface wing. Having a lighter wing loading than the Uno, it has a higher performance with a maximum speed of 43 knots (80 km/h; 50 mph). Latest (1986) version is the Quattro-S. Other details can be found in the table at the end of this section.

FIREBIRD SIERRA

Two versions of the Sierra are produced, the Sierra 155 and Sierra 175. Both have aluminium airframes and 90 per cent double surface wings, and are stressed to $+6/-3g$. The Sierra 155 is the smaller of the two. Set-up time for both is 8 min. Maximum speed of the Sierra 155 is 59 knots (110 km/h; 68 mph), and 58 knots (108 km/h; 67 mph) for the Sierra 175. Further details of both can be found in the table at the end of this section.

FIREBIRD SPIRIT

Newest Firebird glider, introduced in 1986, is the variable geometry Spirit, which has a 95 per cent double surface wing with Mylar leading-edge, speedbar, 'French connection' steering and other advanced features.

ITALY

POLARIS

POLARIS Srl

Via Flaminia 208, 06021 Costacciaro (PG)
Telephone: (075) 917 01 86
MANAGING DIRECTOR: Dr Doi Malingri

POLARIS DELTA

The Delta is an FAI Class 1 hang glider. A powered, water-based Air Dinghy unit for the wing has been developed by powerboat designer Renato ('Sonny') Levi. It features a Kevlar and GRP hydroplane unit with 22·4 kW (30 hp) KFM 107ER engine driving a two-blade wooden pusher propeller and has a fuel capacity of 20 litres (4·4 Imp gallons). The Air Dinghy was designed to be used as a fast dinghy without the Delta wing, and is described in the Sport Aircraft section. The following description applies to the Delta hang glider.

AIRFRAME: Aluminium alloy, stressed to $+6/-3g$, with Dacron single surface sail, vinyl coated stainless steel cables, kingpost standard. Details can be found in the table at the end of this section.

POLARIS GAMMA 177

The Gamma 177, also available with or without the Air Dinghy unit, is essentially similar in construction to the Delta, but has a double surface Dacron sail area. Details can be found in the table.

Moyes Mars

Moyes GTR 148

La Mouette Atlas *(Ivan J. Arthur)*

La Mouette Profil

Finsterwalder Topfex

Firebird Sierra 175

Air Dinghy unit attached to a Polaris hang glider *(Wolfgang Wagner)*

Instytut Lotnictwa Zeta-80B

Instytut Lotnictwa Zeta-84

NEW ZEALAND

FREE FLIGHT

FREE FLIGHT MICROLIGHTS AND HANG GLIDERS NZ

c/o Muriwai Beach PO, Auckland

This company, formerly known as Pacific Kites Ltd, manufactured two hang gliders, the Lancer Mk IV and Vampyre Mk II. The last known details of these were given in the 1985-86 *Jane's*, but no recent news of Free Flight has been received.

POLAND

WARSAW TECHNICAL UNIVERSITY

STUDENTS' HANG GLIDING CLUB, WARSAW TECHNICAL UNIVERSITY

Pl. Jedności Robotniczej 1, 00-661 Warszawa

STRATUS R-10/11/12/15

This family of hang gliders was designed by Mr Grzegorz Rycaj. No recent news of them has been received. Last known details appeared in the 1985-86 *Jane's*.

IL

INSTYTUT LOTNICTWA (Aviation Institute)

Al. Krakowska 110/114, 02-256 Warszawa-Okecie
Telephone: Warszawa 460011 and 460993
Telex: 813537
OFFICERS: see Aircraft section

ZETA-80B

This semi-rigid training hang glider, the first hang glider in Poland to be designed by professionals, was designed and developed at the Instytut Lotnictwa and is now in production by PZL's Warsaw-Okecie factory. It is believed to have flown for the first time in 1980, is stressed to $+4/-2g$, and conforms to the British airworthiness regulations issued by the BHGA in March 1979. It has been awarded two gold medals in recognition of its particularly advanced design. Construction is conventional, and includes a frame of duralumin tube, 15 duralumin ribs (including two pivoting ribs and two sweptback strips) and Dacron covering. Control is by weight shift. Full dimensional and other data are given in the table; max T-O weight is quoted as 130 kg (286 lb), and never-exceed speed as 48 knots (90 km/h; 56 mph).

ZETA-84

Designed by Dr Jerzy Wolf in 1984 and flown for the first time on 3 August 1985, the Zeta-84 is a semi-rigid FAI Class 1 hang glider capable of speeds up to 65 knots (120 km/h; 75 mph). Five prototypes have been built. The airframe is of PA7 duralumin, braced with a kingpost and anodised cables, and stressed to $+6/-3g$. The wing has a central torsion box structure, only the rear and tip portions being flexible, and is Dacron covered. There is no keel pocket, but a floating spar permits a wing displacement of $\pm 7°$ in relation to the keel. Assembly time is 16 min, max T-O weight 140 kg (308 lb).

SWEDEN

KOŁECKI

KOŁECKI NEW AVIATION ENGINEERING

Box 1046, 122 22 Enskede, Stockholm
Telephone: 08 499427
DIRECTOR: Jerzy Kołecki

Mr Kołecki, a Polish aviation engineer, studied aviation and aeronautics at technical colleges in Warsaw and later in Stockholm, where he has lived for the past 15 years. He flew his first powered Rogallo hang glider in December 1975, and by April 1977 had successfully developed a power unit for use with this type of aircraft. The latest version of this is marketed under the name **Motolotnia 80 White Eagle**, utilising a 7·5 kW (10 hp) Chrysler or McCulloch engine driving either a tractor or a pusher two-blade metal propeller via 2:1 reduction gearing. The 'universal' propeller can turn clockwise or anti-clockwise, to suit the installation, and is suitable for use with engines of up to 74·5 kW (100 hp); variants are available with two or more folding or non-folding blades, and with optional adjustable pitch. Fuel is contained in a 2·5 litre (0·5 Imp gallon) tank.

SWITZERLAND

SWISS AEROLIGHT

SWISS AEROLIGHT

PO Box 22, Pt Lancy 1, CH-1213 Geneva

SWISS AEROLIGHT NIMBUS

The Nimbus is a 12·50 m (41 ft 0¼ in) span, 16·20 m² (174·4 sq ft) area 'flying wing' rigid hang glider, stressed to +8/−6*g*. The sweptback wings have constant chord, elliptical dihedral and a Kevlar leading-edge. Glider weight is 36 kg (79 lb), and performance includes a best glide ratio of 18, min rate of sink of 0·75 m (2·46 ft)/s and stalling speed of 16 knots (28 km/h; 18 mph).

Further details were requested, but not received.

UNION OF SOVIET SOCIALIST REPUBLICS

ANTONOV

ANTONOV SLAVUTITCH-UT

The O.K. Antonov design bureau has designed a flex-wing hang glider known as the Slavutitch-UT, the first five examples of which were completed in June 1979. Of conventional appearance and construction, with an air-frame of D-16T duralumin, it has been in series production since about 1983, with more than 400 built by the beginning of 1985. Improvements introduced during that period have included relocation of the end spars and hang frame suspension point, new pilot harness, and (from 1985) an improved steering control system and increased dihedral on the inboard trailing-edge. All known details are given in the table.

A powered version, known as the Slavutitch M-1, is described in the Sport Aircraft section.

UNITED KINGDOM

AIRWAVE

AIRWAVE GLIDERS LTD

Elm Lane, Shalfleet, Newport, Isle of Wight PO30 4JY
Telephone: 0983 78611
Telex: 869188 GLIDER G
MANAGING DIRECTOR: Rory Carter
PRODUCTION DIRECTOR: Graham Deegan
COMPANY SECRETARY: Patsy Carter

Airwave Gliders Ltd has been manufacturing hang gliders since 1980. The current model is the Magic III, which is distributed in the United States by Airwave Gliders USA, PO Box 1153, Mercer Island, Washington 98040.

AIRWAVE GLIDERS MAGIC IV

Certificated to British, German, Swiss and US standards, the Magic IV (previously Magic III) is an FAI Class 1 hang glider, available in three sizes. Details are given in the table. Airframe is of aluminium alloy, with Dacron sail (Mylar optional), plastics coated stainless steel bracing and aerofoil section kingpost standard.

CUNION

EVERARD CUNION

155 Fairmile Road, Christchurch, Dorset BH23 2LD
Telephone: 0202 483847

Mr Cunion's latest aircraft, still in the design stage in February 1985, is a double-surfaced (enclosed crossboom) glider, similar to current popular hang glider configurations but with a reflexed 'sting' tail added to the root area. This 1970s design feature affords increased pitch damping and stability. The aircraft was to have a duralumin airframe stressed to +6·5/−4·5*g*, stainless steel cables, a kingpost and double surfaced Dacron sail. Other details are given in the table. No 1986 update was received.

PEGASUS

PEGASUS TRANSPORT SYSTEMS LTD/ SOLAR WINGS LTD

PO Box 29, Marlborough, Wiltshire SN8 1PF
Telephone: 0672 53504

CHAIRMAN, PEGASUS TRANSPORT SYSTEMS LTD:
Frederick Hogarth

DIRECTORS, SOLAR WINGS LTD:
S. M. G. Rose (Managing)
D. S. Raymond
G. J. Slater
M. S. Southall

Solar Wings is a CAA-approved manufacturing subsidiary of Pegasus Transport Systems Ltd. It was founded in 1979 and first manufactured the **Solar Storm** intermediate hang glider. This was replaced in 1981 with the first of the **Typhoon** series which, benefiting from the **Blade** and **Tempest** R & D gliders, continues through to the 1986 **S4 Plus**, **S4 Racer** and **Racer GP**. An addition to the 1986 product range is the new **Solar Ace**. Airframes are of aluminium alloy with Dacron double surface covering over 55 per cent of the sail area, with Mylar inserts at the leading-edges, plastics coated stainless steel cables and faired kingpost. Faired control-frame sides are optional. Typhoon wings have been adapted for power and are used with various Pegasus trikes (see entry in Sport Aircraft section) and with the Pegasus Minimum System, a simple strap-on power unit which enables a pilot to climb away from level ground and sustain flight when the natural lift sources used in free flight fail. The Typhoons have the Pegasus Towing System facility incorporated as a standard fitting, and were used extensively in the development of the Pegasus Tug, whose XLT wing was designed to match the performance envelope of the S4 series.

Details can be found in the table at the end of this section.

UNITED STATES OF AMERICA

DELTA WING

DELTA WING AVIATION

PO Box 483, Van Nuys, California 91408
Telephone: (818) 787 6000
Telex: 65-1425
PRESIDENT: William Bennett

Details of Delta Wing's Phoenix 6D, Lazor, Viper and X series gliders can be found in the 1982-83 *Jane's*. Most recent models are the 1982 Dream and Streak and the 1985 Mystic. 'Bullet' recovery parachute available for all models.

DELTA WING DREAM

Basic/intermediate glider, designed by Bob England and derived from Phoenix X. Introduced in Spring 1982 and originally available in two models (see table). Dream 185 received USHGMA certification in 1984; Dream 175 (16·26 m²; 175 sq ft wing area) added to range for 1985. Aluminium alloy airframe, Dacron sail (single thickness on 165, double on 185), and vinyl coated stainless steel cables. Kingpost standard. Features include sliding crossbar, leading-edge foam inserts, keel pocket, and enclosed washout struts. Can be flown prone, seated or supine.

DELTA WING STREAK

Also designed by Bob England, and introduced in Autumn 1982, receiving USHGMA certification in 1982 (Streak 160) and 1983 (130 and 180). Airframe is of aluminium alloy, stressed to +8·5/−5*g*, and has a double covering of Dacron (optionally Mylar) over 87 per cent of the wing area, the lower surface being free-floating. Vinyl coated stainless steel cables and a kingpost are standard; battens are of aluminium and Lexan tube. Features include concealed floating crossbar, leading-edge hard foam inserts, and enclosed washout struts. Can be flown prone, seated or supine.

DELTA WING MYSTIC

Three models of the Mystic were introduced in 1985, the 166 and 177 receiving USHGMA certification during that year, with certification of the smaller Mystic 155 being in progress in early 1986. All have an anodised aluminium alloy tube airframe with streamlined kingpost and control bar downtubes, braced by coated stainless steel cables. The wing has six ribs and two half-ribs on top, and three battens underneath, on each side, and is fitted with foam backed leading-edge pockets as standard. Options include a 'variable geometry' system and surfcoat leading-edge pockets, as well as a choice of wing cloth. Set-up time for the Mystic is about 15 minutes.

FLIGHT DESIGNS

FLIGHT DESIGNS INC (a division of Pioneer International Corporation)

PO Box 631, Manchester, Connecticut 06040

Current product in 1984 was the Demon, described in the 1985-86 *Jane's*. No news of hang glider activity has been received since early 1984.

Early example of the Antonov Slavutitch-UT

Kołecki White Eagle (tractor configuration)

Airwave Gliders Magic IV

Pegasus/Solar Wings Typhoon S4

Pacific Windcraft Vision

Delta Wing Streak

Pegasus/Solar Ace

Pacific Windcraft Vision Eclipse

MANTA

MANTA PRODUCTS INC

1647 East 14th Street, Oakland, California 94606
Telephone: (415) 536 1500

SECRETARY AND CHIEF PILOT: William J. Armour

MANTA FLEDGE III

Earlier versions of this rigid sweptwing hang glider have been described in the 1980-81 (Fledge I and IIA) and 1982-83 editions of *Jane's* (Fledge IIB). Sales of these models totalled 1,600 by February 1981.

The improved **Fledge III** won first place in the Open Class of the 1981 US national hang gliding championships, and in 1983 the 1,000th had been sold. No news has been received since that time; consequently it is not known if this well known glider continues in production. Latest known details, and a photograph, can be found in the 1985-86 *Jane's*.

PACIFIC WINDCRAFT

PACIFIC WINDCRAFT LTD

PO Box 4384, Salinas, California 93912
Telephone: (408) 422 2299

PRESIDENT: Jean-Michel Bernasconi

This company was formed in the late Summer of 1982. Its first product is the Vision hang glider, of which production began in the following September; USHGMA certification was granted on 10 November 1982.

PACIFIC WINDCRAFT VISION

Available in three versions, the Vision is claimed to be the only double-surfaced hang glider designed for the intermediate recreational pilot. The aluminium alloy airframe has what the manufacturer calls a '3DCG' above-the-keel suspension system, with a streamlined extrusion forming the kingpost, and is Dacron covered.

By early 1985, a total of 750 Visions had been sold in 13 countries, including Australia, Brazil, Canada, France, West Germany, Guatemala, Israel, Japan, Norway and the USA. Three licenced manufacturers have been established: Delta Sud, in France; Hiway Flight Service (Pacific Windcraft Europe), in England; and Suncoast Hang Gliders in Australia. No dimensions or performance details were received from Pacific Windcraft; all known data are given in the table at the end of this section.

PACIFIC WINDCRAFT VISION ECLIPSE

Intended to be equally suitable for cross-country and high performance flying, the Eclipse is a new version of the Vision designed jointly by Mr Bob England and the President of Pacific Windcraft. After some 300 hours of flight and other testing with six prototypes, the Vision Eclipse 17 received USHGMA certification in November 1985 and the larger Eclipse 19 in January 1986. Major differences from the basic Vision are a 40 per cent wider leading-edge foam pocket, faired downtubes with a rubber trailing-edge, speed bar, a 'variable geometry' system, and deletion of the keel pocket. Known data are included in the table at the end of this section.

PROGRESSIVE

PROGRESSIVE AIRCRAFT COMPANY

4544 Industrial Street, Simi Valley, California 93063
Telephone: (805) 583 1014

PRESIDENT: Richard L. Boone

This company specialises in high performance hang gliders and associated products. Its earlier models (see 1985-86 and previous *Jane's*) included the ProAir, ProStar II and Breez, all sizes of which have USHGMA certification. It is not known whether these continue in production. A **ProDawn 155** model received HGMA approval in 1984, and a **Dawn Comp 160** in 1985, but no details of these were received.

SEEDWINGS

SEEDWINGS

5760 Thornwood Drive No. 3, Santa Barbara, California 93117

Telephone: (805) 967 4848

DIRECTOR: Robert E. Trampenau

SEEDWINGS SENSOR 510-B

This company's Sensor hang glider won a number of US national and regional championships in 1981 and 1982. The variable geometry **Sensor 510-160 VG**, introduced in 1983, features flight-adjustable sail tension to improve soaring performance, half-ribs extended to the double surface line, closer rib spacing, and higher leading-edge tension with redesigned Mylar leading-edge inserts and a wraparound nose fairing. The 510-165 (1985-86 *Jane's*) and 510-160 VG were approved by the USHGMA in 1982 and 1984 respectively. All known details of the latter are given in the table at the end of this section. Current version from 1985 is the **510-B** (HGMA certification May 1985); this has a new suspension system with faired kingpost and downtubes, eight extra half-ribs, and a variable geometry trailing-edge. Sensor 510-Bs took first three places in the 1985 US 'Masters' championship.

UP

UP INC (ULTRALITE PRODUCTS)

PO Box 659, Temecula, California 92390
Telephone: (714) 676 5652
Telex: 910 332 1306
President: Peter Brock
R & D Consultant: J. C. Brown

UP COMET 2B

To enhance the Comet's role as an all-round recreational glider, a detuned variant, the Comet 2B, was introduced for production in 1985. The Dacron/Mylar sandwich covered sail of the Comet II has been replaced with conventional Dacron. USHGMA certificated, it is stressed to +6·5/−3·5*g* and available in two sizes; details are given in the table. Airframe is of anodised aluminium alloy tube, with kingpost as standard, sail double surface over 60 per cent of area, vinyl covered stainless steel cables, enclosed cross-spars, leech tension line and nosecone fairing. Rigging time is 15 min. Manufacture of the Comet II and earlier variants (see 1984-85 *Jane's*) has been discontinued.

In early 1985 the Comet held the NAA US open distance record of 192·4 nm (356·5 km; 221·5 miles), the longest hang glider flight ever made. By January 1985 a total of 3,356 Comets (all versions) had been built and sold. No 1986 details were received.

UP GEMINI

Basically, the Gemini is a single-surface intermediate version of the Comet, with minor variations in the sail and cross-spars. The Mylar leading-edge inserts, introduced in 1984, are now standard. Details of the three sizes available in 1985 (134, 164 and 184) are given in the table at the end of this section.

UP GLIDEZILLA 155

Production of this racing glider began in Spring 1985. Designed by Roy Haggard and J. C. Brown, it is intended for the advanced pilot (USHGMA advanced level or higher). Features include high density batten spacing, enclosed keel, cross-spars, nose plates and wingtips, trailing-edge tension line sewn into hem, European-style rigging system and no keel pocket. Airframe, stressed to +6·5/−3·5*g*, is of anodised aluminium tube, with kingpost as standard, Dacron sail (double surface over 77 per cent of area), and vinyl coated stainless steel cables. An optional faired control bar and kingpost are available.

VOLMER

VOLMER AIRCRAFT

PO Box 5222, Glendale, California 91201
Telephone: (213) 247 8718
President: Volmer Jensen

Plans (but not kits or materials) for the VJ-23 and VJ-24 are available from Volmer Aircraft, and several hundred sets have been sold. Rights to manufacture the VJ-24 in kit form were acquired in the Spring of 1982 by Airway Aircraft of PO Box 3025, Airway Avenue, Glendale, California 91201.

Details of the powered versions of both gliders can be found in the Sport Aircraft section.

VOLMER VJ-23 SWINGWING

This monoplane hang glider was designed in 1971 by Volmer Jensen and Irving Culver, making its first flight towards the end of that year. Subsequent modifications made the aircraft safer and more controllable.

Airframe: Cantilever high-wing monoplane, constructed of steel tube, spruce, mahogany and plywood, with Dacron or other fabric covering. Control by means of ailerons, elevators and rudder.

Dimensions:
- Wing span: 9·93 m (32 ft 7 in)
- Length overall: 5·31 m (17 ft 5 in)
- Height overall: 1·83 m (6 ft 0 in)

Area:
- Wings, gross: 16·63 m² (179·0 sq ft)

Weights:
- Weight empty: 45·5 kg (100 lb)
- Pilot weight range: 45·5-91 kg (100-200 lb)
- Max T-O weight: 136 kg (300 lb)

Performance:
- Best glide ratio at 17 knots (32 km/h; 20 mph): 9
- Cruising speed: 17 knots (32 km/h; 20 mph)
- Stalling speed: 13 knots (24 km/h; 15 mph)
- *g* limits: ±3

VOLMER VJ-24 SUNFUN

The VJ-24 rigid-wing monoplane hang glider is essentially a simplified version of the VJ-23 Swingwing, from which it differs primarily in having wings and tail of fabric covered aluminium tube instead of wooden spars and ribs; rectangular instead of tapered planform wings, of increased span, with V bracing struts; and a pair of ground handling wheels.

Dimensions:
- Wing span: 11·13 m (36 ft 6 in)
- Length overall: 5·54 m (18 ft 2 in)
- Height overall: 1·73 m (5 ft 8 in)

Area:
- Wings, gross: 15·14 m² (163·0 sq ft)

Weights:
- Weight empty: 50 kg (110 lb)
- Max T-O weight: 140·5 kg (310 lb)

Performance: As for VJ-23

FLEXIBLE WING HANG GLIDER DATA

Manufacturer and Model	FAI or other class	Span: m/ft-in	Leading-edge: m/ft-in	Keel: m/ft-in	Nose/Billow angle: degrees	Wing area: m²/sq ft	Wing aspect ratio
AUSTRALIA							
Moyes Delta							
Mars 150	1	8·84/29-0	5·10/16-9	2·54/8-4	125/0·5	13·94/150·0	5·60
Mars 170	1	9·45/31-0	5·51/18-1	2·62/8-7	125/0·5	15·98/172·0	5·58
Mars 190	1	10·06/33-0	5·87/19-3	2·74/9-0	125/0·5	17·65/190·0	5·70
GTR 148	n.k.	9·75/32-0	4·80/15-9	1·98/6-6	130/n.k.	13·75/148·0	6·92
GTR 162	n.k.	10·36/34-0	5·14/16-10½	3·57/11-8½	130/n.k.	15·05/162·0	7·20
GTR 175	n.k.	10·97/36-0	5·49/18-0	2·13/7-0	130/n.k.	16·26/175·0	7·40
GTR 210	n.k.	10·97/36-0	5·49/18-0	2·90/9-6	130/n.k.	19·51/210·0	6·17
FRANCE							
La Mouette							
Atlas 14	1	9·30/30-6¼	5·36/17-7	3·50/11-5¾	120/0·5	13·80/148·5	6·25
Atlas 16	1	9·90/32-5¾	5·70/18-8½	3·50/11-5¾	120/0·5	15·80/170·0	6·20
Atlas 18	1	10·50/34-5½	6·10/20-0	3·50/11-5¾	120/0·5	18·00/193·8	6·10
Hermes 13	n.k.	10·60/34-9¼	n.k.	n.k.	130/n.k.	13·30/143·2	8·45
Hermes 14	n.k.	10·60/34-9¼	n.k.	n.k.	130/n.k.	13·80/148·5	8·14
Hermes 15	n.k.	10·60/34-9¼	n.k.	n.k.	130/n.k.	14·80/159·3	7·59
Hermes 16	n.k.	10·60/34-9¼	n.k.	n.k.	130/n.k.	15·80/170·0	7·11
Profil 15	1	10·00/32-9¾	5·80/19-0¼	3·50/11-5¾	119/0	14·50/156·1	6·90
Profil 17	1	10·60/34-9¼	6·20/20-4	3·50/11-5¾	119/0	16·50/177·6	6·80
GERMANY							
Finsterwalder							
Topfex	n.k.	10·40/34-1½	5·80/19-0¼	n.k.	130/n.k.	16·10/173·3	6·72
Firebird							
World Cup 90-S School Glider	1 (DHV)	8·40/27-6¾	5·85/19-2¼	n.k.	90/n.k.	20·30/218·5	3·47
Uno	1 & 2 (DHV)	9·95/32-7¾	5·75/18-10½	n.k.	125/n.k.	15·50/166·8	6·38
Uno Piccolo	1 & 2 (DHV)	9·35/30-8	5·40/17-8½	n.k.	125/n.k.	14·00/150·7	6·24
Quattro	1 & 2 (DHV)	9·95/32-7¾	5·75/18-10½	n.k.	125/n.k.	15·50/166·8	6·38
Quattro-S	2 & 3 (DHV)	9·95/32-7¾	5·75/18-10½	n.k.	125/n.k.	15·50/166·8	6·39
Sierra 155	3 (DHV)	10·40/34-1½	5·50/18-0½	n.k.	136/n.k.	14·90/160·4	7·26
Sierra 175	3 (DHV)	10·90/35-9	5·75/18-10½	n.k.	136/n.k.	16·70/179·8	7·11
Spirit	3 (DHV)	10·90/35-9	5·80/19-0¼	n.k.	130-133/n.k.	16·00/172·2	7·43
ITALY							
Polaris *(no 1986 update received)*							
Delta 13	1	9·35/30-8	n.k.	n.k.	120/n.k.	13·50/145·3	6·48
Delta 16	1	9·90/32-5¾	n.k.	n.k.	120/n.k.	15·80/170·1	6·20
Delta 19	1	10·50/34-5½	n.k.	n.k.	120/n.k.	19·00/204·5	5·80
Delta 21	1	10·50/34-5½	n.k.	n.k.	120/n.k.	21·00/226·0	5·25
Gamma 177	1	10·60/34-9¼	6·20/20-4	3·60/11-9¾	120/0	16·44/177·0	6·80

n.k. = not known; n.a. = not applicable

Wills Wing Skyhawk

Wills Wing 167 Sport

Wills Wing HP 170

UP Gemini

WILLS WING

WILLS WING INC

1208-H, East Walnut, Santa Ana, California 92701

Telephone: (714) 547 1344

Engineering Officer: Michael Meier

WILLS WING DUCK and ATTACK DUCK

High-performance flex-wing hang glider, with double surface covering over 63 per cent of sail area and enclosed crossbar. Two basic models (160 and 180) currently in production. Certificated by USHGMA in 1982. A version with eight additional half-length pre-cambered top-surface ribs inserted between existing midspan ribs is known as the Attack Duck. Dimensions are identical to the Duck, but there is a 0·9 kg (2 lb) increase in weight and 2 per cent improvement in performance.

WILLS WING SKYHAWK

The Skyhawk superseded the earlier Harrier series of hang gliders (see 1983-84 *Jane's*) in 1984. Produced in two models (see table). Airframe, stressed to +6/−3*g*, is of 6061-T6 aluminium alloy, with vinyl coated stainless steel cables. Foam leading-edge inserts. Dacron sail (single surface).

By 1 January 1985 (no later figure was given) a total of 100 Skyhawks had been built.

WILLS WING HP 170

This high-performance flex-wing hang glider was certificated by the USHGMA in 1984 and won the first three places in the 1984 US Nationals Great Race. In 1985, first place was achieved in the US and Canadian Nationals and 12 other races or championship events held in the USA and Canada. Drag is minimised by a stiff spar, high sail tension, and elimination of the keel pocket. The airframe, stressed to +6/−3*g*, is of aluminium alloy, with vinyl coated stainless steel cables. The double surfaced Dacron sail has twenty chordwise battens. The HP 170 is available ready to fly, and more than 500 had been built by January 1986. A streamlined control bar, kingpost and supine rigging are available as options. Other data are given in the table.

WILLS WING 167 SPORT

First flown in July 1985 and marketed from February 1986, the Sport combines extremely light weight, improved aerodynamic efficiency and high structural strength. The USHGMA certificated airframe is made of 7075-T6 aluminium alloy, claimed to be up to 98 per cent stronger than the 6061-T6 of which most hang gliders are constructed. Other standard features include a double surface Dacron sail, streamlined kingpost, elevated hang point and vinyl coated stainless steel cables, and the aircraft is stressed to +7/−3*g*. Rigging time is 10-15 minutes. A streamlined control bar is available as an option.

Five Sports had been completed by 1 February 1986, of 50 then on order. Other details are given in the following table.

Weight: kg/lb	Glide ratio	Sink rate: m/ft per min	Pilot weight: kg (lb)	Stalling speed: knots (km/h; mph)	Remarks
23·6/52	8·5	61/200	41-82 (90-180)	19 (34; 21)	
28·1/62	8	61/200	57-109 (125-240)	23 (42; 26)	Max speed at min recommended loading 36 knots (67 km/h; 42 mph). Stalling speed at max recommended loading given
n.k.	n.k.	n.k.	n.k.	n.k.	
n.k.	n.k.	n.k.	n.k.	n.k.	
30·8/68	n.k.	n.k.	59-104 (130-230)	15 (28; 18)	Max speed at min recommended loading 42 knots (78 km/h; 49 mph) IAS. Stalling speed at 6·8 kg/m² (1·4 lb/sq ft) loading
n.k.	n.k.	n.k.	n.k.	n.k.	
n.k.	n.k.	n.k.	n.k.	n.k.	
24·5/54	9	60/197	50-175 (110-165)	14 (25; 16)	
26/57·3	9	60/197	65-95 (143-209)	14 (25; 16)	
29/63·9	9	60/197	90-140 (198-308)	14 (25; 16)	
29·8/65·7	n.k.	n.k.	55-65 (121-143)	n.k.	
30/66·1	n.k.	n.k.	60-75 (132-165)	n.k.	
31/68·3	n.k.	n.k.	65-85 (143-187)	n.k.	
31·5/69·4	n.k.	n.k.	75-100 (165-220)	n.k.	
26/57·3	11	54/177	50-80 (110-176)	14 (25; 16)	
29/63·9	11	54/177	65-110 (143-242)	13 (23; 15)	
n.k.	12	54/177	n.k.	18 (32; 20)	
18/39·7	6	n.k.	55-85 (121-187)	14 (25; 16)	
25·5/56·2	8·5	n.k.	50-100 (110-220)	12 (22; 14)	
18/39·7	n.k.	n.k.	75 (165) max	n.k.	
26·5/58·4	10	n.k.	50-125 (110-275)	14 (25; 16)	
27/59·5	n.k.	n.k.	50-125 (110-275)	n.k.	
26/57·3	11	n.k.	75 (165) max	15 (28; 18)	
31/68·3	11	n.k.	60-175 (132-385)	15 (28; 18)	
34/75	n.k.	n.k.	60-110 (132-242)	17 (30; 19)	
24/52·9	n.k.	n.k.	45-68 (99-150)	14 (25; 16)	
27/59·5	n.k.	n.k.	62-95 (137-209)	14 (25; 16)	
32·5/71·7	n.k.	n.k.	85-150 (187-331)	14 (25; 16)	
33·5/73·9	n.k.	n.k.	133-213 (293-469)	14 (25; 16)	
33/72·7	9	54/177	55-95 (121-209)	14 (25; 16)	

FLEXIBLE WING HANG GLIDER DATA, contd

Manufacturer and Model	FAI or other class	Span: m/ft-in	Leading-edge: m/ft-in	Keel: m/ft-in	Nose/Billow angle: degrees	Wing area: m²/sq ft	Wing aspect ratio
POLAND							
Instytut Lotnictwa							
Zeta-80B	1	10·20/33-5½	5·465/17-11¼	3·27/10-8¾	140/0	15·30/164·7	6·80
Zeta-84	1	11·60/38-0¾	6·00/19-8¼	3·60/11-9¾	140/0	17·00/183·0	7·91
USSR							
Antonov							
Slavutitch-UT	n.k.	8·80/28-10½	5·72/18-9¼	4·235/13-10¾	104/1·0	17·60/189·4	4·45
UNITED KINGDOM							
Airwave							
Magic IV 155	1	9·99/32-9¼	5·89/19-4	3·66/12-0	120/n.k.	14·49/156·0	6·72
Magic IV 166	1	10·40/34-1½	5·99/19-8	3·66/12-0	120/n.k.	15·79/170·0	6·80
Magic IV 177	1	10·64/34-11	6·21/20-4½	3·66/12-0	120/n.k.	16·54/178·0	6·84
Cunion							
(no 1986 update received)	1	10·46/34-0	5·79/19-0	3·35/11-0	127/0	16·72/180·0	6·42
Pegasus/Solar Wings							
Ace (medium)	1	9·91/32-6	n.k.	n.k.	122/n.k.	14·86/160·0	6·60
Typhoon S4 (small)	1	9·60/31-6	5·64/18-6	4·00/13-1½	122/n.a.	14·68/158	6·28
Typhoon S4 (medium)	1	9·91/32-6	5·81/19-0¾	4·00/13-1½	122/n.a.	15·42/166	6·40
Typhoon S4 (large)	1	10·36/34-0	6·08/19-11½	4·00/13-1½	122/n.a.	16·72/180	6·45
Typhoon S4 Plus, Racer and GP (small)	1	9·60/31-6	5·64/18-6	4·00/13-1½	122/n.a.	14·21/153	6·49
Typhoon S4 Plus, Racer and GP (medium)	1	9·91/32-6	5·81/19-0¾	4·00/13-1½	122/n.a.	14·96/161	6·56
Typhoon S4 Plus, Racer and GP (large)	1	10·36/34-0	6·08/19-11½	4·00/13-1½	122/n.a.	16·26/175	6·60
UNITED STATES OF AMERICA							
Delta Wing *(no 1986 update received)*							
Dream 165	1	9·55/31-4	n.k.	n.k.	124/1·0	15·33/165	6·40
Dream 185	1	10·31/33-10	n.k.	n.k.	124/1·0	17·19/185	6·20
Mystic 155	n.k.	9·96/32-8	n.k.	n.k.	n.k.	14·49/156	6·72
Mystic 166	n.k.	10·39/34-1	n.k.	n.k.	n.k.	15·42/166	6·80
Mystic 177	n.k.	10·57/34-8	n.k.	n.k.	n.k.	16·26/175	6·84
Streak 130	1	8·84/29-0	n.k.	n.k.	133/0	12·08/130	6·60
Streak 160	1	10·62/34-10	5·56/18-3	3·35/11-0	133/0	14·68/158	7·50
Streak 180	1	11·38/37-4	n.k.	n.k.	133/0	16·72/180	7·60
Pacific Windcraft							
Vision 148	n.k.	n.k.	n.k.	n.k.	122/n.k.	13·75/148·0	5·7
Vision 175	n.k.	n.k.	n.k.	n.k.	122/n.k.	16·26/175·0	5·7
Vision 194	n.k.	n.k.	n.k.	n.k.	122/n.k.	18·02/194·0	5·5
Vision Eclipse 17	n.k.	9·27/30-5	n.k.	n.k.	122/n.k.	15·89/171·0	5·44
Vision Eclipse 19	n.k.	9·75/32-0	n.k.	n.k.	122/n.k.	17·19/185·0	5·53
Seedwings *(no 1986 update received)*							
Sensor 510-160 VG	n.k.	10·57/34-8	n.k.	n.k.	n.k.	14·96/161·0	7·52
Sensor 510-165	n.k.	10·67/35-0	5·18/17-0	n.k.	n.k.	15·33/165·0	7·42
UP *(no 1986 update received)*							
Comet 2B 165	1	9·96/32-8	5·86/19-2¾	2·49/8-2	120/0	15·33/165·0	6·50
Comet 2B 185	1	10·57/34-8	6·22/20-4¾	2·62/8-7	120/0	17·19/185·0	6·60
Gemini M 134	1	8·78/28-9½	5·22/17-1½	2·18/7-2	120/1·0	12·45/134·0	6·19
Gemini M 164	1	9·91/32-6	5·86/19-2¾	2·49/8-2	120/1·0	15·24/164·0	6·44
Gemini M 184	1	10·49/34-5	6·22/20-4¾	2·62/8-7	120/1·0	17·09/184·0	6·43
Glidezilla 155	1	10·36/34-0	5·87/19-3	2·06/6-9	126/0	14·31/154·0	7·50
Wills Wing							
Duck 160	1	9·86/32-4	5·51/18-1⅛	3·30/10-10	130/0	14·40/155·0	6·70
Duck 180	1	10·62/34-10	5·93/19-5½	3·35/11-0	130/0	16·72/180·0	6·80
Skyhawk 168	1	9·19/30-2	5·49/18-0	3·66/12-0	115/0	15·42/166·0	5·50
Skyhawk 188	1	10·01/32-10	5·94/19-6	3·66/12-0	115/0	17·47/188·0	5·70
167 Sport	1	10·21/33-6	5·94/19-6	3·45/11-4	124/0	15·51/167·0	6·72
HP 170	1	10·46/34-4	5·92/19-5	3·45/11-4	128/0	15·61/168·0	7·00

n.k. = not known; n.a. = not applicable

Weight: kg/lb	Glide ratio	Sink rate: m/ft per min	Pilot weight: kg (lb)	Stalling speed: knots (km/h; mph)	Remarks
25/55	10	57/187	60-85 (132-187)	16 (28; 18)	
32/70·5	13	51/167	60-90 (132-198)	13·5 (25; 15)	
25/55	7	78/256	n.k.	14 (25; 16)	
29/64	11	52/171	64-73 (140-160)	16 (29; 18)	
29·9/66	11	52/171	70-79 (155-175)	16 (29; 18)	
32·2/71	11	54/177	79-91 (175-200)	16 (29; 18)	
n.k.	n.k.	n.k.	n.k.	18 (32; 20)	
31·8/70	12·5	n.k.	91 (200) max	n.k.	
29·5/65	11	55/180	76 (168) max	17 (32; 20)	
32·7/72	11	55/180	91 (200) max	17 (32; 20)	
34·5/76	11	55/180	89 (195) min	17 (32; 20)	
28/61·7	12	53/174	76 (168) max	16 (30; 19)	
32·7/72	12	53/174	91 (200) max	16 (30; 19)	
35/77·2	12	53/174	89 (195) min	16 (30; 19)	
28·1/62	n.k.	n.k.	59-91 (130-200)	n.k.	
30·8/68	n.k.	n.k.	n.k.	n.k.	
29/64	n.k.	n.k.	45-77 (100-170)	n.k.	
29·9/66	n.k.	n.k.	64-95 (140-210)	n.k.	
32·2/71	n.k.	n.k.	77-109 (170-240)	n.k.	
24·9/55	n.k.	50/165	n.k.	n.k.	
32·7/72	n.k.	50/165	59-100 (130-220)	n.k.	
37·2/82	n.k.	50/165	n.k.	n.k.	
23·6/52	n.k.	n.k.	45-113 (100-250)	n.k.	
26·8/59	n.k.	45-113 (100-250)	n.k.	n.k.	
29/64	n.k.	n.k.	45-113 (100-250)	n.k.	
27·2/60	n.k.	n.k.	32-64 (70-140)	n.k.	
29/64	n.k.	n.k.	39-84 (86-186)	n.k.	
29·9/66	n.k.	n.k.	n.k.	n.k.	
29·9/66	n.k.	n.k.	n.k.	n.k.	Max diving speed 44 knots (82 km/h; 51 mph)
29/64	10+	55/180	59-104 (130-230)	13·5 (25; 15) IAS	
35·4/78	10+	55/180	68-113 (150-250)	13·5 (25; 15) IAS	
24·9/55	8·5	64/210	43-75 (95-165)	12·5 (23; 14) IAS	
28·6/63	8·5	64/210	57-91 (125-200)	12·5 (23; 14) IAS	
34/75	8·5	64/210	68-104 (150-230)	12·5 (23; 14) IAS	
32·7/72	12·5	52/170	64-104 (140-230)	13 (24; 15)	
30·8/68*	—	—	59-104 (130-230)	22 (41; 25)	* 2·7 kg (6 lb) heavier with optional steel control bar and kingpost
32·7/72*	—	—	73-118 (160-260)	22 (41; 25)	* 2·7 kg (6 lb) heavier with optional steel control bar and kingpost
24·5/54	8·5	69/225	52-75 (115-165)	20 (36; 22)	
29/64	8·5	69/225	66-88 (145-195)	20 (36; 22)	
26·8/59	9	73/240	64-95 (140-210)	18 (33; 20)	
31·8/70	10+	76/250	68-113 (150-250)	22 (41; 25)	

LIGHTER THAN AIR: AIRSHIPS

AUSTRALIA

ADA

AIRSHIP DEVELOPMENTS AUSTRALIA PTY LTD

96 Rankins Road, Kensington, Victoria 3031
Telephone: (03) 376 2450
DESIGNER: Bruce N. Blake

Nearly a decade ago Mr Bruce Blake, then a newly graduated aeronautical engineer, contributed to the design and construction of Australia's first airship, the non-rigid *Ardath*. In the interim, after working at the Department of Aviation, Government Aircraft Factories and Australian Aircraft Consortium, he initiated a series of airship designs under the name of his Airship Developments Australia company. These include a pair of drones, a single- and two-seat non-rigid, a twin-engined, four/six-seat light utility airship, and a 50-passenger tourist craft. The single-seat project was terminated at mockup stage when studies indicated that resources were better committed to refinement of the light utility airship design. As the means of demonstrating the airworthiness of this design, at minimal cost, while generating revenue, a scaled-down drone version, the Model LUA, was funded and built during 1985. First flown in early 1986, the LUA is intended to prove several innovative features, including a lifting outrigger with blown flap similar to one wind-tunnel tested in the USA for the GZ-16 non-rigid of the 1950s. Revenue will be generated at outdoor displays and other promotional opportunities. The ability to carry a small TV camera system may improve market access, as well as pave the way for more advanced guidance and piloting technology. The full size version of the LUA, for which preliminary design work has been completed, is known as the **ADA-1200**. The following description relates to the one-third scale prototype:

The ADA LUA remotely controlled airship, a scale prototype for the ADA-1200, nearing completion in late 1985 *(The Age, Melbourne)*

ADA LUA

ENVELOPE: The envelope is a two-skin type, the inner (gas cell) being made from metallised laminated nylon film while the outer (load carrying) skin is of stabilised polyester fabric. Seams of the outer skin are double sewn, with heat-sealed tapes to attain full fabric strength across the seams. The inner skin, which is highly plastic and roughing tolerant, will eventually conform to the shape of the outer skin as it stretches with use. A single spherical ballonet (volume 8·0 m^3; 283 cu ft) is provided, constructed from nylon film. Automatic pressure control is achieved by the use of a pressure switch, an electric centrifugal blower (with a one-way flow valve) and an outflow valve. An overpressure valve is provided to vent helium, should envelope pressure exceed safe limits. Additionally, a remotely controlled dump valve will enable the initiation of a controlled descent if the propulsion system should fail. The LUA has an X-fin tail unit, each fin being fitted with a 'ruddervator' actuated by servos, with electronic mixing, to provide control in pitch and yaw. The fins are constructed from balsa wood and covered with a heat-shrunk polyester film.

POWER PLANT: Two 2·6 kW (3·5 hp) Robin EY15D single-cylinder four-stroke engines, lightened in weight and each fitted with an electric starter/generator. Engines are mounted on stub-wings, each with direct drive to a two-blade wooden propeller with spinner. Single fuel tank in spine fairing, max capacity 15 litres (3·3 Imp gallons).

GONDOLA, SPINE AND WINGS: The cabin/spine unit is unusually large, in comparison with gondolas fitted to existing non-rigid airships, but is in fact of scale size, and is an innovation of the LUA design. Past non-rigids have generally relied upon cables and catenary curtains fitted into the upper envelope to support the gondola, but by elongating the cabin/spine it is entirely practicable, with modern materials, to introduce vertical loading into the lower envelope surface. In addition, the cabin/spine configuration leads to improved stiffness, in pitch and roll, between it and the envelope, and allows the installation of tricycle landing gear, essential for ground manoeuvring. The LUA prototype is not entirely representative of the full sized ADA-1200, since the CG of the cabin/spine is aft of the appropriate position, and the two-skin envelope precludes a conventional internal suspension system. Instead, cords at the wingtips provide the missing support. Materials used in the cabin/spine are hand layed glass/epoxy/PVC foam sandwich, with aircraft plywood structural reinforcing. The wing, lifting outrigger or lift plane, attached to the rear of the spine, is constructed from light gauge aluminium alloy sheet and provides structural attachment for the engines and main landing gear units. The trailing-edge is formed by a 30% chord flap, servo actuated to ±40° deflection. This provides a useful increment of aerodynamic lift control. Landing gear has gas strut shock absorption and twin wheels, with 5½ in pneumatic tyres, on each unit.

GUIDANCE AND CONTROL: A standard FM radio control unit is used for line-of-sight operation. Minor modification was made to enable the use of a large external battery for the transmitter, with a similar improvement at the receiver. Control is provided for throttles, 'ruddervators', flaps and dump valve; three channels remain unused. The system provides an electronic discriminator for 'fail-safe' operation in the event of signal interference. Advanced RPV television based guidance is a possibility for future out-of-sight operations.

DIMENSIONS, OVERALL:	
Length	12·00 m (39 ft 4½ in)
Height	4·40 m (14 ft 5¼ in)
Width	3·60 m (11 ft 9¾ in)
DIMENSIONS, ENVELOPE:	
Length	12·00 m (39 ft 4½ in)
Max diameter	3·20 m (10 ft 6 in)
Volume	76·0 m^3 (2,684 cu ft)
DIMENSIONS, GONDOLA/WINGS:	
Gondola: Length	3·90 m (12 ft 9½ in)
Height (incl landing gear)	1·00 m (3 ft 3¼ in)
Wing span	2·10 m (6 ft 10¾ in)
Wing chord	0·60 m (1 ft 11½ in)
Wheel track	2·00 m (6 ft 6¾ in)
Wheelbase	2·50 m (8 ft 2½ in)
Propeller diameter	0·76 m (2 ft 6 in)
WEIGHTS:	
Weight empty	64 kg (141 lb)
Max fuel	11 kg (24 lb)
Max payload	11 kg (24 lb)
PERFORMANCE (estimated):	
Max level speed (neutral buoyancy)	41 knots (76 km/h; 47 mph)
Max cruising speed, 75% power	38 knots (70 km/h; 44 mph)

CANADA

HYSTAR

Vancouver, British Columbia

HYSTAR

Hystar is the name of a lenticular hybrid design of toroidal (doughnut) shape, developed by Mr George Ninkovich and designed for use by the Canadian forestry industry. Radio controlled models, one of which was demonstrated during the 1986 Expo 86 World Fair in Vancouver, can vary in size from 4·5 to 17 m (14·76 to 55·77 ft) in length. Piloted versions can be produced varying in length from 17 to 35 m (55·77 to 114·83 ft), with lifting capacities of up to 6,800 kg (14,990 lb) and speeds of up to 56 knots (105 km/h, 65 mph).

MAGNUS

MAGNUS AEROSPACE CORPORATION

200 First Avenue, Second Floor, Ottawa, Ontario K1S 2G6
POSTAL ADDRESS: PO Box 599, Station 'B', Ottawa, Ontario K1P 5P7
Telephone: (613) 236 4798
Telex: 053-4937
PRESIDENT: Fredrick D. Ferguson
DIRECTOR, COMMUNICATIONS: Ann Dempsey

This lighter than air (LTA) project was initiated by Van Dusen Commercial Development (Canada) Ltd (now Magnus Aerospace Corporation) in February 1978. Eight months of market research resulted in a design concept using modern materials to overcome traditional airship problems of ballasting, controllability and changing buoyancy resulting from variations in temperature and altitude. The helium filled lifting envelope is a pressurised sphere made from a high strength Kevlar material, and is able to withstand a sufficiently high internal pressure to maintain constant volume and shape over a wide range of pressure, temperature and wind conditions. The LTA vehicle uses this superpressure balloon concept in conjunction with the so-called Magnus effect, which generates additional lift from rotation of the spherical balloon. (Magnus effect is a force which will raise the flight path of a spinning ball, and was named after the 19th century German physicist who first noted it.)

A 6·1 m (20 ft) radio controlled model was flown at Ottawa for the first time during October 1981. A description of this, and of its successful testing, can be found under the Van Dusen heading in the 1983-84 and previous editions of *Jane's*.

MAGNUS LTA

Under this designation, Magnus is designing a commercial version of its new airship. This heavy lift craft is intended for short- and medium-range transport of oversize loads to remote or normally inaccessible locations. During 1983, work at the Institute for Aerospace Studies in Toronto concentrated on modifications to the craft to provide stable flight characteristics and low drag.

In 1984 three dynamically scaled drone vehicles were built. No news has been received from Magnus since that year, but the largest of these (diameter 5·5 m; 18 ft) was intended to be used in 1985 as a testbed for configuration changes, flight dynamics testing (using an onboard motion sensing package), and in-flight structural testing with strain gauges attached to the airframe.

In 1984, contracts were also awarded to prepare the first stage engineering definition of the LTA 20-1 production craft, including hardware options for the propulsion system, control systems, structure, vehicle dynamics, and weight and cost estimates. Its configuration will be generally similar to that of the drone scale model (see 1983-84 *Jane's*). VTOL capability will be provided by internal ballasting and engine thrust, enabling the craft to take off and land unassisted. Sphere rotation allows de-icing of the entire envelope surface from the gondola. The airship will be powered by four 2,610 kW (3,500 shp) engines, two being mounted at each end of the horizontal axle and each able to rotate independently through 90° to vector thrust from a vertical take-off mode to a horizontal cruising position.

The gondola, suspended from the horizontal axle, will accommodate the operator, utilising controls similar to those of a helicopter, and will carry payload within its cargo hold or as a slung load beneath the gondola. Additional lift will be generated by the vertical thrust of the engines during take-off and by the large Magnus force in horizontal cruising flight. After the payload has been offloaded, neutral buoyancy will be achieved by stopping sphere rotation to eliminate Magnus lift, reducing buoyant volume by expansion of the inner ballonet, and by taking in ballast as required.

Continuing market studies have identified a requirement for a smaller heavy lift craft. A design and development programme has begun on a 30 m (98·5 ft), 16,000 kg (35,274 lb) payload vehicle designated **LTA 20-16**, for which the initial demand would be utilisation in the forest products industry. This new craft is the offspring of the primary heavy lift (54·4 tonne payload) craft, now known as the **LTA 20-1**. Each would carry two pilots plus a loadmaster.

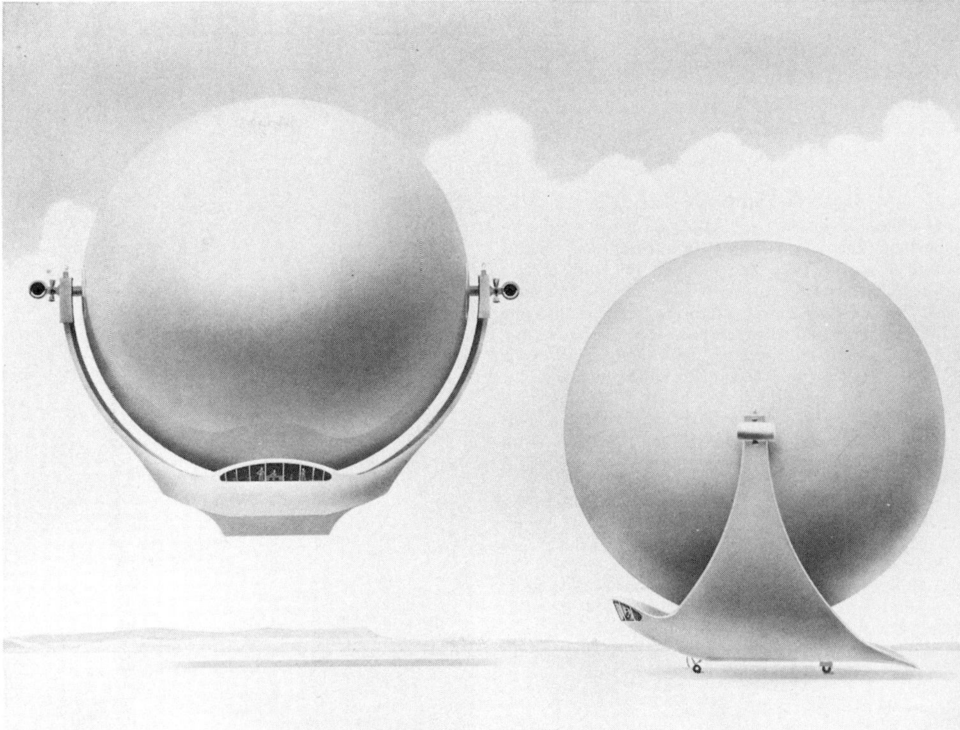

Artist's impression of Magnus LTA 20-1, showing general configuration

DIMENSIONS, ENVELOPE:	
Diameter: 20-16	30·0 m (98 ft 6 in)
20-1	60·96 m (200 ft 0 in)
Volume, gross: 20-16	14,137 m³ (499,244 cu ft)
20-1	118,613 m³ (4,188,785 cu ft)
Fuel capacity: 20-16	3,800 litres (836 Imp gallons)
20-1	18,850 litres (4,146 Imp gallons)
DIMENSIONS, GONDOLA:	
Length overall: 20-1	59·5 m (195 ft 2½ in)
Width: 20-1	31·7 m (104 ft 0 in)
Height: 20-1	4·3 m (14 ft 1¼ in)
WEIGHTS (estimated):	
Weight empty: 20-16	9,000 kg (19,840 lb)
20-1	39,000 kg (85,980 lb)
Max payload: 20-16 at S/L	16,000 kg (35,275 lb)
20-1	54,400 kg (119,930 lb)
Max T-O weight: 20-16 at S/L	25,000 kg (55,115 lb)
20-1	124,300 kg (274,035 lb)
PERFORMANCE (estimated):	
Max level speed:	
20-16	64 knots (120 km/h; 74 mph)
20-1	83 knots (96 km/h; 59 mph)
Cruising speed: 20-1	43 knots (80 km/h; 50 mph)
Range with max payload:	
20-16	280 nm (520 km; 323 miles)
20-1 at 43 knots (80 km/h; 50 mph), ISA	698 nm (804 km; 500 miles)
Typical endurance in logging operation:	
20-16	2 h 30 min

CHINA
(PEOPLE'S REPUBLIC)

HACDC
HANGZHOU AIRSHIP COMPREHENSIVE DEVELOPMENT COMPANY

c/o Lin An Physico-Chemical Research Institute, Hangzhou, Lin An County, Zhejiang Province

MANAGER: Zhang Chuhong

After retiring from the PLA Air Force in 1979, Mr Zhang Chuhong established privately the Physico-Chemical Research Institute in Lin An. Revenue earned as a result of this investment enabled him in March 1983 to begin the design of China's first modern airship. It was built by HACDC, of which Mr Zhang is now the manager.

HACDC XIHU-1 (WEST LAKE 1)

The Xihu-1 is powered by four 22·4 kW (30 hp) Huosai-350 piston engines, and was piloted by its designer on its first flight in May 1984. Subsequent test flights, according to *China Daily* in December 1985, have demonstrated its ability to carry one ton of cargo or 20 passengers.

At the same time it was reported that two other companies, GPSIDC (Guangdong Popular Science and Industrial Development Corporation) and CHTDC (Changzhou Huazhou Technical Development Co) were joining forces with HACDC to produce other airships based on HACDC's technology. Two more dirigibles, one built in Hangzhou and the other in Guangzhou, were due to be completed by October 1986 for commercial demonstration purposes.

The following data apply to the Xihu-1:

DIMENSIONS:	
Length overall	46·4 m (152 ft 2¾ in)
Envelope diameter (max)	13·0 m (42 ft 8 in)
Height overall	17·5 m (57 ft 5 in)
Ballonet diameter	3·5 m (11 ft 5¾ in)
Span over tail-fins	16·0 m (52 ft 6 in)
Volume:	
envelope, gross	4,050 m³ (143,025 cu ft)
ballonet	1,053 m³ (37,186 cu ft)
WEIGHT:	
Max overload T-O weight	1,000 kg (2,204 lb)
PERFORMANCE:	
Max cruising speed	27 knots (50 km/h; 31 mph)
Ceiling	3,000 m (9,840 ft)

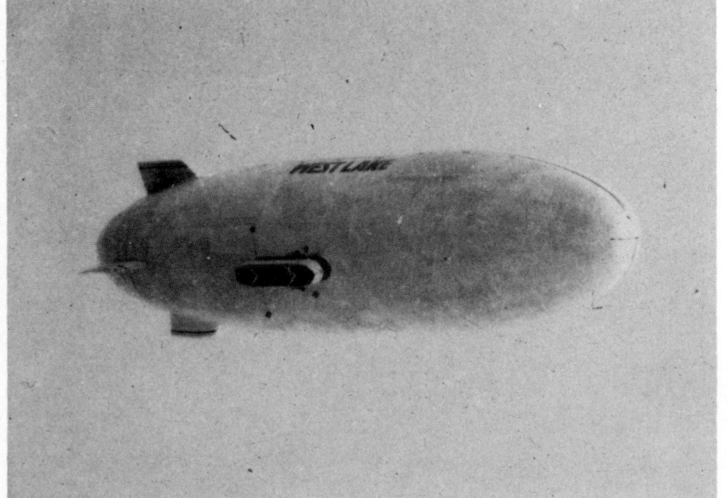

Two views of the Hangzhou Xihu-1, China's first modern commercial airship

CZECHOSLOVAKIA

AVIATIK BRNO

AVIATIK CLUB BRNO

Hlinky 164, 603 00 Brno
Telephone: 331 666
CHAIRMAN: Dr Jan Kunovský

A-1 and AV-1

In addition to its AB-1 and AB-2 balloons (see Balloons subsection), the Aviatik Club at Brno completed a model hot-air airship in 1983, and followed this with a scale prototype intended as a pattern for a larger craft of the same type. This non-man-carrying prototype (see accompanying photograph), designated **A-1**, is being used to evaluate and define the optimum envelope shape and aerodynamic efficiency. Various types of engine are also being tested. The full-size airship, which will be known as the **AV-1**, is projected as having overall length and height of 35 m (114 ft 10 in) and 14 m (46 ft 0 in), with a total volume of about 3,000 m³ (105,944 cu ft).

DIMENSIONS (prototype):

Envelope length	14·78 m (48 ft 6 in)
Height overall	9·97 m (32 ft 8½ in)
Propeller diameter	1·20 m (3 ft 11¼ in)
Volume:	
Hull (excl tail unit)	366·6 m³ (12,946 cu ft)
Total	405·0 m³ (14,302 cu ft)

WEIGHT:

Fuel load (prototype)	30 kg (66 lb)

Non-man-carrying A-1 prototype hot-air airship built by the Aviatik Club at Brno *(via Peter J. Bish)*

FRANCE

AÉRAZUR

AÉRAZUR EFA (Member company of the Groupe Zodiac)

Division Equipements Aéronautiques

58 boulevard Galliéni, 92130 Issy-les-Moulineaux
Telephone: (1) 45 54 92 80
Telex: 270 887 F
CHIEF EXECUTIVE OFFICER: Jean Louis Gerondeau
DIRECTOR GENERAL: Jean Corizzi
GENERAL MANAGER: Michel Roussel
MARKETING MANAGER: Jean-Pierre Fetu

DINOSAURE

Designed in 1975, originally for meteorological applications, the Dinosaure is a twin hulled 'catamaran' airship (hydrogen or helium filled) which, more recently, has been evaluated for remotely piloted surveillance and other potential military missions. The two hulls each have internal air ballonets, a gondola, separate cruciform tail surfaces, and are joined together in 'Siamese twin' fashion by a rigid central structure. A single engine mounted at the rear, between the hulls, drives a pusher propeller.

The **Dino 3** is a small scale test model which has also been evaluated. It carries a 10 kg (22 lb) payload which includes a TV camera, providing real-time video downlink to a ground based VDU, and a seven-channel radio command system. Its actual weight of 120 kg (265 lb) versus aerostatic lift of 105 kg (232 lb) means that, in fact, the Dino 3 is slightly heavier than air, but this is overcome by ability to derive part of its total lift from aerodynamic effects. Manoeuvrability is controlled by the conventional rudders and elevators, climb and descent by means of the ballonets or elasticity of the envelope. Larger versions could be fitted with underhull suction fans to hold the airship down after landing, to minimise ground handling requirements.

The following details apply to Dino 3, which is powered by a 7·5 kW (10 hp) microlight aircraft engine:

The Aérazur Dinosaure twin-hull 'catamaran' airship

DIMENSIONS, ENVELOPE:

Length overall	9·80 m (32 ft 2 in)
Width overall	7·90 m (25 ft 11 in)
Height overall	3·57 m (11 ft 8½ in)
Volume, gross	95·0 m³ (3,355 cu ft)

GERMANY (FEDERAL REPUBLIC)

GEFA-FLUG

Aachen

Gefa-Flug has been operating advertising and passenger-carrying balloons and remotely controlled airships since 1976, and currently has been commissioned by the Belgian government to design a large airship similar to the Airship Industries Skyship 500.

HUNGARY

MÉM RSZ

MÉM REPÜLŐGÉPES SZOLGÁLAT

PO Box 56, Kőérberki út 36, H 1112 Budapest XI
Telephone: 851 344 and 668 450
Telex: 22-5187
COMMERCIAL MANAGER: László Kürtös

MÉM RSZ HOT-AIR AIRSHIP

In addition to its manufacture of balloons (which see), MÉM RSZ completed in early 1981 (c/n 2/1981) the envelope of a BX-5 class hot-air airship, registration HA-B-501, which is illustrated in an accompanying photograph. Similar to, but slightly larger than, the Cameron D-96 described in the UK part of this subsection, the Hungarian airship has an envelope volume of 4,000 m³ (141,260 cu ft) and is of similar construction to this factory's hot-air balloons.

Up to the beginning of 1984 it had been flown only as a free balloon, owing to difficulties with the (unknown) power plant. No update for 1985 or 1986 was received.

The Hungarian hot-air airship built by MÉM RSZ, flying as a free balloon in 1981 *(Peter J. Bish)*

MEXICO

SPACIAL

SERVICIOS PUBLICITARIOS AÉREOS CONSTRUCCIÓN E INGENIERÍA DE AERONAVES LIGERAS

Margaritas 312-8, Colonia Florida, Mexico DF 01030
Telephone: 524 7262
CHAIRMAN OF THE BOARD: Lic Ramón González Parra
DIRECTOR GENERAL: Ing Mario Sánchez Roldán
EXECUTIVE SECRETARY: Dorotea Mahr Kanter
PUBLIC RELATIONS MANAGER: Velino M. Preza

SPACIAL MLA-32-A

Research, development and design work on this unusual rigid airship began in 1973. The MLA-24-A prototype was nearing completion in the Spring of 1985, and it was hoped to make the first flight that Summer, but the prototype and its hangar were destroyed in a tornado before this could take place. Details and illustrations of the MLA-24-A were published in the 1985-86 *Jane's*.

By early 1986 construction of the larger MLA-32-A had begun on a new site at Toluca, 64 km (40 miles) north-east of Mexico City. (MLA is an abbreviation of the Spanish for 'lighter than air').

The envelope/hull of the MLA-32-A consists of an ellipsoid frame of 6068-T6 aluminium tube and steel, with an aluminium box structure at the equator and glassfibre 'stars' connecting the tubular intersections. The hull is covered with a protective layer of foam plastics and an outer skin of nylon fabric, and is of NACA 0012 aerofoil section. Inside the frame are 12 helium cells (six upper and six lower), connected in pairs and each made of four layers of Mylar, Saran and polythene, and the water ballast tanks. At the rear is a wide span tailplane, with a centrally mounted fin and rudder above and below it. Kevlar cables connect the hull to the gondola, which is constructed of aluminium, Styrofoam and acrylic materials with an inner and outer skin of Kevlar. The gondola has accommodation for a pilot and five passengers, with toilet, a bulletproof floor, and provision for carrying an aerial camera.

Power plant comprises a pair of 67 kW (90 hp) McCulloch two-stroke engines, which can be swivelled through 150° (120° down/30° up) to provide thrust vectoring for manoeuvring.

DIMENSIONS, EXTERNAL:
Hull diameter 32·0 m (105 ft 0 in)
Hull depth (max) 10·67 m (35 ft 0 in)
Hull volume 5,944 m³ (209,910 cu ft)
Height overall (incl gondola and wheel) 13·87 m (45 ft 6 in)

WEIGHTS:
Gondola, empty 181 kg (400 lb)
Water ballast 400 kg (882 lb)
Total weight empty (excl ballast) 2,950 kg (6,504 lb)
Max T-O weight (calculated) 5,788 kg (12,760 lb)

LIFT:
Dynamic lift (thrust) 879 kg (1,938 lb)
Useful lift (static) at 305 m (1,000 ft) 2,543 kg (5,606 lb)
Total vertical lift 3,422 kg (7,544 lb)
Gross lift at 4,591 m³ (162,130 cu ft) inflation 4,581 kg (10,099 lb)

PERFORMANCE (estimated):
Cruising speed 60 knots (111 km/h; 69 mph)
Rate of sink, power off 0·20 m (0·66 ft)/s

Gondola and power plant of the Spacial MLA-32-A, in model form

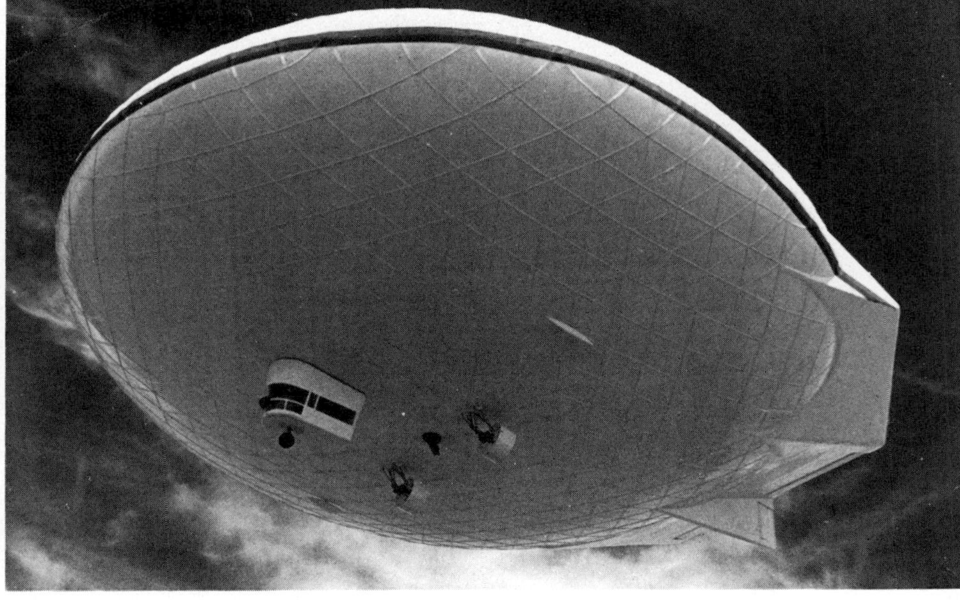

Model of the Spacial MLA-32-A elliptical hull airship, now under construction

NEW ZEALAND

CAC

COMMERCIAL AIRSHIP COMPANY

This company was being formed in early 1986. Subject to the arrangement of satisfactory financing, it hoped to begin building a small two-man advertising airship before the end of the year.

NZA

NEW ZEALAND AIRSHIPS LTD

65A Vogel Street, Cambridge
DIRECTOR: P. W. C. Monk

This company was formed in 1984 to undertake the design and development of a new airship to be known as the **NZ-1**. Design parameters include the ability to accommodate 33 passengers or 3,500 kg (7,716 lb) of cargo.

UNION OF SOVIET SOCIALIST REPUBLICS

ANGREN-84

The USSR is flight testing a radio controlled airship known as the Angren-84, reportedly as a small scale prototype (length 9 m; 29·5 ft, diameter 3 m; 9·8 ft) for planned larger craft to transport freight to Siberia and the Soviet Far East. The production version is intended to be 45 m (147·6 ft) long, carry a 1,360 kg (3,000 lb) payload, and be powered by twin engines mounted on stub wings.

The Angren-84, named after the town in Uzbekhistan where it was developed, has a ventral gondola with mid-mounted stub wings and a non-retractable tricycle landing gear. The engines are mounted in rotatable nacelles near each wingtip; a wide span horizontal tail surface, aft of the gondola and beneath the rear of the envelope, supports dependent endplate fins/rudders. Up to the end of 1984 the airship had been flight tested at altitudes up to 100 m (330 ft) and distances of up to 2·7 nm (5 km; 3·1 miles) from the ground control station.

MAI (YEGER) AIRSHIP

A large cargo airship, possibly lenticular in shape, is reportedly being designed at the Moscow Aviation Institute under the leadership of Sergei Yeger. The helium lift will be supplemented by heated air to help prevent icing during cold weather operations. No other details were known at the time of going to press.

UNITED KINGDOM

AIRSHIP INDUSTRIES

AIRSHIP INDUSTRIES (UK) LTD (Associate company of Bond Corporation)

Bond House, 347-353 Chiswick High Road, London W4 4HS
Telephone: (01) 995 7811
Telex: 299964 SKYSHP G
Managing Director: A. G. Birchmore
Technical Director: J. R. M. Munk
Head of Marketing: G. A. Spyrou
Manager, Public Relations: A. Williams

Airship Industries, an associate company of Bond Corporation Holdings of Perth, Australia, is a CAA approved company for the design and manufacture of non-rigid airships. The first of its range of airships, Skyship 500, made its initial flight on 28 September 1981. A 'stretched' derivative, Skyship 600 (G-SKSC), made its initial flight on 6 March 1984. Preliminary studies have been completed on larger airships, and in mid-1985 Airship Industries announced development programmes for the larger Skyships 1000, 3000 and 9000, with the first of the class anticipated in 1989. Resorts International (USA) is to contribute part of the development costs for a 200-passenger commercial Skyship. Airship Industries is a partner of Westinghouse Electric Corporation in Airship USA Inc (see US part of this section), which is one of the contenders for the US Navy's Naval Airship Program (which see).

Skyship 500 and 600 are intended to satisfy requirements in the civil, military and paramilitary fields. The prime civil applications are for aerial advertising and promotional and pleasure flight operations; defence applications are for surveillance-related activities. The airships have adequate payload volume to house a thorough and sophisticated communications, navigation and sensor system. In particular, the dimensions of the envelope and fins make the internal mounting of large antennae very simple. This gives performance advantages for the avionics designer. The airship has considerable potential in such roles as airborne early warning, anti-submarine warfare, electronic warfare and mine countermeasures.

The paramilitary and civil power roles are essentially surveillance activities, reinforced by the airship's ability to lower a boarding boat/party for inspection or prosecution. General coastguard activities, EEZ (exclusive economic zone) patrol, fishery protection, and search and rescue, are logical applications. In all of these roles the extended endurance, low noise and vibration levels, spacious cabin and attractive operating costs render the airship a cost-effective and viable platform.

The second Skyship 500, G-SKSA, during a flight from its base in North Carolina *(William A. Ford)*

AIRSHIP INDUSTRIES SKYSHIP 500

The Skyship 500 prototype (G-BIHN, c/n 02) made its first flight, at RAE Cardington, Bedfordshire, on 28 September 1981. Four more Skyship 500s had been completed by the end of 1985, including two (G-SKSA, c/n 03, and G-SKSB, c/n 04) assembled in Canada. G-SKSA flew at Toronto for the first time on 26 April 1983; G-SKSB first flew on 13 November 1983 and was temporarily named *Olympia* during its attendance at the Olympic Games in Los Angeles in July/August 1984. Operation of the Skyship 500 was under a British CAA 'aerial work' C of A initially, but a full transport category certificate—the first since the 1930s—was awarded on 21 November 1984. The fourth Skyship 500 (G-SKSE, c/n 05) was shipped to Japan and reassembled at Narita, for advertising use by Japan Air Lines. The first Skyship 500 to be sold outright, it made its first flight on 18 May 1984. On 23 April 1986, Skyship 500-02 (G-BIHN) inaugurated the first scheduled airship passenger service for 49 years when it took off from Leavesden Airport for the first of four daily sightseeing flights over central London. The service continued to run until 15 June 1986, after which the airship was due to resume an advertising lease.

The envelope of the Skyship 500 is manufactured, by the Zodiac division of Aérazur in France, from a strong-in-weft single ply polyester fabric, coated with a titanium dioxide loaded polyurethane to reduce ultra-violet degradation, and with a polyvinylidene chloride film bonded on the inside to minimise loss of helium gas. The nose structure consists of a domed disc, moulded from GRP and carrying the fitting by which the airship is moored to its mast. Two ballonets, which together comprise 26 per cent of the envelope volume, are installed fore and aft, so that differential inflation will provide static fore and aft trim. There is a ballonet air intake aft of each propulsor unit. Four catenary curtains carry 12 main cables of Kevlar within the envelope for suspension of the gondola. The tail unit is of conventional cruciform layout, each surface being attached to the envelope at its root and braced by four wires on each side. All four surfaces are constructed from interlocking ribs and spars of Fibrelam and have GRP skins: their hinged rudder and elevator control surfaces are cable operated and each has a spring tab.

The gondola is a one-piece moulding of Kevlar reinforced plastics, with flooring and bulkheads of Fibrelam panels; those which form the engine compartment at the rear of the gondola are faced with titanium for fire protection. There is accommodation for a pilot and co-pilot, with dual controls, although the airship is designed to be flown by a single pilot. The standard civil configuration seats passengers on seven individual seats and a three-person bunk seat at the rear. Ballast in the form of lead shot is contained in a box situated below the crew seats, and disposable water ballast up to a maximum of 513 kg (1,130 lb) is contained in tanks at the rear of the gondola. On the ground, the airship rests on a single wheel, with double tyres, mounted beneath the rear part of the gondola.

Power plant comprises two 152 kW (204 hp) Porsche 930/10 six-cylinder aircooled piston engines mounted in the rear of the gondola. Each drives, via a modified Lynx helicopter tail rotor gearbox and a lateral driveshaft, a ducted propulsor consisting of a Hoffmann five-blade reversible-pitch propeller rotating within an annular duct constructed of GRP, reinforced with carbonfibre. Each propulsor can be rotated about its pylon attachment to the gondola through an arc of 210°: 90° upward and 120° downward. The vectored thrust available gives the airship a V/STOL capability, as well as in-flight hovering ability. A fuel tank, capacity 545 litres (120 Imp gallons), is mounted at the rear of the engine compartment. Engine modifications include provision of automatic mixture control, fuel injection and electronic ignition. The 28V electrical system is supplied by engine driven alternators. Avionics include King Silver Crown series dual nav/com, ADF, Omega, VOR/ILS and weather radar.

Dimensions, envelope:
- Length overall: 52·00 m (170 ft 7¼ in)
- Max diameter: 14·00 m (45 ft 11¼ in)
- Height overall: 18·66 m (61 ft 2½ in)
- Tail fin span: 17·00 m (55 ft 9 in)
- Volume: gross: 5,153 m³ (181,977 cu ft)
- ballonets (total): 1,334 m³ (47,102 cu ft)

Dimensions, gondola:
- Length overall: 9·24 m (30 ft 3½ in)
- Max width: 2·41 m (7 ft 10¾ in)
- Cabin: Length: 4·20 m (13 ft 9½ in)
- Height: 1·96 m (6 ft 5 in)

Weight:
- Gross disposable load: 1,550 kg (3,417 lb)

Performance:
- Max level speed: 55 knots (101 km/h; 63 mph)
- Cruising speed (50% power): 47 knots (87 km/h; 54 mph)
- Pressure altitude: 3,050 m (10,000 ft)
- Still air range at 40 knots (74 km/h; 46 mph): 470 nm (870 km; 541 miles)
- Endurance: standard fuel: over 12 h
- with long-range tanks: over 24 h

AIRSHIP INDUSTRIES SKYSHIP 600

The Skyship 600 (G-SKSC, c/n 01), which made its initial flight at RAE Cardington on 6 March 1984, is basically a 'stretched' version of the Skyship 500, with accommodation for up to 16 passengers. The increased volume of the envelope provides approximately 740 kg (1,631 lb) more payload capability, and the lengthened gondola has a usable floor area of 12·0 m² (130·0 sq ft). The addition of turbochargers to the Porsche engines increases the available power to 201 kW (270 hp) per engine, fuel capacity is increased to 682 litres (150 Imp gallons) and auxiliary fuel tanks are available as optional equipment. A special category C of A was awarded to Skyship 600 by the UK CAA on 1 September 1984; aerial work certification was received in the Spring of 1986.

Developed to meet the needs of operators who require greater payload and/or endurance than are provided by the Skyship 500, the 600 is considered to be suited to roles which require long endurance patrols or extended time on station. The large cabin permits a high degree of crew comfort and efficiency.

The prototype 600 was evaluated in November 1984 by the French Navy. Carrying British pilots and a four-man French crew, it was under consideration for search and rescue, ship traffic control and surveillance roles. The French Navy is said to have a requirement for up to 20 airships for such duties. Equipment carried for this evaluation included an MEL Marec 2 search radar, Tracor Omega nav system, and a Zodiac two-man inflatable high-speed launch. Skyship 600 has also been proposed to the US Coast Guard, which has a requirement to short-lease an airship for patrol duties.

The size and capability of the Skyship 600 make it particularly suitable for deployment in a surveillance role and other military applications. As a major assistance to handling the Skyship 600 during prolonged sorties, a fly by light (fibre optics) flight control system has been developed by GEC Avionics and was to be installed in Skyship 600-01 by mid-1986.

Skyship 600-03 has been sold to Resorts International in the USA, and 600-02 to Swan Television of Perth, Australia (first flight in Australia 6 May 1986). In early 1986 Skyship 600-04 was being used as a military demonstrator, while

600-05 was hangared in the USA pending sale or lease. At the same time negotiations were under way for the sale of two 600s to Japan Air Lines.

DIMENSIONS, ENVELOPE:

Length overall	59·01 m (193 ft 7 in)
Max diameter	15·20 m (49 ft 10½ in)
Height overall	20·30 m (66 ft 7¼ in)
Tail fin span	19·20 m (63 ft 0 in)
Volume: gross	6,666 m³ (235,400 cu ft)
ballonets	1,800 m³ (63,566 cu ft)

DIMENSIONS, GONDOLA:

Length overall	11·67 m (38 ft 3½ in)
Max width	2·56 m (8 ft 4¾ in)
Cabin: Length	6·89 m (22 ft 7¼ in)
Height	1·92 m (6 ft 3½ in)

WEIGHT (design):

Gross disposable load	2,280 kg (5,026 lb)

PERFORMANCE:

Max level speed	58 knots (107 km/h; 67 mph)
Cruising speed (70% power)	50 knots (93 km/h; 58 mph)
Pressure altitude	3,050 m (10,000 ft)
Still air range at 40 knots (74 km/h; 46 mph), without auxiliary tanks	480 nm (889 km; 552 miles)

Skyship 600 with 4·57 m (15 ft) Zodiac two-man inflatable slung beneath the gondola *(Brian M. Service)*

CAMERON

CAMERON BALLOONS LTD

St John's Street, Bedminster, Bristol BS3 4NH
Telephone: (0272) 637216

DIRECTORS:
D. A. Cameron, BSc (Aero Eng), MIE, MRAeS
Kim Cameron
R. I. M. Kerr, BSc, MRAeS
N. Purvis
Tom Sage, ARPS, AIIP

Cameron Balloons Ltd, which designs and manufactures a wide range of hot-air balloons (which see), also designs and produces hot-air airships, being the first company to develop a craft of this type. Production hot-air airships now include an improved two/three-seat D-96, and the single-seat D-38 and D-50. Helium filled airships are also manufactured: a DG-14 single-seater and DG-25 two-seater.

CAMERON D-96

First flight of the prototype D-96 (G-BAMK), the world's first hot-air airship, was made at Wantage, Berkshire, on 7 January 1973. Considerable work was performed subsequently to improve and develop the airship, and the current production model has two vertical and two horizontal stabilisers. An improved method of suspending the gondola eliminates distortion of the envelope which occurred in the early stages. During 1978, further development led to increases in the length and volume of the envelope. Like the envelopes of Cameron hot-air balloons, this is made from a light but high strength nylon fabric. A lightweight gondola carries the propane burner, gas supply, pilot and power plant. Two passengers can be accommodated.

Power plant is a 33·5 kW (45 hp) 1,600 cc Volkswagen modified motorcar engine, using propane as fuel and driving a large-diameter semi-shrouded pusher propeller.

The first production D-96 airship was completed for a customer in the USA. A total of 17 had been completed by 1 January 1985, for customers in Australia, Belgium, Canada, France, Japan, the Netherlands, Spain, Sweden and the UK.

Cameron DG-19 helium filled airship during early flight trials at RAF Wroughton

The following data apply to the current version:

DIMENSIONS, ENVELOPE:

Length overall	34·14 m (112 ft 0 in)
Max diameter	13·72 m (45 ft 0 in)
Volume, gross	2,917 m³ (103,000 cu ft)

PERFORMANCE:

Max speed	13 knots (24 km/h; 15 mph)
Turning radius at 9 knots (16 km/h; 10 mph)	30·5 m (100 ft)
Endurance	2 h

CAMERON D-38

This hot-air airship, which benefits from experience gained during development of the larger D-96, was first flown in a kite balloon configuration, as illustrated in the 1980-81 *Jane's*. It was the company's original intention to market it in that form, under the designation C-38; but the decision was made subsequently to manufacture only the single-pilot D-38 airship, to complement the two/three-person D-96. The original kite balloon (G-BGEP) served also as the prototype of the powered airship, which flew for

Cameron D-38 hot-air airship for a customer in Hong Kong *(Peter J. Bish)*

Single-seat gondola of the D-38 and D-50 hot-air airships

the first time at Ashton Park, Bristol, on 25 September 1980.

Construction of the envelope is similar to that of the D-96, made from lightweight high strength ripstop nylon, but with only one vertical and two horizontal stabilisers. The gondola has a basic structure of welded steel tube, a plywood floor and fabric enclosure. It accommodates the pilot and two cylinders of propane gas; and the steel frame provides mountings for the single standard Cameron burner and the 250 cc Fuji Robin single-cylinder two-stroke engine which drives, through a V belt reduction gear, a two-blade pusher propeller. Its petrol/oil fuel mixture is contained in a tank mounted alongside the engine.

The first production D-38 airship (G-CULT) was completed for Colt Cars, and two more had been built by early 1985. Flying one of these, on 27 August 1982, Ron Taafe of Australia established FAI duration, distance and altitude records of 1 h 26 min 52 s, 37·07 km (23·03 miles) and 3,159 m (10,364 ft) respectively for all dirigible sub-classes from BX-3 (900-1,600 m³) to BX-10 (100,000 m³ and above).

DIMENSIONS, ENVELOPE:	
Length overall	22·86 m (75 ft 0 in)
Height, incl gondola	15·24 m (50 ft 0 in)
Max diameter	9·96 m (32 ft 8 in)
Volume, gross	1,076 m³ (38,000 cu ft)
DIMENSIONS, GONDOLA:	
Length	1·65 m (5 ft 5 in)
Propeller diameter	1·32 m (4 ft 4 in)
WEIGHTS;	
Envelope	89 kg (196 lb)
Gondola, empty	91 kg (200 lb)
Propane fuel	23·6 kg (52 lb)
PERFORMANCE:	
Max speed	12 knots (22 km/h; 14 mph)

Cameron D-50 hot-air airship, showing clearly the cruciform tail surfaces *(Peter J. Bish)*

CAMERON D-50

Early testing showed that the single-seat D-38 hot-air airship was too small for use in high-altitude/high-temperature locations, so Cameron developed the larger single-seat D-50, which has an envelope volume of 1,416 m³ (50,000 cu ft). It introduced also a revised form of tail unit, shown in the accompanying illustration, which is now applied to Cameron hot-air airships of all sizes. First flight was made on 2 September 1981, and 13 D-50s had been completed by 1 January 1985.

DIMENSIONS, ENVELOPE:	
Length overall	25·00 m (82 ft 0¼ in)
Height, incl gondola	16·80 m (55 ft 1½ in)
Max diameter	10·90 m (35 ft 9 in)
Volume, gross	1,416 m³ (50,000 cu ft)
DIMENSIONS, GONDOLA: As for D-38	
WEIGHTS:	
Envelope	105 kg (231 lb)
Gondola, empty	91 kg (200 lb)
Propane fuel	23·6 kg (52 lb)

Prototype Cameron D-50P during its first flight in April 1986 *(John Christopher)*

CAMERON HELIUM FILLED AIRSHIPS

Extremely successful tests of the two-man helium filled **DG-19** prototype (G-BKIK) during the Summer of 1983 have, according to Cameron Balloons, given confidence that the design offers a new formula for a 'minimum' low-cost airship. It is hoped that applications will be found in sport, advertising, survey, and training of pilots for larger airships.

Production versions are designated **DG-14** (single-seat) and **DG-25** (two-seat). Power plant is a 400 cc Rotax two-stroke engine (rating approx 18·6 kW; 25 hp), driving twin ducted fans aft of the gondola and giving a speed of about 30 knots (55 km/h; 34 mph). Endurance is approx 3 hours, and max ceiling 915 m (3,000 ft). A single ballonet, maintained automatically at flying pressure by ram air, is fitted inside the envelope. The airship has inflatable cruciform fins, and the upper and lower fins are fitted with rudders for directional control; climb and descent are effected by vectoring the thrust of the ducted fans, and the airship is said to be extremely manoeuvrable.

DIMENSIONS, ENVELOPE:	
Length overall: DG-14	16·25 m (53 ft 4 in)
DG-19	17·90 m (58 ft 8¾ in)
DG-25	19·60 m (64 ft 4 in)
Height, incl gondola: DG-14	9·91 m (32 ft 6 in)
DG-19	10·30 m (33 ft 9½ in)
DG-25	12·04 m (39 ft 6 in)
Hangar height (de-rigged): DG-14	7·17 m (23 ft 6 in)
DG-25	8·69 m (28 ft 6 in)
Volume, gross: DG-14	396 m³ (14,000 cu ft)
DG-19	538 m³ (19,000 cu ft)
DG-25	708 m³ (25,000 cu ft)

CAMERON D-50P SKYSTAR

First flown in April 1986, the D-50P is described as the first of a new generation of pressurised hot-air airships, and differs from earlier airships of this kind in utilising a single engine (a 570 cc four-cylinder König driving a three-blade shrouded pusher propeller) for both propulsion and pressure control. In the event of an engine failure it can be flown unpressurised, and landed like a hot-air balloon. Twin silencers are fitted, to minimise the engine noise level.

The D-50P also has a new, specially designed aluminium gondola, and is equipped with an ergonomically designed single-seat cockpit and a unique Cameron self-regulating pressure control system. A two-seat car is being developed. Deliveries were expected to begin during 1986.

Gondola of the D-50P pressurised thermal airship *(John Christopher)*

DIMENSIONS, ENVELOPE:	
Length overall	29·00 m (95 ft 1¾ in)
Volume, gross	1,416 m³ (50,000 cu ft)
PERFORMANCE:	
Max speed	19 knots (35 km/h; 22 mph)
Endurance	1 h 30 min

THUNDER & COLT

THUNDER & COLT LTD

Maesbury Road, Oswestry, Shropshire SY10 8HA
Telephone: (0691) 652216
Telex: 35503 COLT G
MANAGING DIRECTOR: Per Lindstrand
SALES AND MARKETING DIRECTOR: Chris Kirby

COLT AS 105

The Colt AS 105 is the largest of Thunder & Colt's present range of hot-air airships. It is a larger capacity design based on the previous AS 90 (1985-86 *Jane's*) and AS 80 thermal airships, which have now been discontinued.

The envelope of the AS 105 is manufactured from double coated high tenacity nylon, its shape being optimised for greater dynamic stability, and incorporates cruciform tail surfaces which are part envelope-pressurised and part pressurised from the propeller slipstream. Steering is by a rudder mounted at the trailing-edge of the lower vertical tail fin, connected by cables to a servo controlled rudder bar mounted on the roof of the airship's car. The rudder bar is operated by feeding vapour propane to linear pneumatic push/pull cylinders, the servos for this purpose being located on the control column to give one-hand steering capability.

The envelope incorporates twin elliptical deflation parachutes, and the majority of the load is carried internally by a catenary suspension. A simple crossover ensures that the load is distributed evenly, and the car is attached by four hand-tightened shackles. The frame of the car is of high duty chrome molybdenum steel tube; Lexan is used for the windscreen and on the roof to allow easy in-flight inspection. Hatches through the roof panel give access to the burners and control systems. Four wheels suspended on rubber mountings beneath the car allow easy ground handling, running take-offs and landings.

The main engine is a 37·3 kW (50 hp) Honda CX500B, which turns via a shaft-drive linkage a two-blade pusher propeller mounted within a moulded glassfibre duct. To the rear of this duct is a scoop which partly pressurises the tail surface. Superpressure for the hull is provided by a 3·7 kW (5 hp) horizontally mounted engine located immediately beneath the Colt Mk II twin burner unit. The burners are controlled by electric operation, with manual override, and electronic ignition is standard. The airship is inflated by means of the onboard superpressure system and burners, requiring no external equipment. Cold inflation takes five minutes and full buoyancy is achieved with a short burn. Standard equipment includes altimeter, clock, envelope and propane pressure gauges, fuel level gauges, gauges for oil pressure and water temperature (rear engine), oil temperature (front and rear engine) and ambient temperature, tachometer, variometer and voltmeter. King 720-channel com transceiver. Two persons can be carried, including the pilot.

DIMENSIONS, ENVELOPE:

Length overall	34·00 m (111 ft 6½ in)
Max diameter	13·50 m (44 ft 3½ in)
Volume	3,000 m³ (105,944 cu ft)

DIMENSIONS, GONDOLA:

Length overall	4·40 m (14 ft 5¼ in)
Max width	1·70 m (5 ft 7 in)
Height overall	1·60 m (5 ft 3 in)

WEIGHTS:

Envelope	170 kg (375 lb)
Car, empty	275 kg (606 lb)
Gross lift	750 kg (1,653 lb)

PERFORMANCE:

Max level speed	20 knots (37 km/h; 23 mph)
Cruising speed	12-15 knots (22-28 km/h; 14-17 mph)

COLT AS 42 Mk II and AS 56

The Colt AS 42 is a scaled-down design following the principles of the larger AS 105. It was first certificated in the UK in 1984, but only a prototype was completed. Later, alterations to the original specifications were incorporated, resulting in the **AS 42 Mk II**. The **AS 56** has an identical gondola, but a larger envelope.

Envelopes of the AS 42 Mk II and AS 56 follow the same constructional pattern as the earlier AS 80, AS 90 and AS 105, the only major difference being that the smaller envelopes have only a single parachute vent.

The gondola is a tubular spaceframe made from stainless steel. It has a three-wheel landing gear and a single seat with full safety harness. Power plant is an 18 kW (24 hp) König SC430 three-cylinder two-stroke engine, driving a pusher propeller. Pressurisation is by a separate 2·24 kW (3 hp) single-cylinder two-stroke engine, driving a fan, situated beneath the single Colt Mk II burner unit.

DIMENSIONS, ENVELOPE:

Length overall: AS 42 Mk II	25·00 m (82 ft 0½ in)
AS 56	28·00 m (91 ft 10½ in)
Max diameter: AS 42 Mk II	10·00 m (32 ft 9¾ in)
AS 56	11·20 m (36 ft 9 in)
Volume: AS 42 Mk II	1,200 m³ (42,377 cu ft)
AS 56	1,600 m³ (56,504 cu ft)

DIMENSIONS, GONDOLA:

Length overall	2·70 m (8 ft 10¼ in)
Max width	1·40 m (4 ft 7 in)
Height overall	1·50 m (4 ft 11 in)

WEIGHTS:

Envelope: AS 42 Mk II	75 kg (165 lb)
AS 56	95 kg (209 lb)
Gondola	97 kg (214 lb)
Max T-O weight: AS 56	325 kg (716 lb)

PERFORMANCE (AS 56):

Max level speed	20 knots (37 km/h; 23 mph)
Max endurance	2 h

COLT GA 42

This helium filled dirigible is a project in which Thunder & Colt co-operates with Airborne Industries of Southend on Sea (see Balloons subsection). Thunder and Colt is undertaking design and production of the gondola and design of the envelope; Airborne Industries will undertake the envelope manufacture.

The GA 42 has an overall volume of 1,200 m³ (42,377 cu ft), with twin ballonets, and features rigid control surfaces. The aluminium monocoque gondola offers fully enclosed accommodation for two crew. The power plant is a 74·5 kW (100 hp) Continental O-200-B engine driving a pusher propeller. The design will be certificated to BCAR CAP 471 Section Q in the Aerial Work category, and a prototype is scheduled to fly in 1987.

Colt AS 105 operating on behalf of Miller Breweries, in Canada *(Peter J. Bish)*

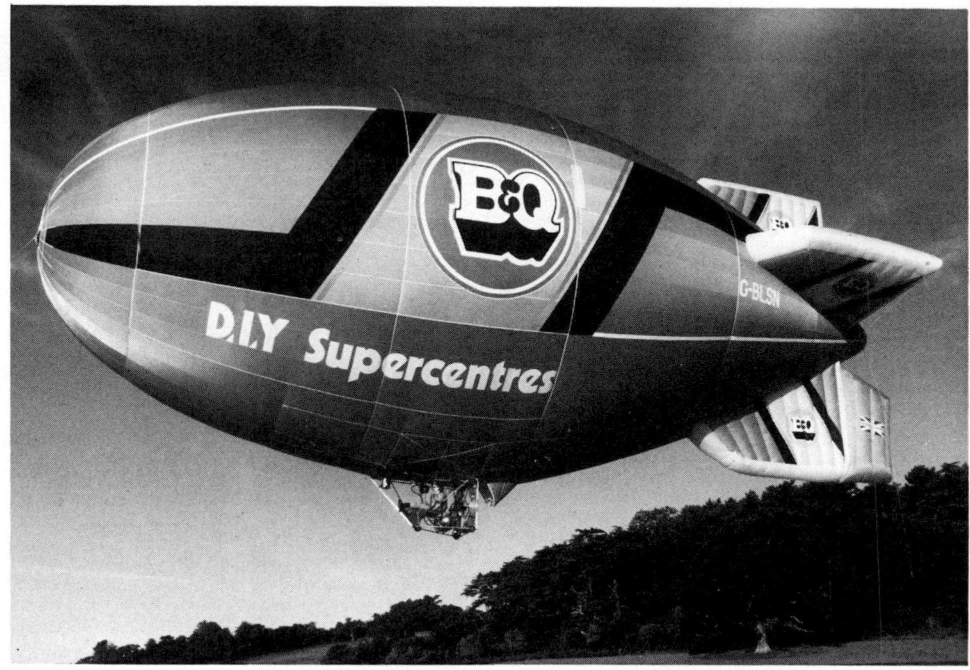

Colt AS 56 thermal airship *(John Christopher)*

Artist's impression of the new GA 42 gas airship, due to fly in 1987

WREN

WREN SKYSHIPS LTD

Meadows Court, West Street, Ramsey, Isle of Man
Telephone: 0624 812894
Telex: 627835 WNSKSP G
CHAIRMAN: Major Malcolm W. Wren
CHIEF DESIGNER: P. W. C. Monk

WREN RS.1

The RS.1 (Rigid Skyship, first generation) was designed by Wren Skyships Ltd to meet what it sees as a growing need for a heavy-lift VTOL form of transportation with greater operating potential than the helicopter, longer service life, and much reduced operating costs. Funds are being sought for a prototype to be built by the company's US subsidiary American Skyship Industries Inc.

Claims made for the RS.1 are that it is extremely fuel-efficient, quiet, and requires minimal land areas from which to operate. It can carry both internal and external/underslung payloads, including standard ISO containers. Since space in an airship is not at a premium, it has a long-term future ability to exploit the use of alternative low-density, high-energy fuels such as natural gas and liquid hydrogen, new low-fuel-consumption power plants such as the regenerative gas turbine, and even nuclear power units. Moreover, rigid airships are capable of extended flight after losing superpressure. It will be possible to repair the envelope in flight by means of prepared patches applied by trained personnel wearing breathing apparatus within the hull, but even with no pressure in the envelope a speed of more than 49 knots (90 km/h; 56 mph) should always be available.

Wren Skyships has concluded that the optimum payload for a 'first generation' modern rigid airship is in the order of 22-23 tonnes, and this has dictated the size of the RS.1 prototype, which will be powered by four conventional gas turbine engines.

TYPE: Heavy-lift rigid airship.

HULL: Conventionally shaped helium-filled, metal-clad rigid structure, of circular cross-section, maintained under slight internal pressure. Main frames, of aluminium, define circular shape, carry concentrated loads (eg engines), and distribute such loads by shear into and throughout the skin. Shaped by the main frames, the 0·25-0·30 mm thick aluminium skin resists these loads in addition to those imposed on the hull by aerodynamic and gas loadings. Aluminium longerons, of which there are 24, support the skin as panel breakers and provide localised structural support. In the event of loss of internal pressure the longerons become the primary load carriers in respect of hull bending loads, and provide sufficient strength for continued flight with reduced performance. The requirement for internal pressure is met by the supply of external air to two ballonets, virtually identical to those of a non-rigid airship, which compensate for altitude and temperature changes. These are located fore and aft, and are connected to the pressurisation fans by large fabric ducts. As the airship climbs, air is emptied from the ballonets by automatic valves to prevent hull overpressure. In the descent phase, each ballonet is re-inflated by an electrically driven fan. Small thrusters at the bow and stern provide precise station-keeping control at low airspeeds during take-off, landing and hover. The helium gas occupies 84·9 per cent of the hull volume at S/L, increasing to 98·5 per cent at the pressure altitude of 1,525 m (5,000 ft). Provision is made for carrying external loads suspended from the hull.

Artist's impression of the Wren RS.1 metal-clad rigid airship

TAIL UNIT: Four cantilever fins and rudders, in cruciform X configuration, mounted on two of the hull main frames. Fixed fins are of two-spar and rib construction covered with a thin, honeycomb-core skin; there are no fin spar carry-through structures. The large-area moving surfaces, used for both yaw and pitch control, are aerodynamically balanced with a nose overhang and tip mounted horn. Construction is similar to that of fins, but with a single spar and the overhung balance portion forming a torsion box.

GONDOLA: Gondola/payload compartment is fitted with a simple landing gear, and can be configured for carrying cargo, passengers, or a combination of the two. Max capacity for 22·6 tonnes of cargo at very low density, or 180-200 passengers in airline-standard comfort.

POWER PLANT: Four 1,227 kW (1,645 shp) Garrett TPE331-15 turboprop engines, each mounted on separate outrigger from hull and driving a tractor propeller. Supplementary lift can be provided by vectoring propeller thrust, with 50 per cent power normally available for this purpose, remainder in reserve for emergencies. Fuel in two main tanks, combined capacity 10,751 litres (2,365 Imp gallons).

DIMENSIONS, EXTERNAL (HULL):
Length overall 127·88 m (419 ft 6¾ in)
Max diameter 25·38 m (83 ft 3 in)
Length/diameter ratio 5·04
Width over propellers 34·44 m (113 ft 0 in)
Height overall (incl gondola) 28·27 m (92 ft 9 in)
Gas volume 45,307 m³ (1,600,000 cu ft)

DIMENSIONS, INTERNAL (provisional):
Cargo hold: Length 36·58 m (120 ft 0 in)
Width 5·18 m (17 ft 0 in)
Height 2·59 m (8 ft 6 in)
Volume 491 m³ (17,340 cu ft)

WEIGHTS:
Weight empty 20,401 kg (44,976 lb)
Fuel load: min 2,041 kg (4,500 lb)
max 6,804 kg (15,000 lb)
Payload: with min fuel 24,947 kg (55,000 lb)
with max fuel 20,185 kg (44,500 lb)
Max T-O weight 47,553 kg (104,836 lb)

PERFORMANCE (estimated at max T-O weight):
Max level speed 124 knots (230 km/h; 143 mph)
Max cruising speed:
four engines 118 knots (218 km/h; 136 mph)
three engines 105 knots (194 km/h; 121 mph)
two engines 88 knots (163 km/h; 101 mph)
Pressure altitude 1,525 m (5,000 ft)
Range with max fuel, no reserves:
three engines, at 100 knots (185 km/h; 115 mph) 813 nm (1,506 km; 936 miles)
one engine, at 50 knots (93 km/h; 57 mph) 1,552 nm (2,876 km; 1,787 miles)

UNITED STATES OF AMERICA

AEROLIFT

AEROLIFT INC

4105 Blimp Boulevard, Tillamook, Oregon 97141-9694
Telephone: (503) 842 8891
PRESIDENT AND CHIEF EXECUTIVE OFFICER:
John R. Aikman
VICE-PRESIDENT AND GENERAL MANAGER:
J. J. Morris

AEROLIFT CYCLO-CRANE

The proof-of-concept version of the Cyclo-Crane was rolled out on 5 August 1982 and successfully accomplished free flight at Tillamook, Oregon, on 23 October 1984. The eventual full scale version is intended primarily for logging use worldwide, and its development is being supported by five Canadian forest products companies and, for initial testing, by the US Forest Service and Defense Advanced Research Projects Agency (DARPA). It is, however, suitable for other ultra-heavy vertical lift applications where precision lifting and placement of heavy and outsize cargo are required. The Cyclo-Crane introduces a new concept for a lighter than air craft, combining fixed-wing and rotating-wing techniques.

As can be seen in the accompanying photograph, the Cyclo-Crane has a helium filled centrebody resembling the envelope of a conventional airship. The entire centrebody is able to rotate at a max 13 rpm about a shaft which passes longitudinally through its axis. This rotation allows an airflow over the wings of 52 knots (96 km/h; 60 mph), creating the required lift necessary for manoeuvring. At the forward end of the shaft is a cylindrical housing for control equipment; at the rear are stabilising surfaces. Initially of inverted Y form, these now comprise a multi-faceted annular structure as shown in accompanying illustrations.

Structure within the envelope supports four external aerofoil surfaces, known as blades. These are attached at 90° intervals around its circumference, which enables them to rotate and so vary their angle of attack in relation to airflow past the vehicle. An articulated symmetrical wing surface is mounted in T form at the outer end of each blade. On the outer side of each of two opposing wings is a pylon mounted pod containing a 112 kW (150 hp) Avco Lycoming AEIO-320 engine, driving a four-blade tractor propeller.

A pilot's cabin is suspended by cables, which are attached at each end to outer race bearings on the central shaft. The load to be airlifted is slung on cables beneath this cabin.

The structure is so designed that the net aerostatic lift of the helium is equal to the sum of all structural weight, fuel, crew, and 50 per cent of the intended sling load. The balance of lift for the sling load, and thrust for control and translation, are created by the external aerofoils.

When the Cyclo-Crane is in a hover mode *(Fig. a)*, the wings are positioned parallel to the shaft on which the centrebody rotates, providing lift via cyclic control enabling the Cyclo-Crane to ascend and descend vertically as well as laterally. The blade aerofoils have both cyclic and collective control systems. The cyclic system allows the aircraft to pitch and yaw; the collective system allows it to move short distances forward and backward. The wing and blade control systems, while rotating, allow the Cyclo-Crane to maintain a position over the ground or over a load. Non-rotating forward flight is accomplished by turning the entire wing/blade assemblies. The wing/blade assemblies continue to turn as the vehicle accelerates *(Fig. b)*. When optimum forward speed is reached, all aerofoil surfaces and engines are aligned with the direction of flight *(Fig. c)* and the centrebody ceases to rotate. Cruising speed is expected to be similar to that of a helicopter hauling a comparable external load.

The proof-of-concept vehicle has a two-ton sling load capacity. Unmanned testing in its current modified form began in August 1984, followed by initial manned test flights starting on 23 October 1984. Minor modifications and further flight testing were continuing in early 1986.

Current flight test data and dynamic computer model analysis have verified earlier Princeton University studies indicating that a Cyclo-Crane should offer controllability equal to that of a helicopter of similar external lift capacity under gust and direct side wind conditions. It can be mast moored and can be designed to float hundreds of feet above the ground on a single line tether. When major storms are predicted, standard aircraft procedures would be followed and the vehicle flown out of the area of danger. Commercial use of Cyclo-Cranes, initially on Vancouver Island, is expected to start as soon as larger capacity vehicles have been built and certificated. Each of these is likely to have a sling load capacity of 16 tons; but AeroLift emphasises that the Cyclo-Rotor concept is valid for sling loads of up to at least 100 tons.

DIMENSIONS (proof-of-concept vehicle):
- Length overall: 54·25 m (178 ft 0 in)
- Height overall, top centre engine nacelle to payload hook: 77·73 m (255 ft 0 in)
- Aerostat diameter (max): 20·73 m (68 ft 0 in)
- Aerostat length: 41·45 m (136 ft 0 in)
- Helium volume (nominal): 9,345 m³ (330,000 cu ft)

WEIGHTS (design):
- Operating weight empty (buoyant): 680 kg (1,500 lb)
- Max gross weight (allowing for combined aerostatic and aerodynamic lift): 1,451 kg (3,200 lb)

Cyclo-Crane proof-of-concept prototype airlifting a slung load beneath the control cabin

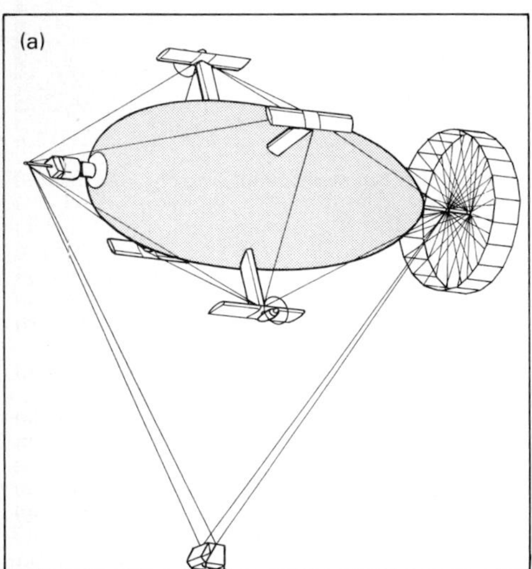

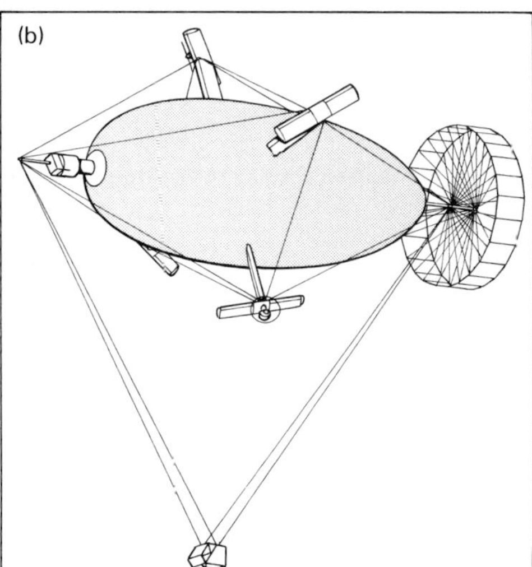

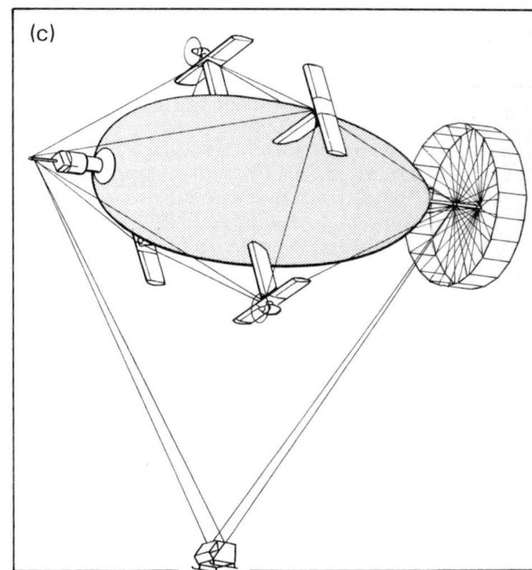

Figure a: Cyclo-Crane in hover mode, with wings parallel to the horizontal axis of rotation. For forward (or reverse) movement, the blade aerofoils are used to generate forces in line with the horizontal axis by turning the entire wing/blade assemblies. Figure b: The wing/blade assemblies continue to turn as the Cyclo-Crane accelerates. Figure c: At maximum forward speed, aerofoils and engines are all aligned directly with the direction of flight, and the centrebody has ceased to rotate *(Michael A. Badrocke)*

AEROSYSTEMS — *see California Airships*

AIRSHIP USA

AIRSHIP USA INC

1801 K Street NW, Washington, DC 20006

DIRECTORS:
J. W. Phipps (President)
J. R. M. Munk (Vice-President and Technical Director)
Alan Bond
A. G. Birchmore
Richard A. Linder
Thomas J. Murrin

Formation of Airship USA Inc, to design and manufacture airships for the US market, was announced in July 1986, following the acquisition by Westinghouse Electric Corporation of shares in the British company Airship Industries (UK) Ltd. Airship USA will maintain facilities at Weeksville, North Carolina, where TCOM, a Westinghouse subsidiary (see Balloons subsection), has been manufacturing tethered aerostats since the early 1970s. In 1986 Airship USA was one of the contenders in the US Navy's Naval Airship Program (which see).

BOLAND

BOLAND BALLOON

Pine Drive, RD 2, Burlington, Connecticut 06013
Telephone: (203) 673 1307

PROPRIETORS:
Brian J. Boland
Mrs K. Boland

Mr Brian Boland has, with his wife Kathy, designed and built several hot-air balloons (see Balloons subsection), as well as a hot-air airship named *Albatross*. Manufacture of a second airship, named *Rover*, began in early 1982. No news of this has been received since the beginning of 1984. A description of *Albatross* can be found in the 1985-86 and earlier editions of *Jane's*.

BOLAND A-2 ROVER

Work began in early 1982 to manufacture the envelope of *Rover*. Benefiting from the 'trial and error' development of *Albatross*, envelope design presented fewer problems, but the final configuration of the control car was to be decided only after several inflations of the envelope.

The envelope, which consists of 10 gores and 311 panels, is fabricated from 1·4 oz polyurethane coated ripstop nylon for the main body, and has similar material of 1·0 to 1·4 oz for the nose and tail sections. Undecided by early 1984 were the number of fins, the fin and rudder configuration, and whether to suspend the control car by internal catenary curtains or external load tapes. Load tapes would consist of 182 kg (400 lb) test flat nylon tape, strengthened in high load/stress areas by heavier nylon tubular webbing. Final volume of the envelope is in excess of 2,265 m³ (80,000 cu ft), and it incorporates a rip system similar to that of the A-1 *Albatross*. This has one seam opening along the backbone of the envelope, its closure reinforced with a series of safety locks.

The control car was intended to have a width and height of about 1·12 m (3 ft 8 in), and length of 2·13 m (7 ft 0 in), and to carry one or two persons, with up to five or three 38 litre (10 US gallon) propane cylinders respectively. Two 8 million BTU gimballed burners were to be used for envelope inflation. It was planned to use initially the 30 kW (40 hp) Rockwell JLO engine from the A-1 *Albatross*, and to fit a tricycle landing gear with steerable nosewheel. Instrumentation was expected to include a pyrometer for envelope heat sensing, ambient thermometer, altimeter, rate of climb indicator, compass, and contents gauges for low pressure gas and engine fuel.

WEIGHTS (estimated):
- Weight empty: 204 kg (450 lb)
- Operating weight empty: 295 kg (650 lb)
- Max T-O weight: 590 kg (1,300 lb)

PERFORMANCE (estimated, A: 3 propane cylinders; B: 5 propane cylinders):
- Range: A: 13 nm (24 km; 15 miles)
- B: 22 nm (40 km; 25 miles)
- Endurance: A: 1 h 30 min
- B: 2 h 30 min

Model of proposed two-seat car for the Boland hot-air airship *Rover*

CALIFORNIA AIRSHIPS

WATSON MODEL WORKS

16140 Covello Street, Van Nuys, California 91406
Telephone: (818) 785 7271
PRESIDENT: Bill Watson

Mr Bill Watson's California Airships company was asked by a TV entertainer named Gallagher to design and build a human powered ultralight airship, mainly as a unique prop for his television shows. Mr Watson had previously been associated with design of the Icarus HPA-1 and Gossamer Albatross man powered aircraft, and also had experience in building small remotely controlled model airships. The aircraft built for Mr Gallagher is known as the White Dwarf, and was flown on its initial trials by Mr Bryan Allen, formerly a test pilot for the Gossamer Condor and Gossamer Albatross.

Inquiries were being solicited in early 1986 to find a purchaser for the design rights and tooling for White Dwarf, which the company had no immediate plans to put into production. Meanwhile a larger, two-person, engine powered airship is being designed, and future development of a solar powered airship is under consideration.

Designer Bill Watson piloting the California Airships White Dwarf. Small propeller at front was deleted after early test flights

CALIFORNIA AIRSHIPS (GALLAGHER) WHITE DWARF

Construction of the White Dwarf started in June 1984, and the first flight was made on 28 August that year. This and other early test flights were made at the end of a nylon tether line; for free flight, a 1·13 kg (2·5 lb) thrust electric motor was originally fitted, as a redundant emergency power source. This was removed for subsequent flights when the White Dwarf proved safer than expected. There is no major tendency to pitch and yaw, but control in these two axes is provided, respectively, by propeller thrust vectoring and a large-area rudder. A combined pressure relief/gas filler valve adjusts envelope buoyancy according to altitude and ambient temperature.

In February 1985 Bryan Allen pedalled the White Dwarf for some 50 nm (93 km; 58 miles) over the Salton Sea desert in California, from Thermal to Brawley. This flight established new records in FAI categories BA-1 to BA-10 inclusive for both distance (50·44 nm; 93·47 km; 58·08 miles) and duration (8 h 50 min 12·56 s).

TYPE: Experimental single-seat human powered airship.

ENVELOPE: Helium filled non-rigid type of polyurethane coated nylon, modified from a standard Raven Industries TIF 6000, with tail fins and some load patches deleted. Helium maintained at slight pressure (approx 0·0013 bars; 0·02 lb/sq in); no ballonets.

FUSELAGE/GONDOLA: Open framework structure of 2024-T3 aluminium tube, stressed to 4·5*g*, attached to envelope by 24 Dacron-sheathed Kevlar support lines, any one of which can support its weight. Two small water ballast tanks (one forward, one aft) and four 7·26 kg (16 lb) lead weights to maintain optimum buoyancy. Large Mylar covered foam and spruce rudder, with balance tab. Two-wheel landing gear. Single open seat, adjustable fore and aft.

POWER SYSTEM: Pedal power (average 0·22 kW; 0·3 hp), producing approx 4·54 kg (10 lb) of cruise thrust via 4:1 gearing and a plastics chain drive to a two-blade pusher propeller, which has ground adjustable pitch, is made of spruce and foam plastics and is mounted on an aluminium tube pylon aft of pilot's seat; pylon head can be swivelled to vector propeller thrust (40° up/60° down) for altitude control.

DIMENSIONS:
- Envelope: Length — 14·63 m (48 ft 0 in)
  - Max diameter — 4·57 m (15 ft 0 in)
  - Volume — 175·56 m³ (6,200 cu ft)
- Height overall — 8·23 m (27 ft 0 in)
- Propeller diameter — 1·63 m (5 ft 4 in)
- Rudder area — 8·36 m² (90 sq ft)

WEIGHTS:
- Weight empty — 63·5 kg (140 lb)
- Max water ballast — 22·7 kg (50 lb)
- Pilot weight range — 41-113 kg (90-250 lb)
- Max T-O weight — 177 kg (390 lb)

PERFORMANCE (measured):
- Max level speed (0·45 kW; 0·6 pedal hp) — 10·4 knots (19·3 km/h; 12 mph)
- Cruising speed (0·22 kW; 0·3 pedal hp) — 7 knots (13 km/h; 8 mph)
- Altitude — 366 m (1,200 ft)

GOODYEAR

GOODYEAR AEROSPACE CORPORATION

1210 Massillon Road, Akron, Ohio 44315-0001
Telephone: (216) 796 3632
PROGRAMME DIRECTOR, ADVANCED AIRSHIPS:
Ronald G. E. Browning
DIRECTOR, PUBLIC RELATIONS: Lyle Schwilling

Goodyear has built over 300 airships, more than any other company in the world. Of these, over 250 were constructed under contract for the US Army and Navy, and included the USS *Akron* and USS *Macon*, the largest rigid airships constructed in the USA. The remainder have been commercial airships, of which the first was the *Pilgrim*, launched in 1925.

Goodyear currently operates four GZ-20A non-rigid airships for public relations and sales promotion activities: *America* (N3A), *Columbia, Europa* (N2A) and *Enterprise* (N1A). *Europa* is based near Rome, Italy, the other three airships in the USA. Details of the more recently constructed *America* follow. In size, equipment and performance it is generally the same as the three other airships in the fleet.

GOODYEAR GZ-20A AMERICA

The *America* (N3A) was constructed during 1982 and erected at Houston, Texas, which is its home base. It was named at a ceremony on 12 July 1982, replacing the earlier *America* (N10A) which was dismantled. Like its sister ships, N3A has a gross volume of 5,740 m³ (202,700 cu ft) and envelope surface area of 2,006 m² (21,600 sq ft). The envelope is made of two-ply rubber coated polyester fabric and is helium filled. On each side is a four-colour sign 32·00 m (105 ft 0 in) long and 7·47 m (24 ft 6 in) high, containing 3,780 lamps to flash static or animated messages. These can be read at a distance of 1·6 km (1 mile) when the airship is cruising at a height of 305 m (1,000 ft). A turbojet APU, mounted in a removable pod on the undersurface of the 'ship's gondola, drives a 500A 28V generator to supply electrical power for the signs and their control equipment. The turbojet is designed to operate without developing any appreciable amount of forward thrust for the airship.

The gondola, attached to the undersurface of the envelope, has accommodation for a pilot and six passengers, and has a single non-retractable landing wheel mounted beneath it.

Power plant consists of two 157 kW (210 hp) Continental IO-360-D22 flat-six engines, each driving a Hartzell BHC-92 WF-3L two-blade metal reversible-pitch pusher propeller. Fuel capacity is 527 litres (138 US gallons).

DIMENSIONS, OVERALL:
- Length — 58·67 m (192 ft 6 in)
- Width — 15·24 m (50 ft 0 in)
- Height — 18·14 m (59 ft 6 in)

DIMENSIONS, ENVELOPE:
- Length — 58·00 m (190 ft 3½ in)
- Max diameter — 14·00 m (45 ft 11½ in)

The Goodyear non-rigid airship *America* (N3A), with *Enterprise* (N1A) in the background

Fineness ratio 14·4
Volume: gross 5,740 m³ (202,700 cu ft)
ballonets 1,662·2 m³ (58,700 cu ft)
DIMENSIONS, GONDOLA:
Length overall 6·93 m (22 ft 9 in)
Height: excl landing gear 2·47 m (8 ft 1¼ in)
incl landing gear 3·59 m (11 ft 9½ in)
Width: at ceiling 2·13 m (7 ft 0 in)
at floor 1·31 m (4 ft 3½ in)
Propeller diameter 2·11 m (6 ft 11 in)
WEIGHTS:
Weight empty 4,252 kg (9,375 lb)
Max design gross weight 5,824 kg (12,840 lb)
PERFORMANCE:
Max speed 43 knots (80 km/h; 50 mph)
Normal cruising speed 30-35 knots (56-64 km/h; 35-40 mph)
Max rate of climb at S/L 732 m (2,400 ft)/min
Max rate of descent 427 m (1,400 ft)/min
Normal operational altitude 305-915 m (1,000-3,000 ft)
Service ceiling 2,285 m (7,500 ft)
Endurance at cruising speed approx 10 h

GOODYEAR GZ-22

This new airship, due to fly in 1987, has a conventional envelope of typical Goodyear construction (a sandwich of Neoprene between two layers of rubber coated polyester fabric), with tail fins set in an X configuration. It will be powered by two 313 kW (420 shp) Allison 250 turboprop engines, each driving a three-blade propeller turning within an annular duct which can be swivelled to vector the thrust. The gondola will be of composite construction, with dual controls for one or two pilots, and the airship will have an electronic fly by wire control system with a mechanical backup.

The GZ-22 is larger than the current Goodyear airships, and the first to be powered by turbine engines. Vectoring of the ducted fans provides more precise control during very slow speed and ground handling manoeuvres. The cabin is larger, with larger windows, and seats nine passengers; an improved night sign, with truer colours and greater resolution, will be mounted on the envelope. After certification the GZ-22 is expected to be assigned to one of three field locations in the USA: Pompano Beach (Florida), Houston (Texas) or Los Angeles. A similar airship is expected to be based at Rome, Italy.

Model of the Goodyear Aerospace Corporation GZ-22, due to fly in 1987

DIMENSIONS, ENVELOPE:
Length overall 63 m (206 ft)
Max diameter 14·33 m (47 ft)
Volume (helium) 7,017 m³ (247,800 cu ft)
WEIGHTS:
Max payload 998 kg (2,200 lb)
Useful load 1,996 kg (4,400 lb)
PERFORMANCE (estimated):
Max cruising speed 56 knots (105 km/h; 65 mph)
Normal cruising speed 39-48 knots (72-89 km/h; 45-55 mph)

GRACE — *see US Airship*

ILC

ILC DOVER (Division of ILC Industries Inc)

PO Box 266, Frederica, Delaware 19946
Telephone: (302) 335 3911
SALES ADMINISTRATOR: Rhonda Ksionek

ILC Dover designs and manufactures a range of unmanned non-rigid aerostats of the tethered, aerodynamically shaped balloon type (see Balloons subsection). It also performs varied R & D programmes on high-altitude long-endurance platforms and inflatable-wing RPVs (see RPVs and Targets section, 1985-86 *Jane's*), hybrid heavy-lift vehicles, and many other inflatable technology products.

ILC DOVER HYBRID HEAVY-LIFT VEHICLES

Several concepts of hybrid heavy-lift vehicle have been prepared which combine the principles of aerostatic and aerodynamic lift to derive a total system lift greater than that attainable by either principle alone.

ILC DOVER HIGH ALTITUDE PLATFORMS

ILC Dover has developed conceptual designs for several high-altitude aerostat RPV platforms. These vehicles are designed to fly at altitudes in the order of 21,350 m (70,000 ft), to take advantage of optimum wind fields to reduce power requirements.

These systems have been evaluated in two configurations. One concept carries its own power source and can be fully mobile, while another maintains a fixed location and has microwave power transmitted up from the ground. Both concepts utilise advanced laminar flow hull shapes to reduce drag, fabricated from lightweight reinforced film laminate materials.

Configurations ranging in size from 70,792 to 141,584 m³ (2·5 to 5·0 million cu ft) have been investigated. Future development of the concept would start with a scale model vehicle in the order of 7,079 to 28,317 m³ (0·25 to 1·0 million cu ft).

MEMPHIS

MEMPHIS AIRSHIPS INC

Isle-A-Port Airport, 1720 Harbor, PO Box 13114, Memphis, Tennessee 38113
Telephone: (901) 775 0386
PRESIDENT: Steve Garner
VICE-PRESIDENT: Jim Groce

Memphis Airships was formed in 1981 as a producer of small unmanned advertising airships and fan supported inflatables. Since 1982 it has been involved with the research and development of a small air recreation vehicle known as the Ultrablimp, designed by Mr Steve Garner.

MEMPHIS ULTRABLIMP

A prototype of the Ultrablimp was flown at the 1985 Sun 'n Fun and Oshkosh meetings. It has a helium filled envelope of nylon, coated with thermoplastic urethane, and double stitched seams coated with heat-sealed load tapes.

Memphis Dreamfinder single-seat non-rigid airship

Memphis Ultrablimp helium filled air recreation vehicle

The single-seat car is built of 6061-T6 bright anodised aluminium tube, with aviation grade hardware and fittings. Other features include a gas release valve mounted at the envelope equator, catenary curtain suspension system, steerable rudder (controlled by a centre mounted stick), and weight shift control of pitch and trim. Power plant is an 11·2 kW (15 hp) Yamaha KT100-S engine, with 4·25:1 reduction drive to a two-blade ground adjustable propeller; fuel tank capacity is 9·5 litres (2·5 US gallons) standard, 19 litres (5 US gallons) optional.

Brief details of the prototype Ultrablimp appeared in the Addenda to the 1985-86 *Jane's*. Manufacture of the production version, which is slightly larger, was scheduled to begin in May 1986.

The following data apply to the production prototype:

DIMENSIONS:
- Envelope: Length — 16·15 m (53 ft 0 in)
- Max diameter — 5·33 m (17 ft 6 in)
- Volume — 232 m³ (8,200 cu ft)
- Propeller diameter — 1·22 m (4 ft 0 in)

WEIGHTS:
- Weight empty — 113 kg (250 lb)
- Max payload — 109 kg (241 lb)
- Total lift (94% helium purity) — 230 kg (508 lb)

PERFORMANCE:
- Max level speed — 24 knots (45 km/h; 28 mph)
- Ceiling — 457 m (1,500 ft)
- Max endurance (standard fuel) — 4 h

MEMPHIS DREAMFINDER

The Dreamfinder is a single-seat, single-engined non-rigid airship powered by a 36 kW (48 hp) Rotax 503 two-stroke engine driving a ducted propeller. It has an envelope of nylon scrim and vinyl laminate, with a single ballonet to regulate pressure of the helium gas. A tail mounted elevator and rudder provide directional control; trim is achieved by pumping water ballast fore and aft. Internal catenary curtains are used to suspend the car, which is constructed from welded 4130 chromoly tubing.

One Dreamfinder has been built, as a centrepiece attraction for the Skyleidoscope air and water show at the Walt Disney World's Epcot Center.

DIMENSIONS:
- Envelope: Length — 24·99 m (82 ft 0 in)
- Max diameter — 8·99 m (29 ft 6 in)
- Volume — 821·2 m³ (29,000 cu ft)
- Fineness ratio — 3·3:1
- Propeller diameter — 0·61 m (2 ft 0 in)

WEIGHTS:
- Weight empty — 689 kg (1,519 lb)
- Max payload — 113 kg (250 lb)
- Total lift (94% helium purity) — 815 kg (1,798 lb)

PERFORMANCE:
- Max level speed — 23 knots (43 km/h; 27 mph)
- Ceiling — 457 m (1,500 ft)

PIASECKI

PIASECKI AIRCRAFT CORPORATION

West Terminus, 2nd Street, Essington, Pennsylvania
ERECTION WORKS: PO Box 1776, Lakehurst, New Jersey 08733
Telephone: (201) 657 4222
PRESIDENT: Frank N. Piasecki
VICE-PRESIDENT: Donald N. Meyers (Engineering)
SECRETARY: Arthur J. Kania
INDUSTRIAL ENGINEERING: K. R. Meenen

The Piasecki Aircraft Corporation was formed in 1955 by Mr Frank Piasecki, who was formerly Chairman of the Board and President of the Piasecki Helicopter Corporation (now the Boeing Vertol Company). The Corporation has a wholly owned subsidiary, Piasecki Aircraft of Canada Ltd, in Ottawa, Ontario.

Heli-Stat hovering on mast, 4·6 m (15 ft) above ground. Note flat coning angle of rotors

PIASECKI HELI-STAT

A Heli-Stat is a hybrid VTOL vehicle which links the envelope of a lighter than air craft with a helicopter power system. The aerostat provides static lift to support approximately the full empty weight of the entire assembly. The helicopters furnish the lift to support the payload, as well as providing propulsion and control, with adequate control forces to enable the Heli-Stat to hover with precision, which is impracticable for conventional airships.

Details of an early Heli-Stat project can be found in the 1977-78 *Jane's*. By 1979 Piasecki had started engineering work on a logging demonstrator, designated **Model 97-34J**, and subsequently received a contract from the US Navy to design, build and fly this vehicle for logging demonstration by the US Forest Service. The Heli-Stat was erected at the company's works in Lakehurst, New Jersey, located at the US Naval Air Engineering Center. Static testing of the Heli-Stat structure has been carried out, and tiedown tests with the four helicopters attached to the interconnecting structure, and with the envelope in place, were completed in March 1985.

During October 1985 the Heli-Stat demonstrated pilot controllability while in tethered flight. Rear mounted variable-pitch propellers were added to the modified helicopters during early 1986, first run-up being made on 19 February. Free-flight testing began at Lakehurst on 26 April 1986, following the start of tethered tests in early March, but the craft was grounded on 28 April after sustaining damage to the port front landing gear. Trials were resumed a few weeks later, but on 1 July 1986, after about 15 successful untethered flights, the Heli-Stat was beginning a turning manoeuvre when the starboard rear helicopter broke away from the mounting frame, destabilising the craft and causing the other three SH-34Js also to break free and crash, killing one occupant of the port rear helicopter. Collapse of the envelope and spaceframe ruptured the fuel tanks and destroyed the craft by fire. Cause of the accident, and the future of the Heli-Stat programme, had not been determined at the time of going to press.

ENVELOPE: Prototype utilised the envelope of a Goodyear ZPG-2 patrol airship, which the US Navy decommissioned in 1961 and stored disassembled in one of the disused airship sheds at Lakehurst.

FUSELAGE: Frame structure of light alloy to provide mountings for four Sikorsky SH-34J helicopters, on outriggers which provided adequate clearance for their rotors and ensured that they were not blanketed by the aerostat envelope. In addition, this structure served as the basic framework on which a cargo hold could be built, and to which the logging tagline was to be attached.

TAIL UNIT: Light alloy frame with fabric covering, mounting a composite control surface which served the dual roles of rudder and elevator.

LANDING GEAR: Four non-retractable units, each with twin castoring wheels, mounted one at each corner of the basic fuselage frame.

POWER PLANT: Basically four Sikorsky SH-34J helicopters without landing gear, each powered by a 1,137 kW (1,525 hp) Wright R-1820-84A radial aircooled engine, and each driving both the conventional main rotor system of the SH-34J (last described in the 1970-71 *Jane's*) and a variable-pitch tail propeller through a fixed gear ratio. Each helicopter had its rear fuselage removed, the tail rotor being replaced by an H-3 tail rotor acting as a 'push/pull' variable-pitch propeller. These propellers were to provide propulsion and controllability when the Heli-Stat was flown in a lightly loaded condition. Total combined fuel capacity 4,164 litres (1,100 US gallons).

ACCOMMODATION: Crew of five, comprising a master pilot and co-pilot in the port rear helicopter, and a flight engineer in each of the other helicopters. Controls of the four helicopters linked by a closed cable system.

SYSTEMS: Duplicated hydraulic system in each helicopter, pressure 103·5 bars (1,500 lb/sq in), for operation of rotor controls. Electrical system included four 28V 400A engine driven DC generators, and eight 115V 400Hz AC inverters in the helicopters.

EQUIPMENT: Included a PCM data instrumentation system for test flights; command transceivers; and a logging tagline with a pilot operated cargo hook.

DIMENSIONS, ENVELOPE:
- Length overall — 104·55 m (343 ft 0 in)
- Max diameter — 23·16 m (76 ft 0 in)
- Volume — 27,590 m³ (975,000 cu ft)

DIMENSIONS, EXTERNAL:
- Rotor diameter (each) — 17·07 m (56 ft 0 in)
- Width overall: rotors turning — 57·30 m (188 ft 0 in)
- rotor blades folded — 42·07 m (138 ft 0 in)
- Height overall — 34·14 m (112 ft 0 in)
- Wheel track — 24·38 m (80 ft 0 in)
- Wheelbase — 11·89 m (39 ft 0 in)
- Propeller diameter (each) — 3·23 m (10 ft 7¼ in)

AREA:
- Rotor discs (total) — 915·3 m² (9,852 sq ft)

WEIGHTS (estimated):
- Weight empty — 24,895 kg (54,885 lb)
- Max payload — 21,773 kg (48,000 lb)
- Max fuel load (no auxiliary fuel) — 2,894 kg (6,382 lb)
- Max hovering weight — 48,558 kg (107,051 lb)
- Max landing weight — 30,268 kg (66,729 lb)

PERFORMANCE (estimated at max T-O weight):
- Max level speed at S/L — 69 knots (128 km/h; 80 mph)
- Max cruising speed at S/L — 60 knots (111 km/h; 69 mph)
- Max rate of climb at S/L — 290 m (950 ft)/min
- Ballonet ceiling — 3,810 m (12,500 ft)
- Range with max payload, 10% reserves — 165 nm (305 km; 190 miles)
- Range with max fuel, 10% reserves — 1,900 nm (3,520 km; 2,188 miles)

Rear view of modified SH-34J helicopter, showing Sikorsky H-3 tail rotor acting as a variable-pitch 'push/pull' propeller

THOMPSON

JAMES THOMPSON, AIAA

1700 Citizens Plaza, Louisville, Kentucky 40202
Telephone: (502) 589 0130
Telex: 204335

THOMPSON AIRSHIP

Most component parts of Mr Thompson's small, two-person sport and advertising airship had been completed by September 1985. It was expected to make its first flight during the first half of 1986.

The airship has a helium filled envelope, inside which are two 56·6 m³ (2,000 cu ft) capacity air ballonets that will be filled unequally to provide pitch trim. The tail unit is a fabric covered aluminium tube inverted Y structure (all three angles 120°), the elevators of which operate differentially to control rolling moment. There are no catenary curtains: cables attached to five finger patches on each side of the envelope suspend the gondola slightly forward of the centre of buoyancy, to compensate for pitch-up. The gondola itself has a steel tube frame, with glassfibre and urethane foam skin panels, and accommodates the crew, power plant and two water ballast tanks. Propulsion is provided by a 1,200 cc Honda liquid-cooled engine, with 2·2:1 toothed-belt reduction drive to a two-blade shrouded wooden pusher propeller. The gondola is stabilised by three cables attached to the propeller shroud.

DIMENSIONS, ENVELOPE:
Length overall 24·91 m (81 ft 9 in)
Max diameter 7·91 m (25 ft 11¼ in)
Volume: helium 695·0 m^3 (24,544 cu ft)
ballonets 97·9 m^3 (3,456 cu ft)
design total 792·9 m^3 (28,000 cu ft)
Fineness ratio 3·15

WEIGHTS:
Envelope 244 kg (538 lb)
Gondola 187 kg (412 lb)
Water ballast 81·5 kg (180 lb)
Max T-O weight 696 kg (1,534 lb)

PERFORMANCE (estimated):
Design speed 30 knots (55 km/h; 34 mph)

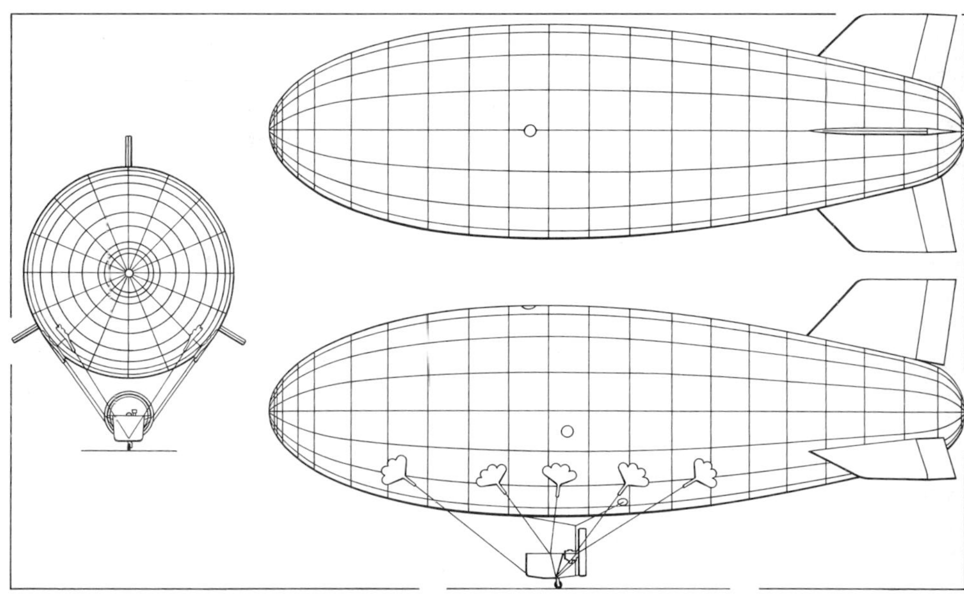
General arrangement of the Thompson two-man airship *(Jane's/Mike Keep)*

ULITA

ULITA INDUSTRIES INC (Manufacturing Division)

PO Box 412, Sheboygan, Wisconsin 53082-0412
Telephone: (414) 458 2842
Telex: 881259 ULITA AIRSHIP
VICE-PRESIDENT, MARKETING: Mark Forss

Ulita has three current light utility airship programmes: the LUA-1 and UM-10, of which prototypes are under construction, and the LUA-2, which is in the design stage.

ULITA UM-10

Optimised for the ARV (air recreational vehicle) category, the UM-10 is intended as a low-cost light utility airship, and will be Ulita's initial lighter than air product. It is hoped that it will appeal to a broad range of markets that larger contemporary airships cannot satisfy, embodying a reasonable degree of sophistication while utilising time- and cost-saving constructional techniques developed for microlight aircraft.

Prototype construction was due to begin in March 1986, with a view to its being ready for exhibition at the Oshkosh EAA Convention in the following August.

ENVELOPE: Non-rigid helium filled hull, of identical design to LUA-1 but with only one ballonet. Tail unit is of inverted V configuration, with vertical fin and rudder at end of each V leg and central tailplane and elevator spanning gap between fins. One landing wheel at base of each fin.

GONDOLA: Generally similar in configuration to LUA-1, with side by side seats for pilot and one passenger. Two landing wheels, mounted on outriggers. Accommodation ventilated, but not heated.

POWER PLANT: Two 18 kW (24 hp) König SC430 three-cylinder two-stroke engines, each driving a three-blade fixed-pitch ducted propeller, mounted on an outrigger from gondola and capable of rotation to provide horizontal or vertical thrust. Fuel tank on each outrigger, combined capacity 38 litres (10 US gallons).

ELECTRICAL SYSTEM: As for LUA-1.

DIMENSIONS, OVERALL:
Length 20·12 m (66 ft 0 in)
Width 5·59 m (18 ft 4 in)
Height 7·51 m (24 ft 7½ in)

DIMENSIONS, ENVELOPE:
Volume: ballonet 17·22 m^3 (608 cu ft)
total 344·7 m^3 (12,173 cu ft)

DIMENSIONS, GONDOLA:
Length 2·95 m (9 ft 8 in)
Max width (excl thrusters) 1·30 m (4 ft 3 in)
Max height 1·98 m (6 ft 6 in)
Volume approx 1·19 m^3 (42 cu ft)

WEIGHTS (estimated):
Weight empty 218 kg (481 lb)
Total gross lift 409 kg (901 lb)

PERFORMANCE (estimated):
Max level speed at S/L 43 knots (80 km/h; 50 mph)
Max cruising speed at S/L 30 knots (56 km/h; 35 mph)
Max rate of climb at S/L 335 m (1,100 ft)/min
Pressure ceiling 610 m (2,000 ft)

ULITA LUA-1

Details of the LUA-1 were released in 1981, and a prototype has been partially completed. By Spring 1985 the control car was 90 per cent complete, with the envelope (by ILC Dover) and tail unit (by Ulita) still to be built. After flight testing and certification, it is intended to use the prototype for aerial advertising within the USA, with production LUA-1s being leased for similar work or training by the company's Airship Operations Division.

Scheduled completion of the prototype has been postponed in order to concentrate effort on the UM-10, but work is expected to resume in late 1987.

ENVELOPE: Non-rigid helium filled airship, with two ballonets. Tail unit, of inverted Y configuration, is a rivited aluminium truss structure with lightweight fabric covering. Trim tab on rudder and each elevator.

GONDOLA: Primary structure is a welded 4130 steel tube truss, with a skin of light gauge aluminium sheet riveted to aluminium angle and channel. It is fitted with a single non-retractable landing gear unit, carrying twin fully castoring and bungee sprung wheels of 9·6 in diameter, and has side by side seats for a pilot and one passenger. Storage space behind seats. Forward opening door on port side, rearward opening door on starboard side. Accommodation is heated and ventilated.

POWER PLANT: One 85·75 kW (115 hp) Avco Lycoming O-235-1E flat-four engine, driving a two-blade reversible-pitch pusher propeller. Single 98 litre (26 US gallon) fuel tank standard; 76 litre (20 US gallon) auxiliary tank optional.

ELECTRICAL SYSTEM: 12V DC battery and alternator.

DIMENSIONS, OVERALL:
Length 32·62 m (107 ft 0⅓ in)
Width 10·10 m (33 ft 1¾ in)
Height 13·14 m (43 ft 1¼ in)

DIMENSIONS, ENVELOPE:
Length 31·95 m (104 ft 10 in)
Max diameter 8·88 m (29 ft 1½ in)
Volume: ballonets (two) 271·8 m^3 (9,600 cu ft)
total 1,359·2 m^3 (48,000 cu ft)

DIMENSIONS, GONDOLA:
Length 4·20 m (13 ft 9½ in)
Max width 1·07 m (3 ft 6 in)
Max height 2·01 m (6 ft 7¼ in)
Volume 2·41 m^3 (85 cu ft)

WEIGHTS (estimated):
Weight empty 934 kg (2,059 lb)
Total gross lift 1,265 kg (2,789 lb)

PERFORMANCE (estimated):
Max level speed at S/L 43 knots (80 km/h; 50 mph)
Max cruising speed at S/L 35 knots (64 km/h; 40 mph)
Nominal max rate of climb at S/L 183 m (600 ft)/min
Pressure ceiling 2,135 m (7,000 ft)
Range at econ cruising speed of 30 knots (56 km/h; 35 mph), no reserves:
with max fuel 364 nm (676 km; 420 miles)
with max payload 212 nm (394 km; 245 miles)

ULITA LUA-2

Still in the design stage, the LUA-2 is a 'second-generation' LUA vehicle intended to offer greater payload capacity and in-flight endurance than the LUA-1, opening up the market to such applications as harbour patrol and short-range maritime surveillance. Features will include vectored thrust propulsion, tricycle landing gear for improved ground handling, gondola accommodation for a pilot and three passengers, composite construction, and a fly by light control system with automated flight control capabilities.

Construction is not anticipated in the near future, and a detailed description is therefore inappropriate, but general parameters include a 41·45 m (136 ft) long envelope with a volume of 2,022 m^3 (71,413 cu ft), empty weight of 1,386 kg (3,055 lb), power plant of one 149 kW (200 hp) Avco Lycoming IO-360 engine, max cruising speed of 48 knots (90 km/h; 56 mph), pressure ceiling of 2,135 m (7,000 ft) and a max endurance with auxiliary fuel of 12 hours.

Three-quarter rear view of LUA-1 gondola, showing pilot's door open

US AIRSHIP

US AIRSHIP CORPORATION

255 Madison Street, Eugene, Oregon 97402
Telephone: (503) 485 5335
Telex: 910 459 2027
Telefax: 503 342 3638
PRESIDENT: Richard K. Meigs

Formerly known as Grace Aircraft Corporation, this company began designing its first commercial airship in January 1983, and its Eugene engineering facility became operational by the end of that year. It adopted the title US Airship Corporation in July 1985. Major components of the USA 100 prototype were built at Eugene; final assembly was intended to take place in the former US Navy airship hangars at Tillamook, Oregon.

US AIRSHIP USA 100

The USA 100 (previously designated GAC-20) is intended for commercial advertising, and as a testbed for further engineering and development of airships and airship systems. It is designed and built in accordance with new FAA airworthiness standards for airships, in the definition of which US Airship Corporation has been actively involved. First flight was scheduled for Summer 1986.

HULL: Non-rigid envelope of ellipsoidal configuration, made of polyurethane coated Dacron with a non-woven material laminated on the inside for bias stability. Seams are heat-sealed inside and out. Nose is stiffened by 16 battens to permit higher airspeeds and distribute mooring loads. Weight of gondola is supported by cables attached to four internal catenary curtains which hang from upper quarter of envelope over half of its length. Side loads and thrust from car are transmitted to envelope via the car catenary, a fabric doubler extending away from car perimeter in all directions to ensure uniform load distribution to envelope. Two air-filled ballonets within helium compartment, to compensate for variations in hull pressure and adjust in-flight trim, are made of heat sealed urethane coated nylon. Air is supplied to ballonets via ram air duct aft of propeller, with mechanically controlled valves to duct air to front or rear ballonet as required. A passive pressure relief valve is fitted to each ballonet and in the helium compartment to control and prevent accidental envelope overpressure. Manual cable control permits controlled venting of helium or air if required. Inverted Y tail unit, comprising three identical aluminium fins, covered with doped fabric; each fin is attached to envelope with 13 fan patches at its base and supported by three guy wires on each side.

GONDOLA: Control car is shaped as an ellipsoidal hyperbola with a circular end section, and has an exterior shell of glassfibre epoxy sandwich construction with a foam core, over a welded steel tube frame. Windows of Plexiglas. The cabin seats eight persons, including the pilot, in pairs, and is separated acoustically from the engine compartment at the rear; it is heated (by exhaust heat exchanger) and ventilated. The single-wheel landing gear is of trailing link type, pivoting about a vertical axis.

Model of the US Airship Corporation USA 100, due to fly in 1986

POWER PLANT: One 224 kW (300 hp) Avco Lycoming IO-540-K1A5 flat-six engine, mounted aft of control car on a 4130 steel tube frame and driving a Hartzell HC-3YR-7LF three-blade constant-speed reversible-pitch pusher propeller within an annular duct. Fuel tanks at rear of car, combined capacity 439 litres (116 US gallons).

SYSTEMS: Electrical system is a standard light aircraft 28V 70A negative ground type, powered by an engine driven alternator. While moored, onboard system is powered by a ground based generator for automatic monitoring and control of envelope pressurisation. Flight control is cable driven and hydraulically boosted, using a conventional stick with pushrods in combination with an adjustable friction damper, hydraulic boost system and mechanical mixer for the tail surfaces. System can be flown manually in the event of hydraulic failure.

AVIONICS AND EQUIPMENT: Avionics include dual nav/com radios with VOR/ILS, Loran, ADF, transponder, marker beacon receivers, and optional autopilot. Standard instrumentation includes ASI, VSI, attitude indicator, barometric and radar altimeters, turn co-ordinator, directional gyro, magnetic compass, engine and fuel system instruments, inside and outside air temperature gauges, ballonet and helium envelope manometers, hydraulic system temperature and pressure gauges, and clock.

DIMENSIONS, OVERALL:
- Length: 48·77 m (160 ft 0 in)
- Width: 12·80 m (42 ft 0 in)
- Height: 17·37 m (57 ft 0 in)
- Envelope volume: 3,908 m³ (138,000 cu ft)

DIMENSIONS, GONDOLA:
- External:
  - Length: incl power plant: 6·55 m (21 ft 6 in)
  - excl power plant: approx 5·79 m (19 ft 0 in)
  - Max width: approx 1·83 m (6 ft 0 in)
  - Max height: approx 2·74 m (9 ft 0 in)
- Internal (cabin):
  - Length: 4·07 m (13 ft 4¼ in)
  - Max width: at floor: 1·65 m (5 ft 4¾ in)
  - at ceiling: 1·77 m (5 ft 9½ in)
  - Max height: 1·93 m (6 ft 4 in)

WEIGHTS:
- Control car, empty: approx 907 kg (2,000 lb)
- Max fuel: 239 kg (528 lb)
- Gross weight: 4,048 kg (8,925 lb)

PERFORMANCE (estimated):
- Max cruising speed: 39 knots (72 km/h; 45 mph)
- With max fuel, cruising at 25 knots (46 km/h; 29 mph):
  - Range: 400 nm (741 km; 460 miles)
  - Endurance: 17 h

US NAVY

NAVAL AIR SYSTEMS COMMAND

Lighter Than Air Project Office, NASC, Warminster, Pennsylvania 18974
Telephone: (215) 441 2456

NAVAL AIRSHIP PROGRAM (NAP)

Six-month study contracts were placed in mid-1985 by the Lighter Than Air Project Office of the NASC with three US companies (Boeing Military Airplane Company, Goodyear Aerospace and Westinghouse Electric Corporation), to investigate the suitability of airships for use by the US Navy in an independent airborne early warning role. Boeing engaged Wren Skyship Ltd of the UK as a consultant in its study; Westinghouse selected Airship Industries of the UK as team partner, subsequently forming a joint venture known as Airship USA Inc (which see).

The Navy's interest lies in development of an independent airborne early warning system capable of operating with surface attack groups anywhere in the world. Primary functions were described by the Naval Air Development Center as "detection, classification, identification and tracking of surface and airborne targets, particularly those of low radar cross-section, flying at low altitude and high speed in a sea clutter environment, and communications connectivity between surface ships in a battle group". The surveillance system would warn surface ships of threats beyond the range of shipboard radars, including long-range sea-skimming cruise missiles.

Because of the independent operations required of the surveillance systems, and the long endurance required to accompany a naval force, an airship is considered the only feasible solution. The airship would be equipped with a large, long-range radar carried internally. Although the size of the radar will largely dictate the size of the airship, the surveillance airship could be larger than any non-rigid airship ever built: according to some estimates, over 152 m (500 ft) long with an envelope volume of 56,634-84,950 m³ (2 to 3 million cu ft).

Boeing artist's impression of a possible USN airship, designed to carry a large AEW radar internally

LIGHTER THAN AIR: BALLOONS

CZECHOSLOVAKIA

AVIATIK BRNO

AVIATIK CLUB BRNO

Hlinky 164, 603 00 Brno
Telephone: 331666
CHAIRMAN: Dr Jan Kunovský

AB-1 and AB-2

An accompanying photograph illustrates OK-3010, the first homebuilt hot-air balloon constructed by this Czech aero club. Designated **AB-1**, it first flew in the Summer of 1983 and was photographed in Hungary in October of that year. Three similar **AB-2** balloons were completed in 1984. Details of both types can be found under the FAI AX-7 class heading in the table at the end of this section. The AB-1 (c/n 1, named *Aviatik*) is a 24-gore balloon with a 'chimney' type rip panel. The fabric making up the chimney is held together during flight in a bunch at the top of the envelope, by means of a steel pin connected to the rip line. Pulling the rip line withdraws the pin, allowing the chimney to open and air to escape. The burner is a modified Cameron double unit. A hot-air airship (which see) is also being developed.

Aviatik Club Brno AB-1 homebuilt hot-air balloon
(Peter J. Bish)

FRANCE

AÉRAZUR

AÉRAZUR EFA (Member company of the Groupe Zodiac)

Division Equipements Aéronautiques

58 boulevard Galliéni, 92130 Issy-les-Moulineaux
Telephone: (1) 45 54 92 80
Telex: 270 887 F
OFFICERS: see Airships subsection

Aérazur began building lighter than air craft before the Second World War, and in the 1960s manufactured the world's largest non-rigid kite balloons (up to 15,000 m³; 529,720 cu ft), which were used for tests in the atmosphere of French nuclear weapons. More recently, it has manufactured envelopes for the Airship Industries Skyship 500 and 600 airships (which see), and is developing the Dinosaure 'catamaran' twin-hulled airship concept (see Airships subsection). Aérazur made a series of small Vénus balloons for the French space agency CNES, as well as very large stratosphere research balloons of up to 1 million m³ (35,314,720 cu ft) in volume.

Recent Aérazur programmes have included development of the OP 2000 kite balloon for parachute training; a surveillance balloon carrying a Thomson-CSF radar; and two sizes of barrage balloon for anti-aircraft defence.

CHAIZE

BALLONS CHAIZE

48 rue Balay, 42000 Saint-Étienne
Telephone: (77) 33 43 76

M Maurice Chaize markets six hot-air balloons, one in the FAI AX-6 class, three in the AX-7 class, and one each in the AX-8 and AX-9 classes. The envelopes are made from high strength nylon, with the lower panels in the throat made from Nomex flame resistant fabric. They are supplied in a ready to fly state, complete with basket, burners and gas cylinders, but without instruments. Several options are available to customer requirements.

The company holds the French Certificat de Navigabilité de Type for all six models, details of which can be found in the accompanying table.

The prototype balloon was flown for the first time in December 1972. Deliveries began in the Summer of 1977, and totalled 47 by February 1984, the latest date for which figures have been received. On 20 October 1979 two Chaize balloons, one of 2,000 m³ (70,630 cu ft) and one of 4,000 m³ (141,260 cu ft) capacity, crossed the Alps from France to Italy, flying directly over Mont Blanc.

On 20 November 1983, at Bagatelle, the 200th anniversary of man's first ascent into the air was commemorated using a modern, and modified, representation (F-WZDC) of the Montgolfier hot-air balloon used by Pilâtre de Rozier and the Marquis d' Arlandes. Brief details of this, and of a 1983 replica of Joseph Montgolfier's larger *Le Flesselles*, have appeared in previous editions of *Jane's*. Demand for hot-air balloons continues. In 1985, two 3,000 m³ (105,944 cu ft) balloons of this type spent six weeks flying over and around Spitzbergen while filming in the Arctic, and one of the same balloons, flown by M Dany Cleyet-Marrel, made an overflight of the Sahara in 1984. In both extremes of temperature the balloons performed excellently.

Maurice Chaize CS.4000 balloon in the FAI AX-9 class

GERMANY (FEDERAL REPUBLIC)

BALLONFABRIK

BALLONFABRIK SEE- UND LUFT-AUSRÜSTUNG GmbH und Co KG

Postfach 101327, Austrasse 35, 8900 Augsburg 1
Telephone: (0821) 41 50 41
Telex: 17/821810
DIRECTORS: Frau Gabriele Hassold
Dipl-Ing Gerhard Endras

Ballonfabrik is currently manufacturing and marketing a range of eight gas balloons, all of which are within the FAI categories AA-3/-4/-5/-6 and take advantage of the rule which allows them to be produced 5 per cent larger than the official maximum volume of this class. All available details of these balloons are given in the accompanying table. The newest balloon is the AA-6 class K 1360/4-Ri.

Ballonfabrik K1050/3-Ri gas balloon in AA-5 class

HUNGARY

MÉM RSZ

MÉM REPÜLŐGÉPES SZOLGÁLAT

PO Box 56, Koérberki út 36, H 1112 Budapest XI
Telephone: 851 344 and 668 450
Telex: 22-5187

COMMERCIAL MANAGER: László Kürtös

MÉM RSZ is the Air Service of the Hungarian Ministry of Agriculture, and operates a fleet of more than 200 fixed-wing aircraft and helicopters. Its headquarters are at Budaörs airfield, near Budapest, where it also has a separate section producing various sizes of hot-air balloon (see AX-4, AX-7, AX-8 and AX-9 classes in the accompanying table). At least six examples of the RSZ-03 (AX-8 class) have been built. The MÉM RSZ balloons are used for sporting purposes, but are also suitable for advertising, aerial photography, airlift of suspended loads, and surveillance.

Construction is conventional, and optional equipment includes an altimeter, gas cylinder content gauge, variometer, spare gas cylinders, and separate burner and ventilator for ground inflation.

MÉM RSZ has also completed the envelope of a hot-air airship. All known details of this, and an illustration, are given in the Airships subsection.

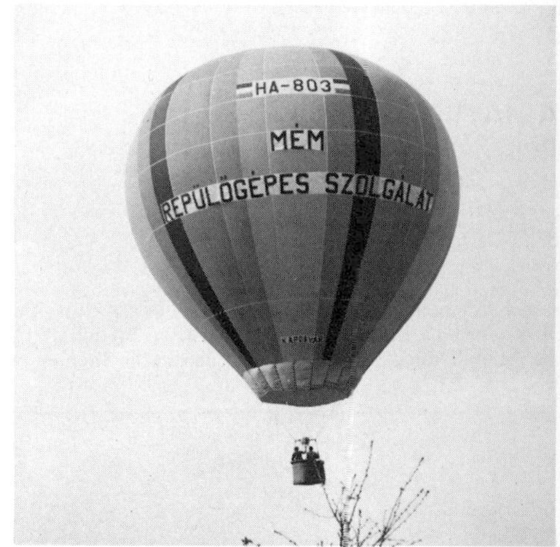

MÉM RSZ-03 AX-8 class hot-air balloon
(Studio of Air Service, Hungary)

ITALY

BONANNO

LETTERIO BONANNO

Via Volo 3/A, 12036 Revello (CN)

BONANNO X-8

One of the world's few homebuilt balloons, the AX-8 Class 2,980 m³ (105,238 cu ft) X-8 (I-PAAM) has been flown to a national record altitude of approx 8,500 m (27,887 ft). It is 23 m (75·46 ft) in height, with an envelope diameter of 19 m (62·34 ft), and carries four people. The twin burners are also designed by Mr Bonanno, and the X-8 has a S/L lift of 662 kg (1,459 lb).

Mr L. Bonanno's homebuilt AX-8 balloon I-PAAM
(Aviodata)

SOUTH AFRICA

FLAMBOYANT

FLAMBOYANT BALLOONS (PTY) LTD

PO Box 1535, Rivonia 2128, Transvaal
Telephone: (011) 659 1370

MANAGING DIRECTOR: Terence A. Adams

Flamboyant Balloons manufactures helium inflatables, and carries out promotions, balloon tours, and balloon pilot training. Eight types of hot-air balloon (one AX-5 class, two AX-6, two AX-7, two AX-8 and one AX-10) are believed to be currently available, although no 1986 update from the company was received. All known details are given in the table.

Flamboyant Balloons AX7-65

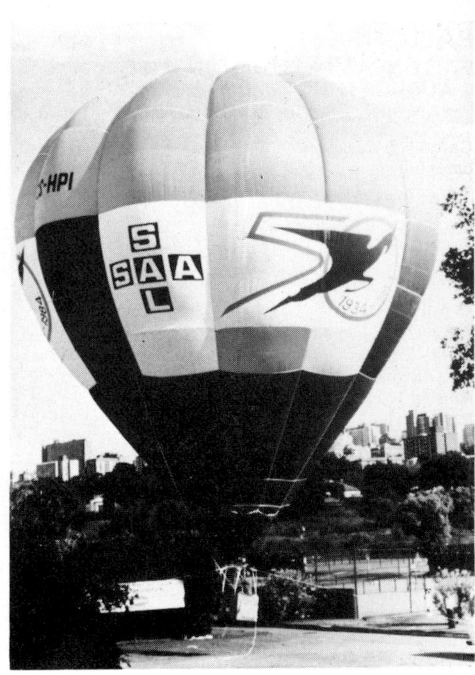

Flamboyant Balloons AX8-85 in the colours of South African Airways

UNITED KINGDOM

AIRBORNE

AIRBORNE INDUSTRIES LIMITED

Airborne Industrial Estate, Arterial Road, Leigh-on-Sea, Essex SS9 4EF
Telephone: 0702 525265
Telex: 99412

Airborne Industries became well known for its manufacture of barrage balloons during the Second World War, and since then has supplied parachute training balloons to many of the world's armed forces. With Thunder & Colt Ltd, with which it merged in December 1985, it is jointly undertaking manufacture of the GA 42 gas airship (which see).

AIRBORNE INDUSTRIES PTB 50

Airborne Industries manufactures a range of military and civil equipment, including a parachutist training balloon system comprising a PTB 50 tethered balloon, gondola, and truck mounted hydraulic winch. The balloon is a conventional 'barrage balloon' streamlined design, with air-inflated fins and rudders and ballonet compartment. The main envelope, which is helium filled, is constructed from high strength nylon fabric, coated with polyurethane for optimum weatherability and gas-holding characteristics. It is tethered by a galvanised steel wire cable to the winch's storage drum, which has a capacity for up to 1,500 m (4,920 ft) of cable.

The balloon's seven-man gondola has a tubular steel framework with a high strength light alloy floor, and can be used with or without a fabric cover. In operation, the exact jumping height is a matter of choice, but a standard figure is 300 m (984 ft) above ground level. The Airborne system, specifically designed for static line training, has been in use for many years by the Royal Air Force and Belgian Army, and has an extremely high record of safety and accuracy of landing in operation.

DIMENSIONS, EXTERNAL:

Envelope: Length overall	28·40 m (93 ft 2 in)
Diameter (max)	10·20 m (33 ft 5½ in)
Volume: nominal	1,420 m³ (50,147 cu ft)
max	1,510 m³ (53,325 cu ft)
Gondola: Length	2·70 m (8 ft 10¼ in)
Width	1·80 m (5 ft 11 in)
Height	2·00 m (6 ft 6¾ in)

WEIGHTS:

Balloon	520 kg (1,146 lb)
Gondola	180 kg (397 lb)

CAMERON

CAMERON BALLOONS LTD

St John's Street, Bedminster, Bristol BS3 4NH
Telephone: (0272) 637216
DIRECTORS: See Airships subsection

Cameron has been manufacturing hot-air balloons in Bristol since 1968 and holds CAA, FAA, Certificat de Navigabilité de Type and the West German Musterzulassungsschein type certificates for its balloons. More than 1,200 balloons had been produced by the beginning of 1985.

Envelopes are made from ripstop nylon which has been treated with a polyurethane sealant to reduce porosity. The lower section of the envelope is made from Nomex flame resistant fabric. The envelopes are available with either a Velcro seal or parachute deflation system, and those with the Velcro seal have also a vertical flap type vent. Cameron offers a wide range of balloons, details of which can be found in the accompanying table. Each is supplied complete with willow and cane basket, burner and gas cylinders and is ready to fly when delivered. Optional items include instrument pack, envelope thermometer, pressure scoop, Nomex skirt, rigid suspension basket, trail rope and additional gas cylinders.

During 1976 the company initiated the design of specially shaped balloons for advertising purposes. Three new sporting balloons were introduced during 1979, comprising the N-65 and Viva-65 in the AX-7 class, and the O-105 in the AX-8 class. It also constructed the world's first hot-air airship, and is now manufacturing such aircraft to order (see Airships subsection).

During 1981 the company built a new balloon, designated A-530, which superseded the earlier *Gerard A. Heineken* as the world's largest hot-air balloon, with a capacity of 15,000 m³ (529,720 cu ft). Subsequently named *Primagaz*, it was used by French balloonists Hélène Dorigny and Michel Arnould to establish on 6-7 July 1984 a new world duration record for hot-air balloons of 40 h 12 min 5 s.

Four new models were introduced during 1983-84, all catering for the trend towards larger balloons; these are designated N-90, O-160, N-180 and A-210. Detail improvements have been made to the Aristocrat basket, which now has raised and curved ends to improve passenger comfort.

On 26-27 January 1985, Harold A. Warner of Canada, with Phillip A. Johnson as co-pilot, set a world distance record in an A-210, covering 794·07 nm (1,470·62 km; 913·80 miles) from Calgary, Alberta, to Arnold, Nebraska. Cameron balloons thus hold all three absolute records for hot-air balloons, including an altitude record of 16,805 m (55,137 ft) set by Julian Nott in a Cameron A-375.

Cameron has also developed a helium filled pressure balloon known as the **ULD 1**, a one-third scale prototype of which (G-BLHF) underwent successful test inflation at Cardington in mid-1984 and subsequently made a successful west-east trial flight across Australia on 20-22 November 1984. In doing so, it set world duration (33 h 8 min 42 s), distance (1,291·28 nm; 2,391·46 km; 1,485·98 miles) and altitude (5,415·4 m; 17,767 ft) records for Class AS pressurised balloons. The full-size balloon, named *Endeavour*, is to be used for an attempted round-the-world flight by Julian Nott, of which further details can be found under the Endeavour entry in this section.

Also completed in 1984 was the envelope for a non-pressurised 'special', using a mixture of helium and hot air. Known as the **R-225**, it has an envelope volume of 6,371 m³ (225,000 cu ft) and was to be used for an attempt by a Dutch crew (Henk and Eveliën Brink and Evert Louwman) at a trans-Atlantic flight to Europe from St John's, Newfoundland. The gondola was adapted from a Dutch lifeboat.

Cameron Balloons representation of the first man-carrying Montgolfier balloon, on a demonstration flight in Lyons

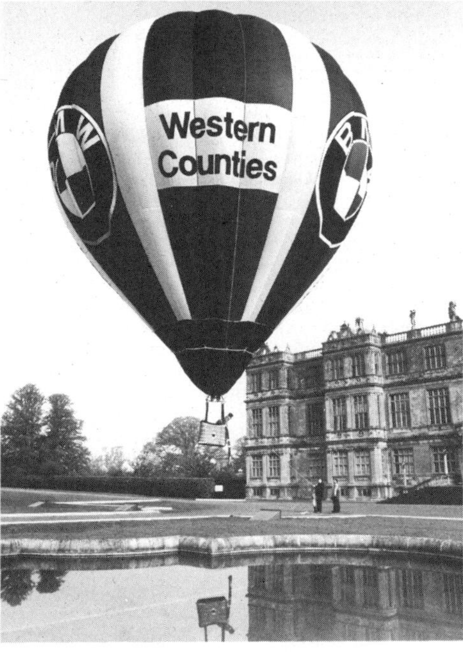

Cameron hot-air balloon G-BKZY *(John Christopher)*

Cameron hot-air balloon to publicise a German truck rental company

ENDEAVOUR

49 Mill Lane, London NW6 1NB
Telephone: (01) 435 3688 and 794 3879
PROJECT MANAGER: Julian Nott

Endeavour is the project name for an attempt at a nonstop round-the-world flight by balloon, to be made by Mr Julian Nott, present holder of the world altitude record for a hot-air balloon. The venture is financed by Western Continental Corporation of Australia, and its patrons include such well known figures as Sir Edmund Hillary, John Bertrand, Lord Hunt, Lord Kings-Norton and Thor Heyerdahl.

NCS ULD 1

Mr Julian Nott, holder of the hot-air balloon world altitude record, is preparing to make the first flight round the world by balloon, accompanied by an Australian, Mr 'Spider' Anderson. It is planned to make the flight nonstop in the jetstream at about 12,200 m (40,000 ft).

The longest manned balloon flight up to January 1986 was a six-day Atlantic crossing by Abruzzo and Anderson. The world flight is expected to take between 12 and 20 days, at much higher altitude. To achieve sufficient endurance, a large superpressure balloon is being constructed. Small meteorological superpressure balloons have achieved very long durations, but success in overcoming the engineering problems of large superpressure balloons has been limited.

A one-third scale prototype balloon, designated NCS ULD 1 (Nott Cameron Smith ULD 1) has already been built. The envelope has external ropes of a very high tensile strength aramid fibre to contain the pressure forces, and an elastic nylon fabric to allow relief from the stresses induced by the manufacturing errors inevitable in large fabric structures. Despite its relatively small volume, Nott and Anderson used it to cross Australia in November 1984 in just over 33 h, the seventh longest distance ever flown by balloon.

Following this success, a substantially larger envelope is being built for the world flight. The high altitude and long duration mean pressurisation is essential, and a pressure cabin is being built from aramid/epoxy, larger but very similar to the one Mr Nott used in 1980 to establish the hot-air balloon altitude record. Mr Nott and his team are in overall charge of the design, but assistance or advice is being received from numerous sources including the RAF Institute of Aviation Medicine, the National Center for Atmospheric Research (USA), NASA (JSC), Airship Industries, and Cameron Balloons. An oxygen rich (not 100 per cent) atmosphere will be used. The full size Endeavour balloon will be tested in the USA, but the world flight attempt will start from Australia.

A set of experiments has been prepared by the UK Meteorological Office, which will be carried to measure ozone, water vapour and other parameters, particularly those associated with the transfer of air across the tropopause. Special forecasts will be prepared at Bracknell by the Meteorological Office, and transmitted to the balloon via the Inmarsat satellite. Equipment includes Telesystems MCS9100 Inmarsat terminal, Litton LTN3000, specially prepared Magnavox Transit receiver, and comprehensive conventional aircraft communications equipment.

MAIN DATA:

NCS ULD 1 PROTOTYPE	
Envelope: Height	10·10 m (33 ft 2 in)
Diameter (measured at ropes)	16·40 m (53 ft 10 in)
Volume	1,600 m³ (56,500 cu ft)
Gross lift at 6,100 m (20,000 ft), ISA	900 kg (1,984 lb)
WORLD FLIGHT BALLOON	
Envelope: Volume	4,250 m³ (150,087 cu ft)
Cabin: Diameter	2·20 m (7 ft 2½ in)
Max internal height	1·98 m (6 ft 6 in)
Structure weight	approx 40 kg (88 lb)
Pressure differential	0·138 bars (2·00 lb/sq in)

NCS ULD 1 superpressure balloon, a scale prototype for the Endeavour world flight balloon. It has broken 24 world and international balloon records

Pressure cabin of the Endeavour world flight balloon under construction, with Mr Julian Nott on left. Black disc is the SATCOM antenna

THUNDER & COLT

THUNDER & COLT LTD

Maesbury Road, Oswestry, Shropshire SY10 8HA
Telephone: (0691) 652216
Telex: 35503 COLT G

MANAGING DIRECTOR: Per Lindstrand

SALES AND MARKETING DIRECTOR: Chris Kirby

The two former companies Thunder Balloons (established 1972) and Colt Balloons (1976) merged to form Thunder & Colt Ltd in December 1983. All production and administration is now centred in Oswestry, Shropshire.

Thunder & Colt manufactures an extensive range of ready to fly hot-air balloons, ranging from the one-person Cloudhopper to the 13-person 280A, details of which can be found in the accompanying tables. All balloons are type certificated by the United Kingdom CAA, the West German LBA, the French Bureau Veritas and the US FAA, among others, and hold several FAI world records.

Balloons with the suffix **Series 1** are 12-gore, semi-bulbous designs. They are utilised mostly by the private owner or syndicate, although in volumes greater than 140 they are operated also by commercial passenger-carrying companies. Balloons with the suffix **A** or **Series 2** are multi-gore designs which are ideal for the placement of advertising and graphics. Again, the larger volume sizes are utilised by commercial passenger-carrying operators.

All Thunder & Colt envelopes are of horizontal panel design with the exception of the Cloudhopper. The A type range can be constructed with either vertical or horizontal panel configuration. Envelopes are constructed from soft coated polyurethane ripstop nylon or polyester fabrics, with lower panels of Nomex flame resistant fabric. In the past two years the company has introduced lightweight, high operating temperature fabrics for specialised balloons such as the 42,475 m³ (1·5 million cu ft) *Skyquest*, the world's largest hot-air balloon, constructed by Thunder & Colt in 1983. Features of Thunder & Colt envelopes include rotation vents and the combination parachute/Velcro deflation system, both introduced in 1983.

The C2 range of burner units, introduced in 1980, is available in single, double, triple and quadruple configurations. Recent developments to the burner include cross-flow valves, liquid fire (quiet burner) and electronic ignition.

Thunder & Colt Cloudhopper *(John Christopher)*

'Flying Tyre' special shape balloon by Thunder & Colt

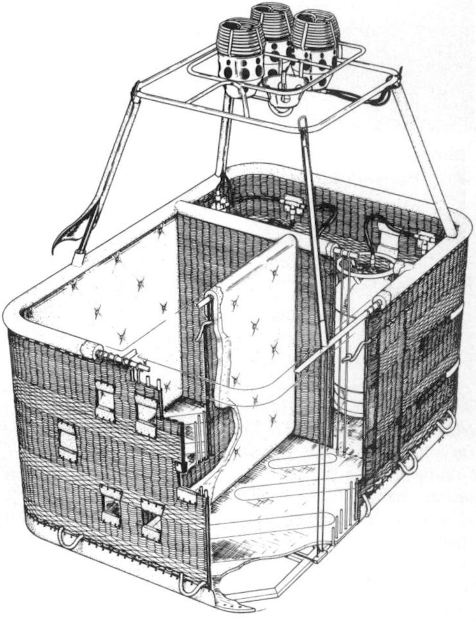

The T-partition basket for Thunder & Colt's larger balloons, which has a stainless steel frame

All major components, with the exception of baskets, are manufactured in-house; they include the introduction in 1982 of 30 kg (66 lb) upright stainless steel cylinders.

Nine sizes of cane and wicker basket are manufactured to complement the wide range of envelopes. These can have solid or wicker floors. Thunder & Colt's unique T-partition basket is used with envelopes greater than 3,964 m³ (140,000 cu ft). This revolutionary design, strengthened with stainless steel subframes, is the first to separate pilot and fuel systems from the passengers and further separate the passengers for comfort on landing.

Apart from sporting hot-air balloons, the company is also noted for the production of large passenger-carrying balloon systems which are operated from locations in Australia, Africa, the USA and Europe. The company also manufactures many special shape balloons which have included replica bottles, tyres, flames and ice cream cones. Over 65 per cent of Thunder & Colt products carry corporate advertising designs. The company is currently manufacturing more than 150 hot-air balloons and airships each year, of which over 80 per cent are exported.

Thunder & Colt also manufactures the world's first successful range of pressurised hot-air airships and, in partnership with Airborne Industries, is undertaking the manufacture of the GA42 gas airship (see Airships sub-section).

Thunder & Colt 56A advertising hot-air balloon

UNITED STATES OF AMERICA

ABC

AMERICAN BALLOON COMPANY

8220 Cooper Street, Alexandria, Virginia 22309
Telephone: (703) 780 6672
PRESIDENT: Carl E. Becker

ABC YANKEE DOODLE

Introduced in late 1983, the Yankee Doodle is a 68 kg (150 lb) dry weight, one-man ultralight aircraft designed to carry a 102 kg (225 lb) pilot. It belongs in the FAI's AX-5 class, and can be set up, inflated and launched by one person.

Yankee Doodle incorporates many unique design features. Among its standard components are a 4,000 hp (10,000,000 BTU) gimbal mounted burner, a 906 m³ (32,000 cu ft) 'floating' ripstop nylon envelope with 20 pre-stressed load tapes, and a para-rip flight control system, a proprietary development by ABC to combine the outstanding features of the ripping top method for deflation with the parachute venting concept for manoeuvring. The envelope design is based on 'natural shape' technology.

The all-aluminium basket consists of a frame with wraparound floor side panels which are riveted or bolted together to retain the integrity of the high strength alloys used in its construction. The upper part of the frame supports the burner and provides the attachment to the envelope. The basket also contains a shock mounted 38 litre (10 US gallon) fuel tank, which is adequate for more than one hour of flight time. The burner is connected to the fuel tank with a single liquid fuel line. It is a self-contained system consisting of a throttle, a miniature pressure regulator used to convert liquid to vapour for the pilot light, and a vapour pressure gauge to indicate the level of burner output.

Yankee Doodle is offered as a flyaway flight system, requiring only the addition of fuel to inflate and become airborne. It is also offered in kit form for the homebuilder, requiring approximately 100 assembly hours from precisely cut and marked fabric panels for the envelope, and preformed hardware components which can be finished with standard workshop tools. The envelope can be assembled with a home sewing machine capable of making zig-zag stitches. The burner, and other components which require special tools or techniques for manufacture, are shipped completely assembled.

Yankee Doodle requires no licensing for the flight system or the pilot.

ABC AMERICANA

Americana, introduced in 1984, is an AX-8 class 2,265 m³ (80,000 cu ft) balloon system designed for a gross load of 544 kg (1,200 lb). It is equipped with twin (optionally four) 4,000 hp (10,000,000 BTU) burners, each completely independent and capable of maintaining a safe flight pattern under full load; both are available when increased flight performance is desired.

The envelope design is based on 'natural shape' technology and 'floats' within its 28 pre-stressed load tapes. It is made of ripstop nylon fabric and incorporates a para-rip control system developed specifically to provide the sport flyer with maximum flight safety.

The basket is all-aluminium, consisting of a frame and wraparound floor side panels which are riveted or bolted together to retain the high inherent strength of the alloys used in its construction. It is equipped with shock mountings for four 38 litre (10 US gallon) fuel tanks (two are furnished as standard equipment), which are connected singly to each burner. The upper part of the basket frame supports the burners and provides the attachment to the envelope. The burners are self-contained systems, similar to those of the Yankee Doodle, and are connected to their respective fuel tanks with single liquid fuel lines.

Americana is offered in kit form for the homebuilder, for whom it was specifically designed. Approximately 150 hours are required to assemble the kit from precision cut and marked fabric panels for the envelope, and from preformed hardware which can be finished with standard workshop tools. The burners, shroud lines, and other components which require special tools for manufacture and assembly, are included in the kit as completed assemblies. A commercial sewing machine is recommended for ease of assembly of the envelope, although this can be accomplished with a home machine capable of zig-zag stitches.

Americana must be licensed as an experimental aircraft, and the pilot must have a lighter than air licence with a rating for hot-air balloons.

All-aluminium basket of the Yankee Doodle

ABC's Americana AX-8 class homebuilt hot-air balloon

Yankee Doodle hot-air ultralight of the American Balloon Company

ADAMS

ADAMS BALLOON LOFT INC

Building 27, Dekalb Peachtree Airport, Atlanta, Georgia 30341
Telephone: (404) 452 8066

Adams Balloon Loft is manufacturing a range of hot-air balloons, of which details can be found in the accompanying table. Latest additions to the range are the A60 and A60S (AX-8 class) and the AX-9 class Model AB.

Envelopes are made from ripstop nylon, which may be coated optionally with a polyurethane or aluminised sealant to reduce porosity. Nomex flame resistant fabric is used to protect the envelope throat. Two manoeuvring vents are located in the crown of the balloon and there is a duffle bag type of deflation system, or an optional Paravent.

The LD models, introduced in 1978, feature a deflation system which the company calls MultiVent. A single control line creates 16 diamond shaped openings which snap shut immediately the control line is released, so providing an improved measure of control.

Adams balloons are supplied complete with a woven rattan basket, burner, aluminium fuel cylinders, and instruments which include a sensitive altimeter, rate of climb indicator, envelope temperature gauge, bubble type compass and fuel gauges. Optional items include tank-mounted pressure gauge, Nomex skirt, Paravent or MultiVent deflation system, inflator fan and additional fuel cylinders.

Adams Balloon Loft Model A55S

AVIAN

AVIAN BALLOON COMPANY

South 3722 Ridgeview Drive, Spokane, Washington 99206
Telephone: (509) 928 6847

Avian Balloon was marketing in 1984 six hot-air balloons: the 32 Calibre and Sparrow (FAI class AX-5), Falcon II (AX-7), Skyhawk and Turbo 8 (AX-8) and Magnum IX (AX-9). No update for 1985 or 1986 was received.

Envelopes are made from coated ripstop nylon, or can optionally be made from aluminised balloon fabric. The Sparrow, Falcon II and Skyhawk have as standard a 20 or 70 gore envelope, with a customer-designed horizontal or vertical pattern in three colours from an 11-colour range; and a choice of parachute or resealable deflation port with side vent. The basket is of wicker and, in addition to the burner and gas cylinders, an instrument panel that includes an altimeter, rate of climb indicator and envelope LCD temperature gauge is standard. The Magnum IX is standard with a customer-designed 24 gore horizontal pattern, deflation port with UltraVent control, dual burners, plus the features listed for the other models. Details of Avian's balloons are given in the accompanying table.

Avian Balloon 20 gore envelope in the AX-7 class

BALLOON WORKS

THE BALLOON WORKS

PO Box 827, 810 Salisbury Road, Statesville, North Carolina 28677
Telephone: (704) 878 9501
DIRECTORS:
Sidney Conn
Elenor Conn

The Balloon Works is currently manufacturing six sizes of triangular basket with three, four and six fuel cylinder configurations, and seven envelope sizes ranging from 1,841 m³ (65,000 cu ft) to 2,973 m³ (105,000 cu ft). The envelopes are available in zig-zag, horizontal, spiral and diamond patterns.

The envelopes are made of a polyester fabric, which tests have shown to be more resistant to ultraviolet and acid rain degradation than other materials, and are coated with a urethane sealant to reduce porosity. Flexnet, a net of panel-isolating tapes to prevent tear propagation, is standard. Rapid deflation is made possible by use of a wide-diameter envelope valve, which is self-sealing immediately the valve line is released. Triangular baskets of the **FireFly** balloons are of coloured wicker and trimmed in suede; those of the **DragonFly** are trimmed in black fabric and hand finished birch.

The FireFly range received approval from the British CAA in 1985 for the issue of standard UK certificates of airworthiness, and are the first US manufactured balloons to receive this approval.

One high output burner with three independent pilot lights, their associated burners, and a Fire 2 quiet backup burner system, are supplied as standard. Other equipment supplied for DragonFly and FireFly balloons includes two fuel cylinders and related fuel lines, apex handling line, altimeter, fuel pressure gauges, rate of climb indicator, thermometer and an envelope pack-up bag. A wide variety of envelope artwork can be provided.

One of the range of hot-air balloons produced by The Balloon Works

BOLAND

BOLAND BALLOON

Pine Drive, RD 2, Burlington, Connecticut 06013
Telephone: (203) 673 1307
PROPRIETORS:
Brian J. Boland
Mrs K. Boland

Mr Brian Boland, designer and builder, with his wife Kathy, of the *Albatross* and *Rover* hot-air airships (described in the Airships subsection) has also designed and built a number of hot-air balloons. Early examples included the very small *Piccolo,* and the somewhat larger *Fred II* of which Mr Boland built six examples. Details of both of these early balloons can be found in the 1978-79 and 1983-84 *Jane's.*

During 1978 the Bolands built three new balloons, two of them in the lower-size FAI categories. These included the XXUS (also known as *Scooter*) in the AX-1 class, *High Fred* in the AX-3 class, and *Spirit of Lake Garda* in the AX-8 class. Details of these can be found in the 1979-80 *Jane's.*

The 1979 *Peaches,* which is in the AX-6 class, was flown by Mr Boland in January 1983 from Gstaad, Switzerland, a distance of 151 km (94 miles) over the Alps to just north of Turin, Italy, in two hours. This is believed to be the smallest hot-air balloon to have overflown the Alps. A second 1979 design was the AX-5 class *Dimples.* In December 1980 a new balloon in the AX-9 class was completed. Known as *Riff Raff,* this was illustrated in the 1984-85 *Jane's,* and a sister balloon, *Fitzgerald,* was completed in May 1980. In the AX-8 class *Mr Snake,* Mr Boland flew to championship victories in the Irish Hot Air Balloon Nationals in 1982 and 1983. For 1983, *Mr Snake* was fitted with a new collapsible/portable three-place gondola. Two other hot-air balloons completed in 1983 were the AX-6 class *Desert Fox* (July) and AX-7 *Circus Maximus* (February). Details of the balloons listed in this paragraph can be found in the 1985-86 and earlier editions of *Jane's.*

Under construction for March 1984 completion was a two-place, 12 gore 1,444 m³ (51,000 cu ft) ultralight hot-air balloon envelope, and by May or early June 1984 Boland Balloon planned to design and construct a 5,663 m³ (200,000 cu ft) hot-air balloon envelope, the carriage for which was completed earlier. However, no information regarding current activities has been received since the beginning of 1984.

All known details of these balloons are given in the accompanying table.

Boland AX-6 *Desert Fox*, completed in 1983

The 1983 Boland AX-7 class *Circus Maximus*

Boland AX-8 *Mr Snake* during the Irish Hot Air Balloon Nationals in 1983, with its new collapsible gondola *(John W. Bond)*

GALAXY

GALAXY BALLOONS INC

820 Salisbury Road, Statesville, North Carolina 28677
Telephone: (704) 878 9147
TECHNICAL MANAGER: Nick Parise

Operating under the authority of two US type certificates, Galaxy was formed to manufacture hot-air balloons, gas and hot-air airships and cold-air inflatables.

One model of hot-air balloon was being certificated by the FAA in January 1986. It is an FAI Class AX-7 with a choice of two carriages, both having a rattan frame with wicker weaving. The smaller will carry a pilot and two passengers, the larger will carry a pilot and three. Both can accept four fuel cylinders and will utilise a triple orifice burner with three pilot lights and a backup burner.

Envelopes are made of ripstop nylon or ripstop polyester, at customer's preference, coated with urethane to reduce porosity, and are available in horizontal pattern with a choice of 15 standard colours. They are constructed using the patented Integral Net method, in which tapes surrounding each panel prevent propagation of tears from panel to panel. In-flight vertical control and rapid deflation for landing are accomplished by the use of a parachute valve. All necessary flight instruments are supplied as standard equipment. Further details are given in the table.

AX-7 class balloon being certificated by Galaxy Balloons in early 1986

HOVERAIR

HOVERAIR LIMITED

1385 Fairfax Drive #B, San Francisco, California 94124
Telephone: (415) 756 0330
PRESIDENT: William Chambers

HOVERAIR DRIFTER

When displayed at the Sun 'N' Fun Fly-in at Lakeland, Florida, in March 1983, this single-seat hot-air balloon/microlight won the 'Most Unique Ultralight Vehicle' award. Its envelope, manufactured by Colt in the UK, is of double ripstop nylon, with 26 four-section gores and a Nomex skirt. Vertical nylon load tapes connect the envelope to stainless steel cables which are locked to a heavy steel ring from which are suspended, on ball bearing runners, the propane tank, burner, and pilot's seat. The 7 million BTU/h burner pack is incorporated in a harness that is strapped to the pilot's back, and also provides him with a sling seat. All harness parts are stressed for 907 kg (2,000 lb) load minimum, and most parts for 2,268 kg (5,000 lb) maximum. An electronic igniter is standard. Safe flying time is one hour. The Drifter packs into two bags which have a combined weight of 43 kg (95 lb). A 453 m³ (16,000 cu ft) envelope is available optionally for advanced pilots. Details of the Drifter with standard 566·3 m³ (20,000 cu ft) envelope can be found in the accompanying table.

ILC

ILC DOVER (Division of ILC Industries Inc)

PO Box 266, Frederica, Delaware 19946
Telephone: (302) 335 3911

As noted in the Airships subsection, ILC Dover manufactures a variety of tethered balloon-type aerostats. The standard range covers balloons from as small as 1·70 m³ (60 cu ft) to large 7,079 m³ (250,000 cu ft) radar carrying platforms, but the company also develops balloon systems to satisfy specific user requirements. Details of three standard types follow:

ILC DOVER AG-60 BALLOON

ILC's AG-60 balloon is designed for any general use where a highly visible ground marker is required for such applications as aerial spraying and surveying. Its envelope is made from heat sealed white urethane coated nylon, and incorporates three inflatable fins forming an inverted 'Y' to ensure stable flight in wind velocities from 0 to 39 knots (72 km/h; 45 mph) on a 91 m (300 ft) nylon tether. The fins are designed so that no rigid members are required to increase stiffness or prevent flutter. It is equipped with an automatic self-closing fill port to provide easy inflation, and a pressure relief valve to prevent overpressurisation. Handled easily by one operator, it can be transported, flown and retrieved from a standard open pickup truck.

DIMENSIONS, ENVELOPE:

Length overall	3·05 m (10 ft 0 in)
Max diameter	1·17 m (3 ft 10 in)
Volume, gross	1·70 m³ (60 cu ft)

WEIGHT:

Unfilled	1·4 kg (3 lb)

ILC DOVER SSP SERIES

The SSP (stable sensor platform) is a non-rigid tethered aerostat based upon the design of the successful Family II D7 developed by the Advanced Research Projects Agency for the surveillance and communications relay requirements of the US Department of Defense. It consists of an elliptically shaped envelope, containing a lenticular shaped ballonet, and incorporating three fins forming an inverted 'Y'. Each fin has 13 spar webs to form an NACA 0018 aerofoil section.

ILC's SSP series aerostats range in size from 85 to 1,076 m³ (3,000-38,000 cu ft). A typical and popular model is the **SSP-6000**, which has a pressure control system that maintains the envelope's design shape, with redundant valves to relieve pressure resulting from superheat, atmospheric pressure drop, or increase in altitude. A battery powered electric blower, with more than five days' sustained in-flight capability, maintains pressure during descent, atmospheric pressure increase, or temperature drop. The fins are air inflated and coupled to the ballonet, so that the complete aerostat is maintained at the same pressure.

Flight loads are taken by 14 confluence lines and patches, seven port and seven starboard; four close-haul lines, two port and two starboard, are provided for ground handling.

An effective low-cost mooring system is available for the SSP series. Details of this were given in the 1985-86 *Jane's*.

DIMENSIONS, ENVELOPE:

Length overall	15·35 m (50 ft 4¼ in)
Max diameter	4·98 m (16 ft 4 in)
Tail fin span: horizontal	5·06 m (16 ft 7¼ in)
vertical	6·10 m (20 ft 0 in)
Max helium volume	170·0 m³ (6,000 cu ft)
Max ballonet volume	28·33 m³ (1,000 cu ft)
Nominal helium volume at S/L	147·25 m³ (5,200 cu ft)
Nominal ballonet volume at S/L	22·65 m³ (800 cu ft)

ILC Dover mooring system in use with one of the company's SSP series balloons

ILC Dover 250,000 cu ft aerostat with RCA AN/DPS-5 radar payload in ventral radome

WEIGHTS:

Gross lift, 95% helium purity	144 kg (317 lb)
Free lift	14·5 kg (32 lb)
Aerostat weight	72·6 kg (160 lb)
Net lift	56·7 kg (125 lb)

PERFORMANCE:

Max design altitude	1,525 m (5,000 ft)
Max wind velocity, operational	45 knots (83 km/h; 52 mph)

ILC DOVER 250,000 CU FT AEROSTAT

This large-volume aerostat can lift a payload of 454 kg (1,000 lb) to an altitude of 3,660 m (12,000 ft). The shape of its envelope is a modification of the Class 'C' developed by the US Air Force as a radar surveillance platform. The envelope incorporates a large ballonet, and has four tail fins in cruciform configuration: these not only provide pitch and yaw stability, but generate additional lift as windspeeds increase. The avionics or other payload is carried beneath the envelope, and a pressurised cover is available to protect the payload and decrease aerodynamic drag. Pressure control is maintained by a system of valves and blowers which add or dump air from the ballonet, tail fins, and pressurised load cover. This pressure maintenance is totally automatic, controlled by pressure switches and logic circuits, but manual control from the ground via onboard telemetry can be used to override any pre-set limits. Onboard power supplies can be matched to the payload requirements but, typically, a 6kW generator will meet radar payload and pressure system requirements.

DIMENSIONS, ENVELOPE:

Length overall	53·34 m (175 ft 0 in)
Max diameter	17·31 m (56 ft 9½ in)
Tail fin span	24·62 m (80 ft 9½ in)
Volume: gross	7,079 m³ (250,000 cu ft)
ballonet	3,030 m³ (107,000 cu ft)

PERFORMANCE:

Design altitude, with 454 kg (1,000 lb) payload 3,660 m (12,000 ft)

Max wind velocity:

operational	60 knots (111 km/h; 69 mph)
moored	90 knots (167 km/h; 103 mph)

RAVEN

RAVEN INDUSTRIES INC

Box 1007, Sioux Falls, South Dakota 57117

Telephone: (605) 336 2750

Raven Industries has been manufacturing hot-air balloons since the early 1960s, and also built the STAR hot-air airship of which details were given in the 1977-78 *Jane's*. It claims to be the world's largest manufacturer of hot-air balloons, details of which can be found in the accompanying table.

Raven envelopes are made from ripstop nylon treated with ultra-violet inhibitors to prolong fabric life. They embody to the customer's choice either a parachute style deflation system or a Velcro rapid deflation port. All models have woven rattan wicker baskets. Standard equipment includes the burner, gas cylinders, and an instrument case containing a sensitive altimeter, rate of climb indicator and envelope temperature gauge. A range of options includes fire retardant Kynol skirt liner, Kynol throat liner, stainless steel or additional aluminium gas cylinders, electric variometer, special colours, designs and decorations for the envelope, banners, bunting and repair fabrics.

In 1982 the company began production of a helium filled balloon known as the MG-1000 Orbiter, the first example of which had flown for the first time in the Summer of 1981. The MG-1000 falls in FAI class AA-5 and has since been complemented by the MG-300 Orbiter Ultralight in the AA-2 class. The envelopes of these gas balloons are of urethane coated nylon, the gores thermal sealed with adhesive bonded seal strip, and incorporate horizontal ripstops, a Reuter manual inflation valve and an easily resealable deflation vent.

Group of balloons made by Raven Industries; largest is the S-77A

RCA

RCA SERVICE COMPANY

Route 38, Cherry Hill, New Jersey 08358

Telephone: (609) 486 5040

Telex: 834357 (US); 222935 (Overseas)

DIVISION VICE-PRESIDENT, GOVERNMENT SERVICES
MARKETING: T. E. Alman

VICE-PRESIDENT, RANGE SERVICES: J. O. Cain

RCA's Aerostat Systems organisation has been active in the design and development of tethered aerostat systems since 1967. RCA developed systems have been deployed for a variety of surveillance applications using radar, electro-optical, video and acoustic sensors. Tethered aerostats used as platforms for these payloads have been designed in sizes varying from 1,274 to 7,079 m³ (45,000 to 250,000 cu ft).

RCA HIGH ALTITUDE SYSTEM

This system is designed to carry a primary radar, a secondary IFF radar, and associated FM command and data equipment. The latest configuration is based on an ILC Dover 250,000 cu ft aerostat (which see) and an RCA designed AN/DPS-5 radar. The ground handling subsystem comprises an RCA developed soft-nose mooring system and a high-speed electric winch platform. The system can be made mobile using a truck mounted hydraulic winch, uniquely designed mooring tower, and transportable instrumentation enclosures.

The AN/DPS-5 surveillance radar provides a detection range of 150 nm (278 km; 173 miles) against 5 m² (54 sq ft) targets flying at an altitude of 30·5 m (100 ft) with a single-scan probability of detection of 90 per cent. Unique sea clutter Doppler correction techniques and improved transmitter pulse circuitry have resulted in the attainment of 55 dB of cancellation in both land and sea clutter. This allows detection and tracking of surface targets (ships) with a radial speed of 10 knots (18·5 km/h; 11·5 mph). A secondary AN/APX-76 IFF radar is capable of obtaining beacon data within a range of 250 nm (463 km; 288 miles).

RCA's high altitude system has been operating for over four years and has consistently surpassed the design goal of 96 per cent average operational availability.

DIMENSIONS, ENVELOPE:

see ILC Dover entry

PERFORMANCE:

Payload coverage at 3,050 m (10,000 ft) altitude:

Radius:

primary	150 nm (278 km; 173 miles)
secondary	250 nm (463 km; 288 miles)

Area:

primary	70,908 nm² (243,524 km²; 94,025 sq miles)
secondary	196,513 nm² (674,889 km²; 260,576 sq miles)

RCA 56,000 cu ft SEA-BASED AEROSTAT

This smaller aerostat system was designed to be deployed from a 58·52 m (192 ft) motor vessel. RCA designed a 1,274 m³ (45,000 cu ft) prototype and later a 1,586 m³ (56,000 cu ft) aerostat to meet the unique requirements of shipboard mooring. An inverted Y tail configuration and a 10-degree-angled, soft-nose docking system permit a lower mooring position and thus improve accessibility for operation and maintenance. The aerostat is flown using a Kevlar 49 strength member tether with integrated electrical wires for primary power and optical fibres for the transmission of telemetered data and command signals. The tether has a break strength of 6,350 kg (14,000 lb) and a power carrying capacity of up to 8kVA. A layer of braiding immediately beneath the tether jacket functions as a lightning protection system.

The payload is a modified Eaton Corporation AN/APS-128J PC airborne surveillance radar. This is a modern solid state system designed specifically for maritime patrol

RCA's sea-based aerostat system, using a 1,586 m³ (56,000 cu ft) tethered balloon on a rotatable ship-mounted platform

applications and is ideally suited for a small aerostat system. Pulse compression, frequency agility, scan-to-scan integration, anti-clutter and CFAR (constant false-alarm rate) are built into the AN/APS-128 PC to enhance detection performance in rough seas. The radar will detect a Swerling class 3, 10 m² (107·6 sq ft) surface target in sea state three at distances from 3 to 60 nm (5·6-111 km; 3·5-69 miles) with a minimum probability of detection of 50 per cent and a false-alarm probability of ·0001 per sweep.

A 58·52 m (192 ft), 269·5 tonne (297 gross ton) motor vessel functions as the platform for mooring and flying the aerostat. RCA designed the rotatable mooring platform, hydraulic winch system, and the soft-nose mooring tower. The vessel can provide mission coverage virtually anywhere in the world for extended periods of up to 30 days without support.

DIMENSIONS, ENVELOPE:

Length overall	33·38 m (109 ft 6 in)
Max diameter	5·56 m (18 ft 3 in)
Tail-fin span	7·80 m (25 ft 7¼ in)
Volume: gross	1,586 m³ (56,000 cu ft)
ballonet	453 m³ (16,000 cu ft)

PERFORMANCE:

Operating altitude	762 m (2,500 ft)
Max wind velocity:	
operational	65 knots (120 km/h; 75 mph)
moored	90 knots (167 km/h; 104 mph)
Payload coverage at 762 m (2,500 ft) altitude:	
Radius	60 nm (111 km; 69 miles)
Area	11,279 nm² (38,738 km²: 14,957 sq miles)

SOLO

SOLO SYSTEM INC

265 Front Street, Mattawan, Michigan 49071
Telephone: (616) 668 4228

SOLO SYSTEM SS-103

As its designation indicates, the SS-103 was designed to comply with the FAA's FAR Pt 103 regulations for microlight aircraft. It has a 16-gore, horizontally cut envelope of ripstop nylon, with a detachable 4·88 m (16 ft) diameter bellmouth skirt, and a parachute-like deflation system. The basket is a seamless structure, made of plastics with interior padding and measuring 0·69 m (27 in) square by 0·99 m (39 in) deep. Other envelope and basket data are given in the AX-4 class table at the end of this section. Envelope weight is 32·7 kg (72 lb); the complete system weighs 69·4 kg (153 lb).

The burner is gimbal mounted, has electric ignition, and is fed by a 38 litre (10 US gallon) fuel tank. Options include an instrument package, 46 m (150 ft) trail line, trailer and inflation fan.

TCOM

TCOM CORPORATION (Subsidiary of Westinghouse Electric Corporation)

Ridgely Building, 5575 Sterrett Place, Columbia, Maryland 21044
Telephone: (301) 992 3300
Telex: 87586

MANAGER, PROPOSALS AND PUBLICATIONS: L. V. Pelletier

OTHER FACILITIES:
Elizabeth City, North Carolina, and Baltimore, Maryland

TCOM Corporation, a wholly owned subsidiary of Westinghouse Electric Corporation, was formed in 1971 to build tethered aerostat systems for a variety of uses including surveillance (both active and passive), communications (including telephony, TV, AM and FM broadcast), and as a platform for a variety of electronic and electro-optical payloads. By 1985 TCOM had contracted for more than 30 systems.

The aerostats are constructed from a laminate of Tedlar, Mylar and Dacron fabric, bonded together with Hytrel polyester resin which produces a strong, lightweight, flexible structure with exceptionally good weathering characteristics. The aerostat is held captive by a unique tether developed by TCOM. The strength member is Kevlar 29 and the tether core contains electrical wires for primary aerostat operating power, as well as optical fibres (optional) for telemetry purposes. Tethers have been produced with break strengths of 5,000 kg (11,023 lb) for the small aerostats to as much as 30,000 kg (66,140 lb), with power carrying capacities of 3·5 kW to 31·5 kW. The power tether concept permits continuous airborne on-station time of up to 30 days, and also functions as part of the lightning protection system.

TCOM 365 (Mark VII-S) aerostat in Nigeria

TCOM 25M (STARS)

Also known as STARS (Small Tethered Aerostat Relocatable System), the TCOM 25M is a completely self-contained system which can be mounted on one or two road trailers, transported quickly to an operating site, and launched by a crew of four or five in about 5 hours. It can remain on station for up to two weeks before being hauled in to replenish helium and service the electronic payload; can operate in steady horizontal winds of up to 50 knots 93 km/h; 57 mph); and withstand horizontal gusts of up to 70 knots (130 km/h; 81 mph).

Approximately the last 3 m (9·8 ft) of the aerostat hull is air inflated and is separated from the main hull by a diaphragm. There are three fins, forming an inverted Y, with the two lower fins each at an anhedral angle of 45°; all three fins are the same size and are air inflated, connecting directly with the air inflated tailcone. The ballonet consists of a flexible fabric membrane attached to the interior lower surface of the hull, into which air can be pumped automatically by a pressure control unit when hull pressure drops to a predetermined level. A fabric tube connects the ballonet to the hull tailcone and allows air to flow freely into or out of the tailcone as required to maintain the proper pressure in the tailcone and fins.

Payloads that can be carried by STARS include a French LMT Radio Professionnelle Rasit battlefield surveillance radar, Litton 504 maritime surveillance radar, or Westinghouse APG-66 air surveillance radar of the kind fitted in the F-16 fighter. In one application, the tether of the aerostat serves as a rapidly deployable and reconstitutable VLF antenna.

The TCOM 25M system has been operated successfully from small ships, including operations above the Arctic Circle (Beaufort Sea) and in the Caribbean area.

DIMENSIONS, ENVELOPE:

Length overall	25·60 m (84 ft 0 in)
Length of hull	24·99 m (82 ft 0 in)
Width over tail fins	8·43 m (27 ft 8 in)
Hull diameter (max)	8·00 m (26 ft 3 in)
Height (bottom of radome to top of fin)	12·85 m (42 ft 2 in)
Volume: helium	738 m³ (26,082 cu ft)
ballonet	200 m³ (7,068 cu ft)

WEIGHTS:

Total weight without payload	381 kg (840 lb)
Payload	125 kg (275 lb)

PERFORMANCE:

Operating altitude, ISA, with 113 kg (250 lb) payload	700-1,000 m (2,300-3,280 ft)
Payload coverage at 750 m (2,460 ft) altitude:	
radius	59 nm (110 km; 68 miles)
area	11,065 nm² (38,000 km²; 14,672 sq miles)

TCOM 365B/H (MARK VII-S)

This larger aerostat is designed to carry surveillance and communications payloads to operating altitudes of 3,000 m (9,850 ft) and above. It has four tail fins, spaced 90° apart, the hull and three fins being filled with helium; the lower vertical fin and the windscreen (radome) are air filled. The fins impart static and dynamic flight stability, returning the aerostat to its designed equilibrium attitude if it is displaced by air currents. A ballonet blower system keeps the pressure within the hull above the ambient atmospheric pressure; ballonet size depends upon the maximum mission altitude required. The mooring system is designed to withstand a wind velocity of 90 knots (167 km/h; 104 mph) at sea level. A lightning protection system is installed, but the Mark VII-S is not intended for service in thunderstorms or during conditions of extreme turbulence.

Payloads for the TCOM 365 include complete television and radio broadcast systems with their associated studio/transmitter links, elint and sigint systems, and airborne radar units. The Westinghouse TPS-63 radar provides a detection range of 150 nm (278 km; 173 miles) against a 5 m² (54 sq ft) target flying at an altitude of 60 m (200 ft), with a single-scan probability of detection of 90 per cent. Surface targets (ships) with a radial speed of 15 knots (28 km/h; 17 mph) or more can also be detected. One such system, known as LASS (low altitude surveillance system) was to be demonstrated in 1986 by TCOM and Westinghouse to the Royal Saudi Air Force, as a potential backup to the RSAF's Boeing E-3A force.

DIMENSIONS, ENVELOPE:

Length overall	69·49 m (228 ft 0 in)
Length of hull	59·19 m (194 ft 2·4 in)
Width over horizontal tail fins	24·85 m (81 ft 6½ in)
Height over vertical tail fins	30·34 m (99 ft 6½ in)
Hull diameter (max)	17·31 m (56 ft 9·6 in)
Windscreen (radome) diameter (max)	9·75 m (32 ft 0 in)
Hull volume (design)	10,336 m³ (365,000 cu ft)
Volume: helium (actual, incl 3 upper fins)	11,638 m³ (411,000 cu ft)
ballonet: 365B	5,324 m³ (188,000 cu ft)
365H	6,258 m³ (221,000 cu ft)

WEIGHTS:

Total weight without payload	3,382 kg (7,457 lb)
Payload for operation at 3,000 m (9,840 ft)	1,814 kg (4,000 lb)

PERFORMANCE:

Operating altitude, ISA:	
365B with 1,814 kg (4,000 lb) payload	3,050-3,660 m (10,000-12,000 ft)
365H with 726 kg (1,600 lb) payload	above 5,485 m (18,000 ft)
Payload coverage at 3,000 m (9,850 ft) altitude	
radius	108 nm (200 km; 124 miles)
area	36,400 nm² (125,000 km²; 48,262 sq miles)

TCOM 25M STARS aerostat

HOT-AIR (AX) AND GAS BALLOON (AA) DATA

Country	Company	Model	Volume m³/cu ft	Diameter m/ft	Height m/ft	Crew	Basket	Fuel Cylinders	Burners
FAI CLASS AA/AX-2 (250-400 m³; 8,829-14,126 cu ft)									
United Kingdom	Thunder & Colt	Cloudhopper Junior	396·4/14,000	8·53/28	8·53/28	1	Harness seat	1	1
United States	Raven	MG-300	300/10,595	8·78/28·8	8·23/27	1	Mixed structure	NA	NA
FAI CLASS AA/AX-3 (400-600 m³; 14,126-21,189 cu ft)									
West Germany	Ballonfabrik	K 630/1-Ri	630/22,248	10·64/34·91	18·0/59	3-4	Rattan	NA	NA
United Kingdom	Cameron	Viva-20	566·3/20,000	9·14/30	9·75/32	1	Harness seat	1	1
United Kingdom	Thunder & Colt	Cloudhopper Midi	481·4/17,000	9·45/31	9·45/31	1	Harness seat	1	1
United Kingdom	Thunder & Colt	Cloudhopper Super	594·7/21,000	10·06/33	10·67/35	1	Harness seat	1	1
United States	Hoverair	Drifter	566·3/20,000	9·14/30	10·67/35	1	Harness seat	1	1
FAI CLASS AA/AX-4 (600-900 m³; 21,189-31,783 cu ft)									
West Germany	Ballonfabrik	K 780/2-Ri	780/27,545	11·5/37·73	19·81/65	4	Rattan	NA	NA
West Germany	Ballonfabrik	B 800/2-Ri	800/28,252	11·5/37·73	20·12/66	4	Rattan	NA	NA
West Germany	Ballonfabrik	K 945/2-Ri	945/33,372	12·17/39·93	20·42/67	5-6	Rattan	NA	NA
Hungary	MÉM RSZ	RSZ-06	896/31,642	12·5/41	15·5/50·9	1	Rattan	1	1
United Kingdom	Cameron	N-31	890/31,430	12·5/41	14·63/48	1	Willow/Cane	2	1
United Kingdom	Cameron	O-31	890/31,430	12·5/41	14·63/48	1	Willow/Cane	2	1
United Kingdom	Cameron	Viva-31	890/31,430	12·5/41	14·63/48	1	Willow/Cane	2	1
United Kingdom	Thunder & Colt	31Z	890/31,430	12·19/40	14·63/48	1	Wicker/Cane	2	1
United States	Raven	S-40	900/31,783	12·19/40	16·76/55	1	Aluminium chair	1	1
United States	Solo	SS-103	793/28,000	—	—	1	Plastics	1	1
FAI CLASS AA/AX-5 (900-1,200 m³; 31,783-42,378 cu ft)									
West Germany	Ballonfabrik	K 1050/3-Ri	1,050/37,080	12·6/41·3	20·7/67·9	5-6	Rattan	NA	NA
West Germany	Ballonfabrik	K 1260/3-Ri	1,260/44,496	13·4/44	22·25/73	6	Rattan	NA	NA
South Africa	Flamboyant	AX5-40M	1,132/40,000	12·9/42·32	14·0/45·93	1	Rattan	1	1
United Kingdom	Cameron	O-42	1,190/42,024	—	—	2	Willow/Cane	2	1
United Kingdom	Thunder & Colt	42 Series 1	1,190/42,024	13·59/44·6	14·30/46·9	2	Wicker/Cane	2	1
United Kingdom	Thunder & Colt	42A	1,190/42,024	13·69/44·9	14·50/47·6	2	Wicker/Cane	2	1
United States	ABC	Yankee Doodle	906/32,000	—	—	1	Aluminium	1	1
United States	Adams	LD	964/34,029	12·95/42·5	15·54/51	1	Rattan	1/2	1
United States	Adams	LD-S	1,104/38,978	12·95/42·5	16·46/54	1-2	Rattan	1/2	1
United States	Avian	32 Calibre	906/32,000	12·19/40	14·02/46	1	Aluminium chair	1	1
United States	Avian	Sparrow	1,189/42,000	13·41/44	16·46/54	1	Wicker	1/2	2
United States	Balloon Works	FireFly 42	1,182/41,740	14·02/46	14·63/48	1-2	Wicker	3	2
United States	Raven	MG-1000	1,047/36,959	13·34/43·76	12·72/41·72	1-3	Rattan	NA	NA
FAI CLASS AA/AX-6 (1,200-1,600 m³; 42,378-56,503 cu ft)									
France	Chaize	CS. 1600	1,600/56,503	14·0/45·93	22·5/73·82	2	Rattan	2	1
West Germany	Ballonfabrik	K 1360/4-Ri	1,360/48,028	13·75/45·11	25·0/82·02	6	Rattan	NA	NA
West Germany	Ballonfabrik	K 1680/4-Ri	1,680/59,329	14·78/48·5	24·4/80	6	Rattan	NA	NA
South Africa	Flamboyant	AX6-56	1,586/56,000	15·0/49·2	18·0/59·0	2	Rattan	2	1
South Africa	Flamboyant	AX6-56M	1,586/56,000	15·0/49·2	18·0/59·0	2	Rattan	2	1
United Kingdom	Cameron	O-56	1,590/56,150	15·24/50	17·07/56	3	Willow/Cane	2	1
United Kingdom	Cameron	Viva-56	1,590/56,150	15·24/50	17·07/56	3	Willow/Cane	2	1
United Kingdom	Cameron	N-56	1,590/56,150	15·24/50	17·07/56	3	Willow/Cane	2	1
United Kingdom	Thunder & Colt	56 Series 1	1,590/56,150	15·39/50·5	16·31/53·5	3	Wicker/Cane	2-3	1
United Kingdom	Thunder & Colt	56A	1,590/56,150	15·61/51·2	16·40/53·8	3	Wicker/Cane	2-3	1
United States	Adams	A50	1,557/54,985	15·24/50	17·68/58	2	Rattan	1-4	1
United States	Balloon Works	GadFly 56	1,576/55,660	15·3/50·1	16·1/52·8	3	Wicker	3	1
United States	Balloon Works	GadFly 560	1,576/55,660	15·24/50	16·46/54	1-3	Wicker	3	1
United States	Balloon Works	DragonFly 56	1,576/55,660	15·24/50	15·85/52	1-3	Wicker	3	1
United States	Balloon Works	DragonFly 560	1,576/55,660	15·24/50	15·85/52	1-3	Wicker	3	1
United States	Raven	S-50A	1,597/56,400	15·24/50	17·68/58	2-4	Wicker	3	1
United States	Raven	RX-6	1,597/56,400	15·24/50	17·68/58	2-3	Wicker	2	1
FAI CLASS AA/AX-7 (1,600-2,200 m³; 56,503-77,692 cu ft)									
Czechoslovakia	Aviatik Brno	AB-1	2,190/77,339	16·0/52·5	22·0/72·2	4	Rattan	2	2
Czechoslovakia	Aviatik Brno	AB-2	2,190/77,339	16·2/53·1	21·0/68·9	4	Rattan	2	2
France	Chaize	CS. 1800	1,800/63,566	15·0/49·2	22·5/73·8	2-3	Rattan	3	1
France	Chaize	CS. 2000	2,000/70,629	16·5/54·1	22·5/73·8	3	Rattan	3	1
France	Chaize	CS. 2200	2,200/77,692	18·0/59	22·5/73·8	3-4	Rattan	4	2
Hungary	MÉM RSZ	RSZ-05	2,200/77,692	17·0/55·77	20·7/68	1-3	Rattan	2-4	2
South Africa	Flamboyant	AX7-65	1,840/65,000	16·0/52·5	20·0/65·6	3	Rattan	2	1
South Africa	Flamboyant	AX7-77M	2,180/77,000	16·0/52·5	20·0/65·6	3	Rattan	2	1

NA: Not applicable (gas balloon)

HOT-AIR (AX) AND GAS BALLOON (AA) DATA

Country	Company	Model	Volume m³/cu ft	Diameter m/ft	Height m/ft	Crew	Basket	Fuel Cylinders	Burners
United Kingdom	Cameron	O-65	1,840/64,980	16·15/53	18·0/59	3	Willow/Cane	3	1
United Kingdom	Cameron	O-77	2,190/77,339	17·07/56	18·9/62	4	Willow/Cane	4	1
United Kingdom	Cameron	N-65	1,840/64,980	16·15/53	18·0/59	3	Willow/Cane	3	1
United Kingdom	Cameron	Viva-65	1,840/64,980	16·15/53	18·0/59	3	Willow/Cane	2	1
United Kingdom	Cameron	Viva-77	2,190/77,339	17·07/56	18·9/62	4	Willow/Cane	2	1
United Kingdom	Cameron	N-77	2,190/77,339	17·07/56	18·9/62	4	Willow/Cane	4	1
United Kingdom	Thunder & Colt	65 Series 1	1,840/64,980	16·18/53·1	17·19/56·4	3	Wicker/Cane	2-3	1
United Kingdom	Thunder & Colt	69A	1,954/69,000	16·31/53·5	17·31/56·8	3	Wicker/Cane	2-3	1
United Kingdom	Thunder & Colt	77 Series 1	2,190/77,339	16·79/55·1	18·11/59·4	4	Wicker/Cane	2-3	1-2
United Kingdom	Thunder & Colt	77A	2,190/77,339	17·01/55·8	18·29/60	4	Wicker/Cane	2-3	1-2
United States	Adams	A50S	1,755/61,977	15·24/50	18·59/61	3	Rattan	1-4	1
United States	Adams	A55	2,123/74,973	16·76/55	19·51/64	3	Rattan	1-4	1
United States	Avian	Falcon II	1,700/60,035	15·54/51	18·6/61	1-3	Wicker	2	1
United States	Balloon Works	DragonFly 65	1,840/65,000	17·07/56	17·68/58	3-4	Wicker	3	1
United States	Balloon Works	DragonFly 650	1,840/65,000	7·07/56	17·68/58	3-4	Wicker	3	1
United States	Balloon Works	DragonFly 77	2,167/76,520	17·07/56	17·68/58	3-4	Wicker	3	1
United States	Balloon Works	DragonFly 770	2,167/76,520	17·07/56	17·68/58	3-4	Wicker	3	1
United States	Balloon Works	FireFly 65	1,840/65,000	17·07/56	17·68/58	3-4	Wicker	3	1
United States	Balloon Works	FireFly 650	1,840/65,000	17·07/56	17·68/58	3-4	Wicker	3	1
United States	Balloon Works	FireFly 77	2,167/76,520	17·07/56	17·68/58	3-4	Wicker	3	1
United States	Balloon Works	FireFly 770	2,167/76,520	17·07/56	17·68/58	3-4	Wicker	3	1
United States	Galaxy	?	2,170/76,633	17·07/56	17·68/58	3-4	Rattan/Wicker	4	1-2
United States	Raven	S-55-A	2,195/77,500	16·76/55	19·2/63	3-4	Wicker	3	1
United States	Raven	RX-7	2,195/77,500	16·76/55	19·2/63	3	Wicker	3	1
FAI CLASS AX-8 (2,200-3,000 m³; 77,692-105,944 cu ft)									
France	Chaize	CS. 3000	3,000/105,944	19·44/63·8	25·0/82	5-6	Rattan	5	2
Hungary	MÉM RSZ	RSZ-03	2,563/90,512	17·26/56·6	22·7/74·5	2-4	Rattan	3-4	2
South Africa	Flamboyant	AX8-85	2,407/85,000	18·0/59	20·0/65·6	4	Rattan	2	1
South Africa	Flamboyant	AX8-105	2,973/105,000	19·0/62·3	21·0/68·9	6	Rattan	3	2
United Kingdom	Cameron	O-84	2,380/84,047	17·68/58	19·5/64	4	Willow/Cane	4	1
United Kingdom	Cameron	N-90	2,548/90,000	17·98/59	19·81/65	4-5	Wicker	6	2
United Kingdom	Cameron	A-105	2,970/104,885	18·9/62	20·72/68	6	Willow/Cane	6	2
United Kingdom	Cameron	N-105	2,970/104,885	18·9/62	20·72/68	6	Willow/Cane	6	2
United Kingdom	Cameron	O-105	2,970/104,885	18·9/62	20·72/68	6	Willow/Cane	6	2
United Kingdom	Thunder & Colt	84 Series 1	2,380/84,047	17·3/56·8	18·41/60·4	4	Wicker/Cane	2-3	1-2
United Kingdom	Thunder & Colt	90A	2,550/90,050	17·5/57·5	17·5/57·5	5	Wicker/Cane	2-4	2
United Kingdom	Thunder & Colt	90 Series 2	2,550/90,050	17·50/57·4	18·59/61	5	Wicker/Cane	2-4	2
United Kingdom	Thunder & Colt	105 Series 1	2,970/104,885	18·44/60·5	18·44/60·5	6	Wicker/Cane	2-6	2
United Kingdom	Thunder & Colt	105A	2,970/104,885	18·90/62	19·90/65·3	6	Wicker/Cane	2-6	2
United Kingdom	Thunder & Colt	105 Series 2	2,970/104,885	18·84/61·8	19·78/64·9	6	Wicker/Cane	2-6	2
United States	ABC	Americana	2,265/80,000	—	—	—	Aluminium	2-4	2-4
United States	Adams	A55S	2,350/82,990	16·76/55	20·42/67	4	Rattan	1-4	1
United States	Adams	A60	2,973/105,000	18·59/61	22·25/73	5	Rattan	4	1-2
United States	Adams	A60S	3,370/119,000	18·59/61	22·86/75	5-6	Rattan	4	1-2
United States	Avian	Skyhawk	2,265/80,000	16·76/55	20·1/66	3-4	Wicker	3	1
United States	Avian	Turbo 8	2,973/105,000	18·29/60	21·34/70	6	Wicker	4	2
United States	Balloon Works	DragonFly 90	2,600/91,818	17·98/59	18·75/61·5	3-4	Wicker	3	1
United States	Balloon Works	DragonFly 105	2,957/104,440	18·90/62	19·51/64	4-5	Wicker	6	2
United States	Balloon Works	DragonFly 900	2,600/91,818	17·98/59	18·75/61·5	3-4	Wicker	3	1
United States	Balloon Works	DragonFly 1050	2,957/104,440	18·90/62	19·51/64	4-5	Wicker	6	2
United States	Balloon Works	FireFly 90	2,600/91,818	17·98/59	18·75/61·5	3-4	Wicker	3	1
United States	Balloon Works	FireFly 105	2,957/104,440	18·90/62	• 19·51/64	4-5	Wicker	6	2
United States	Balloon Works	FireFly 900	2,600/91,818	17·98/59	18·75/61·5	3-4	Wicker	3	1
United States	Balloon Works	FireFly 1050	2,957/104,440	18·90/62	19·51/64	4-5	Wicker	6	2
United States	Raven	S-60A	2,973/105,000	18·29/60	21·03/69	3-4	Wicker	3	2
FAI CLASS AX-9 (3,000-4,000 m³; 105,944-141,259 cu ft)									
France	Chaize	CS.4000	4,000/141,259	22·0/72·2	27·5/90·2	8	Rattan	6	2
Hungary	MÉM RSZ	RSZ-04	4,000/141,259	20/65·6	26·3/86·3	4-5	Rattan	3-6	2
United Kingdom	Cameron	A-140	3,960/139,846	20·73/68	21·95/72	8	Willow/Cane	6	2
United Kingdom	Thunder & Colt	140	3,965/140,023	20·36/66·8	20·36/66·8	8	Stainless steel/Cane*	2-6	2
United States	Adams	AB	3,540/125,000	19·51/64	23·16/76	6	Rattan	6	2
United States	Avian	Magnum IX	3,964/140,000	20·1/66	23·2/76	8	Wicker	6	2
United States	Raven	S-66A	4,000/141,259	20·1/66	23/75	8	Wicker	6	2

*T-partition format

HOT-AIR (AX) AND GAS BALLOON (AA) DATA

Country	Company	Model	Volume m³/cu ft	Diameter m/ft	Height m/ft	Crew	Basket	Fuel Cylinders	Burners
FAI CLASS AX-10 (4,000-6,000 m³; 141,259-211,888 cu ft)									
South Africa	Flamboyant	AX10-150	4,248/150,000	21·0/68·9	22·0/72·2	8	Rattan	4	2
United Kingdom	Cameron	O-160	4,530/160,000	21·0/69	22·25/73	8	Willow/Cane	6	2
United Kingdom	Cameron	N-180	5,097/180,000	27·13/89	29·57/97	9	Willow/Cane	8	3
United Kingdom	Cameron	A-210	5,947/210,000	23·77/78	24·99/82	12	Willow/Cane	8	4
United Kingdom	Thunder & Colt	160 Series 1	4,530/159,976	21·61/70·9	22·71/74·5	9	Stainless steel/Cane*	2-8	3
United Kingdom	Thunder & Colt	160A	4,530/159,976	21·70/71·2	23·01/75·5	9	Stainless steel/Cane*	2-8	3
United Kingdom	Thunder & Colt	180A	5,097/180,000	23·0/75·46	24·0/78·74	10	Stainless steel/Cane*	2-9	3
United States	Raven	S-77A	6,000/211,888	23·47/77	25·3/83	8	Wicker	6	2
FAI CLASS AX-11 (6,000-9,000 m³; 211,888-317,832 cu ft)									
United Kingdom	Thunder & Colt	240A	6,796/240,000	24·51/80·4	25·79/84·6	12	Stainless steel/Cane*	2-10	3-4
United Kingdom	Thunder & Colt	280A	7,929/280,000	(not yet certified)		13	Stainless steel/Cane*	2-11	4

*T-partition format

RPVs and TARGETS

ARGENTINA

QUIMAR

QUIMAR SA, CONSTRUCCIONES AERONÁUTICAS Y ELECTRONICAS

Gorriti, Cordoba 5000
Telephone: 005451 58485
Telex: S 1603 QUI HO AR

This company produces two drones, known as the MQ-1 Chimango and MQ-2 Bigua. The former is a licence built version of the piston engined Meteor Mirach-70 (see Italian part of this section); the latter, a turbojet powered transonic RPV, is a version of the Mirach-100 intended to have both target and RPV applications. A common automatic launcher is used for both vehicles, and for another (as yet unidentified) known as the MQ-4.

QUIMAR MQ-1 CHIMANGO

The Chimango is intended as a target for training the crews of anti-aircraft artillery and low/medium altitude surface-to-air missiles. It can be equipped with smoke or infra-red emitters in underwing pods, or can tow banner targets at the end of a 100 m (330 ft) nylon cable. The airframe is of glassfibre reinforced polyester resin, and zero-length ramp launch is by means of an MQ 8785/NNZ solid propellant rocket booster which gives 18·63 kN (4,189 lb) thrust for 0·7 s before the 53·7 kW (72 hp) piston engine takes over. The target is recovered by parachute. Onboard equipment includes a Rolido y Cabeceo autopilot and a miss distance indicator. Missions are controlled by a Meteor Alamak ground station.

DIMENSIONS, EXTERNAL: As for Mirach-70

WEIGHTS:
Mission equipment 10 kg (22 lb)
Fuel 34 kg (75 lb)
Launching weight 184 kg (406 lb)

PERFORMANCE:
Max level speed at S/L 194 knots (360 km/h; 224 mph)
Min operating altitude 200 m (656 ft)
Range 65 nm (120 km; 74·5 miles)
Max endurance 1 h

QUIMAR MQ-2 BIGUA

Two versions of the Bigua are under development. Version 1 is for use as a recoverable target, or target banner towing vehicle, in the weapons training of gunnery or missile battery crews; to evaluate new weapons systems or special equipment; and as a reconnaissance RPV trainer. Version 2 is intended to undertake such operational missions as battlefield surveillance, intermediate-range reconnaissance, target acquisition, elint, ECM, attack against sea or air targets, defence saturation, infra-red decoy, and close support.

Basic configuration is that of a sweptback low-wing monoplane with a dorsal air intake, dihedral tailplane and twin ventral fins. Construction, including control surfaces, is almost entirely of light alloy except for the wing leading-edges, fins and parachute container, which are of glassfibre reinforced polyester resin. The MQ-2 is normally launched, by JATO booster rockets, from a zero-length ramp, cruising power being provided by a 1·13 kN (253 lb st) turbojet engine. However, provision is also made for air launch from fixed-wing aircraft or helicopters, and a joint Quimar/Meteor programme was under way in 1985 to adapt the Bigua for launch from beneath the fuselage of an IA 58A Pucará close support aircraft.

The Bigua has a two-stage parachute recovery system, and is fitted with impact absorbers to cushion the landing. An inflatable airbag is provided for recovery from water. The drone is equipped with a three-axis autopilot, and can be either remotely piloted (using the Alamak ground control system) or pre-programmed when fitted with an automatic navigation kit. Real-time sensors, mounted in the nose compartment, can include low light level TV, a panoramic camera, an infra-red package, or a secure elint transceiver.

DIMENSIONS, EXTERNAL:
Wing span 1·80 m (5 ft 11 in)
Length overall 3·90 m (12 ft 9½ in)
Height overall 0·80 m (2 ft 7½ in)
Body diameter (max) 0·38 m (1 ft 3 in)

AREA:
Wings, gross 0·82 m² (8·83 sq ft)

WEIGHTS:
Sensors 40-70 kg (88-154 lb)
Max launching weight (excl boosters) 260 kg (573 lb)
Landing weight with 10 litres (2·2 Imp gallons) fuel remaining 195 kg (430 lb)

PERFORMANCE:
Max level speed 458 knots (850 km/h; 521 mph)
Ceiling 9,000 m (29,525 ft)
Range at 2,000 m (6,560 ft):
out and back 216 nm (400 km; 248 miles)
one-way mission 485 nm (900 km; 559 miles)
Endurance at max speed at 9,000 m (29,525 ft) 1 h

AUSTRALIA

GAF

GOVERNMENT AIRCRAFT FACTORIES

Fishermen's Bend, Private Bag No. 4, Post Office, Port Melbourne, Victoria 3207
Telephone: (03) 647 3111
Telex: AA 30252
OFFICERS: see Aircraft section

GAF JINDIVIK Mk 4A

The Jindivik continues to be a standard weapons target for Australia and Great Britain. Design began in March 1948, and the prototype Jindivik Mk 1 flew for the first time on 28 August 1952.

A total of 496 Jindiviks had been delivered by 1 January 1985, including 40 Mk 103BL for the UK and 12 Mk 203B for the Royal Australian Navy. These models, which are no longer in production, cater for low level trials at speeds up to 500 knots (925 km/h; 575 mph). The autopilot is the improved GEC Avionics L4 or L5, and equipment incorporates printed circuit techniques. Jindiviks have flown more than 6,600 sorties at the RAE, Llanbedr, North Wales, and in Australia; one particular Mk 3A drone (WRE 418) was destroyed after successfully completing 285 sorties at Woomera.

An improved Mk 4A Jindivik entered production in March 1981. Fifteen have been ordered by the UK, of which ten had been completed by January 1986. The Mk 4A has a rationalised electrical power supply system, integrated electronic systems, and increased speed, endurance and manoeuvring capability (up to more than 6*g*).

For low altitude work, the standard span Mk 4A is fitted with Mk 9 wingtip pods each containing two cameras, a microwave reflector and a small amount of fuel. For high altitude work, also with Mk 9 wing pods, constant chord 1·02 m (40 in) wing extension panels can be added outboard of the pods. For extra high altitude flying (with Mk 5 pods only), these panels can be replaced by 2·03 m (80 in) panels, tapered on the leading-edge. A ventral fin is fitted for high altitude and maximum turn rate configurations.

TYPE: Recoverable target drone.

AIRFRAME: Cantilever low/mid-wing monoplane. Wing section NACA 64A-106 with modified trailing-edge. Dihedral 2° 30′. Incidence 1°. Bonded multi-spar wing box with integral trailing-edge of aluminium alloy. Replaceable foam filled aluminium alloy leading-edge. Interspar torsion box forms integral fuel tank. Aluminium alloy monocoque flaps and ailerons. Ailerons fitted with inset geared tab and driven by GAF designed twin-motor servo. Flaps operated pneumatically. Aluminium alloy semi-monocoque fuselage. Front portion carries all control equipment, autopilot and telemetry equipment. Pitot head is mounted on nose probe. Moulded glassfibre honeycomb canopy, which lifts off for access to equipment, also forms ram type air intake. Rear end of front fuselage and front end of centre-fuselage form bay for all mission equipment. Centre-fuselage also houses retractable landing skid. Removable rear fuselage carries engine and jetpipe. Cantilever multi-spar light alloy tailplane. Elevators, with inset geared tabs, driven by GAF designed twin-motor servo actuator, operable on one motor. Fin is polyurethane foam filled light alloy skin, bonded to a single spar. No rudder. Ventral fin in max turn rate and high altitude configurations. Pneumatically extended, manually retracted (on ground) central skid. Pneumatic jack acts as shock absorber. Steel auxiliary skids at wingtips. See also paragraph on 'Launch and Recovery'.

POWER PLANT: One Rolls-Royce Viper Mk 201 turbojet engine, rated at 12·36 kN (2,780 lb st). Engine relight capability in the event of flameout. Flexible rubber main fuselage fuel tank, capacity 291 litres (64 Imp gallons), and two integral wing tanks, total capacity 173 litres (38 Imp gallons). Mk 4A has additional 91 litre (20 Imp gallon) fuselage tank. Mk 9 pods each hold 86 litres (19 Imp gallons). Total possible fuel capacity 727 litres (160 Imp gallons). Oil capacity 4·5 litres (1 Imp gallon).

LAUNCH AND RECOVERY: Take-off from aircraft trolley, steered by gyro and servo-controlled nosewheel which responds to signals from ground controller. Aircraft/trolley combination accelerates under normal jet power with flaps retracted and with aircraft set at negative incidence. When unstick speed is reached, aircraft flaps are lowered rapidly. Rotation of aircraft initiates trolley release system and the aircraft climbs away. When Jindivik is in approach run, flaps and skid are selected down for landing. On touchdown, at approx 120 knots (222 km/h; 138 mph), a 'sting' extended below main skid rotates on impact and initiates rapid retraction of flaps. Fuel supply terminated by radio command.

GUIDANCE AND CONTROL: Radio control equipment comprises two UHF receivers and GAF auxiliary control unit. GEC Avionics flight control computer, with gyroscope. Telemetry equipment consists of Australian designed transmitter and data unit.

SYSTEMS: No hydraulic system. Non-regenerative pneumatic system: air stored at 138 bars (2,000 lb/sq in) in power pack which supplies air to flaps and landing skid at reduced pressure of 39·6 bars (575 lb/sq in). Engine driven brushless DC generator, rated at 9 kW at 30V DC. In event of generator failure, a 24V DC battery provides limited power for essential control functions. Automatic orbit and/or destruct systems provided, consistent with range safety requirements.

EQUIPMENT: Transponders and microwave reflectors for trials of active, semi-active or beam riding missiles. Heat sources, including infra-red flare packs mounted on rear of fuselage, can be fitted to provide low-frequency IR output. Transponders in X, S and C bands can be fitted for target acquisition and to enable Jindivik to be tracked to greater range. Provision for recoverable towed target to be carried under each wing. These tow bodies can carry either active radar, in-flight-commanded IR flares, or forward looking Luneberg lens. They can be towed at 15-150 m (50-500 ft) behind aircraft; recovery by electric winch mounted in centre of fuselage. Other types of special tow may also be carried. Cameras fitted with wide angle lenses are carried in wingtip pods, with all-round viewing capability. Variants are Mk 5 pod with cameras only and Mk 9 with cameras, fuel and provision for fitment of microwave reflectors (Luneberg lenses) in leading-edge and/or trailing-edge radomes. By fitting rearward looking prisms to the lower cameras they can record missile performance when Tonic towed targets are used. To simulate different types of aircraft by varying the apparent radar cross-section, Plessey Microwave Ltd has developed a semi-active artificial radar target (SART Mk IV) for operation in a towed configuration with Jindivik as the towing aircraft.

DIMENSIONS, EXTERNAL:
Wing span:
short span, low altitude 6·32 m (20 ft 8·99 in)
extended, high altitude 7·92 m (26 ft 6 in)
extended, extra high altitude 9·78 m (32 ft 1·4 in)
Length overall: incl nose probe 8·15 m (26 ft 8¾ in)
excl nose probe 7·11 m (23 ft 3¾ in)
Height overall, skid extended 2·08 m (6 ft 9·85 in)

AREAS:
Wings, gross: short span 7·06 m² (76·0 sq ft)
extended span, high altitude 9·48 m² (102·0 sq ft)
extended span, extra high altitude 10·68 m² (115·0 sq ft)

WEIGHTS:
Weight empty, equipped (min) 1,315 kg (2,900 lb)
Max payload: short-span version 249 kg (550 lb)
extended-span versions 181 kg (400 lb)
Max T-O weight:
short span, Mk 9 wing pods 1,814 kg (4,000 lb)
high altitude, Mk 9 wing pods 1,814 kg (4,000 lb)
extra high altitude, Mk 5 wing pods 1,496 kg (3,300 lb)

PERFORMANCE (A: short span, Mk 9 pods; B: high altitude, Mk 9 pods; C: extra high altitude, Mk 5 pods):
Max level speed at S/L 540 knots (1,000 km/h; 622 mph)
Min operating height: A 12 m (40 ft)
Max operational ceiling: A 15,850 m (52,000 ft)
B 17,985 m (59,000 ft)
C 19,810 m (65,000 ft)
Time to max operational ceiling: A 26 min
B 30 min
C 34 min
Typical max on-station endurance: A 1 h 35 min
B 2 h 0 min
C 2 h 5 min
Max range: A 825 nm (1,529 km; 950 miles)
B 1,125 nm (2,085 km; 1,295 miles)
C 1,160 nm (2,150 km; 1,335 miles)

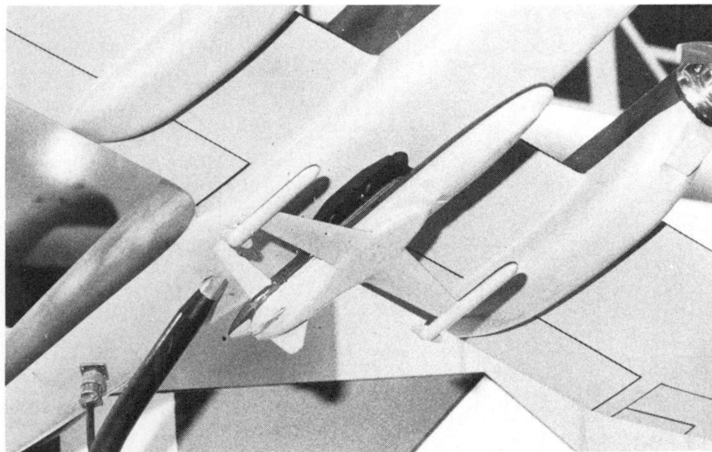

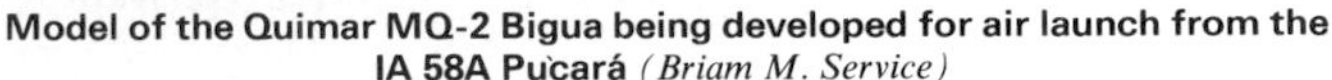

Model of the Quimar MQ-2 Bigua being developed for air launch from the IA 58A Pucará *(Briam M. Service)*

First of two prototypes (N11-800) of the GAF Jindivik Mk 4A

BRAZIL

AEROMOT

AERONAVES E MOTORES LTDA

Aeroporto International, Salgado Filho (PO Box 8031), 9000 Porto Alegre, RS
Telephone: 0512 423344
Telex: 511911
President: Claudio Miguel Barreto Viana
Technical Director: João Claudio Jotz

AEROMOT K1 AM

Produced by Aeromot for the Brazilian Navy, the K1 AM is a modified version of the Northrop Basic Training Target (which see). It is platform launched, fitted with an autopilot, and powered by a piston engine with a two-blade tractor propeller. A large pod at each wingtip houses a radar reflector. See Addenda for further details.

Dimensions, external:
- Wing span over reflector pods 4·00 m (13 ft 1½ in)
- Length overall 3·80 m (12 ft 5½ in)

Weight:
- Weight empty 143 kg (315 lb)

Performance:
- Max level speed at S/L 195 knots (360 km/h; 224 mph)
- Stalling speed 68 knots (125 km/h; 78 mph)
- Ceiling 4,000 m (13,125 ft)
- GCS control range 27 nm (50 km; 31 miles)
- Endurance at S/L 50 min

CBT

COMPANHIA BRASILEIRA DE TRATORES

Caixa Postal 376, 13560 São Carlos, SP

CBT BQM-1 BR

Brazil's first remotely piloted vehicle, the BQM-1 BR was designed and built by the Aeronautical Division of CBT, a long established tractor manufacturer; the power plant was developed by the PMO-Divisão de Mecânica (Mechanics Division) of the CTA (Aerospace Technical Centre) and manufactured by CBT.

General appearance of the BQM-1 BR is shown in an accompanying illustration. Missions envisaged included aerial target, tactical reconnaissance (with TV camera), and attack; a version for civil applications, including crop-dusting, was mentioned.

The BQM-1 BR was intended to make its first flight in 1983, but no confirmation of this, or any other news of the RPV, has been received.

Type: Multi-purpose mini-RPV.

Airframe: All-metal (light alloy) cantilever low-wing monoplane. Wings have 3° dihedral, 4° incidence, and are sweptback 33° over most of span, increasing to 55° at root. Conventional semi-monocoque fuselage, of circular cross-section. Cantilever fixed incidence tailplane, with 5° dihedral and 30° leading-edge sweep. Fin sweptback 45°.

Power Plant: One 0·30 kN (67·5 lb st) PMO/CBT Tietê single-stage centrifugal flow turbojet engine, mounted in nacelle on top of rear fuselage at base of fin.

Launch and Recovery: Takes off on tricycle type landing gear which is jettisoned after take-off.

Guidance and Control: Radio command guidance system, using a six-channel VHF-FM radio with a range of 11 nm (20 km; 12·5 miles).

Dimensions, external:
- Wing span 3·18 m (10 ft 5¼ in)
- Wing chord: at root 0·91 m (3 ft 0 in)
- at tip 0·28 m (11 in)
- Length overall 3·89 m (12 ft 9¼ in)
- Fuselage: Length 3·50 m (11 ft 5¾ in)
- Max diameter 0·28 m (11 in)
- Height overall 1·28 m (4 ft 2½ in)
- Tailplane span 1·10 m (3 ft 7¼ in)

Weight:
- Max T-O weight 93 kg (205 lb)

Performance (estimated):
- Max level speed at 6,100 m (20,000 ft) Mach 0·7
- Max endurance 45 min

CTA

CENTRO TÉCNICO AEROESPACIAL

PO Box 6001, 12200 São José dos Campos, SP
Telephone: 0123 21 1311

The CTA is developing a small, propeller driven RPV of shoulder-wing configuration, having a box-section fuselage, twin tailbooms supporting a twin tail unit, and non-retractable tricycle landing gear. No other details were known at the time of going to press. See Addenda for illustration.

IGAE

INDUSTRIA GAÚCHA DE AERONAVES ESPECIAIS LTDA

Rua Padre Henrique Koelher 87, 90000 Porto Alegre, RS

IGAE LAH/EB

The designation of this delta-winged mini-RPV is derived from the names of its joint designers (1st Lt Luis Arcari and engineer Airton Hoch) and the fact that it was developed for the Brazilian Army (Exército Brasileiro). It is powered by a Japanese 2·6 kW (3·5 hp) OS Max 1·08 model aircraft engine, installed in the nose and driving a two-blade fixed-pitch wooden propeller, with a 1 litre (0·22 Imp gallon) fuel tank. The LAH/EB has a tricycle landing gear, no horizontal tail surfaces, and is operated under line-of-sight radio control. See Addenda for photograph.

Dimensions, external:
- Wing span 1·50 m (4 ft 11 in)
- Length overall 1·20 m (3 ft 11¼ in)

Performance:
- Endurance 35 min

CANADA

BOEING

BOEING OF CANADA LTD (Winnipeg Division)

99 Murray Park Road, Winnipeg, Manitoba R3J 3M6
Telephone: (204) 888 2300
Telex: 07 57309
Technical Sales Manager: Robert D. Palmer

Boeing of Canada also manufactures the DRES Robot series and Targetair TATS 102 target systems, described under those headings in this section.

BOEING 'HIND-D' TARGET

Eight prototypes have been ordered of this one-fifth scale representation of the Mil Mi-24 'Hind-D' attack helicopter, the first one being flown in mid-1985. It was developed to simulate both attack and evasive manoeuvres by the Mi-24, but modular front and rear fuselage sections can be replaced with others to represent any modern single main rotor helicopter.

The target was originally developed, and the first prototype manufactured, by Gorham Model Products of Calabasas, California. Gorham is now teamed with Boeing Canada (which holds a world product mandate for the target) to carry out jointly the advanced development of the system.

Type: Recoverable miniature helicopter target.

Airframe: Glassfibre fuselage shell with replaceable front and rear sections. Two-blade main and tail rotors, with simple but reliable drive train. Non-retractable tricycle landing gear.

Power Plant: One 19·5 kW (26 hp) 360 cc Normalair-Garrett two-cylinder piston engine. Fuel for 30 min operation initially.

Guidance and Control: PCM radio control system. Remote flight operations include jinking, hovering and 'S' turns in slow forward flight. Rate gyro to assist yaw control. Control system may be developed to permit fully automatic flight.

Dimensions, external:
- Fuselage: Length 3·35 m (11 ft 0 in)
- Max width 0·76 m (2 ft 6 in)
- Height overall 1·07 m (3 ft 6 in)

Weights:
- Max payload 30·5 kg (67 lb)
- Normal T-O weight (incl 7·7 kg; 17 lb ballast) 47·5 kg (105 lb)
- Max permissible T-O weight 75 kg (165 lb)

Performance (required by specification):
- Max level speed at 5-25 m (15-80 ft) above S/L 30 knots (55 km/h; 34 mph)
- Min ascent/descent velocity at 5-25 m (15-80 ft) above S/L 55 m (180 ft)/min
- Endurance 1 h

BOEING (CONTINENTAL) MiG-27 'FLOGGER-D' TARGET

Boeing of Canada is producing the C125M and other scale versions of the MiG-27 'Flogger-D' target designed by Continental RPVs of Barstow, California. Details of these can be found under the Continental heading in the US part of this section. The Boeing versions are updated with electronic control and stability systems, have increased flight duration, and are marketed as a low-cost target aircraft recognition training system (TARTS).

BOEING DRAGON FLY

The Dragon Fly was designed in 1980 by Boeing Com-

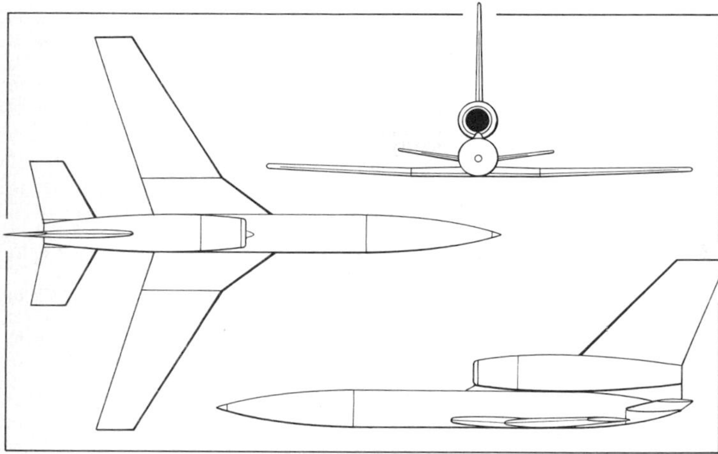

Brazil's first RPV: the CBT BQM-1 BR *(Michael A. Badrocke)*

Canadair CL-89 airborne surveillance/target acquisition drone system

Canadair CL-227 Sentinel (Phase 2) surveillance/target acquisition RPV taking off from its mobile take-off and landing platform

Boeing of Canada 'Hind-D' target

mercial Airplane Company in Seattle, originally as a maritime RPV to provide expendable sea-launched surveillance in various tactical situations. It can be stored complete within a 5·33 × 1·12 × 0·86 m (17 ft 6 in × 3 ft 8 in × 2 ft 10 in) container. Payloads are mounted in port and starboard pods beneath the forward fuselage.

The programme was later transferred to Boeing Canada, which in 1986 had suspended marketing pending completion of further development and updating of the system. A description of the original version appeared under the Boeing Canada heading in the 1985-86 *Jane's*.

CANADAIR

CANADAIR LTD

PO Box 6087, Montreal, Quebec H3C 3G9
Telephone: (514) 744 1511
OFFICERS: see Aircraft section

In addition to its work on manned aircraft, Canadair is developing or producing various drone systems, including the CL-289 described in the International section.

CANADAIR CL-89

NATO designation: AN/USD-501
British Army name: Midge

The Canadair CL-89 (AN/USD-501) airborne surveillance drone system evolved from a need of the western Allied armed forces for an intelligence gathering device for battlefield commanders; details of its early history can be found in the 1977-78 and earlier editions of *Jane's*.

With a very high probability of survival against all known air defence systems, the CL-89 can acquire timely and accurate battlefield intelligence using its photographic and infra-red linescanning equipment. The system, consisting of the air vehicles plus the related ground support and operational maintenance equipment, is totally integrated, mobile, and independent of such external services as electrical power supplies.

The CL-89 system is in service with the armed forces of the UK, the Federal Republic of Germany, France and Italy. More than 500 had been delivered by the beginning of 1985.

TYPE: Recoverable airborne surveillance drone system.

AIRFRAME: Cylindrical metal body, with curved nosecone and tapering tailcone. Three detachable dorsal packs for forward and rear landing bags and flare container; two detachable ventral packs for sensor equipment and parachute recovery system. Four rectangular stub wings at rear of body, in cruciform arrangement at 45° to horizontal and vertical centrelines. Upper pair fold out of way when landing airbags are inflated. Ailerons on port upper and starboard lower stub wings. Two pairs of foreplanes aft of nosecone on horizontal and vertical centrelines, for pitch and yaw trim respectively.

POWER PLANT: One 0·56 kN (125 lb st) Williams International WR2-6 turbojet engine, with variable exhaust nozzle, installed in tailcone aft of wings. Air intake duct on each side of fuselage, forward of wings. Fuel and oil tanks in central body compartment, forward of air intakes. One 22·24 kN (5,000 lb st) average thrust PERME Wagtail booster rocket motor, attached to body of drone by three V shaped thrust arms and cable.

LAUNCH AND RECOVERY: Launched from truck mounted zero-length ramp; booster separates automatically after 2·5 s of flight. Irvin GB recovery system, for release within speed bracket of 310-440 knots (575-815 km/h; 357-506 mph), comprises a 0·91 m (3 ft) diameter flat ribbon drogue 'chute and 5·99 m (19 ft 8 in) diameter flat ribbon main parachute. After final positioning by ground homing beacon, drone is slowed by drogue parachute to approx 61 m (200 ft)/s, when main parachute deploys. Drone is then inverted, and forward and rear airbags are inflated and deployed automatically to absorb landing impact.

GUIDANCE AND CONTROL: Flight path, altitude and sensor on/off commands are controlled by preset programmer which receives information from onboard air distance measuring unit (ADMU) and combines this with preset programme to control flight path. Ground homing beacon positions drone in final stages of flight to ensure accuracy of landing.

EQUIPMENT: Engine driven alternator for electrical power during flight. Two main sensor systems currently in use: Carl Zeiss KRb8/24C camera system and British Aerospace Type 201 infra-red linescan system. Aft of sensor pack is compartment for fuel and oil tanks. Compartment aft of tanks has ventral forward-hinged door providing access to engine start air connector, and dorsal pack containing 12 photoflares just forward of rear landing bag container. Final cylindrical compartment houses rear landing bag container and parachute recovery pack, between dorsal and ventral pairs of wings respectively. Other onboard equipment includes forward and rear landing airbags; air distance measuring unit (ADMU); programmer; static power converter; homing receiver; amplifier; flash detector; directional and vertical gyros; transponder antenna; and air bottle to inflate airbags.

DIMENSIONS, EXTERNAL:
- Span: wings — 0·94 m (3 ft 1 in)
  - foreplanes — 0·48 m (1 ft 7 in)
- Length overall, excl nose probe:
  - with booster — 3·73 m (12 ft 3 in)
  - without booster — 2·60 m (8 ft 6½ in)
- Body diameter — 0·33 m (1 ft 1 in)

WEIGHTS:
- Weight dry (excl fuel, oil and mission equipment) — 78·2 kg (172·4 lb)
- Mission equipment — 17-20 kg (37·5-44 lb)
- Max launching weight: with booster — 156 kg (343 lb)
  - without booster — 108 kg (238 lb)

PERFORMANCE:
- Max speed — 400 knots (741 km/h; 460 mph)
- Max operating altitude — 3,050 m (10,000 ft)
- Max range: standard — 65 nm (120 km; 74 miles)
  - with extended range fuel tank — 75 nm (140 km; 87 miles)

CANADAIR CL-227 SENTINEL

The CL-227 was designed as a highly survivable real-time surveillance and target acquisition RPV for use at medium range. It has VTOL capability, and can translate to horizontal flight or hover. It is launched either from the ground or from a mobile platform. The CL-227 can be landed free, or winched down to a simple landing device to provide an automatic landing capability. It can also fly tethered or untethered from small surface craft. With a CL-227 on a 200 m (655 ft) tether, the craft's horizon would be extended to 26 nm (48 km; 30 miles). With a 500 m (1,640 ft) tether, the range of view would be 43 nm (80 km; 50 miles).

Phase 1 of the system development programme utilised a prototype vehicle powered by a Wankel rotary combustion engine, as described in earlier editions of *Jane's*. This prototype made its first flight, tethered, on 25 August 1978.

The Phase 2 vehicle was slightly larger, carried a bigger load of mission equipment, and was powered by a 24 kW (32 shp) Williams International WR34-15-2 turboshaft engine. Flight demonstrations of the Phase 2 configuration took place in Montreal in October and December 1981, the first completely untethered flight being made on 14 December. Further flight trials in a quasi-tactical environment were conducted at Suffield Canadian Forces Base, Alberta, during January/February 1982, culminating in a series of demonstration flights for NATO observers in March 1982. In May 1983 the Sentinel was demonstrated to representatives of the US Army and NATO.

The full scale development Phase 3 started in 1984 and is due for completion in early 1988. Ten air vehicles, of near production standard, plus two ground control stations and six mission payloads, are being produced for customer evaluation. The air vehicles are each powered by a Williams International 37·3 kW (50 shp) WTS-34 turboshaft engine and have a more sophisticated navigation and control system than the Phase 2 version. Much attention has been paid in the Phase 3 design to increased reliability and survivability. First (tethered) flight by a Phase 3 air vehicle is scheduled for early 1987.

The Canadian government agreed on 7 May 1985 to share initial funding of the final development phase, which could lead to the start of full production in 1988.

The CL-227 has a peanut shaped body made of composite materials, housing the power plant and fuel in the upper segment, with the sensors, data link and autopilot in the lower segment. A non-retractable skid landing gear is fitted. Two Kevlar three-blade contra-rotating rigid rotors/propellers, mounted amidships, provide the lift and attitude control, the main gearbox having a single input from the engine and twin outputs to the rotors. The Phase 3 vehicles are each equipped with a daylight TV camera with zoom lens. Sensors can include daylight or low light level TV, a laser designator, thermal imager, radiation detector or decoy equipment; a starter/alternator provides 1kW of electrical power for all onboard equipment.

DIMENSIONS:
- Rotor diameter (each) 2·54 m (8 ft 4 in)
- Height overall 1·64 m (5 ft 4½ in)
- Body diameter (max) 0·64 m (2 ft 1 in)

AREA:
- Rotor discs (each) 5·17 m² (55·6 sq ft)

WEIGHTS:
- *Mission equipment (typical) 31 kg (68 lb)
- *Fuel weight (typical) 52 kg (115 lb)
- Max T-O weight 175 kg (386 lb)

* *various payload/fuel combinations possible within 83 kg (183 lb) combined total*

PERFORMANCE:
- Max level speed 70 knots (130 km/h; 81 mph)
- Max forward and vertical rate of climb at 1,500 m (4,920 ft) 180 m (591 ft)/min
- Max operating altitude 3,000 m (9,850 ft)
- Typical operating radius 27 nm (50 km; 31 miles)
- Typical mission endurance at 500 m (1,640 ft) 3-4 h

DRES

DEFENCE RESEARCH ESTABLISHMENT SUFFIELD

Ralston, Alberta T0J 2N0

HEAD OF PROGRAMME SUPPORT OFFICE:
B. G. Laidlaw

PRODUCTION: Boeing of Canada Ltd (Winnipeg Division), 99 Murray Park Road, Winnipeg, Manitoba R3J 3M6

Telephone: (204) 888 2300

Telex: 07 57309

TECHNICAL SALES MANAGER: Robert D. Palmer

One of the Defence Research Laboratories of the Canadian Department of National Defence, DRES has been responsible for the Robot series of aerial targets, including the Robot-5 and Robot-9 rocket boosted ballistic targets. Its latest design is the Robot-X, which is built for DRES by the Winnipeg Division of Boeing of Canada Ltd.

DRES ROBOT-X

Newest and most sophisticated addition to the Robot family, the Robot-X is intended primarily to simulate a low-altitude anti-ship missile or invader aircraft, able to exercise point defence missile systems such as Sea Sparrow. It can also be used as a lookdown/shootdown target for aircraft, or as a low level air defence target for ground forces.

Ten Robot-Xs have been ordered. First flight was scheduled to take place at DRES during the first quarter of 1986.

TYPE: Recoverable rocket powered target drone.

AIRFRAME: Bullet shaped body, sweptback rear-mounted wings with endplate fins, and sweptback, all-moving nose-mounted foreplanes; modular construction, entirely of composite materials. Wings have a shockless symmetrical section, 37° sweepback at quarter-chord, and no anhedral or dihedral. Foreplanes and ailerons actuated by Simmonds Precision electric servo. No landing gear.

POWER PLANT: Nineteen 2·75 in RPU-3 rocket motors, fired sequentially to achieve over-the-radar-horizon ranges.

LAUNCH AND RECOVERY: Rocket launch (see preceding paragraph); normally surface launched, but air or seaborne launch optional. Parachute recovery system.

GUIDANCE AND CONTROL: Pre-programmed manoeuvres using onboard three-axis digital autopilot.

MISSION EQUIPMENT: Payload capability for miss distance scoring system, chaff dispenser, infra-red flares or radar or visual augmentation devices. 28V battery supply for DC power.

DIMENSIONS, EXTERNAL:
- Wing span 2·40 m (7 ft 10½ in)
- Wing aspect ratio 4·6
- Foreplane span 1·10 m (3 ft 7¼ in)
- Length overall 3·40 m (11 ft 2 in)
- Length of fuselage 2·80 m (9 ft 2¼ in)
- Body diameter (max) 0·415 m (1 ft 4¼ in)

AREAS:
- Wings, gross 1·25 m² (13·45 sq ft)
- Foreplanes, total 0·35 m² (3·77 sq ft)

WEIGHTS AND LOADING:
- Max payload 22·7 kg (50 lb)
- Max launching weight 250 kg (550 lb)
- Max wing loading 200 kg/m² (41 lb/sq ft)

PERFORMANCE (surface launch):
- Never-exceed speed Mach 0·95
- Max level speed at S/L Mach 0·85
- Operating altitude (surface launch):
  - min 30 m (100 ft)
  - max 4,575 m (15,000 ft)
- Max range at S/L 21 nm (40 km; 25 miles)
- Endurance at S/L 6 min
- Max endurance 30 min

TARGETAIR

TARGETAIR LTD

RR4, Moncton, New Brunswick E1C 8J8

PRODUCTION AND MARKETING: Boeing of Canada Ltd (Winnipeg Division), 99 Murray Park Road, Winnipeg, Manitoba R3J 3M6

Telephone: (204) 888 2300

Telex: 07 57309

TECHNICAL SALES MANAGER: Robert D. Palmer

TARGETAIR TATS 102

The TATS 102 aerial target system was designed and developed by Targetair for Canadian Forces close-range weapons training; it is manufactured under licence, and marketed, by the Winnipeg Division of Boeing of Canada Ltd.

The air vehicle is a low-wing monoplane of typical 'model aeroplane' appearance, built of glassfibre, wood and foam plastics, and is powered by a 13·8 kW (18·5 hp) 100 cc modified Yamaha piston engine. Fuel capacity is 8·2 litres (1·8 Imp gallons). The target is catapult launched, and can be recovered by parachute or fitted with wheels or skids for conventional landing. It is controlled using a binocular based ground control system to a maximum range of 3·2 nm (6 km; 3·7 miles). A light or a 4·5 litre (1 Imp gallon) smoke canister can be carried for visual augmentation. The vehicle is also equipped with a Doppler miss distance scoring system and a 9A electrical power source.

DIMENSIONS, EXTERNAL:
- Wing span 3·35 m (11 ft 0 in)
- Length overall 3·05 m (10 ft 0 in)
- Height overall 0·29 m (11¼ in)

WEIGHTS:
- Basic weight empty 29·5 kg (65 lb)
- Max T-O/launching weight 35·5 kg (78 lb)

PERFORMANCE:
- Max speed in dive 239 knots (444 km/h; 276 mph)
- Max level speed 130 knots (241 km/h; 150 mph)
- Stalling speed 31 knots (57 km/h; 35 mph)
- Max rate of climb at S/L 305 m (1,000 ft)/min
- T-O distance: on wheels 152 m (500 ft)
  - on launcher 12 m (38 ft)
- Landing distance:
  - on wheels 152-305 m (500-1,000 ft)
  - on skids 152 m (500 ft)
- Radio range: whip antenna 1·6 nm (2·9 km; 1·8 miles)
  - linear amp and dipole antenna 7·8 nm (14·5 km; 9 miles)
- Endurance of drone: at full throttle 1 h 15 min
  - at econ power setting 1 h 45 min
- Max battery life after full charge 2 h

ZENAIR

ZENAIR LTD

King Road, Nobleton, Ontario L0G 1N0

Telephone: (416) 859 4556

PRESIDENT: Christophe Heintz

ZENAIR RPV-007

Combining simple and proven construction methods with a well known small power plant, Zenair has designed the RPV-007 pod and boom mini-RPV primarily for such civilian surveillance missions as fishery, coastguard and ice patrol, search and rescue, forest firewatch and pipeline patrol. It has sufficient inbuilt flexibility to perform many other civilian and military reconnaissance or associated missions. Features include simplicity of assembly and operation, low acquisition and operating costs, and an exceptionally good all-round 'view' for the nose mounted sensors.

TYPE: Recoverable surveillance mini-RPV.

AIRFRAME: Low-wing monoplane, with dihedral on outer panels; latter can be folded upward to facilitate storage. Pod type fuselage nacelle, accommodating mission payload at front and engine at rear. Twin tailbooms, each with sweptback fin. Two-axis aerodynamic control (ailerons and one-piece elevator); no rudders. Standard landing gear has 25 cm (10 in) diameter mainwheels and small tailskid. Ski or float gear available optionally. Entire airframe is bolted together from simple components, none of which is more that 1·83 m (6 ft) long.

POWER PLANT: One 20 kW (27 hp) Rotax 277 single-cylinder two-stroke engine, with hand starting; reduction drive to a two-blade fixed-pitch pusher propeller. Two fuel tanks, combined capacity 45·5 litres (10 Imp gallons).

LAUNCH AND RECOVERY: Conventional T-O and landing. Net recovery optional.

EQUIPMENT: According to mission. Payload in vibration damped nose compartment which offers a sensor field of 'view' of 300° in horizontal plane and 270° in vertical plane.

DIMENSIONS, EXTERNAL:
- Wing span 5·49 m (18 ft 0 in)
- Wing aspect ratio 6·0
- Width, wings folded 2·13 m (7 ft 0 in)
- Length overall 3·66 m (12 ft 0 in)
- Fuselage: Max width 0·61 m (2 ft 0 in)
- Height: over tail fins 1·70 m (5 ft 7 in)
  - overall (wings folded) 2·10 m (6 ft 10¾ in)
- Tailplane span (incl fins) 1·83 m (6 ft 0 in)
- Propeller diameter 1·52 m (5 ft 0 in)

AREAS:
- Wings, gross 5·02 m² (54·0 sq ft)
- Horizontal tail surfaces (total) 1·39 m² (15·0 sq ft)

WEIGHTS AND LOADINGS:
- Weight empty 90·7 kg (200 lb)
- Max T-O weight 181·4 kg (400 lb)
- Max wing loading 36·14 kg/m² (7·41 lb/sq ft)
- Max power loading 9·02 kg/kW (14·81 lb/hp)

PERFORMANCE (at max T-O weight):
- Max level speed 104 knots (193 km/h; 120 mph)
- Cruising speed:
  - 75% power 95 knots (177 km/h; 110 mph)
  - 60% power 87 knots (161 km/h; 100 mph)
- Stalling speed 35 knots (65 km/h; 40 mph)
- Max rate of climb at S/L 396 m (1,300 ft)/min
- Ceiling 4,270 m (14,000 ft)
- T-O and landing run (wheel gear, hard surface) 85 m (280 ft)
- *g* limits: ±6 vertical
  - ±10 horizontal (net retrieval)

DRES Robot-X, built by Boeing of Canada

Targetair TATS 102 aerial target on launcher

Fuselage of the pilotless conversion of the Zenair Cricket (see 1985-86 *Jane's* for details)

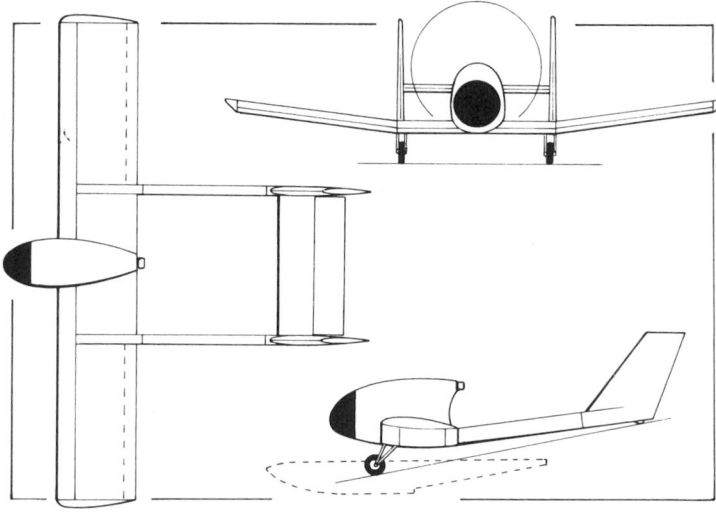

General arrangement of the Zenair RPV-007 *(Michael A. Badrocke)*

CSIF (Changcheng) B-2 glassfibre target drone on its zero-length launcher

NAI ChangKong 1C (CK1C) jet powered recoverable target drone *(Wang Lue)*

CHINA
(PEOPLE'S REPUBLIC)

CSIF

CHANGCHENG SCIENTIFIC INSTRUMENTATION FACTORY

PO Box 2351, Beijing
Telephone: 596291
PRESIDENT/CHIEF ENGINEER: Zhuang Zi Xin

CSIF B-2

Displayed at the Guangzhou Fair in April 1982, the B-2 radio controlled target drone has a compact, rigid airframe constructed of lightweight GRP/honeycomb sandwich, is fitted with conventional three-axis control surfaces, and can be launched from various kinds of surface using a zero-length launcher and rocket assisted take-off. Onboard avionics include the 3W radio command guidance system, an autopilot, heading/azimuth/altitude/distance telemetry, and a number of safety devices. Frequencies used are 49·525MHz (remote control) and 129MHz (telemetry).

Designed for weapon system training and gunnery practice, the B-2 appears to be a variant of the BJ7104 manufactured by the Yuhe Machine Factory (which see) in Nanjing. It is said to be simple to operate, requiring a minimum of crew training. In this configuration operational equipment comprises two towed targets, plus four other devices which give a realistic representation of descending paratroops. The B-2 can also be modified to extend the range of applications, according to individual user requirements.

POWER PLANT: One 12 kW (16 hp) Huosai-16 flat-four two-stroke engine, with pull cord starting, driving a two-blade fixed-pitch wooden propeller. Fuel is a mixture of automobile gasoline and lubrication oil.

DIMENSIONS, EXTERNAL:
- Wing span: 2·70 m (8 ft 10¼ in)
- Length overall: 2·55 m (8 ft 4½ in)
- Height overall: 0·60 m (1 ft 11½ in)

WEIGHTS:
- Fuel: 6 kg (13·2 lb)
- Max launching weight: 56 kg (123·5 lb)

PERFORMANCE:
- Max level speed at 1,000 m (3,280 ft): 119-129 knots (220-240 km/h; 137-149 mph)
- Max rate of climb at S/L: 480-600 m (1,575-1,968 ft)/min
- Max controllable range: 10·75 nm (20 km; 12·5 miles)
- Endurance: 1 h

NAI

NANJING AERONAUTICAL INSTITUTE (Department of RPV Research)

29 Yudaojei Street, Nanjing, Jiangsu Province
Telephone: 41191 and 46443
Telex: 34155 NAINJ CN
PRESIDENT OF NAI: Prof Yu Chenye

DIRECTOR OF AIRCRAFT GENERAL DESIGN GROUP:
Wang Lue

NAI CHANGKONG 1C

The Nanjing Aeronautical Institute began its research work for this series of unmanned aircraft at the end of the 1960s, and finalised the design of a CK1 prototype in late 1976. In the following year it developed a version with underwing equipment pods, known as the CK1A, and in 1982 replaced these pods with non-jettisonable auxiliary fuel tanks, the designation then becoming CK1B.

The definitive version, tested successfully in the Autumn of 1984, is the ChangKong 1C or CK1C. This is described as the first high-manoeuvrability pilotless aircraft researched and developed by the People's Republic of China, and subsequent test flights have demonstrated its ability to meet requirements for use as an aerial target for various types of missile, including a capability for high-manoeuvre flights at bank angles of 70-77°.

The following description applies to the CK1C. Its overall configuration, which outwardly resembles that of the Lavochkin La-17 (see USSR RPVs section of the 1977-78 *Jane's*), is shown in the accompanying illustration.

Type: Subsonic jet powered recoverable target drone.

Airframe: Cantilever mid-wing monoplane. Constant chord wings, with unsymmetrical section, 2° anhedral and 0° 45′ incidence. Fuselage built in three sections, those at front (housing radio control, telemetry and electrical equipment) and rear (autopilot and flares) being of aluminium alloy. Central portion, made from steel sheet, forms integral fuel tank. Rectangular conventional tail surfaces, with tailplane mounted near base of fin. No landing gear.

Power Plant: One 25·5 kN (5,732 lb st) turbojet engine (Shenyang Wopen-6 modified by removal of afterburner section), mounted in nacelle underslung beneath centre of fuselage. Main fuel in steel integral tank forming central portion of fuselage; auxiliary fuel in underwing pods. (See under 'Weights' for capacities.)

Launch and Recovery: Launched from re-usable trolley, upon which drone is mounted on three short guiderails and attached by a single connecting pin at base of engine nacelle. Complete ensemble accelerates along runway under engine power, connecting pin being withdrawn automatically by pneumatic release system when speed reaches 151-154 knots (280-285 km/h; 174-177 mph). Drone then lifts off trolley and enters climbout phase, trolley decelerating and being brought to halt under radio command by brake-chute and wheel brakes. Drone can enter firing area two or three times during mission. If not shot down, it can be directed to a pre-selected landing site, where engine is shut down at a pre-determined speed and altitude and drone completes an unpowered landing. Engine nacelle is reinforced to absorb landing impact, resulting in only minor damage which can be repaired easily before re-use.

Guidance and Control: Four-channel autopilot (pitch, roll, yaw and altitude) in rear of fuselage stabilises aircraft and controls its flight in response to radio commands from ground station; it incorporates gyroscope, directional gyro, three-axis rate gyro, programmer, electrical actuator, amplifier and converter. After drone's separation from trolley, first 85 s of flight are programme controlled; mission then comes under pre-planned radio command from ground controller. Aerodynamic control by ailerons, elevators and rudder.

Avionics and Equipment: Onboard radar transponder for identification and tracking from ground. Airborne radio equipment comprises receiver/decoder which enables up to 24 command signals to be conveyed to autopilot and other components and equipment. A 52-channel telemetry system provides ground controller with continuous indication of altitude, speed, angle of bank, engine rpm and temperature, and other functions. Mission equipment includes miss distance indicator (antenna at rear of fin-tip); infra-red augmentation pod at each wingtip; five corner reflectors for radar signature augmentation; and flares (on undersurface of each wing and on rear edge of engine nacelle fairing) to provide visual augmentation to aid tracking by ground based optical aids. Main electrical power for avionics and equipment provided by engine driven generator, with alternator for AC power; emergency battery supplies DC power for continued safe flight in the event of main system or engine failure.

Dimensions, external:
Wing span	7·50 m (24 ft 7¼ in)
Wing aspect ratio	6·58
Length overall	8·435 m (27 ft 8 in)
Body diameter (max)	0·55 m (1 ft 9¾ in)
Height overall	2·955 m (9 ft 8⅓ in)
Area:	
Wings, gross	8·55 m² (92·03 sq ft)
Weights:	
Fuel: fuselage tank	600 kg (1,323 lb)
underwing tanks (total)	240 kg (529 lb)
Max launching weight	2,450 kg (5,401 lb)
Performance:	
Operating speed range	458-491 knots (850-910 km/h; 528-565 mph)
Operating height range	500-16,500 m (1,640-54,135 ft)
Range	324-485 nm (600-900 km; 373-559 miles)
Endurance at low and medium altitude	45 min

NPU

NORTHWESTERN POLYTECHNICAL UNIVERSITY

Xian, Shaanxi Province
Honorary President: Ji Wenmei
President: Fu Hengzhi
Head of Avionics Dept: Chen Xingen

The NPU was formed in 1957 by amalgamating the aeronautics departments of several Chinese universities. Today it is one of China's major aerospace and avionics institutions, with about 6,000 students on campus and a teaching staff of more than 1,300. It has departments for aircraft, aero engine and astronautical engineering, automatic control systems, avionics, marine equipment engineering, computer and other sciences, and several wind tunnels, including transonic and supersonic.

NPU D-4

Developed by the NPU, the D-4 bears some outward resemblance to early piston engined Beech and Northrop target drones, but is reportedly intended for use as a multi-purpose, radio controlled, camera carrying RPV. The NPU is believed to have built four prototypes of the D-4, which is of honeycomb and GRP construction and is powered by a nose mounted 22·4 kW (30 hp) Huosai-510 piston engine, driving a two-blade propeller. An autopilot is standard. First flight is believed to have taken place on 5 October 1983.

As shown in the accompanying photograph, the D-4 is launched from a mobile zero-length launcher by an under-fuselage rocket booster. Recovery is by parachute stowed in a dorsal compartment near the tail. A small production batch is being built for "urgent needs". Other known details include:

Dimensions, external:
Wing span	4·30 m (14 ft 1¼ in)
Length overall	3·30 m (10 ft 10 in)
Weights:	
Payload	25 kg (55 lb)
Max launching weight	140 kg (308·5 lb)
Performance:	
Max level speed at S/L	92 knots (170 km/h; 106 mph)
Operating height range	100-3,000 m (330-9,850 ft)
Endurance	2 h 40 min

NRIST

NANJING RESEARCH INSTITUTE FOR SIMULATION TECHNIQUES

PO Box 1819, Nanjing, Jiangsu Province
Telephone: 44438
Cables: 0319 Nanjing
Vice-Director: Wu Xiao Chun

The Z-2 remotely piloted helicopter was developed by NRIST as an RPH feasibility study. It was preceded by a small Z-1 model built primarily to train the ground control operator of the Z-2.

NRIST Z-1

The Z-1 was designed in January 1983 and made its first flight in the following May. Its purpose was to train those responsible for ground control of the Z-2 in remote control operating techniques.

Type: Miniature remotely piloted helicopter.

Airframe: Fuselage of aluminium tube and sheet, with non-stressed plastics outer shell. Hiller type main rotor; wooden main and tail rotor blades.

Power Plant: One 10 cc single-cylinder two-stroke glow-plug engine.

Guidance and Control: FM digital proportional radio control system and heading stabiliser.

Dimensions, external:
Main rotor diameter	1·60 m (5 ft 3 in)
Fuselage length	1·44 m (4 ft 8¾ in
Weights:	
Basic weight empty	4·4 kg (9·7 lb)
Fuel	0·6 kg (1·3 lb)
Max T-O weight	5 kg (11 lb)
Performance:	
Max level speed	58 knots (108 km/h; 67 mph)
Endurance	25 min

NRIST Z-2

From 1976 onward, three Chinese organisations developed RPHs with take-off weights of more than 20 kg (44 lb). Two were single main/single tail rotor types, with 3·7 kW (5 hp) and 11·2 kW (15 hp) engines respectively, and the third, also with a 5 hp engine, had a coaxial rotor configuration. None, however, proved capable of stable flight, and their further development was terminated.

The Z-2 research RPH programme began in January 1982, and two prototypes were built, the first of these being flown in June 1983. Preliminary ground and flight tests took place during the remainder of 1983, more than 70 flights being completed by the end of that year. For test flying, the Z-2 was generally flown for 10-15 min at a time, at a height of 10-15 m (33-50 ft). Maximum flying height on test was 120 m (394 ft). A number of modifications were made in 1984, in which year over 20 more flights were made. The results confirmed that the Z-2 had achieved its primary design goals of stability and controllability, without exhibiting unacceptable levels of vibration or dynamic structural stress. The Z-2 is thus the first successful RPH in the 20-30 kg (44-66 lb) class to be developed entirely by the Chinese aviation industry, and the experience gained is expected to be used in the development of more advanced RPHs.

Type: Experimental remotely piloted helicopter.

Airframe: Single two-blade teetering main rotor and two-blade tail rotor. Main rotor is of modified Hiller type, with auxiliary flaps carried on stabilising bar mounted above and at right angles to main blades. Blades are of NPL-9627 unsymmetrical section, with a tapered planform and 7° of linear negative twist, and are each attached to hub by two bolts and a metal bracket. Each blade has a 'C' shape glassfibre spar forming the leading-edge, the rear portion consisting of glassfibre/epoxy cloth (layers reducing gradually from root to tip) wrapping a core of polystyrene foam plastics. Outer leading-edge of each blade has a nose balance weight of lead. Tail rotor (mounted originally on starboard side of tail pylon, later reversed and transferred to port side) is of similar construction. Fuselage has a central load-bearing frame of welded steel alloy tube and a forward section of riveted aluminium, covered with a non-stressed shell of laminated glassfibre; tailboom is a composites monocoque. Sweptback fins above and below end of tailboom; horizontal stabiliser mid-mounted on tailboom forward of fins. Non-retractable aluminium tube landing skids, with legs of steel alloy tubing; optional flotation bags for impact absorption. Tailskid attached to underfin, to protect tail rotor.

Power Plant and Transmission: One 3·7 kW (5 hp) 85 cc single-cylinder two-stroke modified chain-saw engine, driving main rotor via a centrifugal friction clutch and Maximizer belt to main gearbox, and tail rotor via two bevel gears and a driveshaft. Fuel tank in centre-fuselage.

Launch and Recovery: Conventional helicopter take-off and landing.

Guidance and Control: Digital proportional control by FM radio and heading stabiliser. Signals are transmitted to onboard receiver, which decodes them and commands onboard actuators (three for collective pitch, longitudinal and lateral manoeuvres, two others for engine throttle and tail rotor pitch) to produce required control movement. Separate main rotor controls for cyclic and collective pitch; tail rotor has collective pitch function only.

Equipment: Battery pack, radio receiver and control actuators.

Dimensions, external:
Main rotor diameter	3·25 m (10 ft 8 in)
Tail rotor diameter	0·65 m (2 ft 1½ in)
Distance between rotor centres	2·105 m (6 ft 11 in)
Length overall, rotors turning	4·105 m (13 ft 5½ in)
Fuselage: Length	2·74 m (9 ft 0 in)
Max width	0·385 m (1 ft 3¼ in)
Height to top of rotor head	1·10 m (3 ft 7¼ in)
Skid track	1·18 m (3 ft 10½ in)
Areas:	
Main rotor disc	8·30 m² (89·3 sq ft)
Tail rotor disc	0·33 m² (3·6 sq ft)
Weights and Loadings:	
Basic weight empty	23·5 kg (51·8 lb)
Fuel	1·5 kg (3·3 lb)
Max T-O weight	25 kg (55·1 lb)
Max disc loading	3·01 kg/m² (0·62 lb/sq ft)
Max power loading	6·71 kg/kW (11·02 lb/hp)
Performance (calculated):	
Max level speed	60 knots (111 km/h; 69 mph)
Max rate of climb at S/L	262 m (860 ft)/min
Service ceiling	4,785 m (15,700 ft)
Hovering ceiling: IGE	2,195 m (7,200 ft)
OGE	1,278 m (4,195 ft)
Endurance	40 min

YMF

YUHE MACHINE FACTORY

2 Jie Fang Road, Nanjing, Jiangsu Province
Telephone: 42133 and 46462
Cables: 1630 Nanjing
Director: Zhang Bao Xiang

This state-owned factory manufactures the BJ7104, a target drone designed and developed by the Nanjing Research Institute for Simulation Techniques (see NRIST entry in this section).

YMF BJ7104

Design, prototype construction and first flight of the BJ7104 took place in 1971, and series production began two years later. A total of 2,400 had been built by the Yuhe Machine Factory by February 1986, with production continuing, primarily for use as training targets for small and medium sized anti-aircraft artillery weapons. The B-2 drone produced by the Changcheng Scientific Instrument-

D-4 aerial photography RPV developed by the Chinese NPU at Xian
(Hangkong Zhishi)

BJ7104 target/RPV produced by the Yuhe Machine Factory

Aérospatiale C.22 high performance subsonic target drone

The NRIST Z-1 (left), alongside the Z-2 in its modified form with a Puma-like fuselage and port side tail rotor. Both RPHs are fitted with inflated airbags under the landing skids, to cushion landing impact

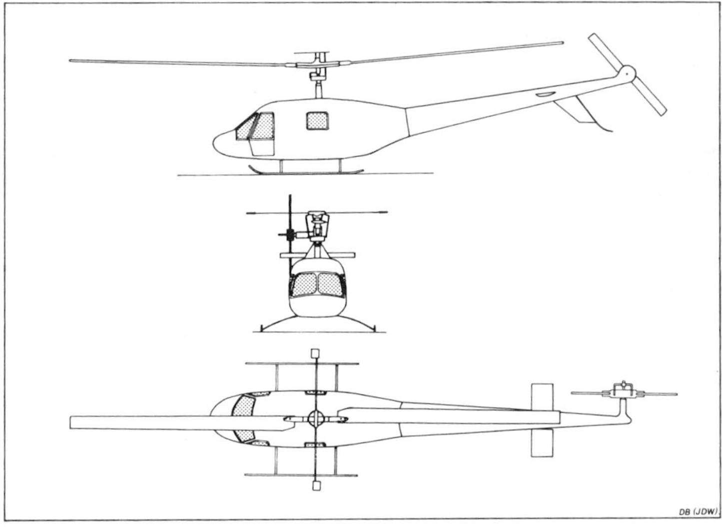

Original design configuration of the NRIST Z-2 remotely piloted helicopter
(Jane's Defence Weekly)

ation Factory (see CSIF entry in this section) appears to be a variant of the BJ7104.

Suitably re-equipped, the BJ7104 is said to have a number of civil applications including geological prospecting/ surveying/mapping, weather monitoring, artificial rain-making, powerline inspection and cropspraying. By adding a microcomputer to the system, the BJ7104 can fly pre-programmed missions, including formation flights by several drones under simultaneous control.

TYPE: Recoverable target drone.

AIRFRAME: Cantilever mid-wing monoplane. Tapered wings, with NACA 2415 aerofoil section, thickness/ chord ratio of 6·4% and 6° dihedral from roots. Circular section fuselage and conventional tail surfaces. Skid under tailcone and each wingtip to minimise damage on landing. Constructional details not stated, but probably similar to those given for Changcheng B-2.

POWER PLANT: One 11·2 kW (15 hp) YH280 (280 cc) four-cylinder two-stroke engine, driving a two-blade wooden propeller.

LAUNCH AND RECOVERY: Rocket assisted take-off from zero-length launcher. Skid landing.

GUIDANCE AND CONTROL: 22-channel radio control system. Provision for pre-programmed flights under microcomputer ground control. Aerodynamic control by ailerons, elevators and rudder.

EQUIPMENT: Onboard autopilot, radio receiver and telemetry.

DIMENSIONS, EXTERNAL:

Wing span	2·70 m (8 ft 10¼ in)
Length overall	2·55 m (8 ft 4½ in)
Fuselage: Max diameter	0·28 m (11 in)
Height overall	0·60 m (1 ft 11½ in)

AREA:

Wings, gross	1·14 m² (12·27 sq ft)

WEIGHTS AND LOADINGS:

Weight empty	34 kg (75 lb)
Fuel	8 kg (17·6 lb)
Payload	10 kg (22 lb)
Max launching weight	52 kg (114·6 lb)
Max wing loading	45·6 kg/m² (9·34 lb/sq ft)
Max power loading	4·65 kg/kW (7·64 lb/hp)

PERFORMANCE:

Max level speed	135 knots (250 km/h; 155 mph)
Max rate of climb at S/L	600 m (1,968 ft)/min
Service ceiling	6,000 m (19,685 ft)
Operating height range	100-2,000 m (330-6,560 ft)
Control range	8·1 nm (15 km; 9·3 miles)
Endurance	1 h

FRANCE

AÉROSPATIALE

AÉROSPATIALE SNI

Division Engins Tactiques

2 rue Béranger, BP 84, 92322 Châtillon Cédex
Telephone: (1) 47 46 21 21
Telex: AISPA 250881 F
PROGRAMME MANAGER, C.22: R. Berroir
OTHER OFFICERS: see Aircraft section

AÉROSPATIALE C.22

The C.22, which first flew on 6 June 1980, was designed in 1977 for use as a variable speed target for anti-aircraft weapons and, especially, for training of fighter pilots and anti-aircraft system crews. Its dimensions, radar signature and high performance enable it to simulate combat aircraft flying at any altitude, and also sea skimming missiles.

Ten prototypes and 24 pre-production C.22s have been built for the French Ministry of Defence. There are two versions: the **C.22T** with remote control only, for use on French ranges, and the **C.22L** with added telemetry and tracking system.

TYPE: High performance variable speed subsonic target.

AIRFRAME: Moulded sweptback plastics wings, with light alloy main spar, glassfibre skin and foam core, symmetrical profile (8% thickness/chord ratio) and no control surfaces. Fuselage of wound glassfibre on a central metal frame, impregnated with epoxy resin, reinforced by metal inserts at attachment points. Nosecone and tailcone of moulded plastics. Cruciform aluminium alloy tail fins, with four control surfaces operated by Labinal electric actuators.

POWER PLANT: One 3·73 kN (838 lb st) Microturbo TRI 60-2 turbojet engine, mounted in pod on top of fuselage; and two jettisonable solid propellant booster rockets (each 28·3 kN; 6,360 lb st for 1¼ s) attached beneath wings on sides of fuselage. Fuel tanks for TRI 60 in centre of fuselage, capacity 240 litres (53 Imp gallons). Oil capacity 4 litres (0·9 Imp gallons).

LAUNCH AND RECOVERY: Launched by jettisonable rockets from ground or ship base. Parachute system for recovery from land or sea. Inflatable airbags beneath fuselage to absorb landing impact.

GUIDANCE AND CONTROL: Radio command digital guidance system. Flight control, based upon a mini-computer, permits complex manoeuvres at more than 6*g*. Aerodynamic control by four movable surfaces inset in cruciform tail fins indexed at 45° from vertical axis.

SPECIAL EQUIPMENT: Operational equipment depends upon weapon systems to be fired at target. Nose compartment available for equipment, including tow winch. Tail compartment includes 25 kg (55 lb) smoke generator tank and recovery parachutes. Nosecone houses up to 60 kg (132 lb) of mission equipment; active or passive countermeasures; recording equipment for assessing the effectiveness of weapon systems during training; two 30 kg (66 lb) underfuselage pods; or equipment for towing successively two 30 kg (66 lb) secondary targets at speeds of more than 485 knots (900 km/h; 559 mph), with 800 m (2,625 ft) cable for each target. Onboard 28V battery (engine driven generator to come later) for electrical power. LCT TTL (Télémesure, Télécommande et Localisation) system for remote control, telemetry and tracking.

DIMENSIONS, EXTERNAL:
- Wing span: 2·50 m (8 ft 2½ in)
- Wing chord: at root: 0·92 m (3 ft 0¼ in)
- at tip: 0·28 m (11 in)
- Span over tail fins: 1·40 m (4 ft 7¼ in)
- Length overall: 5·25 m (17 ft 2¾ in)
- Height overall: 1·15 m (3 ft 9¼ in)
- Body diameter: 0·40 m (1 ft 3¾ in)

AREAS:
- Wings, gross: 1·6 m² (17·22 sq ft)
- Fins, total: 0·6 m² (6·46 sq ft)

WEIGHTS:
- Weight empty: 300 kg (661 lb)
- Max fuel load: 192 kg (423 lb)
- Total internal/external mission load, incl towed targets: 150 kg (331 lb)
- Max launching weight (excl boosters): 650 kg (1,433 lb)

PERFORMANCE:
- Max speed (all altitudes): Mach 0·9
- Max level speed at S/L: 600 knots (1,112 km/h; 691 mph)
- Max rate of climb at S/L: 4,200 m (13,780 ft)/min
- Time to 12,000 m (39,375 ft): less than 6 min
- Service ceiling: 12,000 m (39,375 ft)
- Minimum operating altitude: less than 15 m (50 ft)
- Range with max payload: 593 nm (1,100 km; 683 miles)
- Max endurance at 12,000 m (39,375 ft): 2 h
- *g* limit: more than +6

MATRA

SA MATRA (Branche Militaire)

BP No. 1, 78146 Vélizy-Villacoublay Cédex
Telephone: (03) 946 96 00
Telex: 698 077 F

MATRA SCORPION

The Scorpion experimental battlefield surveillance mini-RPV is being developed for the French government by Matra and Thomson-CSF. As shown in an accompanying illustration, it is of pod and boom configuration with high-mounted wings and twin fins and rudders. Main sensor is a Thomson-CSF TV camera, mounted on a gyro stabilised platform, for real-time video data transmission. Primary roles envisaged are reconnaissance and daytime target designation, with a laser designator as optional equipment.

The Scorpion was originally due to make its first flight in 1983,but Matra has declined to confirm whether it did so, or to provide any other details of the programme. Scorpion experience is expected to be used in the joint MBB/Matra Brevel RPV (see International part of this section).

GERMANY
(FEDERAL REPUBLIC)

DORNIER

DORNIER GmbH

Postfach 1420, 7990 Friedrichshafen 1
Telephone: (07545) 81
Telex: 0734209-0 do d
PRESS MANAGER: Horst Voigt

Activities of Dornier GmbH include the development of helicopter drones, tactical mini-RPVs, reconnaissance systems, standoff missiles and air target systems. Under subcontract to LMSC (see US section), it is supplying the net recovery system for the Aquila mini-RPV under development for the US Army.

Jointly with Canadair and SAT, Dornier is developing the AN/USD-502 (Canadair CL-289), details of which can be found in the International section.

DORNIER ARGUS II/PRIAMOS

Details of the original Argus programme can be found in earlier editions of *Jane's*.

The Argus I was cancelled following French withdrawal, but Dornier has proposed an Argus II, which is based on experience with its experimental MTC II free-flying drone helicopter (see 1985-86 and earlier *Jane's*) equipped with a battlefield radar and radio downlink.

In 1986 integration work began on an Argus II demonstrator, which is due to fly in 1987. This droned radar platform will have coaxial counter-rotating rotors, and will serve as a test vehicle for an advanced standoff battlefield surveillance system known as Priamos. The demonstrator will use a modified Gyrodyne QH-50D drone helicopter airframe, fitted with a French LCT Orphée II radar and powered by a 246 kW (330 shp) Boeing T50-BO-12 turboshaft engine. Principal data of the QH-50D are as follows:

DIMENSION, EXTERNAL:
- Rotor diameter (each): 6·10 m (20 ft 0 in)

WEIGHTS:
- Weight empty: 458 kg (1,010 lb)
- Payload: 272 kg (600 lb)
- Fuel: 327 kg (720 lb)
- Max T-O weight: 1,057 kg (2,330 lb)

PERFORMANCE:
- Endurance at 78 knots (145 km/h; 90 mph): 2 h 42 min

DORNIER MINI-DRONE

Dornier has studied the development of mini-RPVs for many years, and a Dornier vehicle was one of three German RPVs designed for the original US-West German Locust harassment weapon system programme, which was cancelled subsequently for budgetary reasons.

A detailed description of early Dornier test vehicles appeared in the 1984-85 *Jane's*. More recent concept studies have concentrated upon applications for attack missions, and at the 1983 Paris Air Show Dornier displayed a similar mini-RPV, called the Hornisse (Hornet), which was then being developed under Federal Defence Ministry contract and proposed for anti-tank operations, with possible applications also for anti-radar and electronic warfare duties.

Locust was succeeded in 1984 by a German national programme, now known as **KDAR** (Kleindrohne Anti-Radar), for an anti-radar drone for entry into service in the early 1990s, and Dornier has improved its delta-winged Mini-Drone to serve as a platform for the above-mentioned missions. Flight testing began in 1984 and was completed successfully in 1986. Equipment during this period included a broad band seeker; missions with active or passive electronic warfare payloads are under consideration.

The basic Mini-Drone is powered by a 19·4 kW (26 hp) two-cylinder two-stroke engine, and currently has the following characteristics:

DIMENSIONS, EXTERNAL:
- Wing span: 2·00 m (6 ft 6¾ in)
- Length: 2·25 m (7 ft 4½ in)

WEIGHT:
- Max launching weight: 110 kg (242·5 lb)

PERFORMANCE:
- Max level speed at S/L: 135 knots (250 km/h; 155 mph)
- Max operating height: 3,000 m (9,850 ft)
- Max endurance: 3 h

DORNIER KZO

The KZO (Kleinfluggerät für Zielortung) is intended as an all-weather day/night surveillance and target designation mini-RPV for the West German Army. The competitive definition phase, in which MBB is also a contender, was due to be completed in October 1986.

Dornier's contender makes use of an existing airframe, equipped with the relevant mission subsystems for navigation, sensing, launch and recovery. The overall system includes a sophisticated ground control station for mission planning, air vehicle guidance, and imagery interpretation.

No other details were received before going to press.

MBB

MESSERSCHMITT-BÖLKOW-BLOHM GmbH (Marine and Special Products Division)

Postfach 107845, 2800 Bremen 1
Telephone: (0421) 538 1
Telex: 245821 0 mbb d
OFFICERS: see Aircraft section

MBB continues to develop derivatives of the Tucan mini-RPV for various applications, as described in the following entries. With Matra of France, it has completed a definition study of the Brevel RPV (see International part of this section).

MBB RT-900 TUCAN (TOUCAN)

The Tucan experimental mini-RPV has been used to test, on behalf of the Federal German Ministry of Defence, various payloads for reconnaissance, target location and other tasks. Development began in 1978, and the first flight was made in November 1979. Sensor testing started in 1983, and by 1985, when development flying was completed, some 250 test flights had been made (about 30 with 12 full size air vehicles, the rest with two-thirds scale models). Operational derivatives currently being proposed are the KZO and PAD/KDAR, described separately.

The following description applies to the Tucan:

AIRFRAME: Low-wing monoplane, with medium aspect ratio wings. Modular construction, made of glassfibre for low radar cross-section. Outer wing panels are folded downward for storage in launch container.

POWER PLANT: One rear-mounted 16·5 kW (22 hp) Fichtel & Sachs SF 2/330 two-cylinder two-stroke engine, driving a two-blade pusher propeller. Fuel capacity 15 litres (3·3 Imp gallons). Booster motor for launch.

LAUNCH AND RECOVERY: Launched by booster motor from starting ramp or from static or vehicle mounted container. Parachute and airbag recovery system with autonomous emergency mode, independent of ground equipment.

GUIDANCE AND CONTROL: Autonomous onboard navigation system, which can be updated by radio command. Three-axis aerodynamic control (elevons and rudders). Ground control system comprises mission planning and control, air vehicle status control, and real-time observation.

MISSION EQUIPMENT: Nose-integrated stabilisation platform with TV or FLIR camera, tracker, forward/rearward/downward/side looking capability, and command, telemetry and video data link equipment. Can also be fitted with infra-red linescanner, low light level TV or other sensors.

DIMENSIONS, EXTERNAL:
- Wing span: 3·30 m (10 ft 10 in)
- Length overall: 2·055 m (6 ft 9 in)
- Body diameter: 0·35 m (1 ft 1¾ in)

WEIGHTS:
- Payload: 30-50 kg (66-110 lb)
- Launching weight: 100-140 kg (220-308 lb)

PERFORMANCE (at launch weight of 100 kg; 220 lb):
- Max level speed: 135 knots (250 km/h; 155 mph)
- Max operating height: 3,000 m (9,850 ft)
- Operational radius (incl 30 min hold): 38 nm (70 km; 43 miles)
- Max endurance: 4 h 30 min

MBB EXPENDABLE COMBAT DRONE

MBB is continuing to develop from the Tucan a combat weapon system to fulfil two main tasks. One version, known as **PAD** (Panzerabwehrdrohne), is for an anti-tank role; the other, for defence suppression missions, is known as **KDAR** (Kleindrohne Anti-Radar). The latter is the current designation for the former USAF/German Locust programme, which was revived as a purely national programme by the German Ministry of Defence in 1984. MBB's PAD and KDAR proposals are competing for production contracts from the West German Army and the Luftwaffe respectively.

The combat drone was developed as a tail-less cruciform wing configuration with direct force capability, to provide terminal phase accuracy comparable to that of a missile during a high-speed diving approach to its target. By folding the wings, 20 drones can be stored in a single 6·10 m (20 ft) standard container which serves as the storage, transport and launch unit. Zero launch is effected by a booster which detaches from the drone automatically after burnout when the wings of the drone have unfolded after leaving the container. No special separation mechanism is required. The container launch and satisfactory flight characteristics (no banking required for turns and steep dives) have been demonstrated successfully in Tucan test flights.

The attack drone fulfils many important tactical requirements, including high mobility; rapid deployment and operational readiness; low personnel requirements; all-weather capability; long-duration search phase/deep penetration range; high survivability; autonomous target acquisition; automatic target attack; and economical operation (attack is abandoned if target not confirmed as

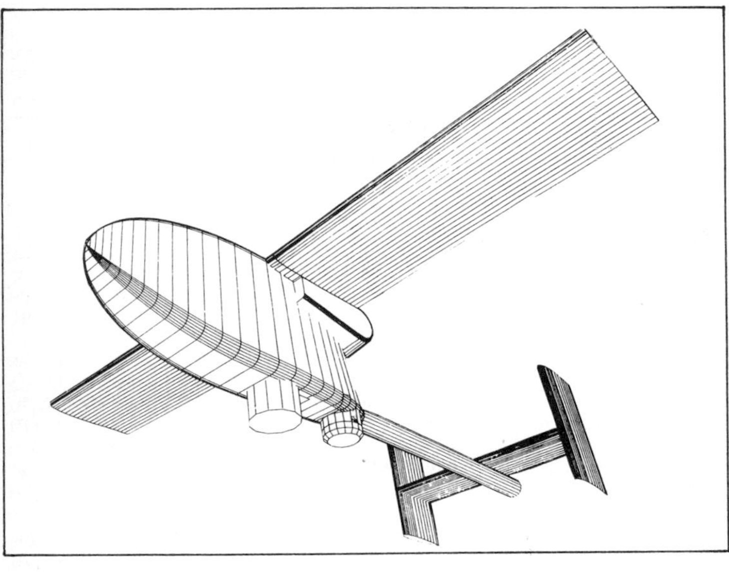

General appearance of the Matra Scorpion mini-RPV

Dornier's proposed Argus II/Priamos

Dornier Mini-Drone (anti-radar version) in cruise configuration

MBB Tucan in KDAR configuration being booster launched from a mobile container; rear (booster) structure is jettisoned after launch

MBB Tucan air vehicles in various configurations; some of the scale flight test models are mounted on wall in background

genuine by terminal guidance sensor). To these advantages can be added low system costs and low logistic support requirements: low production costs, storage as ammunition (containerised drones can be stored for up to 15 years, in the open if necessary), no periodical maintenance necessary, and deployment by all military and civil road, rail, sea and air means of container transport.

DIMENSIONS, EXTERNAL:

Wing span	2·26 m (7 ft 5 in)
Length overall	1·81 m (5 ft 11¼ in)
Body diameter	0·25 m (9¾ in)
Height overall	1·03 m (3 ft 4½ in)

WEIGHTS:

Weight empty, equipped	100 kg (220 lb)
Payload plus fuel	50 kg (110 lb)

PERFORMANCE:

Speed	75-135 knots (140-250 km/h; 87-155 mph)
Cruise altitude	up to 3,000 m (9,850 ft)
Endurance	several hours

MBB KZO

The Tucan system provides a suitable hardware basis for the MBB proposal for an operational target location and acquisition RPV known as KZO (Kleinfluggerät für Zielortung: small flight vehicle for target location), designed especially to meet the stringent requirements of bad weather capability together with high operational readiness under adverse mid-European environmental conditions. The details given here are equally applicable to the MBB/Matra Brevel (see International part of this section). Competitive definition phase of the KZO programme, in which Dornier is also a contender, was due for completion in October 1986.

Powered by a two-cylinder two-stroke engine, mounted in the rear of the fuselage and driving a two-blade pusher propeller, MBB's KZO has a high lift/drag ratio and is fitted with a programmable autopilot. It is launched automatically by booster from a truck mounted and transportable short ramp, recovery being by parachute to an airbag landing. Real-time data acquisition is by roll/pitch stabilised high-resolution FLIR with electronic image processing (onboard recorder optional); target location is by Rho/Theta radio navigation with map/image correlation. The data link is resistant to jamming. Other sensors, such as IR linescanners or LLLTV cameras, can be substituted without difficulty.

Dimensions, external:
Not known

Weight:
Max launching weight 100-140 kg (220-308 lb)

Performance (estimated):
Speed range 75-135 knots (140-250 km/h; 87-155 mph)
Operating height range 300-3,000 m (985-9,850 ft)
Range 27-43 nm (50-80 km; 31-50 miles)
Max endurance more than 3 h 30 min

INDIA

ADE

AERONAUTICAL DEVELOPMENT ESTABLISHMENT

Jeevan Beema Nagar, Bangalore 560075

Director: Air Vice-Marshal H. N. Krishnamurthy

ADE EXPERIMENTAL MINI-RPV

Work on developing this low-cost experimental mini-RPV, with the specific objective of gaining an insight into vehicle technology, remote control and flying, began in 1981-82. Development was continuing in early 1984. A new lightweight wing structure had then been built, and other programmes were in hand to develop assisted launch, net recovery, weight reduction and lower engine noise levels. No later news than this has been received, despite several requests. A description and illustration can be found in the 1985-86 and earlier editions.

ADE PTA

The PTA (Pilotless Target Aircraft) is a re-usable, ship or ground launched variable speed subsonic target drone, developed by the ADE for use by all three Indian armed services. A small batch of experimental launch vehicles (ELVs), one of which is illustrated, has been completed. Test launches from a ground launcher began in 1983, using a Bharat Dynamics JATO bottle for launch assistance. These vehicles, and the two prototype PTAs (first flight of which was due in December 1985), are each powered by a Microturbo TRI 60 turbojet engine.

The production PTA is intended for manufacture by Hindustan Aeronautics Ltd at Bangalore, and is to be powered by a 3·43 kN (771 lb st) PTAE-7 expendable turbojet engine (PTA Engine 7) currently being developed by HAL. This engine is intended to have an operating life of 25 hours. The PTA is designed to tow two HAL infra-red or radar augmented targets, each on a 1,500 m (4,920 ft) cable, and to have an onboard digital data link through which information from the towed targets will be relayed back to the ground controller in real time. A programmable flight computer will provide the PTA with navigation information; recovery is by parachute, with a crushable nosecone to absorb ground impact.

Series production of the PTA is planned to begin in 1987. Although intended primarily for target duties, the design could be adapted for battlefield reconnaissance, coastguard or environmental control, and/or offensive military roles.

Dimension, external:
Length overall approx 6·00 m (19 ft 8 in)

Weights:
Not known

Performance:
Speed range Mach 0·4 to 0·85
265-563 knots (491-1,043 km/h; 305-648 mph)
Operating altitude 300-9,000 m (985-29,525 ft)
Range 54 nm (100 km; 62 miles)
Endurance at 400 knots (741 km/h; 460 mph) at 7,000 m (22,965 ft) 1 h

MT

The MT is an air launched, expendable missile target for evaluating surface-to-air missiles. Flight development and evaluation trials have been completed.

Dimensions and Weights:
Not known

Performance:
Speed range Mach 0·7 to 1·4
Operating altitude 100-13,000 m (330-42,650 ft)
Range 19-38 nm (35-70 km; 22-44 miles)
Endurance 2½ to 5 min

INTERNATIONAL PROGRAMMES

AN/USD-502 (CL-289)

Prime Contractor:
Canadair Ltd, PO Box 6087, Montreal, Quebec H3C 3G9, Canada
Telephone: (514) 744 1511

Principal Subcontractor:
Dornier GmbH, Postfach 1420, 7990 Friedrichshafen 1, Federal Republic of Germany
Telephone: (07545) 81
Telex: 0734209-0 do d

CANADAIR/DORNIER CL-289

NATO designation: AN/USD-502

The CL-289 was designed to meet the needs of army corps commanders for timely and accurate battlefield intelligence. It is a development of the successful Canadair CL-89 (NATO AN/USD-501) system (which see); however, since the CL-89 was designed for intelligence gathering at division level, it does not have the range and target coverage capability needed at corps level. The requirement for increased range led to a larger air vehicle, able to incorporate a more complex navigation system (to achieve the necessary navigational accuracy at greater range); two kinds of sensor (photographic and infra-red linescan), to permit both day and night intelligence gathering; and a real-time data link to provide virtually instant IRLS imagery.

Development of the CL-289 began in July 1976 as a joint programme between the governments of the German Federal Republic and Canada, with Canadair as prime contractor and system manager sharing the work equally with Dornier as principal subcontractor. France joined the programme in March 1977, nominating Société Anonyme de Télécommunications (SAT) of Paris to develop an infra-red linescan (IRLS) sensor with real-time data transmission for ground recording. The SAT work represents approx 15 per cent of the total programme. Canadian Marconi and Lear Siegler supply major elements of the navigation system, and Klöckner-Humboldt-Deutz (KHD) the sustainer engine.

Operation of the CL-289 is similar to that of the CL-89. The drone is launched from a mobile zero length launcher by a jettisonable rocket booster, sustained flight being maintained by a ground started turbojet engine controlled by the onboard computer. The navigation system uses an advanced heading reference unit, together with a Doppler system and a precise airspeed transducer, all supplying data to the airborne computer, to provide accurate navigation. The Doppler system provides a quasi-terrain-following height control mode, which enables the drone to be flown at low altitude with a consequent reduction in vulnerability. The flight mission programme prepared by the mission planning facility is stored in the launcher computer and fed into the drone's computer just before launch.

Towards the end of the flight, the drone's terminal guidance unit is switched on by the onboard computer, and the drone homes on to a ground beacon. At the appropriate point on the homing leg the drone intercepts a radio fan marker beam which initiates the recovery sequence. The drone then makes a heading correction (to arrive upwind of the landing site), and a drogue parachute is deployed to slow it down to a safe speed for main parachute deployment. Emergence of the main parachute initiates inflation of the airbags, which cushion the landing impact. The exposed films are removed from the drone and taken for processing and interpretation, the landed drone being transported to the maintenance area for preparation for its next flight.

The first launch of a CL-289 was made on 3 March 1980, and a major milestone was reached with the conclusion in March 1981 of contractors' flight trials at the US Army Proving Grounds at Yuma, Arizona. The next main stage of the programme, beginning in December 1981 and completed successfully in May 1983, concerned customer evaluation and troop trials, to ensure that the system (a) met its military technical objectives and (b) was acceptable for service use.

Pre-production was approved in January 1986; full scale production is to begin in mid-1987 and will reach peak rate in late 1988. Both the French and West German armies have expressed their intention to procure the system, and evaluation by the latter was nearing completion in the early months of 1986. Other NATO member nations have expressed interest in the system.

Type: Recoverable airborne surveillance drone system.

Airframe: Cylindrical metal body, with ogival nosecone and tailcone of plastics. Four stub wings, with sweptback leading-edges, near rear of body in cruciform arrangement at 45° to vertical and horizontal centrelines; upper pair ejected when landing airbags are inflated. Ailerons on port upper and starboard lower stub wings. Two pairs of small foreplanes aft of nosecone, on vertical and horizontal centrelines, to control pitch and yaw; dorsal foreplane is ejected when airbags are inflated. Detachable dorsal packs for forward and rear airbags; detachable ventral packs for camera and linescan installations (forward), and for ribbon type parachute recovery system (aft of stub wings).

Power Plant: One 1·07 kN (240 lb st) KHD T117 turbojet engine, installed in tailcone, with an air intake duct on each side of body aft of stub wings. Fuel and oil tanks in central body compartment, forward of wings. One 32·0 kN (7,200 lb) max thrust Bristol Aerospace solid propellant booster rocket motor, attached to rear of drone body. Booster is jettisoned a few seconds after launch; turbojet is controlled by onboard computer to allow a near-constant airspeed, and to alter thrust as necessary during programmed turns, climbs and descents.

Launch and Recovery: Launched from mobile (truck mounted) zero length launcher; booster separates automatically shortly after launch. For recovery, drone is slowed down by drogue parachute until main parachute deploys. Drone is then inverted; forward and rear airbags are inflated and deployed automatically to absorb landing impact. Parachute and airbag system (latter of Kevlar fabric) by Irvin GB Ltd.

Guidance and Control: Pre-programmed operation. Navigation and control system comprises a Lear Siegler tuned rotor heading reference, a Canadian Marconi Doppler velocity sensor, and a Dornier System airborne digital computer. Mission programme is stored in computer, which generates the command signals required for navigation, attitude control and sensor activation. Ground homing beacon positions drone in final stages of flight to ensure accuracy of landing.

Equipment: 28V DC regulator for electrical power during flight. Two main sensor systems comprise Carl Zeiss KRb 8/24D three-lens reconnaissance camera and SAT Corsaire infra-red linescan, with SAT real-time video data link transmitter. Other onboard equipment includes air distance measuring unit (ADMU); heading reference unit; power supply unit; barometric altitude reference unit; radar transponder; fuel expulsion unit; non-tactical telemetry for mission equipment; terminal guidance unit; command receiver/decoder; vertical gyro; air reservoir and air pressure regulator for airbag inflation.

Dimensions, external:
Wing span 1·32 m (4 ft 4 in)
Length overall, excl ADMU nose probe:
with booster 4·67 m (15 ft 4 in)
without booster 3·61 m (11 ft 10 in)
Body diameter (max) 0·38 m (1 ft 3 in)

Weights and Performance:
Not released, but performance said to be "considerably higher" than that of CL-89

MBB/MATRA

Participating Companies:
Messerschmitt-Bölkow-Blohm GmbH (Marine and Special Products Division)
Postfach 107845, 2800 Bremen 1, Federal Republic of Germany
Telephone: (0421) 538 1
Telex: 245821 0 mbb d

SA Matra, BP No. 1, 78146 Vélizy-Villacoublay Cédex, France
Telephone: (03) 946 96 00
Telex: 698 077 F

MBB/MATRA BREVEL

Under the name Brevel (coined from their companies' locations at Bremen and Vélizy), MBB of West Germany and Matra of France have begun to develop a new reconnaissance RPV capable of being organised in rapidly deployable mobile batteries with one or more launching vehicles and a single command, control and communic-

MBB expendable combat drone in PAD form (anti-tank role), with wings folded

Experimental Launch Vehicle (ELV) for the Pilotless Target Aircraft (PTA) produced by India's Aeronautical Development Establishment

The Indian ADE's MT expendable air launched missile target

Launch of an AN/USD-502 (CL-289) surveillance drone from a MAN German Army truck platform

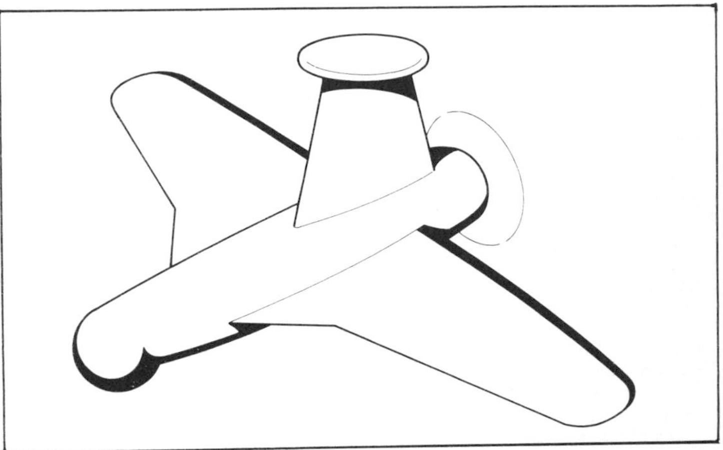
Only illustration so far released of the MBB/Matra Brevel

Mazlat Mastiff Mk III tactical reconnaissance/surveillance mini-RPV *(Brian M. Service)*

Mazlat Scout 800 tactical mini-RPV *(Brian M. Service)*

ations vehicle. The Brevel is in the 100-150 kg (220-330 lb) weight class, with a penetration range of 27-43 nm (50-80 km; 31-50 miles) and an endurance of three hours. It can accommodate TV and/or FLIR sensors and a playback recorder, and has growth potential for additional applications.

Brevel combines the two companies' experience with, respectively, the MBB Tucan and Matra Scorpion (which see). It flew for the first time in April 1984, but by the following April was still awaiting a government decision to go ahead with the programme. Intended in-service date is 1991.

ISRAEL

MAZLAT

MAZLAT LTD (Mini-RPV Systems) (Subsidiary of Tadiran and Israel Aircraft Industries)

Kiryat Weizmann, Science Park, Nes Ziona 70400
Telephone: (08) 472236 and 465353
Telex: 361904 MZLAT IL
General Manager: Zvi Shiller
Vice-President, Marketing: Israel Geva
Marketing Promotion Manager: M. Hevrony

IAI and Tadiran decided in September 1984 to establish a subsidiary company to consolidate their efforts in the mini-RPV business, which had previously concerned the IAI Scout and Tadiran Mastiff. Mazlat Ltd, formed for this purpose, is now the sole manufacturer of these mini-RPVs in Israel. Its new generation Pioneer mini incorporates the best elements of the two earlier systems, and received its first contract, from the US Navy, in early 1986.

MAZLAT PIONEER

Pioneer is a mini-RPV system developed by Mazlat to satisfy future military and civilian requirements. It incorporates the accumulated battlefield and technical experience of the IAI Scout and Tadiran Mastiff systems, which between them have logged more than 4,000 flight hours in about 1,000 sorties, most of them over hostile territory.

The complete Pioneer system consists of a few basic elements, plus additional subsystems that may be used to upgrade the basic system to the specific requirements of the user. The basic system includes the air vehicles; MKD-200 stabilised TV payload; Elta GCS-2000 ground control station (GCS); portable control station (PCS); MRU-2000 mobile receiving unit (MRU); a pneumatic launcher or rocket booster; and recovery system(s). An integrated logistics support provides all necessary logistics to allow independent storage, operation and maintenance of the system by users in the field, and includes training (maintenance and operation), complete set of manuals, spare parts allocation, special test equipment, and maintenance shelters.

It was announced on 7 January 1986 that Naval Air Systems Command had awarded a $25·8 million contract for procurement of three Pioneer short range RPV systems for US Navy (shipboard) and Marine Corps use, with deliveries to begin in May 1986 and continue until the Autumn of 1991. The contract calls for 21 drones (five to eight per system), ground control stations, portable control stations, remote data receiving stations, and launch and recovery equipment. It includes options for two more complete systems in 1987 and four in 1988. The Pioneer will be used by the USN and USMC on reconnaissance and surveillance missions, flying for extended periods of time while observing and transmitting video of surface activity by day or night. Mazlat's partner in the US Navy programme is AAI Corporation (see entry in US part of this section).

Type: Recoverable reconnaissance/surveillance mini-RPV.

Airframe: Cantilever shoulder-wing monoplane with constant chord wings, of similar general configuration to IAI Scout. Central fuselage nacelle of mainly rectangular cross-section, tapered at each end. Slender tailboom extending from each wing, outboard of fuselage, supporting twin inward-canted fins and rudders connected by a central tailplane with elevator. Wings, booms and tail unit detachable to simplify dismantling and assembly in the field and facilitate prompt despatch of several vehicles at one time. Airframe built mainly of composite materials to minimise radar signature. Non-retractable tricycle landing gear, plus arrester hook.

Power Plant: One 19·4 kW (26 hp) Sachs two-cylinder two-stroke engine, driving a two-blade pusher propeller. Fuel capacity 42 litres (9·2 Imp gallons).

Launch and Recovery: Conventional wheeled take-off from short, improvised strips; or catapult launch from pneumatically operated twin-rail launcher, compressed air tank for which is charged by truck's or ship's air compressors. Recovery by wheel landing, using short distance landing system (SDLS) of arrester cable, secured by two energy absorbers, to engage ventral hook; or by retrieval in vertically strung net attached to an energy absorbing system. Retrieval can be carried out from within GCS.

Guidance and Control: Autopilot control in all mission phases, from take-off to landing, ensures platform stability and ease of control. Programmed emergency manoeuvres allow for extreme flight situations. Elta GCS-2000 ground control station operates and controls the aircraft and its payloads, and receives, computes and displays real-time data from the aircraft, including TV pictures of the target area, via an automatic tracking antenna and secure two-way data link. Target co-ordinates are computed for display on the TV screen; alphanumeric and graphic displays allow artillery fire adjustment and improve the commander's control of the battlefield situation. The GCS-2000 is compact enough to be housed in small shelters such as the S-250, or in an armoured personnel carrier, giving it mobility under the most severe environmental conditions. It requires only a two-person crew (aircraft operator and observer); operation and maintenance are simplified by intensive use of microprocessors and software.

Mission Equipment: Main payload compartment in centre-fuselage, with volume of 0·1 m³ (3·6 cu ft). Up to 500W of electrical power available for mission payloads which can include day (TV) or night (FLIR) sensors in transparent underfuselage dome, EW, ECM, decoy, communications relay, and laser target designator and/or rangefinder.

Dimensions, external:

Wing span	5·12 m (16 ft 9½ in)
Length overall	4·96 m (16 ft 3¼ in)
Height overall	1·00 m (3 ft 3¼ in)

Weights:

Mission payload	up to 45 kg (100 lb)
Max T-O weight	195 kg (430 lb)

Performance:

Max level speed (typical)	100 knots (185 km/h; 115 mph)
Cruising speed (typical)	48-70 knots (90-130 km/h; 56-81 mph)
Max rate of climb at S/L	244 m (800 ft)/min
Ceiling	4,575 m (15,000 ft)
Landing distance with SDLS	within 70 m (230 ft)
Range	100 nm (185 km; 115 miles)
Endurance (typical)	6-9 h

MAZLAT (TADIRAN) MASTIFF MK III

The Mastiff Mk III is an RPV of conventional miniature aircraft configuration, for use in reconnaissance, surveillance, target designation and artillery spotting roles. The payload compartment can carry a variety of sensors, including still or TV cameras mounted on gyro stabilised gimbals; high survivability is ensured by the aircraft's small radar cross-section, negligible infra-red signature, and low visibility and noise levels.

The Israeli Army has acquired considerable battlefield experience with the Mastiff system. It has also been produced for export, including eight Mastiff Mk IIIs supplied to the US Navy in 1984-85 for evaluation and to equip the 1st RPV Platoon of the US Marine Corps at Camp Lejeune, North Carolina.

Type: Tactical mini-RPV.

Airframe: High-wing braced monoplane, with high-mounted tailplane and twin fins, supported by two slender tailbooms. Single wing bracing strut each side. Non-retractable tricycle landing gear. Nacelle type fuselage, in which power plant and mission equipment are mounted. Modular construction, with wings, booms and tail detachable to facilitate transportation.

Power Plant: One 16·4 kW (22 hp) two-cylinder two-stroke engine, driving a two-blade pusher propeller. Fuel capacity 35 litres (7·7 Imp gallons).

Launch and Recovery: Non-retractable tricycle gear for conventional take-off and landing. Vehicle mounted hydraulic launcher, activated and controlled automatically by an electronic system, is optional. Recovery by means of arrester wire stretched at near ground level between two energy absorbers. On landing, RPV engages wire with tailhook.

Guidance and Control: Remotely controlled from ground control station (GCS) or portable control station (PCS). The GCS is housed in a standard S-280 shelter which is normally carried on a 2½ ton military vehicle. The functions of this unit are mainly air vehicle and payload control, RPV tracking, video and telemetry data reception, with mini-computer processing of received data for real-time or subsequent analysis. There is a portable control station that permits RPV T-O and landing at a site remote from the GCS; this is used when the latter is located in terrain unsuitable for launch and recovery, and/or when extended mission range is required. All mission phases are under autopilot control. Aerodynamic control by ailerons and elevators.

Mission Equipment: The Mastiff Mk III generates up to 1kW of electrical power, of which some 400W is available for various payloads, depending upon customer requirements. These can include: (1) TV camera on stabilised gimbals, operable in yaw (360°) and pitch (88° down, 5° up) movements, with remote control of camera lens viewing angle and 1:10 zoom; (2) gimbal mounted TV camera and miniature panoramic film camera for detail photography; (3) various electronic warfare and ECM packages (government furnished equipment); (4) certain other electro-optical payloads, such as laser designator and miniature FLIR, to suit specific missions (government furnished equipment).

Dimensions, external:

Wing span	4·25 m (13 ft 11¼ in)
Wing chord (constant)	0·54 m (1 ft 9¼ in)
Length overall	3·30 m (10 ft 10 in)
Height overall	0·89 m (2 ft 11 in)
Propeller diameter	0·72 m (2 ft 4¼ in)

Area:

Wings, gross	2·27 m² (24·4 sq ft)

Weights:

Weight empty	77 kg (170 lb)
Max mission equipment	37 kg (81 lb)
Max fuel	24 kg (53 lb)
Max T-O/launching weight	138 kg (304 lb)

Performance (at 115 kg; 253·5 lb T-O/launching weight):

Max level speed at S/L	100 knots (185 km/h; 115 mph)
Cruising speed	53 knots (98 km/h; 61 mph)
Stalling speed	46 knots (86 km/h; 53 mph)
Max rate of climb at S/L	305 m (1,000 ft)/min
Max operating altitude	4,480 m (14,700 ft)
Range: without PCS	73 nm (135 km; 84 miles)
with PCS	108 nm (200 km; 124 miles)
Endurance	7 h 30 min

MAZLAT (IAI) SCOUT

The Scout mini-RPV system, developed originally by Israel Aircraft Industries, is employed primarily for real-time battlefield reconnaissance and surveillance, and is designed for operation by ground troops after only minimum training. The complete system, operated by a crew of 12, comprises up to eight Scout aircraft, ground control station, launcher and retrieval net. The current version is designated **Scout 800**.

Military and civil applications include missile site reconnaissance, battlefield control, target identification, strike force control, artillery targeting, border patrol, coastal and waterway control, and damage assessment.

Scouts are in service with the Israeli Army and Air Force, which have used them operationally with considerable success, and have also been supplied to a number of export customers, including South Africa and Switzerland (one system for evaluation). Many of the TV pictures of the Lebanon crisis have been filmed from Scout RPVs.

Type: Tactical mini-RPV.

Airframe: Cantilever high-wing monoplane. Fuselage is a rectangular section aluminium nacelle; twin inward-canted fins and rudders, supported by twin tailbooms extending from wings outboard of fuselage. Wings, tailbooms and tail unit are of glassfibre. Aircraft can be delivered with undercarriage and arrester hook for wheeled take-off and landing, and/or 'launching legs' for catapult take-off and net retrieval. Modular construction, with large access panels; wings, booms and tail unit detachable for transportation. Low detection signatures.

Power Plant: One 16·4 kW (22 hp) two-cylinder two-stroke engine, installed in rear of fuselage nacelle, driving a specially designed two-blade pusher propeller. Fuel capacity (20:1 petrol/oil mixture) 33 litres (7·25 Imp gallons).

Launch and Recovery: Catapult launch, from a truck mounted ramp; recovered by flying into retrieval net set up at ground station.

Guidance and Control: Pre-programmed or ground controlled, as situation requires. Control system is organised so that operator has merely to transmit flight path demands to the RPV, rather than using link between RPV and ground station to convey signals for direct operation of air vehicle's aerodynamic control surfaces. Instead, demands transmitted to air vehicle are fed to autopilot, which embodies necessary control logic to translate these demands into appropriate movements of control surfaces. Advantage of this method is that transmission is required only when a fresh flight demand (eg change of altitude or heading) has to be passed to the air vehicle, eliminating the almost continuous ground-to-air use of the command link which would be needed to pilot the air vehicle under full remote control. For recovery, aircraft is guided semi-automatically by an optical device into centre of retrieval net.

Mission Equipment: Tamam TV camera, with telephoto lens, mounted in belly on gyro stabilised platform servo-controlled for vibration damping. Large transparent hemispherical blister under centre of fuselage nacelle. Camera can be controlled remotely by ground operator, and can rotate and scan through 360° in azimuth and 0-90° in pitch. Two payloads are available, differing in field of view adjustment range: Mk I (47·5° to 3·4°) and Mk II (23·8° to 1·7°). Pictures obtained are relayed back to ground station by data link for real-time display. The RPV can also be fitted with a panoramic camera to scan an area within 60° on each side of flight path. Configuration permits installation of other mission equipment packages, such as laser designator/rangefinder and thermal imaging camera, to customer's requirements. Ground control station essentially similar to that for Mastiff (which see), housed in one of a variety of standard military shelters.

Dimensions, external:

Wing span	4·96 m (16 ft 3¼ in)
Length overall	3·68 m (12 ft 1 in)
Height	0·94 m (3 ft 1 in)
Propeller diameter	0·74 m (2 ft 5 in)

Weights:

Weight empty	96 kg (211 lb)
Max mission equipment	38 kg (84 lb)
Max fuel	25 kg (55 lb)
Max launching weight	159 kg (350 lb)

Performance (typical):

Max level speed	95 knots (176 km/h; 109 mph)
Speed for max range	55 knots (102 km/h; 63 mph)
Stalling speed	42 knots (78 km/h; 49 mph)
Rate of climb at S/L	244 m (800 ft)/min
Max operating altitude	4,575 m (15,000 ft)
*Control range	54 nm (100 km; 62 miles)
Max flight endurance	7 h

**Can be doubled if RPV is handed over to a second GCS*

TAMNAR

TAMNAR AVIATION TECHNOLOGY

62 Hailanot Street, Gat Rimon, 49920 Petah Tikva

Telephone: (03) 9325845 or 9325461

Telex: 371561 GDINT or 35317 DAMITIL ATT TAMNAR

Director General: N. Eskenazy

Director of Marketing: David Dinour

Tamnar develops and produces training aids for air defence forces, and has been the exclusive supplier of target drones to the Israeli Defence Forces since 1972. Its latest

Mazlat Pioneer reconnaissance/surveillance RPV, ordered by the US Navy and Marine Corps

Tamnar EDO 'model aircraft' training target

Launch of a Mirach-20 target acquisition/designation, battlefield surveillance and fire adjustment mini-RPV

Shipboard launch of a Mirach-70 RPV

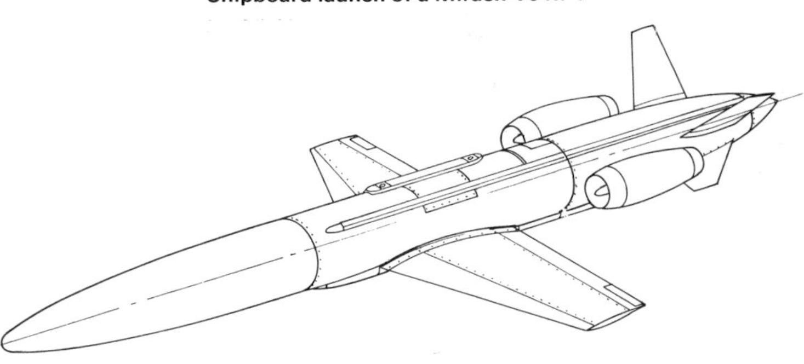

Drawing of proposed Mirach-600

target drone is the EDO; it also produces a half-scale target version of the Mazlat (IAI) Scout mini-RPV, known as the **TM-3 Mosquito**, for training operating crews.

TAMNAR TM-105 EDO

Approved for use by air, ground and naval anti-aircraft units of the IDF, the EDO 'model aircraft' target drone permits realistic AA unit training with guns or missiles. The target can simulate various aircraft attack modes and manoeuvres, and is extremely low-cost and easy to operate. Its name is derived from the initials of the Hebrew names of three anti-aircraft soldiers killed in the Lebanon in 1982.

Design of the EDO began in February 1982, and the first flight was made in September 1983. Production began in December of that year, and by the beginning of 1986 totalled 540 (including exports), of 800 then on order.

TYPE: Air defence target drone.

AIRFRAME: Cantilever shoulder-wing monoplane. Wings have a birch plywood skin with polystyrene core; fuselage is of impact absorbing glassfibre and epoxy; tail unit is of balsa wood. Steel landing skid standard; can also be fitted with tricycle landing gear.

POWER PLANT: One 3 kW (4 hp) Quadra Q-50, Q-82 or Q-100 single-cylinder two-stroke engine, driving a Clark two-blade wooden propeller. Fuel capacity 4·5 litres (1 Imp gallon) standard; extended range tank optional.

LAUNCH AND RECOVERY: By catapult from Tamnar rail launcher, returning to land (if not destroyed during mission) on underfuselage skid. Alternatively, can be fitted with tricycle gear (jettisoned after take-off) for conventional T-O from any suitable 50-80 m (164-262 ft) length of roadway, track or grass. At sea, can be platform launched from any vessel of patrol boat size or larger, and recovered in retrieval net installed at stern.

GUIDANCE AND CONTROL: Radio controlled by operator located within unit training area, using a Kraft 10W transmitter able to control two drones simultaneously. During each exercise, instructions can be transmitted to both AA battery crew and EDO operator. Commander thus remains in control throughout training session, and can initiate or alter strategic situations within seconds.

MISSION EQUIPMENT: Includes hit counter which records 'hits' at up to 6 m (20 ft) from target and relays results in real time to ground control display. For use as missile target, drone can be equipped with devices to activate missile's infra-red homing.

DIMENSIONS, EXTERNAL:

Wing span	2·50 m (8 ft 2½ in)
Length overall	2·31 m (7 ft 7 in)
Length of fuselage	2·25 m (7 ft 4½ in)
Propeller diameter: Q-50	0·46 m (1 ft 6 in)
Q-82	0·51 m (1 ft 8 in)
Q-100	0·56 m (1 ft 10 in)

WEIGHTS:

Weight empty	13·5 kg (29·8 lb)
Max payload (incl fuel)	4·5 kg (9·9 lb)
Max T-O/launching weight	18 kg (39·7 lb)

PERFORMANCE:

Max level speed	162 knots (300 km/h; 186 mph)
Min flying speed	19 knots (35 km/h; 22 mph)
Radio control range	3·2 nm (6 km; 3·7 miles)
Endurance: standard fuel	1 h 30 min
optional fuel	2 h

TAMNAR 'FLOGGER' and 'FROGFOOT'

Target representations of the MiG-27 'Flogger' and Su-25 'Frogfoot' entered production in 1986, the latter apparently varying only slightly in appearance from the EDO. The 'Flogger' target has a deeper fuselage, and altogether resembles the real Soviet aircraft more closely than does the 'Frogfoot' drone. Both are constructed, like the EDO, of impact absorbing glassfibre, have a 7·1 kW (9·5 hp) Quadra Q-100 engine, and are similarly launched and recovered.

DIMENSIONS, EXTERNAL (both):

Wing span	3·30 m (10 ft 10 in)
Length overall	3·05 m (10 ft 0 in)

WEIGHT (both):

Max T-O/launching weight	18 kg (39·7 lb)

PERFORMANCE (both):

Endurance: standard fuel	1 h
optional fuel	1 h 30 min

ITALY

METEOR

METEOR COSTRUZIONI AERONAUTICHE ED ELETTRONICHE SpA

146 Via Nomentana, 00162 Rome

Telephone: (06) 830991
Telex: 680136 Meteor-I
PRESIDENT: Grand'Uff M. O. Avv Furio Lauri
VICE-PRESIDENT: Ing Giovanni Sarzotti
GENERAL MANAGER: Ing Edoardo Dello Siesto

PRODUCTION PLANT: 34074 Monfalcone (Trieste)
Telephone: (0481) 778001
Telex: 460288 METMON-I
PLANT MANAGER: Ing Carlo Spano
TEST CENTRE: Villaputzu (Sardinia)

Centre Manager: P. I. Bruno Pipan
Telephone: (070) 99937
Telex: 790076 AVIELS-I

Meteor was established in Trieste in 1947. It is owned equally by the Italian government, through Aeritalia SpA, and by a private group through Meteor (Holding) SpA; the paid-in capital is 9,000 million Italian lire. Its present head office is in Rome, supported by facilities at Monfalcone (Trieste) and Villaputzu (Sardinia). The former is a production factory, the latter being equipped for flight operations and for technical assistance to the users of the tri-service range at Salto di Quirra.

Meteor is producing for the Italian and foreign armed forces various propeller driven and turbojet powered radio controlled and/or automatic navigating drones covering a speed range from 108 knots (200 km/h; 124 mph) up to Mach 3, and altitudes from 10 m (35 ft) to 25,000 m (82,000 ft) above sea level. Apart from the Andromeda and Aldebaran systems of its own design, Meteor also co-produces the Northrop-Ventura KD2R-5 (as the NVM-1 Meteor 1), MQM-74A (NVM-2 Meteor 2) and USD-1 SD-1(M)); and Beechcraft AQM-37A (BM-1). Under licence from Canadair, Meteor produces 50 per cent of the AN/USD-501 (CL-89) reconnaissance systems for the Italian Army.

METEOR ANDROMEDA SYSTEM

Andromeda is a multi-role system equipped with various types of RPV for combat or training use by air, land and naval forces. It can be supplied with one of five current types of Mirach air vehicle, or adapted to use other types that a customer may already have in his inventory.

Now in operation with many armed forces around the world, the Andromeda system is characterised by completely independent operation, maximum utilisation and considerable mobility. It is composed of the following subsystems:

1st Subsystem (Alamak/Sirah). Ground station for controlling the mission by ground crew (Standard and RID (Reduced) versions) and equipment which keeps air vehicle automatically on a pre-programmed flight.

2nd Subsystem. Equipment for launch, recovery and maintenance of the air vehicles.

3rd Subsystem. Equipment for preparation, recovery, maintenance and operation and/or evaluation of the payload and/or its results.

4th Subsystem. Part of the air vehicle system, comprising five different types of vehicle, all known as **Mirach** (see following entry).

METEOR MIRACH

Two propeller driven and three turbojet powered types of Mirach air vehicle are currently available for use with the Andromeda system, as follows:

Mirach-20 Condor/Pelican. Mini-RPV for target acquisition, location and designation; surveillance; and defence saturation. Powered by single 19·5 kW (26 hp) Herbrandson Dyad two-stroke flat-twin engine driving a two-blade wooden pusher propeller. Twin-boom, twin-tail configuration, with central fuselage nacelle. Skid landing gear. Airframe built mainly of Kevlar and synthetic expanded resin, with minimal use of metal; can remain afloat after ditching for up to 24 hours. Shoulder mounted wings are detachable. Booster rocket fitted under rear of fuselage, for assisted take-off from zero-length launcher, provides 10·79 kN (2,425 lb) of thrust for 0·7 s and is then jettisoned. Fuel load for piston engine is 23 kg (51 lb). Recovery by parachute stored in dorsal compartment forward of engine bay. Ground controlled (radio command) or pre-programmed automatic Omega/VLF navigation, with real-time data uplink and downlink and four-channel hybrid autopilot. Aerodynamic control via ailerons, elevator and rudders. Onboard sensors and other avionics can include over-the-horizon acquisition radar (radius 50 nm; 93 km; 57·5 miles at 915 m; 3,000 ft), TV camera, FLIR, target position computer and data conversion unit, vertical/directional/rate gyros (one of each), speed/altitude/rpm sensors (one of each), emergency locator transmitter, and flux gate. Electrical power (28V DC) from 1·7kW generator. Alternative sensors can include IRLS, photo-reconnaissance cameras and laser designator. In production for Italian Army (Condor) and Navy (Pelican).

Mirach-70. Target drone, or electronic warfare or decoy RPV. Powered by single 52 kW (7 hp) piston engine. Radio command guidance system. Various combat or training payloads. Also produced under licence in Argentina by Quimar (which see) as the **MQ-1 Chimango**.

Mirach-100. Target drone, or RPV for surveillance; reconnaissance; target location and acquisition; electronic warfare; defence saturation; and strike. Powered by single 1·13 kN (253 lb st) turbojet engine. Ground control or automatic navigation with real-time data transmission. Various combat or training payloads. In production for Italy and foreign countries, and produced under licence in Argentina by Quimar (which see) as the **MQ-2 Bigua**. One-way penetration range of 485 nm (900 km; 560 miles). The Agusta A 109/Meteor Mirach-100 combination, consisting of the transport, release and recovery by helicopter of one or two Mirach-100 RPVs, has been delivered to various customers and is now operational. With Quimar, Meteor has developed a mounting enabling a Bigua to be carried underfuselage by the IA 58A Pucará, and flight trials with such an aircraft were due to begin in 1985. The Mirach-100 is equipped with an automatic navigation subsystem called Sirah. With this system installed, the RPV can be programmed to loiter over a battlefield for surveillance purposes. It also has potential applications as a tactical cruise missile, launched from an Aeritalia G222 'mother' aircraft carrying six Mirach-100s.

Mirach-300. Target drone, or RPV for surveillance, reconnaissance, target location and acquisition, electronic warfare, strike, and defence saturation. Powered by single 3·70 kN (832 lb st) turbojet engine. Guidance and automatic navigation as for Mirach-100. Various combat or training payloads. Still under development.

Mirach-600. RPV for area reconnaissance, electronic warfare, strike, and defence suppression. Powered by two 3·70 kN (832 lb st) turbojet engines. Guidance and automatic navigation as for Mirach-100. Various combat or evaluation payloads. Not yet built.

Dimensions, external:	
Span overall (wings or fins):	
20	3·83 m (12 ft 6¾ in)
70	3·57 m (11 ft 8½ in)
100	1·80 m (5 ft 11 in)
300	2·83 m (9 ft 3½ in)
600	3·60 m (11 ft 9¾ in)
Length overall: 20	3·61 m (11 ft 10 in)
70	3·66 m (12 ft 0 in)
100	4·32 m (14 ft 2 in)
300	5·00 m (16 ft 4¾ in)
600	6·10 m (20 ft 0 in)
Height overall: 20	1·25 m (4 ft 1¼ in)
Weights:	
Weight empty: 20	95 kg (210 lb)
70	200 kg (441 lb)
100	210 kg (463 lb)
*300	400 kg (882 lb)
*600	680 kg (1,499 lb)
Combat load (internal): 20	25 kg (55 lb)
70	20 kg (44 lb)
100	40 kg (88 lb)
300	150 kg (330 lb)
600	300-500 kg (661-1,102 lb)
Max T-O weight (incl booster where applicable):	
20	180 kg (397 lb)
70	260 kg (573 lb)
100	310 kg (683 lb)
*300	800 kg (1,763 lb)
*600	1,000 kg (2,204 lb)
Performance:	
Max level speed: 20	108 knots (200 km/h; 124 mph)
70	194 knots (360 km/h; 224 mph)
100	458 knots (850 km/h; 528 mph)
*300, 600	Mach 0·92
Max rate of climb at 1,000 m (3,280 ft):	
20	240 m (787 ft)/min
Ceiling: 20	3,500 m (11,485 ft)
Max endurance: 20	more than 4 h
70, 100	1 h
*300, 600	2 h

**estimated*

JAPAN

FUJI

FUJI JUKOGYO KABUSHIKI KAISHA (Fuji Heavy Industries Ltd)

Subaru Building, 7-2, Nishi-Shinjuku, 1-chome, Shinjuku-ku, Tokyo 160
Telephone: Tokyo (03) 347 2533
Telex: 03-232-2268 FUJI J
Officers: see Aircraft section

Under contract from the Japan Defence Agency, Fuji is building the Teledyne Ryan BQM-34A Firebee I subsonic target drone (see US section) for use in the training of Tartar missile and gunnery crews, and for the evaluation of air-to-air missile systems and Japanese built F-15Js. The first shipboard launch of a Fuji built drone was carried out successfully in 1970, and about 360 flights had been made by the beginning of 1986.

By the end of March 1986 a total of 51 Fuji built BQM-34AJs had been delivered to the JMSDF and 20 to the JASDF. Fuji built BQM-34AJs include four fitted with RALACS (radar altimeter low altitude control system: see Teledyne Ryan Firebee in US section), for training the crews of defensive weapons against attack by anti-shipping missiles.

FUJI RESEARCH MINI-RPV

The Technical Research and Development Institute of the Japan Defence Agency authorised the design, development and construction of the first all-Japanese RPV, a research mini-RPV for JGSDF surveillance and reconnaissance missions.

As the accompanying photograph shows, the air vehicle has a pod shaped fuselage, with high-mounted sweptback wings on which twin fins and rudders are mounted at just over mid span. Power plant is a 13·4 kW (18 hp) DH Enterprises (Herbrandson) Dyad 220 engine, driving a two-blade pusher propeller. Launch is from a mobile ramp, the aircraft being accelerated to flying speed by a JATO booster rocket.

Fuji was prime contractor, with Nippon Avionics providing the onboard guidance equipment, Hitachi the TV camera, and Hitachi and Nippon Electric the ground control equipment. Other Japanese participants were Japan Aviation Electronics and Daicel.

Dimensions, external:	
Wing span	3·50 m (11 ft 5¾ in)
Length overall	2·30 m (7 ft 6½ in)
Weight:	
Basic operating weight empty	90 kg (198 lb)
Performance:	
Max level speed at S/L	120 knots (222 km/h; 138 mph)
Service ceiling	above 2,500 m (8,200 ft)
Endurance	1 h

FUJI MODEL 820

JASDF designation: XJ/AQM-1

This is an expendable air-launched target drone currently being developed for the JASDF under JDA contract. Fuji was selected by the JDA in July 1983 as prime contractor, and is building a static test article and four flying prototypes. Two of the latter had been completed by the end of 1985, and the first of these was due to make its initial flight during the first quarter of 1986. The development programme is scheduled for completion by the end of FY 1986.

General configuration of the XJ/AQM-1 is shown in an accompanying illustration. Construction is virtually all-metal (steel and aluminium).

Type: Expendable target drone.

Airframe: Mid-wing monoplane, with clipped-delta wings interchangeable port/starboard. Four tail fins, of similar planform, indexed in X configuration at 45° to vertical and horizontal axes. Cylindrical metal body, with glass-fibre nosecone and tailcone. Engine suspended on centre-line pylon beneath rear of fuselage. No landing gear.

Power Plant: One 1·96 kN (441 lb st) Mitsubishi Heavy Industries TJM3 turbojet engine in underslung nacelle. Pressurised fuel tank in centre of fuselage.

Launch and Recovery: Can be air launched from underwing pylon (one under each wing) of JASDF McDonnell Douglas F-4EJ Phantom or F-15J/DJ Eagle. Non-recoverable.

Guidance and Control: Pre-programmed guidance system, which can be overridden by radio command from either the launch aircraft or a surface station. Digital flight control system, including engine throttle control.

Mission Equipment: X band reflector in fore and aft body compartments. Smoke or infra-red generators can be attached to wingtips. Miss distance indicator can be installed in forward section of fuselage.

Dimensions, external:	
Wing span (over smoke generator pods)	2·07 m (6 ft 9½ in)
Wing aspect ratio	3·2
Length overall	3·65 m (11 ft 11¾ in)
Height overall	0·92 m (3 ft 0¼ in)
Body diameter (max)	0·35 m (1 ft 1¾ in)
Span over tail fins	0·98 m (3 ft 2½ in)
Areas:	
Wings, gross	1·20 m² (12·92 sq ft)
Tail fins (total)	0·30 m² (3·23 sq ft)
Weights:	
Max mission payload	42·4 kg (93·5 lb)
Fuel	32 kg (70·5 lb)
Max launching weight	235·5 kg (519 lb)
Performance (estimated):	
Max level speed at 9,150 m (30,000 ft)	Mach 0·91
Max sustained turn at 9,150 m (30,000 ft)	3·2*g*
Operating height: min	660 m (2,000 ft)
max	9,150 m (30,000 ft)
Endurance at Mach 0·9 at 9,150 m (30,000 ft)	15 min 42 s
g limits	+5/−2

Meteor Mirach-300 target/RPV on launch trailer

Mirach-100s on an Agusta A 109

Fuji research mini-RPV

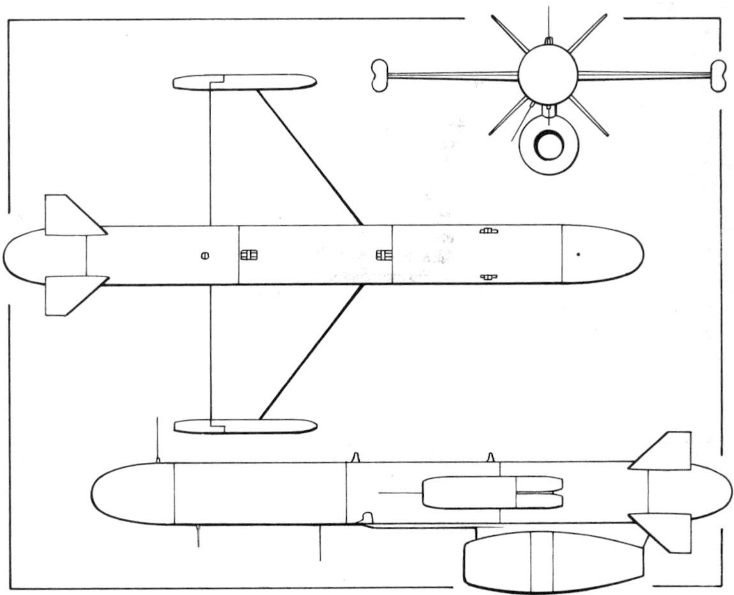
General arrangement of the Fuji Model 820 XJ/AQM-1 *(Michael A. Badrocke)*

MITSUBISHI

MITSUBISHI JUKOGYO KABUSHIKI KAISHA (Mitsubishi Heavy Industries Ltd)

5-1, Marunouchi 2-chome, Chiyoda-ku, Tokyo 100
Telephone: Tokyo (03) 212 3111
Telex: J22282 and J22443

OFFICERS: see Aircraft section

MITSUBISHI QF-104J

Approval was given in the 1985 defence budget for the storage of retired JASDF F-104J Starfighters with a view to their eventual modification into QF-104 target drones, for use in air-to-air combat training and domestically developed missile tests, and possibly also to investigate ECM or decoy RPV technology. Current plans are for two prototype modifications, with an additional 30 QF-104J conversions to follow.

NEC

NEC CORPORATION (Nippon Denki Kabushiki Kaisha)

33-1, Shiba 5-chome, Minato-ku, Tokyo 108
Telephone: Tokyo (03) 454 1111
Telex: NECTOK J22686

PRESIDENT: Tadahiro Sekimoto
MANAGER, OVERSEAS RELATIONS SECTION, 1ST DEPARTMENT LEGAL AND ADMINISTRATION DIVISION: Seiichi Tanahashi

Under licence from Northrop Corporation, USA, NEC is responsible for production and repair of Northrop KD2R-5 Basic Training Target and Chukar II high-speed target drones for the Japan Defence Agency.

Deliveries of the KD2R-5 and Chukar II began in 1961 and 1982 respectively. By the beginning of 1986 a total of 357 KD2R-5s and 74 Chukar IIs had been delivered to the JDA.

SOUTH AFRICA

NATIONAL DYNAMICS

NATIONAL DYNAMICS (PTY) LTD

RCA Division, 38 Dunkeld Road, Westville 3630, Natal
Telephone: Durban (2731) 821131
Telex: 6-28195 SA
WORKS: PO Box 663, 15 Henwood Road, Pinetown 3600
MANAGING DIRECTOR AND CHIEF EXECUTIVE OFFICER:
Maitland Reed, MSc (Eng), PhD, CEng, FIMechE, MRAeS, MIAeE
DIRECTORS:
M. J. Richmond, CA (SA)
J. L. S. Whittle, BSc (Eng)

National Dynamics developed the Eyrie as a private venture multi-role target and advanced mini-RPV system for the export market.

NATIONAL DYNAMICS EYRIE (TARGET VERSION)

The Eyrie is a miniature unmanned aircraft of sturdy construction and low observable signatures, utilising a Warren-Young type rhomboid wing configuration. The rhomboid wing is inherently stable and unstallable, yet very manoeuvrable, with no control surface movement restrictions, and can be assembled quickly. Production is from precision moulds, enabling a packaged system to be delivered promptly. The standard system comprises five air vehicles, a ground control station, launch and recovery subsystems, a test/service shelter, storage/crew shelter, GPUs and antennae, mounted on five trucks and two trailers. The system is designed for rapid emplacement and displacement, high availability, and ease of operation and maintenance.

Design of the Eyrie Mk 1 began in May 1978, and the first of three prototypes made its initial flight in April 1980. These were followed by six prototypes of the Mk 2 (first flight June 1981), three of the Mk 3 (first flight March 1984), and series production of the Mk 3 (first flight September 1984). Details of these early versions have appeared in the 1985-86 and previous editions of *Jane's*. Availability of suitable four-stroke engines, with their inherently lower specific fuel consumptions, has enabled National Dynamics to offer a family of current production models covering a wide spectrum of target and RPV applications. These are the **TD 110** basic training target drone, to which the following description applies, and two mini-RPV models, the **HP 85** and **LE 40**, which are described separately. Details of customers and production quantities are classified.

TYPE: Radio controlled ship-recoverable aerial target.

AIRFRAME: As described for RPV versions.

POWER PLANT: One 82 kW (110 hp) two-cylinder four-stroke turbocharged engine, with twin ignition (optionally, one 112 kW; 150 hp normally aspirated two-stroke engine), driving a two-blade Kevlar pusher propeller with remotely controlled variable pitch. Fuel capacity 55 litres (12 Imp gallons).

LAUNCH AND RECOVERY: Surface launch from land or ship by zero-length launcher (one JATO rocket). Recovery by (a) short stroke travelling net, (b) skids and parafoil with vertical barrier net, or (c) parafoil (released by radio command) steering to tined (spiked) gantry. Guidance aid device for recovery. All recovery systems suitable for shipboard use.

GUIDANCE AND CONTROL: Radio command guidance system, with portable radar tracking control station to control drone via autopilot at distances up to 43 nm (80 km; 50 miles). Radar/transponder link provides accurate positioning, transmission of commands to drone, and transmission of telemetry data from drone. Command and telemetry data are encoded into a PPC (pulse position coded) format. Aerodynamic control via ailerons, elevators and rudder.

MISSION EQUIPMENT: Electrical power provided by 1·2 kW alternator, rectifier/regulator and 28V battery pack. Equipment includes strobe light, remotely controlled smoke generator, recovery guidance aid, and various ECM options.

DIMENSIONS, EXTERNAL:

Wing span	4·27 m (14 ft 0 in)
Length overall	3·81 m (12 ft 6 in)
Height over fins	1·22 m (4 ft 0 in)
Body diameter (max)	0·55 m (1 ft 9¾ in)
Propeller diameter	1·22 m (4 ft 0 in)

DIMENSION, INTERNAL:

Nosecone volume	0·212 m³ (7·5 cu ft)

AREA:

Wings, gross	3·01 m² (32·38 sq ft)

WEIGHTS:

Basic operating weight empty	123 kg (272 lb)
Fuel	40 kg (88 lb)
Electrical payload	36 kg (80 lb)
Max launching weight	200 kg (440 lb)
Max landing weight	190 kg (420 lb)

PERFORMANCE:

Max level speed at S/L	204 knots (378 km/h; 235 mph)
Min flying speed	47 knots (87 km/h; 54 mph)
Max rate of climb at S/L	1,554 m (5,100 ft)/min
Service ceiling	8,230 m (27,000 ft)
Range at S/L with max fuel (110 hp engine)	295 nm (547 km; 340 miles)

NATIONAL DYNAMICS EYRIE (RPV VERSIONS)

As indicated in the preceding entry, two mini-RPV versions of the Eyrie are available, as follows:

HP 85. High performance version, with 85 hp engine and rocket carrying capability.

LE 40. Long endurance version (more than 24 hours), with 40 hp engine but without rocket capability.

TYPE: *(HP 85)* All-weather, day/night, recoverable mini-RPV for the variable tactical aspects of C³I and rocket strike; *(LE 40)* Same, but without all-weather and rocket strike capability.

AIRFRAME (both): Warren-Young type rhomboid wing configuration, with mid-wing front wing and low-wing rear wing/stabiliser. No control surfaces on front wing; rear wing fitted with inboard elevators and outboard ailerons, both operated by electric servos. Ailerons and elevators mass and aerodynamically balanced internally. Streamlined fuselage, of circular cross-section, with sweptback fin and electric servo operated rudder, plus ventral fin and skid. Entire structure of Kevlar, rigid PVC foam, glassfibre and polyester resin.

POWER PLANT: *(HP 85)* One 63 kW (85 hp) two-cylinder four-stroke engine, with twin ignition, driving a two-blade variable-pitch Kevlar pusher propeller via a large-diameter torsion-damped hollow shaft. Engine speed controlled remotely by electric servo operated throttle; propeller pitch varied remotely by electric servo motor. Single fuel cell in fuselage, capacity 63 litres (13·9 Imp gallons). *(LE 40)* One 30 kW (40 hp) two-cylinder four-stroke engine, driving a smaller two-blade propeller; otherwise as described for HP 85. Fuel cell capacity 107 litres (23·5 Imp gallons).

LAUNCH AND RECOVERY (both models): Can be launched from aircraft, zero length launcher or moving truck. Recovery by (a) short stroke travelling net, (b) parafoil and tined gantry, or (c) skids and short stroke vertical barrier net. All three systems are suitable for both land and shipboard recovery.

GUIDANCE AND CONTROL: Radio command with radar tracking, as described for target version. Ground control by crew of three (mission commander, flight controller and terrain analyst) with target control transponder and TV target group set for two TV cameras. Flight controller in GCS is in full control of air vehicle at all times, operating RPV manually according to telemetry and real-time TV imagery and overriding the autopilot, or in supervisory mode with autopilot engaged. Autopilot has magnetic heading sensor and automatic 'return to base' mode. Jamming resistant telemetry of essential data. Aerodynamic control by ailerons, elevators and rudder.

MISSION EQUIPMENT: Electrical power provided by onboard alternator (2·5kW in HP 85, 1·5kW in LE 40) with rectifier/regulator and twin battery pack. Two gimballed TV cameras (one forward looking for navigation and strike, under forward top canopy, and one sideways looking and slewing for target identification, retractable in belly); nose-mounted remotely controlled mini-panoramic camera; and telemetry equipment. Ample volume in forward fuselage for electronic warfare equipment.

ARMAMENT (HP 85 only): Rails for four 2·75 in rockets.

DIMENSIONS, EXTERNAL AND INTERNAL: As for target version except:

Wing span	4·88 m (16 ft 0 in)
Height over fins	1·26 m (4 ft 1½ in)
Propeller diameter: HP 85	1·22 m (4 ft 0 in)
LE 40	0·76 m (2 ft 6 in)

AREA:

Wings, gross	3·29 m² (35·38 sq ft)

WEIGHTS:

Basic operating weight empty:	
HP 85	124 kg (273 lb)
LE 40	100 kg (220 lb)
Fuel: HP 85	45·5 kg (100 lb)
LE 40	77 kg (170 lb)
Electrical payload: HP 85	53 kg (117 lb)
LE 40	45·5 kg (100 lb)
Max launching weight (both)	222 kg (490 lb)

PERFORMANCE:

Max level speed at S/L:	
HP 85	189 knots (351 km/h; 218 mph)
LE 40	134 knots (248 km/h; 154 mph)
Max cruising speed at S/L:	
HP 85	165 knots (306 km/h; 190 mph)
LE 40	113 knots (209 km/h; 130 mph)
Best range speed: LE 40	78 knots (145 km/h; 90 mph)
Loitering speed (both)	61 knots (113 km/h; 70 mph)
Min flying speed (both)	47 knots (87 km/h; 54 mph)
Max rate of climb at S/L:	
HP 85	1,317 m (4,320 ft)/min
LE 40	292 m (960 ft)/min
Service ceiling: HP 85	5,945 m (19,500 ft)
LE 40	3,050 m (10,000 ft)
Radio line of sight range (both)	87 nm (161 km; 100 miles)
Range with max fuel, no reserves:	
HP 85	1,018 nm (1,888 km; 1,173 miles)
LE 40	1,700 nm (3,151 km; 1,958 miles)
Max endurance: HP 85	14 h
LE 40	24 h 36 min

SWEDEN

NORABEL

NORABEL AB (MILITARY PRODUCTS)

PO Box 803, S-713 00 Nora
Telephone: (0587) 11450
Telex: 73451 NORABEL S

NORABEL RIPAN

Ten prototypes of this very small target drone had been completed by the beginning of 1986.

TYPE: Re-usable anti-aircraft gunnery target.

AIRFRAME: Cantilever shoulder-wing monoplane with conventional tail unit. Wings are of symmetrical profile, and have a plywood skin with an expanded polystyrene core. Ailerons and tail surfaces are of balsa wood. Prototypes have a fuselage box structure of plywood, balsa and expanded polystyrene; this would be entirely of polystyrene in production version. No landing gear.

POWER PLANT: One 1·9 kW (2·5 hp) 15 cc Super Tigre piston engine, driving a two-blade propeller. Fuel capacity 0·45 litres (0·1 Imp gallons).

LAUNCH AND RECOVERY: Hand launched; recovery by belly landing.

GUIDANCE AND CONTROL: Radio command guidance system. Aerodynamic control by full span ailerons, rudder and one-piece elevator.

MISSION EQUIPMENT: Three-element hit indicator system comprising dorsally mounted acoustic sensor (microphone), hit recorder and indicator. Microphone can be preset for either 7·62 mm or 5·52 mm ammunition, and six sensitivity levels corresponding to radii from 2 m (6·6 ft) to 12 m (39·4 ft) can be preselected to represent different hit zones (ie target sizes). Sound of passing projectile is registered by microphone, and signals processed electronically by hit recorder. Sensor computer, in centre-fuselage, can be set at different numbers of registered hits (up to 15) required to produce a 'kill'. When required number is reached, computer signals to adjacent indicator unit, which activates a pyrotechnic cartridge, producing a vivid flash that is visible up to at least 0·5 nm (1 km; 0·6 miles) away, indicating to gunners that target has been 'killed'. Hit recorder is powered by 8·4V nickel-cadmium batteries; indicator is a rechargeable cassette containing ten disposable flash cartridges.

DIMENSIONS, EXTERNAL:

Wing span	1·77 m (5 ft 9¾ in)
Length overall	1·40 m (4 ft 7 in)
Height overall	0·15 m (6 in)

WEIGHTS:

Payload	1·5 kg (3·3 lb)
Max launching weight	4·0 kg (8·8 lb)

PERFORMANCE:

Max level speed	108 knots (200 km/h; 124 mph)
Stalling speed	22 knots (40 km/h; 25 mph)
Range	0·5 nm (1 km; 0·6 miles)
Endurance	10-15 min

SWITZERLAND

FARNER

FARNER AIR SERVICE AG

Grenchen Airport, CH-2540 Grenchen
Telephone: 065 525341
Telex: 934565
PRESIDENT: Markus E. Seiler

FARNER/F + W KZD-85 TOPAZ

The KZD-85 (Kleinzieldrohne: small target drone) is produced jointly by Farner Air Service AG and the Swiss Federal Aircraft Factory (F + W) as a line of sight anti-aircraft gunnery target for the Swiss armed forces. Farner produces the airframe, launcher and ground support equipment; F + W supplies the remote control system and acts as prime contractor to the military procurement authority for the total system.

Design started in 1979, and the first of five prototypes made its initial flight in April 1983. A total of 60 production KZD-85s has been ordered. Manufacture of these began on 1 January 1985, and 20 had been completed by the end of February 1986.

TYPE: Re-usable small target drone.

AIRFRAME: Cantilever shoulder-wing monoplane, with Kevlar reinforced GRP sandwich wings and tail and an aluminium alloy fuselage, the underside of which is of vulcanised rubber to cushion the landing impact. Wing and tail surfaces detach to simplify transportation. No landing gear.

POWER PLANT: One 4·85 kW (6·5 hp) 99 cc Husqvarna 2100 CH single-cylinder two-stroke engine, driving a two-blade propeller. Electric engine starting. Fuel capacity 2 litres (0·4 Imp gallons).

LAUNCH AND RECOVERY: Catapult launched from trailer mounted 6·5 m (21·3 ft) ramp. Recovered by 11 m (36 ft) diameter cruciform parachute.

GUIDANCE AND CONTROL: PCM radio command guidance within line of sight. Aerodynamic control by conventional wing and tail control surfaces.

DIMENSIONS, EXTERNAL:

Wing span	2·48 m (8 ft 1⅔ in)
Length overall	2·18 m (7 ft 1⅞ in)
Height overall	0·62 m (2 ft 0½ in)
Propeller diameter	0·51 m (1 ft 8 in)

AREA:

Wings, gross	0·875 m² (9·42 sq ft)

WEIGHTS:

Weight empty, equipped	20·9 kg (46·1 lb)
Fuel	1·6 kg (3·5 lb)
Max launching weight	22·5 kg (49·6 lb)

PERFORMANCE:

Max diving speed	135 knots (250 km/h; 155 mph)
Max level speed	97 knots (180 km/h; 112 mph)
Min flying speed	43 knots (80 km/h; 50 mph)
Max operating altitude	2,500 m (8,200 ft)
Max operating radius	2,000 m (6,560 ft)
Max endurance	30 min
g limit	+7

Photographs of the TD 110, HP 85 and LE 40 versions of National Dynamics' Eyrie are still classified, but the general configuration can be seen in these two pictures. Left is an Eyrie model with special extended-chord low-speed wingtips to facilitate recovery at sea; right is a Mk 3 on its mobile zero length launcher. Neither has the annular propeller shroud seen on earlier versions

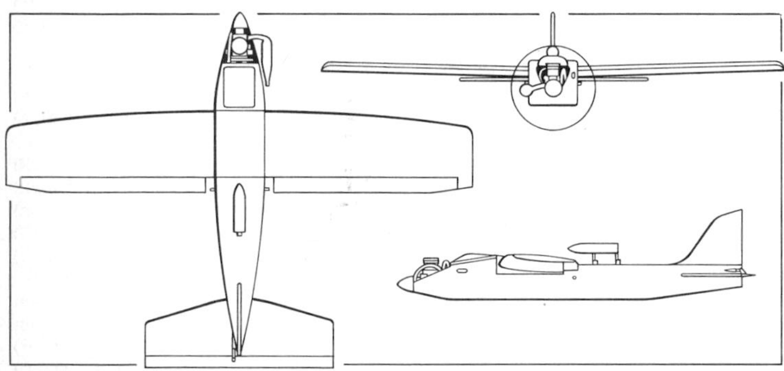

Norabel Ripan anti-aircraft gunnery target *(Jane's/Mike Keep)*

Farner KZD-85 anti-aircraft gunnery target on its launch ramp

UNION OF SOVIET SOCIALIST REPUBLICS

DR-3

The DR-3 is the first known Soviet mini-RPV, its existence having been revealed by the conflict over the Lebanon, where Syrian based examples were first observed in the early part of 1984. Configuration is said to be similar to that of the Israeli Scout and Mastiff and the US Developmental Sciences SkyEye, with a twin-tailboom layout and sweptback wings. Main sensor is a non-gimballed reconnaissance camera with a fixed lens, but an improved version carrying a zoom lens TV camera on a stabilised mounting is also believed to have been developed in the USSR.

No other details were known at the time of going to press.

SS-N-3

NATO reporting name: Shaddock

RPV versions are believed to exist of both 'Shaddock' and the related SS-C-1 'Sepal' missiles which entered service in the early 1970s. 'Sepal' is ground launched; 'Shaddock' is launched from surface vessels or 'Echo II', 'Juliett' and 'Whiskey' class submarines.

The missile is container launched by two solid propellant rocket boosters, having hinged wings that flip out after it leaves the launch tube. Turbojet powered, it can cruise at low altitude over water, and is radio guided, possibly with active radar homing. The RPV version probably carries ballast to make up any difference between its mission payload and the 1,000 kg (2,205 lb) warhead of the original missile.

A 'Shaddock' RPV launched from a Soviet submarine in the Barents Sea inadvertently violated Norwegian airspace in December 1984, subsequently crashing near a lake in Finland when its fuel was exhausted. This vehicle was tracked by radars at a speed of about Mach 1·1, and was flying at "several thousand" feet when it entered Norwegian airspace.

DIMENSIONS, EXTERNAL (estimated):
- Wing span: 4·00 m (13 ft 1½ in)
- Length overall: 10·00 m (32 ft 9¾ in)
- Body diameter (max): 1·00 m (3 ft 3¼ in)

WEIGHT (estimated):
- Max launching weight: 4,700 kg (10,360 lb)

PERFORMANCE (estimated):
- Max range: 243 nm (450 km; 280 miles)

SS-N-12

NATO reporting name: Sandbox

An RPV version of the 'Sandbox' missile reportedly entered service in the late 1970s, presumably intended as a replacement for the older and slower 'Shaddock' and 'Sepal' RPVs, of which it is essentially an improved version. It has the advantage of being launchable from both land based and seaborne platforms, including 'Echo II' class submarines.

DIMENSIONS, EXTERNAL (estimated):
- Wing span: folded: 1·80 m (5 ft 11 in)
- deployed: 2·60 m (8 ft 6½ in)
- Length overall: 10·80 m (35 ft 5¼ in)
- Body diameter (max): 0·90 m (2 ft 11½ in)

WEIGHT (estimated):
- Max launching weight: 5,250 kg (11,575 lb)

PERFORMANCE (estimated):
- Max speed: Mach 1·7
- Operational ceiling: 10,700 m (35,100 ft)
- Max range: 297 nm (550 km; 342 miles)

SUKHOI Su-9/Su-11

NATO reporting name: Fishpot

Some Su-9 and Su-11 fighters withdrawn from operational service in the USSR have been modified as radio controlled target drones for testing anti-aircraft missiles.

UR-1

The Soviet unmanned aircraft to which this designation applies is still something of an enigma, but is evidently of greater significance than was thought when it was first observed in the late 1970s. At that time it was known as a target drone employed during tests of late-model MiG-25 'Foxbat' interceptors equipped with AA-9 radar guided air-to-air missiles. These tests were said to have been successful against UR-1s flying at low level, in ground clutter, and at altitudes up to approx 21,335 m (70,000 ft). The drones, used to simulate targets of some 25 m² (269 sq ft) gross area, are air launched from Tu-16 carrier aircraft. They are said to operate normally between 20,000 m (65,615 ft) and 30,000 m (98,425 ft), but to be capable of flying as high as 40,000 m (131,230 ft). Other reports of the UR-1 have described it as being sophisticated, capable of high speed, and carrying remotely controlled subsystems such as a TV camera or electronic jammers for testing the latest Soviet airborne radars and air-to-air missiles. Its chief limitation is said to be a relatively short range. More recently, it was stated that the Soviet built reconnaissance/elint drone shot down by the Israeli Defence Forces near the Israel/Lebanon border on 13 June 1985 had been identified as a UR-1, and that at least one other Syrian based UR-1 had been destroyed before this.

Configuration of the UR-1 is still a matter for speculation, since no illustrations of the aircraft have yet been published openly. The Soviets are however known to have been particularly interested in the AQM-34 Firebee RPVs air launched from DC-130 Hercules during the Vietnam war, and the UR-1 has been described as "relatively large" and having a specification "not unlike" the Firebee I.

YASTREB (EAGLET)

Yastreb was a major Soviet reconnaissance and elint RPV in the European theatre from the mid-1960s to mid-1970s, but is nowadays deployed over Africa, the Near and Far East, and for target acquisition and ocean surveillance. Developed from the late-1940s T-4A supersonic cruise missile, it is launched atop a rocket booster and powered by a Tumansky R-31 turbojet engine. It can be either pre-programmed or remotely piloted under radio control. With a maximum speed of more than 1,890 knots (3,500 km/h; 2,175 mph), it has a ceiling of 27,500-30,000 m (90,225-98,425 ft) and a range of more than 540 nm (1,000 km; 620 miles).

UNITED KINGDOM

AEL

AEL (RPV) LIMITED

Gatwick House, Horley, Surrey RH6 9SU
Telephone: 0293 785353
Telex: 87116 and 87180 AERO G
MANAGING DIRECTOR: M. H. Nicholas
MARKETING DIRECTOR: J. I. Hunter

This company specialises in the manufacture of low cost radio controlled surveillance RPVs and target drones.

AEL 4800 SPARROWHAWK

The Sparrowhawk surveillance system was designed for use in the field, to give real-time information from which commanders can make decisions. During successful trials in France using five air vehicles, Sparrowhawk, when fitted with an AEL autostabiliser and the unique AEL tracking system, demonstrated a proven radius of operation of more than 19 nm (35 km; 22 miles). In early 1986 this was followed by a contract on behalf of the French Army, and AEL is establishing a facility in France for these Sparrowhawks to be produced locally. Options explored during evaluation included control of the RPVs from Gazelle helicopters of the ALAT.

The basic Sparrowhawk carries a TV camera and data downlink. Other more sophisticated payloads are available, such as still cameras, infra-red or thermal imaging packages, ESM/ECM, or chaff/flare dispensers.

TYPE: Battlefield surveillance mini-RPV.

AIRFRAME: Glassfibre reinforced plastics fuselage; foam core marine ply wings.

POWER PLANT: One 18·6 kW (25 hp) NGL WAM 342 flat-twin engine, driving a two-blade propeller.

LAUNCH AND RECOVERY: Launch by simple rubber bungee catapult, mounted on two-wheel transporting trailer. Recovery normally by belly landing if sufficient space, or by parachute. Fail-safe system closes throttle automatically after 1½ s and deploys parachute after a further 1½ s in event of loss of command signal or heavy radio interference. Independent auxiliary power supply automatically actuates fail-safe sequence in the event of main power failure or receiver malfunction.

GUIDANCE AND CONTROL: Radio command guidance system using long-range transmitter and control console to command RPV route or height changes and to operate onboard sensors. When fitted with tracking system, this provides continuous update of position for navigation and can be fed to monitors for target co-ordinates.

MISSION EQUIPMENT: AEL two-axis autostabiliser and digital proportional PCM command link standard. Basic Sparrowhawk carries TV camera and a data downlink, providing real-time surveillance capability. Other payload options include still cameras, low light IR or thermal imaging packages, electronic surveillance or countermeasures (ESM/ECM), or chaff/flare dispensers.

DIMENSIONS, EXTERNAL:
Wing span 3·21 m (10 ft 6½ in)
Length overall 2·77 m (9 ft 1 in)

WEIGHT:
Max launching weight 59 kg (130 lb)

PERFORMANCE:
Max level speed 162 knots (300 km/h; 186 mph)
Max range 27 nm (50 km; 31 miles)
Endurance 1 h 30 min

AEL SNIPE MARKS IV and V

Two new models of Snipe were introduced in 1986, both developed from the Mk III (see following entry) to incorporate major improvements in airframe design and electronics, reduce turnround times and facilitate maintenance. The **Mark IV** has a high-lift wing section which allows high altitude operation even in high temperatures with a full payload; landing speeds are low. The **Mark V** has a high-speed wing section and is some 20 knots (37 km/h; 23 mph) faster, but remains a 'user-friendly' aircraft. Both versions are in customer service.

Both versions meet the target requirements for large calibre defence guns and medium-range missiles. They are considerably larger and faster than the now-obsolete Mark II (1985-86 *Jane's*), and many of the latter have been upgraded to this standard by existing operators. Construction is similar to that of the Sparrowhawk (which see), and the same command link is used for both models.

The AEL autopilot gives the Mks IV and V a proven out-of-sight range of up to 19 nm (35 km; 22 miles), as required for range operation of medium-range weapon systems. It can be tracked with the AEL tracking unit, allowing deployment away from permanent installations. System reaction time is short, and a target can be launched within 15 minutes of crew arrival. Average turnround time between sorties is less than 10 minutes. Target recovery is by normal belly landing if there is sufficient space, or by parachute if not. A built-in fail-safe mechanism ensures that under conditions of lost command signal, severe interference, loss of main power or destruction of the receiver, the engine will be stopped and the parachute deployed automatically.

DIMENSIONS, EXTERNAL:
Wing span 3·14 m (10 ft 3½ in)
Length overall 2·50 m (8 ft 2½ in)

WEIGHTS AND PERFORMANCE:
No details received

AEL 4700 SNIPE MARK III

Snipe Mark III is a larger, faster target aircraft than the Mark II (see 1985-86 *Jane's*), providing greater realism in tracking and live firing training. The Mark III can be supplied with the AEL tracking system giving range, bearing, height and heading. Together with the onboard autostabiliser, this gives an effective operational range in excess of 27 nm (50 km; 31 miles). A target aircraft can be prepared and launched within 15 min of the crew arriving at the range head; average turnround time between sorties is less than 10 min.

The Mark III is now in service in four countries. A small evaluation batch was ordered by the French Army in early 1986.

AIRFRAME, POWER PLANT, LAUNCH AND RECOVERY, GUIDANCE AND CONTROL: As described for basic Sparrowhawk.

MISSION EQUIPMENT: Standard RDF tracking system, with optional interface to plotting table; autostabiliser; and smoke enhancement flares.

DIMENSIONS, EXTERNAL: As for Mks IV/V

WEIGHT:
Max launching weight 32 kg (70·5 lb)

PERFORMANCE:
Max in-service speed more than 162 knots (300 km/h; 186 mph)
Max range:
in-sight (binoculars) 4·9 nm (9 km; 5·6 miles)
tracking more than 27 nm (50 km; 31 miles)
Average endurance 1 h

AEL 4111 SNIPE MARK II

The AEL Snipe Mk II aerial target system is a dynamic target for use with air defence gun systems of up to 40 mm calibre, and close-range missile systems. It combines simplicity of design with outstanding performance and ease of operation. Its high manoeuvrability enables it to reproduce faithfully any of the complex attack profiles which are normally executed by full size manned ground attack aircraft.

The Mark II entered service with 14 countries worldwide, but is now regarded as obsolete and many customers are upgrading to the Marks III, IV or V (see preceding entries) for more advanced weapons systems. The Mk II shares many common components with the Mark III, thus offering ease of operation and maintenance in the field.

A description and illustration of the Snipe Mark II can be found in the 1985-86 and earlier editions of *Jane's*.

AEL 4600 STREEK

This radio controlled trainer/all arms air defence RPV is a cost-effective and realistic target for small arms and machine-guns used in air defence roles It is also used as an ab initio trainer for personnel using the larger Snipe aerial target systems; as such, Streek is in service with 15 armed forces worldwide.

AIRFRAME: GRP fuselage, veneered polystyrene wings.

POWER PLANT: One Glo-fuel 10 cc piston engine, driving a two-blade propeller. Methanol/castor oil (4 : 1) fuel mixture.

LAUNCH AND RECOVERY: Hand launched by operator or assistant. Recovery by belly landing on any reasonably level ground.

GUIDANCE AND CONTROL: Rugged VHF and UHF transmitter, crystallised to customer specifications.

GROUND SUPPORT EQUIPMENT (GSE): Comprises GRP box incorporating a fuel container (2·5 litres; 0·55 Imp gallons), electric fuel pump, electric engine starter, ammeter, 12V battery to power equipment, and selection of hand tools.

DIMENSIONS, EXTERNAL:
Wing span 1·70 m (5 ft 7 in)
Length overall 1·385 m (4 ft 6½ in)

WEIGHT:
Max launching weight 2·7 kg (6 lb)

PERFORMANCE:
Max level speed 75·5 knots (140 km/h; 87 mph)
Endurance 20 min

ARE

ADMIRALTY RESEARCH ESTABLISHMENT

Department XTW 1, Portsdown, Cosham, Hampshire PO6 4AA
Telephone: 0705 379411

CONTACT: T. Nottingham

The ARE has produced three small unmanned aircraft known as **Alcat**, **Sigu** and **Bus**. Details were awaited at the time of going to press.

ASVEC

ASVEC (UK) LIMITED

Building 1, Blackwater Industrial Estate, Camberley, Surrey GU17 9XX
Telephone: 0276 34433
Telex: 859970
MANAGING DIRECTOR: Trevor Cloughley
SALES DIRECTOR: John Wallis

ASVEC MERLIN

The Merlin is a multi-role RPV designed for military or police type operations such as surveillance, artillery targeting, communications relay, ECM/decoy, payload delivery and NBC 'sniffing'. Individual RPVs can be supplied with specified slide-in mission pods, or the package varied to meet specific customer requirements. Two basic air vehicle models are available, depending upon mission and payload requirements.

In the surveillance role the standard system would comprise six Merlin RPS air vehicles fitted with video and still camera systems, plus a mobile control station based on one of three available types of ground vehicle. The latter contains the control, guidance and navigation systems, tracking equipment, communications links, video surveillance and recording equipment, all housed in a desk console; plus the aircraft launcher and support facilities. Communication with command/HQ is provided by VHF/UHF and HF/SSB radio and 'slow scan' video transmission equipment. A range of options includes night vision equipment, mobile darkroom, facsimile link to command/HQ, speech encryption, teleprinter and other data processing equipment.

The two basic versions of the Merlin air vehicle are:

M100. With 10 kg (22 lb) payload and 50 cc engine.

M200. With 25 kg (55 lb) payload and 70 cc engine.

These are subdivided into the following mission variants:

RPL. Long range surveillance version of M200 (up to 135 nm; 250 km; 155 mile range). Equipped as standard with autonavigator, transponder, video system, still camera and dedicated digital autopilot system. Optional cameras as for RPS.

RPM. Short range surveillance and gunnery target version of M100. Operated under manual control, using binoculars or video display monitor. Standard equipment comprises manual radio control unit, colour TV camera and transmitter; options include SIT (silicon intensifier target) camera.

RPR. 'Repeater' version of either M100 or M200, designed to operate in conjunction with RPL by relaying transmissions between surveillance RPV and mobile ground station. Equipped with stabilised autopilot, autonavigator and radar transponder, video and command transmitters and receivers.

RPS. Medium range surveillance version of M200 (up to 54 nm; 100 km; 62 mile range). Equipped as standard with stabilised autopilot system, autonavigator, radar transponder, colour TV camera with 90 mm lens, video/telemetry transmitter and 35 mm still camera. Options include thermal imaging, infra-red and SIT cameras.

RPT. Training version, for use with Asvec pilot training programme. Slightly smaller than M100. Normally fitted with radio control equipment only, but video system can be installed for more advanced operator training. Also available, with minimal avionics, as low-cost decoy RPV.

RPX. Low-cost expendable version of M100, operated under manual control. Payload comprises monochrome TV camera with two lens head units, positioned at different angles, plus a container for explosives and an impact detonator. Aircraft is flown manually via video display until target is sighted, then switched to sighting lens and flown directly into target.

The following description applies generally to all Merlin variants, except where a specific model is indicated:

TYPE: Multi-role recoverable (except RPX) mini-RPV.

AIRFRAME: High-wing monoplane with central fuselage nacelle, twin tailbooms, and twin fins and rudders bridged at top by tailplane with one-piece elevator. Manufactured from double skinned GRP with a honeycomb core; wings have a foam infill. Main wing comprises centre-section and two outer panels, and can be bolted to fuselage at one of several positions to cater for CG changes caused by different payloads. Fuselage consists of nosecone, main body and engine cowling. Nosecone incorporates optically ground clear plastics windows to permit undistorted video images, and its removal provides access to slide-in tray on which avionics and mission equipment are mounted. Further optical window, for still camera, in underside of main fuselage section. Reinforced skids beneath fuselage for attaching to launching platform and for conventional landings.

POWER PLANT: *(M100)* One 2·7 kW (3·6 hp) 50 cc Quadra single-cylinder two-stroke engine, mounted in rear of fuselage and driving a two-blade wooden pusher propeller. *(M200)* One 5·8 kW (7·75 hp) 70 cc Horner two-cylinder two-stroke, driving a two-blade propeller. Electronic ignition on both engines. Standard fuel capacity 2·5 litres (0·55 Imp gallons) in all versions; RPL version of M200 has provision for two underwing auxiliary tanks, doubling total capacity to 5 litres (1·1 Imp gallons).

LAUNCH AND RECOVERY: Can be launched either by WL 25 pneumatic launcher supplied with system or, in suitable terrain, from wheeled trolley. Recovered by manual radio controlled skid landing, initiated within 2·7 nm (5 km; 3·1 miles) of transmitter to avoid radiation detection. Recovery parachute can be fitted optionally, at expense of some payload capacity.

GUIDANCE AND CONTROL: PCM telecommand guidance system (VHF or UHF). Normally pre-programmed by feeding in predetermined waypoints, airspeeds, heights and bearings from ground based navigation computer to onboard stabilised digital autopilot and autonavigator. Several areas can be visited on one mission, with pre-programmed loiter time over each target (extendable by manual override if required). Final waypoint is location of ground station. Radar tracking, via onboard transponder to ground station telemetry display unit and

AEL Sparrowhawk reconnaissance drone awaiting launch

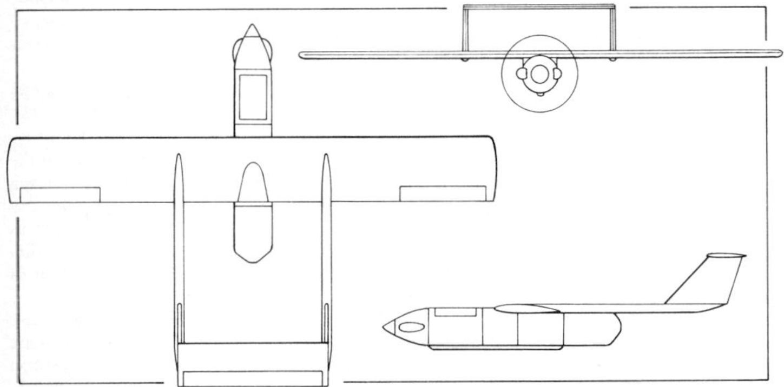

Asvec Swift twin-boom target/RPV *(Michael A. Badrocke)*

AEL Streek trainer/air defence target aircraft in operational use

Launch of an AEL 4700 Snipe Mk IV

Asvec Merlin multi-role mini-RPV

computer map plotter. Mission progress supervised via TVR 10 video receiver with colour monitor and video recorder. Alternatively, aircraft can be flown entirely under manual radio control, either visually using binoculars or via the onboard video camera and TV surveillance monitor. If RPV is required to operate beyond normal control or video transmission range, a 'repeater' RPV can be launched, programmed to fly a holding pattern at about 3,000 m (9,850 ft). This aircraft then acts as airborne relay for telecommand, telemetry and video surveillance systems.

Mission Equipment: Multi-role capability, using interchangeable slide-in mission pods. Engine driven alternator provides 28V DC power for avionics, surveillance and other systems; standby rechargeable battery pack is carried to power control systems. Standard equipment in surveillance versions comprises solid state colour TV camera with 90 mm zoom lens (RPL, RPM and RPS): TVX 20 UHF real-time video/telemetry transmitter (RPL, RPM and RPS); and 100 frame 35 mm still camera for high quality photography of target area (RPL and RPS). Optional cameras as detailed under model listing; monochrome TV camera in RPX. All video cameras, their lens options and positioning can be varied to suit specific locations or targets. At customer's option other mission pods and systems, including ECM, radar jamming, chaff, flares, NBC and other 'sniffing' equipment, can be installed in either M100 or M200.

Dimensions, external (M200):
- Wing span: 3·45 m (11 ft 4 in)
- Length overall: 3·05 m (10 ft 0 in)
- Height overall: 1·02 m (3 ft 4 in)
- Propeller diameter: 0·51 m (1 ft 8 in)

Area:
- Wings, gross: 1.78 m² (19·2 sq ft)

Weights:
- Weight empty: M100: 15 kg (33 lb)
  - M200: 20 kg (44 lb)
- Payload (incl fuel): M100: 10 kg (22 lb)
  - M200: 25 kg (55 lb)
- Max launching weight: M100: 25 kg (55 lb)
  - M200: 45 kg (99 lb)

Performance (M100 and M200 except where indicated):
- Operating speed range: 51-97 knots (95-180 km/h; 59-112 mph)
- Stalling speed: 30 knots (55 km/h; 35 mph)
- Typical rate of climb at S/L: 244 m (800 ft)/min
- Normal operating height range: 250-1,525 m (820-5,000 ft)
- Ceiling: 4,575 m (15,000 ft)
- Range with max fuel:
  - M200 RPS: 54 nm (100 km; 62 miles)
  - M200 RPL: 135 nm (250 km; 155 miles)
- Endurance:
  - M100 and M200, standard fuel: 2 h
  - *M200 RPL, auxiliary fuel: 4 h

**with reduced payload*

ASVEC SWIFT

Developed from the Merlin, the Swift is a low-cost aerial target designed to UK MoD specifications for use with ground-to-air missile and anti-aircraft systems. Chief recognition differences are the circular-section fuselage and tractor propeller. Swift can also be deployed on non-target missions such as ECM, artillery ranging, decoy/chaff dispensing and surveillance.

Type: Recoverable target or RPV.

Airframe: Generally similar to Merlin except for shape of fuselage. Modular construction, using composite materials.

Power Plant: One 7·5 kW (10 hp) Horner 100 cc two-cylinder two-stroke engine, driving a two-blade tractor propeller. Fuel tank in centre of fuselage, capacity 5·34 litres (1·17 Imp gallons).

Launch and Recovery: Can be launched by Asvec pneumatic launcher, or adapted for other suitable existing launch systems. Slow stalling speed permits recovery either by radio controlled landing on reinforced underfuselage skids or by deploying onboard emergency parachute housed in forward fuselage.

Guidance and Control: Manual radio control system, with autopilot optional. Ailerons and one-piece elevator for aerodynamic control. Manual or automatic control ground stations available, including telemetry and video display monitors. Also available is a binocular system enabling the aircraft to be flown manually over a distance of approx 5·4 nm (10 km; 6·2 miles).

Mission Equipment: Can be fitted with 16 sequentially switched smoke canisters, in pod forming rear compartment of fuselage, or with various infra-red flares in the interchangeable pod, to enable it to be used as a target for most types of ground-to-air missile. Safety circuits prevent accidental firing of smoke or infra-red burners. Racal miss distance indicator system can be installed as an option, complete with telemetry downlink and ground display equipment.

Dimensions, external:
- Wing span: 2·74 m (9 ft 0 in)
- Length overall: 2·29 m (7 ft 6 in)
- Propeller diameter: 0·46 m (1 ft 6 in)

Weight:
- Max launching weight: 33·6 kg (74 lb)

Performance:
- Max level speed: 140 knots (259 km/h; 161 mph)
- Stalling speed: 39 knots (73 km/h; 45 mph)
- Max rate of climb at S/L: 588 m (1,930 ft)/min
- Ceiling: 2,970 m (9,750 ft)
- Endurance: 1 h 30 min

BAe

BRITISH AEROSPACE PLC (Naval Weapons Division)

PO Box 5, Filton, Bristol BS12 7QW
Telephone: 0272 693831
Telex: 449452
Asst Chief Project Manager, New Surface Weapons: T. T. Walters

BAe's Naval Weapons Division, and predecessor companies on the Filton site, have a long and established involvement with RPV and target aircraft. This work has included design, development, manufacture and operation of aircraft in both categories. BAe experience includes a long association with UK Jindivik activities (see GAF entry in Australian part of this section), and the company has recently been confirmed in the role of UK co-ordinating design authority for the latest Mk 4 version of this aircraft.

Since the early 1970s, effort has been devoted to the development of surveillance RPVs, funded from both company and MoD contract resources. The work has covered several distinct families of airframes, investigation of payloads which include IR, optical and elint sensors, in addition to active EW and decoy packages. In several cases complete system evaluation has been undertaken, and offers based on these systems, several of which were under discussion in 1986, have been made to potential customers.

BAe STABILEYE Mk 3

The Stabileye family of mini-RPVs has been developed over a number of years for various Ministry of Defence and BAe research programmes. The initial concept was to produce a simple, robust mini-RPV, capable of flight testing a large variety of sensors and other mission equipment loads. A key feature of the airframe/autopilot design was the inclusion of a high level of inherent stability, so that acceptable surveillance images could be recovered from unstabilised sensor packages. The aircraft's name was chosen to reflect the pursuit of this principle, and the concepts described governed the course of development through earlier versions to the Stabileye Mk 3, the prototype of which first flew on 24 September 1980.

A total of 20 Mk 3s have been built, mostly under MoD contract; they are employed in an MoD flight trials programme. The most recent deliveries embodied improvements to the airframe and avionics. BAe development activities include flight trials of digital autopilot systems with stored waypoint navigational facilities, and advanced IRLS systems.

Type: Research mini-RPV.

Airframe: Cantilever high-wing monoplane, with constant chord wings of NACA 4415 section. Twin tailboom configuration, with engine mounted at rear of rectangular section central nacelle. Single sheet of GRP/honeycomb core material is cut and folded to form bottom and sides of fuselage box. Bulkheads then cut from the same material and bonded in position. GRP mouldings form nose and rear body fairings. Hinged 'lid' on top of fuselage allows access to payload bay and recovery parachute. Wings of foam core construction, fitted with conventional ailerons. Twin tailbooms, of square section GRP tube, attached by four bolts to undersurface of wings; another four bolts locate constant chord tailplane at rear end of booms. Single central fin, of honeycomb core, slotted on and bonded to tailplane. Elevator on each half of tailplane; provision for optional rudder. Complete wing, boom and tail assembly secured to top of fuselage by a single strap fastening; removal of this assembly gives access to flight control equipment bay. Configuration is chosen to allow large payload space with unobstructed views forward and downward.

Power Plant: Depending upon payload and mission requirements, various power plants have been used. Generally, BAe has used the 18·6 kW (25 hp) NGL WAM 342 two-cylinder two-stroke, or the 200 cc counterpart from the same manufacturer; the latest fuel injected version of the larger engine can be accommodated. In all cases the engine drives a pusher propeller.

Launch and Recovery: Launch is from a pneumatic catapult. Recovery is by parachute, with an under-fuselage airbag to cushion impact with the ground. Programme for recovery sequence (engine cut/deploy parachute/deploy airbag) is automatic. Sequence can be initiated on command from ground station or by emergence of preselected onboard conditions such as loss of radio contact.

Guidance and Control: Onboard flight control equipment, interfacing with ground station via a pulse code modulated (PCM) telecommand system, includes digital flight control electronics, vertical gyro, yaw rate gyro, magnetometer, telemetry encoder, and command receiver/decoder. Semi-autonomous navigation is available by use of waypoint co-ordinate references stored in digital autopilot. Navigation options include tracking radar with transponder, or Omega, in conjunction with waypoint system. Ground equipment includes plotter unit showing position of RPV relative to a pre-printed map of the area of interest, and a colour TV screen on which the view seen by RPV can be displayed in real time.

Mission Equipment: A variety of commercial TV and photographic cameras has been flown in Stabileye. Such equipment can be switched on or off, exposure sequences initiated, and lens movements controlled, either by onboard sequencers or by ground control. One of the BAe series of IR Linescan equipments has also been flown successfully, and a selection of electronic warfare payloads has been evaluated for use on board. Power for onboard equipment is provided by a directly coupled alternator with regulator and backup batteries.

Dimensions, external:
- Wing span: 3·66 m (12 ft 0 in)
- Length overall: 2·87 m (9 ft 5 in)
- Height overall: 1·03 m (3 ft 4½ in)
- Propeller diameter: 0·56 m (1 ft 10 in)

Area:
- Wings, gross: 2·23 m² (24·0 sq ft)

Weights:
- Max mission load: 25 kg (55 lb)
- Max launching weight: 80 kg (176 lb)

Performance:
- Operating speed range: 52-97 knots (96-180 km/h; 60-112 mph)
- Max operating altitude: 3,050 m (10,000 ft)
- Endurance at 75 knots (140 km/h; 87 mph) with max payload: 4 h

BAe STABILEYE Mk 4

Stabileye Mk 4 was derived from a design prepared for the original British MoD Phoenix competition. This initial design incorporated flip-out wings, to permit launch directly from the storage box, but the version finally built was considerably enlarged to accommodate a stabilised infra-red imager, and dispensed with container launch in favour of a more conventional fixed-wing aircraft using a pneumatic rail launcher. In this form the aircraft retained a place in the Phoenix competition until the final contract award.

The aircraft was designed around the Lotus 225 four-stroke engine, but because of programme difficulties the prototype was flown using a two-stroke engine instead. Up to early 1986 only the one prototype had been flown, further work depending upon a positive market assessment or on a specific enquiry for a vehicle having the capabilities offered by the Mk 4 version.

Type: Prototype mini-RPV.

Airframe: Design philosophy of this air vehicle was to produce a stable flight platform with minimal radar, acoustic and IR signatures. The aircraft is shaped externally to minimise the radar cross-section as presented to a ground based radar system; this effect is achieved by use of a fuselage having a triangular cross-section, formed as a flat floor with two sloping sides. Fuselage is built from a heavy grade GRP honeycomb material, metallised externally to be radar-reflective. These features ensure specular reflection of impinging radar emanations away from the source, thus avoiding detectable reflections such as would be given by a metal box within a radar-transparent skin. Wings are mounted low, dihedralled and swept. Tailplane is also mounted low, with dihedral, and carries twin tail-fins canted inward to minimise radar signature. Prototype wings and tailplane were made of skinned plastics foam; those of production versions would be made as self skinning foam mouldings.

Power Plant: Aircraft is configured to use 18·6 kW (25 hp) NGL WAM 342 two-cylinder two-stroke engine (as originally flown), or the Lotus 225 two-cylinder four-stroke of the same rating, mounted in fuselage centre-section above wing and driving a two-blade pusher propeller via a flexibly coupled shaft. Cooling air intakes are thus shrouded by wing, to minimise radar cross-section contribution from this source and to screen this area from IR detection. An engine driven alternator is mounted on forward end of engine.

Launch and Recovery: Aircraft is designed to be launched from a pneumatic catapult, although a large motorcar fitted with a fixed cradle has been used for flight testing. Recovery is by parachute and airbag, as with Stabileye 3, but in case of Stabileye 4 air vehicle is inverted for recovery sequence. This recovery mode is intended to afford maximum protection on touchdown for relatively fragile payloads such as downward looking IR imagers.

Guidance and Control: Versions of the equipment used with the Stabileye 3 system, with suitable software adjustments, are used in Stabileye 4.

Mission Equipment: Entire range of sensors used in Stabileye 3 can be used in Stabileye 4. In addition, several different proprietary IR imagers can be accommodated.

Dimensions, external:
- Wing span: 3·66 m (12 ft 0 in)
- Length overall: 3·40 m (11 ft 2 in)
- Height over tail-fins: 1·02 m (3 ft 4 in)

Area:
- Wings, gross: 2·69 m² (29·0 sq ft)

Weights:
- Max mission load: 50 kg (110 lb)
- Max launching weight: 131·5 kg (290 lb)

Performance:
- Operating speed range: 68-87 knots (126-162 km/h; 78-101 mph)
- Operational ceiling: 3,960 m (13,000 ft)
- Endurance, depending on engine and payload: 4-7 h

BAe TARGETS and DECOYS

British Aerospace is involved in studies and experimental work for a number of target and decoy systems. Naval target activities have been influenced by budgetary constraints, but prototype testing was in hand in mid-1986 for several off-board decoy systems.

The two most advanced projects feature carrier vehicles designed to be launched from a standard 130 mm mortar. The first of these is an infra-red decoy system. The second, a wrap-around flexible (Rogallo) wing unmanned aircraft known as **Plover**, is 1·70 m (5 ft 7 in) in overall length and has a wing span of 2·50 m (8 ft 2½ in). It will carry a 20 kg (44 lb) payload, and is expected to have an endurance of several hours.

BUCKLE

BEN BUCKLE RPV

9 Islay Crescent, Highworth, Wiltshire SN6 7HL
Telephone: 0793 764017
Owner: Ben Buckle

As an engineer and model aircraft hobbyist, Mr Buckle has more than 30 years' experience of particular value in the design and manufacture of small remotely piloted aircraft, and formed a company in 1982 to exploit this capability. His first production mini-RPVs, the PR 21 and Owl, were described in the 1985-86 *Jane's*.

No news of Mr Buckle's RPV activities has been received since the Spring of 1984.

EYRIE

EYRIE ENTERPRISES

223 Bramhall Moor Lane, Hazel Grove, Stockport, Cheshire SK7 5JL
Telephone: 061 487 1704
Managing Director: Noel Falconer

Eyrie Enterprises was formed to investigate the AX (Advanced eXpendable) flying wing RPV, described in the 1984-85 *Jane's*. When no governmental interest was shown in this, attention was transferred to UMAC (UnManned Aircraft for Civil applications) which, although a much lighter and more limited vehicle, is still an exceptionally 'clean' flying wing.

EYRIE UMAC/MERLIN

The **UMAC I** first prototype (first flight December 1984) was flown initially as a glider, to investigate the aerodynamics of the design. By early 1986 the programme had utilised four prototypes, each reconfigured several times. The version then current was known as the UMAC II-, similar to the intended definitive **UMAC II** but with some cannibalised components pending the installation of those intended for fitment. Some sensor sets had then been tested, cameras flown, and transfer of control while airborne achieved. Performance predictions at that stage appeared conservative rather than otherwise. UMAC II has a slightly greater span than UMAC I, more sweep on the outer panels, and a larger centre-section, to provide useful volume ahead of the CG so that the aircraft can be balanced without a nacelle. Tipsails have been substituted for the downturned wingtips of the UMAC I.

Roles for UMAC have been identified, and potential customers interested, and an economically viable aircraft is expected to result. This is, however, dependent upon provision of funding to 'productionise' the structure. It is intended to give the name **Merlin** to the production version.

UMAC is intended for such local operations as aerial photography or filming for television, where the brief endurance possible with primary electric power is acceptable. Radius of action is limited by control range to about 1·6 nm (3 km; 1·9 miles), although handover from one ground station to another has been demonstrated. Testing of the power system in non-UMAC aircraft indicates an endurance of about 30 min on one battery and 70 min on two. The former is adequate for the typical 40 s run of a 16 mm film camera; the latter can be employed, for example, for direct surveillance of traffic or crowds. Moreover, because UMAC is so slow and light it will not cause major damage on landing, and so can be employed where a lightplane would not be acceptable.

Type: Experimental electric powered mini-RPV.

Airframe: 'Flying wing' monoplane, without tail surfaces. Wings have a Wortmann profile and a NACA zero-pitching-moment centreline, with a thickness/chord ratio of 15%. Sweepback at quarter-chord 11° 36′ on UMAC I, 18° 30′ on UMAC II. No anhedral or dihedral. Down-

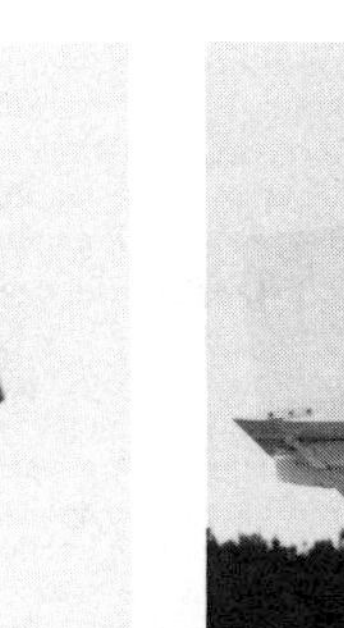

Stabileye Mk 4 prototype, configured for minimal radar, acoustic and infra-red signatures

BAe Stabileye Mk 3

Eyrie UMAC II-, with single electric motor and twin batteries

Close-up of Ferranti Firebird, showing sensor 'ball' mounting between the retracted take-off skids

Ferranti Firebird prototype in flight

turned (Hoerner) wingtips on UMAC I, upturned Spillman tipsails on UMAC II. Construction is of glassfibre on a balsawood core. Two-axis control by elevons, with Futaba controls, hinged by flexing glassfibre skin; yaw control by differential throttle in twin-engined version. Airbrakes under development. 'Fuselage', where applicable, achieved by bulging wing centre-section as required by specific payloads.

Power Plant: One or two Keller 25 or 35 electric motors initially, each of 300 W (0·3 hp) input (single Keller 25/16 in UMAC II). Nylon two-blade pusher propeller.

Launch and Recovery: Launched by short bungee; recovery by belly landing on grass.

Guidance and Control: Futaba PCM radio control system with Colching II downlink.

Avionics and Equipment: Sony XC 37 CCD TV camera, Richer micro-16 mm film camera, or other payloads, fitted in centre-section as required. One or two Ever-Ready AN 220 nickel-cadmium batteries (16-cell, to be increased to 20) installed immediately behind centre-section leading-edge to provide 2·2Ah for electric motors.

Dimensions, external:

Wing span: UMAC I	2·29 m (7 ft 6 in)
UMAC II (excl tipsails):	
single engine	2·64 m (8 ft 8 in)
twin engines	3·30 m (10 ft 10 in)
Length overall: UMAC II	0·74 m (2 ft 5¼ in)
Height overall: wing only (excl tipsails)	5 cm (2 in)
with bulged (camera) 'fuselage'	10 cm (4 in)
Propeller diameter: current	25·4 cm (10 in)
planned	30·5 cm (12 in)

Areas:

Wings, gross: UMAC I	0·70 m² (7·5 sq ft)
UMAC II (excl tipsails):	
single engine	0·77 m² (8·25 sq ft)
Elevons (total): UMAC I	0·04 m² (0·42 sq ft)

Weights (approx):

Flying weight (excl payload):	
single engine	4·5 kg (10 lb)
twin engines	5 kg (11 lb)
Max payload	2·5 kg (5·5 lb)
Batteries (each)	1·36 kg (3 lb)
Max launching weight	6·8 kg (15 lb)

Performance (estimated):

Max level speed at S/L	72 knots (133 km/h; 83 mph)
Max cruising speed at S/L	48 knots (89 km/h; 55 mph)
Stalling speed	24 knots (45 km/h; 28 mph)
Max rate of climb at S/L (single engine)	100 m (328 ft)/min
Control limit ceiling	610 m (2,000 ft)
Launch to 15 m (50 ft)	15 m (50 ft)
Landing from 15 m (50 ft)	50 m (164 ft)
Landing run	10 m (33 ft)
Max range (2 batteries):	
with payload	10 nm (18 km; 11·5 miles)
without payload	22 nm (41 km; 25·3 miles)

FERRANTI

FERRANTI DEFENCE SYSTEMS LTD (Electro-optics Department)

St Andrew's Works, Robertson Avenue, Edinburgh EH11 1PX
Telephone: 031 337 2442
Telex: 72529 FERROB G
Manager, UMA Programmes: D. Hope

Ferranti has worked on unmanned aircraft systems and subsystems since the late 1970s, and was one of two contenders to fulfil the British Army's requirement for a battlefield target acquisition and surveillance RPV system, known as Phoenix. Although unsuccessful in this competition, it is continuing to develop and market an essentially similar RPV, at first known simply as the Reconnaissance UMA and now as the Firebird.

FERRANTI/AEL FIREBIRD

The essential requirements for the Phoenix programme were for a low observable, catapult launched/parachute recoverable mini-RPV, carrying a thermal imaging (infra-red) sensor package for day/night surveillance as the primary payload. Five Phoenix prototypes were built (first flight 1983), with airframes provided by Slingsby Aviation (see Ferranti entry in 1985-86 *Jane's*).

The complete Firebird system comprises the air vehicle, launcher, ground control station and support facilities, and is based on a compact, recoverable fixed-wing RPV carrying either a stabilised electro-optic sensor or stabilised daytime or low light level TV. Other payloads can be accommodated to meet specific customer requirements, the available range being able to provide real-time detection, location and identification of targets by day and night and in conditions of poor visibility.

TYPE: Recoverable reconnaissance RPV.

AIRFRAME: Cantilever low-wing monoplane, of all-glass-fibre modular construction. Constant chord dihedral wings, with ailerons and spoilers. Trapezoidal-section fuselage, to reflect radar away from transmitter. Engine module, at front of aircraft, is designed to minimise thermal radiation and engine noise levels. Removal of corner reflectors, where possible, also helps to reduce radar signature. Engine, fuel cell and payload are concentrated into small volumes to provide payload bays fore and aft, so allowing a variety of payloads to be accommodated. Anhedral tailplane, with elevators; inward canted endplate fins and rudders. Wings and tail unit detachable for transportation and storage. Retractable skids under fuselage.

POWER PLANT: One 19·4 kW (26 hp) NGL WAM 342 two-stroke flat-twin engine, driving a two-blade propeller with spinner.

LAUNCH AND RECOVERY: Pneumatic catapult launch from vehicle mounted ramp. Can be recovered by skid landing; or by parachute, using inflatable airbag to cushion landing. (Drone inverts during landing phase, to protect ventrally mounted payload.) Parachute can be deployed automatically by fuselage mounted actuator in the event of a malfunction.

GUIDANCE AND CONTROL: Choice of uplinks and downlinks available; basic Firebird system uses a UHF uplink and VHF downlink in conjunction with a radar tracker. Flight control and navigation system is Ferranti Type 2001, using a Ferranti FS 60A vertical gyro. Basic two-man ground control station uses an XY plotter for mission planning and progress; a Ferranti moving map display with a graphics overlay is available as an option. Air vehicle is normally pre-programmed using GCS computer to plan flight path by means of waypoints, but this can be overridden by GCS to carry out an en-route search mode in an area of interest. A manual flight mode is also available. Air vehicle will return to launch area if data or command link is lost.

MISSION EQUIPMENT: Basic Firebird payload is a Ferranti Type 233 daylight TV system, consisting of a TV camera with 10:1 zoom lens on a gyro stabilised platform contained in a transparent ventral dome with a full field of view in the hemisphere beneath the aircraft. A variant of this equipment (Type 233A), fitted with an image intensifier, is available for low light applications. Other payloads which can be accommodated include a Ferranti Type 236 four-gimbal stabilised platform containing a FLIR camera and, if required, a boresighted laser. Electronic warfare, ESM and panoramic camera payloads are also available.

DIMENSIONS, EXTERNAL:

Wing span	4·40 m (14 ft 5¼ in)
Length overall	3·40 m (11 ft 1¾ in)
Fuselage: Max depth	0·28 m (11 in)
Propeller diameter	0·66 m (2 ft 2 in)

WEIGHTS:

Max fuel	20 kg (44 lb)
Max payload	45 kg (99 lb)
Max launching weight	140 kg (308 lb)

PERFORMANCE:

Max level speed	93 knots (172 km/h; 107 mph)
Cruising speed	68 knots (126 km/h; 78 mph)
Stalling speed	49 knots (90 km/h; 56 mph)
Max rate of climb at S/L	360 m (1,181 ft)/min
Ceiling	3,000 m (9,845 ft)
Range with max payload	302 nm (560 km; 348 miles)
Max endurance	more than 4 h

FR

FR GROUP PLC

Brook Road, Wimborne, Dorset BH21 2BJ
Telephone: 0202 882121
Telex: 41247

CHAIRMAN: M. J. Cobham, CBE, MA, FRAeS, Barrister
GROUP PUBLIC RELATIONS EXECUTIVE: S. D. Flaherty

For more than 25 years, FR Group (Flight Refuelling) has been engaged, inter alia, in the design and manufacture of control systems for pilotless aircraft. It was responsible for the conversion of more than 250 Gloster Meteor aircraft to pilotless or drone configuration. Some of these aircraft are still in service use for missile development trials and practice firings.

FR is continuing the development of RPVs and target drones, and is currently producing the ASAT and Raven vehicles for the UK Ministry of Defence. It is also teamed with GEC Avionics (which see) in developing the Phoenix surveillance RPV.

FR ASAT

British Army name: Falconet

ASAT (advanced subsonic aerial target) was designed to meet a Ministry of Defence requirement. The first of eight flight vehicles began flight testing on 14 February 1982, and trials included launch and recovery in wind speeds up to 28 knots (52 km/h; 32 mph). Operation of the 'carousel' circular runway launch system, and stability and control of the air vehicle, have been established; a zero-length launch system, using JATO bottles, is also available, which allows the carriage of heavier payloads.

All eight development vehicles had flown by the beginning of 1984. Deliveries of the first 75 production Falconets to the British Army began in late 1983 and were due for completion by mid-1986.

Approach and intercept legs of a typical target mission total about 5·5 nm (10 km; 6·2 miles), over the whole of which the target vehicle may be flown at more than 400 knots (741 km/h; 461 mph) at S/L. Ten such circuits can be repeated at 4·5 min intervals. During less demanding operations, or where more time is required between presentations, the rate of fuel usage can be reduced by loiter at 3,000 m (9,840 ft) altitude.

Other possible applications for ASAT include the towing of banners or sub-targets, short/medium-range reconnaissance (with a suitable payload such as infra-red linescan), ECM, and decoy.

TYPE: Subsonic re-usable target drone or RPV.

AIRFRAME: Cantilever low/mid-wing monoplane. Wings, tailplane and elevators folded from flat aluminium alloy sheet, without compound forming. Wings are each attached to fuselage by four bolts, are fitted with plain ailerons, and are interchangeable port/starboard. Tailplane held in place by GRP fin, via two studs. Aluminium alloy stressed skin fuselage, of circular cross-section, with crushable nosecone to absorb nose-down ground impact. Nosecone attachment and body joints made by band clamps. Nosecone is expendable, and is replaced after each flight. Cylindrical canister in rear fuselage houses recovery parachute. Engine pod attached under fuselage by two bolts.

POWER PLANT: One 1·08 kN (242 lb st) Ames Industrial (Microturbo) TRS 18-075 turbojet engine, mounted in pod under centre of fuselage. Single integral fuel tank in centre of fuselage, between wings; this has a capacity of 77 litres (17 Imp gallons) and is pressurised at 1·0 bar (15 lb/sq in). Refuelling point on top of fuselage. Aft of fuel tank is a smaller tank for oil, which can be injected into jetpipe, on command from ground, to produce smoke for visual enhancement. Two jettisonable JATO boosters, each burning for 1·3 s, can be attached for zero-length launch.

LAUNCH AND RECOVERY: Production Falconet is configured for fixed base operations and takes off under own power from three-wheeled trolley, running clockwise on a circular track 115 m (377 ft) in diameter and tethered to a pylon in the centre. Aircraft reaches T-O speed in three laps of this track, equivalent to a straight line T-O run of 1,000 m (3,280 ft), and with this system can always be launched into wind. Alternative zero-length launcher also available, for mobile or shipboard operations. A phased release Irvin GB parachute recovery system, consisting of a drogue and single RPS/1 cruciform main canopy, is pre-loaded in a cylindrical pack and deployed by tailcone release. Can be recovered on land or from sea.

GUIDANCE AND CONTROL: Radio command PCM guidance system, with Skyleader receiver and GEC Avionics autopilot and ground control console. Programmable ground based control option, using a microprocessor based control station which utilises radar data as the basis for aircraft navigation and control functions. Aerodynamic control by ailerons and elevators, actuators for which are in rear fuselage, between fuel/oil tanks and parachute compartment.

SYSTEMS: Fuel and smoke/oil tanks pressurised by engine compressor bleed air. 400W direct drive alternator/PCU.

MISSION EQUIPMENT: Large bay in forward fuselage, aft of nosecone, for avionics and optional target equipment such as miss distance indicator and radio altimeter. Pylon provision for optical or infra-red flares, radar enhancement devices, subtargets, banners or other external stores. Capability, with suitable payload, for short/medium-range reconnaissance, ECM or decoy duties.

DIMENSIONS, EXTERNAL:

Wing span	3·05 m (10 ft 0 in)
Wing aspect ratio	6·62
Length overall	3·50 m (11 ft 6 in)
Body diameter (max)	0·387 m (1 ft 3¼ in)
Height overall	1·32 m (4 ft 4 in)
Tailplane span	1·32 m (4 ft 4 in)

AREA:

Wings, gross	1·40 m² (15·1 sq ft)

WEIGHTS:

Basic weight empty	123 kg (271 lb)
Max fuel	60 kg (132 lb)
Payload (according to mission)	15-50 kg (33-110 lb)
Max launching weight	230 kg (507 lb)

PERFORMANCE:

Max level speed	450 knots (834 km/h; 518 mph)
Min loitering speed	150 knots (278 km/h; 173 mph)
Max rate of climb at S/L	2,600 m (8,530 ft)/min
Ceiling	3,000 m (9,840 ft)
Radius of action	13·5 nm (25 km; 15·5 miles)
Typical endurance	1 h 0 min
Max endurance	1 h 30 min
g limits	±6

FR RAVEN

The Raven is designed as a low-cost RPV surveillance system to provide real-time TV imagery and gathering of still photographs in daylight, and also the evaluation of alternative payloads and their roles. It was developed from the Royal Aircraft Establishment's XRAE series of equipment testbeds, the concept of which was purchased from the RAE by FR in January 1983. First public showing of the Raven was at the Defence Exhibition in Changi, Singapore, in January 1984, and FR initially developed the system under MoD (PE) contract as an unmanned aircraft applications demonstrator. Initial delivery, in May 1985, comprised one ground station, including radar tracker, and seven fully equipped air vehicles.

AIRFRAME: Cantilever mid-wing monoplane with pod and boom fuselage and cantilever T tail. Constant chord one-piece wing is of polystyrene foam cored GRP and obeche, bolted to fuselage. Tailplane, also attached by bolts, is of similar construction. Fuselage and integral fin are of GRP over a plywood internal structure. Wingtips and triple landing skids are frangible; wings, tailplane and propeller easily detachable.

POWER PLANT: One 1·9 kW (2·5 hp) 15 cc Webra 91 two-stroke engine, driving a two-blade pusher propeller. Max fuel capacity 2·5 litres (0·55 Imp gallons).

LAUNCH AND RECOVERY: Either by dedicated trailer mounted elastic powered rail launcher or, in suitable conditions, direct from ground by stretched elastic cable. Skid landing on smooth ground, net recovery in rough terrain.

GUIDANCE AND CONTROL: VHF or UHF radio command link via PCM (pulse code modulated) digital system using integrated autopilot. Air vehicle is continuously auto-stabilised, and commands can be input either manually or automatically (pre-programmed) via ground based microprocessor (HP 86 or equivalent) working co-operatively with suitable C-band or X-band tracking radar (Plessey WF3, Vega Cantley or similar). Automatic mode includes pre-programming of flight path through designated waypoints. Auto mode can be re-programmed during mission or can be interdicted manually. Three-axis aerodynamic control surfaces; outer aileron segments act as airbrakes.

MISSION EQUIPMENT: Payload bay in nose contains real-time video camera, filming obliquely through nose transparency, and vertical Cosina Compact 35 mm still camera. Video downlink transmitter (1W) and telemetry operate in D band. Onboard receiver/decoder, radar transponder and nickel-cadmium battery pack.

DIMENSIONS, EXTERNAL:

Wing span	2·70 m (8 ft 10¼ in)
Length overall	2·10 m (6 ft 10¾ in)
Height overall (over propeller)	0·50 m (1 ft 7¾ in)
Propeller diameter	0·36 m (1 ft 2 in)

WEIGHTS:

Typical payload	4 kg (8·8 lb)
Typical launching weight	15 kg (33 lb)

PERFORMANCE:

Normal operating speed range, ISA	40-68 knots (74-126 km/h; 46-78 mph)
Stalling speed (attainable only with autopilot disengaged)	25 knots (47 km/h; 29 mph)
Max rate of climb at S/L	209 m (685 ft)/min
Operational ceiling	2,500 m (8,200 ft)
Typical radius of operation	13·5 nm (25 km; 15·5 miles)
Max command operating range	43 nm (80 km; 50 miles)
Max endurance	2 h
g limits	+3/−1

FR RAVEN 2

The production version of the RAE XRAE-2 (which see) will be manufactured by FR and known as the Raven 2.

FR HORNET

The basic version of the Hornet, due to become available in October 1986, is a delta-winged general purpose target drone of GRP modular construction, powered by an 18·6 kW (25 hp) two-stroke engine driving a pusher propeller. It has been submitted as a contender in the British Army programme to replace the Shorts Skeet (which see) as a target for Blowpipe and Javelin missiles.

FR ASAT on 'carousel' launch trolley

FR Raven surveillance mini-RPV

GEC Avionics Phoenix battlefield surveillance and target acquisition RPV

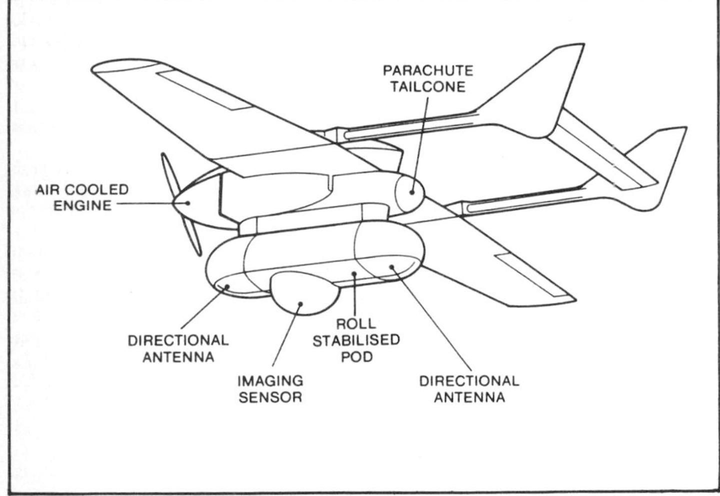

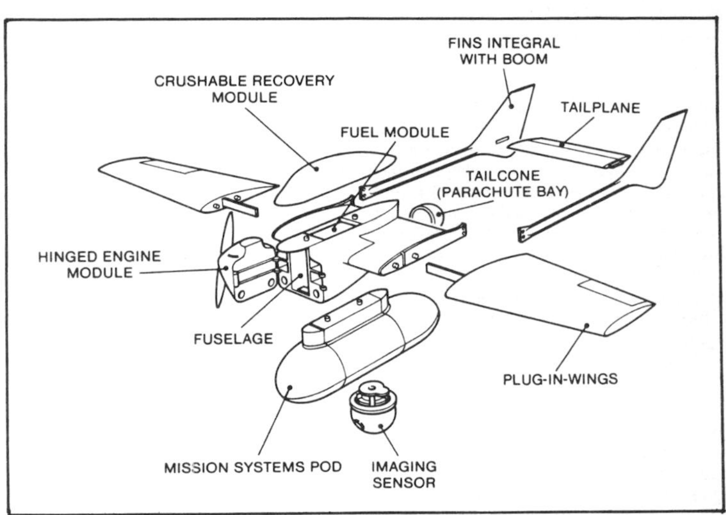

General and exploded views of the GEC Avionics Phoenix RPV, to be built by FR Group. Features include modular construction and low radar, infra-red and acoustic signatures

A sea-skimming variant is due to follow in early 1987, and may be proposed for the US Navy's close-in weapons system target requirement. The Hornet can also be made available in a number of other configurations. It can be launched pneumatically or by bungee, with parachute recovery on land or at sea. Visual and radar enhancement devices and a miss distance indicator are carried, and autostabilisation is available optionally.

Dimensions and Weights:
Not known

Performance:

Max level speed	165 knots (306 km/h; 190 mph)
Operating height range	S/L to 3,660 m (12,000 ft)
Max range	16·2 nm (30 km; 18·6 miles)
Max endurance	more than 1 h

GEC AVIONICS

GEC AVIONICS LIMITED

Airport Works, Rochester, Kent ME1 2XX
Telephone: 0634 44400
Telex: 96333/4

Manager, Flight Controls Division: B. G. S. Tucker
Information Executive: Malcolm Moulton

Phoenix represents one of several involvements by GEC Avionics in unmanned aircraft. Others include the development of control systems; lightweight surveillance equipment, including TV systems; and associated data link equipment.

GEC AVIONICS PHOENIX

Phoenix is the British Army's first fully equipped pilotless aircraft system for real-time remote targeting and battlefield surveillance. After entry into service, it is intended to play a part in supporting long-range artillery.

The requirement for Phoenix arose out of an earlier programme known as Supervisor which was cancelled in 1979. To meet the Army's requirement, Phoenix has to be highly mobile, capable of quick deployment, and flexible in operation, in extreme environments and the demanding conditions of electronic warfare. The complete system comprises a small air vehicle (first flown on 30 May 1986), an air-to-ground data link, a mobile ground station, and logistics vehicles for launch and recovery. The parachute-recoverable fixed-wing air vehicle carries advanced avionics and a thermal imager (stabilised infra-red camera) with a zoom lens. It is designed to have low radar, infra-red and acoustic signatures, to make it hard to detect. Modular construction and small size make it easy for soldiers to assemble, launch and recover.

GEC's contract is a complete package deal covering full development and production of the total number of Phoenix systems currently required. GEC Avionics is overall programme manager for the complete system; the air vehicle is manufactured under subcontract by FR, which is also responsible for the launch and recovery systems.

Type: Battlefield surveillance and target acquisition RPV.

Airframe: Mid-wing monoplane, with central fuselage nacelle and twin tailbooms; detachable underfuselage pod contains the mission-related avionics, including the imaging sensor and data link. Pod is roll-stabilised to minimise demands on the sensor and the directional antenna used for the data link. Modular construction, to facilitate assembly/launch/recovery by soldiers in the field. Wing centre-section integral with fuselage nacelle; tapered 'plug-in' outer panels, with ailerons. Crushable recovery module fairing on top of fuselage. Sweptback endplate fins, integral with tailbooms, fitted with rudders and supporting a central tailplane with one-piece elevator. Airframe components of sandwich composite construction, for low radar signature, manufactured by Herman Smith Hitco Ltd.

Power Plant: One flat-twin aircooled piston engine, in hinged module at front of nacelle, driving a two-blade wooden propeller. Fuel tank in fuselage.

Launch and Recovery: Pneumatic catapult launch from vehicle mounted ramp. Recovery by parachute stored in fuselage. (RPV is inverted during recovery phase, landing on crushable dorsal fairing to protect mission pod and IR sensor on impact.)

Guidance and Control: Flight control and navigation systems derived from those used in earlier Machan research RPV (see 1984-85 and previous *Jane's*); they include Ferranti FS 60 vertical and FDG 60 directional gyros. Air vehicle commands and surveillance data are transmitted via uplink/downlink using advanced component technology. The complex ground control facility interfaces with the Army's Marconi Command and Control Systems Ltd BATES battlefield command and control system and includes a new GEC Avionics digital moving map display; software for this and other GCS installations supplied by Scicon Ltd. Electronic equipment in GCS housed in Hunting Hivolt Ltd Isolator lightweight shelter.

Mission Equipment: Ball mounting beneath ventral mission systems pod houses infra-red camera, based on the GEC Avionics TICM II (thermal imaging common modules) and fitted with a Pilkington PE lens having zoom capability.

Dimensions, Weights and Performance: Classified

MILTRAIN

MILTRAIN LIMITED

West Wing, Building C2, Fairoaks Airport, Chobham, Woking, Surrey GU24 8HX
Telephone: 09905 6385
Telex: 858893 FLETEL G
DIRECTORS:
J. O. G. Paton
M. J. Massy-Beresford

MILTRAIN FLYRT B

Designed and first flown in 1984, the Flyrt B was put into production in 1985.

TYPE: Recoverable airborne small arms target system.

AIRFRAME: Low-wing monoplane of double-delta planform, with triangular fin; no rudder or horizontal tail surfaces. Constructed from composite materials, laminated wood, polyurethane high density foam and epoxy resins.

POWER PLANT: One 0·63 kW (0·85 hp) single-cylinder piston engine, driving a two-blade composite (nylon/glassfibre) propeller. Integral fuel tank in forward fuselage.

LAUNCH AND RECOVERY: Ramp or hand launch, at user's option. Recovery by parachute on command of operator; target can also be recovered safely under operator command, on to a suitable site, without deploying parachute system.

GUIDANCE AND CONTROL: Radio command guidance system, with three servos for precise control by operator within 1·1 nm (2 km; 1·2 miles) of control site. Full span elevons for pitch and roll control; automatic yaw compensation and variable power setting.

DIMENSIONS, EXTERNAL:
Wing span 0·81 m (2 ft 8 in)
Wing aspect ratio 2·05
Length overall 1·22 m (4 ft 0 in)
Fuselage: Max width 10·8 cm (4¼ in)
AREA:
Wings, gross 0·32 m² (3·47 sq ft)
WEIGHTS AND LOADING:
Basic operating weight empty 2·4 kg (5·3 lb)
Max fuel 0·34 kg (0·75 lb)
Max launching weight 3·0 kg (6·6 lb)
Max wing loading 9·28 kg/m² (1·90 lb/sq ft)
PERFORMANCE (at max launching weight):
Never-exceed speed 150 knots (278 km/h; 173 mph)
Max level speed at S/L 110 knots (204 km/h; 127 mph)
Min flying speed 25 knots (47 km/h; 29 mph)
Operating height: min 3 m (10 ft)
max 2,000 m (6,560 ft)
Endurance 30 min
g limit +10

ML

ML AVIATION COMPANY LTD (Flight Systems Division)

White Waltham Aerodrome, Maidenhead, Berkshire SL6 3JG
Telephone: 062 882 3361
DIVISIONAL MANAGER: R. G. Austin
TECHNICAL MANAGER: R. J. Pierce

Founded in the mid-1930s, ML Aviation has design approval for aeroplanes and rotorcraft up to a design gross weight of 6,000 kg (13,227 lb). Its aerospace activities include the design and manufacture of RPVs, aerostructures, bomb carriers and release units, ground handling equipment, and electronic equipment and test sets.

ML's Flight Systems Division activities include the design and development of RPV systems and helicopter rotor test equipment.

ML AVIATION SPRITE

The Sprite is a private venture RPV which derives its name from the initial letters of the six principal roles for which it is intended: surveillance, patrol, reconnaissance, intelligence gathering, target designation, and electronic warfare. Basic role envisaged is that of a 'pop-up' battlefield surveillance RPV; other military, naval and civil uses are also foreseen.

Design began in January 1981, and the first untethered flight was made in January 1983. Trials are continuing, with three Sprites in flight test by early 1986 and five other prototypes under construction.

A large number of military and civilian authorities have expressed interest in the Sprite, and flight demonstrations have been given in the UK, USA and Europe.

AIRFRAME: Two two-blade coaxial counter-rotating rotors, with blades attached to hub by teetering hinges; no rotor brake. Blades are of glassfibre composite construction, with a modified Göttingen aerofoil section. Mechanical transmission via oil lubricated spur gear; rotor/engine rpm ratio 1 : 5. Symmetrical planform body of glassfibre and carbonfibre, with sandwich construction frames, carefully shaped and constructed to offer minimal radar, thermal, noise and optical signatures. Divided internally into four compartments for power plant, fuel tanks, guidance system and sensors. Landing gear comprises four radar-transparent non-retractable glassfibre legs.

POWER PLANT: Two 5·2 kW (7 hp) Piper P.2/80 two-stroke flat-twin engines. Petrol/oil fuel mixture carried in two plastics tanks, combined capacity approx 8 litres (1·75 Imp gallons). Sprite can be maintained airborne on only one engine, thus providing a full 'one engine out' capability. This is considered essential for civil operations.

LAUNCH AND RECOVERY: Vertical take-off and landing, without additional aids.

GUIDANCE AND CONTROL: Skyleader PCM radio command system permits direct ground control through the fully automatic flight control system. Sprite can be pre-programmed for autonomous flight or automatic recovery to base in the event of loss of control link.

MISSION EQUIPMENT: Two 28V 500W alternators provide power for aircraft functioning and for sensors. The sensor pack is one quadrant of the airframe and can be changed easily as required. Many different sensors can be installed, including stabilised TV or infra-red cameras, low light level TV, laser target designator, chemical sensors, elint and ECM. The experimental aircraft are currently fitted with a black and white CCD TV camera with 5:1 zoom lens.

DIMENSIONS, EXTERNAL:
Rotor diameter (each) 1·60 m (5 ft 3 in)
Rotor blade chord (each) 60 mm (2·36 in)
Body diameter (max) 0·65 m (2 ft 1½ in)
Height to top of rotor head 0·90 m (2 ft 11½ in)
WEIGHTS:
Weight empty 24 kg (53 lb)
Max fuel 6 kg (13·2 lb)
Sensor pack (max) 6 kg (13·2 lb)
Max T-O and landing weight 36 kg (79 lb)
PERFORMANCE (at max T-O weight):
Max level speed (estimated) 70 knots (130 km/h; 80 mph)
Max cruising and econ cruising speed 60 knots (111 km/h; 69 mph)
Climb rate at optimum speed of 45 knots (83 km/h; 52 mph) 366 m (1,200 ft)/min
Normal operating height range 250-500 m (820-1,640 ft)
Operating ceiling 3,050 m (10,000 ft)
Maintainable height on one engine 2,440 m (8,000 ft)
Typical mission radius 17 nm (32 km; 20 miles)
Max endurance 2 h 30 min

MoD

MINISTRY OF DEFENCE

Whitehall, London SW1A 2HB

The Royal Navy has a requirement for a sea skimming aerial target system to be used in conjunction with the Goalkeeper close-in weapon system being fitted in Type 22 Batch 3 frigates now being built. Proposals under consideration in 1986 included the Sea Falcon (FR ASAT), Sea Fly (TTL with FR), Sea Star (ML Aviation) and Seawitch (British Aerospace).

A decision on a selected system was not expected to be announced before this section closed for press.

The Royal Air Force is considering a requirement (Air Staff Target 1232) for a drone system, for entry into service in the mid-1990s, fitted with an anti-radar seeker to suppress enemy air defence units in a battlefield area. The drones may also be required to serve as decoys, to allow identification of fire control radars, and to carry radar jamming equipment.

RAE

ROYAL AIRCRAFT ESTABLISHMENT

Radio and Navigation Department (RN2 Division), Building Q146, Farnborough, Hampshire GU14 6TD
Telephone: 0252 24461 extn 2203
SENIOR PRINCIPAL TECHNICAL OFFICER, MECHANICAL SYSTEMS: D. Gordon

RAE XRAE-1

The XRAE-1 was designed originally for homing head trials in 1981; it has also carried video and still cameras, and electronic warfare payloads. The concept was acquired in 1983 by Flight Refuelling (see Raven entry under FR heading).

TYPE: Experimental mini-RPV.

AIRFRAME: Cantilever mid-wing monoplane with pod and boom fuselage and T tail. Tapered wings and non-tapered tailplane are of foam cored GRP and obeche; fuselage is of GRP or Kevlar over a plywood or Kevlar internal structure. Wings and tailplane attached by bolts; with propeller, they can be detached easily for transportation and storage. Landing skids under fuselage.

POWER PLANT: One 1·9 kW (2·5 hp) 15 cc Webra 91 or OS 90 two-stroke engine, driving a two-blade pusher propeller. Max fuel capacity 1·5 litres (0·3 Imp gallons).

LAUNCH AND RECOVERY: Either by dedicated trailer mounted launcher or by stretched elastic cable from suitable sites. Skid landing.

GUIDANCE AND CONTROL: Radio command link via RAE autopilot. Air vehicle is continuously autostabilised, and commands can be input either manually or automatically (pre-programmed) via ground based microprocessor working co-operatively with Plessey WF3 X band tracking radar. Automatic mode includes pre-programming of flight path through designated waypoints. Auto mode can be re-programmed during mission or interdicted manually. Three-axis aerodynamic control surfaces.

MISSION EQUIPMENT: Payload bay in nose can contain real-time JVC video camera, filming obliquely through nose transparency, and vertical Cosina Compact 35 mm still camera. Video transmitter (1W) and PCM telemetry operate in D band. Onboard receiver/decoder, transponder and nickel-cadmium battery.

DIMENSIONS, EXTERNAL:
Wing span 2·70 m (8 ft 10¼ in)
Length overall 2·10 m (6 ft 10¾ in)
Height overall (over propeller) 0·50 m (1 ft 7¾ in)
Propeller diameter 0·36 m (1 ft 2 in)
WEIGHTS:
Typical payload 2·5 kg (5·5 lb)
Typical launching weight 17·5 kg (38·5 lb)
PERFORMANCE (typical):
Operating speed range 32-65 knots (60-120 km/h; 37-74 mph)
Rate of climb at S/L 152 m (500 ft)/min
Endurance 1 h

RAE XRAE-2

Design of the XRAE-2 began in late 1982, and the first flight was made in October 1984. In general terms, it is a scaled-up development of XRAE-1, and its original purpose was to carry a British Aerospace miniature infra-red linescan (MIRLS) to demonstrate the feasibility of a low-cost system. It can also carry a Barr & Stroud MIRLS, an ECM or ESM payload, or chaff. Payloads under development in 1985 included Marconi Defence Systems passive and active EW systems. Equipped with passive ESM, the RPV can be pre-programmed to carry out surveillance in areas of interest and pass the processed data direct to the ground by data link. Control of the onboard system can be exercised by the same method. A range of expendable jammers is also being developed by MDS; these, too, are suitable for use in a ground environment.

Fitment of other electronic warfare payloads was due to take place during 1986.

Thirteen prototypes have been ordered, of which 11 had been completed by early 1986. Production aircraft will be produced by FR with the name Raven 2.

TYPE: Experimental surveillance and electronic warfare RPV.

AIRFRAME: Configuration generally as for XRAE-1. Wings have NACA 4415 or Wortmann FX-63-137 section, 2° 30′ incidence and 2° sweepback at quarter-chord, but no dihedral or anhedral, and are of Kevlar and GRP with a foam core. On trailing-edge between each wingtip and aileron are sheet metal upper and lower surface airbrakes. Fuselage is a glassfibre or Kevlar monocoque, reinforced with foam or Nomex honeycomb and incorporating an integral fin. Movable surfaces are powered by electric servos; later version will have electrically actuated variable tailplane incidence. Fixed energy absorbing skids under fuselage. Interchangeable nose modules, of basically same shape but differing in size depending upon volume of payload required.

POWER PLANT: One 2·2 kW (3 hp) Quadra 50 cc single-cylinder or 3·7 kW (5 hp) Horner 70 cc two-cylinder two-stroke engine, driving a two-blade pusher propeller. Fuel tank in fuselage beneath wing centre-section, capacity 5·56 litres (1·22 Imp gallons). External fuel tanks under development.

LAUNCH AND RECOVERY: As for XRAE-1. Alternative recovery can be made by 5·5 m (18 ft) diameter GQ cruciform parachute.

GUIDANCE AND CONTROL: As for XRAE-1.

MISSION EQUIPMENT: Autopilot, telecommand receiver, payload information transmitter and telemetry transmitter. Chaff cartridge can be fitted to fuselage sides underwing. Engine driven alternator and two 2Ah 28V DC batteries. For other payloads, see opening paragraph.

DIMENSIONS, EXTERNAL:
Wing span 3·62 m (11 ft 10½ in)
Wing chord: at root 0·50 m (1 ft 7¾ in)
at tip 0·415 m (1 ft 4⅓ in)

Miltrain Flyrt B small arms targets

FR ASAT in Sea Falcon configuration (see MoD entry)

Model of the Scicon SOARfly X-wing RPV *(G. R. Wrixon)*

ML Aviation Sprite remotely piloted mini-helicopter in flight. Rotor head fairing has been removed

RAE XRAE-2 surveillance/EW prototype RPV

Wing aspect ratio	7·9
Length overall: standard	2·58 m (8 ft 5½ in)
alternative	2·755 m (9 ft 0½ in) *or* 2·845 m (9 ft 4 in)
Fuselage: Max width	0·50 m (1 ft 7¾ in)
Height overall	0·70 m (2 ft 3½ in)
Tailplane span	1·13 m (3 ft 8½ in)
Propeller diameter (either engine)	0·51 m (1 ft 8 in)
DIMENSIONS, INTERNAL:	
Payload compartment (standard):	
Length	0·635 m (2 ft 1 in)
Max width	0·40 m (1 ft 3¾ in)
Max depth	0·16 m (6·3 in)
Volume	0·033 m³ (1·16 cu ft)
AREA:	
Wings, gross	1·659 m² (17·86 sq ft)
WEIGHTS AND LOADING:	
Max fuel	5 kg (11 lb)
Max payload	10 kg (22 lb)
Max launching weight	40 kg (88 lb)
Max wing loading	24·1 kg/m² (4·9 lb/sq ft)
PERFORMANCE (estimated):	
Never-exceed speed	104 knots (193 km/h; 120 mph)
Max level speed	69 knots (129 km/h; 80 mph)
Max cruising speed	61 knots (113 km/h; 70 mph)
Econ cruising speed	52 knots (96 km/h; 60 mph)
Stalling speed, engine idling	35 knots (65 km/h; 40 mph)
Max rate of climb at S/L	183 m (600 ft)/min
Ceiling	1,525 m (5,000 ft)
Range with max fuel	61 nm (113 km; 70 miles)

SCICON

SCICON LTD

49 Berners Street, London W1P 4AQ
Telephone: 01 580 5599
Telex: 24293
MANAGING DDIRECTOR: W. Werblow

SCICON SOARFLY

To meet airborne reconnaissance needs in a high-intensity battle area, Scicon has conceived the SOARfly as an autonomous battlefield surveillance, electronic warfare and attack vehicle. It was shown in model form at the British Army Equipment Exhibition in June 1986.

Intended as a look at the next stage of RPV development, SOARfly represents the integration of artificial intelligence, terrain-identifying 'map comparison computer' and burst transmission facilities into an airborne battlefield RPV. According to Scicon, the SOARfly could be adapted to carry a variety of payloads, including an electronic countermeasures system, real-time TV, infra-red and thermal surveillance systems, and an offensive payload designed to destroy missile sites in preparation for air strikes by conventional manned aircraft.

SOARfly features rotors for vertical take-off which lock into X-wing configuration for forward flight.

DIMENSIONS, WEIGHTS AND PERFORMANCE:

No details known

SHORTS

SHORT BROTHERS PLC

MISSILE SYSTEMS DIVISION: Montgomery Road, Belfast BT6 9HN, Northern Ireland
Telephone: 0232 59271
Telex: 747087
OFFICERS: see Aircraft section

SHORTS SKEET

The Skeet, now in service with the British Army, provides a realistic, quick-reaction and cost-effective aerial target for use with close range weapon systems. It combines simplicity with high manoeuvrability and ease of operation, but offers the additional advantages of higher speed, greater range and better payload, and has a maximum endurance twice that of the earlier MATS-B. The Skeet completed acceptance trials in September 1979, and was still in production in 1986 for the British Army and for export.

Proposals for a Skeet replacement, including one from Shorts, were being considered by the Army in mid-1986, and a selection was anticipated later in the year.

TYPE: Aerial target system for use with close range weapons.

AIRFRAME: Modular construction cantilever high-wing monoplane. Fuselage of metal and GRP. Polyurethane foam filled glassfibre wings, fin and tailplane.

POWER PLANT: One 13·4 kW (18 hp) NGL WAM 274-6 274 cc two-cylinder two-stroke aircooled engine.

LAUNCH AND RECOVERY: Launched pneumatically from self-contained two-wheel trailer, having a capacity of eight launches from one charging, or from launch rail mounted on a four-wheel truck. Recovery by parachute or by conventional landing, using fuselage underfairing as a skid. Launches can be carried out in crosswinds of up to 25 knots (46 km/h; 29 mph).

GUIDANCE AND CONTROL: Eight-channel (elevator, aileron, throttle, smoke generator firing, height hold, and three spare) radio command system (hand held transmitter and 10W rf amplifier), in the 68MHz band. Automatic barometric height hold available. Visual control sight with binoculars to assist pilot in flying the aircraft visually to over 2·7 nm (5 km; 3·1 miles) range and to enable repeatable tracks to be flown.

SPECIAL EQUIPMENT: X-band reflector in rear fuselage, and parachute in forward fuselage. Sixteen 40 s smoke generators fitted in landing skid. Two wing mounted pods can carry, for example, Simflak for training, and the fuselage can accept either a miss distance indicator or a transponder. An autopilot, complete with heading device, is under development for out of sight operation. An automatic parachute release can be provided. Skeet can accept mission equipment loads of up to 18 kg (40 lb) of a non-target nature (eg, for surveillance and tactical aggression).

DIMENSIONS, EXTERNAL:
Wing span 3·35 m (11 ft 0 in)
Length overall, incl MDI aerial 2·72 m (8 ft 11 in)
Height overall 0·45 m (1 ft 5¾ in)

AREA:
Wings, gross 1·53 m² (16·5 sq ft)

WEIGHTS:
Basic aircraft, empty 42 kg (92·5 lb)
Parachute pack 4 kg (9 lb)
Fuel 9 kg (20 lb)
Mission equipment (normal) 8 kg (17·5 lb)
Max launching weight 63 kg (139 lb)

PERFORMANCE:
Max level speed 130 knots (241 km/h; 150 mph)
Stalling speed 50 knots (93 km/h; 58 mph)
Max in-sight range 2·7 nm (5 km; 3·1 miles)
Max range under control more than 5·4 nm (10 km; 6·2 miles)
Endurance at full throttle 1 h 15 min

SKYLEADER

SKYLEADER RADIO CONTROL LIMITED

Airport House, Purley Way, Croydon CR0 0XZ
Telephone: 01 686 6688 or 0700
MANAGING DIRECTOR: S. E. Uwins

Skyleader was formed in 1965 to manufacture remote control equipment, and today is one of the leading suppliers of telecommand, remote control and associated electronic systems for incorporation in all kinds of unmanned aircraft. It also designed, and continues to produce, the MATS-A aerial target system in use by the British Army.

SKYLEADER MATS-A

MATS-A has been in use for many years by the British Army, and production was continuing in 1986.

TYPE: Aerial target system.

AIRFRAME: Cantilever high-wing monoplane. Fuselage built of glassfibre reinforced resin material with additional strengthening. Wings have polystyrene foam core with veneer covering. Tail surfaces are of balsa. All flying surfaces further covered with tough vinyl.

POWER PLANT: One 10 cc single-cylinder piston engine, driving a two-blade propeller. Methanol/castor oil fuel mixture.

LAUNCH AND RECOVERY: Hand launched. Normal recovery by belly landing on fuselage undersurface; parachute recovery system optional.

GUIDANCE AND CONTROL: Line of sight radio command system, using hand held transmitter. Conventional moving surfaces for aerodynamic control.

MISSION EQUIPMENT: Four-channel superhet receiver, operating on 27MHz bandwidth, within which 12 spot frequencies are available. Rechargeable nickel-cadmium battery pack and three or four proportional feedback servos provide outputs to control surfaces. Transmitter power (1W) is adequate for operating distance of up to 1·1 nm (2 km; 1·25 miles). Other frequencies available up to 72MHz.

DIMENSIONS, EXTERNAL:
Wing span 1·73 m (5 ft 8 in)
Length overall 1·22 m (4 ft 0 in)

WEIGHT:
Max launching weight 3·85 kg (8·5 lb)

PERFORMANCE:
Max level speed 78 knots (145 km/h; 90 mph)
Operating range approx 1·7 nm (3·2 km; 2 miles)
Endurance 15-20 min

TASUMA

TASUMA (UK) LTD

8 South Hill, Alderholt, Fordingbridge, Hampshire
Telephone: 0425 55040
WORKS: Unit A1, Forelle Centre, Ebblake Industrial Estate, Verwood, Dorset
Telephone: 0202 825489
MANAGING DIRECTOR: W. H. Longley

Tasuma (Target And Surveillance UnManned Aircraft) was formed originally to manufacture model aircraft for the hobby trade, but development into higher technology structures led to requests to produce airframe components for major RPV manufacturers. This resulted in disposal of the hobby business to concentrate entirely on RPV work, which has included components and subassemblies for the FR Raven, Shorts MATS-B and Skeet, and Royal Aircraft Establishment XRAE-2.

Such work is still the company's mainstay, but private ventures have led Tasuma to develop designs of its own. These include both surveillance RPVs, for which composite construction methods make possible a high ratio of payload to take-off weight, and high performance target drones. These are available either for direct sale or as an airframe hire service to avionics companies needing air vehicles for flight testing and proofing experiments.

TASUMA T1 WASP

Tasuma's first own-design RPV, the Wasp was produced for the Central Electricity Generating Board and the Cranfield Institute of Technology, a total of ten being manufactured between 1979 and 1982. Wasp was used by the CEGB for altitude air sampling over power stations.

TYPE: Recoverable airborne surveillance mini-RPV.

AIRFRAME: Conventional high-wing monoplane, with tricycle landing gear. Constructed of GRP (fuselage) and epoxy laminated foam (wings).

POWER PLANT: One 1·9 kW (2·5 hp) reciprocating engine, driving a two-blade propeller.

LAUNCH AND RECOVERY: Conventional T-O and landing from smooth terrain.

GUIDANCE AND CONTROL: Manual line of sight, using digital proportional radio on 35 or 68MHz.

DIMENSIONS, EXTERNAL:
Wing span 3·20 m (10 ft 6 in)
Length overall 1·90 m (6 ft 2¾ in)

WEIGHTS:
Max payload 10 kg (22 lb)
Max T-O weight 18 kg (40 lb)

PERFORMANCE:
Cruising speed 51 knots (95 km/h; 59 mph)
Endurance 40 min

TASUMA MINI-TARGET VEHICLE

This aircraft was designed, developed and prototyped in the early 1980s for submission to the UK Ministry of Defence, to meet a requirement of the Admiralty Surface Weapons Establishment.

TYPE: High-speed aerial target.

AIRFRAME: Delta-wing mid-wing monoplane, without horizontal tail surfaces but with optional canard surfaces. Constructed from GRP and Kevlar composites.

POWER PLANT: Single engine (type and power not known), driving a two-blade pusher propeller.

LAUNCH AND RECOVERY: Launched by Tasuma bungee catapult system. Recovered by ventral skid landing on level terrain, or by shipboard retrieval net.

GUIDANCE AND CONTROL: As for T1 Wasp.

DIMENSIONS, EXTERNAL:
Wing span 1·05 m (3 ft 5⅓ in)
Length overall 1·40 m (4 ft 7 in)

WEIGHTS:
Max payload 3 kg (6·6 lb)
Max launching weight 10 kg (22 lb)

PERFORMANCE:
Max level speed 135 knots (250 km/h; 155 mph)
Endurance 30 min

TASUMA T4

TYPE: Recoverable (surveillance) or expendable (hazard threat) mini-RPV.

AIRFRAME: High-wing monoplane, with dihedralled outer wings, nacelle type fuselage, twin-boom/twin-fin-and-rudder tail assembly, and tricycle landing gear. Airframe is of GRP and Kevlar composite construction, and can be assembled and ready to fly in 1 min after unpacking from compact carrying crate.

POWER PLANT: One 2·2 kW (3 hp) engine, mounted in rear of fuselage driving a two-blade pusher propeller.

LAUNCH AND RECOVERY: Can take off conventionally from smooth ground; alternatively, can be given assisted launch by bungee catapult, or by rocket boost from rails on carrying crate. Recovery, when required, by ventral skid landing on smooth ground or by retrieval net.

GUIDANCE AND CONTROL: By simple telemetry control using radar map positioning for location. Aircraft is self-stable in flight and carries height hold facility.

DIMENSIONS, EXTERNAL:
Wing span 2·80 m (9 ft 2¼ in)
Length overall 2·40 m (7 ft 10½ in)

WEIGHTS:
Max payload 10 kg (22 lb)
Max T-O/launching weight 18 kg (40 lb)

PERFORMANCE:
Cruising speed 59 knots (110 km/h; 68 mph)
Endurance 2 h

TASUMA T5

TYPE: Recoverable multi-role surveillance mini-RPV.

AIRFRAME: High-wing pod and boom monoplane with T tail, of Kevlar composite construction.

POWER PLANT: One 3 kW (4 hp) engine, mounted in fuselage pod aft of wing and driving a two-blade pusher propeller.

LAUNCH AND RECOVERY: Three alternative launch systems: (a) from jettisonable T-O dolly on smooth terrain, (b) by bungee assisted take-off from grass field, or (c) by proprietary bungee or compressed air launcher. Recovery by ventral skid landing (smooth terrain) or optional catchnet system.

GUIDANCE AND CONTROL: To customer's requirements.

DIMENSIONS, EXTERNAL:
Wing span 3·30 m (10 ft 10 in)
Length overall 2·30 m (7 ft 6½ in)

WEIGHTS:
Max payload 12 kg (26·5 lb)
Max T-O/launching weight 22 kg (48·5 lb)

PERFORMANCE:
Cruising speed 65 knots (120 km/h; 75 mph)
Endurance 2 h

TASUMA T7

TYPE: Prototype development surveillance RPV with multi-role capability.

AIRFRAME: Twin-boom 'pusher' monoplane of Kevlar composite construction. Optional payload pods according to mission requirements.

POWER PLANT: One 6 kW (8 hp) engine (type not known).

LAUNCH AND RECOVERY: Proprietary bungee or pneumatic launcher. Skid landing or optional catchnet system.

GUIDANCE AND CONTROL: To customer's requirements.

DIMENSIONS, EXTERNAL:
Wing span 3·60 m (11 ft 9¾ in)
Length overall 3·20 m (10 ft 6 in)

WEIGHTS:
Max payload 22 kg (48·5 lb)
Max launching weight 42 kg (93 lb)

PERFORMANCE:
Cruising speed 67 knots (125 km/h; 78 mph)
Endurance (depending on payload) 2-5 h

Shorts Skeet target drone on standard self-contained ground launcher

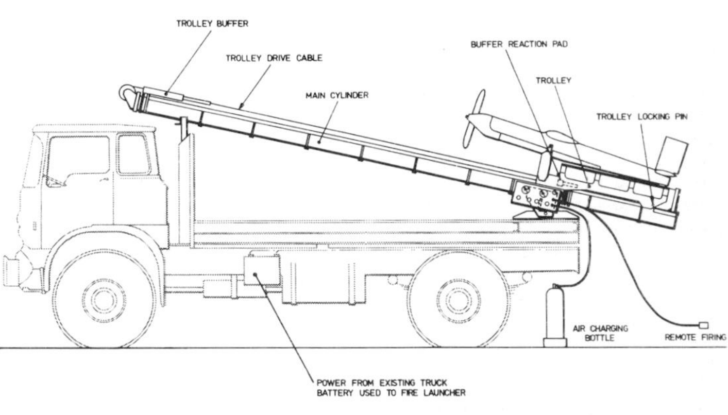

Vehicle mounted variant of Shorts Skeet, now operational

Tasuma Wasp surveillance mini-RPV

Tasuma high-speed mini-target vehicle

Tasuma T4 recoverable or expendable RPVs

Tasuma T5 multi-role surveillance mini-RPV

THORN EMI

THORN EMI ELECTRONICS LTD (Defence Systems Division)

Victoria Road, Feltham, Middlesex TW13 7DZ
Telephone: 01 890 3600
Telex: 23425 EMIFEL G
Managing Director: E. R. Hall
Manager, Sales and Marketing:
Roger Gardner, Albert Drive, Sheerwater, Woking, Surrey GU21 5RU
Telephone: 048 62 76123
Telex: 859615

The Defence Systems Division of Thorn EMI Electronics has built two types of experimental unmanned aircraft, both named Argus (not Argos, as given in the 1985-86 *Jane's*); descriptions of both aircraft follow. The division has also completed a design study for a high altitude, long endurance UMA known as Himet, based on the airframe of a proprietary 15 metre Class sailplane powered by a 1·33 kN (300 lb st) NPT 301 turbojet engine mounted in a dorsal pod.

All three projects have been undertaken as design studies on behalf of the UK Ministry of Defence, and none is a production vehicle. Further information may be obtained by contacting the Marketing Department at the address given.

THORN EMI ARGUS 1

The Argus 1 was developed as a private venture by the Defence Systems Division of Thorn EMI Electronics for applications in which rapid or remote deployment is required, or in which very low thermal and acoustic signatures are necessary. An electric propulsion system was chosen, to offer minimal power plant induced vibration and independence from atmospheric oxygen.

A technology demonstrator prototype flew for the first time in 1979, and a batch of Argus 1s was subsequently built under contract to the UK Ministry of Defence and operated by the Royal Aircraft Establishment. Further improvements are planned.

Type: Experimental electrically powered unmanned aircraft.

Airframe: Conventional high-wing monoplane of stressed skin lightweight construction. Tricycle landing gear.

Power Plant: Thorn EMI purpose-designed DC electric motor, with power range of 300-900W, controlled by a pulse-width modulated throttle and driving a two-blade propeller. Energy source is a battery pack which can be rechargeable or of the primary lithium anode type.

Launch and Recovery: Aircraft can be launched from a tricycle undercarriage or by winch, bungee or vehicle mounted launcher. Recovery can be achieved by skid landing on grass, or wheels on a prepared surface.

Guidance and Control: Range of options available, from manually controlled radio link to full autopilot systems.

Mission Equipment: Various payloads can be accommodated, depending upon particular mission.

Dimensions, external:

Wing span	3·00 m (9 ft 10 in)
Wing area, gross	1·00 m² (10·76 sq ft)

Weights:

Basic weight empty	8 kg (17·6 lb)
Fuel	2 kg (4·4 lb)
Max payload	5 kg (11 lb)
Max T-O/launching weight	15 kg (33 lb)

Performance:

Max level speed	43 knots (80 km/h; 50 mph)
Max range	26·5 nm (49 km; 30·5 miles)
Max endurance	1 h 3 min
g limits	±5

THORN EMI ARGUS 2

Argus 2 was designed to exploit the technology demonstrated by Argus 1, and flew for the first time in January 1984. It has demonstrated improved performance, and has a large bay in the nose which can accommodate a significantly greater payload. Prototype testing has been completed.

TYPE: Experimental electrically powered unmanned aircraft.

AIRFRAME: Square-section fuselage, tail unit and landing gear generally similar to Argus 1, with new high-mounted gull wings of increased span and area. Wings have an Eppler 387 aerofoil section, with constant chord inboard and tapered outer panels, and attached to fuselage by a single plug and socket and six screws.

POWER PLANT: Two DC electric motors of the type that power Argus 1, thus giving a total power which can be varied from 600-1,800W. These drive pusher propellers at the rear end of small trailing-edge pods at the 'knuckles' of the gull wings. Control and energy source as described for Argus 1.

LAUNCH, RECOVERY, GUIDANCE, CONTROL, AND MISSION EQUIPMENT: As described for Argus 1.

DIMENSIONS, EXTERNAL:
Wing span 5·00 m (16 ft 4¾ in)
Wing area, gross 2·00 m² (21·53 sq ft)

WEIGHTS:
Basic weight empty 16 kg (35·3 lb)
Fuel 4 kg (8·8 lb)
Max payload 10 kg (22 lb)
Max T-O/launching weight 30 kg (66·1 lb)

PERFORMANCE:
*Max level speed 43 knots (80 km/h; 50 mph)
Max range 54 nm (100 km; 62 miles)
*Max endurance 1 h 42 min
g limits ±5

**with 6 kg (13·2 lb) payload*

TTL

TARGET TECHNOLOGY LTD

Unit 3, Brunswick Industrial Centre, Ashford, Kent TN24 9QP
Telephone: 0233 39764
Telex: 946240 CWEASY G Ref: 19013070

DIRECTORS:
R. W. Davies
G. C. Dodds
R. J. Gayler

MARKETING MANAGER: Mark Gayler

In addition to its own range of RPVs and targets described in this entry, TTL manufactures a range of launchers, engines, propellers and ground support equipment for a variety of unmanned aircraft. Customers for these items have included AEL, BAe, FR, ML Aviation, Racal and the RAE in the UK, and others in the Middle East, Africa, the USA and Canada.

TTL BTT-1 IMP

The Imp is a hand launched target for use both on land and at sea. By mid-February 1986 a total of 63 had been built. These were in service with the Army, Navy, Air Force and Royal Guard Brigade of the Sultanate of Oman, and had also been purchased by Canada. A further 35 Imps were on order at that time.

TYPE: Training and all-arms air defence target.

AIRFRAME: Mid-wing monoplane of 'cropped delta' planform, with sweptback vertical tail. No horizontal tail surfaces. Fuselage is of glassfibre reinforced resin, with additional strengthening; wings are of plywood over a polystyrene foam core. All flying surfaces are further covered with a tough vinyl material, and parts are interchangeable to simplify replacement.

POWER PLANT: One 12·5 cc glow-plug engine, driving a two-blade propeller.

LAUNCH AND RECOVERY: Hand launch. Recovery by conventional skid landing or, optionally, by parachute. Latter can be commanded manually, or automatically in the event of target damage or failure of command link.

GUIDANCE AND CONTROL: Radio command system (hand held transmitter), developed from a Skyleader four-channel digital system giving independent proportional control of elevons, engine and (optionally) recovery parachute. Variety of frequencies available.

DIMENSIONS, EXTERNAL:
Wing span 1·83 m (6 ft 0 in)
Length overall 1·09 m (3 ft 7 in)
Height overall 0·43 m (1 ft 5 in)
Propeller diameter 0·33 m (1 ft 1 in)

WEIGHTS:
Weight empty 4·5 kg (10 lb)
Max launching weight 5·9 kg (13 lb)

PERFORMANCE:
Max level speed 82 knots (153 km/h; 95 mph)
Stalling speed 13 knots (24 km/h; 15 mph)
Endurance 30 min

TTL BTT-2 DEMON

The Demon has a configuration generally similar to that of the AEL Snipe Mark II. Twelve Demons had been delivered by mid-February 1986, at which time a further ten were on order for a Middle East customer.

TYPE: Basic training target.

AIRFRAME: High-wing monoplane, built of GRP composite materials.

POWER PLANT: One 6·7 kW (9 hp) Piper P.100 single-cylinder two-stroke engine, driving a two-blade propeller. Fuel capacity 5 litres (1·1 Imp gallons).

LAUNCH AND RECOVERY: Similar to those described for Banshee.

GUIDANCE AND CONTROL: By VHF PCM equipment similar to, and compatible with, that used for Banshee.

MISSION EQUIPMENT: Payloads can include a 9-shot smoke flare pod, laser reflectors, infra-red flares, and a miss distance indicator with telemetry downlink.

DIMENSIONS, EXTERNAL:
Wing span 2·59 m (8 ft 6 in)
Length overall 2·13 m (7 ft 0 in)
Height overall 0·63 m (2 ft 1 in)
Propeller diameter 0·51 m (1 ft 8 in)

WEIGHTS:
Weight empty 20·4 kg (45 lb)
Max payload 5·9 kg (13 lb)
Max launching weight 34 kg (75 lb)

PERFORMANCE:
Launching speed 45 knots (84 km/h; 52 mph)
Max level speed 130 knots (241 km/h; 150 mph)
Stalling speed 35 knots (65 km/h; 40 mph)
Visual range with optical tracking system 3·2 nm (6 km; 3·7 miles)
Endurance 1 h 10 min

TTL BTT-3 BANSHEE

The Banshee is a low-cost target system designed primarily to simulate the threat of missiles (including sea skimming weapons) and aircraft for missile and cannon air defence systems. The first of six prototypes made its initial flight in January 1983, and the Banshee is currently in operation in Abu Dhabi, Canada, Egypt, Oman (Army, Navy, Air Force and Royal Guard Brigade), Saudi Arabia and Turkey. In 1985 and 1986 it was the chosen target for the Gulf Co-operation Council's naval exercises, and in July 1986 entered service with the British Army.

By mid-February 1986 production had exceeded 100, with orders outstanding for a further 150. The current version, known as **Banshee B**, has a 381 mm (1½ in) deeper and more streamlined '200 series' fuselage, with increased space available for internal equipment.

TYPE: Remotely controlled aerial target.

AIRFRAME: Low-wing monoplane with clipped delta wings and sweptback fin. No horizontal tail surfaces. Detachable nosecone payload bay. Wings have 45° sweepback at quarter-chord and approx 3° dihedral. Entire airframe of GRP composite material except for elevons, which are of injection moulded epoxy composite. Airframe is watertight for recovery from sea.

POWER PLANT: One 19·4 kW (26 hp) NGL WAM 342 two-cylinder two-stroke engine, driving a two-blade wooden fixed-pitch pusher propeller with spinner. Can also be fitted with Thorn EMI 250W alternator. Fuel in integral fuselage tank, capacity 12 litres (2·6 Imp gallons).

LAUNCH AND RECOVERY: Catapult launch. Launcher is mounted on GSE trailer, but can be removed and used separately (eg, on board ship). Recovery by belly landing on land or water, or by cruciform parachute for braking and vertical descent. Underfuselage smoke pod (faired into overall contour on Banshee B) acts as landing skid; pod also acts as mission payload bay. Parachute mode can be commanded manually or automatically by a fail-safe system in the event of in-flight damage or failure of command link. Turnround times: on land 15 min, at sea 20 min.

GUIDANCE AND CONTROL: High-power PCM radio command guidance system, using VHF radio and line-of-sight optical tracking system incorporating gyrostabilised optics. Autostabiliser incorporates rate gyros controlling yaw, pitch and roll, with height lock; it can be switched in and out during flight with varying degrees of stabilisation. Long-range tracking system available optionally. Elevons are the only moving surfaces for aerodynamic control.

MISSION EQUIPMENT: Onboard battery pack. Alternative mission loads can include a 24-shot underbelly pod of smoke and/or infra-red flares; and Luneberg lenses (one 7·5 in in nose and a second in mid-fuselage, or three 4 in lenses in nose only). Can also be fitted with Firdell 200 (101/103) radar reflectors, each consisting of an optimised triple array of reflective corners with emissions tuned to customer's requirements. Acoustic and Doppler radar miss distance indication systems are available.

DIMENSIONS, EXTERNAL:
Wing span 2·49 m (8 ft 2 in)
Length overall 2·84 m (9 ft 4 in)
Height overall 0·86 m (2 ft 10 in)
Body diameter (max) 0·305 m (1 ft 0 in)
Propeller diameter 0·61 m (2 ft 0 in)

AREA:
Wings, gross 2·14 m² (23·0 sq ft)

WEIGHTS:
Weight empty 38·5 kg (85 lb)
Max payload 16 kg (35 lb)
Max launching weight 70 kg (155 lb)

PERFORMANCE:
Launching speed 52 knots (97 km/h; 60 mph)
Max level speed 174 knots (322 km/h; 200 mph)
Stalling speed 39 knots (73 km/h; 45 mph)
Max range:
optical tracking system 6·5 nm (12 km; 7·5 miles)
long-range tracking system 10·8 nm (20 km; 12·5 miles)
Endurance at full throttle 1 h 15 min

TTL SPECTRE and HAWKEYE

The **Spectre** derivative of Banshee is essentially a flying platform for testing and development of customer payloads; four have been delivered to Racal in the UK for airborne system development of electronic warfare payloads.

Standard packages are also available, one of which is the Adrian March Research TV surveillance system, comprising a solid state TV camera, 35 mm film camera, wide-range zoom lens with sight line stabilised and steered by a gyro-controlled mirror, and a data downlink. The Defence Research Establishment of Canada, in conjunction with Boeing of Canada, has purchased five Spectres fitted with this system and named **Hawkeye**, plus a quantity of Banshees, to study the suitability of RPVs for surveillance in naval operations. Several Middle Eastern countries have also expressed interest in procuring this system.

Spectre power plant and vehicle weights are as quoted for the Banshee, but dimensions and other data differ as follows:

DIMENSIONS, EXTERNAL:
Wing span: min 2·13 m (7 ft 0 in)
max 2·90 m (9 ft 6 in)
Length overall 2·74 m (9 ft 0 in)
Height overall 0·71 m (2 ft 4 in)

WEIGHTS:
Payload: Spectre (max) 20 kg (44 lb)
Hawkeye 15 kg (33 lb)

PERFORMANCE:
Launching speed 49 knots (90 km/h; 56 mph)
Max level speed 148 knots (273 km/h; 170 mph)
Stalling speed 39 knots (73 km/h; 45 mph)
Max range:
optical tracking system 6·5 nm (12 km; 7·5 miles)
long-range tracking system 27 nm (50 km; 31 miles)
Loiter endurance 2 h

TTL JTT-5 VOODOO

Brief details of the Voodoo were released at the Farnborough International air show in September 1986. A development of the Banshee, it is intended for both RPV and target use. It is powered by a 0·525 kN (118 lb st) NGL WAEL 600N turbojet and has a maximum speed of more than 260 knots (483 km/h; 300 mph).

VINTEN

W. VINTEN LTD (Military Division)

Western Way, Bury St Edmunds, Suffolk IP33 3TB
Telephone: 0284 2121
Telex: 81176

CHAIRMAN AND MANAGING DIRECTOR: Michael James

PUBLICITY MANAGER: J. Mulvaney

On 1 March 1981 a collaborative agreement was reached between Wing Commander K. H. Wallis (see UK part of main Aircraft section) and W. Vinten Ltd, permitting the latter to manufacture autogyros to Wallis designs for various military and commercial purposes.

A project to demonstrate the ability of the autogyro as an RPV, known as the Vindicator, has been completed successfully. Details of this programme can be found in the 1985-86 *Jane's*. Vinten retains the ability to re-establish RPV trials if a suitable requirement should occur.

Thorn EMI Argus 1

Thorn EMI Argus 2

Target Technology's hand launched BTT-1 Imp

TTL Banshee B recoverable target during 1986 naval exercises in the Gulf of Oman

TTL Hawkeye surveillance variant of the Spectre for Canadian evaluation

TTL Spectre on mobile ground support trolley

UNITED STATES OF AMERICA

AAI

AAI CORPORATION
(Missiles and Robotics Division)

PO Box 6767, Baltimore, Maryland 21204
Telephone: (301) 666 1400
Telex: 8-7849
President: I. R. Barr
Marketing: Warren E. Mann
Public Relations: Walter A. Friend

AAI is developing a non-ballistic high-speed, high-altitude reconnaissance mini-RPV with VTOL capability, including hovering. For this mission it can be equipped with a miniature TV camera. Its rate of climb is quoted as "about six times that of conventional mini-RPVs", and it is reported to be capable also of acting as an anti-tank and anti-helicopter missile. Another current in-house programme in early 1986 was for a rocket launched drone utilising a lightweight zero-length launcher.

AAI is teamed with Mazlat of Israel (which see) in producing the latter's Pioneer RPV for the US Navy.

AEROBOTICS

AEROBOTICS INC (Subsidiary of Moller International Inc)

1222 Research Park Drive, Davis, California 95616
Telephone: (916) 753 1029
PRESIDENT: Paul Moller
ELECTRONICS GROUP MANAGER: Max Parker

Aerobotics Inc was formed in 1985 as a subsidiary of Moller International (see main Aircraft section) to concentrate the parent company's accumulated knowledge of small VTOL 'flying saucer' aircraft into a specific product line of unmanned models, which are known collectively as Aerobots.

AEROBOTICS AEROBOTS

In early 1985 a 0·81 m (2 ft 8 in) diameter electrically powered Aerobot, with a 2·3 kg (5 lb) payload, was constructed as a demonstrator under contract to the US Naval Ocean Systems Command, flying with an onboard video camera for remote viewing. Subsequently, the company has developed a range of Aerobots designed to carry payloads of up to 363 kg (800 lb) over distances of up to 373 nm (692 km; 430 miles) and at speeds of up to 217 knots (402 km/h; 250 mph). It reports significant interest in these from military groups worldwide.

The Aerobots combine VTOL capability with the extensive use of plastics to minimise radar cross-section, and their power plant systems have a low noise signature. A complex thrust vectoring system within the ducts is used to accomplish stability and control; all models also carry onboard flight stabilisation equipment and various radio or 'wire guidance' control links, depending upon the range and operating altitude required. Surveillance payload packages can include TV cameras and laser equipment, and the Aerobots can transition from vertical to horizontal flight to reach a region of interest, hover or loiter for a period, then return to their launch point.

The announced product range as at Spring 1986 comprised six models, identified as follows:

E410M. Powered by 3 kW (4 hp) electric motor; four fan ducts, each with two-blade fan.

P115M. Powered by 3·7 kW (5 hp) two-cylinder piston engine, driving a two-blade fan in a single duct.

R124M. Powered by 37·3 kW (50 hp) rotary engine, driving a seven-blade fan in a single duct.

R1242RM. As R124M, but powered by twin 37·3 kW (50 hp) rotary engines.

R820M. Powered by 298 kW (400 hp) rotary engine; eight fan ducts, each with a seven-blade fan.

R8202RM. As R820M, but powered by twin 298 kW (400 hp) rotary engines.

DIMENSIONS, EXTERNAL:
- Diameter overall: E410M — 0·86 m (2 ft 10 in)
  - P115M — 0·51 m (1 ft 8 in)
  - R124M, R1242RM — 0·76 m (2 ft 6 in)
  - R820M, R8202RM — 2·84 m (9 ft 4 in)
- Diameter of duct(s): E410M — 0·25 m (10 in)
  - P115M — 0·38 m (1 ft 3 in)
  - R124M, R1242RM — 0·61 m (2 ft 0 in)
  - R820M, R8202RM — 0·51 m (1 ft 8 in)
- Height overall: E410M — 0·25 m (10 in)
  - P115M — 0·46 m (1 ft 6 in)
  - R124M, R1242RM — 0·71 m (2 ft 4 in)
  - R820M, R8202RM — 0·91 m (3 ft 0 in)

WEIGHTS:
- Max payload: E410M, P115M — 4·5 kg (10 lb)
  - R124M — 20·4 kg (45 lb)
  - R1242RM — 56·6 kg (125 lb)
  - R820M — 181 kg (400 lb)
  - R8202RM — 363 kg (800 lb)
- Max T-O weight: E410M — 10·4 kg (23 lb)
  - P115M — 13·6 kg (30 lb)
  - R124M — 91 kg (200 lb)
  - R1242RM — 136 kg (300 lb)
  - R820M — 544 kg (1,200 lb)
  - R8202RM — 907 kg (2,000 lb)

PERFORMANCE (estimated):
- Max level speed:
  - P115M — 56 knots (105 km/h; 65 mph)
  - R124M — 152 knots (282 km/h; 175 mph)
  - R1242RM — 217 knots (402 km/h; 250 mph)
  - R820M — 78 knots (145 km/h; 90 mph)
  - R8202RM — 96 knots (177 km/h; 110 mph)
- *Service ceiling: E410M** — over 61 m (200 ft)
  - all other models — 4,575 m (15,000 ft)
- Typical mission range:
  - P115M — 30·4 nm (56 km; 35 miles)
  - R124M — 278 nm (515 km; 320 miles)
  - R1242RM — 373 nm (692 km; 430 miles)
  - R820M — 104 nm (193 km; 120 miles)
  - R8202RM — 139 nm (257 km; 160 miles)
- Max hover time: E410M — indefinite
  - P115M — 30 min
  - R124M, R1242RM — 1 h 45 min
  - R820M, R8202RM — 1 h 15 min

* *Requires trade-off against payload*
***According to power/control cable: this model designed for local surveillance above ground station*

AERODYNE

AERODYNE SYSTEMS ENGINEERING LTD

1140 19th Street NW, Suite 600, Washington, DC 20036
Telephone: (202) 223 9100
Telex: 46-6169
PRESIDENT: James J. Solano

AERODYNE CH-84 PEGASUS

Aerodyne Systems Engineering has re-engineered the Gyrodyne QH-50 DASH (drone anti-submarine helicopter) of the 1960s by replacing the original 224 kW (300 shp) Boeing T50 engine with a lighter and more powerful Allison 250-C20 and fitting a new electronic control system. Renamed CH-84 Pegasus, it is now configured as a recoverable airborne surveillance RPH. Design modification began in 1981, and construction of a prototype started in 1983. This made its first flight in 1984, in which year Aerodyne Systems also completed one pre-production and one production standard example.

The Pegasus was expected to be submitted during 1986 in response to RFPs (requests for proposals) from the US Army and US Navy. The former requirement is for an off-the-shelf elint/EW RPV, the latter for a medium-range reconnaissance vehicle. Contractor selection was expected to be announced in Autumn 1986 and early 1987 respectively. There is a reported likelihood that the US Navy vehicle may also be purchased by the US Air Force.

TYPE: Recoverable airborne surveillance RPH.

ROTOR SYSTEM: Two two-blade semi-rigid counter-rotating coaxial rotors, with glassfibre blades, incorporating linear taper (in planform and thickness) and negative twist. Rotor controls operated by automatic stabilisation and remote control equipment: pitch and roll via cyclic control of swashplates, collective pitch control by collective movement of swashplates. Control in yaw exercised by movable tip brakes connected to both upper and lower blade tips, which create unequal torque distribution. Lower tip brakes are deflected to turn left, upper tip brakes to turn right.

ROTOR DRIVE: Transmission system consists of two-stage gear reduction, two coaxial rotor driveshafts, integral lubrication system, generator drive and rotary actuator drive. Engine power transmitted to rotors via two-stage reduction, second stage of which divides torque to the two rotor shafts. Generator and rotary actuator driven by accessory drives, in mesh with a single drivegear mounted on lower rotor shaft.

POWER PLANT: One 313 kW (420 shp) Allison 250-C20F turboshaft engine. Single cylindrical fuel tank, capacity 197 litres (52 US gallons). Provision for 303 litre (80 US gallon) auxiliary tank.

LAUNCH AND RECOVERY: Conventional helicopter take-off and landing.

GUIDANCE AND CONTROL: Remote control consists of an airborne four-axis stabilisation system and a receiver/decoder, interfaced with a Vega 6104 ground based target tracking control system. Aircraft is stabilised in pitch, roll, yaw and altitude, with rotor rpm maintained at constant speed by engine governor. Vertical gyro for pitch and roll reference, directional gyro for yaw and barometric altimeter for altitude reference. Lear Siegler autopilot. The CH-84 is equipped with a loss of carrier and/or destruct system. In former case, aircraft will enter a hover mode within 30 s; destruct is a command function shutting off engine fuel supply.

MISSION EQUIPMENT: 'Mini-View' concept for OTH (over the horizon) surveillance utilises a tethered aerostat as a repeater for simultaneous control of two CH-84 drone helicopters. Each drone sends back a TV signal through the aerostat repeater together with telemetry of its 'housekeeping' functions. In addition, two separate command channels, operating at UHF to the drone, are afforded via the aerostat. Using the aerostat as a repeater allows the CH-84s to operate within line of sight up to 130 nm (241 km; 150 miles) from the aerostat tether point. Aerostat-to-ground uplinks/downlinks can be in 2, 4, 6 or 8GHz region, at customer's choice.

DIMENSIONS, EXTERNAL:
- Rotor diameter (each) — 6·10 m (20 ft 0 in)
- Fuselage: Length (basic) — 2·04 m (6 ft 8¼ in)
- Max width — 1·60 m (5 ft 3 in)
- Height to top of rotor head — 2·79 m (9 ft 2 in)
- Skid track — 1·52 m (5 ft 0 in)
- Skid length — 1·62 m (5 ft 3⅔ in)

AREA:
- Rotor discs (each) — 29·19 m² (314·2 sq ft)

WEIGHTS:
- Basic weight empty — 338 kg (745·6 lb)
- Payload: normal — 661·7 kg (1,458·9 lb)
  - military — 463 kg (1,020 lb)
- Max fuel weight (standard tank) — 170 kg (375 lb)
- Max T-O weight — 1,179 kg (2,600 lb)

PERFORMANCE (at max T-O weight):
- Max level speed at S/L — 115 knots (213 km/h; 132 mph)
- Typical cruising speed at S/L — 80 knots (148 km/h; 92 mph)
- Econ cruising speed at S/L — 55 knots (102 km/h; 63 mph)
- Forward rate of climb at 1,525 m (5,000 ft) — 570 m (1,870 ft)/min
- Service ceiling — 4,875 m (16,000 ft)
- Hovering ceiling: IGE — 4,575 m (15,000 ft)
  - OGE — 3,355 m (11,000 ft)
- Endurance at 55 knots (102 km/h; 63 mph) at S/L:
  - standard fuel — 1 h 45 min
  - with auxiliary fuel — 5 h 30 min

AEROMET

AEROMET INC

PO Box 701767, Jones Airport, Tulsa, Oklahoma 74170-1767
Telephone: (918) 299 2621
PRESIDENT: Dr D. Ray Booker, PhD

AEROMET AURA

As indicated briefly under the RAF heading in the 1985-86 *Jane's*, remotely piloted versions of the Rutan Long-EZ are being used by some US armed services. These are known by the acronym AURA (Aeromet Unmanned Reconnaissance Aircraft).

Aeromet developed the AURA for use on national test ranges, for applications where a manned aircraft is unsuitable for reasons of personnel safety, mission duration or operating costs. The AURA offers the capability of being flown manned; a feature which permits operation in populated areas, flight tests for equipment performance evaluation, and use as a surrogate unmanned aircraft. Essentially an IR&D development of Aeromet, the AURA has had some contract support from the US Army Strategic Defense Command and the US Navy Pacific Missile Test Center. The USAF Ballistic Missile Office is sponsoring development of meteorological instrumentation to be on the AURA for missile re-entry tests at Kwajalein Missile Range.

The AURA programme was begun in late 1983, underwent evaluation at the Pacific Missile Range in early 1985, and remotely controlled take-off and landing were demonstrated in August 1985.

TYPE: Recoverable airborne reconnaissance system.

AIRFRAME: Modified Rutan Long-EZ, of all-composite glassfibre construction with rigid foam core (see Sport Aircraft section for full description). It features a canard foreplane, highly swept wings with winglets, and a pusher propeller.

POWER PLANT: Engine used in standard AURA is an 85·75 kW (115 hp) Avco Lycoming O-235 with fixed-pitch wooden propeller. Fuel capacity 197 litres (52 US gallons).

LAUNCH AND RECOVERY: Conventional take-off and landing, controlled by ground pilot through autopilot system.

GUIDANCE AND CONTROL: Independent primary and manual control systems. Primary system controls aircraft in all regimes except take-off and landing, which are performed through the manual system. Manual system also provides backup to primary control. Aircraft is controlled at all times through a rate-based autopilot, mated to a Litton LTN-3000 VLF/Omega navigation system. Vertical flight modes are commanded through a digital interface control. Navigation waypoints are programmed before flight, and can be reprogrammed during flight. Aircraft position and situation data are downlinked, with mission data, to the ground station, which has telemetered displays of flight and performance parameters, aircraft position and mission data. In the manual mode, the ground pilot controls the aircraft through the autopilot. The ground pilot can direct changes in aircraft attitude and heading, and operate aircraft controls such as brakes, throttle, carburettor heat and other functions. The system has built-in limits on bank angle and rate of ascent. In the event of primary control system failure the ground pilot can assume control through the manual system and return the aircraft for landing.

MISSION EQUIPMENT: The AURA payload compartment can accommodate a variety of sensors and other equipment for missions such as reconnaissance, meteorological data gathering and communications relay. Depending on fuel load, equipment weight can be up to 181 kg (400 lb), including the Aeromet distributed data acquisition system of microprocessors and centralised computer. A fast-scan video system is provided for visual surveillance.

P115M Aerobot, with hand held radio control transmitter in foreground

Aerobotics E410M, with Sony miniature video camera mounted on top

The eight-duct Aerobot R820M, known previously as the XM-4

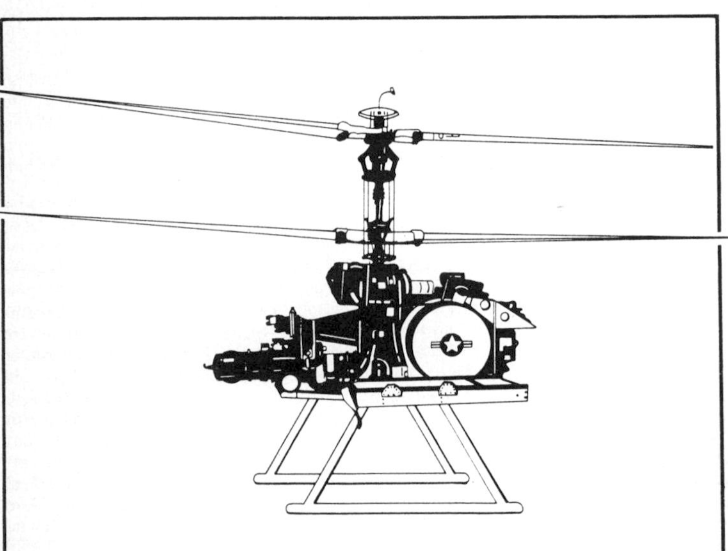

General configuration of the Aerodyne CH-84 Pegasus RPH

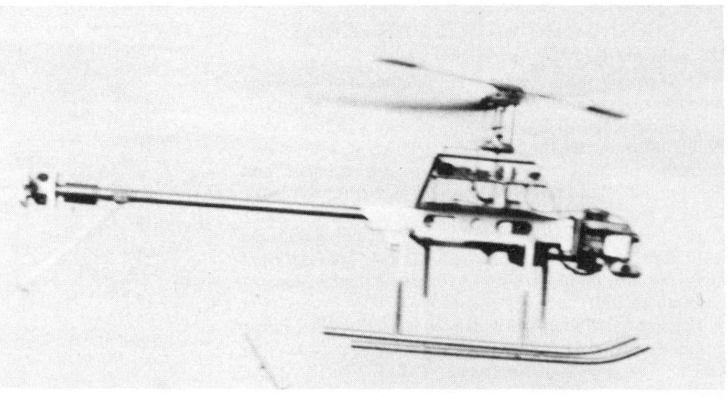

Aerotronics RPH-1 Dragonfly remotely piloted mini-helicopter

Aeromet AURA remotely piloted reconnaissance version of the Rutan Long-EZ

Dimensions, external, and Areas: As for standard Long-EZ

Weights:

Basic operating weight empty	362 kg (800 lb)
Max mission load	181 kg (400 lb)
Max T-O weight	725 kg (1,600 lb)

Performance:

Never-exceed speed, and max level speed at S/L	190 knots (352 km/h; 218 mph)
Normal cruising speed	167 knots (309 km/h; 192 mph)
Econ cruising speed	110 knots (204 km/h; 127 mph)
Min flying speed	65 knots (121 km/h; 75 mph)
Max ceiling	6,100 m (20,000 ft)
Range with max fuel	2,000 nm (3,706 km; 2,303 miles)
Max endurance	12 h
g limits	+5/−2

AEROTRONICS

AEROTRONICS INC

21000 NE 28th Avenue, Suite 109, Miami, Florida 33180
Telephone: (404) 257 1686
President: Paul Fetko

This company has produced and flight demonstrated two small remotely piloted helicopters (RPHs) known as Dragonfly, designed by Mr Michael J. Mas.

AEROTRONICS DRAGONFLY

The Dragonfly was developed as a private venture to demonstrate the feasibility of a lightweight, simple RPV with fundamental reliability and low cost. A helicopter configuration was chosen to eliminate the need for separate launch and recovery systems. The first prototype, designated **RPH-1**, was flown for the first time in 1984 and proved stable, responsive and dependable. A second, identical example confirmed performance repeatability, and was subsequently upgraded to **Modified RPH-2** standard to increase its payload capability to a more useful level. In this latter form it has a slightly enlarged and strengthened airframe and increased engine power.

A wide variety of civil and military applications is foreseen, and the Dragonfly has already demonstrated the carriage of such payloads as a TV camera and radar and infra-red augmentation devices. It was used by Martin Marietta for an eight-month programme measuring guidance-beam cross-sections, and to measure miss distances during test firings of the latter's air defence anti-tank system (ADATS). Presentations have been made to the US Army, Air Force, Navy, Marine Corps and Coast Guard, as well as to the CIA, DIA and FBI.

Type: Remotely piloted mini-helicopter.

Airframe: Simple minimum airframe of weldless aluminium tube, with lightening holes. Two-blade main and tail rotors, former having blades mainly of wood with metal and glassfibre reinforcement at hub end. Stabilised hub of proprietary design. Main landing skids are aluminium; shock mounted tailskid.

Power Plant: One single-cylinder two-stroke marine piston engine, mounted at nose; of increased power on Modified RPH-2.

Launch and Recovery: Conventional helicopter take-off and landing.

Guidance and Control: By HF proportional radio remote control system.

Mission Equipment: Demonstrated payloads have included video cameras, transmitters, instrumentation, and heat and radar augmentation panels. Other potential payloads can include closed circuit TV, ciné and/or still cameras; autopilot; com/nav, infra-red or ECM equipment; laser rangefinder/designator; or military weapons and explosives.

Dimensions, external (A: RPH-1, B: RPH-2):

Main rotor diameter: A	3·05 m (10 ft 0 in)
B	3·66 m (12 ft 0 in)
Tail rotor diameter: A, B	0·99 m (3 ft 3 in)
Length overall: A	2·44 m (8 ft 0 in)
B	2·74 m (9 ft 0 in)

Weights:

Weight empty: A	31·75 kg (70 lb)
B	36·3 kg (80 lb)
Useful load (payload + fuel): A	13·6 kg (30 lb)
B	31·75 kg (70 lb)

Performance:

Max level speed: A, B	109 knots (201 km/h; 125 mph)
Max operating altitude: A, B	3,050 m (10,000 ft)

AMERICAN AIRCRAFT

AMERICAN AIRCRAFT INC

4310 Rankin Lane NE, Albuquerque, New Mexico 87107

Telephone: (505) 344 6366

OFFICERS: see Sport Aircraft section

AMERICAN AIRCRAFT FALCON

A remotely controlled version of the Falcon microlight (see Sport Aircraft section) was developed by American Aircraft Inc, originally to test the aircraft's recovery parachute system. Since then, considerable interest has reportedly been shown in a pilotless version for various applications, and at least three have been sold: two to the US Army as low-level battlefield communications platforms (with radio equipment by Cincinnati Electronics), and one to the Los Alamos Laboratory in New Mexico for atmospheric and environmental tests.

BEECHCRAFT

BEECH AIRCRAFT CORPORATION

PO Box 85, Wichita, Kansas 67201-0085

Telephone: (316) 681 7689

OFFICERS: see Aircraft section

In addition to manufacturing piloted aircraft, Beech has been designing and producing pilotless target drones since 1955. By 1 January 1986 it had built more than 7,000 target drones, including more than 2,200 MQM-61As (now out of production), more than 4,000 AQM-37s, and more than 750 MQM-107s.

BEECHCRAFT MODEL 1104 SERIES

US military designation: AQM-37C

This normally non-recoverable, supersonic air-launched missile target system is designed to simulate invader aircraft and missile threats, and to provide defence weapon system evaluation and crew training. The latest AQM-37C version is currently being used to support development and deployment of the US Navy's Aegis fleet defence missile system. The target provides both active and passive radar augmentation for radar acquisition and tracking; a chemical flare is provided for infra-red homing. Two optional miss distance systems are available. Launch aircraft currently include the A-4, A-6 and F-4.

The original Model 1019 won a 1959 US Navy/Air Force design competition, and has since entered service in a variety of versions with the US Navy (AQM-37A, 20 Model 1019A and 415 Model 1102), US Air Force and US Army (incl 48 recoverable Models 1100/1101), as well as the air forces of France (50 Model 1094/Matra Vanneau), Israel (20 Model 1098), Italy (11 Model 1088) and the UK (190 Model 1072/Shorts SD.2 Stiletto and 40 Model 1095). Details of these earlier models can be found in the 1984-85 and previous editions of *Jane's*. Total deliveries of all versions had reached 4,200 by January 1986, including 3,750 for the US Navy.

The **Model 1104** is the current basic **AQM-37C** target, of which the US Navy ordered a further 56 in 1984, for delivery between March and September 1986. In late 1985 the US Navy ordered an additional 205 of this model, for delivery between October 1986 and March 1988, bringing to 3,950 the total number of AQM-37s (all versions) ordered by the USN.

The current Model 1104/AQM-37C is an improved version of the Model 1019 series for US Navy, for missions at speeds and altitudes up to Mach 3·0 and 24,385 m (80,000 ft). Ordered after a successful demonstration programme of ten vehicles, conducted in 1981, it has a digital autopilot with improved flight control features; greater range and endurance, achieved by an optimum energy management programme; and command control capability which permits dual launch and in-flight heading control. Dives of 15-65°, and pullout from dives, can be initiated upon command from ground. Radar augmentation is improved, covering several frequency bands. A new radome, with nose mounted pitot, increases overall length. Endplate fins are increased in area by 40 per cent. Total of 54 delivered to US Navy; 44 flights made by early 1986, with 95·5 per cent flight reliability.

Other current versions are:

Model 1105 (AQM-37 Variant). Beech designation for a version of AQM-37C for missions at Mach 4·0 and 30,480 m (100,000 ft). Incorporates thermal protection of leading surfaces. US Navy funded eight vehicles for the development programme. All test objectives were achieved in five flights; remainder of flights pushed flight profile to Mach 4·7 at 34,140 m (112,000 ft) after launch from F-4 Phantom aircraft. US Navy is currently funding development of 35 kits to modify AQM-37Cs to Variant configuration.

Model 1108. Training version of UK Model 1095, with single-chamber engine and modified performance. Total of 30 delivered to British Ministry of Defence by late 1984; further 30 ordered, for late 1986 delivery.

The following description applies to current models of the AQM-37, except as noted in the Model 1105 paragraph:

TYPE: Air launched expendable target.

AIRFRAME: Mid-wing monoplane, of canard configuration, with slim-delta main wings (of double-wedge section) at rear having 76° sweep on leading-edges, 0° dihedral, 0° incidence, and full span ailerons. Movable foreplanes, of modified double-wedge section. Fixed endplate fin at tip of each main wing. Cylindrical centre-fuselage, with ogival nose section and tapering rear section over rocket chambers. Underbelly tunnel for rocket engine cartridge operated start valves, plumbing, infra-red flare and miss distance scoring system antenna.

POWER PLANT: One Rocketdyne/AMF LR64 P-4 two-chamber liquid propellant variable thrust rocket motor (2·81 kN; 631 lb st). Three propellant tanks, for nitrogen pressurant, mixed amine fuel (MAF-4) and IRFNA oxidiser, form integral part of centre-fuselage.

LAUNCH AND RECOVERY: Air launched from launcher which is adapted to A-4, A-6, F-4 and other aircraft. Non-recoverable.

GUIDANCE AND CONTROL: Programmed guidance system. Flight normally terminated by automatic destruct system, which also operates in event of a major failure. Command standby destruct system for added range safety.

MISSION EQUIPMENT: Approx 0·04 m³ (1·4 cu ft) of space in nose section for optional scoring and augmentation systems (see introductory paragraph). Target is compatible with most non-co-operative scoring systems.

DIMENSIONS, EXTERNAL (AQM-37C):

Wing span	1·01 m (3 ft 4 in)
Length overall	4·14 m (13 ft 7 in)
Height overall	0·66 m (2 ft 2 in)
Diameter of fuselage	0·33 m (1 ft 1 in)

AREA:

Wings (exposed)	0·87 m² (9·35 sq ft)

WEIGHTS:

Weight empty	109 kg (241 lb)
Max payload	22·7 kg (50 lb)
Max launching weight	295 kg (650 lb)

PERFORMANCE:

Cruising height and speed:

from Mach 0·87 (573 knots; 1,062 km/h; 660 mph) at 305 m (1,000 ft)

to Mach 3·0 (1,719 knots; 3,186 km/h; 1.980 mph) at 24,385 m (80,000 ft)

Range	more than 100 nm (185 km; 115 miles)
Endurance (powered)	8 min

BEECHCRAFT MODELS 999A and 1089

US Army designation: MQM-107A/C/D Streaker

Swedish Air Force designation: RB06 Girun

Beech was awarded a multi-year production contract by the US Army in 1975 for the Model 1089 Variable Speed Training Target, under the designation MQM-107A Streaker. Final assembly is performed at Beech's Boulder Division in Colorado. Beech designed, developed and now delivers ground support equipment, spares and ancillaries; and also provides operation of the system.

The principal function of the Streaker is to provide a variety of threat simulations for training with missiles and automatic weapons. It is the primary subsonic missile training target for the US Army, and is also used in R & D testing of weapon systems. The standard **MQM-107A** is a sweptwing, turbojet powered aerial target that operates at altitudes from sea level up to 12,200 m (40,000 ft) and at speeds of up to 500 knots (925 km/h; 575 mph). It tows gunnery banners and tow targets on cable lengths of up to 2,440 m (8,000 ft). With wingtip augmentation and scoring devices the MQM-107A itself also serves as an aerial target for air defence systems such as Stinger, Chaparral, Redeye, Hawk and Improved Hawk. External mission equipment loads can be carried.

In addition to its use by the US Army and other Department of Defense agencies, the MQM-107A system has been supplied by the US Army to Iran (MQM-107A) and Sweden (999A) through Foreign Military Sales. Taiwan and South Korea have purchased and are now operating the system. Total orders amounted to more than 750 units by early 1986, including the higher powered later **MQM-107C and D versions** (see 'Power Plant' paragraph). A total of 152 MQM-107Cs was delivered in 1985; 90 MQM-107Ds are scheduled for delivery in 1987, followed by 92 more in 1988.

TYPE: Re-usable variable speed target.

AIRFRAME: Low-wing monoplane configuration, with swept-back wings and tail surfaces. Engine suspended on pylon beneath centre of cylindrical fuselage. Modular design throughout, with flat-section wing and tail surfaces of bonded honeycomb (fixed surfaces); foam filled aluminium ailerons and elevators. Ogival nose and tail cones.

POWER PLANT: Standard MQM-107A is powered by a 2·85 kN (640 lb st) Teledyne CAE J402-CA-700 turbojet engine, mounted in an underfuselage pod. The MQM-107C is powered by a Teledyne CAE 372-11A, an uprated version of the J402-CA-700 delivering 3·23 kN (725 lb st), and the MQM-107D, for 1987 delivery, will have the 4·36 kN (980 lb st) TCAE 373-8 engine. Standard fuel capacity is 246 litres (65 US gallons), plus 15 litres (4 US gallons) for a smoke/oil visual identification system. Wing insert fuel tanks, provided as a kit, can add a further 113 litres (30 US gallons). Target can be surface launched from a zero length launcher, using a JATO booster. An improved booster, providing additional thrust, is under development by Thiokol. Payload weights can be increased by use of this new booster.

LAUNCH AND RECOVERY: Lightweight zero length surface launcher and checkout system, easily transportable in two suitcase size containers; can also be air launched from manned aircraft. Drogue and main parachute command recovery system.

GUIDANCE AND CONTROL: Guidance and control systems, either analog or digital, provide for both ground control and pre-programmed flight. The flight controller is provided with all pertinent flight information by radio link from sensors located in the vehicle, and the operator can command vehicle manoeuvres and recovery. In flight, the guidance and control system automatically stabilises around the roll, yaw and pitch attitudes and provides altitude and velocity hold modes. Flight control developments include a terrain following guidance capability which has demonstrated extremely low altitude flight profiles. To provide a greater internal carrying capacity, an extended payload section is available. This also provides easier access to the payload and vehicle electronics, and has specialised waterproofing provisions for sea water recoveries.

MISSION EQUIPMENT: Principal function is to tow a variety of targets for missile training and evaluation. Two TRX-4 radar or two TA-8 infra-red augmentation targets can be carried on each mission and towed separately up to 2,440 m (8,000 ft) behind MQM-107A. Streaker serves as aerial target for such air defence systems as Chaparral, Redeye, Hawk, Roland and Stinger, and the Vulcan rapid-fire gun system. Internal payload capacity for avionics; wingtip payload capacity for decoy augmentation and additional avionics; capacity for up to 113 kg (250 lb) beneath wings.

DIMENSIONS, EXTERNAL AND INTERNAL:

Wing span	3·00 m (9 ft 10 in)
Length: standard version	5·13 m (16 ft 10 in)
extended version	5·51 m (18 ft 1 in)
Height (total)	1·47 m (4 ft 10 in)
Body diameter	0·38 m (1 ft 3 in)
Volume available for mission equipment and core avionics: standard	0·092 m³ (3·26 cu ft)

AREAS:

Wings (total projected)	2·52 m² (27·16 sq ft)
Vertical tail surfaces	0·43 m² (4·63 sq ft)
Horizontal tail surfaces	0·55 m² (5·92 sq ft)

WEIGHTS:

Weight empty	218 kg (480 lb)
Usable fuel	173 kg (381 lb)
Launching weight (incl booster)	460 kg (1,014 lb)

PERFORMANCE (MQM-107A):

Operating speed range

247-500 knots (459-925 km/h; 285-575 mph)

Operating height range	S/L to 12,200 m (40,000 ft)
Endurance	more than 3 h

BEECHCRAFT MODELS 999E and 999H

US Army and Air Force designation: MQM-107B

These new models embody system improvements tested and proven on the MQM-107A. Primary reason for re-designation is the installation of a French Microturbo TRI 60 turbojet engine, the increased thrust of which results in higher operating speed.

Initial deliveries were made to the US Army and US Air Force (ten each). These were standard MQM-107Bs, with the longer fuselage that is available also to increase the payload capacity of the MQM-107A. Under an April 1983 contract, the Army has now ordered 139 production MQM-107Bs and the Air Force 70. Deliveries began in 1984 and were due to be completed in 1986. The MQM-107Bs ordered by Abu Dhabi, and delivered in 1983, combine the shorter fuselage of the standard MQM-107A with a Microturbo TRI 60 turbojet engine, and have a max launching weight of 488 kg (1,075 lb). The short fuselage version was also delivered, in 1984, to Egypt.

The description of the MQM-107A applies also to the standard MQM-107B, except as follows:

TYPE AND AIRFRAME: As recoverable version of MQM-107A, with extended fuselage and increased payload/avionics volume. Improved waterproofing.

POWER PLANT: One 3·68 kN (827 lb st) Ames Industrial built Microturbo TRI 60-2 Model 074 turbojet engine. Fuel capacity and JATO details as for MQM-107A, except for increased smoke/oil tank capacity.

GUIDANCE AND CONTROL: As described for MQM-107A, plus provisions for a high-*g* autopilot, which extends the manoeuvring and high-*g* envelope of the vehicle. Either constant airspeed or constant altitude high-*g* manoeuvres can be selected by the flight controller. Six-*g* manoeuvres can be maintained during use by air-to-air or surface-to-air weapons systems.

MISSION EQUIPMENT: Increased internal capacity compared with MQM-107A.

Beechcraft AQM-37 Variant target, carried by a US Navy QF-4B Phantom

Beechcraft MQM-107A Streaker of the US Army

Beechcraft MQM-107B at White Sands Missile Range, New Mexico

Launch of a Beechcraft Model 997 subsonic target at the Pacific Missile Test Center *(US Navy)*

Beechcraft Raider tactical RPV version of the MQM-107B

DIMENSIONS, EXTERNAL AND INTERNAL: As MQM-107A except:

Length: standard	5·51 m (18 ft 1 in)
optional	5·13 m (16 ft 10 in)
Volume available for mission equipment and core avionics: standard	0·136 m³ (4·79 cu ft)

WEIGHTS (standard version):

Weight empty	245 kg (540 lb)
Usable fuel	199 kg (438 lb)
Mission equipment:	43 kg (95 lb) internal *or* 109 kg (240 lb) external
Launching weight (incl booster)	494 kg (1,090 lb)

PERFORMANCE (standard version):

Operating speed range	275-535 knots (510-991 km/h; 317-615 mph)
Operating height range	15-12,200 m (50-40,000 ft)
Endurance	more than 3 h

BEECHCRAFT MODELS 999D, F and L

These designations apply to various hybrid configurations of the MQM-107 system for delivery to international customers. In early 1984, as noted under MQM-107A/B entries, orders had been received or were pending from South Korea (D), Taiwan (F) and Egypt (L).

BEECHCRAFT MQM-107EP

Announced in 1986, the MQM-107EP (for enhanced performance) is a variant of the MQM-107B with a new high-speed wing aerofoil section and composites construction, resulting in a faster and more manoeuvrable target. The power plant, recovery parachute and watertight payload compartment of the MQM-107B are retained.

WEIGHTS:

Mission equipment	68 kg (150 lb) internal *or* 136 kg (300 lb) external

PERFORMANCE:

Max level speed	580 knots (1,075 km/h; 668 mph)
Ceiling	13,410 m (44,000 ft)
Endurance	1 h 50 min

BEECHCRAFT RAIDER

The Raider, which made its public debut at the 1985 Paris Air Show, is under development as a tactical RPV making use of the airframe and power plant of the MQM-107B. Ground launched, it has both pre-programmed and ground controlled capabilities, and is recoverable.

Special mission payloads, housed in detachable pods, can include passive and active ECM such as radar jammers, flares, chaff and radar enhancement devices for penetration aid decoy missions. Additional future applications could include weapon systems evaluation in an ECM environment, reconnaissance, and intelligence gathering.

DIMENSIONS, EXTERNAL: As for standard length MQM-107B

WEIGHTS:

Max payload	45·5 kg (100 lb) internal *or* 159 kg (350 lb) external

PERFORMANCE:

Max level speed	515 knots (954 km/h; 593 mph)
Operating height range	S/L to 12,200 m (40,000 ft)
Endurance (depending on speed):	
standard fuel	1 h 12 min
with auxiliary fuel tanks	2 h 36 min

BEECHCRAFT MODEL 997

US Navy designation: BQM-126A

The Beechcraft Model 997 system has been selected by the US Navy in its competition for a cost-effective recoverable replacement for the subsonic BQM-34 Firebee I. The programme resulting from this selection will include full scale development, followed by the production of 700 air vehicles. Procurement requirements have been forecast at 200 vehicles per year for 20 years.

An important feature is the ability to perform precise controlled high-*g* manoeuvres. A load factor of 5*g* can be sustained through 720° of orbit, and 7*g* capability through 180°. Operation of the BQM-126A provides target missions for support of test and evaluation, and fleet readiness assessments of anti-air weapons systems. When equipped with particular sets of the various payloads of radar and IR augmentation, ECM or IRCM, and scoring, the BQM-126A will support the requirements of air-to-air missiles, surface-to-air missiles, anti-ship missile defence and surface-to-air gunnery missions.

The airframe makes extensive use of composite materials, and is adaptable for either air or ground launch. It incorporates both a digital autopilot and remote control command capabilities, and has provisions for both pre-programmed missions and Tacan guidance.

The power plant is a 4 kN (899 lb st) Microturbo TRI 60-2 Model 097, which has the US Navy designation J403-MT-400.

DIMENSIONS, EXTERNAL:

Wing span	3·05 m (10 ft 0 in)
Length overall	5·51 m (18 ft 1 in)
Body diameter (max)	0·38 m (1 ft 3 in)

WEIGHTS:

Weight empty	303 kg (667 lb)
Usable fuel	192 kg (424 lb)
Max payload	45·5 kg (100 lb) internal *or* 91 kg (200 lb) external
Launching weight (incl booster)	634 kg (1,398 lb)

PERFORMANCE:

Max level speed	579 knots (1,073 km/h; 667 mph)
Operating height range	S/L to 12,200 m (40,000 ft)
Endurance (depending on speed)	16·5 min to 1 h 36 min

BOEING

BOEING ELECTRONICS COMPANY

625 Andover Park West (Building 5), Corporate Square, Seattle, Washington 98188

Telephone: (206) 575 5755

Telex: 329430

PRESIDENT: R. W. Tharrington

DIRECTOR, SALES DEVELOPMENT: Reynolds Priebe

BOEING EXPERIMENTAL UMA

Boeing has built two prototypes of a very large experimental unmanned aircraft, the first of which was rolled out in late March 1986 at the Moses Lake facility of Boeing Electronics Company in Washington and was expected to begin flight testing shortly afterwards.

The programme is highly classified, although Boeing officials have been quoted as saying that the aircraft is potentially suitable for a number of missions including reconnaissance/surveillance, communications relay and border patrol. Clearly, the main clues to its capabilities are internal, the airframe being very unsophisticated in shape and the power plant modest. It is thought to have been built by Boeing Military Airplane Company, and probably makes extensive use of composite materials. The fuselage is of unrelieved box section throughout most of its approximately 18·3 m (60 ft) length, having a blunt ogival nosecone and tapering at the extreme rear into a smaller tailcone. The wings, of commensurately high span and aspect ratio, are pylon mounted at about one-third of the fuselage length, with considerable anhedral outboard of the engine nacelles. The latter are very large, the twin Teledyne Continental liquid-cooled engines being mounted overwing but with considerable extension of their nacelles behind and below the wing trailing-edges. Each drives a large-diameter three-blade propeller with a blunt conical spinner. Height over the tall, angular fin and rudder is about 5·5 m (18 ft).

The aircraft appears to have a short-wheelbase zero-track landing gear, apparently non-retractable, with a single wheel forward and twin wheels aft, plus a small outrigged balancer wheel inboard of each wingtip. Apart from a long nose boom and wingtip pitot, no external antennae were visible on the only photograph seen at the time of going to press. The overall configuration is suggestive of the ability to fly long endurance, high altitude missions with a low engine noise signature. The USAF is known to have had an active requirement in late 1985 for a high-altitude, subsonic standoff sensor platform for elint and other missions.

BOEING MILITARY AIRPLANE COMPANY

3801 South Oliver, Wichita, Kansas 67277-7730
Telephone: (316) 526 3153
President: Abraham M. S. Goo
RPV Projects Manager: David Sladovnik
Public Relations: Allen F. Hobbs

BOEING BRAVE 200

Brave 200 (Boeing Robotic Air VEhicle) is the designation of a series of low-cost multi-purpose drones, of which the YCGM-121A Pave Tiger (see 1984-85 *Jane's*) was one variant. Powered by a 21 kW (28 hp) engine, the Brave 200 is built of moulded plastics and can be configured for such missions as ECM, defence suppression and reconnaissance.

The central electronics unit, just forward of the fuel tank, interfaces with the payload, located in the nose of the vehicle. The Brave 200 can be surface launched from train, truck or ship, and has 1·1kW of regulated power available for payload use. Zero-length rocket assisted launch was chosen for simplicity, reliability and rapid fire rate.

While a dead reckoning navigation system is an integral part of the Brave 200, alternative navigation systems can also be integrated into the vehicle, if necessary. On a typical mission, Brave 200 would climb to an altitude of 2,500-3,500 m (8,200-11,500 ft) and proceed to the target area. The vehicle can loiter in the target area for the duration of its flight, or move to another area and re-initiate its assigned mission.

The Brave 200 vehicles are designed for long-term storage, and are serviced, programmed and launched on their 'fire and forget' mission by a two-man ground crew.

At the request of the West German Ministry of Defence, BMAC has submitted a proposal (code named Pave Panther) based on the Brave 200 to fulfil Germany's KDAR anti-radar drone requirement. If successful, Bodenseewerk would select and integrate German subsystems in the air vehicle, of which up to 3,000 could be required.

Type: Tactical mini-RPV.

Airframe: Sweptwing monoplane, with wings upswept at tips to form fins and rudders; non-swept canard surfaces, with elevators. Construction mainly of injection moulded composite materials including glassfibre, resin and polyurethane. No anhedral or dihedral. Wings have glassfibre spars and skin with moulded foam core, and fold forward when in launch container, deploying on exit. No flaps or ailerons; roll control spoilers of composite construction above wings. Canard surfaces have same construction as wings and are fitted with elevators. Short, pod shaped monocoque fuselage. No landing gear.

Power Plant: One 21 kW (28 hp) 438 cc Cuyuna two-cylinder two-stroke engine, mounted at rear of fuselage and driving a Boeing fixed-pitch pusher propeller with four blades made of injection moulded thermoplastics. Fuel tank in centre of fuselage. Underfuselage UPC rocket motor boosts aircraft to approx 70 knots (130 km/h; 81 mph) and 61 m (200 ft), when piston engine takes over.

Launch and Recovery: Air vehicles can be surface launched from train, truck or ship, with rocket boost. Alternatively, they can be stored in a GPU powered 2·44 × 2·44 × 6·1 m (8 × 8 × 20 ft) standard international container, in which 15 drones can be stored, if necessary, for 5 to 10 years without maintenance. Each of the 15 compartments contains a drone, launch rail and electric starter motor. To launch a drone, the compartment door is jettisoned and the drone emerges on its zero length launch rail. The wings are then unfolded, the drone elevated to its launch angle, fuelled, electrical power connected, the drone checked out by launcher test equipment, and the mission programme fed in. The rocket booster is then fired electronically to launch the drone. Entire system can be handled by a two-man launch crew. Alternatively, drones can be packaged in groups of 2, 4, 6, 9 or 12; or the equipment can be connected to four containers, enabling 60 drones to be programmed and launched sequentially. By reducing range and/or payload weight, a parachute or other recovery system can be installed if required.

Guidance and Control: Normally pre-programmed, controlled by a Boeing autopilot, but can be re-programmed in the field by tactical commanders. Onboard sensors and microprocessor guide drone along flight path to its destination. Engine driven alternators; passive homing system for some missions. BMAC three-axis control system integrates a yaw-to-turn capability into the digital autopilot, simplifying tracking and target alignment.

Mission Equipment: Payload bay in nose, nearly half of overall fuselage volume. Payloads can include non-nuclear warhead or modular ECM or sensor packages.

Dimensions, external:
Wing span 2·57 m (8 ft 5 in)
Foreplane span 1·12 m (3 ft 8 in)
Length overall 2·12 m (6 ft 11·42 in)
Height overall 0·61 m (2 ft 0 in)
Fuselage: Max depth 0·51 m (1 ft 8·3 in)

Area:
Wings, gross 0·93 m² (10·0 sq ft)

Weights:
Weight empty 70 kg (154 lb)
Fuel 22·7 kg (50 lb)
Max payload approx 27 kg (60 lb)
Max launching weight 120 kg (265 lb)

Performance:
Cruising speed 121 knots (225 km/h; 140 mph)
Loiter speed 78 knots (145 km/h; 90 mph)
Max rate of climb at S/L 488 m (1,600 ft)/min
Ceiling over 3,960 m (13,000 ft)
Range (depending upon payload/fuel ratio)
more than 434 nm (805 km; 500 miles)

BOEING BRAVE 3000

BMAC announced this second member of its Brave family in July 1986. It is a jet powered, container launched expendable drone for battlefield use, designed for easy and rapid deployment coupled with low cost and low maintenance requirements. Construction makes extensive use of composite materials, and the NPT-171 turbojet engine is a joint development by BMAC and Noel Penny Turbines of the UK (see Engines section). After leaving its container, boosted to flight speed by solid propellant rocket bottles, the Brave 3000 transitions to flight by unfolding its wings and fins and starting the turbojet engine.

The drone is equipped with a three-axis digital autopilot and central electronics unit which is the heart of the vehicle control system. All mission data are pre-programmed prior to launch, and once in the air the drone is totally autonomous, completing its assigned mission without any further commands or directions.

Development of the Brave 3000 began in 1980. Concept and validation testing have been completed, and flight tests have verified aerodynamic properties, flight and propulsion controls, engine air start operation, climbout and cruise performance, and Doppler aided navigation performance. The launch concept has been demonstrated via ground launches from an enclosed container mounted on a mobile trailer, including ripple firing at 10 second intervals.

Dimensions, external:
Wing span, spread 2·26 m (7 ft 5 in)
Length overall (excl booster) 3·44 m (11 ft 3½ in)

Weights:
Fuel: min 15·9 kg (35 lb)
max 56·7 kg (125 lb)
Payload: min 74·8 kg (165 lb)
max 115·6 kg (255 lb)

Performance:
Max cruising speed at up to 7,620 m (25,000 ft)
380 knots (704 km/h; 437 mph)
Range at 380 knots (704 km/h; 437 mph) at 3,050 m (10,000 ft) with 131·5 kg (290 lb) fuel/payload mix as follows:
15·9 + 115·6 kg (35 + 255 lb)
65 nm (121 km; 75 miles)
24·9 + 106·6 kg (55 + 235 lb)
110 nm (205 km; 127 miles)
38·5 + 93·0 kg (85 + 205 lb)
178 nm (331 km; 205 miles)
47·6 + 83·9 kg (105 + 185 lb)
224 nm (415 km; 258 miles)
56·7 + 74·8 kg (125 + 165 lb)
269 nm (499 km; 310 miles)

BRANDEBURY

BRANDEBURY AEROSTRUCTURES INC

15734 Crabbs Branch Way, Rockville, Maryland 20855
Telephone: (301) 330 0890
President: William B. Harvey

This company manufactures RPV airframe components for various US government agencies, output being at the rate of six to eight airframes per month in the Spring of 1986. Details of these aircraft are classified, but Brandebury has also developed a mini-RPV of its own, known as the Microdrone.

BRANDEBURY MICRODRONE

The Microdrone embodies an airframe structure of the type developed by Brandebury for all its RPV manufacturing programmes, which consists of a combination of open-cell plastics foam, epoxy impregnated at hardpoints and covered with a glassfibre composite skin. Wing spars are reinforced with carbonfibre.

The Microdrone prototype is of shoulder-wing configuration, with a nose mounted 35 cc two-stroke engine, wide-span tailplane with twin endplate fins and rudders, and a tailwheel type landing gear. As demonstrated to the US Coast Guard in 1985, including launch and recovery from both land and shipboard helicopter platforms, it was equipped with a Paraflight Inc ram air inflated rectangular parachute which could be used either to recover the air vehicle or to enable it to loiter on station at low speeds. Payloads included a pod mounted video or low light level camera, with an onboard transponder to facilitate radar tracking. Guidance and control were by VFR equipment which included airspeed, altitude and magnetic heading telemetry and control centre based display for imagery from the onboard sensor.

It was planned to test, in early 1986, a larger version of the Microdrone, powered by a 100 cc engine. Another Microdrone, designated **VTX-1**, has been designed and was expected to be proposed in 1986 for a US Army requirement known as BOSS (Battalion Operated Surveillance System). Having a max payload capacity of 36·3 kg (80 lb) for a real-time imagery sensor, this has a high-wing configuration, cylindrical-section fuselage with spinnered propeller, anhedral tailplane and single fin and rudder.

No other details of the VTX-1 were received. The following details apply to the two earlier Microdrones:

Dimensions, external (A: 35 cc, B:100 cc):
Wing span: A 2·74 m (9 ft 0 in)
B not stated

Areas:
Wings, gross: A 0·93 m² (10·0 sq ft)
B 1·11 m² (12·0 sq ft)

Weights:
Payload: A not stated
B 7·25 kg (16 lb)
Max launching weight: A 13·6 kg (30 lb)
B not stated

Performance:
Cruising speed (B):
with parafoil 9-26 knots (16-48 km/h; 10-30 mph)
without parafoil
26-78 knots (48-145 km/h; 30-90 mph)

CONTINENTAL

CONTINENTAL RPVs

34924 Victor Street, Barstow, California 92311
Telephone: (619) 252 4741

CONTINENTAL MiG-27 'FLOGGER-D' TARGETS

Following extensive testing at Fort Bliss, Texas, Continental RPVs became a new contractor in 1983 for the US Army Test Center at Fort Irwin, California, to supply RCMAT (HEAT) aerial targets based on a scale representation of the Soviet MiG-27 'Flogger-D' combat aircraft. During these tests, the targets reached an altitude of more than 3,660 m (12,000 ft).

The 'Flogger-D' targets are manufactured in four sizes, ranging from the one-ninth scale **C19M** through the **C17M** and **C17MG** (both one-seventh) to the **C125M** (one-fifth).

'Black' in more senses than for its external paint scheme, this large Boeing RPV is believed to have been built for standoff elint missions by the USAF *(Associated Press)*

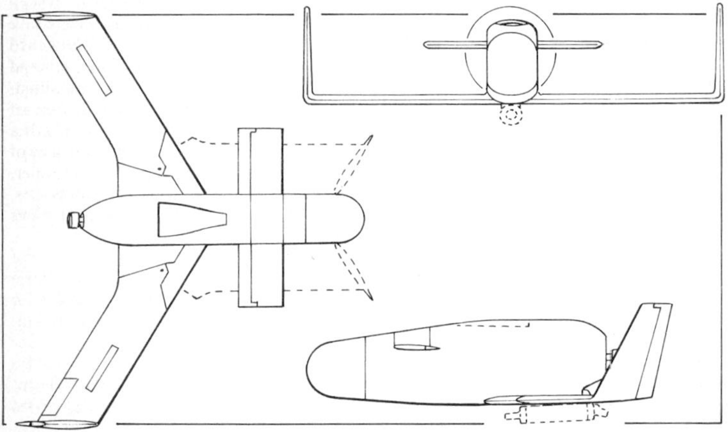

Three-view drawing of the Boeing Brave 200, showing forward folding of wings *(Michael A. Badrocke)*

Continental RPVs 'Flogger-D' aerial target

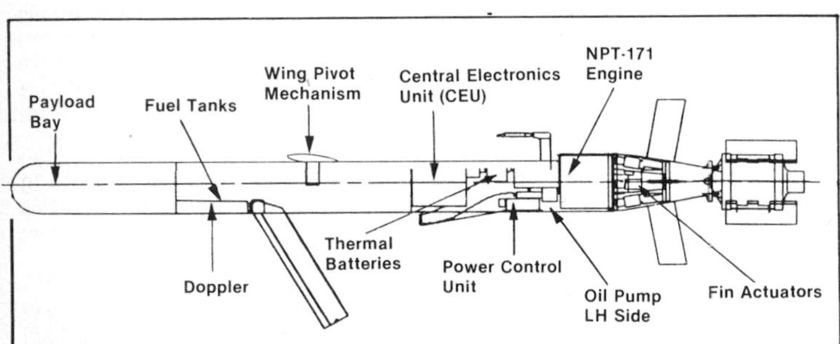

Boeing Brave 3000 container launched expendable drone

E-175 strike RPV, with starboard wing and side-force generator folded back

The C19M runs on nitro-methanol fuel, the others on a petrol/oil mixture. Manoeuvrability is effected by elevator control, and onboard payloads can include a gas or smoke grenade, pyrotechnics, infra-red source, ciné camera, smoke hit indicator, or near-miss indicator. The aircraft have glassfibre fuselages and tail units with plywood wings. A modified version of the C125M is being produced by Boeing of Canada (which see).

The targets are hand launched, returning to a belly landing, and are used in training crews of air defence artillery and small arms air defence, including such weapon systems as Redeye, Stinger, Vulcan and Chapparal.

DIMENSIONS, EXTERNAL:

Wing span: C19M — 1·52 m (5 ft 0 in)
C17M — 2·29 m (7 ft 6 in)
C17MG — 2·54 m (8 ft 4 in)
C125M — 2·84 m (9 ft 4 in)

WEIGHTS:

Weight empty: C19M — 3·2 kg (7 lb)
C17M — 7·7 kg (17 lb)
C17MG — 13·2 kg (29 lb)
C125M — 12·7 kg (28 lb)

Payload: C19M — 2·3 kg (5 lb)
C17M — 2·7 kg (6 lb)
C17MG — 8·2 kg (18 lb)
C125M — 13·6 kg (30 lb)

Fuel (standard): C19M — 0·45 kg (1 lb)
C17M, C17MG, C125M — 0·91 kg (2 lb)

PERFORMANCE:

Speed range:
C19M — 16-82 knots (29-151 km/h; 18-94 mph)
C17M — 17-80 knots (32-148 km/h; 20-92 mph)
C17MG — 35-104 knots (64-193 km/h; 40-120 mph)
C125M — 26-104 knots (48-193 km/h; 30-120 mph)

Endurance at max speed, standard fuel:
C19M — 16 min
C17M — 45 min
C17MG, C125M — 32 min

Control range (each controller):
C19M — 1·08 nm (2 km; 1·24 miles)
C17M, C17MG — 1·62 nm (3 km; 1·86 miles)
C125M — 2·16 nm (4 km; 2·49 miles)

E-SYSTEMS

E-SYSTEMS INC (Melpar Division)

7700 Arlington Boulevard, Falls Church, Virginia 22046
Telephone: (703) 560 5000
Telex: 89 9494

Primary business areas of Melpar Division are electronic combat weapons and reconnaissance systems (ECWRS), remotely controlled intelligence systems (RCIS), information systems, electronic warfare and communications products, and physical security sensors. In the ECWRS area, Melpar Division has designed a number of miniature RPVs in the 16-125 kg (35-275 lb) weight range (see previous editions of *Jane's*), any of which could be produced if required. Three weight configurations of the same basic airframe comprise its current standard aircraft, the E-175, E-260 and E-310.

E-SYSTEMS E-175

The E-175 is an uprated version of the earlier E-130 (see 1983-84 *Jane's*), with increased wing surface area and a slightly more powerful (13·4 kW; 18 hp) engine. Expendable strike and electronic warfare are the principal programme applications, but the E-175 is adaptable to other applications and payloads which are also expendable.

The E-175 has been fully wind tunnel tested at the University of Washington, Seattle, Washington. All major configurations were tested in pitch and yaw. Typical measurement angles included −10° to +14° in pitch and ±20° in yaw. Force data in lift, drag, pitching moment, rolling moment, yawing moment and side force were recorded at each pitch and yaw angle selected.

Features common to the E-90 and E-175 include shoulder-mounted wings, a single-tailboom fuselage and a pusher engine installation. The wings, horizontal tail surfaces, nose equipment pod and engine are removable for transportation and maintenance; mission flexibility is assisted by use of interchangeable equipment pods. A distinctive feature of the E-175 is the provision of a side-force generator panel beneath each wing.

AIRFRAME: Cantilever shoulder-wing monoplane, with NACA 4415 wing section. Non-swept constant chord wings, without anhedral or dihedral; wing incidence depends on mission configuration. Wings are built of glassfibre and foam plastics, and fitted with electrically actuated ailerons; no flaps. Pod and boom fuselage, of glassfibre and polymer fairings over an aluminium frame. Conventional vertical and horizontal tail surfaces, of similar construction to wings. Ventral landing skid. Side-force generator panel beneath each wing at approx mid span.

POWER PLANT: One 220 cc two-cylinder two-stroke engine, developing more than 13·4 kW (18 hp) at 7,400 rpm, with direct drive to a two-blade fixed-pitch pusher propeller. Single fuselage fuel tank, capacity 19 litres (5 US gallons). Fuel is a 20:1 mixture of regular automotive petrol and two-stroke engine oil. Engine is equipped with a Melpar designed muffler.

LAUNCH AND RECOVERY: Launching can be performed from the top of a moving vehicle, by a 6 m (20 ft) pneumatic catapult, or by rocket assistance. Recovery methods include parachute or parafoil, arrester hook, skid landing, and flying the RPV into a special recovery net which can stop the aircraft without damage within a distance of 12 m (40 ft). Fully automated recovery is feasible by the last of these techniques.

GUIDANCE AND CONTROL: A lightweight and simple autopilot, not requiring a vertical gyro, has been developed for flight path control. This is capable of real-time data link update by a ground operator, or can be pre-programmed to carry out an autonomous mission. The autopilot has three independent feedback loops that are used to stabilise the aircraft, and uses a barometric pressure transducer, angle of attack vane, magnetometer, rate gyros and velocity transducer as sensor inputs. The autopilot controls throttle, elevator, ailerons and rudder. Omega (VLF) or Navstar/GPS (Global Positioning System navigation satellites) are the two recommended means of navigation for the RPVs, although other techniques such as Loran, inertial, area correlation or beacons may be considered.

MISSION EQUIPMENT: Military equipment according to mission configuration (principal missions are expendable strike and electronic warfare). Three types of Melpar onboard jammer are available: (1) barrage — wide-band noise and tone, (2) spot — narrow-band noise and tone with remote running or onboard look-through, (3) dart (delay and repeat transmitter), which combines the best features of barrage and spot jamming at low cost. Electrical power is generated by an engine driven alternator producing 1kW at 28V DC.

DIMENSIONS, EXTERNAL:
- Wing span: 3·66 m (12 ft 0 in)
- Length overall: 2·54 m (8 ft 4 in)

WEIGHTS:
- Payload: 18·1 kg (40 lb)
- Fuel load: 13·6 kg (30 lb)
- Launching weight: 79·4 kg (175 lb)

PERFORMANCE:
- Cruising speed: 104 knots (193 km/h; 120 mph)
- Range: 260 nm (482 km; 300 miles)
- Endurance: 4 h

E-SYSTEMS E-260

This is the mid-size member of the E-Systems family of RPVs, and uses a scaled-up E-175 airframe. Design allows for interchangeable payload nose modules, permitting a basic airframe to accommodate a number of different reconnaissance missions in different operating modes. Trade-offs between endurance/fuel weight and payload capability can be accomplished, a typical payload configuration of 24·5 kg (54 lb) having an endurance of more than five hours.

AIRFRAME: A formed and machined aluminium backbone joins the firewall, propulsion unit, tailboom and wing spars. Fuselage structure, tailboom and payload nosecones are of glassfibre. Firewall provides for structural mounting of equipment package. Wings and horizontal tail surfaces are shaped foam cores covered with glassfibre reinforced skin. Nose modules are removable and have interchangeable configurations; wings and horizontal tail surfaces are also removable, and all removable items facilitate transportation. Lifting yoke at CG.

POWER PLANT: One 290 cc two-cylinder two-stroke engine, developing more than 18·6 kW (25 hp) at 8,000 rpm, with direct drive to a two-blade fixed-pitch pusher propeller. Single fuselage fuel tank, capacity 33·3 litres (8·8 US gallons).

LAUNCH AND RECOVERY: 7·62 m (25 ft) hydraulic launcher. Recovery by conventional landing on dual shock absorbing skids mounted under tailboom.

GUIDANCE AND CONTROL: Radio command control for launch and recovery. In-flight guidance by Melpar three-axis autopilot with dead reckoning capability. Aerodynamic control by ailerons, elevator, rudder and throttle. Sensor inputs are angle of attack, magnetic heading, yaw/pitch/roll rates, and altitude. The autopilot is capable of real-time data link update from the ground operator, or can be pre-programmed to carry out an autonomous mission. The same telemetry system can provide data to the control station for monitoring vehicle performance, as well as providing data from the payload package(s). Omega (VLF) or Navstar/GPS are the two recommended navigation systems, but Loran, inertial, area correlation or beacon techniques may be employed.

MISSION EQUIPMENT: A variety of interchangeable nosecones, each with a different equipment configuration, allows for versatility in reconnaissance missions. For remote real-time reconnaissance, Melpar manufactures a low-cost TV camera system in a gimballed mount which can be positioned during flight. Remotely controlled camera functions are from horizon to −45° in pitch, ±90° in yaw, and CAMERA ON/OFF; the camera has a 500 line resolution. Electrical power is generated by an engine driven alternator producing 1·5kW, with an emergency battery backup of 250W for ten minutes.

DIMENSIONS, EXTERNAL:
- Wing span: 4·42 m (14 ft 6 in)
- Length overall: 3·23 m (10 ft 7 in)

WEIGHTS:
- Payload: 22·7 kg (50 lb)
- Fuel load: 24 kg (53 lb)
- Launching weight: 118 kg (260 lb)

PERFORMANCE:
- Cruising speed: 87 knots (161 km/h; 100 mph)
- Range: 260 nm (483 km; 300 miles)
- Endurance: 5-6 h

E-SYSTEMS E-310

Newest member of the E-Systems family, the E-310 was shown in reconnaissance configuration at the 1985 Paris Air Show, equipped with a remotely controlled real-time TV camera. The E-310 is designed for easily interchangeable payloads for a variety of missions, and is configured for repeated recovery by skid landings. A complete system would consist of six RPVs, multiple payloads, a data link and ground support equipment, transported in four M813 or equivalent trucks and operated by a minimum crew of eight people. Typical payloads can include stabilised, unstabilised or LLL TV, FLIR, IRLS, panoramic cameras, or signal collection equipment. The RPV is capable of either real-time control or pre-programmed flight; onboard avionics include an alternator, mission programmer/controller, payload interface unit, mission controller microprocessor, autopilot, and navigation system. Power plant is an 18·6 kW (25 hp) piston engine.

DIMENSIONS, EXTERNAL:
- Wing span: 4·30 m (14 ft 1¼ in)
- Length overall: 3·77 m (12 ft 4½ in)
- Height overall: 0·66 m (2 ft 2 in)

WEIGHTS:
- Typical payload: 27 kg (60 lb)
- Max payload (incl fuel): 50 kg (110 lb)
- Max launching weight: 141 kg (310 lb)

PERFORMANCE:
- Max level speed: 108 knots (200 km/h; 124 mph)
- Cruising speed: 67 knots (125 km/h; 78 mph)
- Stalling speed: 49 knots (90 km/h; 56 mph)
- Max rate of climb at S/L: 300 m (984 ft)/min
- Max range: 97 nm (180 km; 112 miles)
- Endurance: more than 5 h

FAIRCHILD

FAIRCHILD REPUBLIC COMPANY

Farmingdale, Long Island, New York 11735-1793

Telephone: (516) 531 0105
Telex: 96-7735

Fairchild built three prototypes of an advanced tactical mini-RPV designated ATM-100, of which details can be found in the 1984-85 and previous editions of *Jane's*. This programme has been terminated.

FSI

FLIGHT SYSTEMS INC (Subsidiary of Tracor Inc)

1901 Dove Street, PO Box 2400, Newport Beach, California 92660

Telephone: (714) 833 9661

PRESIDENT: Stuart C. Warrick Jr

VICE-PRESIDENT, SPECIAL PROJECTS: P. Aston

FSI has been producing drones for the US Department of Defense since 1975, and currently holds contracts to convert more than 200 aircraft into unmanned aerial target vehicles. These include the North American F-86 and F-100, Convair F-106 and Northrop F-5A.

FSI QF-86E SABRE

FSI demonstrated to the US Army in 1975 two remotely controlled Sabre jet fighters, the converted aircraft being Canadair built Sabre 5s, structurally similar to the US built F-86E. Deliveries began in mid-1977, and 51 target conversions had been delivered by March 1985, with low-quantity production continuing in 1986.

A detailed description of the FSI QF-86E has appeared in the 1983-84 and earlier editions of *Jane's*. The QF-86Es are actively supporting US Army air defence system requirements at White Sands missile range, and can deploy stores, initiate jamming and provide other countermeasures, all under remote control.

FSI (NORTH AMERICAN) QF-100 SUPER SABRE

Conversion of US Air Force /Air National Guard F-100 fighter-bombers for remotely piloted operation as QF-100 aerial targets is currently being performed under contract from the US Air Force Sacramento Air Logistics Center, McClellan AFB, California. This full scale aerial target (FSAT) programme is for a multi-service target to provide air-to-air and ground-to-air missile evaluation and combat crew training. The QF-100 succeeds the Sperry-converted Convair QF-102/PQM-102 target in these roles.

The full scale engineering development and initial production programme conducted by Sperry Corporation involved delivery of 100 Super Sabres (nine prototype and 91 'production') in four different configurations. Of these, configuration No. 2, converted from the single-seat F-100D, is the standard US Air Force target version; No. 1 incorporated additional cockpit controls to permit evaluation of system performance from within the cockpit; No. 3 is the same configuration as No. 2, except that it is converted from the two-seat F-100F; No. 4 incorporates a drone formation control system (DFCS) for multiple-target missions involving up to six QF-100s. The FSED programme included DT & E (development, test and evaluation) and IOT & E (initial operational test and evaluation), and was carried out at Sperry's facility at Phoenix-Litchfield Airport, Arizona. Conversions are now being accomplished at FSI's Aircraft Modification and Test Center at Mojave, California.

Deliveries by Sperry began on 13 March 1981 to Tyndall AFB, Florida, for US Air Force DT & E, and the first unmanned flight was made on 19 November 1981. Development testing for the DFCS was carried out at Holloman AFB, New Mexico; final test and evaluation took place during 1983 at Tyndall AFB. Initial operational capability with Tactical Air Command was achieved in late 1983.

In May 1984 the QF-100 follow-on production contract was awarded to FSI, which is delivering a total of 209 targets over a five-year period from mid-1985.

The QF-100 drone ground control and test equipment is the same as used in PQM-102 operations, together with many PQM-102 airborne subsystems. While sharing a common conversion and operational scheme with the PQM-102 series, the QF-100 utilises an SDP-175 digital flight control computer instead of the PQM-102 analog flight control stabilisation system (FCSS), thus achieving ease of testing and flexibility for future growth of operational modes.

AIRFRAME: As F-100D/F (see 1961-62 *Jane's*).

POWER PLANT: One Pratt & Whitney J57-P-21A turbojet, rated at 75·4 kN (16,950 lb st) with afterburning.

LAUNCH AND RECOVERY: Normal runway T-O and landing. Automatic T-O and landing, utilising the IBM DFCS, has been demonstrated at Holloman AFB, and will be installed on the Eglin AFB Gulf range as part of the latter's drone control update system.

GUIDANCE AND CONTROL: Dual Vega command guidance and telemetry systems. Fully redundant digital tracking and control system for command/telemetry link, in conjunction with AN/FPS-16 ground based range radar. Simultaneous control of multiple targets has been demonstrated. Sperry digital flight control computer (FCC) system incorporates air data sensors, SDP-175 processor, analog/digital and digital/analog converters, a power supply, and necessary interface electronics. FCC provides eight longitudinal/vertical and four lateral/directional modes, and interface between aircraft systems and command/telemetry system. Automatic modes are provided for take-off, loss of command carrier, take-off abort, and other safety modes. Redundant power systems and dual autopilot channels. Digital FCC permits automatic checkout of many primary autopilot functions; it also provides a flexible system for incorporating target system functions, or for adaptation to other target programmes. Control is exercised by a mobile ground station for take-off and recovery, and by a fixed ground site for guidance to, over and from the target range. Manoeuvre programmer can be pre-programmed for multiple manoeuvres, in any required sequence, and provides backup for FCC system.

MISSION EQUIPMENT: Incorporates remotely operated smoke, braking and explosive destruct systems; Digidops miss distance scoring system standard. Two types of scoring camera operational, covering forward and aft areas to provide missile approach angle, velocity and miss distance. Manoeuvre destruct and explosive destruct systems incorporated. Visual augmentation (smoke) system, operable at any altitude or power setting. Radar and infra-red augmentation not required, due to size of aircraft. LVSS (laser vector scoring system), one of several systems tested in 1983, can provide a directional parameter to help further in evaluating missile performance. A DLQ-3B ECM pod and ALE-40 infra-red/chaff pod are incorporated to provide realistic evaluation of missile performance against anticipated countermeasures. Drone formation control system incorporated to permit formation flight of two or more targets, to provide a realistic challenge for missiles equipped with seeker heads.

DIMENSIONS, EXTERNAL:
- Wing span: 11·82 m (38 ft 9⅓ in)
- Length overall, incl probe: 16·54 m (54 ft 3 in)
- Height overall: 4·95 m (16 ft 2⅔ in)

AREA:
- Wings, gross: 35·79 m² (385·2 sq ft)

WEIGHT:
- Mission operational T-O weight: 14,060 kg (31,000 lb)

PERFORMANCE:
- Max speed at altitude: Mach 1·3 (745 knots; 1,381 km/h; 858 mph)

E-Systems E-310 in reconnaissance configuration *(Brian M. Service)*

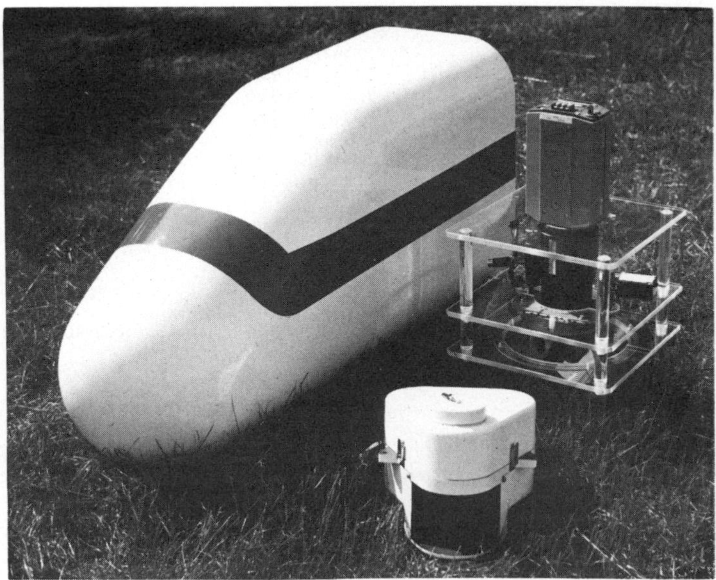

E-Systems E-310 interchangeable nosecone with payloads

Hynes H-5T remotely piloted helicopter for the US Army

QF-100 full scale aerial targets at FSI's Mojave, California, facility

Operating height range 60-15,240 m (200-50,000 ft)
Range, nominal (guidance radar range-limited) 120 nm (222 km; 138 miles)
Normal mission endurance 40-55 min
g limits +8/−2

FSI (CONVAIR) QF-106 DELTA DART

The Aerospace and Marine Group of Sperry Corporation was appointed prime contractor in July 1986 to supply QF-106 full scale aerial targets to the US Air Force. In the following month Sperry awarded FSI a $7·25 million major subcontract to convert six F-106As to prototype QF-106 configuration. The contract contains options to convert up to 192 more of these aircraft for target use over the next five years.

Further details of the conversion had not been received at the time of going to press. The following basic details apply to the manned F-106A:

POWER PLANT: One 109 kN (24,500 lb st) Pratt & Whitney J75-P-17 afterburning turbojet engine.

DIMENSIONS, EXTERNAL:
Wing span 11·67 m (38 ft 3½ in)
Length overall 21·56 m (70 ft 8¾ in)
WEIGHT:
Max T-O weight over 15,875 kg (35,000 lb)
PERFORMANCE:
Max level speed at 11,000 m (36,000 ft) 1,324 knots (2,455 km/h; 1,525 mph)
Service ceiling 17,375 m (57,000 ft)
Range 1,000 nm (1,850 km; 1,150 miles)

GOULD

GOULD INC (Advanced Systems Development Division)

6730 Baymeadow Drive, Dept 750, Glen Burnie, Maryland 21061
Telephone: (301) 787 2884
SENIOR ANALYST: Alan B. Renshaw

Gould Inc provides the mission equipment and US marketing for the **Isis** and **Swallow** RPVs produced by the Canadian company Control Technologies. Isis 1 was demonstrated to the US Army in April 1986, and Gould entered these vehicles in the Army's BOSS (battallion operated surveillance system) competition later that year. All are capable of carrying a lightweight TV and/or 35 mm still camera, although other payloads could be accommodated in the nose bay. Isis has a rectangular-section fuselage with low-mounted main wings at the rear and a high-mounted foreplane with elevators. Twin fins and rudders are mounted on the main wings at approx mid span, and the aircraft takes off and lands on a non-retractable tricycle undercarriage. A zero-length catapult launcher is also being developed.

DIMENSIONS, EXTERNAL:
Wing span: Swallow 1·42 m (4 ft 8 in)
Isis 1 2·54 m (8 ft 4 in)
Isis 2 3·35 m (11 ft 0 in)
Length overall: Swallow 1·36 m (4 ft 5½ in)
Isis 1 2·13 m (7 ft 0 in)
Isis 2 2·79 m (9 ft 2 in)
WEIGHTS:
Max T-O weight: Swallow 15·9 kg (35 lb)
Isis 1 45·4 kg (100 lb)
Isis 2 61·2 kg (135 lb)

HYNES

HYNES HELICOPTER (Division of Hynes Aviation Industries Inc)

PO Box 697, Frederick, Oklahoma 73542
Telephone: (405) 335 7511
OFFICERS: see Aircraft section
RPV PROJECT MANAGER: Humayun Kabir

In the Autumn of 1984 Hynes Helicopter began adapting the airframes of its H-2 and H-5 commercial helicopters (see main Aircraft section) to remotely piloted operation, and now offers a 'rent-a-drone' capability to manufacturers of avionics, weapons and other aircraft equipment. The programme is known as TERT, signifying the RPV's suitability for test and evaluation, educational, R & D and tactical missions. First result of this programme was a September 1984 contract from the US Army Missile Command for four H-5Ts, with options on a further six. The first H-5T was due for delivery in 1986. Since 1984, more than 200 hours have been flown by a manned H-5T drone helicopter trainer.

HYNES H-2T and H-5T

In general, these RPV versions use the standard airframes, power plants and systems of the passenger carrying H-2 and H-5, but modifications can be made to the cabin and avionics, or weapons and other equipment installed, to meet specific customer requirements. For example, the H-5Ts ordered by the US Army have glassfibre fairings over the fuselage to assist in simulating the Soviet Mi-24 'Hind-D' helicopter. Rotor braking is not available for the RPV versions. A non-retractable tricycle landing gear (single mainwheels and twin nosewheels) with optional mainwheel braking is standard, but skid gear or pontoons are available optionally. An electrical power source (12V 33Ah DC in the H-2T, 24V in the H-5T) is available to power a wide range of equipment, but other DC or AC sources can be provided if required. An automatic emergency flight termination system is standard.

In order to improve payload capability in hot and high conditions, Hynes has initiated two engine test programmes with the H-5T. One involves fitting a turbocharger to the existing 250 kW (335 hp) Avco Lycoming IVO-540 piston engine; the other replaces that engine with a Soloy conversion using a 313 kW (420 shp) Allison 250-C20B turboshaft.

DIMENSIONS, EXTERNAL: As for H-2/H-5 except:
Main rotor diameter: 5T 7·82 m (25 ft 8 in)
Length overall, rotors turning: 2T 8·56 m (28 ft 1 in)

5T 9·53 m (31 ft 3 in)
Length of fuselage: 2T 6·53 m (21 ft 5 in)
5T 8·38 m (27 ft 6 in)
Height overall: 2T 2·13 m (7 ft 0 in)
5T 2·44 m (8 ft 0 in)
Wheel track: 2T 1·93 m (6 ft 4 in)
5T 2·03 m (6 ft 8 in)
Wheelbase: 2T 1·73 m (5 ft 8 in)
5T 1·88 m (6 ft 2 in)

WEIGHTS AND LOADINGS (designed):
Weight empty: 2T 386-431 kg (850-950 lb)
5T 680-771 kg (1,500-1,700 lb)
Max fuel: 2T 27·2 kg (60 lb)
5T 49 kg (108 lb)
Max payload: 2T 295-363 kg (650-800 lb)
5T 317-544 kg (700-1,200 lb)
Max T-O weight: 2T 680-748 kg (1,500-1,650 lb)
5T 998-1,225 kg (2,200-2,700 lb)
Disc loading (design goal):
2T 17·09 kg/m² (3·5 lb/sq ft)
5T 19·53 kg/m² (4·0 lb/sq ft)
Power loading (design goal):
2T, 5T 4·87 kg/kW (8·0 lb/hp)

PERFORMANCE (estimated at max T-O weight):
Never-exceed speed:
2T 87 knots (161 km/h; 100 mph)
5T 104 knots (193 km/h; 120 mph)
Max cruising speed:
2T 76 knots (142 km/h; 88 mph)
5T at 915 m (3,000 ft) 91 knots (169 km/h; 105 mph)
Econ cruising speed:
2T, 5T 48 knots (89 km/h; 55 mph)
Rate of climb at 1,525 m (5,000 ft):
2T 183 m (600 ft)/min
5T 305 m (1,000 ft)/min
Service ceiling: 2T 3,050 m (10,000 ft)
5T 3,660 m (12,000 ft)
Hovering ceiling IGE: 2T 1,830 m (6,000 ft)
5T 2,440 m (8,000 ft)
Hovering ceiling OGE: 2T 1,220 m (4,000 ft)
5T 1,830 m (6,000 ft)
Range with max fuel:
2T 217 nm (402 km; 250 miles)
5T 191 nm (354 km; 220 miles)
Max endurance: 2T, 5T more than 3 h

HYNES (BELL) UH-1H DRONE

In the Summer of 1986, Hynes was working on a new R&D programme to drone a UH-1H for an unnamed foreign country. This customer has a large supply of surplus UH-1Hs, for which drone conversions are required. The Hynes demonstrator will embody a modified version of the H-2T/H-5T control system.

KAMAN
KAMAN AEROSPACE CORPORATION

PO Box 2, Old Windsor Road, Bloomfield, Connecticut 06002-0002
Telephone: (203) 242 4461
MARKETING MANAGER: John D. Mimnaugh
OTHER OFFICERS: see Aircraft section

Kaman provides, under US Army contracts, helicopter drone kits for use in defence programmes. These kits provide complete radio remote control from the ground for take-off, performance of mission, return and landing. Kaman designs and manufactures the kits; installs and flight tests them, using an onboard safety pilot; and provides the ground controller to fly the target missions.

Drone kits, to convert surplus Bell UH-1 helicopters into QH-1 target aircraft, have been produced for use at Fort Bliss, Texas, in testing competing designs for the Division Air Defence (DIVAD) gun system for the US Army. Additional kits, also for installation in UH-1s, were used at White Sands missile range, New Mexico, in trials of the Patriot missile and the Stinger man-portable surface-to-air missile. Fabrication of drone kits continues at an irregular pace, depending on US Army requirements.

Additional testing of various forward area defence weapons took place in 1985, using various surplus models of the UH-1; further gun and missile tests were continuing at several weapons test ranges during 1986, including those at Redstone, Huntsville (Alabama) and White Sands.

LMSC
LOCKHEED MISSILES AND SPACE COMPANY INC

1111 Lockheed Way (PO Box 504), Sunnyvale, California 94086
Telephone: (408) 742 6688
MANAGER, HIGH-ALTITUDE RPV PROGRAMMES: David W. Hall
DIRECTOR OF PUBLIC RELATIONS: George Mulherne

LMSC/NASA SOLAR HAPP

In October 1984 NASA's Langley Research Center awarded LMSC a third contract for a Solar High Altitude Powered Platform (Solar HAPP), with a new mission and revised design. Earlier (1982-83) contracts had covered operational needs, systems and structures, with a potential mission to monitor crops in California for the US Department of Agriculture. The unmanned aircraft proposed under the earlier contracts was a 'flying wing' design with an integral central payload pod.

As currently envisaged (see accompanying illustration), the payload pod is underslung, and twin tailbooms/tail unit added. The airframe would be built of graphite epoxy, with Mylar and Teflon wing skins. Vertical stabiliser panels are mounted above the wings at about one-third span, and the outer one-third of each wing is hinged. There are solar cells on each side of the vertical stabilisers and on the top and bottom surfaces of the outer wing panels; the latter would be hinged upward during daylight, to absorb maximum solar energy, and downward at night to improve cruise performance. The aircraft would have an 11·2 kW (15 hp) electric motor, driving a large diameter pusher propeller; this would be powered directly by the solar cells during the day, and at night by fuel cells which had been charged by the Sun during daylight hours.

The 1984 contract covers the study of payload options, and simulation of a potential mission to monitor experimental crops in southern Arizona. The sensor payload would operate in the near-infra-red, far-infra-red and ultraviolet spectra, sending back real-time images to assist farmers in making quick economic and crop decisions. Images transmitted would be much sharper than those from orbiting satellites.

Solar HAPP would be launched in still air, spiralling upward in 4 hours to its operational altitude, where winds are light, and loitering over a designated area using an onboard reference system. Changes of location could be directed by radio command. It could remain airborne for up to a year. First flight is possible by 1993.

DIMENSIONS, EXTERNAL:
Wing span 98 m (322 ft)
Length overall 28 m (92 ft)
Propeller diameter 12·2 m (40 ft)

WEIGHTS (approx):
Payload 113 kg (250 lb)
Launching weight 907 kg (2,000 lb)

PERFORMANCE (estimated):
Max level speed 80 knots (148 km/h; 92 mph)
Cruising speed at altitude 52 knots (97 km/h; 60 mph)

AUSTIN DIVISION

PO Box 17100, Austin, Texas 78760, Org T7-01
Telephone: (512) 448 5555
VICE-PRESIDENT, RPV PROGRAMMES: Robert E. Nettles
MANAGER, RPV MARKET RESEARCH & DEVELOPMENT: Don Gordon
PUBLIC INFORMATION: Sandy Dochen

LMSC AQUILA
US Army designation: YMQM-105

The Aquila (Latin for eagle) mini-RPV provides real-time target acquisition, first round fire for effect, artillery adjustment, laser target designation and aerial reconnaissance. US Army interest in such a vehicle was first expressed in 1974, and resulted in an XMQM-105 programme (first flight December 1975) to quantify the performance, operations and training characteristics for such a system, as detailed in earlier editions of *Jane's*. The Army awarded LMSC contracts for a TADAR (target acquisition, designation and aerial reconnaissance) full scale development programme, beginning on 31 August 1979. Under these contracts, Lockheed was to supply 28 YMQM-105 Aquila air vehicles (first flight July 1982), together with ground control stations (GCS), a remote ground terminal (RGT), hydraulic catapult launchers, Dornier net recovery units, payload subassemblies, maintenance shelters, training simulators and training manuals. The Aquila programme was transferred from LMSC at Sunnyvale, California, to Lockheed-Austin in mid-1983.

During 1985, an early operational capability Aquila system was fielded by the US Army, operated by Army personnel in full scale force-on-force exercises to develop operational techniques. At the end of 1985, the Army restructured the programme to include a month-long capability demonstration in January 1986 and to reschedule the completion of Army operational testing to December 1986. During the testing in January, Aquila successfully demonstrated its capability to perform to its design specifications, and was used to designate tank targets for live Copperhead anti-tank rounds fired from artillery howitzers. Eight direct hits were achieved out of nine rounds fired: four against moving targets and four against stationary tanks. One Copperhead round malfunctioned. Other capabilities demonstrated included: finding a target and determining its specific type and identity at specified ranges and conditions; locking on and tracking a moving target automatically; maintaining a laser spot on a moving target to provide a marker for laser guided munitions; retrieving the Aquila automatically; launching the Aquila at a central launching facility, passing it in flight to a forward facility, and reversing this process for recovery.

By early 1986 some 330 test flights of the FSD Aquila had been completed: 306 were completely successful, 15 ended with parachute recoveries, and 9 crashed. At the time of going to press it was hoped that a production decision would be forthcoming by the Spring of 1987, enabling deliveries to begin in early 1989. The US Army's planned purchase was reported in 1986 to include 376 air vehicles and 53 ground stations.

Sensors for the target acquisition/designation role consist of a stabilised daylight TV camera combined with a laser rangefinder/designator. The air vehicle and its payload are controlled from the GCS; video imagery and target location information are returned via an anti-jam data link. The target acquisition system can be used for conventional artillery as well as for such laser homing munitions as Copperhead, Hellfire and other laser guided projectiles, both cannon and aircraft launched. Real-time TV pictures and damage assessment data can be relayed to a ground station many miles behind the battlefront.

Command and control of the tactical system entail four basic functions: (1) automatic launch and navigation of the air vehicle over enemy territory, and return for recovery; (2) control of an onboard video camera by ground operators to acquire and auto-track targets; (3) accurate determination of target co-ordinates; and (4) processing and transmission of target data to fire direction centres, for use by artillery batteries.

TYPE: Recoverable tactical mini-RPV.

AIRFRAME: Mid-mounted sweptwing tail-less blended fuselage monoplane, built by Hitco from moulded and pre-impregnated Kevlar epoxy laminates with graphite/epoxy laminates for increased strength, shaped and treated for low radar signature. Leading-edge sweepback 28°. Differentially operated elevons on trailing-edges of wings. Airframe dismantles into three major subsections (centrebody and the two wings).

POWER PLANT: One Herbrandson Dyad 280B two-stroke flat-twin piston engine (17·9 kW; 24 hp at 8,000 rpm), driving a two-blade fixed-pitch wooden pusher propeller within an annular duct. Exhaust is directed upward to minimise IR signature. Collapsible, quick-disconnect bladder fuel cell; fuel is a 50:1 (by volume) petrol/oil mixture.

LAUNCH AND RECOVERY: Launched from All American Engineering HP-30 hydraulically actuated catapult mounted on a 5 ton truck. Primary recovery system uses infra-red sensors to retrieve the air vehicle automatically, guiding it into a hydraulically deployed Dornier vertical ribbon net raised on back of M814 truck and capable of being lowered quickly after recovery in order to maintain low profile. Entire ground system can be set up for launch in less than 1 h and taken down in 30 min. For test and training flights, YMQM-105 has an 11·51 m (37 ft 9 in) diameter nylon parachute for emergency backup recovery, from which air vehicle is suspended inverted to protect mission equipment, providing survivability for avionics and payload. Parachute deploys automatically if control link is lost for more than 20 min.

GUIDANCE AND CONTROL: Flight is defined by pre-programmed waypoints stored in air vehicle's LMSC flight control electronic package (FCEP) and ground system's Norden Systems GCS computer. At any time during mission, air vehicle operator can change waypoints or command RPV to go into any of several loiter or jinking modes. If data link transmission is interrupted, RPV continues its flight according to last set of instructions and position data received. At any time when within line of sight, RPV can receive a burst transmission with position update and, if desired, onboard computer can be reloaded with new instructions. Final waypoint is recovery area. In addition to FCEP, flight control subsystem includes a Singer-Kearfott attitude reference assembly (ARA), two air data transducers, three servo-actuators, a power supply, and a near IR source landing aid. FCEP provides computation capability for navigation, guid-

Artist's impression of LMSC/NASA Solar HAPP very long endurance aircraft, with outer wing panels hinged upward

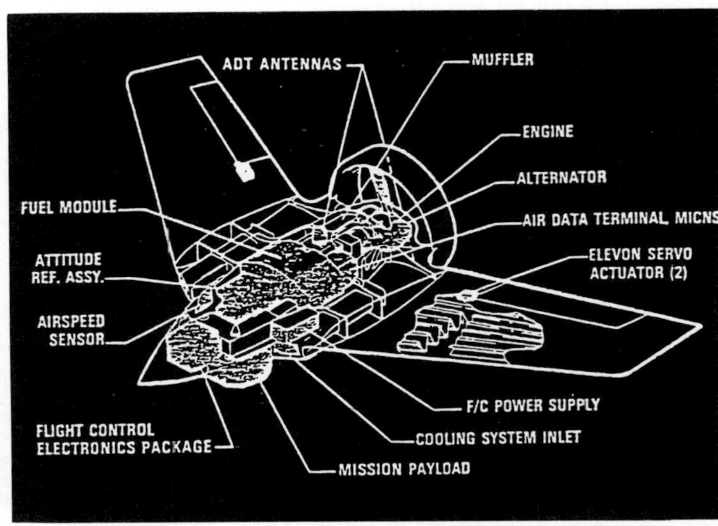

Sectional view of the LMSC YMQM-105 Aquila tactical mini-RPV

LSI/DS SkyEye R4E-40, with 'Eyeball' TV in transparent nosecone, making a skid landing

Launch of an LSI/Developmental Sciences SkyEye R4E-40 with a Texas Instruments FLIR in turreted undernose module

ance and control of the RPV as well as signals for controlling the payload air data terminal and built-in test functions. ARA is a strapdown inertial sensor package, key components of which are a three-axis rate gyro assembly, three-axis accelerometer assembly, and a small computer to provide co-ordinate transformation calculations. System requires periodic position update by burst transmission; this allows the onboard computer to calculate and compensate for gyro and accelerometer errors and calculate a new wind estimate. Computer also points the steerable data link antennae, transfers control from one GCS to another following handoff, and initiates pre-programmed link loss and reacquisition logic following dead reckoning or inadvertent link loss. Air data transducers provide barometric altitude and airspeed information to the FCEP, where it is combined with outputs from the ARA to provide signals to the servo-actuators controlling elevons and throttle and updates to the onboard FCEP computer. Airborne data terminal (ADT) receives command signals from, and returns status and video signals to, the RGT.

The Aquila FSD programme utilises a Harris Inc modular integrated communication and navigation system (MICNS) as its jam-resistant data link. This J-band system provides command uplink, telemetry and video downlinks, and navigation of the RPV relative to the ground station, all in a hostile jamming environment. Location of target with respect to RPV is determined from the mission payload gimbal angles while it is tracking the target; the laser measures slant range. The ARA provides heading and local vertical reference to the onboard computer, which calculates target position relative to local vertical. This vector is transmitted to the GCS and combined with RPV position and the surveyed location of the ground station to determine co-ordinates of the target. GCS is the control centre of the RPV system. Telemetry and video data from the air vehicle are processed and displayed; command data are generated and relayed to the air vehicle via the ground station.

SYSTEM: Electrical power for onboard subsystems provided by a 1·5kW 28V DC engine driven alternator via a power conditioning unit.

MISSION EQUIPMENT: Mission payload subsystem (MPS) is mounted in lower forward fuselage. MPS is a Westinghouse three-axis stabilised daylight TV camera, incorporating a laser rangefinder/designator, autotracker (controlled by a microprocessor), and three-fields-of-view optics. Line of sight stabilisation and tracking is provided throughout lower hemisphere and up to 15° elevation above air vehicle's horizontal reference plane. Azimuth rotation is continuous while observing targets. The TV camera, laser, laser receiver and control electronics are stationary, with image stabilisation provided by a gimballed mirror system. The boresighted laser provides range to target and designation. A turret mounted Kevlar shroud protects the gimballed portion of the MPS, and contains a multi-faceted window through which the optical line of sight is projected. The turret is environmentally sealed. A stabilised, gimbal mounted FLIR MPS has been ordered from Ford Aerospace (Aeronutronic Division), to extend RPV operations to 24 hour day/night and restricted visibility conditions. Ford's main subcontractor is Honeywell (Electro-Optics Division), which will provide the mini-FLIR and dual-mode autotracker.

DIMENSIONS, EXTERNAL:

Wing span	3·88 m (12 ft 8¾ in)
Length overall	2·08 m (6 ft 10 in)
Propeller diameter	0·66 m (2 ft 2 in)

WEIGHTS (A: TADARS Aquila, B: extended range Aquila):

Payload: daylight TV	28 kg (61·7 lb)
FLIR	25 kg (55 lb)
Max payload: A	36·5 kg (80·5 lb)
B	52 kg (114·5 lb)
Max fuel weight: A	15 kg (33 lb)
B	40·5 kg (89 lb)
Usable load: A	51·5 kg (113·5 lb)
B	71 kg (156·5 lb)
Max launching weight: A	132 kg (291 lb)
B	150 kg (331 lb)

PERFORMANCE (A and B except where indicated):

Max level speed	113 knots (210 km/h; 130 mph)
Cruising speed	73-94 knots (135-175 km/h; 84-109 mph)
Loiter speed	70 knots (130 km/h; 81 mph)
Service ceiling	4,500 m (14,765 ft)
Endurance, excl 40 min reserves: A	3 h
B	10 h

LMSC ALTAIR

Lockheed's Austin Division announced the Altair on 5 June 1985 as an international version of the US Army's Aquila. Intended to provide a highly survivable means of providing real-time imaging for target acquisition and artillery adjustment, it will utilise the same basic airframe and power plant as the Aquila. Principal difference will be elimination of the Aquila's laser target designation system; also, the data link in the Altair will be less resistant to jamming than that in the Aquila. A prototype/demonstrator was expected to be completed in 1986.

The Altair will carry a Lockheed adaptive modular payload (LAMP) with a stabilised platform. Initially, the payload choice will consist of a solid state TV or FLIR camera for full day/night imaging capability.

Growth options for Altair include launch from helicopters or ships' platforms. Increased flight endurance, using electronic engine control and additional fuel tanks in the wings, are being developed, and LMSC expects to be able to achieve a mission endurance of more than 10 hours.

DIMENSIONS AND PERFORMANCE:
As for extended range Aquila

LSI/DS

DEVELOPMENTAL SCIENCES
(Astronics Division of Lear Siegler Inc)

1930 South Vineyard Avenue, PO Box 50000, Ontario, California 91761
Telephone: (714) 947 7600 and 947 3368

VICE-PRESIDENT AND GENERAL MANAGER:
Dr Gerald R. Seemann
VICE-PRESIDENT, RESEARCH: Dr Gordon Harris
DIRECTOR OF MARKETING: Dr James A. Gardner

Since 1971 Developmental Sciences, which became the Astronics Division of Lear Siegler Inc in April 1984, has designed and built, under contract to various US agencies and manufacturers, a number of advanced RPVs for research and other purposes. Details of several of these have appeared in previous editions of *Jane's*. Recent designs have included the Gunsight, Locomp and AED air vehicles (1983-84 edition), development of which was continuing in 1986. More recently, however, main activities have been concentrated on the SkyEye R4E-40 RPV system, supporting foreign and domestic operators of this system.

LSI/DS's SkyEye mini-RPV programme started in late 1972, and the prototype flew for the first time on 26 April 1973. Details of the early models can be found in the 1980-81 and previous editions of *Jane's*. First flight of the improved SkyEye R4D was made in 1978, and this model was described and illustrated in the 1982-83 *Jane's*.

LSI/DS SKYEYE R4E-40

From its success with the R4D, and its work on the US Army Aquila programme (see under LMSC in this section), for which it built the first 38 air vehicles, LSI/DS began in 1980 to develop a family of R4E SkyEyes which respond to customers' needs for a variety of missions, payloads and vehicle sizes. The R4E has an entirely different airframe configuration to that of the R4D, and has been in operational service with the Royal Thai Air Force since 1982 (six R4E-30) and with the US Army (R4E-40) since 1984. In late 1985 it was reconfigured to accommodate either a turreted daylight video camera or a turreted common module FLIR.

The SkyEye can perform both day and night missions which include real-time surveillance, reconnaissance, tactical weather observation, artillery and naval gunfire and close air support, laser designation and rangefinding, battle damage assessment, coastal and maritime patrol, elint/sigint/comint, ECM, communications relay, and weapons delivery and emplacement. Operational suitability in many of these roles has already been demonstrated successfully.

The system is completely mobile, being transportable by ground vehicles, military transport aircraft or naval vessels. A typical ground based SkyEye unit consists of four to six RPVs, a mobile command and control shelter, a mobile launch system, and a personnel/equipment transport vehicle.

Joint Lear Siegler/US Army operations in 1984-85 included reconnaissance patrols along the Honduran/Nicaraguan border after launch from airfields at Puerto San Lorenzo and Palmerola in central and southern Honduras. Four SkyEyes were delivered to the US Army in late 1984, with a further four funded in mid-1985. Operations have included night launch and recovery, and the use of both daylight and LLL TV payloads, FLIR sensors, and a panoramic camera. SkyEye was expected to be a major contender in the US Army's IEW-UAV competition (intelligence and electronic warfare unmanned air vehicle), for which RFPs were due to be issued in May 1986.

Brief details of other R4E versions were given in the 1984-85 *Jane's*. The following description applies specifically to the R4E-40:

TYPE: Multi-mission mini-RPV.

AIRFRAME: Cantilever high-wing monoplane with a fuselage pod, twin tailbooms, twin sweptback fins (one with rudder), and an enclosed tailplane with central elevator. Inboard wing panels are sweptback, with ailerons on their trailing-edges; outer panels have swept leading-edges, non-swept trailing-edges, and are set at an anhedral angle. The engine is mounted at the rear of the fuselage pod, driving a pusher propeller, and there is an extendable landing skid beneath the fuselage. Airframe construction is primarily of graphite (carbonfibre) and Kevlar reinforced epoxy, and is fully sealed for long life in hot and humid climates. The SkyEye can be fitted with a rail or pod under each wing, in line with the tailboom, for the carriage of external stores (eg, chaff).

POWER PLANT: One LSI/DS modified Kawasaki 440 cc two-cylinder two-stroke engine (nominal rating 28·3 kW; 38 hp), driving a two-blade fixed-pitch wooden propeller (variable-pitch propeller optional). Bladder fuel tank in each wing.

LAUNCH AND RECOVERY: All American Engineering HP-3403 hydraulic/pneumatic catapult launcher. The HP-3403 is self-contained, can be truck mounted, and can launch a vehicle within ten minutes of being started, so eliminating both the recurring expense of a rocket boost and its associated infra-red, noise and visual signatures. System contains enough engine fuel for 20 launches. The RPV uses a simple extendable-skid landing system which allows a pilot, after brief training, to land the RPV safely by monitoring the TV picture from the RPV's nose camera. The RPV is flown in the landing pattern to a short field; full pitch-up is then applied while the RPV limits elevator position to provide an approach speed safely above stalling speed. A specially designed shock attenuation system compensates for not flaring the RPV, and the vehicle skids to a straight stop in a few hundred feet. As a backup to the skid landing, for use in rough terrain or in an emergency, a low altitude (less than 61 m; 200 ft) 12·8 m (42 ft) diameter cruciform parachute (housed in the wing centre-section between the fuel tanks) is deployed.

GUIDANCE AND CONTROL: Radio/TV command guidance system, with fully equipped three-axis autopilot for stability and precise control, even in very rough air. LSI/DS guidance and control unit includes vertical gyro, yaw rate gyro, barometric altitude transducer, vertical accelerometer, airspeed transducer, and compass. Aircraft can be operated in four different modes, in-flight selected from the command console: (1) rate mode, commanding rate of climb/descent and turn, used for target tracking and other tasks requiring continuous manoeuvring of the RPV; (2) attitude mode (used, for example, to align vehicle weapons with a target, or for landing); (3) automatic (pre-programmed) mode; and (4) manual mode, in which uplink commands are applied directly to the RPV's control surfaces. (Manual is an electrically redundant mode, used in case of autopilot failure; because of SkyEye's low speed and high intrinsic stability, it can be operated safely without autopilot.) The type of data link used depends upon customers' specific requirements, and both analog and digital links can be specified. Avionics and data link equipment are housed in a rear fuselage bay, together with the electrical system equipment, which comprises a 980W engine driven alternator (2kW alternator optional) for 28V DC power, and an emergency battery which provides 5 min flying time in the event of alternator failure.

MISSION EQUIPMENT: The large payload volume and weight capacity permit the accommodation of a wide variety of payloads, carried individually or in combinations. Demonstrated examples of payloads carried by the R4E-40 include gyro stabilised daylight and low light level TV systems in combination with panoramic cameras or communications repeaters; a standard US Army common module gyro stabilised FLIR (Texas Instruments AIR-360/3) in a gimballed 'chin' turret, in combination with infra-red linescanners (Texas Instruments RPV-700); and nose mounted TV with underwing rocket launchers (up to six 10 kg rockets or tubes for 2·75 in rockets). Other payloads can include multiple meteorological sensors, a laser designator/rangefinder, two 33 kg (73 lb) underwing pods of fuel or ejectable items such as chaff, leaflets, flares or communications jammers.

DIMENSIONS, EXTERNAL:
- Wing span: 5·36 m (17 ft 7 in)
- Wing aspect ratio: 7·9
- Length overall: 3·72 m (12 ft 2½ in)
- Propeller diameter: 0·79 m (2 ft 7 in)

AREA:
- Wings, gross: 3·63 m² (39·1 sq ft)

WEIGHTS:
- Weight empty: 127 kg (280 lb)
- Max payload: 63·5 kg (140 lb)
- Max standard fuel: 45·5 kg (100 lb)
- Max launching weight: 236 kg (520 lb)
- Max weight for parachute recovery: 190·5 kg (420 lb)

PERFORMANCE:
- Max level speed ('clean' configuration): 136 knots (252 km/h; 156 mph)
- Max rate of climb at S/L: 305 m (1,000 ft)/min
- Service ceiling:
  - AUW of 227 kg (500 lb): 4,575 m (15,000 ft)
  - AUW of 190·5 kg (420 lb): 6,100 m (20,000 ft)
- Typical command and control range: 80 nm (148 km; 92 miles)
- Max endurance:
  - 63·5 kg (140 lb) payload, at S/L: 7 h 42 min
  - 63·5 kg (140 lb) payload, at 4,875 m (16,000 ft): 6 h 24 min
  - 45·5 kg (100 lb) payload, at S/L: 8 h 12 min

MARTIN MARIETTA

MARTIN MARIETTA ORLANDO AEROSPACE

PO Box 5837, Orlando, Florida 32855
Telephone: (305) 356 2207
DIRECTOR, PUBLIC RELATIONS: Phil Giaramita

MARTIN MARIETTA SLAT

US Navy designation: YAQM-127A

A full scale engineering development contract for this supersonic low-altitude target was awarded to Martin Marietta by the US Navy in September 1984, after consideration also of entries from LTV (Vought) and Teledyne Ryan. The contract calls for delivery of 15 pre-production targets by 1987, with the flight test programme to take place during FYs 1987-88. It is then planned to carry out limited operations at the Pacific Missile Test Center in FY 1989, using targets remaining from the flight test programme. Initial procurement of 30 production targets is planned for FY 1990, followed by a three-year production option for 100 targets per year with IOC for Fleet training coming in FY 1991.

Martin Marietta's partners in this programme are Marquardt (main rocket/ramjet sustainer engine), Morton Thiokol (solid propellant booster rocket), and Northrop (avionics, payload integration, recovery system, and related ground support equipment).

The air vehicle is a derivative of the cancelled advanced strategic air launched missile (ASALM), which made seven test flights during 1978-80 and was last described in the 1980-81 *Jane's*. Primary payload will be an I band seeker simulator, radar cross-section augmentation (1-10 m²; 11-108 sq ft in G, E/F and I/J bands), and scoring equipment.

First flight of a YAQM-127A is expected in about March 1987. The target will be pre-programmed, with a remote command override. It is required to be capable of subsonic launch from an F-4 or QF-4 aircraft at 305 m (1,000 ft) altitude, be capable of recovery from land and water, and have a design life of four flights. It should also demonstrate capability for air launch from a DC-130 aircraft, and compatibility for such launch from the A-6 Intruder, F/A-18 Hornet and P-3 Orion, under the same conditions. Launch speed will be in the order of 200 knots (370 km/h; 230 mph), the SLAT then entering a shallow dive to level out at about 9 m (30 ft) above the surface after reaching its maximum speed of Mach 2·5, to simulate a sea skimming missile. It will be recoverable by parachute and re-usable. Range requirement, all fuel expended, is 55 nm (102 km; 63 miles).

DIMENSIONS, EXTERNAL:
- Length overall: 5·47 m (17 ft 11½ in)
- Body diameter (max): 0·54 m (1 ft 9¼ in)

WEIGHT (estimated):
- Max launching weight: 1,088 kg (2,400 lb)

NASA

NATIONAL AERONAUTICS AND SPACE ADMINISTRATION

400 Mayland Avenue SW, Washington, DC 20546
PUBLIC AFFAIRS OFFICER: Debra J. Rahn

NASA PROJECT DAST

Project DAST (Drones for Aerodynamic and Structural Testing), conducted jointly by NASA's Langley and Dryden Flight Research Centers, utilises modified Firebee IIs as testbeds for high-risk evaluation of various research wing configurations. Primary object of the programme is to demonstrate the ability of advanced flight control systems to control wing flutter. Details of the early ARW-1 (aeroelastic research wing) stages of the programme were given in the 1984-85 *Jane's*.

The ARW-2 phase, in addition to flutter suppression, is intended to study manoeuvre load alleviation, gust load alleviation, and relaxed static stability. Vehicle control is via a rudder and differentially moving horizontal tail surfaces. All wing control surfaces are used for the flutter and load control functions. The ARW-2, which has a high aspect ratio, low sweep angle, and a wing section designed for transonic flight, is similar to wings proposed for use on energy-efficient transports. Flight tests are to study the effectiveness of various load control systems when operating simultaneously. Studies were initiated toward developing an energy absorbing system to allow an alternative recovery mode, in which the approx 1,134 kg (2,500 lb) vehicle would descend to ground impact on a 30·5 m (100 ft) diameter parachute.

No recent news of the ARW-2 phase has been received.

NORTHROP

NORTHROP CORPORATION—VENTURA DIVISION

1515 Rancho Conejo Boulevard, Newbury Park, California 91320
Telephone: (805) 498 3131
Telex: 659 220
VICE-PRESIDENT AND GENERAL MANAGER: L. Bruce James
VICE-PRESIDENT, TARGET SYSTEMS: Frank Caramelli
PUBLIC INFORMATION: A. W. Cantafio, Public Information Director, Northrop Corporation, 1840 Century Park East, Los Angeles, California 90067

Northrop's Ventura Division designs and manufactures pilotless target aircraft and related equipment. It also produces glassfibre wing fairings for the Boeing 747 transport aircraft, as well as various parts and subassemblies for Northrop F-5E/F and McDonnell Douglas/Northrop F/A-18 combat aircraft.

Northrop Ventura (formerly Radioplane) undertook the design, development and construction of its first radio controlled target drone in the mid-thirties. Since then it has become a leader in the field of pilotless aircraft. More than 78,000 drones have been delivered to the US military services and 25 allied nations. It has nearly 2,000 employees engaged in aerial target design and production.

Since 1971, Ventura Division has also been responsible for aerial target services at the NATO Missile Firing Installation (NAMFI) on the island of Crete. The latest

Artist's impression of the Martin Marietta YAQM-127A supersonic low-altitude target (SLAT)

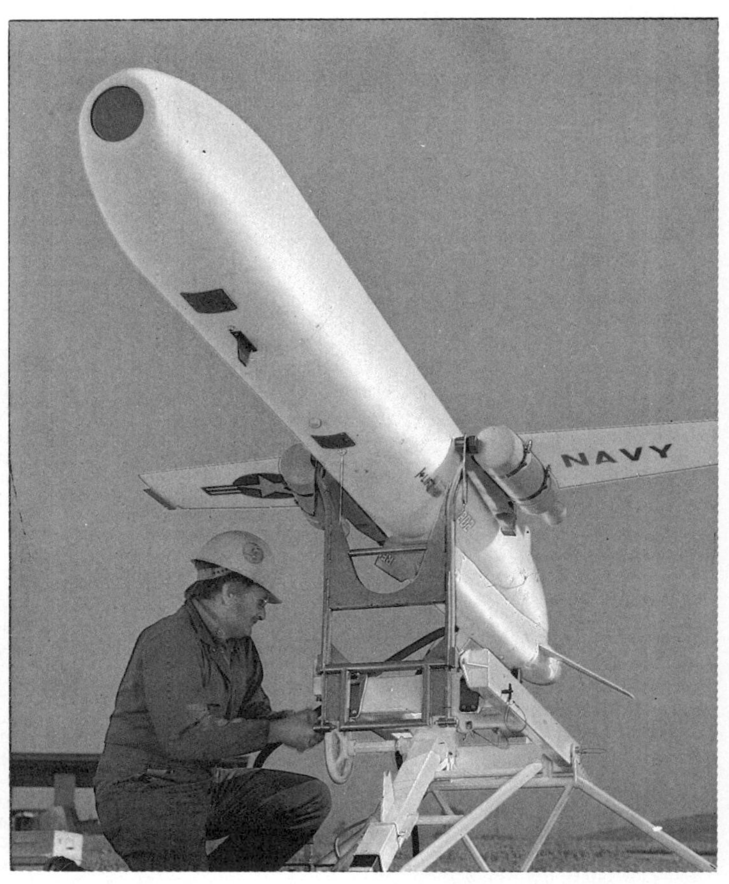

Northrop tactical reconnaissance version of the US Navy BQM-74C

The Northrop BQM-74C Chukar III can be launched from the air, from the deck of a ship, and from the ground

Northrop Basic Training Target (BTT)/MQM-33C being launched at a US Army range

(1983) renewal of this contract calls for these services to be continued until December 1987.

NORTHROP BASIC TRAINING TARGET (BTT)

US military designations: MQM-33C and MQM-36

This target drone is currently in worldwide use, and has been manufactured for the armed forces of 25 countries. Also known as the **Shelduck** or **KD2R-5**, it has been used as a training device for 20 mm, 23 mm, 35 mm, 40 mm, 57 mm, 3 in, 5 in, Vulcan and Bitubes anti-aircraft gunnery, as well as a target for surface-to-air missiles such as Blowpipe, Chaparral, Rapier, RBS-70, Redeye, Seacat, Sea Sparrow, Shahine, Stinger and Tigercat. Design began in 1946 and the prototype was initially flown in 1947. Since then more than 65,000 vehicles of this type have been built, and plans for production continue into the 1990s.

Northrop has delivered a modified version of the BTT to the US Army. Known as the **MQM-33C**, it incorporates a Northrop developed G band command control system; 161 MQM-33Cs and 18 G band ground control stations had been produced by early 1985, and production was continuing in early 1986.

The BTT system has been integrated with a Northrop developed portable tracking system. Towed gunnery sleeves with real-time scoring, and six towed infra-red targets, are also available for use with the BTT.

The following description applies to the standard version:

Type: Remotely controlled recoverable target.

Airframe: High-wing monoplane, of aluminium alloy construction. No dihedral. Wing incidence 1° at root, −2° at tip. Ailerons and elevator servo-operated by D-9 actuators.

Power Plant: One 59·7 kW (80 hp) Northrop O-11-3 flat-four two-stroke engine, driving a two-blade fixed-pitch wooden propeller. Steel integral fuel tank in mid-fuselage, capacity 44 litres (11·6 US gallons). Refuelling point in fuselage forward of wing.

Launch and Recovery: Surface launch from land or ship, by either rotary catapult or zero length launcher. Recovery by parachute released by radio command. Engine is stopped and parachute deploys automatically in event of serious damage by gunfire, or loss of radio control or electrical power.

Guidance and Control: AN/ARW-79 radio command guidance system, with automatic altitude hold. Visual or radar tracking (radar or FM type tracking systems or equivalent).

Mission Equipment: 28V battery for all electrical power. Optional augmentation devices include two wingtip radar reflector pods, visual and infra-red flare kits, and towed banners. An acoustic scoring system and auxiliary decoder can provide three spare command and control links in addition to the single spare channel of the basic system. An altitude hold control, a precision barometric sensor which detects variations in altitude and provides control corrections to secure constant flight altitude, can also be provided.

Dimensions, external:

Wing span	3·50 m (11 ft 6 in)
Length overall	3·85 m (12 ft 7½ in)
Height overall	0·76 m (2 ft 6 in)

Area:

Wings, gross	1·74 m² (18·7 sq ft)

Weights:

Weight empty	123 kg (271 lb)
Max launching weight	181 kg (400 lb)
Max zero-fuel weight	133 kg (292 lb)
Max landing weight	154 kg (340 lb)

Performance:

Max level speed at S/L and max cruising speed	195 knots (360 km/h; 224 mph)
Stalling speed	58 knots (108 km/h; 67 mph)
Max rate of climb at S/L	1,341 m (4,400 ft)/min
Service ceiling	more than 8,230 m (27,000 ft)
Range at S/L with max fuel	183 nm (338 km; 210 miles)
Average flight duration	55 min

NORTHROP CHUKAR II

US military designation: MQM-74C

The MQM-74C is an improved version of the MQM-74A (1974-75 *Jane's*), developed via an MQM-74B experimental model to meet requirements for a 500 knot (926 km/h; 576 mph) target. Since early 1974 more than 1,400 MQM-74Cs have been delivered to the US Navy, making more than 4,300 MQM-74 Chukars manufactured in all. Other Chukar II users include the UK, West Germany, Greece, Japan, Netherlands, Saudi Arabia and Spain. Production of the Chukar II is continuing.

Modified versions of the MQM-74C have been tested and operated as reconnaissance, electronic warfare and strike RPVs under the US Navy's Persistent Anti-Radiation Missile (PARM) and US Air Force's TED programmes. Under US Navy contract, Northrop is producing a version of the MQM-74C known as the **BQM-74C** (described separately), for use by the US Navy as a cruise missile simulator and standard aerial training target.

The basic Chukar II/MQM-74C target aircraft was designed to meet requirements for a small, lightweight target for anti-aircraft gunnery, surface-to-air and air-to-air missile training and weapons system evaluation. Chukar II is in service at the NATO Missile Firing Installation (NAMFI) on the island of Crete in the Mediterranean, where it is used to train crews of radar and non-radar directed anti-aircraft guns, active and semi-active radar guided, visual and infra-red guided surface-to-air and air-to-air missiles which include Hawk, Redeye, Chaparral, Standard Sparrow, Sea Sparrow, Sidewinder, Seacat and Tigercat. Meteor of Italy (which see) was selected by NATO's Hawk management office to provide Chukar II services at the Salto di Quirra range in Sardinia.

Type: Radio controlled recoverable target.

Airframe: Shoulder-wing monoplane, of aluminium construction. No dihedral. Detachable wings, each with electrically actuated aileron. Tapered circular-section body, with underslung air intake duct. Inverted Y tail unit, with 30° anhedral on tailplane, electrically actuated elevators and fixed vertical fin.

Power Plant: One Williams International WR24-7 (J400-WR-401) turbojet engine, rated at 0·80 kN (180 lb st). Fuel tank in centre of fuselage, capacity 61·3 litres (16·2 US gallons).

Launch and Recovery: Zero length launching by means of two Mk 91 Mod 0 JATO rockets and a ZL-5 launcher.

Normal recovery by automatic drone pull-up followed by main parachute deployment, initiated automatically in emergencies such as interruption of continuous radio signal or loss of parachute command channel. Alternative method consists of direct main parachute deployment and is initiated automatically on loss of electrical power. Main parachute housed in fuselage immediately aft of wing, with automatic disconnect on impact.

GUIDANCE AND CONTROL: Radio command guidance system. Out-of-sight control by automatic stabilisation and command, with radar tracking; in-sight control with visual acquisition aids. Proportional feedback stabilisation and control system for pitch and bank. Engine throttle position, altitude hold initiation and recovery system initiation controlled by audio tone signals. Components include receiver, decoder, autopilot, aileron and elevator servos, altitude hold and airspeed pressure transducers. Command control antenna in upper forward fuselage.

MISSION EQUIPMENT (target): Electrical power from engine driven alternator through a rectifier-regulator. 28V nickel-cadmium battery secondary power source used during glide. Onboard acquisition and tracking aids include fore and aft Luneberg lenses for passive radar augmentation, four wingtip mounted Mk 28 Mod 3 infra-red flares, pyrotechnic infra-red plume augmentors, active L-band augmentation, and a smoke system, designed to improve visual detection. Main payload compartment is in front fuselage between control equipment bay and fuel tank. Improved manoeuvrability package (IMP) successfully flight tested in 1976 has closed loop control device installed in flight control system, enabling Chukar II to perform constant *g* manoeuvres at any of five selected levels up to and including 6*g*. A low cost infra-red tow target, for use with the Chukar II system, is in production. One can be attached to each wingtip and towed approx 30 m (100 ft) behind the Chukar. A re-usable active RF augmentation tow target system is in use for various RF guided missile systems. Production of active tow targets began in 1979.

DIMENSIONS, EXTERNAL:
- Wing span — 1·76 m (5 ft 9¼ in)
- Length overall — 3·87 m (12 ft 8½ in)
- Body diameter — 0·38 m (1 ft 3 in)
- Height overall — 0·71 m (2 ft 4 in)

WEIGHTS:
- Weight empty — 128·4 kg (283 lb)
- Fuel — 50·3 kg (111 lb)
- Max launching weight — 223 kg (492 lb)

PERFORMANCE:
- Max level speed at 6,100 m (20,000 ft) — 515 knots (954 km/h; 593 mph)
- Max level speed at S/L — 475 knots (880 km/h; 547 mph)
- Econ cruising speed at S/L — 250 knots (463 km/h; 288 mph)
- Max rate of climb at S/L with full fuel — 1,780 m (5,840 ft)/min
- Service ceiling — 12,200 m (40,000 ft)
- Range at max speed:
  - at S/L — 205 nm (380 km; 236 miles)
  - at 6,100 m (20,000 ft) — 330 nm (611 km; 380 miles)
- Range at econ cruising speed:
  - at S/L — 245 nm (454 km; 282 miles)
- Average flight duration — more than 1 h

NORTHROP CHUKAR III

US Navy designation: BQM-74C

The BQM-74C is a US Navy target version of the MQM-74C Chukar II (which see) with added air launch capability and pre-programmed flight profiles. It can be used as a cruise missile simulator, in training pilots for air-to-air combat, and as a target for anti-aircraft gunnery and surface-to-air missiles. Design began in November 1977, and construction of 16 pre-production examples started in September 1978. Navy technical and operational evaluation tests of the basic BQM-74C configuration were completed successfully in 1980.

Since 1980 Northrop has produced more than 1,000 BQM-74Cs for the US Navy, including 350 in 1985. Continuing contracts are planned through 1987 for an additional 470 targets, and subsequent contracts well into the 1990s. In its first deployment overseas, the Chukar III in 1984 successfully simulated, in France, a sea-skimming anti-ship cruise missile during test firings of the Thomson-CSF Crotale. Export deliveries have been made to France and Spain.

Under a US Navy development contract Northrop successfully flight tested during 1985 a BQM-74C powered by a Williams International YJ400-WR-404 engine, rated at 1·07 kN (240 lb st), which permits the ceiling to be increased to 12,200 m (40,000 ft), speeds to approx 530 knots (982 km/h; 610 mph) at 6,100 m (20,000 ft), and *g* limit during sustained manoeuvres to +4. This power plant became available as the baseline engine for the BQM-74C/Chukar III in early 1986.

The BQM-74C target system includes pylon adaptors for air launching from several types of aircraft, and payload kits for mobile sea range (MSR) operations. MSR enables fleet commanders to conduct realistic 'war games' on open sea. The BQM-74C's role in these exercises is to simulate cruise missiles fired from multiple directions and latitudes. The BQM-74C's missions can be pre-programmed, and the target is capable of air or surface launch from beyond the horizon of target ships. It has been flown at an altitude of 3 m (10 ft) while simulating cruise missile flight profiles.

A **BQM-74C/Recce** version was displayed at the 1985 Paris Air Show. The nose bay of this version, which was developed under US Navy contract, is reconfigured to accommodate a non-gimballed daylight TV camera and zoom lens of the type installed in the Northrop RF-5E TigerEye, a video data link transmitter, a video cassette recorder with in-flight replay capability, and a control and interface unit. Air, ground or ship launchable, and parachute recoverable, this version has a growth potential extending to panoramic photography and real-time infra-red coverage. The reconnaissance kit allows ready conversion to and from target configuration, enabling either training or tactical missions to be flown using the same basic vehicle. Four Recce kits were delivered to the US Navy in 1985, after a successful four-flight Northrop test programme. The USN was evaluating this version in 1986, with an additional six Recce kits due for delivery during that year.

The following description applies to the current standard BQM-74C target version:

TYPE: Radio controlled or programmable automatically recoverable multirole target.

AIRFRAME: Shoulder-wing monoplane of aluminium alloy and GRP construction. Northrop G-9224-080 wing section of 8% thickness/chord ratio. No dihedral. Non-swept wings, each with electrically actuated aileron. Semi-monocoque aluminium body, similar to that of MQM-74C, houses all equipment, power plant and fuel tank. Nose and tail skins removable for access to equipment and power plants. Underslung engine air intake. Inverted Y aluminium tail unit, comprising fixed vertical fin, fixed tailplane halves (anhedral 30°) and two electrically actuated elevators.

POWER PLANT: One Williams International WR24-7A (J400-WR-402) turbojet engine initially, rated at 0·80 kN (180 lb st). Available from 1986 with 1·07 kN (240 lb st) J400-WR-404 as standard. Pressurised fuel tank in centre of fuselage, capacity as for Chukar II.

LAUNCH AND RECOVERY: Can be launched from ground or shipborne launcher in same manner as MQM-74C. Can also be air-launched from Grumman A-6E Intruder or McDonnell Douglas TA-4J Skyhawk (one under each wing); is also compatible with underwing launchers of Lockheed DP-2 Neptune or DC-130A Hercules. Parachute recovery, on land or from water, as for MQM-74C.

GUIDANCE AND CONTROL: Out-of-sight UHF radio control by automatic stabilisation and command; radar tracking in-sight control, with visual acquisition aids. Alternatively, can be pre-programmed. Proportional feedback stabilisation and control system for pitch and bank. Engine throttle position, altitude hold initiation and recovery initiation are controlled by audio tone signals. Components include a Northrop digital avionics processor, vertical and yaw rate gyros, Motorola AN/DKW-3 integrated target control system, aileron and elevator servos, and altitude hold pressure transducer.

MISSION EQUIPMENT: Electrical power from engine driven alternator through a rectifier-regulator. 28V nickel-cadmium battery secondary power source. Onboard acquisition and tracking aids include fore and aft Luneberg lenses, for passive radar augmentation, and a smoke system. Main payload compartment is in forward fuselage section. Equipment includes locator beacon, radar altimeter, seeker simulator (to duplicate cruise missile emissions), radar transponder for IFF, and scoring. Provisions include flight profile programmer with UHF command override; active J-band, B-band, L-band and X-band radar augmentation; and Tacan receiver. System also includes payload kits with flotation gear for mobile sea range (MSR) operations (see introductory paragraph).

DIMENSIONS, EXTERNAL:
- Wing span — 1·76 m (5 ft 9·4 in)
- Length overall — 3·94 m (12 ft 11·4 in)
- Body diameter (max) — 0·36 m (1 ft 2 in)
- Height overall — 0·72 m (2 ft 4·3 in)

AREA:
- Wings, gross — 0·74 m² (8·0 sq ft)

WEIGHTS AND LOADING:
- Basic operating weight empty — 133 kg (294 lb)
- Max mission load — 78·5 kg (173 lb)
- Fuel — 50·3 kg (111 lb)
- Max launching weight — 199 kg (438 lb)
- Max wing loading — 267·3 kg/m² (54·75 lb/sq ft)

PERFORMANCE (at max T-O weight. A: with J400-WR-402 engine, B: with -404):
- Max level speed at 6,100 m (20,000 ft):
  - A — 500 knots (927 km/h; 576 mph)
  - B — 530 knots (982 km/h; 610 mph)
- Econ cruising speed:
  - A — 300 knots (555 km/h; 345 mph)
- Service ceiling: A — 9,150 m (30,000 ft)
  - B — 12,200 m (40,000 ft)
- Max range: A, B — 450 nm (833 km; 518 miles)
- *g* limits: A — +2·3
  - B — +4

NORTHROP NV-144

Northrop developed this new target drone as a private venture, to satisfy requirements identified by the US Navy and US Air Force. Four targets were flight tested successfully during early 1984, but the NV-144 was unsuccessful in the US Navy's YBQM-126A competition, although it met the technical requirements for that programme. In Spring 1986 Northrop was preparing to submit the NV-144 as a candidate for the US Navy's mid-range reconnaissance RPV requirement. It was believed that little if any airframe modification would be involved, since the nose payload bay has adequate volume available for such sensors as a FLIR camera, infra-red linescanner, navigation and data link equipment and an IFF transponder. Fuselage volume is also available for additional payload or fuel tankage, if required.

TYPE: Subsonic recoverable drone.

AIRFRAME: Cantilever high-wing monoplane. Northrop NROC-2 wing section, with 8% thickness/chord ratio. No anhedral or dihedral. Incidence 1° 12′ at root. Sweepback 22° 30′ at quarter-chord. Wings are of vinylester sheet moulding compound; ailerons have a foam core with aluminium wraparound skin, and are operated by Superior electromechanical proportional actuators. Forward fuselage and pressurised fuel tank are of aluminium. Cowlings and fairings are of vinylester, as is the tailplane; twin endplate fins are of aluminium. Elevator actuation similar to that of ailerons. Construction makes use of some components and equipment from Chukar III.

POWER PLANT: One 3·70 kN (831 lb st) Microturbo TRI 60-2 turbojet engine, semi-recessed under rear of fuselage, for initial flight trials. Also test flown with 4·31 kN (970 lb st) Teledyne CAE 373-8. Single fuel tank in centre-fuselage, capacity 250 litres (66 US gallons), with refuelling point on top of fuselage. Oil capacity 1 litre (0·25 US gallons).

LAUNCH AND RECOVERY: Air and surface launchable. Recovery by onboard parachute system.

GUIDANCE AND CONTROL: Can be radio controlled or pre-programmed. Vehicle can operate with a variety of remotely controlled target control systems such as ITCS, Vega, UHF and CTAS.

SYSTEMS AND EQUIPMENT: Ram air pressurisation of fuel tank; 5·2kVA alternator mounted in engine nose bullet; battery; power regulator; radar altimeter; systems and avionics processor; and Northrop digital avionics processor.

DIMENSIONS, EXTERNAL:
- Wing span — 3·26 m (10 ft 8½ in)
- Wing chord: at root — 0·84 m (2 ft 9 in)
  - at tip — 0·51 m (1 ft 8 in)
- Wing aspect ratio — 4·86
- Length overall — 5·93 m (19 ft 5½ in)
- Body diameter (max) — 0·51 m (1 ft 8 in)
- Height overall — 1·04 m (3 ft 5 in)
- Tailplane span (over fins) — 1·46 m (4 ft 9½ in)

DIMENSION, INTERNAL:
- Payload volume — 0·31 m³ (11 cu ft)

AREA:
- Wings, gross — 2·23 m² (24·0 sq ft)

WEIGHTS AND LOADING:
- Weight empty — 431 kg (950 lb)
- Max fuel weight — 181 kg (400 lb)
- Max payload — 91 kg (200 lb)
- Max T-O weight — 635 kg (1,400 lb)
- Max wing loading — 284·75 kg/m² (58·3 lb/sq ft)
- Thrust/weight ratio: TRI 60 — 0·59
  - CAE 373 — 0·69

PERFORMANCE (estimated at max T-O weight):
- Never-exceed speed — Mach 0·975
- Max level speed at S/L — 570 knots (1,056 km/h; 656 mph)
- Econ cruising speed at 11,430 m (37,500 ft) — 300 knots (555 km/h; 345 mph)
- Stalling speed — 130 knots (240 km/h; 150 mph)
- Operating height: min — 6 m (20 ft)
  - max — 15,240 m (50,000 ft)
- Range at Mach 0·8 at 4,575 m (15,000 ft) — 380 nm (703 km; 437 miles)
- Max range at 15,240 m (50,000 ft) — 1,200 nm (2,224 km; 1,382 miles)
- Endurance — 2 h 45 min
- *g* limit — +8

NORTHROP NV-151

The NV-151, under consideration by the US Air Force in early 1986, is a large, high-performance, subsonic drone designed to perform both aerial target and tactical RPV applications. It can be launched from land, ship or aircraft, and can fly air-to-air and surface-to-air weapons system training and evaluation missions.

The NV-151 is a high-wing monoplane with a twin tail. Wings and tail unit are formed of low-cost, high-strength plastics composites. The remainder of the aircraft is constructed of aluminium. Flight equipment, power plant, fuel tank and parachute recovery systems are housed in the

Northrop MQM-74C Chukar II aerial target system

Northrop-Ventura NV-144 on launch pylon of a US Navy A-6E Intruder

PAI's Heron 26 short-range RPV ready to launch

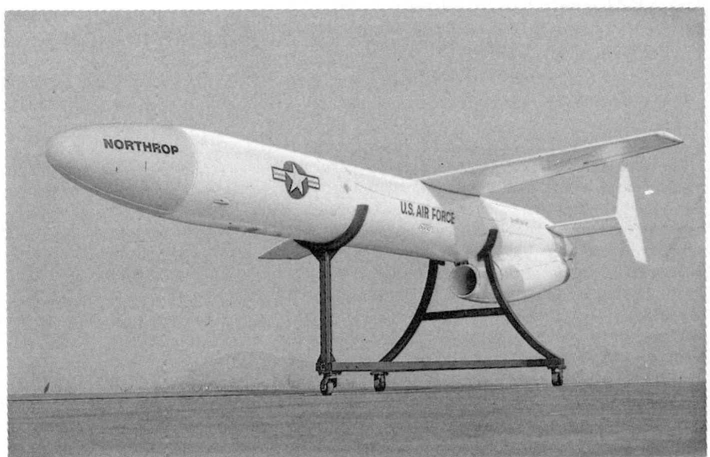

Northrop NV-151 subsonic target/RPV prototype

fuselage. The NV-151 is powered by a turbojet engine in the 4·45 kN (1,000 lb st) class, but can also use other available engines in this class.

The target, a modified version of the NV-144, uses the avionics package originally developed for the Northrop BQM-74C, including the Northrop digital avionics processor, which provides both guidance and control for the drone. The NV-151 can be equipped with a radar altimeter for low altitude flights, a seeker simulator to duplicate cruise missile emissions, a radar transponder for IFF, a miss distance indicator for weapons scoring, and a command override system to assure target ship safety during simulated attacks.

DIMENSIONS, EXTERNAL:
- Wing span: 3·32 m (10 ft 10¾ in)
- Length overall: 5·94 m (19 ft 6 in)
- Body diameter (max): 0·51 m (1 ft 8 in)

DIMENSION, INTERNAL:
- Payload volume: 0·31 m³ (11 cu ft)

WEIGHTS:
- Max payload: 91 kg (200 lb)
- Max launching weight: 635 kg (1,400 lb)

PERFORMANCE:
- Max level speed: 580 knots (1,075 km/h; 668 mph)
- Service ceiling: more than 15,240 m (50,000 ft)
- Max range at 15,240 m (50,000 ft): 1,200 nm (2,223 km; 1,381 miles)
- Max endurance at 15,240 m (50,000 ft): 2 h 35 min
- *g* limit: +8

PAI

PACIFIC AEROSYSTEM INC

8695 Aero Drive, San Diego, California 92123
Telephone: (619) 571 1441
Telex: 472-3028 PAERSY
VICE-PRESIDENT, MARKETING:
Edward V. Dempsey Jr

Pacific Aerosystem was incorporated in 1977 in order to support, with modern technology, unmanned vehicle programmes in which the governments of Italy and other NATO countries have an interest. In particular, PAI has worked closely with Meteor of Italy (which see), whose President, Dr Furio Lauri, was also a co-founder of PAI. The US company has a 4,088 m² (44,000 sq ft) facility close to Montgomery Field municipal airport, and had a 1986 workforce of about 150 people. It collaborated with Meteor in developing and producing the latter's Alamak ground control, tracking and telemetry system, has developed a remotely controlled and/or pre-programmed ocean fast boat for the Italian Navy, and carried out many other R & D programmes for the Italian government. For the US and international market, PAI has produced radio transmitters and receivers for the NASA Space Shuttle Orbiter, aircraft interface units for US Navy QF-86 target drones, and command receivers for the Australian GAF Jindivik target drone. For these markets it has also now developed an unmanned aircraft of its own design, known as the Heron 26.

PAI HERON 26

A primary feature of the Heron 26 is the Mizar avionics system, developed by PAI to enable an unmanned aircraft to determine its own geographical position independently of any ground control station and to perform many of its manoeuvres automatically, thereby ultimately being capable of full pre-programmed 'launch and forget' operation. Mizar currently uses a differential/Omega/VLF system for navigation, backed up by dead reckoning, which will be replaced by GPS navigation when that system can offer worldwide coverage in about 1988. In 1984 the present Mizar system was demonstrated to the Italian government, which adopted it as part of its Sorao battlefield surveillance programme. The air vehicle used for this demonstration was the Meteor Mirach-20 (which see); PAI is a subcontractor in this programme to Meteor, which now produces the Mirach-20 for the Italian Army and Navy.

To cater for US and international markets requiring an aircraft with greater altitude, endurance and payload, PAI developed the Heron 26, starting the design in June 1983 and flying the first of three prototypes in July 1984. Ten production examples, ordered through Meteor by the Italian government, had been completed by February 1986. Demonstrations to potential US and foreign customers were continuing at that time, and the Heron 26 was expected to be a candidate for the US Army's intelligence and electronic warfare RPV competition after the issue of RFPs later in the year.

TYPE: Recoverable multi-role drone/RPV.

AIRFRAME: Shoulder-wing monoplane with central fuselage nacelle, twin tailbooms and twin fins and rudders. Conventional construction, mostly of carbonfibre and epoxy, with some Kevlar in tail unit. Wings have tapered trailing-edge, with ailerons, and can be folded for transportation and storage. No anhedral or dihedral. Mainly rectangular-section fuselage, with crushable keel to absorb landing impact. 'Add-on' wing extension panels to increase altitude capability. Very low radar, infra-red, acoustic and other signatures.

POWER PLANT: One 19·4 kW (26 hp) Herbrandson D-290 two-cylinder two-stroke engine, driving a two-blade fixed-pitch pusher propeller. Fuel tank in fuselage, capacity 30 litres (8 US gallons).

LAUNCH AND RECOVERY: Capability for fully automatic zero length, high angle booster assisted launch (9·8 kN; 2,205 lb thrust solid propellant rocket, burn time 0·7 s), which allows aircraft to be airborne in less than 1 s after clearing any reasonable obstacle in the surrounding area. For missions where mobility is less important and launch area is quite large, a pneumatic launcher installed on a 10 ton truck can be used. Aircraft can fly to a pre-programmed point for precise and automatic unattended recovery by parachute, or acquired and controlled by a portable control station mounted on the launch/checking/recovery vehicle, the PCS operator guiding the Heron down to land on its keel.

GUIDANCE AND CONTROL: Multi-loop four-axis autopilot (pitch, yaw, roll and throttle). In 'launch and forget' mode the Mizar avionics navigator is pre-programmed to allow autonomous flight control in four axes, and to manage payloads. Where real-time data is not required, Heron 26 can fly beyond radio horizon and a ground control station is not needed. GCS can, however, receive any kind of real-time information when aircraft is in radio line of sight, and in this condition can also steer the aircraft. Five levels of redundancy allow mission continuation and/or return home in the event of navigation system and associated mission payload failures; substantial redundancy is also implicit in ability of ground operator to 'fly' vehicle following disruption of onboard navigation.

Mission Equipment: The following alternative payloads can be carried: steerable, stabilised platform with daylight or LLL TV camera or FLIR, with or without laser designator; low or medium altitude panoramic film camera; high altitude vertical camera; infra-red linescan; or packages for communications relay, navigation relay or electronic warfare. Two underwing locations are available for external stores, including auxiliary fuel tanks, within the overall payload limitations.

Dimensions, external:

Wing span: standard	4·00 m (13 ft 1½ in)
extended	6·00 m (19 ft 8¼ in)
Width, wings folded	2·00 m (6 ft 6¾ in)
Length overall	3·93 m (12 ft 10·9 in)
Fuselage: Length	2·72 m (8 ft 11 in)
Max width	0·36 m (1 ft 2·2 in)
Max depth	0·49 m (1 ft 7·3 in)
Height overall	1·16 m (3 ft 9·8 in)
Tailplane span (c/l of tailbooms)	1·37 m (4 ft 6⅓ in)
Propeller diameter	0·74 m (2 ft 5 in)

Dimension, internal:

Payload compartment volume	0·063 m³ (2·24 cu ft)

Areas:

Wings, gross: standard	4·72 m² (50·8 sq ft)
extended	6·30 m² (67·8 sq ft)

Weights (A: standard wings, B: extended span):

Weight empty: A	93·2 kg (205·5 lb)
B	99·2 kg (218·5 lb)
Max payload: A, B	35 kg (77 lb)
Max fuel: A, B	21·8 kg (48 lb)
Max launching weight: A, B	150 kg (330 lb)

Performance (at max launching weight, A and B as above):

Max level speed at S/L:	
A	108 knots (200 km/h; 124 mph)
B	105 knots (195 km/h; 121 mph)
Econ cruising speed at S/L:	
A, B	85 knots (158 km/h; 98 mph)
Stalling speed: A	51 knots (95 km/h; 59 mph)
B	48 knots (89 km/h; 56 mph)
Max rate of climb at S/L: A	240 m (785 ft)/min
B	300 m (985 ft)/min
Service ceiling: A	3,500 m (11,480 ft)
B	6,000 m (19,675 ft)
Landing run: A, B	70 m (230 ft)
Range with max fuel, 20 min reserves:	
B	170 nm (315 km; 196 miles)
Endurance (A and B):	
with 34 kg (75 lb) payload	5 h 0 min
with 22·7 kg (50 lb) payload	7 h 12 min
with 11·3 kg (25 lb) payload	10 h 0 min

PARTNERSHIPS

PARTNERSHIPS LIMITED INC

PO Box 6503, Lawrenceville, New Jersey 08648
Telephone: (609) 896 2193
President: Dr Paul H. Kydd

Partnerships formerly produced the Model A Sport single-engined microlight aircraft (described in the 1984-85 *Jane's*), but has since turned its attention to research RPVs. Its first such design is the C-1, a high altitude test vehicle developed under NASA contract.

PARTNERSHIPS C-1

Development of this aircraft began with a 1983 NASA contract aimed at providing technology for flight test at altitudes above 18,300 m (60,000 ft). There were three major project tasks: the airframe, a power system to carry it to very high altitudes, and a data and control system (DACS) which could fly the aircraft when it was out of sight of the ground, perform a precise flight test pattern, and record the data for analysis on the ground.

The programme has succeeded in its objectives of demonstrating a method of chemically supercharging a two-stroke engine with oxygen which potentially can be used to reach extreme altitudes. Autonomous flight under computer control has been demonstrated, and preliminary flight test data obtained. The system for storing the data in CMOS RAM on board, with automatic downloading to a portable computer on the ground and automatic data reduction and plotting, has been demonstrated.

Since its first flight in December 1984 the airframe has been modified from the original design (see 1985-86 *Jane's*) and now has a shorter wing span with 4° of dihedral and struts. Otherwise it is essentially the same. It has proved reliable in service and had accumulated a total of 56 flights by February 1986.

The current programme objective then was to improve the flight data instrumentation so that better data can be obtained to provide a competitive flight test capability. In addition, Partnerships plans to extend the DACS software to permit long-range autonomous flight. This will involve navigation capability which is not yet complete, as well as development of artificial intelligence concepts to deal with in-flight problems such as weather, ice and traffic.

Type: High-altitude research RPV.

Airframe: Strut braced high-wing monoplane, of typical 'model aircraft' configuration. Constant chord wings, with Eppler 193 section, 2° incidence, 4° dihedral and single bracing strut each side. No ailerons. Box-section forward fuselage, of plywood and spruce with Dacron covering. Rear fuselage, wings and horizontal tail surfaces also of wood construction; fin and rudder made from composites. Elevators are partially mass balanced and controlled by electric servo. Non-retractable tricycle landing gear, with 6 in diameter wheels and tyres on all units.

Power Plant: One 3·73 kW (5 hp) Quadra Q-50 modified two-stroke chain-saw engine, driving a two-blade fixed-pitch wooden propeller. Fuel tank in centre of fuselage, capacity (petrol/oil mixture) 15·1 litres (4 US gallons). Oxygen boost system permits aircraft to attain a ceiling of 18,300 m (60,000 ft).

Launch and Recovery: Conventional T-O and landing.

Guidance and Control: Kraft KPR8FD radio control receiver, mounted in rear fuselage. Autonomous navigation. Two onboard microcomputers, installed in forward fuselage, form part of data acquisition and control system.

Mission Equipment: See introductory paragraphs.

Dimensions, external:

Wing span	4·14 m (13 ft 7 in)
Wing chord, constant	0·457 m (1 ft 6 in)
Wing aspect ratio	9·07
Fuselage: Length	3·66 m (12 ft 0 in)
Max width	0·359 m (1 ft 2¼ in)
Height overall	0·761 m (2 ft 6 in)
Tailplane span	1·82 m (5 ft 11¾ in)
Wheel track	0·675 m (2 ft 2½ in)
Wheelbase	1·06 m (3 ft 5¾ in)
Propeller diameter	0·56 m (1 ft 10 in)

Dimension, internal:

Payload compartment volume	0·0265 m³ (0·936 cu ft)

Areas:

Wings, gross	1·89 m² (20·34 sq ft)
Fin	0·10 m² (1·08 sq ft)
Rudder	0·10 m² (1·08 sq ft)
Tailplane	0·40 m² (4·31 sq ft)
Elevators (total)	0·20 m² (2·15 sq ft)

Weights and Loadings:

Weight empty	19 kg (42 lb)
Max payload	3 kg (6·6 lb)
Fuel: normal	3 kg (6·6 lb)
max	15 kg (33 lb)
T-O weight: normal	25 kg (55 lb)
max	37 kg (81·5 lb)
Wing loading:	
normal	13·22 kg/m² (2·71 lb/sq ft)
max	19·58 kg/m² (4·01 lb/sq ft)
Power loading:	
normal	6·70 kg/kW (11·02 lb/hp)
max	9·92 kg/kW (16·31 lb/hp)

Performance:

Max level speed	70 knots (130 km/h; 81 mph)
Max cruising speed	35 knots (65 km/h; 40 mph)
Stalling speed	23 knots (43 km/h; 27 mph)
Max rate of climb at S/L	300 m (984 ft)/min
*Ceiling	18,300 m (60,000 ft)
Range with max fuel	1,084 nm (2,009 km; 1,248 miles)
g limits	+4/−2

**with chemical supercharging*

PHALANX

PHALANX ORGANIZATION

2600 E Wardlow Road, Long Beach, California 90807
Telephone: (213) 595 0701
Telex: 5106003438 Phalanx LGB
President: William F. Moody Jr

PHALANX MP-9 DRAGONFLEA

The MP-9 Dragonflea, for drone/RPV/cruise missile applications, is one of several announced versions of the Phalanx Dragon family (see main Aircraft section), and was expected to be among the earliest versions to be completed and flown. Published details include:

Power Plant: One 13·34 kN (3,000 lb st) turbojet engine.

Dimensions:

Wing span	2·74 m (9 ft 0 in)
Wing area	4·76 m² (51·25 sq ft)

Weights (estimated):

Weight empty	625 kg (1,378 lb)
Payload	270 kg (595 lb)
Fuel	270 kg (595 lb)
Max T-O weight	1,165 kg (2,568 lb)

Performance (estimated):

Max level speed	Mach 0·96

ROTEC

ROTEC ENGINEERING INC

PO Box 220, Duncanville, Texas 75138
Telephone: (214) 298 2505
Telex: 288777 ROTEC DCVL

Officers: See Sport Aircraft section

Rotec has developed an actuator package for its **Panther 2 Plus** microlight aircraft (see Sport Aircraft section) enabling it to be remotely controlled while carrying a 272 kg (600 lb) civil, military or personnel payload. Flight testing of the radio controlled version was due to start in the Spring of 1986. The electrical actuators are powered by an 8Ah 12V battery, through a 15 × 10 × 4 cm (6 × 4 × 1½ in) control box in the cockpit; provision for manual override is retained for emergency use.

RS

RS SYSTEMS

5301 Holland Drive, Beltsville, Maryland 20705-2383
Telephone: (301) 474 2900
Vice-President and General Manager: Fred Marks
Manager, Training and Field Services:
Lavega J. Green Jr

After supplying more than 50,000 aerial targets to the US Army, US Marine Corps and foreign forces since 1979, RS Systems had in 1986 reorganised its remote controlled miniature aerial target (RCMAT) product line into two main categories. Between those dates the product line has been expanded from a delta-winged gunnery target, the FQM-117A, to state-of-the-art three-dimensional one-ninth and one-fifth scale aerial targets carrying infra-red sources, two-axis stabilisers, sonic hit indicators, payload release devices, and an Airmiles airborne hit recording and signalling system.

Details of the FQM-117A (over 30,000 built), Augmented RCMAT and HEAT series of targets can be found in the 1984-85 and 1985-86 editions of *Jane's*. These are no longer in production. The current products in 1986 are described in the following entries:

RS SYSTEMS ONE-NINTH SCALE TARGETS

At this scale, RS Systems produces '3-D' representations of two Soviet and two Western aircraft: the MiG-27 'Flogger-D' and Su-25 'Frogfoot', and the General Dynamics F-16 and McDonnell Douglas/BAe AV-8B. The one-ninth MiG-27, a replacement for the delta-winged FQM-117A, is produced for the US Army (designation **FQM-117B**) and, in an undesignated version, for the US Marine Corps. Both configurations are used to fly realistic attack profiles, and can be tracked and engaged by air defence units using small arms, 20-40 mm gun systems or infra-red based weapons.

Power Plant: One 1·5 kW (2 hp) 0·6 cu in engine, mounted in nose.

Mission Equipment: Four principal training payloads can be used: a tactical hit indicator (THI), manual hit indicator (MHI), Airmiles, or an IR (infra-red) source. The THI automatically initiates up to ten flash-bang-smoke 'target disabled' indications per flight, its sonic detection system providing users with an adjustable target size from 2-24 m (6·56-78·74 ft) and adjustable 'hits to disable' (1-15 rounds through the hit zone). Each time a pre-set 'disabled' criterion is met, the gunner is rewarded with an instant flash-bang-smoke feedback. The MHI can also provide up to ten similar indications per flight, via push-button actuation at the target pilot's transmitter. Airmiles, which is compatible with US Army MILES (multiple integrated laser engagement system), enables air defence users to conduct training in virtually any open area, without live-fire logistics and costs. It will signal 'target disabled' automatically with the same flash-

Partnerships C-1 high-altitude long-endurance research RPV

RS Systems FQM-117B representation of the MiG-27

Teledyne Ryan BQM-34S Firebee I subsonic target for the US Navy

AQM-81A Firebolt high-altitude high-speed target under the fuselage of a USAF F-4 Phantom II

bang-smoke indication as the THI and MHI, the 'disabled' criteria in its microprocessor varying according to lethality of the weapon fired against the target. Airmiles has an optional eye-safe 'fire back' feature for use in 'cover and concealment' training by air defence units, through its laser gun which is mounted on the target and controlled by the target's pilot. In-flight remotely actuated flares can be carried by the target for infra-red based weapon tracking.

DIMENSIONS, EXTERNAL (MiG-27):
- Wing span: 1·70 m (5 ft 7 in)
- Length overall: 1·85 m (6 ft 1 in)

WEIGHTS (MiG-27):
- Weight empty, incl fuel: 2·7 kg (6 lb)
- Max payload: 2·3 kg (5 lb)
- Max launching weight: 5·4 kg (12 lb)

PERFORMANCE (MiG-27):
- Cruising speed: 65 knots (120 km/h; 75 mph)
- Service ceiling: 3,050 m (10,000 ft)
- Endurance (standard fuel): 12 min

RS SYSTEMS ONE-FIFTH SCALE TARGETS

MiG-27 and Su-25 versions at one-fifth scale are also available, the former being the replacement for RS Systems' earlier one-seventh scale HEAT series (see 1985-86 *Jane's*). The increased size, speed, range and endurance afford air defence trainees a low-cost realistic target that can be hand or mechanically launched from an unprepared training site.

MISSION EQUIPMENT: As described for one-ninth scale targets. In addition, IR source (flares) can be used for live-fire engagements.

WEIGHT:
- Max payload (both): 11·3 kg (25 lb)

PERFORMANCE:
- Visual range (both): 2·2 nm (4 km; 2·5 miles)

SIMULATORS

SIMULATORS LIMITED INC (Target Division)

PO Box 1644, Terre Haute, Indiana 47808
Telephone: (812) 466 2071
Telex: PDIMC IND 11 810 341 3235

PRESIDENT: Wilbur R. Adams

This company was incorporated in May 1982. Its first products were an aerial target representation of the Mikoyan MiG-27 'Flogger-D' ground attack aircraft, and the Falcon and Matador mini-RPVs produced originally by Eglen Hovercraft Inc.

Details of these can be found in the 1985-86 *Jane's*. No communication has been received from the company since the Spring of 1984.

SPERRY

SPERRY CORPORATION (AEROSPACE AND MARINE GROUP)

Defense Systems Division, PO Box 9200, Albuquerque, New Mexico 87119
Telephone: (505) 822 5651
COMMUNICATIONS SUPERVISOR, DEFENSE SYSTEMS DIVISION: Judy Redman

Sperry is one of the world's most experienced producers of full scale aerial targets (FSATs), its past programmes having included remotely controlled versions of the B-17, B-47, F-80, F-104, T-33 and T-38. More recent programmes have involved conversions of the F-86 (1982-83 *Jane's*) and F-102 (1983-84 edition).

Sperry production of QF-100 target drones ended in June 1985, and continued conversion of these aircraft is now undertaken by FSI (which see). Sperry is prime contractor to the USAF for the QF-106 drone programme, with FSI as principal subcontractor.

The project to develop a surveillance/relay drone based on the Schweizer Sprite motor glider, mentioned briefly in the 1985-86 *Jane's*, has been abandoned.

TELEDYNE RYAN

TELEDYNE RYAN AERONAUTICAL

2701 Harbor Drive, PO Box 80311, San Diego, California 92138-9012
Telephone: (619) 291 7311
Telex: 68-31061

PRESIDENT: Hudson B. Drake

SENIOR VICE-PRESIDENTS:
- Darrell A. Cole (Engineering, Business Development)
- C. E. McGill (Administration)

VICE-PRESIDENTS:
- K. Carson (Administration)
- W. Cassidy (Manufacturing)
- Richard G. Huntington (Engineering)
- A. C. Richards (Business Development Programmes)
- R. Scurlock (Contracts)

DIRECTOR, PROJECT ENGINEERING: Frank Oldfield

PUBLIC RELATIONS: Jack G. Broward

The former Ryan Aeronautical Company was an indirect successor to Ryan Airlines Inc, which produced the aeroplane in which Charles A. Lindbergh made the first nonstop flight from New York to Paris in 1927. It was renamed Teledyne Ryan Aeronautical in December 1969.

Current activities include the design, production and field operation of high performance aerial jet targets and RPV systems. Teledyne Ryan is also a major subcontractor to McDonnell Douglas Helicopters on the AH-64 Apache programme, for which it builds the complete airframe.

Major production items at Teledyne Ryan's plant for many years have been the Firebee jet powered targets and special purpose vehicles (pre-programmed and remotely piloted) for various types of reconnaissance mission. The supersonic Firebee II (286 built: see 1979-80 *Jane's*), although not currently in production, remains in service with the US Navy (BQM-34E and T) and Air Force (BQM-34F); a total of 79 remained in the US government inventory in March 1986. US Air Force BQM-34Fs are currently being retrofitted with the Vega drone tracking and control system (DTCS).

TELEDYNE RYAN MODEL 124 FIREBEE I

US Air Force designation: BQM-34A
US Army designation: MQM-34D
US Navy designations: BQM-34A and BQM-34S

The Firebee I remotely piloted vehicle was developed as a joint US Air Force/Army/Navy project, in collaboration with the USAF Air Research and Development Command.

Glide flight tests of the original version began in March 1951, and the first powered flights were made that Summer at the US Air Force Holloman Air Development Center, Alamogordo, New Mexico. A total of 1,280 of these early Q-2A and KDA versions were built eventually for all three US services and for the Royal Canadian Air Force; full details can be found in previous *Jane's*.

Development of the current **BQM-34A** (originally Q-2C) improved Firebee began on 25 February 1958. Construction of the prototype started on 1 May and it flew for the first time on 19 December 1958. The first production model flew on 25 January 1960.

By January 1986 a total of 6,411 Firebee Is had been produced, including the early Q-2A and KDA versions. The total includes Firebees supplied to NATO for use in a missile test programme, and those sold to the Japan Defence Agency to support the training of missile and gunnery crews in both surface-to-air and air-to-air operations. The latter are built under licence by Fuji Heavy Industries. Current 1986 production by Teledyne Ryan comprised 87 Firebee Is for the US Navy, deliveries beginning in May of that year. Firebee Is in the current operational inventory are powered by J69-T-29, J69-T-41A or J85-GE-7 turbojet engines.

Current Firebee targets for the US Navy incorporate a Motorola integrated target control system (ITCS) and have the designation **BQM-34S**; US Air Force BQM-34A targets have a Vega drone tracking and control system (DTCS).

By 1 January 1986 Firebee I targets had provided more than 32,000 flights in support of weapons system and target research, development, test, evaluation, quality assurance, training and annual service practices conducted by the US Army, Navy and Air Force, and foreign governments. Since the current Firebee I and its predecessor models have been in operational use, target presentations have been made to virtually every surface-to-air and air-to-air weapon system in the US arsenal. To reduce the vulnerability of the target, and increase its cost-effectiveness, a 'non-kill' environment has been created and extensive use made of infra-red and/or radar augmented towed targets ('Towbees') or cloth banners, towed behind the Firebee on cables or mounted on the wingtips.

RPVs (remotely piloted vehicles) using airframes developed from that of the Firebee I were described in the 1980-81 and earlier editions of *Jane's*.

The following details refer to the standard BQM-34A:

TYPE: Remotely piloted jet target vehicle.

AIRFRAME: Cantilever mid-wing monoplane, of aluminium alloy semi-monocoque construction. Three-spar wings, with leading-edge droop. No dihedral or incidence. Sweepback at quarter-chord 45°. Single-spar ailerons, with Lear servo-actuators. Wingtips detachable. Provision for wingtip extensions. Tapered, circular-section body, with chemical-etched components. Glassfibre tailcone and nose section. Keel under central portion, to absorb landing impact. All tail surfaces swept 45° at quarter-chord. Multi-spar fin, with glassfibre tip housing guidance and control antenna. Rudder operated electrically by servo-actuator. Single-spar tailplane, with glassfibre tips housing radar echo enhancing antennae. Ventral fin under tailcone, aft of main tail unit. Magnesium elevators powered by Lear servo.

POWER PLANT: One 7·56 kN (1,700 lb st) Teledyne CAE J69-T-29, one 8·54 kN (1,920 lb st) Teledyne CAE J69-T-41A, or one 10·9 kN (2,450 lb st) General Electric J85-GE-7 turbojet. Integral fuel tank in forward fuselage, capacity 378 litres (100 US gallons). Provision for one 68 litre (18 US gallon) auxiliary fuselage tank. Oil capacity 5·75 litres (1·5 US gallons).

LAUNCH AND RECOVERY: Either air launching, from suitably modified aircraft, or surface launching, using 50·3 kN (11,300 lb st) (nominal) solid propellant JATO bottle. US Navy has launched BQM-34As from ships under way at up to 15 knots (27·5 km/h; 17 mph). Two-stage parachute recovery system operates automatically in event of loss of radio wave carrier from remote control station, engine failure, or upon command by remote control operator. To prevent damage by dragging, recovery system incorporates disconnect which releases parachute from Firebee on contact with ground or water.

GUIDANCE AND CONTROL: Remote control methods include choice of radar, UHF radio, active seeker and automatic navigator, developed and designed by Teledyne Ryan. Normal method is through Motorola ITCS (integrated target control system) in BQM-34S; BQM-34A fitted with Vega DTCS (drone tracking and control system). Target can be controlled either from manned aircraft or from surface station. Remote command includes activation of special scoring and augmentation equipment in target. Basic commands consist primarily of on/off functions, received by onboard receiver and relayed to appropriate subsystem. Other types of remote command and tracking system can include microwave command and guidance system to control Firebee beyond line of sight from ground station through airborne relay station. BQM-34A equipped with three-axis flight control system for tactical air combat simulation which gives target capability to perform 4, 5 or 6*g* manoeuvres. Other systems include active and passive radar augmentation, and afterburning plume devices. Radar altimeter low altitude control system (RALACS), when added to Firebee I control system, permits precision low altitude flights at 6 m (20 ft) over water and 30 m (100 ft) over land.

SYSTEMS: Electrical power only. Primary power furnished by 28V 200A DC engine driven generator. Power for control systems furnished by 400Hz 115V 250W AC inverter; 28V 12·5Ah lead-acid battery provides power for electric devices of recovery system and for control during pre-landing glide phase.

MISSION EQUIPMENT: ITCS DKW-2 guidance transponder, or DTCS Model 685-2 guidance system. A/A37G-8A or A/A37G-14 flight control system. Wide range of 'building block' operational equipment includes visual or radar-reflecting banner targets; radar or infra-red Towbee towed targets or wingtip mounted infra-red pods; two underwing drop tanks, 500 lb bombs or bomblet dispensers; AN/ALE-33 or other ECM containers; wingtip tow launchers, camera pods, scoring equipment, flares or other forms of infra-red augmentation, or reflector pods for radar augmentation. BQM-34A can be equipped with adjustable travelling wave tube amplifiers for use as radar echo enhancers in L, S, X and C frequency bands.

DIMENSIONS, EXTERNAL:
- Wing span: 3·93 m (12 ft 10·8 in)
- Length overall: 6·98 m (22 ft 10·8 in)
- Body diameter: 0·94 m (3 ft 1·2 in)
- Height overall: 2·04 m (6 ft 8·4 in)

AREA:
- Wings, gross: 3·34 m² (36·0 sq ft)

*WEIGHTS:
- Weight empty: 680 kg (1,500 lb)
- Basic gross weight: 934 kg (2,060 lb)
- Max launching weight: 1,134 kg (2,500 lb)

*PERFORMANCE:
- Never-exceed speed: Mach 0·96 (635 knots; 1,176 km/h; 731 mph at 15,240 m; 50,000 ft)
- Max level speed at 1,980 m (6,500 ft): 600 knots (1,112 km/h; 690 mph)
- Max cruising speed at 15,240 m (50,000 ft) at 816 kg (1,800 lb) AUW: 547 knots (1,015 km/h; 630 mph)
- Stalling speed, power on, at 816 kg (1,800 lb) AUW: 101 knots (187 km/h; 116 mph)
- Max rate of climb at S/L at 1,000 kg (2,200 lb) AUW: 5,486 m (18,000 ft)/min
- Operating height range: 6 m-18,300 m (20 ft to more than 60,000 ft)
- Endurance at 15,240 m (50,000 ft), incl 2 min 40 s glide after fuel expended: 75 min 30 s
- Max range: 692 nm (1,282 km; 796 miles)
- Flotation time with 25% fuel: 24 h

* *Same for aircraft with J85-GE-7 engine*

TELEDYNE RYAN MODEL 305 FIREBOLT

US Air Force and Navy designation: AQM-81A

Teledyne Ryan conducted, for the US Air Force Armament Division at Eglin AFB, Florida, full scale engineering development of the Firebolt high altitude high speed target. The programme is a continuation and refinement of the high altitude supersonic target (HAST) which was an advanced development programme conducted by Beech Aircraft Corporation. Teledyne Ryan was the winner in a competitive procurement bid for the full scale engineering development of this target, and on 10 December 1979 was awarded a contract to produce and deliver nine test vehicles (later increased to 21, with six each to specific Air Force and Navy configurations). The last of these was delivered in December 1985. The programme included 28 test flights, the first of which took place at Eglin AFB on 13 June 1983. Five subsequent flights that year encompassed altitudes of 12,200 to 30,500 m (40,000 to 100,000 ft) and speeds from Mach 1·2 to Mach 4·0.

Design and production of US Navy Firebolt prototypes was completed in 1983. These vehicles are similar to the USAF Firebolt except for changes made for Navy integrated target control system (ITCS) capability, FPS-16 range radar tracking augmentation, flight profile requirements, and compatibility with Navy water recovery procedures. The FSED phase was completed in 1985.

TYPE: Supersonic air-launched recoverable target drone.

AIRFRAME: Mid-wing monoplane, constructed mainly of stainless steel. Clipped-tip slim delta wings are of constant thickness (thickness/chord ratio 1·287% at exposed root, 3·41% at tip) except for tapered leading-edge, which has sweepback angle of 75°. No anhedral, dihedral or incidence. Full span stainless steel ailerons. Arrow planform stainless steel foreplanes for pitch control. Stainless steel fixed endplate fin at tip of each main wing for lateral stability. Cylindrical body, with 3·5 calibre von Kármán nose section and conical boat-tail rear section, is divided into four portions: forward equipment compartment and oxidiser tank (both pressurised), centre-section (for parachute and ducted power unit), and controlled thrust assembly. Electric servos for control surface actuation are by Superior Manufacturing and Instrument Co.

POWER PLANT: CSD hybrid rocket motor. Propellant comprises 68 kg (150 lb) of polybutadiene and polymethyl-methacrylate, with 227 kg (500 lb) of IRFNA oxidiser. System is inherently safe, since propellants will not burn unless external ignition is applied. Engine is throttleable, with thrust variable from 0·53 to 5·34 kN (120-1,200 lb). The 0·33 m (13 in) thrust chamber forms integral part of fuselage assembly. Oxidiser pressurisation and electrical power provided by Marquardt ducted power unit, powered by ram air turbine with air intake and exit on lower side of fuselage mid-section. Manoeuvring requirements dictate positive expulsion system for oxidiser.

LAUNCH AND RECOVERY: Air launched from F-4 carrier aircraft at speeds between Mach 1·2 and 2·5. Recovery by 13·72 m (45 ft) diameter ring-sail parachute from land, water or mid-air. Flotation bag for water retrieval.

GUIDANCE AND CONTROL: Command and control link. Digital microprocessor for command updates; hybrid digital/analog flight control system; built-in test equipment. Manoeuvres can be either pre-programmed or initiated via ground command radio link. Manoeuvres of between 5*g* at 10,670 m (35,000 ft) and 1·15*g* at 27,400 m (90,000 ft) are part of flight test programme; vehicle also capable of 'S' and 180° turns in horizontal plane and altitude changes in vertical plane.

MISSION EQUIPMENT: Range radar and FAA/GCI augmentation; radar augmentation for weapons users. The flight test vehicles include provisions for a Scaler miss distance scoring system and a point source radar augmentation system.

DIMENSIONS, EXTERNAL:
- Wing span: 1·02 m (3 ft 4 in)
- Length: 5·18 m (17 ft 0 in)
- Height (stabiliser): 0·66 m (2 ft 2 in)
- Body diameter (max): 0·33 m (1 ft 1 in)

VOLUME:
- Mission equipment: 0·033 m³ (1·14 cu ft)

AREAS:
- Wings, gross: 1·71 m² (18·432 sq ft)
- Foreplanes (total): 0·27 m² (2·884 sq ft)

WEIGHTS:
- Max payload: 24 kg (53 lb)
- Solid propellant: 68 kg (150 lb)
- Oxidiser: 227 kg (500 lb)
- Max launching weight: 558 kg (1,231 lb)

PERFORMANCE:
- Max level speed at 30,500 m (100,000 ft): Mach 4·0
- Service ceiling: 30,500 m (100,000 ft)
- Endurance at Mach 3: 5 min

TELEDYNE RYAN MODEL 328

This new mini-RPV entered flight test in February 1985, and systems evaluation was still under way in July, when details of the Model 328 were first made public. At that time it had been evaluated primarily in an airfield damage assessment role at Wendover AFB, Utah, equipped with an infra-red linescanning system. Further development has been postponed indefinitely. A description and illustration of the Model 328 appeared in the 1985-86 *Jane's*.

TELEDYNE RYAN MINI-RPH

Originally conceived as a low-cost Army target for AA artillery weapons, this aircraft took the form of a quarter-scale representation of the Mil Mi-24 'Hind-D', and was in the developmental flight test stage in mid-1985. By the Spring of 1986, however, this mini-RPH programme had been shelved indefinitely. A photograph and all known details can be found in the 1985-86 *Jane's*.

TELEDYNE RYAN SPIRIT

This high-altitude long-endurance (HALE) RPV was designed for a variety of tactical missions, and original plans were for a prototype to be built by Scaled Composites Inc for a first flight in early 1987. Primary missions were intended to include communications relay, elint, sonobuoy monitoring for ASW ships and aircraft, and long-range weather monitoring.

In the Spring of 1986 Teledyne Ryan had suspended further development effort on the Spirit programme. All known details, and an illustration, appeared in the 1985-86 *Jane's*.

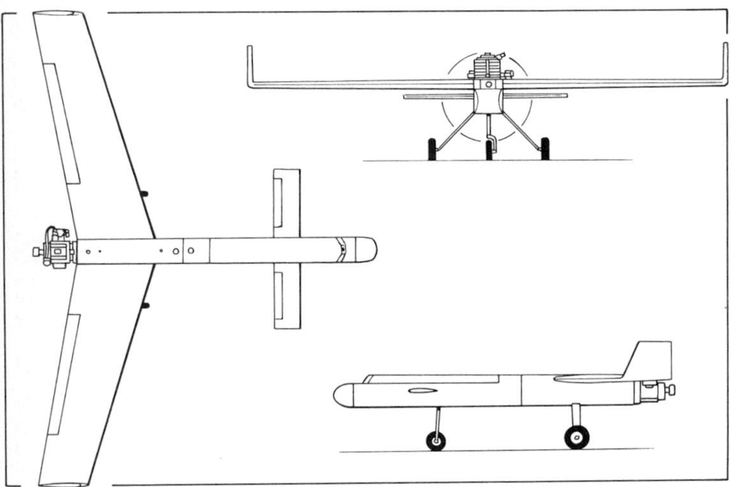

Tractel AMT-RPV1 surveillance mini-RPV *(Michael A. Badrocke)*

Naval Weapons Center QF-86F pilotless target aircraft *(US Navy)*

Naval Weapons Center QF-4 (converted F-4B), with onboard safety pilot *(US Navy)*

TRACTEL

TRACTEL CORPORATION

2761 Laguna Canyon Road, Laguna Beach, California 92651
Telephone: (714) 494 3032
Telex: 9103330317 TRACTEL

TRACTEL AMT-RPV1

The general appearance of the AMT-RPV1 is shown in an accompanying drawing.

Type: Recoverable surveillance mini-RPV.

Airframe: Canard configuration, comprising mid mounted non-swept foreplane with elevators and shoulder mounted sweptback main wing, with ailerons, at rear. Main wingtips upswept to form winglets. Box-section fuselage. Non-retractable tricycle landing gear. Kevlar fuselage and epoxy/foam wings, of modular construction to facilitate in-the-field replacement of individual components.

Power Plant: Single piston engine (type not known), mounted at rear to drive a two-blade pusher propeller. Fuel capacity 7·6 litres (2 US gallons).

Launch and Recovery: Launched from rail launcher; recovered by conventional wheeled landing or, optionally, by net system.

Guidance and Control: Ground control station includes two video monitors with controls for video imaging and for proximal guidance of RPV utilising forward looking dedicated camera for flight control. Two 9·14 m (30 ft) mast antennae, linked with telemetry and remote from base station, provide telemetry link for location and control functions. Computer with logic function, to determine plot and assist control, is linked to plotting board mounted for accepting standard military maps as graphics. Options include distal navigation system, with memory for pre-programmed flight data, and laser disc storage facility for map data and sequencing data link.

Mission Equipment: Standard payload of two infra-red video cameras, one forward looking and one downward looking, with any available 8 mm lens system including telephoto, wide angle or fisheye. All video cameras are solid state and CCD (charged coupled device) technology, available in three configurations: 288 or 560 horizontal line resolution black and white, or 330 line colour. Transmitter in range 400MHz to 1·2GHz. Camera options include 256 greyscale daytime recognition processor (which can be set to night-time sensitivity for anything greater than ambient light, such as muzzle flash or vehicle headlights); passive second generation fixed focal point lens for night observation; or 35 mm motor driven single lens reflex camera with telephoto lens for still photography. Signal options include digitally encrypted transmitter (requiring special receiver), and frequency hopping facility to prevent jamming of signal.

Dimensions, external:

Wing span	3·05 m (10 ft 0 in)
Length overall	2·18 m (7 ft 2 in)

Weights:

Weight empty	12·7 kg (28 lb)
Max launching weight	20·4 kg (45 lb)

Performance:

Endurance	4 h

USAF

UNITED STATES AIR FORCE

Office of Public Affairs, Aeronautical Systems Division (AFSC), Wright-Patterson AFB, Ohio 45433-6503
Telephone: (513) 255 2725

In early 1986 Air Force Systems Command had no RPV or target drone programmes for which prototype/development contracts had not been awarded to industry.

US ARMY

UNITED STATES ARMY

Public Affairs Office, US Army Troop Support Command, 4300 Goodfellow Boulevard, St Louis, Missouri 63120

IEW-UAV

This Army programme, for an intelligence and electronic warfare unmanned air vehicle, was announced in 1986. RFPs (requests for proposals) were due to be issued to industry in May of that year, followed by a possible mid-year fly-off competition and selection of a contractor in the Autumn. The new RPV is understood to be required as a backup to the long-delayed Aquila, which is no longer to be procured in the large numbers originally planned.

USN

UNITED STATES NAVY

Office of Public Affairs, Naval Air Systems Command, Department of the Navy, The Pentagon, Washington, DC 20361

The following entries are based on information received in early 1984. No updates were received from the US Navy in 1985 or 1986.

NAVAL WEAPONS CENTER QF-4

Development of this new QF-4 all-altitude manoeuvring aircraft target was started in 1977, and development testing was completed in June 1983. The Techeval (technical evaluation) flight tests on a production prototype began in March 1983, but were later postponed due to technical difficulties. Design changes are being incorporated into the Techeval aircraft, and testing was scheduled to resume by August 1984.

The NWC QF-4 differs from the NADC QF-4B (see 1984-85 *Jane's*) primarily in having an NWC developed integrated target control system (ITCS) for command and control, and a forward looking TV camera for drone take-off and landing. This ITCS configured QF-4 target aircraft will replace the earlier UHF configured QF-4B, and will be produced by converting existing F-4B, F-4J and F-4N Phantoms.

Rework and drone conversion of the first ten pre-production Phantoms is being accomplished by NWC China Lake, with deliveries scheduled in FYs 1985 and 1986. Full production will begin with the 11th aircraft and will be accomplished by either an organic or commercial rework facility, with deliveries to start in November 1986. The full scale programme provides for rework and conversion of seven F-4s per year until 1990.

Airframe and Power Plant: As F-4B/J/N.

Accommodation: As appropriate F-4 model, with full provision for onboard safety pilot.

Systems: As appropriate F-4 model.

Mission Equipment: Radar deleted; ITCS drone conversion kit installed.

Armament: None installed, but capability retained for launch of missiles and air-to-surface weapons.

Dimensions, Weights and Performance: As appropriate F-4 model.

NAVAL WEAPONS CENTER QF-86

Thirty-one North American F-86H Sabres were converted by the Naval Weapons Center, China Lake, California, into QF-86H pilotless target aircraft, as described in the 1977-78 *Jane's*. Three F-86F Sabres underwent prototype conversion at the NWC in 1979 into QF-86F pilotless target aircraft, and 43 QF-86Fs had been delivered to the USN by early 1984, to support weapons system test and evaluation. They are used as subsonic all-altitude manoeuvring targets. In December 1982 the Navy awarded a $14 million competitive contract to rework and convert 65 additional F-86Fs to QF-86F drone aircraft. Overhaul, modification and flight testing are undertaken by Northrop Services Inc, which re-delivered the first of this batch to the Navy in September 1983. Deliveries are at the rate of 13 per year under the five-year contract.

WING

WING MANUFACTURING

Crystal Lake, Illinois

WING CRUISE 3

This new RPV was designed and built by Wing Manufacturing for testbed use by the US Naval Air Development Center at Warminster, Pennsylvania. It has high-mounted wings with prominent leading-edge root extensions, sweptback tail surfaces, and a fuselage with a long, slender nose. A single piston engine is installed in the rear of the fuselage, driving a pusher propeller, and the Cruise 3 is catapult launched and parachute recovered.

Dimensions:

Not known

Weights:

Weight empty	11 kg (24 lb)
Max payload	9 kg (20 lb)

Performance:

Cruising speed	60 knots (111 km/h; 69 mph)
Ceiling	3,050 m (10,000 ft)
Range	43-78 nm (80-145 km; 50-90 miles)

AIR-LAUNCHED MISSILES

This section of *All the World's Aircraft* is restricted to items of information considered to be of major importance to aircraft designers, manufacturers and operators. More extensive entries, including development history, can be found in *Jane's Weapon Systems*.

ARGENTINA

CITEFA

INSTITUTO DE INVESTIGACIONES CIENTIFICAS Y TECNICAS DE LAS FUERZAS ARMADAS

Zufriategui y Varela, 1603 Villa Martelli, Provincia de Buenos Aires

MARTIN PESCADOR (KINGFISHER)

This supersonic tactical missile was exhibited at the 1981 Paris Air Show, as armament for Agusta A 109 helicopters of the Argentine Army. Guidance is by radio command from the launch aircraft, along a line of sight. It has canard control surfaces, a single-stage solid propellant rocket motor, and a high explosive warhead with impact fuse. When launched from a hovering helicopter, the Martin Pescador has a range of 2·3 nm (4·3 km; 2·7 miles), with a target impact speed of Mach 1·1. It can also be launched from any fixed-wing aircraft capable of a speed of Mach 0·5 or more; performance in this form is given in the table at the end of this section.

The Martin Pescador is reported to be in full production. New versions, with a heavier warhead and increased range, are under development.

ADAPTED TO: Aermacchi MB-339A, IA 58 Pucará and, possibly, A-4 Skyhawk.

BRAZIL

IAE

INSTITUTO DE ATIVIDADES ESPACIAIS

Divisão de Sistemas Bélicos, 12200 São José dos Campos, São Paulo

PIRANHA

Piranha is an infra-red homing air-to-air missile which has been under development since March 1976. The original intention was to produce a weapon similar to the US AIM-9B Sidewinder, but with improved performance, for operation by land, sea and air forces in air-to-air and close-range surface-to-air applications. Staff from the Brazilian Army, Navy and Air Force were seconded to the programme, which was centred at the IAE division of the Centro Tecnico Aeroespacial (CTA).

In 1977, the Army and Navy withdrew from the Piranha project, which was continued and financed by the Air Force until 1982. By the Summer of that year, it was clear that the missile's capability would equal that of second-generation Sidewinders, and the other two services decided to resume funding to speed completion of development and testing. Initial captive flight trials were conducted on an EMB-326GB Xavante ground attack aircraft. Live firings from a Northrop F-5B were scheduled for 1985, and Piranha is expected to arm the Aeritalia/Aermacchi/EMBRAER AMX combat aircraft of the Brazilian Air Force in due course.

The general appearance of Piranha is shown in an accompanying drawing. The D.F. Vasconcelos company, São Paulo State, is prime contractor for production, which has started. The smokeless double-base solid propellant rocket motors are being supplied by the Piquete plant of the Army owned Imbel ordnance industry.

CHINA
(PEOPLE'S REPUBLIC)

CPMIEC

CHINA PRECISION MACHINERY IMPORT AND EXPORT CORPORATION

No. 17 Wenchang Hutong Xidan. PO Box 845, Beijing
Telephone: 895012
Telex: 22484 CPMC CN

AIR-TO-AIR MISSILES

Four types of air-to-air missile have been identified as armament for fighters of the Chinese Air Force and Navy:

Pili 2 or **PL-2**. Infra-red homing missile similar in appearance to the Soviet K-13A (NATO 'Atoll'), operational since 1960s. Acquisition angle 90°. Known in West as **CAA-1**. Equips J-6, J-7 and F-7M Airguard aircraft.

PL-2A. Improved version of the PL-2, with new seeker. Max range for lock-on increased to 4·3-5·4 nm (8-10 km; 5-6·2 miles). Operational.

PL-7. Advanced development of PL-2/2A with delta forward control surfaces, second set of canards immediately behind front set, and less sweptback tail fins. Acquisition angle 180°. Min range for lock-on 500 m (1,640 ft). Max range for lock-on 7·75 nm (14·4 km; 9 miles). Warhead weight 12 kg (26·5 lb).

CAA-2 (Chinese designation not known). Deployed since 1975-76, this missile resembles the British ASRAAM development round in configuration, with no forward control surfaces. Like the CAA-1, it has a solid propellant rocket motor. It has been illustrated on the J-7 and is believed to equip also the Q-5, in alternative infra-red and semi-active radar homing forms.

AIR-TO-SURFACE MISSILE

CAS-N-1 (Chinese designation **C601**). Anti-shipping missile carried by H-6 (Chinese built Tu-16) bomber, to attack surface vessels larger than a light cruiser. Close resemblance to Soviet SS-N-2 (NATO 'Styx') shipborne surface-to-surface missile, but incorporating some AS-5 (NATO 'Kelt') technology. Propulsion by liquid propellant rocket motor, with inertial midcourse guidance and monopulse radar terminal homing. The standard undernose radome of H-6 launch aircraft is replaced by a flat-bottom drum shape radome of much greater size (see Chinese aircraft section).

FRANCE

AÉROSPATIALE

AÉROSPATIALE SOCIÉTÉ NATIONALE INDUSTRIELLE

Division Engins Tactiques

2 rue Béranger, BP 84, 92322 Châtillon Cédex
Telephone: (1) 47 46 21 21
Telex. AISPA 250881 F
PRESS OFFICER: Jocelyne Terrien

AS 15TT

The AS 15TT is a lightweight all-weather missile for attacking surface targets of all tonnages at sea, by day or night in up to Force 6 conditions. Intended for operation from ship based or shore based helicopters and maritime patrol aircraft, it uses an extremely accurate automatic guidance system, and carries a warhead similar to that of the earlier AS 12. Associated surface surveillance radar is the Thomson-CSF Agrion 15, which has a 360° scan, is designed for automatic target tracking and determination of the differential target/missile range and bearing, and is able to operate in an ECM environment. Orders totalled 200, all for Saudi Arabia, in March 1985, at which time deliveries were beginning.

ADAPTED TO: AS 365F Dauphin 2

INTENDED FOR: Several unspecified types of aircraft

AS 30 LASER

This tactical air-to-surface supersonic missile is intended for use against hardened and heavily defended targets on land or at sea, usually in conjunction with a Thomson-CSF Atlis 2 target illuminating pod carried by the launch aircraft. It has a two-stage solid propellant rocket motor and a two-phase guidance system, comprising a pre-guidance phase on gyro reference, followed by automatic (TV) target tracking combined with semi-active laser terminal homing. This is claimed to provide the optimum standoff distance for direct target acquisition. The 240 kg (529 lb) general purpose warhead has a hard steel coating to allow penetration of thick concrete before detonation. Orders totalled 500 in early 1985, of which 64 per cent were for export. Deliveries of 180 to the French Air Force began in September 1984, followed by initial deliveries to two foreign operators, one of them reportedly Iraq.

ADAPTED TO: Jaguar, Mirage F1

INTENDED FOR: F-15 Eagle, Mirage 2000

EXOCET AM39

The AM39 air-launched version of Exocet provides all-weather 'fire and forget' attack capability against surface ships. Propulsion is by a tandem two-stage solid propellant motor, and the warhead is comparable with that of a torpedo. The missile's high subsonic flight profile consists of a pre-guidance phase, during which it travels towards the target, the range and bearing of which have been determined by an airborne radar and fire control computer and set up in the missile pre-guidance before launch; an inertially guided midcourse phase; and a final guidance phase during which the missile homes on the target under the control of its active radar head. Throughout its flight the missile is maintained at a very low altitude above the crests of the waves (2 to 3 m; 6·5 to 10 ft); its homing head is reported to pick up the target over a range of up to 6·5 nm (12 km; 7·5 miles). Exocet is intended to operate efficiently in an ECM (electronic countermeasures) environment.

By early 1986, orders totalled more than 800. Exocets were first used from Iraqi Super Frelon helicopters against Iranian vessels, from October 1980, and then against ships of the Royal Navy and British merchant navy during the Falklands campaign of 1982, from Super Etendard fighters of the Argentine Navy. They have since been launched from Iraqi Super Etendard and Mirage F1 aircraft against shipping in the Gulf War. According to US sources, 52 of the first 53 Exocets launched (to the beginning of 1985) achieved hits on target. Only two failed to detonate. Seven small or medium sized freighter/tankers were sunk, 19 heavily damaged, seven slightly damaged. Eleven tankers of

CITEFA Martin Pescador air-to-surface missile being launched from an Argentine Navy MB-339A

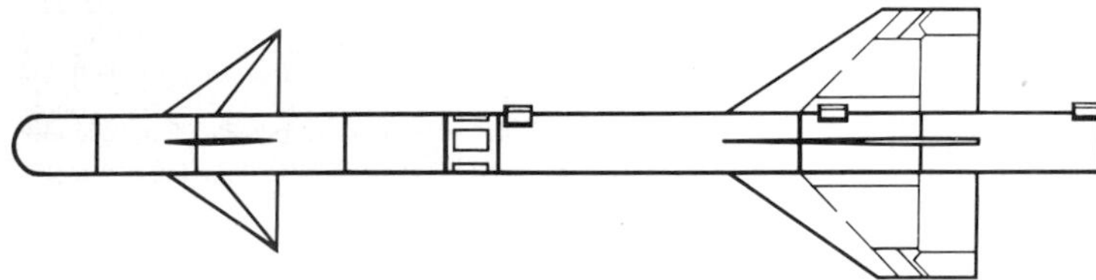

Piranha air-to-air missile *(Roberto Pereira de Andrade)*

PL-2 infra-red homing missiles on J-7 fighter of Chinese Air Force

more than 50,000 deadweight tons were heavily damaged and six slightly damaged. Rounds in service with the French Aéronavale are being updated by replacing their ADAC homing head with a Super ADAC, more resistant to ECM.

ADAPTED TO: Atlantique, Gardian 2, Mirage 50, Mirage F1, Mirage 2000, Super Etendard; Sea King (including Agusta SH-3D), Super Frelon, Super Puma

RANGE:
launched from a helicopter at 60 knots (110 km/h; 69 mph) at a height of 100 m (330 ft)
28 nm (52 km; 32·25 miles)
launched from an Atlantique aircraft at heights between 300 and 5,000 m (1,000 ft and 16,400 ft)
29-32·25 nm (54-60 km; 33·5-37·25 miles)
launched from a Super Etendard aircraft at heights between 100 m (330 ft) and 10,000 m (33,000 ft)
32-37 nm (60-70 km; 37-43 miles)

ASMP

Developed to arm 18 Dassault Mirage IVP bombers, as well as Super Etendard naval fighters and Mirage 2000N tactical fighters, from 1986, the ASMP (Air-Sol Moyenne Portée) is powered in supersonic cruising flight by a kerosene burning ramjet, supplied with air by a pair of two-dimensional side intakes which serve also as wings. It has a Sagem pre-programmed inertial guidance system, with terrain following capability. Range is in the order of 40-54 nm (75-100 km; 46-62 miles). Yield of the nuclear warhead is 150 kT, and ASMP is intended for standoff use against heavily defended targets such as airfields, and command and communications centres.

The power plant has a solid propellant launch booster integrated in the ramjet combustion chamber, forming a two-stage rocket-ramjet.

MATRA

SA MATRA

4 rue de Presbourg, 75116 Paris

MANAGEMENT AND WORKS, POSTAL ADDRESS: BP No. 1, 78146 Vélizy-Villacoublay Cédex

PRESS DEPARTMENT: Centre Montigny les Cadrans, 3 rue du Centre, 78182 Saint Quentin en Yvelines Cédex

Matra weapon systems include the Durandal rocket propelled penetration bomb for attacking runways; the Belouga cluster weapon, which dispenses 151 grenades or other munitions, lowered to the ground on individual brake-chutes; and the BGL kit able to adapt several standard types of bomb for laser guidance.

SUPER 530 F and SUPER 530 D

The Super 530 is an all-weather and all-sector air-to-air weapon, able to attack targets flying 9,000 m (29,500 ft) higher or lower than the launch aircraft. Range limits are from "several hundreds of metres" to "several tens of km". The missile has a semi-active pulse radar homing head, dual-thrust solid-propellant rocket motor, fragmenting warhead with electromagnetic proximity fuse, and advanced ECM anti-jamming circuits. Orders totalled 1,490 in early 1986.

The basic **Super 530 F** is deployed on Mirage F1 interceptors. In 1987 the Mirage 2000 will be armed with the **Super 530 D**, compatible with its Doppler radar and able to attack targets flying at speeds up to Mach 3 and heights from S/L to 24,400 m (80,000 ft).

ADAPTED TO: Mirage F1, Mirage 2000

R.550 MAGIC

The basic version of this highly manoeuvrable short/medium-range 'dogfight' missile has a single-stage solid propellant motor, an infra-red homing head, and a 12·5 kg (27·5 lb) warhead with 6 kg (13·2 lb) of explosive, impact and infra-red proximity fuses. It can be launched at ranges between 500 and 7,000 m (1,640-23,000 ft) in the hemisphere behind the target, is stressed for 50*g* manoeuvres and can be fired from an aircraft in a 7*g* turn, singly or at one second interval between rounds. There is no minimum launch speed; maximum is more than 700 knots (1,300 km/h; 805 mph) IAS.

A **Magic 2** all-sector version entered production in early 1984, and became operational on Mirage 2000 aircraft in 1985. Magic 2 has a new infra-red seeker with a multi-element cell and great sensitivity, and can be slaved to the launch aircraft's AI radar as an alternative to autonomous operation. More than 7,850 Magics had been ordered or delivered by early 1986.

ADAPTED TO: A-4 Skyhawk, Alpha Jet, F-8E(FN) Crusader, Jaguar, MB-339, MiG-21, MiG-23, Mirage III, Mirage 5, Mirage F1, Mirage 2000, Super Etendard, Sea Harrier

MICA

Mica (missile d'interception et de combat aérien) is an all-weather air-to-air missile with thrust vector control for enhanced manoeuvrability at launch, inertial guidance and an active seeker. It is intended for use over intermediate and dogfight ranges, in an extreme ECM environment. First test of a proof-of-concept vehicle was made in October 1982. Under parallel development are ground-to-air and sea-to-air derivatives known as Samat (sol-air-Matra).

ARMAT

This improved high-speed version of the 'fire and forget' AJ37 anti-radiation Martel (see 1978-79 *Jane's*) has an advanced ESD passive homing head and other refinements. It is intended to attack all types of surface radar, on the ground or shipborne, in several frequency bands, overcoming any enemy decoy tactics.

ADAPTED TO: Mirage 2000, Mirage F1

MISTRAL

Developed to intercept high-speed aircraft and helicopters flying at low altitude, the Mistral SATCP (sol-air très courte portée) is basically a tube-launched portable weapon for infantry, which can also be carried by land vehicles on multiple mountings, and by ships and aircraft. A solid propellant rocket motor accelerates the 'fire and forget' missile to a very high speed, enabling it to cover 3 km (1·85 miles) in approximately 5 seconds. The infra-red homing head can detect a helicopter at a range of 4 km (2·5 miles). Terminal effectiveness is ensured by a laser type proximity fused warhead weighing 3 kg (6·6 lb), and the fact that the missile can manoeuvre to intercept a target taking evasive action at up to 8*g*.

An AATCP air-to-air version of Mistral, using twin-round launchers, is under development. Trials have been conducted on an ALAT Gazelle helicopter, and air-to-air Mistral is expected to be ready for service in 1987, linked initially to a SFIM roof mounted sight of the kind used with Hot missiles. When fitted to Eurocopter HAP helicopters, in 1992, Mistral will employ a helmet mounted sight.

ADAPTED TO: Gazelle, Dauphin 2

INTENDED FOR: Ecureuil 2, Eurocopter HAP

GERMANY
(FEDERAL REPUBLIC)

BODENSEEWERK

BODENSEEWERK GERÄTETECHNIK GmbH

Postfach 1120, 7770 Überlingen

Bodenseewerk is prime contractor for European production of the AIM-9L Sidewinder air-to-air missile (see NWC in US section), and is developing an improved version of this weapon that will be available in the second half of the 1980s. Participating countries, in addition to West Germany, are Italy, Norway and the UK. It is also undertaking major development work on the ASRAAM missile (see International part of this section) under contract to BBG, the Überlingen based joint company responsible for development and production of ASRAAM.

MBB

MESSERSCHMITT-BÖLKOW-BLOHM GmbH

Postfach 801149, 8000 München 80

KORMORAN

The basic **Kormoran 1** version of this rail-launched sea-skimming anti-ship missile can be carried by any aircraft which is able to maintain a speed between Mach 0·6 and 0·95 during the attack, and which is equipped with target acquisition radar and an autonomous navigation system such as an inertial platform. On modern aircraft like the Tornado, the Kormoran system requires a minimum of special equipment for signal adaptation and missile control. A Kormoran launcher provides the mechanical interface between a standard 30 in pylon and the missile, and houses missile related electric interface units. Launch information

Chinese PL-7 air-to-air missile on F-7M Airguard fighter

Launch of an Aérospatiale AS 30 Laser missile from a Mirage F1

Matra AATCP Mistral air-to-air missile on a Gazelle helicopter

Matra Magic 2 all-sector infra-red homing missile (foreground) and Armat anti-radar missile on a Mirage 2000

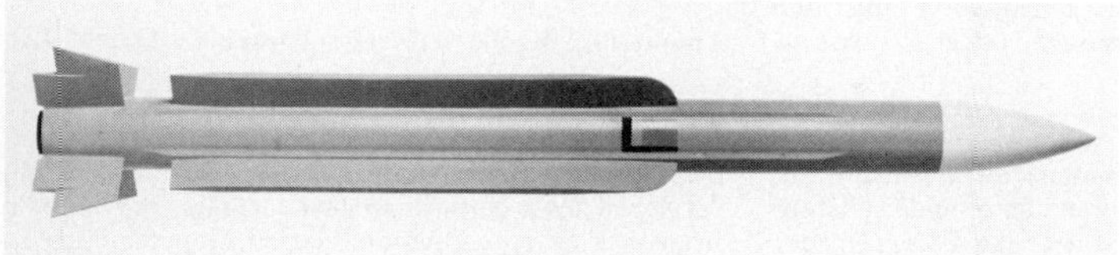

Matra Super 530 D all-weather all-sector air-to-air missile

C601 (CAS-N-1) anti-shipping missile on H-6 bomber of Chinese Air Force

ASMP nuclear air-to-surface missile on Mirage 2000N

Aérospatiale AM39 Exocet air-to-surface missile on a Mirage 2000

Aérospatiale AS 15TT anti-ship missile being test fired from a Dauphin 2

Matra 400 kg laser guided bomb on a SEPECAT Jaguar aircraft

Pair of AIM-9L Sidewinders on a Luftwaffe F-4E of JG 74

Four MBB Kormoran 1 missiles under the wings and fuselage of a Tornado, with air-to-air Sidewinders and other stores

is received from the aircraft's radar and navigation system. The missile can be operated in range-and-bearing and bearing-only modes, the latter being used when firing the missile optically without use of radar.

Two built-in boosters accelerate Kormoran 1 to high subsonic cruising speed, which is maintained by the solid propellant sustainer motor. The 'fire and forget' guidance system employs inertial midcourse guidance and homing phases, using a radar terminal seeker. The high energy warhead weighs 160 kg (352 lb) and is designed for maximum effectiveness against ships up to the size of a destroyer. Kormoran itself is immune to all contemporary types of ECM.

Kormoran 1 was produced for use on F-104s and Tornados of the German Navy and Italian Air Force. An improved version, known as **Kormoran 2**, is being developed by MBB under a contract received from the Federal German Defence Ministry. It will have an entirely new radar seeker, a strapdown inertial navigation system and digital signal processing. Kormoran 2 will offer improved target engagement capability, advanced ECCM, a longer range, better penetration capability and increased warhead weight. It will be fully interchangeable with Kormoran 1 on the Tornado. A MIL 1553B standard interface will make it easy to adapt to other modern aircraft. First firing at a practice target was planned for mid-1986.

ADAPTED TO: F-104G Starfighter, Tornado

INTERNATIONAL PROGRAMMES

AÉROSPATIALE/MBB

PARTICIPATING COMPANIES:

Aérospatiale, Division Engins Tactiques, 2 rue Béranger, BP 84, 92322 Châtillon Cédex, France

Messerschmitt-Bölkow-Blohm GmbH, Dynamics Division, Postfach 801149, Ottobrunn bei München, 8000 München 80, Federal Republic of Germany

ANS

Aérospatiale and MBB are collaborating in the development of a new all-weather 'fire and forget' anti-ship missile known as ANS (anti-navire supersonique) to replace ship-launched and air-launched versions of Exocet in service with the German and French navies in the early 1990s. Aérospatiale is prime contractor, responsible for design, development and testing of the ANS missile. MBB is responsible for the propulsion and warhead.

ANS has a cylindrical body, ogival nosecone, and cruciform tail control surfaces indexed in line with small wings. It is launched with the aid of an integral solid propellant rocket motor and sustained in supersonic cruising flight by a solid rocket-ramjet, supplied with air via four ram intakes, at the base of each wing. Midcourse guidance will be by a strapdown inertial navigation system, with active radar terminal homing. Features will include a 10*g* manoeuvre capability, high resistance to ECM and target impact at very low altitude.

BBG

BODENSEEWERK GERÄTETECHNIK BRITISH AEROSPACE GmbH

Postfach 1120, 7770 Überlingen, Federal Republic of Germany

BBG is owned equally by Bodenseewerk Gerätetechnik and British Aerospace. The company was formed in November 1983 to operate as prime contractor for the development and production of an advanced short-range air-to-air missile (ASRAAM) to replace the AIM-9 Sidewinder in the air forces of the Federal Republic of Germany, Great Britain, Norway and the USA in the 1990s. The intention is to manufacture ASRAAM in both Europe and, under licence, in the USA. Parallel US development of the advanced medium-range air-to-air missile (AMRAAM) is intended to lead to production of this weapon in the USA and, under licence, in Europe, so providing a modern NATO standard air-to-air missile inventory.

ASRAAM

US military designation: AIM-132

ASRAAM will have a solid propellant rocket motor and an all-aspect infra-red homing seeker in order to confer a 'fire and forget' capability. It will be a wingless missile with tail mounted aerodynamic control surfaces, giving enhanced manoeuvrability.

Major subcontractors to BBG under the two-year project definition phase started in 1985 are British Aerospace, Bodenseewerk and Raufoss Ammunisjonsfabrikker of Norway.

EMDG

EUROMISSILE DYNAMICS GROUP

12 rue de la Redoute, 92260 Fontenay-aux-Roses, France
Telephone: (1) 661 73 11
Telex: EUROM 204691 F

Formation of this guided weapons company was announced by Aérospatiale, British Aerospace and MBB on 2 January 1980, following the signing of a memorandum of understanding by the governments of France, the UK and the German Federal Republic. Under a further MOU signed in early 1983, EMDG is defining a new generation of anti-tank missiles for service in the 1990s. These will include a lightweight man-portable infantry weapon, for which Aérospatiale is team leader, and a long-range weapon of which brief details follow:

PARS 3LR

EMDG's long-range weapon, known as PARS 3LR, will be both an air-launched and land-launched 'fire and forget' system, allowing a high rate of fire and evasive manoeuvres by the launch vehicle. British Aerospace has the leading role for the land version, and MBB for the helicopter-launched version. PARS 3LR will have a range of up to 2·4 nm (4·5 km; 2·8 miles), using infra-red passive homing. Its primary role is anti-tank, but with a good capability against helicopter targets. It will offer all-weather capability and a variety of installation options to suit the launch platforms. Development will begin in 1987.

EUROMISSILE

EUROMISSILE GROUPEMENT D'INTÉRÊT ÉCONOMIQUE

12 rue de la Redoute, 92260 Fontenay-aux-Roses, France

Euromissile is a Groupement d'Intérêt Economique formed in 1972 by Aérospatiale of France and MBB of Federal Germany.

HOT

The Hot (High subsonic, optically guided, tube launched) is a wire guided anti-tank missile that can be helicopter launched, with a two-stage solid propellant rocket motor, jet vane steering, automatic command to line of sight guidance, with infra-red tracking, and an HLVS (Hot, stabilised localiser sight) system. To engage a target, the aimer maintains a sighting cross on the target, switches on the firing installation and selects a missile on the control box. During missile flight, the helicopter is able to take evasive action at a turning speed of up to 6°/s. A system known as Venus (Viseur Ecartométrique de Nuit Stabilisé), which includes an infra-red sensor, has been developed to permit firing at night.

ADAPTED TO: BO 105 M (PAH-1), Dauphin 2, Gazelle, Lynx

LOCPOD PROGRAMME

LOCPOD

LOCPOD (low cost powered dispenser) is a projected low altitude, short range, standoff submunition dispenser required primarily by NATO to attack airfields and static targets. It is covered by a memorandum of understanding signed in 1985 by the governments of the USA, Canada, Italy and Spain.

One candidate dispenser is the LD-LAD described under the Brunswick entry in the US section. This is being developed by a consortium that includes, provisionally, Brunswick Defense Division; Garrett Manufacturing Ltd of Canada; Agusta Sistemi SpA and Oto Melara of Italy; and Empresa Nacional Santa Barbara and CASA of Spain.

Model of Aérospatiale/MBB ANS anti-ship missile

Mockup BBG ASRAAM air-to-air missiles on an F-16 Fighting Falcon

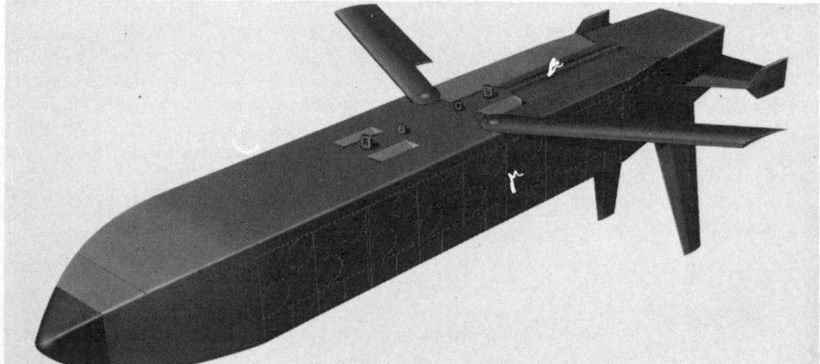

Matra/MBB modular air-to-ground weapon based on Apache and CWS projects

Euromissile Hot anti-tank missile being launched from an SA 342 Gazelle

Experimental version of MoBiDic/SR-SOM undergoing flight tests on an Alpha Jet

LR-SOM PROGRAMME

LR-SOM

Following the signing of a memorandum of understanding between their three governments on 12 July 1984 the USA, Britain and West Germany are to develop a new long-range standoff missile (LR-SOM) for common use. Two international teams have been formed for the initial stage of the programme. One of these involves Boeing Aerospace, BAe, GEC Avionics and MBB, and is undertaking feasibility studies for a subsonic LR-SOM capable of carrying conventional high explosive munitions over ranges of less than 323 nm (600 km; 373 miles). If this leads to a development contract, Boeing will act as prime contractor for the weapon, which will be adaptable to German and British Tornados and to the US B-1B, B-52, F-111 and F-16. Initial operational capability is scheduled for 1994.

The competing team is made up of General Dynamics of the USA, Dornier of Germany and Hunting Engineering of the UK. Its proposal is expected to embody the same types of advanced guidance and dispensing systems as the MoBiDic SR-SOM in which Dornier is also involved (see MoBiDic entry in this section).

Teledyne CAE of the USA and Lucas Aerospace Power Systems Division of the UK are collaborating to develop a propulsion system for the LR-SOM. In competition is a team comprising Williams International of the USA, Rolls-Royce of the UK and KHD of Germany.

MATRA/MBB

PARTICIPATING COMPANIES:

SA Matra, BP No. 1, 78140 Vélizy-Villacoublay Cédex, France

Messerschmitt-Bölkow-Blohm GmbH, Dynamics Division, Postfach 801149, Ottobrunn bei München, 8000 München 80, Federal Republic of Germany

In May 1983 Matra and MBB signed an agreement to develop jointly an air-to-ground dispersal weapon system based on the Apache and CWS projects already studied respectively by the two companies.

APACHE/CWS

The joint Apache/CWS programme is expected to produce a family of winged modular weapons in the 1,000-1,200 kg class, with a deployed span of 2·53 m (8 ft 3½ in) and length of 4·04 m (13 ft 10 in), of which 2·0 m (6 ft 6¾ in) will consist of a rectangular-section container for 750 kg (1,653 lb) of sideways ejected submunitions. The first functional prototype was to be completed by the end of 1985, and first test flights with live missiles are scheduled for early 1987. Three versions of the weapon are being planned initially: an unpowered version with a range of 6·5 nm (12 km; 7·5 miles), a powered version with a range of 13·5 nm (25 km; 15·5 miles), and a further powered version with a larger motor and range of 21·6 nm (40 km; 24·8 miles). All will have an inertial guidance system, with terminal guidance on the longest range version. The submunitions will comprise interchangeable packs of fragmentation, anti-tank, anti-runway and other stores, including mines. Launch will be practicable at speeds up to Mach 0·95, from aircraft in the class of the Tornado, F-16 and Mirage 2000, and all flights will be made at low altitude. Initial operational capability is scheduled for 1992.

MoBiDic/SR-SOM

PARTICIPATING COMPANIES:

Aérospatiale, Division Engins Tactiques, 2 rue Béranger, BP 84, 92322 Châtillon Cédex, France

Diehl GmbH, Heinrich-Diehl-Strasse 2, 8505 Röthenbach, Federal Republic of Germany

Dornier GmbH, PO Box 1420, 7990 Friedrichshafen 1, Federal Republic of Germany

Thomson Brandt Armements, 52 avenue des Champs-Élysées, 75008 Paris, France

MoBiDic/SR-SOM

To meet NATO requirements for new short range standoff missile systems (SR-SOMs) for service in the 1990s, Dornier and its partners are developing a winged container/dispenser that will steer itself automatically to a target after launch from any one of a variety of tactical aircraft. First prototypes of the missile had undergone ground testing and begun flight trials on an Alpha Jet carrier aircraft at the German armed forces' Test Centre 91 (Erprobungsstelle 91) at Meppen by May 1985. Using this missile as a basis, the partner companies are now co-operating in the MoBiDic (*Mo*dular *Bi*rd with *Di*spensing *c*ontainer) programme, which covers the design of a weapon system tailored to the specific joint needs of the German and French air forces.

MoBiDic is proposed in two forms: the shorter **SR-SOM 1** for carriage by aircraft like the Alpha Jet with 14 in bomb racks; the longer **SR-SOM 2** for aircraft in the class of the Tornado and Mirage 2000 with 30 in bomb racks. Both versions will use a solid propellant rocket engine.

Thomson Brandt had earlier studied a family of inertially guided winged dispensers, both powered and unpowered, with ranges of 3·2 to 32 km (6-60 km; 3·7-37 miles) under its Pégase project. Dornier is contributing its so-called 'intelligent sensor system' of midcourse and high precision terminal guidance suitable for use under varying terrain, seasonal and weather conditions; accurate and versatile dispensing mechanisms of low structural weight and simple construction; and submunitions able to destroy different types of hard targets, including moving armoured vehicles and aircraft in shelters.

DIMENSIONS:
- Length overall: SR-SOM 1 — 3·40 m (11 ft 2 in)
- SR-SOM 2 — 4·30 m (14 ft 1¼ in)
- Wing span — 2·60 m (8 ft 6½ in)

WEIGHTS:
- Submunitions: SR-SOM 1 — 350 kg (772 lb)
- SR-SOM 2 — 900 kg (1,984 lb)
- Launch weight: SR-SOM 1 — 720 kg (1,587 lb)
- SR-SOM 2 — 1,400 kg (3,086 lb)

PERFORMANCE:
- Cruising speed: both — Mach 0·8
- Powered range: SR-SOM 1 — 10·8 nm (20 km; 12·4 miles)
- SR-SOM 2 — 21·6 nm (40 km; 24·8 miles)

SRARM PROGRAMME

In September 1985, it was announced that the Air Weapons Division of British Aerospace had been chosen as prime contractor to the US Air Force to lead a seven-nation consortium in a 15-month feasibility study into a short-range anti-radiation missile (SRARM). The consortium comprises British Aerospace; The BDM Corporation, USA; AEG, Federal Republic of Germany; Holland Signaalapparaten, The Netherlands; Philips and MBLE Associated, Belgium; SNIA-BPD, Italy; and Garrett Manufacturing Ltd, Canada.

The contract has been awarded under a seven-nation Memorandum of Understanding, with the Armament Division of US Air Force Systems Command acting as the contracting authority.

SRARM is intended to meet a NATO requirement for the self-defence of aircraft against hostile ground-based air defences. No details of the missile are yet available.

ISRAEL

IAI

ISRAEL AIRCRAFT INDUSTRIES LTD

Ben-Gurion International Airport, 70100 Lydda

GABRIEL III A/S

This all-weather standoff air-to-surface (A/S) weapon is based upon the Gabriel III ship-launched missile with a fully active radar seeker incorporating ECCM features. The basic version has a range of 21 nm (40 km; 25 miles). The extended range Gabriel III A/S ER has a longer solid propellant motor, giving a range of more than 32 nm (60 km; 37 miles). Both versions can be launched in either 'fire and forget' or 'fire and update' mode. The 'fire and forget' Gabriel descends to a low cruising height (reportedly 20 m; 65 ft) and follows an inertial course to the pre-programmed point at which its radar switches on, acquires, locks on and homes on the target. In 'fire and update' mode, the missile receives en route corrections from the launch aircraft, enabling the active search to begin closer to the target, so improving target discrimination and ability to cope with a target ship's defences. Terminal phase altitude in each mode is pre-set at 1·5, 2·5 or 4·0 m (5, 8 or 13 ft).

ADAPTED TO: A-4 Skyhawk, F-4 Phantom II, Kfir-C2/C7, Westwind Sea Scan

RAFAEL

RAFAEL ARMAMENT DEVELOPMENT AUTHORITY

Ministry of Defence, POB 2082, 31021 Haifa
Telephone: 04 706965
Telex: 471508 VERED IL

PYTHON 3

This air-to-air missile is an all-aspect weapon, suitable for use over ranges of 0·25-8 nm (0·5-15 km; 0·3-9·3 miles) and with a 40*g* manoeuvre capability. It offers three modes of target acquisition: boresight, uncaged and radar slaved. Except for its highly swept tail surfaces, its configuration is similar to that of the earlier Shafrir 2 (see 1984-85 *Jane's*), but with a cooled infra-red seeker. Python 3 was first used in combat in Lebanon in 1983, achieving a performance comparable with that of the American AIM-9L Sidewinder.

ADAPTED TO: F-4 Phantom II, F-15 and Kfir-C2/C7

ITALY

OTO MELARA

OTO MELARA SpA

Via Valdilocchi 15, 19100 La Spezia
Telephone: 0187 530111
Telex: 270368 OTO I

MARTE Mk 2

Marte Mk 2 is a 'fire and forget' anti-ship guided weapon system that can be installed on shore-based or shipborne helicopters as well as on fixed-wing aircraft. It utilises a two-stage solid propellant sea skimming missile with midcourse gyroscopic guidance, active radar homing and inherent insensibility to ECM. Its radar altimeter can be pre-set before launch to control the cruising height with regard to sea state and target dimensions. Launch can be in radar mode (target data received from the launch aircraft's radar); manual mode (target data manually pre-set according to information from other sources); or visual mode (after rough alignment of launch aircraft and target). Marte Mk 2 takes slightly more than one minute to reach the enemy ship over a range of 10·8 nm (20 km; 12·4 miles). Its warhead is of high explosive semi-armour-piercing type, with impact/proximity fuse, offering high probability of sinking fast patrol boats and incapacitating larger vessels.

ADAPTED TO: AB 212ASW, ASH-3D/H Sea King
COMPATIBLE WITH: AMX, MB-339 and larger aircraft

SELENIA

SELENIA INDUSTRIE ELETTRONICHE ASSOCIATE SpA

Via Tiburtina km 12.400, 00131 Rome

ASPIDE

This multi-role (air-to-air and surface-to-air) weapon is used as an all-weather all-aspect missile for high performance interceptors, to improve their effectiveness in terms of maximum missile range, operation at very low altitudes, multiple target engagement and resistance to advanced ECM. Aspide has a single-stage solid propellant rocket motor. Its guidance system is of the semi-active radar type (monopulse, inverse receiver), and it has a fragmentation warhead with active radar proximity fuse.

The same missile is used in the Albatros, international NATO Seasparrow and other shipborne joint defence systems, as well as in the Spada land-based point defence system and Skyguard/Aspide battlefield air defence system.

ADAPTED TO: F-104S ASA Starfighter.

JAPAN

MITSUBISHI

MITSUBISHI DENKI KABUSHIKI KAISHA (Mitsubishi Electric Corporation)

2-3, Marunouchi 2-chome, Chiyoda-ku, Tokyo 100

Mitsubishi Electric is prime contractor for licence production of AIM-7F Sparrow air-to-air missiles to arm F-15J fighters of the JASDF (see Raytheon entry in US section).

MITSUBISHI JUKOGYO KABUSHIKI KAISHA (Mitsubishi Heavy Industries Ltd)

5-1 Marunouchi 2-chome, Chiyoda-ku, Tokyo 100

In addition to its responsibility for the ASM-1 and IR-AAM missiles, of which brief details follow, Mitsubishi Heavy Industries is producing AIM-9L Sidewinder air-to-air missiles of US design under licence for the JASDF.

ASM-1

JASDF designation: Type 80

The ASM-1 solid propellant anti-shipping missile is intended to travel to the target at a low altitude, using an inertial system and radio altimeter for midcourse guidance, and an active radar seeker for terminal guidance.

ADAPTED TO: Mitsubishi F-1

IR-AAM

Mitsubishi has begun the development and pre-series manufacture of a highly manoeuvrable infra-red homing dogfight missile known as the IR-AAM. No details are available.

NORWAY

KONGSBERG

A/S KONGSBERG VAAPENFABRIKK

Defence Products Division: Postboks 25, N-3601 Kongsberg

PENGUIN

US Navy designation: AGM-119

This anti-ship missile system can be installed on ships, helicopters and other platforms. The air-launched Penguin Mk 3 has an extended range, higher cruising speed and reduced wing span compared with the ship-launched version. It has a solid propellant rocket motor, a programmed inertial midcourse guidance system, infra-red terminal

Gabriel III A/S on an F-4 Phantom II of the Israeli Air Force

Marte Mk 2 air-to-surface weapon system installed on ASH-3D helicopter

Python 3 air-to-air missile

Aspide multi-role missiles on an Italian Air Force F-104S ASA

Mitsubishi ASM-1 anti-shipping missile

Penguin Mk 3 anti-ship missile on a Norwegian F-16

Armscor V3B on wingtip launcher of Mirage F1

homing (immune to ECM and able to discriminate between real targets and decoys) and a high explosive armour piercing warhead with delayed-action fuse to allow optimum target penetration before detonation. Penguin Mk 3 is expected to enter service in 1987. It can be carried by aircraft flying at speeds up to Mach 1·2 and launched at any height between 45 and 9,150 m (150-30,000 ft).

Meanwhile, the US Navy is adapting the surface-to-surface Penguin Mk 2 to its Sikorsky SH-60B Seahawk helicopter and integrating this missile in its LAMPS III weapon system, of which the SH-60B is part. Grumman is marketing the Penguin in the USA, and has a contract to redesign the missile's wings to fold in the SH-60B application. The booster that is standard on the surface-launched Penguin Mk 2 will be retained, to permit firing of the missile while the helicopter is hovering or flying slowly. Technical and operational evaluation is scheduled for completion in 1988. Present plans envisage procurement of 193 rounds.

Adapted to: F-16 Fighting Falcon (Mk 3)

Intended for: SH-60B Seahawk (Mk 2 Mod 7)

SOUTH AFRICA

ARMSCOR

Private Bag X337, Pretoria 0001

Among current products of the Arms Corporation of South Africa (Armscor) is an air-to-air missile known as V3B/Kukri.

V3B/KUKRI

Development of the original **V3A** version of this highly manoeuvrable infra-red homing dogfight missile began in late 1971, and it went into production in 1975. It was the first air-to-air missile to be coupled to a helmet sight and is still operational with the South African Air Force. Work on the **V3B**, an upgraded version, began in 1975 and it has been in production since 1979. An export version known as **Kukri** is available to selected customers.

V3B and Kukri have an asymmetric double canard aerodynamic configuration reminiscent of that of the French Magic missile, a solid propellant rocket motor and a conventional fragmentation warhead. All controls related to mode switching, target designation and missile firing are located on the pilot's control column and throttle. The pilot simply has to look at the enemy aircraft; when target acquisition is signalled by an audio tone in his headset, he designates the target, thereby putting a missile in the tracking mode. Once the missile is tracking the target the pilot can move his head at will. The missile can be fired whilst tracking or even in the aiming mode, over the entire flight envelope of the clean aircraft.

Adapted to: Cheetah, Mirage III, Mirage F1. Trial installations made on other types.

SWEDEN

BOFORS

AB BOFORS

Ordnance Division: Box 500, S-691 80 Bofors

The RBS 70 helicopter weapon system developed by the Ordnance Division of Bofors is now available to order.

RBS 70

This helicopter self-defence weapon system comprises four-round packs of RBS 70 solid propellant tube launched missiles and a sight/control unit. The basic RBS 70 is a portable or vehicle mounted surface-to-air weapon employing optical beam riding guidance on a laser beam.

RBS 15F under the wing of a Saab 37 Viggen

RBS 70 anti-helicopter missile system fitted to a Lynx helicopter

SAAB

SAAB MISSILES AB

S-581 88 Linköping
Telephone: (46) 13 18 40 00
Telex: 50001 SMABLG S

RBS 15

The Saab RBS 15 is an anti-ship missile with a Microturbo TRI 60-2 turbojet engine for long range at sea skimming height, an ECM resistant radar homing system, and a heavy and effective warhead. It is deployed initially as armament for fast missile craft. Second stage of the programme involves an airborne version known as the **RBS 15F**, ordered in 1982 for the Swedish Air Force's JAS 39 Gripen combat aircraft. A mobile version, for coastal defence, is also being studied.

TAIWAN

STATE ARSENALS

SKY SWORD I

Developed by the Chung Shan Institute of Science and Technology, Taiwan's first indigenous air-to-air missile bears a close resemblance to the US AIM-9L Sidewinder and can be assumed to have similar dimensions, weight and performance. Known as the Sky Sword, it was test fired on 18 May 1986, from the starboard wingtip launch rail of an F-5F fighter. Its infra-red guidance system achieved a hit on a Firebee subsonic target drone on that occasion.

Sky Sword is being developed as a replacement for the Sidewinder in service with the Chinese Nationalist Air Force.

UNION OF SOVIET SOCIALIST REPUBLICS

AIR-TO-AIR MISSILES

K-13A (AA-2)

NATO reporting name: Atoll

This solid propellant missile is almost identical to the first generation American Sidewinder (AIM-9B) in size and configuration and has similar infra-red guidance. Produced also, under licence, in India.

ADAPTED TO: MiG-21, MiG-23, Su-22, Su-25

AA-2-2

NATO reporting name: Advanced Atoll

Multi-role versions of the MiG-21 ('Fishbed-J, K, L and N') carry a mix of standard infra-red 'Atolls' and this later version of the weapon with a radar homing head. Length is increased to more than 3·0 m (9 ft 10 in).

AA-3

NATO reporting name: Anab

'Anab' has a cylindrical body, with small cruciform canard control surfaces indexed in line with very large cruciform tail fins. Both infra-red and I/J band semi-active radar homing versions are operational.

ADAPTED TO: Su-21, Yak-28P

AA-5

NATO reporting name: Ash

'Ash' is the large air-to-air missile carried by Tu-28P ('Fiddler') fighters. It has cruciform wings and tail surfaces indexed in line, and is operational in two versions, which have infra-red and I/J band semi-active radar homing heads respectively.

ADAPTED TO: Tu-28P

AA-6

NATO reporting name: Acrid

The configuration of this air-to-air missile is similar to that of 'Anab' but it is considerably larger. The MiG-25 ('Foxbat-A') carries both infra-red homing and radar homing versions. The wingtip fairings on the fighter, different in shape from those of 'Foxbat-B', are thought to house continuous wave target illuminating equipment for the radar homing missiles.

ADAPTED TO: MiG-25

R-23 (AA-7)

NATO reporting name: Apex

This long-range air-to-air missile has a solid propellant rocket motor and exists in two versions, with infra-red (R-23T) and semi-active radar (R-23R) homing heads.

ADAPTED TO: MiG-23, MiG-25

R-60 (AA-8)

NATO reporting name: Aphid

'Aphid' is a close-range solid propellant weapon with infra-red homing guidance. It has a canard configuration, with small cruciform control surfaces in tandem with nose foreplanes, and indexed in line with cruciform rear mounted wings. This configuration, like that of the Matra R.550 Magic, should ensure high manoeuvrability, with a minimum range of under 500 m (1,640 ft).

ADAPTED TO: MiG-21, MiG-23, MiG-25, Su-21, Su-25, Yak-38.

AA-9

NATO reporting name: Amos

The radar homing long-range missile known in the West as AA-9 is reported to have achieved successes against simulated cruise missiles, after 'lookdown/shootdown' launch from a modified MiG-25 interceptor. It is standard armament of the MiG-31 ('Foxhound'), with a reported range of 21-24 nm (40-45 km; 25-28 miles) at height or 11 nm (20 km; 12·5 miles) at low altitude.

ADAPTED TO: MiG-31

AA-10

The AA-10 has generally similar capabilities to those of the AA-9, but is intended for use over medium ranges.

ADAPTED TO: MiG-29, Su-27

AA-11

This new close-range missile was first mentioned by the US Department of Defense in 1986. No details are yet available.

ADAPTED TO: MiG-23, MiG-25, MiG-29, Su-27

HELICOPTER MISSILES

AT-2

NATO reporting name: Swatter

This standard Soviet anti-tank weapon is controlled by elevons on the trailing-edges of its rear mounted cruciform wings, and embodies terminal homing, guiding the missile via two small, movable canard surfaces at the nose. The motor exhausts through two vents diametrically opposed between the wings. Two more tubes, projecting rearward from opposite wings, house tracking flares.

ADAPTED TO: Mi-8 ('Hip-E'), Mi-24 ('Hind-A/D')

AT-3

NATO reporting name: Sagger

The wire-guided 'Sagger' has a short cylindrical body, with conical nose. Rear mounted cruciform wings, which fold for storage, are swept near the body of the missile but unswept outboard. A hollow charge warhead is fitted.

ADAPTED TO: Mi-2, Mi-8 ('Hip-F'), Gazelle (Yugoslavia)

AT-6

NATO reporting name: Spiral

'Spiral' is tube-launched and radio command guided. It is said to have a range of 3·75-5·3 nm (7-10 km; 4·3-6·2 miles).

ADAPTED TO: Mi-24 ('Hind-E/F')

SA-7

NATO reporting name: Grail

This shoulder-fired infantry surface-to-air weapon has been used worldwide with considerable success. Its first known application as armament for helicopters is on Gazelles of the Yugoslav Air Force. Positioned between and below AT-3 'Saggers', on each side of the fuselage, the 'Grails' probably have both anti-armour and air-to-air roles. A French report suggests that SA-7s are installed on some Mil Mi-24 ('Hind') helicopters.

AIR-TO-SURFACE MISSILES

AS-2

NATO reporting name: Kipper

This aeroplane-configuration missile, with swept wings and underslung turbojet engine, is an anti-shipping weapon. Guidance is believed to comprise pre-programmed flight under autopilot control, with optional command override, and active radar terminal homing.

ADAPTED TO: Tu-16 ('Badger-C')

AS-3

NATO reporting name: Kangaroo

'Kangaroo' is an air-to-surface missile with an airframe similar in size and shape to a sweptwing turbojet powered fighter aircraft. Guidance is assumed to be by initial beam riding and subsequent pre-programmed flight under autopilot control, without terminal homing. A nuclear (800 kT) or high explosive (2,300 kg; 5,070 lb) warhead can be fitted. 'Kangaroo' has been superseded by the AS-4 'Kitchen' on 'Bear-B/Cs' reconfigured as 'Bear-Gs'.

ADAPTED TO: Tu-95 ('Bear-B/C')

AS-4

NATO reporting name: Kitchen

This supersonic standoff missile, which is operational in more than one form, has an aeroplane configuration, with stubby delta wings and cruciform tail surfaces. Propulsion is believed to be by liquid propellant rocket motor. Guidance is reported to be inertial, with radar terminal homing. Choice of nuclear (200 kT) or high explosive (1,000 kg; 2,200 lb) warhead can be assumed. The version with high explosive warhead is operational also with the Iraqi Air Force.

ADAPTED TO: Tu-22, Tu-26, Tu-95 ('Bear-G')

Known as 'Badger-G modified', this version of the Tu-16 carries AS-6 'Kingfish' missiles *(Swedish Air Force)*

AA-2 'Atoll' air-to-air missile under wing of MiG-21

AT-2 'Swatter' missiles on wingtip launchers of Mi-24 ('Hind-D') of Czechoslovak Air Force

AS-5 'Kelt' air-to-surface missile and ground transporter under wing of Egyptian Air Force Tu-16 *(Denis Hughes)*

AA-9 'Amos' missiles on MiG-31 *(Royal Norwegian Air Force)*

Artist's impression of AA-10 missiles on MiG-29 *(US Department of Defense)*

Launch of AS-2 ('Kipper') missile from a Tupolev Tu-16 ('Badger-C')

Infra-red and radar homing versions of AA-3 'Anab' under port and starboard wings, respectively, of Su-21. Note also underbelly gun pods

AA-7 'Apex' missiles under wing gloves of MiG-23, and AA-8 'Aphids' under fuselage

Infra-red (left) and radar versions of the AA-5 'Ash'

AA-6 'Acrid' missiles under wings of a MiG-25 ('Foxbat-A') of Libyan Arab Air Force *(US Navy)*

AS-5
NATO reporting name: Kelt

This liquid propellant rocket powered air-to-surface missile is externally similar to the earlier turbojet powered 'Kennel', which resembled a scaled-down unpiloted MiG-15 fighter with a hemispherical radome above its air intake. On 'Kelt', the ram air intake and radome are replaced by a hemispherical nose fairing, probably housing a larger radar. Guidance is said to be by autopilot on a pre-programmed flight path, with radar terminal homing which can be switched from active to passive as required. A high explosive warhead is fitted. 'Kelt' is operational also with the Iraqi Air Force.

ADAPTED TO: Tu-16 ('Badger-G')

AS-6
NATO reporting name: Kingfish

'Kingfish' has a cylindrical body with ogival nose, two short-span long-chord wings, and a cruciform tail unit with folding ventral fin. Propulsion is said to be by liquid propellant rocket motor, with inertial midcourse guidance and active radar terminal homing, giving exceptional accuracy. The warhead can be either nuclear (200 kT) or 1,000 kg (2,200 lb) high explosive.

ADAPTED TO: Tu-16 ('Badger-G' modified), Tu-26

AS-7
NATO reporting name: Kerry

This tactical air-to-surface missile is said to have a single-stage solid propellant rocket motor, radio command guidance system, and 100 kg (220 lb) high explosive warhead. It is illustrated on an Su-17 in the Soviet aircraft section of this edition.

ADAPTED TO: MiG-23BN, MiG-27, Su-17/20/22, Su-24, Yak-38

AS-X-9

A reported anti-radiation missile to arm the Sukhoi Su-24 ('Fencer').

AS-10
NATO reporting name: Karen

This laser guided weapon has a solid propellant rocket motor. Its configuration is similar to that of the AS-7 'Kerry', from which it may have been developed.

ADAPTED TO: MiG-27, Su-17, Su-24

AS-12
NATO reporting name: Kegler

No details of this tactical air-to-surface missile may yet be published.

AS-14
NATO reporting name: Kedge

This is a Maverick type tactical air-to-surface missile, of which no details may yet be published. It is approx 4 m (13 ft 1½ in) long.

AS-15
NATO reporting name: Kent

Confirmation that the Soviet Union was developing a new generation of air-launched cruise missiles was given on 1 February 1979. US administration officials said that at least eight missiles had been test launched from 'Backfire' bombers during preceding months, over ranges of about 650 nm (1,200 km; 750 miles). First known product of this effort is the AS-15, which is being developed to arm 'Blackjack', and is deployed initially on a new production version of the Tu-95 ('Bear-H'). It provides the Soviet strategic attack force with greatly improved capabilities for low level and standoff attack in both theatre and international operations. Configuration of the AS-15 is similar to that of the USAF's much smaller General Dynamics ground-launched cruise missile. Submarine-launched and ground-launched versions are under development, as the SS-NX-21 and SSC-X-4 respectively. All have a guidance system similar to the US Tercom, making possible a CEP of about 45 m (150 ft), and a nuclear warhead. The AS-15 attained initial operational status during 1984.

BL-10

This supersonic cruise missile, with a reported range of 1,735 nm (3,215 km; 2,000 miles), is being developed for use by the new Tupolev 'Blackjack' strategic bomber.

UNITED KINGDOM

BAe
BRITISH AEROSPACE PUBLIC LIMITED COMPANY

Six Hills Way, Stevenage, Herts SG1 2DA

Air Weapons Division Hatfield

Army Weapons Division Stevenage

Naval Weapons Division Bristol

In addition to its responsibility for weapons listed in this entry, BAe supplies components for European licence manufacture of the AIM-9L Sidewinder air-to-air missile (see Bodenseewerk, Germany). The AIM-9L arms the Royal Air Force's Phantom, Nimrod, Tornado F.2 and Hawk, and Royal Navy Sea Harriers.

SEA SKUA

This lightweight all-weather sea skimming anti-ship missile is operational on the Royal Navy's Lynx helicopter, to meet the threat from missile firing fast patrol craft and to provide a good standoff capability for the helicopter. In addition, Sea Skua has a significant effectiveness against larger warships. It is a quick reaction system, at immediate readiness throughout the helicopter sortie, with full capability in a complex ECM environment. It has a solid propellant boost and sustainer motor, semi-active radar for terminal homing and a high efficiency warhead actuated by a direct action fuse. It has been ordered also for deployment on Sea King helicopters of the Federal German Navy. A ship-launched version is available.

ADAPTED TO: Lynx, Sea King (Federal German Navy) (proposed for other helicopters and fixed-wing aircraft)

SEA EAGLE

Sea Eagle is an all-weather, day and night, 'fire and forget' anti-ship missile, with a Marconi Defence Systems active radar homing head. It is powered by a Microturbo TRI-60 turbojet, which confers a longer range than that of the rocket powered Martel missile which it is replacing. Prior to launch, the onboard microprocessor is supplied with target positional information from the carrier aircraft. The computer controls the flight path of the Sea Eagle until the target is acquired by the seeker during the final sea skimming phase of the attack. The missile can discriminate between several potential targets and is designed to destroy or disable targets protected by sophisticated ECM and decoys, including heavy cruisers and aircraft carriers. A ship-launched version is available; a helicopter-launched version is being developed, with a small additional boost motor.

ADAPTED TO: Buccaneer, Sea Harrier, Sea King (India). May arm Tornado GR.1 later

SKY FLASH
Swedish Air Force designation: RB71

The 'boost and coast' Sky Flash all-weather air-to-air missile has the same general configuration and dimensions as the Raytheon AIM-7E Sparrow, but is fitted with a Marconi Defence Systems semi-active radar homing head of inverse monopulse design. This is only 283 mm (11 in) long and can be fitted on any appropriate missile body of 180 mm (7 in) internal diameter. The Thorn EMI advanced radar proximity fuse is claimed to offer a high single-shot kill capability against targets flying at subsonic and supersonic speeds, singly and in formation, at high, medium and low (75 m; 250 ft) altitudes, in severe ECM environments.

In 1985, BAe and Swedish industry were considering the launch of a programme to develop an improved missile, known as **Sky Flash 90**, to arm the Saab JAS 39 Gripen combat aircraft. This version would have a Marconi active homing head.

ADAPTED TO: F-4 Phantom, F-16 Fighting Falcon, JA 37 Viggen, Tornado F.2

ALARM

The ALARM air-launched defence suppression weapon is being developed to meet a Royal Air Force requirement. When carried by deep penetration strike and close support aircraft, it will enable them to counter enemy surface-to-air

AS-3 'Kangaroo' air-to-surface missile under the fuselage of a Tu-95 ('Bear-B') strategic bomber

One of several types of AS-4 'Kitchen' air-to-surface missile photographed under 'Backfire-B' bombers

British Aerospace Sea Skua anti-ship missiles on Lynx helicopter

Sky Flash air-to-air missiles on inboard underwing hardpoints of JA 37 Viggen

Sea Eagle anti-ship missiles on Royal Navy Sea Harrier

Artist's impression of Tornado GR.1 carrying four ALARM missiles on stub pylons in addition to its normal attack weapon load

gun and missile defences by destroying the associated radars. Weighing only 280 kg (617 lb), complete with launcher, ALARM can be carried by aircraft as small as the Hawk, and military helicopters. The anti-radar seeker is of Marconi Defence Systems design. MBB of West Germany is developing the missile's warhead, and Thorn EMI the proximity fuse. Power plant is a two-stage Nuthatch solid-propellant rocket motor.

ALARM has a number of operational modes. These include direct attack, where the missile flies to a selected target, and a loiter mode, where it climbs to height and deploys a parachute from which it remains suspended until a suitable target has been identified. The parachute is then released and the missile descends on to the target under gravity. Delivery of 750 missiles reportedly required by the Royal Air Force is expected to begin in 1987.

INTENDED FOR: Tornado GR.1

ASRAAM

Details of the ASRAAM programme can be found under the BBG heading in the International part of this section.

SHORTS

SHORT BROTHERS PLC

PO Box 241, Airport Road, Belfast BT3 9DZ, Northern Ireland

BLOWPIPE/JAVELIN

No orders for the projected helicopter-borne versions of these infantry missiles had been received by early 1986.

STARSTREAK

This high velocity close air defence weapon system was announced by Shorts in November 1985. Representing a further development of the Blowpipe/Javelin concept, it will be available in infantry, vehicle-launched, ship-launched and air-to-air versions.

UNITED STATES OF AMERICA

BOEING

BOEING AEROSPACE COMPANY

PO Box 3999, Seattle, Washington 98124

ALCM

USAF designation: AGM-86

The operational AGM-86B air-launched cruise missile (ALCM) is a small unmanned winged air vehicle capable of sustained subsonic flight following launch from an airborne carrier aircraft. It is powered by a Williams International/Teledyne CAE F107-WR-100 turbofan engine (2·67 kN;

600 lb st), incorporates a W80-1 nuclear warhead (150 kT) for 'hard target' kill capability, and is programmed for precision attack on a specific surface target. Guidance is by a combination of inertial and terrain comparison (Tercom) techniques. In the terrain comparison mode the missile is kept on course by a computer which compares pre-programmed geographical features on its flight plan with the geography seen by its sensors during actual flight.

If launched in large numbers, each of the missiles would have to be countered, making defence against them difficult and costly. The missiles are intended both to serve as standoff weapons and to dilute defences and improve the ability of manned aircraft to penetrate to major targets. Small radar signature and low level flight capability would enhance their effectiveness.

The US Air Force is acquiring a total of 1,715 AGM-86s. Initial operational capability was attained in 1982, and the 1,600th ALCM was completed in early 1986, ahead of schedule and below programmed cost. Deliveries were scheduled to end in September 1986.

ADAPTED TO: B-52G/H Stratofortress

BRUNSWICK

BRUNSWICK CORPORATION (DEFENSE DIVISION)

3333 Harbor Boulevard, Costa Mesa, California 92626

Brunswick Corporation manufactures an air-launched Low Altitude Dispenser (LAD) for submunitions. This enables strike aircraft to attack targets while maintaining low-altitude avoidance of air defence systems. Its ability to accept a wide range of submunitions and guidance packages allows it to be equally effective against armour, vehicles, airfields and personnel.

LOW ALTITUDE DISPENSER (LAD)

Launched from any current US strike aircraft, LAD makes a climbing turn behind the aircraft until reaching dispensing altitude, from where it can deliver virtually any submunition currently in service or under development. LAD can attack off-axis targets, and can manoeuvre to provide optimum delivery of its weapon load. The current deliverable load can be increased to 907 kg (2,000 lb), and is limited only by the carrying capability of the parent aircraft. Provision is made for the addition of a small motor to extend the standoff range of the system.

A follow-on LAD-FWETE (foreign weapons equipment technology evaluation) programme began in March 1985. The USAF is evaluating three vehicles, two with MBB, and one with Dornier new submunition ejection systems. Two of the vehicles have low drag configurations (LD-LAD) compatible with F-16 weight and drag parameters. LD-LAD will be offered as an SUU-54 dispenser replacement for the Rockwell International AGM-130, as a candidate for the NATO low cost powered dispenser (LOCPOD, see International section), and as a near-term candidate for a potential NATO modular standoff weapon system programme.

DIMENSIONS (A: LAD, B: LD-LAD):

Wing span: A	1·47 m (4 ft 10 in)
B	approx 1·57 m (5 ft 2 in)
Body width: A	0·58 m (1 ft 11 in)
B	0·66 m (2 ft 2 in)
Body depth: A	0·58 m (1 ft 11in)
B	0·44 m (1 ft 5½ in)
Length: A	4·165 m (13 ft 8 in)
B	4·17 m (13 ft 8¼ in)
Mission equipment volume:	
A	0·530 m³ (18·7 cu ft)
B	0·532 m³ (18·8 cu ft)

WEIGHTS (current):

Max payload: B	744 kg (1,640 lb)
Max launching weight: A	1,406 kg (3,100 lb)
B	1,020 kg (2,250 lb)

PERFORMANCE:

Max speed: A, B	700 knots (1,297 km/h; 806 mph)
Min launch altitude: A, B	30 m (100 ft)
Max range:	
A, B, unpowered	7 nm (13 km; 8 miles)
B, powered	20 nm (37 km; 23 miles)

FORD

FORD AEROSPACE & COMMUNICATIONS CORPORATION

20th Floor, 300 Renaissance Center, PO Box 43342, Detroit, Michigan 48243

Aeronutronic Division

Ford Road, Newport Beach, California 92660

Ford Aerospace & Communications Corporation, and its Philco predecessor, have produced Sidewinder air-to-air missiles for the US armed services for more than 30 years. Current production version is the AIM-9M for the US Navy and US Air Force. Details of the Sidewinder can be found under the NWC entry in this section.

GENERAL DYNAMICS

GENERAL DYNAMICS CORPORATION

Pierre Laclede Center, St Louis, Missouri 63105

Convair Division

5001 Kearny Villa Road, San Diego, California 92123

Pomona Division

PO Box 2507, Pomona, California 91769

Valley Systems Division

PO Box 2507, Pomona, California 91769

Pomona Division is responsible for development and production of the Standard naval surface-to-air missile and Phalanx ship defence system, as well as second source production of the Sparrow air-to-air and surface-to-air missile (see Raytheon entry).

Valley Systems Division concentrates on passive and strategic defence systems, including the Stinger and Stinger-POST infra-red weapons, the ship defence Rolling Airframe Missile (RAM) and terminally guided submunitions.

Convair Division is responsible for the US Navy's sea-launched cruise missile, under the designation BGM-109 Tomahawk, and developments such as the USAF's ground-launched cruise missile.

ACM

In April 1983 it was announced that Convair Division of General Dynamics would develop and manufacture the US Air Force's air-launched advanced cruise missile (ACM) that will be deployed in a mix with the AGM-86B ALCM. The currently anticipated requirement is for about 1,261 ACMs to arm B-52H and B-1B bombers. Few details of the missile are available, except that it will have a Williams International F112 turbofan engine. Range will be at least 10 per cent greater than that of the AGM-86B, accuracy and targeting flexibility will be improved, and 'low observability' techniques will be used to reduce radar and infra-red signatures. It is expected that a 200 kT W80-1 nuclear warhead will be standard.

STINGER

US military designation: FIM-92A

This all-aspect solid propellant tube-launched missile was developed to replace the 'tail-chase' Redeye as the US Army's standard shoulder-fired infantry surface-to-air weapon. An infra-red homing system is retained, but Stinger has a longer range, is more manoeuvrable and is more resistant to countermeasures than the earlier weapon. Under a two-year US Army programme that was scheduled for completion in September 1986, General Dynamics and Bell Helicopter have developed a Stinger missile kit for retrofit on the OH-58C Kiowa light observation helicopter and OH-58D advanced scout helicopter.

GM-HUGHES

GENERAL MOTORS-HUGHES ELECTRONICS CORPORATION

Hughes Aircraft Unit

PO Box 45066, 7200 Hughes Terrace, Los Angeles, California 90045-0066

Missile Systems Group

Canoga Park, California 91304

PHOENIX

US Navy designation: AIM-54

Phoenix has a solid propellant rocket motor, semi-active radar midcourse guidance, active radar terminal guidance, and a large impact or proximity fused high explosive warhead. The launch aircraft's AWG-9 weapon control system is able to track an enemy target, at high or low altitude, in any kind of weather, and launch the Phoenix missile. The data from the radar is displayed to the missile control officer in the launch aircraft on a 254 mm (10 in) cathode ray tube and a 127 mm (5 in) multi-mode storage tube. The long range high power pulse-Doppler radar has a 'lookdown' capability that enables it to pick out moving targets from ground clutter, and a track-while-scan radar mode that makes it possible to launch up to six missiles and keep them on course while searching for other possible targets, all in the presence of sophisticated enemy countermeasures.

There are two versions of Phoenix:

AIM-54A. Initial version. Total of 2,566 built. Production completed 1980.

AIM-54C. Improved version, with much enhanced ECCM capability and reliability. New proximity fuse, digital electronics unit, solid state radar transceiver and strapdown inertial reference system for improved accuracy and greater range. In production; 234 built by February 1986.

ADAPTED TO: F-14A Tomcat

AMRAAM

US military designation: AIM-120A

The 'fire and forget' advanced medium range air-to-air missile (AMRAAM) is intended to replace the AIM-7 Sparrow in USAF and US Navy service, and to be a NATO standard weapon with licence production in Europe. Basic design requirements included an upper weight limit of about 160 kg (350 lb); all-weather capability; snapdown capability; a resistance to ECM at least as good as that offered by current monopulse techniques; all-aspect launch and tracking ability; a minimum range at least equal to that of the AIM-7F Sparrow; and a maximum range as great as the state of the art permits.

In its AIM-120A form, AMRAAM embodies a strapdown midcourse inertial reference system, and active radar terminal homing. It will outperform the Sparrow, cost less to build and be about two-thirds as heavy as the earlier weapon. In combat, it will enable the pilot to make launches against multiple targets with no changes in current cockpit procedures.

Under a full scale development contract awarded in December 1981, Hughes is producing 98 test missiles. In the first guided test of an FSD round, on 14 May 1985, the AMRAAM passed within lethal distance of a QF-100 target drone after launch from an F-16 flying at Mach 0·85 at 6,400 m (21,000 ft). Six subsequent tests up to Spring 1986 had all proved successful, but emphasis in FY 1986 was on reduced production costs. Raytheon has been selected as second production source, and USAF has requested a low rate initial production run of 260 AMRAAMs from both contractors in FY 1987. Total planned USN/USAF procurement is 24,335 missiles.

ADAPTED TO: F-15 Eagle, F-16 Fighting Falcon; will also arm F-14 Tomcat, F/A-18 Hornet, West German F-4F Phantom, RAF Tornado F. Mk2 and Royal Navy Sea Harrier

TOW

US Army designation: BGM-71

The basic characteristics of this high performance anti-tank missile are indicated by its name, as **TOW** is an acronym for Tube launched, Optically tracked, Wire guided. The missile has low aspect ratio wings and tail control surfaces that remain folded while in the launcher and flick open as the missile leaves the launch tube. The wings flick forward during extension, the tail surfaces rearward. There are two separate solid propellant rocket motors. The launch motor fires first to propel the missile from the launcher. The missile coasts for a short period after leaving the mouth of the tube, before the second (boost) motor fires. The operator guides the missile by keeping the target centred in a telescopic sight. Movement of the sight generates electronic signals to correct the missile's course, the signals being passed through two wires. The warhead is a high explosive shaped charge.

TOW is a heavy assault weapon for use against tanks, armoured vehicles and gun emplacements over ranges up to 3,750 m (12,300 ft). When it is used from helicopters, a gyro stabilised sight eliminates the effects of aircraft vibration and manoeuvres. To provide night vision capability, the standard system can be replaced by a FLIR (forward looking infra-red) system embodying a thermal imaging sensor. US Army AH-1S helicopters also have a laser rangefinder. A total of 310,793 TOWs was built in 1969-83.

All existing TOWs are able to be uprated to **ITOW** (improved TOW) standard, by substitution of an improved 127 mm (5 in) diameter warhead, approximately the same size and weight as the current warhead, to provide increased armour penetrating capability, without any changes to the launcher or guidance hardware. The ITOW warhead embodies an extensible probe to provide standoff detonation. By February 1986, a total of 39,924 ITOWs had been delivered. This version has been followed by a more extensively upgraded **TOW 2** with a heavier 152 mm (6 in)

Boeing AGM-86B ALCMs on the underwing pylons of a B-52G

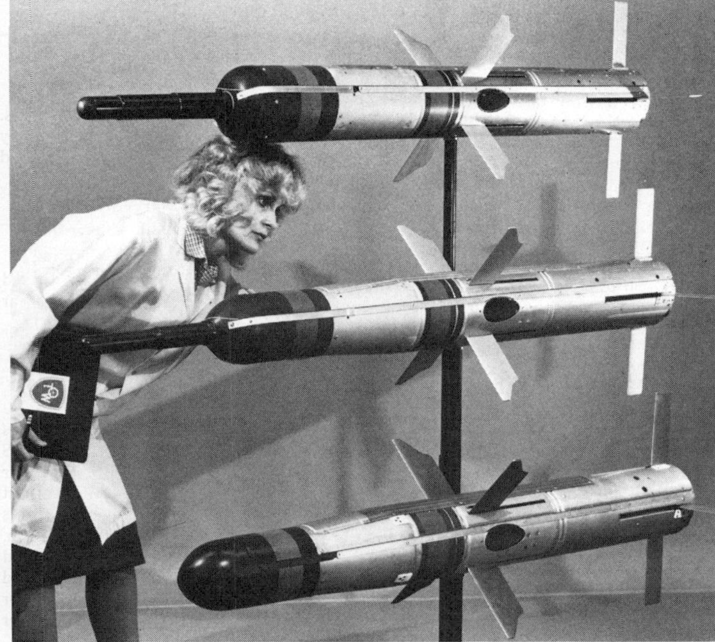

Top to bottom: TOW 2, ITOW (improved TOW) and the basic TOW

First fully guided prototype AIM-120A AMRAAM missile

Boeing AGM-86B air-launched cruise missile in flight

Brunswick Low Altitude Dispenser for submunitions on an F-16

Front to rear: AGM-65D, AGM-65E, AGM-65B and AGM-65F versions of Maverick

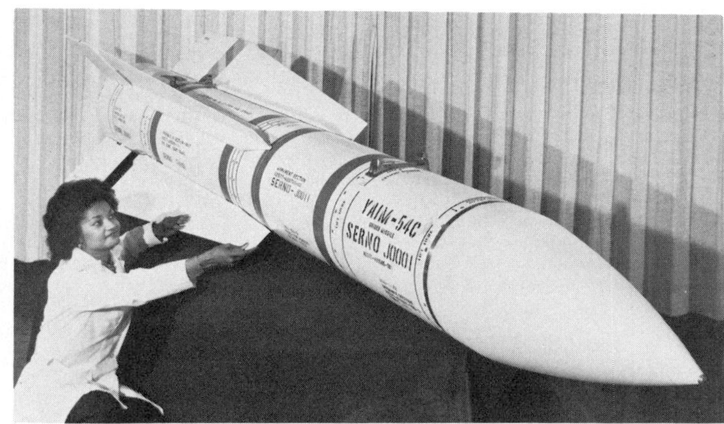

First pre-production AIM-54C Phoenix air-to-air missile

warhead, occupying the full diameter of the missile body, and a microprocessor based digital missile guidance set, which provides greater flexibility in guidance programming and higher precision. In particular, the guidance system can cope better with a 'dirty' battlefield environment, including smoke and countermeasures. The boost motor is loaded with an improved propellant, to provide a higher impulse that will offset the additional weight of the warhead and equipment changes. By February 1986, a total of 33,454 TOW 2s had been built. TOW 2 modifications are applicable by retrofit to early missiles.

ADAPTED TO: Agusta A 109, AH-1 HueyCobra, Bell 206L-1, BK 117, BO 105, Dauphin, Ecureuil, Gazelle, McDonnell Douglas 500MD Defender, Lynx

WILL ARM: Agusta A 129, Sikorsky H-76

MAVERICK

USAF designation: AGM-65

Maverick is a precision guided air-to-surface missile in the 500 lb class. It is possible to adapt existing controls and displays in launch aircraft to operation of the weapon system. The minimum aircraft requirement is a raster scan TV display in the cockpit and conventional control functions. A single-rail launcher has been developed for wing stations which cannot accommodate the standard three-round launcher.

Versions of Maverick are:

AGM-65A. Basic TV guided model with 5° field of view camera in the seeker, centroid tracker and single-stage solid propellant boost/sustain rocket motor. The 57 kg (125 lb) shaped charge warhead is designed to defeat heavy armour and reinforced concrete, making it most suitable for use against tanks and pillbox type targets. Operational use is in the 'fire and forget' mode. The pilot can slew the seeker for rapid lock-on to the target, using a TV visual display, launch the missile and immediately take evasive action. Approximately 19,000 built when production ceased in 1984.

AGM-65B. 'Scene magnification' version of TV Maverick, with 2·5° field of view camera and improved video symbols on cockpit display. Production completed in 1984 with 31,022 AGM-65A/Bs built for customers in 18 countries. In 100 combat launches in Viet-Nam and during 1973 Israeli-Egyptian war, 87 direct hits and 5 deliberate near misses were achieved.

AGM-65D. Has imaging infra-red (IIR) seeker, which tracks passively the natural thermal image of a tactical target and surrounding environment, providing a pictorial display of the target to the pilot in darkness, haze and smoke. Lock-on, launch and 'fire and forget' homing flight as for AGM-65A/B. In production. First of planned 58,864 for USAF delivered in late 1983. Total of 334 built by February 1986.

Raytheon is second source manufacturer of infra-red Maverick missiles.

AGM-65E. Fitted with a laser seeker, which homes on a target illuminated by a ground or airborne laser designator, and a new 135 kg (298 lb) penetrator/blast fragmentation warhead, developed to extend Maverick's capability against larger or heavily fortified targets. Can be used by day or night, as the pilot of the launch aircraft does not need to acquire the target visually. Provision is made for rendering the warhead inert, to protect friendly troops in the event of a designator failure or other loss of lock-on during close support missions. In production for US Marine Corps; 34 built by February 1986.

AGM-65F. Combines the imaging infra-red seeker of the AGM-65D with the warhead and propulsion sections of the AGM-65E. This version has a fine-tuned tracker, to enhance its effectiveness against ships at sea, and selectable delayed or contact fusing of the blast penetration warhead. In production for US Navy.

AGM-65G. Combines IIR seeker of AGM-65D with 135 kg (298 lb) warhead of AGM-65E. USAF plans to procure 1,800.

ADAPTED TO: A-4M Skyhawk II (AGM-65E), A-7D Corsair II, A-10A Thunderbolt II, AJ 37 Viggen, F-4D/E/G Phantom II, F-5E/F Tiger II, F-16 Fighting Falcon, F/A-18 Hornet (AGM-65E), F-111F, Hunter; Teledyne Ryan BGM-34 RPV

WILL ARM: A-6E Intruder (AGM-65F), A-7E Corsair II (AGM-65F), AV-8B Harrier II, Alpha Jet, F/A-18 Hornet (AGM-65F), Fokker Maritime Enforcer, Tornado

LTV

LTV AEROSPACE AND DEFENSE COMPANY
Vought Missiles and Advanced Programs Division

PO Box 650003, Dallas, Texas 75265-0003

ASAT

Under USAF contract, Vought and the Boeing Company are developing and flight testing a small high-technology air-launched anti-satellite (ASAT) weapon capable of destroying enemy satellites at low orbital altitudes. This consists of a modified SRAM first stage, a Thiokol Altair III solid propellant second stage rated at 26·7 kN (6,000 lb st), and a Vought miniature vehicle (MV) with Hughes infra-red terminal seeker and conventional warhead mounted forward of the second stage. The guidance system is by Singer-Kearfott. ASAT is about 5·2 m (17 ft) long, with a launch weight of 1,225 kg (2,700 lb).

ASAT is intended to be carried by designated air defence F-15s, based at Langley AFB, Virginia. In operational form, it would be released from the F-15 in a zoom climb. Immediately before separation from the Altair, the miniature homing vehicle would be spun up to 20 rps for stabilisation. Small solid propellant rocket motors would then provide course corrections as a laser gyro and the infra-red seeker guided it to target impact.

Firing trials from an F-15 began in 1983 and the first live launch against a target in space occurred successfully on 13 September 1985. A total of $322 million is sought for continuation of the ASAT programme in FY 1987.

HVM

Under a US Air Force contract awarded in late 1981, Vought Missiles and Advanced Programs Division of LTV began developing a guided air-to-surface hypervelocity missile (HVM) system capable of defeating all types of vehicle in an armoured assault force, using small low-cost missiles which rely on kinetic energy derived from their speed for penetration. It is now a joint USAF, Marine Corps and Army programme.

The system will consist of pods, each containing launch tubes for up to 18 HVMs, and a laser radar guidance system. The guidance system employs a carbon dioxide laser to provide three-dimensional ranging and Doppler information, and will perform the functions of multiple target detection, classification, identification and allocation of priority in under one second. The rockets will utilise a track-while-guidance system; the laser will provide a coarse beam for rocket capture and a fine beam for terminal guidance. The use of laser guidance is intended to make the system almost impervious to countermeasures.

Each HVM missile is expected to weigh less than 22 kg (48 lb). It will have no moving parts and will be stabilised in flight by spin, aided by a gyro roll sensor and a series of 'squib' rocket motors for attitude control. HVM will reach a speed of more than 2,900 knots (5,400 km/h; 3,355 mph) and will carry an inert warhead of high density, possibly a depleted uranium rod weighing 2·2 to 2·7 kg (4·8-6 lb), able to penetrate most modern armour plate. Estimated maximum range is about 6 km (3·7 miles)

Simultaneous multiple target engagement is an important requirement, and it is hoped to be able to demonstrate firing of several missiles delivered simultaneously against separate stationary and moving targets. Initial ground-launched flight tests in 1982-83 demonstrated the missile's ability to receive laser guidance signals through the rocket motor plume, speed capabilities in excess of 2,900 knots for the air-launch role, and the ability of the missile to respond to signals from a ground-based laser at the launch site and manoeuvre to its target. Launch platforms will include the A-10 and F-16.

MDAC

MCDONNELL DOUGLAS ASTRONAUTICS COMPANY (A Divsion of McDonnell Douglas Corporation)

5301 Bolsa Avenue, Huntington Beach, California 92647

McDonnell Douglas Astronautics Company-St Louis

PO Box 516, St Louis, Missouri 63166

HARPOON

US military designation: AGM-84

The general configuration of the air-launched version of the Harpoon all-weather anti-ship missile is shown in an accompanying illustration. The Teledyne CAE J402-CA-400 turbojet power plant (2·94 kN; 660 lb st) is housed in the rear of the body, with a ventral flush air intake. Prior to launch, targeting data for Harpoon are provided by the command and launch subsystem, which interfaces with onboard systems. After launch, guidance is provided by a Northrop strapdown attitude reference assembly and digital computer. Cruise altitude is monitored by a radar altimeter, enabling the flight to the target to be made at sea skimming altitude, so offering both optimum target acquisition capability, through reduction of clutter effects, and the ability to penetrate enemy defences.

When the target comes within the search area of the active radar seeker, the system detects and locks on to the target, even in rain and high sea states. Seeker lock-on is maintained until impact. Capability to perform high-*g* manoeuvres throughout flight permits successful operation against fast manoeuvring targets. Counter-countermeasures devices are installed. The warhead is a penetration/high explosive blast type.

Four versions of air-launched Harpoon are known to exist, as follows:

AGM-84A. Initial version for US Navy, utilising a terminal 'pop-up' manoeuvre to counter close-in defences and offer maximum warhead effectiveness.

AGM-84B. Terminal 'pop-up' manoeuvre eliminated, following improvements to low-altitude penetration capability. First delivery, to Royal Navy, 8 June 1982.

AGM-84C. Improved AGM-84A, with 'pop-up' mode, for US Navy.

AGM-84D. Current production version, with increases in range, waypoints, and selectable terminal trajectories.

The US Air Force has one squadron of 15 sea control B-52Gs at Loring AFB, Maine, for Atlantic operations, and another squadron at Andersen AFB, Guam, for Pacific operations, with each bomber equipped to carry eight to 12 Harpoons externally.

Advanced versions of Harpoon are under development, including some with an alternative guidance system, using an imaging infra-red seeker.

ADAPTED TO: A-6E Intruder, B-52G Stratofortress, P-3A/B/C Orion, Nimrod, S-3 Viking

WILL ARM: F/A-18 Hornet

NWC

NAVAL WEAPONS CENTER

China Lake, California 93555

Weapons developed at the Naval Weapons Center have included the Mighty Mouse 2·75 in folding fin aircraft rocket, the 11·75 in Tiny Tim rocket, the Zuni 5 in folding fin aircraft rocket, the Sidewinder air-to-air guided missile, the Snakeye 250/500 lb bomb with folding dive-brake retardation system, the Shrike and Standard ARM air-to-surface anti-radar missiles and the Walleye glide bomb. Production of many of these weapons was entrusted to commercial companies.

SIDEWINDER

US military designation: AIM-9

Versions of this simple air-to-air missile are:

AIM-9B. First generation production version manufactured by Philco (now Ford) and General Electric for US Navy and USAF, with Naval Propellant Plant solid propellant rocket motor and uncooled infra-red seeker. Licence-built in Europe. Dead zone around Sun 20° in early models, 5° later.

AIM-9E. Produced by Philco for USAF, by modification of AIM-9Bs to have a new seeker section with thermo-electric cooling, refurbished electronics and wiring. Major increase in capability claimed.

AIM-9G. Higher speed, longer range version, distinguished from 9B by tapering nose, longer chord nose fins and greater sweepback on tail fins. Rocketdyne Mk 36 Mod 5 motor; continuous rod warhead with optional infra-red or HF proximity fuse; off-boresight target acquisition and lock-on. Produced by Raytheon for US Navy.

AIM-9H. Version for US Navy with improved close range dogfight capability, produced by Raytheon and Ford. Basically similar to AIM-9G, but with solid state guidance instead of vacuum tube electronics, decreased minimum ranges and faster angle tracking rates.

AIM-9J. Conversion of AIM-9Bs and 9Es, with new 'front end' to enhance dogfight capability by improved manoeuvring ability. Modified for USAF by Ford.

AIM-9L. Third generation version with all-aspect detection and launch capability. Double delta nose fins for improved inner boundary performance and better manoeuvrability. AM-FM conical scan for increased seeker sensitivity and improved tracking stability. Active infra-red proximity fuse for increased lethality and low susceptibility to countermeasures. Annular blast fragmentation warhead. Produced for USAF and USN by Raytheon and Ford. In production under licence by a consortium of manufacturers in NATO countries and by the Japan Defence Agency.

AIM-9M. Improved version of AIM-9L in production by Ford and Raytheon for US Navy and USAF. Increased IRCCM capability, improved background discrimination, Thiokol/Hercules Mk 36 Mod 11 reduced smoke rocket motor.

AIM-9N. Modified AIM-9B/E servo and electronic subsection for increased manoeuvrability and accuracy, produced by Ford for foreign military sales.

AIM-9P. Improved version of AIM-9J produced by Ford for USAF. Increased lethality due to improvements to guidance section and introduction of reduced smoke rocket motor and active optical fuse. Nose fins of new form, with increased span.

AIM-9R. Development of AIM-9M, with improved control and guidance section for greater target acquisition range and better resistance to countermeasures. Full scale development started in 1986, with planned IOC in 1990.

ADAPTED TO: Most current fighters, some reconnaissance and attack aircraft, operated by the United States, its allies and nations in receipt of US military exports

SIDEARM

US Navy designation: AGM-122A

Sidearm was developed by the NWC as a low-cost lightweight counterpart to HARM for less demanding missions. It combines the airframe and power plant of Sidewinder with a new warhead and anti-radiation seeker modified from the semi-active radar seeker of the non-operational AIM-9C version. It is light enough to be carried by almost all US Navy and Marine Corps combat aircraft, including specifically the AH-1 attack helicopter and AV-8B V/STOL combat aircraft. Procurement of 168 for US Navy was planned in FY 1986, with 256 more requested in FY 1987. The AIM-9C seekers, currently in store, are expected to be modified by Motorola. Launch weight of Sidearm is 113 kg (250 lb).

SKIPPER II

US military designation: AGM-123A

Deployed on US Navy aircraft carriers, Skipper II is a laser guided weapon designed by NWC; production is by Emerson Defense Systems, with procurement of 925 rounds authorised under FY 1986 funding. Intended for anti-ship use, Skipper II is a 582 kg (1,283 lb) missile combining the airframe parts of a Paveway II Mark 83 glide-bomb with a guidance and control package based on that of Paveway II and a solid propellant rocket motor of the kind used in the AGM-45 Shrike anti-radiation missile. Range of Skipper II, limited by its laser homing, is up to 9 nm (16·5 km; 10·35 miles). Length overall is 4·3 m (14 ft 1in).

ADAPTED TO: A-6 Intruder, A-7 Corsair II, F/A-18 Hornet

Vought anti-satellite (ASAT) weapon on an air defence F-15 Eagle *(Erik Simonsen)*

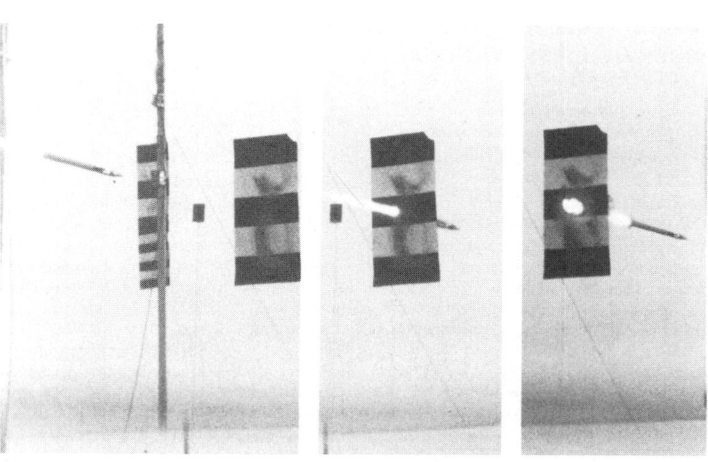

Guided flight test of an LTV hypervelocity missile (HVM)

AIM-9P Sidewinder on an F-5E 'aggressor' aircraft

Harpoon being launched from underwing pylon of a B-52 Stratofortress

Sparrow (lower) and Sidewinder (upper, with protective nosecap) missiles on an F-15 Eagle fighter of the US Air Force

Wingtip mounted AIM-9L Sidewinder on a McDonnell Douglas F/A-18

RAYTHEON

RAYTHEON COMPANY

141 Spring Street, Lexington, Massachusetts 02173

SPARROW

US military designations: AIM-7 and RIM-7

Sparrow is a semi-active radar homing missile capable of being launched from the air or the surface. The air-launched versions carry the designation AIM-7 and the surface-launched versions carry the designation RIM-7. Certain models can be launched from aircraft or ships against surface vessels. The original Raytheon AIM-7C/D/E models were followed in production by the **AIM-7F** which was manufactured by Raytheon, General Dynamics and Mitsubishi of Japan. The AIM-7F has a larger solid propellant motor and a smaller solid state seeker, which significantly improve performance and reliability. A larger continuous rod warhead is activated by a proximity fuse or contact fuse. Manoeuvrability is also improved and Sparrow is now considered an excellent close combat (dogfight) missile as well as a good medium-range weapon with all-aspect capability including lookdown/shootdown.

An advanced monopulse seeker and digital processor have been developed for Sparrow, to improve performance in ECM and lookdown/clutter environments. Together with a new autopilot and active fuse, these improvements are incorporated into a version of the missile designated **AIM/RIM-7M**. This model is in current production by Raytheon and General Dynamics Pomona for both the US Air Force and Navy. More than 14,000 are to be built, including RIM-7Ms for the surface-to-air NATO Seasparrow missile system. AIM/RIM-7Ms entered the inventory in 1983, and procurement has been extended through 1990. Dimensions are the same as those given for the AIM-7F in the table on page 875; launch weight is 231 kg (510 lb).

In addition to aircraft listed below, Sparrow has been fired from the F-20 Tigershark, successfully intercepting a target. Separation tests from the F-16 Fighting Falcon have been conducted.

Adapted to: F-4 Phantom, F-14 Tomcat, F-15 Eagle, F/A-18 Hornet, F-104S Starfighter

SIDEWINDER

US military designation: AIM-9

For more than 20 years, Raytheon Company has participated in the Sidewinder programme, initially as a manufacture of the guidance and control sections of AIM-9G/H models, and later as the designated industrial support contractor to the Naval Weapons Center (NWC) for the development of the AIM-9L and AIM-9M advanced versions of the missile. In total, Raytheon has produced over 35,000 Sidewinders for the US armed forces and foreign military sales. The current production version is the AIM-9M. Details can be found under the NWC entry in this section.

IMAGING INFRA-RED (IIR) MAVERICK

US military designation: AGM-65D

Raytheon completed a 30-month IIR Maverick second source qualification programme in November 1985 and was awarded an FY 1986 production contract for 800 missiles by the US Air Force. The Air Force plans to conduct annual competitions between Raytheon and Hughes Aircraft Company (see GM-Hughes entry) for major and minor shares, beginning with the FY 1987 procurement.

AMRAAM

US military designation: AIM-120A

In July 1982 Raytheon was selected by the US Air Force as the follower in a leader/follower acquisition plan for AMRAAM. In November 1985 it received a $111 million contract to build 15 missiles and qualify as a second source producer. The US Air Force plans to award pilot production contracts to both Raytheon and GM-Hughes (which see) in FY 1987 and FY 1988.

Beginning in FY 1989, competitions will be conducted between Raytheon and Hughes for major and minor shares of the annual production awards.

ROCKWELL INTERNATIONAL

ROCKWELL INTERNATIONAL CORPORATION

Missile Systems Division
Defense Electronics Operations
1800 Satellite Boulevard, Duluth, Georgia 30136

HELLFIRE

US Army designation: AGM-114A

Hellfire (HELicopter Launched, FIRE and forget) is a modular solid propellant missile system which, in its initial form, uses a laser seeker as its guidance module. Hellfire is designed to accept a variety of other terminal homing seeker modules, including imaging infra-red (IIR), radio frequency (RF), and dual mode RF/IIR.

Hellfire can be fired against targets illuminated by ground based or airborne laser designators. It has demonstrated rapid, ripple and indirect fire, and can be launched from a variety of helicopters, ground vehicles and fixed wing aircraft. Its 178 mm (7 in) warhead has a high level of effectiveness against present and near-term future types of armour.

Initial large-scale production, by Rockwell and Martin Marietta Orlando Aerospace, is to provide primary armament for US Army Apache attack helicopters. The US Marine Corps will also use Hellfire on its AH-1J/T SeaCobra helicopters.

Adapted to: AH-64 Apache, UH-60 Black Hawk, Lynx
Will arm: AH-1 SeaCobra (USMC)

GBU-15

The GBU-15 is an air-launched glide bomb fitted with a guidance system which is claimed to give it pinpoint accuracy from low or high altitudes over standoff ranges up to 5 nm (9·25 km; 5·75 miles). It is a modular weapon, intended for tactical use to suppress enemy defences and to destroy heavily defended targets. It is normally built around a standard 2,000 lb Mk 84 general purpose bomb, minus fins, but is adaptable to the CBU-75 cluster munition and other warheads. Guidance is by TV or an imaging infra-red (IIR) seeker 90 per cent common with that of the AGM-65D Maverick; these two versions are designated GBU-15(V)1/B and GBU-15(V)2/B respectively. The control module, with autopilot, and data link module attach to the rear of the warhead. Foreplanes and rear mounted wings and control surfaces complete the weapon. For direct attack trajectories, the weapon is locked on target before launch and flies a near line of sight profile to impact. The indirect profile includes a midcourse glide phase which extends standoff capability. In this profile, the seeker can be locked on to the target after launch, or the operator can fly the weapon manually to impact, using guidance updates provided through the data link. Production deliveries of the TV version to the US Air Force began in January 1982. The first two launches by an operational squadron, during Red Flag readiness evaluation by F-4E fighters at Nellis AFB in January 1985, scored direct hits on ground targets. Follow-on testing and evaluation of the night attack IIR version were under way in early 1986.

Adapted to: F-4E Phantom II, F-111F
Compatible with: F-15 Eagle, F-16 Fighting Falcon, F/A-18 Hornet, AJ 37 Viggen (1,000 lb Mk 83), Tornado

AGM-130A

The AGM-130A is a rocket powered version of the GBU-15, with added radar altimeter, to give USAF tactical combat aircraft improved standoff capability. It retains the Mk 84 military warhead of the GBU-15; initial plans to develop a dispenser version were abandoned due to fiscal restrictions.

One or two solid propellant rockets, mounted under the missile, boost it to near Mach 1 speed, giving a maximum range of about 13 nm (24 km; 15 miles) after release at low altitude. The FY 1987 Department of Defense budget proposals included a request for 159 AGM-130As. Separation tests from an F-4 Phantom II began in Spring 1986. Live firings were planned to start during the Summer.

Adapted to: F-4E Phantom II, F-15E Eagle, F-111F

TEXAS INSTRUMENTS

TEXAS INSTRUMENTS INC

PO Box 660246, 8505 Forest Lane, Dallas, Texas 75266

HARM

US Navy designation: AGM-88A

The HARM (High-speed Anti-Radiation Missile) has a conventional configuration, with a slim cylindrical body, ogival head, cruciform double delta wings at mid-length for simplified roll control, cruciform tail fins, a fixed antenna for proportional navigation in the extreme nose, with the seeker, and a smokeless solid propellant dual-thrust rocket motor. It can cover a wide range of frequency spectra through the use of programmable digital processors in both the aircraft's avionics equipment and the missile. The emphasis on high speed reflects experience gained in Viet-Nam, where Soviet surface-to-air missile radar systems sometimes detected the approach of US anti-radiation missiles such as the first generation Shrike and ceased operation before the missile could lock on to them.

Production deliveries of HARM to the US Navy began in December 1982. By mid-1985, a total of 470 missiles had been delivered, out of 2,805 then ordered. A total of 1,684 was procured in FY 1985. The first operational use was against Libyan SAM-5 radars during the US attack on 24 March 1986. Production is increasing annually, for the USN and US Air Force, and for foreign customers. West Germany has ordered 368, with options on 576 more.

Adapted to: A-7E Corsair II, EA-6B Prowler, F-4G 'Wild Weasel', F/A-18 Hornet, Tornado
Adaptable to: A-6E Intruder, B-52 Stratofortress, EF-111 Raven, F-15 Eagle, F-16 Fighting Falcon

PAVEWAY LASER GUIDED BOMBS

The Paveway laser guided bomb (LGB) concept involves the adaptation of forward guidance and control units and rear wing assemblies to conventional general purpose bomb bodies, to produce a semi-active laser-guided munition. After release, Paveway LGBs acquire and home on laser energy reflected from a target being illuminated by an airborne or ground laser designator. As no intrinsic target signature is required, and since the laser energy is not in the visible spectrum, day and night attacks can be accomplished with little chance of detection. Paveway LGBs can be employed against any target suitable for a particular general purpose warhead, and have been used successfully against anti-aircraft gun and missile installations, tanks, trucks, bridges, power stations, railroads, buildings, ships and caves.

The Paveway laser guidance and rear wing assemblies have been adapted successfully to US Mk 80 series warheads as well as to British Mk 13/18 and 540 lb stores. Standard electrical or electro-mechanical interface is used at the stores pylon, thus enabling any aircraft that can carry conventional bombs to carry the Paveway LGB without aircraft modifications. More than 145,000 Paveway weapons have been delivered for service with the armed forces of 17 countries.

Paveway III, a third generation of Paveway, is in limited production for the US Air Force. Nicknamed the 'low level laser guided bomb (LLLGB)', Paveway III is capable of very low altitude launches and long standoff ranges, and can operate effectively under low ceilings and in poor visibility conditions found frequently in Europe. A digital autopilot optimises the weapon trajectory automatically during mid-course flight, from either dive, level or loft deliveries. Proportional terminal guidance provides Paveway III with extreme accuracy, and terminal trajectory shaping impact angles to optimise weapon effects. Operational test and evaluation in March 1986 resulted in 44 hits in 47 launches.

Adapted to: F-4 Phantom II, F-111

USAF

UNITED STATES AIR FORCE

Aeronautical Systems Division, Wright-Patterson AFB, Ohio 45433

SRAM II

US Air Force designation: XAGM-131A

In February 1985, USAF Aeronautical Systems Division awarded contracts to Boeing Aerospace, Martin Marietta Aerospace and McDonnell Douglas Astronautics for the system definition phase of a new short range attack missile (known provisionally as SRAM II) to replace Boeing's AGM-69A SRAM which is deployed currently on US strategic bombers (see 1977-78 *Jane's*).

SRAM II will be an air-to-surface missile with nuclear capability, able to suppress defences along the flight path of its launch aircraft and to attack hardened primary targets. Propulsion will be by rocket motor, and special care will be taken to ensure a low radar signature. Like the AGM-69A it will be supersonic. Although smaller, its overall capability, including effectiveness against hardened targets, will be increased.

Following system definition, ASD will select one of the contractors during 1987 for full-scale development of SRAM II. Production is scheduled to begin in 1991, giving Strategic Air Command an initial operating capability with the weapon in 1992. Current plans envisage procurement of 1,900 SRAM IIs.

Will equip: B-1B, ATB

F-4 Phantom of 3rd TFS drops a GBU-15 TV guided glide bomb

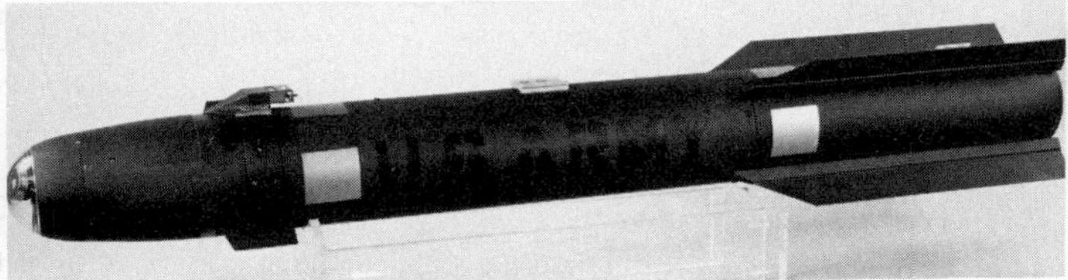

Laser Hellfire modular air-to-surface missile

AGM-88A HARM anti-radar missile on F/A-18 Hornet of US Navy

AGM-130A launch from an F-4 Phantom

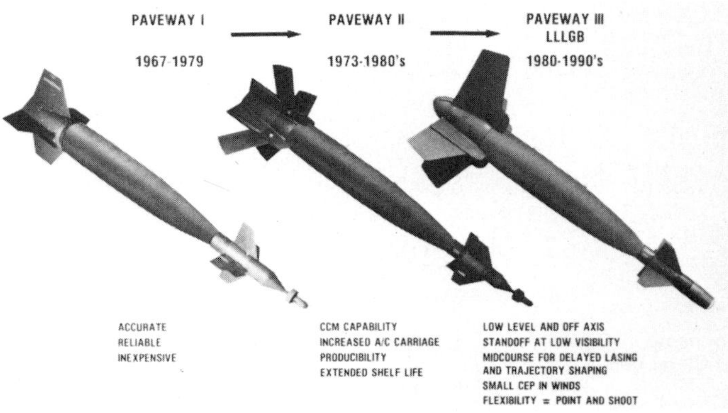

Paveway laser guided bombs

AIR-LAUNCHED MISSILES

Note: entries in italics are estimated

Country	Prime contractor	Model	Length m (ft in)	Body diam cm (in)	Wing span m (ft in)	Launch weight kg (lb)	Cruising speed knots (km/h; mph)	Range	Remarks
Argentina	CITEFA	Martin Pescador	2·94 (9 7¾)	21·85 (8·6)	0·73 (2 4¾)	140 (308)	Mach 2·3	1·3-4·25 nm (2·5-7·9 km; 1·5-4·9 miles)	Warhead 40 kg (88 lb)
Brazil		Piranha	2·72 (8 11)	15 (5·9)	NA	85·5 (188)	Mach 2+	5·4 nm (10 km; 6·2 miles)	Warhead 12 kg (26·5 lb)
China		CAA-1 (PL-2)	2·80 (9 2¼)	12 (4¾)	0·53 (1 9)	70 154	*Mach 2*	2·7-4·2 nm (5-7·8 km; 3·1-4·85 miles)	Min range 1,300 m (4,265 ft) Warhead 11·3 kg (25 lb)
		CAA-2	2·85 (9 4¼)	13 (5¼)	0·55 (1 9¾)	*85 (187)*	*Mach 2*	9·7 nm (18 km; 11·1 miles)	
		CAS-N-1 (C601)	7·38 (24 2½)	90 (35½)	2·40 (7 10½)	2,440 (5,380)	Mach 0·9 at 70-100 m (230-330 ft)	51-54 nm (95-100 km; 59-62 miles)	Warhead 500 kg (1,100 lb)
France	Aérospatiale	AS 15TT	2·30 (7 6½)	18·8 (7·4)	0·56 (1 10)	103 (227)	540 (1,000; 620)	more than 8 nm (15 km; 9·3 miles)	Warhead 30 kg (66 lb). Time of flight (propelled) 45·2 s
	Aérospatiale	AS 30 Laser	3·65 (11 11¾)	34·2 (13½)	1·00 (3 3¼)	520 (1,146)	Supersonic	1·6-5·4 nm (3-10 km; 1·8-6·2 miles)	Warhead 240 kg (529 lb). Time of flight 21 s
	Aérospatiale	ASMP	5·38 (17 8)	NA	0·956 (3 1¾)	*900 (1,985)*	*Mach 3*	*54 nm (100 km; 62 miles)*	Nuclear warhead
	Aérospatiale	Exocet AM39	4·69 (15 4½)	35 (13¾)	1·10 (3 7¼)	652 (1,438)	Mach 0·93	see text	Warhead 160 kg (352 lb)
	Matra	Armat	4·15 (13 7½)	NA	1·20 (3 11¼)	550 (1,213)	NA	8-54 nm (15-100 km; 9-62 miles)	Warhead 150 kg (330 lb)
	Matra	Super 530	3·54 (11 7¼)	26 (10¼)	0·64 (2 1¼)	250 (550)	Mach 3·5	*16-19 nm (30-35 km; 18·5-21·75 miles)*	Fin span 0·90 m (2 ft 11½ in). Operational ceiling above 21,350 m (70,000 ft). Warhead greater than 30 kg (66 lb)
	Matra	Super 530D	3·795 (12 5½)	NA	NA	265 (584)	Mach 4·5	over 22 nm (40 km; 25 miles)	Fin span 0·875 m (2 ft 10½ in). Operational ceiling 24,400 m (80,000 ft)
	Matra	R.550 Magic	2·75 (9 0¼)	16·4 (6½)	0·46 (1 6)	89 (196)	Mach 2+	3·75 nm (7 km; 4·35 miles)	Fin span 0·66 m (2 ft 2 in). Min range 500 m (1,640 ft)
	Matra	Mistral	1·80 (5 10⅞)	9 (3½)	—	17 (38)	Mach 2·6	over 3·2 nm (6 km; 3·7 miles)	Warhead 3 kg (6·6 lb).
Germany, Federal Rep	MBB	Kormoran 1	4·40 (14 5)	34 (13½)	1·00 (3 3¼)	600 (1,320)	*Mach 0·95*	*20 nm (37 km; 23 miles)*	
	MBB	Kormoran 2	4·40 (14 5)	34 (13½)	1·00 (3 3¼)	630 (1,389)	Mach 0·9	NA	Warhead 220 kg (485 lb)
International	Aérospatiale/ MBB	ANS	5·70 (18 8½)	35 (13¾)	NA	950 (2,095)	Mach 2 at S/L Mach 3 at height	approx 100 nm (185 km; 115 miles)	Warhead approx 180 kg (397 lb). Max flight time 4 min
	Euromissile	Hot	1·28 (4 2½)	14·4 (5¾)	*0·31 (1 0¼)	23·5 (51·8)	486 (900; 560)	400-4,000 m (1,310-13,125 ft)	Time of flight to 4,000 m (13,125 ft) 17 s. Warhead 6 kg (13·2 lb)
Israel	IAI	Gabriel III A/S ER	3·85 (12 7½)	34 (13½)	1·10 (3 7¼)	600 (1,322)	Mach 0·73	32 nm (60 km; 37 miles)	Warhead approx 150 kg (330 lb)
	Rafael	Python 3	3·00 (9 10)	16 (6¼)	0·86 (2 9¾)	120 (265)	NA	0·25-8 nm (0·5-15 km; 0·3-9·3 miles)	Warhead 11 kg (24·25 lb)
Italy	Oto Melara	Marte Mk 2	4·48 (14 8½)	31·6 (12·4)	0·98 (3 2½)	330 (727)	High subsonic	over 13·5 nm (25 km; 15·5 miles)	Warhead 70 kg (154 lb)
	Selenia	Aspide	3·70 (12 1½)	20·3 (8)	1·00 (3 3¼)	220 (485)	Mach 2 + speed of launch platform	19-32 nm (35-60 km; 22-37 miles)	Warhead 33 kg (73 lb). Data for air-to-air version
Japan	Mitsubishi	ASM-1	4·00 (13 1½)	35 (13¾)	1·20 (3 11¼)	610 (1,345)	Mach 0·9	*27 nm (50 km; 31 miles)*	
Norway	Kongsberg	Penguin Mk 2	3·05 (10 0)	28 (11)	1·40 (4 7)	330 (727)	Mach 0·8	15 nm (27 km; 17 miles)	
		Penguin Mk 3	3·18 (10 5¼)	28 (11)	1·00 (3 3¼)	372 (820)	Mach 0·8+	over 22 nm (40 km; 25 miles)	Warhead 120 kg (265 lb)
South Africa	Armscor	V3B/Kukri	2·94 (9 7¾)	12·7 (5)	0·56 (1 10)	73·4 (162)	500 (925; 575) + speed of launch platform	0·16-2·15 nm (0·3-4 km; 0·19-2·5 miles)	Warhead 90% effective at 9 m (30 ft)
Sweden	Bofors	RBS 70	1·32 (4 4)	12 (4¾)	0·33 (1 1)	15 (33)	Supersonic	2·7 nm (5 km; 3·1 miles)	
	Saab	RBS 15	4·35 (14 3¼)	50 (19¾)	1·40 (4 7¼)	598 (1,320)	High subsonic	over 38 nm (70 km; 43 miles)	
USSR		AA-2 'Atoll' (K-13A)	2·80 (9 2)	12·0 (4¾)	0·45 (1 5¾)	70 (154)	Mach 2·5	2·5-3·5 nm (5-6·5 km; 3-4 miles)	Fin span 0·53 m (1 ft 8¾ in); 6 kg (13·2 lb) fragmentation warhead
		AA-3 'Anab'	*4·10 (13 5)*	*28·0 (11)*	*1·30 (4 3)*	NA	NA	over 8·75 nm (16 km; 10 miles)	Length for IR version; radar version is *4·0 m (13 ft 1 in)* long
		AA-5 'Ash'	*5·30 (17 4½)*	*30 (12)*	*1·30 (4 3)*	NA	NA	16 nm (30 km; 18·5 miles)	Length for IR version; radar version is *5·2 m (17 ft 0 in)* long
		AA-6 'Acrid'	*6·29 (20 7½)*	NA	NA	*750 (1,650)*	*Mach 2·2*	*at least 20 nm (37 km; 23 miles)*	Length for radar version; IR version is *5·8 m (19 ft)* long. Warhead *100 kg (220 lb)*
		AA-7 'Apex' (R-23R)	*4·60 (15 1¼)*	*22·0 (8¾)*	*1·05 (3 5½)*	*320 (705)*	NA	*18 nm (33 km; 20 miles)*	Warhead *40 kg (88 lb)*
		AA-8 'Aphid' (R-60)	*2·20 (7 2½)*	*12·0 (4¾)*	*0·40 (1 3¾)*	*55 (121)*	NA	*2·7-3·8 nm (5-7 km; 3-4·3 miles)*	Warhead *6 kg (13·2 lb)*
		AT-2 'Swatter'	1·16 (3 9¾)	13·2 (5¼)	0·66 (2 2)	29·4 (65)	290 (540; 335)	500-3,500 m (1,640-11,500 ft)	
		AT-3 'Sagger'	0·86 (2 10)	*12·0 (5)*	0·46 (1 6)	11·3 (24·9)	230 (430; 265)	500-3,000 m (1,640-9,840 ft)	
		SA-7 'Grail'	1·29 (4 2¾)	NA	NA	9·2 (20·3)	Mach 1·5	2 nm (3·6 km; 2·25 miles)	Warhead 2·5 kg (5·5 lb)

Note: entries in italics are estimated

Country	Prime contractor	Model	Length m (ft in)	Body diam cm (in)	Wing span m (ft in)	Launch weight kg (lb)	Cruising speed knots (km/h; mph)	Range	Remarks
USSR		AS-3 'Kangaroo'	*14·96 (49 1)*	*185 (72·8)*	9·00 (29 6)	*8,000 (17,600)*	Supersonic	350 nm (650 km; 400 miles)	*Nuclear or HE warhead*
		AS-4 'Kitchen'	*11·30 (37 0)*	*90 (35·4)*	*3·00 (9 10)*	*6,000+ (13,225)*	*Mach 2+*	*160 nm (300 km; 185 miles)*	Range at low altitude. *Nuclear or HE warhead*
		AS-5 'Kelt'	*8·59 (28 2)*	*100 (39·5)*	*4·30 (14 1¼)*	*3,500 (7,715)*	*Mach 0·9 at low altitude; Mach 1·2 at 9,150 m (30,000 ft)*	*over 85 nm (160 km; 100 miles)*	Range at low altitude; doubled at height. *HE warhead: 1,000 kg (2,200 lb)*
		AS-6 'Kingfish'	*10·50 (34 6)*	NA	*2·50 (8 2½)*	*5,000 (11,000)*	*Mach 3*	*120 nm (220 km; 135 miles)*	Range at low altitude. *Nuclear or HE warhead*
		AS-7 'Kerry'	*3·50 (11 6)*	30·5 *(12)*	NA	*under 400 kg (880 lb)*	*Transonic*	*6 nm (11 km; 7 miles)*	*HE warhead: 100 kg (220 lb)*
		AS-X-9	*6·00 (19 9½)*	*50 (19·5)*	NA	NA	*Mach 0·8*	*48 nm* (88 km; 55 miles)	Anti-radiation homing missile
		AS-10 'Karen'	*3·50 (11 6)*	*30·5 (12)*	NA	NA	*Transonic*	*5·2 nm (9·6 km; 6 miles)*	
		AS-15 'Kent'	*7·00 (23 0)*	NA	*3·25 (10 8)*	NA	NA	1,620 nm (3,000 km; 1,850 miles)	Nuclear warhead
UK	British Aerospace	Sea Eagle	4·14 (13 7)	40 (15¾)	1·20 (3 11¼)	*600 (1,325)*	Mach 0·85	more than 60 nm (110 km; 68 miles)	Warhead weight more than 230 kg (507 lb)
	British Aerospace	Sea Skua	2·50 (8 2½)	25 (9¾)	0·72 (2 4½)	*147 (325)*	High subsonic	over 8 nm (15 km; 9·3 miles)	*Warhead 20 kg (44 lb)*
	British Aerospace	Sky Flash	3·66 (12 0)	20·3 (8)	1·02 (3 4¼)	193 (425)	Mach 4	27 nm (50 km; 31 miles)	
USA	Boeing Aerospace	AGM-86B ALCM	6·32 (20 9)	62 (24½)	3·66 (12 0)	1,450 (3,200)	approx 435 (805; 500)	approx 1,350 nm (2,500 km; 1,550 miles)	Height overall 1·19 m (3 ft 11 in)
	General Dynamics	FIM-92A Stinger	1·52 (5 0)	*7 (2·75)*	0·09 (3 5)	13·5 (30)	Mach 2+	3 nm (5·5 km; (3·5 miles)	Fragmentation warhead 3 kg (6·5 lb)
	Hughes	AIM-54C Phoenix	3·95 (13 0)	38 (15)	0·91 (3 0)	458 (1,008)	Mach 4+	over 108 nm (200 km; 124 miles)	Warhead 60 kg (133 lb)
	Hughes/ Raytheon	AIM-120A AMRAAM	3·58 (11 9)	17·8 (7)	0·635 (2 1)	152 (335)	*Mach 4*	NA	Span is for tail control fins
	Hughes	BGM-71A TOW	1·174 (3 10¼)	14·85 (5·85)	0·34 (1 1½)	18·9 (41·7)	High subsonic	400-3,000 m (1,315-9,840 ft)	Warhead 2·63 kg (5·8 lb).
		BGM-71C ITOW	1·174 (3 10¼)	14·85 (5 85)	0·34 (1 1½)	19·1 (42·1)	High subsonic	400-3,750 m (1,315-12,300 ft)	Warhead as for TOW
		BGM-71D TOW 2	1·177 (3 10⅜)	14·85 (5·85)	0·34 (1 1½)	21·5 (47·4)	High subsonic	400-3,750 m (1,315-12,300 ft)	Warhead 3·63 kg (8·0 lb).
	Hughes	AGM-65A/B Maverick	2·49 (8 2)	30·5 (12)	0·72 (2 4½)	210 (462)	NA	0·5-12 nm (1-22 km; 0·6-14 miles)	AGM-65D weight 220 kg (485 lb); AGM-65E/F 293/ 307 kg (646/677 lb) with heavy warhead
	LTV/Vought	ASAT	5·43 (17 9½)	*50 (20)*	NA	*1,180 (2,600)*	NA		
	MDAC	AGM-84A Harpoon	3·90 (12 7½)	34·3 (13½)	0·91 (3 0)	519 (1,145)	High subsonic	over 50 nm (92 km; 57 miles)	Warhead 221·5 kg (488·5 lb)
	Ford Aerospace	AIM-9J/N/P Sidewinder	3·05 (10 0)	13 (5)	*0·56 (1 10)	81 (178)	Mach 2+	over 8·7 nm (16 km; 10 miles)	Warhead 11·4 kg (25 lb)
	NWC/ Raytheon/ Ford Aerospace	AIM-9L/M Sidewinder	2·87 (9 5)	13 (5)	*0·635 (2 1)	86·6 (191)	Mach 2+	over 8·7 nm (16 km; 10 miles)	Warhead 9·4 kg (20·8 lb)
	Raytheon	AIM-7F Sparrow	3·60 (11 10)	20 (8)	1·02 (3 4)	229 (504)	NA	NA	Warhead 39 kg (86 lb)
	Rockwell	GBU-15(V)/B	3·92 (12 10½)	45·7 (18)	1·50 (4 11)	1,187 (2,617)	Subsonic	—	Warhead 907 kg (2,000 lb)
	Rockwell	AGM-114A Hellfire	1·625 (5 4)	17·8 (7)	0·33 (1 1)	45·7 (101)	NA	NA	Data for laser version
	Texas Instruments	AGM-88A HARM	4·18 (13 8½)	25·4 (10)	1·13 (3 8½)	366 (807)	Supersonic	over 8·5 nm (16 km; 10 miles)	Altitude limits S/L to 12,200 m (40,000 ft)
	Texas Instruments	Paveway LGBs: GBU-10 C/B-F/B	4·32 (14 2)	45·7 (18)	1·68 (5 6)	944 (2,081)	Subsonic	—	Span with wings deployed. Mk 84 warhead (2,000 lb)
		GBU-12 B/B-E/B	3·33 (10 11)	27·4 (10·8)	1·32 (4 4)	277 (611)	Subsonic	—	Span with wings deployed. Mk 82 warhead (500 lb)
		GBU-16 A/B-B/B	3·68 (12 1)	35·6 (14)	1·63 (5 4)	499 (1,100)	Subsonic	—	Span with wings deployed. Mk 83 warhead (1,000 lb)
		GBU-22/B	3·51 (11 6)	27·4 (10·8)	1·40 (4 7)	326 (718)	Subsonic	—	Span with wings deployed. Mk 82 warhead (500 lb)
		GBU-24/B	4·40 (14 5)	45·7 (18)	2·03 (6 8)	1,037 (2,287)	Subsonic	—	Span with wings deployed. Mk 84 warhead (2,000 lb)

*Fin span NA: not available

AERO ENGINES

This section includes all available details of engines of manned aircraft, including microlights, as well as many engines used in air-launched missiles, manned spacecraft, RPVs and targets. Rocket engines and other propulsion systems used purely for surface-launched missiles and unmanned spaceflight are no longer included. Readers are referred for these subjects to *Jane's Weapon Systems* and *Jane's Spaceflight Directory* respectively.

AUSTRALIA

CAC

COMMONWEALTH AIRCRAFT CORPORATION LIMITED

Box 779H, GPO Melbourne, Victoria 3001
Telephone: (03) 647 6111
OFFICERS: See HDH entry in Aircraft section

Now a subsidiary of Hawker de Havilland Ltd, CAC has built more than 2,500 engines since 1936. These included the Rolls-Royce Viper and SNECMA Atar 9C turbojets, which CAC supports in service with the RAAF. Participation in the RAAF F/A-18A programme includes assembly and test of the General Electric F404-400 turbofan and manufacture of fan rotor and stator blades, HP and LP turbine rotor blades, fan case, mount ring, internal ducting, static and rotating seals, power offtake gear and shaft drive, nozzle flaps and fuel manifolds.

CAC also makes components for the GE CF6 and the CFM56, Sikorsky and Aérospatiale transmission parts and cast aluminium cylinder heads.

AUSTRIA

ROTAX

BOMBARDIER-ROTAX GmbH

Postfach 5, A-4623 Gunskirchen
Telephone: (07246) 271-0
Telex: 25 546 bomrot a

This company is one of the world's largest producers of light piston engines. Those listed for light aircraft, microlights and gliders are all aircooled two-strokes using a 1:50 mix of oil with petrol (gasoline) of not below MON 83 or RON 90 grade. Customers have many options, including rewind manual or electric starter. Rotax has agents throughout the world, that for the UK being Andover Norton Ltd, West Portway, Andover, Hants SP10 3LF (*Tel:* 0264 61411).

Rotax 447 with rewind starter (29·4 kW; 39·4 hp)

ROTAX LIGHT AIRCRAFT ENGINES

Engine Model	277	377	447	503	503·2V	462	532
Layout	1 cylinder Piston port	2 cylinder Piston port	2 cylinder Piston port	2 cylinder Piston port	2 cylinder Piston port	2 cylinder Rotary valve	2 cylinder Rotary valve
Bore/stroke mm (in)	72·0/66·0 (2·83/2·60)	62·0/61·0 (2·44/2·40)	67·5/61·0 (2·66/2·40)	72·0/61·0 (2·83/2·40)	72·0/61·0 (2·83/2·40)	69·5/61·0 (2·74/2·40)	72·0/64·0 (2·83/2·52)
Capacity cc (cu in)	268·7 (16·397)	368·3 (22·475)	436·5 (26·637)	496·7 (30·310)	496·7 (30·310)	462·8 (28·242)	521·1 (31·799)
Weight, Dry (1) kg (lb)	19·0 (41·9)	27·5 (60·6)	27·5 (60·6)	30·2 (66·6)	30·2 (66·6)	27·0 (59·5)	28·0 (61·7)
Weight, Dry (2) kg (lb)	24·0 (52·9)	32·5 (71·6)	32·5 (71·6)	36·2 (79·8)	36·2 (79·8)	32·0 (70·5)	33·0 (72·8)
Rating (3) kW (hp)	19 (25·5) 6,500 rpm	26 (34·9) 6,500 rpm	29·4 (39·4) 6,500 rpm	34 (45·6) 6,500 rpm	38 (51·0) 6,500 rpm	38 (51·0) 6,500 rpm	47 (63·0) 6,500 rpm
Rating (4) kW (hp)	14 (18·8)	19 (25·5)	25·7 (34·5)	26·5 (35·5)	—	28 (37·5)	—

Notes: 1, Bare, unequipped; 2, with carburettor (503·2V, twin carburettors), intake silencer and exhaust system; 3, standard bare engine; 4, installed engine with intake silencer and exhaust muffler.

WESTERMAYER

OSKAR WESTERMAYER

Hauptstrasse 11, A-2161 Poysbrunn
Telephone: (02554) 405
Telex: 73379

This engineer has developed a piston engine with air-cooled barrels but liquid-cooled heads. He claims that, compared with the Continental O-200 which was the basis for the engine, fuel consumption is reduced by 25 per cent. Compression ratio is raised to 8·6.

WESTERMAYER W 5/33

This flat-four engine has cylinder heads of cast aluminium alloy, cooled by pure ethylene glycol. The coolant pump feeds via a separate pipe to each head, and the return line passes through an air radiator. Running on 100, 100LL or Mogas fuel, a total of 922 flight hours was recorded in 1985 on seven engines installed in Westermayer WE 04 autogyros (see 1981-82 *Jane's*) and a Cessna 150, plus 626 hours on the bench. Certification to FAR 33 was to be completed in Spring 1986.

The 74·6 kW (100 hp) Westermayer W 5/33

Westermayer W 5/33 engine installation in Cessna 150

DIMENSIONS:
- Length: 730 mm (28·7 in)
- Width: 790 mm (31·1 in)
- Height: carburettor: 625 mm (24·6 in)
- airbox: 700 mm (27·6 in)

WEIGHT, DRY:
- Bare: 85 kg (187 lb)
- With starter, alternator and silencer: 102 kg (225 lb)

PERFORMANCE RATING:
- T-O: 74·6 kW (100 hp) at 2,750 rpm

FUEL CONSUMPTION:
- T-O: 25·5 litres (5·6 Imp gallons)/h

SPECIFIC FUEL CONSUMPTION:
- T-O: 71 μg/J (0·42 lb/h/hp)

BELGIUM

FN

FABRIQUE NATIONALE HERSTAL SA

Voie de Liège 33, B-4400 Herstal
CHAIRMAN: M. Goblet
PRESIDENT: M. Vandestrick
Telephone: 041 640800

FN Moteurs
ENGINE DIVISION: Route de Liers 121, B-4411 Milmort (Herstal)
Telephone: 041 784671
Telex: B 42075 monat
VICE-PRESIDENT AND DIVISION MANAGER: R. Boulanger

With long experience of work on aircraft piston engines, FN entered jet engine production in 1949. After producing more than 1,000 Derwent and 635 Avon engines under Rolls-Royce licence for Meteor and Hunter aircraft, FN assumed a major share in the consortium manufacturing the GE J79 for the Starfighters of Germany, Holland, Italy and Belgium. In co-operation with SNECMA, FN built Atar 9C engines for Belgium's Mirage 5s, and assembled and tested the Larzac for Belgium's Alpha Jets. FN is a member of the consortium (RR, MTU, SNECMA, FN) building the Tyne engine for the Atlantic and the Transall.

Its current major activity is related to the Pratt & Whitney F100 engine for the F-16. FN is the major co-producer of the European consortium, with responsibility for producing the fan and core engine modules and for engine assembly and test. F100 deliveries started in late 1978 and exceeded 420 engines by 1984. Although production rates are tapering off, further co-production, spares manufacture, repair and overhaul will carry F100 activities into the late 'eighties.

FN Moteurs has signed a co-operation agreement with Turboméca for the development and production of critical parts of the TM333.

In the commercial engine field, FN has been a supplier to several major engine manufacturers and currently produces a selection of parts for the Pratt & Whitney JT9D in the latest -7R4 version. FN has entered into a further partnership for a 3 per cent share in the PW4000 series from 1987.

FN has been associated with SNECMA on the CFM56 engine family since the beginning of development. The lubrication modules for both the CFM56-2 and CFM56-3 were developed by FN and are in production. FN Moteurs has increased its participation up to 10 per cent of the SNECMA share (5 per cent overall) in future versions, starting with the CFM56-5, including endurance testing of complete engines.

From the beginning, FN has maintained, repaired and overhauled Belgian operated engines and their accessories. Current maintenance activity is related to Marboré, Atar and F100 engines.

SECA

SOCIÉTÉ D'ENTREPRISES COMMERCIALES ET AÉRONAUTIQUES SA

Box 68, 28d rue Fossé-aux-Loups, 1000 Brussels
Telephone: 02 217 0677

The engineering company SECA announced in April 1984 that it was "reaching the final stage of development" with the GK two-stroke diesel engine, planned for many applications including aircraft propulsion. Under development since 1977, it uses the swashplate principle, with axial cylinders whose compression ratio can be varied from about 22 for starting down to about 14 during cruise. In the 3,000 cc (183 cu in) size the GK engine's light alloy cylinder block with steel sleeves weighs a claimed 19 kg (42 lb), compared with about 100 kg (220 lb) for conventional diesels. The engine is claimed to have no low-speed diesel rattle and extremely low vibration, and to offer doubled aircraft range "without a weight penalty".

The prototype SECA GK lightweight diesel engine

BRAZIL

CELMA

CELMA-CIA ELECTROMECANICA

Rue Alice Hervê 356, PO Box 90341, 25600 Petropolis, RJ
Telephone: (0242) 43 4962
PRESIDENT: Edivio Caldas Sanctos
TECHNICAL DIRECTOR: Carlos A. R. Pereira

This company of 1,400 people has facilities totalling 35,000 m² (376,736 sq ft) in which it overhauls many kinds of jet engine and accessories. It now shares in the production of components for the Rolls-Royce Spey 807 turbofan which powers the AMX attack aircraft produced jointly by Italy and Brazil.

RETIMOTOR

RETIMOTOR ENGENHARIA LTDA

Rua Scipião 98, CEP 05047 Lapa, São Paulo
Telephone: (011) 262 2192

This company produces engines for light aircraft. One objective is to replace imported engines.

RETIMOTOR RM-2000

This aircooled piston engine is a four-cylinder opposed type based on the VW car engine but with a special crankshaft. The RM-2000-A began flight development in a Paulistinha 56 in June 1983. The RM-2000-Z has been certificated by the Brazilian CTA under JAR 22 rules and is in production for autogyros. Retimotor is well advanced with a test programme to clear the RM-2000 to use alcohol from sugar cane, with 8-10 per cent increase in power.

WEIGHT, DRY: 80 kg (176 lb)
PERFORMANCE RATING (T-O): 59·7 kW (80 hp)

RETIMOTOR RM-1000-A

This flat twin is essentially half an RM-2000-A, although it has a new crankshaft, crankcase and cylinder head. Several examples are flying in microlight aircraft.

WEIGHT, DRY: 40 kg (88·2 lb)
PERFORMANCE RATING (T-O): 28-35 kW (38-47 hp)

CANADA

ORENDA

HAWKER SIDDELEY CANADA INC (Orenda Division)

PO Box 6001, Toronto AMF, Ontario L5P 1B3
Telephone: (416) 677 3250
Telex: 06-968727
VICE-PRESIDENT: P. K. Peterson
GENERAL MANAGER: R. J. Munro

Orenda has a 67,262 m² (724,000 sq ft) facility close to Toronto International Airport. It meets the manufacturing, repair, overhaul and technical support needs of the Canadian Forces for General Electric J79, J85 and F404 engines, and performs subcontract manufacture of parts for aero engines currently in production, and for future developments. Orenda also supplies parts to Belgium, Canada, West Germany, Italy, Netherlands, Norway, the USA and Venezuela.

P&WC

PRATT & WHITNEY CANADA (Subsidiary of United Technologies Corporation)

PO Box 10, Longueuil, Quebec J4K 4X9
Telephone: (514) 677 9411
CHAIRMAN: Elvie L. Smith
PRESIDENT AND CHIEF EXECUTIVE OFFICER: L. D. Caplan
VICE-PRESIDENTS:
R. C. Abraham (Production)
J. P. Beauregard (Materials & Procurement)
J. N. Clark (Marketing Administration & Support)
R. P. Dilda (Marketing & Product Support)
J. B. Haworth (Industrial & Marine)
P. Henry (Communications)
R. J. Losch (Product Support)
R. H. McLachlan (Marketing)
G. P. Ouimet (Operations)
C. J. C. Pascoe (Counsel)
W. M. Steath (Quality Assurance)
R. F. Steers (Finance)
C. B. Wrong (Engineering)

Pratt & Whitney Canada is a major subsidiary of United Technologies Corporation, Connecticut, USA, and is the UTC company responsible for engines for general aviation and regional airlines.

Original turbine work by the company was initiated in 1957 by the concept and preliminary design of the JT12 (J60) turbojet, development and manufacture of which were completed subsequently in the USA by Pratt & Whitney. Design, development and manufacture of the PT6, ST6, PT6T, JT15D, PW100 and PW200 series of small turbine aero engines represents more than 70 per cent of the company's activities.

P&WC is owned 97% by United Technologies Corporation. It occupies more than 185,800 m² (2·0 million sq ft) of space and employs 8,000 persons.

In 1985 a total of 1,093 new engines was delivered. By 1 January 1986 P&WC had delivered 28,293 engines.

P&WC JT15D

Following a comprehensive performance study of small turbofan engines carried out by P&WC during 1965, detail design of a definitive engine, the 8·9-11·12 kN (2,000 lb to 2,500 lb st) JT15D was initiated in June 1966. First run of the new turbofan was on 23 September 1967.

Designed to power business aircraft, small transports and training aircraft in the 8,000 lb to 12,500 lb AUW category, the JT15D is an advanced technology two-spool front fan engine having a minimum number of aerodynamic components. Major design features include a significant improvement in sfc, and simplicity of construction to ensure low first cost and maintenance costs. Other advantages are low noise levels, ease of handling, and the attainment of airline standards of reliability.

Initial application for the JT15D was the twin-engined Cessna Citation. Flightworthy prototype engines were delivered in August 1969 for the Citation's first flight in mid-September. Up to 1976 Cessna produced the Citation powered by the **JT15D-1**. Late that year it announced the Citation I powered by the improved performance **JT15D-1A** and the Citation II powered by the **JT15D-4**. During 1983 the D-1A was replaced by the improved **D-1B**, which was certificated in July 1982. More than 1,471 JT15D-1, -1A and -1B and 1,246 JT15D-4 engines had been delivered for these aircraft by January 1986.

Other twin-engined business jets powered by the JT15D-4 are the Aérospatiale Corvette and Mitsubishi Diamond I, for which 265 engines had been delivered by January 1984. TBO is 3,500 h for the JT15D-1/D-1A, and 3,000 h for the JT15D-4. By December 1985 the total operating time was 7,691,278 h.

The **JT15D-4B** is an altitude optimised variant of the D-4. Certificated in 1983, it powers the Citation S/II.

The **JT15D-4C** is derived from the basic D-4 model. Major differences include the incorporation of an aerobatic oil system for sustained inverted flight, and a full throttle electronic supervision fuel control unit. Selected for SIAI-Marchetti S.211. Certificated September 1982.

The **JT15D-4D** is flat rated for improved hot/high performance. Certificated in December 1983, it powers the Mitsubishi Diamond IA.

The **JT15D-5** is a growth version of the JT15D-4. A new fan with higher pressure ratio and flow, plus an improved boost stage and HP compressor, are combined to produce 25 per cent more altitude cruise thrust, with a 3 per cent improvement in specific fuel consumption. HP turbine blades and electronic fuel control are also improved. JT15D-5 development began in 1977, and first flight was in April 1978. This engine was certificated in 1983 and powers the US Navy's Cessna T-47A and Mitsubishi Diamond II.

The following description relates to the JT15D-1B:

TYPE: Two-shaft turbofan.

AIR INTAKE: Direct pitot intake without inlet guide vanes. Hot air anti-icing for nose bullet.

FAN: Single-stage axial fan, aerodynamically related to that of the JT9D but on a much smaller scale. Forged disc fitted with 28 solid titanium blades secured by dovetail fixings riveted to disc. Blades have part-span shrouds. Casing, which forms the engine air intake, of forged stainless steel. Circular splitter ring behind fan, held between two rows of 33 inner wrapped sheet stators and single row of 66 outer stator blades. Total air mass flow, 34 kg (75 lb)/s; bypass ratio about 3·3:1; bypass flow typically 26 kg (57·5 lb)/s; primary core air flow 8 kg (17·5 lb)/s; fan pressure ratio 1·5:1.

COMPRESSOR: Primary airflow enters eye of single stage titanium centrifugal compressor. Single sided impeller, with 16 full vanes and 16 splitter vanes, secured to shaft by special bolt and key-washer. Two-piece casing with diffuser in form of pipes containing straightening vanes. Overall pressure ratio almost 10:1. (JT15D-4 compressor airflow augmented by axial boost stage between fan and compressor.)

COMBUSTION CHAMBER: Annular reverse flow type. Outer casing of heat resistant steel; flame tube of nickel alloy, supported on low pressure turbine stator assembly. Spark igniters at 5 and 7 o'clock (viewed from rear).

FUEL SYSTEM: Engine driven sandwich mounted pump delivering through FCU, flow divider and dual manifolds at 44·8 bars (650 lb/sq in); DP-L2 pneumatic control unit on pump, with dual metering valve.

FUEL GRADES: JP-1, JP-4, JP-5 to CPW 204.

NOZZLE GUIDE VANES: High pressure ring of 15, aircooled, integrally cast in cobalt alloy.

TURBINE: Single-stage HP with 71 solid blades held in fir tree roots. Two-stage LP with nickel alloy discs, first stage being cast integrally with 61 blades and second stage carrying 55 blades in fir tree roots. LP fan shaft drives fan, with ball thrust bearing behind fan and roller gear and intershaft bearings; HP shaft drives centrifugal compressor, with front ball thrust bearing and rear roller bearing. Gas temperature 960°C before turbine, 562°C after turbine.

JETPIPE: Nickel alloy cone and sheet metal pipe. Provision made for adjusting the area to match engines and to trim performance.

ACCESSORY DRIVES: Package under front of engine driven by power offtake from front of HP shaft.

LUBRICATION SYSTEM: Integral oil system, with gear type pump delivering at up to 5·52 bars (80 lb/sq in). Capacity, 9·0 litres (2·4 US gallons; 2·0 Imp gallons).

OIL SPECIFICATION: PWA521 Type II, CPW 202.

MOUNTING: Hard or soft, according to customers' choice. Four main pads on front casing, arranged two on each side at 30° above and below horizontal. One rear mount at top or on either side of centreline.

STARTING: Air turbine starter or electric starter/generator.

DIMENSIONS:

Diameter: JT15D-1	691 mm (27·2 in)
JT15D-4	686 mm (27·0 in)
Length overall: JT15D-1	1,506 mm (59·3 in)
JT15D-4	1,600 mm (63·0 in)

WEIGHT, DRY:

JT15D-1, -1A	232·5 kg (514 lb)
JT15D-1B	235 kg (519 lb)
JT15D-4	253 kg (557 lb)
JT15D-4B	258 kg (568 lb)
JT15D-4C	261 kg (575 lb)
JT15D-4D	255 kg (560 lb)
JT15D-5	291·5 kg (642 lb)

PERFORMANCE RATINGS:

T-O: JT15D-1, -1A, -1B	9·8 kN (2,200 lb st)
JT15D-4, -4B, -4C, -4D	11·12 kN (2,500 lb st)
JT15D-5	12·89 kN (2,900 lb st)
Max continuous:	
JT15D-1, -1A, -1B	9·3 kN (2,090 lb st)
JT15D-4, -4B, -4D	10·56 kN (2,375 lb st)
JT15D-4C	9·45 kN (2,125 lb st)
JT15D-5	12·89 kN (2,900 lb st)

SPECIFIC FUEL CONSUMPTION (T-O):

JT15D-1, -1A, -1B	15·30 mg/Ns (0·540 lb/h/lb st)
JT15D-4, -4C, -5	15·92 mg/Ns (0·562 lb/h/lb st)

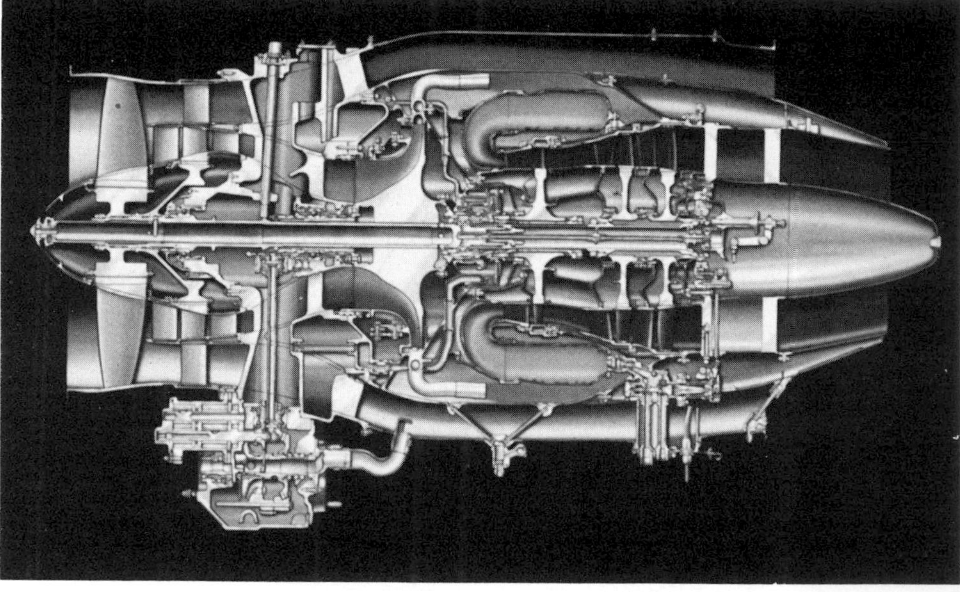

Longitudinal section of the P&WC JT15D-5 turbofan (12·89 kN; 2,900 lb st)

P&WC PW300

Price sensitivity, previously a major factor in the design of the PW200 helicopter engines, is judged to be a future factor in business jet engines, and has dictated the simple approach followed in the PW300 family. Planned for corporate aircraft of the 1990s, this engine is aimed at US coast-to-coast flights at Mach 0·75 at 14,325 m (47,000 ft). MTU of West Germany will be responsible for the LP turbine section, as a partner sharing 25 per cent of the estimated development cost of $Can 500 million.

Component testing at P&WC's Toronto facility began in 1986, but gas generator tests were due at the main Montreal plant, followed by a complete PW300/1 engine test in 1987. Certification is due in 1989. The PW300/3 is a planned uprated growth version.

TYPE: Two-shaft turbofan.

FAN: Single-stage with Kevlar blades, overhung ahead of front bearing. Pointed rotating spinner. Bypass ratio 4·5.

COMPRESSOR: Four axial stages followed by one centrifugal. Core pressure ratio 15.

COMBUSTION CHAMBER: Annular, fed around periphery by ring of separate curved pipes ducting air from diffuser case of centrifugal compressor.

CONTROL SYSTEM: Hamilton Standard full-authority digital, with dual channels.

HP TURBINE: Two axial stages, the first having aircooled blades.

LP TURBINE: Three axial stages joined via centre stage disc to fan shaft. Two main shaft bearings.

DIMENSIONS (estimated):

Diameter	890 mm (35·0 in)
Length	1,650 mm (65·0 in)

WEIGHT, DRY (estimated): 400 kg (880 lb)

PERFORMANCE RATINGS (ISA, estimated):

T-O, S/L: 23·29 kN (5,236 lb st) or flat rated at 21·13 kN (4,750 lb st) to 25°C

Cruise Mach 0·8 at 12,200 m (40,000 ft): 4·95 kN (1,113 lb)

SPECIFIC FUEL CONSUMPTION (estimate):

T-O as above	11·50 mg/Ns (0·406 lb/h/lb st)
Cruise as above	19·12 mg/s (0·675 lb/h/lb)

P&WC PW100

The PW100 is a free turbine turboprop consisting of turbomachine and reduction gearbox modules connected by a torque-measuring driveshaft and integrated structural intake case. The turbomachine is a three-concentric-shaft design incorporating two centrifugal compressors, each driven separately by single-stage turbines, and a two-stage power turbine. The reduction gearbox features a twin-layshaft design with anti-friction bearings and an offset propeller shaft. The combustion system comprises an annular reverse-flow combustor, 14 piloted air blast fuel nozzles and two igniters.

Additional features include a combined hydromechanical and electronic power control system, single oil system designed to prevent cross contamination, provision for motive fuel flow, electric torque signal, concentric exhaust, and automatic power augmentation.

Flight development of the PW100 began in February 1982. Principal versions are as follows:

PW115. T-O rated at 1,256 ekW; 1,193 kW (1,685 ehp; 1,600 shp) at 1,300 propeller rpm to 37·8°C. Selected for EMBRAER EMB-120 Brasilia. Certificated December 1983.

PW120. T-O (reserve) rated at 1,411 ekW (1,892 ehp); 1,566 ekW; 1,491 kW (2,100 ehp; 2,000 shp) at 1,200 propeller rpm to 27·7°C. Selected for de Havilland Canada Dash 8-100 and Aérospatiale/Aeritalia ATR 42. Certificated December 1983.

PW124. Growth version, with T-O (reserve) rating of 1,694 ekW (2,272 ehp); 1,880 ekW; 1,790 kW (2,522 ehp; 2,400 shp) to 34·4°C. Powers BAe ATP and Fokker 50.

PW137. Selected for Dash 8-300 (1,790 kW; 2,400 shp).

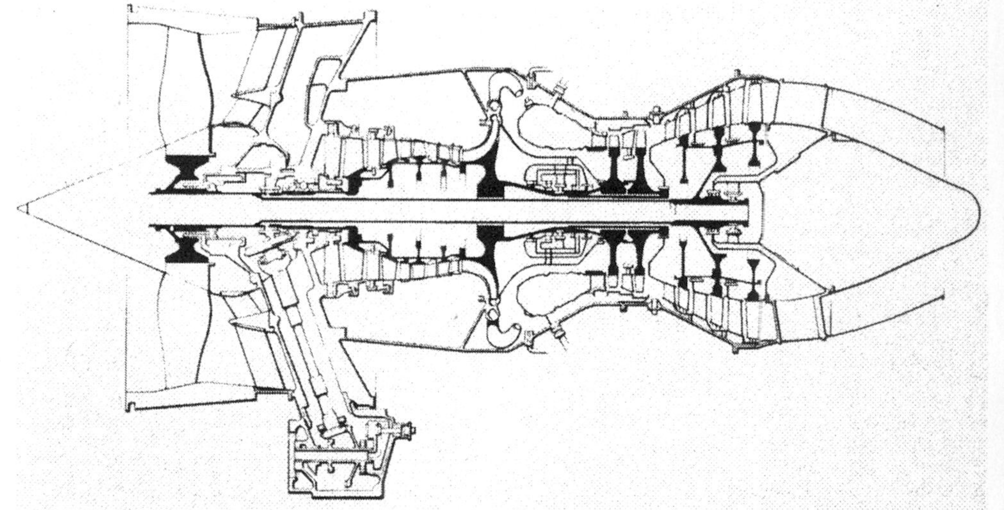

Section through the P&WC PW300/1 turbofan

The following description applies to all PW100 series engines:

TYPE: Free turbine turboprop.

PROPELLER DRIVE: Reduction gearbox consists of a twin-layshaft design, with the propeller shaft centreline offset above that of the turbomachine. Max propeller speeds are 1,300 rpm (PW115) and 1,200 rpm (PW120).

AIR INTAKE: Air enters via a pitot inlet lip and S-bend duct. A secondary duct forms a flowing bypass to prevent foreign object ingestion.

COMPRESSOR: Two-spool assembly of two centrifugal impellers in series, each mounted on its own shaft and driven by its own turbine. Air guided through ring of curved pipes from LP diffuser to HP entry.

COMBUSTION CHAMBER: Annular reverse flow type, as used in PT6 and JT15D engines, with 14 air blast fuel nozzles around periphery. Ignition by two spark igniters which can be powered from airframe DC supply.

FUEL SYSTEM: Hydromechanical unit provides essential fuel control functions; electronic unit provides power management functions. Primary and secondary flow manifolds, each with seven nozzles.

FUEL GRADES: JP-1, JP-4, JP-5 to PWA Spec 522.

NOZZLE GUIDE VANES: High pressure ring of 27, aircooled, integrally cast in cobalt alloy.

TURBINES: Single-stage HP turbine with 47 aircooled blades. Single-stage LP turbine with 53 solid blades. Two-stage power turbine, first stage with 68 blades and second with 74, all with shrouded tips. All blades have fir tree root fixings. Maximum temperatures conservatively low.

BEARINGS: Ball or roller anti-friction bearings in gas generator, power section and reduction gearbox.

JETPIPE: Nickel alloy and sheet metal pipe of approx 993·5 cm² (154 sq in) exhaust area.

ACCESSORY DRIVES: Pads on turbomachine, driven by HP compressor, for starter/generator, hydromechanical fuel control and hand turning. Pads on reduction gearbox for alternator, hydraulic pump, propeller control module, propeller overspeed governor and electric auxiliary pump. Electric torque signal and auto power augmentation.

LUBRICATION SYSTEM: One pressure pump and two scavenge pumps, all gear type and driven off HP rotor. Additional HP-driven scavenge pump on PW120 if oil-cooled alternator fitted. Integral oil tank, capacity 9·44 litres (2·5 US gallons, 2·08 Imp gallons).

OIL SPECIFICATION: CPW202 or PWA521 Type II.

MOUNTING: Supported at both turbomachine and reduction gearbox. Auxiliary mounts may be attached to inlet flange.

STARTING: Electric starter/generator.

DIMENSIONS:

Length: PW115 — 2,057 mm (81 in)
PW120, 124 — 2,134 mm (84 in)
Width: PW115, 120, 124 — 635 mm (25 in)
Height: PW115, 120, 124 — 787 mm (31 in)

WEIGHT, DRY:

PW115 — 391 kg (861 lb)
PW120 — 417·8 kg (921 lb)
PW124 — 481 kg (1,060 lb)

PERFORMANCE RATINGS (S/L, static):

T-O: See under model listings

Alternative (normal) T-O:
PW115 — same as T-O
PW120 — 1,411 ekW; 1,342 kW (1,892 ehp; 1,800 shp) at 1,200 rpm to 27·7°C
PW124 — 1,693 ekW; 1,610 kW (2,272 ehp; 2,160 shp) at 1,200 rpm to 34·4°C

Max continuous:
PW115 — 1,256 ekW; 1,193 kW (1,685 ehp; 1,600 shp) at 1,300 rpm to 37·8°C
PW120 — 1,333 ekW; 1,268 kW (1,787 ehp; 1,700 shp) at 1,200 rpm to 32·7°C

Max cruise:
PW115 — 1,178 ekW; 1,119 kW (1,580 ehp; 1,500 shp) at 1,300 rpm to 20°C
PW120 — 1,271 ekW; 1,207 kW (1,704 ehp; 1,619 shp) at 1,200 rpm to 15°C
PW124 — 1,593 ekW; 1,514 kW (2,136 ehp; 2,030 shp) at 1,200 rpm to 22·2°C

SPECIFIC FUEL CONSUMPTION:

T-O rating:
PW115 — 87·2 μg/J (0·516 lb/h/ehp)
PW120 — 82·0 μg/J (0·485 lb/h/ehp)
PW120 alternative T-O — 84·3 μg/J (0·499 lb/h/ehp)
PW124 — 79·1 μg/J (0·468 lb/h/ehp)

P&WC PT6A

US military designations: T74 (separate entry) and **T101** (PT6A-45R)

The PT6A is a free turbine turboprop, built in many versions. By January 1986 more than 19,500 had logged 96,329,267 h in some 9,157 aircraft registered in 144 countries.

An experimental PT6 ran for the first time in November 1959 and flight trials in the nose of a Beech 18 began in May 1961. Civil certification of the first production model, the 578 ehp PT6A-6, was granted in late 1963. Progressively higher rated versions followed to power a wide variety of aircraft. In September 1977 P&WC introduced the PT6A-10 series, with ratings extending down to 354 kW (475 shp) for light and agricultural aviation.

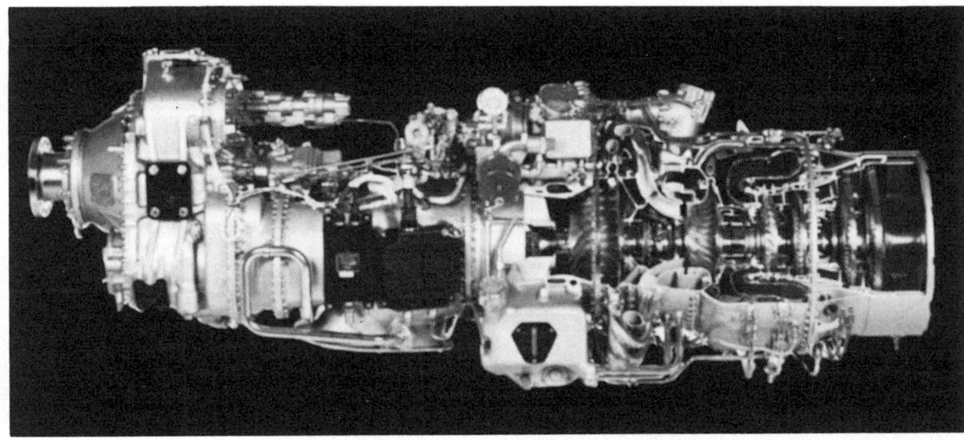

A cutaway PW124 engine (1,790 kW; 2,400 shp)

Current versions of the PT6A are as follows:

PT6A-10. Flat rated at 374 ekW; 354 kW (502 ehp; 475 shp) at 2,200 propeller rpm to 38°C.

PT6A-11. Flat rated at 394 ekW; 373 kW (528 ehp; 500 shp) at 2,200 propeller rpm to 42°C. Certificated December 1977. Fitted to Piper Cheyenne I and T-1040 and Claudius Dornier Seastar. Selected for initial development version of Harbin Y-12.

PT6A-110. Flat rated at 374 ekW; 354 kW (502 ehp; 475 shp) at 1,900 propeller rpm to 38°C. Certificated January 1980. Fitted to Dornier 128-6.

PT6A-11AG. Flat rated at 394 ekW; 373 kW (528 ehp; 500 shp) at 2,200 propeller rpm to 42°C. Certificated in May 1979, it embodies design features for agricultural aviation, including operation on diesel fuel. Fitted to Ayres Turbo-Thrush and Weatherly 620 TP.

PT6A-112. Flat rated at 394 ekW; 373 kW (528 ehp; 500 shp) at 1,900 propeller rpm to 56°C. Certificated October 1978. Fitted to Cessna Conquest I, Reims-Cessna F 406 Caravan II and AAC Turbine P-210 conversion.

PT6A-114. Flat rated at 471 ekW; 447 kW (632 ehp; 600 shp) at 1,900 propeller rpm to 58°C. Certificated January 1984. Fitted to Cessna Caravan I, with single exhaust.

PT6A-15AG. Flat rated at 533 ekW; 507 kW (715 ehp; 680 shp) at 2,200 propeller rpm to 22°C. Certificated October 1977, including operation on diesel fuel. Embodies design features for agricultural aviation. Fitted to Ayres Turbo-Thrush, Frakes Turbo-Cat, Schweizer Turbo Ag-Cat D, Air Tractor AT-400, and prototypes of ICA Brasov IAR-827TP and IAR-825TP Triumf.

PT6A-20. Flat rated at 432 ekW; 410 kW (579 ehp; 550 shp) at 2,200 propeller rpm to 21°C. Early applications listed in 1983-84 *Jane's*; currently fitted in Schafer Comanchero 500A.

PT6A-21. Flat rated at 432·5 ekW; 410 kW (580 ehp; 550 shp) at 2,200 propeller rpm to 21°C, the A-21 offers improved fuel consumption and reliability, mainly by mating the A-27 power unit with the A-20A gearbox. Certificated on 10 December 1974. Fitted to current Beechcraft King Air C90.

PT6A-25. Flat rated at 432·5 ekW; 410 kW (580 ehp; 550 shp) at 2,200 propeller rpm to 33°C. Special oil system for sustained inverted flight. Certificated May 1976. Fitted to Beechcraft T-34C and Norman Firecracker.

PT6A-25A. Identical to -25 except for certain castings being made of magnesium alloy instead of aluminium alloy. Fitted to production Pilatus PC-7.

PT6A-25C. Flat rated at 584 ekW; 559 kW (783 ehp; 750 shp) at 2,200 propeller rpm to 31°C. Basically an A-25 with standard A-34 hot end and A-27 first stage reduction gearing. The A-25C, while maintaining aerobatic capabilities, offers an increased power rating over that of the A-25 and A-25A. Fitted to EMBRAER EMB-312. Selected for production IAR-825TP Triumf.

PT6A-25D. As -25C but aluminium castings. Selected for Australian AAC A10 Wamira trainer.

PT6A-27. Flat rated at 553 ekW; 507 kW (715 ehp; 680 shp) at 2,200 propeller rpm to 22°C, attained by 12½ per cent increase in mass flow provided by larger diameter compressor, at lower turbine temperatures than in PT6A-20. Production began in November 1967 and 2,206 had been delivered by January 1982. Production continues. Applications include the Hamilton Westwind II/III (Beech 18) conversions, Beechcraft Model 99 and 99A, Beechcraft U-21A and U-21D, de Havilland Canada DHC-6 Twin Otter Series 300, Pilatus/Fairchild Industries PC-6/B2-H2 Porter, Frakes Aviation (Grumman) Mallard conversion, Let L-410A Turbolet, Saunders Aircraft ST-27A (de Havilland Heron) conversion, EMBRAER EMB-110 Bandeirante (early models), Harbin Y-12, SAC Spectrum-One, and Schafer Comanchero 500B/Neiva Carajá.

PT6A-28. Similar to the PT6A-27 and with same T-O and max continuous ratings, this version has an additional normal cruise rating of 419 ekW (562 ehp) available up to 21°C, corresponding to the max cruise rating conditions of the -27. In addition the max cruise rating of the -28 gives 486 ekW (652 ehp) up to the higher ambient of 33°C. This model continues in production, with 2,613 engines delivered by the beginning of 1982 for Beechcraft King Air E90 and A100, Piper Cheyenne II and EMBRAER Xingu I. Also powers the Avtek 400.

PT6A-34. Flat rated at 584 ekW; 559 kW (783 ehp; 750 shp) at 2,200 propeller rpm to 31°C, this version has aircooled nozzle guide vanes to allow operation at higher turbine entry temperatures. For the IAI 102/201 Arava, Saunders ST-28, Frakes Aviation (Grumman) Mallard conversion and EMBRAER EMB-110P1/P2 and EMB-111.

PT6A-34B. Identical to -34 except for aluminium alloy replacing magnesium in major castings. Fitted to Beechcraft T-44A.

PT6A-34AG. First model intended specifically for agricultural use, and certificated on diesel fuel. Retrofitted to Frakes conversion of Ag-Cat and Ayres Turbo-Thrush. Selected for PZL-106AT/BT Turbo-Kruk, Schweizer Turbo Ag-Cat and Norman Fieldmaster.

PT6A-135. Flat rated at 587 ekW; 559 kW (787 ehp; 750 shp) at 1,900 rpm. Changed drive ratio reduces propeller noise; hot end modifications to permit higher cycle temperatures. Certificated July 1977. Fitted to JetCrafters Taurus, Beechcraft King Air F90 (-135A), EMBRAER 121A1 Xingu II, Piper Cheyenne IIXL, AAC Regent 1500 (Riley Turbine Eagle 421), Airmaster Avalon 680, and Schafer Comanchero/Comanchero 750 conversions.

PT6A-36. Flat rated at 586 ekW; 559 kW (786 ehp; 750 shp) at 2,200 rpm to 36°C. Similar to -34 but slightly higher ehp rating. Certificated June 1977. Fitted to IAI 101B/202 Arava and Beechcraft C99.

PT6A-41. Higher mass flow, aircooled stage one turbine nozzle guide vanes and two-stage free turbine. T-O rating of 673 ekW; 634 kW (903 ehp; 850 shp) at 2,000 propeller rpm, available up to 41°C. Thermodynamic power is 812 ekW (1,089 ehp). Powers Beechcraft Super King Air 200 and C-12, and Piper Cheyenne III.

PT6A-42. Identical to A-41, but with detailed improvements to give approx 10 per cent increase in cruise performance. Certificated August 1979. Fitted to Beechcraft Super King Air B200.

PT6A-45A. Similar to PT6A-41 but with redesigned gearbox to transmit higher powers at reduced propeller speeds. Rated at 916 ekW; 875 kW (1,229 ehp; 1,173 shp) at 1,700 rpm to 8°C, or to 21°C with water injection. Certificated February 1976. Powers Shorts 330 and Mohawk 298.

PT6A-45B. Identical to PT6A-45A, but with increased water injection to give improved thermodynamic performance. Rated at 916 ekW; 875 kW (1,229 ehp; 1,173 shp) at 1,700 rpm to 11°C or to 30°C with water injection. Certificated March 1979. Powers Shorts 330 and Dornier Do ATT.

PT6A-45R. PT6A-45B with added reserve power rating and deleted water/methanol injection system. Reserve power rated at 935 ekW; 893 kW (1,254 ehp; 1,197 shp) at 1,700 rpm to 23°C. Alternative T-O at 916 ekW; 875 kW (1,229 ehp; 1,173 shp) at 1,700 rpm to 11°C. Certificated 1980. Powers Shorts 330 and Sherpa, USAC DC-3 Turbo Express, prototype Gafhawk 125 and Fairchild Metro IIIA.

T101-CP-100. PT6A-45R for Shorts C-23A.

PT6A-50. Similar to PT6A-41 with a longer, higher ratio reduction gear to give lower propeller tip speed for quieter operation at T-O. Rating at T-O is 875·5 ekW; 835 kW (1,174 ehp; 1,120 shp) available with water injection up to 34°C at 1,210 propeller rpm. Certificated September 1976, and delivered same month for de Havilland Canada DHC-7.

PT6A-60A. Similar to PT6A-45B with jet flap intake and increased compressor mass flow matched for high altitude cruise. Rated at 830 ekW; 783 kW (1,113 ehp; 1,050 shp) at 1,700 rpm to 25°C. Certificated November 1982. Powers Beech Super King Air 300.

PT6A-61. PT6A-60 gas generator matched with A-41

power section with 2,000 rpm gearbox. T-O rating 673 ekW; 634 kW (903 ehp; 850 shp) to 46°C. Certificated November 1982. Powers Piper Cheyenne IIIA.

PT6A-62A. For Pilatus PC-9. Flat rated to 708 kW (950 shp).

PT6A-65B. Identical to PT6A-65R, but without reserve power rating. Flat rated at 875·5 ekW; 820 kW (1,174 ehp; 1,100 shp) at 1,700 rpm to 51°C. Certificated August 1982. Powers Beechcraft 1900.

PT6A-65R. Similar to PT6A-45R, with a new four-stage compressor with jet flap intake, fuel control unit and fuel dump. Improved hot end hardware and exhaust duct. Reserve power rated at 1,087 ekW; 1,026 kW (1,459 ehp; 1,376 shp) at 1,700 rpm to 28°C. Alternative T-O at 975 ekW; 917 kW (1,308 ehp; 1,230 shp) at 1,700 rpm to 24°C. Certificated August 1982. Powers Shorts 360 and Gafhawk 125.

PT6A-66. Flat rated at 674 ekW; 534 kW (905 ehp; 850 shp) at 2,200 rpm to 62·2°C. Powers Piaggio Avanti.

PT6A-67. Flat rated at 870 ekW; 820 kW (1,167 ehp; 1,100 shp) at 1,700 rpm to 60°C. Powers Beechcraft Starship 2000.

The following data apply generally to the PT6A series:

Type: Free turbine axial-plus-centrifugal turboprop engine.

Propeller Drive (all models up to and including PT6A-41): Two-stage planetary gear train. Ratio 15 : 1. Rotation clockwise when viewed from rear. Drive from free turbine. Flanged propeller shaft. Plain bearings. Higher ratio reduction gears developed for PT6A-45R, -50, -60 and -65.

Air Intake: Annular air intake at rear of engine, with intake screen. Aircraft-supplied alcohol anti-icing system or inertial separation anti-icing system.

Compressor: Three axial flow stages, plus single centrifugal stage (-65 series, four axial stages). Single-sided centrifugal compressor, with 26 vanes, made from titanium forging. Axial rotor of disc-drum type, with stainless steel stator and rotor blades. The stator vanes (44 first-stage, 44 second-stage, 40 third-stage) are brazed to casing. The rotor blades (16 first-stage, 32 second-stage and 32 third-stage) are dovetailed to discs. Discs through bolted, with centrifugal compressor, to shaft. Fabricated one-piece stainless steel casing and radial diffuser. PT6A-27: pressure ratio 6·7, mass flow 3·1 kg (6·8 lb/s). PT6A-65: pressure ratio 10, mass flow 4·3 kg (9·5 lb/s).

Combustion Chamber: Annular reverse flow type of stainless steel construction, with 14 simplex burners around periphery of chamber. All versions up to A-34 have two glow plug igniters with option of two spark igniters; A-38 onwards, two spark igniters. PT6A-27 has one plug at 64° on starboard side of vertical centreline and one at 90° on port side.

Fuel System: Bendix DP-F2 pneumatic automatic fuel control system. Pneumatic computing section, fuel metering and regulating section, gas generator governor and free turbine governor. Primary and secondary flow manifolds with seven nozzles per manifold. PT6A-50 has DP-F3 with starting spill valve and motive flow systems.

Fuel Grade: Commercial jet fuels JP-1, JP-4, JP-5, MIL-J-5624. Use of aviation gasolines (MIL-G-5572) grades 80/87, 91/98, 100/130 and 115/145 permitted for a period of up to 150 h during any overhaul period.

Nozzle Guide Vanes: 29 nozzle guide vanes; A-34 onward, 14 aircooled HP vanes.

Turbines: Models up to A-34 have two single-stage axial; HP turbine (with 58 blades) drives compressor, and LP turbine (with 41 shrouded blades) drives output shaft. PT6A-41 onward have two-stage LP turbine. All blades have fir tree root fixings.

Bearings: Each main rotor (gas generator and free turbine) supported by one ball and one roller anti-friction bearing.

Jetpipe: Collector duct surrounding free turbine shaft, exhaust through two ports on horizontal centreline.

Accessories: Mounting pads on accessory case (rear of engine) for starter/generator, hydraulic pump, aircraft accessory drive, vacuum pump and tachometer generator. Mounting pad on the shaft-turbine reduction gear case for propeller overspeed governor, propeller constant speed control unit and tachometer generator.

Lubrication System: One pressure and four scavenge elements in the pump stacks. All are gear type and are driven by the gas generator rotor. Engine has an integral oil tank with a capacity of 8·75 litres (2·3 US gallons). Oil supply pressure is 5·5 bars (80 lb/sq in) on PT6A-11 to -28, 5·85 bars (85 lb/sq in) on -34 to -36, and 7·25 bars (105 lb/sq in) on -38 to -65.

Oil Specification: CPW202, PWA521 Type II (7·5 cs vis) (MIL-L-23699, MIL-L-7808 for military engines).

Mounting: Up to A-34, three-point ring suspension. A-38 onward, four-point mounting, except -50 has base mounting.

Starting: Electric starter/generator on accessory case.

Dimensions:

Max diameter	483 mm (19 in)
Length, excl accessories:	
PT6A-10 to -36	1,575 mm (62 in)
PT6A-41	1,701 mm (67 in)
PT6A-45	1,829 mm (72 in)
PT6A-50	2,133 mm (84 in)
PT6A-65	1,880 mm (74 in)

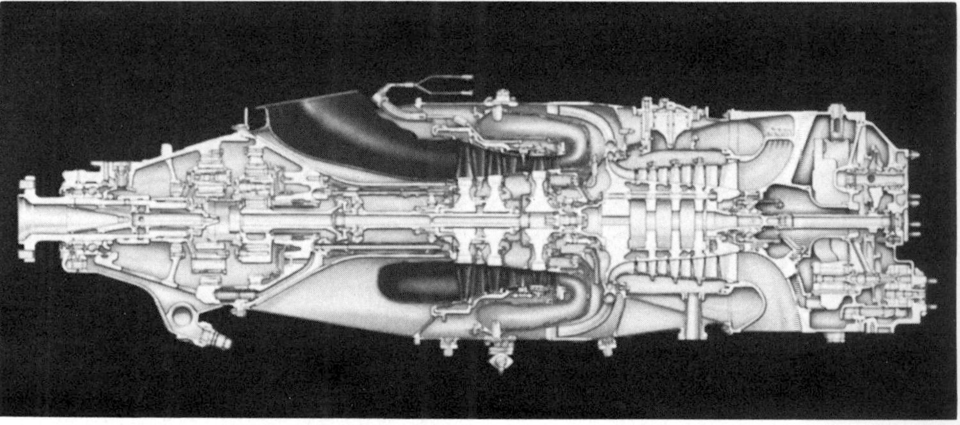

Longitudinal section through PT6A-67 turboprop (870 ekW; 1,167 ehp)

Weight, Dry:

PT6A-10, -11, -27, -28	137·4 kg (303 lb)
PT6A-11AG, -34, -36	141 kg (311 lb)
PT6A-110, -112	144·7 kg (319 lb)
PT6A-15AG	140·2 kg (309 lb)
PT6A-20	130 kg (286 lb)
PT6A-21	144 kg (316 lb)
PT6A-25	150 kg (331 lb)
PT6A-25A, -25C, -135	146 kg (322 lb)
PT6A-135	150 kg (331 lb)
PT6A-40, -41, -42	172 kg (380 lb)
PT6A-45A	192 kg (423 lb)
PT6A-45B, -45R	193 kg (425 lb)
PT6A-50	263 kg (580 lb)
PT6A-60	204 kg (450 lb)
PT6A-65B	208 kg (458 lb)
PT6A-65R	210 kg (463 lb)

Performance Ratings (S/L, static):

T-O: See under model listings

Max continuous:

PT6A-110 374 ekW; 354 kW (502 ehp; 475 shp) at 1,900 rpm (to 38°C)

PT6A-11, -11AG 394 ekW; 373 kW (528 ehp; 500 shp)

PT6A-112 394 ekW; 373 kW (528 ehp; 500 shp) at 1,900 rpm (to 56°C)

PT6A-15AG, -27, -28 533 ekW; 507 kW (715 ehp; 680 shp) at 2,200 rpm (to 22°C)

PT6A-21 432·5 ekW; 410 kW (580 ehp; 550 shp) at 2,200 rpm (to 33°C)

PT6A-25, -25A 432·5 ekW; 410 kW (580 ehp; 550 shp) at 2,200 rpm (to 33°C)

PT6A-25C 584 ekW; 559 kW (783 ehp; 750 shp) at 2,200 rpm (to 31°C)

PT6A-34 584 ekW; 559 kW (783 ehp; 750 shp) at 2,200 rpm (to 30°C)

PT6A-135 587 ekW; 559 kW (787 ehp; 750 shp) at 1,900 rpm (-135 to 29°C, -135A to 34°C)

PT6A-36 586 ekW; 559 kW (786 ehp; 750 shp) at 2,200 rpm (to 36°C)

PT6A-40 558 ekW; 522 kW (749 ehp; 700 shp) at 2,000 rpm (to 57°C)

PT6A-41 673 ekW; 634 kW (903 ehp; 850 shp) at 2,000 rpm (to 41°C)

PT6A-42 674 ekW; 634 kW (904 ehp; 850 shp) at 2,000 rpm (to 41°C)

PT6A-45B, -45R 798 ekW; 761 kW (1,070 ehp; 1,020 shp) at 1,700 rpm (to: -45B, 29°C; -45R, 33°C)

PT6A-50 762 ekW; 725·5 kW (1,022 ehp; 973 shp) at 1,210 rpm (to 32°C)

PT6A-60, -60A 830 ekW; 783 kW (1,113 ehp; 1,050 shp) at 1,700 rpm (to 25°C)

PT6A-61 673 ekW; 634 kW (902 ehp; 850 shp) at 2,000 rpm (to 46°C)

PT6A-65B 931 ekW; 875 kW (1,249 ehp; 1,173 shp) at 1,700 rpm (to 38°C)

PT6A-65R 931 ekW; 875 kW (1,249 ehp; 1,173 shp) at 1,700 rpm (to 26°C)

Max cruise rating:

PT6A-110 374 ekW; 354 kW (502 ehp; 475 shp) at 1,900 rpm (to 19°C)

PT6A-11 394 ekW; 373 kW (528 ehp; 500 shp) at 2,200 rpm (to 37°C)

PT6A-11AG 394 ekW; 373 kW (528 ehp; 500 shp) at 2,200 rpm (to 36°C)

PT6A-112 394 ekW; 373 kW (528 ehp; 500 shp) at 1,900 rpm (to 48°C)

PT6A-15AG as PT6A-27

PT6A-21, -25 432·5 ekW; 410 kW (580 ehp; 550 shp) at 2,200 rpm (to 33°C)

PT6A-25C 545 ekW; 522 kW (731 ehp; 700 shp) at 2,200 rpm (to 19°C)

PT6A-27 486 ekW; 462 kW (652 ehp; 620 shp) at 2,200 rpm (to 21°C)

PT6A-28 486 ekW; 462 kW (652 ehp; 620 shp) at 2,200 rpm (to 33°C)

PT6A-34 545 ekW; 522 kW (731 ehp; 700 shp) at 2,200 rpm (to 19°C)

PT6A-135 548 ekW; 522 kW (735 ehp; 700 shp) at 1,900 rpm (-135 to 37°C, -135A to 41°C)

PT6A-36 548 ekW; 522 kW (735 ehp; 700 shp) at 2,200 rpm (to 28°C)

PT6A-41 673 ekW; 634 kW (903 ehp; 850 shp) at 2,000 rpm (to 28°C)

PT6A-42 674 ekW; 634 kW (904 ehp; 850 shp) at 2,000 rpm (to 33°C)

PT6A-45B, -45R 749 ekW; 713 kW (1,004 ehp; 956 shp) at 1,425 rpm (to 15°C)

PT6A-50 706 ekW; 671 kW (947 ehp; 900 shp) at 1,020-1,160 rpm (to 23°C)

PT6A-60, 60A 791 ekW; 746 kW (1,061 ehp; 1,000 shp) at 1,700 rpm (to 28°C)

PT6A-61 as max continuous

PT6A-65B, -65R 762 ekW; 713 kW (1,022 ehp; 956 shp) at 1,425 rpm (to 27°C)

Specific Fuel Consumption:

At T-O rating:

PT6A-110	111·0 µg/J (0·657 lb/h/ehp)
PT6A-11, -11AG	109·4 µg/J (0·647 lb/h/ehp)
PT6A-112	107·6 µg/J (0·637 lb/h/ehp)
PT6A-15AG, -27, -28	101·3 µg/J (0·602 lb/h/ehp)
PT6A-21	108·5 µg/J (0·642 lb/h/ehp)
PT6A-25	106·5 µg/J (0·630 lb/h/ehp)
PT6A-25C, -34, -34B, -34AG	100·6 µg/J (0·595 lb/h/ehp)
PT6A-135, -135A	98·9 µg/J (0·585 lb/h/ehp)
PT6A-36, -41	99·9 µg/J (0·591 lb/h/ehp)
PT6A-42	101·5 µg/J (0·601 lb/h/ehp)
PT6A-45B	93 5 µg/J (0·554 lb/h/ehp)
PT6A-45R	93 4 µg/J (0·553 lb/h/ehp)
PT6A-50	94 6 µg/J (0·560 lb/h/ehp)
PT6A-60, -60A, -61	90·0 µg/J (0·533 lb/h/ehp)
PT6A-65B, -65R, -67	85·5 µg/J (0·506 lb/h/ehp)
PT6A-66	89·2 µg/J (0·528 lb/h/ehp)

Oil Consumption:

Max	0·091 kg (0·20 lb)/h

P&WC T74

T74 is a US designation for military versions of the PT6A turboprop and PT6B turboshaft.

T74-CP-700. US Army counterpart of the PT6A-20. More than 300 T74-CP-700s were delivered to Beechcraft for 129 U-21A aircraft. Inertial separator system to protect against sand and dust ingestion.

T74-CP-702. Rated at 580 ekW (778 ehp) and retrofitted in Beechcraft U-21.

P&WC PT6B/PT6C

The PT6B is the commercial turboshaft version of the PT6A and has a lower ratio reduction gear. Current versions are:

PT6B-35F. Based upon PT6A-135 but with single-stage reduction gearbox. T-O rating 485 kW (650 shp) at 6,000 rpm to 43°C. Certificated April 1982. Fitted to Lear Fan 2100.

PT6B-36. Based on PT6T-3B with reverse drive 6,050 rpm gearbox. T-O rating 716 kW (960 shp) to 15°C, with 2½-min contingency 760 kW (1,020 shp) to 15°C. Certificated 1984. Fitted to Sikorsky S-76B.

PT6C. This series of engines provides direct drive from the power turbine, with no reduction gearing.

Dimensions:

Max diameter: PT6B-35F	572 mm (22·5 in)
Length, excl accessories:	
PT6B-35F	1,499 mm (59·0 in)
Frontal area	0·18 m² (1·95 sq ft)

Weight, Dry:

PT6B-35F	133 kg (294 lb)
PT6B-36	161 kg (355 lb)

Performance Ratings:

T-O: See under model listings

Max cruise:

PT6B-35F 485 kW (650 shp) at 6,188 rpm (to 43°C)

PT6B-36 716 kW (960 shp) to 15°C

The P&WC PT6B-36, with contingency rating of 760 kW (1,020 shp)

SPECIFIC FUEL CONSUMPTION:
At T-O rating:
PT6B-35F 103·0 μg/J (0·608 lb/h/shp)
PT6B-36 100·5 μg/J (0·594 lb/h/shp)
OIL CONSUMPTION:
Max 0·091 kg (0·20 lb)/h

P&WC PT6T TWIN-PAC

US military designation: T400 (separate entry)

First run in July 1968, the PT6T Twin-Pac comprises two PT6 turboshaft engines mounted side by side and driving into a combining gearbox to provide a single output drive. The engine was launched as a coupled power unit for a family of twin-engined helicopters based on the Bell Helicopter UH-1 series. First of these, jointly financed by Bell, P&WC and the Canadian government, was the 15-seat Bell Model 212, which first flew with the PT6T-3 in April 1969.

PT6T-3. Basic model with T-O rating of 1,342 kW (1,800 shp). In Bell 212, in addition to offering true engine out capability, provides an additional 300 shp over the single-engined 205A and gives enhanced hot day and high altitude performance. Qualified PT6T-3s became available in the third quarter of 1970 coincident with certification of the Model 212, which is also produced under licence by Agusta in Italy.

Another application of the PT6T-3 engine is for conversion from piston engine to turbine power of the Sikorsky S-58. The prototype S-58T flew in August 1970 and certification was received in April 1971.

In these two helicopter applications, total shaft power output is limited by the helicopter transmission. In the Model 212 the 1,342 kW (1,800 shp) PT6T-3 is restricted to a T-O rating of 962 kW (1,290 shp) and 843 kW (1,130 shp) for continuous power. In the S-58T the limits are 1,122 kW (1,505 shp) at T-O and 935 kW (1,254 shp) for continuous operation. The PT6T-3 is easily adapted to such power requirements by a simple setting of its torque control. In the event of a power section failure, torquemeters in the combining gearbox signal the other power section to maximum power. A single-engine 30 min rating is included for use, at pilot discretion, in such contingencies. Current versions are as follows:

PT6T-3B. Certificated late 1979. Introduced as an alternative to the PT6T-3 for installation in the Bell 212. The T-3B is basically a PT6T-3 with some T-6 hardware and improved single-engine performance, and powers the Bell 412.

PT6T-6. Uprated engine, certificated in December 1974. The higher power is achieved by material and aerodynamic improvements to the compressor-turbine nozzle guide vanes and rotor blades. Installed in S-58T and Agusta-Bell 212. By the Autumn of 1984 a total of 12·2 million equivalent PT6 hours had been flown by PT6T engines in 1,869 helicopters in 61 countries.

The following details describe the main features differing from those of the standard PT6:

TYPE: Coupled free turbine turboshaft.

SHAFT DRIVE: Combining gearbox comprises three separate gear trains, two input and one output, each contained within an individual sealed compartment and all interconnected by drive shafts. Overall reduction ratio 5 : 1. Input gear train comprising three spur gears provides speed reduction between power sections and output gearbox. The two drives into the output gearbox are via Formsprag fully phased overrunning clutches with input third gear forming outer member of clutch, and interconnect shaft forming inner, overrunning member. Output gear train comprises three helical spur gears, two input pinions meshing with single output gear.

AIR INTAKES: Additional inertial particle separator fitted upstream of engine to reduce sand and dust ingestion. High frequency compressor noise suppressed.

FUEL SYSTEM: As PT6 with manual backup system, and dual manifold for cool starts. Automatic power sharing and torque limiting. Torquemeters provide signals to Bendix fuel system metering valves to maintain power at level set by pilot's selective collective control. Fuel heaters.

FUEL GRADES: JP-1, JP-4 and JP-5.

JETPIPE: Single upward facing exhaust port on each gas generator.

ACCESSORIES: Starter/generator and tachogenerator mounted on accessory drive case at front of each power section. Other accessory drives on combining gearbox, including individual power turbine speed governors and tachogenerators, and provision for blowers and aircraft accessories.

LUBRICATION SYSTEM: Independent lubrication system on each power section for maximum safety during single-engine operation. Integral oil tanks. Separate oil system for output section of combining gearbox.

OIL SPECIFICATION: PWA Spec 521. For military engines, MIL-L-7808 and -23699.

STARTING: Electrical, with cold weather starting down to −54°C.

DIMENSIONS:
Length 1,702 mm (67·0 in)
Width 1,118 mm (44·0 in)
Height 838 mm (33·0 in)

WEIGHT, DRY (standard equipment):
PT6T-3 292 kg (645 lb)
PT6T-3B, -6 298 kg (657 lb)

PERFORMANCE RATINGS:
T-O (5 min):
Total output, at 6,600 rpm:
PT6T-3, -3B 1,342 kW (1,800 shp)
PT6T-6 1,398 kW (1,875 shp) (to 21°C)
Single power section only, at 6,600 rpm:
PT6T-3, -3B 671 kW (900 shp)
PT6T-6, -3B (2½ min) 764 kW (1,025 shp)
30 min power (single power section), at 6,600 rpm:
PT6T-3B, -6 723 kW (970 shp)
Max continuous:
Total output, at 6,600 rpm:
PT6T-3, -3B 1,193 kW (1,600 shp)
PT6T-6 1,249 kW (1,675 shp) (to 19°C)
Single power section only, at 6,600 rpm:
PT6T-3, -3B 596 kW (800 shp)
PT6T-6 615 kW (825 shp) (to 19°C)
Cruise A:
Total output, at 6,600 rpm:
PT6T-3, -3B 932 kW (1,250 shp)
PT6T-6 1,014 kW (1,360 shp)
Single power section only, at 6,600 rpm:
PT6T-3, -3B 466 kW (625 shp)
PT6T-6 500 kW (670 shp)
Cruise B:
Total output, at 6,600 rpm:
PT6T-3, -3B 820 kW (1,100 shp)
PT6T-6 891 kW (1,195 shp)
Single power section only, at 6,600 rpm:
PT6T-3, -3B 410 kW (550 shp)
PT6T-6 440 kW (590 shp)
Ground idle, at 2,200 rpm 44·7 kW (60 shp) max

SPECIFIC FUEL CONSUMPTION:
At 2½-min rating (single power section):
PT6T-3B 100·7 μg/J (0·596 lb/h/shp)
PT6T-6 101·6 μg/J (0·602 lb/h/shp)
At 30-min rating (single power section):
PT6T-3 101·9 μg/J (0·603 lb/h/shp)
PT6T-3B 101·0 μg/J (0·598 lb/h/shp)
PT6T-6 101·3 μg/J (0·600 lb/h/shp)
T-O, 5-min rating (total output):
PT6T-3 100·6 μg/J (0·595 lb/h/shp)
PT6T-3B 101·3 μg/J (0·600 lb/h/shp)
PT6T-6 100·0 μg/J (0·592 lb/h/shp)
At max continuous rating (total output):
PT6T-3 101·2 μg/J (0·599 lb/h/shp)
PT6T-3B 103·9 μg/J (0·615 lb/h/shp)
PT6T-6 101·9 μg/J (0·603 lb/h/shp)

OIL CONSUMPTION:
Max (for both gas generators) 0·18 kg (0·4 lb)/h

P&WC T400

Military version of the PT6T Twin-Pac, the T400-CP-400 has castings of aluminium instead of magnesium. For military roles, P&WC describes the T400 as producing a minimum infra-red signature. Military Qualification Tests (MQT) were completed in March 1970, and production deliveries started in the same month.

The T400 is used in the US Air Force and Navy Bell UH-1N (military version of the Model 212), the US Marine Corps Bell AH-1J, and the Canadian Armed Forces Bell CH-135. T400 field operations started in the middle of 1970.

TBO on the T400-CP-400 is 2,000 h on both the power section and reduction gearbox. By the beginning of 1983 deliveries totalled 799 CP-400 engines.

The T400-WV-402 is the military counterpart of the PT6T-6 and is used in the AH-1T. By the beginning of 1983 a total of 524 WV-402s had been delivered.

DIMENSIONS (CP-400 and WV-402):
Length 1,659 mm (65·3 in)
Width 1,115 mm (43·5 in)
Height 828 mm (32·6 in)

WEIGHT, DRY:
T400-CP-400 324 kg (714 lb)
T400-WV-402 338 kg (745 lb)

PERFORMANCE RATINGS:
Intermediate:
T400-CP-400 1,342 kW (1,800 shp) at 6,600 rpm
T400-WV-402 1,469 kW (1,970 shp) at 6,600 rpm
Max continuous:
T400-CP-400 1,141 kW (1,530 shp) at 6,600 rpm
T400-WV-402 1,248 kW (1,673 shp) at 6,600 rpm

SPECIFIC FUEL CONSUMPTION (Intermediate rating):
T400-CP-400 100·4 μg/J (0·594 lb/h/shp)
T400-WV-402 99·9 μg/J (0·591 lb/h/shp)

P&WC PW209T

In 1983 P&WC announced the development of a new engine series, with the basic designation PW200. The first

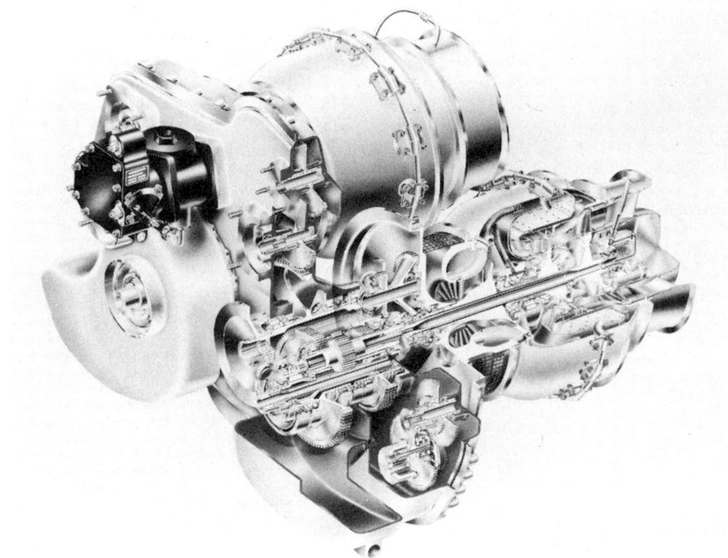

Cutaway drawing of P&WC PW209T twin turboshaft (699 kW; 937 shp)

model of this family, the PW209T, is a twin-engined turboshaft with integral combining gearbox. The engine has been selected to power the Bell 400A and 440 helicopters to be built in Canada. The power section contains fewer than half as many parts as that of previous engines. The PW209T is scheduled for certification in March 1988, with production deliveries beginning in the first half of that year.

AIR INTAKE: Inwards amidships through mesh screen, with integral scroll.

COMPRESSOR: Single-stage centrifugal of machined titanium. Pressure ratio 8.

COMBUSTION CHAMBER: Reverse-flow annular with 12 air blast nozzles. Two capacitor discharge igniters.

FUEL SYSTEM: Full authority digital with dedicated power supply and manual fuel metering backup.

FUEL GRADE: Any turbine type of diesel A or AA.

TURBINES: Single-stage axial compressor and power turbines with blades held in dovetail slots. Cold junction temperature sensing.

ACCESSORY DRIVES: Reduction gearbox at front drives starter-generator, dedicated FADEC alternator, hydraulic pump, phase shift torquemeter, oil cooler blower and airframe accessories.

DIMENSIONS:

Length	894 mm (35·2 in)
Width	991 mm (39·0 in)
Height	737 mm (29·0 in)

WEIGHT, DRY: 211 kg (465 lb)

PERFORMANCE RATINGS:

Both power sections driving:	
T-O (5 min)	699 kW (937 shp)
Max continuous	597 kW (800 shp)
Single power section driving:	
2½ min	390 kW (523 shp)
30 min	380 kW (510 shp)
Take-off (5 min)	343 kW (460 shp)
Max continuous	293 kW (393 shp)

SPECIFIC FUEL CONSUMPTION (both sections driving):

T-O (5 min)	98·0 µg/J (0·580 lb/h/ehp)
Max continuous	102·2 µg/J (0·605 lb/h/ehp)

P&WC PW205B

Utilizing the technology described under the PW209T engine, P&WC is developing a single-version turboshaft, the PW205B, with a front-mounted reduction and accessory gearbox. Certification of the PW205B is due in late 1988, the first application being the MBB BO 105LS helicopter.

DIMENSIONS:

Length	907 mm (35·7 in)
Width	566 mm (22·3 in)
Height	483 mm (19 in)

PERFORMANCE RATINGS:

2½ min	466 kW (625 shp)
30 min and T-O	440 kW (590 shp)
Max continuous	358 kW (480 shp)

SPECIFIC FUEL CONSUMPTIONS:

2½ min	93·8 µg/J (0·555 lb/h/ehp)
30 min and T-O	93·9 µg/J (0·556 lb/h/ehp)
Max continuous	96·8 µg/J (0·573 lb/h/ehp)

CHINA

(PEOPLE'S REPUBLIC)

STATE AIRCRAFT ENGINE FACTORIES

LOCATIONS: Shenyang, Xian, Harbin, Chengdu, Quzhou and Shanghai

PISTON ENGINES

As stated in the 1977-78 *Jane's,* the first aircraft engine made in numbers in the People's Republic of China was the Soviet M-11 radial.

In 1958 licences were obtained by the 2nd Ministry of Machine Building for two additional Soviet aircooled radial engines, the 194 kW (260 hp) Ivchenko AI-14R and 746 kW (1,000 hp) Shvetsov ASh-62IR (both described under Poland), fitted respectively to the locally built Jinge (Chinko) No. 1 (Yak-12) and Y-5 (An-2). Both of these aircraft and their engines were built in large numbers, the engines being known as the HS-6A and HS-5 (Huosai-6A and -5) respectively. By 1959 the 1,268 kW (1,700 shp) Shvetsov ASh-82V 14-cylinder radial and the 104·4 kW (140 hp) Czech M 332 four-in-line were also being produced.

Production is continuing on the Huosai-6A (based now on the Vedeneyev AI-14RF) for the CJ-6 trainer and Y-11 STOL transport.

WP-6 (based on Tumansky RD-9BF) before fitting the afterburner. The oil tank and accessories are above, with access through dorsal doors in the J-6

HUOSAI-16

The HS-16 is the first known aero engine of Chinese design. A small two-stroke piston engine, it has four horizontally opposed cylinders, each of 46 mm (1·81 in) bore and 42 mm (1·65 in) stroke, giving a displacement of 280 cc (17·1 cu in). The twin needle valve carburettor supplies a mix of 20:1 automotive gasoline with lubricating oil, and the screened ignition system is fed by a specially designed magneto. The HS-16 is the power plant of the Changcheng B-2 target drone.

DIMENSIONS:

Length	460 mm (18·11 in)
Width	320 mm (12·60 in)
Height	275 mm (10·83 in)

WEIGHT, DRY:

Bare	about 10 kg (22 lb)
With 125W generator	about 12 kg (26·5 lb)

PERFORMANCE RATING:

Max S/L 11·9 kW (16 hp) at 6,000 rpm

GAS TURBINE ENGINES

During the Korean War (1950-53) large numbers of MiG-15 fighters were ferried through Manchuria. Chinese technicians became familiar with the aircraft and its Klimov RD-45 (Rolls-Royce Nene derivative) engine. In 1955 a licence for Chinese manufacture of the MiG-15 fighter was signed in Moscow. No production was undertaken, but in 1959 the first Chinese J-5 (F-5), a licence built MiG-17F, began a production run of well over 1,000 aircraft, all powered by Chinese built WP-5 (Klimov VK-1F) turbojets rated at 33·2 kN (7,452 lb st). The non-afterburning WP-5D (VK-1A) version powers the JJ-5 trainer and all versions of the H-5 (Chinese Il-28).

Plans to build the Tu-16 bomber and its Mikulin AM-3M engines were drawn up in 1958. The bomber and all spare parts remain in production at Xian, together with Wopen-8 (RD-3M) engines.

In February 1959 the Chinese signed a licence agreement for the manufacture of the MiG-19 supersonic fighter, powered by RD-9 turbojets. Soon afterwards the relationship with the Soviet Union was severed; but the Chinese, working alone, managed to fly a locally built J-6 (F-6) (MiG-19) in 1961, and have since produced this fighter in very large numbers. Thus, several thousand WP-6 (R-9BF-811) engines have been made at Shenyang. Developments of the WP-6 have been used in locally produced military designs. One of these is the Q-5 (NATO 'Fantan') twin-engined attack aircraft, which has been built in quantity. In 1986 the J-6 and Q-5 were believed still to be in production.

CHINESE AERO ENGINES

Class	Factory	Engine	Derivation	Max rating	Application
Piston (Huosai)	Zhuzhou	HS-5	ASh-62IR	746 kW (1,000 hp)	Y-5
	Harbin	HS-5A	ASh-82V	1,268 kW (1,700 hp)	Z-5
	Zhuzhou	HS-6A	AI-14RF	213 kW (285 hp)	CJ-6, Y-11
	?	HS-16	Chinese design	11·9 kW (16 hp)	B-2 target drone
	?	HS-26	Chinese design?	19·4 kW (26 hp)	?
	?	HS-510	Chinese design?	22·4 kW (30 hp)	D-4 reconnaissance drone
	Nanjing	YH-280	Chinese design?	11·2 kW (15 hp)	BJ 7104 target drone
Turboprop (Wojiang)	Shanghai	WJ-5A-1	AI-24A	1,901 ekW (2,550 ehp)	Y-7, Y7-100
	Shanghai	WJ-6	AI-20K	2,983 ekW (4,000 ehp)	Y-8
Turboshaft (Wozhou)	Shanghai	WZ-5	WJ-5A	about 1,790 kW (2,400 shp)	Z-6
	?	WZ-6?	Arriel	about 520 kW (698 shp)	Z-9
Turbojet (Wopen)	Harbin	WP-2	RD-45	22·24 kN (5,000 lb st)	MiG-15, MiG-15UTI
	Harbin	WP-5	VK-1F	33·15 kN (7,452 lb st)*	J-5
	Harbin	WP-5D	VK-1A	26·48 kN (5,952 lb st)	JJ-5, H-5, HJ-5, HZ-5
	Shenyang	WP-6	RD-9BF-811	31·88 kN (7,167 lb st)*	J-6 and variants, Q-5/A-5, CK1C target drone
	Chengdu	WP-7A	R-11	50·01 kN (11,243 lb st)*	Early J-7/F-7
	Chengdu	WP-7B	WP-7A (improved afterburner)	59·82 kN (13,448 lb st)*	Current J-7/F-7, J-8/F-8 I
	Chengdu	WP-7B (BM)	WP-7B (kerosene instead of gasoline starting)	59·82 kN (13,448 lb st)*	F-7M
	Xian	WP-8	RD-3M	93·19 kN (20,950 lb st)	H-6
	?	WP-13A	R-13-300	64·72 kN (14,550 lb st)*	J-8 II
Turbofan (Woshan)	?	WS-9	?	?	?

*With afterburning

A subsequent production programme concerns the J-7 (F-7) MiG-21. As described in the Aircraft section, this fighter and its R-11 axial turbojet were put into production in China without a licence or any Soviet help. Deliveries of the R-11 (WP-7) are thought to have begun in 1965. Various improvements in TBO and afterburning thrust have been made since then, as detailed in the J-7/J-8 descriptions in the Aircraft section. A new engine (designation WP-13A) has been developed for the latest J-8, and is evidently a Chinese version of the Tumansky R-13-300.

In 1975, the Chinese government signed a preliminary contract with Rolls-Royce Ltd for licence manufacture of a supersonic afterburning Spey turbofan. This was not put into production, but one (so far unidentified) turbofan is designated WS-9 (Woshan-9) (see Addenda).

Turboprops manufactured in China include the WJ-5A-1 (Wojiang 5A-1), the Ivchenko AI-24A; the WJ-6 (Ivchenko AI-20K); and a modified WJ-5, the WZ-5 (Wozhou-5), for the Z-6 helicopter. In May 1986 China signed an agreement for licence assembly and testing of the P&WC PT6A used in the Chinese Y-12, and orders for the A310, MD-82 and Challenger civil transports may lead to renewed interest in other P&W engines. Chinese sources have also announced licence production of the Turboméca Arriel turboshaft, for the Harbin Z-9 (Aérospatiale Dauphin 2) helicopter.

WP-7BM afterburning turbojet for the F-7M Airguard fighter

CZECHOSLOVAKIA

OMNIPOL

OMNIPOL FOREIGN TRADE CORPORATION

Nekázanka 11, 112 21 Prague 1
Telephone: (02) 2140 111

Omnipol is responsible for exporting products of the Czechoslovak aviation industry and for supplying information on those products which are available for export.

AEROTECHNIK

68604 Uherské Hradiste 4, Kunovice
Telephone: 5122
Telex: 60380
DEVELOPMENT AND TEST: Petr Kousal

This company is now producing the long established inverted four-cylinder Walter Mikron piston engine, of 2,180 cc (133 cu in) capacity. The factory at Mor. Trebová calls it the **Mikron IIIS (A)**. It is rated at 48·5 kW (65 hp) and powers the Aerotechnik L-13SW Vivat motor glider.

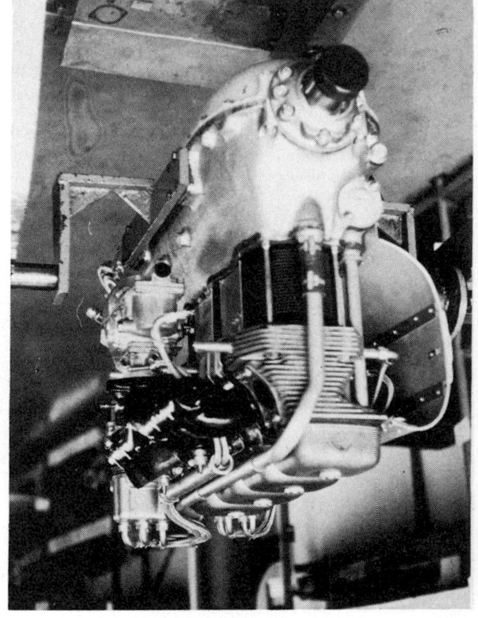

Aerotechnik-built Mikron IIIS (A)

AVIA

AVIA NARODNÍ PODNIK

199 03 Prague 9, Letňany
Telephone: Prague 89 51 21

This company is at present engaged in series production of piston engines, propellers and spare parts.

AVIA M 137 A

Designed to power light aerobatic aircraft, the 134 kW (180 hp) M 137 A piston engine is a modification of the M 337 with fuel and oil systems for aerobatic operation and without a supercharger. It powers the Zlin 42 M and Z 526 F. The **M 137 AZ** is a modified version, with the air intake port at the rear so that a dust filter can be incorporated. Details are as M 337, with the following differences:

CRANKSHAFT: No oil holes for propeller control.

FUEL SYSTEM: Type LUN 5150 pump; system designed for sustained aerobatics.

STARTER: LUN 2131 electric.

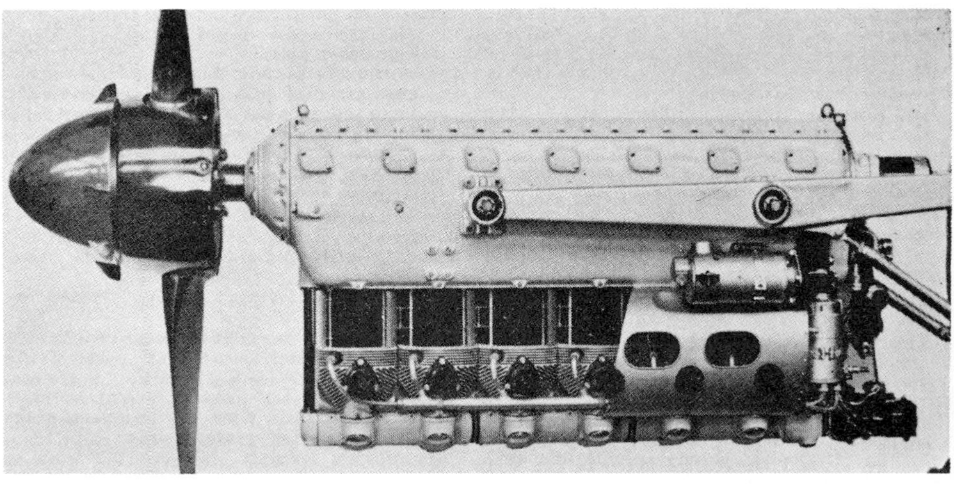

The 134 kW (180 hp) Avia M 137 A six-cylinder aircooled piston engine

DIMENSIONS:

Length	1,344 mm (52·9 in)
Width	443 mm (17·44 in)
Height	630 mm (24·80 in)
WEIGHT (incl starter):	141·5 kg (312 lb)
PERFORMANCE RATINGS:	
T-O	134 kW (180 hp) at 2,750 rpm
Max continuous	119 kW (160 hp) at 2,680 rpm
Max cruise	104·5 kW (140 hp) at 2,580 rpm
SPECIFIC FUEL CONSUMPTION:	
At T-O rating	91·26 µg/J (0·540 lb/h/hp)
At max cruise rating	81·96 µg/J (0·485 lb/h/hp)

AVIA M 337 A

The M 337 A six-cylinder aircooled supercharged engine powers several types of light aircraft that were built in Czechoslovakia, including the L-200D Morava, Zlin 43 and Zlin 726K. It can be supplied with hubs for fixed-pitch or controllable-pitch propellers. The **M 337 AK** is fitted to the Zlin 142.

TYPE: Six-cylinder inverted in-line aircooled, ungeared, supercharged and with direct fuel injection.

CYLINDERS: Bore 105 mm (4·13 in). Stroke 115 mm (4·53 in). Swept volume 5·97 litres (364·31 cu in). Compression ratio 6·3 : 1. Steel cylinders with cooling fins machined from solid. Cylinder bores nitrided. Detachable cylinder heads are aluminium alloy castings.

PISTONS: Aluminium alloy with graphited surfaces.

CONNECTING RODS: Two split big ends bolted together.

CRANKSHAFT: Forged from chrome vanadium steel, machined all over. Nitrided crankpins.

CRANKCASE: Heat treated magnesium alloy (Elektron).

IGNITION: Shielded type. Two plugs per cylinder.

LUBRICATION: Dry sump pressure feed type. The M 337 AK has a system for sustained inverted operation.

SUPERCHARGER: Centrifugal, ratio 7·4 : 1.

FUEL SYSTEM: Low pressure injection system with nozzles in front of inlet valves. The M 337 A has a unified fuel injection pump.

FUEL GRADE: Minimum 72-78 octane.

STARTING: Electric, engaged by an electromagnet.

ACCESSORIES: One 600W 28V dynamo. Electric tachometer. Propeller control unit. Mechanical tachometer on oil pump. Hydraulic pump to special order.

PROPELLER DRIVE: Direct left hand tractor.

DIMENSIONS:

Length, excl propeller boss	1,410 mm (55·51 in)
Width	472 mm (18·58 in)
Height	628 mm (24·72 in)
WEIGHT, DRY:	148 kg (326·3 lb)
PERFORMANCE RATINGS:	
T-O	157 kW (210 hp) at 2,750 rpm
Max cruise at 1,200 m (3,940 ft)	112 kW (150 hp) at 2,400 rpm
SPECIFIC FUEL CONSUMPTION:	
At T-O rating	100·6 µg/J (0·595 lb/h/hp)
At max cruise rating at 1,200 m (3,940 ft)	72·7 µg/J (0·430 lb/h/hp)

MOTORLET

MOTORLET NC, ZÁVOD JANA SVERMY

Prague-Jinonice
Telephone: Prague 520714
GENERAL MANAGER: Zdenek Horcik
ASSISTANTS TO GENERAL MANAGER:
TECHNICAL DIRECTOR: Ing Josef Krca
ECONOMIC DIRECTOR: Alois Svoboda
PRODUCTION DIRECTOR: Václav Jeřábek
HEAD OF DESIGN DEVELOPMENT: Ing Vladimir Pospisil

Motorlet National Corporation operates the main aero engine establishment in Czechoslovakia, based on the former Walter factory at Jinonice, previously well known for its radial and in-line piston engines. Today, the Walter name continues in use only as a trademark for Motorlet piston and turbine engines.

Motorlet started turbine engine manufacture in 1952 with licensed production of the Soviet RD-45 centrifugal turbojet for MiG-15 fighters.

WALTER M 601

Second of Czechoslovakia's small turbine engines to enter production, the M 601 was designed to power the Czech L-410 twin-engined light transport aircraft. It drives an Avia V 508 constant-speed three-blade propeller with hydraulically variable pitch.

The first version of the M 601, rated at 550 ehp, ran in October 1967. Development of the **M 601B**, of increased diameter, started during 1968. The Let L-410M, powered by M 601B engines in place of the Canadian PT6A-34s fitted to the L-410A, was in Aeroflot service in Siberia by early 1979. The M 601B powers the current L-410UVP version which then superseded the L-410M in production.

In 1982 a third variant, the **M 601D**, entered production. This gives increased power and can be operated to longer TBO.

By 1985 the **M 601Z** had entered production to power the Z 37T agricultural aircraft. It drives an Avia VJ 7.508Z three-blade propeller and an auxiliary blower for the spraying/dusting installation. TBO is 1,000 h.

The **M 601E** powers the L-410UVP-E, and has been developed to a TBO of 2,000 h. It drives an Avia VJ 8.508E five-blade propeller, and an alternator for anti-icing windshields and propeller blades.

TYPE: Free turbine combined axial-and-centrifugal turboprop.

PROPELLER DRIVE: Reduction gear at front of engine with drive from free turbine. Reduction ratio 14·9 : 1.

AIR INTAKE: Annular intake at rear of engine, with debris screen, feeds air to compressor plenum chamber.

COMPRESSOR: Two axial stages of stainless steel, plus single centrifugal stage of titanium. Pressure ratio (601B) 6·4, (601D) 6·55, (601 E) 6·65, at 36,660 rpm gas generator speed. Air mass flow (601B) 3·25 kg (7·17 lb)/s, (601D) 3·55 kg (7·83 lb)/s, (601E) 3·6 kg (7·94 lb)/s.

COMBUSTION CHAMBER: Annular combustor with rotary fuel injection and low-voltage LUN 2201.01-08 (601D, 2201.03-08) ignition.

COMPRESSOR TURBINE: Single stage; inlet temperature 952°C.

POWER TURBINE: Single stage.

FUEL SYSTEM: Low pressure LUN 6590 regulator, with three-lever control providing gas generator and power turbine speed controls.

FUEL GRADE: PL4, PL5 kerosene.

JETPIPE: Collector duct surrounding power turbine shaft. Exhaust through two ports on horizontal centreline.

ACCESSORIES: Mounting pads on accessory case at rear of engine. Propeller controls mounted on reduction gear case at front of engine.

LUBRICATION SYSTEM: Pressure gear-pump circulation. Integral oil tank and cooler.

OIL SPECIFICATION: B3V synthetic oil.

MOUNTING: Three elastically supported pins on compressor casing.

STARTING: LUN 2132-8 8kW electric starter/generator.

DIMENSIONS:

Length: 601D	1,658 mm (65·27 in)
601B, E, Z	1,675 mm (65·94 in)
Width	590 mm (23·23 in)
Height	650 mm (25·59 in)
WEIGHT, DRY:	
601B, D, E	193 kg (425·5 lb)
601Z	197 kg (434·3 lb)
PERFORMANCE RATINGS (T-O):	
601B	515 kW (691 shp)
601D	540 kW (724 shp)
601E	560 kW (751 shp)
601Z	360 kW (483 shp)
SPECIFIC FUEL CONSUMPTION (T-O):	
601B	109·55 µg/J (0·648 lb/h/ehp)
601D	109·4 µg/J (0·647 lb/h/ehp)

Left: Walter M 601Z turboprop rated at 360 kW (483 shp). Right: M 601E turboprop, rated at 560 kW (751 shp)

EGYPT

AOI

AOI ENGINE FACTORY (135)

PO Box 12, Helwan
Telephone: 745090, 747984 and 781088
Telex: 92135 Enfac UN
CHAIRMAN: Hassan El Gebali

Known previously as Factory 135, the AOI Engine Factory employs about 3,500 people, mainly in the production of military engine spare parts and in assembly and test of the Larzac 04 turbofan for Alpha Jet aircraft and the P&WC PT6A-25E turboprop for Tucano aircraft, delivery of the first PT6 having been made in 1985. Following selection of a new fighter for the Egyptian Air Force, the factory is expected to assemble either the F100, F404 or M53-P2.

Since 1980 AOI/EF has carried out complete overhaul, repair and test of Soviet APUs and the SNECMA Atar 9C and Larzac, GE T64 and Allison T56.

FRANCE

FAM

FRANCE AÉRO MOTEURS SARL

Roanne

This new company, inaugurated on 29 April 1985, was formed on a 50/50 basis by Avions Pierre Robin and the Motorop division of Besson-Moteurs Sopart, to put into production the PRV (Peugeot-Renault-Volvo) V6 light aircraft engine developed by Robin and the École Nationale des Ingénieurs de Saint-Etienne (ENISE).

PRV V6

The basis of this engine is the watercooled V6 piston engine used in Peugeot, Renault and Volvo cars, of which more than 470,000 have been built by Société Franco-Suédoise de Moteurs. Capacity of the 90° V cylinders is 2,850 cc (173·9 cu in), and overall dimensions 710 mm (27·95 in) long by 680 mm (26·77 in) high. ENISE is running many engines with carburettors and with Bosch K Jetronic electronically controlled fuel injection. Take-off power varies from 89-118 kW (120-160 hp) at a propeller speed reduced to 2,550 rpm by toothed belt, with fuel consumption in cruising flight of 70·64 µg/J (0·418 lb/h/hp). Extremely successful test flying has taken place in a Robin R 3140 (first flight 2 August 1982) and it is planned to offer the PRV engine to constructors of the Aérodis Orion (see Grinvalds in French part of Sport Aircraft section). Flight testing was expected to end in 1985, and certification is planned for 1987. In 1985 development began of a PRV that could be installed with crankshaft vertical in light helicopters.

JPX

ATELIERS JPX

Z.I. Nord, BP 13, 72320 Vibraye
Telephone: (43) 93 61 74

PUL 212

The PUL 212 is a single-cylinder low cost two-stroke, with bore of 66 mm (2·6 in), stroke of 62 mm (2·44 in) and capacity of 212 cc. Weighing 7·9 kg (17·42 lb) with pull cord inertia starter, it gives 11 kW (15 hp) at 6,000 rpm and is cleared to run at up to 6,500 rpm.

PUL 425

This is an opposed engine with two cylinders of the same size as in the PUL 212. Dry weight is 14·5 kg (32 lb), or 16·7 kg (36·8 lb) with silencer. Rated power is 16·4 kW (22 hp) at 4,600 rpm.

PAL 640

Three-cylinder radial using same size cylinders, giving 636 cc. Dry weight with electric starter 21 kg (46 lb). Rated power 22 kW (30 hp) at 4,000 rpm.

PAL 1300

Radial two-stroke with three cylinders of 84 mm bore and 78 mm stroke, giving 1,297 cc. Equipped dry weight 35 kg (77 lb). Rated power 37 kW (50 hp) at 3,200 rpm. Two-cylinder version (swept volume 865 cc, rated power 26 kW; 35 hp at 3,000 rpm) is also under development, with a dry weight (equipped) of 17 kg (37·5 lb).

JPX 4T60/A

Unlike previous JPX engines this is a four-stroke, with four opposed aircooled cylinders with bore 93·0 mm (3·66 in) and stroke 75·4 mm (2·97 in). Capacity 2,050 cc (125 cu in). Compression ratio 8·2. Overall length 650 mm (25·6 in). Width 805 mm (31·7 in). Weight, dry (without propeller hub) 73·0 kg (161 lb). Developed from the Volkswagen VW126A of smaller capacity, the 4T60/A has an electric starter and alternator, and is rated at 47·8 kW (65 hp) at 3,200 rpm, and 42·0 kW (57 hp) at 2,500 rpm. Using 4-star motor fuel or 100LL fuel, this engine was certificated by the DGAC on 9 January 1985, ready for production for the Robin ATL.

MICROTURBO

MICROTURBO SA

Chemin du Pont de Rupé, BP 2089, 31019 Toulouse Cédex
Telephone: (61) 70 11 27
Telex: 531442
DIRECTORATE:
J. G. Bayard (President)
P. F. Calmels (General Manager)
L. A. Pech (Marketing Director)

Microturbo was established in 1960 for the production of small gas turbines. The initial product was the Noelle 60290 free turbine starter for the SNECMA Atar turbojet, and from this a wide range of units has evolved. Today it operates as a division of Précision Mécanique Labinal. In 1985 it committed $3·5 million to upgrade its US subsidiary (see Microturbo North America in this section) to produce TRI 60 turbojets in that country.

MICROTURBO TRB

In 1986 the TRB 13 and TRB 19 turbojets were under development. The former has a diameter of 230 mm (9·06 in), length of 480 mm (18·90 in), weight of 16 kg (35·3 lb) and thrust rating of 0·81 kN (182 lb st) with sfc of 32·5 mg/Ns (1·15 lb/h/lb st). The TRB 19 has a diameter of 280 mm (11·02 in), length of 570 mm (22·44 in), weight of 28 kg (61·7 lb) and thrust rating of 1·2 kN (270 lb st) with sfc of 33·3 mg/Ns (1·18 lb/h/lb st)

MICROTURBO TRS 18-046

The TRS-18 single-shaft turbojet was designed for installation in gliders, to impart a self-launch and climb capability, but has since been adapted for ultralight aeroplanes and unmanned vehicles.

The TRS 18-046 is of modular construction. The forward module incorporates the air intake, gearbox, electronic governing and protection unit and the start sequencing and indication unit. The 28V 600W starter/generator is located in the nose bullet. The oil tank, with submerged pump, is on the underside, and includes provision for inverted flight. The HP oil filter and pressure transducer are on the top of this module. Adjacent to the compressor are the probes for engine speed and air temperature.

The turbine module comprises: the one-piece centrifugal compressor, with diffuser and straightener vanes; the axial turbine rotor and nozzle diaphragm; and the main frame, carrying the rotor assembly on two ball bearings between the compressor and turbine. The aft module comprises: the turbine casing backplate, carrying the annular folded combustion chamber liner, exhaust cone and nozzle; 10 spill type burners; two igniter plugs, used only during starting; and the jetpipe with thermocouple.

The fuel pump is driven electrically. The lubrication system is a closed circuit, with pressure supply to the rotor and gearbox bearings. The engine can be shut down and restarted in flight, and incorporates automatic fault and protection systems.

The following are current versions:

TRS 18-046. Certificated May 1976. Powers various prototypes.

TRS 18-046-1. Certificated October 1982. Powers Microjet 90, A-21SJ Calif, NASA/Ames AD-1, BD-5J, Fairchild scaled NGT, various other prototypes and (uprated) Mirach and Flight Refuelling RPVs and targets.

TRS 18-1. Uprated version, certificated March 1984. Powers Microjet 200B, A-21SJ, C-22J and (uprated) Mirach 100-2 and 100-3 and FR Falconet RPVs and targets.

DIMENSIONS:

Length: TRS 18	578 mm (22·75 in)
TRS 18-1	564 mm (22·20 in)
Width: TRS 18, 18-1	306 mm (12·05 in)
Height: TRS 18	349 mm (13·74 in)
TRS 18-1	339·5 mm (13·36 in)

WEIGHT, DRY:

TRS 18	37·0 kg (81·5 lb)
TRS 18-1	38·5 kg (84·9 lb)

PERFORMANCE RATINGS (T-O, ISA, S/L):

TRS 18 man rated	1 kN (225 lb st)
TRS 18 unmanned	1·13 kN (254 lb st)
TRS 18-1 man rated	1·45 kN (326 lb st)
TRS 18-1 unmanned	1·50 kN (337 lb st)

SPECIFIC FUEL CONSUMPTION (as above):

TRS 18	34·5 mg/Ns (1·22 lb/h/lb st)
TRS 18-1	33·4 mg/Ns (1·18 lb/h/lb st)

MICROTURBO TRI 60

US military designation: J403

Representing a significant French development in the propulsion of cruise type unmanned vehicles, the TRI 60 was designed under a contract from the Direction des Recherches et Moyens d'Essais. It is an extremely simple single-shaft turbojet for use in subsonic missiles and RPVs. The design has been biased towards minimal cost and absence of any maintenance or overhaul requirement, though engine design life exceeds 20 h.

The annular intake contains the accessory gearbox in the central bullet, together with an alternator or starter/generator; the struts house fuel and oil pipes. The simple axial compressor operates at a pressure ratio of about 4 : 1, with airflow of 5·6 kg (12·3 lb)/s, and is carried between front and rear bearings with labyrinth seals. The smokeless combustor is of the axial type, with multiple spray burners fed by a peripheral manifold. The axial turbine is overhung behind the rear bearing on the central diffuser housing.

An air bleed provides up to 1·5 per cent of total airflow. There is an engine driven fuel pump, but lubrication is by either pre-lubricated bearings or a total loss system from a pressurised reservoir. Speed control can be mechanical, electronic, fluidic or pneumatic, according to installation. Starting can be by impingement, electrical, cartridge or other means.

Versions of the TRI 60 announced by early 1985 are as follows:

TRI 60-1 Model 067. For British Aerospace Sea Eagle missile. Hydro-pneumatic fuel control unit to ensure a constant range mission at low altitude. Ignition by two pyro-igniters for windmill start.

TRI 60-2 Model 071. For Aérospatiale C.22 variable speed target drone. Continuous controlled electronic system. Fully throttleable.

TRI 60-2 Model 074. For Beechcraft MQM-107B variable speed target drone. As Model 071, but with 2 kW DC generator driven directly by gas generator shaft.

TRI 60-2 Model 077. For Saab Bofors Missile Corporation RBS 15M long-range anti-ship missile. As TRI 60-1 Model 067, with performance similar to that of TRI 60-2 Model 071.

TRI 60-2 Model 089. For SBMC RBS 15F missile. As Model 077 with adaptation for air launch.

TRI 60-2 Model 097. For Beechcraft BQM-126A (US Navy designation **J403-MT-400**). As Model 074 with enhanced performance. Has 4kW alternator and digital control computer.

A podded TRI 60 has been installed under the wing of the prototype Alpha Jet 01, which is serving as a flight development testbed.

DIMENSIONS (gas generator, no jetpipe):

Length overall	749 mm (29·49 in)
Envelope diameter	330 mm (12·99 in)

WEIGHT, DRY: 47 kg (103·6 lb)

PERFORMANCE RATINGS (ISA, S/L):

T-O: Model 067	3·50 kN (787 lb st)
Model 071	3·70 kN (831 lb st)
Model 097	4·00 kN (900 lb st)

SPECIFIC FUEL CONSUMPTION:

Model 067	34·5 mg/Ns (1·22 lb/h/lb st)
Model 071	35·4 mg/Ns (1·25 lb/h/lb st)
Model 097	34·8 mg/Ns (1·23 lb/h/lb st)

MICROTURBO TRI 80

This new series of engines, under development for unmanned applications, will have a fourth stage added in front of a basic TRI 60-2 axial compressor, to increase performance. Flight testing was due in 1985.

DIMENSIONS (gas generator, no jetpipe):

Length	768 mm (30·24 in)
Diameter	330 mm (12·99 in)

WEIGHT, DRY: 54 kg (119·1 lb)

PERFORMANCE RATING (ISA, S/L):

T-O (min, designed)	4·65 kN (1,040 lb st)
Enhanced version	5·35 kN (1,200 lb st)

SPECIFIC FUEL CONSUMPTION:

T-O	34·0 mg/Ns (1·20 lb/h/lb st)
Enhanced	33·4 mg/Ns (1·18 lb/h/lb st)

MICROTURBO TFA

Two simple turbofans were under study in 1986. The TFA 66 would have a diameter of 350 mm (13·78 in), length of 1,000 mm (39·37 in) and be rated at 360 kN (810 lb st) with sfc of 25·28 mg/Ns (0·892 lb/h/lb st). The TFA 130 would have a diameter of 440 mm (17·32 in), length of 975 mm (38·39 in) and be rated at 3·57 kN (802 lb st) with sfc of 17·48 mg/Ns (0·617 lb/h/lb st). Both engines would weigh (60 kg (132 lb).

Microturbo TRS 18-046 turbojet as prepared for use in Microjet 200

Microturbo TRS 18 for Meteor Mirach 100

Microturbo TRI 60-2 rated at 3·7 kN (831 lb st)

Microturbo TRI 80 rated at up to 5·35 kN (1,200 lb st) *(Brian M. Service)*

MUDRY

MOTEURS MUDRY-BUCHOUX (AVIONS MUDRY et CIE)

Aérodrome de Bernay, BP 47, 27300 Bernay
Telephone: (32) 43 47 34
DIRECTOR: Auguste Mudry

MUDRY MB-4-80

Described as being of highly original design, this aircooled four-stroke flat-four incorporates some parts, such as piston rings, rocker arms, valves and springs, of standard auto industry type, and several design features stem from Le Mans 24-h and other racing experience. Development is continuing.

CYLINDERS: Cast in pairs in light alloy with cast iron liners. Bore 93 mm (3·7 in). Stroke 92 mm (3·6 in). Capacity 2,498 cc (152·4 cu in).

VALVES: Flat cylinder heads with twin vertical overhead valves operated by pushrods and rocker arms.

PISTONS: Hypersilicate alloy, forming combustion chamber in head. Three rings including U-Flex scraper.

CRANKCASE: AS7G-06 alloy divided on vertical centreline.

FUEL GRADE: 100LL or automobile gasoline.

ACCESSORIES: Generator, starter and alternator all mounted on rear case. Two 32 mm carburettors. Bendix dual ignition.

DIMENSIONS:
- Length: 730 mm (28·7 in)
- Width: 710 mm (28·0 in)
- Height: 420 mm (16·5 in)

WEIGHT, DRY (equipped): 83 kg (183 lb)

PERFORMANCE RATING (S/L):
- Max T-O: 59·7 kW (80 hp) at 2,750 rpm

RECTIMO

RECTIMO AVIATION SA

Aérodrome de Chambéry, 73420 Savoie
Telephone: (79) 54 40 06
Telex: 980 202
DIRECTOR: André Rosselot

Rectimo has manufactured more than 500 Type 4 AR 1200 single ignition derivatives of the Volkswagen four-cylinder aircooled car engine, which together with the larger 4 AR 1600 are used in the Sportavia RF4D motor glider and various lightweight aircraft. The 30 kW (40 hp) 4 AR 1200 engine has a 1,192 cc cubic capacity, 7 : 1 compression ratio and weighs 61·5 kg (136 lb). Fuel consumption under cruise conditions is 11 litres (2·4 Imp gal)/h. The 4 AR 1600 produces 45·5 kW (61 hp) at T-O and has a cubic capacity of 1,600 cc and an 8 : 1 compression ratio. Weight is 64 kg (141 lb). Both engines have a maximum speed of 3,600 rpm.

Rectimo 4 AR 1200 piston engine of 30 kW (40 hp)

SNECMA

SOCIÉTÉ NATIONALE D'ÉTUDE ET DE CONSTRUCTION DE MOTEURS D'AVIATION

2 boulevard Victor, 75724 Paris Cédex 15
Telephone: 45 54 92 00
Telex: 202 834 Motav
CHAIRMAN AND CHIEF EXECUTIVE: Jacques Benichou
EXECUTIVE VICE-PRESIDENT, MILITARY PROGRAMME MANAGEMENT AND MARKETING: Jean Péquignot
EXECUTIVE VICE-PRESIDENT, FINANCE, PLANNING AND AFFILIATES: Jean Sollier
SENIOR VICE-PRESIDENT, ENGINEERING AND PRODUCTION: Jean Calmon
SENIOR VICE-PRESIDENT, INDUSTRIAL RELATIONS: André Van Wynsberghe
VICE-PRESIDENT, AFFILIATES AND PLANNING: Raymond Poggi
VICE-PRESIDENT, PRODUCTION: Yves Bonnet
VICE-PRESIDENT, COMMERCIAL PROGRAMME MANAGEMENT AND MARKETING: Dominique Paris
VICE-PRESIDENT, NEW PLANTS: Henri Forsans
VICE-PRESIDENT, ENGINEERING: Pierre Lachaume
PRESS ADVISER TO THE CHAIRMAN: Philippe Dreux

Villaroche Centre: 77550 Moissy-Cramayel
Design, development, assembly and ground test; flight and noise tests at Istres.

Evry-Corbeil:
RN 7, BP 81, 91003 Evry Cédex
Engine parts production, quality control, service, procurement and laboratories for research and development.

Gennevilliers:
291 avenue d'Argenteuil, BP 48, 92234 Gennevilliers
Forging and casting production, and blade machining.

Suresnes—ELECMA Division:
22 quai Galliéni, 92156 Suresnes
Design, development and production of electronic equipment, especially electronic control systems for the aircraft industry.

SNECMA (Société Nationale d'Etude et de Construction de Moteurs d'Aviation) was born on 28 August 1945 from the merger of the following aero-engine companies: Gnome et Rhône, Société Anonyme des Moteurs Renault pour l'Aviation, Société Générale de Mécanique et d'Aviation (former Moteurs Lorraine), and Groupe d'Etudes des Moteurs à Huile Lourde.

These companies already had a long aeronautical tradition and SNECMA has always devoted its main activity to aero-engines. More than 5,000 Atar turbojets have played a significant part in the worldwide success of Mirage fighters. SNECMA is now producing the M53 turbojet for fighters of the 1980s, and developing the M88 for the next generation. It is also participating in the following international collaborative programmes:

The CF6-50 for the Airbus A300, 747 and DC-10 (with MTU), and CF6-80 for the A300-600 and A310-300 under a co-production agreement with General Electric; the CFM56, which SNECMA shares equally with General Electric, but with FN and Kongsberg associated within SNECMA's share; the Larzac, produced in co-operation with Turboméca and with production also involving the German companies MTU and KHD, and FN in Belgium; and the Tyne, produced by a consortium (SNECMA, MTU, Rolls-Royce, FN).

Major subsidiaries are: Sochata SNECMA, engine repair and overhaul; Hispano-Suiza, industrial gas turbines and turbochargers, engine equipment and robotics and turrets for armoured vehicles; Messier-Hispano-Bugatti, complete landing gears and brake systems; and SEP, missile and space propulsion and image processing.

SNECMA ATAR

The Atar is a single-shaft military turbojet first run in 1946 and since developed and cleared for flight at Mach numbers greater than 2. Major versions are:

Atar 9C. Compared with the earlier 9B this introduced a new compressor, a self contained starter and an improved overspeed which comes into operation automatically when the aircraft reaches Mach 1·4, giving power equivalent to a sea level thrust of 62·76 kN (14,110 lb). Equips most Mirage III and 5.

Atar 9K50. Derived from the Atar 9C. Designed to offer improved subsonic specific fuel consumption, increased thrust for supersonic acceleration and improved overhaul life. The main improvements are in an entirely redesigned turbine with blades not forged but cast and coated with refractory metal from the vapour phase. Stages 1 and 8 of the compressor have been redesigned, resulting in pressure ratio raised from 6 to 6·15, coupled with slightly augmented mass flow. The control and electronic equipment have been revised and extended to improve the security of single-engined aircraft. The 9K50 is the power plant of all production Mirage F1 versions, Mirage 50 and 3 NG.

Atar 8K50. This is essentially the 9K50, re-engineered to have a simple unaugmented jetpipe and fixed nozzle, for the Super Etendard. Engines were delivered from May 1977 to June 1982.

DIMENSIONS:
- Diameter: 1,020 mm (40·2 in)
- Length overall:
  - Atar 8K50: 3,936 mm (155 in)
  - Atar 9C, 9K50: 5,944 mm (234 in)

WEIGHTS:
- Dry, complete with all accessories:
  - Atar 8K50: 1,155 kg (2,546 lb)
  - Atar 9C: 1,456 kg (3,209 lb)
  - Atar 9K50: 1,582 kg (3,487 lb)

PERFORMANCE RATINGS:
- Max with afterburner:
  - Atar 9C: 58·9 kN (13,230 lb st) at 8,400 rpm
  - Atar 9K50: 70·6 kN (15,870 lb st) at 8,400 rpm
- Max without afterburner:
  - Atar 8K50: 49 kN (11,025 lb st) at 8,550 rpm
  - Atar 9C: 42 kN (9,430 lb st) at 8,400 rpm
  - Atar 9K50: 49·2 kN (11,055 lb st)

SPECIFIC FUEL CONSUMPTION:
- At max rating with afterburner:
  - Atar 9C: 57·5 mg/Ns (2·03 lb/h/lb st)
  - Atar 9K50: 55·5 mg/Ns (1·96 lb/h/lb st)
- At max rating without afterburner:
  - Atar 8K50: 27·5 mg/Ns (0·97 lb/h/lb st)
  - Atar 9C: 28·6 mg/Ns (1·01 lb/h/lb st)
  - Atar 9K50: 27·5 mg/Ns (0·97 lb/h/lb st)

OIL CONSUMPTION: 1·5 litres (2·64 Imp pints)/h

SNECMA M53

The M53 is a single-shaft turbofan—more strictly a continuous bleed turbojet—capable of propelling fighter aircraft at high altitude at Mach 2·5. The first applications are in the Mirage 2000 and Super Mirage 4000. The engine is of modular construction.

The single shaft comprises a three-stage fan and five-stage compressor driven by a two-stage turbine designed for operation at high gas temperature. There are no inlet guide vanes. Between the fan and compressor is a mid-frame incorporating accessory drives and front roller bearing and ball thrust bearing. The annular combustion chamber is designed for smoke free operation. The turbine delivery casing incorporates the third bearing. Fuel to the combustion chamber and reheat system, and the multi-flap nozzle, are controlled by a fuel system monitored by an Elecma electronic computer.

Flight trials began on 18 July 1973 in the starboard pod of a Caravelle testbed. The supersonic flight envelope was explored with the Mirage F1-M53 flying testbed, which first flew in December 1974. The Mirage 2000 first flew in March 1978 and the Super Mirage 4000 in March 1979. By early 1986, total engine running time had exceeded 38,000 h.

The initial **M53-2** version is rated at 83.4 kN (18,740 lb st). The **M53-5** is in production as the initial engine of the Mirage 2000.

The **M53-P2** is an uprated version developed to power the Mirage 2000 from 1985. The first batch ordered in 1983 power the first 15 Mirage 2000N two-seat attack aircraft.

DIMENSIONS:
- Length, overall: 4,853 mm (191 in)
- Max diameter: 1,055 mm (41·5 in)

WEIGHT, DRY:
- M53-5: 1,450 kg (3,195 lb)
- M53-P2: 1,500 kg (3,307 lb)

SNECMA Atar 9K50 turbojet of 70·6 kN (15,870 lb st) with afterburning

PERFORMANCE RATINGS:
Max with afterburner:
M53-5 88·2 kN (19,850 lb st)
M53-P2 95·0 kN (21,360 lb st)
Max without afterburner:
M53-5 54·4 kN (12,240 lb st)
M53-P2 64·3 kN (14,470 lb st)
SPECIFIC FUEL CONSUMPTION (without afterburner):
M53-5 24·64 mg/Ns (0·87 lb/h/lb st)
M53-P2 25·55 mg/Ns (0·90 lb/h/lb st)

SNECMA M88

This two-shaft turbofan has variable inlet guide vanes, a three-stage LP compressor (fan), six-stage HP compressor, annular combustor, single-stage HP and LP turbines, and an afterburner with convergent/divergent nozzle. Intended to be the basis of a new family of engines for air defence, air superiority and ground attack fighters of the 1990s, it is being developed under contract to the French Defence Ministry. The HP core met test objectives in 1983, and the first complete engine ran at the beginning of 1984. The following data relate to the demonstration programme intended to lead to an engine with a thrust/weight ratio of 10.

DIMENSION:
Length overall 3,800 mm (150 in)
WEIGHT, DRY: 900 kg (1,984 lb)
PERFORMANCE RATINGS:
First stage 1984-85:
Max: with afterburner 73·5 kN (16,540 lb st)
without afterburner 46·8 kN (10,530 lb st)
Second stage 1986-87:
Max: with afterburner 84·7 kN (19,060 lb st)
without afterburner 54·4 kN (12,240 lb st)
SPECIFIC FUEL CONSUMPTION:
First stage 1984-85:
Max: with afterburner 52·77 mg/Ns (1·86 lb/h/lb st)
without afterburner 21·94 mg/Ns (0·775 lb/h/lb st)
Second stage 1986-87:
Max: with afterburner 51·11 mg/Ns (1·805 lb/h/lb st)
without afterburner 22·50 mg/Ns (0·795 lb/h/lb st)

CFM INTERNATIONAL CFM56

SNECMA decided in the Autumn of 1971 to develop the CFM56 subsonic turbofan in co-operation with General Electric. The programme is covered under CFM in the International part of this section.

GE/SNECMA/MTU CF6

To provide engines for the Airbus Industrie A300B and French Boeing 747s, SNECMA and MTU of Federal Germany participate in a co-production programme with General Electric to make the CF6-50 turbofan. SNECMA performs assembly and test, and manufactures parts, with a total share on a cost basis of 27 per cent. Included in the share are parts for engines for the DC-10-30. A similar production agreement applies to the CF6-80A1 and A3 for the A310 aircraft, and has been extended to include the CF6-80C for all applications (A300-600, A310-300, B747 and B767), with a total share on a cost basis of 10 per cent.

SNECMA/TURBOMÉCA LARZAC

This turbofan was designed jointly by SNECMA and Turboméca. It appears under the entry for Turboméca-SNECMA GRTS, in this section.

RR/SNECMA/MTU/FN TYNE

Under Rolls-Royce licence, the Tyne 22 turboprop for the Transall C-160, was put back into production in October 1977, by the original four-nation consortium with the original work split. SNECMA's share is made by Hispano-Suiza, and assembly and test take place at Sochata-SNECMA, Châtellerault. First delivery August 1980. The similar Tyne 21 will be re-ordered, to power the Dassault-Breguet Atlantique. These 4,550 kW (6,100 shp) engines were last described in the 1975-76 *Jane's*.

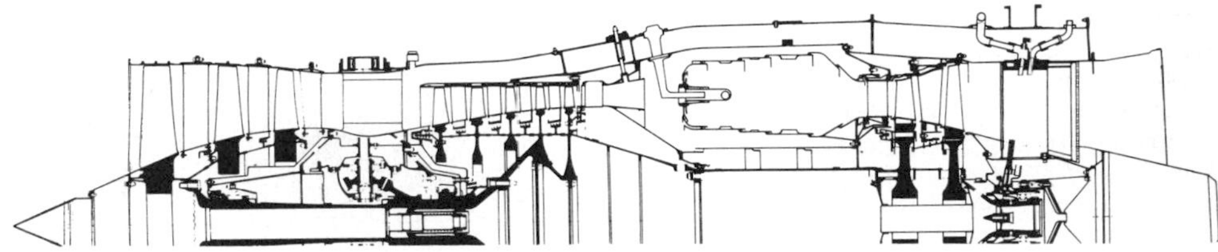

Longitudinal section through the SNECMA M53 showing LP and HP sections on single shaft (pressure ratio, 9·3 at 10,500 rpm) and bypass duct

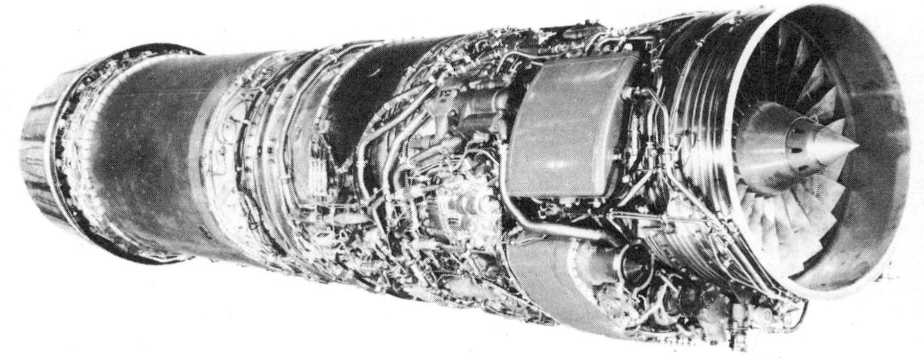

SNECMA M53-P2 augmented bypass turbojet of 95·0 kN (21,360 lb st)

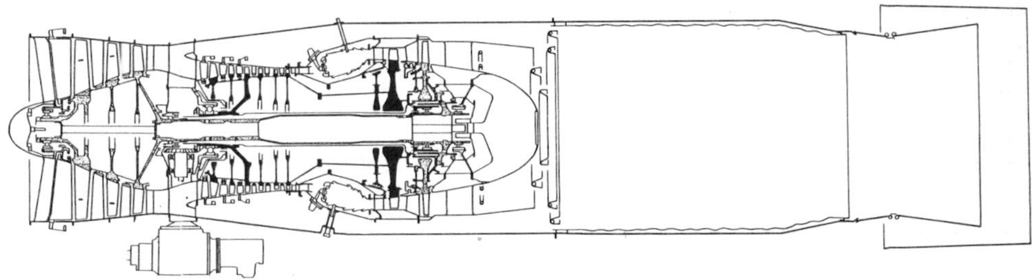

Longitudinal section through SNECMA M88 augmented turbofan

SNECMA M88 demonstration engine (1985 rating 73·5 kN, 16,540 lb st)

SNPE

SOCIÉTÉ NATIONALE DES POUDRES ET EXPLOSIFS

12 Quai Henri IV, 75181 Paris Cédex 04

Telephone: 4277 15 70

SNPE produces solid rocket motors for defence and space applications. Air-launched applications include 68, 70 and 100 mm rockets, the AS 12, AS 15TT, AS 30L, AM 39 Exocet, Martel, Kormoran and ASMP air-to-surface missiles, R.530, R.550 and Super 530 AAMs, Durandal and BAP.100 runway penetrators and boost propulsion of the CT.20 and C.22 targets. In collaboration with Aérospatiale and ONERA work is proceeding on a variable-flow ducted ramrocket with integrated booster.

TURBOMÉCA

SOCIÉTÉ TURBOMÉCA

Bordes, 64320 Bizanos
Telephone: (16-59) 32 84 37
Telex: 560928
OTHER WORKS: Mézières S/Seine (Yvelines) and Tarnos (near Bayonne)
PARIS OFFICE: 1, Rue Beaujon, Paris 8e
PRESIDENT AND DIRECTOR-GENERAL:
J. R. Szydlowski

The Société Turboméca was formed in 1938 by Messieurs Szydlowski and Planiol to develop blowers, compressors and turbines for aeronautical use. Today, it is the leading European manufacturer of small turbine aero engines. Since it first started development of gas turbines in 1947, the company has developed about 50 different types of power plant of which some 15 have entered production and ten types have been manufactured under licence in nine countries.

By 1 January 1985 more than 24,000 Turboméca engines for fixed and rotating-wing applications and aircraft auxiliary duties had been delivered to customers in 110 countries. Approximately 14,000 more engines have been built under licence by what are today Rolls-Royce Ltd in the UK, Teledyne CAE in the USA, ENMASA in Spain, Hindustan Aeronautics Ltd in India, Bet-Shemesh in Israel and state factories in Romania and Yugoslavia. The Arriel helicopter engine is reported by the People's Republic of China to be in production in that country.

A European Small Engines Co-operation Agreement signed in April 1985 joins Turboméca, MTU of West Germany and Rolls-Royce of the UK in promoting three complementary new engines: the Turboméca TM 333, MTU Turboméca MTM 385 and Rolls-Royce Turboméca RTM 322. Other European small engine makers may join the collaboration, in which each partner may share in engines sold to its own government.

Total covered floor area for Turboméca's three plants at Bordes, Mézières and Tarnos is 136,487 m² (1,469,134 sq ft). The company employs about 4,400 people.

Turboméca Arriel 1 free turbine turboshaft, with ratings up to 544 kW (730 shp) *(Michel Isaac)*

Turboméca has 45·6% participation in CGTM, 26% in CGR, 50% in Turboméca-SNECMA, 50% in Astadyne (APU development with ABG-Semca), 50% in MTU-Turboméca, 50% in Rolls-Royce Turboméca, 22·08% in Ormat Turbines and 50% in RR-TM do Brasil.

ROLLS-ROYCE TURBOMÉCA ADOUR

This turbofan was developed jointly by Rolls-Royce and Turboméca. A description is given in the International part of this section.

TURBOMÉCA-SNECMA LARZAC

This small turbofan was developed jointly by Turboméca and SNECMA. A description is given under Turboméca-SNECMA GRTS.

TURBOMÉCA ARRIEL

This turboshaft engine is being used initially in two Aérospatiale helicopters, the single-engined AS 350 Ecureuil and twin-engined SA 365 Dauphin. It could also power a future version of the SA 341/342 Gazelle.

The Arriel is intended to have low first cost, low maintenance cost and low specific weight. It is characterised by modular construction, and is expected eventually to form the basis for a single-shaft turboprop and a turbofan in the 4·90 kN (1,100 lb st) class. The gas generator ran in 1973. The first complete engine ran on the bench on 7 August 1974. Flight development began on 17 December 1974 in the SA 341-02 Gazelle, which had been converted for Arriel development by Aérospatiale and the CGTM. The twin-engined SA 365 first flew on 24 January 1975, and the AS 350 Ecureuil on 14 February 1975. By 1 January 1985 a total of 1,166 Arriels had been delivered, against orders for 1,533. These figures do not include licence production in China.

TYPE: Single-shaft axial-plus-centrifugal free turbine turboshaft.

AIR INTAKE: Direct pitot entry to axial compressor.

COMPRESSOR: Single-stage axial compressor, machined from titanium forging. Supersonic centrifugal stage also machined from titanium. High rotational speed for maximum attainable pressure ratio (9:1).

COMBUSTION CHAMBER: Annular chamber, with flow radially outwards and then inwards. Centrifugal fuel injection without central tube.

GAS-GENERATOR TURBINE: Two integral cast axial stages with solid blades. Turbine shield capable of disc containment.

POWER TURBINE: Single axial stage with inserted blades.

JETPIPE: Exhaust diffuser fabricated by welding.

REDUCTION GEAR: Light alloy gearbox, containing two stages of helical gears, giving drive at 6,000 rpm to output shaft extending whole length of engine, with drive connections to both front and rear. Hydraulic torquemeter.

ACCESSORY DRIVES: Two bevel gears and radial quill shaft drive accessory gearbox at front end, carried between compressor case and output shaft. Main pad provides for optional 12,000 rpm alternator; other drives for oil pumps, tachometer generator, governor and starter.

LUBRICATION SYSTEM: Independent circuit. Oil from tank passes through gear pump and metallic cartridge filter. Return from engine via three gear scavenge pumps. Temperature probe and pressure switch to verify operation.

OIL SPECIFICATION: AIR 3512 (mineral) or AIR 3513A (synthetic).

MOUNTING: Multi-point flanges allow easy mounting in single or twin installation.

STARTING: Electric starter or starter/generator.

DIMENSIONS:

Length, excl accessories	1,090 mm (42·91 in)
Height overall	569 mm (22·40 in)
Width	430 mm (16·93 in)

WEIGHT, DRY:

With all engine accessories	109 kg (240 lb)

PERFORMANCE RATINGS:

Max contingency	520 kW (698 shp)
Max contingency, later	544 kW (730 shp)
T-O and intermediate contingency	478 kW (641 shp)
Max continuous	441 kW (592 shp)

SPECIFIC FUEL CONSUMPTION:

Max contingency	93·1 μg/J (0·551 lb/h/shp)
Intermediate contingency	96·8 μg/J (0·573 lb/h/shp)

TURBOMÉCA ASTAZOU TURBOPROP

The Astazou is the major turboprop in the Turboméca range and is in production in its 761 kW (1,020 ehp) Astazou XVI versions. The Astazou XIV was certificated by the French airworthiness authorities in October 1968, followed by ARB/FAA certification of the Astazou XIVC and C1 in March 1969.

Current versions of the Astazou are:

Astazou XII. Powered Shorts Skyvan Srs 2 at 690 shp and Pilatus Turbo-Porter PC-6/A1-H2 at 700 ehp.

Astazou XIV (alias AZ14). Developed from Astazou XII. Powers early Jetstream business aircraft at 853 ehp.

Astazou XVI (alias AZ16). Higher rated version of Astazou XIV and first engine to enter production with new Turboméca aircooled turbine. The XVID, without starter/generator, powers the former production versions of the Jetstream; the XVIZ powers the Nord 260A. The Astazou XVIG, equipped for sustained inverted flight, powers the Argentine IA 58 Pucará. By early 1985 deliveries of all XVI versions totalled 367, against orders for 440.

DIMENSIONS:

Diameter over intake cowl	546 mm (21·5 in)
Overall length, incl propeller	2,047 mm (80·6 in)

WEIGHTS:

With accessories:	
Astazou XIV	approx 206 kg (454 lb)
Astazou XVID	205 kg (452 lb)
Astazou XVIG	228 kg (502 lb)
Astazou XVIZ	213 kg (468 lb)

PERFORMANCE RATINGS:

T-O: Astazou XIV	636 ekW; 596·5 kW (853 ehp; 800 shp) at 43,000 rpm
Astazou XVID	723 ekW; 681 kW (969 ehp; 913 shp) at 43,089 rpm
Astazou XVIG, XVIZ	761 ekW; 720 kW (1,020 ehp; 965 shp) at 43,000 rpm
Max continuous: Astazou XIV	574 ekW; 537 kW (770 ehp; 720 shp) at 43,000 rpm
Astazou XVID	626 ekW; 586 kW (840 ehp; 786 shp) at 43,089 rpm
Astazou XVIG, XVIZ	696 ekW; 654 kW (934 ehp; 877 shp) at 43,000 rpm

SPECIFIC FUEL CONSUMPTION:

At T-O rating:	
Astazou XIV	92·4 μg/J (0·547 lb/h/shp)
Astazou XVI (all versions)	88·7 μg/J (0·525 lb/h/shp)

TURBOMÉCA ASTAZOU TURBOSHAFT

This turboshaft series of the Astazou family is derived from the early second generation Astazou II turboprop fitted to the Mitsubishi MU-2 and Pilatus Turbo-Porter. Variants are as follows:

Astazou IIA. Rated at 390 kW (523 shp) and powers the Aérospatiale SA 318C Alouette II Astazou helicopter. Total of 732 built by 1977.

Astazou III. Definitive turboshaft for Anglo-French helicopter programme for production SA 341 Gazelle. Derived from Astazou IIA but with revised profile of turbine, using higher temperature alloy to match power needs of SA 341. Astazou IIIA, B, C and N for Gazelle versions all certificated in June 1972; uprated IIIA2, B2, C2 and N2 certificated May 1978. Produced jointly by Turboméca and Rolls-Royce Ltd, with 914 delivered by 1 January 1982.

Astazou XIVB and XIVF. In production for the SA 319B Alouette III; XIVB is civil and XIVF military. Flat rated to 441 kW (591 shp) (1 h) up to 4,000 m (13,125 ft) or +55°C.

Astazou XIVH. In production for SA 341 Gazelle, with much increased power. Flat rated to transmission limit, to remove all altitude and temperature limitations. Certificated October 1974. By 1 January 1985 1,118 of all XIV versions had been delivered, of 1,227 ordered.

Astazou XVIIIA. Further increase in power gained by improved turbine, allowing higher gas temperature. Powers SA 360 Dauphin.

Astazou XX. Fourth axial compressor stage added. Designed for operation in hot and high countries.

The following description relates to the Astazou IIIN except where indicated:

TYPE: Single-shaft axial-plus-centrifugal turboshaft.

REDUCTION GEAR: Mounted in tapered cylindrical casing at front of engine, with two stage epicyclic reduction gear having helical primary gears and straight secondary gears. Reduction ratio 7·039 : 1 (Astazou XIVB/F, 7·345; XVIIIA, 7·375).

AIR INTAKE: Annular air intake at rear of reduction gear casing.

COMPRESSOR: Single-stage axial (IIA, IIN, IIIN), two-stage axial (XIV, XVIII) or three stage-axial (XX) followed by single-stage centrifugal with single-sided impeller. Air mass flow 2·5 kg (5·5 lb)/s.

COMBUSTION SYSTEM: Reverse flow annular type with centrifugal fuel injector using rotary atomiser disc. Ignition by two ventilated torch igniters.

TURBINE: Three-stage axial with blades integral with discs. Discs attached by curvic couplings and bolts.

JETPIPE: Fixed type with curved inner cone.

ACCESSORIES: Five drive pads on casing forming rear of air intake.

Turboméca Astazou XX turboshaft, rated at 749 kW (1,005 shp)

MOUNTING: At front by flange located at power take-off section, and at rear by two lugs on accessory mounting pad section.
FUEL SYSTEM: Automatic constant speed control with speed governor.
LUBRICATION SYSTEM: Pressure type with gear type pumps. Oil tank of 8 litre (14 Imp pint) capacity mounted at front of engine.
STARTING: Electrical, automatic.
DIMENSIONS:

Length overall: Astazou IIA	1,272 mm (50·0 in)
Astazou III, XIVB/F	1,433 mm (56·3 in)
Astazou XIVH	1,470 mm (57·9 in)
Astazou XVIIIA	1,327 mm (52·2 in)
Astazou XX	1,529 mm (60·22 in)
Height: Astazou IIA	458 mm (18 in)
Astazou III, XIVH	460 mm (18·1 in)
Astazou XVIIIA	698 mm (27·48 in)
Astazou XX	721 mm (28·4 in)
Width: Astazou IIA	480 mm (18·8 in)
Astazou III, XIVH	460 mm (18·1 in)

WEIGHTS:

Equipped: Astazou III	147 kg (324 lb)
Astazou III (suffix 2)	150 kg (330 lb)
Astazou XIVB/F	166 kg (366 lb)
Astazou XIVH	160 kg (353 lb)
Astazou XVIIIA	155 kg (341 lb)
Astazou XX	195 kg (430 lb)

PERFORMANCE RATINGS:

Max power: Astazou IIA	390 kW (523 shp)
Astazou III	441 kW (592 shp)
Astazou III (suffix 2)	481 kW (645 shp)
Astazou XX	749 kW (1,005 shp)
One hour: Astazou XIVB/F	441 kW (591 shp)
Astazou XVIIIA	651 kW (873 shp)
	maintained at sea level to 40°C
Max continuous: Astazou IIA	353 kW (473 shp)
Astazou III	390 kW (523 shp)
Astazou III (suffix 2)	441 kW (592 shp)
Astazou XIVB/F	405 kW (543 shp)
Astazou XIVH	flat rated in SA 341 at 440·7 kW (591 shp) to 55°C or 4,000 m (13,125 ft)
Astazou XVIIIA	600 kW (805 shp)
Astazou XX	675 kW (905 shp)

SPECIFIC FUEL CONSUMPTION:
At max power rating:

Astazou IIA	105·3 μg/J (0·623 lb/h/shp)
Astazou III	108·7 μg/J (0·643 lb/h/shp)
Astazou III (suffix 2)	109·9 μg/J (0·650 lb/h/shp)
Astazou XIVB/F	105·5 μg/J (0·624 lb/h/shp)
Astazou XVIIIA	91·3 μg/J (0·540 lb/h/shp)
Astazou XX	85·9 μg/J (0·508 lb/h/shp)

TURBOMÉCA ARTOUSTE III

The Artouste IIIB is a single-shaft turboshaft derived from the Artouste II. It is a member of the second generation of Turboméca engines with two-stage axial-centrifugal compressor and three-stage turbine. The Artouste IIIB has a pressure ratio of 5·2 : 1. Air mass flow is 4·3 kg/s (9·5 lb/s) at 33,300 rpm.

Type approval at the rating quoted was received on 25 May 1961, following completion of a 150-h official type test. Production at Turboméca continues. In addition, Artouste IIIBs are being built under licence in India by Hindustan Aeronautics Ltd.

The Artouste IIIB, which powers the Aérospatiale SA 316B Alouette III, obtained FAA certification in March 1962 and in August 1968 similar certification of the Artouste IIC1, C2, C5 and C6, powering the SE 3130 and 313B Alouette II Artouste, was also obtained.

An uprated version, the Artouste IIID, was certificated on 30 April 1971. It differs in having a reduction gear giving 5,864 rpm at the driveshaft (instead of 5,773 rpm) and in slightly revised equipment. The IIID powers a late version of the Alouette III; data are for this version. A total of 2,514 Artouste III engines had been built by 1 January 1985, of 2,520 ordered.

DIMENSIONS:

Length	1,815 mm (71·46 in)
Height	627 mm (24·68 in)
Width	507 mm (19·96 in)

WEIGHT, DRY: 178 kg (392 lb)
PERFORMANCE RATING (T-O, maintained up to 55°C at S/L or up to approximately 4,000 m; 13,125 ft): 440 kW (590 shp)
SPECIFIC FUEL CONSUMPTION: 126·2 μg/J (0·747 lb/h/shp)

The 1,032 kW (1,384 shp) Turboméca Turmo IIIC$_4$ turboshaft which powers the SA 330 Puma helicopter

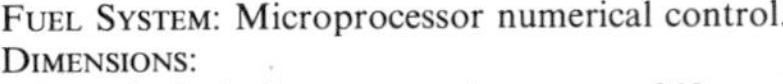

MTU-TURBOMÉCA MTM 385

This helicopter engine is covered in the International part of this section.

TURBOMÉCA TM 333

This turboshaft engine was launched in July 1979 to power advanced versions of the Aérospatiale SA 365 Dauphin and other helicopters in the 4,000 kg (8,800 lb) class including the Indian ALH. A turboprop version is also being developed.

The core engine first ran on 19 August 1981 and the complete engine ran in the following month. Flight testing began on 8 April 1982 and 14 engines had run 4,250 h by 30 September 1984. Production engines were due in late 1985. Two versions have been announced:

TM 333. Basic version, composed of a gas generator module, free turbine module and reduction gear module.

TM 333B. Growth version with aircooled HP turbine, giving T-O rating of 731 kW (980 shp). First run 6 November 1984. Selected for HAL (India) ALH. Deliveries planned to begin in 1988.

The TM 333 is one of three new engines included in the European Small Engines Co-operation Agreement mentioned in the company introductory text. General Electric is marketing the TM 333 in North America and has been collaborating with Turboméca on a turbofan derivative since 1981.

TYPE: Free turbine turboshaft.
AIR INTAKE: Annular with scroll to recover dynamic pressure.
COMPRESSOR: Variable inlet guide vanes, two stage axial compressor, single stage centrifugal.
COMBUSTION CHAMBER: Annular, reverse flow.
GAS GENERATOR TURBINE: Single-stage with uncooled inserted blades.
POWER TURBINE: Single-stage axial with uncooled inserted blades.
JETPIPE: Straight pipe at rear.
GEARBOX: Two stages to give drive at 6,000 rpm to front output shaft.
LUBRICATION: Independent system. Oil from tank passes through gear pump and metallic cartridge filter, returning via two scavenge pumps.
FUEL SYSTEM: Microprocessor numerical control.
DIMENSIONS:

Length, including accessories	943 mm (37·1 in)
Height overall	557 mm (21·9 in)
Width	415 mm (16·3 in)

WEIGHT, DRY: 140 kg (308 lb)
PERFORMANCE RATINGS:

Max contingency	680 kW (912 shp)
T-O	625 kW (838 shp)
Max continuous	560 kW (751 shp)

SPECIFIC FUEL CONSUMPTION:

Max contingency	88 μg/J (0·523 lb/h/shp)
T-O	89·4 μg/J (0·529 lb/h/shp)
Max continuous	91·7 μg/J (0·543 lb/h/shp)

TURBOMÉCA TM 319

This turboshaft engine has been developed since September 1981 to provide a power plant for a helicopter to replace the Alouette family, and to be suitable for a wide range of other light twin and ultralight single engined helicopters. It follows typical Turboméca principles, and is very compact, there being no axial compressor stages. Initial rating is 330 kW (443 shp). The first TM 319 was run on the bench on 21 February 1983. Five engines were on test by 9 May, on which date a 50 h test was completed successfully. All these engines have full authority digital electronic control, which for production 319s will be supplied by Elecma. Flight testing began on 19 May 1983 with two engines installed by CGTM in an AS 355 Ecureuil. By 1985 sixteen engines had run over 1,700 h. The French Air Force will be the first customer for the twin TM 319 Ecureuil. Certification was due in early 1986. The same gas generator is used in the TP 319 turboprop, and also in a forthcoming APU for 150/200-seat aircraft.

DIMENSIONS:

Length	782 mm (30·78 in)
Width	360 mm (14·2 in)
Height	540 mm (21·26 in)

WEIGHT, DRY: 87 kg (192 lb)
PERFORMANCE RATINGS (ISA, S/L):

Max contingency	380 kW (509 shp)
Max T-O	340 kW (456 shp)
Max continuous	295 kW (395 shp)

TURBOMÉCA TP 319

The turboprop version of the 319 family is a fully aerobatic engine aimed at single and twin-engined aircraft. The gas generator and power turbine modules are identical with those of the TM 319. The first TP 319 ran on 11 September 1985, and flight testing in an Epsilon began in December 1985, by which time two ground-test engines had logged 75 hours. Certification is due in 1987.

DIMENSIONS:

Length	826 mm (32·52 in)
Width	476 mm (18·74 in)
Height	590 mm (23·22 in)

WEIGHT, DRY (bare): 111 kg (245 lb)
PERFORMANCE RATINGS (ISA, S/L):

Twin T-O contingency	343 kW (460 shp)
T-O	313 kW (420 shp)
Cruise (6,100 m, 20,000 ft)	179 kW (240 shp)

The 313 kW (420 shp) Turboméca TP 319 turboprop

TURBOMÉCA TURMO

The Turmo free turbine engine is in service in both turboshaft and turboprop versions.

The main variants are as follows:

Turmo IIIC$_3$. This was the original power plant of the three-engined SA 321 Super Frelon helicopter. Maximum contingency rating is 1,104 kW (1,480 shp).

Turmo IIIC$_4$. Developed from Turmo IIIC$_3$ and with a maximum contingency rating of 1,032 kW (1,384 shp), this all-weather version was manufactured jointly by Turboméca and Rolls-Royce to power SA 330 Puma twin-engined helicopters under the Franco-British helicopter agreement of October 1967. Certificated by the Services Officiels Français on 9 October 1970. Total production of IIIC$_4$ and IV by 1 January 1984 was 1,957, of 1,961 ordered.

Turmo IIIC$_5$, IIIC$_6$, IIIC$_7$. Similar to Turmo IIIC$_3$ but with different ratings. The SA 321F and 321J Super Frelons powered by these engines obtained French certification in June 1968. Total production of Super Frelon engines (including E series), 549.

Turmo IIID. Turboprop version, similar in basic construction to Turmo IIIC series but with output speed limited to 6,000 rpm.

Turmo IIIE$_3$. Similar to Turmo IIIC$_3$ but with different ratings. In production for SA 321 Super Frelon.

Turmo IIIE$_6$. Higher turbine temperature.

Turmo IV. The Turmo IVA is a civil engine derived from the IIIC$_4$, with a maximum contingency rating of 1,057 kW (1,417 shp). The IVB is a military version having the same ratings as the IIIC$_4$.

The following description applies generally to the Turmo IIIC$_3$, C$_4$, C$_5$ and E$_3$, except where indicated:

TYPE: Free turbine axial plus centrifugal turboshaft.

REDUCTION GEAR: Turmo IIIC$_3$, C$_5$ and E$_3$ fitted with rear mounted reduction gear mounted in bifurcated exhaust duct with rear facing power take-off shaft. Turmo IIIC$_4$ is a direct drive engine.

AIR INTAKE: Annular forward facing intake, with de-icing in Turmo IIIC$_4$ and C$_5$.

COMPRESSOR: Single-stage axial followed by single-stage centrifugal with single-sided impeller. Two rows of light alloy stator blades aft of axial stage. Centrifugal stage has steel radial and axial diffusers; impeller located by lugs on turbine shaft. Axial rotor blades, titanium in Turmo IIIC$_3$, C$_5$ and E$_3$ and steel in Turmo IIIC$_4$, pin mounted in steel disc with integral shaft. Pressure ratio 5·9 : 1 on Turmo IIIC$_3$. Air mass flow 5·9 kg (13 lb)/s.

COMBUSTION SYSTEM: Reverse flow annular type with centrifugal fuel injector using rotary atomiser disc. Ignition by two ventilated torch igniters.

GAS GENERATOR TURBINE: Two-stage axial unit with integral rotor bades.

POWER TURBINE: Two-stage axial unit in Turmo IIIC$_3$, C$_5$ and E$_3$, and single stage in Turmo IIIC$_4$. In all advanced production engines of IIIC$_4$ derivation the power turbine speed is 22,840 rpm under all high power conditions.

JETPIPE: Fixed type with lateral bifurcated exhaust duct in Turmo IIIC$_3$, C$_5$ and E$_3$, and single lateral duct on Turmo IIIC$_4$.

ACCESSORIES: Mounted above and below intake casing with drive pads for oil pump, fuel control unit, electric starter, tacho-generator and, on Turmo IIIC$_4$, oil cooler fan. Control unit remote drive also provided on Turmo IIIC$_4$ from bevel gear drive on power turbine output shaft.

MOUNTING: Two lateral supports fitted to lower part of turbine casing at rear flange output shaft protection tube. On Turmo IIIC$_4$, also on reduction gear case.

FUEL SYSTEM: Fuel control unit for gas generator on Turmo IIIC$_3$, C$_5$ and E$_3$, with speed limiter for power turbine also fitted on E$_3$. Constant-speed system fitted on Turmo IIIC$_4$ power turbine, with speed limiter also fitted on gas generator.

FUEL GRADE: AIR 3405 for Turmo IIIC$_4$.

LUBRICATION SYSTEM: Pressure type with oil cooler and 13 litre (23 Imp pint) tank at front of engine on Turmo IIIC$_4$, with oil tank only around intake casing on Turmo IIIC$_3$, C$_5$ and E$_3$, and by intake accessory drive gear on Turmo IIIC$_4$.

OIL SPECIFICATION: AIR 3155A, or synthetic AIR 3513, for Turmo IIIC$_4$.

STARTING: Automatic system with electric starter motor.

DIMENSIONS:

Length:

Turmo IIIC$_3$, C$_5$ and E$_3$	1,975·7 mm (78·0 in)
Turmo IIIC$_4$	2,184 mm (85·5 in)
Turmo IIID$_3$	1,868 mm (73·6 in)

Width:

Turmo IIIC$_3$, C$_5$ and E$_3$	693 mm (27·3 in)
Turmo IIIC$_4$	637 mm (25·1 in)
Turmo IIID$_3$	934 mm (36·8 in)

Height:

Turmo IIIC$_3$, C$_5$ and E$_3$	716·5 mm (28·2 in)
Turmo IIIC$_4$	719 mm (28·3 in)
Turmo IIID$_3$	926 mm (36·5 in)

WEIGHT, DRY:

Turmo IIIC$_3$ and E$_3$, fully equipped	297 kg (655 lb)
Turmo IIIC$_5$, IIIC$_6$ and IIIC$_7$	325 kg (716 lb)
Turmo IIIC$_4$, equipped engine	225 kg (496 lb)
Turmo IIID$_3$, basic engine	365 kg (805 lb)

PERFORMANCE RATINGS:

T-O: Turmo IIIC$_3$, D$_3$ and E$_3$	1,104 kW (1,480 shp)
Turmo IIIE$_6$	1,181 kW (1,584 shp)

Max contingency:

Turmo IIIC$_4$ at 33,800 gas generator rpm	1,032 kW (1,384 shp)
Turmo IIIC$_6$ at 33,550 gas generator rpm	1,156 kW (1,550 shp)
Turmo IIIC$_7$ at 33,800 gas generator rpm	1,200 kW (1,610 shp)
Turmo IVA at 33,950 gas generator rpm	1,057 kW (1,417 shp)
Turmo IVC at 33,800 gas generator rpm	1,163 kW (1,560 shp)

T-O and intermediate contingency:

Turmo IIIC$_5$	1,050 kW (1,408 shp)

SPECIFIC FUEL CONSUMPTION:

At T-O rating:

Turmo IIIC$_3$ and E$_3$	101·9 μg/J (0·603 lb/h/shp)
Turmo IIID$_3$	104·1 μg/J (0·616 lb/h/shp)

At max contingency rating:

Turmo IIIC$_4$, C$_5$, C$_6$, C$_7$ and IV	106·8 μg/J (0·632 lb/h/shp)
Turmo IVA	106·3 μg/J (0·629 lb/h/shp)

ROLLS-ROYCE TURBOMÉCA RTM 322

See International part of this section.

TURBOMÉCA MAKILA

This turboshaft engine, rated at 1,368 kW (1,835 shp) for take-off and intermediate contingency, powers the Aérospatiale Super Puma helicopter. Derived partly from the Turmo family, it incorporates all the latest features of the company's advanced engines, including: rapid-strip modular construction; three axial stages of compression plus one centrifugal; centrifugal atomiser; two-stage gas generator turbine with cooled blades; two-stage free power turbine; and lateral exhaust.

During 1974 this engine was confirmed as partner to the Arriel in laying the foundation for the company's marketing in the next 15 years. The world market for this size of engine is put at 10,000 units. The first engine was delivered for bench test in 1976, and gas generator testing began in November 1976. The first complete Makila ran in January and flew in June 1977. French and FAA certification followed in February 1980 and April 1981 respectively. By 1 January 1985 deliveries had reached 396, of 613 ordered.

DIMENSIONS:

Length, intake face to rear face	1,395 mm (54·94 in)
Width	530 mm (20·9 in)
Max diameter	514 mm (20·25 in)

WEIGHT, DRY: Basic	210 kg (463 lb)
Equipped	242 kg (533 lb)

PERFORMANCE RATINGS (ISA, S/L):

Max contingency

1,398 kW (1,875 shp) at 35,300 gas generator rpm

T-O and intermediate

1,368 kW (1,835 shp) at 35,500 gas generator rpm

Max continuous

1,208 kW (1,620 shp) at 34,750 gas generator rpm

SPECIFIC FUEL CONSUMPTION:

Max contingency	84·0 μg/J (0·497 lb/h/shp)
T-O and intermediate	84·7 μg/J (0·501 lb/h/shp)
Max continuous	85·7 μg/J (0·507 lb/h/shp)

Turboméca Makila IA free turbine turboshaft, with initial ratings up to 1,398 kW (1,875 shp)

TURBOMÉCA-SNECMA

GROUPEMENT TURBOMÉCA-SNECMA (GRTS)

1 rue Beaujon, BP 37-08, 75362 Paris Cédex 08
Telephone: 49 24 18 61

ADMINISTRATORS:
P. Ragou
E. Delfour

Announced in March 1969, Groupement Turboméca-SNECMA is a company formed jointly by Société Turboméca and SNECMA to be responsible for the design, development, manufacture, sales and service support of the Larzac all-axial small turbofan launched in 1968 as a joint venture by the two companies. Groupement Turboméca-SNECMA has no capital and comprises primarily a joint management organisation to produce the engine.

TURBOMÉCA-SNECMA LARZAC

In February 1972 the **Larzac 04** turbofan was selected for a joint Franco-German programme to provide propulsion for the Alpha Jet (see International entry in Aircraft section). In addition to the two French partners in GRTS, two West German companies, MTU and KHD, were added to the programme. Both played a part in the manufacture of prototype engines and the achievement of endurance tests. All four companies are sharing in production and post-certification development. Complete engines are assembled in both countries for the Alpha Jet programme.

Bench testing of the Larzac 04 began in May 1972. The first Alpha Jet flew on 26 October 1973, and qualification of the Larzac 04 was accomplished on schedule in May 1975.

Turboméca-SNECMA Larzac 04-C6 two-shaft turbofan, rated at 13·19 kN (2,966 lb st)

Latest versions are as follows:

Larzac 04-C6. Two-stage fan, four-stage HP compressor, annular combustion chamber, single-stage HP turbine with cooled blades and single-stage LP turbine. Maximum airflow is 28 kg (62 lb)/s, pressure ratio 10·6 and bypass ratio 1·13. A single fixed area jetpipe is used. All accessories are driven by the HP spool and grouped under the fan case. The engine is mounted by an isostatic suspension on either side of the centre of gravity. The engine is of modular design and is intended to produce minimum noise and smoke. First production delivery September 1977. Thrust growth exceeding 20 per cent is forecast without dimensional change.

Larzac 04-C20. Growth version with increased mass flow compressor and higher temperature HP turbine. Thrust increased by 7 to 15 per cent according to speed and altitude. First run March 1982; first flight December 1982; production deliveries from September 1984.

DIMENSIONS:
- Overall length of basic engine 1,179 mm (46·4 in)
- Overall diameter 602 mm (23·7 in)

WEIGHT, DRY:
- Larzac 04-C6 290 kg (640 lb)

T-O THRUST (S/L, static):
- Larzac 04-C6 13·19 kN (2,966 lb)
- Larzac 04-C20 14·12 kN (3,175 lb)

SPECIFIC FUEL CONSUMPTION:
- Larzac 04 20·1 mg/Ns (0·71 lb/h/lb st)

GERMANY
(FEDERAL REPUBLIC)

HIRTH
GÖBLER HIRTHMOTOREN GmbH

Postfach 20, Max Eyth Strasse 10, 7141 Benningen
Telephone: 07144 6074
Telex: 7 264 530 ghir d

This company produces small piston engines for microlights and other aircraft. All models listed are two-cylinder upright in-line two-strokes with carburettor, Bosch magneto ignition and direct drive.

HIRTH F 263 R 53

This engine has cylinders of 66 mm (2·598 in) bore and 56 mm (2·205 in) stroke, giving a capacity of 383 cc (23·37 cu in). Compression ratio 9·5, using 25:1 fuel mix. Weight with electric starter 20·0 kg (44 lb), the silencer adding 3 kg (6·6 lb). Max power 17 kW (23 hp) at 5,000 rpm.

HIRTH F 22

This engine has cylinders of 66 mm (2·598 in) bore and 56 mm (2·205 in) stroke, giving a capacity of 383 cc (23·37 cu in). Compression ratio 9·5, using 25:1 fuel mix. Weight with electric starter 20·0 kg (44 lb), the silencer adding 3 kg (6·6 lb). Max power 17 kW (23 hp) at 5,000 rpm.

HIRTH 2701 R 03

This engine has cylinders of 70 mm (2·756 in) bore and 64 mm (2·52 in) stroke, giving a capacity of 493 cc (30·08 cu in). Compression ratio 11, using 50:1 fuel mix. Weight with fan and recoil starter 32·8 kg (72·5 lb). Max power 32 kW (43 hp) at 6,750 rpm.

HIRTH 2702 R 03

This engine has cylinders of 72 mm (2·835 in) bore and 64 mm (2·52 in) stroke, giving a capacity of 521 cc (31·79 cu in). Compression ratio 10·5, using 50:1 fuel mix. Weight with fan and recoil starter 35·0 kg (77 lb). Max power 26·5 kW (36 hp) at 5,500 rpm.

KHD
KHD LUFTFAHRTTECHNIK GmbH

Hohemark Str 60-70, Postfach 246, 6370 Oberursel
Telephone: (0 61 71) 500-1
Telex: 410927

The KHD group is the world's leading producer of aircooled diesel engines. In its subsidiary, the KHD Luftfahrttechnik GmbH at Oberursel, it concentrates its activities in the gas turbine field for aircraft. Its most important product is the SPS (secondary power system) for the Tornado combat aircraft with the T312 gas turbine as APU and high-technology gearboxes. A new SPS generation is under development. The KHD T117 turbojet is being developed to power RPVs. KHD is participating in production and further development of the Larzac 04 turbofan, and is responsible for product support for Larzac engines in the Luftwaffe.

KHD T117

This small turbojet is being developed to power RPVs, especially for surveillance. First application is in the Canadair CL-289.

COMPRESSOR: Centrifugal. Mass flow 1·56 kg (3·44 lb)/s. Pressure ratio 5·5.

TURBINE: Single stage. Exhaust temperature 847°C.

FUEL: JP-1, JP-4, JP-5.

DIMENSIONS:
- Length 770 mm (30·3 in)
- Diameter 350 mm (13·8 in)

WEIGHT, DRY: 21·8 kg (48 lb)

PERFORMANCE RATING (S/L, static):
- Max continuous 1·05 kN (236 lb st)

SPECIFIC FUEL CONSUMPTION:
- Max continuous 33·3 mg/Ns (1·18 lb/h/lb st)

The KHD T117 turbojet for the CL-289 RPV

KÖNIG
KÖNIG MOTORENBAU

Friedrich-Olbricht Damm 72, 1000 Berlin 13
Telephone: 030 344 3071

This company produces small two-stroke piston engines designed specifically for microlights and other aircraft. All except the SF 930 have radial cylinders of 66 mm (2·598 in) bore and 42 mm (1·654 in) stroke, with natural air cooling. A 33:1 fuel mix is used, aspirated through a single bowl carburettor and with separate capacitor discharge ignition for each cylinder. The SC 430 and SD 570 both have an electric starter and are available with direct drive or with 1·75:1 Powergrip belt reduction (no change in model designation).

KÖNIG SC 430

This engine has three cylinders spaced at 120°, giving a capacity of 430 cc (26·24 cu in). Weight with full equipment is 16 kg (35·3 lb) and max power 18 kW (24 hp) at 4,000-4,200 rpm.

KÖNIG SD 570

This engine has four cylinders spaced at 90°, giving a capacity of 570 cc (34·78 cu in). Weight with full equipment is 18·5 kg (41 lb) and max power 21 kW (28 hp) at 4,000-4,200 rpm.

KÖNIG SF 930

Production of this larger four-cylinder radial began in April 1985. Bore and stroke are respectively 70 and 60 mm (2·756 and 2·362 in), giving a capacity of 930 cc (56·75 cu in); equipped weight is 36 kg (79·4 lb) and maximum power 35·8 kW (48 hp) at 4,000-4,200 rpm.

The 35·8 kW (48 hp) König SF 930 driving a four-blade propeller

LIMBACH

LIMBACH FLUGMOTOREN GmbH

Kotthausener Strasse 5, 533 Königswinter 21, Sassenberg
Telephone: (02244) 2322 and 3031
Telex: 889574 plm d
PRESIDENT OF LIMBACH GMBH: Peter Limbach Sen

This company manufactures four-stroke piston engines for very light aeroplanes and powered gliders. A two-cylinder two-stroke engine is under development.

LIMBACH SL 1700

Several variants of this engine have been certificated by the LBA (Federal Office of Civil Aviation).

Limbach SL 1700D. Dual ignition. Not certificated. Fitted to Sportavia RF7.

Sportavia-Limbach SL 1700E. Basic engine of the current range. Fitted to Sportavia RF5 and RF5B.

Limbach SL 1700EA. Front-end starter and different induction system. Fitted to Scheibe SF-25C Falke.

Limbach SL 1700EAI. EA equipped to drive Hoffmann variable-pitch propeller. Fitted to Scheibe SF-28.

Limbach SL 1700EC. Similar to E except for having a carburettor intake heating box.

Limbach SL 1700 ECI. Similar to EC except equipped to drive Hoffmann variable-pitch propeller.

Sportavia-Limbach SL 1700EI. Similar to E except equipped to drive Hoffmann variable-pitch propeller. Optional for Sportavia RF5B.

Unless otherwise stated, the following description refers to the SL 1700E:

TYPE: Four-cylinder opposed aircooled piston engine.

CYLINDERS: Bore 88 mm (3·46 in). Stroke 69 mm (2·71 in). Swept volume 1,680 cc (102·51 cu in). Compression ratio 8 : 1.

INDUCTION: Stromberg-Zenith 150CD carburettor.

FUEL GRADE: 90 octane.

IGNITION: Single Slick 4230 magneto feeding one Bosch WB 240 ERT 1 plug in each cylinder.

STARTING: One Fiat 0·37 kW (0·5 hp) starter (EA, EAI, one Bosch 0·3 kW; 0·4 hp).

ACCESSORIES: Ducellier 250W alternator; APG 17.09.001 fuel pump (EA,EAI, 17.09.001A).

DIMENSIONS:

Length overall: SL 1700D	649 mm (25·6 in)
SL 1700EA, EAI	558 mm (22·0 in)
SL 1700E, EI, EC, ECI	618 mm (24·3 in)
Width overall: SL 1700D	800 mm (31·5 in)
SL 1700EA, EAI	770 mm (30·3 in)
other variants	764 mm (30·1 in)
Height overall: SL 1700D	451 mm (17·8 in)
SL 1700EA, EAI	392 mm (15·4 in)
other variants	368 mm (14·5 in)

WEIGHT, DRY:

SL 1700E, EI	73 kg (161 lb)
SL 1700EA, EAI	70 kg (154 lb)
SL 1700EC, ECI	74 kg (164 lb)

PERFORMANCE RATINGS:

T-O: SL 1700D	48·5 kW (65 hp) at 3,600 rpm
SL 1700E, EI, EC, ECI	51 kW (68 hp) at 3,600 rpm
SL 1700EA, EAI	44·7 kW (60 hp) at 3,550 rpm
Continuous: SL 1700E, EI, EC, ECI	45·5 kW (61 hp) at 3,200 rpm
SL 1700EA, EAI	41·7 kW (56 hp) at 3,300 rpm

LIMBACH L 2000

This family of engines is based on the SL 1700 with increased bore and stroke:

Limbach L 2000EOI. Dimensions as SL 1700EI. Installed in Fournier RF-9 and Valentin Taifun.

Limbach L 2000EAI. Dimensions as SL 1700EAI. Installed in Scheibe SF-25C Falke 2000 and SF-36.

Limbach L 2000EBI. Dimensions as SL 1700EBI. Installed in Grob G 109 and Hoffmann Dimona.

Details as for SL 1700, except for following:

CYLINDERS: Bore 90 mm (3·54 in). Stroke 78·4 mm (3·09 in). Swept volume 1,994 cc (120·26 cu in). Compression ratio 8·7:1 (EAI, 8·9:1).

FUEL GRADE: 100L.

WEIGHT, DRY (with all accessories):

L 2000EOI	70 kg (154 lb)
L 2000EAI	69 kg (152 lb)
L 2000EBI	71·5 kg (157·5 lb)

PERFORMANCE RATINGS:

T-O: all models	59 kW (80 hp) at 3,400 rpm
Continuous:	
L 2000EOI, EAI	52 kW (70 hp) at 3,000 rpm
L 2000EBI	53 kW (72 hp) at 3,000 rpm

LIMBACH L 275E

This engine is intended for low cost propulsion of RPVs and microlight aircraft.

TYPE: Two-cylinder horizontally opposed two-stroke air-cooled piston engine.

CYLINDERS: Cast aluminium alloy with Nicasil liner. Bore 66 mm (2·6 in). Stroke 40 mm (1·57 in). Swept volume 274 cc (16·72 cu in).

INDUCTION: Two all-attitude diaphragm carburettors.

FUEL GRADE: 90 octane, mixed 25:1 with two-stroke oil.

IGNITION: 12V Bosch transistorised, one Bosch WK 175T6 plug per cylinder.

ACCESSORIES: Leistritz type turbo silencer (muffler).

DIMENSIONS:

Length overall	226 mm (8·89 in)
Width overall	390 mm (15·35 in)
Height overall	187 mm (7·36 in)
WEIGHT (with silencer):	7·5 kg (16·5 lb)
PERFORMANCE RATING:	18 kW (24 hp) at 7,300 rpm

Sportavia-Limbach SL 1700E flat-four four-stroke engine, rated at 51 kW (68 hp)

Limbach SL 1700EA flat-four four-stroke engine, rated at 44·7 kW (60 hp)

Limbach L 275E two-stroke for microlight aircraft and RPV applications, rated at 18 kW (24 hp)

MTU

MOTOREN- UND TURBINEN-UNION MÜNCHEN GmbH

Dachauer Str 655, München-Allach, (postal address, Postfach 500640, 8000 München 50)
Telephone: (089) 1489 1
Telex: 529 500-15 mt d
BOARD OF MANAGEMENT, MTU GROUP:
Dr Ernst Zimmermann (President)
Dr Hans Dinger (Executive Vice-President)
Hubert Dunkler
Dr Wolfgang Hansen
Günter Welsch
Dr Peter Beer

MTU München was owned 50/50 by Daimler-Benz AG and MAN, but in Spring 1985 Daimler-Benz bought out MAN's half and is now sole owner. MTU produces aero and industrial gas turbines, and is a party to the European Small Engines Co-operation Agreement described in the introduction to Turboméca of France. It is a partner in Eurojet GmbH (see International part of this section).

MTU handles service support for the J79-MTU-J1K/17A and T64-MTU-7 engines made by MTU under General Electric licence and for Avco Lycoming piston engines. MTU Maintenance GmbH at Hanover-Langenhagen started in 1981 to overhaul, repair and modify CF6 and RB211 engines, the LM2500 marine gas turbine, and modules and parts of JT8D and JT9D engines. MTU Maintenance GmbH will also carry out endurance testing for the CF6-80 and PW2037, and will assemble these engines.

GENERAL ELECTRIC CF6

Under the terms of co-production agreements signed with General Electric, MTU has approximately a 12 per cent share in the manufacture of the CF6-50 engine for the Airbus A300; and approximately an 8 per cent share of the CF6-80A/A1 for the A310 and Boeing 767 and a 7 per cent share of the CF6-80C2 for the A300-600 and Boeing 747 and 767. The main task of MTU is production of HP turbine parts.

PRATT & WHITNEY PW2037

MTU is a partner, with Fiat of Italy, in this new turbofan described in the US part of this section. The company is responsible for the LP turbine, under an 11·2 per cent share.

IAE V 2500

MTU has a 12·1 per cent share in IAE, which, as described under that heading in the International part of this section, is developing the V 2500 turbofan in the 111 kN (25,000 lb st) class.

TURBOMÉCA/SNECMA LARZAC

MTU has a 23 per cent share in production and is participating in development of the 04-C20 and support of the 04-C6.

TURBO-UNION RB199-34R

MTU München's largest programme is a 40 per cent share in this engine, described under Turbo-Union in the International part of this section.

ROLLS-ROYCE TYNE

MTU has a 28 per cent share in the production of a further batch of about 170 Tyne engines for the re-opened Transall production line. In addition MTU has assumed responsibility for service support of all Tyne 21 engines (Atlantique) and Tyne 22 (Transall), as well as Tyne engines used by civil operators. Some 1,700 have been built or overhauled by MTU, which is now the main overhaul centre for this engine.

ALLISON 250-C20B

MTU has licence built more than 700 engines, designated 250-MTU-C20B, for the PAH-1 and VBH helicopter programmes (see MBB in Aircraft section). MTU now supports these engines, as well as C20 and C20B engines used by civil operators.

MTU/TURBOMÉCA MTM 385R

This new turboshaft engine for helicopters is described in the International part of this section.

P&WC PW300

MTU has a 25 per cent share in this new Canadian turbofan aimed at the business jet market. One of its responsibilities will be the LP turbine.

PARODI

PARODI MOTORSEGLERTECHNIK

Hauptstrasse 70, 7895 Klettgau-Erzingen
Telephone: 07742 7689
DIRECTOR: Roland Parodi

This company has developed a family of piston engines for ultralight aircraft and motor gliders. With various designations in the HP 45 and HP 60 series, these are derived from a Honda design, with a new crankcase and lubrication system.

Details were given in the 1984-85 *Jane's* of the HP 60 series engines of 44·7 kW (60 hp). These have since been uprated to the 59·7 kW (80 hp) class, and are being used as test engines to support development of later engines for two-seat aircraft. An automatic constant-speed propeller is being developed, and in 1986 Parodi hoped to produce two definitive engines: one with variable turbo pressure for 74·6 kW (100 hp), cruising at 55·9 kW (75 hp); and the other for 96·9 kW (130 hp), cruising at 74·6 kW (100 hp).

PIEPER

PIEPER MOTORENBAU GmbH

Postfach 1229, 495 Minden/Westf
Telephone: (0571) 34088

STAMO MS 1500

Pieper manufactures the 33·5 kW (45 hp) Stamo MS 1500-1 modified Volkswagen four-cylinder aircooled piston engine, applications for which have included the Scheibe SF-25B Falke two-seat motor glider. The capacity of this is 1,500 cc, compression ratio 7·2 : 1, length 640 mm (25 in), width 745 mm (29·3 in), height 395 mm (15·5 in) and dry weight 52 kg (115 lb). The MS 1500-1 operates on either 80/86 or 90 octane fuel, and is started by a pull-cord. A variant is the MS 1500-2, with electric starter and generator. This increases overall height to 450 mm (17·7 in) and dry weight to 60 kg (132 lb). By 1986 well over 600 engines had been delivered, and the period between complete overhauls had been extended to 1,000 h.

Work on the Stamo 1000, described in the 1985-86 *Jane's*, has been terminated.

Pieper built Stamo MS 1500-1 four-cylinder four-stroke engine, rated at 33·5 kW (45 hp)

PORSCHE

DR ING h c F. PORSCHE AG

Postfach 1140, 7251 Weissach
Telephone: 07044 35 2385
MANAGER, DEVELOPMENT AIRCRAFT ENGINE:
Dipl Ing Heinz Dorsch

PORSCHE PFM 3200

Developed from the well known 911 sports car engine, this piston engine is the first since 1955 designed for aircraft (standard 911S engines power the Airship Industries Skyships). A four-stroke flat-six, the PFM 3200 is aircooled, with a fan, and has a capacity of 3·2 litres (195 cu in). Dry sump lubrication makes the engine fully aerobatic; it has a geared drive of 0·441 ratio with propeller thrust set-off characteristic, single-lever control, and electronic ignition. Rated at 156 kW (212 hp), the PFM can burn Avgas or Mogas, or any mixture, and has fuel consumption 10-20 per cent lower than competitor engines.

Flight development in a Cessna Skylane began in August 1983, and certification was completed in September 1984 by the LBA and in August 1985 by the FAA. Prototype engines are now flying in various aircraft, and a pilot production batch of 50 engines was initiated in August 1985.

CYLINDERS: Bore 74·4 mm (2·93 in). Stroke 95·0 mm (3·74 in). Capacity 3,164 cc (193 cu in). Compression ratio 9·2.
FUEL SUPPLY: K-Jetronic direct injection, two electrical pumps; fuel grade 100LL or Mogas.
ACCESSORIES: Magneti Marelli dual variable timing electronic ignition, power/speed proportional fan cooling, two 24V alternators, two vacuum pumps, drive for hydraulic pump.
DIMENSIONS:

Length	946 mm (37·2 in)
Width	850 mm (33·5 in)
Height (excluding exhaust system)	605 mm (23·8 in)

WEIGHT, DRY:

Equipped	200 kg (441 lb)

The 156 kW (212 hp) Porsche PFM 3200 piston engine

PERFORMANCE RATING:
T-O and max cont at S/L
156 kW (212 hp) at 5,300 rpm

SPECIFIC FUEL CONSUMPTION:

T-O rating	82·8 µg/J (0·49 lb/h/hp)
75% cruise rating	70·1 µg/J (0·415 lb/h/hp)

INDIA

HAL

HINDUSTAN AERONAUTICS LTD

Indian Express Building, Dr Ambedkar Veedhi, PO Box 5150, Bangalore 560 001
Telephone: 76091

OFFICERS: see Aircraft section

The Bangalore and Koraput Engine Divisions of HAL constitute the main aero engine manufacturing elements of the Indian aircraft industry.

BANGALORE COMPLEX (Engine Division)

This Division is engaged in the manufacture of gas turbine engines. Adour 811 engines for all except the initial batch of Jaguars for the Indian Air Force are manufactured under Rolls-Royce Turboméca licence. The Orpheus 701 to power the Kiran II and the Dart 536-2T to power the BAe 748 are manufactured under licence from Rolls-Royce. The Artouste IIIB to power the Chetak and Cheetah is made under licence from Turboméca. The division also overhauls Dart, Avon, Orpheus, Artouste and Gnome engines.

Bangalore is developing the 3·43 kN (771 lb st) PTAE-7 short-life turbojet (Pilotless Target Aircraft Engine 7) for the ADE RPV. On 2 July 1984, DSIC (Dowty & Smiths Industries Controls) announced its first run. The engine nosecone contains a DSIC integrated digital control system complete with fuel pumps, valves, electronics and alternator. The British company stated that "It is anticipated that the success of the project will lead to substantial production orders in the near future".

KORAPUT DIVISION

This Division of HAL is located at Koraput in Orissa. It was established to manufacture under Soviet government licence the Tumansky R-11 afterburning turbojet for HAL built MiG-21 fighters. With help from the Soviet Union, the first engine was run on the bench (which it was used to calibrate) in early 1969. In 1977 production switched to the R-25 for the MiG-21 bis, followed in 1984 by the R-29B for the MiG-27M.

HAL PTAE-7 short-life turbojet *(Brian M. Service)*

GTRE

GAS TURBINE RESEARCH ESTABLISHMENT

Bangalore

This establishment is one of the largest of 42 R&D facilities administered by the DRDO (Defence Research and Development Organisation). By far its biggest challenge is the design of a new fighter engine.

GTRE GTX-35

This engine is a two-spool turbojet with afterburner, planned as the production powerplant of the HAL LCA (Light Combat Aircraft). Although influenced by existing engines, such as the GE F404 and Tumansky R-25 and R-29B, the GTX-35 is a completely Indian project, and no attempt has been made to find a foreign partner. A basic requirement is high dry thrust for good performance with modest fuel burn; another is minimum degradation in thrust under hot or high-altitude conditions.

The engine has no inlet guide vanes or variable stators, but is fitted with ventral accessories, an annular combustor and an afterburner nozzle positioned by a ring translated by six rams. The first of ten prototype engines went on test in January 1986, but high-altitude testing will be subcontracted to a foreign establishment. Flight testing is to begin in 1993-94, and soon afterwards it is hoped that the GTX-35 will replace the F404 in the LCA programme.

PERFORMANCE RATINGS (S/L, T-O, maintained to 30°C):

Max: dry	44·62 kN (10,030 lb st)
with afterburning	86·30 kN (19,400 lb st)

INTERNATIONAL PROGRAMMES

CFM

CFM INTERNATIONAL SA

2 boulevard Victor, 75015 Paris, France
Telephone: (1) 45 54 22 34

CHAIRMAN AND CHIEF EXECUTIVE: J. Chausse

EXECUTIVE OFFICERS:

J. P. Bernard (Vice-President CFM, and SNECMA CFM56 Project General Manager)

F. R. Homan (Vice-President CFM, and GE CFM56 Project General Manager)

CFM International, a joint company, was formed by General Electric (USA) and SNECMA (France) in early 1974 to provide management for the CFM56 engine programme and a single customer interface. Owned and managed on a 50/50 share basis, the company is staffed from the two parent companies. Responsibilities for hardware design, development and production are assigned to the parent companies through CFM International on an equal basis. Each company then assumes responsibility and funding for its assigned task throughout the life of the programme. This is a unique concept among international aerospace co-operative ventures.

GE is responsible for design integration, the core engine and the main engine control. The core engine is derived from that of the F101 turbofan developed for the B-1 bomber. SNECMA is responsible for the low-pressure system, reverser, gearbox, and accessory integration and engine installation. From the outset SNECMA has been agreeable to participation of other European engine companies within its 50% share. Thus, FN of Belgium has joined SNECMA for certain low-pressure system components. In 1985 the co-operation was extended to Kongsberg of Norway on the CFM56-5 engine.

CFM INTERNATIONAL CFM56

US military designation: F108

In the late 1960s General Electric and SNECMA made independent studies of the market requirement for the next generation of high bypass ratio engines. GE studies were centred around an engine designated GE13, the core of which is now being used in the F101 and F110. SNECMA's studies were based on an engine designated M56. Each company concluded that a large market existed for a high bypass ratio engine in the ten tonne class (97·9-106·8 kN; 22,000-24,000 lb st), with low noise, low emissions and low fuel consumption, coupled with ease of maintenance and low operating costs.

In April 1971 SNECMA began a search for possible partners to undertake development of a commercial engine in this class. By December 1971 it had chosen GE as its partner and, after obtaining French government approval, detailed design activity began. A working agreement and management structure were defined leading to the formation of the joint company CFM International.

The first CFM56 demonstrator engine ran at GE's Evendale plant on 20 June 1974. The engine reached its full rated thrust within 10 h of running, with fuel consumption lower than specification. The CFM56 first flew in a US Air Force McDonnell Douglas YC-15 transport prototype. Development flight testing began in March 1977 when an engine installed with a full length fan duct flew in a Caravelle at the SNECMA flight test centre. Flight evaluation of a Boeing 707 equipped with four CFM56 engines was carried out by the Boeing Commercial Airplane Company, demonstrating installed engine performance. As part of its ground and flight testing, the CFM56 demonstrated noise levels enabling aircraft in which it is installed to comply with the latest, most stringent noise regulations.

The CFM56 designation covers a family of engines from 89·0-122·38 kN (20,000-27,500 lb st). By February 1986 a total of 1,170 engines had been delivered against orders for 2,442. Output is stable at 55 per month. The following are current versions:

CFM56-2. This first version received its certification on 8 November 1979. This marked the first time that an engine had been certificated simultaneously to both US and European standards by the French and US certification authorities. As part of its certification, the CFM56 had to comply with FAR Pt 33 for the USA and JAR-E (Joint Airworthiness Requirements-Engine) for France and most of Europe. The CFM56-2 is rated at 106·8 kN (24,000 lb st), but several of its applications use only a 97·9 kN (22,000 lb) T-O rating. CFM56-2 production was launched in 1979 to re-engine the DC-8 Series 60 to Super 70 standard. Scheduled operations began on 24 April 1982. By 1 January 1986, 19 operators had placed contracts to re-engine 110 DC-8s. The 104 aircraft in service had then logged more than 2,100,000 engine flight hours. Engine-caused shop visit rate (three month average) was 0·09, and the aircraft dispatch reliability was 99·82 per cent.

The CFM56-2 exists in several variants, differing by their ratings or configuration details.

CFM56-2A. This version was certificated by the FAA and DGAC on 6 June 1985 at a thrust of 106·8 kN (24,000 lb st), flat-rated to 35°C (95°F). The **CFM56-2A-2** powers the US Navy's E-6A surveillance aircraft and the Royal Saudi Air Force's E-3 advanced warning aircraft and KE-3 tanker; these applications require long duration oil tank, integral reverser and uprated gearbox to drive up to two high capacity IDGs (integrated drive generators). The E-6A programme was launched in April 1983, and the E-3A and KE-3A programmes in October of the same year. The first flight of a Saudi E-3A took place on 19 September 1985 and the Saudi KE-3A on 19 February 1986.

CFM56-2B. This version was certificated on 25 June 1984 at 97·9 kN (22,000 lb st), flat-rated to 32°C (90° F). The **CFM56-2B-1** was selected by the US Air Force for its KC-135A tanker re-engining programme on 22 January 1980, and funding for re-engined KC-135R aircraft was released in FY 1982. First flight of a KC-135R took place on 4 August 1982, and production **F108-CF-100** (military designation) engines power KC-135R aircraft delivered from late 1983. USAF operations began on 2 July 1984. CFM56-2B-1 engines are also being retrofitted to C-135F tankers of the French Armée de l'Air.

CFM56-2C. Version of CFM56-2A for re-engining DC-8; derated to 99·79 kN (22,000 lb st), flat-rated at 30°C (86°F) to 41°C (106°F) in -2C-1 to -2C-6 sub-variants.

CFM56-3B-1. Reduced thrust derivative of CFM56-2, rated at 89·38 kN (20,100 lb st), flat-rated to 30°C (86°F), using the same basic core engine and LP turbine but with a

CFM56-3 turbofan, power plant of the Boeing 737-300 airliner

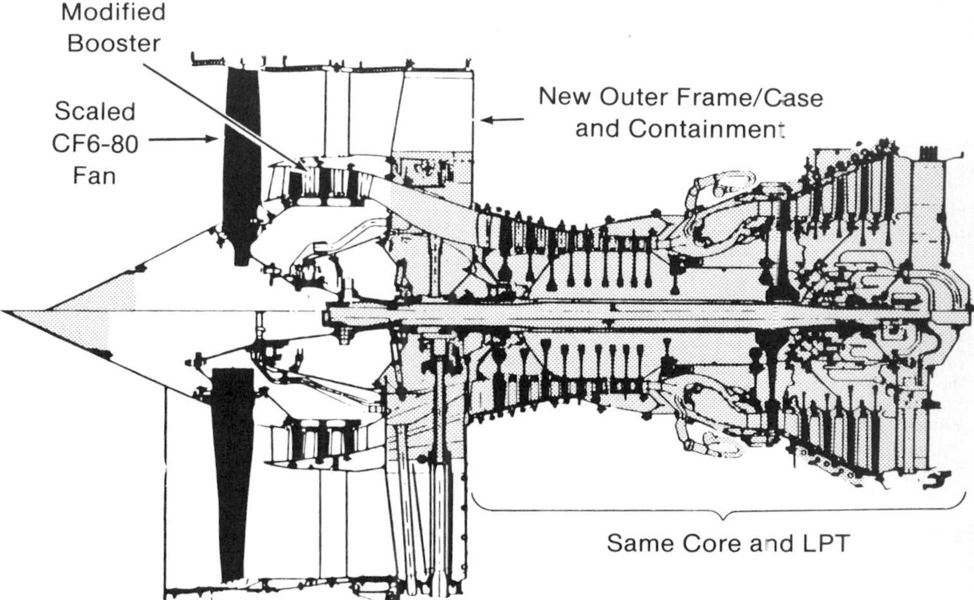

Comparative sections of the CFM56-2 (lower half) and -3 (upper)

reduced-diameter fan based on that of the CF6-80. It powers the Boeing 737-300. The first CFM56-3 ran in March 1982. Development flight tests started in February 1983 on a Boeing 707 flight testbed, and both US and French certification were granted on 12 January 1984. The CFM56-3 programme was launched in March 1981. The first CFM56-3B-1 production engines were delivered in 1983, and the 737-300 entered airline service in November 1984. By the end of February 1986, 444 737-300s had been ordered, of which 95 were in service.

CFM56-3B-2. Uprated version, certificated to 98·27 kN (22,100 lb st), flat-rated to 30°C (86°F), on 20 June 1984. In production, for Boeing 737-300 and 737-400 with improved payload/range from short, hot or high airfields.

CFM56-5. Launched in September 1984, with a formal order from Airbus Industrie for its A320 aircraft. The CFM56-5 retains the proven structure of the CFM56-2 and -3 with improved aerodynamics in all LP and HP components. It also integrates advanced clearance control features throughout the engine, and a full authority digital engine control for improved efficiency and aircraft compatibility. With a nominal rating of 111·25 kN (25,000 lb st), flat-rated to 30°C (86°F) and growth potential to 122·38 kN (27,500 lb st), it provides a fuel saving of 17 per cent on a typical mission compared with the CFM56-2-C1. The first engine went to test on 31 January 1986 at Villaroche, France. After less than 7 hours of testing it exceeded its nominal rating of 25,000 lb and confirmed that the performance levels will be achieved.

The **CFM56-5A-1** was to fly in a 707 testbed in July 1986; it is to be certificated in August 1987, and entry to service on the A320 is scheduled for February 1988. At the Paris Air Show in June 1985, CFM Vice-President Ron Welsch claimed "a 30 to 40 per cent maintenance cost advantage over the competitor's engine", and said "Fuel burn performance status on our CFM56-5 engine is 4 to 5 per cent better than what we've offered".

CFM56-3. The CFM56-3 is a reduced thrust derivative of the CFM56-2, rated at 89 kN (20,000 lb st) and using the same basic core engine and LP turbine but with a reduced diameter fan based on that of the CF6-80. It powers the Boeing 737-300. The first CFM56-3 ran in March 1982. Development flight tests started in February 1983 on a Boeing 707 flight testbed, and both US and French certification were granted on 12 January 1984. The CFM56-3 programme was launched in March 1981, when US Air and Southwest Airlines placed a total of 70 firm orders and options for the Boeing 737-300. The first production engines were delivered in 1983, and the aircraft entered airline service in December 1984.

CFM56-3B. Uprated version, certificated 20 June 1984 at 97·9 kN (22,000 lb st). In production, as **-3B-1**, for Boeing 737-300.

CFM56-5. This version was launched in September 1984, with a formal order from Airbus Industrie for its 150-passenger A320 aircraft. The CFM56-5 will retain the same fan diameter as the CFM56-2, and the same basic core engine as the CFM56-3. It provides fuel savings of at least 19 per cent compared with the CFM56-2-C1, and is equipped with a full authority digital electronic control. It retains the proven Dash-2 basic design but incorporates aerodynamic and other improvements. The **CFM56-5A-1** will be certificated in August 1987 and enter service in March 1988. CFM International claims a 30 to 40 per cent maintenance cost advantage over the competitor engine.

The CFM56-5A-1 turbofan (111·25 kN; 25,000 lb st)

Type: Two-shaft subsonic turbofan.

Air Intake: Direct entry, without inlet guide vanes.

Fan: Single-stage axial. Forged titanium disc holding (CFM56-2) 44 inserted titanium blades, each with a tip shroud to form a continuous peripheral ring; (CFM56-3) 38 titanium blades, each with a part-span shroud. (CFM56-5) 36 titanium blades, each with part-span shroud. Pointed conical spinner. Fan and attached LP compressor (booster) run in front ball bearing, with rear roller bearing. Max airflow (-2A-2) 370 kg (817 lb)/s, (-3B-2) 355 kg (783 lb)/s, (-5A-1) 386 kg (852 lb)/s. Bypass ratio (-2) 6, (-3) 5, (-5) 6.

LP Compressor: Three axial stages, on titanium drum bolted to fan disc, serve as booster to supercharge the core. In this section are main fan frame and sumps, and bearings for front end of both shafts. A ring of bleed doors allows core airflow to escape into fan duct at low power settings only.

HP Compressor: Nine-stage rotor of high strength corrosion resistant alloy, with three stages of titanium blades and the remainder of steel. Stators are steel, with first four stators variable. Split titanium front casing with steel liners. (-2, -3), steel front casing (-5). Overall pressure ratio 25:1 class (-3, 22·6; -5, 26·5).

Combustion Chamber: Machined ring, fully annular, with advanced film cooling giving low metal temperatures and uniform gas temperature distribution. Based upon F101 but modified for reduced emissions. Level of pollution from core is below that of any engine previously in airline service.

HP Turbine: Single-stage axial with aircooled stator and rotor blades, directionally solidified on -3 and -5. Entry gas temperature in 1,260°C class. High stage loading. HP system carried in two bearings (-5, three bearings).

LP Turbine: Four-stage (-5, 4½) axial with tip shrouds.

Exhaust Unit (Fan): Constant diameter duct of sound-absorbent construction. Outer cowl and engine cowl form convergent plug nozzle, with airframe mounted reverser.

Exhaust Unit (Core): Fixed area type with convergent plug nozzle.

Accessory Drive: (CFM56-2 and -5) Gearbox in front sump transmits drive from front of HP spool, via radial shaft in fan frame, to transfer gearbox on underside of fan case, with drive faces front and rear. Air starter at transfer gearbox (-2) or accessory gearbox (-5). (CFM56-3) Side mounted accessory drive gearbox with transfer gearbox; air starter pad on accessory gearbox.

Fuel System: Hydromechanical with electronic trim (-2, -3). Full authority digital control (-5).

Lubrication: Non-pressure-regulated system.

Dimensions:

Length, excl spinner: CFM56-2	2,430 mm (95·7 in)
CFM56-3	2,360 mm (93·0 in)
CFM56-5	2,422 mm (95·35 in)
Fan diameter: CFM56-2	1,733 mm (68·3 in)
CFM56-3	1,522 mm (60·0 in)
CFM56-5	1,733 mm (68·3 in)

Weight, Dry:

CFM56-2A-2	2,185 kg (4,820 lb)
CFM56-2B-1	2,093 kg (4,617 lb)
CFM56-2C series	2,101 kg (4,635 lb)
CFM56-3B-1, -3B-2	1,939 kg (4,276 lb)
CFM56-5A-1	2,204 kg (4,860 lb)

Performance Ratings:

Max T-O, see under model listings

Cruise at 10,670 m (35,000 ft):

CFM56-A2-2, Mach 0·8	25·96 kN (5,830 lb)
CFM56-2B-1, Mach 0·8	22·40 kN (5,030 lb)
CFM56-2C series, Mach 0·8	22·18 kN (4,980 lb)
CFM56-3B-1, Mach 0·72	21·42 kN (4,810 lb)
CFM56-3B-2, Mach 0·72	22·76 kN (5,110 lb)
CFM56-5A-1, Mach 0·8	22·58 kN (5,070 lb)

Specific Fuel Consumption:

Cruise rating as above:

CFM56-2A-2	18·86 mg/Ns (0·666 lb/h/lb)
CFM56-2B-1	18·35 mg/Ns (0·648 lb/h/lb)
CFM56-2C series	18·16 mg/Ns (0·641 lb/h/lb)
CFM56-3B-1	18·44 mg/Ns (0·651 lb/h/lb)
CFM56-3B-2	19·03 mg/Ns (0·672 lb/h/lb)
CFM56-5A-1	16·77 mg/Ns (0·592 lb/h/lb)

EUROJET

EUROJET ENGINES GmbH

Registered Office: Arabellastrasse, 8000 München 81, Federal Republic of Germany

Managing Director: Colin Green (Rolls-Royce)

Technical Director: Arthur Schäffler (MTU)

Commercial Director: Menotti Zinna (Fiat)

Director of Product Assurance: Juan Villate (SENER)

The **EJ200** advanced augmented turbofan engine for the Eurofighter (EFA) will be based fairly closely on the XG-40 described in the Rolls-Royce entry in this section.

Formation of Eurojet Engines GmbH, to manage the EFA engine programme, was announced in September 1986, it will be registered in the Federal Republic of Germany, with its headquarters in Munich.

The partner companies are Rolls-Royce (UK), MTU (West Germany), Fiat (Italy) and SENER (Spain). Shareholdings are: UK and West Germany, 33 per cent each; Italy, 21 per cent; and Spain, 13 per cent. For further details, see Addenda.

IAE

INTERNATIONAL AERO ENGINES AG

Registered Office: General Guisan-Quai 38, 8002 Zurich, Switzerland

Offices: 287 Main Street, East Hartford, Connecticut 06108, USA

Telephone: (203) 280 1800

Telex: 4436031 INTLAERO

Engineering Facility: Eastgate House, Nottingham Road, Derby DE1 3QL, England

Telephone: 0332 40811

Telex: 378260 IAEAG G

President and Chief Executive Officer: Robert E. Rosati

Executive Vice-President: J. M. S. Keen

Public Relations Manager: Alan C. Brothers

(All available at East Hartford)

IAE V2500

The beginning of International Aero Engines (IAE) goes back to an agreement signed by five aero engine companies in Derby, England, on 11 March 1983, to develop an advanced technology turbofan for future 150-passenger airliners. The five companies were Rolls-Royce (UK), United Technologies' Pratt & Whitney (USA), The Japanese Aero Engines Corporation, MTU (West Germany) and Fiat Aviazione of Italy.

The company was registered on 15 December 1983 in Zurich, Switzerland. IAE members announced a 30-year commitment to produce engines in the thrust range 80·1-133·4 kN (18,000-30,000 lb st). The engine, the V2500, was officially launched on 1 January 1984. The V of the designation is intended to be read as the Roman numeral five, for the five companies in five nations which are the shareholders, and the 2500 denotes the 25,000 lb thrust (111·25 kN) rating of the baseline engine. A lower thrust version rated at 23,000 lb (102·35 kN) is also offered.

The higher thrust version meets the power requirements for the 72 tonne version of the Airbus A320, and the lower thrust engine meets those of the 66 tonne version of that aircraft. By mid-June 1986, the V2500 had been selected to power A320s ordered by six airlines. The V2500 is also designated to power the McDonnell Douglas MD-89, late members of the MD-80/90 series and the Airbus A340, and is being offered for future Boeing projects.

Pratt & Whitney and Rolls-Royce each have 30 per cent workshares in the V2500, Japanese Aero Engines has 23 per cent, MTU 11 per cent and Fiat Aviazione six per cent. IAE directs the design, development and manufacture of the V2500 at the shareholders' facilities. The company is responsible for marketing the engine, for providing product support, and keeping close financial controls on the whole project.

Design, development and manufacturing tasks are apportioned to each of the partners by IAE. As examples, JAEC holds responsibility for the fan and LP compressor; Rolls-Royce for the HP compressor; Pratt & Whitney for the combustor and HP turbine; MTU for the LP turbine; and Fiat for the accessory gearbox and turbine exhaust case. Design integration is under the direction of the IAE Engineering group. Engine development testing is being carried out at Pratt & Whitney at East Hartford, Connecticut, USA, and Rolls-Royce, Derby, England.

The partners bring to the V2500 the latest in turbomachinery technology. Component designs are based essentially on those available from the latest generation of turbofan engines, including the PW2037, PW4000, Rolls-Royce 535E4 and RJ500. While the fan is a derivative of that of the 535E4, the HP compressor is derived from the HP compressor research programme by Rolls-Royce which also formed the basis for the HP compressor on the RB401 and RJ500 engines, the latter being a joint development by Rolls-Royce and the companies which now comprise JAEC. Similarly, the turbines, gearbox and electronic engine control are derived from the PW2037 developed by Pratt & Whitney in conjunction with MTU, Fiat and Hamilton Standard.

IAE is offering a complete propulsion system package, including the nacelle. The preliminary engine design was begun in 1983, and detail design was launched formally in January 1984. Testing of the engine began in December 1985, with certification scheduled for April 1988. The V2500 will be certificated to the requirements of the US Federal Aviation Administration, and the airworthiness authorities in the UK, Japan, West Germany and Italy.

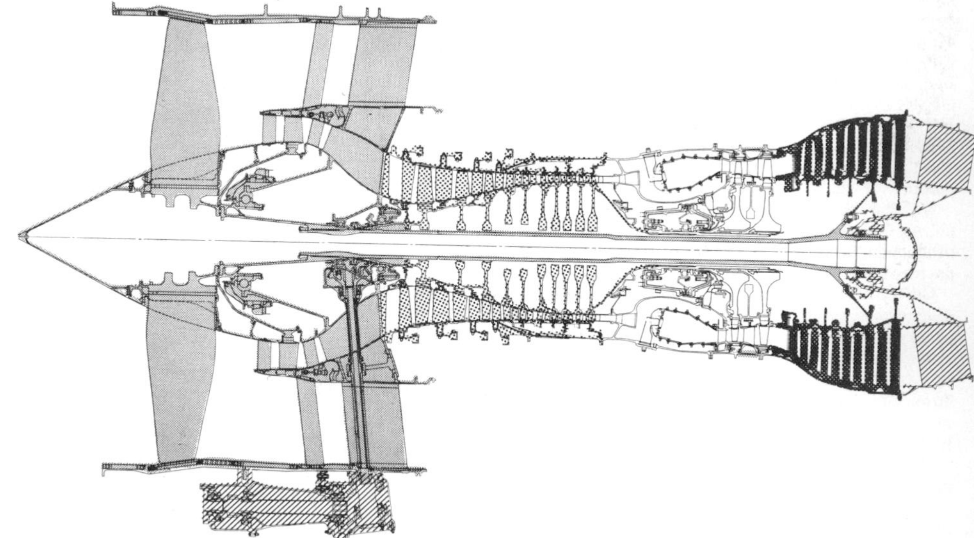

Cross-section of the IAE V2500 turbofan (high and low thrust versions). Different shading identifies areas of responsibility of the five partners

The primary design features of the V2500 are as follows:

TYPE: Two-spool subsonic turbofan.

AIR ENTRY: Direct via a strutless inlet.

FAN: Single-stage with wide-chord shroudless blading. Diameter 1,600 mm (63·0 in). Pressure ratio 1·76. Bypass ratio (climb) 5·8. T-O airflow 358 kg (789 lb)/s.

LP COMPRESSOR: Single-stage, bolted to the rear of the fan discs, serves as a booster to the inlet of the HP compressor.

HP COMPRESSOR: Ten stages of blading supported by a drum rotor. End bend and controlled diffusion aerodynamic improvements are incorporated. The inlet guide vanes and first three stages of compressor vanes are variable. Overall pressure ratio 30.

COMBUSTOR: Full annular segmented construction eliminates hoop stresses and provides low emissions and uniform exit gas temperatures with enhanced turbine durability.

HP TURBINE: Two stages of aircooled single-crystal blading. Active blade tip clearance control will be employed for best efficiency. Blades will be carried in powder metallurgy discs.

LP TURBINE: Five stages of uncooled blading supported by a welded and bolted drum rotor. Active tip clearance control.

GEARBOX: Modular unit, fan-case mounted.

CONTROL SYSTEM: Full-authority digital electronic control (FADEC) to provide command outputs for engine fuel flow, stator-vane angle, bleed modulation, turbine and turbine exhaust-case cooling, oil cooling, ignition and thrust-reverser functions. Supplied by Hamilton Standard.

NACELLE: Baseline full-length nacelle will consist of inlet, fan cowl doors, fan discharge ducts, reverser, common nozzle assembly, engine mounts and engine build unit, to comprise a complete functioning power plant when installed at the aircraft pylon interface. Cowl load sharing is planned to minimise engine-to-rotor case deflections. Acoustically treated. Supplied by Rohr/Shorts.

DIMENSIONS:
- Length (flange to flange) 2,960 mm (122·1 in)
- Fan diameter 1,600 mm (63·0 in)

WEIGHT, DRY:
- Bare engine 2,242 kg (4,943 lb)
- Complete power plant, incl nacelle 3,311 kg (7,300 lb)

PERFORMANCE RATINGS:
- T-O, S/L, ISA:
  - V2500 lower thrust 102·34 kN (23,000 lb st)
  - V2500 higher thrust 111·25 kN (25,000 lb st)
- Cruise Mach 0·8, 10,670 m, 35,000 ft: 22·2 kN (5,000 lb)

SPECIFIC FUEL CONSUMPTION (cruise Mach 0·8, 10,670 m; 35,000 ft, no external fan cowl drag): 15·81 mg/Ns (0·560 lb/h/lb)

MTU-TURBOMÉCA GmbH

PO Box 500640, 8000 München 50, Federal republic of Germany
Telephone: (089) 1489 1
Telex: 529 500-15 mt d
Telefax: (089) 1506147

MTU-TURBOMÉCA MTM 385R

This turboshaft engine is being developed by MTU-Turboméca GmbH, a joint company owned equally by MTU München and Turboméca of France. First application will be in the Eurocopter Franco-German helicopters. This engine is one of the three covered by the European Small Engines Co-operation Agreement described in the introduction to Turboméca of France.

COMPRESSOR: Two axial stages and one centrifugal stage. Variable inlet guide vanes.

COMBUSTION CHAMBER: Reverse flow annular.

TURBINES: Single-stage cooled gas generator turbine. Two-stage free power turbine.

CONTROL SYSTEM: Full-authority digital.

RATING:
Thermodynamic power 900 to 1,100 kW (1,200 to 1,475 shp)

MTU-Turboméca MTM 385R mockup

ROLLS-ROYCE TURBOMÉCA

ROLLS-ROYCE TURBOMÉCA LIMITED

4/5 Grosvenor Place, London SW1X 7HH, England
Telephone: 01 235 3641

Co-operation between Rolls-Royce and Turboméca started in 1965, when Rolls-Royce was licensed to use specified Turboméca patents. It continues under the Anglo French helicopter agreement of 1967. This involves Turmo and Astazou engines, for RAF/Army Puma and Gazelle helicopters, being part manufactured, assembled and supported by Rolls-Royce. In return Gem engines for French Navy Lynx helicopters are part manufactured, assembled and supported by Turboméca.

A joint company, Rolls-Royce Turboméca Limited, was formed in June 1966 to control design, development and production programmes for the Adour two-shaft turbofan.

In 1980 Rolls-Royce Turboméca launched development of the RTM 321 turboshaft demonstrator. This ran for the first time in November 1983, and provided valuable background for the RTM 322, which was launched in May 1984.

ROLLS-ROYCE TURBOMÉCA ADOUR

The Adour was designed originally for the SEPECAT Jaguar. The whole engine is simple and robust and of modular design. The complete propulsion unit was designed for an overhaul life of 1,200 h. Temperatures and rotational speeds are moderate, and a thrust growth of the order of 40 per cent was envisaged.

Bench testing began at Derby on 9 May 1967. Engines for Jaguars are assembled at Derby (R-R) and Tarnos (Turboméca) from parts made at single sources in Britain and France. Turboméca makes the compressors, casings and external pipework (to preserve Anglo-French parity the afterburner is subcontracted to SNECMA); Rolls-Royce makes the remainder.

Following selection of the Adour for the Japanese Mitsubishi T-2 trainer and F-1 fighter/support aircraft, Ishikawajima-Harima Heavy Industries has been producing the Adour since 1970 under a licence agreement. In 1972 a non-afterburning Adour was selected to power the British Aerospace Hawk advanced trainer. The 1,746th Adour from Rolls-Royce Turboméca production was completed at Derby in December 1985. At that time, a further 500 had been manufactured under licence in Japan, India and Finland, flying over 2·3 million hours.

Current versions of the engine are as follows:

Mk 102. Original production engine for Jaguars in service with RAF and Armée de l'Air. Qualified in 1972.

Mk 104. Uprated RT172-26 version similar to Mk 804; RAF Mk 102 engines were converted to this standard.

Mk 151. Non-afterburning version for Hawk. Internal components and certification temperatures identical to Mk 102 and Mk 801A. Qualified in 1975.

Mk 801A. Japanese designation TF40-IHI-801A. For Mitsubishi T-2 and F-1. Qualified in 1972. (See Ishikawajima-Harima in Japanese section.)

Mk 804. Uprated engine for Jaguar International. Installationally interchangeable with Mk 102. General increase in thrust of some 10 per cent, with greater increase at high forward speeds (rating with full afterburner at Mach 0·9 at S/L, ISA, increased by 27 per cent). Qualified in 1976.

Mk 811. Uprated version for Jaguar International, installationally interchangeable with 804. Revised compressor aerodynamics and hot-end improvements to match higher temperatures. Qualified 1981 for Indian Jaguar; engines assembled by Hindustan Aeronautics, with increasing Indian manufactured content.

Mk 815C. The Mk 804 uprated to Mk 811 performance level by conversion at overhaul.

Mk 851. Non-afterburning version of Mk 804 for export Hawk.

Mk 861. Non-afterburning version of Mk 811, installationally interchangeable with 851; first deliveries 1981.

Mk 861-49. Derated version of Mk 861, in development for McDD/BAe T-45A Goshawk for US Navy.

Mk 871. Uprated version matched to 35°C day under development for BAe Hawk Series 200. Engine availability scheduled for 1988.

The following refers to current non-afterburning versions:

TYPE: Two-shaft turbofan for subsonic and, with augmentation, supersonic aircraft.

INTAKE: Formed by forward extension of fan casing. No radial struts or inlet guide vanes.

FAN: Two-stage. Rotating spinner, anti-iced by turbine-bearing cooling air, on front of first stage disc. Individually replaceable blades. Fixed stators and exit vanes. Unit overhung on spring loaded ball bearing of squeeze film type. Full length bypass duct leading to afterburner. Bypass ratio, 0·75-0·80.

COMPRESSOR: Five-stage compressor on HP shaft. Large diameter double-conical shaft for rigidity with bolted curvic couplings. Wide chord blades of titanium. Steel stator blades. Overall pressure ratio 11 : 1.

COMBUSTION CHAMBER: Annular, with straight-through flow. Fitted with 18 air spray fuel nozzles and two igniter plugs. Engine fuel system by Lucas GTE.

HP TURBINE: Single-stage, aircooled.

LP TURBINE: Single-stage. Both turbine bearings of squeeze film type.

JETPIPE: Fixed area stainless steel sheet.

DIMENSIONS:	
Length:	
Mks 102, 801A, 804, 811	2,970 mm (117 in)
Mks 151, 851, 861, 861-49, 871	1,956 mm (77 in)
Inlet diameter (all)	559 mm (22 in)
Max width (all)	762 mm (30 in)
Max height (all)	1,041 mm (41 in)
WEIGHT, DRY:	
Mk 102, 801A	704 kg (1,552 lb)
Mk 104, 804	713 kg (1,571 lb)
Mk 151	553 kg (1,220 lb)
Mk 851	568 kg (1,252 lb)
Mk 861	577 kg (1,273 lb)
Mk 811	738 kg (1,627 lb)
PERFORMANCE RATINGS (S/L T-O):	
Mk 102, 801A	32·5 kN (7,305 lb st)*
Mk 104	35·1 kN (7,900 lb st)*
Mk 151, 851	23·1 kN (5,200 lb st)
Mk 804	35·8 kN (8,040 lb st)*
Mk 861	25·4 kN (5,700 lb st)
Mk 861-49	24·2 kN (5,450 lb st)
Mk 811	37·4 kN (8,400 lb st)*
Mk 871	26·0 kN (5,845 lb st)

**With afterburner*

SPECIFIC FUEL CONSUMPTION (Mk 102):	
S/L static, dry	21 mg/Ns (0·74 lb/h/lb st)
Mach 0·8, 11,890 m (39,000 ft)	27 mg/Ns (0·955 lb/h/lb st)

ROLLS-ROYCE TURBOMÉCA RTM 322

The RTM 322 engine family is the product of studies and programmes conducted by Rolls-Royce and Turboméca. Its technology is derived from existing engine programmes and research projects, and its concept has been proven in jointly managed demonstrator engine programmes.

The launch engine is the **RTM 322-01** turboshaft, which is conservatively rated at 1,566 kW (2,100 shp) with growth potential to 2,240 kW (3,000 shp).

The family, which will include turboprop and turbofan derivatives, is configured to combine simple design, reliability, low fuel consumption, light weight and low cost of ownership, to make the RTM 322 highly attractive for both civil and military applications.

The turboshaft itself has been optimised for flexibility of application by the use of a full-authority digital electronic control system, availability of different output drive configurations, a choice of three starting systems, and options for an inlet particle separator and infra-red suppressor. This gives the engine a wide range of future civil and military applications, including the EH 101, Westland 30 Series 400 and other helicopters in the 7 to 15 tonne class such as the British AST 404 and European NH 90 projects. For added versatility the engine has mountings configured for ease of installation into existing airframes such as the Sikorsky Black Hawk and Seahawk. The RTM 322 has been the subject of a US Army contract to study more powerful versions of the Black Hawk and Apache helicopters, and on 28 May 1985 United Technologies' Pratt & Whitney signed an agreement with Rolls-Royce Turboméca giving the American company rights to manufacture RTM 322 engines for helicopters built in and for sale in the USA and Canada.

The first complete RTM 322-01 engine ran on 4 February 1985, and by the end of that year the design verification part of the development programme had been completed. Over 1,790 kW (2,400 shp) had been demonstrated during the testing, while the engine gave good reliability with low spares utilisation, and exhibited good starting characteristics and power response. A flight clearance test was completed satisfactorily in December 1985, and by early 1986 over 1,000 hours of bench testing had been completed. The programme is planned to continue, with emphasis on developing early maturity by including accelerated mission testing. In February 1986 a Sikorsky S-70C helicopter was procured as a flying testbed, and the first flight was made on 14 June. Certification is targeted for end of 1987.

Turboprop derivatives are suitable for 35/70-seat commuter, general aviation and military aircraft. Turbofan derivatives are projected for primary trainers and executive aircraft. All versions are included in the European Small Engines Co-operation Agreement described in the introduction to Turboméca of France.

The following particulars apply to the RTM 322-01 turboshaft:

COMPRESSOR: Three-stage axial and single-stage centrifugal.

COMBUSTOR: Annular reverse flow. Ignition by Lucas Aerospace exciter.

TURBINES: Two-stage gas generator turbine. Cooling is applied to the 1st and 2nd stage stators and 1st stage rotor. The 2nd stage rotor is made of single crystal material and is uncooled. Two-stage power turbine with drive to front or rear.

DIMENSIONS:	
Length overall	1,143 mm (45 in)
Diameter	524 mm (20·6 in)
WEIGHT, DRY:	240 kg (538 lb)
PERFORMANCE RATINGS (S/L):	
Max contingency	1,721 kW (2,308 shp)
Max T-O	1,566 kW (2,100 shp)
Typical cruise	940 kW (1,260 shp)
SPECIFIC FUEL CONSUMPTION:	
Cruise (as above)	81 µg/J (0·48 lb/shp/h)

Rolls-Royce Turboméca Adour Mk 151 for British Aerospace Hawk T.1, rated at 23·1 kN (5,200 lb st)

Rolls-Royce Turboméca RTM 322-01 turboshaft

TURBO-UNION

TURBO-UNION LTD

PO Box 3, Filton, Bristol BS12 7QE, England
Telephone: 0272 791234
MUNICH OFFICE: Arabellastrasse 4/7, 8 München 81, Federal Republic of Germany
Telephone: (089) 9242 1

CHAIRMAN: Dr G. C. Boffetta

MANAGING DIRECTOR: Kurt Munzenmaier

Formed in October 1969, this international company was established to manage the entire programme for the RB199 engine for the Panavia Tornado. Shares are held in the ratio Fiat Aviazione SpA, 20%; MTU München GmbH, 40%; Rolls-Royce Ltd, 40%.

TURBO-UNION RB199

The RB199 is a three-shaft augmented turbofan of extremely advanced design, offering low fuel consumption for long-range dry cruise, even at sea level, and approximately 100 per cent thrust augmentation with full afterburner for combat manoeuvre and supersonic acceleration. Further design goals included minimal weight, frontal area and volume, and moderate first cost and operating costs. Rapid strip and rebuild are facilitated by modular construction and by the use of advanced manufacturing techniques to reduce the number of separate components.

The first RB199 ran in September 1971, less than two years after go-ahead. The early development of the engine was described in the 1979-80 *Jane's*. The 150 h FQT (Formal Qualification Test) was completed in November 1978. By early 1986 more than 1,480 production engines had been delivered. Total engine production for the initial programme of 809 Tornado aircraft is more than 2,000. The overall work share is intended to be in proportion to the number of aircraft acquired by each nation.

The first production engine for the Tornado was the **RB199 Mk 101**. The **Mk 103** is the current standard, developed under the three-year Post-FQT Programme, which started at the beginning of 1979; this was aimed at modest performance increases and a significant extension of life. First production delivery and flight of the Mk 103 took place in 1983. This engine powers IDS Tornados of Saudi Arabia.

Service experience has confirmed the basic robustness of the design. The ability of the engine to cope with FOD and bird strikes is due largely to the three-spool layout, with its consequent short, rigid rotating assemblies held between small bearing spans.

The **Mk 104** engine entered service with the RAF in the Tornado F.3 (Air Defence Variant) in early 1986. This engine has a jetpipe extended by 360 mm (14 in) to provide a thrust increase of up to 10 per cent whilst giving significant advantages in terms of sfc. The Mk 104 introduces the world's first FADEC (full-authority digital engine control) system in combat service without a hydromechanical backup. FADEC provides optimum performance for any speed or manoeuvre and enhances reliability. ADV Tornados ordered by the air forces of Oman and Saudi Arabia will be powered by the Mk 104 engine.

A slightly modified version of the Mk 104 powers the British Aerospace EAP. The main difference is removal of the reversers, and there is no APU.

A future 'stretched' engine to meet the requirements of combat aircraft for the 1990s would retain the existing small diameter and low sfc. The first 'stretched' demonstrator, called Demo 1A, first ran in December 1982 and has bettered the predicted performance; in both the dry and augmented regimes at altitude the thrust can exceed that of in-service engines by 40 per cent. Upgrading of in-service engines would be facilitated by their modular construction.

The following structural description refers to the Mk 101:

TYPE: Three-shaft turbofan with afterburner and integral thrust reverser.

INTAKE: Annular, without inlet guide vanes.

LP COMPRESSOR: Three-stage axial LP compressor of titanium alloy. Casing of three bolted sections, comprising a ring of stator vanes welded at their outer ends to form the casing and at their inner ends to form the interstage seal. Rotor of three discs welded together. Rotor blades secured by dovetail roots, all with snubbers to control vibration and provide greater resistance to foreign-object damage. Blade containment by local increase of casing thickness. Mass flow approx 70 kg (154 lb)/s. Bypass ratio about 1:1.

IP COMPRESSOR: Three stages of titanium alloy. Rotor has welded discs in which blades are secured by dovetail roots. Stator rings bolted together, with rear pair of flanges forming attachment to intermediate casing, holding blades in dovetail grooves.

HP COMPRESSOR: Six-stage; material changes from titanium at front to heat resisting alloy at rear, except stator blades are heat resisting steel throughout. Casing of six rings bolted together. Each ring forms track of corresponding rotor and each pair of rings forms groove in which stators are located by dovetail roots. Rotor discs secured by ten through-bolts, carrying blades by dovetail roots. Provides bleed air for aircraft services, turbine cooling and air motors for reverser and nozzle. Bevel gear provides radial drive to gearbox. Overall pressure ratio greater than 23:1.

INTERMEDIATE CASING: Fabricated titanium inner and outer casings, with main thrust spigot and front side-mounting links. Inner casing houses IP and HP compressor bearings, supported on eight hollow vanes across bypass and core flows.

BYPASS DUCT: Fabricated in titanium, forms outer shell between intermediate casing and jetpipe.

COMBUSTION CHAMBER: Annular flame tube fabricated from nickel-based alloy, bolted at rear end between outer casing, forged and chemically milled in nickel-iron alloy, and inner casing, fabricated in nickel alloy. Carries 13 double-headed fuel vaporisers which give combustion without visible smoke. Two igniter plugs combined with primary fuel injectors. Hot-streak injector for afterburner ignition.

TURBINES: Rotor blades and stator vanes machined from precision castings in heat resisting nickel-based alloy. All rotor blades shrouded and secured by fir tree fixings. Stator vanes of all four stages carried in single casing machined from nickel forging.

HP TURBINE: Entry temperature over 1,327°C. Rotor blades and stator vanes aircooled. Stator cooling provided by HP air which passes through root and tip of each hollow vane into a perforated sheet metal insert. This cooling air passes through holes in the insert before exhausting into through-holes in the vane leading and trailing edges. Remainder of cooling air is ducted to HP rotor-blade roots via pre-swirl nozzles and a turbine cover plate which increases cooling-air pressure. Air leaves blades through holes in leading edge, at tip and in trailing edge.

IP TURBINE: Aircooled stator vanes and rotor blades. Cooling air from third HP compressor stage passes into perforated central insert in stator vanes. Approximately half air cools vane and exhausts through holes in trailing edge; rest feeds via pre-swirl nozzles into rotor blade roots and via machined holes to exit at tips.

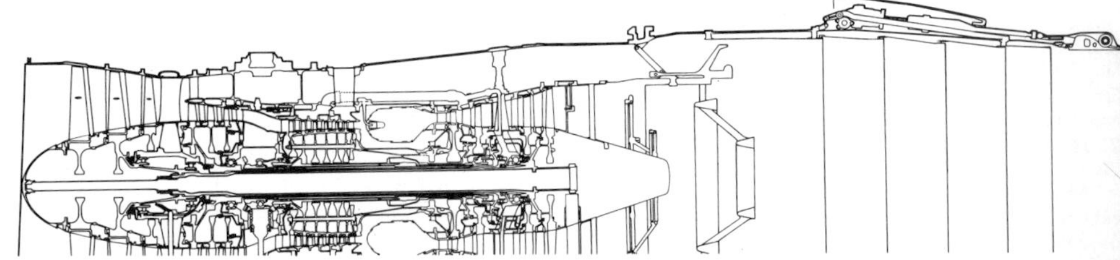

Longitudinal section through RB199 Mk 101, the initial production engine for the Tornado IDS

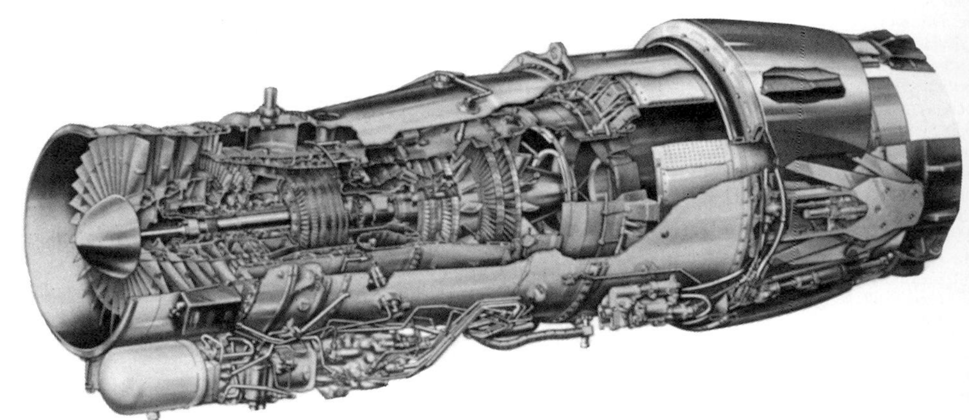

Cutaway drawing of Turbo-Union RB199 Mk 103, the current production engine for Tornado IDS aircraft

LP TURBINE: Two-stage with hollow uncooled rotor blades. First-stage stator vanes cooled by third-stage HP compressor air, and contain support struts for IP/LP bearing.

LP SPOOL: LP compressor rotates clockwise (from rear), overhung on two widely spaced roller bearings, on bearing support welded to inner wall of third-stage stator ring. LP turbine shaft runs in ball thrust bearing in combined IP/LP bearing housing.

IP SPOOL: Front end of shaft, which also has clockwise rotation, runs in ball thrust bearing carried by intermediate casing. Rear end runs in roller bearing supported by IP/LP bearing housing.

HP SPOOL: Rotates anticlockwise in two roller bearings. Front bearing is carried in intermediate casing; rear is a contra-rotating intershaft bearing carried on IP shaft sleeve. Compensating shaft is located at front by ball thrust bearing in intermediate casing and at rear is attached to HP turbine, locating whole spool axially. This shaft of low-expansion steel matches thermal expansion of casings to maintain axial seal clearances.

AFTERBURNER: Front end of titanium fabricated jetpipe carries afterburner in which bypass air and core gas burn concurrently, without a mixing section. For core flow, two gutter flameholders fed by upstream atomisers. For bypass flow, reverse colander with radial extensions, each containing vaporising primary burner, between which multiple jets inject remainder of afterburner fuel. Provides fully modulated augmentation. Aircooled heat shield protects jetpipe from afterburner temperature greater than 1,627°C.

NOZZLE: Variable area, short petal, convergent nozzle operated by shroud actuated by four screwjacks, driven by fourth stage HP air motor via flexible shafting. Each of 14 master and 14 secondary petals is precision casting in cobalt alloy which minimises friction.

REVERSER: External two bucket type driven via flexible shafts by motor using HP air. In stowed position outer skins form aircraft profile. Deployment takes 1 s at any thrust setting from idle to max dry.

ACCESSORY DRIVES: Accessory gearbox on underside of intermediate casing (quick attach/detach coupling) carries hydromechanical portions of main and afterburner fuel systems, oil tank and pump, and output shaft to aircraft gearbox carrying KHD gas turbine starter/APU.

FUEL SYSTEM: The electronic main engine control unit (MECU), which is aircraft mounted, uses signals from pilot's lever and power plant sensors to control hydromechanical engine and afterburner fuel systems, nozzle and reverser. Duplicated electronics provide integrity, with automatic switching. Flow through main gear pump determined by metering orifice commanded by MECU, with recirculation for cooling aircraft and engine systems. Afterburner fuel from engine driven vapour core pump controlled by main and distribution actuators, both under MECU command.

LUBRICATION SYSTEM: Main bearings, with squeeze film damping, in three chambers; each is supplied with pressure oil and scavenged through return pipes which have filters and magnetic detector plugs. Oil samples drawn from tank for spectrographic analysis.

DIMENSIONS:

Length overall	3,230 mm (127 in)
Max diameter	870 mm (34·25 in)

WEIGHT, DRY:

Excl reverser	approx 900 kg (1,980 lb)
Incl reverser	1,084 kg (2,390 lb)

PERFORMANCE RATINGS (Mk 103, S/L, ISA):

Max dry	42·95 kN (9,656 lb st)
Max afterburning	75·26 kN (16,920 lb st)

Rolls-Royce engineers checking the RB199 Demo 1A engine

ISRAEL

BET-SHEMESH

BET-SHEMESH ENGINES LTD

Mobile Post Haela, Bet-Shemesh 99000
Telephone: 02 911661-6
Telex: 25290

The first section of a 12,077 m² (130,000 sq ft) Israeli aero engine factory, Bet-Shemesh Engines Ltd, was inaugurated officially on 15 January 1969. The company is owned by the Israeli government. The manufacturing plant was based on the Turboméca factory at Tarnos. On 1 January 1977 a change in management took place. Over the subsequent year the number of employees increased from 550 to about 1,300, and plant area increased to 22,500 m² (242,000 sq ft).

At first Bet-Shemesh manufactured turboprop components on behalf of Turboméca. By 1973 complete Marboré VI turbojets for CM 170 Super Magister trainers were being produced. The company now manufactures parts of the Marboré II and VI. As the centralised source for all aircraft gas turbine manufacture in Israel, it makes portions of the General Electric J79 (see IAI entry) and parts of the Pratt & Whitney F100, and provides support for the Allison 250-C20. It is prime contractor for the PW1120 engine for the IAI Lavi. With Reshef Systems of Haifa it is developing full authority digital engine controls.

BET-SHEMESH SOREK 4

Also written Sorek IV, this expendable turbojet is the first engine for aerospace propulsion known to have been designed by Bet-Shemesh Engines. Intended for cruise missiles, RPVs and long duration target drones, it is designed for flight at Mach numbers up to 0·9. A particular feature is outstanding autonomy, the only exception being the fuel tank. No flight control instrumentation is needed, and it is claimed that the Sorek 4 is exceptionally compact in relation to the thrust. Bench testing began in June 1982, and deliveries of production engines started in the Summer of 1983.

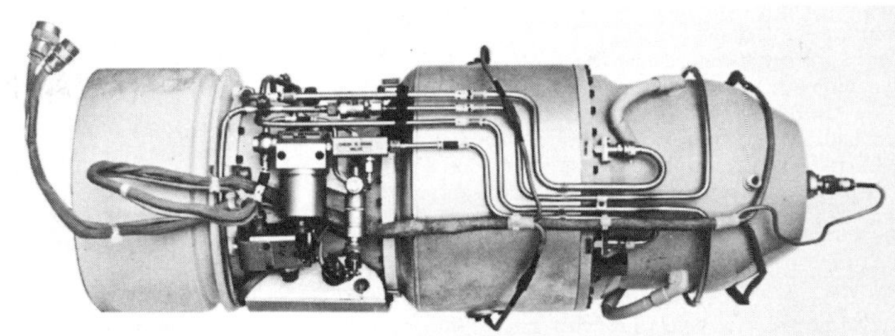

Bet-Shemesh Sorek 4 expendable turbojet

TYPE: Single-shaft expendable turbojet.

COMPRESSOR: Single-stage axial followed by single-stage centrifugal. Overall pressure ratio 5·8. Airflow 5·5 kg (12 lb)/s.

COMBUSTOR: Fully annular fabricated from welded sheet complete with turbine nozzle guide vanes. Centrifugal fuel injection from radial holes in main shaft.

JETPIPE: Fixed area, fabricated from sheet with starter charge in large central bullet.

ACCESSORIES: Automatic starting by pyrotechnic cartridge, windmilling or compressed air, with fuel flow programmed as function of engine speed to give full power within 10 s. FADEC (full authority digital electronic control) fitted as integral part of engine. BIT (built-in test) fuel and oil pumps in inlet bullet, alternator on main shaft inside hub of axial compressor; oil tank surrounds inlet casing.

DIMENSIONS:
- Length: 1,014 mm (43·46 in)
- Diameter (exclusive of piping): 330 mm (13·0 in)

WEIGHT, DRY (dual start): 67·0 kg (147·4 lb)

PERFORMANCE RATING (S/L): 3·6 kN (809 lb st) at 35,000 rpm

SPECIFIC FUEL CONSUMPTION: 34·67 mg/Ns (1·225 lb/h/lb st)

IAI

ISRAEL AIRCRAFT INDUSTRIES LTD

Ben-Gurion International Airport, 70100 Lydda

The Engine Overhaul Plant in IAI's Bedek Division is organised to support and overhaul aircraft engines for civil customers and the Israeli Air Force. More recently the plant has manufactured J79 turbojet engines. The Engine Directorate is responsible for assembly and test of the engine from parts manufactured by subcontractors, including IAI's Manufacturing Division, Bet-Shemesh Engines, Iscar Blades, Amcoram and TAAT.

J79-IAI-J1E

The J79-IAI-J1E powers the IAI Kfir and is produced by IAI under GE licence. It is a J79-GE-19 modified to fit the Kfir's airframe and incorporating 102 per cent engine speed at high aircraft Mach number, smokeless combustors, and a T_5 reset for fast acceleration. Accessories and gearboxes are relocated, and a titanium heatshield covers the afterburner. From 1981 Bedek Division has incorporated a Combat Plus system to increase T-O thrust from 78·9 kN (17,750 lb) to 83·4 kN (18,750 lb).

Data for the J1E include:

MASS FLOW: 77·1 kg (170 lb)/s

IAI Bedek J79-IAI-J1E afterburning turbojet

PRESSURE RATIO: 12·4

DIMENSIONS:
- Max diameter: 995·7 mm (39·2 in)
- Length: 5,283 mm (208 in)

WEIGHT, DRY: 1,699 kg (3,746 lb)

MAX RATINGS (T-O, S/L):
- With augmentation: 83·4 kN (18,750 lb st)
- Dry: 49·4 kN (11,110 lb st)

ITALY

ALFA ROMEO

ALFA ROMEO AVIO SpA

80038 Pomigliano D'Arco, Naples
Telephone: 081 8430111
Telex: 710083 Aravio
CHAIRMAN: Gen Fulvio Ristori
MANAGING DIRECTOR: Ing Filippo De Luca
VICE GENERAL MANAGER: Ing Mario Sala

Alfa Romeo Avio was prime contractor for the manufacture, under General Electric licence, of the J85, J79 and T58. It manufactures CF6 combustors and JT9D components, and assembles the kits and overhauls PT6T engines for the AB 212 helicopter. Under GE licence it is responsible for the hot section of the T64-P4D, co-produced with Fiat, and participates in development and hot section manufacture of the RB199. The company is a partner in Italian production of the Rolls-Royce Spey 807.

In February 1986 it began deliveries of GE T700-401 engines for prototype EH 101 helicopters. Alfa Romeo Avio also supplies components for T700 engines fitted to American helicopters and, under a revenue-sharing agreement, is developing new versions of the T700. It is also involved, with Fiat, in the development of the GE CT7-6 turboshaft, aimed at the NH 90 and a new version of the A 129.

The company is developing, in collaboration with a French manufacturer, a new jet engine to power Mach 2 anti-ship missiles. It overhauls several engines of Rolls-Royce, General Electric, Allison and Pratt & Whitney manufacture.

Since 1 January 1985 Alfa Romeo Avio has belonged to the Aeritalia Group and, through Finmeccanica, to the IRI (Istituto Ricostruzione Industriale).

ALFA ROMEO AR.318

In the mid-1970s Alfa Romeo's Aero Engine Division began collaboration with Rolls-Royce on a small gas turbine for general aviation applications, known as the RB318. By 1979 a successful development programme had led to component and engine testing, including flight testing of a turboprop in a King Air A90.

By 1980 the programme was being transferred entirely to

The 453 kW (608 shp) Alfa Romeo AR.318 turboprop

Alfa Romeo in accordance with an agreed time schedule. The definitive engine, a turboprop covering a range of powers from 298 to 596 kW (400-800 shp), is redesignated AR.318. The programme draws upon Rolls-Royce under a contract for technical support. By early 1982 a total of eleven prototype engines had run 2,000 h on the bench on dynamometer test, 1,500 h with propellers and 300 h in the King Air. By early 1984 two flight engines and 12 on bench test had completed most of the certification programme. RAI (Italian civil) certification was achieved in April 1985, and production engines with FAA certification are now available. Applications are expected to include the Pilatus PC-7.

TYPE: Single-shaft turboprop.

AIR INTAKE: Forward-facing cast integral with gearbox. Can be above or below propeller axis.

REDUCTION GEAR: Epicyclic, driven by muff coupling from compressor forward shaft. Accessory gear train driven from first reduction stage. Phase displacement torquemeter and torque/speed sensing unit.

COMPRESSOR: Single-stage centrifugal, machined from single forging. Surrounded by radial/axial diffuser fabricated in sheet. Pressure ratio 5·4.

COMBUSTION CHAMBER: Annular reverse flow type, with eight T shape vaporiser tubes. Two igniters and three starter spray nozzles. One-piece rear casing carries turbine IGVs and rear bearing. Main fuel manifold inside rear case.

TURBINE: Two-stage axial. Each IGV row is a one-piece investment casting. Rotors and blades are integral solid castings, joined by a curvic coupling. Compressor shaft has curvic coupling and transmits all air for blowing seals.

OIL SYSTEM: One pressure and two scavenge pumps. Provision for engine mounted tank, fuel heater and temperature/pressure transducers.

FUEL SYSTEM: Single assembly of filters, pumps, metering and overspeed protection. Optional beta control, top temperature and torque limiting, and autofeather.

FUEL GRADE: JP-1, JP-4.

DIMENSIONS:

Length	1,061 mm (41·8 in)
Width	534 mm (21·0 in)
Height	658 mm (25·9 in)
WEIGHT, DRY:	140·6 kg (310 lb)
PERFORMANCE RATINGS (S/L, ISA):	
T-O (no time limit)	453 kW (608 shp)
AR.318-T	298 kW (400 shp) to ISA + 30°C
Max continuous	420 kW (564 shp)
Cruise	394 kW (529 shp)
SPECIFIC FUEL CONSUMPTION:	
T-O	97·7 μg/J (0·578 lb/h/shp)
Max continuous	99·2 μg/J (0·587 lb/h/shp)
Cruise	102·4 μg/J (0·606 lb/h/shp)

FIAT

FIAT AVIAZIONE SpA

Via Nizza 312, 10127 Turin

Telephone: (011) 69311
Telex: 221320 Fiatav

CHAIRMAN: G. Gabrielli
MANAGING DIRECTOR: G. C. Boffetta
PRODUCTION DIRECTOR: S. Piola
DESIGN AND ENGINEERING DIRECTOR: L. La Rocca

Fiat Aviazione SpA was incorporated in 1976 as a wholly Fiat owned company. It took over all the aero engine activities carried out formerly by the Fiat Aviation Division, and the participation in Turbo-Union Ltd and Turbomotori Internazionale, as well as control of a plant at Brindisi which overhauls jet and piston engines and makes jet engine parts.

Fiat's main aircraft engine programmes now concern the IAE V2500, Turbo-Union RB199, Rolls-Royce Spey 807 and Viper 600, Pratt & Whitney PW2037 and General Electric CF6 (including CF6-80C2), CT7 and T64. In addition the company produced the J79-19 under General Electric licence and participated in the licence production by Alfa Romeo of the J85-GE-13A. It overhauls many types of engine, including the J79 and Orpheus, and the R-2800 piston engine. It produces the LM 2500 marine gas turbine, in collaboration with General Electric, and designs and produces main gearboxes for helicopters. Fiat is a partner in Eurojet GmbH (see International part of this section).

Fiat assisted Pratt & Whitney Canada and Sikorsky in mating the PT6B-36 turboshaft to the S-76 helicopter. An engine was tested at Sangone, sandwiched between Fiat reduction and power gearboxes, and a testbed aircraft was flown for the first time on 22 June 1984.

TURBO-UNION RB199

Fiat holds 20% of the shares of Turbo-Union Ltd, the joint company set up to produce the RB199 engine for the Panavia Tornado. Fiat's responsibility is the LP turbine and shaft, exhaust diffuser, jetpipe and nozzle. The programme is described under Turbo-Union in the International part of this section.

IAE V2500

The V2500 turbofan is being designed and developed by the IAE consortium formed by Pratt & Whitney, Rolls-Royce, JAEC, MTU and Fiat. Fiat is responsible for design, development and production of the accessory gearbox, oil tank and pumps, exhaust case and No 5 bearing compartment.

ROLLS-ROYCE SPEY 807

This turbofan is produced under a Rolls-Royce licence to the Italian government, by Fiat (prime contractor in Italy) and CELMA (prime contractor in Brazil) as power plant of the AMX tactical fighter. The engine is to undergo type testing in the first half of 1987. Fiat carries out bench testing in support of the prototype aircraft, and rig testing of the engine Group-A parts.

PRATT & WHITNEY PW2037

Since 1974 Fiat has been responsible for design and development of the accessory drive gearbox for the Pratt & Whitney PW2037 civil turbofan engine. The programme is described under Pratt & Whitney in the US part of this section.

GENERAL ELECTRIC CF6

Fiat is engaged in the manufacture of components for the CF6 civil turbofan for both General Electric and SNECMA. For GE the company supplies complete accessory gearboxes, transfer gearboxes, inlet gearboxes and shafts. SNECMA is supplied with various gearbox components and shafts for CF6-50 engines. Fiat is collaborating with GE in the development and production of CF6-80C/C2 engines.

GENERAL ELECTRIC T64-P4D

This free turbine turboprop powers most versions of the Aeritalia G222 military transport aircraft. Under a licence agreement between the General Electric Company and the Italian government, the engine is being manufactured in Italy, with Fiat as prime contractor.

ROLLS-ROYCE VIPER 600

Development of this turbojet was undertaken in collaboration with Rolls-Royce. For most versions, components rearward of the compressor (except turbine discs and blades) are Fiat's responsibility. However, the Mk 632-43 engine for the Aermacchi MB339 is licensed to Piaggio. The Viper 600 is described in the Rolls-Royce entry in the UK part of this section.

IAME

ITAL-AMERICAN MOTOR ENGINEERING

Via Lisbona 15, 24040 Zingonia
Telephone: (035) 883022
Telex: 301205
US ADDRESS:
Italmotion, PO Box 71, Monroe, NY 10950
Telephone: (914) 783 7314
Telex: 646105

IAME is the producer of a growing series of specially designed light piston engines for aircraft. All are known as KFM (Komet Flight Motors) engines. They were launched at the EAA Fly-in at Oshkosh in 1981, the chief market being US homebuilders and microlight aircraft manufacturers.

KFM 104

Four-cylinder four-stroke of advanced modular construction. Available in five versions: **104S**, standard with dual ignition and carburettor; **104E**, adds electric starter and alternator; **104G**, as 104E plus propeller governor and hydraulic feed for propeller control; **104V**, as 104E plus vacuum pump; **104A**, as 104S but with inverted oil and fuel systems for aerobatic use. Flight development began in June 1981 in an INAV Sonerai II, with certification due in 1985

CYLINDERS: Bore 90 mm (3·54 in). Stroke 72 mm (2·83 in). Capacity 1,832 cc (111·79 cu in).

DIMENSIONS:

Length	602·5 mm (23·72 in)
Width	665 mm (26·18 in)
Height	398 mm (15·67 in)
WEIGHT, DRY:	
104S	67·8 kg (149·5 lb)
104E	74·0 kg (163·1 lb)
PERFORMANCE RATINGS:	
Max T-O	57·5 kW (77 hp) at 3,900 rpm
Max continuous	52 kW (69·5 hp) at 3,475 rpm
FUEL CONSUMPTION:	
Max T-O	24·6 litres (6·49 US gal)/h
Cruise	14·2 litres (3·75 US gal)/h

KFM 104 installed in INAV Sonerai II
(Howard Levy)

KFM 105

Two-cylinder engine using same cylinders as KFM 104 and with dual ignition as standard. Pre-production engines in 1982, with certification testing extending into 1985. Capacity is 918 cc (56 cu in).

DIMENSIONS (pre-production; reduced in production engines):

Length	393·5 mm (15·49 in)
Width and height originally as KFM 104	
WEIGHT, DRY:	29·5 kg (65 lb)
PERFORMANCE RATINGS:	
Max T-O	30 kW (40 hp) at 3,800 rpm
Max continuous	26·2 kW (35·1 hp) at 3,465 rpm
FUEL CONSUMPTION:	
Max T-O	12·5 litres (3·3 US gal)/h
Cruise	7·1 litres (1·87 US gal)/h

KFM 107 MAXI

A completely new two-cylinder two-stroke engine for microlights, motor gliders, RPVs and similar uses. Avail-

KFM 107 Maxi two-stroke piston engine

KFM 112 flat-four piston engine *(Aviodata)*

able as: **107E**, direct drive, with electric starter and alternator; and **107ER**, with V belt reduction gear (2 : 1).
CYLINDERS: Bore 64 mm (2·52 in). Stroke 52 mm (2·05 in). Capacity 334 cc (20·38 cu in).
DIMENSIONS:
Length 435 mm (17·13 in)
Width (over plugs) 440 mm (17·32 in)
Height 253 mm (9·96 in)
WEIGHT, DRY:
Maxi 107E 19·0 kg (41·8 lb)
Maxi 107ER 22·5 kg (49·6 lb)
PERFORMANCE RATINGS:
Max T-O 22·4 kW (30 hp) at 6,300 rpm
Max continuous: 20·1 kW (27 hp) at 6,080 rpm
FUEL CONSUMPTION:
Cruise 8·3 litres (2·19 US gal)/h

KFM 112

This flat-four piston engine is similar to the previous KFM 104 but has smaller cylinders (80 × 64 mm) giving a capacity of 1,286 cc (78·4 cu in). Dry weight with starter is 45·0 kg (99 lb) and max T-O rating is 37·5 kW (50 hp). Certification was planned for early 1985, with first deliveries scheduled for September.

PIAGGIO

INDUSTRIE AERONAUTICHE E MECCANICHE RINALDO PIAGGIO SpA

Via Cibrario 4, 16154, Genoa
Telephone: (10) 600 41
Telex: 270695

WORKS AND OFFICERS: see Aircraft section

The Aero Engine Division of Piaggio manufactures the following engines under licence agreements: Rolls-Royce Viper 11, 526, 540 and 632-43 turbojets to power the Aermacchi MB326 and 339 (a sublicence for manufacture of the Viper 11 and 540 was issued to Atlas Aircraft to power South African built MB326 aircraft); Avco Lycoming T53-L-13 turboshafts for various Bell and Agusta-Bell helicopters; Avco Lycoming T55-L-11 and -712 and derivatives for CH-47 Chinook helicopters; and Rolls-Royce Gem 2 Mk 1004D turboshafts for the Agusta A 129 anti-tank helicopter. Piaggio also participates in co-production under licence of the Rolls-Royce Spey 807 turbofan.

JAPAN

IHI

ISHIKAWAJIMA-HARIMA JUKOGYO KABUSHIKI KAISHA (Ishikawajima-Harima Heavy Industries Co Ltd)

Shin Ohtemachi Bldg 2-1, Ohtemachi 2-chome, Chiyoda-ku, Tokyo 100
AERO-ENGINE AND SPACE OPERATIONS (ASO): 5-1, Mukodai-cho 3-chome, Tanashi-shi, Tokyo 188
Telephone: (0424) 66 1252
Telex: 02822561
PRESIDENT: Kosaku Inaba
EXECUTIVE SENIOR MANAGING DIRECTOR AND GENERAL MANAGER, ASO:
Sadao Takahashi

In February 1960 IHI began licence production of the General Electric J79-IHI-11A turbojet for the F-104J, followed by the J79-IHI-17 for the F-4EJ. IHI delivered 610 J79s, ending in 1980.

Under further licensing agreements with General Electric, IHI is producing the T58 turboshaft and T64 turboprop; under agreement with Allison it produces the T56 turboprop. By March 1986 deliveries totalled 798 T58s, 391 T64s and 109 T56s.

In 1979 IHI linked with other Japanese companies in the 50/50 development with Rolls-Royce of the RJ500, described under RRJAEL in the 1982-83 *Jane's*. The experience and technology gained from the RJ500 work with Rolls-Royce will be embodied in the V2500, described under IAE in the International part of this section. In this project, Japanese Aero Engines Corporation (JAEC), representing IHI, KHI and MHI, has a work share of 23 per cent. IHI, with a majority share in JAEC, is responsible for developing the fan.

Licence manufacture of the Rolls-Royce Turboméca Adour began in 1973, under the designation TF40-IHI-801A, to power the Mitsubishi T-2 and F-1. By March 1986 IHI had delivered 412 TF40s.

IHI was nominated in 1978 as prime contractor of the Pratt & Whitney F100 engine for the Japanese built F-15; by March 1986 IHI had delivered 175 F100s.

IHI undertakes overhaul and repair of Pratt & Whitney JT8D and Rolls-Royce RB211 commercial turbofans, General Electric J79, T58 and T64, and R-R Turboméca TF40 military engines, and Turboméca Artouste and Astazou turboshafts.

The 16·37 kN (3,680 lb st) class IHI XF3-30 turbofan

IHI produced 247 J3 turbojets for the Fuji T-1B and Kawasaki P-2J. It helped to develop the XJ11 lift jet, as well as the JR100 and JR200 built under supervision of the NAL. In collaboration with Mitsubishi and Kawasaki, IHI built prototypes of the FJR710 turbofan (see NAL entry).

IHI XF3

Development of this turbofan began in 1976, with funding by the JDA's Technical Research & Development Institute. The Phase 1 (XF3-1) form has a single-stage fan with bypass ratio of 1·9, five-stage transonic compressor, 12-burner combustor and single-stage HP and LP turbines. Rating is 11·79 kN (2,650 lb st).

In 1977 JDA contracted with IHI for the XF3-20, with reduced bypass ratio and higher turbine temperature to give a rating of 16·28 kN (3,660 lb st). This was followed by the XF3-30, which in 1982 was selected by the JASDF as the engine for the XT-4 trainer. Preliminary flight rating tests, completed in 1983, included altitude testing at USAF Arnold Engineering Development Center and flight testing in a modified C-1 transport.

The XT-4, powered by two XF3-30 engines, first flew on 29 July 1985. XF3-30 qualification testing was to be completed by March 1986, but testing of four XT-4 prototypes is scheduled to continue until 1988. The following data refer to the XF3-30:

TYPE: Two-shaft turbofan.
FAN: Two-stage axial. No inlet guide vanes. Airflow 34 kg (75 lb)/s. Pressure ratio 2·6. Bypass ratio 0·9.
COMPRESSOR: Five stages. First two stators variable. Overall pressure ratio 11.
COMBUSTION CHAMBER: Annular, with 12 duplex fuel nozzles.
HP TURBINE: Single-stage, aircooled rotor blades.
LP TURBINE: Two-stage, tip shrouded.
FUEL SYSTEM: Hydromechanical, with electronics supervisor.
DIMENSIONS:
Length 1,340 mm (52·76 in)
Inlet diameter 560 mm (22·0 in)
WEIGHT, DRY: 340 kg (750 lb)
PERFORMANCE RATING (T-O, S/L):
16·37 kN (3,680 lb st) class
SPECIFIC FUEL CONSUMPTION:
19·83 mg/Ns (0·7 lb/h/lb st)

KAWASAKI

KAWASAKI JUKOGYO KABUSHIKI KAISHA (Kawasaki Heavy Industries Ltd)

1-18 Nakamachi-dori 2-chome, Chuo-ku, Kobe 650-91
Telephone: Kobe (078) 341 7731
JET ENGINE DIVISION: 1-1 Kawasaki-cho, Akashi 673
Telephone: (078) 923 1313
Telex: 5628 951 to 953
OFFICERS: see Aircraft section

Kawasaki's factory at Akashi started repair, overhaul and component manufacturing for aircraft engines, on behalf of the US armed forces and the Japan Defence Agency, in 1953. Since then it has overhauled more than 12,468 engines, mainly of the Allison J33, General Electric J47, Rolls-Royce Orpheus, Westinghouse J34, and Kawasaki KT5311A and KT5313B series. Since 1968 the company has also been making spare parts for the J33, and since 1973 for the Orpheus.

In 1967, under a licence agreement with Avco Lycoming, KHI started manufacturing T53 turboshaft engines. Deliveries of the resulting KT5311A, KT5313B and T53-K-13B engines totalled 285 by 1986. KHI is now producing T53-K-703 engines for Japanese built AH-1S HueyCobras and T55-K-712 engines for Japanese built CH-47J Chinooks. KHI also produces Rolls-Royce industrial/marine Olympus, Spey and Tyne engines.

Kawasaki shares in parts manufacturing for the Rolls-Royce Turboméca Adour, the Pratt & Whitney F100 and JT8D and the IHI assembled Allison T56. In 1983 Kawasaki became a member of the IAE consortium responsible for development and manufacture of the V2500 commercial turbofan (see under International heading).

KAWASAKI KJ12

This simple low cost turbojet has been developed by Kawasaki as the core of various future aircraft engine programmes. In its present form it is suited to RPVs and also to sporting aircraft. Component testing began in 1979 and the first complete KJ12 ran in early 1981. It has a centrifugal compressor driven by a single-stage axial turbine; the combustion chamber is annular and the control system of the electronic type.
DIMENSIONS:
Length 653 mm (25·71 in)
Max diameter 314 mm (12·36 in)
WEIGHT DRY: 40 kg (88·2 lb)
PERFORMANCE RATINGS:
T-O 1·47 kN (331 lb st)
Cruise (9,145 m; 30,000 ft at Mach 0·9)
715 N (161 lb)

Full scale display model of Kawasaki KJ12 turbojet

MITSUBISHI

MITSUBISHI JUKOGYO KABUSHIKI KAISHA (Mitsubishi Heavy Industries Ltd)

Head Office: 5-1, Marunouchi 2 chome, Chiyoda-ku, Tokyo 100

Engine Works: Daiko Plant, Nagoya Aircraft Works, 1-1, Daiko-Minami, Higashi-ku, Nagoya 455

Telephone: (052) 721 3111

Komaki North Plant, Nagoya Aircraft Works, 1200, Higashi-Tanaka, Komaki-Shi, Aichi 485

Telephone: (0568) 79 2111

Officers: see Aircraft section

Since 1952 Mitsubishi Heavy Industries (MHI) has repaired and overhauled engines of the Japan Defence Agency and domestic and foreign airlines. In 1967 it began production of the CT63 turboshaft engine to power Hughes 369HM helicopters of the JGSDF, under a licence agreement with Allison. A total of 217 engines was delivered by March 1978. Between January 1973 and June 1981, under licence agreement with Pratt & Whitney Aircraft, MHI delivered 72 JT8D-M-9 turbofans.

In collaboration with IHI and Kawasaki, MHI participates in the V2500 engine programme (see IAE in the International part of this section). It is also developing a small turbojet of its own design to power the SSM-1 surface-to-ship missile being developed for the JGSDF. A slightly different turbojet is being developed to power the Fuji XJ/AQM-1 target drone.

NAL

NATIONAL AEROSPACE LABORATORY

7-44-1 Higashi-machi, Jindiji, Chofu City, Tokyo

Telephone: 0422 47 5911

Director: Hideo Nagasu

Head of Aero Engine Division: Hiroyuki Nouse

The National Aerospace Laboratory (NAL) is a government establishment responsible for research and development in the field of aeronautical and space science. Since 1962 it has extended its activity to include V/STOL techniques. The decision was made in that year to initiate development of an engine, the JR 100, to fulfil the requirement for a lightweight lift jet for VTOL aircraft. The more advanced NAL/IHI JR200 was developed in 1966; the NAL/IHI JR220 was completed in 1971.

In 1971 the Agency of Industrial Science and Technology, Ministry of International Trade and Industry (MITI), funded a high bypass ratio turbofan engine (FJR710) development programme.

MITI/NAL FJR710

In the late 1960s the Japanese government and industry, seeking an engine programme that might remain competitive for many years, decided to embark on the design of a subsonic turbofan of high bypass ratio. After a preliminary study by the NAL, funding was provided by the Ministry of International Trade and Industry in 1971 for a prototype demonstrator and test programme.

NAL has managed the design of the resulting FJR710. Manufacture of the prototype and development engines was subcontracted to IHI, Kawasaki and Mitsubishi. The first engine made its first run in May 1973. By the end of 1978 six engines (three FJR710/10 and three FJR710/20 with small changes) had run a total of 1,300 h.

Phase 2 of the FJR710 programme began in 1976, and the first of three FJR710/600s had been completed by December 1978. This version was followed by the lower-rated FJR710/600S, rated at 47 kN (10,582 lb st), which powers the experimental Asuka QSTOL aircraft. The following description applies to the /600 engine.

Type: Two-shaft high bypass ratio turbofan for subsonic commercial or military aircraft.

Air Intake: Direct annular entry around fan spinner.

The FJR710/600S turbofan (47 kN; 10,582 lb st)

Fan: Single-stage fan, with rotating spinner and inserted titanium blades with part span shrouds. Metal fan duct held by eight aerofoil struts, preceded by ring of flow-straightening vanes. Bypass ratio 6·5 : 1.

Compressor: Mechanically independent HP compressor. Twelve-stage axial assembly with inserted blades of titanium and, at delivery end, high nickel alloy. Several rows of variable stator blades held in upper and lower half casings and operated by peripheral rings scheduled by hydraulic ram.

Combustion Chamber: Smokeless annular type.

Turbine: Two-stage HP gas generator turbine with cooled blades. Four-stage LP fan turbine.

Jetpipe: Fixed area.

Dimensions (approx):
- Length: 3,300 mm (130 in)
- Diameter: 1,520 mm (60 in)

Weight, Dry: 980 kg (2,160 lb)

Performance Ratings (ISA):
- T-O: 50 kN (11,243 lb st)
- Cruise at 7,600 m (25,000 ft) at Mach 0·75: 13·24 kN (2,976 lb)

Specific Fuel Consumption:
- T-O: 10·6 mg/Ns (0·374 lb/h/lb st)
- Cruise, as above: 19·3 mg/Ns (0·680 lb/h/lb st)

ZENOAH

KOMATSU ZENOAH COMPANY

2-142-1 Sakuragaoka, Higashiyamato, Tokyo 189

Telephone: 0425 61 2141

Telex: 2842122

President: Isamu Minami

This company is producing two types of engine for microlight and related aircraft.

ZENOAH G25B

Derived from a snowmobile engine with forced air cooling, this single-cylinder microlight piston engine has free air cooling, a flywheel magneto with capacitor discharge ignition, a float type carburettor and recoil starter. It is a two-stroke, using a 25:1 fuel mix. Cylinder bore is 72 mm (2·835 in) and stroke 59·5 mm (2·343 in), giving a capacity of 242 cc (14·78 cu in). The silencer (muffler) is optional.

Dimensions:
- Length: 300 mm (11·81 in)
- Width: 294 mm (11·57 in)
- Height: 377 mm (14·84 in)

Weight, Dry: 17·5 kg (38·6 lb)

Performance Rating: 16·4 kW (22 hp) at 6,500 rpm

ZENOAH XG50C

This is the opposed twin version of the G25B, with dual carburettors and a cooling fan. It was intended to begin production in 1984. Capacity is 484·5 cc (29·59 cu in).

Dimensions:
- Length: 403 mm (15·87 in)
- Width: 387 mm (15·24 in)
- Height: 580 mm (22·83 in)

Weight, Dry: 25·4 kg (56·0 lb)

Performance Rating: 36 kW (48 hp) at 6,500 rpm

Zenoah G25B-1, complete with carburettor and silencer

POLAND

PZL

POLSKIE ZAKŁADY LOTNICZE

ul. Miodowa 5, 00251 Warsaw

Telephone: Warsaw 261441

Telex: 814281

Pezetel, Foreign Trade Enterprise Co:

00-991 Warsaw 44, Al. Stanów Zjednoczonych 61, PO Box 6

Telephone: 108001

Telex: 813314

The Polish aircraft and diesel engine industry is managed by the association of aviation and engine producers 'PZL'. Pezetel handles all exports of Polish aeronautical material and diesel engines.

BORZECKI

JOZEF BORZECKI

ul. Sernicka 20/4, Wroclaw

BORZECKI JB 2 × 250

This designer's 2RB engine was described in the 1980-81 *Jane's*. Work is now concentrated upon engines comprising two single-cylinder units, each driving a propeller, coupled rigidly together through the cylinder heads by steel rods which offer extremely high stiffness axially. The dual-engine combination offers single-engine or two-engine operation without vibration problems. The engines are handed (rotate in opposite directions).

CYLINDERS: Capacity 250 cc (15·25 cu in) each. Compression ratio 10.

INDUCTION: Two floatless carburettors fed by pump.

FUEL: 30:1 mix of LO 92 petrol and oil.

DIMENSION:

Distance between crankshaft centrelines 820 mm (32·3 in)

PERFORMANCE RATINGS:

T-O 2 × 15 = 30 kW (40·25 hp) at 5,200 rpm

Continuous 2 × 14 = 28 kW (37·5 hp) at 4,900 rpm

The Borzecki JB 2 × 250 dual engine unit (30 kW; 40·25 hp)

SPECIFIC FUEL CONSUMPTION:

Continuous rating 123·4 μg/J (0·73 lb/h/hp)

IL

INSTYTUT LOTNICTWA (Aviation Institute)

HEADQUARTERS: Al. Krakowska 110/114, 02-256 Warsaw-Okecie

Telephone: Warsaw 460993

MANAGING DIRECTOR: Prof Dr Ing Zbigniew Dzygadlo

CHIEF CONSULTANT FOR SCIENTIFIC AND TECHNICAL CO-OPERATION: Dipl Ing Jerzy Grzegorzewski

CHIEF OF SCIENTIFIC, TECHNICAL AND ECONOMIC INFORMATION DIVISION: Dr Ing Tadeusz Kostia

The Aviation Institute is an establishment concerned with aeronautical research, aerodynamic tests, strength tests, test flights of aeroplanes, helicopters and gliders, aviation equipment, materials, technical information and standardisation. The Institute has a special manufacturing plant responsible for constructing prototypes to its own design.

IL SO-3B turbojet rated at 10·8 kN (2,425 lb st)

IL SO-1

The Aviation Institute designed the SO-1 turbojet to power the Polish TS-11 Iskra (Spark) jet basic trainer. It was designed to permit the full range of aerobatics, including inverted flight. Guaranteed overhaul life is 200 h. Production was handled by the WSK-Rzeszów, as noted in that organisation's entry.

TYPE: Single-shaft axial-flow turbojet.

AIR INTAKE: Annular intake casing manufactured as a cast shell. Fixed inlet guide vanes.

COMPRESSOR CASING: Manufactured as a cast shell in two parts, split along horizontal centreline, in aluminium alloy.

COMPRESSOR: Seven-stage axial-flow compressor. Drum type rotor built up of disc assemblies, with constant diameter over tips of rotor blades. Carried in ball bearing at front and roller bearing at rear. Steel stator blades bonded with resinous compound into slots in carrier rings. Rotor originally of steel and duralumin, with first three blade rows of steel and remainder of aluminium alloy. Modified as a result of operating experience; entire compressor rotor and blades on all stages now made of steel. Pressure ratio 4·8.

COMBUSTION CHAMBER: Annular type with 24 integral vaporisers. Outer casing made of welded steel.

FUEL SYSTEM: Two independent systems supplied by one pump. Starting system consists of six injectors, with direct injection. Main system consists of twelve twin injectors with outlets towards the vaporisers.

FUEL SPECIFICATION: Kerosene P-2 or TS-1.

TURBINE: Single-stage axial-flow type. Blades attached to disc by fir tree roots. Supported in roller bearing at front.

JETPIPE: Outer tapered casing and central cone connected by streamlined struts. Nozzle area adjusted by exchangeable inserts.

LUBRICATION SYSTEM: Open type for rear compressor and turbine bearings, supplied by separate pumps. Closed type for all other lubrication points, fed by separate pumps.

OIL SPECIFICATION: Type AP-26 (synthetic).

ACCESSORY DRIVES: Gearbox mounted at bottom of air intake casing and driven by bevel gear shaft from front of compressor.

STARTING: 27V starter/generator and bevel gear shaft, driven by aircraft battery or ground power unit, mounted on air intake casing.

DIMENSIONS:

Length overall 2,151 mm (84·7 in)

Width 707 mm (27·8 in)

Height 764 mm (30·1 in)

WEIGHT, DRY: 303 kg (668 lb)

PERFORMANCE RATINGS:

T-O 9·8 kN (2,205 lb st) at 15,600 rpm

Max continuous 8·7 kN (1,958 lb st) at 15,100 rpm

SPECIFIC FUEL CONSUMPTION:

At T-O rating 29·6 mg/Ns (1·045 lb/h/lb st)

OIL CONSUMPTION: 0·8 litres (1·4 Imp pints)/h

IL SO-3

This improved version of the SO-1 replaced the earlier type in production at the WSK-Rzeszów. The SO-3 is intended for tropical use and incorporates minor changes in compressor, combustion chamber and turbine, data remaining the same as for the SO-1. It is fitted to all Indian TS-11 aircraft. Since 1978 the SO-3B has been developed and qualified, and this is now the standard TS-11 engine, with TBO of 400h. The compressor is entirely steel, and a revised vaporising burner and flame tube result in more uniform gas temperature entering the turbine. Data are as for the SO-1 except:

OIL SPECIFICATION: AW-30 synthetic.

WEIGHT, DRY: 321 kg (708 lb)

PERFORMANCE RATINGS:

T-O 10·8 kN (2,425 lb st) at 15,600 rpm

Max continuous 9·8 kN (2,205 lb st) at 15,100 rpm

OIL CONSUMPTION: 1·0-1·2 litres (1·7-2·1 Imp pints)/h

JANOWSKI

JAROSLAW JANOWSKI

ul. Nowomiejska 2/29, Lodz 11

JANOWSKI SATURN 500

The prototype Saturn 500 was built in 1969. This engine may be used with tractor or pusher propeller, and is intended for ultralight aircraft built by amateurs.

A version of the Saturn 500 with new cylinder heads, improved crankshaft and dual ignition has been reported. Its rating (max T-O) is increased to 22·5 kW (30 hp); dry weight is believed to be about 25 kg (55 lb).

The following description applies to the initial 25 hp version:

TYPE: Two-cylinder two-stroke horizontally opposed air-cooled piston engine.

CYLINDERS: Bore 70 mm (2·76 in). Stroke 65 mm (2·56 in). Capacity 500 cc (30·5 cu in). Compression ratio 8·5 : 1. Steel barrels with aluminium alloy cylinder heads. Cylinder and head assembly attached to crankcase by four studs.

PISTONS: Of aluminium alloy. Two compression rings and one oil scraper ring.

CONNECTING RODS: Steel forgings.

CRANKSHAFT: Steel counterbalanced shaft, supported in two lead-bronze plain bearings and one ball-thrust bearing at the front.

CRANKCASE: Aluminium alloy case, split in the vertical plane, with front and aft covers.

INDUCTION: Two BVF 28N1 carburettors.

FUEL: Petrol/oil mixture using aviation 90 octane.

IGNITION: Two magnetos. One M14-250 14 mm (0·55 in) sparking plug per cylinder.

MOUNTING: Four rubber dampers at rear of crankcase.

PROPELLER DRIVE: Direct tractor or pusher.

DIMENSIONS:

Length overall, with propeller boss 430 mm (16·93 in)

Width, without sparking plugs 515 mm (20·27 in)

WEIGHT, DRY: 27 kg (59·5 lb)

PERFORMANCE RATING:

T-O 18·65 kW (25 hp) at 4,000 rpm

SPECIFIC FUEL CONSUMPTION:

Max T-O rating 118·23 μg/J (0·70 lb/h/hp)

Normal cruising power 111·48 μg/J (0·66 lb/h/hp)

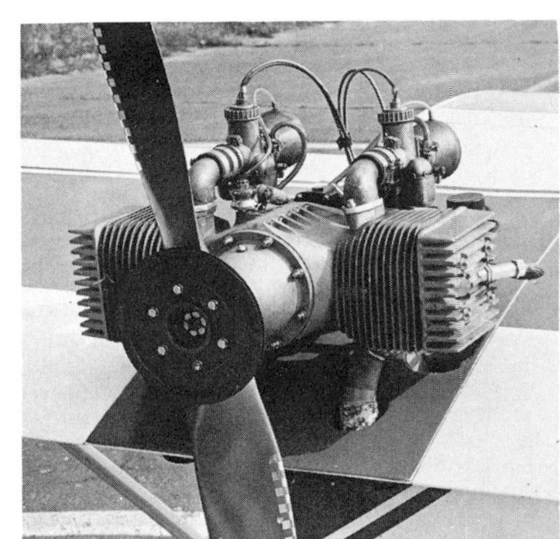

Saturn 500 two-cylinder two-stroke engine designed by Jaroslaw Janowski

REFRIGERATION EQUIPMENT

REFRIGERATION EQUIPMENT WORKS

ul. Metalowców 25, 39-200 Dębica
Telephone: Dębica 2031
Telex: 066617 wuch pl

PZL-F ENGINES

In 1975 Pezetel acquired rights to manufacture and market the entire range of aircooled piston engines formerly produced by the Franklin Engine Company (Aircooled Motors) of the USA. These engines, known as PZL-F, are being produced in Poland for light aircraft and motor gliders. Previously manufactured by WSK-PZL Rzeszów, they were transferred in 1985 to the Dębica works.

Current applications include the SZD-45-2 Ogar F motor glider (2A-120C), PZL-110 Koliber (4A-235B3), and PZL Mielec M-20 Mewa (6A-350C). The 2A-120C, 4A-235B3 and 6A-350C each have a Polish CACA certificate.

All models are of the horizontally opposed type, with cylinders of 117·48 mm (4·625 in) bore and 88·9 mm (3·5 in) stroke. All have direct drive and operate on 100/130 grade fuel. Accessories normally include electric starter, alternator and fuel pump. Other details are tabulated:

PZL-F 4A-235B (93 kW; 125 hp)

PZL-F 6A-350 six-cylinder aircooled piston engine

PZL-F 2A-120C (45 kW; 60 hp)

PZL-F ENGINES

Engine model	Cylinder arrangement	Capacity cc (cu in)	Compression ratio	Max T-O rating at S/L kW (hp) at rpm	Overall dimensions mm (in) length	width	height	Weight dry kg (lb)
2A-120C	2 horiz	1,916 (117)	8·5	45 (60) at 3,200	581 (22·9)	795 (31·3)	515 (20·3)	75·8 (167)
4A-235B	4 horiz	3,850 (235)	8·5	93 (125) at 2,800	774 (30·5)	795 (31·3)	637 (25·1)	117·5 (259)
6A-350C	6 horiz	5,735 (350)	10·5	164 (220) at 2,800	952 (37·5)	795 (31·3)	641 (25·25)	167 (367)

WSK-PZL KALISZ

WYTWÓRNIA SPRZETU KOMUNIKACYJNEGO-PZL KALISZ

ul. Czestochowska 140, 62-800 Kalisz
Telephone: 77351
Telex: 046 384
General Manager: Dipl Ing Jan Kolodziej

In 1952 the Soviet Union transferred responsibility for manufacture and service support of Soviet aircooled radial piston engines to the WSK (transport equipment manufacturing centre) at Kalisz. Current production is centred on the 1,000 hp ASz-62IR and the 260 hp AI-14RA/RC.

PZL (IVCHENKO) AI-14R

The original 260 hp AI-14R version of this nine-cylinder aircooled radial engine has been produced in very large quantities, in both the Soviet Union and Poland. Since 1960 several later versions have gone into production in the Soviet Union for fixed-wing aircraft and helicopters. Kalisz has developed four versions:

AI-14RA. Basic production engine, rated at 194 kW (260 hp); fitted to Yak-12, Yak-18, PZL-101A Gawron and PZL-104 Wilga 35.

AI-14RA-KAF. RA with carburettor further aft, for Wilga 80.

AI-14RC. Version fitted with electric starter.

AI-14RD. Uprated version (209 kW; 280 hp), bench tested in 1982. Was to be flight tested in a PZL-104 in 1983.

The following description refers to the AI-14RA:

Type: Nine-cylinder single-row aircooled radial, geared with blower.

Cylinders: Bore 105 mm (4·125 in). Stroke 130 mm (5·125 in). Capacity 10·16 litres (620 cu in). Nitrided steel barrel; cast light alloy head incorporating air starting valve. Two spark plugs and single inlet and exhaust valves. Compression ratio 5·9.

Pistons: Aluminium forgings, each with two chromium plated compression rings and two scraper rings.

Connecting Rods: One master rod, with lead-bronze big-end bearing; eight link rods articulated by steel cemented knuckle pins fixed in the master rod cheeks against rotation and secured laterally by retaining plates.

Crankshaft: Heat treated steel in two parts, the front portion being gripped in the split cheek of the rear portion and held by a pinch bolt. Both portions carry a counterweight, the rear counterweight being pendulous type which balances inertia forces and also serves as vibration damper. Shaft held in two main roller bearings and ball thrust bearing.

Crankcase: Comprises gearcase, thrust-bearing cover, mid-case, mixture chamber and rear casing.

Valve Gear: Each valve is opened by push/pull rod, from a cam plate geared to rotate in opposition to the crankshaft.

PZL AI-14RA piston engine

Induction System: Carburettor type K-14A, fed by fuel pump type 702M.

Fuel Grade: 91 to 100 octane.

Blower: Aluminium forged impeller. Magnesium cast diffuser

Lubrication: Gear type pressure and scavenge pumps.

Ignition: Two M-9 magnetos; automatic timing and fully screened.

Propeller Drive: Planetary gears, ratio 0·787.

Starting: By compressed air from airborne or ground bottle to cylinder-head valves.

Dimensions:

Length	956 mm (37·63 in)
Diameter	985 mm (38·78 in)

Weight, Dry: 197 kg (434 lb)

Performance Ratings:

T-O	194 kW (260 hp) at 2,350 rpm
Rated	164 kW (220 hp) at 2,050 rpm
Cruise	98·4 kW (132 hp) at 1,730 rpm

Specific Fuel Consumption:

T-O	95-104·3 µg/J (0·562-0·617 lb/h/hp)
Cruise	76·4-83·8 µg/J (0·452-0·496 lb/h/hp)

PZL (SHVETSOV) ASz-62R

Power plant of the An-2 transport biplane, the ASz-62R is a 1,000 hp nine-cylinder aircooled radial engine. It was developed from the Wright Cyclone R-1820 by Arkadiya Shvetsov's bureau in the Soviet Union, as the ASh-62. Several variants have been built in the Soviet Union, including the ASh-62IR/TK driving a turbo-compressor to maintain 634 kW (850 hp) up to a height of 9,500 m (31,000 ft).

PZL ASz-62IR piston engine

ASz-62IR. Standard power plant of all versions of the An-2 except for the An-2M. Transferred to WSK-PZL Kalisz in 1959. In production also for Warszawa PZL-106BS and Mielec M-18 Dromader. M-18 versions have no centrifugal oil filter, and drive a hydraulic pump instead of an air compressor. Polish production for the An-2 exceeds 20,000.

All versions have a cylinder bore of 155·5 mm (6⅛ in), capacity of 29·87 litres (1,823 cu in) and compression ratio of 6·4 : 1.

The planetary reduction gear has a ratio of 0·637 : 1.

Dimensions:

Length overall	1,130 mm (44·50 in)
Diameter	1,375 mm (54·13 in)

Weight, Dry:

Without power take-off	579 kg (1,276 lb)

Performance Ratings:

T-O	746 kW (1,000 hp) at 2,200 rpm
Rated power	611 kW (820 hp) at 2,100 rpm
Cruise (50% power)	306 kW (410 hp) at 1,670 rpm

Specific Fuel Consumption:

T-O	112 µg/J (0·661 lb/h/hp)
Cruise	80 µg/J (0·474 lb/h/hp)

WSK-PZL RZESZÓW

WYTWÓRNIA SPRZETU KOMUNIKACYJNEGO-PZL RZESZÓW

ul. Obrońców Stalingradu 120, 35-078 Rzeszów, PO Box 340
Telephone: 46100
Telex: 0632411
GENERAL MANAGER: Ing Henryk Trzęsicki

WSK Rzeszów, founded in 1938 as PZL Rzeszów, at first produced Bristol Pegasus and Walter Junior and Minor engines under licence. After the second World War the works expanded considerably. The first product was the Soviet M-11D, followed by series production of the ASz-62IR and LiT-3 piston engines and HO-10 and SO-1 turbojets.

Current production is centred on the Soviet designed TVD-10 turboprop and turboshaft, and GTD-350 turboshaft, together with WR-2 reduction gear for Mi-2 helicopters; the tropicalised SO-3 turbojet for the TS-11 Iskra trainer; and the PZL-3S piston engine for agricultural aircraft. The SO-3 is described (with the SO-1) on an earlier page, under the IL heading.

PZL-F (Franklin) engines were in 1985 transferred to Refrigeration Equipment Works, as noted under that heading.

PZL TVD-10B

The Soviet designed Glushenkov TVD-10B turboprop engine, rated at 716 kW (960 shp), is made under licence in Poland for the An-28 STOL light transport built at WSK-PZL Mielec.

TYPE: Free turbine turboprop.

AIR INTAKE: Three radial struts, inlet guide vanes and starter de-iced by bleed air from combustion chamber.

COMPRESSOR: Six axial stages and one centrifugal stage. Stage 1 has front bearing journal, bolted to stages 2 to 6 which are pinched by compressor shaft used as tie bolt. Blades in dovetail roots, as are blades of centrifugal stage, which is bolted to shaft flange. Front ball and rear roller bearings. Pressure ratio 7·4. Mass flow 4·6 kg (10·14 lb)/s at 29,600 rpm.

COMPRESSOR CASING: Forward upper and lower halves in titanium; rear section welded from sheet steel and containing anti-surge bleed valve and radial diffuser.

COMBUSTION CHAMBER: Annular with centrifugal burner, and two starting units each with semiconductor igniter and auxiliary burner.

FUEL SYSTEM: Comprises supply pump, filter, pump governor, acceleration control, signalling block and thermocorrector. The system ensures optimum engine starting, acceleration and deceleration, operation at set ranges, and shutdown.

FUEL GRADE: T-1, T-2, TS-1 or RT.

COMPRESSOR TURBINE: Two-stage axial. Blades held by fir tree roots in aircooled discs. Inlet guide vanes of hollow sheet with air cooling. Casing has ceramic liner. Max temperature behind turbine 740°C.

POWER TURBINE: Single-stage axial, blades with fir tree roots, held in front roller and rear ball bearing.

REDUCTION GEARS: Single-stage spur high speed gear to accessory box and propeller gear; under the high speed gear is the feathering pump oil tank. Accessory box drives 16kW alternator, propeller tachometer and reduction gear oil pump, with propeller brake on the casing. Upper driveshaft consists of front and rear sections inside a titanium tube carrying the propeller reduction gear. The latter is single-stage planetary, and drives the propeller shaft, propeller governor (on rear reduction gear) and power turbine governor (on the pump governor).

ENGINE ACCESSORIES: Mounted on intake casing, box contains oil centrifuge; and drives tachometer, oil pump, fuel pump and pump governor. The starter is on the front of the engine with a claw clutch.

JETPIPE: Two sections joined in the airframe into one elongated pipe.

OIL SYSTEM: Closed and pressurised. Gas generator pump with one delivery and four scavenge gears, and reduction gear pump with one delivery and three scavenge. Oil tank on intake flange; normal content 16 litres (3·5 Imp gallons).

OIL GRADE: Oil mixture: 25 per cent MK-22 or MS-20, 75 per cent MK-8 or MS-8p.

DIMENSIONS:
- Length without airframe jetpipe section: 2,060 mm (81·1 in)
- Width: 555 mm (21·9 in)
- Height: 900 mm (35·4 in)

WEIGHT, DRY: 230 kg (507 lb)
- Complete engine: 295 kg (650 lb)

PERFORMANCE RATINGS:
- T-O: 754 kW (1,011 shp)
- Nominal: 613 kW (823 shp)
- Max cruise: 547 kW (739 shp)

SPECIFIC FUEL CONSUMPTION (T-O): 95·8 μg/J (0·567 lb/h/shp)

PZL TVD-10W

This is the helicopter version of the TVD-10B, two of which power the PZL Swidnik Sokól. It uses the same gas generator, with the following differences:

TYPE: Free turbine turboshaft engine.

Glushenkov TVD-10B licensed to PZL Rzeszów

AIR INTAKE: Annular, cast integral with accessory drive box. Three radial struts, which with inlet guide vanes and starter bullet may be heated by bleed air.

FUEL SYSTEM: Comprises pump governor and thermo-corrector to provide automatic operation at constant helicopter rotor speed through all variations of blade pitch, as well as control of anti-surge bleed valve, maintaining constant fuel flow in starting cycle, limiting maximum shaft speed and gas temperature behind gas-generator turbine and automatic switch-off of faulty engine and selection of emergency power on remaining unit. Synchronises power of both engines and holds helicopter rotor speed within ±5 per cent.

POWER TURBINE: Single-stage axial, with blades held in fir tree roots. Held in front roller and rear ball bearing, with rear extension shaft to main reduction gear. Speed maintained at 22,490 rpm. Small bevel drive via flexible shaft to pump governor.

JETPIPE: Single fixed-area, turned 180° for port or starboard installation.

OIL SYSTEM: Closed and pressurised, with one delivery and four suction pumps, all gear-type. Oil tank airframe-mounted, normal capacity 8 litres (1·76 Imp gallons).

OIL GRADE: B-3W synthetic.

ACCESSORIES: Integral cast box drives 5kW starter, starter unit, electronic temperature limiter, vibration sensor, tachometer generator, oil pumps and centrifuge, phase torquemeter, de-icing valve, power-turbine speed limiter and operation time counter.

DIMENSIONS:
- Length with jetpipe: 1,875 mm (73·8 in)
- Width: 740 mm (29·0 in)

WEIGHT, DRY: 144 kg (317 lb)

PERFORMANCE, RATINGS (ISA):
- T-O: 662 kW (900 shp)
- Max contingency: 846 kW (1,134 shp)
- Max cruise: 515 kW (690 shp)

SPECIFIC FUEL CONSUMPTION:
- T-O: 97 μg/J (0·575 lb/h/hp)

PZL GTD-350

The **GTD-350** is a helicopter turboshaft. In the Mi-2, the drive is taken from the rear, with the twin jetpipes of each engine exhausting to port (port engine) and starboard (starboard engine). Though developed by the Isotov bureau in the Soviet Union, it is in production only in Poland. PZL Rzeszów has developed a new version rated at 331 kW (444 shp) and designated **GTD-350P**. TBO of the GTD-350 is 4,000 h.

TYPE: Axial/centrifugal-flow free turbine turboshaft.

AIR INTAKE: Annular intake casing and inlet guide vanes of stainless steel. Automatic de-icing of inlet guide vanes and central bullet by air bleed from compressor.

COMPRESSOR: Seven axial stages and one centrifugal stage, all of steel, connected with a tie bolt. Discs shrink fitted to shaft. Blades have dovetail roots. Front roller bearing and rear ball bearing. Pressure ratio 6·05 : 1. Mass flow 2·19 kg (4·83 lb)/s at 45,000 rpm.

COMPRESSOR CASING: Horizontally split aluminium alloy casing, with stator blades brazed to semi-rings.

COMBUSTION CHAMBER: Reverse-flow type with air supply through two tubes. Centrifugal duplex single-nozzle burner. Semiconductor igniter plug.

FUEL SYSTEM: NR-40TA pump governor; RO-40TA power turbine governor, DS-40 controlling bleed valves; and electromagnetic starting valve. Provision against power turbine overspeed and (GTD-350P only) transmission overload.

FUEL GRADE: TS-1, TS-2 or Jet A-1.

COMPRESSOR TURBINE: Single stage with aircooled disc. Shrouded blades with fir tree roots. Casing has metal-ceramic insert. Shaft supported in ball bearing at rear. Temperature before turbine 940°C (GTD-350P, 985°C).

POWER TURBINE: Two-stage constant speed (24,000 rpm). Shrouded blades with fir tree roots. Discs bolted together. Turbine stators integrally cast.

JETPIPES: Two fixed area jetpipes.

REDUCTION GEARING: Two sets of gears, with ratio of 0·246 : 1, in cast magnesium alloy casing. Output shaft speed 5,900 rpm.

LUBRICATION SYSTEM: Closed type. Gear type pump with one pressure and four scavenge units. Cooler and tank, capacity 12·5 litres (2·75 Imp gallons).

OIL GRADE: B3-W (synthetic) or Shell Turbine Oil-500.

ACCESSORIES: STG3 3kW starter/generator, NR-40TA governor pump, D1 tachometer and oil pumps driven by gas generator. RO-40TA speed governor, D1 tachometer and centrifugal breather driven by power turbine.

STARTING: STG3 starter/generator suitable for operation at up to 4,000 m (13,125 ft) altitude.

DIMENSIONS:
- Length overall: 1,385 mm (54·53 in)
- Max width: 520 mm (20·47 in)
- Width (with jetpipes): 626 mm (24·65 in)
- Max height: 630 mm (24·80 in)
- Height (with jetpipes): 760 mm (29·9 in)

WEIGHT, DRY:
- Less jetpipes and accessories: 139·5 kg (307 lb)

PERFORMANCE RATINGS:
- T-O rating (6 min) at 96% max gas generator rpm:
  - GTD-350: 298 kW (400 shp)
  - GTD-350P: 331 kW (444 shp)
- Nominal rating (1 h) at 90% gas generator rpm:
  - GTD-350: 238·5 kW (320 shp)
  - GTD-350P: 261 kW (350 shp)
- Cruise rating (I)
  - 212·5 kW (285 shp) at 87·5% gas-generator rpm
- Cruise rating (II)
  - 175 kW (235 shp) at 84·5% gas-generator rpm

SPECIFIC FUEL CONSUMPTION:
- T-O: 136 μg/J (0·805 lb/h/shp)
- Nominal: 146 μg/J (0·861 lb/h/shp)
- Cruise (I): 154 μg/J (0·913 lb/h/shp)
- Cruise (II): 165 μg/J (0·978 lb/h/shp)

OIL CONSUMPTION:
- Max: 0·3 litres (0·53 Imp pints)/h

PZL (Isotov) GTD-350 turboshaft engine (298 kW; 400 shp)

PZL-3S

With ancestry going back via the LiT-3 to the AI-26W, this radial was the only type in its class to be developed in the 1970s. It has FAA, Yugoslav SKSV and Canadian DoT type certificates and Polish CACA certification to BCAR. Applications include the PZL-106A Kruk, Romanian IAR-827A and conversions of the Grumman/Schweizer Ag-Cat A, B and C, Thrush Commander, DHC-2 Beaver and DHC-3 Otter.

TYPE: Seven-cylinder aircooled radial.

CYLINDERS: Bore 155·5 mm (6·12 in). Stroke 155 mm (6·1 in). Capacity 20·6 litres (1,265 cu in). Compression ratio 6·4 : 1.

PISTONS: Forged aluminium.

INDUCTION SYSTEM: Float type carburettor. Mechanically driven supercharger.

FUEL GRADE: Aviation gasoline, minimum 91 octane.

LUBRICATION: Gear type oil pump. Oil grade Aero Shell 100 or other to MIL-L-6082.

PROPELLER DRIVE: Direct. Provision for constant-speed US-132000A or Dowty Rotol propeller.

ACCESSORIES: ANG 6423 Prestolite alternator and two output shafts, one 20 kW; 27 hp (26 kW; 35 hp max) for spraying pump and the other 3·7 kW; 5 hp.

STARTING: Electric.

DIMENSIONS:
- Diameter 1,267 mm (49·88 in)
- Length 1,110 mm (43·72 in)

WEIGHT, DRY: 411 kg (906 lb)

PERFORMANCE RATINGS:
- Max T-O 448 kW (600 hp) at 2,200 rpm
- Max continuous 410 kW (550 hp) at 2,050 rpm
- Cruise (75 per cent) 310 kW (415 hp) at 2,000 rpm

SPECIFIC FUEL CONSUMPTION:
- T-O, max continuous 105 μg/J (0·61 lb/h/hp)
- Cruise 86 μg/J (0·51 lb/h/hp)

PZL-3SR

This is the geared version of the PZL-3S. Applications include the PZL-106AR and BR and M-21. The following are the main differences:

PROPELLER DRIVE: Planetary gear of 0·7 ratio. Provision for constant-speed propeller, Type US-133000.

DIMENSION:
- Length 1,271 mm (50·06 in)

WEIGHT, DRY: 446 kg (983 lb)

Cutaway PZL-3S seven-cylinder radial

ROMANIA

TURBOMECANICA

INTREPRINDEREA TURBOMECANICA BUCURESTI

c/o Central National Aeronautic, Bulevardul Dacia 13, Casuta Postala 22-149, R-70185 Bucharest
Telephone: 12 08 78
Telex: 10660 CNAER

This factory produces under licence the Rolls-Royce Spey 511-14W and Viper 632/633, and the Turboméca Turmo IVC.

SOUTH AFRICA

ATLAS

ATLAS AIRCRAFT CORPORATION OF SOUTH AFRICA (PTY) LTD

PO Box 11, Atlas Road, Kempton Park 1620, Transvaal

Atlas is manufacturing the Rolls-Royce Viper 540 turbojet under sublicence from Piaggio of Italy, for use in Atlas Impala attack trainers.

SPAIN

SENER

SENER-INGENIERIA Y SISTEMAS SA

Edificio Bronce, Plaza Manuel Gomez Moreno S/N, 28020 Madrid
Telephone: (1) 455 8556

At Cosmo 86, a Spanish Aerospace and Defence show, in April 1986, Sener was announced as the Spanish partner in the consortium that will build the engine of the future EFA Eurofighter. This is briefly referred to under the Eurojet entry in the International part of this section. Previously, Sener was concerned chiefly with rockets and spaceflight.

SWEDEN

FLYGMOTOR

VOLVO FLYGMOTOR AB

S-461 81 Trollhättan
Telephone: 0520 (international 46 520) 94000
Telex: 420 40 Volfa s
Telefax: (International) 46 520 94628

The original Flygmotor company was founded in 1930 and began by building under licence the Bristol Pegasus I aero engine, under the designation My VI. Since 1970 Volvo Flygmotor has been a wholly owned subsidiary of AB Volvo.

Volvo Flygmotor AB is engaged in research and development work on turbojet engines, ramjet engines and (see 1984-85 and earlier *Jane's*) rocket engines. Its major current programmes involve production of the B version of the RM8 supersonic turbofan developed from the Pratt & Whitney JT8D to power the Saab JA 37 Viggen; and, in collaboration with General Electric, development and manufacture of the RM12 engine for the JAS 39 Gripen.

Since mid-1980 Volvo Flygmotor has been a risk and revenue sharing partner with General Electric on the CF6-80A and -80C turbofans, for the Boeing 767, Airbus A310, Boeing 747-300 and Airbus A300-600. Volvo Flygmotor has chosen to undertake engineering tasks and to manufacture components mainly in the structural housing section and in the rotating fan and HP compressor spool areas.

Volvo Flygmotor participates in development and production of the Garrett TFE731-5 turbofan, contributing stationary compressor, combustion chamber and turbine parts.

The company has also entered into a risk- and revenue-sharing collaboration with Pratt & Whitney on the JT8D-200; the Swedish company is performing engineering tasks and also makes major structural components and rotating parts.

FLYGMOTOR RM8

The RM8 is a Swedish military version of the Pratt & Whitney JT8D turbofan which Flygmotor developed to power the Saab 37 Viggen supersonic combat aircraft. Following the **RM8A** for the AJ 37, SF 37, SH 37 and SK 37 versions of the Viggen, the **RM8B** was conceived to meet the propulsion requirements of the fighter Viggen, the JA 37. Research showed that a changed design could improve the stability of operation at high altitudes and in severe manoeuvres, as well as increase thrust in all regimes. In collaboration with Pratt & Whitney the design of the RM8B was completed in late 1971. The major change to improve functional stability at high altitude involved replacing the first stage of the LP compressor by a third stage on the fan. To increase thrust the RM8B has a four-nozzle burner combustion system and a new HP turbine. Delivery of

Volvo Flygmotor RM8B augmented turbofan for JA 37 fighter version of Viggen

production RM8B engines began in 1978, and is due for completion in 1988.

The following description refers to the RM8A:

TYPE: Two-spool turbofan with modulated afterburner.

AIR INTAKE: Annular, with 19 fixed inlet guide vanes.

FAN: Two-stage front fan. Titanium blades.

LP COMPRESSOR: Four-stage axial flow, integral with fan stages. Blades of titanium. Steel casing.

HP COMPRESSOR: Seven-stages. Blades of high temperature alloys. Overall pressure ratio 16·5. Bypass ratio approximately 1. Mass flow 145 kg (320 lb)/s.

COMBUSTION CHAMBER: Cannular type with nine cylindrical flame tubes, each downstream of a single Duplex fuel nozzle. Two high energy spark plugs, each with its own igniter box.

HP TURBINE: Single-stage with cast aircooled blades.

LP TURBINE: Three-stage axial flow, with cast blades. Exit guide vanes after turbine.

AFTERBURNER: Outer skin titanium. Inner skin special alloys. One hot streak igniter. Hydraulically actuated fully variable nozzle, using fuel as the operating fluid.

CONTROL SYSTEMS: The main system for the gas generator comprises a Bendix hydromechanical control. A further Bendix unit controls the afterburner and nozzle. A single power lever controls thrust from maximum afterburner down to idle; movement below idle actuates the fuel cutoff valve.

MOUNTING: Three point. Main mountings on each side of compressor casing; one under turbine casing.

ACCESSORY DRIVE: Via gearbox, under engine, driven from HP turbine shaft.

DIMENSIONS:

Length overall: RM8A	6,197 mm (244 in)
RM8B	6,279 mm (247·2 in)
Max diameter (both versions)	1,397 mm (55 in)
Inlet diameter (both)	1,030 mm (40·55 in)

WEIGHT, DRY:

RM8A	2,100 kg (4,630 lb)
RM8B	2,250 kg (4,960 lb)

PERFORMANCE RATINGS (ISA, S/L):

Max T-O, augmented:	
RM8A	115·6 kN (25,990 lb st)
RM8B	125 kN (28,110 lb st)
Max T-O, dry:	
RM8A	65·6 kN (14,750 lb st)
RM8B	72·1 kN (16,200 lb st)

SPECIFIC FUEL CONSUMPTION:

Max augmented:	
RM8A	70·0 mg/Ns (2·47 lb/h/lb st)
RM8B	71·4 mg/Ns (2·52 lb/h/lb st)
Max dry:	
RM8A	17·8 mg/Ns (0·63 lb/h/lb st)
RM8B	18·1 mg/Ns (0·64 lb/h/lb st)
Max continuous (both)	17·3 mg/Ns (0·61 lb/h/lb st)

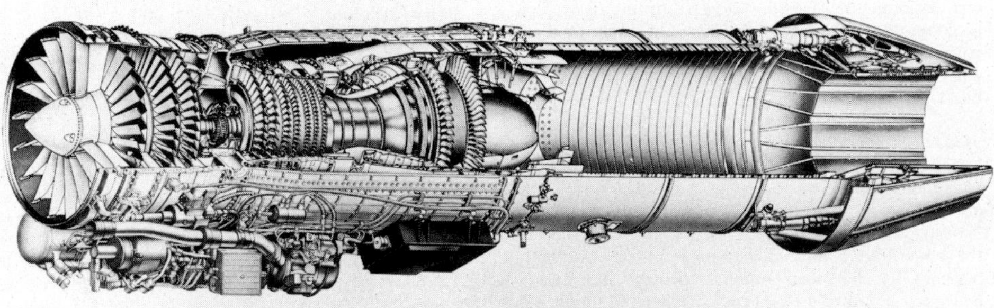

Cutaway drawing of Flygmotor RM12 (80·5 kN; 18,100 lb st)

FLYGMOTOR RM12

The RM12 is a Swedish version of the General Electric F404 augmented turbofan engine to power the single-engined JAS 39 Gripen multi-mission combat aircraft. Its development is a joint undertaking between General Electric and Volvo Flygmotor. General Electric retains all rights to the design and engineering policy in the development phase, and will supply to Sweden approximately 60 per cent by value of engine parts for all the engines. About 40 per cent by value will be covered by Volvo Flygmotor parts manufacturing, final assembly and test.

Under a separate agreement, Volvo Flygmotor is a 20 per cent risk- and revenue-sharing partner in all F404 single-engine aircraft applications, in addition to the JAS 39. Volvo Flygmotor will supply parts to General Electric similar to those parts that it manufactures for the RM12. Vendor substantiation engineering parts were delivered to General Electric in 1984. Deliveries of production parts started in mid-1985.

The RM12 thrust improvement relative to the F404-GE-400 engine has been achieved by increasing the turbine inlet temperature by up to 105°C under extreme mission conditions, and by increasing the fan airflow. The fan has been reinforced to meet more stringent bird strike requirements for the single-engine application, and this has required changes to the engine control system. Increased temperature and pressure have required changes to hot end materials. RM12 testing started at GE's Lynn factory in June 1984, and the official start of testing in Sweden followed on 23 January 1985. Five engines (three at Lynn, two at Trolhättan) had run more than 1,100 hours by the end of 1985. Flight testing should begin in 1987 and production deliveries in 1991.

The following description is confined to changes from the basic F404, which is described in the General Electric entry in the US section:

FAN: Three-stage axial. Variable first-stage stator. Airflow 68 kg (150 lb)/s. Bypass ratio 0·28.

WEIGHT, DRY:	1,050 kg (2,315 lb)
PERFORMANCE RATINGS:	
Max T-O: dry	54 kN (12,140 lb st)
augmented	80·5 kN (18,100 lb st)

UNION OF SOVIET SOCIALIST REPUBLICS

GLUSHENKOV

Little is known of this design bureau, which was first mentioned in 1969 as responsible for the TVD-10 engines of the Be-30 light turboprop transport. Since then it has produced important turboprop and turboshaft engines.

GLUSHENKOV TVD-10

This free turbine engine was developed originally to power the Kamov Ka-25 helicopter, and in that application it received the military designation **GTD-3**. The civil turboshaft engine has been licensed to Poland for production, and a full description appears under WSK-PZL Rzeszów. It is believed that all engines for the Ka-25 have been made in the Soviet Union, the GTD-3 being rated at 671 kW (900 shp) and the later **GTD-3BM** at 738 kW (990 shp).

The **TVD-10B** is the turboprop version, using the same gas generator, and in 1978 this was selected at a rating of 716 kW (960 shp) to power the An-28 STOL utility transport. Again this engine has been licensed to Poland for production, where it is known as the **TVD-10S**, as described under WSK-PZL Rzeszów.

GLUSHENKOV TVD-20

This engine is the turboprop fitted to the An-3 biplane, which has been flying since 1979. Its announced rating is 1,081 kW (1,450 hp), and this is sufficiently greater than that of the TVD-10 to conclude that, instead of being a mere uprated version of the earlier engine, the TVD-20 has a new gas generator. It would also be reasonable to suppose that a turboshaft helicopter version exists. In the An-3 the gearbox has a particularly large reduction ratio to drive a slow-turning propeller. It will be noted from the photograph of the An-3 in the Aircraft section that the exhaust stack is at the front of the engine, confirming the same back-to-front layout as in the TVD-10B. The An-3 is expected to be produced in very large numbers, by conversion of An-2s.

ISOTOV

This bureau, headed by General Designer Sergei Pietrovich Isotov until his death on 6 May 1983 at the age of 65, was responsible for the GTD-350 and TV2-117A turboshaft engines which power Mil Mi-2 and Mi-8 helicopters respectively. The former is in production in Poland, and is described under the WSK-PZL Rzeszów entry in this edition. Isotov was also responsible for the TVD-850 turboprop engines which powered early Antonov An-28 transport aircraft (see Polish Aircraft section).

ISOTOV TV2-117A

The power plant of the Mi-8 comprises two TV2-117A engines coupled through a VR-8A gearbox. As is common with modern Soviet helicopters, the engines and gearbox are delivered and thereafter treated as a single unit. The complete package incorporates a control system (separate from the control system of each gas generator) which maintains desired rotor speed, synchronises the power of both engines, and increases the power of the remaining engine if the other should fail.

The TV2 engine is of conservative design, being biased in favour of long and trouble-free life rather than attempting to rival the small size and weight of some Western engines in the same power class.

TYPE: Free turbine helicopter turboshaft engine.

AIR INTAKE: Direct pitot, with main front casing providing vertical upper and lower driveshafts to accessory packages. Main accessory group above the engine projects ahead of intake face. Casing incorporates variable incidence inlet vanes.

COMPRESSOR: Ten-stage axial. Construction principally in titanium to reduce weight in comparison with the steel that would otherwise be used. Inlet guide vanes and stators of stages 1, 2 and 3 are of variable incidence to facilitate starting and increase compressor efficiency over a wide speed range; for the same reasons the casing incorporates automatic blow-off valves. Pressure ratio 6·6 : 1 at 21,200 rpm.

COMBUSTION CHAMBER: Annular, with eight burner cones. Fabricated from inner and outer diffuser casings, flame tube, casing, burners, and anti-icing bleed air pipe.

FUEL GRADE: T-1 or TS-1 to GOST 10227-62 specification (Western equivalents, DERD.2494, MIL-F-5616).

TURBINE: Two-stage axial compressor turbine bolted to rear of splined shaft with front extension to drive accessories. Solid rotor blades, held by fir tree roots in discs cooled by bleed air (first disc 10th stage air, all other discs 8th stage). First- and second-stage stators have 51 and 47 inserted blades respectively. Free power turbine of similar two stage design; its rotors have 43 and 37 blades respectively.

EXHAUST UNIT: Large fixed-area duct which deflects the gas out at 60°. It comprises a pipe, pipe shroud and tie-band, shroud connector links and exhaust pipe attachments. The exhaust pipe and shroud together form a double-wall assembly which minimises heat transfer into the power plant nacelle, the pipe being cooled by air circulating in the double wall.

OUTPUT SHAFT: The main driveshaft is an extension of the power turbine rotor shaft. It conveys torque from the free turbine to the overrunning clutch of the helicopter main gearbox (VR-8A) and is also coupled to the speed governor of the free turbine rotor. Max output speed 12,000 rpm; main rotor speed 192 rpm.

ACCESSORIES: Mounted on the main drive box above the intake casing, in which a train of bevel and spur gears provides drives for airframe and engine accessories. The engine automatic control system includes a fuel system, hydraulic system, anti-icing system, gas temperature restriction system, engine electric supply and starting

Isotov TV2-117A turboshaft engine (1,267 kW; 1,700 shp)

system, and monitoring instruments. The hydraulic system positions the variable stators according to a preset programme, depending on compressor speed and air temperature at the inlet; it also sends electrical signals to control the starter/generator system, close the starting bleed air valves and restrict peak gas temperature to 600°C. Air up to 1·8 per cent of the total mass flow can be used to heat the intake and other parts liable to icing. Fire extinguishant can be released manually by the pilot, upon receipt of a fire warning, through a series of spray rings and pipes.

LUBRICATION: Pressure circulation type. Oil is supplied by the upper pump and scavenged from the five main bearings by the lower pump, returned through the helicopter mounted air/oil heat exchanger and thence to the helicopter tank. The oil seals and air/oil labyrinth seals are connected to a centrifugal breathing system.

OIL GRADE: Synthetic, permitting operation at oil temperatures above 200°C, combined with easy starting at minus 40°C without heating the oil. Grade B-3V to MRTU 38-1-157-65 (nearest foreign substitute Castrol 98 to DERD.2487). Consumption, not over 0·5 litre per hour per engine.

STARTING: Electrical, fuel, and ignition systems are integrated. The SP3-15 system comprises DC starter/generator, six storage batteries, control panel, ground supply receptacle, and control switches and relays; of these all are airframe mounted except for the GS-18TP starter/generator which cranks the compressor during the starting cycle. The ignition unit comprises a control box, two semiconductor plugs, solenoid valve, and switch. The starting fuel system comprises an automatic starting unit on the NR-40V fuel regulating pump, constant-pressure valve, and two igniters.

DIMENSIONS:
- Length overall: 2,835 mm (111·5 in)
- Width: 547 mm (21·5 in)
- Height: 745 mm (29·25 in)

WEIGHT, DRY:
- Engine, without generator, etc: 330 kg (727 lb)
- VR-8A gearbox, less entrapped oil: 745 kg (1,642 lb)

PERFORMANCE RATINGS:
- Max: 1,267 kW (1,700 shp)
- T-O (S/L, static): 1,118 kW (1,500 shp)
- Max continuous: 895 kW (1,200 shp)
- Cruise (122 knots; 225 km/h; 140 mph at 500 m; 1,640 ft): 746 kW (1,000 shp)

SPECIFIC FUEL CONSUMPTION:
- T-O, as above: 102·4 µg/J (0·606 lb/h/shp)
- Cruise, as above: 115·4 µg/J (0·683 lb/h/shp)

ISOTOV TV3-117

The A-10 (Mi-24) helicopter in which Gourguen Karapetyan set a current speed record for helicopters over a 15/25 km course, on 21 September 1978, was powered by two TV3-117 turboshaft engines, each rated at 1,640 kW (2,200 shp). Similar engines are known to power the Mil Mi-14, Mi-17, Mi-24 and Ka-27/32. They may also power the attack helicopters reported as the Kamov 'Hokum' and Mil Mi-28 'Havoc'.

The Mi-17 helicopter is powered by the **TV3-117MT**, with a normal T-O rating of 1,417 kW (1,900 shp) and emergency 2½ min rating of 1,640 kW (2,200 shp). Pneumatic (air turbine) starters are fitted. The shipboard helicopter called 'Helix' by NATO, and Ka-27 by the US Department of Defense, and the commercial Ka-32, are powered by two **TV3-117V** engines each rated at 1,660 kW (2,225 shp).

The engine's designation and applications suggest that the TV3-117 is an uprated version of the TV2-117, but no other details are available.

ISOTOV TVD-850

Power plant of early Antonov An-28 STOL transports, the TVD-850 turboprop has a rating of 604 kW (810 shp). The cowled engine looks almost identical to the Turboméca Astazou, and the reduction gearbox must be housed in the centre of an annular air intake section. This engine appears to have been unsuccessful in competition with the Glushenkov TVD-10B.

IVCHENKO

GENERAL DESIGNER IN CHARGE OF BUREAU: Vladimir Lotarev

The collective headed by General Designer Alexander G. Ivchenko until his death in June 1968 was based in a factory at Zaporozhye in the Ukraine. The bureau is now headed by General Designer Lotarev, who has his own entry on a later page.

The first engine with which Ivchenko was associated officially was the 41 kW (55 hp) AI-4G piston engine used in the Kamov Ka-10 ultralight helicopter. He progressed ultimately, via the widely used AI-14 and AI-26 piston engines, to become one of the Soviet Union's leading producers of gas turbine engines. Since 1952 all Soviet piston engines have been assigned to Poland (see under WSK-PZL Kalisz in Polish section). Ivchenko turboprops are also produced in China (which see).

Ivchenko AI-20M turboprop of 3,169 ekW (4,250 ehp) *(courtesy of Aviation Magazine International, Paris)*

IVCHENKO AI-20

This engine was developed as the NK-4 at the Kuznetsov bureau in 1947-52, with the assistance of German engineers. Eventually preferred to the VK-2, it was ordered into production, and the Zaporozhye collective was charged with the final refinement and production.

Redesignated AI-20, it was produced from 1955 in several versions for aircraft that included the An-10, An-12, An-32, Be-12, Il-18 and Il-38.

AI-20K. Rated at 2,942 ekW (3,945 ehp). Used in Il-18V, An-10A and An-12. Produced at Shanghai in China as Wojiang-6.

AI-20M. Initial T-O rating of 3,124 ekW (4,190 ehp). Used in Il-18D/E, An-10A and An-12. Probably fitted to Il-20 and Il-38. Capable of operation on a wide range of fuels and lubricating oils. Power increased to 3,169 ekW (4,250 ehp) for later engines as in detailed description.

AI-20D. Rated at 3,124 ekW (4,190 ehp); navalised engine fitted to Beriev M-12.

AI-20DM. Uprated engine with T-O power (S/L, ISA) of 3,862 ekW (5,180 ehp). Fitted to An-32. In ten world record claims in late 1985 this engine was reported to the FAI as the **AM-20**.

The AI-20 was designed to operate reliably in all temperatures from −60°C to +55°C at heights up to 10,000 m (33,000 ft). It is a constant-speed engine, the rotor speed being maintained at 12,300 rpm by automatic variation of propeller pitch. Gas temperature after turbine is 560°C in the AI-20K and -20M. TBO of the AI-20K was 4,000 h in the Spring of 1966; the same life was reached by the -20M in 1968.

In the Il-18 installation, the AI-20 turboprop is supplied as a complete power plant with cowling, mounting and automatically-feathering reversible-pitch four-blade propeller.

The following description refers to the AI-20M:

TYPE: Single-shaft turboprop.

AIR INTAKE: Inner and outer cones connected by six radial struts. Outer casing carries accessories and front mountings. Centre casing carries reduction gear.

COMPRESSOR: Ten-stage assembly of discs running in roller bearing in front casing, joined to first disc by tubular extension shaft, and ball-thrust bearing in combustion chamber casing on through-bolted rear shaft. Magnesium alloy stator casing in upper and lower halves, bolted together. Pressure ratio 9·2 under altitude cruise conditions. Air mass flow 20·7 kg (45·6 lb)/s.

COMBUSTION CHAMBER: Annular chamber with ten burner cones welded to front ring, and separate inner and outer shrouds. Burners anchored by flanges on chamber casing. Pilot burners and ignition plugs at top of casing.

FUEL GRADE: T-1 or TS-1 to GOST-10227-62 (DERD.2492, JP-1 to MIL-F-5616).

TURBINE: Three stages overhung on cantilevered shaft running in roller bearing in tapered cone of combustion chamber casing and splined to compressor drive-shaft. Rotor blades shrouded at inner and outer ends and installed in pairs in slots in aircooled discs. Stator blades secured in grooves in casing, first stage being aircooled and second stage hollow to ensure uniform heating.

JETPIPE: Fixed-area type with five radial struts. Nozzle area 0·225 m² (2·42 sq ft).

REDUCTION GEAR: Planetary type, incorporating six-cylinder torquemeter and negative-thrust transmitter (type IKM), with self-checking device, for autofeathering AV-68I propeller. Ratio 0·08732 (input speed 12,300 rpm except ground-idle 10,400 rpm).

LUBRICATION: Pressure-feed type with full recirculation; hourly consumption not over 0·8 litres (0·175 Imp gal).

OIL GRADE: Mixture 75 per cent transformer oil GOST 982-56 or MK-8 to GOST 6457-66 (equivalent to DERD.2490 or MIL-O-6081B) and 25 per cent MS-20 or MK-22 to GOST 1013-49 (DERD.2472 or MIL-O-6082B).

ACCESSORIES: Engine and airframe accessories driven off compressor front extension shaft, via radial shafts at 6 and 12 o'clock. Full ice protection and fire extinguishing systems.

STARTING: Two electric starter/generators, Type STG-12 TMO-1000, supplied from ground source or from APU Type TG-16.

DIMENSIONS:
- Length: 3,096 mm (121·89 in)
- Width: 842 mm (33·15 in)
- Height: 1,180 mm (46·46 in)

WEIGHT, DRY: 1,040 kg (2,292 lb)

PERFORMANCE RATINGS:
- T-O: 3,169 ekW (4,250 ehp)
- Cruise (350 knots; 650 km/h; 404 mph at 8,000 m; 26,000 ft): 2,013 ekW (2,700 ehp)

SPECIFIC FUEL CONSUMPTION:
- T-O: 104·3 µg/J (0·617 lb/h/ehp)
- Cruise, as above: 73 3 µg/J (0·434 lb/h/ehp)

IVCHENKO AI-24

This turboprop powers the An-24 and its derivatives. Production began in 1960 and the following data refer to engines of the second series, which were in production by the Spring of 1966.

The **AI-24** of 1,875 ekW (2,515 ehp) powered the An-24V Series I, and was followed by the **AI-24A** with provision for water injection in the main production version of that aircraft. The latter is produced at Shanghai in China as the Wojiang-5A.

The 1,875 ekW (2,515 ehp) Ivchenko AI-24 turboprop *(courtesy of Aviation Magazine International, Paris)*

The more powerful **AI-24T** of 2,103 ekW (2,820 ehp) with water injection is used in the An-26 and An-30. This engine has in-flight vibration monitoring, automatic relief of power overloads and gas temperature behind the turbine, and auto-shutdown and feathering. From 1980, engines for these applications were designated **AI-24VT**; ratings are unchanged.

The AI-24 is a constant-speed engine, maintained at 15,100 rpm by automatic variation of propeller pitch. The engine is flat rated to maintain its nominal output to 3,500 m (11,500 ft). TBO was 3,000 h in the Spring of 1966; by 1968 the later AI-24T had reached 4,000 h.

Following the successful flight testing of otherwise conventional propellers with eight blades on an An-24, a major research programme has been under way for three years on multi-blade propfans, with special emphasis on contra-rotating dual configurations. Several model contra-propfans have been tested and two full scale examples have been run with an AI-24 engine. Typical configurations have 6 + 6, 7 + 7 and 8 + 8 blades, each blade being of the wide-chord scimitar shape arrived at in tests by NASA and various Western manufacturers.

TYPE: Single-shaft turboprop.

AIR INTAKE: Large magnesium alloy casting, comprising inner and outer cones joined by four radial struts. Carries accessories, reduction gear, front mountings and compressor inlet guide vanes.

COMPRESSOR: Ten-stage axial. Stainless steel rotor, comprising rigidly connected discs carrying dovetailed blades. Front shaft runs in roller bearing and is bolted to propeller driveshaft of reduction gear; rear shaft runs in ball-thrust bearing and is splined to turbine shaft. Welded steel casing in bolted left and right halves, with welded front and rear connecting flanges. Pressure ratio (max continuous, 6,000 m; 18,300 ft, 272 knots; 505 km/h; 314 mph) 7·85 : 1. Air mass flow 14·4 kg (31·7 lb)/s.

COMBUSTION CHAMBER: Annular, of spot welded heat resistant steel, with eight simplex burners inserted into swirl vane heads. Contains two starting units, each comprising a body, pilot burner and igniter plug.

FUEL GRADE: T-1, TS-1 to GOST 10227-62 (DERD.2494 or MIL-F-5616).

TURBINE: Three-stage axial. Three discs carry solid blades in fir tree roots, and are automatically centred on each other when connected by stay-bolts to the extended flange at the rear of the turbine shaft. Shaft splined to compressor rear shaft and held by tie-rod; runs in roller bearing ahead of first turbine disc. Three stator diaphragms through-bolted together and to combustion chamber casing. First nozzle diaphragm cooled by secondary air from combustion chamber. Rotor/stator sealing effected by soft inserts mounted in grooves in nozzle assemblies. Peak exhaust temperature during starting 750°C.

JETPIPE: Fixed-area type. Inner and outer rings connected by three hollow struts carrying 12 thermocouples.

REDUCTION GEAR: Planetary type, incorporating hydraulic torquemeter and electromagnetic negative thrust transmitter for propeller auto feathering. Magnesium alloy casing. Front flange of propeller shaft has end splines and 12 stud holes for type AV-72 propeller (AI-24T drives AV-72T propeller). Ratio 0·08255.

LUBRICATION: Pressure circulation system; hourly consumption not over 850 g (1·87 lb).

OIL GRADE: Mixture of 75 per cent transformer oil GOST 982-56 or MK-8 (DERD.2490 or MIL-O-6081B) and 25 per cent MS-20 or MK-22 (DERD.2472 or MIL-O-6082B).

ACCESSORIES: Mounted on front casing are starter/generator, alternator, propeller speed governor and centrifugal breather. Below casing are oil unit, air separator and removable box containing LP and HP fuel pumps and drives to hydraulic pump and tachometer generators. Also on front casing are an aerodynamic probe, ice detector, and negative-thrust feathering valve, torque transmitter and oil filter.

STARTING: Electric STG-18TMO starter/generator supplied from ground power or from TG-16 APU.

DIMENSIONS:

Length overall	2,346 mm (92·36 in)
Width	677 mm (26·65 in)
Height	1,075 mm (42·32 in)

WEIGHT, DRY: 600 kg (1,323 lb)

PERFORMANCE RATINGS:

T-O: AI-24A	1,875 ekW (2,515 ehp)
AI-24T	2,103 ekW (2,820 ehp)
Cruise rating at 243 knots (450 km/h; 280 mph) at 6,000 m (18,300 ft):	
AI-24A	1,156 ekW (1,550 ehp)
AI-24T	1,178 ekW (1,580 ehp)

SPECIFIC FUEL CONSUMPTION:

At cruise rating: AI-24A	91·3 μg/J (0·540 lb/h/ehp)
AI-24T	90·1 μg/J (0·533 lb/h/ehp)

OIL CONSUMPTION: 0·85 kg (1·87 lb)/h

IVCHENKO AI-25

This turbofan powers the three-engined Yakovlev Yak-40 STOL transport. Aeroflot Yak-40s have the basic AI-25 engine, but Yak-40Bs of the Soviet Air Force have an AI-25 with an aircooled HP turbine and rating of 17·13 kN (3,850 lb st). The AI-25TL powers the Czechoslovak L-39 trainer.

Emergence of the Polish WSK-PZL Mielec M-15 agricultural aircraft led to transfer of AI-25 activity to Poland, and production was expected to take place in that country to provide engines for the M-15 programme. However, following rejection of this aircraft by Aeroflot, the number to be built did not justify transfer of tooling from Zaporozhye. The AI-25 has been selected for the Semurg light transport by MAI and the Tashkent High School, the single engine being fed via an S-duct.

The Ivchenko bureau planned the engine for small transports, trainers and business jet aircraft. It is claimed to have an exceptional margin of flow stability and to be unusually robust and simple.

TYPE: Two-shaft turbofan.

AIR INTAKE: Fabricated from titanium sheet. Central bullet and intake leading-edges anti-iced by hot bleed air.

FAN: Three-stage axial. Drum/disc construction with pin-jointed blades. Casing and fan duct of magnesium alloy. Pressure ratio, 1·695 at 10,750 rpm. Bypass ratio 2.

COMPRESSOR: Eight-stage axial. Drum/disc construction of titanium, with aluminium and magnesium casing. Dovetailed blades. Peak pressure ratio, 4·68 at 16,640 rpm. Overall pressure ratio, 8.

COMBUSTION CHAMBER: Annular. Inner and outer casings joined upstream to 12 burner heads with stabilisers.

FUEL GRADE: T-1, TS-1 to GOST 10227-62 (DERD.2494, MIL-F-5616).

TURBINE: Single-stage HP turbine; two-stage LP turbine. Shrouded solid rotor blades held by fir tree roots in cooled discs.

JETPIPE: Plain fixed convergent nozzles for core and by-pass airflow. No mixer.

LUBRICATION: Self-contained, pressure circulating.

OIL GRADE: MK-8 to GOST 6457-66 or MK-6 to GOST 10328-63 (Western equivalents, DERD.2490 or MIL-O-6081B). Consumption 0·3 litres (0·53 Imp pints)/h.

ACCESSORIES: All shaft driven accessories mounted on gearbox on underside of engine and driven off HP spool. Equipment includes automatic fire extinguishing (agent can be supplied into oil-contacted labyrinth cavities), ice protection, automatic starting and control system, oil system chip detector and casing vibration monitor.

STARTING: Pneumatic. Air starter type SV-25 is supplied from ground hose coupling or from APU type AI-9 or an operating engine bleed. System claimed to develop high torque for rapid start in any climatic condition, and to be cleared for exceptional number of starts in given overhaul life.

DIMENSIONS:

Length overall	1,993 mm (78·46 in)
Width overall	820 mm (32·28 in)
Height overall	895 mm (35·24 in)

WEIGHT, DRY:

Without accessories	290 kg (639 lb)

PERFORMANCE RATINGS:

T-O	14·71 kN (3,307 lb st)
Long-range cruise rating, 6,000 m (20,000 ft) and 296 knots (550 km/h; 342 mph)	3·49 kN (785 lb st)

SPECIFIC FUEL CONSUMPTION:

T-O	15·86 mg/Ns (0·56 lb/h/lb st)
Cruise, as above	23·71 mg/Ns (0·837 lb/h/lb st)

Ivchenko AI-25TL turbofan (14·71 kN; 3,307 lb st), which powers the Czechoslovak Aero L-39

KOLIESOV

It is reported that this design bureau took over the assets of that of V. A. Dobrynin in the 1950s, and has since concentrated on powerful afterburning turbojets for large supersonic aircraft.

KOLIESOV VD-7

This large single-shaft turbojet was fitted to at least the final Myasishchev M-50 supersonic bomber (NATO reporting name 'Bounder'), with afterburners on the inner engines. No details are known, but the maximum thrust has always been estimated in the 137·3 kN (30,865 lb st; 14 tonne) class. It is commonly supposed that a derived version powers the Tu-22 (NATO 'Blinder') family of supersonic bomber and reconnaissance aircraft.

KOLIESOV Tu-144D ENGINE

In 1973 an American journalist visiting the Soviet aircraft industry was told that the Koliesov bureau was developing an advanced variable geometry variable bypass augmented engine capable of operating both as a turbofan in the subsonic regime and as an augmented turbojet in supersonic flight. It was described as a future alternative engine for the Tu-144 SST. In 1979 the Soviet Civil Aviation Minister announced that the engines of the Tu-144D were "50 per cent more economical in operation" than the Kuznetsov NK-144s originally fitted. It is generally believed that these were single-shaft turbojets by Koliesov. The large bomber called 'Blackjack' by NATO may be powered by similar engines.

KOLIESOV LIFT JET

Koliesov designers are believed to form one of the teams that have produced lift jet engines for V/STOL aircraft. In particular, this bureau has been reported as responsible for the lift engines of the Yak-38 (NATO 'Forger'). See 'Engines of Unknown Design' at the end of Soviet entries.

KUZNETSOV

GENERAL DESIGNER IN CHARGE OF BUREAU:
Nikolai Dmitrievich Kuznetsov

Kuznetsov was deputy to General V. Ya. Klimov during the Second World War. In the late 1940s his own bureau at Kuibyshev developed a series of large turboprop and turbofan engines. One of the first, the NK-4, was transferred to Ivchenko, and is described under that collective's heading, as the AI-20. The much larger NK-12 turboprop was used in the Tu-95, Tu-142 and Tu-126 military aircraft and in the Tu-114 civil transport, and was produced subsequently in smaller numbers for the An-22. The NK-8 and NK-144 may no longer be produced in their original forms.

KUZNETSOV NK-8

One of the first Soviet civil turbofans, the NK-8 has been developed through a number of variants, the most powerful of which is the NK-144 supersonic augmented engine for the Tupolev Tu-144 supersonic transport. Basic versions are the 99·1 kN (22,273 lb st) **NK-8-4**, later uprated to 103 kN (23,150 lb st), which originally powered the Ilyushin Il-62 four-engined transport, and the further developed 93·2 kN (20,950 lb) **NK-8-2** which was the original engine of the Tupolev Tu-154. At one time it was planned to replace the NK-8-2 by the Soloviev D-30K, which replaced the NK-8-4 in the Il-62M. However, it is believed that all current Tu-154A/B aircraft are powered by the **NK-8-2U** of greater thrust. The NK-8-4 remains in service with several Il-62 (not Il-62M) operators, including LOT. It led to the NK-86 described later.

TYPE: Two-shaft turbofan.

AIR INTAKE: Fabricated from outer ring, inner splitter and welded stator blades (15 in core airflow, 30 ahead of fan). Hot-air ice protection.

FAN: Two-stage axial, with anti-flutter sweptback blades on first rotor stage. Pressure ratio 2·15 at 5,350 rpm. Bypass ratio 1·02 (NK-8-2, 1·00).

COMPRESSOR: Two IP stages on fan shaft. Six-stage HP compressor. Construction of rotors and stators, including blading, almost wholly of titanium alloy. Core pressure ratio, 10·8 at 6,950 HP rpm (NK-8-2, 10 at 6,835 rpm).

COMBUSTION CHAMBER: Annular, with 139 burners. Claimed to produce no visible smoke.

FUEL GRADE: T-1 and TS-1 to GOST 10227-62 or T-7 to GOST 12308-66 (equivalent to Avtur 50 to DERD.2494 or MIL-F-5616).

TURBINE: Single-stage HP turbine, two-stage LP turbine, all with shrouded rotor blades, aircooled discs and hollow nozzle blades (stators). All shafting carried between shock absorbing bearings at each end, with labyrinth and contact (rubbing) graphite seals to prevent gas leakage. Gas temperature, not over 870°C (1,143°K) ahead of turbine, not over 670°C (NK-8-2, 650°C) downstream, both values sea level, static.

JETPIPE: Mixer leads bypass flow into common jetpipe which may be fitted with blocker/cascade type reverser giving up to 48 per cent (NK-8-2, 45 per cent) reverse thrust, and noise suppressor.

LUBRICATION: Continuous pressure feed and recirculation. Oil consumption not over 1·3 kg (2·87 lb)/h. Pressure not less than 2·28 bars (33 lb/sq in).

OIL GRADE: Mineral oil MK-8 or MK-8P to GOST 6457-66 (DERD.2490 or MIL-O-6081B). External tank on left side of front casing.

ACCESSORIES: These include automatic flight deck warning of vibration exceeding permissible limit, ice and fire. All accessories grouped beneath fan duct casing. Engine claimed to need no attention for long periods, other than inspection of fuel and oil filters. RTA-26-9-1 turbine gas temperature controller by Smiths Industries.

STARTING: HP spool driven by constant-speed drive type PPO-62M, or started pneumatically by air from APU type TA-6, from ground hose or by air from another engine (NK-8-2, pneumatic starter only). Time to idling speed not over 80 s. Engine can be windmill-started in the air under all conditions, up to altitudes of 11,000 m (36,000 ft).

DIMENSIONS:
NK-8-4: Length, no reverser 5,100 mm (201 in)
NK-8-2: Length, with reverser 5,288 mm (208·19 in)
Length, no reverser 4,762 mm (187·48 in)
Diameter 1,442 mm (56·8 in)

WEIGHT, DRY:
NK-8-4: No reverser 2,100 kg (4,629 lb)
With reverser 2,400 kg (5,291 lb)
NK-8-2: No reverser 2,100 kg (4,629 lb) max
With reverser 2,350 kg (5,180 lb) max

PERFORMANCE RATINGS:
NK-8-4: T-O rating 103·0 kN (23,150 lb st)
Cruise rating at 11,000 m (36,000 ft) and 458 knots (850 km/h; 530 mph) 27·0 kN (6,063 lb st)
NK-8-2: T-O rating 93·2 kN (20,950 lb st)
NK-8-2U: T-O rating 103·0 kN (23,150 lb st)

SPECIFIC FUEL CONSUMPTION:
At cruise rating at 11,000 m (36,000 ft) and 458 knots (850 km/h; 530 mph):
NK-8-4 22·1 mg/Ns (0·78 lb/h/lb st)
NK-8-2 21·53 mg/Ns (0·76 lb/h/lb st)

KUZNETSOV NK-86

Though described by the Ilyushin aircraft bureau as a new engine, this turbofan of 127·5 kN (28,660 lb st) appears to be closely related to the lower-thrust NK-8 series used in the Il-62 and Tu-154. The thrust is the same as the unaugmented rating of the NK-144 (see below) and the NK-86 may bear an even closer resemblance to the supersonic engine, which was itself derived from the NK-8. Four NK-86s power the Il-86 wide-body transport, with combined reversers and noise attenuators.

Kuznetsov NK-8-2 turbofan with thrust reverser (93·2 kN; 20,950 lb st)

Kuznetsov NK-12MV single-shaft turboprop of 11,033 ekW (14,795 ehp)
(courtesy of Aviation Magazine International, Paris)

KUZNETSOV NK-144

This is the two-spool augmented turbofan developed for the Soviet Union's first supersonic transport aircraft, the Tu-144. It is a development of the NK-8, and the first five pre-production NK-144s completed some 1,500 h of bench-testing by October 1965. The engine flew in at least one testbed aircraft before the start of the Tu-144 flight programme in 1968.

Since 1972 the afterburner augmentation has been increased, raising maximum rating from 171·6 kN (38,580 lb) to the figure quoted here. A version of the NK-144 is believed to be the engine of at least the first subtype of the Tupolev Tu-26 supersonic bomber known to NATO as 'Backfire'.

The NK-144 is reported to have a two-stage titanium fan, three-stage IP compressor, eleven-stage HP compressor, annular combustion chamber, single stage HP turbine and two-stage LP turbine. Aircooled blades are used in the HP turbine, and titanium is used extensively in construction of the engine. Bypass ratio is reported to be 1 : 1, maximum mass flow 250 kg (551 lb)/s, and pressure ratio 15 : 1. The jetpipe incorporates an afterburner, with hydraulically actuated variable area nozzle. Gas temperature at turbine entry is 1,050°C.

DIMENSIONS:
Length overall 5,200 mm (204·7 in)
Diameter 1,500 mm (59 in)

WEIGHT:
Without jetpipe, but with afterburner 2,850 kg (6,283 lb)

PERFORMANCE RATINGS:
Max: without afterburning 127·5 kN (28,660 lb st)
with afterburning 196·1 kN (44,090 lb st)

KUZNETSOV NK-12M

Designed at Kuibyshev under the leadership of N. D. Kuznetsov and former German engineers, the NK-12M is the most powerful turboprop engine in the world. In its original form as the **NK-12M** it developed 8,948 ekW (12,000 ehp). The later **NK-12MV** is rated at 11,033 ekW (14,795 ehp) and powered the Tupolev Tu-114 transport, driving four-blade contra-rotating propellers of 5·6 m (18 ft 4 in) diameter. As the **NK-12MA**, rated at 11,185 kW (15,000 shp), it powers the Antonov An-22 military transport, with propellers of 6·2 m (20 ft 4 in) diameter. A further application is in the Tupolev Tu-95 bomber and its derivatives, and Tu-126, both believed to be powered by the NK-12MV.

The NK-12M has a single 14-stage axial-flow compressor. Compression ratio varies from 9 : 1 to 13 : 1 according to altitude, and variable inlet guide vanes and blow-off valves are necessary. A cannular type combustion system is used: each flame tube is mounted centrally on a downstream injector, but all tubes merge at their maximum diameter to form an annular secondary region. The single turbine is a five-stage axial. Mass flow is 65 kg (143 lb)/s.

The casing is made in four portions, from sheet steel, precision welded. An electric control for variation of propeller pitch is incorporated, to maintain constant engine speed.

DIMENSIONS:
Length 6,000 mm (236·2 in)
Diameter 1,150 mm (45·3 in)

WEIGHT, DRY: 2,350 kg (5,181 lb)

PERFORMANCE RATINGS (NK-12MV):
T-O 11,033 ekW (14,795 ehp)
Nominal power 8,826 ekW (11,836 ehp) at 8,300 rpm
Idling speed 6,600 rpm

LOTAREV

GENERAL DESIGNER IN CHARGE OF BUREAU:
Vladimir A. Lotarev

LOTAREV D-36

As successor to Alexander Ivchenko at Zaporozhye, Vladimir Lotarev has developed the three-shaft turbofan engine that powers the An-72, An-74 and Yak-42. With a bypass ratio of 5·6 : 1 the D-36 is the first avowed turbofan—as distinct from a bypass turbojet—to emerge in the Soviet Union. Bench testing was in progress by September 1973, and flights in a pod carried beneath a Tu-16 testbed aircraft preceded the Yak-42 first flight by several years.

TYPE: Three-shaft turbofan for subsonic transport applications.

AIR INTAKE: Direct entry to fan, without inlet guide vanes.

FAN: Single-stage; 29 inserted titanium blades with part-span shrouds (snubbers). Bypass ratio 5·6 at S/L ISA static.

LP COMPRESSOR: Multi-stage axial with variable inlet guide vanes.

HP COMPRESSOR: Multi-stage axial housed in intermediate case. Overall engine pressure ratio at T-O, S/L ISA static, 20.

COMBUSTION CHAMBER: Annular, with 28 burners and with integral inlet guide vanes to HP turbine. Described as a new concept for low pollution.

HP TURBINE: Single-stage; aircooled blades. Max inlet temperature 1,177°C (1,450°K).

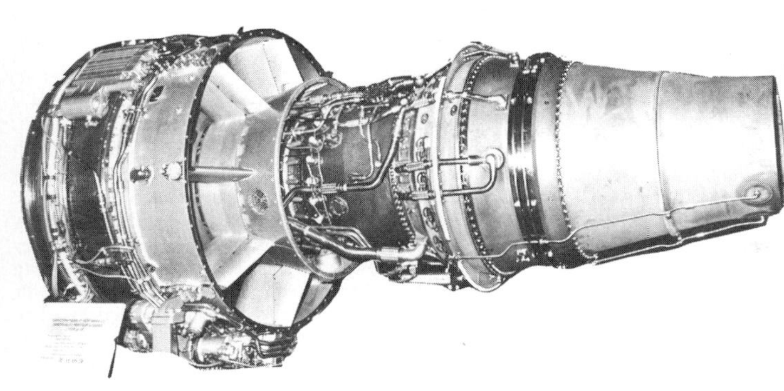
Lotarev D-36 turbofan, rated at 63·74 kN (14,330 lb st)
(Brian M. Service)

Lotarev D-136 free turbine turboshaft, rated at 8,500 kW (11,400 shp)
(Brian M. Service)

LP TURBINE: Single-stage. (Called IP in Western engines.)
FAN TURBINE: Two-stage. (Called LP in Western engines.)
JETPIPE: Called rear support case. No provision for reverser.
BYPASS DUCT: Short-length, comprising forward module (called the fan contravane) and rear module (called intermediate case). Contravane case contains 49 inserted blades, divided into inner and outer sections by ring downstream of fan snubbers to remove residual twist from fan delivery. Provision for sound reducing lining and for reverser downstream of intermediate case.
ACCESSORIES: Shaft driven units mounted on gearbox of banana type mounted around underside of intermediate case.
DIMENSIONS: Not disclosed
WEIGHT, DRY: 1,100 kg (2,425 lb)
PERFORMANCE RATINGS (ISA):
T-O static 63·74 kN (14,330 lb st)
Max continuous 49·0 kN (11,025 lb st)
Max cruise at 8,000 m (26,250 ft) at Mach 0·75 15·7 kN (3,527 lb)
SPECIFIC FUEL CONSUMPTION:
T-O 10·195 mg/Ns (0·360 lb/h/lb st)
At max cont rating 9·83 mg/Ns (0·347 lb/h/lb st)
Max cruise as above 18·4 mg/Ns (0·65 lb/h/lb)

LOTAREV D-18T

For many years the main gap in the spectrum of available Soviet engines was a large HBPR (high bypass ratio) turbofan, of the kind used in the West to power large military freighters and civil wide-body airliners. It is known that attempts were made to purchase Western engines, and possibly a manufacturing licence, but in 1983 it became known not only that the Lotarev bureau had produced such an engine but that it was already powering the An-124 heavy transport. The policy was to develop similar engines in two sizes, the smaller (the D-36) to an earlier timescale. The linear scale is about 2 : 1; so, in terms of airflow and thrust, the ratio is about 4 : 1.

In some respects the bigger engine is even more advanced than the small one, its pressure ratio and turbine entry temperature both being higher. Another significant difference is that, unlike the D-36, the D-18T has an integral fan duct reverser, with a geometry similar to that of the General Electric CF6-50. It is not known for certain how the D-18T was first flight tested, but four were fitted to the An-124 prototype which made its first flight on 26 December 1982.

TYPE: Three-shaft turbofan for large subsonic aircraft.
AIR INTAKE: Direct entry without inlet guide vanes.
FAN: Single-stage with conical rotating spinner and 33 inserted titanium blades with part-span shrouds. Bypass ratio 5·7 at ISA S/L static.
IP COMPRESSOR: Seven-stage axial with variable inlet guide vanes.
HP COMPRESSOR: Seven-stage axial housed in intermediate case. Overall engine pressure ratio at T-O, ISA S/L static, 27·5.
COMBUSTION CHAMBER: Annular, with forged and machined outer case and 28 vaporising burners to give smokeless low-emissions combustion.
FUEL GRADE: T-1, TS-1 or T-7 (Avtur equivalent).
HP TURBINE: Single axial stage with aircooled directionally solidified blades with tip shrouds and raised root platforms. Max inlet temperature 1,327°C (1,600°K); temperature at cruise (as below) 1,080°C (1,353°K).
IP TURBINE: Single axial stage with aircooled blades with tip shrouds.
LP TURBINE: Four axial stages with tip shrouded blades.
JETPIPE: Called rear support case. No reverser.
BYPASS DUCT: Comprises forward module, called contravane, with inserted blades (vanes) to remove twist from flow, followed by rear case with six large radial struts carrying pipes and shaft drives.
REVERSER: Attached to rear fan duct case, with multiple blocker doors pulled inwards by axial movement of translating cowl section, which simultaneously opens peripheral cascade rings directing expelled air forwards.
ACCESSORIES: Oil tank and all shaft driven accessories are grouped around lower half of rear fan case.

Lotarev D-18T three-shaft turbofan engine *(Brian M. Service)*

DIMENSION:
Fan diameter 2,330 mm (91·73 in)
WEIGHT, DRY: 4,100 kg (9,039 lb)
PERFORMANCE RATINGS:
T-O (S/L, ISA + 13°C) 229·77 kN (51,655 lb st)
Max cruise (11,000 m; 36,100 ft, Mach 0·75, ISA) 47·66 kN (10,715 lb)
SPECIFIC FUEL CONSUMPTION:
T-O 10·195 mg/Ns (0·360 lb/h/lb st)
Cruise as above 16·142 mg/Ns (0·570 lb/h/lb)

LOTAREV D-136

Preliminary details are available of this powerful turboshaft engine which is fitted to the Mi-26 helicopter. Like all modern gas turbine engines it is of modular construction, and the Soviet Aviaexport organisation stresses its simplicity, low fuel consumption, environmental acceptance and background of over 20,000 h running prior to certification to standards which included FAR and BCAR.
TYPE: Two-spool free turbine turboshaft.
AIR INTAKE: Fabricated from sheet, with large central bullet and eight long-chord radial struts.
LP COMPRESSOR: Six stages, with one row of variable inlet guide vanes. Faces for very large bleed air ducts, of which three normally used, with pipes facing forward (probably for anti-icing the main inlets, part of the Mi-26 airframe).
HP COMPRESSOR: Six stages, in casing provided with large bleed air pipes and carrying main gearbox and mounting points. Overall pressure ratio 18·3.
COMBUSTION CHAMBER: Annular low-emissions type, with 28 burners and incorporating integral inlet guide vanes for HP turbine.
HP TURBINE: Single-stage with aircooled blades. Max inlet temperature 1,205°C (1,478°K).
LP TURBINE: Single-stage, separated from HP rotor by large intermediate case with 26 guide vanes (stators).
POWER TURBINE: Two stages forming separate module; casing with 12 long-chord radial struts. Large-diameter tube housing rear driveshaft.
JETPIPE: The only handed part of the engine. Large welded steel assembly with oval-section exhaust stack curved to left or right.
DRIVE SHAFT: Flexibly mounted shaft at rear; max speed 8,300 rpm.
ACCESSORIES: Shaft driven units mounted on gearbox above intermediate casing around HP compressor.
DIMENSIONS: Not disclosed
WEIGHT, DRY: 1,050 kg (2,315 lb)
PERFORMANCE RATINGS (ISA, S/L):
Max T-O at 8,300 rpm 8,500 kW (11,400 shp)
Max cont at 7,500 output rpm 8,280 kW (11,100 shp)
SPECIFIC FUEL CONSUMPTION:
Max T-O 73·8 μg/J (0·4365 lb/h/shp)

LOTAREV D-236T

An advanced technology propeller, comprising two eight-blade contra-rotating units with a diameter of 4·6 m (15 ft 1 in), was displayed in the USSR pavilion at the 1985 Paris Air Show. Designed for an engine in the 7,457 kW

Sixteen-blade advanced technology contra-prop for the Lotarev D-236T turboprop engine
(Flight International)

(10,000 shp) class, it was said to have completed about 300 hours of ground test running, and to be due for installation on a flight test aircraft by the end of 1985. The gently curved blades are of composite construction. Other details include a rotational speed of 960 rpm, a duplicated hydromechanical pitch control system (including feathering and reverse pitch), a propulsive efficiency of 0·9 at Mach 0·7, and a thrust of 0·013 kN per kW of input power.

First production engine designed to use this type of propeller will be the Lotarev D-236T, which is intended to power a new Antonov airliner scheduled to enter service in 1989.

LYULKA

During the late 1930s Arkhip Mikhailovich Lyulka, who died on 1 June 1984, worked on the design of an axial turbojet that became an early war casualty. In 1942 he planned a more advanced engine that finally materialised as the TR-1, of 12·75 kN (2,866 lb st), run on the bench in 1944 and used in the Ilyushin Il-22 four-jet bomber and Sukhoi Su-11 twin-jet fighter prototypes, both of 1947. Ultimately, in 1948, this pioneer Soviet designed turbojet was developed to give 14·71 kN (3,307 lb st).

In 1946 Lyulka began the design of a very ambitious axial engine to give a thrust of 44·13 kN (9,920 lb), and in 1950 this began bench trials under the designation AL-5. Although of basically simple, single-shaft configuration, with a seven-stage compressor and single-stage turbine, the AL-5 was more powerful than any Western engine apart from the prototype Olympus and J53. By 1951 it was rated at 45·1 kN (10,140 lb st) and flew in the prototype Ilyushin Il-30 twin-jet bomber. Later in 1951-52 uprated AL-5 engines, giving a static thrust of 49·1 kN (11,032 lb), powered the Il-46 twin-jet bomber and the transonic Lavochkin La-190 and Yakovlev Yak-1000 fighters. An advanced civil version of the same engine, the AL-5 rated at 53·93 kN (12,125 lb st), powered the Tu-110 four-engined derivative of the Tu-104 airliner that did not go into production (at the time, in 1959, this engine was reported in the West as the 'Lu-4').

By the time the AL-5 was running, Lyulka had conducted extensive research with axial compressors having supersonic airflow through some or all of the stages. It was clear that, if problems of flow breakdown and inefficiency could be resolved, such a compressor would enable turbojets to be made much smaller and lighter for a given thrust and with greater thrust per unit frontal area, and thus much better suited to the propulsion of supersonic fighters. By 1952 a supersonic-compressor engine had been designed and built. This, the AL-7, became Lyulka's first major success.

LYULKA AL-7

The first AL-7 ran on the bench in late 1952 and the first production version was cleared for use in 1954 at a design rating of 63·74 kN (14,330 lb st). Its initial application was to power two pioneer supersonic bombers, the Ilyushin Il-54 and the Tupolev Tu-98. The latter, which was slightly larger, was shown to Western visitors in 1956, receiving the name 'Backfin'; it is believed to have been fitted with the **AL-7F** afterburning engine. The same engine was picked in 1954 for the first two products of the re-formed Sukhoi bureau, which eventually went into production as the Su-7 and Su-9.

By 1958 a further developed version of the basic unaugmented engine, the **AL-7RV**, had been chosen by Beriev for the Be-10 reconnaissance flying-boat, which—apart from being the only pure-jet flying-boat ever to go into service anywhere—set world records for speed, load carrying and altitude. Other versions of the AL-7, in both cases of the -7F afterburning family, powered the La-250 interceptor of 1956, and the Sukhoi P-1 interceptor of 1957.

By 1963 production had been transferred to an uprated afterburning version designated **AL-7F-1**. This is fitted to the Su-7BM and BMK, the Su-11 and several prototypes.

Type: Single-shaft axial-flow turbojet, available with or without afterburner.

Air Intake: Central bullet fairing and 14 fixed aerofoil struts anti-iced by compressor bleed air.

Compressor: Nine-stage axial (probably eight stages in original AL-7 design). First two stages widely separated axially, with variable stators ahead of second stage. Each stage has blades inserted in centreless disc held by peripheral spacers at correct distance from adjacent discs, the whole being coupled together finally by the central driveshaft in tension. Pressure ratio probably about 8 : 1.

Combustion Chamber: Annular type with perforated inner flame tube. Multiple downstream fuel injectors inserted through cups in forward face of liner. Liner outer casing provided with multiple inward secondary-air injection ducts.

Turbine: Two-stage axial-flow type. Both wheels overhung behind rear bearing; front disc bolted to flange on hollow tubular driveshaft which, in turn, is splined to rear of compressor shaft running in main centre bearing which locates compressor axially against end loads.

Afterburner (AL-7F): Comprises upstream diffuser and downstream combustion section. Pilot combustor on turbine exit cone includes single nozzle ring and flame holder; main spray ring and gutter flame holder assembly located further downstream at greater radius. Refractory liner in combustion section. Variable-area nozzle, with multiple hinged flaps which govern nozzle size and profile according to signals from reheat control system based on turbine exit temperature and throttle lever position.

Accessories: Fuel pump and control unit, oil pumps, hydraulic pump, electric generator, tachometer and other items grouped into quickly replaceable packages beneath compressor casing.

Performance Ratings:

Max rating:

AL-7F, unaugmented	63·0 kN (14,250 lb st)
AL-7F, afterburning	88·25 kN (19,840 lb st)
AL-7RV	63·74 kN (14,330 lb st)
AL-7F-1, unaugmented	68·65 kN (15,432 lb st)
AL-7F-1, afterburning	98·1 kN (22,046 lb st)

LYULKA AL-21

When continued development of the Su-7 family by the Sukhoi bureau was known to be matched with increased thrust, it was logical to suppose that the engine installed in the later aircraft was a derivative of the AL-7. In fact, the resulting AL-21 resembles the AL-7 closely, and may be installationally interchangeable, but has significant improvements to the compressor and other components. One production version is the **AL-21F-3**, for the Su-17 variable geometry tactical aircraft (Fitter-C, D, E, G and H). It has also been surmised that the AL-21F powers the Su-24, and that an unaugmented vectored thrust version is fitted as main engine to the Yak-38. One of the AL-21 powered prototypes was the Ye-231, the first MiG variable geometry aircraft.

Performance Ratings:

Max S/L, unaugmented	76·5 kN (17,200 lb st)
Max S/L, afterburning	110 kN (24,700 lb st)

MIKULIN

Alexander Alexandrovich Mikulin was a leading designer of Soviet aircraft engines from 1916. Notable V-12 water cooled engines from his designs were the AM-13, AM-34, AM-38 (used in the Il-2 and Il-10 Shturmovik) and AM-42.

The large turbojet described here was designed immediately after the Second World War. Though a version was fitted to M-4 four-engined bombers, it is not known if Mikulin's bureau was involved with the Soloviev D-15 fitted to some later M-4 aircraft.

MIKULIN RD-3M-500

The basic RD-3M (or AM-3M) single-spool axial-flow turbojet was developed under the design leadership of P. F. Zubets from the original Mikulin M-209 (civil RD-3 or AM-3) engine which powers the Tu-16 and early M-4 bombers and was adapted for the USSR's first jet transport, the Tu-104. Current M-4s are believed to have the AM-3D; while the usual engine of Tu-16s is the AM-3M. This engine has been produced at the Xian factory in China as the Wopen-8.

The RD-3M-500 evolved, in turn, from the RD-3M and powered the Tu-104A and Tu-104B commercial transports. It has a simple basic configuration, with an eight-stage axial-flow compressor, annular combustion system with 14 flame tubes, and a two-stage turbine. The compressor casing is made in front, centre and rear portions, the front casing housing a row of inlet guide vanes. A bullet fairing mounted centrally in the annular ram air intake houses a type S-300M gas turbine starter, developing 75 kW (100 hp) at 31,000-35,000 rpm. The jetpipe consists of a central cone and fixed nozzle with an orifice diameter of approximately 840 mm (33 in). Pressure ratio is 6·4 : 1; temperature after turbine 720°C.

Dimensions:

Length overall	5,340 mm (210·23 in)
Diameter	1,400 mm (55·12 in)

Performance Ratings (T-O):

AM-3	85·8 kN (19,285 lb st)
AM-3D	85·3 kN (19,180 lb st)
AM-3M, RD-3M	93·19 kN (20,950 lb st)

SHVETSOV

Founder of Bureau: Arkadiya Dmitrievich Shvetsov

Arkadiya Shvetsov was responsible for the M-11 five-cylinder aircooled radial engines made in enormous numbers in 1928-59 at powers from 74·6 kW (100 hp) to 149 kW (200 hp). He later developed larger radials, the most important being the ASh-82, which at ratings up to 1,491 kW (2,000 hp) powered Lavochkin fighters, the Tu-2 and Tu-4 bombers, Il-12 and -14 transports and Mi-4 and Yak-24 helicopters. The ASh-62 was made in large numbers at ratings in the 750 kW (1,000 hp) class for the Li-2 and An-2. The ASh-62M agricultural version, developed by Vedeneyev, and all An-2 engines after 1952, were transferred with other Soviet aircooled radials to Poland (see WSK-PZL Kalisz and WSK-PZL Rzeszów in Polish part of this section). Another important Shvetsov piston engine was the 545 kW (730 hp) ASh-21, fitted to the Yak-11. All these engines have been described in earlier editions. The ASh-62 and ASh-82 have been produced under licence in China, as described in the Chinese entry in this section.

SOLOVIEV

General Designer in Charge of Bureu: P. A. Soloviev

Engines for which Soloviev's design team is responsible include the turbofans fitted in the Ilyushin Il-62M and Il-76 and Tupolev Tu-124, Tu-134 and Tu-154M transport aircraft, and the turboshafts which power the Mi-6 and Mi-10 helicopters.

SOLOVIEV D-15

This engine was first reported, in 1959, as that fitted to the four-engined Type 201-M aircraft which gained a number of world records for speed and altitude. Over the years it became apparent that the aircraft was a special Myasishchev M-4, and that the engine was standard in some service versions of this aircraft. Details of the D-15 are still unknown in the West, but it is probably safe to deduce that it is a two-shaft turbojet. It is likely that it laid the foundation upon which Soloviev's bureau produced the civil D-20 and D-30, both of which are considerably smaller engines.

Performance Rating:

T-O	128·6 kN (28,660 lb st)

SOLOVIEV D-20P

The D-20P is a two-spool turbofan fitted to the Tupolev Tu-124 twin-engined passenger transport. Of conservative design, it underwent prolonged testing before entering service. It was designed for maximum economy and reliability over the range of ambient temperatures between −40°C and 40°C.

Type: Two-shaft turbofan (bypass turbojet).

Air Intake: Eight radial struts and central bullet fairing, de-iced by hot bleed air from fourth HP stage (from final stage at low rpm).

Fan: Three-stage axial, with supersonic blading in first stage. Mass flow 113 kg (249 lb)/s at 8,550 rpm. Pressure ratio (S/L, static at max continuous 7,900 rpm) 2·4 : 1. Bypass ratio 1.

Compressor: Eight-stage axial. Automatically controlled flap valves downstream of the third and fourth stages bleed air into the fan duct to stabilise behaviour. Pressure ratio (at max continuous, 11,170 rpm) 5 : 1; overall pressure ratio 13 : 1.

Combustion Chamber: Can-annular, with 12 flame tubes each fitted with duplex burner.

Fuel Grade: T-1, TS-1 to GOST 10227-62 (Avtur-50 to DERD.2494, MIL-F-5616).

Turbine: Single-stage HP turbine with cast blades; stator blades and both sides of disc cooled by bleed air. Two-stage LP turbine with forged blades. Max gas temperature downstream of turbine 650°C.

Jetpipe: Concentric pipes for fan airflow and core gas, terminating in supersonic nozzles of fixed-area type.

Lubrication: Open type, with oil returned to tank. Consumption in flight, not over 1 kg (2·2 lb)/h. Typical pressure 3·45-4·41 kg/cm² (50-64 lb/sq in).

Oil Grade: Mineral oil MK-8 or MK-8P to GOST 6457-66 (DERD.2490 or MIL-O-6081B).

Accessories: Two gearboxes provide drives for starter/generator, tachometer, air compressors, hydraulic pump, oil pump and other controls and instruments. For restarting in flight, an altitude sensing device meters fuel flow appropriate to height. An automatic fire extinguishing system is fitted. De-icing of the air intake and inlet guide vanes is controlled automatically. The engine also has oil chip detectors, vibration monitors and turbine gas temperature limiters.

Soloviev D-20P turbofan (52·96 kN; 11,905 lb st)

STARTING: Electric (DC) system, incorporating STG-18TM starter/generator.

DIMENSIONS:

Length overall	3,304 mm (130 in)
Diameter, bare	976 mm (38·3 in)

WEIGHT, DRY: 1,468 kg (3,236 lb)

PERFORMANCE RATINGS:

Max T-O 52·96 kN (11,905 lb st)

Long-range cruise, Mach 0·75, 11,000 m (36,000 ft) 10·79 kN (2,425 lb st)

SPECIFIC FUEL CONSUMPTION:

Max T-O 20·4 mg/Ns (0·72 lb/h/lb st)

Long-range cruise, as above 25·5 mg/Ns (0·90 lb/h/lb st)

SOLOVIEV D-25V

D-25V is the Soloviev bureau designation for the free turbine turboshaft which powers the Mil Mi-6 and Mi-10 helicopters and was also fitted to the Kamov Ka-22 experimental convertiplane and V-12 helicopter. It is usually referred to by its official designation of **TV-2BM**.

The complete helicopter power plant comprises two D-25V engines, identical except for handed jetpipes, and an R-7 gearbox. The latter has four stages of large gearwheels providing an overall ratio of 69·2 : 1. The R-7 is 2,795 mm (110·04 in) high, 1,551 mm (61·06 in) wide and 1,852 mm (72·91 in) long. Its dry weight is 3,200 kg (7,054 lb), more than that of the pair of engines.

The D-25V is flat rated to maintain rated power to 3,000 m (10,000 ft) or to temperatures up to 40°C at sea level.

The **D-25VF** turboshafts fitted to the Mil V-12 helicopter were uprated to 4,847 kW (6,500 shp). These engines were believed to incorporate a zero stage on the compressor and to operate at higher turbine gas temperatures. The same subtype powers the Mi-10K crane helicopter.

The following details apply to the basic D-25V:

TYPE: Single-shaft turboshaft with free power turbine.

AIR INTAKE: Six hollow radial struts, the two vertical struts housing splined shafts driving upper and lower accessory drive boxes. Vertical struts de-iced by oil drained from upper drive box; four inclined struts and bullet fairing de-iced by hot oil returned from engine to tank.

COMPRESSOR: Nine-stage axial. Comprises fixed inlet guide vane assembly, first-stage stator ring, upper and lower casings with dovetailed stator blades, ninth-stage stator ring and exit vanes, rotor, and air blow-off valves. Pressure ratio 5·6 at T-O power, 10,530 rpm.

COMBUSTION CHAMBER: Can-annular. Assembled from diffuser (the structural basis of the engine), inner shroud, 12 flame tubes with transition liners, diaphragm and compressor-shaft shroud.

FUEL GRADE: T-1, TS-1 to GOST 10227-62 (DERD.2494, MIL-F-5616)

TURBINE: Single-stage compressor turbine, overhung behind rear roller bearing. Two-stage power turbine, overhung on end of rear output shaft. Both turbines rotate counter-clockwise, seen from the rear. Normal power turbine rpm, 7,800-8,300; maximum 9,000. Transmission shaft in three universally jointed sections, allowing for 10 mm (0·4 in) misalignment between engine and gearbox.

JETPIPE: Large fabricated assembly in heat resistant steel, curved out to side to allow rotor transmission to pass through duct wall in aircooled protecting pipe.

LUBRICATION: Pressure circulation at 3·45-4·41 bars (50-64 lb/sq in). Separate systems for gas generator and for power turbine, transmission and gearbox.

OIL GRADE: Gas generator, MK-8 to GOST 6457-66 or transformer oil to GOST 982-56. Power turbine and gearbox, mixture (75-25 Summer, 50-50 Winter) of MK-22 or MS-20 to GOST 1013-49 and MK-8 or transformer oil. Hourly oil consumption, gas generator not over 1 kg (2·2 lb), power turbine and transmission not over 2 kg (4·4 lb).

ACCESSORIES: SP3-12TV electric supply and starting system; fuel supply to separate LP and HP systems; airframe accessories driven off upper and lower gearboxes on inlet casing.

STARTING: The SP3-12TV system starts both engines and also generates electric current. It comprises an STG-12TM starter/generator on each engine, igniter unit, two spark plugs with cooling shrouds, two switch-over contactors, solenoid air valve, pressure warning, PSG-12V control panel and electro-hydraulic cutout switch of the TsP-23A centrifugal governor. In the starter mode the system draws current from a ground supply receptacle or from batteries.

DIMENSIONS:

Length overall, bare 2,737 mm (107·75 in)

Length overall with transmission shaft 5,537 mm (218·0 in)

Width 1,086 mm (42·76 in)

Height 1,158 mm (45·59 in)

WEIGHT, DRY:

With engine mounted accessories 1,325 kg (2,921 lb)

PERFORMANCE RATINGS:

T-O 4,101 kW (5,500 shp)

Rated power 3,504 kW (4,700 shp)

Cruise (1,000 m; 3,280 ft, 135 knots; 250 km/h; 155 mph) 2,983 kW (4,000 shp)

SPECIFIC FUEL CONSUMPTION:

T-O, as above 108 µg/J (0·639 lb/h/shp)

Cruise, as above 118·1 µg/J (0·699 lb/h/shp)

SOLOVIEV D-30

This two-spool turbofan powers the Tu-134 twin-engined airliner and is derived from the D-20. Major portions of the core and carcase are similar, but the complete power plant is larger than the D-20, and more powerful and efficient.

In turn the D-30 has been developed into the considerably larger D-30K (described separately) which is a different engine despite its designation. Since about 1972 the standard engine of the Tu-134A has been the D-30 Series II, with reverser. One Tu-134 has flown with D-30 engines with a zero stage on the LP compressor; the existing ratings are obtained at reduced gas temperature and maintained to ISA + 25°C.

TYPE: Two-shaft turbofan (bypass turbojet).

AIR INTAKE: Titanium alloy assembly, incorporating air bleed anti-icing of centre bullet and radial struts.

FAN: Four-stage axial (LP compressor). First stage has shrouded titanium blades held in disc by pinned joints. Pressure ratio (T-O rating, 7,700 rpm, S/L, static), 2·65. Mass flow 125 kg (265 lb)/s. Bypass ratio 1.

COMPRESSOR: Ten-stage axial (HP compressor). Drum and disc construction, largely of titanium. Pressure ratio (T-O rating, 11,600 rpm, S/L, static), 7·1. Overall pressure ratio, 17·4.

COMBUSTION CHAMBER: Can-annular, with 12 flame tubes fitted with duplex burners.

FUEL GRADE: T-1 and TS-1 to GOST 10227-62 (equivalent to DERD.2494 or MIL-F-5616).

TURBINE: Two-stage HP turbine. First stage has cooled blades in both stator and rotor. LP turbine also has two stages. All discs aircooled on both sides, and all blades shrouded to improve efficiency and reduce vibration. All shaft bearings shock mounted.

JETPIPE: Subsonic fixed-area type, incorporating main and bypass flow mixer with curvilinear ducts of optimum shape. D-30-II engine of Tu-134A fitted with twin-clamshell reverser.

LUBRICATION: Open type, with oil returned to tank.

OIL GRADE: Mineral oil MK-8 or MK-8P to GOST 6457-66 (equivalent to DERD.2490 or MIL-O-6081B). Consumption in flight not over 1·0 kg (2·2 lb)/h.

ACCESSORIES: Automatic ice protection system, fire extinguishing for core and bypass flows, vibration detectors on casings, oil chip detectors and automatic limitation of exhaust gas temperature to 620°C at take-off or when starting and to 630°C in flight (5 min limit). Shaft driven accessories driven via radial bevel gear shafts in centre casing, mainly off HP spool, accessory gearboxes being provided above and below centre casing and fan duct. D-30-2 carries constant speed drives for alternators.

STARTING: Electric DC starting system incorporating STG-12TVMO starter/generators.

DIMENSIONS:

Overall length 3,983 mm (156·8 in)

Base diameter of inlet casing 1,050 mm (41·3 in)

WEIGHT, DRY: 1,550 kg (3,417 lb)

PERFORMANCE RATINGS:

T-O 66·68 kN (14,990 lb st)

Long-range cruise rating, 11,000 m (36,000 ft) and Mach 0·75 12·75 kN (2,866 lb st)

SPECIFIC FUEL CONSUMPTION:

T-O 17·56 mg/Ns (0·62 lb/h/lb st)

Cruise, as above 21·81 mg/Ns (0·77 lb/h/lb st)

SOLOVIEV D-30K

Despite its designation, this turbofan is very different from the D-30 described previously. It is larger, and has a much higher rating, a bypass ratio considerably higher, and very few parts (in the core) common to the D-30.

The basic **D-30KU** version, to which the specification details here apply, replaced the Kuznetsov NK-8-4 as power plant of the Ilyushin Il-62M long-range transport. The **D-30KU-154-II** is a version specially configured to suit the Tu-154M, which uses the Tu-154B airframe; the replacement engine is derated to 104 kN (23,380 lb st). The more powerful **D-30KP**, rated at 117·7 kN (26,455 lb st), powers the Ilyushin Il-76 freight transport. Clamshell thrust reversers are fitted to all four engines of this aircraft, and to the outer engines of the Il-62M. These reversers are not an integral part of the engine but are airframe assemblies incorporated in the nacelle.

TYPE: Two-shaft turbofan, with integral flow mixer and reverser.

AIR INTAKE: Fabricated from titanium alloy. Fixed spinner and 26 cambered inlet guide vanes anti-iced by air bled

The 4,101 kW (5,500 shp) Soloviev D-25V turboshaft

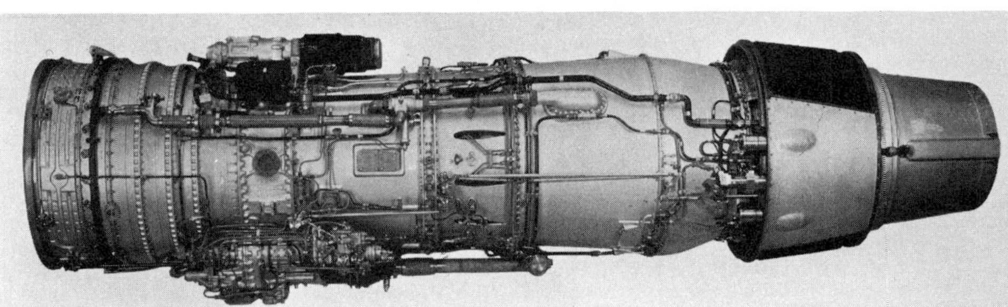

Soloviev D-30 Series II turbofan (66·68 kN; 14,990 lb st) with thrust reverser

from sixth or eleventh stage of HP compressor (depending on rpm). Integral front roller bearing for LP shaft.

FAN (LP COMPRESSOR): Three stages, mainly of titanium alloy. First-stage rotor blades held in dovetail slots, with part-span anti-vibration snubbers. Other two stages have pinned rotor blades. Spool rotates between front roller bearing and rear ball bearing, with additional roller bearing behind LP turbine. Drum/disc construction, coupled with tie-bolt and driven by splined shaft connection. Mass flow at take-off, 269 kg (593 lb)/s at 4,730 rpm (87·9 per cent), with bypass ratio of 2·42.

DIVISION CASING: Linking the LP and HP compressors, this is the main structural attachment band to the aircraft. Magnesium alloy casting, held by front and rear rows of peripheral bolts. Carries LP mid bearing and HP front bearing and incorporates vertical radial drive to front drive box for accessories on underside.

HP COMPRESSOR: Eleven stages. Drum/disc rotor, with discs centred on shaft by rectangular splines. Rotor blades held in dovetail slots, first two stages having part-span snubbers. Construction of titanium alloys, except for shafts, rear casing, and rotor blades and discs of stages 9-11, and stator vanes of stages 10-11, which are steel. To reduce blade vibration inlet guide vanes are turned through up to 30° according to preset programme over speed range of 7,900-9,600 rpm, while air is bled from fifth and sixth stages under transient conditions; in addition a closed peripheral chamber with perforated walls surrounds the first stage rotor blades. HP shaft supported in front roller bearing in division casing, ball thrust bearing at rear of compressor spool and roller bearing ahead of turbine. Casing split horizontally. Overall pressure ratio (S/L, static) 20 at HP speed of 10,460 rpm (96 per cent).

COMBUSTION CHAMBER: Cannular type with 12 flame tubes in annular chamber. Each tube comprises hemispherical head and eight short sections welded with gaps for dilution air. Single swirl type main/pilot burner centred in each tube. Igniter plugs in two tubes. Outer casing and duct shroud provided with longitudinal joints for access to flame tubes and HP turbine nozzle ring.

Soloviev D-30KU turbofan (108 kN; 24,250 lb st) complete with external dressing, tankage and reverser

FUEL GRADE: T-1, TS-1, GOST-10227-62, A-1 (D1655/63t), DERD.2494 or 2498, Air 3405/B or 3-GP-23e.

TURBINES: Two-stage HP turbine with first-stage nozzles, part of second-stage nozzles and both sets of discs and rotor blades cooled by HP bleed air. Second-stage rotor blades tip shrouded. Both discs interchangeable. Take-off inlet gas temperature 1,122°C. Four-stage LP turbine with uncooled shrouded rotor blades carried in four identical discs cooled by bypass air.

JETPIPE: Downstream of LP turbine a rear support frame serves as the rear structural band attaching the engine to the aircraft. This frame incorporates the rear LP shaft roller bearing and 12 thermocouples, and also includes the 16-chute mixer for the core and bypass flows.

LUBRICATION: Closed type, with oil returned to tank. Incorporates fuel/oil heat exchanger and centrifugal air separator with metal particle warning unit.

OIL GRADE: MK-8 or MK-8P to GOST 6467-66 (mineral) or BNII NP-50-1-4F to GOST 13076-67 (synthetic) or Western equivalents.

ACCESSORIES: Front and rear drive boxes under engine carry all shaft driven accessories. Differential constant speed drive to alternator and air turbine starter.

STARTING: Pneumatic air turbine starter fed by ground supply, APU or cross-bleed from running engine. Start cycle time to idling rpm, 40-80 s depending on ambient temperature (limits, −60° to +50°C). In-flight starting up to 9,000 m (27,430 ft) by windmilling.

DIMENSIONS:
- Length with reverser: 5,700 mm (224 in)
- Inlet diameter: 1,464 mm (57·6 in)
- Maximum diameter of casing: 1,560 mm (61·4 in)

WEIGHT, DRY:
- With reverser: 2,650 kg (5,842 lb)
- Without reverser: 2,300 kg (5,071 lb)

PERFORMANCE RATINGS (ISA):
- T-O: 108 kN (24,250 lb st) to 21°C
- Cruise at 11,000 m (36,000 ft) and Mach 0·8: 27 kN (6,063 lb st)

SPECIFIC FUEL CONSUMPTION:
- At T-O rating: 13·88 mg/Ns (0·49 lb/h/lb st)
- Cruise, as above: 19·83 mg/Ns (0·70 lb/h/lb st)

TUMANSKY

Academician Sergei Konstantinovich Tumansky, who died in 1973, was a noted designer of piston engines and supercharging systems, and during the Second World War was appointed deputy to A. A. Mikulin on the AM series of high-power engines. He showed even greater promise with outstanding axial turbojets, the RD-9 going into production in 1953. On Mikulin's political disgrace in 1956, Tumansky was appointed head of the bureau. He designed the series of axial turbojets derived from the RD-9 which continue in production to this day, and on which the MiG series of combat aircraft has been based as well as several recent Sukhoi aircraft. Total production of Tumansky engines easily exceeds that of any other family of aircraft gas turbines in the post-1955 era.

TUMANSKY RD-9

First axial turbojet of wholly Soviet design to be placed in mass production, this engine was designed under Tumansky in the Mikulin bureau in 1950-51 and received the TsIAM designation **AM-5**. The afterburning version, the **AM-5F**, was selected for the MiG-19 and the unaugmented engine for the Yak-25. After Mikulin's removal in 1956 the engine was redesignated **RD-9**, the afterburning type being called **RD-9B**. In 1957 the improved **RD-9BM** entered production, with a hydraulically actuated three-step nozzle. All variants have a nine-stage compressor, annular combustor and two-stage turbine; pressure ratio at take-off is 7·14. Production in the Soviet Union tapered off in about 1958 in favour of a slightly larger and improved design which became the R-11. In China, production of the RD-9BM began in 1960 and has continued for the J-6 and Q-5. Diameter of all models is 813 mm (32·0 in). Maximum T-O rating of the BM is 32·36 kN (7,275 lb st).

TUMANSKY R-11

The first of a long line of R-11 turbojets (known as the R-37 series of engines by the Soviet armed forces) probably ran in 1953 and entered production in 1956. The R-11 is an extremely neat and advanced two-spool engine, with a slim cylindrical external appearance and, in most installations, all its accessories grouped on the underside of the compressor. It was one of the first engines to have an overhung first rotor stage without inlet guide vanes. Other features include a can-annular combustion chamber with ten flame tubes, which in some versions provides large air bleed couplings for flap blowing, and, in most installations, a large afterburner with multi-flap variable nozzle. All early versions (but not the Chinese derivative) are started on petrol (gasoline) fed from a separate starting tank, and gaseous oxygen can be fed to the burners to increase relight altitude from 8 to 11·9 km (26,250 to 39,000 ft). Considerably more than 20,000 of all versions have been delivered from Soviet plants, to power many types of aircraft including versions of the MiG-21, Su-15 and Yak-28. Additional engines have been produced by Hindustan Aeronautics in India and by the Chinese state aircraft industry. Chinese designation is Chengdu WP-7. Known Soviet versions are as follows:

Tumansky R-11F2S-300 built under licence by HAL in India

R-11. Initial production series, rated at 38·25 kN (8,600 lb st) without afterburner and at 50·0 kN (11,240 lb st) with afterburner. Three-stage transonic LP compressor and three-stage HP, each driven by single-stage turbine.

R-11-300. Fitted with enlarged afterburner and new nozzle. First announced at time of 1959 speed record by Ye-66, with dry thrust unchanged but maximum thrust increased to 58·4 kN (13,120 lb st).

R-11F. Original engine uprated, with small afterburner; dry thrust unchanged, maximum thrust 56·4 kN (12,676 lb st).

R-11FS, F2S. Addition of letter signifies provision for flap blowing. The final mass production engine was the **R-11F2S-300**, with maximum rating of 60·8 kN (13,668 lb st). This engine is believed to be still in production in India and China, and is shown in an accompanying illustration.

TUMANSKY R-13

This two-spool turbojet supplanted the R-11 as the usual MiG-21 engine in the late 1960s. It is used also in later versions of the Su-15 and, possibly, in the Yak-28 versions with extended inlet ducts. In all these versions it has an advanced afterburner, and a new five-stage HP compressor handling a greater airflow than that of the R-11. An unaugmented version powers the Su-25 close support aircraft (NATO 'Frogfoot'). The so-called **PDM** engine fitted to the record breaking Ye-66B (MiG-21 variant) of 1974 may have been an R-13. The standard ratings for the R-13-300 are 41·55 kN (9,340 lb st) dry and 64·73 kN (14,550 lb st) with afterburner. Chinese designation is WP-13A.

TUMANSKY RU-19

This small single-shaft turbojet has been used both as the primary engine of aircraft and also as an APU and emergency booster (in the Antonov An-26 and related transports). When used as an APU its thrust is reduced depending upon the amount of shaft power extracted. The fully rated **RU-19-300** has a thrust of 8·83 kN (1,985 lb st). This version is installed in the starboard nacelle of the An-24RV and An-24RT. The **RU-19A-300** is rated at 7·85 kN (1,765 lb st) and is installed in the starboard nacelle of the An-26 and An-30. When providing the full electrical power for the An-24RV (and presumably related aircraft) the residual jet thrust is only 2·16 kN (485 lb st). It is thus assumed that an RU-19 type engine has been selected as the APU/booster for the MAI-Tashkent Semurg light jet transport, the rating in this application being 3·1 kN (697 lb st). Another RU-19, equipped as a plain turbojet and fully rated, powers the La-17 target (see RPVs and Targets in 1977-78 *Jane's*).

TUMANSKY R-25

This two-spool turbojet was an essentially new design, and its advanced compressor of high pressure ratio is said to confer a markedly lower specific fuel consumption than that of the R-13. The R-25 has redesigned accessory systems but is installationally interchangeable with the R-13. The first LP compressor stage has 21 titanium blades of large chord. The afterburner has two stages (the R-11 and R-13 having one) and so can be used in combat at very high altitudes. Maximum S/L thrust is 73·6 kN (16,535 lb st). No longer made, except under licence by HAL of India for MiG-21 bis.

TUMANSKY R-266/R-31

The designation of this engine is almost certainly to be read as R-26 sub-type 6. A single-shaft afterburning turbojet designed for propulsion of the MiG-25 to Mach 3, it probably stemmed from the P-166 afterburning turbojet fitted to the single-engined MiG Ye-166 which set a world speed record in 1962. The P-166 was almost certainly a Tumansky engine in the same family, its thrust with afterburner being 98·06 kN (22,046 lb st). This was also the maximum thrust of the original R-266 engine, announced under its service designation of **R-31** as being fitted to prototypes of the MiG-25 (designated Ye-266).

Constructed mainly of steel, the R-266 has a five-stage compressor with a take-off pressure ratio of about 7, driven by a single-stage turbine with uncooled blades. Special T-6 fuel is used, with freezing point of −62·2°C and flash point of 54·4°C. In the MiG-25, water/methanol is injected into the variable inlet duct upstream of the compressor at supersonic speeds. At Mach 3 most of the thrust is generated by the large three-ring afterburner and multi-flap variable profile nozzle. Ratings are 91·18 kN (20,500 lb st) dry and 120 kN (27,010 lb st) with afterburner.

RD-F. This is the announced designation of an uprated R-266 engine fitted to the Ye-266M (MiG-25 variant) which set time-to-height records in 1975. A military series engine, probably designated **R-31F**, powers advanced versions of the MiG-25, with the same maximum rating of 137·3 kN (30,865 lb st). It is assumed that an advanced version also powers the MiG-31 'Foxhound', and possibly also the Su-27.

TUMANSKY R-27

Using a core similar to that of the highly successful R-25, this basically simple and efficient turbojet was developed for the MiG-23 family (it was not ready in time, the Ye-231 initially having a Lyulka engine). Rated at 68·65 kN (15,430 lb st) dry and 100 kN (22,485 lb st) with afterburner and water injection, the R-27 was produced in modest numbers for early ('Flogger-B') versions of the MiG-23, as well as for all known MiG-23U trainer versions and some export models. Basic features are similar to those of the much more highly-rated R-29B.

Tumansky R-25 turbojet built by HAL in India for the licence-built MiG-21bis

TUMANSKY R-29

One of the most important engines in the Soviet inventory, this augmented turbojet is simpler than the corresponding American F100, with fewer compressor stages and a much lower pressure ratio; but it is more powerful and costs much less. Different subtypes are fitted to all current MiG-23 and MiG-27 versions for Warsaw Pact front-line use, and to the Su-22. In all these aircraft water injection is used on take-off, the MiG-23MF water tank having a capacity of 28 litres (6·2 Imp gallons). The MiG-27 versions are powered by the slightly less powerful R-29-300 with simpler afterburner and nozzle. The following data refer to the R-29B, fitted to the MiG-23MF:

COMPRESSOR: Five-stage LP, six-stage HP. Overall pressure ratio 12·4. Maximum airflow 105 kg (235 lb)/s.
COMBUSTION CHAMBER: Annular, vaporising burners.
TURBINES: HP has single stage with aircooled blades. LP unknown.
AFTERBURNER: Fuel rings with separate light-up give modulated fully variable augmentation. Fully variable nozzles differ in different installations.
WEIGHT, DRY: 1,760 kg (3,880 lb)
PERFORMANCE RATINGS:
- Max S/L unaugmented: 78·45 kN (17,635 lb st)
- Min with afterburner: 97·1 kN (21,825 lb st)
- Max T-O, wet (R-29-300): 112·8 kN (25,350 lb st)
- Max T-O, wet (MiG-23MF): 122·0 kN (27,500 lb st)

TUMANSKY R-33

Designation of the Tumansky turbofans used in the twin-engined MiG-29 counter-air fighter is reported to be R-33D. No details are known, except for the following ratings:
PERFORMANCE RATINGS:
- Max S/L unaugmented: 50·0 kN (11,245 lb st)
- Max T-O with afterburner: 81·4 kN (18,300 lb st)

VEDENEYEV

GENERAL DESIGNER IN CHARGE OF BUREAU:
Ivan M. Vedeneyev

This designer was responsible for the improvement and development of certain models of the AI-14 piston engine designed by the Ivchenko bureau. He also developed the ASh-62M, produced in Poland as the ASz-62M, from Shvetsov's ASh-62IR nine-cylinder radial. He now heads his own bureau.

M-14V-26

Derived from the Ivchenko AI-14 family of engines for fixed-wing aircraft, the M-14V-26 powers the Kamov Ka-26 helicopter. In this installation the stub wing carries an engine on each tip. Beneath the rotor an R-26 gearbox combines the power of the engines and distributes it equally between the two coaxial main rotors turning in opposite directions.

It is said to incorporate all the experience gained in many years of developing engines in this class, and shows numerous areas of refinement compared with the AI-14 series. The engine has forced cooling by an axial fan driven via a friction clutch and extension shaft ahead of the main output bevel box at 1·452 times crankshaft speed. The engine planetary gearbox has a ratio of 0·309 and incorporates friction and ratchet clutches. The central R-26 gearbox has a ratio of 0·34; it also drives the generator, hydraulic pump, oil pump and tachometer generator.

DIMENSIONS:
- Length: 1,145 mm (45·08 in)
- Diameter: 985 mm (38·78 in)

WEIGHT, DRY: 245 kg (540 lb)
PERFORMANCE RATINGS:
- T-O: 242 kW; 325 hp at 2,800 rpm
- Max continuous I: 205 kW; 275 hp at 2,450 rpm
- Max continuous II: 142 kW; 190 hp at 2,350 rpm
- Cruise I: 142 kW; 190 hp at 2,350 rpm
- Cruise II: 108 kW; 145 hp at 2,350 rpm

SPECIFIC FUEL CONSUMPTION:
- At cruise ratings: 77·7 μg/J (0·46 lb/h/hp)

VEDENEYEV M-14P

With this engine Vedeneyev reverted to the original fixed-wing application, apparently independently of the Ivchenko bureau. The M-14P was used with direct drive to a fixed-pitch two-blade propeller in the original version of the Moscow Aviation Institute OSKB-1-3PM Kwant, at a T-O rating of 242 kW (325 hp). Currently, the Kwant has an M-14 II engine of 268 kW (360 hp). The same rating is quoted officially for the M-14P engine fitted to the Yakovlev Yak-18T, -50, 52, 53 and 55 and Sukhoi Su-26, all of which have a controllable-pitch propeller.

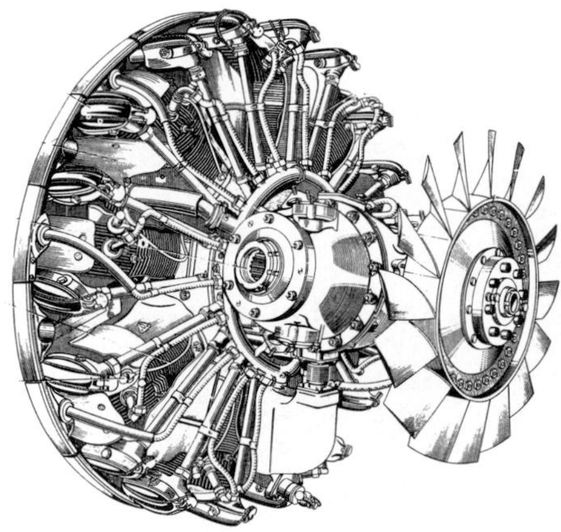

Vedeneyev M-14V-26 radial piston engine, with cooling fan, for Kamov Ka-26 helicopter

SOVIET ENGINES OF UNKNOWN DESIGN

1. TRD Type 57. Jet engine Type 57 is the cryptic designation supplied to the FAI as the power unit of the large four-engined delta known as Aircraft 101. The thrust is given as 20,000 kg (196·1 kN; 44,090 lb st). The Type 57 is probably an augmented turbofan, and may be the Kuznetsov NK-144 or a derived engine.

2. Lift Jet. Soviet design bureaux conducted extensive research into jet lift from the late 1950s, and purpose-designed lift jets were probably flying by 1962 (possibly much earlier). At the 1967 air show at Domodedovo three lift jet V/STOL research aircraft were displayed. A MiG aircraft based on the MiG-21 had two lift jets in the mid-fuselage, with a single large inlet door above. A larger MiG, with fuselage and tail closely similar to the eventual MiG-23 but with a small delta wing, had a similar arrangement, differing in detail design of the dorsal door. A Sukhoi aircraft, similar to the twin-engined Su-15, had three lift engines fed by two upper doors. All these installations had large open slots in the dorsal doors (which were hinged at the rear) and transverse louvres filling the ventral jet aperture (probably hinged and under pilot control to give variable forward thrust). Photographs of these aircraft last appeared in the 1971-72 *Jane's*. The two lift jets used in the Yak-38 V/STOL aircraft carried on board the carriers of the *Kiev* class are probably developments of the same engines, though details are not yet known. They could be turbojets or turbofans. The inlet door has open louvres, and it is safe to assume pilot-controlled exit cascades. Thrust estimates for these engines are agreed at around 35·5 kN (8,000 lb) each. A Czechoslovak magazine in 1984 described them as Koliesov Type ZM.

UNITED KINGDOM

EMDAIR
EMDAIR LTD

Harbour Road, Rye, E Sussex TN31 7TH
Telephone: 0797 223460
Telex: 957116 FOR EMDAIR

Founded in 1984, Emdair purchased the designs of the former Weslake & Co (see 1984-85 *Jane's*) and is now operating with updated facilities at the original Weslake plant. Activities centre on a new range of lightweight four-stroke flat-twin engines designed to meet full international certification requirements. These aircooled engines run on Mogas and have four-valve heads, dual electronic ignition with central and side spark plugs, direct fuel injection, alternator and electric starter. They are intended to combine high specific output at low rpm with low sfc, low costs and long life.

EMDAIR CF 077A

Delivery of this engine was scheduled to start in 1986. Crankshaft rotation is counterclockwise, seen from the front. An exhaust muffler (silencer) is optional.

CYLINDERS: Bore 95·0 mm (3·74 in). Stroke 88·9 mm (3·50 in). Capacity 1,261 cc (76·91 cu in). Compression ratio 9·5.

DIMENSIONS:
- Length 400 mm (15·75 in)
- Width 696 mm (27·4 in)
- Height 447 mm (17·75 in)

WEIGHT, DRY (with starter): 47·27 kg (104 lb)

PERFORMANCE RATINGS:
- Max 44·8 kW (60 hp) at 3,600 rpm
- Max cruise 33·6 kW (45 hp) at 3,090 rpm

FUEL CONSUMPTION:
- Max cruise 11·8 litres (2·6 Imp gallons)/h

EMDAIR CF 077B

This version of the 077A has been chosen to power the De Vore Sunbird Affordable Airplane, which is designed to meet FAR Pt 23. The engine incorporates a geared output shaft with integral torsional vibration damping, reducing propeller speed to 2,600 rpm (clockwise).

EMDAIR CF 100A

This is an enlarged version of the 077A.

CYLINDERS: Bore 101·6 mm (4·0 in). Stroke 99·06 mm (3·9 in). Capacity 1,606 cc (98·0 cu in). Compression ratio 9·5.

DIMENSIONS: Length 400 mm (15·75 in). Width 701 mm (27·6 in). Height 447 mm (17·75 in).

WEIGHT, DRY (with starter): 53 kg (115 lb)

PERFORMANCE RATINGS:
- Max T-O 56 kW (75 hp) at 3,400 rpm
- Alternative (medium speed) 46 kW (62 hp) at 2,800 rpm

EMDAIR CF 150A

This engine has features similar to the CF 100A.

CYLINDERS: Bore 125·0 mm (4·92 in). Stroke 100·0 mm (3·937 in). Capacity 2,454 cc (149·48 cu in). Compression ratio 9·5.

DIMENSIONS:
- Length 424 mm (16·7 in)
- Width 737 mm (29·0 in)
- Height 457·2 mm (18·0 in)

WEIGHT, DRY (with starter): 59·0 kg (130·0 lb)

PERFORMANCE RATINGS:
- Max 82·06 kW (110 hp) at 3,400 rpm
- Alternative (medium speed) 70·87 kW (95 hp) at 2,800 rpm

Emdair CF 077A flat-twin piston engine

FIELDHOUSE
FIELDHOUSE ENGINES LTD

2/4 Latimer St, Anstey, Leicester LE7 7AW

Telephone: 0533 362613
Telex: 341023

Fieldhouse has developed two basic engines, one twice the size of the other but with common cylinders, for microlights, hang gliders and other applications. Both engines are fully navalised, have power variation by tuning over a speed range, and are available with pullstart or 12V electric starting.

HS.260A

This is the single-cylinder unit with direct drive to an output flange.

TYPE: Single-cylinder aircooled two-stroke.

CYLINDER: Bore 72 mm (2·835 in). Stroke 64 mm (2·52 in). Capacity 260 cc (15·85 cu in). Compression ratio 10.

INDUCTION: Through single Amal 28 mm carburettor.

FUEL GRADE: Automotive gasoline plus 2·5 per cent two-cycle oil mix.

IGNITION: Motoplat twin plug, fed by 10A Motoplat.

STARTING: 12V pre-engaged or pullcord.

DIMENSIONS:
- Length 290 mm (11·42 in)
- Width 330 mm (12·99 in)
- Height 380 mm (14·96 in)

WEIGHT, DRY: 20·0 kg (44·1 lb)

PERFORMANCE RATING: 18·65 kW (25 hp) at 6,000 rpm

Fieldhouse FE.525A(F) fan-cooled engine

FE.260AG

This 260 series engine has an integral gearbox to meet requirements of ultralight and microlight aircraft operators. The drive ratio may be altered between 1·1 : 1 and 3·0 : 1. Output power is unchanged.

DIMENSIONS:
- Length 242 mm (9·53 in)
- Width 335 mm (13·19 in)
- Height 398 mm (15·67 in)

WEIGHT, DRY: 26·0 kg (57·3 lb)

Fieldhouse FE.260AG geared engine

Fieldhouse microlight engines: (left) HS.260A, (right) HS.525A

Fieldhouse FE.525AG geared engine

HS.525A

This is the corresponding two-cylinder engine, with cylinders and most other features identical to the HS.260A.

INDUCTION: Twin Amal 34 mm carburettors.

IGNITION: 14A alternator Lumenition. Dual twin plugs.

DIMENSIONS:

Length	470 mm (18·5 in)
Width	350 mm (13·78 in)
Height	400 mm (15·75 in)
WEIGHT, DRY:	36·0 kg (80·0 lb)
PERFORMANCE RATING:	33·57 kW (45 hp) at 6,000 rpm

FE.525A(F)

This fan-cooled version of the 525 is designed for microlight and other aircraft where the environment is hot, such as an enclosed engine bay. Details are as before with the following changes:

DIMENSIONS:

Length	452 mm (17·80 in)
Width	285 mm (11·22 in)
Height	380 mm (14·96 in)
WEIGHT, DRY:	34·0 kg (75·0 lb)

FE.525AG

This is the geared version of the 525, the drive ratio again being selectable between 1·1 : 1 and 3 : 1. Power is unchanged.

DIMENSIONS:

Length	554 mm (21·81 in)
Width	320 mm (12·60 in)
Height	510 mm (20·08 in)
WEIGHT, DRY:	41·0 kg (90·4 lb)

LOTUS

LOTUS CARS LTD

Norwich, Norfolk NR14 8EZ

Telephone: 0953 608000

COMMERCIAL DIRECTOR: Martin Long

LOTUS 225 and 450

The 225 is the two-cylinder and the 450 the four-cylinder version of otherwise similar engines purpose designed for microlight aircraft. Each is designed for 50 h service interval and 500 h between overhauls.

TYPE: Four-stroke aircooled opposed piston engine.

CYLINDERS: Each formed as single die casting incorporating head, barrel and crankcase half, with housings for crankshaft and camshaft bearings. Nicasil base, single carefully profiled inlet and exhaust ports on underside. Bore 72·0 mm (2·83 in). Stroke 59·0 mm (2·32 in). Capacity 480 cc (29·3 cu in) (Type 450, 960 cc; 58·6 cu in).

CONNECTING RODS: Forged alloy steel with needle roller bearing at each end.

CRANKSHAFT: Central flying web (two in Type 450) joined to identical front and rear crank assemblies incorporating balance weights. Front roller and rear deep ball bearing.

VALVE GEAR: Overhead valves driven by push rods from camshaft gear-driven from crankshaft.

INDUCTION: Inlet manifold incorporated in crankcase for heating by sump oil. Single-choke side draught carburettor at front (option, at rear) of engine.

ACCESSORIES: Capacitor discharge ignition, provision for dual plugs optional. Hand starting with electric option. Provision for alternator at rear of crankshaft.

PROPELLER DRIVE: Direct from camshaft at half crankshaft speed. Provision for vibration damper, and for shaft extension for pushers.

WEIGHT, DRY (fully equipped):

225	14 kg (30·9 lb)
450	25·2 kg (55·5 lb)

PERFORMANCE RATINGS:

225	18·65 kW (25 hp) at 2,500 propeller rpm
450	37·3 kW (50 hp) at 2,500 propeller rpm

SPECIFIC FUEL CONSUMPTION (both):

Performance cruise 2,100 rpm	74·4 µg/J (0·44 lb/h/hp)
Economy cruise 1,500 rpm	71·0 µg/J (0·42 lb/h/hp)

Lotus 225 four-stroke piston engine for microlight aircraft

NGL

NORMALAIR-GARRETT LIMITED

Propulsion Division

Yeovil, Somerset, BA20 2YD

Telephone: Yeovil (0935) 75181

Telex: 46132

DIVISIONAL MANAGER: A. J. Purchase

MANAGER, MILITARY SALES: D. P. Short

The Propulsion Division of Normalair-Garrett incorporates Weslake Aeromarine Engines Ltd, which was acquired by Westland in 1979. In 1980 the division was relocated at Yeovil, to take advantage of the high quality manufacturing facility available there for quantity production of lightweight high performance aero engines.

NGL WAEL 342

The WAEL 342 is an ultra-lightweight two-stroke engine. The simultaneously firing twin-cylinder layout offers very low weight and volume, with minimum vibration. The accessories are modular, so the power unit can be tailored to each application. The design incorporates the Schnürle loop scavenge principle. The basic engine can have hand or electric starter, alternator or generator, altitude-compensated fuel injection system and exhaust systems to achieve maximum performance or minimum noise level. Various versions are in production. Applications include such RPVs and targets as the AEL Snipe Mk III, BAe Stabileye, GEC Avionics Phoenix and TTL Banshee.

CYLINDERS: Cast aluminium with plated bores. Bore 66 mm (2·6 in). Stroke 50 mm (1·97 in). Capacity 342 cc (20·9 cu in). Compression ratio 9·2.

CYLINDER HEADS: Cast aluminium, hemispherical chamber; provision for dual ignition.

CONNECTING ROD: Forged steel with caged needle bearings at both ends.

CRANKSHAFT: Three-piece balanced design in forged steel, supported by two deep groove ball and one needle roller bearing. Drive end shaft suitable for rigid mounting of propeller.

CRANKCASE: Two-piece design of cast aluminium.

CARBURETTOR: Single unit mounted directly on reed valve block providing all-altitude operation.

NGL WAEL 342 two-stroke engine (18·65 kW; 25 hp)

IGNITION: Contactorless electronic magneto.

ROTATION: Counter clockwise from power take-off end.

FUEL: Automotive gasoline 92 octane (leaded) plus approved two-cycle lubricating oil.

DIMENSIONS:

Width	390 mm (15·4 in)
Length (over carburettor)	237 mm (9·3 in)
WEIGHT, DRY:	from 8·5 kg (18·7 lb)
PERFORMANCE RATING:	18·65 kW (25 hp) at 7,000 rpm
SPECIFIC FUEL CONSUMPTION:	below 121 µg/J (0·8 lb/h/hp)

NGL WAEL 600N

The WAEL 600N turbojet has been designed for unmanned aircraft, missiles and RPVs. The core is a component common to a mass-produced diesel turbocharger. To this core is fitted a matched diffuser and plenum chamber forming the main carcase of the engine.

CORE: Single shaft carrying centrifugal compressor and radial inflow turbine.

NGL WAEL 600N turbojet (0·525 kN; 118 lb st)

COMBUSTION CHAMBER: Single reverse-flow with low-pressure spill burner. Delivery to light torus with vanes nozzles which direct gas into the turbine.

FUEL SYSTEM: Avtur, Avcat or other fuel is pumped via the oil cooler to the burner via a shut-off valve. Electronic control sensing TET and rpm, giving three-position or fully modulated operation.

ACCESSORIES: Starting by air impingement on compressor. High-energy surface surface-discharge igniter. Alternator in inlet bullet (typically 2·4 kW at 75,000 rpm) supplies power for motor driving fuel and oil pumps. Oil tank wrapped around inlet plenum. Optional air bleed.

DIMENSIONS:

Length, excl jetpipe	470 mm (18·5 in)
Width	274 mm (10·8 in)
Height	384 mm (15·1 in)
WEIGHT, DRY:	21·5 kg (47·4 lb)
PERFORMANCE RATING (S/L, static, ISA):	0·525 kN (118 lb st)
SPECIFIC FUEL CONSUMPTION:	37·5 mg/Ns (1·32 lb/h/lb st)

NORTON

NORTON MOTORS LTD

Lynn Lane, Shenstone, Lichfield, Staffs WS14 0EA

Telephone: 0543 480101

A forerunner of this company, BSA Motorcycles, started investigation of Wankel-type rotary engines in 1969. Since then a two-rotor engine has been developed, initially for motorcycle applications, and is now in production. In addition single- and twin-rotor engines are being developed for aircraft applications, in conjunction with Norton's licensee, Teledyne Continental Motors (TCM, which see in the US part of this section). The smaller engine has outstanding characteristics as an RPV or microlight engine, while the twin-rotor is aimed at conventional light aircraft.

Norton claims the weight and simplicity of a two-stroke, the sfc of a four-stroke, and smoothness and lack of maintenance approaching that of a gas turbine. A major factor in the achievement of low sfc is very low mechanical friction, which stems from the aircooled rotor.

The basic specification appears in the description of the TCM R-18. TCM did not announce any connection with Norton, but in fact the engineering development and drawings were undertaken by Norton, with TCM providing finance.

To amplify the specification, Norton quotes a power output of 26·1 kW (35 hp) at 7,000 rpm without intercooler, 33·57 kW (45 hp) with intercooler, and up to 44·76 kW (60 hp) with an exhaust ejector to augment the rotor cooling. Dry weight is given as from 12·7 to 18·1 kg (28-40 lb) depending on accessories. Specific fuel consumption is currently 91·29 μg/J (0·54 lb/h/hp) at maximum power and 81·15 μg/J (0·48 lb/h/hp) at 50-90 per cent cruise rating.

The twin-rotor engine has been packaged by Norton into a 406 mm (16 in) duct. This encloses all accessories as well as all airflows. In general the twin-rotor engine gives double the power (about 67 kW; 90 hp) for a 50 per cent increase in weight.

For powers up to 134 kW (180 hp) two of the very narrow twin-rotor engines could be situated side-by-side, driving the propeller through a common gearbox. Over-run clutches could provide for engine-out operation.

Norton RPV rotary engine exhibition model

NPT

NOEL PENNY TURBINES LTD

Siskin Drive, Toll Bar End, Coventry CV3 4FE

Telephone: 0203 301528
Telex: 312285 Penny G

DIRECTORS:
R. N. Penny (Chairman and Managing Director)
The Earl of Minto
E. R. Jeynes
S. Penny (Secretary)

Noel Penny has more than 30 years of small gas turbine experience, and derives a major part of its income from packaged research and development programmes for worldwide clients, across the entire spectrum of small gas turbines. Current projects include a turboprop, a single-shaft gas turbine for power generation, an advanced turbocharging system and a heat pump.

The company's range of products has been updated by the introduction of new designs, and manufacture of earlier products is limited to special applications. An example is the NPT 401, which is still produced as an instructional turbojet. The current aerospace programme is concentrated on small, lightweight, low cost, expendable turbojets for unmanned vehicles. The NPT 151 and NPT 301 are in production. A small expendable unit of 0·22 kN (50 lb st), a low cost turbojet of 4 kN (900 lb st) for missiles and targets, and a small 15-30 kW (20-40 shp) turboprop for unmanned vehicles are being developed.

NPT 151

Now in service, this low cost turbojet has been developed for RPV propulsion. It can be adapted for other applications requiring extended life.

TYPE: Single-shaft turbojet.

COMPRESSOR: Centrifugal, aluminium alloy. Maximum airflow 1·2 kg (2·65 lb)/s. Pressure ratio 4·3.

COMBUSTION CHAMBER: Straight through annular with vaporising burners. Ignition by electrically fired pyrotechnic cartridge.

FUEL SYSTEM: LP single-speed pump mounted on compressor shaft. Control by hydromechanical governor and acceleration unit. NPT 151-2 has LP pressurised-inlet electric pump and electronic control.

FUEL GRADES: Jet A-1 or JP-5 preferred.

TURBINE: Inward radial flow, cast nickel alloy. Max inlet temperature 987°C.

LUBRICATION: Total loss pulsed oil flow.

MOUNTING: Three brackets on front casing.

STARTING: Windmilling, or by external air source on compressor.

DIMENSIONS:
Diameter 275 mm (10·83 in)
Length 310 mm (12·20 in)
WEIGHT, DRY: 20 kg (44 lb)
PERFORMANCE RATING: Max S/L 0·667 kN (150 lb st)
SPECIFIC FUEL CONSUMPTION: 35·4 mg/Ns (1·25 lb/h/lb st)

NPT 301

This simple expendable turbojet can be supplied at a range of outputs up to 2 kN (450 lb st). The following description refers to the definitive NPT 301:

TYPE: Single-shaft turbojet.

COMPRESSOR: Single-stage centrifugal. Max airflow 2·27 kg (5·0 lb)/s. Pressure ratio 4·5.

COMBUSTION CHAMBER: Reverse flow annular, with vaporising burners.

FUEL SYSTEM: LP pressurised inlet electric pump. Electronic control.

FUEL GRADES: Kerosene, Jet A-1, JP-5 preferred.

TURBINE: Single-stage axial with integral blades. Cast nickel alloy.

ACCESSORY DRIVE: Alternator to customer's specification.

LUBRICATION: Total loss pulsed oil flow.

DIMENSIONS:
Diameter 343 mm (13·5 in)
Length 577 mm (22·72 in)
WEIGHT, DRY: 40·37 kg (89 lb)
PERFORMANCE RATING (S/L): 1·334 kN (300 lb st)
SPECIFIC FUEL CONSUMPTION: 30·6 mg/Ns (1·08 lb/h/lb st)
STARTING: External air source on compressor.

NPT 151 turbojet

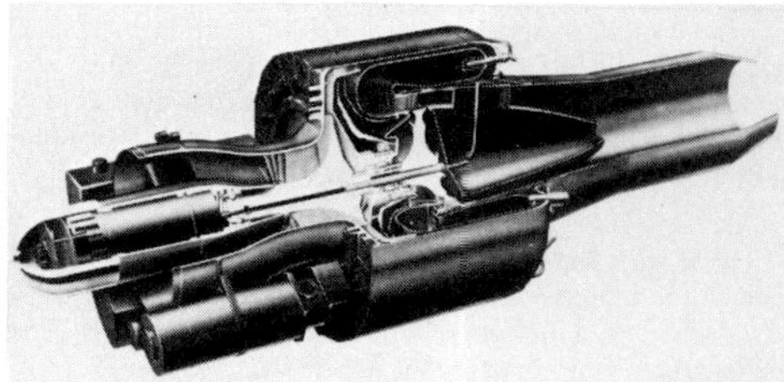

Cutaway of NPT 301 turbojet

PIPER

PIPER FM LTD

Bromley Green Road, Ashford, Kent TN26 2EF

Telephone: 0233 733131
Telex: 946240 CWEASY G

Piper, an engine research and development company associated principally with the automotive industry, also manufactures RPV engines. With the growing need for reduced fuel consumption, and temperature and altitude correction, Piper have developed versions of Pijet, their automotive microprocessor-controlled fuelling system, to suit this duty. Through an associate company, Piper-Mechadyne Ltd, a range of compact lightweight generators is available, with size and weight reduced by half compared with traditional units.

Piper engines are of high power for their size and weight. All are two-stroke piston engines using 25:1 fuel mix, with magnesium alloy crankcase, light alloy cylinder(s) with hard coated liner, caged needle bearings at both ends of the connecting rod(s), Tillotson Walbro floatless carburettor, shielded HT ignition, and starting by hand-held external power source.

Two Piper RPV engines: left, P.100 with Pijet injection; right, P.200

PIPER P.80

Single cylinder of 52·0 mm (2·05 in) bore, 36·0 mm (1·42 in) stroke and 76·5 cc (4·67 cu in) capacity. Dry weight 3·32 kg (7·3 lb). Max power 5·8 kW (7·8 hp) at 7,200 rpm. Flywheel magneto ignition. In service in many countries, but superseded in production by P.100.

PIPER P.80/2

Two cylinders, each 40·0 mm (1·57 in) bore, 32·33 mm (1·27 in) stroke, with total capacity 81·0 cc (4·94 cu in). Dry weight 2·65 kg (5·8 lb). Max power 3·9 kW (5·2 hp) at 7,200 rpm. Solid state (24V supply) electronic ignition, twin carburettors. Powers the ML Aviation Sprite RPV rotorcraft.

PIPER P.100

Single cylinder of 55·6 mm (2·19 in) bore, 40·8 mm (1·61 in) stroke and 99·0 cc (6·04 cu in) capacity. Dry weight 3·59 kg (7·9 lb). Max power 6·6 kW (8·8 hp) at 7,200 rpm. Solid state ignition. In service in many countries powering target RPVs, and also used in BAe Stabileye.

PIPER P.200

Two cylinders, each of P.100 size, giving 198·0 cc (12·08 cu in) capacity. Dry weight 4·78 kg (10·5 lb). Max power 11·9 kW (16·0 hp) at 7,200 rpm. Solid state ignition, twin carburettors.

ROLLS-ROYCE

ROLLS-ROYCE LIMITED

65 Buckingham Gate, London SW1E 6AT
Telephone: 01 222 9020

Main Locations:
PO Box 31, Moor Lane, Derby DE2 8BJ
Telephone: 0332 42424
PO Box 3, Filton, Bristol BS12 7QE
Telephone: 0272 791234
Leavesden, Watford WD2 7BZ
Telephone: 0923 674000

Main Board Directors:
Sir Francis Tombs (Chairman)
R. H. Robins (Managing Director)
S. L. Higginbottom (Chairman, Rolls-Royce Inc)
J. O. Keir (Director, Civil Engines)
S. C. Miller (Director, Corporate Engineering)
J. A. Rigg (Director, Finance)
F. T. Salt (Director, Supply)
J. D. Wragg (Director, Military Engines)

Public Affairs Director:
Dominic Leahy (at Buckingham Gate)

Rolls-Royce, which produces a range of gas turbines and ramjets, retains the experience in aircraft engines built up over more than 70 years. The company also represents British experience in lightweight high power gas turbines for industrial and marine purposes, since such engines were first derived from aircraft gas turbines.

More than 278 million hours of operating experience have been accumulated with Rolls-Royce civil and military gas turbines, which are used by 270 airlines, 122 armed forces and more than 680 executive customers.

In addition to products designed, developed and manufactured solely in Britain, the company works with partners abroad on a number of joint civil and military aircraft engine programmes. Licences for the manufacture of Rolls-Royce engines or components are held by many countries throughout the world.

The main activities are at Derby, Glasgow, Bristol, Coventry and Leavesden, where aircraft gas turbines are produced, and at Ansty, where aircraft gas turbine techniques are applied to industrial and marine uses. Employees total 41,500.

Rolls-Royce engines in commercial service include the RB211, 535, 183, Spey and Conway turbofans, Olympus, Avon, Viper and RB162 turbojets, and Dart and Tyne turboprops. New civil engines include the Tay turbofan. Military engines include the Pegasus vectored thrust turbofan and Odin ramjet, as well as versions of the RB211, Spey, Conway, Avon, Viper, Dart and Tyne. Helicopter engines include the Gem and Gnome. Under the International heading in this section are described the RB199 (Turbo-Union), and Adour and RTM 322 (with Turboméca).

In March 1983 a multinational collaborative agreement was signed to develop an engine for 150-seat aircraft; this is covered under IAE in the International part of this section. Another international agreement was announced in February 1984: General Electric is to participate in the 535E4 programme and future developments, while Rolls-Royce is taking the same percentage share (up to 25 per cent) in the US company's CF6-80C2 engine. As the result of a memorandum of understanding with Garrett (USA), Rolls-Royce expects to make 30 per cent of each TPE 331-12B turboprop for RAF Shorts Tucano trainers. It is also a partner in the Eurojet EJ200 engine (see International section) for the EFA fighter.

In April 1985 Rolls-Royce joined with Turboméca and MTU in the European Small Engines Co-operation Agreement. Aimed at ensuring the preservation of competitive European capability in small gas turbines—primarily for helicopters, but including turboprop and turbofan derivatives—the agreement involves the Rolls-Royce Turboméca RTM 322, MTM Turboméca MTM 385, and Turboméca TM 333. Further details are given under Turboméca in the French part of this section.

In 1983 Rolls-Royce announced that it was engaged in a broad study programme on possible future engines to drive advanced propellers for aircraft speeds of about Mach 0·8. The work includes ground and flight testing of single and contra-rotating propellers and propfans, lightweight gearboxes, inlets and installations, and noise and vibration research.

Versions of several Rolls-Royce aircraft gas turbines are used as power units for large and small ships, hydrofoils, air cushion vehicles, electricity generating sets, gas and oil pumping equipment and for other industrial uses.

ROLLS-ROYCE TURBOMÉCA ADOUR

This turbofan was designed by Rolls-Royce and Turboméca. It is described in the International part of this section.

TURBO-UNION RB199

This advanced augmented turbofan is the power unit for the Panavia Tornado. The RB199 programme is managed by Turbo-Union (see International part of this section).

IAE V2500

This turbofan is being developed by IAE: see International part of this section.

ROLLS-ROYCE RB211

The designation RB211 applies to a family of advanced technology three-shaft turbofans of high bypass ratio and high pressure ratio, with thrusts from 166 kN (37,400 lb) to 249 kN (56,000 lb). The engine was selected by Lockheed in March 1968 to power the L-1011 TriStar, and later by Boeing as an alternative option on the 747.

Rolls-Royce initiated design studies of three-shaft turbofans in 1961 and a twin-spool engine, the RB178, was tested in 1967 to provide relevant component and gas generator experience. Among the advantages afforded by a three-shaft layout are its achievement of a high pressure ratio with fewer compressor and turbine stages while maintaining excellent handling. The need for compressor variable stator mechanisms can also be minimised and the rotating assemblies can be made relatively short and rigid while preserving light construction. As a result the RB211 has demonstrated outstandingly low seal and aerofoil wear, thus maintaining a high level of performance throughout engine life.

For all announced applications Rolls-Royce retains responsibility for the complete propulsion system, comprising the engine, fan airflow reverser, pod cowlings and related systems, and noise attenuation for the intake, fan cowl and turbine exhaust duct.

The engine is built up of seven modules, each changed easily. This enables spare engine holdings to be reduced, and for each module to be individually lifed. Maximum provision is made for in-service monitoring of engine condition and visual inspection of all engine sections.

The RB211 combustion chamber is of annular design, giving significant advantages over tubo-annular systems in terms of reduced cost, weight and length, and improved efficiency. The reduced length makes a two-bearing HP system possible, with both bearings located away from the high temperatures of the combustion area. Detailed design has been aimed at reducing noise and exhaust contaminants to a minimum.

The **RB211-22B**, fitted to the L-1011-1 and -100 TriStar, is flat rated at 187 kN (42,000 lb st) to 28·9°C. Certificated in February 1973 by the CAA and in April 1973 by the FAA. By 1986 more than 630 had been delivered, and engine flight hours in service were in excess of 13 million.

The **RB211-524** series of engines was developed from the RB211-22B and covers a range of thrust from 222 kN (50,000 lb) to 249 kN (56,000 lb). The -524 entered airline service in 1977 with the L-1011 and 747. By the beginning of 1986 more than 610 engines had been delivered and service experience of over 7 million hours achieved.

The **RB211-524B**, which powers the L-1011-200, L-1011-500 and 747, is certificated at 222 kN (50,000 lb) to 28·9°C. Further developments at the same thrust but offering better fuel consumption include the **RB211-524B3**, giving a 3·5 per cent improvement over the -524B, and which entered service in May 1980; and the **RB211-524B4**, which offers up to 4·8 per cent better sfc than the 524B and entered service in February 1981. Further savings for 1987 are obtained from the **524B4 Improved**, with an sfc 6·7 per cent better than the 524B. This engine can be installed new or by modifying existing engines in the L-1011-250.

The **RB211-524C2** is a 229 kN (51,500 lb) engine for the 747 which entered service in April 1980. This engine offers increased thrust ratings with no change in sfc.

The **RB211-524D4** is an improved engine rated at 236 kN (53,000 lb) for the 747, and offering a 4·8 per cent better fuel consumption relative to the -524C2. Certification was followed by entry into service in November 1981.

The **RB211-524D4 Upgrade** offers 2·5 per cent lower sfc than the D4 and is rated at 236 kN (53,000 lb) for the 747. This engine entered service in 1984. Further improvements are under way with two derived engines. The **524D4C** is to be certificated in late 1986 at 242 kN (54,500 lb st), with sfc 4·5 per cent lower than the D4. The **524D4D** incorporates advanced features proven on the 535E4, such as the wide-chord fan, 3-D aerodynamics and integrated nozzle. It is to be rated at 249 kN (56,000 lb st), with sfc 8·0 per cent lower than the D4, and is to be certificated in early 1988 for the 747-400.

The **535** series is described separately.

The following description relates to the RB211-524D4:

Type: Three-shaft axial turbofan.

LP Fan: Single-stage overhung fan driven by LP turbine, the whole rotor assembly being supported on three bearings. Front bearing is large roller, squeeze film supported behind fan. Axial location of rotor is by intershaft ball bearing in rear end of IP compressor drum. LP turbine supported on roller bearing, squeeze film mounted in exhaust cone panel. Composite nosecone. Titanium alloy used for 33 fan rotor blades, and steel for 70 fan outlet guide vanes. Titanium fan disc bolted with curvic coupling to LP shaft. Aluminium fan casing, with Armco containment ring. Total fan airflow (T-O rating), 703 kg (1,550 lb)/s. Bypass ratio 4·4.

IP Compressor: Seven-stage compressor rotor driven by IP turbine and supported on three bearings located directly in support panels. Front squeeze film bearing is roller. Mid bearing at rear of IP compressor is ball bearing providing axial location for IP rotor. Rear bearing is roller, squeeze film supported in panel between HP and IP turbines. Two drums, one of titanium discs welded together and the other of welded steel discs, are bolted to form one rotor, carrying titanium rotor blades. Aluminium and steel casings carry steel stator blades. Single-stage titanium variable inlet guide vanes.

HP Compressor: Six-stage compressor rotor driven by HP turbine connected by large diameter shaft and carried on ball location bearing at front and roller bearing mounted at the rear in panel behind HP turbine disc. Welded titanium discs, a single steel disc and welded nickel alloy discs are bolted together to form the rotor, carrying titanium, steel and nickel alloy blades. Steel casing carries steel and Nimonic stator blades. Overall pressure ratio 29 : 1.

Combustion Chamber: Fully annular, with steel outer casings and Nimonic combustor. Downstream fuel injection by 18 airspray burners with annular atomisers. Ignition by high energy igniter plugs in Nos 8 and 12 burners.

HP Turbine: Single-stage axial unit with nozzle guide vanes and Nimonic cast rotor blades, both convection and film cooled. Blades mounted in Nimonic disc by fir tree roots.

IP Turbine: Single-stage axial unit with Nimonic nozzle guide vanes and Nimonic rotor blades. NGVs aircooled. Rotor blades fir tree mounted in Nimonic disc.

LP Turbine: Three-stage axial unit with Nimonic rotor blades fir tree mounted in steel discs.

Jetpipe: Steel jetpipe without spoiler.

Accessory Drives: Radial drive from HP shaft to gearbox on fan casing. Accessories driven include integrated drive generator and aircraft hydraulic pumps.

Lubrication System: Continuous circulation 'dry sump' system with single gear type pressure and secondary pumps, and multiple gear-type scavenge pumps. Oil tank 27 litres (48 Imp pints) capacity integral with gearbox.

Mounting: Two-point mounting system. Front mount on fan casing takes thrust, vertical and side loads. Rear link mount on exhaust casing takes torsional, side and vertical loads. Both mounts are fail-safe and allow for carcase expansion.

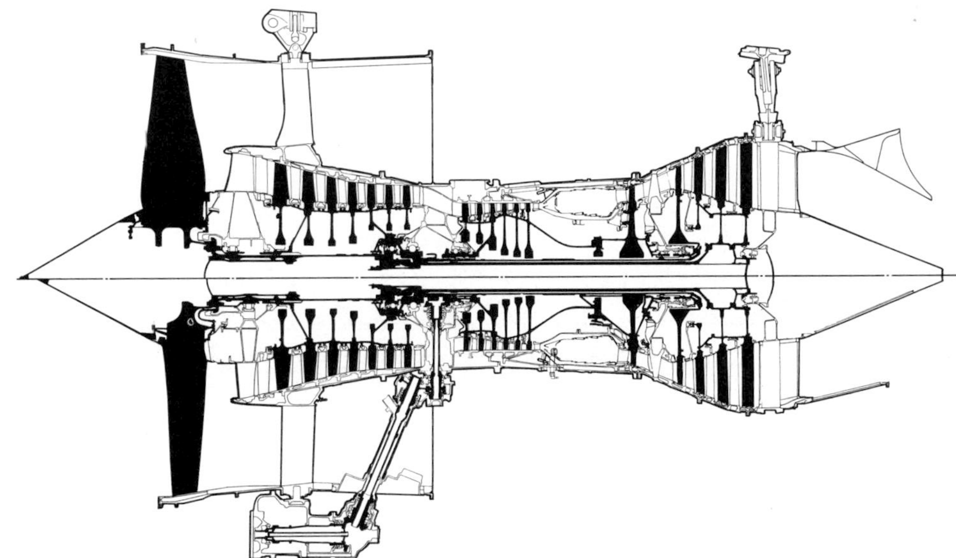

Comparative cross-sections of the Rolls-Royce RB211-524D4 (upper half) and RB211-524D4 Upgrade (lower)

DIMENSIONS:
Length overall:
RB211-22B, -524C2 — 3,033 mm (119·4 in)
RB211-524B4, -524D4 — 3,106 mm (122·3 in)
Inlet diameter:
RB211-22B, -524C2 — 2,182 mm (85·9 in)
RB211-524B4, -524D4 — 2,192 mm (86·3 in)

WEIGHT, DRY:
RB211-22B — 4,171 kg (9,195 lb)
RB211-524C2 — 4,472 kg (9,859 lb)
RB211-524B4, B4 Improved — 4,452 kg (9,814 lb)
RB211-524D4, D4 Upgrade, D4C, D4D — 4,479 kg (9,874 lb)

PERFORMANCE RATINGS:
T-O: see model listings
Cruise at 10,670 m (35,000 ft) and Mach 0·8 (uninstalled):
RB211-22B — 43·1 kN (9,700 lb)
RB211-524B4, B4 Improved — 48·75 kN (10,960 lb)
RB211-524C2 — 50·5 kN (11,360 lb)
RB211-524D4 (all models) — 52·04 kN (11,700 lb)

SPECIFIC FUEL CONSUMPTION (Cruise):
RB211-22B — 17·50 mg/Ns (0·618 lb/h/lb)
RB211-524B4, D4 — 17·00 mg/Ns (0·600 lb/h/lb)
RB211-524B4 Improved — 16·49 mg/Ns (0·582 lb/h/lb)
RB211-524C2 — 17·68 mg/Ns (0·624 lb/h/lb)
RB211-524D4 Upgrade — 16·575 mg/Ns (0·585 lb/h/lb)
RB211-524D4C — 16·23 mg/Ns (0·573 lb/h/lb)
RB211-524D4D — 15·64 mg/Ns (0·552 lb/h/lb)

ROLLS-ROYCE 535

Originally the RB211-535, this simplified engine family has now become important and different enough to be treated separately. The first model, the 535C, was based on major parts of RB211 engines, including the -22B HP module.

The **535C** was launch engine for the Boeing 757. It has a high pressure module based on the -22B, a six-stage IP compressor without variable stator vanes, and a scaled down version of the most advanced of the -524 fans. Fan airflow is 18 per cent lower than that of the -22B, and core airflow 12 per cent lower. The engine runs at moderate temperatures, pressures and velocities, resulting in low noise and optimisation for short-haul operation. The 535C entered service on 1 January 1983. It has been the most trouble free engine ever developed by Rolls-Royce. In the 757's first three years of service the total engine-caused removal rate was 0·045 per 1,000 h, many times better than the previously claimed industry best.

The **535E4** is an advanced technology version of the 535C, available for the Boeing 757 and offering an increased T-O thrust, together with about 10 per cent reduction in fuel consumption relative to the 535C. These improvements have been achieved by the introduction of a new wide chord fan blade without snubbers (only 22 per engine), together with advanced compressor and turbine blading and an integrated nozzle. CAA certification was achieved in November 1983, at a T-O rating of 178 kN (40,100 lb), and revenue service began in October 1984. The E4 reliability rates are similar to those of its predecessor, and its environmental disturbance is so low that the 757 with this engine is the quietest civil aircraft with more than 100 seats. General Electric is contributing to manufacture, further development and marketing of the E4.

The following description relates to the 535E4:

TYPE: Three-shaft turbofan.

FAN: Single-stage, overhung ahead of squeeze film roller bearing. Only 22 very wide chord blades, without part span snubbers, each of accelerated diffusion bonded titanium skins on titanium honeycomb core. Fan case of Rohrbond construction with Kevlar containment. High resistance to impact damage and designed to centrifuge debris away from core. Fan airflow 522 kg (1,150 lb)/s. Bypass ratio 4·1 (535C, 4·4).

IP COMPRESSOR: Six stages of controlled diffusion design, derived from RB211-524 and spaced to minimise foreign object damage. No variable vanes.

Rolls-Royce 535E4 three-shaft turbofan

HP COMPRESSOR: Six stages of advanced design. End-bend blading for higher efficiency, with stage -4, -5 and -6 discs in titanium super alloy. Low expansion casing for improved tip clearance control. Overall engine pressure ratio 28·5 (535C, 21·2).

COMBUSTION CHAMBER: Annular, advanced design for higher efficiency, 18 airspray nozzles, flexible liner mountings, heatshields and thermal barrier coatings for long life.

HP TURBINE: Single-stage. Rotor blades DS (directionally solidified) cast with advanced aircooling. HP leading-edge cooling, HP and LP internal cooling passages both with triple pass system. Nozzle guide vanes with curved stacking for reduced secondary losses, highly cooled and with thermal barrier coating on platforms.

IP TURBINE: Single stage. New cooled NGVs with multi-lean stacking for improved airflow onto high aspect ratio blades.

LP TURBINE: Three stages. Conventional design using RB211-524 technology. Low stage loading, and numbers of blades and vanes matched to give tone cutoff for reduced noise. All turbine casings double wall and cooled.

JETPIPE: Core and bypass flows mixed in integrated nozzle giving lower sfc, increased thrust and 40 per cent increase in reverse thrust.

REVERSER: Fan reverser only, incorporated in top hinged C-ducts which swing open for core access or engine removal. Hydraulic jacks move translating cowl to rear, blocker doors seal fan duct and uncover cascade vanes. Over expansion reduces core thrust.

GEARBOX: Mounted under fan case and driven from HP spool with short shafts of proven design.

Both the fan airflow and the hot exhaust gases leave the 535E4 through this single 'integrated' nozzle

DIMENSIONS:
Length: 535C — 3,010 mm (118·5 in)
535E4 — 2,995 mm (117·9 in)
Inlet diameter: 535C — 1,877 mm (73·9 in)
535E4 — 1,892 mm (74·5 in)

WEIGHT, DRY:
535C — 3,309 kg (7,294 lb)
535E4 — 3,295 kg (7,264 lb)

PERFORMANCE RATINGS (note: flexible T-O ratings involving considerable derating are used in operation):
T-O (S/L, ISA): 535C — 166·4 kN (37,400 lb st)
535E4 — 178·4 kN (40,100 lb st)
Max climb (10,670 m; 35,000 ft, Mach 0·85):
535C — 40·1 kN (9,023 lb)
535E4 — 41·4 kN (9,300 lb)
Max cruise (10,670 m; 35,000 ft, Mach 0·85):
535C — 37·6 kN (8,453 lb)
535E4 — 38·7 kN (8,700 lb)

SPECIFIC FUEL CONSUMPTION (cruise, as above):
535C — 17·33 mg/Ns (0·612 lb/h/lb)
535E4 — 16·09 mg/Ns (0·568 lb/h/lb)

ROLLS-ROYCE RB163 CIVIL SPEY

US military designation: F113

Design of the Spey RB163 began in September 1959, and the first engine ran at the end of December 1960. Civil Speys are in service in the Trident, BAe One-Eleven, Gulfstream II and III and (see RB183 entry) F28 Fellowship, and are the subject of a collaborative production programme between Rolls-Royce and the government of Romania for Rombac 1-11s. The **F113-RR-100** is the Mk 511-8 which powers the Gulfstream C-20A C-SAM aircraft.

The RB183 and military versions are described separately. The following details refer specifically to the Spey Mk 512-14DW, as fitted to the BAe and Rombac One-Eleven Series 500, except where indicated:

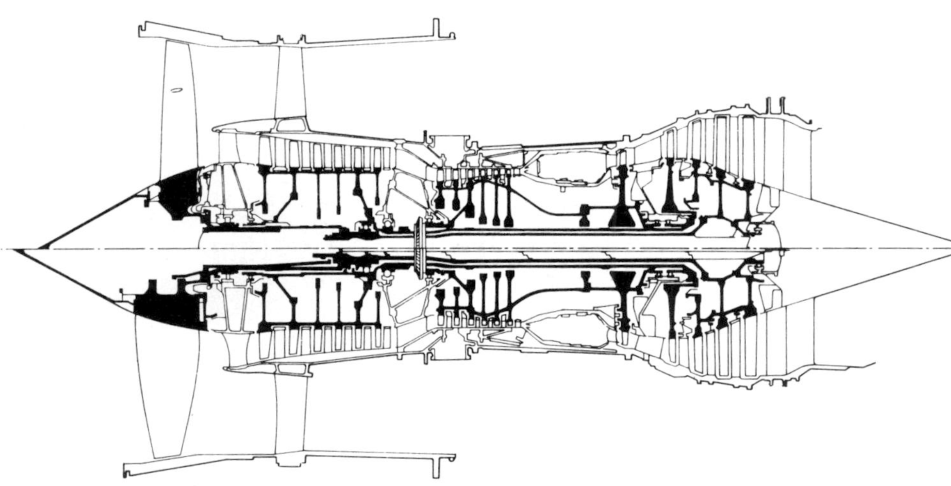
Comparative cross-sections of Rolls-Royce 535C (upper) and 535E4 (lower)

TYPE: Two-spool turbofan engine.
AIR INTAKE: Annular, with bleed air thermal anti-icing.
COMPRESSOR: Two spools. Five-stage (four-stage on Mks 505 and 506) low pressure (LP) and 12-stage high pressure (HP). First-stage HP stator vanes variable incidence. LP compressor steel drum type, pinned to shaft. HP compressor is of the steel disc type, first stage bolted to shaft, remaining stages splined. HP stator blades steel; LP stators aluminium. LP rotor blades aluminium (Mk 512 titanium 1st stage); HP blades titanium. Stators slotted into casing; rotor blades pinned or dovetailed. LP casing two-piece magnesium. HP casing steel. Pressure ratio 21·2 : 1. Air mass flow 94·4 kg (208 lb)/s. Bypass ratio 0·64.
COMBUSTION CHAMBER: Tubo-annular with 10 Nimonic sheet liners. Duplex downstream burners, one per chamber. High energy igniters in chambers 4 and 8.
FUEL SYSTEM: Plessey LP pump feeding through fuel cooled oil cooler and Marston Excelsior fuel heater to LP filter at inlet to Lucas GD pump. HP metered by Lucas regulator, embodying combined speed and acceleration control and fed through Lucas LP governor and shut-off valve to duplex spray nozzles. Maximum pressure 124 bars (1,800 lb/sq in).
FUEL GRADE: DERD.2482 or 2486.
WATER INJECTION SYSTEM (engines bearing 'W' suffix): Water supplied by Lucas air turbopump through engine-mounted automatic shut-off valve to injector passages in fuel spray nozzles (water sprays into primary airflow through flame tube swirlers).
NOZZLE GUIDE VANES: Hollow cast in nickel based alloy. HP aircooled.
TURBINES: Two two-stage. First HP aircooled. HP discs nickel based alloy, bolted to shaft. LP discs creep resisting ferritic steel. Nickel based alloy blades attached by fir tree roots.
BEARINGS: LP compressor supported in roller bearings, plus ball thrust bearing. HP compressor has front roller bearing and ball thrust bearing. Turbine bearings all roller type flexibly mounted.
JETPIPE: Fixed area stainless steel sheet.
REVERSER AND SUPPRESSOR: Normally internal clamshell (Gulfstream II and III target type). Five- or six-chute silencing nozzles available.
ACCESSORY DRIVES: Port gearbox, driven from LP rotor, carries LP governor and LP tacho. Starboard gearbox, driven from HP rotor, carries LP and HP fuel pumps, fuel regulator, main oil pumps, airflow control rpm signal transmitter, starter and HP tacho. Provision in starboard gearbox for aircraft ancillaries.
LUBRICATION SYSTEM: Self-contained continuous circulation. Single pressure pump feeds oil from tank through fuel cooled cooler and HP filter to gearboxes and shaft bearings. Five main scavenge pumps. Tank capacity 6·8 litres (12 Imp pints). Usable oil 5·1 litres (9 Imp pints). Normal pressure 2·41-3·45 bars (35-50 lb/sq in).
OIL SPECIFICATION: DERD.2487.
MOUNTING: Two trunnions, two saddle mountings and one rear mounting.
STARTING: Plessey 220 air turbine starter.
DIMENSIONS:
Length, less tailpipe 2,911 mm (114·6 in)
Diameter 942 mm (37·1 in)
WEIGHT, DRY: 1,168 kg (2,574 lb)
PERFORMANCE RATINGS:
Max T-O 55·8 kN (12,550 lb st)
Max continuous 51·5 kN (11,580 lb st) at 12,450 rpm
Typical cruise rating at 450 knots (834 km/h; 518 mph) at 9,750 m (32,000 ft) 13·7 kN (3,070 lb)
SPECIFIC FUEL CONSUMPTION (cruise as above) 22·7 mg/Ns (0·800 lb/h/lb)
OIL CONSUMPTION:
Max (all Marks) 0·42 litres (0·75 Imp pints)/h

ROLLS-ROYCE RB183

Developed for the Fokker F28, this derivative engine has a similar configuration to the Spey but has numerous significant changes to suit the F28's special requirements. It has a four-stage LP compressor. Pressure ratio is 15·4, mass flow 90·27 kg (199 lb)/s and bypass ratio 1. The RB183 entered service in 1969 and the following versions are in use:

Mk 555-15. Basic model, rated at 43·8 kN (9,850 lb st).

Mk 555-15H. Hot-day version, flat rated at 44·0 kN (9,900 lb st) to 29·7°C. Entered service 1973.

Mk 555-15N. Mk 555-15 with 10-lobe mixer.

Mk 555-15P. More fuel-efficient -15H with 10-lobe mixer. Entered service 1982.

The following data refer to the 555-15P:
DIMENSIONS:
Length 2,553 mm (100·5 in)
Diameter 940 mm (37·0 in)
WEIGHT, DRY: 1,024 kg (2,257 lb)
PERFORMANCE RATINGS:
T-O: see model listings
Cruise at 7,620 m (25,000 ft) at 440 knots (815 km/h; 507 mph) 16·59 kN (3,730 lb)
SPECIFIC FUEL CONSUMPTION:
T-O 15·9 mg/Ns (0·560 lb/h/lb st)
Cruise (as above) 22·7 mg/Ns (0·800 lb/h/lb)

Rolls-Royce Spey Mk 807 turbofan for the Italian/Brazilian AMX combat aircraft

Rolls-Royce RB183 Mk 555-15H turbofan rated at 44·0 kN (9,900 lb st)

ROLLS-ROYCE RB168 SPEY

The RB168 military versions of the Spey are as follow:

Mk 101. Basic engine, but with air offtake for BLC. Fitted to BAe Buccaneer.

Mk 202. Augmented engine for supersonic aircraft, with shaft/disc LP compressor and fully modulated afterburner. Fitted to Phantom FGR.2 (F-4M) and licensed to China. Phantom FG.1 (F-4K) has **Mk 203**.

Mk 250. Fully navalised. Fitted to BAe Nimrod MR.1, R.1 and MR.2.

Mk 251. Mk 250 with strengthened drive for uprated electrical generation. Fitted to Nimrod AEW.3.

Mk 807. Mk 101 rotors within RB183 structure, with BLC deleted and fitted with manual emergency fuel control. To be produced under licence in Italy with Brazilian participation for AMX aircraft.
DIMENSIONS:
Length: Mk 101 2,911 mm (114·6 in)
Mk 202 5,204 mm (204·9 in)
Mk 250, 251 2,972 mm (117·0 in)
Mk 807 2,456 mm (96·7 in)
Diameter 825 mm (32·5 in)
WEIGHT, DRY:
Mk 101 1,121 kg (2,471 lb)
Mk 202 1,857 kg (4,093 lb)
Mk 250, 251 1,243 kg (2,740 lb)
Mk 807 1,083 kg (2,388 lb)
PERFORMANCE RATINGS (max T-O):
Mk 101, 807 49·1 kN (11,030 lb st)
Mk 202: dry 54·5 kN (12,250 lb st)
augmented 91·2 kN (20,515 lb st)
Mk 250, 251 53·3 kN (11,995 lb st)

ROLLS-ROYCE TAY

Repeating the name of a turbojet of 1946, the Tay has the designation RB183-03 and combines the reliable mature core of the Mk 555 with a new LP system using technology from the proven RB211-524.

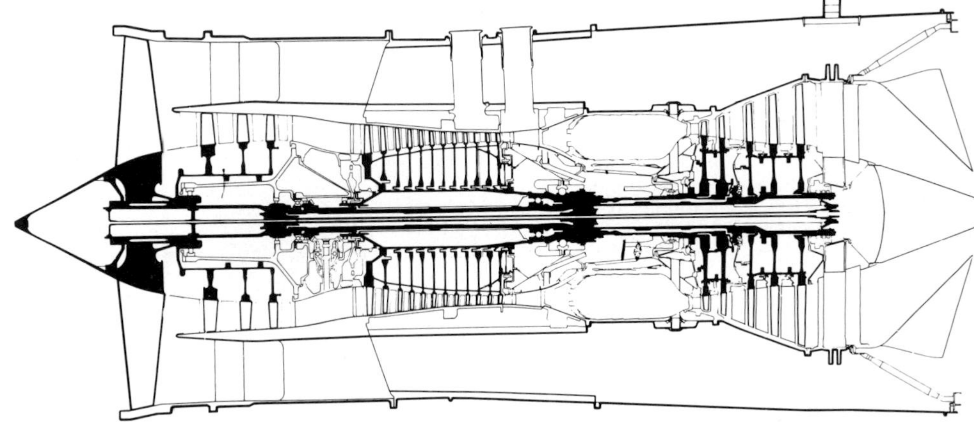
Cross-section of Rolls-Royce Tay turbofan

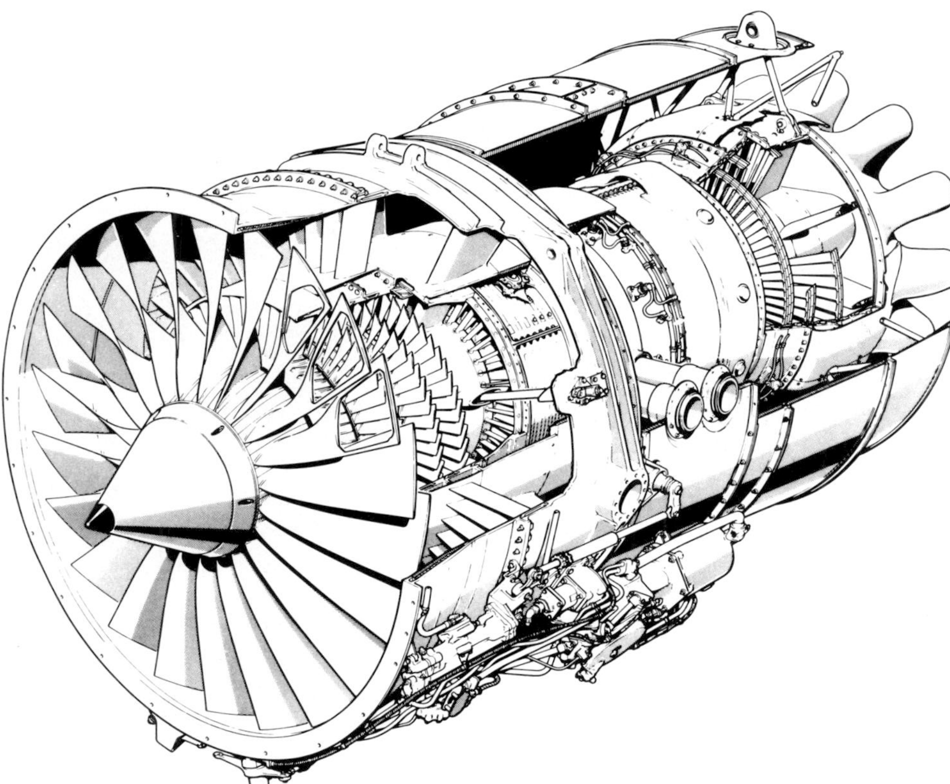
Cutaway drawing of the Rolls-Royce Tay turbofan

In March 1983 Gulfstream Aerospace announced an order for 200 Tays worth $300 million with spares. In November 1983 Fokker announced an order for 100 to power Fokker 100 airliners. The Tay will be about 14 per cent more fuel-efficient than the RB 183-555, will easily meet all emission standards, and will enable aircraft to comply with FAR Pt 36 Stage III noise requirements. It is a strong contender for re-engining the BAe One-Eleven and other short-haul jets. First engine run was in August 1984. By June 1985 six engines had run 70 per cent more test cycles than had been planned. Initial versions are as follows:

Tay 610-8. Selected for Gulfstream IV, and first flown on that aircraft on 19 September 1985. Certificated on 26 June 1986.

Tay 620-15. Selected for Fokker 100. To fly on this aircraft in 1986 and enter service in 1987.

TYPE: Two-shaft turbofan.
FAN: Single-stage with wide chord blades based on other Rolls-Royce advanced technology engines.
LP COMPRESSOR: New design with three stages on fan shaft.
HP COMPRESSOR: 12-stage axial (RB183 Mk 555).
COMBUSTION CHAMBER: Tubo-annular with 10 flame tubes, each with one duplex burner. Modified to meet emission regulations.
FUEL SYSTEM: As RB183 Mk 555 but with improved fuel control unit.
HP TURBINE: All Mks except 650, two stages as RB183 Mk 555. Mk 650, advanced technology two-stage design.
LP TURBINE: New design with three stages.
MIXER: Forced deep chute type with 12 lobes.
DIMENSIONS:
Length 2,405 mm (94·7 in)
Inlet diameter 1,118 mm (44 in)
PERFORMANCE RATING (T-O):
Tay 610-8 55·24 kN (12,420 lb st) to 37°C
Tay 620-15 59·24 kN (13,320 lb st) to 28°C
SPECIFIC FUEL CONSUMPTION:
Both versions, cruise Mach 0·8 at 9,145 m (30,000 ft) 20·1 mg/Ns (0·71 lb/h/lb)

ROLLS-ROYCE TYNE

The 4,570 ekW (6,100 ehp) Tyne 22 two-shaft turboprop was put back into production for the additional Transall C-160 aircraft being built by Aérospatiale/MBB. Like engines for previous Transall aircraft they are made by a consortium comprising Rolls-Royce, SNECMA, MTU and FN. Further engines will be ordered for the Dassault-Breguet Atlantique.

Limited production has been undertaken of the Tyne 20 Mk 801, derated to 4,090 ekW (5,480 ehp) for the Libyan Arab Air Force export version of the Aeritalia G222. Substantially uprated Tynes are projected in future propeller studies.

ROLLS-ROYCE DART

Beginning life in 1945 at 738 kW (990 ehp), this turboprop was developed to give 2,420 ekW (3,245 ehp) in military and 2,256 ekW (3,025 ehp) in civil versions. Current production of new engines is centred on the less powerful **Mk 536-2** for the BAe 748 and **Mk 536-7R** for the Fokker F27. About 7,100 Dart engines have been delivered, flying 108 million hours.

In May 1982 Rolls-Royce announced the Dart **Mk 551** with improved LP and HP compressors and turbine. The Mk 551 has a T-O rating of 1,738 ekW (2,330 ehp) and saves up to 8 per cent in fuel. The Mk 551 ran in November 1982 and was certificated in March 1984. In early 1984 testing began on the **Mk 552**, with the same rating but further improvements saving another 3 per cent in fuel. New Mk 552 engines and kits for modifying RDa.7 engines were available from mid-1985, full CAA certification having been received on 6 June. At that time more than 200 field conversion kits had been ordered. The following description refers to the Mk 536:

TYPE: Single-shaft centrifugal flow turboprop.
REDUCTION GEAR: Double helical high speed train and final helical drive. Ratio in current engines: 0·093.
AIR INTAKE: Circular intake with annular duct leading to impeller eye of first-stage compressor. Oil tank cast integral with casing. Secondary air intake supplies air to oil cooler.
COMPRESSOR: Two-stage centrifugal. Each impeller has nineteen vanes and steel rotating guide vanes. Mass air flow at maximum rpm typically 10·66 kg (23·5 lb)/s at 5·62 : 1 pressure ratio.
COMBUSTION CHAMBERS: Seven inclined flame tubes with atomisers for downstream injection. High energy igniter plugs in Nos. 3 and 7 chambers.
FUEL SYSTEM: Variable stroke pump delivers fuel to burners through flow control unit, which incorporates a filter, throttle valve, shut-off cock and barometric pressure control. Automatically progressive injection of water/methanol to maintain take-off power under high ambient temperature. System linked with throttle lever to prohibit use except at take-off rpm. Fuel filter de-icing by hot air from compressor.
TURBINE: Three-stage axial.
EXHAUST UNIT: Inclined to suit installation.
ACCESSORY DRIVES: Gearbox drive from main shaft centre coupling immediately behind compressor.
LUBRICATION: Integral oil tank (14 litres: 25 Imp pints) feeds via standpipe and feathering pump through tank base, to ensure feathering possible even after prolonged system oil leak. Gear pump supplies oil to all bearings and reduction gear jets.
CONTROLS: Throttle interconnected with propeller controller, and high pressure cock linked with feathering controls. Propeller feathered by moving shut-off cock past closed position.
MOUNTING: Four feet at 90° on compressor casing, although only three need be used.
DIMENSIONS:
Length (no jetpipe) 2,480 mm (97·64 in)
Diameter 963 mm (37·9 in)
WEIGHT, DRY: basic 569 kg (1,257 lb)
PERFORMANCE RATINGS:
T-O: dry 1,551 kW (2,080 shp);
wet 1,700 ekW (2,280 ehp) at 15,000 rpm
Recommended cruise (250 knots; 463 km/h; 288 mph; at 6,100 m; 20,000 ft) 910 kW (1,220 shp)

ROLLS-ROYCE VIPER

This turbojet remains in production for civil and military customers. More than 5,000 Vipers are currently in operation in 29 countries in trainer and light attack aircraft.

Current versions are as follows:

Viper 11 (Mk 200 Series). Single-shaft seven-stage axial flow compressor driven by single-stage turbine. Air mass flow 20 kg (44 lb)/s. Type tested at 11·12 kN (2,500 lb st) and powers Jindivik Mk 3 drone, BAC Jet Provost T.4 and 5, Yugoslav SOKO Galeb and Hindustan HJT-16 Kiran Mk I/IA trainers.

A Viper 11 version, the 22-1, was built under licence in Italy by Piaggio for the Aermacchi MB-326 trainer and by Atlas of South Africa and Commonwealth Aircraft of Australia for local versions of that aircraft.

Viper 500 Series. Development with increased airflow, achieved by zero stage on compressor. Major applications include early HS 125 (Mks 521, 522) and PD-808 executive aircraft (Mk 526) and BAC Strikemaster (Mk 535), Aermacchi MB-326GB (Mk 540) and SOKO Jastreb (Mk 531) training and light combat aircraft. Mk 540 built under licence by Piaggio and Atlas.

Viper 600 Series. Eight-stage axial flow compressor driven by two-stage turbine; annular vaporising combustion chamber. Take-off rating 16·7 kN (3,750 lb st) civil and 17·8 kN (4,000 lb st) military. Agreement signed with Fiat (Italy) in July 1969 for technical collaboration in design, development and production (see Fiat entry).

The civil Viper 601 powers the BAe 125-600; the military Viper 632 is fitted to the SOKO G-4 Super Galeb, Aermacchi MB-326K and MB-339. A version designated 632-41 powers the Orao/IAR-93A and IAR-99. The Viper 632 is now built under licence in Italy, Romania and Yugoslavia. The Viper 633 has an afterburner of the two-gutter type, with hot streak ignition and closed loop nozzle control. Thrust with maximum augmentation is 22·3 kN (5,000 lb).

The **Viper 680** is being developed for military applications. It will produce up to 14·4 per cent more thrust than the Viper 632.

The following details apply to the Viper 600 series:

TYPE: Single-shaft axial turbojet.
AIR INTAKE: Direct pitot. Anti-icing by hot compressor air. No inlet guide vanes.

The 1,700 ekW (2,280 ehp) Rolls-Royce Dart 536 single-shaft turboprop

COMPRESSOR: Eight-stage. Steel drum type rotor with disc assemblies. Magnesium alloy casing with blow-off valve. Stator blades mounted in carrier rings slotted into casing. All stator blades and 0, 1 and 7 stage rotor blades of steel; remainder aluminium alloy. Zero-stage and first-stage rotor blades attached by fir tree roots; stages 2-7 riveted. Pressure ratio 5·8 : 1. Air mass flow 26·5 kg (58·4 lb)/s.

COMBUSTION CHAMBER: Short annular type with 24 vaporising burners and six starting atomisers. Electric ignition.

FUEL SYSTEM: Hydromechanical, consisting primarily of fuel pump, barometric fuel control and air/fuel ratio control.

FUEL GRADE: JP-1 or JP-4.

TURBINE: Two-stage axial. Shrouded blades attached to discs by fir tree roots and locking strips. Discs attached by Hirth couplings.

BEARINGS: Ball thrust type at forward end of compressor, roller bearings at centre section and at rear end of combustion chamber inner casing.

JETPIPE: Cone of heat resisting steel rings butt welded together. (Viper 601: eight-lobe convoluted nozzle to meet FAR Pt 36 noise requirements).

ACCESSORY DRIVES: Gearbox driven from front of compressor by bevel gear.

LUBRICATION SYSTEM: Self contained. Recirculatory system supplying front bearing and gearbox, metered feed supplied to centre and rear bearings by micropumps. Military version fully aerobatic.

OIL SPECIFICATION: Mobil Jet 2, Shell ASTO 500 and Castrol 98.

MOUNTING: Civil: cantilevered, side mounted, single spherical bearing in centre-section casing, with top and bottom links and attachment at intake casing. Military: trunnion mounted at centre-section with additional support at intake casing.

STARTING: 24V starter/generator.

DIMENSIONS:

Length (flange to flange):	
Viper 11	1,626 mm (64·0 in)
Viper 531, 535, 540, 632	1,806 mm (71·1 in)
Max casing diameter:	
all versions	622 mm (24·5 in)

WEIGHT, DRY:

Viper 11	284 kg (625 lb)
Viper 531	345 kg (760 lb)
Viper 535	331 kg (730 lb)
Viper 540	342 kg (755 lb)
Viper 601, 632 and 680	358 kg (790 lb)

PERFORMANCE RATINGS (T-O):

Viper 11	11·12 kN (2,500 lb st)
Viper 531	13·9 kN (3,120 lb st)
Viper 535, 540	14·9 kN (3,360 lb st)
Viper 601	16·7 kN (3,750 lb st)
Viper 632	17·8 kN (4,000 lb st)
Viper 680	19·8 kN (4,450 lb st)

SPECIFIC FUEL CONSUMPTION (T-O):

Viper 11	30·3 mg/Ns (1·07 lb/h/lb st)
Viper 500 series	28·3 mg/Ns (1·00 lb/h/lb st)
Viper 601	26·6 mg/Ns (0·94 lb/h/lb st)
Viper 632	27·5 mg/Ns (0·97 lb/h/lb st)

OIL CONSUMPTION (max):

all versions	0·71 litres (1·25 Imp pints)/h

ROLLS-ROYCE XG-40

The XG-40 is a technology demonstrator engine, centred at Rolls-Royce Bristol and funded jointly by the company and the British Ministry of Defence. Its purpose is to support the development of the EJ200 for the production Eurofighter (EFA), which is expected to be based fairly closely upon the XG-40 though the existing engine is in no sense a prototype. The production engine is expected to be manufactured by a four-nation consortium, as outlined

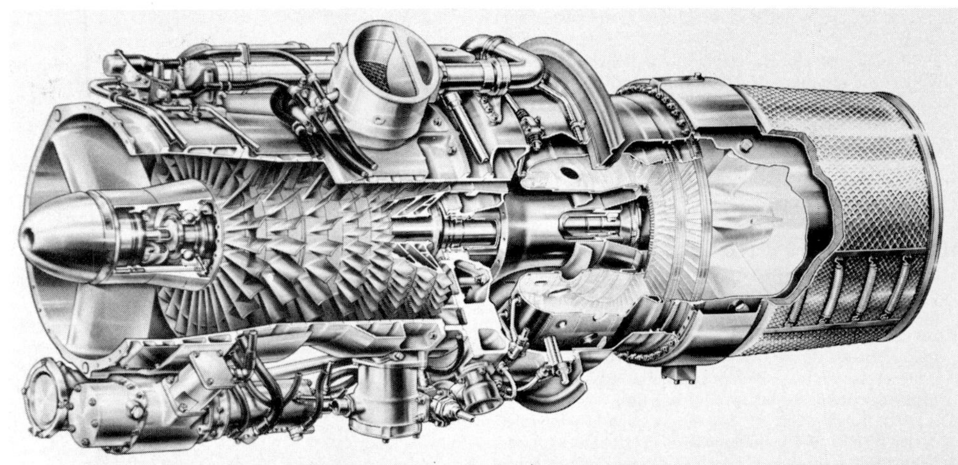

Cutaway drawing of the Rolls-Royce Viper 632 single-shaft turbojet (take-off rating 17·8 kN; 4,000 lb st)

Preparing the first XG-40 core for test at Rolls-Royce Military Engine Group at Bristol

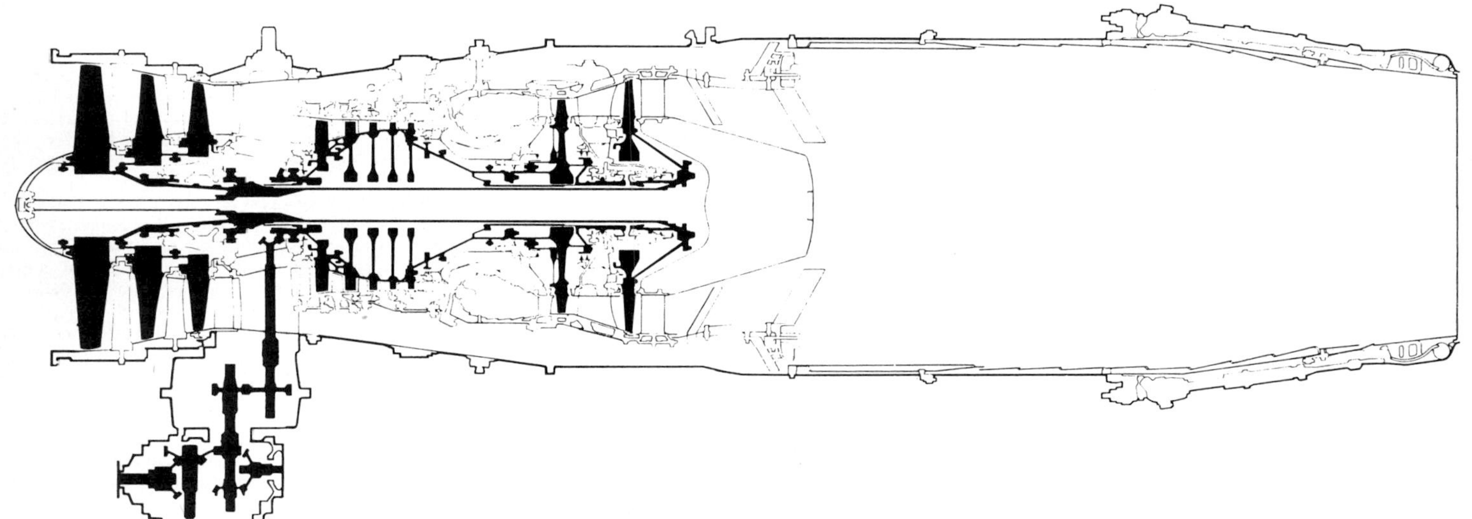

Longitudinal section drawing through the Rolls-Royce XG-40 engine

under the Eurojet heading in the International part of this section.

Following extensive rig testing of components, the XG-40 core began very successful testing at Bristol in April 1986. A complete XG-40 demonstrator engine was to go on test in October 1986, with a second engine following in early 1987.

TYPE: Two-shaft augmented turbofan.

INLET: Direct pitot type with no inlet guide vanes.

FAN: Three stages carried on front of LP shaft. No variable geometry, and progressively reduced outer diameter. Rotating spinner.

HP COMPRESSOR: Five stages; first two fitted with variable stators. Technology derived from ACME (advanced core military engine), with advanced aerodynamic blading and tip clearance control.

COMBUSTION CHAMBER: High-intensity annular, with technology based on ACET (advanced core engine technology) programme which proved ceramic coatings, new forms of cooling and thermal protection.

TURBINES: Single-stage HP and single-stage LP. Features drawn from ACET include shroudless HP blades formed from low-density single-crystal material, high-strength disc materials and new sealing techniques.

AFTERBURNER: High augmentation, with technology based on XG-20 and RB199.

DIMENSIONS: to be smaller than RB199

WEIGHT, DRY: in 900 kg (1,980 lb) class

PERFORMANCE RATING:

Max afterburning 90 kN (20,234 lb st) class

Cutaway drawing of the Rolls-Royce Gem 60 free turbine turboshaft

ROLLS-ROYCE PEGASUS

The Pegasus is a turbofan for V/STOL applications. It has two main rotating systems which are mechanically independent and rotate in opposite directions, thus minimising gyroscopic effects. It has a three-stage axial-flow fan of transonic design and an eight-stage high-pressure compressor, each driven by a two-stage turbine. Thrust vectoring is achieved by four rotatable nozzles simultaneously operated and symmetrically positioned on each side of the engine. The front nozzles discharge by-pass air, whilst the rear nozzles discharge the turbine efflux. The total thrust is divided between the four nozzles, and the resultant thrust passes through a fixed point irrespective of nozzle angle, thus minimising aircraft control problems. HP bleed air is used for aircraft stabilisation. The Pegasus was the first engine designed with an overhung fan, without inlet guide vanes or anti-icing.

The Pegasus ran in August 1959, and flight trials in the Hawker Siddeley P.1127 prototypes began in October 1960. The **Pegasus 3**, which powered prototype P.1127 aircraft, was rated at 60 kN (13,500 lb st). The engine entered service in the BAe Harrier with the RAF in 1969 and later with the AV-8A of the USMC and Matador of the Spanish Navy. These aircraft have the **Pegasus 11 Mk 103**, (US designation **F402-RR-402**), rated at 95·64 kN (21,500 lb st).

A maritime version of the Mk 103 is designated **Mk 104**. Developed for the Sea Harrier, it embodies material changes to the LP and intermediate casings, sacrificial protective coatings on ferrous components, and an increased capacity gearbox. The Sea Harrier entered service with the Royal Navy in June 1979 and with the Indian Navy in January 1983.

The **Pegasus 11-21** developed for the McDonnell Douglas/BAe Harrier II has the US designation **F402-RR-406** and UK designation **Mk 105**; it includes improved HP turbine cooling, a new shrouded LP turbine, revised swanneck intermediate casing and revisions to suit the new airframe. A FADEC digital control is available to replace the hydromechanical system. US engines with digital control are designated **F402-RR-406A**; all UK Mk 105 full production will have this control. Delivery of pilot production AV-8Bs to the Marine Corps began in October 1983, production aircraft with 95·64 kN (21,500 lb st) Dash-406 engines following in mid-1984. Delivery of 96·75 kN (21,750 lb st) development batch Mk 105 engines began in December 1984.

Further development of this V/STOL engine is planned which could, by increments, bring thrust up to the 111·2 kN (25,000 lb) class. This will be achieved with no increase in engine size and will enhance significantly the operational capabilities of the Harrier II, as well as being applicable to existing aircraft. Under an MoD funded programme, a demonstrator engine (with 15 per cent lift rating improvement) was run in mid-1986. This engine incorporates single crystal HP turbine blades and a new, higher pressure ratio (2·6) LP fan.

Work is continuing on a thrust augmentation system known as plenum chamber burning (PCB). Bench testing has demonstrated a thrust increase at the front nozzles of over 100 per cent, equivalent to about 50 per cent overall thrust boost. High altitude PCB tests have indicated that handling and ignition characteristics are compatible with expected flight envelopes for future supersonic V/STOL aircraft. A Pegasus 11 with PCB would have a thrust of 120 kN (27,000 lb st). British Aerospace and McDonnell Douglas are studying demonstrator aircraft configured around this engine.

Testing of a Pegasus/PCB installation in a Harrier airframe began in mid-1983. The Harrier is suspended from a gantry and the tests are investigating gas flow when in ground effect. Current PCB technology programmes will establish standards for production systems.

The following data apply specifically to the Pegasus 11-21 (-406A, Mk 105):

TYPE: Two-shaft vectored thrust turbofan.

AIR INTAKE CASING: One-piece casting in aluminium alloy.

FAN: Three-stage axial, overhung ahead of front bearing. Titanium blades with part-span snubbers. Maximum airflow 196 kg (432 lb)/s. Pressure ratio 2·3 : 1. Bypass ratio 1·4 : 1.

INTERMEDIATE CASING: Houses front fan bearing, accessory drives and HP compressor front bearing. All engine driven accessories mounted above this casing.

HP COMPRESSOR: Eight-stage with titanium rotor blades. Overall pressure ratio 14 : 1.

COMBUSTION SYSTEM: Annular, with low pressure vaporising burner system.

FUEL SYSTEM: DSIC duplicated digital electronic control system with emergency hydromechanical manual backup.

TURBINES: Two-stage HP turbine and two-stage LP turbine. First-stage HP blades and both LP stage blades cast, second HP forged. Both HP stages aircooled.

THRUST NOZZLES: Two steel zero-scarf cold nozzles and two Nimonic hot nozzles, actuated by duplicated air motors through shafts and chains. Vectored thrust control by pilot command lever.

LUBRICATION SYSTEM: Self contained, comprising pressure pump and three scavenge pumps, with fuel cooled oil cooler.

MOUNTING: Four-point suspension, with main trunnions on each side of delivery casing and tie link at rear of turbines.

STARTING: Gas turbine starter/APU on intermediate casing.

DIMENSIONS:

Length, without nozzles	2,510 mm (98·83 in)
Length, with nozzles	3,485 mm (137·2 in)
Diameter, fan casing	1,220 mm (48·05 in)

WEIGHT, DRY (without nozzles):

Mk 103	1,412 kg (3,113 lb)
Mk 104	1,442 kg (3,179 lb)
Mk 105	1,470 kg (3,240 lb)

PERFORMANCE RATINGS:

See under subtype descriptions

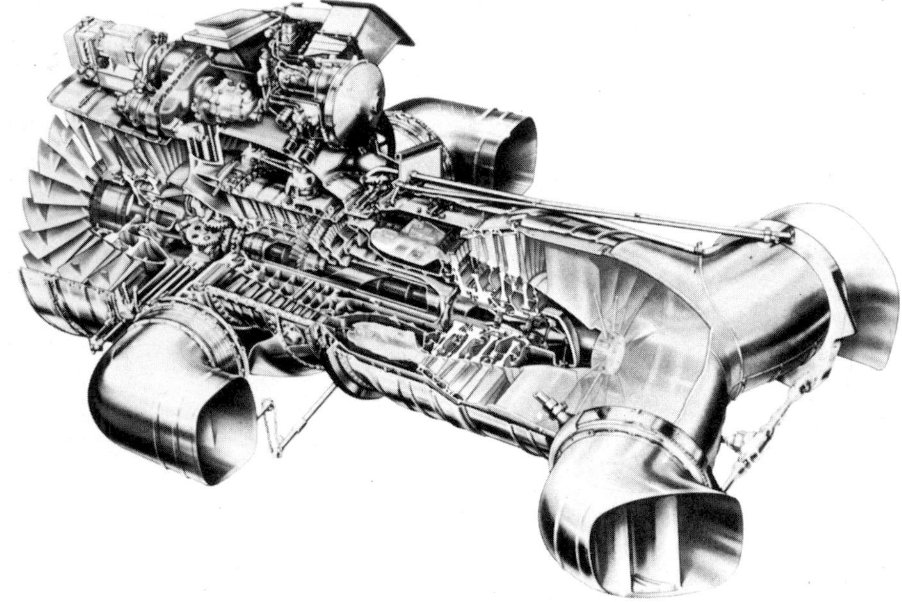

Cutaway drawing of the Rolls-Royce Pegasus 11-21 (F402-RR-406A, Mk 105) turbofan (96·75 kN; 21,750 lb st)

ROLLS-ROYCE TURBOMÉCA RTM 322

This turboshaft engine is described in the International part of this section.

ROLLS-ROYCE GEM

The Gem was designed and developed at Leavesden, for the Westland Lynx helicopter. Subsequent applications are the Westland 30, Westland Lynx 3 and Agusta A 129 helicopters, and the Gem 41 and 60 series have been civil certificated. More than 1,050 engines had been ordered by early 1985.

Choice of a two-spool gas generator gives fast response to power demand without the need for a complex control system. Conservative stressing and thermodynamic loading, and use of proven design and manufacturing techniques, are features which experience has shown to contribute to engine reliability.

The design concept of the engine is based upon seven major modules, each capable of being assembled, tested and released as an interchangeable unit for service use in the interest of reducing the operator's product support commitments.

The nine main bearings each have labyrinth seals pressurised by LP compressor air which also cools the bearings and minimises heat transfer to the oil, and oil cooler and fan requirements.

Provision is made for in-flight and on-ground condition monitoring systems. Features include access ports for intrascope inspection of each LP compressor stage, HP compressor, combustor, LP turbine and power turbine, and mountings for vibration pickups.

The following versions have been announced:

Gem Mk 1001. Engine change unit for Lynx of British services and French Navy. Rated at 671 kW (900 shp). Entered service in 1976.

Gem 2. Export military engine, rated at 671 kW (900 shp).

Gem 2 Mk 1004. Version of Gem 2 being developed for Agusta A 129. Direct drive module in place of reduction gearbox module, and electronic fuel control instead of hydromechanical system. Initial max contingency rating of 682 kW (915 shp). Production under licence by Piaggio.

Gem 41 series. Based on Gem 2, with modified compressor to increase mass flow by about 10 per cent plus small increase in TET to give maximum contingency rating of 835 kW (1,120 shp). In production for Lynx and Westland 30. In service with Royal Netherlands Navy.

Gem Mk 1020. Engine change unit of Gem 41 for uprated Lynx of British and French Navies.

Gem 42 series. Same ratings as Gem 41, but with features to improve reliability and power retention. Conversion of Gem 2 and 41 engines in UK fleet by modification action began 1986.

Gem Mk 510. Civil version of Gem 41 for commercial Westland 30. In service with British and US operators.

Gem 60 series. Further uprating of Gem to 940 kW (1,260 shp), by further increase in mass flow of approximately 26 per cent over Gem 41, derived from new-technology LP compressor incorporating new blades to achieve high work per stage. TET also increased.

Gem Mk 531. Civil Gem 60 for Westland 30. Certificated and delivered from 1983.

The following description relates to the Gem Mk 1001, except where otherwise indicated:

Type: Free turbine turboshaft, with two-spool gas generator.

Air Intake: Annular forward facing.

Shaft Drive: Compact single-stage double-helical reduction gear with rotating planet cage carried by ball bearing at front and roller bearing at rear. Reduction gear mounted within intake casing and driven by power turbine shaft. Gearbox comprises No. 1 module, and power turbine shaft No. 2 module. Alternative of direct drive output at 27,000 rpm or gearbox giving governed output speed of 6,000 rpm. No. 2 module provides for signal to phase displacement torquemeter.

LP Compressor: Four-stage axial. LP compressor and intake case comprise No. 3 module.

HP Compressor: Single-stage centrifugal impeller having alternate inducer and radial vanes. Combined radial and axial diffuser feeds compressor delivery air to annular combustor. Overall pressure ratio 12·0 : 1.

Combustion Chamber: Fully annular reverse flow with air atomiser fuel sprays supplied by external fuel manifold. High energy ignition box mounted on power turbine/jet pipe case.

HP Turbine: Single-stage axial close-coupled to HP impeller. Rotor blades and aircooled nozzle guide vanes based on R-R Dart technology. HP spool with compressor intermediate casing and combustor comprise No. 4 module.

LP Turbine: Single-stage axial with shrouded rotor blades, drives LP compressor. LP turbine and main shaft comprise No. 6 module.

Power Turbine: Two-stage axial with shrouded rotor blades. Rear of power drive shaft drives output speed governor and overspeed fuel cut-off trip mechanism via spur and bevel gear train in exhaust cone. Power turbine and jetpipe form No. 7 module.

Jetpipe: Short-length duct with casing extending forward to combustor rear casing. Four cruciform struts integral with exhaust cone.

Accessory Drives: Bevel gear on front of HP compressor shaft drives accessory shaft extending through compressor intermediate casing to spiral bevel gear drive to accessory wheelcase mounted atop intermediate casing. Drives provided for starter/generator, fuel pump, oil cooler fan and other accessories. Wheelcase forms No. 5 module.

Fuel System: Plessey fuel system with fluidics circuit providing fully automatic control, and power matching for multi-engine installation. Also automatic restoration of power from 'good' engine in event of single engine failure. Incorporates fuel filter. Alternative Hamilton Standard digital electronic control fitted to Gem 1004 and Gem 60.

Lubrication System: Engine mounted oil tank and cooler to provide self contained system. Magnetic chip detectors fitted in each scavenge line. Oil filter incorporated in accessory wheelcase.

Dimensions:

Length overall	1,099 mm (43·2 in)
Width overall	575 mm (22·6 in)
Height overall	596 mm (23·5 in)

Weight, Dry:

Gem 1001, 2	150 kg (330 lb)
Gem 41, 42	156 kg (343 lb)
Gem 2 Mk 1004	140 kg (309 lb)
Gem 60	155 kg (342 lb)

Performance Ratings: see table

Specific Fuel Consumption:

50 per cent max T-O:

Except Gem 60	110 μg/J (0·65 lb/h/shp)
Gem 60	103 μg/J (0·61 lb/h/shp)

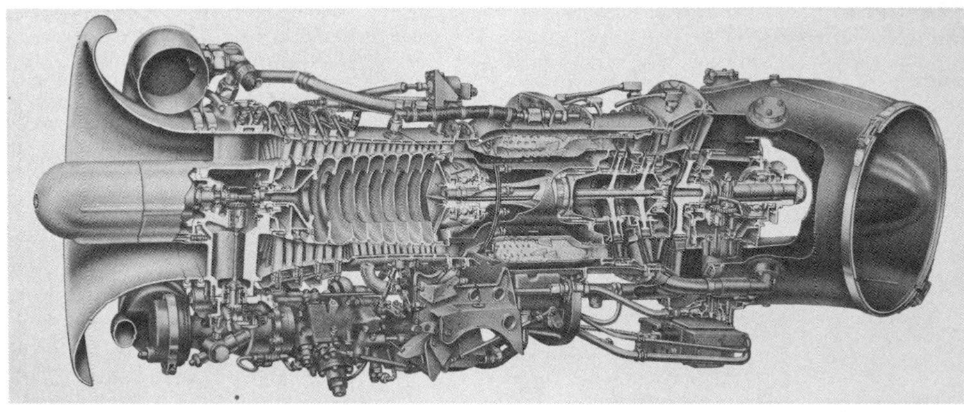

Cutaway drawing of the Rolls-Royce Gnome H.1400-1 free turbine turboshaft

ROLLS-ROYCE GNOME

Gnome is the name given to the versions of the General Electric T58 turboshaft which Rolls-Royce manufactures in the UK. The first ran on 5 June 1959.

More than 2,200 Gnome engines have been delivered to 20 operators in the following versions:

H.1000. Initial version, rated at 783 kW (1,050 shp). Power plant for military and civil versions of the Whirlwind and Agusta-Bell 204B.

H.1200. Rated at 932 kW (1,250 shp). Used in Agusta-Bell 204B, Boeing Vertol 107 and some Kawasaki KV107-II-5s. Coupled version for Wessex comprises two H.1200s driving through a coupling gearbox.

H.1400. Rated at 1,044 kW (1,400 shp). Based on the H.1200, with modified compressor to increase airflow.

H.1400-1. Rated at 1,145 kW (1,535 shp). Uprated from H.1400, without change in size or weight, by increasing gas generator speed and using improved gas generator turbine blade material. In production for current Westland Sea King and Commando.

H.1400-1T. Tropical model; turbine nozzle adjusted for better high ambient performance.

The following description refers to the H.1400-1:

Type: Axial-flow free turbine turboshaft engine.

Air Intake: Annular forward-facing. Centre housing carrying front main bearing supported by four radial struts. Struts and inlet guide vanes anti-iced with hot compressor bleed air and oil drainage.

Compressor: Ten-stage axial. Controlled variable incidence for inlet guide vanes and first three rows of stator blades. Air mass flow 6·26 kg (13·8 lb)/s.

Combustion System: Straight through annular chamber with outer casing split along horizontal centreline. Sixteen Simplex type fuel injectors, eight on each of two sets of manifolds. One Lodge capacitor discharge high energy igniter plug.

Fuel System: Lucas hydromechanical units, comprising variable stroke multi-plunger pump, flow control unit and throttle controlled by BAeD computer.

Fuel Grade: DERD.2452, 2453, 2454, 2486, 2494 and 2498 (NATO F44, F34, F40, F35 and F43).

Gas-Producer Turbine: Two-stage, coupled to compressor shaft by conical shaft. Extended root blading with fir tree attachments.

Power Turbine: Single-stage free turbine. Extended root blading with fir tree attachments.

Exhaust System: Curved exhaust ducting arranged to suit individual applications.

Reduction Gear: Optional double helical gear providing reduction from nominal 19,500 rpm power turbine speed to 6,600 rpm at left or right output shaft.

Accessory Drives: Quill shaft drive through lower intake strut. Fuel and lubrication systems mounted beneath compressor casing. Power take-off shaft up to 100 shp.

Lubrication: Scavenged gear pumps. Serck oil cooler.

Mounting: Three mounting faces on intake casing. Rear mounts on gearbox or output housing.

Starting: Rotax electric starter in nose bullet.

Dimensions:

Length:	
H.1000, H.1200, H.1400-1	1,392 mm (54·8 in)
Coupled H.1200 (Wessex)	1,747 mm (68·8 in)
Max height:	
H.1000, H.1200, H.1400-1	549 mm (21·6 in)
Coupled H.1200 (Wessex)	1,031 mm (40·6 in)
Max width:	
H.1000, H.1200 (ungeared)	462 mm (18·2 in)
H.1400-1 (ungeared)	577 mm (22·7 in)
Coupled H.1200 (Wessex)	1,059 mm (41·7 in)

Weight, Dry:

H.1000 (ungeared)	134 kg (296 lb)
H.1200 (ungeared)	142 kg (314 lb)
H.1400-1 (ungeared)	148 kg (326 lb)
Reduction gearbox	52·6 kg (116 lb)
Coupled H.1200	422 kg (930 lb)

Performance Ratings (at power turbine shaft):

Max contingency (2½ min; multi-engine aircraft only):	
H.1200	1,007 kW (1,350 shp)
H.1400-1	1,238 kW (1,660 shp)
H.1400-1T	1,092 kW (1,465 shp) to 45°C
Max one-hour (single engine):	
H.1000	783 kW (1,050 shp)
H.1200	932 kW (1,250 shp)
H.1400-1	1,145 kW (1,535 shp)
H.1400-1T	1,030 kW (1,380 shp) to 45°C
Max continuous:	
H.1000	671 kW (900 shp)
H.1200	783 kW (1,050 shp)
H.1400-1	932 kW (1,250 shp)
H.1400-1T	783 kW (1,050 shp) to 45°C

Specific Fuel Consumption:

At max contingency rating:

H.1200	104·4 μg/J (0·618 lb/h/shp)
H.1400-1	102·75 μg/J (0·608 lb/h/shp)
H.1400-1T (30°C)	105·8 μg/J (0·626 lb/h/shp)

GEM ENGINE RATINGS, kW (shp) ISA S/L STATIC

Designation	Date In Service	One Engine Inoperative: Emergency (20 s)	Max Contingency (2½ min)	Intermediate Contingency (60 min)	Max (T-O) (30 min)	Normal Twin Operation: Max (T-O) (5 min)	Max Continuous
Gem 2, Mk 1001	1976	N/A	671 (900)	619 (830)	N/A	619 (830)	559 (750)
Gem 2, Mk 1004	1976	772 (1,035)	710 (952)	667·5 (895)	667·5 (895)	N/A	608 (815)
Gem 41-1, Mk 1014	1978	N/A	835 (1,120)	790·5 (1,060)	N/A	746 (1,000)	664 (890)
Gem 42, Mk 1017	1987	N/A	835 (1,120)	790·5 (1,060)	N/A	746 (1,000)	664 (890)
Gem 60-3/1 Mk 530	1983	N/A	897 (1,203)	844 (1,132)	N/A	844 (1,132)	821·75 (1,102)
Gem 60-3/3 Mk 531	1983	N/A	897 (1,203)	844 (1,132)	N/A	821·75 (1,102)	821·75 (1,102)

N/A: Not applicable

TTL
TARGET TECHNOLOGY LTD

Unit 3, Brunswick Industrial Centre, Ashford, Kent TN24 9QP
Telephone: 0233 39764

Piper, described on an earlier page, and TTL operate two factories whose ties are not rigid. This particular engine has been produced at the TTL location.

TTL T-70

Currently being used in three separate RPV programmes, the T-70 is a single-cylinder aircooled two-stroke designed for this application. It has spark ignition and runs on a petrol/oil mix. Rated at 4·5 kW (6 hp) at 7,200 rpm, it weighs 3·2 kg (7 lb) complete with carburettor and propeller. An alternator can be fitted to give 130W at 28V at a cruising speed of 4,500 rpm. Total weight of engine, alternator, spinner and mounting plate is 4·3 kg (9·5 lb).

The TTL T-70 RPV engine, with alternator

UNITED STATES OF AMERICA

AEROJET
AEROJET-GENERAL CORPORATION
(Subsidiary of General Corporation)

10300 N Torrey Pines Road, La Jolla, California 92037
Telephone: (714) 455 8500

CHAIRMAN OF THE BOARD: J. L. Heckel
PRESIDENT: G. W. Leisz
GROUP VICE-PRESIDENT: R. W. Warden
VICE-PRESIDENT, PUBLIC AFFAIRS: Tom Sprague

Aerojet TechSystems Company
PRESIDENT: Roger I. Ramseier
Aerojet Strategic Propulsion Company
PRESIDENT: K. R. Collins
Aerojet Tactical Systems Company
PRESIDENT: C. R. Sebastian

Aerojet-General Corporation has activities in four major areas of business: chemicals, electronics, engineering and mechanical systems, and metal products.

In the chemical area, two organisations produce solid propellant rocket motors for the Department of Defense. The Aerojet Strategic Propulsion Company (see 1984-85 *Jane's*) designs, develops and produces solid propulsion strategic ballistic missile rocket motors; Aerojet Tactical Systems produces a variety of tactical missile motors.

In the mechanical systems area, Aerojet TechSystems Company (formerly known as Aerojet Liquid Rocket Company) is active in research, development, testing and production of liquid propellant rocket engines, waterjet propulsors and lift fan systems for surface effect ships.

AEROJET TECHSYSTEMS CO

Sacramento, California: Development and manufacture of all liquid fuel engines for the US Air Force's Titan family of vehicles; second stage propulsion for the Japanese Space Agency (NASDA) N-II launch vehicles; and Orbiter Manoeuvring System (OMS) engines for the Space Shuttle.

AEROJET SPACE SHUTTLE OMS ENGINE

The Space Shuttle Orbiter has two Orbiter Manoeuvring System (OMS) engines, in pods each side of the vertical stabiliser (fin). The OMS engine, produced by TechSystems, provides thrust for orbit insertion, circularisation and plane change, rendezvous and de-orbit manoeuvres. The propellants are monomethylhydrazine (MMH) and nitrogen tetroxide. At launch the basic system carries 4,087 kg (9,010 lb) of usable MMH and 6,743 kg (14,866 lb) of usable oxidiser. Fully qualified OMS engines have flown on all Shuttle missions to date. The following are chief characteristics:

THRUST (in vacuo):	26·7 kN (6,000 lb)
CHAMBER PRESSURE (in vacuo):	8·62 bars (125 lb/sq in)
SPECIFIC IMPULSE:	316 s
MIXTURE RATIO:	1·65 : 1
NOZZLE AREA RATIO (flight):	55 : 1
WEIGHT, DRY:	118 kg (260 lb)
THRUST VECTOR LIMITS:	± 7°
STORAGE LIFE:	10 years
FIRING LIFE (100 missions):	15 h
NUMBER OF STARTS:	500
LONGEST SINGLE FIRING:	1,250 s

Aerojet Space Shuttle OMS engine

AEROJET TACTICAL SYSTEMS CO (ATSC)

Development and production of motors for Improved Hawk, Sparrow, Sky Flash, Standard Missile, Sidewinder, Shrike, Improved Shrike and Skipper, and booster for Harpoon. Data for many spacecraft motors and other rocket products were given in the 1981-82 *Jane's*.

AEROJET MAVERICK MOTOR

The Aerojet Maverick rocket motor, Type SR115-AJ-1, utilises a reduced smoke HTPB propellant system and is completely interchangeable in all Maverick missile systems. The primary use will be in improved systems following the AGM-65B configuration. Aerojet has completed qualification of this boost/sustain motor.

AEROJET SIDEWINDER MOTOR

Aerojet qualified a rocket motor in 1979 for use on the AIM-9B/E/J/N/P air-to-air missile systems. The motor utilises a reduced smoke HTPB propellant. Production is in progress for US and export customers.

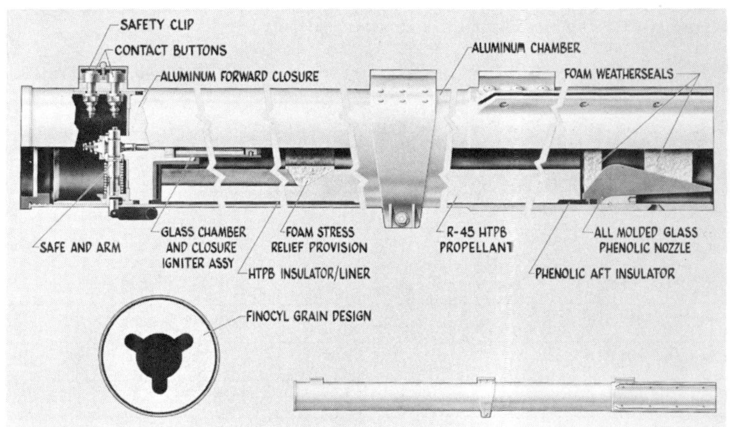

Cross-section of ATSC motor used in advanced models of Sidewinder

AEROJET SPARROW/SHRIKE/SKIPPER MOTORS

The Mk 52 and Mk 53 motors are the 'all boost' thrust units for the Sparrow AIM-7E and Shrike AGM-45A missiles. They are similar in construction and dimensions. The principal difference lies in the performance characteristics, which are tailored to match the air-to-air and air-to-ground missions. Several thousand have been produced to meet US Navy and Air Force requirements. The Mk 78 dual thrust motor greatly enhances the performance of the AGM-45B Improved Shrike. Mk 52 motors are supplied for the BAe Sky Flash. The Skipper motor is a modified Improved Shrike motor on which production was initiated in 1984.

AEROJET TACTICAL SYSTEMS COMPANY MOTORS*

Name	Designation	Fuel	Oxidiser	Max length m (in)	Max dia m (in)	Total weight kg (lb)	Remarks/Primary Application
Tactical Motors							
Phoenix	Mk 60 Mod 0	Polybutadiene	NH_4ClO_4	1·78 (70)	0·38 (15)	199 (439)	Propulsion for Navy's fleet defence air-to-air missile.
Sparrow III, AIM-7E	Mk 52 Mod 2	Polybutadiene	NH_4ClO_4	1·32 (52)	0·2 (8)	68·5 (151)	Propulsion for Navy's Sparrow air-to-air missile.
Sky Flash	Mk 52 Mod 3	Polybutadiene	NH_4ClO_4	1·32 (52)	0·2 (8)	68·5 (151)	Propulsion for BAe Sky Flash air-to-air missile.
Shrike	Mk 53 Mod 2	Polybutadiene	NH_4ClO_4	1·32 (52)	0·2 (8)	71 (157)	Propulsion for Navy's AGM-45 anti-radiation air-to-surface missile.
Shrike, Improved	Mk 78 Mod 0	Polyurethane	NH_4ClO_4	1·30 (51)	0·2 (8)	78 (172)	Dual thrust propulsion for anti-radiation air-to-surface missile.
Skipper	WPU-5B	Polyurethane	NH_4ClO_4	1·30 (51)	0·2 (8)	78 (172)	Dual thrust propulsion for Navy air-to-surface missile.
2·75 in FFAR, Improved	SR105-AJ-1	Polybutadiene	NH_4ClO_4	0·34 (33)	0·07 (2·75)	5·9 (13)	Air-launched forward-firing.
Sidewinder	SR116-AJ-2	HTPB	NH_4ClO_4	1·91 (75)	0·127 (5)	40·4 (89)	Propulsion for AIM-9J/9P Sidewinder air-to-air missiles.
Maverick	SR115-AJ-1	HTPB	NH_4ClO_4	1·00 (39·5)	0·28 (11)	48·4 (107)	Propulsion for AGM-65 Maverick missile.

*For non-military motors and other ATSC products see 1981-82 and 1984-85 *Jane's*.

ALLISON

ALLISON GAS TURBINE DIVISION, GENERAL MOTORS CORPORATION

Indianapolis, Indiana 46206-0420
Telephone: (317) 242 5000
General Manager: Dr F. Blake Wallace
Director, Gas Turbine Research & Engineering: S. M. Hudson
Director, Gas Turbine Sales: William C. Campbell

Allison Gas Turbine Division has extensive facilities on the south-west side of Indianapolis, together with a flight test establishment on the city's north-west side. Its 7,500 employees produce gas turbine engines and components for aircraft, vehicular and industrial/marine applications.

Collaboration on the T800 engine with Garrett is described under LHTEC on a later page.

ALLISON MODEL 250

US military designations: T63 and T703

The Model 250 is a small turboshaft engine in which power is derived from a free power turbine and is delivered through an offset gearbox which includes all accessory drive pads. Deliveries of all versions totalled more than 21,000 by 31 December 1985.

A development contract for the T63 military version was received by Allison in June 1958 and the engine was first run in the Spring of 1959. Details of early versions last appeared in the 1978-79 *Jane's*; the following are current models:

T63-A-720. Military engine with hot-end improvements, increasing T-O rating to 313 kW (420 shp). Corresponds to commercial C20B. In production for the Bell OH-58C.

T703-A-700. Military engine corresponding to 250-C30R. Selected for Bell 406 (AHIP).

250-B17. Announced in 1972, the B17 is an uprated version of the earlier B15 turboprop. The **B17B** operates at 17°C higher turbine gas temperature with hot-end improvements which maintain full power at high ambient temperatures. The B17B entered production in September 1974 for Turbostar 402 conversions, Turbostar 414, GAF Nomad N22 and 24, SIAI-Marchetti SM.1019E and various agricultural aircraft modifications. The **B17C** introduced an improved gearbox allowing the use of 313 kW (420 shp) on T-O. Produced for Nomad N22 and 24, SIAI-Marchetti SF.260TP and 600TP, Turbostar 402, Pilatus Britten-Norman BN-2T Turbine Islander, Windecker Eagle and Partenavia Viator. **B17F**, with new compressor as in -C20R for increased T-O power, introduced in 1985. Certification expected in 1987.

250-C20B. Introduced in 1974, and rated at 313 kW (420 shp). For Bell and Agusta-Bell 206B JetRanger III and 206L LongRanger, MBB BO 105 C, Agusta A 109A and A 109A Mk II, MD 500D and E, PZL Kania, Hiller Aviation FH-1100 and UH-12E conversion, Soloy C20B turboprop and Bell 47G conversions.

250-C20F. For Aérospatiale AS 355 Ecureuil 2/Twinstar.

250-C20J. For current Bell and Agusta-Bell 206B JetRanger III.

250-C20R. Derivative of C20B with new axial-centrifugal compressor. Certification due 1986.

250-C20S. For Soloy Turbine Pac conversions of Cessna 185, 206 and 207.

250-C28. Major redesign with single centrifugal compressor only, with increased airflow. Reduced noise and emissions, and low-velocity exhaust pipe with minimal infra-red signature. The main gearbox has new gears with increased helix and decreased pressure angles. Prototype engines available September 1975. Certificated December 1977.

250-C28B. Improved model with plain inlet; 2½-min rating of 410 kW (550 shp).

250-C28C. Improved model with particle separator; 2½-min rating of 410 kW (550 shp). Powers Bell LongRanger and MBB BO 105 LS.

250-C30. Advanced single-stage compressor and numerous new features, one of which is dual ignition to comply with FAR Pt 29. Initial rating 485 kW (650 shp), with a 2½ min rating of 522 kW (700 shp). Prototype engines delivered 1976. Certification completed March 1978. C30L, M, P (Bell LongRanger III), R and S (Sikorsky S-76 Mk II) variants are detailed in the descriptive text. The C30R, with digital control, powers the AHIP improved Bell OH-58D.

250-C34. Basically C30 with single-stage gas generator turbine allowing increased gas temperatures for higher T-O power. First flown in a Sikorsky S-76 in March 1984. Certification due 1986.

Type: Light turboshaft or turboprop.

Compressor: The C20, C20B and B17B incorporate an axial/centrifugal compressor with six axial stages and one centrifugal. B17F and C20R have four axial stages and one centrifugal. Other models have a single-stage centrifugal compressor only. Pressure ratio: C20, 7·0; C20B, B17, 7·2: C28B/C, C30, C34, 8·4. Air mass flow: C20, 1·5 kg (3·4 lb)/s; C20B, B17C, 1·56 kg (3·45 lb)/s; C28B/C, 2·02 kg (4·45 lb)/s; C30, C34, 2·54 kg (5·6 lb)/s.

Combustion Chamber: Single can type chamber at rear of engine. Single duplex fuel nozzle in rear face of chamber. One igniter on C20, C20B, B17C, C28B/C and C30L/M/P/R. Dual igniters on C30, C30S and C34; optional on C28B/C.

Turbines: Two-stage (C34, new single-stage) gas producer turbine and two-stage free power turbine. Integrally cast rotor blades and wheels. Gas producer turbine outlet temperature: C20B, B17C, 810°C; C28B/C, 730°C; C30, 740°C; C30L/P/R/S, 725°C; C30M, 742°C; C34, 798°C.

Gearcase: Magnesium casting which forms primary structure of engine and contains all power and accessory gear trains, torque sensor and oil pumps. Compressor and turbine assemblies bolted to front and rear faces respectively. Rated shp available at either front or rear output shaft spline or any combination totalling both. Turboshaft output speed, 6,016 rpm. Turboprop output speed, 2,030 rpm.

Control System: Pneumatic-mechanical system consisting essentially of fuel pump and filter assembly, gas producer fuel control and power turbine governor (B17C, hydro-

The 548 kW (735 shp) Allison Model 250-C34 turboshaft engine

The 313 kW (420 shp) Allison Model 250-B17C turboprop engine

mechanical; C20B, C28, C30/30M/P/S, pneumatic-mechanical; C30L, C30R, C34, supervisory electronic).
FUEL: Primary fuels are ASTM-A or A-1 (Model 250-C20, ASTM D-1655) and MIL-T-5624, JP-4, JP-5 and diesel fuel.
LUBRICATION: Dry sump.
OIL SPECIFICATION: MIL-L-7808 and MIL-L-23699.
DIMENSIONS:

Length: B17C	1,143 mm (45·0 in)
C20B, R	985 mm (38·8 in)
C28C	1,201 mm (47·3 in)
C30	1,041 mm (41·0 in)
C34	1,097 mm (43·3 in)
Width: B17C, C20B	483 mm (19·0 in)
C28, C30, C34	557 mm (21·94 in)
Height: B17C	572 mm (22·5 in)
C20B	589 mm (23·2 in)
C28, C30, C34	638 mm (25·13 in)

WEIGHT, DRY: B17C 88·4 kg (195 lb)

C20B	71·5 kg (158 lb)
C20R	76·0 kg (168 lb)
C28	99·3 kg (219 lb)
C28B, C	104 kg (230 lb)
C30	109·3 kg (240 lb)
C34	118·9 kg (262 lb)

PERFORMANCE RATINGS (S/L, ISA):
T-O: B17C, C20B (5 min), C20J, C20S 313 kW (420 shp)
B17F, C20R (5 min, to 26·7°C) 335 kW (450 shp)

C20F	317 kW (425 shp)
C28, 28B, 28C (30 min)	373 kW (500 shp)
C30 (2½ min)	522 kW (700 shp) to 32·2°C
C34	548 kW (735 shp)
Max continuous: B17C (cruise)	275 kW (369 shp)
C20B	298 kW (400 shp)
C20R	283 kW (380 shp)
C28	373 kW (500 shp)
C30	485 kW (650 shp)
C34	469 kW (629 shp)
Cruise B (75 per cent): B17C	206 kW (277 shp)
C20B	207 kW (278 shp)
C20R	236 kW (317 shp)
C28	274 kW (367 shp)
C30	312 kW (418 shp)
C34	352 kW (472 shp)

SPECIFIC FUEL CONSUMPTION:

At T-O rating: B17C	111 µg/J (0·657 lb/h/shp)
C20B	110 µg/J (0·650 lb/h/shp)
C20R	103 µg/J (0·608 lb/h/shp)
C28	102·5 µg/J (0·606 lb/h/shp)
C30	100 µg/J (0·592 lb/h/shp)
C34	100·7 µg/J (0·596 lb/h/shp)
At cruise B rating: B17C	120·8 µg/J (0·715 lb/h/shp)
C20B	120 µg/J (0·709 lb/h/shp)
C20R	112·5 µg/J (0·666 lb/h/shp)
C28	112 µg/J (0·664 lb/h/shp)
C30, C34	111 µg/J (0·657 lb/h/shp)

ALLISON MODEL 225

The Model 225 is essentially a simple derivative of the Model 250, available as the 225-B10 turboprop (derived from the 250-B17C) and the 225-C10 turboshaft (derived from the 250-C20B).

The objective of the programme is to provide worldwide a low-cost multifuel tolerant engine for general aviation and particularly for emergent nations. Parts are predominantly sourced in Asia, calling upon the technology base of China, India, Japan and South Korea. Initial assembly, test and distribution will be in North America, with production commencing in August 1987. Allison plans later to transition to Asian assembly, test and distribution.

BASIC DESCRIPTION: As for Model 250. Compressor pressure ratio 7·2. Mass flow (B10) 1·62 kg (3·57 lb)/s, (C10) 1·59 kg (3·51 lb)/s.
DIMENSIONS:

Length: B10	1,143 mm (45·0 in)
C10	985 mm (38·8 in)
Width; B10, C10	483 mm (19·0 in)
Height: B10	572 mm (22·5 in)
C10	589 mm (23·2 in)

WEIGHT, DRY:

B10	90·7 kg (200 lb)
C10	73·9 kg (163 lb)

PERFORMANCE RATINGS (both, S/L, ISA):

T-O (5 min) and max cont	261 kW (350 shp)
Normal cruise	212·5 kW (285 shp)

ALLISON MODEL 280

Commercial outgrowth of US Army GMA 500 (see 1984-85 *Jane's*). It is a front drive free-turbine turboshaft in the 600 kW (800 shp) class, with two-stage centrifugal compressor, reverse flow transpiration-cooled combustor, two-stage aircooled gas generator turbine and two-stage power turbine.

ALLISON T56 and MODEL 501

Current versions of the T56 are as follows:

T56-A-14 Rated at 3,661 ekW (4,910 ehp). Generally similar to T56-A-15, but seven-point suspension and detail changes. Powers the P-3B and C Orion.

T56-A-15. Rated at 3,661 ekW (4,910 ehp). Introduced aircooled turbine blades. Powers current C-130.

T56-A-423 and **A-16.** Rated at 3,661 ekW (4,910 ehp). Powers US Navy versions of the C-130.

T56-A-425. Rated at 3,661 ekW (4,910 ehp). Powers E-2C Hawkeye and C-2A Greyhound.

T56-A-427. Rated at 3,915 kW (5,250 shp). For delivery from June 1987, initially for E-2C.

Model 501-D22A. Rated at 3,490 ekW (4,680 ehp). Commercial version of T56-A-15. Powers Lockheed L-100 series.

Model 501-M39. Commercial derivative of T56-A-427.

Model 501-M78. Turboprop version of YT701 incorporating modified T56-A-14 gearbox for NASA-sponsored propfan flight testing at Mach numbers to 0·8. One M78 engine, driving a single-rotation propfan in a tractor installation, is mounted on the left wing of a NASA Gulfstream II. Certification of this installation was due in 1986, initially for flight test purposes only.

Model 501-M80. Free turbine front drive 4,476 kW (6,000 shp) class engine, incorporating aerodynamic features of the T56-A-427 and the front-drive free-turbine mechanical arrangement of the T701. Features include full-authority digital electronic control and an oil system capable of operation in a vertical attitude. Flight qualification scheduled for 1987 for JVX (V-22 Osprey) application.

Including the Model 501 commercial engines, production of these engines reached 14,830 by 1 January 1986. They have logged a total of 122 million flying hours. Production is continuing.

The following details apply to the T56-A-15:
TYPE: Axial-flow turboprop engine.
PROPELLER DRIVE: Combination spur/planetary gear type, primary step-down by spur, secondary by planetary. Overall gear ratio 13·54 : 1. Power section rpm 13,820. Cast magnesium reduction gear housing. Gearbox assembly supported from power section by main drive shaft casing 711 mm (28 in) long and two inclined struts. Weight of gearbox assembly approximately 249 kg (550 lb) with pads on rear face for accessory mounting.
AIR INTAKE: Circular duct on engine face. Thermal de-icing.
COMPRESSOR: Fourteen-stage axial-flow. Series of fourteen discs with rotor blades dovetailed in peripheries and locked by adjacent discs. Rotor assembly tie-bolted to shaft which runs on one ball and one roller type bearing. Fifteen rows of stator blades, welded in rings. Disc, rotor and stator blades and four-piece cast casing of stainless steel. Compressor inlet area 1,004 cm² (155·65 sq in). Pressure ratio 9·5 : 1. Air mass flow 14·70 kg (32·4 lb)/s. Constant speed 13,820 rpm.
COMBUSTION CHAMBER: Six stainless steel cannular type perforated combustion liners within one-piece stainless steel outer casing. Fuel nozzles in forward end of each combustor liner. Primary ignition by two igniters in diametrically opposite combustors.
FUEL SYSTEM: High pressure type. Bendix control system. Water/alcohol augmentation system available.
FUEL GRADE: MIL-J-5624, JP-4 or JP-5.
NOZZLE GUIDE VANES: Hollow aircooled blades of special high temperature alloy.
TURBINE: Four-stage. Rotor assembly consists of four stainless steel discs, with first stage having hollow air-cooled blades of special high temperature alloy, secured in peripheries of discs by fir tree roots. Discs splined to rotor shaft which runs on front and rear roller bearings. Steel outer turbine casing. Gas temperature before turbine 1,076°C.
JETPIPE: Fixed. Stainless steel.
ACCESSORY DRIVES: Accessory pads on rear face of reduction gear housing at front end of engine.
LUBRICATION SYSTEM: Low pressure. Dry sump. Pesco dual-element oil pump. Normal oil supply pressure 3·8 bars (55 lb/sq in).
OIL SPECIFICATION: MIL-L-7808.
MOUNTING: Three-point suspension.
STARTING: Air turbine, gearbox mounted.
DIMENSIONS:

Length (all current versions)	3,708 mm (146 in)
Width (all current versions)	686 mm (27 in)
Height: A-15, A-16, A-425, D-22A	991 mm (39 in)
A-14	1,118 mm (44 in)

WEIGHT, DRY: A-14 855 kg (1,885 lb)

A-15	828 kg (1,825 lb)
A-16	835 kg (1,841 lb)
A-425	860 kg (1,895 lb)
D22A	832 kg (1,834 lb)

PERFORMANCE RATINGS (S/L, ISA, static):
T-O: A-14, A-15, A-16, A-425
3,661 ekW; 3,424 kW (4,910 ehp; 4,591 shp)
501-D22A 3,490 ekW (4,680 ehp)
Normal: A-14, A-15, A-16, A-425, D22A
3,255 ekW; 3,028 kW (4,365 ehp; 4,061 shp)
SPECIFIC FUEL CONSUMPTION:
At max rating:
A-14, A-15, D22A 84·67 µg/J (0·501 lb/h/ehp)
At normal rating:
A-14, A-15 87·4 µg/J (0·517 lb/h/ehp)
OIL CONSUMPTION:
A-14, A-15 1·3 litres (0·35 US gallons)/h

ALLISON 501-M62

US military designation: T701-AD-700

Developed from the T56, the T701 is a free turbine turboshaft engine of modular construction and handling substantially greater airflow.

The XT701 appeared in *Jane's* in the 1970s but was removed upon termination of the Boeing Vertol XCH-62 HLH (heavy lift helicopter) programme. The XT701 has completed a preliminary flight rating test and safety demo test, and was intended to power the HLRV (heavy-lift research vehicle).

An industrial variant, the Model 570, is rated for continuous operation at 4,800 kW (6,445 shp). The T701 served as the basis for Allison's 501-M80C engine for the JVX (V-22 Osprey).

The 3,915 kW (5,250 shp) Allison T56-A-427 turboprop engine which powers late versions of the Grumman E-2C Hawkeye

Allison 501-M78 for PTA (Propfan Test Assessment) programme

TYPE: Free-turbine turboshaft engine.

INTAKE: Circular casting incorporating six aerofoil struts with thermal anti-icing. Accessory drive shafts at top and bottom, with main accessory gearbox on underside. This section carries front bearing for output shaft.

COMPRESSOR: Thirteen-stage axial, with variable inlet guide vanes and first five stator rows. Rotor built up from rings and discs, with large-diameter tubular central shaft rearwards from second stage. Rotor supported by front roller bearing and rear ball-thrust bearing. Longitudinally jointed casing incorporates large bleed manifold for 10th stage air. Pressure ratio 12·8. Mass flow 20·1 kg (44·3 lb)/s.

COMBUSTION CHAMBER: Annular, with 16 burners disposed around inner wall of flame tube fed with primary air through narrow annular gap at upstream end of snout section. Smoke-free combustion. Secondary air admitted through peripheral slits in flame tube giving film cooling.

FUEL GRADE: MIL-T-5624 grades JP-4, JP-5.

TURBINE: Gas-generator turbine has two axial stages with aircooled blades, both stages cantilevered behind rear roller bearing. Power turbine has two axial stages assembled by row of bolts at first disc, carried between central ball thrust bearing on mid-frame through centre of combustion chamber and rear roller bearing.

JETPIPE: Fixed-area type, with truncated central bullet and tangential struts carrying rear bearing.

OUTPUT: Power turbine forward shaft is splined to central driveshaft carried in two ball bearings at front end and incorporating torque sensing assembly. Rotation clockwise, viewed from rear. Rated speed 11,500 rpm.

ACCESSORY DRIVES: Main accessory gearcase beneath air intake section. Drives on front for starter/generator and tachometer, and on rear face for fuel pump and fuel control unit.

LUBRICATION SYSTEM: Self-contained integral oil system with external tank carried on left side of compressor casing.

OIL SPECIFICATION: MIL-L-23699, MIL-L-7808.

MOUNTING: Main suspension on each side of intake casing; seven possible mounting pads arranged around jetpipe casing.

DIMENSIONS:	
Length (intake face to jetpipe exit)	1,633 mm (64·3 in)
Length overall	1,880 mm (74·0 in)
Intake diameter	516 mm (20·3 in)
Jetpipe diameter	714 mm (28·1 in)
Width	767 mm (30·2 in)
Height	935 mm (36·8 in)
WEIGHT, DRY:	534 kg (1,179 lb)

PERFORMANCE RATINGS (ISA, S/L, static at gas generator speed of 15,049 rpm):	
Intermediate (30 min)	6,025 kW (8,079 shp)
Max continuous	5,447 kW (7,305 shp)
75%	4,085 kW (5,478 shp)
50%	2,720 kW (3,648 shp)
25%	1,362 kW (1,827 shp)

SPECIFIC FUEL CONSUMPTION (conditions as above):	
Intermediate	79·6 μg/J (0·471 lb/h/ehp)
Max continuous	78·1 μg/J (0·462 lb/h/ehp)
75%	79·1 μg/J (0·468 lb/h/ehp)
50%	85·5 μg/J (0·506 lb/h/ehp)
25%	107·7 μg/J (0·637 lb/h/ehp)

The 6,025 kW (8,079 shp) Allison XT701-AD-700 turboshaft engine

Half scale model of Allison Model 578 propfan shown at 1985 Paris Air Show *(Brian M. Service)*

ALLISON MODEL 578

Allison is developing the Model 578 geared counter-rotation propfan propulsion system for 100 to 150-passenger commercial transport aircraft. The initial flight test demonstrator is the **578-DX** rated at 7,758 kW (10,400 shp). This incorporates a three-stage LP compressor, modified T701 core engine, and an advanced-technology 9,698 kW (13,000 shp) differential planetary counter-rotation gearbox. The latter drives the two 3·5 m (11 ft 6 in) six-bladed Hamilton Standard propfans.

The proven core is capable of being configured for propfan engines rated at from 6,712 to 11,930 kW (9,000-16,000 shp). A full-authority digital control system regulates fuel flow, variable compressor stators and propfan blade angles. System certification is planned for the early 1990s.

ALLISON 912-B52

For almost 20 years Allison, in partnership with Rolls-Royce, produced the TF41 turbofan to power the A-7 Corsair II. Allison is now proposing an uprated derivative to power an upgraded A-7. The 912-B52 comprises a modified TF41-A-1 rated at about 77·43 kN (17,400 lb st), 20 per cent more than the original engine and also offering enhanced durability, coupled to a simplified F100 afterburner providing approximately 60 per cent augmentation. Hardware was being readied for demonstration testing in 1986.

ALTURDYNE

ALTURDYNE

8050 Armour Street, San Diego, California 92111
Telephone: (619) 565 2131
Telex: (910) 335-2000
PRESIDENT: Frank Verbeke

This company, "dedicated to bringing the advantages of the small gas turbine to new areas of industry and commerce", has developed small engines for RPVs and very light aircraft. It was formed in 1970 and employs 100 people.

At present it purchases the basic gas generator and incorporates this into a complete engine for various purposes. The two main products are of 112 kW (150 hp) and 157 kW (210 hp). These are based upon the Solar T62 Titan single-shaft gas turbine (last described in the 1975-76 *Jane's*). Alturdyne is marketing these units in APU, generator and air compressor applications. A company funded lightweight rotary combustion aircraft engine is under development in two sizes up to 186·5 kW (250 hp). The first engines were tested in December 1984 and were exhibited at the EAA Oshkosh meet in 1985. Current pilot production is regarded as experimental.

AMI

AEROMOTION INC

This company has produced a light two-cylinder opposed piston engine tailored to light aircraft. It is not a modification of any existing engine, though it does use many off the shelf automotive parts. The first AeroMotion Twin ran in April 1982 and has shown high reliability since then. Pre-production engines flew in a Heath Parasol in March 1984 and in a Ken Brock autogyro a month later.

AEROMOTION TWIN

TYPE: Two-cylinder opposed four-stroke aircooled piston engine.

CYLINDERS: Bore 104·8 mm (4·125 in). Stroke 95·25 mm (3·75 in). Capacity 1,650 cc (100 cu in).

IGNITION: Twin Slick magnetos, dual plugs.

DIMENSIONS:	
Width	787 mm (31·0 in)
Length	451 mm (17·75 in)
Height	470 mm (18·5 in)
WEIGHT, DRY (equipped):	45 kg (100 lb)
PERFORMANCE RATING (SL):	37-39·5 kW (50-53 hp) at 3,100 rpm

AeroMotion Twin piston engine

AVCO LYCOMING TEXTRON

AVCO LYCOMING TEXTRON STRATFORD DIVISION

550 Main Street, Stratford, Connecticut 06497
Telephone: (203) 385 2000

President of Avco Lycoming Division: J. R. Myers
Vice-Presidents (Stratford):
R. Ainsworth (Engineering)
J. Burns (Quality)
A. J. Burrows (Washington Operation)
J. Ches (Human Resources)
R. Crawford (Finance)
H. Frederick (Contracts and Audit)
R. Gustafson (Customer Operations)
C. Kuintzle (Business Strategies)
M. J. Leff (Marketing and Commercial Engine Programmes)
J. Pellegrino (Procurement and Subcontract)
J. Stanley (Manufacturing Operations)
S. White (Military Engine Programmes)

Avco Lycoming Stratford together with the Lycoming Greer, South Carolina, and Lycoming Williamsport, Pennsylvania, divisions became subsidiaries of Textron Inc in 1985.

Stratford division produces several families of engines, including the T53, T55 and ALF 502, with turboshaft, turboprop, turbofan, vehicular and marine variants. In 1981 the LTP 101 and LTS 101 were transferred to Williamsport.

Avco Lycoming has teamed with Pratt & Whitney to develop the T800-APW-800 advanced technology turboshaft under US Army contract. The engine is a high performance/low fuel consumption unit for use in an LHX demonstrator programme.

Avco Lycoming ALF 502L geared turbofan rated at 33·36 kN (7,500 lb st)

AVCO LYCOMING ALF 502

The ALF 502 turbofan was launched as a company sponsored effort in 1969, primarily as a power plant for commercial and executive aircraft. The core gas generator is the T55, and construction was made totally modular. The ALF 502 has flown in several aircraft, demonstrating low noise signature, and at altitudes up to 14,950 m (49,000 ft).

Current versions are as follows:

ALF 502L. First commercial version, FAA certificated in February 1980. Powers Canadair Challenger 600 in ALF 502L-2 form. L-2A, L-2C and L-3 certificated 1982-3.

ALF 502R. Reduced rating, FAA certificated January 1981 as R-3 to power BAe 146. Improved R-3A, R-4 and R-5 certificated 1982-3. R-6 certificated 1984. R-7 to power BAe 146-300 has FADEC control.

Engine deliveries off production tooling were made in December 1977, with quantity production starting in 1979.

By 1986 a total of 184 engines had flown 200,000 h in the Challenger, while another 190 had flown 350,000 h in the BAe 146. TBO was 4,000 h, but the ALF 502 is usually operated on-condition.

Type: High bypass ratio, two-shaft geared turbofan.

Fan Module: Cast fan frame includes four engine mounts 90° apart, and may be used for mounting thrust reverser. Fan rotor blades are base and part-span shrouded and individually replaceable. Containment ring surrounds rotor. Mounted directly behind rotor (6,700 lb st engines) is a single or (7,500 lb st engines) two stages of compression. Individually replaceable fan exit stators are located to minimise noise. Inlet spinner bolted to fan rotor is anti-iced by oil flow. Anti-icing of LP compressor inlet by bleed air. Accessory gearbox on fan frame takes HP shaft power. Additional services such as fuel, oil, pneumatic and electrical lines, are routed through other hollow struts. Reduction gear within centre of fan frame couples LP turbine to fan. Bypass ratio: 502R-3, 5·71; 502L, 5·0.

Compressor: Core supercharged by one or two LP stages, as described above. HP compressor has seven axial stages and single centrifugal stage, driven by two-stage HP turbine, and supported by ball and (aft) roller bearing. Acceleration bleed control between stages 6 and 7 operated by main fuel control. Upper and lower casings contain stator half rings, removable for maintenance, and borescope ports. Overall engine pressure ratio: R-3, 11·6; L-2, 13·6.

Turbine: HP has two aircooled stages. LP has two stages, splined to fan reduction gear. All rotor blades base shrouded: LP additionally tip shrouded.

Combustion Chamber: One-piece annular combustor wraps around turbine. Atomising nozzles inserted through outer chamber at rear. Four customer bleed ports around exterior. Combustion liner and housing bolted to compressor diffuser. Disconnecting permits removal of combustor/turbine module, providing access to HP turbine. Borescope ports permit inspection of combustor and turbine without removal.

Accessory Drives: Accessory gearbox carries main fuel control, oil pump and filter, tachometer (if required) and provisions for customer accessories.

Exhaust Unit: Fan and core exhaust include flanges for bolted ducts and nozzles.

Data: See table.

AVCO LYCOMING LTC1

US military designation: T53

The T53 is a turboshaft with a free power turbine, which was developed under a joint US Air Force/US Army contract. More than 19,000 units had logged over 41 million hours of operation, with every US armed service and in 29 other countries, by January 1985.

Licences for manufacture of the T53 are held by Klöckner-Humboldt-Deutz in the Federal Republic of Germany, Piaggio in Italy, Kawasaki in Japan, and in Taiwan.

Versions currently in production or under development are as follows:

T53-L-13. Uprated version of L-11, which it superseded in production in August 1966. Redesigned 'hot end' and initial stages of compressor section to provide substantially increased power for hot day and high altitude performance. Four turbine stages, compared with two in earlier models, and variable incidence inlet guide vanes combined with redesigned first two compressor stages, permit greater airflow and lower turbine temperatures. This version has atomising combustor to facilitate operation on a wider range of fuels. Powers Bell UH-1M and UH-1H and AH-1G HueyCobra. The **T5313A** commercial version of the T53-L-13 received FAA type certification in 1968 for the Bell 205A and has been superseded by the **T5313B**.

AVCO LYCOMING GAS TURBINE ENGINES

Manufacturer's and civil designation	Military designation	Type*	T-O Rating kN (lb st) or max kW (hp)	SFC µg/J; ‡ mg/Ns (lb/h/hp; ‡lb/h/lb st)	Weight, Dry less tailpipe kg (lb)	Max diameter mm (in)	Length overall mm (in)	Remarks
T5311A	—	ACFS	820 kW (1,100 shp)	115 (0·68)	225 (496)	584 (23)	1,209 (47·6)	Bell 204B
T5313B	—	ACFS	1,044 kW (1,400 shp)	98 (0·58)	245 (540)	584 (23)	1,209 (47·6)	Bell 205A
T5317A	—	ACFS	1,119 kW (1,500 shp)	99·7 (0·59)	256 (564)	584 (23)	1,209 (47·6)	
—	T53-L-13B	ACFS	1,044 kW (1,400 shp)	98 (0·58)	245 (540)	584 (23)	1,209 (47·6)	Advanced UH-1H, AH-1G
—	T53-L-703	ACFS	1,106 kW (1,485 shp)	101·4 (0·60)	247 (545)	584 (23)	1,209 (47·6)	Bell AH-1S TOW/Cobra
LTC1K-4K	—	ACFS	1,156 kW (1,550 shp)	98·7 (0·584)	234 (515)	584 (23)	1,209 (47·6)	Bell XV-15
—	T53-L-701	ACFP	1,082 ekW (1,451 ehp)	101·4 (0·60)	312 (688)	584 (23)	1,483 (58·4)	Grumman OV-1D
—	YT55-L-9	ACFP	1,887 ekW (2,529 ehp)	102·7 (0·608)	363 (799)	615 (24·2)	1,580 (62·2)	
—	T55-L-7C	ACFS	2,125 kW (2,850 shp)	101·4 (0·60)	267 (590)	615 (24·2)	1,118 (44)	
T5508D (LTC4B-8D)	—	ACFS	2,186 kW (2,930 shp) flat rated at 1,678 kW (2,250 shp)	100·1 (0·592) 106·0 (0·628)	274 (605)	610 (24)	1,118 (44)	Bell 214A, 214B
—	T55-L-712†	ACFS	2,796 kW (3,750 shp)	89·6 (0·53)	340 (750)	615 (24·2)	1,181 (46·5)	Boeing CH-47D
AL5512	—	ACFS	3,039 kW (4,075 shp)	89·6 (0·53)	355 (780)	615 (24·2)	1,118 (44)	Boeing 234
ALF 502R-3	—	ACFF	29·8 kN (6,700 lb)	‡11·64 (‡0·411)	576 (1,270)	1,059 (41·7)	1,443 (56·8)	BAe 146
ALF 502R-3A	—	ACFF	31·0 kN (6,968 lb)	‡11·55 (‡0·408)	576 (1,270)	1,059 (41·7)	1,443 (56·8)	
ALF 502R-5	—	ACFF	31·0 kN (6,968 lb)	‡11·55 (‡0·408)	583 (1,283)	1,059 (41·7)	1,443 (56·8)	BAe 146-200
ALF 502R-6	—	ACFF	33·36 kN (7,500 lb)	‡11·73 (‡0·415)	589 (1,298)	1,059 (41·7)	1,487 (58·56)	BAe 146-300
ALF 502R-7	—	ACFF	33·36 kN (7,500 lb)	‡11·73 (‡0·415)	623 (1,370)	1,059 (41·7)	1,487 (58·56)	BAe 146-300
ALF 502L/L-2	—	ACFF	33·36 kN (7,500 lb)	‡12·1 (‡0·428)	589 (1,298)	1,059 (41·7)	1,487 (58·56)	Canadair Challenger 600
ALF 502L-2A	—	ACFF	33·36 kN (7,500 lb)	‡11·70 (‡0·414)	589 (1,298)	1,059 (41·7)	1,487 (58·56)	
ALF 502L-3	—	ACFF	34·74 kN (7,800 lb)	‡11·73 (‡0·415)	589 (1,298)	1,059 (41·7)	1,487 (58·56)	

*ACFS = axial plus centrifugal, free-turbine shaft; ACFP = axial plus centrifugal, free-turbine propeller; ACFF = axial plus centrifugal, free-turbine fan
†Applies to T55-L-11A, C**, D, E** and 712**, those designated ** having 2½ min contingency rating of 3,357 kW (4,500 shp).

T53-L-701. Turboprop version of the L-13 incorporating the Lycoming 'split power' propeller reduction gear. Produced for Grumman OV-1D previously powered by T53-L-15, and for T-CH-1 (Taiwan).

T53-L-703. Improved durability L-13. Flat rated for AH-1S HueyCobra.

LTC1K-4K. Direct drive version of T53-L-13 suitable for operation from 105° nose up to 90° nose down; rated at 1,156 kW (1,550 shp). Powers Bell XV-15 VTOL aircraft.

T5317A. Latest growth version of T53 turboshaft family. Improvements over L-13 include improved cooling of first gas producer turbine nozzle plus aircooled blades in first turbine rotor. Also incorporates new materials in other turbine stages. Flat rated, with take-off rating limited to 1,119 kW (1,500 shp) by use of standard L-13 reduction gear.

The following details apply to the T53-L-13 and L-701:

TYPE: Free turbine turboshaft engine.

AIR INTAKE: Annular casing of magnesium alloy, with 6 struts supporting reduction gearbox and front main bearings. Anti-icing by hot air tapped from engine.

COMPRESSOR: Five axial stages followed by a single centrifugal stage. Four-piece magnesium alloy casing with one row of variable incidence inlet guide vanes and five rows of steel stator blades, bolted to one-piece steel alloy diffuser casing with tangential outlet to combustion chamber. Rotor comprises one stainless steel disc, and welded titanium drum construction for the four remaining axial stages, with stainless steel blades and one titanium impeller. Rotor shaft supported by front ball thrust bearing and rear roller bearing. Pressure ratio is 7·2, and mass flow 5·53 kg (12·2 lb)/s at 25,150 gas producer rpm. Four aluminium alloy discs with stainless steel blades and one titanium impeller mounted on shaft supported in forward ball thrust and rear roller bearings.

COMBUSTION CHAMBER: Annular reverse flow type, with one-piece sheet steel outer shell and annular liner; 22 atomising fuel injectors.

FUEL CONTROL SYSTEM: Hydromechanical controls for gas generator and for power sections. Chandler Evans TA-2S system with one dual fuel pump. Pump pressure 41·4 bars (600 lb/sq in). Main and emergency flow controls. Separate interstage air bleed control.

FUEL GRADE: ASTM A-1, MIL-J-5624, MIL-F-26005A, JP-1, JP-4, JP-5, CITE.

TURBINE: Four axial flow turbine stages. Casing fabricated from sheet steel. First two stages, driving compressor, use hollow aircooled stator vanes and cored-out cast steel rotor blades and are mounted on outer coaxial shaft to gas producer. Second two stages, driving reduction gearing, have solid steel blades, and are spline mounted to shaft.

EXHAUST UNIT: Fixed area nozzle. Steel outer casing and inner cone, supported by four radial struts.

ACCESSORIES: Electric starter or starter/generator (not furnished). Bendix-Scintilla TGLN high energy ignition unit. Two igniter plugs.

LUBRICATION: Recirculating system, with gear pump with one pressure and one scavenge unit. Filter. Pump pressure 4·83 bars (70 lb/sq in).

OIL GRADE: MIL-L-7808, MIL-L-23699.

DATA: See table.

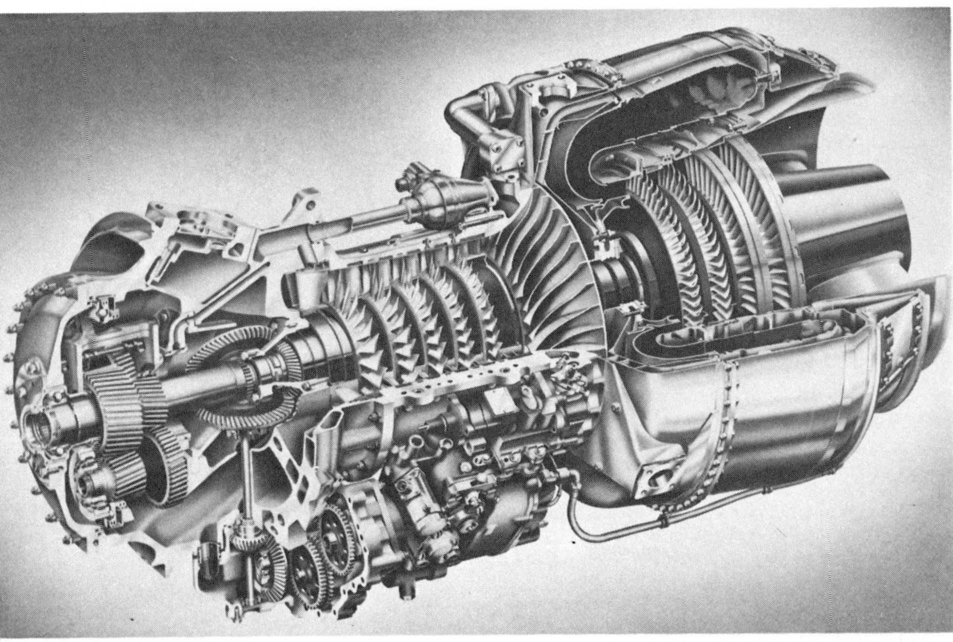

Cutaway drawing of the 1,044 kW (1,400 shp) Avco Lycoming T53-L-13B turboshaft engine

Avco Lycoming T55-L-712 (military) or AL5512 (commercial) turboshaft

AVCO LYCOMING LTC4

US military designation: T55

This engine is based on the T53 design concept but with higher mass flow. It was developed under a joint US Air Force/US Army contract. Total operating time by early 1985 on more than 3,500 engines was 5·0 million hours.

Current production and development versions are as follows:

LTC4B-8D. Modified version of the T55-L-7C. Powers Bell 214A and 214C utility helicopters for Iran, flat rated at transmission limit of 1,678 kW (2,250 shp).

T5508D. Commercial version of LTC4B-8D. Powers Bell 214B.

T55-L-11 (LTC4B-11B) series. Uprated and redesigned version of L-7, with a second stage added to the compressor turbine, and variable incidence inlet guide vanes ahead of the compressor. First two compressor stages transonic. Atomising fuel nozzles. Powers CH-47C Chinook, first deliveries having been made in August 1968.

T55-L-712. Improved T55-L-11D fitted to the US Army's modernised Boeing Vertol CH-47D. Wide chord compressor blades without inlet guide vanes, and one-piece rotor. Emergency (engine out) rating 3,357 kW (4,500 shp). Improvements in design and materials are aimed at achieving a time between overhauls of 2,500 h.

AL5512. Commercial version of L-712, with engine out contingency rating of 3,250 kW (4,355 shp). Certificated in 1980 for Boeing Vertol 234.

LTC4B-12. Proposed growth version with 3,430 kW (4,600 shp) maximum power rating, 3,258 kW (4,370 shp) on hot day. Higher turbine entry temperature and increased turbine cooling.

YT55-L-9A. Turboprop version of L-7C using split-power reduction gears. Rated at 1,887 ekW (2,529 ehp) for Piper Enforcer.

The following description applies to the T55-L-11:

TYPE: Free turbine turboshaft engine.

AIR INTAKE: Annular type casing of magnesium alloy with four struts supporting reduction gearbox and front main bearings. Anti-icing by hot air tapped from engine. Provision for intake screens. Integral oil tank.

COMPRESSOR: Seven axial stages followed by a single centrifugal stage. Two-piece magnesium alloy stator casing with one row of variable inlet guide vanes and seven rows of steel stator blades, bolted to steel diffuser casing to which combustion chamber casing is attached. Late models have wide chord blades in first two stages and no inlet guide vanes. Rotor comprises seven steel discs and one titanium impeller mounted on shaft supported in forward ball thrust bearing and rear roller bearing. Pressure ratio 8·2 : 1. Air mass flow 12·25 kg (27 lb)/s.

COMBUSTION CHAMBER: Annular reverse flow type. Steel outer shell and inner liner. Twenty-eight fuel burners with downstream injection.

FUEL SYSTEM: Hamilton Standard JFC 31 fuel control system. Gear type fuel pump, with gas producer and power shaft governors, flow control with altitude compensation and shut-off valve.

FUEL GRADE: MIL-J-5624 grade JP-4, JP-5, MIL-F-46005A or CITE.

TURBINE: Two mechanically independent axial turbines. Gas generator turbine has two stages with cored-out cast steel blades having inner cooling airflow. Disc flange bolted to drive shaft. Hollow stator vanes. Two-stage power turbine has solid steel blades.

EXHAUST UNIT: Fixed area nozzle, with inner cone, supported by 21 vanes.

ACCESSORIES: Electric starter or starter/generator, or air or hydraulic starter. Bendix-Scintilla TGLN high energy ignition unit. Four igniter plugs.

LUBRICATION: Recirculating type. Integral oil tank and cooler.

OIL GRADE: MIL-L-7808, MIL-L-23699.

DATA: See table.

AVCO LYCOMING PLT34

Avco Lycoming demonstrated the PLT34 under contract to the US Army Aviation Systems Command (AVSCOM) as part of the Advanced Technology Demonstrator Engine programme. From this engine in the 615 kW (825 shp) class is being developed the T800-APW-800, listed under the joint Avco/P&W team on a later page.

WILLIAMSPORT DIVISION

Williamsport, Pennsylvania 17701

Telephone: (717) 323 6181

PRESIDENT: Howard M. Knutson

VICE-PRESIDENTS:
A. E. Light (Engineering)
E. C. Pease (Turbine Engineering)
P. R. Boob (Domestic Sales)
O. Oppliger (International Sales)

The world's largest producer of piston engines for general aviation, this division of Avco Lycoming was in 1981 additionally assigned the LTS 101 turboshaft and LTP 101 turboprop. Production began at Williamsport in mid-1981.

AVCO LYCOMING LT 101

US military designation: YT702-LD-700

The LT 101 is a simple modular gas turbine engine designed to provide low life cycle costs. Each engine is made up of three major modules: the accessory reduction gearbox, the gas generator module and the combustor/power turbine module. The engine has a single axial compressor stage followed by a single centrifugal compressor stage, a reverse flow annular combustor, a single-stage gas generator turbine, and a concentric mounted single-stage free power turbine. Front mounted gearboxes, in three available versions, provide output speeds of 1,925, 6,000 or 9,545 rpm. The 6,000 rpm gearbox has both forward and aft drives. The engine has either a scroll inlet or a radial inlet, each with an optional particle separator. Mass flow is 2·03 kg (4·8 lb)/s, and the pressure ratio is 8·5.

Current production versions of the LT 101 include both turboshaft (LTS) and turboprop (LTP) models, with max power ratings in the 459 to 548 kW (615 to 735 shp) range. All engines are certificated under FAR Pt 33 for 2,400 h TBO or on-condition maintenance. LT 101 operating experience now totals more than 1 million h.

Lycoming has developed a turbofan and an airborne APU for the US government based on the LT 101 core. The military version, designated YT702-LD-700, has completed a 60 h PFRT. In addition, a marine version of the LT 101 is being developed.

AVCO LYCOMING LTS 101

The LTS 101 turboshaft has been certificated in a variety of models. The **LTS 101-600A-2**, certificated in November 1977, is a 6,000 rpm output power plant for the Aérospatiale AS 350D Astar helicopter. The **LTS 101-650C-2/C-3** is a 9,545 rpm power plant used in the twin-engined Bell 222. The **LTS 101-650B-1**, a 6,000 rpm output engine with a radial inlet, powers the twin-engined MBB/Kawasaki BK 117.

Several further versions have been certificated. The **LTS 101-600A-3** was certificated in September 1984 to power the AS 350D Mk 3. A growth version, the **LTS 101-750C-1**, powers the Bell 222B and 222UT. The **LTS 101-750A-1** and **750B-2**, with radial inlet, power the SA 366 and HH-65A Dolphin. The **-750A-3** incorporates a full authority electronic fuel control; it was first flown in the HH-65A in April 1983, and was certificated in September 1984.

Data: See table.

AVCO LYCOMING LTP 101

The LTP 101 modular turboprop incorporates a free power turbine, provisions for tractor or pusher installation, hydraulic propeller governor, radial screened inlet and anti-icing protection. The output shaft speed lies in the range 1,700-1,950 rpm, consistent with available three-blade reversible-pitch propellers.

FAA certification of the **LTP 101-600** was received in 1976. This model has since been selected for the Piaggio P.166-DL3, Air Tractor Turbo Tractor and New Zealand Aerospace Industries/Pacific Aerospace Fletcher agricultural aircraft, Riley conversion of Cessna 421 and Page Aircraft Turbo Thrush and Ag-Cat conversions. It has flown in Piper Brave, Turbo-Islander and Dornier 128-6 prototypes. The **LTP 101-700** is a more powerful model certificated in July 1980. A fully aerobatic version is under development.

Dimensions:
- Length: 914 mm (36·0 in)
- Diameter: 533 mm (21·0 in)

Weight, Dry: 152 kg (335 lb)

Performance Ratings (T-O, S/L):
- LTP 101-600: 462 ekW (620 ehp)
- LTP 101-700: 522 ekW (700 ehp)

Specific Fuel Consumption (T-O, S/L):
- LTP 101-600, -700: 93 μg/J (0·55 lb/h/ehp)

AVCO LYCOMING RC ENGINES

A major new development is the decision of Avco Lycoming to go into partnership with JDTI (John Deere Technologies International) in developing and marketing rotary combustion (RC) engines. John Deere acquired the RC patents and technology of Curtiss-Wright (whose aviation engines were described in *Jane's* until 1984-85). John Deere also leased Curtiss-Wright's Wood Ridge plant and hired a nucleus of about 20 RC engineers who from 1958 had solved many of the RC problems. Deere's rights to important SC (stratified charge) technology were a further reason for Avco Lycoming's decision to collaborate. Further research is now proceeding on a joint basis. Avco paying JDTI a royalty on engines sold and concentrating upon aviation applications.

Full-scale model of Avco Lycoming 298 kW (400 hp) RC engine *(Brian M. Service)*

At the 1985 Paris Air Show Howard Knutson, who became Williamsport general manager two years previously, explained his conviction that the "industry had stood still too long". He ordered an in-depth evaluation of competing engines in the 261 kW (350 hp) S/L power category. Points were awarded for various criteria for the traditional piston engine, turboprop, diesel and SC rotary. The rotary "won hands down, with a 2:1 lead over the nearest alternative".

Accordingly, Williamsport is itself investing more than $30 million in a five-year programme to develop SC/RC engines, initially for general aviation. The initial engine is to be rated at 298 kW (400 hp) maximum continuous power at up to 6,100 m (20,000 ft), with cruise rating of 224 kW (300 hp) at up to 7,620 m (25,000 ft). It will be able to run on any aviation piston or jet fuel. Bench testing is scheduled for the third quarter of 1987, flight testing from late in the same year, and FAA certification is planned for the fourth quarter of 1989. Into-service TBO is to be 2,000 h. Eventually Williamsport expects to produce SC/RC engines to cover the power range 37-1,120 kW (50-1,500 hp).

AVCO LYCOMING O-160

This new light aircraft engine, announced at the 1985 Paris Air Show, is a flat-twin utilising standard O-320 cylinders, pistons and valves combined with a redesigned crankshaft, camshaft and casing with improved vibration damping. In the 52-59·5 kW (70-80 hp) class, it uses 80 octane fuel and is expected to have a TBO of 2,000 h. Certification and production were planned for the second half of 1986.

AVCO LYCOMING O-235 SERIES

Four cylinders of 111 mm (4⅜ in) bore and 98·4 mm (3⅞ in) stroke. The high compression O-235-N is the most recent production version of the O-235, used in several primary trainers. It requires 100 octane (minimum) aviation fuel.

AVCO LYCOMING O-320 and IO-320 SERIES

Cylinder bore increased to 130 mm (5⅛ in). The O-320 is an engine in the 112-119 kW (150-160 hp) class. Both carburetted and fuel injected versions are produced in low and high compression models for use with 80/87 or 100

AVCO LYCOMING LTS 101 ENGINES

Engine Model	Performace Rating (T-O, S/L) kW (shp)	SFC μg/J (lb/h/shp)	Weight, Dry kg (lb)	Length mm (in)	Diameter mm (in)
LTS 101-600A/600B	441·5 (592)	96·5 (0·571)	109·5 (241)	785 (30·9)	472 (18·6)
LTS 101-600A-2/650A-2	459 (615)	96·5 (0·571)	115 (253)	785 (30·9)	599 (23·6)
LTS 101-600A-3	459 (615)	98·4 (0·582)	120 (265)	785 (30·9)	599 (23·6)
LTS 101-650B-1	410 (550)	95·5 (0·565)	120·5 (266)	790 (31·1)	645 (25·4)
LTS 101-650C-2/C-3/C-3A	447 (600)	96·7 (0·572)	109·5 (241)	787 (31·0)	574 (22·6)
LTS 101-750A-1	461 (618)	96·3 (0·570)	122 (268)	820 (32·3)	756 (29·75)
LTS 101-750A-3	461 (618)	96·3 (0·570)	121 (267)	845 (33·2)	755 (29·7)
LTS 101-750B-2	461 (618)	96·3 (0·570)	123 (271)	822 (32·35)	627 (24·7)
LTS 101-750C-1	510 (684)	97·5 (0·577)	110·5 (244)	790 (31·1)	574 (22·6)

Avco Lycoming turbine engines in the 600 shp class (left to right): LTS 101-650B-1, LTP 101-700A-1A and LTS 101-750C-1

AVCO LYCOMING HORIZONTALLY OPPOSED PISTON ENGINES

Engine Model*	No. of Cylinders	Rated output at Sea Level kW (hp) at rpm	capacity litres (cu in)	Compression Ratio	Fuel grade Minimum	Weight Dry kg (lb)	Length Overall mm (in)	Width Overall mm (in)	Height Overall mm (in)	Gear Ratio†
O-160	2	52-59·5 (70-80) at 2,600	2·62 (159·9)	7·0	80	72·5 (160)	483 (19·00)	819 (32·26)	473 (18·62)	D
O-235-C	4	86 (115) at 2,800	3·85 (233)	6·75	80/87	97·5 (215)	751 (29·56)	812 (32·00)	569 (22·40)	D
O-235-L	4	86 (115) at 2,700 78 (105) at 2,400	3·85 (233)	8·5	100	98 (218)	738 (29·05)	812 (32·00)	569 (22·40)	D
O-235-N, P	4	87 (116) at 2,800	3·85 (233)	8·1	100	98 (218)	738 (29·05)	812 (32·00)	569 (22·40)	D
O-320-A	4	112 (150) at 2,700	5·2 (319·8)	7·0	80/87	110 (243)	751 (29·56)	819 (32·24)	584 (22·99)	D
O-320-D	4	119 (160) at 2,700	5·2 (319·8)	8·5	91/96	114 (253)	808 (31·82)	819 (32·24)	488 (19·22)	D
AEIO-320-D	4	119 (160) at 2,700	5·2 (319·8)	8·5	100	123 (271)	780 (30·70)	819 (32·24)	589 (23·18)	D
O-320-E	4	112 (150) at 2,700	5·2 (319·8)	7·0	80/87	113 (249)	738 (29·05)	819 (32·24)	584 (22·99)	D
O-320-H	4	119 (160) at 2,700	5·2 (319·8)	9·0	100	115 (253)	819 (32·26)	830 (32·68)	621 (24·46)	D
O-360-A	4	134 (180) at 2,700	5·92 (361)	8·5	91/96	118 (260)	808 (31·82)	848 (33·37)	488 (19·22)	D
LO-360-A	4	134 (180) at 2,700	5·92 (361)	8·5	91/96	120 (266)	808 (31·82)	848 (33·37)	488 (19·22)	D
O-360-F	4	134 (180) at 2,700	5·92 (361)	8·5	100	122 (269)	808 (31·81)	859 (33·38)	507 (19·96)	D
TO-360-C, F	4	157 (210) at 2,575 to 3,050 m (10,000 ft)	5·92 (361)	7·3	100	154 (343)	876 (34·50)	921 (36·25)	534 (21·02)	D
IO-360-A	4	149 (200) at 2,700	5·92 (361)	8·7	100	133 (293)	757 (29·81)	870 (34·25)	491 (19·35)	D
IO-360-B	4	134 (180) at 2,700	5·92 (361)	8·5	100	122 (268)	757 (29·81)	848 (33·37)	631 (24·84)	D
IO-360-C	4	149 (200) at 2,700	5·92 (361)	8·7	100	134 (298)	855 (33·65)	870 (34·25)	495 (19·48)	D
TIO-360-C	4	210 (282) at 2,575 to 3,050 m (10,000 ft)	5·92 (361)	7·3	100	158 (348)	910 (35·82)	921 (36·25)	550 (21·65)	D
HIO-360-D	4	142 (190) at 3,200 to 1,280 m (4,200 ft)	5·92 (361)	10·0	100	132 (290)	894 (35·23)	904 (35·62)	495 (19·48)	D
HIO-360-E	4	142 (190) at 2,900	5·92 (361)	8·0	100	132 (290)	797 (31·36)	870 (34·25)	507 (19·97)	D
HIO-360-F	4	142 (190) at 3,050	5·92 (361)	8·0	100	133 (293)	797 (31·36)	870 (34·25)	507 (19·97)	D
AEIO-360-A	4	149 (200) at 2,700	5·92 (361)	8·7	100	139 (307)	780 (30·70)	870 (34·25)	492 (19·35)	D
AEIO-360-B	4	134 (180) at 2,700	5·92 (361)	8·5	91/96	125 (277)	738 (29·05)	848 (33·37)	631 (24·84)	D
O-540-B	6	175 (235) at 2,575	8·86 (541·5)	7·2	80/87	166 (366)	945 (37·22)	848 (33·37)	624 (24·56)	D
O-540-E	6	194 (260) at 2,700	8·86 (541·5)	8·5	91/96	167 (368)	976 (38·42)	848 (33·37)	624 (24·56)	D
O-540-G	6	194 (260) at 2,700	8·86 (541·5)	8·5	91/96	174 (386)	999 (39·34)	848 (33·37)	624 (24·56)	D
O-540-J	6	175 (235) at 2,400	8·86 (541·5)	8·5	100	162 (357)	989 (38·93)	848 (33·37)	519 (20·43)	D
VO-540-B	6	227 (305) at 3,200	8·86 (541·5)	7·3	80/87	202 (446)	882 (34·73)	880 (34·70)	617 (24·29)	D V
VO-540-C	6	227 (305) at 3,200 to 915 m (3,000 ft)	8·86 (541·5)	8·7	100	200 (441)	882 (34·73)	880 (34·70)	649 (25·57)	D V
IO-540-C	6	186 (250) at 2,575	8·86 (541·5)	8·5	91/96	170 (375)	976 (38·42)	848 (33·37)	622 (24·46)	D
IO-540-K	6	224 (300) at 2,700	8·86 (541·5)	8·7	100	201 (443)	999 (39·34)	870 (34·25)	498 (19·60)	D
IO-540-W	6	175 (235) at 2,400	8·86 (541·5)	8·5	100	166 (367)	989 (38·93)	848 (33·37)	492 (19·35)	D
AEIO-540-D	6	194 (260) at 2,700	8·86 (541·5)	8·5	91/96	174 (386)	999 (39·34)	848 (33·37)	621 (24·46)	D
AEIO-540-L	6	224 (300) at 2,700	8·86 (541·5)	8·7	100	202 (445)	989 (38·93)	870 (34·25)	622 (24·46)	D
TIO-540-A	6	231 (310) at 2,575 to 4,575 m (15,000 ft)	8·86 (541·5)	7·3	100	232 (511)	1,304 (51·34)	870 (34·25)	577 (22·71)	D
TIO-540-C	6	186 (250) at 2,575 to 4,575 m (15,000 ft)	8·86 (541·5)	7·2	100	205 (456)	1,026 (40·38)	848 (33·37)	770 (30·33)	D
TIO/LTIO-540-F	6	242 (325) at 2,575 to 4,575 m (15,000 ft)	8·86 (541·5)	7·3	100	233 (514)	1,304 (51·34)	870 (34·25)	570 (22·42)	D
TIO/LTIO-540-J	6	261 (350) at 2,575 to 4,575 m (15,000 ft)	8·86 (541·5)	7·3	100	235 (518)	1,308 (51·50)	870 (34·25)	573 (22·56)	D
TIO-540-S	6	224 (300) at 2,700 to 3,660 m (12,000 ft)	8·86 (541·5)	7·3	100	228 (502)	1,004 (39·56)	915 (36·02)	667 (26·28)	D
TIO/LTIO-540-U	6	261 (350) at 2,500 to 4,575 m (15,000 ft)	8·86 (541·5)	7·3	100	248 (547)	1,204 (47·40)	870 (34·25)	574 (22·59)	D
TIO/LTIO-540-V	6	269 (360) at 2,600 to 5,486 m (18,000 ft)	8·86 (541·5)	7·3	100	248 (547)	1,352 (53·21)	886 (34·88)	621 (24·44)	D
TIO-541-E	6	283 (380) at 2,900 to 4,575 m (15,000 ft)	8·86 (541·5)	7·3	100	270 (596)	1,282 (50·70)	905 (35·66)	640 (25·17)	D
TIGO-541-E	6	317 (425) at 3,200 to 4,575 m (15,000 ft)	8·86 (541·5)	7·3	100	319 (704)	1,462 (57·57)	885 (34·86)	575 (22·65)	0·667
IO-720-A	8	298 (400) at 2,650	11·84 (722)	8·7	100	257 (567)	1,179 (46·41)	870 (34·25)	573 (22·53)	D
IO-720-B	8	298 (400) at 2,650	11·84 (722)	8·7	100	252 (556)	1,218 (47·97)	870 (34·25)	530 (20·88)	D
IO-720-D	8	298 (400) at 2,650	11·84 (722)	8·7	100	259 (570)	1,189 (46·80)	870 (34·25)	562 (22·11)	D

*Model designation code: A, Aerobatic; AE, Aerobatic engine; G, Geared; H, Helicopter; I, Fuel injected; L, Left-hand rotation crankshaft; O, Opposed cylinders; S, Supercharged; T, Turbocharged; V, Vertical mounting; †D, Direct drive; V, Vertical mounting

octane minimum grade fuels, respectively. Fully aerobatic models are available.

AVCO LYCOMING O-360 and IO-360 SERIES

The O-360 series is basically the same as the O-320 except for an increase in stroke to 111 mm (4⅜ in). Like the O-320, this engine is manufactured with low or high compression, with carburettor or fuel injection. The various models include aerobatic capability, a specific design for helicopters and a turbocharged version. The IO-360 is built in several versions; the IO-360-A series has fuel injection, tuned induction and high output cylinders, while the IO-360-B series has continuous flow port injection and standard cylinders. In the TIO-360-C the turbocharger is pilot controlled, a mechanical link closing the wastegate as the throttle is advanced.

AVCO LYCOMING O-540 and IO-540 SERIES

The O-540 is basically a direct drive, six-cylinder version of the four-cylinder O-360. It is available in low and high compression versions, and the VO-540 is in production as a helicopter power plant with crankshaft vertical. Fuel injected IO-540 models are manufactured in a variety of configurations, with ratings of 186-224 kW (250-300 hp). An aerobatic version is available. Many of these engines, particularly in the higher horsepower range, have a tuned induction system. Continuous monitoring and computer analysis of engine service records has made it possible to increase the recommended time between overhauls (TBO) for these engines; most models have a TBO of 2,000 h. The most recent members of this family are the -J series of direct drive engines.

AVCO LYCOMING TIO-540 SERIES

This is a turbocharged version of the fuel injected IO-540, with tuned induction. It is manufactured in a wide range of powers for unpressurised Piper Navajo and turbocharged Saratoga aircraft. The turbo can be auto-controlled or, in the 540-S, governed directly by throttle lever position. The latest model, the V2AD, has an intercooler and down-draught cooling.

The 231 kW (310 hp) Avco Lycoming TIO-540 six-cylinder engine fitted to the Piper Navajo C

AVCO LYCOMING TIO-541 SERIES

Although the displacement of this turbocharged, six-cylinder series is the same as that of the TIO-540, the TIO-541 and geared TIGO-541 are totally redesigned. The accessory housing is an integral part of the crankcase, and the new design features allow these engines to operate at the high end of the Lycoming power spectrum. The TIO-541-E is rated at 283 kW (380 hp) and the geared TIGO-541-E at 317 kW (425 hp). Times between overhauls are recommended at 1,600 and 1,200 h, respectively. A double scroll blower is available to provide cabin pressurisation.

AVCO LYCOMING IO-720 SERIES

This eight-cylinder version of the IO-540 is used in a variety of aircraft at ratings from 280 to 298 kW (375 to 400 hp). Time between overhauls is 1,800 h (1,500 in agricultural applications).

Avco Lycoming O-235-L rated at 86 kW (115 hp)

The 175 kW (235 hp) Avco Lycoming O-540-J six-cylinder engine

AVCO LYCOMING/PRATT & WHITNEY

AVCO LYCOMING TEXTRON

Stratford, Connecticut 06497

UNITED TECHNOLOGIES PRATT & WHITNEY

East Hartford, Connecticut 06108

These companies joined forces in August 1984 to submit a proposal for joint development of a new turboshaft engine to power the US Army's LHX next-generation helicopter. In July 1985 the Avco Lycoming and Pratt & Whitney team received one of two competitive development contracts that were awarded. The Army designation of the Avco Lycoming/Pratt & Whitney engine is T800-APW-800.

AVCO/PW T800-APW-800

This 895 kW (1,200 shp class) turboshaft engine is based on the Avco Lycoming PLT34 (Advanced Technology Demonstrator Engine), which by late 1985 had run more than 2,300 component and 1,200 complete engine hours. Dimensions are metric.

Type: Free-turbine turboshaft engine.

Inlet: Large diameter annular with integral particle separator. Folded sheet construction.

Compressor: Drum and disc assembly of two axial stages and one centrifugal. Stators ahead of axial stages are both variable incidence.

Combustion Chamber: High-efficiency folded annular reverse-flow.

Turbines: Two-stage gas generator turbine with single-crystal aircooled blades. Two-stage power turbine with uncooled blades. First power turbine disc connected around front face of second disc, which is overhung downstream of main turbine section ball bearing on central driveshaft, with splined output at front of engine.

Gearcase: Tower shaft takes drive vertically to grouped accessories above engine. All parts combat tolerant.

Control System: Dual redundant digital electronic control. Hamilton Standard is teamed with Lucas Aerospace to develop the integrated engine management system, which incorporates direct turbine blade metal temperature sensing.

Dimensions:
- Length: 986 mm (38·8 in)
- Basic diameter: 470 mm (18·5 in)

Weight, Dry: 185·0 kg (298·0 lb)

Performance Rating (S/L, ISA):
- T-O: 895 kW (1,200 shp)

Mockup of the T800-APW-800 with inlet and particle separator

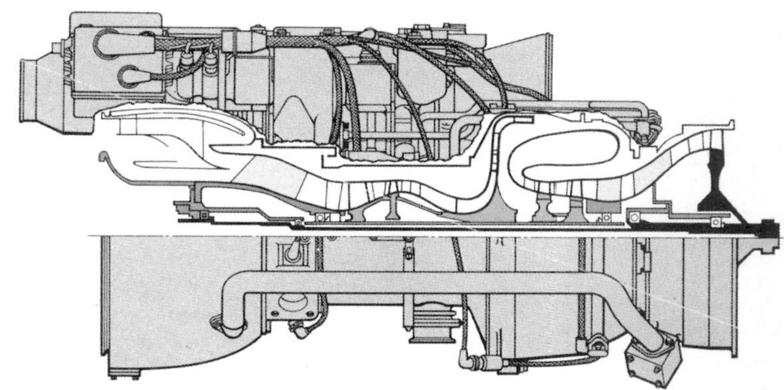

Cross-section of the PLT34 predecessor of the Avco/PW T800 turboshaft engine

Cutaway drawing of the Avco Lycoming/Pratt & Whitney T800-APW-800 turboshaft engine

CSD

CHEMICAL SYSTEMS DIVISION
(A division of United Technologies Corporation)

PO Box 50015, San Jose, California 95150-0015
Telephone: (408) 281 1121
DIVISION EXECUTIVE VICE-PRESIDENT AND GENERAL MANAGER: David E. Lee
DIVISION SENIOR VICE-PRESIDENT: Daniel Nuzzo

In 1983 CSD joined UTC Defense Systems Group as an operating division of Norden Systems. It was re-formed into four sections: Space and Strategic Boosters, Space Maneuvering Systems, Tactical Systems, and Advanced Technology.

Since its founding in the late 1950s, CSD has conducted a continuous programme of rocket technology. It is currently engaged in research, development and production of rockets, rocket propellants and advanced propulsion systems.

CSD IUS

In October 1976 the US Air Force awarded the Boeing/CSD team a contract to develop the Inertial Upper Stage (IUS) for the Space Shuttle and the Titan 34D space launch vehicle. The Boeing/CSD IUS completed its validation phase on 19 December 1977, after a successful test firing of the 2,310 mm (91 in) diameter rocket motor at the Arnold Engineering Development Center (AEDC). During the firing, the 9,979 kg (22,000 lb) motor encountered no difficulties during an unusually long (154 s) burn. Key components, including the advanced flightweight nozzle, proved their survivability. Average thrust was 173·6 kN (39,000 lb) and maximum 249·2 kN (56,000 lb) at a simulated height of 33,800 m (111,000 ft). Full scale development of the IUS propulsion system began on 1 March 1978 under a $32 million contract award from Boeing Aerospace. The propulsion system for the two-stage IUS consists of two solid rocket motors designed by CSD: a 2·31 m (91 in) aft motor, designated SRM-1, containing 9,707 kg (21,400 lb) of propellant, and a 1·6 m (63 in) forward stage motor, designated SRM-2, with 2,722 kg (6,000 lb) of propellant. In May 1978 CSD received an award from Boeing to develop the thrust vector control (TVC) servo actuator system to control the movable nozzle. The basic TVC system consists of two controllers and four actuators powered by 28V batteries. In December 1978 CSD received a contract to produce a servo-actuator system to raise the IUS to deployment position inside the Shuttle Orbiter's cargo bay.

CSD small IUS, motor type SRM-2, showing the EEC (extendible exit cone) in the nested position

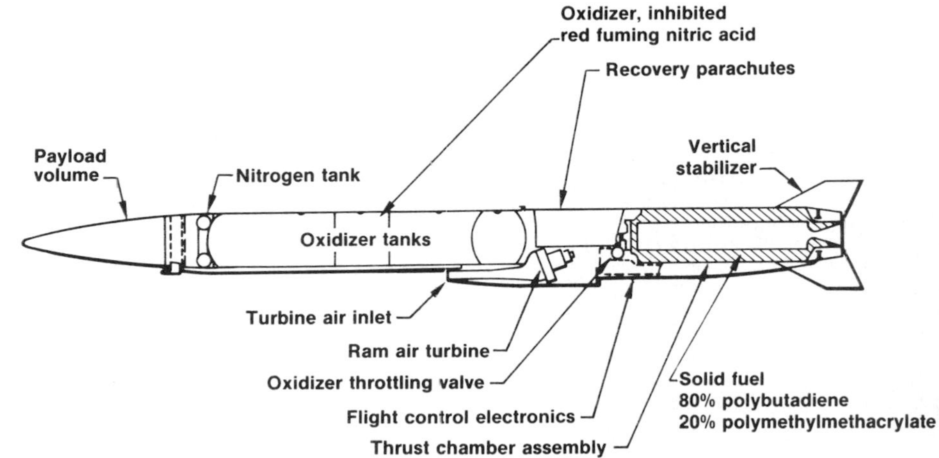

Simplified section of Firebolt showing CSD hybrid propulsion

On 13 August 1980, the first offloaded IUS motor was test fired, with the most extreme propellant offload (50 per cent) of any solid rocket motor ever tested. The motor was fired for approximately 64 s at a simulated altitude of 30,480 m (100,000 ft). It burned 4,808 kg (1,600 lb) of HTPB propellant and generated 275·78 kN (62,000 lb) max thrust.

By January 1986 no failure had occurred in 34 static firings, despite the combination of such advanced features as a Kevlar fibre case, carbon/carbon integrated throat and entrance, igniter for full or reduced propellant loads, the first extensible exit cone for flight, with Techroll seal, and a new nozzle actuation bearing. The first Titan 34D IUS mission flew in October 1982 and the first shuttle IUS mission (STS-6) in April 1983. A flight control anomaly during STS-6 resulted in extensive reviews and SRM-2 tests before Shuttle flights resumed.

The SRM-1 has been selected to power a new Shuttle upper stage being developed by Orbital Sciences and Martin Marietta, and a spin-stabilised derivative has been developed to place the Hughes Intelsat VI comsats in transfer orbit from 1987.

CSD BOOSTER SEPARATION MOTOR

In late 1975 NASA selected CSD to develop and produce solid propellant booster separation motors (BSM) to be used on the first six development flights of the Space Shuttle programme.

The BSMs are used to separate the two reusable solid rocket boosters (SRB) approximately 110 s after launch of the Space Shuttle. Each SRB requires eight BSMs, four forward and four aft, which fire for less than 1 s to achieve safe separation. In September 1978 the motor passed acceptance by NASA. The last of the 104 motors originally ordered was shipped in early 1980. CSD is now producing the BSMs for Shuttle flights Nos. 9 to 35, and is working on BSMs for Nos. 36 to 50.

Each BSM has a length of 838 mm (33·0 in) and a diameter of 327 mm (12·88 in), with a weight of 73·0 kg (161 lb). It uses CSD UTP-19048 (HTPB) propellant, and has 62·5 kN-s (14,000 lb-s) minimum total impulse WEB action time, and 67·0 kN-s (15,000 lb-s) minimum action time. Burn time (WEB) performance time limit is 0·8 s. Maximum thrust called for is 129·5 kN (29,000 lb), with a WEB action time average thrust of 82·6 kN (18,500 lb) minimum.

Each motor consists of solid propellant, motor case with attachments, nozzle, igniter and pyrotechnic initiators. Aft motors are provided with cork insulation for protection from the Shuttle's main engine plumes and solid rocket booster exhaust. Forward separation motors are equipped with an aerodynamic heatshield which opens instantly on motor ignition but does not discharge any debris that could damage the Orbiter.

CSD HYBRID PROPULSION

CSD's hybrid rocket produced for the Department of Defense High Altitude Supersonic Target (HAST) drone weighs 390 kg (860 lb). It uses a polybutadiene and methyl methacrylate fuel grain, and nitric acid as its liquid oxidiser. Ablative cooled, its thrust ranges from 0·88-5·34 kN (200 to 1,200 lb) at altitudes between 10,670 and 30,480 m (35,000 and 100,000 ft). In 1978 the HAST was flown successfully three times by the US Navy.

In 1980 CSD received a contract for full scale development of the propulsion system of the Teledyne Ryan Firebolt, the advanced successor to HAST. A total of 30 flights was completed by March 1984, the vehicles being launched from an F-4 and cruising at Mach 4 at above 30,000 m (100,000 ft). A production decision was then expected, with deliveries to the USAF and Navy beginning in 1986.

CSD AIR-BREATHING PROPULSION

CSD spearheads the efforts of its parent, United Technologies Corporation, in the research and development of ramjet propulsion systems. In 1973 it was awarded a contract by the US Navy to research, design and develop a modern ramjet engine (MRE). Called an integral rocket/ramjet (IRR), the device involves both solid rocket and liquid fuel ramjet technology. It operates as a solid rocket booster until it reaches supersonic speeds. At that point, through a series of mechanical changes that take place in flight, it becomes a ramjet. These changes involve the opening of air inlets, an increase in the nozzle diameter and a switch to the burning of liquid fuel and air in the combustion chamber within a common system.

In 1979 CSD was chosen by Hughes Aircraft to supply the propulsion subsystem for the ducted rocket missile that Hughes is developing for the US Air Force. CSD is responsible for design, development, integration and testing of the gas generator and air induction system.

In the ducted rocket a solid rocket fuel produces a fuel-rich gas. This is injected into a combustion (ramburner) chamber, mixed with ram air and further burned to provide sustained thrust at supersonic speeds. The ram air is introduced through inlet ducts alongside the vehicle. Compared to a conventional rocket, the ducted rocket is claimed to offer many times the thrust duration, permitting powered flight all the way to a target and a greater range with less weight. In 1982 CSD demonstrated 18:1 throttlings adequate for all advanced AAM missions.

In 1980 CSD received a contract to develop advanced high-energy solid fuels for ramjets. The study, for the Naval Weapons Center and Air Force Aeropropulsion Laboratory, calls for fuels offering a greater range of performance for tactical missiles.

In December 1983 CSD announced the first test of a hypervelocity missile with integral solid-fuel rocket/ramjet propulsion. In collaboration with the US Army Missile Command, CSD demonstrated SPARK (solid propellant advanced ramjet kinetic energy missile). Spin stabilised, the 165 mm (6·5 in) diameter missile cruised at sea level at Mach 3·5, to complete initial development of a propulsion system for anti-armour and anti-aircraft missiles.

CSD is testing integral rocket/ramjet combustors which utilise the technology of swirl combustion. CSD engineers expect to realise a significant improvement in combustor performance while reducing combustor length by as much as 50 per cent.

Another programme aims at developing a ramjet capable of cruising at Mach 6, while work is also proceeding on consumable air inlet covers to prevent ejected debris from hitting launch aircraft.

CSD solid fuel ramjet test vehicle mounted in supersonic tunnel at NASA Lewis Laboratory

CUYUNA

CUYUNA ENGINE CO

Box 116, Crosby, Minnesota 56441
Telephone: (218) 546 8313
PRESIDENT: Roger P. Worth

This company is one of the largest suppliers of engines for microlight and ultralight aircraft. By January 1986 well over 10,000 engines had been sold.

CUYUNA 215

Basic single-cylinder two-stroke with axial fan cooling. Accessories can include regulator and/or rectifier, carburetion/exhaust system and reverse-flow fan. Bore 67·5 mm (2·658 in). Stroke 60·0 mm (2·362 in). Capacity 214 cc (13·06 cu in). Dry weight (215D direct drive) 19 kg (42 lb), (215R for indirect speed-reducing drive) 20·4 kg (45 lb). Max power 15 kW (20 hp) at 6,000/6,500 rpm.

CUYUNA 430

Twin version with cylinders of same size. Dry weight (430D and 430R) 29·5 kg (65 lb), (430LC liquid cooled) 28-30·8 kg (62-68 lb). Max power (430D and 430R) 26 kW (35 hp) at 6,200 rpm; (430LC) 30 kW (40 hp); (high-performance 430) 32 kW (43 hp) at 6,800 rpm.

CUYUNA ULII-02

This improved 430R is lighter, because of use of magnesium alloys and a new crankshaft. It has improved (capacitor-discharge) ignition, and the rear cylinder runs cooler. Rated at 26·9 kW (36 hp) at 6,000 to 6,250 rpm, it weighs 26·3 kg (58 lb).

Cuyuna 430D two-cylinder two-stroke engine

CUYUNA PAVE TIGER

This two-cylinder engine was developed to power the now-cancelled Boeing Pave Tiger expendable RPV described in the 1984-85 *Jane's*. A similar 438 cc engine powers the current Brave-200. It has free-air cooling, but cylinders the same size as before. Rated at 20·9 kW (28 hp), it weighs 23·8 kg (52·5 lb) complete with 1,200W alternator.

Cuyuna ULII-02 two-cylinder two-stroke engine

DRAGON

DRAGON ENGINE CORPORATION

14215 NE 193 Place, Woodinville, Washington 98072
Telephone: (206) 487 0420
Telex: 269847 DEC UR
PRESIDENT: Robert E. Davis
CONCEPT DESIGNER: Alex Pong
VICE-PRESIDENT SALES: Daniel T. Krpan

This company began work in 1981 as a public corporation registered in Washington state, but with Universal Technical Services of Houston, Texas, as manufacturing agents, and with major component manufacture and assembly in the Republic of Singapore.

DRAGON 1.7-50

This aircooled four-stroke is a six-cylinder radial notable for large capacity, low rpm and, it is claimed, perfect symmetry and balance.

CYLINDERS: Bore 85·5 mm (3·36 in). Stroke 50 mm (1·97 in). Capacity 1,721 cc (106 cu in). Arranged in two rows of three. Compression ratio 8·5.

CRANKSHAFT: Two throws each with patented connecting rod interface eliminating need for master rods. Direct drive, counterclockwise from front.

SYSTEMS: Supply of auto fuel, min 80 octane. Pumped lubricating oil from tank. Full dual ignition, electric starter and 12V alternator.

DIMENSIONS:

Max width	526 mm (20·7 in)
Max height	500 mm (19·7 in)
Length	438 mm (17·25 in)
WEIGHT, DRY:	35·4 kg (78 lb)
MAX RATING:	37·3 kW (50 hp) at 2,500 rpm

SPECIFIC FUEL CONSUMPTION: 93 μg/J (0·55 lb/h/hp)

Dragon 1.7-50 six-cylinder radial (37·3 kW; 50 hp)

EMG

EMG ENGINEERING COMPANY

PO Box 1368, Hesperia, California 92345

Telephone: (714) 247 8519

Eugene M. Gluhareff, a pioneer of ultra-lightweight rotorcraft, has been developing a unique type of air-breathing jet engine which he considers to offer notable advantages over all other systems for rotor tip drive. The first model is the G8-2, which was designed in 1955 and fully developed over the next ten years for tip drive or sailplane auxiliary propulsion. It has also been used for surface application in a go-kart, and in numerous static rigs sold to universities and other organisations. Production has been hard pressed to keep up with demand, a fast growing market being radio controlled flight vehicles. Manned platforms, hang gliders and small helicopters are also proving to be a large market for EMG engines.

GLUHAREFF G8-2

Although extremely simple, the G8 series corresponds to no prior jet system. The design is based on propane, a readily available volatile fuel. The pressure of the liquid propane in the tank delivers the fuel, via a needle valve serving as the throttle, to the burner unit. The fuel enters the burner duct and is immediately vaporised in a hot heat exchanger. Vapour then passes back down an insulated pipe to the injector where its residual pressure is converted to kinetic energy. The high velocity gas jet induces air through three 'supercharger' intakes, each synchronised to the internal flow, which gives the correct final fuel/air ratio to the mixture entering the combustion chamber. Here the mixture is initially ignited by a spark plug and thereafter burns continuously. The intake ducts are tuned to each other to create one-way flow. Resonance in the tailpipe is undesirable and is prevented by making the propelling nozzle of fishtail shape.

Since 1979 three more models have been available, the G8-2-20, -80 and -130, rated respectively at 0·09, 0·36 and 0·58 kN (20, 80 and 130 lb st). A G8-2-250 (1·1 kN, 250 lb st) was then on bench test. The best specific fuel consumption has been reduced dramatically from 170 mg/Ns (6 lb/h/lb st) to only 21·8 mg/Ns (0·77 lb/h/lb st).

The units are manufactured by Gluhareff's subsidiary EMG Engineering Co. Customers have the option of buying plans only, a construction package, partly prefabricated, or an assembly kit or finished engine.

GARRETT

GARRETT TURBINE ENGINE COMPANY (a division of The Garrett Corporation)

Sky Harbor Airport, 111 S 34th St, PO Box 5217, Phoenix, Arizona 85010
Telephone: (602) 231 1000
PRESIDENT: Malcolm Craig
VICE-PRESIDENT, SALES: Steven Burns

The Garrett Corporation, one of the Allied/Signal Companies, has been called the world's largest producer of small gas turbines. Development of the first Garrett (formerly Garrett-AiResearch) small turbines began in 1946.

At the end of 1984 Garrett announced its collaboration with Allison on the T800-LHT-800 turboshaft for the LHX helicopter programme. This is mentioned briefly under LHTEC in this section.

GARRETT ATF3

US military designation: F104-GA-100

Considered to be the first three-spool engine to run in the USA, the Garrett ATF3 was the first engine in the world to combine the three-spool features with a reverse-flow combustion system and turbines, and mixed-flow exhaust.

The arrangement of components allows the fan design to be determined largely independently of the gas generator compressor requirements, and permits operation at optimum fan speed. Omission of fan inlet guide vanes, mixing of the gas generator exhaust with the fan airflow, and double reversal of the internal airflow, enable the ATF3 to offer significant reductions in overall noise and IR signature.

Other design considerations include reliability, maintainability and elimination of visible smoke. The accessories are revealed by removing the tailcone fairing, and their positioning at the rear of the engine is claimed to reduce installed drag.

The basic design was completed in early 1966, and testing of demonstrator engines was initiated in May 1968. Under US Air Force contract, the ATF3 successfully completed preliminary flight rating tests in 1972 at 18 kN (4,050 lb) thrust. Both the aerodynamic and mechanical design criteria were established around a sea-level, ISA +15°C take-off rating of 22·46 kN (5,050 lb).

In May 1976 it was announced that the **ATF3-6A** had been selected by Dassault-Breguet to power the Falcon 200 business jet. FAA certification was achieved on 24 December 1981, and Falcon 200 deliveries began in 1983. The ATF3-6A is offered under a retrofit programme for Falcon 20 aircraft. It also powers the HU-25A Guardian.

TYPE: Three-shaft axial-flow turbofan.

INTAKE: Direct pitot, fixed type. No inlet vanes or struts. Total airflow 73·5 kg (162 lb)/s.

LOW PRESSURE (FAN) SYSTEM: Single-stage titanium fan, driven by three-stage IP turbine. Bypass ratio 2·8 at take-off.

INTERMEDIATE PRESSURE SYSTEM: Five-stage titanium axial IP compressor, each stage having a separate disc, driven by two-stage LP turbine. Airflow is then delivered to rearward facing HP compressor via eight tubes feeding into an annular duct concentric with the bypass duct. Core airflow 18·15 kg (40 lb)/s.

HIGH PRESSURE SYSTEM: Single-stage titanium centrifugal compressor, driven by single-stage HP turbine. IP airflow enters the single-sided impeller from the rear. Overall pressure ratio (T-O) 21, (high altitude cruise) 25.

COMBUSTION SYSTEM: Reverse-flow annular type.

TURBINES: Single-stage HP, three-stage IP and two-stage LP turbines drive, respectively, the HP, fan (LP) and IP compressors. IP and LP turbines have fully shrouded blades. Aircooled first-stage nozzle vanes and HP rotor blades. Exhaust gases turned 180° through eight sets of cascades to mix with fan bypass flow.

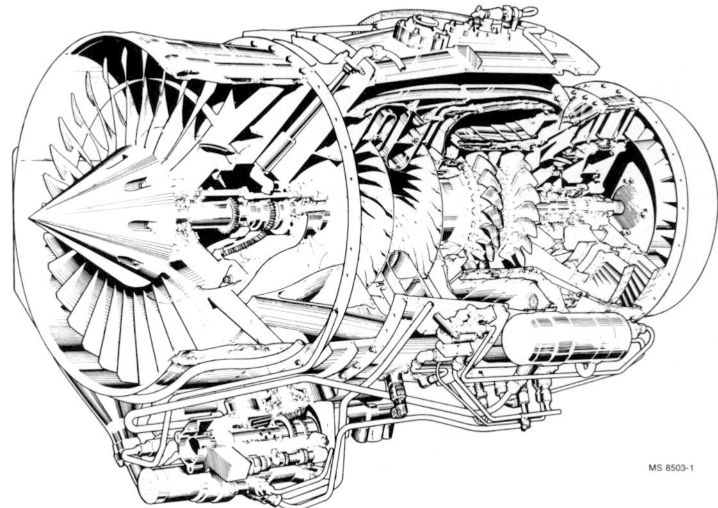

Cutaway drawing of the Garrett F109-GA-100 turbofan (5·92 kN; 1,330 lb st)

FUEL SYSTEM: Electromechanical, incorporating solid state computer. Manual emergency backup system.

ACCESSORY DRIVES: Three drive pads on rear-mounted gearbox driven by HP shaft, providing for hydraulic pump, starter/generator and one spare. Accessory cooling by fan discharge air which is exhausted through a nozzle at the tip of the fairing.

EXHAUST SYSTEM: Mixed fan and turbine exhaust discharged to atmosphere through annular nozzle surrounding combustion section.

LUBRICATION SYSTEM: Self-contained hot tank type; tank integral with gearbox.

MOUNTING: Two-plane pickup system.

STARTING: Electric or pneumatic.

DIMENSIONS:

Length	2,591 mm (102·0 in)
Max diameter	853 mm (33·6 in)

WEIGHT, DRY: 510 kg (1,125 lb)

PERFORMANCE RATINGS (uninstalled):

T-O (ISA, S/L, static)	24·20 kN (5,440 lb st)
Cruise (12,200 m; 40,000 ft at Mach 0·8)	4·69 kN (1,055 lb)

SPECIFIC FUEL CONSUMPTION:

At T-O rating (S/L, ISA static)	14·33 mg/Ns (0·506 lb/h/lb st)
At cruise (as above)	23·51 mg/Ns (0·83 lb/h/lb)

GARRETT TFE76

US military designation: F109-GA-100

Based initially on the core of the T76/TPE331 family of turboprops, with significant performance improvements, this small turbofan was selected in July 1982 as the engine of the US Air Force's next generation trainer, the Fairchild T-46A. Garrett's initial contract was valued at $121 million and covered the development of the F109 and delivery of 29 engines, with an option for a further 119 engines.

The first TFE76 ran in early December 1983, and 6,000 hours had been logged by December 1985, when eleven test engines were involved in the programme. However, the T-46A programme was subsequently cancelled.

The core of the F109 will be used in the ATE109 helicopter engine, described under LHTEC in this section.

TYPE: Two-shaft turbofan.

FAN: Single-stage, with 28 blades with part span shrouds (snubbers) inserted in self-de-icing rotating spinner. Double shell with blade containment features. One row of straightener vanes between fan and flow divider.

COMPRESSOR: Tandem two-stage centrifugal with titanium impellers. LP and HP bleeds, with optimum bleed for environmental control system.

COMBUSTION CHAMBER: Annular reverse flow type, with piloted air blast nozzles for low emissions without visible exhaust.

HP TURBINE: Two-stage axial with low blade count. Low-risk single pass cooling. Single blade replacement.

LP TURBINE: Two-stage axial, with inserted blades with complete tip shrouds. Low exit swirl through exit guide vanes.

JETPIPE: Concentric fan and jetpipes with fixed geometry.

CONTROL SYSTEM: Digital with hydromechanical backup. Auto start sequence, trimless operation with self-test and engine monitoring capability.

ACCESSORIES: Mounted on one-piece gearbox, under intermediate case, with drive from HP shaft taken through one of five main aerofoil struts spaced at 72°.

DIMENSIONS:

Length	942 mm (37·1 in)
Diameter	523 mm (20·6 in)

WEIGHT, DRY: 182 kg (400 lb)

PERFORMANCE RATINGS (ISA):

T-O	5·92 kN (1,330 lb st)
Max continuous (9,145 m; 30,000 ft, Mach 0·5)	1·78 kN (400 lb)

SPECIFIC FUEL CONSUMPTION:

Max T-O as above	11·10 mg/Ns (0·392 lb/h/lb st)

GARRETT TFE731

Announced in April 1969, the TFE731 is a two-spool geared turbofan designed to confer US coast to coast range upon business jet aircraft. Use of a geared fan confers flexibility in operation and yields optimum performance at up to 15,545 m (51,000 ft).

Component testing began in March 1969. The first engine ran in September 1970, and was tested at Phoenix in a Learjet 25. FAA certification and first production deliveries to Dassault for the Falcon 10 took place in August 1972.

In October 1972 it was stated that the Lockheed JetStar would be re-engined with the **TFE731-3**, flat rated at 16·46 kN (3,700 lb st) by a modest increase in turbine inlet temperature. The TFE731-3 was certificated in 1974. The modified aircraft is designated JetStar II, and first flew in July 1974. AiResearch Aviation converted a number of JetStar I aircraft to have TFE731-3 power.

Since 1973 the TFE731, in various subtypes, has been selected for the Gates Learjet 35/36, Cessna Citation III, Dassault-Breguet Falcon 50, BAe 125-700, IAI Westwind 1 and 2 and Astra, Rockwell International's Sabreliner 65A, CASA C-101 and Argentine IA 63 trainer and light attack aircraft and Learjet 54/56; proposals have been made for RPV and other short life programmes.

In 1980 the **731-5** was announced, to offer higher thrust and reduced noise, while maintaining low smoke characteristics. The -5 is installationally similar to earlier models but has a higher bypass ratio fan driven by a new LP turbine, the design of which was demonstrated in a NASA programme. This major improved engine was certificated in November 1983. Its first applications are the BAe 125-800 and the CASA C-101. The **TFE731-5A**, with a mixer nozzle reducing specific fuel consumption and raising standard thrust to that of the previous APR rating, was certificated in December 1984. It powers the Dassault-Breguet Falcon 900. Volvo Flygmotor has a 5·6 per cent share of the 731-5 production programme.

By May 1985 deliveries of TFE731 series engines had reached 5,000. Output had risen to 60 per month.

TYPE: Turbofan with two shafts and geared front fan.

AIR INTAKE: Direct pitot, fixed, without guide vanes.

FAN: Single-stage axial titanium fan, with inserted blades. The fan shaft is connected directly to the planetary gearbox ring gear. Max fan airflow, sea level static, TFE731-2, 51·25 kg (113 lb)/s; -3, 53·7 kg (118·3 lb)/s; -5, 64·86 kg (143 lb)/s. Bypass ratio, -2, 2·66; -3, 2·80; -5, 3·48.

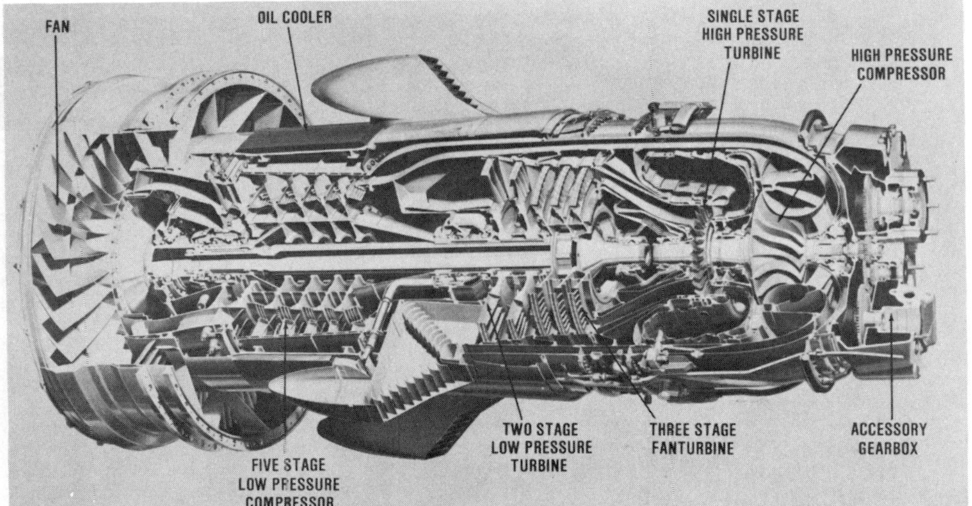

Cutaway of the Garrett ATF3-6A three-shaft turbofan (24·20 kN; 5,440 lb st)

COMPRESSOR: Low pressure compressor has four stages (TFE731-4, five stages), each with a separate disc. Rotors and stators have inserted blades and vanes. High pressure compressor, carried on a separate shaft running at higher speeds, is centrifugal. Overall pressure ratio (S/L, static): -2, 14·0; -3, 14·6.

COMBUSTION CHAMBER: Annular combustion chamber of reverse flow type, with 12 fuel nozzles inserted radially and injecting fuel tangentially.

FUEL SYSTEM: Hydro-electronic, with single lever control to mechanical and electronic elements.

TURBINES: High pressure turbine has a single axial stage with inserted blades. Low pressure turbine has three axial stages, all with inserted blades. Average inlet gas temperature to HP turbine, S/L, max T-O thrust, -2, 860°C; -3, 907°C; -5, 952°C.

JETPIPE: Short fan duct facilitating installation of fan reverser. Fixed core nozzle.

ACCESSORY DRIVES: Accessories driven from HP spool are grouped around underside of the forward section of the fan duct. Pads are provided on the front side of the accessory gearbox for the airframe type accessories: hydraulic pump, starter/generator or starter motor and alternators. Pads on the back side of the gearbox drive the engine accessories: fuel control unit and oil pump.

DIMENSIONS:

Length overall:	
-2, -3	1,520 mm (59·83 in)
-5	1,665 mm (65·54 in)
-5A	2,314 mm (91·10 in)
Intake diameter	716 mm (28·2 in)
Width:	
-2, -3	869 mm (34·20 in)
-5, -5A	858 mm (33·79 in)
Height overall:	
-2, -3	1,000 mm (39·36 in)
-5, -5A	1,029 mm (40·52 in)

WEIGHT, DRY:

-2, -3	329 kg (725 lb)
-5	386 kg (850 lb)

PERFORMANCE RATINGS:

Max T-O (S/L, 24·4°C):	
-2	15·57 kN (3,500 lb st)
-3	16·46 kN (3,700 lb st)
-3B-100	16·24 kN (3,650 lb st)
-5	19·15 kN (4,304 lb st)
-5A	20·02 kN (4,500 lb st)
Max T-O (APR, auto performance reserve):	
-3	17·13 kN (3,850 lb st)
-5	20·02 kN (4,500 lb st)
Cruise (12,200 m; 40,000 ft at Mach 0·8):	
-2	3·36 kN (755 lb)
-3	3·64 kN (817 lb)
-3B-100	3·75 kN (844 lb)
-5	4·25 kN (955 lb)
-5A	4·39 kN (986 lb)

SPECIFIC FUEL CONSUMPTION:

Max T-O (as above):	
-2	13·88 mg/Ns (0·49 lb/h/lb st)
-3	14·33 mg/Ns (0·506 lb/h/lb st)
-3B-100	14·36 mg/Ns (0·507 lb/h/lb st)
-5	13·71 mg/Ns (0·484 lb/h/lb st)
-5A	13·28 mg/Ns (0·469 lb/h/lb st)
Cruise (as above):	
-2	23·08 mg/Ns (0·815 lb/h/lb)
-3	23·65 mg/Ns (0·835 lb/h/lb)
-3B-100	23·11 mg/Ns (0·816 lb/h/lb)
-5	22·72 mg/Ns (0·802 lb/h/lb)
-5A	21·84 mg/Ns (0·771 lb/h/lb)

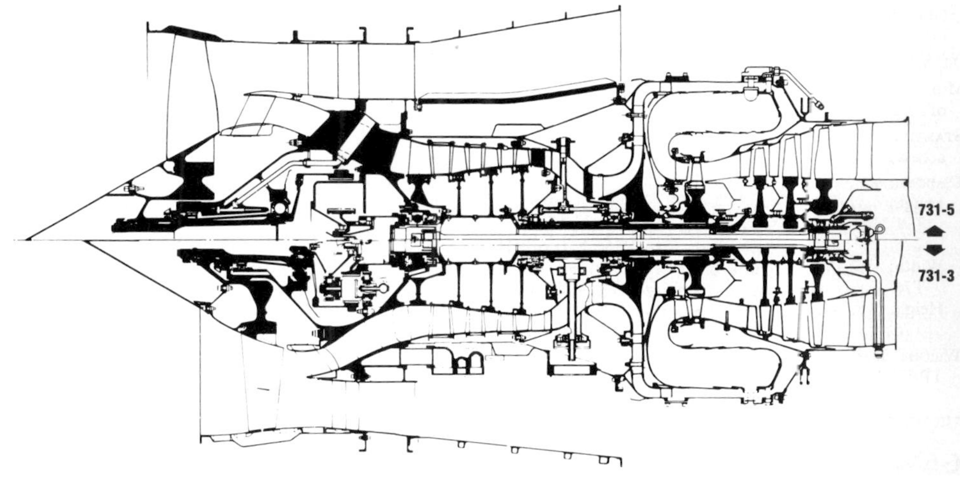

Section of the TFE731-5 (top half) and TFE731-3 (bottom half)

GARRETT TPE331

US military designation: T76

Based originally upon extensive experience with APUs, this was the first Garrett engine for aircraft propulsion. The military T76 achieved only modest sales, but the civil TPE331 has been most successful, in a series of versions. By January 1986 deliveries of all versions had passed 10,000, with 32,000,000 h of service experience. TBO had reached 3,600 h for the early models and 3,000 h for the -8, -9, -10 and -11 (in scheduled airline use, up to 9,000 h).

The following are major versions:

TPE331 series I, II. Initial production version, FAA certificated in February 1965. Rated at 451 ekW; 429 kW plus 0·33 kN (605 ehp; 575 shp plus 75 lb st). Redesignated **TPE331-25/61** and **-25/71** and produced until 1970. Powers Mitsubishi MU-2 (A to E models), Fairchild Industries/Pilatus Porter, Carstedt Jet Liner, Volpar Super Turbo 18, NZ Aerospace FU-24, Rockwell International Hawk Commander and 680, and DHC-2 Turbo Beaver.

TPE331-1 series. Certificated December 1967 at 526 ekW; 496 kW plus 0·44 kN (705 ehp; 665 shp plus 100 lb st). Powers Mitsubishi MU-2 (F and G), Pilatus Turbo-Porter and Fairchild Industries AU-23A Peacemaker, Mid West CJ600, Volpar Turboliner, Interceptor 400, Rockwell International Turbo Commander and (customer option) Thrush Commander, Swearingen Merlin IIB and NZ Aerospace Fletcher 1284, Marsh Turbo Thrush and Marsh Turbo Ag-Cat.

TPE331-2 series. Certificated in December 1967 at 563 ekW; 533 kW plus 0·45 kN (755 ehp; 715 shp plus 102 lb st). Powers Shorts Skyvan, CASA 212 pre-series and Volpar Turbo Goose and Turbo Beaver.

TPE331-3 series. Certificated in March 1970 at 674 ekW; 626 kW plus 0·71 kN (904 ehp; 840 shp plus 159 lb st). Uprated gas generator with increased airflow and pressure ratio, but same turbine temperature as in original TPE 331. Powers Fairchild Merlin III, IV and Metro, and Century Jetstream III.

TPE331-5/6 series. The -5 was certificated in March 1970; this matches the gas generator of the -3 series with the 715 shp gearbox, and is flat rated to 2,134 m (7,000 ft). Powers Mitsubishi MU-2, Beechcraft King Air B100 (-6), CASA 212 Aviocar (-5), Dornier 228 (-5), and Gulfstream Commander 840/900. The -5 designation indicates output speed of 1,591 rpm; the -6 has an output speed of 2,000 rpm.

TPE331-8. Matches compressor and gearbox of -3 with new turbine section. Thermodynamic power of 676 ekW; 645 kW (905 ehp; 865 shp) plus 0·47 kN (105 lb st), but flat rated at 533 kW (715 shp) to 36°C. Certification was received in September 1976. Powers Cessna Conquest II.

TPE331-9. Thermodynamic rating 645 kW (865 shp).

TPE331-10. Rated at 746 kW (1,000 shp). Certificated February 1978. Powers Mitsubishi Marquise and Solitaire, Gulfstream Commander 980/1000, Fairchild Merlin IIIC, CASA 212-200 and BAe Jetstream 31.

TPE331-11. Certificated 1979 at thermodynamic power of 746 kW (1,000 shp). Higher gearbox limit than Dash-10 engine; wet rating 820 kW (1,100 shp). Powers Fairchild Metro III and FMA IA 66 Pucará.

TPE331-12. Same size as -10 but offers 834 kW (1,119 shp). Certificated December 1984. The **TPE331-12B**, which powers the RAF future basic trainer (Shorts Tucano) is the subject of an exclusive offset agreement with Rolls-Royce covering engine parts manufacture, assembly, test and spares, which extends to Shorts' export sales. Rolls-Royce will make up to 30 per cent by value of engines for Shorts, and support RAF engines in service.

TPE331-14/15. Uprated TPE331s, initially for Piper Cheyenne 400 LS and Fairchild 400. They are essentially scaled-up models, with thermodynamic power in the 1,227 kW (1,645 shp) class, with significant improvements in fuel efficiency, component life and maintainability. Certification of the -14 model was obtained on 30 April 1984; it is flat rated at 746 kW (1,000 shp) for the Cheyenne 400 LS.

T76. Military engine, with gas generator similar to TPE331-1 series but with front end inverted, to give inlet above instead of below spinner. All models power Rockwell International OV-10 Bronco.

Except for the TPE331-14, all versions of the TPE331 and T76 are of similar frame size, and the following data apply generally to both models:

TYPE: Single-shaft turboprop.

PROPELLER DRIVE: Two-stage reduction gear, one helical spur and one planetary, with overall ratio of 20·865 : 1 or 26·3 : 1. Rotation clockwise or anticlockwise.

AIR INTAKE: Single scoop intake duct at top (T76) or bottom of engine, at front. Provision for bleed air de-icing.

COMPRESSOR: Tandem two-stage centrifugal type. Each impeller is single sided, and is made from titanium. First-stage casing of magnesium, with aluminium diffuser. Second-stage casing and diffuser of stainless steel. Mass flow, 2·61 kg (5·78 lb)/s for 25/61, 25/71, 2·81 kg (6·2 lb)/s for -1, 2·80 kg (6·17 lb)/s for -2 and T76, 3·52 kg (7·75 lb)/s for -251 and 3·54 kg (7·8 lb)/s for -3. Pressure ratio 8·0 for 25/61, 25/71, 8·34 for -1, 8·54 for -2 and T76, 10·37 for -251 and -3.

COMBUSTION CHAMBER: Annular type of high temperature alloy. High energy capacitor discharge ignition. Igniter plug on turbine plenum.

FUEL SYSTEM: Woodward or Bendix control system for use with Beta propeller governing control system. Five radial primary nozzles in continuous operation. Ten axial nozzles, simplex in early models and duplex in -10, -11, -12, -14/-15. Max fuel pressure 41·4 bars (600 lb/sq in).

FUEL GRADE (TPE331): Aviation turbine fuels ASTM designation D1655-64T types Jet A, Jet B and Jet A-1; MIL-F-5616-1, Grade JP-1.

FUEL GRADE (T76): MIL-L-5624F(2), Grades JP-4 and JP-5; MIL-G-5572, Grade 115/145.

NOZZLE GUIDE VANES: Axial vanes made from Inco 713C castings.

TURBINE: Three-stage axial-flow type. In early models, discs of first two stages of Inco 100, third stage of Inco 713C, attached to shaft by curvic couplings, with blades cast integrally with disc. In -10, -11, -12 forged first-stage disc with inserted blades. In -14/-15 forged discs with inserted blades in all three stages. Turbine inlet gas temperature, 987°C for 25/61, 25/71, 993°C for T76, 1,005°C for all other models.

JET PIPE: Fixed type, stainless steel.

ACCESSORIES: AND 20005 Type XV-B tachometer generator, AND 20002 Type XII-D starter/generator, AND 20010 Type XX-A propeller governor and AND 20001 Type XI-B hydraulic pump, all mounted on aft face of accessories case.

LUBRICATION SYSTEM: Medium pressure dry sump system. Gerotor internal gear type pressure and scavenge pumps.

Cutaway drawing of Garrett TPE331-14 turboprop (932 kW; 1,250 shp, or flat rated at 746 kW; 1,000 shp)

Normal oil supply pressure 6·90 bars (100 lb/sq in). Provision for automatic fuel filter anti-icing.

OIL SPECIFICATION: MIL-L-23699-(1) or MIL-L-7808.

MOUNTING: Five-point suspension. Three pads on aft face of accessory case, two pads at aft end of turbine plenum.

STARTING: Pad for 399A starter/generator on aft face of accessory case.

DIMENSIONS (approx):
- Length overall:
  - TPE331: 1,092 to 1,333 mm (43-52·5 in)
  - T76: 1,118 mm (44 in)
- Width: TPE331: 533 mm (21 in)
  - T76: 483 mm (19 in)
- Height: TPE331: 660 mm (26 in)
  - T76: 686 mm (27 in)

WEIGHT, DRY:
- TPE331-25/61, 71: 152 kg (335 lb)
- TPE331-1, -2: 152·5 kg (336 lb)
- T76: 155 kg (341 lb)
- TPE331-3: 161 kg (355 lb)
- TPE331-5: 163 kg (360 lb)
- TPE331-8: 168 kg (370 lb)
- TPE331-10: 172 kg (380 lb)
- TPE331-11: 182 kg (400 lb)
- TPE331-12: 176 kg (387 lb)
- TPE331-14/15: 256 kg (565 lb)

PERFORMANCE RATINGS:
- T-O: see under model listings
- Military (30 min): T76-G-410/411: 533 kW; 563 ekW (715 shp; 755 ehp)
- Normal: T76-G-410/411: 485 kW; 514·5 ekW (650 shp; 690 ehp)
- Max cruise (ISA, 3,050 m; 10,000 ft and 250 knots; 463 km/h; 288 mph):
  - TPE331-25/61, 71: 332 kW (445 shp)
  - TPE331-1: 404 kW (542 shp)
  - TPE331-2, T76: 430 kW (577 shp)
  - TPE331-3, -5: 530 kW (710 shp)

SPECIFIC FUEL CONSUMPTION:
- At T-O rating:
  - TPE331-25/61, 71: 111·5 μg/J (0·66 lb/h/shp)
  - TPE331-1: 102·2 μg/J (0·605 lb/h/shp)
  - TPE331-2: 99·4 μg/J (0·588 lb/h/shp)
  - TPE331-3: 99·7 μg/J (0·59 lb/h/shp)
  - TPE331-5: 105·8 μg/J (0·626 lb/h/shp)
  - TPE331-8: 96·7 μg/J (0·572 lb/h/shp)
  - TPE331-10: 94·6 μg/J (0·560 lb/h/shp)
  - TPE331-11: 94·3 μg/J (0·558 lb/h/shp)
  - TPE331-12: 92·8 μg/J (0·549 lb/h/shp)
  - TPE331-14/-15: 84·8 μg/J (0·502 lb/h/shp)
  - T76-G-410/411: 101·4 μg/J (0·60 lb/h/shp)

OIL CONSUMPTION:
- Max: 0·009 kg (0·02 lb)/h

GENERAL ELECTRIC

GENERAL ELECTRIC COMPANY AIRCRAFT ENGINE BUSINESS GROUP

Neumann Way, Evendale, Ohio 45215
Telephone: (513) 243 2000

GROUP LOCATIONS: Lynn and Everett, Massachusetts; Evendale, Ohio; Rutland, Vermont; Hooksett, New Hampshire; Wilmington, North Carolina; Albuquerque, New Mexico, and Madisonville, Kentucky. Also test facilities at Edwards Air Force Base, California, and Peebles, Ohio. Further facilities at Seattle, Washington; Arkansas City, Kansas; Ontario, California; Cincinnati, Ohio; Fort Wayne, Indiana; Bromont, Canada; St Nazaire, France; and Singapore

SENIOR VICE-PRESIDENT AND GROUP EXECUTIVE:
B. H. Rowe

Engine Product Operations, Evendale:
VICE-PRESIDENT AND GENERAL MANAGER:
H. C. Stonecipher

Engine Product Operations, Lynn:
VICE-PRESIDENT AND GENERAL MANAGER:
R. C. Hawkins

Advanced Technology Operations:
GENERAL MANAGER: R. C. Turnbull

Business & Market Development Operations:
MANAGER: R. B. Smith

Current products of the GE Aircraft Engine Business Group include the F101, F103, F110, F404, J79, J85, T58, T64, T700, TF34 and TF39 for military use, and the CF6, CF34, CF700, CJ610, CT7 and CT58 for the commercial and general aviation market. In partnership with SNECMA of France a company was formed to develop and market the CFM56 turbofan, as described in the International part of this section under CFM International.

General Electric J79-GE-119 turbojet (83·31 kN; 18,730 lb st with afterburning)

GENERAL ELECTRIC J79

Development of the J79, America's first high compression variable-stator turbojet, began in 1952. In addition to US manufacture, it was produced by Orenda of Canada to power the Canadair CF-104/F-104G (MAP), by Ishikawajima-Harima in Japan for the licence built F-104DJ, and by MTU of West Germany, Fiat of Italy and FN of Belgium for the European built F-104G. The Italian production team, including Alfa Romeo, also produced the J79-GE-19, an improved engine similar to the J79-GE-17 but configured for the F-104S Starfighter. More than 17,200 J79s were built by GE and licensees by January 1986. The latest models are the GE-119 and the J1E made under licence in Israel (see IAI entry in this section).

Versions of the J79 in service are as follows:

J79-GE-7A. Built under licence by Orenda (as J79-OEL-7) for Canadair CF-104.

J79-GE-8. McDonnell Douglas F-4B and RF-4B. Air mass flow 76·5 kg (169 lb)/s. Pressure ratio 12·9 : 1.

J79-GE-10. RA-5C and F-4J. Pressure ratio 13·5 : 1. Improved -10A has smoke free combustor for F-4S.

J79-GE-11A. Lockheed F-104G. Built under licence in Japan (as J79-IHI-11A), West Germany, Italy, Belgium and Canada.

J79-GE-15. Powers F-4C, F-4D and RF-4C for USAF. Similar to J79-GE-8 except for self contained starting.

J79-GE-17. Similar to J79-GE-10, but for F-4E, F-4G, RF-4E, F-4EJ and F-4F. The J1E, a slightly modified -17, powers all versions of IAI Kfir including the US Navy F-21.

J79-GE-19. F-104S and F-104A. Differs from J79-GE-10/17 only in external characteristics. Guided expansion jet nozzle. Afterburner provides continuous fuel flow modulation from 1,225 kg (2,700 lb)/h to 15,420 kg (34,000 lb)/h.

J79-GE-119. Developed to power F-16/79; programme terminated January 1986.

Full details of the J79 can be found in the 1977-78 and 1978-79 editions of *Jane's*.

TYPE: Variable-stator single-shaft turbojet.

COMPRESSOR: Seventeen-stage.

COMBUSTION CHAMBER: Cannular type consisting of 10 combustion cans.

FUEL SYSTEM: Hydromechanical.

FUEL GRADE: JP-4 or JP-5.

TURBINE: Three-stage.

DIMENSIONS:
- Length overall:
  - J79-GE-7A, 11A: 5,283 mm (207·96 in)
  - J79-GE-10, 17, 19, 119: 5,301 mm (208·69 in)
- Diameter at compressor:
  - J79-GE 7A, 11A: 973 mm (38·3 in)
  - J79-GE-10, 17, 19, 119: 992 mm (39·06 in)

WEIGHT, DRY:
- J79-GE-7A: 1,644 kg (3,625 lb)
- J79-GE-10: 1,749 kg (3,855 lb)
- J79-GE-11A: 1,658 kg (3,655 lb)
- J79-GE-17, 19, 119: 1,745 kg (3,847 lb)

PERFORMANCE RATINGS:
- T-O, with afterburning:
  - J79-GE-7A, 11A: 70·3 kN (15,800 lb st)
  - J79-GE-10, 17, 19: 79·24 kN (17,820 lb st)
  - J79-GE-119: 83·31 kN (18,730 lb st)
- Military:
  - J79-GE-7A, 11A: 44·5 kN (10,000 lb st)
  - J79-GE-10, 17, 19, 119: 52·5 kN (11,810 lb st)

SPECIFIC FUEL CONSUMPTION:
- At T-O rating:
  - J79-GE-7A, 11A: 55·8 mg/Ns (1·97 lb/h/lb st)
  - J79-GE-10, 17, 19: 55·66 mg/Ns (1·965 lb/h/lb st)
  - J79-GE-119: 56·08 mg/Ns (1·98 lb/h/lb st)
- At military rating:
  - J79-GE-7A, 10, 11A, 17, 19, 119: 24·08 mg/Ns (0·85 lb/h/lb st)

GENERAL ELECTRIC J85

The following are major versions of the J85 small military turbojet, the -21 still being in production. More than 13,500 J85 engines have been delivered to air forces in 29 nations.

J85-4A. Powers Rockwell T-2C Buckeye.

J85-5. Afterburning; powers Northrop T-38 Talon.

J85-13. Afterburning; powers Northrop F-5A/B and Aeritalia G91Y.

J85-15. J85-13 with improved turbine and nozzle to power CF-5 and NF-5.

J85-17A/B. Powers Saab 105G and Cessna A-37B. Booster for Fairchild UC-123K.

J85-21. Higher airflow version with zero stage, described below; powers Northrop F-5E/F Tiger II.

TYPE: Single-shaft turbojet.

AIR INTAKE: Annular type, surrounding central bullet fairing. Variable incidence inlet guide vanes, with hot air anti-icing.

COMPRESSOR: Nine-stage axial-flow type, with variable inlet guide vanes and first three stator stages. Titanium rotor blades, first two stages having part-span shrouds. Discs joined at periphery. Casing in upper and lower halves. Pressure ratio approximately 8·3 : 1. Air mass flow 24·0 kg (53·0 lb)/s.

COMBUSTION CHAMBER: Annular type with perforated liner. Twelve duplex fuel injectors. Ports in outer casing facilitate inspection of liner.

TURBINE: Two-stage axial-flow type. Casing is in halves, split horizontally. Turbine inlet temperature 977°C.

AFTERBURNER: Consists of a diffuser and a combustor. A pilot burner with four spraybars and a main burner of 12 spraybars are located in the diffuser section. Combustion is initiated by a single igniter plug and is then self-sustained. Nozzle position governs exit area and is regulated automatically by the afterburner control system as a function of turbine exit temperature and throttle lever position.

General Electric J85-21 turbojet (22·2 kN; 5,000 lb st with afterburning)

LUBRICATION: Positive displacement, pressurised recirculating type.

STARTING: Air impingement starter on afterburning engines. Provision for starter/generator on non-afterburning engines.

DIMENSIONS:

Length overall	2,858 mm (112·5 in)
Max diameter	533 mm (21·0 in)

WEIGHT, DRY:

J85-21	310 kg (684 lb)

PERFORMANCE RATINGS (J85-21):

Max rating, with afterburner	22·2 kN (5,000 lb st)
Military rating, without afterburner:	15·6 kN (3,500 lb st)

SPECIFIC FUEL CONSUMPTION (J85-21):

At max rating	60·3 mg/Ns (2·13 lb/h/lb st)
At military rating	28·3 mg/Ns (1·00 lb/h/lb st)

GENERAL ELECTRIC CJ610

Announced in May 1960, the CJ610 turbojet is tailored for executive aircraft of 5,700-7,500 kg (12,500-16,500 lb) gross weight. It is similar to the J85 turbojet, without afterburner.

CJ610-1, CJ610-4. Initial production versions, differing only in accessory gearbox location.

CJ610-5, CJ610-6. Developed versions of -1 and -4 respectively, providing increased T-O thrust. Power Gates Learjet 24D, 25B and 25C, Hansa and IAI Westwind 1121.

CJ610-8, CJ610-9. Developed for production, deliveries beginning in 1969. Power Hansa, IAI Westwind 1123 and NAL (Japan) experimental VTOL.

CJ610-8A. FAA certificated in April 1977 for operation at up to 15,500 m (51,000 ft), to give better economy and over-weather capability to Gates Learjet Century III 24E, 24F, 25D and 25F. Main differences are longer life turbine and turbine nozzle area change.

By early 1986 over 8·8 million hours had been flown by 2,048 CJ610 engines.

DIMENSIONS:

Length overall:	
CJ610-1, -5, -9	1,298 mm (51·1 in)
CJ610-4, -6, -8, -8A	1,153 mm (45·4 in)
Max flange diameter	449 mm (17·7 in)

WEIGHT, DRY:

CJ610-1	181 kg (399 lb)
CJ610-4	176 kg (389 lb)
CJ610-5	183 kg (402 lb)
CJ610-6	180 kg (396 lb)
CJ610-8, -8A	185 kg (407 lb)
CJ610-9	191 kg (421 lb)

PERFORMANCE RATINGS (guaranteed):

T-O:	
CJ610-1, -4	12·7 kN (2,850 lb st)
CJ610-5, -6, -8A	13·1 kN (2,950 lb st)
CJ610-8, -9	13·8 kN (3,100 lb st)
Max continuous:	
CJ610-1, -4	12 kN (2,700 lb st)
CJ610-5, -6	12·4 kN (2,780 lb st)
CJ610-8, -9	13 kN (2,925 lb st)
CJ610-8A	12·7 kN (2,850 lb st)

SPECIFIC FUEL CONSUMPTION:

At T-O rating:	
CJ610-1, -4	28·05 mg/Ns (0·99 lb/h/lb st)
CJ610-5, -6, -8, -9	27·75 mg/Ns (0·98 lb/h/lb st)
CJ610-8A	27·5 mg/Ns (0·97 lb/h/lb st)
At max continuous rating:	
CJ610-1, -4, -8A	27·5 mg/Ns (0·97 lb/h/lb st)
CJ610-5, -6, -8, -9	27·2 mg/Ns (0·96 lb/h/lb st)

GENERAL ELECTRIC CF700

The CF700 is an aft fan turbofan based on the CJ610 gas generator. The **CF700-2D** was certificated on 1 July 1964. The **CF700-2C** has an improved compressor turbine and was certificated in 1968. The **CF700-2D2** incorporates a new design of tailpipe.

CF700 engines power the Dassault-Breguet Falcon 20 and Rockwell Sabreliner 75A executive transports. By 1974 the TBO had reached 3,000 h. By early 1986 more than 1,150 CF700s had flown over 6·4 million hours.

General Electric CF700-2D turbofan (19·24 kN; 4,325 lb st)

The general description of the J85 turbojet applies also to the CF700, with the following additional assembly:

AFT FAN: Single-stage free floating fan. Bypass ratio 1·6. Mass air flow through fan 39·9 kg (88·0 lb)/s.

DIMENSIONS:

Length overall, compressor nose to tailcone tip	1,912 mm (75·57 in)
Length, flange to flange	1,361 mm (53·6 in)
Max diameter	840·4 mm (33·1 in)
Max diameter less fan	447 mm (17·6 in)

WEIGHT, DRY:

CF700-2C	330 kg (725 lb)
CF700-2D, -2D2	334 kg (737 lb)

PERFORMANCE RATINGS:

Max T-O (flat rated to 30°C):	
CF700-2C	18·68 kN (4,200 lb st)
CF700-2D	19·24 kN (4,325 lb st)
CF700-2D2	20·02 kN (4,500 lb st)
Max continuous:	
CF700-2C	17·8 kN (4,000 lb st)
CF700-2D, 2D2	18·3 kN (4,120 lb st)

SPECIFIC FUEL CONSUMPTION:

Max T-O:	
CF700-2C, -2D, -2D2	18·4 mg/Ns (0·65 lb/h/lb st)
Max continuous:	
CF700-2C, -2D	18·4 mg/Ns (0·65 lb/h/lb st)
CF700-2D2	18·1 mg/Ns (0·64 lb/h/lb st)

GENERAL ELECTRIC F404

The F404 is an advanced technology augmented turbofan rated at 71·2-89 kN (16,000-20,000 lb st). It is the US Navy derivative of the YJ101 engine flown in the US Air Force's YF-17 aircraft (see 1975-76 *Jane's*). In May 1975 the US Navy selected the McDonnell Douglas/Northrop team to develop its F/A-18 Hornet, powered by two F404-GE-400 engines.

Compared with that of the J101, the F404 fan diameter is increased less than 25·4 mm (1·0 in) while increasing the bypass ratio from 0·20 to 0·34. The fan is driven by a slightly larger LP turbine.

First F404 engine test took place one month ahead of schedule in December 1976 and soon demonstrated sea-level production performance. Preliminary flight rating test took place in May 1978 and first F/A-18 flight in November 1978. Nine engines were delivered in 1978 and 24 in 1979, and MQT (model qualification test) was completed in July 1979. The first production delivery took place in December 1979.

The following are current versions of the F404:

F404-GE-400. Original production engine for F/A-18A, TF-18A and CF-18. Also powers the Grumman X-29A and Dassault-Breguet Rafale. Probably to power prototypes of the Indian HAL LCA.

F404-GE-100A. Flight-test version with external modifications, new control system and improved turbine materials to permit increased turbine temperature for rating at 75·6 kN (17,000 lb st). Powers F-20 Tigershark.

F404-GE-400D. Unaugmented version of Dash-400. Changes include replacement of augmentor by short exhaust adaptor and bypass airsplitter, removal of augmentor controls and modification of control system and external configuration. To be rated at 48·0 kN (10,800 lb st). Under development to power Grumman A-5F. Deliveries to begin August 1986, for first flight in May 1987. A basically similar engine powers the Lockheed F-19A.

F404-GE-100. Version of Dash-100A uprated to 80·0 kN (18,000 lb st). Would power production F-20A.

F404-GE-100D. Unaugmented version similar to Dash-400D, with new control system as fitted to Dash-100A and RM12. To be rated at 48·9 kN (11,000 lb st). Under development for Singapore A-4S-1 flight test programme, due to start late 1986.

General Electric F404-GE-100A augmented turbofan (75·6 kN; 17,000 lb st)

General Electric CJ610-4 (12·7 kN; 2,850 lb st) and (right) CJ610-5 (13·1 kN; 2,950 lb st) turbojet engines

F404/RM12. Previously F404J. Increased-airflow fan. Different materials permit further increase in turbine temperature of about 42°C. Same control system as F404-100, but engine 'tuned' to increase thrust in extreme mission conditions. To be rated at 80·0 kN (18,000 lb st). Selected for Saab 39 Gripen. Swedish designation **RM12**.

The following description applies to the F404-GE-400, except where otherwise noted:

TYPE: Two-shaft augmented low ratio turbofan (turbojet with continuous bypass bleed).

AIR INTAKE: Plain annular. Fixed central bullet, fixed and variable inlet vanes.

FAN: Three-stage axial. Outer flow diverted to bypass duct. Bypass ratio 0·34. Airflow 64·4 kg (142 lb)/s.

HP COMPRESSOR: Seven-stage axial. Overall pressure ratio, 25 : 1 class.

COMBUSTION CHAMBER: Single-piece annular.

HP TURBINE: Single-stage axial. Highly loaded aircooled blades.

LP TURBINE: Single-stage axial.

EXHAUST SYSTEM: Close coupled high augmentation afterburner. Convergent-divergent exhaust nozzle with hydraulic actuation.

CONTROL SYSTEM: Electrical-hydromechanical.

DIMENSIONS:
- Length overall: 4,030 mm (158·8 in)
- Max diameter: 880 mm (34·8 in)

WEIGHT, DRY: 989 kg (2,180 lb)

PERFORMANCE RATING:
- Max T-O: 71·2 kN (16,000 lb st)

GENERAL ELECTRIC TF34

It was announced in April 1968 that the US Naval Air Systems Command had awarded General Electric a contract for development of the TF34. This high bypass ratio turbofan had won a 1965 US Navy competition aimed at providing a tailor made engine in the 40 kN (9,000 lb st) category for the VS(X) aircraft by 1972 within a budget of $96 million. In August 1972 the **TF34-GE-2**, the initial variant for the VS(X) application (the Lockheed S-3A Viking), completed its Model Qualification Test (MQT) and subsequently entered production. The S-3A entered fleet service in February 1974, and GE and the US Navy have defined a 4,000 h TBO extension programme.

In January 1975 GE began shipment of the **TF34-GE-400A**, which replaced the GE-2 as S-3A engine. The later model incorporates various improvements, with changed external piping, an adaptive control system for optimising accessory power extraction, and a simplified rocket gas ingestion system.

In 1970 the TF34 was selected to power the twin-engined Fairchild Republic A-10A Thunderbolt II attack aircraft to compete in the AX competition. The A-10A application led in July 1972 to an Air Force contract for development of the **TF34-GE-100**. This was re-engineered to minimise unit price. It has a long fan duct and side mountings. The GE-100 flew in the first A-10A in May 1972. The A-10A won the AX competition, and the TF34-GE-100 was formally qualified for production in October 1974.

In 1974 a third version of the TF34, most nearly resembling the GE-2, was selected to provide auxiliary (thrust) power for the Sikorsky S-72 RSRA (rotor systems research aircraft) for NASA and the US Army.

TYPE: Two-shaft high bypass ratio turbofan.

AIR INTAKE: Plain annular intake. No fixed inlet struts or guide vanes. Small spinner rotates with fan.

FAN: Single-stage fan has blades forged in titanium, without part-span shrouds. Blades replaceable with engine installed. Performance at max S/L rating, mass flow 153 kg (338 lb)/s at 7,365 rpm with pressure ratio 1·5. Bypass ratio 6·2.

COMPRESSOR: 14-stage axial on HP shaft. Inlet guide vanes and first five stators variable. First nine rotor stages titanium, remainder high nickel alloy. Performance at max S/L rating, core airflow 21·3 kg (47 lb)/s at 17,900 rpm with pressure ratio 14 : 1, overall engine pressure ratio 21.

COMBUSTION CHAMBER: Annular Hastelloy chamber liner and front dome, providing ports for primer nozzles, igniters and 18 carburetting burners.

TURBINE: Two-stage HP gas generator turbine with convection cooled rotor blades and stator vanes, the first-stage nozzle vanes having film and impingement cooling. Four-stage LP fan turbine with tip-shrouded blades. Turbine entry gas temperature 1,225°C maximum.

FUEL SYSTEM: Contamination resistant, carburetting type. Integrated hydromechanical control unit with electronic amplifier. Fuel grade JP-4 or JP-5.

ACCESSORY DRIVES: Engine and customer accessories mounted around horseshoe shaped gearbox, fitting closely around lower half of compressor casing. Radial shaft drive from front of HP shaft.

LUBRICATION: Enclosed, pressurised, dual system with vent along centre shaft.

DIMENSIONS:
- Max diameter:
  - TF34-GE-400A: 1,321 mm (52·0 in)
  - TF34-GE-100: 1,245 mm (49·0 in)
- Basic length (both): 2,540 mm (100·0 in)

WEIGHT, DRY:
- TF34-GE-400A: 670 kg (1,478 lb)
- TF34-GE-100: 653 kg (1,440 lb)

PERFORMANCE RATINGS:
- Max T-O (S/L, static):
  - TF34-GE-400A: 41·3 kN (9,275 lb st)
  - TF34-GE-100: 40·3 kN (9,065 lb st)

SPECIFIC FUEL CONSUMPTION:
- Max T-O, S/L static:
  - TF34-GE-400A: 10·3 mg/Ns (0·363 lb/h/lb st)
  - TF34-GE-100: 10·5 mg/Ns (0·370 lb/h/lb st)

General Electric CF34-1A turbofan of 40·7 kN (9,140 lb st)

GENERAL ELECTRIC CF34

The CF34-1A turbofan, a commercial adaptation of the TF34, is essentially the same as the TF34-GE-100 except for configuration differences required for individual installations and FAA certification. Total airflow at take-off power with automatic power reserve (APR) is 151 kg (332 lb)/s. A core pressure ratio of 14 and a fan pressure ratio of 1·47 provide an overall pressure ratio of 21. Bypass ratio is 6·3.

Certificated in January 1980, the CF34 powers the Challenger 601 corporate aircraft and has been selected for the AAI FanStar.

DIMENSIONS:
- Length (overall): 2,621 mm (103·2 in)
- Max diameter (at mounts): 1,260 mm (49·6 in)

WEIGHT, DRY: 739 kg (1,625 lb)

PERFORMANCE RATINGS: (S/L static)
- T-O (APR): Thrust: 40·7 kN (9,140 lb st)
- T-O (Normal): Thrust: 38·5 kN (8,650 lb st)

SPECIFIC FUEL CONSUMPTION (as above):
- T-O (APR): 10·35 mg/Ns (0·365 lb/h/lb st)
- T-O (Normal): 10·21 mg/Ns (0·360 lb/h/lb st)

GENERAL ELECTRIC TF39

General Electric's TF39, the world's first high bypass turbofan, was designed to meet the requirements of the US Air Force C-5A heavy airlift transport; it entered service with Military Airlift Command in 1970. The latest TF39, designated **TF39-GE-1C**, is an improved model of that engine. More than two-thirds of the TF39 engines now flying on C-5As have been converted to -1C configuration, and are demonstrating longer on-wing life, improved durability and performance retention levels comparable with commercial experience. The -1C also powers new C-5B transports, with the first engines being delivered to Lockheed-Georgia in 1985.

FAN: '1½-stage', with two stages in the inner flowpath and one in the outer. A flow splitter divides the two flows. Driven by LP turbine, optimised for altitude cruise performance, constructed primarily of titanium. Bypass ratio 8. Mass flow 700 kg (1,541 lb)/s.

COMPRESSOR: 16-stage axial; inlet diameter 749 mm (29·5 in). IGVs and first six stator stages variable. Interstage bleed for airframe use and engine cooling. Overall pressure ratio 26.

COMBUSTOR: High efficiency annular, virtually eliminating visual emissions. All components film cooled. Snout, dome and inner/outer skirts separable; nozzles, igniters and manifold externally removable.

HP TURBINE: Two-stage, with film and convection cooling in first-stage nozzle vanes and blades, and convection cooling in second-stage blades. Gas inlet temperature approx 1,316°C.

LP TURBINE: Six-stage, with uncooled shrouded blades; inlet temperature approx 871°C. Case externally cooled for clearance control.

ACCESSORY DRIVES: Consist of an inlet gearbox, transfer gearbox, and radial and horizontal driveshafts. Power is extracted from the compressor front shaft. Mounting pads for two hydraulic pumps, starter, constant speed drive, forward scavenge pump, lube and scavenge pump, fuel pump, and air/oil separator are provided on the aft section of the transfer gearbox.

REVERSERS: Fan thrust reverser consists of a support assembly, translating cowl, blocker doors, fixed forward fan cowl, inner splitter, and inner cowl assembly. The core reverser is an annular assembly, supported from the engine. The hydraulically actuated system consists of four synchronised actuators, blocker doors and deflectors.

DIMENSIONS:
- Max diameter: 2,540 mm (100 in)
- Length, flange to flange: 4,801 mm (189 in)
- Length overall: 6,880 mm (271 in)

WEIGHT, DRY: 3,583 kg (7,900 lb)

PERFORMANCE RATING (T-O, S/L, ISA):
- Flat rated to 31·94°C: 191·3 kN (43,000 lb st)

GENERAL ELECTRIC CF6

US military designation (CF6-50E): F103-GE-100

On 11 September 1967 General Electric announced the commitment of corporate funding for development of the CF6 turbofan for the then-forthcoming generation of wide-body transports. From the initial family of 142 to 160 kN (32,000 lb to 36,000 lb st) CF6 two-shaft engines announced in September 1967 to cover the anticipated thrust requirements of the Lockheed and McDonnell Douglas airbus projects, the CF6 evolved through a series of variants to the CF6-6D, flat rated at 178 kN (40,000 lb) to 31°C and tailored to the McDonnell Douglas DC-10 Series 10 intermediate range transport. Announcement that this engine had been selected by United Air Lines and American Airlines was made on 25 April 1968. Further orders have since been placed by many airlines for the CF6-6, -45, -50 and -80 series.

Basic configuration of the CF6-6 comprises a '1¼-stage' fan driven by a five-stage LP turbine energised by a slightly modified TF39 core engine, consisting of a 16-stage HP compressor, annular combustor and two-stage turbine. Modifications have been introduced to enable the accessory systems to suit airline installation requirements, while other changes are aimed at enhancing reliability, durability and maintainability.

CF6-6D. Initial 178 kN (40,000 lb st) version of engine produced for intermediate range DC-10 Series 10. First ran on 21 October 1968 and 18 days later attained 203·5 kN (45,750 lb st). Following a series of successful factory and outdoor tests, engine was released for production in February 1969. The second CF6-6D, built to the production configuration, first ran in May 1969. By December 1970 a total of 30 engines had been shipped and flight testing with a single engine hung on the starboard inner pylon of a B-52 had extended to 15,250 m (50,000 ft), Mach 0·896 and 420 knots (779 km/h; 484 mph) indicated airspeed. Delivery of flight test engines to McDonnell Douglas started in late 1969, with aircraft first flight following in September 1970. Certification of the CF6-6D for commercial service was granted by the FAA in September 1970, and the engine entered airline service in the DC-10 Series 10 in August 1971.

CF6-6D1. In August 1971 this growth version was FAA certificated and offered to take advantage of the demonstrated margin of the -6D. The D1 rating is increased by

1,000 lb to 182·4 kN (41,000 lb st) at 28·9°C. By 1981 more than 400 -6D and -6D1 engines had been delivered.

CF6-6K. This version of the -6D1, rated at 178 kN (40,000 lb st) at 31·1°C, was certificated in September 1981. It features improved sfc, improved performance retention and further improved reliability, and is planned for applications currently using CF6-6D1 engines. Mechanical changes include improved fan.

CF6-45A, -50E2-F (-45A2) and -50C2-F (-45B2). Economical derated CF6-50E (described later) giving flat rating of 206·8 kN (46,500 lb st) to 36·1°C (-50E2-F for 747SR) or 43·3°C (-50C2-F for DC-10-15).

CF6-50A. Announced by GE in January 1969, the 218 kN (49,000 lb st) CF6-50A is a growth version of the CF6-6. The increased thrust is achieved by increased flow through the core engine (reducing the bypass ratio from 5·9 to 4·4) at slightly decreased turbine entry temperature. A major change is the introduction of two additional stages behind the single-stage LP compressor of the CF6-6, with no change in the turbofan's external dimensions. To provide for flow matching between the two rotors, variable bypass doors are incorporated between the LP and HP compressors. FAA certification testing was completed in March 1972. The CF6-50A entered airline service in December 1972 in the DC-10 Series 30. The CF6-50 series also powers most Airbus Industrie A300Bs and some versions of the Boeing 747.

CF6-50C. The CF6-50C is rated at 226·8 kN (51,000 lb st) up to 30°C. Higher thrust is provided by an increase in turbine temperature, with improved cooling of hot section components. Certificated November 1973.

CF6-50C1/E1. Rated 233·5 kN (52,500 lb st) to 30°C.

CF6-50C2/E2. Similar to C1 and E1 but improved sfc and EGT margins and new fan case and blades with improved bird strike resistance. Certification 1978. Military -50C2 powers KC-10; -50E2 powers Boeing E-4.

CF6-50E. (Military designation **F103-GE-100).** This engine is rated to give 233·5 kN (52,500 lb st) up to 26°C. Certificated November 1973. Powers some versions of Boeing 747-200.

CF6-80A/A3. Combination of new technology with CF6-50 proven features, resulting in engine of reduced length and weight, with improved sfc and performance retention. Contributors to short length and light weight are the elimination of the turbine mid frame and a reduction in combustor and diffuser length. Engine rated at 213·5 kN (48,000 lb) as the -80A/A1, and 222·4 kN (50,000 lb) as the -80A2/A3. Ratings available with no mechanical configuration changes. Fitted to Boeing 767 and Airbus A310. Programme launched November 1977, first engine ran in October 1979 and certification obtained in October 1981. About 9 per cent of the -80A is built by Volvo Flygmotor.

CF6-80C2. Described separately.

By February 1984 CF6-6 engines had accumulated over 10,000,000 h. During the same time period CF6-50 engines had accumulated over 22,000,000 h.

The following data relate to the CF6-6D, with the differing features of the CF6-50 and -80 series also detailed.

TYPE: Two-shaft high bypass ratio commercial turbofan.

AIR INTAKE: Single forward facing annular configuration.

FAN: Single-stage fan with integrally mounted single-stage LP compressor (described together as a 1¼-stage fan), both driven by LP turbine. Fan has rotating spinner and omits inlet guide vanes. Blade containment shroud provided against possible blade failure. The 38 fan rotor blades are individually removable from the thick section disc bolted to forward conical extension of LP shaft system. Blade aerofoil has anti-vibration shrouds at two-thirds span. Fan exit airflow split between LP compressor and fan slipstream. Fan frame has 12 radial struts across fan slipstream exit. Fan frame provides support for LP and HP rotor front bearings, fan being overhung ahead of large diameter ball thrust bearing with rear roller bearing ahead of core engine. Blades, discs, spool of titanium; exit guide vanes of aluminium; fan frame and shaft of steel; spinner and fan case of aluminium alloy. Total airflow 591 kg (1,303 lb)/s, bypass ratio 5·7. Configuration of CF6-50 is similar but with two added LP stages and bypass doors (described below). CF6-80A/A1 similar to -50 with blade/vane modifications for better efficiency and bird strike resistance, with Kevlar containment system in fan case. Fan diameter 2,195 mm (86·4 in). Total airflow 658 kg (1,450 lb)/s; bypass ratio 4·3. CF6-80A/A1, 651 kg (1,433 lb)/s; -80A2/A3, 663 kg (1,460 lb)/s. Bypass ratio, -80A/A1, 4·7; -80A2/A3, 4·6.

LP COMPRESSOR: Single-stage compressor acting as booster to airflow into core engine. Rotor blades carried on rear rim of tapered drum bolted to rear of fan disc. Stators cantilevered off short chord shroud ring, supported by radial outer struts and radial/tangential inner struts located on fan front frame. Compressor exit flow free to balance between core engine and fan slipstream exit. Configuration of CF6-50 and -80A modified to three compressor booster stages carried on flanged rotor drum. Continuous shroud extends to fan front frame with 12 integral bypass doors located between canted radial struts in fan exit inner casing. These doors maintain proper flow matching between the fan/LP system and core by opening at low power settings to permit LP supercharged flow to bleed into the fan airstream. The doors are closed during take-off and cruise.

HP COMPRESSOR: Sixteen-stage compressor of near constant tip diameter, with inlet guide vanes and first six stator rows having variable incidence. Provision for interstage air bleed for airframe use and engine cooling. Rotor is of combined drum and disc construction with front stage and rear three stages overhung on conical shaft providing location on HP front bearing and HP main shaft. All rotor blades held in rabbeted discs and individually replaceable without dismantling rotor. Stages 1-7 blades forged titanium, 8-16 steel. Stages 1-10 disc titanium, 11-16 and aft casing Inconel 718. Casing split on horizontal centreline: stator vanes held in dovetail slots and replaceable individually. All blading now steel. Double-skin inner casing shrouds the LP main shaft. Outlet frame contains compressor diffuser and incorporates support structure for HP rotor mid-bearings. Overall pressure ratio (T-O), 24·3 (-6D), 24·9 (-6D1). Core airflow (-6D) 88 kg (194 lb)/s. CF6-50A has 15th and 16th stages removed to pass greater core airflow of 125 kg (276 lb)/s and reduce pressure and temperature of air entering combustion chamber. Titanium blades in stages 1-5, steel 6-14. CF6-80A series incorporate bore cooling for blade/casing clearance control, and one-piece steel casing with insulated aft stages and short diffuser section. Overall pressure ratio (T-O), 27·1 (-45B), 28·4 (-50A), 29·13 (-50C), 30·1 (-50E), 28·0 (-80A/A1), 29·0 (-80A2/A3).

COMBUSTOR: Fully annular with comprehensive film cooling. Separate snout, dome and inner/outer skirts, with nozzles, igniter, leads and manifold externally removable. Dome contains ports for two igniters and axial swirler cups for 30 fuel nozzles. Igniters of high voltage surface-gap type with energy level of 2·0 joules, each igniter operated independently. Forged steel nozzles with liner of Hastelloy X. Nozzle and dome designed to minimise smoke, and entrance diffuser has gradual profile to assure low temperature gradient to turbine under all flight conditions. CF6-50 combustor is shorter, of improved material (HS 18-8), and can be removed with fuel nozzles in place. CF6-80A has rolled ring combustor, 152 mm (6·0 in) shorter, mounted at aft flange.

HP TURBINE: Two-stage aircooled turbine with 1,330°C entry temperature. Rotor blades are film and convection cooled. Rotor blades cast from René 80; discs and forward and rear shafts of Inconel 718. First-stage nozzle guide vanes supported at inner and outer ends, second-stage cantilevered from outer ends, with inner ends carrying interstage labyrinth seals. First-stage vanes cast from X40 and film cooled by compressor discharge pressure. Second-stage vanes are cast from René 80 material and are convection cooled. Vanes are welded into pairs to decrease number of gas leakage paths. Thin section discs with heavy-section centreless hubs are bolted to front and rear conical shafts, including conical and arched inter-disc diaphragms. Configuration for CF6-50 is similar but introduces improved materials and cooling, and blades are not Siamesed but individual. CF6-80A has no turbine mid-frame and eliminates one main bearing, and HP case has active clearance control.

LP TURBINE: Five-stage constant tip diameter turbine with nominal 871°C inlet temperature. Rotor blades tip-shrouded and cast in René 77, not aircooled. Forward and rear shafts, case and discs of Inconel 718. First-stage nozzle guide vanes supported at inner and outer ends, remaining stages are cantilevered from outer ends, with inner ends carrying interstage labyrinth seals. Stages 1-3 guide vanes cast in six-vane segments in René 77, stages 4 and 5 cast in pairs in René 41. Vanes held in slots machined in the two half-stator casing. Drum and centreless disc construction, located on LP rotor by front and rear conical shafts attached to third- and fourth-stage discs. Drive to rotor by means of long fan midshaft. On CF6-50 a four-stage LP turbine is used, all stages being modified in geometry and cooled by 7th HP-stage compressor air instead of 9th. CF6-80A, new four-stage turbine with active clearance control.

EXHAUST UNIT (FAN): Fixed area annular duct with outer cowl and engine cowl forming convergent plug nozzle for fan slipstream.

EXHAUST UNIT (TURBINE): Short fixed area exhaust duct with convergent plug nozzle. Provision for exhaust reverser.

THRUST REVERSER (FAN): Annular cascade reverser with blocker doors across fan duct. For reverse thrust, rear portion of fan outer cowl translates aft on rotating ballscrews to uncover cascade vanes. Blocker doors (16) flush-mounted in cowl on link arms hinged in inner cowl, rotate inwards to expose cascade vanes and block fan duct. Reverser hinged at top to open in L/R halves for access to HP casing and combustor. CF6-80A1/A3 (A310) similar to CF6-50; 767 reverser by Boeing.

THRUST REVERSER (TURBINE): Post nozzle exit, cascade type. Two cascade screens are mounted in vertical plane on fixed pivot aft of turbine exhaust and are enclosed in fairing forming aerofoil shaped plug. Aft translation of fairing uncovers cascades which open across nozzle exit and divert turbine exhaust radially outward and slightly forward in horizontal plane. Configuration for CF6-50 similar to fan thrust reverser with nine blocker doors, but not split. CF6-50 available with long fixed core nozzle; short nozzle also designed, for performance improvement. Acoustic treatment is provided in the nozzle flow path. CF6-80, not fitted.

ROTOR SUPPORT SYSTEM: Eight bearings (four for each rotor) at seven locations. Fan and LP compressor carried on ball thrust bearing (1) behind fan disc and roller bearing (2) at front of LP main shaft; both bearings mounted in fan front frame structure, which also supports HP compressor front roller bearing (3). LP turbine carried on roller bearings at front and rear of turbine rotor assembly—rear bearing (7) being mounted in spider structure across turbine exit, and front bearing (6) on major spider structure between HP and LP turbines. HP compressor carried at rear on adjacent roller bearing (4R) and ball thrust bearing (4B) at interconnection with HP turbine front conical shaft, both bearings being mounted on support structure integral with compressor outlet diffuser. A roller bearing (5), mounted in the inter-turbine structure, carries the aft HP conical shaft (absent from CF6-80).

ACCESSORY DRIVE: This consists of the inlet gearbox, radial gearbox, radial driveshaft, transfer gearbox, horizontal driveshaft and accessory gearbox. The inlet gearbox is located in the forward sump of the engine. The gearbox transfers energy from the core-engine (HP) rotor to the radial driveshaft located in a housing aft of the bottom vertical strut of the fan frame. The transfer gearbox is mounted on the bottom of the fan frame. Accessory mounting pads are provided on both the forward and aft faces of the gearbox. The engine accessories mounted on the gearbox are starter, fuel pump, main engine control, lubrication pump and tachometer. Pads are also provided for mounting the aircraft hydraulic pumps, constant speed drive and alternator. CF6-80A gearbox in environmental enclosure on core; -80A1 on fan case.

FUEL SYSTEM: Hydromechanical fuel control system regulates steady state fuel flow and schedules acceleration and deceleration fuel flow. It also schedules and powers variable stator vane position. A governor in the Woodward control provides core engine speed stability during steady state operation. During transient operation, core engine fuel flow is scheduled on the basis of throttle position, compressor inlet temperature, compressor discharge pressure and core engine speed. The fuel control and fuel pump are mounted in the accessory package as an integrated unit which avoids interconnecting high pressure fuel lines and potential leakage points (they are separable for change or maintenance). This configuration provides a single drive mounting flange. The filter, fuel/oil heat exchanger and control pressurising valve may be removed individually without removing the entire assembly. The fuel manifold is double-wall constructed for

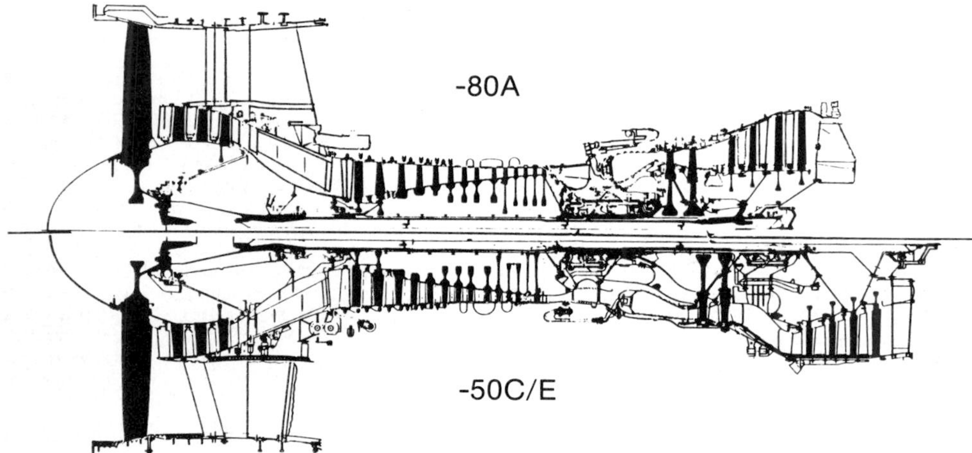

Features of the General Electric CF6-80A (upper half of drawing) compared with the CF6-50C/E (lower half)

safety and mounted on the exterior of the engine. For CF6-50, fuel control is modified to provide scheduling function for LP compressor variable bypass doors. CF6-80, electronic power management trims hydromechanical control.

FUEL GRADES: Fuels conforming to ASTM-1655-65T, Jet A, Jet A1 and Jet B, and MIL-T-5624G2 grades JP-4 or JP-5 are authorised, but Jet A is primary specification.

LUBRICATION SYSTEM: Dry sump centre-vented system in which oil is pressure-fed to each engine component requiring lubrication. Oil is removed from the sump areas by scavenge pumps, passed through a fuel/oil heat exchanger and filter to the engine tank. Nominal lubrication system pressure is 2·07-6·21 bars (30-90 lb/sq in) above sump reference pressure. All pressure and scavenge pumps and filters are located in the lubrication centre on the forward side of the gearbox.

OIL SPECIFICATION: Conforming to General Electric specification D50TFI classes A & B, equivalent to MIL-L-7808 or MIL-L-23699A.

MOUNTING: Main thrust mount located on the inner fan frame; aft mount located on the turbine mid-frame.

STARTING: Air turbine starter mounted on the front of the accessory gearbox at the through shaft.

NOISE SUPPRESSION EQUIPMENT: Acoustic panels integrated with fan casing, fan front frame and thrust reverser.

DIMENSIONS:

Max height (over gearbox)	2,675 mm (105·3 in)
Length overall (cold):	
CF6-6D	4,775 mm (188·0 in)
CF6-50 series	4,394 mm (173·0 in)
CF6-80A	3,998 mm (157·4 in)

WEIGHT, DRY:

Basic engine:	
CF6-6D, -6D1	3,582 kg (7,896 lb)
CF6-50A, -50C, -50C1	3,956 kg (8,721 lb)
CF6-50C2	3,960 kg (8,731 lb)
CF6-50E, -E1	3,851 kg (8,490 lb)
CF6-50E2	3,977 kg (8,768 lb)
CF6-80A	3,826 kg (8,435 lb)
CF6-80A1	3,769 kg (8,310 lb)
Fan and turbine reverser:	
CF6-6D, -6D1	932 kg (2,054 lb)
CF6-50A, -50C	968 kg (2,135 lb)
CF6-50E	962 kg (2,121 lb)

PERFORMANCE RATINGS:

Max T-O, uninstalled, ideal nozzle:
See under model listings

Max altitude and Mach No:
CF6-6 and -50 13,700 m (45,000 ft) at Mach 1·0

Max cruise thrust at 10,670 m (35,000 ft), Mach 0·85, flat rated to ISA + 10°C, uninstalled, real nozzle:

CF6-6D	40·6 kN (9,120 lb)
CF6-6D1	41·1 kN (9,250 lb)
CF6-45A	48·9 kN (11,000 lb)
CF6-50A, -50C	48·0 kN (10,800 lb)
CF6-50C2, -E2	50·3 kN (11,300 lb)
CF6-80A, -80A1	45·9 kN (10,320 lb)

SPECIFIC FUEL CONSUMPTION:

At T-O thrust, as above:	
CF6-6D	9·86 mg/Ns (0·348 lb/h/lb st)
CF6-6D1	9·91 mg/Ns (0·350 lb/h/lb st)
CF6-50A	10·90 mg/Ns (0·385 lb/h/lb st)
CF6-50C	11·05 mg/Ns (0·390 lb/h/lb st)
CF6-50E	10·65 mg/Ns (0·376 lb/h/lb st)
CF6-50C2, -E2	10·51 mg/Ns (0·371 lb/h/lb st)
CF6-80A	9·74 mg/Ns (0·344 lb/h/lb st)
OIL CONSUMPTION:	0·9 kg (2·0 lb)/h

GENERAL ELECTRIC CF6-80C2

This engine is a major redesign for higher thrust and improved sfc, based on the CF6-80A1/A3 configuration but with a 2,362 mm (93 in) diameter fan. It has a new four-stage LP compressor and LP turbine redesigned aerodynamically with 5½ stages. The first engine ran in May 1982, and exceeded 276 kN (62,000 lb) corrected thrust. Flight test on an A300 took place between August and December 1984, leading to certification on 28 June 1985. In February 1984 this engine became the subject of a technical collaboration agreement with Rolls-Royce, as described in the entry on that company. Other programme sharing agreements have been signed with SNECMA of France, MTU of Germany, Volvo Flygmotor of Sweden and Fiat Aviazione of Italy. Applications include the A300-600, A310-200 and -300, 767-200 and -300ER, 747-300 and -400 and MD-II.

The CF6-80C2 differs from earlier CF6 engines in the following features:

FAN: Single-stage, with integrally mounted four-stage booster (LP compressor). Mainly titanium except for steel mid-fan shaft, aluminium spinner and blade-containment shroud of layers of Kevlar around aluminium case. Rotor blades (38) individually removable. Blade shrouds at two-thirds span. Fan frame hub single titanium casting, with 12 radial struts. Eighty composite exit guide vanes canted for better aerodynamic efficiency. Total mass airflow 796 kg (1,754 lb)/s; bypass ratio 5·2.

LP COMPRESSOR: Four stages acting as booster to core engine. Total of 12 integral bypass doors maintain proper flow matching between the fan/LP system and core by opening at lower power settings to bleed into bypass stream. Blades and vanes mounted orthogonally, with dovetail offset from centre of pressure to reduce bending.

HP COMPRESSOR: 14-stage, with inlet guide vanes and first five stator rows with variable incidence. Rotor cooled by LP air to maintain clearances, stator lands recessed and tapered to reduce leakage. Drum supported between two bearings. Blades in stages 1-5 titanium, 6-14 steel; vanes all steel. One-piece steel casing with insulated aft stages. Core airflow 154 kg (340 lb)/s. Overall pressure ratio 30·4.

COMBUSTOR: Annular, rolled ring construction, aft-mounted with film cooling.

HP TURBINE: Two-stage. Stage one blades directionally solidified René 80 Rotating structures overhung by unitised shaft and stage-one disc. Casing with active and passive clearance control. No turbine midframe.

LP TURBINE: Five stages, with cambered struts in the rear frame to reduce exit swirl, effectively producing another half-stage. One-piece welded steel casing. First-stage nozzle has hollow vanes to transport 7th-stage cooling air to discs. Rear hub heated by exhaust gas to reduce thermal stress.

ROTOR SUPPORT SYSTEM: Seven bearings in three sumps. LP system has three bearings, one thrust and two roller. HP has four bearings, one thrust and three roller.

FUEL SYSTEM: Hydromechanical fan speed control with electronic supervision. Governor provides LP shaft speed stability during steady state operation. The electronic supervisory control uses flight inlet conditions to trim the hydromechanical control; thus, one throttle position corresponds to each engine rating in all flight conditions. FADEC (full authority digital electronic control) in development for 1988 release.

DIMENSION:

Length	4,087 mm (160·9 in)
WEIGHT, DRY:	4,058 kg (8,946 lb)

PERFORMANCE RATINGS (uninstalled, ideal nozzle):

Max T-O	268 kN (60,200 lb st)
Max cruise (10,670 m; 35,000 ft, Mach 0·85)	50·4 kN (11,330 lb)

SPECIFIC FUEL CONSUMPTION:

T-O, as above	9·32 mg/Ns (0·329 lb/h/lb st)

General Electric CF6-80C2 turbofan, rated at 268 kN (60,200 lb st)

GENERAL ELECTRIC F101

The F101-GE-100 is the augmented turbofan designed for the US Air Force's original B-1 strategic aircraft competition. It was preceded by the GE9 demonstrator engine under the sponsorship of Air Force Systems Command. From it stemmed the F110, described separately, and the **F101-GE-102** augmented turbofan for the Rockwell B-1B.

Like the earlier model, the F101-GE-102 is a dual-rotor design with a bypass ratio close to 2. Design criteria are durability and operability, while maintaining high turbine temperatures to maximise performance and operating efficiency. The engine incorporates a simplified exhaust nozzle to reduce weight, and neutral position bleed air extraction ports to permit built-up engine assemblies to be installed in any engine position. It provides efficient operation during high altitude cruise and low level penetration.

Much progress has been made on the F101 engine since the original cancellation of B-1 production in June 1977. A continued engineering development (CED) programme was initiated by the Air Force and GE in 1976 and progressed through 1981. CED objectives were: acceleration of engine maturity, extension of component life, and reduction of engine ownership costs. GE also developed engine repair procedures, minimised manufacturing costs, and refined manufacturing techniques, including engine health monitoring and trending.

At the conclusion of the original B-1 flight test programme in May 1981, F101 engines had powered four B-1 aircraft on 347 flights for a total of 7,600 engine flight hours.

From its inception, the F101 has been designed to incorporate technology that would lessen the impact of exhaust emissions and noise, and enhance fuel conservation. The engine is virtually smokeless.

FAN: Inlet guide vanes with variable trailing flaps. The two fan stages have solid titanium blades with tip shrouds. Inlet guide vanes and fan vanes are installed in a horizontally split casing which permits blades and vanes to be individually replaceable. Pressure ratio is over 2. Airflow approximately 159 kg (350 lb)/s.

COMPRESSOR: Nine stages, with pressure ratio over 11. First

General Electric F101-GE-102 augmented turbofan (133 kN; 30,000 lb st class)

three vane stages and inlet guide vanes variable. Horizontally split casing, forward section of titanium and aft section of steel. Inertia welded discs make continuous steel drum. Blades and vanes individually replaceable. Borescope inspection of vanes, blades and clearances.

COMBUSTOR: Very short annular, with dual cone nozzles to inject fuel into dome area.

HP TURBINE: Single-stage, high energy extraction design. Blades and vanes are hollow airfoils which are convective and film cooled. Stationary shroud is segmented and cooled, to provide tip clearance control.

LP TURBINE: Two stages, tip-shrouded and uncooled. Blades individually replaceable, and second-stage vanes replaceable in segmented groups.

AUGMENTOR: Mixed flow type, with convoluted flow mixer to provide efficient mixing and burning of both fan and core streams. Fan and core flows mix in plane of flameholder where ignition begins on inner ring. Radial flameholders in core stream, for lightoff and stable high altitude operation. Smooth and continuous temperature rise over the entire modulation range.

EXHAUST NOZZLE: Convergent-divergent type. Area variations obtained by hydraulic actuators translating actuation ring which positions flaps and seals through cams and links.

DIMENSIONS:
Length 4,598 mm (181 in)
Diameter 1,397 mm (55 in)
WEIGHT, DRY: 1,996 kg (4,400 lb)
PERFORMANCE RATING:
T-O 133 kN (30,000 lb st) class

GENERAL ELECTRIC F110

The **F110** (previously F101 DFE) is a fighter engine derivative of the General Electric F101, incorporating scaled-up fan and exhaust nozzle components from GE's F404.

Based on the F101-X demonstrator programme, the F110 was announced in June 1979. At that time development was funded for a joint US Air Force/US Navy alternative engine for high performance fighters. The first of five engines ran at Evendale in late 1979.

Since that time, the F110 has been flight tested successfully in the USAF F-16/101 (first flight 19 December 1980), the USN F-14 Super Tomcat and the USAF F-16XL. During these flight tests the F110 has accumulated more than 550 engine flight hours with no required engine changes or trim runs. The engine has demonstrated the capability to operate without throttle restrictions in all three aircraft. In early 1984 the USAF selected the F110 to power future F-16 production aircraft.

The initial USAF contract was awarded for 120 **F110-GE-100** engines. A second contract for approximately 184 engines was signed in February 1985. Israel announced selection of the F110 for 100 engines, and Turkey is buying 173 engines. The US Navy selected the Dash-100 to power its planned buy of 26 F-16Ns for the adversary role. This engine has been chosen by LTV as one option for the proposed A-7 Strikefighter.

A similar engine, designated **F110-GE-400**, will power Grumman F-14A + and F-14D Tomcats for the US Navy. Engine qualification was scheduled to begin in late 1986. Test flying is also scheduled for late 1986, with the first F-14A + due for delivery in late 1987.

The F110 is designed for modular assembly to facilitate maintenance and repair. Numerous borescope ports are positioned along the engine for visual inspection of critical areas such as the compressor, combustor and turbine.

FAN: Inlet guide vanes with variable trailing-edge flaps. Three fan stages, a scaled-up F404 design, with solid titanium blades. Inlet guide vanes and fan vanes individually replaceable. Fan pressure ratio over 3. Airflow 113-122 kg (250-270 lb)/s. Bypass ratio 0·87.

HIGH PRESSURE COMPRESSOR: As F101.

COMBUSTOR: As F101.

HP TURBINE: As F101.

LP TURBINE: Based on F101.

AUGMENTOR: Scaled version of F101 mixed flow type, with convoluted flow mixer. Flows mix in plane of flameholder, and 90 per cent of core flow is completely burned before fuelling of any bypass air is initiated.

EXHAUST NOZZLE: Scaled-up version of F404 design. Variable area type, made up of convergent and divergent flaps and seals and outer flaps.

DIMENSIONS:
Length 4,620 mm (181·9 in)
Diameter 1,181 mm (46·5 in)
PERFORMANCE RATING:
T-O 122·8 kN (27,600 lb st)

GENERAL ELECTRIC GE36 (UDF)

In a dramatic unveiling at Farnborough on 2 September 1984, General Electric staked its claim to leadership in the race to beat the best turbofan fuel consumptions by between 40 and 60 per cent with a UDF (unducted fan). Using thin scimitar-like blades with a diameter of 3·57 m (140 in), the new engine in effect forms a new class of propulsion system with a bypass ratio roughly halfway between the 5:1 class of commercial turbofans and the 50:1 of typical turboprops.

Group Executive Brian H. Rowe revealed little of the UDF beyond stating that the proof of concept demonstrator would use an F404 core and be rated in the 18,650 kW (25,000 hp) class. Flight testing on a Boeing 727 is planned for the second half of 1986, for the start of full scale development of a commercial engine in 1987, followed by service in the early 1990s.

At the Paris Air Show, on 30 May 1985, GE and SNECMA signed an agreement assigning to the French company a 35 per cent share in the UDF programme. At that time SNECMA was already participating in manufacture of test hardware, to be shipped to GE in early 1987; the company is now involved in design and development. On the same occasion Bruce Gordon, GE36 programme manager, said "Noise control was a potential problem many sceptics believed we couldn't solve. But we have designed a fan configuration that will enable us to demonstrate by late Summer that the UDF will better the strictest local noise limits in the USA. Moreover, we exceed our goals for design efficiency up to Mach 0·83. While the proof of concept demonstrator is operating, we are now designing an engine with a much higher pressure core and with modern transport engine component efficiencies and loading that will result in considerably improved weight and performance." On the following day it was announced that McDonnell Douglas will participate in a full-scale flight programme using an F404-derived UDF in the left-hand position on an MD-80, to be based at GE's test facility at Mojave from early 1987.

The key to the light weight and low fuel consumption of the GE form of UDF lies in elimination of a drive gearbox. Instead, the gas from the core passes through large multi-stage contra-rotating turbines downstream. This arrangement eliminates the need for stators, and the visible propeller blades are mounted direct on the two halves of the power turbine. A little thought will show that, while one half of the turbine can be of conventional configuration, the other half must have its blades carried projecting inwards from a ring round the outer periphery. Blade loading for the LP power turbines is normal, but speed is low and the

General Electric F110 augmented turbofan (122·8 kN; 27,600 lb st)

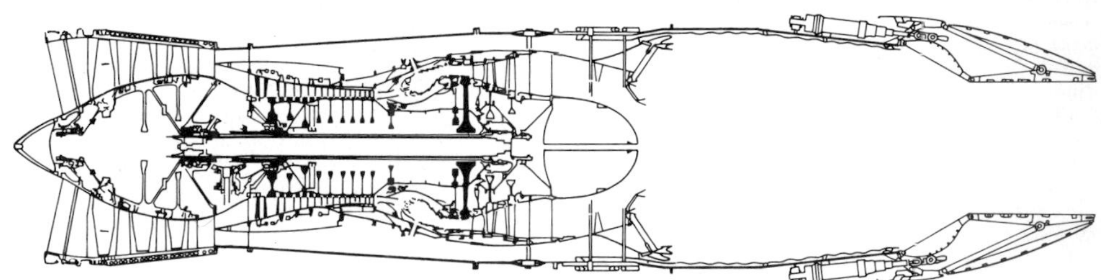

Longitudinal section through the General Electric F110 fighter engine (122·8 kN; 27,600 lb st)

General Electric GE36 UDF engine on outdoor test at Peebles

resulting 'insignificant' stress levels allow the unique construction at low risk.

Up to September 1984 no engineering problem had emerged in running one turbine with blades (vanes) on the outer wall and the other with blades on the inner wall. Stage loading is high, but speed extremely low, in the region of 1,300 rpm. This speed is determined largely by external noise, which cannot be attenuated. The external propulsor blades are designed using techniques established with fan blades, the hub radius ratio of over 0·45 being more than twice that common for propellers. The composite blades change pitch from flight settings through feather to reverse, and the pitch determines the aircraft speed. In practice, the UDF promises to be almost a constant-rpm and constant-temperature engine, and it should be relatively cheap because of the great simplicity of its nacelle and absence of a propeller or reverser.

General Electric is developing the UDF (the initials are a registered trademark) partially under contract to NASA for work which has already led to runs of powered scale models at a Boeing wind tunnel in Seattle, showing fan performance better than prediction, an acoustic test model run at the company's own plant at Evendale, Ohio, and a third model run at NASA Lewis Research Center in early 1985. Design is now going ahead on a 20K (89 kN; 20,000 lb st) class UDF engine, this being a likely size for envisaged markets. The 'super core' for this engine would be much smaller than the F404, and would operate at a high pressure ratio. Overall diameter over the propulsor might be 3 m (10 ft) compared with 2·1 m (7 ft) for a conventional turbofan in this class. It is expected that the eventual UDF will first go into use on a 120/160-passenger aircraft with two engines mounted on the rear fuselage well behind the passenger accommodation.

The 1,394 kW (1,870 shp) General Electric T58-GE-16 turboshaft

GENERAL ELECTRIC GE27

In March 1983 the Department of Defense, on behalf of the US Army, placed a contract to design and build this advanced turboshaft demonstrator engine in the 3,730 kW (5,000 shp) class. A direct rival to the PW3005, it has an inlet particle separator, compressor with five axial and one centrifugal stages, short annular combustor, two-stage compressor turbine and three-stage power turbine. A power : weight ratio of 6·5 is claimed, together with an sfc 15 to 30 per cent better than existing engines. The core engine first ran in December 1983, and the full engine in late 1984. This demonstrator programme is scheduled to last 46 months. An immediate potential application is the Bell-Boeing V-22 Osprey; later turboprop versions may be developed.

GENERAL ELECTRIC T58

The T58 is a small free turbine turboshaft engine which was developed for helicopter propulsion for the US Navy Bureau of Weapons. A civil version, the CT58, was awarded a Type Certificate by the FAA on 1 July 1959 and is described separately.

The hydromechanical constant speed control system featured in the T58 maintains essentially constant rotor speed by regulating the engine power automatically, so eliminating the need for speed adjustment by the pilot during normal operation.

Rolls-Royce Ltd produces modified versions of the T58 under licence in the United Kingdom as the Gnome. The T58 is also licensed for manufacture in Italy and Japan. Industrial and marine version of the T58 is the LM100.

Versions currently in service or in production are as follows:

T58-GE-3. Five-minute rating of 988 kW (1,325 shp). Powers Bell UH-1F.

T58-GE-5. Five-minute rating of 1,119 kW (1,500 shp). Powers Sikorsky CH-3E, HH-3E/F and NASA RSRA (Sikorsky S-72).

T58-GE-8E, F. Rated at 1,007 kW (1,350 shp). Powers Boeing Vertol CH-46A, Kaman SH-2, Sikorsky SH-3A/G and HH-52A.

T58-GE-10. Rated at 1,044 kW (1,400 shp). Powers Sikorsky SH-3D/H, and Boeing Vertol CH-46D/F.

T58-GE-16. Rated at 1,394 kW (1,870 shp). US military qualified. Aircooled gas generator turbine and two-stage power turbine. Powers Boeing Vertol CH-46E.

T58-GE-100. Uprated T58-GE-5. Ten-minute rating 1,119 kW (1,500 shp) to 15°C or 1,100 kW (1,475 shp) to 26°C. Powers selected CH/HH-3E. Qualified 1976.

Type: Free turbine turboshaft.

Air Intake: Annular intake casing with four hollow radial struts supporting central housing for starter drive clutch and front main roller bearing. Casing and struts anti-iced by air bled from compressor.

Compressor: Ten-stage axial-flow. Variable incidence inlet guide vanes. First three of the eleven rows of stator blades also have variable incidence. One-piece steel construction for last eight stages of rotor hub. Casing divided into upper and lower halves. Pressure ratio 8·4 : 1. Air mass flow 5·62 kg (12·4 lb)/s in T58-GE-3 and 8E, 6·21 kg (13·7 lb)/s in T58-GE-5, -10 and -100, 6·30 kg (13·9 lb)/s in T58-GE-16.

Combustion Chamber: Annular type. Sixteen fuel nozzles (eight on each of two manifolds) mounted on front of inner liner. Dual capacitor discharge ignition unit. Outer casing in two halves to facilitate inspection.

Gas Generator Turbine: Two-stage short chord axial flow type, coupled directly to compressor by hollow conical shaft. Centre ball thrust bearing, rear roller bearing. Cooling by air bled from compressor. T58-GE-16 has aircooled first-stage turbine nozzle and blades and second-stage nozzle.

Power Turbine: Single-stage (two-stage in T58-GE-16) axial-flow type, mechanically independent of gas generator turbine. Operated nominally at 19,500 rpm. Engines with single-stage power turbine can have reduction gear giving output at 6,000 rpm. Power turbine accessory drive unit and flexible feedback cable provide a speed signal to the control.

Torque Sensor Speed Decreaser Gearbox (optional except on -16): Integral lubrication system. Reduces power speed to 6,000 rpm. Assembly includes an integral torque sensing system.

Jet Exhaust: Two positions (90° left or right) on all versions. T58-GE-16 can also be supplied with downward ejecting or multiple position exhaust.

Controls (except T58-GE-10 and -16): Free turbine constant speed control. Hydromechanical controls.

Controls (T58-GE-10, -16): Integrated hydro-mechanical/electrical power control system for isochronous speed governing and twin-engine load sharing.

Accessory Drives: Engine accessories driven from compressor shaft. Airframe accessories mounted on free turbine reduction gearbox or rotor hub.

Dimensions:

Max width:	
except T58-GE-16	526 mm (20·7 in)
T58-GE-16	607 mm (23·9 in)
Length overall:	
except T58-GE-16	1,499 mm (59·0 in)
T58-GE-16	1,626 mm (64·0 in)

Weight, Dry:

T58-GE-3	140 kg (309 lb)
T58-GE-5, -100	152 kg (335 lb)
T58-GE-8E, F	138 kg (305 lb)
T58-GE-10	159 kg (350 lb)
T58-GE-16	201 kg (443 lb)

Performance Ratings:

Five-minute: See under model listings

Military:	
T58-GE-3	988 kW (1,325 shp) at 20,960 rpm
T58-GE-5, 10	1,044 kW (1,400 shp) at 19,500 rpm
T58-GE-8E, F	1,007 kW (1,350 shp) at 19,500 rpm
T58-GE-16	1,394 kW (1,870 shp) at 19,500 rpm
T58-GE-100	1,119 kW (1,500 shp) at 19,500 rpm
Cruise:	
T58-GE-3	798 kW (1,070 shp)
T58-GE-5, 10	932 kW (1,250 shp)
T58-GE-8E, F	857·5 kW (1,150 shp)
T58-GE-16	1,320 kW (1,770 shp)
T58-GE-100	1,015 kW (1,360 shp) at 19,500 rpm

Specific Fuel Consumption:

At military rating:	
T58-GE-3	103 µg/J (0·61 lb/h/shp)
T58-GE-5, 8E/F, 10, 100	101 µg/J (0·60 lb/h/shp)
T58-GE-16	89·5 µg/J (0·53 lb/h/shp)
At cruise rating:	
T58-GE-3	106·5 µg/J (0·63 lb/h/shp)
T58-GE-5, 100	103 µg/J (0·61 lb/h/shp)
T58-GE-8E, F	105 µg/J (0·62 lb/h/shp)
T58-GE-10	105 µg/J (0·62 lb/h/shp)
T58-GE-16	91 µg/J (0·54 lb/h/shp)

General Electric GE27 turboshaft demonstrator engine

GENERAL ELECTRIC CT58

The commercial version of the T58 is designated CT58 and was the first US helicopter turbine to receive FAA certification.

Current versions are as follows:

CT58-110. Rated at 932 kW; 1,250 shp (1,007 kW; 1,350 shp for 2½ min) at 19,500 rpm. Air mass flow 5·67 kg (12·7 lb)/s. Pressure ratio 8·2 : 1.

CT58-140. Rated at 1,044 kW; 1,400 shp (1,119 kW; 1,500 shp for 2½ min) at 19,500 rpm. Air mass flow 6·21 kg (13·7 lb)/s. Pressure ratio 8·4 : 1.

The CT58 powers the Sikorsky S-61 and S-62 and Boeing Vertol 107 Model II.

DIMENSIONS:
Max width — 406 mm (16·0 in)
Length overall — 1,500 mm (59·0 in)

WEIGHT, DRY:
CT58-110 — 143 kg (315 lb)
CT58-140 — 154 kg (340 lb)

PERFORMANCE RATINGS:
2½ min and normal T-O:
See under model listings
Cruise:
CT58-110 — 783 kW (1,050 shp)
CT58-140 — 932 kW (1,250 shp)

SPECIFIC FUEL CONSUMPTION:
At normal T-O rating — 103 μg/J (0·61 lb/h/shp)
At cruise rating:
CT58-110 — 108 μg/J (0·64 lb/h/shp)
CT58-140 — 105 μg/J (0·62 lb/h/shp)

GENERAL ELECTRIC T64

The T64 is a versatile aircraft gas turbine engine which was developed initially for the US Navy. The basic T64 turboshaft engine becomes a turboprop with the addition of a two-part speed reduction gearbox.

Current versions include:

T64-GE-7. Direct drive turboshaft rated at 2,928 kW (3,925 shp). Powers US Air Force CH-53B, CH-53C and HH-53C. Also powers VFW built CH-53D/G. Produced under licence by MTU (see entry under Germany, Federal Republic).

T64-GE-7A. Direct drive turboshaft flat rated at 2,935 kW (3,936 shp) to 28°C. Powers Sikorsky S-65.

T64-GE-10. Turboprop engine with propeller gearbox above centreline. Rated at 2,215 kW (2,970 shp). Produced under licence by Ishikawajima-Harima Heavy Industries in Japan for Shin Meiwa PS-1 and US-1 flying-boats (four engines) and Kawasaki P-2J patrol aircraft (two engines).

T64-GE-413A. Direct drive turboshaft rated at 2,935 kW (3,936 shp). Powers the US Navy CH-53D.

T64-GE-415. Growth version with improved combustion liner and turbine cooling. Max rating 3,266 kW (4,380 shp). Powers Sikorsky RH-53D.

T64-GE-416. As -415; powers CH-53E.

T64-GE-100. USAF designation of T64-T4C2. Flat rated at 3,229 kW (4,330 shp) to 29·4°C. Powers S-65C.

CT64-GE-820. CT64-820-1, -2 and -3 turboprops based on early turboshaft versions power DHC-5C Buffalo and prototype Aeritalia G222. FAA certificated CT64-820-4 has improved components of T64-415 and is flat rated at 2,336 kW (3,133 shp) to 38°C; in production for DHC-5D Buffalo.

T64-P4D. Turboprop version flat rated at 2,535 kW (3,400 shp) to 45°C. Two P4D engines power most Aeritalia G222 transports. Production by Fiat, supported by Alfa Romeo, from 1975.

All T64s are qualified to operate from 100° nose-up to 45° nose-down. The T64 was designed for extensive growth: current production engines rated at 3,266 kW (4,380 shp) are a result of growth made possible largely by aircooling of the first-stage gas generator turbine rotor and stator. The addition of aircooling to the second turbine stage provides further horsepower growth beyond 3,729 kW (5,000 shp) without significant change in external dimensions.

By January 1986 a total of nearly 2,800 T64 engines of all kinds had been delivered by GE to customers in 28 countries. Licences to produce the T64 are held by MTU in West Germany, Fiat in Italy and IHI in Japan.

TYPE: Free turbine turboshaft/turboprop engine.

COMPRESSOR: Fourteen-stage axial-flow. Single-spool steel rotor for -10 and -820-1/2/3. Titanium and steel compressor for -7A, -413A, -415, -P4D and CT64-820-4. Inlet guide vanes and first four stages of stator blades variable. Compressor blades can be removed individually without rotor disassembly. Casing flanged along centreline. Stator blades removable. Air mass flow per second: -10, 11·6 kg (25·5 lb); -7A, -413A, 12·8 kg (28·3 lb); -415, 13·3 kg (29·4 lb); -820-4, 11·9 kg (26·2 lb); P4D, 12·2 kg (27·0 lb). Pressure ratio: -10, -820-4, 12·5; -7A, -413A, 14·1; -415/-416, 14·0; P4D, 13·0.

COMBUSTION CHAMBER: Annular type. Double fuel manifold feeds twelve duplex type fuel nozzles with external flow divider. Nozzles mounted on outer diffuser wall of compressor rear frame.

GAS GENERATOR TURBINE: Two-stage, coupled directly to compressor rotor by spline connection.

POWER TURBINE: Two-stage, mechanically independent of gas generator turbine.

REDUCTION GEAR: Remotely mounted basic reduction gear for turboprop versions is offset and accessible for inspection and replacement. Gear driven by power turbine, using co-axial shafting through the compressor. Propeller gear ratio 13·44 : 1.

The 2,935 kW (3,936 shp) General Electric T64-GE-413A turboshaft

STARTING: Mechanical, airframe supplied.

DIMENSIONS:
Length:
T64-GE-7A, -413A, -415, -416 — 2,006 mm (79 in)
T64-GE-10, -P4D — 2,793 mm (110 in)
CT64-820 — 2,870 mm (113 in)
Width:
T64-GE-7A, -413A, -415, -416 — 660 mm (26·0 in)
T64-GE-10, -P4D, -820 — 683 mm (26·9 in)
Height:
T64-GE-7A, -413A, -415, -416 — 825 mm (32·5 in)
T64-GE-10, -P4D — 1,168 mm (46 in)
CT64-820 — 1,026 mm (40·4 in)

WEIGHT, DRY:
T64-GE-7A, -415, -416 — 327 kg (720 lb)
T64-GE-10 — 529 kg (1,167 lb)
T64-GE-413A — 325 kg (716 lb)
CT64-820-1 — 513 kg (1,130 lb)
CT64-820-2, -4 — 520 kg (1,145 lb)
CT64-820-3 — 518 kg (1,140 lb)
T64-P4D — 538 kg (1,188 lb)

PERFORMANCE RATINGS:
Max rating (S/L):
T64-GE-7A, -413A — 2,935 kW (3,936 shp)
T64-GE-10
2,215 kW (2,970 shp) at 1,160 output rpm
T64-GE-415, -416 — 3,266 kW (4,380 shp)
CT64-820-4 — 2,336 kW (3,133 shp)
T64-P4D — 2,535 kW (3,400 shp)

SPECIFIC FUEL CONSUMPTION (S/L):
At max rating:
T64-GE-7A, -415, -416 — 79·4 μg/J (0·47 lb/h/shp)
T64-GE-10 — 84·5 μg/J (0·50 lb/h/shp)
T64-GE-413A, -P4D — 81 μg/J (0·48 lb/h/shp)
CT64-820-4 — 82·8 μg/J (0·49 lb/h/shp)

GENERAL ELECTRIC T700

A competition was conducted in 1971 to provide the power plant for the US Army's utility tactical transport aircraft system (UTTAS), proposed as a replacement for the Bell UH-1 family of Army helicopters. In late 1971 it was announced that the winner was the GE T700.

The first T700 engine was tested in February 1973. Shipment of ground test engines was accomplished on schedule in February 1974, and flight qualification testing was completed ahead of schedule in August 1974. Shipments for UTTAS flight aircraft began immediately, with first flights of the Boeing YUH-61A and Sikorsky YUH-60A following during the autumn of 1974. Identical T700 engines powered the two advanced attack helicopter (AAH) contenders, the Bell YAH-63A and Hughes YAH-64A, of which the latter was selected and was developed into the AH-64A Apache.

The T700 was designed to be compatible with the Army's special operating and environmental conditions, and embodies high reliability, simplicity of maintenance, low vulnerability to combat damage, and high performance combined with compact dimensions. Use is made of higher pressure ratios and turbine entry temperatures than with earlier small turboshafts, to assist in reducing size and weight.

To reduce vulnerability, all external lines and leads are short in length and are grouped compactly for minimum exposure. Self-contained electrical and lubrication systems are fitted. Multiple mounting points allow for ease of installation. The necessary airframe connections have been minimised and are located close to the engine centreline. The engine is of modular construction for swift field maintenance or section replacement without special tools.

The following are current T700 versions:

T700-GE-700. First production model ordered from December 1976 and delivered from early 1978. Following description refers to this version, except where otherwise noted. Powers UH-60A Black Hawk. Over 1 million hours flown by mid-1986.

T700-GE-701. Upgrade of 10 per cent. In production for AH-64A Apache.

T700-GE-401. Navalised and upgraded version with over 95 per cent commonality. Powers SH-60B Seahawk, HH-60A Night Hawk, YSH-2G re-engined Seasprite, AH-1W SuperCobra and prototype EH 101.

T700-GE-405/-705. Models suitable for tri-service application. Being qualified at powers 20 per cent higher than Dash-700.

General Electric T700-401 turboshaft engine for SH-60B

A further growth plan has been defined utilising new aerodynamics, materials and manufacturing processes, as well as a compressor booster stage. This will result in growth T700 models with power about 70 per cent greater than the T700-700.

TYPE: Ungeared free turbine turboshaft engine.

INTAKE: Annular type, with anti-iced integral inlet particle separator containing no moving parts yet designed to remove 95 per cent of sand, dust and foreign object ingestion. Extracted matter discharged by separator blower driven from accessory gearbox.

COMPRESSOR: Combined axial/centrifugal. Five axial stages and single centrifugal stage mounted on same shaft. Each axial stage is one-piece 'blisk' (blades plus disc) in AM355 steel highly resistant to erosion. Inlet guide vanes and first two stator stages are variable. Pressure ratio, about 15 : 1. Airflow about 4·5 kg (10 lb)/s at 44,720 rpm.

COMBUSTION CHAMBER: Fully annular. Short length configuration, designed for maximum reliability and long life. Central fuel injection to maximise acceptance of contaminated fuel and give minimal smoke generation and uniform temperature profile into the turbine. Flame tube is machined ring in Hastelloy X. Ignition system obtains power from separate winding on engine mounted alternator and serves dual plugs.

TURBINE: Two stage gas generator (HP) turbine operates at gas temperatures exceeding 1,100°C. First stage nozzle investment cast in X40. Second stage nozzle investment cast in two-vane segments in R80. Discs, cooling plates, and blades of both stages clamped by five short tiebolts; five larger bolts then tighten turbine to shaft, driving via curvic joint. Rated shaft speed (S/L, ISA, max T-O power), 44,720 rpm. Two stage free power turbine, designed for high efficiency at part power levels (especially 30 and 60 per cent of military power), with tip shrouded blades and segmented nozzles. Power turbine inlet temperature at intermediate power, 827°C. Nozzle guide vanes René 77, rotor discs Inco 718, rotor blades René 80 uncooled. Output speed, 21,000 rpm. Power output shaft for front drive.

CONTROLS: Hydromechanical control can be replaced in less than 12 minutes and requires no adjustment or lockwire. Electrical control, coupled with hydromechanical control, provides twin-engine speed and torque matching.

ACCESSORIES: Grouped at top of engine, together with engine control system, for maximum simplicity, accessibility and combat survivability. Integral lubrication supply tank, plus an emergency supply of mist lubrication following total loss of main supply. Torque sensor provides signal to electrical control system.

DIMENSIONS:
- Length overall: 1,181 mm (46·5 in)
- Width: 635 mm (25 in)
- Height overall: 584 mm (23 in)

WEIGHT, DRY (with particle separator):
- T700-700: 192 kg (423 lb)
- T700-401: 194 kg (427 lb)

PERFORMANCE RATINGS (ISA, S/L, static):
- T700-700:
  - Intermediate: 1,163 kW (1,560 shp)
  - Continuous: 938 kW (1,258 shp)
- T700-401:
  - Contingency: 1,289 kW (1,729 shp)
  - Intermediate: 1,262 kW (1,693 shp)
  - Continuous: 1,071 kW (1,437 shp)

SPECIFIC FUEL CONSUMPTION (ISA, S/L, static):
- T700-700:
  - Intermediate: 81·78 µg/J (0·484 lb/h/shp)
  - Continuous: 80·1 µg/J (0·474 lb/h/shp)
- T700-401:
  - Contingency: 78·4 µg/J (0·464 lb/h/shp)
  - Intermediate: 78·2 µg/J (0·463 lb/h/shp)

General Electric CT7 turboprop (typical of all models)

GENERAL ELECTRIC CT7

In September 1976 General Electric announced a new commercial helicopter engine known as the CT7, based on the T700 military engine developed for the US Army. Certification testing to Federal Aviation Administration standards was completed in April 1977. The **CT7-2A** powers the Bell 214ST and the **CT7-2B** powers the Westland 30 Series 200 and 300.

The **CT7-6**, which represents a 27 per cent increase in power over the T700-GE-700, has been developed in partnership with Alfa Romeo Avio and Fiat Aviazione to power the civil version of the EH 101 and other helicopters in the European market.

The same core is used in the CT7 turboprop, which has a remote gearbox. This engine received FAA certification in August 1983 and is in production in two models: the **CT7-5A2** for the Saab SF 340 and the **CT7-7A** for the Airtech CN-235.

CT7 growth engines include the **CT7-9** to be rated at 1,306-1,395 kW (1,750-1,870 shp), the **CT7-9+** at 1,492 kW (2,000 shp) and the **CT7-11** at 1,642-1,791 kW (2,200-2,400 shp).

Data below are for the current turboshaft versions:

DIMENSIONS:
- Length: 1,168 mm (46·0 in)
- Diameter (max envelope): 635 mm (25·0 in)

WEIGHT, DRY:
- CT7-2A: 196 kg (432 lb)
- CT7-2C: 197 kg (437 lb)
- CT7-2D/2B: 201 kg (442 lb)
- CT7-6: 209 kg (460 lb)

PERFORMANCE RATINGS (S/L, static, 15°C):
- Contingency (2½ min OEI):
  - CT7-2A: 1,209 kW (1,620 shp)
  - CT7-2B: 1,287 kW (1,725 shp)
  - CT7-2D: 1,285 kW 1,723 shp)
  - CT7-6: 1,491 kW (2,000 shp)
- T-O (5 min) and en route contingency (30 min):
  - CT7-2A: 1,164 kW (1,560 shp)
  - CT7-2B: 1,212 kW (1,625 shp)
  - CT7-6: 1,491 kW (2,000 shp)
- Intermediate (30 min):
  - CT7-2C: 1,167 kW (1,565 shp)
- Max cruise: 940 kW (1,260 shp)

Data below are for the current turboprop versions:

DIMENSIONS:
- Length: 2,438 mm (96·0 in)
- Height overall: 737 mm (29·0 in)

WEIGHT, DRY: 351 kg (773 lb)

PERFORMANCE RATINGS (S/L, static):
- T-O: CT7-5A2, -7A: 1,293 ekW (1,735 ehp) to 34°C
- Max continuous:
  - CT7-5A2: 1,192 kW (1,600 shp) to 35°C
  - CT7-7A: 1,267 kW (1,700 shp) to 30°C

SPECIFIC FUEL CONSUMPTION:
- T-O (5 min) as above:
  - CT7-2A, -2B: 80·1 µg/J (0·474 lb/h/shp)
  - CT7-6 (15°C): 76·0 µg/J (0·450 lb/h/shp)
  - CT7-6 (35°C): 78·7 µg/J (0·466 lb/h/shp)
- Maximum continuous:
  - CT7-2A, -2B: 79·9 µg/J (0·473 lb/h/shp)
  - CT7-6 (15°C): 77·4 µg/J (0·458 lb/h/shp)
  - CT7-6 (35°C): 82·8 µg/J (0·490 lb/h/shp)

IN-TECH

IN-TECH INTERNATIONAL, INC

West 7510 Hall Avenue, Spokane, Washington 99204-5708
Telephone: (509) 455 6116

In September 1985 In-Tech International acquired the Merlyn engine (see Machen in 1985-86 *Jane's*) which had had little development since January 1984. This new-technology engine was designed originally with general aviation in mind. It is Intech's objective to continue refining the design for hovercraft, marine and other applications. Due to the present status of product liability exposure, the Merlyn will be available for aircraft only after considerable service and experience indicate that the risk can be minimised. Completion dates have not been established, but development and testing are continuing.

IN-TECH MERLYN

Research shows that there is a need for a new piston engine in the 373-522 kW (500-700 hp) class, with liquid cooling. Design goals for the Merlyn included a power: weight ratio better than 0·34 kg/kW (1 lb/hp); ability to use multifuels (Jet A, JP-4, JP-5, Nos 1 and 2 diesel) rather than aviation or automotive gasoline; an sfc 20 per cent lower than that of small turboprops; low frontal area and drag when installed in aircraft or other applications where space saving is a major parameter; and provision for a minimum of six accessory drive pads.

TYPE: Three-cylinder inline two-stroke diesel.

CYLINDERS: Bore 130 mm (5·125 in). Stroke 86 mm (3·388 in). Capacity 3·47 litres (210 cu in). Twin overhead camshaft and four exhaust valves per cylinder. Offset crankshaft.

In-Tech Merlyn two-stroke diesel (485 kW; 650 hp)

DIMENSIONS:
- Length: 1,283 mm (50·5 in)
- Width: 457 mm (18·0 in)
- Height: 648 mm (25·5 in)

WEIGHT, DRY: 263 kg (580 lb)

PERFORMANCE RATINGS:
- T-O: 485 kW (650 hp) at 4,800 rpm
- Max continuous: 448 kW (600 hp)

JAVELIN

JAVELIN AIRCRAFT COMPANY INC

Municipal Airport, Augusta, Kansas 67010
Telephone: (316) 733 1011

As outlined in the Sport Aircraft section, Javelin is the world's largest producer of special auxiliary fuel systems. This helps to fund other developments, the largest of which is a long-term programme to produce fully engineered liquid cooled aircraft engines. Extensive work has been done on the Javelin Ford 140 (cu in capacity) engine derived from that of the Mustang Cobra motorcar. A completely engineered power plant with turbocharger was flight tested in a Cessna 172. The 140T continues to be in demand for replica fighters, but most homebuilders need a smaller engine, and in Javelin's view the ideal engine is the Ford Escort/Lynx 98 engine of 1,607 cc (98 cu in). Six Javelin Ford 98s are on test, one being a 'hi-drive' model for amphibians with the engine and radiator inside the hull and the propeller above. The conventional (tractor or Long-EZ pusher) installation weighs about 129 kg (285 lb) with toothed belt drive. By early 1982 one 98-size engine was flying in a Cessna 150, held to 93 kW (125 hp) and cruising at 44·8 kW (60 hp) with specific fuel consumption of 62 μg/J (0·37 lb/h/hp). In 1983 intensive flight development was in progress on the Javelin Ford 230 (Windsor) V-6, a remarkable engine with a continuous (max cruise) rating of 149 kW (200 hp) for a weight, with reduction gear and all accessories, of 176 kg (387 lb).

Javelin Ford 230 V-6 (149 kW; 200 hp)

LHTEC

LIGHT HELICOPTER TURBINE ENGINE COMPANY

MEMBER COMPANIES: **Allison Gas Turbine Division**
PO Box 420, Indianapolis 46206
Garrett Turbine Engine Company
Phoenix, Arizona 85010

These two companies have combined their resources in forming the Light Helicopter Turbine Engine Company (LHTEC). This is developing the T800-LHT-800 joint proposal 895 kW (1,200 shp) class turboshaft engine for the multi-service LHX programme. It combines elements of Garrett's F109 and TSE109 engines with technology demonstrated by Allison in the ATDE (Army Advanced Technology Demonstrator Engine) programme.

T800-LHT-800

This advanced helicopter engine stems from programmes that the two partners started prior to 1983. The Garrett TSE109 used a core based on the F109 turbofan and did extensive running before leading to the ATE109, incorporating Allison technology, which exceeded 940 kW (1,260 shp) in December 1984 with lower than the required fuel consumption. The initial flight evaluation of the T800-LHT-800 in a Bell 206 was completed in January 1985, complete with Chandler Evans adaptive fuel control. AESD (AiResearch Electronic System Division) assists in the final control system. Flight development of prototype engines began on 7 March 1985, using a Bell UH-1B. By early 1986 two prototype engines had run 350 h, including sand ingestion and loss of oil.

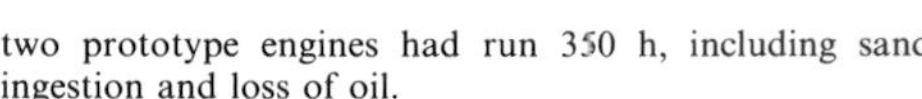

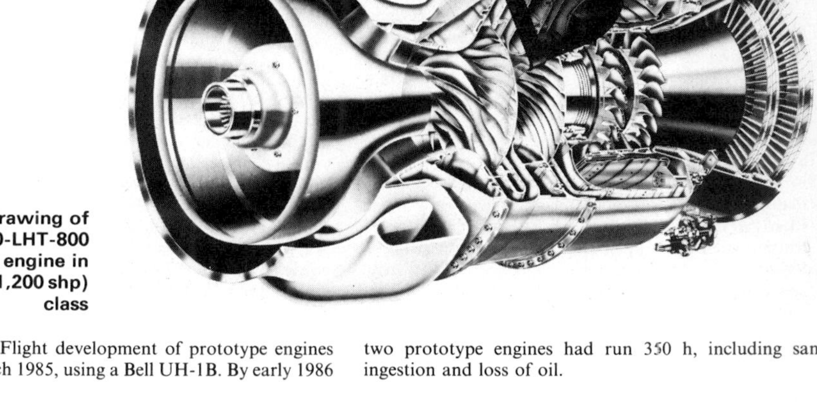

Cutaway drawing of the T800-LHT-800 turboshaft engine in the 895 kW (1,200 shp) class

MARQUARDT

THE MARQUARDT COMPANY (a subsidiary of International Signal and Control Group (ISC))

16555 Saticoy Street, Van Nuys, California 91409
Telephone: (818) 989 6400
CHAIRMAN: K. E. Woodgrift
PRESIDENT: F. X. Marshall
PRODUCT LINE DIRECTORS:
Bob Wilson (Ramjets)
Ted Linton (Rocket Systems)
Ed Wecker (Turbo Products)

The Marquardt company was formed in November 1944 to initiate research and development which produced the first American subsonic ramjet in 1945. Its main engineering business continues to be advanced aerospace propulsion and the supply of ram air turbine power systems. A major portion of sales is associated currently with manufacture of sophisticated structures and components for the aerospace industry, and the production of clustered munitions.

Marquardt is developing composite rocket/air breathing propulsion systems for the US Air Force and Navy. These are regarded by the company as likely to lead to a new generation of power plants for aerospace vehicles, supersonic strategic missiles and expendable tactical vehicles. Marquardt has also been developing precision bipropellant rockets for spacecraft since 1959, as described in the 1984-85 and earlier editions of *Jane's*.

MARQUARDT RAMJETS

Marquardt continues to be a principal developer of advanced ramjet systems. This activity has included the development of an integral rocket/ramjet for an advanced strategic air launched missile, the development of fixed and variable flow ducted rockets and small scale integral rocket/ramjets for air-launched missile applications.

MARQUARDT MA-196

This dual-mode scramjet is designed to operate in both subsonic and supersonic combustion modes as a function of vehicle flight speed. Below Mach 4 the engine operates as a conventional ramjet, and automatically transitions to the supersonic combustion mode above approximately Mach 5. Engine performance in each mode has been demonstrated with both liquid hydrogen and conventional hydrocarbon fuels.

Marquardt MA-196 dual-mode scramjet

DIMENSIONS:
Length overall 2,794 mm (110 in)
Cross section 622·62 cm² (96·5 sq in)
PERFORMANCE (net thrust at dynamic pressure 4,882 kg/m²; 1,000 lb/sq ft)
Subsonic combustion 3·34 kN (750 lb) at Mach 4
Supersonic combustion 1·20 kN (270 lb) at Mach 8
SPECIFIC IMPULSE:
Subsonic combustion 3,000 s at Mach 4
Supersonic combustion 1,800 s at Mach 8

MARQUARDT ROCKETS

Precision bipropellant rocket engines are available in the thrust sizes of 0·004, 0·02, 0·04, 0·06, 0·11, 0·22, 0·44, 0·89 and 4 kN (1, 5, 10, 15, 25, 50, 100, 200 and 900 lb). Thrust sizes to 8 kN (1,800 lb) can be made available on request. Shuttle Orbiter engines are described in more detail in the following entries.

MARQUARDT R-40A

This precision control rocket was developed and qualified for the Space Shuttle Orbiter vehicle and is currently being used as an orbit insertion engine for the US Navy's Shuttle Launch Dispenser.

TYPE: Liquid propellant reaction control rocket.

PROPELLANTS: Nitrogen tetroxide and monomethyl hydrazine.

THRUST CHAMBER ASSEMBLY: Single chamber. Area ratio 20. Made of silicide coated columbium, with welded-on orthogonal and scarfed nozzle extension in same material. Internal film cooling. Exterior insulated for buried installation. Started by electrical signal to on/off solenoid valve. Multiple doublet injector with hypergolic ignition.

Marquardt R-40A reaction control rocket

PROPELLANT FEED SYSTEM: Pressurised tanks, with feed of 0·526 kg (1·16 lb)/s fuel and 0·838 kg (1·85 lb)/s oxidant at 16·4 bars (238 lb/sq in abs).

DIMENSIONS:
Length overall 472 mm (18·6 in)
Nozzle exit diameter 267 mm (10·5 in)
WEIGHT, DRY: 9·5 kg (21·0 lb)
PERFORMANCE RATINGS:
Max thrust (vacuum) 3·87 kN (870 lb)
Chamber pressure 10·5 bars (152 lb/sq in)
Specific impulse: area ratio 20 281
area ratio 120 306

MARQUARDT R-1E

This small high performance rocket was qualified as the vernier engine for the Space Shuttle Orbiter.

TYPE: Liquid bipropellant rocket for use in space.

PROPELLANTS: Nitrogen tetroxide and monomethyl hydrazine.

THRUST CHAMBER: Single chamber. Minimum area ratio 26 with orthogonal and scarfed nozzles. Made of silicide coated columbium. Insulated for buried installation. Started by electrical signal to on/off solenoid valve. Single doublet injector with hypergolic ignition.

PROPELLANT FEED SYSTEM: Pressurised tank. Flow rate 0·016 kg (0·0354 lb)/s fuel and 0·0256 kg (0·565 lb)/s oxidant.

DIMENSIONS:

Length overall	279 mm (11·0 in)
Width	147 mm (5·8 in)
Height (depth)	145 mm (5·7 in)

WEIGHT, DRY: 3·7 kg (8·2 lb)

PERFORMANCE RATINGS:

Max thrust (vacuum)	0·11 kN (25·0 lb)
Chamber pressure	7·45 bars (108 lb/sq in)
Specific impulse (area ratio 100)	290

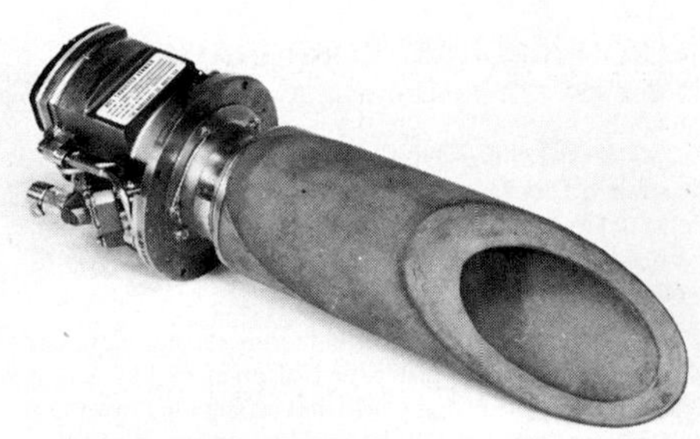

Marquardt R-1E vernier long scarf thruster

MNA

MICROTURBO NORTH AMERICA INC

55 Orville Drive, Bohemia, NY 11716

Telephone: (516) 567 3780

Telex: (510) 228 7320

Facsimile: (516) 567 3763

PRESIDENT: P. Calmels

This company was established in 1970 as the US subsidiary of Microturbo (see under France). It provides overhaul and repair service for Microturbo turbojets and has also conducted research and certification programmes. It is now producing TRI 60 engines for the Beechcraft MQM-107B (see RPVs and Targets section) for the USAF and Army, and also for US Navy Beechcraft BQM-126A targets. Deliveries began in late 1985 and were scheduled to reach 12 to 16 per month in 1986.

MORTON THIOKOL

MORTON THIOKOL INC

3340 Airport Rd, Ogden, Utah 84405

Telephone: (801) 625 4996

SOLID PROPELLANT ROCKET MOTOR PLANTS: Elkton, Maryland; Huntsville, Alabama; Marshall, Texas; Brigham City, Utah

PYROTECHNIC AND ORDNANCE PLANTS: Shreveport, Louisiana; Marshall, Texas; Ogden, Utah

CHAIRMAN AND CHIEF EXECUTIVE OFFICER:
Charles S. Locke

PRESIDENT AND CHIEF OPERATING OFFICER:
Robert C. Hyndman

VICE-PRESIDENTS:
John R. Bowen (Finance)
T. F. Davidson (Technical)
Robert B. Gerrie (Legal)

PRESIDENT, AEROSPACE GROUP: U. E. Garrison

Organised in 1929, Thiokol Chemical Corporation produced and marketed the first synthetic rubber manufactured in the USA. In 1943, the discovery by Thiokol of liquid polymer, a new type of synthetic rubber, paved the way for the practical development of the 'case-bonded' principle of rocket power plant design. The company's polysulphide liquid polymer proved to be the catalyst for the first mass production of efficient solid propellant rocket motors, as well as for the development of large solid propellant motors. Operations were organised into separate groups to serve widening areas of related products, and the name was changed to Thiokol Corporation. It merged with Morton-Norwich Products in September 1982 to form Morton Thiokol Inc.

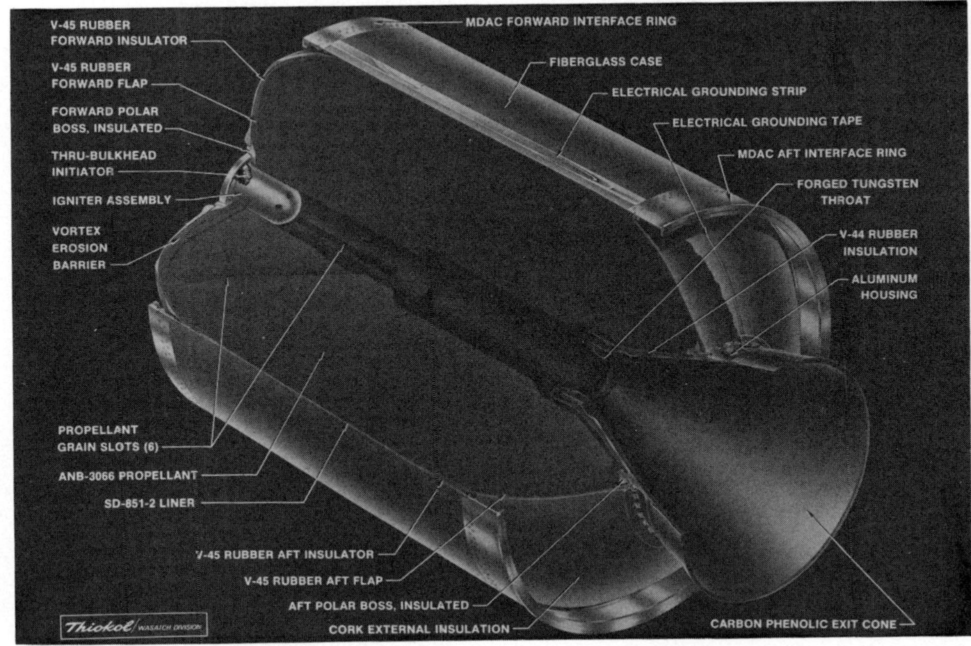

Morton Thiokol SSUS-A motor shown as cutaway drawing

MORTON THIOKOL SPACE SHUTTLE SRM

The Space Shuttle Solid Rocket Motor (SRM) is cast in four segments, which are rail shipped to launch sites at Kennedy Space Center, Florida, and Vandenberg AFB, California, where they are stacked vertically in pairs as part of the solid rocket booster for the Space Shuttle. At lift-off, the two SRMs burn in parallel with the three main engines. Thrust vector control for each SRM is provided by a flexible bearing movable nozzle driven by two hydraulic actuators.

After burnout, the two boosters are separated from the vehicle and fall back into the atmosphere, where parachutes are deployed to control impact velocity into the ocean. The boosters are then towed back to a recovery site, hoisted out of the water, and dismantled. SRM components are preserved and returned to the factory for refurbishment and propellant reloading.

The Space Shuttle SRM is the largest solid rocket propulsion system to reach operational status. It is also the first to be qualified for manned flight, and the first to demonstrate reusability of major components. Performance improvements have been incorporated in the SRM, with the High Performance Motor (HPM) becoming the standard configuration from the eighth shuttle flight in August 1983. Currently development is underway on a graphite epoxy case for the SRM, which will be used for selected Shuttle flights when additional payload capacity is needed. The lighter weight of these composite cases will increase the Shuttle's into-orbit payload by 2,087 kg (4,600 lb). The following data apply to the HPM:

DIMENSIONS:

Length	38·47 m (126·2 ft)
Diameter	3,708 mm (146 in)

WEIGHTS:

Propellant	503,487 kg (1,110,000 lb)
Loaded motor	569,893 kg (1,256,400 lb)

THRUST:

Average vacuum	11,521 kN (2,590,000 lb)

BURN TIME: 123 s

MORTON THIOKOL SSUS-A MOTOR

The Morton Thiokol TU-844 motor provides propulsion for the McDonnell Douglas Spinning Solid Upper Stage (SSUS-A) which launches Atlas-Centaur-class payloads from the Space Shuttle. The motor is a slightly modified third stage Minuteman III with TVC and roll control systems removed. Lengths of the nozzle and case are optimised to minimise Space Shuttle user charges. The motor uses an S-901 glassfibre case and is loaded with CTPB propellant. It is 2,120 mm (83·4 in) long and 1,320 mm (52 in) in diameter, and weighs 3,662 kg (8,074 lb).

MORTON THIOKOL TX-481 (MAVERICK)

TX-481 motors are used in the AGM-65A and AGM-65B Maverick missiles. The motor has an overall length of 1,020 mm (40·16 in), is 272 mm (10·7 in) in diameter, and has a total weight of 47·2 kg (104 lb). The case and blast tube are aluminium. The composite propellant has a Morton Thiokol polysulphide polymer binder with ammonium perchlorate oxidiser. The motor operates with thrust of 44·5 kN (10,017 lb) in boost for 0·575 s and 9·68 kN (2,175 lb) in sustain phase for 3·495 s. The overall impulse is 6,169 kg-s (13,600 lb-s).

Production of motors for the A and B models of Maverick began in 1972 and was continuous until 1978. The total quantity delivered was 26,213.

MORTON THIOKOL TX-633 (MAVERICK)

US military designation: SR-114-TC-1

The TX-633 was developed as a reduced smoke version of the Maverick rocket motor (see TX-481). The propellant and liner for this motor employ a hydroxyl terminated polybutadiene polymer binder; the oxidiser is ammonium perchlorate. Production was initiated in 1981.

MORTON THIOKOL TU-780 HARM

The HARM motor is a reduced smoke dual-thrust rocket that powers the USAF/US Navy High-speed Anti-Radiation Missile. The motor is approximately 254 mm (10 in) in diameter and 2,120 mm (83·5 in) long. It utilises a D6AC steel case loaded with 127 kg (280 lb) of non-aluminised HTPB propellant and has a single fixed nozzle. A single propellant grain provides the boost/sustain thrust profile. Production began in 1981.

MORTON THIOKOL TX657 (HELLFIRE)

The TX657 motor is used as propulsion for the Hellfire missile. It has a length of 594 mm (23·38 in) and a diameter of 178 mm (7 in). The case is aluminium. The blast tube is of composite construction. The reduced smoke composite propellant employs an HTPB binder with AP oxidiser. Production began in 1982.

MORTON THIOKOL TX-683 (Mk 36 Mod 9)

This is a reduced smoke replacement for the Mk 36 Mod 8, used in the AIM-9L Sidewinder. It uses the same case and has the same performance. Propellant is HTPB/AP; diameter is 127 mm (5 in), length 1,803 mm (71 in) and weight about 45·4 kg (100 lb). Production began in 1981.

MORTON THIOKOL TX773 (HELLFIRE)

The TX773 motor is a replacement for the TX657 used currently as propulsion for the Hellfire missile. It incorporates a low cost, minimum smoke propellant. Physical characteristics and performance are identical to those of the TX657. Qualification was completed in 1983.

MORTON THIOKOL TX632

The TX632 is used as a zero-length launch motor for various configurations of the Beech MQM-107 target. Diameter is 210 mm (8·25 in), length 1,140 mm (45 in) and weight about 59 kg (130 lb). Propellant is HTPB/Al/AP. The motor is in production.

NELSON

NELSON AIRCRAFT CORPORATION

PO Box 454, 8075 Pennsylvania Ave, Irwin, Pennsylvania 15642
Telephone: (412) 863 5900
PRESIDENT: Charles R. Rhoades
DEVELOPMENT DEPARTMENT: 420 Harbor Drive, Naples, Florida 33940
Telephone: (813) 261 1670

Nelson Aircraft Corporation, among its many industrial activities, produces to order the Nelson H-63 four-cylinder two-cycle aircooled engine, which is certificated by the FAA as a power unit for single-seat helicopters, and is also available as a power plant for propeller driven aircraft. These engines are capable of sustained inverted flight. Recommended overhaul period is 800 h.

The affiliated Sport Plane Power Inc in Naples, Florida, is the subject of a separate entry.

NELSON H-63

US military designation: YO-65

Developed originally as a power unit for single-seat helicopters, the H-63 is now available in two versions, as follows:

H-63C. Basic helicopter power unit for vertical installation. Battery/electronic ignition and direct drive. Certificated by FAA. Supplied as complete power package, including clutch, cooling fan and shroud.

H-63CP. Basically as H-63C, but without clutch, fan and shroud. Intended primarily for installation in horizontal position, with direct drive to propeller. FAA certificated.

Nelson has developed a 1·07 m (42 in) wooden propeller with glassfibre covering for use with the H-63. It is suitable for either tractor or pusher installation.

TYPE: Four-cylinder horizontally opposed aircooled, two-stroke.

CYLINDERS: Bore 68·3 mm (2¹¹⁄₁₆ in). Stroke 70 mm (2¾ in). Total capacity 1·03 litres (63 cu in). Compression ratio 8:1. Each complete cylinder is machined from an aluminium alloy casting, the bore being porous-chrome plated for wear resistance. Cylinders bolted to and detachable from crankcase.

PISTONS: Aluminium alloy casting. Two piston rings. Two needle roller bearings pressed in boss. Piston (gudgeon) pin pressed into small end of connecting rod.

The 32 kW (43 hp) Nelson H-63C four-cylinder two-stroke engine

CONNECTING RODS: Alloy steel forging. Caged roller bearing at big-end.

CRANKSHAFT: Four-throw. Nitralloy shaft on ball and roller bearings.

CRANKCASE: Two-piece case divided on horizontal centreline. Each half is a magnesium alloy casting.

INDUCTION: Nelson diaphragm type all-angle fuel control carburettor. Hot air anti-icing. Fuel/oil mixture valves from crankcase through specially designed rotary valve driven by crankshaft. Intake to and exhaust from cylinders through ports. Exhaust stacks are of aluminium alloy.

FUEL: 80/87 octane gasoline and SAE 30 ash-free-base oil in 16 : 1 mixture for fuel and lubrication.

IGNITION: Battery/electronic dual ignition with automatic retard for starting. Two Champion D-9 or 5 COM spark plugs per cylinder.

LUBRICATION: See under 'Fuel'.

POWER TAKE-OFF: (H-63C): Hollow shaft extension from Salisbury centrifugal clutch output drive.

STARTING: 12V DC Autolite electric motor and Bendix drive.

COOLING: (H-63C): Centrifugal aluminium fan and two-piece glassfibre shrouding designed to maintain all temperatures within acceptable limits on an FAA hot day of 37·8°C, S/L. (H-63CP): by propeller slipstream.

The 35·8 kW (48 hp) Nelson H-63CP for fixed-wing aircraft

MOUNTING: Four Lord mounts, two on each half of crankcase.

DIMENSIONS (H-63C):
- Length: 508 mm (20·0 in)
- Height: 376 mm (14·8 in)
- Width: 605 mm (23·8 in)

WEIGHT, DRY (with accessories):
- H-63C: 34·5 kg (76 lb)
- H-63CP: 30·8 kg (68 lb)

POWER RATINGS:
- T-O:
  - H-63C: 32 kW (43 hp) at 4,000 rpm
  - H-63CP: 35·8 kW (48 hp) at 4,400 rpm
- Max continuous:
  - H-63C: 32 kW (43 hp) at 4,000 rpm
  - H-63CP: 33·6 kW (45 hp) at 4,000 rpm

NORTHROP

NORTHROP CORPORATION, VENTURA DIVISION

1515 Rancho Conejo Boulevard, Newbury Park, California 91320
Telephone: (805) 498 3131

In 1972 Northrop Corporation acquired the rights to this engine from McCulloch Corporation. The 4318 series continues in production at Ventura Division, to power the KD2R-5 target (see RPVs and Targets section).

NORTHROP MODEL 4318F

US military designation: O-100-3

TYPE: Four-cylinder opposed aircooled two-stroke.

CYLINDERS: Bore 80·8 mm (3³⁄₁₆ in). Stroke 79·4 mm (3⅛ in). Capacity 1·6 litres (100 cu in). Compression ratio 7·8 : 1. Die-cast aluminium with integral head and hard chrome plated walls.

PISTONS: Cast aluminium. Two rings above pins. Piston (gudgeon) pins of case hardened steel.

CONNECTING RODS: Forged steel. 'Free roll' silver plated bearings at big-end. Small-end carries needle bearing.

CRANKSHAFT: Four-throw one-piece steel forging on four anti-friction bearings, two ball and two needle, one with split race for centre main bearing.

CRANKCASE: One-piece heat treated permanent mould aluminium casting, closed at rear end with cast aluminium cover which provides mounting for magneto.

VALVE GEAR: Fuel mixture for scavenging and power stroke introduced to cylinders through crankshaft driven rotary valves and ported cylinders.

INDUCTION: Mechanical or electrical fuel pump. Diaphragm type carburettor with adjustable jet.

FUEL SPECIFICATION: Grade 100/130 aviation fuel (20 parts), two-cycle oil (1 part).

IGNITION: Single magneto and distributor. Directly connected to crankshaft through impulse coupling for easy starting. Radio noise suppressor included. BG type RB 916S, AC type 83P or Champion REM-38R spark plugs. Complete radio shielding.

PROPELLER DRIVE: RH tractor. Keyed taper shaft.

STARTING: By separate portable hydraulic starter.

MOUNTING: Three mounting lugs with rubber bushings.

DIMENSIONS:
- Length: 686 mm (27·0 in)
- Width: 711 mm (28·0 in)
- Height: 381 mm (15·0 in)

WEIGHT, DRY (less propeller hub): 34·9 kg (77 lb)

POWER RATING: 62·6 kW (84 hp) at 4,100 rpm

SPECIFIC CONSUMPTION (fuel/oil mixture at S/L at rated power): 127 µg/J (0·75 lb/h/hp)

Northrop Ventura targets powered by O-100-3 piston engines rated at 62·6 kW (84 hp)

PRATT & WHITNEY

UNITED TECHNOLOGIES PRATT & WHITNEY

HEADQUARTERS: East Hartford, Connecticut 06108
Telephone: (203) 565 4321
PRESIDENT: Arthur E. Wegner
EXECUTIVE VICE-PRESIDENTS:
William C. Missimer Jr, Selwyn D. Berson
VICE-PRESIDENT COMMUNICATIONS:
Curtis G. Linke

Commercial Products Division
East Hartford, Connecticut
DIVISION PRESIDENT: Lawrence W. Clarkson

Government Products Division
West Palm Beach, Florida
DIVISION PRESIDENT: James G. O'Connor

Manufacturing Division
East Hartford, Connecticut
DIVISION PRESIDENT: Karl M. Thomas

Engineering Division
East Hartford, Connecticut
DIVISION PRESIDENT: Irwin Mendelson

Pratt & Whitney Canada
See separate entry under Canada

Pratt & Whitney Aircraft was formed in 1925. Today Pratt & Whitney is the world's largest producer of gas turbine engines.

Commercial Products Division is responsible for commercial aircraft engines. Government Products Division is responsible for military engines. Manufacturing Division provides plant and facilities for making the products of the CPD and GPD. Pratt & Whitney Canada (P&WC), which has its own entry under that country, is responsible for engines for general aviation.

Pratt & Whitney has approximately 45,000 employees at locations in Connecticut, Georgia, Maine, Florida and Canada.

Excluding P&WC, the divisions had by 1986 manufactured over 68,000 gas turbine engines, most of them for aircraft. These engines had accumulated over 1 billion flight hours in military and commercial service. Most of this time has been logged by the JT3D, JT8D and JT9D turbofans on which a major part of the world's air transport is based.

PRATT & WHITNEY JT8

US military designation: J52

The J52 powers the Grumman A-6 Intruder/Prowler attack and ECM aircraft and versions of the McDonnell Douglas A-4 Skyhawk.

J52-P-6A, 6B, 8A, 8B. Rated at 37·8 kN (8,500 lb st) (6A, 6B) or 41·4 kN (9,300 lb st) (8A, 8B). Powers most versions of A-4, and A-6.

J52-P-408. Rated at 49·8 kN (11,200 lb st). Powers A-4F, A-4M, some export A-4 versions, EA-6B.

The J52 is a two-spool turbojet, with total of 12 compressor stages, a 'cannular' type combustion system fed by 36 dual orifice injectors and independent high pressure and low pressure single-stage turbines. Pressure ratio ranges from 12·4 to 14·6 : 1. Burner cans include features for reduced smoke. In the P-408 advanced design features are incorporated to achieve the rating increases with a minimum change in engine envelope and weight compared to other J52 models. These include two-position inlet guide vanes and aircooled first-stage turbine vanes and blades.

Two derivative engine programmes have been initiated. The **PW1216** is an afterburning derivative rated at 71·2 kN (16,000 lb st) and the **PW1212** is rated at 53·4 kN (12,000 lb st).

Data below are for the P-408:

DIMENSIONS:
- Diameter: 814·3 mm (32·06 in)
- Length: 3,020 mm (118·9 in)

WEIGHT, DRY: 1,052 kg (2,318 lb)

PRATT & WHITNEY JT4

US military designation: J75

Last described in the 1970-71 *Jane's*, about 50 of these large two-shaft turbojets, of J75-P-13B type, have been rebuilt by Pratt & Whitney to power Lockheed TR-1 reconnaissance aircraft. Afterburners were removed and other changes made.

PRATT & WHITNEY JT3D

US military designation: TF33

The JT3D is a turbofan version of the J57 turbojet, handling almost 2·5 times more air than the J57 and with pressure ratio ranging from 13 : 1 on the JT3D-1 to 15·6 : 1 on the JT3D-8A (TF33-P-7).

Flight trials in a B-52 Stratofortress bomber and Boeing 707 and DC-8 transports began in 1960. The JT3D powers the B-52H, most 707s and DC-8s, and the Shanghai Y-10. The Lockheed C-141B StarLifter military transport uses the TF33-P-7 version, with an additional stage of compression. In January 1973 the -7 engine, modified to incorporate additional accessory drives, was selected to power the Boeing E-3A (AWACS) aircraft. Designation of the E-3A engine is TF33-PW-100A (JT3D-8B).

More than 8,550 JT3D turbofans, including converted JT3C engines, had been delivered by completion in 1984.

DIMENSIONS:
- Diameter: JT3D-3B: 1,350 mm (53·14 in)
- TF33-PW-100A: 1,373 mm (54·06 in)
- Length: JT3D-3B: 3,479 mm (137 in)
- TF33-PW-100A: 3,607 mm (142 in)

WEIGHT, DRY:
- JT3D-3B: 1,969 kg (4,340 lb)
- TF33-PW-100A: 2,173 kg (4,790 lb)

PERFORMANCE RATINGS (T-O, S/L, static):
- JT3D-3B: 80 kN (18,000 lb st)
- TF33-PW-100A: 93·4 kN (21,000 lb st)

SPECIFIC FUEL CONSUMPTION (T-O rating):
- JT3D-3B: 15·5 mg/Ns (0·535 lb/h/lb st)
- TF33-PW-100A: 15·86 mg/Ns (0·560 lb/h/lb st)

PRATT & WHITNEY JT8D

This turbofan engine was developed as a company sponsored project to power the Boeing 727. It was later selected for other types of aircraft, and supersonic military versions of the JT8D have been developed in Sweden by Volvo Flygmotor (see RM8 in that company's entry).

Construction of the JT8D is largely of steel and titanium. An annular bypass duct runs the full length of the engine, with balanced mixing of the hot and cold air streams in the tailpipe.

The JT8D entered commercial service on 1 February 1964. It has since become the most widely used commercial jet engine, almost 12,000 having logged more than 225 million flight hours by March 1984.

The following are current versions:

JT8D-9, -9A. Develops 64·5 kN (14,500 lb st) to 28·9°C at S/L. Specified for Boeing 727-100, -100C and -200, 737-200, -200C and T-43A, McDonnell Douglas DC-9-20, -30, -40, C-9A, C-9B and VC-9C, Aérospatiale Caravelle 12 and Kawasaki C-1. Deliveries began in July 1967. Produced under licence in Japan (see entry under Mitsubishi) until 1981.

JT8D-11. Develops 66·7 kN (15,000 lb st) to 28·9°C at S/L. Specified for McDonnell Douglas DC-9-20, -30 and -40 series aircraft. Deliveries began in November 1968.

JT8D-15. Develops 69 kN (15,500 lb st) to 28·9°C. FAA certification was received and deliveries began in April 1971. Powers Dassault Mercure, Boeing Advanced 727 and 737, and DC-9. Entered service 1972.

JT8D-15A. In 1982 new components in the Dash-15 engine resulted in a 5·5 per cent reduction in cruise fuel consumption. The same parts in the Dash-17 produce the **JT8D-17A**, and when fitted to the Dash-17R the **JT8D-17AR**. Some can be incorporated in earlier JT8D engines, giving up to 3 per cent reduction in fuel consumption.

JT8D-17. Develops 71·2 kN (16,000 lb st) to 28·9°C. Certificated on 1 February 1974. Entered service July 1974. Powers Advanced versions of Boeing 727 and 737, and DC-9. For JT8D-17A, see JT8D-15A.

JT8D-17R. Normal T-O rating 72·95 kN (16,400 lb st) but has capability of providing 4·448 kN (1,000 lb) additional thrust in the event of significant thrust loss on any other engine. Certificated at 77·40 kN (17,400 lb st) T-O rating in April 1976. Delivery of Advanced 727-200 August 1976 and certification with reserve-thrust feature November 1976. For JT8D-17AR, see JT8D-15A.

Pratt & Whitney J52-P-408 two-shaft turbojet rated at 49·8 kN (11,200 lb st)

Pratt & Whitney TF33-PW-100A turbofan rated at 93·4 kN (21,000 lb st)

Pratt & Whitney JT8D-219 turbofan rated at 93·4 kN (21,000 lb st)

JT8D-200 Series. Described separately.

Since February 1970 all new JT8D engines have incorporated smoke reduction hardware, and conversion kits are available for in-service engines. Two noise reduction options are also available for all JT8D models. Maximum TBO for the JT8D is 16,800 h.

TYPE: Axial flow two-spool turbofan.

AIR INTAKE: Annular with 19 fixed inlet guide vanes.

FAN: Two-stage front fan. First stage has 27 titanium blades dovetailed into discs. First-stage blades have integral shroud at about 61 per cent span. Airflow: -9, -9A, 145 kg (319 lb)/s; -11, -15, 146 kg (322 lb)/s; -17, 147 kg (324 lb)/s. -17R, 148 kg (326 lb)/s. Bypass ratio: -9, -9A, 1·04; -11, 1·05; -15, 1·03; -17, 1·02; -17R, 1·00.

LP COMPRESSOR: Six-stage axial, integral with fan stages, on inner of two concentric shafts. Blades made of titanium. Shaft carried in double ball bearings, either half of each bearing being able to handle the complete loading.

HP COMPRESSOR: Seven-stage axial flow on outer hollow shaft which, like the inner shaft, is carried in double ball bearings. One-piece casing. Blades made of steel or titanium. Overall pressure ratio: -9, -9A, 15·9; -11, 16·2; -15, 16·5; -17, 16·9; -17R, 17·3.

COMBUSTION CHAMBER: Cannular type with nine cylindrical flame tubes, each downstream of a single Duplex burner and discharging into a single annular nozzle.

HP TURBINE: Single-stage axial flow. Solid blades in -9 aircooled in -11 and later; guide vanes hollow and aircooled in all models.

LP Turbine: Three-stage axial flow. Solid blades and guide vanes.

Dimensions:

Diameter	1,080 mm (42·5 in)
Length	3,137 mm (123·5 in)

Weight, Dry:

JT8D-9, -9A	1,532 kg (3,377 lb)
JT8D-11	1,537 kg (3,389 lb)
JT8D-15,	1,549 kg (3,414 lb)
-15A	1,576 kg (3,474 lb)
JT8D-17,	1,556 kg (3,430 lb)
-17A	1,577 kg (3,475 lb)
JT8D-17R,	1,585 kg (3,495 lb)
-17AR	1,588 kg (3,500 lb)

Performance Ratings:

T-O thrust (S/L, static) see model descriptions

Max cruise thrust (10,670 m; 35,000 ft at Mach 0·8):

JT8D-9, -9A	18·2 kN (4,100 lb)
JT8D-11	17·6 kN (3,950 lb)
JT8D-15, -15A	18·2 kN (4,100 lb)
JT8D-17, -17R, -17A, -17AR	18·9 kN (4,240 lb)

Specific Fuel Consumption:

T-O rating:

JT8D-9, 9A	16·85 mg/Ns (0·595 lb/h/lb st)
JT8D-11	17·56 mg/Ns (0·620 lb/h/lb st)
JT8D-15	17·84 mg/Ns (0·630 lb/h/lb st)
-15A	16·63 mg/Ns (0·587 lb/h/lb st)
JT8D-17	18·27 mg/Ns (0·645 lb/h/lb st)
-17A	17·05 mg/Ns (0·602 lb/h/lb st)
JT8D-17R	18·55 mg/Ns (0·655 lb/h/lb st)
-17AR	17·31 mg/Ns (0·611 lb/h/lb st)

Max cruise rating, as above:

JT8D-9, -9A	22·86 mg/Ns (0·807 lb/h/lb)
JT8D-11	23·14 mg/Ns (0·817 lb/h/lb)
JT8D-15	22·97 mg/Ns (0·811 lb/h/lb)
JT8D-17, -17R	23·37 mg/Ns (0·825 lb/h/lb)

PRATT & WHITNEY JT8D-200 SERIES

This reduced noise derivative of the JT8D family is substantially redesigned. The JT8D-200 combines the HP compressor, HP turbine spool and combustion section of the JT8D-9 with advanced LP technology derived from the NASA JT8D refan programme and other modern P&W engines. The 200 Series offers substantially increased thrust with reduced noise and specific fuel consumption, together with the established reliability and low maintenance cost of the JT8D HP spool. The new single-stage fan has increased diameter. The new six-stage LP compressor, integral with the fan, offers increased pressure ratio. The LP turbine has 20 per cent greater annular area and achieves a higher efficiency. Surrounding the engine is a new bypass duct. The exhaust system includes a 12 lobe internal mixer to provide forced mixing of fan and primary streams. A **JT8D-209** prototype engine began flight development in a McDonnell Douglas YC-15 AMST prototype transport aircraft on 4 March 1977. Later that month Pratt & Whitney launched the JT8D-200 series as commercial products, the basic application being the McDonnell Douglas MD-80 family of aircraft. FAA certification of the JT8D-209 was awarded in June 1979. Volvo Flygmotor has a 9 per cent share of the programme, delivering components and spares for the -209, -217 and -219.

The following JT8D-200 engine models are currently certificated or under development:

JT8D-209. This initial model, which is discussed above, is rated at 82·2 kN (18,500 lb st) to 25°C for normal use, and 85·6 kN (19,250 lb st) following loss of thrust on any other engine. It received FAA certification in June 1979, and entered service in October 1980, powering the MD-81.

JT8D-217. Rated at 88·96 kN (20,000 lb st) for normal use, and 92·75 kN (20,850 lb st) following loss of thrust on any other engine. Engine certificated in October 1980; production deliveries began one month later for use in the MD-82.

JT8D-217A. Modifications extend T-O thrust to 28·9°C or up to 1,525 m (5,000 ft). This engine, which also powers the MD-82, received FAA certification in October 1981.

JT8D-217C. This engine, developed in 1985, will power the MD-82, as well as the smaller MD-87. The JT8D-217B has the thrust ratings of the JT8D-217A but incorporates JT8D-219 performance improvements to reduce sfc. FAA certification scheduled for first quarter of 1986.

JT8D-219. Launched to power the MD-83, the JT8D-219 produces 93·4 kN (21,000 lb st) for normal use, with a maximum rating of 96·5 kN (21,700 lb st), while maintaining the same external dimensions as other versions. It was certified in February 1985 and production deliveries started a month later. The -219 provides aerodynamic improvements to reduce sfc. Additional performance improvements to reduce sfc further will be available by January 1987. The JT8D-219 will also be used to power MD-81 aircraft.

Type: Axial flow two-spool turbofan.

Air Intake: Annular, with 23 fixed inlet guide vanes.

Fan: Single-stage front fan has 34 titanium blades, with part-span shrouds, dovetailed into discs. Airflow: at normal T-O rating: -209, 213 kg (469 lb)/s; -217 (all), 219 kg (483 lb)/s; -219, 221 kg (488 lb)/s. Bypass ratio: -209, 1·78; -217 (all), 1·73; -219, 1·77.

LP Compressor: Six-stage axial, integral with fan; blades of titanium.

HP Compressor: Seven-stage axial on outer hollow shaft. One-piece casing. Blades of steel or titanium. Overall pressure ratio: -209, 17·1; -217 (all), 18·6; -219, 19·2.

Combustion Chamber: Nine cannular low-emissions burners with aerating fuel nozzles.

HP Turbine: Single-stage axial. Aircooled guide vanes; solid rotor blades in -209, aircooled in -217/A/C and -219.

LP Turbine: Three-stage axial. Solid blades and guide vanes.

Dimensions:

Diameter	1,250 mm (49·2 in)
Length	3,911 mm (154 in)

Weight, Dry:

JT8D-209	2,001 kg (4,410 lb)
JT8D-217, -217A	2,010 kg (4,430 lb)
JT8D-217C, -219	2,048 kg (4,515 lb)

Performance Ratings:

T-O (S/L static): see model descriptions

Max cruise thrust (10,670 m; 35,000 ft at Mach 0·8):

JT8D-209	22·0 kN (4,945 lb)
JT8D-217, -217A, -217C	23·31 kN (5,240 lb)
JT8D-219	23·35 kN (5,250 lb)

Specific Fuel Consumption:

Max cruise rating, as above:

JT8D-209	20·50 mg/Ns (0·724 lb/h/lb)
JT8D-217, -217A	21·32 mg/Ns (0·753 lb/h/lb)
JT8D-217C	20·84 mg/Ns (0·736 lb/h/lb st)
JT8D-219	20·87 mg/Ns (0·737 lb/h/lb)

PRATT & WHITNEY PW4000

The PW4000 engine series is a third generation high bypass ratio turbofan family, intended for application to existing and future wide-body transports. Ratings cover a thrust range from 213·5 kN (48,000 lb) to 267 kN (60,000 lb). The December 1982 formal announcement of the engine series was preceded by more than one year of design and development. The first engine of the PW4000 series achieved 275 kN (61,800 lb) thrust during initial sea level testing in April 1984. Testing of the same engine in the Pratt & Whitney altitude test chamber showed cruise fuel consumption as predicted to be improved approximately 5 per cent relative to the current JT9D-7R4 and within 2 per cent of 1986 PW4000 guarantee levels. As a result of the very successful testing, the certification date for the 249 kN (56,000 lb) configuration was advanced three months to April 1986. First engine flight test on an Airbus Industrie A300B took place on 31 July 1985. The engine will be introduced into service on the Airbus A310-300 by Pan American World Airways in the Summer of 1987, and has been selected by Singapore Airlines to power a new fleet of A310-300s and Boeing 747-400s. The company designation policy will be applied, with the last two numbers denoting thrust (thus, the initially certificated 56,000 lb st engine will be the PW4056). Programme sharing agreements have been signed with FN (Belgium), Fiat (Italy), Kongsberg (Norway), Kawasaki (Japan) and Samsung (South Korea).

In appearance the new engines resemble the JT9D. Fuel consumption is reduced seven per cent compared with the JT9D-7R4. The configuration contains about half the number of parts of the -7R4, promising reductions in maintenance cost exceeding 25 per cent. Cycle and configuration changes result in a thrust/weight ratio higher than 6·5. Relative to the JT9D, the HP compressor pressure ratio is increased by 10 per cent and the HP rotor system operates at 27 per cent higher rotational speed. The PW4000 embodies the low noise features of the JT9D, with similar rotor/stator geometry and spacing, and corresponding fan tip speed.

The PW4000 incorporates and improves upon technology from the -7R4, E[3], and PW2037 programmes. The design incorporates advanced single-crystal turbine blades, aerodynamically enhanced aerofoils, an efficiency improving Thermatic rotor, and a full authority electronic engine control. The PW4000 is designed to fit into existing -7R4 nacelles with minimum changes.

Type: Two-shaft turbofan of high bypass ratio.

Air Intake: Direct front entry. No inlet guide vanes or anti-icing.

Fan: Single stage. Titanium/alloy hub retains 38 titanium alloy blades with aft part-span shrouds. Downstream is a row of 84 non-structural fan exit guide vanes, followed by nine structural struts supporting the cases. Rotating fan spinner of composite material. Fan diameter 2,373 mm (93·44 in). Data for 249·0 kN (56,000 lb st) rating: airflow 773 kg (1,705 lb)/s. Fan pressure ratio 1·7. Bypass ratio 4·85.

LP Compressor: Four stages with one-piece titanium/alloy rotor, retaining advanced controlled diffusion titanium/alloy aerofoils. Splitter and static-structure axial positioning designed to enhance dirt removal.

HP Compressor: Eleven stages with first four vane rows variable. Thermatic rotor retains advanced controlled-diffusion aerofoils of titanium alloys in first eight rows and nickel alloys in last three. Clearance control accomplished via rotor response to ventilation air temperature. Overall pressure ratio at 249 kN rating, 29·7.

Combustor: Annular, forged nickel alloy roll-ring with double-pass cooling geometry. 24 air-blast single-feed anti-coking fuel injectors, equally spaced between 24 structural struts in cascade/area-ruled diffuser.

HP Turbine: Two stages with aircooled blades cast as single crystal (PWA 1480) in first row and directional crystal (PWA 1422) in second row, retained in double-hub nickel alloy rotor. Vane aerofoils thermal barrier coated. Clearance control by integral system of fan air impingement on cast nickel alloy case. Aerofoil cooling-air supply modulated.

LP Turbine: Four stages with uncooled cast nickel alloy blades in bonded/bolted rotor. Vanes nickel alloy cast in clusters, uncooled but with first two rows coated. Clearance control by fan air impingement on nickel alloy case. Exhaust case has single row of controlled diffusion aerofoils which double as structural struts and exit guide vanes.

Control System: Full authority digital electronic with dual channel computer.

Dimensions:

Length	3,371 mm (132·7 in)
Fan case diameter	2,463 mm (96·98 in)

The Pratt & Whitney PW4000 advanced large turbofan engine

Exhaust case diameter	1,467 mm (57·76 in)
WEIGHT, DRY:	
Basic engine	4,173 kg (9,200 lb)

PRATT & WHITNEY JT9D

Based on technology stemming from the US Air Force heavy freighter propulsion of 1961-63, the JT9D was the first of the new era of very large, high bypass ratio turbofans on which the design of the present generation of wide-body commercial transports rests.

In its basic design the JT9D is compact, being shorter than the JT3D, and has two shafts, each supported in two bearings. In cruising flight the installed sfc is 22-23 per cent lower than for the JT3D or JT8D. Careful attention has been paid to maintenance.

First run of the JT9D was in December 1966, and first engine flight test, with the engine mounted on the starboard inboard pylon of a Boeing B-52E, was in June 1968. The first flight of the Boeing 747 was on 9 February 1969.

Current versions include:

JT9D-3A. Incorporates water injection for wet rating of 200·8 kN (45,150 lb) to 26·7°C. Powers Boeing 747-100 and -200B. Engines delivered from December 1969 and certificated on 9 January 1970.

JT9D-7. Higher thrust version, described in 1981-82 *Jane's*. Certificated June 1971; powers the 747-200B, C, F and SR.

JT9D-7A. Aerodynamic improvements provide increased thrust at the same turbine temperature and reduced specific fuel consumption. Certificated September 1972; powers 747-200 and 747SP.

JT9D-7F, -7J. JT9D-7A with first and second stage turbine rotor blades and second stage stator vanes of directionally solidified material; -7J also has improved cooling, giving -7F T-O rating without water injection. The -7F was certificated in September 1974 and the -7J in August 1976.

JT9D-7Q, -7R. Described later.

JT9D-20. Similar to the D-7A, except for external configuration changes such as accessory gearbox under fan case. Certificated October 1972.

JT9D-59A, -70A. First growth versions. Fan diameter approximately 25·4 mm (one inch) larger, with re-profiled blades; LP compressor has a zero (fourth) stage and is completely redesigned; burners recontoured, an HP turbine carbon seal is added, HP turbine rotor blades are of directionally solidified PWA 1422 superalloy, and HP turbine annulus is of greater area. Both models certificated December 1974; configured for installation in a common nacelle, developed jointly by P&W and Rohr Industries, for the 747 (-70A) or DC-10 and A300B (-59A). The **-59D** and **-70D** are higher thrust versions.

JT9D-7Q Series. These have the same gas path as the -59A and -70A but an exterior configured like the -7 for installation in the Boeing 747-200 nacelle. The combination of improved performance, reduced drag and reduced propulsion system weight significantly improved 747-200 performance. The -7Q was certificated in October 1978. This series spans a thrust range of 236-249 kN (53,000-56,000 lb).

JT9D-7R4 Series. This family comprises seven models (7R4D to 7R4H), with common fan, LP and HP compressor, LP turbine and gearbox modules, incorporating the latest technology and materials. Compared with the 1977 D-7A the -7R4 series has a larger fan with wide chord blades, a zero stage on the LP compressor, improved combustor, single crystal HP turbine blades, increased diameter LP turbine, a supervisory electronic fuel control and many smaller changes. The new engines offer a TSFC reduction of up to eight per cent. The 7R4D, 7R4E and 7R4E4 for the Boeing 767 were certificated in November 1980, June 1982 and March 1985, respectively, the 7R4D1 and 7R4E1 for the A310 were certificated in April 1981, and the -7R4G2 for the 747 and the -7R4H1 for the A300B-600 in July 1982. Engines are offered as a complete package in the PW7R4 nacelle; this propulsion system was selected for the A300-600 and A310.

Since entry to service on 21 January 1970 the JT9D has gained experience more rapidly than any previous engine. Within one year 653 engines had been delivered, and early in 1973 the total exceeded 1,132. Rate of delivery has since slowed but the total now exceeds 3,000 and flight time in early 1986 was in excess of 66 million h.

The following description applies to early versions of the JT9D, with data for later models given in parentheses:

TYPE: Two-shaft turbofan of high bypass ratio.

INTAKE: Direct pitot, annular fixed geometry (except that airframe inlet on early 747 aircraft has blow-in side doors around periphery). No inlet guide vanes ahead of fan. Airflow improved by rotating spinner.

FAN: Single stage, with 46 titanium blades of 4·6 aspect ratio (-7R4, 40 blades of 4·0 a.r.) and two part span shrouds (-7R4, one shroud) dovetailed in titanium LP rotor. Downstream are 108 aluminium alloy exit guide vanes (96 on the -59A, -70A and -7Q, 84 on -7R4), followed by nine discharge case radial struts. Fan case of stainless steel (7R4, titanium) and aluminium alloy, designed to contain fan blades. Discharge case lined with perforated acoustic material. Nominal airflow 684 kg (1,509 lb)/s at 3,650 rpm (-7, 698 kg; 1,540 lb/s at 3,750 rpm; -59A, -70A, -7Q, 744 kg; 1,640 lb/s at 3,430 rpm; -7R4G/H, 769 kg; 1,695 lb/s at 3,530 rpm). Pressure ratio typically 1·6 : 1. Bypass ratio: -3A, 5·17; -7, 5·15; -59A, -70A, 4·9; -7R4D, E, 5·0; -7R4G2, H1, 4·8.

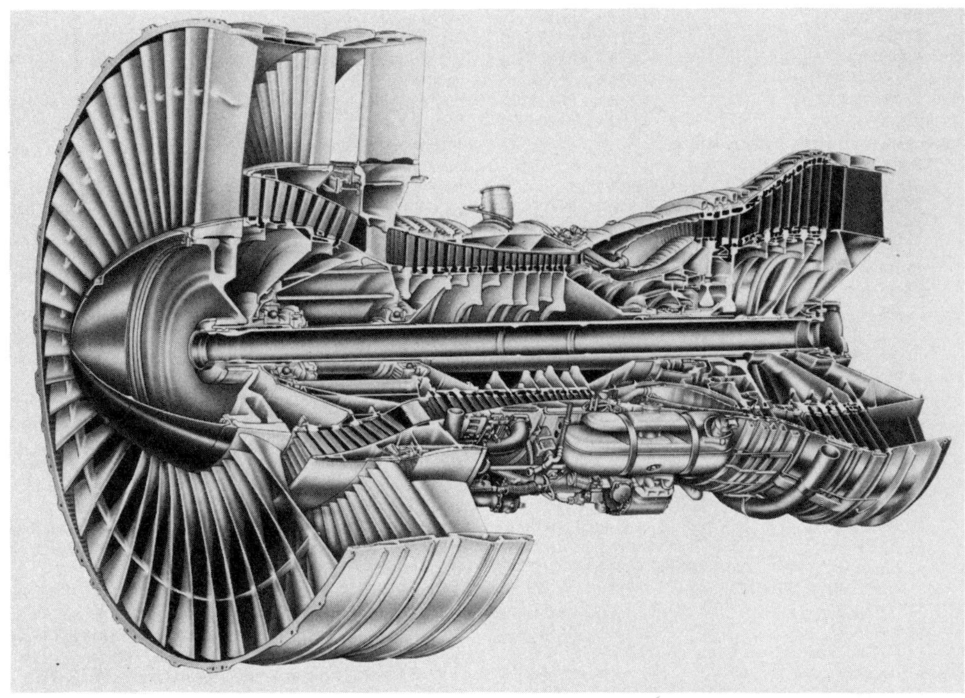

Cutaway drawing of JT9D-7R4 with improved LP turbine introduced in 1982

LP COMPRESSOR: Three stages (JT9D-59A, -70A, -7Q, -7R4, four stages), rotating with fan. Rotor made up of rings, spacers and integral hub/disc splined to steel LP shaft and held by lock-nut ahead of fan and overhung ahead of main LP ball thrust bearing. Hydraulically opened bleed ring at LP exit to increase flight idle stall margin and excess air during deceleration. Rotor stages have 104, 132 and 130 (-7Q, -59A, -70, -7R4, 108, 120, 112, 100) dovetailed blades of titanium alloy. First stator stage (except -7R4) anti-iced by 9th stage bleed air. Stator stages have 88, 128 and 126 (-7Q, -59, -70, 7R4, 96, 114, 116, 104, 88) titanium vanes and 120 (4th stage) nickel alloy vanes, all riveted to outer rings. First stator nickel alloy, remainder corrosion resistant iron alloy. Casing of aluminium alloy. Core airflow typically 118 kg (260 lb)/s (all versions).

HP COMPRESSOR: Eleven stages. All stages have rings or centreless discs with integral spacers carried on titanium hub/disc at third stage and nickel bolted hub at 11th stage. Rotor stages have 60, 84, 102, 100, 110, 108, 104, 94 and 100 dovetailed titanium blades and 102 and 90 nickel alloy blades. Stator has 76, 70, 80, 106, 100 and 112 steel vanes and 126, 146, 154, 158 and 92 vanes of nickel alloy, the last eight stages brazed to inner and outer rings. First three stator stages are variable, plus the intermediate IGV stage, positioned by hydraulic actuator to provide adequate stall margin for starting, acceleration and part power operation. Casing of titanium alloys (last two stages, nickel alloy) has bleed ports supplying 8th stage air for airframe requirements. Max HP speed: -3A, 7,850 rpm; -7, 8,000 rpm; -7R4E4/G/H, 8,080 rpm. Overall engine pressure ratio: -3A, 21·5; -7, 22·2; -7Q, -59A, -70, 24·5; -7R4D, D1, 23·4; -7R4E, E1, E4, 24·2; -7R4G2, 26·3; -7R4H1, 26·7.

COMBUSTION CHAMBER: The diffuser case incorporates two sets of bleed ports for 15th stage air for airframe requirements. The forward set (absent from -7R4) takes air from the outside case via an integral manifold and the rear set bleeds air from the inner diameter via four of the ten radial struts. The combustor itself is fabricated in nickel alloy and is annular. Ignition by dual AC 4-joule capacitor system serving two plugs just above chamber centreline on each side.

FUEL SYSTEM: Pressure type with hydraulic control system operating at up to 76 bars (1,100 lb/sq in). Main components are fuel control, pump, fuel/air heater and fuel/oil heat exchanger. (-7R4 except G2 has digital electronic system to control hydromechanical control; engine is operational with or without electronic system functioning.) Provision for water injection, as customer option, with regulator, piping and spray nozzles, adds 18·1 kg (40 lb) to engine weight (not fitted to -7R4).

FUEL GRADE: P&W specification PWA 522.

HP TURBINE: Two stages. Both have high-nickel discs carrying high-nickel blades in fir tree roots; first stage has 116 aircooled blades and second has 138 solid blades (aircooled in -D7 and all subsequent models). Stators have 66 and 90 high-nickel alloy vanes, both rows aircooled. (-7R4, single crystal alloy in first-stage blades to 222·4 kN, 50,000 lb st, and in first and second blades and second stator (vane) for higher-thrust models.) Turbine inlet temperature (-3A, max T-O), typically 1,243°C (-59A, -70A, 1,350-1,370°C; -7R4, 1,200-1,300°C).

LP TURBINE: Four stages. Stages have 122, 120, 110 and 102 solid nickel alloy blades held in fir tree roots in discs of nickel alloy (fifth disc, iron alloy). Stators have 108, 126, 122 and 116 solid nickel alloy vanes. In 1982 an improved LP turbine was introduced to -7R4 production, consisting of four stages with integral spacers carried on a single bolted hub splined to the LP shaft (see cutaway). Exhaust gas temperature after turbine, typically 452°C (-3A), 482°C (-7, -20), 580°C (-59A, -70, -7Q), 500°C (-7R4D), 535°C (-7R4E), 560°C (-7R4G2) and 575°C (-7R4H1).

JETPIPE: Fixed Inconel assembly.

REVERSER: Fan duct reverser comprises a translating sleeve (the rearmost portion of fan duct) which moves aft, causing long links to close the blocker doors and simultaneously pulling aft the cascade vanes. Primary (core) reverser, largely of Inconel 625, uses fixed cascades which are uncovered by aft movement of translating sleeves to which are hinged blocker doors pulled by links against the central nozzle plug. No primary reverser is used on -59A, -70A, -7Q or -7R4.

ACCESSORY DRIVES: Main accessory gearbox driven by tower bevel shaft from front of HP spool and mounted under central diffuser case (-20, -59A, -70A, under fan discharge case). Main driven accessories include CSD (IDG on -7R4 except G2) fuel pump and control, starter, hydraulic pump, alternator and N_2 tachometer; Boeing 747 includes primary reverser motor and the DC-10-40 a second hydraulic pump and a fuel boost pump. The box also includes numerous lubrication system items, and provides for hand turning the HP spool during borescope inspection.

LUBRICATION SYSTEM: Pressure feed through fuel/oil cooler to four main bearings and return through scavenge pumps (-20 also centrifugal scavenge) to 18·8-37·6 litre (5-10 US gal; 4·16-8·32 Imp gal) tank.

OIL GRADE: PWA 521C (blend of synthetic and/or mineral oils).

MOUNTING: From above, in two planes. Front mount (-3A, -7) is double flange at top of fan discharge case, absorbing vertical and side loads. On -20, -59A, -70A the mount is rectangular block above intermediate case, taking vertical and side loads, and thrust brackets at 40° each side of vertical on intermediate case outer flange.

STARTING: Pneumatic, by HamStan PS 700 or AiResearch ATS100-384 (DC-10, PS 700 only). Supplied at 2·76-3·10 bars (40-45 lb/sq in) from APU, ground cart or cross-bleed.

DIMENSIONS:	
JT9D-3A, -7, -7A, -7F, -7J, -20:	
Diameter	2,427 mm (95·56 in)
Length (flange to flange)	3,255 mm (128·15 in)
JT9D-59A, -70A, -7Q:	
Diameter	2,464 mm (97·0 in)
Length	3,358 mm (132·2 in)
JT9D-7R4D to H:	
Diameter	2,463 mm (96·98 in)
Length	3,371 mm (132·7 in)
WEIGHT, DRY:	
Guaranteed, including standard equipment:	
JT9D-3A	3,905 kg (8,608 lb)
JT9D-7, -7A, -7F, -7J	4,014 kg (8,850 lb)
JT9D-20	3,833 kg (8,450 lb)
JT9D-59A	4,146 kg (9,140 lb)

JT9D-70A	4,153 kg (9,155 lb)
JT9D-7Q	4,216 kg (9,295 lb)
JT9D-7R4D, E, E4	4,039 kg (8,905 lb)
JT9D-7R4D1, E1	4,029 kg (8,885 lb)
JT9D-7R4G2	4,143 kg (9,135 lb)
JT9D-7R4H1	4,029 kg (8,885 lb)

PERFORMANCE RATINGS (ideal nozzles):

T-O thrust, dry:

JT9D-3A	193·9 kN (43,600 lb st) to 26·7°C
JT9D-7	202·8 kN (45,600 lb st) to 26·7°C
JT9D-7A	205·7 kN (46,250 lb st) to 26·7°C
JT9D-7F	213·5 kN (48,000 lb st) to 26·7°C
JT9D-7J	222·4 kN (50,000 lb st) to 30°C
JT9D-20	206·0 kN (46,300 lb st) to 28·9°C
JT9D-59A, -70A, -7Q	236·0 kN (53,000 lb st) to 30°C
JT9D-7R4D, D1	213·5 kN (48,000 lb st) to 33°C
JT9D-7R4E, E1	222·4 kN (50,000 lb st) to 33°C
JT9D-7R4E4	222·4 kN (50,000 lb st) to 45·6°C
JT9D-7R4G2	243·4 kN (54,750 lb st) to 30°C
JT9D-7R4H1	249·0 kN (56,000 lb st) to 30°C

T-O thrust, wet:

JT9D-3A	200·8 kN (45,150 lb st) to 26·7°C
JT9D-7	210·0 kN (47,200 lb st) to 30°C
JT9D-7A	212·4 kN (47,750 lb st) to 30°C
JT9D-7F	222·4 kN (50,000 lb st) to 30°C
JT9D-20	220·0 kN (49,400 lb st) to 30°C

Max cruise thrust, 10,670 m (35,000 ft) at Mach 0·85:

JT9D-3A, -7	45·4 kN (10,200 lb)
JT9D-7A	48·2 kN (10,830 lb)
JT9D-7F, -7J	49·2 kN (11,050 lb)
JT9D-20	47·5 kN (10,680 lb)
JT9D-59A, -70A, -7Q	53·2 kN (11,950 lb)
JT9D-7R4D, D1	50·0 kN (11,250 lb)
JT9D-7R4E, E1	52·0 kN (11,700 lb)
JT9D-7R4G2, H1	54·5 kN (12,250 lb)

SPECIFIC FUEL CONSUMPTION (ideal nozzles):

Max cruise, ISA + 10°C, Mach 0·85 at 10,670 m (35,000 ft):

JT9D-3A	17·67 mg/Ns (0·624 lb/h/lb)
JT9D-7	17·55 mg/Ns (0·620 lb/h/lb)
JT9D-7A	17·69 mg/Ns (0·625 lb/h/lb)
JT9D-7F, -7Q, -59A, -70A	17·87 mg/Ns (0·631 lb/h/lb)
JT9D-20	17·67 mg/Ns (0·624 lb/h/lb)
JT9D-7R4D, D1	17·42 mg/Ns (0·615 lb/h/lb)
JT9D-7R4E, E1	17·55 mg/Ns (0·620 lb/h/lb)
JT9D-7R4G2	18·10 mg/Ns (0·639 lb/h/lb)
JT9D-7R4H1	17·79 mg/Ns (0·628 lb/h/lb)

PRATT & WHITNEY PW2037

US military designation: F117

The PW2037, formerly designated JT10D, is a third generation turbofan, intended for transport aircraft. Work on the engine began in 1972, and the first JT10D flight-weight demonstrator engine ran in August 1974, at a thrust level of 102·3 kN (23,000 lb). Major changes to the engine have been made since that time, to keep abreast of increased thrust requirements and to incorporate advanced technology features.

The development programme on the JT10D-232 began in January 1980. This engine was rated at 142·3 kN (32,000 lb st). In mid-1980 the engine was again scaled up to be compatible with the Boeing 757-200, at 167·2 kN (37,600 lb st). Following company policy it was given the present designation in the PW2000 series, the last two digits denoting thrust.

The PW2037 incorporates technology advancements such as single crystal turbine blades, higher strength disc material, aerodynamically superior aerofoils and full authority digital control. It therefore represents a substantial improvement over the JT10D engines which were proposed earlier.

Specific fuel consumption is reduced nearly 30 per cent compared with first generation turbofans. Configuration changes have lightened the engine, resulting in a thrust: weight ratio higher than 5·3. The PW2037 incorporates the low noise features of the JT9D, including the use of a single-stage fan without inlet guide vanes, wide axial separation between the blade and vane rows, and a moderate fan tip speed.

The engine is designed to be compatible with acoustically treated nacelles, to achieve noise levels below FAR Pt 36 requirements. The engine is also configured with a low-emissions burner. The first engine test run took place in December 1981. FAA certification was achieved in December 1983, at which time 11 engines had run more than 5,000 h. The first flight was made on the prototype Boeing 757 on 14 March 1984.

Companies participating in development of the PW2037 are Motoren- und Turbinen Union GmbH (MTU) of Federal Germany and Fiat SpA of Italy. P&W is expected to bear 84·8 per cent of the programme, MTU 11·2 per cent and Fiat 4 per cent. A collaboration agreement between these companies was signed in July 1977.

P&W has, in conjunction with Boeing, proposed that USAF B-52G and H bombers should each be re-engined with four PW2037 engines. Current applications are the Boeing 757 for Delta, Singapore, Northwest, United Parcel Service and Royal Air Maroc, and the McDonnell Douglas C-17. The PW2037-powered 757 was certificated on 25 October 1984 and entered revenue service on 1 December. Other potential applications are the Airbus Industrie A340 and smaller versions of the Boeing 747.

The PW2000 engine family is expected to consist ultimately of a series of models which will span a take-off thrust range of 133·4 to 195·7 kN (30,000 to 44,000 lb), filling the gap between the JT8D and JT9D.

TYPE: Two-shaft turbofan of high bypass ratio.

AIR INTAKE: Direct front entry. No inlet guide vanes or anti-icing.

FAN: Single-stage. Titanium forged hub, with 36 inserted titanium alloy blades with part-span shrouds. Downstream are radial struts supporting the fan case. Rotating fan spinner. Fan tip diameter 1,994 mm (78·5 in). Max airflow 608 kg (1,340 lb)/s. Fan pressure ratio 1·7. Bypass ratio 6·0.

LP COMPRESSOR: Four stages, with controlled diffusion aerofoils with thick leading- and trailing-edges.

HP COMPRESSOR: Twelve stages, with controlled diffusion aerofoils. Variable vanes on first five stages and active clearance control on last eight stages by using cool fan air to shrink casing in cruising flight. Overall cruise pressure ratio 31·8.

COMBUSTION CHAMBER: Annular, with flame tube fabricated in nickel alloy. Single-pipe fuel nozzles.

HP TURBINE: Two stages with aircooled blades cast as single crystals in PW 1480 alloy. Rotors with active clearance control. Both discs of PW1100 nickel based powder.

LP TURBINE: Five stages, with active clearance control.

CONTROL SYSTEM: Full authority digital electronic with two redundant computers.

DIMENSIONS:

Length	3,591 mm (141·4 in)
Fan case diameter	2,154 mm (84·8 in)

WEIGHT, DRY: 3,248 kg (7,160 lb)

PERFORMANCE RATING:

T-O, S/L: 170·1 kN (38,250 lb st)

SPECIFIC FUEL CONSUMPTION (ideal nozzle, cruise at Mach 0·8 at 10,670 m; 35,000 ft): 15·95 mg/Ns (0·563 lb/h/lb)

PRATT & WHITNEY JTF10A

US military designation: TF30

Development of this high compression two-spool turbofan was begun in 1958 as a private venture, and resulted in testing of the first turbofan with afterburning. It was chosen

Pratt & Whitney PW2037 turbofan engine

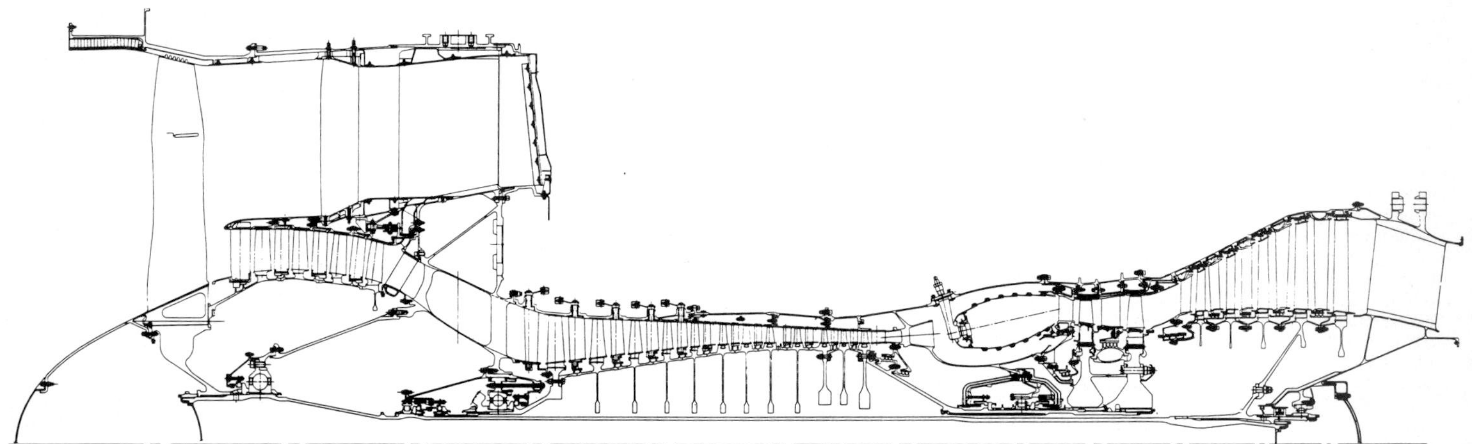

Longitudinal cross-section through Pratt & Whitney PW2037, rated at 170·1 kN (38,250 lb st)

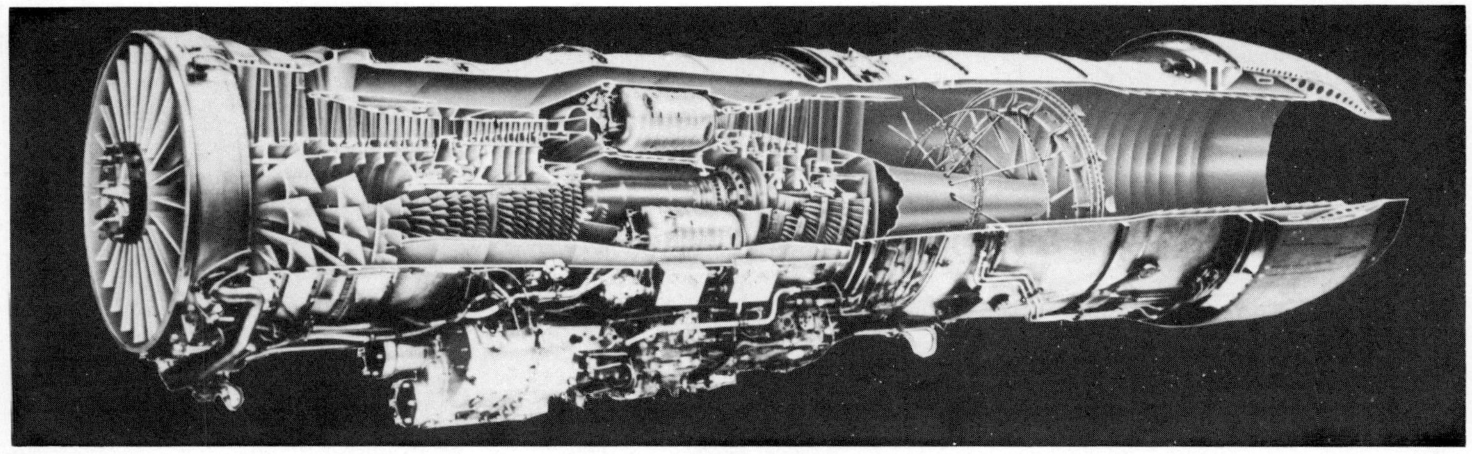

Cutaway drawing of TF30-P-414A, rated at 93 kN (20,900 lb st)

subsequently as the power plant for the General Dynamics F-111, though the first version in service was the unaugmented version in the Vought A-7A.

A third application is the US Navy's Grumman F-14A Tomcat fighter, powered by the **TF30-P-414**, now being converted to **-414A** standard which significantly improves engine stability and extends overhaul interval to 2,400 h.

The following description refers to the P-414A:

TYPE: Two-shaft turbofan.

INTAKE: Direct pitot annular type with 23 fixed inlet guide vanes. Hollow vanes pass anti-icing air.

FAN: Three stages. Rotor and stator and casings all of titanium, except for steel containment case.

LP COMPRESSOR: Six stages constructed integrally with fan to form nine-stage spool. Titanium, except stator blades of steel.

HP COMPRESSOR: Seven stages, mainly nickel alloy.

COMBUSTION CHAMBER: Can-annular, with steel casing and eight Hastelloy combustors, each with four dual-orifice burners.

FUEL SYSTEM: HP system (above 69 bars; 1,000 lb/sq in), with conventional hydromechanical control. Main elements comprise fuel pump, filter, fuel control, P & D valve and nozzles. Separate afterburner system.

FUEL GRADES: JP-4, JP-5, JP-8.

HP TURBINE: Single stage, with 40 aircooled nozzle guide vanes (stators) of single-crystal nickel based material and aircooled rotor blades of nickel-based alloy.

LP TURBINE: Three stages of nickel based alloys. Rotor stages have 94, 96 and 80 fir tree root blades. Gas temperature after turbine, typically 587°C.

AFTERBURNER: Diffuser leads to combustion section comprising double wall outer duct and inner liner carrying five-zone combustion system. Ignition by auxiliary squirt in A/B diffuser, coupled with main squirt in No. 4 burner can which produces hot streak of fuel through the turbine. Max gas temperature 1,677°C.

NOZZLE: Primary nozzle has variable area, with six hinged segments actuated by engine fuel rams. Ejector nozzle has 18 iris segments.

ACCESSORY DRIVES: Main gearbox under compressor, driven by bevel shaft from HP spool.

LUBRICATION SYSTEM: Self contained dry sump system.

OIL GRADE: MIL-L-7808, MIL-L-23699.

STARTING: Air turbine starter on left forward drive pad.

DIMENSIONS:
- Max diameter: 1,293 mm (50·9 in)
- Length overall: 5,987 mm (235·7 in)

WEIGHT, DRY: 1,905 kg (4,201 lb)

PERFORMANCE RATING:
- T-O, S/L: 93 kN (20,900 lb st)

SPECIFIC FUEL CONSUMPTION (T-O): 78·75 mg/Ns (2·78 lb/h/lb st)

PRATT & WHITNEY JTF22

US military designation: F100

Stemming partly from the JTF16 demonstrator engine designed in 1965-66, the JTF22 is an advanced technology military turbofan with afterburner for supersonic applications. Basic development was funded as a demonstrator programme for the US Air Force. In February 1970 the decision was taken to use the JTF22 core engine as the basis for the **F100-PW-100** (JTF22A-25A) to power the twin-engined McDonnell Douglas F-15 Eagle fighter for the US Air Force. Subsequently, the F100 was adopted for the single-engined General Dynamics F-16, production versions of which are powered by a slightly modified engine designated **F100-PW-200**, with a backup fuel control system.

Some 3,000 h of development testing were accomplished between 1968 and the 60 h PFRT (preliminary flight rating test) in February 1972. The 150 h QT (qualification test) was completed in October 1973. By January 1986 more than 4,400 engines had flown more than 3·2 million hours in F-15s and F-16s. Current production engines can operate 1,800 mission cycles without hot section refurbishment.

By mid 1985 the improved **F100-PW-220** had been qualified after a 4,000 cycle accelerated mission test, equivalent to nine years' normal operation. Delivery of the Dash-220 began in November 1985. This digitally controlled engine will power F-15C/D and F-16C/D aircraft.

TYPE: Two-shaft turbofan with high augmentation afterburner.

INTAKE: Direct pitot type. Fabricated titanium, with fixed nose bullet. Single row of 21 inlet guide vanes, with hot air anti-iced leading-edges and variable camber trailing-edge flaps.

FAN: Three stages. Fan blades have part-span shrouds. Discs of titanium 6-2-4-6, blades titanium 8-1-1. Entry diameter 928 mm (36·5 in). Bypass ratio 0·7.

COMPRESSOR: Ten-stage axial, on HP shaft. First three stages have variable stators. Discs 1-2, forged Ti 6-2-4-6; 3, forged Ti 8-1-1; 4, forged PWA 1016; 5, 7 and 9, Waspalloy; 6, 8 and 10, Gatorised (isothermal squeeze forging) IN-100. Blades 1-3, Ti 8-1-1; 4, Ti 6-2-4-6; 5-9 Incoloy 901; 10, Waspalloy. Pressure ratio 8 : 1. Overall engine pressure ratio 25 : 1.

COMBUSTION CHAMBER: Annular. Fabricated in Haynes 188 cobalt based alloy with film cooling throughout. Large diameter air blast fuel nozzles. Capacitor-discharge ignition.

HP TURBINE: Two stages. Discs forged IN-100. Blades and vanes directionally solidified Mar M200/Hf alloy with aluminide coating; first rotor transpiration convectively cooled, second with convective (HP bleed air) only. Maximum gas temperature 1,399°C. Maximum speed 13,450 rpm.

LP TURBINE: Two stages. Discs forged IN-100. Blades, uncooled, cast in IN-100 with aluminide coating. Maximum speed 10,400 rpm.

AFTERBURNER: Five concentric spray rings in flow from core engine; two slightly farther downstream in bypass airflow. Flameholder assembly downstream of spray nozzles, with high energy electrical ignition to give modulated light-up. Outer bypass duct and other major portions fabricated in sheet and stringer titanium. Interior liner of coated Haynes 188.

NOZZLE: Multi-flap balanced beam articulated nozzle giving very wide range in area and profile.

CONTROL SYSTEM: Unified hydromechanical fuel and nozzle area control, with electronic supervisory control. The F100-PW-200 also has a hydromechanical backup control. The Dash-220 includes a new digital electronic control, new gear type main fuel pump, and an ILC (increased life core) with a 4,000 cycle depot refurbishment interval.

DIMENSIONS:
- Overall diameter: 1,181 mm (46·5 in)
- Length:
  - F100-PW-100, excl bullet: 4,855 mm (191·2 in)
  - F100-PW-220: 5,280 mm (208 in)

WEIGHT, DRY:
- F100-PW-100: 1,375 kg (3,033 lb)
- F100-PW-200: 1,400 kg (3,087 lb)
- F100-PW-220: 1,444 kg (3,184 lb)

PERFORMANCE RATINGS (S/L, ISA):
- Max T-O, dry:
  - F100-PW-100: 65·2 kN (14,670 lb st)
  - F100-PW-220: 63·9 kN (14,370 lb st)
- Max T-O, augmented:
  - F100-PW-100: 106·0 kN (23,830 lb st)
  - F100-PW-220: 104·3 kN (23,450 lb st)

PRATT & WHITNEY PW1120

The PW1120 is an afterburning turbojet derivative of the F100 turbofan intended specifically as a fighter engine. Its development was initiated in June 1980.

The PW1120 retains a high degree of commonality with the F100, incorporating the entire F100 core module (HP compressor, combustor and HP turbine), gearbox, fuel pump and forward ducts without change, as well as the F100 DEEC (digital electronic engine control) system with only minor schedule modifications. More than 70 per cent of the PW1120 hardware is identical to, and interchangeable with, the F100.

Unique PW1120 components include a new, low aspect ratio, wide chord blade design LP compressor, a new single-stage uncooled LP turbine, a simplified single stream augmentor, and a lightweight convergent/divergent exhaust nozzle. Mass flow is 80·9 kg (178 lb)/s and overall pressure

Cutaway drawing of the F100-PW-220, rated at 104·3 kN (23,450 lb st)

ratio 26·8. The unique components embody reliability, durability and safety features demonstrated in F100 operational experience.

Full scale PW1120 testing was initiated in June 1982, and the engine completed flight clearance testing in August 1984. Production is scheduled for 1987.

The PW1120 has been selected by the government of Israel to power its new indigenous fighter aircraft, the Lavi, scheduled to become operational in 1989. Engine flight demonstration in an F-4 began on 30 July 1986. In addition, Boeing Military Airplane Co is promoting an F-4 re-engining programme using the PW1120 (see Aircraft section).

DIMENSIONS:

Max diameter	1,021 mm (40·2 in)
Length	4,110 mm (161·8 in)

WEIGHT, DRY: 1,292 kg (2,848 lb)

PERFORMANCE RATINGS (S/L, ISA):

Max T-O	91·7 kN (20,620 lb st)
Intermediate	60·3 kN (13,550 lb st)

SPECIFIC FUEL CONSUMPTION:

Maximum	52·65 mg/Ns (1·86 lb/h/lb)
Intermediate	22·7 mg/Ns (0·8 lb/h/lb)

PRATT & WHITNEY PW5000

This advanced augmented turbofan is competing against the General Electric GE37 as the ATF (advanced tactical fighter) engine for the period after 1995. The US Air Force is expected to select one of these engines.

PRATT & WHITNEY PW1129

The PW1129 is the next-generation fighter engine, aimed at later versions of the F-15 and F-16. It has been designed as a bolt-in replacement for the F100 in existing F-15s and F-16s. Using components of the F100-PW-220 and PW1128 EMD (see 1984-85 *Jane's*), it is an advanced augmented turbofan with many new features including an improved efficiency compressor and Float-wall (registered name) combustor. Thrust will be in the 129 kN (29,000 lb st) class. The combustor went on test in July 1985, full hardware was assembled in January 1986 (six sets being required during that calendar year), the first engine was to run in mid-1986, and the first flight is due in September 1987. This engine immediately precedes the P&W candidate engine for the ATF (USAF advanced tactical fighter) for the 1990s, the PW5000.

PRATT & WHITNEY PW3000

In June 1981 Pratt & Whitney announced this family of shaft drive engines in the power range 2,984-5,968 kW (4,000-8,000 shp). The 3000 series engines are planned in turboshaft and turboprop versions for military helicopters and fixed-wing aircraft and commercial commuter type aircraft. The same core can also be mated with a fan to yield a turbofan engine. The first member of the family on which work is proceeding is the **PW3005**, which is rated at 4,993 kW (6,693 shp) as a turboshaft. Pratt & Whitney's Government Products Division is managing the programme in partnership with two other UTC divisions, Pratt & Whitney Canada and Hamilton Standard.

Applications for the PW3005 include the ACA (advanced cargo aircraft) and advanced P-3 Orions. It could also be used to re-engine the CH-47, C-130, E-2/C-2 and H-53, and there are possible commercial applications. The following data are estimates:

DIMENSIONS:

Length: Turboshaft with inlet particle separator	2,017 mm (79·4 in)
Turboprop	1,580 mm (62·2 in)
Diameter: Turboshaft with IPS	787 mm (31 in)
Turboprop	655 mm (25·8 in)

WEIGHT, DRY:

Turboshaft with IPS	429 kg (946 lb)
Turboprop	385 kg (850 lb)

PERFORMANCE RATINGS (ISA, S/L, static, max power):

Turboshaft	4,993 kW (6,693 shp) to 15°C
Turboprop	3,790 kW (5,080 shp) to 39·5°C

PW1120 augmented turbojet, rated at 91·7 kN (20,620 lb st) *(Brian M. Service)*

Mockup of Pratt & Whitney PW5000, with 2D (two-dimensional) nozzle with limited thrust vectoring

Pratt & Whitney PW3005 turboshaft rated at 4,993 kW (6,693 shp)

ROCKETDYNE

ROCKETDYNE DIVISION OF ROCKWELL INTERNATIONAL

6633 Canoga Avenue, Canoga Park, California 91303
Telephone: (818) 710 6300
Telex: 698478
Other Facilities: Santa Susana, California
President: R. Schwartz
Executive Vice-President: D. J. Sanchini

Rocketdyne is a division of Rockwell International, devoted primarily to the design and manufacture of rocket engines for the US Air Force and the National Aeronautics and Space Administration. It was established as a separate division in November 1955.

Rocketdyne liquid propellant engines have powered more than three-quarters of all large US space vehicle stages.

ROCKETDYNE SSME

On 13 July 1971, the Rocketdyne Division of Rockwell International was selected by NASA to design and develop the main engine for the Orbiter stage of the US Space Shuttle. Three of these engines provide a total of 6,833 kN (1,536,000 lb) vacuum thrust.

Two large solid propellant boosters are strapped on the sides of the Orbiter's expendable propellant tank which carries the liquid oxygen and liquid hydrogen for the three main engines in the Orbiter. The Orbiter rides piggyback on the propellant tank in a parallel configuration. The solid motors and the three Space Shuttle Main Engines (SSME) produce 29,037 kN (6,527,000 lb st) to lift the vehicle from the pad in a conventional vertical flight path. The solid motors burn out at about 40 km (25 miles) altitude, separate from the Orbiter stage, and are lowered by parachutes into the ocean for recovery. The three main engines continue to power the vehicle to near orbit; the external tank then separates and is disposed in a safe area of the ocean. After mission completion the Orbiter re-enters the Earth's atmosphere and manoeuvres to a landing site for an unpowered horizontal landing similar to that of a conventional jet aircraft.

In overall configuration, the SSME is slightly smaller in size than the F-1 engine used in the Saturn V vehicle first stage. It burns liquid oxygen and liquid hydrogen propellants and has been designed for high reliability, reusability, multiple re-start capability and low cost. It is designed for 7½ h of burn time, accrued during 55 flights. Modified airline maintenance procedures are used to service the engine between flights without removing it from the vehicle.

The design combines the merits of high chamber pressure operation, an optimum performance contoured bell shaped nozzle, and a regeneratively cooled thrust chamber, capable of 11° gimballing, for maximum performance and long life. The chamber wall is cooled so efficiently that it is at 567°C, although the combustion temperature is about 3,300°C. No propellants are wasted in the cooling process. The combustion chamber wall is made of slotted metal, rather than tubes, using Rocketdyne developed NARloy-Z, a copper alloy that is easily machined, has higher strength than pure copper, and has very high thermal conductivity. Tubes are incorporated in the lower nozzle section.

The SSME is controlled by a unique system incorporating dual redundant digital computers. This system monitors engine parameters such as pressure and flow rate, and the engine is adjusted automatically to operate at the required thrust and mixture ratio. The system also develops a record of engine operating history for maintenance purposes to improve serviceability and extend total engine life.

Flight certification of the SSME was achieved in December 1980, after two certification cycles had been completed on each of two engines. Each cycle required a minimum of 13 tests and 5,000 s, including simulation of nominal and abort mission profiles. Forty tests, totalling 12,750 s, were made on one engine, and 34 tests, totalling 10,650 s, on the other.

Another cycle in the FPL (full power level) certification programme was completed in April 1983. Certification required four test series of 5,000 s each, involving engine power levels of 104, 105, 109 and 111 per cent. This testing provided flight readiness certification for engine sets for the *Challenger, Columbia, Discovery* and *Atlantis* orbiters.

The Shuttle programme began its operational phase with the STS-5 launch of the *Columbia* at Kennedy Space Center on 11 November 1982. On 4 April 1983 a second shuttle vehicle, *Challenger*, powered by SSMEs rated at 104 per cent thrust, was launched on its maiden voyage, STS-6.

The third Orbiter, *Discovery*, was successfully launched on 30 August 1984 after an abort caused by contamination of hydraulic fluid. Prelaunch checkout was revised to prevent a recurrence. A total of 24 launches, all successful, had been accomplished prior to the loss of *Challenger* on 28 January 1986. Excellent flight-to-flight performance repeatability had been achieved.

Certification extension testing up to 20 equivalent flights has been accomplished on one engine, while another has run 15 equivalent flights at 104 per cent power level. Testing is being continued to extend the life of the HP turbomachinery, increase performance margin by reducing flow losses and investigate other modifications that could allow uprating or life extension.

Combustion Chamber: Channel wall construction with regenerative cooling by the hydrogen fuel. Concentric element injector.

Turbopumps: Two low pressure pumps boost the inlet pressures for two high pressure pumps. Dual pre-burners provide turbine drive gases to power the high-pressure pumps. Hydrogen pump discharge pressure is 485·4 bars (7,040 lb/sq in) at 37,250 rpm; it develops 57,650 kW (77,310 hp).

SSME undergoing FPL test

Controller: Honeywell digital computer controller provides closed loop engine control, in addition to data processing and signal conditioning for control, checkout, monitoring engine status, and maintenance data acquisition.

Controls: A hydraulic actuation control system is used. The dual redundant self-monitoring servo actuators respond to signals from the controller to position the ball valves. A pneumatic system provides backup for the hydraulic system for engine cut-off. Main subcontractors: Honeywell Inc (controller); Hydraulic Research and Manufacturing Co (actuators).

Maintenance: Engine to be maintained using airline type maintenance procedure for on-the-vehicle servicing. Planned life between overhauls is 40 flights.

Dimensions:

Length	4,242 mm (167 in)
Diameter at nozzle exit	2,388 mm (94 in)

Performance:

S/L thrust (one engine)	1,856 kN (417,300 lb)
Vacuum thrust	2,277 kN (512,000 lb)
Specific impulse	455 s
Chamber pressure	224·8 bars (3,260 lb/sq in)
Throttling ratio	1·67
Expansion ratio	77·5

ROTORWAY

ROTORWAY INC

7411 W Galveston, Chandler, Arizona 85224
Telephone: (602) 961 1001

RotorWay Inc is a builder of small helicopters for amateur assembly (see entry in Sport Aircraft section). For a considerable period it has been developing and producing its own power plants, for these and for other light aircraft.

ROTORWAY RW-145

This engine was designed to power the RotorWay Exec and Scorpion light helicopters, with the following objectives in mind: high power/weight ratio; improved fuel economy; reduced noise and emissions; smooth operation; and long, reliable life.

Type: Horizontally opposed, vertical-crankshaft, water-cooled four-stroke piston engine.

Cylinders: Offset left and right for plain connecting rods side by side. Capacity 2·65 litres (162 cu in). Compression ratio 9·6 : 1.

Induction: Through circular air cleaners to dual down-draught carburettors with adjustable high and low speed metering.

Ignition: RotorWay distributor.

Lubrication: Oil temperature 82°-99°C. Oil pressure 2·72-4·1 bars (40-60 lb/sq in).

Cooling: Closed water system, operating temperature 85°C.

Weight, Dry (with starter):	77·1 kg (170 lb)
Performance Rating:	112 kW (150 hp)

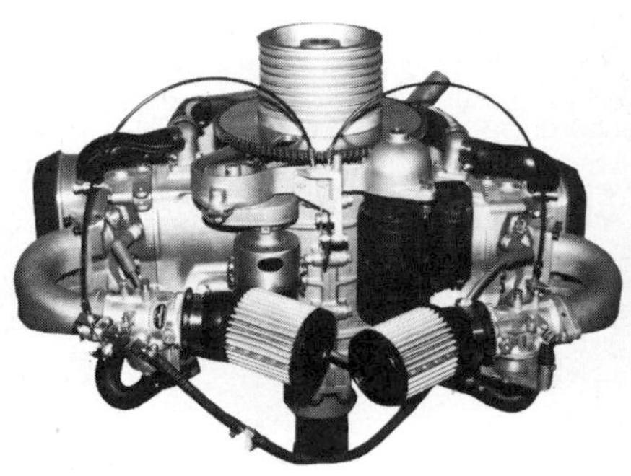

RotorWay RW-145 vertical-crankshaft helicopter engine

SOLOY

SOLOY CONVERSIONS LTD

450 Pat Kennedy Way SW, Olympia, Washington 98502
Telephone: (206) 754 7000
Marketing Group Manager: Randy Furtick

Soloy has developed a Turbine Pac for adapting models of Allison 250 turbine engine to fixed-wing aircraft. The basic gas generator in the initial application, the Cessna 206, which is now in production, is the 250-C20S rated at 313 kW (420 shp). Features include aft facing inlet, downward inclined exhaust (with cabin heat provision without power loss), a remote gearbox with 3,500 h TBO mounted direct on the airframe, and a 1,810 rpm propeller drive with autofeather. The package is suited to Model 250 engines of 298-548 kW (400-735 shp) input power. The Turbine Pac was FAA certificated in May 1984, and production deliveries began two months later. Applications include the Cessna 206, 207, 210 and 185, and also the Beechcraft A36 Bonanza (with B17C basic gas generator) which is available with or without tip fuel pods with winglets.

Further details of this programme can be found in the main US Aircraft section.

The Soloy 206 Turbine Pac, based on the Allison 250-C20S turboprop of 313 kW (420 shp)

SPP

SPORT PLANE POWER INC

3659 Arnold Avenue, Naples, Florida 33942
Telephone: (813) 775 2214

This company is an associate of Nelson (see entry in this section) and shares the same President and Vice-President. Its first product is the K-100A.

SPORT PLANE POWER K-100A

A four-cylinder four-stroke piston engine, the K-100A is an automotive derived high performance unit with liquid cooling, altitude compensation, overhead camshafts, electronic control and speed reducing drive, allowed for in the figure for weight.

WEIGHT, WET: 88·5 kg (195 lb)
PERFORMANCE RATING: 74·6 kW (100 hp)

The Sport Plane Power K-100A piston engine

TELEDYNE CAE

TELEDYNE CAE DIVISION OF TELEDYNE INC

1330 Laskey Road, Toledo, Ohio 43612-0971
Telephone: (419) 470 3000
Telex: Easylink 6 288 4828
PRESIDENT: Robert R. Schwanhausser
SENIOR VICE-PRESIDENT: James H. Wills
Gainesville Division, Georgia:
VICE-PRESIDENT AND GENERAL MANAGER:
Theodore Ivanko

Teledyne CAE is devoted primarily to design, development and production of small gas turbine engines for training aircraft, missiles and RPVs. The Toledo Division continues to be involved in research, design, development and production. The Gainesville Division, opened in January 1986, is equipped for volume production by computer-aided manufacturing (CAM).

In the early 1950s, Teledyne CAE (then Continental Aviation Engineering) produced the Models 140/141 turboshaft engines for USAF starting carts. During the same period it developed the J69-T-25 turbojet and its derivatives. In parallel, Teledyne CAE developed the T65-T-1 and T67 helicopter engines. In September 1978 Teledyne CAE was selected as Williams International's licensee to produce the F107-WR-101 and -400 cruise missile engines. Production of these engines continues.

Since the mid-1960s, Teledyne CAE has been active in advanced development programmes, including the Advanced Turbine Engine Gas Generator (ATEGG), the Aircraft Propulsion Subsystem Integration (APSI), and the Joint Technology Demonstrator Engine (JTDE) Programmes.

Teledyne CAE J402-CA-700 turbojet of 2·85 kN (640 lb st) for MQM-107 variable speed training target

TELEDYNE CAE 352 and 356

US military designation: J69

The J69 was originally the Turboméca Marboré, developed to meet American requirements. Four versions are available, as follows:

J69-T-25 (Teledyne CAE Model 352-5A). Long life version; powers Cessna T-37B. In production.

J69-T-29 (Teledyne CAE Model 356-7A). Powers Teledyne Ryan BQM-34A target. Operational ceiling is 18,300 m (60,000 ft). Marboré II with single-stage transonic axial compressor supercharging centrifugal stage. In production.

J69-T-41A (Teledyne CAE Model 356-29A). Transonic axial compressor and revised centrifugal stage handling airflow of 13·5 kg (29·8 lb)/s with pressure ratio of 5·45 : 1. Operational ceiling in excess of 21,030 m (69,000 ft). Production is now spares only.

YJ69-T-406 (Teledyne CAE Model 356-34A). Produced for US Navy BQM-34E and US Air Force BQM-34F supersonic RPVs. Production is now spares only.

DIMENSIONS (nominal):
Length overall:
J69-T-25: 899 mm (35·39 in)
YJ69-T-406, J69-T-41A and J69-T-29: 1,138 mm (44·8 in)
Width:
J69-T-25: 566 mm (22·30 in)
J69-T-41A, J69-T-29: 568 mm (22·36 in)
YJ69-T-406: 572 mm (22·52 in)

WEIGHT, DRY:
J69-T-25: 165 kg (364 lb)
J69-T-29: 154 kg (341 lb)
J69-T-41A: 159 kg (350 lb)
YJ69-T-406: 163 kg (360 lb)

PERFORMANCE RATINGS:
Max T-O thrust:
J69-T-25: 4·56 kN (1,025 lb) at 21,730 rpm
J69-T-29: 7·56 kN (1,700 lb) at 22,000 rpm
J69-T-41A: 8·54 kN (1,920 lb) at 22,000 rpm
YJ69-T-406: 8·54 kN (1,920 lb) at 22,150 rpm
Normal thrust:
J69-T-25: 3·91 kN (880 lb) at 20,700 rpm
J69-T-29: 6·12 kN (1,375 lb) at 20,790 rpm
J69-T-41A: 7·34 kN (1,650 lb) at 20,900 rpm
YJ69-T-406: 7·65 kN (1,719 lb) at 21,450 rpm

SPECIFIC FUEL CONSUMPTION (max T-O):
J69-T-25: 32·30 mg/Ns (1·14 lb/h/lb st)
J69-T-41A, T-29: 31·16 mg/Ns (1·10 lb/h/lb st)
YJ69-T-406: 31·44 mg/Ns (1·11 lb/h/lb st)

TELEDYNE CAE 370

US military designation: J402-CA-400

This low-cost expendable engine was designed for the propulsion of cruise missiles and is in production for the US Navy AGM-84A and RGM-84A Harpoon missiles. The J402 is noteworthy for its compact component and accessory disposition, giving minimum frontal area. Though the entire design minimises production time and cost, high reliability was a prime requirement. Flight limits are 12,200 m (40,000 ft) and Mach 0·9 continuous or Mach 1·1 for limited periods. Engine life is reported unofficially to be 1 h. By 1986 deliveries of the 370 and 372-2 were close to 4,500 and continuing.

TYPE: Single-shaft turbojet.

INTAKE: Direct pitot inlet with four struts.

COMPRESSOR: Single transonic axial compressor with precision cast construction. Single centrifugal compressor with precision cast construction. Max airflow 4·35 kg (9·6 lb)/s. Pressure ratio 5·8.

COMBUSTION CHAMBER: Annular type.

FUEL SYSTEM: Low-pressure supply to centrifugal injection nozzles in compressor shaft. Electronic control system with automatic sequencing and regulation to meet demands of missile flight profile.

TURBINE: Single stage axial.

JETPIPE: Fixed area.

ACCESSORIES: Pyrotechnic starting and ignition systems. Optional integral alternator and alternator regulator to give 6 kW of DC power.

MOUNTING: Four main mountings disposed radially around main (compressor diffuser) frame.

DIMENSIONS:
Length (excl bullet): 748 mm (29·44 in)
Overall diameter: 318 mm (12·52 in)

WEIGHT, DRY: 45·4 kg (100 lb)

PERFORMANCE RATING:
Max S/L static: 2·94 kN (660 lb) at 41,200 rpm

SPECIFIC FUEL CONSUMPTION (S/L static):
34·0 mg/Ns (1·20 lb/h/lb)

TELEDYNE CAE 370-1

US military designation: J402-CA-401

This derivative of the J402-CA-400 incorporates features for additional tactical missile requirements. A longer-life

Teledyne CAE J69-T-29 turbojet of 7·56 kN (1,700 lb st)

Teledyne CAE J402-CA-400 expendable low-cost turbojet of 2·94 kN (660 lb st)

turbine, external oil reservoir, coated combustor and provision for a 3·2 kW alternator are included. The electronic fuel control is modified to accommodate more complex mission profiles.

DIMENSIONS:
Length (excl bullet) 742 mm (29·2 in)
Overall diameter 317 mm (12·5 in)
WEIGHT, DRY: 51·7 kg (114 lb)

TELEDYNE CAE 372-2

US military designation: J402-CA-700

This turbojet is in production for the Beech MQM-107A variable speed training target. It is based on the Model 370 (J402) but differs in detail engineering and equipment, reflecting the need for repeated missions of extended duration. The electronic fuel control governs engine operation throughout the starting cycle and over the whole operating range. A shaft mounted high-speed alternator provides 1·2 kW of DC power. TBO is 15 h.

DIMENSIONS:
Length (excl bullet) 753 mm (29·65 in)
Overall diameter 317 mm (12·50 in)
WEIGHT, DRY: 52 kg (115 lb)
PERFORMANCE RATING:
Max S/L static 2·85 kN (640 lb) at 40,400 rpm
SPECIFIC FUEL CONSUMPTION (S/L, static):
33·71 mg/Ns (1·19 lb/h/lb)

TELEDYNE CAE 372-11A

US military designation: J402-CA-701

This turbojet is an uprated version of the J402-CA-700, with provision for a 4 kW dc generator, regulated through a power conditioning unit. It is designed for target and RPV applications.

DIMENSIONS: Similar to 372-2
WEIGHT, DRY: 51 kg (113 lb)
PERFORMANCE RATING:
Max S/L static 3·33 kN (725 lb st) at 42,000 rpm
SPECIFIC FUEL CONSUMPTION (S/L, static):
34·0 mg/Ns (1·20 lb/h/lb)

TELEDYNE CAE 373

A growth version of the basic J402 described earlier, the CAE 373 is a turbojet in the 4·00-4·45 kN (900-1,000 lb st) class. Addition of a second axial compressor stage increases pressure ratio to 8·7 : 1 and airflow to 6·2 kg (13·7) lb/s. The engine retains low cost features but is designed for both expendable and long-life applications. It will be available with various starting options and either high speed alternator or a centreline reduction gear and starter/generator. The CAE 373 is a company funded development, and a demonstrator engine ran in 1976. It is intended for missile and RPV applications. The CAE 373-8 (4·36 kN; 980 lb st) has been selected to power US Army MQM-107D Streakers.

TELEDYNE CAE 455

In 1979 preliminary details were disclosed of the Model 455H-2, first of the three rival JTDE (joint technology demonstrator engine) types to complete initial objectives for the US Air Force and Navy APSI (aircraft propulsion subsystem integration) programme. The 455H-2 uses a USAF-sponsored LP (fan) turbine, Navy-sponsored single-stage fan and HP spool based on the Model 555 research core engine. It is intended to lead to a new family of durable, low cost engines in the 22 kN (5,000 lb st) class for cruise missiles, trainers and liaison aircraft until the end of the century.

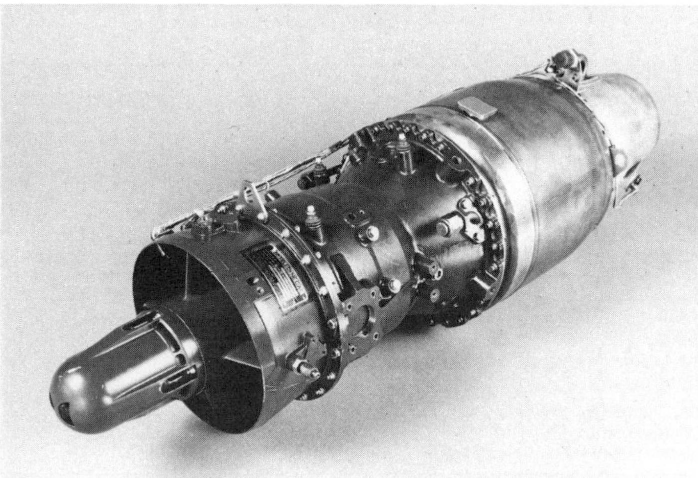

The Teledyne CAE 373-8 turbojet (4·36 kN; 980 lb st)

This slightly retouched photograph remains the only illustration of the Teledyne CAE 455H-2 turbofan demonstrator cleared for publication

TCM

TELEDYNE CONTINENTAL MOTORS
Aircraft Products Division

PO Box 90, Mobile, Alabama 36601
Telephone: (205) 438 3411
Telex: 505519
PRESIDENT: D. G. Bigler
EXECUTIVE VICE-PRESIDENT: J. Ishee
VICE-PRESIDENT AND CHIEF ENGINEER:
I. Swatman
VICE-PRESIDENT, MARKETING: G. Pape
DIRECTOR OF MARKETING: L. Jensen
DIRECTOR OF INTERNATIONAL SALES: D. Crawford
DIRECTOR OF SERVICE: B. Miller

In 1927, the former Teledyne Continental Motors Corporation, one of the largest automobile engine manufacturers in the world, produced its first aero engine, a sleeve valve air-cooled radial incorporating the Argyll (Burt-McCollum) patents, which had been purchased by the Corporation from the British Argyll Company in 1925.

In 1931 the 38 hp A40 flat-four was put on the market. This was followed by the A50, A65, A75, A80 and C90 engines, described in earlier editions of *Jane's*.

At the Paris Air Show in 1985 TCM (as the company now abbreviates itself) unveiled several completely new developments. One is a line of liquid-cooled engines, the first of which (IOL-200 and IOL-300) are described briefly. The second is a family of rotary (or rotating-combustion) engines, also described (R-18 and GR-36) and further mentioned under Norton in the UK part of this section. The third is a regenerative gas turbine, whose many applications are initially non-flying.

CONTINENTAL O-200 SERIES

The O-200-A engine is a four-cylinder horizontally opposed aircooled engine. It is fitted with a single updraught carburettor, dual magnetos and starter and generator.

The O-200-B is similar to the O-200-A, but is designed for pusher installation.

For other details see table.

TELEDYNE CONTINENTAL IOL-200

This is the first of the company's range of liquid-cooled engines which are geometrically similar to the existing range of opposed aircooled units. Derived from the familiar O-200, it has a high-compression cylinder with combustion chamber improvements aimed at minimising fuel consumption. The 60 per cent ethylene glycol coolant can operate at 121°C, and with a well installed radiator shows a significant reduction in cooling drag. The engine is more powerful than the aircooled predecessor (for data see table), and is claimed also to offer improved cooling, reduced wear, longer life and TBO, and higher altitude capability. An sfc of 63·38 µg/J (0·375 lb/h/bhp) can be maintained across a broad operating range, with minimum heat loss to coolant and oil.

TELEDYNE CONTINENTAL IOL-300

The six-cylinder member of the new liquid-cooled family, the IOL-300 uses the same high-turbulence high-compression cylinder as the IOL-200. The maximum rpm given in the table is 2,700, slightly less than for the four-cylinder. The turbocharged version has demonstrated sfc well below 62·5 µg/J (0·37 lb/h/bhp) at altitude. The weight given in the table includes magnetos, plugs, fuel injection system, coolant pump, alternator and starter.

CONTINENTAL IO-360 SERIES

Newest members of this family of flat-six engines include the TSIO and LTSIO-360-E, EB and KB. These are counter-rotating engines for the Piper Seneca II and III.

Teledyne Continental IOL-200 four-cylinder liquid-cooled engine

The Teledyne Continental IOL-300 is the six-cylinder member of the new liquid-cooled family

REPRESENTATIVE TELEDYNE CONTINENTAL HORIZONTALLY OPPOSED ENGINES

Engine Model	No. of Cylinders	Bore and Stroke mm (in)	Capacity litres (cu in)	Power Ratings kW (hp) at rpm		Comp. Ratio	Dry Weight* kg (lb)	Dimensions			Octane Rating
				Take-off	M.E.T.O.			Length mm (in)	Width mm (in)	Height mm (in)	
O-200-A	4	103·2 × 98·4 (4$^{1}/_{16}$ × 3⅞)	3·28 (201)	74·5 (100) at 2,750	74·5 (100) at 2,750	7·0	99·8 (220)	725 (28·53)	802 (31·56)	589 (23·18)	80/87
IOL-200	4	103·2 × 98·4 (4$^{1}/_{16}$ × 3⅞)	3·28 (201)	81·95 (110) at 2,750	81·95 (110) at 2,750	11·4	88·0 (194)	708 (27·86)	819 (32·25)	588 (23·16)	100/ 100LL
IOL-300	6	103·2 × 98·4 (4$^{1}/_{16}$ × 3⅞)	4·93 (301)	127 (170) at 2,700	127 (170) at 2,700	11·4	132 (291)	864 (34·0)	819 (32·25)	533 (21·0)	100/ 100LL
IO-360-D	6	112·7 × 98·4 (4$^{7}/_{16}$ × 3⅞)	5·9 (360)	157 (210) at 2,800	157 (210) at 2,800	8·5	148·3 (327)	877 (34·53)	798 (31·40)	618 (24·33)	100/130
IO-360-KB	6	112·7 × 98·4 (4$^{7}/_{16}$ × 3⅞)	5·9 (360)	145·5 (195) at 2,600	145·5 (195) at 2,600	8·5	148·3 (327)	864 (34·03)	841 (33·11)	781 (30·74)	100/130
TSIO-360-C, D	6	112·7 × 98·4 (4$^{7}/_{16}$ × 3⅞)	5·9 (360)	168 (225) at 2,800	168 (225) at 2,800	7·5	136 (300)	910† (35·84)	838 (33·03)	603 (23·75)	100/130
LTSIO-360-EB TSIO-360-FB	6	112·7 × 98·4 (4$^{7}/_{16}$ × 3⅞)	5·9 (360)	149 (200) at 2,575	149 (200) at 2,575	7·5	175 (385)	1,437¼ (56·58)	795 (31·30)	671 (26·44)	100/130
TSIO-360-LB	6	112·7 × 98·4 (4$^{7}/_{16}$ × 3⅞)	5·9 (360)	156·5 (210) at 2,700	156·5 (210) at 2,700	7·5	175 (386)	902 (35·52)	795 (31·30)	699 (27·53)	100/130
LTSIO-360-KB	6	112·7 × 98·4 (4$^{7}/_{16}$ × 3⅞)	5·9 (360)	164 (220) at 2,800	164 (220) at 2,800	7·5	178 (392)	1,437 (56·58)	795 (31·30)	672 (26·44)	100/130
TSIO-360-LB	6	112·7 × 98·4 (4$^{7}/_{16}$ × 3⅞)	5·9 (360)	156·5 (210) at 2,700	156·5 (210) at 2,700	7·5	180·5 (401)	1,087 (42·78)	860 (33·88)	822 (32·34)	100LL
IO-470-H	6	127 × 101·6 (5 × 4)	7·7 (471)	194 (260) at 2,625	194 (260) at 2,625	8·6	202·5 (446·5)	1,100 (43·31)	852 (33·56)	502 (19·75)	100/130
IO-470-L	6	127 × 101·6 (5 × 4)	7·7 (471)	194 (260) at 2,625	194 (260) at 2,625	8·6	215·40 (474·87)	1,100 (43·31)	852 (33·56)	678 (26·71)	100/130
O-470-R, S	6	127 × 101·6 (5 × 4)	7·7 (471)	172 (230) at 2,600	172 (230) at 2,600	7·0	193·2 (426)	915 (36·03)	852 (33·56)	723 (28·42)	80/87
O-470-U	6	127 × 101·6 (5 × 4)	7·7 (471)	171·5 (230) at 2,400	171·5 (230) at 2,400	8·6	176·4 (388·9)	915 (36·03)	852 (33·56)	732 (28·42)	100LL
IO-520-A	6	133 × 101·6 (5¼ × 4)	8·5 (520)	212·5 (285) at 2,700	212·5 (285) at 2,700	8·5	215·9 (476)	1,053 (41·41)	852 (33·56)	502 (19·75)	100/130
IO-520-BA, -BB	6	133 × 101·6 (5¼ × 4)	8·5 (520)	212·5 (285) at 2,700	212·5 (285) at 2,700	8·5	207·3 (457)	1,009 (39·71)	853 (33·58)	678 (26·71)	100/130
IO-520-CB	6	133 × 101·6 (5¼ × 4)	8·5 (520)	212·5 (285) at 2,700	212·5 (285) at 2,700	8·5	204·7 (451·3)	1,087 (42·81)	852 (33·56)	502 (19·78)	100/130
IO-520-D	6	133 × 101·6 (5¼ × 4)	8·5 (520)	224 (300) at 2,850	212·5 (285) at 2,700	8·5	208·2 (459)	949 (37·36)	901 (35·46)	604 (23·79)	100/130
IO-520-L	6	133 × 101·6 (5¼ × 4)	8·5 (520)	224 (300) at 2,850	212·5 (285) at 2,700	8·5	211·7 (466·7)	1,039 (40·91)	852 (33·56)	591 (23·25)	100/130
IO-520-M, -MB	6	133 × 101·6 (5¼ × 4)	8·5 (520)	212·5 (285) at 2,700	212·5 (285) at 2,700	8·5	188 (415)	1,189 (46·80)	852 (33·56)	518 (20·41)	100/130
TSIO-520-C	6	133 × 101·6 (5¼ × 4)	8·5 (520)	212·5 (285) at 2,700	212·5 (285) at 2,700	7·5	208 (458)	1,040† (40·91)	852 (33·56)	509 (20·04)	100/130
TSIO-520-E, -EB	6	133 × 101·6 (5¼ × 4)	8·5 (520)	224 (300) at 2,700	224 (300) at 2,700	7·5	219 (483)	1,010† (39·75)	852 (33·56)	527 (20·74)	100/130
TSIO-520-J, N, -JB, -NB	6	133 × 101·6 (5¼ × 4)	8·5 (520)	231 (310) at 2,700	231 (310) at 2,700	7·5	221·3 (487·8)	997 (39·25)	852 (33·56)	516 (20·32)	100/130
TSIO-520-L, -LB	6	133 × 101·6 (5¼ × 4)	8·5 (520)	231 (310) at 2,700	231 (310) at 2,700	7·5	244·5 (539)	1,286 (50·62)	852 (33·56)	508 (20·02)	100/130
TSIO-520-M, R	6	133 × 101·6 (5¼ × 4)	8·5 (520)	231 (310) at 2,700	212·5 (285) at 2,600	7·5	198 (436)	1,040† (40·91)	852 (33·56)	598 (23·54)	100/130
TSIO-520-T	6	133 × 101·6 (5¼ × 4)	8·5 (520)	231 (310) at 2,700	231 (310) at 2,700	7·5	193·4 (426·3)	970 (38·2)	852 (33·56)	819 (32·26)	100/130
TSIO-520-VB	6	133 × 101·6 (5¼ × 4)	8·5 (520)	242·5 (325) at 2,700	242·5 (325) at 2,700	7·5	207·2 (456·7)	997 (39·25)	852 (33·56)	518 (20·41)	100/130
TSIO-520-UB	6	133 × 101·6 (5¼ × 4)	8·5 (520)	224 (300) at 2,700	224 (300) at 2,700	7·5	191·63 (422·47)	1,136 (44·73)	852 (33·56)	733 (28·86)	100/130
TSIO-520-WB	6	133 × 101·6 (5¼ × 4)	8·5 (520)	242·5 (325) at 2,700	242·5 (325) at 2,700	7·5	188·75 (416·1)	1,286 (50·62)	852 (33·56)	509 (20·02)	100/130
GTSIO-520-C	6	133 × 101·6 (5¼ × 4)	8·5 (520)	254 (340) at 3,200	254 (340) at 3,200	7·5	252·7 (557)	1,081 (42·56)	880 (34·04)	587 (23·1)	100/130
GTSIO-520-D, H	6	133 × 101·6 (5¼ × 4)	8·5 (520)	280 (375) at 3,400	280 (375) at 3,400	7·5	250 (550·37)	1,081 (42·56)	880 (34·04)	680 (26·78)	100/130
GTSIO-520-F, K	6	133 × 101·6 (5¼ × 4)	8·5 (520)	324 (435) at 3,400	324 (435) at 3,400	7·5	272·0 (600)	1,426 (56·12)	880 (34·04)	664 (26·15)	100/130
GTSIO-520-L, M, N	6	133 × 101·6 (5¼ × 4)	8·5 (520)	280 (375) at 3,350	280 (375) at 3,350	7·5	228 (502)‡	1,114 (43·87)	880 (34·04)	671 (26·41)	100/130
LTSIO-520-AE	6	133 × 101·6 (5¼ × 4)	8·5 (520)	186·5 (250) at 2,400	186·5 (250) at 2,400	8·5	172·2 (379·6)	967 (38·07)	846 (33·29)	543 (21·38)	100/130

REPRESENTATIVE TELEDYNE CONTINENTAL HORIZONTALLY OPPOSED ENGINES

Engine Model	No. of Cylinders	Bore and Stroke mm (in)	Capacity litres (cu in)	Power Ratings kW (hp) at rpm		Comp. Ratio	Dry Weight*	Dimensions			Octane Rating
				Take-off	M.E.T.O.		kg (lb)	Length mm (in)	Width mm (in)	Height mm (in)	
TSIO-520-AF	6	133 × 101·6 (5¼ × 4)	8·5 (520)	231 (210) at 2,700	212·5 (285) at 2,600	7·5	197·83 (436·15)	1,039 (40·91)	852 (33·56)	598 (23·54)	100/130
TSIO-520-B, -BB	6	133 × 101·6 (5¼ × 4)	8·5 (520)	213 (285) at 2,700	213 (285) at 2,700	7·5	219 (483)	1,490· (58·67)	852 (33·56)	516 (20·32)	100/130
TSIO-520-BE	6	133 × 101·6 (5¼ × 4)	8·5 (520)	231 (310) at 2,600	231 (310) at 2,600	7·5	?	1,083 (42·64)	1,079 (42·5)	851 (33·5)	100LL
TSIO-520-CE	6	133 × 101·6 (5¼ × 4)	8·5 (520)	242·5 (325) at 2,700	242·5 (325) at 2,700	7·5	237 (527)	1,039 (40·91)	852 (33·56)	597 (23·54)	100LL
IO-550-B	6	133 × 108 (5¼ × 4¼)	9·0 (550)	224 (300) at 2,700	224 (300) at 2,700	8·5	207·9 (462)	964 (37·97)	852 (33·56)	694 (27·32)	100LL
IO-550-C	6	133 × 108 (5¼ × 4¼)	9·0 (550)	224 (300) at 2,700	224 (300) at 2,700	8·5	211·95 (471)	1,100·1 (43·31)	852 (33·56)	502 (19·78)	100LL

*With accessories; †Not including turbocharger;
‡N weight 220 kg (486 lb)

CONTINENTAL O-470 SERIES

Engines in the O-470 series (including the E-185 and E-225) are all basically similar. Engines prefixed 'IO' have direct fuel injection.

The 168 kW and 172 kW (225 hp and 230 hp) models have a compression ratio of 7 : 1, the 186·5 kW (250 hp) models a ratio of 8 : 1, and the 194 kW (260 hp) models a ratio of 8·6 : 1. The exception is the O-470-U, which has a ratio of 8·6 : 1 and runs on 100LL grade fuel.

CONTINENTAL IO-520 SERIES

These engines are basically similar to the IO-470, but with cylinders of larger bore. They are fitted with an alternator driven either by a belt or by a face gear on the crankshaft. All IO-520 series engines are rated at 213 kW (285 hp) except for the IO-520-D, -E and -F which have a take-off rating of 224 kW (300 hp). IO-520 engines power the Beechcraft Baron and Bonanza, Navion and Cessna 210. New in 1970 were the generally similar IO-520-J, -K and -L, also rated at 213 kW (285 hp) (-K and -L are cleared to 224 kW (300 hp) at 2,850 rpm at take-off). The IO-520-M was developed in 1975 for use in the Cessna 310, replacing the IO-470-V.

The TSIO-520 series are turbocharged. Take-off rating is 213 kW (285 hp) except for the -E and -G, rated at 224 kW (300 hp), and the TSIO-520-J rated at 231 kW (310 hp) and equipped with an intercooler and provision for an over-boost valve. These engines power the Cessna 414, 320D, T210 and 210F, and turbocharged Bonanza. The TSIO-520-L was developed for use in the Beech Pressurised Baron. It develops 231 kW (310 hp) at 2,700 rpm, has a complete exhaust system and an engine mounted turbocharger. The TSIO-520-N is used in the Cessna 340A and 414.

In 1981 Teledyne Continental Motors announced a lightweight series of engines approximately 10 per cent lighter than previous models, with magnesium replacing aluminium in some areas, modified camshaft and cylinder heads (with parallel valves or inclined valves of larger diameter), and a range of turbocharging options. The first production models are the TSIO-520-AE and LTSIO-520-AE for the Cessna Crusader, with initial TBO of 2,000 h. The TSIO-520BE, for the Piper Malibu, has a top intake, dual turbos and two aftercoolers.

For other details see table.

CONTINENTAL GTSIO-520

This is similar to the TSIO-520 range but is geared and uprated. The -C model, rated at 254 kW (340 hp) at 3,200 rpm, powers the Cessna 411. The GTSIO-520-D, rated at 280 kW (375 hp) at 3,400 rpm, powers the Cessna 421. The -K has an integral turbocharger and complete exhaust system; the most powerful Continental engine in production, it powers the Rockwell Commander 685. The -G is used in a military application, the -H powers the Cessna 421A Golden Eagle. The -L is used in the Cessna 421C and the -M in the Cessna Titan.

The Teledyne Continental TSIO-520 (up to 242·5 kW; 325 hp)

CONTINENTAL IO-550

In 1984 this series of fuel-injected engines was introduced, similar to the IO-520 but with greater stroke. Initial applications are the Beechcraft Baron and Bonanza.

TELEDYNE CONTINENTAL R-18

This single-rotor engine is the first of the TCM rotaries (rotating-combustion, popularly called Wankel-type engines). Under development for several years, it is aimed at air and surface applications, chiefly in general aviation and RPVs. Design features include a rotor cooled by the oil/air mixture entering the engine, liquid-cooled housings, dual capacitive-discharge electronic ignition, total loss metered

Teledyne Continental R-18 single-rotor engine

The 149 kW (200 hp) Teledyne Continental TSIO-360-E

The 280 kW (375 hp) Teledyne Continental GTSIO-520-L

oil-injection system, 12V starter and 15A alternator. Compression ratio is 9, and the carburettor type fuel system was in 1985 running on automotive or aviation petrol (gasoline) but in future will have multifuel capability. The R-18 was to fly in early 1986 in an RPV configuration.

ROTOR: Single multilobe with rolling element bearings. Capacity 294 cc (17·9 cu in).

DIMENSIONS:

Length	394 mm (15·5 in)
Width	356 mm (14·0 in)
Height	318 mm (12·5 in)

WEIGHT, DRY (equipped): 23 kg (51 lb)

PERFORMANCE RATING (S/L): 29·8 kW (40 hp) at 7,500 rpm

TELEDYNE CONTINENTAL GR-36

This twin-rotor engine is virtually a double R-18 with a 3:1 reduction gear added. The GR-36 is intended chiefly for general aviation applications. It runs slightly slower than the single-rotor machine, at 6,900 rpm, giving a propeller speed of 2,300 rpm. Capacity is 588 cc (35·8 cu in). The GR-36 will be available with carburettor or fuel injection. TCM claim for their rotary engines compactness, light weight, extremely low vibration and simple construction with few moving parts.

DIMENSIONS:

Length	678 mm (26·70 in)
Width (with coolant pipe)	298 mm (11·75 in)
Height	244 mm (9·60 in)

WEIGHT, DRY: 50 kg (110 lb)

PERFORMANCE RATING (S/L): 85 hp at 6,900 rpm

THERMO-JET

THERMO-JET STANDARD INC

PO Box 55976, Houston, Texas 77055
Telephone: (713) 465 5735

MANAGER: John A. Melenric

This company specialises in the design and manufacture of valveless pulsejet units for remotely piloted vehicles and the homebuilt aircraft market. These engines are devoid of moving parts and are characterised by multiple reverse flow air inlets to a combustion chamber in which is burned propane, butane or compressed natural gas, obviating the need for a fuel pump. Intermittent combustion and expulsion takes place at a cycle frequency determined by the chamber size and geometry and combustion pressure.

Thermo-Jet J13-202 valveless pulsejet (0·40 kN; 90 lb st)

At present Thermo-Jet is offering four sizes of unit, the J7-300 (0·09 kN, 21 lb st at S/L), J8-200 (0·044 kN, 10 lb st at S/L), J10-200 (0·244 kN, 55 lb st at S/L), and J13-202 (0·4 kN, 90 lb st at S/L). Full details were given in the 1979-80 *Jane's*.

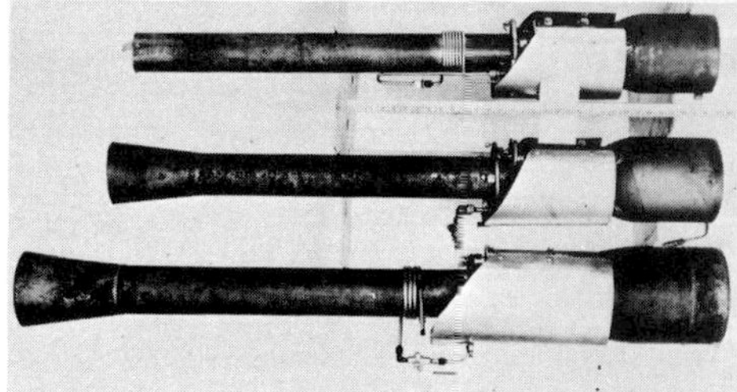

From the top: Thermo-Jet J7-300, J8-200 and J10-200

THUNDER

THUNDER ENGINES INC

7120 Hayvenhurst Avenue, Suite 321, Van Nuys, California 91406
Telephone: (213) 997 0117

This company has used the Can-Am McLaren-Chevrolet racing car engine as the basis for an extremely competitive V-8 aircraft piston engine.

THUNDER TE495-TC700

Following long and successful development, this advanced watercooled piston engine is now in production, with a first batch of 12 assigned to certification. Present Thunder V-8s run on 100/130 grade fuel, an increasing disadvantage, and future models will have multi-fuel capability achieved mainly by electronic engine control. The cylinder head sensors will adapt fuel injection, timing and boost to any gasoline (petrol) grade or to such mixtures as JP-4/alcohol. Later a spark assisted diesel may be developed. Initial market for the present 522 kW (700 hp) engine is put at 2,000 units, mainly for agricultural aircraft. Flight development began in January 1981 in the port position on a Rockwell Commander, the engine matching well with the TPE 331 turboprop except in having much faster throttle response.

TYPE: V-8 watercooled turbocharged four-stroke piston engine.

CYLINDERS: Blocks and pistons of Reynolds 390 Si/Al alloy. Bore 112·78 mm (4·44 in). Stroke 101·60 mm (4·00 in). Capacity 8·12 litres (495 cu in).

INDUCTION: Direct fuel injection, twin exhaust driven turbochargers with liquid cooled intercooler.

Production Thunder TE495 V-8 piston engine with Hartzell propeller hub

FUEL: Avgas 100/130.

IGNITION: Two rear mounted magnetos, two plugs per cylinder.

LUBRICATION: Dry sump system, two pressure segments and eight scavenge segments in pumps.

PROPELLER DRIVE: Reduction gear ratio 2·14.

COOLING: Twin water pumps circulating through radiator at best place on airframe (in Commander in fuselage behind pressure bulkhead).

ACCESSORIES: Nine drive pads available.

MOUNTING: Four anti-vibration mounts (see photograph).

DIMENSIONS:

Length: with turbos	1,625·6 mm (64·0 in)
without turbos	1,174·75 mm (46·25 in)
Width	704·85 mm (27·75 in)
Height	685·80 mm (27·00 in)

WEIGHT, DRY:

Basic	244·27 kg (537·39 lb)
With all accessories	323·61 kg (711·95 lb)

PERFOMANCE RATINGS:

Max continuous	522 kW (700 hp) at 4,400 rpm
Max recommended cruise	392 kW (525 hp) at 4,000 rpm
Rated torque at 4,000 rpm	1,134 N-m (836 lb-ft)

SPECIFIC FUEL CONSUMPTION:

65 per cent power	72·66 μg/J (0·43 lb/h/hp)

WILLIAMS

WILLIAMS INTERNATIONAL

2280 West Maple Road, PO Box 200, Walled Lake, Michigan 48088
Telephone: (313) 624 5200

PRESIDENT: Sam Williams

VICE-PRESIDENTS:
E. L. Klein (Executive V-P and Chief Operating Officer)
John Jones (Technical)
Robert Haas (Engineering)
Robert Katz (Finance)
Myron Goers (Operations)
David C. Jolivette (Public Relations)
Michael Busch (Program Management and Contracts)

Sam Williams believed in 1955 that gas turbine technology could be extended down to very small sizes, and that if a small turbojet were made available it would find a market. The WR2 first ran at a thrust of 0·31 kN (70 lb) in 1962 and has since been developed into the WR2-6 and WR24-6. The more advanced WR19, described in *Jane's* up to 1985-86 used an aerodynamically similar core and Williams is also building a range of shaft drive engines.

Versions of the US Air Force and Navy cruise missiles, ALCM and Tomahawk, are propelled by the F107 turbofan. Additional engine production facilities for the F107 were established in Ogden, Utah, and in September 1978 Teledyne CAE was named as second source producer. Mass production began in 1982.

WILLIAMS WR2 and WR24

US military designation (WR24): J400

These turbojets power the Canadair CL-89 reconnaissance RPV and Northrop RPVs and targets. In the initial WR2 the air enters at the eye of a single-sided light alloy centrifugal compressor which handles an air mass flow of 1 kg (2·2 lb)/s at a pressure ratio of 4·1 : 1. After passing through the diffuser which provides the structural basis for the engine the air divides, part of it flowing radially inwards

Left: Williams WR2-6 turbojet for the Canadair CL-89 (AN/USD-501) reconnaissance drone (0·56 kN; 125 lb st). Right: Williams WR24-7 turbojet (0·76 kN; 170 lb st)

as primary combustion airflow and the main bulk entering the short outward radial annular combustor, through dilution apertures around the outer and rear face of the flame tube.

Fuel is sprayed centrifugally through a group of fine holes in the main compressor driveshaft. Surrounding the fuel pipe along the centreline of the main driveshaft is a cool airflow bled from the diffuser, which escapes through holes in the driveshaft to cool the combustion flames and reduce metal shaft and bearing temperatures, the main bearing being behind the compressor. A single igniter is mounted in the chamber at 12 o'clock. The hot gas, at about 955°C, then turns inward and exits rearward through the single-stage axial turbine and simple jetpipe.

The first production versions are the WR2-6, fitted to the CL-89, and the WR24-6 and -7 (YJ400-WR-400 and J400-WR-401) which power, respectively, the Northrop Chukar I and II target drones. To these have now been added the uprated YJ400-WR-404 (WJ24-8) which powers the BQM-74C Chukar III. The WR2-6 has a variable area exhaust nozzle with translating central bullet, and drives a DC generator. The WR24 family have a minimal fixed area jetpipe and drive a 4,000Hz alternator. The WR24-7 runs at higher temperature than the WR24-6 and has a zero-stage axle compressor and other detail modifications which increase mass flow to 1·36 kg (3 lb)/s and pressure ratio to 5·3.

DIMENSIONS:
- Overall length:
  - WR2-6: 566 mm (22·3 in)
  - WR24-6: 490 mm (19·3 in)
  - WR24-7: about 635 mm (25 in)
  - WJ24-8: 500 mm (19·7 in)
- Max diameter:
  - WR2-6, WR24-6: 274 mm (10·8 in)
  - WR24-7: about 305 mm (12 in)
  - WJ24-8: 302 mm (11·9 in)

WEIGHT, DRY:
- WR2-6, WR24-6: about 13·6 kg (30 lb)
- WR24-7: 20 kg (44·0 lb)
- WJ24-8: 22·7 kg (50 lb)

MAXIMUM RATINGS (S/L):
- WR2-6: 0·56 kN (125 lb st) at 60,000 rpm
- WR24-6: 0·54 kN (121 lb st) at 60,000 rpm
- WR24-7: 0·76 kN (170 lb st)
- WJ24-8: 1·07 kN (240 lb st) at 52,000 rpm

SPECIFIC FUEL CONSUMPTION:
- WR2-6, WR24-6: 35·41 mg/Ns (1·25 lb/h/lb st)
- WJ24-8: 33·99 mg/Ns (1·2 lb/h/lb st)

WILLIAMS WR19-A7

US military designation: F107

The F107 two-shaft turbofan was designed originally to propel the US Air Force/Boeing ALCM (air-launched cruise missile), and now powers also the General Dynamics Tomahawk sea- and ground-launched cruise missile. All versions are basically similar, but differ in mission and equipment, as follows:

F107-WR-100. Also designated WR19-A7, this was the engine selected for the Boeing AGM-86A ALCM, making the first ALCM flight at White Sands on 5 March 1976. Prototype engines only.

F107-WR-101. Selected to power the Boeing AGM-86B (ALCM-B). Improved configuration and performance. Qualification testing began in October 1978 and production deliveries in Spring 1981.

F107-WR-102. This engine powered the General Dynamics AGM-109 Tomahawk ALCM.

F107-WR-103. Uprated engine in 3·74 kN (840 lb st) class under development for Advanced Cruise Missile; scheduled to complete qualification in 1984.

F107-WR-104. Uprated engine to be retrofitted into existing AGM-86B cruise missiles.

F107-WR-400. Selected to power the General Dynamics BGM-109 SLCM (sub/ship launched cruise missile) and the GLCM (ground launched cruise missile) for the US Air Force, both versions of Tomahawk. An early -400 engine powered the first Tomahawk to fly (air launched by A-6A) on 5 June 1976. The missile system completed qualification testing in early 1980 and both SLCM and GLCM had entered the Navy and Air Force inventory by 1983.

Williams F107-WR-400 two-shaft turbofan for BGM-109 Tomahawk SLCM and GLCM

Williams F107-WR-101 two-shaft turbofan for AGM-86B Air Launched Cruise Missile

An engine in this family rated at 2·54 kN (570 lb st) powers the Williams X-Jet (formerly WASP II) manned platform.

TYPE: Two-shaft turbofan.

AIR INTAKE: Direct pitot type.

LP COMPRESSOR: Two-stage fan coupled to two-stage IP compressor.

HP COMPRESSOR: Single-stage centrifugal.

COMBUSTION CHAMBER: Folded annular with rotary fuel injection.

TURBINE: Single-stage HP, two-stage LP.

ACCESSORIES: Grouping varies with subtype. Self contained lubrication system. Solid propellant gas impingement starter.

DIMENSIONS:
- Length overall:
  - F107-WR-100: 800 mm (31·5 in)
  - F107-WR-101: 1,232 mm (48·5 in)
  - F107-WR-102, -400: 937 mm (36·9 in)
- Envelope diameter: 305 mm (12 in)

WEIGHT, DRY:
- F107-WR-100: 58·7 kg (130 lb)
- F107-WR-101: 66·2 kg (146 lb)
- F107-WR-102: 65·8 kg (145 lb)
- F107-WR-400: 65·3 kg (144 lb)

PERFORMANCE RATING: 2·67 kN (600 lb st) class

WILLIAMS F112

This is the first Williams engine to be known only by its military designation. Not yet publicly referred to by Williams, it is described by the US Air Force as "a small turbofan engine for an advanced cruise missile".

WILLIAMS WTS34

This family of simple turboshaft engines is aimed at a wide spectrum of applications, including aviation. Based on a centrifugal compressor, annular combustor and radial inflow turbine, it is robust and reliable, and has unchanged configuration over power outputs from 11-26 kW (15-35 hp) at output speeds of 3,600, 6,000, or 12,000 rpm. Equipped weight is 29·5 kg (65 lb). One version, the **WTS34-16**, powers the Canadair CL-227 (see RPVs and Targets section). This model weighs only 17·25 kg (38 lb), is rated at 24 kW (32 hp), and is 239 mm (9·4 in) in diameter by 450 mm (17·7 in) long. It has multi-fuel and multi-lubricant capability.

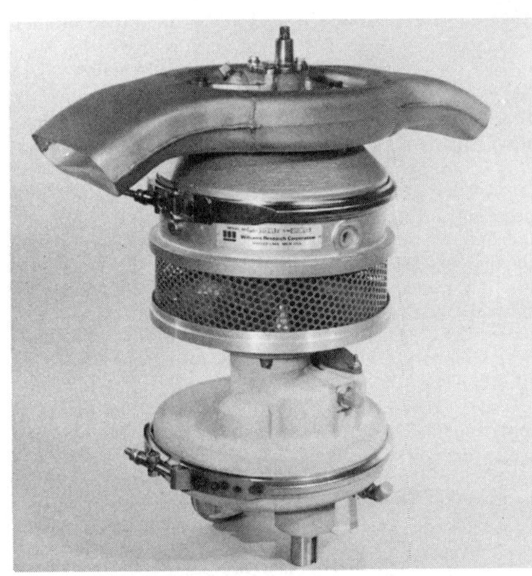

Williams WTS34-16 turboshaft (24 kW; 32 hp)

WILLIAMS FJ44

Development of a turbofan known then as the WR44 began in 1971, using the WR19 as a basis. Bypass ratio was increased to 3, and overall pressure ratio increased. Claimed to be outstandingly quiet and suitable for general aviation applications, the WR44 was flight tested initially in a two-man VTOL system in 1973. It was chosen at a rating of 3·78 kN (850 lb st) for the proposed Foxjet, but was subsequently redesigned to incorporate the latest F107 technology, with bypass ratio of 3·24, resulting in increased thrust and reduced fuel consumption.

In May 1982 it was announced that Hawker Siddeley Dynamics Engineering of the UK had licensed Chandler-Evans Inc to use its digital electronic technology in developing an advanced fuel control system for this engine. The first FJ44, built to meet FAR.33 requirements, achieved design thrust at "a very modest turbine inlet temperature" on its first build. Williams has built a mockup business jet, called the V-Jet from its forward-swept wings, to stimulate interest in twin-FJ44 aircraft.

Williams FJ44 turbofan (8 kN; 1,800 lb st)

DIMENSIONS:
- Length (with tailpipe): 1,227 mm (48·3 in)
- Max diameter: 602 mm (23·7 in)

WEIGHT, DRY: 177 kg (390 lb)

PERFORMANCE RATINGS:
- T-O (S/L) to 24°C: 8·0 kN (1,800 lb st)
- Max cruise (11,000 m; 36,090 ft, Mach 0·6): 1·96 kN (440 lb)

SPECIFIC FUEL CONSUMPTION:
- T-O (S/L): 12·69 mg/Ns (0·448 lb/h/lb st)
- Max cruise (as above): 19·83 mg/Ns (0·70 lb/h/lb)

YUGOSLAVIA

ORAO

ORAO AIR FORCE DEPOT

Federal Directorate of Supply and Procurement
9 Nemanjina St, 11001 Belgrade 9
Telephone: 011 621522

The depot was established in 1944. Today its main task is licence manufacture of the Rolls-Royce Viper 632-41 and 632-46, and the latest afterburning 633-41, used in most of the Orao twin-engined combat aircraft at present flying.

The Orao works has built up a design and development team which, in collaboration with Turbomecanica of Romania, has been developing the afterburning Viper Mk 633-47 engine for production Oraos. The first afterburning engines were overweight, but an Orao 2 flew with afterburning engines on 20 October 1983.

ADDENDA

AIRCRAFT

BRAZIL

EMBRAER (page 10)

EMBRAER EMB-123

Following a co-operation agreement with the Fabricá Militar de Aviones (FMA) of Argentina, signed in January 1986, EMBRAER revealed in April provisional details of a proposed new commuter transport aircraft to be known as the EMB-123. At that time it was planned to use a lengthened version of the EMB-121 Xingu fuselage, fitted with foreplanes, but by the time that a more detailed description was released at the Farnborough International air show in September 1986 it had been decided to delete the canard surfaces and to adopt a shortened version of the EMB-120 Brasilia fuselage. Orders and options for the Brasilia totalled 218 at that time, and the EMB-123 will now share with that aircraft approximately 60 per cent commonality of components, including almost the same flight deck, as well as common maintenance and cabin and crew procedures. Combined with a new supercritical wing, a T tail, and two rear mounted 'pusher' turboprop engines with scimitar propeller blades, the EMB-123 in this configuration is expected to offer an optimum combination of fuel efficiency and speed, as well as an extremely smooth and quiet ride. Certification will be to FAR/JAR Pt 25 (Transport Category), with noise certification to FAR Pt 36 (ICAO Annex 16).

The EMB-123 is expected to enter service in 1990, replacing the EMB-110 Bandeirante, and the Brazilian and Argentine governments have announced their intention to support its launch with the purchase of 36 aircraft each, for military and executive transport or corporate use. The agreement includes purchase by Argentina of an undisclosed number of EMB-312 Tucano turboprop trainers, and collaboration in the EMB-123 programme was being discussed also with Chile and Peru in the Autumn of 1986. Under present arrangements, one-third of the work-split between Brazil and Argentina is allocated to FMA, which will produce the wings, fins and rudders.

TYPE: Twin-turboprop regional and corporate transport aircraft.

WINGS: Cantilever low-wing monoplane. High aspect ratio wings with supercritical section and 8° sweepback, taper being increased on inboard portions by extending chord and sweeping trailing-edges forward. Two-segment flaps and single aileron on each trailing-edge.

FUSELAGE: Pressurised semi-monocoque structure of circular cross-section; generally as for EMB-120, but of reduced length.

TAIL UNIT: Broad chord sweptback fin and rudder, with narrow dorsal fin. Sweptback variable incidence T tailplane with balanced elevators.

LANDING GEAR: Retractable tricycle type, with twin wheels on each unit. Mainwheels retract inward into wing/underfuselage fairing; nose unit retracts rearward.

POWER PLANT: Two 895 kW (1,200 shp) class Pratt & Whitney Canada or Garrett turboprop engines, each driving a slow-turning 'pusher' propeller with reversible pitch, autofeathering, synchrophasing, and six scimitar blades. Engines mounted at rear of fuselage, on pylons set at dihedral angle of approx 30°, and having a cruise/climb rating of 746 kW (1,000 shp). Fuel in two integral wing tanks with combined capacity of 1,211 litres (266·5 Imp gallons). Single-point pressure fuelling/defuelling, and overwing gravity refuelling.

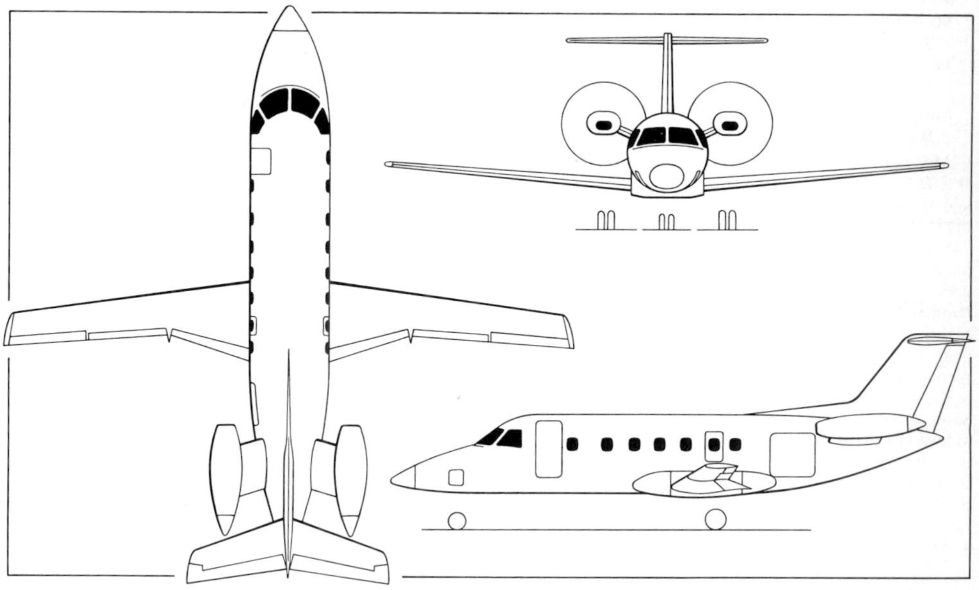

EMBRAER EMB-123 twin-turboprop 19-passenger regional and corporate transport *(Jane's/Mike Keep)*

ACCOMMODATION: Crew of two on flight deck, with optional seat to rear for observer. Standard commuter cabin layout for 19 passengers, in five rows of three and a final four-seat row, at 79 cm (31 in) pitch. Wardrobe, toilet, galley and seat for cabin attendant at front of cabin. Underseat and overhead bin stowage for carry-on baggage; main baggage/cargo compartment aft of rear row of seats. Executive interiors, to customer's requirements, available optionally. Passenger door and baggage/cargo door on port side, at front and rear of cabin respectively. Passenger emergency exit above wing on each side; flight deck side windows serve as emergency exits for crew. Entire accommodation pressurised and air-conditioned. Max pressure differential 0·56 bars (8·2 lb/sq in), giving a S/L cabin atmosphere up to 6,400 m (21,000 ft) and a 2,440 m (8,000 ft) environment at altitudes up to 12,200 m (40,000 ft).

AVIONICS: Generally similar to those for EMB-120 Brasilia. Standard fit will include electronic flight instrumentation system (EFIS), electronic engine and instrument caution advisory system (EICAS), autopilot/flight director, flight data recorder, cockpit voice recorder, and weather radar.

DIMENSIONS, EXTERNAL:
- Wing span: 16·46 m (54 ft 0 in)
- Wing aspect ratio: 12·32
- Wing taper ratio: 0·5
- Length overall: 17·19 m (56 ft 4¾ in)
- Height overall: 5·61 m (18 ft 4¾ in)
- Tailplane span: 5·79 m (19 ft 0 in)
- Wheel track: 3·47 m (11 ft 4½ in)
- Wheelbase: 7·62 m (25 ft 0 in)
- Cargo door: Height: 1·30 m (4 ft 3¼ in)
  - Width: 1·36 m (4 ft 5½ in)

DIMENSIONS, INTERNAL:
- Cabin: Max width: 2·10 m (6 ft 10¾ in)
  - Max height: 1·76 m (5 ft 9¼ in)
- Baggage compartment volume: 6·30 m³ (222·5 cu ft)

AREA:
- Wings, gross: 22·0 m² (236·8 sq ft)

WEIGHTS (estimated):
- Basic operating weight empty: 4,900 kg (10,802 lb)
- Max fuel: 980 kg (2,160 lb)
- Payload with max fuel: 1,820 kg (4,012 lb)
- Max payload: 2,000 kg (4,409 lb)
- Baggage: 450 kg (992 lb)
- Max ramp weight: 7,740 kg (17,064 lb)
- Max T-O weight: 7,700 kg (16,975 lb)
- Max landing weight: 7,550 kg (16,645 lb)
- Max zero-fuel weight: 6,900 kg (15,212 lb)

PERFORMANCE (ISA, estimated at max T-O weight except where indicated):
- Max cruising speed at 9,150 m (30,000 ft), 95% of MTOGW: 340 knots (630 km/h; 391 mph)
- Max rate of climb at S/L: 762 m (2,500 ft)/min
- Rate of climb at S/L, one engine out: 244 m (800 ft)/min
- Max operating altitude: 12,200 m (40,000 ft)
- FAR 25 balanced T-O distance:
  - ISA at S/L: 1,200 m (3,937 ft)
  - ISA + 20°C at 1,525 m (5,000 ft): 1,500 m (4,921 ft)
- FAR 135 landing distance at max landing weight:
  - ISA at S/L: 1,200 m (3,937 ft)
  - ISA + 20°C at 1,525 m (5,000 ft): 1,330 m (4,364 ft)
- Range with max passenger payload at 10,670 m (35,000 ft), IFR reserves for 100 nm (185 km; 115 mile) diversion and 45 min hold: 700 nm (1,296 km; 805 miles)

CANADA

CANADAIR (page 20)

CANADAIR CL-215T

After long deliberation and a detailed market survey, Canadair has decided to go ahead with development of a turboprop version of the CL-215, sales of which had reached 111 by the Autumn of 1986. Known as the CL-215T, it will be offered both as a retrofit kit for existing piston engined CL-215s and as a new-build aircraft. It will also offer a choice of Pratt & Whitney Canada engines: the PW100/47, with a take-off rating of 1,491 kW (2,000 shp), which is expected to meet the requirements of most potential operators; and the PW100/37 for 'hot and high' applications, offering the same level of power up to 50°C.

Other standard improvements will include an upgraded and air-conditioned flight deck, a new fuel system with both pressure and gravity refuelling, nosewheel steering (on new-build aircraft only), and single-point refill and a choice of drop patterns for firefighting missions. An extensive list of options will be available for specialised applications, including underwing hardpoints, and various military and commercial transport versions have been defined.

Canadair expects to continue building the radial engined CL-215 for a few more years, and will begin modifying two as CL-215T prototypes in July and September 1987, with first flight planned for May 1988, followed by certification in March 1989 with the PW100/47 and September 1989 with the PW100/37. Retrofit kits will become available first, in February 1989, followed by new-production CL-215Ts two months later.

General appearance of the CL-215T is shown in the drawing on page 23 of this edition. A more detailed description will appear in the next edition of *Jane's*; the principal specification changes are as follows:

POWER PLANT: Two 1,491 kW (2,000 shp) Pratt & Whitney Canada PW100/47 or PW100/37 (PW123) turboprop engines, each driving a Hamilton Standard 14SF four-blade propeller with spinner. Standard internal fuel capacity of 5,914 litres (1,301 Imp gallons), in 16 identical bladder type cells in wings. Two 1,136 litre (250 Imp gallon) underwing auxiliary tanks optional.

ACCOMMODATION: Crew of two on flight deck. With water tanks removed, transport configurations can include shuttle layout for 35 passenger seats plus toilet; or standard layout for 32 passengers plus toilet, galley and baggage area. Combi layout offers cargo at front, full firefighting capability, and 11 seats at rear. All-cargo and other special mission interiors to customer's requirements.

EQUIPMENT (water bomber): Similar to that of CL-215, comprising two fuselage tanks with combined capacity of 5,346 litres (1,176 Imp gallons), each having an independently openable door in the floor for water dropping; and two hydraulically operated scoops mounted aft of the hull step, fillable also on ground by hose adaptor on each side of fuselage. Feasibility study in progress to increase tank capacity.

DIMENSIONS, EXTERNAL: As for CL-215 except:
- Length overall: 19·94 m (65 ft 5 in)
- Height overall: on land: 8·99 m (29 ft 6 in)
  - on water: 6·88 m (22 ft 7 in)
- Propeller diameter: 3·96 m (13 ft 0 in)
- Propeller/water clearance: 0·99 m (3 ft 3 in)

WEIGHTS AND LOADINGS: (A: water bomber, land based; B: utility, land or water based):
- Manufacturer's weight empty:
  - A, B: 10,977 kg (24,200 lb)
- Typical operating weight empty:
  - A, B: 11,158 kg (24,600 lb)
- Max fuel weight: A, B: 4,817 kg (10,620 lb)
- Max payload: A: 5,443 kg (12,000 lb)
  - B: 5,352 kg (11,800 lb)
- Max ramp weight: A: 19,731 kg (43,500 lb)
  - B: 17,236 kg (38,000 lb)

Max T-O weight:	
A, B (land)	19,731 kg (43,500 lb)
B (water)	17,100 kg (37,700 lb)
Max flying weight (A):	
before scooping	15,195 kg (33,500 lb)
after scooping	19,731 kg (43,500 lb)
Max landing weight: A, B	16,783 kg (37,000 lb)
Max zero-fuel weight: A	18,597 kg (41,000 lb)
B	16,511 kg (36,400 lb)
Max cabin floor loading:	
A, B	732 kg/m² (150 lb/sq ft)
Max wing loading: A	196·55 kg/m² (40·28 lb/sq ft)
B	170·35 kg/m² (34·91 lb/sq ft)
Max power loading: A	6.62 kg/kW (10·87 lb/shp)
B	5·74 kg/kW (9·42 lb/shp)

PERFORMANCE (ISA, estimated, at weights indicated):
Cruising speed at 3,050 m (10,000 ft):
max cruise power, 14,742 kg (32,500 lb
190 knots (352 km/h; 219 mph)
max recommended power, 18,144 kg (40,000 lb)
184 knots (341 km/h; 212 mph)
long-range cruise power, 14,742 kg (32,500 lb)
165 knots (306 km/h; 190 mph)
Patrol speed at S/L, 14,742 kg (32,500 lb)
110 knots (204 km/h; 126 mph)
Stalling speed at S/L, max landing weight
69 knots (128 km/h; 80 mph)
Max rate of climb at S/L, 19,731 kg (43,500 lb), max climb power 254 m (832 ft)/min
Rate of climb at S/L, one engine out, 14,288 kg (31,500 lb), T-O power 113 m (370 ft)/min
Service ceiling, 19,731 kg (43,500 lb) 6,100 m (20,000 ft)
Service ceiling, one engine out, 17,100 kg (37,700 lb)
3,960 m (13,000 ft)
T-O to 10·7 m (35 ft) at S/L:
on land (water bomber), 19,731 kg (43,500 lb)
777 m (2,550 ft)
on land (utility), 17,100 kg (37,700 lb)
677 m (2,220 ft)
on water (utility), 17,100 kg (37,700 lb)
774 m (2,540 ft)
Landing from 15 m (50 ft) at S/L, at MLW:
on land 768 m (2,520 ft)
on water 835 m (2,740 ft)
Range with 1,814 kg (4,000 lb) payload at long-range cruise power
1,150 nm (2,131 km; 1,324 miles)

CHINA (PEOPLE'S REPUBLIC)

HARBIN (page 34)

HARBIN PS-5

As indicated on page 35, the accompanying photograph of the PS-5 (presumably the second prototype) shows it to be a very large aircraft, comparable in size to Japan's Shin Meiwa US-1A. Apart from the elimination of anhedral on the outer wings, the wing/engine combination bears very close resemblance to that of the Shaanxi Y-8 cargo transport (page 38), but mounted to a hump fairing on top of the fuselage. If this assumption is correct, and taking the latter's 4·00 m (13 ft 1½ in) diameter propellers as a guide to scale, overall dimensions do not appear to be significantly different from those of the Y-8.

Hull shape, and method of retracting the single mainwheels/twin nosewheels landing gear, show similarities to the US-1A, including the spray-suppressing strakes on each side of the nose and fuselage-side slots in line with the propellers. The dihedral tailplane and twin oval fins and rudders, mounted on a fairing above the rear fuselage, clearly owe their configuration to the Soviet Beriev Be-12, though they are proportionately larger. Stabilising floats, strut mounted under the outer wings midway between the outboard engines and the wingtips, are non-retractable.

The following data are estimated:

POWER PLANT: Four 3,169 kW (4,250 ehp) Shanghai WJ-6 turboprop engines, each driving a four-blade propeller with spinner.

DIMENSIONS, EXTERNAL:	
Wing span	38·0 m (124 ft 8 in)
Length overall	33·0 m (108 ft 3 in)
Height overall	10·0 m (32 ft 9¾ in)
Wheelbase	10·0 m (32 ft 9¾ in)
Propeller diameter	4·0 m (13 ft 1½ in)
WEIGHT:	
Max T-O weight	55,000 kg (121,250 lb)

Harbin PS-5 patrol and anti-submarine bomber amphibian, now in service with the Chinese Navy *(CATIC)*

POLAND

INSTYTUT LOTNICTWA (page 180)

IL I-22

These photographs of a new jet trainer and light attack aircraft appeared in the Polish aviation press in October 1986. Designated I-22, the aircraft was designed at the Instytut Lotnictwa in Warsaw under the leadership of Mr Alfred Baron, and the 01 prototype had already flown before the 02 was revealed publicly on Polish television on 18 October. The I-22 is presumably intended as a replacement for the PZL Mielec TS-11 Iskra. Of particular interest are the compound sweep on the wing leading-edges, and the underbelly gun pack, probably housing a GSh-23 twin-barrel 23 mm gun *(Lech Zielaskowski/Skrzydlata Polska)*

UNITED STATES OF AMERICA

BELL HELICOPTER TEXTRON INC

(page 351)

BELL/BOEING VERTOL V-22 OSPREY

The Bell/Boeing Vertol team has begun a predesign study of a sea based anti-submarine warfare variant of the V-22 Osprey for the US Navy. Provisionally designated **SV-22**, this aircraft would have a modified fuselage interior for additional avionics and crew stations, and mountings for torpedoes and, possibly, air-to-surface missiles. Radar and FLIR systems are also anticipated in the design. As envisaged, SV-22s would be based on US Navy aircraft carriers for all maintenance and berthing, but would operate for extended periods of time from smaller ships such as DD-963 class destroyers, providing long range ASW protection for non-carrier battle groups. The SV-22 could be available in the mid-1990s.

Commercial variants of the V-22 are also under consideration by the development team, which believes that a certificated 'civil Osprey' could be available for delivery by 1995.

Chadwick C-122S RainBow

CHADWICK
CHADWICK HELICOPTERS INTERNATIONAL INC

11969 SW Herman Road, Sherwood, Oregon 97140
Telephone: (503) 692 0570
Telex: 360652 CHAD SHOD
PRESIDENT AND CHIEF EXECUTIVE OFFICER:
Russell D. Chadwick
VICE-PRESIDENT, ADMINISTRATION: Laurie J. Parson

CHADWICK C-122S RAINBOW

Chadwick Helicopters International is a subsidiary of Chadwick Incorporated, which was founded in 1964 and manufactures a number of helicopter accessories including auxiliary fuel systems, electronic underslung load indicators, firefighting and aerial applications equipment, and computerised weighing devices for aircraft.

Work began on a single-seat ultralight helicopter design during 1983. The development programme included the building and flight testing of a 'flying platform' to define the configuration of the prototype Model C-122S RainBow, which made its public debut at the 38th Helicopter Association International meeting at Anaheim, California, in January 1986, The RainBow is designed to meet FAR Pt 103 certification requirements for ultralight aircraft. Its fuselage structure comprises an aluminium truss to support the engine, main rotor mast, idler shaft assembly, basic control mixer and landing gear, with a composite glassfibre and polyester monocoque cabin and tailboom incorporating a fixed sweptback ventral fin and a 'ring' style tail rotor guard. The fixed twin-skid landing gear is of aluminium tube construction. Power plant is a 47 kW (63 hp) Rotax 503 two-cylinder piston engine, mounted vertically and driving a four-blade fully articulated main rotor, with folding blades, and a two-blade tail rotor.

In late 1986 Chadwick Helicopters was developing a two-seat trainer version of the RainBow designated **C-122T**, an agricultural **C-122AG**, a 'police interceptor' variant to be known as the **C-122PI**, a **C-122R** RPV version, and the **C-122WP** weapons platform. First deliveries of production Model C-122S and C-122T RainBows were anticipated before the end of 1986.

DIMENSIONS, EXTERNAL:
- Main rotor diameter: 5·64 m (18 ft 6 in)
- Tail rotor diameter: 1·01 m (3 ft 4 in)
- Main rotor blade chord: 0·23 m (9 in)
- Tail rotor blade chord: 0·09 m (3½ in)
- Length overall: rotors turning: 6·83 m (22 ft 5 in)
  - main rotor folded: 5·79 m (19 ft 0 in)
- Width overall, main rotor folded: 1·22 m (4 ft 0 in)

AREAS:
- Main rotor disc: 24·97 m² (268·8 sq ft)
- Tail rotor disc: 0·81 m² (8·78 sq ft)

WEIGHTS:
- Weight empty: 115 kg (253 lb)
- Max T-O weight (normal): 227 kg (500 lb)
- Max design weight: 317 kg (700 lb)

PERFORMANCE (at max T-O weight of 227 kg; 500 lb):
- Never-exceed speed: 100 knots (185 km/h; 115 mph)*
- Max cruising speed:
  - at S/L: 82 knots (151 km/h; 94 mph)*
  - at 1,220 m (4,000 ft): 80 knots (148 km/h; 92 mph)*
  - at 2,440 m (8,000 ft): 76 knots (142 km/h; 88 mph)*
- Econ cruising speed at S/L: 64 knots (119 km/h; 74 mph)*
- Vertical rate of climb at S/L: 288 m (945 ft)/min
- Hovering ceiling: OGE: 2,875 m (9,440 ft)
  - IGE: 3,860 m (12,670 ft)
- Service ceiling: 4,110 m (13,480 ft)
- Range, 2 min warmup, no reserves, at S/L: 104 nm (193 km; 120 miles)

**To meet FAR Pt 103 requirements, speed is limited by electronic microprocessor to 55 knots (101 km/h; 63 mph)*

CHRISTEN (page 395)

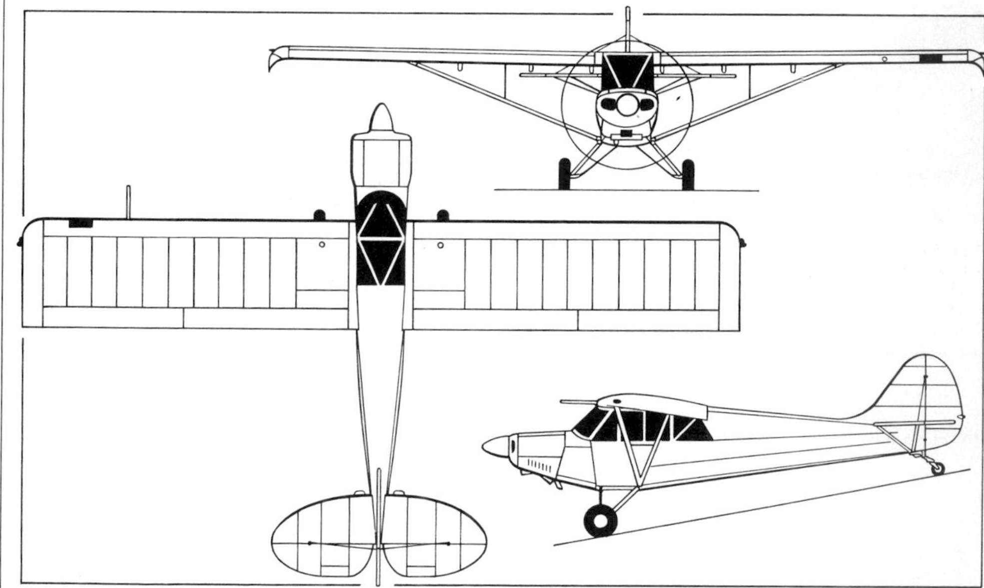

Christen A-1 Husky two-seat light aircraft *(Jane's/Mike Keep)*

MAULE (page 447)

MAULE MX-7 STARCRAFT

Maule has developed a turboprop version of its MX-7 Star Rocket known as the MX-7 Starcraft. The aircraft is powered by a 313 kW (420 shp) Allison 250 turboprop engine, driving a three-blade feathering metal propeller. A prototype (N5666K) was being test flown in the Summer of 1986, with FAA certification of a landplane version anticipated by the end of the year and of a seaplane version early in 1987.

ROBINSON (Page 491)

ROBINSON R44

In the Summer of 1986 Robinson Helicopter Company announced that it was designing a four-seat version of its R22 helicopter, to be designated **R44**. The R44 will be powered by a piston engine, for which the 194 kW (260 hp) Avco Lycoming O-540, 212·5 kW (285 hp) Teledyne Continental IO-520 and 158 kW (212 hp) Porsche PFM 3200 were under consideration. Provisional date for introduction of the R44 is the early 1990s.

SCHAFER (page 504)

Schafer Aircraft Modifications and Aero Mod International have developed jointly a conversion of the Douglas DC-3 which involves replacing the aircraft's piston engines with two 875 kW (1,173 shp) Pratt & Whitney Canada PT6A-65AR turboprops. The conversion also includes a fuselage 'stretch', achieved by insertion of a 1·02 m (3 ft 4 in) plug, and additional fuel capacity. A prototype made its first flight on 1 August 1986, at which time the companies held orders for 25 conversions. FAA certification, by Supplemental Type Certificate, was anticipated at the end of December 1986.

SPORT AIRCRAFT

CANADA

MURPHY
MURPHY AVIATION

2-44335 Yale Road West, Sardis, British Columbia V2R 1A9
Telephone: 792 5855

Murphy Aviation is marketing a new tandem two-seat biplane, known as the Renegade II, in kit form and as a fully assembled aircraft.

MURPHY RENEGADE II

TYPE: Two-seat light sporting biplane.

AIRFRAME: Conventional strut and wire braced biplane of fabric covered all-metal construction. Sweepback 10° on upper wings only. Dihedral 3° on lower wings only. Front spars of 3 in 6061-T6 aluminium alloy tubing; rear spars of C section 2024-T3 aluminium alloy; stamped 2024-T3 ribs. N type cabane structure and I type interplane struts. Frise type ailerons standard on lower wings only; optional on all four wings. No flaps. Fuselage of 6061-T6 aluminium alloy tubing. Conventional wire braced tail unit.

LANDING GEAR: Non-retractable tailwheel landing gear. Mainwheels, with low pressure tyres, carried on side Vs and half-axles with bungee shock absorption. Independent dual brakes, wheel fairings, steerable tailwheel and floats optional.

POWER PLANT: One 34 kW (45·6 hp) Rotax 503 two-cylinder two-stroke engine standard; 47 kW (63 hp) Rotax 532 optional. GSC Systems 68 × 36 two-blade wooden fixed-pitch propeller, driven through 2·58:1 reduction gear. Fuel capacity 29·5 litres (6·5 Imp gallons).

ACCOMMODATION: Two persons in tandem in open cockpits. Windscreen for front cockpit. Small head fairing behind rear cockpit.

AVIONICS AND EQUIPMENT: Provision for radio. Options include agricultural spraygear.

DIMENSIONS, EXTERNAL:

Wing span: upper	6·71 m (22 ft 0 in)
lower	6·30 m (20 ft 8 in)

AREA:

Wings, gross	14·86 m² (160 sq ft)

WEIGHTS:

Weight empty	163 kg (360 lb)
Max T-O weight	363 kg (800 lb)

PERFORMANCE (Rotax 503 engine):

Never-exceed speed	86 knots (160 km/h; 100 mph)
Max level speed	74 knots (136 km/h; 85 mph)
Max cruising speed	65 knots (120 km/h; 75 mph)
Approach speed	39 knots (73 km/h; 45 mph)
Stalling speed, power off	28 knots (52 km/h; 32 mph)
Max rate of climb at S/L	365 m (1,200 ft)/min
T-O run	46 m (150 ft)
Landing run	61 m (200 ft)
g limits	+10/−6 ultimate

Murphy Renegade II two-seat homebuilt biplane *(Peter M. Bowers)*

Scicraft Gambit two-seat homebuilt canard light aircraft *(J. M. G. Gradidge)*

ISRAEL

SCICRAFT
SCICRAFT LTD

D N Misgav 20100
Telephone: (04) 962214
Telex: 46384 CYCLV

This company was established in 1984. After considerable development, via two prototypes named Dove I and Dove II, it is now marketing in kit form a canard light aircraft known as the Gambit.

SCICRAFT GAMBIT

This aircraft is made up of more than 400 prefabricated parts, which can be assembled from four kits in less than 400 hours, using only an electric hand drill and a pop riveter. The Gambit is not aerobatic.

TYPE: Side by side two-seat light aircraft.

AIRFRAME: Sweptwing canard, with removable strut braced wings and cantilever foreplane. High mounted wings have pre-assembled aluminium alloy leading-edge, cambered tips and winglets. Large-span ailerons. No flaps. Composites fuselage of Kevlar and carbonfibre, with composites cockpit interior. Composites foreplane, with elevators. Rudder on each winglet, deflecting outward only. Set-up time about 30 min.

LANDING GEAR: Non-retractable tricycle type. Cantilever mainwheel legs, with optional wheel fairings. Mainwheel brakes standard.

POWER PLANT: Available as **Gambit 600** with 47 kW (63 hp) Rotax 532 liquid cooled two-cylinder two-stroke engine, or **Gambit 900** with 67 kW (90 hp) Limbach 2400 aircooled four-cylinder engine or equivalent, in each case driving a two-blade wooden pusher propeller. Fuel capacity 60 litres (16 US gallons) standard, with optional 30 litre (8 US gallon) auxiliary tank.

ACCOMMODATION: Two persons side by side in fully enclosed cabin, with upward opening canopy door each side. Dual controls optional.

SYSTEM: Electrical system, with battery, standard.

DIMENSIONS, EXTERNAL:

Wing span	10·01 m (32 ft 10 in)
Length overall	5·13 m (16 ft 10 in)
Height overall	2·44 m (8 ft 0 in)

DIMENSIONS, INTERNAL:

Cabin: Max width	1·27 m (4 ft 2 in)
Height: seat to ceiling	1·09 m (3 ft 7 in)
floor to ceiling	1·29 m (4 ft 3 in)

AREAS:

Wings, gross	13·65 m² (147 sq ft)
Foreplanes, gross	2·00 m² (21·5 sq ft)

WEIGHTS (A: Gambit 600, B: Gambit 900):

Weight empty: A	250 kg (550 lb)
B:	270 kg (595 lb)
Max baggage: A	16 kg (35 lb)
B	25 kg (55 lb)
Max T-O weight: A	470 kg (1,036 lb)
B	500 kg (1,102 lb)

PERFORMANCE (A and B as above):

Never-exceed speed, both	126 knots (233 km/h; 145 mph)
Max level speed: A	87 knots (161 km/h; 100 mph)
B	113 knots (209 km/h; 130 mph)
Max cruising speed: A	78 knots (145 km/h; 90 mph)
B	100 knots (185 km/h; 115 mph)
Min flying speed: A	39 knots (73 km/h; 45 mph)
B	42 knots (78 km/h; 48 mph)
Max rate of climb at S/L: A	183 m (600 ft)/min
B	259 m (850 ft)/min
Range with standard fuel:	
A	217 nm (402 km; 250 miles)
B	347 nm (643 km; 400 miles)
g limits: A	+7/−2·8
B	+6·6/−2·64

UNITED STATES OF AMERICA

FREE SPIRIT
FREE SPIRIT AIRCRAFT COMPANY, INC

c/o SOTAAP Inc, 21622 Kanakoa Lane, Huntington Beach, California 92646
Telephone: (714) 968 3571
DESIGNER: Richard Cabrinha

Mr Richard Cabrinha, after serving in the USAF, received his engineering degree from San José State College in 1973 and is currently working on joined-wing prototypes for NASA and the US Navy at ACA Industries (see main US Aircraft section). He has built the prototype of an all-composites two/four-seat light aircraft known as the Free Spirit, which is to be made available in kit form for amateur construction.

FREE SPIRIT

TYPE: Side by side two-seat light aircraft. (Convertible to four-seater.)

AIRFRAME: Cantilever low-wing monoplane of all-composites (glassfibre honeycomb) construction. Wings built in three portions: centre-section and two outer panels, with D type leading-edge spar, main spar and trailing-edge spar integral with lower skin. Centre-section upper skin integral with side panels of semi-monocoque fuselage embodying only two bulkheads and firewall. Cantilever tail surfaces each made in two halves. Control surfaces comprise a top-surface spoiler forward of a slotted flap on each outer wing panel, horn balanced rudder and horn balanced one-piece elevator. Variable incidence tailplane.

LANDING GEAR: Manually retractable tricycle type. Main units retract inward into wing centre-section; nose unit retracts rearward. Gear fully enclosed when retracted. Composites nosewheel leg; oleo-pneumatic mainwheel shock absorption. Dual brakes.

POWER PLANT: One 119 kW (160 hp) Avco Lycoming IO-320 flat-four engine, driving a three-blade metal constant-speed propeller. Integral wing fuel tanks, capacity 189 litres (50 US gallons). Provision for auxiliary tank in freight compartment.

ACCOMMODATION: Two persons side by side, with dual controls, under forward and upward hinged one-piece transparent windscreen/canopy. Space for 90 kg (200 lb) of baggage or freight aft of seats. (Can be converted to four-seater by fitting different wings, adding two seats and a canopy hatch.)

Free Spirit two/four-seat homebuilt aircraft *(J. M. G. Gradidge)*

EQUIPMENT: Provision for radio and full IFR instrumentation.

DIMENSIONS, EXTERNAL:
- Wing span 8·23 m (27 ft 0 in)
- Length overall 6·10 m (20 ft 0 in)
- Propeller diameter 1·525 m (5 ft 0 in)

DIMENSIONS, INTERNAL:
- Cabin: Max width 1·11 m (3 ft 8 in)
- Baggage space: volume 0·57 m³ (20 cu ft)

AREA:
- Wings, gross 7·25 m² (78 sq ft)

WEIGHTS:
- Weight empty approx 385 kg (850 lb)
- Max T-O weight 725 kg (1,600 lb)

PERFORMANCE:
- Max level speed 230 knots (426 km/h; 265 mph)
- Max cruising speed at 1,525 m (5,000 ft) 191 knots (354 km/h; 220 mph)
- Stalling speed: clean, solo 48 knots (89 km/h; 55 mph)
  - flaps down, solo 39 knots (73 km/h; 45 mph)
  - flaps down, max T-O weight 48 knots (89 km/h; 55 mph)
- Max rate of climb at S/L:
  - solo 823 m (2,700 ft)/min
  - max T-O weight 457 m (1,500 ft)/min
- Rate of roll 120-150°/s
- T-O run: solo 119 m (390 ft)
  - max T-O weight 168 m (550 ft)
- Landing run: solo 133 m (435 ft)
  - max T-O weight 153 m (500 ft)
- Range with max standard fuel 955 nm (1,770 km; 1,100 miles)

SAILPLANES

BRAZIL

AEROMOT AERONAVES E MOTORES SA

Aeroporto Internacional, Salgado Filho (PO Box 8031), 90201 Porto Alegre, RS

Telephone: 0512 423344

Telex: (051) 1991 AEMT

PRESIDENT: Claudio Miguel Barreto Viana

OPERATIONAL AND SPECIAL PROGRAMMES MANAGER: Silvio Barreto Viana

AEROMOT AMT-100 XIMANGO

The Ximango is the production version of the Aérostructure (Fournier) RF-10 motor glider, described on pages 742-3 of this edition. Following French certification in October 1984, the French company sold all production rights to Aeromot in July 1985. Brazilian CTA certification was granted on 5 June 1986, and series production is under way, the Aeromot aircraft being known as the AMT-100 Ximango.

By the end of September 1986 Aeromot had completed two of the Civilian Aeronautical Department's order for 100. One of these had been delivered; the other was being certificated with a Brazilian Retimotor RM-2000A version of the Limbach/Volkswagen engine. Other sales and deliveries of the AMT-100 have been made, to private customers in Brazil and Argentina.

Information provided by Aeromot amends the description on pages 742-3 in the following respects:

AIRFRAME: Wing dihedral is 2° 30'.

POWER PLANT: Limbach engine is an L 2000 EOI.

DIMENSIONS, EXTERNAL:
- Width, wings folded 10·15 m (33 ft 3½ in)

WEIGHTS AND LOADINGS:
- Weight empty 600 kg (1,323 lb)
- Max T-O weight 800 kg (1,764 lb)
- Max wing loading 42·78 kg/m² (8·77 lb/sq ft)
- Max power loading 13·42 kg/kW (22·05 lb/hp)

PERFORMANCE, POWERED (at max T-O weight):
- Min rate of sink at 49 knots (90 km/h; 56 mph) 0·96 m (3·15 ft)/s
- Max speed (smooth air) 132 knots (245 km/h; 152 mph)

PERFORMANCE POWERED (at max T-O weight):
- Max cruising speed 108 knots (200 km/h; 124 mph)
- Max rate of climb at S/L 150 m (492 ft)/min
- Range with max fuel 728 nm (1,350 km; 839 miles)
- Max endurance 7 h 30 min

Aeromot AMT-100 Ximango side by side two-seat motor glider, with wings folded

Prototype Stemme S 10 self launching sailplane and motor glider
(Archiv Peter F. Selinger)

GERMANY (FEDERAL REPUBLIC)

STEMME STEMME GmbH & Co KG

Gustav Meyer Allee 25, 1000 Berlin 65

Telephone: (030) 4634071

DIRECTORS:
- Dr Reiner Stemme (Managing)
- Alfred Schulze

SALES OFFICE: Flughafen Lilienthalplatz, 3300 Braunschweig

Telephone: (0531) 351705

SALES MANAGER: Ingo Andresen

Stemme GmbH & Co KG was formed in Berlin in November 1984 by a group of businessmen, with Dr Reiner Stemme as managing shareholder. It offers high performance motor gliders and sailplane propulsion systems, and is currently developing an advanced aircraft of this type known as the S 10.

STEMME S 10

Claimed by Stemme to be the first sailplane to incorporate a fully effective propulsion system without suffering aerodynamic penalties, the S 10 prototype (D-KKST) made its first flight at Braunschweig on 6 July 1986. The propulsion system, invented by Dr Reiner Stemme, mounts the engine in mid-fuselage for CG stability, with an extension shaft to drive a nose-mounted propeller with hinged blades, deployed when required by extending the aircraft's nosecone forward. For gliding flight, the blades are folded and retracted inside the forward fuselage, and the nosecone is restored to its closed position. Thus, only the propeller blades are extended outside the aircraft, instead of the pylon structure associated with most other retractable power plant installations.

Known originally as the HMS (Hochleistungs Motor Segelflugzeug: high performance motor glider), the S 10 was flown as a single-seater in initial flight trials, due mainly to load-bearing limitations of the interim wings, which are essentially those of a Glaser-Dirks DG-500. The stronger HQ-17 section wings developed for the production version will enable the S 10 to realise its full two-seat performance potential.

TYPE: Tandem two-seat high performance motor glider.

AIRFRAME: Cantilever shoulder-wing monoplane with T tail. High aspect ratio wings, with tapered outer panels. Wing section Wortmann FX-73-K-170/20/22 on prototype, with 3° dihedral. (New-design wing with HQ-17 section intended for production version.) Long-span flaps and ailerons on trailing-edges; Schempp-Hirth upper surface airbrakes. Wings are built of CFRP, in four sections, with integral fuel and water ballast tanks. Inboard sections can be folded on to fuselage. Fuselage has a central load-bearing mainframe of welded steel tube, with GRP cladding; forward fuselage and integral fin are of GRP sandwich construction. Tail unit incorporates a damped elevator and a rudder of larger than usual size. Landing gear comprises twin 348 × 122 mm mainwheels on steel tube legs, each sprung and fully retractable into its own bay, and a partially recessed 210 × 65 mm steerable tailwheel. Tandem seats, with optional dual controls, under one-piece canopy which is hinged at front and opens upward. 12V 44Ah battery for engine starting.

POWER PLANT: One 59·7 kW (80 hp) Limbach L2000 four-cylinder four-stroke engine, mounted in centre-fuselage aft of seats and beneath wings, close to CG. Propeller, at front of fuselage, consists of a hub and two hinged blades and is driven via a shaft and gearbox, power transmission occurring, after start-up, via a centrifugal clutch. Start-up is achieved by extending the nosecone forward (on the ground or in flight, by control in cockpit); the propeller blades deploy by centrifugal force, and cause no change in trim. Blades are spring-loaded for retraction, after which they are concealed within fuselage by returning the nosecone to its 'glider' position to restore an aerodynamically clean nose contour. Fuel (mogas) in two integral wing tanks with combined capacity of 120 litres (26·4 Imp gallons).

DIMENSIONS, EXTERNAL:
- Wing span 22·00 m (72 ft 2¼ in)
- Wing aspect ratio 26·46
- Length overall 8·42 m (27 ft 7½ in)
- Height over tail 1·99 m (6 ft 6¼ in)
- Wheel track 1·15 m (3 ft 9¼ in)
- Wheelbase 5·40 m (17 ft 8½ in)
- Propeller diameter 1·53 m (5 ft 0¼ in)

AREAS:
- Wings, gross 18·29 m² (196·9 sq ft)
- Ailerons (total) 1·26 m² (13·56 sq ft)
- Flaps (total) 2·18 m² (23·46 sq ft)
- Airbrakes (total) 0·76 m² (8·18 sq ft)
- Vertical tail surfaces (total) 1·55 m² (16·68 sq ft)
- Horizontal tail surfaces (total) 1·46 m² (15·72 sq ft)

WEIGHTS AND LOADINGS:
- Weight empty approx 540 kg (1,190 lb)
- Max T-O weight 850 kg (1,874 lb)
- Max wing loading 46·47 kg/m² (9·52 lb/sq ft)
- Max power loading 14·26 kg/kW (23·42 lb/hp)

PERFORMANCE, UNPOWERED (at AUW of 695 kg; 1,532 lb, ISA):
- Best glide ratio at 57 knots (105 km/h; 65 mph) 44
- Min rate of sink 0·53 m (1·74 ft)/s
- Stalling speed 38 knots (69 km/h; 43 mph)
- Max speed (smooth air) 162 knots (300 km/h; 186 mph)
- Max speed (rough air) 108 knots (200 km/h; 124 mph)

PERFORMANCE, POWERED (at AUW of 695 kg; 1,532 lb, ISA):
- Max cruising speed 108 knots (200 km/h; 124 mph)
- Max rate of climb at S/L 210 m (689 ft)/min
- Service ceiling 5,600 m (18,375 ft)
- T-O run 195 m (640 ft)
- T-O to 15 m (50 ft) 325 m (1,066 ft)
- Landing from 15 m (50 ft) 370 m (1,214 ft)
- Landing run 205 m (673 ft)
- Range with max fuel 1,079 nm (2,000 km; 1,243 miles)

RPVs and TARGETS

BRAZIL

AEROMOT (page 810)

AEROMOT K1 AM

The K1 AM is an Aeromot design, based on the airframe of imported Northrop KD2R-5 target drones but using a Brazilian engine and equipment. Design began in December 1984, and construction of a prototype started in April 1985; this was due to make its first flight in early January 1987. Ten K1 AMs have been ordered by the Brazilian Navy, including six pre-production examples.

Type: Recoverable target drone.

Airframe: Tapered high-wing monoplane, of duralumin construction, with oval section monocoque fuselage and conventional tail surfaces. Fuel tank, in forward fuselage, is made of stainless steel. Wingtip radar reflector pods are of epoxy resin, reinforced with glassfibre. No landing gear.

Power Plant: One 65·6 kW (88 hp) Aeromot A-164-E1 flat-four two-stroke engine, driving a two-blade fixed-pitch wooden propeller.

Launch and Recovery: Platform launched, using a 12·75 kN (2,866 lb st) solid propellant booster rocket motor. Recovery is made by 11·58 m (38 ft) diameter parachute stowed in fuselage immediately aft of wings; deployment is initiated normally by ground control operator, or automatically in the event of communications or engine failure. Recovery can be made on land or from water.

Guidance and Control: Radio command guidance system, transmitting to digital autopilot via onboard receiver/decoder to eliminate interference from other frequencies. Vertical gyro, distribution box, receiver computer, battery box and dual servos, and their connecting cables, are all sealed against sea water infiltration. Conventional aerodynamic control surfaces. In the event of communications failure, autopilot is programmed to continue flight until link is restored, or to deploy parachute if link is not regained within a specified time.

Aeromot K1 AM target drone, under development for the Brazilian Navy

Dimensions, external:

Wing span:	
without reflector pods	3·502 m (11 ft 5⅞ in)
with reflector pods	4·02 m (13 ft 2¼ in)
Wing aspect ratio	7·01
Length overall	3·80 m (12 ft 5½ in)
Fuselage (oval section): Max depth	0·346 m (1 ft 1½ in)
Max width	0·243 m (9½ in)

Area:

Wings, gross	1·75 m² (18·84 sq ft)

Weights:

Basic operating weight empty	137 kg (302 lb)
Fuel	33 kg (73 lb)
Max launching weight	170 kg (375 lb)

Performance (estimated at max launching weight):

Never-exceed speed	240 knots (444 km/h; 276 mph)
Max level speed at S/L	180 knots (333 km/h; 207 mph)
Stalling speed	60 knots (112 km/h; 69 mph)
Max rate of climb at S/L	1,000 m (3,280 ft)/min
Max operating height	4,575 m (15,000 ft)
Max range at S/L	150 nm (278 km; 173 miles)
Endurance	50 min

CTA (page 810)

Two examples of the small twin-boom piston engined RPV being developed by the Brazilian CTA. Nearer aircraft has its nosecone removed *(M.R.V. Carneiro)*

IGAE (page 810)

IGAE LAH/EB small target drone, of which deliveries to Brazilian Army anti-aircraft artillery units were due to begin in 1986 *(Antonio F. Rosa Dini)*

UNITED KINGDOM

TTL (page 836)

TTL JTT-5 Voodoo jet powered RPV/target, developed from the Banshee

UNITED STATES OF AMERICA

BOEING (page 841)

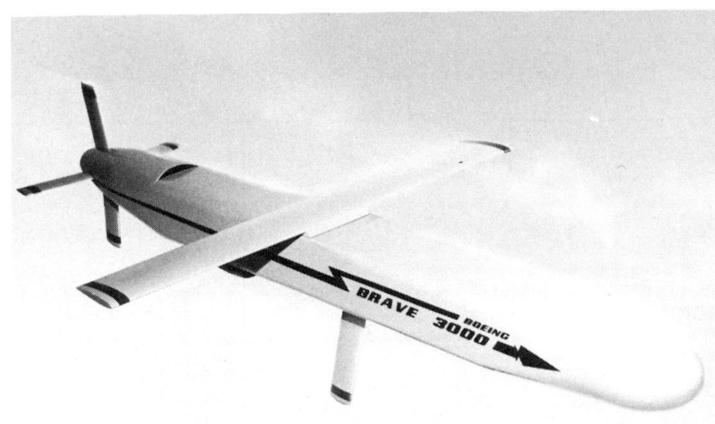

Boeing Military Airplane Company's rocket launched, jet powered Brave 3000 expendable drone, details of which are given on page 842

AIR LAUNCHED MISSILES

CHILE

FERRIMAR

This Chilean weapons manufacturer is developing a submunitions dispenser for air-to-surface use. Already tested in a wind tunnel, it has folding sweptback wings mounted at approximately mid-point on the lower surface of a square-section body, with three conventional fixed tail surfaces. Launch weight is about 900 kg (2,000 lb) loaded with 1,000 submunitions. Its standoff range is between 3·25 and 6·5 nm (6-12 km; 3·75-7·5 miles) depending on launch parameters. The weapon is expected to be operational by mid-1988.

CHINA

CATIC
CHINA NATIONAL AERO TECHNOLOGY IMPORT AND EXPORT CORPORATION

67 Jiao Nan Street, PO Box 1671, Beijing
Telephone: 442444
Telex: 22318 AEROT CN

PL-5B

In addition to the air-to-air missiles listed on page 857, CATIC has given details of a new close-range weapon designated PL-5B which resembles closely the US AIM-9L Sidewinder in appearance and dimensions. In service on a variety of aircraft, it is an infra-red missile, capable of off-boresight launch. The IR seeker is cooled by compressed air and is claimed to offer highly effective CCM capability against background radiation. It can be fitted with a high-explosive fragmentation warhead with IR proximity fuse, or a continuous rod warhead with radio proximity fuse. Dead zone around the Sun is 16°.

DIMENSIONS:
Length 2·892 m (9 ft 5⅞ in)
Body diameter 12·7 cm (5 in)
Wing span 0·657 m (2 ft 1⅞ in)
LAUNCH WEIGHT: 85 kg (187 lb)
PERFORMANCE:
Max speed Mach 4·5
Max range 8·6 nm (16 km; 10 miles)
Effective lethal radius 10 m (33 ft)

UNITED STATES OF AMERICA

MCDONNELL DOUGLAS (page 870)

SLAM

SLAM (standoff land attack missile) is a multi-mission derivative of the AGM-84 Harpoon, intended primarily for deployment on naval carrier based attack aircraft that are Harpoon compatible. It is basically similar to the current AGM-84, with J402 turbojet, Harpoon attitude reference assembly (ARA) midcourse guidance, warhead and control, but utilises a Maverick IIR seeker and Walleye data link for precision use against land targets. SLAM's range is in excess of 50 nm (92 km; 57 miles).

DIMENSIONS:
Length 4·50 m (14 ft 9 in)
Body diameter 34·3 cm (13½ in)
LAUNCH WEIGHT: 628 kg (1,385 lb)

AERO ENGINES

CHINA

CHINA (page 882)

Accompanying illustrations show two previously unknown jet engines marketed by CATIC, the national aviation import and export organisation of the People's Republic. One, the **WP-13** (WP from Wopen, meaning turbojet) is clearly based on a Soviet Tumansky afterburning turbojet, but its exact ancestry is puzzling. The R-11 family, used in early MiG-21s, such as are produced in China, has many different features, and in any case led to the Chinese WP-7 series of engines. The R-13 and R-25, used in later models of MiG-21, again have different features; moreover, the designation WP-13 leaves WPs from 9 to 12 inclusive unaccounted for. The likelihood is that the WP-13 is based on the Soviet R-13, and that this has influenced the numerical designation. The version powering the J-8 II fighter is designated WP-13A II and has an identical afterburning thrust (64·72 kN; 14,550 lb) to the R-13-300.

Even more puzzling is the **WS-9**, the first Chinese turbofan to be revealed. WS comes from Woshan, presumably meaning turbofan. Obviously an afterburning or augmented engine, probably for a supersonic application, the new engine is not a copy of any previously known engine. It appears at first to be in the class of the RB199 and F404, but closer inspection suggests that it is much smaller. The first fan stage has 31 or 32 blades with part-span shrouds, and several features of the engine show similarity to the Pratt & Whitney Canada JT15D, long ago rumoured as the engine picked for the Chinese twin-engined advanced trainer thought to be designated CJ-8. Pratt & Whitney Canada has never mentioned an augmented supersonic version of the JT15D, and the possibility that the WS-9 is such an engine is pure speculation.

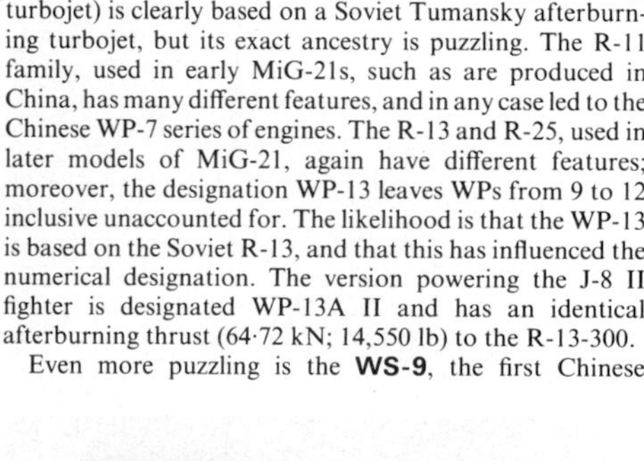

The first illustration of the CATIC Woshan-9 augmented turbofan

A production example of the CATIC Wopen-13 afterburning turbojet

FRANCE

JPX (page 885)

JPX announced in May 1986 certification of the four-stroke 4T75/BC, the uprated 56 kW (75 hp) version of the 4T/60 used in the Robin ATL, as well as the first bench run of the two-stroke 2TV4, which is seen as a possible future engine for the ATL Club version.

TURBOMÉCA (page 887)

The Turboméca TM 333-1A turboshaft engine was awarded French certification on 11 July 1986. Production is due from March 1988.

INTERNATIONAL

CFM INTERNATIONAL (page 894)

On 26 August 1986 the CFM56-5 made its first flight on a Boeing 707 testbed at the General Electric facility at Mojave, California. It was announced that a growth version of the Dash-5 is being developed for a thrust of 127 kN (28,600 lb) for such applications as the A320, A340 and MD-90X; this version could be available in 1990. In September it was announced that continued refinement of the CFM56-3 has resulted in a new thrust rating of 104·5 kN (23,500 lb st), coupled with a 2 per cent reduction in specific fuel consumption. President Jean Bilien described the Dash-3 as "the most reliable turbofan ever to enter service", a claim also made by Rolls-Royce on behalf of the 535.

EUROJET
EUROJET ENGINES GmbH

ADDRESS: To be in Munich, West Germany
MANAGING DIRECTOR: Colin Green (Rolls-Royce)
TECHNICAL DIRECTOR: Arthur Schäffler (MTU)
COMMERCIAL DIRECTOR: Menotti Zinna (Fiat)
PRODUCT ASSURANCE DIRECTOR:
Juan Villate (SENER)

This company was formed in August 1986 to manage the engine programme for the European Fighter Aircraft. Eurojet Engines GmbH will have been registered in the Federal Republic of Germany before this volume is published, with headquarters in Munich (probably in the same building as Turbo-Union). The structure of the company will reflect the experience gained by Turbo-Union, but the shareholding is likely to be: Fiat Aviazione (Italy) 21%; MTU (West Germany) 33%; Rolls-Royce (UK) 33%; SENER (Spain) 13%. The four companies are all contributing staff, initially numbering about 35.

The engine, as described, will be shared out in the above proportions, corresponding to each country's stake in the EFA aircraft programme. Each partner will be entirely responsible for design, development and manufacture of its assigned sections of the engine, the proposed workshare being: Fiat, LP turbine, interstage support, augmentation (reheat) system, gearbox, oil system and (part) intermediate casing; MTU, LP compressor (fan), HP compressor and (part) HP turbine; Rolls-Royce, combustion system, HP turbine and intermediate casing, and (part) LP and HP compressors, LP turbine, interstage support, reheat system and nozzle; SENER, LP shaft, bypass duct, exhaust diffuser, jetpipe and nozzle. Each partner will build and test complete EJ200 engines, and will be responsible for comprehensive support of engines of its own national air force, which (excluding possible exports) are expected to number more than 2,000.

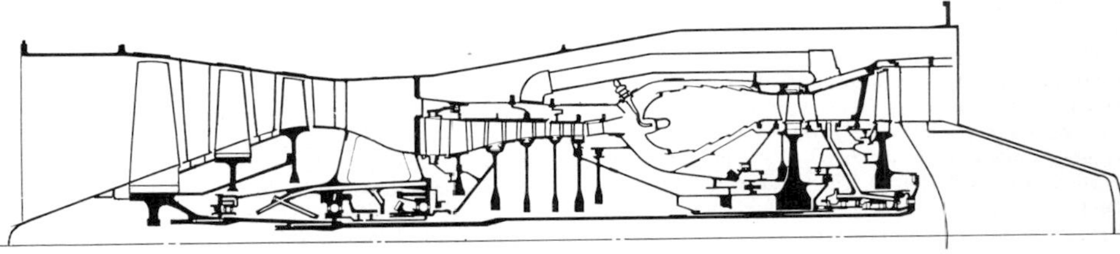

Longitudinal section through the Eurojet EJ200 two-shaft augmented turbofan engine

EUROJET EJ200

This engine will be an advanced turbofan designed for Mach numbers of about 2, with emphasis on supportability, with reliability, component life and ease of maintenance having equal priority with performance and weight. First run is scheduled for 18 months from go-ahead, with flight clearance approximately two years later. Entry into service is expected to be in 1995.

Type: Two-shaft augmented turbofan.

LP Compressor: Three stages, with 3-D transonic blade design. Overhung ahead of high-capacity ball bearing and forward roller bearing. Bypass ratio about 0·4.

HP Compressor: Five stages, with first stage variable inlet guide vanes. Shaft supported between front ball and rear roller bearings. Overall pressure ratio, more than 25.

Combustor: Fully annular, with vaporising burners.

HP Turbine: Single stage, with powder metallurgy disc and single crystal blades.

LP Turbine: Single stage.

Exhaust System: High efficiency augmentor (reheat jetpipe) with fully variable convergent/divergent nozzle.

Accessories: Central gearbox driven via tower shaft in interstage support. Full authority digital electronic control. Integrated health monitoring system.

Dimensions: Generally similar to RB199

Weight: In 900 kg (2,000 lb) class

Performance Rating: In 90 kN (20,000 lb st) class

ROLLS-ROYCE TURBOMECA (page 896)

The RTM 322 made its first flight in a Sikorsky S-70C helicopter at Yeovil on 14 June 1986. Certification is due in late 1987. In September Rinaldo Piaggio SpA of Italy (page 901) signed an agreement under which it will join the RTM 322 programme. The new partner will have a 10% share (which can be increased in the event of an Italian order, as expected for single-engined A 129s), covering design, development and production of components as well as assembly, test and support of complete engines.

ROLLS-ROYCE (page 919) and PRATT & WHITNEY (page 950)

Further to a memorandum of understanding signed in January 1986 between the British Ministry of Defence and the US Department of Defense for collaboration on studies of an advanced STOVL (or V/STOL) aircraft, the above engine companies signed a letter of intent in September covering joint study of engines for such an aircraft. Supersonic speed is a requirement. Flight demonstration is predicted for the late 1990s.

ITALY

ARROW
ARROW snc

via Badiaschi 25, 29100 Piacenza
Telephone: 0523 41932
Telex: 530112 CC PC1
Telefax: 0523 34367
Chairman: Tullio Osellini
Engineering Manager: G. Polidoro

This company produces modular aircooled piston engines for microlights and homebuilts. In 1985 aircraft powered by Arrow won the French ULM championship and the Grande Course for two-seat microlights.

ARROW GT250

Single-cylinder geared two-stroke. Cast light alloy cylinder with ceramic coated interior. Bore 74·6 mm (2·94 in). Stroke 57·0 mm (2·24 in). Capacity 250 cc (15·25 cu in). Induction through 36 mm Dell'Orto carburettor of 100 grade fuel mixed with 2 per cent oil. Electric starter and 12 V electronic ignition with one or two plugs. Planetary reduction gear of 0·335 ratio.

Dimensions:
Length 460 mm (18·12 in)
Width 370 mm (14·60 in)
Height 380 mm (15·0 in)
Weight, ready to run: 26·0 kg (57·26 lb)
Performance Rating: 25·33 kW (34 hp) at 6,800 rpm
Fuel Consumption: 4 to 6 litres (0·88-1·32 Imp gallons)/h

ARROW GT500

This is the opposed-twin version of the GT250. A 38 mm carburettor is used.

Dimensions:
Length 500 mm (19·65 in)
Width 500 mm (19·65 in)
Height 451 mm (17·70 in)
Weight, ready to run: 36·0 kg (79·3 lb)
Performance Rating: 48·5 kW (65 hp) at 6,800 rpm
Fuel Consumption: 6 to 10 litres (1·32-2·20 Imp gallons)/h

ARROW GT1000

This is the flat-four version, using the same cylinders as in the foregoing engines. Two 38 mm carburettors are fitted.

Dimensions:
Length 521 mm (20·45 in)
Width 500 mm (19·65 in)
Height 451 mm (17·70 in)
Weight, ready to run: 54·0 kg (119 lb)
Performance Rating: 82 kW (110 hp) at 6,200 rpm
Fuel Consumption: 8 to 14 litres (1·76-3·08 Imp gallons)/h

ARROW GT654

This is a 90° V-twin four-stroke based on the Moto Guzzi V65 motorcycle engine. The light alloy cylinders have Nicasil liners. Bore 80·0 mm (3·15 in). Stroke 64·0 mm (2·52 in). Capacity 650 cc (39·66 cu in). Fuel is 100 mogas fed through twin 30 mm Dell'Orto carburettors. A 12V starter is fitted, and the planetary geared drive has a ratio of 0·335.

Dimensions:
Length 702 mm (27·6 in)
Width 431 mm (17·0 in)
Height 460 mm (18·12 in)
Weight, ready to run: 60·0 kg (132 lb)
Performance Rating: 41·0 kW (55 hp) at 6,500 rpm
Fuel Consumption: 4 to 6 litres (0·88-1·32 Imp gallons)/h

The Arrow GT250 single-cylinder engine

The Arrow GT500 two-cylinder engine

The Arrow GT1000 four-cylinder engine

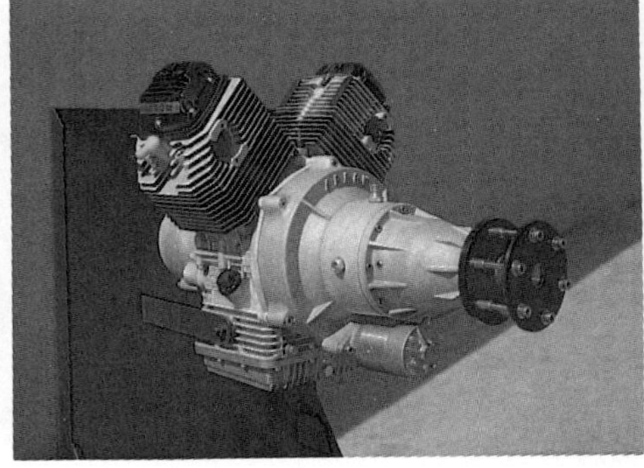

The Arrow GT654 V-twin engine

TURKEY

TUMSAS

This is the new Turkish aero engine industry, to be located at a factory near Eskisehir airbase. It is to build the F110 fighter engine under licence from US General Electric. The latter has a 7% holding in the parent TUSAS aircraft company.

UNION OF SOVIET SOCIALIST REPUBLICS

TUMANSKY (page 914)

Further information is now available on the three families of engine used to power the various models of MiG-21 fighter.

TUMANSKY R-11

This tough and simple afterburning turbojet has a three-stage LP compressor (which, by using transonic flow, achieves a pressure per stage of 1·4, or 2·74 overall) and a three-stage HP compressor. The can-annular combustion chamber has ten flame tubes, two (usually Nos 1 and 6) having igniters, and both the LP and HP turbines have single stages. A separate gasoline (petrol) tank is used for starting, the switch to kerosene taking place after full idling speed has been reached and fuel pressure is adequate for the main fuel to vaporise adequately. Maximum relight altitude is raised from 8,000 m (26,250 ft) to 11,900 m (39,050 ft) by injection of gaseous oxygen. The Chinese WP-7B version eliminates the starting tank, kerosene only being required.

TUMANSKY R-13

This engine came into production in 1965, and is installationally interchangeable with the R-11. The compressor has considerably higher work per stage and handles increased airflow; the HP spool has five stages. Replacing steel by titanium in many parts reduced weight, and fuel burn is little more than that of the R-11 despite the much greater output.

TUMANSKY R-25

Again installationally interchangeable, this engine is started on main aircraft fuel, has an overall pressure ratio of 14·2 (double that of the R-11) and has good combustion in the main chamber and afterburner up to 18,000 m (59,050 ft).

NORTON MOTORS (page 917)

Under Ministry of Defence contract, Wallis Autogyros has since 31 July 1986 been flying a WA-116 powered by a Norton twin-rotor Wankel type engine. It is proving to be extremely smooth, even when mounted rigidly to the airframe, and is demonstrating a high power/weight ratio.

Norton twin-rotor engine installed in a Wallis WA-116

ROLLS-ROYCE (page 919)

On 1 July 1986 Rolls-Royce plc and Garrett Turbine Engine Co (page 937) signed workshare agreements for the TPE331-12B turboprop which powers the Shorts Tucano for the RAF. From early 1987 RR factories at Bristol, Derby, Leavesden and Hillington will make turbine blades and discs, nozzle guide vanes and engine casings, both for RAF engines and for supply to Garrett for engines for other customers. The 140 RAF engines will be assembled and tested at RR East Kilbride from 1987 until 1991.

ROLLS-ROYCE RB211

On 3 June 1986 Cathay Pacific became launch customer for the latest RB211 version, the D4D, to be installed in the airline's Boeing 747-400s. The D4D introduces new wide chord fan blades and an integrated mixer nozzle, both derived from those developed for the smaller 535E4. The core has also been improved, with directionally solidified HP and IP turbine blades and new nozzle guide vanes incorporating 3-D design techniques. Another new feature is a digital control system. The D4D is to be certificated in Spring 1988 at 249·0 kN (56,000 lb st), with specific fuel consumption "at least 8 per cent better" than that of the 524D4.

ROLLS-ROYCE TAY

After one of the most troublefree developments of any engine, the Tay was certificated by Britain's CAA in June 1986. Development, at the East Kilbride factory, was funded entirely by the company. The first of 400 Tays ordered for the Gulfstream IV were to enter service later in 1986, followed in 1987 by engines in the Fokker 100.

ROLLS-ROYCE RB545

Under this designation, project design studies are in hand at Bristol on the unique combined airbreathing and rocket propulsion system for the BAe HOTOL. During the first nine minutes of flight the engine will use oxygen from the atmosphere, thereafter switching to on-board liquid oxygen. Rig testing of critical components began early in 1986 at the company's facility at Ansty, Coventry, as part of a two-year proof of concept study.

ROLLS-ROYCE RB550

Long predicted, this is the new turboprop based on the core of the Rolls-Royce Turboméca RTM 322 turboshaft, mated with the reduction gear of the latest Rolls-Royce Dart (the engine the RB550 is planned to replace). Aimed mainly at the 60/80-passenger transport market, the 550 is expected to pose few risks since all major parts are thoroughly proven. The immediate applications are listed as the BAe ATP, the Fokker 50 development and the Chinese Y-7 development, together with the ATR 72 and 70-seat projects at Airtech and EMBRAER.

Compared with the RTM 322, the RB550 has a greater mass flow and various minor changes Rolls-Royce claims

UNITED KINGDOM

GTi
GAS TURBINE INDUSTRIES LTD

4 Nuttfield Close, Croxley Green, Rickmansworth, Herts
Telephone: 0923 22265

DIRECTORS: M. Gharib, G. Weston, R. Tink, A. Skinner

GTi was formed in 1984 to design, develop and manufacture a series of very small, low cost gas-turbine engines for general aviation. Development began with a much smaller proof of concept unit, run from January 1985. Current work is centred on the TJ-4 and on derived turbofan and turboprop versions.

GTi TJ-4

This small turbojet is being developed as the **TJ-4C** for general aviation and the **TJ-4M** low cost version for expendable RPVs.

COMPRESSOR: Single-stage centrifugal.
COMBUSTION CHAMBER: Reversed flow annular with spray atomisers.
TURBINE: Inward flow radial.
FUEL SYSTEM: Gear type pump, pressure reducing valve for control, with microchip control offered as option on TJ-4C.
LUBRICATION: Pumped recirculating.
STARTING: External air source or windmilling; electric starter/generator under development.
LENGTH: 295 mm (11·6 in)
DIAMETER: 200 mm (7·9 in)

The GTi TJ-4 turbojet

WEIGHT, DRY: 8·2 kg (18 lb)
PERFORMANCE RATING (T-O, S/L):
TJ-4C 0·178 kN (40 lb st) at 72,000 rpm
TJ-4M 0·245 kN (55 lb st) at 72,000 rpm

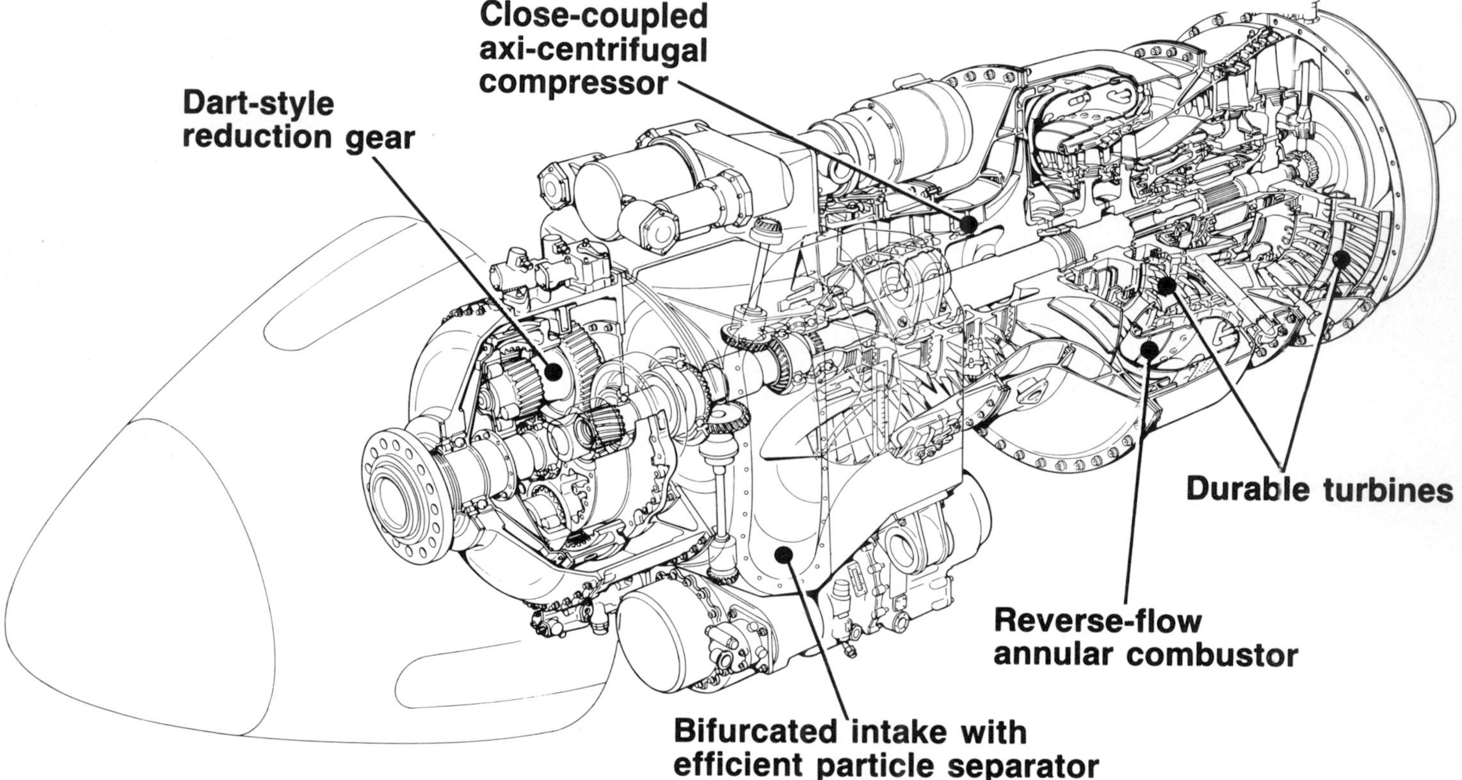

Cutaway drawing of Rolls-Royce RB550-02 turboprop engine

many benefits compared with turboprops which need a flexible chin intake duct, including much lighter and simpler installation and mounting, improved airflow, simpler anti-icing and oil cooling, less external drag and reduced noise. The engine is assembled from seven modules. Pressure ratio will be 12. Certification is due in 1991.

DIMENSIONS:
- Length: 1,918 mm (75·5 in)
- Width: 762 mm (30·0 in)
- Height: 996 mm (39·2 in)

WEIGHT, DRY:
- Fully dressed: 590 kg (1,300 lb)

PERFORMANCE RATING (RB550-02, uninstalled):
- T-O (S/L, static): 2,386 kW (3,200 shp) to 20°C
- Max cruise (Mach 0·45 at 6,100 m; 20,000 ft): 1,517 kW (2,034 shp)

SPECIFIC FUEL CONSUMPTION:
- T-O: 77·7 µg/J (0·46 lb/h/shp)
- Max cruise: 69·3 µg/J (0·41 lb/h/shp)

ROLLS-ROYCE GEM

Confusingly, the engine now in production for the Agusta A 129 helicopter is referred to simply as the Rolls-Royce 1004, the name being dropped.

UNITED STATES OF AMERICA

ALLISON (page 927)

ALLISON T406

In September Allison announced completion of testing of the compressor of the T406-AD-400, the engine selected for the V-22 Osprey tilt-rotor aircraft. Among other results was demonstration of infinite fatigue life for the rotor blades.

AVCO LYCOMING (page 930)

The Williamsport Division ran the first SCORE (stratified-charge omnivorous rotary engine) in October 1986. Offered in powers from 37·3 to 1,119 kW (50-1,500 hp), the initial rating is likely to be 298 kW (400 hp). First flight is expected in 1987, and deliveries could begin in 1990.

GENERAL ELECTRIC (page 939)

GENERAL ELECTRIC UDF

Ground testing of the proof of concept UDF (unducted fan) engine, carried out in co-operation with NASA Lewis Research Center, was completed in July 1986 with 100 flight cycles, and over one million cycles at critical frequencies. Programme manager Bruce Gordon said "The engine ran successfully above its rating of 25,000 lb thrust, and demonstrated an sfc of less than 0·24 lb/h/lb st, better than prediction". This sfc is 6·8 mg/Ns. The single-lever electronic control demonstrated smooth control of fan speed and blade pitch. The engine was then inspected, refurbished, converted to side mounting and installed in the starboard position on a Boeing 727-100. A very successful first flight was made on 20 August from the Mojave test facility. The 75-hour test programme was to be completed by the end of 1986. Meanwhile, in October 1986 an MD-80 arrived at Mojave for modification to flight test a second UDF from mid-1987. This second engine will have ten blades on the front rotor, retaining the original eight on the rear rotor. This configuration, based on McDonnell Douglas research, is expected to meet FAR Pt 36 noise requirements.

GENERAL ELECTRIC GE27

In August 1986 the GE27 MTDE (modern technology demonstrator engine) completed an initial 94 hours of bench testing, configured as a turboprop. The additions included an Allison T56 reduction gearbox and a Grumman E-2 inlet duct. The tests, at the Naval Air Development Center at Trenton, NJ, documented possible capability for re-engining such aircraft as the C-130, E-2 and P-3, as well as the V-22 and CH-47.

GENERAL ELECTRIC CT7

In September 1986 it was announced that the 1,000,000 hours flown by T700 engines have made possible a growth version, the commercial CT7-6. To be developed in partnership with Alfa Romeo Avio and Fiat Aviazione, the Dash-6 will have an increased mass flow and more efficient gas-generator and power turbines. These components are common to the other growth versions, the CT7-9 turboprop and the military T700-401C and -701C. Rated in the 1,491 kW (2,000 shp) class, the Dash-6 is being marketed by GE and Alfa Romeo, with certification due in the first quarter of 1988.

The first flight example of the General Electric UDF engine installed in a Boeing 727-100, seen in flight on the right

LHTEC (page 948)

LHTEC T800

Following more than 600 hours of running on two T800 prototype engines, the first PFRT (preliminary flight rating test) engine, described as the first Metric T800, began its test programme in August 1986. The engine "ran exceptionally well, several weeks ahead of schedule". By mid-1988 the PFRT programme should have logged 3,500 hours.

PRATT & WHITNEY (page 950)

The Government Products Division announced a new mailing address: P.O. Box 109600, West Palm Beach, Florida 33410-9600.

First of two revealing new Pratt & Whitney cutaway drawings, this shows the PW1120 afterburning turbojet, engine of the IAI Lavi and upgraded F-4 Phantom II

Second new Pratt & Whitney cutaway drawing to be released, this depicts the PW1129 augmented turbofan, a future competitor for propulsion of US fighters

INDEXES

(Items in italics refer to the ten previous editions)

AIRCRAFT
(including Homebuilts entries in 1976-86 editions)

B

D

E

F

IT'LL TEACH YOU A LESSON.

C-101

TRAINS FROM CADET TO COMBAT... AND CAN ATTACK!

The first lesson of any good trainer is to aim for the best possible results at the lowest possible cost. The C-101 combines quality of instruction with the best cost/efficiency ratio.

Thanks to its unique versatility, it can give a complete training program, including all stages of tactical training, with just one fleet. This means extraordinary savings in maintenance and purchasing costs.

And if need be you can also teach the enemy a lesson because the C-101 is capable of carrying out ground attack missions.

The C-101 is a good lesson from the company that has overhauled and maintained for 30 years the U.S. Air Force in Europe. CASA's best guarantee of service and technology.

Technical Characteristics:
M.T.O.W. = 6.300 Kg.
Engine Thrust = 4.700 lb.
R/C = 6.100 ft/min.
Outstanding Handling qualities.
Radius (LO-LO-LO. 4xMK 82 + 30 mm. = 270 N.M.).
Enhanced Avionics (H.U.D.).
Operational Safety.
Low fuel consumption (1.100 lb/hr.).
Low maintenance (3.5 M.H/F.H.).

For further information, contact: Construcciones Aeronáuticas, S. A. Rey Francisco, 4. 28008 Madrid. Spain. Phone: 248 53 09. Telex: 44729. Or contact: CASA Inc.: 1215 Jefferson Davis Highway. Suite 404. Crystal City. Arlington, VA 22202.USA. Phone: (703) 486 53 70. Telex: 901109.

G

H

I

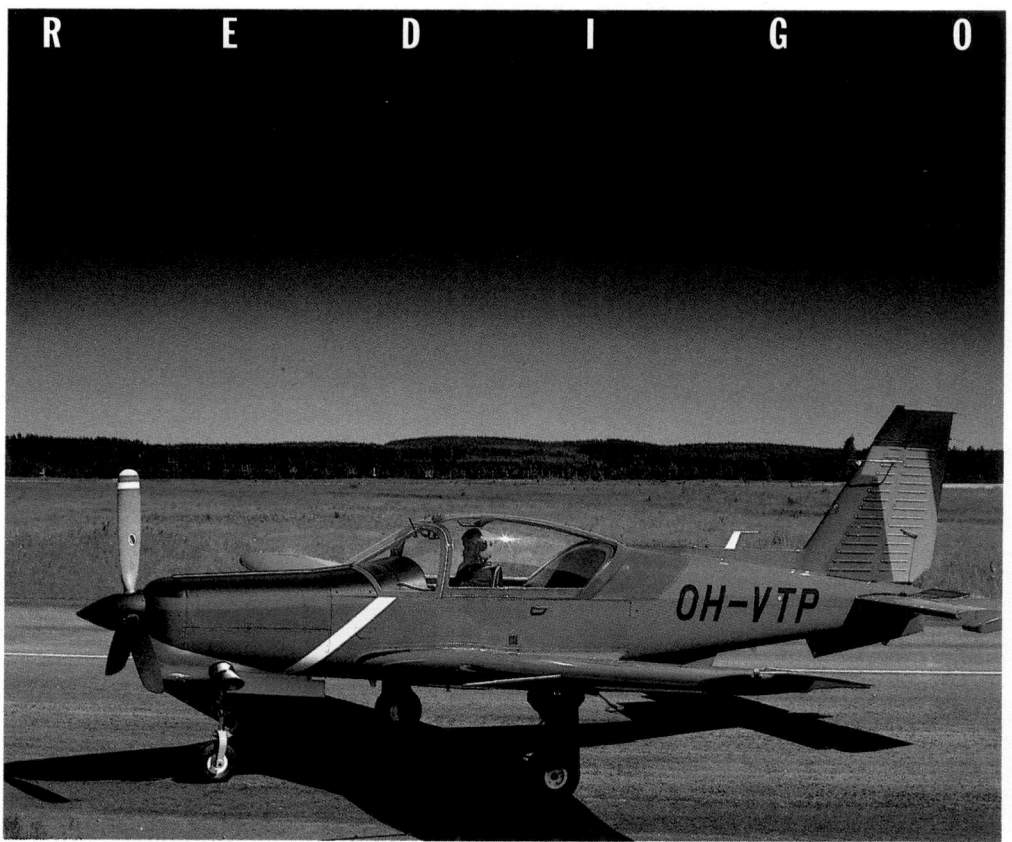

M

Q

R

S

T

SPORT AIRCRAFT

D

E

F

M

N

O

P

Q

R

S

T

U

V

SAILPLANES

C

D

E

F

G

H

I

J

K

L

M

N

O

P

HANG GLIDERS

LIGHTER-THAN-AIR

RPVs AND TARGETS

AIR-LAUNCHED MISSILES

(including Spaceflight entries in 1976-85 editions)

AERO-ENGINES

N

O

P

R

S

Printed and made in the United Kingdom by Netherwood Dalton & Co. Ltd., Huddersfield